CHASE'S
Calendar of Events

2009

New York Chicago San Francisco Lisbon London Madrid Mexico City
Milan New Delhi San Juan Seoul Singapore Sydney Toronto

1 2 3 4 5 6 7 8 9 10 11 12 13 14 15 16 17 18 19 QPD/QPD 0 9 8

ISBN 978-0-07-159954-2 (set)
MHID 0-07-159954-1 (set)
ISBN 978-0-07-159956-6 (book)
MHID 0-07-159956-8 (book)

ISSN 0740-5286

McGraw-Hill books are available at special quantity discounts to use as premiums and sales promotions, or for use in corporate training programs. For more information, please write to the Director of Special Sales, McGraw-Hill Professional, Two Penn Plaza, New York, New York 10121-2298. Or contact your local bookstore.

NOTICE
Events listed herein are not necessarily endorsed by the editors or publisher. Every effort has been made to assure the correctness of all entries, but neither the editors nor the publisher can warrant their accuracy. IT IS IMPERATIVE, IF FINANCIAL PLANS ARE TO BE MADE IN CONNECTION WITH THE DATES OR EVENTS LISTED HEREIN, THAT PRINCIPALS BE CONSULTED FOR FINAL INFORMATION.

This book is printed on acid-free paper.

✦ Contents ✦

Introduction 5

Spotlight on 2009 Anniversaries and Events 9

Spotlight on the Past: 1809, 1859, 1909, 1934, 1959, 1984 9

Spotlight on World and American Anniversaries: *Charles Darwin and* On the Origin of Species *(1809, 1859), The Cuban Revolution (1959), Abraham Lincoln (1809), Oregon Enters the Union (1859), NAACP (1909), Alaska and Hawaii Join the Union (1959)* 40

Spotlight on People 48

Calendar of Events: Jan 1–Dec 31, 2009

January—65
February—108
March—149
April—194
May—243
June—293
July—338
August—385
September—427
October—480
November—532
December—573

Calendar Information for the Years 2009–2011 610

Looking Forward: Future Anniversaries and Major Events 613

Perpetual Calendar 614

National Days of the World for 2009 618

Selected Special Years: 1990–2011 619

Chinese Calendar 619

Wedding Anniversary Gifts 619

World Map of Time Zones 620

Universal, Standard and Daylight Times 621

Leap Seconds 621

Astronomical Phenomena for the Years 2009–2011 622

The Naming of Hurricanes 623

Some Facts About the US Presidents 624

Presidential Proclamations 626

Some Facts About the United States 628

State & Territory Abbreviations: United States 629

State Governors/US Senators/US Supreme Court 630

Some Facts About Canada 631

Province & Territory Abbreviations: Canada 631

Some Facts About Mexico 631

2009 Special Months 632

Major Awards Presented in 2007–2008 634

National Film Registry and National Recording Registry 642

Index 643

✦ Introduction ✦

Welcome to *Chase's Calendar of Events 2009*, the 52nd edition of this publication. Within this book are more than 12,500 entries in a range of subject areas—plus exhaustive appendices. All entries are updated and thoroughly fact-checked, making *Chase's* the most respected and comprehensive reference available on holidays, events and anniversaries and special days, weeks and months.

What's New in 2009

2009 ushers in many milestone anniversaries, many of which are described more fully in the "Spotlight" section. World anniversaries of note include the 150th publication anniversary of Charles Darwin's groundbreaking *On the Origin of Species*, the 100th anniversary of Peary and Henson reaching the North Pole and the 50th anniversary of the Cuban revolution that overthrew dictator Fulgencio Batista.

In America, several states celebrate significant anniversaries of their admission to the Union: Oregon (1859) and Alaska and Hawaii (1959). The NAACP observes its 100th birthday in 2009.

Among the many notable people enjoying a significant birth anniversary are US presidents Zachary Taylor (225), Abraham Lincoln (200) and Harry Truman (125); Samuel Johnson (300); Charles Darwin (200); Robert Burns (225); Edgar Allan Poe (200) and many others.

Types of Entries in *Chase's Calendar of Events*

Astronomical Phenomena

Information about eclipses, equinoxes and solstices, moon phases and other astronomical phenomena is calculated from data prepared by the US Naval Observatory's Nautical Almanac Office and Her Majesty's Nautical Almanac Office. In *Chase's*, universal time has been converted to eastern time.

Religious Observances

Principal observances of the Christian, Jewish, Muslim and Baha'i faiths are presented with background information from their respective calendars. We include anticipated dates for Muslim holidays. When known, religious events of China, Japan and India are also listed. There is no single Hindu calendar and different sects define the Hindu lunar month differently. There is no single lunar calendar that serves as a model for all Buddhists, either. Therefore, we are not able to provide the dates of many religious holidays for these faiths.

National and International Observances and Civic Holidays

Chase's features independence days, national days and public holidays from around the world. Technically, there are no national holidays in the US: holidays proclaimed by the president apply only to federal employees and to the District of Columbia. State governors proclaim holidays for their states. In practice, federal holidays usually are proclaimed by governors as well. Some governors proclaim commemorative days that are unique to their state.

Special Days, Weeks and Months

Whether it's Black History Month, National Police Week or National Grandparents' Day, the annual calendar has myriad special days, weeks and months—and *Chase's* has the most comprehensive listing of them. Until January 1995, Congress had been active in seeing that special observances were commemorated. Members of the Senate and House could introduce legislation for a special observance to commemorate people, events and other activities they thought worthy of national recognition. Because these bills took up a disproportionate amount of time on the part of congressmen and their staffs, Congress decided to discontinue this process in January 1995 when it reviewed and reformed its rules and practices. Congress does from time to time issue commemorative resolutions, which do not have the force of law. The president of the US has the authority to declare any commemorative event by proclamation, but this is done infrequently. (Some state legislatures and governors proclaim special days, as do mayors of cities.)

So where do all these special days, weeks and months come from? The majority come from national organizations that use their observances for public outreach and to plan specific events. For special months regarding health issues, for example, you can expect to see more information disseminated, special commemorative walks and medical screenings during that month. The *Chase's* editorial staff includes a special day, week or month in the annual reference based on the authority of the organization observing it, how many years it has been observed, the amount of promotion and activities that are a part of it, its uniqueness and a variety of other factors. (We've included a list of 2009 special months in our appendix section.)

Presidential Proclamations

As we noted above, the president has the authority to declare any commemorative event by proclamation. A good number of these will be proclamations for which there has been legislation giving continuing authority for a proclamation to be issued each year. Mother's Day, for example, has been proclaimed since 1914 by public resolution. The White House Clerk's Office initiates the issuing of these proclamations each year, since they are mandated by authorizing legislation. Of course, there will be new ones: Patriot Day (created in the wake of the Sept 11, 2001, terrorist attacks) and the 2004 death of former president Ronald Reagan are recent examples. In *Chase's* we list proclamations that have continuing authority and those that have been issued consistently since 2002 in the main calendar of the book. In our text, ♦ indicates a presidential proclamation. In our appendix, we also offer a complete list of proclamations issued from Jan 1, 2007, to June 15, 2008. (The most recent proclamations can be found at the Federal Register online: www.access.gpo.gov.)

Events and Festivals

Chase's includes national and international special events and festivals—defined again by their uniqueness and their finite brief length of time. Sporting events; book, film, food and other festivals; seasonal celebrations; folkloric events (Groundhog Day, for example); music outings and more make up these types of entries. These entries are usually sponsored: they have contact information for the general public and all information in the entry comes from the sponsor (see below on sponsored events).

Anniversaries

Anniversaries include historic (creation of states, battles, inventions, publications of note, popular culture events, etc.) and biographical (birth or death anniversaries of notable personages) milestones.

Birthdays Today

Living celebrities in politics, the arts, sports and popular culture are included in the "Birthdays Today" section following each calendar day. If there is a question about the birth day or year, this is noted. Be aware that US governors and senators listed are current as of July 2008. The November 2008 general elections occur after *Chase's* is published.

Spotlight

The tinted pages starting off *Chase's Calendar of Events* form the "Spotlight" section. In a book as packed as *Chase's*, the reader may need a little help picking out significant anniversaries and events for the current year, and Spotlight is the answer to that need. We cover significant 2009 historical and birth anniversaries as well as major events.

New Style Versus Old Style Dates

Please note: dates for historic events can be assumed to be Gregorian calendar (New Style) dates unless "(OS)" appears after the date. This annotation means that the date in question is an Old Style, or Julian date. Most of America's founders were born before 1752, when Great Britain and its colonies adopted the Gregorian calendar. As an example of this, we list George Washington's birthday as Feb 22, 1732, the Gregorian or New Style date. However, when he was born Great Britain and its colonies began the year on Mar 25, not Jan 1, so his Julian birthdate was Feb 11, 1731.

About Sponsored Events

Events for which there is individual or organizational sponsorship are listed with the name of the event, inclusive dates of observance, a brief description, estimated attendance figures and the sponsor's name and contact information. We obtain information for these events directly from the sponsors. There is no fee to be listed in *Chase's* and sponsors submit events to be chosen at the discretion of the *Chase's* editors. Neither the editors nor the publisher necessarily endorse these events.

About the CD-ROM

For Windows users, this CD-ROM includes all the January through December birthday and event information for 2009. It provides users a quick way to conduct simple or sophisticated searches—either of a single topic or in combined areas. Search by country, US state, attendance, keyword, type of event and much more. Installation instructions are on the disk.

Acknowledgments

A book the size of *Chase's* comes about through the care and attention of many organizations and people. The editors and publisher would like to thank the event sponsors; CVBs; chambers of commerce; tourism agencies; nonprofit organizations; publicists; festival organizers; historians; museum directors; librarians; National Park Service employees; embassy staffs; national, state and local government officials and many others who help us put together this reference every year.

We especially wish to thank Bill and Helen Chase and their families for their ongoing support of and inspiration for the book. Bill Chase continues to be the champion of the unique passion and pastime of creating holidays and his editorial advice and input are greatly appreciated.

Many talented writer/researchers helped us create *Chase's*: Sandy Whiteley provided us a window into the years 1809 and 1859, as did Susan Campanini for 1909 and 1934 and Johnny Loftus for 1959 and 1984. Loftus also contributed the article on Abraham Lincoln's 200th birth centennial, while Campanini researched Alaska and Hawaii and Whiteley sketched John Brown's raid and the history of Oregon. Denise Frank provided a portrait of the NAACP. Betty Schaal penned the history of Charles Darwin and his publication of *On the Origin of Species.*

The CD-ROM was created by the powerhouse team at FMA: Rich Shupe (design), Thomas Yeh (programming) and Steven Hayhurst and Jodi Rotondo (project management).

Finally, special thanks to our editorial and production colleagues at McGraw-Hill Professional, a division of the McGraw-Hill Companies: Marisa L'Heureux, Denise Fieldman, Handel Low, Jeanette Wojtyla, Terry Stone, Martha Best, Gigi Grajdura, Arvydas Valiukenas, Lyzette Austen, Leola Grant-Tucker and publisher Christopher Brown.

Holly McGuire, *Editor in Chief*
Kathryn Keil, *Associate Editor*
July 2008

Spotlight on the Past

1809

200 YEARS AGO

Landmark World Events

JAN 5 Great Britain signed the Treaty of the Dardanelles with the Ottoman Empire.

JAN 14 Spanish insurgents signed a formal alliance with Great Britain that would lead to the defeat of France and the end of the Peninsular War in 1814.

APR War of the Fifth Coalition between Austria and the United Kingdom and France began.

APR 25 The British East India Company signed the Treaty of Amritsar, under which Britain would control east India and the Sikh ruler Ranjit Singh would control the west.

MAY 12 British General Arthur Wellesley defeated the French at Oporto, Portugal. By July 28 he had driven the French out of Portugal and scored a victory in Spain at Talavera. Based on his victories in the Peninsular War, on Aug 20 Wellesley was made Viscount Wellington.

MAY 13 Napoleon entered Vienna.

MAY 17 Napoleon ordered the annexation of the Papal States to the French empire. In response, Pope Pius VII excommunicated him on June 10. The pope was arrested in July by the French.

JULY 5–6 The French defeated the Austrians at the Battle of Wagram. Austria lost 40,000 men and France 34,000.

AUG 10 Ecuador declared independence from Spain, but freedom from Spain was not attained until 1822.

OCT 14 Under the Treaty of Schönbrunn between France and Austria, Austria ceded lands to Bavaria and Russia and much of the Adriatic coast to France.

Landmark US Events

FEB 20 In *The United States v Peters*, the Supreme Court ruled that Pennsylvania could not nullify federal court cases, meaning that the power of the federal government is greater than that of any individual state.

MAR 1 The Illinois Territory was formed from part of the Northwest Territory. It included Illinois and Wisconsin and parts of Minnesota and Michigan.

MAR 1 Outgoing president Thomas Jefferson signed the Non-Intercourse Act, which opened trade with all countries. This repealed the Embargo Acts.

MAR 4 James Madison was inaugurated as the fourth president.

JUNE 27 John Quincy Adams was appointed minister to Russia.

OCT 11 Meriwether Lewis, coleader of the Louisiana Purchase expedition, died of gunshot wounds—either purposefully or accidentally self-inflicted.

Death of a Founding Father

JUNE 8 Founding Father and author of *Common Sense* Thomas Paine died in New York City. Neglected in his later years and wracked by many health problems, Paine was refused burial by the local Quakers and was buried in unconsecrated ground near his New Rochelle cottage attended by six mourners. His bones were dug up in 1819 by an English admirer and dispersed.

■ In the Treaty of Fort Wayne, General William Henry Harrison (governor of the Indiana Territory) obtained 2,500,000 acres from Native Americans.

■ Miami University, Oxford, OH, was chartered.

Culture

Publications

Nonfiction

■ *Zoological Philosophy: An Exposition with Regard to the Natural History of Animals in France*, by Jean-Baptiste Lamarck, was one of the earliest works to explore species inheritance. Lamarck believed in the inheritance of acquired characteristics, which was later disproved.

■ *A History of New York*, by Washington Irving, writing under the name Diedrich Knickerbocker.

■ *Observations on the Geology of the United States*, by William Maclure, contained the first geological survey map of the eastern US.

Poetry

■ *English Bards and Scottish Reviewers*, a satire by Lord Byron

Theater

■ *The Yankey in London* [sic], Royall Tyler

Music

■ *Piano Concerto No 5 in E Flat*, "Emperor," Beethoven

■ *Piano Sonatas No 24 in F Sharp* and *No 25 in G Major*, Beethoven

■ First Lady Dolly Madison purchased the first piano for the White House.

■ The first collegiate orchestra was founded at Harvard.

Popular Song

■ "President Madison's March," Peter Weldon

Art

■ *Malvern Hall*, John Constable

■ *The Surrender of Madrid*, Antoine-Jean Gros

■ *Fishing on the Blythe-Sand*, Joseph Turner

Science and Technology

May 5 Mary Kies was the first American woman to be granted a patent.

Dec 31 Briton George Cayley built and flew an unmanned glider. He founded the science of aerodynamics.

■ René-Just Haüy published *Comparative Table*, one of the first classifications of minerals.

Commerce and New Products

■ Frenchman Nicolas Appert developed a method to preserve food by canning. The next year, he won a prize of 12,000 francs from the French government for his invention, which revolutionized our seasonal diet.

■ The steamboat *Phoenix*, built by Colonel John Stevens, began ocean travel—a first for steamships—with commercial trade between Trenton and Philadelphia.

■ The Denby Pottery was established in Britain.

1809 Deaths

■ Franz Joseph Haydn, Austrian composer

■ Thomas Heyward, signer of the Declaration of Independence

■ Meriwether Lewis, explorer

■ Thomas Paine, pamphleteer, author of *Common Sense*

1859

150 YEARS AGO

Landmark World Events

JAN 24 Wallachia and Moldavia were united under Prince Alexandru Cuza with the name Romania.

APR 25 Ground was broken on the Suez Canal, connecting the Mediterranean with the Red Sea. It was completed 10 years later.

JUNE 6 The British Crown Colony of Queensland in Australia was formed from part of the territory of New South Wales. Brisbane was made the capital.

JUNE 24 At the Battle of Solferino the armies of France and Piedmont-Sardinia defeated an Austrian force, ending Austria's hold on Northern Italy and setting the stage for Italian unity. On July 11, the Armistice of Villafranca between France and Austria furthered the cause of unification. (Italy was unified in 1861.)

JUNE One of the civilian witnesses to the Battle of Solferino was Henri Dunant. He was so unnerved by post-battle medical care that he was inspired to create the Red Cross.

AUG 28–SEPT 2 A solar superstorm shorted out telegraph wires in the US and Europe and started many fires. The northern lights were visible as far south as Rome and Hawaii.

NOV 12 The first flying-trapeze act was performed in Paris by Jules Leótard. He designed the garment that bears his name.

NOV 22 Charles Darwin's *On the Origin of Species* was published, and most of the first printing was sold out the first day. See "Spotlight on World Anniversaries."

■ Russia captured the Chechen rebel leader Shamil. North Caucasus region of Chechnya was incorporated into the Russian empire.

Landmark US Events

FEB 14 Oregon became the 33rd state. See "Spotlight on American Anniversaries."

APR 9 Samuel Clemens (Mark Twain) became a licensed riverboat pilot on the Mississippi River.

MAY 9 The Southern Commercial Convention met in Mississippi to call for the reinstitution of a legal slave trade.

JUNE 30 French acrobat Charles Blondin walked across Niagara Falls on a tightrope, viewed by a crowd of 25,000.

JUNE The Comstock Lode, the first major silver strike in the US, was discovered in Nevada.

JULY Last slave ship docked at Mobile, AL. Although banned in 1808, the slave trade had continued. More than 150 Africans were smuggled into Alabama on the slave ship *Clotilde*. The owner of the ship was arrested, but released for lack of evidence.

AUG 27 Commercial oil well drilling was begun at Titusville, PA, by Edwin Drake. The oil was refined into kerosene and used for lighting.

OCT 16 With two of his sons and 19 others, John Brown attacked the federal arsenal at Harper's Ferry, VA, and rounded up 60 men from the area as hostages. Colonel Robert E. Lee and troops counterattacked and defeated the raiders. Brown was hung Dec 2.

OCT 30 Henry David Thoreau read his "A Plea for Captain John Brown" to the citizens of Concord, MA.

■ An executive order set aside in Arizona the first lands specifically for Indians.

■ Georgia passed a law forbidding owners from freeing slaves in their wills.

■ The Arkansas legislature required free blacks to choose exile or slavery.

- More than 100,000 gold seekers headed to Colorado in the Pike's Peak gold rush. Their chant was "Pike's Peak or bust!"
- The first Indian-head pennies were issued by the US Mint. They were in production until 1909.
- Approximately 2,000 daguerrotype studios were open in the US.
- Valparaiso University, in Indiana, was founded.
- The Cooper Union for the Advancement of Science and Art, a tuition-free college of architecture, art and engineering, was founded in New York City.

Culture

Publications

Fiction

- *A Tale of Two Cities*, Charles Dickens. It was serialized in *All the Year Round*, a new literary magazine founded this year by Dickens.
- *Adam Bede*, George Eliot
- *The Minister's Wooing*, Harriet Beecher Stowe
- *Our Nig; or, Sketches in the Life of a Free Black*, by Harriet E. Wilson, was one of the first novels published by an African-American woman.
- *Home of the Gentry*, Ivan Turgenev

Nonfiction

- *On the Origin of Species*, Charles Darwin
- *On Liberty*, by John Stuart Mill, classic work of political philosophy
- *Self-Help: With Illustrations of Character and Conduct*, Samuel Smiles. This bestseller contained the line "Heaven helps those who help themselves."

Poetry

- *The Rubáiyát of Omar Khayyám* was first translated into English by Edward Fitzgerald, who published it this year anonymously.

John Brown at Harper's Ferry

Born in Connecticut in 1800, John Brown grew up in Ohio. By the 1850s he had become deeply interested in the slavery question. Brown and five of his sons became embroiled in the fight between proslavery and antislavery forces in the Kansas Territory. The conflict in "Bleeding Kansas" was over whether Kansas would enter the Union as a free or slave state. In 1855, civil war broke out there and Brown led the local Free-Soil militia. In 1856, proslavery forces attacked the Free-Soil town of Lawrence, which triggered a bloody retaliation by Brown in which five proslavery men were killed.

From then on, Brown became preoccupied with abolition by slave insurrection. By 1858 he had persuaded a number of prominent abolitionists to finance his project. He chose the federal arsenal at Harpers Ferry, VA (modern-day West Virginia), as his point of attack, intending to arm blacks with weapons from the arsenal and to establish a base in the mountains to which free blacks and slaves could flee. On Aug 19, 1859, he met with Frederick Douglass in Pennsylvania for the last time. On Oct 16, 1859, his armed force of 21 men (16 of them white like Brown and 5 of them black) attacked the arsenal and seized the town, killing 7 men. Local militia soon surrounded the town, and federal troops led by Lt Col Robert E. Lee arrived the following day. Ten of Brown's men (two of them his sons) were killed in the ensuing battle, and Brown was wounded. Arrested and charged with treason, he was found guilty on Nov 2 and hanged in Charles Town on Dec 2, 1859.

Many Northerners saw Brown as a martyr, while Southern whites saw him as a terrorist. Southern Democrats said the raid was a consequence of the Republican Party's political platform, but Abraham Lincoln called Brown "a misguided fanatic." John Brown's raid escalated tensions that led to the Civil War less than two years later. Henry Wadsworth Longfellow wrote "They are leading old John Brown to execution. This is sowing the wind to reap the whirlwind, which will soon come." The song "John Brown's Body" became a Union army marching song during the war.

- The first four narrative poems in *Idylls of the King* by Alfred Lord Tennyson were published.

Children's Literature

- *Boys'* and *Girls' Own Magazine*

Journalism

APR 23 *The Rocky Mountain News*, Colorado's first newspaper, was published in Denver.

Theater and Opera

MAR 19 *Faust*, by Charles Gounod, debuted in Paris.

MAY 9 *Rob Roy*, an operatic drama based on Sir Walter Scott's novel, opened in New York City.

NOV The great Italian singer Adelina Patti made her operatic debut in *Lucia di Lammermoor* at New York City.

- *Un ballo in maschera* (*A Masked Ball*), by Giuseppe Verdi, premiered in Rome.
- *The Octoroon; or, Life in Louisiana*, Dion Boucicault

Music

- *Piano Concerto No 1 in D Minor*, Johannes Brahms
- *Serenade No 2*, "Marianlieder," Johannes Brahms
- *Morgenlied*, Franz Liszt

Popular Songs

- "Hard Times Come No More" and "Thou Art the Queen of My Song," Stephen Foster
- The melody to "Happy Birthday to You" was written by Mildred J. Hill. The lyrics were added in 1924.
- "Dixie," written by Daniel Decatur Emmett, was first performed in New York City by Bryant's Minstrels. Later it was to be the anthem of the Civil War South.

Art

- *The Angelus*, Jean-François Millet, the most reproduced painting of the 19th century
- *The Absinthe Drinker*, Edouard Manet
- *Thunderstorm in the Rockies*, Albert Bierstadt
- *Heart of the Andes*, Frederic Church
- *Approaching Thunder Storm*, Martin Johnson Heade
- Eight nude statues purchased for the Tennessee capitol building had clothing added to them, and even then many people were offended by the skimpy covering.

Science and Technology

OCT 27 German chemists Robert Wilhelm Bunsen and Gustav Kirchhoff, using a spectroscope, discovered that each element emits a characteristic wavelength of light.

- Solar flares were first observed on the sun by English astronomer Richard Carrington.
- A flight from St. Louis, MO, to Henderson, NY, by balloon set a distance record. Mail was carried aboard the balloon but had to be jettisoned along with other cargo to lighten the load.
- French physicist Gaston Planté invented the first lead acid storage battery that could be recharged.
- Belgian inventor Etienne Lenoir built the first internal combustion engine in Paris. Operating on coal gas, it had an efficiency of only 4 percent.

Commerce and New Products

AUG 9 Patent number 25,076 was awarded to Nathan Ames for a revolving staircase—later coined an "escalator" in 1900.

JUNE 7 The Chicago and North Western Railway was chartered.

JULY 12 William Goodale patented a paper bag manufacturing machine.

SEPT 20 The electric stove was patented.

- Charles Diebold founded Diebold, Inc, as a manufacturer of safes and vaults at Cincinnati, OH.
- George Huntington Hartford and George Frances Gilman founded the Great American Tea Company in New York City. It eventually became the Great Atlantic and Pacific Tea Company, the A&P supermarket chain.

■ Alexander Clavel, a French silk maker and dyer, moved to Switzerland to found a dye works. This was the forerunner of CIBA-Geigy, one of the world's largest chemical companies.

■ Rumford Baking Powder was introduced, the first calcium phosphate baking powder.

Sports

Baseball

July 1 First intercollegiate baseball game was played, with Amherst defeating Williams.

■ Government employees formed two baseball teams: the Potomacs and the National Base Ball Club (or "Nationals").

Miscellaneous

July 1 Lacrosse was chosen as Canada's national sport by the Canadian Parliament.

■ The world's first polo club was founded by British officers in India.

■ The Washington Nationals baseball team was founded.

1859 Deaths

■ Karl Baedeker, German guidebook publisher

■ Isambard Kingdom Brunel, English engineer and builder of tunnels, bridges and railways

■ Thomas de Quincey, English author of *Confessions of an English Opium-Eater*

■ Wilhelm Grimm, the younger of the Brothers Grimm

■ Leigh Hunt, English essayist and poet

■ Washington Irving, great American man of letters and diplomat

■ Thomas Babington Macaulay, English essayist and historian

■ Horace Mann, father of American public education

■ Alexis de Tocqueville, French politician and author

■ Alexander von Humboldt, Prussian naturalist and explorer

■ Prince von Metternich, Austrian diplomat

1909

100 YEARS AGO

Landmark World Events

Jan 16 After a perilous journey, suffering snow blindness and severe malnutrition, Australia's great Antarctic explorer, Sir Douglas Mawson, along with T.W. Edgeworth David and Alistair Mackay, raised the Union Jack at the south magnetic pole.

Jan 28 A republican government headed by President José Miguel Gómez took over in Cuba, which had been under US military control.

Apr 6 American polar explorer Robert Edwin Peary and his expedition team, which included African-American Matthew A. Henson and four Eskimo guides, reached the North Pole—the first ever to do so.

Apr 13 Accused of committing massacres of the Armenians in Adana, squandering the wealth of the Ottoman Empire, and burning holy books, Sultan Abdul Hamid II was deposed and replaced with his brother, Mehmed V Hamid.

July 25 The world's first international overseas airplane flight was made from France to England, across the English Channel, by French aviation pioneer Louis Blériot; the flight, in a Type XI Monoplane, took 37 minutes.

Aug 2 The 1909 Wright Flyer was formally accepted and designated Signal Corps Airplane No 1, becoming the world's first military airplane. The US Army bought the plane for $30,000.

Oct 26 A Korean nationalist assassinated Hirobumi Ito, considered the most important Japanese public figure in the late 19th century and the man most responsible for the modernization of Japan. The assassin was protesting the Japanese attempt to control Korea; the assassination gave the Japanese a convenient pretext for the outright annexation of the Korean peninsula.

■ The Nobel Peace Prize was awarded to Auguste Marie François Beernaert (Belgium) and Paul Henri Benjamin Balluet d'Estournelles de Constant (France).

■ Nicaraguan dictator José Santos Zelaya, a disruptive force in Central America and opposed to US influence in the area, resigned after US military intervention.

Landmark US Events

Jan 28 US troops left Cuba for the first time since the beginning of the Spanish-American War.

Feb 12 The National Association for the Advancement of Colored People was founded by W.E.B. DuBois, Ida Wells-Barnett and others to fight racial oppression and challenge segregation. See "Spotlight on American Anniversaries."

Mar 4 William Howard Taft was inaugurated as the 27th president. In his inaugural speech, he said, "The Panama Canal will have a most important bearing upon the trade between the eastern and far western sections of our country, and will greatly increase the facilities for transportation between the eastern and the western seaboard, and may possibly revolutionize the transcontinental rates with respect to bulky merchandise."

Mar 31 Former President Theodore Roosevelt and his son Kermit left for a safari in Africa sponsored by the Smithsonian Institute and the National Geographic Society.

Apr 9 Congress enacted the Republican-sponsored Payne-Aldrich Tariff Act, a bill intended to lower certain tariffs on goods entering the United States but which ended up lowering some, raising others, and leaving some unchanged; it was met by the public, particularly the Progressives, with anger and disappointment.

Nov 13 The Cherry Mine fire in Cherry, IL, killed 259 men and boys—many of them immigrants—in the worst coal mine disaster in US history. One group of miners spent eight days 500 feet underground before digging through to incoming rescuers. The disaster brought about better fire and safety regulations for American mines.

■ Butch Cassidy (born Robert LeRoy Parker) and the Sundance Kid (born Harry Longabaugh), notorious outlaws of the Old West and members of the Wild Bunch Gang, apparently died in a gun battle with Bolivian soldiers at the Concordia Tin Mines in Bolivia. Cassidy and Sundance had moved to South America to prey on the mines there.

■ The US Supreme Court held its first criminal lynching trial and found law enforcement officials (a sheriff and two deputies) responsible for a lynching (Ed Johnson's 1906 lynching at Chattanooga, TN). The sheriff and two deputies were sentenced to 60 days in jail.

Culture

■ The Nobel Prize in Literature was awarded to Selma Lagerlöf (Sweden).

Publications

Fiction

■ "The Machine Stops," E.M. Forster's chilling short story masterpiece about the role of technology

■ *Balthazar*, Anatole France

■ *Martin Eden*, Jack London

■ *Three Lives*, Gertrude Stein

■ *Tono-Bungay*, H.G. Wells

Nonfiction

■ *A Pluralistic Universe*, William James

■ *Italian Hours*, Henry James

Poetry

■ *Ballads of a Cheechako*, Robert Service

■ *Personae and Exultations*, Ezra Pound

Children's Literature

■ *The Road to Oz*, L. Frank Baum

■ *The Secret Garden*, Frances Hodgson Burnett

Theater

- *Strife*, John Galsworthy

Opera

May 5 *Bacchus*, an opera in four acts by Jules Massenet, was first performed at the Paris Opéra in Paris, France.

Oct 7 *The Golden Cockerel*, an opera in three acts by Rimsky-Korsakov, premiered in Moscow. Written in 1907, the opera premiered after the 1908 death of the composer.

- *Elektra*, a one-act opera by Richard Strauss, was first performed at the Dresden State Opera.

Dance

- Serge Diaghilev founded the Ballets Russes in Paris, which began the era of modern ballet. Mikhail Fokine, Anna Pavlova and Nijinsky were members of this troupe.

Film

- D.W. Griffith made a number of short films for the Biograph Company in 1909, including *Lady Helen's Escapade*, *A Corner in Wheat*, *At the Altar*, *Resurrection* and *The Country Doctor*, starring Mary Pickford.
- Matsunosuke Onoe, the first superstar of Japanese cinema, made his film debut in *Goban Tadanobu* ("Tadanobu the Fox"), based on a Kabuki play.
- The first newsreel, the *Pathé Gazette*, was shown in a Paris theater. Charles Pathé was the producer.
- *Les Miserables*, produced by Charles Pathé
- The *New York Times* published the first movie review, a report on D.W. Griffith's *Pippa Passes*.

Radio

Jan 2 The first amateur radio club, The Junior Wireless Club, Limited, of New York City, was organized.

Mar 18 Einar Dessau of Denmark used a shortwave radio transmitter, becoming the first ham radio broadcaster, speaking to a government post six miles away.

- The word *broadcast* appeared in the *Boston Globe* in an article called "Experiment with Wireless," which referred to how information about a ship that was sinking was "sent broadcast" by wireless telegraphers.
- Charles David Herrold began a 24-hour broadcast of music and news from the Herrold's College of Wireless and Engineering in San Jose, CA, using a 15-watt spark transmitter. Herrold has been called "the father of broadcasting."

Music

- *Piano Concerto No 3* and *The Isle of the Dead*, Sergei Rachmaninoff
- The first edition of the *Little Red Songbook* was published in 1909. It included early labor songs, such as "The Red Flag" and "The Internationale," written by Joe Hill, Ralph Chaplin, T-Bone Slim and other early 20th-century labor activists.

Popular Songs

- "Ace in the Hole," George D. Mitchell and James E. Dempsey
- "By the Light of the Silvery Moon," Edward Madden and Gus Edwards
- "I Wonder Who's Kissing Her Now," Will M. Hough, Frank R. Adams, Joseph E. Howard and Harold Orlob
- "On Wisconsin," Carl Beck and W.T. Purdy
- "Put on Your Old Grey Bonnet," Stanley Murphy and Percy Wenrich
- "The Whiffenpoof Song," Meade Minnigerode, George S. Pomeroy and Tod B. Galloway

Art

- The Cubists were active at this time.
- *Woman's Head, Landscape with Bridge*, Pablo Picasso
- *Landscape with Steeple*, Wassily Kandinsky
- *Dance (I)*, Henri Matisse

Photography

- Photographer Lewis Wickes Hine began his exposure of child labor practices with *Child Labor in the Carolinas* and *Day Laborers Before Their Time.*

Architecture

- American architect and pioneering city planner Daniel Hudson Burnham, an advocate of tall fireproof skyscrapers, proposed the Plan of Chicago, also known as the Burnham Plan, a long-range plan for Chicago that resulted in its beautiful lakefront, which balanced urban growth with preservation of green spaces.
- The Robie House, a masterpiece of the Prairie style, designed by Frank Lloyd Wright, was constructed in Chicago.

Science and Technology

- The Nobel Prize in Physics was awarded to Guglielmo Marconi (Italy) and Karl Ferdinand Braun (Germany) in recognition of their contributions to the development of wireless telegraphy.
- The Nobel Prize in Chemistry went to Wilhelm Ostwald (Germany) in recognition of his work on catalysis and for his investigations into the fundamental principles governing chemical equilibria and rates of reaction.
- The Nobel Prize in Physiology or Medicine went to Emil Theodor Kocher (Switzerland) for his work on the physiology, pathology and surgery of the thyroid gland.

Aug German bacteriologist Paul Ehrlich discovered the arsenic-based drug salvarsan, which was used to treat syphilis. It quickly became the most widely prescribed drug in the world, the first blockbuster drug, and remained the most effective drug for syphilis until penicillin became available in the 1940s.

Oct After an earthquake in central Europe, geophysicist Andrija Mohorovicic discovered the zone between the Earth's crust and mantle, which is now named after him.

- The Burgess Shale, one of the most diverse and well-preserved fossil localities in the world, was discovered in an area of the Canadian Rocky Mountains known as the Burgess Pass by Charles D. Walcott of the Smithsonian Institution.
- Bausch and Lomb produced the Darkfield microscope.
- Charles Jules Henri Nicolle at the Pasteur Institute in Tunis, Tunisia, discovered that the body louse was the carrier of typhus *Rickettsia*. This discovery led to the development of the typhus vaccine.
- Brazilian inventor and aviation pioneer Alberto Santos-Dumont produced the *Demoiselle* (Grasshopper) in 1909, which was the forerunner of modern light planes.
- The "true-snouted reptile" Eurhinosaurus, a type of ichthyosaur, was discovered.

Commerce and New Products

Feb 24 The Hudson Motor Car Company was founded. Its first production was the Model 20, which rolled off the line July 3, 1909. The Model 20 cost $900.

Dec 7 Leo Hendrik Baekeland patented the first true plastic and transformed the world: Bakelite was introduced to the general public at a chemical conference. Baekeland has been called "the father of the plastic industry."

- Magazine publishers James Herbert McGraw and John Alexander Hill founded the McGraw-Hill Book Company.
- Future star fashion designer Coco Chanel opened a millinery shop in Paris, France.
- Eugène Schuller, French chemist, founded the Société Française de Teintures Inoffensives pour Cheveux (Harmless Hair Dye Company), later renamed L'Oréal after the hair dye he invented, *Auréole.*
- "Red E Coffee," the first mass-produced instant coffee, was first marketed.
- German hairdresser Karl Nessler patented the permanent wave process.

Sports

Auto Racing

- The Indianapolis Motor Speedway opened in 1909 as a 2.5-mile oval track, after investment and leadership by founders Carl G. Fisher, James A. Allison, Arthur C. Newby and Frank H. Wheeler. The first competitive event to take place at the facility was a gas-filled balloon race June 5, 1909. The first land-based vehicle race was a motorcycle event Aug 14, 1909. The first automobile race at the Speedway took place Aug 19, 1909. The crushed rock surface proved hazardous, and it was paved over with 3.2 million bricks by 1910.

Bicycle Racing

- The Six Days of Berlin bicycle race was inaugurated this year.

Baseball

July 19 Cleveland Blues shortstop Neal Ball recorded the first unassisted triple play in American League history in a game against the Boston Pilgrims.

Oct 8–16 The Pittsburg Pirates defeated the Detroit Tigers in the first seven-game World Series. The matchup between the two greatest ballplayers in the world, Pittsburgh's Honus Wagner and Detroit's Ty Cobb, was highly anticipated, but the star of the series would be neither of them, but a reserve pitcher named Babe Adams (three wins).

- Jim Curry, the youngest player in American League history, made his major-league debut for the Philadelphia Athletics at 16 years of age.
- The first two modern steel-and-concrete ballparks, Shibe Park in Philadelphia and Forbes Field in Pittsburgh, opened their doors.

Basketball

- Glass backboards were developed in 1909 so that fans seated behind a goal could see the action but couldn't help direct a ball into the basket or deflect a ball away for the opposition.

Football

- Yale was the 1909 NCAA football champion team.

Golf

- George Sargent shot a 290 at the 15th US Golf Open at the Englewood Golf Course in New Jersey.
- J.H. Taylor won the British Open.

Hockey

Dec 4 The Montreal Canadiens Hockey Club was founded by Ottawa businessman J. Ambrose O'Brien, with the help of Jack Laviolette, as Le Club de Hockey Canadien.

- The Ottawa Senators won the Stanley Cup as champions of the Eastern Canada Amateur Hockey Association.

Horse Racing

- Wintergreen, ridden by Vincent Powers, was the champion of the 35th Kentucky Derby in 2:08.2.
- Effendi, ridden by Willie Doyle, won the 34th Preakness Stakes in 1:39.8.
- Joe Madden, ridden by Eddie Dugan, won the 43rd Belmont Stakes in 2:21.6.

Running

- "Marathon fever" swept the athletic world in 1909—amateur and professional alike, especially in the United States. This resulted in five successive improvements to the world amateur record within eight months. Robert Fowler ran the world record marathon (2:46:52.6), followed in May by Albert Raines (2:46:04.6) and Frederick Barrett (2:42:31).
- The 13th Boston Marathon was won by Henri Renaud of New Hampshire in 2:53:36.8.

Soccer

Apr 24 Manchester United won its first FA Cup, defeating Bristol City 1–0.

Tennis

- At Wimbledon, Dora Boothby and Arthur Gore were the winners.
- Hazel Hotchkiss Wightman, known as the "Queen Mother of American Tennis," beat Maud Barger-Wallach at the 23rd US Women's Tennis championship. Wightman also won the women's doubles and mixed doubles titles that year.
- At the 29th US Men's Tennis championships, William A. Larned beat William J. Clothier.

Miscellaneous

- Warren Remedy, a smooth fox terrier, was awarded Best in Show for the third consecutive year, a feat never since duplicated at the Westminster Kennel Club Dog Show.

1909 Deaths

- Butch Cassidy, American outlaw
- John Gibson Clarkson, Baseball Hall of Fame pitcher who won 326 games in a 12-year career
- Geronimo, Apache leader
- Cesare Lombrose, first scientific criminologist
- Herman C. ("Germany") Long, baseball player, rated one of the best shortstops of the 19th century
- Simon Newcomb, Canadian astronomer who investigated the planetary orbits and devised planetary tables that were used universally by observatories
- Red Cloud, Sioux chief, courageous leader and defender of Indian rights whose unrelenting determination caused the US abandonment of the Bozeman trail and three forts that interfered with Indian hunting grounds
- Frederic S. Remington, noted artist of the American West
- The Sundance Kid, American outlaw
- Algernon Charles Swinburne, British poet
- John Millington Synge, Irish dramatist and poet, author of *The Playboy of the Western World*

1934

75 YEARS AGO

Landmark World Events

Jan 15 The Bihar-Nepal earthquake was one of the worst in India's history, killing 30,000 people and damaging much of Kathmandu and parts of Darjeeling. The earthquake had a magnitude of 8.4.

Feb 21 Cesar Augusto Sandino, the Nicaraguan guerilla leader after whom the Sandinistas were named, was murdered, along with his brother and several aides at Managua. "The Worthy Saint" was revered as a martyred patriot by many Nicaraguans and widespread anti-US feeling resulted in the Latin American "Good Neighbor Policy."

Mar 1 Changing the name of Manchuria to Manchukuo, Japan created a puppet state there. Manchukuo was proclaimed a monarchy, with Pu Yi, the last emperor of China, assuming the throne under the reign name of Emperor Kang-de.

Apr 12 The highest-velocity wind ever recorded on the Earth's surface reached a speed of 231 miles per hour at the Mount Washington, NH, Observatory.

May 28 Near Callander, ON, Canada, the Dionne quintuplets—Marie, Cécille, Yvonne, Emilie and Annette—were born to Oliva and Elzire Dionne, becoming the first quintuplets to survive infancy.

June 29 The Night of Long Knives, on which German chancellor Adolph Hitler ordered the execution of 77 people, including storm trooper (SA) leader Ernst Röhm, General Von Schleicher and his wife, Gregor Strasser—one of the original members of the Nazi Party and formerly next in importance to Hitler—and Erich Klausenere, a prominent Catholic.

July 25 Austrian Nazis attempted a coup in Austria, taking over the Chancellery in Vienna and killing Austrian chancellor Engelbert Dolfuss. The Austrian army rapidly put down the insurrection.

Sep 17 The USSR was admitted to the League of Nations.

Oct 9 King Alexander I of Yugoslavia was killed in France by a Croatian assassin.

Oct 15 Continued victories by the Kuomintang army under Chiang Kai-Shek compelled the forces under Mao Zedong's control to retreat in order to regroup. They undertook "The Long March," which covered 6,000 miles and ended in Yenan. One hundred thousand set off on the march, but only one-third survived, arriving at Yenan in October 1935.

Oct 24 Mohandas Gandhi formally resigned from politics in India, being replaced as leader of the Congress Party by Jawaharlal Nehru.

Dec 1 Sergei Kirov, a close associate of Joseph Stalin, was assassinated—most certainly at Stalin's instigation, which prompted another great purge of state "enemies." This murder helped consolidate Stalin's power in the USSR. By 1935, close to 3 million people had been executed or sent to labor camps.

■ The Nobel Peace Prize was awarded to Arthur Henderson (UK), president of the 1932 Disarmament Conference.

Landmark US Events

May 11 A strong two-day dust storm removed massive amounts of topsoil in one of the worst dust storms of the Dust Bowl: 100 million acres in Texas, Oklahoma, New Mexico, Colorado and Kansas. Throughout the 1930s, dust storms ravaged the Great Plains; the agricultural and ecological damage was caused by severe drought, decades of extensive farming without crop rotation or other techniques that prevented erosion and the expansion of agriculture.

May 18 As a result of the kidnapping and murder, two years earlier, of the son of Charles A. and Anne Morrow Lindbergh, the Crime Control Act was passed, authorizing the death penalty for kidnappers who take their victims across state lines.

May 23 The two-year crime spree of Clyde Barrow and Bonnie Parker, bank robbers accused of 12 murders, ended when a law enforcement posse, headed by Frank Hamer, ambushed the couple in Gibsland, LA.

June 6 The Securities and Exchange Commission (SEC) was established.

June 15 The Great Smoky Mountains National Park was established.

June 19 Congress created the Federal Communications Commission (FCC). Its mission was to oversee communication by radio, wire and cable.

June 26 The Federal Credit Union Act was signed, enabling the formation of credit unions anywhere in the United States.

July 11 As part of the first presidential visit to South America, Franklin Delano Roosevelt became the first US president to travel through the Panama Canal.

July 22 John Dillinger was shot and killed in Chicago, IL.

Sep 5 Aviator Wiley Hardeman Post, wearing the world's first pressure suit, reached an altitude of 40,000 feet above Chicago. Eventually flying as high as 50,000 feet, Post discovered the jet stream and made the first major practical advances in pressurized flight.

■ At the height of the Great Depression in 1934, one out of every four Americans was unemployed. Through Franklin Delano Roosevelt's New Deal programs, the federal government committed to providing a social safety net to aid those hardest hit.

Public Enemy Number 1

Bank robber, murderer, escaped prisoner and "Public Enemy Number 1," John Dillinger was shot by Federal Bureau of Investigation officers outside the Biograph Theater in Chicago, IL. A cocky Dillinger, who had recently undergone plastic surgery to disguise his features, felt invulnerable enough to catch a movie, *Manhattan Melodrama* starring Clark Gable and Myrna Loy, with his girlfriend Polly Hamilton and her friend Anna Sage. The Biograph featured air-conditioning—perfect for a sweltering July night. Anna Sage, underworld moll, had already tipped the FBI that night. Wearing orange (afterward the press incorrectly dubbed her "the Lady in Red"), she caught the eye of G-man Melvin Purvis, who coordinated with other officers to corner and kill Dillinger. The media exposure was explosive, and the newly formed FBI basked in the attention.

- Franklin Delano Roosevelt was *Time* magazine's Man of the Year for 1934 (announced in January 1935).

Culture

- The Nobel Prize in Literature was awarded to Luigi Pirandello (Italy).

Publications

Fiction

- Boris Pasternak and Korney Chukovsky were among those present at the first Congress of the Soviet Union of Writers.
- The first Nero Wolfe book, *Fer-de-Lance* by Rex Stout, was published.
- *A Handful of Dust*, Evelyn Waugh
- *Claudius the God*, Robert Graves
- *Call It Sleep*, Henry Roth
- *Goodbye, Mr. Chips*, James Hilton
- *Jonah's Gourd Vine*, Zora Neale Hurston
- *Lust for Life*, Irving Stone
- *Murder on the Orient Express*, Agatha Christie
- *Seven Gothic Tales*, Isak Dinesen
- *Tender Is the Night*, F. Scott Fitzgerald
- *The Chinese Orange Mystery*, Ellery Queen
- *The Thin Man*, Dashiell Hammett
- *The Postman Always Rings Twice*, James M. Cain
- *Tropic of Cancer*, Henry Miller

Nonfiction

- *An Experiment in Autobiography*, H.G. Wells
- *The Army of the Future*, Charles de Gaulle

Poetry

Dec 18 Dylan Thomas published *Eighteen Poems*, including "The Force That Through the Green Fuse Drives the Flower."

- The Pulitzer Prize for Poetry went to Robert Hillyer for *Collected Verse*.
- Rudyard Kipling and William Butler Yeats were awarded the Gothenburg Prize for Poetry.

Children's Literature

- *Invincible Louisa: The Story of the Author of Little Women* by Cornelia Meigs, winner of the Newbery Medal
- *Mary Poppins*, P.L. Travers

Journalism, Comics

Jan 7 The comic strip *Flash Gordon* first appeared, created by Alex Raymond.

Aug 13 *Lil' Abner* appeared for the first time, created by Al Capp.

Oct 22 Milton Caniff's *Terry and the Pirates* made its debut.

- Associated Press started the wirephoto service.

Theater

- The Pulitzer Prize for Drama went to *Men in White*, by Sidney Kingsley.
- The Apollo Theater first opened to black customers in Harlem, NY.

- *The Children's Hour*, Lillian Hellman
- *Yerma*, Federico García Lorca
- Musical theater was very popular in 1934 and included the Broadway production *Anything Goes*, which opened at the Alvin Theatre on Nov 21 and ran for 420 performances. The *Ziegfeld Follies of 1934* Broadway revue opened at the Winter Garden Theatre on Jan 4 and ran for 182 performances.

Opera

Jan 22 Dmitry Shostakovich's opera *Lady MacBeth* premiered in Leningrad.

Dance

Jan 2 The School of American Ballet opened with George Balanchine as its director.

Film

- *It Happened One Night* swept the Academy Awards, becoming the first film to win all five major awards: Best Picture, Best Screenplay, Best Director for Frank Capra, Best Actor for Clark Gable and Best Actress for Claudette Colbert. (A scene featuring a carrot-chomping Clark Gable provided a visual inspiration for the animated Bugs Bunny some years later.)

June 9 Donald Duck made his film debut in the *Silly Symphonies* cartoon "The Wise Little Hen."

- The first drive-in movie theater opened in New Jersey.
- *Babes in Toyland*, starring Laurel and Hardy
- *Bright Eyes*, starring Shirley Temple singing "The Good Ship Lollipop"
- *The Barretts of Wimpole Street*, starring Norma Shearer, Fredric March and Charles Laughton
- *The Black Cat*, starring Boris Karloff and Bela Lugosi
- *The Count of Monte Cristo*, starring Robert Donat
- *The Gay Divorcee*, starring Fred Astaire and Ginger Rogers
- *The Man Who Knew Too Much*, directed by Alfred Hitchcock, starring Leslie Banks and Peter Lorre (making his English-language film debut after leaving Germany)
- *Manhattan Melodrama*, starring Clark Gable, William Powell and Myrna Loy
- *The Merry Widow*, starring Maurice Chevalier and Jeanette MacDonald
- *Of Human Bondage*, starring Leslie Howard and Bette Davis
- *Spitfire*, starring Katharine Hepburn
- *Here Comes the Navy*, starring James Cagney
- *Tarzan and His Mate*, starring Johnny Weissmuller and Maureen O'Sullivan

- *The Thin Man*, starring William Powell and Myrna Loy
- *Treasure Island*, starring Wallace Beery and Jackie Cooper

Radio

- In 1934, approximately half of the homes in the United States had radios.

Apr "Major Bowes Amateur Hour" debuted on the New York City station WHN.

June 19 The Federal Communications Commission was created, replacing the Federal Radio Commission.

Oct 14 "Lux Radio Theater" debuted on NBC's Blue network.

Dec 1 Jazz clarinet pioneer Benny Goodman debuted as a regular on the radio variety show "Let's Dance."

Dec 24 Actor Lionel Barrymore began the annual tradition (1934–1951) of playing Ebenezer Scrooge in dramatizations of Charles Dickens's *A Christmas Carol*.

Television

July 11 The Communications Act of 1934 stipulated that commercial television stations "operate in the public interest, convenience, and necessity." The Federal Communications Commission (FCC) was charged with the responsibility of enforcing the act.

Aug 25 Philo Farnsworth gave the world's first public demonstration of an all-electronic television system at the Franklin Institute in Philadelphia.

Nov 5 First television broadcasts in the USSR.

Music

Nov 7 Sergei Rachmaninoff's *Rhapsody on a Theme of Paganini* premiered.

Nov 21 As a shy, impoverished teenager, Ella Fitzgerald made her stage debut and won the Apollo Amateur Night in Harlem, New York City.

- Django Reinhardt and Stéphane Grappelli formed the groundbreaking jazz group Quintette du Hot Club in France.
- RCA Victor released the first 33⅓ rpm recording, Beethoven's Fifth Symphony.

Popular Songs

- "Autumn in New York," Vernon Duke
- "Beer Barrel Polka," Vasek Zeman and Jaromir Vejvoda (English lyrics by Lew Brown)
- "Blue Moon," Lorenz Hart and Richard Rodgers

- "Cocktails for Two," Duke Ellington
- "I Get a Kick out of You," Cole Porter
- "I Only Have Eyes for You," Al Dubin and Harry Warren
- "Moonglow," Eddie DeLange, Will Hudson and Irving Mills
- "Santa Claus Is Coming to Town," Haven Gillespie and J. Fred Coots
- "Stars Fell on Alabama," Mitchell Parish and Frank Perkins
- "Tumbling Tumbleweeds," Bob Nolan
- "The Very Thought of You," Ray Noble
- "Winter Wonderland," Richard B. Smith and Felix Bernard
- "You Oughta Be in Pictures," Edward Heyman and Dana Suesse
- "You're the Top," Cole Porter
- "Zing! Went the Strings of My Heart," James F. Hanley

Art

- *Nude in the Garden*, *Bullfight* and *Femme au Chapeau Rouge*, Pablo Picasso
- *Cape Cod Sunset* and *Jenness House Looking North*, Edward Hopper
- *Interior with Dog*, Henri Matisse
- Aaron Douglas painted four panels in the *Aspects of Negro Life* series for the New York Public Library.

Architecture

- Albert Speer, appointed this year as Nazi architect, designed a new setting for the party's annual Nuremberg rally.
- Openly hostile to the Nazis, architect Walter Gropius (founder of Bauhaus) moved to England.

Science and Technology

Sept 9 "Rocket No 4" broke the sound barrier at Staten Island, NY.

- No Nobel Prize in Physics was awarded in 1934.
- The Nobel Prize in Chemistry went to Harold Clayton Urey (US), for his discovery of heavy hydrogen.
- The Nobel Prize in Physiology or Medicine went to George Hoyt Whipple, George Richards Minot and William Parry Murphy (US), for their discoveries concerning liver therapy in cases of anemia.
- Italian physicist Enrico Fermi worked on the creation of new elements through the bombardment of uranium with neutrons.
- French husband-and-wife scientist team Irene and Frederic Joliot-Curie created the first man-made radioactive substance.
- Pavel A. Cherenkov of Russia discovered that electrons emit light (Cherenkov radiation).

Commerce and New Products

JAN 20 Fujifilm was founded in Japan.

JAN Ferdinand Porsche shared his preliminary designs for the Volkswagen ("people's car") with Adolf Hitler.

APR 18 The first "washateria" opened in Fort Worth, TX.

SEPT 26 The luxurious British ocean liner *Queen Mary* was launched.

■ Wheaties cereal introduced a fictional character on the cereal box, Jack Armstrong, All-American Boy. Later in 1934 Lou Gehrig of the New York Yankees became the first real-life sports hero to grace a Wheaties box. Other heroes that year were Jimmie Foxx, aviator Elinor Smith and tennis star Ellsworth Vines.

■ Ole Kirk Christiansen and his son adopted the company name Lego (meaning "to play well" in Danish) for their carpentry business, whose products included wooden toys.

Sports

Auto Racing

MAY 30 Winner "Wild" Bill Cummings won the Indianapolis 500 in his fifth start.

■ From 1927 to 1934, the number of races considered to have Grand Prix status exploded, jumping from 5 events in 1927 to 18 in 1934—the peak year before World War II.

Baseball

■ The St. Louis Cardinals beat the Detroit Tigers to win the World Series (4–3). Cardinal pitcher Dizzy Dean won two games and lost one. His brother Paul had the other two wins for the Cardinals.

■ In July, Babe Ruth hit the 700th home run of his career against Tommy Bridges of the Detroit Tigers. In September, he played his last game with the New York Yankees at Yankee Stadium, after 15 seasons.

■ The New York Yankees paid the San Francisco Seals $25,000 and four players for Joe DiMaggio.

■ Mildred ("Babe") Didrikson, perhaps the greatest woman athlete of all time, pitched one inning of baseball for the Philadelphia Athletics in an exhibition game against the Brooklyn Dodgers.

■ In baseball's second All-Star Game, National League pitcher Carl Hubbell of the New York Giants struck out Babe Ruth, Lou Gehrig, Jimmie Foxx, Al Simmons and Joe Cronin in succession.

Boxing

JUNE 14 Max Baer knocked out Primo Carnera in the 11th round of a fight at Long Island City, NY, to win the heavyweight title.

■ Winning his first professional fight, Joe Louis burst onto the professional boxing scene.

Football

JAN 1 In college football, Columbia beat Stanford in the Rose Bowl, and Duquesne defeated Miami in the Orange Bowl.

■ The Minnesota Golden Gophers were the National Collegiate Athletic Association football champions.

■ The first College All-Star Game football contest, matching the defending National Football League champion against a team of college seniors from the previous season, was played at Chicago's Soldier Field.

■ After four years in the National Football League, the Portsmouth Spartans were sold to G.A. Richards, who moved the team to Detroit and changed its nickname to the Lions.

■ In November, the Detroit Lions played their first Thanksgiving Day game, the start of a National Football League tradition, and lost to the Chicago Bears.

■ The New York Giants defeated the Chicago Bears to win the National Football League championship in a game that became known as the "Sneakers Game": with the field at the Polo Grounds covered by ice and the temperature at nine degrees Fahrenheit, the Giants donned sneakers in the second half to gain better traction.

Golf

■ Olin Dutra won the US Open at the Merion Cricket Club in Ardmore, PA.

■ Paul Runyan won the PGA Championship at the Park Country Club in Williamsville, NY.

■ Henry Cotton won the British Open at Royal St. Georges, England.

■ Horton Smith shot four-under-par 284 to win the first Augusta National tournament by one stroke over Craig Wood. The Augusta championship was called The Masters starting in 1939.

Hockey

Apr 3–10 The Chicago Blackhawks defeated the Detroit Red Wings for the Stanley Cup.

Horse Racing

■ Cavalcade, ridden by Mark Garner, was the champion of the 60th Kentucky Derby in 2:04.

■ High Quest, ridden by Robert Jones, won the 60th Preakness Stakes in 1:58.2.

■ Peace Chance, ridden by Wayne D. Wright, won the 66th Belmont Stakes in 2:29.2.

Dec 25 Santa Anita Park opened in Arcadia, CA. It was designed by Gordon Kaufmann, who also designed Hoover Dam.

Marathon

■ The 38th Boston Marathon was won by Dave Komonen of Canada in 2:32:53.8.

Soccer

Apr 28 Manchester City took the FA Cup over Portsmouth.

June 10 Italy defeated Czechoslovakia by 2–1 to win the second FIFA World Cup.

Nov 14 England defeated world champion Italy 3–2 in the "Battle of Highbury," a violent exhibition match, at Arsenal Stadium, Highbury, London. Three players suffered broken bones in the match.

Tennis

■ At Wimbledon, Dorothy Round defeated Helen Jacobs, Fred Perry defeated Jack Crawford and Elizabeth Ryan won her 12th Wimbledon doubles championship.

■ At the US Women's Tennis championships, Helen Jacobs beat Sarah Palfrey Cooke.

■ At the US Men's Tennis championships, Fred Perry beat Wilmer Allison.

Miscellaneous

■ Flornell Spicy Bit of Halleston, fox terrier (wire), was awarded Best in Show at the Westminster Kennel Club Dog Show.

1934 Deaths

■ Clyde Barrow and Bonnie Parker, infamous American outlaws

■ Marie Sklodowska Curie, Polish-born scientist and recipient of the Nobel Prize for Physics, of leukemia induced by radiation poisoning

■ John Dillinger, Public Enemy Number 1

■ Frank Nelson Doubleday, American publisher

■ Edward Elgar, English composer

■ Fielder Allison Jones, baseball player and manager

■ Alice Liddell, who, as an English schoolgirl, was the inspiration for *Alice's Adventures in Wonderland*

■ John Joseph McGraw, Baseball Hall of Fame third baseman and manager

■ Wilbert Robinson, Baseball Hall of Fame catcher and manager

■ Thorne Smith Jr, author of humorous supernatural fantasy novels

1959

50 YEARS AGO

Landmark World Events

JAN 1 Fidel Castro took over Cuba after his revolutionary army defeated the forces of Fulgencio Batista upon his flight from Havana. See "Spotlight on World Anniversaries."

JAN 2 The USSR launched *Luna I* into orbit. It was the first man-made object to escape the earth's gravitational area.

JAN 3 President Dwight Eisenhower signed a proclamation admitting Alaska to the Union as the 49th state.

JAN 4 Troops led by Che Guevara and Camilo Cienfuegos entered Havana, Cuba.

JAN 8 Charles de Gaulle was inaugurated as president of France's Fifth Republic.

JAN 13 Cuban communists executed 71 Batista supporters.

JAN 25 Pope John XXIII convened the Second Vatican Council.

FEB 1 The Swiss government rejected a bid for female suffrage.

FEB 19 The United Kingdom granted the island of Cyprus its independence.

MAR 10 Lhasa was the site of a Tibetan uprising against China.

MAR 17 The Dalai Lama fled Chinese suppression in Tibet, disappearing into the mountains.

MAR 31 The Dalai Lama arrived in India after being granted political asylum there.

APR 10 Japan's Prince Akihito married Shoda Michiko, a commoner.

APR 15 Fidel Castro, newly minted as the premier of Cuba, began a goodwill tour of America.

APR 25 The St. Lawrence Seaway was opened to ship traffic between the Great Lakes and the Atlantic Ocean.

JUNE 3 Singapore became a self-governing crown colony of Great Britain.

JUNE 14 A failed coup orchestrated by Castro-backed rebels was launched in the Dominican Republic.

JUNE 26 President Eisenhower and Queen Elizabeth II dedicated the St. Lawrence Seaway in official ceremonies held at Lambert, QC, Canada.

AUG 1 Martial law was declared in Laos.

AUG 24 Cyprus joined the United Nations.

SEPT 26 Typhoon Vera hit the southern coast of Japan. Over 5,000 people were killed in the disaster, which caused nearly $300 million in damage.

SEPT 15 Soviet leader Nikita Krushchev arrived in the US for a 13-day visit.

OCT 27 A hurricane in the Pacific killed almost 2,000 people in Mexico.

OCT 31 The USSR and Egypt agreed to begin building the Aswan High Dam (completed in 1970).

OCT 31 Lee Harvey Oswald announced in Moscow that he would never return to the US.

DEC 1 Twelve nations, including the US and the USSR, signed the Antarctic Treaty, promoting scientific research on the continent and barring any military activity.

DEC 22 The United Nations Committee on the Peaceful Use of Outer Space was established.

■ The Nobel Peace Prize went to Philip J. Noel-Baker.

Landmark US Events

JAN 7 The US recognized the government of Fidel Castro.

JAN 25 American Airlines opened the jet age in the US with the first scheduled transcontinental flight from Los Angeles to New York on a Boeing 707.

FEB 3 An American Airlines Electra crashed in New York's East River on approach to LaGuardia Airport; 65 passengers and crew members perished.

FEB 3 Musicians Buddy Holly, Richie Valens and J.P. "The Big Bopper" Richardson died in a plane crash near Mason City, IA (an event eulogized later by Don McLean in his song "American Pie," which called it "the day the music died").

JUNE 3 The Air Force Academy in Colorado Springs, CO, graduated its first class.

JUNE 8 The submarine *USS Barbero* and the post office attempted delivery of mail via a Regales cruise missile.

JUNE 9 The *USS George Washington* was launched as the first submarine capable of launching ballistic missiles.

JUNE 25 Infamous Midwestern killer Charles Starkweather was executed at Nebraska State Penitentiary.

JULY 8 The first Americans were killed in action in Vietnam: Dale R. Buis and Charles Ovnand.

JULY 13 *Time* magazine labeled stand-up performer Lenny Bruce a "sick comic."

JULY 23 Vice President Richard Nixon visited the USSR.

AUG 7 The explosion of a dynamite truck in the mining compound caused the Roseburg Oregon Blast, destroying millions of dollars of property and killing 14.

AUG 21 President Eisenhower signed legislation admitting Hawaii to the Union.

AUG 24 Hiram L. Fong and Daniel Inouye were sworn in as the first senator and state representative from Hawaii. Fong, a Chinese-American, and Inouye, a Japanese-American, represented the first Asian-Americans in Congress.

SEPT 11 Congress passed a bill authorizing food stamps for low-income Americans.

SEPT 19 During his visit to the US, Soviet premier Nikita Krushchev was denied access to Disneyland.

NOV 14 Kilauea erupted in Hawaii.

Culture

- The Nobel Prize for Literature went to Italian poet Salvatore Quasimodo.

Publications

Fiction

- *Goodbye, Columbus*, Philip Roth
- *The Tin Drum*, Günter Grass
- *Naked Lunch*, William S. Burroughs
- *Hawaii*, James Michener
- *Advise and Consent*, Allen Drury
- *Goldfinger*, Ian Fleming

Nonfiction

- *The Elements of Style*, William Strunk Jr and E.B. White

Children's Literature

- *Eloise in Moscow*, Kay Thompson, illustrations by Hilary Knight

Theater

JUNE 27 *West Side Story* closed on Broadway after 734 performances.

OCT 19 *The Miracle Worker* premiered.

- Notable Broadway debuts included *The Sound of Music*, *Take Me Along*, *Redhead* and *A Raisin in the Sun*.

Film

- Winners of the 32nd Academy Awards included Best Actor: Charlton Heston, *Ben-Hur*; Best Supporting Actor: Hugh Griffith, *Ben-Hur*; Best Actress: Simone Signoret, *Room at the Top*; Best Supporting Actress: Shelley Winters, *The Diary of Anne Frank*; Best Picture: *Ben-Hur*; Best Director: William Wyler, *Ben-Hur*; Best Foreign Language Film: *Black Orpheus* (France); Music (Music Score of a Dramatic or Comedy Picture): Miklos Rozsa, *Ben-Hur*; Best Score: Andre Previn, Ken Darby, *Porgy and Bess*; Best Song: "High Hopes," from *A Hole in the Head*.
- Notable 1959 films included *Sleeping Beauty*, *Ben-Hur*, *The Nun's Story*, *Rio Bravo*, *Auntie Mame*, *The 400 Blows*, *The Diary of Anne Frank*, *Gidget*, *Some Like It Hot*, *North by Northwest*, *Anatomy of a Murder*, *The Shaggy Dog*, *Operation Petticoat*, *Pork Chop Hill* and *Imitation of Life*.

Television

Jan 4 The quiz show "College Bowl" premiered on CBS.

Jan 5 "Bozo the Clown," the famous children's program, premiered.

Jan 9 "Rawhide," the long-running Western, premiered on CBS.

Mar 8 "The Incredible Jewel Robbery" was the last appearance by the Marx Brothers on television.

June 16 George Reeves, popular star of TV's "Superman," died of a gunshot wound to the head—apparently self-inflicted.

June 18 The inaugural telecast from England to the US was transmitted.

Sept 12 "Bonanza" became the first Western to be broadcast in color.

Oct 2 "The Twilight Zone" premiered.

Nov 2 Charles Van Doren admitted during a congressional hearing that "21," the quiz show he hosted, was fixed.

Nov 19 "Rocky and His Friends" premiered. The cartoon starred a talking squirrel named Rocky and a dimwitted moose named Bullwinkle.

Nov 21 Jack Benny and Richard Nixon performed a duet on violin and piano, respectively.

- By 1959, 42,000,000 American homes had a television.

Music

- Winners of the second annual Grammy Awards included Record of the Year: Bobby Darin, "Mack the Knife"; Album of the Year: Frank Sinatra, *Come Dance with Me!*; Song of the Year: Jimmy Driftwood, "The Battle of New Orleans"; Best Vocal Performance, Female: Ella Fitzgerald, *But Not for Me*; Best Vocal Performance, Male: Frank Sinatra, *Come Dance with Me!*; Best Performance by a Dance Band: Duke Ellington, *Anatomy of a Murder*; Best Performance by a "Top 40" Artist: Nat "King" Cole, "Midnight Flyer"; *The Button-Down Mind of Bob Newhart*—first comedy album to hit No 1—also Newhart's debut recording.

Popular Songs

- "Mack the Knife," Bobby Darin
- "La Bamba," Ritchie Valens
- "Lonesome Town," Ricky Nelson
- "Put Your Head on My Shoulder," Paul Anka

- "Beyond the Sea," Bobby Darin
- "What a Difference a Day Makes," Dinah Washington
- "Battle of New Orleans," Johnny Horton
- "(You've Got) Personality," Lloyd Price
- "Crying, Waiting, Hoping," Buddy Holly
- "Dream Lover," Bobby Darin
- "High Hopes," Frank Sinatra
- "I Only Have Eyes for You," The Flamingos
- "Lipstick on Your Collar," Connie Francis
- "Teenager in Love," Dion and the Belmonts
- "The Twist," Hank Ballard
- "Stagger Lee," Lloyd Price
- "What'd I Say," Ray Charles
- "Smoke Gets in Your Eyes," The Platters
- "Venus," Frankie Avalon
- "Peggy Sue Got Married," Buddy Holly
- "Pillow Talk," Doris Day
- "Sleepwalk," Santo and Johnny

Art

- *Buste de femme*, Pablo Picasso
- *Red on Maroon*, Mark Rothko
- *Big Red*, Alexander Calder

Architecture

Oct 21 The Guggenheim Museum, designed by Frank Lloyd Wright, opened in New York City.

Science and Technology

- The Nobel Prize in Physics was awarded to Emilio Gino Segrè and Owen Chamberlain for their discovery of the antiproton.
- The Nobel Prize in Chemistry was awarded to Czech Jaroslav Heyrovsky.
- The Nobel Prize in Physiology or Medicine went to Servero Ochoa and Arthur Kornberg.

Jan 27 NASA selected 110 candidates for Project Mercury astronaut training from the air force, navy and marine corps test pilot schools.

Feb 6 A Titan ICBM was successfully fired at Cape Canaveral, FL.

Feb 17 A USAF committee declared, after study, that no scientific evidence supported that any UFO sightings were, in fact, mystery spacecraft.

Feb 20 NASA was awarded $105 million in contracts for 1959 projects (15 satellites).

Mar 6 Radio signals were received from spacecraft *Pioneer IV* from 406,620 miles away, a new record.

Apr 2 Seven astronauts were selected for Project Mercury after the most rigorous battery of tests ever given to US pilots. They were Capts Leroy G. Cooper Jr, Virgil I. Grissom and Donald K. Slayton (USAF); Lt Malcolm S. Carpenter, Lt Comdr Alan B. Shepard Jr and Lt Comdr Walter M. Schirra Jr (USN); and Lt Col John H. Glenn (USMC).

May 28 The US Army launched a nose cone carrying a rhesus monkey (Able) and squirrel monkey (Baker) to a 300-mile altitude. Both were recovered alive.

June 8 The X-15 rocket aircraft made its maiden flight. It went on to set speed records and gather data through flight tests on the fringes of space.

July 17 Mary Leakey found the nearly complete skull of a 1.75-million-year-old hominid—later termed *Zinjanthropus*.

Aug 7 The US's *Explorer 6* satellite launched. On Aug 14 it transmitted the first pictures of Earth from outer space.

Sept 1 USAF Atlas ICBM officially declared operational.

Sept 14 Soviet *Luna 2* crashed into the moon—the first man-made object to hit a celestial body.

Oct 7 *Luna 3* photographed the dark side of the moon.

Commerce and New Products

Jan 25 American Airlines opened the jet age in the US with the establishment of transcontinental Boeing 707 flights between Los Angeles and New York City.

Mar 9 Barbie, the popular doll, debuted in stores.

Mar 31 Busch Gardens opened in Tampa, FL.

Oct 10 Pan Am airlines began regular around-the-world service.

Nov 1 The hockey mask was invented by Montreal Canadiens goalie Jacques Plante. (It was made from fiberglass and resin.)

Nov 19 Ford Motor Company cancelled production of the Edsel.

- According to NASA, transatlantic air passengers totaled 1,367,000 persons on scheduled flights and 173,000 on charter and special flights for the year, as compared to 884,000 sea passengers.

Sports

Auto Racing

FEB 22 Lee Petty (Richard Petty's father) won the first running of the Daytona 500.

MAY 30 Rodger Ward won the Indianapolis 500.

Baseball

▪ The Los Angeles Dodgers won the World Series, beating the Chicago White Sox, four games to two.

MAY 26 Harvey Haddix of the Pittsburgh Pirates pitched a perfect game for 12 innings before losing to the Milwaukee Braves 1–0 in the 13th inning.

JUNE 2 A game between the Baltimore Orioles and Chicago White Sox at Comiskey Field in Chicago was delayed for nearly half an hour by a swarm of gnats. A smoke bomb eventually dispersed the pests.

JUNE 10 Rocky Colavito hit home runs in four consecutive at-bats for the Cleveland Indians in their 11–8 victory over the Baltimore Orioles.

JULY 29 New York City attorney William A. Shea announced plans to establish the Continental League, a third major baseball league. The league never played a game, but its inaugural host cities—New York, Toronto, Houston, Denver and Minneapolis–St. Paul—eventually got major league teams.

Basketball

▪ The Boston Celtics won the NBA championship over the Minneapolis Lakers four games to none.

▪ California won the NCAA championship over West Virginia, 71–70.

Boxing

JUNE 26 Ingemar Johannson of Sweden knocked out Floyd Patterson in the third round of a fight at Yankee Stadium to win the heavyweight championship.

Football

▪ The Baltimore Colts defeated the New York Giants 31–16 for the NFL Championship. (This game to determine an overall football champion predated the Super Bowl.)

FEB 2 Vince Lombardi signed his first contract to coach the Green Bay Packers.

AUG 14 The formation of the American Football League was announced. There were initial plans for at least six teams.

NOV 22 The AFL held its first draft. The league was set to begin play in 1960. Don Meredith was a notable draft pick of the Dallas franchise.

Golf

▪ Art Wall Jr won the Masters.

▪ Billy Caspar won the US Open.

▪ Gary Player won the British Open.

▪ Bob Rosburg won the PGA Championship.

▪ The United States defeated Great Britain for the Ryder Cup.

▪ Mickey Wright won the US Women's Open.

▪ Besty Rawls won the LPGA Championship.

▪ Bill Wright became the first African-American golfer to win a major tournament, claiming the US Amateur Public Links.

▪ Jack Nicklaus claimed his first two US amateur titles. He was 19.

Hockey

▪ The Montreal Canadiens defeated the Toronto Maple Leafs for the Stanley Cup, four games to one.

Horse Racing

▪ Tomy Lee, ridden by Bill Shoemaker, won the Kentucky Derby in 2:02.

▪ Royal Orbit, ridden by William Harmatz, won the Preakness Stakes in 1:57.

▪ Sword Dancer, ridden by Bill Shoemaker, won the Belmont Stakes in 2:28.

Soccer

▪ Real Madrid won the Europe Cup.

▪ Nottingham Forest won the FA Cup.

■ The St. Louis Billikens defeated the University of Bridgeport 5–2 to win the NCAA soccer championship.

Tennis

■ Alex Olmedo won the men's Australian Open and Wimbledon championships.

■ Nicola Pietrangeli won the men's French Open.

■ Neale Fraser won the men's US Open.

■ Mary Carter-Reitano won the women's Australian Open.

■ Christine Truman won the women's French Open.

■ Maria Bueno won the women's Wimbledon championship and US Open.

Miscellaneous

■ Fontclair Festoon, a standard poodle, took Best in Show at Westminster Kennel Dog Show.

1959 Deaths

■ Max Baer, boxer

■ Ethel Barrymore, actress

■ Raymond Chandler, American author and creator of gumshoe Philip Marlowe

■ Lou Costello, comedian and actor (of Abbott and Costello)

■ Cecil B. DeMille, film pioneer

■ Errol Flynn, actor

■ Mohammed Zakaria Goneim, Egyptian archaeologist

■ Edgar Guest, newspaperman and writer

■ William "Bull" Frederick Halsey, American admiral and fleet commander who helped lead American forces in the Pacific during WWII

■ Billie Holiday, legendary jazz vocalist

■ Buddy Holly, musician

■ Joe Kelly, American TV host ("Quiz Kids")

■ Mario Lanza, tenor

■ George Marshall, American general and chairman of the Joint Chiefs of Staff

■ Blind Willie McTell, blues musician

■ George Reeves, actor ("Adventures of Superman")

■ J.P. "The Big Bopper" Richardson, musician

■ Charles Starkweather, killer

■ James Moore "Big Jim" Tatum, football player and coach

■ Richie Valens, musician

■ Walter Williams, reputed last survivor of the Civil War

■ George LeRoy "Hooks" Wiltse, baseball player and manager

■ Frank Lloyd Wright, American architect

■ Lester Young, American jazz tenor saxophonist and clarinetist

1984

25 YEARS AGO

Landmark World Events

JAN 1 Brunei became an independent state.

FEB 13 Konstantin Chernenko succeeded Yuri Andropov as General Secretary of the Soviet Union's Communist Party.

FEB 29 Canadian Prime Minister Pierre Trudeau retired.

APR 12 Palestinian gunmen took an Israeli bus hostage. Israeli Special Forces eventually stormed the bus; they freed the hostages, but one hostage and two of the hijackers were killed.

MAY 8 The Soviet Union announced its boycott of the 1984 Summer Olympics.

JUNE 6 Indian troops stormed the Golden Temple at Amritsar, the Sikhs' holiest shrine, killing an estimated 2,000 people.

JUNE 30 John Napier Turner became Canada's 17th Prime Minister.

AUG 4 The African republic Upper Volta changed its name to Burkina Faso.

Aug 21 500,000 people demonstrated in Manila against Philippines president Ferdinand Marcos.

Sept 4 Brian Mulroney's Progressive party won 211 seats in the Canadian House of Commons. (The victory formed the largest majority in Canadian government history.)

Sept 4 The Sandinista Front won general elections in Nicaragua.

Sept 20 Hezbollah bombed the US Embassy annex in Beirut, Lebanon; 22 people were killed.

Oct 12 The Irish Republican Army attempted to assassinate the British Cabinet—including Prime Minister Margaret Thatcher—by bombing the Grand Hotel in the English city of Brighton during a political conference.

Oct 31 Indian Prime Minister Indira Gandhi was assassinated by her two Sikh security guards. Riots broke out, and thousands of Sikhs were killed.

Nov 19 More than 300 people were killed when a gas truck explosion set off explosions at a gas storage facility near Mexico City.

Nov 30 Tamil Tigers militants killed 127 during ethnic purges in Sri Lanka.

Dec 3 A Union Carbide pesticide plant in Bhopal, India, began to leak methyl isocyanate, killing 4,000 and sickening thousands more who would go on to die in one of the worst industrial disasters in history.

Dec 4 Hezbollah militants hijacked a Kuwait Airlines jetliner, killing four passengers.

Dec 19 The United Kingdom and the People's Republic of China signed the Sino-British Joint Declaration, establishing the future of Hong Kong.

Dec 28 A Soviet cruise missile plunged into a lake in Finland.

Dec 31 Rajiv Gandhi became Prime Minister of India.

- The Nobel Peace Prize went to Desmond Mpilo Tutu of South Africa.

Landmark US Events

Jan 1 AT&T was broken up into seven regional phone companies. The official action was the result of a 1982 federal antitrust ruling against the company. The original seven companies' names were Ameritech, Bell Atlantic, BellSouth, US West, Southwestern Bell, Pacific Telesis and NYNEX.

Jan 10 The United States reestablished diplomatic relations with the Vatican after a break of 117 years.

Feb 26 US Marines pulled out of Beirut, Lebanon.

Mar 16 William Francis Buckley, CIA station chief in Beirut and noted CIA operative and Korean War veteran, was kidnapped by Hezbollah. He later died in captivity.

Apr 4 President Reagan called for an international ban on chemical weapons.

June 8 An F5 tornado struck Barneveld, WI, killing nine, wounding 200, and causing $25,000,000 in damage.

June 28 Richard Ramirez, the "Night Stalker," murdered his first victim.

July 12 At the Democratic National Convention in San Francisco, Walter Mondale was nominated for US president and Geraldine Ferraro for vice president.

July 17 With lobbying from Mothers Against Drunk Driving (MADD), President Reagan signed federal legislation making 21 the minimum legal drinking age (MLDA law).

July 18 James Oliver Huberty opened fire in a San Ysirdo, CA, McDonald's, killing 21 before being killed.

July 21 A worker in Jackson, MI, was killed by a factory robot in what OSHA called the first robot-related homicide in the United States.

July 23 Vanessa Williams resigned her Miss America crown when nude photos of her appeared in *Penthouse*.

Aug 11 President Reagan's voice-test joke: during a voice level test for a radio broadcast, the president, kidding around, said, "My fellow Americans, I am pleased to tell you I just signed legislation which outlaws Russia forever. The bombing begins in five minutes." Mistakenly picked up by microphones, the statement was heard by millions around the world.

Aug 16 Businessman John DeLorean was acquitted of charges of cocaine possession.

Aug 23 President Reagan and vice president George H.W. Bush were nominated for a second term in office at the Republican National Convention in Dallas, TX.

Nov 2 Velma Barfield became the first woman executed in the US since 1962.

Nov 6 Incumbent Ronald Reagan roundly defeated Democratic candidate Walter Mondale with 59 percent of the popular vote. Reagan carried 49 of 50 states (Mondale won his home state of Minnesota and the District of Columbia) and 525 electoral votes to Mondale's 13. It was to be the second and final term for Reagan and his running mate, vice president George H.W. Bush. Prior to the vote for Mondale, the Democratic nomination had been up for grabs, with Colorado senator Gary Hart and civil rights activist Jesse Jackson figuring heavily into the action.

Nov 9 The Vietnam Veterans Memorial was completed with the unveiling of the statue *Three Servicemen*, sculpted by Frederick Hart.

Dec 22 Bernhard Goetz killed four African-American youths on a New York City subway, spurring a national debate on urban crime and vigilantism.

- 1984 marked the beginning of the crack epidemic in America, with the drug's introduction onto the streets of Los Angeles.

Culture

- The Nobel Prize in Literature went to Czech poet Jaroslav Seifert.

Fiction

Oct 1 In his groundbreaking sci-fi novel *Neuromancer*, author William Gibson coined the now-famous term *cyberspace*. The novel won the Hugo, Nebula and Philip K. Dick awards.

- *The Hunt for Red October*, Tom Clancy
- *The Witches of Eastwick*, John Updike
- *The Fourth Protocol*, Frederick Forsyth
- *The Unbearable Lightness of Being*, Milan Kundera
- *The Sicilian*, Mario Puzo

Nonfiction

- *Iacocca: An Autobiography*, Lee Iacocca
- *Hackers: Heroes of the Computer Revolution*, Steven Levy

Theater

Mar 27 *Starlight Express* opened in the West End.

Film

- Winners of the 57th Academy Awards included Best Picture: *Terms of Endearment*; Best Foreign Language Film: *Dangerous Moves* (Switzerland); Actor in a Leading Role: F. Murray Abraham, *Amadeus*; Actress in a Leading Role: Sally Field, *Places in the Heart*; Actor in a Supporting Role: Haing S. Ngor, *The Killing Fields*; Actress in a Supporting Role: Peggy Ashcroft, *A Passage to India*; Best Director: Milos Forman, *Amadeus*; Best Screenplay: Robert Benson, *Places in the Heart*; Best Screenplay based on material from another medium: Peter Shaffer, *Amadeus*; Best Song: Stevie Wonder, "I Just Called to Say I Love You" (*The Woman in Red*).
- Notable films included *Beverly Hills Cop, Ghostbusters, Indiana Jones and the Temple of Doom, Gremlins, The Karate Kid, Footloose, Romancing the Stone, The Terminator, Star Trek III: The Search for Spock, Splash, 2010, Dune, Purple Rain, Red Dawn* and *This Is Spinal Tap*.

Television

JAN 1 The NBC sitcom "Night Court" premiered. Starring Harry Anderson, John Larroquette, Richard Moll, Selma Diamond and Markie Post, the program would air until 1991.

MAR 4 The Television Academy Hall of Fame announced its first inductees (Lucille Ball, Milton Berle, Paddy Chayefsky, Norman Lear, Edward R. Murrow, William S. Paley and David Sarnoff).

JULY 13 The Showtime sitcom "Brothers" premiered. Originally planned for NBC, the network balked because of one of the ensemble cast's openly gay sexuality.

AUG 27 "Good Sex! with Dr. Ruth Westheimer" premiered on Lifetime with actors appearing as the patients the doctor would counsel.

SEPT 14 The first MTV Video Music Awards were held at Radio City Music Hall in New York City.

SEPT 20 Landmark sitcom "The Cosby Show" premiered on NBC.

SEPT 30 "Murder She Wrote" premiered on CBS. The mystery drama starred Angela Lansbury as Jessica Fletcher.

■ Wendy's premiered its famous "Where's the Beef?" ad campaign starring cranky elderly woman Clara Peller.

Music

■ Winners of the 27th Annual Grammy Awards included Record of the Year: Tina Turner, "What's Love Got to Do with It"; Album of the Year: Lionel Richie, *Can't Slow Down*; Song of the Year: Tina Turner, "What's Love Got to Do with It" (songwriters: Graham Lyle and Terry Britten); Best New Artist: Cyndi Lauper; Best Pop Vocal Performance, Female: Tina Turner, "What's Love Got to Do with It"; Best Pop Vocal Performance, Male: Phil Collins, "Against All Odds (Take a Look at Me Now)"; Best Pop Performance by a Duo or Group: The Pointer Sisters, "Jump (For My Love)"; Best Pop Instrumental Performance: Ray Parker Jr, "Ghostbusters (Instrumental)"; Best Rock Vocal Performance, Female: Tina Turner, "Better Be Good to Me"; Best Rock Vocal Performance, Male: Bruce Springsteen, "Dancing in the Dark"; Best Rock Performance by a Duo or Group: Prince and the Revolution, *Purple Rain—Music from the Motion Picture*.

JAN 27 Michael Jackson's scalp was severely burned by pyrotechnics during the filming of a Pepsi commercial.

MAY 5 The Herreys won the Eurovision Song contest. The Swedish group's song was called "Diggi-Loo, Diggi-Ley."

NOV 25 Top musicians in Great Britain and Ireland gathered to form Band Aid. The group recorded "Do They Know It's Christmas" with a goal to raise money for famine relief in Ethiopia. Participants included Bob Geldof and Midge Ure (the organizers), Phil Collins (Genesis), Duran Duran, Sting, Bananarama, Culture Club and Paul McCartney.

Popular Songs

- Van Halen, "Jump"
- "What's Love Got to Do with It," Tina Turner
- "I Just Called to Say I Love You," Stevie Wonder
- "Relax," Frankie Goes to Hollywood
- "Girls Just Want to Have Fun" and "Time After Time," Cyndi Lauper
- "Say Say Say," Paul McCartney and Michael Jackson
- "Hello," Lionel Richie
- "Wake Me Up Before You Go Go," Wham!
- "Ghostbusters," Ray Parker Jr
- "Dancing in the Dark," Bruce Springsteen

■ "Jump (for My Love)," The Pointer Sisters

■ "Hold Me Now," The Thompson Twins

■ "When Doves Cry," Prince

■ "Footloose," Kenny Loggins

■ "Reflex," Duran Duran

■ "Karma Chameleon," Culture Club

■ "Against All Odds (Take a Look at Me Now)," Phil Collins

■ "Owner of a Lonely Heart," Yes

■ "I Want a New Drug," Huey Lewis and the News

Popular Albums

■ *Footloose*, original motion picture soundtrack

■ *Born in the USA*, Bruce Springsteen

■ *Purple Rain*, Prince

■ *Sports*, Huey Lewis and the News

■ *The Unforgettable Fire*, U2

■ *Reckoning*, REM

■ *Make It Big*, Wham!

■ *Bon Jovi*, Bon Jovi

■ *Like a Virgin*, Madonna

■ *Let It Be*, The Replacements

■ *Stop Making Sense*, Talking Heads

Science and Technology

■ Fred Cohen, a PhD student at the University of Southern California, first coined the term *computer virus* and built the first such program as an experiment to illustrate how it might damage computer systems.

■ The Nobel Prize in Physics was awarded to Carlo Rubbia and Simon van der Meer for their contribution to the discovery of field particles W and Z.

■ The Nobel Prize in Chemistry went to Robert Bruce Merrifield.

■ The Nobel Prize in Physiology or Medicine went to Niels K. Jerne, Georges J.F. Köhler and César Milstein.

Feb 3 Space shuttle mission STS-41B was launched on the *Challenger*. It was the 10th official shuttle mission. The crew included Vance D. Brand, Robert L. Gibson, Bruce McCandless II, Ronald E. McNair and Robert L. Stewart.

Feb 7 Astronauts Robert L. Stewart and Bruce McCandless II make the first untethered space walk. They flew freely in space propelled by their backpack jets.

Apr 6 Space shuttle mission STS-41C was launched on the *Challenger*. The crew included Robert L. Crippen, Francis R. Scobee, George D. Nelson, James D.A. von Hoften, and Terry J. Hart.

July 25 *Salyut 7* cosmonaut Svetlana Savitskaya became the first female astronaut to perform a space walk.

Aug 30 Space shuttle *Discovery* (STS-41D) was launched for the first time. The crew included Henry W. Hartsfield Jr, Michael L. Coats, Judith A. Resnick, Steven A. Hawley, Richard M. Mullane and Charles D. Walker.

Oct 5 Space shuttle mission STS-41G was launched on the *Challenger*. The crew included Robert L. Crippen, Jon A. McBride, Kathryn D. Sullivan, Sally K. Ride, David C. Leestma, Marc Garneau and Paul D. Scully-Power. It was the first shuttle flight to include two female crew members.

Oct 12 Kathryn D. Sullivan, an astronaut aboard the space shuttle *Challenger*, became the first American woman to perform an untethered space walk.

Oct 13 President Reagan signed an executive order creating a National Commission on Space to prepare a 20-year agenda for the civilian space program.

Oct 26 First baboon heart transplant

Nov 8 Space shuttle mission STS-51A was launched on the *Discovery*. The crew included Frederick H. Hauck, David M. Walker, Anna L. Fisher, Dale A. Gardner and Joseph P. Allen.

Dec 15 The USSR spacecraft *Vega* was launched to rendezvous with Halley's Comet in March 1986.

Miscellaneous

- SETI (Search for Extraterrestrial Intelligence) was founded.

Commerce and New Products

- The Nobel Prize in Economics was awarded to Richard Stone.

Jan 22 "1984," one of the most famous advertisements in media history, was broadcast for the first time during the Super Bowl. Directed by Ridley Scott, the ad for Macintosh computers featured an Olympic-like female athlete hurling a giant hammer at "Big Brother" on a screen—the ad's stand-in for IBM, Apple's rival and an industry powerhouse.

Jan 24 The first Apple Macintosh was officially introduced. The initial price was $2,495.

June 22 Virgin Atlantic made its inaugural flight.

Oct 25 The world's largest power plant, the Itaipu power plant, opened on the Brazil/Paraguay border.

Nov 4 Dell Computers was founded in Austin, TX, as PC's Limited.

- Video game system manufacturer Atari was sold after two years of intense competition from upstart rivals in the home gaming market (Coleco, Intellivision, etc.). This was after Atari had pioneered simple, affordable and fun home gaming and computer entertainment and dominated pop and media culture for the first part of the decade with its Atari 2600 game console.
- RadioShack introduced the Tandy 1000, an affordable IBM-compatible personal computer.
- The 3½″, double-sided floppy disc was introduced.
- Sony and Philips introduced the first commercial compact disc players.

Sports

Auto Racing

July 4 Driver Richard Petty won his 200th (and final) NASCAR race, the Firecracker 400 in Daytona, FL.

- Niki Lauda won the Formula One Championship.
- Rick Mears won the Indianapolis 500.
- Cale Yarborough won the Daytona 500 (his second consecutive win at Daytona).
- Terry Labonte won the NASCAR championship.

Baseball

- The Detroit Tigers won the World Series, four games to one over the San Diego Padres.

Mar 3 Peter V. Ueberroth, president of the Los Angeles Olympic Organizing Committee, was voted commissioner of Major League Baseball.

Apr 13 Cincinnati Reds fireplug Pete Rose got the 4,000th hit of his MLB career in a game against the Philadelphia Phillies.

May 8 The Chicago White Sox and Milwaukee Brewers began a baseball game that would go on to last 25 innings. It was played over two days and totaled eight hours and six minutes. It remains the longest game in MLB history.

July 4 After a 19-inning game between the New York Mets and Atlanta Braves that lasted until 4 AM, the victorious Mets launched their scheduled postgame fireworks show. The surrounding neighborhood was startled.

The 1984 Winter and Summer Olympics

Feb 8 The XIV Olympic Winter Games opened in Sarajevo, Yugoslavia. It was the first time the Winter Games were held in a Communist country. Forty-nine nations participated, sending 1,272 athletes to the Games. Medal highlights included Jure Franko's silver medal in giant slalom, the first medal for host country Yugoslavia; Bill Johnson, who became the first (and only) American skier to win the Olympic downhill; Scott Hamilton's gold medal for the US in individual men's figure skating; American skiers Phillip Mahre, Debbie Armstrong and William Johnson receiving gold medals in men's slalom, women's giant slalom and men's downhill, respectively (Mahre's brother Steve won the silver in men's slalom); Katarina Witt's gold medal for Germany in individual women's figure skating; and British skaters Jayne Torvill and Christopher Dean, who became the first ice dancing team to earn nine perfect marks of 6.0. The Winter Olympics closed on Feb 19.

July 28 The Games of the XXIII Olympiad opened in Los Angeles, CA. The Soviet Union boycotted the event, but 140 other nations took part, sending 6,829 athletes to the Games. Medal highlights included American runner Carl Lewis taking home the gold in men's 100 meters, 200 meters and long jump, and American gymnastics, in which Mary-Lou Retton took home the individual all-around women's gold, Bart Conner found gold in men's parallel bars and the US men took gold in the team gymnastics competition. Other highlights included Edwin Moses winning gold in the 400-meter relay and gold medals for the US men's and women's teams in the 4+100-meter relay. The Summer Olympics closed on Aug 12.

July 4 Phil Niekro of the New York Yankees struck out Larry Parrish of the Texas Rangers for the 3,000th strikeout of his career.

Sept 17 Reggie Jackson of the New York Yankees became the 13th player to hit 500 home runs.

Basketball

▪ Georgetown defeated Houston 84–75 to win the NCAA Men's Basketball Championship.

▪ The Boston Celtics defeated the Los Angeles Lakers four games to three to win the NBA Championship.

Apr 5 LA Lakers center Kareem Abdul-Jabbar broke Wilt Chamberlain's scoring record by hitting a sky hook with 8:53 left to play against the Utah Jazz, bringing his total to 31,420.

June 23 Future superstars Michael Jordan and Charles Barkley were drafted.

Boxing

June 15 WBC world junior middleweight champ Tommy Hearns knocked out WBA champ Roberto Duran.

Football

▪ The Oakland Raiders defeated the Washington Redskins 38–9 to win Super Bowl XVIII.

Mar 28 The Baltimore Colts loaded up and moved their team to Indianapolis, IN. The city was left teamless until 1996, when the Cleveland Browns moved to Baltimore and were renamed the Ravens.

Oct 7 Chicago Bears running back Walter Payton broke Jim Brown's rushing record of 12,312 career rushing yards and rushed for 100 yards or more for the 58th time in his career. Both records were broken in a 20–7 Bears win over the New Orleans Saints.

Dec 9 Los Angeles Rams running back Eric Dickerson became the second player to gain more than 2,000 yards in a single season.

▪ Brigham Young won the NCAA National Championship.

▪ Doug Flutie, quarterback for Boston College, won the Heisman Trophy.

Golf

July 22 Kathy Whitworth won the Rochester Open to log her 85th victory, the most ever in professional golf.

- Ben Crenshaw won the Masters.
- Fuzzy Zoeller won the US Open.
- Severiano Ballesteros won the British Open.
- Lee Trevino won the PGA Championship.
- Hollis Stacey won the US Women's Open.
- Patty Sheehan won the LPGA Championship.

Hockey

JAN 27 Wayne Gretzky of the Edmonton Oilers scored a goal against the New Jersey Devils to extend his scoring streak to 51 games.

DEC 19 Center Wayne Gretzky tallied the 1,000th point of his NHL career with an assist in a 7–3 Oilers victory over the Los Angeles Kings.

- The Edmonton Oilers won the Stanley Cup four games to one over the New York Islanders.

Horse Racing

- Swale, ridden by Laffit Pincay Jr, won the Kentucky Derby in 2:02 and the Belmont Stakes in 2:27.
- Gate Dancer won the Preakness Stakes.
- Wild Again won the debut Breeders' Cup race.

Soccer

- France defeated Spain 2–0 to win the European Championship.
- Everton defeated Watford to win the FA Cup.

Tennis

DEC 6 The longest winning streak in women's tennis history ended when Helena Sukova defeated Martina Navratilova, who had won 74 matches in a row.

- Mats Wilander won the men's Australian Open.
- Ivan Lendl won the men's French Open.
- John McEnroe won the men's Wimbledon championship and the US Open.
- Chris Evert won the women's Australian Open.
- Martina Navratilova won the women's French Open, Wimbledon championship and US Open.

Miscellaneous

SEPT 14 Balloonist Joe W. Kittinger completed the first solo transatlantic balloon crossing. It took nearly 84 hours.

- France's Laurent Fignon won the Tour de France bicycle race.
- Seaward's Blackbeard, a Newfoundland, took Best in Show at Westminster Kennel Dog Show.

1984 Deaths

- Ansel Adams, American photographer
- Vincente Aleixandre, Spanish writer
- Walter Alston, baseball player and Hall of Fame manager
- Yuri Andropov, general secretary of the Communist Party of the Soviet Union
- William "Count" Basie, American musician and composer
- Richard Brautigan, American author (*Trout Fishing in America*)
- Richard Burton, stage and film legend
- Truman Capote, novelist
- Mark Clark, US Army general
- Stanley Covaleski, MLB Hall of Fame pitcher
- Joe Cronin, Hall of Fame baseball player, manager and executive
- Michel Foucault, French philosopher
- George Gallup, American statistician and poll-maker
- Indira Gandhi, Indian prime minister
- Janet Gaynor, actress
- Marvin Gaye, American singer. Gaye was shot and killed by his father after an argument.
- Ed Gein, notorious Wisconsin-based killer

- William Dale "Billy" Goodman, major league baseball player
- Mary Hamman, American writer and editor
- Lillian Hellman, American playwright and author
- Waite Hoyt, broadcaster and MLB Hall of Fame pitcher
- Andy Kaufman, American comedian
- Alfred A. Knopf, publisher
- Ray Kroc, entrepreneur, builder of the McDonald's empire
- George "High Pockets" Lane, American baseball player
- Gus Mancuso, American baseball player
- Ethel Merman, musical comedy star
- Sam Peckinpah, American film director
- Walter Pidgeon, actor
- Babe Pinelli, baseball player and major league umpire
- Francois Truffaut, French film director
- Ernest Tubb, country and western singing legend
- Peter John (Johnny) Weissmuller, actor and Olympic champion swimmer
- Jackie Wilson, American R&B singer
- Glenn Wright, major league shortstop
- Meredith Wilson, American musician, playwright and composer
- LeeRoy Yarbrough, auto racer

Spotlight on World Anniversaries

Charles Darwin and *On the Origin of Species*

200TH BIRTH ANNIVERSARY AND 150TH PUBLICATION ANNIVERSARY

His youthful interest in collecting things—shells, rocks, insects—became a passion that eventually led Charles Darwin (born Feb 12, 1809, at Shrewsbury, England) to formulate a revolutionary scientific theory. When his attempt to study medicine failed (Darwin found surgery horrible—there were no anesthetics to shield patients from the agonies), his father packed him off to Cambridge to prepare for the clergy. There he met botanist John Henslow, who trained his student to observe nature in thorough detail. From geologist Adam Sedgwick, Darwin learned that looking for patterns of meaning was just as important as the recording of facts.

At 22, Darwin embarked on an adventure that shaped his entire life. He became an unpaid naturalist aboard the HMS *Beagle* on a mission to survey the coasts of South America. One of the books he took with him on the voyage was Charles Lyell's 1830 *Principles of Geology*, itself a groundbreaking text in terms of Earth's chronology. The around-the-world voyage took five years (1831–1836), during which time the budding scientist collected thousands of shells, sea creatures, bones, birds, animals, insects, and most important, fossils of extinct life-forms that were similar to contemporary ones. Darwin also made an abundance of notes (more than 1,700 pages) and observations.

Witnessing a massive earthquake and tidal wave in Chile and finding fossilized seashells in the Andes—among other evidence—confirmed Darwin's growing conviction that Earth had not been created all at once in a permanent form—a contradiction to a literal interpretation of the biblical account of God's six-day creation. A vexing question, too, was the existence of extinct animals. One religious explanation for such extinctions was that these animals had been too large to fit through the doorway of Noah's ark and thus perished in the flood.

Returning to England in 1836, Darwin began formulating, in secret, his theory of the transmutation of species and the mechanism by which it was brought about—natural selection. More than 20 years later, on Nov 22, 1859, *On the Origin of Species by Means of Natural Selection, or the Preservation of Favoured Races in the Struggle for Life* was published, and all 1,250 copies sold out the first day (at 15 shillings each). Another printing of 3,000 quickly sold out in December.

Giving ample evidence, Darwin's book described evolution (although the word *evolution* did not appear until the 1872 edition of *On the Origin of Species*). Darwin was no abstract-thinking armchair scientist, but a hands-on biologist, one who collected his own specimens, sorted and analyzed them, and did his own experiments with artificial selection. He showed how the struggle to survive forced a species to change over the course of many generations. Those individuals (either animal or plant) that are the best adapted to their unique environment are the ones most likely to survive and go on to produce offspring who inherit those best-suited characteristics. Although Darwin did not

directly address the origin of humans, readers did not fail to see the implication that *Homo sapiens* is just another species. (His *Descent of Man*, published in 1871, would address humans more fully.)

Some Christians were outraged. Angry responses appeared in newspapers and journals, and ministers sermonized against the theory. Most critics viewed the book as a direct attack on religion. Clearly, the established order had been undermined.

There were also prominent scientists who angrily disputed Darwin's theory. Among them was Richard Owen, the scientist who had coined the term *dinosaur* in 1842. Owen had been a mentor to the young Darwin, yet *On the Origin of Species* caused the rupture of their relationship: Owen even wrote an anonymous review attacking the book. The controversy continued for a decade or so but eventually became less volatile. The discovery of the *Archaeopteryx* fossil in 1861—a creature with avian and reptilian traits—seemed to validate Darwin's key points. Other scientific discoveries, inventions, innovations and medical advances during the Victorian era led to broader ways of thinking about human life, and Darwin's proposition began to be seen as less revolutionary and more as the scientific discovery that it was.

Darwin died Apr 19, 1882, in Kent, England, where he had lived quietly for several decades. In spite of playing a central role in the scientific community's divisive declaration of independence from religion, Charles Darwin finished his life as one of the most respected men of science, revered for his achievements, and was buried in Westminster Abbey.

The Cuban Revolution

JANUARY 1959 ✦ 50 YEARS

In the wee hours of Jan 1, 1959, the Batista era ended in Cuba as dictator Fulgencio Batista (carrying much of Cuba's treasury) fled by plane to the Dominican Republic, where fellow caudillo Rafael Trujillo welcomed him. As news of Batista's flight reached his armed forces under siege in cities around the island, the demoralized soldiers surrendered to the July 26 Movement, led by Fidel Castro. Some 30,000 federal troops were conquered by probably not more than 800 rebels. By Jan 3, Castro was in Havana and a new turn in Cuba's history came.

Batista, who had ruled Cuba previously from 1933 to 1944, seized power in March of 1952 in a military coup. His regime was characterized by ruthless suppression of civil rights and underpinned by a brutal secret police force. On July 26, 1953, 160 rebels attacked the Moncada army barracks in Santiago in an attempt to create a 20th-century Bastille Day. They were slaughtered and the few survivors, including young lawyer/leader Fidel Castro and his brother Raúl, were imprisoned. The Castros, released from jail two years later, plotted a revolution from Mexico for three years. They named their force the July 26 Movement.

Their revolution had an unlikely beginning. Fidel Castro led an amateurish invasion squad aboard the boat *Granma* from Mexico for the initial invasion Dec 2, 1956, but the voyage was delayed, no fellow rebels could meet them, they were off target and Batista's men ambushed the debarking rebels. The 82-man force was reduced to 22 men, who fled to the Sierra Maestra—so quickly that they left arms and medicine behind.

But Castro proved to be a charismatic, if Machiavellian, leader and during the next two years wooed new rebels, encouraged downtrodden peasants, reached out to more conservative Cuban city dwellers and charmed overseas reporters, and soon the forces and the message grew. The July 26 Movement fought a guerilla war in the mountains for two years, moving quickly to establish new bases and outmaneuvering federal troops—who often vented their frustration by attacking peasants suspected of collaboration.

The US kept a worried watch over events from 1956 to 1959. Despite Castro's assurances that he was anti-communist, US intelligence noted two hard-line Marxists who were his right-hand men: his brother Raúl and the Argentine adventurer Ernesto "Che" Guevara. Guevara met Castro in Mexico and had been looking for a "social revolution" to join. As Central America and the Caribbean were infested with vicious dictators, Guevara wanted to join a revolt to topple them and install a Soviet-style state. He picked Cuba and never wavered in his Marxist agenda. The wily Castro tried to keep Guevara's visibility low with lower-level positions, but there was no question about who was actually second in command.

Castro assured nervous onlookers that after the revolution, the July 26 Movement would be just one of many political parties and would only "fight with the arms of the Constitution and the law," but privately wrote to his girlfriend, "When this war is over, I'll start a much longer and bigger war of my own: the war I'm going to fight against [the United States]."

The question was what would happen in Cuba in 1959? Castro established a US-pleasing provisional government filled with moderates, but he worked in the background with his revolutionary leaders on more radical policies meant to free Cuba from US economic dependence.

In January 1959, the Cuban people embraced the rebels as liberators of Batista—and even began sporting beards in admiring imitation of the ragged mountain fighters. They began to howl for executions of Batista regime torturers and traitors—in scenes eerily reminiscent of 1793 France. Castro put Guevara in charge of "cleansing" the armed forces of traitors and "enemies of the new state." Although Guevara protested that his tribunals were conducted with witnesses and with fairness, only he had the final say in their fates. Some 550 soldiers were executed from January to May, when Castro suspended the tribunals. The speed and number of executions angered the world—and were an early indicator of Cuba's upcoming fate under the Castro regime.

By February, Prime Minister Miró Cardona resigned and on Feb 16 Castro took the oath as Cuba's prime minister—gaining the public title that reflected the unspoken reality of Castro's rule. By then, moderate President Manuel Urrutia realized that he was only a powerless figurehead and resigned later in the year. Despite Castro's previous public statements, Cuba became a one-party nation.

By the end of the year, Castro had started implementing radical agrarian reform, took control of the universities and public education system, sponsored a revolution in the Dominican Republic (which failed) and began suppressing and imprisoning opponents. In 1960, Cuba seized US- and European-owned oil refineries and formally established diplomatic relations with the Soviet Union, who pledged to buy all of Cuba's eight-ton annual sugar production—thus replacing US dollars with Soviet ones. The Soviet Union, led by Nikita Khrushchev, was gleeful at the prospect of a communist bee buzzing in the backyard of the US. Cuban-US relations deteriorated past the saving point.

Thus, 1959 saw Cuba become a Soviet-style communist state—the first to be established in the Western Hemisphere.

Spotlight on American Anniversaries

Abraham Lincoln

200TH BIRTH ANNIVERSARY

About an hour's drive south from Louisville, KY, lies Hodgenville, the seat of LaRue County and the birthplace of Abraham Lincoln, America's 16th president. Gnarled blue ash and leafy burr oak trees still dot the grassy, rolling hills, and the stacked timber fences that were common when the Lincoln family lived here haven't gone out of style. In these parts, tradition is a virtue.

Lincoln was born Feb 12, 1809, in a log cabin a few miles south of where Hodgenville lies today, and he and his family spent the first few years of his life there before moving to a farm on Knob Creek, 11 miles to the northeast of their original homestead. It was there that young Abraham Lincoln learned to fish, gather wood and berries from the nearby hills and forests, perform chores and enjoy the solitude and hearty challenges that were central to frontier living.

Today, Kentuckians are deservedly proud of having reared a president known as much for his oratory gifts as his principled nature, political tact and vision of a more perfect Union. It's appropriate then that the two-year celebration of his bicentennial began with an inaugural ceremony in Hodgenville on Feb 12, 2008. The event was cut short due to inclement weather. But it was noted that the bitter cold and icy storms were probably very similar to the conditions on that day 199 years before when in a tiny log cabin on the Kentucky frontier Thomas and Nancy Hanks Lincoln welcomed their infant son into the world.

The celebration of Lincoln's birth continues through 2009 and beyond with hundreds of events, exhibitions, gatherings, discussions and tributes planned throughout Kentucky as well as nearby states such as Indiana and Illinois, each with its own close ties to the president's life. The Boy Scouts of America, for example, plan an annual pilgrimage to Springfield, the capital of Illinois, where scouts can walk in the footsteps of the young Abraham Lincoln, who worked in the city as a talented, ambitious and altruistic attorney. Meanwhile, the American Library Association sponsors "Forever Free: Abraham Lincoln's Journey to Emancipation," a traveling panel exhibit that displays reproductions of rare historical documents, period photographs and relevant political materials and draws on the latest scholarship into Lincoln's legacy to present the president in a new and interesting light. Two copies of the exhibit will travel to 63 libraries through May 2010.

On Feb 2, 2009, the Lincoln Bicentennial year will officially open with a gala event in Washington, DC, where military bands will perform 19th-century music. On Feb 12, Lincoln's birthday, there will be a joint meeting of the US Congress, and that spring the Lincoln Memorial will be rededicated, complete with an address by our nation's 44th president.

On Apr 24 and 25, 2009, Harvard University will host "Abraham Lincoln at 200: New Perspectives on his Life and Legacy," a symposium that will explore the principal issues of Lincoln's presidency, including his views on race and slavery, his role in transforming the duties, powers and perception of America's commander-in-chief and his astute use of the press as a political and social tool. Numerous Lincoln scholars are scheduled to participate.

From the Lincoln Bicentennial Jubilee in Grandview, IN, planned for August 2009, all the way to the Lincoln Days Celebration held the following October in Hodgenville itself, the bicentennial celebration of one of our nation's most popular presidents will be in good hands. There will be fellowship and celebrations of Lincoln's life and leadership. Plus, given the number of streets, schools, institutions and towns named for him throughout the country, there are sure to be more than a few Abraham Lincoln look-alike contests.

For more information:

Abraham Lincoln Bicentennial Commission
Phone: (202) 707-6998
Fax: (202) 707-6995
Web: www.lincolnbicentennial.gov

Other useful websites:
www.c-span.org/lincoln200years
www.kylincoln.org
www.in.gov/lincoln
www.lincoln200.net
http://hcl.harvard.edu/libraries/houghton/lincoln.html
www.ala.org/ala/ppo/programs/currentprograms/foreverfree/foreverfreeabraham.cfm

Oregon Enters the Union

FEB 14, 1859 ✦ 150 YEARS

Oregon celebrates its sesquicentennial of statehood in 2009. The origin of the name *Oregon* is uncertain. Many ships touched the Pacific coast of Oregon in the late 1700s and early 1800s but provided little information about the interior. The Lewis and Clark expedition of 1805–1806 made the first land exploration. Although Lewis and Clark only visited the Columbia River region, they learned a lot about the interior from friendly Native American tribes. Their report created a lot of interest in the eastern United States, especially among fur traders. The town of Astoria, OR, was founded in 1811 by John Jacob Astor as a fur trading station.

The first white settlers arrived in Oregon in the 1830s, and the Oregon Country functioned as an independent republic until it was annexed to the United States as the Oregon Territory in 1848. The territory extended from California north to Alaska and from the Rocky Mountains west to the Pacific.

During the 1840s and 1850s, the Oregon Trail, which began in Independence, MO, and stretched 2,000 miles to the Pacific coast, carried thousands of pioneers to the rich farmlands of Oregon's Willamette Valley. By 1846 more than 6,000 people had made the six-month trek. The discovery of gold in California in 1848 reduced somewhat the flow of people to the Oregon Territory.

Oregon was admitted to the Union as the 33rd state on Feb 14, 1859. It entered the Union as a free state, increasing the number of free states to 18 versus 15 slave states. It was the last state admitted to the Union before the Civil War. The remainder of the Oregon Territory eventually became the states of Washington (the Columbia River is the border between Oregon and Washington), Idaho and western Montana and the Canadian province of British Columbia.

Nicknamed the "Beaver State," Oregon ranks 10th in land area among the 50 states and 27th in population. Portland is its largest city; Salem is the capital. Oregon's forests are a leading force in the state's economy, with the processing of lumber and the manufacturing of paper as major industries. Agriculture and salmon fisheries are also important. High-tech companies and corporations such as Intel and Nike are increasingly major employers in the state.

For more information:

Oregon 150
1211 SW Fifth Ave, Ste L17
Portland, OR 97204
Phone: (503) 445-7120
E-mail: info@oregon150.org
Web: www.oregon150.org

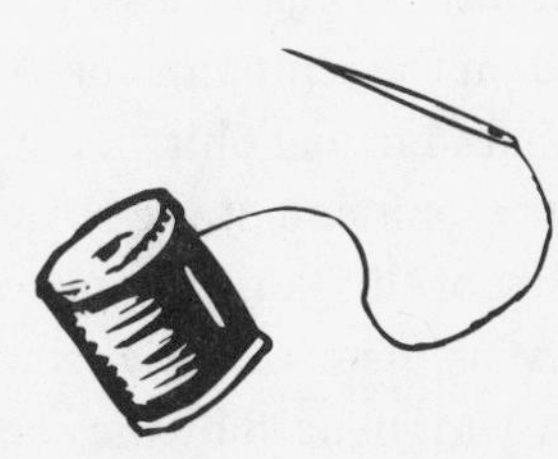

NAACP

1909 ✦ 100 YEARS

The National Association for the Advancement of Colored People (NAACP), the nation's oldest civil rights organization, was founded on the principles of the Declaration of Independence, that "all men are created equal," and the 13th, 14th and 15th Amendments to the US Constitution, calling for an end to slavery, equal protection under the law and universal suffrage. To that end, its mission, to "ensure the political, educational, social, and economic equality of all persons and to eliminate racial hatred and racial discrimination," has helped to correct the injustices and inequalities that led to its inception 100 years ago.

The NAACP was formed in response to the 1908 race riot in Springfield, IL. Sheriffs transferred two black prisoners to another jail to avoid a growing mob of angry whites itching to take justice into their own hands, sparking a riot that resulted in seven deaths and the destruction of black homes and businesses. Following the riot, a small group of white liberals and African-American men and women, including W.E.B. DuBois and Ida B. Wells-Barnett, met to discuss racial violence and injustice. Their ideas, published on the centennial of Abraham Lincoln's birth, put forth the mission of the NAACP.

Some of this nation's greatest achievements in civil rights were directly influenced by the collective power of the NAACP's courageous members that played out on a legal battleground. Rosa Parks, referred to as the "Mother of the Modern-Day Civil Rights Movement" by the US Congress, had been a member of the NAACP since 1943, more than a decade prior to famously refusing to give up her seat on the bus. Other notable achievements include the following:

- *Brown v Board of Education* (1954)—the Supreme Court Decision outlawing segregation in public education
- Civil Rights Act (1964)—signed by President Lyndon B. Johnson
- Voting Rights Act (1965)—ensuring the right to vote for African-American citizens

Young people played an important part in shaping the NAACP's constituency and agenda. The Youth and College Division was founded in 1936. Since then, student-led sit-ins, peaceful protests and mass demonstrations have given voice to the specific concerns of young people. With more than 30,000 members today, the NAACP has one of the largest organized youth groups of any US organization, and it is the only major civil rights group to include the voices of youth on its board of directors. The specific goals of the youth division—to inform and empower, and to advance the economic, educational, social and political status of young people of color—continue to guide the group's action to provoking positive change.

For observances of the NAACP's centennial founding anniversary, visit the official website at www.naacp.org. Students will be interested in exploring links to the NAACP Blog and the NAACP YouTube page from the homepage.

NAACP National Headquarters
4805 Mt Hope Dr
Baltimore, MD 21215
Phone: 877-NAACP-98
Web: www.naacp.org

Alaska and Hawaii Join the Union

1959 ✦ 50 YEARS

In 2009, Alaska and Hawaii celebrate 50 years of statehood.

Alaska was granted statehood Jan 3, 1959, making it the 49th state. Alaska's history and culture have been marked by booms and busts—fur, timber, gold, fishing and oil—each bringing to the Arctic splendor of the "Great Land" a different set of people.

The difficult struggle for statehood began in 1867 when William H. Seward, the US secretary of state, engineered the purchase of Alaska from Russia for $7.2 million; it was called "Seward's Folly" and "Seward's Icebox" at the time. For the next 17 years, Alaska was a US military district. The gold rushes of the 1890s brought thousands of miners and settlers, and Alaska was granted territorial status in 1912. During World War II, three of the outer Aleutian Islands were occupied by the Japanese; their recovery was a matter of national pride.

As it became a strategic military base and a key to the Pacific, Alaska's population increased and the struggle for statehood gained nationwide attention. Legislators were worried that Alaska's population was too sparse and isolated and its economy too unstable, but the discovery of oil soon dispelled those concerns. After statehood and the building of the Alaskan highway system, tourism also emerged as an important source of revenue.

Hawaii was admitted to the Union on Aug 21, 1959, making it the 50th state. Located on an archipelago in the central Pacific Ocean, Hawaii was annexed in 1898 as a US territory. A referendum was held asking residents to vote on the statehood bill; however, the legality of the annexation was not addressed at the time and has since led to criticism. On Dec 7, 1941, Japanese aircraft made a surprise attack on Pearl Harbor. During World War II, the Hawaiian Islands were the chief Pacific base for US forces and were under martial law.

The postwar years ushered in economic and social developments: expansion of labor unionism, the growth of the tourist trade and a construction boom. Famous for its geological features, exotic flora and fauna and tropical climate, Hawaii quickly became a modern state with a rapidly growing economy. In recent decades, the state government has implemented programs to promote Hawaiian culture and language.

At press time, the 50th anniversary of statehood celebrations were still in the planning stages. In Hawaii, there has been continuous dialog as to the nature of the observance—with some constituencies not favoring a celebration.

For more information:

Alaska Statehood Celebration Commission
550 W 7th Ave, Ste 1770
Anchorage, AK 99501
Phone: (907) 269-8492
Fax: (907) 269-8125
Web: www.state.ak.us/commerce/alaska50

State of Hawaii
220 S King St, Ste 2190
Honolulu, HI 96813
Phone: (808) 587-4220
Fax: (808) 587-4218
E-mail: info@ehawaii.gov
Web: www.ehawaii.gov

Spotlight on People

2009 brings many significant birth anniversaries, of which a selection is presented below. See also the main chronology for other significant biographies.

World History

John Calvin

Birth: July 10, 1509 ✦ 500 years

Pastor and theologian John Calvin was born at Noyon, France. After Martin Luther, Calvin was the most important figure of the Protestant Reformation, being the creator of Calvinism. He was the author of the immensely influential *Institutes of the Christian Religion* (1536). Calvin died at Geneva, Switzerland, May 27, 1564.

William Pitt

Birth: May 28, 1759 ✦ 250 years

British prime minister from 1783 to 1801 and from 1804 to 1806, William Pitt was influenced by Adam Smith's economic theories and reduced England's large national debt incurred by the American Revolution. Born at Hayes, Kent, England, he died Jan 23, 1806, at Putney. He was the son of William Pitt, first earl of Chatham, for whom the city of Pittsburgh was named.

Etienne de Silhouette

Birth: July 8, 1709 ✦ 300 years

Born in Limoges, Etienne de Silhouette would become briefly the French controller-general of finances in 1759 under Louis XV. A minor figure in history, de Silhouette was an unimpressive figure at the French court, thus lending his name to the black profile cutouts that are today called silhouettes.

Georges Danton

Birth: Oct 26, 1759 ✦ 250 years

Born at Arcis-sur-Aube, Georges Danton was a lawyer who gradually emerged as a leader in the French revolutionary movement. In the chaos after the August 1792 overthrow of the French monarchy, Danton boasted of being a key player. He held a variety of positions in the revolutionary government, yet represented a more moderate line. Despite his charisma, though, he was unable to rein in the murderous factions swirling in the movement. On Mar 29, 1794, Danton and his moderate followers were arrested. His last words before his execution by guillotine on Apr 5 were "Show my head to the people. It is worth the trouble."

Louis Braille

Birth: Jan 4, 1809 ✦ 200 years

Louis Braille, the inventor of a widely used touch system of reading and writing for the blind, was born at Coupvray, France. Permanently blinded at the age of three by a leather-working awl in his father's saddle-making shop, Braille developed a system of writing that used, ironically, an awl-like stylus to punch marks in paper that could be felt and interpreted by the blind. The system was largely ignored until after Braille died in poverty, suffering from tuberculosis, at Paris, Jan 6, 1852.

Charles Darwin

Birth: Feb 12, 1809 ✦ 200 years

See "Spotlight on World Anniversaries."

William Ewart Gladstone

Birth: Dec 29, 1809 ✦ 200 years

William Ewart Gladstone was the English statesman and author for whom the Gladstone (luggage) bag was named. Inspiring orator, eccentric individual, intensely loved or hated by all who knew him (cheered from the streets and jeered from the balconies), Gladstone is said to have left more writings (letters, diaries, journals, books) than any other major English politician. However, his preoccupation with the charitable rehabilitation of prostitutes was perhaps easily misunderstood. Born at Liverpool, England, he was four times Britain's prime minister. Gladstone died at Hawarden, Wales, May 19, 1898.

Wilhelm II

Birth: Jan 27, 1859 ✦ 150 years

Wilhelm II, grandson of England's Queen Victoria, was born to Crown Prince Frederick and Victoria's daughter of the same name in Potsdam. Wilhelm II became kaiser of Germany and king of Prussia at age 29 and ruled from 1888 to 1918. His militaristic posturing helped fan the flames of World War I. At the end of the war, he was forced into exile in the Netherlands. He died at Doorn, the Netherlands, on June 4, 1941.

Alfred Dreyfus

Birth: Oct 9, 1859 ✦ 150 years

French army officer Alfred Dreyfus, born at Mulhouse, France, was the center of a military scandal from 1894 to 1906. From when he was accused of treason in 1894 (forged documents were used to convict him) and sentenced to life imprisonment at Devil's Island in 1895, the Dreyfus affair was a lightning rod for rival factions in France and exposed the virulent anti-Semitism in the country (Dreyfus was Jewish). The case was notable for the involvement of France's major literary figures in Dreyfus's defense, most famously Emile Zola, who published "J'Accuse" in 1898 in a periodical and accused the French army of a massive cover-up. Public outrage ensured two more trials for Dreyfus. He was still found guilty but was pardoned at his last trial in 1899. A 1906 civilian court finally cleared Dreyfus, who eventually returned to the military. He died July 12, 1935, at Paris, France.

Isoroku Yamamoto

Birth: Apr 4, 1884 ✦ 125 years

Considered Japan's greatest naval strategist, Admiral Isoroku Yamamoto, who planned the attack on Pearl Harbor, was born at Nagaoka, Honshu. Yamamoto also devised the complex attack on Midway Island, which ended in defeat for the Japanese because the Allies had the key to the Imperial fleet code and were prepared for the June 4, 1942, attack. The US intercepted reports of Yamamoto's proposed 1943 tour of the Western Solomons and shot down his plane Apr 18 while he was touring Japanese installations in the area.

Simone Weil

Birth: Feb 3, 1909 ✦ 100 years

Simone Weil was a French philosopher and social activist whose impact came posthumously with the publication of her many notebooks. Born at Paris, France, Weil was a teacher of philosophy who later traveled Europe investigating industrial situations. She was a member of the French Resistance in World War II working in London, England. She insisted on eating the same rations as her suffering compatriots in France, and that, coupled with poor health and tuberculosis, brought about her death at Ashford, England, on Aug 24, 1943. Her 20 volumes of writings include these thoughts: "Man alone can enslave man" and "What a country calls its vital economic interests are not the things which enable its citizens to live, but the things which enable it to make war. Gasoline is much more likely than wheat to be a cause of international conflict."

Andrei Gromyko

Birth: July 18, 1909 ✦ 100 years

Soviet diplomat and statesman, born at Belorussia, USSR, Andrei Gromyko played a leading role in Soviet history from World War II until the early days of Mikhail Gorbachev's reform programs. He entered diplomatic service in 1939 with a post in the Soviet Embassy in Washington, DC, and four years later was promoted to ambassador at the age of 34. He was instrumental in bringing the US, Britain and the

USSR together for conferences in Yalta, Potsdam and Tehran. He became deputy foreign minister and permanent representative to the United Nations in 1946. Appointed foreign minister in February 1957, he became the voice of the Soviet Union in international debate. He was given the mostly ceremonial post of state president after Gorbachev's ascension in 1985 and retained that post until his death July 2, 1989, at Moscow.

US History

Robert Morris

Birth: Jan 31, 1734 ✦ 275 years

Robert Morris was a signer of the Declaration of Independence, the Articles of Confederation and the Constitution. He was one of only two men who signed all three documents. He was born at Liverpool, England, and died May 7, 1806, at Philadelphia, PA.

Daniel Boone

Birth: Nov 2, 1734 ✦ 275 years

Daniel Boone was an American frontiersman, explorer and militia officer, born at Berks County, near Reading, PA. In February, 1778, he was captured at Blue Licks, KY, by Shawnee Indians, under Chief Blackfish, who adopted Boone when he was inducted into the tribe as "Big Turtle." Boone escaped after five months and in 1781 was captured briefly by the British. He experienced a series of personal and financial disasters during his life but continued a rugged existence, hunting until his 80s. Boone died at St. Charles County, MO, Sept 26, 1820. The bodies of Daniel Boone and his wife, Rebecca, were moved to Frankfort, KY, in 1845.

Parson Weems

Birth: Oct 11, 1759 ✦ 250 years

Mason Locke Weems was born at Anne Arundel County, MD. An Episcopal clergyman and traveling bookseller, Weems is remembered for the fictitious stories he presented as historical fact. Best known of his fables is the story describing George Washington cutting down his father's cherry tree with a hatchet. Weems's fictionalized histories, however, delighted many readers who accepted them as true. They became immensely popular and were bestsellers for many years. Weems died May 23, 1825, at Beaufort, SC.

Zachary Taylor

Birth: Nov 24, 1784 ✦ 225 years

This career soldier became the 12th president of the US from Mar 4, 1849, to July 9, 1850. Taylor, born at Orange County, VA, was involved in the War of 1812 and various battles with Native American tribes before becoming major general in 1846. It was during the Mexican-American War that he made his name. After winning the Battle of Buena Vista in February 1847 with a vastly outnumbered force, Taylor caught the attention of the Whig Party. He was nominated at the Whig Party convention in 1848 and defeated Democrat Lewis Cass in the general election. His short term of office was marked by the increasing tension surrounding the decision whether to make incoming states slave or free. Becoming ill July 4, 1850, he died at the White House, July 9. His last words: "I am sorry that I am about to leave my friends."

Abraham Lincoln

Birth: Feb 12, 1809 ✦ 200 years

See "Spotlight on American Anniversaries."

William Barret Travis

Birth: Aug 9, 1809 ✦ 200 years

Born at Saluda County, SC, William Barret Travis was one of many young American men who sought fortune in the Mexican territory of Texas. In 1831, leaving behind his wife and children, he practiced law in Texas and became part of the militant activities by American settlers to secede from Mexico. As tensions escalated into skirmishes and then into battles, Travis and James Bowie, with volunteer soldiers, barricaded themselves in the Alamo at San Antonio, TX. As commander at the Alamo, Travis released an earnest plea for aid in February 1836 but none came. Mexican troops, led by General Santa Anna, overwhelmed the small forces on Mar 6, 1836, and all the Texans were killed.

Oliver Wendell Holmes

Birth: Aug 29, 1809 ✦ 200 years

Oliver Wendell Holmes, physician, poet, author, and father of Supreme Court Justice Oliver Wendell Holmes, was born at Cambridge, MA. As a young law student Oliver Wendell Holmes dashed off a poem in protest when he heard that Congress was to have the USS *Constitution* (popularly known as "Old Ironsides") sent to a scrap yard. "Old Ironsides," published anonymously Sept 16, 1830, in the *Boston Daily Advertisor*, stirred up national outrage, and Congress instead appropriated money for the frigate's reconstruction. Holmes died at Boston, MA, Oct 7, 1894. "A moment's insight," he wrote, "is sometimes worth a life's experience."

Raphael Semmes

Birth: Sept 27, 1809 ✦ 200 years

Raphael Semmes was born at St. Charles County, MD, and died Aug 30, 1877, at Mobile, AL. Semmes was a daring Confederate naval officer, best known for his incredible raids on Union merchant ships during the middle two years of the Civil War. As commander of the *Alabama*, he captured, sank or burned 82 Union ships valued at more than $6 million.

Carrie Lane Chapman Catt

Birth: Jan 9, 1859 ✦ 150 years

Carrie Lane Chapman Catt was an American women's rights leader, founder (in 1919) of the National League of Women Voters. In a 1911 speech at Stockholm, she said, "When a just cause reaches its flood tide . . . whatever stands in its way must fall before its overwhelming power." Born at Ripon, WI, she died at New Rochelle, NY, Mar 9, 1947.

William H. Bonney (Billy the Kid)

Birth: Nov 23, 1859 ✦ 150 years

Billy the Kid was a legendary outlaw of the western US. Probably named Henry McCarty at birth (New York, NY), he was better known as William H. Bonney. A ruthless killer and a failure at everything legal, he escaped from jail at age 21 while under sentence of hanging. Recaptured at Stinking Springs, NM, and returned to jail, he again escaped, only to be shot through the heart by in-pursuit Lincoln County Sheriff Pat Garrett at Fort Sumner, NM, during the night of July 14, 1881. His last words, answered by two shots, reportedly were "Who is there?"

Harry S Truman

Birth: May 8, 1884 ✦ 125 years

The 33rd president of the US—"the Man from Missouri"—Harry S Truman succeeded to that office upon the death of Franklin D. Roosevelt, Apr 12, 1945, and served until Jan 20, 1953. Born at Lamar, MO, Truman was the last of the nine US presidents who did not attend college. He was a farmer and haberdasher who later served as a Missouri senator from 1935 to 1945 before becoming FDR's vice presidential running mate. During his presidency, the atomic bomb was dropped in Japan, the Cold War was fought

The Quotable Harry S Truman

"The buck stops here."

"If you can't stand the heat, get out of the kitchen."

"The release of atomic energy constitutes a new force too revolutionary to consider in the framework of old ideas."

"A President needs political understanding to run the government, but he may be elected without it."

"There is a right kind and wrong kind of victory."

and the Marshall Plan was enacted. The Truman Doctrine, announced Mar 12, 1947, was his effort to contain the spread of Soviet communism. The Korean War broke out during his second term. Truman fired General Douglas MacArthur, and the unpopularity of this action forced Truman to not seek reelection in the 1952 campaign. Affectionately nicknamed "Give 'em Hell Harry" by admirers, Truman died at Kansas City, MO, Dec 26, 1972.

Anna Eleanor Roosevelt

Birth: Oct 11, 1884 ✦ 125 years

Wife of Franklin Delano Roosevelt, 32nd president of the US, Eleanor Roosevelt was born at New York, NY. She led an active and independent life and was the first wife of a president to give her own news conference in the White House (1933). Widely known throughout the world, she was affectionately called "the first lady of the world." She served as US delegate to the United Nations General Assembly for a number of years before her death at New York, NY, Nov 7, 1962. A prolific writer, she wrote in *This Is My Story*, "No one can make you feel inferior without your consent."

Roger Nash Baldwin

Birth: Jan 21, 1884 ✦ 125 years

Founder of the American Civil Liberties Union, Roger Nash Baldwin was called the "country's unofficial agitator for, and defender of, its civil liberties." Born at Wellesley, MA, he died Aug 26, 1981, at Ridgewood, NJ.

Literature

Samuel Johnson

Birth: Sept 18, 1709 ✦ 300 years

Samuel Johnson was an English lexicographer and literary lion, creator of the first great dictionary of the English language (1755)—a labor of nine years—and author of poems, novels, biographical studies and essays. Johnson was born at Lichfield, Staffordshire, England, and died at London, England, Dec 13, 1784. Johnson, master of the quip, stated, "Patriotism is the last refuge of a scoundrel."

Robert Burns

Birth: Jan 25, 1759 ✦ 250 years

In his 37-year life span, Robert Burns was a farmer, lover of women, father of at least 11 children, Freemason, sparkling conversationalist, songwriter and beloved poet. He wove the folk traditions and dialects of Scotland into lovely lyrics and ballads. Poems and songs include "Tam O'Shanter," "To a Mouse," "Green Grow the Rushes, O" and most of "Auld Lang Syne." The lines he penned that live on in the public imagination are too numerous to list: "Oh wad some power the giftie gie us / To see oursels as others see us!" Born at Ayrshire, Scotland, he died at Dumfries, Scotland, July 21, 1796.

Mary Wollstonecraft

Birth: Apr 27, 1759 ✦ 250 years

Writer and advocate of equality for women, Mary Wollstonecraft was born at London, England. Rebelling against her father, she left home at age 18 and served as a lady's companion, opened a school and worked as a governess. Beginning with *Thoughts on the Education of Daughters* in 1787, Wollstonecraft attracted notice as a writer in favor of women's rights. Her *A Vindication of the Rights of Woman* (1792) argued that women should be given an education that would allow them to gain economic independence. She died at London on Sept 10, 1797, 11 days after giving birth to her second daughter, Mary Wollstonecraft Shelley, the author of *Frankenstein*.

Friedrich von Schiller

Birth: Nov 10, 1759 ✦ 250 years

Born at Marbach, Württemberg, von Schiller was the leading German dramatist of his age. His works include *Don Carlos* (1787), the *Wallenstein* trilogy (1798–1801) and *Wilhelm Tell*

(1804). His "An die Freude" ("Ode to Joy") was used by Beethoven in the choral finale to his *Symphony No 9 in D Minor*. He died May 9, 1805, at Weimer, Germany.

Edgar Allan Poe

Birth: Jan 19, 1809 ✦ 200 Years

Edgar Allan Poe, American poet, critic, magazine editor and story writer, has been called "America's most famous man of letters." Born at Boston, MA, he was orphaned in dire poverty in 1811 and was raised by Virginia merchant John Allan. Poe's tales of suspense

Notable Literary Centennials in 2009

James Agee

James Agee was a poet, critic, novelist (*A Death in the Family*), social historian (*Let Us Now Praise Famous Men*) and scriptwriter. Agee was born at Knoxville, TN, Nov 27, 1909, and died at New York, NY, May 16, 1955.

Nelson Algren

Nelson Algren was a "novelist of the city," famous for *The Man with the Golden Arm* (1949). Born Mar 28, 1909, at Detroit, MI; died May 9, 1981, at Sag Harbor, NY.

Eric Ambler

Eric Ambler was an influential novelist of realistic espionage tales that were critically and popularly embraced. Many of his novels were filmed, including *A Coffin for Dimitrios* and *Journey into Fear*. Born June 18, 1909, at London, England, he died there Oct 22, 1998.

Chester Himes

Chester Himes was a groundbreaking African-American author who challenged American racism in such novels as *If He Hollers Let Him Go* (1945). In the 1950s, after he relocated to a more tolerant France, Himes created a series of hard-boiled mystery novels set in Harlem, including *Cotton Comes to Harlem* (1965), that featured black detectives "Coffin Ed" Johnson and "Grave Digger" Jones. Born July 29, 1909, at Jefferson City, MO, Himes died Nov 12, 1984, at Moraira, Spain.

Malcolm Lowry

English author and poet Malcolm Lowry's reputation rests on his surrealistic masterpiece *Under the Volcano* (1947), one of the 20th century's towering novels. Unfortunately, the acclaim for Lowry came posthumously. Born July 28, 1909, at Birkenhead, England, Lowry died June 27, 1957, at Ripe, England.

Stephen Spender

Stephen Spender was an English poet, critic and professor who was very influential in the 1930s working alongside W.H. Auden and Christopher Isherwood. Also known for his memoir, *World Within World* (1951), Spender was knighted in 1983. Born in London, England, Feb 28, 1909, he died there July 16, 1995.

Wallace Stegner

Wallace Stegner was an award-winning writer of the American West. He was the author of *Angle of Repose* (1971), which was awarded the Pulitzer Prize. Born Feb 18, 1909, at Ames, IA, Stegner died Apr 13, 1993, at Santa Fe, NM.

Eudora Welty

Eudora Welty was a novelist and short-story writer whose characters lived in the rural south. Her short stories are considered the zenith of the art. Welty wrote *The Ponder Heart* (1954). She lived her entire life in Jackson, MS: born Apr 13, 1909; died July 23, 2001.

and horror are what he's best remembered for (many of which have been made into films), but he was also the creator of the detective story (featuring Auguste Dupin) and the author of one of the most famous 19th-century poems, "The Raven" (for which he received only $15). His criticism outlined the necessary ingredients of poetry. Poe died under mysterious circumstances at Baltimore, MD, Oct 7, 1849.

Nikolai Gogol

Birth: Mar 31, 1809 ✦ 200 years

Nikolai Gogol was a Ukrainian-Russian author of plays, novels and short stories. Born at Sorochintsy, in what is now the Ukraine, he died at Moscow, Russia, Mar 4, 1852. Gogol's most famous works are the novel *Dead Souls*, the play *The Inspector General* and the short story "The Overcoat."

Alfred, Lord Tennyson

Birth: Aug 6, 1809 ✦ 200 years

Alfred, Lord Tennyson was an English poet, born at Somersby, Lincolnshire, England. His celebrated works include the poems "The Lady of Shalott," "The Charge of the Light Brigade" and "Ulysses" (which contains the line "To strive, to seek, to find, and not to yield"). He also penned the verse novelettes *Maud*, *Enoch Arden*, *In Memoriam* and *The Idylls of the King*. Tennyson was appointed English poet laureate in 1850 in succession to William Wordsworth and made a peer in 1884. He died at Aldworth, England, Oct 6, 1892.

Solomon Aleicheim

Birth: Feb 18, 1859 ✦ 150 years

Solomon Aleicheim is the pen name of Russian-born author and humorist Solomon Rabinowitz. The musical *Fiddler on the Roof* drew from Aleicheim's short stories about Tevye the Milkman. Rabinowitz is affectionately known in the US as the "Jewish Mark Twain." He died at New York, NY, May 13, 1916.

Sir Arthur Conan Doyle

Birth: May 22, 1859 ✦ 150 years

British physician Sir Arthur Conan Doyle, born at Edinburgh, Scotland, is best remembered as a mystery author and the creator of Sherlock Holmes and Dr. Watson. Sherlock Holmes, the consulting detective of 221 B Baker Street, first appeared in the serialized novel *A Study in Scarlet* (1887) and in short tales in the *Strand* magazine. Doyle grew weary of Holmes and attempted to kill him off, but the clamoring public soon brought the detective back. In his later years, Conan Doyle was deeply interested in and lectured on the subject of spiritualism. He died at Crowborough, Sussex, England, July 7, 1930.

Thomas J. Wise

Birth: Oct 7, 1859 ✦ 150 years

Thomas J. Wise, English bibliophile and literary forger, was born at Gravesend, England. One of England's most distinguished bibliographic experts, he was revealed, in 1934, to have forged dozens of first editions and unique publications over a period of more than 20 years. Many of them had been sold at high prices to collectors and libraries. The forgeries in some cases purported to predate the real first editions. Wise died at Hampstead, England, May 13, 1937.

Maxwell Perkins

Birth: Sept 20, 1884 ✦ 125 years

The most powerful and influential editor of the early 20th century, Maxwell Perkins discovered, nurtured, cajoled, guided and edited such authors as F. Scott Fitzgerald, Ernest Hemingway, Thomas Wolfe and others at publisher Charles Scribner's Sons. Born at New York, NY, Perkins died June 17, 1947, at Stamford, CT.

Children's Literature

Horatio Alger

Birth: Jan 13, 1834 ✦ 175 years

Horatio Alger was an American clergyman and author of more than 100 popular books for boys (some 20 million copies sold). His most famous title was *Ragged Dick; or, Street Life in New York with the Bootblacks* (1868), in which a shoeshine boy eventually finds riches. Honesty, frugality and hard work assured that the heroes of his books would find success, wealth and fame. Born at Revere, MA, Alger died at Natick, MA, July 18, 1899.

Kenneth Grahame

Birth: Mar 8, 1859 ✦ 150 years

Kenneth Grahame was a Scottish author, born at Edinburgh. He wrote the classic children's book *The Wind in the Willows*, which has as its main characters a mole, a rat, a badger and a toad. He died July 6, 1932, at Pangbourne, Berkshire.

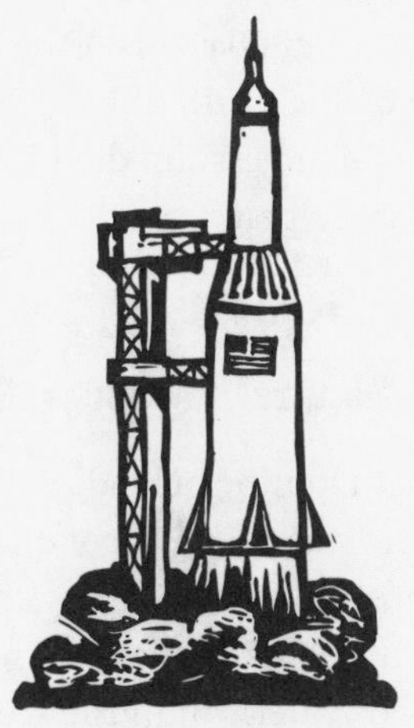

Journalism, Comics

Al Capp

Birth: Sept 28, 1909 ✦ 100 years

The creator of the fictitious village of Dogpatch, KY, Al Capp was born Alfred Gerald Caplin at New Haven, CT. The comic strip "Li'l Abner" appeared in daily newspapers from 1934 until its final episode was published Nov 13, 1977. Along with the misadventures of Abner Yokum, Capp lampooned famous public figures. The minor American institution of Sadie Hawkins Day made its debut in "Li'l Abner." Al Capp died Nov 5, 1979, at Cambridge, MA.

Alex Raymond

Birth: Oct 2, 1909 ✦ 100 Years

Influential comic strip artist Alex Raymond, born at New Rochelle, NY, was the creator in 1934 of the science fiction strip "Flash Gordon." The strip's huge popularity led to Hollywood serials starring Buster Crabbe a few years later. Raymond also created "Secret Agent X-9" and "Rip Kirby," but his career was cut short by a fatal automobile accident on Sept 6, 1956, at Westport, CT.

Damon Runyan

Birth: Oct 4, 1884 ✦ 125 years

American newspaperman and author Damon Runyan was born at Manhattan, KS, and died at New York, NY, Dec 10, 1946. The musical *Guys and Dolls* was based on one of his short stories. "Always try to rub up against money," he wrote, "for if you rub up against money long enough, some of it may rub off on you."

Art and Architecture

Frederic Bartholdi

Birth: Apr 2, 1834 ✦ 175 years

Frederic Bartholdi was the French sculptor who created *Liberty Enlightening the World* (better known as the Statue of Liberty), which stands at New York Harbor. He is also remembered for the *Lion of Belfort* at Belfort, France. Bartholdi was born at Colman, at Alsace, France, and died at Paris, Oct 4, 1904.

James Abbott McNeill Whistler

Birth: July 10, 1834 ✦ 175 years

James McNeill Whistler was an American painter based in England. He was born at Lowell, MA. Whistler's work foreshadowed later abstract act and generated controversy in his day. Whistler even went so far as to sue critic John Ruskin for libel after a scathing essay appeared (Whistler won only a farthing, and the court costs bankrupted him). He is famous for *Arrangement in Grey and Black: The Artist's Mother* (also known as *Whistler's Mother*, 1871). Whistler was also famous for his acerbic wit: When a woman declared that a landscape reminded her of Whistler's paintings, he reportedly said, "Yes, madam, Nature is creeping up." He died at London, England, July 17, 1903.

Edgar Degas

Birth: July 19, 1834 ✦ 175 years

Edgar Degas was a leading French impressionist painter, sculptor and printmaker, especially noted for his paintings and drawings of dancers in motion. He was born at Paris, France, and died there Sept 26, 1917.

Childe Hassam

Birth: Oct 17, 1859 ✦ 150 years

Childe Hassam was the artist who brought French impressionism to America. Hassam's luminous works feature scenes of New York City. He was born at Boston, MA, and died Aug 17, 1935, at East Hampton, NY.

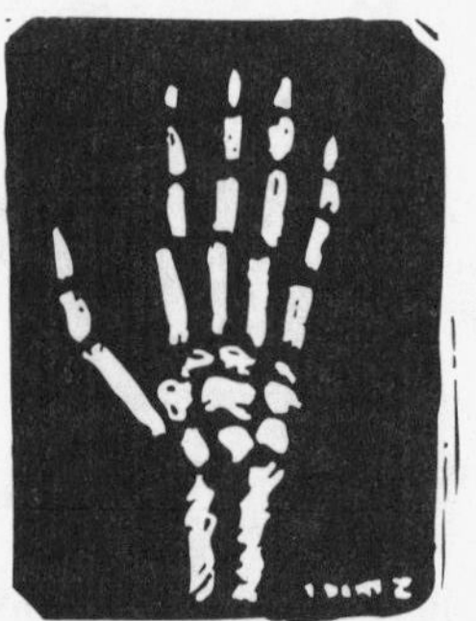

Georges Seurat

Birth: Dec 2, 1859 ✦ 150 years

French neo-impressionist painter born at Paris, France. He died there Mar 29, 1891. Seurat is known for his style of painting with small spots of color, called pointillism, as in *Sunday Afternoon on the Island of Grand Jatte.*

Sister Maria Innocentia Hummel

Birth: May 21, 1909 ✦ 100 years

Born at Massing, Bavaria, Sister Maria Innocentia Hummel attended Munich's Academy of Fine Arts. She entered Siessen Convent, run by the Sisters of the Third Order of St. Francis, and began teaching art to kindergarten children. In 1934 Franz Goebel obtained an exclusive license to translate her drawings into three-dimensional figurines. The first M.I. Hummel figurines were displayed at the Leipzig Trade Fair in 1935; they made their first appearance in the American market in May 1935. Hummel died Nov 6, 1946, at Siessen, Germany. Many M.I. Hummel Clubs across the country commemorate her birth date with special events and fundraisers for local charities.

Music

Henry Purcell

Birth: 1659 ✦ 350 Years

Henry Purcell, the great English composer of the late 17th century, born at London, England, had a tragically short life yet was quite prolific. His fame rests on the proto-operas *Dido and Aeneas* (1689) and *The Fairy Queen* (1692, based on Shakespeare's *A Midsummer's Night Dream*), ceremonial odes for the court of King Charles II and more than 100 songs. The holder of various court musical positions, Purcell died Nov 21, 1695, also at London.

Felix Mendelssohn

Birth: Feb 3, 1809 ✦ 200 years

Born at Hamburg, Germany, Mendelssohn was one of the great early Romantic composers, besides being a talented conductor and pianist. His famous works include the music to *A Midsummer's Night Dream* (the "Wedding March" from that work became traditional wedding music), the *Italian Symphony*, *Scottish Symphony* and the *Hebrides Overture.* Overcome by the death of his sister, Fanny, Mendelssohn died Nov 4, 1847, at Leipzig.

Victor Herbert

Birth: Feb 1, 1859 ✦ 150 years

Born at Dublin, Ireland, Victor Herbert was a cellist, conductor and prolific composer of operettas who dominated the popular American music scene in the late 19th and early 20th centuries. Among his many popular operettas were *Babes in Toyland* (1903) and *Naughty Marietta* (1910). "Ah, Sweet Mystery of Life" is only one of the many songs for which he set the music. Herbert also helped found the American Society of Composers, Artists, and Publishers (ASCAP), which helped protect artists' intellectual property rights. Herbert died May 26, 1924, at New York, NY.

Elie Siegmeister

Birth: Jan 15, 1909 ✦ 100 years

American composer Elie Siegmeister was born at New York, NY. He composed eight symphonies and eight operas and a number of concertos, chamber pieces and orchestral works using folk, jazz and street songs to create a contemporary American classical music. He died Mar 10, 1991, at Manhasset, NY.

Ethel Merman

Birth: Jan 16, 1909 ✦ 100 years

Ethel Merman was a musical comedy star famous for her belting voice and brassy style. Her 1930 debut in *Girl Crazy* singing "I Got Rhythm" drove the fans and critics crazy. She received a special Tony Award in 1972 for lifetime achievement. Born Ethel Agnes Zimmerman on Jan 16, 1909 (or 1912—the date changed the older she got, but most sources say 1909), at Queens, NY, she died Feb 15, 1984, at New York, NY.

Kate Smith

Birth: May 1, 1909 ✦ 100 years

One of America's most popular singers, Kate Smith, who never took a formal music lesson, recorded more songs than any other performer (more than 3,000), made more than 15,000 radio broadcasts and received more than 25 million fan letters. On Nov 11, 1938, she introduced a new song during her regular radio broadcast, written especially for her by Irving Berlin: "God Bless America." It soon became the unofficial national anthem. Born Kathryn Elizabeth Smith at Greenville, VA, she began her radio career May 1, 1931, with "When the Moon Comes Over the Mountain," a song identified with her throughout her career. She died at Raleigh, NC, June 17, 1986.

Maybelle Carter

Birth: May 10, 1909 ✦ 100 years

Maybelle Carter, the matriarch of the singing Carter Family, was born at Nickelsville, VA. She married Ezra Carter in 1926 and in 1927 became part of the Carter Family with brother-in-law A.P. Carter and his wife, Sara. The Carter Family were the first country music stars in America, reigning from 1927 to the 1950s and combining the influences of folk, bluegrass, rural country and gospel. Their hits included "Wabash Cannonball" and "Will the Circle Be Unbroken." Maybelle Carter played guitar, autoharp and banjo. She died Oct 23, 1978, at Nashville, TN.

Benny Goodman

Birth: May 30, 1909 ✦ 100 years

Jazz clarinetist and bandleader Benny Goodman was born Benjamin David Goodman at Chicago, IL. The "King of Swing" reigned in popularity, especially in the 1930s and 1940s. On Jan 16, 1938, Goodman's band was the first to play jazz at New York's Carnegie Hall. "Sing, Sing, Sing" was a signature piece and featured the drumming of Gene Krupa. Goodman and his big band also appeared in Hollywood films throughout the 1940s. He died June 13, 1986, at New York, NY.

Burl Ives

Birth: June 14, 1909 ✦ 100 years

American singer and actor Burl Icle Ivanhoe Ives was born at Hunt, IL. He helped to reintroduce Anglo-American folk music in the 1940s and 1950s. Ives won an Academy Award for his supporting role in *The Big Country* (1958), and he is well known for his role as Big Daddy in both the film and Broadway productions of *Cat on a Hot Tin Roof.* He died Apr 14, 1995, at Anacortes, WA.

Johnny Mercer

Birth: Nov 18, 1909 ✦ 100 years

American songwriter, singer, radio performer and actor Johnny Mercer was born at Savannah, GA. Mercer wrote lyrics (and often the music) for many of the great American popular songs from the 1930s through the 1960s, including "Autumn Leaves," "One for My Baby," "Satin Doll," "On the Achison, Topeka, and the Santa Fe," "You Must Have Been a Beautiful Baby," "Come Rain or Come Shine," "Hooray for Hollywood" and "Jeepers Creepers." Mercer died June 25, 1976, at Bel Air, CA.

Entertainment

Robert Joseph Flaherty

Birth: Feb 16, 1884 ✦ 125 years

American filmmaker, explorer and author Robert J. Flaherty has been called the "father of the documentary film." His films included *Nanook of the North*, *Moana* and *Man of Aran*. He was born at Iron Mountain, MI; died at Dunnerston, VT, July 23, 1951.

Joseph L. Mankiewicz

Birth: Feb 11, 1909 ✦ 100 years

Oscar-winning American film writer, director and producer Joseph L. Mankiewicz was born at Wilkes-Barre, PA. He coined the famous W.C. Fields phrase "my little chickadee" in his screenplay for the 1932 film *If I Had a Million*. In 1935 he turned to producing and subsequently made *The Philadelphia Story* and *Woman of the Year*. He began directing in 1946, and his stature grew with such films as *The Late George Apley*, *The Ghost and Mrs Muir*, *A Letter to Three Wives*, *All About Eve*, *Guys and Dolls*, *Cleopatra* and *Sleuth*. Mankiewicz won four Academy Awards for directing and screenwriting. He died Feb 5, 1993, at Mount Kisco, NY.

James Mason

Birth: May 15, 1909 ✦ 100 years

Born at Huddersfield, England, James Mason was nominated for an Oscar three times without being awarded the statuette. Notable roles were in *Odd Man Out*, *North by Northwest*, *Lolita* and *The Desert Fox*. Mason's velvety voice was a trademark. He died July 27, 1984, at Lausanne, Switzerland.

Jessica Tandy

Birth: June 7, 1909 ✦ 100 years

Born June 7, 1909, at London, England, Jessica Tandy was an acclaimed stage actress who often collaborated with her husband of 52 years, Hume Cronyn. She originated the stage role of Blanche DuBois in Tennessee Williams's *A Streetcar Named Desire* (1947) and was awarded a Tony (she was passed over for the film role; it was given to Vivien Leigh). Her other Tony Awards came for her work in *The Gin Game* (1977) and *Foxfire* (1982). Also a frequent film actress, she won an Academy Award for her leading role in *Driving Miss Daisy* (1989). She continued to work up until her death on Sept 11, 1994, at Easton, CT.

"Colonel" Tom Parker

Birth: June 26, 1909 ✦ 100 years

He was neither a colonel nor an American, but "Colonel" Tom Parker guided the career of America's greatest superstar, Elvis Presley. Born at Breda, Netherlands, as Andreas Cornelis van Kuijk, he picked up the "colonel" and the alias when he came to America, where he became a music promoter. As agent/manager to Presley beginning in 1955, Parker rewrote the rules and made artist management big business—often to accusations of exploitation as he took up to 50 percent of Presley's earnings and pushed the rock idol into an unimpressive film career. Presley credited his superstardom to Parker, and Parker was tireless in his promotion of Presley. Parker died Jan 21, 1997, at Las Vegas, NV.

Ruby Keeler

Birth: Aug 25, 1909 ✦ 100 years

Ruby Keeler, musical star of Broadway and Hollywood, was born Ethel Hilda Keeler at Halifax, NS, Canada (some sources say 1910 was her birth year). Famous films she appeared in (often teaming with Dick Powell) were *42nd Street*, *Gold Diggers of 1933*, *Footlight Parade* and *Dames*. She had an 11-year marriage to entertainer Al Jolson. She died Feb 28, 1993, at Rancho Mirage, CA.

Elia Kazan

Birth: Sept 7, 1909 ✦ 100 years

Born Elia Kazanjoglou at Constantinople, Turkey, Elia Kazan was one of the most influential directors in the history of American stage and film. He directed the Broadway premieres of Arthur Miller's *Death of a Salesman* and Tennessee Williams's *A Streetcar Named Desire* as well as many other Williams plays. He won directing Oscars for the films *On the Waterfront* and *Gentleman's Agreement*. Kazan discovered and promoted actors such as Marlon Brando, Warren Beatty and James Dean, whom he directed in *East of Eden*. In 1952 he angered and outraged much of Hollywood by testifying before the House Un-American Activities Committee, naming persons he thought to be members of the Communist Party, causing many of those named to be blacklisted and kept from working in the film industry for many, many years, or never again. Kazan died at New York, NY, Sept 7, 2003.

Jacques Tati

Birth: Oct 9, 1909 ✦ 100 years

Born at Le Pecq, France, Jacques Tati was a French filmmaker and performer who made internationally beloved comic masterpieces—often combining the best of silent comedy in films that depicted the average Joe's misalliance with modern industrialized society. Tati's filmic alter ego was the pipe-smoking, rumpled hat–wearing Monsieur Hulot, who was always out of step wherever he was. Tati's six films included *Mr. Hulot's Holiday* (1953), *Mon Oncle* ("My Uncle," 1958) and *Playtime* (1967). Tati died Nov 5, 1982, at Paris, France.

Business/Industry

Cyrus H. McCormick

Birth: Feb 15, 1809 ✦ 200 years

Cyrus McCormick, inventor of the reaper, was born at Rockbridge County, VA. It is said that the invention of the reaper rates second only to the railroad as far as contributing greatly in the development of the United States. Continuing the dream of his father, McCormick constructed a horse-operated reaper, which was demonstrated for the first time in a Virginia wheat field in July 1831. He moved his operation to Chicago, IL, in 1847, to be closer to the Midwest's expanding wheat fields. His business prospered despite two decades of constant litigation over patent rights. He died May 13, 1884, at Chicago, IL. In 1902–1903, his McCormick Harvesting Machine Company was consolidated with other firms to become the International Harvester Company.

George Washington Gale Ferris

Birth: Feb 14, 1859 ✦ 150 years

George Washington Gale Ferris, American engineer and inventor, was born at Galesburg, IL. Among his many accomplishments as a civil engineer, Ferris is best remembered as the inventor of the Ferris wheel, which he developed for the World's Columbian Exposition at Chicago, IL, in 1893. Built on the Midway Plaisance, the 250-foot-diameter Ferris wheel (with 36 coaches, each capable of carrying 40 passengers) proved one of the greatest attractions of the fair. It was America's answer to the Eiffel Tower of the Paris International Exposition of 1889. Ferris died at Pittsburgh, PA, Nov 22, 1896.

Edwin Herbert Land

Birth: May 7, 1909 ✦ 100 years

Edwin Herbert Land was an American scientist, founder of the Polaroid Corporation (1937) and inventor, whose study of polarized light led to immense advances in photography. In 1932 (on leave from Harvard), he created what he called the Polaroid sheet. On Feb 21, 1947, Land demonstrated the Polaroid Land Camera, which took, developed and printed photographs on one sheet of paper in one minute. Soon, Land's Polaroids were the most popular cameras in the world. Born at Bridgeport, CN, Land died Mar 1, 1991, at Cambridge, MA.

Leo Fender

Birth: Aug 10, 1909 ✦ 100 years

Leo Fender, founder of the Fender Electric Instruments Company (1946), cocreated in 1948 the first solid-body electric guitar to go into mass production. This model, the Telecaster, was soon joined by the first electric bass guitar (1951) and the Stratocaster (1954), which featured a vibrato bridge that players could use to bend strings and achieve a sound closer to that produced by a steel guitar. All these models and more are still in production. Born at Anaheim, CA, Fender died Mar 21, 1991, at Fullerton, CA.

Peter Drucker

Birth: Nov 19, 1909 ✦ 100 years

Born at Vienna, Austria, Peter Drucker was an economist, theorist, consultant, journalist, professor and author. Arriving in America in 1937 (after leaving his Nazi-occupied homeland), Drucker grew to be one of the most important business thinkers of the century, practically inventing the idea of management as a profession. In 1954, he published his most famous work, *The Practice of Management*—one of almost 40 works. In his long career, he moved from thinking of the corporation as a community builder to being a critical gadfly in the wake of business scandals at the end of the century. He died Nov 11, 2005, at his home in Claremont, CA.

Science

Franz Anton Mesmer

Birth: May 23, 1734 ✦ 275 years

Franz Anton Mesmer was a physician born at Iznang am Bodensee, Germany. Mesmer invented the psychotherapy method mesmerism and used it (as well as magnetism) to treat ailing wealthy socialites throughout Europe to great controversy. Louis XVI of France went so far as to establish a scientific commission in 1784 to study mesmerism, which was the precursor to hypnotism and helped open the door to psychoanalysis late in the next century. Mesmer died Mar 5, 1815, at Meersburg, Swabia, Germany.

John Wesley Powell

Birth: Mar 24, 1834 ✦ 175 years

John Wesley Powell was an American geologist, explorer and ethnologist. He is best known for his explorations of the Grand Canyon by boat on the Colorado River. He published an account of these travels in *Exploration of the Colorado River of the West and Its Tributaries* (1875). Powell provided groundbreaking research into Native American languages and was later the first director of the Smithsonian's US Bureau of Ethnology (founded 1879). Born at Mount Morris, NY, Powell died at Haven, ME, Sept 23, 1902.

Pierre Curie

Birth: May 15, 1859 ✦ 150 years

Born at Paris, France, Pierre Curie was one of the founders of modern physics. As a young man, his research had already brought important results (in heat waves, crystals, magnetism, symmetry) and the formulation of Curie's Law before he met and married Marie Sklowdowska in 1894 and 1895. Together, the Curies discovered polonium and radium while conducting research in radioactivity. With Henri Becquerel, the Curies were awarded the Nobel Prize for Physics in 1903. Tragically, Pierre Curie was struck by a dray in Paris and died Apr 19, 1906.

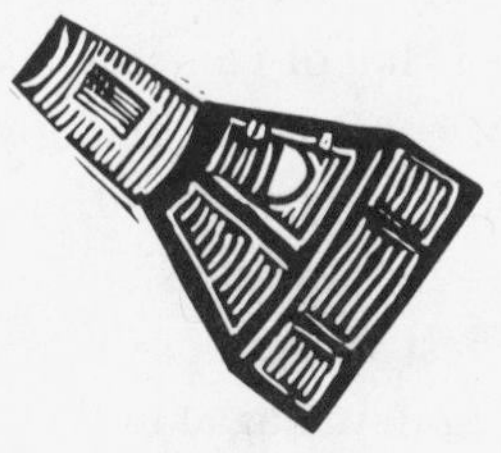

Auguste Piccard and Jean Felix Piccard

Births: Jan 28, 1884 ✦ 125 years

Twin brothers Auguste and Jean Felix Piccard were scientists, engineers and explorers born at Basel, Switzerland. In their study of cosmic rays, the brothers made several epic balloon ascents. Auguste made a record-setting balloon ascent into the stratosphere on May 27, 1931, and also made ocean-depth descents and explorations. He developed the bathyscaphe for deep-sea research. Jean Felix reached 57,579 feet (11 miles) in a sealed gondola piloted by his wife, Jeannette, in October 1934. Jean Felix made several improvements in balloon gondolas. Auguste died at Lausanne, Switzerland, Mar 24, 1962. Jean Felix died at Minneapolis, MN, Jan 28, 1963.

Virginia Apgar

Birth: June 7, 1909 ✦ 100 years

Apgar developed the simple assessment method that permits doctors and nurses to evaluate newborns while they are still in the delivery room to identify those in need of immediate medical care. The Apgar score was first published in 1953, and the Perinatal Section of the American Academy of Pediatrics is named for Apgar. Born at Westfield, NJ, Apgar died Aug 7, 1974, at New York, NY.

Education

John Dewey

Birth: Oct 20, 1859 ✦ 150 years

American psychologist, philosopher and educational reformer John Dewey was born at Burlington, VT. His philosophical views of education have been termed pragmatism, instrumentalism and experimentalism. Died at New York, NY, June 1, 1952.

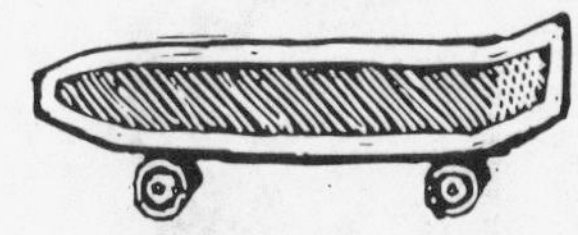

Ludwik Lejzer Zamenhof

Birth: Dec 15, 1859 ✦ 150 years

Born at Bialystok in what is now Poland, Zamenhof was an oculist who invented the language Esperanto (first published in 1887) in an effort to find a way to promote international tolerance and expanded communication. Zamenhof, who adopted the pen name Doktoro Esperanto (which means "Doctor Hopeful" in the language), created his vocabulary from the major Western languages—especially Latin. For example, *mano* means hand. *Esperanto estasĉies propraĵo* translates as "Esperanto is everybody's property." The popularity of the artificial language grew as Zamenhof translated major works of literature and spoke widely about it. The first Esperanto congress took place in 1905 in France. Zamenhof died Apr 14, 1917, at Warsaw, Poland.

Hermann Rorschach

Birth: Nov 8, 1884 ✦ 125 years

Zürich, Switzerland–born psychiatrist Hermann Rorschach used his youthful interest in art and sketching to create the unusual and controversial inkblot test that now bears his name. Drawing on the earlier work of Szyman Hens, in 1918 Rorschach showed his patients inkblots on cards—created at random—and asked for their interpretations to gain insight into their unconscious. Rorschach, a psychoanalyst, continued his experimentation before publishing a comprehensive volume of his findings in 1921. He died Apr 2, 1922, before his methods had gained the international attention that they still hold today.

Sports

Walter Camp

Birth: Apr 7, 1859 ✦ 150 years

Walter Chauncey Camp, college athlete, coach and administrator, was born at New Britain, CT. Camp played football and several other sports at Yale, but he gained prominence for helping to reshape the rules of rugby football into American football. Among his innovations were reducing the number of players on a side from 15 to 11, introducing the scrimmage, giving one team definite possession of the ball and proposing the downs system. He served as a volunteer coach at Yale and became a national figure as a promoter of football; each year from 1889 until his death, he selected an all-American team. He died at New York, NY, Mar 14, 1925.

Charles Comiskey

Birth: Aug 15, 1859 ✦ 150 years

Charles Albert Comiskey, Baseball Hall of Fame first baseman, manager and executive, was born at Chicago, IL. Comiskey's career spanned 50 years, 30 of them as founding owner of the Chicago White Sox. Before that, he was an outstanding and innovative player and a tough, successful manager. Comiskey was inducted into the Hall of Fame in 1939. He died at Eagle River, WI, Oct 26, 1931.

Buck Ewing

Birth: Oct 17, 1859 ✦ 150 years

William Buckingham (Buck) Ewing, Baseball Hall of Fame catcher, was born at Hoagland, OH. Ewing was one of the best catchers of the 19th century and is credited by some with being the first to crouch directly under the batter. Ewing was inducted into the Hall of Fame in 1939. He died at Cincinnati, OH, Oct 20, 1906.

Charles Ebbets

Birth: Oct 29, 1859 ✦ 150 years

Charles Hercules Ebbets, baseball executive, was born at New York, NY. Ebbets bought into the Brooklyn baseball club in 1890 and became controlling owner in 1898. He sold 50 percent of the team to build Ebbets Field, the park whose enduring reputation has been the model for the new, old-fashioned parks constructed in recent years. Ebbets died at New York, Apr 18, 1925.

Billy Evans

Birth: Feb 10, 1884 ✦ 125 years

William George (Billy) Evans, Baseball Hall of Fame umpire and executive, was born at Chicago, IL. Evans was an American League umpire from 1906 to 1927, arguing successfully for using four umpires in the World Series. He wrote *Knotty Problems of Baseball*, a casebook. After retiring, he became general manager of the Cleveland Indians and, later, the Detroit Tigers. Evans was inducted into the Hall of Fame in 1973. He died at Miami, FL, Jan 23, 1956.

Pop Lloyd

Birth: Apr 25, 1884 ✦ 125 years

John Henry ("Pop") Lloyd, Baseball Hall of Fame shortstop, was born at Palatka, FL. Lloyd was often compared to Honus Wagner and was considered one of the best shortstops ever. He played and managed in the Negro Leagues and made quite a career in Cuba, where the fans nicknamed him "Cuchara" (scoop or shovel) for his big hands. Lloyd was inducted into the Hall of Fame in 1977. He died at Atlantic City, NJ, Mar 19, 1965.

Eddie Cicotte

Birth: June 19, 1884 ✦ 125 years

Edward Victor (Eddie) Cicotte, baseball player, was born at Detroit, MI. Pitching for the Chicago White Sox, Cicotte won 28 games in 1917 and 29 in 1919, using his knuckleball to great effectiveness. He was implicated in the Black Sox scandal of 1919 and banned from baseball for life. He died at Detroit, May 5, 1969.

Bob Douglas

Birth: Nov 4, 1884 ✦ 125 years

Robert L. (Bob) Douglas, Basketball Hall of Fame executive, was born at St. Kitts, British West Indies. Douglas came to the US in 1888 and played basketball before founding the New York Renaissance, one of the game's greatest teams, in 1922. The Rens got their name from the Harlem Renaissance ballroom, where they played their home games, but they barnstormed extensively as well. Over 22 years, they won 2,381 games, including the 1931 World Professional Championship. The Rens were inducted into the Hall of Fame as a team in 1963. Douglas followed as an individual contributor in 1971. He died at New York, NY, July 16, 1979.

Max Baer

Birth: Feb 11, 1909 ✦ 100 years

Maximillian Adalbert (Max) Baer, boxer, was born at Omaha, NE. Baer possessed awesome punching power and once knocked out a fighter who collapsed into a coma and died from his injuries, an event that almost caused Baer to drop out of boxing. Baer won the heavyweight title from Primo Carnera on June 14, 1934, and lost it a year later to James Braddock, a severe underdog. He died at Hollywood, CA, Nov 21, 1959.

Mel Ott

Birth: Mar 2, 1909 ✦ 100 years

Melvin Thomas (Mel) Ott, Baseball Hall of Fame outfielder, was born at Gretna, LA. Playing for the New York Giants, Ott hit 511 home runs, third on the all-time list when he retired and a National League record until Willie Mays surpassed it in 1966. Ott's swing was characterized by an unusual, high leg kick that helped him reach the short fences of the Polo Grounds for two-thirds of his homers. Ott was inducted into the Hall of Fame in 1951. He died at New Orleans, LA, Nov 21, 1958.

Luke Appling

Birth: Apr 2, 1909 ✦ 100 years

Lucius Benjamin (Luke) Appling, Baseball Hall of Fame shortstop, was born at High Point, NC. Appling won two American League batting titles, hitting .310 over 20 years with the Chicago White Sox. He was inducted into the Hall of Fame in 1964. Appling died at Cumming, GA, Jan 3, 1991.

Jimmy Cannon

Birth: Apr 10, 1909 ✦ 100 years

Jimmy Cannon, sportswriter, was born at New York, NY. Cannon covered the Lindbergh kidnapping case and then switched to sports, eventually being ranked as New York City's leading sportswriter. He specialized in baseball, boxing and horse racing and was particularly critical of baseball and other sports for their racism. He died at New York, Dec 5, 1973.

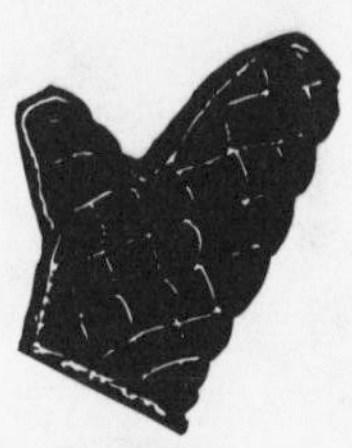

Matthew Busby

Birth: May 26, 1909 ✦ 100 years

Matthew Busby, born at Orbiston, Scotland, went from being a talented soccer player to becoming one of the legendary managers/executives of the game at Manchester United, where he developed the "Busby Babes," a team of wonderfully talented young players. As a manager, he survived a devastating 1958 air crash that killed most of his starting players and then made Manchester United the dominant club of the English premier league, with five league titles in the 1950s and 1960s. Knighted in 1968, Busby died Jan 20, 1994, at Manchester, England.

Bill France

Birth: Sept 26, 1909 ✦ 100 years

William Henry Getty (Bill) France Sr, stock car racing executive, was born at Washington, DC. While running a service station at Daytona Beach, FL, France took an interest in the auto races contested on the beach. He got involved in race promotion and organization and founded NASCAR in 1948. France remained at the helm long enough to see the once-primitive sport evolve into a series of high-profile spectator extravaganzas. He died at Ormond Beach, FL, June 7, 1992.

Glenn Cunningham

Birth: Aug 4, 1909 ✦ 100 years

Glenn V. Cunningham, track and field athlete, was born at Atlanta, KS. Cunningham overcame severe burns to his legs in a schoolhouse fire to become a great middle-distance runner. He won the Sullivan Award for 1933 and starred in the mile run as it became the premier track event. Cunningham set a world record, 4:06.7, in 1934 that lasted three years. After World War II, he and his wife opened a youth ranch and cared for more than 10,000 foster children plus 10 of their own. He died at Menifee, AR, Mar 10, 1988.

✦ January ✦

January 1 — Thursday

DAY 1 364 REMAINING

THURSDAY, JANUARY ONE, 2009. Jan 1. First day of the first month of the Gregorian calendar year, Anno Domini 2009, being a Common Year, and (until July 4) 233rd year of American independence. 2009 will be year 6722 of the Julian Period, a time frame consisting of 7,986 years that began at noon, universal (Greenwich) time, Jan 1, 4714 BC. Astronomers will note that Julian Day number 2,452,647 begins at noon, universal time (representing the number of days since the beginning of the Julian Period). New Year's Day is a public holiday in the US and in many other countries. Traditionally, it is a time for personal stocktaking, for making resolutions for the coming year and sometimes for recovering from the festivities of New Year's Eve. Financial accounting begins anew for businesses and individuals whose fiscal year is the calendar year. Jan 1 has been observed as the beginning of the year in most English-speaking countries since the British Calendar Act of 1751, prior to which the New Year began Mar 25 (approximating the vernal equinox). Earth begins another orbit of the sun, during which it, and we, will travel some 583,416,000 miles in 365.2422 days. New Year's Day has been called "Everyman's Birthday," and in some countries a year is added to everyone's age on Jan 1 rather than on the anniversary of each person's birth.

ACADIA NATIONAL PARK ESTABLISHED: 90th ANNIVERSARY. Jan 1, 1919. Maine's Sieur de Monts National Monument, authorized in 1916, was established as Lafayette National Park in 1919. The name was changed to Acadia National Park by an act of Congress in 1929.

AUSTRALIA: COMMONWEALTH FORMED: ANNIVERSARY. Jan 1, 1901. On this day, the six colonies of Victoria, New South Wales, Queensland, South Australia, Western Australia and Northern Territory were united into one nation. The British Parliament had passed the Commonwealth Constitution Bill in the spring of 1900, and Queen Victoria signed the document Sept 17, 1900.

BONZA BOTTLER DAY™. Jan 1. (also Feb 2, Mar 3, Apr 4, May 5, June 6, July 7, Aug 8, Sept 9, Oct 10, Nov 11 and Dec 12). To celebrate when the number of the day is the same as the number of the month. Bonza Bottler Day™ is an excuse to have a party at least once a month. Created by the late Elaine Fremont and continued by her family, Bonza Bottler Day is now celebrated in many countries. For info: Gail M. Berger, Bonza Bottler Day, 14 Fernwood Dr, Taylors, SC 29687. E-mail: bonza@bonzabottlerday.com. Web: www.bonzabottlerday.com.

BOOK BLITZ MONTH. Jan 1–31. Focuses attention on improving authors' relationships with the media in order to create a bestselling book. Free book PR evaluation available. Annually, the month of January. For info: Barbara Gaughen, Media 21, 7456 Evergreen Dr, Santa Barbara, CA 93117. Phone: (805) 968-8567. Fax: (805) 968-5747. E-mail: bgaughenmu@aol.com. Web: www.goodmorningworld.org.

BRYCE CANYON NATIONAL PARK ESTABLISHED: ANNIVERSARY. Jan 1, 1928. Utah's Bryce Canyon National Monument, created in 1923, was established as a national park and preserve.

CALIFORNIA DRIED PLUM DIGESTIVE HEALTH MONTH. Jan 1–31. Dried plums have a unique combination of nutrients, such as soluble and insoluble fiber, potassium, magnesium and iron; furthermore, dried plums are high in plant substances called pholyphenols, which are strong antioxidants that protect DNA against damage, decrease inflammation and prevent cancer. By combining the fruit's health benefits with a conscientious diet, you will be on track toward protecting your health! For info: Richard Peterson, California Dried Plum Board, 3840 Rosin Ct, Ste 170, Sacramento, CA 95834. Phone: (916) 565-6232. Fax: (916) 565-6237. E-mail: rpeterson@cdpb.org. Web: www.californiadriedplums.org.

CAPITAL ONE BOWL. Jan 1. Florida Citrus Bowl Stadium, Orlando, FL. 63rd annual. Postseason college football game matching two teams selected from the Big Ten Conference and the SEC. Est attendance: 70,000. For info: Florida Citrus Sports, One Citrus Bowl Pl, Orlando, FL 32805. Phone: (407) 423-2476. Fax: (407) 425-8451. E-mail: contactfcs@fcsports.com. Web: www.fcsports.com.

CELEBRATION OF LIFE MONTH. Jan 1–31. The month of January, being the first month of the year, signifies a new beginning, a new life, a new happiness in many lives each year. Every community has a new hope to begin a new page in the book of life. Remember always to value the gift of life for all Americans pursuing life, liberty, happiness and justice for all citizens. For info: Judith Natale, NCAC America, PO Box 493703, Redding, CA 96049-3703. E-mail: childaware@aol.com.

CERVICAL CANCER SCREENING MONTH. Jan 1–31. During January, the National Cervical Cancer Public Education campaign gives women and their doctors information about what causes cervical cancer and the best ways to prevent or detect it. Women are encouraged to get screened for cervical cancer and pledge their commitment to preventing the disease by visiting the campaign's website at www.cervicalcancercampaign.org. For info: The Gynecologic Cancer Foundation, 230 W Monroe, Ste 2528, Chicago, IL 60606. Phone: (312) 578-1439. Fax: (312) 578-9769. E-mail: info@thegcf.org. Web: www.thegcf.org.

CIRCUMCISION OF CHRIST. Jan 1. Holy day in many Christian churches. Celebrates Jesus's submission to Jewish law; on the octave day of Christmas. See also: "Solemnity of Mary, Mother of God" (Jan 1) for Roman Catholic observance since the 1969 calendar reorganization.

COPYRIGHT REVISION LAW SIGNED: ANNIVERSARY. Jan 1, 1976. The first major revision since 1909 of laws governing intellectual property in the US was signed by President Ford. It took effect two years later on Jan 1, 1978. The act (Public Law 94–553) contains substantial revisions of the principles governing acquisition and duration of copyright and deals with issues that have been raised in recent years concerning photocopying and the use of copyrighted works by public broadcasting and cable television systems.

CUBA: 50th ANNIVERSARY OF THE REVOLUTION. Jan 1. National holiday celebrating the overthrow of the government of Fulgencio Batista in 1959 by the revolutionary forces of Fidel Castro, which had begun a civil war in 1956.

CUBA: LIBERATION DAY. Jan 1. A national holiday that celebrates the end of Spanish rule in 1899. Cuba, the largest island of the West Indies, was a Spanish possession from its discovery by Columbus (Oct 27, 1492) until 1899. Under US military control 1899–1902 and 1906–09, a republican government took over Jan 28, 1909, and controlled the island until overthrown Jan 1, 1959, by Fidel Castro's revolutionary movement.

CZECH-SLOVAK DIVORCE: ANNIVERSARY. Jan 1, 1993. As Dec 31, 1992, gave way to Jan 1, 1993, the 74-year-old state of Czechoslovakia separated into two nations—the Czech Republic and Slovakia. The Slovaks held a celebration through the night in the streets of Bratislava amid fireworks, bell ringing, singing of the new country's national anthem and the raising of the Slovak flag. In the new Czech Republic no official festivities took place, but later in the day the Czechs celebrated with a solemn oath by their parliament. The nation of Czechoslovakia ended peacefully though polls showed that most Slovaks and Czechs would have preferred that it survive. Before the split Czech prime minister Vaclav Klaus and Slovak prime minister Vladimir Meciar reached an agreement on dividing everything from army troops and gold reserves to the art on government building walls.

DIET RESOLUTION WEEK. Jan 1–7. This week emphasizes the importance of watching your weight by focusing on the type—not the amount—of food you put on your plate. Resolve to consume minimally processed, less-refined carbohydrate foods. Slim down permanently with whole grains, legumes, fresh fruits and vegetables. Eat more but weigh less for life. Delete meat and other animal foods to make minuscule meals and calorie counting obsolete. Start your year off right by eating light with every bite! For info: Vegetarian Awareness Network, PO Box 3545, Washington, DC 20027-0045. Phone: (877) VEG-DIET.

ELLIS ISLAND OPENED: ANNIVERSARY. Jan 1, 1892. Ellis Island was opened on New Year's Day in 1892. Over the years more than 20 million individuals were processed through the stations. The island was used as a point of deportation as well: in 1932 alone, 20,000 people were deported from Ellis Island. When the US entered WWII in 1941, Ellis Island became a Coast Guard Station. It closed Nov 12, 1954, and was declared a national park in 1956. After years of disuse it was restored, and in 1990 it was reopened as a museum.

EMANCIPATION PROCLAMATION TAKES EFFECT: ANNIVERSARY. Jan 1, 1863. Abraham Lincoln, by executive proclamation of Sept 22, 1862, declared that on this date " . . . all persons held as slaves within any state or designated part of a state, the people whereof shall then be in rebellion against the United States, shall be then, thenceforward, and forever, free. . . ." Slaves in the four slave states that had not seceded from the Union (Delaware, Maryland, Kentucky and Missouri) were not freed until the passage of the 13th Amendment in 1865. See also: "Thirteenth Amendment to the US Constitution Ratified" (Dec 6).

ENGLAND: THE NEW YEAR'S DAY PARADE—LONDON. Jan 1. London. The biggest parade of its kind in the world attracts a million people on the streets of the capital. The route starts at noon in Parliament Square and goes along Whitehall, around Trafalgar Square and up Piccadilly. Dozens of the world's top marching bands, thousands of cheerleaders and the amazing eight-story-high cartoon character balloons all add to the fun. Est attendance: 1,000,000. For info: Bob Bone, The New Year's Day Parade—London, Research House, Fraser Rd, Greenford, Middlesex, England UB6 7AQ. Phone: (44) (20) 8566-8586. Fax: (44) (20) 8566-8494. E-mail: info@londonparade.co.uk. Web: www.londonparade.co.uk.

EURO INTRODUCED: 10th ANNIVERSARY. Jan 1, 1999. The euro, the common currency of members of the European Union, was introduced for use by financial institutions. The value of the currencies of the 11 nations (Austria, Belgium, Finland, France, Germany, Ireland, Italy, Luxembourg, the Netherlands, Portugal and Spain) was locked in at a permanent conversion rate to the euro. Greece joined the eurozone the following year. On Jan 1, 2002, euro bills and coins began circulating; other currencies were phased out as of Feb 28, 2002.

FAMILY FIT LIFESTYLE MONTH. Jan 1–31. Healthy living is achievable. Try, for one month, to move your body and reduce the fat, sugar and salt in your diet while balancing your meals with healthy nutrition. Use moderation and portion control, and try to prevent many of the diseases associated with high-fat/high-cholesterol diets. Help your kids learn proper nutrition and a regular exercise routine. The first month of the new year is the perfect time to change your life. For info: Family Fit Lifestyle, Inc, 15202 N 50th Pl, Scottsdale, AZ 85254. Phone: (866) 548-3348. E-mail: Jyl@AmericasHealthiestMom.com. Web: www.AmericasHealthiestMom.com.

January 2009	S	M	T	W	T	F	S
					1	2	3
	4	5	6	7	8	9	10
	11	12	13	14	15	16	17
	18	19	20	21	22	23	24
	25	26	27	28	29	30	31

FEDEX ORANGE BOWL. Jan 1. Dolphins Stadium, Miami, FL. 75th annual. Part of the BCS. Est attendance: 75,000. For info: Orange Bowl Committee, 14360 NW 77th Ct, Miami Lakes, FL 33016. Phone: (305) 341-4733. Fax: (305) 341-4750. E-mail: info@orangebowl.org. Web: www.orangebowl.org.

FINANCIAL WELLNESS MONTH. Jan 1–31. For people to establish financial balance after credit card bills pour in from the holidays. This is a time to set new goals for financial freedom and moderation in spending. See a financial adviser. Create money management goals. Set up a savings plan. Figure out how to pay off old loans. Get out of debt. Spend less money. Give up a little luxury and donate the savings to charity. Buy in bulk, shop at discount stores, wait for sales and bargains. Shop garage sales, flea markets and online auctions. For info: Angela Brown Oberer, Words of Wellness, PO Box 49266, Charlotte, NC 28277. Phone: (704) 849-2900. E-mail: angela@wordsofwellness.com. Web: www.wordsofwellness.com.

FIRST BABY BOOMER BORN: ANNIVERSARY. Jan 1, 1946. Kathleen Casey Wilkens, born at one minute after midnight at Philadelphia, PA, was the first of the almost 78 million baby boomers born between 1946 and 1964.

FORSTER, E.M.: BIRTH ANNIVERSARY. Jan 1, 1879. Edward Morgan Forster, English author born at London, England, is remembered for his six novels: *Where Angels Fear to Tread* (1905), *The Longest Journey* (1907), *A Room with a View* (1908), *Howard's End* (1910), *A Passage to India* (1924) and the posthumously published *Maurice* (1971). He also achieved eminence for his short stories and essays, and he collaborated on the libretto for an opera, Benjamin Britten's *Billy Budd* (1951). Forster died at Coventry, England, June 7, 1970.

GET ORGANIZED MONTH. Jan 1–31. Is your New Year's resolution to get more organized? This is an opportunity to streamline your life, create more time, lower your stress and increase your profit. For info: National Assn of Professional Organizers, 15000 Commerce Pky, Ste C, Mount Laurel, NJ 08054. Phone: (856) 380-6828. E-mail: napo@napo.net. Web: www.napo.net.

GREENBERG, HANK: BIRTH ANNIVERSARY. Jan 1, 1911. Henry Benjamin (Hank) Greenberg, Baseball Hall of Fame first baseman and outfielder, born at New York, NY. One of the game's most prodigious sluggers, Greenberg hit 331 home runs and drove in 1,276 runs in only nine full seasons. Baseball's first Jewish superstar, Greenberg entered the army after playing just 19 games in 1941 and did not return to the Detroit Tigers until midway through the 1945 season. His grand slam on that season's last day won the pennant for the Tigers and propelled them toward a World Series triumph. Inducted into the Hall of Fame in 1956. Died at Beverly Hills, CA, Sept 4, 1986.

HAITI: INDEPENDENCE DAY. Jan 1. A national holiday commemorating the proclamation of independence in 1804. Haiti, occupying the western third of the island Hispaniola (second largest of the West Indies), was a Spanish colony from its discovery by Columbus in 1492 until 1697. Then it was a French colony until the proclamation of independence in 1804.

HANGOVER HANDICAP RUN. Jan 1. Veteran's Park, Klamath Falls, OR. Two-mile fun run at 9 AM New Year's Day. The first-place male and female finishers each take home a beer can trophy. Est attendance: 100. For info: Hangover Handicap, 1800 Fairmount, Klamath Falls, OR 97601. Phone: (541) 882-6922. Fax: (541) 883-6481.

HOOVER, J. EDGAR: BIRTH ANNIVERSARY. Jan 1, 1895. John Edgar Hoover, born at Washington, DC. He led the Palmer Raids and was director of the FBI, 1924–72. During his time as director, Hoover practiced modern investigative techniques, improved FBI agent training and increased FBI funding from Congress. He died May 2, 1972, at Washington, DC.

INTERNATIONAL CHANGE YOUR STARS MONTH. Jan 1–31. The perfect time to remember and recognize that we can choose our own destiny and through our choices we can change our stars! For info: Jace Carlton. Phone: (925) 640-9756. E-mail: JaceCarlton@changeyourstars.com. Web: www.changeyourstars.com.

INTERNATIONAL CREATIVITY MONTH. Jan 1–31. A month to remind individuals and organizations around the globe to capitalize on the power of creativity. Unleashing creativity and innovation is vital for personal and business success in this age of accelerating change. The first month of the year provides an opportunity to take a fresh approach to problem solving and renew confidence in our creative capabilities. For info: Randall Munson, Pres, Creatively Speaking, 508 Meadow Run Dr SW, Rochester, MN 55902-2337. Phone: (507) 286-1331. Fax: (507) 286-1331. E-mail: Creativity@CreativelySpeaking.com. Web: www.CreativityMonth.com.

INTERNATIONAL NEW YEARS' RESOLUTIONS MONTH FOR BUSINESSES. Jan 1–31. Set in motion a successful year by focusing on PR and marketing efforts guaranteed to make your cash register ring and your bank statements sing. Resolve to get your business and message in front of your target market. For marketing and PR ideas: Raleigh Pinskey. Phone: (800) 249-7322. E-mail: raleigh@promoteyourself.com. Web: www.promoteyourself.com.

INTERNATIONAL QUALITY OF LIFE MONTH. Jan 1–31. An international recognition of the importance of a high quality of life and that this encompasses family, community, education, work, finances, health, leisure and spirituality. Recognition and achievement of quality of life is a worldwide issue. For info: H. Stanley Jones, Dir, Quality of Life Institute, 92-1501 Hoalii St, Kapolei, HI 96707-2511. Phone: (808) 672-0777. Fax: (808) 672-0775. E-mail: PRSpeakers@aol.com.

INTERNATIONAL WAYFINDING MONTH. Jan 1–31. Celebrating the spatial and environmental information systems that help you find your way in the built environment. It's what gets you to the airport gate, through a parking lot, around a museum! For info: Ann Makowski, Society for Environmental Graphic Design, 1000 Vermont Ave NW, Ste 400, Washington, DC 20005. Phone: (202) 638-5555. Fax: (202) 638-0891. E-mail: ann@segd.org. Web: www.segd.org.

INTERNATIONAL WEALTH MENTALITY MONTH. Jan 1–31. The start of the new year provides a great opportunity to examine your financial position and, more important, your beliefs and behavior regarding your financial goals. The International Center for Strategic Planning hosts this monthlong effort each year to draw attention to the importance of having a wealth mentality (thoughts that encourage and support wealth building) and getting your personal finances in order. For info: Sherrin Ross Ingram, International Center for Strategic Planning, 3 Grant Sq, #101, Hinsdale, IL 60521. Phone: (800) 962-4750. E-mail: info@wealthmentality.com. Web: www.wealthmentality.com.

JAPANESE ERA NEW YEAR. Jan 1–3. Celebration of the beginning of the year Heisei Twenty-one, the 21st year of Emperor Akihito's reign.

KLIBAN, B(ERNARD): BIRTH ANNIVERSARY. Jan 1, 1935. Cartoonist B. Kliban was born at Norwalk, CT. He was known for his satirical drawings of cats engaged in human pursuits, which appeared in the books *Cat* (1975), *Never Eat Anything Bigger than Your Head & Other Drawings* (1976) and *Whack Your Porcupine* (1977) and on T-shirts, greeting cards, calendars, bedsheets and other merchandise, creating a $50 million industry before his death at San Francisco, CA, Aug 12, 1990.

MEXICO: ZAPATISTA REBELLION: 15th ANNIVERSARY. Jan 1, 1994. Declaring war against the government of President Carlos Salinas de Gortari, the Zapatista National Liberation Army seized four towns in the state of Chiapas in southern Mexico in 1994. The rebel group, which took their name from the early-20th-century Mexican revolutionary Emiliano Zapata, issued a declaration stating that they were protesting discrimination against the Indian population of the region and against their severe poverty.

MUMMERS PARADE. Jan 1. Philadelphia, PA. World-famous New Year's Day parade of 20,000 spectacularly costumed Mummers in a colorful parade that goes on all day. This celebration has taken place since the 1700s. Est attendance: 100,000. For info: Mummers Parade, 1100 S 2nd St, Philadelphia, PA 19147. Phone: (215) 636-1666. E-mail: parade@mummers.com. Web: www.mummers.com.

NATIONAL BE ON-PURPOSE MONTH. Jan 1–31. An observance to encourage us to start the new year by putting our good intentions into action, personally and professionally, and to trade confusion for clarity as we integrate our lives with more meaning and purpose. For info: Kevin W. McCarthy, CEO, On-Purpose Partners, PO Box 1568, Winter Park, FL 32790-1568. Phone: (407) 657-6000. Fax: (407) 645-1345. E-mail: info@on-purpose.com.

NATIONAL CLEAN UP YOUR COMPUTER MONTH. Jan 1–31. Dedicated to the education of computer users with simple tips and methods to increase the efficiency of their systems. For info: Denise Hall, PO Box 687, Loxley, AL 36551. Phone: (251) 986-6650. Fax: (251) 986-6652. E-mail: denise@specterweb.com. Web: specterweb.com.

NATIONAL ENVIRONMENTAL POLICY ACT: ANNIVERSARY. Jan 1, 1970. The National Environmental Policy Act of 1969 established the Council on Environmental Quality and made it federal government policy to protect the environment.

NATIONAL GLAUCOMA AWARENESS MONTH. Jan 1–31. More than 2 million Americans aged 40 and older suffer from glaucoma. Nearly half do not know they have the disease—it causes no early symptoms. Prevent Blindness America® will provide valuable information about this "sneak thief of sight." Organizations are encouraged to educate the community through screenings, forums and programs. For info: Prevent Blindness America®, 211 W Wacker Dr, Ste 1700, Chicago, IL 60606. Phone: (800) 331-2020. E-mail: info@preventblindness.org. Web: www.preventblindness.org.

NATIONAL HOT TEA MONTH. Jan 1–31. To celebrate one of nature's most popular, soothing and relaxing beverages; the only beverage in America commonly served hot or iced, anytime, anywhere, for any occasion. For info: The Tea Council of the USA, 362 Fifth Ave, Ste 801, New York, NY 10001. Phone: (212) 986-9415. Fax: (212) 697-8658. E-mail: info@teausa.org. Web: www.teausa.org.

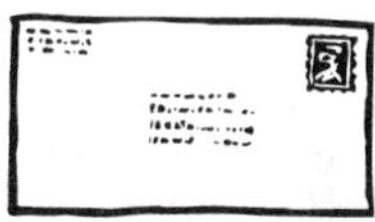

NATIONAL MAILORDER GARDENING MONTH. Jan 1–31. There's no better way to beat the winter blahs than by curling up with a few colorful garden catalogs and spending some time dreaming and scheming about next spring's garden. Many catalogs offer tips and information on how to create a beautiful garden. For a listing of more than 135 garden catalogs and magazines, visit our website. For info: Mailorder Gardening Assn, 5836 Rockburn Woods Way, Elkridge, MD 21075. Phone: (410) 540-9830. Fax: (410) 540-9827. E-mail: info@mailordergardening.com. Web: www.mailordergardening.com.

NATIONAL MENTORING MONTH. Jan 1–31. Goals include raising awareness of mentoring in its various forms; recruiting individuals to mentor, especially in programs that have a waiting list of young people; and promoting the rapid growth of mentoring by recruiting organizations to help find mentors for young people. Each January, this monthlong campaign will provide nationwide publicity and information about mentoring programs in various communities that need volunteers. For info: MENTOR/National Mentoring Partnership, 1600 Duke St, Ste 300, Alexandria, VA 22314. Phone: (703) 224-2200. Web: www.mentoring.org.

NATIONAL PERSONAL SELF-DEFENSE AWARENESS MONTH. Jan 1–31. To educate women and teens about realistic self-defense options that could very well save their lives. Sponsored by the National Self-Defense Institute, Inc, a not-for-profit 501(c)(3) corporation. NSDI/SAFE Program™ seminars and related events nationally emphasize being totally prepared by realizing that awareness + risk reduction = 90 percent of self-defense while the other 10 percent is physical and wake women up to the fact that the key to their own safety lies in themselves. For info: National Self-Defense Institute, Inc, PO Box 398355, Miami Beach, FL 33239-8355. Phone: (305) 868-NSDI. Fax: (305) 867-6634. E-mail: nsdi@worldnet.att.net. Web: www.nsdi.org.

NATIONAL POVERTY IN AMERICA AWARENESS MONTH. Jan 1–31. To promote public awareness of the continuing existence of poverty and social injustice in America. Individuals are encouraged to support efforts to eradicate poverty by increasing their understanding of the causes and practical solutions and by active participation and support for antipoverty programs. Sponsored by the Catholic Campaign for Human Development, the largest private funder of self-help programs for the poor and disenfranchised in the US regardless of religion, race or ethnic origin. For info: Barbara Stephenson, CCHD, US Conference of Catholic Bishops, 3211 Fourth St NE, Washington, DC 20017-1194. Phone: (202) 541-3364. Web: www.povertyusa.org.

NATIONAL RADON ACTION MONTH. Jan 1–31. To increase the public's awareness of the effects of radon. For info: Environmental Protection Agency, 1200 Pennsylvania Ave NW, Washington, DC 20460. Radon Hotline: (800) SOS-RADON. Web: www.epa.gov.

NATIONAL SKATING MONTH. Jan 1–31. During this month, US Figure Skating member clubs and Basic Skill Programs reach out to new members in their community by offering the fundamentals of ice-skating from professionally trained instructors across the US. For info: US Figure Skating, 20 First St, Colorado Springs, CO 80906. Phone: (719) 635-5200. Fax: (719) 635-9548. E-mail: info@usfigureskating.org. Web: www.usfsa.org.

NEW YEAR'S DAY. Jan 1. Legal holiday in all states and territories of the US and in most other countries. The world's most widely celebrated holiday.

NEW YEAR'S DISHONOR LIST. Jan 1. Since 1976, America's dishonor list of words banished from the Queen's English. Overworked words and phrases (e.g., *metrosexual, red states/blue states, bling-bling, embedded journalist* and combined celebrity names like *Brangelina*). Send nominations to following address. For info: Public Relations Office, Lake Superior State University, Sault Ste. Marie, MI 49783. Phone: (906) 635-2315. Fax: (906) 635-2623. Web: www.lssu.edu/banished.

OATMEAL MONTH. Jan 1–31. Oatmeal is a delicious and nutritious way to start the day, and it is also a versatile ingredient to use in your baking and other favorite recipes. When eaten daily as a part of a diet low in saturated fat and cholesterol, three grams of soluble fiber from oatmeal may reduce the risk of heart disease. For delicious, sweet and savory recipes and more info: The Oat Expert. Web: quakeroatmeal.com. E-mail: oatexpert@mpfood.com.

OUTBACK BOWL. Jan 1. Raymond James Stadium, Tampa, FL. The Outback Bowl game brings together college football teams from the SEC and the Big Ten. In addition, the bowl is highlighted by a variety of special events, sports activities and private functions. Est attendance: 65,000. For info: Mike Schulze, Tampa Bay Bowl Assn, 4211 W Boy Scout Blvd, Ste 560, Tampa, FL 33607. Phone: (813) 874-2695. Fax: (813) 873-1959. Web: www.outbackbowl.com.

PHILIPPINES: BLACK NAZARENE FIESTA. Jan 1–9. Manila. This traditional nine-day fiesta honors Quiapo district's patron saint. Cultural events, fireworks and parades culminate in a procession with the life-size statue of the Black Nazarene. Procession begins at the historic Quiapo Church.

POETRY CONTEST. Jan 1–Apr 1. El Paso, TX. 19th annual. Every year the El Paso Public Library sponsors a poetry contest for children in grades 1–12. Entries may be submitted Jan 1–31. Judging will be held Feb 12–15. Award ceremonies will be held on Mar 25. There are two awards given for each grade in both English and Spanish. Each child receives a new book of poetry in English or Spanish. For info: Laurel Indalecio, El Paso Public Library, 501 N Oregon, El Paso, TX 79901. Phone/fax: (915) 543-5470. E-mail: indaleciol@elpasotexas.gov. Web: www.elpasolibrary.org.

***PROFILES IN COURAGE* PUBLISHED: ANNIVERSARY.** Jan 1, 1956. Senator John F. Kennedy of Massachusetts published his book to great praise and sales. It won a Pulitzer Prize in 1957.

REVERE, PAUL: BIRTH ANNIVERSARY. Jan 1, 1735. (Old Style date.) American patriot, silversmith and engraver; maker of false teeth, eyeglasses, picture frames and surgical instruments. Best remembered for his famous ride Apr 18, 1775, celebrated in Longfellow's poem "The Midnight Ride of Paul Revere." Born at Boston, MA; died there May 10, 1818. See also: "Paul Revere's Ride: Anniversary" (Apr 18).

ROSE BOWL GAME. Jan 1. Pasadena, CA. Football conference champions meet in the 95th Rose Bowl game at 2 PM, EST. Tournament of Roses has been an annual New Year's event since 1890; Rose Bowl football game since 1902. Michigan defeated Stanford 49–0 in what was the first postseason football game. Called the Rose Bowl since 1923, it is preceded each year by the Tournament of Roses Parade. Est attendance: 100,000. For info: Program Coordinator, Tournament of Roses, 391 S Orange Grove Blvd, Pasadena, CA 91184. Phone: (626) 449-ROSE. Fax: (626) 449-9066. Web: www.tournamentofroses.com.

ROSS, BETSY: BIRTH ANNIVERSARY. Jan 1, 1752. (Old Style date.) According to legend based largely on her grandson's revelations in 1870, needleworker Betsy Ross created the first Stars and Stripes flag in 1775, under instructions from George Washington. Her sewing and her making of flags were well known, but there is little corroborative evidence of her role in making the first Stars and Stripes. The account is generally accepted, however, in the absence of any documented claims to the contrary. She was born Elizabeth Griscom at Philadelphia, PA, and died there Jan 30, 1836.

RUSSIA: NEW YEAR'S DAY OBSERVANCE. Jan 1–2. National holiday. Modern tradition calls for setting up New Year's trees in homes, halls, clubs, palaces of culture and the hall of the Kremlin Palace. Children's parties with Granddad Frost and his granddaughter, Snow Girl. Games, songs, dancing, special foods, family gatherings and exchange of gifts and New Year's cards.

SAINT BASIL'S DAY. Jan 1. St. Basil's or St. Vasily's feast day observed by Eastern Orthodox churches. Special traditions for the day include serving St. Basil cakes, each of which contains a coin. Feast day observed Jan 14 by those churches using the Julian calendar.

SILENT RECORD WEEK. Jan 1–7. To commemorate the anniversary of the invention of the silent record in 1960, which was played on Detroit jukeboxes. The following year a Silent Record Concert and Recording Session featured emcee Henry Morgan, Soupy Sales and the 120-piece Hush Symphonic Band. (Originated by the late W.T. Rabe of Sault Ste. Marie, MI.)

January 2009

S	M	T	W	T	F	S
				1	2	3
4	5	6	7	8	9	10
11	12	13	14	15	16	17
18	19	20	21	22	23	24
25	26	27	28	29	30	31

SOLEMNITY OF MARY, MOTHER OF GOD. Jan 1. Holy Day of Obligation in the Roman Catholic Church since calendar reorganization of 1969, replacing the Feast of the Circumcision, which had been recognized for more than 14 centuries. See also: "Circumcision of Christ" (Jan 1).

STOCK EXCHANGE HOLIDAY (NEW YEAR'S DAY). Jan 1. The holiday schedules for the various exchanges are subject to change if relevant rules, regulations or exchange policies are revised. If you have questions, contact: American Stock Exchange (866) 422-2639 (www.amex.com), Chicago Board of Trade (312) 435-3500 (www.cbot.com), Chicago Board Options Exchange (312) 786-5600 (www.cboe.com), NASDAQ Stock Market (646) 441-5200 (www.nasdaq.com), New York Stock Exchange (212) 656-3000 (www.nyse.com), Philadelphia Stock Exchange (800) THE-PHLX (www.phlx.com).

SUDAN: INDEPENDENCE DAY. Jan 1. National holiday. Sudan was proclaimed a sovereign independent republic in 1956, ending its status as an Anglo-Egyptian condominium (since 1899).

TAIWAN: FOUNDATION DAYS. Jan 1–2. Public holiday. Commemorates the founding of the Republic of China on Jan 1, 1912.

TOURNAMENT OF ROSES PARADE. Jan 1. Pasadena, CA. 120th annual parade. Rose Parade starting at 8 AM, EST, includes floats, bands and equestrians. 2009 theme is "Hats Off to Entertainment." Est attendance: 1,000,000. For info: Pasadena Tournament of Roses Assn, 391 S Orange Grove Blvd, Pasadena, CA 91184. Phone: (626) 449-4100. Fax: (626) 449-9066. E-mail: rosepr@rosemail.org. Web: www.tournamentofroses.com.

UNITED KINGDOM: NEW YEAR'S HOLIDAY. Jan 1.

UNITED NATIONS: INTERNATIONAL YEAR OF ASTRONOMY. Jan 1–Dec 31. The UN Genereal Assembly designates the United Nations Educational, Scientific and Cultural Organization (UNESCO) as lead agency and focal point for the Year, and invites UNESCO to organize activities to be realized during the Year, in collaboration with other relevant entities of the United Nations system, the International Astronomical Union, the European Southern Observatory, and astronomical societies and groups throughout the world. Resolution 62/200 of Dec 19, 2007. For info: United Nations, Dept of Public Info, New York, NY 10017. Web: www.un.org.

UNITED NATIONS: INTERNATIONAL YEAR OF HUMAN RIGHTS LEARNING. Jan 1–Dec 9. The General Assembly has proclaimed that this year be devoted to activities to broaden and deepen human rights learning based on the principles of universality, indivisibility, interdependency, impartiality, objectivity and non-selectivity, constructive dialogue and cooperation (resolution 62/171 of Dec 18, 2007). It aims to enhance the promotion and protection of all human rights and fundamental freedoms, including the right to development. Began on Dec 10, 2008. For info: United Nations, Dept of Public Info, New York, NY 10017. Web: www.un.org.

UNITED NATIONS: INTERNATIONAL YEAR OF NATURAL FIBERS. Jan 1–Dec 31. Noting that the diverse range of natural fibers produced in many countries provides an important source of income for farmers and can thus play an important role in improving food security, eradicating poverty and contributing to achievement of the Millennium Development Goals, the Assembly has proclaimed 2009 as the International Year of Natural Fibers (resolution 61/189, Dec 20, 2006). For info: United Nations, Dept of Public Info, New York, NY 10017. Web: www.un.org.

UNITED NATIONS: INTERNATIONAL YEAR OF RECONCILIATION. Jan 1–Dec 31. On Nov 20, 2006, the General Assembly proclaimed 2009 as the International Year of Reconciliation (resolution 61/17). The Assembly expressed its steadfast determination to pursue reconciliation processes in those societies affected or divided by conflicts, describing such processes as necessary for the establishment of firm and lasting peace. They invite concerned governments and international and non-governmental organizations to support reconciliation processes among such societies. They also invite them to implement adequate cultural, educational and social programs to promote the concept of reconciliation, including the holding of conferences and seminars, and the dissemination of information on the subject. For info: United Nations, Dept of Public Info, New York, NY 10017. Web: www.un.org.

WALKER, DOAK: BIRTH ANNIVERSARY. Jan 1, 1927. Ewell Doak Walker, Jr, Pro Football Hall of Fame and Heisman Trophy running back, born at Dallas, TX. Walker won the Heisman Trophy in 1948, playing for SMU, and went on to an outstanding pro career with the Detroit Lions. He was a handsome, humble player during a time when football players could become national heroes. Inducted into the Hall of Fame in 1986. Died at Steamboat Springs, CO, Sept 27, 1998.

WAYNE, "MAD ANTHONY": BIRTH ANNIVERSARY. Jan 1, 1745. (Old Style date.) American Revolutionary War general whose daring, sometimes reckless, conduct earned him the nickname "Mad." His courage and shrewdness as a soldier made him a key figure in capturing Stony Point, NY (1779), preventing Benedict Arnold's "delivery" of West Point to the British and subduing hostile Indians of the Northwest Territory (1794). He was born at Waynesboro, PA, and died at Presque Isle, PA, Dec 15, 1796.

WESTERN PACIFIC HURRICANE SEASON. Jan 1–Dec 31. Most hurricanes occur from June 1 through Oct 1, though the season lasts all year. (Western Pacific: West of the International Date Line.) Info from: US Dept of Commerce, National Oceanic and Atmospheric Administration, Rockville, MD 20852.

Z DAY. Jan 1. To give recognition on the first day of the year to all persons and places whose names begin with the letter *Z* and who are always listed or thought of last in any alphabetized list. For info: Tom Zager. E-mail: tee_zee@excite.com.

ZWINGLI, ULRICH: 525th BIRTH ANNIVERSARY. Jan 1, 1484. Swiss clergyman, theologian and reformer, born at Wildhaus, St. Gall, Switzerland. Ordained a Catholic priest, he converted to Protestantism. While serving as a military chaplain in the Second War of Kappel, Zwingli was killed on Oct 11, 1531. A monument marks the place where he fell during the battle.

Birthdays Today

Chet Culver, 44, Governor of Iowa (D), born Washington, DC, Jan 1, 1965.

Jon Corzine, 62, Governor of New Jersey (D), born Taylorville, IL, Jan 1, 1947.

Ernest F. Hollings, 87, retired US Senator (D, South Carolina), born Charleston, SC, Jan 1, 1922.

Michael Imperioli, 43, actor ("The Sopranos"), born Mount Vernon, NY, Jan 1, 1966.

Helmut Jahn, 69, architect, born Nuremberg, Germany, Jan 1, 1940.

Frank Langella, 69, actor (*The Twelve Chairs, Lolita*), born Bayonne, NJ, Jan 1, 1940.

James McAvoy, 30, actor (*Atonement, Becoming Jane, The Last King of Scotland*), born Glasgow, Scotland, Jan 1, 1979.

Robert Menendez, 55, US Senator (D, New Jersey), born New York, NY, Jan 1, 1954.

Don Novello, 66, actor, comedian ("The Smothers Brothers Show," "Saturday Night Live": Father Guido Sarducci), born Ashtabula, OH, Jan 1, 1943.

J.D. Salinger, 90, author (*Catcher in the Rye, Franny & Zooey, Seymour: An Introduction*), born New York, NY, Jan 1, 1919.

January 2 — Friday

DAY 2 **363 REMAINING**

ALLSTATE SUGAR BOWL. Jan 2. Louisiana Superdome, New Orleans, LA. 75th annual. Part of the BCS. Game time is 7 PM, EST. The Sugar Bowl originated in 1935. Est attendance: 75,000. For info: Allstate Sugar Bowl, Sugar Bowl Office, 110 Veterans Memorial Blvd, Ste 500, Metairie, LA 70005. Phone: (504) 828-2440. Web: www.allstatesugarbowl.com.

AMERICAN HISTORICAL ASSOCIATION: ANNUAL MEETING. Jan 2–5. New York, NY. 123rd annual. Approximately 325 sessions will be held covering a wide range of scholarly, professional and pedagogical topics dealing with all areas of history. Est attendance: 5,500. For info: Sharon K. Tune, Convention Director, American Historical Assn, 400 A St SE, Washington, DC 20003. Phone: (202) 544-2422. Fax: (202) 544-8307. E-mail: aha@historians.org. Web: www.historians.org.

ASIMOV, ISAAC: BIRTH ANNIVERSARY. Jan 2, 1920. Although Isaac Asimov was one of the world's best-known writers of science fiction, his almost 500 books dealt with subjects as diverse as the Bible, works for preschoolers, college course work, mysteries, chemistry, biology, limericks, Shakespeare, Gilbert and Sullivan and modern history. During his prolific career he helped to elevate science fiction from pulp magazines to a more intellectual level. Some of his works include the *Foundation Trilogy, The Robots of Dawn, Robots and Empire, Nemesis, Murder at the A.B.A.* (in which he himself was a character), *The Gods Themselves* and *I, Robot*, in which he posited the famous Three Laws of Robotics. His *The Clock We Live On* is an accessible explanation of the origins of calendars. Asimov was born near Smolensk, Russia, and died at New York, NY, Apr 6, 1992.

AT&T COTTON BOWL CLASSIC. Jan 2. Cotton Bowl Stadium, Dallas, TX. Since 1937. Postseason football game matching the number two team from the Big 12 with the Southeastern Conference (SEC) division champion, division runner-up or a team with a comparable record. Game time is 10 AM, EST. Est attendance: 70,000. For info: Cotton Bowl Athletic Assn, PO Box 569420, Dallas, TX 75356-9420. Phone: (214) 634-7525 or (888) 792-BOWL. E-mail: coach@attcottonbowl.com. Web: www.attcottonbowl.com.

COIN & STAMP EXPO/ARIZONA. Jan 2–4. Holiday Inn, Mesa, AZ. Annual expo. Est attendance: 5,000. For info: Israel Bick, Exec Dir, Intl Stamp & Coin Collectors Society, PO Box 854, Van Nuys, CA 91408. Phone: (818) 997-6496. Fax: (818) 988-4337. E-mail: iibick@sbcglobal.net. Web: www.bick.net.

55-MPH SPEED LIMIT: 35th ANNIVERSARY. Jan 2, 1974. President Richard Nixon signed a bill requiring states to limit highway speeds to a maximum of 55 mph. This measure was meant to conserve energy during the crisis precipitated by the embargo imposed by the Arab oil-producing countries. A plan, used by some states, limited sale of gasoline on odd-numbered days for cars whose plates ended in odd numbers and even-numbered days for even-numbered plates. Some states limited purchases to $2–$3 per auto, and lines as long as six miles resulted in some locations. See also: "Arab Oil Embargo Lifted: Anniversary" (Mar 13).

January 2009	S	M	T	W	T	F	S
					1	2	3
	4	5	6	7	8	9	10
	11	12	13	14	15	16	17
	18	19	20	21	22	23	24
	25	26	27	28	29	30	31

GEORGIA: RATIFICATION DAY. Jan 2, 1788. By unanimous vote, Georgia became the fourth state to ratify the Constitution.

HAITI: ANCESTORS' DAY. Jan 2. Commemoration of the ancestors. Also known as Hero's Day. Public holiday.

HAPPY MEW YEAR FOR CATS DAY. Jan 2. Felines, ever above mere humans in the great chain of being, have a day unto themselves to celebrate the "mewness" of a new time. Annually, Jan 2. (©2006 by WH.) For info: Thomas & Ruth Roy, Wellcat Holidays, 2418 Long Ln, Lebanon, PA 17046. Phone: (717) 279-0184. E-mail: info@wellcat.com. Web: www.wellcat.com.

JAPAN: KAKIZOME. Jan 2. Traditional Japanese festival gets under way when the first strokes of the year are made on paper with the traditional brushes.

MILLER, ROGER: BIRTH ANNIVERSARY. Jan 2, 1936. Country and western singer, songwriter and musician ("King of the Road"), Roger Miller was born at Fort Worth, TX. Miller won 11 Grammy Awards and a Tony Award (1986 for the score to the Broadway play *Big River*). He died Oct 25, 1992, at Los Angeles, CA.

NATIONAL GEOGRAPHIC BEE, SCHOOL LEVEL. Jan 2–16. (Began Nov 10, 2008. Principals must have registered their schools by Oct 15, 2008.) Nationwide contest involving millions of students at the school level. The Bee is designed to encourage the teaching and study of geography. There are three levels of competition. A student must win a school-level Bee in order to win the right to take a written exam. The written test determines the top 100 students in each state who are eligible to go on to the state level. National Geographic brings each state winner and a teacher from his or her school to Washington for the national-level Bee in May. Alex Trebek moderates the national level. For info: Natl Geographic Bee, Natl Geographic Society, 1145 17th St NW, Washington, DC 20036. Phone: (202) 828-6659. Web: www.nationalgeographic.com/geographicbee.

RUSSIA: PASSPORT PRESENTATION. Jan 2. A ceremony for 16-year-olds, who are recognized as citizens of the country. Always on the first working day of the New Year.

SCOTLAND: NEW YEAR'S BANK HOLIDAY. Jan 2. Public holiday. The working day after New Year's Day.

"SOMEDAY WE'LL LAUGH ABOUT THIS" WEEK. Jan 2–9. 32nd annual. We've all used the expression, "Someday we'll laugh about this!" Why wait? It usually takes less than seven days for people to violate 90 percent of their New Year's resolutions. This week helps us to remember the art of laughing at ourselves. This week tickles the yoke and joke of perfectionism while encouraging people to strive for excellence at the same time. This week is a great way to start the new year—laughing at the humorous human condition. For info on the positive power of humor: Dr. Joel Goodman, The Humor Project, Inc, 480 Broadway, Ste 210-C, Saratoga Springs, NY 12866. Phone: (518) 587-8770. E-mail: chase@HumorProject.com. Web: www.HumorProject.com.

SPACE MILESTONE: *LUNA 1* (USSR): 50th ANNIVERSARY. Jan 2, 1959. Launch of robotic moon probe that missed the moon and became the first spacecraft from Earth to orbit the sun.

SPAIN CAPTURES GRANADA: ANNIVERSARY. Jan 2, 1492. Spaniards took the city of Granada from the Moors, ending seven centuries of Muslim rule in Spain.

SWITZERLAND: BERCHTOLDSTAG. Jan 2. Holiday in many cantons. Commemorates the founding of the city of Bern by Duke Berchtold V in the 12th century. Now mainly a children's holiday.

TAFT, HELEN HERRON: BIRTH ANNIVERSARY. Jan 2, 1861. Wife of William Howard Taft, 27th president of the US, born at Cincinnati, OH. Died at Washington, DC, May 22, 1943.

THOMAS, MARTHA CAREY: BIRTH ANNIVERSARY. Jan 2, 1857. The second president of Bryn Mawr College, Martha Carey Thomas gained a reputation for her insistence that the education of women should be as rigorous as that of men. A zealous suffragist, she served as the first president of the National College Women's Equal Suffrage League. Thomas promoted Bryn Mawr's Summer School for Women in Industry (opened in 1921) to provide a liberal education for working women. Born at Baltimore, MD, she died at Philadelphia, PA, Dec 2, 1935.

WOLFE, JAMES: BIRTH ANNIVERSARY. Jan 2, 1727. English general who commanded the British army's victory over Montcalm's French forces on the Plains of Abraham at Quebec City in 1759. As a result, France surrendered Canada to England. Wolfe was born at Westerham, Kent, England. He died at the Plains of Abraham of battle wounds, Sept 13, 1759.

Birthdays Today

Jim Bakker, 70, former TV evangelist, born James Orsen at Muskegon, MI, Jan 2, 1939.

Kate Bosworth, 26, actress (*21, Superman Returns, Blue Crush*), born Los Angeles, CA, Jan 2, 1983.

Brian Boucher, 32, hockey player, born Woonsocket, RI, Jan 2, 1977.

Tia Carrere, 42, actress (*Wayne's World, True Lies*), born Honolulu, HI, Jan 2, 1967.

David Cone, 46, former baseball player, born Kansas City, MO, Jan 2, 1963.

Taye Diggs, 37, actor (*Rent, How Stella Got Her Groove Back*), born Rochester, NY, Jan 2, 1972.

Christopher Durang, 60, playwright, actor, born Montclair, NJ, Jan 2, 1949.

Cuba Gooding, Jr, 41, actor (*Jerry Maguire, As Good as It Gets*), born the Bronx, NY, Jan 2, 1968.

Dennis Hastert, 67, former US Congressman, former Speaker of the House (1999–2007), born Aurora, IL, Jan 2, 1942.

Edgar Martinez, 46, former baseball player, born New York, NY, Jan 2, 1963.

Wendy Phillips, 57, actress ("Big Love," "Homefront"), born Brooklyn, NY, Jan 2, 1952.

Christy Turlington, 40, model, born Walnut Creek, CA, Jan 2, 1969.

January 3 — Saturday

DAY 3 — 362 REMAINING

ALASKA: ADMISSION DAY: 50th ANNIVERSARY. Jan 3, 1959. Alaska, which had been purchased from Russia in 1867, became the 49th state. The area of Alaska is nearly one-fifth the size of the rest of the US.

ARIZONA ANTIQUE SHOW AND SALE. Jan 3–4. Yuma Civic Center, Yuma, AZ. A fine collection of antiques and collectibles. Est attendance: 2,000. For info: Yuma Civic Center, 1440 Desert Hills Dr, Yuma, AZ 85365. Phone: (928) 373-5040. Fax: (928) 344-9121. E-mail: ycc@yumaaz.gov. Web: www.yumaaz.gov.

"THE ARSENIO HALL SHOW" TV PREMIERE: 20th ANNIVERSARY. Jan 3, 1989. Arsenio Hall became the first African American to host a successful syndicated late-night talk show. The show attracted a younger audience than that of Johnny Carson's "The Tonight Show" and effectively limited the impact of CBS's 1989 late-night entry, "The Pat Sajak Show." Hall was successful in booking soul and rap music acts that had rarely been seen on other shows. His was also the show on which presidential candidate Bill Clinton appeared, playing the saxophone in dark glasses. Hall was named by *TV Guide* (June 1990) as its first "TV Person of the Year."

ATTLEE, CLEMENT RICHARD: BIRTH ANNIVERSARY. Jan 3, 1883. English leader of the Labour Party and prime minister (July 1945–October 1951). Born at London, England; died there Oct 8, 1967.

COOLIDGE, GRACE ANNA GOODHUE: BIRTH ANNIVERSARY. Jan 3, 1879. Wife of Calvin Coolidge, 30th president of the US, born at Burlington, VT. Died at Northampton, MA, July 8, 1957.

DAKAR RALLY 2009. Jan 3–18. Held since 1978, when it was the Paris–Dakar Rally, the Dakar Rally, the legendary event of the off-road rally discipline, will for the first time go to South America in 2009. It will take place in Argentina and Chile on an amazing course: a 9,000 km loop including 6,000 of specials between Buenos Aires, Valparaiso and Buenos Aires. An estimated one million spectators line the route; some 150 million will follow on television. Est attendance: 1,000,000. For info: Amaury Sport Organisation, 2 rue Rouget de L'Isle, F92137 Issy les Moulineaux, France. Phone: (33) (141) 33-14-80. Fax: (33) (141) 33-15-39. E-mail: service.presse@dakar.com. Web: www.dakar.com or www.aso.fr.

DAVIES, MARION: BIRTH ANNIVERSARY. Jan 3, 1897. Born at Brooklyn, NY, Marion Cecilia Douras became Marion Davies and made her first appearance on film in 1917. Her romantic and professional involvement with newspaper magnate William Randolph Hearst ensured the type of publicity that would launch her to stardom. Her films included *When Knighthood Was in Flower, The Patsy* and *Show People.* Davies died at Hollywood, CA, Sept 23, 1961.

DRINKING STRAW PATENTED: ANNIVERSARY. Jan 3, 1888. A drinking straw made out of paraffin-covered paper was patented by Marvin Stone of Washington, DC. It replaced natural rye straws.

FIRST FEMALE CONGRESSIONAL PAGE: 70th ANNIVERSARY. Jan 3, 1939. Gene Cox, 13, served on the House floor as aide to her father, Representative Eugene Cox (D-GA), on opening day of the 76th Congress. She was paid $4 for three hours of work and there were no objections to her one-day service. More than 30 years later, however, there was much debate when Senator Jacob Javits (R-NY) nominated a female to be a real Senate page.

GREAT FRUITCAKE TOSS. Jan 3. Manitou Springs, CO. What do you do with leftover fruitcake? Toss, hurl, launch competitions. Est attendance: 1,500. For info: Manitou Springs Chamber of Commerce, 354 Manitou Ave, Manitou Springs, CO 80829. Phone: (800) 642-2567. Web: www.manitousprings.org.

LENNON-ONO ALBUM CONFISCATION: 40th ANNIVERSARY. Jan 3, 1969. John Lennon and Yoko Ono posed nude for the cover of their album *Two Virgins.* On this day, a shipment of 30,000 of the albums was confiscated by police at Newark, NJ, as a violation of pornography statutes.

"LOOK UP AND LIVE" TV PREMIERE: 55th ANNIVERSARY. Jan 3, 1954. CBS broadcast this inspirational show on Sunday mornings for 24 years. The Reverend Lawrence McMasters appeared in the early years and Merv Griffin hosted the show in 1955. Pamela Ilott, executive producer, was also director of religious programming for CBS News.

MEMENTO, MORI. Jan 3. *Memento, mori,* Latin for "Remember, you die," is also the title of a novel by Muriel Spark. We suggest posting the words at home and at work, not to be morbid, but to remind us to cherish all that we have today . . . for tomorrow may never arrive. (©2006 by WH.) For info: Thomas & Ruth Roy, Wellcat Holidays, 2418 Long Ln, Lebanon, PA 17046. Phone: (717) 279-0184. E-mail: info@wellcat.com. Web: www.wellcat.com.

MOTT, LUCRETIA (COFFIN): BIRTH ANNIVERSARY. Jan 3, 1793. American teacher, minister, antislavery leader and (with Elizabeth Cady Stanton) one of the founders of the women's rights movement in the US. Born at Nantucket, MA, she died near Philadelphia, PA, Nov 11, 1880.

"QUEEN FOR A DAY" TV PREMIERE: ANNIVERSARY. Jan 3, 1956. Game show on which prizes were awarded to the contestant who evoked the most sympathy from the studio audience. The show began some 11 years earlier on the radio with Jack Bailey hosting. Five women were chosen from the audience to appear on stage. Each related her story of misfortune and explained what she needed to remedy the situation, and the audience would vote by applause. The lucky winner was then given the royal treatment—crown, scepter and red robe—plus a prize to help with her problem. This soon became the top-rated daytime show. In 1969 the show went into syndication with Dick Curtis as host, but it didn't last long.

RAUH, JOSEPH L., JR: BIRTH ANNIVERSARY. Jan 3, 1911. Political activist Joseph L. Rauh, Jr, was born at Cincinnati, OH. In 1947 he cofounded Americans for Democratic Action (ADA), which supports liberal causes. Rauh helped create the minority civil rights plank at the 1948 Democratic National Convention—a foundation for the federal civil rights legislation in the 1960s. He served on the executive board of the NAACP and was general counsel to the Leadership Conference on Civil Rights. He died Sept 3, 1992, at Washington, DC.

SPACE MILESTONE: *MARS EXPLORATION ROVER SPIRIT* (US): 5th ANNIVERSARY. Jan 3, 2004. After traveling 302.6 million miles from its June 10, 2003, launch at Cape Canaveral Air Force Station, FL, the *Mars Exploration Rover Spirit* landed at Gusev Crater on Mars. The robotic rover's mission was to examine the soil and environment of the red planet. By Jan 6, *Spirit* had taken the sharpest color photograph of Mars ever achieved. *Spirit*'s twin rover, *Opportunity*, landed Jan 24, 2004.

STURGES, JOHN: BIRTH ANNIVERSARY. Jan 3, 1911. Motion picture director John Sturges, born at Oak Park, IL, was known for his action movies. He received an Academy Award nomination in 1955 for *Bad Day at Black Rock*. He also directed *Gunfight at the O.K. Corral* (1956), *The Magnificent Seven* (1960), *The Great Escape* (1963) and his last film *The Eagle Has Landed* (1977). He died Aug 18, 1992, at San Luis Obispo, CA.

TOLKIEN, J.R.R.: BIRTH ANNIVERSARY. Jan 3, 1892. John Ronald Reuel Tolkien, author of *The Hobbit* (1937) and the trilogy *The Lord of the Rings*. Though best known for his fantasies, Tolkien was also a serious philologist. Born at Bloemfontein, South Africa, he died at Bournemouth, England, Sept 2, 1973.

WIND CAVE NATIONAL PARK ESTABLISHED: ANNIVERSARY. Jan 3, 1903. President Theodore Roosevelt signed a bill on this date establishing South Dakota's Wind Cave as a national park and preserve. It was the first national park established for the preservation of a cave.

January 2009	S	M	T	W	T	F	S
					1	2	3
	4	5	6	7	8	9	10
	11	12	13	14	15	16	17
	18	19	20	21	22	23	24
	25	26	27	28	29	30	31

Birthdays Today

Joan Walsh Anglund, 83, author, illustrator of children's books (*Crocus in the Snow, Bedtime Book*), born Hinsdale, IL, Jan 3, 1926.

Dabney Coleman, 77, actor ("Buffalo Bill," *Nine to Five, Tootsie*), born Austin, TX, Jan 3, 1932.

Mel Gibson, 53, actor (*Braveheart, Lethal Weapon*), director (*The Passion of the Christ*), born Peekskill, NY, Jan 3, 1956.

Robert Marvin (Bobby) Hull, 70, Hall of Fame hockey player, born Point Anne, ON, Canada, Jan 3, 1939.

Robert Loggia, 79, actor (*An Officer and a Gentleman, Scarface*), born Staten Island, NY, Jan 3, 1930.

Eli Manning, 28, football player, born New Orleans, LA, Jan 3, 1981.

Danica McKellar, 34, actress ("The Wonder Years," *Sidekicks*), born La Jolla, CA, Jan 3, 1975.

Victoria Principal, 59, actress ("Dallas"), born Fukuoka, Japan, Jan 3, 1950.

Stephen Stills, 64, musician, songwriter, born Dallas, TX, Jan 3, 1945.

January 4 — Sunday

DAY 4 — 361 REMAINING

AMNESTY FOR POLYGAMISTS: ANNIVERSARY. Jan 4, 1893. President Benjamin Harrison issued a proclamation granting full amnesty and pardon to all persons who had since Nov 1, 1890, abstained from unlawful cohabitation of a polygamous marriage. This was intended in the main for a specific group of elderly Mormons who had continued in the practice of contracting serial marriages. Amnesty was based on the condition that those pardoned must obey the law in the future or be "vigorously prosecuted." The practice of polygamy was a factor interfering with attainment of statehood for Utah.

BRAILLE, LOUIS: 200th BIRTH ANNIVERSARY. Jan 4, 1809. The inventor of a widely used touch system of reading and writing for the blind was born at Coupvray, France. Permanently blinded at the age of three by a leatherworking awl in his father's saddlemaking shop, Braille developed a system of writing that used, ironically, an awl-like stylus to punch marks in paper that could be felt and interpreted by the blind. The system was largely ignored until after Braille died in poverty, suffering from tuberculosis, at Paris, Jan 6, 1852.

"THE CATHOLIC HOUR" TV PREMIERE: ANNIVERSARY. Jan 4, 1953. Produced in cooperation with the National Council of Catholic Men, this show ran for 17 years, alternating from week to week with "The Eternal Light" and "Frontiers of Faith."

"COLLEGE BOWL" TV PREMIERE: 50th ANNIVERSARY. Jan 4, 1959. Originally, a quiz show on CBS. Two colleges sent a team of their best and brightest to the academic competition. "College Bowl" was sponsored by General Electric and hosted by Allen Ludden (1959–62) and Robert Earle (1962–70). More recent incarnations of "College Bowl" have appeared on NBC and Disney with Pat Sajak and Dick Cavett as hosts.

DIMPLED CHAD DAY. Jan 4. This is a day to commemorate all the dimpled chads of the world, left over from various and sundry contested elections. Chads, roasted in garlic, make an excellent sprinkle topping for salads. (©2006 by WH.) For info: Thomas & Ruth Roy, Wellcat Holidays, 2418 Long Ln, Lebanon, PA 17046. Phone: (717) 279-0184. E-mail: info@wellcat.com. Web: www.wellcat.com.

EARTH AT PERIHELION. Jan 4. At approximately 10 AM, EST, planet Earth will reach perihelion, that point in its orbit when it is closest to the sun (about 91,400,000 miles). The Earth's mean distance from the sun (mean radius of its orbit) is reached early in the months of April and October. Note that Earth is closest to the sun during Northern Hemisphere winter. See also: "Earth at Aphelion" (July 3).

GENERAL TOM THUMB: BIRTH ANNIVERSARY. Jan 4, 1838. Charles Sherwood Stratton, perhaps the most famous midget in history, was born at Bridgeport, CT. He eventually reached a height of three feet, four inches and a weight of 70 pounds. Discovered by P.T. Barnum in 1842, Stratton, as "General Tom Thumb," became an internationally known entertainer and performed before Queen Victoria and other heads of state. On Feb 10, 1863, he married another midget, Lavinia Warren. Stratton died at Middleborough, MA, July 15, 1883.

GRIMM, JACOB: BIRTH ANNIVERSARY. Jan 4, 1785. Librarian, mythologist and philologist, born at Hanau, Germany. Best remembered for *Grimm's Fairy Tales* (in collaboration with his brother Wilhelm). Died at Berlin, Germany, Sept 20, 1863.

MOON PHASE: FIRST QUARTER. Jan 4. Moon enters First Quarter phase at 6:56 AM, EST.

MYANMAR: INDEPENDENCE DAY. Jan 4. National Day. The British controlled the country from 1826 until 1948, when it was granted independence. The country's name was changed from Burma to the Union of Myanmar in 1989 to reflect that the population is made up not just of the Burmese but of many other ethnic groups as well.

NEW YEAR'S RESOLUTIONS WEEK. Jan 4–10. To show people how, why and what resolutions and goals should be set and the necessary action steps to make this new year the best ever! For info: Gary Ryan Blair, The GoalsGuy, 36181 E Lake Rd, Ste 139, Palm Harbor, FL 34685. Phone: (877) GOALSGUY. Fax: (813) 435-2022. E-mail: info@goalsguy.com. Web: www.10millionresolutions.com.

NEWTON, ISAAC: BIRTH ANNIVERSARY. Jan 4, 1643. Sir Isaac Newton was the chief figure of the scientific revolution of the 17th century, a physicist and mathematician who laid the foundations of calculus, studied the mechanics of planetary motion and discovered the law of gravitation. Born at Woolsthorpe, England, he died at London, England, Mar 31, 1727. Newton was born before Great Britain adopted the Gregorian calendar. His Julian (Old Style) birth date is Dec 25, 1642.

"NIGHT COURT" TV PREMIERE: 25th ANNIVERSARY. Jan 4, 1984. NBC sitcom set in an urban courtroom. The cast included Harry Anderson as Judge Harry T. Stone, John Larroquette as prosecutor Dan Fielding, Richard Moll as court officer Bull Shannon and Selma Diamond as court officer Selma Hacker. Markie Post joined the cast in 1985 as PD Christine Sullivan. Mel Tormé made a few appearances as himself, Harry's idol. The last telecast was July 1, 1992.

NIXON'S REJECTION OF SENATE ORDER: 35th ANNIVERSARY. Jan 4, 1974. President Richard Nixon rejected the Senate Watergate Committee's subpoenas seeking White House tapes and documents.

PATTERSON, FLOYD: BIRTH ANNIVERSARY. Jan 4, 1935. Dominant heavyweight boxer of the 1950s and early '60s, born at Waco, NC. Patterson was the gold middleweight medalist at the 1952 Helsinki Olympics (winning all his matches by knockouts), and in 1956 he became the youngest-ever world heavyweight champion. In 1960, he became the first boxer to regain the title (after he had lost it in 1959). Shy and good natured, Patterson was admired by sportswriters and fans. He died May 11, 2006, at New Paltz, NY.

POP MUSIC CHART INTRODUCED: ANNIVERSARY. Jan 4, 1936. *Billboard* magazine published the first list of bestselling pop records, covering the week that ended Dec 30, 1935. On the list were recordings by the Tommy Dorsey and the Ozzie Nelson orchestras.

RUSH, BENJAMIN: BIRTH ANNIVERSARY. Jan 4, 1746. Physician, patriot and humanitarian of the American Revolution, born on a plantation at Byberry, PA. Rush was a signer of the Declaration of Independence, and his writings on mental illness earned him the title "Father of Psychiatry." His tract *Inquiry* attacked the common wisdom of the time that alcohol was beneficial. He was the first American to call alcoholism a chronic disease. Benjamin Rush died at Philadelphia, PA, Apr 19, 1813.

SETON, ELIZABETH ANN BAYLEY: FEAST DAY. Jan 4. First American-born saint (beatified Mar 17, 1963; canonized Sept 14, 1975). Born at New York, NY, Aug 28, 1774, Seton was the founder of the American Sisters of Charity, the first American order of Roman Catholic nuns. She died at Baltimore, MD, Jan 4, 1821.

TRIVIA DAY. Jan 4. In celebration of those who know all sorts of facts and/or have doctorates in uselessology. For info: Robert L. Birch, Puns Corps, 3108 Dashiell Rd, Falls Church, VA 22042. Phone: (703) 533-3668.

UTAH: ADMISSION DAY: ANNIVERSARY. Jan 4. Utah became the 45th state in 1896.

WORLD HYPNOTISM DAY. Jan 4. 5th annual. A day when hypnotism professionals promote the truth and benefits of hypnotism to the people of the world while removing the myths and misconceptions. Free and low-cost events on and off the Internet. For info: Thomas Nicoli, World Hypnotism Day Committee, 16 Faith Rd, Windham, NH 03087. Phone: (603) 598-8389. E-mail: TomNicoli@WHDCommittee.com. Web: www.worldhypnotismday.com.

Birthdays Today

Dyan Cannon, 72, actress (*Heaven Can Wait, Bob and Carol and Ted and Alice*), born Tacoma, WA, Jan 4, 1937.

Dave Foley, 47, actor ("NewsRadio"), born Toronto, ON, Canada, Jan 4, 1962.

Ann Magnuson, 53, performance artist, actress ("Anything but Love," *Clear and Present Danger*), born Charleston, WV, Jan 4, 1956.

Julia Ormond, 44, actress (*Legends of the Fall, Sabrina*), born Surrey, England, Jan 4, 1965.

Barbara Rush, 82, actress ("Seventh Heaven," "Peyton Place," *Hombre*), born Denver, CO, Jan 4, 1927.

Donald Francis (Don) Shula, 79, Hall of Fame football coach and player, born Painesville, OH, Jan 4, 1930.

Michael Stipe, 49, singer (REM), born Decatur, GA, Jan 4, 1960.

January 5 — Monday

DAY 5 | **360 REMAINING**

AILEY, ALVIN: BIRTH ANNIVERSARY. Jan 5, 1931. Born at Rogers, TX, Alvin Ailey began his noted career as a choreographer in the late 1950s after a successful career as a dancer. He founded the Alvin Ailey American Dance Theater, drawing from classical ballet, jazz, Afro-Caribbean and modern dance idioms to create the 79 ballets of the company's repertoire. He and his work played a central part in establishing a role for blacks in the world of modern dance. Ailey died Dec 1, 1989, at New York, NY.

"ALL MY CHILDREN" TV PREMIERE: ANNIVERSARY. Jan 5, 1970. This ABC show, created by Agnes Nixon, became TV's top-rated soap opera by the 1978–79 season and still keeps viewers glued to the screen. Set in Pine Valley, NY, the show originally focused on the Tyler and Martin families. The story includes Erica Kane (Susan Lucci), one of daytime TV's most popular characters. Lucci won an Emmy Award in 1999 for her work. Other award-winning or long-time cast members have included Ruth Warrick as Phoebe Tyler Wallingford, Julia Barr as Brooke English, Michael E. Knight as Tad Martin, David Canary as twin brothers Adam and Stuart Chandler, and John Callahan and Eva LaRue as Edmund and Maria Grey. The show has also launched the careers of such stars as Kim Delaney, Sarah Michelle Gellar and Kelly Ripa. The 9,000th episode aired Dec 16, 2004.

CARVER, GEORGE WASHINGTON: DEATH ANNIVERSARY. Jan 5, 1943. Black American agricultural scientist, author, inventor and teacher. Born into slavery at Diamond Grove, MO, probably in 1864. His research led to the creation of synthetic products made from peanuts, potatoes and wood. Carver died at Tuskegee, AL. His birthplace became a national monument in 1953.

CONGRESS ASSEMBLES. Jan 5. The Constitution provides that "the Congress shall assemble at least once in every year . . . ," and the 20th Amendment specifies "and such meeting shall begin at noon on the third day of January, unless they shall by law appoint a different day." If Jan 3 happens to fall on a weekend, Congress by resolution will meet on the following Monday or Tuesday.

DECATUR, STEPHEN: BIRTH ANNIVERSARY. Jan 5, 1779. American naval officer (whose father and grandfather, both also named Stephen Decatur, were also seafaring men) born at Sinepuxent, MD. In a toast at a dinner in Norfolk in 1815, Decatur spoke his most famous words: "Our country! In her intercourse with foreign nations may she always be in the right; but our country, right or wrong." Mortally wounded in a duel with Commodore James Barron, at Bladensburg, MD, on the morning of Mar 22, 1820, Decatur was carried to his home in Washington, where he died a few hours later.

FIVE-DOLLAR-A-DAY MINIMUM WAGE: 95th ANNIVERSARY. Jan 5, 1914. Henry Ford announced that all worthy Ford Motor Company employees would receive a minimum wage of $5 a day. Ford explained the policy as "profit sharing and efficiency engineering." The more cynical attributed it to an attempt to prevent unionization and to obtain a docile workforce that would accept job speedups. To obtain this minimum wage an employee had to be of "good personal habits." Whether an individual fit these criteria was determined by a new office created by Ford Motor Company—the Sociological Department.

HOME OFFICE SAFETY AND SECURITY WEEK. Jan 5–9. One week each year dedicated to ensuring that the more than 30 million American home offices are safeguarded and protected against break-ins, theft, workplace injury, computer virus and hacking, natural disaster and any other malady that can impact the at-home worker. For info: Jeff Zbar, PO Box 8263, Coral Springs, FL 33075. Phone: (954) 346-4393. E-mail: jeff@chiefhomeofficer.com. Web: www.chiefhomeofficer.com.

ITALY: EPIPHANY FAIR. Jan 5. Piazza Navona, Rome, Italy. On the eve of Epiphany a fair of toys, sweets and presents takes place among the beautiful Bernini Fountains.

NATIONAL THANK GOD IT'S MONDAY! DAY. Jan 5. Besides holidays, such as Presidents' Day, being celebrated on Mondays, people everywhere start new jobs, have birthdays, celebrate promotions and begin vacations on Mondays. A day in recognition of this first day of the week. For info: Dorothy Zjawin, 61 W Colfax Ave, Roselle Park, NJ 07204.

PICCARD, JEANNETTE RIDLON: BIRTH ANNIVERSARY. Jan 5, 1895. First American woman to qualify as a free balloon pilot (1934). One of the first women to be ordained as an Episcopal priest (1976). Pilot for record-setting balloon ascent (57,579 ft) into the stratosphere (from Dearborn, MI, Oct 23, 1934) with her husband, Jean Felix Piccard. Identical twin married to identical twin. See also: "Piccard, Jean Felix: Birth Anniversary" (Jan 28). Born at Chicago, IL. Died at Minneapolis, MN, May 17, 1981.

ROMAN CATHOLIC/EASTERN ORTHODOX MEETING: 45th ANNIVERSARY. Jan 5, 1964. Pope Paul VI and Patriarch Athenagoras of Jerusalem met in the Holy Land for the first meeting in five centuries between a Roman Catholic pontiff and an Eastern Orthodox patriarch.

January 2009

S	M	T	W	T	F	S
				1	2	3
4	5	6	7	8	9	10
11	12	13	14	15	16	17
18	19	20	21	22	23	24
25	26	27	28	29	30	31

RUFFIN, EDMUND: BIRTH ANNIVERSARY. Jan 5, 1794. Born at Prince George County, VA, Edmund Ruffin was an American agriculturist whose discoveries about crop rotation and fertilizer were influential in the early agrarian culture of the US. He published the *Farmer's Register* from 1833 to 1842, a journal that promoted scientific agriculture. A noted politician as well as a farmer, he was an early advocate of Southern secession whose views were widely circulated in pamphlets. As a member of the Palmetto Guards of Charleston, he was given the honor of firing the first shot on Fort Sumter on Apr 12, 1861. According to legend, after the South's defeat he became despondent and, wrapping himself in the Confederate flag, took his own life on June 18, 1865, at Amelia County, VA.

TWELFTH NIGHT. Jan 5. Evening before Epiphany (Jan 6). Twelfth Night marks the end of medieval Christmas festivities. Also called Twelfth Day Eve. See also "Epiphany or Twelfth Day" (Jan 6).

WOMEN'S SELF-EMPOWERMENT WEEK. Jan 5–11. Women wear many hats these days, and this week is a time to stop, take stock of your life and recognize all that you have accomplished. It's an occasion to pat yourself on the back and feel good about your role in society and the opportunities that have come your way through hard work and dedication. Let it inspire you to establish new goals and reach for the sky. For info: Robin Gorman Newman, The Love Coach, 44 Somerset Dr N, Great Neck, NY 11020. Phone: (516) 773-0911. E-mail: robin@lovecoach.com. Web: www.ibwc.org.

WYOMING INAUGURATES FIRST WOMAN GOVERNOR IN US: ANNIVERSARY. Jan 5, 1925. Nellie Tayloe (Mrs William B.) Ross became the first woman to serve as governor upon her inauguration in Wyoming. She had previously finished out the term of her husband, who had died in office. In 1974 Ella Grasso of Connecticut became the first woman to be elected governor in her own right.

Birthdays Today

Bradley Cooper, 34, actor ("Alias," *Failure to Launch*), born Philadelphia, PA, Jan 5, 1975.

Warrick Dunn, 34, football player, born Baton Rouge, LA, Jan 5, 1975.

Robert Duvall, 78, actor (*A Civil Action, The Godfather*), born San Diego, CA, Jan 5, 1931.

Umberto Eco, 77, author (*In the Name of the Rose*), born Alessandria, Italy, Jan 5, 1932.

Carrie Ann Inaba, 41, choreographer, television personality ("Dancing with the Stars"), born Honolulu, HI, Jan 5, 1968.

Diane Keaton, 63, actress (*The First Wives Club, Looking for Mr. Goodbar, Reds,* Oscar for *Annie Hall*), born Diane Hall at Los Angeles, CA, Jan 5, 1946.

Pamela Sue Martin, 55, actress (*The Poseidon Adventure,* "The Nancy Drew Mysteries," "Dynasty"), born Westport, CT, Jan 5, 1954.

Walter Frederick (Fritz) Mondale, 81, 42nd vice president of the US, former senator, born Ceylon, MN, Jan 5, 1928.

Ed Rendell, 65, Governor of Pennsylvania (D), born New York, NY, Jan 5, 1944.

Charlie Rose, 67, newscaster, TV host, born Henderson, NC, Jan 5, 1942.

W.D. Snodgrass, 83, poet, born Wilkinsburg, PA, Jan 5, 1926.

January 6 — Tuesday

DAY 6 359 REMAINING

ARMENIAN CHRISTMAS. Jan 6. Christmas is observed in the Armenian Church, the oldest Christian national church.

ASARAH B'TEVET. Jan 6. Hebrew calendar date: Tevet 10, 5769. The Fast of the 10th of Tevet begins at first morning light and commemorates the beginning of the Babylonian siege of Jerusalem in the sixth century BC. Began at sunset Jan 5. Asarah B'Tevet occurs twice in the 2009 calendar year.

BUSH, GEORGE H.W. AND BARBARA, WEDDING: ANNIVERSARY. Jan 6, 1945. George Herbert Walker Bush was 20 and Barbara Pierce was 19 when they married. They had four sons and two daughters (one of whom died in childhood). Bush served as the 41st president of the US. Their son George W. Bush became the 43rd president of the US.

CARNIVAL SEASON. Jan 6–Feb 24. A secular festival preceding Lent. A time of merrymaking and feasting before the austere days of Lenten fasting and penitence (40 weekdays between Ash Wednesday and Easter Sunday). The word *carnival* probably is derived from the Latin *carnem levare*, meaning "to remove meat." Depending on local custom, the carnival season may start any time between Nov 11 and Shrove Tuesday. Conclusion of the season is much less variable, being the close of Shrove Tuesday in most places. Celebrations vary considerably, but the festival often includes many theatrical aspects (masks, costumes and songs) and has given its name (in the US) to traveling amusement shows that may be seen throughout the year. Observed traditionally in Roman Catholic countries from Epiphany through Shrove Tuesday.

EPIPHANY or TWELFTH DAY. Jan 6. Known also as Old Christmas Day and Twelfthtide. On the 12th day after Christmas, Christians celebrate the visit of the Magi, the first Gentile recognition of Christ. Epiphany of Our Lord, one of the oldest Christian feasts, is observed in Roman Catholic churches in the US on a Sunday between Jan 2 and 8. Theophany of the Eastern Orthodox Church is observed in churches using the Gregorian calendar (Jan 19 in those churches using the Julian calendar). This feast day celebrates the manifestation of the divinity of Jesus at the time of his baptism in the Jordan River by John the Baptist. Note: In centuries past, the day began at sunset. This custom has often led to confusion between Twelfth Night and Twelfth Day.

GIBRAN, KAHLIL: BIRTH ANNIVERSARY. Jan 6, 1883. Lebanese-American poet (*The Prophet*) and artist. Born at Bsherri, Lebanon, he died Oct 10, 1931, at New York, NY.

"HALLMARK HALL OF FAME" TV PREMIERE: ANNIVERSARY. Jan 6, 1952. Carried at different times by ABC, CBS, NBC and PBS, this was a top-quality dramatic anthology series. Originally titled "Hallmark Television Playhouse," the program was sponsored by Hallmark Cards and hosted by Sarah Churchill until 1955. A few of the presentations were *Hamlet*, with Maurice Evans and Ruth Chatterton (Apr 26, 1953); *Moby Dick*, with Victor Jory (May 16, 1954); *Macbeth*, with Maurice Evans, Dame Judith Anderson and House Jameson (Nov 28, 1954); and *Alice in Wonderland*, with Eva LeGallienne, Elsa Lanchester and Reginald Gardiner (Oct 23, 1955). The list goes on with splendid performances by many highly acclaimed actors and actresses.

ITALY: LA BEFANA. Jan 6. Epiphany festival in which the "Befana," a kindly witch, bestows gifts on children—toys and candy for those who have been good, but a lump of coal or a pebble for those who have been naughty. The festival begins on the night of Jan 5 with much noise and merrymaking (when the Befana is supposed to come down the chimneys on her broom, leaving gifts in children's stockings) and continues with joyous fairs, parades and other activities throughout Jan 6.

JAMAICA: MAROON FESTIVAL. Jan 6. Commemorates the 18th-century Treaty of Cudjoe. While Jamaica was a Spanish colony, its native inhabitants (Arawaks) were exterminated. The Spanish then imported African slaves to work their plantations. When the Spanish were driven out (1655), the black slaves fled to the mountains. The "Maroons" (fugitive slaves) were permitted to settle in the north of the island in 1738.

JOAN OF ARC: BIRTH ANNIVERSARY. Jan 6, 1412. Born at the village of Domrémy, in the Meuse River valley of France (probably in 1412). Turned over to an ecclesiastical court by the British, she was tried for heresy and burned to death at the stake May 30, 1431, at age 19; in reality, she was executed for the military action she'd taken against the British on behalf of Charles VII of France.

JOHNSON, BAN: BIRTH ANNIVERSARY. Jan 6, 1863. Byron Bancroft (Ban) Johnson, Baseball Hall of Fame executive, born at Cincinnati, OH. Johnson transformed the minor league Western League into the major league American League in 1901. He ruled as president with an iron hand and was eased out of power by the league's owners in 1927. Inducted into the Hall of Fame in 1937. Died at St. Louis, MO, Mar 28, 1931.

MALESKA, EUGENE T.: BIRTH ANNIVERSARY. Jan 6, 1916. *New York Times* crossword puzzle editor, Maleska was born at Jersey City, NJ. He invented new puzzle formats and clue styles for crossword puzzles in 1977 after a career in education. Maleska died Aug 3, 1993, at Daytona Beach, FL.

MIX, TOM: BIRTH ANNIVERSARY. Jan 6, 1880. American motion picture actor, especially remembered for cowboy films. Born at Driftwood, PA. Died near Florence, AZ, Oct 12, 1940.

NEW MEXICO: ADMISSION DAY: ANNIVERSARY. Jan 6, 1912. Became 47th state in 1912.

PAN AM CIRCLES EARTH: ANNIVERSARY. Jan 6, 1942. A Pan American Airways plane arrived in New York to complete the first around-the-world trip by a commercial aircraft.

SALOMON, HAYM: DEATH ANNIVERSARY. Jan 6, 1785. American Revolutionary War patriot and financier was born at Lissa, Poland, in 1740 (exact date unknown). Salomon died at Philadelphia, PA.

SANDBURG, CARL: BIRTH ANNIVERSARY. Jan 6, 1878. American poet, biographer of Lincoln, historian and folklorist, born at Galesburg, IL. Died at Flat Rock, NC, July 22, 1967.

SMITH, JEDEDIAH STRONG: BIRTH ANNIVERSARY. Jan 6, 1799. Mountain man, fur trader and one of the first explorers of the American West, Smith helped develop the Oregon Trail. He was the first American to reach California by land and the first to travel by land from San Diego up the West Coast to the Canadian border. Smith was born at Jericho (now Bainbridge), NY, and was killed by Comanche Indians along the Santa Fe Trail in what is now Kansas on May 27, 1831.

SPACE MILESTONE: *LUNAR EXPLORER* (US). Jan 6, 1998. NASA headed back to the moon for the first time since the *Apollo 17* flight 25 years before. This unmanned probe searched for evidence of frozen water on the moon and found evidence of ice in late 1998.

THOMAS, DANNY: BIRTH ANNIVERSARY. Jan 6, 1912. Comedian Danny Thomas was born Muzyad Yakhoob, later Amos Jacobs, at Deerfield, MI. Thomas began his entertainment career as a radio actor and nightclub comedian and then went on to movies in the late 1940s and early 1950s. His greatest fame came from his television show "Make Room for Daddy" (1953–64) and later as a television producer. He was also a tireless philanthropist who founded St. Jude Children's Research Hospital at Memphis, TN. Thomas died Feb 6, 1991, at Los Angeles, CA.

THREE KINGS DAY. Jan 6. Major festival of the Christian Church observed in many parts of the world with gifts, feasting, last lighting of Christmas lights and burning of Christmas greens. Twelfth and last day of the Feast of the Nativity. Commemorates the visit of the Three Wise Men (Kings or Magi) to Bethlehem.

"WHEEL OF FORTUNE" TV PREMIERE: ANNIVERSARY. Jan 6, 1975. This daytime quiz show was originally hosted by Chuck Woolery. In 1981 Pat Sajak became host, assisted by Vanna White. A nighttime version was added in 1983. Not to be confused with the human-interest show rewarding people who had done good deeds, hosted by Todd Russell, that premiered in 1952.

YOUNG, LORETTA: BIRTH ANNIVERSARY. Jan 6, 1913. Academy Award–winning actress, born at Salt Lake City, UT. She won an Oscar as Best Actress in 1947 for *The Farmer's Daughter* and several Emmys for her television show, "The Loretta Young Show," which ran from 1953 to 1961. She died Aug 12, 2000, at Los Angeles, CA.

Birthdays Today

Joey Lauren Adams, 38, actress (*Chasing Amy, Big Daddy*), born Little Rock, AR, Jan 6, 1971.

Gilbert Arenas, 27, basketball player, born Los Angeles, CA, Jan 6, 1982.

Rowan Atkinson, 54, British actor ("Mr Bean," "Blackadder"), born Newcastle-upon-Tyne, England, Jan 6, 1955.

E.L. Doctorow, 78, writer (*Ragtime, The March*), born New York, NY, Jan 6, 1931.

Bonnie Franklin, 65, actress ("One Day at a Time," *The Kettles in the Ozarks*), born Santa Monica, CA, Jan 6, 1944.

Louis Leo (Lou) Holtz, 72, former Notre Dame football coach, born Follansbee, WV, Jan 6, 1937.

Howard M. (Howie) Long, 49, sportscaster, Hall of Fame football player, born Somerville, MA, Jan 6, 1960.

Nancy Lopez, 52, Hall of Fame golfer, born Torrance, CA, Jan 6, 1957.

Gabrielle Reece, 39, pro volleyball player, born La Jolla, CA, Jan 6, 1970.

Earl Scruggs, 85, musician, born Flint Hill, NC, Jan 6, 1924.

John Singleton, 41, director, screenwriter (*Shaft, Boyz N the Hood*), born Los Angeles, CA, Jan 6, 1968.

January 2009	S	M	T	W	T	F	S
					1	2	3
	4	5	6	7	8	9	10
	11	12	13	14	15	16	17
	18	19	20	21	22	23	24
	25	26	27	28	29	30	31

January 7 — Wednesday

DAY 7 **358 REMAINING**

ADDAMS, CHARLES: BIRTH ANNIVERSARY. Jan 7, 1912. The prolific cartoonist with a macabre sense of humor was born at Westfield, NJ. He became a full-time staff member of *The New Yorker* in 1935 and stayed there for his entire career, producing some 1,300 cartoons. His most famous creation was the ghoulish "Addams Family," who escaped print into television and film. Author of numerous bestselling cartoon collections and the *Charles Addams Mother Goose* (1967), Addams died Sept 29, 1988, at New York, NY. See also: "'The Addams Family' TV Premiere: Anniversary" (Sept 18).

ASHURA: TENTH DAY. Jan 7. Islamic calendar date: Muharram 10, 1430. For Shia Muslims, commemorates death of Muhammad's grandson at the Battle of Karbala. A time of fasting, reflection and meditation. Jews of Medina fasted on the 10th day in remembrance of their salvation from Pharoah. Different methods for "anticipating" the visibility of the new moon crescent at Mecca are used by different groups. US date may vary. Began at sunset the preceding day.

EMPEROR HIROHITO: 20th DEATH ANNIVERSARY. Jan 7, 1989. After ruling Japan for 62 years as its longest-reigning ruler, Emperor Hirohito died at Tokyo of cancer at 6:33 AM on Jan 7, 1989. His only son, Crown Prince Akihito, succeeded him to the throne later that day.

"FAME" TV PREMIERE: ANNIVERSARY. Jan 7, 1982. NBC series centered on life at New York's High School of the Performing Arts. Based on the movie, it featured four of the film's actors in the same parts: Debbie Allen as dance teacher Lydia Grant, Albert Hague as music instructor Benjamin Shorofsky, Lee Curreri as student Bruno Martelli and Gene Anthony Ray as dancing student Leroy Johnson. The last telecast aired on Aug 4, 1987.

FILLMORE, MILLARD: BIRTH ANNIVERSARY. Jan 7, 1800. 13th president of the US (July 10, 1850–Mar 3, 1853). Fillmore succeeded to the presidency upon the death of Zachary Taylor, but he did not get the hoped-for nomination from his party in 1852. He ran for president in 1856 as candidate of the "Know-Nothing Party," whose platform demanded, among other things, that every government employee (federal, state and local) should be a native-born citizen. Fillmore was born at Summerhill, NY, and died at Buffalo, NY, Mar 8, 1874. Now his birthday is often used as an occasion for parties for which there is no other reason.

FIRST BALLOON FLIGHT ACROSS ENGLISH CHANNEL: ANNIVERSARY. Jan 7, 1785. Dr. John Jeffries, a Boston physician, and Jean-Pierre François Blanchard, French aeronaut, crossed the English Channel from Dover, England, to Calais, France, landing in a forest after being forced to throw overboard all ballast, equipment and even most of their clothing to avoid a forced landing in the icy waters of the English Channel. Blanchard's trousers are said to have been the last article thrown overboard.

FIRST US COMMERCIAL BANK: ANNIVERSARY. Jan 7, 1782. The first commercial bank in the US, the Bank of North America, was opened at Philadelphia.

GARDENIA, VINCENT: BIRTH ANNIVERSARY. Jan 7, 1922. Stage, screen and television performer Vincent Gardenia was born Vincent Scognamiglio at Naples, Italy. Gardenia once estimated he had played 500 parts in his lifetime. He received two Oscar nominations, one for playing a baseball manager in *Bang the Drum Slowly* and again for the role of patriarch of a goofy Brooklyn family in *Moonstruck*. He won a Tony for his part in *The Prisoner of Second Avenue* and an Emmy for his portrayal in *Age Old Friends*. Vincent Gardenia died Dec 9, 1992, at Philadelphia, PA.

GERMANY: MUNICH FASCHING CARNIVAL. Jan 7–Feb 24. Munich. From Jan 7 through Shrove Tuesday is Munich's famous carnival season. Costume balls are popular throughout carnival. The high points of the festival occur on Fasching Sunday (Feb 22) and Shrove Tuesday (Feb 24), with great carnival revelry outside at the Viktualienmarkt and on Pedestrian Mall.

HARLEM GLOBETROTTERS PLAY FIRST GAME: ANNIVERSARY. Jan 7, 1927. Basketball promoter Abe Saperstein's "New York Globetrotters" took the floor on this date at Hinckley, IL. Despite the "New York" in their name, the Globetrotters (who included Inman Jackson, Lester Johnson and Walter Wright) hailed from Chicago's South Side. The talented African-American players—unable to play in white professional leagues—barnstormed the nation in serious basketball promotional events. They changed to "Harlem Globetrotters" in the 1930s and added humor to their games in the 1940s.

HURSTON, ZORA NEALE: BIRTH ANNIVERSARY. Jan 7, 1891. One of the most important African-American writers of the 20th century was born at Eatonville, FL, to a preacher and former schoolteacher. Hurston attended Barnard College and then became an integral part of the Harlem Renaissance of the 1920s and 1930s. Hurston published four novels in her lifetime, including the classic *Their Eyes Were Watching God* (1937), as well as important anthropological works, short stories, plays and a moving memoir. She was a trailblazer in collecting regional black folklore. Hurston died at Fort Pierce, FL, on Jan 28, 1960.

I'M NOT GOING TO TAKE IT ANYMORE DAY. Jan 7. A day to fight back and take control of all events that happen in one's life. Stand up for your rights—it's so easy to walk away. For info: Bob O'Brien, Consumer Advocate, 1061 Koelle Blvd, Secaucus, NJ 07094. Phone: (646) 233-6610. E-mail: robtfobrien@aol.com.

JAPAN: NANAKUSA. Jan 7. Festival dates back to the seventh century and recalls the seven plants served to the emperor that are believed to have great medicinal value—shepherd's purse, chickweed, parsley, cottonweed, radish, hotoke-no-za and aona.

JAPAN: USOKAE (BULLFINCH EXCHANGE FESTIVAL). Jan 7. Dazaifu, Fukuoka Prefecture. "Good Luck"-gilded wood bullfinches, mixed among many plain ones, are sought after by the throngs as priests of the Dazaifu Shrine pass them out in the dim light of a small bonfire.

MARIAN ANDERSON PERFORMS WITH THE METROPOLITAN OPERA: ANNIVERSARY. Jan 7, 1930. Contralto Marian Anderson made her debut with New York's Metropolitan Opera in Verdi's *Un ballo in maschera*, becoming the first African American to perform with that organization. She was 57 years old. The audience gave her repeated ovations.

MONTGOLFIER, JACQUES ETIENNE: BIRTH ANNIVERSARY. Jan 7, 1745. Merchant and inventor, born at Vidalon-lez Annonay, Ardèche, France. With his older brother, Joseph Michel, in November 1782, conducted experiments with paper and fabric bags filled with smoke and hot air, which led to the invention of the hot-air balloon and a human's first flight. Died at Serrieres, France, Aug 2, 1799. See also: "First Balloon Flight: Anniversary" (June 5); "Aviation History Month" (Nov 1).

NEW ORLEANS BOAT SHOW. Jan 7–11. New Orleans, LA. Annual show of boat and marine products, fishing equipment and resort info. Informative boating and fishing seminars. For info: Barbara Sclafani, Natl Marine Manufacturers Assn, 3925 N I-10 Service Rd, Ste 209, Metairie, LA 70002. Phone: (504) 780-1818. Fax: (504) 780-1813. E-mail: bsclafani@nmma.org. Web: www.neworleansboatshow.com.

ONASSIS, ARISTOTLE: BIRTH ANNIVERSARY. Jan 7, 1906. Larger-than-life billionaire Greek shipping magnate who married Jackie Kennedy in 1968. Born in Smyrna (now Izmir), Turkey, Onassis died Mar 15, 1975, near Paris, France.

POL POT OVERTHROWN: 30th ANNIVERSARY. Jan 7, 1979. Pol Pot's Cambodian government fell to combined forces of Cambodian rebels and Vietnamese soldiers.

RUSSIA: CHRISTMAS OBSERVANCE. Jan 7. National holiday.

TRANSATLANTIC PHONING: ANNIVERSARY. Jan 7, 1927. Commercial transatlantic telephone service between New York and London was inaugurated. There were 31 calls made the first day.

 Birthdays Today

William Blatty, 81, novelist (*The Exorcist*), screenwriter, born New York, NY, Jan 7, 1928.

Nicolas Cage, 45, actor (*National Treasure, Adaptation, Leaving Las Vegas, Moonstruck*), born Long Beach, CA, Jan 7, 1964.

David Caruso, 53, actor ("NYPD Blue," "CSI: Miami"), born Forest Hills, NY, Jan 7, 1956.

Katie Couric, 52, journalist ("The CBS Evening News," "The Today Show"), born Arlington, VA, Jan 7, 1957.

Dustin Diamond, 32, actor ("Saved by the Bell"), born San Jose, CA, Jan 7, 1977.

Eric Gagne, 33, baseball player, born Montreal, QC, Canada, Jan 7, 1976.

Erin Gray, 59, actress ("Buck Rogers in the 25th Century," "Silver Spoons"), born Honolulu, HI, Jan 7, 1950 (some sources say 1952).

Kenny Loggins, 61, singer, songwriter ("What a Fool Believes" with Michael McDonald, won three Grammys), born Everett, WA, Jan 7, 1948.

Paul Revere, 71, singer, pianist (Paul Revere & the Raiders), born Harvard, NE, Jan 7, 1938.

Alfonso Soriano, 31, baseball player, born San Pedro de Macoris, Dominican Republic, Jan 7, 1978.

John R. Thune, 48, US Senator (R, South Dakota), born Pierre, SD, Jan 7, 1961.

Jann Wenner, 62, journalist, publisher, *Rolling Stone* magazine, born New York, NY, Jan 7, 1947.

January 8 — Thursday

DAY 8 — **357 REMAINING**

AT&T DIVESTITURE: ANNIVERSARY. Jan 8, 1982. In the most significant antitrust suit since the breakup of Standard Oil in 1911, American Telephone and Telegraph agreed to give up its 22 local Bell System companies ("Baby Bells"). These companies represented 80 percent of AT&T's assets. This ended the corporation's virtual monopoly on US telephone service.

BATTLE OF NEW ORLEANS: ANNIVERSARY. Jan 8, 1815. British forces suffered crushing losses (more than 2,000 casualties) in an attack on New Orleans, LA. Defending US troops were led by General Andrew Jackson, who became a popular hero as a result of the victory. Neither side knew that the War of 1812 had ended two weeks previously with the signing of the Treaty of Ghent, Dec 24, 1814. Battle of New Orleans Day is observed in Louisiana.

BCS NATIONAL CHAMPIONSHIP GAME. Jan 8. Miami, FL. College football's top two teams in the nation will vie for the national title in the annual BCS National Championship game. The contest will be telecast on FOX Sports. For info: BCS National Championship Game. Web: www.bcsfootball.org.

BIDDLE, NICHOLAS: BIRTH ANNIVERSARY. Jan 8, 1786. American lawyer, diplomat, statesman and financier who served as president of the Second Bank of the United States. Born at Philadelphia, PA, he died there Feb 27, 1844.

CHICAGO SKETCH COMEDY FESTIVAL. Jan 8–18. Chicago, IL. Eighth annual event that celebrates the best in local and national sketch comedy. Over two weeks, audiences can take in more than 100 events, including performances and discussions. This is the world's largest sketch comedy festival, with hundreds of funny people in one convenient location—laughter guaranteed. For info: Jill Valentine, Executive Director, Chicago Sketch Comedy Festival. E-mail: jill@chicagosketchfest.net. Web: www.chicagosketchfest.net.

CHOU EN-LAI: DEATH ANNIVERSARY. Jan 8, 1976. Anniversary of the death of Chou En-Lai, premier of the State Council of the People's Republic of China. He was born in 1898 (exact date unknown).

COLLINS, WILLIAM WILKIE: BIRTH ANNIVERSARY. Jan 8, 1824. English novelist, author of *The Moonstone* (one of the first examples of detective fiction), *The Woman in White* and *The Dead Secret*. Born at London, England, he died there Sept 23, 1889.

EARTH'S ROTATION PROVED: ANNIVERSARY. Jan 8, 1851. In his Paris home using a device now known as Foucault's pendulum, physicist Jean Foucault demonstrated that Earth rotates on its axis.

ELVIS PRESLEY'S BIRTHDAY CELEBRATION. Jan 8–11. Graceland, Memphis, TN. Special birthday proclamation on Jan 8 as well as other Elvis birthday events at Graceland. For info: Graceland, 3734 Elvis Presley Blvd, Memphis, TN 38116. Phone: (800) 238-2000 or (901) 332-3322. E-mail: glsales@elvis.com. Web: www.elvis.com.

FERRER, JOSE: BIRTH ANNIVERSARY. Jan 8, 1912. Award-winning actor, producer, writer and director was born at Santurce, Puerto Rico. Nominated three times for an Academy Award, he won Best Actor for his role in *Cyrano de Bergerac*. In addition, Ferrer was awarded Tonys and Critics' Circle prizes during half a century in the entertainment world. He died Jan 26, 1992, at Coral Gables, FL.

FOURTEEN POINTS PROPOSED: ANNIVERSARY. Jan 8, 1918. In a speech before a hastily convened joint session of Congress, President Woodrow Wilson presented Fourteen Points for a just peace. The proposal called for reduction of armaments to the lowest point consistent with domestic safety, "open covenants openly arrived at," self-determination of governments and the creation of a League of Nations to preserve peace. Wilson was unable to obtain Allied agreement to his proposals.

GREECE: MIDWIFE'S DAY or WOMEN'S DAY. Jan 8. Midwife's Day or Women's Day is celebrated Jan 8 each year to honor midwives and all women. "On this day women stop their housework and spend their time in cafés, while the men do all the housework chores and look after the children." In some villages, men caught outside "will be stripped . . . and drenched with cold water."

INTERNATIONAL CONSUMER ELECTRONICS SHOW. Jan 8–11. Las Vegas, NV. The world's largest annual trade show for consumers and America's largest annual tradeshow of any kind. Exhibitors are manufacturers, developers and suppliers of consumer technology hardware, content, technology delivery systems and related products and services. Attendees representing more than 115 countries include manufacturers, retailers, content providers and creators, broadband developers, wireless carriers, cable and satellite TV providers, installers, engineers, corporate buyers, government leaders, financial analysts and the media from around the world. Held since 1967. Est attendance: 130,000. For info: Consumer Electronics Assn, 1919 S Eads St, Arlington, VA 22202. Phone: (866) 858-1555. E-mail: CESinfo@CE.org. Web: www.CE.org or www.cesweb.org.

NATIONAL JOYGERM DAY. Jan 8. A day devoted to sending rousing ripples of joy and good cheer, kindness and courtesy, happiness and humor, sacredness and silliness to those you meet and greet. You'll be spreading that contagious "disease" called Joygerm Fever. For info: Joygerm Joan E. White, Founder, Joygerms Unlimited, PO Box 555, Syracuse, NY 13206-0555. Phone: (315) 472-2779. E-mail: joygerms@gmail.com.

January 2009

S	M	T	W	T	F	S
				1	2	3
4	5	6	7	8	9	10
11	12	13	14	15	16	17
18	19	20	21	22	23	24
25	26	27	28	29	30	31

PRESLEY, ELVIS AARON: BIRTH ANNIVERSARY. Jan 8, 1935. Popular American rock singer, born at Tupelo, MS. Although his middle name was spelled incorrectly as "Aron" on his birth certificate, Elvis had it legally changed to "Aaron," which is how it is spelled on his gravestone. Died at Memphis, TN, Aug 16, 1977.

SAINT GUDULA: FEAST DAY. Jan 8. Virgin, patron saint of the city of Brussels. Died Jan 8, probably in the year 712. Her relics were transferred to the church of St. Michael in Brussels.

SAN DIEGO BOAT SHOW. Jan 8–11. San Diego Convention Center and Marriott Marina, San Diego, CA. Annual show is largest one-stop nautical sports event on the West Coast and features a wide selection of boats and accessories, plus informative boating and fishing seminars. For info: Natl Marine Mfgrs Assn (NMMA), 200 E Randolph St, Ste 5100, Chicago, IL 60601. Phone: (312) 946-6200. Web: www.boatshows.com or www.sandiegoboatshow.com.

SHOW AND TELL DAY AT WORK. Jan 8. Students have show-and-tell at school, so adults should get to do the same. (©2006 by WH.) For info: Thomas & Ruth Roy, Wellcat Holidays, 2418 Long Ln, Lebanon, PA 17046. Phone: (717) 279-0184. E-mail: info@wellcat.com. Web: www.wellcat.com.

ULTIMATE FISHING SHOW—DETROIT. Jan 8–11. Rock Financial Showplace, Novi, MI. This event brings together buyers and sellers of boating, fishing and outdoor sporting products. US and Canadian hunting and fishing trips, as well as other vacation travel destinations, are featured. Est attendance: 25,000. For info: Adam Starr, ShowSpan, Inc, 2121 Celebration Dr NE, Grand Rapids, MI 49525. Phone: (616) 447-2860. Fax: (616) 447-2861. E-mail: events@showspan.com. Web: www.showspan.com.

WAR ON POVERTY: 45th ANNIVERSARY. Jan 8, 1964. President Lyndon Johnson declared a War on Poverty in his State of the Union address. He stressed improved education as one of the cornerstones of the program. The following Aug 20, he signed a $947.5 million antipoverty bill designed to assist more than 30 million citizens.

Birthdays Today

Shirley Bassey, 72, singer ("Goldfinger"), born Cardiff, Wales, Jan 8, 1937.

David Bowie, 62, musician, actor (*The Labyrinth*), born David Robert Jones at London, England, Jan 8, 1947.

Bob Eubanks, 72, game-show host ("The Newlywed Game"), born Flint, MI, Jan 8, 1937.

Vladimir Feltsman, 57, Russian pianist, born Moscow, USSR (now Russia), Jan 8, 1952.

Jeff Francoeur, 25, baseball player, born Atlanta, GA, Jan 8, 1984.

Jason Giambi, 38, baseball player, born West Covina, CA, Jan 8, 1971.

Stephen Hawking, 67, physicist, author (*A Brief History of Time*), born Oxford, England, Jan 8, 1942.

Kathleen Noone, 63, actress ("Party of Five," "Sunset Beach"), born Hillsdale, NJ, Jan 8, 1946.

Charles Osgood, 76, television journalist, born New York, NY, Jan 8, 1933.

Soupy Sales, 83, comedian ("The Soupy Sales Show"), born Morton Supman at Wake Forest, NC, Jan 8, 1926.

January 9 — Friday

DAY 9 356 REMAINING

AVIATION IN AMERICA: ANNIVERSARY. Jan 9, 1793. A Frenchman, Jean-Pierre François Blanchard, made the first manned free-balloon flight in America's history at Philadelphia, PA. The event was watched by President George Washington and many other high government officials. The hydrogen-filled balloon rose to a height of about 5,800 feet, traveled some 15 miles and landed 46 minutes later in New Jersey. Reportedly Blanchard had one passenger on the flight—a little black dog.

BEAUVOIR, SIMONE DE: BIRTH ANNIVERSARY. Jan 9, 1908. French feminist and writer. *The Second Sex* lays out her theories of feminism. Born at Paris, France; died there on Apr 15, 1986.

CATT, CARRIE LANE CHAPMAN: 150th BIRTH ANNIVERSARY. Jan 9, 1859. American women's rights leader, founder (in 1919) of National League of Women Voters. Born at Ripon, WI, she died at New Rochelle, NY, Mar 9, 1947.

CONNECTICUT RATIFIES CONSTITUTION: ANNIVERSARY. Jan 9, 1788. By a vote of 128 to 40, Connecticut became the fifth state to ratify the Constitution.

DENVER, BOB: BIRTH ANNIVERSARY. Jan 9, 1935. Television actor born at New Rochelle, NY. He worked as a mailman and a high school teacher before landing the role—Maynard G. Krebs—that made him famous on "The Many Loves of Dobie Gillis" in 1959. Krebs was one of the first beatniks portrayed on television. When that series ended in 1963, Denver took on the memorable lead character in "Gilligan's Island." That series is one of the most popular in television history. Denver died at Winston-Salem, NC, on Sept 2, 2005.

ENGLAND: LONDON BOAT SHOW. Jan 9–18. ExCeL, London's Docklands, London. The Show promises to be a great day out with a host of features and a wide range of exhibitors. Est attendance: 130,000. For info: British Marine Federation/Natl Boat Shows Ltd, Marine House, Thorpe Lea Rd, Egham, Surrey, England TW20 8BF. Phone: (44) (1784) 223-600 or (44) (1784) 473-377. Fax: (44) (1784) 439-678. E-mail: info@britishmarine.co.uk. Web: www.londonboatshow.com.

FAKE HOWARD HUGHES BIOGRAPHY: ANNIVERSARY. Jan 9, 1972. Reclusive billionaire Howard Hughes held a telephone news conference to state that the biography about him written by Clifford Irving was a fake.

"IT TAKES A THIEF" TV PREMIERE: ANNIVERSARY. Jan 9, 1968. ABC's adventure series starred Robert Wagner as Alexander Mundy, an unlikely thief who agrees to conduct secret government missions instead of serving out his prison term. Malachi Throne costarred as Noah Bain, chief of the SIA and Mundy's employer. Fred Astaire made cameo appearances as Mundy's father.

NIXON, RICHARD MILHOUS: BIRTH ANNIVERSARY. Jan 9, 1913. Richard Nixon served as 36th vice president of the US (under President Dwight D. Eisenhower) Jan 20, 1953, to Jan 20, 1961. He was the 37th president of the US, serving Jan 20, 1969, to Aug 9, 1974, when he resigned the presidency while under the threat of impeachment. First US president to resign that office. He was born at Yorba Linda, CA, and died at New York, NY, Apr 22, 1994.

PANAMA: MARTYRS' DAY. Jan 9. Public holiday.

PHILIPPINES: FEAST OF THE BLACK NAZARENE. Jan 9. Culmination of a nine-day fiesta. Manila's largest procession takes place in the afternoon of Jan 9, in honor of the Black Nazarene, whose shrine is at the Quiapo Church.

"RAWHIDE" TV PREMIERE: 50th ANNIVERSARY. Jan 9, 1959. CBS western that kept them dogies (cattle) rollin' home from northern Texas to Sedalia, KS, for seven years. The series featured Eric Fleming as trail boss Gil Favor; Clint Eastwood as Rowdy Yates, ramrod and trail boss after Fleming's departure from the show; Jim Murdock as Mushy; Paul Brinegar as the cook, Wishbone; Steve Raines as Quince; Rocky Shahan as Joe Scarlett; Sheb Wooley as scout Pete Nolan; Robert Cabal as Hey Soos; John Ireland as Jed Colby; David Watson as Ian Cabot; and Raymond St. Jacques as Solomon King. Also remembered for its rollicking theme song.

ST. PETERSBURG MASSACRE: ANNIVERSARY. Jan 9, 1905. Guards at St. Petersburg's Winter Palace opened fire on some 150,000 unarmed protesting workers, killing at least 200. This event was the major catalyst for revolution in Russia that year, prompting more strikes and uprisings.

"3rd ROCK FROM THE SUN" TV PREMIERE: ANNIVERSARY. Jan 9, 1996. In this Emmy Award–winning comedy a quartet of space aliens who had taken on human form came to Earth to spy on its natives. They were led by Dick Solomon, played by John Lithgow, who fell in love with earthling Mary Albright, played by Jane Curtin. Other cast members included Kristen Johnston, French Stewart and Joseph Gordon-Levitt. The series ended its run after six seasons.

US LANDING ON LUZON: ANNIVERSARY. Jan 9, 1945. US forces began the final push to retake the Philippines by attacking at the same location where the Japanese had begun their invasion nearly four years earlier. General Douglas MacArthur landed 67,000 troops in the Gulf of Lingayen on the western coast of the big island of Luzon. The Japanese offered little opposition to the landing itself but fought fiercely against Allied advancement, particularly around Clarke Field, the major air base in the islands.

VAN CLEEF, LEE: BIRTH ANNIVERSARY. Jan 9, 1925. Actor Lee Van Cleef was born at Somerville, NJ. He appeared in many westerns and action films including *High Noon* (1952), *The Man Who Shot Liberty Valance* (1962), *The Good, the Bad and the Ugly* (1967) and *Escape from New York* (1981). Van Cleef died on Dec 16, 1989, at Oxnard, CA.

YORBA LINDA, CALIFORNIA: NIXON BIRTHDAY HOLIDAY. Jan 9. Yorba Linda, the birthplace in 1913 of former president Richard M. Nixon, became the first community officially to declare his birth anniversary a public holiday. In announcing the declaration Sept 20, 1989, Mayor Henry Wedaa said, "We're not here to judge history—we're here to recognize it." The first observance by Yorba Linda's municipal employees took place in 1990.

YOUNG, MURAT BERNARD "CHIC": BIRTH ANNIVERSARY. Jan 9, 1901. The comic strip "Blondie" was created by Murat Bernard "Chic" Young in 1930. Originally about a jazz-age flapper who marries a playboy from a socially prominent family, "Blondie" soon changed its direction: two children and a dog were added to the cast, Dagwood became a working stiff and the strip focused on middle-class family situations and problems. "Blondie" introduced America to the "dagwood," an enormous sandwich made during Dagwood's late-night forays in the refrigerator. Chic Young was born at Chicago, IL, and died at St. Petersburg, FL, Mar 14, 1973.

Birthdays Today

Joan Baez, 68, folksinger, born Staten Island, NY, Jan 9, 1941.

Tyrone Curtis "Muggsy" Bogues, 44, former basketball player, born Baltimore, MD, Jan 9, 1965.

Richard Allen (Dick) Enberg, 74, sportscaster, born Mount Clemens, MI, Jan 9, 1935.

Sergio Garcia, 29, golfer, born Borriol, Spain, Jan 9, 1980.

Crystal Gayle, 58, singer, born Brenda Gayle Webb at Paintsville, KY, Jan 9, 1951.

Mat Hoffman, 37, BMX bike racer, born Oklahoma City, OK, Jan 9, 1972.

Judith Krantz, 81, author (*Dazzle, Scruples*), born Judith Tarcher at New York, NY, Jan 9, 1928.

Dave Matthews, 42, singer, musician (The Dave Matthews Band), born Johannesburg, South Africa, Jan 9, 1967.

Joely Richardson, 44, actress (*The Patriot,* "Nip/Tuck"), born London, England, Jan 9, 1965.

J.K. Simmons, 54, actor ("Law & Order," *Spiderman*), born Detroit, MI, Jan 9, 1955.

Byron Bartlett (Bart) Starr, 75, Hall of Fame football player and former coach, born Montgomery, AL, Jan 9, 1934.

Imelda Staunton, 53, actress (*Harry Potter and the Order of the Phoenix, Vera Drake*), born London, England, Jan 9, 1956.

Susannah York, 68, actress (*Tom Jones; They Shoot Horses, Don't They?; Superman*), born London, England, Jan 9, 1941.

January 10 — Saturday

DAY 10 — **355 REMAINING**

***COMMON SENSE* PUBLISHED: ANNIVERSARY.** Jan 10, 1776. More than any other publication, *Common Sense* influenced the authors of the Declaration of Independence. Thomas Paine's 50-page pamphlet sold 150,000 copies within a few months of its first printing.

FIRST UNITED NATIONS GENERAL ASSEMBLY: ANNIVERSARY. Jan 10, 1946. On the 26th anniversary of the establishment of the unsuccessful League of Nations, delegates from 51 nations met at London, England, for the first meeting of the United Nations General Assembly.

FLORIDA MANATEE FESTIVAL. Jan 10–11. Crystal River, FL. Manatee boat tours, helicopter tours, kayak races and wildlife education are just a little of what this festival offers. Juried fine arts show, live entertainment, special children's events, beer and wine garden and lots more. Est attendance: 35,000. For info: Citrus County Chamber of Commerce, 401 Tompkins St, Inverness, FL 34450. Phone: (352) 726-2801. Fax: (352) 637-6498. Web: www.citruscountychamber.com.

HENRIED, PAUL: BIRTH ANNIVERSARY. Jan 10, 1908. Actor Paul Henried once estimated that he had played in or directed more than 300 films. Though he was a staunch anti-Nazi, his early film parts included a number of German roles, including those in *Goodbye, Mr Chips* and *Night Train.* He eventually moved away from the German stereotype in such films as *Of Human Bondage, The Four Horsemen of the Apocalypse* and as Victor Laslo in *Casablanca.* His film career cut short by the anti-Communist blacklist in Hollywood during the 1940s, Henried found a second calling as a director, with more than 80 episodes of TV's "Alfred Hitchcock Presents" to his credit. Born at Trieste, Austria, he died Mar 29, 1992, at Pacific Palisades, CA.

January 2009

S	M	T	W	T	F	S
				1	2	3
4	5	6	7	8	9	10
11	12	13	14	15	16	17
18	19	20	21	22	23	24
25	26	27	28	29	30	31

JEFFERS, ROBINSON: BIRTH ANNIVERSARY. Jan 10, 1887. American poet and playwright. Born at Pittsburgh, PA, he died at Carmel, CA, Jan 20, 1962.

LEAGUE OF NATIONS FOUNDING: ANNIVERSARY. Jan 10, 1920. Through the Treaty of Versailles, the League of Nations came into existence. Fifty nations entered into a covenant designed to avoid war. The US never joined the League of Nations, which was dissolved Apr 18, 1946.

"MASTERPIECE THEATRE" TV PREMIERE: ANNIVERSARY. Jan 10, 1971. Television at its best, PBS's long-running anthology series consists of many highly acclaimed original and adapted dramatizations. Many are produced by the BBC. Alistair Cooke and Russell Baker have hosted the program. The first presentation was "The First Churchills." Other notable programs include: "The Six Wives of Henry VIII" and "Elizabeth R" (1972); "Upstairs Downstairs" (1974–77); "I, Claudius" (1978); "The Jewel in the Crown" (1984); "The Buccaneers" (1995); and "White Teeth" (2002).

MOON PHASE: FULL MOON. Jan 10. Moon enters Full Moon phase at 10:27 PM, EST.

NATIONAL CUT YOUR ENERGY COSTS DAY. Jan 10. A day to educate people on the ways they can stay warm in the winter and cool in the summer while saving money on their energy bills. By following a few easy steps, home owners and renters can put a reasonable ceiling on their heating and cooling costs and stay comfortable. For info: Tom Peric, Natl Cut Your Energy Costs Day, 2040 Fairfax Ave, Cherry Hill, NJ 08003. Phone: (856) 874-0049. Fax: (856) 874-0052. E-mail: tom@cutyourenergycosts.com. Web: www.cutyourenergycosts.com.

NATIONAL WESTERN STOCK SHOW AND RODEO. Jan 10–25. Denver, CO. 103rd annual. It's a rodeo and more! See horse shows, Colorado's largest trade show, Western art and educational displays and the Super Bowl of livestock shows. Est attendance: 650,000. For info: Natl Western Stock Show and Rodeo, 4655 Humboldt St, Denver, CO 80216. Phone: (303) 297-1166 or (800) 336-6977. Fax: (303) 292-1708. Web: www.nationalwestern.com.

PENNSYLVANIA FARM SHOW. Jan 10–17. Harrisburg, PA. The largest indoor agricultural event in America. Est attendance: 400,000. For info: Pennsylvania Dept of Agriculture, State Farm Products Show Commission, 2300 N Cameron St, Harrisburg, PA 17110. Phone: (717) 787-5373. Fax: (717) 783-8710. Web: www.agriculture.state.pa.us/farmshow.

POSITIVELY PENGUINS. Jan 10. Jenkinson's Aquarium, Point Pleasant Beach, NJ. Learn all about the African penguin families at Jenkinson's Aquarium and the status of penguins in the wild. Children will enjoy penguin storytelling as well as appearances by our mascot, Perky the Penguin. Penguins are fed at 11 AM and 3:30 PM. Free activities with paid admission from 1 to 4 PM. Est attendance: 800. For info: Jenkinson's Aquarium, 300 Ocean Ave, Point Pleasant Beach, NJ 08742. Phone: (732) 899-1212. Fax: (732) 899-1717. E-mail: jenkinsonsaquarium@comcast.net. Web: www.jenkinsons.com.

US AND VATICAN REESTABLISH DIPLOMATIC RELATIONS: 25th ANNIVERSARY. Jan 10, 1984. The US and the Vatican established full diplomatic relations after a break of 117 years.

WELCOME BACK SNOWBIRDS PANCAKE BREAKFAST. Jan 10. El Centro, CA. Annually, the second Saturday in January. Est attendance: 2,500. For info: El Centro Chamber of Commerce, Box 3006, El Centro, CA 92244. Phone: (760) 352-3681. Fax: (760) 352-3246. E-mail: generalinfo@elcentrochamber.com. Web: www.elcentrochamber.com.

WOLF MOON. Jan 10. So called by Native American tribes of New England and the Great Lakes because at this time of winter, the wolves howl in hunger. The January Full Moon.

WOMEN'S SUFFRAGE AMENDMENT INTRODUCED IN CONGRESS: ANNIVERSARY. Jan 10, 1878. Senator A.A. Sargent of California, a close friend of Susan B. Anthony, introduced into the US Senate a women's suffrage amendment known as the Susan B. Anthony Amendment. It wasn't until Aug 26, 1920, 42 years later, that the amendment was signed into law.

 **Birthdays Today**

Pat Benatar, 56, singer, born Patricia Andrejewski at Brooklyn, NY, Jan 10, 1953.

George Foreman, 60, boxer, born Marshall, TX, Jan 10, 1949.

Mark Pryor, 46, US Senator (D, Arkansas), born Fayetteville, AR, Jan 10, 1963.

Glenn Robinson, 36, former basketball player, born Gary, IN, Jan 10, 1973.

Rod Stewart, 64, singer, musician ("Maggie May," "Do Ya Think I'm Sexy?"), born London, England, Jan 10, 1945.

William Anthony (Bill) Toomey, 70, Olympic gold medal decathlete, born Philadelphia, PA, Jan 10, 1939.

January 11 — Sunday

DAY 11 354 REMAINING

CUCKOO DANCING WEEK. Jan 11–17. To honor the memory of Laurel and Hardy, whose theme, "The Dancing Cuckoos," shall be heard throughout the land as their movies are seen and their antics greeted with laughter by old and new fans of these unique masters of comedy. (Originated by the late William T. Rabe of Sault Ste Marie, MI.)

"DESIGNATED HITTER" RULE ADOPTED: ANNIVERSARY. Jan 11, 1973. American League adopted the "designated hitter" rule, whereby an additional player is used to bat for the pitcher.

GOLDEN GLOBE AWARDS. Jan 11. Beverly Hilton Hotel, Beverly Hills, CA. 66th annual. Sponsored by the Hollywood Foreign Press Association and honoring achievement in film and television. Telecast live by NBC. For info: The Hollywood Foreign Press Assn, 646 N Robertson Blvd, West Hollywood, CA 90069. Phone: (310) 657-1731. Fax: (310) 657-5576. E-mail: info@hfpa.org. Web: www.hfpa.org.

HAMILTON, ALEXANDER: BIRTH ANNIVERSARY. Jan 11, 1755. American statesman, an author of *The Federalist* papers, first secretary of the Treasury, born at British West Indies. Engaged in a duel with Aaron Burr the morning of July 11, 1804, at Weehawken, NJ. Mortally wounded there and died July 12, 1804.

HOSTOS, EUGENIO MARIA: BIRTH ANNIVERSARY. Jan 11, 1839. Puerto Rican patriot, scholar and author of more than 50 books. Born at Rio Canas, Puerto Rico, he died at Santo Domingo, Dominican Republic, Aug 11, 1903.

INTERNATIONAL PRINTING WEEK. Jan 11–17. To develop public awareness of the printing/graphic arts industry. Annually, the week including Ben Franklin's birthday, Jan 17. For info: Intl Assn of Printing House Craftsmen, 7042 Brooklyn Blvd, Minneapolis, MN 55429-1370. Phone: (800) 466-4274. Web: www.iaphc.org.

JAMES, WILLIAM: BIRTH ANNIVERSARY. Jan 11, 1842. American psychologist and philosopher of distinguished family that included his brother, novelist Henry James. "There is no worse lie," he wrote in *Varieties of Religious Experience* (1902), "than a truth misunderstood by those who hear it." Born at New York City, he died at Chocorua, NH, Aug 26, 1910.

MacDONALD, JOHN A.: BIRTH ANNIVERSARY. Jan 11, 1815. Canadian statesman, first prime minister of Canada. Born at Glasgow, Scotland, he died June 6, 1891, at Ottawa. His birth anniversary is observed in Canada.

MOROCCO: INDEPENDENCE DAY. Jan 11. National holiday. Commemorates the date in 1944 when the Independence Party submitted a memo to the Allied authorities asking for independence under a constitutional regime. Morocco gained independence from France in 1956.

NEPAL: NATIONAL UNITY DAY. Jan 11. Celebration paying homage to King Prithvinarayan Shah (1723–75), founder of the present house of rulers of Nepal and creator of the unified Nepal of today.

NORTH AMERICAN INTERNATIONAL AUTO SHOW. Jan 11–25. COBO Center, Detroit, MI. 93rd annual Detroit show; 21st annual international show. One of the premier auto shows, the NAIAS is a showcase for the world's vehicle introductions. An estimated 70 introductions will take place during the show. Press Preview Days Jan 11–13, Industry Preview Days Jan 14–15, Charity Preview Jan 16 and Public Days Jan 17–25. Est attendance: 760,000. For info: NAIAS, 1900 W Big Beaver, Troy, MI 48084. Phone: (248) 643-0250. Fax: (248) 637-0784. E-mail: naiasmail@dada.org. Web: www.naias.com.

PAUL, ALICE: BIRTH ANNIVERSARY. Jan 11, 1885. Women's rights leader and founder of the National Woman's Party in 1913, advocate of an equal rights amendment to the US Constitution. Born at Moorestown, NJ, she died there July 10, 1977.

PERIGEAN SPRING TIDES. Jan 11. Spring tides, the highest possible tides, occur when New Moon or Full Moon takes place within 24 hours of the moment the moon is nearest Earth (perigee) in its monthly orbit. The word *spring* refers not to the season but comes from the German word *springen*, "to rise up."

STEPHEN FOSTER DAY. Jan 11. Stephen Foster Folk Culture Center State Park, White Springs, FL. A musical program and carillon recital in honor of the legendary American composer Stephen Foster. For info: Mitzi Nelson, Florida Park Service, PO Drawer G, White Springs, FL 32096. Phone: (386) 397-7005. Fax: (386) 397-4262. E-mail: margaret.a.nelson@dep.state.fl.us. Web: www.floridastateparks.org.

SWITZERLAND: MEITLISUNNTIG. Jan 11. On Meitlisunntig, the second Sunday in January, the girls of Meisterschwanden and Fahrwangen, in the Seetal district of Aargau, Switzerland, stage a procession in historical uniforms and a military parade before a female General Staff. According to tradition, the custom dates from the Villmergen War of 1712, when the women of both communes gave vital help that led to victory. Popular festival follows the procession.

THEODOSIUS I: BIRTH ANNIVERSARY. Jan 11, 347. Roman emperor known as Theodosius the Great was born at Cauca, Gallaecia, in Spain. In 379 Theodosius was summoned by the emperor Gratian to become emperor of the East. On Feb 28, 380, without consulting religious authorities, he issued the edict that made the Nicene Creed (in which God the Father, the Son and the Holy Spirit are all of the same substance) binding on all subjects. Only those who accepted it would be considered Christians; this was the first recorded use of that designation. Theodosius engaged in a continuing struggle with the West for power. He prohibited pagan worship, but the emperors of the West had strong connections with pagan aristocracy. The two sides came to blows in 394. His final victory in September of that year was seen as a divine victory in which the Christian god had triumphed over the Roman gods. Theodosius died in January 395.

US SURGEON GENERAL DECLARES CIGARETTES HAZARDOUS: 45th ANNIVERSARY. Jan 11, 1964. US Surgeon General Luther Terry issued the first government report saying that smoking may be hazardous to one's health.

Birthdays Today

Mary J. Blige, 38, pop singer, born the Bronx, NY, Jan 11, 1971.

Jean Chretien, 75, 20th prime minister of Canada (1993–2003), born Shawinigan, QC, Canada, Jan 11, 1934.

Clarence Clemons, 67, musician, singer, born Norfolk, VA, Jan 11, 1942.

Ben Daniel Crenshaw, 57, golfer, born Austin, TX, Jan 11, 1952.

Jim Hightower, 66, radio host, author (*Eat Your Heart Out, There's Nothing in the Middle of the Road but Yellow Stripes and Dead Armadillos*), born Denison, TX, Jan 11, 1943.

Naomi Judd, 63, country singer ("Have Mercy," "Why Not Me"), born Ashland, KY, Jan 11, 1946.

Christine Kaufmann, 64, actress (*Taras Bulba, Bagdad Cafe*), born Lansdorf Graz, Austria, Jan 11, 1945.

Amanda Peet, 37, actress (*A Lot Like Love, Something's Gotta Give*), born New York, NY, Jan 11, 1972.

Rod Taylor, 79, actor (*The Birds*, "Masquerade"), born Sydney, Australia, Jan 11, 1930.

Grant Tinker, 83, TV executive, born Stamford, CT, Jan 11, 1926.

Stanley Tucci, 49, actor (*Big Night*, "Murder One"), born Katonah, NY, Jan 11, 1960.

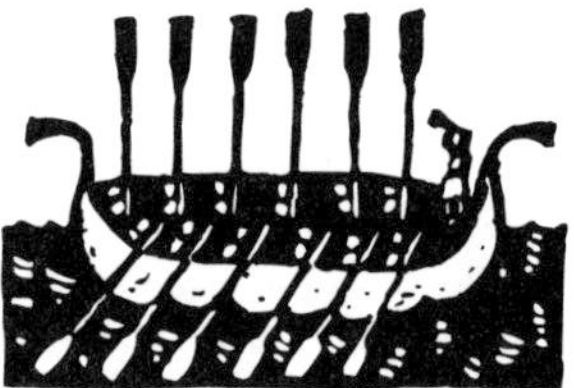

January 12 — Monday

DAY 12 353 REMAINING

"ALL IN THE FAMILY" TV PREMIERE: ANNIVERSARY. Jan 12, 1971. Based on the success of the British comedy "Till Death Us Do Part," Norman Lear created CBS's controversial sitcom "All in the Family." The series was the first of its kind to realistically portray the prevailing issues and taboos of its time with a wickedly humorous bent. From bigotry to birth control, few topics were considered too sacred to discuss on air. Ultraconservative Archie Bunker (played by Carroll O'Connor) held court from his recliner, spewing invective at any who disagreed with him. Jean Stapleton portrayed Archie's dutiful wife, Edith. Sally Struthers and Rob Reiner rounded out the cast as Archie's liberal daughter and son-in-law, Gloria and Mike "Meathead" Stivic. All three characters often fell victim to Archie's zinging one-liners and insults. The series had a 12-year run.

"BATMAN" TV PREMIERE: ANNIVERSARY. Jan 12, 1966. ABC's crime-fighting show gained a place in Nielsen's top 10 ratings in its first season. The series was based on the DC Comics characters created by Bob Kane in 1939. Adam West starred as millionaire Bruce Wayne and his superhero alter ego, Batman. Burt Ward costarred as Dick Grayson/Robin, the Boy Wonder. An assortment of villains guest-starring each week included: Cesar Romero as the Joker, Eartha Kitt and Julie Newmar as Catwoman, Burgess Meredith as the Penguin and Frank Gorshin as the Riddler. Some other stars making memorable appearances included Liberace, Vincent Price, Milton Berle, Tallulah Bankhead and Ethel Merman. The series played up its comic-strip roots with innovative and sharply skewed camera angles, bright bold colors and wild graphics. Although the last telecast was Mar 14, 1968, the show's memorable theme song, composed by Neal Hefti, can be heard today with some 120 episodes in syndication.

January 2009

S	M	T	W	T	F	S
				1	2	3
4	5	6	7	8	9	10
11	12	13	14	15	16	17
18	19	20	21	22	23	24
25	26	27	28	29	30	31

BURKE, EDMUND: BIRTH ANNIVERSARY. Jan 12, 1729. British orator, politician and philosopher, born at Dublin, Ireland. "Superstition is the religion of feeble minds," he wrote in 1790, but best remembered is "The only thing necessary for the triumph of evil is for good men to do nothing," not found in his writings but almost universally attributed to Burke. Died at Beaconsfield, England, July 9, 1797.

CONGRESS AUTHORIZED USE OF FORCE AGAINST IRAQ: ANNIVERSARY. Jan 12, 1991. The US Congress passed a resolution authorizing the president of the US to use force to expel Iraq from Kuwait. This was the sixth congressional vote in US history declaring war or authorizing force on another nation.

"DYNASTY" TV PREMIERE: ANNIVERSARY. Jan 12, 1981. The popular ABC prime-time serial focused on the high-flying exploits of the Denver-based Carrington family. The series had a weekly wardrobe budget of $10,000 with many elegant costumes designed by Nolan Miller. In addition to following the juicy storylines, many people tuned in worldwide to view the palatial mansions and lavish sets. John Forsythe played patriarch Blake Carrington with Linda Evans as his wife, Krystle. Joan Collins played Alexis, Blake's scheming ex-wife and arch business rival.

ENGLAND: PLOUGH MONDAY. Jan 12. Always the Monday after Twelfth Day. Work on the farm is resumed after the festivities of the 12 days of Christmas. On the preceding Sunday ploughs may be blessed in churches. Celebrated with dances and plays.

FARMER, JAMES: BIRTH ANNIVERSARY. Jan 12, 1920. Civil rights leader, born at Marshall, TX. Farmer was one of the founders of CORE, the Congress of Racial Equality, a volunteer organization established in 1942 to improve race relations and eliminate discriminatory practices. Farmer led the nonviolent fight to desegregate buses and terminals in 1961, known as the Freedom Rides. He received the Presidential Medal of Freedom in 1998. Died at Fredericksburg, VA, July 9, 1999.

FIRST ELECTED WOMAN SENATOR: ANNIVERSARY. Jan 12, 1932. Hattie W. Caraway, a Democrat from Arkansas, was the first woman elected to the US Senate. Born in 1878, Caraway was appointed to the Senate on Nov 13, 1931, to fill out the term of her husband, Senator Thaddeus Caraway, who had died a few days earlier. On Jan 12, 1932, she won a special election to fill the remaining months of his term. Subsequently elected to two more terms, she served in the Senate until January 1945. She was an adept and tireless legislator (once introducing 43 bills on the same day) who worked for women's rights (once cosponsoring an equal rights amendment) and supported New Deal policies. She died Dec 21, 1950, at Falls Church, VA. The first woman appointed to the Senate was Mrs W.H. Felton, who in 1922 served for two days. The first woman to be elected to the Senate without having been appointed first was Margaret Chase Smith of Maine, who had served first in the House. She was elected to the Senate in 1948.

HAYES, IRA HAMILTON: BIRTH ANNIVERSARY. Jan 12, 1922. Ira Hayes was one of six US Marines who raised the American flag on Iwo Jima's Mount Suribachi, Feb 23, 1945, following a US assault on the Japanese stronghold. The event was immortalized by AP photographer Joe Rosenthal's famous photo and later by a Marine War Memorial monument at Arlington, VA. Hayes was born on a Pima Indian Reservation at Arizona. He returned home after WWII a much celebrated hero but was unable to cope with fame. He was found dead of "exposure to freezing weather and overconsumption of alcohol" on the Sacaton Indian Reservation at Arizona, Jan 24, 1955.

JAPAN: COMING-OF-AGE DAY. Jan 12. National holiday for youth of the country who reached adulthood during the preceding year. Annually, the second Monday in January.

KIDFILM® FESTIVAL. Jan 12–25. Dallas, TX. 25th annual. Oldest and largest-attended international children's film festival in the world. Fifty shorts and features shown with filmmakers in attendance. Each year, a major figure in media (for all ages) is honored. Est attendance: 24,000. For info: USA Film Festival, 6116 N Central Expressway, Ste 105, Dallas, TX 75206. Phone: (214) 821-6300 or (214) 821-FILM. Fax: (214) 821-6364. E-mail: info@usafilm festival.com. Web: www.usafilmfestival.com.

LONDON, JACK: BIRTH ANNIVERSARY. Jan 12, 1876. American author of more than 50 books: short stories, novels and travel stories of the sea and of the far north, many marked by brutal realism. His most widely known work is *The Call of the Wild*, the great dog story published in 1903. London was born at San Francisco, CA. He died of gastrointestinal uremia on Nov 22, 1916, near Santa Rosa, CA.

MISSION SANTA CLARA DE ASIS: FOUNDING ANNIVERSARY. Jan 12, 1777. California mission built by followers of Father Junipero Serra to educate the Indians. In the 1850s, the mission became Santa Clara University, the oldest university in California. The current building, used by the university as its chapel, is a replica of an older building that was destroyed by fire in 1926.

NATIONAL CLEAN-OFF-YOUR-DESK DAY. Jan 12. To provide one day early each year for every desk worker to see the top of the desk and prepare for the following year's paperwork. Annually, the second Monday in January. For info: A.C. Vierow, Box 71, Clio, MI 48420-0071.

ORGANIZE YOUR HOME DAY. Jan 12. Organize your life by clearing the clutter at home. Start today by organizing your kitchen, kid's room, closets or family room. Devote an entire day to your New Year's resolution of "getting it together!" OrganizedTimes.com, the sponsor, will offer advice and giveaways. Annually, the second Monday in January. For info: Debbie Williams, OrganizedTimes .com, PO Box 590860, Houston, TX 77259. Phone: (281) 286-9512. E-mail: debbie@organizedtimes.com. Web: www.organizedtimes .com.

PEDDLER'S VILLAGE ANNUAL QUILT COMPETITION AND DISPLAY. Jan 12–Apr 5. Peddler's Village, Lahaska, PA. Handmade quilt entries compete for $1,400 in cash prizes in such categories as traditional, Amish, creative, clothing, children's and amateur. A distinguished panel of judges chooses the winners, and quilts are displayed in the Village Gazebo. Open daily to public. Free admission. Est attendance: 250,000. For info: Peddler's Village, Routes 202 and 263, Lahaska, PA 18931. Phone: (215) 794-4000. Fax: (215) 794-4001. Web: www.peddlersvillage.com.

SARGENT, JOHN SINGER: BIRTH ANNIVERSARY. Jan 12, 1856. Born in Florence, Italy, of American parents, Sargent became one of the most famous portrait artists of the late Victorian and Edwardian ages in Britain and the US. His best-known paintings include *Madame X* (1884), *Carnation, Lily, Lily, Rose* (1885–86) and *Ellen Terry as Lady Macbeth* (1889). Sargent died Apr 15, 1925, at London, England.

TANZANIA: ZANZIBAR REVOLUTION DAY. Jan 12. National day. Zanzibar became independent in December 1963, under a sultan; the sultan was overthrown on this day in 1964.

WINTHROP, JOHN: BIRTH ANNIVERSARY. Jan 12, 1588. (Old Style date.) American colonial governor of Massachusetts Bay Colony, born at Edwardston, England. Governor Winthrop kept a diary of events in the Massachusetts Bay Colony, published nearly two centuries later (in 1825–26), titled *The History of New England from 1630 to 1649*. Died at Boston, MA, Mar 26, 1649 (OS).

WOMEN DENIED VOTE: ANNIVERSARY. Jan 12, 1915. The US House of Representatives rejected a proposal to give women the right to vote. Women gained the right to vote in 1920.

Birthdays Today

Kirstie Alley, 54, actress ("Cheers," "Veronica's Closet," *Look Who's Talking*), born Wichita, KS, Jan 12, 1955.

Jeff Bezos, 45, founder, Amazon.com, born Albuquerque, NM, Jan 12, 1964.

Joe Frazier, 65, former boxer, born Beaufort, SC, Jan 12, 1944.

HAL, 17, computer in *2001: A Space Odyssey*, by Arthur C. Clarke, "born" Urbana, IL, Jan 12, 1992.

Marian Hossa, 30, hockey player, born Stara Lubovna, Czechoslovakia, Jan 12, 1979.

Rush Limbaugh, 58, talk-show host ("The Rush Limbaugh Show"), author, born Cape Girardeau, MO, Jan 12, 1951.

Oliver Platt, 49, actor ("Huff," "The West Wing," *Dr. Dolittle*), born Windsor, ON, Canada, Jan 12, 1960.

Ray Price, 83, country singer, born Perryville, TX, Jan 12, 1926.

Luise Rainer, 99, actress (Oscars for *The Great Ziegfield* and *The Good Earth*), born Vienna, Austria, Jan 12, 1910 (some sources say 1912).

Howard Stern, 55, radio and TV personality ("The Howard Stern Show"), born Queens, NY, Jan 12, 1954.

January 13 — Tuesday

DAY 13 — 352 REMAINING

ALGER, HORATIO, JR: 175th BIRTH ANNIVERSARY. Jan 13, 1834. American clergyman and author of more than 100 popular books for boys (some 20 million copies sold). Honesty, frugality and hard work assured that the heroes of his books would find success, wealth and fame. Born at Revere, MA, he died at Natick, MA, July 18, 1899.

CHASE, SALMON PORTLAND: BIRTH ANNIVERSARY. Jan 13, 1808. American statesman, born at Cornish, NH. US senator, secretary of the Treasury and chief justice of the US. Salmon P. Chase spent much of his life fighting slavery (he was popularly known as "attorney general for runaway Negroes"). He was one of the founders of the Republican Party, and his hopes for becoming candidate for president of the US in 1856 and 1860 were dashed because his unconcealed antislavery views made him unacceptable. Died at New York, NY, May 7, 1873.

CORRIDOR OF DEATH: ANNIVERSARY. Jan 13, 1943. The suffering of the people of Leningrad during the German siege of that city was one of the greatest tragedies of WWII. More than half the population of Russia's second-largest city died during the winter of 1942. On Jan 13, 1943, Soviet troops broke through German lines and opened a 10-mile-wide corridor south of Lake Ladoga. Within a week supplies were arriving in the city by way of this narrow opening. Because fierce German bombardment of the passage continued for another year, the pass came to be called the "Corridor of Death." The siege finally ended Jan 27, 1944, after 880 days.

FULLER, ALFRED CARL: BIRTH ANNIVERSARY. Jan 13, 1885. Founder of the Fuller Brush Company, born at Kings County, NS, Canada. In 1906 the young brush salesman went into business on his own, making brushes at a bench between the furnace and the coal bin in his sister's basement. Died at Hartford, CT, Dec 4, 1973.

JOHNNY CASH AT FOLSOM PRISON: ANNIVERSARY. Jan 13, 1968. In a landmark concert, country music star Johnny Cash performed in front of 2,000 inmates at Folsom Prison at Folsom, CA. Backed by the Tennessee Three and accompanied by June Carter, Carl Perkins and the Statler Brothers, Cash performed in the prison cafeteria. The concert was recorded as a live album and was a worldwide hit. Cash's choice to play for prisoners cemented his reputation as a hero to the downtrodden.

NORWAY: TYVENDEDAGEN. Jan 13. "20th Day," the traditional end of the Christmas season. Also commemorated as St. Knut's Day (Tjugondag Knut, or "The 20th Day of Knut") in Sweden.

RADIO BROADCASTING: ANNIVERSARY. Jan 13, 1910. Radio pioneer and electron tube inventor Lee De Forest arranged the world's first radio broadcast to the public at New York, NY. He succeeded in broadcasting the voice of Enrico Caruso along with other stars of the Metropolitan Opera to several receiving locations in the city where listeners with earphones marveled at wireless music from the air. Though only a few were equipped to listen, it was the first broadcast to reach the public and the beginning of a new era in which wireless radio communication became almost universal. See also: "First Scheduled Radio Broadcast: Anniv" (Nov 2).

RUSSIA: OLD NEW YEAR'S EVE. Jan 13. Although Jan 1 is the official New Year's Day in Russia, some Russians still celebrate on the old Julian date of Jan 13–14. Also celebrated in Belarus and Ukraine.

"THE SOPRANOS" TV PREMIERE: 10th ANNIVERSARY. Jan 13, 1999. The thinking viewer's mob drama, "The Sopranos" featured James Gandolfini as Tony Soprano, whose panic attacks drive him to seek out a psychiatrist (Lorraine Bracco). The HBO drama revolved around Tony's home and crime lives. *TV Guide* named the series one of the greatest TV shows of all time. The final episode aired June 10, 2007.

TOGO: LIBERATION DAY. Jan 13. National holiday. Commemorates 1967 uprising.

VERDON, GWEN: BIRTH ANNIVERSARY. Jan 13, 1926. One of Broadway's premier female dancers and actresses; many of her most successful roles were choreographed by her husband, Bob Fosse. She won Tony Awards for *Can-Can, Damn Yankees, New Girl in Town* and *Redhead*. She also acted in movies, including *Cocoon* and the film adaptation of *Damn Yankees*. Born at Los Angeles, CA, she died Oct 18, 2000, at Woodstock, VT.

Birthdays Today

Kevin Anderson, 49, actor (*Hoffa, Rising Sun*), born Gurnee, IL, Jan 13, 1960.

Orlando Bloom, 32, actor (*Pirates of the Caribbean, The Lord of the Rings* trilogies), born Canterbury, Kent, England, Jan 13, 1977.

Keith Coogan, 39, actor (*Adventures in Babysitting, Cousins*), born Palm Springs, CA, Jan 13, 1970.

Patrick Dempsey, 43, actor ("Grey's Anatomy," *Enchanted, Sweet Home Alabama*), born Lewiston, ME, Jan 13, 1966.

Nicole Eggert, 37, actress ("Baywatch," "Charles in Charge"), born Glendale, CA, Jan 13, 1972.

Frank Gallo, 76, artist, sculptor, born Toledo, OH, Jan 13, 1933.

Julia Louis-Dreyfus, 48, actress ("Seinfeld," "The New Adventures of Old Christine"), born New York, NY, Jan 13, 1961.

Jay McInerney, 54, writer (*Bright Lights, Big City*), born Hartford, CT, Jan 13, 1955.

Penelope Ann Miller, 45, actress (*Adventures in Babysitting, The Freshman, Carlito's Way*), born Los Angeles, CA, Jan 13, 1964.

Richard Moll, 66, actor ("Night Court," *Wicked Stepmother, The Flintstones*), born Pasadena, CA, Jan 13, 1943.

Frances Sternhagen, 79, actress ("Cheers," *Misery*; stage: *The Good Doctor, The Heiress*), born Washington, DC, Jan 13, 1930.

January 2009	S	M	T	W	T	F	S
					1	2	3
	4	5	6	7	8	9	10
	11	12	13	14	15	16	17
	18	19	20	21	22	23	24
	25	26	27	28	29	30	31

January 14 — Wednesday

DAY 14 — 351 REMAINING

ARNOLD, BENEDICT: BIRTH ANNIVERSARY. Jan 14, 1741. (Old Style date.) American officer who deserted to the British during the Revolutionary War and whose name has since become synonymous with treachery. Born at Norwich, CT. Died June 14, 1801, at London, England.

FIRST CAESAREAN SECTION: ANNIVERSARY. Jan 14, 1794. Dr. Jesse Bennett, of Edom, VA, performed the first successful caesarean section. The patient was his wife.

MAURY, MATTHEW FONTAINE: BIRTH ANNIVERSARY. Jan 14, 1806. Naval officer, born at Fredericksburg, VA. Maury established oceanography as a branch of science and revolutionized the recording of oceanographic data as a superintendent of the Naval Observatory. Died at Lexington, VA, Feb 1, 1873.

NATIONAL NO-TILLAGE CONFERENCE. Jan 14–17. Indianapolis, IN. Attracts innovative farmers interested in reducing tillage to protect the environment and boost profits. Est attendance: 800. For info: Frank Lessiter, Natl No-Tillage Conference, PO Box 624, Brookfield, WI 53008-0624. Phone: (262) 782-4480. Fax: (262) 782-1252. E-mail: info@lesspub.com. Web: www.no-tillfarmer.com.

NATIONAL SOCCER COACHES ASSOCIATION OF AMERICA NATIONAL CONVENTION. Jan 14–18. St. Louis, MO. The NSCAA is the largest single-sport coaching organization in the US. The NSCAA convention is the largest annual gathering of soccer coaches in the world. The convention features clinics, lectures, exhibits and national awards. Est attendance: 7,500. For info: NSCAA, 800 Ann Ave, Kansas City, KS 66101. Phone: (800) 458-0678 or (913) 362-1747. Fax: (913) 362-3439. E-mail: info@nscaa.com. Web: www.nscaa.com.

OUTCAULT, RICHARD FELTON: BIRTH ANNIVERSARY. Jan 14, 1863. When Richard Felton Outcault was asked by the *New York World*'s Sunday editor to submit drawings for use with their new color printing process, the "funny papers" were born. Outcault's first color drawing, titled "Origin of a New Species," was published Nov 18, 1894. The first regular colored cartoon, "Hogan's Alley," drawn by Outcault, began appearing with its main character's blustery comments written across his yellow nightshirt—thus making him the "Yellow Kid." The term "yellow journalism" was coined for newspapers featuring the Kid. Outcault's strip "Buster Brown" brought him celebrity and fortune. Outcault was born at Lancaster, OH, and died Sept 25, 1928, at Flushing, NY.

RATIFICATION DAY. Jan 14, 1784. Anniversary of the act that officially ended the American Revolution and established the US as a sovereign power. On Jan 14, 1784, the Continental Congress, meeting at Annapolis, MD, ratified the Treaty of Paris, thus fulfilling the Declaration of Independence of July 4, 1776.

ROACH, HAL: BIRTH ANNIVERSARY. Jan 14, 1892. American film writer, director and producer Harold Eugene (Hal) Roach was born at Elmira, NY. He pioneered film comedy as chief of his own studio for nearly 40 years. During that time he produced, and sometimes directed and wrote, nearly 1,000 movies. Roach is noted for originating the *Our Gang* comedies in 1922 and for introducing Laurel and Hardy to film audiences. He won Academy Awards for the short films *The Music Box* (1931) and *Bored of Education* (1936). Roach produced the film version of Steinbeck's novel *Of Mice and Men* in 1939. In 1984 he won an honorary Academy Award for career achievement. Roach died Nov 2, 1992, at Los Angeles, CA.

"SANFORD AND SON" TV PREMIERE: ANNIVERSARY. Jan 14, 1972. NBC sitcom that gained immediate popularity depicting an African-American father and son engaged in the junkyard business. Norman Lear and Bud Yorkin developed the comedy series based on the British "Steptoe and Son." Comedian Redd Foxx played Fred Sanford. His son, Lamont, was played by Demond Wilson. Others appearing on the show included Whitman Mayo as Grady, Slappy White as Melvin, LaWanda Page as Aunt Esther and Gregory Sierra as Julio. The last telecast was Sept 2, 1977.

SCHWEITZER, ALBERT: BIRTH ANNIVERSARY. Jan 14, 1875. Alsatian philosopher, musician, physician and winner of the 1952 Nobel Peace Prize was born at Kayserberg, Upper Alsace, and died at Lambarene, Gabon, Sept 4, 1965.

SPACE MILESTONE: *SOYUZ 4* (USSR): 40th ANNIVERSARY. Jan 14, 1969. First docking of two manned spacecraft (with *Soyuz 5*) and first interchange of spaceship personnel in orbit by means of space walks.

"TODAY" TV PREMIERE: ANNIVERSARY. Jan 14, 1952. NBC program that started the morning news format we know today. Captained by Dave Garroway, the show was segmented with bits and pieces of news, sports, weather, interviews and other features that were repeated so that viewers did not have to stop their morning routine to watch. The segments were brief and to the point. Sylvester Weaver devised this concept to capitalize on television's unusual qualities. What used to take three hours to broadcast live across the country was done in two with videotape on a delayed basis. The addition of chimpanzee J. Fred Muggs in 1953 helped push ratings up. There have been a number of hosts over the years, from John Chancellor and Hugh Downs to Tom Brokaw, Bryant Gumbel and Matt Lauer. Female hosts (originally called "Today Girls") have included Betsy Palmer, Florence Henderson, Barbara Walters, Jane Pauley, Katie Couric and Meredith Viera.

UZBEKISTAN: ARMY DAY. Jan 14. National holiday.

WHIPPLE, WILLIAM: BIRTH ANNIVERSARY. Jan 14, 1730. American patriot and signer of the Declaration of Independence. Born at Kittery, ME, he died at Portsmouth, NH, Nov 10, 1785.

 Birthdays Today

Jason Bateman, 40, actor ("Arrested Development"), born Rye, NY, Jan 14, 1969.

Julian Bond, 69, legislator, civil rights leader, born Nashville, TN, Jan 14, 1940.

Kristin Cavallari, 22, actress ("Laguna Beach: The Real Orange County"), born Chicago, IL, Jan 14, 1987.

Faye Dunaway, 68, actress (Oscar for *Network*; *Bonnie and Clyde, Chinatown*), born Bascom, FL, Jan 14, 1941.

Lawrence Kasdan, 60, filmmaker (*The Bodyguard, The Big Chill, Mumford*), born Miami Beach, FL, Jan 14, 1949.

Shannon Lucid, 66, astronaut, born Shanghai, China, Jan 14, 1943.

Andy Rooney, 90, writer, columnist ("60 Minutes," *Pieces of My Mind*), born Albany, NY, Jan 14, 1919.

Shepard Smith, 45, news anchor, born David Shepard Smith, Jr, at Holly Springs, MS, Jan 14, 1964.

Steven Soderbergh, 46, filmmaker (*Traffic, Ocean's Eleven, Erin Brockovich*), born Atlanta, GA, Jan 14, 1963.

Holland Taylor, 66, actress ("The Practice," *The Truman Show*), born Philadelphia, PA, Jan 14, 1943.

Nina Totenberg, 65, broadcast journalist, correspondent ("Nightline"), born New York, NY, Jan 14, 1944.

Emily Watson, 42, actress (*Gosford Park, Angela's Ashes, Hilary and Jackie*), born London, England, Jan 14, 1967.

Carl Weathers, 61, actor (*Rocky, Happy Gilmore*), born New Orleans, LA, Jan 14, 1948.

January 15 — Thursday

DAY 15 | **350 REMAINING**

ACE, GOODMAN: BIRTH ANNIVERSARY. Jan 15, 1899. Radio and TV writer, actor, columnist and humorist. With his wife, Jane, created and acted in the popular series of radio programs (1928–45) "Easy Aces." Called "America's greatest wit" by Fred Allen. Born at Kansas City, MO; died at New York, NY, Mar 25, 1982, soon after asking that his tombstone be inscribed "No flowers, please, I'm allergic."

ALPHA KAPPA ALPHA SORORITY FOUNDED: ANNIVERSARY. Jan 15, 1908. Founded at Howard University at Washington, DC, by Ethel Hedgeman Lyle, Alpha Kappa Alpha was the first organization of its type for black women. It was incorporated Jan 29, 1913.

AUGUSTA FUTURITY. Jan 15–24. Augusta, GA. 30th annual. Brings together the top cutting horses and riders in the world to compete for purse and awards of more than $1 million. Sponsors: Wrangler, John Deere, Ariat Boots, *Augusta Chronicle*, E-Z-Go Textron, Gist Silversmiths, Horseware, Inc, Circle R Custom Hat Works, Circle Y of Yoakum, Marsh Co, Horsecity.com, Dodge Trucks, Fort Dodge Animal Health, BellSouth, Reveal 4-N-1, Quarter Horse News, K.O. Trading Co, Barnmaster, Beasley Broadcast Group, WAGT Television, SRP Federal Credit Union, Double C Saddlery, New York Life and Augusta Metro Convention and Visitors Bureau. Est attendance: 50,000. For info: Noell Inman, Dir of Mktg, Augusta Futurity, PO Box 936, Augusta, GA 30903. Phone: (706) 823-3362 or (706) 823-3417. Web: www.augustafuturity.com.

BLACK DAHLIA MURDER: ANNIVERSARY. Jan 15, 1947. On this day, the body of Elizabeth Short was found in an empty lot in Los Angeles, CA. Short, nicknamed the Black Dahlia for her striking looks, had been murdered and mutilated, and her body's discovery sparked a media frenzy. Although dozens of men (and women) confessed to the crime, those confessions were discounted. The murder remains LA's most famous unsolved murder and one that evokes the noirish aura of postwar LA's corruption and crime problems.

BRITISH MUSEUM: 250th ANNIVERSARY. Jan 15, 1759. On this date, the British Museum opened its doors at Montague House in London. Incorporated by an act of Parliament in 1753, following the death of British medical doctor and naturalist Sir Hans Sloane, who had bequeathed his personal collection of books, manuscripts, coins, medals and antiquities to Britain. As the national museum of the United Kingdom, the British Museum houses many of the world's most prized treasures. The national library moved to separate facilities in 1997.

FIRST SUPER BOWL: ANNIVERSARY. Jan 15, 1967. The Green Bay Packers won the first NFL–AFL World Championship Game, defeating the Kansas City Chiefs, 35–10, at the Los Angeles Memorial Coliseum. Packers quarterback Bart Starr was named the game's Most Valuable Player. Pro football's title game later became known as the Super Bowl.

GET TO KNOW YOUR CUSTOMER DAY. Jan 15 (also Apr 16, July 16 and Oct 15). Set aside the third Thursday of each quarter to get to know your customers even better. For example, salespeople might plan to take a customer out to lunch, not to sell, but to learn more about their needs and why they like doing business with them. Executives could get out from behind the desk and go into the field. For info: Shep Hyken, Shepard Presentations, LLC, 711 Old Ballas Rd, Ste 215, St. Louis, MO 63141. Phone: (314) 692-2200. Fax: (314) 692-2222. E-mail: Shep@hyken.com. Web: www.hyken.com or www.GetToKnowYourCustomerDay.com.

"HAPPY DAYS" TV PREMIERE: 35th ANNIVERSARY. Jan 15, 1974. This nostalgic comedy set in Milwaukee in the 1950s starred Ron Howard as teenager Richie Cunningham with Anson Williams and Don Most as his friends "Potsie" Weber and Ralph Malph. Tom Bosley and Marion Ross played Richie's parents, and his sister, Joanie, was played by Erin Moran. The most memorable character was The Fonz—Arthur "Fonzie" Fonzarelli—played by Henry Winkler. "Happy Days" remained on the air until July 12, 1984. "Laverne and Shirley" was a spin-off.

"HILL STREET BLUES" TV PREMIERE: ANNIVERSARY. Jan 15, 1981. Immensely popular NBC police series created by Stephen Bochco and Michael Kozoll that focused more on police officers than crime. The realistic show was highly praised by actual police officers. It won a slew of Emmys and ran for seven seasons. The cast featured Daniel J. Travanti as Captain Frank Furillo, Veronica Hamel as public defender Joyce Davenport and Michael Conrad as Sergeant Phil "Let's be careful out there" Esterhaus. Other cast members included Barbara Bosson, Bruce Weitz, Taurean Blacque, Joe Spano, James B. Sikking, Michael Warren, Betty Thomas, Ed Marinaro and Charles Haid. The last telecast was on May 19, 1987.

HUMANITARIAN DAY. Jan 15. The birth anniversary of Rev Dr. Martin Luther King, Jr, is one of the three Days of Respect. Humanitarian Day visually affirms the principles of human and civil rights. See also: "Victims of Violence Wholly Day" (Apr 4) and "Dream Day Quest and Jubilee" (Aug 28). For info: EvAngel Mamadee YHWHnewBN, Global Committee Commemorating King Days of Respect, PO Box 21050, Chicago, IL 60621. Phone: (773) RESPECT. E-mail: YHWHnewBN@aol.com.

KING, MARTIN LUTHER, JR: 80th BIRTH ANNIVERSARY. Jan 15, 1929. Black civil rights leader, minister, advocate of nonviolence and recipient of the Nobel Peace Prize (1964). Born at Atlanta, GA, he was assassinated at Memphis, TN, Apr 4, 1968. After his death many states and territories observed his birthday as a holiday. In 1983 the Congress approved HR 3706, "A bill to amend Title 5, United States Code, to make the birthday of Martin Luther King, Jr, a legal public holiday." Signed by the president on Nov 2, 1983, it became Public Law 98–144. The law sets the third Monday in January for observance of King's birthday. First observance was Jan 20, 1986. See also: "King, Martin Luther, Jr: Birthday Observed" (Jan 19).

LIVINGSTON, PHILIP: BIRTH ANNIVERSARY. Jan 15, 1716. Merchant and signer of the Declaration of Independence, born at Albany, NY. Died at York, PA, June 12, 1778.

MOLIÈRE DAY: BAPTISM ANNIVERSARY. Jan 15, 1622. Most celebrated of French authors and dramatists, Jean Baptiste Poquelin, baptized at Paris, France, Jan 15, 1622, took the stage name Molière when he was about 22 years old. While playing in a performance of his last play, *Le Malade Imaginaire* (about a hypochondriac afraid of death), Molière became ill and died within a few hours at Paris, Feb 17, 1673.

PENTAGON COMPLETED: ANNIVERSARY. Jan 15, 1943. The world's largest office building with 6.5 million square feet of usable space, the Pentagon is located in Virginia across the Potomac River from Washington, DC, and serves as headquarters for the Department of Defense.

QUARTERLY ESTIMATED FEDERAL INCOME TAX PAYERS' DUE DATE. Jan 15. For those individuals whose fiscal year is the calendar year and who make quarterly estimated federal income tax payments, today would be one of the due dates (Jan 15, Apr 15, June 15 and Sept 15, 2009).

SIEGMEISTER, ELIE: 100th BIRTH ANNIVERSARY. Jan 15, 1909. American composer Elie Siegmeister was born at New York, NY. He composed eight symphonies and eight operas and a number of concertos, chamber pieces and orchestral works using folk, jazz and street songs to create a contemporary American classical music. He died Mar 10, 1991, at Manhasset, NY.

SLAMDANCE. Jan 15–23. Park City, Utah. 15th annual. Independent film festival "by filmmakers for filmmakers." Feature-length films and shorts. Numerous awards given. Screenplay competition during the year. For info: Slamdance, 5634 Melrose Ave, Los Angeles, CA 90038. Phone: (323) 466-1786. Fax: (323) 466-1784. E-mail: mail@slamdance.com. Web: www.slamdance.com.

January 2009

S	M	T	W	T	F	S
				1	2	3
4	5	6	7	8	9	10
11	12	13	14	15	16	17
18	19	20	21	22	23	24
25	26	27	28	29	30	31

SUNDANCE FILM FESTIVAL. Jan 15–25. Park City, UT. "The premier US festival for independent filmmakers." More than 120 feature-length films and more than 80 short films screened. Est attendance: 53,000. For info: Sundance Institute, PO Box 684429, Park City, UT 84068. Phone: (435) 658-3456. Fax: (435) 658-3457. Web: www.sundance.org/festival.

TELLER, EDWARD: BIRTH ANNIVERSARY. Jan 15, 1908. Born at Budapest, Hungary, Edward Teller was a physicist who worked on the Manhattan Project at Los Alamos, NM, in the 1940s. He promoted the first hydrogen fusion bomb, work that was considered secondary to the atomic bomb research taking place at the same time. He was a vocal critic of Robert Oppenheimer, director of the Manhattan Project, and his comments eventually destroyed Oppenheimer's career. Teller's hydrogen bomb research ultimately proved feasible but was never used in wartime. Throughout his life he remained a profound influence on America's defense and energy policies. He died at Stanford, CA, Sept 9, 2003.

WINGS OVER WILLCOX/SANDHILL CRANE CELEBRATION. Jan 15–18. Willcox, AZ. Tours to the Willcox Playa and Wetlands to see sandhill cranes, hawks, plovers, longspurs and much more. Visit Cochise Lake and see the waders. Workshops on wildlife. Seminars on bird-watching by various experts, a banquet, silent auction and a whole lot more. Est attendance: 1,000. For info: Willcox Chamber of Commerce. Phone: (800) 200-2272 or (520) 384-2272. Web: www.wingsoverwillcox.com or www.willcoxchamber.com.

WOMEN IN BLUE JEANS DAYS. Jan 15–17. A time to celebrate the women of rural America and their contributions to their families, friends and communities. Women involved in agriculture recognize the value of their family farms to the world that they help feed. For info: Diana Goldammer, Women in Blue Jeans, PO Box 53, Mitchell, SD 57301. Phone: (605) 996-8089. E-mail: diana789456@yahoo.com. Web: www.womeninbluejeans.org.

Birthdays Today

Drew Brees, 30, football player, born Austin, TX, Jan 15, 1979.

Ernest J. Gaines, 76, author (*The Autobiography of Miss Jane Pittman, A Lesson Before Dying*), born at River Lake Plantation, Oscar, LA, Jan 15, 1933.

Chad Lowe, 41, actor ("Now and Again," "Life Goes On," *Nobody's Perfect*), born Dayton, OH, Jan 15, 1968.

Andrea Martin, 62, actress (*Wag the Dog, Anastasia*, "SCTV"), born Portland, ME, Jan 15, 1947.

Margaret O'Brien, 72, actress (*Little Women, Meet Me in St. Louis*), born San Diego, CA, Jan 15, 1937.

Mario Van Peebles, 52, actor (*Love Kills, Judgment Day*), director, born Mexico City, Mexico, Jan 15, 1957.

January 16 — Friday

DAY 16 — 349 REMAINING

APPRECIATE A DRAGON DAY. Jan 16. In school and public libraries everywhere, children will have the opportunity to choose dragons from popular literature and participate in activities to share their enthusiasm for the dragon of their choice. For info: Donita Tompkins, 9223 Wolf Pack Terrace, Colorado Springs, CO 80920-7675. Phone: (719) 635-3940. E-mail: donitakpaul@msn.com. Web: www.dragonkeeper.us.

ARBOR DAY IN FLORIDA. Jan 16. The third Friday in January is Arbor Day in Florida, a ceremonial day.

ART DECO WEEKEND. Jan 16–18. Miami Beach, FL. 32nd annual. Features parade, jazz entertainment and plenty of food. The 2009 event explores the rich culture of Argentina. Includes art deco antiques, vendors and artists, from national and local talent. Est attendance: 455,000. For info: Art Deco Weekend, PO Box 190180,

Miami Beach, FL 33119-0180. Phone: (305) 672-2014. Fax: (305) 672-4319. Web: www.artdecoweekend.com.

BALD EAGLE APPRECIATION DAYS. Jan 16–18. River City Mall, Keokuk, IA. Features trained personnel stationed at observation points for viewing the American bald eagle. Indoor activities include a wood-carver's show. Also featuring live eagle demonstrations. Est attendance: 10,000. For info: Keokuk Area Convention and Tourism Bureau, 329 Main St, Keokuk, IA 52632. Phone: (800) 383-1219 or (319) 524-5599. E-mail: info@keokukiowatourism.org. Web: www.keokukiowatourism.org.

BRITISH AIR RAID ON BERLIN: ANNIVERSARY. Jan 16, 1943. In the first bombing of Germany since the Casablanca Conference, the British Royal Air Force began heavy bombing of Germany by day and night to bring about "the progressive destruction and dislocation of the German military, industrial and economic system, and for the undermining of the morale of the German people." The RAF used their new "target indicator" bombs to mark targets for their bombers.

CIVIL SERVICE CREATED: ANNIVERSARY. Jan 16, 1883. The US Congress passed a bill creating the civil service.

DEAN, DIZZY: BIRTH ANNIVERSARY. Jan 16, 1911. Jay Hanna "Dizzy" Dean, major league pitcher (St. Louis Cardinals) and Baseball Hall of Fame member, was born at Lucas, AR. Following his baseball career, Dean established himself as a radio and TV sports announcer and commentator, becoming famous for his innovative delivery. "He slud into third," reported Dizzy, who on another occasion explained that "Me and Paul [baseball player brother Paul "Daffy" Dean] . . . didn't get much education." Died at Reno, NV, July 17, 1974.

DR. MARTIN LUTHER KING, JR, CELEBRATION. Jan 16–18. Hollywood, FL. Friday Fun Fest features children's activities and VIP evening dinner featuring a celebrity speaker. Sunday features a tribute. Est attendance: 3,000. For info: Marketing, City of Hollywood, Department of Parks, Recreation & Cultural Arts, 1405 S 28th Ave, Hollywood, FL 33020. Phone: (954) 921-3404.

"DONNY AND MARIE" TV PREMIERE: ANNIVERSARY. Jan 16, 1976. ABC show hosted by brother-and-sister act Donny and Marie Osmond. There were seven other talented siblings in the Osmond family who appeared on the show at times along with regulars Jim Connell and Hank Garcia. The sister-and-brother team could sing, dance and perform on ice skates.

EISENHOWER ASSUMES COMMAND: 65th ANNIVERSARY. Jan 16, 1944. General Dwight D. Eisenhower arrived in London to assume command of the Supreme Headquarters Allied Expeditionary Forces in Europe (SHAEF). Having demonstrated his organizational abilities in North Africa as well as his strength as an arbitrator of inter-Allied rivalries, Eisenhower was charged with the most far-reaching push of the war—the invasion of France.

EL SALVADOR: NATIONAL DAY OF PEACE. Jan 16. A peace treaty was signed in Mexico City on this date in 1992 ending the 12-year civil war that had claimed 75,000 lives. On Feb 1, a cease-fire went into effect.

FOSSEY, DIAN: BIRTH ANNIVERSARY. Jan 16, 1932. Born at San Francisco, CA, Fossey went to the Virunga Mountains at Rwanda, Africa, to study the endangered mountain gorillas. Her work, conducted in isolation among the primates, was groundbreaking in terms of increasing science's understanding of the gorillas' social world. Fossey was a vigorous crusader against the poachers who decimate the gorilla population, and she was probably murdered by them: her body was discovered on Dec 26, 1985, at Mount Visoke, Rwanda.

GULF WAR BEGINS: ANNIVERSARY. Jan 16, 1991. Allied forces launched a major air offensive against Iraq to begin the Gulf War. The strike was designed to destroy Iraqi air defenses and command, control and communication centers. As Desert Shield became Desert Storm, the world was able to see and hear for the first time an initial engagement of war as CNN broadcasters, stationed at Baghdad, covered the attack live.

JAPAN: HARU-NO-YABUIRI. Jan 16. Employees and servants who have been working over the holidays are given a day off.

LEE-JACKSON DAY IN VIRGINIA. Jan 16. Annually, the Friday in January that precedes Martin Luther King Day. To commemorate the January birthdays of Robert E. Lee and Thomas Jonathan "Stonewall" Jackson.

MALAWI: JOHN CHILEMBWE DAY. Jan 16. National holiday. Honors a leader for independence who led an uprising against the British in 1915.

MERMAN, ETHEL: 100th BIRTH ANNIVERSARY. Jan 16, 1909. Musical comedy star famous for her belting voice and brassy style. Born Ethel Agnes Zimmerman on Jan 16, 1909 (or 1912—the date changed the older she got, but most sources say 1909), at Queens, NY. Died Feb 15, 1984, at New York, NY.

MICHELIN, ANDRE: BIRTH ANNIVERSARY. Jan 16, 1853. French industrialist who, along with his brother Edouard, started the Michelin Tire Company in 1888, manufacturing bicycle tires. They were the first to use demountable pneumatic tires on cars. Born at Paris, France; died there Apr 4, 1931.

MILWAUKEE BOAT SHOW. Jan 16–25. Wisconsin Expo Center, Milwaukee, WI. This event brings together buyers and sellers of sail- and powerboats, including fishing boats, pontoons and boating accessories, as well as vacation property and travel destinations. Est attendance: 25,000. For info: Henri Boucher, ShowSpan, Inc, 2121 Celebration Dr NE, Grand Rapids, MI 49525. Phone: (616) 447-2860. Fax: (616) 447-2861. E-mail: events@showspan.com. Web: www.showspan.com.

NATIONAL NOTHING DAY: ANNIVERSARY. Jan 16, 1973. Anniversary of National Nothing Day, an event created by newspaperman Harold Pullman Coffin and first observed "to provide Americans with one national day when they can just sit without celebrating, observing or honoring anything." Since 1975, though many other events have been listed on this day, lighthearted traditional observance of Coffin's idea has continued. Coffin, a native of Reno, NV, died at Capitola, CA, Sept 12, 1981, at the age of 76.

PROHIBITION (18th AMENDMENT): 90th ANNIVERSARY. Jan 16, 1919. When Nebraska became the 36th state to ratify the prohibition amendment, the 18th Amendment became part of the US Constitution. One year later, Jan 16, 1920, the 18th Amendment took effect and the sale of alcoholic beverages became illegal in the US with the Volstead Act providing for enforcement. This was the first time that an amendment to the Constitution dealt with a social issue. The 21st Amendment, repealing the 18th, went into effect Dec 6, 1933.

✦ **RELIGIOUS FREEDOM DAY.** Jan 16. Commemorates the adoption of a religious freedom statute by the Virginia legislature in 1786.

RELIGIOUS FREEDOM DAY. Jan 16, 1786. The legislature of Virginia adopted a religious freedom statute that protected Virginians against any requirement to attend or support any church and against discrimination. This statute, which had been drafted by Thomas Jefferson and introduced by James Madison, later was the model for the First Amendment to the US Constitution.

SERVICE, ROBERT WILLIAM: BIRTH ANNIVERSARY. Jan 16, 1874. Canadian poet, born at Preston, England. Lived in the Canadian northwest for many years and perhaps is best remembered for such ballads as "The Shooting of Dan McGrew" and "The Cremation of Sam McGee" and for such books as *Songs of a Sourdough, Rhymes of a Rolling Stone* and *The Spell of the Yukon.* Died at France, Sept 11, 1958.

SOUTHWESTERN EXPOSITION LIVESTOCK SHOW AND RODEO. Jan 16–Feb 8. Fort Worth, TX. Western-flavored extravaganza. World's first indoor professional rodeo began in 1918 (45 acres under one roof). Ranch Rodeo, prize livestock (more than 22,000 head) displays, horse shows, midway, commercial exhibits and quality family-oriented entertainment. Est attendance: 955,000. For info: Bradford S. Barnes, PO Box 150, Fort Worth, TX 76101-0150. Phone: (817) 877-2400. Fax: (817) 877-2499. Web: www.fwssr.com.

TIP-UP TOWN USA™. Jan 16–18 (also Jan 23–25). Houghton Lake, MI. 59th annual. Michigan's largest winter family festival featuring ice-fishing contests, softball on the ice, polar bear dip, parade, carnival, vendors, arts and crafts, fireworks, poker runs, radar runs, scavenger hunts and much more. Annually, the last two full weekends of January. Est attendance: 35,000. For info: Chamber of Commerce, 1625 W Houghton Lake Dr, Houghton Lake, MI 48629. Phone: (800) 248-5253. E-mail: hlcc@houghtonlakemichigan.net. Web: www.hougtonlakechamber.org.

YUMA HOME & GARDEN SHOW. Jan 16–18. Yuma Civic Center, Yuma, AZ. Public exhibit—home improvement, construction, renovation, remodeling and decorating. Est attendance: 17,000. For info: Yuma Civic Center, 1440 Desert Hills Dr, Yuma, AZ 85365. Phone: (928) 373-5040. Fax: (928) 344-9121. E-mail: ycc@yumaaz.gov. Web: www.yumaaz.gov.

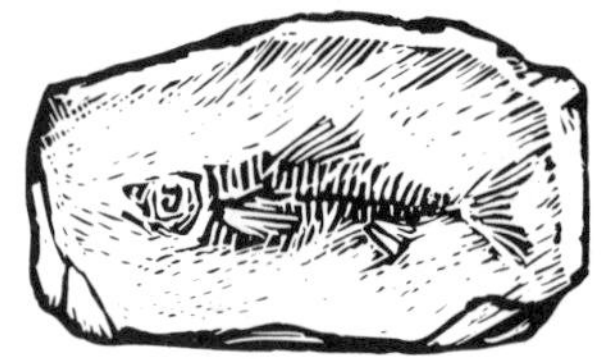

Birthdays Today

Debbie Allen, 59, dancer, choreographer, singer, actress ("Fame"), born Houston, TX, Jan 16, 1950.

John Carpenter, 61, movie director (*Halloween, The Thing*), born Carthage, NY, Jan 16, 1948.

David Chokachi, 41, actor ("Baywatch"), born Plymouth, MA, Jan 16, 1968.

Anthony Joseph (A.J.) Foyt, Jr, 74, former auto racer, born Houston, TX, Jan 16, 1935.

Marilyn Horne, 75, opera singer, born Bradford, PA, Jan 16, 1934.

William Kennedy, 81, author (*Ironweed, Roscoe*), born Albany, NY, Jan 16, 1928.

Jack Burns McDowell, 43, former baseball player, born Van Nuys, CA, Jan 16, 1966.

Ronnie Milsap, 65, country singer, born Robinsville, NC, Jan 16, 1944.

Albert Pujols, 29, baseball player, born Santo Domingo, Dominican Republic, Jan 16, 1980.

January 2009

S	M	T	W	T	F	S
				1	2	3
4	5	6	7	8	9	10
11	12	13	14	15	16	17
18	19	20	21	22	23	24
25	26	27	28	29	30	31

January 17 — Saturday

DAY 17 | 348 REMAINING

THE BUSINESS OF AMERICA QUOTATION: ANNIVERSARY. Jan 17, 1925. President Calvin Coolidge, in a speech to the American Society of Newspaper Editors, described America in a way that was to define the country in the 20th century and beyond—not just for the prosperous 1920s. "The chief business of the American people," he said, "is business."

CABLE CAR PATENT: ANNIVERSARY. Jan 17, 1871. Andrew Hallikie received a patent for a cable car system that began service in San Francisco in 1873.

CAPONE, AL: BIRTH ANNIVERSARY. Jan 17, 1899. Gangster Alphonse ("Scarface") Capone was born this date at Brooklyn, NY, to immigrants from Naples, Italy. Capone dominated organized crime in Chicago throughout Prohibition. Targeted by the "Untouchables" after 1929's St. Valentine's Day Massacre (which he allegedly ordered), Capone was finally imprisoned on tax evasion charges. He died Jan 25, 1947, at Miami, FL, after suffering from syphilis.

EAGLE DAY AT THE LAKE. Jan 17. Wyandotte County Lake Park, Kansas City, KS. The public is invited to the environmental learning center to see a live bald eagle presentation and other wildlife presentations. Eagle viewing over the lake and children's activities will be available all day. For info: Mr & Mrs F.L. Schlagle Library, 4051 West Dr, Wyandotte County Lake Park, Kansas City, KS 66109. Phone: (913) 299-2384. Fax: (913) 299-9967. E-mail: aporter@kckpl.lib.ks.us. Web: www.kckpl.lib.ks.us/schlagle.

EAGLE DAYS. Jan 17–18. Milford Nature Center/Fish Hatchery, Junction City, KS. Learn more about the magnificent bird that is our national emblem. Meet both a live bald eagle and a golden eagle! Guides with spotting scopes and binoculars will be waiting to show you eagles as they roost and soar around Milford Lake. Sponsors: Kansas Wildlife and Parks; US Army Corps of Engineers. Est attendance: 700. For info: Milford Nature Center, 3415 Hatchery Dr, Junction City, KS 66441. Phone: (785) 238-5323. Fax: (785) 238-5775.

EAGLE DAYS IN SPRINGFIELD. Jan 17–18. Springfield Conservation Nature Center, Springfield, MO. Celebrate the return of bald eagles to Springfield through indoor programs with a live eagle and outdoor viewing opportunities. Est attendance: 1,000. For info: Springfield Conservation Nature Center, 4600 S Chrisman Ave, Springfield, MO 65804. Phone: (417) 888-4237. Fax: (417) 888-4241. Web: www.missouriconservation.org.

FIRST NUCLEAR-POWERED SUBMARINE VOYAGE: ANNIVERSARY. Jan 17, 1955. At 11 AM, EST, the commanding officer of the world's first nuclear-powered submarine, the *Nautilus*, ordered all lines cast off and sent the historic message: "Under way on nuclear power." Highlights of the *Nautilus*: keel laid by President Harry S Truman June 14, 1952; christened and launched by Mrs Dwight D. Eisenhower Jan 21, 1954; commissioned to the US Navy Sept 30, 1954. It now forms part of the *Nautilus* Memorial Submarine Force Library and Museum at the Naval Submarine Base New London at Groton, CT.

FRANKLIN, BENJAMIN: BIRTH ANNIVERSARY. Jan 17, 1706. "Elder statesman of the American Revolution," oldest signer of both the Declaration of Independence and the Constitution, scientist, diplomat, author, printer, publisher, philosopher, philanthropist and self-made, self-educated man. Author, printer and publisher of *Poor Richard's Almanack* (1733–58). Born at Boston, MA, Franklin died at Philadelphia, PA, Apr 17, 1790. His birthday is commemorated each year by the Poor Richard Club of Philadelphia with graveside observance. In 1728 Franklin wrote a premature epitaph for himself. It first appeared in print in Ames's 1771 almanac: "The Body of BENJAMIN FRANKLIN/Printer/Like a Covering of an old Book/Its contents torn out/And stript of its Lettering and Gilding,/Lies here, Food for Worms;/But the work shall not be lost,/It will (as he believ'd) appear once more/In a New and more beautiful Edition/Corrected and amended/By the Author."

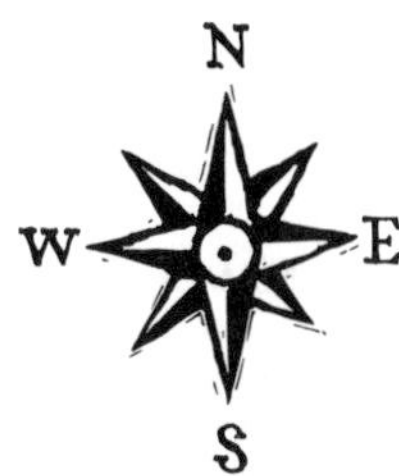

"FRONTLINE" TV PREMIERE: ANNIVERSARY. Jan 17, 1983. PBS hour-long independently produced documentaries. The programs often create controversy, focusing on a variety of political, military and social issues.

"THE GOLDBERGS" TV PREMIERE: 60th ANNIVERSARY. Jan 17, 1949. Originally broadcast by CBS, this show was one of the earliest TV sitcoms. The show centered around a Jewish mother and her family living in the Bronx and later in the suburbs. Gertrude Berg created the hit radio show before she wrote, produced and starred as Molly Goldberg in the television version. Contributing actors and actresses included Philip Loeb, Arlene McQuade, Tom Taylor, Eli Mintz, Menasha Skulnik and Arnold Stang.

HOT HEADS CHILI COOK-OFF. Jan 17–18. NELA Lincoln Expo Center, Ruston, LA. Hottest chili cook-off in Louisiana! CASI sanctioned. Awards for the top 10 cooks as well as people's choice awards. Raises money for non-profit organizations. This year's recipients: NELA Wish I Could and Relay for Life. Est attendance: 5,000. For info: Horace Ketchens, Hot Heads Chili Cook-off, 510 Thomas St, Farmerville, LA 71241. Phone: (318) 368-8935. E-mail: pegasusfestivals@bellsouth.net. Web: hotheadschili.org.

HUTCHINS, ROBERT MAYNARD: BIRTH ANNIVERSARY. Jan 17, 1899. American educator, foundation executive and civil liberties activist, born at Brooklyn, NY. He was president and later chancellor of the University of Chicago, where he introduced many educational concepts, including the Great Books program. Died at Santa Barbara, CA, on May 14, 1977.

IKE'S FAREWELL: ANNIVERSARY. Jan 17, 1961. President Dwight D. Eisenhower, in his farewell address to the nation on national radio and television, spoke the sentences that would be the most quoted and remembered of his presidency. In a direct warning, he said, "In the councils of government, we must guard against the acquisition of unwarranted influence, whether sought or unsought, by the military-industrial complex. The potential for the disastrous rise of misplaced power exists and persists."

JAPAN SUFFERS MAJOR EARTHQUAKE: ANNIVERSARY. Jan 17, 1995. Japan suffered its second most deadly earthquake in the 20th century when a 20-second temblor left 5,500 people dead and more than 21,600 injured. The epicenter was six miles beneath Awaji Island at Osaka Bay. This was just 20 miles west of Kobe, Japan's sixth-largest city and a major port that accounted for 12 percent of the country's exports. Measuring 7.2 on the Richter scale, the quake collapsed or badly damaged more than 30,400 buildings and left 275,000 people homeless.

JUDGMENT DAY. Jan 17. No need to wait 'til it's too late. All you need to do to see how you measure up to the standards of your God is simple: look in the mirror. There's your judgment. (©2006 by WH.) For info: Thomas & Ruth Roy, Wellcat Holidays, 2418 Long Ln, Lebanon, PA 17046. Phone: (717) 279-0184. E-mail: info@wellcat.com. Web: www.wellcat.com.

KID INVENTORS' DAY. Jan 17. Water skis. Earmuffs. The Popsicle. What do these have in common? All were invented by kids! Some 500,000 children and teens invent gadgets and games each year to make our lives easier—and more fun. Celebrate the ingenuity and value of these young brainstormers on the birthday of Benjamin Franklin, who invented the first swim fins at age 12. To learn more about Kid Inventors' Day (KID), or to receive teachers' guides, book lists and links, and information about inventor contests, camps, and clubs for kids, visit www.kidinventorsday.com or contact Lee Wardlaw. E-mail: author@leewardlaw.com.

MEXICO: BLESSING OF THE ANIMALS AT THE CATHEDRAL. Jan 17. Church of San Antonio at Mexico City or Xochimilco provide best sights of chickens, cows and household pets gaily decorated with flowers. (Saint's day for San Antonio Abad, patron saint of domestic animals.)

MOON PHASE: LAST QUARTER. Jan 17. Moon enters Last Quarter phase at 9:46 PM, EST.

PALOMARES HYDROGEN BOMB ACCIDENT: ANNIVERSARY. Jan 17, 1966. At 10:16 AM, according to villagers, fire fell from the sky over Palomares, Spain. An American B-52 bomber carrying four hydrogen bombs collided with its refueling plane, spilling the bombs (two of which had "chemical explosions," scattering radioactive plutonium over the area). In a cleanup, American soldiers burned crops, slaughtered animals and removed tons of topsoil (which was sent to South Carolina for burial). More than 19 years later, in November 1985, the Nuclear Energy Board permitted villagers to see their medical reports for the first time.

PGA OF AMERICA FOUNDED: ANNIVERSARY. Jan 17, 1916. Golf great Walter Hagen and some 30 other pro golfers met and formed the Professional Golfers' Association of America and also developed the idea for a national championship. Rodman Wanamaker provided the trophy and the $2,580 purse for the first PGA Championship, which was played Apr 10, 1916, at the Siwanoy course at Bronxville, NY. The winner was British golfer Jim Barnes, who also won the second competition—not held until 1919 because of WWI. In 1921 Walter Hagen became the first American to win, a feat he accomplished four more times—in 1924, '25, '26 and '27.

PHILIPPINES: ATI-ATIHAN FESTIVAL. Jan 17–18. Kalibo, Aklan. One of the most colorful celebrations in the Philippines, the Ati-Atihan Festival commemorates the peace pact between the Ati of Panay (pygmies) and the Malays, who were early migrants in the islands. The townspeople blacken their bodies with soot, don colorful and bizarre costumes and sing and dance in the streets. The festival also celebrates the Feast Day of Santo Niño (the infant Jesus). Annually, the third weekend in January.

POLAND: LIBERATION DAY. Jan 17. Celebration of 1945 liberation of the city of Warsaw from Nazi oppression on this day by Soviet troops. Special ceremonies at the Monument to the Unknown Soldier in Warsaw's Victory Square (which had been called Adolf Hitler Platz during the German occupation).

POPEYE DEBUTS: 80th ANNIVERSARY. Jan 17, 1929. In E.C. Segar's newspaper comic strip "Thimble Theatre," a new character, Popeye, appeared on the scene and was an immediate success. Olive Oyl quickly dumped her beau, Ham Gravy, for the colorful sailor. Popeye's signature line was to be "Tha's all I can stands, 'cause I can't stands no more!"

QUEEN LILIUOKALANI DEPOSED: ANNIVERSARY. Jan 17, 1893. Queen Liliuokalani, the last monarch of Hawaii, lost her throne when the monarchy was abolished by the "Committee of Safety," with the foreknowledge of US minister John L. Stevens, who encouraged the revolutionaries. The Queen's supporters were intimidated by the 300 US Marines sent to protect American lives and property. Judge Sanford B. Dole became president of the republic and later was Hawaii's first governor after the US annexed it by joint resolution of Congress on July 7, 1898. Hawaii held incorporated territory status for 60 years. President Dwight D. Eisenhower signed the proclamation making Hawaii the 50th state on Aug 21, 1959.

RUSH, WILLIAM: DEATH ANNIVERSARY. Jan 17, 1833. First American-born sculptor. William Rush's work in wood and clay included busts of many notables, American and European alike; carved wooden female figureheads for ships; the masks of Tragedy and Comedy seen at the Actor's House outside Philadelphia, PA; and the *Spirit of Schuylkill* in Fairmount Park in Philadelphia. In 1805 Rush and others founded the Pennsylvania Academy of the Fine Arts. Rush was born at Philadelphia in 1756.

SAINT ANTHONY'S DAY. Jan 17. Feast day honoring Egyptian hermit who became the first Christian monk and who established communities of hermits; patron saint of domestic animals and patriarch of all monks. Lived about AD 251–354.

SOUTHERN CALIFORNIA EARTHQUAKE: 15th ANNIVERSARY. Jan 17, 1994. An earthquake measuring 6.6 on the Richter scale struck the Los Angeles area about 4:20 AM. The epicenter was at Northridge in the San Fernando Valley, about 20 miles northwest of downtown Los Angeles. A death toll of 51 was announced Jan 20. Sixteen of the dead were killed in the collapse of one apartment building. More than 25,000 people were made homeless by the quake and 680,000 lost electric power. Many buildings were destroyed and others made uninhabitable due to structural damage. A section of the Santa Monica Freeway, part of the Simi Valley Freeway and three major overpasses collapsed. Hundreds of aftershocks occurred in the following several weeks. Costs to repair the damages were estimated at $15–30 billion.

WISCONSIN DELLS FLAKE OUT FESTIVAL. Jan 17–18. Wisconsin Dells, WI. One of the largest winter festivals in the Midwest, Flake Out Festival is also Wisconsin's only state-sanctioned snow-sculpting competition. Families can warm up to winter with great activities like horse-drawn wagon and pony rides, arts and crafts fair, Kids Craft Corner, live music, fireworks, food and, of course, world-class snow sculptures. Est attendance: 30,000. For info: Wisconsin Dells Visitors & Convention Bureau, PO Box 390, Wisconsin Dells, WI 53965. Phone: (800) 223-3557. E-mail: info@wisdells.com. Web: www.wisdells.com.

 Birthdays Today

Muhammad Ali, 67, former heavyweight champion boxer, born Cassius Marcellus Clay, Jr, at Louisville, KY, Jan 17, 1942.

Naveen Andrews, 40, actor ("Lost," *The English Patient*), born at London, England, Jan 17, 1969.

Cuauhtemoc Blanco, 36, soccer player, born Mexico City, Mexico, Jan 17, 1973.

Jim Carrey, 47, actor (*Dumb and Dumber, The Truman Show, Ace Ventura*), comedian ("In Living Color"), born Newmarket, ON, Canada, Jan 17, 1962.

James Earl Jones, 78, actor (*The Great White Hope; Roots: The Next Generations*), born Arktabula, MS, Jan 17, 1931.

Eartha Kitt, 82, singer, actress, born North, SC, Jan 17, 1927.

Ruth Ann Minner, 74, Governor of Delaware (D), born Milford, DE, Jan 17, 1935.

Newton Minow, 83, former head of the Federal Communications Commission (1961–63), called television a "vast wasteland," born Milwaukee, WI, Jan 17, 1926.

Maury Povich, 70, talk-show host, born Washington, DC, Jan 17, 1939.

Vidal Sassoon, 81, hair stylist, born London, England, Jan 17, 1928.

Dwyane Wade, 27, basketball player, born Chicago, IL, Jan 17, 1982.

Betty White, 85, actress ("Mary Tyler Moore," "The Golden Girls"), animal rights activist, born Oak Park, IL, Jan 17, 1924 (some sources say 1922).

Donald William (Don) Zimmer, 78, baseball manager and former player, born Cincinnati, OH, Jan 17, 1931.

January 2009

S	M	T	W	T	F	S
				1	2	3
4	5	6	7	8	9	10
11	12	13	14	15	16	17
18	19	20	21	22	23	24
25	26	27	28	29	30	31

January 18 — Sunday

DAY 18 — 347 REMAINING

FIRST BLACK US CABINET MEMBER: ANNIVERSARY. Jan 18, 1966. Robert Clifton Weaver was sworn in as Secretary of Housing and Urban Development, becoming the first black cabinet member in US history. He was nominated by President Lyndon Johnson. Weaver died at New York, NY, July 17, 1997.

FLOOD, CURT: BIRTH ANNIVERSARY. Jan 18, 1938. Curtis Charles (Curt) Flood, baseball player, born at Houston, TX. Flood was one of baseball's best center fielders in the 1960s, batting .293 over 15 seasons and playing spectacular defense. After the 1969 season, he refused to accept a trade from the St. Louis Cardinals to the Philadelphia Phillies. "I am not a piece of property to be bought and sold irrespective of my wishes," he said in a letter to Commissioner Bowie Kuhn. The resulting lawsuit went to the Supreme Court, where Flood lost. But his stand, taken because he did not want to switch teams, paved the way for the end of baseball's reserve clause and the advent of free agency. Died at Los Angeles, CA, Jan 20, 1997.

GRANT, CARY: BIRTH ANNIVERSARY. Jan 18, 1904. Known as a romantic leading actor, Grant was born at Bristol, England. For more than three decades Grant entertained with his wit, charm, sophistication and personality. His films include *Topper, The Awful Truth, Bringing Up Baby* and *Holiday*. Died at Davenport, IA, Nov 29, 1986.

HARDY, OLIVER: BIRTH ANNIVERSARY. Jan 18, 1892. Born at Atlanta, GA, Hardy teamed up with Stan Laurel in 1926 to form the comedy team of Laurel and Hardy. Among their most popular films: *From Soup to Nuts, Babes in Toyland, Swiss Miss.* Hardy died at Hollywood, CA, Aug 7, 1957.

HEALTHY WEIGHT WEEK. Jan 18–24. 16th annual. People who diet the first week in January and binge the second are ready for better living by the third week: Healthy Weight Week. This is a week to promote healthy lifestyle habits that last a lifetime and prevent weight and eating problems (not cause them, as dieting does); a time to move on to Health at Every Size. News release, 2009 awards and consumer handouts available on website. For info: Francie M. Berg, Healthy Weight Network, 402 S 14th St, Hettinger, ND 58639. E-mail: fmberg@healthyweight.net (please put "Berg-Healthy Weight Week" in subject line). Web: www.healthyweight.net.

HOUSTON MARATHON. Jan 18. Houston, TX. 37th annual city-wide race. Also features 2009 USA Half Marathon Championships and 5k run. Est attendance: 23,000. For info: Houston Marathon, 720 N Post Oak Rd, #100, Houston, TX 77024. Phone: (713) 957-3453. Fax: (713) 957-3406. E-mail: marathon@houstonmarathon.com. Web: www.houstonmarathon.com.

HUNT FOR HAPPINESS WEEK. Jan 18–24. Celebrate the eighth annual Hunt for Happiness Week sponsored by the Secret Society of Happy People. Activities, suggestions and ideas for teachers, youth leaders and parents to encourage kids and teens to discover more happy moments are available on our website. Annually, the third full week in January. For info: Secret Society of Happy People, 425 Busher Dr, Lewisville, TX 75067. Phone: (972) 459-7031. E-mail: pamelagail@sohp.com. Web: www.sohp.com.

"THE JEFFERSONS" TV PREMIERE: ANNIVERSARY. Jan 18, 1975. CBS sitcom about an African-American family (formerly neighbors of the Bunkers on "All in the Family") who moved to Manhattan's East Side, thanks to the success of George Jefferson's chain of dry cleaning stores. Having a format similar to "All in the Family," the show featured a black bigot, George Jefferson. Cast included Sherman Hemsley as George Jefferson, Isabel Sanford as Louise Jefferson and Marla Gibbs as maid Florence. The last episode aired July 23, 1985.

KAYE, DANNY: BIRTH ANNIVERSARY. Jan 18, 1913. American entertainer Danny Kaye was born David Daniel Kaminski at Brooklyn, NY. Kaye became a star in films, international stage performances and television. His most notable films are *The Secret Life of Walter Mitty* (1947) and *Hans Christian Andersen* (1952), as well as the classic *White Christmas*. He hosted the television show "The Danny Kaye Show" in the 1960s. In addition, Kaye helped raise millions of dollars for the United Nations International Children's Emergency Fund (UNICEF) and musicians' pension plans. He died Mar 3, 1987, at Los Angeles, CA.

LEWIS AND CLARK EXPEDITION COMMISSIONED: ANNIVERSARY. Jan 18, 1803. Seeking information on what lay west of the young US, President Thomas Jefferson sent a confidential letter to Congress on Jan 18, 1803, requesting funds for an exploratory expedition to be led by Captain Meriwether Lewis and Lieutenant William Clark. After the Louisiana Purchase was signed on Apr 30, 1803, the expedition's mission changed: it became a survey of new American land. The "Corps of Discovery" set off May 14 from St. Louis and returned with much information about the land, flora and fauna and peoples there on Sept 23, 1806. (See also May 14, Sept 23 and Nov 16.)

NATIONAL FRESH SQUEEZED JUICE WEEK. Jan 18–23. Drinking fresh-squeezed juice is a great, healthy way of living. For info: Bob O'Brien, Consumer Advocate, 1061 Koelle Blvd, Secaucus, NJ 07094. Phone: (646) 233-6610. E-mail: robtfobrien@aol.com.

PASADENA DOO DAH PARADE. Jan 18. Pasadena, CA. Held in Old Pasadena, this spoof of the more traditional parade is a wacky and humorous celebration that attracts thousands. Includes entries like the precision marching Briefcase Drill Team. For info: Light Bringer Project. Phone: (626) 205-4029. Web: www.pasadenadoodahparade.info.

POOH DAY: A.A. MILNE: BIRTH ANNIVERSARY. Jan 18, 1882. Anniversary of the birth of A(lan) A(lexander) Milne, English author, especially remembered for his children's stories: *Winnie the Pooh* and *The House at Pooh Corner*. Also the author of *Mr Pim Passes By*, *When We Were Very Young* and *Now We Are Six*. Born at London, England; died at Hartfield, England, Jan 31, 1956.

ROGET, PETER MARK: BIRTH ANNIVERSARY. Jan 18, 1779. English physician, best known as author of Roget's *Thesaurus of English Words and Phrases*, first published in 1852. Roget was also the inventor of the "log-log" slide rule. He was born at London and died at West Malvern, Worcestershire, England, Sept 12, 1869.

RUFFIN, DAVIS ELI (DAVID): BIRTH ANNIVERSARY. Jan 18, 1941. American popular singer David Ruffin was born at Meridian, MS. He was one of the original members of the Motown singing group the Temptations, which began in Detroit in the 1960s. Ruffin left the group in 1968 to pursue a solo career. He and the other original members of the Temptations were inducted into the Rock and Roll Hall of Fame in 1989. Ruffin died June 1, 1991, at Philadelphia, PA.

"TED MACK'S ORIGINAL AMATEUR HOUR" TV PREMIERE: ANNIVERSARY. Jan 18, 1948. This immensely popular show, featuring host Ted Mack, introduced amateurs performing their talents on live television. It debuted as a regularly scheduled broadcast on the DuMont network. The show had been a long-running success on radio as "Major Bowes' Original Amateur Hour" until the death of Edward Bowes. Mack became host of the radio show a year later. While a few episodes were televised in 1947, the show did not air weekly until this date. The program ran until 1970 and also continued on radio until 1952.

VERSAILLES PEACE CONFERENCE: 90th ANNIVERSARY. Jan 18, 1919. French president Raymond Poincare formally opened the (WWI) peace conference at Versailles, France. It proceeded under the chairmanship of Georges Clemenceau. In May the conference disposed of Germany's colonies and delivered a treaty to the German delegates on May 7, 1919, fourth anniversary of the sinking of the *Lusitania*. Final treaty-signing ceremonies were completed at the palace at Versailles, June 28, 1919.

WEBSTER, DANIEL: BIRTH ANNIVERSARY. Jan 18, 1782. American statesman and orator who said, on Apr 6, 1830, "The people's government, made for the people, made by the people, and answerable to the people." Born at Salisbury, NH; died at Marshfield, MA, Oct 24, 1852.

WEEK OF CHRISTIAN UNITY. Jan 18–25. From the Conversion of St. Peter (Jan 18) to the Conversion of St. Paul (Jan 25).

WORLD RELIGION DAY. Jan 18. To proclaim the oneness of religion and the belief that world religion will unify the peoples of the earth. Baha'i-sponsored observance established in 1950 by the Baha'is of the US. Annually, the third Sunday in January. For info: Baha'is of the US, Office of Communications, 1233 Central St, Evanston, IL 60201. Phone: (847) 733-3559. Fax: (847) 733-3578. E-mail: ooc@usbnc.org. Web: www.bahai.us.

Birthdays Today

John Boorman, 76, filmmaker (*Deliverance, Excalibur*), born Shepperton, England, Jan 18, 1933.

Kevin Costner, 54, actor, director (*Field of Dreams, Dances with Wolves, Bull Durham*), born Lynwood, CA, Jan 18, 1955.

Ray Dolby, 76, inventor of the Dolby Sound System for sound recording, born Portland, OR, Jan 18, 1933.

Jane Horrocks, 45, actress (*Little Voice*, "Absolutely Fabulous"), born Lancashire, England, Jan 18, 1964.

Evelyn Lear, 78, opera singer, born New York, NY, Jan 18, 1931.

Jesse L. Martin, 40, actor ("Law & Order," "Ally McBeal"), born Rocky Mountain, VA, Jan 18, 1969.

Mark Messier, 48, hockey player, born Edmonton, AB, Canada, Jan 18, 1961.

Martin O'Malley, 46, Governor of Maryland (D), born Bethesda, MD, Jan 18, 1963.

Jason Segel, 29, actor ("Freaks and Geeks," "How I Met Your Mother"), born Los Angeles, CA, Jan 18, 1980.

January 19 — Monday

DAY 19 346 REMAINING

BOB HOPE CHRYSLER CLASSIC. Jan 19–25. Palm Springs, CA. 50th annual. The nation's largest sports event for charity. It features PGA tour pros, celebrities and amateurs. Est attendance: 110,000. For info: Pat Bennett, PR and Production, Bob Hope Chrysler Classic, 39000 Bob Hope Dr, Rancho Mirage, CA 92270. Phone: (760) 346-8184. Fax: (760) 346-6329. E-mail: info@bhcc.com. Web: www.bhcc.com.

CÉZANNE, PAUL: BIRTH ANNIVERSARY. Jan 19, 1839. Postimpressionist painter, born at Aix-en-Provence, France. Still lifes and landscapes were his preferred subjects. Cézanne died Oct 23, 1906, at Aix.

CONFEDERATE HEROES DAY IN TEXAS. Jan 19. Also called Confederate Memorial Day, observed on anniversary of Robert E. Lee's birthday. Official holiday in Texas.

ETHIOPIA: TIMKET. Jan 19. National holiday. Epiphany in the Ethiopian and Coptic churches. Occurs some years on Jan 20. Also a holiday in Eritrea.

"48 HOURS" TV PREMIERE: ANNIVERSARY. Jan 19, 1988. CBS prime-time newsmagazine program airing each week with first Dan Rather as host, then Leslie Stahl. Recently, the focus has been on crime mysteries.

HELMS, EDGAR J.: BIRTH ANNIVERSARY. Jan 19, 1863. Born near Malone, NY, Reverend Dr. Helms became a minister to a parish of poor immigrants in Boston's South End. In that capacity he developed the philosophy and organization that eventually became Goodwill Industries. Helms died Dec 23, 1942, at Boston.

JOHNSON, JOHN H.: BIRTH ANNIVERSARY. Jan 19, 1918. Born at Arkansas City, AR, the grandson of a slave, John H. Johnson rose from abject poverty to become one of the most influential black businessmen in America. In 1942, he launched the first of his successful magazines, *Negro Digest*, which reached a circulation of 50,000 within eight months. In 1945 came *Ebony*, followed by *Jet* in 1951. By the time of his death at Chicago, IL, on Aug 8, 2005, Johnson's company was the world's largest African-American-owned-and-operated publishing operation. He served the US as goodwill ambassador and received numerous honors, the most important of which was the Presidential Medal of Freedom in 1996 for "building self-respect in the black community."

JOPLIN, JANIS: BIRTH ANNIVERSARY. Jan 19, 1943. Possibly the most highly regarded white female blues singer of all time, Janis Joplin was born at Port Arthur, TX. Joplin's appearance with Big Brother and the Holding Company at the Monterey International Pop Festival in August 1967 launched her to superstar status. Among her recording hits were "Get It While You Can," "Piece of My Heart" and "Ball and Chain." She died of a heroin overdose Oct 4, 1970, at Hollywood, CA, at the age of 27.

KING, MARTIN LUTHER, JR: BIRTHDAY OBSERVED. Jan 19. Public Law 98–144 designates the third Monday in January as an annual legal public holiday observing the birth of Martin Luther King, Jr. First observed in 1986. In New Hampshire, this day is designated Civil Rights Day. See also: "King, Martin Luther, Jr: Birth Anniversary" (Jan 15).

LEE, ROBERT E.: BIRTH ANNIVERSARY. Jan 19, 1807. Greatest military leader of the Confederacy, son of Revolutionary War general Henry (Light-Horse Harry) Lee. His surrender Apr 9, 1865, to Union general Ulysses S. Grant brought an end to the Civil War. Born at Westmoreland County, VA, he died at Lexington, VA, Oct 12, 1870. His birthday is observed in Florida, Kentucky, Louisiana, South Carolina and Tennessee. Observed on third Monday in January in Alabama, Arkansas and Mississippi.

✦ **MARTIN LUTHER KING, JR, FEDERAL HOLIDAY.** Jan 19. Presidential Proclamation has been issued without request each year for the third Monday in January since 1986.

"THE MILLIONAIRE" TV PREMIERE: ANNIVERSARY. Jan 19, 1955. The CBS drama that had all of America hoping to find Michael Anthony on their doorstep. Mr John Beresford Tipton was a millionaire who made a hobby of giving away million-dollar checks anonymously to unknown people to see how they handled the sudden wealth. Michael Anthony, played by Marvin Miller, was Mr Tipton's personal secretary and the star of "The Millionaire." No one ever saw Mr Tipton, but his voice would greet Anthony at the opening of each show and issue instructions for delivery of the next check. Anthony would then find the recipient and give him or her the check, explaining that the recipient had to agree never to divulge the amount or how it was acquired.

NATIONAL MEDICAL GROUP PRACTICE WEEK. Jan 19–23. A week to advance the awareness and understanding of medical group practices as a premier form of health care delivery. This week also honors those physicians, administrators and staff who dedicate their professional careers to the administration of quality health care. Annually, the fourth week of January. For info: Medical Group Management Assn, 104 Inverness Terrace E, Englewood, CO 80112. Phone: (303) 799-1111. Fax: (303) 643-4420. Web: www.medicalgrouppracticeweek.com.

POE, EDGAR ALLAN: 200th BIRTH ANNIVERSARY. Jan 19, 1809. American poet and story writer, called "America's most famous man of letters." Born at Boston, MA, he was orphaned in dire poverty in 1811 and was raised by Virginia merchant John Allan. In 1836 he married his 13-year-old cousin, Virginia Clemm. A magazine editor of note, he is best remembered for his poetry (especially "The Raven") and for his tales of suspense. Died at Baltimore, MD, Oct 7, 1849.

STOCK EXCHANGE HOLIDAY (MARTIN LUTHER KING DAY). Jan 19. The holiday schedules for the various exchanges are subject to change if relevant rules, regulations or exchange policies are revised. If you have questions, contact: American Stock Exchange (866) 422-2639 (www.amex.com), Chicago Board of Trade (312) 435-3500 (www.cbot.com), Chicago Board Options Exchange (312) 786-5600 (www.cboe.com), NASDAQ Stock Market (646) 441-5200 (www.nasdaq.com), New York Stock Exchange (212) 656-3000 (www.nyse.com), Philadelphia Stock Exchange (800) THE-PHLX (www.phlx.com).

TIN CAN PATENT: ANNIVERSARY. Jan 19, 1825. Ezra Daggett and Thomas Kensett obtained a patent for a process for storing food in tin cans.

WAR CRIMES TRIBUNAL APPOINTED (JAPAN): ANNIVERSARY. Jan 19, 1946. An international tribunal for the trial of far eastern war criminals was appointed by General Douglas MacArthur on Jan 19, 1946. The trial began at Tokyo on May 3, 1946, and ended more than two years later when the judgments were read, Nov 4–12, 1948. Of the 28 defendants 25 were brought to trial. Seven were sentenced to death by hanging, 16 were sentenced to life imprisonment and 2 were given lesser prison terms. See also: "Tojo Hideki: Execution Anniversary" (Dec 23).

WATT, JAMES: BIRTH ANNIVERSARY. Jan 19, 1736. (Old Style date.) Scottish engineer and inventor, born at Greenock, Scotland. The modern steam engine grew out of his efficiency-improving inventions. Died at Heathfield, England, Aug 25, 1819.

Birthdays Today

Desi Arnaz, Jr, 56, singer, actor, born Los Angeles, CA, Jan 19, 1953.

Michael Crawford, 67, actor, singer (*Phantom of the Opera*), born Salisbury, Wiltshire, England, Jan 19, 1942.

Drea de Matteo, 37, actress ("The Sopranos," "Joey"), born Queens, NY, Jan 19, 1972.

Phil Everly, 70, singer, with brother Don (The Everly Brothers), born Chicago, IL, Jan 19, 1939.

Shelley Fabares, 67, actress ("The Donna Reed Show," "Coach"), born Santa Monica, CA, Jan 19, 1942 (some sources say 1944).

Richard Lester, 77, director (*The Four Musketeers, Superman II & III*), born Philadelphia, PA, Jan 19, 1932.

Robert MacNeil, 78, broadcast journalist, born Montreal, QC, Canada, Jan 19, 1931.

Dolly Parton, 63, singer ("Jolene"), actress (*Nine to Five*), born Sevier County, TN, Jan 19, 1946.

William Ragsdale, 48, actor ("Brother's Keeper," "Herman's Head"), born El Dorado, AR, Jan 19, 1961.

Simon Rattle, 54, orchestra conductor, born Liverpool, England, Jan 19, 1955.

Jean Stapleton, 86, actress (*Klute*; Emmy for "All in the Family"), born Jeanne Murray at New York, NY, Jan 19, 1923.

Jeff Van Gundy, 47, basketball coach, born Inkster, MI, Jan 19, 1962.

Shawn Wayans, 38, actor (*Scary Movie*, "In Living Color"), born New York, NY, Jan 19, 1971.

Fritz Weaver, 83, actor (*Holocaust, Marathon Man*), born Philadelphia, PA, Jan 19, 1926.

January 2009

S	M	T	W	T	F	S
				1	2	3
4	5	6	7	8	9	10
11	12	13	14	15	16	17
18	19	20	21	22	23	24
25	26	27	28	29	30	31

January 20 — Tuesday

DAY 20 345 REMAINING

AQUARIUS, THE WATER CARRIER. Jan 20–Feb 19. In the astronomical/astrological zodiac, which divides the sun's apparent orbit into 12 segments, the period Jan 20–Feb 19 is traditionally identified as the sun sign of Aquarius, the Water Carrier. The ruling planet is Uranus or Saturn.

AZERBAIJAN: MARTYRS' DAY. Jan 20. National holiday. Commemorates the Azeris killed by Soviet troops, Jan 20, 1990, as they fought for independence.

BRAZIL: NOSSO SENHOR DO BONFIM FESTIVAL. Jan 20–30. Salvador, Bahia. Our Lord of the Happy Ending Festival is one of Salvador's most colorful religious feasts. Climax comes with people carrying water to pour over church stairs and sidewalks to cleanse them of impurities.

BRAZIL: SAN SEBASTIAN'S DAY. Jan 20. Patron saint of Rio de Janeiro.

BURNS, GEORGE: BIRTH ANNIVERSARY. Jan 20, 1896. Comedian George Burns was born at New York City. He began in vaudeville without much success until he teamed up with Gracie Allen, who became his wife. As Burns and Allen, the two had a long career on radio, in film and with their hit TV show, "The George Burns and Gracie Allen Show." Later he played the roles of God and the Devil in the *Oh, God!* movies. He lived to be 100 and died Mar 9, 1996, at Los Angeles, CA.

CAMCORDER DEVELOPED: ANNIVERSARY. Jan 20, 1982. Five companies (Hitachi, JVC, Philips, Matsushita and Sony) agreed to cooperate on the construction of a camera with a built-in videocassette recorder.

FELLINI, FEDERICO: BIRTH ANNIVERSARY. Jan 20, 1920. Director and screenwriter Federico Fellini was born at Rimini, Italy. Four of Fellini's movies won Oscars for best foreign-language film: *La Strada* (1956), *The Nights of Cabiria* (1957), *8½* (1963) and *Amarcord* (1974). He received an honorary Oscar in 1993 in recognition of his cinematic accomplishments. Fellini died Oct 31, 1993, at Rome.

GRAY, HAROLD LINCOLN: BIRTH ANNIVERSARY. Jan 20, 1894. The creator of "Little Orphan Annie" was born at Kankakee, IL. The comic strip featuring the 12-year-old Annie, her dog, Sandy, and her mentor and guardian, Oliver "Daddy" Warbucks, began appearing in the *Chicago Tribune* in 1924. While controversial for its strong conservative views, the strip was highly popular for its stories demonstrating the values of perseverance, independence and courage. Gray created the strip for 44 years until his death May 9, 1968, at La Jolla, CA, at age 74.

GUINEA-BISSAU: NATIONAL HEROES DAY. Jan 20. National holiday.

INAUGURATION DAY. Jan 20. The 20th Amendment provides that "The terms of the President and Vice President shall end at noon on the 20th day of January . . . and the terms of their successors shall then begin . . ." A quadrennial event and holiday in the District of Columbia. See also: "Old Inauguration Day" (Mar 4).

INAUGURATION DAY PUBLIC HOLIDAY OBSERVANCE. Jan 20. The US Code, Title 5, Section 6103(c) declares "January 20 of each fourth year after 1965, Inauguration Day, is a legal public holiday for the purpose of statutes relating to pay and leave of employees." Note: Title 5 concerns Government Organization and Employees.

JOHN MARSHALL APPOINTED CHIEF JUSTICE: ANNIVERSARY. Jan 20, 1801. John Marshall was appointed the fourth chief justice of the US.

LEE, RICHARD HENRY: BIRTH ANNIVERSARY. Jan 20, 1732. Signer of the Declaration of Independence. Born at Westmoreland County, VA, he died June 19, 1794, at his birthplace.

LESOTHO: ARMY DAY. Jan 20. Lesotho.

RID THE WORLD OF FAD DIETS AND GIMMICKS DAY. Jan 20. The 20th annual Slim Chance Awards for the "worst" weight loss products of the year are announced. Diet quackery defrauds, disables and kills. Listing of 2009 awards, diet quackery information and consumer handouts available on website. For info: Francie M. Berg, Healthy Weight Network, 402 S 14th St, Hettinger, ND 58639. E-mail: fmberg@healthyweight.net (please put "Berg-Healthy Weight Week" in subject line). Web: www.healthyweight.net.

US HOSTAGES IN IRAN RELEASED: ANNIVERSARY. Jan 20, 1981. The Iran hostage crisis ended with the release of 52 US citizens after 444 days of captivity. The deal was announced minutes after the swearing in of President Ronald Reagan.

US REVOLUTIONARY WAR: CESSATION OF HOSTILITIES: ANNIVERSARY. Jan 20, 1783. The British and US commissioners signed a preliminary "Cessation of Hostilities," which was ratified by England's King George III Feb 14 and led to the treaties of Paris and Versailles, Sept 3, 1783, ending the war.

ZORA NEALE HURSTON FESTIVAL OF THE ARTS AND HUMANITIES. Jan 20–25. Eatonville, FL. Festival celebrates Hurston, her work, her hometown, Eatonville (popularly known as the oldest incorporated African-American municipality in the country) and the cultural contributions Africa-descended people have made to the US and to world culture, with arts and humanities programming highlighting theater, music, folklore and literature through seminars, symposia, master classes, intellectual conversations/dialogues, art exhibitions, workshops, self-tours, concert fare and performances. Festival attracts both "domestic and international travelers looking for 'the other Florida'—the Africa-descendant cultural matrix." Est attendance: 75,000. For info: Zora! Festival Office, 227 E Kennedy Blvd, Eatonville, FL 32751. Phone: (407) 647-3307. Fax: (407) 647-4436. E-mail: info@zorafestival.com. Web: www.zoranealehurstonfestival.com.

Birthdays Today

Edwin "Buzz" Aldrin, 79, former astronaut, one of first three men on moon, born Montclair, NJ, Jan 20, 1930.

James Denton, 46, actor ("The Pretender," "Desperate Housewives"), born Nashville, TN, Jan 20, 1963.

Arte Johnson, 75, comedian, actor (Emmy for "Rowan & Martin's Laugh-In"), born Benton Harbor, MI, Jan 20, 1934 (some sources say 1929).

Lorenzo Lamas, 51, actor ("Falcon Crest," "Renegade"), born Los Angeles, CA, Jan 20, 1958.

David Lynch, 63, director ("Twin Peaks," *Blue Velvet*), writer, producer, born Missoula, MT, Jan 20, 1946.

Bill Maher, 53, comedian, TV host ("Politically Incorrect with Bill Maher"), born New York, NY, Jan 20, 1956.

Patricia Neal, 83, actress (*Breakfast at Tiffany's, Hud, The Subject Was Roses*), born Packard, KY, Jan 20, 1926.

Geovany Soto, 26, baseball player, born San Juan, PR, Jan 20, 1983.

Skeet Ulrich, 39, actor ("Jericho," *Scream*), born New York, NY, Jan 20, 1970 (some sources say 1969).

Otis Dewey "Slim" Whitman, 85, singer (first country performer to play at the London Palladium), born Tampa, FL, Jan 20, 1924.

Rainn Wilson, 41, actor ("The Office," "Six Feet Under," *The Last Mimzy*), born Seattle, WA, Jan 20, 1968.

January 21 — Wednesday

DAY 21 344 REMAINING

ALLEN, ETHAN: BIRTH ANNIVERSARY. Jan 21, 1738. Revolutionary War hero and leader of the Vermont "Green Mountain Boys." Born at Litchfield, CT, he died at Burlington, VT, Feb 12, 1789.

BALDWIN, ROGER NASH: 125th BIRTH ANNIVERSARY. Jan 21, 1884. Founder of the American Civil Liberties Union, called the "country's unofficial agitator for, and defender of, its civil liberties." Born at Wellesley, MA, he died Aug 26, 1981, at Ridgewood, NJ.

BRECKINRIDGE, JOHN CABELL: BIRTH ANNIVERSARY. Jan 21, 1821. 14th vice president of the US (1857–61), serving under President James Buchanan. Born at Lexington, KY; died there May 17, 1875.

BROWNING, JOHN MOSES: BIRTH ANNIVERSARY. Jan 21, 1855. World-famous gun maker and inventor who was taught gunsmithing by his Mormon pioneer father, Jonathan Browning, was born at Ogden, UT. Starting the J.M. & M.S. Browning Arms Company with his brother, he designed guns for Winchester, Remington, Stevens and Colt arms companies, as well as American and European armies. Browning had more gun patents than any other gunsmith in the world. He is best known for inventing the machine gun in 1890 and the automatic pistol in 1896. He died suddenly Nov 26, 1926, at age 71, while at Belgium on business. The company he founded, known now as Browning Arms Company, is located at Morgan, UT.

DIOR, CHRISTIAN: BIRTH ANNIVERSARY. Jan 21, 1905. Influential French fashion designer who was the world's premier style maker after WWII up until the 1950s. He was also one of the first designers to utilize licensing to help create his own brand. Born at Granville, France, Dior died on Oct 24, 1957, at Montecatini, Italy.

FIRST CONCORDE FLIGHT: ANNIVERSARY. Jan 21, 1976. The supersonic Concorde airplane was put into service by Britain and France. The Concorde ended flights on Oct 24, 2003—bringing an end to supersonic air travel.

ILLINOIS SNOW SCULPTING COMPETITION. Jan 21–24. Rockford, IL. Teams from around the state create enormous works of frozen art, as they compete to represent Illinois in national snow-sculpting competition. In case of inclement weather, event may be postponed. Sponsor: Rockford Park District. Est attendance: 20,000. For info: Jan Davis, Rockford Park District, 401 S Main St, Rockford, IL 61101. Phone: (815) 987-8800. Fax: (815) 987-0376. E-mail: rpdmail@RockfordParkDistrict.org. Web: www.snowsculpting.org.

JACKSON, THOMAS JONATHAN "STONEWALL": BIRTH ANNIVERSARY. Jan 21, 1824. Confederate general and one of the most famous soldiers of the American Civil War, best known as "Stonewall" Jackson. Born at Clarksburg, VA (now WV). He died of wounds received in battle near Chancellorsville, VA, May 10, 1863.

January 2009	S	M	T	W	T	F	S
					1	2	3
	4	5	6	7	8	9	10
	11	12	13	14	15	16	17
	18	19	20	21	22	23	24
	25	26	27	28	29	30	31

KIWANIS INTERNATIONAL: ANNIVERSARY. Jan 21, 1915. First Kiwanis Club chartered at Detroit, MI.

MARGARET BRENT DEMANDS A POLITICAL VOICE: ANNIVERSARY. Jan 21, 1648. Margaret Brent made her claim as America's first feminist by demanding a voice and vote for herself in the Maryland colonial assembly. Brent came to America in 1638 and was the first woman to own property in Maryland. At the time of her demands she was serving as secretary to Governor Leonard Calvert. She was ejected from the meetings, but when Calvert died she became his executor and acting governor, presiding over the general assembly.

NATIONAL HUGGING DAY™. Jan 21. Because hugging is something everyone can do and because it is a healthful form of touching, this day should be spent hugging anyone who will accept a hug, especially family and friends. The most "Huggable People" of the year will be announced. Nominations accepted through Jan 10. For more info, please send SASE to: Kevin C. Zaborney, 2023 Vickory Rd, Caro, MI 48723. Phone: (989) 673-6696. E-mail: kevin@nationalhuggingday.com. Web: www.nationalhuggingday.com.

SOUTH FLORIDA SENIOR GAMES. Jan 21–Feb 4. Hollywood, FL. 19th annual. Hollywood observance includes bocce, shuffleboard and sailing. For info: Marketing, City of Hollywood, Dept of Parks, Recreation & Cultural Arts, 1405 S 28th Ave, Hollywood, FL 33020. Phone: (954) 921-3404.

STONEWALL JACKSON'S BIRTHDAY CELEBRATION. Jan 21. Stonewall Jackson House, Lexington, VA. Celebrates the birthday of Stonewall Jackson. For info: Stonewall Jackson House, 8 E Washington St, Lexington, VA 24450. Phone: (540) 463-2552. E-mail: development@stonewalljackson.org. Web: www.stonewalljackson.org.

WOLFMAN JACK: BIRTH ANNIVERSARY. Jan 21, 1938. Wolfman Jack was born Robert Smith at Brooklyn, NY. He became famous as a disc jockey for radio stations at Mexico in the 1960s. Wolfman Jack was influential as a border radio voice because the Mexican station broadcast at 250,000 watts, five times the legal limit for American stations at the time, and therefore he was heard over a vast part of the US. During his night shift he played blues, hillbilly and other black and white music that wasn't getting a lot of exposure. He later appeared on American radio, in movies and on television as an icon of 1960s radio. Wolfman Jack died July 1, 1995, at Belvidere, NC.

ZEHNDER'S SNOWFEST (WITH ICE CARVING AND STATE OF MICHIGAN SNOW SCULPTING COMPETITIONS). Jan 21–26. Frankenmuth, MI. Annual festival also includes ice demonstrations, snow exhibitions by international teams from 6–10 countries and many children's activities such as a petting zoo, rides and music. Est attendance: 150,000. For info: Linda Kelly, Zehnder's of Frankenmuth, 730 S Main St, Frankenmuth, MI 48734. Phone: (800) 863-7999. Fax: (517) 652-3544. Web: www.zehnders.com.

Birthdays Today

Robby Benson, 53, actor ("Search for Tomorrow," *Ode to Billie Joe*), born Robin Segal, Dallas, TX, Jan 21, 1956.

Geena Davis, 52, actress ("Commander in Chief," *Thelma and Louise*, Oscar for *The Accidental Tourist*), born Ware, MA, Jan 21, 1957.

Mac Davis, 67, actor, songwriter ("The Mac Davis Show," *North Dallas Forty*), born Lubbock, TX, Jan 21, 1942.

Placido Domingo, 68, opera singer, one of the "Three Tenors," born Madrid, Spain, Jan 21, 1941.

Jill Eikenberry, 62, actress ("LA Law"), born New Haven, CT, Jan 21, 1947.

Jack William Nicklaus, 69, golfer, born Columbus, OH, Jan 21, 1940.

Billy Ocean, 59, musician, songwriter, born Leslie Charles at Trinidad, West Indies, Jan 21, 1950.

Hakeem Abdul Olajuwon, 46, former basketball player, born Lagos, Nigeria, Jan 21, 1963.

Detlef Schrempf, 46, former basketball player, born Leverkusen, West Germany, Jan 21, 1963.

January 22 — Thursday

DAY 22 **343 REMAINING**

ALLIED LANDING AT ANZIO: 65th ANNIVERSARY. Jan 22, 1944. A predominately American Allied force of 36,000 men was landed at Anzio on Italy's western coast. Commanding officer John P. Lucas failed to take the initiative but instead fortified his original position and thus possibly missed an early opportunity to retake Rome. The Allies entered Rome, June 4, 1944.

ALLIES TAKE NEW GUINEA: ANNIVERSARY. Jan 22, 1943. In the first land victory over the Japanese in WWII, American and Australian soldiers overcame the last pockets of resistance west and south of Sananda on New Guinea. Three thousand Allies were killed in the battle. The Japanese lost 7,000. Of the 350 prisoners taken, most were Chinese and Korean laborers attached to the Japanese forces. Almost no Japanese allowed themselves to be taken prisoner, preferring to commit hara-kiri.

AMPÈRE, ANDRE: BIRTH ANNIVERSARY. Jan 22, 1775. Physicist, student of electrical and magnetic phenomena, founder of the science of electrodynamics. Born at Lyons, France, from his early childhood, tragedy and depression pursued him. His father was executed during the French Revolution. Ampère died at Marseilles, France, June 10, 1836. The epitaph he selected for his tombstone was *tandem felix* ("happy at last"). The ampere, a unit of electrical current, is named for him.

ANSWER YOUR CAT'S QUESTION DAY. Jan 22. If you will stop what you are doing and take a look at your cat, you will observe that the cat is looking at you with a serious question. Meditate upon it, then answer the question! Annually, Jan 22. (©2006 by WH.) For info: Thomas & Ruth Roy, Wellcat Holidays, 2418 Long Ln, Lebanon, PA 17046. Phone: (717) 279-0184. E-mail: info@wellcat.com. Web: www.wellcat.com.

BACON, FRANCIS: BIRTH ANNIVERSARY. Jan 22, 1561. (Old Style date.) Statesman and essayist, born at London, England. One may guess that Bacon was of short stature, as he wrote (*Apothegms*), "Wise nature did never put her precious jewels into a garret four stories high: and therefore . . . exceeding tall men had ever very empty heads." Died at London, Apr 9, 1626 (OS).

BALANCHINE, GEORGE: BIRTH ANNIVERSARY. Jan 22, 1904. Born Georgi Militonovitch Balanchivadze at St. Petersburg, Russia, George Balanchine became one of the leading influences in 20th-century ballet. He choreographed more than 200 ballets including *Concerto Barocco, Apollo, Orpheus, Firebird, Swan Lake, Waltz Academy* and *The Nutcracker*. In 1933 he was invited to the US by Boston philanthropist Lincoln Kirstein to establish a school for American dancers. Together they founded the School of American Ballet in 1934 and then formed several ballet companies, including the New York City Ballet, which was led by Balanchine. Died at New York, NY, Apr 30, 1983.

BYRON, GEORGE GORDON: BIRTH ANNIVERSARY. Jan 22, 1788. Romantic poet, born at London, England. Described as "Mad, bad, and dangerous to know" by Lady Caroline Lamb. Byron died of fever at Missolonghi, Greece, Apr 19, 1824, while fighting for Greek independence.

CELEBRATION OF LIFE DAY. Jan 22. A time to honor our children and grandchildren in America. Each child and each life is to be held as a precious gift and should be treated with the highest respect and dignity. For info: Judith Natale, Women of Freedom, USA, PO Box 493703, Redding, CA 96049-3703. E-mail: WomenofFreedom @aol.com.

"EMERGENCY!" TV PREMIERE: ANNIVERSARY. Jan 22, 1972. This NBC program was introduced in midseason up against "All in the Family." It surprised everyone by becoming quite popular. The fast-paced action of the fire department paramedics saving lives by giving victims emergency treatment and then taking them to the hospital demonstrated the steps taken during actual emergency situations. The last episode aired Sept 3, 1977.

GRIFFITH, DAVID (LLEWELYN) WARK: BIRTH ANNIVERSARY. Jan 22, 1875. D.W. Griffith, pioneer producer-director in the American motion picture industry, best remembered for his film *Birth of a Nation* (1915). Born at LaGrange, KY. Died at Hollywood, CA, July 23, 1948.

HOWARD, ROBERT E.: BIRTH ANNIVERSARY. Jan 22, 1906. Born at Peaster, TX, Howard was to become one of the great and prolific pulp fiction writers of the 1920s and 1930s. He is most famous for creating Conan the Barbarian. Committed suicide at Cross Plains, TX, Jan 11, 1936.

"LAUGH-IN" TV PREMIERE: ANNIVERSARY. Jan 22, 1968. Actually the name of this NBC comedy was "Rowan and Martin's Laugh-In." Funny men Dan Rowan and Dick Martin hosted the show, but they seemed staid next to the show's other regulars, most of whom were young unknowns, including Dennis Allen, Chelsea Brown, Judy Carne, Ruth Buzzi, Ann Elder, Richard Dawson, Teresa Graves, Arte Johnson, Goldie Hawn, Alan Sues, Jo Anne Worley and Lily Tomlin. The show moved fast from gag to gag with heads popping out of bushes or doors in the big wall. The show brought a new energy to comedy as well as new phrases to our vocabulary ("You bet your sweet bippy," "Sock it to me"). The last telecast was May 14, 1973.

MONTANA WINTER FAIR. Jan 22–25. Fergus County Fairgrounds, Lewistown, MT. Fair featuring farm forums, commercial booths, youth education, open exhibits, dog clinic and trials, fiddlers' contest, art swap and shop, 4-H and FFA livestock exhibits and more. Est attendance: 10,000. For info: Montana Winter Fair, PO Box 3507, Lewistown, MT 59457. Phone: (406) 538-3007 or (406) 423-5297.

"OZARK JUBILEE" TV PREMIERE: ANNIVERSARY. Jan 22, 1955. ABC country and western music show hosted by Red Foley from Springfield, MO. Brenda "(Open Up Your Heart and) Let the Sunshine In" Lee appeared on the show at age 10 as one of the regulars. Other regulars included Smiley Burnette, Bobby Lord, Wanda Jackson, Suzi Arden and Webb Pierce.

PONSELLE, ROSA: BIRTH ANNIVERSARY. Jan 22, 1897. Formerly Rosa Melba Ponzilla, soprano Ponselle was born at Meriden, CT. Her career changed direction from vaudeville to opera when she was discovered by Enrico Caruso at the age of 21. Ponselle made her operatic debut at the Met in Verdi's *La forza del destino*. Her career spanned 19 seasons at the Met and included performances at London and Florence. Ponselle died May 25, 1981, at Baltimore, MD.

QUEEN VICTORIA: DEATH ANNIVERSARY. Jan 22, 1901. Queen Victoria died at age 82 after a reign of 64 years, the longest in British history. She had ruled over the one-quarter of the world that was the British Empire. Born May 24, 1819, at London, she died at Osborne, England.

***ROE v WADE* DECISION: ANNIVERSARY.** Jan 22, 1973. In the case of *Roe v Wade*, the US Supreme Court struck down state laws restricting abortions during the first six months of pregnancy. In the following decades debate has continued to rage between those who believe a woman has a right to choose whether to continue a pregnancy and those who believe that aborting such a pregnancy is murder of an unborn child.

SAINT PAUL WINTER CARNIVAL. Jan 22–Feb 1. St. Paul, MN. One of Minnesota's largest tourist attractions and the nation's oldest and largest winter festival. The 123-year-old Saint Paul Winter Carnival provides the "Coolest Celebration on Earth" with many indoor and outdoor events celebrating the thrills and chills of wintertime fun. Est attendance: 350,000. For info: Saint Paul Festival and Heritage Foundation, 429 Landmark Ctr, 75 W 5th St, St. Paul, MN 55102. Phone: (651) 223-4700. Fax: (651) 223-4707. E-mail: info@winter-carnival.com. Web: www.winter-carnival.com.

SAINT VINCENT: FEAST DAY. Jan 22. Spanish deacon and martyr who died AD 304. Patron saint of wine growers. Old weather lore says if there is sun on this day, good wine crops may be expected in the ensuing season.

STRINDBERG, AUGUST: BIRTH ANNIVERSARY. Jan 22, 1849. Swedish novelist and dramatist often called Sweden's greatest playwright. Born at Stockholm and died there of cancer on May 14, 1912, at age 63.

UKRAINE: UKRAINIAN DAY. Jan 22. National holiday. Commemorates the proclamation of the Ukrainian National Republic, Jan 22, 1918. Independence was short lived, however; by 1921 Ukraine had become part of the Soviet Union. It gained its independence from the Soviet Union in 1991.

UPJOHN, RICHARD: BIRTH ANNIVERSARY. Jan 22, 1802. American architect and founder of the American Institute of Architects in 1857. A Gothic revivalist, he designed many churches. Among his works were Trinity Chapel, New York, NY; Corn Exchange Bank Building, New York, NY; Central Congregational Church, Boston, MA. Born at Shaftesbury, England, he died Aug 17, 1878, at Garrison, NY.

VINSON, FRED M.: BIRTH ANNIVERSARY. Jan 22, 1890. The 13th chief justice of the US, born at Louisa, KY. Served in the House of Representatives, appointed director of war mobilization during WWII and secretary of the Treasury under Harry Truman. Nominated by Truman to succeed Harlan F. Stone as chief justice of the US. Died at Washington, DC, Sept 8, 1953.

WASHINGTON'S BIRTHDAY CELEBRATION™. Jan 22–Feb 22. Laredo, TX. Founded in 1898, Laredo's Washington's Birthday Celebration is the largest celebration of its kind in the US. This month-long festival includes two parades, a carnival, an air show, fireworks, live concerts, a jalapeño festival and many other fun, family events. Est attendance: 400,000. For info: Selina Villarreal, Washington's Birthday Celebration Assn, 1819 E Hillside Rd, Laredo, TX 78041. Phone: (956) 722-0589. Fax: (956) 722-5528. E-mail: publicity@wbcalaredo.org. Web: www.wbcalaredo.org.

WOMEN'S HEALTHY WEIGHT DAY. Jan 22. A day to honor American women of all sizes and confirm that beauty, talent and love cannot be weighed. Winners of the Women's Healthy Weight Day awards will be announced—businesses that portray size diversity and reject the national obsession with thinness that is shattering the lives of women, young girls and their families. News releases, awards and consumer handouts available on website. For info: Francie M. Berg, Healthy Weight Network, 402 S 14th St, Hettinger, ND 58639. E-mail: fmberg@healthyweight.net (please put "Berg-Healthy Weight Week" in subject line). Web: www.healthyweight.net.

Birthdays Today

Linda Blair, 50, actress (*The Exorcist, Airport*), born Westport, CT, Jan 22, 1959.

Seymour Cassel, 72, actor (*Faces, Dick Tracy, Honeymoon in Vegas*), born Detroit, MI, Jan 22, 1937.

Olivia D'Abo, 42, actress ("The Wonder Years," "The Single Guy"), born London, England, Jan 22, 1967.

Balthazar Getty, 34, actor (*Lost Highway*), born Los Angeles, CA, Jan 22, 1975.

John Hurt, 69, actor ("And the Band Played On," *The Elephant Man*), born Lincolnshire, England, Jan 22, 1940.

Diane Lane, 44, actress (*Unfaithful, A Walk on the Moon, A Little Romance*), born New York, NY, Jan 22, 1965.

Piper Laurie, 77, actress (*Fighting for My Daughter*, "Twin Peaks"), born Rosetta Jacobs at Detroit, MI, Jan 22, 1932.

Christopher Masterson, 29, actor ("Malcolm in the Middle"), born Long Island, NY, Jan 22, 1980.

Greg Oden, 21, basketball player, born Buffalo, NY, Jan 22, 1988.

Steve Perry, 60, singer (Journey), born Hanford, CA, Jan 22, 1949.

Joseph Wambaugh, 72, former police officer, author (*The Onion Field, The Choir Boys*), born East Pittsburgh, PA, Jan 22, 1937.

January 2009	S	M	T	W	T	F	S
					1	2	3
	4	5	6	7	8	9	10
	11	12	13	14	15	16	17
	18	19	20	21	22	23	24
	25	26	27	28	29	30	31

January 23 — Friday

DAY 23 **342 REMAINING**

"BARNEY MILLER" TV PREMIERE: ANNIVERSARY. Jan 23, 1975. ABC sitcom about a New York precinct captain starred Hal Linden as Captain Barney Miller. The 12th Precinct gang included Barbara Barrie as Miller's wife, Abe Vigoda as Detective Phil Fish, Max Gail as Sergeant Stan Wojciehowicz, Gregory Sierra as Sergeant Chano Amenguale, Jack Soo as Sergeant Nick Yemana, Ron Glass as Detective Ron Harris and a host of others. The last episode aired in 1982.

BIG BAND/SWING DANCE WEEKEND. Jan 23–25. Grove Park Inn, Asheville, NC. 17th annual. Delve into a world of music with evening and afternoon concerts in the Grand Ballroom and numerous jazz artists performing in the Great Hall all weekend. The Glenn Miller Orchestra and The Charles Goodwin Orchestra headline in 2009. Also includes Meet the Artists receptions and a Saturday morning jazz clinic. Annually, the last full weekend in January. Est attendance: 1,500. For info: The Grove Park Inn Resort & Spa, 290 Macon Ave, Asheville, NC 28804. Phone: (800) 438-5800 or (828) 252-2711. Fax: (828) 252-5585. E-mail: jwiner@groveparkinn.com. Web: www.groveparkinn.com.

BLACKWELL, ELIZABETH, AWARDED MD: ANNIVERSARY. Jan 23, 1849. Dr. Elizabeth Blackwell became the first woman to receive an MD degree. The native of Bristol, England, was awarded her degree by the Medical Institution of Geneva, NY.

BULGARIA: BABIN DEN. Jan 23. Celebrated throughout Bulgaria as Day of the Midwives or Grandmother's Day. Traditional festivities.

HANCOCK, JOHN: BIRTH ANNIVERSARY. Jan 23, 1737. American patriot and statesman, first signer of the Declaration of Independence. Because of his conspicuous signature on the Declaration, Hancock's name has become part of the American language, referring to any handwritten signature, as in "Put your John Hancock on that!" Born at Braintree, MA, he died at Quincy, MA, Oct 8, 1793. (Some sources cite Hancock's Old Style birth date of Jan 12, 1736/7.)

HEWES, JOSEPH: BIRTH ANNIVERSARY. Jan 23, 1730. Signer of the Declaration of Independence. Born at Princeton, NJ, he died Nov 10, 1779, at Philadelphia, PA.

"THE KING FAMILY SHOW" TV PREMIERE: ANNIVERSARY. Jan 23, 1965. ABC musical variety show featuring the singing and playing of the King sisters and other descendents of William King

Driggs, who organized the family musical group in the 1930s. Including spouses, children, grandchildren and great-grandchildren, some three dozen members of the King family have appeared on camera at one time.

KOVACS, ERNIE: 90th BIRTH ANNIVERSARY. Jan 23, 1919. Comedian and television pioneer, born at Trenton, NJ. Throughout the '40s and '50s Ernie Kovacs made a name for himself hosting his own shows, including "The Ernie Kovacs Show" and "Ernie In Kovacsland" and a variety of quiz shows. He died in an automobile accident at Los Angeles, Jan 13, 1962.

MANET, ÉDOUARD: BIRTH ANNIVERSARY. Jan 23, 1832. Painter, born at Paris, France. Among his best-known paintings are *Olympia* and *Déjeuner sur l'herbe*. Manet died Apr 30, 1883, at Paris.

NATIONAL HANDWRITING DAY. Jan 23. Popularly observed on birthday of John Hancock to encourage more legible handwriting. (Some sources cite Hancock's Old Style birth date of Jan 12, 1736/7.)

SNOWPLOW MAILBOX HOCKEY DAY. Jan 23. It's wintertime and time for snowplow drivers everywhere to see how many rural mailboxes they can knock over. Twenty extra points for boosting one into the next township! (©2006 by WH.) For info: Thomas & Ruth Roy, Wellcat Holidays, 2418 Long Ln, Lebanon, PA 17046. Phone: (717) 279-0184. E-mail: info@wellcat.com. Web: www.wellcat.com.

STENDHAL: BIRTH ANNIVERSARY. Jan 23, 1783. French author Marie Henri Beyle, whose best-known pseudonym was Stendhal. Best remembered are his novels *The Red and the Black* (1831) and *The Charterhouse of Parma* (1839). Born at Grenoble, France, he died at Paris, Mar 23, 1842.

STEWART, POTTER: BIRTH ANNIVERSARY. Jan 23, 1915. Associate justice of the Supreme Court of the US, nominated by President Eisenhower Jan 17, 1959. (Oath of office, May 15, 1959.) Born at Jackson, MI, he retired in July 1981 and died Dec 7, 1985, at Putney, VT, five days after suffering a stroke. Buried at Arlington National Cemetery.

TWENTIETH AMENDMENT TO US CONSTITUTION RATIFIED: ANNIVERSARY. Jan 23, 1933. The 20th Amendment was ratified, fixing the date of the presidential inauguration at the current Jan 20 instead of the previous Mar 4. It also specified that were the president-elect to die before taking office, the vice president–elect would succeed to the presidency. In addition, it set Jan 3 as the official opening date of Congress each year.

TWENTY-FOURTH AMENDMENT TO US CONSTITUTION RATIFIED: 45th ANNIVERSARY. Jan 23, 1964. Poll taxes and other taxes were eliminated as a prerequisite for voting in all federal elections by the 24th Amendment.

USS *PUEBLO* SEIZED BY NORTH KOREA: ANNIVERSARY. Jan 23, 1968. North Korea seized the USS *Pueblo* in the Sea of Japan, claiming the ship was on a spy mission. The crew was held for 11 months. The vessel was confiscated. Accompanying the crew when they were released—on Dec 22, 1968—was the body of Seaman Duane D. Hodges, the only crewman killed.

VEGASPEX. Jan 23–25. Las Vegas, NV. Coin, stamp, antique watch, jewelry and collectibles expo. Est attendance: 10,000. For info: Israel Bick, Exec Dir, Intl Coin & Stamp Collectors Society, PO Box 854, Van Nuys, CA 91408. Phone: (818) 997-6496. Fax: (818) 988-4337. E-mail: iibick@sbcglobal.net. Web: www.bick.net.

Birthdays Today

Richard Dean Anderson, 59, actor ("Stargate SG-1," "MacGyver"), born Minneapolis, MN, Jan 23, 1950.

Princess Caroline, 52, born Monte Carlo, Monaco, Jan 23, 1957.

Tom Carper, 62, US Senator (D, Delaware), born Beckley, WV, Jan 23, 1947.

Gil Gerard, 66, actor ("Buck Rogers," "Sidekicks"), born Little Rock, AR, Jan 23, 1943.

Patrick Capper (Pat) Haden, 56, sportscaster, former football player, born Westbury, NY, Jan 23, 1953.

Mariska Hargitay, 45, actress ("Law & Order: Special Victims Unit"), born Los Angeles, CA, Jan 23, 1964.

Rutger Hauer, 65, actor (*Blade Runner*), born Breukelen, Netherlands, Jan 23, 1944.

Frank Lautenberg, 85, US Senator (D, New Jersey), born Paterson, NJ, Jan 23, 1924.

Jeanne Moreau, 81, actress (*Jules and Jim, Viva Maria*), born Paris, France, Jan 23, 1928.

Gail O'Grady, 46, actress ("NYPD Blue"), born Detroit, MI, Jan 23, 1963.

Chita Rivera, 76, singer, actress (*The Kiss of the Spider Woman*), born Conchita del Rivero at Washington, DC, Jan 23, 1933.

Tiffani-Amber Thiessen, 35, actress ("Beverly Hills 90210," "Saved by the Bell"), born Long Beach, CA, Jan 23, 1974.

January 24 — Saturday

DAY 24 — **341 REMAINING**

ACHELIS, ELISABETH: BIRTH ANNIVERSARY. Jan 24, 1880. Calendar reform advocate, author of *The World Calendar*, born at Brooklyn, NY. Her proposed calendar made every year the same, with equal quarters, each year beginning on Sunday, Jan 1, and each date falling on the same day of the week every year. Died at New York, NY, Feb 11, 1973.

AFRMA FANCY RAT AND MOUSE ANNUAL SHOW. Jan 24. Riverside, CA. Annual show where trophies are awarded to the winners. Rats and mice are emerging as ideal pets: they provide all the pleasure and satisfaction of a warm, cuddly, intelligent and friendly pet companion. The American Fancy Rat and Mouse Association (AFRMA) was founded in 1983 to promote the breeding and exhibition of fancy rats and mice, to educate the public on their positive qualities as companion animals and to provide information on their proper care. Est attendance: 100. For info: AFRMA (CAE), PO Box 2589, Winnetka, CA 91396-2589. Phone: (951) 685-2350 or (818) 992-5564 or (909) 238-5231. E-mail: afrma@afrma.org. Web: www.afrma.org.

AMHERST RAILWAY SOCIETY RAILROAD HOBBY SHOW. Jan 24–25. West Springfield, MA. Now expanded to three buildings, nearly 5½ acres with dealers, displays, art, more than 30 operating layouts and railroads including Shortline, Tourist, Class 1 and more. Est attendance: 24,000. For info: Amherst Railway Society, PO Box 247, Monson, MA 01057-0247. Phone: (413) 267-4555. Web: www.amherstrail.org.

BELLY LAUGH DAY. Jan 24. Belly Laugh Day is a day to celebrate the great gift of laughter. Smiling and laughing are permitted, encouraged and celebrated. How? Smile, throw your arms in the air and laugh out loud. Join the Belly Laugh Bounce 'Round the World, as people from Fiji to Alaska and Hawaii in kitchens, schools, hospitals, offices, plants and stores stop at 1:24 PM (local time) to bounce a smile and a laugh around the world. For info: Elaine Helle, 13413 Vermeer Dr, Lake Oswego, OR 97035. Phone: (503) 344-6428. E-mail: jan24@bellylaughday.com. Web: www.bellylaughday.com.

BELUSHI, JOHN: 60th BIRTH ANNIVERSARY. Jan 24, 1949. Actor, comedian ("Saturday Night Live," *Animal House, The Blues Brothers*), born at Chicago, IL. Died Mar 5, 1982, at Hollywood, CA.

BOLIVIA: ALACITIS FAIR. Jan 24–26. La Paz. Traditional annual celebration by Aymara Indians with prayers and offerings to the god of prosperity.

BRICKHOUSE, JACK: BIRTH ANNIVERSARY. Jan 24, 1916. Born John Beasley Brickhouse at Peoria, IL. A legend in Chicago broadcasting, Brickhouse was the play-by-play voice for the first baseball game televised by WGN, an exhibition game between the Cubs and the White Sox on Apr 16, 1948. He broadcast Cubs games for 40 years, Chicago Bears games for 24 years and some Chicago Bulls and White Sox games. In 1983 he received the Ford C. Frick Award. Died at Chicago, IL, Aug 6, 1998.

CALIFORNIA GOLD DISCOVERY: ANNIVERSARY. Jan 24, 1848. James W. Marshal, an employee of John Sutter, accidentally discovered gold while building a sawmill near Coloma, CA. Efforts to keep the discovery secret failed, and the gold rush of 1849 was under way.

CHINESE NEW YEAR FESTIVAL AND PARADE. Jan 24–Feb 8. San Francisco, CA. North America's largest Chinese community salutes the Year of the Ox, Lunar Year 4707. Activities include Chinatown Flower Fair (Jan 24–25); Miss Chinatown USA Pageant (Jan 31) with Coronation Ball (Feb 6); Southwest Airlines Chinese New Year Parade (Feb 7); Chinatown Community Street Fair (Feb 7–8). These events showcase the diversity of Chinese culture from Chinese opera and ballet, traditional dance and ancient dynastic costumes to martial arts. Booths feature cooking demonstrations, calligraphy and arts and crafts. Est attendance: 700,000. For info: Chinese Chamber of Commerce, Chinese New Year Festival & Parade, 730 Sacramento, San Francisco, CA 94108. Phone: (415) 982-3000. Fax: (415) 986-1933. Web: www.chineseparade.com.

FDR's "UNCONDITIONAL SURRENDER" STATEMENT: ANNIVERSARY. Jan 24, 1943. At the end of the Casablanca Conference, 1943, Franklin D. Roosevelt and Winston Churchill held a press conference. Roosevelt stated, "Peace can come to the world only by the total elimination of German and Japanese war power. That means the unconditional surrender of Germany, Italy and Japan." This position calling for "unconditional surrender" has subsequently been criticized by some as having prolonged the war.

GASPARILLA EXTRAVAGANZA AND PIRATE FEST. Jan 24 and Feb 7. Tampa, FL. As any Tampa resident can attest, "Gasparilla" means boats, pirates, parades, merriment and more. On Jan 24, the "Extravaganza" is an alcohol-free family event featuring the Children's Gasparilla Parade and one of the largest fireworks displays in the country. Saturday, Feb 7, The Gasparilla Pirate Fest features 700 citizens, members of Ye Mystic Krewe, reenacting the 1904 invasion of Tampa by a band of pirates. For info: EventMakers Corp of Tampa, 3701 W Azeele St, Tampa, FL 33609. Phone: (813) 353-8108. E-mail: info@Eventmakers-FL.com. Web: www.gasparillapiratefest.com and gasparillaextravaganza.com.

GOODSON, MARK: BIRTH ANNIVERSARY. Jan 24, 1915. Producer and creator of TV game shows, Mark Goodson was born at Sacramento, CA. His career in entertainment began in radio where he created his first game show, "Pop the Question." He later teamed with Bill Todman, and that partnership led to "I've Got a Secret," "Password," "The Price Is Right," "What's My Line?" and "Family Feud." He died Dec 18, 1992, at New York, NY.

HOGGETOWNE MEDIEVAL FAIRE. Jan 24–25 (also Jan 30–31, Feb 1). Alachua County Fairgrounds, Gainesville, FL. 23rd annual fair features jousting, birds of prey, medieval arts and crafts, food and continuous entertainment on eight stages. Est attendance: 60,000. For info: Linda Piper, City of Gainesville, Dept of Cultural Affairs, PO Box 490 Station 30, Gainesville, FL 32602. Phone: (352) 334-5064. Fax: (352) 334-2249. E-mail: piperLr@cityofgainesville.org. Web: www.gvlculturalaffairs.org.

ICE FEST. Jan 24–25. Ligonier, PA. A weekend of ice-carving demonstrations as blocks of ice are turned into works of art. Est attendance: 5,000. For info: Rachel Roehrig, Ligonier Chamber of Commerce, 120 E Main St, Ligonier, PA 15658. Phone: (724) 238-4200. Fax: (724) 238-4610. E-mail: thechamber@ligonier.com.

LONGWOOD GARDENS ORCHID EXTRAVAGANZA. Jan 24–Mar 31. Kennett Square, PA. Indoor conservatory display features thousands of colorful, fragrant orchids. Est attendance: 90,000. For info: Longwood Gardens, PO Box 501, Kennett Sqare, PA 19348-0501. Phone: (610) 377-1000. Web: www.longwoodgardens.org.

NATIONAL COMPLIMENT DAY. Jan 24. This day is set aside to compliment at least five people. Not only are compliments appreciated by the receiver, they lift the spirit of the giver. Compliments provide a quick and easy way to connect positively with those you come in contact with. Giving compliments forges bonds, dispels loneliness and just plain feels good. For info: Debby Hoffman, Positive Results Seminars, PO Box 3478, Concord, NH 03302-3478. Phone: (603) 783-4446. E-mail: Debby@DebbyHoffman.com. Or Kathy Chamberlin, Respectful Communication, 724 Park Ave, Hopkinton, NH 03229-3089. Phone: (603) 746-3602. E-mail: KathyChamberlin@aol.com. Web: www.complimentday.com.

NATIONAL COWBOY POETRY GATHERING. Jan 24–31. Elko, NV. 25th annual. Soulful poetry and music performed by working cowboys. The event, which includes workshops, jam sessions, Western art and buckaroo trappings exhibits, attracts an international audience. For info: Western Folklife Center, 501 Railroad St, Elko, NV 89801. Phone: (775) 738-7508. Fax: (775) 738-2900. E-mail: wfc@westernfolklife.org. Web: www.westernfolklife.org.

ROLEX 24 AT DAYTONA GRAND-AM SERIES RACE. Jan 24–25. Daytona International Speedway, Daytona Beach, FL. 47th annual running of the most prestigious endurance race in North America. For info: Daytona International Speedway, PO Box 2801, Daytona Beach, FL 32120-2801. Phone: (800) PIT-SHOP. Fax: (386) 947-6791. Web: www.daytonainternationalspeedway.com.

SENIOR BOWL. Jan 24. Ladd-Peebles Stadium, Mobile, AL. 60th annual. All-star football game featuring the nation's top collegiate seniors on teams coached by National Football League coaching staffs. Proceeds go to charities. Sponsored by Under Armour. Est attendance: 40,700. For info: Senior Bowl, PO Box 1408, Mobile, AL 36633-1408. Phone: (251) 438-2276. Fax: (251) 432-0409. E-mail: srbowl@seniorbowl.com. Web: www.seniorbowl.com.

SPACE MILESTONE: *COSMOS 954* (USSR) FALLS. Jan 24, 1978. Nuclear-equipped reconnaissance satellite launched Sept 18, 1977, fell into Earth's atmosphere and burned over northern Canada. Some radioactive debris reached ground on Jan 24, 1978.

SPACE MILESTONE: *DISCOVERY* (US). Jan 24, 1985. Space shuttle *Discovery* launched from Kennedy Space Center, FL. On its secret, all-military mission, Jan 24–27, 1985, it deployed an eavesdropping satellite.

WHARTON, EDITH: BIRTH ANNIVERSARY. Jan 24, 1862. American author (*The Age of Innocence, Ethan Frome*) and Pulitzer Prize winner. Born at New York, NY. Died at Pavillon Colombe, France, Aug 11, 1937, of a stroke.

Birthdays Today

Mischa Barton, 23, actress ("The O.C."), born London, England, Jan 24, 1986.

Ernest Borgnine, 92, actor ("McHale's Navy," *Marty*), born Hamden, CT, Jan 24, 1917.

Neil Diamond, 68, singer, composer, born Coney Island, NY, Jan 24, 1941.

Ed Helms, 35, writer, comedian ("The Daily Show"), born Atlanta, GA, Jan 24, 1974.

January 2009

S	M	T	W	T	F	S
				1	2	3
4	5	6	7	8	9	10
11	12	13	14	15	16	17
18	19	20	21	22	23	24
25	26	27	28	29	30	31

Nastassja Kinski, 49, actress (*Tess, The Hotel New Hampshire*), born Berlin, Germany, Jan 24, 1960.

Matthew Lillard, 39, actor (*Scream, Scooby-Doo*), born Lansing, MI, Jan 24, 1970.

Aaron Neville, 68, singer, songwriter, born New Orleans, LA, Jan 24, 1941.

Michael Ontkean, 63, actor ("Twin Peaks," *Slap Shot*), born Vancouver, BC, Canada, Jan 24, 1946.

Mary Lou Retton, 41, Olympic gold medal gymnast, born Fairmont, WV, Jan 24, 1968.

Oral Roberts, 91, evangelist, born Tulsa, OK, Jan 24, 1918.

Yakov Smirnoff, 58, comedian, born Odessa, USSR (now Ukraine), Jan 24, 1951.

Maria Tallchief, 84, former ballet dancer, born Fairfax, OK, Jan 24, 1925.

January 25 — Sunday

DAY 25 — **340 REMAINING**

AROUND THE WORLD IN 72 DAYS: ANNIVERSARY. Jan 25, 1890. Newspaper reporter Nellie Bly (pen name used by Elizabeth Cochrane Seaman) set off from Hoboken, NJ, Nov 14, 1889, to attempt to break Jules Verne's imaginary hero Phileas Fogg's record of voyaging around the world in 80 days. She did beat Fogg's record, taking 72 days, 6 hours, 11 minutes and 14 seconds to make the trip, arriving back in New Jersey on Jan 25, 1890.

BOYLE, ROBERT: BIRTH ANNIVERSARY. Jan 25, 1627. (Old Style date.) Irish physicist, chemist and author who formulated Boyle's Law in 1662. Born at Lismore, Ireland, he died at London, England, Dec 30, 1691 (OS).

BURNS, ROBERT: 250th BIRTH ANNIVERSARY. Jan 25, 1759. Beloved Scottish poet ("Oh wad some power the giftie gie us/To see oursels as others see us!"). Born at Ayrshire, Scotland, he died at Dumfries, Scotland, July 21, 1796. His birthday is widely celebrated as Burns' Nights, especially in Scotland, England and Newfoundland.

CARLSBAD MARATHON AND HALF MARATHON. Jan 25. Plaza Camino Real, Carlsbad, CA. Race open to runners, walkers, race walkers and the disabled. Postrace festival with refreshments, entertainment, massages and more. Est attendance: 12,000. For info: Carlsbad Marathon, In Motion, Inc, 6355 Corte del Abeto, Ste C-103, Carlsbad, CA 92011. Phone: (760) 692-2900. E-mail: info@inmotionevents.com. Web: www.carlsbadmarathon.com.

CATHOLIC SCHOOLS WEEK. Jan 25–31. A national celebration focusing on the uniqueness of Catholic schools. Many schools plan special activities celebrating their Catholic heritage. Jointly sponsored by the National Catholic Educational Association and the US Conference of Catholic Bishops. Annually, beginning on the last Sunday in January. For info: Natl Catholic Educational Assn, 1077 30th St NW, Ste 100, Washington, DC 20007-3852. Phone: (888) 467-7453. E-mail: csw@specworks.com. Web: www.catholicschoolsweek.org.

CRAFT & HOBBY ASSOCIATION WINTER CONVENTION AND TRADE SHOW. Jan 25–28. Anaheim Convention Center, Anaheim, CA. The world's largest trade show for the craft and hobby industry. The CHA show also offers extensive educational programs and workshops. Est attendance: 20,000. For info: Craft & Hobby Assn, 319 E 54th St, Elmwood Park, NJ 07407. Phone: (800) 822-0494. Fax: (201) 835-1278. E-mail: info@craftandhobby.org. Web: www.chashow.org or www.craftandhobby.org.

CURTIS, CHARLES: BIRTH ANNIVERSARY. Jan 25, 1860. The 31st vice president of the US (1929–33). Born at Topeka, KS, he died at Washington, DC, Feb 8, 1936.

FIRST SCHEDULED TRANSCONTINENTAL FLIGHT: 50th ANNIVERSARY. Jan 25, 1959. American Airlines opened the jet age in the US with the first scheduled transcontinental flight on a Boeing 707 nonstop from California to New York.

FIRST TELEVISED PRESIDENTIAL NEWS CONFERENCE: ANNIVERSARY. Jan 25, 1961. Beginning a tradition that survives to this day, John F. Kennedy held the first televised presidential news conference five days after being inaugurated the 35th president.

FIRST WINTER OLYMPICS: 85th ANNIVERSARY. Jan 25, 1924. The first Winter Olympic Games opened at Chamonix, France, with athletes representing 16 nations. The ski jump, previously unknown, thrilled spectators. The Olympics offered a boost to skiing, which became enormously popular in the next decade.

GROUNDHOG RUN. Jan 25. Kansas City, MO. 27th annual. The world's only 10k and 5k underground run takes place at the Hunt Midwest SubTropolis. 3,000 runners from across the country participate in this MARA Grand Prix event to benefit Children's TLC. Est attendance: 3,000. For info: Children's TLC, 3101 Main St, Kansas City, MO 64111-1921. Phone: (816) 756-0780. Fax: (816) 756-1677. E-mail: dlowland@childrenstlc.org. Web: www.childrenstlc.org.

MACINTOSH DEBUTS: 25th ANNIVERSARY. Jan 25, 1984. Apple's Macintosh computer went on sale this day for $2,495. It wasn't until mid-1985, however, that sales began to take off and this computer began to replace the Apple II model.

MAUGHAM, W. SOMERSET: BIRTH ANNIVERSARY. Jan 25, 1874. English short story writer, novelist and playwright, born at Paris, France. Among his best-remembered books: *Of Human Bondage, Cakes and Ale* and *The Razor's Edge.* Died at Cap Ferrat, France, Dec 16, 1965.

MILLS, FLORENCE: BIRTH ANNIVERSARY. Jan 25, 1896. The leading black American singer and dancer of the Jazz Age and the Harlem Renaissance was born Florence Winfree at Washington, DC. She appeared in Langston Hughes's *Shuffle Along* in 1921 and *Plantation Review* on Broadway in 1922, then at the London Pavilion in *Dover Street to Dixie* in 1923. Offered a spot in the *Ziegfeld Follies*, she turned it down and joined in creating a rival show with an all-black cast. Mills was the first black woman to appear as a headliner at the Palace Theatre. She was so revered for her efforts to create opportunities for black entertainers and to bring the unique culture of blacks to Broadway that more than 150,000 people filled the streets of Harlem to mourn her when she died at New York City, Nov 1, 1927, at age 31.

NATIONAL NURSE ANESTHETISTS WEEK. Jan 25–31. To provide recognition for the nation's 37,000 certified registered nurse anesthetists (CRNAs), who have been providing safe anesthesia care for more than 125 years. CRNAs administer approximately 30 million anesthetics to patients in the US each year. For info: Amer Assn of Nurse Anesthetists, 222 S Prospect, Park Ridge, IL 60068. Phone: (847) 692-7050. Fax: (847) 692-6968. Web: www.aana.com.

"ROBOT" ENTERS WORLD LEXICON: ANNIVERSARY. Jan 25, 1921. On this date, the play *R.U.R.* premiered at the National Theater in Prague, Czechoslovakia. "R.U.R." stood for "Rossum's Universal Robots," and the play concerned artificial human workers who rebel against their human masters. Czech dramatist Karel Capek and his brother, Josef Capek, derived "robot" from the Czech noun *robota*, which means "labor" and "servitude." As the play became a hit worldwide (with an English translation published in 1923), the concept of the robot took hold. Capek's robots were chemically created; today's real and fictional robots are metallic machines.

A ROOM OF ONE'S OWN DAY. Jan 25. For anyone who knows or longs for the sheer bliss and rightness of having a private place, no matter how humble, to call one's own. (©2006 by WH.) For info: Thomas & Ruth Roy, Wellcat Holidays, 2418 Long Ln, Lebanon, PA 17046. Phone: (717) 279-0184. E-mail: info@wellcat.com. Web: www.wellcat.com.

WOOLF, VIRGINIA: BIRTH ANNIVERSARY. Jan 25, 1882. English writer, critic and novelist, author of *Jacob's Room* and *To the Lighthouse.* Born at London, England. After completing her last novel, *Between the Acts,* she collapsed under the strain and drowned herself in the River Ouse near Rodmell, England, on Mar 28, 1941.

Birthdays Today

Corazon "Cory" Aquino, 76, former president of the Philippines, born Tarlac Province, Philippine Islands, Jan 25, 1933.

Vince Carter, 32, basketball player, born Daytona Beach, FL, Jan 25, 1977.

Chris Chelios, 47, hockey player, born Chicago, IL, Jan 25, 1962.

Ernie Harwell, 91, sportscaster, born Washington, GA, Jan 25, 1918.

Dean Jones, 78, actor (*Tea and Sympathy, The Love Bug, Beethoven*), born Decatur, AL, Jan 25, 1931 (some sources say 1935).

Alicia Keys, 28, musician, singer (*Songs in A Minor*), born Harlem, NY, Jan 25, 1981.

Dinah Manoff, 51, actress ("Soap," "Empty Nest," Tony Award for *I Ought to Be in Pictures*), born New York, NY, Jan 25, 1958.

Edwin Newman, 90, journalist, author ("Comet," *A Civil Tongue*), born New York, NY, Jan 25, 1919.

Ana Ortiz, 38, actress ("Ugly Betty"), born New York, NY, Jan 25, 1971.

Leigh Taylor-Young, 64, actress ("Peyton Place," "Dallas," *I Love You, Alice B. Toklas*), born Washington, DC, Jan 25, 1945.

January 26 — Monday

DAY 26 — 339 REMAINING

AUSTRALIA: AUSTRALIA DAY—FIRST BRITISH SETTLEMENT: ANNIVERSARY. Jan 26, 1788. A shipload of convicts arrived briefly at Botany Bay (which proved to be unsuitable) and then at Port Jackson (later the site of the city of Sydney). Establishment of an Australian prison colony was to relieve crowding of British prisons. Australia Day, formerly known as Foundation Day or Anniversary Day, has been observed since about 1817 and has been a public holiday since 1838.

AUSTRALIA: AUSTRALIA DAY COCKROACH RACES. Jan 26. Brisbane, Queensland. 28th annual. "The greatest gathering of thoroughbred cockroaches in the known universe." Cockroach race enthusiasts celebrate Australia Day at the Story Bridge Hotel, where icky insects (Cocky Balboa, Lord of the Drains or other such) compete. Race includes steeplechase. Also: music, "Miss Cocky" pageant, "Best Dressed" contest and more. Proceeds benefit charity. For info: Story Bridge Hotel, 200 Main St, Kangaroo Point, Queensland 4169 Australia. Phone: (07) 3391-2266. Fax: (07) 3393-0926. Web: www.storybridgehotel.com.au.

January 2009

S	M	T	W	T	F	S
				1	2	3
4	5	6	7	8	9	10
11	12	13	14	15	16	17
18	19	20	21	22	23	24
25	26	27	28	29	30	31

BETTER BUSINESS COMMUNICATION DAY. Jan 26. This is a day set aside to encourage all workers to acknowledge the importance of effective communication in the workplace. Tips, workshops and seminars will be offered around this day to help workers improve their communication skills. Annually, the fourth Monday in January. For info: Corporate Speech Pathology Network (Corspan). E-mail: info@corspan.org. Web: www.corspan.org.

BUBBLE WRAP® APPRECIATION DAY. Jan 26. A day to celebrate the joy that Bubble Wrap® brings to our lives. A day to learn the history and snapping etiquette and to gain a new appreciation of the country's favorite shipping material (invented in 1960). Also, a day to snap and share Bubble Wrap® with coworkers, classmates and loved ones. Annually, the last Monday in January. For info: Sealed Air Corp, 301 Mayhill St, Saddlebrook, NJ 07663. Phone: (201) 712-7000. Fax: (201) 712-7019. Web: www.sealedair.com. Also for info: High Octane, Spirit 95 Radio WVNI, PO Box 1628, Bloomington, IN 47402. Phone: (812) 335-9500. Fax: (812) 335-8880. E-mail: spirit95@spirit95fm.com. Web: www.SPIRIT95FM.com.

CHINESE NEW YEAR. Jan 26. Traditional Chinese Lunar Year 4707 begins at sunset on the day of the second New Moon following the winter solstice. Outside China, the date of the New Year may differ by a day. The New Year can begin anytime from Jan 21 through Feb 21. Begins the Year of the Ox. Generally celebrated until the Lantern Festival 15 days later, but merchants usually reopen their stores and places of business on the fifth day of the first lunar month. This holiday is celebrated as Tet in Vietnam. See also: "China: Lantern Festival" (Feb 9).

COLEMAN, BESSIE: BIRTH ANNIVERSARY. Jan 26, 1893. Born at Atlanta, TX, Bessie Coleman would not take no for an answer, especially where it concerned her dreams of flying. Because of her race and gender, she was denied admission to aviation school programs in the US. She therefore worked as a manicurist earning her way to Paris. There she received an international pilot's license from the Fédération Aéronautique Internationale in 1921. Upon return, "Queen Bess" took part in numerous acrobatic air exhibitions where her stunt flying and "figure eights" won her many admirers. She avidly encouraged others to follow in her footsteps. Coleman, however, perished in a plane crash during a practice session, at Jacksonville, FL, Apr 30, 1926.

DENTAL DRILL PATENT: ANNIVERSARY. Jan 26, 1875. George F. Green, of Kalamazoo, MI, patented the electric dental drill.

DOMINICAN REPUBLIC: NATIONAL HOLIDAY. Jan 26. An official public holiday celebrates the birth anniversary of Juan Pablo Duarte, one of the fathers of the republic.

"THE DUKES OF HAZZARD" TV PREMIERE: 30th ANNIVERSARY. Jan 26, 1979. This comedy/action show ran for seven seasons and featured car chases. Brothers Bo Duke (John Schneider) and Luke Duke (Tom Wopat) were the good guys, fighting crooked law enforcement in their rural southern community. Other characters included Daisy Duke (Catherine Bach), Uncle Jesse Duke (Denver Pyle), Sheriff Roscoe P. Coltrane (James Best), Deputy Enos Strate (Sonny Shroyer) and Boss Hogg (Sorrell Booke).

FRANKLIN PREFERS TURKEY: 225th ANNIVERSARY. Jan 26, 1784. In a letter to his daughter, Benjamin Franklin expressed his unhappiness over the choice of the eagle as the symbol of America. He preferred the turkey.

GRANT, JULIA DENT: BIRTH ANNIVERSARY. Jan 26, 1826. Wife of Ulysses Simpson Grant, 18th president of the US. Born at St. Louis, MO; died at Washington, DC, Dec 14, 1902.

HITLER YOUTH DEPLOYED: ANNIVERSARY. Jan 26, 1943. Due to the need for more men at the front, the Nazis began manning antiaircraft batteries within Germany with members of the Hitler Youth who were aged 15 and up. This was 10 days after the British had begun the heavy bombing of Berlin and other German cities. See also: "British Air Raid on Berlin: Anniversary" (Jan 16).

INDIA: REPUBLIC DAY. Jan 26. National holiday. Anniversary of Proclamation of the Republic, Basant Panchmi. In 1929, Indian National Congress resolved to work for establishment of a sovereign republic, a goal that was realized Jan 26, 1950, when India became a democratic republic and its constitution went into effect.

INDIAN EARTHQUAKE: ANNIVERSARY. Jan 26, 2001. An earthquake that struck the state of Gujarat in India left more than 15,000 dead. The quake was estimated to be 7.7 on the Richter scale. India's largest port at Kandla suffered severe damage.

LOTUS 1-2-3 RELEASED: ANNIVERSARY. Jan 26, 1983. This spreadsheet software drove demand for the IBM PC, just as the introduction of VisiCalc had for the Apple II in 1979.

MacARTHUR, DOUGLAS: BIRTH ANNIVERSARY. Jan 26, 1880. US general and supreme commander of Allied forces in Southwest Pacific during WWII. Born at Little Rock, AR, he served as commander of the Rainbow Division's 84th Infantry Brigade in WWI, leading it in the St. Mihiel, Meuse-Argonne and Sedan offensives. Remembered for his "I shall return" prediction when forced out of the Philippines by the Japanese during WWII, a promise he fulfilled. Relieved of Far Eastern command by President Harry Truman on Apr 11, 1951, during the Korean War. MacArthur died at Washington, DC, Apr 5, 1964.

MICHIGAN: ADMISSION DAY: ANNIVERSARY. Jan 26. Became 26th state in 1837.

MOON PHASE: NEW MOON. Jan 26. Moon enters New Moon phase at 2:55 AM, EST.

NATIONAL TAKE BACK YOUR TIME WEEK. Jan 26–30. Good time-management habits are not enough. You also need clear values to direct how you spend your time. Prioritize and say "no" to unwanted activities and demands. Annually, the last full week (Monday through Friday) of January. For info: Jan Jasper. Phone: (212) 465-7472. E-mail: JanJasper52@hotmail.com. Web: www.janjasper.com.

***PHANTOM OF THE OPERA* BROADWAY PREMIERE: ANNIVERSARY.** Jan 26, 1988. This multiple award-winning musical, based on the classic Gaston Leroux novel about the tortured soul haunting the Paris Opera House, premiered in London on Oct 9, 1986. Its music and lyrics are by Andrew Lloyd Webber and Charles Hart, with book by Lloyd Webber and Richard Stilgoe. It premiered on Broadway in 1988 and in January 2006 became the longest-running show in Broadway history. On Apr 4, 2007, it became the first Broadway show to reach 8,000 performances.

ROCKY MOUNTAIN NATIONAL PARK ESTABLISHED: ANNIVERSARY. Jan 26, 1915. Under President Woodrow Wilson, the area covering more than 1,000 square miles in Colorado became a national park.

SOLAR ECLIPSE. Jan 26. Annular eclipse of the sun. Visible in southern Africa, Antarctica, southeast Asia and Australia.

TOAD HOLLOW DAY OF ENCOURAGEMENT. Jan 26. A day to give and receive a word of encouragement. For info: Ralph Morrison, Director, Toad Hollow, PO Box 2132, Garden City, MI 48135. Phone: (800) 574-8623.

UNITED ARAB EMIRATES: DUBAI DESERT (GOLF) CLASSIC. Jan 26–Feb 1. Majlis Course, Emirates Golf Club, Dubai. A key event on the PGA European Tour calendar, the Dubai Desert Classic will once again attract the leading European Tour players as well as invited world stars. For info: UAE Golf Assn, PO Box 31410, Dubai, UAE. Phone: (971) 4-295-6440. Fax: (971) 4-295-6026. E-mail: Adrian@dubaidesertclassic.com. Web: www.dubaidesertclassic.com.

VAN HEUSEN, JIMMY: BIRTH ANNIVERSARY. Jan 26, 1913. Jimmy Van Heusen was born Edward Chester Babcock at Syracuse, NY. He was a composer of many popular songs with his lyricist partners Johnny Burke and Sammy Cahn. One of his 76 songs that Frank Sinatra recorded was "My Kind of Town." Van Heusen won four Academy Awards for songs in movies such as *Going My Way* (1944). He was inducted into the Songwriters Hall of Fame when it was founded in 1971. Van Heusen died Feb 7, 1990, at Rancho Mirage, CA.

Birthdays Today

Anita Baker, 51, singer, born Toledo, OH, Jan 26, 1958.

Father George Harold Clements, 77, Roman Catholic priest, civil rights leader, born Chicago, IL, Jan 26, 1932.

Angela Davis, 65, political activist, born Birmingham, AL, Jan 26, 1944.

Ellen DeGeneres, 51, comedienne, actress ("Ellen"), talk-show host ("The Ellen DeGeneres Show"), born New Orleans, LA, Jan 26, 1958.

Philip Jose Farmer, 91, science fiction writer, born Peoria, IL, Jan 26, 1918.

Jules Feiffer, 80, cartoonist, writer, born New York, NY, Jan 26, 1929.

Scott Glenn, 67, actor (*The Right Stuff, Silverado*), born Pittsburgh, PA, Jan 26, 1942.

Wayne Gretzky, 48, Hall of Fame hockey player, born Brantford, ON, Canada, Jan 26, 1961.

Paul Newman, 84, actor (Oscar for *The Color of Money; Cat on a Hot Tin Roof, Butch Cassidy and the Sundance Kid*), director (*The Glass Menagerie*), born Cleveland, OH, Jan 26, 1925.

Andrew Ridgeley, 46, singer, musician (Wham!), born Bushey, England, Jan 26, 1963.

David Strathairn, 59, actor (*Good Night, and Good Luck*; *LA Confidential*), born San Francisco, CA, Jan 26, 1950.

Robert George (Bob) Uecker, 74, sportscaster, former baseball player, actor ("Mr Belvedere"), born Milwaukee, WI, Jan 26, 1935.

Eddie Van Halen, 54, guitarist, born Nijmegen, Netherlands, Jan 26, 1955.

January 27 — Tuesday

DAY 27 | **338 REMAINING**

***APOLLO I*: SPACECRAFT FIRE: ANNIVERSARY.** Jan 27, 1967. Three American astronauts, Virgil I. Grissom, Edward H. White and Roger B. Chaffee, died when fire suddenly broke out at 6:31 PM, EST in *Apollo I* during a launching simulation test, as it stood on the ground at Cape Kennedy, FL. First launching in the Apollo program had been scheduled for Feb 27, 1967.

AUSCHWITZ LIBERATED: ANNIVERSARY. Jan 27, 1945. The Soviet army liberated about 6,000 prisoners of the Nazi concentration camp Auschwitz. It is estimated that 1.5 million inmates were killed at Auschwitz between 1941 and liberation—95 percent of them were Jewish.

DODGSON, CHARLES LUTWIDGE (LEWIS CARROLL): BIRTH ANNIVERSARY. Jan 27, 1832. English mathematician and author, better known by his pseudonym, Lewis Carroll, creator of *Alice's Adventures in Wonderland*, was born at Cheshire, England. *Alice* was written for Alice Liddell, daughter of a friend, and first published in 1886. *Through the Looking-Glass*, a sequel, and *The Hunting of the Snark* followed. Dodgson's books for children proved equally enjoyable to adults, and they overshadowed his serious works on mathematics. Dodgson died at Guildford, Surrey, England, Jan 14, 1898.

GERMANY: DAY OF REMEMBRANCE FOR VICTIMS OF NAZISM. Jan 27. Since 1996 commemorated on this day, the date in 1945 that Soviet soldiers liberated the Auschwitz concentration camp in Poland.

GOMPERS, SAMUEL: BIRTH ANNIVERSARY. Jan 27, 1850. Labor leader, first president of the American Federation of Labor, born at London, England. Died Dec 13, 1924, at San Antonio, TX.

KERN, JEROME: BIRTH ANNIVERSARY. Jan 27, 1885. American composer born at New York City; died there Nov 11, 1945. In addition to scores for stage and screen, Kern wrote many memorable songs, including "Ol' Man River," "Smoke Gets in Your Eyes," "I Won't Dance," "The Way You Look Tonight," "All the Things You Are" and "The Last Time I Saw Paris."

"LAVERNE AND SHIRLEY" TV PREMIERE: ANNIVERSARY. Jan 27, 1976. This ABC sitcom was a spin-off of the popular TV show "Happy Days" that was also set during the late '50s in Milwaukee, WI. Penny Marshall (sister of series cocreator Garry Marshall) starred as Laverne DeFazio with Cindy Williams as Shirley Feeney. The two friends worked at a brewery and shared a basement apartment. Also featured in the cast were Phil Foster as Laverne's father, Frank DeFazio; David L. Lander as Andrew "Squiggy" Squiggman; Michael McKean as Lenny Kosnowski; Betty Garrett as landlady Edna Babish and Eddie Mekka as Carmine Ragusa, Shirley's sometime boyfriend.

LENINGRAD LIBERATED: 65th ANNIVERSARY. Jan 27, 1944. The seige of Leningrad began with German bombing of the city on Sept 4, 1941. The bombing continued for 430 hours. The suffering of the people of Leningrad during the 880-day seige was one of the greatest tragedies of WWII. More than half the population of Russia's second-largest city died during the winter of 1942. The seige finally ended on Jan 27, 1944.

MOZART, WOLFGANG AMADEUS: BIRTH ANNIVERSARY. Jan 27, 1756. One of the world's greatest music makers. Born at Salzburg, Austria, into a gifted musical family, Mozart began performing at age three and composing at age five. Some of the best known of his more than 600 compositions include the operas *Marriage of Figaro*, *Don Giovanni*, *Cosi fan tutte* and *The Magic Flute*; his unfinished Requiem Mass; his C major symphony known as the "Jupiter" and many of his quartets and piano concertos. He died at Vienna, Dec 5, 1791.

NATIONAL SPEAK UP AND SUCCEED DAY. Jan 27. Fewer than 3 percent of Americans have no fear of public speaking or have never felt shy. Yet, the top-rated skill for success is effective communication skills. On National Speak Up and Succeed Day, face your fear of public speaking and speak out anyway—speak up at a committee meeting, voice your opinion to a group of colleagues, give the toast at a special event, volunteer to chair a program, join Toastmasters. You have nothing to lose and everything to gain. Annually, the fourth Tuesday in January. For info: Mary-Ellen Drummond, Polished Presentations Intl, PO Box 2104, Rancho Santa Fe, CA 92067. Phone: (858) 756-4248. Fax: (858) 756-9621. E-mail: medrummond@aol.com. Web: www.medrummond.com.

RICKOVER, HYMAN GEORGE: BIRTH ANNIVERSARY. Jan 27, 1900. American naval officer, known as the "Father of the Nuclear Navy." Admiral Rickover directed development of nuclear reactor–powered submarines, the first of which was the *Nautilus*, launched in 1954. Rickover was noted for his blunt remarks: "To increase the efficiency of the Department of Defense," he said, "you must first abolish it." The four-star admiral retired (unwillingly) at the age of 81, after 63 years in the Navy. Born in Russia, Rickover died at Arlington, VA, July 9, 1986, and was buried at Arlington National Cemetery.

SCOTLAND: UP HELLY AA. Jan 27. Lerwick, Shetland Islands. Norse galley burned in impressive ceremony symbolizing sacrifice to the sun. Old Viking custom. A festival marking the end of Yule. Annually, the last Tuesday in January. For info: Tourist Information Centre, Market Cross, Lerwick, Shetland, Scotland ZE1 0LU. Phone: (44) (8701) 999-440. Fax: (44) (1595) 695-807. E-mail: info@visitshetland.com. Web: www.visitshetland.com.

January 2009

S	M	T	W	T	F	S
				1	2	3
4	5	6	7	8	9	10
11	12	13	14	15	16	17
18	19	20	21	22	23	24
25	26	27	28	29	30	31

SIOUX EMPIRE FARM SHOW. Jan 27–31. Sioux Falls, SD. Winter farm and livestock show featuring all classes of livestock, commercial exhibits and a horse pull. Est attendance: 30,000. For info: Sioux Empire Farm Show, Sioux Falls Area Chamber of Commerce, 200 N Phillips Ave, #102, Sioux Falls, SD 57104. Phone: (605) 373-2016. Fax: (605) 336-6499. E-mail: cchristensen@siouxfalls.com. Web: www.siouxempirefarmshow.org.

THOMAS CRAPPER DAY: DEATH ANNIVERSARY. Jan 27, 1910. Born at Thorne, Yorkshire, England, in 1836 (exact date unknown), Crapper is often described as the prime developer of the flush toilet mechanism as it is known today. The flush toilet had been in use for more than 100 years; Crapper perfected it. Founder, London, 1861, of Thomas Crapper & Co, later patentees and manufacturers of sanitary appliances.

UNITED KINGDOM: HOLOCAUST MEMORIAL DAY. Jan 27. Commemorates the day in 1945 that Soviet troops liberated the Auschwitz concentration camp. For more info: www.holocaustmemorialday.gov.uk.

VIETNAM PEACE AGREEMENT SIGNED: ANNIVERSARY. Jan 27, 1973. US and North Vietnam, along with South Vietnam and the Viet Cong, signed an "Agreement on ending the war and restoring peace in Vietnam." Signed at Paris, France, to take effect Jan 28 at 8 AM Saigon time, thus ending the US combat role in a war that had involved American personnel stationed in Vietnam since defeated French forces had departed under terms of the Geneva Accords in 1954. This was the longest war in US history, with more than one million combat deaths (US: 47,366). However, within weeks of the departure of American troops the war between North and South Vietnam resumed. For the Vietnamese, the war didn't end until Apr 30, 1975, when Saigon fell to Communist forces.

Birthdays Today

Mikhail Baryshnikov, 61, ballet dancer, actor (*White Nights, The Turning Point*), born Riga, Latvia (at the time part of the USSR), Jan 27, 1948.

(Anthony) Cris Collinsworth, 50, sportscaster, former football player, born Dayton, OH, Jan 27, 1959.

Mairead Corrigan, 65, pacifist, Nobel Peace Prize winner, born Belfast, Northern Ireland, Jan 27, 1944.

James Cromwell, 67, actor (*The People vs. Larry Flynt, Babe, LA Confidential*), born Los Angeles, CA, Jan 27, 1942.

Alan Cumming, 44, actor (Tony for *Cabaret*; *Spy Kids, The Anniversary Party, Emma*), director, born Perthshire, Scotland, Jan 27, 1965.

Bridget Fonda, 45, actress (*Single White Female, Lake Placid*), born Los Angeles, CA, Jan 27, 1964.

Julie Foudy, 38, former soccer player, born San Diego, CA, Jan 27, 1971.

John G. Roberts, Jr, 54, Chief Justice of the US Supreme Court, born Buffalo, NY, Jan 27, 1955.

Mimi Rogers, 53, actress (*The Doors, The Rapture*), born Coral Gables, FL, Jan 27, 1956.

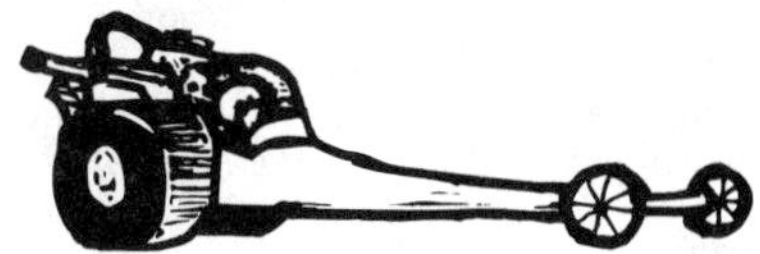

January 28 — Wednesday

DAY 28 337 REMAINING

"BARNABY JONES" TV PREMIERE: ANNIVERSARY. Jan 28, 1973. CBS drama about a mild-mannered, milk-drinking private eye who comes out of retirement following his son's murder. Cast included Buddy Ebsen as Barnaby Jones; Lee Meriwether as Barnaby's widowed daughter-in-law, Betty Jones; John Carter as Lieutenant Biddle; and Mark Shera as Jedediah Jones. The last episode aired in 1980.

***CHALLENGER* SPACE SHUTTLE EXPLOSION: ANNIVERSARY.** Jan 28, 1986. At 11:39 AM, EST, the space shuttle *Challenger STS-51L* exploded, 74 seconds into its flight and about 10 miles above the earth. Hundreds of millions around the world watched television replays of the horrifying event that killed seven people. The billion-dollar craft was destroyed, all shuttle flights suspended and much of the US manned space flight program temporarily halted. Killed were teacher Christa McAuliffe (who was to have been the first ordinary citizen in space) and six crew members: Francis R. Scobee, Michael J. Smith, Judith A. Resnik, Ellison S. Onizuka, Ronald E. McNair and Gregory B. Jarvis.

"FANTASY ISLAND" TV PREMIERE: ANNIVERSARY. Jan 28, 1978. Ricardo Montalban starred as the prescient guide, Mr Roarke, with Hervé Villechaize as his faithful assistant, Tattoo. Each week, guest stars played characters anxious to live out their fantasies in camp splendor. The show's run of 130 episodes, ending on Aug 18, 1984, was produced by Aaron Spelling and Leonard Goldberg. Best remembered is Tattoo's opening line each week: "De plane, de plane!"

GREAT SEAL OF THE US: AUTHORIZATION ANNIVERSARY. Jan 28, 1782. Congress resolved that the secretary of the Congress should "keep the public seal, and cause the same to be affixed to every act, ordinance or paper, which Congress shall direct . . . ." Although the Great Seal did not exist yet, the Congress recognized the need for it. See also: "Great Seal of the United States Proposed: Anniversary" (July 4 and Sept 16).

ISRAELI SIEGE OF SUEZ CITY ENDS: 35th ANNIVERSARY. Jan 28, 1974. The Israeli army lifted its siege of Suez City, freed encircled Egyptian troops and turned over 300,000 square miles of Egyptian territory to the UN, thereby ending the occupation that started during the October 1973 war.

MacKENZIE, ALEXANDER: BIRTH ANNIVERSARY. Jan 28, 1822. The man who became the first Liberal prime minister of Canada (1873–78) was born at Logierait, Perth, Scotland. He died at Toronto, Apr 17, 1892.

MARTÍ, JOSÉ JULIAN: BIRTH ANNIVERSARY. Jan 28, 1853. Cuban author and political activist, born at Havana, Cuba, Martí was exiled to Spain, where he studied law before coming to the US in 1890. He was killed in battle at Dos Rios, Cuba, May 19, 1895.

PICCARD, AUGUSTE: 125th BIRTH ANNIVERSARY. Jan 28, 1884. Scientist and explorer, born at Basel, Switzerland. Made a record-setting balloon ascent into the stratosphere on May 27, 1931, and also ocean-depth descents and explorations. Twin brother of Jean Felix Piccard. Died at Lausanne, Switzerland, Mar 24, 1962. See also: "Piccard, Jean Felix: Birth Anniversary" (Jan 28).

PICCARD, JEAN FELIX: 125th BIRTH ANNIVERSARY. Jan 28, 1884. Scientist, engineer, explorer, born at Basel, Switzerland. Noted for cosmic-ray research and record-setting balloon ascensions into the stratosphere. Reached 57,579 feet in a sealed gondola piloted by his wife, Jeannette, in 1934. Twin brother of Auguste Piccard. Died at Minneapolis, MN, Jan 28, 1963. See also: "Piccard, Jeannette Ridlon: Birth Anniversary" (Jan 5) and "Piccard, Auguste: Birth Anniversary" (Jan 28).

STANLEY, HENRY MORTON: BIRTH ANNIVERSARY. Jan 28, 1841. Explorer, born at Denbigh, Wales, and leader of the expedition to find the missing missionary-explorer David Livingstone, who had not been heard from for more than two years. Stanley began the search in Africa on Mar 21, 1871, finally finding the explorer at Ujiji, near Lake Tanganyika, on Nov 10, 1871, whereupon he asked the now famous question: "Dr. Livingstone, I presume?" Stanley died at London, England, May 10, 1904.

Birthdays Today

Alan Alda, 73, actor (*Paper Lion, The Four Seasons,* "M*A*S*H"), director, born Alphonso D'Abruzzo at New York, NY, Jan 28, 1936.

John Beck, 66, actor ("Dallas," *Sleeper, The Big Bus*), born Chicago, IL, Jan 28, 1943.

Susan Howard, 66, actress ("Dallas"), born Jeri Lynn Mooney, Marshall, TX, Jan 28, 1943.

Harley Jane Kozak, 52, actress (*When Harry Met Sally . . . , Parenthood*), born Wilkes-Barre, PA, Jan 28, 1957.

Sarah McLachlan, 41, singer, born Halifax, NS, Canada, Jan 28, 1968.

Kathryn Morris, 40, actress (*Mindhunters,* "Cold Case"), born Cincinnati, OH, Jan 28, 1969.

Claes Oldenburg, 80, artist, sculptor, born Stockholm, Sweden, Jan 28, 1929.

Nicolas Sarkozy, 54, President of France, born at Paris, France, Jan 28, 1955.

Elijah Wood, 28, actor (the *Lord of the Rings* trilogy, *The Ice Storm*), born Cedar Rapids, IA, Jan 28, 1981.

January 29 — Thursday

DAY 29 336 REMAINING

CHEKHOV, ANTON PAVLOVICH: BIRTH ANNIVERSARY. Jan 29, 1860. Russian playwright and short story writer, especially remembered for *The Sea Gull, The Three Sisters* and *The Cherry Orchard.* Born at Taganrog, Russia; died July 15, 1904, at the Black Forest spa at Badenweiler, Germany.

FIELDS, W.C.: BIRTH ANNIVERSARY. Jan 29, 1880. Stage and motion picture actor (*My Little Chickadee*), screenwriter and expert juggler. Born Claude William Dukenfield at Philadelphia, PA; died Dec 25, 1946, at Pasadena, CA. He wrote his own epitaph: "On the whole, I'd rather be in Philadelphia."

FREETHINKER'S DAY. Jan 29. Annual celebration of the birth of Thomas Paine. For info: Truth Seeker Co, 239 S Juniper St, Escondido, CA 92025. Phone: (760) 489-5211. Fax: (760) 489-5311. E-mail: tseditor@aol.com. Web: www.truthseeker.com.

GROUNDHOG DAYS. Jan 29–Feb 2. Historic Woodstock Square, Woodstock, IL. Thanks to Bill Murray and the *Groundhog Day* movie, Woodstock celebrates with groundhogs on parade, dinner dance, walking tour of filming sites, breakfast and Woodstock Willie's prognostication (Feb 2). Est attendance: 500. For info: Woodstock Chamber of Commerce, 136 Cass St, Woodstock, IL 60098. Phone: (815) 338-2436. Fax: (815) 338-2927. E-mail: chamber@woodstockilchamber.com. Web: www.woodstockilchamber.com.

KANSAS: ADMISSION DAY: ANNIVERSARY. Jan 29. Became the 34th state in 1861.

McKINLEY, WILLIAM: BIRTH ANNIVERSARY. Jan 29, 1843. 25th president of the US (1897–1901), born at Niles, OH. Died in office, at Buffalo, NY, Sept 14, 1901, as the result of a gunshot wound by an anarchist assassin Sept 6, 1901, while he was attending the Pan-American Exposition.

MILITARY BAN ON HOMOSEXUALS EASED: ANNIVERSARY. Jan 29, 1993. An interim policy on ending the ban on homosexuals in the US military was announced by President William Clinton. The policy ended the questioning of military recruits regarding their sexual orientation but allowed removal of openly homosexual members from active service. President Clinton's announced policy of "don't ask, don't tell, don't pursue" was intended to allow homosexuals to serve in the armed forces as long as they were discreet.

MORMON BATTALION ARRIVAL IN CALIFORNIA: ANNIVERSARY. Jan 29, 1847. The 500 men of the US Mormon Battalion, along with 50 women and children, arrived at San Diego, CA, on this date, having marched 2,000 miles—the longest march in modern military history—since leaving Council Bluffs, IA, on July 16, 1846, to fight in the war against Mexico. In the course of their trek they established the first wagon route from Santa Fe to southern California. Their historic arrival is commemorated each year with a military parade in San Diego's Old Town.

PAINE, THOMAS: BIRTH ANNIVERSARY. Jan 29, 1737. American Revolutionary leader, a corset maker by trade, author of *Common Sense*, *The Age of Reason* and many other influential works, was born at Thetford, England. "These are the times that try men's souls" are the well-known opening words of his inspirational tract *The Crisis*. Paine died at New York, NY, June 8, 1809, but 10 years later his remains were moved to England by William Cobbett for reburial there. Reburial was refused, however, and the location of Paine's bones, said to have been distributed, is unknown.

PROVIDENCE BOAT SHOW. Jan 29–Feb 1. Providence, RI. The boating season starts at this show, featuring power boats, small sailing craft, kayaks, inflatables and more. Seminars, children's section and a special area with a focus on fishing. For info: Nancy Piffard, Providence Boat Show, PO Box 698, Newport, RI 02842. Phone: (401) 846-1115. Fax: (401) 848-0455. E-mail: neginfo@newportexhibition.com. Web: www.providenceboatshow.com.

"THE RAVEN" PUBLISHED: ANNIVERSARY. Jan 29, 1845. One of the most famous poems in American literature was published on this date in New York's *Evening Mirror* newspaper. The author was anonymous, but the poem was such a sensation (it would be reprinted at least 16 times in various periodicals and books that year) that soon the author was revealed as literary critic and author Edgar Allan Poe. Despite the celebrity status Poe enjoyed as a result of "The Raven," it did not relieve his poverty: Poe received $15 for the poem. The classic lines "Once upon a midnight dreary . . ." and "Quoth the Raven, 'Nevermore'" resound in countless anthologies and dramatic readings as well as in parodies.

THE SEEING EYE ESTABLISHED: 80th ANNIVERSARY. Jan 29, 1929. The Seeing Eye, North America's first guide dog school, was incorporated on this date at Nashville, TN. The first class took place in February and included Buddy, the "seeing eye" dog brought from Europe. The Seeing Eye was the first program in the US that enabled people with disabilities to be full participants in society. Its mission is to enhance the independence, self-confidence and dignity of people who are blind through the use of Seeing Eye dogs. Since its founding, The Seeing Eye has matched more than 13,000 specially bred dogs with blind people from the US and Canada. In 1931 the school moved to New Jersey, where it continues to breed, raise and train Seeing Eye dogs and instruct blind and visually impaired people in the use and care of their dogs. For info: Teresa Davenport, Dir of Communications, The Seeing Eye, PO Box 375, Morristown, NJ 07963-0375. Phone: (973) 539-4425. Fax: (973) 539-0922. E-mail: info@seeingeye.org. Web: www.seeingeye.org.

SWEDENBORG, EMANUEL: BIRTH ANNIVERSARY. Jan 29, 1688. (Old Style date.) Born at Stockholm, Sweden, Swedenborg is remembered as a scientist, inventor, writer and religious leader. Swedenborg made plans for machine guns, submarines and airplanes and published Sweden's first scientific journal. His study of human anatomy and his search for the soul led him to begin thinking about religion. His writings interpreting the scriptures formed the basis of the Church of the New Jerusalem, which was established by his devotees soon after his death. He died at London, England, Mar 29, 1772.

SWITZERLAND: CARTIER POLO WORLD CUP ON SNOW. Jan 29–Feb 1. St. Moritz. 25th annual. Spectacular winter polo on the frozen lake of St. Moritz 2,000 meters above sea level. Est attendance: 20,000. For info: St. Moritz Polo AG, Via Maistra 24, CH-7500 St. Moritz, Switzerland. Phone: (41) (81) 839-92-92. Fax: (41) (81) 839-92-00. E-mail: info@polostmoritz.com. Web: www.polostmoritz.com.

THOMAS PAINE DAY. Jan 29. The words of Thomas Paine inspired many to strive for political, economic and social advancement. He was among the first to call for an end to slavery and the establishment of human rights around the world. In appreciation, the Freethought Society of Greater Philadelphia celebrates the birthday of Thomas Paine on Jan 29, a Thomas Paine Day proclamation on June 8 and other Paine-themed events during the year. For info: Freethought Society of Greater Philadelphia, PO Box 5054, West Chester, PA 19380. Phone: (610) 430-7719. E-mail: fsgp@freethought.org. Web: www.fsgp.org/tpf.htm. Or Institute for Humanist Studies, 48 Howard St, Albany, NY 12207. E-mail: Mcherry@HumanistStudies.org.

Birthdays Today

John Forsythe, 91, actor ("Bachelor Father," Charlie's voice on "Charlie's Angels," "Dynasty"), born John Freund at Penn's Grove, NJ, Jan 29, 1918.

Sara Gilbert, 34, actress ("The Big Bang Theory," "Roseanne"), born Santa Monica, CA, Jan 29, 1975.

Heather Graham, 39, actress (*Lost in Space, Boogie Nights*), born Milwaukee, WI, Jan 29, 1970.

Germaine Greer, 70, author (*Daddy We Hardly Knew You, The Female Eunuch*), born Melbourne, Australia, Jan 29, 1939.

Dominik Hasek, 44, former hockey player, born Pardubice, Czechoslovakia, Jan 29, 1965.

Ann Jillian, 58, actress ("It's a Living," *The Ann Jillian Story*), born Cambridge, MA, Jan 29, 1951.

Andrew Keegan, 30, actor (*Independence Day*), born Los Angeles, CA, Jan 29, 1979.

Gregory Efthimios (Greg) Louganis, 49, actor, Olympic gold medal diver, born San Diego, CA, Jan 29, 1960.

Bobbie Phillips, 41, actress ("Murder One," *Red Shoe Diaries*), born Charleston, SC, Jan 29, 1968 (some sources say 1972).

Katharine Ross, 66, actress (*The Graduate*), born Los Angeles, CA, Jan 29, 1943.

Tom Selleck, 64, actor ("Magnum, PI," *Three Men and a Baby, Mr Baseball*), born Detroit, MI, Jan 29, 1945.

Nick Turturro, 47, actor ("NYPD Blue"), born Queens, NY, Jan 29, 1962.

Oprah Winfrey, 55, TV talk-show host ("The Oprah Winfrey Show"), actress (*The Color Purple*), producer (owner of Harpo Studios), born Kosciusko, MS, Jan 29, 1954.

January 2009

S	M	T	W	T	F	S
				1	2	3
4	5	6	7	8	9	10
11	12	13	14	15	16	17
18	19	20	21	22	23	24
25	26	27	28	29	30	31

January 30 — Friday

DAY 30 335 REMAINING

AMERICANA INDIAN AND WESTERN ART SHOW AND SALE. Jan 30–Feb 1. Yuma, AZ. Indian and Western paintings, rugs and jewelry. Est attendance: 1,800. For info: Yuma Civic Center, 1440 Desert Hills Dr, Yuma, AZ 85365. Phone: (928) 373-5040. Fax: (928) 344-9121. E-mail: ycc@yumaaz.gov. Web: www.yumaaz.gov.

BEATLES LAST CONCERT: 40th ANNIVERSARY. Jan 30, 1969. On this day the Beatles performed together in public for the last time. The show took place on the roof of their Apple Studios in London, England, but it was interrupted by police after they received complaints from the neighbors about the noise.

BLACK HILLS STOCK SHOW AND RODEO. Jan 30–Feb 8. Rapid City, SD. Events include PRCA rodeos, ranch rodeo, timed sheepdog trials, cattle cutting, ranch horse competition, livestock shows and sales, buffalo show and sale, team penning, bucking horse and bull sale, stockman banquet and ball and commercial exhibits. Est attendance: 250,000. For info: Black Hills Stock Show & Rodeo, 800 San Francisco, Rapid City, SD 57701. Phone: (605) 355-3861.

BLOODY SUNDAY: ANNIVERSARY. Jan 30, 1972. In Londonderry, Northern Ireland, 13 Roman Catholics were shot dead by British troops during a banned civil rights march. During 1972, the first year of British direct rule, 467 people were killed in the fighting.

CHARLES I: EXECUTION ANNIVERSARY. Jan 30, 1649. English king beheaded by order of Parliament under Oliver Cromwell on this date; considered a martyr by some.

CHENEY, RICHARD (DICK): BIRTHDAY. Jan 30, 1941. 46th vice president of the US, born at Lincoln, NE.

EAGLES ET CETERA FESTIVAL. Jan 30–Feb 1. Bismarck, AR. See bald eagles in the wild and learn about and observe birds of prey. Est attendance: 500. For info: Park Naturalist, DeGray Lake Resort State Park, 2027 State Park Entrance Rd, Bismarck, AR 71929-8194. Phone: (800) 737-8355. Fax: (501) 865-4436. E-mail: degray@arkansas.com. Web: www.degray.com.

FIRST BRAWL IN THE US HOUSE OF REPRESENTATIVES: ANNIVERSARY. Jan 30, 1798. The first brawl to break out on the floor of the US House of Representatives occurred at Philadelphia, PA. The fight was precipitated by an argument between Matthew Lyon of Vermont and Roger Griswold of Connecticut. Lyon spat in Griswold's face. Although a resolution to expel Lyon was introduced, the measure failed and Lyon maintained his seat.

FUN AT WORK DAY. Jan 30. Inject some laughter into your workplace by planning a fun and relaxing activity. Do something to encourage enthusiasm and openness and to help build rapport and release tension. When we enjoy our work, we are more productive and creative. Annually, the last Friday of January. For info: Diane C. Decker. Phone: (847) 394-0994. E-mail: dcdecker@msn.com. Web: www.qualitytransitions.com.

GANDHI ASSASSINATED: ANNIVERSARY. Jan 30, 1948. Indian religious and political leader, assassinated at New Delhi, India. The assassin was a Hindu extremist, Ram Naturam. See also: "Gandhi, Mohandas Karamchand (Mahatma): Birth Anniversary" (Oct 2).

GATOR KNAP-IN. Jan 30–Feb 1. Stephen Foster Folk Culture Center State Park, White Springs, FL. 2nd annual. An education experience geared at bringing those interested in prehistoric technologies. Demonstrations and classes in flint knapping, cordage and carving of stone, shell, bone and wood will be held. For info: Mitzi Nelson, Florida Park Service, PO Drawer G, White Springs, FL 32096. Phone: (386) 397-7005. Fax: (386) 397-4262. E-mail: margaret.a.nelson@dep.state.fl.us. Web: www.floridastateparks.org/stephenfoster.

INANE ANSWERING MESSAGE DAY. Jan 30. Annually, the day set aside to change, shorten, replace or delete those ridiculous and/or annoying answering machine messages that waste the time of anyone who must listen to them. (©2006 by WH.) For info: Thomas & Ruth Roy, Wellcat Holidays, 2418 Long Ln, Lebanon, PA 17046. Phone: (717) 279-0184. E-mail: info@wellcat.com. Web: www.wellcat.com.

JORDAN: KING'S BIRTHDAY. Jan 30. National holiday. Honors King Abdullah II, son of the late King Hussein, who was born Jan 30, 1962, and assumed the throne June 9, 1999.

MARYLAND ADOPTS ARTICLES OF CONFEDERATION: ANNIVERSARY. Jan 30, 1781. Maryland became the last of the 13 original states to adopt the Articles of Confederation.

OSCEOLA: DEATH ANNIVERSARY. Jan 30, 1838. Osceola was a leader during the Second Seminole War (1835–42). During the first two years of the war, he led the fight against removal of the Florida Seminoles to Indian territory. He was captured under a flag of truce in 1837 and imprisoned at Fort Marion in St. Augustine, FL. He was moved to Fort Moultrie at Charleston Harbor, SC, where he died. He was born near present-day Tuskegee, AL, circa 1804.

RAF BOMBS HITLER CELEBRATION: ANNIVERSARY. Jan 30, 1943. British Royal Air Force Mosquito bombers ran a daylight raid on Berlin timed to coincide with a speech being given by Joseph Goebbels in honor of Hitler's 10th year in power.

ROOSEVELT, FRANKLIN DELANO: BIRTH ANNIVERSARY. Jan 30, 1882. 32nd president of the US (Mar 4, 1933–Apr 12, 1945). The only president to serve more than two terms, FDR was elected four times. He supported the Allies in WWII before the US entered the struggle by supplying them with war materials through the Lend-Lease Act; he became deeply involved in broad decision making after the Japanese attack on Pearl Harbor Dec 7, 1941. Born at Hyde Park, NY, he died a few months into his fourth term at Warm Springs, GA, Apr 12, 1945.

SUGARLOAF CRAFTS FESTIVAL. Jan 30–Feb 1. Dulles Expo Center, Chantilly, VA. This show, now in its 11th year, features more than 350 nationally recognized craft designers and fine artists displaying and selling their original creations. Includes craft demonstrations, live music, specialty foods, hourly gift certificate drawings and more. Est attendance: 18,000. For info: Sugarloaf Mountain Works, 200 Orchard Ridge Dr, #215, Gaithersburg, MD 20878. Phone: (800) 210-9900. Fax: (301) 253-9620. Web: www.sugarloafcrafts.com.

TET OFFENSIVE BEGINS: ANNIVERSARY. Jan 30, 1968. After calling for a cease-fire during the Tet holiday celebrations, North Vietnam and the National Liberation Front launched a major offensive throughout South Vietnam on that holiday. Attacks erupted in 36 of the 44 provincial capitals and five of the six major cities. In addition, the Viet Cong attacked the US embassy in Saigon, Tan Son Nhut Air Base, the presidential palace and South Vietnamese general staff headquarters. Costing as many as 40,000 battlefield deaths, the offensive was a tactical defeat for the Viet Cong and North Vietnam. The South Vietnamese held their ground, and the US was able to airlift troops into the critical areas and quickly regain control. However, the offensive is credited as a strategic success in that it continued the demoralization of American public opinion. After Tet, American policy toward Vietnam shifted from winning the war to seeking an honorable way out.

THOMAS, ISAIAH: BIRTH ANNIVERSARY. Jan 30, 1749. American printer, editor, almanac publisher, historian and founder of the American Antiquarian Society. Born at Boston, MA; died Apr 4, 1831, at Worcester, MA.

TUCHMAN, BARBARA W.: BIRTH ANNIVERSARY. Jan 30, 1912. Historian and journalist Barbara Tuchman's most famous works were her Pulitzer Prize–winning books *The Guns of August* (1962) and *Stilwell and the American Experience in China, 1911–45* (1971). Tuchman was known for making history lively. Other well-known books included *The Proud Tower* (1966) and *The First Salute* (1988). Barbara Wertheim Tuchman was born at New York, NY, and died at Greenwich, CT, Feb 6, 1988.

WINTER GAMES OF IDAHO. Jan 30–Feb 28. Idaho Falls, Sun Valley, Boise, McCall, Donnelly, Wallace, Salmon and Kellogg, ID. Idaho's official winter sports competition—five weeks of competition in ice hockey, figure skating, alpine skiing, telemark skiing, snowboarding and cross-country skiing with 3,000 participants. For info: Winter Games of Idaho, PO Box 9046, Boise, ID 83707. Phone: (800) 442-3794. Fax: (208) 343-6725. Web: www.wintergamesofidaho.com.

Birthdays Today

John Baldacci, 54, Governor of Maine (D), born Bangor, ME, Jan 30, 1955.

Christian Bale, 35, actor (*3:10 to Yuma, The Prestige, Rescue Dawn, Batman Begins*), born Pembrokeshire, West Wales, Jan 30, 1974.

Brett Butler, 51, comedienne, actress ("Grace Under Fire"), born Montgomery, AL, Jan 30, 1958.

Richard (Dick) Cheney, 68, 46th vice president of the US, born Lincoln, NE, Jan 30, 1941.

Phil Collins, 58, musician, singer, songwriter, born Chiswick, England, Jan 30, 1951.

Peter Crouch, 28, soccer player, born Macclesfield, England, Jan 30, 1981.

Charles S. Dutton, 58, actor ("Roc," *Mississippi Masala, Menace II Society*), born Baltimore, MD, Jan 30, 1951.

Gene Hackman, 79, actor (Oscars for *The French Connection* and *Unforgiven*; *The Royal Tenenbaums*), born San Bernardino, CA, Jan 30, 1930.

Johnathan Lee Iverson, 33, circus ringmaster, born New York, NY, Jan 30, 1976.

Davey Johnson, 66, baseball manager and former player, born Orlando, FL, Jan 30, 1943.

Dorothy Malone, 84, actress ("Peyton Place"; Oscar for *Written on the Wind*), born Chicago, IL, Jan 30, 1925.

Vanessa Redgrave, 72, actress (*Mary, Queen of Scots; Julia*), born London, England, Jan 30, 1937.

Jalen Rose, 36, former basketball player, born Detroit, MI, Jan 30, 1973.

Boris Spassky, 72, former chess player, journalist, born Leningrad, USSR (now St. Petersburg, Russia), Jan 30, 1937.

Curtis Strange, 54, golfer, broadcaster, born Norfolk, VA, Jan 30, 1955.

Jody Watley, 50, singer, born Chicago, IL, Jan 30, 1959.

January 2009	S	M	T	W	T	F	S
					1	2	3
	4	5	6	7	8	9	10
	11	12	13	14	15	16	17
	18	19	20	21	22	23	24
	25	26	27	28	29	30	31

January 31 — Saturday

DAY 31 — 334 REMAINING

BROOKFIELD ICE HARVEST. Jan 31. Brookfield, VT. Demonstrations of ice harvesting using the original equipment near the Brookfield Floating Bridge, one of only two such bridges remaining in the US today. This 30th annual harvest will feature many special activities. Annually, the last Saturday in January. Est attendance: 1,000. For info: Al Wilder, PO Box 405, Brookfield, VT 05036. Phone: (802) 276-3959. Fax: (802) 276-3023.

FIRST SOCIAL SECURITY CHECK ISSUED: ANNIVERSARY. Jan 31, 1940. Ida May Fuller of Ludlow, VT, received the first monthly retirement check in the amount of $22.54. Ms Fuller had worked for three years under the Social Security program (which had been established by legislation in 1935). The accumulated taxes on her salary over those three years were $24.75. She lived to be 100 years old, collecting $22,888 in Social Security benefits. See also: "Social Security Act: Anniv" (Aug 14).

GOLDWYN, SAMUEL: 35th DEATH ANNIVERSARY. Jan 31, 1974. Motion picture producer and industry pioneer Goldwyn died at Los Angeles, CA. He was born Samuel Goldfish, at Warsaw, Poland, probably in July 1879 (although he always claimed Aug 27, 1882, as his birthday). Famous for his confusing outbursts, Goldwyn is claimed to have said such things as "Anybody who goes to see a psychiatrist ought to have his head examined."

GREATER SPRINGFIELD GARAGE SALE. Jan 31–Feb 1. Missouri Entertainment and Event Center, Springfield, MO. Indoor garage sale featuring more than 400 booths of treasures for shoppers to seek out. For info: Missouri Entertainment and Event Center, 3001 N Grant, Springfield, MO 65803. Phone: (417) 833-2660. Fax: (417) 833-3769. Web: www.entertainmo.com.

GREY, ZANE: BIRTH ANNIVERSARY. Jan 31, 1872. Zane Grey (original name Pearl Grey), American dentist and prolific author of tales of the Old West, was born at Zanesville, OH. Grey wrote more than 80 books that were translated into many languages and sold more than 10 million copies. The novel *Riders of the Purple Sage* (1912) was the most popular. Grey died Oct 23, 1939, at Altadena, CA.

GROUNDHOG DAY CELEBRATION AND PROGNOSTICATION. Jan 31–Feb 2. Sun Prairie, WI. Celebration includes breakfast, entertainment, vendors and more. Prognostication is Feb 2 at 7:15 AM, EST, to see if Jimmy the Groundhog has seen his shadow. Est attendance: 1,000. For info: Sun Prairie Chamber of Commerce, 109 E Main St, Sun Prairie, WI 53590. Phone: (608) 837-4547. Fax: (608) 837-8765. Web: www.sunprairiechamber.com.

INSPIRE YOUR HEART WITH THE ARTS DAY. Jan 31. A day to experience art in your life. Food sustains you as a human; art inspires you to be divine. Go to an art museum, browse through an art book at the library, enroll in an art class or commission an artist. Read your favorite poem out loud. Go to a concert or play. Sign up for dance lessons. Today is a day to inspire your heart with the arts! For info: Rev Jayne Howard Feldman, Angel Heights, PO Box 95, Upperco, MD 21155. Phone: (410) 833-6912. Fax: (410) 429-5425. E-mail: earthangel4peace@aol.com. Web: www.earthangel4peace.com.

MARSHALL ISLANDS LANDINGS: 65th ANNIVERSARY. Jan 31, 1944. After two months of saturation bombing (the heaviest to precede an attack thus far in the Pacific), the 23rd and 24th Marine Regiments attacked the Marshall Islands. In four days Kwajalein was taken, providing the Allies with a major staging area. The dead numbered 8,122 Japanese and 356 Americans.

MOORE, GARRY: BIRTH ANNIVERSARY. Jan 31, 1915. American television host Garry Moore was born Thomas Garrison Morfit at Baltimore, MD. His best-known shows were "I've Got a Secret" (1952–67) and "To Tell the Truth" (1969–76). He gave Carol Burnett her break on TV when he made her a regular on "The Garry Moore Show." He died Nov 28, 1993, at Hilton Head Island, SC.

MORRIS, ROBERT: 275th BIRTH ANNIVERSARY. Jan 31, 1734. Signer of the Declaration of Independence, the Articles of Confederation and the Constitution. He was one of only two men who signed all three documents. He was born at Liverpool, England, and died May 7, 1806, at Philadelphia, PA.

NATIONAL SEED SWAP DAY. Jan 31. Washington, DC. Bring your extra seeds and swap them with other gardeners. Everyone will leave with a bag full of seeds, new garden friends and expert planting advice. Seed swap categories include natives, edibles, herbs, exotics, annuals, perennials and woodies (trees/shrubs). Learn, network and prepare for next year's seed collecting! If you are outside of the DC area, celebrate seed swapping by setting up an event in your area. Annually, the last Sunday in January. For info: Kathy Jentz, *Washington Gardener Magazine*, 826 Philadelphia Ave, Silver Spring, MD 20910. Phone: (301) 588-6894. E-mail: editor@washingtongardener.com. Web: www.washingtongardener.com.

NAURU: NATIONAL HOLIDAY. Jan 31. Republic of Nauru. Commemorates independence in 1968 from a UN trusteeship administered by Australia, New Zealand and the UK.

ORCHID SHOW. Jan 31–Mar 15. Missouri Botanical Garden, St. Louis, MO. Spectacular display of the garden's vast orchid collection. For info: Missouri Botanical Garden, 4344 Shaw Blvd, St. Louis, MO 63110. Phone: (314) 577-9400 or (800) 642-8842. Web: www.mobot.org.

ROBINSON, JACKIE: 90th BIRTH ANNIVERSARY. Jan 31, 1919. Jack Roosevelt Robinson, athlete and business executive, first black to enter professional major league baseball (Brooklyn Dodgers, 1947–56). Voted National League's Most Valuable Player in 1949 and elected to the Baseball Hall of Fame in 1962. Born at Cairo, GA, Jackson died at Stamford, CT, Oct 24, 1972.

SCHUBERT, FRANZ: BIRTH ANNIVERSARY. Jan 31, 1797. Composer, born at Vienna, Austria, and died there of typhus Nov 19, 1828, at age 31. Buried, at his request, near the grave of Beethoven. Schubert last worked on his "Unfinished Symphony" (No 8) in 1822. On the 100th anniversary of his death in 1928 a $10,000 prize was offered to "finish" the work. The protests were so great that the offer was withdrawn.

SLOVIK, EDDIE D.: EXECUTION ANNIVERSARY. Jan 31, 1945. Anniversary of execution by firing squad of 24-year-old Private Eddie D. Slovik. Born at Detroit, MI, Feb 18, 1920, Slovik was assigned to Company G, 109th Infantry, 28th Division, US Army. His death sentence, the first for desertion since the Civil War, has been a subject of controversy. First buried in France, Slovik's remains were exhumed in 1987 for reburial beside his wife, Antoinette, who died in 1979, after years of effort to clear Slovik's name and have his body returned to the US.

SPACE MILESTONE: *APOLLO 14* (US). Jan 31, 1971. Launch date of *Apollo 14*. Five days later on Feb 5 astronauts Alan B. Shepard, Jr, and Edgar D. Mitchell landed on the moon (lunar module *Antares*). Command module *Kitty Hawk* was piloted by Stuart A. Roosa. Pacific splashdown on Feb 9.

SPACE MILESTONE: *EXPLORER 1* (US). Jan 31, 1958. The first successful US satellite. Although launched four months later than the Soviet Union's *Sputnik*, *Explorer* reached a higher altitude and detected a zone of intense radiation inside Earth's magnetic field. This was later named the Van Allen radiation belts. More than 65 subsequent *Explorer* satellites were launched through 1984.

SPACE MILESTONE: *LUNA 9* (USSR). Jan 31, 1966. Launch of unmanned mission that accomplished the first soft landing on the moon three days later on Feb 3. Relayed TV photos of the lunar surface.

SPACE MILESTONE: PROJECT MERCURY TEST (US). Jan 31, 1961. A test of Project Mercury spacecraft accomplished the first US recovery of a large animal from space. Ham, the chimpanzee, successfully performed simple tasks in space.

Birthdays Today

Ernest (Ernie) Banks, 78, Hall of Fame baseball player, born Dallas, TX, Jan 31, 1931.

Queen Beatrix, 71, Queen of the Netherlands, born Sostdijk, Netherlands, Jan 31, 1938.

Carol Channing, 86, actress (stage: *Hello, Dolly!; Thoroughly Modern Millie*), born Seattle, WA, Jan 31, 1923.

Portia de Rossi, 36, actress ("Ally McBeal," "Arrested Development"), born Geelong, Victoria, Australia, Jan 31, 1973.

Minnie Driver, 38, actress (*Gross Pointe Blank, Good Will Hunting*), born London, England, Jan 31, 1971.

Philip Glass, 72, composer, born Baltimore, MD, Jan 31, 1937.

John Lydon, 53, singer (as Johnny Rotten, The Sex Pistols), composer, born near London, England, Jan 31, 1956.

Kelly Lynch, 50, actress (*Drugstore Cowboy*), born Minneapolis, MN, Jan 31, 1959.

Stuart Margolin, 69, actor, director, writer ("The Rockford Files," *The Big Blue*), born Davenport, IA, Jan 31, 1940.

(Lynn) Nolan Ryan, 62, Hall of Fame baseball player, born Refugio, TX, Jan 31, 1947.

Jean Simmons, 80, actress (*Black Narcissus, The Robe, Elmer Gantry*), born London, England, Jan 31, 1929.

Justin Timberlake, 28, singer, actor (*Alpha Dog, Black Snake Moan*), born Memphis, TN, Jan 31, 1981.

Jessica Walter, 68, actress ("Arrested Development," *Play Misty for Me, The Flamingo Kid*), born Brooklyn, NY, Jan 31, 1941.

✦ February ✦

February 1 — Sunday

DAY 32 333 REMAINING

AMD/LOW VISION AWARENESS MONTH. Feb 1–28. Macular degeneration is a leading cause of vision loss. Low vision aids can make the most of remaining vision. Information on eye disease warning signs and on low vision aids will be available. For info: Prevent Blindness America®, 211 W Wacker Dr, Ste 1700, Chicago, IL 60606. Phone: (800) 331-2020. E-mail: info@preventblindness.org. Web: www.preventblindness.org.

✦ **AMERICAN HEART MONTH.** Feb 1–28. Presidential Proclamation issued each year for February since 1964. (PL88–254 of Dec 30, 1963.)

AMERICAN HEART MONTH. Feb 1–28. During this month, the American Heart Association will focus on women with "Go Red for Women," an educational movement about women and cardiovascular disease. Each year cardiovascular diseases claim the lives of nearly 500,000 women. For all of the women you know who have been affected by cardiovascular disease, participate in National Wear Red Day on Friday, Feb 6. For information on American Heart Month and Go Red for Women: American Heart Assn, 7272 Greenville Ave, Dallas, TX 75231. Phone: (800) 242-8721. Fax: (214) 369-3685. Web: www.americanheart.org or www.goredforwomen.org.

BAKE FOR FAMILY FUN MONTH. Feb 1–28. The Home Baking Association has designated February as Bake for Family Fun Month, dedicated to the great taste, good nutrition, economy and family fun of traditional home baking. For info: Charlene Patton, 2931 SW Gainsboro Rd, Topeka, KS 66614. Phone: (785) 478-3283. Fax: (785) 478-3024. Web: www.homebaking.org.

BLACK MARIA STUDIO: ANNIVERSARY. Feb 1, 1893. The first moving picture studio was built at Thomas Edison's laboratory compound at West Orange, NJ, at a cost of less than $700. The wooden structure of irregular oblong shape was covered with black tar paper. It had a sharply sloping roof hinged at one edge so that half of it could be raised to admit sunlight. Fifty feet in length, it was mounted on a pivot enabling it to be swung around to follow the changing position of the sun. There was a stage draped in black at one end of the room. Though the structure was officially called a Kinetographic Theater, it was nicknamed the "Black Maria" because it resembled the old-fashioned black police wagons, also called "Black Marias," that were common earlier in the century.

CAR INSURANCE FIRST ISSUED: ANNIVERSARY. Feb 1, 1898. Travelers Insurance Company issued the first car insurance against accidents with horses.

CARAWAY, HATTIE WYATT: BIRTH ANNIVERSARY. Feb 1, 1878. Born at Bakersville, TN, Hattie Caraway became a US senator from Arkansas in 1931 when her husband died and she was appointed to fill out his term. The following year, she ran for the seat herself and became the first woman elected to the US Senate. She served 14 years there, becoming an adept and tireless legislator (once introducing 43 bills on the same day) who worked for women's rights (once cosponsoring an equal rights amendment), supported New Deal policies as well as Prohibition and opposed the increasing influence of lobbyists. Caraway died at Falls Church, VA, Dec 21, 1950. See also: "First Elected Woman Senator: Anniversary" (Jan 12).

February 2009	S	M	T	W	T	F	S
	1	2	3	4	5	6	7
	8	9	10	11	12	13	14
	15	16	17	18	19	20	21
	22	23	24	25	26	27	28

CHILDREN'S AUTHORS & ILLUSTRATORS WEEK. Feb 1–7. To celebrate and recognize authors and illustrators who create books for young people and promote literacy by inspiring enjoyment of quality literature. During this week, members of the Children's Authors Network speak at schools, libraries and children's shelters. Motivate children to read and write: invite authors and illustrators to school and venues near you! Annually, the first full week in February. For info: Children's Authors Network! (CAN!), 23291 Mobile St, West Hills, CA 91307. Phone: (818) 615-0857. Web: www.childrensauthorsnetwork.com.

FEBRUARY IS FABULOUS FLORIDA STRAWBERRY MONTH. Feb 1–28. Strawberries in February? You bet your snow boots! Though it's cold and dreary in many parts of the country, February is fabulous in Florida, where strawberry growers are harvesting their winter crop and shipping handpicked fruit to key markets. Strawberries dipped in chocolate or champagne are a Valentine's Day delight. Consider using the ripe, luscious berry in a variety of recipes from salads to shortbread. For info: Florida Strawberry Growers Assn, PO Drawer 2550, Plant City, FL 33564. Phone: (813) 752-6822. Fax: (813) 752-2167. E-mail: info@flastrawberry.com. Web: www.flastrawberry.com.

FESTIVAL OF CAMELLIAS. Feb 1–28. Massee Lane Gardens, Fort Valley, GA. Focal event of Camellia Days, which run from January through March each year. Annual celebration of the lovely flower, the camellia. Festival events include garden tours and workshops, plant sale and more. Call for more details and ticket prices. Sponsor: The American Camellia Society. Est attendance: 8,000. For info: Massee Lane Gardens, 100 Massee Ln, Fort Valley, GA 31030. Phone: (478) 967-2358. E-mail: ask@camellias-acs.org. Web: www.camellias-acs.org.

FESTIVAL OF THE NORTH. Feb 1–28. Ketchikan, AK. A cultural event encompassing performing, visual and literary arts, including an annual Wearable Art Show and a variety of workshops. Annually, the month of February. Est attendance: 2,000. For info: Ketchikan Area Arts and Humanities Council, 716 Totem Way, Ketchikan, AK 99901. Phone: (907) 225-2211. Fax: (907) 225-4330. E-mail: info@ketchikanarts.org.

FIRST SESSION OF SUPREME COURT: ANNIVERSARY. Feb 1, 1790. The Supreme Court of the US met for the first time in New York City, with Chief Justice John Jay presiding.

FLAGSTAFF WINTERFEST. Feb 1–28. Flagstaff, AZ. This festival, now in its 23rd year, celebrates the many facets of a Flagstaff winter. Family fun for everyone: concerts, performances, art shows, snow sports, wacky sports, winter workshops, children's events and much more. The fun will go on with or without snow. Est attendance: 20,000. For info: Joe Galli, VP of Government Affairs, Flagstaff Chamber of Commerce, 101 W Rte 66, Flagstaff, AZ 86001. Phone: (928) 774-4505. Fax: (928) 779-1209. Web: www.flagstaffchamber.com.

FORD, JOHN: BIRTH ANNIVERSARY. Feb 1, 1895. Film director John Ford was born at Cape Elizabeth, ME, as Sean Aloysius O'Feeney; he changed his name after moving to Hollywood. Ford won his first Academy Award in 1935 for *The Informer*. Among his many other films: *Stagecoach, Young Mr. Lincoln, The Grapes of Wrath, How Green Was My Valley, Rio Grande, What Price Glory?* and *Mister Roberts*. During WWII he served as chief of the Field Photographic Branch of the Office of Strategic Services (OSS). Two documentaries made during the war earned him Academy Awards. He died Aug 31, 1973, at Palm Desert, CA.

FREEDOM DAY: ANNIVERSARY. Feb 1, 1865. Anniversary of President Abraham Lincoln's approval of the 13th Amendment to the US Constitution (abolishing slavery): "1. Neither slavery nor involuntary servitude, except as a punishment for crime whereof the party shall have been duly convicted, shall exist within the United States or any place subject to their jurisdiction. 2. Congress shall have power to enforce this article by appropriate legislation." The amendment had been proposed by Congress Jan 31, 1865; ratification was completed Dec 6, 1865.

"FROM AFRICA TO VIRGINIA" MONTH. Feb 1–28. Jamestown Settlement, Williamsburg, VA. Guided gallery tours and a special gallery brochure highlight the culture of the first known Africans in Virginia, from the kingdom of Ndongo in Angola, and the experience of Africans in 17th-century Virginia. Tours of the museum's outdoor riverfront discovery area will compare boatbuilding, fishing and metalworking skills of Africans in Angola with technology used in 17th-century Virginia. For info: Jamestown-Yorktown Foundation, PO Box 1607, Williamsburg, VA 23187. Phone: (757) 253-4838 or (888) 593-4682. Fax: (757) 253-5299. Web: www.historyisfun.org.

GABLE, CLARK: BIRTH ANNIVERSARY. Feb 1, 1901. Actor William Clark Gable's first film was *The Painted Desert* in 1931, when talking films were replacing silent films. He won an Academy Award for his role in the comedy *It Happened One Night*, which established him as a romantic screen idol. Other films included *China Seas, Mutiny on the Bounty, Saratoga* and *Gone with the Wind*, for which his casting as Rhett Butler seemed a foregone conclusion due to his popularity as the acknowledged "King of Movies." Gable was born at Cadiz, OH, and died Nov 16, 1960, at Hollywood, CA, shortly after completing his last film, Arthur Miller's *The Misfits*, in which he starred with Marilyn Monroe.

"GENERAL ELECTRIC THEATER" TV PREMIERE: ANNIVERSARY. Feb 1, 1953. CBS's half-hour dramatic anthology series was hosted by Ronald Reagan (in between his movie and political careers). Making their television debuts were Joseph Cotten (1954); Fred MacMurray, James Stewart and Myrna Loy (1955); Bette Davis, Anne Baxter, Tony Curtis and Fred Astaire (1957); Sammy Davis, Jr (1958); and Gene Tierney (1960). Other memorable stars who appeared on the series included Joan Crawford, Harry Belafonte, Rosalind Russell, Ernie Kovacs, the Marx Brothers and Nancy Davis (Reagan), who starred with husband Ronald Reagan in an episode titled "A Turkey for the President" (1958).

G.I. JOE INTRODUCED: 45th ANNIVERSARY. Feb 1, 1964. This toy action figure was introduced by Hasbro and sold for $2.49. It was the first mass-market doll intended for boys and was a great success. The figure's name came from a film, *The Story of G.I. Joe* (1945), that starred Robert Mitchum and Burgess Meredith.

"GOOD TIMES" TV PREMIERE: 35th ANNIVERSARY. Feb 1, 1974. A CBS spin-off of "Maude," which was a spin-off of "All in the Family," "Good Times" featured an African-American family living in the housing projects of Chicago and struggling to improve its lot. The cast featured Esther Rolle and John Amos as Florida and James Evans, Jimmie Walker as son J.J., BernNadette Stanis as daughter Thelma, Ralph Carter as son Michael, Johnny Brown as janitor Mr Bookman, Ja'Net DuBois as neighbor Willona Woods, Janet Jackson as Willona's adopted daughter Penny and Ben Powers as Thelma's husband, Keith Anderson.

GREENSBORO SIT-IN: ANNIVERSARY. Feb 1, 1960. Commercial discrimination against blacks and other minorities provoked a nonviolent protest. At Greensboro, NC, four students from the Agricultural and Technical College (Ezell Blair, Jr; Franklin McCain; Joseph McNeill and David Richmond) sat down at a F.W. Woolworth store lunch counter and ordered coffee. Refused service, they remained all day. In the following days similar sit-ins took place at Woolworth's lunch counter. Before the week was over, they were joined by a few white students. The protest spread rapidly, especially in Southern states. More than 1,600 people were arrested before the year was over for participating in sit-ins. Civil rights for all became a cause for thousands of students and activists. In response, equal accommodation regardless of race became the rule at lunch counters, hotels and business establishments in thousands of places.

HERBERT, VICTOR: 150th BIRTH ANNIVERSARY. Feb 1, 1859. Born at Dublin, Ireland, Herbert was a cellist, conductor and prolific composer of operettas who dominated the popular American music scene in the late 19th and early 20th centuries. Among his many popular operettas were *Babes in Toyland* (1903) and *Naughty Marietta* (1910). Herbert also helped found the American Society of Composers, Artists, and Publishers (ASCAP), which helped protect artistsí intellectual property rights. Herbert died May 26, 1924, at New York, NY.

HUGHES, LANGSTON: BIRTH ANNIVERSARY. Feb 1, 1902. African-American poet and author, born at Joplin, MO. Among his works are the poetry collection *Montage of a Dream Deferred*, plays, a novel, memoirs and short stories. He wrote, "My soul has grown deep like the rivers," and asked, "What happens to a dream deferred?" Hughes died May 22, 1967, at New York, NY.

HULA IN THE COOLA DAY. Feb 1. A day for those longing to escape the winter doldrums to laugh at the cold with a luau party. Put away your winter coats, get out your shorts and flip-flops, play limbo and say, "Aloha!" For info: iParty, 270 Bridge St, Ste 301, Dedham, MA 02026. Phone: (781) 329-3952. E-mail: fun@iparty.com. Web: www.iparty.com.

INTERNATIONAL BOOST SELF-ESTEEM MONTH. Feb 1–28. A month to focus on the importance of nurturing and cultivating self-esteem to beat the winter blahs, to boost morale and to inspire yourself and others to seize new challenges. For info: Valla Dana Fotiades, MEd, PO Box 133, Waverly, FL 33877. Phone: (863) 875-0759. E-mail: Valladana@verizon.net.

INTERNATIONAL COACHING WEEK. Feb 1–7. To provide a week each year to educate the public about the value of working with a personal, business or executive coach and to provide an opportunity for coaches and their clients to acknowledge the progress and results made through the coaching process. Annually, the first full week in February. For info: Jerri N. Udelson, MCC, Entrepreneurial Coaching & Consulting, 20 Tanoito, Santa Fe, NM 87506. Phone: (505) 988-5533. E-mail: Jerri@JerriUdelson.com. Web: www.coachfederation.org or www.coachingweek.org.

"LATE NIGHT WITH DAVID LETTERMAN" TV PREMIERE: ANNIVERSARY. Feb 1, 1982. This is when it all began: stupid pet tricks, stupid human tricks and the legendary top ten lists. "Late Night" premiered on NBC as a talk/variety show appearing after "The Tonight Show with Johnny Carson." Host David Letterman was known for his irreverent sense of humor and daffy antics. The offbeat show attained cult status among college crowds and insomniacs, as many tuned in to see a Velcro-suited Letterman throw himself against a wall. The show also featured bandleader-sidekick Paul Shaffer, writer Chris Elliott and Calvert DeForest as geezer Larry "Bud" Melman. In 1993 Letterman made a highly publicized exit from NBC and began hosting "The Late Show" on CBS.

LIBRARY LOVERS' MONTH. Feb 1–28. A monthlong celebration of school, public and private libraries of all types. This is a time for everyone, especially library support groups, to recognize the value of libraries and to work to ensure that the nation's libraries will continue to serve. For info: Library Lovers' Month. Web: www.librarysupport.net/librarylovers.

MARFAN SYNDROME AWARENESS MONTH. Feb 1–28. Volunteers across the country distribute educational information about Marfan syndrome and related connective-tissue disorders that can result in life-threatening cardiovascular problems as well as orthopedic and ophthalmologic handicaps. Marfan affects about 200,000 Americans. Annually, the month of February. For info: Cathie Tsuchiya, Natl Marfan Foundation, 22 Manhasset Ave, Port Washington, NY 11050. Phone: (800) 862-7326 or (516) 883-8712. Fax: (516) 883-8040. E-mail: ctsuchiya@marfan.org. Web: www.marfan.org.

✦ **NATIONAL AFRICAN AMERICAN HISTORY MONTH.** Feb 1–28.

NATIONAL BIRD FEEDING MONTHS. Feb 1–Mar 31. To spread the word of how difficult it can be for birds to survive North American winters. In 1993 the National Bird-Feeding Society named February and March National Bird Feeding Months. The widespread awareness generated by this event has contributed to the safe passage of winter for our feathered friends. Providing wild birds with food, water and shelter supplements their natural diet and helps them survive. For info: National Bird Feeding Month, 7370 MacArthur Blvd, Glen Echo, MD 20812. Phone: (301) 229-9585. E-mail: info@birdfeeding.org. Web: www.birdfeeding.org.

NATIONAL BLACK HISTORY MONTH. Feb 1–28. Traditionally the month containing Abraham Lincoln's birthday (Feb 12) and Frederick Douglass's presumed birthday (Feb 14). Observance of a special period to recognize achievements and contributions by African Americans dates from February 1926, when it was launched by Dr. Carter G. Woodson. The 2009 theme: "The Quest for Black Citizenship in the Americas." Variously designated Negro History, Black History, Afro-American History, African-American History, the observance period was initially one week, but since 1976 the entire month of February. The ASALH will host its annual Black History Luncheon on Feb 21, 2009, at the Omni Shoreham Hotel, Washington, DC. For info: Assn for the Study of African American Life and History, Inc, Howard University, C.B. Powell Building, 525 Bryant St, Ste C142, Washington, DC 20059. Phone: (202) 865-0053. Fax: (202) 265-7920. E-mail: info@asalh.net. Web: www.asalh.org.

NATIONAL CARE ABOUT YOUR INDOOR AIR MONTH. Feb 1–28. According to the EPA, indoor air can be two to five times more polluted (and sometimes as much as 100 times more polluted!) than outdoor air. This month was created to increase consumer awareness of the dangers of indoor air pollution and the steps people can take to protect their families' well-being. Annually, each February. For info: Cheri Wright, Honeywell, 250 Turnpike Rd, Southborough, MA 01772. Phone: (508) 490-7162. E-mail: cheri.wright@kaz.com. Web: www.honeywellcleanair.com/care.html.

NATIONAL CHERRY MONTH. Feb 1–28. To publicize the colorful red tart cherry. For info: Cherry Marketing Institute, PO Box 30285, Lansing, MI 48909-7785. E-mail: info@choosecherries.com. Web: www.choosecherries.com.

NATIONAL CHILDREN'S DENTAL HEALTH MONTH. Feb 1–28. To increase dental awareness and stress the importance of regular dental care. For info: American Dental Assn, 211 E Chicago Ave, Chicago, IL 60611. Phone: (312) 440-2500. E-mail: ncdhm@ada.org. Web: www.ada.org.

February 2009

S	M	T	W	T	F	S
1	2	3	4	5	6	7
8	9	10	11	12	13	14
15	16	17	18	19	20	21
22	23	24	25	26	27	28

NATIONAL LAUGH-FRIENDLY MONTH. Feb 1–28. Laughter and humor are essential elements when creating a laugh-friendly business—for both employees and customers. This month encourages businesses and individuals to promote exceptional customer service with smiles, humor and laughter. Who wouldn't want a laugh-friendly company? Annually, the month of February. For info: Elena Patrice, VP, ee publishing & productions, llc, PO Box 7006, Fairfax Station, VA 22039. Phone: (703) 256-1721. E-mail: elena@laughfriendly.com. Web: www.laughfriendly.com.

NATIONAL MEND A BROKEN HEART MONTH. Feb 1–28. An annual observance sponsored by the nonprofit My Stuff Bags Foundation, National Mend a Broken Heart Month encourages individuals and groups to support America's children who have been abused, neglected and abandoned by the very people who should love them most. These children must be rescued from their homes, often entering crisis shelters and foster care with no personal belongings. Suggested activities include volunteering or donating funding and new belongings to support America's foster children through local organizations. For info: Diann Neill, My Stuff Bags Foundation, 5347 Sterling Center Dr, Westlake, CA 91361. Phone: (866) 369-7883. Fax: (818) 865-3865. E-mail: dneill@mystuffbags.org. Web: www.mystuffbags.org.

NATIONAL PARENT LEADERSHIP MONTH. Feb 1–28. In order to recognize, honor and celebrate parents for their vital leadership roles in their homes and communities and in state, national and international arenas, Parents Anonymous® Inc has designated the month of February as National Parent Leadership Month. This annual event acknowledges the strengths of parents as leaders and generates awareness about the important roles parents can play in shaping the lives of their families and communities. Founded in 1969, Parents Anonymous® Inc is dedicated to strengthening families by preventing child abuse and neglect all around the world. For info: Parents Anonymous® Inc, 675 W Foothill Blvd, Ste 220, Claremont, CA 91711. Phone: (909) 621-6184. E-mail: parentsanonymous@parentsanonymous.org. Web: www.parentsanonymous.org.

NATIONAL PATIENT RECOGNITION WEEK. Feb 1–7. The day when health care providers, professionals and personnel make a special effort to recognize their patients through planned interactions and events. Annually, the first seven days of February. For info: John O'Malley, NPRW, 337 Turnberry Rd, Birmingham, AL 35244. Phone: (205) 995-8495. E-mail: jom@strategvisioninc.com. Web: www.nprw.com.

NATIONAL PET DENTAL HEALTH MONTH. Feb 1–28. A nationwide effort cosponsored by veterinary dental groups and Hill's Pet Nutrition, Inc, to educate consumers on the importance of good dental care for pets. For info: Hill's Pet Nutrition. Web: www.petdental.com.

NATIONAL SENIOR INDEPENDENCE MONTH. Feb 1–28. A month to increase awareness of and celebrate seniors who choose to age with dignity in their own homes and maintain their independence. In a national Home Instead Senior Care survey, 83 percent of seniors surveyed said they were very or somewhat likely to remain at home rather than move to a care facility. For info: Mahnaz Pourian, Home Instead Senior Care, 459 N Gilbert Rd, Ste C-120, Gilbert, AZ 85234. Phone: (602) 292-8112. Fax: (480) 827-1101. E-mail: mpourian@homeinstead.com. Web: www.homeinstead.com.

NATIONAL TIME MANAGEMENT MONTH. Feb 1–28. This is the month when those noble plans made in January start to go awry. This observance is dedicated to renewing those best-laid plans; breaking out those new calendars that have yet to be opened; and reevaluating and reprioritizing harried, out-of-balance lives—making specific commitments to balance them. For info: Sylvia Henderson, Springboard Training, PO Box 588, Olney, MD 20830-0588. Phone: (301) 260-1538. E-mail: sylvia@springboardtraining.com. Web: www.springboardtraining.com.

NATIONAL WEDDINGS MONTH. Feb 1–28. As the wedding season gets into high gear, this observance is to call attention to the fact that more than 2.5 million weddings are celebrated in the US each year. For info: Assn of Bridal Consultants, 56 Danbury Rd,

Ste 11, New Milford, CT 06776. Phone: (860) 355-0464. Fax: (860) 354-1404. E-mail: office@BridalAssn.com. Web: www.BridalAssn.com.

PLANT THE SEEDS OF GREATNESS MONTH. Feb 1–28. Think globally—build for the future—Plant the Seeds of Greatness. If you're unhappy with your present situation, discover how you can remove the barriers and make a change in your life for the better. Use this month to put to use your own unique prosperity consciousness and plant the seeds for your new career, life objectives or goals. Make a difference for yourself, your family, your business or your community. Get outside of your comfort zone and take action on your ideas and dreams. Info available for $2. For info: Lorrie Walters Marsiglio, Lorimar Communications, PO Box 284-CC, Wasco, IL 60183-0284. Phone: (630) 584-9368.

PUBLICITY FOR PROFIT WEEK. Feb 1–7. Harness the power of free publicity for yourself, your business or your organization. Spend each day this week getting free publicity by doing one task to promote whatever you deem important. For free and easy-to-follow publicity plans, send e-mail request or SASE. Free publicity newsletter also available. For info: Tom Peric, Publicity for Profit, 2040 Fairfax Ave, Cherry Hill, NJ 08003. Phone: (856) 874-0049. Fax: (856) 874-0052. E-mail: tom@thegalileo.com. Web: www.wackydays.com.

RELATIONSHIP WELLNESS MONTH. Feb 1–28. Recapture the spark and zeal of personal relationships. Rekindle the flame with your partner or spouse. Get close, communicate, laugh, love and live. This is a time of forgiveness, harmony and trust. Set new goals as a couple, and establish relationship priorities. Go out on a date once a week. Be irresistible. Be patient. Seek forgiveness. Avoid nagging and complaining. Give bear hugs and gentle kisses. For info: Angela Brown Oberer, Words of Wellness, PO Box 49266, Charlotte, NC 28277. Phone: (704) 849-2900. E-mail: angela@WordsofWellness.com. Web: www.WordsofWellness.com.

RETURN SHOPPING CARTS TO THE SUPERMARKET MONTH. Feb 1–28. A monthlong opportunity to return stolen shopping carts, milk crates, bread trays and ice cream baskets to supermarkets and to avoid the increased food prices that these thefts cause. Annually, the month of February. Sponsor: Illinois Food Retailers Association. For info: Anthony A. Dinolfo, Grocer-Retired, 163 Fairfield Dr, New Lenox, IL 60451-3523. Phone: (815) 463-9136.

ROBINSON CRUSOE DAY: 300th ANNIVERSARY. Feb 1, 1709. (Old Style date.) Anniversary of the rescue of Alexander Selkirk, a Scottish sailor who had been put ashore (in September 1704) on the uninhabited island Juan Fernáandez, at his own request, after a quarrel with his captain. His adventures formed the basis for Daniel Defoe's book *Robinson Crusoe.* A day to be adventurous and self-reliant.

ST. LAURENT, LOUIS STEPHEN: BIRTH ANNIVERSARY. Feb 1, 1882. Canadian lawyer and prime minister, born at Compton, QC. Died at Quebec City, July 25, 1973.

"THE SECRET STORM" TV PREMIERE: 55th ANNIVERSARY. Feb 1, 1954. "The Secret Storm" lathered up homes for 20 years. The first soap on television, it revolved around the Ames family in fictional Woodbridge and featured a variety of actors and actresses who have moved on to bigger things. Among them are Bibi Besch, Roy Scheider, Diana Muldaur, Nicolas Coster, Robert Loggia, Laurence Luckinbill, Christina Crawford, Diane Ladd, Troy Donahue and Frances Sternhagen.

SOLO DINERS EAT OUT WEEK. Feb 1–7. Treat yourself to a meal in a restaurant—all by yourself. Settle in at a communal table, nab a stool at a counter or opt for a select table for one. Revel in a meal entirely of hors d'oeuvres or even desserts! It's your choice during this special week. For info: Marya Alexander, PO Box 2664, Carlsbad, CA 92018. Phone: (760) 720-1011. Fax: (760) 720-1049. E-mail: editor@solodining.com. Web: www.solodining.com.

SPACE SHUTTLE *COLUMBIA* DISASTER: ANNIVERSARY. Feb 1, 2003. Minutes before space shuttle *Columbia* was due to land after a successful 16-day scientific mission, it disintegrated 40 miles above the state of Texas, killing its seven-member crew. Commander Rick Husband, pilot William McCool, Michael Anderson, David Brown, Kalpana Chawla (first woman astronaut from India), Laurel Clark and Ilan Ramon (first Israeli astronaut) lost their lives and were mourned worldwide. *Columbia* was the first shuttle to fly in space (1981).

SPUNKY OLD BROADS MONTH. Feb 1–28. A monthlong celebration for all women over 50 who are interested in living a regret-free life. For info: Gayle Carson, SOB, 2957 Flamingo Dr, Miami Beach, FL 33140-3916. Phone: (305) 534-8846. Fax: (305) 532-8826. E-mail: Gayle@spunkyoldbroad.com. Web: www.spunkyoldbroad.com.

SUPER BOWL XLIII. Feb 1. Raymond James Stadium, Tampa Bay, FL. The battle between the NFC and AFC champions. For info: PR Dept, The Natl Football League, 280 Park Ave, New York, NY 10017. Phone: (212) 450-2000. Web: www.nfl.com and www.tampabaysuperbowl.com.

SWEET POTATO MONTH. Feb 1–28. Sweet potatoes—the vegetable with super food powers! Discover the benefits of sweet potatoes this month and every month. They're not just for the holidays anymore. And sweet potatoes from North Carolina, the nation's largest sweet potato producer, are available year-round. Sweet potatoes are fat free, cholesterol free, low in sodium and loaded with beta-carotene, fiber and vitamins C and E. The North Carolina Stroke Association, American Heart Association and American Cancer Society endorse sweet potatoes as a nutritious food helpful in disease prevention. So whether it's breakfast, lunch or dinner, appetizer, entrée or dessert, sweet potatoes fit any course and any occasion. Join the Sweet Potato Recipe Club for more ideas and free e-newsletters. For info: Sue Johnson-Langdon, North Carolina Sweet Potato Commission, 1327 N Brightleaf Blvd, Ste H, Smithfield, NC 27577. Phone: (919) 989-7323. Fax: (919) 989-3015. E-mail: ncsweetsue@aol.com. Web: www.ncsweetpotatoes.com.

SWITZERLAND: HOMSTROM. Feb 1. Scuol. Burning of straw men on poles as a symbol of winter's imminent departure. Annually, the first Sunday in February.

WISE HEALTH CARE CONSUMER MONTH. Feb 1–28. Teaching consumers to make better health care decisions is a proven way to reduce health care costs. For this reason, companies, hospitals and HMOs are offering medical self-care programs for employees, subscribers and patients. Wise Health Care Consumer Marketing packet available. For info: American Institute for Preventive Medicine, 30445 Northwestern Hwy, Ste 350, Farmington Hills, MI 48334. Phone: (248) 539-1800. Fax: (248) 539-1808. E-mail: aipm@HealthyLife.com. Web: www.aipm.net/wise.

WOMEN'S HEART WEEK. Feb 1–7. Women's Heart Foundation's nationally recognized program to raise awareness about the number one killer of American women: heart disease. The program introduces fun activities to promote healthier living. View the Women's Heart Week video online at www.womensheart.org. This is a turnkey program for health sites around the country to commemorate using the Seven Focus Days for women's heart wellness and awareness and the Women's Heart Week Kit. The kit includes a risk assessment tool, symptoms awareness brochure and health tracker card. For info: Women's Heart Foundation, PO Box 7827, West Trenton, NJ 08628. Phone: (609) 771-9600. Fax: (609) 771-3778. E-mail: Bonnie@womensheart.org. Web: www.womensheart.org.

WORLDWIDE RENAISSANCE OF THE HEART MONTH. Feb 1–28. This month is dedicated to compassionately thinking with your heart as well as your intellect. During this month, you are asked to take a heartfelt look at the way you think. Special events on Feb 14 and 15. For info: Deborah Kulkkula, 381 Billings Rd, Fitchburg, MA 01420-1407. Phone: (978) 343-4009. E-mail: RenaissanceLady@RenaissanceoftheHeart.com. Web: www.RenaissanceoftheHeart.com.

YELTSIN, BORIS: BIRTH ANNIVERSARY. Feb 1, 1931. First president of the Russian Federation, born at Butka, Sverdlovsk, Russia. He worked in construction in his youth and rose through the Communist Party ranks to become mayor of Moscow. Estranged from the party for his criticism of Mikhail Gorbachev but popular with the people, he was elected president by the Russian parliament in 1989, and in 1991, after the breakup of the Soviet Union, he was reelected in the first popular election to take place in that nation's history. His work focused on transforming the Russian economy and on establishing a constitution and revising systems of parliament within the Russian government. His administration was fraught with controversy, and he survived two impeachment attempts before he resigned on Dec 31, 1999, appointing Vladimir Putin as his successor. Yeltsin died at Moscow, Apr 23, 2007.

"YOU ARE THERE" TV PREMIERE: ANNIVERSARY. Feb 1, 1953. The program began as an inventive radio show in 1947. News correspondents would comb the annals of history and "interview" the movers and shakers of times past. Walter Cronkite hosted the series on CBS for four seasons. The show's concept was revived for a season in 1971, with Cronkite gearing the program toward children.

YOUTH LEADERSHIP MONTH. Feb 1–28. This month is dedicated to celebrating young people who take on leadership roles in their lives. It is also dedicated to encouraging those who have not yet done so to consider doing so because they can. Programs that focus on youth leadership opportunities and effective leadership skill building are appropriate for this month. For info: Sylvia Henderson, Springboard Training, PO Box 588, Olney, MD 20830-0588. Phone: (301) 260-1538. E-mail: sylvia@springboardtraining.com. Web: www.springboardtraining.com.

Birthdays Today

Michelle Akers, 43, former soccer player, born Santa Clara, CA, Feb 1, 1966.

Big Boi, 34, singer, musician (Outkast), born Antwan Patton, Savannah, GA, Feb 1, 1975.

Lauren Conrad, 23, television personality ("The Hills," "Laguna Beach"), born Laguna Beach, CA, Feb 1, 1986.

Michael B. Enzi, 65, US Senator (R, Wyoming), born Bremerton, WA, Feb 1, 1944.

Don Everly, 72, singer, musician ("Bye Bye Love"), with brother Phil (The Everly Brothers), born Brownie, KY, Feb 1, 1937.

Sherilyn Fenn, 44, actress ("Twin Peaks," *Wild at Heart*), born Detroit, MI, Feb 1, 1965.

Michael C. Hall, 38, actor ("Six Feet Under," "Dexter"), born Raleigh, NC, Feb 1, 1971.

Sherman Hemsley, 71, actor ("The Jeffersons," "Amen"), born Philadelphia, PA, Feb 1, 1938.

Bob Jamieson, 66, broadcast journalist, born Streator, IL, Feb 1, 1943.

Terry Jones, 67, actor, director ("Monty Python's Flying Circus"), born Colwyn Bay, Wales, Feb 1, 1942.

Garrett Morris, 72, comedian ("Saturday Night Live"), born New Orleans, LA, Feb 1, 1937.

Bill Mumy, 55, actor, born El Centro, CA, Feb 1, 1954.

Lisa Marie Presley, 41, singer, born Memphis, TN, Feb 1, 1968.

Pauly Shore, 39, comedian, actor, born Los Angeles, CA, Feb 1, 1970.

Stuart Whitman, 80, actor ("Cimarron Strip," *The Seekers*), born San Francisco, CA, Feb 1, 1929.

February 2009

S	M	T	W	T	F	S
1	2	3	4	5	6	7
8	9	10	11	12	13	14
15	16	17	18	19	20	21
22	23	24	25	26	27	28

February 2 — Monday

DAY 33 — 332 REMAINING

BAN ON AFRICAN NATIONAL CONGRESS LIFTED: ANNIVERSARY. Feb 2, 1990. The 30-year ban on the African National Congress was lifted by South African president F.W. de Klerk. De Klerk also vowed to free Nelson Mandela and lift restrictions on 33 other opposition groups.

BASEBALL HALL OF FAME'S CHARTER MEMBERS: ANNIVERSARY. Feb 2, 1936. The five charter members of the brand-new Baseball Hall of Fame at Cooperstown, NY, were announced. Of 226 ballots cast, Ty Cobb was named on 222, Babe Ruth on 215, Honus Wagner on 215, Christy Mathewson on 205 and Walter Johnson on 189. A total of 170 votes were necessary to be elected to the Hall of Fame.

BENÉT, WILLIAM ROSE: BIRTH ANNIVERSARY. Feb 2, 1886. American poet and critic. Born at Fort Hamilton, NY; died at New York, NY, May 4, 1950.

BONZA BOTTLER DAY™. Feb 2. To celebrate when the number of the day is the same as the number of the month. Bonza Bottler Day™ is an excuse to have a party at least once a month. For more information see Jan 1. For info: Gail M. Berger, 14 Fernwood Dr, Taylors, SC 29687. E-mail: bonza@bonzabottlerday.com. Web: www.bonzabottlerday.com.

CANDLEMAS DAY or PRESENTATION OF THE LORD. Feb 2. Observed in the Roman Catholic Church. Commemorates presentation of Jesus in the Temple and the purification of Mary 40 days after his birth. Candles have been blessed since the 11th century. This marks the end of the Christmas liturgical season. Formerly called the Feast of Purification of the Blessed Virgin Mary. Old Scottish couplet proclaims: "If Candlemas is fair and clear/There'll be two winters in the year."

GERMAN SURRENDER AT STALINGRAD: ANNIVERSARY. Feb 2, 1943. Two pockets of starving German soldiers remained in Stalingrad on this date. They had received few supplies since Soviet soldiers had encircled the city the previous November. Friedrich Paulus, whom Hitler had promoted to field marshal only the day before, was forced to seek surrender terms, thereby becoming the first German marshal to surrender. Hitler was furious with Paulus, believing he should have preferred suicide to surrender. Approximately 160,000 Germans died in the Stalingrad Battle; 34,000 were evacuated by air. Of the 90,000 captured and sent to Siberia on foot, tens of thousands died on the way. This Allied victory is generally considered the psychological turning point of the war.

GETZ, STAN: BIRTH ANNIVERSARY. Feb 2, 1927. American jazz saxophonist Stan Getz was born at Philadelphia, PA. He introduced the cool-jazz style, which became a major movement in the 1950s, and the bossa nova (new wave) style of the 1960s. Getz received 11 Grammy Awards and was the first jazz musician to win the Grammy Award for Record of the Year (1965), for "The Girl from Ipanema." Died at Malibu, CA, June 6, 1991.

GROUNDHOG DAY. Feb 2. Old belief that if the sun shines on Candlemas Day, or if the groundhog sees his shadow when he emerges on this day, six weeks of winter will ensue.

GROUNDHOG DAY IN PUNXSUTAWNEY, PENNSYLVANIA. Feb 2. Punxsutawney, PA. Widely observed traditional annual Candlemas Day event at which "Punxsutawney Phil, king of the weather prophets," is the object of a search. Tradition is said to have been established by early German settlers. The official trek (which began in 1887) is followed by a weather prediction for the next six weeks. Phil made his dramatic film debut with Bill Murray in *Groundhog Day*.

GROUNDHOG JOB SHADOW DAY. Feb 2. 12th annual. Students spend part of the day in the workplace "shadowing" an employee as he or she goes through a normal day on the job. Job Shadow Day demonstrates the connection between academics and careers and introduces students to the requirements of professions and industries. Local contacts can be found on the website. Planning kit available. For info: Groundhog Job Shadow Day. Phone: (800) 373-3174. E-mail: info@jobshadow.org. Web: www.jobshadow.org.

HALAS, GEORGE: BIRTH ANNIVERSARY. Feb 2, 1895. George "Papa Bear" Halas, Pro Football Hall of Fame coach and team owner, born at Chicago, IL. After playing football at the University of Illinois and baseball with the New York Yankees, Halas helped to found the National Football League and the Chicago Bears in 1920. As coach of the Bears for 40 years, he compiled a record of 324 wins, 151 losses and 31 ties. Charter member of the Hall of Fame, 1963. Died at Chicago, Oct 31, 1983.

HEDGEHOG DAY. Feb 2. This ancient Roman tradition was the inspiration for Groundhog Day in the US. Romans observed whether a hedgehog emerging from hibernation could see its shadow in the moonlight—if it could, then six more weeks of winter were expected. Later observed as a folk holiday in Europe and the British Isles.

IMBOLC. Feb 2. (Also called Imbolg, Candlemas, Lupercalia, Feast of Pan, Feast of Torches, Feast of Waxing Light, Brigit's Day and Oimelc.) One of the "Greater Sabbats" during the Wiccan year, Imbolc marks the recovery of the Goddess (after giving birth to the Sun, or the God, at Yule) and celebrates the anticipation of spring. Annually, Feb 2.

INTERNATIONAL NETWORKING WEEK. Feb 2–6. To celebrate the key role that networking plays in the development and success of businesses around the world, recognizing networking as an essential tool for success. Simultaneous events will be held globally, bringing together representatives of government, businesses and the community to network with each other, understand the concept of good networking and listen to talks by networking specialists from around the world. For info: Ivan Misner, PhD, BNI, 545 College Commerce Way, Upland, CA 91786. Phone: (800) 825-8286 or (909) 608-7575. Fax: (909) 608-7676. E-mail: internationalnetworkingweek@bni.com. Web: www.internationalnetworkingweek.com or www.bni.com.

INTIMATE APPAREL MARKET WEEK. Feb 2–6. (Also May 4–8, Aug 3–7 and Nov 2–6.) Market week dates for the intimate apparel industry. For info: Mary Howell, Vice President Industry Relations, American Apparel & Footwear Assn, 1601 N Kent St, Ste 1200, Arlington, VA 22209. Phone: (703) 524-1864. Fax: (703) 522-6741. Web: www.apparelandfootwear.org.

JOYCE, JAMES: BIRTH ANNIVERSARY. Feb 2, 1882. Irish novelist and poet, author of *Dubliners, A Portrait of the Artist as a Young Man, Ulysses* and *Finnegans Wake*, was born at Dublin, Ireland. "A man of genius," he wrote in *Ulysses*, "makes no mistakes. His errors are volitional and are portals of discovery." Of *Finnegans Wake*, Joyce is reported to have replied to an academic whose letter had asked for clues to its meaning, "If I can throw any obscurity on the subject, let me know." Joyce died at the age of 58 of peritonitis Jan 13, 1941, at Zurich, Switzerland, and was buried there.

LINCOLN, ABRAHAM: OREGON BIRTHDAY OBSERVANCE. Feb 2. Observed annually in Oregon on the first Monday in February. See also: "Lincoln, Abraham: 200th Birth Anniversary" (Feb 12).

LUXEMBOURG: CANDLEMAS. Feb 2. Traditional observance of Candlemas. At night children sing a customary song wishing health and prosperity to their neighbors and receive sweets in return. They carry special candles called *Lichtebengel*, symbolizing the coming of spring.

MEXICO: DIA DE LA CANDELARIA. Feb 2. "Day of the Light." All Mexico celebrates. Dances, processions, bullfights.

MOON PHASE: FIRST QUARTER. Feb 2. Moon enters First Quarter phase at 6:13 PM, EST.

NEW AMSTERDAM (NEW YORK) INCORPORATED AS CITY: ANNIVERSARY. Feb 2, 1653. The magistrates of the Dutch colony on Manhattan Island signed a municipal charter making New Amsterdam a city. This was the official birth of New York City, as New Amsterdam was renamed in August 1664, when the English took the colony over. New York was named in honor of James, the Duke of York, brother to the English king Charles II.

RAND, AYN: BIRTH ANNIVERSARY. Feb 2, 1905. Novelist (*The Fountainhead, Atlas Shrugged*), born Alyssa Rosenbaum at St. Petersburg, Russia. Founded the Objectivism school of philosophy. Died Mar 6, 1982, at New York, NY.

***THE RECORD OF A SNEEZE*: ANNIVERSARY.** Feb 2, 1893. One day after Thomas Edison's "Black Maria" studio was completed at West Orange, NJ, a studio cameraman took the first "close-up" in film history. *The Record of a Sneeze*, starring Edison's assistant Fred P. Ott, was also the first motion picture to receive a copyright (1894). See also: "Black Maria Studio: Anniversary" (Feb 1).

SLED DOGS SAVE NOME: ANNIVERSARY. Feb 2, 1925. When a diphtheria outbreak was diagnosed in Nome, AK (population 1,500), on Jan 21, the nearest large amount of antitoxin serum was in Anchorage. Bitter winter temperatures made air delivery impossible, so a heroic dog sled relay was set up. Some 300,000 units of serum were delivered by train to Nenana, AK, and on Jan 27—in temperatures of 40–50 degrees below zero (Fahrenheit)—20 mushers drove scores of dogs on a 674-mile journey to Nome in 127 hours. Togo was the lead dog for the first 350 miles, and Balto was the lead dog on the final 53 miles. The frozen serum arrived at 5:30 AM, and once it was thawed and administered, there were no more diphtheria deaths. Balto became a national hero, and a statue was erected in his honor in New York City's Central Park.

TREATY OF GUADALUPE HIDALGO: ANNIVERSARY. Feb 2, 1848. The war between Mexico and the US formally ended with the Treaty of Guadalupe Hidalgo, signed in the village for which it was named. The treaty provided for Mexico's cession to the US of the territory that became the states of California, Nevada, Utah, most of Arizona, and parts of New Mexico, Colorado and Wyoming in exchange for $15 million from the US. In addition, Mexico relinquished all rights to Texas north of the Rio Grande. The Senate ratified the treaty Mar 10, 1848.

WALTON, GEORGE: DEATH ANNIVERSARY. Feb 2, 1804. Signer of the Declaration of Independence. Born at Prince Edward County, VA, 1749 (exact date unknown). Died at Augusta, GA.

"WHAT'S MY LINE?" TV PREMIERE: ANNIVERSARY. Feb 2, 1950. This popular game show premiered on CBS and ran for 17 years in prime time. A panel of four celebrities figured out the professions of the contestants and the identities of the mystery guests by asking yes-or-no questions. The first panel consisted of poet Louis Untermeyer, columnist Dorothy Kilgallen, former New Jersey governor Harold Hoffman and psychiatrist Dr. Richard Hoffman. Yankee Phil Rizzuto was the first mystery guest. John Daly hosted.

Birthdays Today

Christie Brinkley, 56, model, born Monroe, MI, Feb 2, 1953.

John Cornyn, 57, US Senator (R, Texas), born Houston, TX, Feb 2, 1952.

Sean Michael Elliott, 41, former basketball player, born Tucson, AZ, Feb 2, 1968.

Farrah Fawcett, 62, actress, model ("Charlie's Angels," *The Burning Bed*), born Corpus Christi, TX, Feb 2, 1947.

Ina Garten, 61, chef, cookbook author, television celebrity ("The Barefoot Contessa"), born Brooklyn, NY, Feb 2, 1948.

Bo Hopkins, 67, actor, born Greenwood, SC, Feb 2, 1942.

Robert Mandan, 77, actor ("Soap," "Days of Our Lives"), born Clever, MO, Feb 2, 1932.

Graham Nash, 67, musician, singer, born Blackpool, England, Feb 2, 1942.

Liz Smith, 86, journalist, author, born Fort Worth, TX, Feb 2, 1923.

Tom Smothers, 72, comedian, folksinger ("The Smothers Brothers Comedy Hour"), born New York, NY, Feb 2, 1937.

Elaine Stritch, 84, singer, actress (*Company, Elaine Stritch at Liberty*), born Birmingham, MI, Feb 2, 1925.

Michael T. Weiss, 47, actor ("The Pretender"), born Chicago, IL, Feb 2, 1962.

February 3 — Tuesday

DAY 34 — **331 REMAINING**

AFRICAN-AMERICAN COACHES DAY. Feb 3. To provide a day each year to educate the African-American community about the value of working with a personal or business coach and to provide an opportunity for coaches and their clients to acknowledge the results and progress made through the coaching process. Annually, the first Tuesday in February. For info: Monique Belton, PhD, 35 Dix Hills Rd, Huntington, NY 11743. Phone: (631) 549-7314.

BLACKWELL, ELIZABETH: BIRTH ANNIVERSARY. Feb 3, 1821. First woman physician. Born near Bristol, England, she and several other members of her family were active abolitionists, women's suffrage advocates and pioneers in women's medicine. Her family moved to New York State in 1832, and she received a medical doctor's degree at Geneva, NY, in 1849. She established a hospital in New York City with an all-woman staff, where she recruited nurses and trained them for service in the Civil War. Returning to England in 1869, she continued to teach and practice medicine until her death at Hastings, England, May 31, 1910.

CIVIL WAR PEACE TALKS: ANNIVERSARY. Feb 3, 1865. Abraham Lincoln and his secretary of state, William Seward, met to discuss peace with Confederate vice president Alexander Stephens and others at Hampton Roads, VA. The meeting, which took place on board the ship *River Queen*, lasted four hours and produced no positive results. The Confederates sought an armistice first and discussion of reunion later, while Lincoln was insistent that recognition of Federal authority must be the first step toward peace.

February 2009

S	M	T	W	T	F	S
1	2	3	4	5	6	7
8	9	10	11	12	13	14
15	16	17	18	19	20	21
22	23	24	25	26	27	28

"THE DAY THE MUSIC DIED": 50th ANNIVERSARY. Feb 3, 1959. The anniversary of the death of rock-and-roll legend Charles Hardin "Buddy" Holly. "The Day the Music Died," so called in singer Don McLean's song "American Pie," is the date on which Holly was killed in a plane crash in a cornfield near Mason City, IA, along with J.P. Richardson (otherwise known as "The Big Bopper") and Richie Valens. Holly was born Sept 7, 1936, at Lubbock, TX.

FIFTEENTH AMENDMENT TO US CONSTITUTION RATIFIED: ANNIVERSARY. Feb 3, 1870. The 15th Amendment granted that the right of citizens to vote shall not be denied on account of race, color or previous condition of servitude.

FOUR CHAPLAINS MEMORIAL DAY: ANNIVERSARY. Feb 3, 1943. Commemorates four chaplains (George Fox, Alexander Goode, Clark Poling, John Washington) who sacrificed their life belts and lives when the SS *Dorchester* was torpedoed off Greenland during WWII.

GREELEY, HORACE: BIRTH ANNIVERSARY. Feb 3, 1811. Newspaper editor, born at Amherst, NH. Founder of the *New York Tribune* and one of the organizers of the Republican Party, Greeley was an outspoken opponent of slavery. Best remembered for his saying, "Go West, young man." Died Nov 29, 1872, at New York City.

INCOME TAX BIRTHDAY: SIXTEENTH AMENDMENT TO US CONSTITUTION RATIFIED. Feb 3, 1913. The 16th Amendment was ratified, granting Congress the authority to levy taxes on income. (Church bells did not ring throughout the land, and no dancing in the streets was reported.)

INTERNATIONAL HOOF-CARE SUMMIT. Feb 3–6. Cincinnati, OH. This annual meeting attracts highly innovative foot-care professionals interested in learning new ways to provide quality hoof care. Est attendance: 800. For info: Frank Lessiter, International Hoof-Care Summit, PO Box 624, Brookfield, WI 53008-0624. Phone: (262) 782-4480. Fax: (262) 782-1252. E-mail: info@lesspub.com. Web: www.americanfarriers.com.

JAPAN: BEAN-THROWING FESTIVAL (SETSUBUN). Feb 3. Setsubun marks the last day of winter according to the lunar calendar. Throngs at temple grounds throw beans to drive away imaginary devils.

JOHNSTON, JOSEPH: BIRTH ANNIVERSARY. Feb 3, 1807. Born near Farmville, VA, and died Mar 21, 1891, at Washington, DC. Confederate general in the Civil War whose troops were never directly defeated. Long-standing differences with Jefferson Davis, president of the Confederacy, prevented him from reaching his full potential as a military leader.

MICHENER, JAMES: BIRTH ANNIVERSARY. Feb 3, 1907. American author, born at New York, NY. His *Tales of the South Pacific* was the basis for the popular musical *South Pacific*. A prolific author, his works included *Sayonara, Iberia, Hawaii, Centennial* and *Texas*. Died at Austin, TX, Oct 17, 1997.

MOZAMBIQUE: HEROES' DAY. Feb 3. National holiday. Honors all heroic citizens, especially Eduardo Mondlane, leader of the fight for independence, assassinated on Feb 3, 1969.

NAUVOO LEGION CHARTERED: ANNIVERSARY. Feb 3, 1841. Created by Illinois charter and composed of 5,000 Mormon men under the command of Lieutenant General Joseph Smith, the Nauvoo Legion was considered the "largest trained soldiery in the US" except for the US Army.

ROCKWELL, NORMAN: BIRTH ANNIVERSARY. Feb 3, 1894. American artist and illustrator especially noted for his realistic and homey magazine cover art for the *Saturday Evening Post*. Born at New York, NY, he died at Stockbridge, MA, Nov 8, 1978.

SPACE MILESTONE: *CHALLENGER* STS-10 (US): 25th ANNIVERSARY. Feb 3, 1984. Shuttle *Challenger* launched from Kennedy Space Center, FL, with a crew of five—Vance Brand, Robert Gibson, Ronald McNair, Bruce McCandless and Robert Stewart. On Feb 7 McCandless and Stewart became the first to fly freely in space (propelled by their backpack jets), untethered to any craft. Landed at Cape Canaveral, FL, Feb 11.

STEIN, GERTRUDE: BIRTH ANNIVERSARY. Feb 3, 1874. Avant-garde expatriate American writer, perhaps best remembered for her poetic declaration (in 1913): "Rose is a rose is a rose is a rose." Born at Allegheny, PA; died at Paris, France, July 27, 1946.

VIETNAM: NATIONAL HOLIDAY. Feb 3. National holiday. Anniversary of the founding of the Vietnamese Communist Party, Feb 3, 1930.

WEIL, SIMONE: 100th BIRTH ANNIVERSARY. Feb 3, 1909. French philosopher and social activist whose impact came posthumously with the publication of her many notebooks. Born at Paris, France, Weil died at Ashford, England, on Aug 24, 1943. Her 20 volumes of writings include these thoughts: "What a country calls its vital economic interests are not the things which enable its citizens to live, but the things which enable it to make war. Gasoline is much more likely than wheat to be a cause of international conflict."

Birthdays Today

Shelley Berman, 83, comedian ("Mary Hartman, Mary Hartman"), born Chicago, IL, Feb 3, 1926.

Thomas Calabro, 50, actor ("Melrose Place"), born Brooklyn, NY, Feb 3, 1959.

Blythe Danner, 66, actress (*Butterflies Are Free, Brighton Beach Memoirs*), born Philadelphia, PA, Feb 3, 1943.

Vlade Divac, 41, former basketball player, born Prijepolje, Yugoslavia, Feb 3, 1968.

Morgan Fairchild, 59, actress ("Dallas," "Falcon Crest," "Flamingo Road"), born Patsy McClenny at Dallas, TX, Feb 3, 1950.

Isla Fisher, 33, actress (*Wedding Crashers, The Lookout*), born Muscat, Oman, Feb 3, 1976.

Keith Gordon, 48, actor (*Dressed to Kill, A Midnight Clear*), director, born New York, NY, Feb 3, 1961.

Robert Allen (Bob) Griese, 64, sportscaster, Hall of Fame football player, born Evansville, IN, Feb 3, 1945.

Nathan Lane, 53, actor (Tonys for *A Funny Thing Happened on the Way to the Forum, The Producers*; *The Birdcage*), born Jersey City, NJ, Feb 3, 1956.

Francis Asbury (Fran) Tarkenton, 69, Hall of Fame football player, born Richmond, VA, Feb 3, 1940.

Maura Tierney, 44, actress ("NewsRadio," "ER"), born Boston, MA, Feb 3, 1965.

February 4 — Wednesday

DAY 35 — **330 REMAINING**

ANGOLA: ARMED STRUGGLE DAY. Feb 4. National holiday. Commemorates the beginning of the struggle for independence from Portugal in 1961.

APACHE WARS BEGAN: ANNIVERSARY. Feb 4, 1861. The period of conflict known as the Apache Wars began at Apache Pass, AZ, when army lieutenant George Bascom arrested Apache chief Cochise for raiding a ranch. Cochise escaped and declared war. The wars lasted 25 years under the leadership of Cochise and, later, Geronimo.

ARIZONA MUSICFEST. Feb 4–Mar 1. Carefree/Cave Creek, North Scottsdale, North Phoenix Valley, AZ. Arizona's premier winter classical music festival celebrates the music of the masters with 13 events over a five-week period. Est attendance: 8,000. For info: Arizona Musicfest, PO Box 5254, Carefree, AZ 85377. Phone: (480) 488-0806. Fax: (480) 488-1401. E-mail: info@azmusicfest.org. Web: www.azmusicfest.org.

CANADA: VANCOUVER INTERNATIONAL BOAT SHOW. Feb 4–8. British Columbia Place Stadium, Vancouver, BC. Sail- and powerboats, sailboards, inflatables, canoes, personal watercraft, marine electronics and accessories, marine services, charters, sailing schools, water skis, sporting goods, travel and resort destinations, fishing equipment and Marine Facts Stage. Est attendance: 38,000. For info: NMMA Canada, 18 King St E, Unit E9, Toronto, ON, Canada L7E 1E8. Phone: (905) 951-0009. Fax: (905) 951-0018. Web: www.vancouverboatshow.ca.

FRIEDAN, BETTY: BIRTH ANNIVERSARY. Feb 4, 1921. The cofounder and first president of the National Organization for Women (NOW) was born Bettye Naomi Goldstein at Peoria, IL. She was an outspoken feminist who spent her entire career crusading for women's rights. Her book *The Feminine Mystique* chronicled the frustrations of the 1960s American housewife, to which she referred as "the problem that has no name." The book struck a chord with millions of women and is widely regarded as one of the most influential books of the 20th century. Friedan died at Washington, DC, on Feb 4, 2006, her 85th birthday.

KOŚCIUSZKO, TADEUSZ: BIRTH ANNIVERSARY. Feb 4, 1746. Polish patriot and American Revolutionary War figure. Born at Lithuania, he died at Solothurn, Switzerland, Oct 15, 1817.

LIBERACE COMMEMORATION. Feb 4. Las Vegas, NV. To honor Liberace's passing on Feb 4, 1987, the Liberace Museum will celebrate Liberace's life and legacy with special programs. "Mr Showmanship" was known throughout the world for his beautiful music, costumes and candelabra. He was honored with an astounding array of awards, including two Emmys, six gold albums and two stars on the Hollywood Walk of Fame. For info: Liberace Museum, 1775 E Tropicana Ave, Las Vegas, NV 89119-6529. Phone: (702) 798-5595. Web: www.liberace.org.

LINDBERGH, CHARLES AUGUSTUS: BIRTH ANNIVERSARY. Feb 4, 1902. American aviator Charles "Lucky Lindy" Lindbergh was the first to fly solo and nonstop over the Atlantic Ocean, New York to Paris, May 20–21, 1927. Born at Detroit, MI; died at Kipahulu, Maui, HI, Aug 27, 1974. See also: "Lindbergh Flight: Anniversary" (May 20).

NATIONAL GIRLS AND WOMEN IN SPORTS DAY. Feb 4. 23rd annual. Celebrates and honors all girls and women participating in sports. Recognizes the passage of Title IX in 1972, the law that guarantees gender equity in federally funded school programs, including athletics. Sponsored by the American Association of University Women, Girls Incorporated, the Girl Scouts, the National Association for Girls and Women in Sports, the National Women's Law Center, the Women's Sports Foundation and the YWCA. For info: Women's Sports Foundation, Eisenhower Park, East Meadow, NY 11554. Phone: (516) 542-4700 or (800) 227-3988. E-mail: Info@WomensSportsFoundation.org.

NELSON, BYRON: BIRTH ANNIVERSARY. Feb 4, 1912. "Lord Byron" was the premier golfer of the 1930s and '40s, whose spectacular play in 1945 enshrined him as one of the legendary sportsmen of all time. In 1945 Nelson won 11 consecutive tournaments, with the season's total coming to 18. That single-season victory record has never been equaled. In all, Nelson had 52 PGA victories in a professional career that began in 1932. He retired from full-time play in 1946. Nelson's golf swing is still considered the one to emulate today. Born John Byron Nelson, Jr, near Waxahachie, TX, he died Sept 26, 2006, at Roanoke, TX.

PARKS, ROSA: BIRTH ANNIVERSARY. Feb 4, 1913. Born Rosa Louise McCauley in Tuskegee, AL, Rosa Parks was a seamstress who was active with the NAACP. On a fateful day in Montgomery, AL, in 1955, a time when African Americans were obligated by law to ride in the back of a bus, she refused to give up her seat to a white man during a ride home from work. Parks was subsequently arrested, found guilty of disorderly conduct and fined $14. This simple act sparked the modern civil rights movement, leading to a 381-day boycott of the Montgomery bus system, lawsuits and an eventual Supreme Court decision decreeing segregation to be unconstitutional. A hero to blacks and whites alike, Parks continued work on civil rights until her death on Oct 25, 2005, at Detroit, MI. She was awarded the Presidential Medal of Freedom and the Congressional Gold Medal, and she is the only American woman to lie in state at the US Capitol Rotunda. Many municipalities consider Dec 1, the day of her arrest in 1955, a holiday: Rosa Parks Day.

SRI LANKA: INDEPENDENCE DAY: ANNIVERSARY. Feb 4. Democratic Socialist Republic of Sri Lanka observes National Day. Public holiday. On Feb 4, 1948, Ceylon (as it was then known) obtained independence from Great Britain. The country's name was changed to Sri Lanka in 1972.

US NATIONAL SNOW SCULPTING COMPETITION. Feb 4–8. Lake Geneva, WI. 14th annual. Snow sculpting competition where each three-person team creates a work of art out of a 7-foot × 9-foot block of snow. Several awards given. For info: Lake Geneva Area CVB, 201 Wrigley Dr, Lake Geneva, WI 53147-2004. Phone: (262) 248-4416 or (800) 345-1020. E-mail: lgcc@lakegenevawi.com. Web: www.lakegenevawi.com.

USO FOUNDED: ANNIVERSARY. Feb 4, 1941. This civilian agency was founded in 1941 to provide support worldwide for US service people and their families. The United Service Organizations (USO) centers have served as a home away from home for hundreds of thousands of Americans.

Birthdays Today

Gabrielle Anwar, 38, actress (*Scent of a Woman*, "The Tudors," "Burn Notice"), born Laleham, England, Feb 4, 1971.

Clint Black, 47, country singer, songwriter, born Katy, LA, Feb 4, 1962.

David Brenner, 64, comedian, born Philadelphia, PA, Feb 4, 1945.

Gary Conway, 73, actor ("Burke's Law," *I Was a Teenage Frankenstein*), born Boston, MA, Feb 4, 1936.

Alice Cooper, 61, singer, songwriter, born Vincent Damon Furnier, Detroit, MI, Feb 4, 1948.

Rob Corddry, 38, writer, comedian ("The Daily Show"), born Weymouth, MA, Feb 4, 1971.

Oscar De La Hoya, 36, boxer, born Los Angeles, CA, Feb 4, 1973.

Lisa Eichhorn, 57, actress (*The Vanishing, King of the Hill*), born Reading, PA, Feb 4, 1952.

Pamela Franklin, 59, actress (*The Prime of Miss Jean Brodie, The Legend of Hell House*), born Tokyo, Japan, Feb 4, 1950.

Michael Goorjian, 38, actor ("Party of Five"), born San Francisco, CA, Feb 4, 1971.

J. Danforth (Dan) Quayle, 62, 44th vice president of US, born Indianapolis, IN, Feb 4, 1947.

John Schuck, 69, actor ("McMillan and Wife," *McCabe and Mrs Miller, Dick Tracy*), born Boston, MA, Feb 4, 1940.

Lawrence Taylor, 50, Hall of Fame football player, born Williamsburg, VA, Feb 4, 1959.

February 2009

S	M	T	W	T	F	S
1	2	3	4	5	6	7
8	9	10	11	12	13	14
15	16	17	18	19	20	21
22	23	24	25	26	27	28

February 5 — Thursday

DAY 36 — 329 REMAINING

CARRADINE, JOHN: BIRTH ANNIVERSARY. Feb 5, 1906. American film actor John Carradine was born Richmond Reed Carradine at Greenwich Village, NY. He appeared in more than 200 films. Frequently observed wandering the streets in a velvet suit and satin cape while reciting Shakespeare, he became known as "the Bard of the Boulevard." Died Nov 27, 1988, at Milan, Italy.

FAMILY-LEAVE BILL: ANNIVERSARY. Feb 5, 1993. President William Clinton signed legislation requiring companies with 50 or more employees (and all government agencies) to allow employees to take up to 12 weeks of unpaid leave in a 12-month period to deal with the birth or adoption of a child or to care for a relative with a serious health problem. The bill became effective Aug 5, 1993.

FLORIDA STATE FAIR. Feb 5–16. Florida State Fairgrounds, Tampa, FL. 105th annual. The fair features the best arts, crafts, competitive exhibits, equestrian shows, livestock, entertainment, midway rides and food found in Florida. Also not to be missed is Cracker Country, a rural-history living museum where cultural and architectural history has been preserved. Est attendance: 500,000. For info: Florida State Fair, PO Box 11766, Tampa, FL 33680. Phone: (813) 621-7821 or (800) 345-FAIR. Web: www.floridastatefair.com.

GERMANY: BERLIN INTERNATIONAL FILM FESTIVAL. Feb 5–15. Potsdamer Platz, Berlin. The 59th festival. One of the premier international film festivals since its inaugural opening in 1951. Includes film competition, children's film festival and other special programs. The awarding of Golden and Silver Bears by the international jury marks the conclusion of the festival. Est attendance: 200,000. For info: Internationale Filmfestspiele Berlin, Potsdamer Strasse 5, D-10785 Berlin, Germany. Phone: (49) 30-259-20-0. Fax: (49) 30-259-20-299. E-mail: info@berlinale.de. Web: www.berlinale.de.

LONGEST WAR IN HISTORY ENDS: ANNIVERSARY. Feb 5, 1985. The Third Punic War, between Rome and Carthage, started in the year 149 BC. It culminated in the year 146 BC, when Roman soldiers led by Scipio razed Carthage to the ground. The desolate site was cursed and rebuilding forbidden. On this date, 2,131 years after the war began, Ugo Vetere, mayor of Rome, and Chedli Klibi, mayor of Carthage, met at Tunis to sign a treaty of friendship officially ending the Third Punic War.

MEXICO: CONSTITUTION DAY. Feb 5. National holiday. Present constitution, embracing major social reforms, adopted in 1917.

MOVE HOLLYWOOD & BROADWAY TO LEBANON, PENNSYLVANIA, DAY. Feb 5. There's lots of room, friendly folks and Amish farms. Lebanon is a haven for residents and tourists to serenely indulge in the city's world-famous bologna and the Wertz family homemade candies. (©2006 by WH.) For info: Thomas & Ruth Roy, Wellcat Holidays, 2418 Long Ln, Lebanon, PA 17046. Phone: (717) 279-0184. E-mail: info@wellcat.com. Web: www.wellcat.com.

PEEL, ROBERT: BIRTH ANNIVERSARY. Feb 5, 1788. English statesman who established the Irish constabulary (known as the "Peelers"). Later, as England's home secretary, he reorganized the London police, thereafter known as "Bobbies." Born at Lancashire, England, he died July 2, 1850, at London from injuries received in a fall from his horse.

STEVENSON, ADLAI EWING: BIRTH ANNIVERSARY. Feb 5, 1900. American statesman, governor of Illinois, Democratic candidate for president in 1952 and 1956, US representative to the UN, 1961–65. Born at Los Angeles, CA. Died at London, England, July 14, 1965. Not to be confused with his grandfather, Vice President Adlai Ewing Stevenson. See also: "Stevenson, Adlai Ewing: Birth Anniversary" (Oct 23).

WEATHERMAN'S [WEATHERPERSON'S] DAY. Feb 5. Commemorates the birth of one of America's first weathermen, John Jeffries, a Boston physician who kept detailed records of weather conditions, 1774–1816. Born at Boston, MA, Feb 5, 1744, and died there Sept 16, 1819. See also: "First Balloon Flight Across English Channel: Anniversary" (Jan 7).

WITHERSPOON, JOHN: BIRTH ANNIVERSARY. Feb 5, 1723. Clergyman, signer of the Declaration of Independence and reputed coiner of the word *Americanism* (in 1781). Born near Edinburgh, Scotland. Died at Princeton, NJ, Nov 15, 1794.

Birthdays Today

Henry Louis (Hank) Aaron, 75, Hall of Fame baseball player, baseball executive, 755 career home-run hitter, born Mobile, AL, Feb 5, 1934.

Roberto Alomar, 41, former baseball player, born Ponce, Puerto Rico, Feb 5, 1968.

Bobby Brown, 40, singer, dancer, born Roxbury, MA, Feb 5, 1969.

Sara Evans, 38, country singer, born Bookville, MO, Feb 5, 1971.

Jennifer Granholm, 50, Governor of Michigan (D), born Vancouver, BC, Canada, Feb 5, 1959.

Father Andrew Greeley, 81, Roman Catholic priest and author (*Happy Are the Merciful, An Occasion of Sin*), born Oak Park, IL, Feb 5, 1928.

Christopher Guest, 61, writer, comedian (Emmy for writing *Lily Tomlin*; *Spinal Tap, Best in Show*), born New York, NY, Feb 5, 1948.

Barbara Hershey, 61, actress (*Hannah and Her Sisters*), born Barbara Hertzstein at Los Angeles, CA, Feb 5, 1948.

David Alan Ladd, 62, actor, producer (*A Dog of Flanders, The Day of the Locust*), born Los Angeles, CA, Feb 5, 1947.

Jennifer Jason Leigh, 47, actress (*Miami Blues, Rush, Backdraft*), born Los Angeles, CA, Feb 5, 1962.

Laura Linney, 45, actress (*The Savages, You Can Count on Me, Kinsey*, "John Adams"), born New York, NY, Feb 5, 1964.

Jane Bryant Quinn, 68, financial writer (*Everyone's Money Book*), born Niagara Falls, NY, Feb 5, 1941.

Charlotte Rampling, 63, actress (*Georgy Girl, Farewell My Lovely*), born Sturmer, England, Feb 5, 1946.

Cristiano Ronaldo, 24, soccer player, born Funchal, Portugal, Feb 5, 1985.

David Selby, 68, actor ("Falcon Crest," *Rich and Famous*), born Morgantown, WV, Feb 5, 1941.

Roger Thomas Staubach, 67, Hall of Fame football player, born Cincinnati, OH, Feb 5, 1942.

Darrell Waltrip, 62, auto racer, born Owensboro, KY, Feb 5, 1947.

February 6 — Friday

DAY 37 — **328 REMAINING**

ACCESSION OF QUEEN ELIZABETH II: ANNIVERSARY. Feb 6, 1952. Princess Elizabeth Alexandra Mary succeeded to the British throne (becoming Elizabeth II, Queen of the United Kingdom of Great Britain and Northern Ireland and Head of the Commonwealth) upon the death of her father, King George VI, Feb 6, 1952. Her coronation took place June 2, 1953, at Westminster Abbey at London.

BUBBLE GUM DAY. Feb 6. Imagine being able to chew bubble gum at school while helping a worthy cause! Today children across the country will be doing just that. Kids who donate 50¢ or more get to chew gum at school. The money collected is donated to a charity chosen by the school. Don't forget to get your principal's permission! Annually, the first Friday in February. For info: Ruth Spiro, PO Box 1023, Deerfield, IL 60015. Web: www.bubblegumday.com.

BURR, AARON: BIRTH ANNIVERSARY. Feb 6, 1756. third vice president of the US (Mar 4, 1801–Mar 3, 1805). While vice president, Burr challenged political enemy Alexander Hamilton to a duel and mortally wounded him July 11, 1804, at Weehawken, NJ. Indicted for the challenge and for murder, he returned to Washington to complete his term of office (during which he presided over the impeachment trial of Supreme Court Justice Samuel Chase). In 1807 Burr was arrested, tried for treason (in an alleged scheme to invade Mexico and set up a new nation in the West) and acquitted. Born at Newark, NJ, he died at Staten Island, NY, Sept 14, 1836.

CANADA: ONTARIO WINTER CARNIVAL BON SOO. Feb 6–15. Sault Ste. Marie, ON. One of Canada's largest winter carnivals features more than 75 festive indoor and hearty outdoor events for all ages during an annual 10-day winter extravaganza that includes winter sports, festive dances, entertainment, fireworks and winter playground. Est attendance: 75,000. For info: Bon Soo Winter Carnival Inc, PO Box 781, Sault Ste. Marie, ON, Canada P6A 5N3. Phone: (705) 759-3000 or (866) 899-1607. Fax: (705) 759-6950. E-mail: mrbonsoo@bonsoo.on.ca. Web: www.bonsoo.on.ca.

CANADA: WINTERLUDE. Feb 6–22. Ottawa, ON. Annual celebration of Canadian winter and traditions for the whole family. Skating on Rideau Canal, the world's longest skating rink; snow and ice sculptures; world-class figure skating; North America's largest snow playground and exciting Winter Triathlon. Est attendance: 700,000. For info: Natl Capital Commission, 202-40 Elgin St, Ottawa, ON, Canada K1P 1C7. Phone: (613) 239-5000 or (800) 465-1867. E-mail: info@ncc-ccn.ca. Web: www.capcan.ca/winterlude.

MANCHESTER UNITED PLANE CRASH: ANNIVERSARY. Feb 6, 1958. A British European Airways jet crashed on takeoff in Munich, killing 21 people on board, including 8 Manchester United football players: team captain Roger Byrne, Mark Jones, Eddie Colman, Duncan Edwards, Tommy Taylor, Liam Whelan, David Pegg and Geoff Bent. When the survivors arrived later in Manchester, citizens lined the streets for the 12 miles from the airport to the soccer stadium in tribute.

MARLEY, BOB: BIRTH ANNIVERSARY. Feb 6, 1945. With his group, the Wailers, Bob Marley was one of the most popular and influential performers of reggae music. Marley was born at Rhoden Hall in northern Jamaica. Died of cancer at Miami, FL, May 11, 1981.

MASSACHUSETTS RATIFIES CONSTITUTION: ANNIVERSARY. Feb 6, 1788. By a vote of 187 to 168, Massachusetts became the sixth state to ratify the Constitution.

MIDWINTER'S DAY CELEBRATION. Feb 6. Ann Arbor, MI. To create euphoria by fiat in celebration that winter is half over. For info: Richard Ankli, Allen Creek Hydro, Inc, 100 S 4th Ave #608, Ann Arbor, MI 48104.

NATIONAL WEAR RED DAY. Feb 6. During American Heart Month in February, the American Heart Association will focus on women with "Go Red for Women," a national movement about women and cardiovascular disease. Each year cardiovascular diseases claim the lives of nearly 500,000 women. For all of the women you know who have been affected by cardiovascular disease, participate in Wear Red Day. Annually, the first Friday in February. For info: American Heart Assn, 7272 Greenville Ave, Dallas, TX 75231. Phone: 888-MY-HEART. Web: www.americanheart.org or www.goredforwomen.org.

NEW YORK COMIC CON. Feb 6–8. Jacob Javits Center, New York, NY. 4th annual. A trade and consumer show devoted to all facets of comics. Includes exhibits, panels, movie screenings and more. Est attendance: 40,000. For info: New York Comic Con, Reed Exhibitions. Phone: (888) 605-6059. Web: www.nycomiccon.com.

NEW ZEALAND: WAITANGI DAY. Feb 6. National Day. Commemorates signing of the Treaty of Waitangi in 1840 (at Waitangi, Chatham Islands, New Zealand). The treaty, between the native Maori and the European peoples, provided for development of New Zealand under the British Crown.

REAGAN, RONALD WILSON: BIRTH ANNIVERSARY. Feb 6, 1911. 40th president of the US (1981–89). Former sportscaster, motion picture actor, governor of California (1967–74); he was the oldest and the first divorced person to become US president. Born at Tampico, IL. Married actress Jane Wyman in 1940 (divorced in 1948); married actress Nancy Davis, Mar 4, 1952. The "Great Communicator" ushered in a decade of conservative policies upon his election in 1980 and was an indefatigable critic of communist states: he famously challenged Soviet president Mikhail Gorbachev to "tear down this wall!" at the Berlin Wall in 1987. He died at his Los Angeles, CA, home on June 5, 2004.

RUTH, "BABE": BIRTH ANNIVERSARY. Feb 6, 1895. One of baseball's greatest heroes, George Herman "Babe" Ruth was born at Baltimore, MD. The left-handed pitcher—"the Sultan of Swat"—hit 714 home runs in 22 major league seasons of play and played in 10 World Series. Died at New York, NY, Aug 16, 1948.

SARANAC LAKE WINTER CARNIVAL. Feb 6–15. Saranac Lake, NY. 112th annual. The oldest winter festival in the eastern US. Come and join the family fun with fireworks, entertainment and much more. For info: Saranac Lake Winter Carnival, Saranac Lake Chamber of Commerce, 39 Main St, Saranac Lake, NY 12983. Phone: (518) 891-1990 or (800) 347-1992. Web: www.saranaclakewintercarnival.com.

SPECIAL OLYMPICS WORLD WINTER GAMES. Feb 6–13. Boise, ID. The Special Olympics movement offers one of the world's greatest platforms for acceptance and inclusion of all people transcending physical, cultural and geographic boundaries. More than 3,000 athletes from 85 nations will compete in seven Olympic-style sporting events, with thousands of coaches and volunteers on hand to support them. Est attendance: 150,000. For info: Special Olympics World Winter Games, 3150 W Main St, Boise, ID 83702. Phone: (208) 938-5505. Web: www.specialolympics.org.

TRUFFAUT, FRANÇOIS: BIRTH ANNIVERSARY. Feb 6, 1932. Born at Paris, France, Truffaut was the most popular and successful French film director of his time. His films include *The 400 Blows, Jules and Jim, The Last Metro* and *The Story of Adele H.* He died at Paris, Oct 21, 1984.

February 2009

S	M	T	W	T	F	S
1	2	3	4	5	6	7
8	9	10	11	12	13	14
15	16	17	18	19	20	21
22	23	24	25	26	27	28

Birthdays Today

Sarah Brady, 67, handgun control activist, born Alexandria, VA, Feb 6, 1942.

Tom Brokaw, 69, journalist, born Yankton, SD, Feb 6, 1940.

Natalie Cole, 59, singer, born Los Angeles, CA, Feb 6, 1950.

Fabian, 66, singer, actor, born Fabian Forte at Philadelphia, PA, Feb 6, 1943.

Mike Farrell, 70, actor ("M*A*S*H," "Providence"), born St. Paul, MN, Feb 6, 1939.

Zsa Zsa Gabor, 90, actress (*Ninotchka, Special Tonight*), born Budapest, Hungary, Feb 6, 1919.

Gayle Hunnicutt, 66, actress ("Dallas," *The Wild Angels, Marlowe*), born Fort Worth, TX, Feb 6, 1943.

Barry Miller, 51, stage and screen actor (Tony Award for *Biloxi Blues; Saturday Night Fever, The Last Temptation of Christ*), born Los Angeles, CA, Feb 6, 1958.

Kathy Najimy, 52, actress ("Veronica's Closet," *Sister Act*), born San Diego, CA, Feb 6, 1957.

Gigi Perreau, 68, actress (*Bonzo Goes to College, Tammy Tell Me True*), born Los Angeles, CA, Feb 6, 1941.

Rip Torn, 78, actor ("The Larry Sanders Show," *Men in Black*), born Elmore Torn, Jr, at Temple, TX, Feb 6, 1931.

Robert Townsend, 52, actor, director (*The Five Heartbeats, The Mighty Quinn*), born Chicago, IL, Feb 6, 1957.

Michael Tucker, 65, actor ("LA Law"), born Baltimore, MD, Feb 6, 1944.

Mamie Van Doren, 76, actress (*High School Confidential, Three Nuts in Search of a Bolt*), born Rowena, SD, Feb 6, 1933.

February 7 — Saturday

DAY 38 — 327 REMAINING

AMERICAN COUNCIL ON EDUCATION ANNUAL MEETING. Feb 7–10. Omni Shoreham Hotel, Washington, DC. 91st annual meeting. Est attendance: 1,600. For info: Stephanie Marshall, American Council on Education, One Dupont Circle, Washington, DC 20036. Phone: (202) 939-9410. Fax: (202) 833-5692. E-mail: annualmeeting@ace.nche.edu. Web: www.acenet.edu.

"AMERICA'S MOST WANTED" TV PREMIERE: ANNIVERSARY. Feb 7, 1988. One of the longest-running shows in television history, "America's Most Wanted" asks viewers to help find fugitives from the law by airing dramatic reenactments of crimes and interviewing law enforcement officials for insight. It also highlights cases of missing children. The show has led to more than 900 arrests. Popular host John Walsh closes by addressing viewers, "And remember, you can make a difference." The 900th episode aired July 21, 2007.

ARIZONA RENAISSANCE FESTIVAL. Feb 7–Mar 29. (Saturdays, Sundays and Presidents' Day [Feb 16] only.) Apache Junction, AZ. Enjoy your best day out in history. Find yourself surrounded by medieval merriment with knights, kings, maidens and minstrels as we celebrate our 21st season. Stroll through acres of amusements, shoppes and nonstop revelry as you join our village celebration. The official sister event to the Robin Hood Festival in Sherwood Forest, England. Est attendance: 265,000. For info: Arizona Renaissance Festival, 12601 E Hwy 60, Apache Junction, AZ 85218. Phone: (520) 463-2600. Web: www.renfestinfo.com.

BALLET INTRODUCED TO THE US: ANNIVERSARY. Feb 7, 1827. Renowned French danseuse Mme Francisquy Hutin introduced ballet to the US with a performance of *The Deserter*, staged at the Bowery Theater, New York, NY. A minor scandal erupted when the ladies in the lower boxes left the theater upon viewing the light and scanty attire of Mme Hutin and her troupe.

BLAKE, EUBIE: BIRTH ANNIVERSARY. Feb 7, 1883. James Hubert "Eubie" Blake, American composer and pianist, writer of nearly 1,000 songs (including "I'm Just Wild About Harry" and "Memories of You"). Born at Baltimore, MD. Recipient of the Presidential Medal of Freedom in 1981. Last professional performance was in January 1982. Died at Brooklyn, NY, five days after his 100th birthday, Feb 12, 1983.

CHAPLIN'S "TRAMP" DEBUTS: 95th ANNIVERSARY. Feb 7, 1914. Charlie Chaplin, vaudeville star-turned-comedic actor, debuted a new character in *Kid Auto Races at Venice*, a Keystone Studios short released on this date. The mischievous but innocent "Tramp," sporting a tiny mustache and twirling cane and wearing a little derby, tight-fitting jacket, baggy trousers and floppy shoes, was an immediate success with audiences, and soon mass-produced Tramp dolls were selling all over the US and the world.

CHINESE NEW YEAR PARADE IN SAN FRANCISCO. Feb 7. San Francisco, CA. North America's largest Chinese community salutes the Year of the Ox, Lunar Year 4707. Sponsored by Southwest Airlines. For info: Chinese Chamber of Commerce, 730 Sacramento St, San Francisco, CA 94108. Phone: (415) 982-3000. Fax: (415) 982-4720. Web: www.chineseparade.com.

COLONIAL FAIRE AND MUSTER. Feb 7–8. Wormsloe Historic Site, Savannah, GA. Experience colonial life through participation in military and Indian camps, craft demonstations, vendors, period music and dance. Hours 10 AM to 4 PM. For info: Wormsloe Historic Site, 7601 Skidaway Rd, Savannah, GA 31406. Phone: (912) 353-3023. E-mail: wormsloe@bellsouth.net. Web: www.wormsloe.org.

CONGENITAL HEART DEFECT AWARENESS WEEK. Feb 7–14. Public relations/media campaign, special events in cities throughout the US. Annually, Feb 7–14. For info: Mona Barmash, Congenital Heart Information Network, 1561 Clark Dr, Yardley, PA 19067. Phone: (215) 493-3068. E-mail: mb@tchin.org. Web: www.tchin.org.

CORVETTE AND HIGH PERFORMANCE MEET. Feb 7–8. Puyallup, WA. 35th annual. 1,000-booth swap meet with new and used car parts and automobilia. Vehicles for sale, Corvette invitational display area. Est attendance: 10,000. For info: Larry Johnson, Show Organizer, PO Box 7753, Olympia, WA 98507. Phone: (360) 786-8844. Fax: (360) 754-1498. Web: www.corvhp.com.

DICKENS, CHARLES: BIRTH ANNIVERSARY. Feb 7, 1812. English social critic and novelist, born at Portsmouth, England. Among his most successful books: *Oliver Twist, The Posthumous Papers of the Pickwick Club, A Tale of Two Cities, David Copperfield* and *A Christmas Carol.* Died at Gad's Hill, England, June 9, 1870, and was buried at Westminster Abbey.

DOLL SHOW. Feb 7. Yuma Civic Center, Yuma, AZ. Assorted antique, handmade and collector's dolls on display and for sale. Also, miniature furniture and doll-making supplies for sale. Sponsor: Yuma Doll Club. Annually, the first Saturday in February. Est attendance: 750. For info: Yuma Civic Center, 1440 Desert Hills Dr, Yuma, AZ 85365. Phone: (928) 373-5040. Fax: (928) 344-9121. E-mail: ycc@yumaaz.gov. Web: www.yumaaz.gov.

DUMP YOUR "SIGNIFICANT JERK" WEEK. Feb 7–13. It's time to take out the garbage and get rid of that "jerk" boyfriend or girlfriend. This year will be the 16th annual call to arms. Annually, the week before Valentine's Day. For info: Marcus P. Meleton, Jr, Sharkbait Press, PO Box 11300, Costa Mesa, CA 92627. Phone: (949) 413-3052. E-mail: mm@sharkbaitpress.com. Web: www.sharkbaitpress.com.

ELEVENTH AMENDMENT TO US CONSTITUTION (SOVEREIGNTY OF THE STATES): RATIFICATION ANNIVERSARY. Feb 7, 1795. The 11th Amendment to the Constitution was ratified, curbing the powers of the federal judiciary in relation to the states. The amendment reaffirmed the sovereignty of the states by prohibiting suits against them.

GRENADA: INDEPENDENCE DAY: 35th ANNIVERSARY. Feb 7. National Day. Commemorates independence from Great Britain in 1974.

JAMES DEAN BIRTHDAY CELEBRATION. Feb 7–8. Fairmount, IN. The town where James Dean grew up celebrates his birthday with a movie showing, exhibits, refreshments and more. *East of Eden* will be screened, and the Fairmount Museum will be open all weekend. For info: Fairmount Historical Museum, Inc, 203 E Washington St, PO Box 92, Fairmount, IN 46928. Phone: (765) 948-4555. Web: www.jamesdeanartifacts.com.

LEWIS, SINCLAIR: BIRTH ANNIVERSARY. Feb 7, 1885. American novelist and social critic. Recipient of Nobel Prize for Literature (1930). Among his novels: *Main Street, Babbitt* and *It Can't Happen Here.* Born Harry Sinclair Lewis at Sauk Center, MN. Died at Rome, Italy, Jan 10, 1951.

MOBIUS ADVERTISING AWARDS. Feb 7. Los Angeles, CA. Selection and recognition of the world's most outstanding television and radio commercials, print advertising and package designs. Founded in 1971. The entry deadline is annually on Oct 1. Est attendance: 200. For info: Lee W. Gluckman, The Mobius Advertising Awards, 713 S Pacific Coast Hwy, Ste A, Redondo Beach, CA 90277-4233. Phone: (310) 540-0959. Fax: (310) 316-8905. E-mail: mobiusinfo@mobiusawards.com. Web: www.mobiusawards.com.

MORE, SIR THOMAS: BIRTH ANNIVERSARY. Feb 7, 1478. Anniversary of the birth of the lawyer, scholar, author, lord chancellor of England, martyr and saint at London, England. Refusing to recognize Henry VIII's divorce from Queen Catherine, the "Man for All Seasons" was found guilty of treason and imprisoned in the Tower of London, Apr 17, 1534. He was beheaded at Tower Hill on July 6, 1535, and his head displayed from Tower Bridge. Canonized in 1935. Memorial observed on June 22.

PERRY'S "BRR" (BIKE RIDE TO RIPPEY). Feb 7. Perry, IA. Winter bike riding. Twenty-two miles of frigid fun. Annually, the first Saturday in February. Est attendance: 3,000. For info: Sara Truesdell, Chamber of Commerce, 1226 Second St, Perry, IA 50220. Phone: (515) 465-4601. Fax: (515) 465-2256. E-mail: perrychmbr@aol.com. Web: www.perryia.org.

REJECTION/RISK AWARENESS WEEK. Feb 7–14. An annual event celebrating the risk that leads to love. Syndicated advice columnist Harlan Cohen founded RAW in 2003 to help expose the unspoken truth about dating and relationships—that relationship rejection is an unavoidable, normal and natural part of the search for true love. Celebrate RAW by taking the risk that leads to love. Annually, the week leading up to Valentine's Day. For info: Harlan Cohen, Help Me, Harlan!, 2506 N Clark St, Ste 223, Chicago, IL 60614. Phone: (212) 455-4180. E-mail: raw@helpmeharlan.com. Web: www.helpmeharlan.com.

SHOOTOUT AT DAYTONA SPRINT CUP SERIES RACE. Feb 7. Daytona International Speedway, Daytona Beach, FL. Dash for the cash featuring NASCAR Sprint Cup stars. For info: Daytona International Speedway, PO Box 2801, Daytona Beach, FL 32120-2801. Phone: (800) PIT-SHOP. Web: www.daytonainternationalspeedway.com.

SPACE MILESTONE: *STARDUST* (US): 10th ANNIVERSARY. Feb 7, 1999. *Stardust* began its three-billion-mile journey to collect comet dust on this date. The unmanned mission met up with *Comet Wild-2* on Jan 2, 2004, and returned to Earth on Jan 15, 2006, with a 100-pound canister of comet dust samples. This was the first US mission devoted solely to a comet.

TWIN CITIES' KREWE OF JANUS MARDI GRAS PARADE. Feb 7. Monroe, LA. The streets of Monroe and West Monroe come alive to celebrate Mardi Gras. Bands, music and elaborate floats light up the twin cities with fun for all. For info: Monroe/West Monroe CVB, 601 Constitution Dr, West Monroe, LA 71292. Phone: (800) 843-1872. Fax: (318) 324-1752. E-mail: ssnow@monroe-westmonroe.org. Web: www.monroe-westmonroe.org.

WAVE ALL YOUR FINGERS AT YOUR NEIGHBORS DAY. Feb 7. After all the challenges our neighbors and we have faced, it's time to put it all aside for at least one day. Wave "hello" to everybody and mean it. Annually, Feb 7. (©2006 by WH.) For info: Thomas & Ruth Roy, Wellcat Holidays, 2418 Long Ln, Lebanon, PA 17046. Phone: (717) 279-0184. E-mail: info@wellcat.com. Web: www.wellcat.com.

Birthdays Today

Hector Babenco, 63, director (*Ironweed, Kiss of the Spider Woman*), born Buenos Aires, Argentina, Feb 7, 1946.

Oscar Brand, 89, folksinger, born Winnipeg, MB, Canada, Feb 7, 1920.

Garth Brooks, 47, country singer, born Tulsa, OK, Feb 7, 1962.

Miguel Ferrer, 55, actor ("Crossing Jordan," "Twin Peaks," *RoboCop*), born Santa Monica, CA, Feb 7, 1954.

Juwan Howard, 36, basketball player, born Chicago, IL, Feb 7, 1973.

Eddie Izzard, 47, performer, actor ("The Riches"), born Edward John Izzard at Aden, Yemen, Feb 7, 1962.

Herb Kohl, 74, US Senator (D, Wisconsin), born Milwaukee, WI, Feb 7, 1935.

Ashton Kutcher, 31, actor ("That 70s Show," *Dude, Where's My Car?*), born Cedar Rapids, IA, Feb 7, 1978.

Steve Nash, 35, basketball player, born Johannesburg, South Africa, Feb 7, 1974.

Pete Postlethwaite, 64, actor (*Amistad; The Lost World: Jurassic Park; Brassed Off*), born London, England, Feb 7, 1945.

Chris Rock, 43, actor, comedian, born Brooklyn, NY, Feb 7, 1966.

James Spader, 49, actor ("Boston Legal," *Secretary, Stargate*), born Boston, MA, Feb 7, 1960.

Gay Talese, 77, author (*The Kingdom and the Power, Unto the Sons*), born Ocean City, NJ, Feb 7, 1932.

February 8 — Sunday

DAY 39 — 326 REMAINING

BOY SCOUTS OF AMERICA FOUNDED: ANNIVERSARY. Feb 8, 1910. The Boy Scouts of America was founded at Washington, DC, by William Boyce, based on the work of Sir Robert Baden-Powell with the British Boy Scout Association.

DAYTONA 500 POLE DAY. Feb 8. Daytona International Speedway, Daytona Beach, FL. Fastest qualifiers have the front row for the Daytona 500. For info: Daytona International Speedway, PO Box 2801, Daytona Beach, FL 32120-2801. Phone: (800) PIT-SHOP. Web: www.daytonainternationalspeedway.com.

DEAN, JAMES: BIRTH ANNIVERSARY. Feb 8, 1931. American stage, film and television actor who achieved immense popularity during a brief career. Born at Fairmount, IN. Best remembered for his role in *Rebel Without a Cause*. Died in an automobile accident near Cholame, CA, Sept 30, 1955, at age 24.

FREELANCE WRITERS APPRECIATION WEEK. Feb 8–14. Freelance writers do more than query editors and write and submit articles and books (nonfiction and fiction). They provide overworked editors with material, as well as inform and entertain readers. Annually, the second week of February. Visit www.profitable-pen.com for ideas and discussions—registration is free. For info: Dorothy Zjawin, Dir, 61 W Colfax Ave, Roselle Park, NJ 07204.

THE GRAMMY AWARDS. Feb 8. Staples Center, Los Angeles, CA. 51st annual. Celebrating the best in recording arts and sciences, the Grammys cover 104 categories—from classical to jazz to pop and rock. Awarded by and to artists and technical professionals. For info: National Academy of Recording Arts & Sciences, 3402 Pico Blvd, Santa Monica, CA 90405. Phone: (310) 392-3777. Fax: (310) 392-2778. Web: www.grammy.com.

JAPAN: HA-RI-KU-YO (NEEDLE MASS). Feb 8. For Ha-Ri-Ku-Yo, a Needle Mass, observed on Feb 8, women gather their old and broken needles and take them to their temples to offer a prayer of thanks for their hard work. Girls pray to Awashima Myozin (their protecting deity) that their needlework, symbolic of love and marriage, will be good. Girls hope that participation in the Needle Mass will lead to a happy marriage.

JAPAN: SNOW FESTIVAL. Feb 8–12. Sapporo, Hokkaido. Huge, elaborate snow and ice sculptures are erected on the Odori-Koen Promenade.

JELL-O® WEEK. Feb 8–14. Celebrated annually the second full week in February. The first Jell-O® Week was officially declared by the Utah legislature in 2001. For info: Hunter Public Relations, 41 Madison Ave, 5th Fl, New York, NY 10010. Phone: (212) 679-6600. Web: www.hunterpr.com.

LAUGH AND GET RICH DAY. Feb 8. Recognition of laughter's power to add to the bottom line. People who laugh are more effective and tend to remember things better, and laughter helps to lower the turnover rate. For info: Rick Segel, 543 Davinci Pass, Poinciana, FL 34759. Phone: (781) 272-9995. Fax: (800) 847-9411. E-mail: rick@ricksegel.com.

LEMMON, JACK: BIRTH ANNIVERSARY. Feb 8, 1925. Stage, screen and television actor, born John Uhler Lemmon III at Boston, MA. Often paired with actor Walter Matthau, he starred in such films as *The Odd Couple, The Fortune Cookie* and *The Front Page*. He was nominated for seven Academy Awards, winning in 1955 for his supporting role in *Mister Roberts* and in 1974 for his leading role in *Save the Tiger*. Other films included *Some Like It Hot, Days of Wine and Roses* and *Grumpy Old Men*. He also starred in television versions of *Inherit the Wind* and *Twelve Angry Men* and won an Emmy in 2000 for the TV movie *Tuesdays with Morrie*. He died at Los Angeles, CA, June 27, 2001.

LOVE MAY MAKE THE WORLD GO 'ROUND, BUT LAUGHTER KEEPS US FROM GETTING DIZZY WEEK. Feb 8–14. 32nd annual. This week is dedicated to Victor Borge's notion that "Laughter is the shortest distance between two people" and Joel Goodman's notion that "Seven days without laughter makes one weak." This is a chance to lighten your relationships and to reinforce the connection between "heart" and "hearty laughter." Annually, the week leading up to and including Valentine's Day. For info on the positive power of humor: The HUMOR Project, Inc, 480 Broadway, Ste 210-C, Saratoga Springs, NY 12866-2288. Phone: (518) 587-8770. E-mail: chase@HumorProject.com. Web: www.HumorProject.com.

MAN DAY. Feb 8. A day for celebration by friends, family and associates of the men of the world. Annually, the Sunday before Valentine's Day. (©2002 C. Daniel Rhodes.) For info: C. Daniel Rhodes, 1900 Crossvine Rd, Hoover, AL 35244. Phone: (205) 908-6781. E-mail: rhodan@charter.net.

February 2009

S	M	T	W	T	F	S
1	2	3	4	5	6	7
8	9	10	11	12	13	14
15	16	17	18	19	20	21
22	23	24	25	26	27	28

MARY, QUEEN OF SCOTS: EXECUTION ANNIVERSARY. Feb 8, 1587. Mary Stuart, the queen regent of Scotland, was beheaded at Fotheringhay, England, after being accused of plotting Queen Elizabeth I's death. Mary, the daughter of James V of Scotland by his second wife, Mary of Guise, was born Dec 7 or 8, 1542, at Linlithgow, Scotland, and became queen a week later upon the death of her father, although she did not begin governing until after her mother's death in 1561. Accused of knowingly marrying the alleged murderer of her second husband, Lord Darnley, she was forced to abdicate in favor of her son (James VI) and fled to England for protection, only to find herself a prisoner for the rest of her life—a victim of Elizabethan political intrigue.

OCEAN COUNTY BLUEGRASS FESTIVAL. Feb 8 (also Sept 13). Waretown, NJ. A family-oriented bluegrass festival where no alcoholic beverages or smoking are allowed. Two shows each year, one in February and one in September. Est attendance: 400. For info: Albert Music Hall, PO Box 657, Waretown, NJ 08758. Phone: (609) 971-1593. Web: www.alberthall.org.

OPERA DEBUT IN THE COLONIES: ANNIVERSARY. Feb 8, 1735. The first opera produced in the colonies was performed at the Courtroom, at Charleston, SC. The opera was *Flora; or the Hob in the Well*, written by Colley Cibber.

REENACTMENT OF COWTOWN'S LAST OLD WEST GUNFIGHT. Feb 8. White Elephant Saloon, Fort Worth, TX. Annual reenactment of Fort Worth's last Old West gunfight, which took place on Feb 8, 1887, between White Elephant Saloon owner Luke Short and former marshal T.I. "Longhaired Jim" Courtright. Annually, Feb 8. Est attendance: 400. For info: Jason Tighe, Dir of Operations, 108 E Exchange Ave, Fort Worth, TX 76164. Phone: (817) 624-9712. Fax: (817) 625-9663. E-mail: info@whiteelephantsaloon.com. Web: www.whiteelephantsaloon.com.

SHERMAN, WILLIAM TECUMSEH: BIRTH ANNIVERSARY. Feb 8, 1820. Born at Lancaster, OH, General Sherman is especially remembered for his devastating march through Georgia during the Civil War and his statement "War is hell." Died at New York, NY, Feb 14, 1891.

SLOVENIA: CULTURE DAY. Feb 8. National holiday. Honors France Preseren, Slovenia's national poet, who died Feb 8, 1849.

SPACE MILESTONE: *ARABSAT-1* AND *BRASILSAT-1* (BRAZIL). Feb 8, 1985. League of Arab States and Brazilian communications satellites launched into geosynchronous orbit from Kourou, French Guiana, by the European Space Agency.

VERNE, JULES: BIRTH ANNIVERSARY. Feb 8, 1828. French writer, sometimes called the "father of science fiction," born at Nantes, France. Author of *Around the World in Eighty Days, Twenty Thousand Leagues Under the Sea* and many other novels. Died at Amiens, France, Mar 24, 1905.

WORLD MARRIAGE DAY. Feb 8. World Marriage Day honors husband and wife as head of the family, the basic unit of society. It salutes the beauty of their faithfulness, sacrifice and joy in daily married life. Sponsored by WorldWide Marriage Encounter since 1981. Annually, second Sunday in February. For info: WorldWide Marriage Encounter, 2210 E Highland, #106, San Bernardino, CA 92404. Phone: (301) 871-1595. Fax: (909) 863-9986. E-mail: office@wwme.org. Web: www.wwme.org.

Birthdays Today

Brooke Adams, 60, actress (*Days of Heaven, Gas Food Lodging*), born New York, NY, Feb 8, 1949.

Gary Coleman, 41, actor ("Diff'rent Strokes," *The Kid from Left Field*), born Zion, IL, Feb 8, 1968.

Seth Green, 35, actor ("Family Guy," "Greg the Bunny," *Austin Powers*), born Overbrook Park, PA, Feb 8, 1974.

John Grisham, 54, author (*The Firm, The Client*), born Jonesboro, AR, Feb 8, 1955.

Robert Klein, 67, comedian, actor ("Comedy Tonight," *They're Playing Our Song*), born New York, NY, Feb 8, 1942.

Ted Koppel, 69, journalist, born Lancashire, England, Feb 8, 1940.

Alonzo Mourning, 39, basketball player, born Chesapeake, VA, Feb 8, 1970.

Nick Nolte, 68, actor (*Affliction, Prince of Tides*, "Rich Man, Poor Man"), born Omaha, NE, Feb 8, 1941.

Mary Steenburgen, 56, actress (*Melvin and Howard, Parenthood, Back to the Future Part III*), born Newport, AR, Feb 8, 1953.

John Williams, 77, pianist, conductor (formerly with Boston Pops), composer (scores for *Jaws, Star Wars, Jurassic Park, Schindler's List*), born New York, NY, Feb 8, 1932.

February 9 — Monday

DAY 40 — 325 REMAINING

ALLIES RETAKE GUADALCANAL: ANNIVERSARY. Feb 9, 1943. In a major strategic victory, the American 161st and 132nd Regiments retook Guadalcanal in the Solomon Islands on this date after a six-month-long battle. More than 9,000 Japanese and 2,000 Americans were killed. The fierce resistance by the Japanese was an indication to the Allies of things to come. Guadalcanal put the Allies within striking distance of Rabaul, the major Japanese base in the area.

THE BEATLES APPEAR ON "THE ED SULLIVAN SHOW": 45th ANNIVERSARY. Feb 9, 1964. British pop phenomenon the Beatles began the "British Invasion" of America with their appearance on America's top television variety show. They performed five songs before a screaming studio audience of 728. The estimated viewership for that night's show was 73 million people—making it the most-viewed US TV program in history up to that time. See also: "Beatles Take Over Music Charts" (Apr 4).

BEHAN, BRENDAN: BIRTH ANNIVERSARY. Feb 9, 1923. Irish playwright and poet, born at Dublin, Ireland. Died there Mar 20, 1964.

CHINA: LANTERN FESTIVAL. Feb 9. Traditional Chinese festival falls on the 15th day of the first month of the Chinese lunar calendar year. Lantern processions mark the end of the Chinese New Year holiday season. Also celebrated in Taiwan and Korea. Date in other countries will differ from China's by up to one day. See also: "Chinese New Year" (Jan 26).

GYPSY ROSE LEE: 95th BIRTH ANNIVERSARY. Feb 9, 1914. American ecdysiast and author whose real name was Rose Louise Hovick, born at Seattle, WA. Her autobiography, *Gypsy*, was made into a Broadway musical and a motion picture. Died at Los Angeles, CA, Apr 26, 1970.

HARRISON, WILLIAM HENRY: BIRTH ANNIVERSARY. Feb 9, 1773. 9th president of the US (Mar 4–Apr 4, 1841). His term of office was the shortest in our nation's history—32 days. He was the first president to die in office (of pneumonia contracted during inaugural ceremonies). Born at Berkeley, VA, he died at Washington, DC, Apr 4, 1841. His grandson, Benjamin Harrison, was the 23rd president of the US.

INTERNATIONAL FLIRTING WEEK. Feb 9–15. Celebrating the ancient art of flirting and recognizing the role it plays in the lives of singles seeking a mate, couples looking to sustain their love and those simply exchanging a playful glance with a stranger, acquaintance, colleague, etc. For info: Robin Gorman Newman, 44 Somerset Dr N, Great Neck, NY 11020. Phone: (516) 773-0911. E-mail: robin@lovecoach.com. Web: www.lovecoach.com.

JUST SAY NO TO POWERPOINT® WEEK. Feb 9–13. All across America businesspeople are being asked to make presentations without the use of PowerPoint®. We challenge them to communicate with their audiences rather than merely slideswiping them (reading one boring, words-only slide after another, after another). For info: Nancy Stern. Phone: (800) 280-2666. Fax: (858) 792-2745. E-mail: nancy@nancystern.com. Web: www.nancystern.com.

LEBANON: ST. MARON'S DAY. Feb 9. Holiday of Lebanon's Maronite Christian community. St. Maron was a Syrian hermit of the fourth–fifth centuries.

LOWELL, AMY: BIRTH ANNIVERSARY. Feb 9, 1874. American poet born at Brookline, MA. Died there May 12, 1925.

LUNAR ECLIPSE. Feb 9. Penumbral eclipse of the moon. Visible in eastern Europe, Asia, Australia, the Pacific Ocean region and western North America.

MOON PHASE: FULL MOON. Feb 9. Moon enters Full Moon phase at 9:49 AM, EST.

NATIONAL FIELD TRIAL CHAMPIONSHIP. Feb 9–19 (end date tentative). Ames Plantation, Grand Junction, TN. To select the national champion all-age bird dog. Est attendance: 4,000. For info: R.J. Carlisle, Secy/Treas, Natl Field Trial Champion Assn, Box 389, Grand Junction, TN 38039. Phone: (901) 878-1067. Fax: (901) 878-1068. E-mail: info@amesplantation.org. Web: www.amesplantation.org.

READ IN THE BATHTUB DAY. Feb 9. Set aside a day each year to be spent in the bathtub reading a novel. For info: Christine Rogers, 8098 Regents Rd, #301, San Diego, CA 92122. Phone: (858) 412-3687. E-mail: flidais95350@hotmail.com.

RUSK, (DAVID) DEAN: 100th BIRTH ANNIVERSARY. Feb 9, 1909. US diplomat Dean Rusk was born at Cherokee County, GA. He served as US secretary of state from 1961 to 1969, during which time he supported US involvement in the Vietnam War. He died Dec 20, 1994, at Athens, GA.

SNOW MOON. Feb 9. So called by Native American tribes of New England and the Great Lakes because this time of year sees heavy snowfalls. Also called the Hunger Moon, because of the meager hunting at this time of winter. The February Full Moon.

TU B'SHVAT. Feb 9. Hebrew calendar date: Shebat 15, 5769. The 15th day of the month of Shebat in the Hebrew calendar year is set aside as Hamishah Asar (New Year of the Trees, or Jewish Arbor Day), a time to show respect and appreciation for trees and plants. Began at sundown on Feb 8.

TUBB, ERNEST: 95th BIRTH ANNIVERSARY. Feb 9, 1914. Country and western singer, born at Crisp, TX. Ernest Tubb was the sixth member to be elected to the Country Music Hall of Fame and the headliner on the first country music show ever to be presented at Carnegie Hall. His first major hit, "Walking the Floor over You," gained him his first appearance at the Grand Ole Opry in 1942, and he attained regular membership in 1943. He died Sept 6, 1984, at Nashville, TN.

UNION OFFICERS ESCAPE LIBBY PRISON: ANNIVERSARY. Feb 9, 1864. On this date 109 Union officers escaped from Libby Prison at Richmond, VA, in the largest and most dramatic prisoner of war escape of the Civil War. The Libby Prison was the former Libby and Sons candle factory. Forty-eight of the men were recaptured, two drowned and fifty-nine successfully made it back to Federal lines.

February 2009	S	M	T	W	T	F	S
	1	2	3	4	5	6	7
	8	9	10	11	12	13	14
	15	16	17	18	19	20	21
	22	23	24	25	26	27	28

VEECK, BILL: 95th BIRTH ANNIVERSARY. Feb 9, 1914. William Louis (Bill) Veeck, Jr, Baseball Hall of Fame executive born at Chicago, IL. Veeck was baseball's premier promoter and showman as an owner of several teams. He integrated the American League, sent a midget to the plate to start a game and, in general, sought to provide fans with entertainment in addition to baseball. Inducted into the Hall of Fame in 1991. Died at Chicago, Jan 2, 1986.

WAR TIME: ANNIVERSARY. Feb 9, 1942. US clocks were advanced one hour at 2 AM as the nation went on War Time to conserve electricity. President Roosevelt had signed this daylight saving bill on Jan 20.

WESTMINSTER KENNEL CLUB DOG SHOW. Feb 9–10. Madison Square Garden, New York, NY. 133rd annual. America's first and only all-champions dog show. Entry limited to 2,500 dogs. Group and Best in Show competitions televised live on USA Network. For info: Westminster Kennel Club, 149 Madison Ave, Ste 803, New York, NY 10016. Web: westminsterkennelclub.org.

Birthdays Today

Mia Farrow, 64, actress ("Peyton Place," *Rosemary's Baby, Hannah and Her Sisters*), born Maria de Lourdes Villers at Los Angeles, CA, Feb 9, 1945.

Kathryn Grayson, 86, actress (*Kiss Me Kate, The Kissing Bandit*), born Zelma Hedrick at Winston-Salem, NC, Feb 9, 1923.

Vladimir Guerrero, 33, baseball player, born Nizao Bani, Dominican Republic, Feb 9, 1976.

Carole King, 67, singer, songwriter, born Brooklyn, NY, Feb 9, 1942.

Judith Light, 60, actress ("Ugly Betty," "One Life to Live," "Who's the Boss?"), born Trenton, NJ, Feb 9, 1949.

Roger Mudd, 81, journalist, born Washington, DC, Feb 9, 1928.

Joe Pesci, 66, actor (*Raging Bull, Goodfellas, My Cousin Vinny*), born Newark, NJ, Feb 9, 1943.

Shakira, 32, singer, born Shakira Isabelle Mebarak Ripoll at Barranquilla, Colombia, Feb 9, 1977.

Charles Shaughnessy, 54, actor ("Days of Our Lives," "The Nanny"), born London, England, Feb 9, 1955.

Mena Suvari, 30, actress (*American Beauty, Loser*), born Newport, RI, Feb 9, 1979.

Janet Suzman, 70, actress (*Nicholas and Alexandra, A Dry White Season*), born Johannesburg, South Africa, Feb 9, 1939.

Travis Tritt, 46, country and western singer, born Marietta, GA, Feb 9, 1963.

Alice Walker, 65, author (*The Color Purple*), born Eatonton, GA, Feb 9, 1944.

James Webb, 63, US Senator (D, Virginia), born St. Josph, MO, Feb 9, 1946.

Ziyi Zhang, 30, actress (*Crouching Tiger, Hidden Dragon; House of Flying Daggers*), born Beijing, China, Feb 9, 1979.

February 10 — Tuesday

DAY 41 — **324 REMAINING**

"ALL THE NEWS THAT'S FIT TO PRINT": ANNIVERSARY. Feb 10, 1897. The familiar slogan "All the News That's Fit to Print" has appeared on page one of the *New York Times* since Feb 10, 1897. It had first appeared on the editorial page on Oct 25, 1896. Although in 1896 a $100 prize was offered for a slogan, owner Adolph S. Ochs concluded that his own slogan was best.

ANDERSON, DAME JUDITH: BIRTH ANNIVERSARY. Feb 10, 1898. Film and stage actress Dame Judith Anderson was born Frances Margaret Anderson at Adelaide, Australia. She was nominated for an Academy Award in 1941 for her role in Alfred Hitchcock's film *Rebecca*. In 1960 she was made dame commander of the

British Empire by Queen Elizabeth II. She died Jan 3, 1992, at Santa Barbara, CA.

BRECHT, BERTOLT: BIRTH ANNIVERSARY. Feb 10, 1898. German playwright born at Augsburg, Germany. His plays, such as *Mother Courage*, reflect his Marxist and antimilitary world view. Also wrote *The Threepenny Opera* in collaboration with composer Kurt Weill. Died at East Berlin, Aug 14, 1956.

CIVILIAN AUTO PRODUCTION HALTED: ANNIVERSARY. Feb 10, 1942. The production of civilian automobiles was halted on this date. Auto plants were used exclusively to build tanks, jeeps and aircraft until 1945. Contracts were determined on a cost-plus basis under the direction of the War Production Board.

***DEATH OF A SALESMAN* PREMIERE: 60th ANNIVERSARY.** Feb 10, 1949. Arthur Miller's postwar dramatic masterpiece opened at Broadway's Morosco Theater on this day. Elia Kazan was the director, and Lee J. Cobb (Willy Loman), Arthur Kennedy (Biff) and Cameron Mitchell (Happy) starred. The play garnered six Tony Awards and was also awarded the 1949 Pulitzer Prize for Drama.

DURANTE, JIMMY: BIRTH ANNIVERSARY. Feb 10, 1893. "The Schnozz," Jimmy Durante, was born at New York City. His break into show biz came when he was 17 and got a regular job playing ragtime at a saloon at Coney Island. Later his friend Eddie Cantor urged him to try comedy. Durante developed a unique comedic style as a short-tempered but lovable personage. His shtick included slamming down his hat and flapping his arms. His clothing, enormous nose, craggy face, gravelly singing voice and mispronunciations were all part of the persona. Durante, whose career spanned six decades, appeared on TV, stage and screen. His television sign-off, "Good night, Mrs Calabash, wherever you are!" became a trademark. Jimmy Durante died at Santa Monica, CA, Jan 29, 1980.

FIRST ACTOR TO PERFORM IN TWO CITIES ON THE SAME DAY: ANNIVERSARY. Feb 10, 1887. Nathaniel Carr Goodwin performed at an 11:30 AM matinee of *Turned Up* at Boston, MA, and then, following the closing curtain, he returned to New York City on the 1 PM train and that evening performed in *The Mascot* at the Bijou Theatre at 8 PM.

FIRST COMPUTER CHESS VICTORY OVER HUMAN: ANNIVERSARY. Feb 10, 1996. IBM's Deep Blue computer defeated world champion Garry Kasparov in 34 moves on this date in Philadelphia, PA—the first such victory by a computer in tournament conditions. Kasparov, however, went on to win the tournament, defeating the computer three times (the other two matches were draws). In May 1997, in a six-game rematch, Deep Blue emerged the overall victor. Deep Blue, an RS/6000 supercomputer, can evaluate 200 million chess positions a second but is not capable of using artificial intelligence to "learn." Kasparov was reigning World Chess Champion from 1985 to 2000.

FIRST WORLD WAR II MEDAL OF HONOR: ANNIVERSARY. Feb 10, 1942. Second Lieutenant Alexander Ramsey "Sandy" Nininger, Jr, was posthumously awarded WWII's first Medal of Honor for heroism at the Battle of Bataan. He had graduated from West Point in 1941 and was on his first assignment after being commissioned.

LAMB, CHARLES: BIRTH ANNIVERSARY. Feb 10, 1775. Literary critic, poet and essayist, born at London, England. "The greatest pleasure I know," he wrote in 1834, "is to do a good action by stealth, and to have it found out by accident." Died at Edmonton, England, Dec 27, 1834.

MALTA: FEAST OF ST. PAUL'S SHIPWRECK. Feb 10. Valletta. Holy day of obligation. Commemorates the shipwreck of St. Paul on the north coast of Malta in AD 60.

"MY FRIEND FLICKA" TV PREMIERE: ANNIVERSARY. Feb 10, 1956. CBS series about a boy and his horse based on the children's book by Mary O'Hara. The series was set in the early 1900s on the Goose Bar Ranch in Montana. Johnny Washbrook starred as Ken McLaughlin; Gene Evans as Ken's father, Rob; Anita Louise as Ken's mother, Nell; Frank Ferguson as Gus, the ranch hand; and Wahama, the beautiful Arabian horse, as Flicka.

PASTERNAK, BORIS LEONIDOVICH: BIRTH ANNIVERSARY. Feb 10, 1890. Russian poet and novelist, born at Moscow, Russia. Best-known work: *Doctor Zhivago*. Died at Moscow, May 30, 1960.

PLIMSOLL DAY (SAMUEL PLIMSOLL BIRTH ANNIVERSARY). Feb 10, 1824. A day to remember Samuel Plimsoll, "the Sailor's Friend," a coal merchant turned reformer and politician, who was elected to the British parliament in 1868. He attacked the practice of overloading heavily insured ships, calling them "coffin ships." His persistence brought about amendment of Britain's Merchant Shipping Act. The Plimsoll Line, named for him, is a line on the side of ships marking maximum load allowed by law. Born at Bristol, England; died at Folkestone, England, June 3, 1898.

TILDEN, BILL: BIRTH ANNIVERSARY. Feb 10, 1893. William Tatem (Bill) Tilden, Jr, tennis player, born at Philadelphia, PA. Generally considered one of the greatest players of all time, Tilden won more tournaments than the record books can count. A nearly flawless player, he was also an egotistical showman on the court with an interest in show business. He turned pro in 1930 and continued to win regularly. Died at Hollywood, CA, June 5, 1953.

TREATY OF PARIS ENDS FRENCH AND INDIAN WAR: ANNIVERSARY. Feb 10, 1763. Known in Europe as the Seven Years' War, this conflict ranged from North America to India, with many European nations involved. In North America, French expansion in the Ohio River Valley in the 1750s led to conflict with Great Britain. Some Indians fought alongside the French; a young George Washington fought for the British. As a result of the signing of the Treaty of Paris, France lost all claims to Canada and had to cede Louisiana to Spain. Fifteen years later, French bitterness over the loss of its North American colonies to Britain contributed to its supporting the colonists in the American Revolution.

TWENTY-FIFTH AMENDMENT TO US CONSTITUTION RATIFIED (PRESIDENTIAL SUCCESSION, DISABILITY): ANNIVERSARY. Feb 10, 1967. Procedures for presidential succession were further clarified by the 25th Amendment, along with provisions for continuity of power in the event of a disability or illness of the president.

WORLD AG EXPO. Feb 10–12. Tulare, CA. 42nd annual. The largest farm equipment show in North America. Est attendance: 100,000. For info: Intl Agri-Center, PO Box 1475, Tulare, CA 93275. Phone: (800) 999-9186 or (559) 688-1751. Fax: (559) 686-5065. E-mail: info@farmshow.org. Web: www.farmshow.org.

 Birthdays Today

Jim Cramer, 54, financial analyst, broadcaster ("Mad Money with Jim Cramer"), born Wyndmoor, PA, Feb 10, 1955.

Laura Dern, 42, actress (*Blue Velvet, Rambling Rose*), born Los Angeles, CA, Feb 10, 1967.

Donovan, 63, singer, songwriter, born Donovan P. Leitch at Glasgow, Scotland, Feb 10, 1946.

Leonard Kyle (Lenny) Dykstra, 46, former baseball player, born Santa Ana, CA, Feb 10, 1963.

Roberta Flack, 70, singer, born Black Mountain, NC, Feb 10, 1939.

Justin Gatlin, 27, sprinter, born Brooklyn, NY, Feb 10, 1982.

Frances Moore Lappe, 65, author (*Diet for a Small Planet, Rediscovering America's Values*), born Pendleton, OR, Feb 10, 1944.

Gregory John (Greg) Norman, 54, golfer, born Melbourne, Australia, Feb 10, 1955.

Leontyne Price, 82, opera singer, born Laurel, MS, Feb 10, 1927.

Mark Andrew Spitz, 59, Olympic gold medal swimmer, born Modesto, CA, Feb 10, 1950.

Robert Wagner, 79, actor ("It Takes a Thief," "Hart to Hart"), born Detroit, MI, Feb 10, 1930.

February 11 — Wednesday

DAY 42 | **323 REMAINING**

BAER, MAX: 100th BIRTH ANNIVERSARY. Feb 2, 1909. Maximillian Adalbert (Max) Baer, boxer, born at Omaha, NE. Baer possessed awesome punching power and once knocked out a fighter who collapsed into a coma and died from his injuries. He won the heavyweight title from Primo Carnera on June 14, 1934, and lost it a year later to James Braddock, a severe underdog. Died at Hollywood, CA, Nov 21, 1959.

BE ELECTRIFIC DAY. Feb 11. A day to honor the birth of Thomas Alva Edison and recognize his electrical inventions, including the lightbulb. It is also the day to discover our own "body electricity." Annually, Feb 11. For info: Carolyn Finch, Electrific Solutions, 51 Cedar Dr, Danbury, CT 06811. Phone: (203) 791-2756. Fax: (203) 742-5675. E-mail: carolynf@electrific.com. Web: www.electrific.com.

CAMEROON: YOUTH DAY. Feb 11. Public holiday.

CHILD, LYDIA MARIA: BIRTH ANNIVERSARY. Feb 11, 1802. Born at Medford, MA. A writer whose works included *Hobomok*, about early Salem and Plymouth life, and *The Rebels*, which described pre-Revolutionary Boston. In addition, she produced several practical works, including *The Frugal Housewife*, which enjoyed 21 editions, and *The Mother's Book*. In 1833 she and her husband, David Lee Child, published the controversial abolitionist document "An Appeal in Favor of That Class of Americans Called Africans," which called for educating the slaves. Their work for abolition continued with the weekly newspaper *The National Anti-Slavery Standard*, which they published at New York City during 1840–44. Lydia died Oct 20, 1880, at Wayland, MA.

DUNNE, PHILIP: BIRTH ANNIVERSARY. Feb 11, 1908. American screenwriter and director Philip Dunne was born at New York, NY. In 1947 he joined directors John Huston and William Wyler to found the Committee for the First Amendment, which campaigned against the "blacklisting" in Hollywood of anyone suspected of being a communist by the House Un-American Activities Committee. He was also a founder of the Screen Writers Guild. Dunne died June 2, 1992, at Malibu, CA.

February 2009	S	M	T	W	T	F	S
	1	2	3	4	5	6	7
	8	9	10	11	12	13	14
	15	16	17	18	19	20	21
	22	23	24	25	26	27	28

EDISON, THOMAS ALVA: BIRTH ANNIVERSARY. Feb 11, 1847. American inventive genius and holder of more than 1,200 patents (including the incandescent electric lamp, phonograph, electric dynamo and key parts of many now-familiar devices such as the movie camera, telephone transmitter, etc.). Edison said, "Genius is 1 percent inspiration and 99 percent perspiration." His birthday is now widely observed as Inventor's Day. Born at Milan, OH, and died at Menlo Park, NJ, Oct 18, 1931.

FIRST WOMAN EPISCOPAL BISHOP: 20th ANNIVERSARY. Feb 11, 1989. The presiding bishop of the Episcopal Church, Bishop Edmond L. Browning, consecrated the Reverend Barbara Clementine Harris as a bishop of the Episcopal Church.

"THE FRENCH CHEF" TV PREMIERE: ANNIVERSARY. Feb 11, 1963. Beginning on this date, Julia Child demystified French cooking and entertained viewers as "The French Chef" on WGBH-TV, Boston, MA. The show was a great success in syndication on PBS stations, and Child filmed 200 programs—always with her trademark trilling voice and at times slapping around the poultry—signing off with a cheery "Bon appétit!" Child's show, along with her book *Mastering the Art of French Cooking* (1961, authored with Simone Beck and Louisette Bertholle), are credited with awakening Americans to the joy of continental cuisine. See also: "Child, Julia: Birth Anniversary" (Aug 15).

FULLER, MELVILLE WESTON: BIRTH ANNIVERSARY. Feb 11, 1833. 8th chief justice of the US. Born at Augusta, ME, he died at Sorrento, ME, July 4, 1910.

IRAN: VICTORY OF ISLAMIC REVOLUTION. Feb 11. National holiday. Commemorates the revolution that overthrew the shah in 1979.

JAPAN: NATIONAL FOUNDATION DAY. Feb 11. Marks the founding of the Japanese nation. In 1872 the government officially set Feb 11, 660 BC, as the date of accession to the throne of the Emperor Jimmu (said to be Japan's first emperor) and designated the day a national holiday by the name of Empire Day. The holiday was abolished after WWII but was revived as National Foundation Day in 1966. Ceremonies are held with Their Imperial Majesties the Emperor and Empress, the prime minister and other dignitaries attending. National holiday.

MANDELA, NELSON: PRISON RELEASE ANNIVERSARY. Feb 11, 1990. After serving more than 27 years of a life sentence (convicted, with eight others, of sabotage and conspiracy to overthrow the government), South Africa's Nelson Mandela, 71 years old, walked away from the Victor Verster prison farm at Paarl, South Africa, a free man. He had survived the governmental system of apartheid. Mandela greeted a cheering throng of well-wishers, along with hundreds of millions of television viewers worldwide, with demands for an intensification of the struggle for equality for blacks, who make up nearly 75 percent of South Africa's population.

MANKIEWICZ, JOSEPH L.: 100th BIRTH ANNIVERSARY. Feb 11, 1909. Oscar-winning American film writer, director and producer was born at Wilkes-Barre, PA. He coined the famous W.C. Fields phrase "my little chickadee" in his screenplay for the 1932 film *If I Had a Million*. In 1935 he turned to producing and subsequently made *The Philadelphia Story* and *Woman of the Year*. He began directing in 1946, and his stature grew with such films as *The Late George Apley, The Ghost and Mrs Muir, A Letter to Three Wives, All About Eve, Guys and Dolls, Cleopatra* and *Sleuth*. Mankiewicz won four Academy Awards for directing and screenwriting. He died Feb 5, 1993, at Mount Kisco, NY.

NATIONAL SHUT-IN VISITATION DAY. Feb 11. Visit and entertain shut-ins. For info: Natl Shut-In Visitation Day, 237 Franklin St, Reading, PA 19602. Phone: (610) 373-5579.

PRO SPORTS WIVES DAY. Feb 11. This national day of observance will give polite recognition to nearly a half million active and retired sports wives throughout the country for their public service in the estimated $213 billion professional sports industry. Unknown to the public, pro sports wives are the household managers and silent partners who keep their favorite athletes motivated, focused and determined to win and create the feeling of being a winner within us all. Annually, Feb 11. For info: Gena Pitts, *Pro Sports Wives* Magazine, The Terrace at Windward, 3070 Windward Parkway, Ste F-352, Alpharetta, GA 30005. Phone: (770) 619-0383. Fax: (770) 619-5777. E-mail: gjpitts@prosportswives.com. Web: www.prosportswives.com.

SATISFIED STAYING SINGLE DAY. Feb 11. As Valentine's Day approaches, some single folks would like to point out that they're quite content buying candy and flowers for no one but themselves. Live it up. Shadow dance! (©2006 by WH.) For info: Thomas & Ruth Roy, Wellcat Holidays, 2418 Long Ln, Lebanon, PA 17046. Phone: (717) 279-0184. E-mail: info@wellcat.com. Web: www.wellcat.com.

SHELDON, SIDNEY: BIRTH ANNIVERSARY. Feb 11, 1917. Writer born Sidney Schectel at Chicago, IL. After his college years at Northwestern University, he moved to Hollywood and found work as a screenwriter. B movies led to Broadway musicals, and by the mid-1940s he was one of the most prolific and successful writers of his generation. He earned an Academy Award for *The Bachelor and the Bobby Soxer* in 1947 and a Tony Award for *Redhead* in 1959. He also wrote for television, creating several successful series, including "The Patty Duke Show" and "I Dream of Jeannie." In 1969 he moved to writing novels and shortly became one of the best-selling novelists in history, as titles such as *Rage of Angels, Windmills of the Gods* and *The Other Side of Midnight* were translated into 51 languages, adapted as made-for-TV movies and in all sold more than 300 million copies. He died at Rancho Mirage, CA, Jan 30, 2007.

SPACE MILESTONE: *ENDEAVOUR* MAPPING MISSION (US). Feb 11, 2000. This manned flight spent 11 days in space creating a 3-D map of more than 70 percent of the Earth's surface—the most accurate and complete topographic map of Earth ever produced.

SPACE MILESTONE: FIRST SOVIET COMMERCIAL SATELLITE MISSION. Feb 11, 1990. Anatoly Solovyov and Aleksandr Balandin departed the Baikonur launching site on the Soviet Union's first satellite mission designed for profit—by producing industrial crystals in the weightlessness of space. The craft arrived at the *Mir* orbital space station on Feb 13. Launching of the *Soyuz TM-9* capsule was witnessed by four American astronauts and televised live. The mission was hailed as initiating a new level of openness of information about Soviet space projects.

SPACE MILESTONE: *OSUMI* (JAPAN). Feb 11, 1970. First Japanese satellite launched. Japan became the fourth nation to send a satellite into space.

VATICAN CITY: 80th INDEPENDENCE ANNIVERSARY. Feb 11, 1929. The Lateran Treaty, signed by Pietro Cardinal Gasparri and Benito Mussolini, guaranteed the independence of the State of Vatican City and recognized the sovereignty of the Holy See over it. Area is about 109 acres.

WHITE SHIRT DAY: ANNIVERSARY. Feb 11, 1937. Anniversary of UAW-GM agreement following 44-day sit-down strike at General Motors' Flint, MI, factories. Blue-collar workers traditionally wear white shirts to work on this day, symbolic of workingman's dignity won. Has been observed by proclamation at Flint.

YALTA AGREEMENT SIGNED: ANNIVERSARY. Feb 11, 1945. President Franklin D. Roosevelt, British prime minister Winston Churchill and Soviet leader Joseph Stalin signed an agreement at Yalta, a Soviet city on the Black Sea in the Crimea. The agreement contained plans for new blows at the heart of Germany and for occupying Germany at the end of the war. It also called for a meeting in San Francisco to draft a charter for the United Nations.

Birthdays Today

Jennifer Aniston, 40, actress ("Friends," *The Good Girl*), born Sherman Oaks, CA, Feb 11, 1969.

Paul Bocuse, 83, chef, born Collonges-au-Mont-d'Or, France, Feb 11, 1926.

Brandy, 30, singer, actress ("Cinderella," "Moesha"), born Brandy Norwood at Macomb, MS, Feb 11, 1979.

Sheryl Crow, 47, singer, musician, born Kennett, MO, Feb 11, 1962.

Natalie Dormer, 27, actress ("The Tudors"), born Reading, England, Feb 11, 1982.

Mike Leavitt, 58, US Secretary of Health and Human Services, former governor of Utah (R), born Cedar City, UT, Feb 11, 1951.

Tina Louise, 75, actress ("Gilligan's Island," *The Stepford Wives*), born New York, NY, Feb 11, 1934.

Carey Lowell, 48, actress ("Law & Order"), born New York, NY, Feb 11, 1961.

Sergio Mendes, 68, musician, bandleader, born Niteroi, Brazil, Feb 11, 1941.

Leslie Nielsen, 87, actor (*Naked Gun* films, *Airplane!*, "Peyton Place"), born Regina, SK, Canada, Feb 11, 1922.

Sarah Palin, 45, Governor of Alaska (R), born Sandpoint, ID, Feb 11, 1964.

Burt Reynolds, 73, actor (*Hooper, Deliverance, Cannonball Run*, "Evening Shade"), born Waycross, GA, Feb 11, 1936.

February 12 — Thursday

DAY 43 — 322 REMAINING

ADAMS, LOUISA CATHERINE JOHNSON: BIRTH ANNIVERSARY. Feb 12, 1775. Wife of John Quincy Adams, 6th president of the US. Born at London, England. Died at Washington, DC, May 14, 1852.

AMERICAN ASSOCIATION FOR THE ADVANCEMENT OF SCIENCE ANNUAL MEETING. Feb 12–16. Chicago, IL. 175th annual meeting. Est attendance: 9,000. For info: AAAS, 1200 New York Ave NW, Washington, DC 20005. Phone: (202) 326-6450. Fax: (202) 289-4021. Web: www.aaas.org/meetings.

CANADA: CALGARY BOAT AND SPORTSMEN'S SHOW. Feb 12–15. Roundup Centre, Stampede Park, Calgary, AB. Sail-, power- and fishing boats; hunting, fishing and camping supplies; resort destinations and outdoor recreation; four-wheel-drive vehicles; family entertainment. Est attendance: 25,000. For info: Canadian Natl Sportsmen's Shows, 340 1032-17th Ave SW, Calgary, AB, Canada T2T 0A5. Phone: (403) 245-9008. Fax: (403) 245-5100. Web: www.sportshows.ca.

DARWIN, CHARLES ROBERT: 200th BIRTH ANNIVERSARY. Feb 12, 1809. Author and naturalist, born at Shrewsbury, England. Best remembered for his books *On the Origin of Species by Means of Natural Selection, or the Preservation of Favoured Races in the Struggle for Life* and *The Descent of Man and Selection in Relation to Sex.* Died at Down, Kent, England, Apr 19, 1882.

DARWIN DAY. Feb 12. Darwin Day is an international celebration of science and humanity. Events are coordinated around the world to commemorate the life and work of Charles Darwin and the theory of evolution by natural selection and to recognize the contributions and achievements of science and reason. On a broad scale, the program is an effort to advance science literacy, champion the efforts to humanize science and celebrate the adventurous spirit. Events are held on the anniversary of Darwin's birth. For info: Matt Cherry, Institute for Humanist Studies, 48 Howard St, Albany, NY 12207. Phone: (518) 432-7820. Fax: (518) 432-7821. E-mail: info@darwinday.org. Web: www.darwinday.org or HumanistStudies.org.

***DRACULA* PREMIERE: ANNIVERSARY.** Feb 12, 1931. The horror film classic starring Bela Lugosi premiered on this day at the Roxy Theatre in New York City. It had been slated to premiere on Friday, Feb 13, but director Tod Browning, confessing to a superstitious nature, asked for the opening to be moved up a day. *Dracula* made the Hungarian actor Lugosi a star, but at a price: he was offered only horror film roles the rest of his career.

GATORADE DUEL QUALIFYING RACES FOR THE DAYTONA 500. Feb 12. Daytona International Speedway, Daytona Beach, FL. 51st annual running. Drivers battle to set the Daytona 500 field. For info: Daytona International Speedway, PO Box 2801, Daytona Beach, FL 32120-2801. Phone: (800) PIT-SHOP. Web: www.daytona internationalspeedway.com.

HARRIS, ROY: BIRTH ANNIVERSARY. Feb 12, 1898. Born at Chandler, OK, Harris was one of the most important composers of the 20th century. He was known for his use of Anglo-American folk tunes. He composed more than 200 works, including 13 symphonies, several ballet scores and much chamber and choral music. His best-known work is his Third Symphony (1939). He died at Santa Monica, CA, Oct 1, 1979.

LEWIS, JOHN LLEWELLYN: BIRTH ANNIVERSARY. Feb 12, 1880. American labor leader born near Lucas, IA. His parents came to the US from Welsh mining towns, and Lewis left school in the seventh grade to become a miner himself. Became leader of United Mine Workers of America and champion of all miners' causes. Died at Washington, DC, June 11, 1969.

LINCOLN, ABRAHAM: 200th BIRTH ANNIVERSARY. Feb 12, 1809. 16th president of the US (Mar 4, 1861–Apr 15, 1865) and the first to be assassinated (on Good Friday, Apr 14, 1865, at Ford's Theatre at Washington, DC). His presidency encompassed the tragic Civil War. Especially remembered are his Emancipation Proclamation (Jan 1, 1863), his Gettysburg Address (Nov 19, 1863) and his proclamation establishing the last Thursday of November as Thanksgiving Day. Born at Hardin County, KY, he died at Washington, DC, Apr 15, 1865. Lincoln's birthday is observed as part of Presidents' Day in most states but is a legal holiday in Illinois and an optional bank holiday in Iowa, Maryland, Michigan, Pennsylvania, Washington and West Virginia. See also: "Presidents' Day" (Feb 16).

LINCOLN'S BIRTHPLACE CABIN WREATH LAYING. Feb 12. Abraham Lincoln Birthplace National Historic Site, Hodgenville, KY. A wreath is placed at the door of the symbolic "Birthplace Cabin" in commemoration of the birth of Abraham Lincoln. The year 2009 marks the 200th anniversary of his birth. For info: Sandy Brue, Abraham Lincoln Birthplace NHS, 2995 Lincoln Farm Rd, Hodgenville, KY 42748. Phone: (270) 358-3137. E-mail: Sandy_Brue@nps.gov. Web: www.nps.gov/abli.

MIAMI INTERNATIONAL BOAT SHOW. Feb 12–16. Miami Beach Convention Center, Miami Beach, FL. 67th annual boat show, the biggest in the US and considered the main event for product introductions. With more than 3,000 boats, this show offers an unparalleled opportunity to view the sport's latest products. Est attendance: 175,000. For info: NMMA, 200 E Randolph St, Ste 5100, Chicago, IL 60601. Phone: (312) 946-6200. Fax: (312) 946-0388. Web: www.MiamiBoatShow.com.

MYANMAR: UNION DAY. Feb 12. National holiday. Commemorates the founding of the Union of Burma, Feb 12, 1947. The country changed its name to Union of Myanmar in 1989.

NAACP FOUNDED: 100th ANNIVERSARY. Feb 12, 1909. The National Association for the Advancement of Colored People was founded by W.E.B. DuBois and Ida Wells-Barnett, among others, to wage a militant campaign against lynching and other forms of racial oppression. Its legal wing brought many lawsuits that successfully challenged segregation in the 1950s and '60s.

February 2009

S	M	T	W	T	F	S
1	2	3	4	5	6	7
8	9	10	11	12	13	14
15	16	17	18	19	20	21
22	23	24	25	26	27	28

NEW MEXICO: EXTRATERRESTRIAL CULTURE DAY. Feb 12. New Mexico. A day "to celebrate and honor all past, present and future extraterrestrial visitors in ways to enhance relationships among all citizens of the cosmos, known and unknown." Passed as a memorial (not law) by the New Mexico state legislature in acknowledgment that ever since the Roswell UFO incident of 1947, New Mexico is recognized worldwide as a nexus of sightings and unexplained mysteries. Annually, the second Thursday of February.

OGLETHORPE DAY. Feb 12. General James Edward Oglethorpe (born at London, England, Dec 22, 1696), with some 100 other Englishmen, landed at what is now Savannah, GA, on Feb 12, 1733. Naming the new colony Georgia for England's King George II, Oglethorpe was organizer and first governor of the colony and founder of the city of Savannah. Oglethorpe Day and Georgia Day observed on this date.

PAVLOVA, ANNA: BIRTH ANNIVERSARY. Feb 12, 1881. Russian ballerina Anna Pavlova, thought by some to have been the greatest dancer of all time, was born at St. Petersburg, Russia. After performing with great success with the Ballet Russe and other companies, she formed her own company in 1910 and performed on tour for enthusiastic audiences in nearly every country in the world. Pavlova died at The Hague, Netherlands, Jan 23, 1931.

SAFETYPUP'S® BIRTHDAY. Feb 12. This year Safetypup®, created by the National Child Safety Council, joyously celebrates his birthday by bringing safety awareness/education messages to children and their parents in a positive, nonthreatening manner. Age-appropriate materials available through local law enforcement departments on topics including bike safety, drug abuse prevention, child abduction prevention and farm safety. For info: NCSC, Box 1368, Jackson, MI 49204-1368. Phone: (517) 764-6070. E-mail: tlusby@nfcd.org.

SENATE ACQUITS CLINTON: 10th ANNIVERSARY. Feb 12, 1999. After President William Clinton was impeached by the US House of Representatives, the Senate began a January trial on the charges of perjury and obstruction of justice. On this date the Senate acquitted Clinton. See also: "Clinton Impeachment Proceedings: Anniversary" (Dec 20).

SIMENON, GEORGES: BIRTH ANNIVERSARY. Feb 12, 1903. Simenon was the best-selling author of the 20th century, selling more than 500 million copies of his novels in more than 50 languages. The prodigious Simenon wrote up to six novels per year, specializing in dark, intellectual crime works. He garnered worldwide acclaim for his Inspector Maigret novels. He also gained worldwide notoriety in 1977 when he claimed to have had sexual relations with at least 10,000 women. Simenon, born at Liège, Belgium, died at Lausanne, France, on Sept 4, 1989.

UTAH WOMEN GIVEN THE VOTE: ANNIVERSARY. Feb 12, 1870. The women in the Utah Territory were granted the right to vote in political elections—50 years before the 19th Amendment was ratified.

Birthdays Today

Maud Adams, 64, actress (*Killer Force, Octopussy*), born Lulea, Sweden, Feb 12, 1945.

Joe Don Baker, 73, actor (*Charlie Varrick, Cool Hand Luke*), born Groesbeck, TX, Feb 12, 1936.

Ehud Barak, 67, former Israeli prime minister, born Mishmar, Hasharon, Israel, Feb 12, 1942.

Judy Blume, 71, author (*Blubber, Superfudge*), born Elizabeth, NJ, Feb 12, 1938.

Josh Brolin, 41, actor (*No Country for Old Men*), born Los Angeles, CA, Feb 12, 1968.

Cliff De Young, 62, actor (*Blue Collar, F/X*), born Inglewood, CA, Feb 12, 1947.

Joseph Henry (Joe) Garagiola, 83, sportscaster, former baseball player, born St. Louis, MO, Feb 12, 1926.

Arsenio Hall, 54, comedian, actor (*Coming to America*), former TV talk-show host, born Cleveland, OH, Feb 12, 1955.

Joanna Kerns, 56, actress ("Growing Pains"), former gymnast, born San Francisco, CA, Feb 12, 1953.

Simon MacCorkindale, 57, actor, producer, screenwriter ("Falcon Crest," *Death on the Nile, Jaws 3-D*), born Isle-of-Ely, England, Feb 12, 1952.

Chynna Phillips, 41, singer (Wilson Phillips), born Los Angeles, CA, Feb 12, 1968.

Christina Ricci, 29, actress (*Sleepy Hollow, Ice Storm*), born Santa Monica, CA, Feb 12, 1980.

William Felton (Bill) Russell, 75, Hall of Fame basketball player and former coach, born Monroe, LA, Feb 12, 1934.

Arlen Specter, 79, US Senator (R, Pennsylvania), born Wichita, KS, Feb 12, 1930.

Jesse Spencer, 30, actor ("House"), born Melbourne, Victoria, Australia, Feb 12, 1979.

Franco Zeffirelli, 86, stage and film director (*Otello, Romeo and Juliet*), born Florence, Italy, Feb 12, 1923.

February 13 — Friday

DAY 44 — 321 REMAINING

BLAME SOMEONE ELSE DAY. Feb 13. To share the responsibility and the guilt for the mess we're in. Blame someone else! Annually, the first Friday the 13th of the year. For info: A.C. Vierow, Box 71, Clio, MI 48420-0071.

CHURCHILL, RANDOLPH HENRY SPENCER: BIRTH ANNIVERSARY. Feb 13, 1849. English politician and the father of Winston Churchill. Born at Blenheim, Woodstock, Oxfordshire, England, he died at London, Jan 24, 1895.

COIN & STAMP EXPO. Feb 13–15. Pasadena Convention Center, Pasadena, CA. Est attendance: 5,000. For info: Israel Bick, Exec Dir, Intl Stamp & Coin Collectors Society, PO Box 854, Van Nuys, CA 91408. Phone: (818) 997-6496. Fax: (818) 988-4337. E-mail: iibick@sbcglobal.net. Web: www.bick.net.

DRESDEN FIREBOMBING: ANNIVERSARY. Feb 13, 1945. Dresden, Germany. Allied firebombing caused a firestorm that destroyed the city and killed 135,000 people.

EMPLOYEE LEGAL AWARENESS DAY. Feb 13. A day emphasizing the importance of legal education for employees so that large and small businesses reduce their risk of legal problems. For info: Paul Brennan, PO Box 27, Mooloolaba, Queensland 4557, Australia. E-mail: paul.brennan@brennanlaw.com.au.

FIRST MAGAZINE PUBLISHED IN AMERICA: ANNIVERSARY. Feb 13, 1741. (Old Style date.) Andrew Bradford published *The American Magazine* just three days ahead of Benjamin Franklin's *General Magazine*.

FRANCE: NICE CARNIVAL. Feb 13–24. Dates from the 14th century and is celebrated each year during the 12 days ending with Shrove Tuesday. Derived from ancient rites of spring, the carnival offers parades, floats, battles of flowers and confetti and a fireworks display lighting up the entire Baie des Anges. King Carnival is burned on his pyre at the end of the event.

FRIDAY THE THIRTEENTH. Feb 13. Variously believed to be a lucky or an unlucky day. Every year has at least one Friday the 13th, but never more than three. There are three Friday the 13ths in 2009: Feb 13, Mar 13 and Nov 13. Fear of the number 13 is known as triskaidekaphobia.

GET A DIFFERENT NAME DAY. Feb 13. For the pity of the millions of us who hate our birth names. On this day we may change our names to whatever we wish and have the right to expect colleagues, family and friends to so address us. (©2006 by WH.) For info: Thomas & Ruth Roy, Wellcat Holidays, 2418 Long Ln, Lebanon, PA 17046. Phone: (717) 279-0184. E-mail: info@wellcat.com. Web: www.wellcat.com.

GOLD RUSH DAYS. Feb 13–15. Wickenburg, AZ. 61st annual communitywide celebration of the Old West: rodeo, parade, carnival, gold panning. Named one of the top 100 events in North America by the American Bus Association. Annually, the second full weekend in February. Est attendance: 50,000. For info: Chamber of Commerce, 216 N Frontier St, Wickenburg, AZ 85390. Phone: (928) 684-5479 or (928) 684-0977. Fax: (928) 684-5470. E-mail: events@wickenburgchamber.com. Web: www.wickenburgchamber.com.

GREAT BACKYARD BIRD COUNT. Feb 13–16. Thousands of volunteers nationwide track the number and types of birds that live near their homes. Results help researchers monitor species in trouble. Cosponsored by the National Audubon Society and the Cornell University Lab of Ornithology. For info: National Audubon Society, 700 Broadway, 4th Fl, New York, NY 10003. Phone: (212) 979-3000. Web: www.birdsource.org/gbbc.

IRWIN EARNS FIRST MEDAL OF HONOR: ANNIVERSARY. Feb 13, 1861. Colonel Bernard Irwin distinguished himself while leading troops in a battle with Chiricahua Apache Indians at Apache Pass, AZ (at the time part of the territory of New Mexico). For those actions Irwin later became the first person awarded the new US Medal of Honor, although he didn't actually receive it until three years later (Jan 24, 1864).

NASCAR CRAFTSMAN TRUCK SERIES CHEVY SILVERADO 250. Feb 13. Daytona International Speedway, Daytona, FL. NASCAR trucks on the Superspeedway. For info: Daytona International Speedway, PO Box 2801, Daytona Beach, FL 32120-2801. Phone: (800) PIT-SHOP. Web: www.daytonainternationalspeedway.com.

NATIONAL DATE FESTIVAL. Feb 13–22. Indio, CA. America's most exotic county fair features Arabian Nights theme, camel and ostrich races, satellite horse wagering, nightly musical pageant, date exhibits and sampling, thousands of competitive exhibits and carnival. Headliner entertainment included with admission. Est attendance: 300,000. For info: Riverside County Fair and National Date Fest, 82-503 Hwy 111, Indio, CA 92201. Phone: (760) 863-8247 or (800) 811-FAIR. Web: www.datefest.org.

NEWPORT WINTER FESTIVAL. Feb 13–22. Newport, RI. More than 160 individual events from food, music and entertainment to skating, snow sculptures, ice carving, scavenger hunt and all-you-can-eat chili cook-off—fun for all ages. Est attendance: 25,000. For info: Newport Winter Festival, 28 Pelham St, Newport, RI 02840. Phone: (401) 847-7666. E-mail: events@newportevents.com. Web: www.newportwinterfestival.com.

PIAZZETTA, GIOVANNI BATTISTA: BIRTH ANNIVERSARY. Feb 13, 1682. Prominent 18th-century Venetian painter. Notable among his works are the *Ecstasy of St. Francis* and *Fortune Teller*. Born at Venice, Italy, and died there Apr 28, 1754.

REENACTMENT OF THE BATTLE OF OLUSTEE. Feb 13–15. Olustee Battlefield Historic State Park, Olustee, FL. Join us for the 145th anniversary of the largest Civil War battle fought in Florida. Est attendance: 22,000. For info: Mitzi Nelson, Florida Park Service, PO Drawer G, White Springs, FL 32096. Phone: (386) 397-7005. Fax: (386) 397-4262. E-mail: margaret.a.nelson@dep.state.fl.us. Web: www.floridastateparks.org/olustree or www.BattleofOlustee.org.

SOUTH COAST WRITERS CONFERENCE. Feb 13–14. Event Center on the Beach and Gold Beach High School, Gold Beach, OR. Intensive writing workshops, author readings and informational seminars concerning writing techniques, preparing for publication, marketing and genre-specific topics. Fireman's Fish Fry will take place on Feb 14. Est attendance: 125. For info: Janet Pretti, Southwestern Oregon Community College, PO Box 590, Gold Beach, OR 97444. Phone: (541) 247-2741. Fax: (541) 247-6247. E-mail: scwc@socc.edu. Web: www.socc.edu/scwriters.

TRUMAN, BESS (ELIZABETH) VIRGINIA WALLACE: BIRTH ANNIVERSARY. Feb 13, 1885. Wife of Harry S Truman, 33rd president of the US. Born at Independence, MO, and died there Oct 18, 1982.

WOOD, GRANT: BIRTH ANNIVERSARY. Feb 13, 1892. American artist, especially noted for his powerful realism and satirical paintings of the American scene, was born near Anamosa, IA. He was a printer, sculptor, woodworker and high school and college teacher. Among his best-remembered works are *American Gothic, Fall Plowing* and *Stone City.* Died at Iowa City, IA, Feb 12, 1942.

YUMA SQUARE AND ROUND DANCE FESTIVAL. Feb 13–15. Yuma Civic Center, Yuma, AZ. Square and round dance enthusiasts from Southern California and Arizona participate. Est attendance: 2,000. For info: Yuma Civic Center, 1440 Desert Hills Dr, Yuma, AZ 85365. Phone: (928) 373-5040. Fax: (928) 344-9121. E-mail: ycc@yumaaz.gov. Web: www.yumaaz.gov.

Birthdays Today

Stockard Channing, 65, actress (*Six Degrees of Separation, The House of Blue Leaves*, "The West Wing"), born Susan Stockard at New York, NY, Feb 13, 1944.

Peter Gabriel, 59, singer, songwriter, born London, England, Feb 13, 1950.

Kelly Hu, 42, actress ("Martial Law," "Nash Bridges"), born Honolulu, HI, Feb 13, 1967.

Carol Lynley, 67, actress (*Harlow, Bunny Lake Is Missing*), born New York, NY, Feb 13, 1942.

Randy Moss, 32, football player, born Rand, WV, Feb 13, 1977.

David Naughton, 58, singer, actor (*An American Werewolf in London, Overexposed*), born Hartford, CT, Feb 13, 1951.

Kim Novak, 76, actress (*Bell, Book and Candle*; *Vertigo*), born Marilyn Novak at Chicago, IL, Feb 13, 1933.

George Segal, 75, actor (*A Touch of Class*, "Just Shoot Me"), born Great Neck, NY, Feb 13, 1934.

Jerry Springer, 65, TV host ("The Jerry Springer Show"), born London, England, Feb 13, 1944.

Bo Svenson, 68, actor (*North Dallas Forty, Heartbreak Ridge*), born Goteborg, Sweden, Feb 13, 1941.

Peter Tork, 65, actor, singer (The Monkees), born Peter Thorkelson at Washington, DC, Feb 13, 1944 (some sources say 1942).

Aníbál Acevedo Vilá, 47, Governor of Puerto Rico, born Hato Rey, Puerto Rico, Feb 13, 1962.

Chuck Yeager, 86, pilot who broke sound barrier, born Myra, WV, Feb 13, 1923.

February 2009

S	M	T	W	T	F	S
1	2	3	4	5	6	7
8	9	10	11	12	13	14
15	16	17	18	19	20	21
22	23	24	25	26	27	28

February 14 — Saturday

DAY 45 — **320 REMAINING**

ARIZONA: ADMISSION DAY: ANNIVERSARY. Feb 14. Became 48th state in 1912.

BENNY, JACK: BIRTH ANNIVERSARY. Feb 14, 1894. American comedian. Born Benjamin Kubelsky, Jack Benny entered vaudeville at Waukegan, IL, at age 17, using the violin as a comic stage prop. His radio show first aired in 1932 and continued for 20 years with little change in format. He also had a long-running television show. One of his most well-known comic gimmicks was his purported stinginess. Benny was born at Chicago, IL, and died Dec 26, 1974, at Beverly Hills, CA.

BULGARIA: VITICULTURISTS' DAY (TRIFON ZAREZAN). Feb 14. Celebrated since Thracian times. Festivities are based on cult of Dionysus, god of merriment and wine.

CAMPING WORLD 300 PRESENTED BY CHEVY NASCAR NATIONWIDE SERIES RACE. Feb 14. Daytona International Speedway, Daytona Beach, FL. 51st annual race. Nationwide Series' richest and most competitive event. For info: Daytona International Speedway, PO Box 2801, Daytona Beach, FL 32120-2801. Phone: (800) PIT-SHOP. Web: www.daytonainternationalspeedway.com.

CANADA: YUKON QUEST INTERNATIONAL 1,000-MILE SLED DOG RACE. Feb 14–28. Fairbanks, AK, and Whitehorse, YT. Two weeks and 1,000 miles through true northern wilderness in the depths of Arctic winter, between Fairbanks, AK, and Whitehorse, YT, Canada. Top mushers from North America and around the world compete for $200,000 in prize money. Est attendance: 10,000. For info: Yukon Quest International Assn (Canada), #2-1109 First Ave, Whitehorse, YT Y1A 5G4, Canada. Phone: (867) 668-4711. Fax: (867) 668-6674. E-mail: questadmin@polarcom.com. Web: www.yukonquest.com.

CHOCOLATE FESTIVAL. Feb 14–15. Galesburg Antiques Mall, Galesburg, IL. A chocolate lover's dream! Homemade and commercially made chocolates, tortes, cakes, pies and creams—all you can eat for a small admission fee. Est attendance: 1,500. For info: Galesburg Area CVB, PO Box 60, Galesburg, IL 61402-0060. Phone: (309) 343-2485. Fax: (309) 343-2521. E-mail: visitors@visitgalesburg.com. Web: www.visitgalesburg.com.

ENIAC COMPUTER INTRODUCED: ANNIVERSARY. Feb 14, 1946. J. Presper Eckert and John W. Mauchly demonstrated the Electronic Numerical Integrator and Computer (ENIAC) for the first time at the University of Pennsylvania. This was the first electronic digital computer. It occupied a room the size of a gymnasium and contained nearly 18,000 vacuum tubes. The army commissioned the computer to speed the calculation of firing tables for artillery. By the time the computer was ready, WWII was over. However, ENIAC prepared the way for future generations of computers.

FARM TOY SHOW AND AUCTION. Feb 14 (date subject to change). Sauk Centre, MN. More than 30 vendors display farm toy equipment from 9 AM to 3:30 PM, with a consignment auction starting at 4:30 PM. Est attendance: 800. For info: Sauk Centre Chamber of Commerce, PO Box 222, Sauk Centre, MN 56378. Phone: (320) 352-5201. Fax: (320) 352-5202. E-mail: chamber@saukcentrechamber.com. Web: www.saukcentrechamber.com.

FERRIS WHEEL DAY: GEORGE FERRIS'S 150th BIRTH ANNIVERSARY. Feb 14, 1859. Anniversary of the birth of George Washington Gale Ferris, American engineer and inventor, at Galesburg, IL. Among his many accomplishments as a civil engineer, Ferris is best remembered as the inventor of the Ferris wheel, which he developed for the World's Columbian Exposition at Chicago, IL, in 1893. Built on the Midway Plaisance, the 250-feet-diameter Ferris wheel (with 36 coaches, each capable of carrying 40 passengers) proved one of the greatest attractions of the fair. It was America's answer to the Eiffel Tower of the Paris International Exposition of 1889. Ferris died at Pittsburgh, PA, Nov 22, 1896.

FIRST PRESIDENTIAL PHOTOGRAPH: ANNIVERSARY. Feb 14, 1849. President James Polk became the first US president to be photographed while in office. The photographer was Mathew B. Brady, who would become famous for his photography during the American Civil War.

GEORGE WASHINGTON BIRTHNIGHT BANQUET AND BALL. Feb 14. Alexandria, VA. Re-creation of dinner, dancing and toasts offered to George Washington in Alexandria. Staged in original setting—Gadsby's Tavern. Eighteenth-century dancing, clothing. Alexandrians portray historic characters including George and Martha Washington. Advance reservations required. Annually, the Saturday of the federal holiday weekend. Est attendance: 85. For info: George Washington Birthday Celebration Committee, 1108 Jefferson St, Alexandria, VA 22314. Phone/fax: (703) 991-4474. E-mail: gwbcc@email.com. Web: www.washingtonbirthday.net.

HANCOCK, WINFIELD SCOTT: BIRTH ANNIVERSARY. Feb 14, 1824. Born at Montgomery, PA; died Feb 9, 1886, at Governor's Island, NY. After his service as a Union general in the Civil War, his command of the military division of Texas and Louisiana won him much favor from the Democratic Party because he allowed local civil authorities to retain their power. He pleased the Democrats so well that they made him their presidential candidate in 1880. He lost to James A. Garfield by a narrow margin.

HINES, GREGORY: BIRTH ANNIVERSARY. Feb 14, 1946. One of the best tap dancers of his generation, Gregory Hines was born at New York, NY. He was a child star, performing regularly at the Apollo Theater in Harlem, NY, by the age of six. As an adult, he turned to acting, working in film, on television and on the Broadway stage. He was nominated for several Tony Awards, winning in 1993 for *Jelly's Last Jam*. His films included *Running Scared* and *The Cotton Club*, and he was nominated for several Emmy Awards for his television dance specials. He died at Los Angeles, CA, Aug 9, 2003.

LEAGUE OF WOMEN VOTERS FORMED: ANNIVERSARY. Feb 14, 1920. While meeting in Chicago to celebrate the imminent ratification of the 19th Amendment to the Constitution, leaders of the National American Woman Suffrage Association (NAWSA) approved the formation of a new organization—the League of Women Voters. With the vote for women just a few months away, the new organization was created to help American women exercise their new political rights and responsibilities. For info: League of Women Voters of Illinois, 332 S Michigan Ave, Ste 1142, Chicago, IL 60604. Phone: (312) 939-5935. Web: www.lwv.org.

LOVE A MENSCH WEEK. Feb 14–20. Mensches are decent, responsible men or women. During this week, singles look to meet a mensch as well as take time to appreciate how mensches enhance our lives. For info: Robin Gorman Newman, 44 Somerset Dr N, Great Neck, NY 11020. Phone: (516) 773-0911. E-mail: robin@lovecoach.com. Web: www.lovecoach.com.

***THE MALTESE FALCON*: PUBLICATION ANNIVERSARY.** Feb 14, 1930. Former Pinkerton agent–turned author Dashiell Hammett's crime novel introducing Sam Spade was published on this day by Alfred A. Knopf in New York, NY. (The novel had been serialized in *Black Mask* magazine in the fall of 1929, but Hammett revised the text.) The novel was a milestone in American literature, offering the model that all "hard-boiled" crime fiction would follow. And in terse tough-guy Sam Spade (who "looked rather pleasantly like a blond satan"), the world found a new pop icon. The notably dark-haired Humphrey Bogart played Spade in the 1941 film version directed by John Huston.

NATIONAL CONDOM WEEK. Feb 14–21. To educate consumers, patients, students and professionals about the prevention of sexually transmitted diseases, AIDS and teenage pregnancies. For info: Fred S. Mayer, Pharmacists Planning Service, Inc, 101 Lucas Valley Rd, Ste 382, San Rafael, CA 94903. Phone: (415) 479-8628. Fax: (415) 479-8608. E-mail: ppsi@aol.com. Web: www.ppsinc.org.

NATIONAL HAVE-A-HEART DAY. Feb 14. The goal of this celebration of life is to create a new consciousness concerning the impact of our food choices on the environment, world hunger, animal welfare and human health—especially heart health. Vegetarian diets increase longevity and help prevent—and even reverse—heart disease. Total vegetarians live about 15 years longer than nonvegetarians and suffer less than one-tenth the heart disease death rate of nonvegetarians. For info: Vegetarian Awareness Network, PO Box 3545, Washington, DC 20027-0045. Phone: (800) USA-VEGE.

NATIONAL NESTBOX WEEK. Feb 14–21. National Nestbox Week presents an educational opportunity to teach about cavity-nesting birds and encourages the public to put up a nest box (birdhouse). In coordination with the British Trust for Ornithology, this week kicks off the National Nestbox Challenge in North America and in the UK. For info: Marsha Pearson, The Avian Promise, 8785 Duveen Dr, Wyndmoor, PA 19038. Phone: (215) 402-9082. Fax: (215) 701-4557. E-mail: marsha@theavianpromise.org. Web: www.theavianpromise.org.

OREGON: ADMISSION DAY: 150th ANNIVERSARY. Feb 14. Became 33rd state in 1859.

PROUT, MARY ANN ("AUNT MARY PROUT"): BIRTH ANNIVERSARY. Feb 14, 1801. It is believed most likely that Mary Prout—social activist, humanitarian, educator—was born free on this date at Baltimore, MD. Prout became a teacher and in 1830 founded a day school. Actively involved in her church, she founded a secret society that became the Independent Order of St. Luke to help with the cost of medical care and burial services for needy blacks, an organization that grew to have 1,500 chapters across the nation by 1900. Prout died at Baltimore in 1884.

RACE RELATIONS DAY. Feb 14. A day designated by some churches to recognize the importance of interracial relations. Formerly was observed on Abraham Lincoln's birthday or on the Sunday preceding it. Since 1970 observance has generally been Feb 14.

SAINT VALENTINE'S DAY. Feb 14. St. Valentine's Day celebrates the feasts of two Christian martyrs of this name. One, a priest and physician, was beaten and beheaded on the Flaminian Way at Rome, Italy, Feb 14, AD 269, during the reign of Emperor Claudius II. Another Valentine, the bishop of Terni, is said to have been beheaded, also on the Flaminian Way at Rome, Feb 14 (possibly in a later year). Both history and legend are vague and contradictory about details of the Valentines, and some say that Feb 14 was selected for the celebration of Christian martyrs as a diversion from the ancient pagan observance of Lupercalia. An old legend has it that birds choose their mates on Valentine's Day. Now it is one of the most widely observed unofficial holidays. It is an occasion for the exchange of gifts (usually books, flowers or sweets) and greeting cards with affectionate or humorous messages. See also: "Lupercalia" (Feb 15).

SAINT VALENTINE'S DAY MASSACRE: 80th ANNIVERSARY. Feb 14, 1929. Anniversary of Chicago gangland executions, when gunmen posing as police shot seven members of the George "Bugs" Moran gang.

SALMAN RUSHDIE'S DEATH SENTENCE: 20th ANNIVERSARY. Feb 14, 1989. Iranian leader Ayatollah Ruholla Khomeini, offended by *The Satanic Verses*, called on Muslims to kill the book's British author, Salman Rushdie. On the following day the ayatollah offered a $1 million reward for execution of his sentence. Rushdie, fearful for his life, went into hiding. Worldwide protests against the efforts to abridge academic and literary freedoms, countered by protests of Muslim and other religious fundamentalists, stimulated the sales of *The Satanic Verses*, but Rushdie remained virtually a prisoner, unable to resume a public life. In 1998 the Iranian government rescinded the death sentence.

SPACE MILESTONE: *NEAR* ORBITS ASTEROID. Feb 14, 2000. The robot spacecraft *Near Earth Asteroid Rendezvous* (now called *NEAR Shoemaker*) finished circling the asteroid Eros for the first time on this day. Eros is called a near-Earth asteroid because its orbit crosses that of Earth and poses a potential collision danger. *NEAR* continued orbiting the asteroid for a year, moving closer to the surface to make more precise measurements and transmit thousands of pictures. In October 2000 it passed within three miles of Eros. Though it was never designed for landing, on Feb 12, 2001, *NEAR* touched down on Eros, history's first landing of an object on an asteroid. *NEAR* was launched from Cape Canaveral, FL, Feb 17, 1996.

SPACE MILESTONE: 100th SPACE WALK. Feb 14, 2001. Two astronauts from the space shuttle *Atlantis* took the 100th space walk; the first had been taken by American Edward White in 1965. On their excursion Thomas Jones and Robert Curbeam, Jr, put the finishing touches on the International Space Station's new science lab *Destiny*. See also: "Space Milestone: *Gemini 4*" (June 3).

WALLET, SKEEZIX: "BIRTHDAY." Feb 14. Comic strip character in "Gasoline Alley," by Frank King. First cartoon character to grow and age with the years of publication. Foundling child of Walt and Phyllis Wallet, discovered on doorstep Feb 14, 1921. Skeezix grew through childhood, marriage and military service in WWII, returning home to parenthood and business after the war. Comic strip began in the *Chicago Tribune*, Aug 23, 1919.

WASHINGTON'S BIRTHDAY AT MOUNT VERNON. Feb 14–16. Mount Vernon, VA. George Washington's home is the site of a variety of events in honor of his birthday. Each day of the celebration is kicked off by "America's Smallest Hometown Parade" on Mount Vernon's Bowling Green. The parade features 18th-century music, costumed interpreters and animals from the farm. Visitors can partake of the first president's favorite breakfast each morning: hoecakes swimming in butter and honey. On Monday, Feb 16, there will be a wreath-laying ceremony at Washington's tomb. Admission is free on Washington's birthday. For info: Public Affairs Department, Mount Vernon Ladies' Assn, PO Box 110, Mount Vernon, VA 22121. Phone: (703) 780-2000. E-mail: info@mountvernon.org. Web: www.mountvernon.org.

WASHINGTON'S BIRTHDAY PARTY. Feb 14–16. Ferry Farm, Fredericksburg, VA. Birthday celebration for our first president at his childhood home. Features appearance by George Washington and the annual Stone Toss at Fredericksburg's City Dock on the Rappahannock River. For info: George Washington's Fredericksburg Foundation, 268 Kings Hwy, Fredericksburg, VA 22405. Phone: (540) 370-0732. Fax: (540) 371-3398. E-mail: mailroom@kenmore.org. Web: www.kenmore.org/ferryfarm_homepage.html.

WINGS OVER THE PLATTE SPRING MIGRATION CELEBRATION. Feb 14–Apr 12. Grand Island, NE. Celebrate the arrival of the world's largest concentration of sandhill cranes. Each spring up to 500,000 cranes gather along the Platte River during their northward migration. Seminars, tours, nature hikes, films. Est attendance: 100,000. For info: Renee Seifert, Grand Island/Hall County CVB, 2424 S Locust St, Ste C, Grand Island, NE 66801. Phone: (800) 658-3178 or (308) 382-4400. Fax: (308) 382-4908. E-mail: info@visitgrandisland.com. Web: www.visitgrandisland.com.

WMAS 94.7 FM VALENTINE'S BALL. Feb 14. Springfield, MA. A formal affair for both couples and singles. An evening of music, dancing and prizes. Est attendance: 2,000. For info: Promotions Dept, WMAS 94.7 FM, PO Box 9500, Springfield, MA 01102. Phone: (413) 737-1414. Fax: (413) 737-1488.

February 2009

S	M	T	W	T	F	S
1	2	3	4	5	6	7
8	9	10	11	12	13	14
15	16	17	18	19	20	21
22	23	24	25	26	27	28

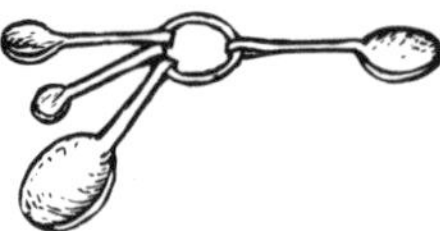

Birthdays Today

Carl Bernstein, 65, journalist, author (*All the President's Men* with Bob Woodward), born Washington, DC, Feb 14, 1944.

Drew Bledsoe, 37, former football player, born Ellensburg, WA, Feb 14, 1972.

Michael Bloomberg, 67, Mayor of New York City (R), born Brighton, MA, Feb 14, 1942.

Enrico Colantoni, 46, actor ("Just Shoot Me," "Veronica Mars"), born Toronto, ON, Canada, Feb 14, 1963.

Hugh Downs, 88, broadcaster ("Today," "20/20"), born Akron, OH, Feb 14, 1921.

Zach Galligan, 45, actor (*Gremlins*), born New York, NY, Feb 14, 1964.

Judd Gregg, 62, US Senator (R, New Hampshire), born Nashua, NH, Feb 14, 1947.

Richard Hamilton, 31, basketball player, born Coatesville, PA, Feb 14, 1978.

Milan Hejduk, 33, hockey player, born Usti-nad-Labem, Czechoslovakia, Feb 14, 1976.

Florence Henderson, 75, singer, actress ("The Brady Bunch"), born Dale, IN, Feb 14, 1934.

Andrew Prine, 73, actor (*The Miracle Worker, Chisum*), born Jennings, FL, Feb 14, 1936.

Teller, 61, magician (Penn and Teller), born Raymond Joseph Teller at Philadelphia, PA, Feb 14, 1948.

Meg Tilly, 49, actress (*Agnes of God, Two Jakes*), born Long Beach, CA, Feb 14, 1960.

Jessica Yu, 43, filmmaker, born Los Altos Hills, CA, Feb 14, 1966.

February 15 — Sunday

DAY 46 — **319 REMAINING**

AFGHANISTAN: SOVIET TROOP WITHDRAWAL: 20th ANNIVERSARY. Feb 15, 1989. The USSR's target of withdrawal of all Soviet troops from Afghanistan by this date was essentially met, ending more than nine years of intervention in a civil war.

ARLEN, HAROLD: BIRTH ANNIVERSARY. Feb 15, 1905. American composer and songwriter, born at Buffalo, NY. Arlen wrote many popular songs, including "Over the Rainbow" (for which he won the 1939 Oscar for Best Song), "That Old Black Magic," "Blues in the Night" and "Stormy Weather." Died at New York, NY, Apr 23, 1986.

BARRYMORE, JOHN: BIRTH ANNIVERSARY. Feb 15, 1882. American actor of famous acting family, brother of Ethel and Lionel. Born John Blythe at Philadelphia, PA, and died at Los Angeles, CA, May 29, 1942.

BUILD A BETTER TRADE SHOW IMAGE WEEK. Feb 15–21. For companies that exhibit at trade shows, this week is set aside to evaluate and improve exhibit strategies for the upcoming trade show season. For "10 Steps to a Better Trade Show Image" tip sheet, send #10 SASE. Annually, the third full week of February. For info: Marlys K. Arnold, ImageSpecialist, PO Box 901808, Kansas City, MO 64190-1808. Phone: (816) 746-7888. E-mail: marnold@imagespecialist.com. Web: www.imagespecialist.com.

CANADA: MAPLE LEAF FLAG ADOPTED: ANNIVERSARY. Feb 15, 1965. The new Canadian national flag was raised at Ottawa, Canada's capital, on this day. The red-and-white flag with a red maple leaf in the center replaced the Red Ensign flag, which had the British Union Jack in the upper left-hand corner.

CERMAK, ANTON J.: ASSASSINATION ANNIVERSARY. Feb 15, 1933. At Bay Front Park, Miami, FL, an assassin aiming at President-elect Franklin D. Roosevelt had his aim deflected by a spectator. Cermak, mayor of Chicago, IL, born May 9, 1873, at Kladno, Bohemia, Czechoslovakia, was struck and killed instead. Giuseppe (Joe) Zangara, the 32-year-old assassin, who had emigrated from Italy in 1923, was electrocuted at the Raiford, FL, state prison Mar 20, 1933.

CLARK, ABRAHAM: BIRTH ANNIVERSARY. Feb 15, 1726. Signer of the Declaration of Independence, farmer and lawyer. Born at Elizabethtown, NJ, and died there Sept 15, 1794.

DAYTONA 500 NASCAR SPRINT CUP SERIES RACE. Feb 15. Daytona International Speedway, Daytona Beach, FL. 51st annual running of the "world's greatest race." For info: Daytona International Speedway, PO Box 2801, Daytona Beach, FL 32120-2801. Phone: (800) PIT-SHOP. Web: www.daytonainternationalspeedway.com.

GALILEI, GALILEO: BIRTH ANNIVERSARY. Feb 15, 1564. Physicist and astronomer who helped overthrow medieval concepts of the world, born at Pisa, Italy. He proved the theory that all bodies, large and small, descend at equal speed and gathered evidence to support Copernicus's theory that Earth and other planets revolve around the sun. Galileo died at Florence, Italy, Jan 8, 1642.

KREWE OF CARROLLTON PARADE. Feb 15. New Orleans, LA. Founded in 1924, the Krewe of Carrollton is the fourth-oldest marching krewe and kicks off the New Orleans carnival season with this popular parade in the Carrollton neighborhood. Annually, the second Sunday before Mardi Gras. For info: Krewe of Carrollton. Web: www.kreweofcarrollton.com.

LUPERCALIA. Feb 15. Anniversary of ancient Roman fertility festival. Thought by some to have been established by Romulus and Remus, who, legend says, were suckled by a she-wolf at Lupercal (a cave in Palestine). Goats and dogs were sacrificed. Lupercalia celebration persisted until the fifth century of the Christian era. Possibly a forerunner of Valentine's Day customs.

McCORMICK, CYRUS H.: 200th BIRTH ANNIVERSARY. Feb 15, 1809. Inventor of the reaper, born at Rockbridge County, VA. It is said that Cyrus McCormick's invention of the reaper rates second only to the railroad in the development of the US. Continuing the dream of his father, McCormick constructed a horse-operated reaper, which was demonstrated for the first time in a Virginia wheat field in July 1831. He moved his operation to Chicago, IL, in 1847 in order to be closer to the Midwest's expanding wheat fields. His business prospered despite two decades of constant litigation over patent rights. He died May 13, 1884, at Chicago. In 1902–03, his McCormick Harvesting Machine Company was consolidated with other firms to become the International Harvester Company.

MENENDEZ DE AVILES, PEDRO: BIRTH ANNIVERSARY. Feb 15, 1519. Spanish explorer and naval adventurer. Explored Florida coastal regions for the king of Spain and established a fort at St. Augustine in September 1565. Died Sept 17, 1574, at Santander, Spain.

MONTE CASSINO BOMBED: 65th ANNIVERSARY. Feb 15, 1944. The monastery and abbey at Monte Cassino, Italy, were attacked by 228 heavy and medium American bombers. The abbey, which was built in AD 529, was destroyed after several hours of bombardment. US commanders reported 200 German soldiers were seen fleeing the fortress during the assault. Benedictine monks were also seen scrambling for cover.

NATIONAL ENGINEERS WEEK. Feb 15–21. The 58th annual observance, cosponsored by more than 140 national engineering societies, federal agencies and major corporations, will feature classroom programs in elementary and secondary schools throughout the US, hands-on activities in science centers and museums, engineering workplace tours, the Future City Competition (www.futurecity.org) and the annual "Introduce a Girl to Engineering Day." 2009 chairs are Intel Corporation and the National Society of Professional Engineers. Annually, the week that includes George Washington's birthday (observed). For info: Natl Engineers Week Headquarters, 1420 King St, Alexandria, VA 22314. Phone: (703) 684-2852. E-mail: eweek@nspe.org. Web: www.eweek.org.

NBA ALL-STAR GAME. Feb 15. US Airways Center, Phoenix, AZ. 58th annual. For info: Brian McIntyre, Sr VP, Basketball Communications, Natl Basketball Assn, Olympic Tower, 645 Fifth Ave, New York, NY 10022. Phone: (212) 407-8000. Web: www.nba.com.

REMEMBER THE *MAINE* DAY: ANNIVERSARY. Feb 15, 1898. American battleship *Maine* was blown up while at anchor in Havana Harbor, at 9:40 PM, on this day in 1898. The ship, under the command of Captain Charles G. Sigsbee, sank quickly, and 260 members of its crew were lost. Inflamed public opinion in the US ignored the lack of evidence to establish responsibility for the explosion. "Remember the *Maine*" became the war cry, and a formal declaration of war against Spain followed on Apr 25, 1898.

SERBIA: NATIONAL DAY. Feb 15.

SHACKLETON, ERNEST: BIRTH ANNIVERSARY. Feb 15, 1874. The Antarctic explorer was born at Kilkea, Ireland. His fame rests not on reaching the South Pole (he tried three times), but on his leadership and bravery. During the British Imperial Trans-Arctic expedition of 1914, the icy seas crushed his ship, *Endurance*, but Shackleton protected his men and buoyed their morale for the two years they were marooned. In 1916 he led a six-man team in a lifeboat on a 17-day, 600-mile journey (without sleep) in search of help. Upon arrival at South Georgia Island, he rounded up a rescue effort, and three months later all his men were rescued without a death. Shackleton died Jan 5, 1922, at Grytviken, South Georgia Island, while beginning a fourth expedition to the South Pole.

SPANISH WAR MEMORIAL DAY AND *MAINE* MEMORIAL DAY. Feb 15. Massachusetts.

SUSAN B. ANTHONY DAY. Feb 15. Honors one of the first women's rights advocates, working especially for the right to vote. Anthony was born on this day in 1820 at Adams, MA. She died Mar 13, 1906, at Rochester, NY.

SUTTER, JOHN AUGUSTUS: BIRTH ANNIVERSARY. Feb 15, 1803. Born at Kandern, Germany, Sutter established the first white settlement on the site of Sacramento, CA, in 1839, and owned a large tract of land there, which he named New Helvetia. The first great gold strike in the US was on his property, at Sutter's Mill, Jan 24, 1848. His land was soon overrun by gold seekers who, he claimed, slaughtered his cattle and stole or destroyed his property. Sutter was bankrupt by 1852. Died at Washington, DC, June 18, 1880.

TIFFANY, CHARLES LEWIS: BIRTH ANNIVERSARY. Feb 15, 1812. American jeweler whose name became synonymous with high standards of quality. Born at Killingly, CT, and died at New York, NY, Feb 18, 1902. Father of artist Louis Comfort Tiffany. See also: "Tiffany, Louis Comfort: Birth Anniversary" (Feb 18).

Birthdays Today

Adolfo, 76, fashion designer, born Adolfo F. Sardina at Havana, Cuba, Feb 15, 1933.

Marisa Berenson, 61, actress (*Cabaret, Barry Lyndon*), model, born New York, NY, Feb 15, 1948.

Claire Bloom, 78, actress (*A Doll's House, The Spy Who Came in from the Cold*), born London, England, Feb 15, 1931.

Susan Brownmiller, 74, author, feminist (*Against Our Will, Femininity*), born Brooklyn, NY, Feb 15, 1935.

Matt Groening, 55, cartoonist ("The Simpsons"), born Portland, OR, Feb 15, 1954.

Jaromir Jagr, 37, hockey player, born Kladno, Czechoslovakia, Feb 15, 1972.

Melissa Manchester, 58, singer ("Don't Cry Out Loud"), born the Bronx, NY, Feb 15, 1951.

Kevin McCarthy, 95, actor (*Invasion of the Body Snatchers, Buffalo Bill and the Indians*), born Seattle, WA, Feb 15, 1914.

William Mark Price, 45, former basketball player, born Bartlesville, OK, Feb 15, 1964.

Jane Seymour, 58, actress (Emmy for "East of Eden"; "Dr. Quinn: Medicine Woman"), born Hillingdon, England, Feb 15, 1951.

February 16 — Monday

DAY 47 — 318 REMAINING

BERGEN, EDGAR: BIRTH ANNIVERSARY. Feb 16, 1903. Actor, radio entertainer and ventriloquist, voice of Charlie McCarthy, Mortimer Snerd and Effie Klinker. Father of Emmy Award–winning actress Candice Bergen. Born at Chicago, IL; died at Las Vegas, NV, Sept 30, 1978.

CANADA: FAMILY DAY IN ALBERTA. Feb 16. Annually, the third Monday in February.

FLAHERTY, ROBERT JOSEPH: 125th BIRTH ANNIVERSARY. Feb 16, 1884. American filmmaker, explorer and author, called "father of the documentary film." Films included *Nanook of the North, Moana of the South Seas* and *Man of Aran*. Born at Iron Mountain, MI; died at Dunnerston, VT, July 23, 1951.

GEORGE WASHINGTON BIRTHDAY CELEBRATION PARADE. Feb 16. Alexandria, VA. Nation's largest parade honoring George Washington, staged by his hometown. Floats, bands, antique cars, equestrian and military units and bagpipers. Route goes through historic district. Est attendance: 50,000. For info: George Washington Birthday Celebration Committee, 1108 Jefferson St, Alexandria, VA 22314. Phone: (703) 549-7662. E-mail: gwbcc@email.com or GWParade@gmail.com. Web: www.washingtonbirthdayparade.net.

February 2009

S	M	T	W	T	F	S
1	2	3	4	5	6	7
8	9	10	11	12	13	14
15	16	17	18	19	20	21
22	23	24	25	26	27	28

KENNAN, GEORGE: BIRTH ANNIVERSARY. Feb 16, 1904. US diplomat who coined the phrase "containment policy," Kennan was born at Milwaukee, WI. He served as a diplomat during WWII and was briefly arrested by the Nazis. After the war, he wrote an article for *Foreign Affairs* magazine that had a great influence on America's Cold War policy. The article, entitled "The Sources of Soviet Conduct" and submitted under the pseudonym "Mr. X," called upon the US and its allies to prevent the territorial spread of communism, either by shows of military force or by economic and technological intervention in at-risk nations. Both the Marshall Plan and the Truman Doctrine were heavily influenced by the ideas expressed in the article. Kennan later had a controversial turn as ambassador to the Soviet Union. He died at Princeton, NJ, at the age of 101, Mar 17, 2005.

LITHUANIA: INDEPENDENCE DAY. Feb 16. National Day. The anniversary of Lithuania's declaration of independence in 1918 is observed as the Baltic state's Independence Day. In 1940 Lithuania became a part of the Soviet Union under an agreement between Joseph Stalin and Adolf Hitler. On Mar 11, 1990, Lithuania declared its independence from the Soviet Union, the first of the Soviet republics to do so. After demanding independence, Lithuania set up a border police force and aided young men in efforts to avoid the Soviet military draft, prompting then Soviet leader Mikhail Gorbachev to send tanks into the capital of Vilnius and impose oil and gas embargoes. In the wake of the failed coup attempt in Moscow, Aug 19, 1991, Lithuanian independence finally was recognized.

MOON PHASE: LAST QUARTER. Feb 16. Moon enters Last Quarter phase at 4:37 PM, EST.

PRESIDENTS' DAY. Feb 16. Presidents' Day observes the birthdays of George Washington (Feb 22) and Abraham Lincoln (Feb 12). With the adoption of the Monday Holiday Law (which moved the observance of George Washington's birthday from Feb 22 to the third Monday in February), some of the specific significance of the event was lost and added impetus was given to the popular description of that holiday as Presidents' Day. Present usage often regards Presidents' Day as a day to honor all former presidents of the US, though the federal holiday is still Washington's Birthday. Annually, the third Monday in February. See also "Washington, George: Birthday Observance (Legal Holiday)" below.

PRESIDENTS' DAY: LIVE FROM DELAWARE STREET. Feb 16. Indianapolis, IN. Visit President Benjamin Harrison Home and listen to the conversations and gossip of the day as you enter each room and speak with family members and household staff, whose roles are re-created by actors. For info: PR Dept, President Benjamin Harrison Home, 1230 N Delaware St, Indianapolis, IN 46202. Phone: (317) 631-1888. Fax: (317) 632-5488. E-mail: harrison@pbhh.org. Web: www.pbhh.org.

STOCK EXCHANGE HOLIDAY (WASHINGTON'S BIRTHDAY). Feb 16 (observed). The holiday schedules for the various exchanges are subject to change if relevant rules, regulations or exchange policies are revised. If you have questions, contact: American Stock Exchange (866) 422-2639 (www.amex.com), Chicago Board of Trade (312) 435-3500 (www.cbot.com), Chicago Board Options Exchange (312) 786-5600 (www.cboe.com), NASDAQ Stock Market (646) 441-5200 (www.nasdaq.com), New York Stock Exchange (212) 656-3000 (www.nyse.com), Philadelphia Stock Exchange (800) THE-PHLX (www.phlx.com).

SURRENDER OF FORT DONELSON: ANNIVERSARY. Feb 16, 1862. With Confederate troops evacuating Bowling Green, KY, and other points along the Kentucky line, General Ulysses S. Grant's forces encircled Fort Donelson, KY. After hard fighting on land and on the Cumberland River, Grant requested surrender of Fort Donelson, stating that "No terms except unconditional and immediate surrender can be accepted." This earned him the nickname "Unconditional Surrender" Grant. Confederate general Simon Buckner surrendered the fort, in essence giving the Union army control of Tennessee and Kentucky and the Tennessee and Cumberland rivers. Disruption ensued and civilians attempted to flee the area occupied by Federal troops.

WASHINGTON, GEORGE: BIRTHDAY OBSERVANCE (LEGAL HOLIDAY). Feb 16. Legal public holiday. (Public Law 90–363 sets

Washington's birthday observance on the third Monday in February each year—applicable to federal employees and to the District of Columbia.) Observed in all states. See also: "Washington, George: Birth Anniversary" (Feb 22).

WILSON, HENRY: BIRTH ANNIVERSARY. Feb 16, 1812. 18th vice president of the US (1873–75). Born at Farmington, NH; died at Washington, DC, Nov 22, 1875.

Birthdays Today

Jerome Bettis, 37, former football player, born Detroit, MI, Feb 16, 1972.

LeVar Burton, 52, actor, host ("Roots," "Star Trek: The Next Generation," "Reading Rainbow"), born Landsthul, Germany, Feb 16, 1957.

Christopher Eccleston, 45, actor ("Doctor Who," "Heroes," *Shallow Grave*), born Salford, Lancashire, England, Feb 16, 1964.

Richard Ford, 65, author (*Independence Day, The Sportswriter*), born Jackson, MS, Feb 16, 1944.

Ice T, 50, rap singer, actor ("Law & Order: Special Victims Unit," *New Jack City*), born Tracy Morrow at Newark, NJ, Feb 16, 1959.

James Ingram, 53, singer, songwriter, born Akron, OH, Feb 16, 1956.

William Katt, 59, actor ("The Greatest American Hero," *Perry Mason Returns, Carrie*), born Los Angeles, CA, Feb 16, 1950 (some sources say 1955 or 1951).

John Patrick McEnroe, Jr, 50, former tennis player, born Wiesbaden, West Germany, Feb 16, 1959.

Barry Primus, 71, actor ("Cagney and Lacey," *Absence of Malice, Down and Out in Beverly Hills*), born New York, NY, Feb 16, 1938.

February 17 — Tuesday

DAY 48 **317 REMAINING**

BARBER, WALTER LANIER "RED": BIRTH ANNIVERSARY. Feb 17, 1908. One of the first broadcasters inducted into the Baseball Hall of Fame, "Red" Barber was born at Columbus, MS. Barber's first professional play-by-play experience was announcing the Cincinnati Reds' opening day on radio in 1934. That game was also the first major league game he had ever seen. His other notable broadcasts include baseball's first night game (in Brooklyn) on Aug 26, 1939, the 1947 game in which Jackie Robinson broke the color barrier and Roger Maris's 61st home run in 1961. Red Barber died Oct 22, 1992, at Tallahassee, FL.

CHICAGO FLAG EXHIBIT CONTROVERSY: 20th ANNIVERSARY. Feb 17, 1989. An exhibit at the School of the Art Institute of Chicago, titled *What Is the Proper Way to Display a US Flag?*, consisted of a ledger for viewers to write their impressions but required the viewers to stand on a US flag mounted on the floor to reach the ledger. The exhibit by art student Scott Tyler prompted protests from veterans' groups, a failed lawsuit and an introduction of legislation by Senator Bob Dole to make displaying a US flag on the floor or ground a crime. Although that legislation didn't pass, Congress periodically continues to introduce legislation against flag desecration.

CORELLI, ARCANGELO: BIRTH ANNIVERSARY. Feb 17, 1653. Italian composer and virtuoso violinist, born at Fusignano, Italy. From his home in Rome, Corelli made extensive and popular concert tours throughout much of Europe. Died at Rome, Jan 8, 1713.

CRABBE, BUSTER: BIRTH ANNIVERSARY. Feb 17, 1908. Clarence Lindon "Buster" Crabbe, Olympic gold medal swimmer, born at Oakland, CA. Crabbe's first-place finish in the 400-meter freestyle was the only swimming medal won by an American at the 1932 Olympic Games at Los Angeles. After his swimming career was over, he played Tarzan, Flash Gordon and Buck Rogers in the movies. Died at Scottsdale, AZ, Apr 23, 1983.

FORT SUMTER RETURNED TO UNION CONTROL: ANNIVERSARY. Feb 17, 1865. After a siege that lasted almost a year and a half, Fort Sumter in South Carolina returned to Union hands on this date. The site of the first shots fired in the American Civil War on Apr 12, 1861, the fort had become a symbol for both sides. As Union attempts to retake it by shelling diminished the fort's capacity with large bombardments, Southern forces managed to hold out with few casualties.

GERONIMO: 100th DEATH ANNIVERSARY. Feb 17, 1909. American Indian of the Chiricahua (Apache) tribe was born about 1829 in Arizona. He was the leader of a small band of warriors whose devastating raids in Arizona, New Mexico and Mexico caused the US Army to send 5,000 men to recapture him after his first escape. He was confined at Fort Sill, OK, where he died after dictating the story of his life for publication.

LAENNEC, RENE THEOPHILE HYACINTHE: BIRTH ANNIVERSARY. Feb 17, 1781. Famed French physician, author and inventor of the stethoscope, called "father of chest medicine." He wrote extensively about respiratory and heart ailments. Born at Quimper, France, he died there Aug 13, 1826.

LEAGUE OF UNITED LATIN AMERICAN CITIZENS (LULAC) FOUNDED: 80th ANNIVERSARY. Feb 17, 1929. Delegates from the Corpus Christi Order of the Sons of America, Knights of America of San Antonio and the League of Latin America Citizens from the Rio Grande Valley met at Obreros Hall, Corpus Christi, TX, to form LULAC. It is now the oldest and largest Hispanic-American civic organization.

***MADAMA BUTTERFLY* PREMIERE: ANNIVERSARY.** Feb 17, 1904. Giacomo Puccini's *Madama Butterfly* was performed for the first time in Milan. The sold-out crowd, restive at what they saw as Puccini's lack of originality, gave boos, moos, groans and heckling to the extent that the performers couldn't hear the orchestra. Rosina Storchio, the soprano portraying Madama Butterfly, began crying on stage. Puccini, enraged at the opera's reception (saying the opera was "daisies thrown to swine"), nevertheless revised the work, and it had a successful performance on May 24.

MALTHUS, THOMAS: BIRTH ANNIVERSARY. Feb 17, 1766. English economist, author and demographer, born near Dorking, England. Malthusian population theories (especially that population growth exceeds growth of production) provoked great controversy when published in 1798. Died near Bath, England, Dec 23, 1834.

McCLURE, SAMUEL SIDNEY: BIRTH ANNIVERSARY. Feb 17, 1857. Irish-American newspaper editor and publisher, founder of newspaper syndicate. Born at County Antrim, Ireland. Died at New York, NY, Mar 21, 1949.

MY WAY DAY. Feb 17. Hundreds of people have their opinions as to who we are. Today is the day we decide who's right. Today we determine our identities all by ourselves. (©2006 by WH.) For info: Thomas & Ruth Roy, Wellcat Holidays, 2418 Long Ln, Lebanon, PA 17046. Phone: (717) 279-0184. E-mail: info@wellcat.com. Web: www.wellcat.com.

NATIONAL PTA FOUNDERS' DAY: ANNIVERSARY. Feb 17, 1897. Celebrates the PTA's founding by Phoebe Apperson Hearst and Alice McLellan Birney. For info: Natl PTA, 541 N Fairbanks, Ste 1300, Chicago, IL 60611-3396. Phone: (312) 670-6782. Fax: (312) 670-6783. E-mail: info@pta.org. Web: www.pta.org.

"A PRAIRIE HOME COMPANION" PREMIERE: 30th ANNIVERSARY. Feb 17, 1979. This popular live variety show debuted locally on Minnesota Public Radio in 1974 and was first broadcast nationally on Feb 17, 1979, as part of National Public Radio's Folk Festival USA. It became a regular Saturday-night program in early 1980. Host Garrison Keillor's monologues about the mythical Lake Wobegon and his humorous ads for local businesses such as Bertha's Kitty Boutique, Powdermilk Biscuits and the Chatterbox Cafe were accompanied by various musical groups. Broadcast from the World Theater in St. Paul, MN, the show went off the air in 1986. A series of programs were done for cable TV, and Keillor continues to write works of fiction (*Lake Wobegon Days*). In 1994 "A Prairie Home Companion" went back on the air on Public Radio International.

UNITED STATES: TELEVISION SWITCHES FROM ANALOG TO DIGITAL. Feb 17, 2009. Today, federal law requires that all full-power television broadcast stations stop broadcasting in analog format and broadcast only in digital format. Congress mandated the conversion because all-digital broadcasting will free up frequencies for public safety communications (such as police, fire, and emergency rescue) and because digital is a more efficient transmission technology that allows broadcast stations to offer improved picture and sound quality.

WORLD HUMAN SPIRIT DAY. Feb 17. Fort Lauderdale, FL. At 3 PM, EST, we will hold two minutes of silent meditation throughout the world and beyond, to focus on the true spirit that flows through everything. Please join us in silence to bring the energy of universal healing and peace into the hearts and minds of all humanity. For info: Michael Levy, Point of Life Foundation, PO Box 7, 3032 E Commercial Blvd, Fort Lauderdale, FL 33308. Phone/fax: (954) 785-8439. E-mail: mikmikl@aol.com. Web: www.pointoflife.com or www.polfoundation.org.

Birthdays Today

Vanessa Atler, 27, former gymnast, born Valencia, CA, Feb 17, 1982.

James Nathaniel (Jim) Brown, 73, Hall of Fame football player, activist, actor, born St. Simons Island, GA, Feb 17, 1936.

Ronald DeVoe, 42, singer (Bell Biv DeVoe), born Boston, MA, Feb 17, 1967.

Michelle Forbes, 42, actress ("Homicide: Life on the Street," "Prison Break"), born Austin, TX, Feb 17, 1967.

Brenda Fricker, 64, actress (Oscar for *My Left Foot*; *The Field*), born Dublin, Ireland, Feb 17, 1945.

Joseph Gordon-Levitt, 28, actor ("3rd Rock from the Sun," *The Lookout, Mysterious Skin, Brick*), born Los Angeles, CA, Feb 17, 1981.

Paris Hilton, 28, socialite, television personality ("The Simple Life"), born New York, NY, Feb 17, 1981.

Lee Hoiby, 83, composer, concert pianist, born Madison, WI, Feb 17, 1926.

Hal Holbrook, 84, actor (*Magnum Force, All the President's Men*), born Harold Rowe, Jr, at Cleveland, OH, Feb 17, 1925.

Barry Humphries, 75, actor, comedian, aka Dame Edna Everidge, born Melbourne, Australia, Feb 17, 1934.

Michael Jordan, 46, former basketball player, sports executive, born Brooklyn, NY, Feb 17, 1963.

Richard Karn, 50, actor ("Home Improvement"), game-show host ("Family Feud"), born Seattle, WA, Feb 17, 1959.

Lou Diamond Phillips, 47, actor (*La Bamba, Stand and Deliver*), born Corpus Christi, TX, Feb 17, 1962.

Denise Richards, 38, actress (*Wild Things, The World Is Not Enough*), born Downers Grove, IL, Feb 17, 1971.

Rene Russo, 55, actress (*Lethal Weapon 3, Ransom*), born Burbank, CA, Feb 17, 1954.

February 2009

S	M	T	W	T	F	S
1	2	3	4	5	6	7
8	9	10	11	12	13	14
15	16	17	18	19	20	21
22	23	24	25	26	27	28

February 18 — Wednesday

DAY 49 — **316 REMAINING**

ALEICHEM, SHOLEM: 150th BIRTH ANNIVERSARY. Feb 18, 1859. (Old Style date.) Pen name of Russian-born author and humorist Solomon Rabinowitz. The musical *Fiddler on the Roof* drew from Aleichem's short stories about Tevye the Milkman. Affectionately known in the US as the "Jewish Mark Twain." Died at New York, NY, May 13, 1916.

CARNIVAL DE PONCE. Feb 18–24. Ponce, PR. Carnival, artisans, parade with floats and colorfully dressed people with papier-mâché masks (*vejigantes*). Also featuring kiosks with typical Puerto Rican foods and drinks. Annually, the week before Ash Wednesday. Est attendance: 100,000. For info: Vangie Rivera, Director, Culture and Tourism Office, Municipality of Ponce, PO Box 331709, Ponce, PR 00733-1709. Phone: (787) 284-4141. E-mail: cultponce@hotmail.com. Web: www.visitponce.com.

COW MILKED WHILE FLYING IN AN AIRPLANE: ANNIVERSARY. Feb 18, 1930. Elm Farm Ollie became the first cow to fly in an airplane. During the flight, which was attended by reporters, she was milked, and the milk was sealed in paper containers and parachuted over St. Louis, MO.

DAVIS, JEFFERSON: INAUGURATION ANNIVERSARY. Feb 18, 1861. In the years before the Civil War, Senator Jefferson Davis was the acknowledged leader of the Southern bloc and a champion of states' rights, but he had little to do with the secessionist movement until after his home state of Mississippi seceded from the Union and joined the Confederacy Jan 9, 1861. Davis withdrew from the Senate that same day. He was unanimously chosen as president of the Confederacy's provisional government and was inaugurated at Montgomery, AL, Feb 18. Within the next year he was elected to a six-year term by popular vote and inaugurated a second time Feb 22, 1862, at Richmond, VA.

GAMBIA: INDEPENDENCE DAY. Feb 18, 1965. National holiday. Independence from Britain granted. Referendum in April 1970 established Gambia as a republic within the Commonwealth.

GRAND RAPIDS BOAT SHOW. Feb 18–22. DeVos Place, Grand Rapids, MI. This event brings together buyers and sellers of powerboats from 16 to 50 feet, fishing boats, ski boats and motor yachts, boating accessories, docks, dockominiums and vacation properties. Est attendance: 30,000. For info: ShowSpan, Inc, 2121 Celebration Dr NE, Grand Rapids, MI 49525. Phone: (616) 447-2860. Fax: (616) 447-2861. E-mail: events@showspan.com. Web: www.showspan.com.

NEPAL: NATIONAL DEMOCRACY DAY. Feb 18. National holiday. Anniversary of the 1952 constitution.

PEABODY, GEORGE: BIRTH ANNIVERSARY. Feb 18, 1795. American merchant and philanthropist, born at South Danvers, MA. He endowed the Peabody Institute in Baltimore, MD, museums at Harvard and Yale and the George Peabody College for Teachers at Nashville, TN. Died at London, England, Nov 4, 1869.

PLUTO DISCOVERY: ANNIVERSARY. Feb 18, 1930. Pluto was discovered by astronomer Clyde Tombaugh at the Lowell Observatory at Flagstaff, AZ. It was given the name of the Roman god of the underworld. It was considered the ninth planet of the solar system until 2006, when astronomers reclassified it as a dwarf planet. See also: "Pluto Demoted: Anniversary" (Aug 24).

TIFFANY, LOUIS COMFORT: BIRTH ANNIVERSARY. Feb 18, 1848. American artist, son of famed jeweler Charles L. Tiffany. Best remembered for his remarkable work with decorative iridescent "favrile" glass. Born at New York, NY; died there Jan 17, 1933. See also: "Tiffany, Charles Lewis: Birth Anniversary" (Feb 15).

WILLKIE, WENDELL LEWIS: BIRTH ANNIVERSARY. Feb 18, 1892. American lawyer, author, public utility executive and politician, born at Elwood, IN. Presidential nominee of the Republican Party in 1940. Remembered for his book, *One World*, published in 1943. Died at New York, NY, Oct 8, 1944.

Birthdays Today

Helen Gurley Brown, 87, author (*Sex and the Single Girl*), publisher (*Cosmopolitan*), born Green Forest, AR, Feb 18, 1922.

Aldo Ceccato, 75, conductor, born Milan, Italy, Feb 18, 1934.

Matt Dillon, 45, actor (*Crash, There's Something About Mary, Drugstore Cowboy*), born Westchester, NY, Feb 18, 1964.

Milos Forman, 77, film director (Oscars for *Amadeus* and *One Flew Over the Cuckoo's Nest*), born Caslaz, Czechoslovakia, Feb 18, 1932.

John Hughes, 59, producer, director, screenwriter (*Sixteen Candles, Pretty in Pink, Home Alone*), born Lansing, MI, Feb 18, 1950.

George Kennedy, 82, actor (Oscar for *Cool Hand Luke*; "The Blue Knight"), born New York, NY, Feb 18, 1927.

Toni Morrison, 78, Nobel Prize–winning novelist (*Beloved, Jazz, Tar Baby, Sula*), born Lorain, OH, Feb 18, 1931.

Juice Newton, 57, singer (*Juice, Quiet Lives*), born Judy Cohen at Virginia Beach, VA, Feb 18, 1952.

Yoko Ono, 76, artist, musician, born Tokyo, Japan, Feb 18, 1933.

Molly Ringwald, 41, actress (*Sixteen Candles, The Breakfast Club, Pretty in Pink*), born Roseville, CA, Feb 18, 1968.

Greta Scacchi, 49, actress (*White Mischief, Presumed Innocent*), born Milan, Italy, Feb 18, 1960.

Cybill Shepherd, 59, actress (*The Last Picture Show*, "Moonlighting," "Cybill"), born Memphis, TN, Feb 18, 1950.

John Travolta, 54, actor (*Pulp Fiction, Urban Cowboy, Saturday Night Fever*, "Welcome Back, Kotter"), born Englewood, NJ, Feb 18, 1955.

John William Warner, 82, US Senator (R, Virginia), born Washington, DC, Feb 18, 1927.

Vanna White, 52, TV personality ("Wheel of Fortune"), born Conway, SC, Feb 18, 1957.

February 19 — Thursday

DAY 50 | **315 REMAINING**

AMERICAN BIRKEBEINER RACE. Feb 19–21. Cable to Hayward, WI. The largest and most prestigious cross-country ski marathon in North America attracts more than 5,000 participants for the 51k trek. Starting off with the Birkie, which finishes on Main St in Hayward, skiers of the 23k Kortelopet finish at Telemark Lodge. A Nordic festival of related ski events and activities begins Feb 19. Est attendance: 18,000. For info: American Birkebeiner Ski Foundation, Inc, Box 911, Hayward, WI 54843. Phone: (715) 634-5025. Fax: (715) 634-5663. E-mail: birkie@birkie.com. Web: www.birkie.com.

BIG TEN WOMEN'S SWIMMING AND DIVING CHAMPIONSHIPS. Feb 19–21. University of Michigan, Ann Arbor, MI. Est attendance: 1,500. For info: Big Ten Conference, 1500 W Higgins Rd, Park Ridge, IL 60068-6300. Phone: (847) 696-1010. Fax: (847) 696-1110. Web: www.bigten.org.

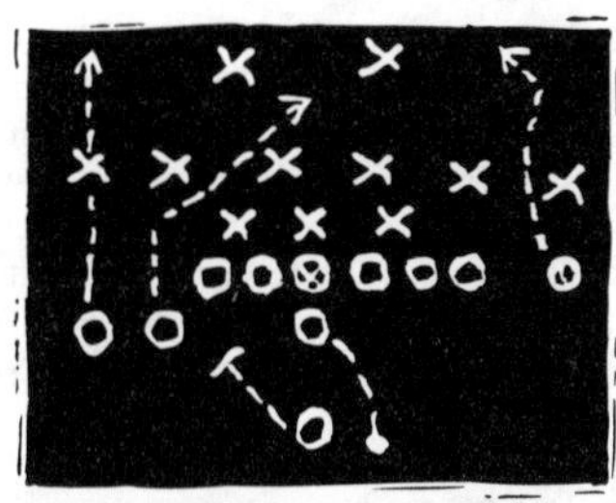

BOLLINGEN PRIZE: 60th ANNIVERSARY. Feb 19, 1949. On this date the first Bollingen Prize for poetry was awarded to Ezra Pound for his collection *The Pisan Cantos.* This first award was steeped in controversy because Pound had been charged with treason after making pro-Fascist broadcasts in Italy during WWII.

COPERNICUS, NICOLAUS: BIRTH ANNIVERSARY. Feb 19, 1473. Polish astronomer and priest who revolutionized scientific thought with what came to be called the Copernican theory that placed the sun instead of Earth at the center of our planetary system. Born at Torun, Poland, he died at East Prussia, May 24, 1543.

***THE FEMININE MYSTIQUE* PUBLISHED: ANNIVERSARY.** Feb 19, 1963. Betty Friedan published *The Feminine Mystique* this month, a call for women to achieve their full potential. Her book generated enormous response and revitalized the women's movement in the US.

GARRICK, DAVID: BIRTH ANNIVERSARY. Feb 19, 1717. English actor, theater manager and playwright. Born at Hereford, England; died Jan 20, 1779, at London.

INTRODUCE A GIRL TO ENGINEERING DAY. Feb 19. 10th annual. During National Engineers Week, the engineering community is asked to mobilize women and men engineers to reach more than one million girls and encourage them to pursue the fields that lead to engineering careers. Website includes links for teachers. For info: Natl Engineers Week Headquarters, 1420 King St, Alexandria, VA 22314. Phone: (703) 684-2852. E-mail: eweek@nspe.org. Web: www.eweek.org/site/News/Eweek/girlsday.shtml.

ITALY: FEAST OF THE INCAPPUCCIATI. Feb 19. Gradoli (near Viterbo). On the Thursday before Ash Wednesday the members of the Confraternity of Purgatory make the rounds of the town dressed in traditional hooded robes, bearing a banner and walking to the beat of a drum. They stop at every house to collect foodstuffs in the name of the souls in purgatory; the food is then served at the banquet on Ash Wednesday.

JAPANESE INTERNMENT: ANNIVERSARY. Feb 19, 1942. As a result of President Franklin Roosevelt's Executive Order 9066, some 110,000 Japanese Americans living in coastal Pacific areas were placed in concentration camps in remote areas of Arizona, Arkansas, inland California, Colorado, Idaho, Utah and Wyoming. The interned Japanese Americans (two-thirds of whom were US citizens) lost an estimated $400 million in property. They were allowed to return to their homes Jan 2, 1945.

KNIGHTS OF PYTHIAS: FOUNDING ANNIVERSARY. Feb 19, 1864. The social and fraternal order of the Knights of Pythias was founded at Washington, DC.

SIMPLOT GAMES. Feb 19–21. Holt Arena, Idaho State University, Pocatello, ID. One of the nation's largest indoor high school track-and-field events, featuring 2,000 top high school athletes from the US and Canada. Est attendance: 20,000. For info: Rebecca Anderson, Exec Dir, Simplot Games, PO Box 912, Pocatello, ID 83204. Phone: (208) 235-5604. Fax: (208) 235-5699. E-mail: simplotgames@simplot.com. Web: www.simplotgames.com.

US LANDING ON IWO JIMA: ANNIVERSARY. Feb 19, 1945. Beginning at dawn, the landing of 30,000 American troops took place on the barren 12-square-mile island of Iwo Jima. Initially there was little resistance, but 21,500 Japanese stood ready underground to fight to the last man to protect massive strategic fortifications linked by tunnels. See also: "Iwo Jima Day: Anniversary" (Feb 23).

WASHINGTON BOAT SHOW. Feb 19–22. Washington Convention Center, Washington, DC. 48th annual. Biggest indoor boat show in the mid-Atlantic region: more than 400 boats—from express cruisers to motor yachts to dinghies. Also hundreds of booths with every possible accessory, from electronics and foul-weather gear to marinas and destinations. For info: Dee Stafford, Washington Boat Show, 6017 Tower Ct, Alexandria, VA 22304. Phone: (703) 823-7960. E-mail: tjsevents@aol.com. Web: www.washingtonboatshow.com.

Birthdays Today

Prince Andrew, 49, Duke of York, born London, England, Feb 19, 1960.

Justine Bateman, 43, actress ("Family Ties," "Men Behaving Badly"), born Rye, NY, Feb 19, 1966.

Lou Christie, 66, singer, born Glen Willard, PA, Feb 19, 1943.

Jeff Daniels, 54, actor (*The Purple Rose of Cairo, Something Wild, Dumb and Dumber*), born Chelsea, MI, Feb 19, 1955.

Benicio Del Toro, 42, actor (Oscar for *Traffic*; *Che, 21 Grams, The Usual Suspects*), born Santurce, Puerto Rico, Feb 19, 1967.

Haylie Duff, 24, actress ("7th Heaven," *Napolean Dynamite*), born Houston, TX, Feb 19, 1985.

Jonathan Lethem, 45, author (*Motherless Brooklyn, Fortress of Solitude*), born Brooklyn, NY, Feb 19, 1964.

Stephen Nichols, 58, actor ("Days of Our Lives," "General Hospital"), born Cincinnati, OH, Feb 19, 1951.

Smokey Robinson, 69, singer, songwriter, born William Robinson, Jr, at Detroit, MI, Feb 19, 1940.

Seal, 46, singer, songwriter, born Sealhenry Samuel at London, England, Feb 19, 1963.

Andrew Shue, 42, actor ("Melrose Place"), born South Orange, NJ, Feb 19, 1967.

Amy Tan, 57, author (*The Joy Luck Club*), born Oakland, CA, Feb 19, 1952.

Ray Winstone, 52, actor (*Indiana Jones and the Kingdom of the Crystal Skull, The Departed, Sexy Beast*), born London, England, Feb 19, 1957.

February 20 — Friday

DAY 51 | **314 REMAINING**

ADAMS, ANSEL: BIRTH ANNIVERSARY. Feb 20, 1902. American photographer, known for his photographs of Yosemite National Park, born at San Francisco, CA. Adams died at Monterey, CA, Apr 22, 1984.

ALTMAN, ROBERT: BIRTH ANNIVERSARY. Feb 20, 1925. This iconoclastic filmmaker was master of satire, ensemble casts and the long take. His long and lauded career included such classic films as *M*A*S*H* (1970), *McCabe and Mrs Miller* (1971), *Nashville* (1975), *The Player* (1992) and *Gosford Park* (2001). Altman received a Lifetime Achievement Oscar in 2006. Born at Kansas City, MO, Altman died Nov 20, 2006, at Los Angeles, CA.

CANADA: YUKON SOURDOUGH RENDEZVOUS. Feb 20–22. Whitehorse, YT. Mad trapper competitions, flour packing, beard-growing contests, old-time fiddle show, sourdough pancake breakfasts, cancan dancers, talent shows and much more. Visitors welcome to participate. Est attendance: 20,000. For info: Yukon Sourdough Rendezvous, Box 31721, Whitehorse, YT, Canada Y1A 6L3. Phone: (867) 667-2148. Fax: (867) 668-6755. E-mail: ysr@polarcom.com. Web: www.yukonrendezvous.com.

CLOSEST APPROACH OF A COMET TO EARTH: ANNIVERSARY. Feb 20, 1491. An unnamed comet came within 860,000 miles (.0094 AU) of Earth on this date. By comparison, the closest approach that Halley's comet made to Earth was on Apr 10, 837 AD, at three million miles.

DOUGLASS, FREDERICK: DEATH ANNIVERSARY. Feb 20, 1895. American journalist, orator and antislavery leader. Born at Tuckahoe, MD, probably in February 1817. Died at Anacostia Heights, DC. His original name before his escape from slavery was Frederick Augustus Washington Bailey.

JEFFERSON, JOSEPH: BIRTH ANNIVERSARY. Feb 20, 1829. Distinguished American actor, born at Philadelphia, PA, in a family of actors. Jefferson made his stage debut at the age of three in Kotzebue's *Pizarro*. After many successes, his search for a character both humorous and pathetic centered on Rip van Winkle, about whom he wrote a short play. Later revised by Dion Boucicault, the play opened with Jefferson in the leading role at London, England, in 1865 and was an immediate success. Rip van Winkle became the signature role for which he was known. Jefferson died at Palm Beach, FL, Apr 23, 1905. He is remembered each year in Chicago when the Joseph Jefferson (Jeff) Awards are presented to recognize excellence in theatrical productions.

LOST DUTCHMAN DAYS. Feb 20–22. Apache Junction, AZ. Arts and crafts show and sale. Three-day rodeo competiton, dance, carnival, parade, business vendors in celebration of the legend of the Superstition Mountains and the Lost Dutchman Mine. Free musical entertainment. Annually, the last full weekend in February. Est attendance: 30,000. For info: Apache Junction Chamber of Commerce, PO Box 1747, Apache Junction, AZ 85217-1747. Phone: (480) 982-3141. Fax: (480) 982-3234. Web: www.apachejunctioncoc.com or www.lostdutchmandays.org.

NEWPORT SEAFOOD AND WINE FESTIVAL. Feb 20–22. Newport, OR. Central coastal festival featuring seafood and wines from Oregon, Washington, California and Idaho. Arts and crafts exhibits as well. Annually, the last full weekend in February. Est attendance: 15,000. For info: Laura Castaldo, Events Coordinator, Greater Newport Chamber of Commerce, 555 SW Coast Hwy, Newport, OR 97365. Phone: (541) 265-5883. Fax: (541) 265-5589. Web: www.newportchamber.org/swf.

NORTHERN HEMISPHERE HOODIE-HOO DAY. Feb 20. At high noon (local time) citizens are asked to go outdoors and yell "Hoodie-Hoo" to chase away winter and make ready for spring, one month away. (©2006 by WH.) For info: Thomas & Ruth Roy, Wellcat Holidays, 2418 Long Ln, Lebanon, PA 17046. Phone: (717) 279-0184. E-mail: info@wellcat.com. Web: www.wellcat.com.

PISCES, THE FISH. Feb 20–Mar 20. In the astronomical/astrological zodiac, which divides the sun's apparent orbit into 12 segments, the period Feb 20–Mar 20 is traditionally identified as the sun sign of Pisces, the Fish. The ruling planet is Neptune.

PRESCOTT, WILLIAM: BIRTH ANNIVERSARY. Feb 20, 1726. American Revolutionary soldier, born at Groton, MA. Died at Pepperell, MA, Oct 13, 1795. Credited with the order "Don't one of you fire until you see the whites of their eyes," at the Battle of Bunker Hill, June 17, 1775.

SPACE MILESTONE: *FRIENDSHIP 7* (US): FIRST AMERICAN TO ORBIT EARTH: ANNIVERSARY. Feb 20, 1962. John Herschel Glenn, Jr, became the first American and the third person to orbit Earth. Aboard the capsule *Friendship 7*, he made three orbits of Earth. Spacecraft was *Mercury-Atlas 6*. In 1998 the 77-year-old

February 2009	S	M	T	W	T	F	S
	1	2	3	4	5	6	7
	8	9	10	11	12	13	14
	15	16	17	18	19	20	21
	22	23	24	25	26	27	28

Glenn went into space again on the space shuttle *Discovery* to test the effects of aging.

SPACE MILESTONE: *MIR* SPACE STATION (USSR). Feb 20, 1986. A "third-generation" orbiting space station, *Mir* (Peace), was launched without crew from the Baikonur space center at Leninsk, Kazakhstan. Believed to be 40 feet long, weigh 47 tons and have six docking ports. Both Russian and American crews have used the station. After many equipment failures and financial problems, the Russians took *Mir* out of service Mar 23, 2001. See also: "Space Milestone: *Mir* Abandoned (USSR)" (Mar 23).

STOTZ, CARL E.: BIRTH ANNIVERSARY. Feb 20, 1920. Carl E. Stotz shaped the summers of millions of kids as the founder of Little League baseball. Born at Williamsport, PA, he organized the first three-team league there in 1939. Died at Williamsport, June 4, 1992.

UNITED NATIONS: WORLD DAY FOR SOCIAL JUSTICE. Feb 20. Annually, Feb 20, beginning in 2009. Resolution 62/10 of Nov 26, 2007.

Birthdays Today

Charles Barkley, 46, former basketball player, born Leeds, AL, Feb 20, 1963.

Brenda Blethyn, 63, actress (*Secrets and Lies, A River Runs Through It*), born Ramsgate, England, Feb 20, 1946.

Gordon Brown, 58, Prime Minister of Great Britian, born Glasgow, Scotland, Feb 20, 1951.

Cindy Crawford, 43, model, actress, born DeKalb, IL, Feb 20, 1966.

Sandy Duncan, 63, actress (*Funny Face*, "The Hogan Family," *Peter Pan*), born Henderson, TX, Feb 20, 1946.

Ron Eldard, 46, actor ("Men Behaving Badly," "ER"), born Long Island, NY, Feb 20, 1963.

Philip Anthony (Phil) Esposito, 67, hockey executive, former coach and Hall of Fame hockey player, born Sault Ste. Marie, ON, Canada, Feb 20, 1942.

Stephon Marbury, 32, basketball player, born New York, NY, Feb 20, 1977.

Mitch McConnell, 67, US Senator (R, Kentucky), born Colbert County, AL, Feb 20, 1942.

Jennifer O'Neill, 61, actress (*The Summer of '42*, "Cover-Up"), born Rio de Janeiro, Brazil, Feb 20, 1948.

Sidney Poitier, 82, actor (*In the Heat of the Night*; Oscar for *Lilies of the Field*), born Miami, FL, Feb 20, 1927.

Buffy Sainte-Marie, 68, folksinger, born Craven, SK, Canada, Feb 20, 1941.

Patty Hearst Shaw, 55, newspaper heiress who was kidnapped by radical group Symbionese Liberation Army; actress (*Cry-Baby*), born San Francisco, CA, Feb 20, 1954.

French Stewart, 45, actor ("3rd Rock from the Sun"), born Albuquerque, NM, Feb 20, 1964.

Peter Strauss, 62, actor ("Rich Man, Poor Man," *Soldier Blue*), born Croton-on-Hudson, NY, Feb 20, 1947.

Lili Taylor, 42, actress ("Six Feet Under," *I Shot Andy Warhol, Ransom, Mystic Pizza*), born Glencoe, IL, Feb 20, 1967.

Robert William (Bobby) Unser, 75, auto racer, born Albuquerque, NM, Feb 20, 1934.

Gloria Vanderbilt, 85, fashion designer, artist, born New York, NY, Feb 20, 1924.

Justin Verlander, 26, baseball player, born Manakin Sabot, VA, Feb 20, 1983.

James Wilby, 51, actor (*DreamChild, Howard's End*), born Rangoon, Burma, Feb 20, 1958.

Nancy Wilson, 72, singer, born Chillicothe, OH, Feb 20, 1937.

February 21 — Saturday

DAY 52 — **313 REMAINING**

AUDEN, W.H.: BIRTH ANNIVERSARY. Feb 21, 1907. Pulitzer Prize–winning Anglo-American poet was born Wystan Hugh Auden at York, England. "Some books," he wrote in *The Dyer's Hand* (1962), "are undeservedly forgotten; none are undeservedly remembered." Died at Vienna, Austria, Sept 28, 1973.

BANGLADESH: MARTYRS DAY. Feb 21. National mourning day in memory of martyrs of the Bengali Language Movement in 1952. Mourners gather at the Azimpur graveyard.

BATTLE OF VERDUN: ANNIVERSARY. Feb 21, 1916. The German High Command launched an offensive on the Western Front at Verdun, France, which became WWI's single longest battle. An estimated one million men were killed, decimating both the German and French armies, before the battle ended on Dec 15, 1916.

BOMBECK, ERMA: BIRTH ANNIVERSARY. Feb 21, 1927. Humorist and writer, born at Dayton, OH. Authored many books, including *The Grass Is Always Greener over the Septic Tank*. Bombeck died at San Francisco, CA, Apr 22, 1996.

BRAZIL: CARNIVAL. Feb 21–24. Especially in Rio de Janeiro, this carnival is said to be one of the last great folk festivals and the big annual event in the life of Brazilians. Begins on Saturday night before Ash Wednesday and continues through Shrove Tuesday.

CIA AGENT ARRESTED AS SPY: 15th ANNIVERSARY. Feb 21, 1994. Aldrich Hazen Ames and his wife, Maria del Rosario Casas Ames, were arrested on charges they had spied for the Soviet Union beginning in 1985 and had continued to spy for Russia after the Soviet collapse in 1991. Aldrich Ames had worked as a counterintelligence officer for the CIA at its headquarters at Langley, VA. Prosecutors said that the pair had been paid about $2.5 million for their activities and were probably responsible for the deaths of at least 10 CIA agents whom Ames had identified for the Soviets. The government considered this to be one of the most serious spy cases ever uncovered in the US. On Apr 28 Aldrich Ames was sentenced to life in prison. Rosario Ames was sentenced to a 63-month prison term in return for her husband's promise to cooperate with authorities.

CLAM CHOWDER COOK-OFF. Feb 21. Santa Cruz Beach Boardwalk, Santa Cruz, CA. Who makes the world's greatest clam chowder? Up to 60 teams compete to find out. Prizes for best booth encourage wacky costumes and elaborate props! Separate categories for restaurants, media and individuals, Boston- and Manhattan-style chowder. Free admission. Est attendance: 15,000. For info: Santa Cruz Beach Boardwalk, 400 Beach St, Santa Cruz, CA 95060-5491. Phone: (831) 423-5590. Fax: (831) 460-3336. E-mail: publicity@scseaside.com. Web: www.beachboardwalk.com.

LA FIESTA DE LOS VAQUEROS. Feb 21–Mar 1. Tucson, AZ. 84th annual. Tucson celebrates its Old West heritage with a parade, a PRCA rodeo and other related rodeo events, including an Extreme bull-riding event. Est attendance: 55,000. For info: Tucson Rodeo Committee, Inc, PO Box 11006, Tucson, AZ 85734. Phone: (520) 741-2233 or (800) 964-5662. Fax: (520) 741-7273. E-mail: info@tucsonrodeo.com. Web: www.tucsonrodeo.com.

FRENCH WEST INDIES: CARNIVAL. Feb 21–25. Martinique. For five days ending on Ash Wednesday, business comes to a halt. Streets spill over with parties and parades. A Carnival Queen is elected.

On Dimanche Gras, or Fat Sunday, revelers dressed as red devils parade in the streets. King Carnival is "buried" on Ash Wednesday.

HATSUME FAIR. Feb 21–22. Morikami Museum and Japanese Gardens, Delray Beach, FL. Celebrates the coming of spring with demonstrations and performances of Japanese *taiko* drums, folk dancing, martial arts, plants, orchids and bonsai exhibits. Annually, the last weekend in February. Est attendance: 12,000. For info: The Morikami Museum and Japanese Gardens, 4000 Morikami Park Rd, Delray Beach, FL 33446. Phone: (561) 495-0233. Fax: (561) 499-2557. Web: www.morikami.org.

ICE FISHING DERBY. Feb 21. Fort Peck, MT. 13th annual contest held on Fort Peck Lake. Entry fee of $50 per hole or three holes for $100. Subject to cancellation if no ice. For info: Glasgow Area Chamber of Commerce, PO Box 832, Glasgow, MT 59230. Phone: (406) 228-2222. Fax: (406) 228-2244. E-mail: chamber@glasgowmt.net. Web: www.glasgowmt.net.

KLONDIKE DAYS. Feb 21–22. Northland Pines High School and Rocking W Stables, Eagle River, WI. A re-creation of primitive camps used by early buck-skinners, pioneers, trappers and traders. Additional attractions include a two-day horse weight-pull reminiscent of Wisconsin's logging days, a chain saw carving competition, a Native American cultural presentation featuring a ceremonial dance exhibition, lumberjack competition, craft show, dog weight-pull and much more. Wisconsin's premier multifaceted winter festival. Est attendance: 12,000. For info: Christine Schilling, Exec Dir, Klondike Days, Inc, PO Box 1166, Eagle River, WI 54521. Phone: (800) 359-6315. Web: www.klondikedays.org.

KREWE OF ENDYMION PARADE. Feb 21. New Orleans, LA. Formed in 1966, the Krewe of Endymion puts on a spectacular carnival parade the Saturday before Mardi Gras. For info: Krewe of Endymion. Web: www.endymion.org.

MALCOLM X: ASSASSINATION ANNIVERSARY. Feb 21, 1965. Just as he began a speech to his newly formed Organization of Afro-American Unity, black activist leader Malcolm X was gunned down by several men standing among the 400-plus crowd at the Audubon Ballroom in Harlem, New York City. The assassination occurred barely a week after Malcolm X's Queens home was firebombed. Three men were convicted of the murder in 1966 and sentenced to life in prison. See also: "Malcolm X: Birth Anniversary" (May 19).

MALTA: CARNIVAL. Feb 21–24. Valletta. Festival dates from 1535 when Knights of St. John of Jerusalem introduced Carnival at Malta. Dancing (featuring the sword dance, or *Il Parata*, and other national dances), bands, decorated trucks and grotesque masks. Annually, the Saturday through Tuesday before Ash Wednesday.

MARDI GRAS FIESTA TROPICALE. Feb 21–24. Hollywood, FL. A New Orleans–style music and food festival featuring music of New Orleans, a Taste of New Orleans, evening parades with bead throws and Arti Gras for Kids Quarter. Fat Tuesday on Hollywood Beach is Feb 23–24. Est attendance: 75,000. For info: Fiesta Tropicale of Hollywood, Inc, PO Box 510, Hollywood, FL 33022-0510. Phone: (954) 926-3377. E-mail: david@mardigrasfiesta.com. Web: www.mardigrasfiesta.com.

NEW ENGLAND MID-WINTER SURFING CHAMPIONSHIP. Feb 21. Narragansett Town Beach, Narragansett, RI. 41st annual. Competition in all age categories and specialty events with prizes and trophies. Est attendance: 125. For info: Peter Panagiotis, ESA Dir, 126 Sayles Ave, Pawtucket, RI 02860. E-mail: bicsurf@hotmail.com.

***NEW YORKER* PUBLISHED: ANNIVERSARY.** Feb 21, 1925. First issue of the magazine published on this date.

NIXON'S TRIP TO CHINA: ANNIVERSARY. Feb 21, 1972. Richard Nixon became the first US president to visit any country not diplomatically recognized by the US when he went to the People's Republic of China for meetings with Chairman Mao Tse-tung and Premier Chou En-lai. Nixon arrived at Peking on this date and departed China on Feb 28. The "Shanghai Communiqué" was issued Feb 27. See also: "Shanghai Communiqué: Anniversary" (Feb 27).

PALMER, ALICE FREEMAN: BIRTH ANNIVERSARY. Feb 21, 1855. Born at Colesville, NY, Alice Freeman Palmer became president of Wellesley College at the age of 27. Under her leadership the school grew into one of the leading women's colleges. She was also instrumental in bringing the women's school Radcliffe College into its association with Harvard University. One of the organizers of the American Association of University Women, she served as its president for two terms. She was appointed the first dean of women at the University of Chicago when it opened in 1892. Palmer died Dec 6, 1902, at Paris, France.

PARKE COUNTY MAPLE FAIR. Feb 21–22 (also Feb 28–Mar 1). Rockville, IN. Headquarters at the 4-H Fairgrounds, one mile north of Rockville on US 41. Pancakes, sausage and maple syrup meals. Covered Bridge Art Association, gift shop and butcher shop. Parke County Maple Producers feature the unique process of making maple syrup. Annually, the last weekend in February and the first weekend in March. Est attendance: 10,000. For info: Parke County Inc, PO Box 165, Rockville, IN 47872. Phone: (765) 569-5226. E-mail: pci@ticz.com. Web: www.coveredbridges.com.

SANDINO, CESAR AUGUSTO: 75th ASSASSINATION ANNIVERSARY. Feb 21, 1934. Nicaraguan guerrilla leader after whom the Sandinistas are named. Sandino, born in 1893 (exact date unknown), was murdered along with his brother and several aides at Managua on this date. He and his followers had eluded the occupying force of US Marines as well as the Nicaraguan National Guard from 1927 until 1933. Regarded by the US as an outlaw and a bandit, he is revered as a martyred patriot hero by many Nicaraguans. His successful resistance and the resulting widespread anti-US feeling were largely responsible for inauguration of a US counteraction—the "Good Neighbor Policy"—toward Latin American nations during the administration of President Franklin Roosevelt.

SIMONE, NINA: BIRTH ANNIVERSARY. Feb 21, 1933. The blues and jazz singer was born Eunice Waymon at Tryon, NC. Initially determined to become a concert pianist, Simone instead found a career as a singer of a wide range of musical genres where she could put her uniquely raw and emotional voice on display. Simone was an ardent supporter of the 1950s and '60s civil rights movement. She died at Carry-le-Rouet, France, on Apr 21, 2003.

SINGLE-TASKING DAY. Feb 21. Multitasking is ineffective—and may cause brain damage! Today, do only one thing at a time without feeling guilty. For info: Theresa Gabriel, 2914 E 38th St, Columbus, NE 68601. Phone: (402) 910-4563. E-mail: tree.gabriel@gmail.com.

UNITED NATIONS: INTERNATIONAL MOTHER LANGUAGE DAY. Feb 21. To help raise awareness among all peoples of the distinct and enduring value of their languages. Annually, on Feb 21. For info: United Nations, Dept of Public Info, New York, NY 10017. Web: www.un.org.

WASHINGTON MONUMENT DEDICATED: ANNIVERSARY. Feb 21, 1885. Monument to the first US president was dedicated at Washington, DC.

February 2009

S	M	T	W	T	F	S
1	2	3	4	5	6	7
8	9	10	11	12	13	14
15	16	17	18	19	20	21
22	23	24	25	26	27	28

Birthdays Today

Christopher Atkins, 48, actor ("Dallas," *The Blue Lagoon*), born Rye, NY, Feb 21, 1961.

William Baldwin, 46, actor (*Born on the Fourth of July, Backdraft*), born Massapequa, NY, Feb 21, 1963.

Corbin Bleu, 20, singer, actor (*High School Musical*), born Brooklyn, NY, Feb 21, 1989.

Mary Chapin Carpenter, 51, singer, musician, born Princeton, NJ, Feb 21, 1958.

Charlotte Church, 23, singer, born Cardiff, Wales, Feb 21, 1986.

Jack Coleman, 51, actor ("Heroes," "Dynasty"), born Easton, PA, Feb 21, 1958.

Tyne Daly, 62, actress ("Judging Amy," Emmy for "Cagney and Lacey"; *Gypsy*), born Madison, WI, Feb 21, 1947.

Christine Ebersole, 56, actress (*Richie Rich, Amadeus*, "Saturday Night Live"), born Chicago, IL, Feb 21, 1953.

David Geffen, 65, record company executive (Geffen Records), born New York, NY, Feb 21, 1944.

Hubert de Givenchy, 82, fashion designer, born Beauvais, France, Feb 21, 1927.

Kelsey Grammer, 54, actor ("Cheers," "Frasier"), born St. Thomas, US Virgin Islands, Feb 21, 1955.

Jennifer Love Hewitt, 30, actress ("Ghost Whisperer," "Party of Five," "Time of My Life"), born Waco, TX, Feb 21, 1979.

Gary Lockwood, 72, actor (*Splendor in the Grass; 2001: A Space Odyssey*), born Van Nuys, CA, Feb 21, 1937.

Rue McClanahan, 75, actress ("Maude," "The Golden Girls"), born Healdton, OK, Feb 21, 1934.

Ellen Page, 22, actress (*Juno*; *X-Men: The Last Stand*), born Halifax, NS, Canada, Feb 21, 1987.

William Petersen, 56, actor ("C.S.I.," *Manhunter, To Live and Die in LA*), born Evanston, IL, Feb 21, 1953.

Olympia J. Snowe, 62, US Senator (R, Maine), born Augusta, ME, Feb 21, 1947.

February 22 — Sunday

DAY 53 — **312 REMAINING**

ACADEMY AWARDS PRESENTATION. Feb 22. Kodak Theatre, Los Angeles, CA. 81st annual. Honoring film achievements of the previous year. Begins at 5:30 PM, EST. Also televised live by ABC. For info: Academy of Motion Picture Arts and Sciences, 8949 Wilshire Blvd, Beverly Hills, CA 90211-1972. Phone: (310) 247-3000. Web: www.oscars.org.

BADEN-POWELL, ROBERT: BIRTH ANNIVERSARY. Feb 22, 1857. British army officer who founded the Boy Scouts and Girl Guides. Born at London, England, he died at Kenya, Africa, Jan 8, 1941.

FASCHING SUNDAY. Feb 22. Germany and Austria. The last Sunday before Lent.

FLORIDA ACQUIRED BY US: ANNIVERSARY. Feb 22, 1819. Secretary of State John Quincy Adams signed the Florida Purchase Treaty, under which Spain ceded Florida to the US. As payment, the US assumed $5 million of claims by US citizens against Spain. Florida became a state in 1845.

***IT HAPPENED ONE NIGHT* FILM RELEASE: 75th ANNIVERSARY.** Feb 22, 1934. Frank Capra's romantic screwball comedy, starring Claudette Colbert as a spoiled runaway heiress and Clark Gable as a cocky reporter on to a good story, was the first film to sweep all the major Academy Awards, winning Best Picture, Best Director, Best Actor, Best Actress and Best Screenplay. (A scene in which Clark Gable leans on a fence munching a carrot inspired the Warner Bros. animation team when they were creating Bugs Bunny.)

ITALY: CARNIVAL WEEK. Feb 22–28. Milan. Carnival week is held according to local tradition, with shows and festive events for children on Tuesday and Thursday. Parades of floats, figures in the costume of local folk characters Meneghin and Cecca, parties and more traditional events are held on Saturday. Annually, the Sunday–Saturday of Ash Wednesday week.

JOE CAIN PROCESSION. Feb 22. Mobile, AL. 43rd year. Led by Slacabamorinico IV for the 24th time, it honors the man who revived the Mardi Gras in Mobile in 1866 following the War Between the States. Annually, the Sunday before Shrove Tuesday. Est attendance: 100,000. For info: The Rev Wayne Dean, Sr, VP, Joe Cain Society, 1064 Palmetto St, Mobile, AL 36604-3041. Phone: (251) 753-0546. E-mail: joecain50@gmail.com.

KREWE OF BACCHUS PARADE. Feb 22. New Orleans, LA. This legendary social club, formed in 1968, throws one of the highlight parades of carnival season. Annually, the Sunday before Mardi Gras. For info: Krewe of Bacchus. Web: www.kreweofbacchus.org.

LOWELL, JAMES RUSSELL: BIRTH ANNIVERSARY. Feb 22, 1819. American essayist, poet and diplomat. Born at Cambridge, MA, he died there Aug 12, 1891.

MILLAY, EDNA ST. VINCENT: BIRTH ANNIVERSARY. Feb 22, 1892. American poet ("My candle burns at both ends . . ."), born at Rockland, ME. She died Oct 19, 1950, at Austerlitz, NY.

MILLS, JOHN: BIRTH ANNIVERSARY. Feb 22, 1908. Popular actor, born at North Elmham, England, who played stalwart, everyman heroes. His career ranged from 1932 to 2004, and his memorable films included *In Which We Serve* (1942), *Great Expectations* (1946), *Tunes of Glory* (1960) and *Ryan's Daughter* (1970)—for which he received a Best Supporting Actor Oscar. Mills was knighted in 1976. He died Apr 23, 2005, at Denham, England.

MIRACLE ON ICE: US HOCKEY TEAM DEFEATS USSR: ANNIVERSARY. Feb 22, 1980. The US Olympic hockey team upset the team from the Soviet Union, 4–3, at the Lake Placid Winter Games to earn a victory often called the "Miracle on Ice." Led by coach Herb Brooks, the Americans went on to defeat Finland two days later and win the gold medal.

MONTGOMERY BOYCOTT ARRESTS: ANNIVERSARY. Feb 22, 1956. On Feb 20 white city leaders of Montgomery, AL, issued an ultimatum to black organizers of the three-month-old Montgomery bus boycott. They said if the boycott ended immediately, there would be "no retaliation whatsoever." If it did not end, it was made clear they would begin arresting black leaders. Two days later, 80 well-known boycotters, including Rosa Parks, Martin Luther King, Jr, and E.D. Nixon, marched to the sheriff's office in the county courthouse, where they gave themselves up for arrest. They were booked, fingerprinted and photographed. The next day the story was carried by newspapers all over the world.

NATIONAL EATING DISORDERS AWARENESS WEEK. Feb 22–28. NEDAW provides opportunities for eating disorders organizations, mental health professionals, educators, families and concerned individuals around the world to join together to distribute information and plan events relating to eating disorders. For info: National Eating Disorders Assn, 603 Stewart St, Ste 803, Seattle, WA 98101. Phone: (206) 382-3587. E-mail: info@NationalEatingDisorders.org. Web: www.NationalEatingDisorders.org.

NATIONAL PANCAKE WEEK. Feb 22–28. Traditional celebration surrounding Shrove, or Pancake, Tuesday to recognize the history and continuing popularity of pancakes. For info: Pam Becker, Bisquick Baking Mix, General Mills, Inc, #1 General Mills Blvd, Minneapolis, MN 55426. Phone/fax: (763) 764-2470. E-mail: pam.becker@genmills.com.

ORTHODOX MEATFARE SUNDAY. Feb 22. Meatfare Sunday begins Meatfare Week, a time of abstaining from meat in preparation for Lent. Some Orthodox communities call this Butterweek.

SAINT LUCIA: INDEPENDENCE DAY: 30th ANNIVERSARY. Feb 22. National holiday. Commemorates independence of the island in the West Indies from Britain in 1979.

SCHOPENHAUER, ARTHUR: BIRTH ANNIVERSARY. Feb 22, 1788. Philosopher and author, born at Danzig, Germany, and died at Frankfurt am Main, Germany, Sept 21, 1860. Generally regarded as a misanthrope, the never-married Schopenhauer wrote in 1819, "To marry is to halve your rights and double your duties."

SHROVETIDE. Feb 22–24. The three days before Ash Wednesday: Shrove Sunday, Monday and Tuesday—a time for confession and festivity before the beginning of Lent.

WADLOW, ROBERT PERSHING: BIRTH ANNIVERSARY. Feb 22, 1918. Tallest man in recorded history, born at Alton, IL. Though only 9 pounds at birth, by age 10 Wadlow already stood more than 6 feet tall and weighed 210 pounds. When Wadlow died at age 22, he was a remarkable 8 feet 11.1 inches tall, 490 pounds. His gentle, friendly manner in the face of constant public attention earned him the name "Gentle Giant." Wadlow died July 15, 1940, at Manistee, MI, of complications resulting from a foot infection.

WASHINGTON, GEORGE: BIRTH ANNIVERSARY. Feb 22, 1732. First president of the US ("first in war, first in peace, and first in the hearts of his countrymen" in the words of Henry "Light-Horse Harry" Lee). Born at Westmoreland County, VA, Feb 22, 1732 (New Style). However, the Julian (Old Style) calendar was still in use in the colonies, when he was born and the year began in March, so the date on the calendar when he was born was Feb 11, 1731. He died at Mount Vernon, VA, Dec 14, 1799. See also: "Washington, George: Birthday Observance (Legal Holiday)" (Feb 16) and "Washington, George: Death Anniversary" (Dec 14).

WOOLWORTH'S FIRST OPENED: ANNIVERSARY. Feb 22, 1879. First chain store, F.W. Woolworth, opened at Utica, NY. In 1997 the closing of the chain was announced.

Birthdays Today

Amy Strum Alcott, 53, golfer, born Kansas City, MO, Feb 22, 1956.

George Lee "Sparky" Anderson, 75, Hall of Fame baseball manager and player, born Bridgewater, SD, Feb 22, 1934.

Drew Barrymore, 34, actress (*Charlie's Angels; E.T. The Extra-Terrestrial*), born Los Angeles, CA, Feb 22, 1975.

James Blunt, 32, singer, born Tidworth, Hamphire, England, Feb 22, 1977.

Michael Te Pei Chang, 37, former tennis player, born Hoboken, NJ, Feb 22, 1972.

Jonathan Demme, 65, director (*Silence of the Lambs*), born Centre, MD, Feb 22, 1944.

Paul Dooley, 81, actor (*Slap Shot, Breaking Away, The Player*), born Parkersburg, WV, Feb 22, 1928.

Julius Winfield "Dr. J" Erving, 59, Hall of Fame basketball player, born Roosevelt, NY, Feb 22, 1950.

Edward Moore (Ted) Kennedy, 77, US Senator (D, Massachusetts), born Boston, MA, Feb 22, 1932.

Kyle MacLachlan, 50, actor ("Twin Peaks," *Blue Velvet, The Flintstones*), born Yakima, WA, Feb 22, 1959.

Miou-Miou, 59, actress (*Entre Nous, La Lectrice*), born Paris, France, Feb 22, 1950.

Jeri Ryan, 41, actress ("Shark," "Boston Public," "Star Trek: Voyager"), born Munich, Germany, Feb 22, 1968.

Kazuhiro Sasaki, 41, baseball player, born Sendai, Japan, Feb 22, 1968.

Vijay Singh, 46, golfer, born Lautoka, Fiji, Feb 22, 1963.

Julie Walters, 59, actress (*Calendar Girls, Billy Elliot, Educating Rita*), born Birmingham, England, Feb 22, 1950.

Jayson Williams, 41, former basketball player, born Ritter, SC, Feb 22, 1968.

February 2009	S	M	T	W	T	F	S
	1	2	3	4	5	6	7
	8	9	10	11	12	13	14
	15	16	17	18	19	20	21
	22	23	24	25	26	27	28

February 23 — Monday

DAY 54 — 311 REMAINING

BRUNEI DARUSSALAM: NATIONAL DAY. Feb 23. National holiday observed in Brunei Darussalam, located on the island of Borneo. Commemorates independence from Britain, Feb 23, 1984.

CARNIVAL. Feb 23–24. Period of festivities, feasts, foolishness and gaiety immediately before Lent begins on Ash Wednesday. Ordinarily Carnival includes only Fasching (the Feast of Fools), being the Monday and Tuesday immediately preceding Ash Wednesday. The period of Carnival may also be extended in some areas.

CURLING IS COOL DAY. Feb 23. Offer up a worldwide embrace for an Olympic sport the entire family can play! If you don't get it, you ain't cool. (©2006 by WH.) For info: Thomas & Ruth Roy, Wellcat Holidays, 2418 Long Ln, Lebanon, PA 17046. Phone: (717) 279-0184. Fax: (240) 332-4886. E-mail: info@wellcat.com. Web: www.wellcat.com.

DIESEL ENGINE PATENTED: ANNIVERSARY. Feb 23, 1893. Rudolf Diesel received a patent in Germany for the engine that bears his name. The diesel engine burns fuel oil rather than gasoline and is used in trucks and heavy industrial machinery.

DuBOIS, W.E.B.: BIRTH ANNIVERSARY. Feb 23, 1868. William Edward Burghardt DuBois, American educator and leader of the movement for black equality. Born at Great Barrington, MA, he died at Accra, Ghana, Aug 27, 1963. "The cost of liberty," he wrote in 1909, "is less than the price of repression."

FASCHING. Feb 23–24. In Germany and Austria, Fasching, also called Fasnacht, Fasnet or Feast of Fools, is a Shrovetide festival with processions of masked figures, both beautiful and grotesque. Always the two days (Rose Monday and Shrove Tuesday) between Fasching Sunday and Ash Wednesday.

FIRST CLONING OF AN ADULT ANIMAL: ANNIVERSARY. Feb 23, 1997. Researchers in Scotland announced the first cloning of an adult animal, a lamb they named Dolly with a genetic makeup identical to that of her mother. This led to worldwide speculation about the possibility of human cloning. On Mar 4 President William Clinton imposed a ban on the federal funding of human cloning research.

GROUND WAR AGAINST IRAQ BEGINS: ANNIVERSARY. Feb 23, 1991. After an air campaign lasting slightly more than a month, Allied forces launched the ground offensive against Iraqi forces as part of Desert Storm. The relentless air attacks had devastated troops and targets in both Iraq and Kuwait. A world that had watched and anticipated "the mother of all battles" was surprised at the swiftness and ease with which Allied forces were able to subdue Iraqi forces in 100 hours.

GUYANA: ANNIVERSARY OF REPUBLIC. Feb 23. National holiday. Guyana in South America became a republic within the British Commonwealth, Feb 23, 1970.

HANDEL, GEORGE FREDERICK: BIRTH ANNIVERSARY. Feb 23, 1685. (Old Style date.) Born at Halle, Saxony, Germany. Handel and Bach, born the same year, were perhaps the greatest masters of Baroque music. Handel's most frequently performed work is the oratorio *Messiah*, which was first heard in 1742. He died at London, England, Apr 14, 1759. See also: "Premiere of Handel's *Messiah*: Anniversary" (Apr 13).

ICELAND: BUN DAY. Feb 23. Children invade homes in the morning with colorful sticks and receive gifts of whipped cream buns. On Shrove Monday.

IWO JIMA DAY: ANNIVERSARY. Feb 23, 1945. Anniversary of the day that the US flag was raised on the Pacific island of Iwo Jima by US Marines. Almost 20,000 American soldiers lost their lives before the island was finally taken from the Japanese on Mar 16, 1945.

JAPANESE ATTACK US MAINLAND: ANNIVERSARY. Feb 23, 1942. In the first attack on the US mainland, a Japanese submarine fired 25 shells at an oil refinery at the edge of Ellwood Oil Field 12 miles west of Santa Barbara, CA. One shell made a direct hit of the rigging, causing minor damage. President Franklin Roosevelt was giving a fireside chat at the time of the attack.

NATIONAL PERSONAL CHEF DAY. Feb 23. A national day for clients to honor the hardworking, creative personal chefs who provide them with delicious, affordable, custom-designed meals from fresh ingredients on a regular basis that may be enjoyed in the comfort of the client's own home. Our clients don't have to be celebrities to eat like celebrities! (Formally observed in July.) For info: American Personal & Private Chef Assn, 4572 Delaware St, San Diego, CA 92116. Phone: (800) 644-8389. Fax: (619) 294-2823. E-mail: info@personalchef.com. Web: www.personalchef.com.

PEPYS, SAMUEL: BIRTH ANNIVERSARY. Feb 23, 1633. (Old Style date.) Diarist, born at London, England. Wrote Pepys in his diary (Mar 10, 1666): "The truth is, I do indulge myself a little the more in pleasure, knowing that this is the proper age of my life to do it; and, out of my observation that most men that do thrive in the world do forget to take pleasure during the time that they are getting their estate, but reserve that till they have got one, and then it is too late for them to enjoy it." Died at London, May 26, 1703 (OS).

READ ME WEEK. Feb 23–27. National and local celebrities and other volunteers read in classrooms wearing readable clothing with school-appropriate messages. In 2007, 50 schools and more than 500 volunteers participated. For info: Book'em! Phone: (615) 834-7323. Fax: (615) 834-7323. Web: www.bookem-kids.org.

RUSSIA: ARMY AND NAVY DAY. Feb 23. Also known as Defender of the Fatherland Day. Wreaths are laid at the Tomb of the Unknown Soldier. Commemorates a 1918 clash with German troops that went down in history as the birthday of the Red Army.

SHIRER, WILLIAM L.: BIRTH ANNIVERSARY. Feb 23, 1904. American journalist and author William L. Shirer was born at Chicago, IL. As the European correspondent from 1927 to 1934 for the *Chicago Tribune* he became a friend of Mohandas K. Gandhi, the leader of India's independence movement. As a result of this he published *Gandhi: A Memoir* in 1980. His best-known book is *The Rise and Fall of the Third Reich* (1960), in which he used his experiences in Europe with the *New York Herald Tribune*, the Universal News Service and CBS Radio. He died Dec 28, 1993, at Boston, MA.

SHROVE MONDAY. Feb 23. The Monday before Ash Wednesday. In Germany and Austria, this is called Rose Monday.

TAYLOR, GEORGE: DEATH ANNIVERSARY. Feb 23, 1781. Signer of the Declaration of Independence. Born 1716 at British Isles (exact date unknown). Died at Easton, PA.

TRINIDAD AND TOBAGO: CARNIVAL. Feb 23–24. Port of Spain. Called by islanders "the mother of all carnivals," a special tradition that brings together people from all over the world in an incredibly colorful setting that includes the world's most celebrated calypsonians, steel band players, costume designers and masqueraders. Annually, the two days before Ash Wednesday. For info: Natl Carnival Commission, Corporate Head Office, Queens Park Savannah, Port of Spain, Trinidad, West Indies. Phone: (868) 627-1350. Fax: (868) 623-1391. E-mail: nccmac@tstt.net.tt or tourism-info@tidco.co.tt. Web: www.ncctt.org or www.visittnt.com.

WILLARD, EMMA HART: BIRTH ANNIVERSARY. Feb 23, 1787. Pioneer in higher education for women, born at Berlin, CT. Intent on improving educational opportunities for women, she sent her *Plan for Improving Female Education* to the governor of New York. In it she described her ideal for a girls' school, including the instruction usually offered the girls of her day (music, drawing, penmanship, dancing), as well as adding religious and moral instruction, natural philosophy and domestic science. The New York legislature granted her a charter for the Waterford Academy for Young Ladies. The school later moved to Troy, NY, where it was first named the Troy Female Seminary and later the Emma Willard School. She assisted in the founding of a teachers' training school for girls at Athens, Greece, in 1832. She began the Willard Association for the Mutual Improvement of Female Teachers in 1837, and she authored several textbooks on geography, history and astronomy. Willard died at Troy, Apr 15, 1870.

Birthdays Today

Emily Blunt, 26, actress (*The Devil Wears Prada,* "Gideon's Daughter"), born London, England, Feb 23, 1983.

Roberto Martin Antonio (Bobby) Bonilla, 46, former baseball player, born New York, NY, Feb 23, 1963.

Sylvia Chase, 71, newscaster, born Northfield, MN, Feb 23, 1938.

Peter Fonda, 70, actor (*Easy Rider, Ulee's Gold*), born New York, NY, Feb 23, 1939.

Edward Lee "Too Tall" Jones, 58, former football player and boxer, born Jackson, TN, Feb 23, 1951.

Howard Jones, 54, singer, born Southampton, England, Feb 23, 1955.

Patricia Richardson, 58, actress ("Double Trouble," "Home Improvement"), born Bethesda, MD, Feb 23, 1951.

Johnny Winter, 65, singer, musician, born John Dawson III at Beaumont, TX, Feb 23, 1944.

February 24 — Tuesday

DAY 55 — **310 REMAINING**

ENGLAND: SHROVETIDE PANCAKE RACE. Feb 24. Olney, Buckinghamshire. The pancake race at Olney has been run since 1445. Competitors must be women over 16 years of age, wearing a traditional housewife's costume, including apron and head covering. With a toss and flip of the pancake on the griddle that each must carry, the women dash from the marketplace to the parish church, where the winner receives a kiss from the ringer of the Pancake Bell. Shriving service follows. Annually, on Shrove Tuesday.

ESTONIA: INDEPENDENCE DAY. Feb 24. National holiday. Commemorates declaration of independence from Soviet Union in 1918. Independence was brief, however; Estonia was again under Soviet control until 1991.

GREGORIAN CALENDAR DAY: ANNIVERSARY. Feb 24, 1582. Pope Gregory XIII, enlisting the expertise of distinguished astronomers and mathematicians, issued a bull correcting the Julian calendar that was then 10 days in error. The correction was a minor one, changing the rule about leap years. The new calendar named for him, the Gregorian calendar, became effective Oct 4, 1582, in most Catholic countries, in 1752 in Britain and the American colonies, in 1918 in Russia and in 1923 in Greece. It is the most widely used calendar in the world today. See also: "Calendar Adjustment Day: Anniversary" (Sept 2) and "Gregorian Calendar Adjustment: Anniversary" (Oct 4).

GRIMM, WILHELM CARL: BIRTH ANNIVERSARY. Feb 24, 1786. Mythologist and author, born at Hanau, Germany. Best remembered for *Grimm's Fairy Tales,* in collaboration with his brother, Jacob. Died at Berlin, Germany, Dec 16, 1859. See also: "Grimm, Jacob: Birth Anniversary" (Jan 4).

HADASSAH FOUNDED: ANNIVERSARY. Feb 24, 1912. Twelve members of the Daughters of Zion Study Circle met at New York City under the leadership of Henrietta Szold. A constitution was drafted to expand the study group into a national organization called Hadassah (Hebrew for "myrtle" and the biblical name of Queen Esther) to foster Jewish education in America and to create public health nursing and nurses' training in Palestine. Hadassah is now the largest women's volunteer organization in the US, with 1,500 chapters rooted in health care delivery, education and vocational training, children's villages and services, and land reclamation in Israel.

HOMER, WINSLOW: BIRTH ANNIVERSARY. Feb 24, 1836. American artist, born at Boston, MA. Noted for the realism of his work, from the Civil War reportage to the highly regarded rugged outdoor scenes of hunting and fishing. Died at his home at Prouts Neck, ME, Sept 29, 1910.

ICELAND: BURSTING DAY. Feb 24. Feasts with salted mutton and thick pea soup. On Shrove Tuesday.

INTERNATIONAL PANCAKE DAY. Feb 24. Liberal, KS. The 2009 International Pancake Race will be the 60th annual competition between the women of Liberal, KS, and Olney, Buckinghamshire, England. The women, wearing the traditional dress, apron and scarf, run a 415-yard S-shaped course, carrying a pancake in a skillet. Other events taking place include a breakfast, parade, talent show, eating and flipping contests and the Miss Liberal scholarship pageant. Annually on Shrove Tuesday, the day before Ash Wednesday. Est attendance: 5,000. For info: JoAnn Combs, Exec Secy, PO Box 665, Liberal, KS 67905. Phone: (620) 624-6423. Web: www.pancakeday.net.

JOHNSON IMPEACHMENT PROCEEDINGS: ANNIVERSARY. Feb 24, 1867. In a showdown over reconstruction policy following the Civil War, the House of Representatives voted to impeach President Andrew Johnson. During the two years following the end of the war, the Republican-controlled Congress had sought to severely punish the South. Congress passed the Reconstruction Act, which divided the South into five military districts headed by officers who were to take their orders from General Grant, the head of the army, instead of from President Johnson. In addition, Congress passed the Tenure of Office Act, which required Senate approval before Johnson could remove any official whose appointment was originally approved by the Senate. Johnson vetoed this act, but the veto was overridden by Congress. To test the constitutionality of the act, Johnson dismissed Secretary of War Edwin Stanton, triggering the impeachment vote. On Mar 5, 1868, the Senate convened as a court to hear the charges against the president. The Senate vote of 35–19 fell one vote short of the two-thirds majority needed for impeachment.

KREWE OF REX MARDI GRAS PARADE. Feb 24. New Orleans, LA. The Krewe of Rex parade is the main event of New Orleans's Mardi Gras festivities. The parade passes through the Garden District and downtown New Orleans. King Rex presides and is considered the King of New Orleans's Carnival. The Rex motto is "Pro bono publico." Annually, Mardi Gras day.

MARDI GRAS. Feb 24. Celebrated especially at New Orleans, LA, Mobile, AL, and certain Mississippi and Florida cities. Last feast before Lent. Although Mardi Gras (Fat Tuesday, literally) is properly limited to Shrove Tuesday, it has come to be popularly applied to the preceding two weeks of celebration.

MEXICO: FLAG DAY. Feb 24. *El Día de la Bandera.* National holiday honoring the Mexican flag, which was created in 1821 after Mexico achieved independence.

MOON PHASE: NEW MOON. Feb 24. Moon enters New Moon phase at 8:35 PM, EST.

NIMITZ, CHESTER: BIRTH ANNIVERSARY. Feb 24, 1885. Commander of all Allied naval, land and air forces in the southwest Pacific during a portion of WWII, Admiral Chester William Nimitz was born at Fredericksburg, TX. During the final assault on Japan in April 1945, Nimitz resumed command of the entire naval operation in the Pacific, which he had shared with General Douglas MacArthur for some time. Nimitz was one of the signers of the Japanese document of surrender Sept 2, 1945, aboard the USS *Missouri* in Tokyo Bay. Nimitz died Feb 20, 1966, at Treasure Island, San Francisco Bay, CA. The USS *Nimitz* was named in his honor.

SHROVE TUESDAY. Feb 24. Always the day before Ash Wednesday. Sometimes called Pancake Tuesday. This day is a legal holiday in some counties in Florida.

SPAY DAY USA. Feb 24. 15th annual. Yearly nationwide campaign to end the tragedy of pet overpopulation by encouraging every humane American to take responsibility for having at least one cat or dog spayed or neutered, be that pet his or hers, a neighbor's or a shelter animal. Veterinary clinics, humane societies/shelters, businesses and individuals are encouraged to participate. Annually, the last Tuesday of February. For info: Vicki Stevens, National Coordinator, Spay Day USA, Humane Society of the US, 2100 L St NW, Washington, DC 20037. Phone: (301) 721-6482. Fax: (301) 258-3081. E-mail: SpayDay@HumaneSociety.org. Web: www.HumaneSociety.org/SpayDay.

WAGNER, HONUS: BIRTH ANNIVERSARY. Feb 24, 1874. American baseball great, born John Peter Wagner at Carnegie, PA. Nicknamed the "Flying Dutchman," Wagner was among the first five players elected to the Baseball Hall of Fame in 1936. Died at Carnegie, Dec 6, 1955.

ZULU MARDI GRAS PARADE. Feb 24. New Orleans, LA. The Zulu Social Aid and Pleasure Club, one of New Orleans's oldest social clubs (formally established in 1916), has one of the most anticipated parades of the Mardi Gras season in the city. Annually, Mardi Gras day. For info: Zulu Social Aid and Pleasure Club, Inc, 732 N Broad St, New Orleans, LA 70119.

February 2009

S	M	T	W	T	F	S
1	2	3	4	5	6	7
8	9	10	11	12	13	14
15	16	17	18	19	20	21
22	23	24	25	26	27	28

Birthdays Today

Barry Bostwick, 64, actor (*The Rocky Horror Picture Show*, "Spin City"), born San Mateo, CA, Feb 24, 1945.

James Farentino, 71, actor ("Dynasty," "Cool Million," *The Story of a Woman*), born New York, NY, Feb 24, 1938.

Jeff Garcia, 39, football player, born Gilroy, CA, Feb 24, 1970.

Lleyton Hewitt, 28, tennis player, born Adelaide, Australia, Feb 24, 1981.

Steven Hill, 87, actor ("Law & Order"), born Seattle, WA, Feb 24, 1922.

Rupert Holmes, 62, musician, songwriter, born Tenafly, NJ, Feb 24, 1947.

Steven Jobs, 54, founder of Apple computer company, born Los Altos, CA, Feb 24, 1955.

Mark Lane, 82, lawyer, author (*Rush to Judgment, Eyewitness Chicago*), assassination buff, born New York, NY, Feb 24, 1927.

Michel Legrand, 77, composer, conductor, born Paris, France, Feb 24, 1932.

Joseph I. Lieberman, 67, US Senator (D, Connecticut), born Stamford, CT, Feb 24, 1942.

Floyd Mayweather, Jr, 32, boxer, born Las Vegas, NV, Feb 24, 1977.

Eddie Clarence Murray, 53, former baseball player, born Los Angeles, CA, Feb 24, 1956.

Edward James Olmos, 62, actor (*Stand and Deliver*, "Battlestar Galactica"; Emmy for "Miami Vice"), born East Los Angeles, CA, Feb 24, 1947.

Renata Scotto, 73, soprano, born Savona, Italy, Feb 24, 1936.

Helen Shaver, 58, actress (*Desert Hearts, The Color of Money*), born St. Thomas, ON, Canada, Feb 24, 1951.

Abe Vigoda, 88, actor ("Barney Miller," "Fish"), born New York, NY, Feb 24, 1921.

Paula Zahn, 53, TV newscaster, born Naperville, IL, Feb 24, 1956.

Billy Zane, 43, actor (*Titanic, The Phantom*), born Chicago, IL, Feb 24, 1966.

February 25 — Wednesday

DAY 56 | **309 REMAINING**

ASH WEDNESDAY. Feb 25. Marks the beginning of Lent. Forty weekdays and six Sundays (Saturday considered a weekday) remain until Easter Sunday. Named for use of ashes in ceremonial penance.

BACKUS, JIM: BIRTH ANNIVERSARY. Feb 25, 1913. Born James Gilmore Backus at Cleveland, OH. An actor whose career encompassed radio, television and film, Jim Backus is most remembered as the voice behind the nearsighted bumbler Mr Magoo and for his portrayal of Thurston Howell III on the popular TV show "Gilligan's Island." Backus died July 3, 1989, at Santa Monica, CA.

BASCOM, "TEXAS ROSE": BIRTH ANNIVERSARY. Feb 25, 1922. A Cherokee-Choctaw Indian born at Covington County, MS, Rose Flynt married rodeo cowboy Earl Bascom and learned trick roping, becoming known as the greatest female trick roper in the world. She appeared on stage, in movies and on early TV. She toured with the USO during WWII, performing at every military base and military hospital in the US. After the war she entertained servicemen stationed overseas. In 1981 she was inducted into the National Cowgirl Hall of Fame (located at Fort Worth, TX). She died Sept 23, 1993, at St. George, UT.

BURGESS, ANTHONY: BIRTH ANNIVERSARY. Feb 25, 1917. Author (*A Clockwork Orange*). Born at Manchester, England. Died Nov 25, 1993, at London.

CARUSO, ENRICO: BIRTH ANNIVERSARY. Feb 25, 1873. Operatic tenor of legendary voice and fame, born at Naples, Italy. Died there Aug 2, 1921.

CLAY BECOMES HEAVYWEIGHT CHAMP: 45th ANNIVERSARY. Feb 25, 1964. Twenty-two-year-old Cassius Clay (later Muhammad Ali) became world heavyweight boxing champion by defeating Sonny Liston. At the height of his athletic career Ali was well known for both his fighting ability and personal style. His most famous saying was "I am the greatest!" Ali is the only fighter to win the heavyweight fighting title three separate times. He defended that title nine times.

FENWICK, MILLICENT HAMMOND: BIRTH ANNIVERSARY. Feb 25, 1910. Fashion model, author, member NJ General Assembly and US congresswoman, Millicent Fenwick was born at New York, NY. A champion of liberal causes, Fenwick pointed to her sponsorship of the resolution creating the commission to monitor the 1975 Helsinki accords on human rights as her proudest achievement. She fought for civil rights, peace in Vietnam, aid for the poor, reduction of military programs, gun control and restrictions on capital punishment. Fenwick, the inspiration for Garry Trudeau's "Doonesbury" character Lacey Davenport, died at Bernardsville, NJ, Sept 16, 1992.

FIRST NATIONAL BANK CHARTERED BY CONGRESS: ANNIVERSARY. Feb 25, 1791. The First Bank of the US at Philadelphia, PA, was chartered. Proposed as a national bank by Alexander Hamilton, it lost its charter in 1811. The Second Bank of the US received a charter in 1816, which expired in 1836. Since that time, the US has had no central bank. Central banking functions are carried out by the Federal Reserve System, established in 1913. See also: "Federal Reserve System: Anniversary" (Dec 23).

FREER, CHARLES LANG: BIRTH ANNIVERSARY. Feb 25, 1856. American art collector who built and endowed the Freer Gallery, which was presented to the Smithsonian Institution in 1906. Born at Kingston, NY, he died at New York, NY, Sept 25, 1919.

HARRISON, GEORGE: BIRTH ANNIVERSARY. Feb 25, 1943. Musician and singer born at Liverpool, England, Harrison was the lead guitarist and co-songwriter for the Beatles, alongside John Lennon, Paul McCartney and Ringo Starr. The band is considered to be the most influential rock-and-roll group of all time. Harrison is credited with introducing Eastern musical styles and instrumentation to Western pop. After the breakup of the Beatles, Harrison embarked on a successful solo career, became an independent film producer (*Time Bandits*) and created one of the first charity rock concerts with his Concert for Bangladesh, which brought relief to flood victims of that country. He died at Los Angeles, CA, on Nov 29, 2001.

HEBRON MASSACRE: 15th ANNIVERSARY. Feb 25, 1994. An American-born Jewish settler in Hebron, Israel, Baruch Goldstein, opened fire with an assault rifle in a crowded mosque, part of a complex sacred to both Jews and Muslims because it is believed to contain the tomb of Abraham and his wife, Sarah. Of the more than 400 Muslims gathered for early-morning prayers during the holy month of Ramadan, 29 were killed immediately and 150 were wounded. Others, including Goldstein, were crushed in the panic to flee or during subsequent rioting.

INCONVENIENCE YOURSELF™ DAY. Feb 25. A day to think about how your actions affect others and to look for ways to inconvenience yourself while making the lives of others better/easier. Enrich your own life as you focus on ways to show respect to others, the environment and the world you live in. Annually, the fourth Wednesday in February. For info: Julie Thompson, 8255 W Sunrise Blvd, #179, Plantation, FL 33322. Phone: (954) 693-4604. Fax: (954) 370-0083. E-mail: julie@InconvenienceYourself.com. Web: www.InconvenienceYourself.com.

ITALY: PURGATORY BANQUET. Feb 25. Gradoli (near Viterbo). On Ash Wednesday, gourmands are on hand for the banquet of penitence for the souls in purgatory, held on the premises of the cooperative winery.

KUWAIT: NATIONAL DAY. Feb 25. National holiday. Commemorates the 1978 accession of King Shaykh Sir 'abdullah Al-Salim al-Sabah.

LEARNING DISABILITIES ASSOCIATION OF AMERICA INTERNATIONAL CONFERENCE. Feb 25–28. Salt Lake City, UT. 46th annual. Est attendance: 2,300. For info: Learning Disabilities Assn of America, 4156 Library Rd, Pittsburgh, PA 15234. Phone: (412) 341-1515. Fax: (412) 344-0224. E-mail: info@ldaamerica.org. Web: www.ldaamerica.org.

LENT. Feb 25–Apr 11. Most Christian churches observe a period of fasting and penitence (40 weekdays and six Sundays—Saturday considered a weekday) beginning on Ash Wednesday and ending on the Saturday before Easter. The word *Lent* comes from "lengthen," referring to the lengthening of the day that occurs in the spring.

RENOIR, PIERRE AUGUSTE: BIRTH ANNIVERSARY. Feb 25, 1841. Impressionist painter, born at Limoges, France. Renoir's paintings are known for their joy and sensuousness as well as the light techniques he employed in them. In his later years he was crippled by arthritis and would paint with the brush strapped to his hand. He died at Cagnes-sur-Mer, Provence, France, Dec 17, 1919.

SPACE MILESTONE: *SOYUZ 32* (USSR): 30th ANNIVERSARY. Feb 25, 1979. Launched from Baikonur space center in Soviet Central Asia. Cosmonauts Vladimir Lyakhov and Valery Ryumin docked at *Salyut 6* space station Feb 26. Returned to Earth in *Soyuz 34* after what was then a record 175 days in space Aug 19, 1979.

UI LIONEL HAMPTON JAZZ FESTIVAL. Feb 25–28. University of Idaho, Moscow, ID. Each year, college, high school, junior high school and elementary school vocal and instrumental jazz ensembles come from all over the US to compete in the festival and attend concerts and clinics given by the world's greatest jazz artists. Annually, Wednesday–Saturday the last full week of February. Est attendance: 40,000. For info: Dr. Lynn J. Skinner, Exec Dir, UI Lionel Hampton Jazz Fest, PO Box 444257, Moscow, ID 83844-4257. Phone: (208) 885-6765. Fax: (208) 885-6513. E-mail: jazzinfo@uidaho.edu.

"YOUR SHOW OF SHOWS" TV PREMIERE: ANNIVERSARY. Feb 25, 1950. Sid Caesar and Imogene Coca starred in the NBC 90-minute variety program along with Carl Reiner and Howard Morris. The show included monologues, improvisations, parodies, pantomimes and sketches of varying length. Some of its writers were Mel Tolkin, Lucille Kallen, Mel Brooks, Larry Gelbart, Neil Simon and Woody Allen.

Birthdays Today

Sean Astin, 38, actor (the *Lord of the Rings* trilogy, *Rudy, Courage Under Fire*), born Santa Monica, CA, Feb 25, 1971.

Diane Baker, 71, actress (*Silence of the Lambs*), born Hollywood, CA, Feb 25, 1938.

Tom Courtenay, 72, actor (*The Dresser, The Loneliness of the Long Distance Runner, Otley*), born Hull, England, Feb 25, 1937.

Ric Flair, 60, former professional wrestler, born Richard Fliehr at Memphis, TN, Feb 25, 1949.

Larry Gelbart, 81, writer, producer ("M*A*S*H"), born Chicago, IL, Feb 25, 1928.

Karen Grassle, 65, actress ("Little House on the Prairie"), born Berkeley, CA, Feb 25, 1944.

Neil Jordan, 59, director, writer (*The Crying Game, Interview with the Vampire*), born County Sligo, Ireland, Feb 25, 1950.

Tea Leoni, 43, actress (*Jurassic Park III, Deep Impact, Flirting with Disaster*), born New York, NY, Feb 25, 1966.

Sally Jessy Raphael, 66, talk-show host, born Easton, PA, Feb 25, 1943.

Bob Schieffer, 72, TV newscaster, born Austin, TX, Feb 25, 1937.

Josh Wolff, 32, soccer player, born Stone Mountain, GA, Feb 25, 1977.

February 2009

S	M	T	W	T	F	S
1	2	3	4	5	6	7
8	9	10	11	12	13	14
15	16	17	18	19	20	21
22	23	24	25	26	27	28

February 26 — Thursday

DAY 57 — **308 REMAINING**

BIG TEN MEN'S SWIMMING AND DIVING CHAMPIONSHIPS. Feb 26–28. Purdue University, West Lafayette, IN. Est attendance: 2,000. For info: Big Ten Conference, 1500 W Higgins Rd, Park Ridge, IL 60068-6300. Phone: (847) 696-1010. Fax: (847) 696-1110. Web: www.bigten.org.

CANADA: MONTREAL HUNTING, FISHING & CAMPING SHOW. Feb 26–Mar 1. Place Bonaventure, Montreal, QC. Manufacturers' representatives, distributors and retailers of the outdoors, including camping, fishing, ATVs, hunting, marine (fishing boats, canoes, kayaks, etc), tourism offices, outfitters (lodges), RVs and entertainment. Est attendance: 37,000. For info: Canadian National Sportsmen's Shows, 30 Village Centre Pl, Mississauga, ON, Canada L4Z 1V9. Phone: (905) 361-2677 or (888) 695-2677. Fax: (905) 361-2679. Web: www.sportshows.ca.

CANADA: OTTAWA BOAT AND SPORTSMEN SHOW. Feb 26–Mar 1. Civic Centre, Coliseum and Aberdeen Pavilion, Lansdowne Park, Ottawa, ON. Boating, hunting, fishing and archery information. Products displayed: powerboats, runabouts, inflatables, personal watercraft, fishing tackle, travel info, cottage products, canoes, kayaks, camping and family entertainment. Est attendance: 30,000. For info: Canadian Natl Sportsmen's Shows, 30 Village Centre Pl, Mississauga, ON, L4Z 1V9 Canada. Phone: (905) 361-2677. Fax: (905) 361-2679. Web: www.sportshows.ca.

CASH, JOHNNY: BIRTH ANNIVERSARY. Feb 26, 1932. The iconic country music star was born J.R. Cash at Kingsland, AR. His career spanned the 1950s through the year he died, and he recorded more than 1,500 songs, including such hits as "I Walk the Line," "Ring of Fire," "Folsom Prison Blues" and "A Boy Named Sue." He was called the "Man in Black" because he wore a black long-tailed suit in sympathy for those who suffered. The recipient of numerous awards and honors, Cash died at Nashville, TN, on Sept 12, 2003. Cash and Elvis Presley are the only music stars to be inducted into both the Country Music and Rock and Roll halls of fame.

CHARRO DAYS FIESTA. Feb 26–Mar 1. Brownsville, TX. Two Nations—Twin Cultures, a true example of international harmony and cooperation between Brownsville, TX, and Matamoros, Mexico. Starts the last Thursday in February. Colorful celebration of the *charro* horsemen of Mexico, men of great riding skills. Dances, parades and carnival. Est attendance: 150,000. For info: Charro Days, Inc, PO Box 3247, Brownsville, TX 78523-3247. Phone: (956) 542-4245. Fax: (956) 542-6771. Web: www.charrodaysfiesta.com.

CODY, WILLIAM FREDERIC "BUFFALO BILL": BIRTH ANNIVERSARY. Feb 26, 1846. American frontiersman born at Scott County, IA, who claimed to have killed more than 4,000 buffalo. Subject of many heroic Wild West yarns, Cody became successful as a showman, taking his acts across the US and to Europe. Died Jan 10, 1917, at Denver, CO.

***COMMUNIST MANIFESTO* PUBLISHED: ANNIVERSARY.** Feb 26, 1848. Written by Karl Marx and Friedrich Engels on the eve of the revolutions of 1848, the *Manifesto* provided ideas for socialist and communist movements.

DAUMIER, HONORE: BIRTH ANNIVERSARY. Feb 26, 1808. French painter and caricaturist famous for his satirical and comic lithographs. Once spent six months in prison for a caricature of Louis Philippe shown as Gargantua consuming the heavy taxes of the citizens. Born at Marseilles, France, he died Feb 11, 1879, at Volmondois, France.

FEDERAL COMMUNICATIONS COMMISSION CREATED: 75th ANNIVERSARY. Feb 26, 1934. President Franklin Roosevelt ordered the creation of a Communications Commission, which became the FCC. It was established by Congress June 19, 1934, to oversee communication by radio, wire or cable. TV and satellite communication later became part of its charge.

FLORIDA STRAWBERRY FESTIVAL. Feb 26–Mar 8. Plant City, FL. Celebration of winter strawberry harvest. For info: Patsy Brooks, Gen Mgr, Florida Strawberry Fest, PO Drawer 1869, Plant City, FL 33564-1869. Phone: (813) 752-9194. Fax: (813) 754-4297. Web: www.flstrawberryfestival.com.

FOR PETE'S SAKE DAY. Feb 26. A world wonders: after all these years, who is Pete and why do we do or not do things for his sake? (©2006 by WH.) For info: Thomas & Ruth Roy, Wellcat Holidays, 2418 Long Ln, Lebanon, PA 17046. Phone: (717) 279-0184. E-mail: info@wellcat.com. Web: www.wellcat.com.

GLEASON, JACKIE: BIRTH ANNIVERSARY. Feb 26, 1916. American musician, comedian and actor, Herbert John "Jackie" Gleason was born at Brooklyn, NY. Best known for his role as Ralph Kramden in the long-running television series "The Honeymooners." Died at Fort Lauderdale, FL, June 24, 1987.

GRAND CANYON NATIONAL PARK ESTABLISHED: 90th ANNIVERSARY. Feb 26, 1919. By an act of Congress, Grand Canyon National Park was established. An immense gorge cut through the high plateaus of northwest Arizona by the raging Colorado River and covering 1,218,375 acres, Grand Canyon National Park is considered one of the most spectacular natural phenomena in the world.

GRAND TETON NATIONAL PARK ESTABLISHED: 80th ANNIVERSARY. Feb 26, 1929. Grand Teton, in Wyoming, was established as a national park and preserve by Congress. On Sept 14, 1950, Congress authorized enlarging the park to include areas of Jackson Hole National Monument.

HUGO, VICTOR: BIRTH ANNIVERSARY. Feb 26, 1802. One of the most popular 19th-century authors, born at Besançon, France. His most well-known work is the novel *Les Misérables* and his most famous character is Quasimodo, the Hunchback of Notre Dame. "An invasion of armies can be resisted," Hugo wrote in 1852, "but not an idea whose time has come." He died at Paris, May 22, 1885, and more than two million people thronged to his state funeral.

NATIONAL CHILI DAY. Feb 26. A day to recognize chili as an American staple and to celebrate our love for a great bowl of red—especially in the cold winter months. Annually, the last Thursday in February. For info: Doug Welsh, Hard Times Café, 124 Harrison Circle, Locust Grove, VA 22508. Phone: (703) 608-7725. Fax: (540) 972-4313. E-mail: dougwelsh@mac.com.

RANDALL, TONY: BIRTH ANNIVERSARY. Feb 26, 1920. Born Leonard Rosenberg at Tulsa, OK, actor Tony Randall had a career that spanned five decades. He was a successful film actor, starring in 1957's *Will Success Spoil Rock Hunter?* and 1959's *Pillow Talk* and performed extensively on the stage. He launched the National Actors Theatre, a company dedicated to performing classic works of theater. He is perhaps best remembered for his role opposite Jack Klugman in television's "The Odd Couple," playing Felix Unger, the tidy, hypochondriac photographer forced by circumstance to share an apartment with slob sportswriter Oscar Madison. The wildly popular series ran from 1970 to 1975. Randall died at New York, NY, May 17, 2004.

STRAUSS, LEVI: BIRTH ANNIVERSARY. Feb 26, 1829. Bavarian immigrant Levi Strauss created the world's first pair of jeans—Levi's 501 jeans—for California's gold miners in 1850. Born at Buttenheim, Bavaria, Germany, he died in 1902, at San Francisco, CA.

VERCORS, JEAN: BIRTH ANNIVERSARY. Feb 26, 1902. Jean Vercors was the author of the first clandestine novel published during the Nazi occupation of France. Vercors, whose real name was Jean-Marcel de Bruller, was best known for his novel *Silence of the Sea*, which he published with Pierre de Lescure for their publishing house, Les Editions de Minuit, after the Nazis occupied France in 1941. Vercors was born at Paris, France, and died there June 10, 1991.

WORLD TRADE CENTER BOMBING OF 1993: ANNIVERSARY. Feb 26, 1993. A 1,210-pound bomb packed in a van exploded in the underground parking garage of the World Trade Center in New York City, killing six people and injuring more than 1,000 (mostly from smoke inhalation). The powerful blast left a crater 200 feet wide and several stories deep. The cost for damage to the building and disruption of business for the 350 companies with offices in the Center exceeded $591 million. Fifteen people—the fundamentalist Muslim cleric Sheik Omar Abdul Rahman and 14 of his followers—were indicted for the bombing. Rahman was given a life sentence, and the others received prison terms of up to 240 years each.

Birthdays Today

Erykah Badu, 37, pop singer, born Dallas, TX, Feb 26, 1972.

Fats Domino, 81, singer, songwriter ("Ain't That a Shame," "I'm in Love Again," "Blueberry Hill"), born Antoine Domino at New Orleans, LA, Feb 26, 1928.

Marshall Faulk, 36, former football player, born New Orleans, LA, Feb 26, 1973.

Jennifer Grant, 43, actress (*The Evening Star*), born Burbank, CA, Feb 26, 1966.

Tim Kaine, 51, Governor of Virginia (D), born St. Paul, MN, Feb 26, 1958.

February 27 — Friday

DAY 58 | 307 REMAINING

AFRICAN BURIAL GROUND NATIONAL MONUMENT ESTABLISHED: ANNIVERSARY. Feb 27, 2006. On this date President George W. Bush signed a proclamation declaring a seven-acre plot at the corners of Duane and Elk Streets in Lower Manhattan, New York, to be a national monument. From the 1690s to the 1790s, this land served as a cemetery for both free and enslaved Africans and is believed to be the resting place of more than 15,000 people.

ALL-NORTHWEST BARBERSHOP BALLAD CONTEST. Feb 27–28 (tentative). Forest Grove High School, Forest Grove, OR. Barbershop quartets from throughout the Pacific Northwest compete in an 1890s setting. Est attendance: 3,000. For info: Forest Grove Chamber of Commerce, 2417 Pacific Ave, Forest Grove, OR 97116. Phone: (503) 357-3006. Fax: (503) 357-2367. E-mail: info@fgchamber.org.

AMERICAN CROSSWORD PUZZLE TOURNAMENT. Feb 27–Mar 1. Brooklyn Bridge Marriott Hotel, Brooklyn, NY. Seven hundred solvers from the US and Canada compete on eight puzzles during this 32nd annual event. Points are awarded for accuracy and speed. The final puzzle is played on giant white boards for everyone to watch. Prizes are awarded in 22 skill, age and geographic categories and the grand prize is $5,000. The weekend also includes group word games, guest speakers and appearances by celebrity crossword solvers. Solvers can compete at home for fun, either online or by mail, and receive a ranking in all their solving categories. Est attendance: 1,000. For info: Will Shortz, Director, American Crossword Puzzle Tournament, 55 Great Oak Ln, Pleasantville, NY 10570. Phone: (718) 797-0264. Web: www.crosswordtournament.com.

ANDERSON, MARIAN: BIRTH ANNIVERSARY. Feb 27, 1897. Born at Philadelphia, PA (some sources say in 1899 or 1902). Anderson's talent was evident at an early age. Her career stonewalled by the prejudice she encountered in the US, she moved to Europe, where the magnificence of her voice and her versatility as a performer began to establish her as one of the world's finest contraltos. Preventing Anderson's performance at Washington's Constitution Hall in 1939 on the basis of her color, the Daughters of the American Revolution secured for her the publicity that would lay the foundation for her success in the States. Her performance was rescheduled, and on Apr 9 (Easter Sunday), 75,000 people showed up to hear her sing from the steps of the Lincoln Memorial. The performance was simultaneously broadcast by radio. In 1955 Anderson became the first African American to perform with the New York Metropolitan Opera. The following year President Dwight Eisenhower named her a delegate to the United Nations. She performed at President John F. Kennedy's inauguration and in 1963 received the Presidential Medal of Freedom. Anderson died Apr 8, 1993, at Portland, OR.

BENNETT, JOAN: BIRTH ANNIVERSARY. Feb 27, 1910. American film and television actress was born at Palisades, NJ. Her film career was mostly during the 1930s and 1940s in such films as *Father of the Bride* (1950), after which she became a star of the television cult hit "Dark Shadows" (originally broadcast 1966–71). Died Dec 7, 1990, at Scarsdale, NY.

February 2009

S	M	T	W	T	F	S
1	2	3	4	5	6	7
8	9	10	11	12	13	14
15	16	17	18	19	20	21
22	23	24	25	26	27	28

DOMINICAN REPUBLIC: INDEPENDENCE DAY. Feb 27. National Day. Independence gained in 1844 with the withdrawal of Haitians, who had controlled the area for 22 years.

ENGLAND: WORDS BY THE WATER: A CUMBRIAN LITERATURE FESTIVAL. Feb 27–Mar 8. Lake District. The Theatre by the Lake at Keswick, sitting on the banks of Derwentwater, is the perfect setting for a lively literature festival. For info: Ways with Words, Droridge Farm, Dartington, Totnes, Devon, England TQ9 6JG. Phone: (44) (1803) 867-373. E-mail: office@wayswithwords.co.uk. Web: www.wayswithwords.co.uk.

FARRELL, JAMES THOMAS: BIRTH ANNIVERSARY. Feb 27, 1904. American author, novelist and short story writer, best known for his Studs Lonigan trilogy. Born at Chicago, IL, he died at New York, NY, Aug 22, 1979.

HAMILTON, ALICE: BIRTH ANNIVERSARY. Feb 27, 1869. American pathologist Alice Hamilton was born at New York, NY. She contributed to the workmen's compensation laws by reporting on the dangers to workers of industrial toxic substances. She taught at Harvard Medical School from 1919 until 1935. Hamilton died Sept 22, 1970, at Hadlyme, CT.

KUWAIT LIBERATED AND 100-HOUR WAR ENDS: ANNIVERSARY. Feb 27, 1991. Allied troops entered Kuwait City, Kuwait, four days after launching a ground offensive. President George H.W. Bush declared Kuwait to be liberated and ceased all offensive military operations in the Gulf War. The end of military operations at midnight EST came 100 hours after the beginning of the land attack. Feb 26 is commemorated as Liberation Day in Kuwait.

LONGFELLOW, HENRY WADSWORTH: BIRTH ANNIVERSARY. Feb 27, 1807. American poet and writer, born at Portland, ME. He is best remembered for his classic narrative poems, such as *The Song of Hiawatha, Paul Revere's Ride* and *The Wreck of the Hesperus.* Died at Cambridge, MA, Mar 24, 1882.

RABI' I: THE MONTH OF THE MIGRATION. Feb 27. Begins on Islamic calendar date Rabi al-Awal 1, 1430. The third month of the Islamic calendar, the month of the migration of the Prophet Muhammad from Mecca to Medina in AD 622, the event that was used as the starting year of the Islamic lunar calendar. Different methods for "anticipating" the visibility of the new moon crescent at Mecca are used by different Muslim groups. US date may vary. Began at sunset the preceding day.

SARAZEN, GENE: BIRTH ANNIVERSARY. Feb 27, 1902. Gene Sarazen, golfer, born Eugenio Saraceni at Harrison, NY. Sarazen was one of the game's greatest players and in his later years one of its greatest goodwill ambassadors. The inventor of the sand wedge, Sarazen was also the first to win the modern grand slam (the Masters, US Open, British Open and PGA), although not in the same year. During the 1935 Masters, he hit one of golf's most famous shots, a four-wood for a double eagle on the par-5 15th hole of the final round. The shot enabled him to tie Craig Wood for the lead and defeat him in a play-off. Sarazen's last shot was the traditional ceremonial tee shot to open the 1999 Masters. Died at Marco Island, FL, May 13, 1999.

SHANGHAI COMMUNIQUÉ: ANNIVERSARY. Feb 27, 1972. On this day President Richard Nixon and Premier Chou En-lai released a joint communiqué (the Shanghai Communiqué) after Nixon's weeklong visit to the People's Republic of China. The two nations agreed to work toward normalizing relations. Stopping short of establishing diplomatic relations, this was the first step in that direction. The two nations entered full diplomatic relations on Jan 1, 1979, during the Carter administration.

TERRY, ELLEN: BIRTH ANNIVERSARY. Feb 27, 1847. Popular English actress (Alice) Ellen Terry was born at Coventry, Warwickshire. Terry was best known for her portrayal of Shakespeare's heroines, especially Portia, and as theatrical partner of English actor Henry Irving. Together she and Irving dominated both the British and American theater of their day. She died at Small Hythe, Kent, July 21, 1928.

TEXAS COWBOY POETRY GATHERING. Feb 27–Mar 1. Sul Ross State University, Alpine, TX. 23rd annual. Cowboys from Texas and neighboring states gather for poetry readings and music. Est attendance: 2,000. For info: Betty Tanksley, Texas Cowboy Poetry Gathering Committee, PO Box 395, Alpine, TX 79831. Phone: (432) 294-1576. Web: www.cowboy-poetry.org.

TWENTY-SECOND AMENDMENT TO US CONSTITUTION (TWO-TERM LIMIT): RATIFICATION ANNIVERSARY. Feb 27, 1950. After the four successive presidential terms of Franklin Roosevelt, the 22nd Amendment limited the tenure of presidential office to two terms.

Birthdays Today

Adam Baldwin, 47, actor (*My Bodyguard, Full Metal Jacket*), born Chicago, IL, Feb 27, 1962.

Michael Bolton, 56, singer, born New Haven, CT, Feb 27, 1953.

Josh Groban, 28, singer, born Los Angeles, CA, Feb 27, 1981.

Alan Guth, 62, physicist, born New Brunswick, NJ, Feb 27, 1947.

Howard Hesseman, 69, actor ("WKRP in Cincinnati," "Head of the Class"), born Salem, OR, Feb 27, 1940.

Charlayne Hunter-Gault, 67, broadcast journalist, born Due West, SC, Feb 27, 1942.

Ralph Nader, 75, consumer advocate, lawyer, former presidential candidate, born Winsted, CT, Feb 27, 1934.

Grant Show, 46, actor ("Swingtown," "Melrose Place," "Ryan's Hope"), born Detroit, MI, Feb 27, 1963.

Elizabeth Taylor, 77, actress (Oscar for *Who's Afraid of Virginia Woolf?; National Velvet, Cleopatra, Cat on a Hot Tin Roof*), AIDS activist, born London, England, Feb 27, 1932.

Joanne Woodward, 79, actress (Oscar for *The Three Faces of Eve; Mr and Mrs Bridge*), born Thomasville, GA, Feb 27, 1930.

James Ager Worthy, 48, former basketball player, born Gastonia, NC, Feb 27, 1961.

February 28 — Saturday

DAY 59 — **306 REMAINING**

BIG TEN MEN'S INDOOR TRACK AND FIELD CHAMPIONSHIPS. Feb 28–Mar 1. Penn State University, University Park, PA. Est attendance: 1,500. For info: Big Ten Conference, 1500 W Higgins Rd, Park Ridge, IL 60068-6300. Phone: (847) 696-1010. Fax: (847) 696-1110. Web: www.bigten.org.

BIG TEN WOMEN'S INDOOR TRACK AND FIELD CHAMPIONSHIPS. Feb 28–Mar 1. Indiana University, Bloomington, IN. Est attendance: 1,500. For info: Big Ten Conference, 1500 W Higgins Rd, Park Ridge, IL 60068-6300. Phone: (847) 696-1010. Fax: (847) 696-1110. Web: www.bigten.org.

BLONDIN, CHARLES: BIRTH ANNIVERSARY. Feb 28, 1824. Daring French acrobat and aerialist (whose real name was Jean François Gravelet), born at St. Omer, France. Especially remembered for his conquest of Niagara Falls on a tightrope. Died Feb 19, 1897, at London, England. See also: "Charles Blondin's Conquest of Niagara Falls: Anniversary" (June 30).

CANIFF, MILTON: BIRTH ANNIVERSARY. Feb 28, 1907. Creator of the comic strips "Terry and the Pirates®" and "Steve Canyon," Milton Caniff was born at Hillsboro, OH. His strips were noted for their fine draftsmanship and action/adventure story lines. Caniff died Apr 3, 1988, at New York City.

FLORAL DESIGN DAY. Feb 28. A day to commemorate floral designing as an art form. Annually, on Feb 28. For info: Dr. Stephen Rittner, Rittners School of Floral Design, 345 Marlborough St, Boston, MA 02115. Phone: (617) 267-3824. E-mail: stevrt@tiac.net. Web: www.floralschool.com.

HECHT, BEN: BIRTH ANNIVERSARY. Feb 28, 1894. In the course of his career Ben Hecht wrote in many genres. His newspaper column, "1,001 Afternoons in Chicago," popularized human interest sketches. His play *The Front Page*, written with Charles MacArthur, was a hit on Broadway (1928) and on film (1931). He was a successful reporter and his first novel, *Eric Dorn*, resulted partly from his time reporting from Berlin after WWI. Hecht wrote or cowrote a number of successful movie scripts, including *Notorious* and *Wuthering Heights*. Born at New York City, he died there Apr 18, 1964.

INTERNATIONAL SWORD SWALLOWERS AWARENESS DAY. Feb 28. Sword swallowers have been risking their lives for 4,000 years! Today we recognize this ancient art that is still being carried on by a few dozen surviving practitioners. Sword swallowers around the world are encouraged to do what they do best: swallow swords! Annually, Feb 28. For info: Dan Meyer, Sword Swallowers Assn Intl (SSAI), PO Box 882, Hartselle, AL 35640. Phone: (615) 969-2568. E-mail: dan@swordswallow.com. Web: www.swordswallow.org/ssad.php.

LYON, MARY: BIRTH ANNIVERSARY. Feb 28, 1797. Mary Lyon, born near Buckland, MA, became a pioneer in the field of higher education for women. She founded Mount Holyoke Seminary (forerunner of Mount Holyoke College) in South Hadley, MA, in 1837 at a time when American women were educated primarily by ministers in classes held in their homes. Mount Holyoke was one of the first permanent women's colleges. Lyon died Mar 5, 1849, at South Hadley.

"M*A*S*H": THE FINAL EPISODE: ANNIVERSARY. Feb 28, 1983. Concluding a run of 255 episodes, this 2½-hour finale was the most-watched television show at that time—77 percent of the viewing public was tuned in. The show premiered in 1972. See also: "'M*A*S*H' TV Premiere: Anniversary" (Sept 17).

MONTAIGNE, MICHEL DE: BIRTH ANNIVERSARY. Feb 28, 1533. French essayist and philosopher, born at Perigord, France. "And if you have lived a day," he wrote in Book I of his *Essays*, "you have seen everything. One day is equal to all days. There is no other light, no other night. This sun, this moon, these stars, the way they are arranged, all is the very same your ancestors enjoyed and that will entertain your grandchildren." Died at Montaigne, France, Sept 13, 1592.

NATIONAL TOOTH FAIRY DAY. Feb 28. Why shouldn't the tooth fairy have her own day? Every kid in the country knows about her and every parent is her assistant. Celebrate the hard work she does on the graveyard shift and brush, floss and read books about the tooth fairy in her honor! For info: Katie Davis, PO Box 551, Bedford Hills, NY 10507. Phone/fax: (914) 244-8777. E-mail: katiedavis@katiedavis.com. Web: www.toothfairyday.com.

NATO PLANES DOWN SERB JETS: 15th ANNIVERSARY. Feb 28, 1994. In the first military action by the North Atlantic Treaty Organization (NATO) in the two-year-old Bosnian civil war and the first combat action by NATO in its 45-year history, UN-designated American fighter planes shot down four of six Bosnian Serb jets operating in a no-fly zone.

OPEN THAT BOTTLE NIGHT. Feb 28. 10th annual. A night to finally drink that bottle of wine that you've been saving for a special occasion that never seems to come. Annually, the last Saturday in February. For info: Dorothy J. Gaiter and John Brecher, *Wall Street Journal*. E-mail: wine@wsj.com.

PALME, OLOF: ASSASSINATION ANNIVERSARY. Feb 28, 1986. The popular prime minister of Sweden was shot to death as he left a movie theater in Stockholm with his wife. A courageous and dominant figure in Swedish politics, Palme, an aristocrat turned socialist, had earned international respect. On the day of his death he had signed (with five other world leaders) an appeal to the leaders of the US and the Soviet Union to forgo nuclear testing until the next summit meeting. Born on Jan 30, 1927, Palme was the third European head of government to be assassinated since the beginning of WWII (the others: Prime Minister Armand Calinescu of Romania in 1939 and Prime Minister Luis Carrero Blanco of Spain in 1973).

SAINT OSWALD OF WORCESTER FEAST DAY. Feb 28. Bishop of Worcester, England, from 961, and archbishop of York from 972. Oswald died Feb 29, 992, but Feb 28 is generally celebrated as his feast day.

SIEGEL, "BUGSY": BIRTH ANNIVERSARY. Feb 28, 1906. The gangster Benjamin "Bugsy" Siegel was born in Brooklyn, NY. He was a contemporary of and in cahoots with Meyer Lansky and Lucky Luciano. Siegel moved to Hollywood, CA, in 1937 to lay low after committing a murder. Expanding on his petty gambling operations, Siegel began to construct a hotel and casino called The Flamingo in remote Las Vegas, NV. The hotel, opened in 1946, was initially a failure, until Lansky and Luciano poured more money into the venture. Siegel was shot and died at his girlfriend Virginia Hill's Hollywood home on June 20, 1947; no one was ever convicted of the murder.

TENNIEL, JOHN: BIRTH ANNIVERSARY. Feb 28, 1820. Illustrator and cartoonist, born at London, England. Best remembered for his illustrations for Lewis Carroll's *Alice's Adventures in Wonderland*. Died at London, Feb 25, 1914.

USS *PRINCETON* EXPLOSION: ANNIVERSARY. Feb 28, 1844. The newly built "war steamer," USS *Princeton*, cruising on the Potomac River with top government officials as its passengers, fired one of its guns (known, ironically, as the "Peacemaker") to demonstrate the latest in naval armament. The gun exploded, killing Abel P. Upshur, secretary of state; Thomas W. Gilmer, secretary of the navy; David Gardiner, of Gardiners Island, NY; and several others. Many were injured. The president of the US, John Tyler, was on board and narrowly escaped death.

Birthdays Today

Svetlana Allilueva, 83, daughter of Joseph Stalin, author (*The Faraway Music*), born Moscow, USSR, Feb 28, 1926.

Mario Gabrielle Andretti, 69, former auto racer, born Montona, Trieste, Italy, Feb 28, 1940.

Charles Durning, 86, actor (*Dog Day Afternoon*, "Evening Shade"), born Highland Falls, NY, Feb 28, 1923.

Frank Gehry, 80, architect, born Toronto, ON, Canada, Feb 28, 1929.

Jelena Janković, 24, tennis player, born Belgrade, Yugoslavia (now Serbia), Feb 28, 1985.

Ali Larter, 33, actress ("Heroes," *Final Destination*), born Cherry Hill, NJ, Feb 28, 1976.

Robert Sean Leonard, 40, actor ("House," *The Manhattan Project*, *Dead Poets Society*), born Westwood, NJ, Feb 28, 1969.

Eric Lindros, 36, hockey player, born London, ON, Canada, Feb 28, 1973.

Bernadette Peters, 65, singer, actress (*Dames at Sea*, *Annie Get Your Gun*), born Queens, NY, Feb 28, 1944.

Charles Aaron "Bubba" Smith, 64, actor, former football player, born Beaumont, TX, Feb 28, 1945.

Jamaal Tinsley, 31, basketball player, born Brooklyn, NY, Feb 28, 1978.

Tommy Tune, 70, actor, singer, dancer (Tony for *My One and Only*; *Will Rogers Follies*), director, choreographer, born Wichita Falls, TX, Feb 28, 1939.

John Turturro, 52, actor (*O Brother, Where Art Thou?*; *Quiz Show*), born Brooklyn, NY, Feb 28, 1957.

✦ March ✦

March 1 — Sunday

DAY 60 **305 REMAINING**

✦ **AMERICAN RED CROSS MONTH.** Mar 1–31. Presidential Proclamation for Red Cross Month issued each year for March since 1943. Issued as American Red Cross Month since 1987.

THE ARRIVAL OF MARTIN PINZON: ANNIVERSARY. Mar 1, 1493. Martin Alonzo Pinzon (1440–1493), Spanish shipbuilder and navigator (and co-owner of the *Niña* and the *Pinta*), accompanied Christopher Columbus on his first voyage, as commander of the *Pinta*. Storms separated the ships on their return voyage, and the *Pinta* first touched land at Bayona, Spain, where Pinzon gave Europe its first news of the discovery of the New World (before Columbus's landing at Palos). Pinzon's brother, Vicente Yanez Pinzon, was commander of the third caravel of the expedition, the *Niña*.

ARTICLES OF CONFEDERATION RATIFIED: ANNIVERSARY. Mar 1, 1781. This compact made among the original 13 states had been adopted by Congress Nov 15, 1777, and submitted to the states for ratification Nov 17, 1777. Maryland was the last state to approve, Feb 27, 1781, but Congress named Mar 1, 1781, as the day of formal ratification. The Articles of Confederation remained the supreme law of the nation until Mar 4, 1789, when the US Constitution went into effect.

"BELIEVE IT OR NOT" TV PREMIERE: 60th ANNIVERSARY. Mar 1, 1949. The series was originally a radio show based on Robert L. Ripley's comic strips describing curiosities. Both the radio program and the NBC TV show were hosted by Robert Ripley until his death in 1949. Robert St. John became Ripley's successor. ABC re-created the show in 1982 with Jack Palance as host.

BOSNIA AND HERZEGOVINA: INDEPENDENCE DAY. Mar 1. Commemorates independence in 1992.

CARAY, HARRY: 95th BIRTH ANNIVERSARY. Mar 1, 1914. Born Harry Christopher Carabina at St. Louis, MO (some sources say 1917 or 1920). Caray began his baseball broadcasting career with the St. Louis Cardinals in 1945. He then was the announcer for the Oakland A's, the Chicago White Sox and finally the Chicago Cubs. He became a legend at Wrigley Field with his seventh-inning stretch "Take Me out to the Ball Game" and his quirky phrase "Holy Cow." Caray was inducted into the Broadcasters Hall of Fame in 1989. Died at Rancho Mirage, CA, Feb 18, 1998.

CELEBRATE YOUR NAME WEEK!. Mar 1–7. Who would you be if you didn't have a name? Your name identifies you to the world. Celebrate Your Name Week is about not neglecting your name. It's about making sure your name isn't an ignored part of your personhood. Use this week to become connected to your name! See also related events each day this week. Annually, the first full week in March. For info: Jerry Hill. E-mail: celebrateyournameweek@gmail.com. Web: www.namesuniverse.com.

CRANE WATCH '09. Mar 1–Apr 10. Kearney, NE. "World's Largest Concentration of Cranes." Each spring some 500,000 sandhill cranes (80 percent of the world's population of this species) gather on the Platte River "staging area" during their northward migration. For info: Kearney Visitors Bureau, PO Box 607, Kearney, NE 68848-0607. Phone: (800) 652-9435. Web: www.visitkearney.org.

ELLISON, RALPH WALDO: 95th BIRTH ANNIVERSARY. Mar 1, 1914. American writer and educator, born at Oklahoma City, OK. Author of the acclaimed novel *Invisible Man* (1952), the story of a young black man's struggle for his own identity in the face of rejection from both whites and blacks. Quickly recognized as a classic of 20th-century literature, it won the National Book Award in 1953. While only one of his novels was published, Ellison published collections of his essays, reviews and stories in *Shadow and Act* (1964) and *Going to the Territory* (1986). He died Apr 16, 1994, at New York City.

EMPLOYEE SPIRIT MONTH. Mar 1–31. This month seeks to inspire the most vital part of any organization: the employees. Motivate your employees this month—create employee spirit. Annually, the month of March. For info and free tips, newsletter and employee morale assessment: Harriet Meyerson, The Confidence Center. Phone: (214) 373-0080. Fax: (469) 854-2957. E-mail: Harriet@ConfidenceCenter.com. Web: www.ConfidenceCenter.com.

EXPANDING GIRLS' HORIZONS IN SCIENCE AND ENGINEERING MONTH. Mar 1–31. Expanding Your Horizons Network is an international non-profit, encourages middle and high school girls to pursue careers in science, technology, engineering and mathematics. During the month of March, we promote increased awareness of girls excelling in these areas. For info: Stacey Roberts-Ohr, Expanding Your Horizons Network, 5000 MacArthur Blvd, Oakland, CA 94613. Phone: (510) 430-2222. Fax: (510) 430-2090. E-mail: msneyh@mills.edu. Web: www.expandingyourhorizons.org.

GAINES, WILLIAM M.: BIRTH ANNIVERSARY. Mar 1, 1922. The magazine *Mad*, especially popular in the 1960s and 1970s, was founded and published by William Gaines. Alfred E. Neuman, the loony, freckle-faced mascot of the publication, became a pop-culture hero. The magazine, known for its parodies of movies, comic strips and celebrities as well as its satire of politics and social mores, greatly influenced dozens of humorists. Gaines was born at the Bronx, NY. He died June 3, 1992, at New York City.

HONOR SOCIETY AWARENESS MONTH. Mar 1–31. Promote the students of honor societies and recognize superior scholarship, promote intelligent learning and living and promote equal opportunities for all people. Support the staff, faculty and advisers of honor societies and professional fraternities through the exchange of meaningful ideas, celebration of diversity, understanding and service. For info: Charlin Jones, UTSA, One UTSA Circle, San Antonio, TX 78249. Phone: (210) 458-4160. E-mail: charlin.jones@utsa.edu.

HUMORISTS ARE ARTISTS MONTH (HAAM). Mar 1–31. To recognize the important contributions made by various types of humorists to the high art of living. For info: Lone Star Publications of Humor, 8452 Fredericksburg Rd, PMB 103, San Antonio, TX 78229. E-mail: lspubs@aol.com. Web: members.aol.com/lspubs/lsindex.html.

ICELAND: BEER DAY. Mar 1. Reykjavik. This event began on Mar 1, 1989, when a 75-year-long prohibition of beer was lifted. Features celebrations in pubs and restaurants all over Reykjavik.

INTERNATIONAL EXPECT SUCCESS MONTH. Mar 1–31. Make good things happen! If you want good things to happen to you in the new year, you must "Expect success—then work like there is no other option." For ideas and information check the website below. For info: Karla Brandau, 4985 Chartley Circle, Lilburn, GA 30047. Phone: (770) 923-0883. Fax: (770) 931-2530. E-mail: karla@karlaspeaks.com. Web: www.karlaspeaks.com.

INTERNATIONAL IDEAS MONTH. Mar 1–31. Everybody has ideas! Many people need to be encouraged or motivated or need to build skills in order to communicate and get their ideas out in the open for consideration and/or action. This month is dedicated to all ideas—large, small, great, not-so-great, past, current and ideas yet to come. Without constant new ideas, progress and people stagnate. For info: Sylvia Henderson, Springboard Training, PO Box 588, Olney, MD 20830-0588. Phone: (301) 260-1538. E-mail: sylvia@springboardtraining.com. Web: www.springboardtraining.com.

INTERNATIONAL LISTENING AWARENESS MONTH. Mar 1–31. Dedicated to learning more about the impact that listening has on all human activity. To promote the study, development and teaching of effective listening in all settings. For info: Nanette Johnson-Curiskis, Intl Listening Assn, PO Box 164, Belle Plaine, MN 56011. Phone: (877) 854-7836 or (952) 594-5697. Fax: (952) 856-5100. Web: www.listen.org.

INTERNATIONAL MIRTH MONTH. Mar 1–31. The merry month of March is set aside to encourage more mirthful moments. Its focus is to show people how to use humor to deal with not-so-funny stuff. Mirth Month was founded by Allen Klein, professional speaker and past president of the Association for Applied and Therapeutic Humor (www.aath.org). Free monthly mirth e-mail memo available; request through e-mail listed. For info: Allen Klein, 1034 Page St, San Francisco, CA 94117. Phone: (415) 431-1913. Fax: (415) 431-8600. E-mail: humor@allenklein.com. Web: www.allenklein.com.

✦ **IRISH-AMERICAN HERITAGE MONTH.** Mar 1–31. Presidential Proclamation called for by House Joint Resolution 401 (PL 103–379).

JAMESTOWN AND BERMUDA: THE VIRGINIA COMPANY COMPANIES. Mar 1–Oct 15. Jamestown Settlement, Williamsburg, VA. Bermuda, settled in 1609 as the result of a shipwreck that inspired Shakespeare's *The Tempest*, is the focus of a 400th-anniversary exhibition that also explores governmental, religious and trade connections between England's second permanent colony in the New World and its first—Jamestown, VA, founded in 1607. The exhibition illuminates Bermuda's unique character: strategic location and historic stone forts, extraordinary importance of sports and recreation, and land and seascapes immortalized by internationally renowned artists, leading to Bermuda's rise in the 20th century as a premier travel destination. For info: Jamestown-Yorktown Foundation, PO Box 1607, Williamsburg, VA 23187. Phone: (757) 253-4838 or (888) 593-4682. Fax: (757) 253-5299. Web: www.historyisfun.org.

JAPAN: OMIZUTORI (WATER-DRAWING FESTIVAL). Mar 1–14. Todaiji, Nara. At midnight, a solemn rite is performed in the flickering light of pine torches. People rush for sparks from the torches, which are believed to have magic power against evil. Most spectacular on the night of Mar 12. The ceremony of drawing water is observed at 2 AM on Mar 13, to the accompaniment of ancient Japanese music.

KOKOSCHKA, OSKAR: BIRTH ANNIVERSARY. Mar 1, 1886. Born at Pochlarn, Austria. Avant-garde artist, playwright, teacher and humanitarian, his work evoked violent reaction. After viewing a 1911 exhibition of Kokoschka's work, the Archduke Franz Ferdinand is reported to have declared, "This man deserves to have every bone in his body broken." Kokoschka's work was featured in a 1937 Nazi exhibit of "Degenerate Art." Died at Montreux, Switzerland, Feb 22, 1980.

KOREA: SAMILJOL or INDEPENDENCE MOVEMENT DAY. Mar 1. Koreans observe the anniversary of the independence movement against Japanese colonial rule in 1919.

March 2009

S	M	T	W	T	F	S
1	2	3	4	5	6	7
8	9	10	11	12	13	14
15	16	17	18	19	20	21
22	23	24	25	26	27	28
29	30	31				

LAND MINE BAN: 10th ANNIVERSARY. Mar 1, 1999. A United Nations treaty banning land mines took effect on this date. More than 130 nations signed the treaty; the US, Russia, India and China did not.

LINDBERGH KIDNAPPING: ANNIVERSARY. Mar 1, 1932. Twenty-month-old Charles A. Lindbergh, Jr, the son of Charles A. and Anne Morrow Lindbergh, was kidnapped from their home at Hopewell, NJ. Even though the Lindberghs paid a $50,000 ransom, their child's body was found in a wooded area less than five miles from the family home on May 12. Bruno Richard Hauptmann was charged with the murder and kidnapping. He was executed in the electric chair Apr 3, 1936. As a result of the kidnapping and murder of the Lindbergh baby, the Crime Control Act was passed on May 18, 1934. It authorized the death penalty for kidnappers who take their victims across state lines.

LUXEMBOURG: BÜRGSONNDEG. Mar 1. Young people build a huge bonfire on a hill to celebrate the victorious sun, marking the end of winter. A tradition dating to pre-Christian times. On the Sunday after Ash Wednesday.

MILLER, GLENN: BIRTH ANNIVERSARY. Mar 1, 1904. American bandleader and composer (Alton) Glenn Miller was born at Clarinda, IA. He enjoyed great popularity preceding and during WWII. His hit recordings included "Moonlight Serenade," "String of Pearls," "Jersey Bounce" and "Sleepy Lagoon." Major Miller, leader of the US Army Air Force band, disappeared Dec 15, 1944, over the English Channel, on a flight to Paris where he was scheduled to give a show. There were many explanations of his disappearance, but 41 years later, in December 1985, crew members of an aborted RAF bombing said they believed they had seen Miller's plane go down, the victim of bombs being jettisoned by the RAF over the English Channel.

MUSIC IN OUR SCHOOLS MONTH. Mar 1–31. To increase public awareness of the importance of music education as part of a balanced curriculum. Additional information and awareness items are available. For info: MENC: The Natl Assn for Music Education, 1806 Robert Fulton Dr, Reston, VA 20191. Phone: (800) 336-3768. Web: www.menc.org.

NAMESAKE DAY. Mar 1. Today is for more than just pondering the existence of your namesakes (people with the same name as you). Consult a telephone directory and/or go online to find namesakes. Make polite, sincere, gentle contact with any namesake(s) you locate. Annually, the Sunday of Celebrate Your Name Week. For info: Jerry Hill. E-mail: celebrateyournameweek@gmail.com. Web: www.namesuniverse.com.

NATIONAL CAFFEINE AWARENESS MONTH. Mar 1–31. Reduce dependency on caffeine through education. Seminars and other events focus on coffee alternatives and on the harm caffeine causes. For info: CaffeineAwareness.org, PO Box 96775, Las Vegas, NV 89193. Phone: (815) 572-8007. E-mail: info@caffeineawareness.org. Web: www.caffeineawareness.org.

NATIONAL CHRONIC FATIGUE SYNDROME AWARENESS MONTH. Mar 1–31. To educate patients, their families, the public and the medical profession about the nature and impact of CFS, "the Thief of Vitality," and related disorders, as well as to encourage and provide research funding. Annually, the month of March. For info: Natl Chronic Fatigue Syndrome and Fibromyalgia Assn, PO Box 18426, Kansas City, MO 64133. Phone: (816) 737-1343. Fax: (816) 524-6782. E-mail: information@ncfsfa.org. Web: www.ncfsfa.org.

NATIONAL CLEAN UP YOUR IRS ACT MONTH. Mar 1–31. Special month to focus on resolving problems with IRS. Specialists offer multiple "clean-up" gifts to taxpayers in need of assistance. Sponsored by the American Society of Tax Problem Solvers, a national non-profit professional organization. For info: Lawrence Lawler, American Society of Tax Problem Solvers, 2250 Wehrle Dr, Ste 3, Williamsville, NY 14221. Phone: (716) 630-1650. Fax: (716) 630-1651. E-mail: larry@astps.org. Web: www.astps.org.

NATIONAL COLORECTAL CANCER AWARENESS MONTH. Mar 1–31. To generate widespread awareness about colorectal cancer and to encourage people to learn more about how to prevent the disease through a healthy lifestyle and regular screening. Founding partners include the Cancer Research and Prevention Foundation, the American Society for Gastrointestinal Endoscopy, the National Colorectal Cancer Roundtable and The Foundation for Digestive Health and Nutrition. For info: Cancer Research and Prevention Foundation, 1600 Duke St, Ste 500, Alexandria, VA 22314. Phone: (703) 836-4413 or (800) 227-2732. E-mail: jasmine.greenamyer@preventcancer.org. Web: www.preventcancer.org/colorectal.

✦ **NATIONAL CONSUMER PROTECTION WEEK.** Mar 1–7 (tentative).

NATIONAL CRAFT MONTH. Mar 1–31. Promoting the fun and creativity of crafts and hobbies. For info: National Craft Month, Craft & Hobby Assn, 319 E 54th St, Elmwood Park, NJ 07407. Phone: (800) 822-0494. Fax: (201) 835-1279. E-mail: info@craftandhobby.org. Web: www.craftandhobby.org or www.craftplace.org.

NATIONAL ETHICS AWARENESS MONTH. Mar 1–31. An annual event during March in which ethics organizations and businesses nationwide promote ethics awareness. Ethics is a set of values that consistently guides our behaviors. Today our personal and professional world grows at a pace more rapid than our ability to cope and process the changes, and so looking at how we make our decisions becomes crucial. For info: Patricia Clason, 2437 N Booth St, Milwaukee, WI 53212. Phone: (414) 374-5433. Fax: (414) 374-3997. E-mail: patricia@lightly.com.

NATIONAL EYE DONOR MONTH. Mar 1–31. For info: Eye Bank Assn of America, 1015 18th St NW, Ste 1010, Washington, DC 20036. Phone: (202) 775-4999. Web: www.restoresight.org.

NATIONAL FROZEN FOOD MONTH. Mar 1–31. Promotes national awareness of the convenience, quality and nutritional benefits of frozen foods. Annually, the month of March. For info: Julie Henderson, VP Communications, Natl Frozen & Refrigerated Foods Assn, 4755 Linglestown Rd, Ste 300, Harrisburg, PA 17112. Phone: (717) 657-8601. Fax: (717) 657-9862. E-mail: info@nfraweb.org. Web: www.nfraweb.org.

NATIONAL GHOSTWRITERS WEEK. Mar 1–7. Almost 50 percent of all books are written by ghostwriters. This week honors those people who do the work but don't get the credit. One way to celebrate is to do something nice for someone and don't let them know you did it. For info: Mahesh Grossman, 4398 Nicker Ct, Soquel, CA 95073. Phone: (831) 479-7555. Fax: (831) 576-4449. E-mail: GetPublished@AuthorsTeam.com. Web: www.AuthorsTeam.com.

NATIONAL KIDNEY MONTH. Mar 1–31. Kidney disease may often be silent for many years until it has reached an advanced stage. The National Kidney Foundation urges everyone to get regular checkups that include tests for blood pressure, blood sugar, urine protein and kidney function. World Kidney Day is Mar 12. For info: Ellie Schlam, National Kidney Foundation, 30 E 33rd St, New York, NY 10016. Phone: (800) 622-9010 or (212) 889-2210. Web: www.kidney.org.

NATIONAL MARCH INTO LITERACY MONTH. Mar 1–31. This month celebrates the love of reading among children and promotes awareness of literacy as a fundamental skill for success. According to the National Center for Educational Statistics 2007 Reading Report, 33 percent of all fourth graders in the US cannot read at even the basic level. Sponsored by the Toys for Tots Literacy Program, National March into Literacy Month encourages reading among children through a variety of activities and events. The Toys for Tots Literacy Program is a year-round initiative that offers our nation's most economically disadvantaged children direct access to books and educational resources that will enhance their ability to read and to communicate effectively. For info: Toys for Tots Literacy Program, 4300 Tullamore Estates, Gainesville, VA 20155. Phone: (410) 263-5312. Fax: (419) 793-1106. E-mail: mdragano@1stdegree.com. Web: www.toysfortotsliteracy.org.

NATIONAL MULTIPLE SCLEROSIS EDUCATION AND AWARENESS MONTH. Mar 1–31. This month focuses on raising awareness of and compassion for those diagnosed with multiple sclerosis. A series of national events takes place and educational materials and publications are circulated upon request from the Multiple Sclerosis Foundation. For info: Multiple Sclelosis Foundation, 6350 N Andrews Ave, Fort Lauderdale, FL 33309. Phone: (800) 225-6495. Fax: (954) 938-8708. E-mail: awareness@msfocus.org. Web: www.msfocus.org.

NATIONAL NUTRITION MONTH®. Mar 1–31. To educate consumers about the importance of good nutrition by providing the latest practical information on how simple it can be to eat healthfully. For info: American Dietetic Assn, 120 S Riverside Plaza, Ste 2000, Chicago, IL 60606-6995. Phone: (312) 899-0040. Fax: (312) 899-4739. E-mail: nnm@eatright.org. Web: www.eatright.org.

NATIONAL ON-HOLD MONTH. Mar 1–31. A month to recognize everyone who has been placed "on hold" after calling a place of business, and to honor those businesses who make this hold time more enjoyable by supplying informative messages and music for their callers waiting on hold. For info: Audiomax, 470 Sentry Pkwy East, Blue Bell, PA 19422. Phone: (800) 284-4653 or (610) 825-9100. Fax: (610) 825-0703. E-mail: ajs@audiomax.com. Web: www.audiomax.com.

NATIONAL PIG DAY. Mar 1. To accord to the pig its rightful, though generally unrecognized, place as one of man's most intelligent and useful domesticated animals. Annually, Mar 1. For further information send SASE to: Ellen Stanley, 7006 Miami Ave, Lubbock, TX 79413.

NATIONAL SLEEP AWARENESS WEEK. Mar 1–8. All Americans are urged to recognize the importance of proper sleep to their health, safety and productivity and the dangers of untreated sleep disorders. For info: Natl Sleep Foundation, 1522 K St NW, Ste 500, Washington, DC 20005. Phone: (202) 347-3471, ext 214. Web: www.sleepfoundation.org.

NATIONAL SOCIAL WORK MONTH. Mar 1–31. First commissioned by President Reagan, the National Association of Social Workers and our members spend this month celebrating the accomplishments of social workers and the services they provide to vulnerable populations. For info: Allison Nadelhaft, Natl Assn of Social Workers, 750 First St NE, Ste 700, Washington, DC 20002. Phone: (202) 336-8228. Fax: (202) 336-8307. E-mail: anadelhaft@naswdc.org. Web: www.naswdc.org.

NATIONAL UMBRELLA MONTH. Mar 1–31. In honor of one of the most versatile and underrated inventions of the human race, this month is dedicated to the purchase of, use of and conversation about umbrellas. Annually, the month of March. For info: Thomas Edward Knibb, 1450 Key Pkwy, #101, Frederick, MD 21702-3703. E-mail: tomknibb@juno.com.

NATIONAL WOMEN'S HISTORY MONTH. Mar 1–31. A time for reexamining and celebrating the wide range of women's contributions and achievements that are too often overlooked in the telling of US history. For info: Natl Women's History Project, 3440 Airway Dr, Ste F, Santa Rosa, CA 95403. Phone: (707) 636-2888. Fax: (707) 636-2909. E-mail: nwhp@aol.com. Web: www.nwhp.org.

NATIONAL WORDS MATTER WEEK. Mar 1–7. Online at www.naiwe.com and Facebook; with other celebrations at libraries and schools nationwide. This special week is sponsored by the National Association of Independent Writing Evaluators to highlight the value of words in communication. Participants are encouraged to share stories on the "event board" about Word Super-Heroes—people or organizations that work to shore up the standards of written English; funny errors they've spotted in print; or recommendations of good resources for logophiles (word lovers). NAIWE requests that all submissions be family-friendly. Annually, the first full week in March. For info: Janice Campbell, NAIWE, 13041 Hill Club Ln, Ashland, VA 23005. Phone: (804) 752-7655. Fax: (804) 752-2517. E-mail: director@naiwe.com. Web: www.naiwe.com.

NATIONAL WRITE A LETTER OF APPRECIATION WEEK. Mar 1–7. Send a letter expressing your gratitude to others, acknowledging the goodness that we find all around us. For info: Larry McManus, 1504 N Richmond Rd, McHenry, IL 60050-1410. Phone: (815) 344-4934. Fax: (815) 344-4934. E-mail: faithhealer@ameritech.net. Web: www.appreciation.org.

NEBRASKA: ADMISSION DAY: ANNIVERSARY. Mar 1. Became 37th state in 1867.

OHIO: ADMISSION DAY: ANNIVERSARY. Mar 1. Became 17th state in 1803.

OPTIMISM MONTH. Mar 1–31. To encourage people to boost their optimism. Research proves optimists achieve more health, prosperity and happiness than pessimists. Use this monthlong celebration to practice optimism and turn optimism into a delightful, permanent habit. Free tip sheets available. For info: Dr. Michael Mercer & Dr. Maryann Troiani, The Mercer Group, Inc, 25597 Drake Rd, Barrington, IL 60010. Phone: (847) 382-0690. E-mail: drmercer@mercersystems.com. Web: www.DrMercer.com.

ORLANDO FAMILY SPRING BREAK®. Mar 1–Apr 30. Orlando, FL. Each year more than 600,000 families gather to experience the Orlando Family Spring Break®, a celebration of reconnecting as a family. The destination offers more than 95 attractions ranging from the largest and most diverse collection of theme parks in the world to a multitude of smaller attractions sure to appeal to everyone in the family. For info: Orlando/Orange County CVB, 6700 Forum Dr, Ste 100, Orlando, FL 32821. Phone: (407) 363-5800. Web: www.orlandoinfo.com/springbreak.

ORTHODOX CHEESEFARE SUNDAY. Mar 1. The last day for dairy and fish before Clean Monday, which begins Great Lent in the Eastern Orthodox churches.

PARAGUAY: NATIONAL HEROES' DAY. Mar 1. National holiday. Honors those who have died for the country, especially Mariscal Francisco Solano López, who died Mar 1, 1870.

PEACE CORPS FOUNDED: ANNIVERSARY. Mar 1, 1961. Official establishment of the Peace Corps by President John F. Kennedy's signing of executive order. The Peace Corps has sent more than 170,000 volunteers to 136 countries to help people help themselves. The volunteers assist in projects such as health, education, water sanitation, agriculture, nutrition and forestry. For info: Peace Corps, 1111 20th St NW, Washington, DC 20526. Web: www.peacecorps.gov.

PHILADELPHIA FLOWER SHOW. Mar 1–8. PA Convention Center, Philadelphia, PA. The largest flower show in the US. The premier event of its kind in the world. Est attendance: 265,000. For info: Pennsylvania Horticultural Society, 100 N 20th St, 5th Fl, Philadelphia, PA 19103-1495. Phone: (215) 988-8800. Web: www.theflowershow.com.

PLAN A SOLO VACATION DAY. Mar 1. Wanderlust stirring? Tired of waiting for friends' timetables to coincide with yours? Unable to agree with your spouse on the perfect vacation? This is the day to follow the lead of 34.8 million US adults who have taken a vacation by themselves in the past three years. Indulge yourself by spending the day checking out your growing opportunities for solo travel, including tours, cruises and travel clubs that either match roommates or charge little or no supplement. For info: Marya Alexander, Solo Travel Portal, PO Box 2664, Carlsbad, CA 92018. Phone: (760) 720-1011. Fax: (760) 720-1049. E-mail: editor@solotravelportal.com. Web: www.solotravelportal.com.

March 2009	S	M	T	W	T	F	S
	1	2	3	4	5	6	7
	8	9	10	11	12	13	14
	15	16	17	18	19	20	21
	22	23	24	25	26	27	28
	29	30	31				

PLAY-THE-RECORDER MONTH. Mar 1–31. American Recorder Society members all over the continent will celebrate the organization's annual Play-the-Recorder Month by performing in public places such as libraries, bookstores, museums and shopping malls. Some will offer workshops on playing the recorder or demonstrations in schools. Founded in 1939, the ARS is the membership organization for all recorder players, including amateurs to leading professionals. Annually, the month of March. For info: American Recorder Society, 1129 Ruth Dr, St. Louis, MO 63122-1019. Phone: (800) 491-9588 or (314) 966-4082. Fax: (314) 966-4649. Web: www.americanrecorder.org.

POISON PREVENTION AWARENESS MONTH. Mar 1–31. To educate parents, grandparents, schoolchildren and PTAs about accidental poisoning and how to prevent it. PPSI is a nonprofit organization. There is a $15 charge for kit materials. Annually, the month of March. For info: Frederick Mayer, Pres, Pharmacists Planning Service, Inc, 101 Lucas Valley Rd, Ste 382, San Rafael, CA 94903. Phone: (415) 479-8628. Fax: (415) 479-8608. E-mail: ppsi@aol.com. Web: www.ppsinc.org.

PROFESSIONAL PET SITTERS WEEK. Mar 1–7. A week to show appreciation for professional pet sitters who often work 365 days a year for customers. Annually, the first full week (Sunday through Saturday) in March. For info: Pet Sitters Intl (PSI), 201 E King St, King, NC 27021. Phone: (336) 983-9222. Fax: (336) 983-5266. E-mail: info@petsit.com. Web: www.petsit.com.

RAID ON RICHMOND: ANNIVERSARY. Mar 1, 1864. Believing the Confederate capital of Richmond, VA, to be lightly fortified, President Abraham Lincoln ordered a surprise raid to capture the city and free Union prisoners. Federal troops under General Judson Kilpatrick and Colonel Ulric Dahlgren led the attack on this date, but failed when the plan was discovered by Southern forces. In the wake of their retreat, Dahlgren was killed, and two documents were discovered on his body. The incriminating documents contained plans to burn the city and kill Confederate President Jefferson Davis and his cabinet. Confederate General Robert E. Lee complained to the Union commander, George Meade, but a Federal investigation was inconclusive.

RED CROSS MONTH. Mar 1–31. To make the public aware of American Red Cross service in the community. There are nearly 900 Red Cross offices nationwide; each local office plans its own activities. For info on activities in your area, contact your local Red Cross. For info: American Red Cross. Web: www.redcross.org.

REFIRED, NOT RETIRED, DAY. Mar 1. This is a day for retirees (or those soon to be retired) to decide that this is the beginning of "Life, Part II," and to make a commitment to make this an exciting adventure. For info: Phyllis May, 1800 Atlantic Blvd, Ste A-312, Key West, FL 33040. Phone: (305) 295-7501. Fax: (305) 294-7095. E-mail: info@refiredretired.com. Web: www.refiredretired.com.

RETURN THE BORROWED BOOKS WEEK. Mar 1–7. To remind you to make room for those precious old volumes that will be returned to you by cleaning out all that worthless trash that your friends are waiting for. Annually, the first seven days of March. For info: Inter-Global Society for Prevention of Cruelty to Cartoonists, 4626 Richelieu Terrace, Los Angeles, CA 90032. Phone: (323) 222-7944.

ROZELLE, PETE: BIRTH ANNIVERSARY. Mar 1, 1926. Alvin Ray ("Pete") Rozelle, commissioner of the National Football League, born at South Gate, CA. Rozelle began his career in the public relations department of the Los Angeles Rams, became general manager and was elected commissioner in 1960. He built the NFL into a sporting power through the use of television. He helped engineer the NFL's merger with the American Football League, created the Super Bowl as America's greatest sports extravaganza, conceived the idea for Monday Night Football and persuaded NFL owners to accept revenue sharing. Died at Rancho Santa Fe, CA, Dec 6, 1996.

SAINT-GAUDENS, AUGUSTUS: BIRTH ANNIVERSARY. Mar 1, 1848. Sculptor, born at Dublin, Ireland. His works include the statue of Lincoln in Lincoln Park, Chicago, and of Admiral Farragut in Madison Square, New York. Saint-Gaudens died at Cornish, NH, Aug 3, 1907.

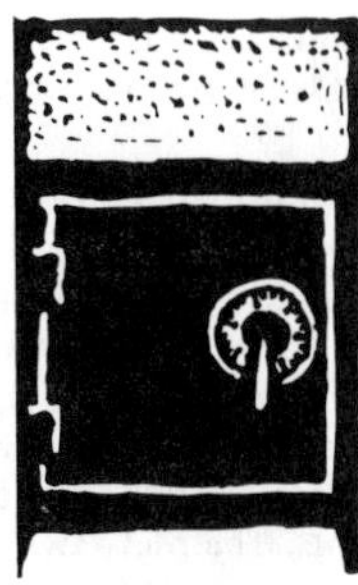

SALEM WITCH HYSTERIA BEGINS: ANNIVERSARY. Mar 1, 1692. The Massachusetts Bay Colony village of Salem had experienced a strange February in which several teenaged girls exhibited bizarre behavior and attributed their ailments to witches. Three women were then arrested on Feb 29, 1692. One of the accused, Tituba, a West Indian slave, broke down under questioning on Mar 1 and admitted to being a witch. Soon the teenaged girls accused four other residents, and by the end of April, 19 women had been accused of witchcraft and were languishing in jail—including a four-year-old child. Massachusetts governor Sir William Phips, seeking to control the growing terror, ordered trials held. In October, the special court was dissolved after growing protests of the trials' unjust proceedings. By then, 19 people had been hanged, 5 had died in jail, 1 had been tortured to death and more than 150 had been imprisoned. Two dogs were also executed. On Jan 14, 1697, Judge Samuel Sewall publicly apologized and a court-ordered day of atonement began. In 1711, all those accused of witchcraft were pardoned by the colony's legislature. See also: "Salem Witch Trials Begin: Anniversary" (June 2).

✦ **SAVE YOUR VISION WEEK.** Mar 1–7. Presidential Proclamation issued for the first week of March since 1964, except 1971 and 1982 when issued for the second week of March. (PL88–1942, of Dec 30, 1963.)

SAVE YOUR VISION MONTH. Mar 1–31. To remind Americans of the importance of eye health and regular exams. For info: American Optometric Assn, 243 N Lindbergh Blvd, St. Louis, MO 63141. Phone: (314) 991-4100. Fax: (314) 991-4101. E-mail: jmmahoney@aoa.org. Web: www.aoa.org.

SHORE, DINAH: BIRTH ANNIVERSARY. Mar 1, 1917. American radio and television personality Dinah Shore was born Frances Rose Shore at Winchester, TN. In addition to recording many hit songs in the 1930s and 1940s, she was one of the first women to be successful as a television host, beginning in the 1950s with the "Dinah Shore Chevy Show." She received 10 Emmys before she died Feb 24, 1994, at Beverly Hills, CA.

SLAYTON, DONALD "DEKE" K.: 85th BIRTH ANNIVERSARY. Mar 1, 1924. Deke Slayton, longtime chief of flight operations at the Johnson Space Center, was born at Sparta, WI. Slayton was a member of the Mercury Seven, the original group of young military aviators chosen to inaugurate America's sojourn into space. Unfortunately, a heart problem prevented him from participating in any of the Mercury flights. When in 1971 the heart condition mysteriously went away, Slayton flew on the last Apollo mission. The July 1975 flight, involving a docking with a Soviet *Soyuz* spacecraft, symbolized a momentary thaw in relations between the two nations. During his years as chief of flight operations, Slayton directed astronaut training and selected the crews for nearly all missions. He died June 13, 1993, at League City, TX.

SMALL PRESS MONTH. Mar 1–31. Small Press Month honors the quality of work being produced in independent publishing, a part of the industry that is growing at a tremendous rate. The estimated 70,000 US independent publishers create a million-plus books. These publishers are publishing unknown authors, enhancing the careers of established writers, constantly taking risks, exploring innovative ideas and, through their diverse titles, reaching new audiences. Individual expression is the driving force behind these publishers. Manhattan will feature a Small Press Book Fair during this month, and posters and materials about small presses and the month are available. Sponsored by the New York Center for Independent Publishing, CLMP (Council for Literary Magazines and Presses) and PMA. For info: Small Press Month, The New York Center for Independent Publishing, 20 W 44th St, New York, NY 10036. Phone: (212) 764-7021. Fax: (212) 840-2046. E-mail: info@smallpress.org. Web: www.smallpress.org.

SPIRITUAL WELLNESS MONTH. Mar 1–31. As spring approaches, this is a time for a new beginning, a time for spiritual renewal and inner peace. Discover a new you as you focus on telling the truth, being honest in all endeavors. Be true to yourself and build your character. Make a list of the values you cherish and work toward incorporating them in your life. Create a life of order, prayer, fasting, faith, learning and respect. For info: Angela Brown Oberer, Words of Wellness, PO Box 49266, Charlotte, NC 28277. Phone: (704) 849-2900. E-mail: Angela@WordsofWellness.com. Web: www.WordsofWellness.com.

SWITZERLAND: CHALANDRA MARZ. Mar 1. Engadine. Springtime traditional event when costumed young people, ringing bells and cracking whips, drive away the demons of winter.

TELECOMMUTER APPRECIATION WEEK. Mar 1–7. Sponsored by the American Telecommuting Association, this week is designed to call attention to the benefits of telecommuting: the individual and family as well as the employer and society benefit in a win-win situation. For info: American Telecommuting Assn, 1220 L St NW, Ste 100, Washington, DC 20005. Phone: (800) ATA-4-YOU. E-mail: YourATA@YourATA.com.

WALES: SAINT DAVID'S DAY. Mar 1. Celebrates patron saint of Wales (Dewi Sant). Welsh tradition calls for the wearing of a leek on this day.

✦ **WOMEN'S HISTORY MONTH.** Mar 1–31.

WORKPLACE EYE HEALTH AND SAFETY MONTH. Mar 1–31. Can you see the dangers at your workplace? Accidents at work are a major cause of preventable blindness. Contact Prevent Blindness America® for information on the Wise Owl® program, which promotes eye safety in the workplace. For info: Prevent Blindness America®, 211 W Wacker Dr, Ste 1700, Chicago, IL 60606. Phone: (800) 331-2020. E-mail: info@preventblindness.org. Web: www.preventblindness.org.

WORLD FOLK TALES AND FABLES WEEK. Mar 1–7. To encourage children and adults to explore the cultural background and lessons learned from folk tales, fables, myths and legends from around the world. For info: Anneke Forzani, Language Lizard, PO Box 421, Basking Ridge, NJ 07920. Phone: (888) 554-9273. Fax: (908) 613-3639. E-mail: info@LanguageLizard.com. Web: www.LanguageLizard.com.

YELLOWSTONE NATIONAL PARK ESTABLISHED: ANNIVERSARY. Mar 1, 1872. The first area in the world to be designated a national park, most of Yellowstone is in Wyoming, with small sections in Montana and Idaho. It was established by an act of Congress.

YOUTH ART MONTH. Mar 1–31. To emphasize the value and importance of art and art education in the development of all children and young people. For info: Council for Art Education, Inc, 1280 Main St, PO Box 479, Hanson, MA 02341. Phone: (781) 293-4100. Fax: (781) 294-0808. Web: acminet.org/youth_art_month.htm.

 Birthdays Today

Catherine Bach, 55, actress ("The Dukes of Hazzard"), born Warren, OH, Mar 1, 1954.

Javier Bardem, 40, actor (Oscar for *No Country for Old Men*; *Love in the Time of Cholera, Before Night Falls*), born Las Palmas de Gran Canaria, Canary Islands, Spain, Mar 1, 1969.

Harry Belafonte, 82, singer, born New York, NY, Mar 1, 1927.

Robert Conrad, 74, actor ("The Wild Wild West"), born Chicago, IL, Mar 1, 1935.

Roger Daltrey, 65, singer (The Who), born London, England, Mar 1, 1944.

Timothy Daly, 53, actor (*Diner*, "Wings"), born New York, NY, Mar 1, 1956.

George Eads, 42, actor ("CSI"), born Fort Worth, TX, Mar 1, 1967.

Ron Francis, 46, former hockey player, born Sault Ste. Marie, ON, Canada, Mar 1, 1963.

Mark-Paul Gosselaar, 35, actor ("NYPD Blue," "Saved by the Bell"), born Panorama City, CA, Mar 1, 1974.

Yolanda Griffith, 39, former basketball player, born Chicago, IL, Mar 1, 1970.

Ron Howard, 55, actor ("The Andy Griffith Show," "Happy Days"), director (Oscar for *A Beautiful Mind; The Da Vinci Code, Apollo 13*), born Duncan, OK, Mar 1, 1954.

Alan Thicke, 62, actor ("Growing Pains"), host ("Thicke of the Night"), born Kirkland Lake, ON, Canada, Mar 1, 1947.

Chris Webber, 36, basketball player, born Detroit, MI, Mar 1, 1973.

Richard (Purdy) Wilbur, 88, former poet laureate of the US, born New York, NY, Mar 1, 1921.

March 2 — Monday

DAY 61 | **304 REMAINING**

AHRMA VINTAGE MOTORCYCLE RACES. Mar 2–3. Daytona Speedway, Daytona Beach, FL. Vintage and historic motorcycles visit the Superspeedway. For info: Daytona International Speedway, PO Box 2801, Daytona Beach, FL 32120-2801. Phone: (800) PIT-SHOP. Web: www.daytonainternationalspeedway.com.

ARNAZ, DESI: BIRTH ANNIVERSARY. Mar 2, 1917. Born at Santiago, Cuba, as Desidero Alberto Arnaz y Acha III, to a wealthy family. The 1933 revolution sent them (now impoverished) to Miami, FL, and the young Arnaz sought a music career. Arnaz led his own band and introduced the conga line to America. He had several musical hits including "Babalu." He moved into acting, meeting his future wife, Lucille Ball, at RKO. Ball and Arnaz created one of the great TV comedies, "I Love Lucy" (1951–57), and started the innovative Desilu TV production company. Ball and Arnaz divorced in 1960. Arnaz died on Dec 2, 1986, at Del Mar, CA.

AUSTRALIA: EIGHT HOUR DAY or LABOR DAY. Mar 2. Western Australia and Tasmania. Parades and celebrations commemorate trade union efforts during the 19th century to limit working hours. Their slogan: "Eight hours labor, eight hours recreation, eight hours rest!" Annually, the first Monday in March.

BATTLE OF BISMARCK SEA: ANNIVERSARY. Mar 2–4, 1943. Protected by American and Australian fighters, 137 American Flying Fortress and Liberator bombers attacked a Japanese convoy en route from its base at Rabaul to New Guinea on Mar 2, 1943. In the convoy were eight transports carrying 7,000 reinforcements, which were escorted by eight destroyers. All the transports and four of the destroyers were sunk and 3,500 Japanese troops were drowned. Of the 150 Japanese aircraft involved in the fighting, 102 were shot down. The Battle of Bismarck Sea was a major victory for the Allies, ending any efforts by the Japanese to send reinforcements to New Guinea.

March 2009	S	M	T	W	T	F	S
	1	2	3	4	5	6	7
	8	9	10	11	12	13	14
	15	16	17	18	19	20	21
	22	23	24	25	26	27	28
	29	30	31				

CHASE'S DEADLINE APPROACHING. Mar 2. Time to plan ahead. Schedule 2010 celebrations and observances and submit information to *Chase's Calendar of Events 2010* by Apr 15, 2009. Sponsors/information suppliers of events in this book should have received confirmation/revision forms for the 2010 edition by this time. To submit new entries for consideration, go to www.chases.com or use a copy of the form on the last page of this book. Send to: Editor, Chase's Calendar of Events, The McGraw-Hill Companies, 130 E Randolph St, Ste 900, Chicago, IL 60601.

CORAY, MELISSA BURTON: BIRTH ANNIVERSARY. Mar 2, 1828. Coray was born at Mersey, ON, Canada. At the age of 18 she accompanied her Mormon Battalion soldier husband, William Coray, on a 2,000-mile military march on foot from Council Bluffs, IA, to San Diego, CA, then 1,500 more miles across the Sierra Nevada Mountains and the Nevada desert to Salt Lake City, UT, the only woman to make the entire trip. On July 30, 1994, a mountain peak near Carson Pass was named for her, the second peak in California to be named for a woman.

ETHIOPIA: ADWA DAY. Mar 2. Ethiopian forces under Menelik II inflicted a crushing defeat on the invading Italians at Adwa in 1896.

FUN FACTS ABOUT NAMES DAY. Mar 2. Celebrate names today by finding (at a library or online) fun facts about names. Does the doll we call "Barbie" have a last name? Does the dog game piece from Monopoly have a name? What was the name of the White House before it was renamed the White House? Annually, the Monday of Celebrate Your Name Week. For info: Jerry Hill. E-mail: celebrateyournameweek@gmail.com. Web: www.namesuniverse.com.

GEISEL, THEODOR "DR. SEUSS": BIRTH ANNIVERSARY. Mar 2, 1904. Theodor Seuss Geisel, the creator of *The Cat in the Hat* and *How the Grinch Stole Christmas*, was born at Springfield, MA. Known to children and parents as Dr. Seuss, his books have sold more than 200 million copies and have been translated into 20 languages. His career began with *And to Think That I Saw It on Mulberry Street*, which was turned down by 27 publishing houses before being published by Vanguard Press. His books included many messages, from environmental consciousness in *The Lorax* to the dangers of pacifism in *Horton Hatches the Egg* and *Yertle the Turtle*'s thinly veiled references to Hitler as the title character. He was awarded a Pulitzer Prize in 1984 "for his contribution over nearly half a century to the education and enjoyment of America's children and their parents." He died Sept 24, 1991, at La Jolla, CA.

GUAM: DISCOVERY DAY or MAGELLAN DAY. Mar 2. Commemorates discovery of Guam in 1521 by Magellan. Annually, the first Monday in March.

HIGHWAY NUMBERS INTRODUCED: ANNIVERSARY. Mar 2, 1925. A joint board of state and federal highway officials created the first system of interstate highway numbering in the US. Standardized road signs identifying the routes were also introduced. Later the system would be improved with the use of odd and even numbers that distinguish between north-south and east-west routes, respectively.

HOUSTON, SAM: BIRTH ANNIVERSARY. Mar 2, 1793. American soldier and politician, born at Rockbridge County, VA, is remembered for his role in Texas history. Houston was a congressman (1823–27) and governor (1827–29) of Tennessee. He resigned his office as governor in 1829 and rejoined the Cherokee Indians (with whom he had lived for several years as a teenage runaway), who accepted him as a member of their tribe. Houston went to Texas in 1832 and became commander of the Texan army in the War for Texan Independence, which was secured when Houston routed the much larger Mexican forces led by Santa Anna, Apr 21, 1836, at the Battle of San Jacinto. After Texas's admission to the Union, Houston served as US senator and later as governor of the state. He was deposed in 1861 when he refused to swear allegiance to the Confederacy. Houston, the only person to have been elected governor of two different states, failed to serve his full term of office in either. The city of Houston, TX, was named for him. He died July 26, 1863, at Huntsville, TX.

KING KONG FILM PREMIERE: ANNIVERSARY. Mar 2, 1933. One of the greatest adventure movies of all time premiered on this date at New York City's Radio City Music Hall and the RKO Roxy. It was to be an immediate hit—the biggest film blockbuster up to that time. Directed by Merion Cooper and Ernest Schoedsack, *King Kong* was a variation of "Beauty and the Beast," with the Beast being the 50-foot ape (actually, an 18-inch model) and Beauty portrayed by actress Fay Wray, who became known as the "Queen of Scream" after this film. Kong climbing the newly completed Empire State Building clutching Wray as biplanes attack him is one of the iconic images of cinema. Technician Willis O'Brien used state-of-the-art stop-motion photography for the film's special effects.

MOUNT RAINIER NATIONAL PARK ESTABLISHED: ANNIVERSARY. Mar 2, 1899. Located in the Cascade Mountains of Washington State, this is the fourth oldest national park.

MULTIPLE SCLEROSIS AWARENESS WEEK. Mar 2–8. For info: National MS Society, 733 Third Ave, New York, NY 10017. Phone: (212) 476-0420. Fax: (212) 989-7981. E-mail: msawarenessweek@nmss.org. Web: www.nationalmssociety.org.

NATIONAL CHEERLEADING WEEK. Mar 2–8. Various cheer activites conducted on a daily basis throughout the week. Annually, the first full week in March. For info: Linda Lundy, 59 County Rd 3474, Cleveland, TX 77327. Phone: (877) 68-CHEER or (281) 399-8357. E-mail: linda@ncwinfo.com. Web: www.ncwinfo.com.

NATIONAL PROCRASTINATION WEEK. Mar 2–8. To promote the benefits of relaxing through putting off until tomorrow everything that needn't be done today. For info: Les Waas, Pres, Procrastinators' Club of America Inc, PO Box 712, Bryn Athyn, PA 19009. Phone: (215) 947-9020. Fax: (215) 947-7210. E-mail: procrastinators_club_of_america@yahoo.com. Web: www.geocities.com/procrastinators_club_of_america.

NATIONAL SCHOOL BREAKFAST WEEK. Mar 2–6. To focus on the importance of a nutritious breakfast served in the schools, giving children a good start to their day. Annually, the first full week in March. For info: School Nutrition Assn, 700 S Washington St, Ste 300, Alexandria, VA 22314. Phone: (703) 739-3900. Fax: (703) 739-3915. E-mail: servicecenter@schoolnutrition.org. Web: www.schoolnutrition.org.

NEA'S READ ACROSS AMERICA DAY. Mar 2. A national reading campaign that advocates that all children read a book on this day. Celebrated on or near Dr. Seuss's birthday (Mar 2). For info: Natl Education Assn, 1201 16th St NW, Washington, DC 20036. Phone: (202) 833-4000. E-mail: readacross@nea.org. Web: www.nea.org/readacross.

NEWSPAPER IN EDUCATION WEEK. Mar 2–6. A weeklong celebration of using newspapers in the classroom as living textbooks. Annually, the first full week in March (weekdays). For info: Newspaper Assn of America, 1921 Gallows Rd, Ste 600, Vienna, VA 22182-3900. Phone: (703) 902-1698. E-mail: james.abbott@naa.org. Web: www.naafoundation.org.

ORTHODOX GREEN MONDAY. Mar 2. Green, or Clean, Monday is the first Monday of Lent on the Orthodox Christian calendar. Lunch in the fields, with bread, olives and uncooked vegetables and no meat or dairy products.

ORTHODOX LENT. Mar 2–Apr 18. Great Lent or Easter Lent, observed by Eastern Orthodox churches, lasts until Holy Saturday (Apr 18). The first day is known as Clean Monday which begins the Great Fast when Orthodox Christians abstain from eating meat, dairy and fish.

OTT, MELVIN (MEL): 100th BIRTH ANNIVERSARY. Mar 2, 1909. Baseball Hall of Fame outfielder, born at Gretna, LA. Playing for the New York Giants, Ott hit 511 home runs, a National League record until Willie Mays surpassed it in 1966. Inducted into the Hall of Fame in 1951. Died at New Orleans, LA, Nov 21, 1958.

POPE PIUS XII: BIRTH ANNIVERSARY. Mar 2, 1876. Eugenio Maria Giovanni Pacelli, 260th pope of the Roman Catholic Church, born at Rome, Italy. Elected pope Mar 2, 1939. Died at Castel Gandolfo, near Rome, Oct 9, 1958.

RITT, MARTIN: 95th BIRTH ANNIVERSARY. Mar 2, 1914. American film and television director Martin Ritt was born at New York, NY. His best-known films are *Hud* (1963), *Sounder* (1972) and *Norma Rae* (1979). During the 1950s he was blacklisted by McCarthy's anti-Communist crusade. Died Dec 8, 1990, at Santa Monica, CA.

SCHURZ, CARL: BIRTH ANNIVERSARY. Mar 2, 1829. American journalist, political reformer and army officer in Civil War. Born near Cologne, Germany, he died at New York, NY, May 14, 1906.

THE SOUND OF MUSIC FILM PREMIERE: ANNIVERSARY. Mar 2, 1965. The perennially popular family film musical, starring Julie Andrews as Maria Von Trapp, premiered on this date at New York City. Nominated for ten Academy Awards, the film won five Oscars, including awards for Best Picture and Best Director (Robert Wise).

SPACE MILESTONE: _PIONEER 10_ (US). Mar 2, 1972. This unmanned probe began a journey on which it passed and photographed Jupiter and its moons, 620 million miles from Earth, in December 1973. It crossed the orbit of Pluto, and then in 1983 become the first known Earth object to leave our solar system. On Sept 22, 1987, *Pioneer 10* reached another space milestone at 4:19 PM, when it reached a distance 50 times farther from the sun than the sun is from Earth.

SPACE MILESTONE: _SOYUZ 28_ (USSR). Mar 2, 1978. Cosmonauts Alexi Gubarev and Vladimir Remek linked with *Salyut 6* space station Mar 3, visiting crew of *Soyuz 26*. Returned to Earth Mar 10. Remek, from Czechoslovakia, was the first person in space from a country other than the US or USSR.

TEXAS INDEPENDENCE DAY. Mar 2, 1836. Texas adopted Declaration of Independence from Mexico.

Birthdays Today

Jon Bon Jovi, 47, singer, songwriter, actor, born John Bongiovi at Sayreville, NJ, Mar 2, 1962.

Reggie Bush, 24, football player, born Spring Valley, CA, Mar 2, 1985.

Daniel Craig, 41, actor (*Casino Royale, The Golden Compass, Munich*), born Chester, England, Mar 2, 1968.

John Cullum, 79, stage and screen actor (*Shenandoah, On the Twentieth Century*; "Northern Exposure"), born Knoxville, TN, Mar 2, 1930.

Russell D. Feingold, 56, US Senator (D, Wisconsin), born Janesville, WI, Mar 2, 1953.

Mikhail Sergeyvich Gorbachev, 78, former Soviet political leader, born Privolnoye, Stavropol, Russia, Mar 2, 1931.

John Irving, 67, author (*Cider House Rules, The World According to Garp*), born Exeter, NH, Mar 2, 1942.

Jennifer Jones, 90, actress (Oscar for *The Song of Bernadette*), born Phyllis Isley at Tulsa, OK, Mar 2, 1919.

Chris Martin, 32, singer, songwriter (Coldplay), born Exeter, Devon, England, Mar 2, 1977.

Eddie Money, 60, musician, born Brooklyn, NY, Mar 2, 1949.

Laraine Newman, 57, comedienne ("Saturday Night Live"), born Los Angeles, CA, Mar 2, 1952.

Ken Salazar, 54, US Senator (D, Colorado), born San Luis Valley, CO, Mar 2, 1955.

Doc Watson, 86, singer, musician (*Riding the Midnight Train, Then and Now*), born Deep Gap, NC, Mar 2, 1923.

Tom Wolfe, 78, author, journalist (*The Bonfire of the Vanities, The Right Stuff*), born Richmond, VA, Mar 2, 1931.

March 3 — Tuesday

DAY 62 303 REMAINING

BELL, ALEXANDER GRAHAM: BIRTH ANNIVERSARY. Mar 3, 1847. Inventor of the telephone, born at Edinburgh, Scotland, Bell acquired his interest in the transmission of sound from his father, Melville Bell, a teacher of the deaf. Bell's use of visual devices to teach articulation to the deaf contributed to the theory from which he derived the principle of the vibrating membrane used in the telephone. On Mar 10, 1876, Bell spoke the first electrically transmitted sentence to his assistant in the next room: "Mr Watson, come here, I want you." Bell's other accomplishments include a refinement of Edison's phonograph, the first successful phonograph record and the audiometer, and he continued exploring the nature and causes of deafness. He died near Baddeck, NS, Canada, Aug 2, 1922.

BETHUNE, NORMAN: BIRTH ANNIVERSARY. Mar 3, 1890. Canadian physician who worked in the front lines during WWI, the Spanish Civil War and the Chinese Revolution. Bethune was born at Gravenhurst, ON; he died at age 49 at China while treating a soldier of Mao's Eighth Route Army, Nov 11, 1939. He is said to be the only Western man recognized as a hero of the Chinese Revolution.

BONZA BOTTLER DAY™. Mar 3. To celebrate when the number of the day is the same as the number of the month. Bonza Bottler Day™ is an excuse to have a party at least once a month. For more information see Jan 1. For info: Gail M. Berger, 14 Fernwood Dr, Taylors, SC 29687. E-mail: bonza@bonzabottlerday.com. Web: www.bonzabottlerday.com.

BULGARIA: LIBERATION DAY. Mar 3. Grateful tribute to the Russian, Romanian and Finnish soldiers and Bulgarian volunteers who, in the Russo-Turkish War, 1877–78, liberated Bulgaria from five centuries of Ottoman rule.

FLORIDA: ADMISSION DAY: ANNIVERSARY. Mar 3. Became 27th state in 1845.

HOUSTON LIVESTOCK SHOW AND RODEO™. Mar 3–22. Reliant Park, Houston, TX. 77th annual. First held in 1932. Livestock show with more than 30,000 entries. Rodeo action and top-name musical entertainment. Est attendance: 1,800,000. For info: Houston Livestock Show and Rodeo, Box 20070, Houston, TX 77225-0070. Phone: (832) 667-1000. Fax: (832) 667-1134. Web: www.rodeohouston.com.

I WANT YOU TO BE HAPPY DAY. Mar 3. A day dedicated to reminding people to be thoughtful of others by showing love and concern, even if things are not going well for them. For info: Harriette W. Grimes, Grandmother, PO Box 545, Winter Garden, FL 34777-0545. Fax: (407) 656-2790. E-mail: LAGRIMES@embarqmail.net.

JAPAN: HINAMATSURI (DOLL FESTIVAL). Mar 3. This special festival for girls is observed throughout Japan. Annually, Mar 3.

March 2009	S	M	T	W	T	F	S
	1	2	3	4	5	6	7
	8	9	10	11	12	13	14
	15	16	17	18	19	20	21
	22	23	24	25	26	27	28
	29	30	31				

MALAWI: MARTYR'S DAY. Mar 3. Public holiday in Malawi.

MISSOURI COMPROMISE: ANNIVERSARY. Mar 3, 1820. In February of 1819 a bill was introduced into Congress that would admit Missouri to the Union as a state that prohibited slavery. At the time there were 11 free states and 10 slave states. Southern congressmen feared this would upset the balance of power between North and South. As a compromise, on this date Missouri was admitted as a slave state but slavery was forever prohibited in the northern part of the Louisiana Purchase. In 1854 this act was repealed when Kansas and Nebraska were allowed to decide on slave or free status by popular vote.

"MR WIZARD" TV PREMIERE: ANNIVERSARY. Mar 3, 1951. Don Herbert as Mr Wizard explained the mysteries of science while performing experiments in front of wide-eyed children. The series ran on NBC for 14 continuous years. In 1983 Herbert returned to host "Mr Wizard's World" on Nickelodeon.

"MOONLIGHTING" TV PREMIERE: ANNIVERSARY. Mar 3, 1985. Cybill Shepherd and Bruce Willis starred in this ABC comedy-adventure hour about the Blue Moon Detective Agency owned by former model Maddie Hayes (Shepherd) who is partnered with wisecracking detective David Addison (Willis). The two find themselves in a series of madcap adventures. The show featured narrative innovations: having characters directly address the camera, shooting sequences in black and white or by going completely off-concept (as in an episode based on Shakespeare's *The Taming of the Shrew*). Last telecast on May 14, 1989.

NATIONAL ANTHEM DAY: ANNIVERSARY. Mar 3, 1931. The bill designating "The Star-Spangled Banner" as our national anthem was adopted by the US Senate and went to President Herbert Hoover for signature. The president signed it the same day.

NORTH DAKOTA WINTER SHOW. Mar 3–8. Valley City, ND. Six-day agricultural expo featuring world's largest crop show, eight-breed cattle show, three-performance PRCA Rodeos, horse pulls, pickup pull, old-time tractor pull (tractors built prior to 1955), crafts and antique shows, farm toy show and single performance headliner country concert. Annually, the first week in March. Est attendance: 50,000. For info: ND Winter Show, PO Box 846, Valley City, ND 58072. Phone: (701) 845-1401 or (800) 437-0218. Fax: (701) 845-3914. E-mail: ndws@northdakotawintershow.com. Web: www.northdakotawintershow.com.

PEACE CORPS DAY. Mar 3. Commemorates the founding of the Peace Corps on Mar 1, 1961, by President John F. Kennedy. Observed on the first Tuesday in March.

PULLMAN, GEORGE: BIRTH ANNIVERSARY. Mar 3, 1831. Born at Brocton, NY, George Mortimer Pullman was an inventor and industrialist who became famous for his design and production of the "Pullman" railroad sleeping car. His first attempt at improving railroad sleeping accommodations began in 1858, while working as a contractor for the Chicago & Alton Railroad at Chicago, IL. His initial model was not adopted, but in 1863 a new design was enthusiastically received. He secured a patent for the folding upper berth design in 1864 and one for the lower berth design in 1865. By 1867 Pullman and his partner organized the Pullman Palace Car Company, which became the greatest railroad car-building organization in the world. In 1881 the town of Pullman, IL, south of Chicago, was formed by Pullman to house his employees. Because rents were not lowered when wages were cut, a strike was initiated against Pullman's company in May 1894. Pullman was eventually forced to give up control of all property in the town not directly required for manufacturing. Pullman died Oct 19, 1897, at Chicago, IL.

RIDGWAY, MATTHEW BUNKER: BIRTH ANNIVERSARY. Mar 3, 1895. American Army officer Matthew Bunker Ridgway was born at Fort Monroe, VA. As major general commanding the newly formed 82nd Airborne Division, he led it in the invasion of Sicily in July 1943 and the invasion of the Italian mainland in 1944. Ridgway replaced MacArthur as commander of the US Eighth Army in Korea in 1951 and succeeded Eisenhower as Supreme Allied Commander of the North Atlantic Treaty Organization in 1952. He became US Army Chief of Staff in 1953. Ridgway died at Fox Chapel, PA, July 26, 1993.

TIME **MAGAZINE FIRST PUBLISHED: ANNIVERSARY.** Mar 3, 1923. The first issue of *Time* bore this date. The magazine was founded by Henry Luce and Briton Hadden.

TOWN MEETING DAY. Mar 3. Vermont. The first Tuesday in March is an official state holiday in Vermont. Nearly every town elects officers, approves budget items and deals with a multitude of other items in a daylong public meeting of the voters.

UNIQUE NAMES DAY. Mar 3. This is a day for all people to appreciate friends, acquaintances and loved ones who have unique names. This is an opportunity for those of us who can buy mass-produced name items to celebrate the beauty of unique names. Annually, the Tuesday of Celebrate Your Name Week. For info: Jerry Hill. E-mail: celebrateyournameweek@gmail.com. Web: www.namesuniverse.com.

WHAT IF CATS AND DOGS HAD OPPOSABLE THUMBS DAY. Mar 3. We are grateful today that the infinite wisdom of the universe has not allowed cats and dogs to have thumbs. Imagine the cat, able to operate the can opener! Imagine the dog, able to open the refrigerator door! (©2006 by WH.) For info: Thomas & Ruth Roy, Wellcat Holidays, 2418 Long Ln, Lebanon, PA 17046. Phone: (717) 279-0184. E-mail: info@wellcat.com. Web: www.wellcat.com.

WOMAN SUFFRAGE PARADE ATTACKED: ANNIVERSARY. Mar 3, 1913. A parade held by the National American Woman Suffrage Association at Washington, DC, on the day before Woodrow Wilson's inauguration turned into a near riot when people in the crowd began jeering and shoving the marchers. The 5,000 women and their supporters were spit upon, struck in the face and pelted with burning cigar stubs while police looked on and made no effort to intervene. Secretary of War Henry Stimson was forced to send soldiers from Fort Myer to restore order.

Birthdays Today

Jessica Biel, 27, actress (*The Illusionist,* "7th Heaven"), born Ely, MN, Mar 3, 1982.

Julie Bowen, 39, actress (*Joe Somebody*, "Ed"), born Baltimore, MD, Mar 3, 1970.

David Faustino, 35, actor ("Married . . . With Children"), born Los Angeles, CA, Mar 3, 1974.

Ira Glass, 50, radio host ("This American Life"), born Baltimore, MD, Mar 3, 1959.

Jacqueline (Jackie) Joyner-Kersee, 47, Olympic gold medal heptathlete, born East St. Louis, IL, Mar 3, 1962.

Tim Kazurinsky, 59, actor, comedian, writer ("Saturday Night Live"), born Johnstown, PA, Mar 3, 1950.

Brian Leetch, 41, former hockey player, born Corpus Christi, TX, Mar 3, 1968.

Lee Radziwill, 76, sister of the late Jacqueline Kennedy Onassis, born Caroline Lee Bouvier at New York, NY, Mar 3, 1933.

Miranda Richardson, 51, actress (*The Crying Game, Enchanted April*), born Lancashire, England, Mar 3, 1958.

Herschel Walker, 47, former football player, born Wrightsville, GA, Mar 3, 1962.

March 4 — Wednesday

DAY 63 **302 REMAINING**

ADAMS, JOHN QUINCY: RETURN TO CONGRESS: ANNIVERSARY. Mar 4, 1830. On this day, John Quincy Adams returned to the House of Representatives to represent the district of Plymouth, MA. He was the first former president to do so and served for eight consecutive terms.

AMA GRAND NATIONAL SINGLES CHAMPIONSHIP DIRT TRACK RACE. Mar 4–5. Daytona Beach Municipal Stadium, Daytona Beach, FL. Dirt track series race. For info: Daytona International Speedway, Box 2801, Daytona Beach, FL 32120-2801. Phone: (800) PIT-SHOP. Web: www.daytonainternationalspeedway.com.

BENJAMIN HARRISON DAY. Mar 4. Indiana State Capitol Building, Indianapolis, IN. Presentation of Harrison Day awards, and a reenactment of a Harrison court case in the Supreme Court. For info: President Benjamin Harrison Home, 1230 N Delaware St, Indianapolis, IN 46202. Phone: (317) 631-1888. Fax: (317) 632-5488. E-mail: harrison@presidentbenjaminharrison.org. Web: www.pbhh.org.

CITY OF CHICAGO INCORPORATED: ANNIVERSARY. Mar 4, 1837. The Illinois state legislature enacted into law a city charter for Chicago on this date. William B. Ogden became the first mayor of this city of 4,170 people. Chicago had been incorporated as a town on Aug 12, 1833. The name "Chicago" was formed from a Native American word, but its meaning is disputed. It probably means "strong" or "great."

CLEVELAND'S SECOND PRESIDENTIAL INAUGURATION: ANNIVERSARY. Mar 4, 1893. Grover Cleveland was inaugurated for a second but nonconsecutive term as president. In 1885 he had become the 22nd president of the US and in 1893 the 24th. Originally a source of some controversy, the Congressional Directory for some time listed him only as the 22nd president. The Directory now lists him as both the 22nd and 24th presidents though some historians continue to argue that one person cannot be both. Benjamin Harrison served during the intervening term, defeating Cleveland in electoral votes, though not in the popular vote.

CONGRESS: ANNIVERSARY OF FIRST MEETING UNDER CONSTITUTION. Mar 4, 1789. The first Congress met at New York, NY. A quorum was obtained in the House Apr 1 and in the Senate Apr 5, and the first Congress was formally organized Apr 6. Electoral votes were counted, and George Washington was declared president (69 votes) and John Adams vice president (34 votes).

COURAGEOUS FOLLOWER DAY. Mar 4. We are a country built on the myth of "rugged individualism," in love with the concept of leadership. But all leaders require followers and, in fact, virtually all of us are followers at some times and leaders at others. This day honors the too-often disparaged role of follower. Its purpose is to dispell the myth that followers are passive and to raise awareness that good followership is energetic and at times courageous. In fact, only through active and courageous followership can leaders be counted on to use their power wisely and well. For info: Ira Chaleff, Exec Coaching & Consulting Assoc. Phone: (301) 933-3752. E-mail: ira.chaleff@exe-coach.com. Web: www.exe-coach.com.

"THE DICK CAVETT SHOW" TV PREMIERE: ANNIVERSARY. Mar 4, 1968. Dick Cavett began his television career on ABC with a daytime talk show that subsequently became a late-night program competing with Johnny Carson. Cavett, with his Yale background, had a reputation as an "intellectual" host and was particularly adept at the one-man interview. He has since appeared on the CBS, PBS and USA networks hosting a variety of shows.

DING LING: DEATH ANNIVERSARY. Mar 4, 1986. Writer and champion of women's rights, born at Hunan Province, China, in 1904. Ding was a prolific author, having written nearly 300 novels as well as plays, short stories and essays. She received the 1951 Stalin Prize for Literature for her novel *The Sun Shines Over the Sanggan River* (1949). She fell from favor in the 1950s, was exiled and in 1970 was imprisoned. After the death of Chairman Mao she was freed and during her last years she enjoyed renewed attention and favor. Died at age 82 at Beijing, China.

HOT SPRINGS NATIONAL PARK ESTABLISHED: ANNIVERSARY. Mar 4, 1921. To protect the hot springs of Arkansas the government set aside Hot Springs Reservation on Apr 20, 1832. In 1921 the area became a national park.

INTERNATIONAL SCRAPBOOKING INDUSTRY DAY. Mar 4. On this day, we celebrate the growth of the scrapbooking industry and the dedicated entrepreneurs who have worked so hard to make it happen. We seek to increase awareness of the scrapbooking industry and to reflect on the ways we can advance this industry to share the gift of scrapbooking with everyone. For info: Sue DiFranco, Fun Facts Publishing, 30 Fox Hill Ln, Enfield, CT 06082. Phone: (212) 604-4562. E-mail: info@funfactspublishing.com. Web: www.funfactspublishing.com.

LEARN WHAT YOUR NAME MEANS DAY. Mar 4. Celebrate your name today by looking up (online or at a library) its meaning. Annually, the Wednesday of Celebrate Your Name Week. For info: Jerry Hill. E-mail: celebrateyournameweek@gmail.com. Web: www.namesuniverse.com.

MARCH FORTH—DO SOMETHING DAY. Mar 4. Stop procrastinating and march forth toward your goals. Just do something, anything, that will move you forward in life. For info: Allison Carter, 180 Worthington Dr, Marietta, GA 30068. Phone: (770) 579-9866. Fax: (770) 579-0314. E-mail: organizer@TheProfessionalOrganizer.com. Web: www.TheProfessionalOrganizer.com.

MOON PHASE: FIRST QUARTER. Mar 4. Moon enters First Quarter phase at 2:46 AM, EST.

NAIA MEN'S AND WOMEN'S SWIMMING AND DIVING NATIONAL CHAMPIONSHIPS. Mar 4–7. Lindenwood University, St. Louis, MO. Individuals compete for the national championship. 29th annual for women; 53rd annual for men. For info: Natl Assn of Intercollegiate Athletics, 1200 Grand Blvd, Kansas City, MO 64106. E-mail: dgreen@naia.org. Web: www.naia.org.

NATIONAL GRAMMAR DAY. Mar 4. On National Grammar Day, we honor our language and its rules, which help us communicate clearly with each other. In turn, clear communication helps us understand each other—a critical component of peaceful relations. The day is sponsored by The Society for the Promotion of Good Grammar, a rapidly growing worldwide organization with more than 6,000 members. Annually, Mar 4th—both a date and an imperative. For info: Martha Brockenbrough, Society for the Promotion of Good Grammar, 1609 37th Ave, Seattle, WA 98122. Phone: (206) 328-7374. E-mail: info@nationalgrammarday.com. Web: www.nationalgrammarday.com.

OLD INAUGURATION DAY. Mar 4. Anniversary of the date set for beginning the US presidential term of office, 1789–1933. Although the Continental Congress had set the first Wednesday of March 1789 as the date for the new government to convene, a quorum was not present to count the electoral votes until Apr 6. Though George Washington's term of office began on Mar 4, he did not take the oath of office until Apr 30, 1789. All subsequent presidential terms (except successions following the death of an incumbent), until Franklin D. Roosevelt's second term, began Mar 4. The 20th Amendment (ratified Jan 23, 1933) provided that "the terms of the President and Vice President shall end at noon on the 20th day of January . . . and the terms of their successors shall then begin."

PENNSYLVANIA DEEDED TO WILLIAM PENN: ANNIVERSARY. Mar 4, 1681. To satisfy a debt of £16,000, King Charles II of England granted a royal charter, deed and governorship of Pennsylvania to William Penn.

***PEOPLE* MAGAZINE: 35th ANNIVERSARY.** Mar 4, 1974. The popular magazine highlighting celebrities was officially launched with the Mar 4, 1974, issue featuring a cover photo of Mia Farrow.

March 2009

S	M	T	W	T	F	S
1	2	3	4	5	6	7
8	9	10	11	12	13	14
15	16	17	18	19	20	21
22	23	24	25	26	27	28
29	30	31				

PERKINS, FRANCES: CABINET APPOINTMENT: ANNIVERSARY. Mar 4, 1933. Frances Perkins became the first woman appointed to the president's cabinet when she was appointed secretary of labor by President Franklin D. Roosevelt.

PULASKI, CASIMIR: BIRTH ANNIVERSARY. Mar 4, 1747. American Revolutionary hero, General Kazimierz (Casimir) Pulaski, born at Winiary, Mazovia, Poland, the son of a count. He was a patriot and military leader in Poland's fight against Russia of 1770–71 and went into exile at the partition of Poland in 1772. He came to America in 1777 to join the Revolution, fighting with General Washington at Brandywine and also serving at Germantown and Valley Forge. He organized the Pulaski Legion to wage guerrilla warfare against the British. Mortally wounded in a heroic charge at the siege of Savannah, GA, he died aboard the warship *Wasp* Oct 11, 1779. Pulaski Day is celebrated on the first Monday of March in Illinois.

ROCKNE, KNUTE: BIRTH ANNIVERSARY. Mar 4, 1888. Legendary Notre Dame football coach, born at Voss, Norway. Known for such sayings as "Win one for the Gipper," he died at Cottonwood Falls, KS, Mar 31, 1931.

SPACE MILESTONE: *OGO 5* (US). Mar 4, 1968. Orbiting Geophysical Observatory (OGO) collected data on the sun's influence on Earth. Launched Mar 4, 1968. Six OGOs were launched in all.

TELEVISION ACADEMY HALL OF FAME: FIRST INDUCTEES ANNOUNCED: 25th ANNIVERSARY. Mar 4, 1984. The Television Academy of Arts and Sciences announced the formation of the Television Academy Hall of Fame at Burbank, CA. The first inductees were Lucille Ball, Milton Berle, Paddy Chayefsky, Norman Lear, Edward R. Murrow, William S. Paley and David Sarnoff.

VERMONT: ADMISSION DAY: ANNIVERSARY. Mar 4. Became 14th state in 1791.

Birthdays Today

Landon Donovan, 27, soccer player, born Redlands, CA, Mar 4, 1982.

Emilio Estefan, 56, percussionist for the Miami Sound Machine, born Havana, Cuba, Mar 4, 1953.

Patricia Heaton, 50, actress ("Everybody Loves Raymond"), born Bay Village, OH, Mar 4, 1959.

Kevin Johnson, 43, former basketball player, born Sacramento, CA, Mar 4, 1966.

Patsy Kensit, 41, actress (*The Great Gatsby, Blame It on the Bellboy*), born London, England, Mar 4, 1968.

Kay Lenz, 56, actress (*Rich Man, Poor Man*), born Los Angeles, CA, Mar 4, 1953.

Miriam Makeba, 77, actress, singer, antiapartheid activist, born Johannesburg, South Africa, Mar 4, 1932.

Catherine O'Hara, 55, comedienne, writer ("SCTV Network 90"), actress (*Home Alone*), born Toronto, ON, Canada, Mar 4, 1954.

Rick Perry, 59, Governor of Texas (R), born Haskell, TX, Mar 4, 1950.

Paula Prentiss, 70, actress ("He & She," *What's New Pussycat?*), born Paula Ragusa at San Antonio, TX, Mar 4, 1939.

Steven Weber, 48, actor ("Wings"), born Queens, NY, Mar 4, 1961.

Mary Wilson, 65, singer (original member of the Supremes), born Detroit, MI, Mar 4, 1944.

March 5 — Thursday

DAY 64 **301 REMAINING**

BIG TEN WOMEN'S BASKETBALL TOURNAMENT. Mar 5–8. Conseco Fieldhouse, Indianapolis, IN. Est attendance: 2,500. For info: Big Ten Conference, 1500 W Higgins Rd, Park Ridge, IL 60068-6300. Phone: (847) 696-1010. Fax: (847) 696-1110. Web: www.bigten.org.

BLACKSTONE, WILLIAM: BIRTH ANNIVERSARY. Mar 5, 1595. William Blackstone, born at Durham County, England, was the first settler in what is now Boston, MA, and also the first in what is now Rhode Island. Blackstone came to New England with the Captain Robert Gorges expedition in 1623. When the expedition failed and most returned to England, he stayed and settled on what later became Beacon Hill. In 1634, he sold most of his Boston property and moved to the shores of the river that now bears his name. He died there at what is now Cumberland, RI, May 26, 1675.

BOSTON MASSACRE: ANNIVERSARY. Mar 5, 1770. A skirmish between British troops and a crowd at Boston, MA, became widely publicized and contributed to the unpopularity of the British regime in America before the American Revolution. Five men were killed and six more were injured by British troops commanded by Captain Thomas Preston.

CHANNEL ISLANDS NATIONAL PARK ESTABLISHED: ANNIVERSARY. Mar 5, 1980. California's Channel Islands Monument, authorized in 1938 by President Franklin D. Roosevelt, consisted of the islands of Anacapa and Santa Barbara. In 1980 President Jimmy Carter signed a bill establishing the Channel Islands National Park consisting of the islands Anacapa, San Miguel, Santa Barbara, Santa Cruz and Santa Rosa.

CRISPUS ATTUCKS DAY: DEATH ANNIVERSARY. Mar 5, 1770. Honors Crispus Attucks, possibly a runaway slave, who was the first to die in the Boston Massacre.

CULLIGAN, EMMETT J.: BIRTH ANNIVERSARY. Mar 5, 1893. Emmett J. Culligan, founder of the world's largest water treatment organization, was born at Yankton, SD. Culligan first experimented with a water-softening device in the early 1920s—to soften water used to wash his baby's diapers. In 1936 he launched the company from a Northbrook, IL, blacksmith shop. Recipient of the Horatio Alger Award in 1969, Culligan died at San Bernardino, CA, June 3, 1970.

DAYTONA 200 BY HONDA QUALIFYING DAY. Mar 5. Daytona International Speedway, Daytona Beach, FL. For info: Daytona International Speedway, PO Box 2801, Daytona Beach, FL 32120-2801. Phone: (800) PIT-SHOP. Web: www.daytonainternationalspeedway.com.

ENGLAND: CRUFTS DOG SHOW. Mar 5–8. National Exhibition Centre, Birmingham, West Midlands. The World's Greatest Dog Show where more than 23,000 top pedigree dogs compete to achieve the title of "Best in Show," the most prestigious award in the world of dogs. Held since 1891. Est attendance: 160,000. For info: Events Department, The Kennel Club, 1 Clarges St, London, England W1J 8AB. Phone: (44) (870) 606-6750. Fax: (44) (207) 5181058. Web: www.crufts.org.uk.

HARRISON, REX: BIRTH ANNIVERSARY. Mar 5, 1908. Born Reginald Carey at Huyton, England. Rex Harrison's career as an actor encompassed more than 40 films and scores of plays. He won both a Tony and an Oscar for the role of Henry Higgins in *My Fair Lady*, perhaps his most famous role. Among other films, he appeared in *Dr. Dolittle, Cleopatra, Blithe Spirit* and *Major Barbara*. He claimed he would never retire from acting, and he was appearing in a Broadway revival of Somerset Maugham's *The Circle* three weeks before his death June 2, 1990, at his home at New York, NY.

"IRON CURTAIN" SPEECH: ANNIVERSARY. Mar 5, 1946. Winston Churchill, speaking at Westminster College, Fulton, MO, established the cold war boundary with these words: "From Stettin in the Baltic to Trieste in the Adriatic an iron curtain has descended across the continent." Though Churchill was not the first to use the phrase *iron curtain*, his speech gave it a new currency and its usage persisted.

LOUISIANA SPORTSMEN'S SHOW AND FESTIVAL. Mar 5–8. Lamar Dixon Expo Center, Gonzales, LA. 30th annual. Louisiana's original sportfishing, hunting and boat show covering New Orleans, Baton Rouge and the Gulf Coast. Est attendance: 100,000. For info: Bob Del Giorno, Louisiana Sportsmen's Show, PO Box 2116, Kenner, LA 70063. Phone: (504) 464-7363. E-mail: bob@lasportsmenshow.com. Web: www.lasportsmenshow.com.

MERCATOR, GERHARDUS: BIRTH ANNIVERSARY. Mar 5, 1512. Cartographer-geographer Mercator was born at Rupelmonde, Belgium. His Mercator projection for maps provided an accurate ratio of latitude to longitude and is still used today. He also introduced the term *atlas* for a collection of maps. He died at Duisberg, Germany, Dec 2, 1594.

NAIA MEN'S AND WOMEN'S INDOOR TRACK AND FIELD NATIONAL CHAMPIONSHIPS. Mar 5–7. Site TBD. Individuals compete for All-America honors while teams compete for the national championship. 44th annual competition for men; 29th annual for women. Est attendance: 2,500. For info: Natl Assn Intercollegiate Athletics, 1200 Grand Blvd, Kansas City, MO 64106. E-mail: rstein@naia.org. Web: www.naia.org.

NAIA WRESTLING NATIONAL CHAMPIONSHIPS. Mar 5–7. Oklahoma City University, Oklahoma City, OK. Individuals compete for All-America honors in 10 weight divisions, while teams compete for the national championship. 52nd annual competition. Est attendance: 10,000. For info: Natl Assn of Intercollegiate Athletics, 1200 Grand Blvd, Kansas City, MO 64106. E-mail: smcclure@naia.org. Web: www.naia.org.

NAMETAG DAY. Mar 5. Today's celebration of names stipulates that wherever you are, whatever you're doing, you wear a "Hello, I'm [your name here]" nametag. (Note: this event is not for children.) Annually, the Thursday of Celebrate Your Name Week. For info: Jerry Hill. E-mail: celebrateyournameweek@gmail.com. Web: www.namesuniverse.com.

NATIONAL WEEK OF THE OCEAN FESTIVAL SEA-SON. Mar 5–June 13. Fort Lauderdale, FL. 30th annual. This multiweek celebration includes school marine fair, marine flea market, waterway cleanup, a plywood regatta, Mother Ocean Day, dive expo and a Reef Sweep. Est attendance: 50,000. For info: Cynthia Hancock, Pres, Natl Week of the Ocean, Inc, PO Box 179, Ft Lauderdale, FL 33302. Phone: (954) 462-5573. Web: www.national-week-of-the-ocean.org.

SAINT PIRAN'S DAY. Mar 5. Celebrates the birthday of St. Piran, the patron saint of Cornish tinners. Cornish worldwide celebrate this day.

UNITED STATES BANK HOLIDAY: ANNIVERSARY. Mar 5, 1933. On his first full day in office (Sunday, Mar 5, 1933), President Franklin Roosevelt proclaimed a national "Bank Holiday" to help save the nation's faltering banking system. Most banks were able to reopen after the 10-day "holiday" (Mar 4–14), but in the meantime, "scrip" had temporarily replaced money in many American households.

 **Birthdays Today**

Kevin Connolly, 35, actor ("Entourage"), born New York, NY, Mar 5, 1974.

Samantha Eggar, 70, actress ("Samantha and the King," *The Collector*), born London, England, Mar 5, 1939.

Penn Jillette, 54, magician, born Greenfield, MA, Mar 5, 1955.

Paul Sand, 65, actor ("St. Elsewhere"; Tony Award for *Story Theatre*), born Paul Sanchez at Los Angeles, CA, Mar 5, 1944.

Dean Stockwell, 73, actor (*The Boy with Green Hair*, "Quantum Leap"), born Los Angeles, CA, Mar 5, 1936.

Marsha Warfield, 55, actress ("Night Court," "Empty Nest"), born Chicago, IL, Mar 5, 1954.

Michael Warren, 63, actor ("Paris," "Hill Street Blues"), born South Bend, IN, Mar 5, 1946.

Fred Williamson, 71, actor ("Julia," "Half Nelson"), former professional football player, born Gary, IN, Mar 5, 1938.

March 6 — Friday

DAY 65 — 300 REMAINING

ALDO LEOPOLD WEEKEND. Mar 6–8. Statewide, Wisconsin. Communities across Wisconsin come together to demonstrate their individual and combined commitment to the "Land Ethic" put forth by renowned environmentalist Aldo Leopold in his famous book, *A Sand County Almanac*. He wrote, "That land is a community is the basic concept of ecology, but that land is to be loved and respected is an extension of ethics." Annually, the first full weekend in March. For info: Jennifer Kobylecky, The Aldo Leopold Foundation, PO Box 77, Baraboo, WI 53913. Phone: (608) 355-0279. Fax: (608) 356-7309. E-mail: jennifer@aldoleopold.org. Web: www.aldoleopold.org.

BROWNING, ELIZABETH BARRETT: BIRTH ANNIVERSARY. Mar 6, 1806. English poet, author of *Sonnets from the Portuguese*, wife of poet Robert Browning and subject of the play *The Barretts of Wimpole Street*, was born near Durham, England. She died at Florence, Italy, June 29, 1861.

COSTELLO, LOU: BIRTH ANNIVERSARY. Mar 6, 1906. Born at Paterson, NJ, partner with Bud Abbott in the legendary comedy duo Abbott and Costello. The team formed in 1936 and were popular on radio, TV and film. Films included *Buck Privates* and *Abbott and Costello Meet Frankenstein*. "Who's On First?" was their legendary comedy routine. Costello died Mar 3, 1959, at East Los Angeles, CA.

CRAFTSMEN'S CLASSIC ARTS & CRAFTS FESTIVAL. Mar 6–8. South Carolina State Fairgrounds, Columbia, SC. 26th annual. Features work from more than 300 talented artists and craftspeople. All juried exhibitors' work has been handmade by the exhibitors and must be their own original design and creation. See the creative process in action with several exhibitors demonstrating through the weekend. Something for every style, taste and budget with items from the most contemporary to the most traditional. Est attendance: 20,000. For info: Gilmore Enterprises, 3514-A Drawbridge Pkwy, Greensboro, NC 27410-8584. Phone: (336) 282-5550. E-mail: contact@gilmoreshows.com. Web: www.CraftShow.com or www.gilmoreshows.com.

DAYTONA SUPERCROSS BY HONDA. Mar 6. Daytona International Speedway, Daytona Beach, FL. One of the most famous and toughest supercross races in the world. For info: Daytona International Speedway, PO Box 2801, Daytona Beach, FL 32120-2801. Phone: (800) PIT-SHOP. Web: www.daytonainternationalspeedway.com.

DRED SCOTT DECISION: ANNIVERSARY. Mar 6, 1857. This was the most famous US Supreme Court decision during the prewar slavery controversy. Dred Scott, a slave, had successfully petitioned for his freedom based on his previous residence in a free state and territory. On this date, the Supreme Court overturned Missouri's Supreme Court decision and declared the 1820 Missouri Compromise unconstitutional. Chief Justice Roger Taney wrote that slaves were property, not citizens, and that Congress had no power to restrict slavery in the territories.

EISNER, WILL: BIRTH ANNIVERSARY. Mar 6, 1917. One of the greatest comic book/graphic artists, William Erwin Eisner was born today at Brooklyn, NY, to Jewish immigrant parents. In a career spanning eight decades, Eisner created the popular and innovative *Spirit* comic book, started an educational comic book business, taught legions of students graphic narrative techniques and created the first graphic novel, *A Contract with God* (1978). He brought cinematic touches—including German Expressionist style—to comics. The Eisner Awards were created in his honor in 1988 to recognize other bright lights in the field. Eisner died Jan 3, 2005, at Fort Lauderdale, FL.

FALL OF THE ALAMO: ANNIVERSARY. Mar 6, 1836. Anniversary of the fall of the Texan fort, the Alamo. The siege, led by Mexican general Santa Anna, began Feb 23 and reached its climax Mar 6, when the last of the defenders was slain. Texans, under General Sam Houston, rallied with the war cry "Remember the Alamo" and, at the Battle of San Jacinto, Apr 21, defeated and captured Santa Anna, who signed a treaty recognizing Texas's independence.

GHANA: INDEPENDENCE DAY. Mar 6. National holiday. Commemorates independence from Great Britain in 1957.

INTERNATIONAL FESTIVAL OF OWLS. Mar 6–8. Houston, MN. Immerse yourself in owls at this all-owl family event. Kids will delight in the owl face painting, owl crafts and owl storytelling. Adults will enjoy presentations by prominent "owlologists," including a banquet address by snowy owl researcher Norman Smith, and the presentation of the World Owl Hall of Fame awards. Live owl presentations with six or more species of owls, hooting contest, owl prowls, a raffle, auction, owl merchandise, owl-themed food and a special reservation-only photography sessions with the owls. Annually, the first weekend in March. For info: Karla Kinstler, International Festival of Owls, 215 W Plum St, PO Box 667, Houston, MN 55943. Phone: (507) 896-4668. Fax: (507) 896-5668. E-mail: nature@acegroup.cc. Web: www.festivalofowls.com.

LARDNER, RING: BIRTH ANNIVERSARY. Mar 6, 1885. Ringgold Wilmer (Ring) Lardner, sportswriter, born at Niles, MI. Lardner wrote about sports for a variety of newspapers, mostly in Chicago. In both his columns and his short stories, he reproduced ballplayers' vernacular speech patterns with great success, thereby laying the groundwork for generations of baseball fiction to come. Lardner abandoned baseball after the Black Sox scandal was exposed. He wrote songs, plays and magazine articles but never the novel that some of his friends thought he should. Taciturn and solemn with a biting sense of humor, Lardner drank and smoked to excess, even after contracting tuberculosis in 1926. Posthumously given the J.G. Taylor Spink Award in 1963 for his baseball writing. Died at East Hampton, NY, Sept 25, 1933.

MARYLAND HOME AND GARDEN SHOW. Mar 6–8 (also Mar 13–15). Timonium Fairgrounds, Baltimore, MD. The largest display of home building, remodeling and home decorating exhibits

March 2009

S	M	T	W	T	F	S
1	2	3	4	5	6	7
8	9	10	11	12	13	14
15	16	17	18	19	20	21
22	23	24	25	26	27	28
29	30	31				

in the Baltimore area. Includes educational exhibits, crafts, plant marketplace and displays of landscaped gardens and floral arrangements. Est attendance: 72,000. For info: S & L Productions Inc, Crain Overlook, 1916 Crain Hwy, Ste 16, Glen Burnie, MD 21061. Phone: (410) 863-1180. Fax: (410) 863-1187. E-mail: jayp@slprod .com.

MICHELANGELO: BIRTH ANNIVERSARY. Mar 6, 1475. Anniversary of the birth, at Caprese, Italy, of Michelangelo di Lodovico Buonarroti Simoni, a prolific Renaissance painter, sculptor, architect and poet who had a profound impact on Western art. Michelangelo's fresco painting on the ceiling of the Sistine Chapel at the Vatican at Rome, Italy, is often considered the pinnacle of his achievement in painting, as well as the highest achievement of the Renaissance. Also among his works were the sculptures *David* and *The Pieta*. Appointed architect of St. Peter's in 1542, a post he held until his death Feb 18, 1564, at Rome.

MIDDLE NAME PRIDE DAY. Mar 6. Today's name celebration requires honesty and boldness. Tell three people who don't already know it what your middle name is (even if it's Egbert). Annually, the Friday of Celebrate Your Name Week. For info: Jerry Hill. E-mail: celebrateyournameweek@gmail.com. Web: www.names universe.com.

MIDNIGHT AT THE OASIS. Mar 6–8. Ray Kroc Complex/Desert Sun Stadium, Yuma, AZ. 17th annual. Stroll down memory lane at an incredible nostalgic festival featuring the cars and music of the '50s and '60s. Limited to 850 '72 and older American cars and trucks and foreign classics. Show & Shine, rock 'n' roll concerts and dances, vendors, activities and entertainment for the whole family. Est attendance: 50,000. For info: Caballeros de Yuma, PO Box 5987, Yuma, AZ 85366. Phone: (928) 343-1715. Fax: (928) 783-1609. E-mail: caballeros@beamspeed.net. Web: www.caballeros.org.

NATURAL BRIDGE BATTLE REENACTMENT. Mar 6–7. Tallahassee, FL. 32nd annual. Reenactment of the Confederate army's victory at the Natural Bridge site, which kept Tallahassee (the state capital) from falling into Union hands. Annually, first full weekend in March. Est attendance: 4,500. For info: Natural Bridge Battlefield Historic State Park, 1022 DeSoto Park Dr, Tallahassee, FL 32301. Phone: (850) 922-6007. Web: www.floridastateparks.org/ naturalbridge.

PEALE, ANNA CLAYPOOLE: BIRTH ANNIVERSARY. Mar 6, 1791. American painter of miniatures and a member of the famous Peale family of artists. Born at Philadelphia, PA; died Dec 25, 1878.

SHERLOCK HOLMES WEEKEND. Mar 6–8 (also Nov 6–8). Cape May, NJ. A weekend of mystery and intrigue awaits amateur sleuths when Cape May celebrates the works of Sir Arthur Conan Doyle, creator of Sherlock Holmes. Offered twice annually. Est attendance: 200. For info: Mid-Atlantic Center for the Arts, 1048 Washington St, Cape May, NJ 08204. Phone: (609) 884-5404 or (800) 275-4278. Fax: (609) 884-0574. E-mail: mac4arts@capemaymac.org. Web: www.capemaymac.org.

WILLS, BOB: BIRTH ANNIVERSARY. Mar 6, 1905. The Father of Western Swing was born at Kosse, TX. Originally a performer (fiddler) with the Light Crust Doughboys, Wills later formed the popular Texas Playboys. Bob Wills and the Texas Playboys appeared on film and at the Grand Ole Opry and made western swing popular with such hits as "San Antonio Rose." Wills died May 13, 1975, at Fort Worth, TX.

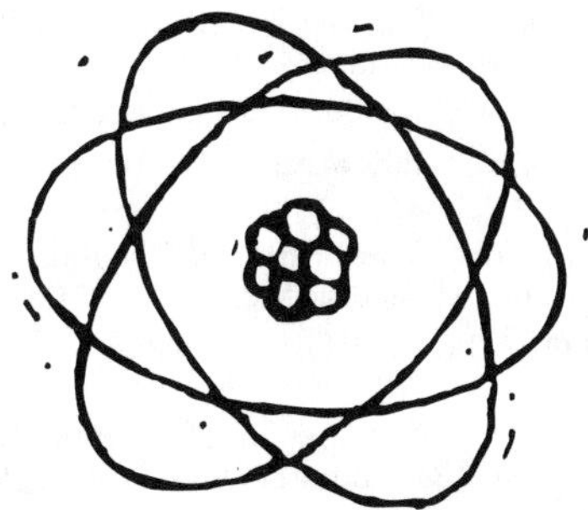

WORLD DAY OF PRAYER. Mar 6. 122nd annual. An ecumenical event that reinforces bonds among peoples of the world as they join in a global circle of prayer. Annually, the first Friday in March. Sponsor: International Committee for World Day of Prayer. Church Women United is the National World Day of Prayer Committee for the US. For info: Church Women United, 475 Riverside Dr, Ste 1626, New York, NY 10115. Phone: (212) 870-2347 or (800) 298-5551. Fax: (212) 870-2338. Web: www.churchwomen.org.

Birthdays Today

Tom Arnold, 50, actor ("Roseanne," *McHale's Navy, True Lies*), born Ottumwa, IA, Mar 6, 1959.

Christopher Samuel Bond, 70, US Senator (R, Missouri), born St. Louis, MO, Mar 6, 1939.

Connie Britton, 41, actress ("Friday Night Lights," "Spin City"), born Boston, MA, Mar 6, 1968.

Gabriel Garcia-Marquez, 81, Nobel Prize–winning author (*A Hundred Years of Solitude, Love in the Time of Cholera*), born Aracaracca, Colombia, Mar 6, 1928.

Dave Gilmour, 65, singer, guitarist (Pink Floyd), born Cambridge, England, Mar 6, 1944.

Alan Greenspan, 83, economist, former Chairman of the Federal Reserve Board, born New York, NY, Mar 6, 1926.

D.L. Hughley, 46, comedian, actor ("The Hughleys," *The Original Kings of Comedy*), born Los Angeles, CA, Mar 6, 1963.

Kiri Te Kanawa, 65, opera singer, born Gisborne, New Zealand, Mar 6, 1944.

Ed McMahon, 86, actor, TV host ("The Tonight Show," "Star Search"), born Detroit, MI, Mar 6, 1923.

Ben Murphy, 67, actor ("Alias Smith and Jones," *Yours, Mine and Ours*), born Jonesboro, AR, Mar 6, 1942.

Ryan Nyquist, 30, BMX bike racer, born Los Gatos, CA, Mar 6, 1979.

Shaquille Rashan O'Neal, 37, basketball player, born Newark, NJ, Mar 6, 1972.

Amy Pietz, 40, actress ("Caroline in the City"), born Oakcreek, WI, Mar 6, 1969.

Rob Reiner, 62, actor ("All in the Family"), director (*When Harry Met Sally . . . , This Is Spinal Tap*), born New York, NY, Mar 6, 1947 (some sources say 1945).

Valentina Tereshkova-Nikolaeva, 72, cosmonaut, born Maslennikovo, USSR, Mar 6, 1937.

March 7 — Saturday

DAY 66 **299 REMAINING**

BIG TEN WRESTLING CHAMPIONSHIPS. Mar 7–8. Penn State University, University Park, PA. Est attendance: 1,000. For info: Big Ten Conference, 1500 W Higgins Rd, Park Ridge, IL 60068-6300. Phone: (847) 696-1010. Fax: (847) 696-1110. Web: www.bigten.org.

BURBANK, LUTHER: BIRTH ANNIVERSARY. Mar 7, 1849. Anniversary of the birth of American naturalist and author, creator and developer of many new varieties of flowers, fruits, vegetables and trees. Luther Burbank's birthday is observed in California as Bird and Arbor Day. Born at Lancaster, MA, he died at Santa Rosa, CA, Apr 11, 1926.

DAYTONA 200 BY HONDA CLASSIC. Mar 7. Daytona International Speedway, Daytona Beach, FL. 68th annual. For info: Daytona International Speedway, PO Box 2801, Daytona Beach, FL 32120-2801. Phone: (800) PIT-SHOP. Web: www.daytonainter nationalspeedway.com.

DISTINGUISHED SERVICE MEDAL: ANNIVERSARY. Mar 7, 1918. With US troops fighting in the trenches in France during the First World War, President Woodrow Wilson authorized the creation of a new bronze, beribboned medal to be given to US Army personnel who performed "exceptionally meritorious service."

FESTIVAL OF THE SUGAR MAPLES. Mar 7–8 (also Mar 14–15). Coral Woods Conservation Area, near Marengo, IL. The flowing of the maple sap is a sure sign that spring is just around the corner! Celebrate with McHenry County Conservation District and learn the fascinating history of maple sugaring and the evolution of the sap collection process. Satisfy your sweet tooth with a taste of pure Coral Woods maple syrup. Half-mile tours begin every 15 minutes and last an hour. Est attendance: 2,500. For info: McHenry County Conservation District, 18410 US Hwy 14, Woodstock, IL 60098. Phone: (815) 338-6223. E-mail: mccd@MCCDistrict.org. Web: www.MCCDistrict.org.

FLORAL CITY STRAWBERRY FESTIVAL. Mar 7–8. Floral City, FL. Art and crafts festival, children's activities, princess pageants, entertainment, car show and, of course, tons of strawberries! Annually, the first full weekend in March. Est attendance: 28,000. For info: Citrus County Chamber of Commerce, 401 Tompkins St, Inverness, FL 34452. Phone: (352) 726-2801. Fax: (352) 637-6498. Web: www.citruscountychamber.com.

GENEALOGY DAY. Mar 7. Join in on one of the world's fastest growing hobbies and celebrate names at the same time. Get genealogy tips, hints and ideas, then begin the journey to knowing your heritage name by name, one ancestor at a time. Annually, the Saturday of Celebrate Your Name Week. For info: Jerry Hill. E-mail: celebrateyournameweek@gmail.com. Web: www.namesuniverse.com.

HOPKINS, STEPHEN: BIRTH ANNIVERSARY. Mar 7, 1707. Colonial governor (Rhode Island) and signer of the Declaration of Independence. Born at Providence, RI, and died there July 13, 1785.

IDITAROD TRAIL SLED DOG RACE. Mar 7–15. 37th running of "The Last Great Race on Earth" (first run on Mar 3, 1973). 1,150 miles through Alaskan wilderness from Anchorage to Nome, AK, along the historic Iditarod Trail. More than 60 16-dog teams competing. Finishers' banquet on Sunday, Mar 15. Est attendance: 25,000. For info: Iditarod Trail Committee, PO Box 870800, Wasilla, AK 99687. Phone: (907) 376-5155, ext 108. Fax: (907) 373-6998. Web: www.iditarod.com.

NATCHEZ SPRING PILGRIMAGE. Mar 7–Apr 11. Natchez, MS. Annual tour of 25 antebellum mansions—many of them private homes of which some have been in the same family for more than 150 years. The owners will be dressed in period costumes to greet visitors. Carriage and bus sightseeing tours daily. Est attendance: 35,000. For info: Natchez Pilgrimage Tours, PO Box 347, Natchez, MS 39121. Phone: (800) 647-6742 or (601) 446-6631. Fax: (601) 446-8687. E-mail: eugeniel@natchezpilgrimage.com. Web: www.natchezpilgrimage.com.

NATIONAL BE HEARD DAY. Mar 7. There are more than 145 million small businesses in the US, but often, small business owners are less likely to get the media coverage they deserve. National Be Heard Day celebrates and empowers each business owner and entrepreneur who can find their voice, tell their story and be heard through publicity efforts. More information and a free Be Heard publicity kit is available at www.beheardsolutions.com. For info: Shannon Cherry, Be Heard Solutions, 184 Lancaster St, Albany, NY 12210. Phone: (518) 632-6212. E-mail: assist@beheardsolutions.com. Web: www.beheardsolutions.com.

NENANA TRIPOD RAISING FESTIVAL. Mar 7–8. Nenana, AK. Festival centers around the guessing of the exact time of the ice breakup on the Tanana River. Highlights include the Raising of the Tripod, Nenana Banana Eating, sled dog races, arm wrestling, turkey shoot, craft bazaar and much more. Est attendance: 2,500. For info: Nenana Ice Classic, PO Box 272, Nenana, AK 99760. Phone: (907) 832-5446. Fax: (907) 832-5888. E-mail: classic@mtaonline.net. Web: www.nenanaakiceclassic.com.

REMAGEN BRIDGE CAPTURE: ANNIVERSARY. Mar 7, 1945. On this date in 1945, a small advance force of the US First Army captured the Ludendorff railway bridge across the Rhine River at Remagen (between Bonn and Coblenz)—the only bridge across the Rhine that had not been blown up by the German defenders—thus acquiring the first bridgehead onto the east bank and the beginning of the Allied advance into Germany, a turning point in WWII.

SAINT PIRAN'S DAY CELEBRATION. Mar 7. Location available after Jan 1. Celebration in honor of St. Piran, patron saint of Cornwall and Cornish peoples. Held to help preserve history and culture of the Cornish (Celtic). Annually, the Saturday nearest Mar 5. For info: Donald Whitman, Ed, Greater Kansas City Cornish Society, 24 E 68th St, Kansas City, MO 64113-2414. Phone: (816) 361-1956. E-mail: donwhitman1@aol.com.

SUEZ CANAL OPENS: ANNIVERSARY. Mar 7, 1869. This waterway across Egypt connecting the Mediterranean and Red seas was built by the French. In 1956 Egyptian president Nasser nationalized the canal, prompting an invasion by the British, French and Israelis. The Six-Day War in 1967 shut down the canal for eight years.

UNITED STATES NATIONAL SNOWSHOE CHAMPIONSHIPS. Mar 7. Location TBD. 9th annual. Men, women and children compete in snowshoe racing at 5k and 10k lengths and at different ability levels. For info: United States Snowshoe Assn, 678 County Rt 25, Corinth, NY 12822. Phone: (518) 654-7648. Web: www.snowshoeracing.com.

Birthdays Today

Anthony Armstrong-Jones (Lord Snowdon), 79, photographer, born London, England, Mar 7, 1930.

Bryan Cranston, 53, actor ("Malcolm in the Middle," "Breaking Bad"), born San Fernando Valley, CA, Mar 7, 1956.

Taylor Dayne, 47, singer ("Love Will Send You Back"), born Long Island, NY, Mar 7, 1962.

Michael Eisner, 67, media executive, born Mount Kisco, NY, Mar 7, 1942.

Jenna Fischer, 35, actress ("The Office," *Walk Hard: The Dewey Cox Story*), born Fort Wayne, IN, Mar 7, 1974.

Janet Guthrie, 71, former auto racer, born Iowa City, IA, Mar 7, 1938.

Franco Harris, 59, Hall of Fame football player, born Fort Dix, NJ, Mar 7, 1950.

John Heard, 63, actor (*The Milagro Beanfield War, Rambling Rose, The Pelican Brief*), born Washington, DC, Mar 7, 1946.

Jeff Kent, 41, baseball player, born Bellflower, CA, Mar 7, 1968.

Ivan Lendl, 49, former tennis player, born Ostrava, Czechoslovakia, Mar 7, 1960.

Willard Herman Scott, 75, weatherman ("The Today Show"), friend of centenarians, born Alexandria, VA, Mar 7, 1934.

Daniel J. Travanti, 69, actor ("Hill Street Blues"), born Kenosha, WI, Mar 7, 1940.

Rachel Weisz, 38, actress (Oscar for *The Constant Gardener*; *The Runaway Jury, About a Boy*), born London, England, Mar 7, 1971.

Peter Wolf, 63, singer (J. Geils Band), born Boston, MA, Mar 7, 1946.

March 2009

S	M	T	W	T	F	S
1	2	3	4	5	6	7
8	9	10	11	12	13	14
15	16	17	18	19	20	21
22	23	24	25	26	27	28
29	30	31				

March 8 — Sunday

DAY 67 298 REMAINING

BEAVERS, LOUISE: BIRTH ANNIVERSARY. Mar 8, 1902. The Hollywood career of Louise Beavers spanned 30 years and more than 125 films. Though she was forced to play stereotypical roles, such as those of maids, her authentic talent was always apparent. Her starring role in the film *Imitation of Life* earned her high praise. Beavers was a member of the Black Filmmakers Hall of Fame. She also played the title role in the TV series "Beulah" (1951–53). Born at Cincinnati, OH; died at Los Angeles, Oct 26, 1962.

CAXTON'S *MIRROR OF THE WORLD* TRANSLATION: ANNIVERSARY. Mar 8, 1481. William Caxton, England's first printer, completed the translation from French into English of *The Mirror of the World*, a popular account of astronomy and other sciences. In print soon afterward, *Mirror of the World* became the first illustrated book printed in England.

CHECK YOUR BATTERIES DAY. Mar 8. A day set aside for checking the batteries in your smoke detector, carbon monoxide detector, HVAC thermostat, audio/visual remote controls and other electronic devices. This could save your life! Annually, the second Sunday in March (with Daylight Saving Time).

DAYLIGHT SAVING TIME BEGINS. Mar 8–Nov 1. Daylight Saving Time begins at 2 AM. The Energy Policy Act of 2005 extended the period of Daylight Saving Time as originally outlined in the Uniform Time Act of 1966 (amended in 1986 by Public Law 99–359). Standard Time in each zone is advanced one hour from 2 AM on the second Sunday in March until 2 AM on the first Sunday in November (except where state legislatures provide exemption). Prior to 1986, Daylight Saving Time began on the last Sunday in April. Many use the popular rule "spring forward, fall back" to remember which way to turn their clocks. See also: "Daylight Saving Time Ends; Standard Time Resumes" (Nov 1).

GIRLS WRITE NOW DAY. Mar 8. International Women's Day (also Mar 8) celebrates the story of ordinary women as makers of history; it is rooted in the centuries-old struggle of women to participate in society on an equal footing with men. Girls Write Now Day honors the younger generation as makers of the future! It is a day and an event to encourage girls of all ages everywhere in the world to put pen to paper and explore the beauty and power of their unique, creative voices. It is a day to celebrate girls, girl writers and overall girl awesomeness. For info: Michele Thomas, Girls Write Now, 520 Eighth Ave, Ste 2020, New York, NY 10018. Phone: (212) 691-6590, ext 212. Fax: (212) 675-0171. E-mail: media@girlswritenow.org. Web: www.girlswritenow.org.

GRAHAME, KENNETH: 150th BIRTH ANNIVERSARY. Mar 8, 1859. Scottish author, born at Edinburgh. His children's book *The Wind in the Willows* has as its main characters a mole, a rat, a badger and a toad. He died July 6, 1932, at Pangbourne, Berkshire.

INTERNATIONAL (WORKING) WOMEN'S DAY. Mar 8. A day to honor women, especially working women. Said to commemorate an 1857 march and demonstration at New York, NY, by female garment and textile workers. Believed to have been first proclaimed for this date at an international conference of women held at Helsinki, Finland, in 1910, "that henceforth Mar 8 should be declared International Women's Day." The 50th anniversary observance, at Peking, China, in 1960, cited Clara Zetkin (1857–1933) as "initiator of Women's Day on Mar 8." This is perhaps the most widely observed holiday of recent origin and is unusual among holidays originating in the US in having been widely adopted and observed in other nations, including socialist countries. In Russia it is a national holiday, and flowers or gifts are presented to women workers.

READ AN E-BOOK WEEK. Mar 8–14. A week set aside to learn about and/or read an electronic book (e-book). For info: Rita Toews, 9 Esker Pl, East St Paul, MB, Canada, R2E 0K2. Phone: (204) 661-2734. E-mail: r.toews@shaw.ca. Web: www.domokos.com/readebookweek.html.

RUSSIA: INTERNATIONAL WOMEN'S DAY. Mar 8. National holiday.

SYRIAN ARAB REPUBLIC: REVOLUTION DAY. Mar 8, 1963. Official public holiday commemorating assumption of power by Revolutionary National Council.

TEEN TECH WEEK. Mar 8–14. Sponsored by the Young Adult Library Services Association, Teen Tech Week is a celebration aimed at getting teens to discover the different technologies offered by their libraries, such as DVDs, databases, audiobooks, electronic games and more. For info: Young Adult Library Services Assn (YALSA), American Library Assn, 50 E Huron St, Chicago, IL 60611. Phone: (800) 545-2433, ext. 4390. E-mail: yalsa@ala.org. Web: www.ala.org/teentechweek.

UNITED NATIONS: DAY FOR WOMEN'S RIGHTS AND INTERNATIONAL PEACE. Mar 8. An international day observed by the organizations of the United Nations system. In some years, known as International Women's Day. For info: United Nations, Dept of Public Info, New York, NY 10017. Web: www.un.org.

UNITED STATES INCOME TAX: ANNIVERSARY. Mar 8, 1913. The Internal Revenue Service began to levy and collect income taxes. The 16th Amendment to the Constitution, ratified Feb 3, 1913, gave Congress the authority to tax income. The US had also levied an income tax during the Civil War. See also: "Lincoln Signs Income Tax" (July 1).

VAN BUREN, HANNAH HOES: BIRTH ANNIVERSARY. Mar 8, 1783. Wife of Martin Van Buren, 8th president of the US. Born at Kinderhook, NY, she died at Albany, NY, Feb 5, 1819.

Birthdays Today

Susan Clark, 69, actress ("Webster," *Babe*), born Sarnia, ON, Canada, Mar 8, 1940.

Micky Dolenz, 64, singer, actor ("The Monkees"), director, born Los Angeles, CA, Mar 8, 1945.

Kathy Ireland, 46, model, born Santa Barbara, CA, Mar 8, 1963.

Camryn Manheim, 48, actress ("Ghost Whisperer," "The Practice"), born Caldwell, NJ, Mar 8, 1961.

Marcia Newby, 21, gymnast, born Virginia Beach, VA, Mar 8, 1988.

Freddie Prinze, Jr, 33, actor (*Scooby-Doo, She's All That*), born Albuquerque, NM, Mar 8, 1976.

Aidan Quinn, 50, actor (*Desperately Seeking Susan*; stage: *A Streetcar Named Desire*), born Chicago, IL, Mar 8, 1959.

Lynn Redgrave, 66, actress (*Georgy Girl*, "House Calls"), born London, England, Mar 8, 1943.

James Edward (Jim) Rice, 56, former baseball player, born Anderson, SC, Mar 8, 1953.

Carole Bayer Sager, 62, singer, songwriter ("That's What Friends Are For," with Burt Bacharach), born New York, NY, Mar 8, 1947.

Raynoma Gordy Singleton, 72, cofounder of Motown Records, born Detroit, MI, Mar 8, 1937.

James Van Der Beek, 32, actor ("Dawson's Creek"), born Cheshire, CT, Mar 8, 1977.

March 9 — Monday

DAY 68 297 REMAINING

BARBIE DEBUTS: 50th ANNIVERSARY. Mar 9, 1959. The popular girls' doll debuted in stores. More than 800 million dolls have been sold.

BELIZE: BARON BLISS DAY. Mar 9. Official public holiday. Celebrated in honor of Sir Henry Edward Ernest Victor Bliss, a great benefactor of Belize.

GAGARIN, YURI ALEXSEYEVICH: 75th BIRTH ANNIVERSARY. Mar 9, 1934. Russian cosmonaut Yuri Gagarin, the first person to travel in space, was born at Gzhatsk, USSR. The 27-year-old Soviet Air Force major made his flight Apr 12, 1961, lasting 108 minutes and orbiting Earth in a rocket-propelled, five-ton space capsule, 187 miles above the Earth's surface. Gagarin was killed in an airplane crash near Moscow, USSR, Mar 27, 1968. After his death the town in which he was born was renamed Gagarin, and the Gagarin Museum was established in the frame house where he spent his childhood.

GRANT COMMISSIONED COMMANDER OF ALL UNION ARMIES: ANNIVERSARY. Mar 9, 1864. At Washington, DC, Ulysses S. Grant accepted his commission as Lieutenant General, becoming the commander of all the Union armies.

JOE FRANKLIN DAY. Mar 9. A day to honor the king of radio, television and entertainment for all his contributions on the anniversary of his birth. Franklin appeared on late-night television in New York from 1950–93 and continues to entertain people today. For info: Bob O'Brien, "The Answer Man", 1061 Koelle Ave, Secaucus, NJ 07094. Phone: (646) 233-6610. E-mail: robtfobrien@aol.com.

JULIA, RAUL: BIRTH ANNIVERSARY. Mar 9, 1940. Born at San Juan, Puerto Rico, Julia won acclaim and four Tony nominations for roles he played on Broadway. Most widely known of his many film roles are Gomez in *The Addams Family* and Valentín in *Kiss of the Spider Woman.* Julia died Oct 24, 1994, at Manhasset, NY.

MAWLID AL NABI: THE BIRTHDAY OF THE PROPHET MUHAMMAD. Mar 9. Mawlid al Nabi (Birth of the Prophet Muhammad) is observed on Muslim calendar date Rabi al-Awal 12, 1430. Different methods for calculating the visibility of the new moon crescent at Mecca are used by different Muslim groups. US date may vary. Began at sunset the preceding day.

NATIONAL NAPPING DAY. Mar 9. This is a day for employees to "lie down and be counted" in support of napping at the workplace. This day occurs on the Monday following the advent of daylight saving time. For info: The Napping Co. Inc, 26 Orchard Park Dr, Reading, MA 01867. Phone: (781) 944-3506. Web: www.napping.com.

PANIC DAY. Mar 9. Run around all day in a panic, telling others you can't handle it anymore. (©2006 by WH.) For info: Thomas & Ruth Roy, Wellcat Holidays, 2418 Long Ln, Lebanon, PA 17046. Phone: (717) 279-0184. E-mail: info@wellcat.com. Web: www.wellcat.com.

March 2009	S	M	T	W	T	F	S
	1	2	3	4	5	6	7
	8	9	10	11	12	13	14
	15	16	17	18	19	20	21
	22	23	24	25	26	27	28
	29	30	31				

SAINT FRANCES OF ROME: FEAST DAY. Mar 9. Patron of motorists and model for housewives and widows (1384–1440). After 40 years of marriage she was widowed in 1436 and later joined the community of Benedictine Oblates. Canonized in 1608.

TA'ANIT ESTHER (FAST OF ESTHER). Mar 9. Hebrew calendar date Adar 13, 5769. Commemorates Queen Esther's fast, in the 6th century BC, to save the Jews of ancient Persia. Began at sundown Mar 8.

TOKYO BLANKET BOMBING: ANNIVERSARY. Mar 9, 1945. The Japanese capital of Tokyo was bombed by 343 Superfortresses carrying all the incendiary bombs they could hold. Within the targeted areas of the city, population densities were four times greater than those of most American cities, and homes were made primarily of wood and paper. Carried by the wind, the fires leveled 16 sq miles. More than a quarter million buildings were destroyed. The death toll was 83,000; 41,000 were injured. For the balance of WWII American strategic bombing followed this pattern.

UNITED KINGDOM: COMMONWEALTH DAY. Mar 9. Replaces Empire Day observance recognized until 1958. Observed on second Monday in March. Also observed in the British Virgin Islands, Gibraltar and Newfoundland, Canada.

VESPUCCI, AMERIGO: BIRTH ANNIVERSARY. Mar 9, 1454. Italian navigator, merchant and explorer for whom the Americas were named. Born at Florence, Italy (some sources cite his birth year as 1451). He participated in at least two expeditions between 1499 and 1502 which took him to the coast of South America, where he discovered the Amazon and Plata rivers. Vespucci's expeditions were of great importance because he believed that he had discovered a new continent, not just a new route to the Orient. Neither Vespucci nor his exploits achieved the fame of Columbus, but the New World was to be named for Amerigo Vespucci by an obscure German geographer and mapmaker, Martin Waldseemuller. Ironically, in his work as an outfitter of ships, Vespucci had been personally acquainted with Christopher Columbus. Vespucci died at Seville, Spain, Feb 22, 1512. See also: "Waldseemuller, Martin: Remembrance Day" (Apr 25).

WORLD GOLF CHAMPIONSHIPS—CA CHAMPIONSHIP. Mar 9–15. Doral Golf Resort and Spa, Miami, FL. A PGA Tour golf tournament with a full week of events, including outdoor concerts, celebrity pro-ams and the four-day tournament, which features 144 of the top golfers in the world. Est attendance: 200,000. For info: PGA Tour, 100 PGA Tour Blvd, Ponte Vedra Beach, FL 32082. Phone: (904) 285-3700. Web: www.pgatour.com.

Birthdays Today

Juliette Binoche, 45, actress (Oscar for *The English Patient; Chocolat*), born Paris, France, Mar 9, 1964.

Linda Fiorentino, 49, actress (*Men in Black*), born Philadelphia, PA, Mar 9, 1960.

Mickey Gilley, 73, singer, musician, born Natchez, MS, Mar 9, 1936.

Marty Ingels, 73, actor (*A Guide for the Married Man*), born Brooklyn, NY, Mar 9, 1936.

David Hume Kennerly, 62, photographer, born Rosenburg, OR, Mar 9, 1947.

Emmanuel Lewis, 38, actor ("Webster"), born Brooklyn, NY, Mar 9, 1971.

Terence John (Terry) Mulholland, 46, baseball player, born St. Paul, MN, Mar 9, 1963.

Jeffrey Osborne, 61, musician, songwriter, born Providence, RI, Mar 9, 1948.

Benito Santiago, 44, baseball player, born Ponce, Puerto Rico, Mar 9, 1965.

Trish Van Devere, 66, actress (*Where's Poppa?, One Is a Lonely Number*), born Tenafly, NJ, Mar 9, 1943.

Joyce Van Patten, 75, actress (*Monkey Shines*, "The Goodbye Guys"), born Queens, NY, Mar 9, 1934.

March 10 — Tuesday

DAY 69 296 REMAINING

"BUFFY THE VAMPIRE SLAYER" TV PREMIERE: ANNIVERSARY. Mar 10, 1997. The popular WB show mixed B-movie horror with teen drama. Buffy Summers, played by Sarah Michelle Gellar, is a chosen slayer of vampires, but she still has to get through high school. The witty series was a spin-off of the 1992 film of the same name. After changing networks, the series ended in May 2003.

ENGLAND: CHELTENHAM HUNT FESTIVAL. Mar 10–13. Cheltenham Racecourse, Prestbury, Cheltenham, Gloucestershire. Est attendance: 230,000. For info: Cheltenham Racecourse, Prestbury Park, Cheltenham, Gloucestershire, England GL50 4SH. Phone: (44) (1242) 513014 or (44) (1242) 226226. Fax: (44) (1242) 224227. Web: www.cheltenham.co.uk.

"THE INCREDIBLE HULK" TV PREMIERE: ANNIVERSARY. Mar 10, 1978. A wonderfully campy action series based on the popular Marvel comic book as well as a modern-day Jekyll and Hyde story. Bill Bixby played the erudite scientist, Dr. David Banner, who accidentally exposed himself to gamma radiation. When provoked, Banner metamorphosed into the shirt-shredding, body-baring, green-skinned, snarling neanderthal Hulk. The 6′5″, 275-lb former Mr Universe, Lou Ferrigno, played the largely nonspeaking part of the Hulk.

JUPITER EFFECT: ANNIVERSARY. Mar 10, 1982. The much-talked-about and sometimes-feared planetary configuration of a semi-alignment of the planets on the same side of the sun occurred on this date without causing any of the disasters or unusual natural phenomena that some had predicted.

LUCE, CLARE BOOTHE: BIRTH ANNIVERSARY. Mar 10, 1903. Playwright and politician Clare Boothe Luce was born at New York City. Luce wrote for and edited *Vogue* and *Vanity Fair* as well as writing plays, three of which were later adapted into motion pictures—*The Women* (1936), *Kiss the Boys Goodbye* (1938) and *Margin of Error* (1939). She served in the US House of Representatives (1943–47) and as ambassador to Italy (1953–56)—the first woman appointed ambassador to a major country. Luce died Oct 9, 1987, at Washington, DC.

MARIO DAY. Mar 10. A day for all persons named Mario. Using the abbreviation for the month of March, i.e., MAR, with the day, i.e., 10, you get the name spelled out: MAR10. Annually, Mar 10. For info: Mario Fascitelli, 8800 Natalie NE, Albuquerque, NM 87111. Phone: (505) 293-2634. Fax: (505) 323-6333. E-mail: C21Allied@aol.com.

MOON PHASE: FULL MOON. Mar 10. Moon enters Full Moon phase at 10:38 PM, EDT.

ORGANIZE YOUR HOME OFFICE DAY. Mar 10. One day each year for the more than 34 million home office households to find files, purge papers and tackle to-do lists. Annually, the second Tuesday in March. For info: Lisa Kanarek, HomeOfficeLife.com, 660 Preston Forest Ctr, #120, Dallas, TX 75230. Phone: (214) 361-0556. E-mail: info@homeofficelife.com. Web: www.homeofficelife.com.

PURIM. Mar 10. Hebrew calendar date: Adar 14, 5769. Feasts, gifts, charity and the reading of the Book of Esther mark this joyous commemoration of Queen Esther's intervention, in the 6th century BC, to save the Jews of ancient Persia. Haman's plot to exterminate the Jews was thwarted, and he was hanged on the very day he had set for execution of the Jews. Began at sundown Mar 9.

SALVATION ARMY IN THE US: ANNIVERSARY. Mar 10, 1880. Commissioner George Scott Railton and seven women officers landed at New York to officially begin the work of the Salvation Army in the US.

TELEPHONE INVENTION: ANNIVERSARY. Mar 10, 1876. Alexander Graham Bell transmitted the first telephone message to his assistant in the next room: "Mr Watson, come here, I want you," at Cambridge, MA. See also: "Bell, Alexander Graham: Birth Anniversary" (Mar 3).

TUBMAN, HARRIET: DEATH ANNIVERSARY. Mar 10, 1913. American abolitionist, Underground Railroad leader, born a slave at Bucktown, Dorchester County, MD, about 1820 or 1821. She escaped from a Maryland plantation in 1849 and later helped more than 300 slaves reach freedom. Died at Auburn, NY.

US PAPER MONEY ISSUED: ANNIVERSARY. Mar 10, 1862. The first paper money was issued in the US on this date. The denominations were $5 (Hamilton), $10 (Lincoln) and $20 (Liberty). They became legal tender by Act of Mar 17, 1862.

WORM MOON. Mar 10. So called by Native American tribes of New England and the Great Lakes because at this time of year there are signs of earthworms as the ground thaws in preparation for spring. The March Full Moon.

 **Birthdays Today**

Edie Brickell, 43, singer, born Oak Cliff, TX, Mar 10, 1966.

Kim Campbell, 62, first woman prime minister of Canada (for five months in 1993), born Vancouver Island, BC, Canada, Mar 10, 1947.

Prince Edward, 45, son of Queen Elizabeth II, born London, England, Mar 10, 1964.

Bob Greene, 62, journalist, born Columbus, OH, Mar 10, 1947.

Jasmine Guy, 45, singer, actress ("A Different World"), born Boston, MA, Mar 10, 1964.

Jon Hamm, 38, actor ("Mad Men," "The Division"), born St. Louis, MO, Mar 10, 1971.

Shannon Miller, 32, former Olympic gymnast, born Rolla, MO, Mar 10, 1977.

Chuck Norris, 69, actor (*Missing in Action*, "Walker, Texas Ranger"), born Ryan, OK, Mar 10, 1940.

David Rabe, 69, playwright, born Dubuque, IA, Mar 10, 1940.

Sharon Stone, 51, actress (*Basic Instinct, The Specialist, Casino*), born Meadville, PA, Mar 10, 1958.

Shannon Tweed, 52, actress ("Pacific Blue," *Detroit Rock City*), born St. John's, NF, Canada, Mar 10, 1957.

Carrie Underwood, 26, singer ("American Idol"), born Muskogee, OK, Mar 10, 1983.

March 11 — Wednesday

DAY 70 295 REMAINING

BUREAU OF INDIAN AFFAIRS ESTABLISHED: ANNIVERSARY. Mar 11, 1824. The US War Department created the Bureau of Indian Affairs.

CAMPBELL, MALCOLM: BIRTH ANNIVERSARY. Mar 11, 1885. Record-making British auto racer, the first man to travel five miles a minute (300 mph) in an automobile. Born at Chislehurst, Kent, England, Mar 11, 1885. Died at his home at Surrey, England, Dec 31, 1948.

"COPS" TV PREMIERE: 20th ANNIVERSARY. Mar 11, 1989. This long-running gritty series follows real-life cops in departments across the US as they answer calls, patrol, question suspects and make arrests. The handheld camera operators only wear bulletproof vests as they follow the action. The theme song, "Bad Boys," by Inner Circle, is as famous as the show.

DREAM 2009 DAY. Mar 11. To focus attention on the new millennium—so that all humans, nations and institutions devote this year to unparalleled dreams for a better world and thinking, action, inspiration, determination and love to solve the remaining problems and to achieve a peaceful, united human family on Earth. As envisioned by Robert Muller, called the Millennium Man. For info: Barbara Gaughen-Muller, Pres, Gaughen Global Public Relations, 7456 Evergreen Dr, Santa Barbara, CA 93117. Phone: (805) 968-8567. Fax: (805) 968-5747. E-mail: robert@robertmuller.org. Web: www.robertmuller.org and www.goodmorningworld.org.

INDIA: HOLI. Mar 11. In this spring festival people run through the streets throwing brightly hued powders and colored water at each other. This is observed by Indians without regard to caste. Huge bonfires are built on the eve of Holi. Because there is no one universally accepted Hindu calendar, this holiday may be celebrated on a different date in some parts of India but it usually falls in March.

JOHNNY APPLESEED DAY (JOHN CHAPMAN DEATH ANNIVERSARY). Mar 11, 1845. Anniversary of the death of John Chapman, better known as Johnny Appleseed, believed to have been born at Leominster, MA, Sept 26, 1774. The planter of orchards and friend of wild animals was regarded by the Indians as a great medicine man. He died at Allen County, IN. See also: "Appleseed, Johnny: Birth Anniversary" (Sept 26).

LITHUANIA: RESTITUTION OF INDEPENDENCE DAY. Mar 11. National holiday. Commemorates independence from the Soviet Union in 1990. Lithuania had initially declared its independence in 1918 but lost it to the Soviet Union in 1940.

MADRID TRAIN BOMBINGS: 5th ANNIVERSARY. Mar 11, 2004. Ten terrorist bombs exploded on four commuter trains in Spain's busy capital on this date, killing 191 people and injuring 1,800. It was the worst loss of life by violence in Europe since WWII. Nations around the world expressed their sorrow, and demonstrations against terrorism were held in Brussels, Paris, Helsinki, Geneva, Berlin and Stockholm. Spain observed a three-minute period of silence at noon on Mar 15 in order to remember the wounded and slain. Several European countries arrested suspects in the case, and seven militants considered major suspects blew themselves up at Madrid to avoid capture on Apr 3. The terrorists responsible were believed to be allied with Al Qaeda.

***MILWAUKEE JOURNAL SENTINEL* SPORTS SHOW.** Mar 11–15. Milwaukee, WI. Travel and resort exhibits, hunting, fishing, boating, family travel, outdoor recreation. Largest outdoor show in Wisconsin. Est attendance: 150,000. For info: Great Outdoors, LLC, 113 McHenry Rd, #268, Buffalo Grove, IL 60089. Phone: (847) 540-8000 or (800) 472-2070. Fax: (847) 540-8884. E-mail: go2show@msn.com.

March 2009	S	M	T	W	T	F	S
	1	2	3	4	5	6	7
	8	9	10	11	12	13	14
	15	16	17	18	19	20	21
	22	23	24	25	26	27	28
	29	30	31				

NAIA DIVISION II MEN'S BASKETBALL NATIONAL CHAMPIONSHIP. Mar 11–17. Point Lookout, MO. 32-team field competes for the national championship. 18th annual. Est attendance: 30,000. For info: Natl Assn of Intercollegiate Athletics, II MBKB, 1200 Grand Blvd, Kansas City, MO 64106. E-mail: smcclure@naia.org. Web: www.naia.org.

NAIA DIVISION II WOMEN'S BASKETBALL NATIONAL CHAMPIONSHIP. Mar 11–17. Sioux City, IA. 32-team field competes for the national championship. 18th annual. Est attendance: 12,500. For info: Natl Assn of Intercollegiate Athletics, II WBKB, 1200 Grand Blvd, Kansas City, MO 64106. E-mail: balmeida@naia.org. Web: www.naia.org.

NATIONAL COLLEGIATE MEN'S AND WOMEN'S SKIING CHAMPIONSHIPS. Mar 11–14. Bethel/Rumford, ME. Est attendance: 1,500. For info: NCAA, 700 W Washington St, PO Box 6222, Indianapolis, IN 46206-6222. Phone: (317) 917-6222. Fax: (317) 917-6826. Web: www.NCAAsports.com.

PAINE, ROBERT TREAT: BIRTH ANNIVERSARY. Mar 11, 1731. Jurist and signer of the Declaration of Independence. Born at Boston, MA; died there May 11, 1814.

PANDEMIC OF 1918 HITS US: ANNIVERSARY. Mar 11, 1918. The first cases of the "Spanish" influenza were reported in the US when 107 soldiers became sick at Fort Riley, KS. By the end of 1920 nearly 25 percent of the US population had had it. As many as 500,000 civilians died from the virus, exceeding the number of US troops killed abroad in WWI. Worldwide, more than 1 percent of the global population, or 22 million people, had died by 1920. The origin of the virus was never determined absolutely, though it was probably somewhere in Asia. The name "Spanish" influenza came from the relatively high number of cases in that country early in the epidemic. Due to the panic, cancellation of public events was common and many public service workers wore masks on the job. Emergency tent hospitals were set up in some locations due to overcrowding.

REGISTERED DIETITIAN DAY. Mar 11. This day will commemorate the dedication of RDs as advocates for advancing the nutritional status of Americans and people around the world. For info: Sharon Denny, American Dietetic Assn, 120 South Riverside Plaza, #2000, Chicago, IL 60606. Phone: (312) 899-4854. Fax: (312) 899-4845. E-mail: sdenny@eatright.org. Web: www.eatright.org.

TASSO, TORQUATO: BIRTH ANNIVERSARY. Mar 11, 1544. Poet of the late Renaissance, born at Sorrento, Italy. His violent outbursts and acute sensitivity to criticism led to his imprisonment for seven years, during which the "misunderstood genius" continued his literary creativity. Died at Rome, Italy, Apr 25, 1595.

TURKEY VULTURES RETURN TO THE LIVING SIGN. Mar 11–17. Entire Canisteo Valley, Canisteo, NY. Traditionally turkey vultures return on St. Pat's Day to their roosting sites in and around the world-famous living sign, as mentioned in "Ripley's Believe It or Not." The sign spells out "Canisteo" using 250 trees in a ridge above Greenwood Street. For info: Bill Berry, 6950 Lain Rd, Hornell, NY 14843-9419. Phone: (607) 324-1086. E-mail: thepaperwolf@gmail.com.

WELK, LAWRENCE: BIRTH ANNIVERSARY. Mar 11, 1903. Bandleader Lawrence Welk was born at Strasburg, ND. He learned to play the accordion and at 17 formed his first band. After playing all over the Midwest, he moved to Los Angeles where in 1955 his show began its nationwide television broadcast of "Champagne Music." The longest-running primetime program in TV history, "The Lawrence Welk Show" played each Saturday evening on ABC from 1955 until 1971 when it was dropped because sponsors thought its audience was too old. Welk kept the show on a network of more than 250 independent stations for 11 more years and it still can be seen in reruns. Welk's entertainment empire included the purchase of royalty rights to songs, including the entire collection of songs by Jerome Kern. Welk died at Santa Monica, CA, May 17, 1992.

WILSON, HAROLD: BIRTH ANNIVERSARY. Mar 11, 1916. British statesman and twice prime minister (1964–70 and 1974–76), leader of the Labour Party. Born at Huddersfield, Yorkshire. He died May 24, 1995, at London.

 **Birthdays Today**

Elton Brand, 30, basketball player, born Peekskill, NY, Mar 11, 1979.

Curtis Brown, Jr, 53, astronaut, born Elizabethtown, NC, Mar 11, 1956.

Sam Donaldson, 75, journalist, born El Paso, TX, Mar 11, 1934.

Didier Drogba, 31, soccer player, born Abidjan, Ivory Coast, Mar 11, 1978.

Terrence Howard, 40, actor (*Hustle & Flow, Get Rich or Die Tryin'*), born Chicago, IL, Mar 11, 1969.

Alex Kingston, 46, actress ("ER"), born London, England, Mar 11, 1963.

Bobby McFerrin, 59, jazz musician, singer, songwriter, conductor, born New York, NY, Mar 11, 1950.

Rupert Murdoch, 78, media executive, born Melbourne, Australia, Mar 11, 1931.

Dominique Sanda, 58, actress (*The Garden of the Finzi-Continis, 1900*), born Paris, France, Mar 11, 1951 (some sources say 1948).

Antonin Scalia, 73, Associate Justice of the US Supreme Court, born Trenton, NJ, Mar 11, 1936.

Jerry Zucker, 59, writer, (*Naked Gun* movies with brother David), producer (*Airplane!*), born Milwaukee, WI, Mar 11, 1950.

March 12 — Thursday

DAY 71 — 294 REMAINING

ATATÜRK, MUSTAFA KEMAL: BIRTH ANNIVERSARY. Mar 12, 1881. The founder of modern Turkey was born at Salonika, Greece (then part of the Ottoman Empire). After a distinguished army career, he led the Turkish revolution after WWI and was elected Turkey's first president. He died at Istanbul, Nov 10, 1938.

AUSTRIA INVADED BY NAZI GERMANY: ANNIVERSARY. Mar 12, 1938. As a test of its own war readiness and of the response of the other major powers, Germany occupied Austria. A year later Germany invaded Czechoslovakia and, in September 1939, Poland, beginning WWII.

BERMUDA COLONIZED BY ENGLISH: 400th ANNIVERSARY. Mar 12, 1609. The ship of Admiral Sir George Somers, taking settlers to Virginia, was wrecked on the reefs of Bermuda. The islands had been discovered in the early 1500s but were uninhabited until 1609.

BIG TEN MEN'S BASKETBALL TOURNAMENT. Mar 12–15. Conseco Fieldhouse, Indianapolis, IN. For info: Big Ten Conference, 1500 W Higgins Rd, Park Ridge, IL 60068-6300. Phone: (847) 696-1010. Fax: (847) 696-1110. Web: www.bigten.org.

BOYCOTT, CHARLES CUNNINGHAM: BIRTH ANNIVERSARY. Mar 12, 1832. Charles Cunningham Boycott, born at Norfolk, England, has been immortalized by having his name become part of the English language. In County Mayo, Ireland, the Tenants' "Land League" in 1880 asked Boycott, an estate agent, to reduce rents (because of poor harvest and dire economic conditions). Boycott responded by serving eviction notices on the tenants, who retaliated by refusing to have any dealings with him. Charles Stewart Parnell, then president of the National Land League and agrarian agitator, retaliated against Boycott by formulating and implementing the method of economic and social ostracism that came to be called a "boycott." Boycott died at Suffolk, England, June 19, 1897.

CANADA: QUEBEC CITY HUNTING, FISHING, CAMPING AND BOAT SHOW. Mar 12–15. Centre de foires d'ExpoCitè, Quebec City. Major manufacturers, distributors and retailers of the outdoors, including camping, fishing and hunting, marine (fishing boats, canoes, kayaks and other craft), tourism offices, outfitters (lodges) and entertainment. Est attendance: 36,000. For info: Canadian National Sportsmen's Shows, 8150 Metropolitan Blvd E, Ste 330, Anjou, Montreal, QC, Canada H1K 1A1. Phone: (514) 866-5409 or (418) 622-8118. Fax: (514) 866-4092. Web: www.sportshows.ca or www.salonshassepeche.ca.

CHURCH OF ENGLAND ORDAINS WOMEN PRIESTS: 15th ANNIVERSARY. Mar 12, 1994. The Church of England for the first time ordained 32 women at Bristol Cathedral. About 700 male members of the clergy and unknown thousands of members indicated they would leave the Church of England and join the Roman Catholic Church. The Catholic Church responded to the ordination by saying that it "constitutes a profound obstacle to every hope of reunion between the Catholic Church and the Anglican Communion." This day's ordinations were not the first. In early 1994 about 1,380 women priests were ordained in churches of the Anglican Communion outside of Great Britain.

FDR'S FIRST FIRESIDE CHAT: ANNIVERSARY. Mar 12, 1933. President Franklin Delano Roosevelt made the first of his Sunday evening "fireside chats" to the American people. Speaking by radio from the White House, he reported rather informally on the economic problems of the nation and on his actions to deal with them.

GABON: NATIONAL DAY. Mar 12. Observes founding of Gabonese Democratic Party on Mar 12, 1968.

GIRL SCOUTS OF THE USA FOUNDING: ANNIVERSARY. Mar 12, 1912. Juliette Low founded the Girl Scouts of the USA at Savannah, GA.

GREAT BLIZZARD OF '88: ANNIVERSARY. Mar 12, 1888. One of the most devastating blizzards to hit the northeastern US began in the early hours of Monday, Mar 12, 1888. A snowfall of 40–50 inches, accompanied by gale-force winds, left drifts as high as 30–40 feet. More than 400 persons died in the storm (200 at New York City alone). Some survivors of the storm, "The Blizzard Men of 1888," held annual meetings at New York City as late as 1941 to recount personal recollections of the event.

KEROUAC, JACK: BIRTH ANNIVERSARY. Mar 12, 1922. American poet and novelist Jack (Jean-Louis) Kerouac, leader and spokesman for the Beat movement, was born at Lowell, MA. Kerouac is best known for his novel *On the Road*, published in 1957, which celebrates the Beat ideal of nonconformity. Kerouac published *The Dharma Bums* in 1958, followed by *The Subterraneans* the same year, *Doctor Sax* and its sequel *Maggie Cassidy* in 1959, *Lonesome Traveler* in 1960, *Big Sur* in 1962 and *Desolation Angels* in 1965. Kerouac died at St. Petersburg, FL, at age 47, Oct 21, 1969. A previously unpublished part of *On the Road* called *Visions of Cody* was published posthumously in 1972.

LESOTHO: MOSHOESHOE'S DAY. Mar 12. National holiday. Commemorates the great leader Chief Moshoeshoe I, who unified the Basotho people, beginning in 1820.

MAURITIUS: INDEPENDENCE DAY: ANNIVERSARY. Mar 12. National holiday commemorates attainment of independent nationhood (within the British Commonwealth) on Mar 12, 1968.

NEWCOMB, SIMON: BIRTH ANNIVERSARY. Mar 12, 1835. Astronomer, born at Wallace, NS, Canada. Newcomb investigated the orbits of Uranus, Neptune and the inner planets and devised planetary tables that were used universally by observatories. Died at Washington, DC, July 11, 1909.

PIERCE, JANE MEANS APPLETON: BIRTH ANNIVERSARY. Mar 12, 1806. Wife of Franklin Pierce, 14th president of the US. Born at Hampton, NH. Died at Concord, NH, Dec 2, 1863.

SCHIRRA, WALLY: BIRTH ANNIVERSARY. Mar 12, 1923. One of the original seven *Mercury* astronauts, born Walter Marty Schirra,

Jr, at Hackensack, NJ. A US Navy pilot during WWII and the Korean conflict, Schirra entered the US space program in 1959. He was the only man to fly all three of the first manned space missions (*Mercury, Gemini* and *Apollo*), logging a total 295 hours, 15 minutes in space. He won an Emmy Award for the footage he sent back from *Apollo 7*, the first televised pictures from space, and later worked with Walter Cronkite on broadcasts of other NASA missions. He died at La Jolla, CA, May 3, 2007.

SPAIN: FIESTA DE LAS FALLAS. Mar 12–19. Valencia. This festival of burning effigies and fireworks has been celebrated for more than 150 years.

SUN YAT-SEN: DEATH ANNIVERSARY. Mar 12, 1925. The heroic leader of China's 1911 revolution is remembered on the anniversary of his death at Peking, China. Observed as Arbor Day in Taiwan.

WORLD KIDNEY DAY. Mar 12. The purpose of this day is to raise awareness about the importance of our kidneys—amazing organs that play a crucial role in keeping us alive and well—and to spread the message that kidney disease is common, harmful and treatable. Observed since 2006 by 65 countries. Annually, the second Thursday of March. For info: World Kidney Day, Ave de Tervueren, 300, B-1150 Brussels, Belgium. Phone: (32) (2) 743-4411. Fax: (32) (2) 743-1550. E-mail: info@worldkidneyday.org. Web: www.worldkidneyday.org.

Birthdays Today

Edward Albee, 81, playwright, born Washington, DC, Mar 12, 1928.

Rob Cohen, 60, producer (*Bird on a Wire*), director (*Dragonheart*), born Cornwall-on-Hudson, NY, Mar 12, 1949.

Kent Conrad, 61, US Senator (D, North Dakota), born Bismarck, ND, Mar 12, 1948.

Aaron Eckhart, 41, actor (*Thank You for Smoking, The Black Dahlia*), born Cupertino, CA, Mar 12, 1968.

Barbara Feldon, 68, actress ("Get Smart," *Smile*), born Pittsburgh, PA, Mar 12, 1941.

Marlon Jackson, 52, singer (Jackson 5), born Gary, IN, Mar 12, 1957.

Al (Alwin) Jarreau, 69, singer, songwriter, born Milwaukee, WI, Mar 12, 1940.

Liza Minnelli, 63, singer, actress (Oscar for *Cabaret*; *The Sterile Cuckoo, Arthur*), born Los Angeles, CA, Mar 12, 1946.

Raul Mondesi, 38, baseball player, born San Cristobal, Dominican Republic, Mar 12, 1971.

Dale Murphy, 53, former baseball player, born Portland, OR, Mar 12, 1956.

Mitt Romney, 62, former Governor of Massachusetts (R), born Detroit, MI, Mar 12, 1947.

Darryl Strawberry, 47, former baseball player, born Los Angeles, CA, Mar 12, 1962.

James Taylor, 61, singer, musician ("You've Got a Friend," "Handy Man"), born Boston, MA, Mar 12, 1948.

Andrew Young, 77, civil rights leader, former mayor of Atlanta, GA, born New Orleans, LA, Mar 12, 1932.

March 2009

S	M	T	W	T	F	S
1	2	3	4	5	6	7
8	9	10	11	12	13	14
15	16	17	18	19	20	21
22	23	24	25	26	27	28
29	30	31				

March 13 — Friday

DAY 72 **293 REMAINING**

ANNENBERG, WALTER: BIRTH ANNIVERSARY. Mar 13, 1908. Publisher, philanthropist and ambassador, Walter Annenberg was born at Milwaukee, WI. He inherited *The Philadelphia Inquirer* from his father and built the newspaper into the cornerstone of a publishing empire that included newspapers, magazines and radio and television stations. He founded many enduring publications, including *Seventeen* (1944) and *TV Guide* (1953). He served as US ambassador to the United Kingdom 1969–76. As a philanthropist, Annenberg gave billions to charities. He died at Wynnewood, PA, on Oct 1, 2002.

ARAB OIL EMBARGO LIFTED: 35th ANNIVERSARY. Mar 13, 1974. The oil-producing Arab countries agreed to lift their five-month embargo on petroleum sales to the US. During the embargo prices went up 300 percent and a ban was imposed on Sunday gasoline sales. The embargo was in retaliation for US support of Israel during the October 1973 Middle East War.

CAMEX. Mar 13–17. Anaheim, CA. The only national conference and trade exhibit designed exclusively for collegiate retailers. College store buyers and suppliers gather at CAMEX to preview products to be seen on college campuses in the coming year. Est attendance: 7,000. For info: Jennifer Libertowski, Public Relations Specialist, Natl Assn of College Stores (NACS), 500 E Lorain St, Oberlin, OH 44074. Phone: (440) 775-7777 or (800) 622-7498. E-mail: jlibertowski@nacs.org. Web: www.camex.org.

CLARENCE DARROW DEATH COMMEMORATION. Mar 13. Jackson Park, Chicago, IL. Annually, on the anniversary of his death, a wreath is tossed from the Jackson Park Clarence Darrow Bridge, named in honor of the famed lawyer and civil libertarian at 10 AM. At 11 AM a discussion follows in the Columbian Room of the Museum of Science and Industry, Chicago. Est attendance: 100. For info: Herb Kraus, 333 N Michigan Ave, Ste 2032, Chicago, IL 60601. Phone: (312) 578-9114. Fax: (312) 726-9520.

CRAFTSMEN'S CLASSIC ARTS & CRAFTS FESTIVAL. Mar 13–15. Richmond Raceway Complex (formerly Virginia State Fairgrounds), Richmond, VA. 25th annual. Features work from more than 410 talented artists and craftspeople. All juried exhibitors' work has been handmade by the exhibitors and must be their own original design and creation. See the creative process in action with several exhibitors demonstrating throughout the weekend. Something for every style, taste and budget with items from the most contemporary to the most traditional. Est attendance: 20,000. For info: Gilmore Enterprises, Inc, 3514-A Drawbridge Pkwy, Greensboro, NC 27410-8584. Phone: (336) 282-5550. E-mail: contact@gilmoreshows.com. Web: www.CraftShow.com or www.gilmoreshows.com.

DEAF HISTORY MONTH. Mar 13–Apr 15. Observance of three of the most important anniversaries for deaf Americans: Apr 15, 1817, establishment of the first public school for the deaf in America, later known as The American School for the Deaf; Apr 8, 1864, charter signed by President Lincoln authorizing the Board of Directors of the Columbia Institution (now Gallaudet University) to grant college degrees to deaf students; Mar 13, 1988, the victory of the Deaf President Now movement at Gallaudet. For info: Natl Literary Society of the Deaf, 2930 Craiglawn Rd, Silver Spring, MD 20904-1816. Web: www.folda.net/nlsd.

DELMONICO, LORENZO: BIRTH ANNIVERSARY. Mar 13, 1813. Famed restaurateur and gastronomic authority. Born at Marengo, Switzerland. Operated a number of restaurants at New York, NY, where he died, Sept 3, 1881.

EARMUFFS PATENTED: ANNIVERSARY. Mar 13, 1887. Chester Greenwood of Maine received a patent for earmuffs.

FILLMORE, ABIGAIL POWERS: BIRTH ANNIVERSARY. Mar 13, 1798. First wife of Millard Fillmore, 13th president of the US. Born at Stillwater, NY. It is said that the White House was without any books until Abigail Fillmore, formerly a teacher, made a room on the second floor into a library. Within a year, Congress appropriated $250 for the president to spend on books for the White House. Died at Washington, DC, Mar 30, 1853.

GOOD SAMARITAN INVOLVEMENT DAY. Mar 13. A day to emphasize the importance of unselfish aid to those who need it. Recognized on the anniversary of the killing of Catherine (Kitty) Genovese, Mar 13, 1964, in the Kew Gardens community, Queens, NY. Reportedly no fewer than 38 of her neighbors, not wanting "to get involved," witnessed and watched for nearly 30 minutes as the fleeing girl was pursued and repeatedly stabbed by her 29-year-old attacker.

HUBBARD, L. RON: BIRTH ANNIVERSARY. Mar 13, 1911. Lafayette Ronald Hubbard, science fiction writer, recluse and founder of the Church of Scientology, was born at Tilden, NE. His best-known book was *Dianetics: The Modern Science of Mental Health*. Died at San Luis Obispo County, CA, Jan 24, 1986.

"THE LARRY KING SHOW" TV PREMIERE: ANNIVERSARY. Mar 13, 1983. Radio talk-show host Larry King brought his topical interview program to syndicated TV in 1983. Using a telephone hookup, viewers called in to speak to particular guests. King has been appearing on CNN since 1985 interviewing a variety of newsmakers and celebrities.

LOWELL, PERCIVAL: BIRTH ANNIVERSARY. Mar 13, 1855. American astronomer, founder of the Lowell Observatory at Flagstaff, AZ. Born at Boston, MA, he died at Flagstaff, Nov 12, 1916. Lowell was initiator of the search that resulted (25 years after the search began and 14 years after his death) in discovery of Pluto. The discovery was announced on Lowell's birthday, Mar 13, 1930, by the Lowell Observatory.

MICHIGAN HOME AND GARDEN SHOW AT FORD FIELD. Mar 13–15. Ford Field, Detroit, MI. Products and services for home building/remodeling, home furnishings and interior design, lawn and garden and related areas. On-site constructions, theme gardens, seminars and demonstrations, plus The Standard Flower Show sponsored by Michigan Garden Clubs, Inc. Est attendance: 20,000. For info: Mike Wilbraham, ShowSpan, Inc, 2121 Celebration Dr NE, Grand Rapids, MI 49525. Phone: (616) 447-2860. Fax: (616) 447-2861. E-mail: events@showspan.com. Web: www.showspan.com.

NATIONAL MONEY SHOW. Mar 13–15. Oregon Convention Center, Portland, OR. Numismatic education programs, exhibits and family activities. Buy, sell and trade coins, paper money, medals and tokens. For info: American Numismatic Assn, 818 N Cascade Ave, Colorado Springs, CO 80903. Phone: (800) 367-9723. E-mail: pr@money.org. Web: www.money.org.

NATIONAL OPEN AN UMBRELLA INDOORS DAY. Mar 13. The purpose of this day is for people to open umbrellas indoors and note whether they have any bad luck. Annually, Mar 13. For info: Thomas Edward Knibb, 1450 Key Pkwy, #101, Frederick, MD 21702-3703. E-mail: tomknibb@juno.com.

NCAA DIVISION I MEN'S & WOMEN'S INDOOR TRACK AND FIELD CHAMPIONSHIPS. Mar 13–14. College Station, TX. Annually, the second weekend in March. Est attendance: 7,000. For info: NCAA, 700 W Washington St, PO Box 6222, Indianapolis, IN 46206-6222. Phone: (317) 917-6222. Fax: (317) 917-6826. Web: www.NCAAsports.com.

NETHERLANDS: THE EUROPEAN FINE ART FAIR (MAASTRICHT 2009). Mar 13–22. MECC, Maastricht. Old Master paintings, antiques, textile arts, modern paintings and sculptures, antiquities, books and prints. Annually, in March. Est attendance: 75,000. For info: The European Fine Art Foundation, Broekwal 64, 5268 HD Helvoirt, The Netherlands. Phone: (31) (41) 645090. E-mail: info@tefaf.com. Web: www.tefaf.com.

OPERATION FLASH: ANNIVERSARY. Mar 13, 1943. Disillusioned German officers planned to take the life of Adolf Hitler on this date. Hitler was to stop at Smolensk on his way to his headquarters and an officer who was not involved in the plot had been commissioned to deliver a package to Hitler's plane, which he was told contained two bottles of liquor for a friend in Rastenburg. A bomb in the package was timed to go off over Minsk, but it reached Rastenburg without detonating. The package was later recovered and a defective detonator was found. See also: "Gersdorff Hitler Assassination Attempt: Anniversary" (Mar 21).

PLANET URANUS DISCOVERY: ANNIVERSARY. Mar 13, 1781. German-born English astronomer Sir William Herschel discovered the seventh planet from the sun, Uranus.

PRIESTLY, JOSEPH: BIRTH ANNIVERSARY. Mar 13, 1733. (Old Style date.) English clergyman and scientist, discoverer of oxygen, born at Fieldhead, England. He and his family narrowly escaped an angry mob attacking their home because of his religious and political views. They moved to the US in 1794. Died at Northumberland, PA, Feb 6, 1804.

RIO GRANDE VALLEY LIVESTOCK SHOW. Mar 13–22. Mercedes, TX. 70th annual. PRCA rodeo, open cattle show and carnival. For the youth of the four counties in the valley to exhibit their projects. Est attendance: 200,000. For info: Sam Magee, Rio Grande Valley Livestock Show Inc, Box 867, Mercedes, TX 78570. Phone: (956) 565-2456. Fax: (956) 565-3005. E-mail: info@rgvlivestockshow.com. Web: www.rgvlivestockshow.com.

SAINT AUBIN, HELEN "CALLAGHAN" CANDAELE: 80th BIRTH ANNIVERSARY. Mar 13, 1929. Helen Candaele Saint Aubin, known as Helen Callaghan during her baseball days, was born at Vancouver, BC, Canada. Saint Aubin and her sister, Margaret Maxwell, were recruited for the All-American Girls Professional Baseball League, which flourished in the 1940s when many major league players were off fighting WWII. She first played at age 15 for the Minneapolis Millerettes, an expansion team that moved to Indiana and became the Fort Wayne Daisies. For the 1945 season the left-handed outfielder led the league with a .299 average and 24 extra base hits. In 1946 she stole 114 bases in 111 games. Her son Kelly Candaele's documentary on the women's baseball league inspired the film *A League of Their Own*. Saint Aubin, known as the "Ted Williams of women's baseball," died Dec 8, 1992, at Santa Barbara, CA.

SOUTH BY SOUTHWEST (SXSW). Mar 13–22. Austin, TX. Annual, internationally recognized music, new media and film conference. Hundreds of music, film and interactive events and panels. Est attendance: 40,000. For info: SXSW Headquarters, Box 4999, Austin, TX 78765. Phone: (512) 467-7979. Fax: (512) 451-0754. E-mail: sxsw@sxsw.com. Web: www.sxsw.com.

SUGARLOAF CRAFTS FESTIVAL. Mar 13–15. Garden State Exhibit Center, Somerset, NJ. This show, now in its 16th year, features 300 nationally recognized craft designers and fine artists displaying and selling their original creations. Includes craft demonstrations, live music, specialty foods, children's entertainment, hourly gift certificate drawings and more! Est attendance: 16,000. For info: Sugarloaf Mountain Works, 200 Orchard Ridge Dr, #215, Gaithersburg, MD 20878. Phone: (800) 210-9900. Fax: (301) 253-9620. Web: www.SugarloafCrafts.com.

VIRGINIA SPRING SHOW. Mar 13–15. Showplace Exhibition Center, Richmond, VA. 22nd annual. Features hundreds of artisans and craftspeople, specialty food shops, boutiques and spring entertainment. Holiday Cooking Theatre. Est attendance: 25,000. For info: Virginia Show Productions, PO Box 305, Chase City, VA 23924. Phone: (434) 372-3996. Fax: (434) 372-3410. E-mail: vashowsinc@aol.com. Web: www.vashowsinc.com.

WORLD'S LARGEST RATTLESNAKE ROUNDUP. Mar 13–15. Sweetwater, TX. 51st annual. Educational programs about rattlesnakes; flea market; gun, knife and coin show; Texas's second largest cook-off; dances; numerous pounds of live rattlesnakes on display; snake meat available to eat and snake articles for sale. Snake hunts and bus tours available. More than 750 booth spaces are available. Annually, the second weekend in March. Est attendance: 30,000. For info: Sweetwater Chamber of Commerce, PO Box 1148, Sweetwater, TX 79556. Phone: (325) 235-5488 or (800) 658-6757. Fax: (325) 235-1026. E-mail: chamber@sweetwatertexas.org. Web: www.sweetwatertexas.org or rattlesnakeroundup.net.

YO-YO AND SKILL TOY CONVENTION. Mar 13–22. Spinning Top Museum, Burlington, WI. 14th annual. Featuring an exhibition of more than 2,000 yo-yos, plus videos, demonstration of classic yo-yo tricks and an I Spy hunt. Mar 15 is Gizmo Day with science and action toys for families, and the weekend of Mar 21–22 features old-fashioned yo-yo contests, juggling, a hula hoop contest, paddleball marathon and the Worldwide Yo-Yo Contests with prizes and awesome yo-yo shows. Learn Walk-the-Dog, Rock-the-Baby, Boingy-Boingy and more! All events are for both participants and spectators, and are sponsored by the American Yo-Yo Association. For info: Spinning Top & Yo-Yo Museum, 533 Milwaukee Ave (Hwy 36), Burlington, WI 53105. Phone: (262) 763-3946. E-mail: thetopmuseum@hotmail.com. Web: www.topmuseum.org.

 Birthdays Today

Thomas Andrew (Andy) Bean, 56, golfer, born Lafayette, GA, Mar 13, 1953.

Caron Butler, 29, basketball player, born Racine, WI, Mar 13, 1980.

Charo, 58, singer, actress ("Chico and the Man"), born Maria Martinez at Murcia, Spain, Mar 13, 1951.

Adam Clayton, 49, musician (U2), born Dublin, Ireland, Mar 13, 1960.

Dana Delany, 53, actress ("Desperate Housewives," "China Beach," *Moon Over Parador*), born New York, NY, Mar 13, 1956.

Glenne Headly, 52, actress (*The Purple Rose of Cairo, Dick Tracy, Mortal Thoughts*), born New London, CT, Mar 13, 1957 (some sources say 1955).

Emile Hirsch, 24, actor (*Speed Racer, Into the Wild, Alpha Dog*), born Palms, CA, Mar 13, 1985.

John Hoeven, 52, Governor of North Dakota (R), born Bismarck, ND, Mar 13, 1957.

William H. Macy, 59, actor (*Door to Door, Fargo, Pleasantville, Boogie Nights*, "ER"), born Miami, FL, Mar 13, 1950.

Deborah Raffin, 56, actress ("Foul Play"), born Los Angeles, CA, Mar 13, 1953.

Neil Sedaka, 70, singer, songwriter ("Breaking Up Is Hard to Do," with Howard Greenfield), born Brooklyn, NY, Mar 13, 1939.

March 2009

S	M	T	W	T	F	S
1	2	3	4	5	6	7
8	9	10	11	12	13	14
15	16	17	18	19	20	21
22	23	24	25	26	27	28
29	30	31				

March 14 — Saturday

DAY 73 **292 REMAINING**

CANADA: MAPLE FESTIVAL OF NOVA SCOTIA. Mar 14–Apr 11 (Saturdays only). Northern Nova Scotia. Promotion of the maple industry. Pancake suppers with entertainment, industry equipment displays and crafts displays. Est attendance: 5,000. For info: Lorna A. Crowe, RR1, Southampton, Cumberland County, NS, Canada B0M 1W0. Phone: (902) 546-2844. Web: www.novascotiamaplesyrup.com.

EINSTEIN, ALBERT: BIRTH ANNIVERSARY. Mar 14, 1879. Theoretical physicist best known for his theory of relativity. Born at Ulm, Germany, he won the Nobel Prize in 1921. Died at Princeton, NJ, Apr 18, 1955.

HIGHLAND COUNTY MAPLE FESTIVAL. Mar 14–15 (also Mar 21–22). Highland County, VA. 51st annual. Festival welcomes visitors to view the process of syrup making. Large arts and crafts shows and antiques. Est attendance: 50,000. For info: Highland County Chamber of Commerce, PO Box 223, Monterey, VA 24465. Phone: (540) 468-2550. Fax: (540) 468-2551. E-mail: highcc@cfw.com. Web: www.highlandcounty.org.

INDIANA FLOWER AND PATIO SHOW. Mar 14–22. Indiana State Fairgrounds, Indianapolis, IN. The oldest show of its kind in the Midwest, featuring more than 30 landscaped gardens and products and services for home, yard and patio. Est attendance: 106,000. For info: HSI Show Productions, Box 502797, Indianapolis, IN 46250. Phone: (317) 576-9933. Fax: (317) 576-9955. Web: www.hsishows.com.

INTERNATIONAL ASK A QUESTION DAY. Mar 14. A day to promote critical thinking/collaborative conversation in education, science and research, business, politics, community, family and relationships. Annually, Mar 14. For info: Marilee Adams, Inquiry Institute, PO Box 339, Lambertville, NJ 08530. Phone: (609) 397-9100. Fax: (609) 397-2998. E-mail: Marilee@InquiryInstitute.com. Web: www.questionday.com.

INTERNATIONAL DAY OF THE SEAL CELEBRATION. Mar 14. Jenkinson's Aquarium, Point Pleasant Beach, NJ. Learn all about seals and help us celebrate our seals' birthdays! Seals are fed at 10 AM, 1 PM and 4 PM. Free activities with paid admission from 1–4 PM. Est attendance: 600. For info: Jenkinson's Aquarium, 300 Ocean Ave, Point Pleasant Beach, NJ 08742. Phone: (732) 899-1212. Fax: (732) 899-1717. E-mail: jenkinsonsaquarium@comcast.net. Web: www.jenkinsons.com.

INTERNATIONAL FANNY PACK DAY. Mar 14. Over the centuries a form of the fanny pack has been used to carry items for easy access. On Mar 8, 2008, more than fifty people came together in Boise, ID, to pay tribute to this fashion essential, but 2009 marks the moment for international celebration. Annually, the second Saturday in March. For info: Nick Yates, International Fanny Pack Day, 6614 W Baron Dr, Boise, ID 83714. Phone: (208) 863-1414. E-mail: yates_nick@hotmail.com.

JONES, CASEY: BIRTH ANNIVERSARY. Mar 14, 1864. Railroad engineer and hero of ballad, whose real name was John Luther Jones. Born near Cayce, KY, he died in a railroad wreck near Vaughn, MS, Apr 30, 1900.

MARSHALL, THOMAS RILEY: BIRTH ANNIVERSARY. Mar 14, 1854. 28th vice president of the US (1913–21). Born at North Manchester, IN, he died at Washington, DC, June 1, 1925.

MOTH-ER DAY. Mar 14. A day set aside to honor moth collectors and specialists. Celebrated in museums or libraries with moth collections. For info: Bob Birch, Puns Corps Grand Punscorpion, 3108 Dashiell Rd, Falls Church, VA 22042. Phone: (703) 533-3668.

NATIONAL TOAD HOLLOW WEEK. Mar 14–21. A community outreach program encouraging people to nourish their imagination, pursue their dreams and practice old-fashioned values in their relationships with others. For info: Ralph Morrison, Director, Toad Hollow, PO Box 2132, Garden City, MI 48135. Phone: (800) 574-8623.

PI DAY. Mar 14. A day to celebrate pi—the ratio of a circle's circumference to its diameter. Since that mathematical constant is about 3.14, Mar 14 became the day to observe it.

SAINT PATRICK'S DAY PARADE. Mar 14. Downtown Hornell, NY. 22nd annual. It's a "come as you are" line of march, open to anyone, with no entry fee, no judges, no prizes. Hornell's parade is designed as purely a fun affair, especially for those people who've always wanted to be in a parade but never had the opportunity. It's larger and longer every year, with more and more "would-be Irish" strolling down Main Street. Est attendance: 5,000. For info: Wolf Berry, 6950 Lain Rd, Hornell, NY 14843-9419. Phone: (607) 324-1086. E-mail: thepaperwolf@gmail.com. Web: www.hornellradio.com.

SAINT PATRICK'S DAY PARADE: "THE WEARIN' OF THE GREEN." Mar 14. Baton Rouge, LA. 24th annual parade includes floats, precision marching bands and bagpipers. Largest St. Patrick's Day celebration in the region rolls through historic Hundred Oaks area in the heart of the city starting at 10 AM. Est attendance: 135,000. For info: Parade Group, LLC, 6906 Moniteau Ct, Baton Rouge, LA 70809. Phone: (225) 925-8295. Fax: (225) 925-8295. E-mail: mabyn@futurebound.com or irishclub@futurebound.com. Web: www.paradegroup.com.

SEOUL RECAPTURED BY UN FORCES: ANNIVERSARY. Mar 14, 1951. Seoul, Korea, which had fallen to Chinese forces in January 1951, was retaken by United Nations troops during the Korean War.

TAYLOR, LUCY HOBBS: BIRTH ANNIVERSARY. Mar 14, 1833. Lucy Beaman Hobbs, first woman in America to receive a degree in dentistry (Ohio College of Dental Surgery, 1866) and to be admitted to membership in a state dental association. Born at Franklin County, NY. In 1867 she married James M. Taylor, who also became a dentist (after she instructed him in the essentials). Active women's rights advocate. Died at Lawrence, KS, Oct 3, 1910.

"10 MOST WANTED" LIST DEBUTS: ANNIVERSARY. Mar 14, 1950. The Federal Bureau of Investigation instituted the "10 Most Wanted Fugitives" list in an effort to publicize particularly dangerous criminals who were at large. From 1950 to 2007, 487 fugitives have appeared on the list; 457 have been located. Generally, the only way to get off the list is to die or be captured. The FBI cooperates with the producers of TV's "America's Most Wanted" to further publicize these fugitives.

Birthdays Today

Frank Borman, 81, former astronaut, airline executive, born Gary, IN, Mar 14, 1928.

Michael Caine, 76, actor (Oscars for *The Cider House Rules* and *Hannah and Her Sisters*), born Maurice Micklewhite, London, England, Mar 14, 1933.

Tom Coburn, 61, US Senator (R, Oklahoma), born Casper, WY, Mar 14, 1948.

Billy Crystal, 62, actor ("Soap," *When Harry Met Sally . . ., City Slickers*), born Long Beach, NY, Mar 14, 1947.

Rick Dees, 58, disc jockey, comedian, born Jacksonville, FL, Mar 14, 1951.

Bobby Jenks, 28, baseball player, born Mission Hills, CA, Mar 14, 1981.

Quincy Jones, 76, composer, producer, born Chicago, IL, Mar 14, 1933.

Grace Park, 35, actress ("Battlestar Galactica"), born Los Angeles, CA, Mar 14, 1974.

Tamara Tunie, 50, actress ("24," "Law & Order: SVU," "As the World Turns"), born McKeesport, PA, Mar 14, 1959.

Rita Tushingham, 67, actress (*Dr. Zhivago, A Taste of Honey*), born Liverpool, England, Mar 14, 1942.

March 15 — Sunday

DAY 74 — 291 REMAINING

BELARUS: CONSTITUTION DAY. Mar 15. National holiday. Commemorates the adoption of the constitution on Mar 15, 1994.

BRUTUS DAY. Mar 15. No matter where you work, you must admit there's as much intrigue, plotting and backstabbing as was found in ancient Rome or is found today inside the Washington Beltway. (©2006 by WH.) For info: Thomas & Ruth Roy, Wellcat Holidays, 2418 Long Ln, Lebanon, PA 17046. Phone: (717) 279-0184. E-mail: info@wellcat.com. Web: www.wellcat.com.

"EIGHT IS ENOUGH" TV PREMIERE: ANNIVERSARY. Mar 15, 1977. This one-hour comedy-drama was set in Sacramento and starred Dick Van Patten as Tom Bradford, a columnist for a local paper and a widower with eight children. Diana Hyland played his wife, Joan; she died from cancer after filming five shows. The children were played by Grant Goodeve, Lani O'Grady, Laurie Walters, Susan Richardson, Dianne Kay, Connie Needham, Willie Aames and Adam Rich. In the fall of 1977 Betty Buckley joined the cast as tutor Abby Abbott, who later married Tom. Most of the cast was reunited for Tom's 50th birthday on "Eight Is Enough: A Family Reunion" shown on Oct 18, 1987.

***THE GODFATHER* FILM PREMIERE: ANNIVERSARY.** Mar 15, 1972. Francis Ford Coppola directed what many consider the greatest American film—perhaps only challenged by the sequel released two years later. Based on the Mario Puzo novel that traced the fortunes of the Corleone crime family, *The Godfather* was nominated for 11 Oscars, picking up three for Best Picture, Best Adapted Screenplay and Best Actor (Marlon Brando in a legendary performance). Costars Al Pacino, James Caan and Robert Duvall were all nominated for Best Supporting Actor. *The Godfather: Part II*, which premiered in New York City on Dec 12, 1974, was also nominated for 11 Oscars and won 6, including Best Picture. A third film was released on Dec 25, 1990.

HUNGARY: ANNIVERSARY OF THE 1848 REVOLUTION. Mar 15. National day. Commemorates when the country briefly attained autonomy from Austria.

IDES OF MARCH. Mar 15. In the Roman calendar the days of the month were not numbered sequentially. Instead, each month had three division days: kalends, nones and ides. Days were numbered from these divisions: e.g., IV Nones or III Ides. The ides occurred on the 15th of the month (or on the 13th in months that had less than 31 days). Julius Caesar was assassinated on this day in 44 BC. This system was used in Europe well into the Renaissance. When Shakespeare wrote "Beware the ides of March" in *Julius Caesar* his audience knew what he meant.

JACKSON, ANDREW: BIRTH ANNIVERSARY. Mar 15, 1767. 7th president of the US (Mar 4, 1829–Mar 3, 1837) was born in a log cabin at Waxhaw, SC. Jackson was the first president since George Washington who had not attended college. He was a military hero in the War of 1812. His presidency reflected his democratic and egalitarian values. Died at Nashville, TN, June 8, 1845. His birthday is observed as a holiday in Tennessee.

LIBERIA: J.J. ROBERTS DAY. Mar 15. National holiday. Commemorates the birth in 1809 of the country's first president.

MAINE: ADMISSION DAY: ANNIVERSARY. Mar 15. Became 23rd state in 1820. Prior to this date, Maine had been part of the state of Massachusetts.

NATIONAL AGRICULTURE WEEK. Mar 15–21. A Celebration of Agriculture. Annually, the week that includes the first day of spring. For info: Agriculture Council of America, 11020 King St, Ste 205, Overland Park, KS 66210. Phone: (913) 491-1895. Fax: (913) 491-6502. E-mail: info@agday.org. Web: www.agday.org.

NATIONAL ANIMAL POISON PREVENTION WEEK. Mar 15–21. In conjunction with National Poison Prevention Week, the ASPCA sponsors this important week to educate Americans about common household products, plants and foods that can be dangerous or even deadly to pets. For info: Media & Communications Dept,

ASPCA, New York, NY. Phone: (212) 876-7700, ext 4565. E-mail: shonalib@aspca.org. Web: www.aspca.org.

✦ **NATIONAL POISON PREVENTION WEEK.** Mar 15–21. Presidential Proclamation issued each year for the third week of March since 1962. (PL87–319 of Sept 26, 1961.)

NATIONAL POISON PREVENTION WEEK. Mar 15–21. To aid in encouraging the American people to learn of the dangers of unintentional poisoning and to take preventive measures against it. Annually, the third full week in March. For info: Kim Dulic, Secy, Poison Prevention Week Council, Box 1543, Washington, DC 20013. E-mail: kdulic@cpsc.gov. Web: www.cpsc.gov or www.poisonprevention.org.

PEDIATRIC NURSE PRACTITIONER WEEK. Mar 15–21. The National Association of Pediatric Nurse Practitioners, an association of more than 7,000 pediatric nurse practitioners and specialty nurses in advanced practice providing primary health care to infants, children, adolescents and young adults, proclaims this week in honor of nearly 11,000 practitioners dedicated to improving children's health. For info: NAPNAP, 20 Brace Rd, Ste 200, Cherry Hill, NJ 08034. Phone: (856) 857-9700. Fax: (856) 857-1600. E-mail: info@napnap.org. Web: www.napnap.org.

TAIWAN: BIRTHDAY OF KUAN YIN, GODDESS OF MERCY. Mar 15. A Buddhist deity, Kuan Yin is also the patron goddess of Taiwan. Nineteenth day of Second Moon of the lunar calendar, celebrated at Taipei's Lungshan (Dragon Mountain) and other temples.

"THREE'S COMPANY" TV PREMIERE: ANNIVERSARY. Mar 15, 1977. This half-hour comedy featured two girls and a guy sharing an apartment. In order for the landlord to go along with the living arrangements, Jack Tripper, played by John Ritter, had to pretend he was gay. Cast included Joyce DeWitt, Suzanne Somers, Norman Fell, Audra Lindley, Richard Kline, Don Knotts and Priscilla Barnes. The last telecast aired on Sept 18, 1984.

TRUE CONFESSIONS DAY. Mar 15. Confession is good for the soul. Go in to work today and tell all. If you plan to stay home, make an appointment with your mirror. (©2006 by WH.) For info: Thomas & Ruth Roy, Wellcat Holidays, 2418 Long Ln, Lebanon, PA 17046. Phone: (717) 279-0184. E-mail: info@wellcat.com. Web: www.wellcat.com.

VAN BROCKLIN, NORM: BIRTH ANNIVERSARY. Mar 15, 1926. Norman Van Brocklin, Pro Football Hall of Fame quarterback and coach, born at Eagle Butte, SD. Van Brocklin played college football at Oregon and then signed with the Los Angeles Rams. He helped the Rams win their only NFL title in 1951. After finishing his playing career with the Philadelphia Eagles, he coached the Minnesota Vikings and the Atlanta Falcons. Inducted into the Pro Football Hall of Fame in 1979. Died at Social Circle, GA, May 2, 1983.

WASHINGTON'S ADDRESS TO CONTINENTAL ARMY OFFICERS: ANNIVERSARY. Mar 15, 1783. George Washington addressed a meeting at Newburgh, NY, of Continental army officers who were dissatisfied and rebellious for want of back pay, food, clothing and pensions. General Washington called for patience, opening his speech with the words "I have grown gray in your service. . . ." Congress later acted to satisfy most of the demands.

"THE WONDER YEARS" TV PREMIERE: ANNIVERSARY. Mar 15, 1988. A coming-of-age tale set in suburbia in the 1960s and 1970s. This drama/comedy starred Fred Savage as Kevin Arnold; Josh Saviano as his best friend, Paul, and Danica McKellar as girlfriend Winnie. Kevin's dad was played by Dan Lauria, his homemaker mom by Alley Mills, his hippie sister by Olivia d'Abo and his bully brother by Jason Hervey. Narrator Daniel Stern was the voice of the grown-up Kevin. The last episode ran Sept 1, 1993, but it remains popular in syndication.

March 2009	S	M	T	W	T	F	S
	1	2	3	4	5	6	7
	8	9	10	11	12	13	14
	15	16	17	18	19	20	21
	22	23	24	25	26	27	28
	29	30	31				

Birthdays Today

Harold Douglas Baines, 50, former baseball player, born St. Michael's, MD, Mar 15, 1959.

Alan Bean, 77, former astronaut, born Wheeler, TX, Mar 15, 1932.

Robert Terrell (Terry) Cummings, 48, former basketball player, born Chicago, IL, Mar 15, 1961.

Fabio, 48, model, born Fabio Lanzoni at Milan, Italy, Mar 15, 1961.

Ruth Bader Ginsburg, 76, Associate Justice of the US Supreme Court, born Brooklyn, NY, Mar 15, 1933.

Judd Hirsch, 74, actor (Emmy for "Taxi"; "Numb3rs," *Ordinary People*), born New York, NY, Mar 15, 1935.

Eva Longoria, 34, actress ("Desperate Housewives," "The Young and the Restless"), born Corpus Christi, TX, Mar 15, 1975.

Mike Love, 68, singer, musician (The Beach Boys), born Los Angeles, CA, Mar 15, 1941.

Mark McGrath, 41, singer (Sugar Ray), born Newport Beach, CA, Mar 15, 1968.

Park Overall, 52, actress ("Empty Nest," *Mississippi Burning*), born Nashville, TN, Mar 15, 1957.

Kim Raver, 40, actress ("Third Watch," "24"), born New York, NY, Mar 15, 1969.

Dee Snider, 54, singer (Twisted Sister), composer, born Massapequa, NY, Mar 15, 1955.

Sly Stone, 65, singer, musician (Sly & the Family Stone), born Sylvester Stewart at Dallas, TX, Mar 15, 1944.

Craig Wasson, 55, actor ("Phyllis," *Body Double, Malcolm X*), born Ontario, OR, Mar 15, 1954.

March 16 — Monday

DAY 75 — **290 REMAINING**

ACT HAPPY WEEK. Mar 16–22. Method acting techniques are prescribed by physicians to release chemicals in the body that aid health, wealth and friendship. During this week, select your own Act Happy Day and celebrate! Annually, the week beginning with the third Monday in March. For info: Dale L. Anderson, MD, 2982 W Owasso Blvd, St Paul, MN 55113. Phone: (651) 484-5162. Fax: (651) 486-8860. E-mail: drdla@acthappy.com. Web: www.acthappy.com.

AUSTRALIA: CANBERRA DAY. Mar 16. Australian Capital Territory. Public holiday the third Monday in March.

BLACK PRESS DAY: ANNIVERSARY OF THE FIRST BLACK NEWSPAPER. Mar 16, 1827. Anniversary of the founding of the first black newspaper in the US, *Freedom's Journal*, on Varick Street at New York, NY.

BONHEUR, ROSA: BIRTH ANNIVERSARY. Mar 16, 1822. French painter and sculptor best known for her paintings of animals, Rosa (Marie-Rosalie) Bonheur was born at Bordeaux. With the income from the sale of her art she purchased the castle of By near Fontainebleau at Melun, France, where she died May 25, 1899. Bonheur's *The Horse Fair*, which she painted in 1853, was purchased by the American millionaire Cornelius Vanderbilt for $53,600, a record price at the time. In 1865 Bonheur was awarded the Grand Cross of the Légion d'Honneur, the first woman so honored. An early Bohemian and feminist, Bonheur defied female convention of the day by dressing in pants and smoking cigarettes.

CAMP FIRE USA BIRTHDAY WEEK. Mar 16–22. To celebrate the 99th anniversary of Camp Fire USA (founded in 1910 as Camp Fire Girls). For info: Camp Fire USA, 1100 Walnut St, Ste 1900, Kansas City, MO 64106-2197. Phone: (816) 285-2010. Fax: (816) 285-9444. E-mail: info@campfireusa.org. Web: www.campfireusa.org.

CLYMER, GEORGE: BIRTH ANNIVERSARY. Mar 16, 1739. Signer of the Declaration of Independence and of the US Constitution. Born at Philadelphia, PA, and died there Jan 24, 1813.

CURLEW DAY. Mar 16. Traditional arrival date for the long-billed curlew at the Umatilla (Oregon) National Wildlife Refuge. More than 500 of the long-billed curlews have been reported at this location during their nesting season.

FREEDOM OF INFORMATION DAY. Mar 16. The American Library Association supports free and open access to government information created at taxpayer expense. On or near the birthday of James Madison (Mar 16), ALA urges libraries and librarians to join in celebrating the public's "right to know" by sponsoring activities to educate their communities about the importance of promoting and protecting freedom of information. Sponsored by the Freedom Forum and the American Library Association. For info: American Library Assn Washington Office, 1301 Pennsylvania Ave NW, Ste 403, Washington, DC 20004. Phone: (202) 628-8410. E-mail: alawash@alawash.org. Web: www.ala.org.

GODDARD DAY: ANNIVERSARY. Mar 16, 1926. Commemorates first liquid-fuel-powered rocket flight launched by Robert Hutchings Goddard (1882–1945) at Auburn, MA.

"THE GUMBY SHOW" TV PREMIERE: ANNIVERSARY. Mar 16, 1957. This kids' show was a spin-off from "Howdy Doody," where the character of Gumby was first introduced in 1956. Gumby and his horse, Pokey, were clay figures whose adventures were filmed using the process of "claymation." "The Gumby Show," created by Art Clokey, was first hosted by Bobby Nicholson and later by Pinky Lee. It was syndicated in 1966 and again in 1988.

INTERNATIONAL BRAIN AWARENESS WEEK. Mar 16–22. Brain Awareness Week is an international effort to advance public awareness about the progress, promise and benefits of brain research. The Dana Alliance is joined in the campaign by partners in the US and around the world, including medical and research organizations; patient advocacy groups; the National Institutes of Health and other government agencies; service groups; hospitals and universities; K–12 schools and professional organizations. For info: Dana Alliance for Brain Initiatives, 745 Fifth Ave, Ste 900, New York, NY 10151. Phone: (212) 223-4040. Fax: (212) 317-8721. E-mail: bawinfo@dana.org. Web: www.dana.org/brainweek.

LIPS APPRECIATION DAY. Mar 16. Where would all those lovely teeth we paid a bundle for be without a lovely frame? Do something nice for your lips today. Buy a lip balm. Better yet, kiss somebody! (©2006 by WH.) For info: Thomas & Ruth Roy, Wellcat Holidays, 2418 Long Ln, Lebanon, PA 17046. Phone: (717) 279-0184. E-mail: info@wellcat.com. Web: www.wellcat.com.

MADISON, JAMES: BIRTH ANNIVERSARY. Mar 16, 1751. 4th president of the US (Mar 4, 1809–Mar 3, 1817), born at Port Conway, VA. He was president when British forces invaded Washington, DC, requiring Madison and other high officials to flee while the British burned the Capitol, the president's residence and most other public buildings (Aug 24–25, 1814). Died at Montpelier, VA, June 28, 1836.

MY LAI MASSACRE: ANNIVERSARY. Mar 16, 1968. Most-publicized atrocity of the Vietnam War. According to findings of US Army's investigating team, approximately 300 noncombatant Vietnamese villagers (at My Lai and Mykhe, near the South China Sea) were killed by infantrymen of the American Division.

NATIONAL SPRING FEVER WEEK. Mar 16–22. Annually, the week including the first day of spring. Recognizing the special socialization rites single people face during this season of revitalization. For info: Robin Gorman Newman, 44 Somerset Dr N, Great Neck, NY 11020. Phone: (516) 773-0911. E-mail: robin@lovecoach.com. Web: www.lovecoach.com.

NIXON, THELMA CATHERINE PATRICIA (PAT) RYAN: BIRTH ANNIVERSARY. Mar 16, 1912. Wife of Richard Milhous Nixon, 37th president of the US. Born at Ely, NV, she died at Park Ridge, NJ, June 22, 1993.

POPE, JOHN: BIRTH ANNIVERSARY. Mar 16, 1822. Pope, a Union general in the Civil War, was born at Louisville, KY, graduated from West Point in 1842 and fought in the Mexican War. During the Civil War President Lincoln put Pope in charge of the Army of Virginia. He led the Union forces at the second Battle of Bull Run (August 1862) to a disastrous defeat, losing about 15,000 troops. He was immediately relieved of his command and sent to Minnesota to handle rioting Sioux Indians. Pope continued to deal with Indian matters until 1883 and eventually espoused the goal of assimilation into white culture. He died at Ohio, Sept 23, 1892.

SPACE MILESTONE: *GEMINI 8* (US). Mar 16, 1966. Executed (with *Agena*) first docking of orbiting spacecraft. Safe emergency landing after malfunction. Launched Mar 16, 1966.

US MILITARY ACADEMY FOUNDED: ANNIVERSARY. Mar 16, 1802. President Thomas Jefferson signed legislation establishing the US Military Academy to train officers for the army. The college is located at West Point, NY, on the site of the oldest continuously occupied military post in America. Women were admitted to West Point in 1976. The Academy's motto is "Duty, Honor, Country." For more info: www.usma.edu.

WELLDERLY WEEK. Mar 16–22. Celebration and recognition of senior citizens who never act their age. During this week, select your own Wellderly Day and celebrate in style. Annually, the week that begins on the third Monday in March. For info: Dale L. Anderson, MD, 2982 W Owasso Blvd, St. Paul, MN 55113. Phone: (651) 484-5162. Fax: (651) 486-8860. E-mail: drdla@acthappy.com. Web: www.acthappy.com.

Birthdays Today

Bernardo Bertolucci, 68, filmmaker (Oscar for *The Last Emperor; Last Tango in Paris*), born Parma, Italy, Mar 16, 1941.

Erik Estrada, 60, actor ("CHiPS," *Honey Boy*), born New York, NY, Mar 16, 1949.

Judah Friedlander, 40, actor ("30 Rock," *American Splendor*), born Gaithersburg, MD, Mar 16, 1969.

Victor Garber, 60, actor (*Godspell*, "Alias"), born London, ON, Canada, Mar 16, 1949.

Lauren Graham, 42, actress (*Sweet November*, "The Gilmore Girls"), born Honolulu, HI, Mar 16, 1967.

Alice Hoffman, 57, writer (*Practical Magic, Aquamarine*), born New York, NY, Mar 16, 1952.

Isabelle Huppert, 54, actress (*Violette, Story of Women*), born Paris, France, Mar 16, 1955.

Jerry Lewis, 83, comedian, actor (*My Friend Irma*), director (*The Bellboy*), born Newark, NJ, Mar 16, 1926.

Kate Nelligan, 58, actress (*Eye of the Needle, Frankie and Johnny, The Prince of Tides*), born London, ON, Canada, Mar 16, 1951.

Chuck Woolery, 67, game-show host ("Love Connection," "Scrabble"), born Ashland, KY, Mar 16, 1942.

March 17 — Tuesday

DAY 76 289 REMAINING

BRIDGER, JIM: BIRTH ANNIVERSARY. Mar 17, 1804. American fur trader, frontiersman and scout, born at Richmond, VA, and died July 17, 1881, near Kansas City, MO. Believed to be the first white man to visit (in 1824) the Great Salt Lake, he also established Fort Bridger in southwestern Wyoming as a fur-trading post and as a way station for pioneers heading west on the Oregon Trail. Bridger National Forest in western Wyoming is named for him.

CAMP FIRE USA: ANNIVERSARY. Mar 17. To commemorate the anniversary of the founding of Camp Fire USA and the service given to children and youth across the nation. Founded in 1910 as Camp Fire Girls. For info: Camp Fire USA, 1100 Walnut St, Ste 1900, Kansas City, MO 64106-2197. Phone: (816) 285-2010. Fax: (816) 285-9444. E-mail: info@campfireusa.org. Web: www.campfireusa.org.

COLE, NAT "KING" (NATHANIEL ADAMS COLE): 90th BIRTH ANNIVERSARY. Mar 17, 1919. Nat King Cole was born at Montgomery, AL, and began his musical career at an early age, playing the piano at age four. He was the first black entertainer to host a national television show. His many songs included "The Christmas Song," "Nature Boy," "Mona Lisa," "Ramblin' Rose" and "Unforgettable." Although he was dogged by racial discrimination throughout his career, including the cancellation of his television show because opposition from Southern white viewers decreased advertising revenue, Cole was criticized by prominent black newspapers for not joining other black entertainers in the civil rights struggle. Cole contributed more than $50,000 to civil rights organizations in response to the criticism. Nat King Cole died Feb 25, 1965, at Santa Monica, CA.

CORBETT-FITZSIMMONS TITLE FIGHT: ANNIVERSARY. Mar 17, 1897. In one of boxing's greatest fights—and the first heavyweight title fight to be filmed—"Gentleman Jim" Corbett lost the world title to "Ruby Robert" Fitzsimmons at Carson City, NV. Fitzsimmons, seemingly a long shot at 34 years of age, hung on for 13 rounds before landing the "solar plexus punch" that felled Corbett. Western legends in attendance were Bat Masterson (overseeing security) and Wyatt Earp.

EVACUATION DAY: ANNIVERSARY. Mar 17, 1776. A public holiday at Boston and Suffolk County, MA, celebrates the anniversary of the evacuation from Boston of British troops.

FEMALE RELIEF SOCIETY OF NAUVOO ORGANIZED: ANNIVERSARY. Mar 17, 1842. Twenty Mormon women formally initiated this organization at Nauvoo, IL, which is now known as the Relief Society and has grown to almost four million members. Information furnished by Church of Jesus Christ of Latter-day Saints, Public Affairs Department.

March 2009	S	M	T	W	T	F	S
	1	2	3	4	5	6	7
	8	9	10	11	12	13	14
	15	16	17	18	19	20	21
	22	23	24	25	26	27	28
	29	30	31				

HOWARD, SHEMP: BIRTH ANNIVERSARY. Mar 17, 1895. A member of the original Three Stooges (with Moe Howard and Larry Fine), Howard was born Samuel Horwitz at Brooklyn, NY. He teamed with brother Moe as comic relief with vaudeville entertainer Ted Healy in the early 1920s. In 1925, Larry Fine joined them to create the Three Stooges. Shemp left the trio in 1932—little brother Curly replaced him—and had roles in many films. Upon Curly's retirement in 1946, Shemp rejoined the Stooges until his death on Nov 23, 1955, at Hollywood, CA.

IRELAND: NATIONAL DAY. Mar 17. St. Patrick's Day is observed in the Republic of Ireland as a legal national holiday.

JONES, BOBBY: BIRTH ANNIVERSARY. Mar 17, 1902. Golfing great Robert Tyre Jones, Jr, first golfer to win the grand slam (the four major British and American tournaments in one year). Born at Atlanta, GA, he died there Dec 18, 1971.

NORTHERN IRELAND: SAINT PATRICK'S DAY HOLIDAY. Mar 17. National holiday.

NUREYEV, RUDOLF HAMETOVICH: BIRTH ANNIVERSARY. Mar 17, 1938. Rudolf Nureyev, one of the most charismatic ballet stars of the 20th century, was born on a train in southeastern Siberia. Nureyev's defection from the Soviet Union on June 17, 1961, while on tour with the Kirov Ballet, made headlines worldwide. The dancer was known for his ability to combine passion with a high level of perfectionism. His long partnership with Dame Margot Fonteyn of the Royal Ballet was legendary, and he also performed frequently with the Martha Graham Dance Company. Nureyev also choreographed and restaged many classics and served as the Paris Opera Ballet's artistic director. He died Jan 6, 1993, at Levallois, France, a suburb of Paris.

PARKER, GEORGE: DEATH ANNIVERSARY. Mar 17, 1764. George Parker, the second Earl of Macclesfield, was born in 1697 (exact date unknown). The eminent English astronomer was president of the Royal Society from 1752 until his death. He was one of the principal authors of the Bill for Regulating the Commencement of the Year (British Calendar Act of 1751), which was introduced in Parliament by Lord Chesterfield. That act caused the adoption, in 1752, of the "New Style" Gregorian calendar, which is still in use today. Parker died at Shirburn Castle, England.

RUSTIN, BAYARD: BIRTH ANNIVERSARY. Mar 17, 1910. Black pacifist and civil rights leader, Bayard Rustin was an organizer and participant in many of the great social protest marches—for jobs, freedom and nuclear disarmament. He was arrested and imprisoned more than 20 times for his civil rights and pacifist activities. Born at West Chester, PA, Rustin died at New York, NY, Aug 24, 1987.

SAINT PATRICK'S DAY. Mar 17. Commemorates the patron saint of Ireland, Bishop Patrick (AD 389–461) who, about AD 432, left his home in the Severn Valley, England, and introduced Christianity into Ireland. Feast day in the Roman Catholic Church. A national holiday in Ireland and Northern Ireland.

SAINT PATRICK'S DAY PARADE. Mar 17. Fifth Avenue, New York, NY. Held since 1762, the parade of 200,000 begins the two-mile march at 11:00 AM and lasts about six hours. Starts on 44th St and 5th Ave and ends at 86th St and First Ave. Est attendance: 700,000. For info: NYC & Company, 810 7th Ave, 3rd Fl, New York, NY 10019. Phone: (800) NYC-VISIT or (212) 484-1222.

SOUTH AFRICAN WHITES VOTE TO END MINORITY RULE: ANNIVERSARY. Mar 17, 1992. A referendum proposing ending white minority rule through negotiations was supported by a whites-only ballot. The vote of 1,924,186 (68.6 percent) whites in support of President F.W. de Klerk's reform policies was greater than expected.

SPACE MILESTONE: *VANGUARD 1* (US). Mar 17, 1958. Established "pear shape" of Earth. At only three pounds it was the first solar-powered satellite.

TANEY, ROGER B.: BIRTH ANNIVERSARY. Mar 17, 1777. Fifth chief justice of the Supreme Court, born at Calvert County, MD. Served as attorney general under President Andrew Jackson. Nominated as secretary of the treasury, he became the first presidential nominee to be rejected by the Senate. His rejection centered on his strong stance against the Bank of the United States as a central bank and his role in urging President Jackson to veto the congressional bill extending its charter. A year later, he was nominated to the Supreme Court as an associate justice by Jackson, but his nomination was stalled until the death of Chief Justice John Marshall July 6, 1835. Taney was nominated to fill Marshall's place on the bench and after much resistance he was sworn in as chief justice in March 1836. His tenure on the Supreme Court is most remembered for the Dred Scott decision. He died at Washington, DC, Oct 12, 1864.

Birthdays Today

Daniel Ray (Danny) Ainge, 50, basketball coach, former basketball and baseball player, born Eugene, OR, Mar 17, 1959.

Lesley-Anne Down, 55, actress ("Upstairs, Downstairs," *The Pink Panther Strikes Again*), born London, England, Mar 17, 1954.

Patrick Duffy, 60, actor ("Step by Step," "Dallas"), born Townsend, MT, Mar 17, 1949.

Paul Horn, 79, composer, musician, born New York, NY, Mar 17, 1930.

Vicki Lewis, 49, actress ("NewsRadio," *Godzilla*), born Cincinnati, OH, Mar 17, 1960.

Rob Lowe, 45, actor (*St. Elmo's Fire, About Last Night . . .*, "Brothers & Sisters," "The West Wing"), born Charlottesville, VA, Mar 17, 1964.

Kurt Russell, 58, actor (*Backdraft, Elvis*), born Springfield, MA, Mar 17, 1951.

Gary Sinise, 54, stage and screen actor (*Forrest Gump, Apollo 13*, "CSI: New York"), born Chicago, IL, Mar 17, 1955.

March 18 — Wednesday

DAY 77 | **288 REMAINING**

ARUBA: FLAG DAY. Mar 18. Aruba national holiday. Display of flags, national music and folkloric events.

AWKWARD MOMENTS DAY. Mar 18. Celebrate the humor in life's uncomfortable situations. Recognize those moments that make us feel unsure and embarrassed, then harness the power of humor, laughter and fun to cope with them. For info: Wayne & Laura Gignac, 30 Slater Ave, Norwich, CT 06360. Phone: (860) 887-7054. Fax: (860) 892-1951. E-mail: wayne@theshowworks.com. Web: www.theshowworks.com.

CALHOUN, JOHN CALDWELL: BIRTH ANNIVERSARY. Mar 18, 1782. American statesman and first vice president of the US to resign that office (Dec 28, 1832). Born at Abbeville District, SC, died at Washington, DC, Mar 31, 1850.

CANADA: TORONTO SPORTSMEN'S SHOW. Mar 18–22. Direct Energy Centre, Exhibition Place, Toronto, ON. Fishing manufacturers and retailers, fishing seminars, travel/vacation exhibits, cottages, camping products, boats and marine accessories, wildlife art, pet products and breeders, conservation and outdoor organizations, sporting goods, retriever trials, arena show and family entertainment. Est attendance: 125,000. For info: Canadian Natl Sportsmen's Shows, 30 Village Centre Pl, Mississauga, ON, L4Z 1V9 Canada. Phone: (905) 361-2677. Fax: (905) 361-2679. E-mail: info@sportshows.ca. Web: www.sportshows.ca.

CLEVELAND, GROVER: BIRTH ANNIVERSARY. Mar 18, 1837. The 22nd and 24th president of the US was born Stephen Grover Cleveland at Caldwell, NJ. Terms of office as president: Mar 4, 1885–Mar 3, 1889, and Mar 4, 1893–Mar 3, 1897. He ran for president for the intervening term and received a plurality of votes cast but failed to win electoral college victory. Only president to serve two nonconsecutive terms. Also the only president to be married in the White House. He married 21-year-old Frances Folsom, his ward. Their daughter, Esther, was the first child of a president to be born in the White House. Died at Princeton, NJ, June 24, 1908.

FIRST ELECTRIC RAZOR MARKETED: ANNIVERSARY. Mar 18, 1931. The first electric razor was marketed by Schick, Inc.

FORGIVE MOM AND DAD DAY. Mar 18. Is there a parent alive who has not made mistakes? It's time to let Mom and Dad down off the wedding cake and into the world of mere humans. Besides, you're an alleged grown-up now, and it's time to stop living your life as a reaction to what used to be. (©2006 by WH.) For info: Thomas & Ruth Roy, Wellcat Holidays, 2418 Long Ln, Lebanon, PA 17046. Phone: (717) 279-0184. E-mail: info@wellcat.com. Web: www.wellcat.com.

JOHNSON, WILLIAM H.: BIRTH ANNIVERSARY. Mar 18, 1901. African-American artist, born at Florence, SC; died Apr 13, 1970, at Islip, NY. Johnson spent many years in Europe painting expressionist works. He was strongly influenced by the vivid styles and brushstrokes of Henry O. Tanner, Vincent van Gogh, Paul Gauguin, Edvard Munch and Otto Dix. He left Europe when Hitler began destroying art that had primitivist or African themes. Back in the US, Johnson developed a new, flatter style and delved into subjects of his own experience as well as historical African-American figures and events. *Going to Church* (1940–41) and *Mom and Dad* (1944) are examples of his later work.

MOON PHASE: LAST QUARTER. Mar 18. Moon enters Last Quarter phase at 1:47 PM, EDT.

NAIA DIVISION I MEN'S BASKETBALL NATIONAL CHAMPIONSHIP. Mar 18–24. Municipal Auditorium, Kansas City, MO. 72nd annual tournament. Sponsored by Buffalo Funds. Est attendance: 45,000. For info: Natl Assn of Intercollegiate Athletics, 1200 Grand Blvd, Kansas City, MO 64106. E-mail: jmccarthy@naia.org. Web: www.naia.org or www.naiahoops.com.

NAIA DIVISION I WOMEN'S BASKETBALL NATIONAL CHAMPIONSHIP. Mar 18–24. Jackson, TN. 32-team field competes for the national championship. 29th annual. Est attendance: 38,000. For info: Natl Assn of Intercollegiate Athletics, I WBKB, 1200 Grand Blvd, Kansas City, MO 64106. E-mail: dgreen@naia.org. Web: www.naia.org.

NATIONAL BIODIESEL DAY. Mar 18. Birthday of Rudolph Diesel, who invented the diesel engine and unveiled it at the World Fair in 1900. Diesel originally designed the engine to run on peanut oil and was a big believer in the role vegetable oils could play in fueling America. Biodiesel is a cleaner-burning, petroleum-free alternative to diesel that can be made from any fat or vegetable oil, such as soybean oil. This day honors the man whose vision comes full circle as biodiesel becomes an increasingly popular fuel. For info: National Biodiesel Board, PO Box 104898, Jefferson City, MO 65110-4898. Phone: (800) 841-5849. Fax: (573) 635-7913. E-mail: info@biodiesel.org. Web: www.biodiesel.org.

NJCAA DIVISION II MEN'S BASKETBALL NATIONAL FINALS. Mar 18–22. Danville, IL. Junior College Division II national men's basketball finals tournament. Est attendance: 8,000. For info: Jeanie Cooke, Exec Dir, Danville Area Conv/Visitors Bureau, PO Box 992, Danville, IL 61834. Phone: (800) 383-4386. E-mail: dacvb@danvilleareainfo.com.

PLIMPTON, GEORGE: BIRTH ANNIVERSARY. Mar 18, 1927. Born at New York, NY, writer and editor George Plimpton called himself a "participatory" journalist, going to great lengths to research his narratives. After training with the 1963 Detroit Lions, he wrote *Paper Lion* based on his experiences; the book is widely considered one of the best pieces of sports writing ever published. He also founded *The Paris Review*, a highly regarded literary quarterly that published the first works of such writers as Philip Roth and Jack Kerouac. The American Academy of Arts and Letters called him a "central figure in American letters" when they inducted him in 2002. He died at New York, NY, Sept 25, 2003.

SPACE MILESTONE: *VOSKHOD 2* (USSR). Mar 18, 1965. Colonel Leonov stepped out of the capsule for 20 minutes in a special space suit, the first man to leave a spaceship. It was two months prior to the first US space walk. See also: "Space Milestone: *Gemini 4* (US)" (June 3).

"TALES OF WELLS FARGO" TV PREMIERE: ANNIVERSARY. Mar 18, 1957. This half-hour western starred Dale Robertson as Jim Hardie, agent for the Wells Fargo transport company. In the fall of 1961, the show expanded to an hour. Hardie bought a ranch, and new cast members were added including Jack Ging as Beau McCloud, another agent; Virginia Christine as Ovie, a widow owning a nearby ranch; Lory Patrick and Mary Jane Saunders as Ovie's daughters and William Demarest as Jeb, Hardie's ranch foreman. Jack Nicholson appeared in one of his first major TV roles in the episode "The Washburn Girl."

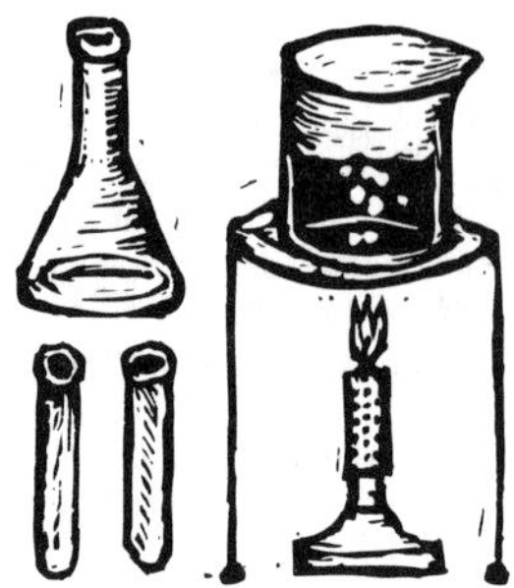

Birthdays Today

Bonnie Blair, 45, Olympic gold medal speed skater, born Cornwall, NY, Mar 18, 1964.

Irene Cara, 50, singer ("Fame," "The Dream"), actress (*Ain't Misbehavin'*), born the Bronx, NY, Mar 18, 1959.

Dane Cook, 37, comedian, actor (*Good Luck Chuck*), born Boston, MA, Mar 18, 1972.

Frederik Willem de Klerk, 73, former president of South Africa, born Johannesburg, South Africa, Mar 18, 1936.

Kevin Dobson, 65, actor ("Kojak," "Knots Landing"), born New York, NY, Mar 18, 1944.

Brad Dourif, 59, actor (*One Flew Over the Cuckoo's Nest, Blue Velvet, Jungle Fever*), born Huntington, WV, Mar 18, 1950.

Peter Graves, 83, actor ("Mission: Impossible," "The Winds of War"), born Peter Aurness at Minneapolis, MN, Mar 18, 1926.

John Kander, 82, composer (*Cabaret, Chicago*), born Kansas City, MO, Mar 18, 1927.

Shashi Kapoor, 71, actor (*Heat and Dust, Sammy and Rosie Get Laid*), born Calcutta, India, Mar 18, 1938.

Queen Latifah, 39, rap artist, actress (*Bringing Down the House, Chicago*), born Dana Owens at East Orange, NJ, Mar 18, 1970.

Charley Pride, 71, singer, former minor league baseball player, born Sledge, MS, Mar 18, 1938.

John Updike, 77, author (*Rabbit Run, The Witches of Eastwick*), born Shillington, PA, Mar 18, 1932.

Vanessa Williams, 46, singer, actress ("Ugly Betty," *Bye, Bye Birdie; Kiss of the Spider Woman*), born New York, NY, Mar 18, 1963.

Alexei Yagudin, 29, figure skater, born Leningrad, Russia, Mar 18, 1980.

March 2009	S	M	T	W	T	F	S
	1	2	3	4	5	6	7
	8	9	10	11	12	13	14
	15	16	17	18	19	20	21
	22	23	24	25	26	27	28
	29	30	31				

March 19 — Thursday

DAY 78 **287 REMAINING**

ABSOLUTELY INCREDIBLE KID DAY. Mar 19. 13th annual. Camp Fire USA, one of the nation's oldest and largest youth development organizations, sponsors this day of appreciation for America's youth. Celebrate by writing letters of love and encouragement to the absolutely incredible children in your life. Annually, the third Thursday of March. For info: Camp Fire USA, 1100 Walnut St, Ste 1900, Kansas City, MO 64106-2197. Phone: (816) 285-2010. Fax: (816) 285-9444. E-mail: kidday@campfireusa.org. Web: www.campfireusa.org.

BRADFORD, WILLIAM: BIRTH ANNIVERSARY. Mar 19, 1589. (Old Style date.) Pilgrim father, governor of Plymouth Colony. Born at Yorkshire, England, and baptized Mar 19, 1589. Sailed from Southampton, England, on the *Mayflower* in 1620. Died at Plymouth, MA, May 9, 1657 (OS).

BRYAN, WILLIAM JENNINGS: BIRTH ANNIVERSARY. Mar 19, 1860. American political leader, member of Congress, Democratic presidential nominee (1896), "free silver" advocate, assisted in prosecution at Scopes trial, known as "the Silver-Tongued Orator." Born at Salem, IL, he died at Dayton, TN, July 26, 1925.

COMPANIES THAT CARE DAY. Mar 19. An annual event, celebrated by companies that prize employees and are committed to ongoing community service. This day encourages employers to highlight and expand their staff and community initiatives as well as highlight their caring activities. Examples of how companies have celebrated the day can be found at our website. For info: Marci Koblenz, Center for Companies That Care, 500 N Dearborn St, 2nd Fl, Chicago, IL 60610. Phone: (312) 661-1010. Fax: (847) 869-2465. E-mail: info@companies-that-care.org. Web: www.companies-that-care.org.

EARP, WYATT: BIRTH ANNIVERSARY. Mar 19, 1848. Born at Monmouth, IL, and died Jan 13, 1929, at Los Angeles, CA. A legendary figure of the Old West, Earp worked as a railroad hand, saloon keeper, gambler, lawman, gunslinger, miner and real estate investor at various times. Best known for the gunfight at the OK Corral Oct 26, 1881, at Tombstone, AZ.

FESTIVAL OF HOUSES AND GARDENS. Mar 19–Apr 18. Charleston, SC. Held annually since 1947. Provides a rare opportunity to explore the private dwellings and gardens of historic Charleston. Est attendance: 14,000. For info: Historic Charleston Foundation, 40 E Bay St, Charleston, SC 29401. Phone: (843) 722-3405. Web: www.historiccharleston.org.

IRAN: NATIONAL DAY OF OIL. Mar 19. National holiday. Commemorates the nationalization of Iran's oil fields in 1963.

LIVINGSTONE, DAVID: BIRTH ANNIVERSARY. Mar 19, 1813. Scottish physician, missionary and explorer, born at Blantyre, Scotland. Subject of a famous search by Henry M. Stanley, who found him at Ujiji, near Lake Tanganyika in Africa, on Nov 10, 1871. Dr. Livingstone died at Africa, May 1, 1873. See also: "Stanley, Henry Morton: Birth Anniversary" (Jan 28).

McKEAN, THOMAS: 275th BIRTH ANNIVERSARY. Mar 19, 1734. Signer of the Declaration of Independence and governor of Pennsylvania. Born at Chester County, PA, he died June 24, 1817.

NAPNAP ANNUAL CONFERENCE. Mar 19–22. San Diego, CA. The National Association of Pediatric Nurse Practitioners, an association of more than 7,000 pediatric nurse practioners and specialty nurses in advanced practice providing primary health care to infants, children, adolescents and young adults, holds their 30th annual conference. For info: NAPNAP, 20 Brace Rd, Ste 200, Cherry Hill, NJ 08034. Phone: (856) 857-9700. Fax: (856) 857-1600. E-mail: info@napnap.org. Web: www.napnap.org.

NATIONAL FESTIVAL OF THE WEST AND LOG HOME SHOW. Mar 19–22. Scottsdale, AZ. Four days of western lifestyle fun with plenty of shopping, log homes, decorative items, clothing, fine art, furniture and more. Four stages of live music, Western Writers of America, movie stars, chuck wagon cookin' competition, historical reenactments. Fun for the whole family. Est attendance: 50,000. For info: Festival of the West, PO Box 12966, Scottsdale, AZ 85267. Phone: (602) 996-4387. Fax: (602) 867-4887. E-mail: email@festivalofthewest.com. Web: www.festivalofthewest.com.

NCAA DIVISION I WOMEN'S SWIMMING AND DIVING CHAMPIONSHIPS. Mar 19–21. College Station, TX. Est attendance: 3,000. For info: NCAA, 700 W Washington St, PO Box 6222, Indianapolis, IN 46206-6222. Phone: (317) 917-6222. Fax: (317) 917-6888. Web: www.ncaa.org.

NCAA DIVISION I WRESTLING CHAMPIONSHIPS. Mar 19–21. Scottrade Center, St. Louis, MO. For info: NCAA, 700 W Washington St, PO Box 6222, Indianapolis, IN 46206-6222. Phone: (317) 917-6222. Web: www.NCAAsports.com.

OPERATION IRAQI FREEDOM: ANNIVERSARY. Mar 19, 2003. At 9:30 PM, EST, two hours past a deadline for Iraqi dictator Saddam Hussein to step down from power, US and British forces began air strikes against his regime. A ground campaign (adding Australian forces) followed quickly, and by Apr 9, Baghdad was in allied control and Hussein had disappeared. On May 1, President George W. Bush announced the end of major military operations in Iraq, although a peacekeeping force remains and faces violent and fatal attacks from insurgents. Hussein was captured by US forces on Dec 13, 2003. On June 28, 2004, Iraq regained its sovereignty. And on Dec 15, 2005, 70 percent of Iraq's registered voters turned out for parliamentary elections—one of the freest elections on record in the Arab world. Still, sectarian and terrorist violence has prevented the withdrawal of US and other national forces. Some 500,000 Iraqis fled the country in 2007.

ROGERS, EDITH NOURSE: BIRTH ANNIVERSARY. Mar 19, 1881. Edith Nourse Rogers was a YMCA and Red Cross volunteer in France during WWI. In 1925 she was elected to the US Congress to fill the vacancy left by the death of her husband. An able legislator, she was reelected to the House of Representatives 17 times and became the first woman to have her name attached to major legislation. She was a major force in the legislation creating the Women's Army Auxiliary Corps (May 14, 1942) during WWII. Rogers was born at Saco, ME, and died Sept 10, 1960, at Boston.

RUSSELL, CHARLES M.: BIRTH ANNIVERSARY. Mar 19, 1864. Born at St. Louis, MO, Charles M. Russell moved to Montana at about age 16 and became a cowboy. Considered one of the greatest Western artists, he recorded the life of the cowboy in his artwork. He died Oct 26, 1926, at Great Falls, MT.

RYDER, ALBERT PINKHAM: BIRTH ANNIVERSARY. Mar 19, 1847. Painter Albert Pinkham Ryder was born at New Bedford, MA, where he gained a great love for the sea, the subject of many of his works. Ryder was a misanthrope and recluse. He dedicated himself to his painting, working slowly and piling layer after layer of paint on his canvases until he achieved the look he was after. In his lifetime Ryder created only 150 paintings. Three of his best-known works are *The Race Track*, *Toilers of the Sea* and *Siegfried and the Rhine Maidens*. Ryder died Mar 28, 1917, at Elmhurst, NY. Because of his method of painting, many of his works have deteriorated since their creation.

SAINT JOSEPH'S DAY. Mar 19. Feast day of Joseph, husband of the Virgin Mary and foster father of Jesus. Patron of the Catholic Church, fathers and carpenters.

SIRICA, JOHN JOSEPH: BIRTH ANNIVERSARY. Mar 19, 1904. John Sirica, "the Watergate Judge," was born at Waterbury, CT. During two years of trials and hearings, Sirica relentlessly pushed for the names of those responsible for the June 17, 1972, burglary of the Democratic National Committee headquarters in Washington's Watergate Complex. His unwavering search for the truth ultimately resulted in the toppling of the Nixon administration. Judge John Sirica died Aug 15, 1992, at Washington, DC.

SWALLOWS RETURN TO SAN JUAN CAPISTRANO. Mar 19. Traditional date (St. Joseph's Day), since 1776, for swallows to return to old mission of San Juan Capistrano, CA. See also: "Saint John of Capistrano: Death Anniversary" (Oct 23).

ULTIMATE SPORT SHOW—GRAND RAPIDS. Mar 19–22. DeVos Place, Grand Rapids, MI. This event brings together buyers and sellers of fishing boat equipment and their accessories, as well as other outdoor sporting goods. US and Canadian hunting and fishing trips and other vacation travel destinations are featured. All aspects of fishing, including tackle boats, seminars, demonstrations and displays are emphasized. Est attendance: 35,000. For info: Adam Starr, ShowSpan, Inc, 2121 Celebration Dr NE, Grand Rapids, MI 49525. Phone: (616) 447-2860. Fax: (616) 447-2861. E-mail: events@showspan.com. Web: www.showspan.com.

US STANDARD TIME ACT: ANNIVERSARY. Mar 19, 1918. Anniversary of passage by Congress of the Standard Time Act, which authorized the Interstate Commerce Commission to establish standard time zones for the US. The act also established "daylight saving time," to save fuel and to promote other economies in a country at war. Daylight saving time first went into operation on Easter Sunday, Mar 31, 1918. The Uniform Time Act of 1966, as amended in 1986 and again in 2005, now governs standard time in the US. See also: "Daylight Saving Time Begins" (Mar 8).

WARREN, EARL: BIRTH ANNIVERSARY. Mar 19, 1891. American jurist, 14th chief justice of the US Supreme Court. Born at Los Angeles, CA; died at Washington, DC, July 9, 1974.

WASHINGTON HOME, GARDEN & FLOWER SHOW. Mar 19–22. Washington Convention Center, Washington, DC. 49th annual. Six acres of everything for the home and garden including full-size blooming gardens created by the area's best landscapers. The show also has demonstrations, lectures and a Spring Marketplace where visitors can purchase anything from orchids to a whole new kitchen. For info: Dee Stafford, Washington Home & Garden Show, 6017 Tower Ct, Alexandria, VA 22304. Phone: (703) 823-7960. E-mail: tjsevents@aol.com. Web: www.washingtonhomeandgardenshow.com.

Birthdays Today

Ursula Andress, 73, actress (*Dr. No, What's New Pussycat?*), born Bern, Switzerland, Mar 19, 1936.

Michael Bergin, 40, actor ("Baywatch"), born Naugatuck, CT, Mar 19, 1969.

Glenn Close, 62, actress ("Damages," *The Big Chill, Fatal Attraction*; stage: *Sunset Boulevard*), born Greenwich, CT, Mar 19, 1947.

Ornette Coleman, 79, composer, saxophonist, born Fort Worth, TX, Mar 19, 1930.

Patrick McGoohan, 81, director, actor ("The Prisoner"), born New York, NY, Mar 19, 1928.

Philip Roth, 76, author (*The Great American Novel, Portnoy's Complaint*), born Newark, NJ, Mar 19, 1933.

Brent Scowcroft, 84, business executive, consultant, born Ogden, UT, Mar 19, 1925.

Renee Taylor, 74, actress ("The Nanny," *The Producers, A New Leaf*), born New York, NY, Mar 19, 1935.

Hedo Turkoglu, 30, basketball player, born Hiyadet Turkoglu at Istanbul, Turkey, Mar 19, 1979.

Bruce Willis, 54, actor (*Sin City, The Sixth Sense, Die Hard*), born Idar-Oberstein, West Germany, Mar 19, 1955.

March 20 — Friday

DAY 79 **286 REMAINING**

CHARLESTON INTERNATIONAL ANTIQUES SHOW. Mar 20–22. Historic Charleston Foundation Headquarters, Charleston, SC. A world-class antiques show featuring a roster of more than 30 dealers exhibiting museum-quality objects in every category with a concentration on period furnishings and decorative pieces. Est attendance: 3,000. For info: Leigh Handal, Historic Charleston Foundation, PO Box 1120, Charleston, SC 29402. Phone: (843) 722-3405. Fax: (843) 577-2067. E-mail: lhandal@historiccharleston.org. Web: www.historiccharleston.org.

GREAT AMERICAN MEATOUT. Mar 20. Every year since 1985, Meatout has become the largest grassroots diet education campaign. Promotes a meat-free diet to improve health, protect the environment and save animals. "Kick the Meat Habit" for at least one day. A thousand events in all 50 US states and two dozen other countries throughout March. Free Vegetarian Starter Kits with recipes available to all. For info: Meatout, 10101 Ashburton Ln, Bethesda, MD 20817. Phone: (301) 530-1737 or (800) MEATOUT. Fax: (301) 530-5747. E-mail: info@meatout.org. Web: www.meatout.org.

IBSEN, HENRIK: BIRTH ANNIVERSARY. Mar 20, 1828. Norwegian playwright born at Skien, Norway. Among his best-remembered plays: *Peer Gynt, The Pillars of Society, The Wild Duck, An Enemy of the People* and *Hedda Gabler*. Died at Oslo, Norway, May 23, 1906.

JAPAN: VERNAL EQUINOX DAY. Mar 20. National holiday in Japan.

MACON, GEORGIA'S INTERNATIONAL CHERRY BLOSSOM FESTIVAL. Mar 20–29. Macon, GA. 27th annual Cherry Blossom Festival features concerts, exhibits, parades, children's events, hot-air balloons, street party, fireworks, food, fun and family entertainment. 300,000 Yoshino cherry trees. Est attendance: 700,000. For info: Macon Cherry Blossom Fest, 794 Cherry St, Macon, GA 31201. Phone: (478) 751-7429. Fax: (478) 751-7408. Web: www.cherryblossom.com.

NATIONAL AGRICULTURE DAY. Mar 20. A day when producers, agricultural associations, corporations, universities, government agencies and countless others across America gather to recognize and celebrate the abundance provided by agriculture. Annually, the first day of spring. Week of celebration: Mar 15–21. For info: Agriculture Council of America, 11020 King St, Ste 205, Overland Park, KS 66210. Phone: (913) 491-1895. Fax: (913) 491-6502. E-mail: info@agday.org. Web: www.agday.org.

NATIONAL BUBBLE WEEK. Mar 20–26. A chance for Americans of all ages to celebrate the classic play and enhancement of bubbles, a favorite hobby in this country for the past 60 years. At the first sign of spring, children and adults alike have headed outside with bubble solution and wands to create the season's first stream of translucent, glimmering bubbles. National Bubble Week was first observed on Mar 20, 2000. Annually, beginning on the first day of spring. For info: Melissa Fogarty, Litzky Public Relations, 88 Garden St, Hoboken, NJ 07030. Phone: (201) 222-9118. Fax: (201) 222-9418. E-mail: mfogarty@litzkypr.com.

NERVE GAS ATTACK ON JAPANESE SUBWAY: ANNIVERSARY. Mar 20, 1995. Twelve people were killed and 5,000 injured in a nerve gas attack on the Tokyo subway system during rush hour. Suspected in the attack was the Japanese religious sect Aum Shinrikyo, founded and led by Shoko Asahara (real name Chizuo Matsumoto). The group, which professes belief in a hybrid of Buddhist-Hindu teachings, predicts an apocalypse. In a raid conducted against the sect's main compound in Kamikuishiki on Mar 25, police seized literature that predicted 90 percent of the people in the world would be killed by poison gas. Also seized were two tons of chemicals for making sarin, the poison used in the Mar 20 attack. This cache was reported to contain enough material to kill five million people. In a second raid, Asahara was arrested.

OSTARA. Mar 20. (Also called Alban Eilir.) One of the "Lesser Sabbats" during the Wiccan year, Ostara is a fire and fertility festival that marks the beginning of spring. Annually, on the spring equinox.

PROPOSAL DAY! ®. Mar 20 (also Sept 22). A holiday for those who seek marriage. Single adults who are ready to marry are encouraged to propose marriage to their true love on the days of the vernal equinox and the autumnal equinox. Thousands of men and women are married today as a result of a marriage proposal made on a "Proposal Day!"®, including the creator of the holiday. For info: John Michael O'Loughlin, 3124 Chisolm Trail, Irving, TX 75062. Phone: (972) 258-4996. E-mail: lldjohn@aol.com. Web: www.proposalday.com.

ROGERS, FRED: BIRTH ANNIVERSARY. Mar 20, 1928. Born Fred McFeely Rogers at LaTrobe, PA, Rogers first began producing television for children in 1953. His first program, "The Children's Hour," was the precursor to "Mister Rogers' Neighborhood," which premiered in Canada in 1966 and the US in 1968. The show ran on public television until Rogers's death, and he became known worldwide for his dedication to the well-being of children and for his demonstrations of the importance of kindness, compassion and learning. He authored a number of books for parents and children, wrote more than 200 songs and won dozens of awards, including Emmys, Peabodys and the Presidential Medal of Freedom. He died Feb 27, 2003, at his home in Pittsburgh, PA.

SHABBAT ACROSS AMERICA/CANADA. Mar 20. More than 600 participating synagogues (Conservative, Orthodox, Reform and Reconstructionist) encourage Jews to observe the Sabbath on this Friday night. Est attendance: 60,000. For info: Natl Jewish Outreach Program, 989 Sixth Ave, 10th Fl, New York, NY 10018. Phone: (888) SHABBAT or (646) 871-4444. Web: www.njop.org.

SKINNER, B.F.: BIRTH ANNIVERSARY. Mar 20, 1904. American psychologist Burrhus Frederic Skinner was born at Susquehanna, PA. He was a pioneer in behaviorism and is best known for developing the "Skinner box" (an enclosed experimental environment). He died Aug 18, 1990, at Cambridge, MA.

SNOWMAN BURNING. Mar 20. Reading of poetry heralding the end of winter and the arrival of spring, followed by sacrifice in effigy, toasts and cheers. Annually, on or near the first day of spring. Est attendance: 300. For info: Public Relations Office, Lake Superior State University, Sault Ste. Marie, MI 49783. Phone: (906) 635-2315 or (906) 635-2314. Fax: (906) 635-2623. Web: www.lssu.edu/snowman.

SPRING. Mar 20–June 21. In the Northern Hemisphere spring begins today with the vernal equinox, at 7:44 AM, EDT. Note that in the Southern Hemisphere today is the beginning of autumn. Sun rises due east and sets due west everywhere on Earth (except near poles) and the daylight length (interval between sunrise and sunset) is virtually the same everywhere today: 12 hours, 8 minutes.

March 2009

S	M	T	W	T	F	S
1	2	3	4	5	6	7
8	9	10	11	12	13	14
15	16	17	18	19	20	21
22	23	24	25	26	27	28
29	30	31				

TAYLOR, FREDERICK WINSLOW: BIRTH ANNIVERSARY. Mar 20, 1856. Villified and praised, Frederick Winslow Taylor changed the face of business forever as the "Father of Scientific Management." Born at Philadelphia, PA, Taylor was a chief engineer at Philadelphia's Midvale Steel Company, when he introduced time-and-motion studies in 1881, which helped companies find efficiencies in worker movement and drive out time wasting on the assembly lines. Henry Ford, in particular, put Taylor's theories to work. Taylor died at Philadelphia, Mar 21, 1915.

TUNISIA: INDEPENDENCE DAY. Mar 20. Commemorates treaty in 1956 by which France recognized Tunisian autonomy.

Birthdays Today

Holly Hunter, 51, actress (Oscar for *The Piano; Broadcast News, The Firm*), born Conyers, GA, Mar 20, 1958.

William Hurt, 59, actor (*The Accidental Tourist, Broadcast News*), born Washington, DC, Mar 20, 1950.

Spike Lee, 52, director, producer, writer, actor (*She's Gotta Have It, Do the Right Thing, Malcolm X*), born Atlanta, GA, Mar 20, 1957.

Hal Linden, 78, actor ("Barney Miller," "Blacke's Magic"), born Harold Lipshitz at the Bronx, NY, Mar 20, 1931.

Marian McPartland, 89, jazz pianist (*After Hours, Personal Choice, In My Life*), born Slough, England, Mar 20, 1920.

Brian Mulroney, 70, Canadian statesman and 18th prime minister of Canada, born Baie Comeau, QC, Canada, Mar 20, 1939.

Robert Gordon (Bobby) Orr, 61, Hall of Fame hockey player, born Parry Sound, ON, Canada, Mar 20, 1948.

Jerry Reed, 72, actor, singer, songwriter ("When You're Hot, You're Hot"), born Jerry Hubbard at Atlanta, GA, Mar 20, 1937.

Carl Reiner, 87, actor ("The Dick Van Dyke Show," "Your Show of Shows"), writer, director, born the Bronx, NY, Mar 20, 1922.

Patrick James (Pat) Riley, 64, basketball coach and former player, born Schenectady, NY, Mar 20, 1945.

Theresa Russell, 52, actress (*Straight Time, Black Widow*), born San Diego, CA, Mar 20, 1957.

David Thewlis, 46, actor ("Dinotopia"), born Blackpool, Lancashire, England, Mar 20, 1963.

Fernando Torres, 25, soccer player, born Fuenlabrada, Spain, Mar 20, 1984.

Paul Junger Witt, 66, producer (*Three Kings*, "Everything's Relative"), director, born New York, NY, Mar 20, 1943.

March 21 — Saturday

DAY 80 | **285 REMAINING**

ARIES, THE RAM. Mar 21–Apr 19. In the astronomical/astrological zodiac, which divides the sun's apparent orbit into 12 segments, the period Mar 21–Apr 19 is traditionally identified as the sun sign of Aries, the Ram. The ruling planet is Mars.

BABE DIDRIKSON PITCHES FOR ATHLETICS: 75th ANNIVERSARY. Mar 21, 1934. Mildred ("Babe") Didrikson, perhaps the greatest women athlete of all time, pitched one inning of baseball for the Philadelphia Athletics in an exhibition game against the Brooklyn Dodgers. Didrikson hit the first batter she faced and walked the next. The third hit into a triple play.

BACH, JOHANN SEBASTIAN: BIRTH ANNIVERSARY. Mar 21, 1685. (Old Style date.) Organist and composer, one of the most influential composers in musical history. Born at Eisenach, Germany; he died at Leipzig, Germany, July 28, 1750.

BIG TEN WOMEN'S GYMNASTICS CHAMPIONSHIPS. Mar 21. University of Illinois, Champaign-Urbana, IL. For info: Big Ten Conference, 1500 W Higgins Rd, Park Ridge, IL 60068-6300. Phone: (847) 696-1010. Fax: (847) 696-1110. Web: www.bigten.org.

ENGLAND: HEAD OF THE RIVER RACE. Mar 21. Mortlake to Putney, River Thames, London. Processional race for 420 eight-oared crews, starting at 10-second intervals. Est attendance: 7,000. For info: Dr. A. Ruddle, 59 Berkeley Ct, Weybridge, Surrey, UK KT13 9HY. Phone: (44) (1932) 220-401. Web: www.horr.co.uk.

FIRST ROUND-THE-WORLD BALLOON FLIGHT: 10th ANNIVERSARY. Mar 21, 1999. Swiss psychiatrist Bertrand Piccard and British copilot Brian Jones landed in the Egyptian desert on this date, having flown 29,056 miles nonstop around the world in a hot-air balloon. Leaving from Chateau d'Oex in the Swiss Alps on Mar 1, the trip took 19 days, 21 hours and 55 minutes. Piccard is the grandson of balloonist Auguste Piccard, who was the first to ascend into the stratosphere in a balloon. See also: "First Solo Round-the-World Balloon Flight: Anniversary" (July 2) and "Piccard, Auguste: Birth Anniversary" (Jan 28).

GALLO, JULIO: BIRTH ANNIVERSARY. Mar 21, 1910. American vintner Julio Gallo was born at Oakland, CA. He is best known for his role in the Ernest and Julio Gallo Winery, of Modesto, CA, which at one time claimed about 26 percent of the US wine industry. He died May 2, 1993, near Tracy, CA.

GERSDORFF HITLER ASSASSINATION ATTEMPT: ANNIVERSARY. Mar 21, 1943. In a suicide/assassination attempt planned for this date, Major General Baron von Gersdorff was to carry a bomb in the pocket of his greatcoat to the "Heroes Memorial Day" annual dedication to the dead of the First World War. Hitler was to attend this event to inspect some weaponry taken from captured Russian soldiers. The bomb was to go off within 10 minutes of Hitler's arrival at the event as he was not expected to be there for very long. The conspirators were unable to locate the necessary short time fuse and the attempt had to be called off. This was the second serious plan to assassinate Hitler in 1943.

IRANIAN NEW YEAR: NORUZ. Mar 21. National celebration for all Iranians, this is the traditional Persian New Year. (In Iran spring comes Mar 20 or 21.) It is a celebration of nature's rebirth. Every household spreads a special cover with symbols for the seven good angels on it. These symbols are sprouts, wheat germ, apples, hyacinth, fruit of the jujube, garlic and sumac heralding life, rebirth, health, happiness, prosperity, joy and beauty. A fishbowl is also customary, representing the end of the astrological year, and wild rue is burned to drive away evil and bring about a happy New Year. This pre-Islamic holiday, a legacy of Zoroastrianism, is also celebrated as Navruz, Nau-Roz or Noo Roz in Afghanistan, Albania, Azerbaijan, Kazakhstan, Kyrgyzstan, Tajikistan, Turkmenistan and Uzbekistan. For info: Mahvash Tafreshi, Librarian, Farmingdale Public Library, 116 Merritts Rd, Farmingdale, NY 11735. Phone: (516) 249-9090. Fax: (516) 694-9697 or Yassaman Djalali, Librarian, West Valley Branch Library, 1243 San Tomas Aquino Rd, San Jose, CA 95117. Phone: (408) 244-4766.

JUAREZ, BENITO: BIRTH ANNIVERSARY. Mar 21. A full-blooded Zapotec Indian, Benito Pablo Juarez was born at Oaxaca, Mexico, in 1806 and grew up to become the president of Mexico. He learned Spanish at age 12. Juarez became judge of the civil court in Oaxaca in 1842, a member of congress in 1846 and governor in 1847. In 1858, following a rebellion against the constitution, the presidency was passed to Juarez. He died at Mexico City, July 18, 1872. A symbol of liberation and of Mexican resistance to foreign intervention, his birthday is a public holiday in Mexico.

LESOTHO: NATIONAL TREE PLANTING DAY. Mar 21. Lesotho.

LEWIS, FRANCIS: BIRTH ANNIVERSARY. Mar 21, 1713. Signer of the Declaration of Independence, born at Wales. Died Dec 31, 1802, at Long Island, NY.

LUNSFORD, BASCOM LAMAR: BIRTH ANNIVERSARY. Mar 21, 1882. Folk song writer and folklorist who authored the folk song "Mountain Dew," Lunsford started the first folk music festival in 1928 at Asheville, NC. This event, which led to the formation of the National Clogging and Hoedown Council, is held to this day. He was known as the "father of clogging dance" and the "king of folk music." He recorded some 320 folk songs, tunes and stories for the Library of Congress. Born at Mars Hill, NC, Lunsford died Sept 4, 1973, at South Turkey Creek, NC.

MAPLE SYRUP SATURDAY. Mar 21. Gordon Bubolz Nature Preserve, Appleton, WI. Find out how to make maple syrup. Est attendance: 600. For info: Gordon Bubolz Nature Preserve, 4815 N Lynndale Dr, Appleton, WI 54913. Phone: (920) 731-6041. Fax: (920) 731-9593. E-mail: info@bubolzpreserve.org.

MEMORY DAY. Mar 21. To encourage awareness of the traditional memory system using pattern t,d = 1; n = 2; m = 3; r = 4; l = 5; j,ch = 6; k,q,g-hard = 7; f,v = 8; b,p = 9. Study historic examples of the use of the memory system in the writings of Milton, Thomas Gray, Longfellow, Lincoln and others. For info: Robert L. Birch, Coord, Puns Corps, 3108 Dashiell Rd, Falls Church, VA 22042. Phone: (703) 533-3668.

MILITARY THROUGH THE AGES. Mar 21–22. Jamestown Settlement, Williamsburg, VA. Centuries of military history unfold as reenactors depicting soldiers and military encounters throughout history demonstrate camp life, military tactics and weaponry. For info: Jamestown-Yorktown Foundation, PO Box 1607, Williamsburg, VA 23187. Phone: (757) 253-4838 or (888) 593-4682. Fax: (757) 253-5299. Web: www.historyisfun.org.

NAMIBIA: INDEPENDENCE DAY. Mar 21. National Day. Commemorates independence from South Africa in 1990.

NATIONAL COMMON COURTESY DAY. Mar 21. Citizens of our country reflect on what it means to demonstrate common courtesy. We live in a society where it seems that we have forgotten how to display such behaviors in our everyday lives, be it at work, home or simply driving down the highway. On National Common Courtesy Day, stories will be collected from individuals who have demonstrated common courtesy or who have been the recipients of such acts. For info: Lefiest H. Galimore, 3139 Plymouth Rd, Ann Arbor, MI 48105. Phone: (734) 502-5775. E-mail: lefiest@aol.com.

NATIONAL QUILTING DAY. Mar 21. 18th annual celebration. Sponsored by NQA since 1992, this day is a grassroots effort to unite quilters and quilt lovers everywhere, not only in this country, but also around the world. Individuals, groups of quilters, shop owners, publishers and the entire community of quiltmaking are invited to join NQA in recognizing and promoting the tradition of quiltmaking. Annually, the third Saturday in March. For info: The Natl Quilting Assn, Inc, PO Box 12190, Columbus, OH 43212-0190. Phone: (614) 488-8520. E-mail: nqaquilts@sbcglobal.net. Web: www.nqaquilts.org.

NAW-RUZ. Mar 21. Baha'i New Year's Day. Astronomically fixed to commence the year on the spring equinox. One of the nine days of the year when Baha'is suspend work. For info: Baha'is of the US, Office of Communications, 1233 Central St, Evanston, IL 60201. Phone: (847) 733-3559. Fax: (847) 733-3578. E-mail: ooc@usbnc.org. Web: www.bahai.us.

NORWAY: BIRKEBEINERRENNET. Mar 21. Rena and Lillehammer. Since 1932, ski marathon of 54 km between the cities of Rena and Lillehammer in which competitors carry a backpack weighing 3.5 kg. The race and the backpack commemorate an epic journey in Norwegian history: On Christmas Day in 1205, in the midst of a power struggle for the Norwegian throne, two birkebeiners (warriors who wore birch-bark leg coverings) smuggled baby prince Hakon Hakonsson by ski over mountainous terrain to safety away from a rival faction. The baby survived to become King Hakon Hakonson IV, and he ended the civil war. For info: Birkebeinerrennet, Pb 144, Rena 2451, Norway. Phone: (47) (41) 77-29-00. Fax: (47) (62) 44-07-35. E-mail: renn@birkebeiner.no. Web: www.birkebeiner.no.

March 2009	S	M	T	W	T	F	S
	1	2	3	4	5	6	7
	8	9	10	11	12	13	14
	15	16	17	18	19	20	21
	22	23	24	25	26	27	28
	29	30	31				

POCAHONTAS (REBECCA ROLFE): DEATH ANNIVERSARY. Mar 21, 1617. Pocahontas, daughter of Powhatan, born about 1595, near Jamestown, VA, leader of the Indian union of Algonkin nations, helped to foster goodwill between the colonists of the Jamestown settlement and her people. Pocahontas converted to Christianity, was baptized with the name Rebecca and married John Rolfe Apr 5, 1614. In 1616, she accompanied Rolfe on a trip to his native England, where she was regarded as an overseas "ambassador." Pocahontas's stay in England drew so much attention to the Virginia Company's Jamestown settlement that lotteries were held to help support the colony. Shortly before she was scheduled to return to Jamestown, Pocahontas died at Gravesend, Kent, England, of either smallpox or pneumonia.

SAVE THE FLORIDA PANTHER DAY. Mar 21. Florida. A ceremonial holiday on the third Saturday in March.

SECOND BATTLE OF SOMME: ANNIVERSARY. Mar 21–Apr 4, 1918. General Erich Ludendorff launched the Michael offensive, the biggest German offensive of 1918, on Mar 21 with a five-hour artillery barrage. The Central Powers' objective was to drive a wedge between the British and French forces and drive the British to the sea. Although they did not accomplish this objective, in the south they captured Montdidier and advanced to a depth of 40 miles. They managed to create a bulge in the front south of Somme and end what had effectively been a stalemate. The Allies lost nearly 230,000 men and the Germans almost as many in the Battle of Somme.

SELMA CIVIL RIGHTS MARCH: ANNIVERSARY. Mar 21, 1965. More than 3,000 civil rights demonstrators led by Dr. Martin Luther King, Jr, began a four-day march from Selma, AL, to Montgomery, AL, to demand federal protection of voting rights. There were violent attempts by local police, using fire hoses and dogs, to suppress the march. A march two weeks before on Mar 7, 1965, was called "Bloody Sunday" because of the use of nightsticks, chains and electric cattle prods against the marchers by the police.

SOUTH AFRICA: HUMAN RIGHTS DAY. Mar 21. National holiday. Commemorates the Mar 21, 1960, massacre at Sharpeville and all those who lost their lives in the struggle for equal rights as citizens of South Africa.

STRANG, JAMES JESSE (KING STRANG): BIRTH ANNIVERSARY. Mar 21, 1813. Perhaps America's only crowned king was born at Scipio, NY, and christened Jesse James Strang (which he later changed to James Jesse Strang). He was crowned king of Mormons at Beaver Island, MI, July 8, 1850, and ruled his kingdom until his death. Elected to the Michigan legislature in 1852 and 1854. Wounded by assassins June 16, 1856, at Beaver Island, he died June 19, 1856, at Voree, WI.

UNITED NATIONS: INTERNATIONAL DAY FOR THE ELIMINATION OF RACIAL DISCRIMINATION. Mar 21. Initiated by the

United Nations General Assembly in 1966 to be observed annually Mar 21, the anniversary of the killing of 69 African demonstrators at Sharpeville, South Africa, in 1960, as a day to remember "the victims of Sharpeville and those countless others in different parts of the world who have fallen victim to racial injustice" and to promote efforts to eradicate racial discrimination worldwide. For info: United Nations, Dept of Public Info, New York, NY 10017. Web: www.un.org.

UNITED NATIONS: WEEK OF SOLIDARITY WITH THE PEOPLES STRUGGLING AGAINST RACISM AND RACIAL DISCRIMINATION. Mar 21–27. Annual observance initiated by the United Nations General Assembly as part of its program of the Decade for Action to Combat Racism and Racial Discrimination. For info: United Nations, Dept of Public Info, New York, NY 10017. Web: www.un.org.

USA MEMORY CHAMPIONSHIP. Mar 21 (tentative). Site TBA. 12th annual. "Mental Athletes" will exercise their memories in events featuring a string of 200 random digits, a double deck of shuffled cards, 200 random words, 99 names and faces and an unpublished 50-line poem. Competitors (ages 12 and up) from all over the country will vie for the title of "National Memory Champion." The winner will automatically qualify to compete against champions of other countries in the World Memory Championships held in Oxford, England. To compete, register on the website. For media info: Renee Sall, Maximum Exposure PR, 50 Tice Blvd, Woodcliff Lake, NJ 07677. Phone: (201) 573-0300. E-mail: renee@maximumexposurepr.com. Web: www.usamemorychampionship.com.

WILD AZALEA FESTIVAL. Mar 21. White Springs, FL. 9th annual. Celebrate the blooming of Florida's wild azaleas with music and dance by Florida entertainers, a wagon ride into the park, arts and crafts and regional foods. Annually, the third Saturday in March. For info: Mitzi Nelson, Florida Park Service, PO Drawer G, White Springs, FL 32096. Phone: (386) 397-7005. Fax: (386) 397-4262. E-mail: margaret.a.nelson@dep.state.fl.us. Web: www.floridastateparks.org/stephenfoster.

Birthdays Today

Matthew Broderick, 47, actor (*Godzilla, Inspector Gadget, Election*; stage: *The Producers*), born New York, NY, Mar 21, 1962.

Peter Brook, 84, theater director, born London, England, Mar 21, 1925.

Timothy Dalton, 63, actor (James Bond movies, *Cleopatra, Centennial*), born Colwyn Bay, Wales, Mar 21, 1946.

Kevin Federline, 31, dancer, born Fresno City, CA, Mar 21, 1978.

Al Freeman, Jr, 75, actor (*A Patch of Blue; Roots: The Next Generations*), born San Antonio, TX, Mar 21, 1934.

Rosie O'Donnell, 47, actress (*A League of Their Own*), host ("The Rosie O'Donnell Show"), born Commack, NY, Mar 21, 1962.

Gary Oldman, 51, actor (*Sid and Nancy, JFK*), born South London, England, Mar 21, 1958.

Ronaldinho, 29, soccer player, born Ronaldo de Assis Moreira at Porto Alegre, Brazil, Mar 21, 1980.

March 22 — Sunday

DAY 81 — **284 REMAINING**

AS YOUNG AS YOU FEEL DAY. Mar 22. Now more than ever you are as young as you feel. So stop acting your chronological age and get out there and start feeling peppy! (©2006 by WH.) For info: Thomas & Ruth Roy, Wellcat Holidays, 2418 Long Ln, Lebanon, PA 17046. Phone: (717) 279-0184. E-mail: info@wellcat.com. Web: www.wellcat.com.

ASSOCIATION OF AMERICAN GEOGRAPHERS ANNUAL MEETING. Mar 22–27. Las Vegas, NV. 105th annual national meeting of members with workshops, paper and poster sessions and field trips. Est attendance: 3,000. For info: Assn of American Geographers, 1710 16th St NW, Washington, DC 20009-3198. Phone: (202) 234-1450. E-mail: gaia@aag.org. Web: www.aag.org.

DOCTOR-PATIENT TRUST WEEK. Mar 22–28. To rekindle the once-revered sanctity of the doctor-patient relationship. For info: Dr. Frank H. Boehm, Vanderbilt Medical Center, B-1000 Medical Center North, Nashville, TN 37232. Phone: (615) 322-2071. E-mail: frank.boehm@vanderbilt.edu. Web: www.dr-boehm.com.

ENGLAND: MOTHERING SUNDAY. Mar 22. Fourth Sunday of Lent, formerly occasion for attending services at Mother Church, family gatherings and visits to parents. Now popularly known as Mother's Day and a time for visiting and taking gifts to mothers.

EQUAL RIGHTS AMENDMENT SENT TO STATES FOR RATIFICATION: ANNIVERSARY. Mar 22, 1972. The Senate passed the 27th Amendment, prohibiting discrimination on the basis of sex, sending it to the states for ratification. Hawaii led the way as the first state to ratify and by the end of the year 22 states had ratified it. On Oct 6, 1978, the deadline for ratification was extended to June 30, 1982, by Congress. The amendment still lacked three of the required 38 states for ratification. This was the first extension granted since Congress set seven years as the limit for ratification. The amendment failed to achieve ratification as the deadline came and passed and no additional states ratified the measure.

FIRST WOMEN'S COLLEGIATE BASKETBALL GAME: ANNIVERSARY. Mar 22, 1893. The first women's collegiate basketball game was played at Smith College at Northampton, MA. Senda Berenson, then Smith's director of physical education and "mother of women's basketball," supervised the game, in which Smith's sophomore team beat the freshman team 5–4. For info: Dir of Media Relations, Smith College, Office of College Relations, Northampton, MA 01063. Phone: (413) 585-2700. Fax: (413) 585-2174. Web: www.smith.edu.

INDIA: NEW YEAR'S DAY. Mar 22. This is the first day of the New Year on the Saka calendar adopted by India after independence from Great Britain. The Saka calendar is a solar calendar with the same Leap Year schedule as the Gregorian calendar. In Common Years, the New Year is Mar 22; in Leap Years, the New Year falls on Mar 21.

INTERNATIONAL DAY OF THE SEAL: ANNIVERSARY. Mar 22. In 1982 Congress declared an International Day of the Seal to draw attention to the cruelty of seal hunts and the virtual inevitability of these creatures' extinction. Zoos and aquariums around the world observe this day with special programs and activities; contact your local affiliate for a schedule of activities.

INTERNATIONAL GOOF-OFF DAY. Mar 22. A day of relaxation and a time to be oneself; a day for some good-humored fun and some good-natured silliness. Everyone needs one special day each year to goof off. For info: Monica A. Dufour, PO Box 71, Clio, MI 48420.

L'AMOUR, LOUIS: BIRTH ANNIVERSARY. Mar 22, 1908. Popular author Louis Dearborn LaMoore was born at Jamestown, ND. He began writing stories in the 1930s, initially selling them to pulp magazines; despite an interruption by military service during WWII, L'Amour was a quite successful writer of adventure stories, Westerns and scripts for television and film. He eventually authored 116 Western novels that sold 20 million copies in 20 different languages. He was the first novelist to be awarded the Congressional Medal of

Freedom (1983) and was also given the Presidential Medal of Freedom (1984). L'Amour died June 10, 1988, at Los Angeles, CA.

LASER PATENTED: ANNIVERSARY. Mar 22, 1960. The first patent for a laser (light amplification by stimulated emission of radiation) granted to Arthur Schawlow and Charles Townes.

LUXEMBOURG: BRETZELSONNDEG. Mar 22. The fourth Sunday in Lent is an occasion for boys to give pretzel-shaped cakes to sweethearts who may respond, on Easter Sunday, with a gift of a decorated egg or sweet.

NATIONAL CLEANING WEEK. Mar 22–28. National Cleaning Week serves as a reminder to tackle spring cleaning. Dedicate each day to a specific chore. Annually, the last week in March. For info: Monica Nassif, The Caldrea Company, 420 N 5th St, Ford Centre, Ste 600, Minneapolis, MN 55401. Phone: (612) 371-0003 or (877) 576-8808. Fax: (612) 371-9995.

PUERTO RICO: EMANCIPATION DAY. Mar 22. Holiday commemorates the end of slavery on Mar 22, 1873.

SPACE MILESTONE: RECORD TIME IN SPACE. Mar 22, 1995. Russian cosmonaut Valery Polyakov returned to Earth after setting a record of 438 days in space aboard *Mir.* Previous records include three Soviet cosmonauts who spent 237 days in space at *Salyut 7* space station in 1984, a Soviet cosmonaut who spent 326 days aboard *Mir* in 1987 and two Soviets who spent 366 days aboard *Mir* in 1988. The US space endurance record was set by Carl Walz and Daniel Bursch, who stayed 196 days in space aboard *Endeavor*, completing their mission on June 19, 2002. US astronaut Shannon Lucid set the record for women in space with her 188-day stay on *Mir* in 1996.

SPRING FAIRY FUN DAY. Mar 22. A Fairy Fun Day is held once each season on the fourth Sunday. Spring Fairy Fun Day is where fairy friends dress up, enjoy picnics, fairy hunts, gardening events and just get together to sparkle, laugh, delight and appreciate fairies, children and nature. Events are organized worldwide—come join us! For info: Fairy Society Artist Community Network, 4128 Bye Way, Santa Cruz, CA 95060. Phone: (408) 564-5550. E-mail: michelle@elementaljoy.net. Web: http://thefairysociety.ning.com/.

TUSKEGEE AIRMEN ACTIVATED: ANNIVERSARY. Mar 22, 1941. This pioneering and highly decorated WWII African-American aviator unit gained their name during training at the US Army airfield near Tuskegee, AL, and at the Tuskegee Institute. They were activated as the 99th Pursuit Squadron and later formed the 332nd Fighter Group (with the 100th, 301st and 302nd squadrons). 992 black pilots emerged from training to fly P-39, P-40, P-47 and P-51 aircraft in more than 15,000 sorties in North Africa, Sicily and Europe. On escort missions, they were the only unit that never lost a US bomber. They shot down 111 enemy planes and destroyed 273 planes on the ground. Lieutenant Colonel Benjamin O. Davis, Jr—later the US Air Force's first black general—was their commander. When President Harry Truman integrated the US military, the all-black group was deactivated. See also: "Davis, Benjamin O., Jr: Birth Anniversary" (Dec 18).

UNITED NATIONS: WORLD DAY FOR WATER. Mar 22. The General Assembly declared this observance (Res 47/193) to promote public awareness of how water resource development contributes to economic productivity and social well-being. Annually, on Mar 22.

WSBA/WARM 103/WSOX 96.1 EASTER CRAFT SHOW. Mar 22. York, PA. More than 125 quality craft displays will be presented with everything from country to contemporary dolls, jewelry, pottery and much more. Admission fee. Est attendance: 3,000. For info: Joe Alfano, Special Events, 5989 Susquehanna Plaza Dr, York, PA 17406. Phone: (717) 764-1155. Fax: (717) 252-4708. E-mail: joe.alfano@cumulus.com. Web: www.warm103.com.

March 2009

S	M	T	W	T	F	S
1	2	3	4	5	6	7
8	9	10	11	12	13	14
15	16	17	18	19	20	21
22	23	24	25	26	27	28
29	30	31				

Birthdays Today

George Benson, 66, singer, guitarist ("On Broadway," "Give Me the Night"), born Pittsburgh, PA, Mar 22, 1943.

Robert Quinlan (Bob) Costas, 57, sportscaster, born New York, NY, Mar 22, 1952.

Bruno Ganz, 68, actor (*The American Friend, Wings of Desire*), born Zurich, Switzerland, Mar 22, 1941.

Orrin Grant Hatch, 75, US Senator (R, Utah), born Pittsburgh, PA, Mar 22, 1934.

Andrew Lloyd Webber, 61, composer (*Cats, Phantom of the Opera*), born London, England, Mar 22, 1948.

Karl Malden, 95, actor (*A Streetcar Named Desire*, "The Streets of San Francisco"), born Mladen Sekulovich at Gary, IN, Mar 22, 1914 (some sources say 1912 or 1913).

Matthew Modine, 50, actor (*Full Metal Jacket*, "And the Band Played On"), born Loma Linda, CA, Mar 22, 1959.

Allen Neuharth, 85, founder of *USA Today*, born Eureka, SD, Mar 22, 1924.

James Patterson, 62, author (*Kiss the Girls, Along Came a Spider*), born Newburgh, NY, Mar 22, 1947.

Cristen Powell, 30, race car driver, born Portland, OR, Mar 22, 1979.

Pat Robertson, 79, TV evangelist, born Lexington, VA, Mar 22, 1930.

William Shatner, 78, actor ("Star Trek," "Boston Legal"), author (*Star Trek* novels), born Montreal, QC, Canada, Mar 22, 1931.

Stephen Sondheim, 79, composer (*A Little Night Music*), born New York, NY, Mar 22, 1930.

Elvis Stojko, 37, former figure skater, born Newmarket, ON, Canada, Mar 22, 1972.

M. Emmet Walsh, 74, actor (*Serpico, Blood Simple, Raising Arizona*), born Ogdensburg, NY, Mar 22, 1935.

Reese Witherspoon, 33, actress (Oscar for *Walk the Line*; *Vanity Fair, Legally Blonde, Election*), born Nashville, TN, Mar 22, 1976.

March 23 — Monday

DAY 82 — 283 REMAINING

"BEAT THE CLOCK" TV PREMIERE: ANNIVERSARY. Mar 23, 1950. On this game show from the team of Mark Goodson and Bill Todman, couples performed stunts within a specified time period with the winners being given a chance to try a special stunt. Special stunts were very difficult, and the same one was attempted every week until a couple got it right. In 1952, James Dean got his first TV job testing stunts and warming up the audience. Bud Collyer was the host, assisted by Roxanne (real name Dolores Rosedale). A 1969 syndicated version hosted by Jack Narz and then by Gene Wood had celebrities to help the contestants. A 1979 revival was hosted by Monty Hall.

"BIG BERTHA" PARIS GUN: ANNIVERSARY. Mar 23, 1918. Germany initiated use of a terrifying new weapon—the Paris Gun—so called because it was first used against that city. The great gun, with a 25-foot carriage, was first used in combat when it was fired from a wooded location near Laon on Mar 23, 1918. It took 176 seconds for a shell to reach the city from a distance of 75 miles. On that first day 15 shots killed 16 individuals. Ridiculing the designers and manufacturers of the weapon, Parisians nicknamed it "Big Bertha" after the wife of the head of the munitions corporation. On Good Friday, Mar 29, a shell from the armament struck the church of Saint Gervais, which was crowded with worshipers. The casualty toll was 88 dead and 68 injured.

"THE BOLD AND THE BEAUTIFUL" TV PREMIERE: ANNIVERSARY. Mar 23, 1987. A continuing daytime serial created by William Bell and Lee Phillip Bell to be "young and hip." It is set in the fashion industry of Los Angeles with two central families, the Logans and the Forresters. The cast has included, as the Forresters: John McCook, Susan Flannery, Clayton Norcross, Jeff Trachta, Ronn Moss, Teri Ann Linn, Colleen Dion and as the Logans: Robert Pine, Judith Baldwin, Nancy Burnette, Nancy Sloan, Carrie Mitchum, Ethan Wayne, Brian Patrick Clarke, Katherine Kelly Lang and Lesley Woods.

CLARK, BARNEY: DEATH ANNIVERSARY. Mar 23, 1983. Barney Clark died after living almost 112 days with an artificial heart. The heart, made of polyurethane plastic and aluminum, was implanted in Clark at the University of Utah Medical Center, Salt Lake City, Dec 2, 1982. Clark was the first person ever to receive a permanent artificial heart. Born at Provo, UT, Jan 21, 1921, Clark was 62 when he died.

COLFAX, SCHUYLER: BIRTH ANNIVERSARY. Mar 23, 1823. 17th vice president of the US (1869–73). Born at New York, NY. Died Jan 13, 1885, at Mankato, MN.

CRAWFORD, JOAN: BIRTH ANNIVERSARY. Mar 23, 1905 (some sources say 1904 or 1907). Actress, born Lucille Fay LeSueur at San Antonio, TX. Crawford became a Hollywood star with her performance in *Our Dancing Daughters.* She won an Oscar in 1945 for her role in *Mildred Pierce.* Events of Crawford's life are chronicled in *Mommie Dearest.* Other films included *The Women, Whatever Happened to Baby Jane?* and *Twelve Miles Out.* She died at New York, NY, May 10, 1977.

DICK CLARK RETIRES FROM "AMERICAN BANDSTAND": 20th ANNIVERSARY. Mar 23, 1989. After 33 years, 59-year-old Dick Clark retired from hosting the television program "American Bandstand."

KUROSAWA, AKIRA: BIRTH ANNIVERSARY. Mar 23, 1910. Acclaimed filmmaker (*Rashomon, The Seven Samurai, Kagemusha, Ran*), born at Tokyo, Japan. The ambassador of Japanese cinema to the West, Kurosawa is considered one of the greatest film directors of all time. Died at Tokyo, Sept 6, 1998.

LIBERTY DAY: ANNIVERSARY. Mar 23, 1775. Anniversary of Patrick Henry's speech for arming the Virginia militia at St. John's Church, Richmond, VA. "I know not what course others may take, but as for me, give me liberty or give me death."

NATIONAL PROTOCOL OFFICERS WEEK. Mar 23–28. Recognizes protocol officers—the trusted advisers who plan and orchestrate international VIP visits, meetings, ceremonies and special events for the military, government, academia and business world. This week acknowledges those who influence worldwide diplomacy by understanding and embracing customs such as forms of address, flag etiquette, titles and more. Annually, the last full week of March. For info: The Protocol School of Washington, PO Box 676, Columbia, SC 29202. Phone: (877) 766-3757. E-mail: info@psow.com. Web: www.psow.com.

NATIONAL PUPPY DAY. Mar 23. To celebrate the puppies in our lives and rescue the ones who need a good home. Our goal is to have 10,000 puppies adopted across the US on National Puppy Day! For info: Animal Miracle Foundation, PO Box 2061, Kingston, WA 98346. Phone: (877) 205-0871. E-mail: puppyday@animalmiraclefoundation.org. Web: www.nationalpuppyday.com.

NEAR MISS DAY: 20th ANNIVERSARY. Mar 23, 1989. A mountain-sized asteroid passed within 500,000 miles of Earth, a very close call according to NASA. Impact would have equaled the strength of 40,000 hydrogen bombs, created a crater the size of the District of Columbia and devastated everything for 100 miles in all directions.

NEW ZEALAND: OTAGO AND SOUTHLAND PROVINCIAL ANNIVERSARY. Mar 23. In addition to the statutory public holidays of New Zealand, there is in each provincial district a holiday for the provincial anniversary. This day is observed in Otago and Southland.

"O.K." FIRST APPEARANCE IN PRINT: ANNIVERSARY. Mar 23, 1839. *The Boston Morning Post* printed the first known "o.k." on this day in 1839. It derived from a jovial misspelling of "all correct"—"oll korrect." Etymologist Allen Read doggedly tracked down the word's origin in the 1960s. "O.K." is now used in most languages.

PAKISTAN: REPUBLIC DAY. Mar 23, 1940. National holiday. In 1940 the All-India-Muslim League adopted a resolution calling for a Muslim homeland. On the same day in 1956 Pakistan declared itself a republic.

RALLY FOR DECENCY: 40th ANNIVERSARY. Mar 23, 1969. Anita Bryant, Jackie Gleason and Kate Smith rallied with 30,000 others in Miami on this day in reaction to Jim Morrison's arrest for indecent exposure.

SPACE MILESTONE: *MIR* ABANDONED (USSR). Mar 23, 2001. The 140-ton *Mir* space station, launched in 1986, was brought down into the South Pacific near Fiji, about 1,800 miles east of New Zealand, just before 1 AM, EST. Two-thirds of the station burned up during its controlled descent. *Mir's* core component had been aloft for more than 15 years and orbited Earth 86,330 times. Nearly 100 people, seven of them American, had spent some time on *Mir*. See also: "Space Milestone: *Mir* Space Station (USSR)" (Feb 20).

UNITED NATIONS: WORLD METEOROLOGICAL DAY. Mar 23. An international day observed by meteorological services throughout the world and by the organizations of the UN system. Annually, on Mar 23. For info: United Nations, Dept of Public Info, New York, NY 10017. Web: www.un.org.

Birthdays Today

Louie Anderson, 56, comedian, actor ("Life with Louie"), born Minneapolis, MN, Mar 23, 1953.

Dr. Roger Bannister, 80, distance runner, broke the four-minute-mile record in 1954, born Harrow, Middlesex, England, Mar 23, 1929.

Mike Easley, 59, Governor of North Carolina (D), born Nash County, NC, Mar 23, 1950.

Richard Grieco, 44, actor (*Ultimate Deception, Blackheart*), born Watertown, NY, Mar 23, 1965.

Perez Hilton, 31, gossip columnist, blogger, born Mario Lavandeira at Miami, FL, Mar 23, 1978.

Chaka Khan, 56, singer, born Yvette Marie Stevens at Chicago, IL, Mar 23, 1953.

Jason Kidd, 36, basketball player, born San Francisco, CA, Mar 23, 1973.

Moses Eugene Malone, 55, Hall of Fame basketball player, born Petersburg, VA, Mar 23, 1954.

Amanda Plummer, 52, actress (Tony for *Agnes of God*; *The Fisher King*), born New York, NY, Mar 23, 1957.

Keri Russell, 33, actress (*Waitress, Mission: Impossible III*, "Felicity"), born Fountain Valley, CA, Mar 23, 1976.

March 24 — Tuesday

DAY 83 **282 REMAINING**

AMERICAN DIABETES ASSOCIATION ALERT DAY. Mar 24. A one-day "wake-up call" to raise awareness about the seriousness of diabetes and its risk factors. The centerpiece of the alert is the diabetes risk test, which is distributed and promoted through national and local media. Annually, the fourth Tuesday in March. For info: 800-DIABETES (342-2383) or www.diabetes.org/alert.

ANN ARBOR FILM FESTIVAL. Mar 24–29. Ann Arbor, MI. 47th annual. Independent digital, 16mm and 35mm film festival. Genres represented include experimental, animation, documentary, narrative, avant-garde. Entry deadline: Oct 1, 2008. $20,000 awarded in prizes. Est attendance: 8,000. For info: Chrisstina Hamilton, Ann Arbor Film Festival, PO Box 8232, Ann Arbor, MI 48107. Phone: (734) 995-5356. Fax: (734) 995-5396. E-mail: info@aafilmfest.org. Web: aafilmfest.org.

ARGENTINA: NATIONAL DAY OF MEMORY FOR TRUTH AND JUSTICE. Mar 24. Public holiday since 2002 commemorating victims of the military coup d'etat of 1976.

BARBERA, JOE: BIRTH ANNIVERSARY. Mar 24, 1911. Joseph Roland Barbera, born at New York, NY, was one-half of the world's most prolific and beloved animation teams: Hanna-Barbera. Working with Bill Hanna, Barbera created the Tom and Jerry theatrical shorts for MGM that garnered 7 Oscars. Moving to television, Hanna-Barbera produced some 100 cartoon series, including the ground-breaking sitcom-style shows "The Flintstones" and "The Jetsons." Barbera continued working in animation almost to his death, creating a Tom and Jerry short in 2005. He died at Los Angeles, CA, on Dec 18, 2006.

***EXXON VALDEZ* OIL SPILL: 20th ANNIVERSARY.** Mar 24, 1989. The tanker *Exxon Valdez* ran aground at Prince William Sound, leaking 11 million gallons of oil into one of nature's richest habitats.

HOUDINI, HARRY: BIRTH ANNIVERSARY. Mar 24, 1874. Magician and escape artist. Born Erik Weisz at Budapest, Hungary, died at Detroit, MI, Oct 31, 1926. Lecturer, athlete, author, expert on history of magic, exposer of fraudulent mediums and motion picture actor. Was best known for his ability to escape from locked restraints (handcuffs, straitjackets, coffins, boxes and milk cans). Anniversary of his death (Halloween) has been the occasion for meetings of magicians and attempts at communication by mediums.

"LETTER FROM AMERICA" RADIO PREMIERE: ANNIVERSARY. Mar 24, 1946. Acclaimed news correspondent and broadcaster Alistair Cooke began his weekly observations on American life on this date, with a story about British war brides traveling to America on the *Queen Mary*. Broadcast from Radio 4 and the BBC World Service, "Letter from America" would become the world's longest continuous running radio talk program. Cooke created 2,869 "letters." His last broadcast was Feb 20, 2004, and the BBC announced his retirement on Mar 2, 2004.

MELLON, ANDREW W.: BIRTH ANNIVERSARY. Mar 24, 1855. American financier, industrialist, government official (secretary of the treasury), art and book collector, born at Pittsburgh, PA. Died Aug 26, 1937, at Southhampton, NY.

MORRIS, WILLIAM: 175th BIRTH ANNIVERSARY. Mar 24, 1834. English poet, artist and social reformer. Born at Walthamstow, England; died at Hammersmith, London, Oct 3, 1896.

March 2009	S	M	T	W	T	F	S
	1	2	3	4	5	6	7
	8	9	10	11	12	13	14
	15	16	17	18	19	20	21
	22	23	24	25	26	27	28
	29	30	31				

PHILIPPINE INDEPENDENCE. Mar 24, 1934. President Franklin Roosevelt signed a bill granting independence to the Philippines. The bill, which took effect July 4, 1946, brought to a close almost half a century of US control of the islands.

POWELL, JOHN WESLEY: 175th BIRTH ANNIVERSARY. Mar 24, 1834. American geologist, explorer, ethnologist. He is best known for his explorations of the Grand Canyon by boat on the Colorado River. Born at Mount Morris, NY, he died at Haven, ME, Sept 23, 1902.

PRESLEY INDUCTED INTO THE ARMY: ANNIVERSARY. Mar 24, 1958. Teenagers across the US mourned as rock idol Elvis Presley was inducted into the US Army on this date at Memphis, TN. Presley completed basic training and then was posted overseas to Germany. He left active service on Mar 5, 1960.

RHODE ISLAND VOTERS REJECT CONSTITUTION: ANNIVERSARY. Mar 24, 1788. In a popular referendum, Rhode Island rejected the new Constitution by a vote of 2,708 to 237. The state later ratified the Constitution (May 29, 1790) and the Bill of Rights (June 7, 1790).

SAINT GABRIEL: FEAST DAY. Mar 24. Saint Gabriel the Archangel, patron saint of postal, telephone and telegraph workers.

STRATTON, DOROTHY CONSTANCE: BIRTH ANNIVERSARY. Mar 24, 1899. Dorothy Constance Stratton, born at Brookfield, MO, was instrumental during WWII in organizing the SPARS, the women's branch of the US Coast Guard (authorized Nov 23, 1942). Under Lieutenant Commander Stratton's command some 10,000 women were trained for supportive noncombat roles in the Coast Guard. SPARS was dissolved in 1946 after the war had ended. Stratton worked with many women's organizations, including the Girl Scouts as national executive director in the '50s. Stratton died at the age of 107 on Sept 17, 2006, at West Lafeyette, IN.

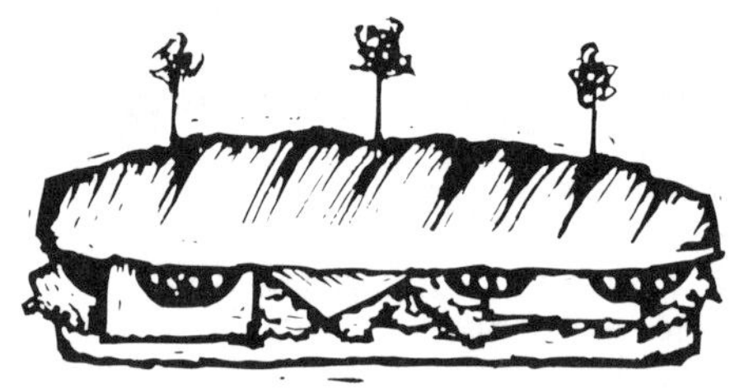

Birthdays Today

Chris Bosh, 25, basketball player, born Dallas, TX, Mar 24, 1984.

Lara Flynn Boyle, 39, actress ("Twin Peaks," "The Practice," *Dead Poets Society*), born Davenport, IA, Mar 24, 1970.

R. Lee Ermey, 65, actor (*Full Metal Jacket, Mississippi Burning*), born Emporia, KS, Mar 24, 1944.

Lawrence Ferlinghetti, 90, "Beat" poet, author (*Coney Island of the Mind*), born Yonkers, NY, Mar 24, 1919.

Christine Gregoire, 62, Governor of Washington (D), born Adrian, MI, Mar 24, 1947.

Byron Janis, 81, pianist, born McKeesport, PA, Mar 24, 1928.

Star Jones, 47, television personality, born Badin, NC, Mar 24, 1962.

Bob Mackie, 69, costume and fashion designer, born Monterey Park, CA, Mar 24, 1940.

Peyton Manning, 33, football player, born New Orleans, LA, Mar 24, 1976.

Donna Pescow, 55, actress (*Saturday Night Fever*, "Angie"), born Brooklyn, NY, Mar 24, 1954.

Annabella Sciorra, 45, actress (*The Hand That Rocks the Cradle, Jungle Fever*), born Wethersfield, CT, Mar 24, 1964.

March 25 — Wednesday

DAY 84 **281 REMAINING**

BARTOK, BELA: BIRTH ANNIVERSARY. Mar 25, 1881. Hungarian composer, born at Nagyszentmiklos (now in Romania). Died at New York, NY, Sept 26, 1945.

BED-IN FOR PEACE: 40th ANNIVERSARY. Mar 25–31, 1969. After their Mar 20 wedding, John Lennon (of the Beatles) and Yoko Ono celebrated their honeymoon with a "happening": a bed-in for peace at their hotel room. In Room 902 of the Hilton Hotel in Amsterdam, pajama-clad Lennon and Ono received the world's print, radio and TV media while sitting up in bed: singing and talking for seven days encouraging the world to choose peace. The couple held another bed-in May 26–June 2 in Montreal, during which "Give Peace a Chance" was recorded.

BORGLUM, GUTZON: BIRTH ANNIVERSARY. Mar 25, 1867. American sculptor who created the huge sculpture of four American presidents (Washington, Jefferson, Lincoln and Theodore Roosevelt) at Mount Rushmore National Memorial in the Black Hills of South Dakota. Born John Gutzon de la Mothe Borglum at Bear Lake, ID, the son of Mormon pioneers, he worked the last 14 years of his life on the Mount Rushmore sculpture. He died at Chicago, IL, Mar 6, 1941.

"CAGNEY & LACEY" TV PREMIERE: ANNIVERSARY. Mar 25, 1982. "Cagney & Lacey" broke new ground as the first TV crime show in which the central characters were both female. The series was based on a made-for-TV movie that aired Oct 8, 1981, starring Loretta Swit and Tyne Daly. Meg Foster played Swit's character, Chris Cagney, but after one season she was replaced by Sharon Gless. Daly and Gless won six Emmys together for their roles. The last telecast aired on Aug 25, 1988.

CHARLIE PARKER AT THE LA PHILHARMONIC: ANNIVERSARY. Mar 25, 1946. One of the most influential solos of jazz alto saxophonist Charlie ("Bird") Parker's career was his rendition of "Lady Be Good," performed at the Los Angeles Philharmonic Auditorium. Every aspect of the performance became part of the language of modern jazz.

COSELL, HOWARD: BIRTH ANNIVERSARY. Mar 25, 1918. Howard Cosell, broadcaster, born at New York, NY. After earning a law degree, Cosell began his broadcasting career as the host of "Howard Cosell Speaking of Sports." He achieved national prominence and a great deal of notoriety for his support of Muhammad Ali's stand against the Vietnam War and then as cohost of ABC's "Monday Night Football." Died at New York, Apr 23, 1994.

FEAST OF ANNUNCIATION. Mar 25. Celebrated in the Roman Catholic Church in commemoration of the message of the Angel Gabriel to Mary that she was to be the mother of Christ.

GREECE: INDEPENDENCE DAY. Mar 25. National holiday. Celebrates the beginning of the Greek revolt for independence from the Ottoman Empire, Mar 25, 1821 (OS). Greece attained independence in 1829.

✦ **GREEK INDEPENDENCE DAY: A NATIONAL DAY OF CELEBRATION OF GREEK AND AMERICAN DEMOCRACY.** Mar 25.

LEAN, SIR DAVID: BIRTH ANNIVERSARY. Mar 25, 1908. British film director Sir David Lean was born at London. He directed 16 films and won two Best Director Academy Awards. His films include *Bridge on the River Kwai* (1957), *Lawrence of Arabia* (1962) and *Dr. Zhivago* (1965). He died Apr 16, 1991, at London.

MARYLAND DAY. Mar 25. Commemorates arrival of Lord Baltimore's first settlers at Maryland in 1634.

NATO FORCES ATTACK YUGOSLAVIA: 10th ANNIVERSARY. Mar 25, 1999. After many weeks of unsuccessful negotiations with Serb leader Slobodan Milosevic over the treatment of ethnic Albanians by Serb forces in the Kosovo Province of Yugoslavia, NATO forces began bombing Serbia and Kosovo. In response, the Serb army forced hundreds of thousands of ethnic Albanians to flee Kosovo for neighboring Albania, Macedonia and Montenegro. On June 10, 1999, NATO and Yugoslav officials signed an agreement providing for withdrawal of Serb troops from Kosovo, the end of Allied air strikes and the return of Kosovo refugees.

OLD NEW YEAR'S DAY. Mar 25. In Great Britain and its North American colonies this was the beginning of the new year up through 1751, when with the adoption of the Gregorian calendar the beginning of the year was changed to Jan 1.

PECAN DAY. Mar 25, 1775. Anniversary of the planting by George Washington of pecan trees (some of which still survive) at Mount Vernon. The trees were a gift to Washington from Thomas Jefferson, who had planted a few pecan trees from the southern US at Monticello, VA. The pecan, native to southern North America, is sometimes called "America's own nut." First cultivated by Native Americans, it has been transplanted to other continents but has failed to achieve wide use or popularity outside the US.

ROME EXECUTIONS: 65th ANNIVERSARY. Mar 25, 1944. Nazis occupying Rome during WWII executed 300 Italian priests, Jews, women and two 14-year-old boys in retaliation for the deaths of 33 German soldiers who had been killed by Italian partisans. Hitler demanded 50 Italian lives for each German life that had been taken, but German officials in Italy lowered the number.

SLAVE TRADE ABOLISHED BY ENGLAND: ANNIVERSARY. Mar 25, 1807. The English Parliament abolished the slave trade after a long campaign against it.

TOSCANINI, ARTURO: BIRTH ANNIVERSARY. Mar 25, 1867. Italian opera and symphony conductor Arturo Toscanini was born at Parma, Italy. He had an all-encompassing repertoire but was famous primarily for the operas of Verdi and the symphonies of Beethoven. Toscanini died at New York City, Jan 16, 1957.

TRIANGLE SHIRTWAIST FIRE: ANNIVERSARY. Mar 25, 1911. At about 4:30 PM, fire broke out at the Triangle Shirtwaist Company at New York, NY, minutes before the seamstresses were to go home. Some workers were fatally burned while others leaped to their deaths from the windows of the 10-story building. The fire lasted only 18 minutes but left 146 workers dead, most of them young immigrant women. Some of the deaths were a direct result of workers being trapped on the ninth floor by a locked door. Labor law forbade locking factory doors while employees were at work, and owners of the company were indicted on charges of first- and second-degree manslaughter. The tragic fire became a turning point in labor history, bringing about reforms in health and safety laws.

Birthdays Today

Bonnie Bedelia, 63, actress (*My Sweet Charlie, Die Hard, Die Hard 2*), born New York, NY, Mar 25, 1946 (some sources say 1952).

Anita Bryant, 69, singer ("The George Gobel Show"), former Miss America, born Barnsdall, OK, Mar 25, 1940.

Marcia Cross, 47, actress ("Melrose Place," "Everwood," "Desperate Housewives"), born Marlborough, MA, Mar 25, 1962.

John Ensign, 51, US Senator (R, Nevada), born Roseville, CA, Mar 25, 1958.

Eileen Ford, 87, model agency executive, born New York, NY, Mar 25, 1922.

Aretha Franklin, 67, singer ("Respect," "Think"), born Memphis, TN, Mar 25, 1942.

Paul Michael Glaser, 66, actor ("Starsky and Hutch"), director (*Butterflies Are Free*), born Cambridge, MA, Mar 25, 1943.

Tom Glavine, 43, baseball player, born Concord, MA, Mar 25, 1966.

Cammi Granato, 38, former hockey player, born Maywood, IL, Mar 25, 1971.

Mary Gross, 56, comedienne, actress ("Saturday Night Live"), born Chicago, IL, Mar 25, 1953.

Elton John, 62, musician, singer, songwriter, born Reginald Kenneth Dwight at Pinner, England, Mar 25, 1947.

Avery Johnson, 44, basketball coach, former player, born New Orleans, LA, Mar 25, 1965.

James Lovell, 81, astronaut, born Cleveland, OH, Mar 25, 1928.

Lee Pace, 30, actor ("Pushing Daisies," "Wonderfalls"), born Chickasha, OK, Mar 25, 1979.

Sarah Jessica Parker, 44, actress (*LA Story, Honeymoon in Vegas*, "Sex and the City"), born Nelsonville, OH, Mar 25, 1965.

Danica Patrick, 27, race car driver, born Beloit, WI, Mar 25, 1982.

Gloria Steinem, 74, feminist (original publisher of *Ms* magazine), journalist, author, born Toledo, OH, Mar 25, 1935.

John Stockwell, 48, actor, writer, director (*Top Gun, Under Cover*), born Galveston, TX, Mar 25, 1961.

Sheryl Swoopes, 38, basketball player, US Olympic basketball team, born Brownfield, TX, Mar 25, 1971.

March 26 — Thursday

DAY 85 **280 REMAINING**

BANGLADESH: INDEPENDENCE DAY. Mar 26. Commemorates East Pakistan's independence in 1971 as the state of Bangladesh. Celebrated with parades, youth festivals and symposia.

BOWDITCH, NATHANIEL: BIRTH ANNIVERSARY. Mar 26, 1773. American mathematician and astronomer, author of the *New American Practical Navigator*. Born at Salem, MA, he died at Boston, MA, Mar 16, 1838.

CAMP DAVID ACCORD SIGNED: 30th ANNIVERSARY. Mar 26, 1979. Israeli Prime Minister Menachem Begin and Egyptian President Anwar Sadat signed the Camp David peace treaty, ending 30 years of war between their two countries. The agreement was fostered by President Jimmy Carter.

DELANO, JANE: BIRTH ANNIVERSARY. Mar 26, 1862. Jane Arminda Delano, dedicated American nurse and teacher, superintendent of the US Army Nurse Corps, chairman of the American Red Cross Nursing Service and recipient (posthumously) of the Distinguished Service Medal of the US, was born near Townsend, NY. While on an official visit to review Red Cross activities, she died Apr 15, 1919, in an army hospital at Savenay, France. Her last words: "What about my work? I must get back to my work." Originally buried at Loire, France, her remains were reinterred at Arlington National Cemetery in 1920.

FROST, ROBERT LEE: BIRTH ANNIVERSARY. Mar 26, 1874. American poet who tried his hand at farming, teaching, shoemaking and editing before winning acclaim as a poet. Pulitzer Prize winner. Born at San Francisco, CA, he died at Boston, MA, Jan 29, 1963.

LEGAL ASSISTANTS DAY. Mar 26. A day recognizing the many contributions made to the legal profession by legal assistants. For info: Claudia A. Evart, 30 Park Ave, #2-P, New York, NY 10016. Phone: (212) 779-2227. E-mail: paralegalcaevart@earthlink.net.

MAKE UP YOUR OWN HOLIDAY DAY. Mar 26. This day is a day you may name for whatever you wish. Reach for the stars! Make up a holiday! Annually, Mar 26. (©2006 by WH.) For info: Thomas & Ruth Roy, Wellcat Holidays, 2418 Long Ln, Lebanon, PA 17046. Phone: (717) 279-0184. E-mail: info@wellcat.com. Web: www.wellcat.com.

MIAEYC EARLY CHILDHOOD CONFERENCE. Mar 26–28. Amway Grand Plaza Hotel and DeVos Place, Grand Rapids, MI. This three-day conference sponsored by the Michigan Association for the Education of the Young Child (MiAEYC) focuses on issues affecting children from birth to age eight. Invited are educators, students, advocates and parents; participants can attend one, two or all three days. Each day includes a keynote address, two full-day focus sessions and 75+ workshops. For info: Laurie Nickson, MiAEYC, Beacon Pl, 4572 S Hagadorn Rd, Ste 1-D, East Lansing, MI 48823. Phone: (800) 336-6424. Fax: (517) 336-9790. E-mail: MiAEYC@MiAEYC.org. Web: www.MiAEYC.org.

MOON PHASE: NEW MOON. Mar 26. Moon enters New Moon phase at 12:06 PM, EDT.

NCAA DIVISION I MEN'S SWIMMING AND DIVING CHAMPIONSHIPS. Mar 26–28. College Station, TX. For info: NCAA, 700 W Washington St, PO Box 6222, Indianapolis, IN 46206-6222. Phone: (317) 917-6222. Fax: (317) 917-6888. Web: www.ncaa.org.

"ORIGINAL" WESTERN MASSACHUSETTS HOME AND GARDEN SHOW. Mar 26–29. West Springfield, MA. The largest home show in New England with more than 700 booths and a large outside area covering more than six acres of exhibits. Annually, third or fourth week of March. For info: Tina Smith, Home Builders Assn of Western Massachusetts, 240 Cadwell Dr, Springfield, MA 01104. Phone: (413) 747-7976. Fax: (413) 781-8416. E-mail: tsmith@hbawm.com. Web: www.hbawm.com.

PRINCE JONAH KUHIO KALANIANOLE DAY. Mar 26. Hawaii. Commemorates the man who, as Hawaii's delegate to the US Congress, introduced the first bill for statehood in 1919. Not until 1959 did Hawaii become a state.

THE SAVANNAH TOUR OF HOMES AND GARDENS. Mar 26–29. Savannah, GA. Residents of Savannah open their homes to visitors to view 18th- and 19th-century architecture. The beauty of spring makes this tour of homes and gardens even more breathtaking. Est attendance: 4,000. For info: The Savannah Tour of Homes and Gardens, 18 Abercorn St, Savannah, GA 31401. Phone: (912) 234-8054. Fax: (912) 234-2123. E-mail: tourinfo@savannahtourofhomes.org. Web: www.savannahtourofhomes.org.

SOVIET COSMONAUT RETURNS TO NEW COUNTRY: ANNIVERSARY. Mar 26, 1992. After spending 313 days in space in the Soviet *Mir* space station, cosmonaut Serge Krikalev returned to Earth and to what was for him a new country. He left Earth May 18, 1991, a citizen of the Soviet Union, but during his stay aboard the space station, the Soviet Union crumbled and became the Commonwealth of Independent States. Originally scheduled to return in October 1991, Krikalev's return was delayed by five months due to his country's disintegration and the ensuing monetary problems.

WILLIAMS, TENNESSEE: BIRTH ANNIVERSARY. Mar 26, 1911. Tennessee Williams was born at Columbus, MS. He was one of America's most prolific playwrights, producing such works as *The Glass Menagerie; A Streetcar Named Desire*, which won a Pulitzer Prize; *Cat on a Hot Tin Roof*, which won a second Pulitzer; *Night of the Iguana; Summer and Smoke; The Rose Tattoo* and *Sweet Bird of Youth*, among others. Williams died at New York, NY, Feb 25, 1983.

"THE YOUNG AND THE RESTLESS" TV PREMIERE: ANNIVERSARY. Mar 26, 1973. This daytime serial is generally thought of as TV's most artistic soap and has won numerous Emmys for out-

March 2009	S	M	T	W	T	F	S
	1	2	3	4	5	6	7
	8	9	10	11	12	13	14
	15	16	17	18	19	20	21
	22	23	24	25	26	27	28
	29	30	31				

standing daytime drama series. Its original storylines revolved around the Brooks and Foster families, but by the early '80s most of them were gone and the Abbott and Williams families were highlighted. The serial's very large and changing cast has included now-famous actors David Hasselhoff, Tom Selleck, Wings Hauser, Deidre Hall and Michael Damian. In 1980, "Y&R" expanded from a half-hour to an hour. Its theme music is well known as "Nadia's Theme," as it was played during Nadia Comaneci's routine at the 1976 Olympics.

 Birthdays Today

Marcus Allen, 49, former football player, TV commentator, born San Diego, CA, Mar 26, 1960.

Alan Arkin, 75, actor (*Catch-22, Little Miss Sunshine*), director (*Little Murders*), born New York, NY, Mar 26, 1934.

Pierre Boulez, 84, composer, conductor, born Montbrison, France, Mar 26, 1925.

James Caan, 69, actor (*Thief, The Godfather, Mickey Blue Eyes*), born New York, NY, Mar 26, 1940.

Elaine Lan Chao, 56, US Secretary of Labor, born Taipei, Taiwan, Mar 26, 1953.

Kenny Chesney, 41, country singer, born Knoxville, TN, Mar 26, 1968.

Leeza Gibbons, 52, TV hostess ("Extra"), born Hartsville, SC, Mar 26, 1957.

Jennifer Grey, 49, actress (*Dirty Dancing*), born New York, NY, Mar 26, 1960.

John Huntsman, Jr, 49, Governor of Utah (R), born Palo Alto, CA, Mar 26, 1960.

Erica Jong, 67, author, poet (*Fear of Flying, Becoming Light*), born New York, NY, Mar 26, 1942.

Catherine Keener, 49, actress (*Capote, The 40 Year Old Virgin, Being John Malkovich*), born Miami, FL, Mar 26, 1960.

T.R. Knight, 36, actor ("Grey's Anatomy"), born Minneapolis, MN, Mar 26, 1973.

Keira Knightley, 24, actress (*Atonement, Pride and Prejudice, Pirates of the Caribbean*), born Teddington, Middlesex, England, Mar 26, 1985.

Vicki Lawrence, 60, singer, actress ("The Carol Burnett Show," "Mama's Family"), born Inglewood, CA, Mar 26, 1949.

Josh Lucas, 37, actor (*Sweet Home Alabama, American Psycho*), born Little Rock, AR, Mar 26, 1972.

Leonard Nimoy, 78, actor ("Star Trek"), director (*Three Men and a Baby*), writer, born Boston, MA, Mar 26, 1931.

Sandra Day O'Connor, 79, former Associate Justice of the US Supreme Court, born El Paso, TX, Mar 26, 1930.

Nancy Pelosi, 69, Speaker of the US House of Representatives (D, California), born Baltimore, MD, Mar 26, 1940.

Teddy Pendergrass, 59, singer, born Philadelphia, PA, Mar 26, 1950.

Diana Ross, 65, singer, actress (*Lady Sings the Blues, The Wiz*), born Detroit, MI, Mar 26, 1944.

Martin Short, 59, actor (*The Three Amigos, Inner Space*), comedian ("SCTV Network 90," "Saturday Night Live"), born Hamilton, ON, Canada, Mar 26, 1950.

John Stockton, 47, former basketball player, born Spokane, WA, Mar 26, 1962.

Bob Woodward, 66, journalist, author (*All the President's Men* with Carl Bernstein, *Plan of Attack*), born Geneva, IL, Mar 26, 1943.

March 27 — Friday

DAY 86 **279 REMAINING**

CANARY ISLANDS PLANE DISASTER: ANNIVERSARY. Mar 27, 1977. The worst accident in the history of civil aviation. Two Boeing 747s collided on the ground; 570 people lost their lives—249 on the KLM Airlines plane and 321 on the Pan Am plane.

CELEBRATE EXCHANGE: NATIONAL EXCHANGE CLUB BIRTHDAY. Mar 27, 1911. Anniversary of the day when the first Exchange Club was founded at Detroit, MI, by Charles A. Berkey. Since 1911, Exchange clubs have been working to improve their communities through service projects, by promoting patriotism and pride of country and through their national project, Child Abuse Prevention. Celebrated annually by nearly 26,000 Exchangites in the US and Puerto Rico. For info: The Natl Exchange Club, 3050 Central Ave, Toledo, OH 43606-1700. Phone: (800) 924-2643. Fax: (419) 535-1989. Web: www.nationalexchangeclub.org.

COIN & STAMP EXPO. Mar 27–29. Wilshire Ebell Convention Complex, Los Angeles, CA. Est attendance: 4,000. For info: Israel Bick, Exec Dir, Intl Stamp & Coin Collectors Society, PO Box 854, Van Nuys, CA 91408. Phone: (818) 997-6496. Fax: (818) 988-4337. E-mail: iibick@sbcglobal.net. Web: www.bick.net.

CRAFTSMEN'S CLASSIC ARTS & CRAFTS FESTIVAL. Mar 27–29. Dulles Expo and Convention Center, Chantilly, VA. 13th annual. Features work from more than 375 talented artists and craftspeople. All juried exhibitors' work has been handmade by the exhibitors and must be their own original design and creation. See the creative process in action with several exhibitors demonstrating throughout the weekend. Something for every style, taste and budget with items from the most contemporary to the most traditional. Est attendance: 20,000. For info: Gilmore Enterprises, Inc, 3514-A Drawbridge Pkwy, Greensboro, NC 27410-8584. Phone: (336) 282-5550. E-mail: contact@gilmoreshows.com. Web: www.CraftShow.com or www.gilmoreshows.com.

EARTHQUAKE STRIKES ALASKA: 45th ANNIVERSARY. Mar 27, 1964. The strongest earthquake in North American history (8.4 on the Richter scale) struck Alaska, east of Anchorage; 117 people were killed. This was the world's second worst earthquake of the 20th century in terms of magnitude.

✦ **EDUCATION AND SHARING DAY.** Mar 27. Proclaimed for the last week in March or the first week in April.

FDA APPROVES VIAGRA: ANNIVERSARY. Mar 27, 1998. The US Food and Drug Administration approved the drug Viagra for treatment of male impotence on this date. It had been patented in 1996.

FUNKY WINKERBEAN: ANNIVERSARY. Mar 27, 1972. Anniversary of the nationally syndicated comic strip. For info: Tom Batiuk, Creator, 2750 Substation Rd, Medina, OH 44256. Phone: (330) 722-8755.

HILL, PATTY SMITH: BIRTH ANNIVERSARY. Mar 27, 1868. Patty Smith Hill, schoolteacher, author and education specialist, was born at Anchorage (suburb of Louisville), KY. She was author of the lyrics of the song "Good Morning to All," which later became known as "Happy Birthday to You." Her older sister, Mildred J. Hill, composed the melody for the song, which was first published in 1893 as a classroom greeting in the book *Song Stories for the Sunday School*. A stanza beginning "Happy Birthday to You" was added in 1924, and the song became arguably the most frequently sung song in the world. Hill died at New York, NY, May 25, 1946. See also: "Happy Birthday to 'Happy Birthday to You'" (June 27).

LUXEMBOURG: OSWEILER. Mar 27. Blessing of horses, tractors and cars.

MYANMAR: RESISTANCE DAY. Mar 27. National holiday. Commemorates the day in 1945 when Burma officially joined the Allies in WWII. Also called Armed Forces Day.

NORTH SEA OIL RIG DISASTER: ANNIVERSARY. Mar 27, 1980. The Alexander L. Keilland Oil Rig capsized during a heavy storm in the Norwegian sector of the North Sea. The pentagon-type,

French-built oil rig had about 200 persons aboard, and 123 lives were lost.

PALMETTO SPORTSMEN'S CLASSIC. Mar 27–29. South Carolina State Fairgrounds, Columbia, SC. 25th annual. Largest family-oriented wildlife show in the Carolinas with information on natural resources education and conservation, hunting, fishing and outdoor recreation. You will find activities for kids and adults throughout the show. Est attendance: 40,000. For info: Donna Swygert, Palmetto Sportsmen's Classic, PO Box 167, Columbia, SC 29202. Phone: (803) 734-4008. E-mail: swygertd@dnr.sc.gov.

PITTSBURGH ARTS & CRAFTS SPRING FEVER FESTIVAL. Mar 27–29. Monroeville, PA. Approximately 150 booths, including pottery, flowers, jewelry, quilts, furniture, tole and decorative painting, leather, toys and much more. Find that perfect gift. Est attendance: 10,000. For info: Debbie & Dave Stoner, Family Festivals Assn, PO Box 166, Irwin, PA 15642. Phone: (724) 863-4577. E-mail: family festivals@hotmail.com. Web: www.familyfestivals.com.

QUIRKY COUNTRY MUSIC SONG TITLES DAY. Mar 27. We love those old country music quirky song titles, and it's time to create some new ones. How about "Put me out at the curb darlin', 'cause the recycling truck's a-comin', and you done throwed me out," for starters? (©2006 by WH.) For info: Thomas & Ruth Roy, Wellcat Holidays, 2418 Long Lane, Lebanon, PA 17046. Phone: (717) 279-0184. E-mail: info@wellcat.com. Web: www.wellcat.com.

RÖNTGEN, WILHELM KONRAD: BIRTH ANNIVERSARY. Mar 27, 1845. German scientist who discovered X-rays (1895) and won a Nobel Prize in 1901. Born at Lennep, Prussia, he died at Munich, Germany, Feb 10, 1923.

ROSTROPOVICH, MSTISLAV: BIRTH ANNIVERSARY. Mar 27, 1927. Russian composer and conductor, perhaps the finest cellist of the 20th century. Born at Baku, USSR (now Azerbaijan), to parents who were also musicians, he studied under Shostokovich and Prokofiev and was performing all over the world by the early 1950s. Fiercely dedicated to human rights and freedom of speech and expression, he was forced to flee the Soviet Union in the early 1970s when the government attempted to interfere with his travels due to his support of dissident writer Alexander Solzhenitsyn. He became an American citizen and was named the musical director of the US National Symphony Orchestra in 1977, a job he held until 1994. He is also remembered for his impromptu performance at the Berlin Wall in 1989, and his trip to Moscow in 1991 to support the new Russian government. He died at Moscow, Russia, Apr 27, 2007.

SCHMECKFEST. Mar 27–28 (also Apr 3–4). Freeman, SD. Sausage and sauerkraut, kuchen and pluma moos. These are just a few of the dishes served at this German "festival of tasting" where visitors can also watch cooking and craft demonstrations and an evening musical. Est attendance: 5,000. For info: DelVonna Wentz, Schmeckfest, PO Box S, Freeman, SD 57029. Phone: (605) 660-8369.

March 2009	S	M	T	W	T	F	S
	1	2	3	4	5	6	7
	8	9	10	11	12	13	14
	15	16	17	18	19	20	21
	22	23	24	25	26	27	28
	29	30	31				

***SINGIN' IN THE RAIN* FILM PREMIERE: ANNIVERSARY.** Mar 27, 1952. MGM's joyous, comic film musical premiered on this date at New York, NY. Starring Gene Kelly, Debbie Reynolds and Donald O'Connor and featuring the songs "Singin' in the Rain," "Good Morning" and "Make 'Em Laugh," *Singin' in the Rain* depicted a Hollywood romance at the time the talkies arrived. Directed by Kelly and Stanley Donen, and written by Betty Comden and Adolph Green, the film was only nominated for two Oscars, yet is now regarded as one of the greatest movie musicals.

SMITH, THORNE: BIRTH ANNIVERSARY. Mar 27, 1892. Perhaps the most critically neglected popular author of the 20th century, he was born James Thorne Smith, Jr, at Annapolis, MD, educated at Dartmouth, and died at Sarasota, FL, June 21, 1934. Author of numerous humorous supernatural fantasy novels, including *Rain in the Doorway, The Stray Lamb* and *Topper*, he was the master of the pointless conversation. The "Thorne Smith" touch has inspired several motion pictures and television series, including "Bewitched." For info: George H. Scheetz, Exec Secy, The Thorne Smith Society, 406 Wolcott Ln, Batavia, IL 60510-2838.

SPACE MILESTONE: *VENERA 8* (USSR). Mar 27, 1972. Launched on this date, this unmanned probe made a soft landing on Venus July 22 and sent back radio transmissions of surface data.

STEICHEN, EDWARD: BIRTH ANNIVERSARY. Mar 27, 1879. Celebrated American photographer. Born at Luxembourg, Germany, and died Mar 25, 1973, at West Redding, CT.

SUGARLOAF CRAFTS FESTIVAL. Mar 27–29. Connecticut Expo Center, Hartford, CT. Now in its 6th year, this show features 250 nationally recognized craft designers and fine artists displaying and selling their original creations. Includes craft demonstrations, live music, specialty foods, children's entertainment, hourly gift certificate drawings and more. Est attendance: 15,000. For info: Sugarloaf Mountain Works, 200 Orchard Ridge Dr, #215, Gaithersburg, MD 20878. Phone: (800) 210-9900. Fax: (301) 253-9620. Web: www.SugarloafCrafts.com.

SWANSON, GLORIA: BIRTH ANNIVERSARY. Mar 27, 1899. American film actress (*Sunset Boulevard*) and businesswoman. Born Gloria May Josephine Svensson at Chicago, IL. Author of an autobiography, *Swanson on Swanson*, published in 1980. Died at New York, NY, Apr 4, 1983.

TEMPE SPRING FESTIVAL OF THE ARTS. Mar 27–28. Downtown Tempe, AZ. Features 500 artists and craftspeople, continuous entertainment and children's activity area. Est attendance: 240,000. For info: Emily Bradley, Festival and Event Dir, Downtown Tempe Community, 310 S Mill Ave, Ste A-201, Tempe, AZ 85281. Phone: (480) 921-2300. E-mail: info@tempefestivalofthearts.com. Web: www.tempefestivalofthearts.com.

VAUGHAN, SARAH: 85th BIRTH ANNIVERSARY. Mar 27, 1924. Legendary jazz singer, born at Newark, NJ, renowned for her melodic improvising, wide vocal range and extraordinary technique. She began her career by winning an amateur contest at New York's Apollo Theater in 1943. She was hired by Earl Hines to accompany his band as his relief pianist as well as singer. She was given the nickname "The Divine One" by Chicago disc jockey Dave Garroway, a moniker that would remain with her the rest of her life. Died at Los Angeles, CA, Apr 3, 1990.

Birthdays Today

Mariah Carey, 39, singer ("Vision of Love," "I'll Be There"), born Long Island, NY, Mar 27, 1970.

Randall Cunningham, 46, former football player, born Santa Barbara, CA, Mar 27, 1963.

Fergie, 34, singer, musician (The Black-Eyed Peas), born Stacy Ferguson at Hacienda Heights, CA, Mar 27, 1975.

Nathan Fillion, 38, actor ("Firefly," *Serenity*), born Edmonton, AB, Canada, Mar 27, 1971.

Anthony Lewis, 82, journalist, author (*Gideon's Trumpet; Make No Law: The Sullivan Case and the First Amendment*), born New York, NY, Mar 27, 1927.

Austin Pendleton, 69, actor (*Mr and Mrs Bridge, Guarding Tess*), born Warren, OH, Mar 27, 1940.

Maria Schneider, 57, actress (*Last Tango in Paris*), born Paris, France, Mar 27, 1952.

Quentin Tarantino, 46, actor, director (*Pulp Fiction, Jackie Brown*), born Knoxville, TN, Mar 27, 1963.

William Caleb (Cale) Yarborough, 69, former auto racer, born Timmonsville, SC, Mar 27, 1940.

Michael York, 67, actor (*Cabaret, The Three Musketeers*), born Fulmer, England, Mar 27, 1942.

March 28 — Saturday

DAY 87 **278 REMAINING**

BARTHOLOMEW, FREDDIE: 85th BIRTH ANNIVERSARY. Mar 28, 1924. Child star of the 1930s, Freddie Bartholomew was born Frederick Llewellyn at Great Britain. He appeared in 24 films and became the second-highest-paid child star after Shirley Temple. He died Jan 23, 1992, at Sarasota, FL.

BATTLE OF LA GLORIETTA PASS: ANNIVERSARY. Mar 28, 1862. At Pigeon's Ranch, a stagecoach stop on the Santa Fe Trail (about 19 miles southeast of Santa Fe, NM), Confederate forces briefly prevailed over Union troops in what some have called the most important battle of the Civil War in the Southwest. It was feared that if Union troops failed to hold here, the Confederate forces would proceed to Fort Union and on to control the rich gold fields of Colorado and California.

CHERRY BLOSSOM FESTIVAL. Mar 28–Apr 12. Various sites in Washington, DC. 97th annual celebration. See more than 6,000 Japanese cherry trees in blossom. Festivities include daily local and international cultural performances, sporting events, arts and crafts, art exhibits and delectable cuisine. Highlights include the National Cherry Blossom Festival Parade® (Apr 4) and the Sakuri Matsuri—Japanese Street Festival. For info: National Cherry Blossom Festival, 1250 H St NW, Ste 1000, Washington, DC 20005. Phone: (202) 661-7585. Web: www.nationalcherryblossomfestival.org.

COLTS SNEAK OUT OF BALTIMORE: 25th ANNIVERSARY. Mar 28, 1984. With little or no warning, the Baltimore Colts loaded moving vans in the dead of night and left for Indianapolis. Baltimore was left without an NFL team until 1996 when the Cleveland Browns moved there and were renamed the Ravens.

CZECH REPUBLIC: TEACHERS' DAY. Mar 28. Celebrates birth on this day of Jan Amos Komensky (Comenius), Moravian educational reformer (1592–1671).

EGGSIBIT. Mar 28–29. Firth Youth Center, Phillipsburg, NJ. 39th annual show to encourage the art of decorating eggshells. Annually, the weekend prior to Palm Sunday. Est attendance: 2,000. For info: Dawn Slifer, Firth Youth Center, 108 Anderson St, Phillipsburg, NJ 08865. Phone: (908) 454-7281. E-mail: eggsoriginal@aol.com.

"GREATEST SHOW ON EARTH" FORMED: ANNIVERSARY. Mar 28, 1881. P.T. Barnum and James A. Bailey merged their circuses to form the "Greatest Show on Earth."

***HAIR* BROADWAY OPENING: ANNIVERSARY.** Mar 28, 1968. The controversial rock musical *Hair*, produced by Michael Butler, opened at the Biltmore Theatre at New York City, after playing off-Broadway. For those who opposed the Vietnam War and the "Establishment," this was a defining piece of work—as evidenced by some of its songs, such as "Aquarius," "Hair" and "Let the Sunshine In."

KEEP NORFOLK BEAUTIFUL DAY. Mar 28. Norfolk, VA. City-wide volunteer cleanup effort. Volunteers improve the quality of life in Norfolk as they clean up litter-strewn streets and waterways, and fix up and beautify public spaces as part of the Great American Cleanup, the nation's largest annual community improvement program. Civic organizations, youth groups, businesses and individuals roll up their sleeves and support clean communities. Annually, the fourth Saturday in March. Est attendance: 1,000. For info: Holly Carson, Keep Norfolk Beautiful Day, 3500-A Granby St, Norfolk, VA 23504. Phone: (757) 441-1347. Fax: (757) 441-5285. E-mail: nec@norfolkbeautiful.org. Web: www.norfolkbeautiful.org.

LAZAR, IRVING "SWIFTY": BIRTH ANNIVERSARY. Mar 28, 1907. Hollywood talent agent whose clients included Ernest Hemingway, Lillian Hellman, Cole Porter, Richard Nixon and Humphrey Bogart (who nicknamed him "Swifty" after Lazar met Bogart's challenge to make him five film deals in one day in 1955). He died Dec 30, 1993, at Beverly Hills, CA.

LIBYA: BRITISH BASES EVACUATION DAY. Mar 28. National holiday. Commemorates the closing of British bases on this day in 1970.

MAROONE HISPANICFEST. Mar 28. Broward County, FL. Latin festival featuring music and dance as well as popular headliners, traditional foods and crafts, community exhibits and children's activities. Est attendance: 20,000. For info: Margaret Delmont-Sanchez or Jameli Bedran, Hispanic Unity of Florida, Inc. Phone: (954) 964-8884 or (954) 342-0425 (Jameli Bedran, Marketing and Development). Email: jbedran@hispanicunity.org. Web: www.hispanicfest.org.

NATCHEZ POWWOW. Mar 28–29. Natchez, MS. Native American dancing and crafts. Admission fee. Est attendance: 3,500. For info: Grand Village of the Natchez Indians, 400 Jefferson Davis Blvd, Natchez, MS 39120. Phone: (601) 446-6502. Fax: (601) 446-6503. E-mail: gvni@mdah.state.ms.us. Web: groups.msn.com/natchezpowwow.

SAINT JOHN NEPOMUCENE NEUMANN: BIRTH ANNIVERSARY. Mar 28, 1811. First male saint of the US. Born at Prachatice, Bohemia, came to the US in 1836. As bishop of Philadelphia, he was affectionately known as the "Little Bishop." Died at Philadelphia, PA, Jan 5, 1860. Beatified Oct 13, 1963. Canonized June 19, 1977.

SFCC SPRING ARTS FESTIVAL. Mar 28–29. Gainesville, FL. Artists and craftspeople from all areas of the US display their work. Also, Kids Art Jungle—a complete art fest for kids. Est attendance: 124,000. For info: Santa Fe Community College, Spring Arts Fest, 3000 NW 83rd St, Gainesville, FL 32606. Phone: (352) 395-5355. Fax: (352) 336-2715. E-mail: kathryn.lehman@sfcc.edu.

SHEEP TO SHAWL FESTIVAL. Mar 28. Savannah, GA. A "Fantastic Fibers" Festival! Visitors will see the magical transformation of wool, from sheep shearing to finished shawl. Members of The Fiber Guild of the Savannahs will demonstrate carding, spinning, dyeing and weaving the wool. A variety of other fiber arts demonstrations will show visitors how fibers can be made into many useful items. Other activities include pony and hay rides, children's crafts and games and our two-mile-long "Native Animal Nature Trail." Est attendance: 1,900. For info: Oatland Island Wildlife Center, 711 Sandtown Rd, Savannah, GA 31410. Phone: (912) 898-3980. Fax: (912) 898-3983. Web: www.oatlandisland.org.

SPACE MILESTONE: *NOAA 8* (US). Mar 28, 1983. Search and Rescue Satellite (SARSAT) launched from Vandenburg Air Force Base, CA, to aid in locating ships and aircraft in distress. *Kosmos 1383*, launched July 1, 1982, by the USSR, in a cooperative rescue effort, is credited with saving more than 20 lives.

SWITZERLAND: LUCERNE FESTIVAL AT EASTER. Mar 28–Apr 5. Lucerne. Sacred and concert music at truly unique sites: in the beautiful churches and at the concert hall of the KKL Lucerne. For the period of this festival, the Symphonieorchester des Bayerischen Rundfunks conducted by Mariss Jansons is orchestra-in-residence. For info: Lucerne Festival, PO Box CH-6002, Lucerne, Switzerland. Phone: (41) 41-226-44-00. Fax: (41) 41-226-44-60. E-mail: info@lucernefestival.ch. Web: www.lucernefestival.ch.

TARPON SPRINGS FINE ARTS FESTIVAL. Mar 28–29. Tarpon Springs, FL. Est attendance: 30,000. For info: Tarpon Springs Chamber of Commerce, 11 E Orange St, Tarpon Springs, FL 34689. Phone: (727) 937-6109. Fax: (727) 937-2879. E-mail: chamber@tarponspringschamber.org. Web: www.TarponSpringsChamber.com.

THREE MILE ISLAND NUCLEAR POWER PLANT ACCIDENT: 30th ANNIVERSARY. Mar 28, 1979. A series of accidents beginning at 4 AM, EST, at Three Mile Island on the Susquehanna River about 10 miles southeast of Harrisburg, PA, was responsible for extensive reevaluation of the safety of existing nuclear power generating operations. Equipment and other failures reportedly brought Three Mile Island close to a meltdown of the uranium core, threatening extensive radiation contamination.

VIETNAM MORATORIUM CONCERT: ANNIVERSARY. Mar 28, 1970. A seven-hour concert at Madison Square Garden at New York City featured many stars who donated their services for the antiwar cause. Among them were Jimi Hendrix; Dave Brubeck; Harry Belafonte; Peter, Paul and Mary; Judy Collins; the Rascals; Blood, Sweat and Tears and the Broadway cast of *Hair.*

Birthdays Today

Conchata Ferrell, 66, actress ("Two and a Half Men," "LA Law," *Edward Scissorhands*), born Charleston, WV, Mar 28, 1943.

Ken Howard, 65, actor ("Crossing Jordan," "The White Shadow"), born El Centro, CA, Mar 28, 1944.

Reba McEntire, 55, singer, actress ("Reba"), born Chockie, OK, Mar 28, 1954.

Henry M. Paulson, Jr., 63, US Secretary of the Treasury, born Palm Beach, FL, Mar 28, 1946.

Jerry Sloan, 67, basketball coach, born McLeansboro, IL, Mar 28, 1942.

Earnie Stewart, 40, former soccer player, born Veghal, Holland, Mar 28, 1969.

Julia Stiles, 28, actress (*The Prince & Me, The Bourne Identity, Save the Last Dance, O*), born New York, NY, Mar 28, 1981.

Keith Tkachuk, 37, hockey player, born Melrose, MA, Mar 28, 1972.

Vince Vaughn, 39, actor (*Wedding Crashers, Old School, Swingers*), born Minneapolis, MN, Mar 28, 1970.

Dianne Wiest, 61, actress (Oscars for *Hannah and Her Sisters* and *Bullets Over Broadway*; "Law & Order"), born Kansas City, MO, Mar 28, 1948.

March 29 — Sunday

DAY 88 — 277 REMAINING

BAILEY, PEARL MAE: BIRTH ANNIVERSARY. Mar 29, 1918. American singer and Broadway musical star Pearl Bailey was born at Newport News, VA. She began her career in vaudeville and won a special Tony Award in 1968 and the Presidential Medal of Freedom in 1988. Bailey died Aug 17, 1990, at Philadelphia, PA.

CANADA: BRITISH NORTH AMERICA ACT: ANNIVERSARY. Mar 29, 1867. This act of the British Parliament established the Dominion of Canada, uniting Ontario, Quebec, Nova Scotia and New Brunswick. The remaining colonies in Canada were still ruled directly by Great Britain until Manitoba joined the Dominion in 1870, British Columbia in 1871, Prince Edward Island in 1873, Alberta and Saskatchewan in 1905 and Newfoundland in 1949. Union was proclaimed July 1, 1867. See also: "Canada: Canada Day" (July 1).

CENTRAL AFRICAN REPUBLIC: BOGANDA DAY. Mar 29. National holiday. Commemorates the death of Barthelemy Boganda, the first president, in 1959.

COMMITTEE ON ASSASSINATIONS REPORT: 30th ANNIVERSARY. Mar 29, 1979. The House Select Committee on Assassinations released on this day the final report on its investigation into the assassinations of President John F. Kennedy, Martin Luther King, Jr, and Robert Kennedy. Based on available evidence, the committee concluded that President Kennedy was assassinated as a result of a conspiracy, although no trail of a conspiracy could be established. They also concluded that on the basis of scientific acoustical evidence two gunmen fired at the President, although no second gunman could be identified. [Note: In December 1980, the FBI released a report discounting the two-gunmen theory, stating that the distinguishable sounds of two separate guns were not proven scientifically.] In addition the committee concluded that the possibility of conspiracy did exist in the cases of Dr. King and Robert Kennedy, although no specific individuals or organizations could be pinpointed as being involved. See also: "Warren Commission Report: Anniversary" (Sept 27).

CONSIDER CHRISTIANITY WEEK. Mar 29–Apr 4. A week to encourage Christians to examine the evidence and reasons for their faith and for non-Christians to take another look at the faith that has played such an important role in shaping the history and culture in which we live. Annually, beginning two Sundays before Easter. For info: Hanna Hushbeck, PR, Aletheia, 408 3rd St, Ste 401, Wausau, WI 54403. Phone: (715) 849-8328. Fax: (715) 849-8329. E-mail: elgin@consider.org. Web: www.consider.org.

DOW JONES TOPS 10,000: 10th ANNIVERSARY. Mar 29, 1999. The Dow Jones Index of 30 major industrial stocks topped the 10,000 mark for the first time.

ENGLAND: CARE SUNDAY. Mar 29. The fifth Sunday of Lent, also known as Carling Sunday and Passion Sunday. First day of Passiontide, remembering the sorrow and passion of Christ.

EUROPE: SUMMER DAYLIGHT SAVING TIME. Mar 29–Oct 25. All members of the European Union observe daylight saving (summer) time from the last Sunday in March until the last Sunday in October.

HOOVER, LOU HENRY: BIRTH ANNIVERSARY. Mar 29, 1875. Wife of Herbert Clark Hoover, 31st president of the US. Born at Waterloo, IA, she died at Palo Alto, CA, Jan 7, 1944.

KNIGHTS OF COLUMBUS FOUNDER'S DAY. Mar 29. The first Knights of Columbus charter was granted in 1882 by the state of Connecticut. This Catholic, family, fraternal service organization has grown into a volunteer force of Knights and family members totaling nearly six million who annually donate tens of millions of dollars and volunteer hours to countless charitable projects. For info: Knights of Columbus, 1 Columbus Plaza, New Haven, CT 06510. E-mail: info@kofc.org. Web: www.kofc.org.

MADAGASCAR: COMMEMORATION DAY. Mar 29. Memorial day for those who died in the rebellion of 1947 against French colonization.

MCCARTHY, EUGENE: BIRTH ANNIVERSARY. Mar 29, 1916. Born at Watkins, MN, the longtime congressman and senator from Minnesota is best remembered for his campaign for the 1968 Democratic presidential nomination. McCarthy ran on a strong antiwar platform, garnering support from those opposed to American involvement in the Vietnam Conflict, but ultimately lost the nomination to Hubert Humphrey. McCarthy never held public office again, despite four more tries at the presidency, and died at Washington, DC, Dec 10, 2005.

"MUTT AND JEFF" DEBUT: ANNIVERSARY. Mar 29, 1908. "Mutt and Jeff," the first comic strip to appear daily with the same protagonists, debuted today in William Randolph Hearst's *San Francisco Examiner.*

March 2009

S	M	T	W	T	F	S
1	2	3	4	5	6	7
8	9	10	11	12	13	14
15	16	17	18	19	20	21
22	23	24	25	26	27	28
29	30	31				

NATIONAL MOM AND POP BUSINESS OWNERS DAY. Mar 29. A day recognizing those very special husband-and-wife business owner teams that work and commune together. Take this day to strike a balance between business and love. For info: Rick and Margie Segel, 543 Davinci Pass, Poinciana, FL 34759. Phone: (781) 272-9995. Fax: (800) 847-9411. E-mail: rick@ricksegel.com.

NIAGARA FALLS RUNS DRY: ANNIVERSARY. Mar 29, 1848. A massive assemblage of ice blocks formed upstream of Niagara Falls late on Mar 29, 1848, and by midnight had stopped water flow over the Falls (which are actually three falls: the American, the Horseshoe [or Canadian] and the Bridal Veil). The ice jam held until Apr 1, when the waters of Lake Erie punched through and things got back to normal. Until that happened, hundreds of the curious swarmed into the now-waterless gorge to hunt for geological souvenirs while thousands of spectators watched from above. Although the American Falls has stopped flowing before, this 1848 stoppage was the first and only time the entire falls was affected.

PASSION WEEK. Mar 29–Apr 4. The week beginning on the fifth Sunday in Lent; the week before Holy Week.

PASSIONTIDE. Mar 29–Apr 11. The last two weeks of Lent (Passion Week and Holy Week), beginning with the fifth Sunday of Lent (Passion Sunday) and continuing through the day before Easter (Holy Saturday or Easter Even).

QUINLAN, KAREN ANN: 55th BIRTH ANNIVERSARY. Mar 29, 1954. Born at Scranton, PA, Karen Ann Quinlan became the center of a legal, medical and ethical controversy over the right to die. She became irreversibly comatose on Apr 14, 1975. A petition filed by her adoptive parents in New Jersey's Superior Court, Sept 12, 1975, sought permission to discontinue use of a respirator, allowing her to die "with grace and dignity." In 1976 the petition was upheld by New Jersey's Supreme Court. Quinlan lived nearly a decade without the respirator, until June 11, 1985. Her plight brought into focus the ethical dilemmas of advancing medical technology—the need for a new understanding of life and death; the right to die; the role of judges, doctors and hospital committees in deciding when not to prolong life.

ROOT CANAL AWARENESS WEEK. Mar 29–Apr 4. 3rd annual. To calm the fears of Americans across the country and to educate the public about misconceptions of root canal treatment and the true benefits of the procedure, the American Association of Endodontists (AAE) has established this week. AAE hopes to teach patients that root canals are virtually painless and can have important implications for overall health. Endodontists, the root canal specialists, perform 25 root canals per week on average and root canal treatment saves more than 16 million natural teeth each year, making the procedure more hero than villain. For info: Dan Aske, PR Coordinator, AAE. Phone: (800) 872-3636 in North America or (312) 266-7255, ext 3035 worldwide. Web: www.rootcanalspecialists.org.

TAIWAN: YOUTH DAY. Mar 29.

TEXAS LOVE THE CHILDREN DAY. Mar 29. A day recognizing every child's right and need to be loved. Promoting the hope that one day all children will live in loving, safe environments and will be given proper health care and equal learning opportunities. Precedes the start of National Child Abuse Prevention Month (April). Think SHELL: Safety, Health, Education, Laughter, Love. For info: Patty Murphy, 1204 Briarwood Blvd, Arlington, TX 76013. Phone: (817) 469-8198. E-mail: MURPH0@swbell.net.

TWENTY-THIRD AMENDMENT TO US CONSTITUTION RATIFIED: ANNIVERSARY. Mar 29, 1961. District of Columbia residents were given the right to vote in presidential elections under the 23rd Amendment.

TYLER, JOHN: BIRTH ANNIVERSARY. Mar 29, 1790. Tenth president of the US (Apr 6, 1841–Mar 3, 1845). Born at Charles City County, VA, Tyler succeeded to the presidency upon the death of William Henry Harrison. Tyler's first wife died while he was president, and he remarried before the end of his term in office, becoming the first president to marry while in office. Fifteen children were born of the two marriages. In 1861 he was elected to the Congress of the Confederate States but died at Richmond, VA, Jan 18, 1862, before being seated. His death received no official tribute from the US government.

UNITED KINGDOM: SUMMER TIME. Mar 29–Oct 25. "Summer Time" (one hour in advance of Standard Time), similar to daylight saving time, is observed from the last Sunday in March until the last Sunday in October.

WALTON, SAM: BIRTH ANNIVERSARY. Mar 29, 1918. Founder of Wal-Mart discount stores, born at Kingfisher, OK. One of the wealthiest men in America, he died at Little Rock, AR, Apr 5, 1992.

YOUNG, DENTON TRUE (CY): BIRTH ANNIVERSARY. Mar 29, 1867. Baseball Hall of Fame pitcher, born at Gilmore, OH. Young is baseball's all-time winningest pitcher, having accumulated 511 victories in his 22-year career. The Cy Young Award is given each year in his honor to Major League Baseball's best pitcher. Inducted into the Hall of Fame in 1937. Died at Peoli, OH, Nov 4, 1955.

Birthdays Today

Earl Christian Campbell, 54, Hall of Fame football player, born Tyler, TX, Mar 29, 1955.

Jennifer Capriati, 33, tennis player, born New York, NY, Mar 29, 1976.

Bud Cort, 59, actor (*Harold and Maude, Brewster McCloud*), born New Rochelle, NY, Mar 29, 1950 (some sources say 1948).

Eric Idle, 66, actor ("Monty Python's Flying Circus," "Suddenly Susan"), author, born Durham, England, Mar 29, 1943.

Christopher Lambert, 52, actor (*Greystoke: The Legend of Tarzan, Lord of the Apes*), born New York, NY, Mar 29, 1957.

Lucy Lawless, 41, actress ("Xena"), born Mount Albert, Auckland, New Zealand, Mar 29, 1968.

Elle Macpherson, 45, model, actress (*Sirens*), born Sydney, Australia, Mar 29, 1964.

John Major, 66, former British prime minister, born Brixton, England, Mar 29, 1943.

John Joseph McLaughlin, 82, editor, columnist, TV host, born Providence, RI, Mar 29, 1927.

Kurt Thomas, 53, former gymnast, born Miami, FL, Mar 29, 1956.

March 30 — Monday

DAY 89 — **276 REMAINING**

ANESTHETIC FIRST USED IN SURGERY: ANNIVERSARY. Mar 30, 1842. Dr. Crawford W. Long, having seen the use of nitrous oxide and sulfuric ether at "laughing gas" parties, observed that individuals under their influence felt no pain. On this date, he removed a tumor from the neck of a man who was under the influence of ether.

DOCTORS' DAY. Mar 30. Traditional annual observance since 1933 to honor America's physicians on the anniversary of the occasion when Dr. Crawford W. Long became the first acclaimed physician to use ether as an anesthetic agent in a surgical technique, Mar 30, 1842. The red carnation has been designated the official flower of Doctors' Day.

GOYA, FRANCISCO JOSE de: BIRTH ANNIVERSARY. Mar 30, 1746. Spanish painter and etcher. It is estimated that he executed more than 1,800 paintings, drawings and lithographs during his lifetime. Born at Aragon, Spain; died at Bordeaux, France, Apr 16, 1828.

GRASS IS ALWAYS BROWNER ON THE OTHER SIDE OF THE FENCE DAY. Mar 30. A day to honor all of those who did not jump ship, did not quit the same old job, did not leave the same old relationship because things appeared to look better somewhere else. (©2006 by WH.) For info: Thomas & Ruth Roy, Wellcat Holidays, 2418 Long Ln, Lebanon, PA 17046. Phone: (717) 279-0184. E-mail: wellcat@comcast.net. Web: www.wellcat.com.

"JEOPARDY" TV PREMIERE: 45th ANNIVERSARY. Mar 30, 1964. The "thinking person's" game show, "Jeopardy" has a reputation as an intelligent and classy program. Art Fleming was the original host of the show, in which three contestants won cash by attempting to give the correct question to an answer in six different categories. Contestants go through two rounds and "final jeopardy," where they can wager up to all their earnings on one question. The series returned in 1984 with Alex Trebek as the popular host.

KRAFT NABISCO CHAMPIONSHIP. Mar 30–Apr 5. Mission Hills Country Club, Rancho Mirage, CA. The first major of the year on the LPGA tour. Held since 1972, this tournament is often called the Master's of women's professional golf. For info: Kraft Nabisco Championship. Web: www.kncgolf.com.

NICKERSON, CAMILLE ("THE LOUISIANA LADY"): BIRTH ANNIVERSARY. Mar 30, 1888. Camille Nickerson, music arranger, composer, musician and educator, is remembered for her musical talent and her work as a music collector who gathered and transcribed Creole music. Born at the French Quarter, New Orleans. Of Creole extraction herself, Nickerson performed for a time in the US and Europe using the stage name "The Louisiana Lady." She died at Washington, DC, at age 94.

O'CASEY, SEAN: BIRTH ANNIVERSARY. Mar 30, 1880. Irish playwright (*Juno and the Paycock*). Born at Dublin, Ireland, he died at Torquay, England, Sept 18, 1964.

PENCIL PATENTED: ANNIVERSARY. Mar 30, 1858. First pencil with the eraser top was patented by Hyman Lipman.

REAGAN, RONALD: ASSASSINATION ATTEMPT: ANNIVERSARY. Mar 30, 1981. President Ronald Reagan was shot in the chest by a 25-year-old gunman at Washington, DC. Three other persons were wounded. John W. Hinckley, Jr, the accused attacker, was arrested at the scene. On June 21, 1982, a federal jury in the District of Columbia found Hinckley not guilty by reason of insanity and he was committed to St. Elizabeth's Hospital at Washington, DC, for an indefinite time.

SEWARD'S DAY: ANNIVERSARY OF THE ACQUISITION OF ALASKA. Mar 30. Observed in Alaska near the anniversary of its acquisition from Russia in 1867. The treaty of purchase was signed between the Russians and the Americans Mar 30, 1867, and ratified by the Senate May 28, 1867. The territory was formally transferred Oct 18, 1867. Annually, the last Monday in March.

TRINIDAD AND TOBAGO: SPIRITUAL BAPTIST LIBERATION SHOUTER DAY. Mar 30. Public holiday. For info: Information Dept, Tourism Div, Tourism and Industrial Development Co, 10-14 Phillips St, Port of Spain, Trinidad, West Indies.

March 2009	S	M	T	W	T	F	S
	1	2	3	4	5	6	7
	8	9	10	11	12	13	14
	15	16	17	18	19	20	21
	22	23	24	25	26	27	28
	29	30	31				

VAN GOGH, VINCENT: BIRTH ANNIVERSARY. Mar 30, 1853. Dutch post-Impressionist painter, especially known for his bold and powerful use of color. Born at Groot Zundert, Holland, he died at Auvers-sur-Oise, France, July 29, 1890.

 Birthdays Today

John Astin, 79, actor ("The Addams Family"; stage: *The Three Penny Opera*), director, born Baltimore, MD, Mar 30, 1930.

Warren Beatty, 71, actor (*Bonnie and Clyde*), director (*Reds, Dick Tracy*), producer, born Richmond, VA, Mar 30, 1938.

Tracy Chapman, 45, singer ("Fast Car"), born Cleveland, OH, Mar 30, 1964.

Eric Clapton, 64, singer, songwriter, guitarist, born Ripley, England, Mar 30, 1945.

Robbie Coltrane, 59, actor (*GoldenEye*, the Harry Potter films), born Anthony Robert McMillan, Rutherglen, Scotland, Mar 30, 1950.

Celine Dion, 41, pop singer, Grammy winner, born Charlemagne, QC, Canada, Mar 30, 1968.

Jason Dohring, 27, actor ("Veronica Mars," *Black Cadillac*), born in Ohio, Mar 30, 1982.

Richard Dysart, 80, actor ("LA Law"), born Augusta, ME, Mar 30, 1929.

M.C. Hammer, 46, rapper, born Stanley Kirk Burrell at Oakland, CA, Mar 30, 1963.

Norah Jones, 30, singer, born New York, NY, Mar 30, 1979.

Peter Marshall, 82, TV host, actor, born Pierre La Cock at Huntington, WV, Mar 30, 1927.

Paul Reiser, 52, actor (*Diner*, "Mad About You"), born New York, NY, Mar 30, 1957.

March 31 — Tuesday

DAY 90 — **275 REMAINING**

BUNSEN BURNER DAY. Mar 31. A day to honor the inventor of the Bunsen burner, Robert Wilhelm Eberhard von Bunsen, who provided chemists and chemistry students with one of their most indispensable instruments. The Bunsen burner allows the user to regulate the proportions of flammable gas and air to create the most efficient flame. Bunsen was born at Gottingen, Germany, Mar 31, 1811, and was a professor of chemistry at the universities at Kassel, Marburg, Breslau and Heidelberg. He died at Heidelberg, Germany, Aug 16, 1899.

CHAVEZ, CESAR ESTRADA: BIRTH ANNIVERSARY. Mar 31, 1927. Labor leader who organized migrant farm workers in support of better working conditions. Chavez initiated the National Farm Workers Association in 1962, attracting attention to the migrant farm workers' plight by organizing boycotts of products including grapes and lettuce. He was born at Yuma, AZ, and died Apr 23, 1993, at San Luis, AZ. His birthday is a holiday in California.

CHESNUT, MARY BOYKIN MILLER: BIRTH ANNIVERSARY. Mar 31, 1823. Born at Pleasant Hill, SC, and died Nov 22, 1886, at Camden, SC. During the Civil War Chesnut accompanied her husband, a Confederate staff officer, on military missions. She kept a journal of her experiences and observations, which was published posthumously as *A Diary from Dixie*, a perceptive portrait of Confederate military and political leaders and an insightful view of Southern life during the Civil War.

DALAI LAMA FLEES TIBET: 50th ANNIVERSARY. Mar 31, 1959. The Dalai Lama fled Chinese suppression and was granted political asylum in India. In 1950 Tibet had been invaded by China and in 1951 an agreement was signed under which Tibet became a "national autonomous region" of China. Tibetans suffered under China's persecution of Buddhism, and after years of scattered protest a full-scale revolt broke out in 1959. The Dalai Lama fled and with the beginning of the Chinese Cultural Revolution the Chinese took brutal repressive measures against the Tibetans, with the practice of religion banned and thousands of monasteries destroyed. The ban was lifted in 1976 with the end of the Cultural Revolution. The Dalai Lama received the Nobel Peace Prize in 1989 for his commitment to the nonviolent liberation of his country.

DESCARTES, RENE: BIRTH ANNIVERSARY. Mar 31, 1596. French philosopher and mathematician, known as the "father of modern philosophy," born at La Haye, Touraine, France. Cartesian philosophical precepts are often remembered because of his famous proposition "I think, therefore I am" (*Cogito ergo sum . . .*). Died of pneumonia at Stockholm, Sweden, Feb 11, 1650.

EIFFEL TOWER: ANNIVERSARY. Mar 31, 1889. Built for the Paris Exhibition of 1889, the tower was named for its architect, Alexandre Gustave Eiffel, and is one of the world's best-known landmarks.

FITZGERALD, EDWARD: 200th BIRTH ANNIVERSARY. Mar 31, 1809. English author, born at Bredfield, England, perhaps best known for his translation of Omar Khayyam's *Rubaiyat.* Died at Merton, Norfolk, June 14, 1883.

GOGOL, NIKOLAI VASILEVICH: 200th BIRTH ANNIVERSARY. Mar 31, 1809. Russian author of plays, novels and short stories. Born at Sorochinsk, Russia, he died at Moscow, Russia, Mar 4, 1852. Gogol's most famous work was the novel *Dead Souls.*

HAYDN, FRANZ JOSEPH: BIRTH ANNIVERSARY. Mar 31, 1732. "Father of the symphony," born at Rohrau, Austria-Hungary. Composed about 120 symphonies, more than a hundred works for chamber groups, a dozen operas and hundreds of other musical works. Died at Vienna, Austria, May 31, 1809.

JOHNSON, JOHN (JACK) ARTHUR: BIRTH ANNIVERSARY. Mar 31, 1878. In 1908 Jack Johnson became the first black to win the heavyweight boxing championship when he defeated Tommy Burns at Sydney, Australia. Unable to accept a black man's triumph, the boxing world tried to find a white challenger. Jim Jeffries, former heavyweight title holder, was badgered out of retirement. On July 4, 1910, at Reno, NV, the "battle of the century" proved to be a farce when Johnson handily defeated Jeffries. Race riots swept the US, and plans to exhibit the film of the fight were canceled. Johnson was born at Galveston, TX, and died in an automobile accident June 10, 1946, at Raleigh, NC. He was inducted into the Boxing Hall of Fame in 1990. The film *The Great White Hope* is based on his life.

MARVELL, ANDREW: BIRTH ANNIVERSARY. Mar 31, 1621. English poet. Born at Winestead, Yorkshire, England. From his poem "To His Coy Mistress": "Had we but world enough and time/ this coyness, lady, were no crime. . . . But at my back I always hear/ time's winged chariot drawing near. . . ." Died at London, England, Aug 18, 1678.

NATIONAL "SHE'S FUNNY THAT WAY" DAY. Mar 31. On this day, individuals will pay tribute to the humorous nature of women, by listing the top five ways in which women in our lives make us laugh. For info: Brenda Meridith, Dahomey Publishing Company, 50 Hall Rd, Winchendon, MA 01475. Phone: (978) 297-1820. Fax: (978) 297-2519. E-mail: BMeridith@aol.com. Web: www.Dahomey Publishing.com.

***OKLAHOMA!* BROADWAY PREMIERE.** Mar 31, 1943. Rodgers and Hammerstein's landmark musical (their first collaboration) opened at the St. James Theatre on this date in 1943. (It had its world premiere under the title *Away We Go* at the Shubert Theatre in New Haven, CT, on Mar 11, 1943.) *Oklahoma!* is considered significant because it was the first musical in which songs, music, characterization and story are integrated into an emotional whole. It changed musicals forever. It was also the first musical to run more than 2,000 performances and to have a cast album recorded. Agnes de Mille was the choreographer. It received a special Pulitzer Prize for drama on May 2, 1944. In May 1953, "Oklahoma!" became that state's official song.

PEARSE, RICHARD: ANNIVERSARY OF MONOPLANE FLIGHT. Mar 31, 1903. Richard Pearse, a farmer and inventor, flew a monoplane of his own design several hundred yards along a road near Temuka, New Zealand, and then landed it on top of a 12-foot-high hedge. Pearse had built the craft, which consisted of a steerable tricycle undercarriage and an internal combustion engine. A Pearse commemorative medal was issued on Sept 19, 1971, by the Museum of Transport and Technology, Auckland, New Zealand.

SOVIET GEORGIA VOTES FOR INDEPENDENCE: ANNIVERSARY. Mar 31, 1991. On this date the Soviet Republic of Georgia voted to declare its independence from the Soviet Union. Georgia followed the Baltic states of Lithuania, Estonia and Latvia by becoming the fourth republic to reject Mikhail Gorbachev's new vision of the Soviet Union as espoused in a new Union Treaty. Totals revealed that 98.9 percent of those voting favored independence from Moscow. Hours after the election, troops were dispatched from Moscow to Georgia under a state of emergency.

US VIRGIN ISLANDS: TRANSFER DAY. Mar 31. Commemorates transfer resulting from purchase of the Virgin Islands by the US from Denmark, Mar 31, 1917, for $25 million.

Birthdays Today

Herb Alpert, 74, musician (Tijuana Brass), born Los Angeles, CA, Mar 31, 1935.

Pavel Bure, 38, hockey player, born Moscow, USSR, Mar 31, 1971.

Richard Chamberlain, 74, actor ("Dr. Kildare," *Shogun*), born Los Angeles, CA, Mar 31, 1935.

William Daniels, 82, actor (Emmy for "St. Elsewhere"; "Boy Meets World"), born Brooklyn, NY, Mar 31, 1927.

Al Gore, 61, 45th vice president of the US, born Albert Gore, Jr, at Washington, DC, Mar 31, 1948.

Gordon (Gordie) Howe, 81, Hall of Fame hockey player, born Floral, SK, Canada, Mar 31, 1928.

John Jakes, 77, author (*North and South*, the Kent Family Chronicles), born Chicago, IL, Mar 31, 1932.

James Earl (Jimmy) Johnson, 71, Hall of Fame football player, born Dallas, TX, Mar 31, 1938.

Shirley Jones, 75, singer, actress ("The Partridge Family," Oscar for *Elmer Gantry; The Music Man*), born Smithton, PA, Mar 31, 1934.

Gabe Kaplan, 63, actor ("Welcome Back, Kotter"), born Brooklyn, NY, Mar 31, 1946.

Patrick J. Leahy, 69, US Senator (D, Vermont), born Montpelier, VT, Mar 31, 1940.

Edward Francis (Ed) Marinaro, 59, actor ("Hill Street Blues," "Sisters"), former football player, born New York, NY, Mar 31, 1950.

Marc McClure, 52, actor (*Freaky Friday, Back to the Future*), born San Mateo, CA, Mar 31, 1957.

Ewan McGregor, 38, actor (*Miss Potter, The Island, Moulin Rouge, Trainspotting, Star Wars* films), born Crieff, Scotland, Mar 31, 1971.

Rhea Perlman, 61, actress ("Cheers" [three Emmy Awards]; *Carpool*), born Brooklyn, NY, Mar 31, 1948.

Steve Smith, 40, basketball player, born Highland Park, MI, Mar 31, 1969.

Christopher Walken, 66, actor (*Hairspray, Catch Me If You Can, The Deer Hunter*), born Queens, NY, Mar 31, 1943.

✦ April ✦

April 1 — Wednesday

DAY 91 — **274 REMAINING**

ALCOHOL AWARENESS MONTH. Apr 1–30. To help raise awareness among community prevention leaders and citizens about the problem of underage drinking. Concentrates on community grassroots activities. For info: Public Info Dept, Natl Council on Alcoholism and Drug Dependence, Inc, 244 E 58th St, 4th Fl, New York, NY 10022. Phone: (212) 269-7797. Fax: (212) 269-7510. E-mail: national@ncadd.org. Web: www.ncadd.org.

APRIL FOOLS' or ALL FOOLS' DAY. Apr 1. April Fools' Day seems to have begun in France in 1564. Apr 1 used to be New Year's Day, but the New Year was changed to Jan 1 that year. People who insisted on celebrating the "old" New Year became known as April fools and it became common to play jokes and tricks on them. The general concept of a feast of fools is, however, an ancient one. The Romans had such a day, and medieval monasteries also had days when the abbot or bishop was replaced for a day by a common monk, who would order his superiors to do the most menial or ridiculous tasks. "The joke of the day is to deceive persons by sending them upon frivolous and nonsensical errands; to pretend they are wanted when they are not, or, in fact, any way to betray them into some supposed ludicrous situation, so as to enable you to call them 'An April Fool.'"—Brady's *Clavis Calendaria*, 1812.

AZALEA FESTIVAL. Apr 1–30. Muskogee, OK. One of the oldest and most celebrated public parks in the southwest: 122 acres, 40 acres of manicured gardens with 30,000 azaleas of 625 varieties. Ranked in the top 100 events by the National Bus Association. Annually in April since 1967. Many related events take place during the month, including a parade and a chili cook-off. Est attendance: 300,000. For info: Muskogee Chamber of Commerce, PO Box 797, Muskogee, OK 74402. Phone: (918) 682-2401. Fax: (918) 682-2404. Web: www.muskogeechamber.org.

BATTLE OF OKINAWA BEGINS: ANNIVERSARY. Apr 1, 1945. On Easter Sunday, the US 10th Army began operation *Iceberg*, the invasion of the Ryukyu Islands of Okinawa. Ground troops numbering 180,000 plus 368,000 men in support services made a total of 548,000 troops involved—the biggest amphibious operation of the Pacific war.

BOOMER BONUS DAY. Apr 1. Aging baby boomers do not look forward to birthdays. This is a nonthreatening (no extra years added) day to celebrate for the over-50 crowd only! On Apr 1 because the whole thing gets to be a joke: the body goes—but the mind still thinks it's 21! For info: Gaye Andersen, Davenport University, 8200 Georgia St, Merrillville, IN 46410. Phone: (219) 650-5218. Fax: (219) 756-8911. E-mail: gaye.andersen@davenport.edu.

BRIDGE OVER THE NEPONSET: 375th ANNIVERSARY. Apr 1, 1634. The first bridge built in the US spanned the Neponset River between Milton and Dorchester, MA. The authority to build the bridge and an adjoining mill was issued to Israel Stoughton on this date by the Massachusetts General Court.

BULGARIA: SAINT LASARUS'S DAY. Apr 1. Ancient Slavic holiday of young girls, in honor of the goddess of spring and love.

April 2009

S	M	T	W	T	F	S
			1	2	3	4
5	6	7	8	9	10	11
12	13	14	15	16	17	18
19	20	21	22	23	24	25
26	27	28	29	30		

CANADA: NUNAVUT INDEPENDENCE: 10th ANNIVERSARY. Apr 1, 1999. Nunavut became Canada's third independent territory. This self-governing territory with an Inuit majority was created from the eastern half of the Northwest Territories.

✦ **CANCER CONTROL MONTH.** Apr 1–30.

CAR CARE MONTHS. Apr 1–30 and Oct 1–31. A nationwide effort to focus motorists' attention on the importance of vehicle maintenance and care. Annually, the months of April and October. For info: Car Care Council, 7101 Wisconsin Ave, Ste 1300, Bethesda, MD 20814. Phone: (240) 333-1088. Fax: (301) 654-3299. E-mail: info@carcare.org. Web: www.carcare.org.

CELEBRATE DIVERSITY MONTH. Apr 1–30. A new national observance that celebrates all diversity that exists within our workplaces, schools and communitites. Date subject to congressional approval. For info: ProGroup, One Main St SE, Ste 200, Minneapolis, MN 55414. Phone: (800) 651-4093. Fax: (612) 379-7048. Web: www.celebratediversitymonth.org.

CHANEY, LON: BIRTH ANNIVERSARY. Apr 1, 1883. The "Man of a Thousand Faces" was born Leonidas Chaney at Colorado Springs, CO. One of the biggest box office stars of the silent era, Chaney was a master of disguise and makeup (he kept his transformation tools and methods a closely guarded secret) who specialized in playing tortured, tragic and often menacing characters. He is best known for his gripping portrayals of Quasimodo in *The Hunchback of Notre Dame* (1923) and of the Phantom in *The Phantom of the Opera* (1925). He died of cancer on Aug 26, 1930, at Hollywood, CA—only one month after his first sound film was released. His impact on films was such that all Hollywood studios observed a moment of silence in his honor to commemorate his death.

CHILD ABUSE PREVENTION MONTH. Apr 1–30. In 1979 the National Exchange Club adopted the prevention of child abuse as its national project and established the National Exchange Club Foundation. The Foundation is a chartered nonprofit corporation in Ohio. The Foundation has established nearly 120 Exchange Club Child Abuse Prevention Centers throughout the US. More than 225,000 families and 300,000 children have received services from the Exchange Club Child Abuse Prevention network. For info: The Natl Exchange Club Foundation, 3050 Central Ave, Toledo, OH 43606-1700. Phone: (419) 535-3232 or (800) 924-2643. Fax: (419) 535-1989. E-mail: cap@nationalexchangeclub.org. Web: www.preventchildabuse.com.

CIGARETTE ADVERTISING BANNED: ANNIVERSARY. Apr 1, 1970. Radio and television ads for cigarettes were banned by legislation signed by President Richard Nixon on this date. The ban went into effect Jan 1, 1971.

COMMUNITY SPIRIT DAYS. Apr 1–30. Any town may observe this period by doing a special project to help those in need or by having a ceremony to present that community's Spirit of America Foundation Awards for outstanding volunteerism. For info: Spirit of America Foundation, PO Box 5637, Augusta, ME 04332.

COUPLE APPRECIATION MONTH. Apr 1–30. To show thanks for each other's love and emotional support. Do something special to reinforce and celebrate your relationship. Annually, the month of April. For info: Donald Etkes, PhD, 11693 San Vicente Blvd, #491, Los Angeles, CA 90049. Phone: (310) 979-0245. E-mail: drdonetkes@aol.com.

DEFEAT AT FIVE FORKS: ANNIVERSARY. Apr 1, 1865. After withdrawing to Five Forks, VA, Confederate troops under George Pickett were defeated and cut off by Union troops. This defeat, according to many military historians, sealed the immediate fate of Robert E. Lee's armies at Petersburg and Richmond. On Apr 2, Lee informed Confederate president Jefferson Davis that he would have to evacuate Richmond. Davis and his cabinet fled by train to Danville, VA.

"THE DOCTORS" TV PREMIERE: ANNIVERSARY. Apr 1, 1963. "The Doctors" premiered on NBC on the same day as ABC's long-running soap "General Hospital," providing viewers with a double dose of medical drama. The show was set at Hope Memorial Hospital and began as an anthology series that was subsequently transformed into a serial in 1964. "The Doctors" ran for 19 years. Ellen Burstyn, Anna Stuart, Nancy Pinkerton, Jonathan Hogan, Julia Duffy and Alec Baldwin are some of its famous alums.

EMOTIONAL OVEREATING AWARENESS MONTH. Apr 1–30. Millions overeat in an attempt to numb unpleasant feelings with food. The challenge this month is to experience your feelings without anesthetizing yourself with sugars and simple carbohydrates. Try to recognize these urges to eat for emotional reasons and deal with them in more appropriate and satisfying ways. Use the month of April to pay attention to your emotional appetite! For info: Dr. Denise Lamothe, PO Box 933, 49 Main St, Epping, NH 03042. Phone: (603) 493-6043 or (603) 778-4814. E-mail: Denise@DeniseLamothe.com. Web: www.DeniseLamothe.com or emotionaloverеatingawarenessmonth.com.

FRESH FLORIDA TOMATO MONTH. Apr 1–30. To publicize the Florida tomato as a versatile, nutritious, flavorful food. For info: Florida Tomato Committee, 800 Trafalgar Ct, Ste 300, Maitland, FL 32751. Phone: (407) 660-1949. Fax: (407) 660-1656. E-mail: samantha@floridatomatoes.org. Web: www.floridatomatoes.org.

"GENERAL HOSPITAL" TV PREMIERE: ANNIVERSARY. Apr 1, 1963. "General Hospital," ABC's longest-running soap, revolves around the denizens of fictional Port Charles, NY. "GH" was created by Doris and Frank Hursley. John Beradino, who was with the show from the beginning until his death in May 1996, played the role of Dr. Steve Hardy, upstanding director of medicine and pillar of the community. In the '80s, story lines became unusual with plots involving international espionage, mob activity and aliens. The wedding of supercouple Luke and Laura (Anthony Geary and Genie Francis) was a ratings topper. By the '90s, stories moved away from high-powered action to more conventional romance. Many actors received their big break on the show, including Demi Moore, Janine Turner, Jack Wagner, Richard Dean Anderson, Rick Springfield, John Stamos, Emma Samms, Mark Hamill, Finola Hughes, Ricky Martin and Tia Carrere.

GRANGE MONTH. Apr 1–30. State and local recognition for Grange's contribution to rural/urban America. Celebrated at National Headquarters at Washington, DC, and in all states with local, county and state Granges. Begun in 1867, the National Grange is the oldest US rural community-service, family-oriented organization with a special interest in agriculture. Annually, the month of April. For info: The Natl Grange of the Patrons of Husbandry, 1616 H St NW, Washington, DC 20006. Phone: (202) 628-3507 or (888) 4-GRANGE. Fax: (202) 347-1091. E-mail: info@nationalgrange.org. Web: www.nationalgrange.org.

HARVEY, WILLIAM: BIRTH ANNIVERSARY. Apr 1, 1578. (Old Style date.) Physician, born at Folkestone, England. The first to discover the mechanics of the circulation of the blood. Died at Roehampton, England, June 3, 1657 (OS).

HOLY HUMOR MONTH. Apr 1–30. To recognize the healing power of Christian joy, humor and celebration; to celebrate "Holy Humor Sunday," the Sunday after Easter (Apr 19) and to be "Fools for Christ" on April Fools' Day (Apr 1). Churches and prayer groups nationwide participate. For info: Cal Samra, The Joyful Noiseletter, PO Box 895, Portage, MI 49081-0895. Phone: (269) 324-0990. Fax: (269) 324-3984. E-mail: joyfulnz@aol.com. Web: www.joyfulnoiseletter.com.

HOME IMPROVEMENT TIME. Apr 1–Sept 30. To explain the investment advantages of spending disposable income for home improvement to create better family living and improved community environment. Editorial package includes approximately 50 camera-ready stories and photos free to editors. Also available on website. (May is a promotion focal point.) For info: James A. Stewart, Jr, Home Improvement Time, PO Box 247, Oakdale, PA 15071-0247. Phone: (412) 787-2881. Fax: (412) 787-3233. Web: homeimprovementtime.com.

INFORMED WOMAN MONTH. Apr 1–30. You owe it to yourself to feel happy and fulfilled. To have confidence that you're in charge of your life and you're guiding it in the right direction. You can have whatever you want, but you need to determine what you need to know, where to go and whom to contact. Discover how to enjoy better living today and learn how to become a more informed and aware individual for the future. Ideas and tips for the month available for $2.50. For info: Lorrie Marsiglio, PO Box 284-CC, Wasco, IL 60183-0284. Phone: (630) 584-9368.

INTERNATIONAL CUSTOMER LOYALTY MONTH. Apr 1–30. We highlight this month to honor and generate customer loyalty! Even though building customer loyalty should be a year-round thing, not just a month, take this month to strategize on how you can improve on relationships with your customers through better service, higher quality, etc. For info: Shep Hyken, Shepard Presentations, LLC, 711 Old Ballas Rd, #215, St. Louis, MO 63141. Phone: (314) 696-2200. E-mail: Shep@hyken.com. Web: www.CustomerLoyaltyMonth.com.

INTERNATIONAL PET FIRST AID AWARENESS MONTH. Apr 1–30. Sponsored by Pet Tech, Inc, the first national training center for pet first aid and care. To help pet owners everywhere in understanding the importance of knowing the skills and techniques of pet first aid, CPR and care for their pets. For info: Pet Tech, Inc, PO Box 2285, Carlsbad, CA 92018. Phone: (760) 930-0309. E-mail: info@pettech.net. Web: www.pettech.net.

INTERNATIONAL POOPER-SCOOPER WEEK. Apr 1–7. The Association of Professional Animal Waste Specialists (aPaws) was founded in February 2002 by a group of pooper-scoopers who believe that every dog should have its day. In recognition of a growing problem in our communities, aPaws has established a special week of educating pet owners on the importance of cleaning up after their dogs—it's no joke! Annually, Apr 1–7. For info: aPaws. Web: www.apaws.org.

INTERNATIONAL TWIT AWARD MONTH. Apr 1–30. Any famous name (celebrity with the worst sense of humor) is eligible to be designated most Tiresome Wit (TWIT) of 2009. For info: Lauren Barnett, Lone Star Publications of Humor, 8452 Fredericksburg Rd, #103, San Antonio, TX 78229. E-mail: lspubs@aol.com. Web: members.aol.com/lspubs/lsindex.html.

IRAN: ISLAMIC REPUBLIC DAY. Apr 1. National holiday. Commemorates the approval of the new constitution of the Islamic Republic of Iran in 1979.

JAZZ APPRECIATION MONTH. Apr 1–30. Every April, Jazz Appreciation Month (JAM) highlights the glories of jazz as both a historical and a living treasure. Here is one special month to draw greater public attention to the extraordinary heritage and history of jazz and its importance to American culture. Musicians, concert halls, schools, colleges, museums, libraries and public broadcasters are encouraged to offer special programs during this month. The Smithsonian Institution's National Museum of American History (which operates the world's most comprehensive set of jazz programs) leads this initiative in concert with a distinguished roster of federal agencies, nongovernmental organizations and broadcasting networks. For info: The Smithsonian Institution, National Museum of American History, PO Box 37012 MRC 616, Washington, DC 20013. Phone: (202) 633-3604. E-mail: jazz@si.edu. Web: www.smithsonianjazz.org.

LAUGH AT WORK WEEK. Apr 1–7. Laughter and humor are vital to a healthy, productive workplace. Benefits of laughing at work include improved productivity, teamwork, communication, stress relief, job satisfaction and employee retention. This week, which begins on April Fools' Day, focuses on the very serious business of humor. For info: Randall Munson, Creatively Speaking, 508 Meadow Run Dr SW, Rochester, MN 55902-2337. Phone: (507) 286-1331. Fax: (507) 286-1331. E-mail: humor@CreativelySpeaking.com. Web: www.LaughAtWorkWeek.com.

LONGWOOD GARDENS SPRING BLOOMS. Apr 1–May 22. Kennett Square, PA. Thousands of spring bulbs, flowering shrubs and trees bloom throughout 1,050 acres of formal gardens, woodlands and meadows. Est attendance: 150,000. For info: Longwood Gardens, PO Box 501, Kennett Square, PA 19348-0501. Phone: (610) 388-1000. Web: www.longwoodgardens.org.

MEDICATION SAFETY WEEK. Apr 1–7. Starting on April Fool's Day, this week serves to raise awareness about medication safety and improving health communication. When it comes to taking medications and supplements—don't be fooled. A free "Medication Safety" presentation for community education is available to partnering health organizations upon request. For info: Women's Heart Foundation, PO Box 7827, West Trenton, NJ 08628. Phone: (609) 771-9600. Fax: (609) 771-3778. Web: www.womensheart.org.

MONTH OF THE MILITARY CHILD. Apr 1–30. All military posts. This month celebrates the special lives and sacrifices of military children! For info: Danielle Hamilton, 246 Creek Nation Dr, Auburn, AL 36830. Phone: (334) 332-5333. E-mail: danielle.hamilton@us.army.mil.

MONTH OF THE YOUNG CHILD®. Apr 1–30. Michigan. To promote awareness of the importance of young children and their specific needs in today's society. Many communities celebrate with special events for children and families. For info: Michigan Assn for Education of Young Children, Beacon Pl, 4572 S Hagadorn Rd, Ste 1D, East Lansing, MI 48823-5385. Phone: (800) 336-6424 or (517) 336-9700. Fax: (517) 336-9790. E-mail: moyc@miaeyc.org. Web: www.miaeyc.org.

NATIONAL AFRICAN-AMERICAN WOMEN'S FITNESS MONTH. Apr 1–30. A national event designed to encourage health awareness through physical activity for African-American women. The event will increase awareness of the health risks associated with a sedentary lifestyle and promote the benefits of an active lifestyle. For info: Sheila Madison, Natl African-American Women's Fitness Month, PO Box 2733, Washington, DC 20013-2733. Phone: (281) 750-2767. Web: www.sheilamadison.com.

NATIONAL CARD AND LETTER WRITING MONTH. Apr 1–May 10. An annual effort to promote literacy and celebrate the art of letter writing. The writing, sending and receiving of letters, postcards and greeting cards is a tradition that has preserved our nation's history and changed lives. Unlike other forms of communications, card and letter writing is timeless, personal and immediately tangible. Postmasters and managers of customer service at post offices across the country are encouraging card and letter writing by hosting friendly competitions among local youth or by supporting activities at local libraries or schools. Annually, from Apr 1 until Mother's Day. For info: US Postal Service. Web: www.usps.com/communications/community/nclwm.htm.

✦ **NATIONAL CHILD ABUSE PREVENTION MONTH.** Apr 1–30.

NATIONAL CHILD ABUSE PREVENTION MONTH. Apr 1–30. For info: Prevent Child Abuse America, 500 N Michigan Ave, Ste 200, Chicago, IL 60611. Phone: (312) 663-3520. Web: www.preventchildabuse.org.

April 2009	S	M	T	W	T	F	S
				1	2	3	4
	5	6	7	8	9	10	11
	12	13	14	15	16	17	18
	19	20	21	22	23	24	25
	26	27	28	29	30		

NATIONAL DAY OF HOPE. Apr 1. During National Child Abuse Prevention Month, this day asks all Americans to keep victims of abuse and neglect in their thoughts and prayers, to seek to break the cycle of child abuse and neglect, and to give victimized children hope for the future. This is also a day when the faith community, nonprofit organizations and volunteers across America should recommit themselves and mobilize their resources to assist abused and neglected children. Observed since 2000. Annually, the first Wednesday of April. For info: National Day of Hope, Childhelp, 15757 N 78th St, Scottsdale, AZ 85260. Phone: (480) 922-8212. Fax: (480) 922-7061. E-mail: Nationaldayofhope@childhelp.org. Web: www.childhelp.org.

NATIONAL DECORATING MONTH. Apr 1–30. This month is dedicated to learning more about the many aspects of home decor while promoting the fun and creativity of DIY decorating. For info: Donna Babylon, PO Box 1603, Westminster, MD 21158. Phone: (410) 876-3121. Fax: (410) 848-3293.

NATIONAL DNA, GENOMICS & STEM CELL EDUCATION AND AWARENESS MONTH. Apr 1–30. Pharmicists Planning Service, Inc (PPSI), along with the Pharmacy Council on Genomics, Stem Cells & DNA, declare April as our education and awareness month. For posters, pamphlets, literature or any additional information, please contact us! For info: Fred Mayer, Pharmacists Planning Service, Inc, 101 Lucas Valley Rd, Ste 382, San Rafael, CA 94903. Phone: (415) 479-8628. E-mail: ppsi@aol.com. Web: www.ppsinc.org.

✦ **NATIONAL DONATE LIFE MONTH.** Apr 1–30.

NATIONAL DONATE LIFE MONTH. Apr 1–30. Formerly known as National Organ and Tissue Donor Awareness Week, this observance expanded to a full month in 2003. The purpose is to encourage Americans to consider organ and tissue donation and to sign donor cards when getting a driver's license. For info: US Dept of Health and Human Services, 200 Independence Ave SW, Washington, DC 20201. Phone: (877) 696-6775 or (202) 619-0257. Web: www.organdonor.gov.

NATIONAL FUN DAY. Apr 1. A day to laugh and reminisce about the good old days when April 1 meant an exploding pen, a hand buzzer, a nice stick of pepper gum or maybe some fake doggie poo. Play a prank on a friend, family member or coworker to keep the spirit of April Fools' alive. For info: iParty, 270 Bridge St, Ste 301, Dedham, MA 02026. Phone: (781) 329-3952. E-mail: fun@iparty.com. Web: www.iparty.com.

NATIONAL FUN AT WORK DAY. Apr 1. Today and every day the workplace should be spiced with fun, laughter and a playful attitude. Morale will increase, productivity will soar and the bottom line will improve. Annually, Apr 1 (or the following Thursday, if April 1 falls on a weekend). For info: Matt Weinstein, Playfair, 2207 Oregon St, Berkeley, CA 94705. Phone/fax: (510) 540-8768. E-mail: playfair1@aol.com. Web: www.playfair.com.

NATIONAL HUMOR MONTH. Apr 1–30. 33rd anniversary. Special events in Canada and the US will focus on the joy and therapeutic value of laughter and how it can reduce stress, improve job performance and enrich the quality of life. For info send 68-cent SASE to: Larry Wilde, Dir, The Carmel Institute of Humor, 25470 Canada Dr, Carmel, CA 93923-8926. Web: www.larrywilde.com.

NATIONAL KITE MONTH. Apr 1–30. Celebrates kiting with more than 600 events throughout the country, including kite festivals, kite-making classes for kids and adults, kite-making classes in schools, kite displays in museums and public libraries and "fun flys" at local parks and beaches. For info: Mel Hickman, American Kitefliers Assn, PO Box 1614, Walla Walla, WA 99362. Phone/fax: (800) 252-2550. E-mail: Admin@NationalKiteMonth.org. Web: www.NationalKiteMonth.org.

NATIONAL KNUCKLES DOWN MONTH. Apr 1–30. To recognize and revive the American tradition of playing and collecting marbles and keep it rolling along. Please send SASE with inquiries. For info: Cathy C. Runyan-Svacina, The Marble Lady, 7812 NW Hampton Rd, Kansas City, MO 64152. Phone: (816) 587-8687. Web: www.themarblelady.com.

NATIONAL LANDSCAPE ARCHITECTURE MONTH. Apr 1–30. Investigate what landscapers do to beautify our grounds—both personal and public. Many architects will have site tours, exhibits, school visits and community projects this week. Annually, during April, as Apr 26 is the birth anniversary of Frederick Law Olmsted. Olmsted is widely regarded as the founder of the profession of landscape architecture in North America. For info: ASLA, 636 Eye Street NW, Washington, DC 20001. Phone: (202) 898-2444. Fax: (202) 898-1185. E-mail: aowens@asla.org. Web: www.asla.org/lamonth.

NATIONAL OCCUPATIONAL THERAPY MONTH. Apr 1–30. To recognize the services and accomplishments of occupational therapy practitioners and promote awareness of the benefits of occupational therapy. For info: The American Occupational Therapy Assn, Inc, 4720 Montgomery Lane, PO Box 31220, Bethesda, MD 20824-1220. Phone: (301) 652-2682. TDD (800) 377-8555. Fax: (301) 652-7711. E-mail: praota@aota.org. Web: www.aota.org.

NATIONAL PARKINSON AWARENESS MONTH. Apr 1–30. To help enhance public education and awareness about Parkinson disease by providing information on treatment, medication, support and research, as well as providing these resources to patients with the disease and their caregivers, helping to improve the quality of life for both. For info: Natl Parkinson Foundation, 1501 NW 9th Ave, Miami, FL 33136. Phone: (800) 327-4545. Fax: (305) 243-5595. E-mail: contact@parkinson.org. Web: www.parkinson.org.

NATIONAL PECAN MONTH. Apr 1–30. A celebration of the great taste, health benefits and versatility of pecans. This delicious tree nut native to North America adds unmistakable flavor, crunch and texture to just about any meal or snack. Pecans have proven cholesterol-lowering properties and contain more than 19 important vitamins and minerals. Almost 90 percent of the fats in pecans are of the heart-healthy, unsaturated variety. For info: Natl Pecan Shellers Assn, 1100 Johnson Ferry Rd, Ste 300, Atlanta, GA 30342. Phone: (404) 252-3663. Fax: (404) 252-0774. E-mail: info@ilovepecans.org. Web: www.ilovepecans.org.

NATIONAL POETRY MONTH. Apr 1–30. Annual observance to pay tribute to the great legacy and ongoing achievement of American poets and the vital place of poetry in American culture. In a proclamation issued in honor of the first observance, President Bill Clinton called it "a welcome opportunity to celebrate not only the unsurpassed body of literature produced by our poets in the past, but also the vitality and diversity of voices reflected in the works of today's American poets. . . . Their creativity and wealth of language enrich our culture and inspire a new generation of Americans to learn the power of reading and writing at its best." Spearheaded by the Academy of American Poets, this is the largest and most extensive celebration of poetry in American history. For info: Academy of American Poets, 584 Broadway, Ste 604, New York, NY 10012-5243. Phone: (212) 274-0343. Fax: (212) 274-9427. Web: www.poets.org.

NATIONAL SEXUAL ASSAULT AWARENESS AND PREVENTION MONTH. Apr 1–30. Every two and a half minutes, somewhere in America, another person is sexually assaulted. During this month, efforts are focused on raising awareness of sexual assault, promoting legislative efforts to address sexual violence, lauding efforts of more than 10,000 volunteers across the US who assist in crisis services and related areas, promoting resources for victims such as the National Sexual Assault Hotline (800-656-HOPE) and, above all, demonstrating solidarity with victims of sexual assault. Celebrated nationally by RAINN, state sexual assault coalitions, local rape crisis centers and other similar organizations. Passed by House/Senate; signed by president. For info: Rape, Abuse & Incest Natl Network (RAINN), 2000 L St NW, Ste 406, Washington, DC 20036. Phone: (202) 544-3064 or (800) 656-HOPE. Fax: (202) 544-3556. E-mail: info@rainn.org. Web: www.rainn.org.

NATIONAL SEXUALLY TRANSMITTED DISEASES (STDs) EDUCATION AND AWARENESS MONTH. Apr 1–30. To educate consumers, patients, students and professionals about the prevention of sexually transmitted diseases. Kits available for $15. For info: Frederick Mayer, Pharmacists Planning Service, Inc, 101 Lucas Valley Rd, Ste 382, San Rafael, CA 94903. E-mail: ppsi@aol.com. Web: www.ppsinc.org.

NATIONAL YOUTH SPORTS SAFETY MONTH. Apr 1–30. Bringing public attention to the prevalent problem of injuries in youth sports. This event promotes safety in sports activities and is supported by more than 60 national sports and medical organizations. Resource material available on website. For info: Natl Youth Sports Safety Foundation, One Beacon St, Ste 3333, Boston, MA 02108. Phone: (617) 367-6677. Fax: (617) 722-9999. E-mail: NYSSF@aol.com. Web: www.nyssf.org.

PARAPROFESSIONAL APPRECIATION DAY. Apr 1. Originally established several years ago by the governor of Missouri, this holiday honors the contributions of paraprofessionals, especially in education. Annually, the first Wednesday in April. For info: Valerie Pennington, Upper Elementary School, 607 S Third St, Odessa, MO 64076. Phone: (816) 633-5396. E-mail: vpennington@odessa.k12.mo.us.

PHARMACISTS' WAR ON DIABETES. Apr 1–30. To educate consumers, patients and health care professionals about prevention of diabetes, especially focusing on "Know Your Numbers for Diabetes" and screening along with awareness and interest in the diabetes epidemic. Kits available for $15. For info: Frederick Mayer, Pharmacists Planning Service, Inc, c/o the Pharmacy Council on Diabetes Education (PCDE), 101 Lucas Valley Rd, Ste 382, San Rafael, CA 94903. E-mail: ppsi@aol.com. Web: www.ppsinc.org.

PHYSICAL WELLNESS MONTH. Apr 1–30. Time to get in shape for summer! Shed those winter clothes and extra pounds, and rejuvenate your body with healthy eating, restful sleep, vigorous exercise and a new look. Jog, swim, bike, roller-skate, play tennis, go hiking or backpacking. Spend time daily outdoors breathing in fresh air, and take time to relax. Retire to bed early for restful sleep and wake up early feeling refreshed and energized. For info: Angela Brown Oberer, Words of Wellness, PO Box 49266, Charlotte, NC 28277. Phone: (704) 849-2900. E-mail: Angela@WordsofWellness.com. Web: www.WordsofWellness.com.

POETRY & THE CREATIVE MIND. Apr 1. Alice Tully Hall, Lincoln Center, New York, NY. Some of America's leading artists, scholars and public figures participate in this extraordinary evening celebrating the role of contemporary poetry in American culture. Poetry & the Creative Mind kicks off National Poetry Month, established by the Academy of American Poets in 1996 and now the largest literary celebration in the world. Participating in 2006 were Meryl Streep, Wynton Marsalis, Alan Alda, Wendy Whelan, Mike Wallace, Dianne Wiest, Oliver Sacks, Gloria Vanderbilt, William Wegman and Christopher Durang. Est attendance: 1,100. For info: Academy of American Poets, 584 Broadway, Ste 604, New York, NY 10012. Phone: (212) 274-0343. Fax: (212) 274-9427. Web: www.poets.org.

PREVENT LYME IN DOGS MONTH. Apr 1–30. An educational campaign to raise awareness of canine Lyme disease and prevention available with an annual vaccination and use of tick control products. Sponsored by Merial, a world-leading animal health company and makers of RECOMBITEK® Lyme vaccine. Annually, the month of April. For info: Merial Ltd, 3239 Satellite Blvd, Duluth, GA 30096. Phone: (888) MERIAL-1. Web: www.LymePrevention.com.

PREVENTION OF ANIMAL CRUELTY MONTH. Apr 1–30. Sponsored by the ASPCA, this crucial month is designed to educate Americans about animal cruelty and to urge them to not only report instances of violence toward animals, but also to "Go Orange for Animals" on Apr 10, the ASPCA's birthday. For info: ASPCA Media & Communications Dept, New York, NY. Phone: (212) 876-7700, ext 4565. E-mail: shonalib@aspca.org. Web: www.aspca.org.

RAM, JAGJIVAN: BIRTH ANNIVERSARY. Apr 1, 1908. Indian political leader and coworker with Mohandas K. Gandhi and Jawaharlal Nehru in the fight for Indian independence. Born into a family of "untouchables" at the village of Chandwa, Bihar, India, Ram was one of the first of that class to attend school and university. Known as the champion and spokesman for India's 100 million untouchables, he overcame most of the handicaps of caste. He served in a number of ministerial cabinet posts and twice was a candidate for prime minister. Ram died at New Delhi, India, July 6, 1986.

ROBERT THE HERMIT: DEATH ANNIVERSARY. Apr 1, 1832. One of the most famous hermits in American history died in his hermitage at Seekonk, MA. Robert was a bonded slave, the son of an African mother and probably an Anglo-Saxon father. After obtaining his freedom, he was swindled out of it and shipped to a foreign slave market, then later escaped to America. He was separated from his first wife by force and rejected by his second wife after a long sea voyage, before withdrawing from society.

ROSACEA AWARENESS MONTH. Apr 1–30. Rosacea Awareness Month has been designated by the National Rosacea Society to raise awareness and understanding of this increasingly common disease. Rosacea is a facial skin condition that can cause permanent physical and psychological damage if it is not diagnosed and treated. For info: Natl Rosacea Society, 800 S Northwest Hwy, Ste 200, Barrington, IL 60010. Phone: (847) 382-8971 or (888) NO-BLUSH. Fax: (847) 382-5567. E-mail: rosaceas@aol.com. Web: www.rosacea.org.

SCHOOL LIBRARY MEDIA MONTH. Apr 1–30. Celebrates the work of school library media specialists in our nation's elementary and secondary schools. For info: American Assn of School Librarians, American Library Assn, 50 E Huron St, Chicago, IL 60611. Phone: (800) 545-2433. E-mail: AASL@ala.org. Web: www.ala.org/aasl.

SKAGIT VALLEY TULIP FESTIVAL. Apr 1–30. Skagit County, La Conner, Mount Vernon, Burlington, WA. To celebrate and share the spectacular beauty of more than 1,000 acres of blooming daffodils and tulips that herald the arrival of spring in the Skagit Valley of Washington state. Est attendance: 350,000. For info: Cindy Verge, SVTF Exec Dir, PO Box 1784, Mount Vernon, WA 98273. Phone: (360) 428-5959. Fax: (360) 428-6753. E-mail: info@tulipfestival.org. Web: www.tulipfestival.org.

SORRY CHARLIE DAY. Apr 1. To honor Charlie the Tuna, who has been rejected for decades and still keeps his spunk. A day to recognize anyone who has been rejected and lived through it. Join the "Sorry Charlie, No-Fan-Club-for-You Club" by sending in your best rejection story. Please send SASE with inquiries. For info: Cathy Runyan-Svacina, 7812 NW Hampton Rd, Kansas City, MO 64152. Phone: (816) 587-8687. Fax: (816) 587-8687. Web: www.themarblelady.com.

SOUTHERN BELLES MONTH. Apr 1–30. Honoring all Southern Belles—whether born or reborn to the title. For info: Susan E. Reno, PO Box 2736, Cartersville, GA 30120. Phone: (770) 546-0095.

STRAW HAT MONTH. Apr 1–30. A month of celebration during which the felt hat is put aside in favor of the straw or fabric hat by both men and women. Local businesses and the media are encouraged to plan hat-related activities. Widely observed in the fashion industry. Originally sponsored by the Headwear Information Bureau.

STRESS AWARENESS MONTH. Apr 1–30. To promote public awareness of what stress is, what causes it to occur and what can be done about it. A month-long focus on the dangers of stress, successful coping strategies and the myths about stress that are prevalent in our society. For info: Morton C. Orman, MD, Dir, The Health Resource Network, 908 Cold Bottom Rd, Sparks, MD 21152. Web: www.stresscure.com.

TESTICULAR CANCER AWARENESS WEEK. Apr 1–7. This public awareness and education program was conceived in 1997 to create a better public understanding of the dangers of undetected testicular cancer in young men aged 15–34. The campaign is designed to promote the importance of early detection, which saves hundreds of young men's lives each year. A free self-exam reminder is available at menstuff-testicular-exam-subscribe@topica.com, so that a monthly self-exam becomes a habit for health. Information is made available to high school and college health centers to ensure correct diagnosis. For info: Gordon Clay, PO Box 1080-CH, Brookings, OR 97415-0024. Web: www.tcaw.org.

US AIR FORCE ACADEMY ESTABLISHED: 55th ANNIVERSARY. Apr 1, 1954. President Dwight Eisenhower signed the bill this day that created the US Air Force Academy to train officers for the Air Force. Construction on the Colorado Springs, CO, academy began July 11, 1955, and ended in 1958. The academy was accredited in 1959. Women were admitted in 1976. For more info: www.usafa.edu.

US HOUSE OF REPRESENTATIVES ACHIEVES A QUORUM: ANNIVERSARY. Apr 1, 1789. First session of Congress was held Mar 4, 1789, but not enough representatives arrived to achieve a quorum until Apr 1.

WOMEN'S EYE HEALTH AND SAFETY MONTH. Apr 1–30. Women often manage family health concerns. Do you know how to protect your sight? Hormonal changes, age and smoking can endanger sight. Information on women's and family eye-health issues will be provided. For info: Prevent Blindness America®, 211 W Wacker Dr, Ste 1700, Chicago, IL 60606. Phone: (800) 331-2020. E-mail: info@preventblindness.org. Web: www.preventblindness.org.

WORKPLACE CONFLICT AWARENESS MONTH. Apr 1–30. At today's harried pace, workplace conflict is increasing. Many of us try to avoid this conflict, but instead we take it home with us. This month, we try to make people aware that trying to avoid conflict is futile; we must learn to deal with it and manage it. For info: Richard Brenner, Chaco Canyon Consulting, 700 Huron Ave, Ste 11J, Cambridge, MA 02138. Phone: (617) 491-6289. Fax: (617) 395-2628. E-mail: rbrenner@ChacoCanyon.com. Web: www.ChacoCanyon.com.

WORLD HABITAT AWARENESS MONTH. Apr 1–30. A worldwide observance for the need to protect the habitat of all Earth's creatures, to make a conscious effort to preserve nature's ecosystems. Annually, the entire month of April. For info: PALS Foundation, PO Box 1271, San Luis Obispo, CA 93406. Phone: (805) 544-0984. Fax: (805) 544-2027. Web: www.PALS.R8.org.

April 2009

S	M	T	W	T	F	S
			1	2	3	4
5	6	7	8	9	10	11
12	13	14	15	16	17	18
19	20	21	22	23	24	25
26	27	28	29	30		

Birthdays Today

Samuel A. Alito, Jr, 59, Associate Justice of the US Supreme Court, born Trenton, NJ, Apr 1, 1950.

David Eisenhower, 62, author (*Eisenhower at War*), lawyer, grandson of former president Dwight Eisenhower, born West Point, NY, Apr 1, 1947.

Ali MacGraw, 70, actress (*Goodbye, Columbus*; *Love Story*), born Pound Ridge, NY, Apr 1, 1939.

Annette O'Toole, 56, actress (*Smile, 48 Hrs*), born Houston, TX, Apr 1, 1953.

Jane Powell, 80, actress (*Seven Brides for Seven Brothers*), born Suzanne Burce at Portland, OR, Apr 1, 1929.

Debbie Reynolds, 77, actress (*Singin' in the Rain, Mother*), born El Paso, TX, Apr 1, 1932.

Libby Riddles, 53, first woman to win the 1,135-mile Iditarod Alaskan dogsled race, born Madison, WI, Apr 1, 1956.

Daniel Joseph "Rusty" Staub, 65, former baseball player, born New Orleans, LA, Apr 1, 1944.

April 2 — Thursday

DAY 92 | 273 REMAINING

ANDERSEN, HANS CHRISTIAN: BIRTH ANNIVERSARY. Apr 2, 1805. Author chiefly remembered for his more than 150 fairy tales, many of which are regarded as classics of children's literature. Andersen was born at Odense, Denmark, and died at Copenhagen, Denmark, Aug 4, 1875.

ARGENTINA: MALVINAS DAY. Apr 2. Public holiday. Full name is Day of the War Veterans and the Fallen in the Malvinas Islands. Commemorates the Argentine dead and wounded during the attempt to regain the Falkland Islands in 1982. Observed since 2001.

"AS THE WORLD TURNS" TV PREMIERE: ANNIVERSARY. Apr 2, 1956. One of the longest-running soaps currently on the air, "ATWT" premiered on CBS. The series is set in midwestern Oakdale and revolves around the Hughes family and their neighbors. Irma Phillips was the show's creator and head writer. Some of its cast members who made it big are: Meg Ryan, Julianne Moore, Michael Nader, Steven Weber and Swoosie Kurtz.

BARTHOLDI, FREDERIC AUGUSTE: 175th BIRTH ANNIVERSARY. Apr 2, 1834. French sculptor who created *Liberty Enlightening the World* (better known as the Statue of Liberty), which stands at New York Harbor. Also remembered for the *Lion of Belfort* at Belfort, France. Born at Colman, at Alsace, France. Died at Paris, Oct 4, 1904.

CASANOVA, GIOVANNI GIACOMO GIROLAMO: BIRTH ANNIVERSARY. Apr 2, 1725. Celebrated Italian writer-librarian and, by his own account, philanderer, adventurer, rogue, seminarian, soldier and spy, was born at Venice, Italy. As the Chevalier de Seingalt, he died at Dux, Bohemia, June 4, 1798, while serving as librarian and working on his lively and frank *History of My Life*, a brilliant picture of 18th-century life.

"DALLAS" TV PREMIERE: ANNIVERSARY. Apr 2, 1978. Oil tycoons battled for money, power and prestige in this prime-time CBS drama that ran for nearly 13 years. The Ewings and Barneses were Texas's modern-day Hatfields and McCoys. Larry Hagman starred as the devious, scheming womanizer J.R. Ewing. When J.R. was shot in the 1980 season-ending cliffhanger, the revelation of the mystery shooter was the single most-watched episode of its time (it was Kristin, J.R.'s sister-in-law, played by Mary Crosby). Cast members included Jim Davis, Barbara Bel Geddes, Donna Reed, Ted Shackelford, Joan Van Ark (who, along with Shackelford, starred in the spin-off "Knots Landing"), Patrick Duffy, Linda Gray, Charlene Tilton, David Wayne, Keenan Wynn, Ken Kercheval, Victoria Principal and Steve Kanaly.

EBSEN, BUDDY: BIRTH ANNIVERSARY. Apr 2, 1908. Born Christian Rudolph Ebsen, Jr, at Belleville, IL. Buddy Ebsen started his career as a vaudeville "song-and-dance" man, then was popular throughout the 1930s on film as well. He almost played the Tin Man in *The Wizard of Oz* (1939) but had a serious allergic reaction to the makeup and was forced to stop filming. In the 1950s, he played Davy Crockett's sidekick on television and in film. He played Jed Clampett in "The Beverly Hillbillies" (1962–71) and starred as "Barnaby Jones" (1973–80). He died at Torrance, CA, July 6, 2003.

"THE EDGE OF NIGHT" TV PREMIERE: ANNIVERSARY. Apr 2, 1956. "The Edge of Night" premiered on CBS along with "As the World Turns." Though the plots initially revolved around crime and courtroom drama, the serial's format soon developed along more conventional soap story lines of romance. The soap shifted to ABC in 1975 but was canceled in 1984. Larry Hagman, Dixie Carter, Lori Loughlin, Willie Aames and Amanda Blake were some of the show's most prominent players.

ENGLAND: GRAND NATIONAL. Apr 2–4. Aintree Racecourse, Liverpool. Often called the world's greatest steeplechase, the Grand National is one of the most famous steeplechases in the world. It is a unique test of horsemanship for the rider and also a test of great significance for a horse. The course is nearly two and a quarter miles in length and has 16 unique fences. First held in 1839. For info: Media Relations, Grand National, Aintree Racecourse, Ormskirk Rd, Aintree, England. Web: www.aintree.co.uk or www.grand-national-world.co.uk.

FALKLAND ISLANDS WAR: ANNIVERSARY. Apr 2–June 15, 1982. Argentina, claiming sovereignty over the nearby Falkland Islands (called the Malvinas by Argentina), invaded and occupied the British Crown colony on Apr 2, 1982. British forces defeated the Argentinians on June 15, 1982. About 250 British and 600 Argentine lives were lost in the conflict. In 1986 three military officers, including General Leopoldo Galtieri (who was president of Argentina at the time of the invasion), were convicted and sentenced for the military crime of negligence. Commemorative ceremonies are observed as Malvinas Day in Argentina.

FIRST WHITE HOUSE EASTER EGG ROLL: ANNIVERSARY. Apr 2, 1877. The first White House Easter Egg Roll took place during the administration of Rutherford B. Hayes. The traditional event was discontinued by President Franklin D. Roosevelt in 1942 and reinstated Apr 6, 1953, by President Dwight D. Eisenhower.

GUINNESS, SIR ALEC: 95th BIRTH ANNIVERSARY. Apr 2, 1914. Academy Award–winning actor (for *The Bridge on the River Kwai*) born at London, England. An active performer on stage, he also appeared in many films, including *Star Wars, A Passage to India* and *Kind Hearts and Coronets.* He died at West Sussex, England, Aug 5, 2000.

INTERNATIONAL CHILDREN'S BOOK DAY. Apr 2. Observes Hans Christian Andersen's birthday and commemorates the international aspects of children's literature. Sponsor: Intl Board on Books for Young People, Nonnenweg 12, Postfach, CH-4003 Basel, Switzerland. For info: USBBY Secretariat, PO Box 8139, Newark, DE 19714-8139. Phone: (302) 731-1600, ext 297. E-mail: usbby@reading.org.

KINGSVILLE INTERNATIONAL YOUNG PERFORMERS' COMPETITIONS. Apr 2–4. Texas A&M University–Kingsville, TX. 28th annual international music competition for performers of classical music. Prodigies and aspiring concert artists under age 26 compete in separate contests for bowed instruments. Cash prizes total about $23,000. Performance awards with orchestra. All contest events are free and open to the public. Contestant's entry fee $40; deadline Jan 21, 2009. Sponsor: Music Club of Kingsville, Inc (affiliate of National Federation and Texas Federation of Music Clubs). Est attendance: 1,000. For info: Mary or James Tryer, 1222 W Lee, Kingsville, TX 78363. Phone: (361) 592-2374. E-mail: youngperf@hotmail.com. Web: www.kingsvillemusic.org.

MOON PHASE: FIRST QUARTER. Apr 2. Moon enters First Quarter phase at 10:34 AM, EDT.

MULE DAY. Apr 2–5. Columbia, TN. Started in 1934 as Breeders Day when mules were brought into town to be sold and traded. Today this homecoming is celebrated with arts and crafts, a flea market, a knife show, a huge parade and several mule shows. Est attendance: 40,000. For info: Mule Day, PO Box 66, Columbia, TN 38402. Phone: (931) 381-9557. E-mail: muleday@bellsouth.net.

NICKELODEON DEBUT: 30th ANNIVERSARY. Apr 2, 1979. Nickelodeon, the cable TV channel for kids owned by MTV Networks, debuted on this date.

PASCUA FLORIDA DAY. Apr 2. A legal holiday in Florida, designated as State Day. When it falls on a Saturday or Sunday, the governor may declare either the preceding Friday or the following Monday as State Day. Florida also observes Pascua Florida Week during Mar 27–Apr 2. Commemorates the sighting of Florida by Ponce de Leon in 1513. He named the land Pascua Florida because of its discovery at Easter, the "Feast of the Flowers."

PONCE DE LEON DISCOVERS FLORIDA: ANNIVERSARY. Apr 2, 1513. Juan Ponce de Leon discovered Florida, landing at the site that became the city of St. Augustine. He claimed the land for the King of Spain.

POPE JOHN PAUL II: DEATH ANNIVERSARY. Apr 2, 2005. Karol Wojtyla, 264th pope of the Roman Catholic Church, elected Oct 16, 1978, died at Vatican City on Apr 2, 2005.

RECONCILIATION DAY. Apr 2. Columnist Ann Landers wrote, "Since 1989, I have suggested that April 2 be set aside to write that letter or make that phone call and mend a broken relationship. Life is too short to hold grudges. To forgive can be enormously life-enhancing. . . ."

SWITZERLAND: NAFELS PILGRIMAGE. Apr 2. Canton Glarus. Commemoration of the Battle of Nafels, fought on Apr 9, 1388. Observed annually on first Thursday in April, with processions, prayers, sermon and a reading out of the names of those killed in the battle.

US MINT: ANNIVERSARY. Apr 2, 1792. The first US Mint was established at Philadelphia, PA, as authorized by an act of Congress.

WHITE, CHARLES: BIRTH ANNIVERSARY. Apr 2, 1918. Renowned African-American artist, born at Chicago, IL; died Oct 3, 1979. Charles White began his professional career by painting murals for the WPA during the Depression. He was influenced by Mexican muralists Diego Rivera and David Alfaro Siqueiros. Among his most notable creations are: *J'Accuse* (1966), a series of charcoal drawings depicting a variety of African Americans from all ages and walks of life; the *Wanted* posters (c. 1969), a series of paintings based on old runaway slave posters; and *Homage to Langston Hughes* (1971).

ZOLA, ÉMILE: BIRTH ANNIVERSARY. Apr 2, 1840. Prolific French novelist of the naturalist school, remembered especially for his role in the Dreyfus case (resulting in retrial and vindication of Alfred Dreyfus). Émile Edouard Charles Antoine Zola was born at Paris, France. Defective venting of a stove flue in his bedroom (which some believed to be the work of political enemies) resulted in his death from carbon monoxide poisoning at Paris, Sept 28, 1902.

April 2009

S	M	T	W	T	F	S
			1	2	3	4
5	6	7	8	9	10	11
12	13	14	15	16	17	18
19	20	21	22	23	24	25
26	27	28	29	30		

Birthdays Today

Bethany Joy Galeotti, 28, actress ("One Tree Hill," "Guiding Light"), born Hollywood, FL, Apr 2, 1981.

Emmylou Harris, 62, singer, born Birmingham, AL, Apr 2, 1947.

Linda Hunt, 64, actress ("The Practice"; Oscar for *The Year of Living Dangerously*), born Morristown, NJ, Apr 2, 1945.

Christopher Meloni, 48, actor (*Runaway Bride*, "Law & Order: SVU," "Oz"), born Washington, DC, Apr 2, 1961.

Camille Paglia, 62, literature professor and literary and cultural critic, born Endicott, NY, Apr 2, 1947.

Pamela Reed, 56, actress (*The Right Stuff, Bob Roberts*), born Tacoma, WA, Apr 2, 1953 (some sources say 1949).

Leon Russell, 68, musician, born Lawton, OK, Apr 2, 1941.

April 3 — Friday

DAY 93 — 272 REMAINING

ALCOHOL-FREE WEEKEND. Apr 3–5. Observance to increase public awareness of the problems associated with drinking alcoholic beverages by asking Americans to refrain from drinking them for this weekend. A part of Alcohol Awareness Month, sponsored by the National Council on Alcohol and Drug Dependence since 1987 to encourage local communities to focus on alcoholism and alcohol-related issues. For info: Public Info Office, NCADD, 244 E 58th St, 4th Fl, New York, NY 10022. Phone: (212) 269-7797. Fax: (212) 269-7510. Web: www.ncadd.org.

BIG TEN MEN'S GYMNASTICS CHAMPIONSHIPS. Apr 3–4. University of Michigan, Ann Arbor, MI. For info: Big Ten Conference, 1500 W Higgins Rd, Park Ridge, IL 60068-6300. Phone: (847) 696-1010. Fax: (847) 696-1110. Web: www.bigten.org.

BIRMINGHAM RESISTANCE: ANNIVERSARY. Apr 3, 1962. In retaliation against a black boycott of downtown stores, the Birmingham, AL, city commission voted not to pay the city's $45,000 share of a $100,000 county program that supplied surplus food to the needy. More than 90 percent of the recipients of aid were black. When the NAACP protested the commission's decision, Birmingham mayor Arthur J. Hanes dismissed the complaint as a "typical reaction from New York Socialist radicals."

BLACKS RULED ELIGIBLE TO VOTE: 65th ANNIVERSARY. Apr 3, 1944. The US Supreme Court, in an 8–1 ruling, declared that blacks could not be barred from voting in the Texas Democratic primaries. The high court repudiated the contention that political parties are private associations and held that discrimination against blacks violated the 15th Amendment.

BOSTON PUBLIC LIBRARY: ANNIVERSARY. Apr 3, 1848. The Massachusetts legislature passed legislation enabling Boston to levy a tax for a public library. This created the funding model for all public libraries in the US. The Boston Public Library opened its doors in 1854.

BRANDO, MARLON: 85th BIRTH ANNIVERSARY. Apr 3, 1924. Born at Omaha, NE, Marlon Brando was perhaps the most influential film actor of his generation. Using the Method style of acting as taught by Stella Adler, his powerful performances in *A Streetcar Named Desire* (1951) and *Viva Zapata!* (1952) established his presence as a star, and *On the Waterfront* (1953) earned him an Academy Award. Later films included *Last Tango in Paris* (1972) and *Apocalypse Now* (1979), but he is perhaps best-remembered for his role as Vito Corleone from *The Godfather* (1972), for which he won his second Oscar. Somewhat of a recluse later in his life, he died July 1, 2004, at Los Angeles, CA.

BURROUGHS, JOHN: BIRTH ANNIVERSARY. Apr 3, 1837. American naturalist and author, born at Roxbury, NY. "Time does not become sacred to us until we have lived it," he wrote in 1877. Died en route from California to New York, Mar 29, 1921.

CLEAR LAKE CRAWFISH FESTIVAL. Apr 3–4. Landolt Pavilion, Clear Lake Park, Seabrook, TX. 14th annual. The festival will have crawfish-eating contests, gumbo cook-off, food, games, silent auction and live music. Sponsored by the Clear Lake Area Chamber of Commerce. Proceeds fund the annual July 4th fireworks over Clear Lake. Est attendance: 3,000. For info: Shari Sweeney, Clear Lake Area Chamber of Commerce, 1201 NASA Pkwy, Houston, TX 77058. Phone: (281) 488-7676. Fax: (281) 488-8981. Web: www.clearlakearea.com.

FALL OF RICHMOND: ANNIVERSARY. Apr 3, 1865. After the withdrawal of Robert E. Lee's troops, the Confederate capital of Richmond and nearby Petersburg surrendered to Union forces on this day. Richmond had survived four years of continuous threats from the North. On Apr 4, the city was toured by President Abraham Lincoln.

GRAHAM, CALVIN "BABY VET": BIRTH ANNIVERSARY. Apr 3, 1930. The man who became known as WWII's "baby vet," Calvin Graham was born at Canton, TX, and enlisted in the Navy at the age of 12. As a gunner on the USS *South Dakota*, he was struck by shrapnel during the battle of Guadalcanal in 1942 but still helped pull fellow crew members to safety. The Navy gave Graham a dishonorable discharge, revoked his disability benefits and stripped him of his decorations, including a Purple Heart and Bronze Star, after discovering his age. Eventually, through congressional efforts, he was granted an honorable discharge and won back all but the Purple Heart. His benefits were restored in 1988. Graham died Nov 6, 1992, at Fort Worth, TX.

GUINEA: ANNIVERSARY OF THE SECOND REPUBLIC. Apr 3. National holiday. Commemorates the establishment of the Second Republic in 1984.

HAUPTMANN EXECUTION: ANNIVERSARY. Apr 3, 1936. Bruno Richard Hauptmann, found guilty of the kidnapping and murder of Charles A. Lindbergh, Jr, was executed on this date in the electric chair. The kidnapping and trial gripped the nation, who mourned the death of aviation heroes Charles and Anne Lindbergh's baby. See also: "Lindbergh Kidnapping: Anniversary" (Mar 1).

HOSPITAL ADMITTING CLERKS DAY. Apr 3. A day set aside to recognize the worthwhile contribution made by admitting clerks in hospitals across the US and Canada. Annually, first Friday in April. For info: Shannon Ouwendyk, 705-6 Ave SE, High River, AB, T1V 1K7 Canada. Phone: (403) 652-4892. E-mail: solo99@shaw.ca.

HOWARD, LESLIE: BIRTH ANNIVERSARY. Apr 3, 1893. Romantic actor of Hollywood's Golden Age who became a casualty of WWII. During the return trip from a British government–sponsored tour of Spain, a plane transporting Leslie Howard was shot down by German raiders. Rumors that he was serving on a spy mission circulated at the time, but in the biography (*A Quite Remarkable Father*), Howard's daughter expressed doubt that her father was the sort to get involved in espionage. Howard's most-remembered film role is that of Ashley Wilkes in *Gone with the Wind*. Born at London, England; died at sea June 1, 1943.

INAUGURATION OF PONY EXPRESS: ANNIVERSARY. Apr 3, 1860. The Pony Express began when the first rider left St. Joseph, MO, heading west. The following day another rider headed east from Sacramento, CA. For $5 an ounce, letters were delivered within 10 days. There were 190 way stations between 10 and 15 miles apart, and each rider had a "run" of between 75 and 100 miles. The Pony Express lasted less than two years, ceasing operation in October 1861, when the overland telegraph was completed.

IRVING, WASHINGTON: BIRTH ANNIVERSARY. Apr 3, 1783. American author, attorney and onetime US minister to Spain, Irving was born at New York, NY. Creator of *Rip Van Winkle* and *The Legend of Sleepy Hollow*, he was also the author of many historical and biographical works, including *A History of the Life and Voyages of Christopher Columbus* and the *Life of Washington*. Died at Tarrytown, NY, Nov 28, 1859.

ISLE ROYALE NATIONAL PARK ESTABLISHED: ANNIVERSARY. Apr 3, 1940. Isle Royale is the largest of a group of more than 200 islands that make up this national park preserve. To preserve upper Michigan's flora and fauna, Congress authorized a national park in 1931 and it was established in 1940.

LUCE, HENRY: BIRTH ANNIVERSARY. Apr 3, 1898. American editor and publisher, born to missionary parents at Penglai, China. He built his publishing empire with *Time, Fortune, Life* and *Sports Illustrated*. Luce also was involved in broadcasting. Died at Phoenix, AZ, Feb 28, 1967.

MARSHALL PLAN: ANNIVERSARY. Apr 3, 1948. Suggested by Secretary of State George C. Marshall in a speech at Harvard, June 5, 1947, the legislation for the European Recovery Program, popularly known as the Marshall Plan, was signed by President Truman on Apr 3, 1948. After distributing more than $12 billion, the program ended in 1952.

MEDIEVAL FAIR. Apr 3–5. Reaves Park, Norman, OK. Arts and crafts and living-history fair. The Middle Ages come alive with dancers, music, theater, jousting, knights in combat and a human chess match. Feasts and follies include games and food "fit for a king." Meet such characters as King Arthur, Sir Lancelot and Merlin. Admission is free. Est attendance: 250,000. For info: Linda Linn, 1700 Asp, Norman, OK 73072. Phone: (405) 288-2536. Fax: (405) 325-7698. E-mail: llinn@ou.edu. Web: www.medievalfair.org.

NATIONAL GEOGRAPHIC BEE, STATE LEVEL. Apr 3. Site is different in each state—many are in the state capital. Winners of school-level competitions who scored in the top 100 in their state on a written test compete in the State Geographic Bees. The winner of each state bee will go to Washington, DC, for the national level in May. Est attendance: 300. For info: Natl Geographic Bee, Natl Geographic Society, 1145 17th St NW, Washington, DC 20036. Phone: (202) 828-6659. Web: www.nationalgeographic.com/geographicbee.

POTEET STRAWBERRY FESTIVAL. Apr 3–5. Poteet, TX. One of the oldest and largest festivals in Texas, established to promote Poteet's crop—strawberries. Great food and family entertainment. Est attendance: 100,000. For info: Nita Harvey, Festival Coord, Poteet Strawberry Festival Assn, PO Box 227, Poteet, TX 78065. Phone: (830) 742-8144. Fax: (830) 742-3608. E-mail: nitaharvey@sbcglobal.net. Web: www.strawberryfestival.com.

RAINEY, MA (GERTRUDE BRIDGET): BIRTH ANNIVERSARY. Apr 3, 1888. Known as the "Mother of the Blues," Gertrude "Ma" Rainey was born at Columbus, GA. She made her stage debut at the Columbus Opera House in 1900 in a talent show called "The Bunch of Blackberries." After touring together as "Rainey and Rainey, the Assassinators of the Blues," she and her husband eventually separated and she toured on her own. She made her first recording in 1923 and her last on Dec 28, 1928, after being told that the rural southern blues she sang had gone out of style. She died Dec 22, 1939, at Columbus, GA.

RAND, SALLY: BIRTH ANNIVERSARY. Apr 3, 1904. American actress, ecdysiast and inventor of the fan dance, which gained fame at the 1933 Chicago World's Fair. Born Helen Gould Beck at Hickory County, MO. Died at Glendora, CA, Aug 31, 1979.

STUDENT GOVERNMENT DAY IN MASSACHUSETTS. Apr 3. Annually, the first Friday of April.

SUGARLOAF CRAFTS FESTIVAL. Apr 3–5. Montgomery County Fairgrounds, Gaithersburg, MD. This show, now in its 34th year, features more than 400 nationally recognized craft designers and fine artists displaying and selling their original creations. Craft demonstrations, live music, hourly gift certificate drawings, specialty foods and more! Est attendance: 15,000. For info: Sugarloaf Mountain Works, Inc, 200 Orchard Ridge Dr, #215, Gaithersburg, MD

20878. Phone: (800) 210-9900. Fax: (310) 253-9620. Web: www.sugarloafcrafts.com.

TWEED DAY: ANNIVERSARY. Apr 3, 1823. Day to consider the cost of political corruption. Birthday of William March Tweed, New York City political boss, whose "Tweed Ring" is said to have stolen $30 million to $200 million from the city. Born at New York, NY, Apr 3, 1823, he died in his cell at New York's Ludlow Street Jail, Apr 12, 1878. Cartoonist Thomas Nast deserves much credit for Tweed's arrests and convictions.

***2001: A SPACE ODYSSEY* PREMIERE: ANNIVERSARY.** Apr 3, 1968. Directed by Stanley Kubrick, this influential film has elicited many different interpretations. Sci-fi novelist Arthur C. Clarke based the screenplay on his 1966 book, which was prescient in several ways. Writing before men had landed on the moon, Clarke describes an expedition launched to Jupiter to track a mysterious signal emanating from the moon. Clarke gave the world's population as six billion (achieved in 1999) and described a space station. During flight, a character reads the news on his electronic news pad. The film starred Keir Dullea, William Sylvester, Gary Lockwood, Daniel Richter and HAL 9000, the creepy computer that had human emotions. The theme music was Richard Strauss's *Also Sprach Zarathustra.*

WOMAN PRESIDES OVER US SUPREME COURT: ANNIVERSARY. Apr 3, 1995. Supreme Court Justice Sandra Day O'Connor became the first woman to preside over the US high court when she sat in for Chief Justice William H. Rehnquist and second-in-seniority Justice John Paul Stevens when both were out of town.

Birthdays Today

Alec Baldwin, 51, actor ("30 Rock," *The Cooler, The Hunt for Red October*), born Massapequa, NY, Apr 3, 1958.

Jamie Bamber, 36, actor ("Battlestar Galactica"), born Hammersmith, London, England, Apr 3, 1973.

Amanda Bynes, 23, actress (*Big Fat Liar*, "What I Like About You"), born Thousand Oaks, CA, Apr 3, 1986.

Doris Day, 85, actress, singer ("Young at Heart," *The Man Who Knew Too Much, Pillow Talk*, "The Doris Day Show"), born Doris Von Kappelhoff at Cincinnati, OH, Apr 3, 1924.

Max Frankel, 79, journalist, born Gera, Germany, Apr 3, 1930.

Jennie Garth, 37, actress ("Beverly Hills 90210"), born Champaign, IL, Apr 3, 1972.

Jane Goodall (Baroness Van Lawick-Goodall), 75, anthropologist known for study of chimpanzees, born London, England, Apr 3, 1934.

Leona Lewis, 24, singer, born Islington, London, England, Apr 3, 1985.

Jonathan Lynn, 66, writer, actor, director (*Into the Night, Nuns on the Run, My Cousin Vinny*), born Bath, England, Apr 3, 1943.

Marsha Mason, 67, actress (*The Goodbye Girl, Cinderella Liberty*), born St. Louis, MO, Apr 3, 1942.

Eddie Murphy, 48, comedian ("Saturday Night Live"), actor (*Dreamgirls, Trading Places, Beverly Hills Cop*), born Brooklyn, NY, Apr 3, 1961.

Wayne Newton, 67, singer ("Danke Schoen," "Daddy Don't You Walk So Fast"), born Norfolk, VA, Apr 3, 1942.

Michael Olowokandi, 34, basketball player, born Lagos, Nigeria, Apr 3, 1975.

Tony Orlando, 65, singer (Tony Orlando and Dawn), born Michael Orlando Cassivitis at New York, NY, Apr 3, 1944.

Bernie Parent, 64, Hall of Fame hockey player, born Montreal, QC, Canada, Apr 3, 1945.

David Hyde Pierce, 50, actor (Tony for *Curtains*; Emmys for "Frasier"), born Albany, NY, Apr 3, 1959.

Cobie Smulders, 27, actress ("How I Met Your Mother," "The L Word"), born Vancouver, BC, Canada, Apr 3, 1982.

Picabo Street, 38, Olympic skier, born Triumph, ID, Apr 3, 1971.

April 4 — Saturday

DAY 94 — **271 REMAINING**

BEATLES TAKE OVER MUSIC CHARTS: 45th ANNIVERSARY. Apr 4, 1964. On this date the Beatles held the top five positions of the Billboard Hot 100 chart: "Can't Buy Me Love" was number one, followed by (in order) "Twist and Shout," "She Loves You," "I Want to Hold Your Hand" and "Please, Please Me." The Beatles had made their first US appearance barely two months before. In the same week, they held the top six places on the Australian music chart.

BONZA BOTTLER DAY™. Apr 4. To celebrate when the number of the day is the same as the number of the month. Bonza Bottler Day™ is an excuse to have a party at least once a month. For more information see Jan 1. For info: Gail M. Berger, 14 Fernwood Dr, Taylors, SC 29687. E-mail: bonza@bonzabottlerday.com. Web: www.bonzabottlerday.com.

CANADA: ELMIRA MAPLE SYRUP FESTIVAL. Apr 4. Elmira, ON. Tours of maple bush by hay wagon, sugaring-off shanty in operation, Pennsylvania Dutch cuisine, handcrafted goods, arts and crafts and antiques. Est attendance: 60,000. For info: Woolwich Visitor Services, 5 First St E, Elmira, ON, Canada N3B 2E3. Phone: (519) 669-2605. Fax: (519) 669-0503. Web: www.elmiramaplesyrup.com.

CHINA: QING MING FESTIVAL OR TOMB SWEEPING DAY. Apr 4. This Confucian festival was traditionally celebrated on the fourth or fifth day of the third month but is now on fixed dates (Apr 4 or 5) in China. It is observed by the maintenance of ancestral graves, the presentation of food, wine and flowers as offerings and the burning of paper money at gravesides to help ancestors in the afterworld. People also picnic and gather for family meals. Also observed in Taiwan.

DIX, DOROTHEA LYNDE: BIRTH ANNIVERSARY. Apr 4, 1802. American social reformer and author, born at Hampden, ME. Left home at age 10, was teaching at age 14 and founded a home for girls at Boston while still in her teens. In spite of frail health, she was a vigorous crusader for humane conditions in insane asylums, jails and almshouses and for the establishment of state-supported institutions to serve those needs. Named superintendent of women nurses during the Civil War. Died at Trenton, NJ, July 17, 1887.

FLAG ACT OF 1818: ANNIVERSARY. Apr 4, 1818. Congress approved the first flag of the US.

GIAMATTI, ANGELO BARTLETT: BIRTH ANNIVERSARY. Apr 4, 1938. Baseball commissioner and former president of Yale University. Born at Boston, MA, Giamatti was the youngest person to be named president of Yale, at the age of 39, in 1978. He became the president of Major League Baseball's National League in 1986 and served in that capacity until he was appointed Commissioner of Baseball Apr 1, 1989. An accomplished author, he moved freely between the worlds of literature and baseball, often linking the two

April 2009

S	M	T	W	T	F	S
			1	2	3	4
5	6	7	8	9	10	11
12	13	14	15	16	17	18
19	20	21	22	23	24	25
26	27	28	29	30		

in the many articles he wrote. One week prior to his death, he suspended Pete Rose for life for betting on baseball games. Giamatti died at Martha's Vineyard, MA, Sept 1, 1989.

HATE WEEK. Apr 4–10. Recognizes the day on which the fictional character Winston Smith started his secret diary and wrote the words "DOWN WITH BIG BROTHER," Wednesday, Apr 4, 1984. From George Orwell's dystopian novel, *1984*, portraying the end of human privacy and the destruction of the individual in a totalitarian state (first published in 1949). "Hates" varied from the daily two-minute concentrated hate to the grand culmination observed during Hate Week.

HISTORIC PENDLETON SPRING JUBILEE. Apr 4–5. Pendleton, SC. 32nd annual. Come and join the fun in historic Pendleton with arts and crafts displays, food booths, entertainment and much more. Annually, the first full weekend in April. Est attendance: 30,000. For info: Historic Pendleton Spring Jubilee, PO Box 565, Pendleton, SC 29670. Phone: (864) 646-3782 or (800) 862-1795. Fax: (864) 646-7768. E-mail: jomc5@bellsouth.net. Web: www.pendleton-district.org.

KING, MARTIN LUTHER, JR: ASSASSINATION: ANNIVERSARY. Apr 4, 1968. The Reverend Dr. Martin Luther King, Jr, was shot at Memphis, TN. James Earl Ray was serving a 99-year sentence for the crime at the time of his death in 1998. See also: "King, Martin Luther, Jr: Birth Anniversary" (Jan 15).

***LADY BE GOOD* LOST: ANNIVERSARY.** Apr 4, 1943. The nine-man crew of the WWII American Liberator bomber *Lady Be Good* bailed out 200 miles off course over the Sahara Desert and disappeared. They were returning to their base in Libya after a raid over southern Italy. On Nov 9, 1958, 15 years after the plane went down and more than 13 years after the war had ended, a pilot flying across the Sahara south of Tobruck sighted wreckage of an aircraft in the sand. Eight skeletons and a diary describing the final days of the crew were recovered near the wreckage. The radio, guns and ammunition in the plane were in working order.

NATIONAL LOVE OUR CHILDREN DAY. Apr 4. National Love Our Children Day is celebrated annually across the US to honor children and strengthen families and raise awareness for efforts to protect children. Please e-mail for event details. For info: Ross Ellis, Love Our Children USA, 220 E 57th St, 9th Fl, Ste G, New York, NY 10022. Phone: (888) 347-KIDS. E-mail: info@loveourchildrenusa.org. Web: www.loveourchildrenusa.org.

NCAA DIVISION I MEN'S BASKETBALL CHAMPIONSHIP (FINAL FOUR). Apr 4 and 6. Detroit, MI. For info: NCAA, 700 W Washington St, PO Box 6222, Indianapolis, IN 46206-6222. Phone: (317) 917-6222. Fax: (317) 917-6827. Web: www.NCAAsports.com.

NORTH ATLANTIC TREATY RATIFIED: 60th ANNIVERSARY. Apr 4, 1949. The North Atlantic Treaty Organization was created by this treaty, which was signed by 12 nations, including the US. (Other countries joined later.) The NATO member nations are united for common defense. The treaty went into effect Apr 24, 1949, and the first session of the North Atlantic Council was held Sept 17, 1949.

PERKINS, ANTHONY: BIRTH ANNIVERSARY. Apr 4, 1932. American actor Anthony Perkins was born at New York, NY. Best known for his movie role as homicidal innkeeper Norman Bates in the film *Psycho* (1960), Perkins appeared in many Broadway plays in addition to his numerous film roles. He received an Oscar nomination for his supporting role in *Friendly Persuasion* (1956). Perkins died Sept 12, 1992, at Hollywood, CA.

PRAIRIE DOG CHILI COOK-OFF AND WORLD CHAMPIONSHIP OF PICKLED QUAIL-EGG EATING. Apr 4. Traders Village, Grand Prairie, TX. Tongue-in-cheek salute to the official state dish of Texas, chili con carne, or "Texas Red." World championship of pickled quail-egg eating featuring contestants devouring as many of these gourmet delights as possible in the 60-second time limit. Est attendance: 85,000. For info: Allan Hughes, Traders Village, 2602 Mayfield Rd, Grand Prairie, TX 75052-7246. Phone: (972) 647-2331. E-mail: dfwinfo@tradersvillage.com. Web: www.tradersvillage.com.

SALTER ELECTED FIRST WOMAN MAYOR IN US: ANNIVERSARY. Apr 4, 1887. The first woman elected mayor in the US was Susanna Medora Salter, who was elected mayor of Argonia, KS. Her name had been submitted for election without her knowledge by the Women's Christian Temperance Union, and she did not know she was a candidate until she went to the polls to vote. She received a two-thirds majority vote and served one year for the salary of $1.

SENEGAL: INDEPENDENCE DAY. Apr 4. National holiday. Commemorates independence from France in 1960.

SMOTHERS BROTHERS FIRED: 40th ANNIVERSARY. Apr 4, 1969. CBS canceled the brothers' popular comedy series on this date. The hour-long show strongly influenced television humor during the two years it aired. Tom and Dick, however, frequently found themselves at odds with the censors over material that would be considered tame today. Guests and cast members frequently knocked the Vietnam War and the Nixon Administration. Acts featuring antiwar protestors such as Harry Belafonte were often cut.

SPACE MILESTONE: *CHALLENGER STS-6* (US). Apr 4, 1983. Shuttle *Challenger* launched from Kennedy Space Center, FL, with four astronauts (Paul Weitz, Karol Bobko, Storey Musgrave and Donald Peterson). Four-hour space walk by Musgrave and Peterson. Landed at Edwards Air Force Base, CA, Apr 9.

SPRING SWING CITY ELECTRA-QUANAH-WIDE GARAGE SALE. Apr 4. Electra, TX. More than 50 miles of garage sales throughout the Electra area. Chamber of commerce will provide free coffee and maps at 7 AM; sales start at 8 AM. The chamber of commerce office will close at 8 AM so that we too may enjoy all of the bargains. Est attendance: 500. For info: Sherry Strange, Electra Chamber of Commerce, 112 W Cleveland, Electra, TX 76360. Phone: (940) 495-3577. E-mail: electracoc@electratel.net. Web: www.electratexas.org.

SWAYZE, JOHN CAMERON: BIRTH ANNIVERSARY. Apr 4, 1906. Pioneering television journalist whose catchphrase was "hop-scotching the world for news." Swayze was one of the first reporters to do on-air interviews and report on breaking news stories. Born at Wichita, KS, he died at Sarasota, FL, Aug 15, 1995.

TANGIBLE KARMA™ DAY. Apr 4. Giving of your time, of your love, of your talents, of your "extras"—Tangible Karma™ Day celebrates when giving feels as good as receiving. Groups and individuals set aside one hour of this day to purposefully become aware of the needs of those they are in contact with and actively do something to help fulfill those needs. Annually, the first Saturday in April. For info: Tangible Karma, 742 S Gammon, Madison, WI 53719. Phone: (773) 844-2022. E-mail: info@tangiblekarma.com. Web: www.tangiblekarma.com.

UNITED NATIONS: INTERNATIONAL DAY FOR MINE AWARENESS AND ASSISTANCE IN MINE ACTION. Apr 4. Calling for continued efforts by member states, with the assistance of the United Nations and relevant organizations, to foster the establishment and development of national mine-action capacities in countries where mines and explosive remnants of war constitute a serious threat to the safety, health and lives of the civilian population, or an impediment to social and economic development at the national and local levels. UN Resolution 60/97 of Dec 8, 2005. For info: United Nations, Dept of Public Info, New York, NY 10017. Web: www.un.org.

VICTIMS OF VIOLENCE WHOLLY DAY. Apr 4. The anniversary of the assassination of Rev Dr. Martin Luther King, Jr, is one of the three Days of Respect. Victims of Violence Wholly Day visually affirms the principles of nonviolence. See also: "Humanitarian Day" (Jan 15) and "Dream Day Quest and Jubilee" (Aug 28). For info: EvAngel Mamadee YHWHnewBN, Global Committee Commemorating King Days of Respect, PO Box 21050, Chicago, IL 60621. Phone: (888) 399-9494. E-mail: YHWHnewBN@aol.com.

VITAMIN C ISOLATED: ANNIVERSARY. Apr 4, 1932. Vitamin C was first isolated by C.C. King at the University of Pittsburgh.

WATERS, MUDDY: BIRTH ANNIVERSARY. Apr 4, 1915. Born McKinley Morganfield at Rolling Fork, MS, American blues guitarist and singer Muddy Waters played a significant part in developing modern rhythm and blues that came to be known as Chicago, or urban, blues. It was predominantly from this music that later forms such as rock and roll and soul sprang. Muddy Waters died at Westmont, IL, Apr 30, 1983.

YALE, LINUS: BIRTH ANNIVERSARY. Apr 4, 1821. American portrait painter and inventor of the lock that is named for him was born at Salisbury, NY. He was creator of the Yale Infallible Bank Lock and developer of the cylinder lock. Yale died at New York, NY, Dec 25, 1868.

YAMAMOTO, ISOROKU: 125th BIRTH ANNIVERSARY. Apr 4, 1884. Considered Japan's greatest naval strategist, Admiral Isoroku Yamamoto, who planned the attack on Pearl Harbor, was born at Nagaoka, Honshu. Yamamoto also devised the complex attack on Midway Island, which ended in defeat for the Japanese because the Allies had the key to the Imperial fleet code and were prepared for the June 4, 1942, attack. The US intercepted reports of Yamamoto's proposed 1943 tour of the Western Solomons and shot down his plane Apr 18, while he was touring Japanese installations in the area.

Birthdays Today

Maya Angelou, 81, poet, author (*I Know Why the Caged Bird Sings*), born St. Louis, MO, Apr 4, 1928.

David Blaine, 36, magician, born Brooklyn, NY, Apr 4, 1973.

Robert Downey, Jr, 44, actor (*Iron Man, Zodiac, Chaplin, Natural Born Killers*), born New York, NY, Apr 4, 1965.

Kitty Kelley, 67, author (*Jackie Oh!, Nancy Reagan*), born Hartford, CT, Apr 4, 1942.

Christine Lahti, 59, actress (Emmys for "Chicago Hope"; *Swing Shift*), director (Oscar for "Lieberman in Love"), born Birmingham, MI, Apr 4, 1950.

Richard G. Lugar, 77, US Senator (R, Indiana), born Indianapolis, IN, Apr 4, 1932.

Nancy McKeon, 43, actress ("The Facts of Life," "The Division"), born Westbury, NY, Apr 4, 1966.

Dave Mirra, 37, BMX bike racer, born Syracuse, NY, Apr 4, 1972.

Craig T. Nelson, 63, actor ("Coach," *Private Benjamin, The Killing Fields, The Family Store*), born Spokane, WA, Apr 4, 1946.

Michael Parks, 71, actor ("Then Came Bronson," "Twin Peaks," *The Happening*), born Corona, CA, Apr 4, 1938.

Barry Pepper, 39, actor (*Saving Private Ryan, Enemy of the State*), born Campbell River, BC, Canada, Apr 4, 1970.

Scott Rolen, 34, baseball player, born Evansville, IN, Apr 4, 1975.

April 2009

S	M	T	W	T	F	S
			1	2	3	4
5	6	7	8	9	10	11
12	13	14	15	16	17	18
19	20	21	22	23	24	25
26	27	28	29	30		

April 5 — Sunday

DAY 95 **270 REMAINING**

DAVIS, BETTE: BIRTH ANNIVERSARY. Apr 5, 1908. American actress Bette Davis was born Ruth Elizabeth Davis at Lowell, MA. In addition to acting in more than 80 films, earning 10 Academy Award nominations and winning the Academy Award twice, for Best Actress in *Dangerous* (1935) and *Jezebel* (1938), Davis claimed to have nicknamed the Academy Award "Oscar" after her first husband, Harmon Oscar Nelson, Jr. She died Oct 6, 1989, at Neuilly-sur-Seine, France.

DR. PEPPER DALLAS CUP XXX. Apr 5–12. Pizza Hut Park, Frisco, TX. 30th annual. International invitation-only boys' (under 13 to under 19) soccer competition, sanctioned by the USSF and FIFA. In past years, more than 98 countries and all six continents have been represented. Many of the world's premier teams participate. Annually, from Palm Sunday to Easter Sunday. Est attendance: 120,000. For info: Dallas Cup, 12700 Park Central Dr, Ste 507, Dallas, TX 75251-1500. Phone: (214) 221-3636. Fax: (214) 221-4636. E-mail: bucki@dallascup.com. Web: www.dallascup.com.

EXPLORE YOUR CAREER OPTIONS WEEK. Apr 5–11. Maybe you're aspiring to a new career or merely interested in more opportunities in your present career. Get a fresh start by taking stock of all available options. For info: Dorothy Zjawin, Dir, 61 W Colfax Ave, Roselle Park, NJ 07204.

"FIRESIDE THEATRE" TV PREMIERE: 60th ANNIVERSARY. Apr 5, 1949. Gene Raymond and later Jane Wyman hosted this NBC anthology program consisting of 15- and 30-minute dramas. One of its most acclaimed presentations was "The Reign of Amelika Jo" on Oct 12, 1954. It was set in the South Pacific during WWII and had a mostly black and Asian cast.

FIRST US CHAMBER OF COMMERCE FOUNDED: ANNIVERSARY. Apr 5, 1768. The first chamber of commerce in the US was founded at New York City.

GREECE: DUMB WEEK. Apr 5–11. The week preceding Holy Week on the Orthodox calendar is known as Dumb Week, as no services are held in churches throughout this period except on Friday, eve of the Saturday of Lazarus.

HELEN KELLER'S MIRACLE: ANNIVERSARY. Apr 5, 1887. Anne Sullivan went to Tuscumbia, AL, in March 1887 to teach the "unteachable" deaf and blind Helen Keller. Although Keller was resistant, Sullivan was determined, and after only one month she succeeded in reaching her: she placed Keller's hand under a gushing water pump and used sign language to spell "w-a-t-e-r" into her palm. Helen grasped the meaning—spelling the word back into Sullivan's palm—and excitedly learned 30 more words that day. Keller's life changed at that breakthrough moment, as she recalled later: "As the cool stream gushed over one hand . . . I felt a misty consciousness as of something forgotten, a thrill of returning thought, and somehow the mystery of language was revealed to me." Keller would go on to become the first deaf and blind person to graduate from college, write books and crusade for the disabled. See also: "Keller, Helen: Birth Anniversary" (June 27).

HOLY WEEK. Apr 5–11. Christian observance dating from the fourth century, known also as Great Week. The seven days beginning on the sixth and final Sunday in Lent (Palm Sunday), consisting of: Palm Sunday, Monday of Holy Week, Tuesday of Holy Week, Spy Wednesday (or Wednesday of Holy Week), Maundy Thursday, Good Friday and Holy Saturday (or Great Sabbath or Easter Even). A time of solemn devotion to and memorializing of the suffering (passion), death and burial of Christ. Formerly a time of strict fasting.

LISTER, JOSEPH: BIRTH ANNIVERSARY. Apr 5, 1827. English physician who was the founder of aseptic surgery, born at Upton, Essex, England. Died at Walmer, England, Feb 10, 1912.

"MARRIED . . . WITH CHILDREN" TV PREMIERE: ANNIVERSARY. Apr 5, 1987. This raunchy FOX TV show premiered as the antidote to Cosby-style family shows. Ed O'Neill starred as boorish, luckless shoe salesman Al Bundy; Katey Sagal portrayed Al's big-haired, spandex-clad, sex-starved wife Peggy; Christina Applegate played airheaded bombshell daughter Kelly and David Faustino played hormone-driven son Bud. The last episode aired Apr 20, 1997.

NATIONAL BLUE RIBBON WEEK. Apr 5–11. National Blue Ribbon Week encourages everyone to wear and distribute Blue Ribbon pins or cutouts in a national effort to raise awareness and funds for child abuse prevention. The Blue Ribbon symbolizes more than 3.2 million abused children reported each year to Child Protective Services. Annually, the first full week of April. For info: The National Exchange Club Foundation, 3050 Central Ave, Toledo, OH 43606-1700. Phone: (800) 924-2643. E-mail: cap@nationalexchangeclub.org. Web: www.preventchildabuse.com.

NATIONAL WEEK OF THE OCEAN. Apr 5–11. 26th annual. A week focusing on humanity's interdependence with the ocean, asking each of us to appreciate, protect and make wise use of the ocean. For info: Natl Week of the Ocean, Inc, PO Box 179, Fort Lauderdale, FL 33302. Phone: (954) 462-5573. Web: www.national-week-of-the-ocean.org.

NATIONAL WOMEN'S NUTRITION WEEK. Apr 5–11. To recognize the importance and value of health in all phases of a woman's life. A woman's biochemistry needs nutritional support when a woman is on the pill, during pregnancy, during lactation, when she is under stress and during menopause. This week is designed to educate women about the importance of nutrition for their ongoing health and well-being. For info: Dr. Lois M. Vanderhoof, Applied Nutrition Concepts, 2828 W Parker Rd, #A205, Plano, TX 75075. Phone: (972) 612-5505. E-mail: drlois@appliednutritionconcepts.com. Web: www.appliednutritionconcepts.com.

NCAA DIVISION I WOMEN'S BASKETBALL CHAMPIONSHIP (FINAL FOUR). Apr 5 & 7. Scottrade Center, St. Louis, MO. 28th annual. Est attendance: 20,000. For info: NCAA, PO Box 6222, Indianapolis, IN 46206-6222. Phone: (317) 917-6222. Web: www.NCAAsports.com.

NEWSPAPER ASSOCIATION OF AMERICA ANNUAL CONVENTION. Apr 5–7. Manchester Grand Hyatt, San Diego, CA. For info: Newspaper Assn of America, 1921 Gallows Rd, Ste 600, Vienna, VA 22182. Phone: (703) 902-1600. Web: www.naa.org.

PALM SUNDAY. Apr 5. Commemorates Christ's last entry into Jerusalem, when His way was covered with palms by the multitudes. Beginning of Holy (or Great) Week in Western Christian churches.

PECK, GREGORY: BIRTH ANNIVERSARY. Apr 5, 1916. Born Eldred Gregory Peck at La Jolla, CA, Gregory Peck was one of Hollywood's most popular and likable leading men. Nominated five times for Best Actor, he finally won the Oscar for his role as Atticus Finch in 1962's *To Kill a Mockingbird*. Other popular films included *Roman Holiday, Gentlemen's Agreement* and Alfred Hitchcock's *Spellbound*. He also founded the La Jolla Playhouse with Dorothy McGuire and Mel Ferrer in 1947 and appeared there throughout his career. He died at his home in La Jolla on June 11, 2003.

PHILIPPINES: HOLY WEEK. Apr 5–11. National observance. Flagellants in the streets, *cenaculos* (passion plays) and other colorful and solemn rituals mark the country's observance of Holy Week.

RESNIK, JUDITH A.: 60th BIRTH ANNIVERSARY. Apr 5, 1949. Dr. Judith A. Resnik, the second American woman in space (1984), was born at Akron, OH. The 36-year-old electrical engineer was mission specialist on space shuttle *Challenger*. She perished with all others aboard when *Challenger* exploded Jan 28, 1986. See also: "*Challenger* Space Shuttle Explosion: Anniversary" (Jan 28).

"SECRET AGENT" TV PREMIERE: ANNIVERSARY. Apr 5, 1961. Before Patrick McGoohan became the star of "The Prisoner," he played the role of intelligence agent John Drake on this CBS adventure series. Produced in England by ATV, it also aired there as "Danger Man."

TAIWAN: NATIONAL TOMB-SWEEPING DAY. Apr 5. National holiday since 1972. According to Chinese custom, the tombs of ancestors are swept "clear and bright" and rites honoring ancestors are held. Tomb-Sweeping Day is observed Apr 5, which is also the anniversary of the death of Chiang Kai-Shek.

"THE TRACEY ULLMAN SHOW" TV PREMIERE: ANNIVERSARY. Apr 5, 1987. This Emmy Award–winning comedy-variety show was one of the FOX network's early critical hits. Tracey Ullman starred with Julie Kavner, Dan Castellaneta, Joe Malone and Sam McMurray. The show, produced by James L. Brooks, contained sketches, songs and satire. Animated snippets in between segments introduced us to the Simpsons, executed by Matt Groening, creator of the "Life in Hell" comic strip. "The Simpsons" spun off from the show in 1990.

TRACY, SPENCER: BIRTH ANNIVERSARY. Apr 5, 1900. Born at Milwaukee, WI, Spencer Tracy was one of the most respected actors in film history. He won Academy Awards for Best Actor for 1937's *Captains Courageous* and 1938's *Boys Town* and was nominated seven other times. In 1942, he met actress Katharine Hepburn, and they shared a relationship that lasted until his death, although they never married. Together, they starred in nine films, including *Adam's Rib* in 1949 and *Guess Who's Coming to Dinner* in 1967. Tracy died June 10, 1967, at Hollywood Hills, CA.

WASHINGTON, BOOKER TALIAFERRO: BIRTH ANNIVERSARY. Apr 5, 1856. Black educator and leader born at Franklin County, VA. "No race can prosper," he wrote in *Up from Slavery*, "till it learns that there is as much dignity in tilling a field as in writing a poem." Died at Tuskegee, AL, Nov 14, 1915.

 Birthdays Today

Roger Corman, 83, filmmaker, born Detroit, MI, Apr 5, 1926.

Max Gail, 66, actor ("Barney Miller," *Pearl*), born Grosse Point, MI, Apr 5, 1943.

Michael Moriarty, 67, actor (*The Last Detail, Bang the Drum Slowly*, "Law & Order"), born Detroit, MI, Apr 5, 1942.

Mitch Pileggi, 57, actor ("The X-Files"), born Portland, OR, Apr 5, 1952.

Colin Luther Powell, 72, former US Secretary of State, general, former Chairman US Joint Chiefs of Staff, born New York, NY, Apr 5, 1937.

Gale Storm, 87, actress ("My Little Margie," "NBC Comedy Hour," "The Gale Storm Show"), born Bloomington, TX, Apr 5, 1922.

April 6 — Monday

DAY 96 — 269 REMAINING

"BARNEY & FRIENDS" TV PREMIERE: ANNIVERSARY. Apr 6, 1992. Although most adults find it hopelessly saccharine, this PBS program is hugely popular with preschoolers. Purple dinosaur Barney; his pals, dinosaurs Baby Bop and B.J.; and a multiethnic group of children sing, play games and learn simple lessons about getting along with one another.

BATTLE OF SHILOH: ANNIVERSARY. Apr 6, 1862. General Ulyssess S. Grant's Union forces at Shiloh, or Pittsburgh Landing, TN, were attacked by a large force under General Albert Sidney Johnston on this date. After heavy fighting, the first day of the battle ended without a conclusive victory for either side. Grant was reinforced before the Confederates on the second day, and Confederate general Beauregard, in command after Johnston's death the previous day, ordered a retreat back to Corinth, MS, leaving the Federal troops in a stronger position in Tennessee than before the battle. Losses on both sides totaled more than 23,000.

BRIGHAM YOUNG'S LAST MARRIAGE: ANNIVERSARY. Apr 6, 1868. Brigham Young, Mormon Church leader, married his 27th, and last, wife on this day.

CHURCH OF JESUS CHRIST OF LATTER-DAY SAINTS: ANNIVERSARY. Apr 6, 1830. Under the leadership of Joseph Smith, Jr, The Church of Jesus Christ of Latter-day Saints was founded with six members in a log cabin at Fayette, NY. For info: Church of Jesus Christ of Latter-day Saints, Public Affairs Dept, 15 E South Temple St, Salt Lake City, UT 84150. Phone: (801) 240-4395. Fax: (801) 240-1167.

DROWSY DRIVER AWARENESS DAY. Apr 6. Annual memorial for people who have died in collisions related to drowsy driving. This is an official state-recognized "day" in the state of California. Annually, on Apr 6. For info: Phil Konstantin, PO Box 17515, San Diego, CA 92177-7515. Phone: (858) 505-5014. E-mail: chpofficerphil@yahoo.com. Web: www.drowsydriverawarenessday.com.

FIRST MODERN OLYMPICS: ANNIVERSARY. Apr 6, 1896. The first modern Olympics formally opened at Athens, Greece, after a 1,500-year hiatus. Thirteen nations participated, represented by 235 male athletes.

FIRST TONY AWARDS PRESENTED: ANNIVERSARY. Apr 6, 1947. The American Theatre Wing bestowed the first annual Tony Awards for distinguished service to the theater.

GANDHI MAKES SALT: ANNIVERSARY. Apr 6, 1930. Mohandas Gandhi, frustrated by British indifference to Indian civil rights demands, planned a symbolic, peaceful protest by conducting a 241-mile march from Sabarmati Ashram to the coast at Dandi. Leaving on Mar 12, Gandhi and his followers arrived at Dandi on Apr 5, and on Apr 6, he made salt by boiling seawater—a violation of the salt law, which granted royal monopoly in its manufacture and levied heavy taxes on its purchasers. His peaceful act and the two-mile-long procession that accompanied it gained worldwide headlines. Besides Gandhi, thousands of Indians were arrested as they, too, made salt in protest.

MULLIGAN, GERRY: BIRTH ANNIVERSARY. Apr 6, 1927. American jazz saxophonist Gerry Mulligan was born at New York, NY. He performed with many great jazz musicians, including Miles Davis, Dave Brubeck, Chet Baker and Duke Ellington, and is credited with helping create the cool-jazz movement with Miles Davis. Mulligan died Jan 20, 1996, at Darien, CT.

NATIONAL NETWORKING WEEK. Apr 6–12. Whether the goal is to grow a business or enrich your personal life, networking is invaluable. One can never meet enough new people; exchange business cards and share goals and desires with others who may offer leads. Camaraderie is another benefit that can result from successfully connecting with others through a concerted, consistent effort. For info: Robin Gorman Newman, Independent Business Women's Circle, 44 Somerset Dr N, Great Neck, NY 10020. Phone: (516) 773-0911. E-mail: robin@lovecoach.com. Web: www.ibwc.org.

April 2009

S	M	T	W	T	F	S
			1	2	3	4
5	6	7	8	9	10	11
12	13	14	15	16	17	18
19	20	21	22	23	24	25
26	27	28	29	30		

NORTH POLE DISCOVERED: 100th ANNIVERSARY. Apr 6, 1909. Robert E. Peary reached the North Pole after several failed attempts. The team consisted of Peary, leader of the expedition; Matthew A. Henson, a black man who had served with Peary since 1886 as ship's cook, carpenter and blacksmith, and then as Peary's coexplorer and valuable assistant; and four Eskimo guides—Coquesh, Ootah, Eginwah and Seegloo. They sailed July 17, 1908, on the ship *Roosevelt*, wintering on Ellesmere Island. After a grueling trek with dwindling food supplies, Henson and two of the Eskimos were first to reach the Pole. An exhausted Peary arrived 45 minutes later and confirmed their location. Dr. Frederick A. Cook, surgeon on an earlier expedition with Peary, claimed to have reached the Pole first, but that could not be substantiated and the National Geographic Society credited the Peary expedition.

PORTLAND, OREGON: BIRTHDAY. Apr 6, 1851. The "City of Roses" adds a year today.

RAPHAEL: BIRTH ANNIVERSARY. Apr 6, 1483. Raffaello Santi (Sanzio), Italian painter and architect. Probably born Apr 6, 1483, at Urbino, Italy. Died on his birthday, at Rome, Italy, Apr 6, 1520.

SCHNEIDERMAN, ROSE: BIRTH ANNIVERSARY. Apr 6, 1882. A pioneer in the battle to increase wages and improve working conditions for women, Rose Schneiderman was born at Saven, Poland, and her family immigrated to the US six years later. At age 16 she began factory work in New York City's garment district and quickly became a union organizer. Opposed to the open-shop policy, which permitted nonunion members to work in a unionized shop, Schneiderman organized a 1913 strike of 25,000 women shirtwaist makers. She worked as an organizer for the International Ladies Garment Workers Union (ILGWU) and for the Women's Trade Union League (WTUL), serving as president for more than 20 years. During the Great Depression President Roosevelt appointed her to his Labor Advisory Board—the only woman member. Died Aug 11, 1972, at New York, NY.

SCOTLAND: EDINBURGH INTERNATIONAL SCIENCE FESTIVAL. Apr 6–18. Edinburgh. A massive public celebration of science and technology, with more than 120 events at 15 venues. Includes workshops, talks, tours and exhibitions. Est attendance: 120,000. For info: Media Officer, Edinburgh Intl Science Festival, 4 Gayfield Place Ln, Edinburgh, Scotland EH1 3NZ. Phone: (44) 131-558-7666. Fax: (44) 131-557-9177. E-mail: jen@scifest.co.uk. Web: www.sciencefestival.co.uk.

SCOTTSBORO TRIAL: ANNIVERSARY. Apr 6, 1931. In what became a cause célèbre, nine black youths went on trial at Scottsboro, AL, accused of raping two white women on a freight train. All were convicted in a hasty trial but by 1950 were free by parole, appeal or escape.

TARTAN DAY. Apr 6. Groups and societies throughout North America take the anniversary of the Declaration of Arbroath (1320) as the day to celebrate their Scottish roots. For more info: www.tartanday.com.

TEFLON INVENTED: ANNIVERSARY. Apr 6, 1938. Polytetraflouroethylene resin was invented by Roy J. Plunkett while he was employed by E.I. Du Pont de Nemours & Co. Commonly known as Teflon, it revolutionized the cookware industry. This substance or something similar coated three-quarters of the pots and pans in America at the time of Plunkett's death in 1994.

THAILAND: CHAKRI DAY. Apr 6. Commemorates the foundation of the present dynasty by King Rama I (1782–1809), who also established Bangkok as the country's capital.

THOMAS, LOWELL: BIRTH ANNIVERSARY. Apr 6, 1892. World traveler, reporter, editor and radio newscaster, whose broadcasts spanned more than half a century, 1925–76. His radio sign-off, "So long until tomorrow," was known to millions of listeners, and he is said to have been the first to broadcast from a ship, an airplane, a submarine and a coal mine. Born at Woodington, OH, he died at Pawling, NY, Aug 29, 1981.

TRAGEDY IN RWANDA: 15th ANNIVERSARY. Apr 6, 1994. A plane carrying the presidents of Rwanda and Burundi was shot down near Kigali, the Rwandan capital, exacerbating a brutal ethnic war that led to the massacre of hundreds of thousands. Presidents Juvenal Habyarimana of Rwanda and Cyprien Ntaryamira of Burundi were returning from a summit in Tanzania where they discussed ways of ending the killing in their countries sparked by ethnic rivalries between the Hutu and Tutsi tribes. Following the attack on the two leaders, Rwanda descended into chaos as the two tribes began killing each other in a genocidal battle for power, leading to a mass exodus of civilians caught in the maelstrom.

US ENTERS WORLD WAR I: ANNIVERSARY. Apr 6, 1917. Congress approved a declaration of war against Germany and the US entered WWI, which had begun in 1914. The first US "doughboys" landed in France June 27, 1917.

US SENATE ACHIEVES A QUORUM: ANNIVERSARY. Apr 6, 1789. The US Senate was formally organized after achieving a quorum.

Birthdays Today

Bret Boone, 40, baseball player, born El Cajon, CA, Apr 6, 1969.

Zach Braff, 34, actor ("Scrubs," *Garden State*), born South Orange, NJ, Apr 6, 1975.

Candace Cameron Bure, 33, actress ("Full House"), born Canoga Park, CA, Apr 6, 1976.

Merle Haggard, 72, singer, songwriter ("Okie from Muskogee"), born Bakersfield, CA, Apr 6, 1937.

Marilu Henner, 57, actress ("Taxi," "Evening Shade"), born Chicago, IL, Apr 6, 1952.

Olaf Kolzig, 39, former hockey player, born Johannesburg, South Africa, Apr 6, 1970.

Barry Levinson, 67, director, producer, writer, actor ("The Carol Burnett Show," *Rain Man, Avalon, Bugsy*), born Baltimore, MD, Apr 6, 1942.

Andre Previn, 80, composer, conductor, born Berlin, Germany, Apr 6, 1929.

John Ratzenberger, 62, actor ("Cheers"), born Bridgeport, CT, Apr 6, 1947.

Paul Rudd, 40, actor (*The 40 Year Old Virgin, Anchorman, Clueless*), born Passaic, NJ, Apr 6, 1969.

Roy Thinnes, 71, actor ("The Invaders," "The Outer Limits"), born Chicago, IL, Apr 6, 1938.

James Watson, 81, discoverer (with Francis Crick) of the structure of DNA, born Chicago, IL, Apr 6, 1928.

Billy Dee Williams, 72, actor (*Brian's Song, Lady Sings the Blues, Return of the Jedi*), born New York, NY, Apr 6, 1937.

April 7 — Tuesday

DAY 97 **268 REMAINING**

BATTLE OF LYS RIVER: ANNIVERSARY. Apr 7, 1918. Having failed to break through Allied lines at Somme in March, General Erich Ludendorff made another attempt by attacking Flanders along the Lys River. On the hot, misty, sticky mornings of Apr 7 and 8, 1918, the Germans released mustard gas. On Apr 9 the Central Powers began a high-explosive bombardment along the 12-mile front from LaBasse to Armentieres. The British managed to avoid a break in their line, and finally Ferdinand Foch sent nine French divisions to take over a portion of it. On Apr 30, realizing that "further attacks promised no success," Ludendorff ended the offensive. As a result of this battle the British were unable to initiate an offensive for three months. The Allies suffered 240,000 casualties while the German losses exceeded 348,000.

CAMP, WALTER: 150th BIRTH ANNIVERSARY. Apr 7, 1859. Walter Chauncey Camp, college athlete, coach and administrator, was born at New Britain, CT. Camp played football and several other sports at Yale, but he gained prominence for helping to reshape the rules of rugby football into American football. Among his innovations were reducing the number of players on a side from 15 to 11, introducing the scrimmage, giving one team definite possession of the ball and proposing the downs system. He served as a volunteer coach at Yale and became a national figure as a promoter of football. He selected an All-American team member from 1889 until his death. Died at New York, NY, Mar 14, 1925.

CHANNING, WILLIAM ELLERY: BIRTH ANNIVERSARY. Apr 7, 1780. Well-known abolitionist and leader of the Unitarian movement in the US, born at Newport, RI. He stood for religious liberalism and influenced such people as Longfellow, Bryant, Emerson, Lowell and Holmes. Died at Bennington, VT, Oct 2, 1842.

FAIRCHILD, DAVID GRANDISON: BIRTH ANNIVERSARY. Apr 7, 1869. American botanist, government official and explorer, born at East Lansing, MI. Noted for scientific studies on importation of tropical plant species such as avocados and mangoes. Died at Miami, FL, Aug 6, 1954.

HOLIDAY, BILLIE: BIRTH ANNIVERSARY. Apr 7, 1915. Billie Holiday (born Eleanora Fagan, nicknamed "Lady Day") is considered by many jazz critics to have been the greatest jazz singer ever recorded. In her 26-year career, despite having received no formal training, she demonstrated a unique style with sophisticated and dramatic phrasing. Among her best-known songs are "Lover Man," "God Bless the Child," "Don't Explain" and "Strange Fruit." Holiday was born at Philadelphia, PA. She died at New York, NY, July 17, 1959.

KING, WILLIAM RUFUS DEVANE: BIRTH ANNIVERSARY. Apr 7, 1786. 13th vice president of the US died on Apr 18, 1853, the 46th day after taking the Oath of Office, of tuberculosis, at Cahaba, AL. The Oath of Office had been administered to King at Havana, Cuba, as authorized by a special act of Congress (the only presidential or vice presidential oath to be administered outside the US). Born on this day at Sampson County, NY, King was the only vice president who had served in both the House of Representatives and the Senate. King's term as vice president was Mar 4–Apr 18, 1853.

MALINOWSKI, BRONISLAW: 125th BIRTH ANNIVERSARY. Apr 7, 1884. Leading British anthropologist, author and teacher, born at Krakow, Poland. His pioneering anthropological fieldwork in Melanesia inspired his colleagues and students. In 1939 he became a visiting professor at Yale University. Died at New Haven, CT, May 16, 1942.

McGRAW, JOHN: BIRTH ANNIVERSARY. Apr 7, 1873. John Joseph McGraw, Baseball Hall of Fame third baseman and manager, born at Truxton, NY. Generally regarded as the best manager ever or close to it, McGraw ran the New York Giants with an iron hand from 1902 to 1932. A scrappy ballplayer with the Baltimore Orioles in the 1890s, McGraw demanded and got total effort from his players. Inducted into the Hall of Fame in 1937. Died at New Rochelle, NY, Feb 25, 1934.

METRIC SYSTEM: ANNIVERSARY. Apr 7, 1795. The metric system was adopted in France, where it had been developed.

NEW YORK SLAVE REVOLT: ANNIVERSARY. Apr 7, 1712. Nine whites were killed in a slave revolt in New York City. Planned by 27 slaves, the rebellion was begun by setting fire to an outhouse; as whites came to put the fire out, they were shot. The state militia was called out to capture the rebels, and the city of New York responded to the event by strengthening its slave codes. Twenty-one blacks were executed as participants, and six alleged participants committed suicide. New York outlawed slavery in 1799, though the last slaves were not freed until 1827.

NO HOUSEWORK DAY. Apr 7. No trash. No dishes. No making of beds or washing of laundry. And no guilt. Give it a rest. (©2006 by WH.) For info: Thomas & Ruth Roy, Wellcat Holidays, 2418 Long Ln, Lebanon, PA 17046. Phone: (717) 279-0184. E-mail: info@wellcat.com. Web: www.wellcat.com.

RWANDA: GENOCIDE REMEMBRANCE DAY. Apr 7. National holiday. Commemorates massacres of 1994.

SPACE MILESTONE: *MARS ODYSSEY* (US). Apr 7, 2001. *Odyssey* was launched on this day and successfully entered Mars's orbit on Oct 23, 2001. The one-way trip was 286 million miles. The two-and-one-half-year mission monitored space radiation, sought out underground water and identified minerals on the Red Planet.

UNITED NATIONS: WORLD HEALTH DAY. Apr 7. A UN observance commemorating the establishment of the World Health Organization in 1948. For info: United Nations, Dept of Public Info, New York, NY 10017. Web: www.un.org.

WINCHELL, WALTER: BIRTH ANNIVERSARY. Apr 7, 1897. Journalist, broadcaster, reporter and gossip columnist Walter Winchell was born at New York, NY, and died at Los Angeles, CA, Feb 20, 1972. He was admired for his way with turning a phrase. His show business columns were voraciously read by millions of Americans between 1924 and 1963.

WORDSWORTH, WILLIAM: BIRTH ANNIVERSARY. Apr 7, 1770. English Lake Poet and philosopher, born at Cumberland, England. "Poetry," he said, "is the spontaneous overflow of powerful feelings: it takes its origin from emotion recollected in tranquility." Wordsworth died Apr 23, 1850, at Rydal Mount, Westmorland.

WORLD HEALTH ORGANIZATION: ANNIVERSARY. Apr 7, 1948. This agency of the UN was founded to coordinate international health systems. It is headquartered at Geneva. Among its achievements is the elimination of smallpox.

Birthdays Today

(William) Hodding Carter III, 74, television and newspaper journalist, born New Orleans, LA, Apr 7, 1935.

Jackie Chan, 55, martial artist, actor (*The Forbidden Kingdom, Rush Hour, Shanghai Noon*), born Hong Kong, Apr 7, 1954.

Francis Ford Coppola, 70, filmmaker (*Godfather* movies, *Apocalypse Now*), born Detroit, MI, Apr 7, 1939.

Russell Crowe, 45, actor (Oscar for *Gladiator*; *Cinderella Man, LA Confidential, A Beautiful Mind*), born Auckland, New Zealand, Apr 7, 1964.

Mitchell Daniels, 60, Governor of Indiana (R), born Monogahela, PA, Apr 7, 1949.

Anthony Drew (Tony) Dorsett, 55, Hall of Fame football player, born Rochester, PA, Apr 7, 1954.

Daniel Ellsberg, 78, author (released the "Pentagon Papers" to *The New York Times*), born Chicago, IL, Apr 7, 1931.

David Frost, 70, entertainer ("That Was the Week That Was"), interviewer, born Tenterden, England, Apr 7, 1939.

James Garner, 81, actor (*Space Cowboys*, "Maverick," "The Rockford Files"), born James Baumgardner at Norman, OK, Apr 7, 1928.

John Oates, 61, singer (Hall & Oates), born New York, NY, Apr 7, 1948.

Wayne Rogers, 76, actor ("M*A*S*H," "House Calls"), born Birmingham, AL, Apr 7, 1933.

Gerhard Schroeder, 65, former chancellor of Germany, born Mossenberg, Germany, Apr 7, 1944.

April 2009	S	M	T	W	T	F	S
				1	2	3	4
	5	6	7	8	9	10	11
	12	13	14	15	16	17	18
	19	20	21	22	23	24	25
	26	27	28	29	30		

April 8 — Wednesday

DAY 98 — **267 REMAINING**

BIRTHDAY OF THE BUDDHA: BIRTH ANNIVERSARY. Apr 8. Among Buddhist holidays, this day is the most important, as it commemorates the birthday of the Buddha. It is also known as the Day of Vesak. The founder of Buddhism had the given name Siddhartha, the family name Gautama and the clan name Shaka. He is commonly called the Buddha, meaning in Sanskrit "the enlightened one." He is thought to have lived in India from c. 563 BC to 483 BC. Some countries celebrate this holiday on the lunar calendar, so the date changes from year to year, but it always occurs in either April or May. This day is a holiday in Indonesia, Korea, Singapore and Thailand.

BLACK SENATE PAGE APPOINTED: ANNIVERSARY. Apr 8, 1965. Sixteen-year-old Lawrence Bradford of New York City was the first black page appointed to the US Senate.

FEDERAL GOVERNMENT SEIZURE OF STEEL MILLS: ANNIVERSARY. Apr 8, 1952. On this date President Harry S Truman seized control of the nation's steel mills by presidential order in an attempt to prevent a shutdown by strikers. On Apr 29, a US district court declared the seizure unconstitutional and workers immediately walked out. Production dropped from 300,000 tons a day to less than 20,000. After 53 days the strike ended July 24, with steelworkers receiving a 16-cent hourly wage raise plus a 5.4-cent hourly increase in fringe benefits.

FIRST INTERCOLLEGIATE RODEO: 70th ANNIVERSARY. Apr 8, 1939. The first Intercollegiate Rodeo was held at historic Godshall Ranch, Apple Valley, CA. The student cowboys and cowgirls, who hailed from California and Arizona colleges and universities, were assisted by world champion professional cowboys including Harry Carey, Dick Foran, Curley Fletcher, Tex Ritter and Errol Flynn from Hollywood. Collegiate rodeos had been held since 1919 at Texas A&M University. College cowboys and cowgirls organized a national association in Texas in 1949 named National Intercollegiate Rodeo Association, which continues today as the only national college rodeo organization.

HENIE, SONJA: BIRTH ANNIVERSARY. Apr 8, 1912. Sonja Henie, Olympic gold medal figure skater, born at Oslo, Norway. Henie competed in the 1924 Winter Olympics when she was just 11, but finished last in ladies' singles. She won gold medals at the Winter Games of 1928, 1932 and 1936. She became a professional skater and an actress (*Sun Valley Serenade*). Died Oct 13, 1969.

HOME RUN RECORD SET BY HANK AARON: 35th ANNIVERSARY. Apr 8, 1974. Henry ("Hammerin' Hank") Aaron hit the 715th home run of his career, breaking the record set by Babe Ruth in 1935. Playing for the Atlanta Braves, Aaron broke the record at Atlanta in a game against the Los Angeles Dodgers. He finished his career in 1976 with a total of 755 home runs. At the time of his retirement, Aaron also held records for first in RBIs, second in at-bats and runs scored and third in base hits. On Aug 7, 2007, Barry Bonds of the San Francisco Giants hit his 756th home run to break Aaron's record.

HUNTER, "CATFISH": BIRTH ANNIVERSARY. Apr 8, 1946. James Augustus ("Catfish") Hunter, Baseball Hall of Fame pitcher, born at Hertford, NC. Died Sept 9, 1999, at Hertford.

JAPAN: FLOWER FESTIVAL (HANA MATSURI). Apr 8. Commemorates Buddha's birthday. Ceremonies in all temples.

KNIGHT, O. RAYMOND: BIRTH ANNIVERSARY. Apr 8, 1872. The "Father of Canadian Rodeo," O. Raymond Knight was born at Payson, UT. His father, the Utah mining magnate Jesse Knight, founded the town of Raymond, AB, in 1901. In 1902 Raymond produced Canada's first rodeo, "Raymond Stampede." He also built rodeo's first grandstand and first chute in 1903. O. Raymond Knight died Feb 7, 1947.

McRAE, CARMEN: BIRTH ANNIVERSARY. Apr 8, 1920. After winning an amateur contest at Harlem's legendary Apollo Theatre in her hometown of New York City, McRae went on to become a noted jazz singer, singing with the Earl Hines, Mercer Ellington and Benny Carter bands, among others, and recording more than 20 albums. She died Nov 10, 1994, at Beverly Hills, CA.

MORRIS, LEWIS: BIRTH ANNIVERSARY. Apr 8, 1726. Signer of the Declaration of Independence, born at Westchester County, NY. Died Jan 22, 1798, at Morrisania Manor at NY.

PASSOVER BEGINS AT SUNDOWN. Apr 8. See "Pesach" (Apr 9).

POLL TAX OUTLAWED: ANNIVERSARY. Apr 8, 1966. In the last of a series of moves to abolish poll taxes, a three-judge federal court at Jackson, MS, outlawed Mississippi's $2 poll tax as a voting requirement for state and local elections.

SEVENTEENTH AMENDMENT TO US CONSTITUTION RATIFIED: ANNIVERSARY. Apr 8, 1913. Prior to the 17th Amendment, members of the Senate were elected by each state's respective legislature. The advent and popularity of primary elections during the last decade of the 19th century and the early 20th century and a string of senatorial scandals, most notably a scandal involving William Lorimer, an Illinois political boss in 1909, forced the Senate to end its resistance to a constitutional amendment requiring direct popular election of senators.

VOYAGEURS NATIONAL PARK ESTABLISHED: ANNIVERSARY. Apr 8, 1975. Minnesota's Voyageurs land was preserved by Congress on Jan 8, 1971. Four years later, it became the 36th US national park.

WILLIAMS, WILLIAM: BIRTH ANNIVERSARY. Apr 8, 1731. Signer of the Declaration of Independence, born at Lebanon, CT. Died there Aug 2, 1811.

Birthdays Today

Kofi Annan, 71, former UN secretary general (1997–2006), born Kumasi, Ghana, Apr 8, 1938.

Patricia Arquette, 41, actress ("Medium," *Lost Highway, Flirting with Disaster*), born Chicago, IL, Apr 8, 1968.

Gary Edmund Carter, 55, sportscaster, Hall of Fame baseball player, born Culver City, CA, Apr 8, 1954.

William D. Chase, 87, librarian and chronicler of contemporary civilization as cofounder and coeditor of *Chase's Annual Events*, born Lakeview, MI, Apr 8, 1922.

Elizabeth (Betty) Ford, 91, former First Lady, wife of Gerald Ford, 38th president of the US, born Chicago, IL, Apr 8, 1918.

Shecky Greene, 84, comedian, actor, born Chicago, IL, Apr 8, 1925.

John J. Havlicek, 69, Hall of Fame basketball player, born Lansing, OH, Apr 8, 1940.

Seymour Hersh, 72, journalist, born Chicago, IL, Apr 8, 1937.

Julian Lennon, 46, musician, singer, son of John Lennon, born Liverpool, England, Apr 8, 1963.

Stuart Pankin, 63, actor ("Not Necessarily the News," *Irreconcilable Differences, Arachnophobia*), born Philadelphia, PA, Apr 8, 1946.

Terry Porter, 46, former basketball player, born Milwaukee, WI, Apr 8, 1963.

Katee Sackhoff, 29, actress ("Battlestar Galactica," "The Bionic Woman"), born Portland, OR, Apr 8, 1980.

John Schneider, 55, actor ("Dukes of Hazzard," *Smokey and the Bandit*), born Mount Kisco, NY, Apr 8, 1954 (some sources say 1960).

Robin Wright, 43, actress (*Breaking and Entering, White Oleander, The Princess Bride*), born Dallas, TX, Apr 8, 1966.

April 9 — Thursday

DAY 99 — **266 REMAINING**

AFRICAN METHODIST EPISCOPAL CHURCH ORGANIZED: ANNIVERSARY. Apr 9, 1816. The first all-black US religious denomination, the AME church was organized at Philadelphia with Richard Allen, a former slave who had bought his freedom, as the first bishop.

BLACK PAGE APPOINTED TO US HOUSE OF REPRESENTATIVES: ANNIVERSARY. Apr 9, 1965. Fifteen-year-old Frank Mitchell of Springfield, IL, was the first black page appointed to the US House of Representatives.

CIVIL RIGHTS BILL OF 1866: ANNIVERSARY. Apr 9, 1866. The Civil Rights Bill of 1866, passed by Congress over the veto of President Andrew Johnson, granted blacks the rights and privileges of American citizenship and formed the basis for the 14th Amendment to the US Constitution.

CIVIL WAR ENDING: ANNIVERSARY. Apr 9, 1865. At 1:30 PM General Robert E. Lee, commander of the Army of Northern Virginia, surrendered to General Ulysses S. Grant, commander in chief of the Union Army, ending four years of civil war. The meeting took place in the house of Wilmer McLean at the village of Appomattox Court House, VA. Confederate soldiers were permitted to keep their horses and go free to their homes, while Confederate officers were allowed to retain their swords and sidearms as well. Grant wrote the terms of surrender. Formal surrender took place at the courthouse on Apr 12. Death toll for the Civil War is estimated at 500,000 men.

DENMARK: OBSERVATION OF NAZI OCCUPATION. Apr 9. Flag-flying day to observe the anniversary of the 1940 Nazi invasion and occupation of the country.

ECKERT, J(OHN) PRESPER, JR: 90th BIRTH ANNIVERSARY. Apr 9, 1919. Coinventor with John W. Mauchly of ENIAC (Electronic Numerical Integrator and Computer), which was first demonstrated at the Moore School of Electrical Engineering at the University of Pennsylvania at Philadelphia Feb 14, 1946. This is generally considered the birth of the computer age. Originally designed to process artillery calculations for the army, ENIAC was also used in the Manhattan Project. Eckert and Mauchly formed Electronic Control Company, which later became Unisys Corporation. Eckert was born at Philadelphia and died at Bryn Mawr, PA, June 3, 1995.

IRAQ: NATIONAL DAY. Apr 9. National holiday commemorating anniversary of dictator Saddam Hussein's fall from power in 2003.

ITALY: PROCESSION OF THE ADDOLORATA AND PROCESSION OF THE MYSTERIES. Apr 9–10. Taranto. Procession of the Addolorata is held on Holy Thursday, while the Procession of the Mysteries takes place on Good Friday. Both processions have in common the very slow pace of the participants and their unusual costumes.

JENKINS'S EAR DAY: ANNIVERSARY. Apr 9, 1731. Spanish *guardacosta* boarded and plundered the British ship *Rebecca* off Jamaica and among other outrages, cut off the ear of English master mariner Robert Jenkins. Little notice was taken until seven years later, when Jenkins exhibited the detached ear and described the atrocity to a committee of the House of Commons. In consequence, Britain declared war on Spain in October 1739, a war that lasted until 1743 and is still known as the "War of Jenkins's Ear." Nothing else is known of him.

JUMBO THE ELEPHANT ARRIVES IN AMERICA: ANNIVERSARY. Apr 9, 1882. The most famous elephant in history was captured as a calf near Lake Chad, Africa, in 1861. He was a tremendously popular part of the London Zoo from 1865 to 1882. At London, he gained the name Jumbo (from a West African word for elephant). In 1882, American circus impresario P.T. Barnum bought the 11½-ft-tall and seven-ton animal for $10,000. Jumbo arrived at Manhattan, NY, on Easter Sunday. In an amazing spectacle, Jumbo paraded up Broadway in a crate pulled by 16 horses. Jumbo was just as popular in the US as he was in Britain, and his name entered the English language to describe anything oversized.

KING, FRANK: BIRTH ANNIVERSARY. Apr 9, 1883. Created by Frank King in 1919 as a comic strip about men's interest in autos, *Gasoline Alley* had a tremendous jump in popularity in 1921 when its main character, Walt, adopted a foundling called Skeezix. Devoid of melodrama, this strip sympathetically described the day-to-day lives of Walt, Skeezix and their friends and family, and it was the first American cartoon in which the characters actually aged. Frank King was born at Cashton, WI, and died at Winter Park, FL, June 24, 1969.

LUDENDORFF, ERICH: BIRTH ANNIVERSARY. Apr 9, 1865. German general who, during the last years of WWI, was chiefly responsible for military policy and strategy. Born near Pozen, Prussia, and died at Tutzing, Dec 20, 1937.

MARIAN ANDERSON EASTER CONCERT: 70th ANNIVERSARY. Apr 9, 1939. On this Easter Sunday, black American contralto Marian Anderson sang an open-air concert from the steps of the Lincoln Memorial at Washington, DC, to an audience of 75,000, after having been denied use of the Daughters of the American Revolution (DAR) Constitution Hall. The event became an American antidiscrimination cause célèbre and led First Lady Eleanor Roosevelt to resign from the DAR.

MAUNDY THURSDAY or HOLY THURSDAY. Apr 9. The Thursday before Easter, originally "dies mandate," celebrates Christ's injunction to love one another, "Mandatus novum do vobis. . . ." ("A new commandment I give to you. . . .")

MOON PHASE: FULL MOON. Apr 9. Moon enters Full Moon phase at 10:56 AM, EDT.

MUYBRIDGE, EADWEARD: BIRTH ANNIVERSARY. Apr 9, 1830. English photographer famed for his studies of animals in motion. Born Edward James Muggeridge, at Kingston-on-Thames, England. Died there May 8, 1904.

NATIONAL ALCOHOL SCREENING DAY. Apr 9. To increase awareness of alcohol's effect on health and connect people with alcohol problems to treatment. Free, anonymous, nationwide. For info: Screening for Mental Health, One Washington St, Ste 304, Wellesley Hills, MA 02481-1706. Phone: (781) 239-0071. Fax: (781) 431-7447. Web: www.mentalhealthscreening.org.

NATIONAL CHERISH AN ANTIQUE DAY. Apr 9. Celebrate when items were made by loving hands and not machines. Honor the past and timeworn traditions by incorporating an antique into your home, lifestyle or wardrobe. For info: Vintage Interiors, 169 S Fairfax Ave, Los Angeles, CA 90036. Phone: (310) 291-1430. Fax: (323) 932-0645. E-mail: vintageweave@aol.com.

✦ **NATIONAL D.A.R.E. DAY.** Apr 9. The Drug Abuse Resistance Education (D.A.R.E.) Program, founded in 1983 by the Los Angeles Police Department and the Los Angeles Unified School District, helps give children in grades K–12 the skills they need to avoid involvement in drugs, gangs and violence. Nearly 75 percent of American school districts offer D.A.R.E. training.

✦ **NATIONAL FORMER PRISONER OF WAR RECOGNITION DAY.** Apr 9.

NCAA DIVISION I MEN'S ICE HOCKEY CHAMPIONSHIP (FROZEN FOUR). Apr 9 & 11. Verizon Center, Washington, DC. For info: NCAA, 700 W Washington St, PO Box 6222, Indianapolis, IN 46206-6222. Web: www.NCAAsports.com.

PESACH or PASSOVER. Apr 9–16. Hebrew calendar dates: Nisan 15–22, 5769. The first day of Passover begins an eight-day celebration of the delivery of the Jews from slavery in Egypt. Unleavened bread (matzoh) is eaten at this time. Began at sundown Apr 8.

April 2009

S	M	T	W	T	F	S
			1	2	3	4
5	6	7	8	9	10	11
12	13	14	15	16	17	18
19	20	21	22	23	24	25
26	27	28	29	30		

PHILIPPINES: ARAW NG KAGITINGAN. Apr 9. Day of Valor. National observance to commemorate the fall of Bataan in 1942. The infamous "Death March" is reenacted at the Mount Samat Shrine, the Dambana ng Kagitingan.

PHILIPPINES: MORIONE'S FESTIVAL. Apr 9–12. Marinduque Island. Provincewide masquerade, Lenten plays and celebrations. Annually, Holy Thursday through Easter Sunday.

PINK MOON. Apr 9. So called by Native American tribes of New England and the Great Lakes because at this time of the season wildflowers—especially the pink ground phlox—herald the newly arrived spring. The April Full Moon.

ROBESON, PAUL BUSTILL: BIRTH ANNIVERSARY. Apr 9, 1898. Paul Robeson, born at Princeton, NJ, was an All-American football player at Rutgers University and received his law degree from Columbia University in 1923. After being seen by Eugene O'Neill in an amateur stage production, he was offered a part in O'Neill's play *The Emperor Jones*. His performance in that play with the Provincetown Players established him as an actor. Without ever having taken a voice lesson, he also became a popular singer. His stage credits include *Show Boat, Porgy and Bess, The Hairy Ape* and *Othello*, which enjoyed the longest Broadway run of a Shakespeare play. In 1950 he was denied a passport by the US for refusing to sign an affidavit stating whether he was or ever had been a member of the Communist Party. The action was overturned by the Supreme Court in 1958. His film credits include *Emperor Jones, Show Boat, King Solomon's Mines* and *Song of Freedom*. Robeson died at Philadelphia, PA, Jan 23, 1976.

SPACE MILESTONE: *SOYUZ 35* (USSR). Apr 9, 1980. Two cosmonauts (Valery Ryumin and Leonid Popov) were launched from Baikonur space center at Kazakhstan, USSR. Docked at *Salyut 6* Apr 10. Ryumin and Popov returned to Earth Oct 11, 1980, after setting a new space endurance record of 185 days.

TEXAS PANHANDLE TORNADO: ANNIVERSARY. Apr 9, 1947. A monster tornado clearing a 1.5-mile-long path struck through at least 12 towns in Texas, Oklahoma and Kansas, killing 169 people and causing more than $15 million in damage. The tornado traveled 221 miles across the three states.

TUNISIA: MARTYRS' DAY. Apr 9.

WINSTON CHURCHILL DAY. Apr 9. Anniversary of enactment of legislation in 1963 that made the late British statesman an honorary citizen of the US.

Birthdays Today

Severiano (Seve) Ballesteros, 52, former golfer, born Pedrena, Spain, Apr 9, 1957.

Hugh Hefner, 83, founder of *Playboy*, born Chicago, IL, Apr 9, 1926.

Taylor Kitsch, 28, actor ("Friday Night Lights"), born Kelowna, BC, Canada, Apr 9, 1981.

Paul Krassner, 77, editor, journalist, born Brooklyn, NY, Apr 9, 1932.

Michael Learned, 70, actress ("The Waltons"), born Washington, DC, Apr 9, 1939.

Tom Lehrer, 81, songwriter ("Vatican Rag," "New Math"), pianist, mathematician, born New York, NY, Apr 9, 1928.

Leighton Meester, 23, actress ("Surface," "Gossip Girl"), born Marco Island, FL, Apr 9, 1986.

Cynthia Nixon, 43, actress ("Sex and the City," *Amadeus*), born New York, NY, Apr 9, 1966.

Keshia Knight Pulliam, 30, actress ("The Cosby Show"), born Newark, NJ, Apr 9, 1979.

Dennis Quaid, 55, actor (*Far from Heaven, The Rookie, Traffic*), born Houston, TX, Apr 9, 1954.

Jacques Villeneueve, 38, race car driver, born St. Jean d'Iberville, QC, Canada, Apr 9, 1971.

April 10 — Friday

DAY 100 | **265 REMAINING**

AFRMA DISPLAY AT AMERICA'S FAMILY PET EXPO. Apr 10–12 (tentative). Costa Mesa, CA. Rats and mice are emerging as ideal pets: they provide all the pleasure and satisfaction of a warm, cuddly, intelligent and friendly pet companion. The American Fancy Rat and Mouse Association (AFRMA) was founded in 1983 to promote the breeding and exhibition of fancy rats and mice, to educate the public on their positive qualities as companion animals and to provide information on their proper care. For info: AFRMA (CAE), PO Box 2589, Winnetka, CA 91396-2589. Phone: (951) 685-2350 or (818) 992-5564 or (909) 238-5231. E-mail: afrma@afrma.org. Web: www.afrma.org.

BATAAN DEATH MARCH: ANNIVERSARY. Apr 10, 1942. On this morning American and Filipino prisoners were herded together by Japanese soldiers on Mariveles Airfield on Bataan (in the Philippine islands) and began the Death March to Camp O'Donnell, near Cabanatuan. During the six-day march they were given only one bowl of rice. More than 5,200 Americans and many more Filipinos lost their lives in the course of the march.

THE BEATLES BREAK UP: ANNIVERSARY. Apr 10, 1970. In a press release accompanying promotional copies of his new solo album, Paul McCartney announced that he had no plans for working with the Beatles because of "personal differences, business differences, musical differences." He stated that he didn't know if the break was temporary or permanent, but the years-long tension in the group coupled with the musicians' solo work brought about the end of the band that year. McCartney sued to dissolve the Beatles on Dec 31, 1970, and the group was formally dissolved four years later.

BOOTH, WILLIAM: BIRTH ANNIVERSARY. Apr 10, 1829. General William Booth, founder of the movement that became known, in 1878, as the Salvation Army, was born at Nottingham, England. Apprenticed to a pawnbroker at the age of 13, Booth experienced firsthand the misery of poverty. He broke with conventional church religion and established a quasi-military religious organization with military uniforms and ranks. Recruiting from the poor, from converted criminals and from many other social outcasts, his organization grew rapidly and its influence spread from England to the US and to other countries. At revivals in slum areas the itinerant evangelist offered help for the poor, homes for the homeless, sobriety for alcoholics, rescue homes for women and girls, training centers and legal aid. Booth died at London, England, Aug 20, 1912. See also: "Salvation Army Founder's Day" (Apr 10).

BRAHMS' *REQUIEM* PREMIERE: ANNIVERSARY. Apr 10, 1868. Composer Johannes Brahms fortified his reputation as one of the leading figures in 19th-century German Romantic music with the success of his *Requiem*, which premiered at Bremen Cathedral on this date. The choral piece, at turns both melancholy and exuberant, is one of the more recognized and often-sung funerary works in the musical canon.

CHINCOTEAGUE ISLAND EASTER DECOY SHOW. Apr 10–11. Chincoteague Island, VA. Wildfowl carving and wildlife art exhibits. Annually, Easter weekend. Est attendance: 2,000. For info: Chincoteague Chamber of Commerce, 6733 Maddox Blvd, Chincoteague Island, VA 23336. Phone: (757) 336-6161. Fax: (757) 336-1242. E-mail: chincochamber@verizon.net. Web: www.chincoteaguechamber.com.

COMMODORE PERRY DAY. Apr 10, 1794. Birth anniversary of Matthew Calbraith Perry, commodore in the US Navy, negotiator of first treaty between US and Japan (Mar 31, 1854). Born at South Kingston, RI. Died Mar 4, 1858, at New York, NY.

CONNORS, CHUCK (KEVIN JOSEPH): BIRTH ANNIVERSARY. Apr 10, 1921. "The Rifleman" of television fame, Chuck Connors played that title role from 1958 to 1963. His portrayal of a slave owner in the miniseries *Roots* won him an Emmy nomination. Connors acted in more than 45 films and appeared on many TV series and specials. He played professional basketball and baseball before becoming an actor. Born at Brooklyn, NY; died Nov 10, 1992, at Los Angeles, CA.

ENGLAND: BRITISH AND WORLD MARBLES CHAMPIONSHIP. Apr 10. Greyhound Public House, Tinsley Green, West Sussex. Since 1932, more than 100 competitors have vied for team and individual titles in the marbles tournament. Annually, on Good Friday. For info: British Marbles Board of Control. Phone: (44) (1403) 730-602. Fax (44) (1403) 733-877. E-mail: marblesam@hotmail.com. Or Bognor Regis Visitor's Centre, Belmont St, Bognor Regis, West Sussex, England PO21 1BJ. Phone: (44) (1243) 823-140.

ENGLAND: DEVIZES TO WESTMINSTER INTERNATIONAL CANOE RACE. Apr 10–13. 61st year. Starts from Wharf Car Park, Wharf St, Devizes, Wiltshire. Canoes race along 125 miles of the Kennet and Avon canals and the River Thames, ending at County Hall Steps, Westminster Bridge Rd, London. Annually, Good Friday to Easter Monday. Est attendance: 6,000. For info: Competition Secretary, Boscombe Forge, Church Road, Bookham, Surrey, England KT23 3JG. Phone: (44) (020) 7620-0298. Web: www.dwrace.org.uk.

FIRST PGA CHAMPIONSHIP: ANNIVERSARY. Apr 10, 1916. The then-recently formed Professional Golfers' Association of America held its first championship at Siwanoy golf course at Bronxville, NY. The trophy and the lion's share of the $2,580 purse were won by British golfer Jim Barnes.

GOOD FRIDAY. Apr 10. Observed in commemoration of the crucifixion. Oldest Christian celebration. Possible corruption of "God's Friday." Observed in some manner by most Christian sects and as a public holiday or part holiday in Canada and in Delaware, Florida, Hawaii, Illinois, Indiana, New Jersey, North Carolina, Pennsylvania and Tennessee.

GOOD FRIDAY PEACE AGREEMENT IN NORTHERN IRELAND: ANNIVERSARY. Apr 10, 1998. Protestant and Catholic factions agreed to a power-sharing agreement on Good Friday, 1998. It was endorsed by referenda in Northern Ireland and the Republic of Ireland on May 22, 1998. As a result, a provincial government was established in Northern Ireland to replace direct rule by Britain. The Northern Ireland Assembly met for the first time June 5, 2000.

GROTIUS, HUGO: BIRTH ANNIVERSARY. Apr 10, 1583. (Old Style date.) Anniversary of the birth of Hugo Grotius, the Dutch theologian, attorney, scholar and statesman whose beliefs profoundly influenced American thinking, especially with regard to the conscience of humanity. Born at Delft, Holland, he died at Rostock, Germany, Aug 28, 1645 (OS).

NATIONAL SIBLINGS DAY. Apr 10. A commemorative day to honor, appreciate and celebrate all brothers and sisters and memorialize those who are no longer with us. Recognizing the bond between siblings for the special gift it is. A day to hug, honor and enjoy your sibling. Founded by Claudia A. Evart of New York City through her nonprofit charity, Siblings Day Foundation, to honor the memory of her sister Lisette and brother Alan; they both died from accidents early in their lives. Forty governors have signed proclamations recognizing this day. Presidents Clinton (2000) and Bush (2008) have issued proclamations. Annually, Apr 10. For info: Claudia A. Evart, Siblings Day Foundation, 30 Park Ave, Ste 2-P, New York, NY 10016-3833. Phone: (212) 779-2227. E-mail: siblingsday@earthlink.net. Web: www.siblingsday.org.

ODESSA RETAKEN: 65th ANNIVERSARY. Apr 10, 1944. The Red Army retook the Ukrainian city of Odessa, the port on the northwest coast of the Black Sea that had been in the hands of the Nazis since October 1941.

OZARK UFO CONFERENCE. Apr 10–12. Inn of the Ozarks Conference Center, Eureka Springs, AR. 21st annual meeting of researchers from various states and foreign countries to inform the public of the latest news concerning UFOs. Speakers include authors of books on the subject and people who have investigated UFO cases; program includes audiovisual presentations of UFO evidence. Est attendance: 400. For info: Lucius Farish, Ozark UFO Conference, #2 Caney Valley Dr, Plumerville, AR 72127-8725. Phone: (501) 354-2558. E-mail: ozarkufo@webtv.net. Web: www.ozarkufo.com.

PERKINS, FRANCES: BIRTH ANNIVERSARY. Apr 10, 1880. First woman member of a US presidential cabinet. Born at Boston, MA, she was married in 1915 to Paul Caldwell Wilson but used her maiden name in public life. She was appointed secretary of labor by President Franklin D. Roosevelt in 1933, a post in which she served until 1945. Died at New York, NY, May 14, 1965.

PULITZER, JOSEPH: BIRTH ANNIVERSARY. Apr 10, 1847. American journalist and newspaper publisher, founder of the Pulitzer Prizes, born at Budapest, Hungary. Died at Charleston, SC, Oct 29, 1911. Pulitzer Prizes awarded annually since 1917. Write for entry and deadline info. (Please specify Book, Journalism, Drama or Music Competition.) For info: Pulitzer Prize Board, Columbia University, 709 Journalism Bldg, 2950 Broadway, New York, NY 10027. Phone: (212) 854-3841. Web: www.pulitzer.org.

SAFETY PIN PATENTED: ANNIVERSARY. Apr 10, 1849. Walter Hunt of New York patented the first safety pin.

SALVATION ARMY FOUNDER'S DAY. Apr 10, 1829. Birth anniversary of William Booth, a Methodist minister who began an evangelical ministry in the East End of London in 1865 and established mission stations to feed and house the poor. In 1878 he changed the name of the organization to the Salvation Army. Booth was born at Nottingham, England; he died at London, Aug 20, 1912. See also: "Booth, William: Birth Anniversary" (Apr 10).

STOCK EXCHANGE HOLIDAY (GOOD FRIDAY). Apr 10. The holiday schedules for the various exchanges are subject to change if relevant rules, regulations or exchange policies are revised. If you have questions, contact: American Stock Exchange (866) 422-2639 (www.amex.com), Chicago Board of Trade (312) 435-3500 (www.cbot.com), Chicago Board Options Exchange (312) 786-5600 (www.cboe.com), NASDAQ Stock Market (646) 441-5200 (www.nasdaq.com), New York Stock Exchange (212) 656-3000 (www.nyse.com), Philadelphia Stock Exchange (800) THE-PHLX (www.phlx.com).

UNITED KINGDOM: GOOD FRIDAY BANK HOLIDAY. Apr 10. Bank and public holiday in England, Wales, Scotland and Northern Ireland.

WOODWARD, ROBERT BURNS: BIRTH ANNIVERSARY. Apr 10, 1917. Nobel Prize–winning (1965) Harvard University science professor whose special field of study was molecular structure of complex organic compounds. Called "one of the most outstanding scientific minds of the century." Born at Boston, MA, he died at Cambridge, MA, July 8, 1979.

April 2009	S	M	T	W	T	F	S
				1	2	3	4
	5	6	7	8	9	10	11
	12	13	14	15	16	17	18
	19	20	21	22	23	24	25
	26	27	28	29	30		

Birthdays Today

Kenneth "Babyface" Edmonds, 52, singer, songwriter, born Indianapolis, IN, Apr 10, 1957.

Dolores Huerta, 79, cofounder, with Cesar Chavez, of the United Farm Workers Union, born Dawson, NM, Apr 10, 1930.

Peter MacNicol, 55, actor ("Numb3rs,""Ally McBeal," *Ghostbusters II*), born Dallas, TX, Apr 10, 1954.

John Earl Madden, 73, sportscaster, former football coach, born Austin, MN, Apr 10, 1936.

Joe Don Meredith, 71, former sportscaster, actor and football player, born Mount Vernon, TX, Apr 10, 1938.

Harry Morgan, 94, actor (Emmy for "M*A*S*H"; "Dragnet"), born Harry Bratsburg at Detroit, MI, Apr 10, 1915.

Haley Joel Osment, 21, actor (*The Sixth Sense, Bogus*), born Los Angeles, CA, Apr 10, 1988.

Steven Seagal, 58, actor, producer (*Hard to Kill, On Deadly Ground*), born Lansing, MI, Apr 10, 1951.

Omar Sharif, 77, actor (*Lawrence of Arabia, Dr. Zhivago*), born Michael Shalhoub at Alexandria, Egypt, Apr 10, 1932.

Paul Edward Theroux, 68, author (*The Mosquito Coast, Millroy the Magician*), born Medford, MS, Apr 10, 1941.

Max Von Sydow, 80, actor (*The Seventh Seal, The Emigrants*), born Lund, Sweden, Apr 10, 1929.

April 11 — Saturday

DAY 101 — **264 REMAINING**

BABY MASSAGE DAY. Apr 11. In honor of the growing trend of baby massage, this day serves to increase awareness of the practice that is so beneficial to babies. Annually, the second Saturday in April. For info: Palmer's Skin Care Products. Web: www.etbrowne.com.

BARBERSHOP QUARTET DAY. Apr 11. Commemorates the gathering of 26 persons at Tulsa, OK, Apr 11, 1938, and the founding there of the Society for the Preservation and Encouragement of Barbershop Quartet Singing in America.

BLISS, LIZZIE "LILLIE": BIRTH ANNIVERSARY. Apr 11, 1864. Lizzie "Lillie" Bliss was born at Boston, MA. She was one of the three founders (all women) of the Museum of Modern Art at New York City in 1929. She died Mar 12, 1931, at New York City.

BOLIN, JANE MATILDA: 100th BIRTH ANNIVERSARY. Apr 11, 1908. Jane Matilda Bolin, born at Poughkeepsie, NY, was the first black woman to graduate from the Yale School of Law (1931) and went on to become the first black woman judge in the US. She served as assistant corporation counsel for the city of New York before being appointed to the city's Domestic Relations Court and the Family Court of the State of New York. Bolin died Jan 8, 2007, at New York, NY.

CIMARRON TERRITORY CELEBRATION AND WORLD COW CHIP-THROWING® CHAMPIONSHIP CONTEST. Apr 11–19. Beaver, OK. 40th annual. A highly specialized international organic sporting event which draws dung flingers from around the world.

Also featuring a craft fair, carnival, poker run, food vendors and a parade. Est attendance: 2,000. For info: Beaver County Chamber of Commerce, PO Box 878, Beaver, OK 73932-0878. Phone: (580) 625-4726. E-mail: bvrchamber@ptsi.net. Web: www.BeaverCountyChamberofCommerce.com.

CIVIL RIGHTS ACT OF 1968: ANNIVERSARY. Apr 11, 1968. Exactly one week after the assassination of Martin Luther King, Jr, the Civil Rights Act of 1968 (protecting civil rights workers, expanding the rights of Native Americans and providing antidiscrimination measures in housing) was signed into law by President Lyndon B. Johnson, who said: "[T]he proudest moments of my presidency have been times such as this when I have signed into law the promises of a century."

COSTA RICA: JUAN SANTAMARÍA DAY. Apr 11. National holiday. Commemorates the 1856 Battle of Rivas.

CYPRUS: THE PROCESSION OF ICON OF SAINT LAZARUS. Apr 11. Larnaca, Cyprus. The tomb of Lazarus (the man raised from the dead by Christ) resides in the Ayios Lazaros Church—built by Emperor Leo VI in the ninth century. Eight days before the Orthodox Easter Sunday, his icon is taken through the streets of Larnaca.

EASTER BEACH RUN. Apr 11. Daytona Beach, FL. The 42nd annual beach run on "the world's most famous beach" includes a four-mile and two-mile run for various age divisions, a two-mile fun health walk and several different kids' runs. Ribbons are awarded to all participants. Est attendance: 1,200. For info: Easter Beach Run, Daytona Beach Leisure Services Dept, PO Box 2451, Daytona Beach, FL 32115-2451. Phone: (386) 671-3420. Fax: (386) 671-3410. Web: www.easterbeachrun.org.

EASTER EVEN. Apr 11. The Saturday before Easter. Last day of Holy Week and of Lent.

HAROLD WASHINGTON ELECTED FIRST BLACK MAYOR OF CHICAGO: ANNIVERSARY. Apr 11, 1983. Harold Washington defeated Bernard Epton and became the first black mayor of Chicago. Of the city's 1.6 million voters, a record 82 percent voted. Washington won 51 percent of the votes, which split along racial lines. He was reelected in April 1987 but died suddenly seven months later at his office, Nov 25, 1987.

HUGHES, CHARLES EVANS: BIRTH ANNIVERSARY. Apr 11, 1862. 11th chief justice of the US. Born at Glens Falls, NY. Died at Osterville, MA, Aug 27, 1948.

INTERNATIONAL "LOUIE LOUIE" DAY. Apr 11. Apr 11 provides an annual opportunity to celebrate the song that has been called the greatest party song of all time, has been recorded more times than any other rock song in history and was very nearly declared the official state song of Washington. Annually, Apr 11, the birthday of composer Richard Berry in 1935. For info: Michael Hintze, 621 27th Ave E, Seattle, WA 98112. E-mail: llamas@louielouie.net. Web: louielouieweb.tripod.com/LLAMAS/LL-day.htm or www.louieday.org.

JOHN WILKES BOOTH ESCAPE ROUTE TOUR. Apr 11 & 18, May 2. Clinton, MD. A 12-hour bus tour over the route used by Lincoln's assassin. Bookings begin no earlier than Jan 15, 2009. For info: Surratt House Museum, Box 427, Clinton, MD 20735. Phone: (301) 868-1121. Fax: (301) 868-8177. Web: www.surratt.org.

JULIAN, PERCY: BIRTH ANNIVERSARY. Apr 11, 1899. Percy Julian, producer of a synthetic progesterone using soybeans, was born at Montgomery, AL. He also developed a cheaper method of producing cortisone, a drug to treat glaucoma and a chemical foam to fight petroleum fires. Julian died Apr 19, 1975, at Waukegan, IL.

LAZARUS SATURDAY. Apr 11. Orthodox celebration of Christ raising Lazarus from the dead. Only time the resurrection liturgy is used on a day other than Sunday.

LIBERATION OF BUCHENWALD CONCENTRATION CAMP: ANNIVERSARY. Apr 11, 1945. Buchenwald, north of Weimar, Germany, was entered by Allied troops. It was the first of the Nazi concentration camps to be liberated. It had been established in 1937, and about 56,000 people died there.

LONGWOOD GARDENS EASTER CELEBRATION. Apr 11–12. Kennett Square, PA. Fragrant Easter lilies trumpet the season, while brilliant freesias, orchids and other colorful plants fill acres of indoor gardens. Est attendance: 40,000. For info: Longwood Gardens, PO Box 501, Kennett Square, PA 19348-0501. Phone: (610) 388-1000. Web: www.longwoodgardens.org.

MESSICK, DALE: BIRTH ANNIVERSARY. Apr 4, 1906. Dalia (Dale) Messick, born at South Bend, IN, was the creator of the intrepid, glamorous globe-trotting reporter Brenda Star in the comic strip of the same name that debuted in June 1940. It is still syndicated today. Messick, one of the first women to break into comics, retired from the strip in the 1980s and died at Sonoma County, CA, on Apr 5, 2005.

SPACE MILESTONE: *APOLLO 13* (US). Apr 11, 1970. Astronauts Lovell, Haise and Swigert were endangered when an oxygen tank ruptured.The planned moon landing was canceled, and details of the accident were made public. The entire world shared concern for the crew, who splashed down successfully in the Pacific Apr 17.

SPELMAN COLLEGE ESTABLISHED: ANNIVERSARY. Apr 11, 1881. Spelman College, with funding from the Rockefeller family, opened its doors for the first time with the purpose of educating young African-American women. The institution, located at Atlanta, GA, was dubbed "the Radcliffe for Negro women."

STRAWBERRY HILL RACES. Apr 11. Colonial Downs, New Kent, VA. Annual steeplechase horse race featuring a week of festivities leading up to the event. Elegant, yet fun, pre-race entertainment and railspace competition on race day. $70,000 in purses. Sponsored by SFVA. Est attendance: 20,000. For info: Sue Mullins, Race Dir, Strawberry Hill Races, PO Box 26805, Richmond, VA 23261. Phone: (804) 569-3238. Fax: (804) 569-3252. E-mail: smullins@statefairva.org.

UGANDA: LIBERATION DAY. Apr 11. Republic of Uganda celebrates anniversary of overthrow of Idi Amin's dictatorship in 1979.

Birthdays Today

Tony Brown, 76, television journalist, born Charleston, WV, Apr 11, 1933.

Ellen Goodman, 61, Pulitzer Prize–winning columnist, born Newton, MA, Apr 11, 1948.

Joel Grey, 77, actor (Oscar for *Cabaret; The Seven Per Cent Solution*), born Joe Katz at Cleveland, OH, Apr 11, 1932.

Tricia Helfer, 35, actress ("Battlestar Galactica"), born Donalda, AB, Canada, Apr 11, 1974.

Bill Irwin, 59, actor, choreographer (*The Regard of Flight*), born Santa Monica, CA, Apr 11, 1950.

Ethel Kennedy, 81, widow of Robert Kennedy, born Greenwich, CT, Apr 11, 1928.

Louise Lasser, 70, actress ("Mary Hartman, Mary Hartman"), born New York, NY, Apr 11, 1939.

Peter Riegert, 62, actor (*Local Hero, Crossing Delancey*), born New York, NY, Apr 11, 1947.

Bret William Saberhagen, 45, former baseball player, born Chicago Heights, IL, Apr 11, 1964.

Meshach Taylor, 62, actor ("Dave's World," "Designing Women"), born Boston, MA, Apr 11, 1947.

April 12 — Sunday

DAY 102 263 REMAINING

ATTACK ON FORT SUMTER: ANNIVERSARY. Apr 12, 1861. After months of escalating tension, Major Robert Anderson refused to evacuate Fort Sumter at Charleston, SC. Confederate troops under the command of General P.T. Beauregard opened fire on the harbor fort at 4:30 AM and continued until Major Anderson surrendered on Apr 13. No lives were lost despite the firing of some 40,000 shells in the first major engagement of the American Civil War.

THE BIG WIND: 75th ANNIVERSARY. Apr 12, 1934. The highest-velocity natural wind ever recorded occurred in the morning at the Mount Washington, NH, Observatory. Three weather observers, Wendell Stephenson, Alexander McKenzie and Salvatore Pagliuca, observed and recorded the phenomenon in which gusts reached 231 mph—"the strongest natural wind ever recorded on the earth's surface." The 50th anniversary was observed at the site in 1984, with the three original observers participating in the ceremony.

CLAY, HENRY: BIRTH ANNIVERSARY. Apr 12, 1777. Statesman, born at Hanover County, VA. Served as the Speaker of the House of Representatives and later became the leader of the new Whig Party. He was defeated for the presidency three times. Clay died at Washington, DC, June 29, 1852.

COCA-COLA SPRING SPLASH. Apr 12. Winter Park Resort, Winter Park, CO. One of Winter Park's most anticipated events, the wet and wild Spring Splash celebrates the joy of spring skiing. Spectators cheer as skiers and snowboarders struggle through a hilarious and challenging obstacle course that includes skimming across a pond of icy water to cross the finish line. Est attendance: 2,000. For info: Winter Park Resort, PO Box 36, Winter Park, CO 80482. Phone: (970) 726-1564. Fax: (970) 726-1572. E-mail: wpinfo@winterparkresort.com. Web: www.winterparkresort.com.

EASTER SUNDAY. Apr 12. Commemorates the Resurrection of Christ. Most joyous festival of the Christian year. The date of Easter, a movable feast, is derived from the lunar calendar: the first Sunday following the first ecclesiastical full moon on or after Mar 21—always between Mar 22 and Apr 25. The Council of Nicaea (AD 325) prescribed that Easter be celebrated on the Sunday after Passover, as that feast's date had been established in Jesus's time. After 1582, when Pope Gregory XIII introduced the Gregorian calendar, Orthodox Christians continued to use the Julian calendar, so Easter can sometimes be as much as five weeks apart in the Western and Eastern churches. Easter in 2010 will be Apr 4; in 2011 it will be Apr 24; in 2012 it will be Apr 8. Many other dates in the Christian year are derived from the date of Easter. See also: "Orthodox Easter Sunday or Pascha" (Apr 19).

FDR COMMEMORATIVE CEREMONY. Apr 12. Little White House, Warm Springs, GA. Annual ceremony honoring Franklin Delano Roosevelt on the anniversary of his death in Warm Springs. Keynote speaker and Marine color guard highlight this impressive ceremony. Est attendance: 1,000. For info: Little White House, 401 Little White House Rd, Warm Springs, GA 31830. Phone: (706) 655-5870.

April 2009

S	M	T	W	T	F	S
			1	2	3	4
5	6	7	8	9	10	11
12	13	14	15	16	17	18
19	20	21	22	23	24	25
26	27	28	29	30		

HALIFAX INDEPENDENCE DAY: ANNIVERSARY. Apr 12, 1776. North Carolina. Anniversary of the resolution adopted by the Provincial Congress of North Carolina at Halifax, NC, authorizing the delegates from North Carolina to the Continental Congress to vote for a Declaration of Independence.

HALL, LYMAN: BIRTH ANNIVERSARY. Apr 12, 1724. Signer of the Declaration of Independence. Born at Wallingford, CT, he died at Burke County, GA, Oct 19, 1790.

HAUTE DOG CHARITY EASTER PARADE. Apr 12. Belmont Shore, Long Beach, CA. Just about every breed from bulldog to poodle will take over Belmont Shore for this annual parade. The event has raised thousands of dollars for animal shelters and rescue organizations. About 600 pooches—some colorfully costumed in Easter attire—are expected to pack Livingston Park for a Yappy Hour before beginning their parade down Second Street. Prizes awarded for best outfits and canine bonnets. Annually, Easter Sunday. Est attendance: 3,000. For info: Justin Rudd. Phone: (562) 439-3316. E-mail: justin@justinrudd.com. Web: www.EasterParade.org.

ITALY: EXPLOSION OF THE CART. Apr 12. Florence. At noon on Easter Sunday in Piazza del Duomo a cart full of fireworks is exploded, perpetuating a ceremony of ancient origin and recalling the fire that used to be kindled during the *Gloria* at Easter mass and was then distributed to all of Florence's households. The tradition is held to date back to the time of the First Crusade, when the valorous Pazzino dei Pazzi was awarded some pieces of flint from the Holy Sepulcher. After his return to Florence the holy fire was kindled with these flints, now preserved in the church of Santi Apostoli.

MARKSVILLE EASTER EGG KNOCKING CONTEST. Apr 12. Marksville, LA. Competition among owners of chicken and guinea eggs that have been boiled and dyed. Annually, on Easter Sunday 9 AM–noon. Est attendance: 500. For info: Chamber of Commerce, Box 767, Marksville, LA 71351. Phone: (318) 253-9222 or (318) 253-0284.

MASSACRE AT FORT PILLOW: ANNIVERSARY. Apr 12, 1864. After surrounding Fort Pillow, TN, Confederate general Nathan Bedford Forrest attacked the stronghold on this date. The ensuing Confederate victory led to many casualties, many of them black Union soldiers. Although Forrest claimed that the large amount of casualties was a result of the fort's refusal to surrender, most believe that Forrest's men massacred the defenseless troops after the fort was surrendered. The action inflamed Northern sentiments and is considered one of the most controversial events of the Civil War.

MERRIE MONARCH FESTIVAL WITH WORLD'S LARGEST HULA COMPETITION. Apr 12–18. Hilo, HI. Cultural event honoring King David Kalakaua. Festival culminates with the world's largest hula competition. Hawaii's finest hula schools compete in ancient and modern divisions. Annually, beginning on Easter Sunday. Est attendance: 6,000. For info: Hawaii Naniloa Hotel, Merrie Monarch Office, 93 Banyan Dr, Hilo, HI 96720. Phone: (808) 935-9168.

MORAVIAN EASTER SUNRISE SERVICE. Apr 12. Winston-Salem, NC. Held since 1771. Outdoor religious service featuring Moravian brass bands playing in streets to awaken sleepers. Service begins in Salem Square and concludes in God's Acre, the Moravian Graveyard, at daybreak. Est attendance: 8,000. For info: Salem Congregation, 501 S Main St, Winston-Salem, NC 27101-5314. Phone: (336) 722-6504. Fax: (336) 725-2514. E-mail: facilitiesmgr@mcsp.org.

NATIONAL LIBRARY WEEK. Apr 12–18. A nationwide observance sponsored by the American Library Association. Celebrates libraries and librarians, the pleasures and importance of reading and invites library use and support. For info: American Library Assn, Public Info Office, 50 E Huron St, Chicago, IL 60611. Phone: (312) 280-5044. Fax: (312) 280-5274. E-mail: pio@ala.org. Web: www.ala.org.

NATIONAL LICORICE DAY. Apr 12. Celebrating black licorice, its history, health benefits and world reknown as a delightful confection. Throughout the entire month of April, Licorice International will present seminars and other special events to educate and entertain the public. For info: Elizabeth Erlandson, Licorice International, 803 Q St, Ste 300, Lincoln, NE 68508. Phone: (402) 488-2230. E-mail: elizabeth@licoriceinternational.com. Web: www.licoriceinternational.com or www.ilovelicorice.com.

NATIONAL PERSONAL TRAINING WEEK. Apr 12–18. Personal trainers help build bodies and minds by guiding people through safe strength-building workouts while offering encouragement along the way. Consider personal trainers as guides to better health. Seek out their expertise to get moving and grow stronger and thus enjoy a healthier, more confident life. Annually, the third week in April. For info: Gail Sideman, Publiside, 333 W Brown Deer Rd, Ste 127, Milwaukee, WI 53217. Phone: (262) 240-7433. E-mail: gsideman@aol.com. Web: www.personaltrainingweek.com.

ORTHODOX PALM SUNDAY. Apr 12. Celebration of Christ's entry into Jerusalem, when his way was covered with palms by the multitudes. Beginning of Holy Week in the Orthodox Church.

✦ **PAN AMERICAN WEEK.** Apr 12–18. Presidential Proclamation customarily issued as "Pan American Day and Pan American Week." Always issued for the week including Apr 14, except in 1965, from 1946 through 1948, 1955 through 1977 and 1979.

POLIO VACCINE: ANNIVERSARY. Apr 12, 1955. Anniversary of announcement that the polio vaccine developed by American physician Dr. Jonas E. Salk was "safe, potent and effective." Incidence of the dreaded infantile paralysis, or poliomyelitis, declined by 95 percent following introduction of preventive vaccines. The first mass innoculations of children with the Salk vaccine had begun in Pittsburgh, Feb 23, 1954.

ROOSEVELT, FRANKLIN DELANO: DEATH ANNIVERSARY. Apr 12, 1945. With the end of WWII only months away, the nation and the world were stunned by the sudden death of the president shortly into his fourth term of office. Roosevelt, 32nd president of the US (Mar 4, 1933–Apr 12, 1945), was the only president to serve more than two terms—he was elected to four consecutive terms. He died at Warm Springs, GA.

SPACE MILESTONE: *COLUMBIA STS-1* (US) FIRST SHUTTLE FLIGHT. Apr 12, 1981. First flight of shuttle *Columbia*. Two astronauts (John Young and Robert Crippen), on first manned US space mission since *Apollo-Soyuz* in July 1976, spent 54 hours in space (36 orbits of Earth) before landing at Edwards Air Force Base, CA, Apr 14.

SPACE MILESTONE: *DISCOVERY* (US). Apr 12, 1985. On its 16th mission (from Kennedy Space Center, FL) shuttle *Discovery* was launched carrying US Senator Jake Garn as a member of its crew of seven.

SPACE MILESTONE: *VOSTOK I*, FIRST MAN IN SPACE. Apr 12, 1961. Yuri Gagarin became the first man in space when he made a 108-minute voyage, orbiting Earth in a 10,395-pound vehicle, *Vostok I*, launched by the USSR.

TRUANCY LAW: ANNIVERSARY. Apr 12, 1853. The first truancy law was enacted at New York. A $50 fine was charged against parents whose children between the ages of 5 and 15 were absent from school.

"21 JUMP STREET" TV PREMIERE: ANNIVERSARY. Apr 12, 1987. Youthful big-city cops busted crime in the local schools and colleges in this FOX police drama. Starred Johnny Depp as Tom Hanson, Holly Robinson Peete as Judy Hoffs, Dustin Nguyen as H.T. Ioki, Peter DeLuise as Doug Penhall, Frederic Forrest as Captain Jenko, Steven Williams as Captain Adam Fuller and Richard Grieco as Dennis Booker. It was one of the FOX network's early hits.

WALK ON YOUR WILD SIDE DAY. Apr 12. Time's wasting, friends. It's high time you went out and did some things no one expects you to do. Be unpredictable for once. Go to work dressed like a gorilla, get a master's degree—do something "they" said you'd never ever do. (©2006 by WH.) For info: Thomas & Ruth Roy, Wellcat Holidays, 2418 Long Ln, Lebanon, PA 17046. Phone: (717) 279-0184. E-mail: info@wellcat.com. Web: www.wellcat.com.

WELLS FARGO GOLDEN BUNNY EGG HUNT AND RACE. Apr 12. Winter Park Resort, Winter Park, CO. Winter Park Willie and the Easter Bunny give kids some holiday fun with an on-mountain egg hunt and traditional fun race for children 10 and under. Est attendance: 500. For info: Winter Park Resort, PO Box 36, Winter Park, CO 80482. Phone: (970) 726-1564. Fax: (970) 726-1572. E-mail: wpinfo@winterparkresort.com. Web: www.winterparkresort.com.

"YOUR HIT PARADE" RADIO PREMIERE: ANNIVERSARY. Apr 12, 1935. This program debuted on radio in 1935 with its countdown of the week's top songs. In 1950 it became a TV program. See also: "Your Hit Parade TV Premiere: Anniversary" (Oct 7).

Birthdays Today

David Cassidy, 59, singer ("Cherish"), actor ("The Partridge Family"), born New York, NY, Apr 12, 1950.

Tom Clancy, 62, author (*The Hunt for Red October, Red Storm Rising*), born Baltimore, MD, Apr 12, 1947.

Beverly Cleary, 93, author (*Ramona* series for children; winner of the Newbery Medal for *Dear Mr Henshaw*), born McMinnville, OR, Apr 12, 1916.

Claire Danes, 30, actress (*Shopgirl, The Hours, Little Women*), born New York, NY, Apr 12, 1979.

Shannen Doherty, 38, actress ("Beverly Hills 90210," *Night Shift, Heathers*), born Memphis, TN, Apr 12, 1971.

Andy Garcia, 53, actor (*Ocean's Eleven, The Untouchables*), born Havana, Cuba, Apr 12, 1956.

Herbie Hancock, 69, musician, born Chicago, IL, Apr 12, 1940.

Dan Lauria, 62, actor ("The Wonder Years," *Stakeout*), born Brooklyn, NY, Apr 12, 1947.

David Letterman, 62, comedian, TV talk-show host ("Late Show with David Letterman"), born Indianapolis, IN, Apr 12, 1947.

Sarah Jane Morris, 32, actress ("Brothers & Sisters," "Felicity"), born Memphis, TN, Apr 12, 1977.

Ed O'Neill, 63, actor ("Married . . . With Children," *Deliverance, Wayne's World*), born Youngstown, OH, Apr 12, 1946.

Saoirse Ronan, 15, actress (*Atonement*), born New York, NY, Apr 12, 1994.

April 13 — Monday

DAY 103 | **262 REMAINING**

BECKETT, SAMUEL: BIRTH ANNIVERSARY. Apr 13, 1906. Author, critic and playwright, born at Foxrock, County Dublin, Ireland. Beckett is best remembered for his plays, including *Waiting for Godot, Endgame, Krapp's Last Tape* and *Happy Days*. Beckett settled at Paris, France, in 1937 and served with an underground resistance group during the early years of WWII. In the years following the war, he wrote the challenging novels *Molloy, Malone Dies* and *The Unnamable* and two plays, *Eleutheria* and *Waiting for Godot. Waiting for Godot* received an acclaimed production at Paris in January 1953, and with it Beckett achieved worldwide renown. Awarded the Nobel Prize for Literature in 1969, he died Dec 22, 1989, at Paris.

BUTTS, ALFRED M.: BIRTH ANNIVERSARY. Apr 13, 1899. Alfred Butts was a jobless architect in the Depression when he invented the board game Scrabble. The game was just a fad for Butts's friends until a Macy's executive saw the game being played at a resort in 1952, and the world's largest store began carrying it. Manufacturing of the game was turned over to Selchow & Righter when 35 workers were producing 6,000 sets a week. Butts received three cents per set for years. He said, "One-third went to taxes. I gave one-third away, and the other third enabled me to have an enjoyable life." Butts was born at Poughkeepsie, NY. He died Apr 4, 1993, at Rhinebeck, NY.

CASSIDY, BUTCH: BIRTH ANNIVERSARY. Apr 13, 1866. Born Robert Leroy Parker at Beaver, UT, son of Mormon pioneer Maximillian Parker, he became a notorious outlaw of the Old West and leader of the Wild Bunch gang. Some believed he died in a gun battle at Bolivia in 1909, while others are certain he returned and died in the US.

EASTER MONDAY. Apr 13. Holiday or bank holiday in many places, including England, Northern Ireland, Wales, Canada and North Carolina in the US.

EGG SALAD WEEK. Apr 13–19. Dedicated to the many delicious uses for all of the Easter eggs that have been cooked, colored, hidden and found. Annually, the full week after Easter. For info: Linda Braun, Consumer Serv Dir, American Egg Board, 1460 Renaissance Dr, Park Ridge, IL 60068. Web: www.aeb.org.

ENGLAND: HALLATON BOTTLE KICKING. Apr 13. Hallaton, Leicestershire. Ancient custom dating back at least 600 years. Annually, Easter Monday.

FIRST BASEBALL STRIKE ENDS: ANNIVERSARY. Apr 13, 1972. Major league baseball players and owners agreed on a settlement in which owners added $500,000 to the players' pension fund. This ended the first baseball strike, which had begun Apr 5 when the season opener was canceled.

GREAT CHICAGO FLOOD: ANNIVERSARY. Apr 13, 1992. On this morning Chicagoans awoke to one of the most unusual disasters of modern times: the Chicago River broke through a rupture in an old underground freight tunnel wall, sending millions of gallons of water flooding into the tunnel system beneath the downtown business district. The water poured into basements of buildings that previously had been connected to the tunnel system. The greater Loop area had to be evacuated as electricity was cut off ahead of the rising water. A hectic effort that was mounted to plug the leak in the river eventually succeeded. Once the flow of water had stopped, the city began the slow and expensive process of draining the water.

INDIA: VAISAKHI. Apr 13. Sikh holiday (also known as Khalsa Day) that commemorates the founding of the brotherhood of the Khalsa in 1699. This harvest festival is regarded as the Sikh New Year. Usually Apr 13, it falls on Apr 14 every 36 years.

JEFFERSON, THOMAS: BIRTH ANNIVERSARY. Apr 13, 1743. Third president of the US (Mar 4, 1801–Mar 3, 1809), second vice president (1797–1801), born at Albermarle County, VA. Jefferson, who died at Charlottesville, VA, July 4, 1826, wrote his own epitaph: "Here was buried Thomas Jefferson, author of the Declaration of American Independence, of the statute of Virginia for religious freedom, and father of the University of Virginia." A holiday in Alabama and Oklahoma. See also: "Adams, John, and Jefferson, Thomas: Death Anniversary" (July 4).

LUXEMBOURG: EMAISHEN. Apr 13. Luxembourg (city). Popular traditional market and festival at the "Marche-aux-Poissons." Young lovers present each other with earthenware articles, sold only on this day. Annually, Easter Monday.

April 2009	S	M	T	W	T	F	S
				1	2	3	4
	5	6	7	8	9	10	11
	12	13	14	15	16	17	18
	19	20	21	22	23	24	25
	26	27	28	29	30		

PREMIERE OF HANDEL'S *MESSIAH*: ANNIVERSARY. Apr 13, 1742. In a charity performance at Dublin, Ireland's New Musick Hall on Fishamble Street, George Frederick Handel sat at the harpsichord and conducted the first concert of his masterpiece, *Messiah.* This sacred oratorio became Handel's most popular work and has been performed every year since 1742. Newspapers of the day anticipated the popularity of the first performance and asked ladies not to wear hoops under their skirts and gentlemen not to wear swords so that 700 people could fit into a hall designed for 600. Some years later, King George II stood up in admiration of the Hallelujah Chorus, starting a tradition still followed by audiences to this day.

***SILENT SPRING* PUBLICATION: ANNIVERSARY.** Apr 13, 1962. Rachel Carson's *Silent Spring* warned humankind that for the first time in history every person is subjected to contact with dangerous chemicals from conception until death. Carson painted a vivid picture of how chemicals—used in many ways but particularly in pesticides—have upset the balance of nature, undermining the survival of countless species. This enormously popular and influential book was a soft-spoken battle cry to protect our natural surroundings. Its publication signaled the beginning of the environmental movement.

SOUTH AFRICA: FAMILY DAY. Apr 13. National holiday. Annually, Easter Monday.

SRI LANKA: SINHALA AND TAMIL NEW YEAR. Apr 13–14. This New Year festival includes traditional games, the wearing of new clothes in auspicious colors and special foods. Public holiday.

SWITZERLAND: EGG RACES. Apr 13. Rural northwest Swiss Easter Monday custom. Race among competitors carrying large numbers of eggs while running to neighboring villages.

THAILAND: SONGKRAN FESTIVAL. Apr 13–15. Public holiday. Thai New Year festival (also known as the "Water Festival"). To welcome the new year, the image of Buddha is bathed with holy or fragrant water and lustral water is sprinkled on celebrants. Joyous event, especially observed at Buddhist temples.

✦ **THOMAS JEFFERSON DAY.** Apr 13. Honoring the birth of our nation's third president. Presidential Proclamation 2276, of Mar 21, 1938, covers all succeeding years. (Pub Res No 60 of Aug 16, 1937.)

UNITED KINGDOM: EASTER MONDAY BANK HOLIDAY. Apr 13. Bank and public holiday in England, Wales and Northern Ireland. (Scotland not included.)

WELTY, EUDORA: 100th BIRTH ANNIVERSARY. Apr 13, 1909. Great novelist and short-story writer whose characters lived in the rural south. Her short stories are considered the zenith of the art. Wrote *The Ponder Heart* (1954), among other works. Lived her entire life in Jackson, MS: born Apr 13, 1909; died July 23, 2001.

WHITE HOUSE EASTER EGG ROLL. Apr 13. Traditionally held at executive mansion's south lawn on Easter Monday. Custom said to have started at Capitol grounds about 1810. Transferred to White House lawn in 1870s.

Birthdays Today

Peabo Bryson, 58, singer, born Greenville, SC, Apr 13, 1951.

Jack Casady, 65, musician, born Washington, DC, Apr 13, 1944.

Robert Casey, 49, US Senator (D, Pennsylvania), born Scranton, PA, Apr 13, 1960.

Bill Conti, 67, composer (Oscar for *The Right Stuff*; "Falcon Crest," "Inside Edition"), born Providence, RI, Apr 13, 1942.

Baron Davis, 30, basketball player, born Los Angeles, CA, Apr 13, 1979.

Tony Dow, 64, actor ("Leave It to Beaver"), born Hollywood, CA, Apr 13, 1945.

Al Green, 63, singer ("Let's Stay Together"), born Forrest City, AR, Apr 13, 1946.

Garry Kasparov, 46, International Grandmaster chess player, born Baku, Azerbaijan, Apr 13, 1963.

Davis Love III, 45, golfer, born Charlotte, NC, Apr 13, 1964.

Ron Perlman, 59, actor (*Hellboy*, "Beauty and the Beast"), born New York, NY, Apr 13, 1950.

Saundra Santiago, 52, actress ("Miami Vice"), born the Bronx, NY, Apr 13, 1957.

Rick Schroder, 39, actor ("Silver Spoons," "NYPD Blue," *The Champ*), born Staten Island, NY, Apr 13, 1970.

Paul Sorvino, 70, actor ("Law & Order"), born Brooklyn, NY, Apr 13, 1939.

Lyle Waggoner, 74, actor ("The Carol Burnett Show," "Wonder Woman"), born Kansas City, KS, Apr 13, 1935.

Max M. Weinberg, 58, musician, bandleader ("Late Night with Conan O'Brien"), born South Orange, NJ, Apr 13, 1951.

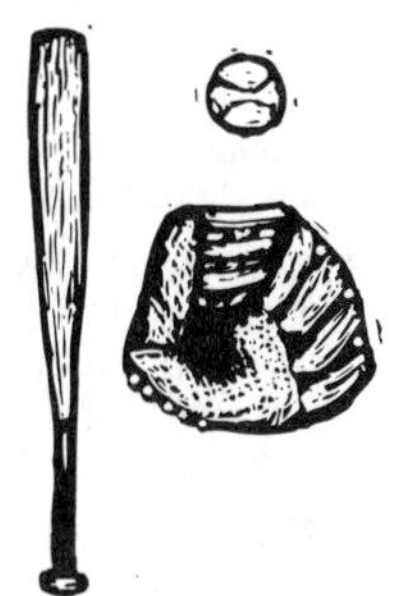

April 14 — Tuesday

DAY 104 **261 REMAINING**

CAMPBELL BECOMES FIRST AMERICAN AIR ACE: ANNIVERSARY. Apr 14, 1918. Lieutenant Douglas Campbell became the first American pilot to achieve the designation of ace when he shot down his fifth German aircraft.

CHILDREN WITH ALOPECIA DAY. Apr 14. If you are a child (or have a child) who is losing hair because of the autoimmune hair-loss disease alopecia areata, today is your day to stand up and be proud of not having hair while still being you! For info: Jeffery Woytovich, The Children's Alopecia Project, PO Box 6036, Wyomissing, PA 19610. Phone: (610) 741-5552. E-mail: jeff.woytovich@childrensalopeciaproject.org. Web: www.childrensalopeciaproject.org.

CHILDREN'S DAY IN FLORIDA. Apr 14. A legal holiday in Florida commemorated on the second Tuesday in April.

FIRST AMERICAN ABOLITION SOCIETY FOUNDED: ANNIVERSARY. Apr 14, 1775. The first abolition organization formed in the US was The Society for the Relief of Free Negroes Unlawfully Held in Bondage, founded at Philadelphia, PA.

FIRST DICTIONARY OF AMERICAN ENGLISH PUBLISHED: ANNIVERSARY. Apr 14, 1828. Noah Webster published his *American Dictionary of the English Language.*

GIELGUD, SIR JOHN: BIRTH ANNIVERSARY. Apr 14, 1904. Director and actor, born at London, England. A legend of the stage, he played the role of Hamlet more than 500 times. He made his professional film debut in 1924 in *Who Is the Man?* Other film credits include *Arthur, Murder on the Orient Express* and *Plenty.* He won the Tony Award for Best Director in 1961 for *Big Fish Little Fish.* He died at Buckinghamshire, England, May 21, 2000.

***GRAPES OF WRATH* PUBLISHED: 70th ANNIVERSARY.** Apr 14, 1939. John Steinbeck's novel of the Great Depression, *Grapes of Wrath*, won the 1940 Pulitzer Prize. It chronicled the mass migration to California of dispossessed farmers from the Dust Bowl region of the Great Plains.

HONDURAS: DIA DE LAS AMERICAS. Apr 14. Pan-American Day, a national holiday.

HUYGENS, CHRISTIAAN: BIRTH ANNIVERSARY. Apr 14, 1629. Scientist, born at The Hague, Netherlands. He discovered the rings of Saturn and the wave theory, or pulse theory, of light. In 1656 he invented the pendulum clock. He died at The Hague, June 8, 1695.

INTERNATIONAL MOMENT OF LAUGHTER DAY. Apr 14. Laughter is a potent and powerful way to deal with the difficulties of modern living. Since the physical, emotional and spiritual benefits of laughter are widely accepted, this day is set aside for everyone to take the necessary time to experience the power of laughter. For info: Izzy Gesell, Head Honcho of Wide Angle Humor, PO Box 962, Northampton, MA 01061. Phone: (413) 586-2634. E-mail: izzy@izzyg.com. Web: www.izzyg.com.

LINCOLN, ABRAHAM: ASSASSINATION ANNIVERSARY. Apr 14, 1865. President Abraham Lincoln was shot while watching a performance of *Our American Cousin* at Ford's Theatre, Washington, DC. He died the following day. The assassin was John Wilkes Booth, a young actor.

NATIONAL BE KIND TO LAWYERS DAY. Apr 14. Lawyers are perhaps the most reviled and ridiculed profession in America today, and yet people flock to lawyers the moment they need help writing a will, running a business or avoiding jail time. This is the one day out of the year to give an ounce or two of respect to the men and women who daily tip the scales of justice. Whether you take your favorite lawyer out to lunch or simply refrain from telling lawyer jokes for 24 hours, this is the day to give a little love to the attorneys in your life. Annually, the second Tuesday in April. For info: Steve Hughes, 412 Luther Ct, St. Louis, MO 63122. Phone: (314) 821-8700. E-mail: info@hityourstride.com. Web: www.BeKindToLawyers.com.

NATIONAL CATHOLIC EDUCATIONAL ASSOCIATION CONVENTION AND EXPOSITION. Apr 14–17. Anaheim, CA. 106th annual meeting for NCEA members and anyone working in, or interested in, the welfare of Catholic education. Annually, the week after Easter Sunday. For info: Sue Arvo, Conv Dir, Natl Catholic Educational Assn, 1077 30th St NW, Ste 100, Washington, DC 20007-3852. Phone: (202) 337-6232. Fax: (202) 333-6706.

✦ **PAN-AMERICAN DAY.** Apr 14. Presidential Proclamation 1912, of May 28, 1930, covers every Apr 14 (required by Governing Board of Pan-American Union). Proclamation issued each year since 1948. Commemorates the first International Conference of American States in 1890.

PAN-AMERICAN DAY IN FLORIDA. Apr 14. A ceremonial day in Florida that is observed in the public schools as a day honoring the republics of Latin America. When Apr 14 does not fall on a school day, the governor may designate the preceding Friday or the following Monday as Pan-American Day.

PRESIDENT TAFT OPENS BASEBALL SEASON: ANNIVERSARY. Apr 14, 1910. President William Howard Taft began a sports tradition by throwing out the first baseball of the season at an American League game between Washington and Philadelphia. Washington won 3–0.

SCOTTSDALE CULINARY FESTIVAL™. Apr 14–19. Scottsdale, AZ. Thirteen spectacular culinary events including Food and Wine Best New Chef Reunion Dinner, On and Off the Rocks cocktail parties, Best of the Fest featuring 11 of the valley's best chefs, Great Arizona Picnic featuring 50 of the valley's best restaurants and more. Proceeds benefit arts education programs for youth in the community. Est attendance: 50,000. For info: Scottsdale Culinary Festival, 7309 E Evans, Scottsdale, AZ 85260. E-mail: info@scottsdaleculinaryfestival.org. Web: www.scottsdaleculinaryfestival.org.

SULLIVAN, ANNE: BIRTH ANNIVERSARY. Apr 14, 1866. Anne Sullivan, born at Feeding Hills, MA, became well known for "working miracles" with Helen Keller, who was blind and deaf. Nearly blind herself, Sullivan used a manual alphabet communicated by the sense of touch to teach Keller to read, write and speak and then to help her go on to higher education. Anne Sullivan died Oct 20, 1936, at Forest Hills, NY.

TOYNBEE, ARNOLD JOSEPH: BIRTH ANNIVERSARY. Apr 14; 1889. English historian, author of monumental *Study of History.* Born at London, England; died at York, England, Oct 22, 1975.

VAN CLIBURN CONQUERS MOSCOW: ANNIVERSARY. Apr 14, 1958. Young Texan pianist Van Cliburn won the first International Tchaikovsky Competition in Moscow—sparking a music frenzy that brought a brief thaw to the Cold War. Embraced by Muscovites, Cliburn was also treated to a ticker tape parade in New York City (the only musician so honored). His subsequent recording of Tchaikovsky's Piano Concerto No. 1 was the first classical music album to go platinum.

Birthdays Today

Abigail Breslin, 13, actress (*Little Miss Sunshine, Signs*), born New York, NY, Apr 14, 1996.

Adrien Brody, 36, actor (Oscar for *The Pianist*; *The Darjeeling Limited, King Kong*), born New York, NY, Apr 14, 1973.

Robert Carlyle, 48, actor (*Angela's Ashes, The Full Monty*), born Glasgow, Scotland, Apr 14, 1961.

Julie Christie, 69, actress (*Dr. Zhivago, Shampoo, Away from Her*), born Chukua, India, Apr 14, 1940.

Cynthia Cooper, 46, former basketball player, born Chicago, IL, Apr 14, 1963.

Brad Garrett, 49, comedian, actor ("Everybody Loves Raymond"), born Woodland Hills, CA, Apr 14, 1960.

Sarah Michelle Gellar, 32, actress (*Scooby-Doo*, "Buffy the Vampire Slayer"), born New York, NY, Apr 14, 1977.

Anthony Michael Hall, 41, actor, comedian ("The Dead Zone," "Saturday Night Live," *Sixteen Candles, The Breakfast Club*), born Boston, MA, Apr 14, 1968.

David Christopher Justice, 43, former baseball player, born Cincinnati, OH, Apr 14, 1966.

Loretta Lynn, 74, singer/songwriter, born Butcher's Hollow, KY, Apr 14, 1935.

Gregory Alan (Greg) Maddux, 43, baseball player, born San Angelo, TX, Apr 14, 1966.

Peter Edward (Pete) Rose, 68, former baseball manager and player, born Cincinnati, OH, Apr 14, 1941.

Emma Thompson, 50, actress (Oscar for *Howards End*; *Wit, Sense and Sensibility*), screenwriter (Oscar for *Sense and Sensibility*), born London, England, Apr 14, 1959.

April 15 — Wednesday

DAY 105 — **260 REMAINING**

ASTRONOMERS FIND NEW SOLAR SYSTEM: 10th ANNIVERSARY. Apr 15, 1999. Astronomers from San Francisco State University working at an observatory in Arizona announced the discovery of the first multiplanet system ever found orbiting around a star other than our own. Three planets orbit the star Upsilon Andromedae, which can be seen with the naked eye. This suggests that the Milky Way probably teems with similar planetary systems.

BENTON, THOMAS HART: BIRTH ANNIVERSARY. Apr 15, 1889. Thomas Hart Benton was an artist whose work was indicative of the American style of painting known as Regionalism. His works of life in the Midwest and South were not always flattering to their subjects, but his style became known as a truly American style of painting. He was born at Neosho, MO, and died at Kansas City, MO, Jan 19, 1975.

April 2009

S	M	T	W	T	F	S
			1	2	3	4
5	6	7	8	9	10	11
12	13	14	15	16	17	18
19	20	21	22	23	24	25
26	27	28	29	30		

"BUCK ROGERS" TV PREMIERE: ANNIVERSARY. Apr 15, 1950. At first a radio show, "Buck Rogers" premiered on ABC with Kem Dibbs. Buck was an average American who woke up from a cave behind Niagara Falls to find himself in the year 2430. The show featured Lou Prentis as Lieutenant Wilma Deering, Harry Sothern as Dr. Huer and Harry Kingston as Black Barney Wade. Buck was later played by Robert Pastene.

CHINA: CANTON SPRING TRADE FAIR. Apr 15–May 15. The Guangzhou (Canton) Spring Trade Fair is held on the same dates each year.

FDA APPROVES BOTOX: ANNIVERSARY. Apr 15, 2002. The US Food and Drug Administration approved the cosmetic use of Botox (an injected preparation of purified botulism) on this date.

FIRST MCDONALD'S OPENS: ANNIVERSARY. Apr 15, 1955. The first franchised McDonald's was opened at Des Plaines, IL, by Ray Kroc, who had gotten the idea from a hamburger joint at San Bernardino, CA, run by the McDonald brothers. On opening day a hamburger was 15 cents. The Big Mac was introduced in 1968 for 49 cents and the Quarter Pounder in 1971 for 53 cents. By the 21st century, there were more than 31,000 McDonald's in 119 countries.

FIRST SCHOOL FOR DEAF FOUNDED: ANNIVERSARY. Apr 15, 1817. Thomas Hopkins Gallaudet and Laurent Clerc founded the first US public school for the deaf, Connecticut Asylum for the Education and Instruction of Deaf and Dumb Persons (now the American School for the Deaf), at Hartford, CT.

"IN LIVING COLOR" TV PREMIERE: ANNIVERSARY. Apr 15, 1990. FOX's sketch comedy series, created by Keenen Ivory Wayans, was modeled after "Saturday Night Live." Between skits, the Fly Girls would entertain the studio audience with hip-hop dance (choreographed by soon-to-be film actress Rosie Perez). The show featured Wayans, his brothers Damon, Marlon and Shawn, his sister Kim, Tommy Davidson, David Alan Grier, T'Keyah "Crystal" Keymáh, Kelly Coffield, Kim Coles and Jim Carrey before he was Ace Ventura. Some of the most popular recurring characters were Homey, the embittered clown, the flammable Fire Marshall Bill and the effeminate movie critics of "Men on Film."

INCOME TAX PAY DAY. Apr 15. A day all Americans need to know—the day by which taxpayers are supposed to make their accounting of the previous year and pay their share of the cost of government. The US Internal Revenue Service provides free forms.

JAMES, HENRY: BIRTH ANNIVERSARY. Apr 15, 1843. Novelist and critic, born at New York, NY. Among his best-known works are *The Portrait of a Lady, Washington Square* and *The Ambassadors.* James died Feb 28, 1916, at London, England.

LONGYEAR, JOHN MUNROE: BIRTH ANNIVERSARY. Apr 15, 1850. American capitalist, landowner, philanthropist and onetime mayor of Marquette, MI. Disapproving of a railway route through Marquette, he caused his home, a stone castle-like showplace, to be torn down in 1903 and moved, stone by stone and stick by stick, in more than 190 freight cars and reerected at Brookline, MA. Born at Lansing, MI, he died May 28, 1922.

NATIONAL TAKE A WILD GUESS DAY. Apr 15. The day honoring guesses, hunches, inspirations, speculations and other forms of "intuitive intelligence." For info: Jim Barber, 1101 Marcano Blvd, Fort Lauderdale, FL 33322. Phone: (954) 476-9252. Fax: (954) 424-0309. E-mail: wildguessday@thebarbershop.com. Web: www.thebarbershop.com.

NATIONAL THAT SUCKS DAY. Apr 15. Today is income tax pay day, quarterly estimated federal income tax payers' due date and the anniversary of the sinking of the *Titanic*. These events and more support a designation for a National That Sucks Day. Visit our website's history of things that suck. Annually, Apr 15. For info: Bruce Novotny, PO Box 1270, Bandon, OR 97411. Phone: (541) 347-5452. Fax: (541) 347-5468. E-mail: novovet@kcnet.com. Web: www.thatsucks.net.

PEALE, CHARLES WILLSON: BIRTH ANNIVERSARY. Apr 15, 1741. (Old Style date.) American portrait painter (best known for his many portraits of colonial and American Revolutionary War figures) was born at Queen Anne County, MD. His children Raphaelle, Rembrandt, Titian, Rubens and his niece Sarah were also artists. Died at Philadelphia, PA, Feb 22, 1827.

QUARTERLY ESTIMATED FEDERAL INCOME TAX PAYERS' DUE DATE. Apr 15. For those individuals whose fiscal year is the calendar year and who make quarterly estimated federal income tax payments, today is one of the due dates (Jan 15, Apr 15, June 15 and Sept 15, 2009).

ROBINSON BREAKS BASEBALL COLOR LINE: ANNIVERSARY. Apr 15, 1947. Jackie Robinson became the first African American to play in the major leagues in the 20th century when he made his debut for the Brooklyn Dodgers against the Boston Braves. Robinson went 0-for-3 but scored the deciding run as the Dodgers prevailed, 5–3. He was later voted 1947's Rookie of the Year.

SIMMS, HILDA: BIRTH ANNIVERSARY. Apr 15, 1920. American stage and film actress, born Hilda Moses at Minneapolis, MN. She joined the American Negro Theater at Harlem, NY, in 1943 and was given the title role in *Anna Lucasta*. When the production moved to Broadway in 1944, it became the first all-black production to be performed on Broadway without a racial theme. Simms was the creative arts director of New York State's human rights division, through which she was instrumental in bringing discrimination against black actors to public attention during the 1960s. She died at Buffalo, NY, Feb 6, 1994.

SINKING OF THE *TITANIC*: ANNIVERSARY. Apr 15, 1912. The "unsinkable" luxury liner *Titanic* on its maiden voyage from Southampton, England, to New York, NY, struck an iceberg just before midnight Apr 14, and sank at 2:27 AM, Apr 15. The *Titanic* had 2,224 persons aboard. Of these, more than 1,500 were lost. About 700 people were rescued from the icy waters off Newfoundland by the liner *Carpathia*, which reached the scene about two hours after the *Titanic* went down. See also: "*Titanic* Discovered: Anniversary" (Sept 1).

SMITH, BESSIE: BIRTH ANNIVERSARY. Apr 15, 1894. The "Empress of the Blues," Bessie Smith, was born at Chattanooga, TN (year varies as late as 1900). She was assisted in her efforts to break into show business by Ma Rainey, the first great blues singer. Her first recording was made in February 1923. Smith died of injuries she sustained in an automobile accident at Clarksdale, MS, Sept 26, 1937.

WASHINGTON, HAROLD: BIRTH ANNIVERSARY. Apr 15, 1922. Illinois legislator and mayor of Chicago (1983–87). Born at Chicago, IL, and died there Nov 25, 1987. Harold Washington was one of the first African Americans to head a major US city. He was instrumental in tearing down Chicago's famed Democratic machine, a holdover from the many decades of domination by the Richard J. Daley administration.

Birthdays Today

Evelyn Ashford, 52, Olympic gold medal track athlete, born Shreveport, LA, Apr 15, 1957.

Linda Bloodworth-Thomason, 62, producer, writer ("Designing Women," "Evening Shade"), born Poplar Bluff, MO, Apr 15, 1947.

Roy Clark, 76, singer and guitarist, former cohost of "Hee Haw," born Meherrin, VA, Apr 15, 1933.

Heloise Cruse Evans, 58, newspaper columnist ("Hints from Heloise"), born Waco, TX, Apr 15, 1951.

Jason Sehorn, 38, former football player, born Mt Shasta, CA, Apr 15, 1971.

Emma Watson, 19, actress (the Harry Potter films), born Oxford, England, Apr 15, 1990.

Amy Wright, 59, actress (*Breaking Away, Wise Blood, The Accidental Tourist*), born Chicago, IL, Apr 15, 1950.

April 16 — Thursday

DAY 106 — **259 REMAINING**

AMIS, KINGSLEY: BIRTH ANNIVERSARY. Apr 16, 1922. Author (*The Old Devils, Lucky Jim*), born at London, England, and died there Oct 22, 1995.

CENTRAL FLORIDA FAIR. Apr 16–26. Orlando, FL. 97th annual. Eleven days of the finest family fun in central Florida. The best of the best in food, music, livestock, animal shows, fine art, crafts, Hollywood star appearances and thrill rides for all ages to enjoy. Est attendance: 250,000. For info: Central Florida Fair, 4603 W Colonial Dr, Orlando, FL 32808. Phone: (407) 295-3247. E-mail: tiffany@centralfloridafair.com. Web: www.centralfloridafair.com.

CHAPLIN, CHARLES SPENCER: BIRTH ANNIVERSARY. Apr 16, 1889. Celebrated film comedian who portrayed "The Little Tramp" was born at London, England. Film debut in 1914. Knighted in 1975. Died at Vevey, Switzerland, Dec 25, 1977. In his autobiography Chaplin wrote: "There are more valid facts and details in works of art than there are in history books." See also: "Chaplin's 'Tramp' Debuts: Anniversary" (Feb 7).

DENMARK: QUEEN MARGRETHE II'S BIRTHDAY. Apr 16. Thousands of children gather to cheer the queen (born 1940) at Amalienborg Palace, and the Royal Guard wears scarlet gala uniforms.

DIEGO, JOSE de: BIRTH ANNIVERSARY. Apr 16, 1866. Puerto Rican patriot and political leader Jose de Diego was born at Aguadilla, PR. His birthday is a holiday in Puerto Rico. He died July 16, 1918, at New York, NY.

DOGWOOD FESTIVAL. Apr 16–19. Camdenton, MO. This annual rite of spring features music, carnival, food, parade, arts and crafts, art exhibitions and more. For info: Bruce Mitchell, Exec Dir, Camdenton Area Chamber of Commerce, PO Box 1375, Camdenton, MO 65020. Phone: (573) 346-2227 or (800) 769-1004. Fax: (573) 346-3496. E-mail: cchamber@thelake.net. Web: www.camdentonchamber.com.

MANCINI, HENRY: 85th BIRTH ANNIVERSARY. Apr 16, 1924. Born at Cleveland, OH, Mancini made his mark in Hollywood composing film scores and songs. He won 20 Grammy Awards and four Oscars (song "Moon River" and score for *Breakfast at Tiffany's*; song "Days of Wine and Roses" for the same-titled film; score for *Victor/Victoria*). He also composed *The Pink Panther*, "Peter Gunn" and "Mr Lucky" themes. Died June 14, 1994, at Beverly Hills, CA.

NATIONAL COLLEGIATE WOMEN'S GYMNASTICS. Apr 16–18. Bob Devaney Sports Center, Lincoln, NE. For info: NCAA, PO Box 6222, Indianapolis, IN 46206-6222. Phone: (317) 917-6222. Fax: (317) 917-6826. Web: www.NCAAsports.com.

NATIONAL HIGH FIVE DAY. Apr 16. 8th annual. National High Five Day is devoted to celebration of the high five and occurs annually on the third Thursday in April. Each year, there are numerous parties, newspaper articles, television appearances and radio interviews. For info: Greg Harrell-Edge, Natl High Five Day, 6732 Franklin Pl, Apt 110, Los Angeles, CA 90028. Phone: (703) 328-4553. E-mail: gregharrelledge@hotmail.com. Web: www.nationalhighfive day.com.

NATIONAL STRESS AWARENESS DAY. Apr 16. To focus public awareness on one of the leading health problems in the world today. Health-related organizations throughout the country are encouraged to sponsor stress education programs and events. Annually, the first day after income taxes due. For info: Morton C. Orman, MD, Dir, The Health Resource Network, 908 Cold Bottom Rd, Sparks, MD 21152. Web: www.stresscure.com.

NATIONAL WEAR YOUR PAJAMAS TO WORK DAY. Apr 16. Relieve that stress and relax after staying up late working on your taxes! Bring the comforts of home to the office for at least one day. Annually, following the day income taxes are due. For info: The PajamaGram Company, 6655 Shelburne Rd, Shelburne, VT 05482. Phone: (800) GIVE-PJS. Fax: (802) 985-1382. Web: www.Pajama Gram.com.

NATURAL BRIDGES NATIONAL MONUMENT: ANNIVERSARY. Apr 16, 1908. Utah. Natural Bridges National Monument was established on this date.

PUYALLUP SPRING FAIR. Apr 16–19. Puyallup Fair and Events Center, Puyallup, WA. 21st annual. Fair to celebrate spring, including exhibits, animals, flowers, rides, demonstrations, gardening, Kid-Zone, lots of entertainment, food and much more. Est attendance: 100,000. For info: Puyallup Spring Fair, 110 9th Ave SW, Puyallup, WA 98371. Phone: (253) 841-5045. Fax: (253) 841-5390. E-mail: info@thefair.com. Web: www.thefair.com.

SELENA: BIRTH ANNIVERSARY. Apr 16, 1971. Tejana singer, born Selena Quintanilla at Lake Jackson, TX. Died Mar 31, 1995, at Corpus Christi, TX, murdered by the president of her fan club.

SLAVERY ABOLISHED IN DISTRICT OF COLUMBIA: ANNIVERSARY. Apr 16, 1862. Congress abolished slavery in the District of Columbia. One million dollars was appropriated to compensate owners of freed slaves, and $100,000 was set aside to pay district slaves who wished to emigrate to Haiti, Liberia or any other country outside the US.

SLOANE, HANS: BIRTH ANNIVERSARY. Apr 16, 1660. British medical doctor and naturalist whose personal collection became the nucleus of the British Museum, born at County Down, Ireland. Upon his death at Chelsea, England, Jan 11, 1753, his collections of books, manuscripts, medals and antiquities were bequeathed to Britain and accepted by an act of Parliament that incorporated the British Museum. It was opened to the public at London, England, Jan 15, 1759. It is the national museum of the United Kingdom.

SPACE MILESTONE: *APOLLO 16* (US). Apr 16, 1972. Astronauts John W. Young, Charles M. Duke, Jr and Thomas K. Mattingly II (command module pilot) began an 11-day mission that included 71-hour exploration of moon (Apr 20–23). Landing module named *Orion*. Splashdown in Pacific Ocean within a mile of target, Apr 27.

SYNGE, JOHN MILLINGTON: BIRTH ANNIVERSARY. Apr 16, 1871. Irish dramatist and poet, most of whose plays were written in the brief span of six years before his death at age 37 of lymphatic sarcoma. His best-known work was *The Playboy of the Western World* (1907), which caused protests and rioting at early performances. Synge (pronounced "Sing") was born near Dublin, Ireland, and died there Mar 24, 1909.

TEXAS CITY DISASTER: ANNIVERSARY. Apr 16–17, 1947. The worst industrial disaster in US history. The French-owned *Grandcamp*, docked at the oil and port town of Texas City, TX, and carrying a load of ammonium nitrate, was discovered to have a smoldering fire in the hold. At 9:12 AM, as onlookers gathered and a small firefighting team attempted to extinguish the blaze, the ship exploded with tremendous force, immediately killing everyone at the dock area. The resulting fires destroyed the nearby Monsanto Chemical Company and spread through oil pipelines into the city. At 1 AM, another ship, the *High Flyer*, exploded. The city was left defenseless due to the deaths of almost the entire fire department. There were 576 known casualties, but most estimate that at least 100 more died in the conflagrations. Thousands were injured. The fires burned for a week. The disaster prompted new regulations on handling chemicals. With thousands of lawsuits, the US Congress passed a special act to settle claims in 1956.

TEXAS HILL COUNTRY WINE & FOOD FESTIVAL. Apr 16–19. Austin, TX. 24th annual. Come on down to Austin and join world-renowned superstar chefs and sommeliers for four days of Texas-flavored events dedicated to the wine and food that have inspired us for more than two decades. Festivities include cooking classes, tastings, kitchen presentations and lots more. For info: Texas Hill Country Wine & Food Festival, 12731 Research Blvd, Ste 112A, Austin, TX 78759. Phone: (512) 249-6300. Fax: (512) 249-6320. E-mail: info@texaswineandfood.org. Web: www.texaswineandfood .org.

USTINOV, PETER: BIRTH ANNIVERSARY. Apr 16, 1921. British actor and playwright born at London, England, Peter Ustinov wrote his first play at age 19. He performed on stage, television and the screen, winning two Oscars (for 1961's *Spartacus* and 1965's *Topkapi*) and several Emmys. He wrote dozens of plays, screenplays and novels and also directed several films, including the highly regarded 1962 version of *Billy Budd*. He played Agatha Christie's detective Hercule Poirot in several screen adaptations. He was knighted by Queen Elizabeth II and dedicated many years to fundraising for UNICEF. He died at Geneva, Switzerland, Mar 28, 2004.

VIRGINIA TECH SHOOTINGS: ANNIVERSARY. Apr 16, 2007. In the worst shooting in US history, a disturbed college student shot and killed 32 people on the Virginia Tech University campus at Blacksburg, VA.

WRIGHT, WILBUR: BIRTH ANNIVERSARY. Apr 16, 1867. Aviation pioneer, born at Millville, IN. Died at Dayton, OH, May 30, 1912. See also: "Wright Brothers First Powered Flight" (Dec 17).

Birthdays Today

Kareem Abdul-Jabbar, 62, Hall of Fame basketball player, born Lewis Ferdinand Alcindor, Jr, at New York, NY, Apr 16, 1947.

Edie Adams, 78, singer, actress, born Elizabeth Edith Enke at Kingston, PA, Apr 16, 1931.

Ellen Barkin, 54, actress (*Tender Mercies, Diner*), born New York, NY, Apr 16, 1955.

Jon Cryer, 44, actor ("Two and a Half Men," *Pretty in Pink, Hot Shots!*), born New York, NY, Apr 16, 1965.

Merce Cunningham, 90, dancer, choreographer, born Centralia, WA, Apr 16, 1919.

Luol Deng, 24, basketball player, born Wow, the Sudan, Apr 16, 1985.

Lukas Haas, 33, actor (*Witness, Rambling Rose*), born West Hollywood, CA, Apr 16, 1976.

Martin Lawrence, 44, comedian, actor (*Wild Hogs, Bad Boys, Big Momma's House*), born Frankfurt-am-Main, Germany, Apr 16, 1965.

Freddie Ljungberg, 32, soccer player, born Vittsjo, Sweden, Apr 16, 1977.

Pope Benedict XVI, 82, leader of the Roman Catholic Church, born Joseph Ratzinger at Marktl Am Inn, Germany, Apr 16, 1927.

Jay O. Sanders, 56, actor ("Crime Story," *Tucker: The Man and His Dream*), born Austin, TX, Apr 16, 1953.

Bobby Vinton, 74, singer, born Canonsburg, PA, Apr 16, 1935.

April 2009

S	M	T	W	T	F	S
			1	2	3	4
5	6	7	8	9	10	11
12	13	14	15	16	17	18
19	20	21	22	23	24	25
26	27	28	29	30		

April 17 — Friday

DAY 107 **258 REMAINING**

AMERICAN SAMOA: FLAG DAY. Apr 17. National holiday commemorating first raising of American flag in what was formerly Eastern Samoa in 1900. Public holiday with singing, dancing, costumes and parades.

ANSON, CAP: BIRTH ANNIVERSARY. Apr 17, 1852. Adrian Constantine ("Cap") Anson, Baseball Hall of Fame player and manager, born at Marshalltown, IA. Anson played professional baseball from 1871 through 1897 and is considered one of the game's greatest first basemen. As a manager, he piloted the Chicago White Stockings (today's Cubs) to five National League pennants and a .575 winning percentage. Inducted into the Hall of Fame in 1939. Died at Chicago, IL, Apr 18, 1922.

BAY OF PIGS INVASION LAUNCHED: ANNIVERSARY. Apr 17, 1961. More than 1,500 Cuban exiles invaded Cuba in an ill-fated attempt to overthrow Fidel Castro.

BLAH BLAH BLAH DAY. Apr 17. Today's the day to do any of the following, or whatever. Stop smoking, take out the trash, empty the cat litter, lose weight, pick up your clothes, put dirty dishes in the sink, get a job or quit your job. Annually, Apr 17. (©2006 by WH.) For info: Thomas & Ruth Roy, Wellcat Holidays, 2418 Long Ln, Lebanon, PA 17046. Phone: (717) 279-0184. E-mail: info@wellcat.com. Web: www.wellcat.com.

CAMBODIA FALLS TO THE KHMER ROUGE: ANNIVERSARY. Apr 17, 1975. Cambodia fell when its capital, Phnom Penh, was captured by the Khmer Rouge. The Pol Pot regime inaugurated "Year One," and the wholesale slaughter of intellectuals, political enemies and peasants began. As many as two million Cambodians perished. See also: "Pol Pot Overthrown: Anniversary" (Jan 7).

CHASE, SAMUEL: BIRTH ANNIVERSARY. Apr 17, 1741. Signer of the Declaration of Independence. Born at Somerset County, MD, he died June 19, 1811.

DOW JONES TOPS 3,000: ANNIVERSARY. Apr 17, 1991. The Dow Jones Index of 30 major industrial stocks topped the 3,000 mark for the first time.

ELLIS ISLAND FAMILY HISTORY DAY. Apr 17. By official proclamation of our nation's governors, Apr 17 has been designated as "Ellis Island Family History Day." Sponsored by The Statue of Liberty–Ellis Island Foundation, Inc, this annual day recognizes the achievements and contributions made to America by Ellis Island immigrants and their descendants. Historically, Apr 17 marks the day in 1907 when more immigrants were processed through the island than on any other day in its colorful history: 11,747 people. In addition, the Foundation has established the "Ellis Island Family Heritage Awards," which are given annually to a select number of Ellis Island immigrants or their descendants who have made a significant contribution to the American experience. For info: Elizabeth Oravetz, Statue of Liberty–Ellis Island Foundation, Inc, 17 Battery Pl, Ste 210, New York, NY 10004. Phone: (212) 561-4500. Fax: (212) 779-1990. E-mail: eoravetz@ellisisland.org. Web: www.ellisisland.org.

ETHNIC AWARENESS PROGRAMS. Apr 17–18 (also Apr 24–25). Macon, GA. 11th anniversary. To unite, educate and draw this diverse country together and to help its citizens understand one another's cultures, respect one another's differences and share one another's likenesses. Program will include informative films, racial discussions, skits, talent showcases, social events and the 11th annual Ethnic Awards Gala & Film Exposure Feast. Nominating rules available. Must submit by Jan 15, 2009. For info: Betty Jean Slater, Willis-Slater Productions, 2806 Kent, Macon, GA 31206. Phone: (478) 788-5419.

FIESTA SAN ANTONIO. Apr 17–26. San Antonio, TX. Ten days of culture, heritage, beauty and remembrance. Parades, carnivals, sports, fireworks, music, ethnic feasts, art exhibits, dances—more than 100 events. This colorful fiesta originated in 1891 with the Battle of Flowers parade honoring the memory of Texas heroes who fought against General Santa Anna for Texan independence at the Alamo and San Jacinto. Est attendance: 3,500,000. For info: Fiesta San Antonio Commission, Inc, 2611 Broadway, San Antonio, TX 78215-1022. Phone: (210) 227-5191 or (877) 723-4378. Fax: (210) 227-1139. Web: www.fiesta-sa.org.

"THE FRED WARING SHOW" TV PREMIERE: 60th ANNIVERSARY. Apr 17, 1949. Fred Waring was leader of the big band called the Pennsylvanians, which featured about 65 musicians and singers. The show aired on Sunday nights until 1954.

FRENCH QUARTER FESTIVAL. Apr 17–19. New Orleans, LA. This festival focuses on all that makes the Quarter special—art, antiques, food, music, shopping, lifestyles and the people. Free concerts on 16 stages, historic patio tours, parade, children's and other family activities. Est attendance: 450,000. For info: French Quarter Festivals, Inc, 400 N Peters St #205, New Orleans, LA 70130. Phone: (504) 522-5730 or (800) 673-5725. Fax: (504) 522-5711. E-mail: feedback@fqfi.org. Web: www.fqfi.org.

HISTORY MEETS THE ARTS. Apr 17–19. Gettysburg, PA. More than 75 artists, authors and artisans with history-related original artwork, special tours, historical films, book and print signings. Est attendance: 25,000. For info: Gettysburg CVB, PO Box 4117, Gettysburg, PA 17325. Phone: (717) 334-6274. Fax: (717) 334-1166. E-mail: info@gettysburg.travel. Web: www.gettysburg.travel.

HOLDEN, WILLIAM: BIRTH ANNIVERSARY. Apr 17, 1918. William Holden's first starring role was in *Golden Boy*. The actor, born at O'Fallon, IL, won an Oscar for his role in *Stalag 17* in 1953. He was found dead at Los Angeles, CA, Nov 16, 1981.

HOLIDAY IN DIXIE. Apr 17–26. Shreveport and Bossier City, LA. Ten days in April celebrating the beginning of spring with more than 50 events including carnival, tournaments, a treasure hunt and parades. Takes place throughout both cities. Est attendance: 200,000. For info: Holiday in Dixie, 220 Carroll St, Ste C-2, Shreveport, LA 71105. Phone: (318) 865-5555. Fax: (318) 868-9577. E-mail: doodah@holidayindixie.com. Web: www.holidayindixie.com.

INTERNATIONAL FORD MUSTANG DAY. Apr 17. Ford Mustang enthusiasts are encouraged to have car shows, cruises, parties and other events to celebrate the birthday of the Mustang automobile. For info: Mustang Club of America, 4051 Barrancas Ave, PMB 102, Pensacola, FL 32507. Phone: (850) 438-0626. Web: www.mustang.org.

KENTUCKY DERBY FESTIVAL. Apr 17–May 1. Louisville, KY. Civic celebration since 1956 as Louisville warms up for the Kentucky Derby. About 70 events, two-thirds of which are free to the public. Est attendance: 1,500,000. For info: Kentucky Derby Festival, Inc, 1001 S Third St, Louisville, KY 40203. Phone: (502) 584-6383. Fax: (502) 589-4674. E-mail: info@kdf.org. Web: www.kdf.org.

MENNONITE RELIEF SALE. Apr 17–18. Kansas State Fair Grounds, Hutchinson, KS. More than 70 Mennonite, Brethren in Christ and Amish congregations in Kansas sponsor this annual festival and benefit auction for the worldwide hunger-relief and community-aid programs of the Mennonite Central Committee. Auctions of quilts, grandfather clocks, furniture, tools and crafts. Great food and lots more. No vendors. Est attendance: 24,000. For info: Rod Chrystie, 6113 S Broadacres Rd, Hutchinson, KS 67501. Phone: (620) 665-7406. Web: www.kansas.mccsale.org.

MOON PHASE: LAST QUARTER. Apr 17. Moon enters Last Quarter phase at 9:36 AM, EDT.

MORGAN, JOHN PIERPONT: BIRTH ANNIVERSARY. Apr 17, 1837. American financier and corporation director, born at Hartford, CT. Morgan died Mar 31, 1913, at Rome, Italy, leaving an estate valued at more than $70 million.

NAB 2009/NATIONAL BROADCASTERS CONVENTION. Apr 17–23. Las Vegas Convention Center, Las Vegas, NV. World's largest convention of radio, television and other types of multimedia. The awards for the National Broadcasting Hall of Fame are also presented at the convention. For info: Natl Assn of Broadcasters, 1771 N St NW, Washington, DC 20036-2891. Phone: (202) 429-5300. Fax: (202) 429-4199. E-mail: nab@nab.org. Web: www.nab.org/conventions.

NATCHITOCHES JAZZ FESTIVAL. Apr 17–18. Natchitoches, LA. The event features numerous bands and food vendors. Annually, the third weekend of April. Est attendance: 25,000. For info: Calendar of Events, Natchitoches Parish Tourism Commission, 781 Front St, Natchitoches, LA 71457. Phone: (318) 352-8072 or (800) 259-1714. Fax: (318) 352-2415. Web: www.natchitoches.net or www.natchjazzfest.com.

NETHERLANDS AND SCILLY ISLES PEACE: ANNIVERSARY. Apr 17, 1986. The 335-year "state of war" that had existed between the Netherlands and the Scilly Isles came to an end on this date when Dutch ambassador Jonkheer Huydecoper flew to the Scilly Isles to deliver a proclamation terminating the war that had started in 1651. Though hostilities had ceased three centuries earlier, a standing joke in the islands was that no one had bothered to declare an end to the war.

REASONER, HARRY: BIRTH ANNIVERSARY. Apr 17, 1923. American television journalist Harry Reasoner was born at Dakota City, IA. In 1956 Reasoner joined CBS News, where he anchored the "CBS Sunday News" (1963–70) and was one of the two original anchors, along with Mike Wallace, of the newsmagazine show "60 Minutes." He was coanchor of the "ABC Evening News" from 1970 until 1978, when he returned to CBS and "60 Minutes." He died Aug 6, 1991, at Norwalk, CT.

SOLIDARITY GRANTED LEGAL STATUS: 20th ANNIVERSARY. Apr 17, 1989. After nearly a decade of struggle and suppression the Polish labor union Solidarity was granted legal status, clearing the way for the downfall of the Polish Communist Party. Solidarity and the Polish people surprised the government by winning 99 of the 100 parliamentary seats in the election. General Wojciech Jaruzelski was elected president on July 19 and nominated Czelaw Kiszczak prime minister, enraging the Lech Walesa–led Solidarity. On Aug 7 Walesa swayed the traditional allies of the Communist Party—the United Peasant and Democratic parties—to switch sides. Kiszczak resigned as prime minister a week later after failing to form a government, forcing Jaruzelski to accept the principle of a government led by Solidarity.

SPACE MILESTONE: *COLUMBIA NEUROLAB* (US). Apr 17, 1998. Seven astronauts and scientists were launched with 2,000 animals (crickets, mice, snails and fish) to study the nervous system in space.

STAMP & COIN EXPO. Apr 17–19. Hotel Pennsylvania, New York, NY. Annual expo. Est attendance: 10,000. For info: Israel Bick, Exec Dir, Intl Stamp & Coin Collectors Society, PO Box 854, Van Nuys, CA 91408. Phone: (818) 997-6496. Fax: (818) 988-4337. E-mail: iibick@sbcglobal.net. Web: www.bick.net.

STEIGER, ROD: BIRTH ANNIVERSARY. Apr 17, 1925. The magnetic character actor was born at Westhampton, NY. In a 50-year career, Steiger played a wide range of roles for some of the best directors of the day. He won a Best Actor Oscar for *In the Heat of the Night* and was also nominated for *On the Waterfront* and *The Pawnbroker*. He died at Los Angeles, CA, July 9, 2002.

SUGARLOAF ART FAIR. Apr 17–19. Rock Financial Showplace, Novi, MI. This show, now in its 15th year, features more than 200 nationally recognized craft designers and fine artists displaying and selling their original creations. Includes craft demonstrations, live music, specialty foods, children's entertainment, hourly gift certificate drawings and more. Est attendance: 15,000. For info: Sugarloaf Mountain Works, 200 Orchard Ridge Dr, #215, Gaithersburg, MD 20878. Phone: (800) 210-9900. Fax: (310) 253-9620. Web: www.sugarloafcrafts.com.

SYRIAN ARAB REPUBLIC: INDEPENDENCE DAY. Apr 17. Official holiday. Proclaimed independence from League of Nations mandate under French administration in 1946.

VERRAZANO DAY: ANNIVERSARY. Apr 17, 1524. Celebrates discovery of New York harbor by Giovanni Verrazano, Florentine navigator, 1485–1527.

WILDER, THORNTON: BIRTH ANNIVERSARY. Apr 17, 1897. Pulitzer Prize–winning American playwright (*Our Town*) and novelist, born at Madison, WI. Died at Hamden, CT, Dec 7, 1975.

WORLD'S LARGEST TRIVIA CONTEST. Apr 17–19. Stevens Point, WI. More than 12,000 players, including more than 500 teams, compete to answer eight questions every hour for 54 hours straight. Prize: Oscar-like trophy. Est attendance: 15,000. For info: Jim Oliva, WWSP Radio, 105 CAC Reserve St, Stevens Point, WI 54481. Phone: (715) 344-8471. E-mail: theoz@dwave.net. Web: www.90fmtrivia.org.

Birthdays Today

Sean Bean, 51, actor (*Lord of the Rings: Fellowship of the Ring; Stormy Monday, Patriot Games*), born Sheffield, Yorkshire, England, Apr 17, 1958.

Victoria Adams Beckham, 34, actress, singer (Posh Spice of Spice Girls), born Hertfordshire, England, Apr 17, 1975.

Norman Julius "Boomer" Esiason, 48, broadcaster and former football player, born West Islip, NY, Apr 17, 1961.

Jennifer Garner, 37, actress (*Juno, 13 Going on 30,* "Alias," "Felicity"), born Houston, TX, Apr 17, 1972.

Olivia Hussey, 58, actress (*Romeo and Juliet*), born Buenos Aires, Argentina, Apr 17, 1951.

Don Kirshner, 75, music publisher, promoter, born the Bronx, NY, Apr 17, 1934.

Cynthia Ozick, 81, feminist, writer, born New York, NY, Apr 17, 1928.

Liz Phair, 42, rock singer/songwriter, born New Haven, CT, Apr 17, 1967.

Lela Rochon, 43, actress (*Waiting to Exhale, Boomerang*), born Los Angeles, CA, Apr 17, 1966.

April 2009

S	M	T	W	T	F	S
			1	2	3	4
5	6	7	8	9	10	11
12	13	14	15	16	17	18
19	20	21	22	23	24	25
26	27	28	29	30		

April 18 — Saturday

DAY 108 **257 REMAINING**

ADULT AUTISM AWARENESS DAY. Apr 18. This day recognizes the challenges faced by those aging with autism, including higher education, independent living and career development. Annually, Apr 18. For info: Christina Koshzow, AHEADD, 353 Spahr St, Pittsburgh, PA 15232. E-mail: christina@aheadd.org. Web: www.aheadd.org.

CANADA: CONSTITUTION ACT OF 1982: ANNIVERSARY. Apr 18, 1982. Replacing the British North America Act of 1867, the Canadian Constitution Act of 1982 provided Canada with a new set of fundamental laws and civil rights. Signed by Queen Elizabeth II, at Parliament Hill, Ottawa, Canada, it went into effect at 12:01 AM, Sunday, Apr 19, 1982.

CRAWFORD, SAMUEL EARL "WAHOO SAM": BIRTH ANNIVERSARY. Apr 18, 1880. Major league baseball player with the Detroit Tigers, born at Wahoo, NE. Wahoo Sam played pro ball for 20 years, racking up a career batting average of .309. His record of 312 career triples still stands. He was inducted into the Baseball Hall of Fame in 1957. Crawford died June 15, 1968, at Hollywood, CA.

DARROW, CLARENCE SEWARD: BIRTH ANNIVERSARY. Apr 18, 1857. American attorney often associated with unpopular causes, from the Pullman strike in 1894 to the Scottsboro case in 1932, born at Kinsman, OH. At the Scopes trial, July 13, 1925, Darrow said: "I do not consider it an insult, but rather a compliment, to be called an agnostic. I do not pretend to know where many ignorant men are sure—that is all that agnosticism means." Darrow died at Chicago, IL, Mar 13, 1938.

GEORGIA RENAISSANCE SPRING FESTIVAL. Apr 18–June 7. Atlanta, GA. A rollicking rendition of a 16th-century English faire. Jousting knights, jugglers, Shakespearean parodies and more than 100 shows daily. Feast like a king and shop like royalty. Saturdays, Sundays and Memorial Day. Est attendance: 200,000. For info: Sarah Petermann, Georgia Renaissance Festival, PO Box 986, Fairburn, GA 30213. Phone: (770) 964-8575. Fax: (770) 964-1477.

HISTORIC GARDEN WEEK IN VIRGINIA. Apr 18–26. This annual statewide event, celebrating its 76th anniversary, is billed as "America's Largest Open House." Showcases more than 250 of Virginia's finest homes, gardens, plantations and landmark properties on more than 30 separate tours on different days of the week. A 225-page guidebook is available February 2009. Please mail a contribution of $6 to cover postage and handling. Est attendance: 40,000. For info: Historic Garden Week, Garden Club of Virginia, 12 E Franklin St, Richmond, VA 23219. Phone: (804) 644-7776. Fax: (804) 644-7778. E-mail: gdnweek@verizon.net. Web: www.VAGardenweek.org.

THE HOUSE THAT RUTH BUILT: ANNIVERSARY. Apr 18, 1923. More than 74,000 fans attended Opening Day festivities as the New York Yankees inaugurated their new stadium. Babe Ruth christened it with a game-winning three-run homer into the right-field bleachers. In his coverage of the game for the *New York Evening Telegram* sportswriter Fred Lieb described Yankee Stadium as "The House That Ruth Built," and the name stuck.

INTERNATIONAL AMATEUR RADIO DAY. Apr 18. Annual, international day recognizing the services and accomplishments of amateur radio operators in wireless technology, emergencies and education. Sponsored by the ARRL, the national association for amateur radio. For info: Allen Pitts, ARRL, 225 Main St, Newington, CT 06111. Phone: (860) 594-0328. Fax: (860) 594-0259. E-mail: apitts@arrl.org. Web: www.arrl.org.

JAPAN BOMBED: ANNIVERSARY. Apr 18, 1942. For the first time during WWII, the mainland of Japan was bombed. Brigade General James Doolittle led a squadron of B-25s from the US carrier *Hornet*. Cities bombed included Tokyo, Yokohama, Kobe and Nagoya. Doolittle said that they flew so low that "one of our party observed a ball game in progress." Although the bombers did little damage, the psychological victory was enormous.

JUST PRAY NO: WORLDWIDE WEEKEND PRAYER AND FASTING. Apr 18–19. 19th annual. Churches throughout the world. Concerts of prayer, fasting, street rallies and marches to gain media attention. Bible studies and sermons concerning alcoholism and drug abuse and revival meetings aimed at those bound by addiction. For info: Just Pray No, Ltd, 1875 Sunset Point Rd, #704, Clearwater, FL 33765. E-mail: justprayno@aol.com. Web: www.justprayno.org.

MOSSY CREEK BARNYARD FESTIVAL. Apr 18–19 (also Oct 17–18). Warner Robins, GA. Arts and crafts chosen from best in the nation; heritage crafts, country and folk music and folk tales in relaxed atmosphere. Semiannually, the third weekend of April (usually) and of October. Est attendance: 25,000. For info: Carolyn Chester, Mossy Creek Barnyard Festival, Inc, 106 Anne Dr, Warner Robins, GA 31093. Phone: (478) 922-8265. E-mail: echester@bellsouth.net. Web: www.mossycreekfestival.com.

NATIONAL AUCTIONEERS DAY. Apr 18. Recognizes the auction profession and its contribution to American commerce. Annually, the third Saturday in April. For info: Natl Auctioneers Assn, 8880 Ballentine, Overland Park, KS 66214. Phone: (913) 541-8084. Fax: (913) 894-5281. E-mail: publicrelations@auctioneers.org. Web: www.auctioneers.org.

NATIONAL WILDLIFE WEEK. Apr 18–26. Children, teens and adults are invited to connect with nature during National Wildlife Week. Activities include environmental service projects addressing climate change, healthy habitats and connecting with the environment. Participants are also encouraged to participate in the National Wildlife Watch. National Wildlife Week has been observed since 1938. For info: Natl Wildlife Federation, 11100 Wildlife Center Dr, Reston, VA 20190. Phone: (703) 438-6000. E-mail: nationalwildlifeweek@nwf.org. Web: www.nwf.org.

PAUL REVERE'S RIDE: ANNIVERSARY. Apr 18, 1775. The "Midnight Ride" of Paul Revere and William Dawes started at about 10 PM to warn American patriots between Boston, MA, and Concord, MA, of the approaching British.

PET OWNERS INDEPENDENCE DAY. Apr 18. Dog and cat owners take the day off from work and the pets go to work in their place, since most pets are jobless, sleep all day and do not even take out the trash. (©2006 by WH.) For info: Thomas & Ruth Roy, Wellcat Holidays, 2418 Long Ln, Lebanon, PA 17046. Phone: (717) 279-0184. E-mail: info@wellcat.com. Web: www.wellcat.com.

"REAL PEOPLE" TV PREMIERE: 30th ANNIVERSARY. Apr 18, 1979. Real people do the darnedest things—from making paintings out of lint to making houses out of aluminum cans. NBC developed the program to spotlight the achievements, funny inventions and extraordinary stunts of ordinary Americans. Hosts of the show included Fred Willard, Sarah Purcell, John Barbour, Skip Stephenson, Byron Allen and Peter Billingsley. The show aired until 1984.

RECORD STORE DAY. Apr 18. 2nd annual. Hundreds of independently owned music stores across the country will celebrate Record Store Day. On this day, all of these stores will simultaneously link and act as one with the purpose of celebrating the culture and unique place that they occupy both in their local communities and nationally. Check your local record store for special events—including artist appearances. Brought to you by AIMS, CIMS, MMN, Newbury Comics and the Value Music Group of Indie Stores. Annually, the third Saturday in April. For info: Record Store Day. E-mail: information@recordstoreday.com. Web: www.recordstoreday.com.

RESPECT YOUR MOTHER. Apr 18. Jenkinson's Aquarium, Point Pleasant Beach, NJ. Celebrate Earth Day in a positive way—learn what you can do to help the environment. Free activities with paid admission 1–4 PM. Est attendance: 1,200. For info: Jenkinson's Aquarium, 300 Ocean Ave, Point Pleasant Beach, NJ 08742. Phone: (732) 899-1212. Fax: (732) 899-1717. E-mail: jenkinsonsaquarium@comcast.net. Web: www.jenkinsons.com.

SAN FRANCISCO 1906 EARTHQUAKE: ANNIVERSARY. Apr 18, 1906. Business section of San Francisco, some 10,000 acres, destroyed by earthquake. First quake at 5:13 AM, followed by fire. Nearly 4,000 lives lost.

SURRENDER AT DURHAM STATION: ANNIVERSARY. Apr 18, 1865. Union general William Tecumseh Sherman and Confederate general Joseph Johnston signed a broad political peace agreement at Durham Station, NC. The agreement promised a general amnesty for all Southerners and pledged federal recognition of all Southern state governments after their officials took an oath of allegiance to the US. Sherman was roundly criticized for his role in drawing up the agreement, although he based it on an earlier conversation with Lincoln and Grant. The agreement was rejected by President Andrew Johnson, and Sherman and Johnston were forced to reach a new agreement with terms virtually the same as those given Robert E. Lee.

TEACH YOUR DAUGHTER TO VOLUNTEER DAY. Apr 18. On this day we are encouraging awareness of volunteerism by "stepping out and volunteering together" with our daughters or younger women. By volunteering, they are helping others while also building stronger characters. The younger woman, stepping out with enthusiasm, compassion and charity to volunteer, improves her community and builds a stronger nation. Annually, the third Saturday in April. For info: Brenda Anderson, Women Empowering Women and Inspiring Now!, 1745 Pennsylvania Ave NW, Ste 218, Washington, DC 20006. Phone: (281) 537-1993. E-mail: StepOutVolunteer@aim.com. Web: www.womenempoweringwomen.homestead.com.

"THIRD WORLD" DAY: ANNIVERSARY. Apr 18, 1955. Anniversary of the first use of the phrase "third world," which was by Indonesia's President Sukarno in his opening speech at the Bandung Conference. Representatives of nearly 30 African and Asian countries (2,000 attendees) heard Sukarno praise the American war of independence, "the first successful anticolonial war in history." More than half the world's population, he said, was represented at this "first intercontinental conference of the so-called colored peoples, in the history of mankind." The phrase and the idea of a "third world" rapidly gained currency, generally signifying the aggregate of nonaligned peoples and nations—the nonwhite and underdeveloped portion of the world.

***TITAN 34-D* ROCKET FAILURE: ANNIVERSARY.** Apr 18, 1986. Launched from Vandenburg Air Force Base, CA, the $65 million *Titan* exploded when it was only a few hundred feet into flight, destroying the $500 million *KH-11* reconnaissance satellite payload. Poisonous fumes were released by the explosion, causing concern for the safety of people in nearby communities.

ZIMBABWE: INDEPENDENCE DAY. Apr 18. National holiday commemorates the recognition by Great Britain of Zimbabwean independence on this day in 1980. Prior to this, the country had been the British colony of Southern Rhodesia.

April 2009

S	M	T	W	T	F	S
			1	2	3	4
5	6	7	8	9	10	11
12	13	14	15	16	17	18
19	20	21	22	23	24	25
26	27	28	29	30		

Birthdays Today

America Ferrera, 25, actress ("Ugly Betty," *The Sisterhood of the Traveling Pants*), born Los Angeles, CA, Apr 18, 1984.

Barbara Hale, 88, actress ("Perry Mason"), born DeKalb, IL, Apr 18, 1921.

Melissa Joan Hart, 33, actress ("Sabrina the Teenage Witch"), born Long Island, NY, Apr 18, 1976.

Cheryl Ann Haworth, 26, weight lifter, born Savannah, GA, Apr 18, 1983.

Robert Hooks, 72, actor, director, producer (*Star Trek III: The Search for Spock*; stage: *Day of Absence*), born Washington, DC, Apr 18, 1937.

John James, 53, actor ("Search for Tomorrow," "Dynasty"), born Minneapolis, MN, Apr 18, 1956.

Jane Leeves, 48, actress ("Murphy Brown," "Frasier"), born East Grinstead, England, Apr 18, 1961.

Dorothy Lyman, 62, actress ("All My Children," "Mama's Family"), director, born Minneapolis, MN, Apr 18, 1947.

Eric McCormack, 46, actor ("Lonesome Dove," "Will & Grace"), born Toronto, ON, Canada, Apr 18, 1963.

Hayley Mills, 63, actress (*Pollyana, The Parent Trap, The Moon Spinners*), born London, England, Apr 18, 1946.

Rick Moranis, 55, actor, writer (*Ghostbusters*; *Honey, I Shrunk the Kids*), born Toronto, ON, Canada, Apr 18, 1954.

Conan O'Brien, 46, host ("Late Night with Conan O'Brien"), born Brookline, MA, Apr 18, 1963.

John Pankow, 55, actor ("Law & Order," "Mad About You"), born St. Louis, MO, Apr 18, 1954.

Eric Roberts, 53, actor (*Runaway Train, Star 80*), born Biloxi, MS, Apr 18, 1956.

David Tennant, 38, actor ("Doctor Who," *Harry Potter and the Goblet of Fire*), born Bathgate, West Lothian, Scotland, Apr 18, 1971.

James Woods, 62, actor ("Shark," *Holocaust, The Onion Field*), born Vernal, UT, Apr 18, 1947.

April 19 — Sunday

DAY 109 **256 REMAINING**

ADMINISTRATIVE PROFESSIONALS WEEK. Apr 19–25. Acknowledgment of the contributions of all administrative professionals and their vital roles in business, industry, education and government. Annually, the last full week (Sunday–Saturday) in April. Administrative Professionals Day is observed on Wednesday of this week (Apr 22 in 2009). For info: Intl Assn of Administrative Professionals, 10502 NW Ambassador Dr, PO Box 20404, Kansas City, MO 64195-0404. Phone: (816) 891-6600, ext 2239. Fax: (816) 891-9118. E-mail: rstroud@iaap-hq.org. Web: www.iaap-hq.org.

BATTLE OF LEXINGTON AND CONCORD: ANNIVERSARY. Apr 19, 1775. Massachusetts. Start of the American Revolution as the British fired the "shot heard 'round the world."

BRANCH DAVIDIAN FIRE AT WACO: ANNIVERSARY. Apr 19, 1993. After a 51-day standoff between the Branch Davidians and law-enforcement groups, the compound of the religious cult burned to the ground with 86 of its members inside, near Waco, TX, after federal agents began battering the compound with armored vehicles. Nine people escaped, but the 86 who perished included 17 children and the cult's leader, David Koresh.

CONSUMER AWARENESS WEEK. Apr 19–24. Consumer advocate Bob O'Brien kicks off a weeklong event aimed at advising and helping consumers with their rights. For info: Bob O'Brien, Consumer Advocate, 1061 Koelle Blvd, Secaucus, NJ 07094. Phone: (646) 233-6610. E-mail: robtfobrien@aol.com.

EXPLOSION ON THE USS *IOWA*: 20th ANNIVERSARY. Apr 19, 1989. In one of the worst naval disasters since the war in Vietnam, a freak explosion rocked the battleship USS *Iowa*, killing 47 sailors. The explosion occurred in the number 2 gun turret as the *Iowa* was participating in gunnery exercises about 300 miles northeast of Puerto Rico.

GARFIELD, LUCRETIA RUDOLPH: BIRTH ANNIVERSARY. Apr 19, 1832. Wife of James Abram Garfield, 20th president of the US, born at Hiram, OH. Died at Pasadena, CA, Mar 14, 1918.

JOHN PARKER DAY. Apr 19. Remembering John Parker's order, at Lexington Green, Apr 19, 1775: "Stand your ground. Don't fire unless fired upon; but if they mean to have a war, let it begin here." Parker, revolutionary soldier, captain of minutemen, born at Lexington, MA, July 13, 1729. Died Sept 17, 1775.

MOORE, DUDLEY: BIRTH ANNIVERSARY. April 19, 1935. British comedian, actor and classically trained pianist born at Dagenham, near London. Initially pursuing a career as a concert and jazz pianist, Moore was invited by Peter Cook to join the comedy revue *Beyond the Fringe*. Moore was best known for his movies *10* and *Arthur*, for which he was nominated for an Oscar. Moore died at New Jersey on Mar 27, 2002.

NATIONAL COIN WEEK. Apr 19–25. 87th annual. Discover the world of money and the hobby of coin collecting. Annually, the third full week of April, Sunday through Saturday. For info: Andy Dickes, American Numismatic Assn, 818 N Cascade Ave, Colorado Springs, CO 80903. Phone: (719) 632-2646 or (800) 367-9723. E-mail: pr@money.org. Web: www.money.org.

✦ **NATIONAL CRIME VICTIMS' RIGHTS WEEK.** Apr 19–25 (tentative). Date varies—a week in April.

NATIONAL HANGING OUT DAY. Apr 19. Project Laundry List joins hundreds of organizations from around the country to educate communities about energy consumption. National Hanging Out Day was created to demonstrate how it is possible to save money and energy by using a clothesline. Annually, Apr 19. For info: Project Laundry List, Inc, 27 Holly St, Ste A, Concord, NH 03301. Phone/fax: (603) 226-3098. E-mail: info@laundrylist.org. Web: www.laundrylist.org.

NATIONAL INSPIRATIONAL NEWS WEEK. Apr 19–25. Organizations across the country are encouraged to pitch inspiring stories that make a difference in their communities. Local media are also encouraged to participate and promote the week through local public service announcements. This designated week coincides with National Volunteer Week. For info: Shawne Duperon, 29558 English Way, Novi, MI 48377. Phone: (248) 669-1868. Fax: (248) 669-5509. E-mail: shawne@shawnetv.com. Web: www.shawnetv.com.

NATIONAL KARAOKE WEEK. Apr 19–25. Karaoke has grown by leaps and bounds in the US. Though it was once thought to be a fad, more and more people are recognizing the benefits of karaoke —increased self-esteem, confidence and stress release. Annually, the fourth week in April. For info: Visual Perspectives, 1083 W 124th Dr, Westminster, CO 80234-1757. E-mail: shirai2@comcast.net.

✦ **NATIONAL PARK WEEK.** Apr 19–25 (tentative).

NATIONAL PLAYGROUND SAFETY WEEK. Apr 19–25. An opportunity for families, community parks, schools and child-care facilities to focus on preventing public playground–related injuries. Sponsored by the National Program for Playground Safety (NPPS), this event helps educate the public about the more than 200,000 children (that's one child every 2½ minutes) that require emergency room treatment for playground-related injuries each year. For info: Natl Program for Playground Safety, WRC 205, University of Northern Iowa, Cedar Falls, IA 50614-0618. Phone: (800) 554-PLAY. Fax: (319) 273-7308. Web: www.playgroundsafety.org.

✦ **NATIONAL VOLUNTEER WEEK.** Apr 19–25.

NESS, ELIOT: BIRTH ANNIVERSARY. Apr 19, 1903. The legendary Prohibition Era lawman was born at Chicago, IL. He gained lasting fame as the leader of the "Untouchables": young, dedicated federal agents handpicked by Ness who could not be bribed by the mobsters they were targeting. Ness especially went after Chicago gangster Al Capone's bootlegging business, which was finally brought down in 1931. After stints in other federal and municipal agencies, Ness died May 7, 1957, at Coudersport, PA—just before publication of his memoirs, *The Untouchables*, which went on to inspire a TV series and later a film.

NETHERLANDS–US DIPLOMATIC RELATIONS: ANNIVERSARY. Apr 19, 1782. Anniversary of establishment of America's oldest continuously peaceful diplomatic relations. On this date, the States General of the Netherlands United Provinces admitted John Adams (later to become second president of the US) as minister plenipotentiary of the young American republic. This was the second diplomatic recognition of the US as an independent nation. Within six months Adams had succeeded in bringing about the signing of the first Treaty of Amity and Commerce between the two countries (Oct 8, 1782).

NICARAGUA: CIVIL WAR TRUCE: ANNIVERSARY. Apr 19, 1990. The Contra guerrillas, the leftist Sandinistas and the incoming Chamorro government agreed to a truce, ending a nine-year civil war.

OKLAHOMA CITY BOMBING: ANNIVERSARY. Apr 19, 1995. A car bomb exploded outside the Alfred P. Murrah Federal Building at Oklahoma City, OK, at 9:02 AM, killing 168 people, 19 of them children at a day-care center; a nurse died of head injuries sustained while helping in rescue efforts. The bomb, estimated to have weighed 5,000 pounds, had been placed in a rented truck. The blast ripped off the north face of the nine-story building, leaving a 20-foot-wide crater and debris two stories high. Structurally unsound and increasingly dangerous, the bombed building was razed May 23. Timothy J. McVeigh, a decorated Gulf War army vet who is alleged to have been angered by the Bureau of Alcohol, Tobacco and Firearms (ATF) attack on the Branch Davidian compound at Waco, TX, exactly two years before, was convicted of the bombing and was executed June 11, 2001. The ATF had offices in the federal building. Terry L. Nichols, an army buddy of McVeigh's, was convicted of murder and conspiracy charges and was sentenced to life in prison.

ORTHODOX EASTER SUNDAY OR PASCHA. Apr 19. Observed by Eastern Orthodox churches on this date. Normally Easter falls on different Sundays in the Eastern and Western churches. See also: "Easter Sunday" (Apr 12).

PATRIOTS' DAY IN FLORIDA. Apr 19. A ceremonial day to commemorate the first blood shed in the American Revolution at Lexington and Concord in 1775.

POLICE OFFICERS WHO GAVE THEIR LIVES IN THE LINE OF DUTY WEEK. Apr 19–24. A week of events remembering all police officers nationwide who gave their lives to protect others. In addition, lectures on how famous crimes were solved. For info: Bob O'Brien, Consumer Advocate, 1061 Koelle Blvd, Secaucus, NJ 07094. Phone: (646) 233-6610. E-mail: robtfobrien@aol.com.

POPE BENEDICT XVI: ELECTION ANNIVERSARY. Apr 19, 2005. German cardinal Joseph Ratzinger was elected 265th pope of the Roman Catholic Church by a papal conclave of 115 cardinals after the death of Pope John Paul II.

RICARDO, DAVID: BIRTH ANNIVERSARY. Apr 19, 1772. Economist David Ricardo, whose writings greatly influenced later economic theory, was born at London, England. He is recognized as the man who first systematized economics. In his best-known work, *Principles of Political Economy and Taxation* (1817), he discussed wages and rent and the economic relationships among landlords, workers and owners of capital. In 1819 Ricardo purchased his own seat in the House of Commons and became a member of Parliament. He died Sept 11, 1823, at Gatcombe Park, Gloucestershire.

SHERMAN, ROGER: BIRTH ANNIVERSARY. Apr 19, 1721. (Old Style date.) American statesman, member of the Continental Congress (1774–81 and 1783–84), signer of the Declaration of Independence and of the Constitution, was born at Newton, MA. He also calculated astronomical and calendar information for an almanac. Sherman died at New Haven, CT, July 23, 1793.

SIERRA LEONE: NATIONAL HOLIDAY. Apr 19. Sierra Leone became a republic in 1971.

SKY AWARENESS WEEK. Apr 19–25. A celebration of the sky and an opportunity to appreciate its natural beauty, to understand sky and weather processes and to work together to protect the sky as a natural resource (it's the only one we have). Events are held at schools, nature centers, etc, all across the US. For info: Barbara G. Levine and H. Michael Mogil, How The Weatherworks, 1104 6th St S, Naples, FL 34102. Phone: (239) 592-6636. Web: www.weatherworks.com.

SPACE MILESTONE: *SALYUT* (USSR). Apr 19, 1971. The Soviet Union launched *Salyut*, the first manned orbiting space laboratory. It was replaced in 1986 by *Mir*, a manned space station and laboratory.

SWAZILAND: KING'S BIRTHDAY. Apr 19. National holiday. Commemorates the birth of King Mswati III, born Apr 19, 1968.

URUGUAY: LANDING OF THE 33 PATRIOTS DAY. Apr 19. National holiday. Commemorates the arrival in 1825 of Juan Lavelleja, an anticolonial leader, and his 33 fighters. This landing marked the first stage in the fight for independence from Brazil in 1828.

WARSAW GHETTO REVOLT: ANNIVERSARY. Apr 19, 1943. A prolonged revolt began at Warsaw, Poland, when German troops tried to resume deportation of Jewish residents of the Warsaw Ghetto to the Treblinka concentration camp. With only 17 rifles and handmade grenades, for almost a month 1,200 Jewish fighters resisted 2,100 German troops who were armed with machine guns. When the uprising ended on May 16, 300 Germans and 7,000 Jews had died and the Warsaw Ghetto lay in ruins.

WEEK OF THE YOUNG CHILD. Apr 19–25. To focus on young children and the importance of quality early childhood education. For info: Natl Assn for the Education of Young Children, 1313 L St NW, Ste 500, Washington, DC 20005. Phone: (800) 424-2460. Fax: (202) 328-1846. E-mail: naeyc@naeyc.org. Web: www.naeyc.org.

WOC NURSE WEEK. Apr 19–25. A national observance to honor wound ostomy and continence nurses. WOC Nurses Day is Apr 16. Annually, the third week in April. For info: Wound Ostomy and Continence Nurse Society, 15000 Commerce Pkwy, Ste C, Mount Laurel, NJ 08054. Phone: (888) 224-9626. Fax: (856) 439-0525. Web: www.wocn.org.

Birthdays Today

Hayden Christensen, 28, actor (*Shattered Glass; Star Wars* films), born Vancouver, BC, Canada, Apr 19, 1981.

Tim Curry, 63, actor (*The Rocky Horror Picture Show*; stage: *Amadeus, My Favorite Year, Spamalot*), born Cheshire, England, Apr 19, 1946.

Elinor Donahue, 72, actress ("Father Knows Best," "The Andy Griffith Show"), born Tacoma, WA, Apr 19, 1937.

James Franco, 31, actor (*Spider-Man* films, *James Dean, Annapolis*), born Palo Alto, CA, Apr 19, 1978.

Kate Hudson, 30, actress (*Fool's Gold; You, Me & Dupree; Almost Famous*), born Los Angeles, CA, Apr 19, 1979.

Ashley Judd, 41, actress (*High Crimes, Double Jeopardy, Kiss the Girls*), born Los Angeles, CA, Apr 19, 1968.

Hugh O'Brian, 79, actor ("The Life and Legend of Wyatt Earp," *Broken Lance, Ten Little Indians*), born Rochester, NY, Apr 19, 1930.

Tony Plana, 55, actor ("Ugly Betty," "Resurrection Boulevard"), born Havana, Cuba, Apr 19, 1954.

Alan Price, 67, singer, songwriter, born Fairfield, England, Apr 19, 1942.

Maria Sharapova, 22, tennis player, born Nyagan, Russia, Apr 19, 1987.

Al Unser, Jr, 47, race car driver, born Albuquerque, NM, Apr 19, 1962.

April 2009	S	M	T	W	T	F	S
				1	2	3	4
	5	6	7	8	9	10	11
	12	13	14	15	16	17	18
	19	20	21	22	23	24	25
	26	27	28	29	30		

April 20 — Monday

DAY 110 — **255 REMAINING**

BOSTON MARATHON—113th RUNNING. Apr 20. Boston, MA. The marathon begins in the rural New England town of Hopkinton, winds through eight cities and towns and finishes near downtown Boston. Always the third Monday in April. 20,000 participants. Athletes qualify by meeting time standards that correspond to age. Est attendance: 500,000. For info: Boston Athletic Assn, Boston Marathon, 40 Trinity Place, 4th Fl, Boston, MA 02116. Phone: (617) 236-1652. E-mail: mile27@baa.org. Web: www.baa.org.

CANADA: NEWFOUNDLAND: SAINT GEORGE'S DAY. Apr 20. Holiday observed at Newfoundland on Monday nearest Feast Day (Apr 23) of Saint George.

COLUMBINE HIGH SCHOOL KILLINGS: 10th ANNIVERSARY. Apr 20, 1999. At this high school at Littleton, CO, students Eric Harris and Dylan Klebold killed 12 other students, a teacher and then themselves.

ENGLAND: LONDON BOOK FAIR. Apr 20–22. Earls Court, London. One of the world's most important publishing events. Est attendance: 25,000. For info: London Book Fair, Oriel House, 26 The Quadrant, Richmond, England TW9 1DL. Web: www.londonbookfair.co.uk.

FRENCH, DANIEL CHESTER: BIRTH ANNIVERSARY. Apr 20, 1850. American sculptor, born at Exeter, NH. One of the most important artists of the 19th and early 20th centuries as a sculptor of public monuments, French is best known for his 1875 "Minute Man" statue at Concord, MA, and his 1922 statue of the seated Abraham Lincoln in the Lincoln Memorial at Washington, DC. French died at Stockbridge, MA, Oct 7, 1931. His home and studio at Stockbridge were donated to the National Trust for Historic Preservation and are open to the public. For info: Chesterwood, PO Box 827, Stockbridge, MA 01262-0827.

HAMPTON, LIONEL: BIRTH ANNIVERSARY. Apr 20, 1908. The jazz great was born at Louisville, KY. Hampton started out on piano and drums, but Louis Armstrong urged him to take up the vibraphone in 1930. Hampton went on to make that his signature instrument. He recorded and played with Armstrong, Benny Goodman, Dizzy Gillespie, Benny Carter and other legends before becoming a bandleader himself. He played almost up until his death on Aug 31, 2002, at New York, NY.

HITLER, ADOLF: BIRTH ANNIVERSARY. Apr 20, 1889. German dictator, obsessed with superiority of the "Aryan race." Hitler was born at Braunau am Inn, Austria. He rose in politics (despite a brief time in prison during which he wrote *Mein Kampf*) quickly as leader of the Nazis, feeding on German anger over the economy and WWI defeat. He also fanned violent anti-Semitism, which later resulted in millions of Jewish deaths in concentration camps. A German plebiscite vested sole executive power in Führer Adolf Hitler Aug 19, 1934. In seeking to increase German power, he started WWII in 1939. Facing certain defeat by the Allied Forces, he shot himself Apr 30, 1945, in a Berlin bunker where he had been hiding for more than three months.

LLOYD, HAROLD: BIRTH ANNIVERSARY. Apr 20, 1893. A comic genius of early American film, Harold Lloyd frequently played the boy-next-door whose distinguishing feature was his round horn spectacles. This character thrilled audiences in "daredevil" comedy featuring dangerous stunts (Lloyd never used a double). Lloyd's hits included *Safety Last* (1923), where he dangled from a building's clock face, *The Freshman* (1925) and *Speedy* (1928). The biggest box-office star of the 1920s, Lloyd survived with lesser success in the talkie 1930s. He was given an honorary Oscar in 1953 for being a "master comedian and good citizen." Born at Burchard, NE, Lloyd died on Mar 8, 1971, at Hollywood, CA.

LUDLOW MINE INCIDENT: 95th ANNIVERSARY. Apr 20, 1914. Miners struggling for recognition of their United Mine Workers Union were attacked at Ludlow, CO, by National Guard troops. The guardsmen were paid by the mining company. A tent colony was destroyed, five men and one boy were killed by machine-gun fire and 11 children and two women were burned to death.

NATIONAL PAPERBOARD PACKAGING WEEK. Apr 20–26. The Paperboard Packaging Council (PPC) sponsors this week to raise awareness of the environmental benefits of paperboard packaging. As part of this campaign, PPC publicizes municipal paperboard recycling programs to increase recycling rates nationwide. A program for school children demonstrates how paperboard packaging can be recycled and reused in planting saplings. Annually, beginning the third Monday in April. For info: Greg Erickson, PPC, 700 Princess St, Ste 202, Alexandria, VA 22314. Phone: (703) 836-3300. Fax: (703) 628-1173. E-mail: gerickson@ppcnet.org. Web: www.ppcnet.org.

NATIONAL WINDOW SAFETY WEEK. April 20–26. Designed to increase awareness of the importance of windows in home safety plans, including their use as emergency escape routes. This week will also address issues of children falling out of windows. For info: Terry Haycock, Public Relations, Natl Safety Council, 1121 Spring Lake Dr, Itasca, IL 60143-3201. Phone: (800) 621-7615. Web: www.nsc.org.

PATRIOTS' DAY IN MASSACHUSETTS AND MAINE. Apr 20. Commemorates battles of Lexington and Concord, 1775. Annually, the third Monday in April.

PUENTE, TITO: BIRTH ANNIVERSARY. Apr 20, 1923. The King of the Mambo—or "El Rey"—was born Ernesto Antonio Puente, Jr, at Spanish Harlem, New York City, to Puerto Rican parents. The legendary Puente had a career that spanned more than six decades, starting in 1937. He popularized the timbale but played many percussion instruments and was also a composer, arranger and bandleader. His album *Dance Mania* (1958) was an international bestseller, and he released more than 100 albums. His song "Oye Como Va" was covered by Carlos Santana and has become a classic. Puente won five Grammys, was inducted into the Jazz and Hispanic halls of fame and received a Smithsonian Lifetime Achievement Award. President Jimmy Carter pronounced him "The Goodwill Ambassador of Latin American Music." Puente died on May 31, 2000, at New York, NY.

SMITH, HOLLAND: BIRTH ANNIVERSARY. Apr 20, 1882. Considered the father of amphibious warfare, Holland "Howling Mad" Smith was born at Hatchechubie, AL. Smith developed techniques for amphibious assaults that involved coordination of land, sea and air forces. During WWII he led troops in assaults in the Marshall and Mariana Islands and also directed forces at Guam, Iwo Jima and Okinawa. Smith died Jan 12, 1967, at San Diego, CA.

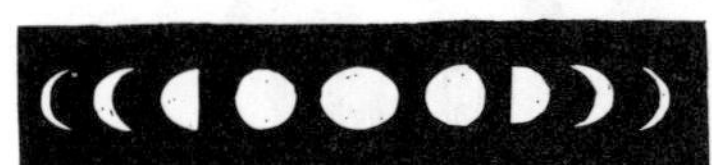

TAURUS, THE BULL. Apr 20–May 20. In the astronomical/astrological zodiac that divides the sun's apparent orbit into 12 segments, the period Apr 20–May 20 is traditionally identified as the sun sign of Taurus, the Bull. The ruling planet is Venus.

TUCSON INTERNATIONAL MARIACHI CONFERENCE. Apr 20–25. Tucson Convention Center, Tucson, AZ. An exciting festival that showcases the best in *baile folklórico* and mariachi. There are four events open to the public: the Participant Showcase, the Espectacular Concert, the Mariachi Mass and the Fiesta de Garibaldi. Contact us for the dates, times and locations of these events. The conference also includes workshops giving students of all ages the opportunity to study the music and dance of Mexico and learn from the masters. Est attendance: 50,000. For info: Lolie Gomez, Tucson Intl Mariachi Conference, 502 W 29th St, PO Box 3035, Tucson, AZ 85702. Phone: (520) 838-3908. Fax: (520) 792-9854. E-mail: lgomez@lafrontera.org. Web: www.tucsonmariachi.org.

WORLD'S BIGGEST FISH FRY. Apr 20–25. Henry County Fairgrounds, Paris, TN. Since 1953. More than 10,000 pounds of catfish will be served. Includes parades, arts and crafts show, auto shows and more. All-you-can-eat dinners are served at the fairgrounds. For info: Paris Chamber of Commerce, 2508 E Wood Rd, Paris, TN 38242. Phone: (731) 642-3431. E-mail: pariscoc@charterbn.com. Web: paristnchamber.com.

Birthdays Today

Carmen Electra, 36, actress ("Baywatch," "Singled Out"), born Cincinnati, OH, Apr 20, 1973.

Nina Foch, 85, actress (*Scaramouche*), born Leyden, Holland, Apr 20, 1924.

Crispin Glover, 45, actor (*Back to the Future, The People vs. Larry Flynt*), born New York, NY, Apr 20, 1964.

Jessica Lange, 60, actress (Oscars for *Tootsie* and *Blue Skies*; *Frances, Sweet Dreams*), born Cloquet, MN, Apr 20, 1949.

Joey Lawrence, 33, actor ("Blossom," "Brotherly Love"), born Strawbridge, PA, Apr 20, 1976.

David Leland, 62, actor (*Time Bandits*), writer, director (*Mona Lisa, Wish You Were Here*), born Cambridge, England, Apr 20, 1947.

Donald Arthur (Don) Mattingly, 48, former baseball player, born Evansville, IN, Apr 20, 1961.

Shemar Moore, 39, actor ("Criminal Minds"), host ("Soul Train"), born Oakland, CA, Apr 20, 1970.

Ryan O'Neal, 68, actor ("Peyton Place," *Love Story, Paper Moon*), born Los Angeles, CA, Apr 20, 1941.

Pat Roberts, 73, US Senator (R, Kansas), born Topeka, KS, Apr 20, 1936.

Steve Spurrier, 64, football coach and former player, born Miami Beach, FL, Apr 20, 1945.

John Paul Stevens, 89, Associate Justice of the US Supreme Court, born Chicago, IL, Apr 20, 1920.

April 21 — Tuesday

DAY 111 254 REMAINING

AGGIE MUSTER. Apr 21. Texas A&M University, College Station, TX, and around the world. A ceremony where current and former students (Aggies) of Texas A&M University gather together to recall their days at the university and to honor fellow Aggies who have died in the past year. During the ceremony, a Roll Call for the Absent is read and a comrade answers "here" for the deceased. The school's most sacred and time-honored tradition. First held in 1883, but in 1903 the Muster date was moved to Apr 21—San Jacinto Day. Celebrated on the school campus and at more than 400 locations around the world. Annually, Apr 21. Est attendance: 100,000. For info: The Assn of Former Students, 505 George Bush Dr, College Station, TX 77840-2918. Phone: (979) 845-7514. Fax: (979) 845-9263. E-mail: afs@aggienetwork.com. Web: www.aggienetwork.com.

BRASÍLIA INAUGURATED: ANNIVERSARY. Apr 21, 1960. At 9:30 AM, Brazil's new federal capital, Brasília, was inaugurated. The futuristic-looking city, located on the country's central plain and featuring the bold architecture of Oscar Niemeyer and others, was built in four years under the master plan of Lúcio Costa, who won a national contest to create a plan. The former capital was Rio de Janeiro.

BRAZIL: TIRADENTES DAY. Apr 21. National holiday commemorating execution of national hero, dentist Jose da Silva Xavier, nicknamed Tiradentes (tooth-puller), a conspirator in revolt against the Portuguese in 1789.

BRONTË, CHARLOTTE: BIRTH ANNIVERSARY. Apr 21, 1816. English novelist, born at Hartshead, Yorkshire, England. "Conventionality," she wrote in the preface to *Jane Eyre*, "is not morality. Self-righteousness is not religion. To attack the first is not to assail the last." She died Mar 31, 1855, at Haworth, Yorkshire, England.

CRAFT BREWERS CONFERENCE & BREWEXPO AMERICA®. Apr 21–24. Boston, MA (tentative). This conference (sponsored by the Brewers Association) is the number-one environment in North America for professional brewers, brewery owners and brewery marketing directors for concentrated, affordable brewing education and idea sharing to improve brewery quality and performance. This is the only industry event that serves both brewpubs and breweries. BrewExpo America allows exhibitors and buyers to develop profitable business relationships and helps them encounter the latest and the best that industry vendors have to offer. Est attendance: 1,200. For info: Brewers Assn, 736 Pearl St, Boulder, CO 80302. Phone: (303) 447-0816. Fax: (303) 447-2825. E-mail: events@brewersassociation.org. Web: www.CraftBrewersConference.com.

EIGHTY-NINER CELEBRATION. Apr 21–25. Guthrie, OK. 80th annual. In celebration of its heritage, this historically restored town features Old West gunfights, chuckwagon feed, professional rodeo and Oklahoma's largest parade of bands, floats and roundup clubs from across the state. Est attendance: 30,000. For info: American Legion, Post 58, 123 N 21st St, Guthrie, OK 73044. Phone: (405) 282-2589. Web: www.guthrieok.com or www.89erdays.com.

FESTIVAL OF RIDVAN. Apr 21–May 2. Annual Baha'i festival commemorating the 12 days (Apr 21–May 2, 1863) when Baha'u'llah, the prophet-founder of the Baha'i Faith, resided in a garden called Ridvan (Paradise) in Baghdad, at which time he publicly proclaimed his mission as God's messenger for this age. The first, ninth (Apr 29) and twelfth days are celebrated as holy days and are three of the nine days of the year when Baha'is suspend work. For info: Baha'is of the US, Office of Communications, 1233 Central St, Evanston, IL 60201. Phone: (847) 733-3559. Fax: (847) 733-3578. E-mail: ooc@usbnc.org. Web: www.bahai.us.

April 2009

S	M	T	W	T	F	S
			1	2	3	4
5	6	7	8	9	10	11
12	13	14	15	16	17	18
19	20	21	22	23	24	25
26	27	28	29	30		

FROEBEL, FRIEDRICH: BIRTH ANNIVERSARY. Apr 21, 1782. German educator and author Friedrich Froebel, who believed that play is an important part of a child's education, was born at Oberwiessbach, Thuringia. Froebel invented the kindergarten, founding the first one at Blankenburg, Germany, in 1837. Froebel also invented a series of toys that he intended to stimulate learning. (The American architect Frank Lloyd Wright as a child received these toys [maplewood blocks] from his mother and spoke throughout his life of their value.) Froebel's ideas about the role of directed play, toys and music in children's education had a profound influence in England and the US, where the nursery school became a further extension of his ideas. Froebel died at Marienthal, Germany, June 21, 1852.

HERITAGE ARTISANS WEEK. Apr 21–25. New Harmony, IN. Head to this historic village and watch crafters create 19th-century-style candles, baskets and pottery. Annually, the third week in April. Est attendance: 5,000. For info: Education Coordinator, Historic New Harmony, PO Box 579, New Harmony, IN 47631. Phone: (812) 682-4488. Fax: (812) 682-4313. E-mail: jkahle@usi.edu.

INDONESIA: KARTINI DAY. Apr 21. Republic of Indonesia. Honors the birth in 1879 of Raden Adjeng Kartini, pioneer in the emancipation of the women of Indonesia.

ISRAEL: HOLOCAUST DAY (YOM HASHOAH). Apr 21. Hebrew calendar date: Nisan 27, 5769. A day established by Israel's Knesset as a memorial to the Jewish dead of WWII. Anniversary in Jewish calendar of Nisan 27, 5705 (corresponding to Apr 10, 1945, in the Gregorian calendar), the day on which Allied troops liberated the first Nazi concentration camp, Buchenwald, north of Weimar, Germany, where about 56,000 prisoners, many of them Jewish, perished. Began at sundown Apr 20.

ITALY: BIRTHDAY OF ROME. Apr 21. Celebration of the founding of Rome, traditionally thought to be in 753 BC.

KINDERGARTEN DAY. Apr 21. A day to recognize the importance of play, games and "creative self-activity" in children's education and to note the history of the kindergarten. Observed on the anniversary of the birth of Friedrich Froebel, in 1782, who established the first kindergarten in 1837. German immigrants brought Froebel's ideas to the US in the 1840s. The first kindergarten in a public school in the US was started in 1873, at St. Louis, MO.

MANGANO, SILVANA: BIRTH ANNIVERSARY. Apr 21, 1930. Italian actress Silvana Mangano was born at Rome, Italy. She is best known for her role in the film *Bitter Rice* (1948). Mangano died Dec 16, 1989, at Madrid, Spain.

MUIR, JOHN: BIRTH ANNIVERSARY. Apr 21, 1838. American naturalist, explorer, conservationist and author for whom the 550-acre Muir Woods National Monument (near San Francisco, CA) is named. Muir, born at Dunbar, Scotland, emigrated to the US in 1849, where he urged establishment of national parks and profoundly influenced US forest conservation. Died at Los Angeles, CA, Dec 24, 1914.

NATIONAL TEACH CHILDREN TO SAVE DAY. Apr 21. More than 10,000 bankers visit classrooms across America to teach children of all ages the importance of saving and making fiscal fitness a lifetime habit. For info: American Bankers Assn Education Foundation, 1120 Connecticut Ave NW, Washington, DC 20036. Phone: (202) 663-5418. Fax: (202) 663-7578. Web: www.abaef.com.

QUINN, ANTHONY: BIRTH ANNIVERSARY. Apr 21, 1915. Actor, sculptor and painter, Anthony Rudolf Oaxaca Quinn was born at Chihuahua, Mexico, and moved to the US as a child. He became a US citizen in 1947. He won Academy Awards for Best Supporting Actor in 1952 for *Viva Zapata!* and in 1956 for *Lust for Life.* His best-remembered role was that of the title character in *Zorba the Greek*, for which he was nominated for Best Actor in 1964. He died at Boston, MA, on June 3, 2001.

RED BARON SHOT DOWN: ANNIVERSARY. Apr 21, 1918. German flying ace Baron Manfred von Richtofen was shot down and killed during the Battle of the Somme. The "Red Baron," so named for the color of his Fokker triplane, was credited with 80 kills in less than two years. Royal Flying Corps pilots recovered his body, and the Allies buried him with full military honors. Asked about his fighting philosophy, he was quoted as saying, "I am a hunter. My brother Lothar is a butcher. When I have shot down an Englishman, my hunting passion is satisfied for a quarter of an hour."

SAN JACINTO DAY. Apr 21. Texas. Commemorates Battle of San Jacinto in 1836, in which Texas won independence from Mexico. A 570-foot monument, dedicated on the 101st anniversary of the battle, marks the site on the banks of the San Jacinto River, about 20 miles from present-day Houston, TX, where General Sam Houston's Texans decisively defeated the Mexican forces led by Santa Anna in the final battle between Texas and Mexico.

SPACE MILESTONE: *COPERNICUS, OAO 4* (US). Apr 21, 1972. Launch of Orbiting Astronomical Observer, named in honor of the Polish astronomer.

Birthdays Today

Ed Belfour, 44, hockey player, born Carman, MB, Canada, Apr 21, 1965.

Tony Danza, 58, actor ("Taxi," "Who's the Boss?"), born Brooklyn, NY, Apr 21, 1951.

Queen Elizabeth II, 83, Queen of the United Kingdom, born London, England, Apr 21, 1926.

Charles Grodin, 74, actor (*Midnight Run, Beethoven*), director, host ("The Charles Grodin Show"), born Pittsburgh, PA, Apr 21, 1935.

Patti LuPone, 60, singer, stage and screen actress (Tonys for *Gypsy, Sweeney Todd* and *Evita*), born Northport, NY, Apr 21, 1949.

Andie MacDowell, 51, actress (*sex, lies, and videotape; Groundhog Day*), born Gaffney, SC, Apr 21, 1958.

Elaine May, 77, actress, writer (comedy with Mike Nichols), director (*A New Leaf*), born Philadelphia, PA, Apr 21, 1932.

Iggy Pop, 62, singer, born James Newell Osterberg, Jr, Ann Arbor, MI, Apr 21, 1947.

Tony Romo, 29, football player, born San Diego, CA, Apr 21, 1980.

April 22 — Wednesday

DAY 112 — **253 REMAINING**

ADMINISTRATIVE PROFESSIONALS DAY. Apr 22. Annually, the Wednesday of Administrative Professionals Week. For info: Emily Hoffman, Intl Assn of Administrative Professionals, 10502 NW Ambassador Dr, PO Box 20404, Kansas City, MO 64195-0404. Phone: (816) 891-6600, ext 2239. E-mail: ehoffman@iaap-hq.org. Web: www.iaap-hq.org.

AMERICAN QUILTER'S SOCIETY QUILT SHOW. Apr 22–25. Paducah, KY. 25th annual. More than 400 quilts are exhibited with $100,000 awarded in prizes. Lectures, workshops, quilt auction and fashion shows. Est attendance: 35,000. For info: American Quilter's Society, PO Box 3290, Paducah, KY 42002. Phone: (270) 898-7903. Fax: (270) 898-1173. Web: www.americanquilter.com.

BABE RUTH'S PITCHING DEBUT: 95th ANNIVERSARY. Apr 22, 1914. Babe Ruth made his professional pitching debut, playing for the Baltimore Orioles in his hometown. Allowing just six hits and contributing two singles himself, Ruth shut out the Buffalo Bisons, 6–0.

BRAZIL: DISCOVERY OF BRAZIL DAY. Apr 22. Commemorates discovery by Pedro Alvarez Cabral in 1500.

CHEMISTS CELEBRATE EARTH DAY. Apr 22. An environmental awareness campaign designed to enhance public awareness of important contributions made through chemistry in preserving our planet and improving our environment. The 2009 theme, "Air—The Sky's the Limit," focuses on the atmosphere. The American Chemical Society provides contests, resources, products and various other activities to engage local communities in the national celebration. For info: Office of Community Activities, American Chemical Society, 1155 16th St NW, Washington, DC 20036. Phone: (800) 227-5558, ext 6097. Fax: (202) 872-4353. E-mail: earthday@acs.org. Web: www.acs.org/earthday.

COINS STAMPED "IN GOD WE TRUST": ANNIVERSARY. Apr 22, 1864. By act of Congress, the phrase "In God We Trust" began to be stamped on all US coins.

EARTH DAY. Apr 22. Earth Day, first observed Apr 22, 1970, with message "New Energy for a New Era" and attention to accelerating the transition to renewable energy worldwide. Note: Earth Day activities are held by many groups on various dates, often on the weekends before and after Apr 22. Search for events online. For info: Earth Day Network, 1616 P St NW, Ste 340, Washington, DC 20036. Phone: (202) 518-0044. Fax: (202) 518-8794. Web: www.earthday.net.

FIRST SOLO TRIP TO NORTH POLE: 15th ANNIVERSARY. Apr 22, 1994. Norwegian explorer Borge Ousland became the first person to make the trip to the North Pole alone. The trip took 52 days, during which he pulled a 265-pound sled. Departing from Cape Atkticheskiy at Siberia Mar 2, he averaged about 18½ miles per day over the 630-mile journey. Ousland had traveled to the Pole on skis with Erling Kagge in 1990.

INTERNATIONAL WHISTLERS CONVENTION. Apr 22–26. Louisburg, NC. Music festival. Assemblage and contest of professional and amateur whistlers and whistle collectors. Contests for children, teens and adults. Est attendance: 2,500. For info: Allen de Hart, Dir, Franklin County Arts Council, Inc, PO Box 758, Louisburg, NC 27549. Phone: (919) 496-4771. Fax: (919) 496-1191.

LENIN, NIKOLAI: BIRTH ANNIVERSARY. Apr 22, 1870. Russian socialist and revolutionary leader (real name: Vladimir Ilyich Ulyanov), ideological follower of Karl Marx, born at Simbirst, on the Volga, Russia. Leader of the Great October Socialist Revolution of 1917. Died at Gorky, near Moscow, Jan 21, 1924. His embalmed body, in a glass coffin at the Lenin Mausoleum, has been viewed by millions of visitors to Moscow's Red Square.

NATIONAL JELLY BEAN DAY. Apr 22. A day to celebrate the colorful candy that has been around since Biblical times. For info: Natl Confectioners Assn, 8320 Old Courthouse Rd, Ste 300, Vienna, VA 22182. Phone: (730) 790-5750. Fax: (730) 790-5752. E-mail: info@CandyUSA.org. Web: www.CandyUSA.org.

OKLAHOMA DAY. Apr 22. Oklahoma.

OKLAHOMA LAND RUSH: ANNIVERSARY. Apr 22, 1889. At noon a gunshot signaled the start of the Oklahoma land rush as thousands of settlers rushed into the territory to claim land. Under pressure from cattlemen, the federal government opened 1,900,000 acres of central Oklahoma that had been bought from the Creek and Seminole tribes.

ROGER EBERT'S FILM FESTIVAL (EBERTFEST). Apr 22–26. Virginia Theatre, Champaign, IL. Spring film festival hosted by Roger Ebert, University of Illinois journalism graduate and Pulitzer Prize–winning film critic. Ebert selects 12 films representing a cross section of important cinematic works. He introduces each film and leads discussions on stage afterward for general audiences, distributors and international critics. Often in attendance are the films' producers, writers, actors or directors. Festival includes panel discussions. Sponsored by the College of Communications, University of Illinois. For info: Mary Susan Britt, University of Illinois,

College of Communications, 119 Gregory Hall, 810 S Wright St, Urbana, IL 61801. Phone: (217) 244-0552. Fax: (217) 333-9882. E-mail: marsue@uiuc.edu. Web: www.ebertfest.com.

 **Birthdays Today**

Byron Allen, 48, comedian, TV host ("Byron Allen Show," "Real People"), actor (*Case Closed*), born Detroit, MI, Apr 22, 1961.

Glen Campbell, 74, singer ("Gentle on My Mind," "By the Time I Get to Phoenix"), born Billstown, AR, Apr 22, 1935.

Francis Capra, 26, actor ("Veronica Mars," *A Bronx Tale*), born New York, NY, Apr 22, 1983.

Peter Frampton, 59, singer ("Show Me the Way," "Do You Feel Like We Do"), born Beckenham, England, Apr 22, 1950.

Eric Mabius, 38, actor ("Ugly Betty," "The L Word"), born Harrisburg, PA, Apr 22, 1971.

Chris Makepeace, 45, actor (*My Bodyguard*), born Montreal, QC, Canada, Apr 22, 1964.

Jack Nicholson, 73, actor (Oscars for *One Flew Over the Cuckoo's Nest, Terms of Endearment* and *As Good as It Gets*), born Neptune, NJ, Apr 22, 1936.

Charlotte Rae, 83, actress ("Diff'rent Strokes," "Facts of Life"), born Milwaukee, WI, Apr 22, 1926.

Ryan Stiles, 50, actor ("The Drew Carey Show," "Whose Line Is It Anyway?"), born Seattle, WA, Apr 22, 1959.

John Waters, 63, filmmaker (*Pink Flamingoes*), born Baltimore, MD, Apr 22, 1946.

April 23 — Thursday

DAY 113 — 252 REMAINING

"BAYWATCH" TV PREMIERE: 20th ANNIVERSARY. Apr 23, 1989. Set on a California beach, this program starred David Hasselhoff and a changing cast of nubile young men and women as lifeguards. Later the program was moved to Hawaii; the last episode was made in 2001. The most widely viewed TV series in the world, the program aired in 142 countries with an estimated weekly audience of 1.1 billion.

BERMUDA: PEPPERCORN CEREMONY. Apr 23. St. George. Commemorates the payment of one peppercorn in 1816 to the governor of Bermuda for rental of Old State House by the Masonic Lodge.

BIG TEN MEN'S TENNIS CHAMPIONSHIP. Apr 23–26. University of Michigan, Ann Arbor, MI. For info: Big Ten Conference, 1500 W Higgins Rd, Park Ridge, IL 60068-6300. Phone: (847) 696-1010. Fax: (847) 696-1110. Web: www.bigten.org.

April 2009

S	M	T	W	T	F	S
			1	2	3	4
5	6	7	8	9	10	11
12	13	14	15	16	17	18
19	20	21	22	23	24	25
26	27	28	29	30		

BIG TEN WOMEN'S TENNIS CHAMPIONSHIP. Apr 23–26. University of Wisconsin, Madison, WI. For info: Big Ten Conference, 1500 W Higgins Rd, Park Ridge, IL 60068-6300. Phone: (847) 696-1010. Fax: (847) 696-1150. Web: www.bigten.org.

BUCHANAN, JAMES: BIRTH ANNIVERSARY. Apr 23, 1791. 15th president of the US, born at Cove Gap, PA. Buchanan was the only president who never married. He served one term in office, Mar 4, 1857–Mar 3, 1861, and died at Lancaster, PA, June 1, 1868.

CERVANTES SAAVEDRA, MIGUEL DE: DEATH ANNIVERSARY. Apr 23, 1616. Spanish poet, playwright and novelist, died at Madrid, Spain. The exact date of his birth at Alcala de Henares is unknown, but he was baptized Oct 9, 1547. As soldier and tax collector, Cervantes traveled widely. He spent more than five years in prisons in Spain, Italy and North Africa. His greatest creation was Don Quixote, the immortal Knight of La Mancha whose profession was chivalry. Riding his nag, Rozinante, and accompanied by Squire Sancho Panza, Don Quixote tilts at windmills of the mind in the world's best-known novel. Nearly a thousand editions of *Don Quixote* (a bestseller since its first appearance in 1605) have been published, and it has been translated into more languages than any other book except the Bible.

ENGLAND: HARROGATE SPRING FLOWER SHOW. Apr 23–26. Great Yorkshire Showground, Harrogate, North Yorkshire. Spectacular exhibits and displays at Britain's premier spring show. Est attendance: 60,000. For info: Roger Brownbridge, Show Dir, North of England Horticultural Society, 4A South Park Rd, Harrogate, North Yorkshire, England HG1 5QU. Phone: (44) (1423) 561-049. Fax: (44) (1423) 536-880. E-mail: info@flowershow.org.uk. Web: www.flowershow.org.uk.

FIRST MOVIE THEATER OPENS: ANNIVERSARY. Apr 23, 1896. The first movie was shown at Koster and Bials Music Hall at New York City. Up until this time, people saw films individually by looking into a kinetoscope, a boxlike "peep show." This was the first time in the US that an audience sat in a theater and watched a movie together.

FIRST PUBLIC SCHOOL IN AMERICA: ANNIVERSARY. Apr 23, 1635. (New Style date.) The Boston Latin School opened—America's oldest public school.

ICELAND: "FIRST DAY OF SUMMER." Apr 23. A national public holiday, *Sumardagurinn fyrsti*, with general festivities, processions and much street dancing, especially at Reykjavik, greets the coming of summer. Flags are flown. Annually, the Thursday between Apr 19 and 25.

PEARSON, LESTER B.: BIRTH ANNIVERSARY. Apr 23, 1897. 14th prime minister of Canada, born at Toronto, Canada. He was Canada's chief delegate at the San Francisco conference where the UN charter was drawn up and later served as president of the General Assembly. He wrote the proposal that resulted in the formation of the North Atlantic Treaty Organization (NATO). He was awarded the Nobel Peace Prize. Died at Rockcliffe, Canada, Dec 27, 1972.

PHYSICISTS DISCOVER TOP QUARK: 15th ANNIVERSARY. Apr 23, 1994. Physicists at the Department of Energy's Fermi National Accelerator Laboratory found evidence for the existence of the subatomic particle called the top quark, the last undiscovered quark of the six predicted to exist by current scientific theory. The discovery provides strong support for the quark theory of the structure of matter. Quarks are subatomic particles that make up protons and neutrons found in the nuclei of atoms. The five other quark types that had already been proven to exist are the up quark, down quark, strange quark, charm quark and bottom quark. Further experimentation over many months confirmed the discovery, and it was publicly announced Mar 2, 1995.

PLANCK, MAX: BIRTH ANNIVERSARY. Apr 23, 1858. Formulator of the quantum theory, which revolutionized physics, born at Kiel, Germany. Einstein's application of quantum theory to light led to the theories of relativity. Planck died at Gottingen, Germany, Oct 3, 1947.

SAINT GEORGE: FEAST DAY. Apr 23. Martyr and patron saint of England, who died Apr 23, AD 303. Hero of the St. George and the dragon legend. The story says that his faith helped him slay a vicious dragon that demanded daily sacrifice after the king's daughter became the intended victim.

SHAKESPEARE, WILLIAM: BIRTH AND DEATH ANNIVERSARY. Apr 23. England's most famous and most revered poet and playwright. He was born at Stratford-on-Avon, England, Apr 23, 1564 (OS), was baptized there three days later and died there on his birthday, Apr 23, 1616 (OS). Author of at least 36 plays and 154 sonnets, Shakespeare created the most influential and lasting body of work in the English language, an extraordinary exploration of human nature. His epitaph: "Good frend for Jesus sake forbeare, To digg the dust enclosed heare. Blese be ye man that spares thes stones, And curst be he that moves my bones."

SPAIN: BOOK DAY AND LOVER'S DAY. Apr 23. Barcelona. Saint George's Day and the anniversary of the death of Spanish writer Miguel de Cervantes have been observed with special ceremonies in the Palacio de la Disputacion and throughout the city since 1714. Book stands are set up in the plazas and on street corners. This is Spain's equivalent of Valentine's Day. Women give books to men; men give roses to women.

TAKE OUR DAUGHTERS AND SONS TO WORK® DAY. Apr 23. A national public education campaign sponsored by the Ms. Foundation for Women in which children aged 8–12 go to work with adult hosts—parents, grandparents, cousins, aunts, uncles, friends. More than 16 million employed Americans participated in 2005 by bringing a boy or girl to work. Annually, the fourth Thursday in April. For info: Take Our Daughters and Sons To Work® Day, Ms. Foundation for Women, 120 Wall St, 33rd Fl, New York, NY 10005. Phone: (800) 676-7780. Fax: (212) 742-1531. E-mail: tods@ms.foundation.org. Web: www.DaughtersandSonstoWork.org.

TURKEY: NATIONAL SOVEREIGNTY AND CHILDREN'S DAY. Apr 23. Commemorates Grand National Assembly's inauguration in 1923.

UNITED NATIONS: WORLD BOOK AND COPYRIGHT DAY. Apr 23. By celebrating this day throughout the world, UNESCO seeks to promote reading, publishing and the protection of intellectual property through copyright. It was a natural choice for UNESCO's General Conference to pay a worldwide tribute to books and authors on Apr 23, because on this date and in the same year of 1616, Cervantes, Shakespeare and Inca Garcilaso de la Vega all died. It is also the date of birth or death of other prominent authors such as Maurice Druon, Halldor Laxness, Vladimir Nabokov, Josep Pla and Manuel Mejía Vallejo. Observed throughout the United Nations system. For info: United Nations, Dept of Public Info, New York, NY 10017. Web: www.un.org.

WASHINGTON STATE APPLE BLOSSOM FESTIVAL. Apr 23–May 3. Wenatchee, WA. 90th annual. To showcase the greater Wenatchee Valley and its people and heritage by producing an ongoing community celebration. Parades, arts and crafts, food concessions, entertainment in the park, theatrical productions, Youth Day and carnival. More than 40 events. Annually, the last weekend in April through the first weekend in May. Est attendance: 100,000. For info: Washington State Apple Blossom Festival, Box 2836, Wenatchee, WA 98807. Phone: (509) 662-3616. Fax: (509) 665-0347. E-mail: festival@appleblossom.org. Web: www.appleblossom.org.

WOODS, GRANVILLE T.: BIRTH ANNIVERSARY. Apr 23, 1856. Granville T. Woods was born at Columbus, OH. He invented the Synchronous Multiplex Railway Telegraph, which allowed communication between dispatchers and trains while the trains were in motion, which decreased the number of train accidents. In addition, Woods is credited with several other electrical inventions. Died Jan 30, 1910, at New York, NY.

Birthdays Today

Valerie Bertinelli, 49, actress ("One Day at a Time," *Silent Witness*), born Wilmington, DE, Apr 23, 1960.

David Birney, 69, actor ("Love Is a Many Splendored Thing," "Bridget Loves Bernie"), born Washington, DC, Apr 23, 1940.

Shirley Temple Black, 81, former ambassador to Ghana, child actress (*Heidi, Curly Top, Little Miss Marker*), TV hostess ("Shirley Temple's Storybook" and "Shirley Temple Theatre"), born Santa Monica, CA, Apr 23, 1928.

John Cena, 32, professional wrestler, born West Newbury, MA, Apr 23, 1977.

Judy Davis, 54, actress ("Life with Judy Garland," *Husbands and Wives, A Passage to India, My Brilliant Career*), born Perth, Australia, Apr 23, 1955.

Joyce Dewitt, 60, actress ("Three's Company"), born Wheeling, WV, Apr 23, 1949.

Jan Hooks, 52, actress ("Saturday Night Live," "Designing Women"), born Atlanta, GA, Apr 23, 1957.

Andruw Jones, 32, baseball player, born Wellemstad, Curacao, Netherlands Antilles, Apr 23, 1977.

Melina Kanakaredes, 42, actress ("CSI: New York," "Providence," "Guiding Light"), born Akron, OH, Apr 23, 1967.

Lee Majors, 69, actor ("The Six Million Dollar Man," "The Fall Guy"), born Wyandotte, MI, Apr 23, 1940.

Bernadette Devlin McAliskey, 62, political activist, born Cookstown, Northern Ireland, Apr 23, 1947.

Michael Moore, 55, author (*Dude, Where's My Country?*), filmmaker (Oscar for *Bowling for Columbine*; *Sicko, Fahrenheit 9/11*), born Flint, MI, Apr 23, 1954.

Kal Penn, 32, actor (*The Namesake, Harold & Kumar Go to White Castle*, "House"), born Montclair, NJ, Apr 23, 1977.

April 24 — Friday

DAY 114 | **251 REMAINING**

ARBOR DAY FESTIVAL. Apr 24–26. Nebraska City, NE. Celebrate Arbor Day, the tree planters' holiday, in the hometown of J. Sterling Morton, the founder of Arbor Day in 1872. Citywide events include the new community tree planting, commemorative tree planting and reception, tree-planting demonstrations and Arbor Day Farm Tree Adventure. Also featured: 5k run and walk, parade, children's festival, barbecue and a variety of live music venues. Est attendance: 25,000. For info: Nebraska City Tourism and Commerce, 806 1st Ave, Nebraska City, NE 68410. Phone: (800) 514-9113. Fax: (402) 873-6701. E-mail: tourism@nebraskacity.com. Web: www.nebraskacity.com.

ARBOR DAY IN ARIZONA. Apr 24. The last Friday in April is proclaimed as Arbor Day in Arizona. It is not a legal holiday.

ARMENIA: ARMENIAN MARTYRS DAY. Apr 24. Commemorates the massacre of Armenians under the Ottoman Turks in 1915. Deportations from Turkey began. Also called Armenian Genocide Memorial Day. Adolf Hitler, in a speech at Obersalzberg, Aug 22, 1939, is reported to have said, "Who today remembers the Armenian extermination?" in an apparent justification of the Nazis' use of genocide.

BASCOM, GEORGE N.: BIRTH ANNIVERSARY. Apr 24, 1836. West Point graduate Lieutenant George N. Bascom was assigned to search out Apache chief Cochise, believed to be responsible for an 1861 raid on an Arizona ranch. He arrested Cochise at Apache Pass, but the chief escaped and declared war, launching a reign of terror known as the Apache Wars. Bascom was born at Owingsville, KY, and died the year following his Apache adventure when he became a casualty of the Civil War battle at Fort Craig, Valverde, NM, Feb 21, 1862.

BIG TEN WOMEN'S GOLF CHAMPIONSHIPS. Apr 24–26. Purdue University, West Lafayette, IN. For info: Big Ten Conference, 1500 W Higgins Rd, Park Ridge, IL 60068-6300. Phone: (847) 696-1010. Fax: (847) 696-1110. Web: www.bigten.org.

CARTWRIGHT, EDMUND: BIRTH ANNIVERSARY. Apr 24, 1743. English cleric and inventor (developed the power loom and other weaving inventions) born at Nottinghamshire, England. He died at Hastings, Sussex, England, Oct 30, 1823.

CIVIL WAR REENACTMENT. Apr 24–26. Rand Park, Keokuk, IA. Battle reenactment, military ball, historic encampment, ladies' tea and style show and Civil War memorial service. Est attendance: 15,000. For info: Keokuk Area Conv and Tourism Bureau, 329 Main, Keokuk, IA 52632. Phone: (800) 383-1219 or (319) 524-5599. E-mail: info@keokukiowatourism.org. Web: www.keokukiowatourism.org.

DAFFODIL FESTIVAL WEEKEND. Apr 24–26. Nantucket Island, MA. Nantucket's traditional welcome to spring, when more than three million daffodils bloom and turn the countryside into a vivid, yellow tapestry. Events include the annual antique car parade, flower show, tailgate picnic and activities such as hiking, fishing, birdwatching and seal cruises. Est attendance: 6,000. For info: Nantucket Island Chamber of Commerce, Zero Main St, Nantucket, MA 02554-3595. Phone: (508) 228-1700. Web: www.nantucketchamber.org.

FORT MOORE ESTABLISHED: ANNIVERSARY. Apr 24, 1847. At the conclusion of the Mexican War, the Mormon Battalion of the Army of the West established Fort Moore overseeing the pueblo of Los Angeles. The fort was named in honor of their captain who had perished in the Battle of San Pascual.

GLOBAL YOUTH SERVICE DAYS. Apr 24–26. This 21st annual observance offers thousands of volunteer opportunities in all 50 states for young people, kindergarten and up. More than three million young Americans will serve in 3,000 communities. This is the world's largest volunteer event. More than 55 national organizations serve as partners for this event, which runs in conjunction with Global Youth Service Day. For info: Youth Service America, 1101 15th St NW, Ste 200, Washington, DC 20005-5002. Phone: (202) 296-2992. Web: www.ysa.org/nysd/.

HOLY SEE: NATIONAL HOLIDAY. Apr 24. The state of Vatican City and the Holy See observe Apr 24 as a national holiday (on the anniversary of the coronation day of the current pope).

INTERSTATE MULLET TOSS. Apr 24–26. Pensacola, FL. 25th annual. Intrepid fish flingers compete to see who can throw a dead, one-pound mullet the farthest, starting from a 10-foot-diameter circle in Alabama, into the state of Florida. A contribution for each fish flung goes to Local Youth Charities. Shuttles run between both states to the competition area. Annually, the last full weekend in April. For info: Flora-Bama, 17401 Perdido Key Dr, Pensacola, FL 32507. Phone: (850) 492-0611. Web: www.florabama.com.

IRELAND: EASTER RISING: ANNIVERSARY. Apr 24, 1916. Irish nationalists seized key buildings in Dublin and proclaimed an Irish republic. The rebellion collapsed, however, and it wasn't until 1922 that the Irish Free State, the predecessor of the Republic of Ireland, was established.

April 2009	S	M	T	W	T	F	S
				1	2	3	4
	5	6	7	8	9	10	11
	12	13	14	15	16	17	18
	19	20	21	22	23	24	25
	26	27	28	29	30		

LIBRARY OF CONGRESS: ANNIVERSARY. Apr 24, 1800. Congress approved an act providing "for the purchase of such books as may be necessary for the use of Congress . . . and for fitting up a suitable apartment for containing them." Thus began one of the world's greatest libraries.

MISSISSIPPI RIVER VALLEY SCENIC DRIVE. Apr 24–25. Mississippi River valley of southeast Missouri. Homemade goodies, quilt shows, history and tours, entertainment, demonstrations; several small towns participate. Annually, the fourth weekend in April. For info: Frank Nickell, One University Plaza, Southeast Missouri State University, Cape Girardeau, MO 63701. Phone: (573) 651-2555. Fax: (573) 651-5114. E-mail: fnickell@semo.edu.

MOON PHASE: NEW MOON. Apr 24. Moon enters New Moon phase at 11:23 PM, EDT.

NATIONAL ARBOR DAY. Apr 24. Since 1872, a day to honor and plant trees. Observed the last Friday in April (although some states have different dates), which is generally a good planting date throughout the country. First observance of Arbor Day was in Nebraska, Apr 10, 1872, where it is still a state holiday. For info: Natl Arbor Day Foundation, 100 Arbor Ave, Nebraska City, NE 68410. Web: www.arborday.org.

NATIONAL DREAM HOTLINE®. Apr 24–26. Now in its 21st year, the National Dream Hotline® is sponsored by the School of Metaphysics as an educational service to people throughout the world. Faculty and staff of the College and Schools of Metaphysics throughout the Midwest offer the benefits of more than 30 years of research into the significance and meaning of dreams by manning the hotline phones from 6 PM EDT, Friday until midnight Sunday. Annually, the last weekend in April. For info: Dr. Teresa Martin, School of Metaphysics, World Headquarters, 163 Moon Valley Rd, Windyville, MO 65783. Phone: (417) 345-8411. Fax: (417) 345-6668. E-mail: som@som.org. Web: www.som.org or www.dreamschool.org.

NATIONAL HAIRBALL AWARENESS DAY. Apr 24. A day to recognize and take steps to eliminate hairballs in cats. Hairballs are more than an inconvenience for cat owners: they cause great discomfort and irritation in our cat companions. Take steps now to stop this injustice of nature for our feline friends. Annually, the last Friday in April. For info: Dr. Blake Hawley, Hill's Pet Nutrition, Sherbourne House, Croxley Business Park, Hatters Lane, Watford, Herts WD18 8WX, United Kingdom. E-mail: Blake_Hawley@HillsPet.com. Web: www.ScienceDiet.com.

NATIONAL SCOOP THE POOP WEEK. Apr 24–30. Between the snowy storms of winter and the backyard barbecues of summer, now is the perfect time for dog owners to catch up on all those "canine calling cards" that have accumulated during the cold months. Besides creating a nasty mess in your yard, it's a health hazard, it pollutes the groundwater and it annoys the neighbors. It doesn't go away by itself, so get it cleaned up this week. And remind your dog-owning friends! Your family, neighbors and dog will love you for it. For info: Matthew Osborn, PO Box 28412, Columbus, OH 43228. E-mail: matthew@pooper-scooper.com. Web: www.pooper-scooper.com.

NEW ORLEANS JAZZ & HERITAGE FESTIVAL. Apr 24–May 3. New Orleans, LA. A two-weekend festival with hundreds of musicians playing. Evening concerts, outdoor daytime activities, Louisiana specialty foods and handmade crafts. Est attendance: 500,000. For info: New Orleans Jazz & Heritage Festival, 1205 N Rampart St, New Orleans, LA 70116. Phone: (504) 522-4786. Web: www.nojazzfest.com.

PANOPLY® 2009. Apr 24–26. Big Spring International Park, Huntsville, AL. Comprehensive arts festival celebrating its 28th year. Showcases the performing arts through a variety of music, theatre and dance. The festival includes five performance stages, family hands-on activities, juried art show and choreography competition. Children under 12 years of age have free admission. Est attendance: 70,000. For info: The Arts Council, 700 Monroe St, Ste 2,

Huntsville, AL 35801. Phone: (256) 519-ARTS. Fax: (256) 533-3811. Web: www.panoply.org.

POLK COUNTY RAMP TRAMP FESTIVAL. Apr 24–25. Polk County 4-H Camp, Camp McCroy, near Benton, TN. A tribute to the ramp, a wild leek that grows only in the Appalachian Mountains. Bluegrass music and feast of the ramps. Est attendance: 1,500. For info: Polk County Ramp Festival, Box 189, Benton, TN 37307. Phone: (423) 338-4503. Web: www.polkagextension.com/ramppage.html.

RATTLESNAKE DERBY. Apr 24–26. Mangum, OK. Hunters stalk these wily reptiles and attempt to bring in the most snakes and the longest snake. Snakeskins and meat will be sold, and entertainment will include live music, a carnival and flea market. Annually, the last full weekend in April. Est attendance: 40,000. For info: Shortgrass Rattlesnake Assn. Phone: (580) 782-2434.

SPACE MILESTONE: *CHINA 1* (PEOPLE'S REPUBLIC OF CHINA). Apr 24, 1970. China became the fifth nation to orbit a satellite with the launch of its own rocket. The satellite broadcast the Chinese song "Tang Fang Hung" ("The East Is Red") and telemetric signals.

SPRING FESTIVAL. Apr 24–May 3. Cape May, NJ. Experience and appreciate the Victorian lifestyle with 10 days of spring activities at America's first seashore resort. Special events include a Vintage Dance Weekend, Victorian Murder Mystery Dinners, outdoor crafts, antiques and collectibles shows, free glassblowing demonstrations on the lawn of Cape May's only Victorian House Museum, the 1879 Emlen Physick Estate and much more. Est attendance: 15,000. For info: Mid-Atlantic Center for the Arts, 1048 Washington St, PO Box 340, Cape May, NJ 08204. Phone: (609) 884-5404 or (800) 275-4278. Fax: (609) 884-0574. E-mail: mac4arts@capemaymac.org. Web: www.capemaymac.org.

SUGARLOAF CRAFTS FESTIVAL. Apr 24–26. Maryland State Fairgrounds, Timonium, MD. This show, now in its 31st year, features more than 300 nationally recognized craft designers and fine artists displaying and selling their original creations. Includes craft demonstrations, live music, specialty food, hourly gift certificate drawings and more. Est attendance: 16,000. For info: Sugarloaf Mountain Works, Inc, 200 Orchard Ridge Dr, #215, Gaithersburg, MD 20878. Phone: (800) 210-9900. Fax: (310) 253-9620. Web: www.sugarloafcrafts.com.

THOMAS, ROBERT BAILEY: BIRTH ANNIVERSARY. Apr 24, 1766. Founder and editor of *The Farmer's Almanac* (first issue for 1793) was born at Grafton, MA. Thomas died May 19, 1846, while working on the 1847 edition.

TROLLOPE, ANTHONY: BIRTH ANNIVERSARY. Apr 24, 1815. English novelist (*Barchester Towers*), born at London, England, and died there Dec 6, 1882. "Of the needs a book has," he wrote in his autobiography, "the chief need is that it be readable."

US ATTEMPT TO FREE IRAN HOSTAGES: ANNIVERSARY. Apr 24, 1980. US Marines attempted to stage a surprise raid to free citizens held at the US embassy in Tehran, Iran, but their helicopters collided at the desert staging area. Eight were killed and five were wounded. No further military rescues were attempted, and the hostages were later released in January 1981 after 444 days of captivity.

VERMONT MAPLE FESTIVAL. Apr 24–26. St. Albans, VT. The 43rd annual festival includes carnival, talent show, entertainment, arts and crafts, antiques, maple exhibits and demonstrations, sugarhouse tours and sap run. Est attendance: 50,000. For info: Vermont Maple Festival, PO Box 255, St. Albans, VT 05478. Phone: (802) 524-5800. Web: www.vtmaplefestival.org.

WARD WORLD CHAMPIONSHIP WILDFOWL CARVING COMPETITION AND ART FESTIVAL. Apr 24–26. Roland E. Powell Convention Center, Ocean City, MD. 39th annual. Lifesize, miniature, interpretive wildfowl carving and sculpture competitions. Festival includes vendors selling carvings, folk art, paintings, home decorating items and art supplies. Est attendance: 10,000. For info: Helen Rogan, Special Events Coord, Ward Museum of Wildfowl Art, 909 S Schumaker Dr, Salisbury, MD 21804. Phone: (410) 742-4988, ext 106. Fax: (410) 742-3107. E-mail: ward@wardmuseum.org. Web: www.wardmuseum.org.

WARREN, ROBERT PENN: BIRTH ANNIVERSARY. Apr 24, 1905. American poet, novelist, essayist and critic. America's first official poet laureate, 1986–88, Robert Penn Warren was born at Guthrie, KY. Warren was awarded the Pulitzer Prize for his novel *All the King's Men*, as well as for his poetry in 1958 and 1979. He died of cancer Sept 15, 1989, at Stratton, VT.

Birthdays Today

Eric Balfour, 32, actor (*Rescue Me, No One Would Tell*), musician, born Los Angeles, CA, Apr 24, 1977.

Eric Bogosian, 56, actor (*Under Siege 2*), playwright, performance artist, born Boston, MA, Apr 24, 1953.

Cedric the Entertainer, 45, comedian, actor (*Street Kings, Barbershop, Be Cool*), born Cedric Kyles at Jefferson City, MO, Apr 24, 1964.

Kelly Clarkson, 27, singer, born Fort Worth, TX, Apr 24, 1982.

Richard M. Daley, 67, Mayor of Chicago, born Chicago, IL, Apr 24, 1942.

Sue Grafton, 69, author (*L Is for Lawless, M Is for Malice*), born Louisville, KY, Apr 24, 1940.

Djimon Hounsou, 45, actor (*Blood Diamond, In America*), born Cotonou, Benin, Apr 24, 1964.

Chipper Jones, 37, baseball player, born DeLand, FL, Apr 24, 1972.

Stanley J. Kauffmann, 93, critic, born New York, NY, Apr 24, 1916.

Shirley MacLaine, 75, author, actress (Oscar for *Terms of Endearment; The Turning Point, Being There*), born Richmond, VA, Apr 24, 1934.

Michael O'Keefe, 54, actor (*The Great Santini, Caddyshack*; stage: *Mass Appeal*), born Larchmont, NY, Apr 24, 1955.

Barbra Streisand, 67, singer, actress (Oscar for *Funny Girl; The Way We Were, Yentl*), director (*Prince of Tides*), born Brooklyn, NY, Apr 24, 1942.

April 25 — Saturday

DAY 115 — **250 REMAINING**

ABORTION FIRST LEGALIZED: ANNIVERSARY. Apr 25, 1967. The first law legalizing abortion in the US was signed by Colorado governor John Arthur Love. The law allowed therapeutic abortions in cases in which a three-doctor panel unanimously agreed.

ANZAC DAY. Apr 25. Australia, New Zealand and Samoa. Memorial day and veterans' observance, especially to mark WWI ANZAC (Australia and New Zealand Army Corps) landing at Gallipoli, Turkey, in 1915 .

BATTLE OF GALLIPOLI: ANNIVERSARY. Apr 25, 1915–Jan 1916. During WWI the Gallipoli Expedition, or the Dardanelles Campaign, combined Allied naval and military forces tried to capture the Gallipoli peninsula in Turkey in order to effect an open route to Russia via the Black Sea. One French and four British divisions were forced back by a strong Turkish-German defense after almost nine months of fighting. The Australian and New Zealand Army Corps (ANZAC) took much of the brunt of the battle.

BOB WILLS DAY. Apr 25. Turkey, TX. Celebration of the creator of western swing, with music, fiddlers contest, parade and barbecue lunch. Appearances by his former band, the Texas Playboys. Annually, the last Saturday in April. Est attendance: 10,000. For info: Bob Wills Foundation, PO Box 306, Turkey, TX 79261. Phone: (806) 423-1253. E-mail: turkey@caprock-spur.com. Web: www.turkeytexas.net.

BRENNAN, WILLIAM: BIRTH ANNIVERSARY. Apr 25, 1906. US Supreme Court Associate Justice William J. Brennan was appointed to the Supreme Court in 1956 by President Dwight Eisenhower. His liberal leanings and judicial activism raised the ire of many conservatives, even leading Eisenhower to call his appointment his "worst mistake." Brennan believed that the courts should go beyond strict constructionism and original intent doctrines in interpreting the law. He was responsible for many landmark decisions, including the decision requiring the Little Rock, AR, schools to desegregate that contained the controversial assertion that it is not only the Constitution that is the "supreme law of the land," but the Supreme Court's interpretation of it as well. His legacy also includes major decisions upholding affirmative action, a losing battle to declare the death penalty unconstitutional, decisions broadening free speech and free press guarantees, expansion of the due process guarantees under the 14th Amendment, and protection of flag burning as a form of expression. Brennan's resignation provided President George Bush with an opportunity to swing the balance of the Supreme Court to a more conservative, constructionist majority for the first time since the days of Franklin D. Roosevelt's presidency. Brennan was born at Newark, NJ; he died at Arlington, VA, July 25, 1997.

CALIFORNIA POPPY FESTIVAL. Apr 25–26. Lancaster, CA. Celebrating the golden poppy as the state flower of California, the California Poppy Festival features unique homemade crafts, a variety of musical entertainers, delicious food booths, cultural demonstrations and exotic animals. Visitors can stop by the Wildflower Information Center to get maps of the best poppy fields. Both kids and adults will enjoy the carnival, crafts and live music. Est attendance: 55,000. For info: City of Lancaster, 44933 Fern Ave, Lancaster, CA 93534. Phone: (661) 723-6077. Fax: (661) 723-5913. Web: www.poppyfestival.com.

***COSMOGRAPHIAE INTRODUCTIO*: PUBLICATION ANNIVERSARY.** Apr 25, 1507. Little is known about the obscure scholar now called the "godfather of America," the German geographer and mapmaker Martin Waldseemuller, who gave America its name. In a book titled *Cosmographiae Introductio*, published Apr 25, 1507, Waldseemuller wrote: "Inasmuch as both Europe and Asia received their names from women, I see no reason why any one should justly object to calling this part Amerige, i.e., the land of Amerigo, or America, after Amerigo, its discoverer, a man of great ability." Believing it was the Italian navigator and merchant Amerigo Vespucci who had discovered the new continent, Waldseemuller sought to honor Vespucci by placing his name on his map of the world, published in 1507. First applied only to the South American continent, it soon was used for both the American continents. Waldseemuller did not learn about the voyage of Christopher Columbus until several years later. Of the thousand copies of his map that were printed, only one is known to have survived. Waldseemuller probably was born at Radolfzell, Germany, about 1470. He died at St. Die, France, about 1517–20. See also: "Vespucci, Amerigo: Birth Anniversary" (Mar 9).

EGYPT: SINAI DAY. Apr 25. National holiday celebrating the return of Sinai to Egypt in 1982 after the peace treaty between Egypt and Israel.

FARRAGUT CAPTURES NEW ORLEANS: ANNIVERSARY. Apr 25, 1862. Union forces under the command of Flag Officer David Farragut seized the city of New Orleans, LA, resulting in the surrender of several Confederate forts along the Mississippi in subsequent days. This action removed any Confederate resistance to Northern action on the Mississippi River as far north as New Orleans. General Benjamin Butler arrived on Apr 27 and took command of the management of the captured city.

FIRST LICENSE PLATES: ANNIVERSARY. Apr 25, 1901. New York began requiring license plates on automobiles, the first state to do so.

FITZGERALD, ELLA: BIRTH ANNIVERSARY. Apr 25, 1917. "First Lady of Song," born at Newport News, VA. Jazz singer known for her treatments of Rogers and Hart, Gershwin, Irving Berlin, Cole Porter and Duke Ellington. Fitzgerald died at Beverly Hills, CA, June 15, 1996.

FOXFIELD RACES. Apr 25 (also Sept 27). Charlottesville, VA. Steeplechase horse racing. Est attendance: 20,000. For info: W. Patrick Butterfield, Racing Mgr, Foxfield Racing Assn, PO Box 5187, Charlottesville, VA 22905. Phone: (434) 293-9501. Fax: (434) 293-8169. E-mail: wpbutterfield@foxfieldraces.com.

HERB FESTIVAL. Apr 25. Mattoon, IL. Fresh herbs, everlasting plants, scented geraniums and lots of perennials. Annually, the last Saturday in April. Est attendance: 7,000. For info: The Picket Fence, 901 Broadway, Mattoon, IL 61938. Phone: (217) 258-6364.

ITALY: LIBERATION DAY. Apr 25. National holiday. Commemorates the liberation of Italy from German troops in 1945.

LLOYD, POP: 125th BIRTH ANNIVERSARY. Apr 25, 1884. John Henry "Pop" Lloyd, Baseball Hall of Fame shortstop, born at Palatka, FL. Lloyd was often compared to Honus Wagner and considered one of the best shortstops ever. He played with and managed black teams and made quite a career in Cuba, where the fans nicknamed him "Cuchara" (scoop or shovel) for his big hands. Inducted into the Hall of Fame in 1977. Died at Atlantic City, NJ, Mar 19, 1965.

✦ **MALARIA AWARENESS DAY.** Apr 25. To promote awareness of this devastating disease, and to promote inititatives to combat the spread of the disease across Africa and around the world. Annually, Apr 25.

MARCONI, GUGLIELMO: BIRTH ANNIVERSARY. Apr 25, 1874. Inventor of wireless telegraphy (1895), born at Bologna, Italy. Died at Rome, Italy, July 20, 1937.

MURROW, EDWARD R.: BIRTH ANNIVERSARY. Apr 25, 1908. Among the greatest journalists in American history, Edward R. Murrow was born at Greensboro, NC. He was a European war correspondent for CBS during WWII and rose to prominence with his dramatic and vivid radio broadcasts. After the war, CBS moved him to television, where he was the trusted host of "See It Now," a news magazine show spotlighting hot-button issues of the day. He died at Pawling, NY, Apr 27, 1965.

NATIONAL BULLDOGS ARE BEAUTIFUL DAY. Apr 25. In addition to recognizing the beauty in our portly pets, National Bulldogs Are Beautiful Day celebrates people's differences whether they're big, small, short, tall, skinny or stout or have names like Stinky or Lulu. For info: Jackie Valent, 2013 N 81st St, Wauwatosa, WI 53213. Phone: (414) 232-1443. E-mail: info@bulldogsarebeautiful.com. Web: www.bulldogsarebeautiful.com.

NATIONAL REBUILDING DAY. Apr 25. 270,000 volunteers come together to rehabilitate the homes of low-income, elderly or disabled people and nonprofit facilities. Annually, the last Saturday in April. For info: Rebuilding Together, 1536 16th St NW, Washington, DC 20036-1402. Phone: (202) 483-9083 or (800) 4-REHAB-9. Fax: (202) 483-9081. Web: www.rebuildingtogether.org.

April 2009

S	M	T	W	T	F	S
			1	2	3	4
5	6	7	8	9	10	11
12	13	14	15	16	17	18
19	20	21	22	23	24	25
26	27	28	29	30		

PORTUGAL: LIBERTY DAY. Apr 25. Portugal. Public holiday. Anniversary of the 1974 revolution.

REDBUD TRAIL RENDEZVOUS. Apr 25–26. Rochester, IN. Reenactment of a pre-1840 gathering to trade furs on the Tippecanoe River, featuring tepee and wigwam villages, traditional music and crafts, pioneer and Indian dances and foods cooked over wood fires. Seven Years' War field day; Hoosier Ladies Aside demonstrate riding sidesaddle. Museum, round barn and Living History Village at north end of grounds. For frontier fun, follow the redbuds blooming along the Tippecanoe River. Est attendance: 2,000. For info: Fulton County Historical Society, 37 E 375 N, Rochester, IN 46975. Phone: (574) 223-4436. E-mail: fchs@rtcol.com. Web: www.icss.net/~fchs.

ROMANCE READER'S LUNCHEON. Apr 25. Portland, OR. A fundraiser for Oregon Literacy. Come meet your favorite romance authors and hobnob with other readers. Get cool free stuff (lots of books!) at the giveaways and raffles, and have a delicious lunch, all in the name of literacy. $35 to attend, and the book signing is free and open to anyone. Est attendance: 200. For info: Kim Wollenburg, 16950 S Redland Rd, Oregon City, OR 97045. Phone: (503) 631-7868. E-mail: rwakw@yahoo.com. Web: www.rosecityromancewriters.com.

SOUTHERN MARYLAND CELTIC FESTIVAL & HIGHLAND GATHERING. Apr 25. Jefferson Patterson Park, St. Leonard, MD. 31st annual. Scottish fiddling championship, bagpipe competition, Scottish heptathlon, Highland dancing competition, Celtic marketplace and crafts, parade of clans and nations, Celtic harp competition, Celtic folk music, demonstrations and Celtic foods. Annually, the last Saturday in April. Est attendance: 15,000. For info: Celtic Society of Southern Maryland, PO Box 209, Prince Frederick, MD 20678. Phone: (443) 404-7319. E-mail: Festival@cssm.org. Web: www.cssm.org.

SPACE MILESTONE: HUBBLE SPACE TELESCOPE DEPLOYED (US). Apr 25, 1990. Deployed by *Discovery*, the telescope is the largest on-orbit observatory to date and is capable of imaging objects up to 14 billion light-years away. The resolution of images was expected to be seven to ten times greater than images from Earth-based telescopes, since the Hubble Space Telescope is not hampered by Earth's atmospheric distortion. Launched Apr 12, 1990, from Kennedy Space Center, FL. Unfortunately, the telescope's lenses were defective, so the anticipated high quality of imaging was not possible. In 1993, however, the world watched as a shuttle crew successfully retrieved the Hubble from orbit, executed the needed repair and replacement work and released it into orbit once more. In December 1999 the space shuttle *Discovery* was launched to do extensive repairs on the telescope.

SWAZILAND: NATIONAL FLAG DAY. Apr 25. National holiday.

THEODORE ROOSEVELT NATIONAL PARK ESTABLISHED: ANNIVERSARY. Apr 25, 1947. Located in North Dakota, the Theodore Roosevelt National Park includes two sections of the Badlands on the Missouri River as well as Theodore Roosevelt's Elkhorn Ranch.

WORLD MALARIA DAY. Apr 25. A day to provide education and understanding of malaria as a global scourge that is preventable and a disease that is curable. For info: Mobilising 4 Malaria, c/o Malaria Consortium, Development House, 56-64 Leonard Street, London EC2A 4LT, United Kingdom. Phone: (44) (20) 7549-0210. Fax: (44) (20) 7549-0211. Email: info@mobilising4malaria.org. Web: www.mobilising4malaria.org.

WORLD TAI CHI AND QIGONG DAY. Apr 25. World Tai Chi and Qigong Day (also spelled T'ai Chi and Ch'i Kung) is an annual event held the last Saturday of April each year to promote the related disciplines of tai chi and qigong in 60 countries since 1999. The mission of this multinational effort is ongoing: to expose people to the growing body of medical research related to traditional Chinese medicine and direct them to teachers in their hometowns. For info: Bill Douglas, World Tai Chi and Qigong Day, PO Box 7786, Shawnee Mission, KS 66207. Phone: (913) 648-2256. E-mail: billdouglas@worldtaichiday.org. Web: www.worldtaichiday.org.

WWII: EAST MEETS WEST: ANNIVERSARY. Apr 25, 1945. US Army Lieutenant Albert Kotzebue encountered a single Soviet soldier near the German village of Lechwitz, 75 miles south of Berlin. Patrols of General Leonard Gerow's V Corps saluted the advance guard of Marshall Ivan Konev's Soviet 58th Guards Division. Soldiers of both nations embraced and exchanged toasts. The Allied armies of East and West had finally met.

Birthdays Today

Hank Azaria, 45, actor ("Huff," *The Birdcage*, many voices on "The Simpsons"), born Forest Hills, NY, Apr 25, 1964.

Emily Bergl, 34, actress ("Men in Trees"), born Milton Keynes, Buckinghamshire, England, Apr 25, 1975.

Johan Cruyff, 62, soccer executive and former player, born Amsterdam, Netherlands, Apr 25, 1947.

Jeffrey DeMunn, 62, actor (*Ragtime, Frances*), born Buffalo, NY, Apr 25, 1947.

Tim Duncan, 33, basketball player, born St. Croix, Virgin Islands, Apr 25, 1976.

Jon Kyl, 67, US Senator (R, Arizona), born Oakland, NE, Apr 25, 1942.

Jason Lee, 39, actor ("My Name Is Earl," *Almost Famous, Chasing Amy*), born Orange, CA, Apr 25, 1970.

Meadow George "Meadowlark" Lemon III, 77, Hall of Fame basketball player, born Lexington, SC, Apr 25, 1932.

Paul Mazursky, 79, director (*Harry and Tonto, An Unmarried Woman, Scenes from a Mall*), born Brooklyn, NY, Apr 25, 1930.

Al Pacino, 69, actor (Oscar for *Scent of a Woman; Dog Day Afternoon, Godfather* movies), born New York, NY, Apr 25, 1940.

Talia Shire, 63, actress (the *Godfather* movies, the *Rocky* movies), born Jamaica, NY, Apr 25, 1946.

Renee Zellweger, 40, actress (Oscar for *Cold Mountain*; *Miss Potter, Chicago, Bridget Jones's Diary*), born Katy, TX, Apr 25, 1969.

April 26 — Sunday

DAY 116 — **249 REMAINING**

AUDUBON, JOHN JAMES: BIRTH ANNIVERSARY. Apr 26, 1785. American artist and naturalist, best known for his *Birds of America*, born at Haiti. Died Jan 27, 1851, at New York, NY.

CHERNOBYL NUCLEAR REACTOR DISASTER: ANNIVERSARY. Apr 26, 1986. At 1:23 AM, local time, an explosion occurred at the Chernobyl atomic power station at Pripyat in the Ukraine. The resulting fire burned for days, sending radioactive material into the atmosphere. More than 100,000 persons were evacuated from a 300-square-mile area around the plant. Three months later 31 people were reported to have died and thousands exposed to dangerous levels of radiation. Estimates projected an additional 1,000 cancer cases in nations downwind of the radioactive discharge. The plant was encased in a concrete tomb in an effort to prevent the still-hot reactor from overheating again and to minimize further release of radiation.

"CHINA BEACH" TV PREMIERE: ANNIVERSARY. Apr 26, 1988. The stories of "China Beach" revolved around the lives of the women serving at a Da Nang armed forces hospital during the Vietnam War. The theme and background music of the series evoked plenty of nostalgia from the turbulent era. The ABC drama was created by William Broyles, Jr, and John Sacret Young. The cast featured Dana Delany, Michael Boatman, Nancy Giles, Jeff Kober, Robert Picardo, Concetta Tomei, Brian Wimmer, Marg Helgenberger, Chloe Webb, Nan Woods, Megan Gallagher, Ned Vaughn and Ricki Lake.

CONFEDERATE MEMORIAL DAY IN FLORIDA AND GEORGIA. Apr 26. Observed on the anniversary of Confederate general Joseph E. Johnston's surrender to General William T. Sherman in Durham, NC, in 1865. Other Southern states observe this day on different dates.

ENGLAND: FLORA LONDON MARATHON. Apr 26. London. Held since 1981 and awarded a road race Gold Label by the International Association of Athletics Federations, the London Marathon hosts more than 46,000 participants in 26 miles from Greenwich to The Mall. For info: Nicola Okey, London Marathon Ltd. Phone: (44) 207-902-0182. E-mail: nicolao@london-marathon.co.uk. Web: www.london-marathon.co.uk or www.worldmarathonmajors.com.

FAUSET, JESSIE REDMON: BIRTH ANNIVERSARY. Apr 26, 1882. African-American poet, editor and novelist, born at Fredericksville, NJ, and died in 1961. Fauset, as literary editor of *Crisis* (a publication of the NAACP), was a patron to so many writers of the Harlem Renaissance that her efforts prompted Langston Hughes to dub her the "midwife of the so-called New Negro Literature." Along with W.E.B. Du Bois, Fauset also published and edited the children's magazine *The Brownie Book*. Her novels about the African-American middle-class experience dealt with issues of identity, autonomy and struggles for fulfillment. Her most recognized works include *The Chinaberry Tree* (1931) and *Comedy, American Style* (1933).

GUERNICA MASSACRE: ANNIVERSARY. Apr 26, 1937. Late in the afternoon, the ancient Basque town of Guernica, in northern Spain, was attacked without warning by German-made airplanes. Three hours of intensive bombing left the town in flames, and citizens who fled to the fields and ditches around Guernica were machine-gunned from the air. This atrocity inspired Pablo Picasso's mural *Guernica*. Responsibility for the bombing was never officially established, but the suffering and anger of the victims and their survivors are still evident at anniversary demonstrations. Intervention by Nazi Germany in the Spanish Civil War has been described as practice for WWII.

HELENA RAILROAD FAIR. Apr 26. Civic Center, Helena, MT. 29th annual. Largest railroad hobby event in Montana features a mix of scale and tin-plate trains; railroad memorabilia and collectibles; real-life train watching at the MRL Helena depot. Annually, the last Sunday in April. Est attendance: 2,500. For info: Helena Railroad Fair, PO Box 4914, Helena, MT 59604-4914. Phone: (406) 443-1578 or (406) 227-7469. E-mail: rrfair@mt.net.

April 2009	S	M	T	W	T	F	S
				1	2	3	4
	5	6	7	8	9	10	11
	12	13	14	15	16	17	18
	19	20	21	22	23	24	25
	26	27	28	29	30		

HESS, RUDOLF: BIRTH ANNIVERSARY. Apr 26, 1894. One of the most bizarre figures of WWII Germany, Walter Richard Rudolf Hess was born at Alexandria, Egypt. He was a close friend, confidant and personal secretary to Adolf Hitler, who had dictated much of *Mein Kampf* to Hess while both were prisoners at Landsberg Prison. Third in command in Nazi Germany, Hess surprised the world on May 10, 1941, by flying alone to Scotland and parachuting from his plane on what he called a "mission of humanity": offering peace to Britain if it would join Germany in attacking the Soviet Union. He was immediately taken prisoner of war. At the Nuremberg Trials (1946), after questions about his sanity, he was convicted and sentenced to life imprisonment at Spandau Allied War Crimes Prison at Berlin, Germany. Outliving all other prisoners there, he was the only inmate from 1955 until he succeeded (in his fourth attempt) in committing suicide. He died at West Berlin, Germany, Aug 17, 1987.

HUG AN AUSTRALIAN DAY. Apr 26. To show our great appreciation for all the love and support the Aussies have given us over the years. (©2006 by WH.) For info: Thomas & Ruth Roy, Wellcat Holidays, 2418 Long Ln, Lebanon, PA 17046. Phone: (717) 279-0184. E-mail: info@wellcat.com. Web: www.wellcat.com.

LOOS, ANITA: BIRTH ANNIVERSARY. Apr 26, 1893. American author and playwright, born at Sisson, CA. She is best remembered for her book *Gentlemen Prefer Blondes*, published in 1925. Loos, a brunette, died at New York, NY, Aug 18, 1981.

MONTGOMERY WARD SEIZED: 65th ANNIVERSARY. Apr 26, 1944. Montgomery Ward chairman Sewell Avery was physically removed from his office when federal troops seized Ward's Chicago offices after the company refused to obey President Franklin D. Roosevelt's order to recognize a CIO union. Government control ended May 9, shortly before the National Labor Relations Board announced the United Mail Order Warehouse and Retail Employees Union had won an election to represent the company's workers.

MOTHER, FATHER DEAF DAY. Apr 26. A day to honor deaf parents and recognize the gifts of culture and language they give to their hearing children. Annually, the last Sunday of April. Sponsored by Children of Deaf Adults International Inc (CODA). For info: T. Teske, Deaf Awareness Events. E-mail: tteske2724@aol.com.

OLMSTED, FREDERICK LAW: BIRTH ANNIVERSARY. Apr 26, 1822. Known as the "father of landscape architecture in America," Olmsted participated in the designing of Yosemite National Park, New York City's Central Park and parks for Boston, Hartford and Louisville. Born at Hartford, CT; died at Waverly, MA, Aug 28, 1903. Olmsted's home and studio, Fairsted Estate, outside of Boston, is now preserved as a National Historic Site and is open to the public: 99 Warren St, Brookline, MA 02146.

RICHTER SCALE DAY. Apr 26. A day to recognize the importance of Charles Francis Richter's research and his work in development of the earthquake magnitude scale that is known as the Richter scale. Richter, an American author, physicist and seismologist, was born Apr 26, 1900, near Hamilton, OH. An Earthquake Awareness Week was observed in recognition of his work. Richter died at Pasadena, CA, Sept 30, 1985.

ST. LOUIS EARTH DAY FESTIVAL. Apr 26. St. Louis, MO. An educational event with hundreds of exhibitors related to environmental issues and their solutions. Est attendance: 20,000. For info: St. Louis Earth Day, PO Box 19863, St Louis, MO 63144. Phone: (314) 961-5838. E-mail: info@stlouisearthday.org. Web: www.stlouisearthday.org.

SIRK, DOUGLAS: BIRTH ANNIVERSARY. Apr 26, 1900. Film director Douglas Sirk was born Detlef Sierck at Hamburg, Germany. His films include *Magnificent Obsession* (1954), *Written on the Wind* (1956) and *Imitation of Life* (1959). He died Jan 14, 1987, at Lugano, Switzerland.

SOUTH AFRICAN MULTIRACIAL ELECTIONS: 15th ANNIVERSARY. Apr 26–29, 1994. For the first time in the history of South Africa, the nation's approximately 18 million blacks voted in multiparty elections. This event marked the definitive end of apartheid, the system of racial separation that had kept blacks and other minorities out of the political process. The election resulted in Nelson Mandela of the African National Congress being elected president and F.W. de Klerk (incumbent president) of the National Party vice president.

SWITZERLAND: LANDSGEMEINDE. Apr 26. In one of the last examples of direct democracy, the citizens of Switzerland's smallest canton, Appenzell Inner Rhoden, gather annually on the last Sunday of April to vote. Uniquely, they don't cast secret ballots but raise their arms in full view of their neighbors. About 2,000 to 3,000 voters of 18 years and older come to the square of the canton capital, Appenzell, after attending a morning church service. Once affairs of the canton are voted on, festivities begin. As part of the tradition, which dates back to the 14th century, men wear swords.

TANZANIA: UNION DAY. Apr 26. Celebrates union between mainland Tanzania (formerly Tanganyika) and the islands of Zanzibar and Pemba, in 1964.

Birthdays Today

Carol Burnett, 73, actress ("Garry Moore Show," "Carol Burnett Show," *The Four Seasons*), born San Antonio, TX, Apr 26, 1936.

Joan Chen, 48, actress ("Twin Peaks," "Golden Gate"), born Shanghai, China, Apr 26, 1961.

Joe Crede, 31, baseball player, born Jefferson City, MO, Apr 26, 1978.

Michael Damian, 47, actor ("Young and the Restless"; stage: *Joseph and the Amazing Technicolor Dreamcoat*), born San Diego, CA, Apr 26, 1962.

Duane Eddy, 71, musician, born Corning, NY, Apr 26, 1938.

Giancarlo Esposito, 51, actor (*Do the Right Thing, Twilight*), born Copenhagen, Denmark, Apr 26, 1958.

Kosuke Fukudome, 32, baseball player, born Osaki, Japan, Apr 26, 1977.

Kevin James, 44, actor ("The King of Queens"), born Stony Brook, NY, Apr 26, 1965.

Jet Li, 46, actor (*The Forbidden Kingdom, Hero, Kiss of the Dragon*), former martial arts champion, born Li Lian Jie at Beijing, China, Apr 26, 1963.

Boyd Matson, 62, television journalist (host of "National Geographic Explorer"), born Oklahoma City, OK, Apr 26, 1947.

Bobby Rydell, 67, singer ("Wild One," "Volare"), born Philadelphia, PA, Apr 26, 1942.

Tom Welling, 32, actor ("Smallville"), born New York, NY, Apr 26, 1977.

Gary Wright, 66, musician, born Englewood, NJ, Apr 26, 1943.

April 27 — Monday

DAY 117 — **248 REMAINING**

ASTRONOMY WEEK. Apr 27–May 3. To take astronomy to the people. Astronomy Week is observed during the calendar week in which Astronomy Day falls. See also: "Astronomy Day" (May 2).

BABE RUTH DAY: ANNIVERSARY. Apr 27, 1947. Babe Ruth Day was celebrated in every ballpark in organized baseball in the US as well as Japan. Mortally ill with throat cancer, Ruth appeared at Yankee Stadium to thank his former club for the honor.

CONFEDERATE MEMORIAL DAY IN ALABAMA. Apr 27. On the fourth Monday in April. Other Southern states observe Confederate Memorial Day on different dates.

CONFEDERATE MEMORIAL DAY IN MISSISSIPPI. Apr 27. Annually, on the last Monday in April. Observed on other dates in some states.

DENNIS, SANDY: BIRTH ANNIVERSARY. Apr 27, 1937. American actress Sandy Dennis was born Sandra Dale Dennis at Hastings, NE. In addition to two Tony Awards, she won an Academy Award for her supporting role in *Who's Afraid of Virginia Woolf* (1966). She died Mar 2, 1992, at Westport, CT.

GIBBON, EDWARD: BIRTH ANNIVERSARY. Apr 27, 1737. (Old Style date.) English historian and author. His *History of the Decline and Fall of the Roman Empire* remains a model of historical writing. From his description of the Roman emperor Gordianus II: "Twenty-two acknowledged concubines, and a library of sixty-two thousand volumes, attested the variety of his inclinations; and from the productions which he left behind him, it appears that the former as well as the latter were designed for use rather than for ostentation." Born at Putney, Surrey, England, Gibbon died at London, Jan 6, 1794.

GRANT, ULYSSES SIMPSON: BIRTH ANNIVERSARY. Apr 27, 1822. 18th president of the US (Mar 4, 1869–Mar 3, 1877), born Hiram Ulysses Grant at Point Pleasant, OH. He graduated from the US Military Academy in 1843. President Lincoln promoted Grant to lieutenant general in command of all the Union armies Mar 9, 1864. On Apr 9, 1865, Grant received General Robert E. Lee's surrender, at Appomattox Court House, VA, which he announced to the secretary of war as follows: "General Lee surrendered the Army of Northern Virginia this afternoon on terms proposed by myself. The accompanying additional correspondence will show the conditions fully." Nicknamed "Unconditional Surrender Grant," he died at Mount McGregor, NY, July 23, 1885, just four days after completing his memoirs. He was buried at Riverside Park, New York, NY, where Grant's Tomb was dedicated in 1897.

INTERNATIONAL HOME FURNISHINGS MARKET. Apr 27–May 3 (also Oct 19–25). High Point and Thomasville, NC. The largest wholesale home furnishings market in the world. (Not open to the general public.) Est attendance: 82,000. For info: High Point Market Authority, PO Box 5243, High Point, NC 27262. Phone: (336) 869-1000. Fax: (336) 869-6999. Web: www.highpointmarket.org.

KING, CORETTA SCOTT: BIRTH ANNIVERSARY. Apr 27, 1927. The wife of Dr. Martin Luther King, Jr, was born on a farm near Heiberger, AL. She picked cotton as a child but was able to go to college, where she met and married the young minister-turned-civil-rights-activist. She worked by his side, establishing Freedom Concerts and other social-change movements, while also raising the couple's four children. After King's 1968 assassination, she took on his mission, founding the Martin Luther King Jr Center for Non-Violent Social Change in Atlanta, and also spearheading the efforts to have a national holiday established in her late husband's honor. The American Library Association established a prestigious children's literature award for African-American writers and illustrators in her name in 1970, and in her later years she was a tireless advocate for gay and lesbian rights. She died at Rosarito, Mexico, Jan 30, 2006.

LANTZ, WALTER: BIRTH ANNIVERSARY. Apr 27, 1900. Originator of Universal Studios' animated opening sequence for their first major musical film, *The King of Jazz.* Walter Lantz is best remembered as the creator of Woody Woodpecker, the bird with the wacky laugh and the taunting ways. Lantz received a lifetime-achievement Academy Award for his animation in 1979. He was born at New Rochelle, NY, and died Mar 22, 1994, at Burbank, CA.

MAGELLAN, FERDINAND: DEATH ANNIVERSARY. Apr 27, 1521. Portuguese explorer Ferdinand Magellan was probably born near Oporto, Portugal, about 1480, but neither the place nor the date is certain. Usually thought of as the first man to circumnavigate the earth, he died before completing the voyage; thus, his coleader, Basque navigator Juan Sebastian de Elcano, became the world's first circumnavigator. The westward, 'round-the-world expedition began Sept 20, 1519, with five ships and about 250 men. Magellan was killed by natives of the Philippine island of Mactan.

MATANZAS MULE DAY. Apr 27, 1898. In one of the first naval actions of the Spanish-American War, US naval forces bombarded the Cuban village of Matanzas. It was widely reported that the only casualty of the bombardment was one mule. The "Matanzas Mule" became instantly famous and remains a footnote in the history of the Spanish-American War.

MORSE, SAMUEL FINLEY BREESE: BIRTH ANNIVERSARY. Apr 27, 1791. American artist and inventor, after whom the Morse code is named, was born at Charlestown, MA, and died at New York, NY, Apr 2, 1872. Graduating from Yale University in 1810, he went to the Royal Academy of London to study painting. After returning to America he achieved success as a portraitist. Morse conceived the idea of an electromagnetic telegraph while on shipboard, returning from art instruction in Europe in 1832, and he proceeded to develop his idea. With financial assistance approved by Congress, the first telegraph line in the US was constructed, between Washington, DC, and Baltimore, MD. The first message tapped out by Morse from the Supreme Court Chamber at the US Capitol building on May 24, 1844, was: "What hath God wrought?"

SIERRA LEONE: INDEPENDENCE DAY. Apr 27. National Day. Commemorates independence from Britain in 1961.

SLOVENIA: INSURRECTION DAY. Apr 27. National holiday. Commemorates the founding of the Liberation Front in 1941 to resist Slovenia's occupation by the Axis powers.

SOUTH AFRICA: FREEDOM DAY. Apr 27. National holiday. Commemorates the day in 1994 when, for the first time, all South Africans had the opportunity to vote.

***SULTANA* STEAMSHIP EXPLOSION: ANNIVERSARY.** Apr 27, 1865. Early in the morning on this day, America's worst steamship disaster occurred. The *Sultana*, heavily overloaded with an estimated 2,300 passengers, exploded in the Mississippi River, just north of Memphis, en route to Cairo, IL. Most of the passengers were Union soldiers who had been prisoners of war and were eagerly returning to their homes. Although there was never an accurate accounting of the dead, estimates range from 1,450 to nearly 2,000. Cause of the explosion was not determined, but the little-known event is unparalleled in US history.

TOGO: INDEPENDENCE DAY. Apr 27. National holiday. In 1960 Togo gained its independence from French administration under a UN trusteeship.

WOLLSTONECRAFT, MARY: 250th BIRTH ANNIVERSARY. Apr 27, 1759. Writer and advocate of equality for women, Mary Wollstonecraft was born at London, England. Rebelling against her father, she left home at age 18 and served as a lady's companion, opened a school and worked as a governess. Beginning with *Thoughts on the Education of Daughters* in 1787, Wollstonecraft attracted notice as a writer in favor of women's rights. Her *A Vindication of the Rights of Woman* (1792) argued that women should be given an education that would allow them to gain economic independence. She died at London on Sept 10, 1797, 11 days after giving birth to her second daughter (Mary Wollstonecraft Shelley, the author of *Frankenstein*).

April 2009	S	M	T	W	T	F	S
				1	2	3	4
	5	6	7	8	9	10	11
	12	13	14	15	16	17	18
	19	20	21	22	23	24	25
	26	27	28	29	30		

Birthdays Today

Anouk Aimee, 75, actress (*Justine, A Man and a Woman, 8½, La Dolce Vita*), born Paris, France, Apr 27, 1934.

Sheena Easton, 50, singer ("Morning Train"), born Sheena Shirley Orr at Bellshill, Scotland, Apr 27, 1959.

Casey Kasem, 77, radio, TV host ("America's Top 40"), born Detroit, MI, Apr 27, 1932.

Jack Klugman, 87, actor ("The Odd Couple," "Quincy, ME"), born Philadelphia, PA, Apr 27, 1922.

April 28 — Tuesday

DAY 118 — 247 REMAINING

BARRYMORE, LIONEL: BIRTH ANNIVERSARY. Apr 28, 1878. Famed American actor of celebrated acting family, Lionel Barrymore was born Lionel Blythe, at Philadelphia, PA. Brother of Ethel and John Barrymore. He died at Van Nuys, CA, Nov 15, 1954.

BIOLOGICAL CLOCK GENE DISCOVERED: 15th ANNIVERSARY. Apr 28, 1994. Northwestern University announced that the so-called biological clock, that gene governing the daily cycle of waking and sleeping called the circadian rhythm, had been found in mice. Never before pinpointed in a mammal, the biological clock gene was found on mouse chromosome 5.

CANADA: NATIONAL DAY OF MOURNING. Apr 28. A national day of mourning for workers killed or injured on the job in Canada. The Canadian Labour Congress first officially recognized the day in 1986. Pointing to the nearly one million workplace injuries each year in Canada, the CLC has called for stricter health and safety regulations and for annual recognition of this day throughout Canada. Federal legislation (Bill D–223) first recognized this day in 1991.

GIBBS, MIFFLIN WISTER: BIRTH ANNIVERSARY. Apr 28, 1828. Mifflin Wister Gibbs was born at Philadelphia, PA. In 1873 he became the first black man to be elected a judge in the US, winning an election for city judge at Little Rock, AR.

HOMER, LOUISE DILWORTH: BIRTH ANNIVERSARY. Apr 28, 1871. The mesmerizing Louise Dilworth Homer was one of the most formidable contraltos of her time. Her plum roles in *Aïda, Tristan und Isolde, Hänsel und Gretel* and *Samson et Dalilah* (with the legendary Caruso) brought her tremendous acclaim. She was born at Sewickley, PA, and died at Winter Park, FL, May 6, 1947.

HUSSEIN, SADDAM: BIRTH ANNIVERSARY. Apr 28, 1937. Military dictator Saddam Hussein Abd al-Majid al-Tikriti was born at Al-Awja, Iraq. A member of the Ba'ath Party that took control of the Iraqi government in 1968, he became president of Iraq in 1979 and served in that role until he was overthrown in a US-led multinational military action in 2003. During his tenure he was considered a major threat to Western interests and waged wars against Iran and Kuwait, and he was tried by an Iraqi Special Tribunal in 2006 for crimes against humanity. He was executed Dec 30, 2006, at Kadhimiya, Iraq.

ISRAEL: REMEMBRANCE DAY (YOM HA'ZIKKARON). Apr 28. Hebrew calendar date: Iyar 4, 5769. Honors the more than 20,000 soldiers killed in battle since the start of the nation's war for independence in 1947. Began at sundown Apr 27.

MARYLAND CONSTITUTION RATIFICATION: ANNIVERSARY. Apr 28, 1788. Maryland became the seventh state to ratify the Constitution, by a vote of 63 to 11.

MONROE, JAMES: BIRTH ANNIVERSARY. Apr 28, 1758. 5th president of the US, was born at Westmoreland County, VA, and served two terms in that office (Mar 4, 1817–Mar 3, 1825). Monrovia, the capital city of Liberia, is named after him, as is the Monroe Doctrine, which he enunciated at Washington, DC, Dec 2, 1823. Last of three presidents to die on US Independence Day, Monroe died at New York, NY, July 4, 1831.

MUSSOLINI EXECUTED: ANNIVERSARY. Apr 28, 1945. Italian partisans shot Benito Mussolini near the lakeside village of Dongo. Leaders of the Fascist Party, several of his friends and his mistress Clara Petacci also were executed. The 23-year-long Fascist rule of Italy was ended.

MUTINY ON THE *BOUNTY*: ANNIVERSARY. Apr 28, 1789. The most famous of all naval mutinies occurred on board HMS *Bounty*. Captain of the *Bounty* was Lieutenant William Bligh, an able seaman and a mean-tempered disciplinarian. The ship, with a load of breadfruit tree plants from Tahiti, was bound for Jamaica. Fletcher Christian, leader of the mutiny, put Bligh and 18 of his loyal followers adrift in a 23-foot open boat. Miraculously Bligh and all of his supporters survived a 47-day voyage of more than 3,600 miles, before landing on the island of Timor, June 14, 1789. In the meantime, Christian had put all of the remaining crew (excepting 8 men and himself) ashore at Tahiti, where he picked up 18 Tahitians (6 men and 12 women) and set sail again. Landing at Pitcairn Island in 1790 (probably uninhabited at the time), they burned the *Bounty* and remained undiscovered for 18 years, when an American whaler, the *Topaz*, called at the island (1808) and found only one member of the mutinous crew surviving. However, the little colony had thrived and, when counted by the British in 1856, numbered 194 persons.

SPACE MILESTONE: FIRST TOURIST IN SPACE. Apr 28, 2001. Millionaire US businessman Dennis Tito reportedly paid the Russian space agency $20 million to accompany *Soyuz TM* to the International Space Station. The rocket with Tito and two Russian cosmonauts was launched this day from the Baikonur launch site in Kazakhstan and arrived at the ISS on Apr 30, 2001. The crew returned to Earth in a week. NASA initially objected to the inclusion of the 60-year-old tycoon on the mission but dropped its opposition.

WORKERS MEMORIAL DAY. Apr 28. First proclaimed in 1989 to commemorate the founding of the Occupational Safety and Health Administration (OSHA) on Apr 28, 1970 (signed into law in 1971). In some places this holiday is observed on the fourth Friday of April.

Birthdays Today

Jessica Alba, 28, actress (*Good Luck Chuck, Fantastic Four, Into the Blue, Sin City,* "Dark Angel"), born Pomona, CA, Apr 28, 1981.

Ann-Margret, 68, actress (*Carnal Knowledge, Tommy, Grumpy Old Men*), born Ann-Margaret Olsson at Stockholm, Sweden, Apr 28, 1941.

Penelope Cruz, 35, actress (*Volver, Bandidas, Sahara, Vanilla Sky*), born Madrid, Spain, Apr 28, 1974.

John Daly, 43, golfer, born Carmichael, CA, Apr 28, 1966.

Jorge Garcia, 36, actor ("Lost," "Becker"), born Omaha, NE, Apr 28, 1973.

Barry Larkin, 45, former baseball player, born Cincinnati, OH, Apr 28, 1964.

Harper Lee, 83, author (*To Kill a Mockingbird*), born Nelle Harper Lee at Monroeville, AL, Apr 28, 1926.

Jay Leno, 59, TV talk-show host ("The Tonight Show"), comedian, born New Rochelle, NY, Apr 28, 1950.

Mary McDonnell, 57, actress ("Battlestar Galactica," *Independence Day, Dances with Wolves*), born Wilkes-Barre, PA, Apr 28, 1952.

Ian Rankin, 49, author (*Black and Blue, The Hanging Garden*), born Cardenden, Fife, Scotland, Apr 28, 1960.

Marcia Strassman, 61, actress ("Welcome Back, Kotter"; *Honey, I Shrunk the Kids*), born New York, NY, Apr 28, 1948.

April 29 — Wednesday

DAY 119 **246 REMAINING**

EARNHARDT, DALE: BIRTH ANNIVERSARY. Apr 29, 1952. Stock car racer, born at Kannapolis, NC. He was one of NASCAR's most popular personalities, winning the Winston Cup seven times. He was killed while driving in the Daytona 500 at Daytona Beach, FL, Feb 18, 2001.

ELLINGTON, "DUKE" (EDWARD KENNEDY): BIRTH ANNIVERSARY. Apr 29, 1899. "Duke" Ellington, one of the most influential individuals in jazz history, was born at Washington, DC. Ellington's professional career began when he was 17, and by 1923 he was leading a small group of musicians at the Kentucky Club at New York City who became the core of his big band. Ellington is credited with being one of the founders of big band jazz. He used his band as an instrument for composition and orchestration to create big band pieces, film scores, operas, ballets, Broadway shows and religious music. Ellington was responsible for more than 1,000 musical pieces. He drew together instruments from different sections of the orchestra to develop unique and haunting sounds such as that of his famous "Mood Indigo." Ellington died May 24, 1974, at New York City.

ELLSWORTH, OLIVER: BIRTH ANNIVERSARY. Apr 29, 1745. (Old Style date.) Third chief justice of the US, born at Windsor, CT. Died there, Nov 26, 1807.

EWELL, TOM: 100th BIRTH ANNIVERSARY. Apr 29, 1909. Born Samuel Yewell Tompkins at Owensboro, KY, Ewell acted in many films and TV series. He won a Tony Award for his Broadway role as the husband in *The Seven Year Itch*, a role he reprised in the film version costarring Marilyn Monroe. In the '60s he starred in his own TV show, "The Tom Ewell Show." He died Sept 12, 1994, at Woodland Hills, CA.

HEARST, WILLIAM RANDOLPH: BIRTH ANNIVERSARY. Apr 29, 1863. American newspaper editor and publisher, born at San Francisco, CA. Died at Beverly Hills, CA, Aug 14, 1951.

HIROHITO MICHI-NO-MIYA, EMPEROR: BIRTH ANNIVERSARY. Apr 29, 1901. Former emperor of Japan, born at Tokyo. Hirohito's death, Jan 7, 1989, ended the reign of the world's longest-ruling monarch. He became the 124th in a line of monarchs when he ascended to the Chrysanthemum Throne in 1926. Hirohito presided over perhaps the most eventful years in the 2,500 years of recorded Japanese history, including the attempted military conquest of Asia; the attack on the US that brought that country into WWII, leading to Japan's ultimate defeat after the US dropped atomic bombs on Hiroshima and Nagasaki; and the amazing economic restoration following the war that led Japan to a preeminent position of economic strength.

ISRAEL: INDEPENDENCE DAY (YOM HA'ATZMA'UT). Apr 29. Hebrew calendar date: Iyar 5, 5769. Celebrates proclamation of independence from British mandatory rule by Palestinian Jews and establishment of the state of Israel and the provisional government May 14, 1948 (Hebrew calendar date: Iyar 5, 5708). Dates in the Hebrew calendar vary from their Gregorian equivalents from year to year. Began at sundown Apr 28.

JAPAN: GOLDEN WEEK HOLIDAYS. Apr 29–May 5. National holidays. This period includes Showa Day (Apr 29), Constitution Memorial Day (May 3), Greenery Day (May 4) and Children's Day (May 5).

JAPAN: SHOWA DAY. Apr 29. Formerly celebrated as Greenery Day until 2007. Honors Emperor Hirohito (1901–89) and is observed on his birthday. "Showa" refers to Japan's postwar era. Part of the Golden Week Holidays.

LIBERATION OF DACHAU: ANNIVERSARY. Apr 29, 1945. The Charlie Battery of the 522nd Field Artillery Battalion liberated the concentration camp at Dachau, Germany. The 522nd, part of the legendary 442nd (Go for Broke) regimental combat team, was made up of Nisei–second-generation Japanese Americans.

LOS ANGELES RIOTS: ANNIVERSARY. Apr 29, 1992. A jury in Simi Valley, CA, failed to convict four Los Angeles police officers accused in the videotaped beating of Rodney King, providing the spark that set off rioting, looting and burning at South Central Los Angeles, CA, and other areas across the country. The anger unleashed during and after the violence was attributed to widespread racism, lack of job opportunities and the resulting hopelessness of inner-city poverty.

NATIONAL DANCE DAY. Apr 29. Concurrent with World Dance Day and as part of World Dance Week, participants across the country organize events in every community to celebrate the spirit and diversity of dance of all kinds. For info: Sharon King, 480 Park Ave, New York, NY 10022. Phone: (212) 751-3293. Fax: (212) 750-4979. E-mail: info@nationaldanceday.org. Web: www.nationaldanceday.org.

'PEACE' ROSE INTRODUCED TO WORLD: ANNIVERSARY. Apr 29, 1945. The 20th century's most popular rose was publicly released by the Pacific Rose Society at Pasadena, CA, just as Berlin was falling to the Allies. The history of 'Peace' is interwoven with events of WWII, and for many the hybrid tea rose has symbolized the hope that grew out of terrible conflict. French rose grower Frances Meilland bred the cream and pink rose (then called 'Mme A. Meilland') in the late 1930s and knew he had something extraordinary. A seedling was smuggled out of France in an American diplomatic pouch on one of the last planes to leave that country before Nazi occupation. American rose company Conrad-Pyle carefully cultivated it. To note Germany's surrender, 'Peace' blooms were presented to all delegates during the first United Nations Conference that May of 1945.

SAINT CATHERINE OF SIENA: FEAST DAY. Apr 29, 1347. St. Catherine of Siena was born at Tuscany, Italy. Patron saint of Italy. She died Apr 29, 1380, at Rome, Italy.

SPACE MILESTONE: *CHALLENGER STS-51B* (US). Apr 29, 1985. *Challenger* launched from Kennedy Space Center, FL, with a crew of seven and an animal menagerie including monkeys and rats. Landed after 111 orbits of Earth on May 6, 1985, at Edwards Air Force Base, CA.

SUNFEST. Apr 29–May 3. West Palm Beach, FL. Florida's largest music, art and waterfront festival features some of the best acts in jazz, rock, blues and more. Family-oriented event includes a juried art show, fireworks, water and youth park activities and fabulous foods. Annually, the first weekend in May. Est attendance: 300,000. For info: SunFest of Palm Beach County, Inc, 525 Clematis St, West Palm Beach, FL 33401. Phone: (561) 659-5980. Fax: (561) 659-3567. E-mail: info@sunfest.com. Web: www.sunfest.com.

April 2009	S	M	T	W	T	F	S
				1	2	3	4
	5	6	7	8	9	10	11
	12	13	14	15	16	17	18
	19	20	21	22	23	24	25
	26	27	28	29	30		

TAIWAN: CHENG CHENG KUNG LANDING DAY. Apr 29. Commemorates landing in Taiwan in 1661 of Ming Dynasty loyalist Cheng Cheng Kung (Koxinga), who ousted Dutch colonists who had occupied Taiwan for 37 years. Main ceremonies held at Tainan, in south Taiwan, where the Dutch had their headquarters and where Cheng is buried.

USA FILM FESTIVAL. Apr 29–May 3. Dallas, TX. 39th annual. Major showcase of new studio and independent films (features and shorts), filmmaker discussions with audience, Master Screen Artist, Great Director and other tributes and retrospectives. Festival is noncompetitive except for Annual National Short Film and Video Competition with cash awards in multiple categories. Est attendance: 15,000. For info: USA Film Festival, 6116 N Central Expressway, Ste 105, Dallas, TX 75206. Phone: (214) 821-6300 or (214) 821-FILM (for 24-hour updates of film programming). Fax: (214) 821-6364. E-mail: usafilmfestival@aol.com. Web: www.usafilmfestival.com.

ZIPPER PATENTED: ANNIVERSARY. Apr 29, 1913. Gideon Sundbach of Hoboken, NJ, received a patent for the zipper.

Birthdays Today

Andre Kirk Agassi, 39, former tennis player, born Las Vegas, NV, Apr 29, 1970.

Daniel Day-Lewis, 52, actor (Oscars for *My Left Foot* and *There Will Be Blood*; *Gangs of New York, The Unbearable Lightness of Being*), born London, England, Apr 29, 1957.

Nora Dunn, 57, actress (*Three Kings*, "Saturday Night Live"), born Chicago, IL, Apr 29, 1952.

Robert Gottlieb, 78, editor, born New York, NY, Apr 29, 1931.

Celeste Holm, 90, actress (*All About Eve*; Oscar for *Gentleman's Agreement*), born New York, NY, Apr 29, 1919.

Rod McKuen, 76, poet, singer, born San Francisco, CA, Apr 29, 1933.

Zubin Mehta, 73, conductor, born Bombay, India, Apr 29, 1936.

Kate Mulgrew, 54, actress ("Star Trek: Voyager," "Ryan's Hope"), born Dubuque, IA, Apr 29, 1955.

Michelle Pfeiffer, 51, actress (*What Lies Beneath, Batman Returns, Dangerous Liaisons*), born Santa Ana, CA, Apr 29, 1958.

Eve Plumb, 51, actress ("The Brady Bunch," "Fudge"), born Burbank, CA, Apr 29, 1958.

Jerry Seinfeld, 55, comedian, actor ("Seinfeld"), born Brooklyn, NY, Apr 29, 1954.

Debbie Stabenow, 59, US Senator (D, Michigan), born Clare, MI, Apr 29, 1950.

Uma Thurman, 39, actress (*Pulp Fiction, Sweet and Lowdown, Kill Bill* films), born Boston, MA, Apr 29, 1970.

Carnie Wilson, 41, singer, born Bel Air, CA, Apr 29, 1968.

April 30 — Thursday

DAY 120 — **245 REMAINING**

BELTANE. Apr 30. (Also called Bealtaine, May Eve, Walpurgis Night, Cyntefyn, Roodmass and Cethsamhain.) One of the "Greater Sabbats" during the Wiccan year, Beltane celebrates the union or marriage of the Goddess and God. In Scotland Beltane was one of the quarter days, or terms when rents were due and debts settled. On the eve of Beltane, two fires were built close together and cattle were driven between them to ward off disease prior to putting the stock out to pasture for the new season. Annually, on Apr 30.

BUGS BUNNY'S DEBUT: ANNIVERSARY. Apr 30, 1938. Warner Bros.' "wascally wabbit" first appeared on screen in the theatrical short "Porky's Hare Hunt," directed by Ben "Bugs" Hardaway and released on this date. Chuck Jones and Tex Avery further developed him into the character we know now—in such cartoons as "A Wild Hare" (1940), in which Bugs asks, "What's up, Doc?" for the first time and first kisses perennial foe Elmer Fudd. The rabbit's noisy carrot munching was based on Clark Gable's carrot chewing in the film *It Happened One Night* (1934).

CAMBODIA INVADED BY US: ANNIVERSARY. Apr 30, 1970. President Richard Nixon announced the US was sending troops into Cambodia in an attempt to destroy the "sanctuaries" from which men and materiel were infiltrated into South Vietnam. This sparked widespread protests on the home front, including a march on Washington and the closure of many American colleges and universities. See also: "Kent State Students' Memorial Day: Anniversay" (May 4).

CHARLIE PARKER FIRST RECORDED: ANNIVERSARY. Apr 30, 1941. The first commercially recorded work of Charlie (Bird) Parker, alto saxophonist and originator of the bebop style of modern jazz, was cut this date at Decca Records. During the recording session, picking up from the last two bars of "Swingmatism," Parker took off into a flowing improvisation that included "Hootie Blues," an example of a Parker blues chorus complete with a characteristic riff figure.

FESTIVAL OF NATIONS. Apr 30–May 3. River Centre, St. Paul, MN. Celebration by 90 ethnic groups, each presenting cultural exhibits, food specialties, folk dances and folk arts to the public. First held in 1932. Est attendance: 85,000. For info: Intl Institute of Minnesota, 1694 Como Ave, St. Paul, MN 55108. Phone: (651) 647-0191. Fax: (651) 647-9268. Web: www.festivalofnations.com.

FIRST PRESIDENTIAL TELECAST: 70th ANNIVERSARY. Apr 30, 1939. Franklin D. Roosevelt became the first president to appear on television when he was televised at the New York World's Fair. However, the appearance was only beamed to 200 TV sets in a 40-mile radius. See also: "First Scheduled Television Broadcast: Anniversary" (July 1).

HAIRSTYLIST APPRECIATION DAY. Apr 30. The personalized service of hairstylists makes customers look great and feel great about themselves. Hairstyling is the art of creating a self-image to help boost self-esteem while lending an ear to customers' problems, thereby lessening their stress. For info: Anne Camilleri, 1220 Arroyo St, San Carlos, CA 94070. Phone: (650) 593-3733 or (650) 568-0565.

HARRISON, MARY SCOTT LORD DIMMICK: BIRTH ANNIVERSARY. Apr 30, 1858. Second wife of Benjamin Harrison, 23rd president of the US, born at Honesdale, PA. Died at New York, NY, Jan 5, 1948.

INTERNATIONAL SCHOOL SPIRIT SEASON. Apr 30–Sept 30. To recognize everyone who has helped to make school spirit better and to provide time to plan improved spirit ideas for the coming school year. For info: Jim Hawkins, Chairman, Pepsters, Committee for More School Spirit, PO Box 122652, San Diego, CA 92112-2652. Phone: (619) 280-0999.

LILLY, WILLIAM: BIRTH ANNIVERSARY. Apr 30, 1602. (Old Style date.) English astrologer, author and almanac compiler, born at Diseworth, Leicestershire. His almanacs were among the most popular in Britain from 1644 until his death, June 9, 1681 (OS), at Hersham, Surrey, England.

LOUISIANA: ADMISSION DAY: ANNIVERSARY. Apr 30. Became 18th state in 1812.

LOUISIANA PURCHASE DAY: ANNIVERSARY. Apr 30, 1803. One of the greatest real estate deals in history was completed in 1803, when more than 820,000 square miles of the Louisiana Territory were turned over to the US by France, for $15 million. This almost doubled the size of the US, extending its western border to the Rocky Mountains.

MUHAMMAD ALI STRIPPED OF TITLE: ANNIVERSARY. Apr 30, 1967. Muhammad Ali was stripped of his world heavyweight boxing championship when he refused to be inducted into military service. Said Ali, "I have searched my conscience, and I find I cannot be true to my belief in my religion by accepting such a call." He had claimed exemption as a minister of the Black Muslim religion. He was convicted of violating the Selective Service Act, but the Supreme Court reversed this decision in 1971.

NATIONAL HONESTY DAY (WITH HONEST ABE AWARDS). Apr 30. To celebrate honesty and those who are honest and honorable in their dealings with others. Nominations accepted for most honest people and companies. Winners to be awarded "Honest Abe" awards and given "Abies" on National Honesty Day. Also presented are dishonorable mentions for notables who have been less than honest. Schools, religious organizations and the media are encouraged to make honesty a subject of discussion on or near this day. Annually, Apr 30. For info: M. Hirsh Goldberg, Founder and author of *The Book of Lies*, 3103 Szold Dr, Baltimore, MD 21208. Phone: (410) 486-4150. E-mail: mhgoldberg@comcast.net.

NETHERLANDS: QUEEN'S BIRTHDAY. Apr 30. A public holiday in celebration of the birthday of former queen Juliana in 1909, the accession of current monarch Beatrix (1980) and the Dutch National Day. The whole country parties as young and old participate in festivities such as markets, theater, music and games.

ORGANIZATION OF AMERICAN STATES FOUNDED: ANNIVERSARY. Apr 30, 1948. The OAS regional alliance was founded by 21 nations of the Americas at Bogota, Colombia. Its purpose is to further economic development and integration among nations of the Western hemisphere, to promote representative democracy and to help overcome poverty. The Pan-American Union, with offices at Washington, DC, serves as the General Secretariat for the OAS.

SMITH, MICHAEL J.: BIRTH ANNIVERSARY. Apr 30, 1945. Forty-year-old pilot of the space shuttle *Challenger* on Jan 28, 1986. It was to have been Commander Smith's first space flight. Born at Beaufort, NC, Smith perished with all others on board when *Challenger* exploded. See also: "*Challenger* Space Shuttle Explosion Anniversary" (Jan 28).

SOUTH VIETNAM FALLS TO VIETCONG: ANNIVERSARY. Apr 30, 1975. The president of South Vietnam announced the country's unconditional surrender to the Vietcong. Communist troops moved into Saigon, and 1,000 Americans in the city were hastily evacuated. Thousands of South Vietnamese also tried to flee. The surrender announcement came 21 years after the 1954 Geneva agreements divided Vietnam into North and South. The last American troops had left South Vietnam in March 1973.

SPANK OUT DAY USA. Apr 30. A day on which all caretakers of children—parents, teachers and day-care workers—are asked not to use corporal punishment as discipline and to become acquainted with positive, effective disciplinary alternatives. For info: Nadine Block, EPOCH-USA, 155 W Main St, Ste 1603, Columbus, OH 43215. Phone: (614) 221-8829. E-mail: nblock@att.net. Web: www.stophitting.org.

SWEDEN: FEAST OF VALBORG. Apr 30. An evening celebration in which Sweden "sings in the spring" by listening to traditional hymns to the spring, often around community bonfires. Also known as Walpurgis Night, the Feast of Valborg occurs annually Apr 30.

THEATER IN NORTH AMERICA FIRST PERFORMANCE: ANNIVERSARY. Apr 30, 1598. On the banks of the Rio Grande, near present-day El Paso, TX, the first North American theatrical performance was acted. The play was a Spanish commedia featuring an expedition of soldiers. On July 10 of the same year, the same group produced *Moros y Los Cristianos* (*Moors and Christians*), an anonymous play.

VIETNAM: LIBERATION DAY. Apr 30. National holiday. Commemorates the fall of Saigon to the Communists in 1975, ending the Vietnam War.

WALPURGIS NIGHT. Apr 30. The eve of May Day, which is the feast day of St. Walpurgis, the protectress against the magic arts. According to German legend, witches gather this night and celebrate their sabbath on the highest peak in the Harz Mountains. Celebrated particularly by university students in northern Europe.

WASHINGTON, GEORGE: PRESIDENTIAL INAUGURATION ANNIVERSARY. Apr 30, 1789. George Washington was inaugurated as the first president of the US under the new Constitution at New York, NY. Robert R. Livingston administered the oath of office to Washington on the balcony of Federal Hall, at the corner of Wall and Broad streets.

WILSON, ELLIS: BIRTH ANNIVERSARY. Apr 30, 1899. African-American artist born at Mayfield, KY, and died at New York, NY, Jan 1, 1977. Wilson painted realistic portrayals of African Americans at work and at play. In 1944 he was awarded a Guggenheim fellowship. He visited South Carolina, painting city scenes and fishing towns. In the 1950s, Wilson took a revelatory trip to Haiti, which changed the way he painted. Unable to note any facial features on the Haitians he painted from a distance, Wilson began painting flat, stylized silhouettes. *Haitian Funeral Procession* remains Wilson's most popular and accessible painting.

Birthdays Today

Jane Campion, 55, film director (*The Piano*), born Wellington, New Zealand, Apr 30, 1954.

Jill Clayburgh, 65, actress (*Fools Rush In, Luna, An Unmarried Woman*), born New York, NY, Apr 30, 1944.

Gary Collins, 71, actor, talk-show host, born Boston, MA, Apr 30, 1938.

Kirsten Dunst, 27, actress (*Spider-Man* films, *Marie Antoinette, The Cat's Meow*), born Point Pleasant, NJ, Apr 30, 1982.

Johnny Galecki, 34, actor ("Roseanne," *Suicide Kings*), born Bree, Belgium, Apr 30, 1975.

Stephen Harper, 50, 22nd Prime Minister of Canada (2006–), born Toronto, ON, Canada, Apr 30, 1959.

Perry King, 61, actor (*Slaughterhouse Five, The Lords of Flatbush, Switch*), born Alliance, OH, Apr 30, 1948.

Cloris Leachman, 79, actress (Oscar for *The Last Picture Show*; "Phyllis"), born Des Moines, IA, Apr 30, 1930.

Willie Nelson, 76, singer ("Always on My Mind," "On the Road Again"), actor (*Honeysuckle Rose*), born Abbott, TX, Apr 30, 1933.

Adrian Pasdar, 44, actor ("Heroes," "Judging Amy"), born Pittsfield, MA, Apr 30, 1965.

Isiah Thomas, 48, Hall of Fame basketball player, basketball coach, born Chicago, IL, Apr 30, 1961.

Burt Young, 69, writer, actor (*Chinatown, Rocky, Once Upon a Time in America*), born New York, NY, Apr 30, 1940.

✦ May ✦

May 1 — Friday

DAY 121 **244 REMAINING**

ADDISON, JOSEPH: BIRTH ANNIVERSARY. May 1, 1672. (Old Style date.) English essayist born at Milston, Wiltshire, England. Died at London, June 17, 1719 (OS). "We are," he wrote in *The Spectator*, "always doing something for Posterity, but I would fain see Posterity do something for us."

AMTRAK: ANNIVERSARY. May 1, 1971. Amtrak, the national rail service that combined the operations of 18 passenger railroads, went into service.

✦ **ASIAN/PACIFIC AMERICAN HERITAGE MONTH.** May 1–31. Presidential Proclamation issued honoring Asian/Pacific Americans each year since 1979. Public Law 102-450 of Oct 28, 1992, designated the observance for the month of May each year.

AWARENESS OF MEDICAL ORPHANS MONTH. May 1–31. A month dedicated to the awareness of medical orphans—rare disorders/diseases. Includes "Adopt a Medical Orphan" in AmericaCares AmericaCan Project; "Unsolved Cases," spotlighting real stories; and publishing of "Hope and Healing" from submissions sent in by the public. Encourages and sponsors internship/study/volunteer programs for credit or noncredit. For info: The ForGoodnessSake! Center, 427 E 7th St, Michigan City, IN 46360. E-mail: ForGood@adsnet.com.

BATMAN DEBUTS: 70th ANNIVERSARY. May 1, 1939. In the May issues of *Detective Comics* #27 that appeared on newsstands on this day, a new crime fighter, the "Batman," debuted, created by Bob Kane (collaborating with Bill Finger). The caped hero was an immediate success. See also: "Superman Debuts: Anniversary" (June 1).

BELGIUM: PLAY OF SAINT EVERMAAR. May 1. Annual performance (for more than 1,000 years) of a mystery play, in its original form, by the village inhabitants.

BETTER HEARING AND SPEECH MONTH. May 1–31. A nationwide public information campaign held each May to inform the 41 million Americans with hearing and speech problems that help is available. Annually, the month of May. For info: American Speech-Language-Hearing Assn, 2200 Research Blvd, Rockville, MD 20850-3289. Phone: (800) 638-8255. Web: www.asha.org.

BIG TEN MEN'S GOLF CHAMPIONSHIPS. May 1–3. Penn State University, University Park, PA. For info: Big Ten Conference, 1500 W Higgins Rd, Park Ridge, IL 60068-6300. Phone: (847) 696-1010. Fax: (847) 696-1110. Web: www.bigten.org.

BREAD PUDDING RECIPE EXCHANGE. May 1–7. A week dedicated to the exchange of creative bread pudding recipes. For sample recipes send SASE. For info: Bread Pudding Update, PO Box 416, Denver, CO 80201. Phone: (303) 575-5676. E-mail: mail@breadpudding.net. Web: www.breadpudding.net.

CANADA: CANADIAN TULIP FESTIVAL. May 1–18. Ottawa, ON. The world's largest tulip festival with more than three million tulips in bloom. The International Pavilion features the food, culture and entertainment of more than 25 countries. This event grew out of a thank-you gift of bulbs for providing refuge to the Dutch royal family. Est attendance: 1,000,000. For info: Canadian Tulip Festival, 130 Albert St, Ste 1705, Ottawa, ON, K1P 5G4 Canada. Phone: (613) 567-5757 or (800) 66-TULIP. Fax: (613) 567-6216. E-mail: info@tulipfestival.ca. Web: www.tulipfestival.ca.

***CITIZEN KANE* FILM PREMIERE: ANNIVERSARY.** May 1, 1941. Orson Welles's directorial masterpiece premiered at New York City's RKO Palace. The premiere had been delayed almost three months due to studio jitters about what media magnate William Randolph Hearst's reaction would be—since the film was a thinly disguised version of his life. The film's multiple points of view, deep-focus photography and witty script made it a favorite with critics at the time: John O'Hara in *Newsweek* said, "Your faithful bystander reports that he has just seen a picture which he thinks must be the best picture he ever saw." Nominated for nine Academy Awards, *Citizen Kane* won for best original screenplay by Herman J. Mankiewicz and Welles. The film did not perform well commercially (due in part to Hearst's influence) but is now regarded as the greatest American film.

CLARK, MARK: BIRTH ANNIVERSARY. May 1, 1896. US general who served in both world wars, Mark Clark was born at Madison Barracks, NY. In November 1942 he commanded the US forces taking part in the invasion of North Africa, and in January 1943 he became commander of the US Fifth Army, which invaded Italy in September 1943, taking Rome in June 1944. After the Germans capitulated in Italy, Clark was appointed commander of US occupation forces in Austria. He died at Charleston, SC, Apr 17, 1984.

COIN & STAMP EXPO. May 1–3. Radisson Hotel, Anaheim, CA. Est attendance: 4,000. For info: Israel Bick, Exec Dir, Intl Stamp & Coin Collectors Society, PO Box 854, Van Nuys, CA 91408. Phone: (818) 997-6496. Fax: (818) 988-4337. E-mail: iibick@sbcglobal.net. Web: www.bick.net.

COLUMBIAN EXPOSITION OPENING: ANNIVERSARY. May 1, 1893. At 12:08 PM President Grover Cleveland, in the presence of nearly a quarter of a million people, placed his finger on a golden key opening the Columbian Exposition at Chicago, IL. Amid the unfurling of thousands of flags, sounding of trumpets and booming of cannons, the key activated an electromagnetic valve, steam rushed into great cylinders, and an immense pump began its enormous burden of pumping 15 million gallons of water a day to provide the 685-acre fair and its visitors with an ample water supply.

CREATIVE BEGINNINGS MONTH. May 1–31. How are you creative? Have you tapped into your full potential? Enjoy the budding month of May while discovering something new about yourself. Enroll in a course, write a poem, plant a garden, coordinate a social event. While developing your gifts, encourage others to cultivate their own creative beginnings. For info: Christina Bergenholtz, PO Box 301, Grafton, MA 01519. Phone: (508) 839-5139. Fax: (508) 887-9556. E-mail: chrismhb@aol.com.

DANDELION MAY FEST. May 1–2. Der Marktplatz, Dover, OH. Old-fashioned festival includes finals in a nationwide dandelion recipe contest, cooking demonstrations, live entertainment and food booths featuring dishes made from dandelions, such as dandelion coffee ice cream, dandelion pizza, dandelion bread and dandelion gravy. Also, dandelion wine and jelly tasting, family entertainment and 5k fun run. Festival highlight is 16th Great Dandelion Cook-Off; for entry forms for cook-off call: (800) 843-9463. Est attendance: 15,000. For info: Anita Davis, Coord, Der Marktplatz-Breitenbach Wine Cellars, 5934 Old Rte 39 NW, Dover, OH 44622.

Phone: (330) 343-3603. Fax: (330) 343-8290. E-mail: info@breitenbachwine.com. Web: www.breitenbachwine.com.

DENMARK: TIVOLI GARDENS SEASON. May 1–Sept 20. Copenhagen. World famous for its variety of entertainment, symphony concerts, pantomime and ballet. Beautiful flower arrangements and excellent restaurants. Traditional season: May 1 until the third Sunday in September.

EMMETT KELLY CLOWN FESTIVAL. May 1–3 (tentative). Downtown Houston, MO. Houston was the home of Emmett Kelly, and this festival in his honor features a carnival, clown school, parade on Saturday, arts and crafts, Big Top performances, souvenir sales and clown competition. Appearance by the daughters of Emmett Kelly, Sr, Stasia Kelly and Monika Kelly, and his grandson, Joey Kelly. Est attendance: 5,000. For info: Houston Area Chamber of Commerce, PO Box 374, Houston, MO 65483. Phone: (417) 967-2220. Fax: (417) 967-2178. E-mail: chamber004@centurytel.net.

EXECUTIVE COACHING DAY. May 1. Workers deserve the best leaders they can get! Our sports stars have skill and strength coaches, our great actors have speech and movement coaches, our politicians have media coaches. Why don't more of our corporate and union executives who are responsible for effectively leading thousands of employees and members utilize the power of coaching? This is a day to applaud all organizational leaders who take their profession seriously enough to improve their skills through coaching. A day to raise the awareness of those who do not use coaching to improve their capacity to effectively lead their organizations. For info: Ira Chaleff, Pres, Executive Coaching & Consulting Assoc, 9621 Hillridge Dr, Kensington, MD 20895. Phone: (301) 933-3752. E-mail: ira.chaleff@exe-coach.com. Web: www.exe-coach.com.

FAMILY WELLNESS MONTH. May 1–31. Spend more time with family and appreciate those closest to you. Hold a family meeting and resolve differences and disputes. Set family goals and share dreams. Call up estranged family and reunite. Remember that your family members are just human, not superhuman, and tell them that you love them. For info: Angela Brown Oberer, Words of Wellness, PO Box 49266, Charlotte, NC 28277. Phone: (704) 289-2900. E-mail: Angela@WordsofWellness.com. Web: www.WordsofWellness.com.

FIBROMYALGIA EDUCATION AND AWARENESS MONTH. May 1–31. To promote education and awareness of the dangers of fibromyalgia, which is also known as the fibromyalgia syndrome, fibrositis or chronic muscle pain syndrome. Fibromyalgia affects more than 10 million American women. Kit of materials available for $15. For info: Pharmacists Planning Services, Inc, c/o Fibromyalgia Council of America, 101 Lucas Valley Rd, Ste 382, San Rafael, CA 94903. Phone: (415) 479-8628. Fax: (415) 479-8608. E-mail: ppsi@aol.com. Web: www.ppsinc.org.

FIRST SKYSCRAPER: 125th ANNIVERSARY. May 1, 1884. Construction was begun on the Home Insurance Company building on this date in Chicago, IL. The 10-story building was completed in 1885. Designed by William Le Baron Jenney, it had a steel frame that carried the weight of the building. The walls provided no support but hung like curtains on the metal frame. This method of construction revolutionized American architecture and allowed architects to build taller and taller buildings. The Home Insurance Building was demolished in 1931.

May 2009	S	M	T	W	T	F	S
						1	2
	3	4	5	6	7	8	9
	10	11	12	13	14	15	16
	17	18	19	20	21	22	23
	24	25	26	27	28	29	30
	31						

FORD, GLENN: BIRTH ANNIVERSARY. May 1, 1916. Born at Sainte-Christine, QC, Canada, Ford was a popular Hollywood actor who appeared in more than 100 films. Important films included *Gilda* with Rita Hayworth, *Blackboard Jungle* with Sidney Poitier, *3:10 to Yuma* and *The Rounders*. He won a Golden Globe Award in 1962 for his leading role in Frank Capra's *Pocketful of Miracles*. He died at Hollywood, CA, Aug 30, 2006.

FREEDOM SHRINE MONTH. May 1–31. The Freedom Shrine is an exclusive program of the National Exchange Club. It is a collection of 30 original historic documents photographically reproduced and attractively displayed in thousands of locations across the nation. The purpose of the Freedom Shrine is to remind all Americans that the freedoms they enjoy today are gifts from the past—forged from idealism, determination and the sacrifice of the many courageous men and women who preceded us. It also serves to remind us that so precious a gift as freedom must be continually guarded and protected. For info: The National Exchange Club, 3050 Central Ave, Toledo, OH 43606-1700. Phone: (800) 924-2643. E-mail: info@nationalexchangeclub.org. Web: www.nationalexchangeclub.org.

GET CAUGHT READING MONTH. May 1–31. Celebrities appear in ads appealing to people of all ages to remind them of the joys of reading. Events will be held throughout the country to celebrate reading. For info: Assn of American Publishers, 71 Fifth Ave, New York, NY 10003. Phone: (212) 255-0200. Web: www.publishers.org or www.getcaughtreading.org.

GIFTS FROM THE GARDEN MONTH. May 1–31. May is the month to celebrate the many ways gardens and gardening benefit people. From flowers and fitness to color and conversation, many treasures are growing in your own backyard. For info: C.L. Fornari, PO Box 355, Osterville, MA 02655. Phone: (508) 428-5895. E-mail: clfornari@yahoo.com. Web: www.gardenlady.com.

GO FETCH! NATIONAL FOOD DRIVE FOR HOMELESS ANIMALS. May 1–31. An annual, monthlong national food drive to raise awareness about starving and malnourished stray animals. These animals may live on the streets, be abused or neglected, be feral, or be homeless pets living with their homeless families in shelters. For info: Go Fetch!, PALS Foundation, PO Box 1271, San Luis Obispo, CA 93406. Phone: (805) 544-0984. Web: www.gofetch.r8.org.

GREAT BRITAIN FORMED: ANNIVERSARY. May 1, 1707. (Old Style date.) A union between England and Scotland resulted in the formation of Great Britain. (Wales had been part of England since the 1500s.) Today's United Kingdom consists of Great Britain and Northern Ireland.

HAITIAN HERITAGE MONTH. May 1–31. Boston, MA. A series of events is organized throughout the month of May in the Boston Haitian American community featuring exhibits, flag raisings, concerts, games, parades and presentations. The events are organized to honor Haitian general Toussaint Louverture, to remember the consensus reached by black and mulatto officers to fight for Haitian independence in 1803 and to celebrate the Haitian flag created that same year. The flag-raising ceremony will take place on May 15, and the Haitian-American Unity Day Parade will take place on May 17. For info: Haitian-Americans United, Inc, 10 Fairway St, PO Box 260440, Mattapan, MA 02126. Phone: (617) 298-2976. E-mail: unity@hauinc.org. Web: www.hauinc.org or www.haitianheritagemonth.net.

HEAL THE CHILDREN MONTH. May 1–31. To encourage survivors of childhood abuse and neglect to speak out. By revealing their painful experiences, they can inspire others to prevent children from suffering the same ordeals. Annually, the month of May. For info: Donald Etkes, PhD, 11693 San Vicente Blvd, #491, Los Angeles, CA 90049. Phone: (310) 979-0245. Web: www.AbuseHealing.com.

HEALTHY VISION MONTH. May 1–31. Although it is believed that half of all blindness can be prevented, the number of people in the US who suffer from vision loss continues to increase. Healthy Vision Month informs the public that preventive eye care is important because eye conditions, diseases and injuries that can rob a person of vision can strike at any time in life, from newborn to old age. For info: American Academy of Ophthalmology, PO Box 7424, San

Francisco, CA 94120-7424. Phone: (415) 447-0258. Fax: (415) 561-8533. E-mail: eyemd@aao.org. Web: www.geteyesmart.org.

HUNTINGTON'S DISEASE AWARENESS MONTH. May 1–31. For info: Huntington's Disease Society of America, 505 Eighth Ave, Ste 902, New York, NY 10018. Phone: (212) 242-1968 or (800) 345-4372. Fax: (212) 239-3430. Web: www.hdsa.org.

INTERNATIONAL BUSINESS IMAGE IMPROVEMENT MONTH. May 1–31. The image of your business sets the tone for how successful your company will be. Just as we judge others within the first few seconds of meeting, we do the same for a business. Receive information on how to improve your business image and take the free online business card quiz. For info: Debbie Allen, Pres, Allen & Assoc Consulting, Inc, PO Box 27946, Scottsdale, AZ 85255-0149. Phone: (800) 359-4544. Web: www.debbieallen.com.

INTERNATIONAL INTERNAL AUDIT AWARENESS MONTH. May 1–31. This month promotes awareness of the internal audit profession and its important role in organizational effectiveness and efficiency, internal control, risk management and corporate governance. Annually, the month of May, since 2003. For info: The Institute of Internal Auditors, 247 Maitland Ave, Altamonte Springs, FL 32701. Phone: (407) 937-1100. Fax: (407) 937-1101. E-mail: Trish.Harris@theiia.org. Web: www.theiia.org.

INTERNATIONAL VICTORIOUS WOMAN MONTH. May 1–31. Celebrating the woman who has shaped life's challenges into distinct victories. Acknowledging the Victorious Woman encourages others to strive toward overcoming difficulties and influences them to achieve their own personal victories. For info: Annmarie Kelly, SkillBuilder Systems. Phone: (610) 738-8225. E-mail: info@victoriouswoman.com. Web: www.victoriouswoman.com.

ISLE OF EIGHT FLAGS SHRIMP FESTIVAL. May 1–3. Fernandina Beach, FL, on beautiful Amelia Island. Florida commemorates Fernandina's role as the birthplace of the modern shrimping industry. Multievent festival includes juried fine arts and crafts show, entertainment, antiques, pirates, children's fun zone and food. Est attendance: 125,000. For info: Isle of Eight Flags Shrimp Festival, PO Box 6146, Fernandina Beach, FL 32035. Phone: (866) 4-AMELIA (toll-free). E-mail: 4info@shrimpfestival.com. Web: www.shrimpfestival.com.

ITALY: FESTIVAL OF SAINT EFISIO. May 1–4. Cagliari. Said to be one of the biggest and most colorful processions in the world. Several thousand pilgrims on foot, in carts and on horseback wearing costumes dating from the 17th century accompany the statue of the saint through the streets.

✦ **JEWISH AMERICAN HERITAGE MONTH.** May 1–31. Formerly celebrated as Jewish Heritage Week.

JONES, MARY HARRIS (MOTHER JONES): BIRTH ANNIVERSARY. May 1, 1830. Irish-born American labor leader. After the death of her husband and four children (during the Memphis yellow fever epidemic of 1867) and loss of her belongings in the Chicago Fire in 1871, Jones devoted her energies and her life to organizing and advancing the cause of labor. It seemed she was present wherever there were labor troubles. She gave her last speech on her 100th birthday. Born at Cork, Ireland, she died Nov 30, 1930, at Silver Spring, MD.

KANSAS BARBED WIRE SWAP/SELL. May 1–2. La Crosse, KS. Barbed Wire Collectors Association show and meeting. Est attendance: 200. For info: Kansas Barbed Wire Collectors Assn, PO Box 578, La Crosse, KS 67548. Phone: (785) 222-9900. Web: www.rushcounty.org/barbedwiremuseum.

KEEP KIDS ALIVE—DRIVE 25® DAY. May 1. 3rd annual. Keep Kids Alive—Drive 25® Day is a call to action on the part of citizens in communities of all sizes across the US to commit to safe driving behaviors on neighborhood streets. Communities develop activities to educate and engage citizens in the efforts through neighborhoods, schools, businesses and civic organizations. In many communities law enforcement and public officials take the lead. Annually, May 1. For info: Tom Everson, Keep Kids Alive—Drive 25, 12418 C St, Omaha, NE 68144. Phone: (402) 334-1391. E-mail: Tom@kkad25.org. Web: www.KeepKidsAliveDrive25.org.

LABOR DAY. May 1. In 140 countries, May 1 is observed as a workers' holiday. When it falls on a Saturday or Sunday, the following Monday is observed as a holiday. Bermuda, Canada and the US are the only countries that observe Labor Day in September. The Bahamas observe Labor Day in June.

LATINO BOOKS MONTH. May 1–31. In its ongoing efforts to promote books by and for Latinos, the Association of American Publishers (AAP) has designated May as Latino Books Month. During the monthlong celebration, booksellers, librarians and others in the book industry will encourage people in their communities to read books by and for Latinos, in both English and Spanish. For info: Tina Jordan, AAP, 71 Fifth Ave, 2nd Fl, New York, NY 10003. Phone: (212) 255-0200. E-mail: tjordan@publishers.org. Web: www.publishers.org.

✦ **LAW DAY, USA.** May 1. Presidential Proclamation issued each year for May 1 since 1958 at request. (PL87–20 of Apr 7, 1961.)

LAW ENFORCEMENT APPRECIATION MONTH IN FLORIDA. May 1–31. Law Enforcement Appreciation Day is May 15 in Florida, a ceremonial day.

LEI DAY. May 1. Hawaii. On this special day—the Hawaiian version of May Day—leis are made, worn, given, displayed and entered in lei-making contests. One of the most popular Lei Day celebrations takes place at Honolulu at Kapiolani Park at Waikiki. Includes the state's largest lei contest, the crowning of the Lei Day Queen, Hawaiian music, hula and flowers galore.

✦ **LOYALTY DAY.** May 1. Presidential Proclamation issued annually for May 1 since 1959 at request. (PL85–529 of July 18, 1958.) Note that an earlier proclamation was issued in 1955.

MAGIC DRAGON STREET MEET NATIONALS AND EXTREME CAR SHOWS. May 1–3. Lake Ozark, MO. 21st annual meet features more than 750 street rods, customs, trucks, street machines and motorcycles from throughout the US. Always the first weekend in May. Est attendance: 10,000. For info: Lake Area Chamber of Commerce, PO Box 1570, Lake Ozark, MO 65049. Phone: (800) 451-4117 or (573) 964-1008. Fax: (573) 964-1010. E-mail: mcook@lakeareachamber.com.

MARSHALL ISLANDS, REPUBLIC OF THE: CONSTITUTION DAY. May 1. National holiday.

MAY DAY. May 1. The first day of May has been observed as a holiday since ancient times. Spring festivals, maypoles and maying are still common, but the political importance of May Day has grown since the 1880s, when it became a workers' day in the US. Now widely observed in countries as a workers' holiday or as Labor Day. (Bermuda, Canada and the US observe Labor Day in September.) In most European countries, when May Day falls on Saturday or Sunday, the Monday following is observed as a holiday, with bank and store closings, parades and other festivities.

MAY DAY FAIRIE FESTIVAL. May 1–3. Spoutwood Farm, Glen Rock, PA. 18th annual. A celebration of spring, featuring nature spirits of all kinds. Entertaining and educational. Annually, the first full weekend in May. Est attendance: 15,000. For info: Dana Stout, Sproutwood Farm, 4255 Pierceville Rd, Glen Rock, PA 17327. Phone: (717) 249-1805. E-mail: posie@posiefairy.com. Web: www.fairiefestival.net.

MELANOMA/SKIN CANCER DETECTION AND PREVENTION MONTH. May 1–31. For info: American Academy of Dermatology, PO Box 4014, Schaumburg, IL 60168-4014. Phone: (866) 503-7546. Web: www.aad.org.

MOON PHASE: FIRST QUARTER. May 1. Moon enters First Quarter phase at 4:44 PM, EDT.

MOTHER GOOSE DAY. May 1. To reappreciate the old nursery rhymes. Motto: "Either alone or in sharing, read childhood nursery favorites and feel the warmth of Mother Goose's embrace." Website has ideas for celebrating, including recipes. Annually, May 1. For info: Gloria T. Delamar, Founder, Mother Goose Society. E-mail: mothergoosesociety@delamar.org. Web: www.delamar.org/mothergoosesociety.html.

MOTORCYCLE SAFETY MONTH. May 1–31. This month is dedicated to encouraging safe motorcycle riding practices. Learn safe riding practices through state and local motorcycle safety courses and continue improving skills through advanced riding courses. Set a safe environment this month to prepare for a safe riding season. For info: Sylvia Henderson, Springboard Training, PO Box 588, Olney, MD 20830-0588. Phone: (301) 260-1538. E-mail: sylvia@springboardtraining.com. Web: www.springboardtraining.com.

NATIONAL ALLERGY/ASTHMA AWARENESS MONTH. May 1–31. Kit of materials available for $15 from this nonprofit organization. For info: Frederick S. Mayer, Pharmacists Planning Service, Inc, c/o Allergy Council of America (ACA), 101 Lucas Valley Rd, Ste 382, San Rafael, CA 94903. Phone: (415) 479-8628. Fax: (415) 479-8608. E-mail: ppsi@aol.com. Web: www.ppsinc.org.

NATIONAL ARTHRITIS MONTH. May 1–31. Increases awareness of the more than 100 forms of arthritis and related diseases and increases support for the 66 million Americans with arthritis. During the month, various communities will sponsor Arthritis Walks™ to raise money for education and research. Participants may choose 5k or 1-mile courses, and men, women and children with arthritis will wear special blue "hero" caps to show that they are taking control of their disease. To join an Arthritis Walk in your area, call (877) 232-2898. For info: Arthritis Foundation, 1330 W Peachtree St NW, Ste 100, Atlanta, GA 30309. Phone: (404) 872-7100. Fax: (404) 872-8694. Web: www.arthritis.org.

NATIONAL BARBECUE MONTH. May 1–31. To encourage people to start enjoying barbecuing early in the season when daylight saving time lengthens the day. Annually, the month of May. For info: Hearth, Patio & Barbecue Assn, 1901 N Moore St, Ste 600, Arlington, VA 22209. Phone: (703) 522-0086. Fax: (703) 522-0548. Web: www.hpba.org.

NATIONAL BIKE MONTH. May 1–31. 53rd annual celebration of bicycling for fun, fitness and transportation. Local activities sponsored by bicycling organizations, environmental groups, PTAs, police departments, health organizations and civic groups. About five million participants nationwide. Annually, the month of May. For info: League of American Bicyclists, 1612 K St, Ste 800, Washington, DC 20006. Phone: (202) 822-1333. Fax: (202) 822-1334. E-mail: bikeleague@bikeleague.org. Web: www.bikemonth.com or www.bikeleague.org.

NATIONAL EGG MONTH. May 1–31. Dedicated to the versatility, convenience, economy and good nutrition of "The incredible edible egg™." Annually, the month of May. For info: Linda Braun, American Egg Board, 1460 Renaissance Dr, Park Ridge, IL 60068. Web: www.aeb.org.

May 2009

S	M	T	W	T	F	S
					1	2
3	4	5	6	7	8	9
10	11	12	13	14	15	16
17	18	19	20	21	22	23
24	25	26	27	28	29	30
31						

NATIONAL GOOD CAR-KEEPING MONTH. May 1–31. To promote increased safety and value through good car maintenance. For info: Sander Allen, Good Car-Keeping Institute, 990 N Lake Shore Dr, Ste 11-A, Chicago, IL 60611.

NATIONAL HAMBURGER MONTH. May 1–31. Sponsored by White Castle, the original fast-food hamburger chain (founded in 1921), to pay tribute to one of America's favorite foods. With or without condiments, on or off a bun or bread, hamburgers have grown in popularity since the early 1920s and are now an American meal mainstay. For info: White Castle Management Co, Marketing Dept, 555 W Goodale St, Columbus, OH 43215-1158. Phone: (614) 228-5781. Fax: (614) 228-8841. Web: www.whitecastle.com.

NATIONAL HEPATITIS AWARENESS MONTH. May 1–31. A month to raise awareness of and increase research for viral hepatitis, while also promoting prevention through schools, health departments, churches, community organizations and other groups. For info: Hepatitis Foundation Intl, 504 Blick Dr, Silver Spring, MD 20904. Phone: (800) 891-0707. E-mail: HFI@comcast.net. Web: www.HepatitisFoundation.org.

NATIONAL MEDITATION MONTH. May 1–31. A monthlong campaign to educate the public about the physical, emotional and mental benefits of meditation. Sponsored by The Deep Calm, an organization committed to creating awareness about meditation and its link to inner peace and peace in the world. Annually, in May. For info: Elesa Commerse, The Deep Calm, 721 Howard St, Evanston, IL 60202. Phone: (773) 777-7754. E-mail: elesa@thedeepcalm.com. Web: www.thedeepcalm.com.

NATIONAL MENTAL HEALTH MONTH. May 1–31. For info: Mental Health America, 2000 N Beauregard St, 6th Fl, Alexandria, VA 22311. Phone: (800) 969-NMHA or (703) 684-7722. Web: www.nmha.org.

NATIONAL MILITARY APPRECIATION MONTH. May 1–31. 11th annual. This month honors, remembers, recognizes and appreciates all military personnel—those men and women who have served throughout our history and all who now serve in uniform and their families as well as those Americans who have given their lives in defense of the freedoms we all enjoy today. For info: Duncan Munro, MSgt USAF (Ret), Natl Events Coordinator, Natl Military Appreciation Month, PO Box 123, Bena, VA 23018-0123. E-mail: nmam@nmam.org. Web: www.nmam.org.

NATIONAL MOVING MONTH. May 1–31. Recognizing America's mobile roots and kicking off the busiest moving season of the year. Each year more than 40 million Americans pack up their belongings and relocate to new homes and communities. More than half of these moves take place between May and September. During National Moving Month, moving experts will be educating Americans on how to plan a successful move, pack efficiently and handle the uncertainties and questions that children may have. For info: Allied Van Lines. Web: www.allied.com.

NATIONAL OSTEOPOROSIS AWARENESS AND PREVENTION MONTH. May 1–31. Osteoporosis is not a natural part of aging. Find out what you can do to prevent, diagnose and treat it by joining the NOF family. For info: Natl Osteoporosis Foundation, 1232 22nd St NW, Washington, DC 20037. Phone: (202) 223-2226. Fax: (202) 223-2237. E-mail: communications@nof.org. Web: www.nof.org.

NATIONAL PHOTO MONTH. May 1–31. This monthlong celebration of the memories market is the perfect opportunity to capture special moments. Visit your local photo retailer for prints or other photo memorabilia. Annually, every May. For info: PMA, 3000 Picture Pl, Jackson, MI 49201. Phone: (517) 788-8100. Fax: (517) 788-8371. Web: www.pmai.org.

NATIONAL PHYSICAL FITNESS AND SPORTS MONTH. May 1–31. Encourages individuals and organizations to promote fitness activities and programs. Popularly known as "May Month," it was established by the President's Council on Physical Fitness and Sports in 1983. For info: President's Council on Physical Fitness and Sports, Dept W, 200 Independence Ave SW, Room 738H, Washington, DC 20201-0004. Phone: (202) 690-9000. Fax: (202) 690-5211. Web: www.fitness.gov or www.presidentschallenge.org.

NATIONAL PRESERVATION MONTH. May 1–31. To draw public attention to historic preservation, including neighborhoods, districts, landmark buildings, open space and maritime heritage. For info: Natl Trust for Historic Preservation, 1785 Massachusetts Ave NW, Washington, DC 20036. Phone: (202) 588-6000. Fax: (202) 588-6038. Web: www.preservationnation.org.

NATIONAL SALAD MONTH. May 1–31. Celebrate healthy eating and good nutrition with salads and salad dressing. For info: Traci Gibson, The Assn for Dressings and Sauces, 1100 Johnson Ferry Rd, Ste 300, Atlanta, GA 30342. Phone: (404) 252-3663. Fax: (404) 252-0774. E-mail: tgibson@kellencompany.com. Web: www.dressings-sauces.org or www.saladaday.org.

NATIONAL SALSA MONTH. May 1–31. Recognizing salsa as America's favorite way to add flavor to all kinds of food, such as eggs, burgers, chicken, tacos, chips, potatoes, rice and much more. Celebrates more than 60 years of picante sauce, a salsa created in 1947, and celebrates Cinco de Mayo, a major Mexican holiday now recognized across North America. For info: Pace Foods, c/o Dublin & Assoc, 3015 San Pedro, San Antonio, TX 78212. Phone: (210) 227-0221. Web: www.pacefoods.com.

NATIONAL SMILE MONTH. May 1–31. Smiling can change your life, which is why the American Academy of Cosmetic Dentistry® (AACD) reminds you to smile throughout this month. Virtually all Americans say an attractive smile is an important social asset. It has the power to give you more confidence in your job, in your personal relationships and in virtually everything you do. For info: American Academy of Cosmetic Dentistry, 5401 World Dairy Dr, Madison, WI 53718. Phone: (608) 222-8583 or (800) 543-9220. Fax: (608) 222-9540. E-mail: pr@aacd.com. Web: www.aacd.com.

NATIONAL STROKE AWARENESS MONTH. May 1–31. A time to educate the nation and spread awareness about stroke prevention, symptom recognition and recovery. For info: Natl Stroke Assn, 9707 E Easter Ln, Englewood, CO 80112. Phone: (800) STROKES. Web: www.stroke.org.

NATIONAL SWEET VIDALIA® ONION MONTH. May 1–31. America's favorite sweet onions come into season each year at about this time and are available fresh in the market through Labor Day. These hand-planted, hand-harvested sweeties are low in pyruvate, the chemical that makes onions hot and causes cooks to tear up when cutting. Vidalia onions grow only in a 20-county area in southeast Georgia. In fact, the Georgia Department of Agriculture has registered the name *Vidalia* as it pertains to onions. The temperate climate and unique soil ensure the onions will have a mild and sweet taste—folks have even been known to bite into a Vidalia onion as if it were an apple. Vidalia onions were a favorite of James Beard, the father of American cuisine. For info and recipes: Wendy Brannen, Exec Dir, Vidalia Onion Committee, PO Box 1609, Vidalia, GA 30475. Phone: 912-537-1918. Web: www.vidaliaonion.org.

NATIONAL VINEGAR MONTH. May 1–31. Celebrate the season of cleaning and cooking with one of the home's most versatile products. For info: Traci Gibson, The Vinegar Institute, 1100 Johnson Ferry Rd, Ste 300, Atlanta, GA 30342. Phone: (404) 252-3663. Fax: (404) 252-0774. E-mail: tgibson@kellencompany.com. Web: www.versatilevinegar.org.

NEW HOME OWNER'S DAY. May 1. You have faced all the challenges—now take the time as a new home owner to stand back and reflect on your new home and savor the feeling. For info: Dorothy Zjawin, Dir, 61 W Colfax Ave, Roselle Park, NJ 07204.

NO PANTS DAY. May 1. A growing international event, held annually on the first Friday in May, based on the simple idea of relishing the joy inherent in not wearing pants. A day on which everyone, be they students, respectable businesspeople or cherished community leaders, parades around in public without pants. Usually, people wear thick, colorful boxers, but bloomers, slips, briefs and other underwear all work as well. For info: Roy Janik, No Pants Day, 507 Sacramento Dr, Austin, TX 78704. Phone: (512) 916-4246. E-mail: info@nopantsday.com. Web: www.nopantsday.com.

✦ **OLDER AMERICANS MONTH.** May 1–31. Presidential Proclamation; from 1963 through 1973 this was called "Senior Citizens Month." In May 1974 it became Older Americans Month. In 1980 the title included Senior Citizens Day, which was observed May 8, 1980. Issued annually since 1963.

ORANGEBURG FESTIVAL OF ROSES. May 1–3. Edisto Memorial Gardens, Orangeburg, SC. To celebrate the beauty of the roses and the gardens. Est attendance: 35,000. For info: Orangeburg County Chamber of Commerce, PO Box 328, Orangeburg, SC 29116-0328. Phone: (803) 534-6821 or (800) 545-6153. Fax: (803) 531-9435. E-mail: chamber@orangeburgsc.net. Web: www.festivalofroses.com.

PAAR, JACK: BIRTH ANNIVERSARY. May 1, 1918. Radio personality, actor and humorist Jack Paar began hosting the "Tonight Show" on NBC in 1957. With his catchphrase, "I kid you not," he revolutionized late-night television, changing the format of traditional late shows from variety hours to talk shows and charming his audience and celebrity guests with a witty interviewing style. Paar introduced dozens of new stars to the American public, including Bill Cosby, Woody Allen, Carol Burnett and the Smothers Brothers. He left the show in 1962, handing it over to Johnny Carson, and retired from show business a few years later. Born at Canton, OH, he died at Greenwich, CT, Jan 27, 2004.

PERSONAL HISTORY MONTH. May 1–31. Members of the Association of Personal Historians across the US, Canada and beyond raise awareness of and appreciation for preserving life stories by providing professional services to help record and publish those stories. Activities include informational events and workshops for individuals, organizations and communities. Many members also donate their services to charitable causes and community organizations during this month. For info: Jurgen Mollers, 1819 Polk St, San Francisco, CA 94109. Web: www.personalhistorians.org.

PHILIPPINES: FEAST OF OUR LADY OF PEACE AND GOOD VOYAGE. May 1–31. Pilgrimage to the shrine of Nuestra Sra de la Paz y Buen Viaje at Antipolo, Rizal.

PHILIPPINES: SANTACRUZAN. May 1–31. Maytime pageant-procession that recalls the quest of Queen Helena and Prince Constantine for the Holy Cross.

REACT MONTH. May 1–31. Highlights the radio safety efforts of Radio Emergency Associated Communications Team (REACT) volunteers worldwide. REACT communications specialists receive emergency radio calls and relay them to authorities. REACTers also teach correct emergency radio procedure to the public. (This includes cell phone emergencies, since cells are really two-way radios.) REACT teams provide two-way radio safety communications for local events, parades, walkathons, etc, on request. Teams also offer speakers on radio safety to local groups. For info: REACT Intl, 403-5210 Auth Rd, Suitland, MD 20746-4330. Phone: (301) 316-2900. Fax: (301) 316-2903. E-mail: REACT@REACTintl.org. Web: www.REACTintl.org.

REVISE YOUR WORK SCHEDULE MONTH. May 1–31. To increase awareness, exploration and implementation of nontraditional work schedules such as flextime, telecommuting, job sharing and compressed workweeks. Annually, the month of May. For info: Center for WorkTime Options, 1286 University Ave, #192, San Diego, CA 92103-3312. Phone: (619) 232-0404. E-mail: info@worktimeoptions.com.

RICHMOND'S MUSHROOM FESTIVAL. May 1–2. Richmond, MO. Parade, arts and crafts, carnival, sanctioned barbecue contest, bike and car show, bands and stage shows. Est attendance: 5,000. For info: Exec Dir, Chamber of Commerce, 104 W North Main, Richmond, MO 64085. Phone: (816) 776-6916. Fax: (816) 776-6917. E-mail: cofcommerce@mchsi.com. Web: www.richmondchamber.org.

RUSSIA: INTERNATIONAL LABOR DAY. May 1–2. Public holiday in Russian Federation. "Official May Day demonstrations of working people."

SCHOOL PRINCIPALS' DAY. May 1. A day of recognition for all elementary, middle and high school principals for their leadership and dedication to providing the best education possible for their students. Annually, May 1. For info: Janet M. Dellaria, PO Box 39, Trout Creek, MI 49967. Phone: (906) 852-3539.

SMITH, KATE: 100th BIRTH ANNIVERSARY. May 1, 1909. One of America's most popular singers. Kate Smith, who never took a formal music lesson, recorded more songs than any other performer (more than 3,000), made more than 15,000 radio broadcasts and received more than 25 million fan letters. On Nov 11, 1938, she introduced a new song during her regular radio broadcast, written especially for her by Irving Berlin: "God Bless America." It soon became the unofficial national anthem. Born Kathryn Elizabeth Smith at Greenville, VA, she began her radio career May 1, 1931, with "When the Moon Comes over the Mountain," a song identified with her throughout her career. She died at Raleigh, NC, June 17, 1986.

SOWERBY, LEO: BIRTH ANNIVERSARY. May 1, 1895. Pulitzer Prize–winning composer of more than 550 compositions, born at Grand Rapids, MI, and died July 7, 1968, at Port Clinton, OH.

STEPMOTHERS DAY. May 1. A day to honor stepmothers who care! Annually, May 1. For info: Susan Wilkins-Hubley, 3650 Hammonds Plains Rd, Unit 14, Ste 113, Upper Tantallon, NS, B3Z 4R3, Canada. E-mail: secondwivesclub.com@gmail.com. Web: www.secondwivesclub.com.

STRIKE OUT STROKES MONTH. May 1–31. Dedicated to the prevention of strokes. Factors resulting from heredity or natural processes can't be changed, but with proper medical treatment and healthful lifestyle adjustments, some risk factors can be eliminated. Kit materials available for $15. For info: Pharmacy Council on Stroke Prevention, c/o Pharmacists Planning Service, Inc, 101 Lucas Valley Rd, #382, San Rafael, CA 94903. Phone: (415) 479-8628. Fax: (415) 479-8608. E-mail: ppsi@aol.com. Web: www.ppsinc.org.

SUGARLOAF CRAFTS FESTIVAL. May 1–3. Dulles Expo Center, Chantilly, VA. This show, now in its ninth year, features more than 300 nationally recognized craft designers and fine artists displaying and selling their original creations. Includes craft demonstrations, live music, specialty food, children's entertainment, hourly gift certificate drawings and more. Est attendance: 15,000. For info: Sugarloaf Mountain Works, 200 Orchard Ridge Dr, #215, Gaithersburg, MD 20878. Phone: (800) 210-9900. Fax: (301) 253-9620. Web: www.sugarloafcrafts.com.

TEEN SELF-ESTEEM MONTH. May 1–31. May is a month of excitement and frenzy as teens graduate, go to proms, get summer jobs and gear up for college. These life-changing events and transitions, combined with a strong dose of hormones and the vacations and parties that come along with springtime, can challenge even the most sensible teenagers. By setting aside the entire month of May and turning our focus and attention toward helping teens understand that their power and sense of self comes from within, we better equip these youths to make decisions that not only can lead to life success but also can save lives. For info: Kathleen Hassan, PO Box 570, Milton, MA 02186. Phone: (617) 698-1976. E-mail: inspire@kathleenhassan.com. Web: www.teenselfesteemmonth.com.

TENNIS MONTH. May 1–31. A month to promote the benefits of playing tennis, sponsored by the United States Tennis Association. Established in 1881, the USTA is the national governing body for the sport of tennis and is the largest tennis organization in the world, with 17 geographic sections, more than 700,000 individual members and 7,000 organizational members, thousands of volunteers, and a professional staff dedicated to growing the game. For info: United States Tennis Assn, 70 W Red Oak Ln, White Plains, NY 10604. Phone: (914) 696-7000. Web: www.usta.com or www.tennismonth.com.

May 2009

S	M	T	W	T	F	S
					1	2
3	4	5	6	7	8	9
10	11	12	13	14	15	16
17	18	19	20	21	22	23
24	25	26	27	28	29	30
31						

TOAD SUCK DAZE. May 1–3. Downtown Conway, AR. 28th annual event features toad-jumping contests, concerts, parade, street dancing, carnival, softball tournament, 5k and 10k runs, arts and crafts and more. Annually, the first weekend in May. Est attendance: 160,000. For info: Conway Chamber of Commerce, 900 Oak St, Conway, AR 72032. Phone: (501) 327-7788. Fax: (501) 327-7790. Web: www.toadsuck.org.

ULTRAVIOLET AWARENESS MONTH. May 1–31. Exposure to UV rays can burn delicate eye tissue and raise the risk of developing cataracts and cancers of the eye. Protecting your eyes from UV dangers by choosing the right sunglasses is the message of this month. For info: Prevent Blindness America®, 211 W Wacker Dr, Ste 1700, Chicago, IL 60606. Phone: (800) 331-2020. E-mail: info@preventblindness.org. Web: www.preventblindness.org.

U-2 INCIDENT: ANNIVERSARY. May 1, 1960. On the eve of a summit meeting between US president Dwight D. Eisenhower and Soviet premier Nikita Khrushchev, a U-2 espionage plane flying at about 60,000 feet was shot down over Sverdlovsk, in central USSR. The pilot, CIA agent Francis Gary Powers, survived the crash, as did large parts of the aircraft, a suicide kit and sophisticated surveillance equipment. The sensational event, which US officials described as a weather reconnaissance flight gone astray, resulted in cancellation of the summit meeting. Powers was tried, convicted and sentenced to 10 years in prison by a Moscow court. In 1962 he was returned to the US in exchange for an imprisoned Soviet spy. He died in a helicopter crash in 1977. See also: "Powers, Francis Gary: Birth Anniversary" (Aug 17).

VEGETARIAN RESOURCE GROUP'S ESSAY CONTEST FOR KIDS. May 1. Children aged 18 and under are encouraged to submit a two- to three-page essay on topics related to vegetarianism. Essays accepted up to May 1. Winners, announced Sept 15, will receive a $50 savings bond. For info: The Vegetarian Resource Group, PO Box 1463, Baltimore, MD 21203. Phone: (410) 366-8343. E-mail: vrg@vrg.org. Web: www.vrg.org.

WILLIAMS, ARCHIE: BIRTH ANNIVERSARY. May 1, 1915. Archie Williams, along with Jesse Owens and others, debunked Hitler's theory of the superiority of Aryan athletes at the 1936 Berlin Olympics. As a black member of the US team, Williams won a gold medal by running the 400-meter in 46.5 seconds (0.4 second slower than his own record of earlier that year). Williams, who was born at Oakland, CA, earned a degree in mechanical engineering from the University of California–Berkeley in 1939 but had to dig ditches for a time because companies weren't hiring black engineers. He became an airplane pilot and for 22 years trained Tuskegee Institute pilots, including the black air corps of WWII. When asked during a 1981 interview about his treatment by the Nazis during the 1936 Olympics, he replied, "Well, over there at least we didn't have to ride in the back of the bus." Archie Williams died June 24, 1993, at Fairfax, CA.

WOMEN'S HEALTH CARE MONTH. May 1–31. To initiate a public education campaign devoted to increasing awareness of the many health concerns unique to women. Focus will be on the prevention of the major causes of death and poor health among women—heart disease, cancer, arthritis, osteoporosis and bone fractures—as well as on depression and alcoholism in women. There is a $15 charge for kit materials. Annually, the month of May. For info: Pharmacists Planning Service, Inc, c/o Pharmacists Council for Women's Health, 101 Lucas Valley Rd, Ste 382, San Rafael, CA 94903. Phone: (415) 479-8628. Fax: (415) 479-8608. E-mail: ppsi@aol.com. Web: www.ppsinc.org.

YOUNG ACHIEVERS/LEADERS OF TOMORROW MONTH. May 1–31. International Leadership Network's Young Achievers/Leaders of Tomorrow Program recognizes and encourages positive achievement, behavior, leadership and service. Community and national recognition events honor student leaders in grades 5–11. Annually, the month of May. For info: Tom Eichhorst, 1750 S Brentwood Blvd, Ste 404, St. Louis, MO 63144. Phone: (314) 961-5978. Fax: (314) 961-8716. E-mail: inleadnet@aol.com. Web: www.ilnleadnet.com.

 BIRTHDAYS TODAY

Wes Anderson, 40, film director/screenwriter (*The Darjeeling Limited, The Life Aquatic with Steve Zissou, The Royal Tenenbaums, Rushmore*), born Houston, TX, May 1, 1969.

Charles (Chuck) Bednarik, 84, Hall of Fame football player, born Bethlehem, PA, May 1, 1925.

Steve Cauthen, 49, former jockey, born Walton, KY, May 1, 1960.

Judy Collins, 70, singer ("Send in the Clowns"), born Seattle, WA, May 1, 1939.

Rita Coolidge, 64, singer, born Nashville, TN, May 1, 1945.

Sonny James, 80, singer, born Jimmy Loden at Hackleburg, AL, May 1, 1929.

Curtis Martin, 36, former football player, born Pittsburgh, PA, May 1, 1973.

Bobbie Ann Mason, 69, writer (*In Country, Spence and Lila*), born Mayfield, KY, May 1, 1940.

Tim McGraw, 42, country singer, born Delhi, LA, May 1, 1967.

Charlie Schlatter, 43, actor ("Diagnosis Murder"), born Englewood, NJ, May 1, 1966.

Paul Teutul, Sr, 60, motorcycle designer, television personality ("American Chopper"), born Yonkers, NY, May 1, 1949.

May 2 — Saturday

DAY 122 — **243 REMAINING**

APPLE BLOSSOM FESTIVAL. May 2–3. Gettysburg, PA. An annual event held the first weekend in May at the South Mountain Fairgrounds. Est attendance: 20,000. For info: Gettysburg CVB, PO Box 4117, Gettysburg, PA 17325. Phone: (717) 334-6274 or (717) 677-9413. Fax: (717) 334-1166. E-mail: info@gettysburg.travel. Web: www.gettysburg.travel.

ASTRONOMY DAY. May 2. To take astronomy to the people. International Astronomy Day is observed on a Saturday near the first quarter moon between mid-April and mid-May. Cosponsored by 14 astronomical organizations. For info: Gary E. Tomlinson, Coord, Astronomy Day Headquarters, 30 Stargazer Ln, Comstock Park, MI 49321. Phone: (616) 456-3537. E-mail: gtomlins@sbcglobal.net. Web: www.astroleague.org. See also: "Astronomy Week" (Apr 27–May 3).

BARK IN THE PARK. May 2. Lincoln Park, Chicago, IL. In recognition of Be Kind to Animals Week, thousands of paws and feet will hit the ground walking for this 5k event to raise funds for the animals. Entrance fee. Est attendance: 3,500. For info: The Anti-Cruelty Society, 157 W Grand Ave, Chicago, IL 60610. Phone: (312) 329-8726. E-mail: info@anticruelty.org. Web: www.barkinthepark.org.

BERLIN SURRENDERS: ANNIVERSARY. May 2, 1945. At 6:45 AM, Soviet marshal Georgi Zhukov accepted the surrender of Berlin, the German capital. The victory came at a terrible cost for the Red Army, with 304,887 men killed, wounded or missing—10 percent of its soldiers. About 125,000 Berliners died in the siege, many by suicide.

BIG TEN WOMEN'S ROWING CHAMPIONSHIPS. May 2. Ohio State University, Columbus, OH. For info: Big Ten Conference, 1500 W Higgins Rd, Park Ridge, IL 60068-6300. Phone: (847) 696-1010. Fax: (847) 696-1150. Web: www.bigten.org.

CHINA: BIRTHDAY OF LORD BUDDHA. May 2. Religious observances are held in Buddhist temples and Buddha's statue is bathed. Annually, eighth day of fourth lunar month. Date in other countries will differ from China's.

COTTON PICKIN' FAIR. May 2–3 (also Oct 3–4). Gay, GA. Skilled artisans feature art, antiques and crafts in a 1910-era venue. The Peach Packing Shed, Cotton Gin and Warehouse, 1891 Farmhouse and a number of smaller buildings create a unique backdrop for a great day of family fun in the country. Includes a wonderful variety of great food plus live entertainment on six stages. Biannually: the first weekends of May and October. Est attendance: 35,000. For info: Cotton Pickin' Fair. Phone: (706) 538-6814. E-mail: info@cpfair.org. Web: www.cpfair.org.

ETHNIC FESTIVAL. May 2. Whittier School, Oak Park, IL. Sponsored by Elementary School District 97's Multicultural Education Department, this 29th annual event is a villagewide celebration of diversity. It kicks off with a parade and culminates with performances by local and professional musicians, dancers and tumblers. A highlight of the festival is the sale of ethnic foods and artifacts. Annually, the first Saturday in May. For info: Lynn Allen or Pearl Hall, Multicultural Education Dept, c/o Percy Julian Middle School, 416 S Ridgeland, Oak Park, IL 60302. Phone: (708) 524-7700. E-mail: lallen@op97.org or phall@op97.org.

FISHING CONTEST. May 2. Lake Shenandoah County Park, Lakewood, NJ. Catch the longest fish of a specific species. Novice or expert. Prizes awarded. Bait and tackle shop on premises. Picnic area. Rain or shine. Children $2, adults $4. Est attendance: 300. For info: Fred Lesser, Wells Mills County Park, 905 Wells Mills Rd, Waretown, NJ 08758. Phone: (609) 971-3085. Fax: (609) 971-9540. Web: www.oceancountyparks.org.

GALVESTON HISTORIC HOMES TOUR. May 2–3 (also May 9–10). Galveston Island, TX. Discover Galveston Island's great treasures of Victorian and post-Victorian architecture as privately owned homes are opened to the public for tours. Annually, the first two full weekends in May. Est attendance: 5,000. For info: Galveston Historical Foundation, 502 20th St, Galveston, TX 77550. Phone: (409) 765-7834. Fax: (409) 765-7851. E-mail: foundation@galvestonhistory.org. Web: www.galvestonhistory.org.

HOLLAND TULIP TIME FESTIVAL. May 2–9. Holland, MI. A celebration of Dutch culture and heritage as well as the queen of the festival, the tulip. Est attendance: 500,000. For info: Holland Tulip Time Festival, Inc, 238 S River Ave, Holland, MI 49423. Phone: (616) 396-4221 or (800) 822-2770. Fax: (616) 396-4545. E-mail: tulip@tuliptime.com. Web: www.tuliptime.com.

JOIN HANDS DAY. May 2. A national day of volunteering that brings youths and adults together to improve their own communities. Sponsored by America's Fraternal Benefit Societies. Annually, the first Saturday in May. For info: Join Hands Day, 1315 W 22nd St, Ste 400, Oak Brook, IL 60523. Phone: (630) 522-6322, ext 116. Fax: (630) 522-6327. Web: www.joinhandsday.org.

KENTUCKY DERBY. May 2. Churchill Downs, Louisville, KY. The running of America's premier Thoroughbred horse race, inaugurated in 1875. First jewel in the Triple Crown, traditionally followed by the Preakness (second Saturday after the Derby) and the Belmont Stakes (fifth Saturday after the Derby). Annually, the first Saturday in May. Est attendance: 150,000. For info: Churchill Downs, 700 Central Ave, Louisville, KY 40208. Phone: (502) 636-4400. Web: kentuckyderby.com.

KING JAMES BIBLE PUBLISHED: ANNIVERSARY. May 2, 1611. King James I had appointed a committee of learned men to produce a new translation of the Bible in English. This version, popularly called the King James Version, is known in England as the Authorized Version.

LEONARDO DA VINCI: DEATH ANNIVERSARY. May 2, 1519. Italian artist, scientist and inventor. Painter of the famed *Last Supper*, perhaps the first painting of the High Renaissance, and of the *Mona Lisa*. Inventor of the first parachute. Born at Vinci, Italy, in 1452 (exact date unknown), he died at Amboise, France.

LOW COUNTRY SHRIMP FESTIVAL. May 2. McClellanville, SC. Seafood, arts, crafts, civic display, entertainment and blessing of the fleet. Annually, the first Saturday in May. Est attendance: 15,000. For info: The Archibald Rutledge Academy, 1011 Old Cemetery Rd, McClellanville, SC 29458. Phone: (843) 887-3323. Web: www.lowcountryshrimpfestival.com.

LUCKY MAY SHOW AND SALE. May 2–3 (also May 9–10; 16–17; 23–25; 30–31). Chapel Hill, NC. Each Saturday and Sunday in May, plus Memorial Day. Unique architectural antiques, featuring an extensive collection of period wrought-iron artifacts (especially iron gates, garden art and home embellishments). For info: Gaines Steer, The Last Unicorn, 536 Edwards Ridge Rd, Chapel Hill, NC 27517. Phone: (919) 968-8440. E-mail: info@thelastunicorn.com. Web: www.thelastunicorn.com.

NATIONAL HOMEBREW DAY. May 2. Each year on the first Saturday in May, homebrewers unite nonbrewing and brewing friends and family to celebrate National Homebrew Day, joining with thousands of homebrewers from around the world in brewing the same recipes and sharing a simultaneous toast at noon, EST. For info: Cindy Jones, Brewers Assn, 736 Pearl St, Boulder, CO 80302. Phone: (303) 447-0816. Fax: (303) 885-2825. E-mail: cindy@brewersassociation.org. Web: www.beertown.org.

RAY, SATYAJIT: BIRTH ANNIVERSARY. May 2, 1921. Film director Satyajit Ray was born at Calcutta, India. Possibly India's best-known film director, he made more than 30 films and won numerous international awards, including an Academy Award for lifetime achievement. His films include the trilogy *Pather Panchali* (1956), *Aparajito* (1956) and *The World of Apu* (1959). Ray died Apr 23, 1992, at Calcutta.

ROBERT'S RULES DAY. May 2, 1837. Anniversary of the birth of Henry M. Robert (General, US Army), author of *Robert's Rules of Order*, a standard parliamentary guide. Born at Robertville, SC. Died at Hornell, NY, May 11, 1923.

SEQUIM IRRIGATION FESTIVAL. May 2–10 (tentative). Sequim, WA. 114th annual. Come and join the fun at this unique festival. Includes amusement rides, a parade, arts and crafts displays, entertainment, food booths and much more. Est attendance: 20,000. For info: Sequim Chamber of Commerce, Sequim Irrigation Festival, PO Box 2073, Sequim, WA 98382. Phone: (360) 683-6197. Fax: (360) 683-6349. Web: www.irrigationfestival.com.

SOUTHERN APPALACHIAN DULCIMER FESTIVAL. May 2. Tannehill Ironworks Historical State Park, McCalla, AL. Festival highlighting old-time dulcimer music. Est attendance: 1,500. For info: Tannehill Ironworks Historical State Park, 12632 Confederate Pkwy, McCalla, AL 35111. Phone: (205) 477-5711. Fax: (205) 477-9400.

SPOCK, BENJAMIN: BIRTH ANNIVERSARY. May 2, 1903. Pediatrician and author, born at New Haven, CT. His book on child rearing, *Common Sense Book of Baby and Child Care* (later called *Baby and Child Care*), has sold more than 30 million copies. In 1955 he became professor of child development at Western Reserve University at Cleveland, OH. He resigned from this position in 1967 to devote his time to the pacifist movement. Spock died at San Diego, CA, Mar 15, 1998.

May 2009	S	M	T	W	T	F	S
						1	2
	3	4	5	6	7	8	9
	10	11	12	13	14	15	16
	17	18	19	20	21	22	23
	24	25	26	27	28	29	30
	31						

STRAWBERRY FESTIVAL. May 2–3. Lahaska, PA. Strawberries served up in various forms—dipped in chocolate, in assorted pastries and shortcake, in jams, in fritters, and fresh and unadorned. Craftspeople gather to show their wares and demonstrate their skills. Live entertainment and pie-eating contests add to the festivities of this traditional spring celebration. Free admission. Est attendance: 18,000. For info: Peddler's Village, Rtes 202 and 263, Lahaska, PA 18931. Phone: (215) 794-4000. Fax: (215) 794-4001. Web: www.peddlersvillage.com.

TOWSONTOWN SPRING FESTIVAL. May 2–3. Towson, MD. 42nd annual. Four stages with continuous entertainment and 450 food, craft and display vendors on the street. Art and photography exhibit and antique auto display. Annually, the first Saturday and Sunday in May. Est attendance: 250,000. For info: Towsontown Spring Fest, 23 W Chesapeake Ave, Towson, MD 21204. Phone: (410) 825-1144. Fax: (410) 832-5863. Web: www.towsontownspringfestival.com.

VIRGINIA GOLD CUP. May 2. Great Meadow, The Plains, VA. Race day features seven steeplechase races, terrier races, and hat and tailgate competitions. The $100,000 Virginia Gold Cup race is run over a challenging four-mile post-and-rail course of 23 fences. Hospitality and sponsorship packages available. Annually, the first Saturday in May. Est attendance: 50,000. For info: Virginia Gold Cup Assn, PO Box 840, Warrenton, VA 20188. Phone: (540) 347-2612. Fax: (540) 349-1829. Web: www.vagoldcup.com.

VIRGINIA STATE CHAMPIONSHIP CHILI COOK-OFF. May 2. Historic Market area, Roanoke, VA. Live entertainment, pepper-eating contest, children's festival area, costume contest and the best chili samples from across the US and the Commonwealth of Virginia. All compete for the state title. Est attendance: 10,000. For info: Jenny Lee, Greenvale School, 627 Westwood Blvd, Roanoke, VA 24017. Phone: (540) 342-4716. Fax: (540) 344-0876. E-mail: jlee@greenvale-school.org.

BIRTHDAYS TODAY

Christine Baranski, 57, stage and screen actress (Tony Awards for *The Real Thing* and *Rumors*; *Mame*), born Buffalo, NY, May 2, 1952.

David Beckham, 34, soccer player, born Leytonstone, London, England, May 2, 1975.

Elizabeth Berridge, 47, actress ("The John Larroquette Show"), born Westchester, NY, May 2, 1962.

Theodore Bikel, 85, singer, actor (*Man on the Run, My Fair Lady*), born Vienna, Austria, May 2, 1924.

Larry Gatlin, 60, singer, songwriter ("Broken Lady," "All the Gold in California"), born Odessa, TX, May 2, 1949.

Lesley Gore, 63, singer ("I'll Cry if I Want To"), born Tenafly, NJ, May 2, 1946.

Sarah Hughes, 24, Olympic gold medal figure skater, born Manhasset, NY, May 2, 1985.

Bianca Jagger, 64, actress, political activist, ex-wife of Mick Jagger, born Managua, Nicaragua, May 2, 1945.

David Suchet, 63, actor ("The Way We Live Now," "Hercule Poirot Mysteries"), born London, England, May 2, 1946.

Jenna Von Oy, 32, actress ("Blossom"), born Newtown, CT, May 2, 1977.

May 3 — Sunday

DAY 123 **242 REMAINING**

BE KIND TO ANIMALS WEEK®. May 3–9. To promote kindness and humane care toward animals. Annually, the first full week of May. Features "Be Kind to Animals Kid Contest" with grand prize. Observed since 1915. For info: American Humane, 63 Inverness Dr E, Englewood, CO 80112. Phone: (303) 792-9900. Fax: (303) 925-9455. E-mail: info@americanhumane.org. Web: www.americanhumane.org.

BROWN, JAMES: BIRTH ANNIVERSARY. May 3, 1933. Singer and songwriter born at Barnwell, SC. Brown began singing gospel while in reform school. He quickly moved into pop music and by the early 1960s was a hugely successful performer. Transcending musical genres, he called himself the "Godfather of Soul" but was equally prominent in rock, gospel and rhythm and blues. He was a spectacular dancer and showman, known for outlandish costumes and energy-filled performances. One of the greatest influences on American music in the 20th century, the "hardest working man in show business" died Dec 25, 2006, at Atlanta, GA.

"CBS EVENING NEWS" TV PREMIERE: ANNIVERSARY. May 3, 1948. The news program began as a 15-minute telecast with Douglas Edwards as anchor. Walter Cronkite succeeded him in 1962 and expanded the show to 30 minutes; Eric Sevareid served as commentator. Dan Rather anchored the newscasts upon Cronkite's retirement in 1981. Rather retired in March 2005, with Katie Couric assuming the anchor seat in 2006.

COMMERCE BANK FIVE BORO BIKE TOUR. May 3. New York, NY. The largest recreational cycling event in America. Share a truly unique adventure with 30,000 cyclists and experience 42 traffic-free miles through the five boroughs of New York City. Venture with fellow cyclists onto the Madison Ave, Third Ave, Queensboro, Pulaski and majestic Verrazano-Narrows bridges—what better way is there to see the sights of New York City? Preregistration required. Annually, the first Sunday in May. Est attendance: 30,000. For info: Bike New York, 891 Amsterdam Ave, New York, NY 10025. Phone: (212) 932-2453. Fax: (212) 932-3206. E-mail: info@BikeNewYork.org. Web: www.BikeNewYork.org.

CROSBY, HARRY LILLIS "BING": BIRTH ANNIVERSARY. May 3, 1903. Bing Crosby, born at Tacoma, WA, was the best-selling artist, most popular radio star and biggest box office draw in his day—even beyond the emergence of rock in the mid-1950s. His "White Christmas" was one of the best-selling single records of the 20th century. He appeared in numerous comedic and dramatic film roles. He earned an Oscar for his performance in *Going My Way* (1944) and was also known for his *Road* films with Bob Hope. Crosby died on Oct 14, 1977, directly after shooting an 85 on 18 holes at La Moraleja Golf Course in Madrid, Spain.

DOW JONES TOPS 11,000: ANNIVERSARY. May 3, 1999. The Dow Jones Index of 30 major industrial stocks topped the 11,000 mark for the first time.

FLEXIBLE WORK ARRANGEMENTS WEEK. May 3–9. To promote experimentation with alternate work schedules and working at home. Annually, the week beginning with the first Sunday in May. For info: Center for WorkTime Options, 1286 University Ave, #192, San Diego, CA 92103-3312. Phone: (619) 232-0404. E-mail: info@worktimeoptions.com.

GARDEN MEDITATION DAY. May 3. Let go of your concerns and center your full attention on the garden for even a few minutes today. Focusing on weeding, tilling the soil or cleaning up the garden is a relaxing way to direct your concentration to just one thing. Annually, May 3. For info: C.L. Fornari, PO Box 355, Osterville, MA 02655. Phone: (508) 428-5895. E-mail: clfornari@yahoo.com. Web: www.gardenlady.com.

GOODWILL INDUSTRIES WEEK. May 3–9. To call international attention to Goodwill Industries as a leader in job training and employment services for people with disabilities and other barriers to employment. Annually, the first full week in May. For info: Goodwill Industries Intl, Communications Dept, 15810 Indianola Dr, Rockville, MD 20855. Phone: (301) 530-6500. Fax: (301) 530-1516. E-mail: contactus@goodwill.org. Web: www.goodwill.org.

HERITAGE GREEN CONCERTS BY THE SPRINGS. May 3 (also June 7, July 5, Aug 2 and Sept 6). Sandy Springs, GA. Celebrating its 13th anniversary, this free outdoor concert series features a diversity of music showcasing local entertainers. Coolers and blankets are welcome; concessions are sold. The concerts begin at 7 PM. Est attendance: 5,000. For info: Christy Nickles, Heritage Sandy Springs, 135 Hilderbrand Dr, Sandy Springs, GA 30328. Phone: (404) 851-9111. Fax: (404) 851-9807. E-mail: events@heritagesandysprings.org. Web: www.heritagesandysprings.org.

HOME AND GARDEN FESTIVAL. May 3. Chestnut Hill, PA. Lively street festival in charming urban village. Garden-related merchandise and handcrafts, live entertainment, food court and children's activities. Annually, the first Sunday in May. Est attendance: 40,000. For info: Peggy Miller, Chestnut Hill Business Assn, 8426 Germantown Ave, Philadelphia, PA 19118. Phone: (215) 247-6696. E-mail: inquiry@chestnuthillpa.com. Web: www.chestnuthillpa.com.

JAPAN: CONSTITUTION MEMORIAL DAY. May 3. National holiday commemorating adoption of the constitution in 1947. Part of the Golden Week Holidays.

KENT STATE COMMEMORATION. May 3–4. Kent State University, Kent, OH. 39th annual commemoration remembering the victims of the May 4, 1970, shootings at Kent State during an antiwar rally. Candlelight vigil and march begin at 11:00 PM on May 3 and continue through the night until the afternoon of May 4. May 4 ceremony includes ringing the Victory Bell at 12:24 PM, the time of the shootings. For info: May 4 Task Force, PO Box 49, CSI, KSC, Kent State University, Kent, OH 44242. Phone: (330) 672-3096. E-mail: may4taskforce@yahoo.com. Web: dept.kent.edu/May4.

LUMPY RUG DAY. May 3. To encourage the custom of teasing bigots and trigots for shoving unwelcome facts under the rug. When many cans of worms have been shoved under the rug, the defenders of the status quo obtain a new rug high enough to cover the unwanted facts. For info: Robert L. Birch, Puns Corps, 3108 Dashiell Rd, Falls Church, VA 22042. Phone: (703) 533-3668.

MACHIAVELLI, NICCOLO: BIRTH ANNIVERSARY. May 3, 1469. Italian writer and statesman, born at Florence, Italy. Author of *The Prince*, a book of advice for a ruler that prescribes strong, absolute government. Died at Florence, June 22, 1527.

MEIR, GOLDA: BIRTH ANNIVERSARY. May 3, 1898. Born at Kiev, Russia, Meir was prime minister of Israel from 1969 to 1974. She died at Jerusalem, Dec 8, 1978.

MEXICO: DAY OF THE HOLY CROSS. May 3. Celebrated especially by construction workers and miners, a festive day during which anyone who is building must give a party for the workers. A flower-decorated cross is placed on every piece of new construction in the country.

MOTORCYCLE MASS AND BLESSING OF THE BIKES. May 3. Paterson, NJ. 40th annual. Since 1969, a blessing of motorcycles, their riders and friends. Annually, the first Sunday in May. For info: Cathedral of St. John the Baptist, 381 Grand St, Paterson, NJ 07505. Est attendance: 2,000.

NATIONAL ANXIETY AND DEPRESSION AWARENESS WEEK. May 3–9. Educational programs and screenings for anxiety and depressive disorders. For info: Freedom from Fear, 308 Seaview Ave,

Staten Island, NY 10305. Phone: (718) 351-1717 for screening locations. Fax: (718) 980-5022. E-mail: help@freedomfromfear.org. Web: freedomfromfear.org.

NATIONAL FAMILY WEEK. May 3–9. Traditionally the first Sunday and the first full week in May are observed as National Family Week in many Christian churches.

NATIONAL HUG HOLIDAY WEEK. May 3–9. Huggers of all ages are invited to make a difference one hug at a time! The Hugs 4 Health movement needs your help to increase hugs, friendship and volunteer support for elderly people living in senior care and residential communities. Send SASE for a "Hugger's Package." For info: Hugs 4 Health, PO Box 896, Seal Beach, CA 90740-0896. Web: www.hugs4health.org.

NATIONAL INFERTILITY SURVIVAL DAY™. May 3. Beat the Mother's Day blues the week *before* Mother's Day. Here is the chance for infertile women to celebrate themselves, too! Infertility survivors also are encouraged to reach out to those struggling to find resolution to their challenges, through friendship, fund-raising and other supportive and creative endeavors. Infertility Survival Day™ is for those who want to use their experiences to attain positive outcomes for themselves and others. Annually, the first Sunday in May. For info: Beverly Barna. E-mail: infertilitysucks@aol.com. Web: www.infertilitysurvivalday.com.

NATIONAL PET WEEK. May 3–9. To promote responsible pet ownership and public awareness of veterinary medical service for animal health and care. Annually, the first full week in May. For info: The American Veterinary Medical Assn, 1931 N Meacham Rd, Ste 100, Schaumburg, IL 60173. Phone: (800) PET-WEEK. E-mail: info@avmaaux.co. Web: www.petweek.org.

NATIONAL PUBLIC RADIO FIRST BROADCAST: ANNIVERSARY. May 3, 1971. National noncommercial radio network, financed by Corporation for Public Broadcasting, began programming.

NATIONAL SPORTING GOODS ASSOCIATION MANAGEMENT CONFERENCE. May 3–6. The Westin La Cantera Resort, San Antonio, TX. 45th annual management conference and 11th annual Team Dealer Summit. The premier educational and networking event for the sporting goods industry. Attracts leading retailers, dealers, manufacturers, agents, media and industry organizations. Est attendance: 400. For info: Larry Weindruch, Dir of Communications, Natl Sporting Goods Assn, 1601 Feehanville Dr, Ste 300, Mount Prospect, IL 60056-6035. Phone: (847) 296-6742. Fax: (847) 391-9827. E-mail: info@nsga.org. Web: www.nsga.org.

NATIONAL TWO DIFFERENT COLORED SHOES DAY. May 3. A day to recognize and celebrate the uniqueness and diversity of humanity. The simple and lighthearted act of purposely wearing two different colored shoes demonstrates the courage to take a risk and step outside of one's daily routine. Annually, May 3. For info: Arlene Kaiser, EdD, 3424 Spring Creek Ln, Milpitas, CA 95035. Phone: (408) 946-4444. Fax: (408) 946-6664. E-mail: drarlenekaiser@mac.com.

PARANORMAL DAY. May 3. A day for all paranormal enthusiasts to get together and share their unique experiences with each other. Seminars, radio broadcasts and readings will take place worldwide. For info: Bob O'Brien, Consumer Advocate, 1061 Koelle Blvd, Seacaucus, NJ 07094. Phone: (646) 233-6610. E-mail: robtfobrien@aol.com.

POLAND: CONSTITUTION DAY (SWIETO TRZECIEGO MAJA). May 3. National Day. Celebrates ratification of Poland's first constitution, 1791.

ROBINSON, SUGAR RAY: BIRTH ANNIVERSARY. May 3, 1921. Ray "Sugar Ray" Robinson, boxer, born Walker Smith, Jr, at Detroit, MI. Generally considered "pound for pound the greatest boxer of all time," Robinson was a welterweight and middleweight champion who won 175 professional fights and lost only 19. A smooth and precise boxer, he fought until he was 45, dabbled in show business and established the Sugar Ray Robinson Youth Foundation to counter juvenile delinquency. To this day, his name connotes class, style and dignity. Died at Los Angeles, CA, Apr 12, 1989.

May 2009	S	M	T	W	T	F	S
						1	2
	3	4	5	6	7	8	9
	10	11	12	13	14	15	16
	17	18	19	20	21	22	23
	24	25	26	27	28	29	30
	31						

TEACHER APPRECIATION WEEK. May 3–9. PTAs across the country conduct activities to strengthen respect and support for teachers and the teaching profession. Founded in 1984. Annually, the first full week of May. For info: Natl PTA, 541 N Fairbanks Ct, Ste 1300, Chicago, IL 60611-3396. Phone: (312) 670-6782. Fax: (312) 670-6783. E-mail: info@pta.org. Web: www.pta.org.

TRADITIONAL PLOWING MATCH. May 3. Woodstock, VT. This annual event features a horse- and oxen-drawn plowing competition as well as demonstrations of different plowing techniques. Est attendance: 700. For info: Billings Farm and Museum, Rte 12 N, Woodstock, VT 05091. Phone: (802) 457-2355. Fax: (802) 457-4663. E-mail: info@billingsfarm.org. Web: www.billingsfarm.org.

UNITED NATIONS: WORLD PRESS FREEDOM DAY. May 3. A day to recognize that a free, pluralistic and independent press is an essential component of any democratic society and to promote press freedom in the world. For info: United Nations, Dept of Public Info, New York, NY 10017. Web: www.un.org.

UPDATE YOUR REFERENCES WEEK. May 3–9. A reminder to all job seekers to update their references annually because people are always moving or changing jobs. Additionally, it reminds former supervisors, etc, of who you are. Keeping an updated list of references means job seekers can be ready when the opportunity presents itself. For info: Laura DeCarlo, Career Directors International, 1665 Clover Circle, Melbourne, FL 32935. Phone: (888) 867-7972. Fax: (801) 752-7517. E-mail: info@careerdirectors.com.

BIRTHDAYS TODAY

Joseph Addai, 26, football player, born Houston, TX, May 3, 1983.

Greg Gumbel, 63, TV personality, sportscaster, born New Orleans, LA, May 3, 1946.

Dulé Hill, 35, actor ("The West Wing"), born Orange, NJ, May 3, 1974.

Jeffrey John Hornacek, 46, former basketball player, born Elmhurst, IL, May 3, 1963.

Engelbert Humperdinck, 73, singer ("After the Lovin'," "Release Me"), born Gerry Dorsey at Madras, India, May 3, 1936.

C.L. (Butch) Otter, 67, Governor of Idaho (R), born Caldwell, ID, May 3, 1942.

Pete Seeger, 90, folksinger, songwriter ("Where Have All the Flowers Gone?"), born New York, NY, May 3, 1919.

Frankie Valli, 72, singer ("Can't Take My Eyes Off You," "Grease"), born Newark, NJ, May 3, 1937.

David Vitter, 48, US Senator (R, Louisiana), born New Orleans, LA, May 3, 1961.

Ron Wyden, 60, US Senator (D, Oregon), born Wichita, KS, May 3, 1949.

May 4 — Monday

DAY 124 241 REMAINING

"ANOTHER WORLD" TV PREMIERE: 45th ANNIVERSARY. May 4, 1964. Created by Irna Phillips and sponsored by P&G, this soap was set in fictional Bay City. It was the first soap to air for a full hour and the first to beget two spin-offs ("Somerset" and "Texas"). Charles Durning, Ted Shackelford, Eric Roberts, Ray Liotta, Kyra Sedgwick, Faith Ford, Morgan Freeman, Jackée Harry, Victoria Wyndham and Valarie Pettiford are some of its well-known alums. The show was canceled in 1999 and the last episode aired June 25, 1999.

CHINA: YOUTH DAY. May 4. Annual public holiday "recalls the demonstration on May 4, 1919, by thousands of patriotic students in Beijing's Tiananmen Square to protest imperialist aggression in China."

CURAÇAO: MEMORIAL DAY. May 4. Victims of WWII are honored on this day. Military ceremonies at the War Monument. Not an official public holiday.

DATING AND LIFE COACH RECOGNITION WEEK. May 4–10. Coaches love to help people lead joyful, purposeful, successful lives. Whether the goals are to find love, pursue passions, embrace challenges, cultivate a career or achieve personal gratification, a coach's job is to empower, guide and inform. This week is a time to recognize the contributions dating and life coaches make to the well-being of society. For info: Robin Gorman Newman, 44 Somerset Dr N, Great Neck, NY 10020. Phone: (516) 773-0911. E-mail: robin@lovecoach.com. Web: www.lovecoach.com.

DISCOVERY OF JAMAICA BY CHRISTOPHER COLUMBUS: ANNIVERSARY. May 4, 1494. Christopher Columbus discovered Jamaica. The Arawak Indians were its first inhabitants.

FIRST WOMAN BRITISH PRIME MINISTER: 30th ANNIVERSARY. May 4, 1979. With the Conservative Party victory in the British election of May 3, 1979, Margaret Thatcher accepted Queen Elizabeth's appointment as prime minister on May 4. She thus became the first woman prime minister in 700 years of English parliamentary history. Thatcher, dubbed by her party the "Iron Maiden" for her toughness, held the office until forced to resign on Nov 22, 1990.

FREEDOM RIDERS: ANNIVERSARY. May 4, 1961. Militant students joined James Farmer of the Congress of Racial Equality (CORE) to conduct "freedom rides" on public transportation from Washington, DC, across the Deep South to New Orleans. The trips were intended to test Supreme Court decisions and Interstate Commerce Commission regulations prohibiting discrimination in interstate travel. In several places riders were brutally beaten by local people and policemen. On May 14 members of the Ku Klux Klan attacked the Freedom Riders in Birmingham, AL, while local police watched. In Mississippi, Freedom Riders were jailed. They never made it to New Orleans. The rides were patterned after a similar challenge to segregation, the 1947 Journey of Reconciliation, which tested the US Supreme Court's June 3, 1946, ban against segregation in interstate bus travel.

HAYMARKET SQUARE RIOT: ANNIVERSARY. May 4, 1886. Labor union unrest at Chicago, IL, led to violence when a crowd of unemployed men tried to enter the McCormick Reaper Works, where a strike was under way. Although no one was killed, anarchist groups called a mass meeting in Haymarket Square to avenge the "massacre." When the police advanced on the demonstrators, a bomb was thrown and several policemen were killed. Four leaders of the demonstration were hanged, and another committed suicide in jail. Three others were given jail terms. The case aroused considerable controversy around the world. See also: "Haymarket Pardon: Anniversary" (June 26).

HEPBURN, AUDREY: 80th BIRTH ANNIVERSARY. May 4, 1929. Audrey Hepburn, whose first major movie role in *Roman Holiday* (1953) won her an Academy Award as best actress, was born Edda Van Heemstra Hepburn-Rusten near Brussels, Belgium. She made 26 movies during her career and received four additional Oscar nominations. During the latter years of her life, Hepburn served as spokesperson for the United Nations Children's Fund, traveling worldwide raising money for the organization. Audrey Hepburn died Jan 20, 1993, at Tolochenaz, Switzerland.

INTERNATIONAL RESPECT FOR CHICKENS DAY. May 4. Launched in 2005, International Respect for Chickens Day (IRCD) is a project of United Poultry Concerns, a nonprofit organization that promotes the compassionate and respectful treatment of domestic fowl. IRCD is a day to celebrate chickens throughout the world by encouraging people to do an *action* for chickens on May 4, showing the world that chickens matter. Ideas include arranging a library display/video presentation, an IRCD school celebration, letters to the editor, radio talk-show participation, a local mall exhibit, etc. UPC supplies posters, brochures, videos and event ideas. For info: United Poultry Concerns, PO Box 150, Machipongo, VA 23405. Phone: (757) 678-7875. Fax: (757) 678-5070. E-mail: karen@upc-online.org. Web: www.upc-online.org.

IRELAND: MAY DAY BANK HOLIDAY. May 4. Bank holiday in the Republic of Ireland the first Monday in May.

JAPAN: GREENERY DAY. May 4. National holiday.

KENT STATE STUDENTS' MEMORIAL DAY: ANNIVERSARY. May 4, 1970. Four students (Allison Krause, 19; Sandra Lee Scheuer, 20; Jeffrey Glenn Miller, 20; and William K. Schroeder, 19) were killed by the National Guard during demonstrations against the Vietnam War at Kent (Ohio) State University.

MANN, HORACE: BIRTH ANNIVERSARY. May 4, 1796. American educator, author and public servant, known as the "father of public education in the US," was born at Franklin, MA. Founder of Westfield (MA) State College, president of Antioch College and editor of the influential *Common School Journal*. Mann died at Yellow Springs, OH, Aug 2, 1859.

MELANOMA MONDAY. May 4. Also known as National Skin Self-Examination Day. People are encouraged to examine their skin for skin cancer. Annually, the first Monday in May. For info: American Academy of Dermatology, PO Box 4014, Schaumburg, IL 60168-4014. Phone: (866) 503-7546. Web: www.aad.org or www.melanomamonday.org.

NATIONAL WILDFLOWER WEEK. May 4–9. A week "to encourage the observation, cultivation and study of native wildflowers as a means of deepening humankind's relationship, responsibility and commitment to protect and care for the ecological integrity of Mother Earth." Annually, the first full week in May. For info: Lady Bird Johnson Wildflower Center, 4801 La Crosse Ave, Austin, TX 78739-1702. Phone: (512) 232-0100. E-mail: wildflower@wildflower.org. Web: www.wildflower.org.

RHODE ISLAND: INDEPENDENCE DAY. May 4. Rhode Island abandoned allegiance to Great Britain in 1776.

SPACE MILESTONE: *ATLANTIS* (US): 20th ANNIVERSARY. May 4, 1989. First American planetary expedition in 11 years. Space shuttle *Atlantis* was launched, its major objective to deploy the *Magellan* spacecraft on its way to Venus to map the planet's surface. The shuttle was on its 65th orbit when it landed May 8, mission accomplished.

TYLER, JULIA GARDINER: BIRTH ANNIVERSARY. May 4, 1820. Second wife of John Tyler, 10th president of the US, born at Gardiners Island, NY. Died at Richmond, VA, July 10, 1889.

UNITED KINGDOM: MAY DAY BANK HOLIDAY. May 4. Bank and public holiday in England, Wales, Scotland and Northern Ireland. Annually, the first Monday in May.

WADE-DAVIS RECONSTRUCTION BILL PASSES THE HOUSE: ANNIVERSARY. May 4, 1864. Over the objections of President Abraham Lincoln, the House of Representatives on this date passed the Wade-Davis Reconstruction Bill, containing stiff punitive measures against the South that if put into law would have destroyed Lincoln's more moderate reconstruction aims. The bill was also adamantly opposed by radical Republicans led by Thaddeus Stevens, for whom it was insufficiently severe in its treatment of the Southern rebels. Lincoln eventually killed the bill by using the pocket veto.

BIRTHDAYS TODAY

Nickolas Ashford, 67, singer, songwriter ("Ain't No Mountain High Enough"), born Fairfield, SC, May 4, 1942.

Francesc "Cesc" Fabregas, 22, soccer player, born Vilessoc de Mar, Spain, May 4, 1987.

Ben Grieve, 33, baseball player, born Arlington, TX, May 4, 1976.

David Guterson, 53, author (*Snow Falling on Cedars*), born Seattle, WA, May 4, 1956.

Jackie Jackson, 58, singer (Jackson 5), born Sigmund Esco Jackson at Gary, IN, May 4, 1951.

Roberta Peters, 79, opera singer (retired), born Bronx, NY, May 4, 1930.

Dawn Staley, 39, former basketball player, born Philadelphia, PA, May 4, 1970.

Randy Travis, 50, country and western musician ("Forever and Ever, Amen"), born Marshville, NC, May 4, 1959.

George F. Will, 68, editor, columnist, baseball executive, born Champaign, IL, May 4, 1941.

Pia Zadora, 53, actress, singer, dancer, born Hoboken, NJ, May 4, 1956.

May 5 — Tuesday

DAY 125 240 REMAINING

AMERICAN MEDICAL ASSOCIATION FOUNDED: ANNIVERSARY. May 5, 1847. The American Medical Association was organized at a meeting at Philadelphia attended by 250 delegates. This was the first national medical convention in the US.

BATTLE OF THE WILDERNESS: ANNIVERSARY. May 5, 1864. The Battle of the Wilderness was the first major encounter between opposing troops under Robert E. Lee and Ulysses S. Grant. So named for the area of dense forest and underbrush of northern Virginia where the battle occurred, the fighting was especially fierce, with opposing armies often fighting at point-blank range as the battle lines became obscured in the smoke-filled forest. Both sides suffered heavy casualties totaling more than 28,000, and after the fighting had ceased on the second day, more than 200 wounded Federal troops were trapped and killed by the flames of fires started by the battle.

May 2009	S	M	T	W	T	F	S
						1	2
	3	4	5	6	7	8	9
	10	11	12	13	14	15	16
	17	18	19	20	21	22	23
	24	25	26	27	28	29	30
	31						

BEARD, JAMES: BIRTH ANNIVERSARY. May 5, 1903. The "father of American cooking" was born at Portland, OR. In a long and busy culinary career, he penned more than 20 classic cookbooks, appeared on television's first cooking show in 1946 and was an enthusiastic ambassador for American regional cooking. He died Jan 21, 1985. His Greenwich Village brownstone is America's only culinary historic landmark and serves as the headquarters of the James Beard Foundation.

BLY, NELLIE: BIRTH ANNIVERSARY. May 5, 1867. Born at Cochran's Mills, PA. Nellie Bly was the pseudonym used by pioneering American journalist Elizabeth Cochrane Seaman. Like her namesake in a Stephen Foster song, Nellie Bly was a social reformer and human rights advocate. As a journalist, she is best known for her exposé of conditions in what were then known as "insane asylums," where she posed as an "inmate." As an adventurer, she is best known for her 1889–90 around-the-world tour in 72 days, in which she bettered the time of Jules Verne's fictional character Phileas Fogg by eight days. She died at New York, NY, Jan 27, 1922.

BONZA BOTTLER DAY™. May 5. To celebrate when the number of the day is the same as the number of the month. Bonza Bottler Day™ is an excuse to have a party at least once a month. For more information see Jan 1. For info: Gail M. Berger, 14 Fernwood Dr, Taylors, SC 29687. E-mail: bonza@bonzabottlerday.com. Web: www.bonzabottlerday.com.

CARTOONISTS DAY. May 5. To honor all cartoonists in the industry: animation, magazines, comic strips, etc. For info: Polly Keener, 400 W Fairlawn Blvd, Akron, OH 44313. Phone: (330) 836-4448. E-mail: hamsteralley@aol.com.

CHILDHOOD DEPRESSION AWARENESS DAY. May 5. Also known as Green Ribbon Day. Annually, the Tuesday of the first full week in May. For info: Mental Health America, 2000 N Beauregard St, 6th Fl, Alexandria, VA 22311. Phone: (800) 969-6642 or (703) 684-7722. Web: www.mentalhealthamerica.net.

DENMARK: OBSERVATION OF 1945 LIBERATION. May 5. Flag-flying day to commemorate the 1945 liberation of Denmark from the Nazi occupation.

ETHIOPIA: PATRIOTS VICTORY DAY. May 5. National holiday. Commemorates the 1941 liberation of Addis Ababa by British and Ethiopian forces.

JAPAN: CHILDREN'S DAY. May 5. National holiday. Observed on the fifth day of the fifth month each year.

JOHNSON, AMY: FLIGHT ANNIVERSARY. May 5, 1930. Yorkshire-born Amy Johnson began the first successful solo flight by a woman from England to Australia. Leaving Croydon Airport in a de Havilland Tiger Moth named *Jason*, she flew 9,960 miles to Port Darwin, Australia, arriving May 28. The song "Amy, Wonderful Amy" celebrated the fame of this "wonder girl of the air," who became a legend in her own lifetime. Serving as an air ferry pilot during WWII, she was lost over the Thames Estuary in 1941.

MARX, KARL: BIRTH ANNIVERSARY. May 5, 1818. German socialist, founder and father of modern communism, author of *Das Kapital* and (with Friedrich Engels) the *Communist Manifesto*. Born at Treves, Germany, he died at London, England, Mar 14, 1883, at age 64.

MEXICO: BATTLE OF PUEBLA: ANNIVERSARY. May 5, 1862. The Mexican army defeated French troops at the city of Puebla. This day is commemorated as a national holiday in Mexico.

MEXICO: CINCO DE MAYO: ANNIVERSARY. May 5. Mexican national holiday recognizing the anniversary of the Battle of Puebla in 1862, in which Mexican troops under General Ignacio Zaragoza, outnumbered three to one, defeated invading French forces of Napoleon III. Anniversary is observed by Mexicans everywhere with parades, festivals, dances and speeches.

NATIONAL TEACHER DAY. May 5. To pay tribute to American educators, sponsored by the National Education Association, Teacher

Day falls during the National PTA's Teacher Appreciation Week. Local communities and organizations are encouraged to use this opportunity to honor those who influence and inspire the next generation through their work. Annually, the Tuesday of the first full week in May. For info: Natl Education Assn, 1201 16th St NW, #710, Washington, DC 20036. Phone: (202) 833-4000. Web: www.nea.org.

NETHERLANDS: LIBERATION DAY. May 5. Marks liberation of the Netherlands from Nazi Germany in 1945.

POWER, TYRONE: BIRTH ANNIVERSARY. May 5, 1913. American actor, best known for his motion picture action-adventure roles. Tyrone Power was born at Cincinnati, OH; he died Nov 15, 1958, at Madrid, Spain.

PRIMARY DAY: LIVE FROM DELAWARE STREET. May 5. Indianapolis, IN. Visit President Benjamin Harrison Home and listen to the conversations and gossip of the day as you enter each room and meet and speak with all the family members and household staff, whose roles are re-created by exceptional actors. Est attendance: 300. For info: PR Dept, President Benjamin Harrison Home, 1230 N Delaware St, Indianapolis, IN 46202. Phone: (317) 631-1888. Fax: (317) 632-5488. E-mail: harrison@pbhh.org. Web: www.pbhh.org.

SOUTH KOREA: CHILDREN'S DAY. May 5. A time for families to take their children on excursions. Parks and children's centers throughout the country are packed with excited and colorfully dressed children. A national holiday since 1975.

SPACE MILESTONE: *FREEDOM 7* (US). May 5, 1961. First US astronaut in space, second man in space, Alan Shepard, Jr, projected 115 miles into space in suborbital flight reaching a speed of more than 5,000 miles per hour. This was the first piloted *Mercury* mission.

STOCK MARKET CRASH OF 1893: ANNIVERSARY. May 5, 1893. Wall Street stock prices took a sudden drop. By the end of the year, 600 banks had closed. The Philadelphia and Reading, the Erie, the Northern Pacific, the Union Pacific and the Atchison, Topeka and Santa Fe railroads had gone into receivership; 15,000 other businesses went into bankruptcy. Other than the Great Depression of the 1930s, this was the worst economic crisis in US history; 15–20 percent of the workforce was unemployed.

"STOP THE MUSIC" TV PREMIERE: 60th ANNIVERSARY. May 5, 1949. ABC's prime-time musical-game show hosted by Bert Parks. Featured the singing talents of Kay Armen, Jimmy Blaine, Betty Ann Grove, Estelle Loring, Jaye P. Morgan and June Valli, and the dancing numbers of Sonja and Courtney Van Horne. Harry Salter conducted the band.

THAILAND: CORONATION DAY. May 5. National holiday. Commemorates the crowning of the current king in 1946.

TOTALLY CHIPOTLE DAY. May 5. To help trumpet what is proving to be one of the most popular "new" flavors in the US. Totally Chipotle Day helps familiarize the uninitiated with the delectable chipotle—a smoked jalapeño pepper—and its somewhat difficult pronunciation. Celebrated alongside Cinco de Mayo to honor its exclusively Mexican-Indian heritage. For info: M. Larkin. E-mail: info@TotallyChipotle.com. Web: www.TotallyChipotle.com.

BIRTHDAYS TODAY

Pat Carroll, 82, actress (Emmy for "Caesar's Hour"; "The Ted Knight Show"), born Shreveport, LA, May 5, 1927.

Henry Cavill, 26, actor ("The Tudors," *I Capture the Castle*), born Jersey, Channel Islands, May 5, 1983.

Richard E. Grant, 52, actor (*Henry and June, LA Story, The Age of Innocence*), born Mbabane, Swaziland, May 5, 1957.

Lance Henriksen, 66, actor (*Dog Day Afternoon, The Terminator, Near Dark*), born New York, NY, May 5, 1943 (some sources say 1940).

Paul Konerko, 33, baseball player, born Providence, RI, May 5, 1976.

Jean-Pierre Leaud, 65, actor (*The 400 Blows, Stolen Kisses, Bed and Board*), born Paris, France, May 5, 1944.

Michael Murphy, 71, actor (*Nashville, Manhattan, Salvador*), born Los Angeles, CA, May 5, 1938.

Ziggy Palffy, 37, hockey player, born Skalica, Czechoslovakia, May 5, 1972.

Michael Palin, 66, actor, comedian ("Monty Python's Flying Circus," *Life of Brian*), born Sheffield, Yorkshire, England, May 5, 1943.

Tina Yothers, 36, singer, actress ("Family Ties"), born Whittier, CA, May 5, 1973.

May 6 — Wednesday

DAY 126 239 REMAINING

BABE RUTH'S FIRST MAJOR LEAGUE HOME RUN: ANNIVERSARY. May 6, 1915. George Herman "Babe" Ruth of the Boston Red Sox hit his first major league home run in a game against the New York Yankees in New York.

BANNISTER BREAKS FOUR-MINUTE MILE: 55th ANNIVERSARY. May 6, 1954. Running for the British Amateur Athletic Association in a meet at Oxford University, Roger Bannister broke the four-minute barrier with a time of 3:59.4. Four minutes for a mile at the time was considered not only a physical barrier but also a psychological one.

FREUD, SIGMUND: BIRTH ANNIVERSARY. May 6, 1856. Austrian physician, born at Freiberg, Moravia. Founder of psychoanalysis. Freud died at London, England, Sept 23, 1939.

GREAT AMERICAN GRUMP OUT. May 6. We are asking America to go 24 hours without being grumpy, crabby or rude. Can *you* meet the challenge? Schoolchildren, parents, businesses and the community will be involved in promoting peace, harmony and lighthearted humor on this day. For info: Janice Hathy, Smile Mania, 1300 N River Rd, C-15, Venice, FL 34293. E-mail: jan1smile@aol.com. Web: www.smilemania.com.

***HINDENBURG* DISASTER: ANNIVERSARY.** May 6, 1937. At 7:20 PM, the dirigible *Hindenburg* exploded as it approached the mooring mast at Lakehurst, NJ, after a transatlantic voyage. Of its 97 passengers and crew, 36 died in the accident, which ended the dream of mass transportation via dirigible.

JOSEPH BRACKETT DAY. May 6. Day honoring the Shaker religious leader, born May 6, 1797, at Cumberland, ME. In 1848 he composed the popular Shaker song "Simple Gifts" (also known as "'Tis the Gift to Be Simple") while at the Shaker community in Alfred, ME. This Shaker dance song became known worldwide after Aaron Copland used it in his score for the ballet *Appalachian Spring* in 1944. Elder Joseph Brackett died at New Gloucester, ME, July 4, 1882. For info: PineTree Productions, 235 Prospect St, Stoughton, MA 02072. E-mail: pinetreemusic@aol.com. Web: www.americanmusicpreservation.com/home.htm.

NATIONAL NURSES WEEK. May 6–12. A week to honor the outstanding efforts of nurses everywhere to strengthen the health of the nation. Annually, beginning May 6, National Nurses Day, and ending May 12, Florence Nightingale's birthday. Call or write for a free catalog. For info: American Nurses Assn, 8515 Georgia Ave, Ste 400, Silver Spring, MD 20910. Phone: (301) 628-5000 or (800) 244-4ANA. Fax: (301) 628-5001. Web: www.nursingworld.org.

NATIONAL SCHOOL NURSE DAY. May 6. Established to foster a better understanding of the role of school nurses in the educational setting. Annually, the Wednesday of National Nurses Week (May 6–12). For info: NASN, 8484 Georgia Ave, Ste 420, Silver Spring, MD 20910. Phone: (240) 821-1130. E-mail: nasn@nasn.org. Web: www.nasn.org.

NO DIET DAY. May 6. A day to stop dieting, stop hazardous weight-loss attempts. International No Diet Day celebrates a paradigm shift to the nondiet Health at Every Size approach to health and well-being, to acceptance and respect for oneself and others. Discover the top 10 reasons not to diet and the risks of weight loss on website. For info: Francie M. Berg, Healthy Weight Network, 402 S 14th St, Hettinger, ND 58639. E-mail: fmberg@healthyweight.net (please put "Berg—No Diet Day" in subject line). Web: www.healthyweight.net.

NO HOMEWORK DAY. May 6. Millions of kids, all of them overloaded with homework, get a much-needed night off tonight. Give 'em a break, teachers! These young folks are working harder than Mom 'n' Dad. (©2006 by WH.) For info: Thomas & Ruth Roy, Wellcat Holidays, 2418 Long Ln, Lebanon, PA 17046. Phone: (717) 279-0184. E-mail: info@wellcat.com. Web: www.wellcat.com.

PEARY, ROBERT E.: BIRTH ANNIVERSARY. May 6, 1856. Born at Cresson, PA. Peary served as a cartographic draftsman in the US Coast and Geodetic Survey for two years and then joined the US Navy's Corps of Civil Engineers in 1881. He first worked as an explorer in tropical climates as he served as subchief of the Inter-Ocean Canal Survey in Nicaragua. After reading of the inland ice of Greenland, Peary became attracted to the Arctic. He organized and led eight Arctic expeditions and is credited with the verification of Greenland's island formation, proving that the polar ice cap extended beyond 82° north latitude, and the discovery of the Melville meteorite on Melville Bay, in addition to his famous discovery of the North Pole, Apr 6, 1909. Peary died Feb 20, 1920, at Washington, DC.

PENN, JOHN: BIRTH ANNIVERSARY. May 6, 1740. Signer of the Declaration of Independence, born at Caroline County, VA. Died Sept 14, 1788.

SACK OF ROME: ANNIVERSARY. May 6, 1527. The Renaissance ended with the Sack of Rome, which began on this date. As part of a series of wars between the Hapsburg Empire and the French monarchy, German troops killed some 4,000 inhabitants of Rome and looted works of art and libraries. Pope Clement VII, who supported the French, was imprisoned at the Castel St. Angelo. Nearly a year passed before order could be restored in the city.

TAGORE, RABINDRANATH: BIRTH ANNIVERSARY. May 6, 1861. Hindu poet, mystic and musical composer born at Calcutta, India. Received Nobel Prize (literature) in 1913. Died at Calcutta, Aug 7, 1941. His birthday is observed in Bangladesh on the 25th day of the Bengali month of Baishakha (second week of May), when the poet laureate is honored with songs, dances and discussions of his works.

VALENTINO, RUDOLPH: BIRTH ANNIVERSARY. May 6, 1895. Rodolpho Alfonzo Rafaello Pietro Filiberto Guglieimi Di Valentina D'Antonguolla, whose professional name was Rudolph Valentino, was born at Castellaneta, Italy. Popular cinema actor. For years press reports claimed that "at least one weeping veiled woman in black brought flowers to his tomb" (at Hollywood Memorial Park) every year on the anniversary of his death at New York, NY, Aug 23, 1926.

May 2009	S	M	T	W	T	F	S
						1	2
	3	4	5	6	7	8	9
	10	11	12	13	14	15	16
	17	18	19	20	21	22	23
	24	25	26	27	28	29	30
	31						

WELLES, ORSON: BIRTH ANNIVERSARY. May 6, 1915. Actor and director born at Kenosha, WI. *Citizen Kane*, which he directed and in which he played the title role, is one of the most influential films ever made. Other films in which he had a role include *The Third Man* and *The Magnificent Ambersons*. Welles died at Los Angeles, CA, Oct 10, 1985.

BIRTHDAYS TODAY

Tom Bergeron, 54, television personality and host ("Hollywood Squares," "America's Funniest Home Videos," "Dancing with the Stars"), born Haverhill, MA, May 6, 1955.

Tony Blair, 56, former British prime minister (1997–2007), born Edinburgh, Scotland, May 6, 1953.

Martin Brodeur, 37, hockey player, born Montreal, QC, Canada, May 6, 1972.

George Clooney, 48, actor (Oscar for *Syriana*; *Ocean's Eleven, Three Kings, Michael Clayton*), born Lexington, KY, May 6, 1961.

Alan Dale, 62, actor ("Ugly Betty"), born Dunedin, South Island, New Zealand, May 6, 1947.

Roma Downey, 45, actress ("Touched by an Angel"), born Derry, Northern Ireland, May 6, 1964.

Leslie Hope, 44, actress ("24," *Talk Radio*), born Halifax, NS, Canada, May 6, 1965.

Ben Masters, 62, actor (*All That Jazz, Making Mr Right*), born Corvallis, OR, May 6, 1947.

Willie Mays, 78, Hall of Fame baseball player, born Westfield, AL, May 6, 1931.

Bob Seger, 64, singer, musician, born Ann Arbor, MI, May 6, 1945.

Richard C. Shelby, 75, US Senator (R, Alabama), born Birmingham, AL, May 6, 1934.

Lynn Whitfield, 56, actress (*Stepmom, Eve's Bayou*), born Baton Rouge, LA, May 6, 1953.

May 7 — Thursday

DAY 127 — 238 REMAINING

BEAUFORT SCALE DAY (FRANCIS BEAUFORT BIRTH ANNIVERSARY). May 7, 1774. A day to honor the British naval officer, Sir Francis Beaufort, who in 1806 devised a scale of wind force from 0 (calm) to 12 (hurricane) that was based on observation, not requiring any special instruments. The scale was adopted for international use in 1874 and has since been enlarged and refined. Beaufort was born at Flower Hill, Meath, Ireland, and died at Brighton, England, Dec 17, 1857.

BEETHOVEN'S NINTH SYMPHONY PREMIERE: ANNIVERSARY. May 7, 1824. Beethoven's Ninth Symphony in D Minor was performed for the first time at Vienna, Austria. Known as the *Choral* because of his use of voices in symphonic form for the first time, the Ninth was his musical interpretation of Schiller's *Ode to Joy*. Beethoven was completely deaf when he composed it, and it was said a soloist had to tug on his sleeve when the performance was over to get him to turn around and see the enthusiastic response he could not hear.

BRAHMS, JOHANNES: BIRTH ANNIVERSARY. May 7, 1833. Regarded as one of the greatest composers of 19th-century music, Johannes Brahms was born at Hamburg, Germany. His works were firmly rooted in traditional classical principles and truly Romantic in spirit. When Brahms was 17, his talent was discovered and promoted by the Hungarian violinist Eduard Remenyi, who took him on a national concert tour. During this tour Brahms met composer Robert Schumann and his wife, Clara Schumann, who was also a composer and the most brilliant concert pianist of her day. The endorsement and support of the Schumanns quickly established his musical reputation. After Schumann's death in 1856,

Brahms became devoted to Clara, supporting her and her children. Brahms completed his most important work, *Ein Deutsches Requiem* (*The German Requiem*), after his mother's death in 1865. It is considered one of the best examples of 19th-century choral music and was presented with great success throughout Germany. Brahms died at Vienna, Austria, Apr 3, 1897.

BROWNING, ROBERT: BIRTH ANNIVERSARY. May 7, 1812. English poet and husband of poet Elizabeth Barrett Browning, born at Camberwell, near London. Known for his dramatic monologues. Died at Venice, Italy, Dec 12, 1889.

COOPER, GARY: BIRTH ANNIVERSARY. May 7, 1901. Frank James Cooper was born at Helena, MT. He changed his name to Gary at the start of his movie career. He is best known by baseball fans for his portrayal of Lou Gehrig in *The Pride of the Yankees*. Other films included *Wings, The Virginian, The Plainsman, Beau Geste, Sergeant York* (for which he won his first Academy Award), *High Noon* (winning his second Oscar for best actor), *The Court Martial of Billy Mitchell* and *Friendly Persuasion*. He died May 13, 1961, at Hollywood, CA.

DIEN BIEN PHU FALLS: 55th ANNIVERSARY. May 7, 1954. Vietnam's victory over France at Dien Bien Phu ended the Indochina War.

EL SALVADOR: DAY OF THE SOLDIER. May 7. National holiday. Anniversary of the founding of the country's armed forces in 1824.

ENGLAND: MITSUBISHI MOTORS BADMINTON HORSE TRIALS. May 7–10. Badminton, Gloucestershire. Famous international horse trials consisting of show jumping, cross-country and dressage. Est attendance: 200,000. For info: Box Office, Badminton Horse Trials, Badminton, Glos, England GL9 1DF. Phone: (44) (1454) 21-8375. Fax: (44) (1454) 21-8596. E-mail: info@badminton-horse.co.uk. Web: www.badminton-horse.co.uk.

FIRST PRESIDENTIAL INAUGURAL BALL: ANNIVERSARY. May 7, 1789. Celebrating the inauguration of George Washington, the first Presidential Inaugural Ball was held at New York, NY.

GERMANY: HAMBURG HARBOR BIRTHDAY. May 7, 1189. "Hafengeburtstag" celebrates establishment of Hamburg as a free city.

GERMANY'S FIRST SURRENDER: ANNIVERSARY. May 7, 1945. Russian, American, British and French ranking officers crowded into a second-floor recreation room of a small red-brick schoolhouse (which served as General Dwight Eisenhower's headquarters) at Reims, Germany. Representing Germany, Field Marshal Alfred Jodl signed an unconditional surrender of all German fighting forces. After a signing that took almost 40 minutes, Jodl was ushered into Eisenhower's presence. The American general asked the German if he fully understood what he had signed and informed Jodl that he would be held personally responsible for any deviation from the terms of the surrender, including the requirement that German commanders sign a formal surrender to the USSR at a time and place determined by that government.

HOMEFEST. May 7–9. Bald Knob, AR. School reunions, homecomings, sports events, antique autos, crafts, parade, beauty pageant and more. Est attendance: 2,000. For info: Bald Knob Area Chamber of Commerce, PO Box 338, Bald Knob, AR 72010. Phone: (501) 724-3140. Fax: (501) 724-3140. E-mail: baldknobchamber@centurytel.net. Web: www.baldknobchamber.com.

"KRAFT TELEVISION THEATRE" TV PREMIERE: ANNIVERSARY. May 7, 1947. Live theatrical programs appearing on both the NBC and ABC networks. The show was a gold mine for discovering new talent. Among the playwrights getting their big breaks were Rod Serling, Paddy Chayefsky and Tad Mosel. Some of the show's most notable plays included "The Easy Mark" (1951) with Jack Lemmon, "Double in Ivory" (1953) with Lee Remick, "To Live in Peace" (1953) with Anne Bancroft, "The Missing Years" (1954) with Anthony Perkins and Mary Astor and "A Profile in Courage" (1956) with James Whitmore. The last play was based on a book by Senator John F. Kennedy, who appeared on the program to introduce the drama.

***LUSITANIA* SINKING: ANNIVERSARY.** May 7, 1915. British passenger liner *Lusitania*, on its return trip from New York to Liverpool, carrying nearly 2,000 passengers, was torpedoed by a German submarine off the coast of Ireland, sinking within minutes; 1,198 lives were lost. US president Woodrow Wilson sent a note of protest to Berlin on May 13, but Germany, which had issued a warning in advance, pointed to *Lusitania*'s cargo of ammunition for Britain. The US maintained neutrality for the time being.

MacLEISH, ARCHIBALD: BIRTH ANNIVERSARY. May 7, 1892. American poet and librarian of Congress (1939–44), born at Glencoe, IL. MacLeish, who was also a playwright, Pulitzer Prize winner, editor, lawyer, professor and farmer, died at Boston, MA, Apr 20, 1982.

MARTIN Z. MOLLUSK DAY. May 7. Moorlyn Terrace Beach, Ocean City, NJ. If Martin Z. Mollusk, a hermit crab, sees his shadow at 11 AM, EST, summer comes a week early in Ocean City—if he doesn't, summer begins on time. For info: Mark Soifer, City Hall, 9th St and Asbury Ave, Ocean City, NJ 08226. Phone: (609) 525-9300. Fax: (609) 399-0374. E-mail: MTSoifer@aol.com.

✦ **NATIONAL DAY OF PRAYER.** May 7. Presidential Proclamation always issued for the first Thursday in May since 1981. (PL100–307 of May 5, 1988.) Beginning in 1957, a day in October was designated, except in 1972 and 1975 through 1977.

NATIONAL DAY OF REASON. May 7. The event is used to promote reason and critical thought. Participants across the world are encouraged to celebrate the life of the thoughtful mind and inject rational thought into their actions and behaviors. Annually, the first Thursday in May. For info: American Humanist Assn, 1777 T St NW, Washington, DC 20009-7125. Phone: (202) 238-9088. Fax: (202) 238-9003. E-mail: aha@americanhumanist.org. Web: www.nationaldayofreason.org.

TCHAIKOVSKY, PETER ILICH: BIRTH ANNIVERSARY. May 7, 1840. (New Style date.) One of the outstanding composers of all time, Peter Ilich Tchaikovsky was born at Vatkinsk, Russia. Among his famous works are the symphony *Pathétique*; the opera *Eugene Onegin*; and the ballets *Swan Lake, Sleeping Beauty* and *The Nutcracker*. He was the first to turn the ballet into a sustained dramatic expression. Tchaikovsky died of cholera during an epidemic at St. Petersburg, Nov 6, 1893—nine days after conducting his *Pathétique* symphony for the first time.

TWENTY-SEVENTH AMENDMENT RATIFIED: ANNIVERSARY. May 7, 1992. The 27th Amendment to the Constitution was ratified, prohibiting Congress from giving itself midterm pay raises.

UNITAS, JOHNNY: BIRTH ANNIVERSARY. May 7, 1933. Born at Pittsburgh, PA, Johnny Unitas played football for the University of Louisville. After college, he went to work as a construction worker but continued to play football (for $6 per game) for the Bloomfield Rams, a semipro team that played on dirt, not grass. Based on a fan's letter, the Baltimore Colts gave him a conditional contract, and soon he was a star. He played 17 seasons for the Colts, was the MVP three times, went to 10 Pro Bowls and led his team to three NFL championships. He was inducted into the Pro Football Hall of Fame in 1979 and has often been called the greatest quarterback ever to play the game. He died at Baltimore, MD, Sept 11, 2002.

 **BIRTHDAYS TODAY**

Pete V. Domenici, 77, US Senator (R, New Mexico), born Albuquerque, NM, May 7, 1932.

Amy Heckerling, 55, filmmaker (*Fast Times at Ridgemont High, Look Who's Talking*), born New York, NY, May 7, 1954.

Shawn Marion, 31, basketball player, born Waukegan, IL, May 7, 1978.

Peter Reckell, 54, actor ("Days of Our Lives"), born Elkhart, IN, May 7, 1955.

May 8 — Friday

DAY 128 **237 REMAINING**

ALBANY TULIP FESTIVAL. May 8–10. Washington Park, Albany, NY. 61st annual. A celebration of spring, the Tulip Festival features thousands of tulips abloom throughout the city and honors Albany's Dutch heritage. Events include crowning of a Tulip Queen, arts and crafts vendors, food vendors, entertainment on three stages, children's activities and Dutch dancers in costume. Est attendance: 100,000. For info: Susan T. Cleary, City of Albany Office of Special Events, City Hall, Room 402, Eagle St, Albany, NY 12207. Phone: (518) 434-2032. Fax: (518) 426-0759. E-mail: info@albanyevents.org. Web: www.albanyevents.org.

BATTLE OF THE CORAL SEA: ANNIVERSARY. May 8, 1942. Beginning on this date, the Battle of the Coral Sea impeded Japanese expansion and introduced a new form of naval warfare. None of the surface vessels exchanged fire—the entire battle was waged by aircraft. The US lost a carrier, destroyer and tanker. The Japanese lost seven warships, including a carrier.

BLUEBERRY HILL OPEN DART TOURNAMENT. May 8–10. St. Louis, MO. 37th annual. America's oldest pub dart tournament open to everyone. Est attendance: 200. For info: Joe Edwards, Blueberry Hill, 6504 Delmar in The Loop, St. Louis, MO 63130. Phone: (314) 727-4444. Web: www.blueberryhill.com.

CZECH REPUBLIC: LIBERATION DAY. May 8. Commemorates the liberation of Czechoslovakia from the Germans in 1945.

DENMARK: COMMON PRAYER DAY. May 8. Public holiday. The fourth Friday after Easter, known as "Store Bededag," is a day for prayer and festivity.

DUNANT, JEAN-HENRI: BIRTH ANNIVERSARY. May 8, 1828. Author and philanthropist, founder of the Red Cross, born at Geneva, Switzerland. Nobel Prize winner in 1901. Died at Heiden, Switzerland, Oct 30, 1910.

May 2009

S	M	T	W	T	F	S
					1	2
3	4	5	6	7	8	9
10	11	12	13	14	15	16
17	18	19	20	21	22	23
24	25	26	27	28	29	30
31						

ELECTRA GOAT BBQ COOK-OFF. May 8–9. Electra Goat Grounds, Electra, TX. Goat brisket, pork ribs, chicken cook-off, Cow Patty Drop, live band, Jackpot Steak & Beans Competition, tug-of-war, eating contest, children's games and crafts. Little Mr and Miss Goat Competition, Friday-night dance and salsa contest. Est attendance: 2,000. For info: Sherry Strange, Electra Chamber of Commerce, 112 W Cleveland, Electra, TX 76360. Phone: (940) 495-3577. E-mail: electracoc@electratel.net. Web: www.electratexas.org.

ENGLAND: HELSTON FURRY DANCE. May 8. Helston, Cornwall. The world-famous Helston Furry Dance is held each year on May 8 (except when the 8th is a Sunday or Monday, in which case it is held on the preceding Saturday). Dancing around the streets begins early in the morning and continues throughout the day. The dance leaves Guildhall at the stroke of noon and winds its way in and out of many of the larger buildings.

FRANCE: VICTORY DAY. May 8. Commemorates the surrender of Germany to Allied forces and the cessation of hostilities in 1945.

GERMANY'S SECOND SURRENDER: ANNIVERSARY. May 8, 1945. Stalin refused to recognize the document of unconditional surrender signed at Reims the previous day, so a second signing was held near Berlin. The event was turned into an elaborate formal ceremony by the Soviets, who had lost some 20 million lives during the war. As in the Reims document, the end of hostilities was set for 12:01 AM local time on May 9.

GOTTSCHALK, LOUIS MOREAU: BIRTH ANNIVERSARY. May 8, 1829. American pianist of international fame who toured the US during the Civil War. Gottschalk composed for the piano, combining American and Creole folk themes and rhythms in his work. Born at New Orleans, LA, he died Dec 18, 1869, at Rio de Janeiro, Brazil.

JOHNSON, ROBERT: BIRTH ANNIVERSARY. May 8, 1911. Born at Hazelhurst, MS, and murdered at age 27, Aug 16, 1938, at Greenwood, MS (poisoned by a jealous husband), in his short life Johnson was a master blues guitarist, a singer and songwriter of great influence. He developed a unique guitar style of such skill that it was said he acquired his ability by selling his soul to the devil—the film *Crossroads* is based very loosely on this myth. Johnson's only two recording sessions captured the classics "Sweet Home Chicago," "Cross Road Blues," "Me and the Devil Blues" and others. Johnson was inducted posthumously into the Blues Hall of Fame in 1980 and the Rock and Roll Hall of Fame in 1986.

LAVOISIER, ANTOINE-LAURENT: EXECUTION ANNIVERSARY. May 8, 1794. French chemist and the "father of modern chemistry." Especially noted for having first explained the real nature of combustion and for showing that matter is not destroyed in chemical reactions. Born at Paris, France, Aug 26, 1743, Lavoisier was guillotined at the Place de la Révolution for his former position as a tax collector. The Revolutionary Tribunal is reported to have responded to a plea to spare his life with the statement: "We need no more scientists in France."

LILAC FESTIVAL. May 8–17. Highland Park, Rochester, NY. Developed by renowned park designer Frederick Law Olmsted, Highland Park is the site of the Lilac Festival, the largest celebration of its kind in North America. In addition to the spectacle of more than 500 varieties of lilacs in bloom, the festival provides free admission, free entertainment, free children's entertainment, a parade, a 10k race, two juried art shows, a senior citizens' day and music concerts. Est attendance: 400,000. For info: Susan LeBeau, Lilac Festival, 333 N Plymouth Ave, Rochester, NY 14608. Phone: (585) 325-4720. Fax: (585) 232-3453. E-mail: info@lilacfestival.com. Web: www.lilacfestival.com.

LISTON, SONNY: BIRTH ANNIVERSARY. May 8, 1932. Charles "Sonny" Liston, boxer born at St. Francis County, AR. Liston rose above a record of criminal activity to defeat Floyd Patterson for the heavyweight title on Sept 25, 1962. He defeated Patterson in a rematch but then lost the title to Cassius Clay, who later changed his name to Muhammad Ali. In a rematch Ali knocked Liston out with a punch few observers saw. Died at Las Vegas, NV, Dec 30, 1970.

✦ **MILITARY SPOUSE APPRECIATION DAY.** May 8. First proclaimed by President Ronald Reagan in 1984 to recognize and honor the contributions and sacrifices of military spouses. Annually, the Friday before Mother's Day.

MILITARY SPOUSE APPRECIATION DAY. May 8. Observed on US military posts worldwide, this day celebrates the strength and patriotism of the spouses of members of the military. They are true unsung heroes. Annually on the Friday before Mother's Day, events are commonly sponsored to recognize the husbands and wives of our men and women in uniform for their support, contributions and sacrifices. For info: Danielle Hamilton, 246 Creek Nation Dr, Auburn, AL 36830. Phone: (334) 332-5333. E-mail: danielle.hamilton@us.army.mil.

MOUNT PELÉE ERUPTION: ANNIVERSARY. May 8, 1902. In the worst volcanic disaster of the 20th century, Mount Pelée erupted on the tiny French Caribbean island of Martinique. In minutes, a cloud of ashes, gases and rocks destroyed the thriving port city of Saint-Pierre, killing all but one of its 30,000 inhabitants.

NO SOCKS DAY. May 8. If we give up wearing socks for one day, it will mean a little less laundry, thereby contributing to the betterment of the environment. Besides, we will all feel a bit freer, at least for one day. Annually, May 8. (©2006 by WH.) For info: Thomas & Ruth Roy, Wellcat Holidays, 2418 Long Ln, Lebanon, PA 17046. Phone: (717) 279-0184. E-mail: info@wellcat.com. Web: www.wellcat.com.

OUIMET, FRANCIS DESALES: BIRTH ANNIVERSARY. May 8, 1893. American amateur golfer who is credited with establishing the popularity of golf in the US. Born at Brookline, MA, he began his golfing career as a caddy. In 1913, at age 20, he generated national enthusiasm for the game when he became the first American and first amateur to win the US Open Golf Championship. He won the US Amateur Championship in 1914 and 1931 and was a member of the US Walker Cup team from its first tournament in 1922 until 1949, serving as its nonplaying captain for six of those years. In 1951 he became the first American to be elected captain of the Royal and Ancient Golf Club of St. Andrews, Scotland. Ouimet died at Newton, MA, Sept 2, 1967.

SLOVAKIA: LIBERATION DAY. May 8. Commemorates the liberation of Czechoslovakia from the Germans in 1945.

TRUMAN, HARRY S: 125th BIRTH ANNIVERSARY. May 8, 1884. The 33rd president of the US, succeeded to that office upon the death of Franklin D. Roosevelt, Apr 12, 1945, and served until Jan 20, 1953. Born at Lamar, MO, Truman was the last of the nine US presidents who did not attend college. Affectionately nicknamed "Give 'em Hell Harry" by admirers. Truman died at Kansas City, MO, Dec 26, 1972. His birthday is a holiday in Missouri.

UNITED NATIONS: TIME OF REMEMBRANCE AND RECONCILIATION FOR THOSE WHO LOST THEIR LIVES DURING THE SECOND WORLD WAR. May 8–9. By its Resolution 59/26 of Nov 22, 2004, the General Assembly declared these days as a time of remembrance and reconciliation and invited member states, United Nations bodies, nongovernmental organizations and individuals to observe annually either one or both of those days in an appropriate manner to pay tribute to all those who lost their lives in WWII. For info: United Nations, Dept of Public Info, New York, NY 10017. Web: www.un.org.

V-E DAY: ANNIVERSARY. May 8, 1945. Victory in Europe Day commemorates unconditional surrender of Germany to Allied forces. The surrender document was signed by German representatives at General Dwight D. Eisenhower's headquarters at Reims to become effective, and hostilities to end, at one minute past midnight May 9, 1945, which was 9:01 PM, EDT on May 8 in the US. President Harry S Truman on May 8 declared May 9, 1945, to be "V-E Day," but it later came to be observed on May 8. A separate German surrender to the USSR was signed at Karlshorst, near Berlin, May 8. See also: "Russia: Victory Day" (May 9).

WORLD RED CROSS DAY. May 8. A day for commemorating the birth of Jean-Henri Dunant, the Swiss founder of the International Red Cross Movement in 1863, and for recognizing the humanitarian work of the Red Cross around the world. For info on activities in your area, contact your local Red Cross chapter. For info: American Red Cross Natl Headquarters, 2025 E St NW, Washington, DC 20006. Web: www.redcross.org.

BIRTHDAYS TODAY

David Attenborough, 83, author, naturalist (*Life on Earth, Trials of Life*), born London, England, May 8, 1926.

Bill Cowher, 52, football coach and former player, born Pittsburgh, PA, May 8, 1957.

Melissa Gilbert, 45, actress ("Little House on the Prairie," *The Miracle Worker*), born Los Angeles, CA, May 8, 1964.

Enrique Iglesias, 34, singer, born Madrid, Spain, May 8, 1975.

David Keith, 55, actor (*The Great Santini, An Officer and a Gentleman*), director, born Knoxville, TN, May 8, 1954.

Bobby Labonte, 45, race car driver, born Corpus Christi, TX, May 8, 1964.

Ronald Mandel (Ronnie) Lott, 50, Hall of Fame football player, born Albuquerque, NM, May 8, 1959.

Janet McTeer, 48, actress (*Tumbleweeds*), born Newcastle, England, May 8, 1961.

Thomas Pynchon, 72, writer (*V, Gravity's Rainbow*), born Glen Cove, NY, May 8, 1937.

Don Rickles, 83, comedian, actor (*Blazing Saddles*, "The Dean Martin Show"), born New York, NY, May 8, 1926.

Toni Tennille, 66, singer (with husband Daryl Dragon made up Captain and Tennille), born Montgomery, AL, May 8, 1943.

May 9 — Saturday

DAY 129 — **236 REMAINING**

BLUEGRASS FESTIVAL. May 9. Hope, AR. The 13th annual Hope/Hempstead County Chamber of Commerce Free Bluegrass Festival is the only free bluegrass festival in the state of Arkansas. Features local, regional and nationally known bluegrass acts. Annually, the Saturday of Mother's Day weekend. Est attendance: 3,000. For info: Hope/Hempstead Chamber of Commerce, PO Box 250, Hope, AR 71802. Phone: (870) 777-3640. Fax: (870) 722-6154. E-mail: hopemelonfest@yahoo.com. Web: www.hopemelonfest.com.

BOYD, BELLE: BIRTH ANNIVERSARY. May 9, 1843. Notorious Confederate spy who later became an actress and lecturer was born at Martinsburg, VA. Author of the book *Belle Boyd in Camp and Prison*, she died June 11, 1900, at Kilbourne, WI.

BRITISH CAPTURE ENIGMA MACHINE: ANNIVERSARY. May 9, 1941. During WWII, when a German U-110 submarine attacked a British convoy, two British vessels, the *Bulldog* and *Aubretia*, were able to retaliate so quickly with depth charges that the submarine was disabled and unable to dive. With the submarine captured, British sailors investigated the radio room and discovered the typewriter-like Enigma, a ciphering machine that enabled safe German communication, and documents of tables that helped explain how it worked. The U-110's capture was kept secret, and British cryptographers used this break to begin unraveling German code during the war.

BROWN, JOHN: BIRTH ANNIVERSARY. May 9, 1800. Abolitionist leader born at Torrington, CT, and hanged Dec 2, 1859, at Charles Town, WV. Leader of attack on Harpers Ferry, VA, Oct 16, 1859, which was intended to give impetus to movement for escape and freedom for slaves. His aim was frustrated and in fact resulted in increased polarization and sectional animosity. Legendary martyr of the abolitionist movement.

CELLULAR SOUTH GUM TREE FESTIVAL. May 9–10. Tupelo, MS. A juried art show with arts, crafts and live entertainment. 10k run. Annually, Mother's Day weekend. Est attendance: 25,000. For info: Gum Tree Museum of Art, PO Box 786, Tupelo, MS 38802. Phone: (662) 844-ARTS. E-mail: tina@gumtreemuseum.com. Web: www.gumtreemuseum.com.

EUROPEAN UNION: ANNIVERSARY OBSERVANCE. May 9, 1950. Member countries of the European Union commemorate the announcement by French statesman Robert Schuman of the "Schuman Plan" for establishing a single authority for production of coal, iron and steel in France and Germany. The European Coal and Steel Community was founded in 1952. This organization was a forerunner of the European Economic Community, founded in 1958, which later became the European Union. At the European Summit at Milan in 1985, this day was proclaimed the Day of Europe.

FLOWER MOON. May 9. So called by Native American tribes of New England and the Great Lakes because by this time of the year, flowers are everywhere. The May Full Moon.

GONZALES, PANCHO: BIRTH ANNIVERSARY. May 9, 1928. Richard Alonzo "Pancho" Gonzales, tennis player born at Los Angeles, CA. A self-taught player, Gonzales won the 1948 US National Singles Championship and repeated in 1949. He turned pro and won the world championship from 1954 through 1962. Gonzales was an aggressive, temperamental player who rarely trained. Died at Las Vegas, NV, July 3, 1995.

HOUSTON ART CAR PARADE. May 9. Houston, TX. 22nd annual. The world's oldest and largest art car parade, featuring mobile masterpieces from the surreal to the sublime. Est attendance: 200,000. For info: Media/Marketing Coordinator, Orange Show Center for Visionary Art, 2402 Munger, Houston, TX 77023. Phone: (713) 926-6368. Fax: (713) 926-1506. Web: www.orangeshow.org.

HUNTER FREES THE SLAVES: ANNIVERSARY. May 9, 1862. At Hilton Head, SC, General David Hunter, commander of the Department of the South, issued orders freeing slaves in South Carolina, Florida and Georgia. Not having congressional or presidential approval, the orders were countermanded by President Abraham Lincoln on May 19.

INTERNATIONAL MIGRATORY BIRD CELEBRATION. May 9. Chincoteague, VA. Walks, talks, workshops, boat tours, children's activities and an art celebration, all conducted outdoors with the birds. Annually, Mother's Day weekend. Est attendance: 10,000. For info: Chincoteague Chamber of Commerce, 6733 Maddox Blvd, Chincoteague, VA 23336. Phone: (757) 336-6161. Fax: (757) 336-1242. E-mail: chincochamber@verizon.net. Web: www.chincoteaguechamber.com.

May 2009	S	M	T	W	T	F	S
						1	2
	3	4	5	6	7	8	9
	10	11	12	13	14	15	16
	17	18	19	20	21	22	23
	24	25	26	27	28	29	30
	31						

INTERNATIONAL MIGRATORY BIRD DAY. May 9. To educate the public about migratory birds and the preservation of their habitats in the US and Central America. Annually, the second Saturday in May.

INTERNATIONAL WILDLIFE FILM FESTIVAL. May 9–16. Missoula, MT. 32nd annual juried international wildlife film festival. This eight-day gathering will involve the world's top wildlife filmmakers, producers, scientists and conservation leaders sharing their ideas, techniques and products with interested members of the public and filmmaking profession. The festival provides films for viewing by people of all ages, with special sections for children. Community celebrations such as a wildlife parade, workshops and panel discussions are also part of this annual festival. Festival venues are located at various sites in downtown Missoula. Est attendance: 12,000. For info: Exec Dir, Intl Wildlife Film Festival, 718 S Higgins, Missoula, MT 59801. Phone: (406) 728-9380. Fax: (406) 728-2881. E-mail: iwff@wildlifefilms.org. Web: www.wildlifefilms.org.

LETTER CARRIERS "STAMP OUT HUNGER" FOOD DRIVE. May 9. Every year since 1993, on the second Saturday in May, letter carriers in more than 10,000 cities and towns across the 50 states, the District of Columbia, Puerto Rico, Guam and the Virgin Islands collect nonperishable food items left by mailboxes and in post offices from their postal customers. The National Association of Letter Carriers "Stamp Out Hunger" Food Drive is the largest one-day food drive in the nation. The US Postal Service, Campbell Soup Company and Valpak are major sponsors among many others. For info: Drew Von Bergen, Natl Assn of Letter Carriers, 100 Indiana Ave NW, Washington, DC 20001-2144. Phone: (202) 662-2489. E-mail: vonbergen@nalc.org. Web: www.nalc.org.

MEET THE ARTISTS AND ARTISANS SHOW. May 9–10. Milford Green, CT. 47th annual. More than 200 juried, award-winning artists and crafters from throughout the nation. One of the Top 100 Events for the Millennium in North America. For info: Meet the Artists & Artisans Show. Phone: (203) 874-5672. E-mail: ctlimner@snet.net. Web: www.meettheartistsandartisans.com or www.ctlimner.com. For additional info: Greater New Haven CVB, 59 Elm St, New Haven, CT 06510. Phone: (203) 777-8550 or (800) 332-STAY.

MOON PHASE: FULL MOON. May 9. Moon enters Full Moon phase at 12:01 AM, EDT.

MOTHER OCEAN DAY. May 9. To celebrate the wonder, vastness and beauty of the ocean. Casting of roses into the sea from the beach and from the water. Annually, on the day before Mother's Day. For info: Cynthia Hancock, Pres, Natl Week of the Ocean, Inc, PO Box 179, Fort Lauderdale, FL 33302. Phone: (954) 462-5573. Web: www.national-week-of-the-ocean.org.

MOTHER'S DAY ANNUAL RHODODENDRON SHOW. May 9–10. Crystal Springs Rhododendron Gardens, Portland, OR. Spectacular display of rhododendron and azalea blooms and plant sale. Est attendance: 6,000. For info: Kathy Van Veen, American Rhododendron Society, Portland Chapter, PO Box 86424, Portland, OR 97286. Phone: (503) 777-1734. Fax: (503) 777-2048.

NATIONAL BABYSITTERS DAY. May 9. To give babysitters across the nation appreciation and special recognition for their quality child care. Annually, the Saturday before Mother's Day. For info: Barbara Baldwin, RN, Safety Whys, PO Box 1177, Helotes, TX 78023-1177. Phone: (210) 695-9838. Fax: (210) 695-5673. E-mail: bbaldwin@satx.rr.com. Web: www.safetywhys.com.

NATIONAL MINIATURE GOLF DAY. May 9. Celebrate the game of miniature golf! Annually, the second Saturday in May. For info: Adventure Landing, 2315 Beach Blvd, Ste 203, Jacksonville Beach, FL 33250. Phone: (904) 249-9784. E-mail: juliedion@comcast.net. Web: adventurelanding.com.

NATIONAL TOURISM WEEK. May 9–17. 26th annual week promoting and enhancing awareness of travel and tourism's importance to the economic, social and cultural well-being of the US. For info: Travel Industry Assn of America, 1100 New York Ave NW, Ste 450, Washington, DC 20005-3934. Phone: (202) 408-2183. Fax: (202) 408-1255. E-mail: ckeefe@tia.org. Web: www.tia.org.

NATIONAL TRAIN DAY. May 9. 2nd annual. On May 10, 1869, in Promontory Summit, UT, the "golden spike" was driven into the final tie that joined 1,776 miles of the Central Pacific and Union Pacific railways, ceremonially creating the nation's first transcontinental railroad. And America was transformed. Now, 140 years after the golden spike connected east and west, there's never been a better time to take the train. Huge crowds and the frustrations that go with them burden our highways and airports. Trains are a more energy-efficient mode of travel than either autos or airplanes. Riding the rails is a great way to reduce your carbon footprint. Not to mention meet interesting people and see breathtaking scenery. National Train Day celebrates the way trains connect people and places—with events from coast to coast and at the Golden Spike National Historical site in Utah. Annually, the second Saturday in May. For info: Natl Railroad Passenger Corp. E-mail: info@nationaltrainday.com. Web: www.nationaltrainday.com.

NETHERLANDS: NATIONAL WINDMILL DAY. May 9. About 950 windmills still survive, and some 300 still are used occasionally and have been designated national monuments by the government. As many windmills as possible are in operation on National Windmill Day for the benefit of tourists. Annually, the second Saturday in May.

OCCONEECHEE STATE PARK NATIVE AMERICAN FESTIVAL AND POW WOW. May 9. Clarksville, VA. Gates open at 10 AM, Grand Entry at noon and continues until 7 PM. Native American artists and crafters show and sell their wares. Dancers, singers and drummers perform intertribal songs and dances. Annually, the second Saturday in May. Est attendance: 3,000. For info: Occoneechee State Park, 1192 Occoneechee Park Rd, Clarksville, VA 23927. Phone: (434) 374-2210. E-mail: occoneechee@dcr.virginia.gov. Web: www.dcr.state.va.us/parks/occoneec.htm.

PENINSULA CAMPAIGN INTENSIFIED: ANNIVERSARY. May 9, 1862. Confederate forces at Norfolk, VA, evacuated the city in a costly move, leaving valuable matériel for the Union army. Norfolk and Portsmouth were occupied on May 10, and the naval yard at Gosport, VA, was burned. President Abraham Lincoln was personally involved in this action, supervising the Federal expeditionary force.

RENO, NEVADA: ANNIVERSARY. May 9, 1868. First known as Fullers Crossing, and then Lakes Crossing, on this date it officially became Reno, known today as "the Biggest Little City in the World." Its six-week residency requirement for divorce became law on May 1, 1931.

RUSSIA: VICTORY DAY. May 9. National holiday observed annually to commemorate the 1945 Allied forces' defeat of Nazi Germany in WWII and to honor the 20 million Soviet people who died in that war. Hostilities ceased and the German surrender became effective at one minute after midnight on May 9, 1945. See also: "V-E Day: Anniversary" (May 8).

STAY UP ALL NIGHT NIGHT. May 9. A night when people are encouraged to stay awake through the night, reliving the excitement of staying up late as a child. It's a chance to catch up on chores, do some cleaning, watch films, read, cook, drink or chat with friends. There is something incredibly satisfying in staying up to see the sun rise—and everyone should do it at least once a year. Annually, the second Saturday in May. For info: George Mahood, 82 Derby Rd, Northampton, England NN1 4JS. E-mail: george@georgemahood.com.

UZBEKISTAN: DAY OF MEMORY AND HONOR. May 9. Honors Uzbek citizens killed in WWII. Formerly Victory Day when Uzbekistan was part of the Soviet Union.

"VAST WASTELAND" SPEECH: ANNIVERSARY. May 9, 1961. Speaking before the bigwigs of network TV at the annual convention of the National Association of Broadcasters, Newton Minow, the new chairman of the Federal Communications Commission, exhorted those executives to sit through an entire day of their own programming. He suggested that they "will observe a vast wasteland." Further, he urged them to try for "imagination in programming, not sterility; creativity, not imitation; experimentation, not conformity; excellence, not mediocrity."

WORLD FAIR TRADE DAY. May 9. A day to promote Fair Trade as an alternative economic model. "Fair Trade" means that trading partnerships are based on reciprocal benefits and mutual respect; that prices paid to producers reflect the work they do; that workers have the right to organize; that national health, safety and wage laws are enforced; and that products are environmentally sustainable and conserve natural resources. Celebrated worldwide in 70 countries with a variety of events from live music to symposia. Annually, the second Saturday in May. For info: International Fair Trade Assn, Prijssestraat 24, 4101 CR Culemborg, The Netherlands. Phone: (31) (345) 53-59-14. Fax: (31) (847) 47-44-01. E-mail: info@ifat.org. Web: www.ifat.org or www.wftday.org.

BIRTHDAYS TODAY

Candice Bergen, 63, actress (*Starting Over, The Group*, "Murphy Brown," "Boston Legal"), daughter of ventriloquist Edgar Bergen, born Beverly Hills, CA, May 9, 1946.

James L. Brooks, 69, director, producer, screenwriter (Oscar for *Terms of Endearment*; *As Good as It Gets*, "Taxi," "The Mary Tyler Moore Show"), born Brooklyn, NY, May 9, 1940.

Rosario Dawson, 30, actress (*He Got Game, Sin City*), born New York, NY, May 9, 1979.

Albert Finney, 73, actor (*Tom Jones, Shoot the Moon, Annie, The Dresser*), born Salford, England, May 9, 1936.

Anthony Keith (Tony) Gwynn, 49, former baseball player, born Los Angeles, CA, May 9, 1960.

Glenda Jackson, 72, actress (Oscars for *Women in Love* and *Touch of Class*), born Cheshire, England, May 9, 1937.

Billy Joel, 60, singer, composer ("It's Still Rock and Roll to Me," "Just the Way You Are"), born Hicksville, NY, May 9, 1949.

Mike Wallace, 91, TV journalist ("60 Minutes"), born Brookline, MA, May 9, 1918.

Steve Yzerman, 44, hockey player, born Cranbrook, BC, Canada, May 9, 1965.

May 10 — Sunday

DAY 130 | **235 REMAINING**

ASTAIRE, FRED: BIRTH ANNIVERSARY. May 10, 1899. Actor, dancer and choreographer, born at Omaha, NE. Astaire began dancing with his sister, Adele, and in the mid-1930s began dancing with Ginger Rogers. After Astaire's first Hollywood screen test, a producer noted of him: "Can't act. Slightly bald. Can dance a little." Despite this, Astaire starred in more than 40 films, including *Holiday Inn, The Gay Divorcée, Silk Stockings* and *Easter Parade*. Died at Los Angeles, CA, June 22, 1987.

ASTOR PLACE RIOT: ANNIVERSARY. May 10, 1849. A riot erupted outside the Astor Place Opera House at New York, NY, where the British actor William Charles Macready was performing. Led by the American actor Edwin Forrest, angry crowds revolted against dress requirements for admission and against Macready's public statements on the vulgarity of American life. On May 8 Macready's performance of *Macbeth* was stopped by Forrest's followers. Two days later, a mob led by Ned Buntline shattered the windows of the theater during a performance. Troops were summoned and ordered to fire, killing 22 and wounding 26.

CARTER, MAYBELLE: 100th BIRTH ANNIVERSARY. May 10, 1909. The guitar/banjo-playing cofounder of the singing Carter Family was born at Nickelsville, VA. The Carter Family were the first country music stars in America, reigning from 1927 to the 1950s and combining the influences of folk, bluegrass, rural country and gospel. Their hits included "Wabash Cannonball" and "Will the Circle Be Unbroken." Carter died Oct 23, 1978, at Nashville, TN.

CONFEDERATE MEMORIAL DAY IN NORTH AND SOUTH CAROLINA. May 10. Observed on the anniversary of the capture of Jefferson Davis by Union troops in 1865. Other Southern states observe Confederate Memorial Day on different dates.

GOLDEN SPIKE DRIVING: ANNIVERSARY. May 10, 1869. Anniversary of the meeting of Union Pacific and Central Pacific railways at Promontory Point, UT. On that day a golden spike was driven by Leland Stanford, president of the Central Pacific, to celebrate the linkage. The golden spike was promptly removed for preservation. Long called the final link in the ocean-to-ocean railroad, this event cannot be accurately described as completing the transcontinental railroad, but it did complete continuous rail tracks between Omaha and Sacramento. See also: "Transcontinental US Railway Completion: Anniversary" (Aug 15).

MANDELA INAUGURATION: 15th ANNIVERSARY. May 10, 1994. In a dramatic and historic exchange of power, former political prisoner Nelson Mandela was inaugurated as president of South Africa. Long the focal point of apartheid foes' attempts to end the enforced policy of discrimination in South Africa, Mandela handily won the first free election in South Africa despite many attempts by various political factions to either stop the electoral process or alter the outcome.

MICRONESIA, FEDERATED STATES OF: CONSTITUTION DAY. May 10. Proclamation of the Federated States of Micronesia in 1979. National holiday.

✦ **MOTHER'S DAY.** May 10. Presidential Proclamation always issued for the second Sunday in May. (Pub Res No. 2 of May 8, 1914.)

MOTHER'S DAY. May 10. Observed first in 1907 at the request of Anna Jarvis of Philadelphia, PA, who asked her church to hold a service in memory of all mothers on the anniversary of her mother's death. In 1909, two years after her mother's death, Jarvis and friends began a letter-writing campaign to create a Mother's Day observance. Congress passed legislation in 1914 designating the second Sunday in May as Mother's Day. Some say the predecessor of Mother's Day was the ancient spring festival dedicated to mother goddesses: Rhea (Greek) and Cybele (Roman).

MOTHER'S DAY AT THE WALL. May 10. Washington, DC. Annual observance at the Vietnam Veterans Memorial since 2000 honoring the mothers of those who died in combat. Area schoolchildren offer cards.

MOTHER'S DAY CELEBRATION. May 10. Jenkinson's Aquarium, Point Pleasant Beach, NJ. Calling all kids! Bring your mom for a special day to learn about the roles of mothers in the marine environment. One mother admitted free with each paid child's admission. Est attendance: 800. For info: Jenkinson's Aquarium, 300 Ocean Ave, Point Pleasant Beach, NJ 08742. Phone: (732) 899-1212. Fax: (732) 899-1717. E-mail: jenkinsonsaquarium@comcast.net. Web: www.jenkinsons.com.

NATIONAL FAMILY MONTH®. May 10–June 21. A month-long national observance to celebrate and promote strong, supportive families. Sponsored by KidsPeace®, a private children's charity that helps kids overcome crisis. Annually, Mother's Day through Father's Day. For info: Kids Peace, 5300 KidsPeace Dr, Orefield, PA 18069. Phone: (800) 25-PEACE. E-mail: kpinfo@kidspeace.org. Web: www.familymonth.net.

NATIONAL NURSING HOME WEEK. May 10–16. A community outreach program designed to familiarize the public with nursing facilities and the services they provide. Activities are conducted locally by individual nursing facilities. Annually, Mother's Day through the following Saturday. For info: American Health Care Assn, Natl Nursing Home Week, 1201 L St NW, Washington, DC 20005. Phone: (202) 842-4444. Fax: (202) 842-3860. Web: www.nnhw.org.

NATIONAL POLICE WEEK. May 10–16. For info: American Police Hall of Fame and Museum, 6350 Horizon Dr, Titusville, FL 32780. Phone: (321) 264-0911. E-mail: policeinfo@aphf.org. Web: www.aphf.org. See also: "Peace Officer Memorial Day" (May 15).

NATIONAL RETURN TO WORK WEEK. May 10–16. Annually 4.1 million employees are injured; 2.1 million employees lose at least 7 days from work. Annually there are 80 million lost workdays due to occupational injury or illness. This week will focus on implementing proactive return-to-work programs that will get injured employees back to work successfully. Annually, the second week in May. For info: Margaret Spence, 1600 NW 2nd Ave, Ste 19, Boca Raton, FL 33432. Phone: (561) 795-3036. Fax: (561) 423-9207. E-mail: mspence@workcompseminars.com.

✦ **NATIONAL TRANSPORTATION WEEK.** May 10–16. Presidential Proclamation issued for week including third Friday in May since 1960. (PL86–475 of May 20, 1960, first requested; PL87–449 of May 14, 1962, requested an annual proclamation.)

✦ **POLICE WEEK.** May 10–16. Presidential Proclamation 3537 of May 4, 1963, covers all succeeding years. (PL87–726 of Oct 1, 1962.) Always the week including May 15 since 1962.

PREPARE TOMORROW'S PARENTS MONTH. May 10–June 21. To celebrate mothers and fathers, do at least one activity between Mother's Day and Father's Day to help prepare a child or teen to become a better parent in the future. To get ideas for parenting-preparation activities for this month and year-round, visit www.preparetomorrowsparents.org, which posts easy, fun steps to take at home as well as classroom-ready learning experiences for teachers, parents and youth organization leaders. For info: Prepare Tomorrow's Parents, 454 NE 3rd St, Boca Raton, FL 33432. Phone: (888) PARENTS. E-mail: info@preparetomorrowsparents.org. Web: www.preparetomorrowsparents.org.

READING IS FUN WEEK. May 10–16. To highlight the importance and fun of reading. Annually, the second full week of May. For info: Reading Is Fundamental, Inc, 1825 Connecticut Ave NW, Ste 400, Washington, DC 20009. Phone: (202) 536-3400 or (877) RIF-READ. Web: www.rif.org.

"THE REST OF THE STORY" RADIO PREMIERE: ANNIVERSARY. May 10, 1976. Radio legend Paul Harvey, whose "News and Comment" radio program had been on the air since 1951, spun off a popular segment into its own show on this date. "The Rest of the Story" was created to look at the story behind the story of famous people and events.

ROSS, GEORGE: BIRTH ANNIVERSARY. May 10, 1730. Signer of the Declaration of Independence. Born at New Castle, DE, he died July 14, 1779, at Philadelphia, PA.

SALUTE TO 35+ MOMS WEEK. May 10–16. Motherhood is challenging at any age, and if you become a mom when you're 35 or older, it can be quite an adjustment. This week is dedicated to moms

May 2009

S	M	T	W	T	F	S
					1	2
3	4	5	6	7	8	9
10	11	12	13	14	15	16
17	18	19	20	21	22	23
24	25	26	27	28	29	30
31						

with more life experience than baby experience. Now, and throughout the year, it is empowering to connect with peers and share the joys and trials and tribulations that child rearing may encompass when you parent later in life. For info: Robin Gorman Newman, 44 Somerset Dr N, Great Neck, NY 11020. Phone: (516) 773-0911. E-mail: rgnewman@optonline.net. Web: www.motherhoodlater.com.

SINGAPORE: VESAK DAY. May 10. Public holiday. Monks commemorate their Lord Buddha's entry into nirvana by chanting holy sutras and freeing captive birds.

TYBEE 500. May 10–11 (tentative). Hollywood, FL. A 540-mile endurance race for 18- and 20-foot beach catamarans. The race will begin in the Florida Keys, with checkpoints along the eastern seaboard of the Florida coastline, and will end at Tybee Island, GA. The public is invited to meet and greet the sailors at several receptions. For info: Marketing, City of Hollywood Dept of Parks & Recreation, 1405 S 28th Ave, Hollywood, FL 33020. Phone: (954) 921-3404. Web: www.hollywoodfl.org.

WORLD LUPUS DAY. May 10. An international call to action has been issued by more than 100 lupus organizations based in countries around the world. Goal is to call attention to the confusing characteristics of this potentially fatal autoimmune disease that mimics other, less serious illnesses. In addition, observing World Lupus Day offers lupus patients the comfort of knowing their condition is recognized and being addressed on a global level. For info: VP of Communications and Advocacy, Lupus Foundation of America, 2000 L St NW, Ste 710, Washington, DC 20036. Phone: (202) 349-1145. Fax: (202) 349-1156. Web: www.lupus.org or www.worldlupusday.org.

BIRTHDAYS TODAY

Bono, 49, singer (U2), humanitarian activist, born Paul Hewson at Dublin, Ireland, May 10, 1960.

Barbara Taylor Bradford, 76, author (*A Woman of Substance, Hold the Dream*), born Upper Armley, Leeds, Yorkshire, England, May 10, 1933.

T. Berry Brazelton, 91, pediatrician, author, born Waco, TX, May 10, 1918.

Jason Brooks, 43, actor ("Days of Our Lives"), born Colorado Springs, CO, May 10, 1966.

Dave Mason, 63, singer, musician, songwriter, born Worcester, England, May 10, 1946.

Gary Owens, 73, actor ("Rowan & Martin's Laugh-In," "The Gong Show"), born Mitchell, SD, May 10, 1936.

Ara Raoul Parseghian, 86, former football coach and sportscaster, born Akron, OH, May 10, 1923.

Marie-France Pisier, 65, actress (*Cousin Cousine, French Postcards*), born Dalat, Vietnam, May 10, 1944.

Ronald F. (Rony) Seikaly, 44, former basketball player, born Beirut, Lebanon, May 10, 1965.

May 11 — Monday

DAY 131 **234 REMAINING**

BATTLE OF HAMBURGER HILL: 40th ANNIVERSARY. May 11, 1969. Beginning of one of the most infamous battles that signified the growing frustration with America's involvement in the Vietnam War. Attempting to seize Dong Ap Bia mountain, American troops repeatedly scaled the hill over a 10-day period, often engaging in bloody hand-to-hand combat with the North Vietnamese. After finally securing the objective, American military decision makers chose to abandon it, and the North Vietnamese retook it shortly thereafter. The heavy casualties in the struggle to take the hill inspired the name "Hamburger Hill."

BERLIN, IRVING: BIRTH ANNIVERSARY. May 11, 1888. Songwriter born Israel Isidore Baline at Tyumen, Russia. Irving Berlin moved to New York, NY, with his family when he was four years old. After the death of his father, he began singing in saloons and on street corners in order to help his family and worked as a singing waiter as a teenager. Berlin became one of America's most prolific songwriters, authoring such songs as "Alexander's Ragtime Band," "White Christmas," "God Bless America," "There's No Business like Show Business," "Doin' What Comes Naturally," "Puttin' on the Ritz," "Blue Skies" and "Oh! How I Hate to Get Up in the Morning," among others. He could neither read nor write musical notation. Berlin died Sept 22, 1989, at New York.

CHILDREN'S BOOK WEEK. May 11–17. An annual event, sponsored by The Children's Book Council, to encourage the enjoyment of reading for young people. (Formerly in November.) For info: The Children's Book Council, Inc, 12 W 37th St, 2nd Fl, New York, NY 10018-7480. Phone: (800) 999-2160. Fax: (888) 807-9355. E-mail: info@cbcbooks.org. Web: www.cbcbooks.org or www.bookweekonline.com.

DALI, SALVADOR: BIRTH ANNIVERSARY. May 11, 1904. A leading painter in the surrealist movement, Salvador Dali was equally well known for his baffling antics and attempts to shock his audiences. The largest collection of his works resides in the Salvador Dali Museum at St. Petersburg, FL. Born at Figueras, Spain, Dali died there Jan 23, 1989.

EAT WHAT YOU WANT DAY. May 11. Here's a day you may actually enjoy yourself. Ignore all those on-again, off-again warnings. (©2006 by WH.) For info: Thomas & Ruth Roy, Wellcat Holidays, 2418 Long Ln, Lebanon, PA 17046. Phone: (717) 279-0184. E-mail: info@wellcat.com. Web: www.wellcat.com.

ELKIN, STANLEY: BIRTH ANNIVERSARY. May 11, 1930. Born at Brooklyn, NY, Stanley Elkin became a professor at Washington University at St. Louis, MO, where he lectured on fiction writing for more than 30 years. In addition to his teaching, Elkin was a novelist of particular acclaim. Author of 17 books, he was awarded the National Book Critics Circle Award in 1983 for his novel *George Mills*. Elkin died at St. Louis, May 31, 1995.

FAIRBANKS, CHARLES WARREN: BIRTH ANNIVERSARY. May 11, 1852. 26th vice president of the US (1905–09), born at Unionville Center, OH. Died at Indianapolis, IN, June 4, 1918.

GLACIER NATIONAL PARK ESTABLISHED: ANNIVERSARY. May 11, 1910. Located in northwest Montana on the Canadian border. In 1932 Glacier National Park and Waterton Lakes National Park in Alberta were joined together by the governments of the US and Canada as Waterton-Glacier International Peace Park.

GRAHAM, MARTHA: BIRTH ANNIVERSARY. May 11, 1894. Martha Graham was born at Allegheny, PA, and became one of the giants of the modern dance movement in the US. She began her dance career at the comparatively late age of 22 and joined the Greenwich Village Follies in 1923. Her new ideas began to surface in the late '20s and '30s, and by the mid-1930s she was incorporating the rituals of the southwestern American Indians in her work. She is credited with bringing a new psychological depth to modern dance by exploring primal emotions and ancient rituals in her work. She performed until the age of 75 and premiered in her 180th ballet, *The Maple Leaf Rag*, in the fall of 1990. Died Apr 1, 1991, at New York, NY.

HART, JOHN: DEATH ANNIVERSARY. May 11, 1779. Signer of the Declaration of Independence, farmer and legislator, born about 1711 (exact date unknown), at Stonington, CT; died at Hopewell, NJ.

JAPAN: CORMORANT FISHING FESTIVAL. May 11–Oct 15. Cormorant fishing on the Nagara River, Gifu. "This ancient method of catching ayu, a troutlike fish, with trained cormorants, takes place nightly under the light of blazing torches."

***MERRIMAC* DESTROYED: ANNIVERSARY.** May 11, 1862. After a standoff with the Union ironclad *Monitor* on Mar 9, the Confederate ironclad *Merrimac* was destroyed by the Confederate navy on May 11. In the wake of advancing Union troops in the Peninsular Campaign, the South was forced to destroy the valuable vessel to prevent its capture by Union forces. See also: "Battle of Hampton Roads: Anniversary" (Mar 9).

MINNESOTA ADMISSION DAY: ANNIVERSARY. May 11. Became 32nd state in 1858.

NAIA MEN'S & WOMEN'S TENNIS NATIONAL CHAMPIONSHIPS. May 11–15. Mobile, AL. 58th annual for men, 29th annual for women. Est attendance: 500. For info: Natl Assn of Intercollegiate Athletics, 1200 Grand Blvd, Kansas City, MO 64106. E-mail: lthomas@naia.org. Web: www.naia.org.

NATIONAL ETIQUETTE WEEK. May 11–15. National Etiquette Week is the national recognition of etiquette and protocol in all areas of American life—business, social, dining, travel, technology, wedding and international protocol. The week will raise awareness of all people to act with courtesy, civility, kindness and manners as well as rally people to act with good manners in their everyday life. Annually, the workweek beginning with the second Monday in May. For info: Cindy Haygood, Two S Main St, Town Center North, Watkinsville, GA 30677. Phone: (888) 769-5150. Fax: (706) 310-0003. E-mail: cindyh@etiquetteleadership.com.

NATIONAL STUTTERING AWARENESS WEEK. May 11–17. Annually, the second full week of May. For info: Stuttering Foundation of America, 3100 Walnut Grove Rd, Ste 603, Memphis, TN 38111-0749. Phone: (800) 992-9392 or (901) 452-7343. E-mail: info@stutteringhelp.org. Web: www.stutteringhelp.org or www.tartamudez.org in Spanish.

SUTTON HOO SHIP BURIAL DISCOVERED: 70th ANNIVERSARY. May 11, 1939. On this date, in a large mound at Sutton Hoo in rural Suffolk, England, archaeologist Basil Brown discovered an undisturbed royal Anglo-Saxon ship burial. The ship—the largest ever found—was 90 feet long and 14 feet wide (the wood had rotted away, leaving only an outline and rivets). Also discovered were gold, bronze, silver and gemmed artifacts and weapons. The buried ship is believed to be that of King Raedwald of East Anglia, who ruled in the early AD 600s.

May 2009	S	M	T	W	T	F	S
						1	2
	3	4	5	6	7	8	9
	10	11	12	13	14	15	16
	17	18	19	20	21	22	23
	24	25	26	27	28	29	30
	31						

BIRTHDAYS TODAY

Louis Farrakhan, 76, Nation of Islam leader, born New York, NY, May 11, 1933.

Bernard Fox, 82, actor ("Bewitched," *Titanic*), born Portalbot, South Wales, May 11, 1927.

Jonathan Jackson, 27, actor (*The Deep End of the Ocean*, "General Hospital"), born Orlando, FL, May 11, 1982.

Robert Jarvik, 63, physician, inventor of artificial heart that went into Barney Clark, born Midland, MI, May 11, 1946.

Matt Leinart, 26, football player, born Santa Ana, CA, May 11, 1983.

Natasha Richardson, 46, actress (*The Handmaid's Tale, Nell*), born London, England, May 11, 1963.

Mort Sahl, 82, comic actor (*Don't Make Waves*; *Doctor, You've Got to Be Kidding*), born Montreal, QC, Canada, May 11, 1927.

May 12 — Tuesday

DAY 132 — 233 REMAINING

BATTLE OF SPOTSYLVANIA: ANNIVERSARY. May 12, 1864. After the Battle of the Wilderness, Grant and Lee next engaged at the Battle of Spotsylvania (VA). Lee had positioned his troops in breastworks along a horseshoe formation, utilizing the natural features of the landscape. During Grant's attack on this strong defensive position, both sides suffered losses of more than 12,000 in what became known as "the Bloody Angle." Lee was forced to use every available man in order to protect the position and so ordered his troops to pull back during the night.

GEORGE VI'S CORONATION: ANNIVERSARY. May 12, 1937. George VI was crowned at Westminster Abbey at London, England, following the abdication of his brother, Edward VIII. Born Dec 14, 1895, King George died Feb 6, 1952. He was succeeded by his daughter Elizabeth, the current reigning monarch.

HEPBURN, KATHARINE: BIRTH ANNIVERSARY. May 12, 1907. American actress Katharine Houghton Hepburn was born at Hartford, CT. Nominated for 12 Oscars over the course of her career, she won four times: for 1933's *Morning Glory,* 1967's *Guess Who's Coming to Dinner,* 1968's *The Lion in Winter* and 1981's *On Golden Pond.* She is best remembered for her on- and offscreen pairing with Spencer Tracy. Together, they made nine films, including *Adam's Rib* and *Woman of the Year*, and enjoyed a 27-year personal relationship. There is often confusion regarding her date of birth: in her 1991 autobiography, *Me: Stories of My Life*, she confirmed the May date and admitted often giving out a late brother's birth date as her own. She died at Old Saybrook, CT, June 29, 2003.

LAG B'OMER. May 12. Hebrew calendar date: Iyar 18, 5769. Literally, the 33rd day of the omer (harvest time), the 33rd day after the beginning of Passover. Traditionally a joyous day for weddings, picnics and outdoor activities. Began at sundown May 11.

LEAR, EDWARD: BIRTH ANNIVERSARY. May 12, 1812. English artist and author, best remembered for his light verse and limericks. Lear was born at Highgate, England, and died at San Remo, Italy, Jan 29, 1888. See also: "Limerick Day" (below).

LIBRARY LEGISLATIVE DAY. May 12. Librarians go to Washington and to their state capitals to talk to legislators about important library issues. For info: Public Information Office, American Library Assn, 1301 Pennsylvania Ave NW, Ste 403, Washington, DC 20004. Phone: (202) 628-8410. E-mail: alawash@alawash.org. Web: www.ala.org.

LIMERICK DAY. May 12. Observed on the birthday of one of its champions, Edward Lear. The limerick, which dates from the early 18th century, has been described as the "only fixed verse form indigenous to the English language." It gained its greatest popularity following the publication of Edward Lear's *Book of Nonsense* (and its sequels). Write a limerick today! Example: There was a young poet named Lear/Who said, it is just as I fear/Five lines are enough/For this kind of stuff/Make a limerick each day of the year. See also: "Lear, Edward: Birth Anniversary" (above).

NAIA WOMEN'S GOLF NATIONAL CHAMPIONSHIPS. May 12–15. Rapid City, SD. 15th annual. Est attendance: 400. For info: Natl Assn of Intercollegiate Athletics, 1200 Grand Blvd, Kansas City, MO 64106. E-mail: balmeida@naia.org. Web: www.naia.org.

NATIVE AMERICAN RIGHTS RECOGNIZED: ANNIVERSARY. May 12, 1879. When the US tried to forcibly remove the Poncas from their homeland in Nebraska to an Oklahoma reservation, their chief, Standing Bear, brought suit to prevent it. The US claimed that Standing Bear could not bring suit because as a Native American he had no legal standing in US law. In *Standing Bear v George Crook* at US District Court, Judge J. Dundy ruled on this day that "an Indian is a PERSON within the meaning of the laws of the United States." This landmark decision was appealed by the US to the Supreme Court, which dismissed it. Standing Bear was not forced to move his tribe, but other Native Americans were unable to use the decision to their advantage in other disputes with the US.

NIGHTINGALE, FLORENCE: BIRTH ANNIVERSARY. May 12, 1820. English nurse and public health activist who, through her unselfish devotion to nursing, contributed perhaps more than any other single person to the development of modern nursing procedures and the dignity of nursing as a profession. Founder of the Nightingale training school for nurses. Author of *Notes on Nursing*. Born at Florence, Italy. Died at London, England, Aug 13, 1910.

ODOMETER INVENTED: ANNIVERSARY. May 12, 1847. Anniversary of the invention of the odometer by Mormon pioneer William Clayton while crossing the plains in a covered wagon. Previous to this, mileage was calculated by counting the revolutions of a rag tied to a spoke of a wagon wheel.

PORTUGAL: PILGRIMAGE TO FATIMA. May 12–13. Commemorates first appearance of the Virgin of the Rosary to little shepherd children May 13, 1917. Pilgrims come to Cova da Iria—religious center, candlelit procession, mass of the sick—for annual observance.

BIRTHDAYS TODAY

MacKenzie Astin, 36, actor (*The Last Days of Disco*), born Los Angeles, CA, May 12, 1973.

Burt Bacharach, 80, composer ("Walk on By," "Close to You," "Raindrops Keep Fallin' on My Head," many film scores), born Kansas City, MO, May 12, 1929.

Stephen Baldwin, 43, actor (*The Usual Suspects*), born Massapequa, NY, May 12, 1966.

Lawrence Peter "Yogi" Berra, 84, Hall of Fame baseball player, former baseball coach and manager, born St. Louis, MO, May 12, 1925.

Jason Biggs, 31, actor (*American Pie, Loser*), born Pompton Plains, NJ, May 12, 1978.

Bruce Boxleitner, 58, actor (*How the West Was Won*, "Scarecrow and Mrs King"), born Elgin, IL, May 12, 1951.

Cheryl Burke, 25, professional dancer, television personality ("Dancing with the Stars"), born San Francisco, CA, May 12, 1984.

Gabriel Byrne, 59, actor ("In Treatment," *The Usual Suspects*), born Dublin, Ireland, May 12, 1950.

Christian Campbell, 37, actor ("Malibu Shores," *Cold Hearts*), born Toronto, ON, Canada, May 12, 1972.

Lindsay Crouse, 61, actress (*The Verdict, Places in the Heart, House of Games*), born New York, NY, May 12, 1948.

Emilio Estevez, 47, actor (*Breakfast Club, Repo Man*), born New York, NY, May 12, 1962.

Kim Fields, 40, actress ("The Facts of Life," "Living Single"), born Los Angeles, CA, May 12, 1969.

Kim Greist, 51, actress (*Brazil, Throw Momma from the Train*), born Stamford, CT, May 12, 1958.

Tony Hawk, 40, skateboarder, born Carlsbad, CA, May 12, 1969.

Dave Heineman, 61, Governor of Nebraska (R), born Falls City, NE, May 12, 1948.

Jamie Luner, 38, actress ("Melrose Place," "Profiler"), born Los Angeles, CA, May 12, 1971.

Millie Perkins, 71, actress ("Knots Landing," *The Diary of Anne Frank, Wall Street*), born Passaic, NJ, May 12, 1938.

Ving Rhames, 48, actor ("Kojak," *Pulp Fiction*), born New York, NY, May 12, 1961.

Frank Stella, 73, artist (*Empress of India*), born Malden, MA, May 12, 1936.

Emily VanCamp, 23, actress ("Brothers & Sisters," "Everwood"), born Port Perry, ON, Canada, May 12, 1986.

Steve Winwood, 61, musician, singer, born Birmingham, England, May 12, 1948.

May 13 — Wednesday

DAY 133 — **232 REMAINING**

ATTEMPTED ASSASSINATION OF POPE JOHN PAUL II: ANNIVERSARY. May 13, 1981. Pope John Paul II was shot twice at close range while riding in an open automobile at St. Peter's Square at Rome, Italy. Two other persons also were wounded. An escaped terrorist, Mehmet Ali Agca (already under sentence of death for the murder of a Turkish journalist), was arrested immediately and was convicted July 22, 1981, of attempted murder of the pope. After convalescence Pope John Paul II was pronounced recovered by his doctors Aug 14, 1981. In 2000 Agca was released from prison and extradited to Turkey.

CALAVERAS COUNTY FAIR AND JUMPING FROG JUBILEE. May 13–17. Calaveras Fairgrounds, Angels Camp, CA. County fair and reenactment of Mark Twain's "Celebrated Jumping Frog of Calaveras County." This "Super Bowl" of the sport of frog jumping attracts more than 2,000 frogs annually from around the country. Est attendance: 45,000. For info: Frogtown, 101 Frogtown Rd, PO Box 489, Angels Camp, CA 95222. Phone: (209) 736-2561. Fax: (209) 736-2476. E-mail: info@frogtown.org. Web: www.frogtown.org.

CANNES FILM FESTIVAL. May 13–24. Cannes, France. 62nd annual. Premier international film festival, with hundreds of screenings (in competition and out), critical panels, director spotlights, Cannes Market for film distribution and numerous other cultural and artistic activities. Palme d'Or, Caméra d'Or, Grand Prix and other awards presented on the last day of the festival. The festival was first held in September 1946, and there have been only three cancellations since then, in 1948, 1950 and 1968. For info: Assoc Française du Festival Intl du Film, 3, rue Amelie, F-75007 Paris, France. Phone: (33) 0-53-59-61-00. E-mail: festival@festival-cannes.fr. Web: www.festival-cannes.org.

CRUISIN' DOWNTOWN 2009. May 13 (also June 10, July 8, Aug 12 and Sept 9). Toms River, NJ. Enjoy classic automobiles and motorcycles along Washington St. Live entertainment, crafters and food. Est attendance: 2,500. For info: Downtown Toms River, 218 Main St, Toms River, NJ 08753. Phone: (732) 341-8738. Fax: (732) 341-8748. E-mail: trbidstaff@verizon.net. Web: www.downtowntomsriver.com.

DOUGLAS, VIRGINIA O'HANLON: DEATH ANNIVERSARY. May 13, 1971. Virginia O'Hanlon Douglas lived a long and productive life as an educator and a loving mother. However, to the reading public she is reintroduced year after year at Christmastime as the disheartened eight-year-old who asked the staff of the *New York Sun* whether Santa Claus exists. In a famous 1897 editorial Francis P. Church answered her question and reassured Virginia that yes, indeed "there is a Santa Claus." Douglas died at Valatie, NY, at the age of 81.

LOUIS, JOE: 95th BIRTH ANNIVERSARY. May 13, 1914. World heavyweight boxing champion, 1937–49, nicknamed the "Brown Bomber," Joseph Louis Barrow was born near Lafayette, AL. He died Apr 12, 1981, at Las Vegas, NV. Buried at Arlington National Cemetery. (Louis's burial there, by presidential waiver, was the 39th exception ever to the eligibility rules for burial in Arlington National Cemetery.)

MEXICAN WAR DECLARED: ANNIVERSARY. May 13, 1846. Although fighting had begun days earlier, Congress officially declared war on Mexico on this date. The struggle cost the lives of 11,300 American soldiers and resulted in the annexation by the US of land that became parts of Oklahoma, New Mexico, Arizona, Nevada, California, Utah and Colorado. The war ended in 1848. See also: "Treaty of Guadalupe Hidalgo: Anniversary" (Feb 2).

NATIONAL NIGHTSHIFT WORKERS DAY. May 13. To honor those workers who reverse their natural circadian rhythm to keep business running 24 hours a day. Annually, the second Wednesday of May. For info: Velcea Kae, 3 Chester Rd, Springfield, VT 05156.

NATIONAL RECEPTIONISTS DAY. May 13. Day of recognition for our nation's frontline personnel in business because you get only one chance to make a good first impression. Receptionists may have other titles such as host/hostess, maître d', front desk clerk, operator, customer service representative or information desk personnel and include anyone responsible for creating or maintaining a favorable image for the company by greeting clients and guests. There are some 892,000 receptionists in the US. Annually, the second Wednesday in May. For info: Jennifer Alexander, Natl Receptionists Assn, PO Box 1187, Washington, CT 06793. Phone: (203) 273-1179. Fax: (888) 292-5782. E-mail: jennifer@nationalreceptionists.com. Web: www.nationalreceptionists.com.

NATIONAL THIRD SHIFT WORKERS DAY. May 13. To show appreciation for and to honor those often-forgotten workers who toil through the night to keep countless companies and businesses running smoothly. Annually, the second Wednesday in May. For info: Jeff Corbett, PO Box 2, Statesville, NC 28687.

PHILADELPHIA POLICE BOMBING: ANNIVERSARY. May 13, 1985. During the siege of the radical group MOVE at Philadelphia, PA, police in a helicopter reportedly dropped a bomb containing the powerful military plastic explosive C-4 on the building in which the group was housed. The bomb and the resulting fire left 11 persons dead (including four children) and destroyed 61 homes.

ROOT CANAL APPRECIATION DAY. May 13. A special day whose goal is to reverse common negative misconceptions of a routine dental procedure. The root canal, which has evolved into a simple, painless procedure, should be held in high esteem for the millions of teeth it saves—42 million American teeth this year alone. This day will provide dentists around the country with an opportunity to plan concurrent public educational events. Ceremonies can include performing a root canal filling at various locations around the country. Madison, WI, will serve as the national headquarters for Root Canal Appreciation Day. Annually, the second Wednesday in May. For info: Chris Kammer, DDS, 2275 Deming Way, Ste 180, Middleton, WI 53562. Phone: (608) 827-6453. E-mail: DrChris@TheSmileExperts.com. Web: www.TheSmileExperts.com.

May 2009

S	M	T	W	T	F	S
					1	2
3	4	5	6	7	8	9
10	11	12	13	14	15	16
17	18	19	20	21	22	23
24	25	26	27	28	29	30
31						

SAINT LAWRENCE SEAWAY ACT: 55th ANNIVERSARY. May 13, 1954. President Dwight D. Eisenhower signed legislation authorizing US-Canadian construction of a waterway that would make it possible for oceangoing ships to reach the Great Lakes.

SPACE MILESTONE: *ENDEAVOUR* (US). May 13, 1992. Three astronauts from the shuttle *Endeavour* simultaneously walked in space for the first time.

SULLIVAN, ARTHUR: BIRTH ANNIVERSARY. May 13, 1842. English composer best known for light operas (with Sir William Gilbert), born at London, England. Died there Nov 22, 1900.

TUNIS CAMPAIGN VICTORY: ANNIVERSARY. May 13, 1943. General Sir Harold Alexander telegraphed Winston Churchill, who was in Washington attending a conference, "It is my duty to report that the Tunis campaign is over. All enemy resistance has ceased. We are masters of the North African shores." About 250,000 Germans and Italians surrendered in the last few days of the campaign. This Allied victory in North Africa helped open Mediterranean shipping lanes.

WELLS, MARY: BIRTH ANNIVERSARY. May 13, 1943. Motown's first big star, Mary Wells was born at Detroit, MI. She was known for such hits as "You Beat Me to the Punch," "Two Lovers" and her signature song, "My Guy." She was one of a group of black artists of the '60s who helped end musical segregation by being played on white radio stations. Mary Wells died July 26, 1992, at Los Angeles, CA.

BIRTHDAYS TODAY

Franklyn Ajaye, 60, actor ("Deadwood," *Car Wash*), born Brooklyn, NY, May 13, 1949.

Beatrice Arthur, 83, actress (*Mame*, "Maude," "Golden Girls"), born Bernice Frankel at New York, NY, May 13, 1926.

Frances Barber, 52, actress (*Sammy and Rosie Get Laid, We Think the World of You*), born Wolverhampton, England, May 13, 1957.

Clive Barnes, 82, critic, born London, England, May 13, 1927.

Mike Bibby, 31, basketball player, born Cherry Hill, NJ, May 13, 1978.

Stephen Colbert, 45, writer, comedian ("The Daily Show," "The Colbert Report"), born Charlestown, SC, May 13, 1964.

Harvey Keitel, 70, actor (*Mean Streets, Blue Collar, Bugsy, The Piano*), born Brooklyn, NY, May 13, 1939.

Julianne Phillips, 47, actress (*Allie & Me*, "Sisters"), born Lake Oswego, OR, May 13, 1962.

Tim Pigott-Smith, 63, actor ("The Jewel in the Crown," *Remains of the Day*), born Rugby, England, May 13, 1946.

Dennis Rodman, 48, former basketball player, born Trenton, NJ, May 13, 1961.

Darius Rucker, 41, lead singer (Hootie and the Blowfish), born Charleston, SC, May 13, 1968.

Bobby Valentine, 59, former baseball player and manager, broadcaster, born Stamford, CT, May 13, 1950.

Stevie Wonder, 59, singer, musician (19 Grammy Awards; "I Just Called to Say I Love You"), born Steveland Morris Hardaway at Saginaw, MI, May 13, 1950.

May 14 — Thursday

DAY 134 **231 REMAINING**

ASPENCASH MOTORCYCLE RALLY. May 14–17. Ruidoso, NM. $10,000 cash poker run, trade show, poker run pin. Est attendance: 12,000. For info: Golden Aspen Rally Assn, PO Box 1467, Ruidoso, NM 88355. Phone: (800) 452-8045. E-mail: info@motorcyclerally.com. Web: www.motorcyclerally.com.

BONNIE BLUE NATIONAL HORSE SHOW. May 14–17. Virginia Horse Center, Lexington, VA. Major all-breed event, "A"-rated show of the American Horse Show Association. For info: Lexington Visitors Bureau, 106 E Washington St, Lexington, VA 24450. Phone: (540) 463-3777. Fax: (540) 463-1105. E-mail: lexington@rockbridge.net. Web: www.horsecenter.org.

CARLSBAD CAVERNS NATIONAL PARK ESTABLISHED: ANNIVERSARY. May 14, 1930. Located in southwestern New Mexico, Carlsbad Caverns was proclaimed a national monument, Oct 25, 1923, and was later established as a national park and preserve.

ENGLAND: ROYAL WINDSOR HORSE SHOW. May 14–17. Home Park, Private Windsor, Berkshire. Major annual show jumping and showing event with royal pageantry and color. Est attendance: 65,000. For info: Penelope Henderson, Sec'y, Royal Windsor Horse Show, The Royal Mews, Windsor Castle, Windsor, Berkshire, England SL4 1NG. Phone: (44) (1753) 860-633. E-mail: info@rwhs.co.uk. Web: www.rwhs.co.uk.

"ERNIE KOVACS" TV PREMIERE: ANNIVERSARY. May 14, 1951. Comedian Ernie Kovacs first hosted "It's Time for Ernie," a 15-minute afternoon program on NBC, in May 1951 before replacing "Kukla, Fran and Ollie" with "Ernie in Kovacsland." "The Ernie Kovacs Show" debuted on Dec 30, 1952. Kovacs also appeared on a variety of daytime and prime-time series and was a fill-in for Steve Allen on the "Tonight" show. His early shows featured his wife, Edie Adams.

FAHRENHEIT, GABRIEL DANIEL: BIRTH ANNIVERSARY. May 14, 1686. German physicist whose name is attached to one of the major temperature measurement scales. He introduced the use of mercury in thermometers and greatly improved their accuracy. Born at Danzig, Germany, he died at Amsterdam, The Netherlands, Sept 16, 1736.

FIRST FORMAL FEMALE HOUSE PAGE APPOINTMENT: 35th ANNIVERSARY. May 14, 1973. The House of Representatives received formal approval of the appointment of female pages in 1972. On May 14, 1973, in the 93rd Congress, Felda Looper was appointed as the successor to Gene Cox, who, for three hours, had served as the first female page 34 years earlier.

GAINSBOROUGH, THOMAS: BIRTH ANNIVERSARY. May 14, 1727. (Old Style date.) English landscape and portrait painter. Among his most remembered works: *The Blue Boy*, *The Watering Place* and *The Market Cart*. Born at Sudbury, Suffolk, England, he was baptized on May 14, 1727 (OS), and he died at London, Aug 2, 1788.

JAMESTOWN, VIRGINIA: FOUNDING ANNIVERSARY. May 14, 1607. (Old Style date.) The first permanent English settlement in what is now the US took place at Jamestown, VA (named for England's King James I), on this date. Captains John Smith and Christopher Newport were among the leaders of the group of royally chartered Virginia Company settlers who had traveled from Plymouth, England, in three small ships: *Susan Constant*, *Godspeed* and *Discovery*.

LEWIS AND CLARK EXPEDITION SETS OUT: ANNIVERSARY. May 14, 1804. Charged by President Thomas Jefferson with finding a route to the Pacific, Captain Meriwether Lewis and Lieutenant William Clark left St. Louis with a 33-member group skilled in botany, zoology, outdoor survival and other scientific skills. They arrived at the Pacific coast of Oregon in November 1805 and returned to St. Louis, Sept 23, 1806. (See also Jan 18 and Sept 23.)

LOST IN THE '50s. May 14–17. Sandpoint, ID. Dance and show with '50s and '60s stars, vintage car parade, car show, car rally and 5K run. Est attendance: 10,000. For info: Lost in the '50s, Carolyn Gleason, Chair, 215 S 2nd Ave, Sandpoint, ID 83864. Phone: (208) 263-9321 or (208) 265-LOST. E-mail: lost50s@sandpoint.net.

MILES CITY BUCKING HORSE SALE. May 14–17. Miles City, MT. Miles City is real "Lonesome Dove" country and its annual bucking horse sale is where rodeo stock operators from around the nation and Canada come to purchase their bucking horses for the coming rodeo season. A festive event, the sale not only involves cowboys trying to ride some of the wildest horses in the country but also includes Western artists displaying and creating works in a weekend art show, a Western trade show featuring practical and gift items, a Saturday morning parade and Miles City's Western attractions such as the Range Riders Museum. (Miles City is the community featured in the novel and two television miniseries about "Lonesome Dove.") Est attendance: 10,000. For info: Miles City Bucking Horse Sale, 511 Pleasant, Miles City, MT 59301. Phone: (406) 874-BUCK.

NCAA DIVISION I MEN'S AND WOMEN'S TENNIS CHAMPIONSHIPS. May 14–25. College Station, TX. For info: Natl Collegiate Athletic Assn, 700 W Washington St, PO Box 6222, Indianapolis, IN 46206-6222. Phone: (317) 917-6222. Web: www.NCAAsports.com.

NORWAY: MIDNIGHT SUN AT NORTH CAPE. May 14–July 30. North Cape. First day of the season with around-the-clock sunshine. At North Cape, the sun never dips below the horizon from May 14 to July 30, but the night is bright long before and after these dates.

OWEN, ROBERT: BIRTH ANNIVERSARY. May 14, 1771. English progressive owner of spinning works, philanthropist, utopian socialist, founder of New Harmony, IN, born at Newtown, Wales. Died there Nov 17, 1858.

PHILIPPINES: CARABAO FESTIVAL. May 14–15. Pulilan, Bulacan; Nueva Ecija; Angono, Rizal. Parade of farmers to honor their patron saint, San Isidro, with hundreds of "dressed-up" *carabaos* (water buffalo) participating.

SMALLPOX VACCINE DISCOVERED: ANNIVERSARY. May 14, 1796. In the 18th century, smallpox was a widespread and often fatal disease. Edward Jenner, a physician in rural England, heard reports of dairy farmers who apparently became immune to smallpox as a result of exposure to cowpox, a related but milder disease. After two decades of studying the phenomenon, Jenner injected cowpox into a healthy eight-year-old boy, who subsequently developed cowpox. Six weeks later, Jenner inoculated the boy with smallpox. He remained healthy. Jenner called this new procedure *vaccination*, from *vaccinia*, another term for cowpox. Within 18 months, 12,000 people in England had been vaccinated and the number of smallpox deaths dropped by two-thirds.

SPACE MILESTONE: *SKYLAB* (US). May 14, 1973. The US launched *Skylab*, its first manned orbiting laboratory.

"THE STARS AND STRIPES FOREVER" DAY. May 14, 1897. Anniversary of the first public performance of John Philip Sousa's march "The Stars and Stripes Forever," at Philadelphia, PA. The occasion was the unveiling of a statue of George Washington, and President William McKinley was present.

WAAC: ANNIVERSARY. May 14, 1942. During WWII women became eligible to enlist for noncombat duties in the Women's Auxiliary Army Corps (WAAC) by an act of Congress. Women also served as Women Accepted for Voluntary Emergency Service (WAVES), Women's Auxiliary Ferrying Squadron (WAFS) and Coast Guard or Semper Paratus Always Ready Service (SPARS), the Women's Reserve of the Marine Corps.

BIRTHDAYS TODAY

Cate Blanchett, 40, actress (Oscar for *The Aviator*; *I'm Not There, Elizabeth, Babel*), born Melbourne, Australia, May 14, 1969.

David Byrne, 57, singer, composer, born Dumbarton, Scotland, May 14, 1952.

Byron L. Dorgan, 67, US Senator (D, North Dakota), born Dickinson, ND, May 14, 1942.

Meg Foster, 61, actress ("Cagney & Lacey," *The Emerald Forest, They Live*), born Reading, PA, May 14, 1948.

Roy Halladay, 32, baseball player, born Denver, CO, May 14, 1977.

George Lucas, 65, filmmaker (*Star Wars* films), born Modesto, CA, May 14, 1944.

Jose Dennis Martinez, 54, former baseball player, born Granada, Nicaragua, May 14, 1955.

Patrice Munsel, 84, opera singer, born Spokane, WA, May 14, 1925.

Ralph Neas, 63, president, People for the American Way, born Brookline, MA, May 14, 1946.

Atanasio (Tony) Perez, 67, Hall of Fame baseball player, born Camaguey, Cuba, May 14, 1942.

Tim Roth, 48, actor (*The Incredible Hulk, Youth Without Youth, Pulp Fiction*), born London, England, May 14, 1961.

Valerie Still, 48, basketball player, born Lexington, KY, May 14, 1961.

Amber Tamblyn, 26, actress (*The Sisterhood of the Traveling Pants*, "Joan of Arcadia"), born Santa Monica, CA, May 14, 1983.

Ronan Tynan, 49, opera singer (The Irish Tenors), born Dublin, Ireland, May 14, 1960.

Robert Zemeckis, 57, director (*Forrest Gump, Back to the Future*), born Chicago, IL, May 14, 1952.

May 15 — Friday

DAY 135 **230 REMAINING**

ART FAIR AND WINEFEST. May 15–17. Washington, MO. The largest Missouri wine tasting of state wines as well as a juried art show featuring 60 Midwestern artists. Art fair is free. Admission to the wine pavilion includes a commemorative wineglass. For info: Downtown Washington, Inc, PO Box 144, Washington, MO 63090. Phone: (636) 239-1743. Fax: (636) 239-4832. E-mail: events@downtownwashmo.org. Web: www.downtownwashmo.org.

AVEDON, RICHARD: BIRTH ANNIVERSARY. May 15, 1923. Influential photographer born at New York, NY. Avedon began his career with the merchant marines, taking personnel identification photos and images of shipwrecks. Later, he worked for *Harper's Bazaar* and *Vogue*, where his artistic style of shooting fashion models against famous backgrounds revolutionized that industry's approach to fashion layouts. He was known for taking memorable, while not necessarily flattering, portraits and was honored with retrospectives and exhibits at many museums. He received the National Medal for the Arts in 2003 and died at New York, Oct 1, 2004.

BAUM, LYMAN FRANK: BIRTH ANNIVERSARY. May 15, 1856. American newspaperman who wrote the Wizard of Oz stories was born at Chittenango, NY. Although *The Wonderful Wizard of Oz* is the most famous, Baum also wrote many other books for children, including more than a dozen about Oz. He died at Hollywood, CA, May 6, 1919.

May 2009

S	M	T	W	T	F	S
					1	2
3	4	5	6	7	8	9
10	11	12	13	14	15	16
17	18	19	20	21	22	23
24	25	26	27	28	29	30
31						

BIG TEN MEN'S/WOMEN'S OUTDOOR TRACK AND FIELD CHAMPIONSHIPS. May 15–17. University of Iowa, Iowa City, IA. Est attendance: 1,500. For info: Big Ten Conference, 1500 W Higgins Rd, Park Ridge, IL 60068-6300. Phone: (847) 696-1010. Fax: (847) 696-1110. Web: www.bigten.org.

COTTEN, JOSEPH: BIRTH ANNIVERSARY. May 15, 1905. Stage and screen star Joseph Cotten was born at Petersburg, VA. Among Cotten's movie credits were *Citizen Kane, The Magnificent Ambersons* and *The Third Man*. Among his most noted performances on Broadway were *The Philadelphia Story* and *Once More with Feeling*. Joseph Cotten died Feb 6, 1994, at Los Angeles, CA.

CURIE, PIERRE: 150th BIRTH ANNIVERSARY. May 15, 1859. Born at Paris, France, Curie was one of the founders of modern physics. His research had already brought important results (in heat waves, crystals, magnetism, symmetry) and the formulation of Curie's law before he married Marie Sklowdowska in 1895. Together, the Curies discovered polonium and radium while conducting research in radioactivity. With Henri Becquerel, the Curies were awarded the Nobel Prize for Physics in 1903. Tragically, Pierre Curie was struck by a dray in Paris and died Apr 19, 1906.

DERMOTT'S ANNUAL CRAWFISH FESTIVAL. May 15–16. Dermott, AR. 26th annual. To publicize and popularize crawfish as a delicacy, to promote the area and to raise funds for industrial expansion. Family fun, arts, crafts, exotic foods, carnival, live music and street dances. Annually, the third weekend in May. Est attendance: 20,000. For info: Dermott Area Chamber of Commerce, Box 147, Dermott, AR 71638. Phone: (870) 538-5656. E-mail: dermottcoc@sbcglobal.net.

EASTERN PACIFIC HURRICANE SEASON. May 15–Nov 30. Eastern Pacific defined as: Coast to 140 degrees west longitude. Info from: US Dept of Commerce, Natl Oceanic and Atmospheric Admin, Rockville, MD 20852.

FIRST FLIGHT ATTENDANT: ANNIVERSARY. May 15, 1930. Ellen Church became the first airline stewardess (today's flight attendant), flying on a United Airlines flight from San Francisco, CA, to Cheyenne, WY.

FISHING HAS NO BOUNDARIES—HAYWARD EVENT. May 15–17. Lake Chippewa Campgrounds, Hayward, WI. A three-day fishing experience for disabled persons. Any disability, age, sex, race, etc, eligible. Fishing with experienced guides on one of the best fishing waters in Wisconsin, attended by 150 participants and 350 volunteers. Advance registration by Apr 27. Est attendance: 2,000. For info: Fishing Has No Boundaries, PO Box 375, Hayward, WI 54843. Phone: (715) 634-3185. Fax: (715) 634-1305. E-mail: hayfhnb@cheqnet.net.

FRISCH, MAX: BIRTH ANNIVERSARY. May 15, 1911. Max Frisch was one of Europe's leading post-WWII literary figures. His work includes the novels *Homo Faber, I'm Not Stiller* and *Juerg Reinhardt* and the plays *The Firebugs* and *Andorra*. In addition to his writing, he was a controversial critic of his native Switzerland. Born at Zurich, he died there Apr 4, 1991.

GEORGE WALLACE SHOT: ANNIVERSARY. May 15, 1972. George Wallace, a former governor of Alabama and a symbol of segregation, was shot by Arthur Bremer while Wallace was at Laurel, MD, campaigning for the US presidency. For the remainder of his life (until he died in 1998), Wallace was paralyzed from the waist down. On Aug 4, 1972, Bremer was sentenced to 67 years in prison for the shooting.

INTERNATIONAL VIRTUAL ASSISTANTS DAY. May 15. This day acknowledges the dedication, experience, expertise and determination of virtual professionals to succeed and exemplifies their integrity and commitment to provide superior administrative and other business support services—virtually. This day is celebrated during the Online International Virtual Assistants Convention and sponsored by the Alliance for Virtual Businesses, a consortium of international virtual assistant organizations. Annually, the third Friday in May. For info: Alliance for Virtual Businesses. Phone: (410) 521-7001. Fax: (410) 521-9742. E-mail: info@oivac.com. Web: www.oivac.com.

JAPAN: AOI MATSURI (HOLLYHOCK FESTIVAL). May 15. Kyoto. The festival features a pageant reproducing imperial processions of ancient times that paid homage to the shrine of Shimogamo and Kamigamo.

LEWIS AND CLARK HERITAGE DAYS. May 15–17. St. Charles, MO. Authentic reenactment of Lewis and Clark's 1804 encampment prior to embarking on the exploration of the Louisiana Purchase. Activities include a parade with fife and drum corps, church service, 19th-century crafts, music, food and demonstrations. Est attendance: 25,000. For info: Greater St. Charles CVB, 230 S Main St, St. Charles, MO 63301-2855. Phone: (800) 366-2427 or (636) 946-7776. Web: www.lewisandclark.net.

MAIFEST. May 15–17. MainStrasse Village, Covington, KY. MainStrasse celebrates the German tradition of welcoming the first spring wines and the beginning of the festival season. Artist and crafts exhibits, food and drink, live music and entertainment. Est attendance: 150,000. For info: Donna Kremer, Administrative Coord, MainStrasse Village, 406 W 6th St, Ste 201, Covington, KY 41011. Phone: (859) 491-0458. Fax: (859) 655-7932. E-mail: dkremer@mainstrasse.org. Web: www.mainstrasse.org.

MEXICO: SAN ISIDRO DAY. May 15. Day of San Isidro Labrador celebrated widely in farming regions to honor St. Isidore, the Plowman. Livestock gaily decorated with flowers. Celebrations usually begin about May 13 and continue for about a week.

NAIA SOFTBALL NATIONAL CHAMPIONSHIP. May 15–20. Site TBD. 29th annual. Est attendance: 2,000. For info: Natl Assn of Intercollegiate Athletics, 1200 Grand Blvd, Kansas City, MO 64106. E-mail: dgreen@naia.org. Web: www.naia.org.

NATIONAL BIKE TO WORK DAY. May 15. At the state or local level, Bike to Work events are conducted by small and large businesses, city governments, bicycle clubs and environmental groups. Annually, the third Friday in May. Est attendance: 2,000,000. For info: Patrick McCormick, Communications Dir, League of American Bicyclists, 1612 K St NW, Ste 800, Washington, DC 20006. Phone: (202) 822-1333. Fax: (202) 822-1334. E-mail: bikeleague@bikeleague.org. Web: www.bikeleague.org.

✦ **NATIONAL DEFENSE TRANSPORTATION DAY.** May 15. Presidential Proclamation customarily issued as "National Defense Transportation Day and National Transportation Week." Issued each year for the third Friday in May since 1957. (PL85–32 of May 16, 1957.)

NATIONAL PIZZA PARTY DAY. May 15. As the school year winds down, students and parents should celebrate with pizza parties! Local promotions will support the day within classrooms and at home. Annually, the third Friday in May. For info: Dwayne Northrup, Garlic Jim's Famous Gourmet Pizza, 802 134th St SW, Ste 130, Everett, WA 98204. Phone: (425) 918-1900. Fax: (425) 918-1700. E-mail: dwayne@garlicjims.com. Web: www.garlicjims.com.

NEWPORT SPRING BOAT SHOW. May 15–17. Newport, RI. New England's largest venue for buying and selling pre-owned boats and new clearance models. Hundreds of powerboats, sailboats, multihulls, kayaks and dinghies on display. Large show tent houses more than 100 booths with marine-related equipment, accessories and services. New marine consignment tent, educational seminars and giveaways. For info: Nancy Piffard, Newport Boat Show, PO Box 698, Newport, RI 02840. Phone: (401) 846-1115. Fax: (401) 848-0455. E-mail: npiffard@newportexhibition.com. Web: www.newportspringboatshow.com.

NYLON STOCKINGS: ANNIVERSARY. May 15, 1940. Nylon hose went on sale at stores throughout the country. Competing producers bought their nylon yarn from E.I. du Pont de Nemours and Company (later DuPont). W.H. Carothers, of DuPont, developed nylon, called "Polymer 66," in 1935. It was the first totally man-made fiber and over time was substituted for other materials and came to have widespread application.

PARAGUAY: INDEPENDENCE DAY. May 15. Commemorates independence from Spain, attained 1811.

✦ **PEACE OFFICER MEMORIAL DAY.** May 15. Presidential Proclamation 3537, of May 4, 1963, covers all succeeding years. (PL87–726 of Oct 1, 1962.) Always May 15 of each year since 1963; however, first issued in 1962 for May 14.

PEACE OFFICER MEMORIAL DAY. May 15. An event honored by some 21,000 police departments nationwide. Memorial ceremonies at 10 AM in American Police Hall of Fame and Museum, Titusville, FL. Sponsor: National Association of Chiefs of Police. For info: American Police Hall of Fame and Museum, 6350 Horizon Dr, Titusville, FL 32780. Phone: (321) 264-0911. E-mail: policeinfo@aphf.org. Web: www.aphf.org. See also: "National Police Week" (May 10–16).

PORTER, KATHERINE ANNE: BIRTH ANNIVERSARY. May 15, 1890. American prose writer Katherine Anne Porter was born at Indian Creek, TX. Her one long novel, *Ship of Fools* (1962), is considered by some to be one of the greatest allegorical works in English. She won the Pulitzer Prize and the National Book Award in 1966 for *Collected Stories*. Died Sept 18, 1980, at Silver Spring, MD.

RED, WHITE & BLUEGRASS. May 15–17 (tentative). Hollywood, FL. Traditional and contemporary bluegrass. Est attendance: 15,000. For info: Marketing, City of Hollywood, 1405 S 28th Ave, Hollywood, FL 33020. Phone: (954) 921-3404. Fax: (954) 921-3572. Web: www.hollywoodfl.org.

RHODODENDRON FESTIVAL. May 15–17. Florence, OR. Abundance of springtime rhododendron blooms celebrated with a Grand Floral Parade, arts and crafts fair, show and shine, car cruise and carnival. Held annually the third weekend of May since 1908. Est attendance: 15,000. For info: Florence Area Chamber of Commerce, 290 Hwy 101, Florence, OR 97439. Phone: (541) 997-3128. E-mail: florence@oregonfast.net. Web: www.florencechamber.com.

RHUBARB FESTIVAL. May 15–16. Intercourse, PA. A lighthearted celebration honoring rhubarb, which grows abundantly in the Pennsylvania Dutch country. Food, games and contests all featuring rhubarb—pie-baking contest, rhubarb derby, rhubarb pick up sticks and more—plus entertainment. Annually, the third Friday and Saturday in May. Est attendance: 20,000. For info: Kitchen Kettle Village, Rte 340, Box 380, Intercourse, PA 17534. Phone: (800) 732-3538 or (717) 768-8261. Fax: (717) 768-2795. Web: www.kitchenkettle.com.

SCHNITZLER, ARTHUR: BIRTH ANNIVERSARY. May 15, 1862. Austrian playwright, novelist and medical doctor, Arthur Schnitzler was born at Vienna. Noted for his psychoanalytic examination of Viennese society. Died at Vienna, Oct 21, 1931.

SPACE MILESTONE: *FAITH 7* (US). May 15, 1963. Launched with Major Gordon Leroy Cooper and orbited Earth 22 times.

TEACHER'S DAY IN FLORIDA. May 15. A ceremonial day observed on the third Friday in May.

UNITED NATIONS: INTERNATIONAL DAY OF FAMILIES. May 15. The general assembly (Resolution 47/237) on Sept 20, 1993, voted this as an annual observance beginning in 1994. For info: United Nations, Dept of Public Info, New York, NY 10017. Web: www.un.org.

WILSON, ELLEN LOUISE AXSON: BIRTH ANNIVERSARY. May 15, 1860. First wife of Woodrow Wilson, 28th president of the US. Born at Savannah, GA; died at Washington, DC, Aug 6, 1914.

BIRTHDAYS TODAY

Anna Maria Alberghetti, 73, singer, actress (*Cinderfella, Carnival*), born Pesaro, Italy, May 15, 1936.

Madeleine Albright, 72, former US Secretary of State (Clinton administration), born Prague, Czechoslovakia, May 15, 1937.

George Howard Brett, 56, Hall of Fame baseball player, executive, born Glen Dale, WV, May 15, 1953.

David Charvet, 37, actor ("Melrose Place," "Baywatch"), born Lyon, France, May 15, 1972.

David Cronenberg, 66, filmmaker (*The Fly, Naked Lunch, Eastern Promises*), born Toronto, ON, Canada, May 15, 1943.

Dwayne De Rosario, 31, soccer player, born Scarborough, ON, Canada, May 15, 1978.

Brian Eno, 61, avant-garde musician, born Woodbridge, England, May 15, 1948.

Giselle Fernandez, 48, TV host, actress, born Mexico City, Mexico, May 15, 1961.

Lee Horsley, 54, actor ("Nero Wolfe," "Matt Houston"), born Muleshoe, TN, May 15, 1955.

Jasper Johns, 79, artist, born Augusta, GA, May 15, 1930.

Kaká, 27, soccer player, born Ricardo Izecson dos Santos Leite at Brasilia, Brazil, May 15, 1982 (some sources say Apr 22, 1982).

Lainie Kazan, 67, singer, actress (*My Favorite Year, Beaches, My Big Fat Greek Wedding*), born New York, NY, May 15, 1942.

David Krumholtz, 31, actor ("Numb3rs"), born New York, NY, May 15, 1978.

Trini Lopez, 72, actor, singer (*Marriage on the Rocks, The Dirty Dozen*), born Dallas, TX, May 15, 1937.

Justin Morneau, 28, baseball player, born New Westmister, BC, Canada, May 15, 1981.

Chazz Palminteri, 58, actor (*Bullets Over Broadway*), playwright, screenwriter (*A Bronx Tale*), born the Bronx, NY, May 15, 1951.

Dan Patrick, 53, sportscaster (ESPN's "SportsCenter"), radio personality, born Zanesville, OH, May 15, 1956.

Kathleen Sebelius, 61, Governor of Kansas (D), born Cincinnati, OH, May 15, 1948.

Jamie-Lynn Sigler, 28, actress ("The Sopranos"), born Jericho, NY, May 15, 1981.

Emmitt Smith, 40, former football player, born Pensacola, FL, May 15, 1969.

John Smoltz, 42, baseball player, born Warren, MI, May 15, 1967.

May 2009	S	M	T	W	T	F	S
						1	2
	3	4	5	6	7	8	9
	10	11	12	13	14	15	16
	17	18	19	20	21	22	23
	24	25	26	27	28	29	30
	31						

May 16 — Saturday

DAY 136 **229 REMAINING**

AMCORE BANK FAIRE ON THE SQUARE ART & CRAFT FAIR. May 16 (also Oct 10). Downtown Baraboo, WI. Biannual outdoor event. Features all-handmade work of 200 artists and crafters, local cuisine food stands, farmers' market, live entertainment, community court, carnival and kids' activities. Visit the unique specialty shops in historic downtown Baraboo. The October Fair is held during the peak fall-color time. Est attendance: 10,000. For info: Cindy Doescher, Fan Faire Promotions, LLC, 1801 Jefferson St, Baraboo, WI 53913. Phone: (608) 356-7995. E-mail: cindy@fan-faire.com. Web: www.faireonthesquare.com.

BIOGRAPHERS DAY. May 16. Anniversary of the meeting, at London, England, May 16, 1763, of James Boswell and Samuel Johnson, beginning history's most famous biographer-biographee relationship. Boswell's *Journal of a Tour to the Hebrides* (1785) and his *Life of Samuel Johnson* (1791) are regarded as models of biographical writing. Thus, this day is recommended as one on which to start reading or writing a biography.

CALIFORNIA ARTICHOKE FESTIVAL. May 16–17. Castroville, CA. 50th annual. Annually, in the Artichoke Capital of the World. Events include wine tasting, agro-art contest, vintage car show and 10k run. Est attendance: 15,000. For info: North Monterey County Chamber of Commerce, PO Box 744, Castroville, CA 95012. Phone: (831) 633-2465. Fax: (831) 633-0485. E-mail: info at artichoke-festival.org. Web: www.artichoke-festival.org.

CANADA: UPPER CANADA VILLAGE. May 16–Oct 4. Morrisburg, ON. One of Canada's premier attractions. Visitors enter the world of the 1860s. Costumed interpreters bring history to life in this fully operational rural community as they perform period activities of townsfolk or of tradespeople who apply their skills in restored buildings ranging from homes to trade shops. Many special events and programs offered throughout the season. Est attendance: 150,000. For info: Upper Canada Village, Parks of the St. Lawrence, 13740 County Rd 2, Morrisburg, ON, Canada K0C 1X0. Phone: (800) 437-2233 or (613) 543-4328. Web: www.uppercanadavillage.com.

EIGHTEENTH-CENTURY SPRING MARKET FAIR. May 16–17. McLean, VA. Learn 18th-century crafts, music and games. Period wares, food and drink for sale. Est attendance: 3,500. For info: Claude Moore Colonial Farm at Turkey Run, 6310 Georgetown Pike, McLean, VA 22101. Phone: (703) 442-7557. Fax: (703) 442-0714. Web: www.1771.org.

FIRST ACADEMY AWARDS: 80th ANNIVERSARY. May 16, 1929. About 270 people attended a dinner at the Hollywood Roosevelt Hotel at which the first Academy Awards were given in 12 categories. The silent film *Wings* won Best Picture. A committee of only 20 members selected the winners that year. By the third year the entire membership of the Academy voted. The Academy Awards were first televised in 1953.

FIRST WOMAN TO CLIMB MOUNT EVEREST: ANNIVERSARY. May 16, 1975. Japanese climber Junko Tabei, leading an all-woman expedition to Mount Everest, became the first woman to reach the summit on this date in 1975. Taking the South-East Ridge route, Tabei was delayed by an avalanche before her last leg up the mountain. "Even after reaching the peak," she later recalled, "instead of shouting with excitement, I was simply happy that I didn't have to go any higher!"

FISHING HAS NO BOUNDARIES. May 16–17. Freeman Lake, Monticello, IN. A two-day event for disabled persons to experience fishing on the lake. Any disability, sex, age, race, etc, eligible. For info: Fishing Has No Boundaries, PO Box 325, Battle Ground, IN 47920. Phone: (765) 567-2567. E-mail: smlinder2000@yahoo.com.

FONDA, HENRY: BIRTH ANNIVERSARY. May 16, 1905. American stage, TV and screen actor (*The Grapes of Wrath, Mister Roberts*), Academy Award winner, born Henry Jaynes Fonda at Grand Island, NE. Began his acting career at the Omaha (NE) Playhouse. Fonda died at Los Angeles, CA, Aug 12, 1982.

GETTYSBURG OUTDOOR ANTIQUE SHOW. May 16. Gettysburg, PA. Features 150 dealers in antiques with exhibits and displays. Annually, a Saturday in May. Est attendance: 25,000. For info: Gettysburg CVB, PO Box 4117, Gettysburg, PA 17325. Phone: (717) 334-6274. Fax: (717) 334-1166. E-mail: info@gettysburg.travel. Web: www.gettysburg.travel.

GWINNETT, BUTTON: DEATH ANNIVERSARY. May 16, 1777. Signer of the Declaration of Independence, born at Down Hatherley, Gloucestershire, England, about 1735 (exact date unknown). Died following a duel at St. Catherine's Island, off of Savannah, GA.

JAMESTOWN DAY. May 16. Jamestown Settlement and Historic Jamestowne, Williamsburg, VA. Maritime demonstrations, military drills, archaeology and programs on English and Powhatan Indian contact and exploration and discovery mark the anniversary of the 1607 founding of Jamestown, America's first permanent English colony. Separate admission. For info: Jamestown-Yorktown Foundation, PO Box 1607, Williamsburg, VA 23187. Phone: (757) 253-4838 or (888) 593-4682. Fax: (757) 253-5299. Web: www.historyisfun.org.

LIBERACE: 90th BIRTH ANNIVERSARY. May 16, 1919. Wladziu Valentino Liberace, concert pianist who began with a piano, a candelabra, a brother named George and a huge engaging smile, threw in extravagant clothes and jewels and became a Las Vegas headliner and the winner of two Emmy Awards, six gold albums and two stars on the Hollywood Walk of Fame. Liberace was born at West Allis, WI; he died Feb 4, 1987, at Palm Springs, CA.

MARTIN, BILLY: BIRTH ANNIVERSARY. May 16, 1928. Baseball player and manager born at Berkeley, CA. Billy Martin's baseball career included managerial stints with five major league teams: the New York Yankees, Minnesota Twins, Detroit Tigers, Texas Rangers and Oakland Athletics. After a successful playing career, he compiled a record of 1,258 victories to 1,018 losses in his 16 seasons as a manager. His combative style both on and off the field kept him in the headlines, and he will long be remembered for his on-again, off-again relationship with Yankees owner George Steinbrenner, for whom he managed the Yankees five different times. Martin died in an auto accident near Fenton, NY, Dec 25, 1989.

MEMORY DAYS. May 16–23. Grayson, KY. Parade, art show and horse show. Est attendance: 10,000. For info: Robert L. Caummisar, Chamber of Commerce, 301 W Main St, Grayson, KY 41143. Phone: (606) 474-9522. Fax: (606) 474-4422. E-mail: barrister9@yahoo.com.

MOREL MUSHROOM FESTIVAL. May 16–17. Muscoda, WI. Wisconsin's "Morel Mushroom Capital" celebrates the end of the morel mushroom's two-week peak season. The 27th annual celebration includes the buying and selling of morels, food vendors, softball tournament, arts and crafts, antique tractor pull, flea market and many fun activities for the whole family. Saturday evening is the annual Fireman's steak feed followed by music and fireworks; Sunday brings a huge parade. Annually, the weekend after Mother's Day. Est attendance: 2,000. For info: Village of Muscoda, Morel Mushroom Fest, PO Box 206, Muscoda, WI 53573-0206. Phone: (608) 739-3182. Fax: (608) 739-3183. E-mail: cljohnson@wppisys.org. Web: www.muscoda.com.

MORTON, LEVI PARSONS: BIRTH ANNIVERSARY. May 16, 1824. 22nd vice president of the US (1889–93), born at Shoreham, VT. Died at Rhinebeck, NY, May 16, 1920.

✦ **NATIONAL SAFE BOATING WEEK.** May 16–22. Presidential Proclamation during May since 1995. From 1958 through 1977, issued for a week including July 4 (PL85–445 of June 4, 1958). From 1981 through 1994, issued for the first week in June (PL96–376 of Oct 3, 1980). From 1995, issued for a seven-day period ending on the Friday before Memorial Day. Not issued from 1978 through 1980.

NATIONAL SAFE BOATING WEEK. May 16–22. Brings boating safety to the public's attention, decreases the number of boating fatalities and makes the waterways safer for all boaters. Sponsors: National Safe Boating Council and US Coast Guard. For info: Natl Safe Boating Council. E-mail: nsbcdirect@safeboatingcouncil.org. Web: www.safeboatingcouncil.org.

NEW JERSEY STATE CHILI & SALSA COOK-OFF. May 16. Washington St, Toms River, NJ. NJ's only ICS-santioned state competition! The 20th annual chili and salsa cook-off features contestants from all over the tristate area competing for prize money, plus live entertainment, children's rides, games, vendors and crafters. Annually, the Saturday after Mother's Day. Est attendance: 6,000. For info: Downtown Toms River, 218 Main St, Toms River, NJ 08753. Phone: (732) 341-8738. Web: www.chili-nj.com.

O. HENRY MUSEUM PUN-OFF (WORLD CHAMPIONSHIP). May 16. The O. Henry Museum, Austin, TX. Pundits and punographers match wits for a wordy cause in two separate pun-filled competitions (Punniest of Show and High Lies & Low Puns). Sponsors: The City of Austin Parks and Recreation Dept and Punsters United Nearly Yearly (PUNY). Est attendance: 2,000. For info: Valerie Bennett, Curator, O. Henry Museum, 409 E Fifth St, Austin, TX 78701. Phone: (512) 472-1903. Fax: (512) 472-7102. Web: www.ci.austin.tx.us/parks/ohenry.htm or www.punpunpun.com

OUACHITA RIVER BIG BASS FISHING TOURNAMENT. May 16–17. Lazarre Point, West Monroe, LA. Join family and friends at this fun event for fishermen across the South! The Kids Korner, a special place for kids sponsored by the Monroe Jaycees, has expanded to both days this year by popular demand. For info: Ronald McDonald House Charities of Northeast LA, 200 S Third St, Monroe, LA 71202. Phone: (318) 387-7933. E-mail: rmh@bayou.com. Web: www.bayou.com/rmh.

PEABODY, ELIZABETH PALMER: BIRTH ANNIVERSARY. May 16, 1804. Born at Billerica, MA, Peabody was an innovative educator, author and publisher. She opened her first school at Lancaster, MA, when only 16. In 1839 Peabody opened a bookstore that quickly became the intellectuals' hangout. With her own printing press, Peabody became the first woman publisher in Boston, MA, and possibly the US. She published three of her brother-in-law Nathaniel Hawthorne's books. For two years she published and wrote for *The Dial*, the literary magazine and voice of the transcendental movement. Peabody's enduring accomplishment was the establishment of the first kindergarten in the US, in 1860 at Boston. She created a magazine, *Kindergarten Messenger*, in 1873. Died Jan 3, 1894, at Jamaica Plain, MA.

PEC THING. May 16–17 (also Sept 19–20). Pecatonica, IL. Semiannual antique show with more than 400 exhibitors. Est attendance: 20,000. For info: Amy Webster, Winnebago County Fair Assn, PO Box 810, Pecatonica, IL 61063-0670. Phone: (815) 239-1641 or (800) 238-3587. Fax: (815) 239-1653. E-mail: pecthing@winnebagocountyfair.com. Web: www.winnebagocountyfair.com.

PREAKNESS STAKES. May 16. Pimlico Race Course, Baltimore, MD. Preakness Stakes, the middle jewel in Thoroughbred racing's Triple Crown, was inaugurated in 1873. Annually, the third Saturday in May—two Saturdays after the Kentucky Derby—and followed, three Saturdays later, by the Belmont Stakes. Est attendance: 120,000. For info: Maryland Jockey Club, Pimlico Race Course, Baltimore, MD 21215. Phone: (410) 542-9400. Web: www.preakness.com.

RAF BOMBS RUHR DAMS: ANNIVERSARY. May 16–17, 1943. Over these two days Royal Air Force Lancasters attacked three dams in the German Ruhr Valley. They dropped 4.5-ton bombs designed specifically for this mission. The Mohne and the Eder (the largest dam in Europe at the time) were both damaged. These two dams provided drinking water for four million people and supplied 75 percent of the electrical power for industry. Widespread flooding and many deaths resulted.

REY, MARGARET: BIRTH ANNIVERSARY. May 16, 1906. Children's author, born at Hamburg, Germany. Together with her illustrator husband, H.A. Rey, she produced the Curious George series. Rey died at Cambridge, MA, Dec 21, 1996.

RIVERBOAT FESTIVAL. May 16. Columbia, LA. Poker Run on the River, antique car show, music, good food, craft booths and more. For info: Riverboat Festival, 601 Constitution Dr, West Monroe, LA 71292. Phone: (318) 649-0726. E-mail: ssnow@monroe-westmonroe.org. Web: www.monroe-westmonroe.org.

WISCONSIN DELLS AUTOMOTION. May 16–17. Noah's Ark Waterpark, Wisconsin Dells, WI. With signs of spring popping up all around, come take in the warmer weather at this showcase of more than 1,000 classic cars! Show features great live music, fire truck rides, fabulous food and a whole "trunkload" of other great family activities. Est attendance: 45,000. For info: Wisconsin Dells Visitor & Convention Bureau, Box 390, Wisconsin Dells, WI 53965. Phone: (800) 223-3557. E-mail: info@wisdells.com. Web: www.wisdells.com.

WRIGHT PLUS. May 16. Oak Park, IL. The Frank Lloyd Wright Preservation Trust's annual house walk features rare interior tours of privately owned homes designed by Frank Lloyd Wright and his contemporaries in the historic community of Oak Park, IL. Tickets are limited; they are available beginning in October. For info: Wright Plus, Frank Lloyd Wright Preservation Trust, 931 Chicago Ave, Oak Park, IL 60302. Phone: (877) 848-3559. Fax: (708) 848-1248. E-mail: info@gowright.org. Web: www.gowright.org.

XTERRA VAIL LAKE XDURO. May 16. Vail Lake, Temecula, CA. The XTERRA Trail Run Series boasts more than 50 events across the country with runs ranging from 5k to 25k. These extreme, off-road trail runs give runners the chance to prove their skills against a variety of terrain. From calf-burning hills to slippery, mud-covered paths athletes will face the ultimate test of endurance. This race features off-road 5k, 10k and half-marathon distance Xduro trail runs. For info: Ann Mickey, XTERRA/TEAM Unlimited, 720 Iwilei Rd #290, Honolulu, HI 96817. Phone: (877) 751-8880. E-mail: info@xterraplanet.com. Web: www.xterratrailrun.com.

BIRTHDAYS TODAY

David Boreanaz, 38, actor ("Angel," "Buffy the Vampire Slayer," "Bones"), born Philadelphia, PA, May 16, 1971.

Pierce Brosnan, 56, actor (*The Matador, The Thomas Crown Affair,* "Remington Steele," James Bond films), born County Meath, Ireland, May 16, 1953.

Jean-Sebastien Giguere, 32, hockey player, born Montreal, QC, Canada, May 16, 1977.

Tracey Gold, 40, actress ("Shirley," "Goodnight Beantown," "Growing Pains"), born New York, NY, May 16, 1969.

Janet Jackson, 43, singer ("What Have You Done for Me Lately"), born Gary, IN, May 16, 1966.

Olga Korbut, 54, Olympic gold medal gymnast, born Grodno, USSR, May 16, 1955.

John Scott (Jack) Morris, 54, former baseball player, born St. Paul, MN, May 16, 1955.

Gabriela Sabatini, 39, former tennis player, born Buenos Aires, Argentina, May 16, 1970.

Joan (Benoit) Samuelson, 52, Olympic gold medal runner, born Cape Elizabeth, ME, May 16, 1957.

Bill Smitrovich, 62, actor ("Crime Story," *Splash, Manhunter*), born Bridgeport, CT, May 16, 1947.

May 2009	S	M	T	W	T	F	S
						1	2
	3	4	5	6	7	8	9
	10	11	12	13	14	15	16
	17	18	19	20	21	22	23
	24	25	26	27	28	29	30
	31						

Tori Spelling, 36, actress ("Beverly Hills 90210"), born Beverly Hills, CA, May 16, 1973.

Jim Sturgess, 28, actor (*Across the Universe, 21*), born London, England, May 16, 1981.

Studs Terkel, 97, author, journalist (*Hard Times, Working*), born Louis Terkel, New York, NY, May 16, 1912.

Mare Winningham, 50, actress (*The Thornbirds, St. Elmo's Fire*), born Phoenix, AZ, May 16, 1959.

May 17 — Sunday

DAY 137 **228 REMAINING**

✦ **ARMED FORCES DAY.** May 17. Presidential Proclamation 5983, of May 17, 1989, covers the third Saturday in May in all succeeding years. Originally proclaimed as "Army Day" for Apr 6, beginning in 1936 (S.Con.Res. 30 of Apr 2, 1936). S.Con.Res. 5 of Mar 16, 1937, requested annual Apr 6 issuance, which was done through 1949. Always the third Saturday in May since 1950. Traditionally issued once by each administration.

BELL, JAMES "COOL PAPA": BIRTH ANNIVERSARY. May 17, 1903. Negro League baseball player James "Cool Papa" Bell was born at Starkville, MS. He played 25 seasons from 1922 to 1946 (one year before Jackie Robinson broke the "color barrier" in major league baseball) with a career average of .338. Regarded as the fastest man ever to play the game—he could round the bases in 13 seconds—he was inducted into the Baseball Hall of Fame in 1974. Bell died Mar 7, 1991, at St. Louis, MO.

***BROWN v BOARD OF EDUCATION* DECISION: 55th ANNIVERSARY.** May 17, 1954. The US Supreme Court ruled unanimously that segregation of public schools "solely on the basis of race" denied black children "equal educational opportunity" even though "physical facilities and other 'tangible' factors may have been equal. Separate educational facilities are inherently unequal." The case was argued before the Court by Thurgood Marshall, who would go on to become the first black appointed to the Supreme Court.

CAPE MAY MUSIC FESTIVAL. May 17–June 14. Cape May, NJ. 20th annual. Enjoy world-class orchestral and chamber music performances along with internationally acclaimed guest artists. Also features world traditions music: Latin jazz, zydeco, klezmer and more. Est attendance: 10,000. For info: Mid-Atlantic Center for the Arts, 1048 Washington St, Cape May, NJ 08204. Phone: (800) 275-4278 or (609) 884-5404. Fax: (609) 884-0574. E-mail: mac4arts@capemaymac.org. Web: www.capemaymac.org.

FIRST KENTUCKY DERBY: ANNIVERSARY. May 17, 1875. The first running of the Kentucky Derby took place at Churchill Downs, Louisville, KY. Jockey Oliver Lewis rode the horse Aristides to a winning time of 2:37.25.

FIRST US SAME-SEX MARRIAGES: 5th ANNIVERSARY. May 17, 2004. Massachusetts became the first US state to sanction gay marriage on this date. Hundreds of gay and lesbian couples received licenses and were married.

ING BAY TO BREAKERS RACE. May 17. San Francisco, CA. Largest footrace in the world attracts 70,000 runners each year, from world-class athletes to fun runners; postrace festival, live concert, food and beverages. Annually, the third Sunday in May. Established in

1912. Est attendance: 150,000. For info: Ing Bay to Breakers, 365 Vermont St, Ste F, San Francisco, CA 94103. Phone: (415) 359-2800. E-mail: info@ingbaytobreakers.com. Web: www.ingbaytobreakers.com.

INTERNATIONAL NEW FRIENDS, OLD FRIENDS WEEK. May 17–23. A week to celebrate and make time for old friends and new friends and remember how vital friends are for our emotional and physical health and well-being and even professional or career success. Friendshifts® is the word coined by author and sociologist Jan Yager to denote the way our ideas about friendships as well as who our friends are may change as we go through different stages of life. But at every stage, friendship is crucial, for children, teenagers, young adults, singles, couples, new mothers, the middle-aged and especially those who are older, retired or widowed. For info: Jan Yager, PhD, PO Box 8038, Stamford, CT 06905-8038. Fax: (203) 968-0193. E-mail: jyager@aol.com. Web: www.JanYager.com/friendship.

JENNER, EDWARD: BIRTH ANNIVERSARY. May 17, 1749. English physician, born at Berkeley, England. He was the first to establish a scientific basis for vaccination with his work on smallpox. Jenner died at Berkeley, Jan 26, 1823.

MOON PHASE: LAST QUARTER. May 17. Moon enters Last Quarter phase at 3:26 AM, EDT.

NATIONAL DOG BITE PREVENTION WEEK. May 17–23. To promote safety with dogs—especially among children, who are the number one victims of dog bites. Humane Society Youth has developed a dog bite prevention program for kids. Annually, third full week in May. For info: Heidi O'Brien, Humane Society Youth, 67 Norwich Essex Turnpike, East Haddam, CT 06423. Phone: (860) 434-8666, ext 17. Fax: (860) 434-9579. E-mail: hobrien@humanesociety.org. Web: www.nodogbites.org or www.humanesociety.org/youth.

NATIONAL STATIONERY SHOW. May 17–20. Jacob K. Javits Center, New York, NY. 62nd annual. For info: George Little Management, 10 Bank St, White Plains, NY 10606. Phone: (914) 421-3200. Fax: (914) 948-6088. Web: www.glmshows.com or www.nationalstationeryshow.com.

NEW YORK STOCK EXCHANGE ESTABLISHED: ANNIVERSARY. May 17, 1792. Some two dozen merchants and brokers agreed to establish what is now known as the New York Stock Exchange. In fair weather they operated under a buttonwood tree on Wall St, at New York, NY. In bad weather they moved to the shelter of a coffeehouse to conduct their business.

NORWAY: CONSTITUTION DAY OR INDEPENDENCE DAY. May 17. National holiday. Constitution signed and Norway separated from Denmark in 1814. Parades and children's festivities.

ROGATION SUNDAY. May 17. The fifth Sunday after Easter is the beginning of Rogationtide (Rogation Sunday and the following three days before Ascension Day). Rogation Day rituals date from the fifth century.

RURAL LIFE SUNDAY OR SOIL STEWARDSHIP SUNDAY. May 17. With an increase in ecological and environmental concerns, Rural Life Sunday emphasizes the concept that Earth belongs to God, who has granted humanity the use of it, along with the responsibility of caring for it wisely. At the suggestion of the International Association of Agricultural Missions, Rural Life Sunday was first observed in 1929. The day is observed annually by churches of many Christian denominations and includes pulpit exchanges by rural and urban pastors. Under the auspices of the National Association of Soil and Water Conservation Districts, the week beginning with Rural Life Sunday is now widely observed as Soil Stewardship Week, with the Sunday itself alternatively termed Soil Stewardship Sunday. Traditionally, Rural Life Sunday is Rogation Sunday, the Sunday preceding Ascension Day.

TOMS RIVER CANOE AND KAYAK RACE. May 17. Old Toms River Bus Terminal, Toms River, NJ. 8½-mile downriver race, 11 categories and five open-water kayak categories. Prizes are awarded. Preregistration to enter the contest, or pay a late-registraton fee if you register the morning of the race. Or just come and observe! Est attendance: 500. For info: Mickey Coen, Coord, Wells Mills County Park, 905 Wells Mills Rd, Waretown, NJ 08758. Phone: (609) 971-3085. Fax: (609) 971-9540. Web: www.oceancountyparks.org.

UNITED NATIONS: WORLD INFORMATION SOCIETY DAY. May 17. On March 27, 2006, the UN General Assembly proclaimed this annual day to help to raise awareness of the possibilities that the use of the Internet and other information and communication technology can bring to societies and economies, as well as of ways to bridge the digital divide (Resolution 60/252). For info: United Nations, Dept of Public Info, New York, NY 10017. Web: www.un.org.

UNITED NATIONS: WORLD TELECOMMUNICATION DAY. May 17. A day to draw attention to the necessity and importance of further development of telecommunications in the global community. For info: United Nations, Dept of Public Info, New York, NY 10017. Web: www.un.org.

USS *STARK* ATTACKED: ANNIVERSARY. May 17, 1987. The US Navy's guided missile frigate *Stark*, sailing off the Iranian coast in the Persian Gulf, was struck and set afire by two Exocet sea-skimming missiles fired from an Iraqi warplane at 2:10 PM, EDT. Also struck was a Cypriot flag tanker. At least 28 American naval personnel were killed. Only hours earlier a Soviet oil tanker in the Gulf had struck a mine.

✦ **WORLD TRADE WEEK.** May 17–23. Presidential Proclamation has been issued each year since 1948 for the third week of May with three exceptions: 1949, 1955 and 1966.

BIRTHDAYS TODAY

Craig Ferguson, 47, comedian, actor ("The Drew Carey Show"), television personality ("The Late Late Show with Craig Ferguson"), born Glasgow, Scotland, May 17, 1962.

Mia Hamm, 37, Hall of Fame soccer player, born Selma, AL, May 17, 1972.

Dennis Hopper, 73, actor ("24," *Blue Velvet, Easy Rider, Giant, Rebel Without a Cause*), born Dodge City, KS, May 17, 1936.

Christian Lacroix, 59, French couturier, born Arles, France, May 17, 1950.

Ray Charles (Sugar Ray) Leonard, 53, former boxer, born Washington, DC, May 17, 1956.

Daniel Ricardo (Danny) Manning, 43, former basketball player, born Hattiesburg, MS, May 17, 1966.

Ben Nelson, 68, US Senator (D, Nebraska), born McCook, NE, May 17, 1941.

Tony Parker, 27, basketball player, born Bruges, Belgium, May 17, 1982.

Bill Paxton, 54, actor (*Aliens, One False Move, Twister*), born Fort Worth, TX, May 17, 1955.

Sendhil Ramamurthy, 35, actor ("Heroes"), born Chicago, IL, May 17, 1974.

Trent Reznor, 44, singer (Nine Inch Nails), born Mercer, PA, May 17, 1965.

Bob Saget, 53, actor ("Full House"), host ("America's Funniest Home Videos"), born Philadelphia, PA, May 17, 1956.

Debra Winger, 54, actress (*Terms of Endearment, Shadowlands*), born Columbus, OH, May 17, 1955.

May 18 — Monday

DAY 138 **227 REMAINING**

ALLIES CAPTURE MONTE CASSINO: 65th ANNIVERSARY. May 18, 1944. Between Oct 12, 1943, and Jan 17, 1944, there were five Allied attempts to take the German position at the Benedictine abbey at Monte Cassino. Although the abbey had been reduced to rubble, it served as a bunker for the Germans. In the spring of 1944 Marshal Alphonse Pierre Juin devised an operation that crossed the mountainous regions behind the fortresslike structure, using Moroccan troops of the French Expeditionary Force. Specially trained for mountain operations, they climbed 4,850 feet to locate a pass. On May 15, 1944, they attacked the Germans from behind. On May 18 Polish troops attached to this force took Monte Cassino.

BIRTHDAY OF MOTHER'S WHISTLER. May 18. Birthday of the world's most melodious human whistler, who not only duplicates the songs of rare, exotic and extinct birds, but in many cases, does so better than the birds themselves. For info: Mother's Whistler, Warfield and Twin Silo Lns, Huntingdon Valley, PA 19006. Phone: (215) 947-0500. Fax: (215) 947-7210. E-mail: motherswhistler1@yahoo.com.

CANADA: VICTORIA DAY. May 18. Commemorates the birth of Queen Victoria May 24, 1819. Observed annually on the Monday preceding May 25.

CAPRA, FRANK: BIRTH ANNIVERSARY. May 18, 1897. The Academy Award–winning director whose movies were suffused with affectionate portrayals of the common man and the strengths and foibles of American democracy. Capra was born at Palermo, Sicily. He bluffed his way into silent movies in 1922 and, despite total ignorance of moviemaking, directed and produced a profitable one-reeler. He was the first to win three directorial Oscars—for *It Happened One Night* (1934), *Mr Deeds Goes to Town* (1936) and *You Can't Take It with You* (1938). The Motion Picture Academy voted the first and third of these as Best Picture. Capra said his favorite of the films he made was *It's a Wonderful Life* (1946). He died at La Quinta, CA, Sept 3, 1991.

FONTEYN, MARGOT: 90th BIRTH ANNIVERSARY. May 18, 1919. Born Margaret Hookman at Reigate, Surrey, England, Dame Margot Fonteyn thrilled ballet audiences for 45 years. She emerged from the Sadler's Wells company during the 1930s and 1940s as a solo artist and followed those successes by partnering with Soviet exile Rudolph Nureyev in the 1960s. She died Feb 21, 1991, at Panama City, Panama.

HAITI: FLAG AND UNIVERSITY DAY. May 18. Public holiday.

INTERNATIONAL MUSEUM DAY. May 18. To pay tribute to museums of the world. "Museums are an important means of cultural exchange, enrichment of cultures and development of mutual understanding and peace among people." Observed annually on May 18 since 1977. Sponsor: International Council of Museums (ICOM), Paris, France. For info: ICOM-US, 1575 Eye St NW, Ste 400, Washington, DC 20005. Phone: (202) 289-9115. Fax: (202) 289-6578. E-mail: aam-icom@aam-us.org.

May 2009

S	M	T	W	T	F	S
					1	2
3	4	5	6	7	8	9
10	11	12	13	14	15	16
17	18	19	20	21	22	23
24	25	26	27	28	29	30
31						

MOUNT SAINT HELENS ERUPTION: ANNIVERSARY. May 18, 1980. A major eruption of Mount Saint Helens volcano, in southwestern Washington, blew steam and ash more than 11 miles into the sky. First major eruption of Mount Saint Helens since 1857, though on Mar 26, 1980, there had been a warning eruption of smaller magnitude.

NATIONAL BACKYARD GAMES WEEK. May 18–25. Observance to celebrate the unofficial start of summer by fostering social interaction and family togetherness through backyard games. Get outside and be both physically and mentally stimulated, playing classic games of the past while discovering and creating new ways to be active and interact with friends and neighbors. For info: Beth Muehlenkamp, Patch Products, 1400 E Inman Pkwy, Beloit, WI 53511. Phone: (608) 362-6896. Fax: (608) 362-8178. E-mail: patch@patchproducts.com. Web: www.patchproducts.com.

NATIONAL EFFECTIVENESS WEEK. May 18–22. Neatness and tidiness do not make you effective. Likewise, messiness does not make you ineffective. What matters is that you get the important things done with a minimum of stress. This week, promote tolerance of different styles of getting things done. Annually, the third full week (Monday through Friday) in May. For info: Jan Jasper. Phone: (212) 465-7472. E-mail: JanJasper52@hotmail.com. Web: www.janjasper.com.

POPE JOHN PAUL II: BIRTH ANNIVERSARY. May 18, 1920. Karol Wojtyla, 264th pope of the Roman Catholic Church, born at Wadowice, Poland. Elected pope Oct 16, 1978, he was the first non-Italian to be elected pope in 456 years and the first Polish pope. His theology was conservative and traditional, and he was known for his worldwide travels to bring the message of the Catholic Church to people around the world. He survived an assassination attempt in 1981 and died at Vatican City on Apr 2, 2005.

SPACE MILESTONE: *APOLLO 10* (US): 40th ANNIVERSARY. May 18, 1969. Launched with astronauts Colonel Thomas Stafford and Commander Eugene Cernan, who brought lunar module (LM) "Snoopy" within nine miles of the moon's surface on May 22. *Apollo 10* circled the moon 31 times and returned to Earth May 26.

SWITZERLAND: PACING THE BOUNDS. May 18. Liestal. Citizens set off at 8 AM and march along boundaries to the beating of drums and firing of pistols and muskets. Occasion for fetes. Annually, the Monday before Ascension Day.

TURKMENISTAN: REVIVAL AND UNITY DAY. May 18. National holiday. Commemorates the 1992 adoption of the constitution.

URUGUAY: BATTLE OF LAS PIEDRAS DAY. May 18. National holiday. Commemorates battle fought for independence from Spain in 1811.

VISIT YOUR RELATIVES DAY. May 18. A day to renew family ties and joys by visiting often-thought-of-seldom-seen relatives. Annually, May 18. For info: A.C. Vierow, Box 71, Clio, MI 48420-0071.

WILLSON, MEREDITH: BIRTH ANNIVERSARY. May 18, 1902. American musician, playwright and composer best known for *The Music Man.* Born at Mason City, IA, Willson received Oscar nominations for *The Little Foxes* and *The Great Dictator*. Many of his songs, including "It's Beginning to Look a Lot like Christmas," "Seventy-Six Trombones" and "Till There Was You" have become standards. Willson died at Santa Monica, CA, June 15, 1984.

WOMAN INDUCTED INTO NATIONAL INVENTORS HALL OF FAME: ANNIVERSARY. May 18, 1991. Gertrude Belle Elion, corecipient of the 1988 Nobel Prize in Medicine, became the first woman inducted as a member of the National Inventors Hall of Fame. Elion's research led to the development of leukemia-fighting drugs and immunosuppressant Imuran, which is used in kidney transplants.

WORK AT HOME MOMS WEEK. May 18–24. The challenge of motherhood and working at home can be a balancing act. To all women who do it every day, you are applauded this week and always. For info: Robin Gorman Newman, 44 Somerset Dr N, Great Neck, NY 11020. Phone: (516) 773-0911. E-mail: rgnewman@optonline.net. Web: www.motherhoodlater.com.

BIRTHDAYS TODAY

Chow Yun-Fat, 54, actor (*Crouching Tiger, Hidden Dragon; Anna and the King; Bulletproof Monk*), born Lamma Island, Hong Kong, May 18, 1955.

Tina Fey, 39, writer, comedienne ("30 Rock," *Baby Mama, Mean Girls,* "Saturday Night Live"), born Upper Darby, PA, May 18, 1970.

Brad Friedel, 38, soccer player, born Lakewood, OH, May 18, 1971.

Dwayne Hickman, 75, actor ("The Many Loves of Dobie Gillis"), born Los Angeles, CA, May 18, 1934.

Reginald Martinez (Reggie) Jackson, 63, Hall of Fame baseball player, born Wyncote, PA, May 18, 1946.

Jari Kurri, 49, Hall of Fame hockey player, born Helsinki, Finland, May 18, 1960.

Yannick Noah, 49, former tennis player, born Sedan, France, May 18, 1960.

Pernell Roberts, 81, actor (*Ride Lonesome*, "Bonanza," "Trapper John, MD"), born Waycross, GA, May 18, 1928.

Brooks Robinson, 72, Hall of Fame baseball player, born Little Rock, AR, May 18, 1937.

James Stephens, 58, actor ("The Paper Chase"), born Mount Kisco, NY, May 18, 1951.

George Strait, 57, country singer, musician, born Poteet, TX, May 18, 1952.

Vince Young, 26, football player, born Houston, TX, May 18, 1983.

May 19 — Tuesday

DAY 139 226 REMAINING

BOLEYN, ANNE: EXECUTION ANNIVERSARY. May 19, 1536. Born around 1501, Anne Boleyn captured the eye of England's King Henry VIII in 1527. Her demand that he make her a wife, not a mistress, caused the married Henry's break with the Catholic Church (which wouldn't allow a divorce), which in turn led to decades of religious turmoil in England. Henry had his marriage to Catherine of Aragon annulled and wed Boleyn in 1533. Boleyn's inability to bear a male heir (although her daughter with Henry was to be Queen Elizabeth I) and court intrigue caused her arrest on charges of adultery. She was executed by sword at the Tower of London. The morning of her execution she said, "I heard say the executioner was very good, and I have a little neck."

BOYS' CLUBS FOUNDED: ANNIVERSARY. May 19, 1906. The Federated Boys' Clubs, which later became the Boys' and Girls' Clubs of America, was founded.

DARK DAY IN NEW ENGLAND: ANNIVERSARY. May 19, 1780. At midday near-total darkness unaccountably descended on much of New England. Candles were lit, fowls went to roost and many fearful persons believed that doomsday had arrived. At New Haven, CT, Colonel Abraham Davenport opposed adjournment of the town council in these words: "I am against adjournment. The day of judgment is either approaching or it is not. If it is not, there is no cause for an adjournment. If it is, I choose to be found doing my duty. I wish therefore that candles may be brought." No scientifically verifiable cause for this widespread phenomenon was ever discovered.

ENGLAND: RHS CHELSEA FLOWER SHOW. May 19–23. Royal Hospital, Chelsea, London. The world's most famous flower show with specially designed gardens and spectacular floral displays. Est attendance: 157,000. For info: Royal Horticultural Society, 80 Vincent Sq, London, England SW1P 2PE. Phone: (44) (20) 7834-4333. E-mail: info@rhs.org.uk. Web: www.rhs.org.uk/flowershows.

***GONE WITH THE WIND* PUBLISHED: ANNIVERSARY.** May 19, 1936. Margaret Mitchell's epic novel of the Civil War South was published on this date. It would be awarded the Pulitzer Prize and National Book Award as best novel of 1936. It has been a best-seller since publication, and 40 countries have published translations. See also: "*Gone with the Wind* Film Premiere: Anniversary" (Dec 15).

HANSBERRY, LORRAINE: BIRTH ANNIVERSARY. May 19, 1930. American playwright Lorraine Hansberry was born at Chicago, IL. For her now classic play *A Raisin in the Sun*, she became the youngest American and first black to win the Best Play Award from the New York Critics' Circle. The play, titled after the Langston Hughes poem, deals with issues such as racism, cultural pride and self-respect and was the first stage production written by a black woman to appear on Broadway (1959). *To Be Young, Gifted, and Black*, a book of excerpts from her journals, letters, speeches and plays, was published posthumously in 1969. Lorraine Hansberry died of cancer Jan 12, 1965, at New York, NY.

HO CHI MINH: BIRTH ANNIVERSARY. May 19, 1890. Vietnamese leader and first president of the Democratic Republic of Vietnam, born at Kim Lien, a central Vietnamese village (Nghe An Province), probably May 19, 1890. His original name was Nguyen That Thanh. Died at Hanoi, Vietnam, Sept 3, 1969. The anniversary of his birth is a national holiday in Vietnam, as is the anniversary of his death.

MALCOLM X: BIRTH ANNIVERSARY. May 19, 1925. Black nationalist and civil rights activist Malcolm X was born Malcolm Little at Omaha, NE. While serving a prison term he resolved to transform his life. On his release in 1952 he changed his name to Malcolm X and worked for the Nation of Islam until he was suspended by Black Muslim leader Elijah Muhammed Dec 4, 1963. Malcolm X later made the pilgrimage to Mecca and became an orthodox Muslim. He was assassinated as he spoke to a meeting at the Audubon Ballroom at New York, NY, Feb 21, 1965.

MAY RAY DAY. May 19. To celebrate the beginning of the warm outside days the sun gives us. Also, a day for people named Ray. Annually, May 19. For info: Richard Ankli, Allen Creek Hydro, Inc, 100 S 4th Ave #608, Ann Arbor, MI 48104.

NAIA MEN'S GOLF NATIONAL CHAMPIONSHIPS. May 19–22. Moline, IL. 58th annual. Est attendance: 500. For info: Natl Assn of Intercollegiate Athletics, 1200 Grand Blvd, Kansas City, MO 64106. E-mail: balmeida@naia.org. Web: www.naia.org.

NATIONAL GEOGRAPHIC BEE: NATIONAL FINALS. May 19–20. National Geographic Society Headquarters, Washington, DC. The first-place winner from each state-level competition (that took place on Apr 3) advances to the national level. Alex Trebek of "Jeopardy!" fame moderates the finals, which are televised on the National Geographic Channel and public television stations. Contestants compete for scholarships and prizes totaling more than $50,000. Est attendance: 400. For info: Natl Geographic Bee, Natl Geographic Society, 1145 17th St NW, Washington, DC 20036. Phone: (202) 828-6659. Web: www.nationalgeographic.com/geographicbee.

NCAA DIVISION I WOMEN'S GOLF CHAMPIONSHIPS. May 19–22. Caves Valley Golf Club, Owings Mills, MD. For info: NCAA, 700 W Washington St, PO Box 6222, Indianapolis, IN 46206-6222. Phone: (317) 917-6222. Web: www.NCAAsports.com.

SCOBEE, FRANCIS R.: 70th BIRTH ANNIVERSARY. May 19, 1939. Commander of the ill-fated space shuttle *Challenger*, 46-year-old pilot Francis R. Scobee had been in the astronaut program since 1978 and had been pilot of the *Challenger* in 1984. Born at Cle Elum, WA, Scobee perished with all others on board when the *Challenger* exploded on Jan 28, 1986. See also: "*Challenger* Space Shuttle Explosion: Anniversary" (Jan 28).

SIMPLON TUNNEL OPENING: ANNIVERSARY. May 19, 1906. Tunnel from Brig, Switzerland, to Iselle, Italy, officially opened on this day. Construction started in 1898.

SPACE MILESTONE: *MARS 2* AND *MARS 3* (USSR). May 19 and 28, 1971. Entered Martian orbits on Nov 27 and Dec 2, respectively. *Mars 3* sent down a TV-equipped capsule that soft-landed and transmitted pictures for 20 seconds.

TURKEY: YOUTH AND SPORTS DAY. May 19. Public holiday commemorating the beginning of a national movement for independence in 1919, led by Mustafa Kemal Ataturk.

BIRTHDAYS TODAY

Nora Ephron, 68, writer, screenwriter, director (*You've Got Mail, Sleepless in Seattle*), born New York, NY, May 19, 1941.

James Fox, 70, actor (*A Passage to India, The Russia House, Patriot Games*), born London, England, May 19, 1939.

Kevin Garnett, 33, basketball player, born Mauldin, SC, May 19, 1976.

David Hartman, 72, actor, broadcaster (Emmy for "Good Morning America"; *Hello Dolly*), born Pawtucket, RI, May 19, 1937.

Grace Jones, 57, model, singer, actress (*A View to a Kill*), born Spanishtown, Jamaica, May 19, 1952.

William (Bill) Laimbeer, Jr, 52, WNBA coach, former basketball player, born Boston, MA, May 19, 1957.

James Lehrer, 75, journalist, anchor ("The Newshour with Jim Lehrer"), born Wichita, KS, May 19, 1934.

Eric Lloyd, 23, actor ("Jesse," *Dunston Checks In*), born Glendale, CA, May 19, 1986.

Pete Townshend, 64, musician (The Who), born London, England, May 19, 1945.

May 20 — Wednesday

DAY 140 — 225 REMAINING

AMELIA EARHART ATLANTIC CROSSING: ANNIVERSARY. May 20, 1932. Leaving Harbor Grace, Newfoundland, Canada, at 7 PM, Amelia Earhart landed near Londonderry, Ireland. The 2,026-mile flight took 13 hours and 30 minutes. She was the first woman to fly solo across the Atlantic.

BALZAC, HONORE DE: BIRTH ANNIVERSARY. May 20, 1799. French author of a huge cycle of stories and novels known as *The Human Comedy*, born at Tours, France. "It is easier," Balzac wrote in 1829, "to be a lover than a husband for the simple reason that it is more difficult to be witty every day than to say pretty things from time to time." Died at Paris, Aug 18, 1850.

BIG TEN BASEBALL TOURNAMENT. May 20–23. Site of conference champion. Est attendance: 1,500. For info: Big Ten Conference, 1500 W Higgins Rd, Park Ridge, IL 60068-6300. Phone: (847) 696-1010. Fax: (847) 696-1110. Web: www.bigten.org.

May 2009

S	M	T	W	T	F	S
					1	2
3	4	5	6	7	8	9
10	11	12	13	14	15	16
17	18	19	20	21	22	23
24	25	26	27	28	29	30
31						

CAMEROON: NATIONAL HOLIDAY. May 20. Republic of Cameroon. Commemorates adoption of constitution in 1972.

COUNCIL OF NICAEA I: ANNIVERSARY. May 20–Aug 25, 325. First ecumenical council of Christian Church, called by Constantine I, first Christian emperor of Roman Empire. Nearly 300 bishops are said to have attended this first of 21 ecumenical councils (latest, Vatican II, began Sept 11, 1962), which was held at Nicaea, in Asia Minor (today's Turkey). The council condemned Arianism (which denied the divinity of Christ), formulated the Nicene Creed and fixed the day of Easter—always on a Sunday.

EAST TIMOR: INDEPENDENCE: ANNIVERSARY. May 20, 2002. East Timor became fully independent from Indonesia on this day. Indonesia had controlled the tiny nation since 1975. It had previously been a colony of Portugal for 450 years.

ELIZA DOOLITTLE DAY. May 20. To honor Miss Doolittle (heroine of George Bernard Shaw's *Pygmalion*) for demonstrating the importance and the advantage of speaking one's native language properly. For info: H.M. Chase, Doolittle Day Committee, 2460 Devonshire Rd, Ann Arbor, MI 48104-2706.

HERZL, THEODOR: BIRTH ANNIVERSARY. May 20, 1860. Founder of the modern Zionist movement, born at Budapest, Hungary. Herzl died at Edlach, Austria, July 3, 1904.

HOMESTEAD ACT: ANNIVERSARY. May 20, 1862. President Abraham Lincoln signed the Homestead Act opening millions of acres of government-owned land in the West to settlers, or "homesteaders," who had to reside on the land and cultivate it for five years.

LINDBERGH FLIGHT: ANNIVERSARY. May 20–21, 1927. Anniversary of the first solo trans-Atlantic flight. Captain Charles Augustus Lindbergh, 25-year-old aviator, departed from rainy, muddy Roosevelt Field, Long Island, NY, alone at 7:52 AM, May 20, 1927, in a Ryan monoplane named *Spirit of St. Louis*. He landed at Le Bourget airfield, Paris, France, at 10:24 PM, Paris time (5:24 PM, NY time), May 21, winning a $25,000 prize offered by Raymond Orteig for the first nonstop flight between New York City and Paris (3,600 miles). The "flying fool," as he had been dubbed by some doubters, became "Lucky Lindy," an instant world hero. See also: "Lindbergh, Charles Augustus: Birth Anniversary" (Feb 4).

MADISON, DOLLY (DOROTHEA) DANDRIDGE PAYNE TODD: BIRTH ANNIVERSARY. May 20, 1768. Wife of James Madison, 4th president of the US, born at Guilford County, NC. Died at Washington, DC, July 12, 1849.

MECKLENBURG DAY. May 20. North Carolina. Commemorates claimed signing of a declaration of independence from England by citizens of Mecklenburg County on this day, 1775.

MOTOR VOTER BILL SIGNED: ANNIVERSARY. May 20, 1993. The latest effort to remove barriers to voter registration resulted in the passage of the Motor Voter Bill, which was signed into law by President William Clinton. This bill requires the states to allow voter registration by mail or when a citizen applies for or renews a driver's license.

NORMAN ROCKWELL'S FIRST *SATURDAY EVENING POST* COVER: ANNIVERSARY. May 20, 1916. Norman Rockwell's first cover for the *Post*, depicting a boy having to care for his infant sibling—pushing the baby carriage while his buddies set off to play ball—appeared on the May 20 edition. His last *Post* cover appeared in 1963.

ROUSSEAU, HENRI JULIEN FELIX: BIRTH ANNIVERSARY. May 20, 1844. Henri Rousseau, nicknamed "Le Douanier" because of his onetime post as customs tollkeeper, was a celebrated French painter born at Laval, Mayenne, France. Painted deceptively "primitive" pictures of exotic foliage, flowers and fruit of the jungle, with stilted human and animal figures. Died at Hospital Necker, Paris, Sept 4, 1910.

SPACE MILESTONE: *PIONEER VENUS I* (US). May 20, 1978. Launched this date, became first Venus orbiter the following Dec 4.

STEWART, JIMMY: BIRTH ANNIVERSARY. May 20, 1908. Film actor born James Stewart at Indiana, PA. Best known for his everyman roles and work with directors Frank Capra and Alfred Hitchcock. Starred in *Mr Smith Goes to Washington*, *It's a Wonderful Life*, *Rear Window* and many classic Westerns. Stewart won a Best Actor Oscar for *The Philadelphia Story*. He died July 2, 1997, at Beverly Hills, CA.

TURN BEAUTY INSIDE OUT DAY. May 20. Is beauty only skin-deep? Not if you turn it inside out. This day serves as a reminder that inner beauty is more important than outer beauty. On this day, people challenge the usual definition of beauty as portrayed in popular media and advertising by recognizing the wonderful actions and attitudes of people who are beautiful on the inside. Annually, the third Wednesday in May. For info: Mind on the Media, 710 St Olaf Ave, Ste 200, Northfield, MN 55057. Phone: (952) 210-1625. E-mail: tbio@mindonthemedia.org. Web: www.tbio.org.

WEIGHTS AND MEASURES DAY. May 20. Anniversary of international treaty, signed May 20, 1875, providing for the establishment of an International Bureau of Weights and Measures. The bureau was founded on international territory at Sèvres, France.

BIRTHDAYS TODAY

Iker Casillas, 28, soccer player, born Madrid, Spain, May 20, 1981.

Cher, 63, singer ("Believe"), actress (*Moonstruck*), born Cherilyn Sarkisian at El Centro, CA, May 20, 1946.

Joe Cocker, 65, singer ("You Are So Beautiful"), born Sheffield, England, May 20, 1944.

Michael Crapo, 58, US Senator (R, Idaho), born Idaho Falls, ID, May 20, 1951.

Tony Goldwyn, 49, actor (*Ghost, Kiss the Girls*), born Los Angeles, CA, May 20, 1960.

Stan Mikita, 69, Hall of Fame hockey player, born Sokolce, Czechoslovakia, May 20, 1940.

David Paterson, 55, Governor of New York (D), born Brooklyn, NY, May 20, 1954.

Bronson Pinchot, 50, actor ("Perfect Strangers," "Step by Step"), born New York, NY, May 20, 1959.

Ronald Prescott Reagan, 51, TV host, commentator, son of former President Ronald Reagan, born Los Angeles, CA, May 20, 1958.

Anthony Zerbe, 73, actor ("Harry-O," *Cool Hand Luke, Papillon*), born Long Beach, CA, May 20, 1936.

May 21 — Thursday

DAY 141 **224 REMAINING**

AMERICAN RED CROSS FOUNDED: ANNIVERSARY. May 21, 1881. Commemorates the founding of the American Red Cross by Clara Barton, its first president. The Red Cross had been founded in Switzerland in 1864 by representatives from 16 European nations. It is a voluntary, not-for-profit organization governed and directed by volunteers and provides disaster relief at home and abroad. Its 1.1 million volunteers are involved in community services such as collecting and distributing donated blood and blood products, teaching health and safety classes and acting as a medium for emergency communication between Americans and their armed forces.

ASCENSION DAY. May 21. Commemorates Christ's ascension into heaven. Observed since AD 68. Ascension Day is the 40th day after the Resurrection, counting Easter as the first day.

BELGIUM: PROCESSION OF THE HOLY BLOOD. May 21. Religious historical procession. Recalls adventurous crusaders, including Count Thierry of Alsace, who carried back relics of the Holy Blood. Always on Ascension Day.

BURR, RAYMOND WILLIAM STACY: BIRTH ANNIVERSARY. May 21, 1917. Stage, film and TV actor best known for the role of Perry Mason in the long-running series of the same name. His films include *Rear Window* and *Godzilla*, and he was also the star of TV's "Ironside." Born at New Westminster, BC, Canada, Burr died near Healdsburg, CA, Sept 12, 1993.

CHILE: BATTLE OF IQUIQUE DAY. May 21. Commemorates a naval battle in 1879, part of the War of the Pacific with Peru and Bolivia.

CURTISS, GLENN HAMMOND: BIRTH ANNIVERSARY. May 21, 1878. American inventor and aviator, born at Hammondsport, NY. The aviation pioneer died at Buffalo, NY, July 23, 1930.

DÜRER, ALBRECHT: BIRTH ANNIVERSARY. May 21, 1471. German painter and engraver, one of the greatest artists of the Renaissance, was born at Nuremberg, Germany, and died there Apr 6, 1528.

FRY, ELIZABETH GURNEY: BIRTH ANNIVERSARY. May 21, 1780. English reformer who dedicated her life to improving the condition of poor people and especially of women in prison, born at Earlham, Norfolk, England. Died at Ramsgate, Oct 12, 1845.

GEMINI, THE TWINS. May 21–June 20. In the astronomical/astrological zodiac, which divides the sun's apparent orbit into 12 segments, the period May 21–June 20 is traditionally identified as the sun sign of Gemini, the Twins. The ruling planet is Mercury.

HAMMER, ARMAND: BIRTH ANNIVERSARY. May 21, 1898. American industrialist Armand Hammer was born at New York, NY. He built the Occidental Petroleum Company into a $20 billion conglomerate after he invested $100,000 in it in 1956 and it was awarded two oil concessions in Libya. He was a trained physician who was sympathetic to the Soviet people and gave away millions of dollars through philanthropy to cancer research. Hammer died Dec 10, 1990, at Los Angeles, CA.

HERRINFESTA ITALIANA. May 21–25. Herrin Civic Center, Herrin, IL. Authentic Italian food, name Italian and American entertainers, bocce tournament, Midwest Pasta Sauce Contest, road races, grape stomp and more. Est attendance: 55,000. For info: Herrinfesta Italiana, PO Box 2005, Herrin, IL 62948. Phone: (800) ITF-ESTA. Web: www.herrinfesta.com.

HUMMEL, SISTER MARIA INNOCENTIA: 100th BIRTH ANNIVERSARY. May 21, 1909. Born at Massing, Bavaria, Sister Maria Innocentia Hummel attended Munich's Academy of Fine Arts. She entered Siessen Convent, run by the Sisters of the Third Order of St. Francis, and began teaching art to kindergarten children. In 1934 Franz Goebel obtained an exclusive license to translate her drawings into three-dimensional figurines. The first M.I. Hummel figurines were displayed at the Leipzig Trade Fair in 1935; they made their first appearance in the American market in May 1935. She died Nov 6, 1946, at Siessen, Germany. Many M.I. Hummel Clubs across the country commemorate her birth date with special events and fund-raisers for local charities.

"I NEED A PATCH FOR THAT" DAY. May 21. They have patches for nicotine and they have patches for heart patients. How about a patch for runny noses or bad hair? (©2006 by WH.) For info: Thomas & Ruth Roy, Wellcat Holidays, 2418 Long Ln, Lebanon, PA 17046. Phone: (717) 279-0184. E-mail: info@wellcat.com. Web: www.wellcat.com.

KODIAK CRAB FESTIVAL. May 21–25. Kodiak, AK. 51st annual. A celebration of spring on the Emerald Isle. Delectable food, exciting midway rides, carnival booths and entertaining events, such as parades, running and bicycle races, survival suit race, bed races, a blessing of the fleet ceremony and memorial services. Annually, Memorial Day weekend. Est attendance: 15,000. For info: Kodiak Crab Festival, 100 E Marine Way, Ste 300, Kodiak, AK 99615. Phone: (907) 486-5557. Fax: (907) 486-7605. Web: www.kodiak.org/crabfest.html.

MONACO: GRAND PRIX DE MONACO. May 21–24. Monte Carlo. One of the premier sporting events in the world. Thrilling Formula

1 race: 77 laps through the streets of Monte Carlo, held since Apr 14, 1929. For info: Automobile Club de Monaco, 23 blvd Albert 1er, BP 464, Monaco. Web: www.acm.mc.

MUDBUG MADNESS. May 21–24. Riverfront, Shreveport, LA. The state's delectable crustacean, the crawfish, and Cajun heritage are celebrated during this four-day festival. Est attendance: 150,000. For info: DSU, 401 Edwards, Ste 205, Shreveport, LA 71101. Phone: (318) 222-7403. E-mail: mbacon@downtownshreveport.com. Web: www.mudbugmadness.com.

NAIA MEN'S AND WOMEN'S OUTDOOR TRACK AND FIELD NATIONAL CHAMPIONSHIPS. May 21–23. St. Louis, MO. 58th annual men's and 29th annual women's competition. Est attendance: 2,500. For info: Natl Assn of Intercollegiate Athletics, 1200 Grand Blvd, Kansas City, MO 64106. E-mail: rstein@naia.org. Web: www.naia.org.

NATIONAL WAITSTAFF DAY. May 21. A day for restaurant managers and patrons to recognize and to express their appreciation for the many fine and dedicated waitresses and waiters. For info: Gaylord F. Ward, Promotion Dir, 1505 E Bristol Rd, Burton, MI 48529-2214.

PGA SENIORS' CHAMPIONSHIP. May 21–24. Canterbury Golf Club, Beechwood, OH. 70th competition for the oldest major championship in senior golf. Conducted by the Professional Golfers' Association of America. For info: PGA of America, 100 Ave of the Champions, Palm Beach Gardens, FL 33418. Phone: (561) 624-8400. Fax: (561) 624-8448. Web: www.pga.com.

POPE, ALEXANDER: BIRTH ANNIVERSARY. May 21, 1688. (Old Style date.) English poet born at London, England. "A man," Pope wrote in 1727, "should never be ashamed to own he has been in the wrong, which is but saying, in other words, that he is wiser today than he was yesterday." Died at Twickenham, May 30, 1744 (OS).

RAJIV GANDHI ASSASSINATED: ANNIVERSARY. May 21, 1991. Former Indian prime minister Rajiv Gandhi was assassinated in the midst of a reelection campaign. He was killed when a bomb, hidden in a bouquet of flowers given by admirers, exploded as he approached a dais to begin a campaign rally. He had served as prime minister between 1984 and 1989 after succeeding his mother, Indira Gandhi, who was assassinated in 1984.

SAKHAROV, ANDREY DMITRIYEVICH: BIRTH ANNIVERSARY. May 21, 1921. Soviet physicist, human rights activist and environmentalist Andrey Sakharov was born at Moscow, Russia. A collaborator in producing the first Soviet atomic bomb and later the hydrogen bomb, Sakharov denounced shortcomings of his country's government and was exiled to Gorky, Russia, 1980–86. He was a formulator of the reform and restructuring concept known as *perestroika* and of *glasnost* (freedom). He was named to the Soviet Congress of People's Deputies eight months before his death at Moscow on Dec 14, 1989. As a physicist, he was the developer of destructive weapons; as a humanitarian, he was courageous as a dissident from militarism and an advocate of human rights.

UNITED NATIONS: WORLD DAY FOR CULTURAL DIVERSITY FOR DIALOGUE AND DEVELOPMENT. May 21. Recognizing the need to enhance the potential of culture as a means of achieving prosperity, sustainable development and global peaceful coexistence, the General Assembly, on Dec 20, 2002, proclaimed May 21 to serve as this day. The Assembly acknowledged the close link between protecting cultural diversity and the larger framework of the dialogue among civilizations. For info: United Nations, Dept of Public Info, New York, NY 10017. Web: www.un.org.

May 2009

S	M	T	W	T	F	S
					1	2
3	4	5	6	7	8	9
10	11	12	13	14	15	16
17	18	19	20	21	22	23
24	25	26	27	28	29	30
31						

WALES: HAY-ON-WYE FESTIVAL OF LITERATURE. May 21–31. Hay-on-Wye, Powys. Largest annual festival of literature takes place in the beautiful market town of Hay-on-Wye in the Black Mountains of the Welsh Marches. Est attendance: 80,000. For info: The Hay Festival, Hay-on-Wye, Wales, United Kingdom HR3 5AD. Phone: (44) (870) 990-1299. Fax: (44) (149) 782-1066. E-mail: admin@hayfestival.com. Web: www.hayfestival.com.

BIRTHDAYS TODAY

Bobby Cox, 68, baseball manager, former executive and player, born Tulsa, OK, May 21, 1941.

Robert Creeley, 83, author, poet (*Have a Heart, Windows*), born Arlington, MA, May 21, 1926.

Janet Dailey, 65, romance novelist (*Tangled Vines*), born Storm Lake, IA, May 21, 1944.

Lisa Edelstein, 42, actress ("House," "Felicity"), born Boston, MA, May 21, 1967.

Al Franken, 58, comedian, writer (*Rush Limbaugh Is a Big Fat Idiot and Other Observations*), actor ("Saturday Night Live"), born New York, NY, May 21, 1951.

Josh Hamilton, 28, baseball player, born Raleigh, NC, May 21, 1981.

Heinz Holliger, 70, oboist, composer, conductor, born Langenthal, Switzerland, May 21, 1939.

Ian McEwan, 61, author (*On Chesil Beach, Atonement, Amsterdam*), born Aldershot, Hampstead, England, May 21, 1948.

William "Spike" O'Dell, 56, Chicago radio personality, born Moline, IL, May 21, 1953.

Judge Reinhold, 52, actor (*Beverly Hills Cop*), born Wilmington, DE, May 21, 1957.

Leo Sayer, 61, singer ("You Make Me Feel Like Dancing"), songwriter, born Shoreham, England, May 21, 1948.

Mr T, 57, actor (*Rocky III*, "The A-Team"), born Lawrence Tero or Tureaud at Chicago, IL, May 21, 1952.

May 22 — Friday

DAY 142 — **223 REMAINING**

BEST, GEORGE: BIRTH ANNIVERSARY. May 22, 1946. Mercurial soccer star of the 1960s and '70s. Beginning his professional career at 17, Best played mainly for Manchester United, for whom he scored 178 goals in 466 appearances. His playboy lifestyle off field was as famous as his quicksilver brilliance on it. Born at Belfast, Northern Ireland, Best died at London, England, on Nov 22, 2005. More than 100,000 mourners lined the streets of Belfast for his funeral procession, and at British soccer matches a minute of silence (or applause) was observed in his honor.

BROOKINGS-HARBOR AZALEA FESTIVAL. May 22–25. Brookings, OR. 70th festival. Parade, street fair, art shows, seafood, 10k run, bonsai exhibit, regional quilt show, crafts fair, Coast Guard demonstration, live music. Annually, Memorial Day weekend. Est attendance: 12,000. For info: Brookings-Harbor Chamber of Commerce, PO Box 940, Brookings, OR 97415. Phone: (800) 535-9469. Fax: (541) 469-4094. E-mail: chamber@brookingsor.com. Web: www.brookingsor.com.

CANADA: IMMIGRANTS' DAY. May 22. A day to celebrate and recognize the contributions made by immigrants to Canada and to discuss the Canadian immigration policy and experience. For info: Sergio R. Karas, BA, LLB, Barrister and Solicitor, Karas & Assoc, 65 Queen St W, Ste 1505, Toronto, ON, Canada M5H 2M5. Phone: (416) 506-1800. Fax: (416) 506-1305. E-mail: karas@karas.ca. Web: www.karas.ca.

CASSATT, MARY: BIRTH ANNIVERSARY. May 22, 1844. Leading American artist of the Impressionist school, Mary Cassatt was born May 22, 1844 (some sources give 1845), at Allegheny City, PA (now part of Pittsburgh). She settled in Paris, France, in 1874, where she was influenced by Degas and the Impressionists. She was later instrumental in their works' becoming well known in the US. The majority of her paintings and pastels were based on the theme of mother and child. After 1900 her eyesight began to fail, and by 1914 she was no longer able to paint. Cassatt died at Chateau de Beaufresne near Paris, June 14, 1926.

COIN & STAMP EXPO. May 22–24. Pasadena Convention Center, Pasadena, CA. Annual expo. Est attendance: 5,000. For info: Israel Bick, Exec Dir, Intl Stamp & Coin Collectors Society, Box 854, Van Nuys, CA 91408. Phone: (818) 997-6496. Fax: (818) 988-4337. E-mail: iibick@sbcglobal.net. Web: www.bick.net.

CRATER LAKE NATIONAL PARK ESTABLISHED: ANNIVERSARY. May 22, 1902. One of the world's deepest lakes, Crater Lake was first discovered in 1853. In 1885 William Gladstone Steele saw the Oregon lake and made it his personal goal to establish the lake and surrounding areas as a national park. His goal was attained 17 years later.

DOWN EAST SPRING BIRDING FESTIVAL. May 22–25. Cobscook Bay area (Eastport, Whiting, Lubec), ME. See more than one-third of Maine's bird species during spring migration and the breeding season—including Atlantic puffins up close and (almost) touchable! Annually, the Friday through Monday of Memorial Day weekend. For info: Down East Spring Birding Festival, c/o Cobscook Community Learning Center, 10 Commissary Point Rd, Trescott Twp, ME 04652. Phone: (207) 733-2233. E-mail: birdfest@thecclc.org. Web: www.downeastbirdfest.org.

DOYLE, SIR ARTHUR CONAN: 150th BIRTH ANNIVERSARY. May 22, 1859. British physician Sir Arthur Conan Doyle is best remembered as a mystery author and the creator of Sherlock Holmes and Dr. Watson. Doyle was born at Edinburgh, Scotland. He was deeply interested in and lectured on the subject of spiritualism. Died at Crowborough, Sussex, England, July 7, 1930.

FARMINGTON INVITATIONAL BALLOON FESTIVAL. May 22–24. Farmington, NM. Hot-air balloons launch off the banks of Farmington Lake. Famous Splash and Dash and Hare and Hound races included in this weekend event. Est attendance: 2,000. For info: Farmington CVB, 3041 E Main St, Farmington, NM 87402. Phone: (800) 448-1240 or (505) 326-7602. Fax: (505) 327-0577. E-mail: fmncvb@earthlink.net. Web: www.farmingtonnm.org.

FLORIDA FOLK FESTIVAL. May 22–24. Stephen Foster Folk Culture Center State Park, White Springs, FL. To celebrate Florida's folk heritage with music, song, dance and stories. Est attendance: 30,000. For info: Stephen Foster Folk Culture Center State Park, PO Drawer G, White Springs, FL 32096. Phone: (877) 6FL-FOLK.

ISRAEL: JERUSALEM DAY (YOM YERUSHALAYIM). May 22. Hebrew calendar date: Iyar 28, 5769. Commemorates the liberation of the old city, June 7, 1967. Began at sundown May 21.

JOHNNY CARSON'S FINAL SHOW: ANNIVERSARY. May 22, 1992. After almost 30 years as host of the "Tonight Show," Johnny Carson hosted his last show. Carson became host of the late-night talk show, which began as a local New York program hosted by Steve Allen, on Oct 1, 1962. Over the years Carson occasionally made headlines with such extravaganzas as the marriage of Tiny Tim and Miss Vicki. Carson received Emmys for his work four years in a row, 1976–79. Ed McMahon, his sidekick of 30 years, and Doc Severinsen, longtime bandleader, left the show with Carson. Jay Leno, the show's exclusive guest host, became the new regular host.

"MISTER ROGERS' NEIGHBORHOOD" TV PREMIERE: ANNIVERSARY. May 22, 1967. Presbyterian minister Fred Rogers hosted this long-running PBS children's program. Puppets and human characters interacted in the neighborhood of make-believe. Rogers played the voices of many of the puppets and educated young viewers on a variety of important subjects. The last episodes of the program were made in 2001. Almost 1,000 episodes were produced over the show's history. Rogers died in 2003. See also "Rogers, Fred: Birth Anniversary" (Mar 20).

NAIA BASEBALL WORLD SERIES. May 22–29. Lewiston, ID. 53rd annual competition. Est attendance: 35,000. For info: Natl Assn of Intercollegiate Athletics, 1200 Grand Blvd, Kansas City, MO 64106. E-mail: smcclure@naia.org. Web: www.naia.org.

✦ **NATIONAL MARITIME DAY.** May 22. Presidential Proclamation always issued for May 22 since 1933. (Pub Res No. 7 of May 20, 1933.)

NATIONAL MARITIME DAY. May 22. Anniversary of departure for first steamship crossing of Atlantic from Savannah, GA, to Liverpool, England, by steamship *Savannah* in 1819.

NATIONAL WIG OUT DAY. May 22. Wig Out Day is an annual celebration of wigs. Like Halloween, but with better weather, Wig Out Day lets people across the country experience the beauty of a bob or the might of a mullet. Annually, the Friday before Memorial Day. For info: June Hathaway, Natl Wig Out Day, 2314 Ellis St, Bellingham, WA 98225. Phone: (360) 739-3545. E-mail: info@thewigout.com.

NCAA DIVISION I WOMEN'S LACROSSE CHAMPIONSHIP. May 22 and 24. Johnny Unitas Stadium, Towson, MD. Est attendance: 8,000. For info: NCAA, 700 W Washington St, Indianapolis, IN 46206-6222. Phone: (317) 917-6222. Web: www.NCAAsports.com.

NIXON FIRST AMERICAN PRESIDENT TO VISIT MOSCOW: ANNIVERSARY. May 22, 1972. President Richard Nixon became the first American president to visit Moscow. Four days later on May 26, Nixon and Soviet leader Leonid Brezhnev signed a treaty on antiballistic missile systems and an interim agreement on limitation of strategic missiles.

NORTHWEST FOLKLIFE FESTIVAL. May 22–25. Seattle Center, Seattle, WA. Ethnic and traditional arts event celebrating world cultures in the Northwest region. Includes music, dance, food, crafts, visual arts exhibits, children's programs, demonstrations, films and more. More than 6,000 performers. Annually, Friday–Monday of Memorial Day weekend. Est attendance: 250,000. For info: Northwest Folklife, 305 Harrison St, Seattle, WA 98109-4623. Phone: (206) 684-7300. Fax: (206) 684-7190. E-mail: folklife@nwfolklife.org. Web: www.nwfolklife.org.

OLIVIER, LAURENCE: BIRTH ANNIVERSARY. May 22, 1907. Actor, director and theater manager, born at Dorking, England. Thought by many to be the most influential actor of the 20th century. Olivier's theatrical and film career shaped the art forms in which he participated. Honored with nine Academy Award nominations, three Oscars and five Emmy Awards, his repertoire included most of the prime Shakespearean roles and roles in such films as *Rebecca, Pride and Prejudice, Marathon Man* and *Wuthering Heights*. Olivier was an innovative theater manager with London's Old Vic company and the National Theatre of Great Britain. The National Theatre's largest auditorium and Britain's equivalent of Broadway's Tony Awards carry his name. He was knighted in 1947 and made a peer of the throne in 1970. Olivier died at Ashurst, England, July 11, 1989.

RA, SUN: 95th BIRTH ANNIVERSARY. May 22, 1914. Born Herman (Sonny) Blount, Sun Ra was a pioneering and innovative jazz musician whose avant-garde performances mixed elements of theater with his surreal composition and performance style. Ra was born at Birmingham, AL, and died there May 30, 1993.

RIVERFEST. May 22–24. Riverfront Park, Little Rock, and North Shore Riverwalk, North Little Rock, AR. 32nd annual outdoor festival of the visual and performing arts with 100 acts on five stages, food vendors, visual artists, kid stuff. Est attendance: 247,000. For info: Riverfest, 500 President Clinton Ave, Ste 217, Little Rock, AR 72201. Phone: (501) 255-FEST. Fax: (501) 255-3379. E-mail: director@riverfestarkansas.com. Web: www.riverfestarkansas.com.

SACRAMENTO JAZZ JUBILEE. May 22–25. Sacramento, CA. More than 100 bands from the US, Canada and foreign countries perform American traditional jazz music in approximately 30 venues around Sacramento at the world's largest traditional jazz festival. Est attendance: 80,000. For info: Gene Berthelsen, Exec Dir, Sacramento Traditional Jazz Society, 2787 Del Monte St, Sacramento, CA 95691. Phone: (916) 372-5277. Fax: (916) 372-3429. E-mail: info@sacjazz.com. Web: www.sacjazz.com.

SHAKER MUSEUM OPENING DAY. May 22. Sabbathday Lake Shaker Village, New Gloucester, ME. The 79th season of the Shaker Museum opens with tours, exhibits and special events. Open through Columbus Day (closed on Sundays). For info: Leonard Brooks, Sabbathday Lake Shaker Village, Rte 26, New Gloucester, ME 04260. Phone: (207) 926-4597. E-mail: usshakers@aol.com. Web: www.shaker.lib.me.us.

SPOLETO FESTIVAL USA. May 22–June 7. Charleston, SC. Comprehensive arts festival with a mix of more than 130 performances of opera, dance, theater, chamber and symphonic music, jazz and visual arts set in one of America's most beautiful and historic cities. For info: Spoleto Festival USA, PO Box 157, Charleston, SC 29402. Phone: (843) 579-3100. Web: www.spoletousa.org.

SRI LANKA: NATIONAL HEROES DAY. May 22. Commemorates the struggle of the leaders of the National Independence Movement to liberate the country from colonial rule in 1971. Public holiday.

STRONGEST EARTHQUAKE OF THE 20th CENTURY: ANNIVERSARY. May 22, 1960. An earthquake of a magnitude of 9.5 struck southern Chile, killing 2,000 people and leaving 2 million homeless. The earthquake also caused damage in Hawaii, Japan and the Philippines. While 20th-century earthquakes in Mexico City, Japan and Turkey resulted in far more deaths, this earthquake in Chile was of the highest magnitude.

SUMNER ATTACKED IN THE SENATE: ANNIVERSARY. May 22, 1856. Two days after he decried the "Crime Against Kansas," US senator Charles Sumner of Massachusetts was attacked with a walking cane by South Carolina congressman Preston Brooks in the Senate Chamber (the Senate was not in session). Abolitionist Sumner needed three years to recuperate.

SUMTER IRIS FESTIVAL. May 22–24. Swan Lake, Sumter, SC. In the largest Japanese iris gardens in the world. South Carolina's oldest continuously running festival. Annually, the weekend before Memorial Day. For info: Iris Festival Commission, PO Box 1802, Sumter, SC 29151. Phone: (803) 436-2640 or (800) 688-4748. Fax: (803) 436-2652. Web: www.irisfestival.org.

TRUMAN DOCTRINE: ANNIVERSARY. May 22, 1947. Congress approved the Truman Doctrine on this day. In order to contain Communism after WWII, it provided for US aid to Greece and Turkey. A corollary of this doctrine was the Marshall Plan, which began sending aid to war-torn European countries in 1948.

UNITED NATIONS: INTERNATIONAL DAY FOR BIOLOGICAL DIVERSITY. May 22. On Dec 19, 1994, the General Assembly proclaimed this observance for Dec 29, the date of entry into force of the Convention on Biological Diversity (Resolution 49/119). In 2000 the date was changed to May 22. This day is an opportunity to strengthen people's commitment and actions for the conservation of the world's biological diversity. For info: United Nations, Dept of Public Info, New York, NY 10017. Web: www.un.org.

VAN CLIBURN INTERNATIONAL PIANO COMPETITION. May 22–June 7. Bass Performance Hall, Fort Worth, TX. 13th annual. Thirty finalists from worldwide qualifying rounds perform; 12 will compete in the semifinal round; and six will vie for top honors in the final round. All six finalists will receive a prize package offering three years of managed concert tours. Cliburn winners perform in hundreds of venues across the US and abroad. Open to the public and televised. Held every four years, this year's competition application deadline was Oct 15, 2008. For info: Sevan Melikyan, Director of PR, Van Cliburn Foundation, Inc, 2525 Ridgmar Blvd, Ste 307, Fort Worth, TX 76116. Phone: (817) 738-6536. Fax: (817) 738-6534. Web: www.cliburn.org.

WAGNER, RICHARD: BIRTH ANNIVERSARY. May 22, 1813. German composer born at Leipzig who made revolutionary changes in the structure of opera. Best known for his Ring Cycle (*Der Ring des Nibelungen*). Died at Italy, Feb 13, 1883.

WORLD CHAMPIONSHIP OLD-TIME PIANO PLAYING CONTEST. May 22–24. Hotel Père Marquette, Peoria, IL. Competition and festival of ragtime, honky-tonk and old-time music. Includes Old-Time Orchestry, workshops and dealers rooms. Annually, Memorial Day weekend. Sponsor: Old-Time Music Preservation Association (OMPA) Inc. Est attendance: 1,000. For info: Judy Leschewski, PO Box 883, Decatur, IL 62525. Phone: (217) 428-2403. E-mail: pianoctest@aol.com. Web: oldtimepiano.com.

YEMEN: NATIONAL DAY. May 22. Public holiday. Commemorates the reunification of Yemen in 1990.

BIRTHDAYS TODAY

Charles Aznavour, 85, singer, songwriter, actor (*Shoot the Piano Player, Candy, The Tin Drum*), born Paris, France, May 22, 1924.

Richard Benjamin, 71, actor (*Goodbye Columbus, Diary of a Mad Housewife*, "He & She"), born New York, NY, May 22, 1938.

Naomi Campbell, 39, model, born London, England, May 22, 1970.

Frank Converse, 71, actor ("Movin' On," *Hurry Sundown*), born St. Louis, MO, May 22, 1938.

Judith Crist, 87, critic, born New York, NY, May 22, 1922.

Thomas Edward (Tommy) John, 66, former baseball player, born Terre Haute, IN, May 22, 1943.

A.J. Langer, 35, actress ("My So-Called Life," "Brooklyn South"), born Columbus, OH, May 22, 1974.

Lisa Murkowski, 52, US Senator (R, Alaska), born Ketchikan, AK, May 22, 1957.

Peter Nero, 75, conductor, composer, pianist, born Brooklyn, NY, May 22, 1934.

Michael Sarrazin, 69, actor (*The Flim Flam Man, The Reincarnation of Peter Proud*), born Quebec City, QC, Canada, May 22, 1940.

Garry Wills, 75, author (*John Wayne's America, Lincoln at Gettysburg*), born Atlanta, GA, May 22, 1934.

May 2009

S	M	T	W	T	F	S
					1	2
3	4	5	6	7	8	9
10	11	12	13	14	15	16
17	18	19	20	21	22	23
24	25	26	27	28	29	30
31						

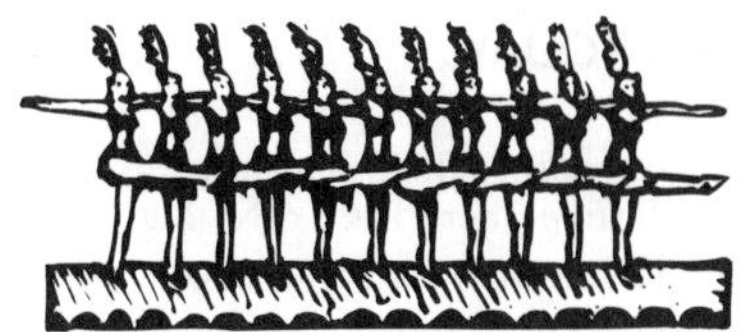

May 23 — Saturday

DAY 143 **222 REMAINING**

ALMA HIGHLAND FESTIVAL AND GAMES. May 23–24. Alma College, Alma, MI. 42nd annual. Old-world pageantry honoring Scottish traditions—Highland dancing, piping, drumming, athletic competitions, clan tents and grand parade. Annually, Memorial Day weekend. Est attendance: 15,000. For info: Alma Highland Festival, 110 W Superior St, PO Box 516, Alma, MI 48801. Phone: (989) 463-8979. Fax: (989) 463-6588. E-mail: highland@almahighlandfestival.com. Web: www.almahighlandfestival.com.

BONNIE AND CLYDE: 75th DEATH ANNIVERSARY. May 23, 1934. The two-year crime spree of Bonnie Parker and Clyde Barrow, bank robbers accused of at least 12 murders, came to an end when a law enforcement posse led by Frank Hamer opened fire on the couple in an ambush at Gibsland, LA. The couple had operated in Texas, Oklahoma, Missouri, Louisiana and other states, and had sent ballads to local newspapers chronicling their exploits, making them two of the most notorious—and romanticized—of many Depression-era gangsters. Some 20,000 people lined up to see the body of Clyde Barrow put on display in a mortuary in downtown Dallas, TX.

CLOONEY, ROSEMARY: BIRTH ANNIVERSARY. May 23, 1928. The beloved pop and jazz singer was born at Maysville, KY. She became popular in the 1950s for singing the novelty song "Come-on-a-My House" and pop standards. She also starred in the holiday film *White Christmas* (1954). She died June 29, 2002, at Beverly Hills, CA.

DECLARATION OF THE BAB. May 23. Baha'i commemoration of May 23, 1844, when the Bab, the prophet-herald of the Baha'i faith, announced in Shiraz, Persia, that he was the herald of a new messenger of God. One of the nine days of the year when Baha'is suspend work. For info: Baha'is of the US, Office of Communications, 1233 Central St, Evanston, IL 60201. Phone: (847) 733-3559. Fax: (847) 733-3578. E-mail: ooc@usbnc.org. Web: www.bahai.us.

FAIRBANKS, DOUGLAS ELTON: BIRTH ANNIVERSARY. May 23, 1883. Douglas Fairbanks was born at Denver, CO. He made his professional debut as an actor at Richmond, VA, Sept 10, 1900, in *The Duke's Jester.* His theatrical career turned to Hollywood, and he became a movie idol, appearing in such films as *The Mark of Zorro, The Three Musketeers, Robin Hood, The Thief of Bagdad, The Black Pirate* and *The Gaucho.* He married "America's Sweetheart," Mary Pickford, in 1918, and in 1919 they joined with D.W. Griffith and Charlie Chaplin to form the production company United Artists. He died at Santa Monica, CA, Dec 12, 1939.

FIRST BLACK RECEIVES CONGRESSIONAL MEDAL OF HONOR: ANNIVERSARY. May 23, 1900. Sergeant William H. Carney, of the 54th Massachusetts Colored Infantry, was the first black to win the Congressional Medal of Honor. He was cited for his efforts, although wounded twice, during the Battle of Fort Wagner, SC, June 18, 1863.

FULLER, MARGARET: BIRTH ANNIVERSARY. May 23, 1810. Journalist and author Sarah Margaret Fuller, born at Cambridgeport, MA, began reading Virgil at age six. Her conversational powers won her the admiration of students at Harvard University, and she was befriended by Ralph Waldo Emerson. She shared editorial duties with Emerson on the transcendentalist quarterly *The Dial* and was hired by Horace Greeley as literary critic for the *New York Tribune.* Her book *Women in the Nineteenth Century*, the first feminist statement by an American writer, brought her international acclaim. In 1846, as a foreign correspondent for the *Tribune*, she became caught up in the Italian revolutionary movement and secretly married a young Roman nobleman, the Marquis Giovanni Angelo Ossoli. En route to the US, Fuller and her husband and child died July 19, 1850, when their ship was wrecked off Fire Island near New York, NY.

GRUBSTAKE DAYS. May 23. Yucca Valley, CA. 59th annual. Includes parade, gold-panning demonstrations, community carnival. Annually, the Saturday of Memorial Day Weekend. Est attendance: 15,000. For info: Yucca Valley Chamber of Commerce, 56711 29 Palms Hwy, Yucca Valley, CA 92284. Phone: (760) 365-6323. Fax: (760) 365-0763. E-mail: chamber@yuccavalley.org. Web: www.yuccavalley.org.

HEAD-OF-THE-MON-RIVER HORSESHOE TOURNAMENT. May 23–25. Fairmont, WV. Open to horseshoe pitchers with a current State/National Horseshoe Pitchers Association membership card. Est attendance: 300. For info: Tri-County Horseshoe Club Dir, Beverly Tiano, 1133 Sunset Dr, Fairmont, WV 26554. Phone: (304) 366-3819. E-mail: btiano1133@aol.com.

INTERNATIONAL JAZZ DAY. May 23. Jazz lovers worldwide attend local festivals (or can start their own) to celebrate jazz on the Saturday of the Memorial Day weekend. Originated by the New Jersey Jazz Society and sanctioned by the American Federation of Jazz Societies, the United Nations Jazz Society and the Sacramento Traditional Jazz Society. For info: Web: www.geocities.com/BourbonStreet/4270.

JULIA PIERPONT DAY. May 23. Julia Pierpont is recognized by many historians for having originated "Decoration Day" in May 1866, which is now the US federal holiday Memorial Day. This day pays tribute to Pierpont by readying veterans' graves for Memorial Day. It was proclaimed in the state of West Virginia in 2005. For info: JoAnn Lough, 200 Locust Ave, Fairmont, WV 26554. Phone: (304) 363-9341. E-mail: joann.lough@verizon.net.

LOBSTER DAYS. May 23–25. Mystic Seaport, Mystic, CT. A New England lobster bake on the banks of the Mystic River over the Memorial Day weekend, put on by the Rotary Club of Mystic. Est attendance: 10,000. For info: Mystic Seaport, 75 Greenmanville Ave, PO Box 6000, Mystic, CT 06355-0990. Phone: (860) 572-5315 or (888) 973-2767. Web: www.mysticseaport.org.

LONGWOOD GARDENS FESTIVAL OF FOUNTAINS. May 23–Sept 6. Kennett Square, PA. A magical mixture of rainbow-hued fountains, alfresco concerts, fireworks and leisurely evenings in the conservatory. Est attendance: 275,000. For info: Longwood Gardens, PO Box 501, Kennett Square, PA 19348-0501. Phone: (610) 388-1000. Web: www.longwoodgardens.org.

MANSFIELD, ARABELLA: BIRTH ANNIVERSARY. May 23, 1846. Arabella Mansfield, born Belle Aurelia Babb near Burlington, IA, was the first woman admitted to the legal profession in the US. In 1869 while teaching at Iowa Wesleyan College, Mansfield was certified as an attorney and admitted to the Iowa bar. According to the examiners, "she gave the very best rebuke possible to the imputation that ladies cannot qualify for the practice of law." Mansfield never did practice law, however, continuing her career as an educator. She joined the faculty of DePauw University, at Greencastle, IN, where she became dean of the schools of art and music. One of the first woman college professors and administrators in the US, Mansfield was also instrumental in the founding of the Iowa Woman Suffrage Society in 1870. She died Aug 2, 1911, at Aurora, IL.

MESMER, FRANZ ANTON: 275th BIRTH ANNIVERSARY. May 23, 1734. German physician after whom mesmerism was named. Magnetism and hypnotism were used by him in treating disease. Born at Iznang, Swabia, Germany. Died Mar 5, 1815, at Meersburg, Swabia.

MOROCCO: NATIONAL DAY. May 23. National holiday. Commemorates referendum on the majority of the king in 1980.

NEW YORK PUBLIC LIBRARY: ANNIVERSARY. May 23, 1895. New York's then governor Samuel J. Tilden was the driving force that resulted in the combining of the private Astor and Lenox libraries with a $2 million endowment and 15,000 volumes from the Tilden Trust to become the New York Public Library. The main branch of the library opened to the public on this day in 1911.

SLOVO, JOE: BIRTH ANNIVERSARY. May 23, 1926. South African Communist Party leader Joe Slovo was a longtime friend and ally of Nelson Mandela. The first white to become a member of the African National Congress Executive Committee, he lived in exile from 1963 to 1990, serving as head of the military arm of the ANC during that period. Born at Obelai, Lithuania, he died Jan 6, 1995, at Johannesburg, South Africa.

SOUTH CAROLINA CONSTITUTION RATIFICATION: ANNIVERSARY. May 23, 1788. By a vote of 149 to 73, South Carolina became the eighth state to ratify the Constitution.

SUPREME COURT UPHOLDS BAN ON ABORTION COUNSELING: ANNIVERSARY. May 23, 1991. In the case *Rust v Sullivan*, the Supreme Court, in a 5–4 ruling, upheld federal regulations that barred federally funded family planning clinics from providing any information about abortion.

SWEDEN: LINNAEUS DAY. May 23, 1707. Stenbrohult. Commemorates birth of Carolus Linnaeus (Carl von Linne), Swedish naturalist, born May 23, 1707 (OS), and died at Uppsala, Sweden, Jan 10, 1778.

TASTE OF CINCINNATI. May 23–25. Cincinnati, OH. 31st annual. Cincinnati is famous for its fine food, from elegant five-star dining to five-way chili. This popular eating extravaganza presents a taste of the most delicious culinary delights available. Annually, Memorial Day weekend. Est attendance: 500,000. For info: Cincinnati USA Regional Chamber, 441 Vine St, Ste 300, Cincinnati, OH 45202. Phone: (513) 579-3100. Fax: (513) 579-3101. E-mail: info@cincinnatichamber.com. Web: www.tasteofcincinnati.com.

TIVOLI FEST. May 23–24. Elk Horn, IA. Annual Danish celebration with parade, Danish folk dancers, Danish foods, unique gift shops, historical tours and much more. Annually, Memorial Day weekend. Sponsor: Better Elk Horn Club. Est attendance: 5,000. For info: Lisa Riggs, Danish Windmill, PO Box 245, Elk Horn, IA 51531. Phone: (712) 764-7472 or (800) 451-7960. Fax: (712) 764-7475. E-mail: info@danishwindmill.com. Web: www.danishwindmill.com.

UTICA OLD-FASHIONED ICE CREAM FESTIVAL. May 23–25. Utica, OH. Saluting "America's favorite dessert," ice cream, with a weekend of fun and entertainment: parade, queen contest, arts and crafts, antique gas engines, sheepherding with border collies and plenty of delicious ice cream. Est attendance: 30,000. For info: Utica Ice Cream Festival, State Rte 13, Utica, OH 43080. Phone: (740) 892-3921. Web: www.velveticecream.com.

WAR OF JENKIN'S EAR: LIVING HISTORY. May 23. Wormsloe State Historic Site, Savannah, GA. A colonial living-history event focusing on the conflict between England and Spain. Features musket demonstrations, military drill, tomahawk throwing and more. Annually, the Saturday of Memorial Day weekend. Hours 11 AM to 4 PM. Est attendance: 500. For info: Wormsloe State Historic Site, 7601 Skidaway Rd, Savannah, GA 31406. Phone: (912) 353-3023. E-mail: wormsloe@bellsouth.net. Web: www.wormsloe.org.

WORLD TURTLE DAY. May 23. An observance sponsored by American Tortoise Rescue to help people celebrate and protect turtles and tortoises, as well as their habitats around the world. For info: Susan Tellem, American Tortoise Rescue, 23852 Pacific Coast Hwy, Malibu, CA 90265. E-mail: info@tortoise.com. Web: www.tortoise.com.

May 2009	S	M	T	W	T	F	S
						1	2
	3	4	5	6	7	8	9
	10	11	12	13	14	15	16
	17	18	19	20	21	22	23
	24	25	26	27	28	29	30
	31						

BIRTHDAYS TODAY

Mitch Albom, 51, journalist, author (*Tuesdays with Morrie, The Five People You Meet in Heaven*), born Passaic, NJ, May 23, 1958.

Barbara Barrie, 78, actress ("Suddenly Susan," *One Potato, Two Potato; Breaking Away*), born Chicago, IL, May 23, 1931.

Drew Carey, 48, actor ("The Drew Carey Show"), host ("The Price Is Right") born Cleveland, OH, May 23, 1961 (some sources say 1958).

Joan Collins, 76, actress ("Dynasty"), born London, England, May 23, 1933.

"Marvelous" Marvin Hagler, 55, former boxer, born Newark, NJ, May 23, 1954.

Jewel, 35, singer, born Jewel Kilcher at Payson, UT, May 23, 1974.

Charles Kimbrough, 73, actor ("Murphy Brown"), born St. Paul, MN, May 23, 1936.

May 24 — Sunday

DAY 144 — **221 REMAINING**

ANDERSONVILLE MEMORIAL DAY CEREMONIES. May 24. Andersonville, GA. Ceremonies pay tribute to our country's men and women who paid for our freedom with their lives. Annually, the Sunday before Memorial Day. For info: Park Ranger, Andersonville National Historic Site, 496 Cemetery Rd, Andersonville, GA 31711. Phone: (229) 924-0343.

ANTIQUES AT MEMORIAL DAY. May 24. Cape May, NJ. Antiques and collectibles dealers from the mid-Atlantic region with a large and varied selection of fine furniture, silver, porcelain, crystal and glass accessories, estate and antique jewelry and vintage clothing. Est attendance: 1,000. For info: Mid-Atlantic Center for the Arts, 1048 Washington St, Cape May, NJ 08204. Phone: (800) 275-4278. Fax: (609) 884-0574. E-mail: mac4arts@capemaymac.org. Web: www.capemaymac.org.

ANTI-SALOON LEAGUE FOUNDED: ANNIVERSARY. May 24, 1893. The Anti-Saloon League was founded by Howard H. Russell at Oberlin, OH. Efforts in that state were so successful that the Anti-Saloon League of America was organized in 1895. The league's permanent home became Otterbein College at Westerville, OH, in 1909.

BASEBALL FIRST PLAYED UNDER LIGHTS: ANNIVERSARY. May 24, 1935. The Cincinnati Reds defeated the Philadelphia Phillies by a score of 2–1, as more than 20,000 fans enjoyed the first night baseball game in the major leagues. The game was played at Crosley Field, Cincinnati, OH.

BELIZE: COMMONWEALTH DAY. May 24. Public holiday.

BROOKLYN BRIDGE OPENED: ANNIVERSARY. May 24, 1883. Nearly 14 years in construction, the $16 million Brooklyn Bridge over the East River opened. Designed by John A. Roebling, the steel suspension bridge has a span of 1,595 feet.

BROTHER'S DAY. May 24. Celebration of brotherhood for biological brothers, fraternity brothers and brothers bonded by union affiliation or lifetime experiences. Annually, May 24. (©2001 C. Daniel Rhodes.) For info: C. Daniel Rhodes, 1900 Crossvine Rd, Hoover, AL 35244. Phone: (205) 908-6781. E-mail: rhodan@charter.net.

BULGARIA: CULTURE DAY. May 24. National holiday festively celebrated by schoolchildren, students and people of science and art.

COAL MINER DAYS. May 24–25. Downtown and fairgrounds, Novinger, MO. Turn-of-the-century coal mining boomtown celebrates its heritage with old-time contests, music, dancing and displays. Est attendance: 3,000. For info: Glenna Daniels, Novinger Renewal Inc, 15892 State Hwy 6, Novinger, MO 63559. Phone: (660) 488-5280. E-mail: ddaniels@nemr.net.

ECUADOR: BATTLE OF PICHINCHA. May 24. National holiday. Commemorates battle in 1822 that marked the final defeat of Spain in Ecuador.

ERITREA: INDEPENDENCE DAY: ANNIVERSARY. May 24. National Day. Gained independence from Ethiopia in 1993 after 30-year civil war.

INDIANAPOLIS 500-MILE RACE. May 24. Indianapolis, IN. Recognized as the world's largest single-day sporting event. First race was in 1911. Annually, the Sunday of Memorial Day weekend. For info: Indianapolis Motor Speedway Corp, 4790 W 16th St, Indianapolis, IN 46222. Phone: (317) 481-8500. Web: www.indy500.com.

ITALY: WEDDING OF THE SEA. May 24. Venice. The feast of the Ascension is the occasion of the ceremony recalling the "Wedding of the Sea" performed by Venice's doge, who cast his ring into the sea from the ceremonial ship known as the *Bucintoro* to symbolize eternal dominion. Annually, on the Sunday following Ascension.

LEUTZE, EMANUEL: BIRTH ANNIVERSARY. May 24, 1816. Obscure itinerant painter, born at Württemberg, Germany, came to the US when he was nine years old, began painting by age 15. Painted some of the most famous of American scenes, such as *Washington Crossing the Delaware, Washington Rallying the Troops at Monmouth* and *Columbus Before the Queen*. Died July 18, 1868, at Washington, DC.

MOON PHASE: NEW MOON. May 24. Moon enters New Moon phase at 8:11 AM, EDT.

MORSE OPENS FIRST US TELEGRAPH LINE: ANNIVERSARY. May 24, 1844. The first US telegraph line was formally opened between Baltimore, MD, and Washington, DC. Samuel F.B. Morse sent the first officially telegraphed words—"What hath God wrought?"—from the Capitol building to Baltimore. Earlier messages had been sent along the historic line during testing, and one, sent May 1 from a meeting in Baltimore, contained the news that Henry Clay had been nominated as president by the Whig Party. This message reached Washington one hour prior to a train carrying the same news.

NEIGHBOR DAY. May 24. A "Day of Special Observance" in Rhode Island, declared by the General Assembly. Annually, the Sunday of Memorial Day weekend. For info: Mary Jane DiMaio, Town of Westerly Coordinator, 101 Shore Rd, Westerly, RI 02891. E-mail: mjdimaio1@cox.net. Web: www.neighbordayworldwide.com.

NEWHOUSE, SAMUEL I.: BIRTH ANNIVERSARY. May 24, 1895. Multimillionaire businessman who built family publishing and communications empire. Born to immigrant parents in a New York City tenement, Newhouse became "America's most profitable publisher." He accumulated 31 newspapers, seven magazines, six television stations, five radio stations and 20 cable television systems. He died at New York, NY, Aug 29, 1979.

PALMER, LILLI: 95th BIRTH ANNIVERSARY. May 24, 1914. Stage, screen and television actress Lilli Palmer was born Lillie Marie Peiser, at Poznan, Poland. She also painted and was the author of several novels and an autobiography titled *Change Lobsters—And Dance*. She died at Los Angeles, CA, Jan 27, 1986.

SPACE MILESTONE: *AURORA 7* MERCURY SPACE CAPSULE (US). May 24, 1962. With this launch Scott Carpenter became the second American to orbit Earth, circling it three times.

BIRTHDAYS TODAY

DaMarcus Beasley, 27, soccer player, born Fort Wayne, IN, May 24, 1982.

Jim Broadbent, 60, actor (*Moulin Rouge, Topsy-Turvy*, Oscar for *Iris*), born Lincoln, Lincolnshire, England, May 24, 1949.

Gary Burghoff, 66, actor (Emmy for "M*A*S*H"), born Bristol, CT, May 24, 1943.

Tommy Chong, 71, actor (*Up in Smoke, The Corsican Brothers*), born Edmonton, AB, Canada, May 24, 1938.

Joe Dumars III, 46, former basketball player, born Shreveport, LA, May 24, 1963.

Bob Dylan, 68, composer, singer, born Robert Zimmerman at Duluth, MN, May 24, 1941.

Alyson Hannigan, 35, actress ("How I Met Your Mother," "Buffy the Vampire Slayer," *American Pie*), born Washington, DC, May 24, 1974.

Patti LaBelle, 65, singer ("Since I Don't Have You"), born Patricia Louise Holte at Philadelphia, PA, May 24, 1944.

Tracy McGrady, 30, basketball player, born Bartow, FL, May 24, 1979.

Alfred Molina, 56, actor (*Frida, Chocolat, Letter to Brezhnev*), born London, England, May 24, 1953.

Frank Oz, 65, director, puppeteer, born Hereford, England, May 24, 1944.

Priscilla Beaulieu Presley, 64, actress ("Dallas," *Naked Gun* movies), born Brooklyn, NY, May 24, 1945.

Kristin Scott Thomas, 49, actress (*Gosford Park, The English Patient, The Horse Whisperer*), born Cornwall, England, May 24, 1960.

May 25 — Monday

DAY 145 — **220 REMAINING**

AFRICAN FREEDOM DAY. May 25. Public holiday in Chad, Zambia and some other African states. Members of the Organization for African Unity (formed May 25, 1963) commemorate their independence from colonial rule. Sports contests, political rallies and tribal dances.

AMERICAN FLIGHT CRASHES AT O'HARE: 30th ANNIVERSARY. May 25, 1979. An American Airlines DC-10 lost an engine upon takeoff and crashed seconds later, killing all 272 aboard and three people on the ground.

ARGENTINA: REVOLUTION DAY. May 25. National holiday. Commemoration of revolt against Spanish rule in 1810.

BOLDER BOULDER 10K. May 25. Boulder, CO. 31st annual. A 10k race of walkers, joggers and world-class runners through the streets of Boulder. Annually, on Memorial Day. Est attendance: 50,000. For info: Bolder Boulder, 5500 Central Ave, Ste 110, Boulder, CO 80301. Phone: (303) 444-7223. Fax: (303) 444-6411. E-mail: race@bolderboulder.com. Web: www.bolderboulder.com.

CARVER, RAYMOND: BIRTH ANNIVERSARY. May 25, 1938. American poet and short-story writer who chronicled the lives of America's working poor. Born at Clatskanie, OR, he died Aug 2, 1988, at his home at Port Angeles, WA, soon after finishing a book of poetry titled *A New Path to the Waterfall*.

CONSTITUTIONAL CONVENTION: ANNIVERSARY. May 25, 1787. At Philadelphia, PA, delegates from seven states, forming a quorum, opened the Constitutional Convention, which had been proposed by the Annapolis Convention Sept 11–14, 1786. Among those who were in attendance: George Washington, Benjamin Franklin, James Madison, Alexander Hamilton and Elbridge Gerry. See also: "1786 Annapolis Convention: Anniversary" (Sept 11).

DAVIS, MILES: BIRTH ANNIVERSARY. May 25, 1926. Jazz trumpeter Miles Davis was born at Alton, IL. He was influenced by the bebop music style of Charlie Parker and Dizzy Gillespie and ended up leaving the Juilliard School of Music to join Parker's quintet in 1945. He experimented with different styles throughout his career, exploring new voicings in jazz with arranger Gil Evans and musicians John Coltrane and Red Garland, delving into modal music with Tony Williams and Wayne Shorter and moving into a fusion sound in the '60s. His career was beset with bouts of drug addiction, but in the 1970s his return to the music scene found him creating a sound that melded his bebop origins, modal chord progressions and driving rock rhythms. He died Sept 28, 1991, at Santa Monica, CA.

DOWIE, JOHN ALEXANDER: BIRTH ANNIVERSARY. May 25, 1847. Evangelist and claimant of the title "Elijah the Restorer" was born at Edinburgh, Scotland. He established the Christian Catholic Church at Zion, IL, where some 5,000 followers created a unique community without pharmacies, physicians, theaters or dance halls and where smoking, drinking and the eating of pork were prohibited. Dowie's ostentatiously expensive personal lifestyle and his unsuccessful attempt to convert New York City were partially responsible for the falling away of his followers. He was expelled from the Church in 1906 and died at Chicago, IL, Mar 9, 1907.

EMERSON, RALPH WALDO: BIRTH ANNIVERSARY. May 25, 1803. American author and philosopher born at Boston, MA, and died there Apr 27, 1882. It was Emerson who wrote (in his essay "Self-Reliance," 1841), "A foolish consistency is the hobgoblin of little minds, adored by little statesmen and philosophers and divines. With consistency a great soul has simply nothing to do."

ENGLAND: GLOUCESTERSHIRE CHEESE ROLLING. May 25. Cooper's Hill, near Gloucester, Stroud and Cheltenham in the Cotswolds. Ancient tradition dating to pre-Roman times and held continuously for the last 200 years in which contestants race down a steep, 300-yard hill after a 7–9-pound wheel of double Gloucester cheese. The races (four in total, with 10–15 participants) begin at noon, with a top-hatted master of ceremonies beginning the countdown: "One to be ready, two to be steady, three to prepare and four to be off!" Spectators lining the hill chant, "Roll that cheese!" The unusual festival is marked by many injuries of racers and spectators. The winner gets the cheese. Annually, the last Monday in May—the second May bank holiday. Est attendance: 4,000.

GREATEST DAY IN TRACK AND FIELD: JESSE OWENS'S REMARKABLE RECORDS: ANNIVERSARY. May 25, 1935. During the Big Ten Championships at the University of Michigan at Ann Arbor, Jesse Owens, representing Ohio State University, broke three world records and tied a fourth in the space of 45 minutes—from 3:15 PM to 4:00 PM. The "Buckeye Bullet" (who was suffering from an injured back) set records in the running broad jump, the 220-yard dash and the 220-yard hurdles and tied the record for the 100-yard dash. See also: "Owens, Jesse: Birth Anniversary" (Sept 12).

JORDAN: INDEPENDENCE DAY. May 25. National holiday. Commemorates treaty in 1946, proclaiming independence from Britain and establishing monarchy.

MEMORIAL DAY. May 25. Legal public holiday. (PL90–363 sets Memorial Day on last Monday in May. Applicable to federal employees and District of Columbia.) Also known as Decoration Day because of the tradition of decorating the graves of servicepeople. An occasion for honoring those who have died in battle. (Observance dates from Civil War years in US: first documented observance at Waterloo, NY, May 5, 1866.) See also: "Confederate Memorial Day" (Apr 27, May 10 and June 3).

MEMORIAL DAY PARADE. May 25. Aurora, IL. Annual parade featuring veterans groups, scouts, bands, floats and more. The parade begins at noon. Est attendance: 7,000. For info: City of Aurora, Mayor's Office of Special Events, 5 E Downer Pl, Ste A, Aurora, IL 60505. Phone: (630) 844-4731. Fax: (630) 844-4797.

May 2009	S	M	T	W	T	F	S
						1	2
	3	4	5	6	7	8	9
	10	11	12	13	14	15	16
	17	18	19	20	21	22	23
	24	25	26	27	28	29	30
	31						

MEMORIAL DAY PARADE AND CEREMONIES. May 25. Gettysburg National Cemetery, Gettysburg, PA. Two thousand schoolchildren scatter flowers over the unknown graves. Memorial services follow parade. Est attendance: 5,000. For info: Gettysburg CVB, PO Box 4117, Gettysburg, PA 17325. Phone: (717) 334-6274. Fax: (717) 334-1166. E-mail: info@gettysburg.travel. Web: www.gettysburg.travel.

MURRAY, PHILIP: BIRTH ANNIVERSARY. May 25, 1886. American labor leader and founder of the Congress of Industrial Organizations, also active in and a leader of the United Mine Workers, was born near Blantyre, Scotland. Murray died at San Francisco, CA, Nov 9, 1952.

NATIONAL MISSING CHILDREN'S DAY. May 25. To promote awareness of the problem of missing children, to offer a forum for change and to offer safety information for children in school and the community. Annually, May 25. For info: Child Find of America, Inc, PO Box 277, New Paltz, NY 12561-0277. Phone: (845) 883-6060 or (800) I-AM-LOST. E-mail: information@childfindofamerica.org. Web: www.childfindofamerica.org.

NATIONAL TAP DANCE DAY. May 25. To celebrate this unique American art form that represents a fusion of African and European cultures and to transmit tap to succeeding generations through documentation and archival and performance support. Held on the anniversary of the birth of Bill "Bojangles" Robinson to honor his outstanding contribution to the art of tap dancing on stage and in films through the unification of diverse stylistic and racial elements.

POETRY DAY IN FLORIDA. May 25. In 1947 the legislature decreed this day to be "Poetry Day in all of the public schools of Florida."

✦ **PRAYER FOR PEACE, MEMORIAL DAY.** May 25. Presidential Proclamation issued each year since 1948. PL81–512 of May 11, 1950, asks the president to proclaim annually this day as a day of prayer for permanent peace. PL90–363 of June 28, 1968, requires that beginning in 1971 it will be observed the last Monday in May. Often titled "Prayer for Peace Memorial Day," and traditionally requests the flying of the flag at half-staff "for the customary forenoon period."

ROBINSON, BILL "BOJANGLES": BIRTH ANNIVERSARY. May 25, 1878. Born at Richmond, VA, the grandson of a slave, Robinson is considered one of the greatest tap dancers. He is best known for a routine in which he tap-danced up and down a staircase. He appeared in several films with Shirley Temple and starred in *Stormy Weather*. Died at New York, NY, Nov 25, 1949.

SIKORSKY, IGOR: BIRTH ANNIVERSARY. May 25, 1889. Aeronautical engineer best remembered for his development of the first successful helicopter in 1939. Also pioneered in multiengine airplanes and large flying boats that made transoceanic air transportation possible. Born at Kiev, Russia, he died Oct 26, 1972, at Easton, CT.

SILLS, BEVERLY: 80th BIRTH ANNIVERSARY. May 25, 1929. The great coloratura soprano was born Belle Silverman at Brooklyn, NY. Signature roles were the title roles in *Lucia di Lammermoor* and *Anna Bolena*, as well as Queen Elizabeth I in *Roberto Devereux*. She was a great ambassador of opera in America and was instrumental in making it accessible both as a singer and later as a television personality and opera executive. She died July 2, 2007, at New York, NY.

SOLZHENITSYN GOES HOME: 15th ANNIVERSARY. May 25, 1994. After 20 years living in exile, mostly in the US, Russian author Aleksandr Solzhenitsyn returned to his homeland. The author had been expelled from the Soviet Union in 1974 after his three-volume work exposing the Soviet prison camp system, *The Gulag Archipelago*, was published in the West. After the collapse of the Soviet Union late in 1991, he announced his intention to go back. He died at Moscow, Aug 4, 2008.

SPACE MILESTONE: *SKYLAB 2* (US). May 25, 1973. Joseph P. Kerwin, Paul J. Weitz and Charles (Pete) Conrad, Jr, spent 28 days in experimentation on this space station, which had been launched May 14. Pacific splashdown occurred June 22.

***STAR WARS* RELEASED: ANNIVERSARY. May 25, 1977.** "May the Force be with you" entered the modern lexicon as a new kind of science fiction film opened at 32 theaters. George Lucas's space epic, starring Mark Hamill as Luke Skywalker, Harrison Ford as Han Solo and Carrie Fisher as Princess Leia, featured stunning special effects and was a smash hit worldwide. It went on to win six Academy Awards out of ten nominations—plus an additional special Academy Award for sound effects. The film was part of a larger saga and in later years was retitled *Star Wars—Episode IV: A New Hope* as prequels were released.

STOCK EXCHANGE HOLIDAY (MEMORIAL DAY). May 25. The holiday schedules for the various exchanges are subject to change if relevant rules, regulations or exchange policies are revised. If you have questions, contact: American Stock Exchange (866) 422-2639 (www.amex.com), Chicago Board of Trade (312) 435-3500 (www.cbot.com), Chicago Board Options Exchange (312) 786-5600 (www.cboe.com), NASDAQ Stock Market (646) 441-5200 (www.nasdaq.com), New York Stock Exchange (212) 656-3000 (www.nyse.com), Philadelphia Stock Exchange (800) THE-PHLX (www.phlx.com).

TITO (JOSIP BROZ): BIRTH ANNIVERSARY. May 25, 1892. Josip Broz, Yugoslavian soldier and political leader, born near Zagreb, Yugoslavia. Died May 4, 1980, at Ljubljana, Yugoslavia (now Slovenia), and was interred in the garden of his home at Belgrade. Tito, a Croat, had managed to keep the many nationalities and religions that made up Yugoslavia in one state, but in the early 1990s the nation broke up as Croats, Serbs and others went to war against each other.

TOUR OF SOMERVILLE. May 25. Somerville, NJ. 66th running. The oldest continuously run major bicycle race in America. Attracts more than 500 top amateur cyclists for four events. Annually, on Memorial Day. Est attendance: 40,000. For info: Dan Puntillo, Middle Earth, PO Box 8045, Bridgewater, NJ 08807. Phone: (908) 725-7223. Fax: (908) 722-5411. Web: www.tourofsomerville.org.

TUNNEY, JAMES JOSEPH (GENE): BIRTH ANNIVERSARY. May 25, 1898. Heavyweight boxing champion, business executive. The famous "long count" occurred in the seventh round of the Jack Dempsey–Gene Tunney world championship fight, Sept 22, 1927, at Soldier Field, Chicago, IL. Tunney was born at New York, NY, and died Nov 7, 1978, at Greenwich, CT.

UNITED KINGDOM: SPRING BANK HOLIDAY. May 25. Bank and public holiday in England, Wales, Scotland and Northern Ireland. Annually, the last Monday in May.

UNITED NATIONS: WEEK OF SOLIDARITY WITH THE PEOPLE OF NON-SELF-GOVERNING TERRITORIES. May 25–31. On Dec 6, 1999 (Resolution 54/91) the General Assembly requested the Special Committee on Decolonization to observe this week beginning on May 25, Africa Liberation Day. For info: United Nations, Dept of Public Info, New York, NY 10017. Web: www.un.org.

BIRTHDAYS TODAY

Dixie Carter, 70, actress ("Designing Women," "Family Law"), born McLemoresville, TN, May 25, 1939.

Jessi Colter, 62, singer, songwriter, born Miriam Johnson at Phoenix, AZ, May 25, 1947.

Tom T. Hall, 73, singer ("P.S. I Love You"), songwriter ("Harper Valley PTA"), born Olive Hill, KY, May 25, 1936.

Anne Heche, 40, actress (*Wag the Dog; Six Days, Seven Nights*; "Men in Trees"), born Aurora, OH, May 25, 1969.

Justin Henry, 38, actor (*Kramer vs Kramer, Sixteen Candles*), born Rye, NY, May 25, 1971.

Lauryn Hill, 34, singer, actress (*Sister Act 2*), born South Orange, NJ, May 25, 1975.

K.C. Jones, 77, Hall of Fame basketball player, former coach, born Tyler, TX, May 25, 1932.

Jamie Kennedy, 39, actor ("JKX: The Jamie Kennedy Experiment," *Malibu's Most Wanted*), born Upper Darby, PA, May 25, 1970.

Amy Klobucher, 49, US Senator (D, Minnesota), born Plymouth, MN, May 25, 1960.

Sir Ian McKellen, 70, actor (stage: *Amadeus* [Tony Award]; *Lord of the Rings* trilogy, *Gods and Monsters*), born Burnley, England, May 25, 1939.

Mike Myers, 46, comedian, actor ("Saturday Night Live," *Wayne's World, Austin Powers* films), born Scarsborough, ON, Canada, May 25, 1963.

Connie Sellecca, 54, actress ("Hotel," *While My Pretty One Sleeps*), born the Bronx, NY, May 25, 1955.

Gordon Smith, 57, US Senator (R, Oregon), born Pendleton, OR, May 25, 1952.

Ethan Suplee, 33, actor ("My Name Is Earl," "Boy Meets World," *Art School Confidential*), born New York, NY, May 25, 1976.

Leslie Uggams, 66, singer ("Sing Along with Mitch"), actress, born New York, NY, May 25, 1943.

Brian Urlacher, 31, football player, born Lovington, NM, May 25, 1978.

Karen Valentine, 62, actress ("Room 222"), born Sebastopol, CA, May 25, 1947.

May 26 — Tuesday

DAY 146 | **219 REMAINING**

AUSTRALIA: SORRY DAY. May 26. A day to express sorrow for the forced removal of aboriginal children from their families.

DUNKIRK EVACUATED: ANNIVERSARY. May 26, 1940. The British Expeditionary Force had become trapped by advancing German armies near this port on the northern coast of France. On this date the evacuation of 200,000 British and 140,000 French and Belgian soldiers began. Sailing on every kind of transport available, including fishing boats and recreational craft, these men were safely brought across the English Channel by June 2.

FEAST OF SAINT AUGUSTINE OF CANTERBURY. May 26. Pope Gregory sent Augustine to convert the pagan English. Augustine became the first archbishop of Canterbury. He died May 26, AD 604.

GEORGIA: INDEPENDENCE DAY. May 26. National Day. Commemorates declaration of independence from Russia in 1918. Was absorbed by the Soviet Union in 1922.

JOLSON, AL: BIRTH ANNIVERSARY. May 26, 1886. Actor (*The Jazz Singer*) and singer, born Asa Yoelson at St. Petersburg, Russia. Died at San Francisco, CA, Oct 23, 1950.

LEE, PEGGY: BIRTH ANNIVERSARY. May 26, 1920. Singer, songwriter and actress Peggy Lee was born Norma Deloris Egstrom at

Jamestown, ND. She got her start singing on a Fargo, ND, radio station and was soon hired by Benny Goodman to sing with his band. Known for her simple, jazzy style as well as her sex appeal. Her biggest hits were 1958's "Fever" and 1969's "Is That All There Is?" She is perhaps best remembered for the songs that she cowrote and performed in Disney's *Lady and the Tramp.* She continued to perform until the 1990s, when poor health forced her to retire. She died Jan 21, 2002, at Los Angeles, CA.

MORLEY, ROBERT: BIRTH ANNIVERSARY. May 26, 1908. British actor Robert Morley was born at Semley, England. Among his best-known film credits are *Major Barbara* (1939) and *The African Queen* (1951). He died June 3, 1992, at Reading, England.

RIDE, SALLY KRISTEN: BIRTHDAY. May 26, 1951. Dr. Sally Ride, one of the first women in the US astronaut corps and the first American woman in space, was born at Encino, CA. Her flight aboard the space shuttle *Challenger* was launched from Cape Canaveral, FL, June 18 and landed at Edwards Air Force Base, CA, June 24, 1983. The six-day flight was termed "nearly a perfect mission."

SPACE MILESTONE: *PHOENIX* LANDS ON MARS (US). May 26, 2008. NASA's *Phoenix* spacecraft landed successfully on the northern plains of Mars. Designed to be stationary, *Phoenix* analyzed soil and permafrost samples and transmitted photographs back to Earth.

VIETNAM AND US RESUME RELATIONS: 15th ANNIVERSARY. May 26, 1994. Nearly 20 years after the end of the Vietnam War, the US and Vietnam agreed to resume diplomatic relations. In the early 1990s Vietnam had become one of the fastest-growing economies in Asia after giving up Communist controls and allowing economic reform. Earlier in 1994 President William Clinton had lifted the American embargo that hindered Americans from doing business in Vietnam.

WAYNE, JOHN: BIRTH ANNIVERSARY. May 26, 1907. American motion picture actor, born Marion Michael Morrison, at Winterset, IA. The quintessential Western actor for five decades. Among his films were *Stagecoach* (1939), *Red River* (1948), *The Searchers* (1956) and *True Grit* (1969), for which he won a Best Actor Oscar. He died at Los Angeles, CA, June 11, 1979. "Talk low, talk slow and don't say too much" was his advice on acting.

BIRTHDAYS TODAY

James Arness, 86, actor ("Gunsmoke," "How the West Was Won"), born James Aurness at Minneapolis, MN, May 26, 1923.

Helena Bonham Carter, 43, actress (*Harry Potter* films, *Sweeney Todd, A Room with a View, Howard's End*), born London, England, May 26, 1966.

Genie Francis, 47, actress ("General Hospital"), born Englewood, NJ, May 26, 1962.

Pam Grier, 60, actress (*Jackie Brown, Mars Attacks, Something Wicked This Way Comes*), born Winston-Salem, NC, May 26, 1949.

Lenny Kravitz, 45, singer, musician, songwriter, born New York, NY, May 26, 1964.

Brent Musburger, 70, sportscaster, born Portland, OR, May 26, 1939.

Stevie Nicks, 61, singer (Fleetwood Mac), songwriter, born Phoenix, AZ, May 26, 1948.

Sally K. Ride, 58, astronaut, first American woman in space, born Los Angeles, CA, May 26, 1951.

Philip Michael Thomas, 60, actor ("Miami Vice," *Hair*), born Los Angeles, CA, May 26, 1949.

Hank Williams, Jr, 60, singer, born Shreveport, LA, May 26, 1949.

May 2009

S	M	T	W	T	F	S
					1	2
3	4	5	6	7	8	9
10	11	12	13	14	15	16
17	18	19	20	21	22	23
24	25	26	27	28	29	30
31						

May 27 — Wednesday

DAY 147 **218 REMAINING**

BEEF EMPIRE DAYS. May 27–June 14. Finney County Fairgrounds, Garden City, KS. 41st annual celebration of the beef industry. Live and carcass show; PRCA rodeo (three nights); parade; beef tasting for the public; feedlot roping and riding; walk/run; golf, softball and tennis tournaments; children's events. Est attendance: 50,000. For info: Beef Empire Days, 206 E Fulton Terrace, Garden City, KS 67846-1197. Phone: (620) 275-6807. E-mail: beefempiredays@gcnet.com. Web: www.beefempiredays.com.

BENNETT, ARNOLD: BIRTH ANNIVERSARY. May 27, 1867. English novelist, playwright and critic Enoch Arnold Bennett was born at Hanley, in the pottery-manufacturing district of North Staffordshire, England. Best known of his novels is *The Old Wives' Tale* (1908). His *Journals* from 1896 until near the time of his death in 1931 provide insight into Bennett's thought. "The price of justice," Bennett wrote, "is eternal publicity." He contracted typhoid fever in France and died at London, England, May 27, 1931.

BLOOMER, AMELIA JENKS: BIRTH ANNIVERSARY. May 27, 1818. American social reformer and women's rights advocate, born at Homer, NY. Her name is remembered especially because of her work for more sensible dress for women and her recommendation of a costume that had been introduced about 1849 by Elizabeth Smith Miller but came to be known as the "Bloomer Costume" or "bloomers." Amelia Bloomer died at Council Bluffs, IA, Dec 30, 1894.

CANADA: ANNAPOLIS VALLEY APPLE BLOSSOM FESTIVAL. May 27–June 1. Windsor to Digby, NS. Annual festival with barbecues, sports events, art show, Princess Tea, coronation ceremonies, dances, concerts, fireworks, craft fair, children's parade, Grand Street Parade and "Family Fun Day at Scotian Gold." Annually, since 1933. Est attendance: 125,000. For info: Mrs Frances Anderson, Annapolis Valley Apple Blossom Fest, 217 Belcher St, Kentville, NS, Canada B4N 1E2. Phone: (902) 678-8322. Fax: (902) 678-3710. E-mail: info@appleblossom.com. Web: www.appleblossom.com.

CARSON, RACHEL LOUISE: BIRTH ANNIVERSARY. May 27, 1907. American scientist and author, born at Springdale, PA. Author of *Silent Spring* (1962), a book that provoked widespread controversy over the use of pesticides. Died Apr 14, 1964, at Silver Spring, MD.

CELLOPHANE TAPE PATENTED: ANNIVERSARY. May 27, 1930. Richard Gurley Drew received a patent for his adhesive tape, later manufactured by 3M as Scotch tape.

DUNCAN, ISADORA: BIRTH ANNIVERSARY. May 27, 1878. American-born interpretive dancer who revolutionized the entire concept of dance. Barefooted, freedom-loving, liberated woman and rebel against tradition, she experienced worldwide professional success and profound personal tragedy (her two children drowned, her marriage failed and she met a bizarre death when the long scarf she was wearing caught in a wheel of the open car in which she was riding, strangling her). Born at San Francisco, CA; died at Nice, France, Sept 14, 1927.

FIRST FLIGHT INTO THE STRATOSPHERE: ANNIVERSARY. May 27, 1931. In a balloon launched from Augsburg, Germany, Paul Kipfer and Auguste Piccard became the first to reach the stratosphere. In a pressurized cabin they rose almost 10 miles during their flight.

FIRST RUNNING OF PREAKNESS: ANNIVERSARY. May 27, 1873. The first running of the Preakness Stakes at Pimlico, MD, was won by Survivor with a time of 2:43. The winning jockey was G. Barbee.

GOLDEN GATE BRIDGE OPENED: ANNIVERSARY. May 27, 1937. Some 200,000 people crossed San Francisco's Golden Gate Bridge on its opening day.

HAMMETT, DASHIELL: BIRTH ANNIVERSARY. May 27, 1894. The man who brought realism to the genre of mystery writing, Samuel Dashiell Hammett was born at St. Mary's County, MD. His first two novels, *Red Harvest* (1929) and *The Dain Curse* (1929), were based on his eight years spent as a Pinkerton detective. Hammett is recognized as the founder of the "hard-boiled" school of detective fiction. Three of his novels have been made into films: *The Maltese Falcon* (1930), considered by many to be his finest work; *The Thin Man* (1932), which provided the basis for a series of five movies starring William Powell and Myrna Loy; and *The Glass Key* (1931). Hammett was called to testify but refused to name members of an alleged subversive organization during House Un-American Activities Committee hearings. He died Jan 10, 1961, at New York City.

HICKOK, WILD BILL: BIRTH ANNIVERSARY. May 27, 1837. Born at Troy Grove, IL, and died Aug 2, 1876, at Deadwood, SD. American frontiersman, legendary marksman, lawman, army scout and gambler. Hickok's end came when he was shot dead at a poker table by a drunk in the Number Ten saloon.

HUMPHREY, HUBERT HORATIO: BIRTH ANNIVERSARY. May 27, 1911. Born at Wallace, SD. The 38th vice president of the US (1965–69). Democratic candidate for president in 1968 who lost to Richard Nixon. Died at Waverly, MN, Jan 13, 1978.

NATIONAL SENIOR HEALTH AND FITNESS DAY. May 27. More than 1,000 local events held on the same day in all 50 states. 16th annual event to promote the value of fitness and exercise for older adults. During this day—as part of Older Americans Month activities—seniors across the country are involved in locally organized health-promotion activities. Call the toll-free number for further info and a list of local sites. Annually, the last Wednesday in May. In 2008 more than 120,000 older adults participated in fitness activities at more than 1,000 events nationwide. Est attendance: 150,000. For info: Tina Godin, Program Mgr, Mature Market Resource Center, 1850 W Winchester Rd, Ste 213, Libertyville, IL 60048. Phone: (800) 828-8225. Fax: (847) 816-8662. E-mail: info@fitnessday.com. Web: www.fitnessday.com.

NCAA DIVISION I MEN'S GOLF CHAMPIONSHIPS. May 27–30. Toledo, OH. For info: NCAA, 700 W Washington St, PO Box 6222, Indianapolis, IN 46206-6222. Phone: (317) 917-6222. Web: www.NCAAsports.com.

PRICE, VINCENT: BIRTH ANNIVERSARY. May 27, 1911. Actor, best known for his portrayal of sinister villains in horror films and as host for the TV series "Mystery!" Born at St. Louis, MO, and died at Los Angeles, CA, Oct 25, 1993.

RMS *QUEEN MARY*: MAIDEN VOYAGE: ANNIVERSARY. May 27, 1936. Anniversary of the maiden voyage from Southampton, England, to New York Harbor. In 1967 the ship sailed to Long Beach, CA, where it is permanently berthed and used as a hotel.

ST. PETERSBURG FOUNDED: ANNIVERSARY. May 27, 1703. Czar Peter the Great founded the city of St. Petersburg on the banks of the Neva River by laying the first stone of the Peter and Paul Fortress. It became the capital of Russia in 1712. See also: "St. Petersburg Name Restored: Anniversary" (Sept 6).

SCRIPPS NATIONAL SPELLING BEE FINALS. May 27–28 (tentative). Washington, DC. Newspapers and other sponsors across the country send 240–250 youngsters to the finals at Washington, DC. Annually, Wednesday and Thursday of Memorial Day week. Est attendance: 1,000. For info: Scripps Natl Spelling Bee, 312 Walnut St, 28th Fl, Cincinnati, OH 45202. Phone: (513) 977-3040. Fax: (513) 977-3803. E-mail: bee@scripps.com. Web: www.spellingbee.com.

SNEAD, SAM: BIRTH ANNIVERSARY. May 27, 1912. The winningest US Tour golfer of the 20th century was born at Hot Springs, VA. He turned pro in 1934 and went on to become the only golfer to win tournaments in six different decades. He won 84 US Tour events and 182 tournaments in total. Snead always wore a snappy straw hat and was a favorite on the Tour. He was one of the founders of the US Senior Tour. Snead died at Hot Springs, on May 23, 2002.

BIRTHDAYS TODAY

Jeff Bagwell, 41, baseball player, born Boston, MA, May 27, 1968.

John Barth, 79, author (*Last Voyage of Somebody the Sailor, Letters*), born Cambridge, MD, May 27, 1930.

André Benjamin, 34, singer, musician (André 3000, Outkast), actor, born Atlanta, GA, May 27, 1975.

Todd Bridges, 44, actor ("Diff'rent Strokes"), born San Francisco, CA, May 27, 1965.

Pat Cash, 44, former tennis player, born Melbourne, Australia, May 27, 1965.

Christopher J. Dodd, 65, US Senator (D, Connecticut), born Willimantic, CT, May 27, 1944.

Joseph Fiennes, 39, actor (*Shakespeare in Love*), born Salisbury, England, May 27, 1970.

Peri Gilpin, 48, actress ("Frasier"), born Waco, TX, May 27, 1961.

Louis Gossett, Jr, 73, actor (Emmy for "Roots"; Oscar for *An Officer and a Gentleman*), born Brooklyn, NY, May 27, 1936.

Henry Kissinger, 86, former secretary of state, author, born Fuerth, Germany, May 27, 1923.

Christopher Lee, 87, actor (*The Lord of the Ring* films, *Dracula, The Mummy*), born London, England, May 27, 1922.

Ramsey Lewis, 74, jazz musician, born Chicago, IL, May 27, 1935.

Jack McBrayer, 36, actor ("30 Rock"), born Macon, GA, May 27, 1973.

Lee Meriwether, 74, actress ("Barnaby Jones," "Batman"), former Miss America ('55), born Los Angeles, CA, May 27, 1935.

Jamie Oliver, 34, chef, television personality ("The Naked Chef"), born Clavering, Essex, England, May 27, 1975.

Richard Schiff, 54, actor ("The West Wing"), born Bethesda, MD, May 27, 1955.

Frank Thomas, 41, baseball player, born Columbus, GA, May 27, 1968.

Bruce Weitz, 66, actor ("Hill Street Blues"), born Norwalk, CT, May 27, 1943.

Herman Wouk, 94, writer (*Marjorie Morningstar, The Winds of War*), born New York, NY, May 27, 1915.

May 28 — Thursday

DAY 148 **217 REMAINING**

AGASSIZ, LOUIS: BIRTH ANNIVERSARY. May 28, 1807. Professor of zoology and geology at Harvard, born at Motier, Switzerland. He was a major influence in spawning American interest in natural history and helped to establish the Harvard Museum of Comparative Zoology. "The eye of the trilobite," Agassiz wrote in 1870, "tells us that the sun shone on the old beach where he lived; for there is nothing in nature without a purpose, and when so complicated an organ was made to receive the light, there must have been light to enter it." Died at Cambridge, MA, Dec 14, 1873.

AMNESTY INTERNATIONAL FOUNDED: ANNIVERSARY. May 28, 1961. This Nobel Prize–winning human rights organization was founded by London lawyer Peter Benenson after he read about two Portuguese students arrested simply for drinking a toast to freedom. He realized that people around the world were at risk daily for peacefully expressing their views. AI currently has more than 2.2 million members in every corner of the world. Its mission is to undertake research and action focused on preventing and ending grave abuses of the rights of physical and mental integrity, freedom of conscience and expression and freedom from discrimination, within the context of its work to promote all human rights. For info: Amnesty International USA, 5 Penn Plaza, New York, NY 10001. Phone: (212) 807-8400. Web: www.amnestyusa.org.

AZERBAIJAN: DAY OF THE REPUBLIC. May 28. Public holiday. Commemorates the declaration of the Azerbaijan Democratic Republic in 1918.

BOOKEXPO AMERICA TRADE EXHIBIT. May 28–31. Jacob K. Javits Center, New York, NY. Publishers display fall titles for booksellers and all interested in reaching the retail bookseller. Book-related items also on display. For info: BookExpo America, 383 Main Ave, Norwalk, CT 06851-1543. Phone: (800) 840-5614. Web: www.bookexpoamerica.com.

CHINA: DRAGON BOAT FESTIVAL. May 28. An important Chinese observance, the Dragon Boat Festival commemorates a hero of ancient China, poet Qu Yuan, who drowned himself in protest against injustice and corruption. It is said that rice dumplings were cast into the water to lure fish away from the body of the martyr, and this is remembered by the eating of *zhong zi*, glutinous rice dumplings filled with meat and wrapped in bamboo leaves. Dragon boat races are held on rivers. The Dragon Boat Festival is observed in many countries by their Chinese populations (date will differ from China's). Also called Fifth Month Festival, or Summer Festival. Annually, the fifth day of the fifth lunar month.

DIONNE QUINTUPLETS: 75th BIRTHDAY. May 28, 1934. Five daughters (Marie, Cecile, Yvonne, Emilie and Annette) were born to Oliva and Elzire Dionne, near Callander, ON, Canada. They were the first quints known to have lived for more than a few hours after birth. Emilie died in 1954, Marie in 1970, Yvonne in 2001. The other two sisters are still living.

ETHIOPIA: NATIONAL DAY. May 28. National holiday. Commemorates the downfall of the Dergue, the military government that ruled Ethiopia from 1974 to 1991.

FLEMING, IAN: BIRTH ANNIVERSARY. May 28, 1908. English journalist, novelist, creator of the James Bond series, beginning with *Casino Royale* in 1953. Fleming also penned the children's classic *Chitty Chitty Bang Bang*. Born at London, died Aug 12, 1964, at Sandwich, England.

GUILLOTIN, JOSEPH IGNACE: BIRTH ANNIVERSARY. May 28, 1738. French physician and member of the Constituent Assembly who urged the use of a machine that was sometimes called the "Maiden" for the execution of death sentences—a less painful, more certain way of dispatching those sentenced to death. The guillotine was first used on Apr 25, 1792, for the execution of a highwayman, Nicolas Jacques Pelletier. Other machines for decapitation had been in use in other countries since the Middle Ages. Guillotin was born at Saintes, France, and died at Paris, Mar 26, 1814.

KOREA: TANO DAY. May 28. Fifth day of fifth lunar month. Summer food offered at the household shrine of the ancestors. Also known as Swing Day, since girls, dressed in their prettiest clothes, often compete in swinging matches. The Tano Festival usually lasts from the third through eighth day of the fifth lunar month.

NCAA DIVISION I SOFTBALL CHAMPIONSHIP. May 28–June 3. ASA Hall of Fame Stadium, Oklahoma City, OK. For info: NCAA, PO Box 6222, Indianapolis, IN 46206-6222. Phone: (317) 917-6222. Fax: (317) 917-6210. Web: www.NCAAsports.com.

ORTHODOX ASCENSION DAY. May 28. Observed by Eastern Orthodox Churches.

PITT, WILLIAM: 250th BIRTH ANNIVERSARY. May 28, 1759. British prime minister from 1783 to 1801 and from 1804 to 1806, Pitt was influenced by Adam Smith's economic theories and reduced England's large national debt caused by the American Revolution. Born at Hayes, Kent, England, he died Jan 23, 1806, at Putney. He was the son of William Pitt, first earl of Chatham, for whom the city of Pittsburgh was named.

PORTLAND ROSE FESTIVAL. May 28–June 7. Portland, OR. Annual celebration includes more than 50 events featuring three parades, dragon boat races, a waterfront village with amusement rides and navy fleet visits. Est attendance: 2,000,000. For info: Portland Rose Festival Assn, 5603 SW Hood Ave, Portland, OR 97239. Phone: (503) 227-2681. Fax: (503) 227-6603. E-mail: info@rosefestival.org. Web: www.rosefestival.org.

SAINT BERNARD OF MONTJOUX: FEAST DAY. May 28. Patron saint of mountain climbers, founder of Alpine hospices of the Great and Little St. Bernard, died at age 85, probably on May 28, 1081.

SHAVUOT BEGINS AT SUNDOWN. May 28. Jewish Pentecost. See also: "Shavuot or Feast of Weeks" (May 29).

SIERRA CLUB FOUNDED: ANNIVERSARY. May 28, 1892. Founded by famed naturalist John Muir, the Sierra Club promotes conservation of the natural environment by influencing public policy. It has been especially important in the founding and protection of our national parks. For info: Sierra Club, 85 Second St, 2nd Fl, San Francisco, CA 94105-3441. Phone: (415) 977-5500. Fax: (415) 977-5799. E-mail: information@sierraclub.org. Web: www.sierraclub.org.

SLUGS RETURN FROM CAPISTRANO DAY. May 28. It's a little-known secret that slimy slugs spend their winters in lovely Capistrano and return to our patios and gardens on this date. Bare feet are not a good idea now through first frost. (©2006 by WH.) For info: Thomas & Ruth Roy, Wellcat Holidays, 2418 Long Ln, Lebanon, PA 17046. Phone: (717) 279-0184. E-mail: info@wellcat.com. Web: www.wellcat.com.

THORPE, JAMES FRANCIS (JIM): BIRTH ANNIVERSARY. May 28, 1888. Jim Thorpe, Pro Football Hall of Famer, distinguished Native American athlete, winner of pentathlon and decathlon events at the 1912 Olympic Games, professional baseball and football player. Born near Prague, OK, and died at Lomita, CA, Mar 28, 1953.

"ZOO PARADE" TV PREMIERE: ANNIVERSARY. May 28, 1950. NBC's half-hour program on animals and animal behavior was hosted by Marlin Perkins and Jim Hurlbut. Initially, it was broadcast from Lincoln Park Zoo in Chicago, IL, but after 1955, the show was broadcast from other locales throughout the country. A successor program, "Mutual of Omaha's Wild Kingdom," was shot almost entirely in the wild and ran into the 1980s.

May 2009

S	M	T	W	T	F	S
					1	2
3	4	5	6	7	8	9
10	11	12	13	14	15	16
17	18	19	20	21	22	23
24	25	26	27	28	29	30
31						

BIRTHDAYS TODAY

Carroll Baker, 78, actress (*Baby Doll, Harlow*), born Johnstown, PA, May 28, 1931.

Barry Commoner, 92, biologist, politician, born Brooklyn, NY, May 28, 1917.

Kirk Harold Gibson, 52, former baseball player, born Pontiac, MI, May 28, 1957.

Armon Louis Gilliam, 45, former basketball player, born Pittsburgh, PA, May 28, 1964.

Rudolph Giuliani, 65, former mayor of New York City, born Brooklyn, NY, May 28, 1944.

Gladys Knight, 65, singer (and the Pips; "Neither One of Us," "If I Were Your Woman"), born Atlanta, GA, May 28, 1944.

Sondra Locke, 62, actress (*The Heart Is a Lonely Hunter, Bronco Billy*), director (*Ratboy*), born Shelbyville, TN, May 28, 1947.

Christa Miller, 45, actress ("The Drew Carey Show"), born New York, NY, May 28, 1964.

Glen Rice, 42, basketball player, born Flint, MI, May 28, 1967.

Mark Sanford, 49, Governor of South Carolina (R), born Fort Lauderdale, FL, May 28, 1960.

May 29 — Friday

DAY 149 **216 REMAINING**

AMNESTY ISSUED FOR SOUTHERN REBELS: ANNIVERSARY. May 29, 1865. President Andrew Johnson issued a proclamation giving a general amnesty to all who participated in the rebellion against the US. High-ranking members of the Confederate government and military and those who owned more than $20,000 worth of property were excepted and had to apply individually to the president for a pardon. Once an oath of allegiance was taken, all former property rights, except those in slaves, were returned to the former owners.

ASCENSION OF BAHA'U'LLAH: ANNIVERSARY. May 29, 1892. Baha'i observance of the anniversary of the death in exile of Baha'u'llah (the prophet-founder of the Baha'i faith). One of the nine days of the year when Baha'is suspend work. For info: Baha'is of the US, Office of Communications, 1233 Central St, Evanston, IL 60201. Phone: (847) 733-3559. Fax: (847) 733-3578. E-mail: ooc@usbnc.org. Web: www.bahai.us.

CENTRALIA ANCHOR FESTIVAL. May 29–31. City Square, Centralia, MO. Continuous entertainment, crafts, concessions, carnival, 3-on-3 basketball, softball, pedal pull, tractor show, car show, fun run, anchor driving, parade, kids' corner and archery shoot. Est attendance: 20,000. For info: Centralia Anchor Festival, PO Box 235, Centralia, MO 65240. Phone: (573) 682-2272. Fax: (573) 682-1111. Web: www.centralia.missouri.org.

CHARLES II: RESTORATION ANNIVERSARY. May 29, 1660. Restoration of Charles II to English throne. Also his birthday (May 29, 1630). English monarchy restored after Commonwealth period under Oliver Cromwell.

CHESTERTON, GILBERT KEITH: BIRTH ANNIVERSARY. May 29, 1874. English author and critic born at London, England. Died June 14, 1936, at Beaconsfield, Buckinghamshire, England.

CONSTANTINOPLE FALLS TO THE TURKS: ANNIVERSARY. May 29, 1453. The city of Constantinople was captured by the Turks, who later renamed it Istanbul. This conquest marked the end of the Byzantine Empire; the city became the capital of the Ottoman Empire.

ENGLAND: ENGLISH RIVIERA DANCE FESTIVAL. May 29–June 5. Torquay, Devon. Demonstrations by world champions and participatory events including modern, ballroom, disco and Latin American dance styles. Est attendance: 2,000. For info: Philip Wylie, 73 Hoylake Crescent, Ickenham, Middlesex, England UB10 8JQ. Phone: (44) (1895) 632-143. Fax: (44) (1895) 635-684. E-mail: info@holidayanddance.co.uk Web: www.holidayanddance.co.uk.

HENRY, PATRICK: BIRTH ANNIVERSARY. May 29, 1736. American Revolutionary leader and orator, born at Studley, VA, and died near Brookneal, VA, June 6, 1799. Especially remembered for his speech (Mar 23, 1775) for arming the Virginia militia, at St. Johns Church, Richmond, VA, when he declared: "I know not what course others may take, but as for me, give me liberty or give me death."

HOPE, BOB: BIRTH ANNIVERSARY. May 29, 1903. The comedic actor was born Leslie Townes Hope at Eltham, England. Hope had a long career in vaudeville, stage, radio, film and TV. His first film appearance was in *The Big Broadcast of 1938* (in which he sang his signature song, "Thanks for the Memory"). Hope went on to appear in more than 75 films—most memorably with crooner Bing Crosby in their series of *Road* movies. He received five honorary Oscars (among them the Jean Hersholt Humanitarian Award) and numerous other honors. Hope tirelessly entertained US troops during every war from WWII to the Gulf War. President Lyndon Johnson presented him with the Medal of Freedom, and he was knighted in 1998. Hope died July 27, 2003, at Toluca Lake, CA.

HUG YOUR CAT DAY. May 29. Cats act as if they don't want or need attention—but they do. Apricat, the pampered star of her own book series, has created a special day for humans to hug their cats without fear of scratches or hisses. For info: Marisa D'Vari, 25 Columbus Circle, Apt ST-55E, New York, NY 10019. E-mail: mdvari@deg.com. Web: www.hugyourcatday.com.

KENNEDY, JOHN FITZGERALD: BIRTH ANNIVERSARY. May 29, 1917. 35th president of the US (1961–63), born at Brookline, MA. Assassinated while riding in an open automobile at Dallas, TX, Nov 22, 1963. (Accused assassin Lee Harvey Oswald was killed at the Dallas police station by a gunman, Jack Ruby, two days later.) Kennedy was the youngest man ever elected to the presidency, the first Roman Catholic and the first president to have served in the US Navy. He was the fourth US president to be killed by an assassin and the second to be buried at Arlington National Cemetery (first was William Howard Taft).

MOSCOW COMMUNIQUE: ANNIVERSARY. May 29, 1972. President Richard Nixon and Soviet Party leader Leonid Brezhnev released a joint communique after Nixon's weeklong visit to Moscow. During the visit the two men acknowledged their major differences on the Vietnam War and signed a treaty on antiballistic missile systems, as well as an interim agreement on limitation of strategic missiles, and an agreement for a joint space flight in 1975. This was the first visit ever to Moscow by a US president (May 22–30, 1972).

MOUNT EVEREST SUMMIT REACHED: ANNIVERSARY. May 29, 1953. New Zealand explorer Sir Edmund Hillary and Tensing Norgay, a Sherpa guide, became the first team to reach the summit of Mount Everest, the world's highest mountain.

RHODE ISLAND: RATIFICATION DAY. May 29. The last of the 13 original states to ratify the Constitution in 1790.

***THE RITE OF SPRING* PREMIERE AND RIOT: ANNIVERSARY.** May 29, 1913. In the most notorious world premiere in any of the arts, Igor Stravinsky's *The Rite of Spring* received a rough reception at the Théatre des Champs-Elysées at Paris, France, on this date. Performed by Sergey Diaghilev's Ballets Russes and choreographed by the legendary Vaslav Nijinsky, the ballet and music presented scenes from pagan Russia. The audience began to boo at Stravinsky's challenging and dissonant music, and before long fistfights between different camps of music lovers broke out. The police were called to restore order. Despite its inauspicious beginning, *The Rite of Spring* is now regarded as a masterpiece.

SHAVUOT or FEAST OF WEEKS. May 29–30. Jewish Pentecost holy days. Hebrew dates, Sivan 6–7, 5769. Celebrates giving of Torah (the Law) to Moses on Mount Sinai. Began at sundown May 28.

SOCCER TRAGEDY: ANNIVERSARY. May 29, 1985. A riot at Heysel stadium at Brussels, Belgium, killed 39 people. Fans attending the European Cup Final, between Liverpool and Juventus of Turin, clashed before the match started. Some 400 people were injured in the riot. The incident was televised and viewed by millions throughout Europe. More than two years later, Sept 2, 1987, the British government announced that 26 British soccer fans (identified from television tapes) would be extradited to Belgium for trial. Hooliganism at soccer matches became the target of increased security measures for England's professional teams following the 1985 tragedy.

SPENGLER, OSWALD: BIRTH ANNIVERSARY. May 29, 1880. German historian, author of *The Decline of the West*, born at Blankenburg-am-Harz, Germany. Died at Munich, Germany, May 8, 1936.

UNITED NATIONS: INTERNATIONAL DAY OF UNITED NATIONS PEACEKEEPERS. May 29. The Assembly has designated May 29 of each year as a day to pay tribute to all the men and women who have served in United Nations peacekeeping operations for their high level of professionalism, dedication and courage, and to honor the memory of those who have lost their lives in the cause of peace (Resolution 57/129, Dec 11, 2002). The Assembly invited all member states, organizations of the United Nations system, non-governmental organizations and individuals to observe the day in an appropriate manner. For info: United Nations, Dept of Public Info, New York, NY 10017. Web: www.un.org.

VIRGINIA PLAN PROPOSED: ANNIVERSARY. May 29, 1787. Just five days after the Constitutional Convention met at Philadelphia, PA, the "Virginia Plan" was proposed. It called for establishment of a new governmental organization consisting of a legislature with two houses, an executive (chosen by the legislature) and a judicial branch.

WISCONSIN: ADMISSION DAY: ANNIVERSARY. May 29. Became 30th state in 1848.

BIRTHDAYS TODAY

Carmelo Anthony, 25, basketball player, born New York, NY, May 29, 1984.

Annette Bening, 51, actress (*Being Julia, American Beauty, The Grifters*), born Topeka, KS, May 29, 1958.

Kevin Conway, 67, actor (*When You Comin' Back, Red Ryder?, Of Mice and Men, Other People's Money*), born New York, NY, May 29, 1942.

Eric Davis, 47, former baseball player, born Los Angeles, CA, May 29, 1962.

Paul Ehrlich, 77, population biologist, born Philadelphia, PA, May 29, 1932.

Melissa Etheridge, 48, singer, guitarist, born Leavenworth, KS, May 29, 1961.

Rupert Everett, 50, actor (*An Ideal Husband, My Best Friend's Wedding*), born Norfolk, England, May 29, 1959.

Anthony Geary, 61, actor ("General Hospital"), born Coalville, UT, May 29, 1948.

Adrian Paul, 50, actor ("Highlander" series), born London, England, May 29, 1959.

Alfred (Al) Unser, Sr, 70, former auto racer, born Albuquerque, NM, May 29, 1939.

Francis Thomas (Fay) Vincent, Jr, 71, former commissioner of baseball, born Waterbury, CT, May 29, 1938.

Lisa Whelchel, 46, actress ("Facts of Life"), born Fort Worth, TX, May 29, 1963.

May 2009	S	M	T	W	T	F	S
						1	2
	3	4	5	6	7	8	9
	10	11	12	13	14	15	16
	17	18	19	20	21	22	23
	24	25	26	27	28	29	30
	31						

May 30 — Saturday

DAY 150 — **215 REMAINING**

BATTLE OF THE ALEUTIAN ISLANDS: ANNIVERSARY. May 30, 1943. The islands of Kiska and Attu in the Aleutian Islands off the coast of Alaska were retaken by the US 7th Infantry Division. The battle (Operation Landgrab) began when an American force of 11,000 landed on Attu May 12. In three weeks of fighting, US casualties numbered 552 killed and 1,140 wounded. Only 28 wounded Japanese were taken prisoner. Japan's dead amounted to 2,352, of whom 500 committed suicide.

BLANC, MEL: BIRTH ANNIVERSARY. May 30, 1908. The greatest voice artist in history, Mel Blanc was born at San Francisco, CA. He performed more than 400 voices in his career, but he is best remembered for "Loonie Tunes" and "Merrie Melodies" in which he performed the voices of Bugs Bunny, Elmer Fudd, Porky Pig, Sylvester, Tweetie Pie and Road Runner. He died on June 10, 1989, at Los Angeles, CA.

CULLEN, COUNTEE: BIRTH ANNIVERSARY. May 30, 1903. One of the leading poets of the Harlem Renaissance (*Color*, 1925). He died at New York City, Jan 9, 1946.

FABERGÉ, CARL: BIRTH ANNIVERSARY. May 30, 1846. The goldsmith, designer and jeweler Peter Carl Fabergé was born on this date at St. Petersburg, Russia. He made the House of Fabergé an internationally known name with fantastical bejeweled decorative objects. His workshop began creating the famous imperial Easter eggs for czars Alexander III and Nicholas II in 1885. After the Russian Revolution, the Bolsheviks shut down the House of Fabergé, and the family fled the country. Fabergé died at Lausanne, France, on Sept 24, 1920. (His birth date was May 18 on the Old Style [Julian] calendar.)

FAIRMOUNT ACADEMY 1800s FESTIVAL. May 30. Fairmount, MD. Rain date the following Saturday. Restored school, spelling bees, square dancing, quilt show, folk arts and crafts, music and plenty of good food. Annually, the last Saturday in May. Est attendance: 2,500. For info: Nevette Muir, Fairmount Academy Historical Assn, PO Box 134, Upper Fairmount, MD 21867. Phone: (410) 651-0351 or (410) 651-3945.

FIRST AMERICAN DAILY NEWSPAPER PUBLISHED: ANNIVERSARY. May 30, 1783. *The Pennsylvania Evening Post* became the first daily newspaper published in the US. The paper was published at Philadelphia, PA, by Benjamin Towne.

GOODMAN, BENNY: 100th BIRTH ANNIVERSARY. May 30, 1909. Jazz clarinetist and bandleader, born Benjamin David Goodman at Chicago, IL. The "King of Swing" reigned in popularity, especially in the 1930s and 1940s. His band was the first to play jazz at New York's Carnegie Hall. He died June 13, 1986, at New York, NY.

INDIANAPOLIS 500: ANNIVERSARY. May 30, 1911. Ray Harroun won the first Indy 500, averaging 74.6 mph. The race was created by

Carl Fisher, who in 1909 replaced the stone surface of his 2.5-mile racetrack with a brick one—hence the nickname "The Brickyard."

ISLE OF MAN: TOURIST TROPHY. May 30–June 12. For two weeks of every year the eyes of the world focus on the Isle of Man as the finest road racers on the planet pit their skills against the 37¾ miles of public roads that form the legendary TT circuit. Starting at the capital, Douglas, up to 600 competitors rocket around the "Jewel of the Irish Sea" at speeds of up to 200 mph. First held in 1907. Est attendance: 35,000. For info: Isle of Man Department of Tourism and Leisure, IOM TT Team, 2nd Fl, St. Andrew's House, Finch Rd, Isle of Man IM1 2PX. E-mail: info@iomtt.com. Web: www.iomtt.com.

LINCOLN MEMORIAL DEDICATION: ANNIVERSARY. May 30, 1922. The memorial is made of marble from Colorado and Tennessee and limestone from Indiana. It stands in West Potomac Park at Washington, DC. The memorial was designed by architect Henry Bacon and its cornerstone was laid in 1915. A skylight lets light into the interiors where the compelling statue *Seated Lincoln*, by sculptor Daniel Chester French, is situated.

LOOMIS DAY. May 30. To honor Mahlon Loomis, a Washington, DC, dentist who received a US patent on wireless telegraphy in 1872 (before Marconi was born). Titled "An Improvement in Telegraphing," the patent described how to do without wires; this patent was backed up by experiment on the Massanutten Mountains of Virginia. For info: Robert L. Birch, Puns Corps, 3108 Dashiell Rd, Falls Church, VA 22042. Phone: (703) 533-3668.

MEMORIAL DAY (TRADITIONAL). May 30. This day honors the tradition of making memorial tributes to the dead, especially remembering those who have died in battle. Observed as a legal public holiday on the last Monday in May.

MOON PHASE: FIRST QUARTER. May 30. Moon enters First Quarter phase at 11:22 PM, EDT.

PETER I: BIRTH ANNIVERSARY. May 30, 1672. Peter I (Peter the Great), Czar and Emperor of all the Russias. His primary aim was to make Russia a major power equal to its size and potential, and the way he saw to do this was through education and technology. He established printing presses and published translations of foreign books, particularly scientific and technical material. The Russian alphabet was simplified, and Arabic numerals were introduced. Peter encouraged trade with foreign countries, mercantilism within Russia and the entrepreneurial skills of resident foreigners; he allowed industrialists to own serfs, a right previously limited to landholders. He completely overhauled the government, the Russian Orthodox Church, the military system and the structure of taxes, ultimately increasing the power of the monarchy at the expense of the nobility and the national church. Upon his death, Jan 28, 1725, he was succeeded by his wife, Catherine.

RIPKEN STREAK BEGINS: ANNIVERSARY. May 30, 1982. Baltimore Oriole Cal Ripken took the baseball field on this date and began a consecutive-games-played streak that lasted for 2,130 games—a major league record. His streak ended Sept 6, 1995.

SAINT JOAN OF ARC: FEAST DAY. May 30. French heroine and martyr, known as the "Maid of Orleans," led the French against the English invading army. Captured, found guilty of heresy and burned at the stake in 1431 (at age 19). Innocence declared in 1456. Canonized in 1920.

SPACE MILESTONE: *MARINER 9* (US). May 30, 1971. Unmanned spacecraft was launched, entering Martian orbit the following Nov 13. The craft relayed temperature and gravitational field information and sent back spectacular photographs of both the surface of Mars and its two moons. First spacecraft to orbit another planet.

TRINIDAD: INDIAN ARRIVAL DAY. May 30. Port of Spain, West Indies. Public holiday. For info: Info Dept, Tourism Div, Tourism and Industrial Development Co, Trinidad and Tobago Ltd, 10–14 Phillips St, West Indies. Phone: (800) 595-1868.

WORLD TRADE CENTER RECOVERY AND CLEANUP ENDS: ANNIVERSARY. May 30, 2002. New York, NY. A solemn and mostly silent ceremony marked the symbolic end of recovery operations at Ground Zero, the former site of the World Trade Center, after the Sept 11, 2001, terrorist attacks. The last standing steel girder was cut down on May 28. An honor guard carried an empty stretcher draped with an American flag to represent those victims who were not recovered from the ruins. Members of the NYFD and NYPD and city, state and federal workers, as well as family members and Ground Zero recovery teams, participated in the ceremony.

BIRTHDAYS TODAY

Blake Bashoff, 28, actor (*Bushwhacked, Big Bully*), born Philadelphia, PA, May 30, 1981.

Keir Dullea, 73, actor (*David and Lisa, 2001: A Space Odyssey*), born Cleveland, OH, May 30, 1936.

Bob Evans, 91, restaurant executive, born Sugar Ridge, OH, May 30, 1918.

Steven Gerrard, 29, soccer player, born Liverpool, England, May 30, 1980.

Wynonna Judd, 45, singer (*Wynonna*, "Tell Me Why"), winner of six Grammy awards, born Ashland, KY, May 30, 1964.

Ted McGinley, 51, actor ("Married . . . With Children," *Revenge of the Nerds*), born Newport Beach, CA, May 30, 1958.

Colm Meaney, 56, actor ("Star Trek: Deep Space Nine,""Star Trek: The Next Generation," *Layer Cake, Last of the Mohicans*), born Dublin, Ireland, May 30, 1953.

Trey Parker, 37, director, creator ("South Park"), born Auburn, AL, May 30, 1972.

Michael J. Pollard, 70, actor (*Bonnie and Clyde*, "Leo & Liz in Beverly Hills"), born Passaic, NJ, May 30, 1939.

Manny Ramirez, 37, baseball player, born Santo Domingo, Dominican Republic, May 30, 1972.

Gale Eugene Sayers, 66, Hall of Fame football player, born Wichita, KS, May 30, 1943.

Stephen Tobolowsky, 58, actor (*The Grifters, Groundhog Day*), born Dallas, TX, May 30, 1951.

Clint Walker, 82, actor (*The Dirty Dozen*, "Cheyenne"), born Hartford, IL, May 30, 1927.

May 31 — Sunday

DAY 151 | **214 REMAINING**

AMECHE, DON: BIRTH ANNIVERSARY. May 31, 1908. Film, stage, radio and TV actor. Born Dominic Felix Amici at Kenosha, WI, and died Dec 6, 1993, at Scottsdale, AZ.

BLACK SINGLE PARENTS' WEEK. May 31–June 6. This week is to honor all the black single parents who have successfully raised their sons and daughters despite poor schools, crime and drug-infested neighborhoods to be responsible, self-sufficient (and sometimes famous) citizens. For info: Will Barnes, Exec Dir, The Black Single Parents' Network, 7732 S Cottage Grove, #431, Chicago, IL 60619. Phone: (773) 933-1061. Fax: (773) 933-1059. E-mail: wwillbar@gmail.com.

COPYRIGHT LAW PASSED: ANNIVERSARY. May 31, 1790. President George Washington signed the first US copyright law. It gave protection for 14 years to books written by US citizens. In 1891 the law was extended to cover books by foreign authors as well.

HARRIS, PATRICIA ROBERTS: 85th BIRTH ANNIVERSARY. May 31, 1924. Born at Matoon, IL. The first African-American woman to serve in an ambassadorial post, the first African American to hold a cabinet position (Secretary of Housing and Urban Development) and the first woman to serve as dean of a law school. Died Mar 23, 1985.

INTERNATIONAL CARILLON FESTIVAL. May 31–June 6. Springfield, IL. A week of recitals by the world's best carillonneurs on Washington Park's carillon of 67 bronze bells. Since it began in 1961, this has become the world's best-known carillon festival. Est attendance: 25,000. For info: Karl Keldermans, Springfield Park District, 2500 S 11th St, Springfield, IL 62703. Phone: (217) 753-6219. E-mail: KKRees@Carillon-Rees.org.

ITALY: PALIO DEI BALESTRIERI. May 31. Gubbio. The last Sunday in May is set aside for a medieval crossbow contest between Gubbio and Sansepolcro; medieval costumes, arms.

JOHNSTOWN FLOOD: ANNIVERSARY. May 31, 1889. Heavy rains caused the Connemaugh River Dam to burst. At nearby Johnstown, PA, the resulting flood killed more than 2,300 people and destroyed the homes of thousands more. Nearly 800 unidentified drowning victims were buried in a common grave at Johnstown's Grandview Cemetery. So devastating was the flood and so widespread the sorrow for its victims that "Johnstown Flood" entered the language as a phrase to describe a disastrous event. The valley city of Johnstown, in the Allegheny Mountains, has been damaged repeatedly by floods. Floods in 1936 (25 deaths) and 1977 (85 deaths) were the next most destructive.

PEALE, NORMAN VINCENT: BIRTH ANNIVERSARY. May 31, 1898. American religious leader Norman Vincent Peale was born at Bowersville, OH. He is best known for his book *The Power of Positive Thinking* (1952), which combines religion and psychiatry. He was a minister at the Marble Collegiate Church at New York, NY. He died Dec 24, 1993, at Pawling, NY.

PENTECOST. May 31. The Christian feast of Pentecost commemorates the descent of the Holy Spirit unto the Apostles, 50 days after Easter. Observed on the seventh Sunday after Easter. Recognized since the third century. See also: "Whitsunday" (below).

POPE PIUS XI: BIRTH ANNIVERSARY. May 31, 1857. Ambrogio Damiano Achille Ratti, 259th pope of the Roman Catholic Church, born at Desio, Italy. Elected pope Feb 6, 1922. Died Feb 10, 1939, at Rome, Italy.

PRINCE RAINIER OF MONACO: BIRTH ANNIVERSARY. May 31, 1923. Born Prince Rainier Louis Henri Maxence Bertrand in the small principality of Monaco, he ascended the throne in 1949. In 1956 he married Hollywood actress Grace Kelly and Monaco soon became the glamour destination for the rich and famous. By changing tax shelter laws and encouraging the casino industry, Rainier changed the destiny of his country, bringing it back from the brink of bankruptcy to become one of the wealthiest nations in Europe. He was Europe's longest-reigning monarch when he died at Monaco on Apr 6, 2005.

"SEINFELD" TV PREMIERE: ANNIVERSARY. May 31, 1990. "Seinfeld"—the show about nothing—premiered on NBC to wide acclaim. The show revolved around the everyday lives of its four main leads, whose story lines intertwined for some surprising plot twists. Some of the programs concerned relationships, valet parking, annoying dogs and waiting for Chinese food. The cast featured Jerry Seinfeld as himself; Michael Richards as his neighbor, Cosmo Kramer; Julia Louis-Dreyfus as his ex-girlfriend, Elaine Benes; and Jason Alexander as his best friend, George Costanza. The series ended with the May 14, 1998, episode.

May 2009

S	M	T	W	T	F	S
					1	2
3	4	5	6	7	8	9
10	11	12	13	14	15	16
17	18	19	20	21	22	23
24	25	26	27	28	29	30
31						

"SURVIVOR" TV PREMIERE: ANNIVERSARY. May 31, 2000. On this immensely popular "reality TV" show, 16 people were sequestered on a deserted island in Malaysia for 39 days. They competed for the right to remain on the island, with the final survivor winning $1 million. Hosted by Jeff Probst, the show drew a total audience of 51 million people. On Jan 28, 2001, another group of "Survivor" contestants began their stay in the Australian outback; later that year another group went to Africa.

UNITED NATIONS: WORLD NO-TOBACCO DAY. May 31.

WHAT YOU THINK UPON GROWS DAY. May 31. A day to remind people of the power of positive thinking. For info: Stephanie West Allen, PO Box 9311, Denver, CO 80209. Phone: (303) 935-8866. E-mail: stephanie@westallen.com. Web: www.westallen.com.

WHITMAN, WALT: BIRTH ANNIVERSARY. May 31, 1819. Poet and journalist, born at West Hills, Long Island, NY. Whitman's best-known work, *Leaves of Grass* (1855), is a classic of American poetry. His poems celebrated all of modern life, including subjects that were considered taboo at the time. Died Mar 26, 1892, at Camden, NJ.

WHITSUNDAY. May 31. Whitsunday, the seventh Sunday after Easter, is a popular time for baptism. "White Sunday" is named for the white garments formerly worn by the candidates for baptism and occurs at the Christian feast of Pentecost. See also: "Pentecost" (above).

BIRTHDAYS TODAY

Tom Berenger, 59, actor (*Born on the Fourth of July, Major League, Gettysburg*), born Chicago, IL, May 31, 1950.

Clint Eastwood, 79, actor, director (Oscars for *Unforgiven* and *Million Dollar Baby*), born San Francisco, CA, May 31, 1930.

Chris Elliott, 49, writer ("Late Night with David Letterman"), actor ("Get a Life"), born New York, NY, May 31, 1960.

Colin Farrell, 33, actor (*In Bruges, Miami Vice, Alexander, The Recruit*), born Castleknock, Dublin, Ireland, May 31, 1976.

Sharon Gless, 66, actress (Emmy for "Cagney & Lacey"), born Los Angeles, CA, May 31, 1943.

Gregory Harrison, 59, actor ("Logan's Run," "Trapper John, MD"), born Avalon, Catalina Island, CA, May 31, 1950.

Phil Keoghan, 42, television personality, host ("The Amazing Race"), born Christchurch, New Zealand, May 31, 1967.

Kenny Lofton, 42, baseball player, born East Chicago, IN, May 31, 1967.

Roma Maffia, 51, actress ("Chicago Hope," "Nip/Tuck," *Holes*), born New York, NY, May 31, 1958.

Joseph William (Joe) Namath, 66, Hall of Fame football player, former sportscaster, actor, born Beaver Falls, PA, May 31, 1943.

Kyle Secor, 51, actor ("Homicide: Life on the Streets"), born Tacoma, WA, May 31, 1958.

Brooke Shields, 44, actress (*Pretty Baby, The Blue Lagoon*, "Suddenly Susan"), born New York, NY, May 31, 1965.

Lea Thompson, 48, actress ("Caroline in the City," *Back to the Future, Howard the Duck*), born Rochester, MN, May 31, 1961.

Terry Waite, 70, Church of England special envoy, former hostage in Lebanon (1987–91), born Bollington, Cheshire, England, May 31, 1939.

Peter Yarrow, 71, composer, singer (Peter, Paul and Mary), born New York, NY, May 31, 1938.

✦ June ✦

June 1 — Monday

DAY 152 **213 REMAINING**

ADOPT-A-SHELTER-CAT MONTH. June 1–30. To promote the adoption of cats from local shelters, the ASPCA sponsors this important observance. "Make Pet Adoption Your First Option®" is a message the organization promotes throughout the year in an effort to end the euthanasia of all adoptable animals. For info: Media & Communications Dept, ASPCA, New York, NY. Phone: (212) 876-7700, ext 4565. E-mail: shonalib@aspca.org. Web: www.aspca.org.

ATLANTIC, CARIBBEAN AND GULF HURRICANE SEASON. June 1–Nov 30. For info: US Dept of Commerce, Natl Oceanic and Atmospheric Admin, Rockville, MD 20852.

CANCER FROM THE SUN MONTH. June 1–30. To promote education and awareness of the dangers of skin cancer from too much exposure to the sun. Kit of materials available for $15 from this nonprofit organization. For info: Frederick Mayer, Pharmacy Council on Dermatology (PCD), 101 Lucas Valley Rd, Ste 382, San Rafael, CA 94903. Phone: (415) 479-8628. Fax: (415) 479-8608. E-mail: ppsi@aol.com. Web: www.ppsinc.org.

CELIBACY AWARENESS MONTH. June 1–30. A celebration of the "Celibate in the City" club's desire to encourage and reaffirm the Christian commitment to remain celibate until marriage. For info: Audrey Miller, Celibate in the City, 165-08 Liberty Ave, Ste 127, Jamaica, NY 11433. Phone: (877) 422-2782. Fax: (718) 849-4696. E-mail: info@celibateinthecity.com. Web: www.celibateinthecity.com.

CENTRAL PACIFIC HURRICANE SEASON. June 1–Oct 31. Central Pacific is defined as 140° west longitude to the International Date Line (180° west longitude). For info: Natl Dept of Commerce, Natl Oceanic and Atmospheric Admin, Rockville, MD 20852.

CHILD VISION AWARENESS MONTH. June 1–30. To better educate and counsel the public on children's vision problems and detection of eye diseases in infants and children, to increase the number of school-aged children who have an eye exam by an eye doctor and to increase the number of children with learning disabilities having a developmental vision exam to rule out vision problems. There is a $15 charge for kit materials. For info: PPSI, c/o Pharmacy Council on Vision Care, 101 Lucas Valley Rd, Ste 382, San Rafael, CA 94903. Phone: (415) 479-8628. Fax: (415) 479-8608. E-mail: ppsi@aol.com. Web: www.ppsinc.org.

CHILDREN'S AWARENESS MONTH. June 1–30. A monthlong celebration of America's children in our everyday lives and communities. We choose to remember our children and grandchildren during the month of June by celebrating the gift of children. For info: Judith Natale, CEO & Founder, NCAC America-USA, PO Box 493703, Redding, CA 96049-3703. E-mail: childaware@aol.com.

CHINA: INTERNATIONAL CHILDREN'S DAY. June 1. Shanghai.

CNN DEBUT: ANNIVERSARY. June 1, 1980. The Cable News Network, TV's first all-news service, went on the air.

DAIRY ALTERNATIVES MONTH. June 1–30. This event encourages consumers to eliminate dairy products from their diets and explore alternative foods made from beans, nuts or grains. For info: VEGANET, PO Box 3545, Washington, DC 20027-0045. Phone: (800) 280-8343.

EFFECTIVE COMMUNICATIONS MONTH. June 1–30. The most important cog in the wheel of interpersonal relationships is communication. Active listening, verbal language, paralanguage, body language and written communication skills are the essence of how humans relate to each other personally and professionally. This month is dedicated to learning how to, improving upon, and committing to communicating more effectively in our lives. For info: Sylvia Henderson, Springboard Training, PO Box 588, Olney, MD 20830-0588. Phone: (301) 260-1538. E-mail: sylvia@springboardtraining.com. Web: www.springboardtraining.com.

ENGLAND: DICING FOR BIBLES. June 1. An old Whitmonday ceremony at All Saints Church, St. Ives, Huntingdonshire. A bequest (in 1675) with the intent of providing Bibles for poor children of the parish required winning them at a dice game played in the church. In recent years the dicing has been moved from the altar to a "more suitable" place. Six Bibles are given on Whitmonday each year.

ENTREPRENEURS "DO IT YOURSELF" MARKETING MONTH. June 1–30. Stand out from your competition and get media attention and more clients, while achieving your goals. Are you looking for better results from your marketing efforts? Would you like to become a new resource the media calls? Remember, your success is a matter of choice, not chance. Discover and apply creative and effective problem-solving marketing ideas that will help you gain the competitive edge. Act now and remove the barriers that are stopping you from achieving your goals. Pamphlet available for $5. For info: Lorrie Walters Marsiglio, Lorimar Communications, PO Box 284-CC, Wasco, IL 60183-0284. Phone: (630) 584-9368.

FIREWORKS SAFETY MONTHS. June 1–July 31. Activities during this period will alert parents and children about the dangers of playing with fireworks. Prevent Blindness America® will offer suggestions for safer ways to celebrate the Fourth of July. For info: Prevent Blindness America®, 211 W Wacker Dr, Ste 1700, Chicago, IL 60606. Phone: (800) 331-2020. E-mail: info@preventblindness.org. Web: www.preventblindness.org.

GAY AND LESBIAN PRIDE MONTH. June 1–30. Observed this month because on June 28, 1969, the clientele of a gay bar at New York City rioted after the club was raided by the police. President Clinton issued presidential proclamations for this month, but President Bush did not declare it during his administration. See also: "Stonewall Riot: Anniversary" (June 28).

✦ **GREAT OUTDOORS MONTH.** June 1–30. To celebrate the rich blessings of our nation's natural beauty and renew our commitment to protecting the environment, to keep our country's open spaces beautiful and accessible to our citizens.

HEIMLICH MANEUVER INTRODUCED: 35th ANNIVERSARY. June 1, 1974. The June issue of the journal *Emergency Medicine* published an article by Dr. Henry Heimlich outlining a better method for aiding choking victims. Instead of the prevailing method of backslaps (which merely pushed foreign objects farther into the airways), Dr. Heimlich advocated "subdiaphragmatic pressure" to force objects out. Three months later, the method was dubbed "the Heimlich Maneuver" by the *Journal of the American Medical Association.*

INTERNATIONAL CHILDHOOD CANCER CAMPAIGN MONTH. June 1–30. Optimist Clubs worldwide will plan and hold special events that benefit patients, families and caregivers associated with pediatric oncology. Events will range from picnics to fund-raisers. For info: Optimist International, 4494 Lindell Blvd, St. Louis, MO 63106. Phone: (800) 500-8130. Fax: (314) 371-6006. Web: www.optimist.org.

INTERNATIONAL MEN'S MONTH. June 1–30. This program was initiated in 1996 to increase media and local community awareness of the many unique issues that impact men's lives and that are of concern to the people who love them. In an effort to promote positive changes in male roles and relationships, a different issue is addressed each day of the month during June, and information and resources on that issue are provided on the website. This free information can be received automatically by signing up at menstuff-html-subscribe@topica.com. For info: Gordon Clay, PO Box 1080-CH, Brookings, OR 97415-0024. E-mail: menstuff@aol.com. Web: www.menstuff.org.

JUNE DAIRY MONTH. June 1–30. Observed since 1937. Promotes national awareness of the quality and nutritional benefits of refrigerated dairy foods. For info: Julie Henderson, Natl Frozen & Refrigerated Foods Assn, 4755 Linglestown Rd, Ste 300, Harrisburg, PA 17112. Phone: (717) 657-8601. Fax: (717) 657-9862. E-mail: info@nfraweb.org. Web: www.nfraweb.org.

JUNE IS PERENNIAL GARDENING MONTH. June 1–30. June is the perfect month to celebrate the versatility and beauty of perennial garden plants. We'll offer some good gardening tips on how to keep your perennial garden beautiful all season long and highlight many individual perennials that bloom for the month of June. For info: Steven Still, 3383 Schrirtzinger Rd, Hilliard, OH 43026. Phone: (614) 771-8431. E-mail: ppa@perennialplant.org. Web: www.perennialplant.org.

JUNE IS TURKEY LOVERS' MONTH. June 1–30. Monthlong campaign to promote awareness and increase turkey consumption at a nonholiday time. Annually, the month of June. For info: Natl Turkey Federation, 1225 New York Ave NW, Ste 400, Washington, DC 20005. Phone: (202) 898-0100. Fax: (202) 898-0203. E-mail: info@turkeyfed.org. Web: www.eatturkey.com.

KENTUCKY: ADMISSION DAY: ANNIVERSARY. June 1. Became 15th state in 1792.

KENYA: MADARAKA DAY. June 1. Madaraka Day (Self-Rule Day) is observed as a national public holiday. Commemorates attainment of self-government in 1963.

LITTLE, CLEAVON: 70th BIRTH ANNIVERSARY. June 1, 1939. Best known for his role as the black sheriff who cleaned up a town of bumbling redneck toughs in the movie *Blazing Saddles*, Cleavon Little was born at Chickasha, OK. Little was the winner of a Tony award for the 1970 musical *Purlie* and an Emmy in 1989 for a guest appearance on the television series "Dear John." Died Oct 22, 1992, near Sherman Oaks, CA.

June 2009	S	M	T	W	T	F	S
		1	2	3	4	5	6
	7	8	9	10	11	12	13
	14	15	16	17	18	19	20
	21	22	23	24	25	26	27
	28	29	30				

MARQUETTE, JACQUES: BIRTH ANNIVERSARY. June 1, 1637. Father Jacques Marquette (Père Marquette), Jesuit missionary-explorer of the Great Lakes region. Born at Laon, France. Died at Ludington, MI, May 18, 1675.

MONROE, MARILYN: BIRTH ANNIVERSARY. June 1, 1926. American actress and sex symbol of the '50s, born at Los Angeles as Norma Jean Mortensen or Baker. She had an unstable childhood in a series of orphanages and foster homes. Her film career came to epitomize Hollywood glamour. In 1954 she wed Yankee legend "Jolting Joe" DiMaggio, but the marriage didn't last. Monroe remained fragile and insecure, tormented by the pressures of Hollywood life. Her death from an overdose Aug 5, 1962, at Los Angeles shocked the world. Among her films: *The Seven Year Itch, Bus Stop, Some Like It Hot, Gentlemen Prefer Blondes* and *The Misfits.*

NATIONAL ACCORDION AWARENESS MONTH. June 1–30. To increase public awareness of this multicultural instrument and its influence and popularity in today's music. For info: Tom Torriglia, All Things Accordion, PO Box 475136, San Francisco, CA 94147-5136. Phone: (415) 440-0800. E-mail: tom@ladyofspain.com. Web: www.ladyofspain.com.

NATIONAL APHASIA AWARENESS MONTH. June 1–30. More than one million Americans have acquired aphasia. Aphasia is a language-processing disorder that impairs a person's ability to speak or understand speech. The mission of the National Aphasia Association (NAA) is to reduce the social and emotional consequences of aphasia by raising awareness of and giving a voice to people who cannot use their own. Annually, the month of June. For info: National Aphasia Assn, 350 Seventh Ave, Ste 902, New York, NY 10001. Phone: (800) 922-4622. E-mail: naa@aphasia.org. Web: www.aphasia.org.

NATIONAL BATHROOM READING MONTH. June 1–30. Since 1988, the Bathroom Readers' Institute has led the movement to stand up for those who sit down and read in the bathroom. National Bathroom Reading Month celebrates the 66 percent of Americans who proudly admit to this time-honored pastime. For info: Bathroom Readers' Institute, PO Box 1117, Ashland, OR 97520. Phone: (212) 465-1290. Fax: (212) 465-1299. E-mail: bathroomreader@stylegroup.com. Web: www.bathroomreader.com.

NATIONAL CANDY MONTH. June 1–30. Celebrated throughout the confectionary industry. Retailers will host special events in stores, and there will be special promotions and merchandising contests. Get the facts on these fun products: candy is good food and can definitely be enjoyed as part of a balanced diet. A great month to host a special candy event. Logo available for use. For info: Lisbeth Echeandia, American Consulting Corporation, PO Box 388, Savoy, TX 75479. Phone: (903) 965-9300. Fax: (903) 965-9144. E-mail: lisbeth@texoma.net.

NATIONAL GLBT BOOK MONTH. June 1–30. Created to increase the recognition of gay, lesbian, bisexual and transgender writing. Begun in 1992 by the Publishing Triangle, June was selected in honor of the anniversary of the 1969 Stonewall Riot in New York City. It was this brave resistance to police harassment that kick-started the gay pride movement in the US. Libraries, bookstores, publishers and bibliophiles everywhere are invited to form a chorus line and celebrate with the community. Annually, the month of June. For info: Gay Lesbian Bisexual Transgender Roundtable, c/o American Library Assn, Office for Literacy and Outreach Services, 50 E Huron St, Chicago, IL 60611. Web: www.ala.org/ala/glbtrt/welcomeglbtround.htm.

NATIONAL GO BAREFOOT DAY. June 1. Nashville-based charity Soles4Souls™ Inc, the global organization dedicated to providing free footwear to people in need all over the world, invites people to go barefoot and show their support in putting shoes on the feet of the more than 300 million children around the world without footwear. For info: Kim Dettwiller, Soles4Soles Inc, 2900 Lebanon Rd, Suite 410, Nashville, TN 37214. Phone: (615) 391-5723. Fax: (615) 391-5730. E-mail: kimd@soles4soles.org. Web: www.soles4soles.org or www.giveshoes.org.

NATIONAL ICED TEA MONTH. June 1–30. To celebrate one of the most widely consumed beverages in the world and one of nature's most perfect beverages, and to encourage Americans to refresh themselves with this all-natural, low-calorie, refreshing thirst-quencher. For info: The Tea Council of the USA, 362 Fifth Ave, Ste 801, New York, NY 10001. Phone: (212) 986-6998. Fax: (212) 697-8658. E-mail: info@teausa.org. Web: www.teausa.org.

NATIONAL RIVERS MONTH. June 1–30. Commemorated by local groups in many states.

NATIONAL ROSE MONTH. June 1–30. To recognize American-grown roses, our national floral emblem. America's favorite flower is grown in all 50 states and more than 1.2 billion fresh-cut roses are sold at retail each year. For info: International Cut Flower Growers. Web: www.rosesinc.org.

NATIONAL SAFETY MONTH. June 1–30. Founded in 1913 and chartered by the US Congress in 1953, the National Safety Council is the nation's only organization committed to promoting safety in all aspects of American life. National Safety Month addresses the nation's safety issues in the home and community, on our roads and highways and in our workplaces. For info: Natl Safety Council, 1121 Spring Lake Dr, Itasca, IL 60143-3201. Phone: (800) 621-7615. Web: www.nsc.org.

NATIONAL SOUL FOOD MONTH. June 1–30. A month to recognize, educate and celebrate the heritage and history of the foods and foodways of African Americans and peoples from the African diaspora. The culinary contributions of this group have had an indelible impact on the menu of the American table and on mainstream American life and culture. For info: Culinary Historians of Chicago, PO Box 805987, Chicago, IL 60680. E-mail: chc2001@earthlink.net. Web: www.culinaryhistorians.org.

NATIONAL STEAKHOUSE MONTH. June 1–30. To celebrate the steakhouse, that uniquely American restaurant, and to recognize and promote the art of expert grilling. Sponsored by Morton's, The Steakhouse, the world's leading fine-dining restaurant brand. For info: Patty Pleuss, VP, Sales & Mktg, Morton's, The Restaurant, 325 N LaSalle, Ste 500, Chicago, IL 60610. Phone: (312) 755-4202. E-mail: ppleuss@mortons.com. Web: www.mortons.com.

PHARMACISTS DECLARE WAR ON ALCOHOLISM. June 1–30. To encourage pharmacists, health care professionals and consumers to better educate and counsel the public on alcoholism and other substance abuse illnesses. By promoting alcohol abuse awareness and education to health care professionals and the general public, PCAA strives to break the stereotype surrounding alcoholism that keeps millions of Americans from receiving proper treatment. There is a $15 charge for kit materials. For info: Pharmacists Planning Service, Inc, Pharmacy Council on Alcohol Abuse, 101 Lucas Valley Rd, Ste 382, San Rafael, CA 94903. Phone: (415) 479-8628. Fax: (415) 479-8608. E-mail: ppsi@aol.com. Web: www.ppsinc.org.

PLYMOUTH PLANTATION EARTHQUAKE: ANNIVERSARY. June 1, 1638. The first earthquake in the US to have been recorded and described in writing occurred at Plymouth, MA, at 2 PM. Governor William Bradford described the event in his *History*: "It was very terrible for ye time; and as ye men were set talking in ye house, some women and others were without ye doors, and ye earth shooke with ye violence as they could not stand without catching hold of ye posts . . . but ye violence lasted not long. And about halfe an hower, or less, came an other noyse & shaking, but neither so loud nor strong as ye former, but quickly passed over, and so it ceased."

POTTY TRAINING AWARENESS MONTH. June 1–30. Potty training can be an exciting yet frustrating time for parents. That's why Pull-Ups® Training Pants sponsors this month devoted to educating parents about the potty training process and helping make this milestone in a child's life easier. Annually, the month of June. For info: Sara Corbett, Edelman Public Relations, 200 E Randolph St, 63rd Fl, Chicago, IL 60601. Phone: (312) 616-1697. Fax: (312) 240-1501. E-mail: sara.corbett@edelman.com. Web: www.pull-ups.com.

"THE PRISONER" TV PREMIERE: ANNIVERSARY. June 1, 1968. "The Prisoner" was one of the most imaginative shows on TV, regarded by some as the finest dramatic series in TV history. Patrick McGoohan, who produced and starred in the series, also wrote and directed some episodes. In the series, McGoohan found himself in a self-contained community known as "the village" where he was referred to, not by name, but as Number 6. Number 6 realized he was a prisoner and spent most of the series trying to escape or to learn the identity of the leader, Number 1.

PROFESSIONAL WELLNESS MONTH. June 1–30. Increase your worth in the marketplace. Add value to your company and your customers. Be accessible, reliable and fair. Update your resume, increase your skills and learn your business completely. Become a source of reference: be visible, attend meetings and company or community socials. For info: Angela Brown Oberer, Words of Wellness, PO Box 49266, Charlotte, NC 28277. Phone: (704) 849-2900. E-mail: Angela@WordsofWellness.com. Web: www.WordsofWellness.com.

REBUILD YOUR LIFE MONTH. June 1–30. This is an opportunity for adults neglected and/or abused as children to celebrate their self-worth and discover inner power. They can learn to heal their lives and emotional pain by helping others. For info send SASE: Donald Etkes, PhD, 11693 San Vicente Blvd, #491, Los Angeles, CA 90049. Phone: (310) 979-0245. E-mail: drdonetkes@aol.com. Web: www.abusehealing.com.

SAMOA: INDEPENDENCE DAY. June 1. National holiday. Commemorates independence from New Zealand in 1962. The former Western Samoa changed its name in 1997.

***SGT PEPPER'S LONELY HEARTS CLUB BAND* RELEASED: ANNIVERSARY.** June 1, 1967. After 700 hours of studio work, the Beatles released what many consider one of the greatest rock albums of the 20th century. No singles were released, but the album included such popular tracks as "Lucy in the Sky with Diamonds," "With a Little Help from My Friends," "When I'm Sixty-Four" and "A Day in the Life."

SPORTS AMERICA KIDS MONTH. June 1–30. To encourage the health and well-being of all America's children. Physical fitness and healthy thinking, through the efforts of teamwork with individual self-esteem, can help America's children to appreciate the gift of life and the value of respecting the lives of others. A time for adults and kids to embrace the wonderful outdoors and the benefits of healthy living with physical fitness. For info: Judith Natale, NCAC America-USA, PO Box 493703, Redding, CA 96049-3703. E-mail: childaware@aol.com.

STUDENT SAFETY MONTH. June 1–30. Heightening the awareness of safety and making sound decisions following graduations, parties, senior proms and other special events. Encourages young people everywhere not to drink and drive and to use good judgment while celebrating throughout the month. For info: Carole Copeland Thomas, 400 W Cummings Pk, Ste 1725-154, Woburn, MA 01801. Phone: (508) 947-5755. Fax: (508) 947-3903. E-mail: carole@TellCarole.com. Web: www.TellCarole.com.

SUPERMAN DEBUTS: ANNIVERSARY. June 1, 1938. Ohio teenagers Joe Shuster and Jerry Siegel wowed the comic book world with a new kind of pulp hero: Superman. Superman, a refugee with super powers from the planet Krypton, appeared in the June issue of *Action Comics* #1 (issues probably hit the newsstands in late May of 1938). Now a pop culture icon, Superman was then a smash hit who ushered in many more fantastical superheroes. See also: "Batman Debuts: Anniversary" (May 1).

TENNESSEE: ADMISSION DAY: ANNIVERSARY. June 1. Became 16th state in 1796. Observed as a holiday in Tennessee.

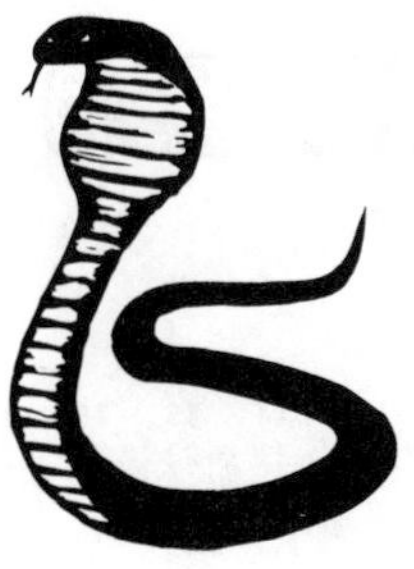

TOOLS OF THE TRADE. June 1–30. Jamestown Settlement, Williamsburg, VA, and Yorktown Victory Center, Yorktown, VA. Implements used for farming, fishing, hunting, defense, navigation and building by people of 17th- and 18th-century Virginia are examined through interpretive programs and hands-on activities. For info: Jamestown-Yorktown Foundation, PO Box 1607, Williamsburg, VA 23187. Phone: (757) 253-4838 or toll-free (888) 593-4682. Fax: (757) 253-5299. Web: www.historyisfun.org.

VISION RESEARCH MONTH. June 1–30. While millions of Americans benefit from vision research, many eye diseases have no effective treatments or cures. An overview of vision research successes and the urgent need for future studies will be offered. For info: Prevent Blindness America®, 211 W Wacker Dr, Ste 1700, Chicago, IL 60606. Phone: (800) 331-2020. E-mail: info@preventblindness.org. Web: www.preventblindness.org.

WHITMONDAY. June 1. The day after Whitsunday is observed as a public holiday in some countries.

YOUNG, BRIGHAM: BIRTH ANNIVERSARY. June 1, 1801. Mormon church leader born at Whittingham, VT. Known as "the American Moses," having led thousands of religious followers across 1,000 miles of wilderness to settle more than 300 towns in the West. He died at Salt Lake City, UT, Aug 29, 1877, and was survived by 17 wives and 47 children. Utah observes, as a state holiday, the anniversary of his entrance into the Salt Lake Valley, July 24, 1847.

BIRTHDAYS TODAY

Rene Auberjonois, 69, stage and screen actor (*M*A*S*H*, "Benson"; Tony Award for *Coco*), born New York, NY, June 1, 1940.

James Hadley Billington, 80, Librarian of Congress, born Bryn Mawr, PA, June 1, 1929.

Lisa Hartman Black, 53, actress ("Tabitha," "Knots Landing"), born Houston, TX, June 1, 1956.

Pat Boone, 75, singer, actor (*State Fair*), author, born Jacksonville, FL, June 1, 1934.

Mark Curry, 45, comedian, actor ("Hangin' with Mr Cooper"), born Oakland, CA, June 1, 1964.

Morgan Freeman, 72, stage and film actor (Oscar for *Million Dollar Baby*; *The Shawshank Redemption, Driving Miss Daisy*), born Memphis, TN, June 1, 1937.

Andy Griffith, 83, actor ("Matlock," "The Andy Griffith Show"), born Mount Airy, NC, June 1, 1926.

Justine Henin, 27, tennis player, born Liege, Belgium, June 1, 1982.

Alexi Lalas, 39, soccer executive and former player, born Detroit, MI, June 1, 1970.

Alanis Morissette, 35, singer, born Ottawa, ON, Canada, June 1, 1974.

Jonathan Pryce, 62, actor (*Glengarry Glen Ross*; stage: *Miss Saigon*, Tony Award for *Hamlet*), born Holywell, North Wales, June 1, 1947.

Frederica von Stade, 64, opera mezzo-soprano, born Somerville, NJ, June 1, 1945.

Ron Wood, 62, musician (guitarist with the Rolling Stones), born London, England, June 1, 1947.

Edward Woodward, 79, actor, singer ("The Equalizer," *Wicker Man, Breaker Morant*), born Croydon, England, June 1, 1930.

Carlos Zambrano, 28, baseball player, born Puerto Cabello, Venezuela, June 1, 1981.

June 2009

S	M	T	W	T	F	S
	1	2	3	4	5	6
7	8	9	10	11	12	13
14	15	16	17	18	19	20
21	22	23	24	25	26	27
28	29	30				

June 2 — Tuesday

DAY 153 — **212 REMAINING**

BELGIUM: PROCESSION OF THE GOLDEN CHARIOT. June 2. Mons. Horse-drawn coach carrying a reliquary of St. Waudru circles the town of Mons. Procession commemorates delivery of Mons from the plague in 1349. In the town square, in the afternoon, St. George fights the dragon.

BHUTAN: CORONATION DAY. June 2. National holiday. Commemorates the crowning of the fourth king in 1974.

BLACK HILLS PASSION PLAY—SOUTH DAKOTA. June 2–Aug 30. Passion Play Amphitheater, Spearfish, SD. On Sunday, Tuesday and Thursday evenings. Spectacular outdoor drama on a huge stage depicts the last seven days in the life of Christ. It features a professionally led cast of more than 200 and live animals. Est attendance: 50,000. For info: Black Hills Passion Play—South Dakota, PO Box 489, Spearfish, SD 57783. Phone: (605) 642-2646 or (800) 457-0160. Fax: (605) 642-7993. E-mail: bhpp@blackhills.com. Web: www.theblackhillspassionplay.com.

BULGARIA: HRISTO BOTEV DAY. June 2. Poet and national hero Hristo Botev fell fighting Turks, 1876.

GERMANY: WALDCHESTAG. June 2. Frankfurt. Since the 19th century Frankfurters have spent the Tuesday after Whitsunday in their forest. See also: "Whitsunday" (May 31).

ITALY: REPUBLIC DAY. June 2. National holiday. Commemorates 1946 referendum in which republic status was selected instead of return to monarchy.

MAINE LAW: ANNIVERSARY. June 2, 1851. America's first statewide statute prohibiting the sale of alcoholic beverages was enacted in the state of Maine. The following Independence Day the mayor of Bangor showed his support of the new law by smashing 10 kegs of confiscated booze.

MARQUIS DE SADE: BIRTH ANNIVERSARY. June 2, 1740. Donatien-Alphonse-François, Comte de Sade, was born at Paris, France. French military man, governor-general and author, who spent much of his life in prison because of his acts of cruelty and violence, outrageous behavior and debauchery. The word *sadism* was created from his name to describe gratification in inflicting pain. He died near Paris, at the Charenton lunatic asylum, Dec 2, 1814.

NATIONAL BUBBA DAY. June 2. Comedian T. Bubba Bechtol has created a holiday for Bubbas everywhere. Annually, June 2. For info: T. Bubba Bechtol, 339 Panferio Dr, Pensacola Beach, FL 32561. Phone: (850) 932-3162. E-mail: tbubba@tbubba.com. Web: www.tbubba.com.

NATIONAL LEAVE THE OFFICE EARLIER DAY. June 2. Employees commit to working productively all day so they can get their work done, leave the office earlier and get home to their families. For info: John Stack, The Productivity Pro, 9948 S Cottoncreek Dr, Highlands Ranch, CO 80130. Phone: (303) 471-7401. Fax: (303) 471-4702. E-mail: Laura@TheProductivityPro.com. Web: www.TheProductivityPro.com.

SAINT ERASMUS DAY. June 2. Feast day of Erasmus, also known as Elmo, bishop of Formiae, Campagna, Italy, who was martyred around AD 303. Patron saint of sailors. The blue light seen around ship masts that marks atmospheric electricity is popularly called St. Elmo's Fire from the ancient belief that it signifies the saint's protection of sailors during storms.

SAINT PIUS X: BIRTH ANNIVERSARY. June 2, 1835. Giuseppe Melchiorre Sarto, 257th pope of the Roman Catholic Church, born at Riese, Italy. Elected pope Aug 4, 1903. Died Aug 20, 1914, at Rome. Canonized May 29, 1954.

SALEM WITCH TRIALS BEGIN: ANNIVERSARY. June 2, 1692. As the village of Salem was gripped by terror of witches, Massachusetts Bay Colony governor Sir William Phips ordered a special court created on May 27, 1692, to expedite judgment of the more than 150 people accused of witchcraft. Unpopular resident Bridget Bishop, first accused in April, was the first of the jailed brought to trial on June 2. At her April examination her accusers—teenaged girls—had collapsed in fits as she appeared, but Bishop adamantly denied the charges: "I am no witch—I know not what a witch is." She was convicted June 2 and hung June 10. See also: "Salem Witch Hysteria Begins: Anniversary" (Mar 1).

UNITED KINGDOM: CORONATION DAY: ANNIVERSARY. June 2. Commemorates the crowning of Queen Elizabeth II in 1953.

WEISSMULLER, JOHNNY: BIRTH ANNIVERSARY. June 2, 1904. Peter John (Johnny) Weissmuller, actor and Olympic gold medal swimmer, born at Windber, PA. Weissmuller won three gold medals at the 1924 Olympics and two more at the 1928 games. He set 24 world records and in 1950 was voted the best swimmer of the first half of the 20th century. After retiring from amateur competition, he appeared as Tarzan in a dozen movies and as "Jungle Jim" in the movies and on television. Died at Acapulco, Mexico, Jan 20, 1984.

YELL "FUDGE" AT THE COBRAS IN NORTH AMERICA DAY. June 2. Anywhere north of the Panama Canal. In order to keep poisonous cobra snakes out of North America, all citizens are asked to go outdoors at noon, local time, and yell "Fudge." Fudge makes cobras gag and the mere mention of it makes them skedaddle. Annually, June 2. (©2006 by WH.) For info: Thomas & Ruth Roy, Wellcat Holidays, 2418 Long Ln, Lebanon, PA 17046. Phone: (717) 279-0184. E-mail: info@wellcat.com. Web: www.wellcat.com.

BIRTHDAYS TODAY

Diana Canova, 56, actress ("Soap," "I'm a Big Girl Now"), born West Palm Beach, FL, June 2, 1953.

Dana Carvey, 54, comedian, actor (*Wayne's World*, "Saturday Night Live"), born Missoula, MT, June 2, 1955.

Nikolay Davydenko, 28, tennis player, born Severodonezk, Ukraine, June 2, 1981.

Gary Grimes, 54, actor (*Summer of '42, Class of '44*), born San Francisco, CA, June 2, 1955.

Charles Haid, 66, actor ("Hill Street Blues," "Delvecchio"), producer, born San Francisco, CA, June 2, 1943.

Marvin Hamlisch, 65, composer (Oscars for *The Sting, The Way We Were*; Tony for *A Chorus Line*), born New York, NY, June 2, 1944.

Dennis Haysbert, 55, actor ("24," *Waiting to Exhale, Major League*), born San Mateo, CA, June 2, 1954.

Stacy Keach, Jr, 68, actor (*Conduct Unbecoming*, "Mickey Spillane's Mike Hammer"), born Savannah, GA, June 2, 1941.

Sally Kellerman, 73, actress (*M*A*S*H, Back to School*), born Long Beach, CA, June 2, 1936.

Jerry Mathers, 61, actor ("Leave It to Beaver"), born Sioux City, IA, June 2, 1948.

Wentworth Miller, 37, actor ("Prison Break," *The Human Stain*), born Chipping Norton, Oxfordshire, England, June 2, 1972.

Milo O'Shea, 83, actor (*The Purple Rose of Cairo*), born Dublin, Ireland, June 2, 1926.

Zachary Quinto, 32, actor ("Heroes," "24"), born Pittsburgh, PA, June 2, 1977.

Charlie Watts, 68, musician (drummer with the Rolling Stones), born Islington, England, June 2, 1941.

June 3 — Wednesday

DAY 154 — 211 REMAINING

BAKER, JOSEPHINE: BIRTH ANNIVERSARY. June 3, 1906. The sensation of 1920s Paris, Baker was born into poverty at St. Louis, MO. She began working as a dancer at age 16 and went to Paris in 1925, where her semi-nude "danse sauvage," became a hit. She was the first American-born woman to be awarded the Croix de Guerre and the Legion of Honor for her Red Cross work during WWII. Baker performed up until her death on Apr 12, 1975, at Paris, France.

BATTLE OF COLD HARBOR: ANNIVERSARY. June 3, 1864. Although Confederate Gen Robert E. Lee had placed his troops behind considerable breastworks, Union Gen Ulysses S. Grant launched an all-out attack on the Southern army in Virginia. More than 7,000 Federal troops were killed within one-half hour of battle on the first attack. After a second unsuccessful attack, Grant's orders for a third assault were all but ignored. Battlefield tradition held that the first commander who sought a truce in order to tend to the wounded was the loser. Grant refused to admit defeat by seeking such a truce and the wounded were left on the ground for three days following the battle. As a consequence, all but two of the thousands of wounded men died either from their wounds, hunger, thirst or exposure.

CANADA: THE NATIONAL TOURNAMENT. June 3–7. Spruce Meadows, Calgary, AB. The National Tournament features the Spruce Meadows Show Jumping Championship, including the CN Reliable Grand Prix and the Nexen Cup. Enjoy country atmosphere in the Agrium Country Fair on the Spruce Meadows Plaza. Live entertainment and activities daily. First week of June, Wednesday through Sunday. Est attendance: 85,750. For info: Spruce Meadows, RR 9, Calgary, AB, Canada T2J 5G5. Phone: (403) 974-4200. Fax: (403) 974-4270. E-mail: information@sprucemeadows.com. Web: www.sprucemeadows.com.

CHIMBORAZO DAY. June 3. To bring the shape of the Earth into focus by publicizing the fact that Mount Chimborazo, Ecuador, near the equator, pokes farther out into space than any other mountain on earth, including Mount Everest. (The distance from sea level at the equator to the center of the Earth is 13 miles greater than the radius to sea level at the North Pole. This means that New Orleans is about six miles farther from the center of the Earth than is Lake Itasca at the headwaters of the Mississippi, so the Mississippi flows uphill.) For info: Robert L. Birch, Puns Corps, 3108 Dashiell Rd, Falls Church, VA 22042. Phone: (703) 533-3668.

CONFEDERATE MEMORIAL DAY IN KENTUCKY, LOUISIANA AND TENNESSEE. June 3. Ceremonial holiday on the birthday of Jefferson Davis. Also observed as Jefferson Davis Day in Kentucky and Confederate Decoration Day in Tennessee.

DAVIS, JEFFERSON: BIRTH ANNIVERSARY. June 3, 1808. American statesman, US senator, only president of the Confederate States of America. Imprisoned May 10, 1865–May 13, 1867, but never brought to trial, deprived of rights of citizenship after the Civil War. Davis was born at Todd County, KY, and died at New Orleans, LA, Dec 6, 1889. His citizenship was restored, posthumously, Oct 17, 1978, when President Carter signed an Amnesty Bill. This bill, he said, "officially completes the long process of reconciliation that has reunited our people following the tragic conflict between the states." Davis's birth anniversary is observed in Florida, Kentucky and South Carolina on this day, in Alabama on the first Monday in June and in Mississippi on the last Monday in May. Davis's birth anniversary is observed as Confederate Decoration Day in Tennessee.

DEWHURST, COLLEEN: 85th BIRTH ANNIVERSARY. June 3, 1924. Colleen Dewhurst was born at Quebec, Canada. Her 40-year career as an actress spanned stage, screen and television. After making her Broadway debut in Eugene O'Neill's *Desire Under the Elms* in 1952, she became the actress most associated with O'Neill's works in the later part of the 20th century, also performing in *Long Day's Journey into Night; Mourning Becomes Electra; Ah, Wilderness!* and *A Moon for the Misbegotten*, for which she won her second Tony award. At the time of her death, she was president of Actor's Equity Association, the union for professional actors. She won three Emmy awards. She died Aug 22, 1991, at South Salem, NY.

DREW, CHARLES RICHARD: BIRTH ANNIVERSARY. June 3, 1904. African-American physician who discovered how to store blood plasma and who organized the blood bank system in the US and UK during WWII. Born at Washington, DC, he was killed in an automobile accident near Burlington, NC, Apr 1, 1950.

DUKE OF WINDSOR MARRIAGE: ANNIVERSARY. June 3, 1937. The Duke of Windsor who, as King Edward VIII, had abdicated the British throne on Dec 11, 1936, was married to Mrs Wallis Warfield Simpson of Baltimore, MD, at Monts, France. The couple made their home in France after their marriage and had little contact with the royal family. The Duke died at Paris on May 28, 1972, and was buried near Windsor Castle in England. The Duchess died Apr 24, 1986.

FIRST WOMAN RABBI IN US: ANNIVERSARY. June 3, 1972. Sally Jan Priesand was ordained the first woman rabbi in the US. She became assistant rabbi at the Stephen Wise Free Synagogue, New York City, Aug 1, 1972.

GINSBERG, ALLEN: BIRTH ANNIVERSARY. June 3, 1926. Poet of the Beat Generation ("Howl"), born Newark, NJ. Died Apr 5, 1997, at New York, NY.

HOBART, GARRET AUGUSTUS: BIRTH ANNIVERSARY. June 3, 1844. 24th vice president of the US (1897–99), born at Long Branch, NJ. Died at Paterson, NJ, Nov 21, 1899.

IRELAND: BANK HOLIDAY. June 3. National holiday in the Republic of Ireland.

JACK JOUETT'S RIDE: ANNIVERSARY. June 3, 1781. Jack Jouett made a heroic 45-mile ride on horseback during the night of June 3–4, 1781, to warn Virginia Governor Thomas Jefferson and the legislature that the British were coming. Jouett rode from a tavern in Louisa County to Charlottesville, VA, in about 6½ hours, arriving at Jefferson's home at dawn on June 4. Lieutenant Colonel Tarleton's British forces raided Charlottesville, but Jouett's warning gave the Americans time to escape. Jouett was born at Albemarle County, VA, Dec 7, 1754, and died at Bath, KY, in 1822 (exact date unknown).

KHOMEINI, AYATOLLAH RUHOLLA: 20th DEATH ANNIVERSARY. June 3, 1989. The Ayatollah Ruholla Khomeini, leader of the Islamic Revolution, lifelong foe of the Shah of Iran, was arrested in 1963 after giving a speech accusing the Shah of seeking to destroy Islam. He was exiled to Turkey in 1964, following which he spent 13 years in Iraq and Paris, where he gained exposure to the world press for his cause. On Jan 16, 1979, the Shah of Iran left the country for a supposed vacation, setting the stage for Khomeini's triumphant return on Jan 31. The monarchy fell on Feb 11, 1979. Khomeini proceeded to reorganize the government based on Islamic principles. On Nov 11, 1979, a group of students loyal to Khomeini occupied the American Embassy in Teheran after the Shah was given admittance to the US for medical treatment, placing the Ayatollah at the center of a diplomatic crisis that consumed the presidency of Jimmy Carter. Khomeini focused attention on the US as the "Great Satan" and blamed many of his country's problems on imperialistic intervention. The anniversary of his death is a national holiday in Iran.

MIGHTY CASEY HAS STRUCK OUT: ANNIVERSARY. June 3, 1888. The famous comic baseball ballad "Casey at the Bat" was printed in the Sunday *San Francisco Examiner*. Appearing anonymously, it was written by Ernest L. Thayer. Recitation of "Casey at the Bat" became part of the repertoire of actor William DeWolf Hopper. The recitation took 5 minutes and 40 seconds. Hopper claimed to have recited it more than 10,000 times, the first being at Wallack's Theater at New York, NY, in 1888. See also: "Thayer, Ernest Lawrence: Birth Anniversary" (Aug 14).

MISSION SAN CARLOS BORROMEO DE CARMELO: FOUNDING ANNIVERSARY. June 3, 1770. California mission to the Indians founded on this date.

NATIONAL TAILORS DAY. June 3. To honor tailors across the US. Annually, the first Wednesday in June. For info: Doug Foley, Tom James Clothiers, 501 Congressional Blvd, Ste 150, Carmel, IN 46032. Phone: (317) 571-9191.

SPACE MILESTONE: *GEMINI 4* (US). June 3, 1965. James McDivitt and Edward White made 66 orbits of Earth. White took the first space walk by an American and maneuvered 20 minutes outside the capsule.

ZOOT SUIT RIOTS: ANNIVERSARY. June 3–8, 1943. In Los Angeles, CA, simmering racial unease exploded as 200 white sailors stormed into East LA and began beating Hispanics in response to an earlier altercation between a few sailors and some street kids. The sailors targeted Zoot Suiters—youths outfitted in the defiant, exaggerated suit of their community (long jackets, wide trousers and ankle-length watch chains). The rioting grew as police either stood by or arrested the victims. The media, antagonistic to the Hispanic community, spurred on the violence with sensational headlines. Finally, military brass declared Los Angeles off-limits to its personnel and the LA City Council banned zoot suits. There were no deaths, but the injuries and mayhem were such that a special state committee was convened and First Lady Eleanor Roosevelt wrote in her newspaper column that the riots were symptomatic of a problem with deep roots.

BIRTHDAYS TODAY

Chuck Barris, 80, TV producer ("Dating Game," "Newlywed Game," "Gong Show"), born Philadelphia, PA, June 3, 1929.

Raúl Castro, 78, President of Cuba, born Holguín, Cuba, June 3, 1931.

Anderson Cooper, 42, television journalist, personality ("Anderson Cooper 360," "The Mole"), born New York, NY, June 3, 1967.

Tony Curtis, 84, actor (*Some Like It Hot, The Boston Strangler, The Defiant Ones*), born Bernard Schwartz at New York, NY, June 3, 1925.

Jan-Michael Gambill, 32, tennis player, born Spokane, WA, June 3, 1977.

Charles Hart, 48, lyricist, composer, born London, England, June 3, 1961.

Hale S. Irwin, 64, golfer, born Joplin, MO, June 3, 1945.

Larry McMurtry, 73, author (*Terms of Endearment, Lonesome Dove, The Last Picture Show*), born Wichita Falls, TX, June 3, 1936.

Rafael Nadal, 23, tennis player, born Manacor, Spain, June 3, 1986.

Scott Valentine, 51, actor ("Family Ties"), born Saratoga Springs, NY, June 3, 1958.

Deniece Williams, 58, singer ("Free," "It's Gonna Take a Miracle"), born Gary, IN, June 3, 1951.

June 2009

S	M	T	W	T	F	S
	1	2	3	4	5	6
7	8	9	10	11	12	13
14	15	16	17	18	19	20
21	22	23	24	25	26	27
28	29	30				

June 4 — Thursday

DAY 155 **210 REMAINING**

BATTLE OF MIDWAY: ANNIVERSARY. June 4–6, 1942. A Japanese task force attempted to capture Midway Island in the Central Pacific, but American bombers from Midway and from two nearby aircraft carriers sent the Japanese into retreat. The Japanese lost four carriers, two large cruisers and three destroyers. Midway was one of the most decisive naval battles of WWII. Japan never regained its margin in carrier strength and the Central Pacific was made safe for American troops.

CANADA: SHELBURNE COUNTY LOBSTER FESTIVAL. June 4–7. Shelburne County, NS. Four days of activities in celebration of the lobster-fishing industry. Local community groups and businesses throughout the county host lobster suppers, sporting events, craft shows, yacht, boat and dorey races and much more. "Shelburne County—The Lobster Capital of Canada." Est attendance: 5,000. For info: Marilyn Johnston, Lobster Fest Secy, PO Box 280, Shelburne, NS, Canada B0T 1W0. Phone: (902) 875-3544, ext 225. Fax: (902) 875-1278. E-mail: mjohnston@municipalityofshelburne.ca. Web: www.municipalityofshelburne.ca or www.auracom.com/tn shelb.

CANADA: WINNIPEG INTERNATIONAL CHILDREN'S FESTIVAL. June 4–7. The Forks, Winnipeg, MB. Festival features song, dance, theater, mime, puppetry and music by local, national and international artists. Est attendance: 20,000. For info: Winnipeg Intl Children's Fest, 201-One Forks Market Rd, Winnipeg, MB, Canada R3L 4C9. Phone: (204) 958-4733 or (800) 527-1515. Fax: (204) 943-7915. E-mail: kidsfest@kidsfest.ca. Web: www.kidsfest.ca.

"CAVALCADE OF STARS" TV PREMIERE: 60th ANNIVERSARY. June 4, 1949. Although the Dumont network was not very successful, it was around long enough to launch this popular show. The one-hour variety show was hosted by Jack Carter (1949–50), Jackie Gleason (1950–52) and Larry Storch (in the summer of 1952). It also served as a showcase for the soon-to-be immortal "The Honeymooners" with Gleason and Pert Kelton starring as the Kramdens.

CHINA: TIANANMEN SQUARE MASSACRE: 20th ANNIVERSARY. June 4, 1989. After almost a month and a half of student demonstrations for democracy, the Chinese government ordered its troops to open fire on the unarmed protestors at Tiananmen Square in Beijing. Under the cover of darkness, early June 4, troops opened fire on the assembled crowds and armored personnel carriers rolled into the square crushing many of the students as they lay sleeping in their tents. Although the government claimed that few died in the attack, estimates range from several hundred to several thousand casualties. In the following months thousands of demonstrators were rounded up and jailed.

CURWOOD FESTIVAL. June 4–7. Owosso, MI. Homecoming celebration commemorating James Oliver Curwood, Owosso-born author and conservationist (June 12, 1878–Aug 13, 1927). The Curwood castle was built for a studio. Open to the public. 40 events including parades, races and music. Annually, the first full weekend in June. Est attendance: 40,000. For info: Owosso Curwood Festival, Box 461, Owosso, MI 48867. Phone: (989) 723-2161. Fax: (989) 729-6098. E-mail: curwood.festivalinc@verizon.net. Web: www.curwoodfestival.com.

FENDER, FREDDY: BIRTH ANNIVERSARY. June 4, 1937. Born Baldemar Huerta at San Benito, TX, to migrant farm workers, Fender was a Grammy-winning balladeer who worked in country, R&B and Tex-Mex music styles—singing in both Spanish and English. In the 1970s, Fender had several number-one country hits, including "Before the Next Teardrop Falls" and "Wasted Days and Wasted Nights." He died Oct 14, 2006, at Corpus Christi, TX.

FINLAND: FLAG DAY. June 4. Finland's armed forces honor the June 4, 1867, birth anniversary of Carl Gustaf Mannerheim.

FIRST FREE FLIGHT BY A WOMAN: 225th ANNIVERSARY. June 4, 1784. Marie Thible, of Lyons, France, accompanied by a pilot (Monsieur Fleurant), became the first woman in history to fly in a free balloon. She drifted across Lyons in a balloon named *Le Gustave* (for King Gustav III of Sweden, who was watching the ascent). The balloon reached a height of 8,500 feet in a flight that lasted about 45 minutes. The event occurred one day short of a year after the first flight in history by a man. See also: "First Balloon Flight: Anniversary" (June 5).

GEORGE III: BIRTH ANNIVERSARY. June 4, 1738. The English king against whom the American Revolution was directed. Born at London, England, died Jan 29, 1820, at Windsor Castle, near London.

PULITZER PRIZES FIRST AWARDED: ANNIVERSARY. June 4, 1917. The first Pulitzer Prizes were awarded on this date: for biography, *Julia Ward Howe* by Laura E. Richards and Maude H. Elliott assisted by Florence H. Hall; for history, *With Americans of Past and Present Days* by Jean Jules Jusserand, the French ambassador to the US. Prizes were also awarded for journalistic achievement.

ROME LIBERATED: 65th ANNIVERSARY. June 4, 1944. The US 9th Army, commanded by General Mark Clark, entered the southern suburbs of Rome as the last of the German rear guard retreated from Mussolini's former capital. Fearful of a last-ditch effort by the Germans to hold the city, the populace remained behind closed doors as Clark's forces entered the Eternal City.

SMOKY MOUNTAINS STORYTELLING FESTIVAL. June 4–6. Pigeon Forge, TN. 18th annual. The region's finest yarn-spinners and folklore specialists. Est attendance: 2,500. For info: Office of Special Events, Pigeon Forge Dept of Tourism, 3107 Pkwy, PO Box 1390, Pigeon Forge, TN 37868. Phone: (800) 251-9100 or (865) 429-7350. Fax: (865) 429-7392. E-mail: inquire@cityofpigeonforge.com. Web: www.mypigeonforge.com.

TONGA: EMANCIPATION DAY. June 4. National holiday. Commemorates independence from Britain in 1970.

UNITED NATIONS: INTERNATIONAL DAY OF INNOCENT CHILDREN VICTIMS OF AGGRESSION. June 4. On Aug 19, 1982, the General Assembly decided to commemorate June 4 of each year as a day to call attention to the urgent need to protect the rights of chidren. It reminds people that throughout the world there are many children suffering from different forms of abuse. For info: United Nations, Dept of Public Info, New York, NY 10017. Web: www.un.org.

BIRTHDAYS TODAY

Cecilia Bartoli, 43, opera singer (mezzo-soprano), born Rome, Italy, June 4, 1966.

James Callis, 38, actor ("Battlestar Galactica," *Bridget Jones's Diary*), born London, England, June 4, 1971.

Keith David, 53, actor (*Platoon, Barbershop*, "Jazz"), born New York, NY, June 4, 1956.

Eldra DeBarge, 48, singer, musician, lead singer (DeBarge), born Grand Rapids, MI, June 4, 1961.

Bruce Dern, 73, actor (*Coming Home, The Burbs*), born Chicago, IL, June 4, 1936.

Bettina Gregory, 63, journalist, born New York, NY, June 4, 1946.

Andrea Jaeger, 44, former tennis player, born Chicago, IL, June 4, 1965.

Angelina Jolie, 34, actress (Oscar for *Girl, Interrupted*; *A Mighty Heart, Mr. & Mrs. Smith, Lara Croft:Tomb Raider*), born Los Angeles, CA, June 4, 1975.

Linda Lingle, 56, Governor of Hawaii (R), born St. Louis, MO, June 4, 1953.

Michelle Phillips, 64, singer (with The Mamas and the Papas), actress ("Knots Landing"), born Long Beach, CA, June 4, 1945.

Parker Stevenson, 56, actor ("Falcon Crest," "Baywatch," *Lifeguard*), born Philadelphia, PA, June 4, 1953.

Dr. Ruth Westheimer, 80, TV, radio host for shows on sexual relationships, born Frankfurt, Germany, June 4, 1929.

Scott Wolf, 41, actor ("Party of Five," *The Evening Star*), born Boston, MA, June 4, 1968.

Noah Wyle, 38, actor (*A Few Good Men*, "ER"), born Hollywood, CA, June 4, 1971.

June 5 — Friday

DAY 156 **209 REMAINING**

AIDS FIRST NOTED: ANNIVERSARY. June 5, 1981. The Centers for Disease Control first described a new illness striking gay men in a newsletter on June 5, 1981. On July 27, 1982, Acquired Immune Deficiency Syndrome was adopted as the official name for the new disease by the CDC. The virus that causes AIDS was identified in 1983 and in May 1985 was named Human Immunodeficiency Virus (HIV) by the International Committee on the Taxonomy of Viruses. The first person killed by this disease in the developed world died in 1959. More than 524,000 Americans have died of AIDS. Worldwide, more than 22 million people have died of AIDS. About 40 million people worldwide are living with HIV/AIDS.

AMERICAN BAHA'I COMMUNITY: ANNIVERSARY. June 5, 1894. The first formal classes on the Baha'i were held at Chicago, IL.

APPLE II COMPUTER RELEASED: ANNIVERSARY. June 5, 1977. The Apple II computer, with 4K of memory, went on sale for $1,298. Its predecessor, the Apple I, was sold largely to electronic hobbyists the previous year. Apple released the Macintosh computer Jan 24, 1984.

BAHAMAS: LABOR DAY. June 5. Public holiday. First Friday in June celebrated with parades, displays and picnics.

BOYD, WILLIAM: BIRTH ANNIVERSARY. June 5, 1895. Born at Hendrysburg, OH, Boyd went to Hollywood in 1919 and got a job as a film extra. In 1935 he got the role of Hopalong Cassidy in a series of popular westerns. He made 66 of these films between 1935 and 1948. Some of them were edited and shown on television; Boyd then made some episodes especially for TV. Died at Hollywood, CA, Sept 12, 1972. See also: "Hopalong Cassidy TV Premiere" (June 24).

BUFFALO DAYS CELEBRATION (WITH BUFFALO CHIP THROWING). June 5–7. Luverne, MN. Parade, Arts in the Park, auto shows, free barbecued buffalo burgers (while they last) and unique buffalo chip throwing contest. Annually, the first weekend in June. Est attendance: 8,000. For info: June Wilding, Exec Dir, Luverne Area Chamber of Commerce, 211 E Main, Luverne, MN 56156. Phone: (507) 283-4061. Fax: (507) 283-4061. E-mail: luvernechamber@iw.net. Web: www.luvernechamber.org.

CHICKEN AND EGG FESTIVAL. June 5–6. Prescott, AR. Two days of athletic events, shows and entertainment for the entire family. Come and watch our famous Cackling and Crowing contest in southwest Arkansas's friendliest city. Other activities include 5k run and walk, tennis tournament, softball, Little Miss Hen and Little Mr Rooster Beauty Pageants, bunco tournament and much more. Est attendance: 2,000. For info: Brandy Jones, PO Box 307, Prescott, AR 71857. Phone: (870) 887-2102. Fax: (870) 887-5317. E-mail: bjones@pnpartnership.org. Web: www.pnpartnership.org.

DENMARK: CONSTITUTION DAY. June 5. National holiday. Commemorates Denmark's becoming a constitutional monarchy in 1849 and the new constitution adopted in 1953.

FARMINGTON COUNTRY DAYS. June 5–7. Farmington, MO. Three-day event featuring amusement rides, a free "oldies" concert and a Nashville country star concert, craft show and lots more fun for the whole family. Est attendance: 30,000. For info: Farmington Chamber of Commerce, PO Box 191, Farmington, MO 63640. Phone: (573) 756-3615. Fax: (573) 756-1003. E-mail: ursulak@farmingtonmo.org.

FIRST BALLOON FLIGHT: ANNIVERSARY. June 5, 1783. The first public demonstration of a hot-air balloon flight took place at Annonay, France, where brothers Joseph and Jacques Montgolfier succeeded in launching the 33-foot-diameter *globe aerostatique* that they had invented. The unmanned balloon rose an estimated 1,500 feet and traveled, wind-borne, about 7,500 feet before landing after a 10-minute flight—the first sustained flight of any object achieved by man.

FORT SISSETON HISTORICAL FESTIVAL. June 5–7. Fort Sisseton State Park, Lake City, SD. Fort Sisseton comes alive the first weekend in June every year. See life as it was in 1864 when the fort was established. Cavalry drills, military costume ball, Indian dancing, Dakota Dan's medicine show, wagon train, muzzle-loader shoot, rendezvous, draft-horse pulls, fiddlers, square dancing, melodramas and arts and crafts are popular features of the festival. Est attendance: 30,000. For info: Fort Sisseton State Park, Dept of Game, Fish and Parks, 11907 434th Ave, Lake City, SD 57247. Phone: (605) 448-5474. Fax: (605) 448-5492. Web: www.state.sd.us/gfp.

GREAT WISCONSIN CHEESE FESTIVAL. June 5–7. Little Chute, WI. Festival features cheese breakfast, parade, cheese tasting, cheese-carving demo and cheesecake contest. Est attendance: 10,000. For info: Great Wisconsin Cheese Festival, 1940 Buchanan St, Little Chute, WI 54140-1414. Phone: (920) 788-7390. Fax: (920) 788-7820.

HARVARD MILK DAYS™ FESTIVAL. June 5–7. Harvard, IL. This salute to the dairy farmer includes a parade, evening entertainment, show featuring crafts and "udder" neat stuff, horse show, grilling competition, farm tours, Market Place, milk-drinking contest, antique farm tractor display, carnival, fireworks, 2-mile milk run, 2-mile milk walk, 10k milk run, junior dairy cattle show, talent show, hot-air balloon launch and wee farm. Est attendance: 100,000. For info: Harvard Milk Days, Inc, PO Box 325, Harvard, IL 60033-0325. Phone: (815) 943-4614. Fax: (815) 943-7404. E-mail: info@milkdays.com. Web: www.milkdays.com.

IRAN: FIFTEENTH OF KHORDAD. June 5. National holiday. Commemorates the deaths of Islamic clerics in a clash with the shah's forces in 1963.

KENNEDY, ROBERT F.: ASSASSINATION ANNIVERSARY. June 5, 1968. Senator Kennedy was shot while campaigning for the Democratic presidential nomination at Los Angeles, CA; he died the following day. Sirhan Sirhan was convicted of his murder.

KEYNES, JOHN MAYNARD: BIRTH ANNIVERSARY. June 5, 1883. British economist born at Cambridge, England. Author of *Treatise on Money* and *The General Theory of Employment, Interest and Money* that focused on "expansionist" economic policy. Died at Firle, England, Apr 21, 1946.

June 2009

S	M	T	W	T	F	S
	1	2	3	4	5	6
7	8	9	10	11	12	13
14	15	16	17	18	19	20
21	22	23	24	25	26	27
28	29	30				

LILAC FESTIVAL. June 5–14. Mackinac Island, MI. This summer festival provides an excellent chance to see the various lilacs on Mackinac Island. Includes a parade and entertainment. Est attendance: 30,000. For info: Mackinac Island Tourism Bureau, PO Box 451, Mackinac Island, MI 49757. Phone: (906) 847-3783 or (800) 4-LILACS. Fax: (906) 847-3571. Web: www.mackinacislandlilac festival.com.

MOROCCO: FÈS FESTIVAL OF WORLD SACRED MUSIC. June 5–15 (tentative). Fès. Since 1994, the Fès Festival has sought to build bridges through music, with the world's leading musicians performing sacred music reflecting spiritual traditions of the East and West. In 2001, the United Nations recognized the festival as one of seven major world events that fosters dialogue between civilizations. Annually, beginning on the first Friday of June. For info: Fès Musiques Sacrees du Monde, Foundation Spirit of Fès, Sidi El Khayat BP 629 Fès-Médina, 30200 Morocco. Phone: (212) 35-74-05-35. Fax: (212) 35-63-39-89. Web: www.espritdefes.com.

RIVERBEND FESTIVAL. June 5–13. Chattanooga, TN. Nine-day festival on the banks of the Tennessee River includes world-class entertainment, sporting events and an evening finale on the final night featuring musically synchronized fireworks. More than 100 artists perform a variety of musical styles before a diverse audience. Est attendance: 650,000. For info: Friends of the Festival, Inc, 180 Hamm Rd, Chattanooga, TN 37405. Phone: (423) 756-2212. Fax: (423) 756-2719. E-mail: info@riverbendfestival.com. Web: www .riverbendfestival.com.

ROUTE 66 SUMMERFEST. June 5–6. Rolla, MO. Annual citywide celebration including car shows, crafts, entertainment and food. Est attendance: 4,000. For info: Nick Barrack, Summerfest Chairman, Central Security & Electric. Phone: (573) 341-2562. E-mail: cse@fidmail.com. Web: www.route66summerfest.com.

SCARRY, RICHARD McCLURE: 90th BIRTH ANNIVERSARY. June 5, 1919. Author and illustrator of children's books was born at Boston, MA. Two widely known books of the more than 250 Scarry authored are *Richard Scarry's Best Word Book Ever* (1965) and *Richard Scarry's Please & Thank You* (1973). The pages are crowded with small animal characters who live like humans. More than 100 million copies of his books have sold worldwide. Died Apr 30, 1994, at Gstaad, Switzerland.

SITKA SUMMER MUSIC FESTIVAL. June 5–26. (Tuesdays, Fridays and Saturdays) Sitka, AK. Sitka hosts a highly acclaimed chamber music festival that attracts performers and spectators from around the world. Est attendance: 5,000. For info: Sitka Summer Music Festival, PO Box 201988, Anchorage, AK 99520-1988. Phone: (907) 277-4852. Fax: (907) 277-4842. E-mail: director@sitkamusicfestival .org. Web: www.sitkamusicfestival.org.

SMITH, ADAM: BIRTH ANNIVERSARY. June 5, 1723. (Old Style date.) Scottish economist and philosopher, author of *An Enquiry into the Nature and Causes of the Wealth of Nations* (published in 1776), born at Kirkaldy, Fifeshire, Scotland. Died at Edinburgh, Scotland, July 17, 1790. "Consumption," he wrote, "is the sole end and purpose of production; and the interest of the producer ought to be attended to only so far as it may be necessary for promoting that of the consumer."

SOUTH CAROLINA FESTIVAL OF FLOWERS. June 5–28. Greenwood, SC. Come and see the beautiful flowers of South Carolina. Includes arts and crafts displays, entertainment, sports events and more. Est attendance: 30,000. For info: Greenwood Chamber of Commerce, SC Festival of Flowers, PO Box 980, Greenwood, SC 29648. Phone: (864) 223-8411. Fax: (864) 229-9785. E-mail: kay@ greenwoodscchamber.org. Web: www.scfestivalofflowers.org.

SPACE MILESTONE: *SOYUZ T-2* (USSR). June 5, 1980. Launched on this date, cosmonauts Yuri Malyshev and Vladimir Aksenov docked at *Salyut 6* on June 6 and returned to Earth June 9. First piloted flight of new T (Transport) spacecraft.

SUMMER FARM TOY SHOW. June 5–6. Beckman HS and National Farm Toy Museum, Dyersville, IA. Features tractor parade, citywide garage sales, antique tractors and farm machinery and indoor/outdoor farm toy show. Annually, the first full weekend in June. Est attendance: 5,000. For info: National Farm Toy Museum, 1110 16th Ave Ct SE, Dyersville, IA 52040. Phone: (563) 875-2727. E-mail: farmtoys@dyersville.com. Web: www.nationalfarmtoymuseum.com.

TAIWAN: BIRTHDAY OF CHENG HUANG. June 5. Thirteenth day of fifth moon. Celebrated with a procession of actors on stilts doing dragon and lion dances.

TELLURIDE BALLOON FESTIVAL. June 5–7. Town Park, Telluride, CO. 26th annual. A small balloon event with free rides for volunteers; Main Street GLO on Saturday evening. Annually, the first full weekend in June. Est attendance: 2,000. For info: Marilyn Branch, PO Box 1295, Telluride, CO 81435. Phone: (970) 708-2202. Fax: (970) 728-4769. E-mail: balloons@telluridecolorado.net.

UNITED NATIONS: WORLD ENVIRONMENT DAY. June 5. Observed annually June 5, the anniversary of the opening of the UN Conference on the Human Environment held in Stockholm in 1972, which led to establishment of UN Environment Programme, based in Nairobi. The General Assembly has urged marking the day with activities reaffirming concern for the preservation and enhancement of the environment. For info: United Nations, Dept of Public Info, New York, NY 10017. Web: www.un.org.

US INTERNATIONAL FILM AND VIDEO FESTIVAL AWARDS PRESENTATIONS AND SCREENINGS. June 5–6. Los Angeles, CA. World's largest awards competition honoring business, television, documentary, informational and industrial productions. Entry deadline is Mar 1. Founded in 1968. Est attendance: 200. For info: Lee W. Gluckman, Jr, Chairman, US Intl Film and Video Festival Awards, 713 S Pacific Coast Hwy, Ste A, Redondo Beach, CA 90277-4233. Phone: (310) 540-0959. Fax: (310) 316-8905. E-mail: filmfest info@filmfestawards.com. Web: www.filmfestawards.com.

 BIRTHDAYS TODAY

Chad Allen, 35, actor ("Dr. Quinn, Medicine Woman"), born Cerritos, CA, June 5, 1974.

Margaret Drabble, 70, British novelist (*The Gates of Ivory*), born Sheffield, Yorkshire, England, June 5, 1939.

Ken Follett, 60, British novelist (*The Eye of the Needle*), born Wales, UK, June 5, 1949.

Brian McKnight, 40, singer, born Buffalo, NY, June 5, 1969.

Bill Moyers, 75, journalist ("Bill Moyers' Journal"), born Hugo, OK, June 5, 1934.

Mark Wahlberg, 38, actor (*Boogie Nights, The Departed*), rapper Marky Mark (Marky Mark and the Funky Bunch), born Dorchester, MA, June 5, 1971.

June 6 — Saturday

DAY 157 | **208 REMAINING**

BELMONT STAKES. June 6. Belmont Park, NY. 141st annual. Final race of the "Triple Crown" was inaugurated in 1867. Traditionally run on the fifth Saturday after Kentucky Derby (third Saturday after Preakness). Est attendance: 60,000. For info: Press Office, New York Racing Assn, PO Box 90, Jamaica, NY 11417. Phone: (718) 641-4700. Web: www.nyra.com.

BONZA BOTTLER DAY™. June 6. To celebrate when the number of the day is the same as the number of the month. Bonza Bottler Day™ is an excuse to have a party at least once a month. For more information see Jan 1. For info: Gail M. Berger, 14 Fernwood Dr, Taylors, SC 29687. E-mail: bonza@bonzabottlerday.com. Web: www .bonzabottlerday.com.

CAPITOL HILL PEOPLE'S FAIR. June 6–7. Civic Center Park, Denver, CO. More than 500 arts and crafts and other exhibit booths; live entertainment featuring local talent on six stages. Est attendance: 250,000. For info: Capitol Hill United Neighborhoods, 1290 Williams St, Ste 101, Denver, CO 80218-2657. Phone: (303) 830-1651. Fax: (303) 830-1782. E-mail: production@chundenver.org. Web: www.chundenver.org.

CHEER COACH DAY. June 6. Show appreciation for the hard work and dedication of those who coach our cheerleaders. Annually, the first Saturday in June. For info: Lindy Lundy, 59 County Rd 3474, Cleveland, TX 77327. Phone: (281) 399-8357 or (877) 68-CHEER. E-mail: linda@cheerintegrity.com.

D-DAY: 65th ANNIVERSARY. June 6, 1944. In the early-morning hours Allied forces landed in Normandy on the north coast of France. In an operation that took months of planning, a fleet of 2,727 ships of every description converged from British ports from Wales to the North Sea. Operation *Overlord* involved 2,000,000 tons of war materials, including more than 50,000 tanks, armored cars, jeeps, trucks and half-tracks. The US alone sent 1,700,000 fighting men. The Germans believed the invasion would not take place under the adverse weather conditions of this early June day. But as the sun came up the village of Saint Mère Eglise was liberated by American parachutists, and by nightfall the landing of 155,000 Allies attested to the success of D-Day. The long-awaited second front had at last materialized.

DO-DAH PARADE. June 6. Kalamazoo, MI. "Salute to Silliness." Since 1981 offbeat entries have included a precision grill team (complete with spatulas) and a herbie curbie brigade. Annually, the first Saturday in June. Sponsored by Downtown Kalamazoo, Inc, and WKFR Radio. Est attendance: 40,000. For info: Downtown Kalamazoo Inc, 157 S Kalamazoo Mall, Kalamazoo, MI 49007. Phone: (269) 344-0795. Fax: (269) 344-0898. Web: www.central-city.net.

ENGLAND: THE DERBY. June 6. Epsom Downs. Horse races. Annually, the Saturday after the first Wednesday in June.

FIRST DRIVE-IN MOVIE OPENS: ANNIVERSARY. June 6, 1933. Richard M. Hollingshead, Jr, opened America's first drive-in movie theater in Camden, NJ, on this date. At the height of their popularity in 1958, there were more than 4,000 drive-ins across America. Today there are fewer than 600 open.

FOUNDERS' DAY STREET FAIR—THE GOOD LIFE. June 6 (rain date June 7). Toms River, NJ. Street fair for Toms River Township nonprofit organizations with a parade, vendor booths, entertainment, prizes, food, literature and games. Crafters welcome. Est attendance: 30,000. For info: Toms River-Ocean County Chamber of Commerce, 1200 Hooper Ave, Toms River, NJ 08753. Phone: (732) 349-0220. Fax: (732) 349-1252. Web: www.oc-chamber.com.

HALE, NATHAN: BIRTH ANNIVERSARY. June 6, 1755. American patriot Nathan Hale was born at Coventry, CT. During the battles for New York in the American Revolution, he volunteered to seek military intelligence behind enemy lines and was captured on the night of Sept 21, 1776. In an audience before General William Howe, Hale admitted he was an American officer and was ordered hanged the following morning. Although some question them, his dying words, "I only regret that I have but one life to lose for my country," have become a symbol of American patriotism. He was hung Sept 22, 1776, at Manhattan, NY.

INTERNATIONAL CLOTHESLINE WEEK. June 6–13. The public is encouraged to save energy by hanging clothes to dry instead of using their electric dryer. Annually, the first week in June, Saturday to Saturday. For info: Gary Drisdelle. E-mail: gdrisdelle@rogers.com. Web: www.hangtodry.com.

June 2009

S	M	T	W	T	F	S
	1	2	3	4	5	6
7	8	9	10	11	12	13
14	15	16	17	18	19	20
21	22	23	24	25	26	27
28	29	30				

KHACHATURIAN, ARAM (ILICH): BIRTH ANNIVERSARY. June 6, 1903. Armenian musician and composer, noted for compositions based on folk music and legend, born at Tbilisi, Georgia, USSR. Died at Moscow, May 1, 1978.

KOREA: MEMORIAL DAY. June 6. Nation pays tribute to the war dead and memorial services are held at the National Cemetery in Seoul. Legally recognized Korean holiday.

MALAYSIA: HEAD OF STATE'S OFFICIAL BIRTHDAY. June 6. National holiday. The first Saturday in June.

MARITIME GIG FESTIVAL. June 6–7. Gig Harbor, WA. This annual family event begins with the parade route that follows the edge of the beautiful harbor with the marina and view of majestic Mount Rainier. The event is jam-packed with family entertainment, a 5-mile run, crafts and games for children, foods of every description, open markets, live music, arts and fine crafts. Annually, the first Saturday and Sunday in June. Est attendance: 20,000. For info: Gig Harbor Peninsula Area Chamber of Commerce, 3311 Harborview Dr, Ste 101, Gig Harbor, WA 98332. Phone: (253) 851-6865 or (800) 359-8804. E-mail: info@gigharborchamber.com. Web: www.maritimegig.com.

MISSOURI STATE CHAMPIONSHIP RACKING HORSE SHOW. June 6. Stoddard County Fairgrounds, Dexter, MO. At this 32nd annual event elegant showmanship by both horse and rider provides an afternoon and evening of spectator pleasure. Annually, the first Saturday in June. Est attendance: 500. For info: Missouri State Championship Racking Horse Show, PO Box 21, Dexter, MO 63841. Phone: (573) 624-7458 or (800) 332-8857. Fax: (573) 624-7459. E-mail: info@dexterchamber.com.

NATIONAL TRAILS DAY. June 6. National Trails Day celebrates trails and the volunteers who maintain them. The first Saturday of every June more than 1,200 trail organizations, agencies and businesses across the country host a variety of events including new trail dedications, workshops, educational exhibits, equestrian and mountain bike rides, boat paddling, trail maintenance projects and, as always, hikes on backcountry trails in America's wild lands. For info: American Hiking Society, 1422 Fenwick Ln, Silver Spring, MD 20910. Phone: (301) 565-6704, ext 208. E-mail: ilevin@americanhiking.org. Web: www.americanhiking.org.

PEDDLER'S VILLAGE FINE ART & CONTEMPORARY CRAFTS SHOW. June 6–7. Lahaska, PA. Juried competition of paintings, prints, photography and more created by fine artists, plus contemporary crafts. Hands-on art activities for children. Shops offer various art-related events. Live music, face painting and balloons. Free admission. Est attendance: 12,000. For info: Peddler's Village, Routes 202 and 263, Lahaska, PA 18931. Phone: (215) 794-4000. Fax: (215) 794-4001. Web: www.peddlersvillage.com.

PROPOSITION 13: ANNIVERSARY. June 6, 1978. California voters (65 percent of them) supported a primary election ballot initiative to cut property taxes 57 percent. Regarded as a possible omen of things to come across the country—a taxpayer's revolt against high taxes and government spending.

PUSHKIN, ALEXANDER: BIRTH ANNIVERSARY. June 6, 1799. Russian poet (*Eugene Onegin*, a novel in verse), born at Moscow. Died Feb 10, 1837 at St. Petersburg as the result of a duel.

SCOTT, ROBERT FALCON: BIRTH ANNIVERSARY. June 6, 1868. British naval officer and polar explorer, born at Devonport, England. Led the ill-starred expedition to the South Pole that arrived on Jan 18, 1912—one month after Norwegian Roald Amundsen's team became the first humans to set foot on the South

Pole. Scott and four team members died on the return journey and their bodies were found November 1912. Scott's diary, with a final entry of Mar 29, 1912, had a message to the public: "Had we lived, I should have had a tale to tell of the hardihood, endurance, and courage of my companions which would have stirred the heart of every Englishman. These rough notes and our dead bodies must tell the tale."

SECURITIES AND EXCHANGE COMMISSION CREATED: 75th ANNIVERSARY. June 6, 1934. President Franklin D. Roosevelt signed the Securities Exchange Act that established the SEC. Wall Street had operated almost unfettered since the end of the 18th century. However, the stock market crash of 1929 necessitated regulation of the exchanges. The Securities and Exchange Commission is composed of five members appointed by the president of the US.

"SEX AND THE CITY" TV PREMIERE: ANNIVERSARY. June 6, 1998. HBO's modern comedy of manners focused on four fashionable women navigating the perilous waters of New York City's dating scene. Starred Sarah Jessica Parker (Carrie Bradshaw), Kristin Davis (Charlotte York), Kim Cattrall (Samantha Jones) and Cynthia Nixon (Miranda Hobbes). More than 10 million viewers tuned in to watch the 94th and final episode air on Feb 22, 2004.

SPACE MILESTONE: *SOYUZ 11* (USSR). June 6, 1971. Launched with cosmonauts G.T. Dobrovolsky, V.N. Volkov and V.I. Patsayev, who died during the return landing June 30, 1971, after a 24-day space flight. *Soyuz 11* had docked at *Salyut* orbital space station June 7–29; the cosmonauts entered the space station for the first time and conducted scientific experiments. First humans to die in space.

STRAWBERRY FESTIVAL. June 6. Vaile Mansion, Independence, MO. Outdoor Victorian-type festival featuring strawberry treats, crafts, antiques, children's activities, carriage rides, flea market and entertainment. Annually, first Saturday in June. Est attendance: 900. For info: Stephanie Roush, Tourism Dir, 111 E Maple, Independence, MO 64050. Phone: (816) 325-7111. Fax: (816) 325-7932. Web: www.visitindependence.com.

SUMMER READING CLUB. June 6–July 18. El Paso, TX. Every summer the El Paso Public Library has a summer reading club program. The program is open to all children from birth through sixth grade. Children are required to read/have been read to eight books or eight hours during the program to receive a certificate. The 14 libraries plus Bookmobile feature weekly special programs in the libraries for the children. For info: Laurel Indalecio, El Paso Public Library, 501 N Oregon, El Paso, TX 79901. Phone: (915) 543-5470. Fax: (915) 543-5410. E-mail: indaleciol@elpasotexas.gov. Web: www.elpasolibrary.org.

SUSAN B. ANTHONY FINED FOR VOTING: ANNIVERSARY. June 6, 1872. Seeking to test for women the citizenship and voting rights extended to black males under the 14th and 15th Amendments, Susan B. Anthony led a group of women who registered and voted at a Rochester, NY, election. She was arrested, tried and sentenced to pay a fine. She refused to do so and was allowed to go free by a judge who feared she would appeal to a higher court.

SWEDEN: FLAG DAY. June 6. Commemorates the day upon which Gustavus I (Gustavus Vasa) ascended the throne of Sweden in 1523.

TOPPENISH MURAL SOCIETY'S "MURAL-IN-A-DAY." June 6. Toppenish, WA. 12 professional artists paint a complete, historically authentic mural in eight hours. Starting at 9 AM they work until finished, usually until 4 PM. Accompanied by an arts and crafts show and a food fair. Annually, the first Saturday in June. Est attendance: 1,200. For info: Toppenish Mural Society, PO Box 1172, Toppenish, WA 98948. Phone: (509) 865-6516. E-mail: chamber@toppenish.net. Web: www.toppenish.net.

"20/20" TV PREMIERE: ANNIVERSARY. June 6, 1978. An hourly newsmagazine developed by ABC to compete with CBS's "60 Minutes." Its original hosts, Harold Hayes and Robert Hughes, were cut after the first show and replaced by Hugh Downs. Barbara Walters became coanchor in 1984. The show consisted of investigative and background reports. Contributors to the show have included Tom Jarriel, Sylvia Chase, Geraldo Rivera, Thomas Hoving, John Stossel, Lynn Sherr and Stone Phillips.

XTERRA OAK MOUNTAIN XDURO. June 6. Pelham, AL. The XTERRA Trail Run Series boasts over 50 events across the country with runs ranging from 5k to 25k. These extreme, off-road trail runs give runners the chance to prove their skills against a variety of terrain. From calf-burning hills to slippery, mud-covered paths athletes will face the ultimate test of endurance. This race features off-road 5k, 10k and half-marathon distance trail runs. For info: Ann Mickey, XTERRA/TEAM Unlimited, 720 Iwilei Road #290, Honolulu, HI 96817. Phone: (877) 751-8880. E-mail: info@xterraplanet.com. Web: www.xterraplanet.com.

BIRTHDAYS TODAY

Sandra Bernhard, 54, comedienne, actress ("The L Word," "Roseanne," *The King of Comedy*), born Flint, MI, June 6, 1955.

Gary U.S. Bonds, 70, singer ("Quarter to Three"), songwriter, born Gary Anderson at Jacksonville, FL, June 6, 1939.

Bjorn Borg, 53, former tennis player, born Sodertalje, Sweden, June 6, 1956.

Marian Wright Edelman, 70, president of Children's Defense Fund, civil rights activist, born Bennettsville, SC, June 6, 1939.

Harvey Fierstein, 55, actor, playwright (Tony Awards for *Hairspray, Torch Song Trilogy*), born Brooklyn, NY, June 6, 1954.

Kenny G, 53, saxophone player, born Kenny Gorelick at Seattle, WA, June 6, 1956.

Paul Giamatti, 42, actor ("John Adams," *Sideways, American Splendor*), born New York, NY, June 6, 1967.

Amanda Pays, 50, actress ("Max Headroom," *Exposure*), born Berkshire, England, June 6, 1959.

Billie Whitelaw, 77, actress (*The Dressmaker*, "Masterpiece Theater"), born Coventry, England, June 6, 1932.

June 7 — Sunday

DAY 158 **207 REMAINING**

APGAR, VIRGINIA: 100th BIRTH ANNIVERSARY. June 7, 1909. Dr. Apgar developed the simple assessment method that permits doctors and nurses to evaluate newborns while they are still in the delivery room to identify those in need of immediate medical care. The Apgar score was first published in 1953, and the Perinatal Section of the American Academy of Pediatrics is named for Dr. Apgar. Born at Westfield, NJ, Apgar died Aug 7, 1974, at New York, NY.

BOONE DAY. June 7. Each year on June 7, the Kentucky Historical Society celebrates the anniversary of the day in 1767 when Daniel Boone, America's most famous frontiersman, reportedly first sighted the land that would become Kentucky. The June 7 date is taken from the book *The Discovery, Settlement and Present State of Kentucky*, by John Filson, published in 1784, with an appendix titled "The Adventures of Colonel Daniel Boone." The information in the appendix supposedly originated with Boone, although Filson is the actual author. The work is not considered completely reliable by historians.

BRADDOCK, JAMES: BIRTH ANNIVERSARY. June 7, 1906. James Walter Braddock, boxer, born at New York, NY. Braddock rose from the ranks of undistinguished fighters to win three key bouts in 1934 and 1935 that propelled him to a match for the heavyweight title. He upset the defending champion, Max Baer, on June 13, 1935, remained inactive for two years and then lost his first title defense to Joe Louis. Died at North Bergen, NJ, Nov 29, 1974.

BRUMMELL, GEORGE BRYAN "BEAU": BIRTH ANNIVERSARY. June 7, 1778. Born at London, England, Beau Brummell was, early in his life, a popular English men's fashion leader, the "arbiter elegantarium" of taste in dress. His extravagance and lack of tact (it was he who reportedly said—indicating the Prince of Wales, later George IV—"Who's your fat friend?") led him from wealth and popularity to poverty and disrepute. Once imprisoned for debt, he became careless of dress and personal appearance. He died in a charitable asylum at Caen, France, Mar 30, 1840.

CHILDREN'S AWARENESS MEMORIAL DAY. June 7. A day set aside each year to remember all of America's children who have died from violence. A day to bring flowers to the gravesite, have memorial services, spend time with or write a letter to a grieving parent or grandparent. A day to mourn and reach out with healing hands of love to those in need of support. Annually, the first Sunday in June. For info: Judith Natale, NCAC America-USA, PO Box 493703, Redding, CA 96049-3703. E-mail: childaware@aol.com.

GAUGUIN, (EUGENE HENRI) PAUL: BIRTH ANNIVERSARY. June 7, 1848. French painter born at Paris, France. Formerly a stockbroker, he became a painter in his middle age and three years later renounced his life at Paris to move to Tahiti. He is remembered best for his broad, flat tones and bold colors. Gauguin died May 8, 1903, at Atoana on the island of Hiva Oa in the Marquesas.

ITALY: GIOCO DEL PONTE. June 7. Pisa. The first Sunday in June is set aside for the Battle of the Bridge, a medieval parade and a contest for possession of the bridge.

JAPAN: DAY OF THE RICE GOD. June 7. Chiyoda. Annual rice-transplanting festival observed on first Sunday in June. Centuries-old rural folk ritual revived in 1930s and celebrated with colorful costumes, parades, music, dancing and prayers to the Shinto rice god Wbai-sama.

MALTA: NATIONAL DAY. June 7. National day or (in Maltese) Sette Giugno.

MARTIN, DEAN: BIRTH ANNIVERSARY. June 7, 1917. Actor/singer Dean Martin was born Dino Paul Crocetti, at Steubenville, OH. Martin's career was barely moving in 1946, when he met Jerry Lewis. Together they formed an unforgettable comedy act that carried them to dizzying heights of success. When the team broke up, Martin found continued success as a singer as well as a Hollywood film star. He died Dec 25, 1995, at Beverly Hills, CA.

MOON PHASE: FULL MOON. June 7. Moon enters Full Moon phase at 2:12 PM, EDT.

NATIONAL BUSINESS ETIQUETTE WEEK. June 7–13. A week to recognize the need for proper business etiquette/business intelligence necessary to compete in the growing global marketplace. Review everything from how to network to the proper handshake to how to remember names. Review the proper forms of address in business as well as government, military and academic areas. Annually, the first full week in June. For info: The Protocol School of Washington, PO Box 676, Columbia, SC 29202. Phone: (877) 766-3757. E-mail: info@psow.com. Web: www.psow.com.

NATIONAL CANCER SURVIVORS DAY. June 7. Hundreds of communities nationwide honor survivors who are living with and beyond cancer. The 22nd annual celebration of life. Annually, the first Sunday in June. For info: Natl Cancer Survivors Day Foundation, PO Box 682285, Franklin, TN 37068-2285. Phone: (615) 794-3006. Fax: (615) 794-0179. E-mail: info@ncsdf.org. Web: www.ncsdf.org.

NATIONAL HEADACHE AWARENESS WEEK. June 7–13. Educating the public about the reality and severity of headache pain as a legitimate neuro-biologic disease. Encouraging sufferers to consult with a health care provider for proper diagnosis and treatment, and to let sufferers know that there are new treatments available. Annually, the first full week in June. For info: Suzanne E Simons, Exec Dir, National Headache Foundation, 820 N Orleans, Ste 217, Chicago, IL 60610-3132. Phone: (312) 274-2651. Fax: (312) 640-9049.

ORTHODOX PENTECOST. June 7. Observed by Eastern Orthodox churches.

"THE $64,000 QUESTION" TV PREMIERE: ANNIVERSARY. June 7, 1955. This game show was a big hit, and the first of prime time's big money shows. Contestants, each an expert in one area, answered questions; each time a question was answered correctly, contestants doubled their money and the questions became harder. Players, if successful, could come back the following week. For the $64,000 question, a player could bring along an expert, but if neither got the correct answer, the player left with $4,000. The host was Hal March, assisted by Lynn Dollar and later Pat Donovan, and questions were compiled by Dr. Bergen Evans. Some famous contestants were Dr. Joyce Brothers, Barbara Feldon and Jack Benny (as a joke). The show was dropped in 1958 amid the game show scandals.

STRAWBERRY MOON. June 7. So called by Native American tribes of New England and the Great Lakes because at this time of the year the strawberry ripened. The June Full Moon.

SUPREME COURT STRIKES DOWN CONNECTICUT LAW BANNING CONTRACEPTION: ANNIVERSARY. June 7, 1965. In *Griswold v Connecticut*, the Supreme Court guaranteed the right to privacy, including the freedom from government intrusion into matters of birth control.

TANDY, JESSICA: 100th BIRTH ANNIVERSARY. June 7, 1909. Born June 7, 1909, at London, England, Tandy was an acclaimed stage actress who often collaborated with husband Hume Cronyn. She originated the role of Blanche DuBois in Tennessee Williams's *A Streetcar Named Desire* (1947) and was awarded a Tony. Her other Tony Awards came for her work in *The Gin Game* (1977) and *Foxfire* (1982). Also a frequent film actress, she won an Academy Award for her leading role in *Driving Miss Daisy* (1989). She continued to work up until her death on Sept 11, 1994, at Easton, CT.

TRINITY SUNDAY. June 7. Christian Holy Day on the Sunday after Pentecost commemorates the Holy Trinity, the three divine persons—Father, Son and Holy Spirit—in one God. See also: "Pentecost" (May 31).

VCR INTRODUCED: ANNIVERSARY. June 7, 1975. The Sony Corporation released its videocassette recorder, the Betamax, which sold for $995. Eventually, another VCR format, VHS, proved more successful and Sony stopped making the Betamax.

WRITE TO YOUR FATHER DAY. June 7. This is a challenge to all citizens to write a letter to their fathers. Ask, "What do you do (or have you done) that is most exciting to you, most scary, most enjoyable and/or most satisfying?" Don't expect a response, but ask anyway. Annually, the Sunday before Father's Day. For info: Evelyn Cole, 1748 Deer Canyon Rd, Arroyo Grande, CA 93420. Phone: (805) 473-0230. E-mail: evycole@hughes.net.

June 2009

S	M	T	W	T	F	S
	1	2	3	4	5	6
7	8	9	10	11	12	13
14	15	16	17	18	19	20
21	22	23	24	25	26	27
28	29	30				

BIRTHDAYS TODAY

Louise Erdrich, 55, author (*Love Medicine, The Beet Queen*), born Little Falls, MN, June 7, 1954.

Bear Grylls, 35, television personality ("Man vs. Wild"), author, born Isle of Wight, June 7, 1974.

Allen Iverson, 34, basketball player, born Hampton, VA, June 7, 1975.

Jenny Jones, 63, talk-show host, born London, ON, Canada, June 7, 1946.

Tom Jones, 69, singer ("It's Not Unusual"), born Thomas Woodward at Pontypridd, Wales, UK, June 7, 1940.

Anna Kournikova, 28, tennis player, born Moscow, Russia, June 7, 1981.

Bill Kreutzmann, Jr, 63, drummer, singer, cofounder of The Grateful Dead, born Palo Alto, CA, June 7, 1946.

Mike Modano, 39, hockey player, born Livonia, MI, June 7, 1970.

Liam Neeson, 57, actor (*Excalibur, Ethan Frome, Schindler's List*), born Ballymena, Northern Ireland, June 7, 1952.

Orhan Pamuk, 57, author (*Snow, My Name Is Red*, 2006 Nobel Prize for Literature), born Istanbul, Turkey, June 7, 1952.

Prince, 51, musician, singer, born Prince Rogers Nelson at Minneapolis, MN, June 7, 1958.

John Napier Turner, 80, Canada's 17th prime minister (served June 30, 1984–Sept 17, 1984), born Richmond, Surrey, England, June 7, 1929.

June 8 — Monday

DAY 159 | **206 REMAINING**

AMERICAN HEROINE REWARDED: ANNIVERSARY. June 8, 1697. On Mar 16, 1697, in an attack on Haverhill, MA, Indians captured Hannah Duston and killed her baby, killing or capturing 39 others in addition. After being taken to an Indian camp, she escaped on Apr 29 after killing 10 Indians with a tomahawk and scalping them as proof of her deed. On June 8 her husband was awarded, on her behalf, the sum of 25 pounds for her heroic efforts, the first public award to a woman in America.

ATTACK ON THE USS *LIBERTY*: ANNIVERSARY. June 8, 1967. At 2 PM local time, the unescorted US intelligence ship USS *Liberty*, sailing in international waters off the Egyptian coast, was attacked without warning by Israeli jet planes and three Israeli torpedo boats. It was strafed and hit repeatedly by rockets, cannon, napalm and finally a torpedo. Casualties: out of a crew of 294 Americans, there were 34 dead and 171 wounded. Israel apologized, claiming mistaken identity, but surviving crew members charged deliberate attack by Israel and cover-up by US authorities.

BILL OF RIGHTS PROPOSED: ANNIVERSARY. June 8, 1789. The Bill of Rights, which led to the first 10 amendments to the US Constitution, was first proposed by James Madison.

COCHISE: DEATH ANNIVERSARY. June 8, 1874. Born around 1810 in the Chiricahua Mountains of Arizona, Cochise became a fierce and courageous leader of the Apache. After his arrest in 1861, he escaped and launched the Apache Wars, which lasted for 25 years. He died 13 years later near his stronghold in southeastern Arizona.

CRICK, FRANCIS: BIRTH ANNIVERSARY. June 8, 1916. Discoverer with James Watson of the structure of DNA in 1953. Born at Northampton, England, Crick died at San Diego, CA, July 28, 2004.

ICELAND: LAKI VOLCANO ERUPTION: ANNIVERSARY. June 8, 1783. One of the most violent and important volcanic eruptions of recorded history began on this date. Laki, or Skafta, volcano in southern Iceland continued erupting for eight months, expelling an estimated 4½ cubic miles of lava, ultimately causing a famine and the deaths of nearly 10,000 persons. Acid rain reached western Europe, and other climatic and atmospheric changes were worldwide. English naturalist Gilbert White described some of the "horrible phenomena" of the summer of 1783, including the "peculiar haze, or smokey fog . . . unlike anything known within the memory of man." The effects of this volcanic eruption and its possible long-term consequences are still being studied by scientists. See also: "White, Gilbert: Birth Anniversary" (July 18).

MAINLY MOZART FESTIVAL. June 8–21. San Diego County and Baja California, Mexico. 21st annual. David Atherton conducts the festival's all-star orchestra and leading soloists and ensembles in a celebration of Mozart and the music of his contemporaries in San Diego and Escondito, CA, and Tijuana, Mexico. Chamber orchestra, chamber ensembles and recitals are featured. Est attendance: 10,000. For info: Public Relations, Mainly Mozart, 2802 Juan St, San Diego, CA 92110. Phone: (619) 239-0100. Fax: (619) 233-4292. E-mail: admin@mainlymozart.org. Web: www.mainlymozart.org.

McKINLEY, IDA SAXTON: BIRTH ANNIVERSARY. June 8, 1847. Wife of William McKinley, 25th president of the US, born at Canton, OH. Died at Canton, OH, May 26, 1907.

NATIONAL AUTOMOTIVE SERVICE PROFESSIONALS WEEK. June 8–14. Sponsored by the National Institute for Automotive Service Excellence (ASE), which was incorporated on June 12, 1972. ASE was founded to improve the quality of automotive service through voluntary testing and certification of service professionals. The goal of this week is to recognize automotive service professionals nationwide for their contribution to keeping America's cars and trucks running. The nonprofit organization also serves as an information source for professionals and consumers about automotive repair and related topics. For info: Trish Serratore, 101 Blue Seal Dr, Leesburg, VA 20175. Phone: (703) 669-6600. Fax: (703) 669-6127. E-mail: tmolla@ase.com. Web: www.ase.com.

QUEEN'S OFFICIAL BIRTHDAY. June 8. A holiday in Australia (except for Western Australia), Belize, Cayman Islands, Fiji and Papua New Guinea on the second Monday in June. In New Zealand and Tuvalu it is commemorated on the first Monday in June. Celebrating Queen Elizabeth II's "official" birthday, not the day she was actually born (which is Apr 21).

SPACE MILESTONE: *VENERA 9* AND *10* (USSR). June 8 and 14, 1975. Launched on these dates, unmanned exploration vehicles landed on Venus Oct 22 and 25, respectively. Sent first pictures ever transmitted from Venus, atmospheric analysis and other data.

STEVENSON DEPOT DAYS. June 8–14. Stevenson, AL. Depot Days brings back the days when the Iron Horse of the Rails was the King of Transportation. Activities are focused around the historic Stevenson Depot, an important junction during the Civil War now listed on the National Register of Historic Places. Activities include rides to Civil War fort, square dancing, storytelling contests, clogging, museum tours and big band entertainment. Street dance on Saturday night. Est attendance: 10,000. For info: Stevenson Depot Museum, PO Box 894, Stevenson, AL 35772. Phone: (205) 437-3012.

UPSY DAISY DAY. June 8. A day to remind people to get up gloriously, gratefully and gleefully each morning. For info: Stephanie West Allen, PO Box 9311, Denver, CO 80209. Phone: (303) 935-8866. E-mail: stephanie@westallen.com. Web: www.westallen.com.

WHITE, BYRON RAYMOND: BIRTH ANNIVERSARY. June 8, 1917. One of the longest serving justices of the Supreme Court of the US, Byron White was born June 8, 1917, at Fort Collins, CO. He was a football star in college (College Football Hall of Fame) and in the National Football League, as well as an academic standout: he was a Rhodes Scholar among other honors. A graduate of Yale Law

School, White was a successful lawyer and director of the Justice Department before being nominated by President Kennedy for the highest court on Apr 3, 1962. White took the oath of office Apr 16, 1962, and served 31 years before retiring in 1993. He died on April 15, 2002, at Denver, CO.

WRIGHT, FRANK LLOYD: BIRTH ANNIVERSARY. June 8, 1867. American architect born at Richland Center, WI. In his autobiography Wright wrote: "No house should ever be *on* any hill or on anything. It should be *of* the hill, belonging to it, so hill and house could live together each the happier for the other." Wright died at Phoenix, AZ, Apr 9, 1959.

WYTHE, GEORGE: DEATH ANNIVERSARY. June 8, 1806. Signer of the Declaration of Independence. Born at Elizabeth County, VA, about 1726 (exact date unknown). Died at Richmond, VA.

BIRTHDAYS TODAY

Scott Adams, 52, cartoonist ("Dilbert"), born Windham, NY, June 8, 1957.

Kathy Baker, 59, actress ("Picket Fences," *The Right Stuff*), born Midland, TX, June 8, 1950.

Tim Berners-Lee, 54, inventor of the World Wide Web, born London, England, June 8, 1955.

Barbara Pierce Bush, 84, former First Lady, wife of George H.W. Bush, 41st president of the US, born Rye, NY, June 8, 1925.

Bernie Casey, 70, former football player, actor (*I'm Gonna Git You Sucka*), born Wyco, WV, June 8, 1939.

Kim Clijsters, 26, tennis player, born Bilzen, Belgium, June 8, 1983.

James Darren, 73, singer ("Goodbye Cruel World"), actor (*Gidget*), born Philadelphia, PA, June 8, 1936.

Lindsay Davenport, 33, tennis player, born Palos Verdes, CA, June 8, 1976.

Griffin Dunne, 54, actor (*Straight Talk*), producer, born New York, NY, June 8, 1955.

Don Grady, 65, actor ("My Three Sons," "Mickey Mouse Club"), born San Diego, CA, June 8, 1944.

Julianna Margulies, 43, actress ("ER"), born Spring Valley, NY, June 8, 1966.

Sara Paretsky, 62, writer (*Killing Orders, Burn Marks*), born Ames, IA, June 8, 1947.

Joan Rivers, 72, comedienne, talk-show host, born New York, NY, June 8, 1937.

Boz Scaggs, 65, singer, musician, songwriter (*Silk Degrees, Middle Man*), born Dallas, TX, June 8, 1944.

Nancy Sinatra, 69, singer ("These Boots Are Made for Walkin'," "Something Stupid"), born Jersey City, NJ, June 8, 1940.

Jerry Stiller, 80, comedian, actor (*Hairspray*, "Seinfeld," "The King of Queens"), born Brooklyn, NY, June 8, 1929.

Keenen Ivory Wayans, 51, actor ("In Living Color"), born New York, NY, June 8, 1958.

Andrew Weil, MD, 67, physician and writer on natural healing, born Philadelphia, PA, June 8, 1942.

Kanye West, 32, singer, producer, born Atlanta, GA, June 8, 1977.

June 2009

S	M	T	W	T	F	S
	1	2	3	4	5	6
7	8	9	10	11	12	13
14	15	16	17	18	19	20
21	22	23	24	25	26	27
28	29	30				

June 9 — Tuesday

DAY 160 **205 REMAINING**

CUMMINGS, ROBERT: BIRTH ANNIVERSARY. June 9, 1908. American actor Robert Cummings was born Charles Clarence Robert Orville Cummings at Joplin, MO. His best-known role was in the film *Dial M for Murder* (1954). He won an Emmy for his role in the television version of *Twelve Angry Men* (1954) and starred in the popular comedy "The Bob Cummings Show" (1955–59). He died Dec 2, 1990, at Woodland Hills, CA.

DONALD DUCK: 75th BIRTHDAY. June 9, 1934. Donald Duck made his screen debut on this date with the release of "The Wise Little Hen," a short film in the Disney series of "Silly Symphonies."

HONG KONG: LEASE SIGNING ANNIVERSARY. June 9, 1898. Hong Kong, consisting of about 400 square miles (islands and mainland) with more than five million persons, was administered as a British Crown Colony after a 99-year lease was signed on June 9, 1898. In 1997 Hong Kong's sovereignty reverted to the People's Republic of China.

JORDAN: ACCESSION DAY. June 9. National holiday. Commemorates the accession to the throne of King Abdullah II in 1999, following the death of his father, King Hussein.

KUTNER, LUIS: BIRTH ANNIVERSARY. June 9, 1908. Human rights attorney Luis Kutner was born at Chicago, IL. Responsible for the release of many unjustly confined prisoners, he came to be known as "The Springman." He helped free Hungarian Cardinal Josef Mindszenty, poet Ezra Pound and former Congo president Moise Tshombe. He was the author of the living will and founded the World Habeas Corpus. Kutner was nominated nine times for the Nobel Peace Prize. He died Mar 1, 1993, at Chicago, IL.

LOLOMA, CHARLES: BIRTH ANNIVERSARY. June 9, 1921. Charles Loloma was a major influence on modern Native American art and was famous for changing the look of American Indian jewelry. A painter, sculptor and potter, he was best known for his jewelry, which broke tradition with previous Indian styles using materials such as coral, fossilized ivory, pearls and diamonds. Loloma was born at Hotevilla on the Hopi Indian Reservation and died June 9, 1991, at Scottsdale, AZ.

PAYNE, JOHN HOWARD: BIRTH ANNIVERSARY. June 9, 1791. American author, actor, diplomat, born at New York, NY. Died at Tunis, Apr 9, 1852. Author of opera libretto (*Clari, or The Maid of Milan*) that contained the song "Home, Sweet Home."

PORTER, COLE: BIRTH ANNIVERSARY. June 9, 1891. Cole Porter published his first song, "The Bobolink Waltz," at the age of 10. His career as a composer and lyricist for Broadway was launched in 1928 when five of his songs were used in the musical play *Let's Do It*. His prolific contributions to the Broadway stage include *Fifty Million Frenchmen, Wake Up and Dream, The Gay Divorcée, Anything Goes, Leave It to Me, Du Barry Was a Lady, Something for the Boys, Kiss Me Kate, Can Can* and *Silk Stockings*. Porter was born at Peru, IN, and died at Santa Monica, CA, Oct 15, 1964.

STEPHENSON, GEORGE: BIRTH ANNIVERSARY. June 9, 1781. English inventor, developer of the steam locomotive, born near Newcastle, England. Died near Chesterfield, England, Aug 12, 1848.

THAYER, SYLVANUS: BIRTH ANNIVERSARY. June 9, 1785. A military engineer and educator, born at Braintree, MA. He was appointed superintendent of West Point at 32 and became known as the "Father of the Military Academy." Thayer died at Braintree, MA, Sept 7, 1872.

BIRTHDAYS TODAY

Patricia Cornwell, 53, mystery writer (*All That Remains, Postmortem*), born Miami, FL, June 9, 1956.

Johnny Depp, 46, actor (*Pirates of the Caribbean* films; *Sweeney Todd, Ed Wood*), born Owensboro, KY, June 9, 1963.

Michael J. Fox, 48, actor ("Family Ties," "Spin City," *Back to the Future* films), born Edmonton, AB, Canada, June 9, 1961.

Marvin Kalb, 79, educator, journalist, born New York, NY, June 9, 1930.

Miroslav Klose, 31, soccer player, born Opole, Poland, June 9, 1978.

Jackie Mason, 75, comedian ("Chicken Soup," *The World According to Me*), born Yacov Moshe Maza at Sheboygan, WI, June 9, 1934.

Robert S. McNamara, 93, banker, former cabinet member, born San Francisco, CA, June 9, 1916.

David Gene (Dave) Parker, 58, former baseball player, born Calhoun, MS, June 9, 1951.

Les Paul, 94, guitar player, born Waukesha, WI, June 9, 1915.

Natalie Portman, 28, actress (*Star Wars* films; *The Other Boleyn Girl, Closer*), born Jerusalem, June 9, 1981.

Ashley Postell, 23, gymnast, born Cheverly, MD, June 9, 1986.

Gloria Reuben, 45, actress ("ER"), born Toronto, ON, Canada, June 9, 1964.

Peja Stojakovic, 32, basketball player, born Predrag Stojakovic at Belgrade, Yugoslavia, June 9, 1977.

Dick Vitale, 70, sportscaster, ESPN and ABC analyst, born East Rutherford, NJ, June 9, 1939.

June 10 — Wednesday

DAY 161 — **204 REMAINING**

ALCOHOLICS ANONYMOUS: FOUNDING ANNIVERSARY. June 10, 1935. On this day at Akron, OH, Dr. Robert Smith completed his first day of permanent sobriety. "Doctor Bob" and William G. Wilson are considered to have founded Alcoholics Anonymous on that day.

BALLPOINT PEN PATENTED: ANNIVERSARY. June 10, 1943. Hungarian Laszlo Biro patented the ballpoint pen, which he had been developing since the 1930s. He was living in Argentina, where he had gone to escape the Nazis. In many languages, the word for ballpoint pen is *biro*.

BELLOW, SAUL: BIRTH ANNIVERSARY. June 10, 1915. Born at Lachine, Canada, Bellow would become one of America's great postwar authors, examining the urban antiheroes at war with the society they live in. His novels included *The Adventures of Augie March* (1953), *Herzog* (1964) and *Mr Sammler's Planet* (1970). Garnered numerous National Book Awards as well as a Pulitzer. Winner of the Nobel Prize for Literature in 1976. Died at Brookline, MA, Apr 5, 2005.

CONGO (BRAZZAVILLE): DAY OF NATIONAL RECONCILIATION. June 10. National holiday. Commemorates official conference in 1991.

CZECHOSLOVAKIA: RAPE OF LIDICE: ANNIVERSARY. June 10, 1942. Nazi German troops executed, by shooting, all male inhabitants of the Czechoslovakian village of Lidice (total population about 500 persons), burned every house and deported the women and children to Germany for "reeducation." One of the most-remembered atrocities of WWII. June 10, Lidice Memorial Day, is observed in New Jersey.

FIRST MINT IN AMERICA: ANNIVERSARY. June 10, 1652. In defiance of English colonial law, John Hull, a silversmith, established the first mint in America. The first coin issued was the Pine Tree Shilling, designed by Hull.

GARLAND, JUDY: BIRTH ANNIVERSARY. June 10, 1922. American actress and singer born Frances Gumm at Grand Rapids, MN. While Garland played in many films and toured widely as a singer, she is probably most remembered for her portrayal of Dorothy Gale in the now-classic *The Wizard of Oz*. Died June 22, 1969, at London, England.

JORDAN: GREAT ARAB REVOLT AND ARMY DAY. June 10. Commemorates the beginning of the Great Arab Revolt in 1916. National holiday.

McDANIEL, HATTIE: BIRTH ANNIVERSARY. June 10, 1889. Hattie McDaniel was the first African American to win an Academy Award. She won it in 1940 for her role in the 1939 film *Gone with the Wind*. Her career spanned radio and vaudeville in addition to her screen roles in *Judge Priest, The Little Colonel, Showboat* and *Saratoga*, among others. She was born at Wichita, KS, and died Oct 26, 1952, at Los Angeles, CA.

NCAA DIVISION I MEN'S & WOMEN'S OUTDOOR TRACK & FIELD CHAMPIONSHIPS. June 10–13. Fayetteville, AR. Est attendance: 20,000. For info: NCAA, 700 W Washington St, PO Box 6222, Indianapolis, IN 46206-6222. Phone: (317) 917-6222. Fax: (317) 917-6826. Web: www.NCAAsports.com.

PORTUGAL: DAY OF PORTUGAL. June 10. National holiday. Anniversary of the death in 1580 of Portugal's national poet, Luis Vas de Camoes (Camoens), born in 1524 (exact date unknown) at either Lisbon or Coimbra. Died at Lisbon, Portugal.

BIRTHDAYS TODAY

F. Lee Bailey, 76, lawyer, born Waltham, MA, June 10, 1933.

John Edwards, 56, former US Senator (D, North Carolina), born Seneca, SC, June 10, 1953.

Linda Evangelista, 44, model, born St. Catharines, ON, Canada, June 10, 1965.

Jeff Greenfield, 66, author, journalist, born New York, NY, June 10, 1943.

Nat Hentoff, 84, music critic, journalist, born Boston, MA, June 10, 1925.

Elizabeth Hurley, 44, model, actress (*Austin Powers: International Man of Mystery*), born Basingstoke, England, June 10, 1965.

Bobby Jindal, 38, Governor of Louisiana (R), born Piyush Jindal at Baton Rouge, LA, June 6, 1971.

Tara Lipinski, 27, figure skater, born Philadelphia, PA, June 10, 1982.

Doug McKeon, 43, actor (*On Golden Pond*), born Pomptain Plains, NJ, June 10, 1966.

Prince Philip, 88, Duke of Edinburgh, husband of Queen Elizabeth II, born Corfu, Greece, June 10, 1921.

Maurice Sendak, 81, author, illustrator (*Chicken Soup with Rice, Where the Wild Things Are*), born Brooklyn, NY, June 10, 1928.

Leelee Sobieski, 27, actress (*The Glass House, A Soldier's Daughter Never Cries*), born New York, NY, June 10, 1982.

Jeanne Tripplehorn, 46, actress (*The Firm, Waterworld, Mickey Blue Eyes*), born Tulsa, OK, June 10, 1963.

June 11 — Thursday

DAY 162 203 REMAINING

"AMERICAN IDOL" TV PREMIERE: ANNIVERSARY. June 11, 2002. FOX's phenomenally successful talent show was based on a British program. Talented singers compete for a major label record deal while being judged by a panel of highly critical music experts: Simon Cowell, Paula Abdul and Randy Jackson. The audience participates by phoning in votes for favorites. Ryan Seacrest hosts. The first "American Idol" was Kelly Clarkson, who has gone on to top-charting success and Grammys.

CHICAGO BLUES FESTIVAL. June 11–14. Grant Park, Chicago, IL. 26th annual. Largest free blues festival in the world. Est attendance: 800,000. For info: Mayor's Office of Special Events, City Hall, 121 N LaSalle St, #806, Chicago, IL 60602. Phone: (312) 744-3370. Fax: (312) 744-8523. E-mail: SpecialEvents@cityofchicago.org. Web: www.chicagobluesfestival.us.

CONSTABLE, JOHN: BIRTH ANNIVERSARY. June 11, 1776. English landscape painter. Born at East Bergholt, Suffolk, England, he died at London, Mar 31, 1837.

CORPUS CHRISTI. June 11. Roman Catholic festival celebrated in honor of the Eucharist. A solemnity observed on the Thursday following Trinity Sunday since 1246. In the US Corpus Christi is celebrated on the Sunday following Trinity Sunday. See also: "Corpus Christi (US Observance)" (June 14).

COUSTEAU, JACQUES: BIRTH ANNIVERSARY. June 11, 1910. French undersea explorer, writer and filmmaker born at St. Andre-de-Cubzac, France. He invented the Aqualung, which allowed him and his colleagues to produce more than 80 documentary films about undersea life, two of which won Oscars. This scientist and explorer was awarded the French Legion of Honor for his work in the Resistance in WWII. He died June 25, 1997, at Paris.

GERMANY: BACH FESTIVAL. June 11–21. Leipzig. Since 1904, the Festival has been held in Leipzig, where Johann Sebastian Bach lived in his later years and composed some of his best-known works. Est attendance: 50,000. For info: Bach-Archiv Leipzig, PO Box 101349, 04013 Leipzig, Germany. E-mail: bachfest@bach-leipzig.de. Web: www.bachfestleipzig.de.

GLENN MILLER BIRTHPLACE SOCIETY FESTIVAL. June 11–14. Clarinda, IA. To commemorate Glenn Miller's contribution to big band music through exhibits, concerts, films, performances by winners of Glenn Miller scholarships and a big band dance. Annually, the second full weekend in June. Est attendance: 5,500. For info: Glenn Miller Birthplace Society, PO Box 61, Clarinda, IA 51632. Phone: (712) 542-2461. Fax: (712) 542-2461. E-mail: gmbs@heartland.net. Web: www.glennmiller.org.

GREAT AMERICAN BRASS BAND FESTIVAL. June 11–14. Centre College Campus, Danville, KY. Brass bands and ensembles from throughout the country in concert Saturday and Sunday. Free to the public. Est attendance: 40,000. For info: Great American Brass Band Festival, c/o Danville/Boyle CVB, 105 E Walnut St, Danville, KY 40422. Phone: (800) 755-0076. Fax: (859) 236-9134. E-mail: carolyn@danvillekentucky.com. Web: www.gabbf.org.

June 2009	S	M	T	W	T	F	S
		1	2	3	4	5	6
	7	8	9	10	11	12	13
	14	15	16	17	18	19	20
	21	22	23	24	25	26	27
	28	29	30				

JONSON, BEN: BIRTH ANNIVERSARY. June 11, 1572. (Old Style date.) English playwright and poet. "Talking and eloquence," he wrote, "are not the same: to speak and to speak well, are two things." Born at London, England, he died there Aug 6, 1637 (OS). The epitaph written on his tombstone in Westminster Abbey: "O rare Ben Jonson."

KING KAMEHAMEHA I DAY. June 11. Designated state holiday in Hawaii honors memory of Hawaiian monarch (1737–1819). Governor appoints state commission to plan annual celebration.

LIBYA: EVACUATION DAY. June 11. National day. Commemorates the closing of US base in 1970.

LOMBARDI, VINCE: BIRTH ANNIVERSARY. June 11, 1913. Vincent Thomas (Vince) Lombardi, Pro Football Hall of Fame coach, born at New York, NY. Lombardi played football for Fordham's famed "Seven Blocks of Granite" line in the mid-1930s, became a teacher and began to coach high school football. He became offensive line coach at West Point in 1949 and moved to the New York Giants in 1954. Five years later, he was named head coach of the Green Bay Packers. His Packers won five NFL titles and two Super Bowls in nine years, and Lombardi was generally regarded as the greatest coach and the finest motivator in pro football history. He retired in 1968, but was lured back to coach the Washington Redskins a year later. Inducted into the Pro Football Hall of Fame in 1971. Died at Washington, DC, Sept 3, 1970.

MOUNT PINATUBO ERUPTS IN PHILIPPINES: ANNIVERSARY. June 11, 1991. Long-dormant volcano Mount Pinatubo erupted with a violent explosion, spewing ash and gases that could be seen for more than 60 miles. The surrounding areas were covered with ash and mud created by rainstorms. US military bases Clark and Subic Bay were also damaged. On July 6, 1992, Ellsworth Dutton of the National Oceanic and Atmospheric Administration's Climate Monitoring and Diagnostics Laboratory announced that a layer of sulfuric acid droplets released into the Earth's atmosphere by the eruption had cooled the planet's average temperature by about 1 degree Fahrenheit. The greatest difference was noted in the Northern Hemisphere with a drop of 1.5 degrees. Although the temperature drop was temporary, the climate trend made determining the effect of greenhouse warming on the Earth more difficult.

NATIONAL NURSING ASSISTANTS DAY AND WEEK. June 11–18. 32nd annual. Recognizes those nursing assistants who provide care to all ill, elderly and long-term residents in nursing homes and other long-term nursing care centers. Begins on Career Nurse Assistants' Day, June 11, 2009, which focuses on these specialists in the art of caring. For info: Natl Network of Career Nursing Assistants, 3577 Easton Rd, Norton, OH 44203. Phone: (330) 825-9342. Fax: (330) 825-9378. E-mail: cnajeni@aol.com. Web: www.cna-network.org.

RANKIN, JEANNETTE: BIRTH ANNIVERSARY. June 11, 1880. First woman elected to the US Congress, a reformer, feminist and pacifist, was born at Missoula, MT. She was the only member of Congress to vote against a declaration of war against Japan in December 1941. Died May 18, 1973, at Carmel, CA.

RED ARMY DEPARTS BERLIN: 15th ANNIVERSARY. June 11, 1994. After 49 years, the Russian military occupation of the region once called East Germany ended. At one time there had been 337,800 Soviet troops stationed in Germany. The departure was celebrated with a parade in Wupnsdorf south of Berlin, which was the Soviet Union's military headquarters in the former German Democratic Republic.

"SPACE ODDITY" SONG RELEASE: 40th ANNIVERSARY. June 11, 1969. This single recorded by David Bowie was released to coincide with the *Apollo 11*'s trip to the moon, during which Neil Armstrong and Edwin Aldrin, Jr, landed and walked on the surface of the moon.

STRAUSS, RICHARD GEORG: BIRTH ANNIVERSARY. June 11, 1864. German composer, musician and conductor whose best-remembered works are *Till Eulenspiegel* (1895), *Also Sprach Zarathustra* (1896) and *Don Quixote* (1898). Born at Munich, he died at Garmisch-Partenkirchen, Germany, after a heart attack Sept 8, 1949, at age 85.

STYRON, WILLIAM: BIRTH ANNIVERSARY. June 11, 1925. Winner of both the National Book Award and the Pulitzer Prize for Literature, Styron was born at Newport News, VA. His acclaimed 1967 novel, *The Confessions of Nat Turner,* a fictionalized memoir of the leader of an 1831 slave rebellion, drew upon his knowledge of Virginia. *Sophie's Choice* (1979), chronicled the life of a non-Jewish Nazi victim. He also chronicled his own struggles with debilitating depression in *Darkness Visible* (1990). Styron died at Martha's Vineyard, MA, Nov 1, 2006.

SUPERMAN CELEBRATION. June 11–14. Metropolis, IL. Weekend full of Super activities. See 15-ft Superman Statue, live entertainment, super museum, road race, carnival, tennis tourney, Supertrek bicycle ride, super car show, washer pitch tournament, weight lifting, arm wrestling, children's games and food fair. Est attendance: 50,000. For info: Metropolis Area Chamber of Commerce, Tourism & Economic Development, PO Box 188, Metropolis, IL 62960. Phone: (618) 524-2714 or (800) 949-5740. Fax: (618) 524-4780. E-mail: metrochamber@hcis.net. Web: www.metropolischamber.com.

BIRTHDAYS TODAY

Adrienne Barbeau, 64, actress ("Maude"), born Sacramento, CA, June 11, 1945.

Peter Bergman, 56, actor ("All My Children," "The Young & the Restless"), born Guantanamo Bay, Cuba, June 11, 1953.

Chad Everett, 73, actor ("The Dakotas," "Medical Center"), born Raymond Cramton at South Bend, IN, June 11, 1936.

Joshua Jackson, 31, actor ("Dawson's Creek," *Scream 2*), born Vancouver, BC, Canada, June 11, 1978.

Hugh Laurie, 50, actor ("House," "Jeeves & Wooster"), born Oxford, Oxfordshire, England, June 11, 1959.

Joseph C. (Joe) Montana, Jr, 53, former sportscaster and Hall of Fame football player, born New Eagle, PA, June 11, 1956.

Jackie Stewart, 70, former auto racer, born Dunbartonshire, Scotland, June 11, 1939.

Gene Wilder, 70, actor (*The Producers, Willy Wonka & the Chocolate Factory, Blazing Saddles, Young Frankenstein*), director, born Milwaukee, WI, June 11, 1939 (some sources say 1935 or 1933).

June 12 — Friday

DAY 163 — **202 REMAINING**

BANANA SPLIT FESTIVAL. June 12–13. JW Denver Williams Memorial Park, Wilmington, OH. 15th annual. A festival celebrating Wilmington as the birthplace of the banana split. Enjoy live concerts, crafters, vendors, great food, games and kids activities and a make-your-own banana split booth. Est attendance: 14,000. For info: Clinton County CVB, 13 N South St, Wilmington, OH 45177. Phone: (877) 428-4748. Fax: (937) 382-1738. E-mail: info@clintoncountyohio.com. Web: www.clintoncountyohio.com.

BASEBALL'S FIRST PERFECT GAME: ANNIVERSARY. June 12, 1880. Lee Richmond of the Worcester Ruby Legs (National League) pitched baseball's first perfect game (not allowing a single opposing player to reach first base), 1–0, against the Cleveland Indians.

BELL TOWER FESTIVAL. June 12–15. Jefferson, IA. Community pride is at its best at the Bell Tower Festival! Celebrating the community's most visible and unique tourist attraction, the Mahanay Memorial Bell Tower. Most of the events take place on the town square, right under the bell tower. The Saturday morning parade starts the festival; there's entertainment on Plaza Stage throughout the day and a bistro on both Friday and Saturday nights with live music. Everyone enjoys the booth vendors that line the square selling their wares and great "fair" food. Annually, the second weekend in June. Est attendance: 7,000. For info: Jefferson Area Chamber of Commerce, 220 N Chestnut, Jefferson, IA 50129. Phone: (515) 386-2155. Fax: (515) 386-2156. E-mail: commerce@jeffersoniowa.com. Web: belltowerfestival.org.

BIG BEND NATIONAL PARK ESTABLISHED: 65th ANNIVERSARY. June 12, 1944. Area on the "big bend" of the Rio Grande River in western Texas along the Mexican border was established as a national park (authorized June 20, 1935). For further park info: Big Bend Natl Park, Big Bend Natl Park, TX 79834.

BLUES ON THE FOX. June 12–13. Aurora, IL. Blues on the Fox is the celebration of the historical blues recordings done in Aurora. It brings famous blues musicians from around the country. Annually, the second weekend in June. For info: City of Aurora, Mayor's Office of Special Events, 5 E Downer Pl, Ste A, Aurora, IL 60507. Phone: (630) 844-4731. Fax: (630) 844-4797. E-mail: info@bluesonthefoxaurora.com. Web: www.bluesonthefoxaurora.com.

BUSH, GEORGE HERBERT WALKER: 85th BIRTHDAY. June 12, 1924. 41st president of US (1989–93), 43rd vice president of US (1981–89), born at Milton, MA.

COIN & STAMP EXPO. June 12–14. Radisson Hotel, Sherman Oaks, CA. Est attendance: 5,000. For info: Israel Bick, Exec Dir, Intl Stamp & Coin Collectors Society, PO Box 854, Van Nuys, CA 91408. Phone: (818) 997-6496. Fax: (818) 988-4337. E-mail: iibick@sbcglobal.net. Web: www.bick.net.

CRAWFORDSVILLE STRAWBERRY FESTIVAL. June 12–14. Crawfordsville, IN. Festival at historic Lane Place includes three days of arts and crafts, food, music and children's activities. Great music, classic car show (Sunday), softball and tennis tournaments, antique tractor exhibits and 4-mile run. All city museums open. Est attendance: 20,000. For info: Montgomery County Visitors & Conv Bureau, Inc, 218 E Pike St, Crawfordsville, IN 47933. Phone: (800) 866-3973. Fax: (317) 362-5215. E-mail: request@crawfordsville.org. Web: www.thestrawberryfestival.com.

CROWDED NEST AWARENESS DAY. June 12. More adult children are coming home, aging parents are moving in or you're raising grandchildren. Survival, humor and support is the key for CNS sufferers. For info: Kathleen Shaputis, PO Box 11056, Olympia, WA 98508. Phone: (360) 791-2041. E-mail: Kathleen@Shaputis.com. Web: www.crowdednestsyndrome.com.

FIRST MAN-POWERED FLIGHT ACROSS ENGLISH CHANNEL: 30th ANNIVERSARY. June 12, 1979. Bryan Allen, 26-year-old Californian, pedaled the 70-1b *Gossamer Albatross* 22 miles across the English Channel, from Folkestone, England, to Cape Gris-Nez, France, in 2 hours, 49 minutes, winning (with the craft's designer, Paul MacCready of Pasadena, CA) the £100,000 prize offered by British industrialist Henry Kremer for the first man-powered flight across the English Channel.

FRANK, ANNE: 80th BIRTH ANNIVERSARY. June 12, 1929. Born at Frankfurt, Germany. Anne Frank's family moved to Amsterdam to escape the Nazis, but after Holland was invaded by Germany, they had to go into hiding. In 1942 Anne began to keep a diary. She died at Bergen-Belsen concentration camp in 1945. After the war, her father published her diary, on which a stage play and movie were later based. See also: "Diary of Anne Frank: The Last Entry: Anniversary" (Aug 1).

***LOVING v VIRGINIA*: ANNIVERSARY.** June 12, 1967. The US Supreme Court decision in *Loving v Virginia* swept away all 16 remaining state laws prohibiting interracial marriages.

MAINSTRASSE VILLAGE "ORIGINAL" GOETTAFEST. June 12–14. MainStrasse Village, Covington, KY. A celebration of goetta, a favorite regional food. Arts & crafts, great entertainment, plenty of goetta and other favorite festival food makes this a fun-filled weekend for the entire family. Est attendance: 25,000. For info: Donna Kremer,

MainStrasse Village, 406 West 6th St, Ste 201, Covington, KY 41011. Phone: (859) 491-0458. Fax: (859) 655-7932. E-mail: dkremer@mainstrasse.org. Web: www.mainstrasse.org.

MINNESOTA INVENTORS CONGRESS. June 12–13. Redwood Falls, MN. 52nd Congress. Promoting innovation and the development of ideas into marketable products. Inventors are supported at this trade show by finding ways to test-market their ideas, selling their market-ready products and connecting with reliable resources. Highlights include more than 50–80 inventions from around the world, student inventors, the Minnesota Inventors Hall of Fame exhibit and Inventing Success workshops. Est attendance: 3,500. For info: Minnesota Inventors Congress, PO Box 71, Redwood Falls, MN 56283-0071. Phone: (507) 627-2344 or (800) IN VENT-1. Fax: (507) 637-4082. E-mail: mic@inventhelper.org. Web: www.inventhelper.org.

MISS OHIO SCHOLARSHIP PROGRAM PAGEANT. June 12–20. Renaissance Theatre, Mansfield, OH. Part of the Miss America Organization. For info: Miss Ohio Scholarship Program, PO Box 1818, Mansfield, OH 44901. Phone: (419) 522-6677. Fax: (419) 522-0054. E-mail: info@missohio.org. Web: www.missohio.org.

NATIONAL BASEBALL HALL OF FAME DEDICATED: 70th ANNIVERSARY. June 12, 1939. The National Baseball Hall of Fame and Museum, Inc, was dedicated at Cooperstown, NY. More than 200 individuals have been honored for their contributions to the game of baseball by induction into the Baseball Hall of Fame. The first players chosen for membership (1936) were Ty Cobb, Honus Wagner, Babe Ruth, Christy Mathewson and Walter Johnson. Relics and memorabilia from the history of baseball are housed at this shrine of America's national sport.

OK MOZART FESTIVAL. June 12–20. Bartlesville, OK. Festival features world-class artists performing with Amici New York Orchestra. Est attendance: 15,000. For info: Mandy Brummett, Public Relations Director, OK Mozart Intl Festival, Box 2344, Bartlesville, OK 74005. Phone: (918) 336-9900. Fax: (918) 336-9525. Web: www.okmozart.com.

PARAGUAY: PEACE WITH BOLIVIA DAY. June 12. Commemorates the end of the Chaco War in 1935.

PHILIPPINES: INDEPENDENCE DAY. June 12. National holiday. Declared independence from Spain in 1898.

RUSSIA: INDEPENDENCE DAY. June 12. National holiday. Commemorates the election in 1991 of the first popularly elected leader (Yeltsin) in the 1,000-year history of the Russian state.

SEA MUSIC FESTIVAL. June 12–14. Mystic, CT. World-famous musicians perform aboard Mystic Seaport's tall ships or in concert. Est attendance: 6,000. For info: Mystic Seaport, 75 Greenmanville Ave, Box 6000, Mystic, CT 06355. Phone: (860) 572-5315 or (888) 973-2767. Web: www.mysticseaport.org.

SPACE MILESTONE: *VENERA 4* (USSR). June 12, 1967. Launched on this date, this instrumental capsule landed on Venus by parachute on Oct 18 and reported a temperature of 536°F.

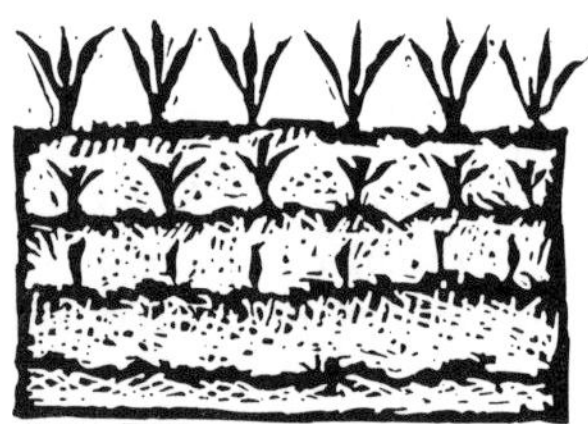

June 2009	S	M	T	W	T	F	S
		1	2	3	4	5	6
	7	8	9	10	11	12	13
	14	15	16	17	18	19	20
	21	22	23	24	25	26	27
	28	29	30				

"TEAR DOWN THIS WALL" SPEECH: ANNIVERSARY. June 12, 1987. US President Ronald Reagan, standing at the Brandenburg Gate and the Berlin Wall, gave one of the most powerful speeches of his career when he challenged Soviet President Mikhail Gorbachev to give liberalization in the Eastern Bloc more than lip service: "General Secretary Gorbachev, if you seek peace, if you seek prosperity for the Soviet Union and Eastern Europe, if you seek liberalization: Come here to this gate! Mr Gorbachev, open this gate! Mr Gorbachev, tear down this wall!" The speech was audible to East Berliners, but East German police made a gathering crowd at the Wall disperse. The State Department had sought to make the speech more conciliatory, but Reagan and his speechwriter, Peter Robinson, refused. The wall was finally opened in 1989. See also: "Berlin Wall Opened: Anniversary" (Nov 9).

***TECUMSEH!*: THE EPIC OUTDOOR DRAMA.** June 12–Sept 5 (Mondays through Saturdays). Chillicothe, OH. Witness the spectacular reenactment of the life and death of the great Shawnee leader Tecumseh. Held in the large, tiered amphitheater nestled in the hardwood forest of Sugarloaf Mountain. Take a backstage tour, visit the Prehistoric Museum, dine in the open-air Tecumseh Restaurant Terrace. Est attendance: 60,000. For info: Tecumseh!, PO Box 73, Chillicothe, OH 45601-0073. Phone toll-free after Mar 1: (866) 775-0700. Fax: (740) 775-4349. E-mail: tecumseh@bright.net. Web: www.tecumsehdrama.com.

TEXAS FOLKLIFE FESTIVAL. June 12–14. San Antonio, TX. Provides an entertaining and historic understanding of the crafts, art, food, music, history and heritage of the more than 40 different cultures and ethnic groups that settled and developed the state of Texas. Est attendance: 50,000. For info: Texas Folklife Festival, Institute of Texan Cultures, 801 S Bowie St, San Antonio, TX 78205-3296. Phone: (210) 458-2390. Fax: (210) 458-2213. Web: www.texasfolklifefestival.org.

WINDSURFING REGATTA/UNVARNISHED MUSIC FESTIVAL. June 12–14. Worthington, MN. Windsurfing on Lake Okabena. Regatta, surfing instruction, swap meet. Traditional music. At sunset, "unvarnished and unamplified" music on the beach. Beer garden and food vendors. Est attendance: 8,000. For info: Worthington Conv & Visitors Bureau, 1121 Third Ave, Worthington, MN 56187. Phone: (800) 279-2919 or (507) 372-2919. Fax: (507) 372-2827. E-mail: wcofc@frontiernet.net.

BIRTHDAYS TODAY

Marv Albert, 66, sportscaster, born Marvin Philip Aufrichtig at New York, NY, June 12, 1943.

Timothy Busfield, 52, actor ("thirtysomething," *Field of Dreams*), born Lansing, MI, June 12, 1957.

George Herbert Walker Bush, 85, 41st president of the US, born Milton, MA, June 12, 1924.

Chick Corea, 68, musician, born Chelsea, MA, June 12, 1941.

Vic Damone, 81, singer ("On the Street Where You Live"), born Vito Farinola at New York, NY, June 12, 1928.

Hideki Matsui, 35, baseball player, born Ishikawa, Japan, June 12, 1974.

Jim Nabors, 77, actor ("The Andy Griffith Show," "Gomer Pyle, U.S.M.C."), singer, born Sylacauga, AL, June 12, 1932.

Frances O'Connor, 40, actress (*The Importance of Being Earnest, Mansfield Park*), born Oxford, England, June 12, 1969.

David Rockefeller, 94, banker, born New York, NY, June 12, 1915.

June 13 — Saturday

DAY 164 201 REMAINING

ANTIQUES ON THE DIAMOND. June 13. Ligonier, PA. 70 quality antique dealers from six states set up their products along the Diamond. Est attendance: 10,000. For info: Ligonier Chamber of Commerce, 120 E Main St, Ligonier, PA 15658. Phone: (724) 238-4200. Fax: (724) 238-4610. E-mail: thechamber@ligonier.com. Web: www.ligonier.com.

BATTLE CREEK CEREAL FESTIVAL (WITH WORLD'S LARGEST BREAKFAST TABLE). June 13. Battle Creek, MI. Featuring a festival parade, arts and crafts, 5k and 10k races, family fun walk, food bank fund-raiser, vendor booths and children's games. The World's Largest Breakfast Table will be from 8 AM–noon, featuring 600 volunteers serving free breakfasts to more than 60,000 people. Annually, the second Saturday in June. Est attendance: 60,000. For info: Battle Creek Cereal Festival, Arts & Industry Council, 77 E Michigan Ave, Ste 190, PO Box 1079, Battle Creek, MI 49016. Phone: (269) 441-2700. Web: www.battlecreekvisitors.org.

BIG MAC SHORELINE SPRING SCENIC BIKE TOUR. June 13–14. Mackinaw City, MI. Bike tours of 25-, 50-, 75- and 100-mile routes along the Lake Michigan shoreline past sparkling water, windswept dunes, through the renowned "Tunnel of Trees," over rolling hills and through quaint resort towns. The weekend concludes with a Sunday morning bike ride across the Mighty Mackinac Bridge. For info: Mackinaw Chamber of Commerce, PO Box 856, Mackinaw City, MI 49701. Phone: (231) 436-5574. Fax: (231) 436-7989. E-mail: info@mackinawchamber.com. Web: www.mackinawchamber.com.

BUZZARD DAY FESTIVAL. June 13. Makoshika State Park, Glendive, MT. Festival activities include 5k and 10k runs, a pancake breakfast, kids' fun fest, nature walks, FOLF (frisbee golf) tournament and lots more. Est attendance: 600. For info: Makoshika State Park, 1301 Snyder Ave, PO Box 1242, Glendive, MT 59330. Phone: (406) 377-6256. Fax: (406) 377-8043. E-mail: makoshika@mt.gov. Web: www.makoshika.org.

CAMBRIDGE POTTERY FESTIVAL AND US POTTERY GAMES. June 13–14. Cambridge, WI. An all-clay event. A nationally recognized art fair featuring potters from all over the US. Professional potters compete in timed events in the US Pottery Games and auction off pottery for scholarships. The hands-on learning center lets you try your hand at wheel-throwing. Lots of food, fun and Raku firing by the local Clay Guild. Est attendance: 5,000. For info: Cambridge Pottery Festival and US Pottery Games, PO Box 393, Cambridge, WI 53523. Web: www.cambridgepotteryfestival.org.

ENGLAND: TROOPING THE COLOUR—THE QUEEN'S OFFICIAL BIRTHDAY PARADE. June 13 (tentative). Horse Guards Parade, Whitehall, London. Colorful ceremony with music and pageantry during which Her Majesty The Queen takes the salute from her Household Division. Observance dates from 1805 in the reign of King George III. Starts at 11 AM. When requesting info, send SASE. Trooping the Colour is always the second or third Saturday in June; The Queen's real birthday is Apr 21. For info: The Ticket Office, HQ Household Division, Horse Guards, Whitehall, London, England SW1A 2AX. Phone: (44) (020) 7414-2479. Web: www.army.mod.uk/ceremonialandheritage/household. Est attendance: 6,500.

EVERS, MEDGAR ASSASSINATED: ANNIVERSARY. June 13, 1963. Civil rights leader Medgar Wiley Evers was active in seeking integration of schools and voter registration. He was assassinated by Byron de la Beckwith. The public outrage following his death was one of the factors that led President John F. Kennedy to propose a comprehensive civil rights law.

FIRST ROLLER COASTER OPENS: 125th ANNIVERSARY. June 13, 1884. The world's first roller coaster opened today in 1884 at Coney Island, Brooklyn, NY. Built and later patented by LaMarcus Thompson, the "Gravity Pleasure Switchback Railway" boasted two parallel 600-foot tracks that descended from 50 feet. The cars traveled at six miles per hour. Riders paid five cents for their ride. The roller coaster was a sensation and soon amusement parks all over the US and the world featured them.

FRANCE: 24 HOURS OF LE MANS. June 13–14 (tentative). Le Mans. 77th annual. Organized on a regular basis since 1923, it is the biggest sporting challenge for car manufacturers because it is based on "being the best over 24 hours." More than 55 teams compete in this storied road test. Est attendance: 250,000. For info: Automobile Club de l'Ouest, Circuit des 24 Heures, 72019 Le Mans, France. Web: www.lemans.org.

GRANGE, RED: BIRTH ANNIVERSARY. June 13, 1903. Harold Edward ("Red") Grange, Pro Football Hall of Fame halfback and broadcaster, born at Forskville, PA. Perhaps the most famous football player of all time, Grange had a spectacular college career at the University of Illinois, being named an All-American in 1923, 1924 and 1925. When Illinois dedicated its Memorial Stadium on Oct 18, 1924, Grange scored four touchdowns against Michigan in the game's first 12 minutes. Known as the "Galloping Ghost," Grange joined the Chicago Bears in 1925 for what amounted to a barnstorming tour, the start of a professional career dictated by Grange and his manager, Charles C. ("Cash and Carry") Pyle. He retired in 1934 following a knee injury, having put pro football on the sports map. Grange entered business and did announcing work on radio and television. In retirement, he lived quietly and humbly. Inducted into the Hall of Fame as a charter member in 1963. Died at Lake Wales, FL, Jan 28, 1991.

HERITAGE DAYS FESTIVAL. June 13–14. Cumberland, MD. 41st annual. Held in historic downtown Cumberland, the festival showcases more than 200 arts and crafts booths. Also, music, entertainment, children's activities, carnivals, tours of historic homes and buildings as well as historic reenactments. Annually, the second weekend in June. Est attendance: 20,000. For info: Heritage Days Festival, PO Box 6349, Cumberland, MD 21501. Phone: (301) 722-0037. E-mail: bkcenter@pennswoods.net. Web: www.heritagedaysfestival.com.

HOME OWNERS LOAN ACT: ANNIVERSARY. June 13, 1933. The Federal Savings and Loan Association was authorized with the passage of the Home Owners Loan Act. The purpose of the legislation was to provide a convenient place for investment and to lend money on first mortgages. The first association was the First Federal Savings and Loan Association of Miami, FL, which was chartered on Aug 8, 1933.

HORSERADISH FESTIVAL. June 13–14 (tentative). Collinsville, IL. Join in the fun at the horseradish capital of the world. "Root Derby" (build a race car out of a horseradish root and win prizes), races, food, great bands and more. For info: Collinsville Chamber of Commerce, 221 W Main St, Collinsville, IL 62234. Phone: (618) 344-2884. E-mail: dcordle@yourjournal.com.

MELROSE PLANTATION ARTS AND CRAFTS FESTIVAL. June 13–14. Melrose, LA. Held on the grounds of Historic Melrose Plantation, this event features quality handcrafted items from more than 150 juried exhibitors. Food, including famous meat pies and soft drinks, will be available. Annually, the second full weekend in June. Est attendance: 20,000. For info: Calendar of Events, Natchitoches Parish Tourist Commission, 781 Front St, Natchitoches, LA 71457. Phone: (318) 379-0055 or (800) 259-1714. Fax: (318) 352-2415. Web: www.natchitoches.net.

***MIRANDA* DECISION: ANNIVERSARY.** June 13, 1966. The US Supreme Court rendered a 5–4 decision in the case of *Miranda v Arizona*, holding that the Fifth Amendment of the Constitution "required warnings before valid statements could be taken by police." The decision has been described as "providing basic legal protections to persons who might otherwise not be aware of their rights." Ernesto Miranda, the 23-year-old whose name became nationally known, was retried after the Miranda Decision, convicted and sent back to prison. Miranda was stabbed to death in a card game dispute at Phoenix, AZ, in 1976. A suspect in the killing was released by police after he had been read his "Miranda rights." Police procedures now routinely require the reading of a prisoner's constitutional ("Miranda") rights before questioning.

MISSION SAN LUIS REY DE FRANCIA: FOUNDING ANNIVERSARY. June 13, 1798. California mission to the Indians founded on this date. Abandoned by 1846; restoration begun in 1892.

NCAA DIVISION I MEN'S COLLEGE WORLD SERIES. June 13–23. Rosenblatt Stadium, Omaha, NE. For info: NCAA, 700 W Washington St, PO Box 6222, Indianapolis, IN 46206-6222. Phone: (317) 917-6222. Web: www.NCAAsports.com.

ORIGINAL RAGGEDY ANN & ANDY FESTIVAL. June 13–14 (tentative). Arcola, IL. 20th annual. A celebration of Raggedy Ann and Andy with a parade, arts and crafts, collectibles, food and free entertainment. Est attendance: 7,000. For info: Arcola Chamber of Commerce, PO Box 274, Arcola, IL 61910. Phone: (800) 336-5456. Web: www.arcolachamber.com.

QUAD CITY AIR SHOW. June 13–14 (tentative). Davenport Municipal Airport, Davenport, IA. 22nd annual. Largest family aviation fun-filled weekend in the area featuring the very best of civilian and military aviation. Sat and Sun: gates open at 8 AM, and flying starts at 9 AM with the WWII Dawn Patrol. Action continues nonstop both in the sky and on the ground. For info: Phone: (563) 285-7469. Web: www.quadcityairshow.com. For info on the Quad Cities: Quad Cities CVB. Phone: (800) 747-7800. Web: www.visitquadcities.com.

SAINT ANTHONY OF PADUA: FEAST DAY: DEATH ANNIVERSARY. June 13. Born at Lisbon, Portugal, Aug 15, 1195, St. Anthony is patron of the illiterate and the poor. Died at Padua, June 13, 1231. Public holiday, Lisbon.

SCOTT, WINFIELD: BIRTH ANNIVERSARY. June 13, 1786. American army general, negotiator of peace treaties with Indians and twice nominated for president (1848 and 1852). Leader of brilliant military campaign in Mexico in 1847. Scott was born at Petersburg, VA, and died at West Point, NY, May 29, 1866.

TURTLE RACES. June 13. Knights of Columbus, Danville, IL. More than 100 turtles compete in 45th annual races throughout the day. Concessions available. Food and fun. Proceeds go to help people in the area with disabilities. Annually, the second Saturday in June. Est attendance: 3,000. For info: Michael Puhr, President, Turtle Club, 512 W Woodlawn, Danville, IL 61832. Phone: (217) 443-6034 or (217) 260-1983. E-mail: michaelpuhr@sbcglobal.net.

THE WICKET WORLD OF CROQUET®. June 13. President Benjamin Harrison Home, Indianapolis, IN. 40 teams wearing white play competitive Victorian croquet. Est attendance: 150. For info: President Benjamin Harrison Home, 1230 N Delaware St, Indianapolis, IN 46202. Phone: (317) 631-1888. Fax: (317) 632-5488. E-mail: harrison@presidentbenjaminharrison.org. Web: www.pbhh.org.

XTERRA RICHMOND XDURO AND JAMES RIVER SCRAMBLE. June 13. Richmond, VA. The XTERRA Trail Run Series boasts over 50 events across the country with runs ranging from 5k to 25k. These extreme, off-road trail runs give runners the chance to prove their skills against a variety of terrain. From calf-burning hills to slippery, mud-covered paths, athletes will face the ultimate test of endurance. These two races feature an off-road half-marathon distance trail run and an off-road 10k. For info: Ann Mickey, XTERRA/TEAM Unlimited, 720 Iwilei Road #290, Honolulu, HI 96817. Phone: (877) 751-8880. E-mail: info@xterraplanet.com. Web: www.xterraplanet.com.

June 2009	S	M	T	W	T	F	S
		1	2	3	4	5	6
	7	8	9	10	11	12	13
	14	15	16	17	18	19	20
	21	22	23	24	25	26	27
	28	29	30				

YEATS, WILLIAM BUTLER: BIRTH ANNIVERSARY. June 13, 1865. Nobel Prize–winning Irish poet and dramatist, born at Dublin, Ireland. He once wrote: "If a poet interprets a poem of his own he limits its suggestibility." Yeats died at France, Jan 28, 1939. After WWII his body was returned, as he had wished, for reburial in a churchyard at Drumcliff, Ireland.

BIRTHDAYS TODAY

Tim Allen, 56, comedian, actor ("Home Improvement," *Galaxy Quest*), born Denver, CO, June 13, 1953.

Ban Ki-Moon, 65, UN Secretary-General, born Eumseong, Korea, June 13, 1944.

Christo, 74, conceptual artist (*Running Fence, Valley Curtain*), born Christo Javacheff at Babrovo, Bulgaria, June 13, 1935.

Malcolm McDowell, 66, actor (*A Clockwork Orange, O Lucky Man*), born Leeds, England, June 13, 1943.

Ashley Olsen, 23, actress ("Full House," "Two of a Kind"), born Los Angeles, CA, June 13, 1986.

Mary-Kate Olsen, 23, actress ("Full House," "Two of a Kind"), born Los Angeles, CA, June 13, 1986.

Ally Sheedy, 47, actress (*St. Elmo's Fire, The Breakfast Club*), born New York, NY, June 13, 1962.

Richard Thomas, 58, actor ("The Waltons," *Roots: The Next Generations*), born New York, NY, June 13, 1951.

June 14 — Sunday

DAY 165 — 200 REMAINING

ABUSED WOMEN AND CHILDREN'S AWARENESS DAY. June 14. A day to reflect on how we can help stop the violence in America that is destroying the lives and well-being of women and children. A day to prayerfully put an end to violent behavior in American homes, schools, workplaces and communities. Annually, the second Sunday in June. For info: Judith Natale, CEO & Founder, NCAC America-USA, PO Box 493703, Redding, CA 96049-3703. E-mail: childaware@aol.com.

ALZHEIMER, ALOIS: BIRTH ANNIVERSARY. June 14, 1864. The German psychiatrist and pathologist Alois Alzheimer was born at Markbreit am Mainz, Germany. In 1907 an article by Alzheimer appeared in *Allgemeine Zeitschrift für Psychiatrie*, first describing the disease that was named for him. It was thought of as a kind of presenile dementia, usually beginning at age 40–60. Alzheimer died Dec 19, 1915, at Breslau, Germany.

BARTLETT, JOHN: BIRTH ANNIVERSARY. June 14, 1820. American editor and compiler (Bartlett's *Familiar Quotations* [1855]) was born at Plymouth, MA. Though he had little formal education, he created one of the most-used reference works of the English language. No quotation of his own is among the more than 22,000 listed today, but in the preface to the first edition he wrote that the object of this work "originally made without any view of publication" was to show "the obligation our language owes to various authors for numerous phrases and familiar quotations which have become 'household words.'" Bartlett died at Cambridge, MA, Dec 3, 1905.

BELGIUM: MILITARY MUSIC FESTIVAL. June 14. Tournai. Traditional cultural observance. Annually, the second Sunday in June.

BOURKE-WHITE, MARGARET: BIRTH ANNIVERSARY. June 14, 1904. Margaret Bourke was born at New York City. One of the original photojournalists, she developed her personal style while photographing the Krupp Iron Works in Germany and the Soviet Union during the first Five-Year Plan. Bourke-White was one of the four original staff photographers for *Life* magazine in 1936. The first woman attached to the US armed forces during WWII, she covered the Italian campaign, the siege of Moscow and American soldiers' crossing of the Rhine into Germany, and she shocked the world with her photographs of the concentration camps. Bourke-White photographed Mahatma Gandhi and covered the migration of millions of people after the Indian subcontinent was divided into Hindu India and Muslim Pakistan. She served as a war correspondent during the Korean War. Among her several books, the most famous was her collaboration with her second husband, novelist Erskine Caldwell, a study of rural poverty in the American South called *You Have Seen Their Faces*. She died Aug 27, 1971, at Stamford, CT.

CHICAGO BULLS WIN THIRD STRAIGHT TITLE FOR THE SECOND TIME: ANNIVERSARY. June 14, 1998. The Chicago Bulls defeated the Utah Jazz to win their third consecutive NBA championship. This was their second "three-peat." They had accomplished this feat the first time with wins in 1991, 1992 and 1993.

CHILDREN'S DAY IN MASSACHUSETTS. June 14. Annually, the second Sunday in June. The governor proclaims this day each year.

CHILDREN'S SUNDAY. June 14. Traditionally the second Sunday in June is observed as Children's Sunday in many Christian churches.

CORPUS CHRISTI (US OBSERVANCE). June 14. A movable Roman Catholic celebration commemorating the institution of the Holy Eucharist. The solemnity has been observed on the Thursday following Trinity Sunday since 1246, except in the US, where it is observed on the Sunday following Trinity Sunday.

FAMILY HISTORY DAY. June 14. Every summer family reunions are so busy with games and activities that most of us forget the true purpose: to share the folklore, legends and myths that bind us together. Each participant should share at least one good recollection (fact or fiction). Don't forget the hot dogs and lemonade. (©2006 by WH.) For info: Thomas & Ruth Roy, Wellcat Holidays, 2418 Long Ln, Lebanon, PA 17046. Phone: (717) 279-0184. E-mail: info@wellcat.com. Web: www.wellcat.com.

FIRST NONSTOP TRANSATLANTIC FLIGHT: 90th ANNIVERSARY. June 14–15, 1919. Captain John Alcock and Lieutenant Arthur W. Brown flew a Vickers Vimy bomber 1,900 miles nonstop from St. Johns, Newfoundland, to Clifden, County Galway, Ireland. In spite of their crash landing in an Irish peat bog, their flight inspired public interest in aviation. See also: "Lindbergh Flight: Anniversary" (May 20).

FIRST US BREACH OF PROMISE SUIT: ANNIVERSARY. June 14, 1623. The first breach of promise suit in the US was filed in the Virginia Council of State, at Charles City, VA. Reverend Greville Pooley brought suit against Cicely Jordan, who had jilted him in favor of another man. (Jordan won the suit.)

✦ **FLAG DAY.** June 14. Presidential Proclamation issued each year for June 14. Proclamation 1335, of May 30, 1916, covers all succeeding years. Has been issued annually since 1941. (PL81–203 of Aug 3, 1949.) Customarily issued as "Flag Day and National Flag Week," as in 1986; the president usually mentions "a time to honor America," Flag Day to Independence Day (89 Stat. 211). See also: "National Flag Day USA: Pause for the Pledge" (below).

FLAG DAY: ANNIVERSARY OF THE STARS AND STRIPES. June 14, 1777. John Adams introduced the following resolution before the Continental Congress, meeting at Philadelphia, PA: "Resolved, That the flag of the thirteen United States shall be thirteen stripes, alternate red and white; that the union be thirteen stars, white on a blue field, representing a new constellation." Legal holiday in Pennsylvania.

"THE GONG SHOW" TV PREMIERE: ANNIVERSARY. June 14, 1976. This popular show featured a panel of three celebrities judging amateur and professional acts, from the ordinary to the unusual. At any time, a judge could bang a gong to end the act; this was often done with gusto. Completed acts were then rated and the winner received a cash prize. Chuck Barris created (along with Chris Bearde) and hosted the show for all seasons and in syndication with the exception of one syndicated season hosted by Gary Owens. Celebrities who frequently appeared were Jaye P. Morgan, Rex Reed, Arte Johnson, Phyllis Diller and Jamie Farr.

GRANT WOOD ART FESTIVAL. June 14. Downtown Anamosa, IA. Juried art exhibits, demonstrations, stage entertainment, roaming performance artists, craft and art workshops, street chalk drawings, antique tractor rides to points of interest, Grant Wood look-alike on Main Street and more—including Grant Wood original art on display as well as lectures on his work. Annually, the second Sunday in June. Est attendance: 10,000. For info: Grant Wood Art Festival, Inc, Anamosa Chamber of Commerce, 124 E Main St, Anamosa, IA 52205. Phone: (319) 462-4879. Web: www.anamosachamber.org.

IVES, BURL: 100th BIRTH ANNIVERSARY. June 14, 1909. American singer and actor Burl Icle Ivanhoe Ives was born at Hunt, IL. He helped to reintroduce Anglo-American folk music in the '40s and '50s. Ives won an Academy Award for his supporting role in *The Big Country* (1958), and he is well known for his role as Big Daddy in both the film and Broadway productions of *Cat On a Hot Tin Roof*. He died Apr 14, 1995, at Anacortes, WA.

JAPAN: RICE PLANTING FESTIVAL. June 14. Osaka. Ceremonial transplanting of rice seedlings in paddy field at Sumiyashi Shrine, Osaka.

MALAWI: FREEDOM DAY. June 14. National holiday. Commemorates free elections in 1994.

MULTICULTURAL AMERICAN CHILD AWARENESS DAY. June 14. Celebrated every second Sunday in June. All children of every culture have been gifted with many talents and uniqueness. As Americans we can all benefit from the sharing of our individual cultural contributions that bring real character and greatness to a nation where all children are precious and deserve our praise. A time to share our many individual talents and treasures. For info: Judith Natale, NCAC America-USA, PO Box 493703, Redding, CA 96049-3703. E-mail: childaware@aol.com.

MUNICH FOUNDED: ANNIVERSARY. June 14, 1158. Traditional date of the founding of Munich (or, "Home of the Monks"), when a marketplace was founded on the banks of the Isar River by Benedictine monks with the blessing of Henry the Lion, Duke of Bavaria.

NATIONAL FLAG DAY USA: PAUSE FOR THE PLEDGE. June 14. Held simultaneously across the country at 7 PM, EDT. PL 99–54 recognizes the Pause for the Pledge as part of National Flag Day ceremonies. The concept of the Pause for the Pledge of Allegiance was conceived as a way for all citizens to share a patriotic moment. National ceremony at Fort McHenry National Monument and Historic Shrine.

✦ **NATIONAL FLAG WEEK.** June 14–20. Presidential Proclamation issued each year since 1966 for the week including June 14. (PL89–443 of June 9, 1966.) In addition, the president often calls upon the American people to participate in public ceremonies in which the Pledge of Allegiance is recited.

ORTHODOX FESTIVAL OF ALL SAINTS. June 14. Observed by Eastern Orthodox churches on the Sunday following Orthodox Pentecost (June 7 in 2009). Marks the end of the 18-week Triodion cycle.

RACE UNITY DAY. June 14. Baha'i-sponsored observance promoting racial harmony and understanding and the essential unity of humanity. Annually, the second Sunday in June. Established in 1957 by the Baha'is of the US. For info: Baha'is of the US, Office of Communications, 1233 Central St, Evanston, IL 60201. Phone: (847) 733-3487. Fax: (847) 733-3578. E-mail: ooc@usbnc.org. Web: www.bahai.us.

SPACE MILESTONE: *MARINER 5* (US). June 14, 1967. Launched on this date, interplanetary probe established that 72.5–87.5 percent of Venus's atmosphere is carbon dioxide on Oct 18 flyby of the planet.

STOWE, HARRIET BEECHER: BIRTH ANNIVERSARY. June 14, 1811. American writer Harriet Beecher Stowe, daughter of the Reverend Lyman Beecher and sister of Henry Ward Beecher. Author of *Uncle Tom's Cabin*, an antislavery novel that provoked a storm of protest and resulted in fame for its author. Two characters in the novel attained such importance that their names became part of the English language—the Negro slave, Uncle Tom, and the villainous slaveowner, Simon Legree. The reaction to *Uncle Tom's Cabin* and its profound political impact are without parallel in American literature. It is said that during the Civil War, when Harriet Beecher Stowe was introduced to President Abraham Lincoln, his words to her were, "So you're the little woman who wrote the book that made this great war." Stowe was born at Litchfield, CT, and died at Hartford, CT, July 1, 1896.

UNIVAC COMPUTER: ANNIVERSARY. June 14, 1951. Univac 1, the world's first commercial computer, designed for the US Bureau of the Census, was unveiled, demonstrated and dedicated at Philadelphia, PA. Though this milestone of the computer age was the first commercial electronic computer, it had been preceded by ENIAC (Electronic Numeric Integrator and Computer). It was completed under the supervision of J. Presper Eckert, Jr, and John W. Mauchly at the University of Pennsylvania in 1946.

US ARMY ESTABLISHED BY CONGRESS: ANNIVERSARY. June 14, 1775. Anniversary of Resolution of the Continental Congress establishing the army as the first US military service.

WARREN G. HARDING BECOMES FIRST PRESIDENT TO BROADCAST ON RADIO: ANNIVERSARY. June 14, 1922. Warren G. Harding became the first president to broadcast a message over the radio. The event was the dedication of the Francis Scott Key Memorial at Baltimore, MD. The first official government message was broadcast Dec 6, 1923.

BIRTHDAYS TODAY

Gene Barry, 88, actor (*War of the Worlds*, stage: La Cage aux folles, "Bat Masterson"), born Eugene Klass at New York, NY, June 14, 1921.

Yasmine Bleeth, 41, actress ("Baywatch," "Nash Bridges"), born New York, NY, June 14, 1968.

Boy George, 48, lead singer (Culture Club), born George Alan O'Dowd at London, England, June 14, 1961.

Marla Gibbs, 63, actress ("227," "The Jeffersons"), born Chicago, IL, June 14, 1946 (some sources say 1931 or 1941).

Stephanie Maria (Steffi) Graf, 40, former tennis player, born Bruhl, West Germany, June 14, 1969.

Eric Arthur Heiden, 51, Olympic gold medal speed skater, born Madison, WI, June 14, 1958.

Traylor Howard, 43, actress ("Monk," "Two Guys and a Girl"), born Orlando, FL, June 14, 1966.

Eddie Mekka, 57, actor ("Laverne and Shirley"), born Worcester, MA, June 14, 1952.

Will Patton, 55, actor ("The Agency," *Remember the Titans, Armageddon, No Way Out*), born Charleston, SC, June 14, 1954.

Samuel Bruce (Sam) Perkins, 48, former basketball player, born New York, NY, June 14, 1961.

Patricia (Pat) Summitt, 57, college basketball coach and former player, born Clarksville, TN, June 14, 1952.

Donald Trump, 63, real estate mogul, born New York, NY, June 14, 1946.

June 15 — Monday

DAY 166 — **199 REMAINING**

ARKANSAS: ADMISSION DAY: ANNIVERSARY. June 15. Became 25th state in 1836.

DONNA REED PERFORMING ARTS FESTIVAL. June 15–20. Denison, IA. Performing arts festival in Donna Reed's hometown. Focus of the festival is educational workshops in various areas of the performing arts taught by Hollywood and New York professionals. Also included are theatrical performances for the general public. Annually, the third full week in June. Est attendance: 2,000. For info: Kenny Kahl, Festival Coordinator, Donna Reed Foundation for the Performing Arts, 1305 Broadway, Denison, IA 51442. Phone: (712) 263-3334. Fax: (712) 263-8026. E-mail: info@donnareed.org. Web: www.donnareed.org.

FIRST FATAL AVIATION ACCIDENT: ANNIVERSARY. June 15, 1785. Two French aeronauts, Jean François Pilatre de Rozier and P.A. de Romain, attempting to cross the English Channel from France to England in a balloon, were killed when their balloon caught fire and crashed to the ground—the first fatal accident in aviation history. Pilatre de Rozier was the first man to fly.

GREAT SMOKY MOUNTAINS NATIONAL PARK ESTABLISHED: 75th ANNIVERSARY. June 15, 1934. Area along southern section of Tennessee–North Carolina boundary was authorized May 22, 1926, established for administration and protection only Feb 6, 1930, and finally established for full development as a national park in 1934. For further park info: Great Smoky Mountains Natl Park, Gatlinburg, TN 37738.

GRIEG, EDVARD: BIRTH ANNIVERSARY. June 15, 1843. Pianist, composer, conductor and teacher, the first Scandinavian to compose nationalistic music. Born at Bergen, Norway, and died there Sept 4, 1907.

"HEE HAW" TV PREMIERE: 40th ANNIVERSARY. June 15, 1969. "Hee Haw" has been described as a country-western version of "Laugh-In," composed of fast-paced sketches, silly jokes and songs. Though critics didn't like it, it had popular appeal and did well as a syndicated show. It was cohosted by Buck Owens and Roy Clark, alternating with guest hosts. Regular performers included Louis M. "Grandpa" Jones, Junior Samples, Jeannine Riley, Lulu Roman, David "Stringbean" Akeman, Sheb Wooley, Marianne Gordon, Minnie Pearl and Gordie Tapp.

HUSBAND CAREGIVER DAY. June 15. Coinciding with Father's Day, today we will honor husbands who give health care to their wives or children. For info: Richard Boyd, MD, 1111 W Spruce St, #30, Yakima, WA 98902. Phone: (509) 575-1922. Fax: (509) 248-2501. E-mail: rboyd@cwmed.com. Web: www.richardboydmd.com.

JACKSON, RACHEL DONELSON ROBARDS: BIRTH ANNIVERSARY. June 15, 1767. Wife of Andrew Jackson, 7th president of the US, born at Halifax County, NC. Died at Nashville, TN, Dec 22, 1828.

June 2009

S	M	T	W	T	F	S
	1	2	3	4	5	6
7	8	9	10	11	12	13
14	15	16	17	18	19	20
21	22	23	24	25	26	27
28	29	30				

MAGNA CARTA DAY: ANNIVERSARY. June 15. Anniversary of King John's sealing, in 1215, of the Magna Carta "in the meadow called Ronimed between Windsor and Staines on the fifteenth day of June in the seventeenth year of our reign." This document is regarded as the first charter of English liberties and one of the most important documents in the history of political and human freedom. Four original copies of the 1215 charter survive.

MEET A MATE WEEK. June 15–21. To inspire singles seeking a mate to take advantage of summer by pursuing warm-weather meeting opportunities. Options include singles travel, sports activities, New Blood parties and volunteer work. For info: Robin Gorman Newman, 44 Somerset Dr N, Great Neck, NY 11020. Phone: (516) 773-0911. E-mail: robin@lovecoach.com. Web: www.lovecoach.com.

MOON PHASE: LAST QUARTER. June 15. Moon enters Last Quarter phase at 6:15 PM, EDT.

"MY LITTLE MARGIE" TV PREMIERE: ANNIVERSARY. June 15, 1952. "My Little Margie" was a half-hour sitcom about a "womanizing widower and his meddlesome daughter." Margie was played by Gale Storm and Charles Farrell played her father, Vern Albright.

NATIVE AMERICAN CITIZENSHIP DAY. June 15. Commemorates the day in 1924 when the US Congress passed legislation recognizing the citizenship of Native Americans.

NATURE PHOTOGRAPHY DAY. June 15. A day to promote the art and science of nature photography as a medium of communication, inspiration, nature appreciation and environmental protection. Annually, June 15. For info: North American Nature Photography Assn, 10200 W 44th St, Ste 304, Wheat Ridge, CO 80033. Phone: (303) 422-8527. Fax: (303) 422-8894. E-mail: info@nanpa.org. Web: www.nanpa.org.

NORWAY: CELEBRATION OF EDVARD GRIEG'S BIRTH ANNIVERSARY. June 15. Special celebrations at Lofthus on the Hardanger fjord where Grieg's cabin still stands.

QUARTERLY ESTIMATED FEDERAL INCOME TAX PAYERS' DUE DATE. June 15. For those individuals whose fiscal year is the calendar year and who make quarterly estimated federal income tax payments, today is one of the due dates (Jan 15, Apr 15, June 15 and Sept 15, 2009).

TWELFTH AMENDMENT TO US CONSTITUTION RATIFIED: ANNIVERSARY. June 15, 1804. The 12th Amendment to the Constitution was ratified. It changed the method of electing the president and vice president after a tie in the electoral college during the election of 1800. Rather than each elector voting for two candidates with the candidate receiving the most votes elected president and the second-place candidate elected vice president, each elector was now required to designate his choice for president and vice president, respectively.

US LANDING ON SAIPAN: 65th ANNIVERSARY. June 15, 1944. In a continued effort to penetrate the Japanese inner defenses, US amphibious forces invaded the Mariana Islands. A huge fleet of 800 ships from Guadalcanal and Hawaii carried the 2nd and 4th Marine Divisions, consisting of 162,000 men. By the end of the day 20,000 of these men had established a 5½-mile-long beachhead on the island of Saipan. Though the American forces suffered heavy losses during an overnight counterattack, on the morning of June 16 the Marines still held the area they had taken the day before.

US VIRGIN ISLANDS: ORGANIC ACT DAY. June 15. Commemorates the enactment by the US Congress, July 22, 1954, of the Revised Organic Act, under which the government of the Virgin Islands is organized. Observed annually on the third Monday in June.

BIRTHDAYS TODAY

Courteney Cox Arquette, 45, actress ("Friends," *Scream*), born Birmingham, AL, June 15, 1964.

Jim Belushi, 55, actor ("Saturday Night Live," "According to Jim"), born Chicago, IL, June 15, 1954.

Wade Anthony Boggs, 51, former baseball player, born Omaha, NE, June 15, 1958.

Simon Callow, 60, actor (*A Room with a View, Howards End*), author, born London, England, June 15, 1949.

Julie Hagerty, 54, actress (*Airplane!, Lost in America, Reversal of Fortune*), born Cincinnati, OH, June 15, 1955.

Neil Patrick Harris, 36, actor ("Doogie Howser, MD," "How I Met Your Mother," *Clara's Heart*), born Albuquerque, NM, June 15, 1973.

Mike Holmgren, 61, football coach, born San Francisco, CA, June 15, 1948.

Helen Hunt, 46, actress (*Then She Found Me, Cast Away*, Oscar for *As Good As It Gets*, "Mad About You"), born Los Angeles, CA, June 15, 1963.

Justin Leonard, 37, golfer, born Dallas, TX, June 15, 1972.

Nicola Pagett, 64, actress ("Upstairs Downstairs," *There's a Girl in My Soup*), born Cairo, Egypt, June 15, 1945.

Leah Remini, 39, actress ("The King of Queens," "Saved by the Bell"), born Brooklyn, NY, June 15, 1970.

June 16 — Tuesday

DAY 167 | **198 REMAINING**

BLOOMSDAY: ANNIVERSARY. June 16, 1904. Anniversary of events in Dublin recorded in James Joyce's *Ulysses*, whose central character is Leopold Bloom.

BURLINGTON STEAMBOAT DAYS/AMERICAN MUSIC FESTIVAL. June 16–21. Mississippi Riverfront at Port of Burlington, IA. 47th annual. Weeklong event offers community and visitors a chance to enjoy top-name entertainment and a carnival setting. Est attendance: 100,000. For info: Steamboat Days, PO Box 271, Burlington, IA 52601. Phone: (319) 754-4334. Fax: (319) 752-1299. E-mail: sales@steamboatdays.com. Web: www.steamboatdays.com.

ENGLAND: ROYAL ASCOT. June 16–19. Ascot, Berkshire. Horse races. Annually, the third Tuesday to Friday in June.

GRIFFIN, JOHN HOWARD: BIRTH ANNIVERSARY. June 16, 1920. American author and photographer deeply concerned about racial problems in US. To better understand blacks in the American South, Griffin blackened his skin by the use of chemicals and ultraviolet light, keeping a journal as he traveled through the South, resulting in his best-known book, *Black Like Me*. Born at Dallas, TX. Died at Fort Worth, TX, Sept 9, 1980.

HOMESTEAD DAYS. June 16–21. Beatrice, NE. This community-wide celebration recognizes the importance of the Homestead Act of 1862 to the settlement of Nebraska. Entertainment, parades and special museum exhibits. Est attendance: 30,000. For info: Homestead Days, Beatrice Area Chamber of Commerce, 226 S 6th St, Beatrice, NE 68310. Phone: (402) 223-2338 or (800) 755-7745. E-mail: info@beatricechamber.com. Web: www.beatricechamber.com.

"HOUSE DIVIDED" SPEECH: ANNIVERSARY. June 16, 1858. Political newcomer Abraham Lincoln, beginning his campaign for the Illinois US senate seat, addressed the Republican State Convention at Springfield, IL, and made a controversial speech that has come to be known as the "House Divided" speech. Attacking the Kansas-Nebraska Act of 1854, Lincoln said, "A house divided against itself cannot stand. I believe this government cannot endure, permanently, half slave and half free. I do not expect the Union to be dissolved; I do not expect the house to fall; but I do expect it will cease to be divided. It will become all one thing, or all the other."

LADIES' DAY INITIATED IN BASEBALL: ANNIVERSARY. June 16, 1883. The New York Giants hosted the first Ladies' Day baseball game. Both escorted and unescorted ladies were admitted to the game free.

LAUREL, STAN: BIRTH ANNIVERSARY. June 16, 1890. Worked with Oliver Hardy as the comedy team of Laurel & Hardy for more than 30 years. Born at Ulverston, England, Laurel died Feb 23, 1965, at Santa Monica, CA.

PETIT JEAN ANTIQUE AUTO SHOW AND SWAP MEET. June 16–20. Petit Jean Mountain, Morrilton, AR. 51st annual show and meet with more than 125 antique and classic cars competing for awards, from turn-of-the-century to 1982 models. More than 1,500 vendor spaces filled with antique cars, parts and related items. Also, arts and crafts. Est attendance: 85,000. For info: Alan Hoelzeman, Museum of Automobiles, 8 Jones Ln, Morrilton, AR 72110. Phone: (501) 727-5427. Fax: (501) 727-6482. E-mail: motaa@ipa.net. Web: www.motaa.com.

***PSYCHO* FILM PREMIERE: ANNIVERSARY.** June 16, 1960. Millions of filmgoers (and star Janet Leigh) avoided the shower after this thriller's debut in 1960. Alfred Hitchcock's shocker, punctuated by shrieking violins and sudden knife attacks, juxtaposed the old-timey horror of the dark gothic mansion with a new locus of fear: the isolated postwar roadside motel. *Psycho* led the way to the "slasher" films of the 1970s and later. Anthony Perkins starred as motel proprietor and bird lover Norman Bates.

SOUTH AFRICA: YOUTH DAY. June 16. National holiday. Commemorates a student uprising in Soweto against "Bantu Education" and the enforced teaching of Afrikaans in 1976.

SPACE MILESTONE: *VOSTOK 6* (USSR): FIRST WOMAN IN SPACE. June 16, 1963. Valentina Tereshkova, 26, former cotton-mill worker, born on collective farm near Yaroslavl, USSR, became the first woman in space when her spacecraft, *Vostok 6*, took off from the Tyuratam launch site. She manually controlled *Vostok 6* during the 70.8-hour flight through 48 orbits of Earth and landed by parachute (separate from her cabin) June 19, 1963. In November 1963 she married cosmonaut Andrian Nikolayev, who had piloted *Vostok 3* through 64 Earth orbits, Aug 11–15, 1962. Their child Yelena (1964) was the first born to space-traveler parents.

BIRTHDAYS TODAY

Sonia Braga, 59, actress ("American Family," *Kiss of the Spider Woman*), born Maringá, Paraná, Brazil, June 16, 1950.

Roberto Duran, 58, former boxer, born Chorillo, Panama, June 16, 1951.

Cobi Jones, 39, former soccer player, played in 1994, 1998 and 2002 World Cups, born Westlake Village, CA, June 16, 1970.

Laurie Metcalf, 54, actress (Emmy for "Roseanne"; "The Norm Show"), born Edwardsville, IL, June 16, 1955.

Phil Mickelson, 39, golfer, born San Diego, CA, June 16, 1970.

Joyce Carol Oates, 71, writer (*Triumph of the Spider Monkey, The Time Traveler*), born Lockport, NY, June 16, 1938.

Irving Penn, 92, photographer, born Plainfield, PA, June 16, 1917.

M. Jodi Rell, 63, Governor of Connecticut (R), born Norfolk, VA, June 16, 1946.

Erich Segal, 72, author (*Acts of Faith, Love Story*), born Brooklyn, NY, June 16, 1937.

Joan Van Ark, 66, actress ("Knots Landing"), born New York, NY, June 16, 1943.

Kerry Wood, 32, baseball player, born Irving, TX, June 16, 1977.

June 2009	S	M	T	W	T	F	S
		1	2	3	4	5	6
	7	8	9	10	11	12	13
	14	15	16	17	18	19	20
	21	22	23	24	25	26	27
	28	29	30				

June 17 — Wednesday

DAY 168 — 197 REMAINING

BELLAMY, RALPH: BIRTH ANNIVERSARY. June 17, 1904. American actor Ralph Rexford Bellamy was born at Chicago, IL. He appeared in more than 100 films and was best known for his stage and film portrayals of President Franklin D. Roosevelt. He was a founder of the Screen Actors' Guild and president of Actors' Equity. Bellamy was awarded an honorary Academy Award in 1987. He died Nov 29, 1991, at Los Angeles, CA.

BUNKER HILL DAY. June 17. Suffolk County, MA. Legal holiday in the county in commemoration of the Battle of Bunker Hill that took place in 1775.

FAIN, SAMMY: BIRTH ANNIVERSARY. June 17, 1902. American composer Sammy Fain was born Samuel Feinberg at New York, NY. He won an Academy Award for his song "Secret Love" from *Calamity Jane* (1953) and for "Love Is a Many-Splendored Thing" from the film of the same name (1955). He died Dec 6, 1989, at Los Angeles, CA.

HERSEY, JOHN: 95th BIRTH ANNIVERSARY. June 17, 1914. American novelist, born at Tientsin, China, who wrote *A Bell for Adano*, which won the Pulitzer Prize in 1945. *The Wall* and *Hiroshima* are both based on fact and set in Poland and Japan, respectively, in WWII. Died at Key West, FL, Mar 24, 1993.

HOOPER, WILLIAM: BIRTH ANNIVERSARY. June 17, 1742. Signer of the Declaration of Independence, born at Boston, MA. Died Oct 14, 1790, at Hillsboro, NC.

ICELAND: INDEPENDENCE DAY: 65th ANNIVERSARY. June 17. National holiday. Anniversary of founding of republic and independence from Denmark in 1944 is major festival, especially in Reykjavik. Parades, competitions, street dancing.

MISS TENNESSEE PAGEANT. June 17–20. Carl Perkins Civic Center, Jackson, TN. Part of the Miss America Organization. For info: Miss Tennessee Pageant, PO Box 938, Jackson, TN 38302. Phone: (731) 425-8590. Fax: (731) 668-2758. E-mail: MissTNED@bellsouth.net. Web: www.misstennessee.org.

SOUTH AFRICA REPEALS LAST APARTHEID LAW: ANNIVERSARY. June 17, 1991. The Parliament of South Africa repealed the Population Registration Act, removing the law that was the foundation of apartheid. The law, first enacted in 1950, required the classification by race of all South Africans at birth. It established four compulsory racial categories: white, mixed race, Asian and black. Although this marked the removal of the last of the apartheid laws, blacks in South Africa still could not vote.

STRAVINSKY, IGOR FYODOROVICH: BIRTH ANNIVERSARY. June 17, 1882. Russian composer and author, born at Oranienbaum (near Leningrad). Among his best-known music: the ballets *The Firebird, Petrushka* and *The Rite of Spring*; the choral work *Symphony of Psalms*; and *Abraham and Isaac, A Sacred Ballet.* Died at New York, NY, Apr 6, 1971.

UNITED NATIONS: WORLD DAY TO COMBAT DESERTIFICATION AND DROUGHT. June 17. Proclaimed by the General Assembly Dec 19, 1994 (Res 49/115). States were invited to promote public awareness of the need for international cooperation to combat desertification and the effects of drought and the implementation of the UN Convention to Combat Desertification. For info: United Nations, Dept of Public Info, New York, NY 10017. Web: www.un.org.

WATERGATE DAY: ANNIVERSARY. June 17, 1972. Anniversary of arrests at Democratic Party Headquarters (in Watergate complex, Washington, DC) that led to revelations of political espionage, threats of imminent impeachment of the president and, on Aug 9, 1974, the resignation of President Richard M. Nixon.

WESLEY, JOHN: BIRTH ANNIVERSARY. June 17, 1703. Born at Epworth, England. Wesley, along with his younger brother Charles, was the founder of Methodism. John Wesley died Mar 2, 1791.

BIRTHDAYS TODAY

Thomas Haden Church, 49, actor (*Sideways*, "Wings"), born Thomas McMillen, El Paso, TX, June 17, 1960.

Dermontti Dawson, 44, former football player, born Lexington, KY, June 17, 1965.

Tommy R. Franks, 64, retired general, US Army, born Wynnewood, OK, June 17, 1945.

Dan Jansen, 44, former speed skater, sportscaster, born West Allis, WI, June 17, 1965.

Greg Kinnear, 46, actor (*Little Miss Sunshine, The Matador, As Good as It Gets*), born Logansport, IN, June 17, 1963.

Mark Linn-Baker, 56, actor ("Perfect Strangers," *My Favorite Year*), born St. Louis, MO, June 17, 1953.

Barry Manilow, 63, singer ("Mandy," "I Write the Songs"), songwriter, born Brooklyn, NY, June 17, 1946.

Joe Piscopo, 58, comedian ("Saturday Night Live"), born Passaic, NJ, June 17, 1951.

Venus Williams, 29, tennis player, born Lynwood, CA, June 17, 1980.

June 18 — Thursday

DAY 169 — **196 REMAINING**

BATTLE OF WATERLOO: ANNIVERSARY. June 18, 1815. Date of the decisive defeat of Napoleon by British generals Wellington and Blucher, near Waterloo in central Belgium.

CAHN, SAMMY: BIRTH ANNIVERSARY. June 18, 1913. Tin Pan Alley legend Sammy Cahn was born Samuel Cohen at New York City. He was nominated for 26 Academy Awards and won four times for "Three Coins in the Fountain" (1954), "All the Way" (1957), "High Hopes" (1959) and "Call Me Irresponsible" (1963). In the late 1940s he began working with composer Jimmy Van Heusen, and the two in essence were the personal songwriting team for Frank Sinatra. Cahn wrote the greatest number of Sinatra hits, including "Love and Marriage," "The Second Time Around" and "The Tender Trap." Sammy Cahn died Jan 15, 1993, at Los Angeles, CA.

CANADA: SAM STEELE DAYS. June 18–21. Cranbrook, BC. Parade, Sweetheart Pageant, banquet and ball, railway museum tours, bocce tournament, wild west show, ball tournament, soccer tournament, live entertainment, climbing wall, children's festival, Taste of Cranbrook and arts and crafts show. Est attendance: 19,000. For info: Sam Steele Society, PO Box 115, Cranbrook, BC, Canada V1C 4H6. Phone: (250) 426-4161. Fax: (250) 426-3873. E-mail: info@samsteeledays.org. Web: www.samsteeledays.org.

CZECH DAYS. June 18–20. Tabor, SD. 61st annual. Czechs dressed in their festive costumes gather with people from all parts of the world in this gala celebration. Fine Czech foods, dancing, music and entertainment. Est attendance: 15,000. For info: Tabor Area Chamber of Commerce, Inc, PO Box 21, Tabor, SD 57063. Phone: (605) 463-2476. E-mail: czechdays@yahoo.com. Web: www.byelectric.com/~tabor.

EGYPT: EVACUATION DAY. June 18. Public holiday celebrating the anniversary of the withdrawal of the British Army from the Suez Canal area of Egypt in 1954.

FOLGER, HENRY CLAY, JR: BIRTH ANNIVERSARY. June 18, 1857. American businessman and industrialist who developed one of the finest collections of Shakespeareana in the world and bequeathed it (The Folger Shakespeare Library, Washington, DC) to the American people. Born at New York, NY. Died June 11, 1930, at Brooklyn, NY.

FORT UNION TRADING POST RENDEZVOUS. June 18–21. 25 miles southwest of Williston, ND. Re-creation of the fur trade era. Fur trade fair, music, blacksmith and craft demonstrations plus Trader's Row. Sponsor: National Park Service, Fort Union Trading Post National Historic Site. Est attendance: 3,000. For info: Fort Union Trading Post NHS, 15550 Hwy 1804, Williston, ND 58801. Phone: (701) 572-9083. Fax: (701) 572-7321. Web: www.nps.gov/fous.

GETTYSBURG BRASS BAND FESTIVAL. June 18–21. Gettysburg, PA. Brass bands, ensembles, drum and bugle corps converge on Gettysburg for many musical events along Gettysburg's "Historical Pathways." Workshops, concerts and performances culminate in one grand finale at the Gettysburg College Stadium on Saturday evening. Est attendance: 8,000. For info: Gettysburg Brass Band Festival, 35 Carlisle St, Gettysburg, PA 17325. Phone: (717) 334-0853 or (866) 994-8881. E-mail: info@gettysburgfestival.org. Web: www.gettysburgbrassbandfestival.org.

KIAMICHI OWA-CHITO FESTIVAL OF THE FOREST. June 18–20. Beavers Bend State Park, Broken Bow, OK. A celebration of American Indian culture and of the forest industry. Compete in ax throwing, cross-buck sawing and logging to become the "Bull of the Woods." Also kids' games, food booths, Miss Owa-Chito contest, photography contest, golf tournament, canoe races, archery contest, turkey-calling contest, 5k road race, talent contest and more. Est attendance: 30,000. For info: Broken Bow Chamber of Commerce, 113 W Martin Luther King Dr, Broken Bow, OK 74728. Phone: (580) 584-3393. Fax: (580) 584-7698. E-mail: bchamber@pine-net.com. Web: www.brokenbowchamber.com.

KYSER, KAY: BIRTH ANNIVERSARY. June 18, 1906. American bandleader whose radio show, "Kay Kyser's Kollege of Musical Knowledge," enjoyed immense popularity in the swing era. He was born James King Kern Kyser at Rocky Mount, NC. A shrewd showman and performer, he said he never learned to read music or play an instrument. Among his hit recordings were "Three Little Fishes" and "Praise the Lord and Pass the Ammunition," a WWII favorite. Kyser retired from show business in 1951 and died at Chapel Hill, NC, July 23, 1985.

MALLORY, GEORGE LEIGH: BIRTH ANNIVERSARY. June 18, 1886. English explorer and mountain climber born at Mobberley, Cheshire, England. Last seen climbing through the mists toward the summit of the highest mountain in the world, Mount Everest, on the morning of June 8, 1924. Best remembered for his answer when asked why he wanted to climb Mount Everest: "Because it is there." In 1999 Mallory's body was found by an expedition to Mount Everest, 75 years after his death at age 37.

PORTER, SYLVIA: BIRTH ANNIVERSARY. June 18, 1913. American financial journalist Sylvia Feldman Porter was born at Patchogue, NY. Her column was syndicated by the *Los Angeles Times*, reaching 450 newspapers worldwide. She also wrote more than 20 books and was noted for her ability to turn complex economic language into readable prose. Porter died June 5, 1991, at Pound Ridge, NY.

PRAIRIE VILLA RENDEZVOUS. June 18–21. Prairie du Chien, WI. Rendezvous with history and learn about life during the fur trading days and experience the fur trader lifestyle firsthand. Many participants come from around the country to display furs, others demonstrate the cumbersome process of loading a rifle with gunpowder and some prepare Indian fry bread and buffalo burgers. Workshops offer information on a variety of subjects including plants and medicines, basket weaving and beadworking. With more than 600 lodges and teepees, this is one of the largest Midwest trading rendezvous. Est attendance: 25,000. For info: Prairie du Chien Area Chamber of Commerce, PO Box 326, Prairie du Chien, WI 53821. Phone: (800) 732-1673. Web: www.prairieduchien.org.

RECESS AT WORK DAY. June 18. It's time for a break from the norm today. Call it team building, call it employee morale, call it professional development—just make sure you call it fun. It's time for recess! Annually, the third Thursday in June. For info: Rich DiGirolamo, PO Box 584, Marion, CT 06444. Phone: (203) 879-5970. E-mail: rich@RichDiGirolamo.com. Web: www.RecessAtWorkDay.com.

SEYCHELLES: CONSTITUTION DAY. June 18. National holiday commemorating adoption of constitution in 1993.

SHAKESPEARE ON THE GREEN. June 18–21 (also June 25–28; July 1–3, 5). Elmwood Park, University of Nebraska, Omaha, NE. Nonprofit professional presentations of the works of William Shakespeare in a beautiful outdoor setting for the families of the Great Plains region. One of the largest donation-driven festivals across the country. Includes preshow seminars and workshops. Picnic area and concessions, Elizabethan entertainment featuring music, dancing, singing, juggling and acrobatics. Est attendance: 35,000. For info: Mary Ann Bamber, Managing Director, Nebraska Shakespeare Festival, Dept of Fine Arts, Creighton University, Omaha, NE 68178. Phone: (402) 280-2391. Fax: (402) 280-2320. E-mail: info@nebraskashakespeare.com. Web: www.nebraskashakespeare.com.

SPACE MILESTONE: FIRST AMERICAN WOMAN IN SPACE. June 18, 1983. Dr. Sally Ride, 32-year-old physicist and pilot, functioned as a "mission specialist" and became the first American woman in space when she began a six-day mission aboard the space shuttle *Challenger*. The "near-perfect" mission was launched from Cape Canaveral, FL, and landed June 24, 1983, at Edwards Air Force Base, CA. See also: "Space Milestone: *Vostok 6* (USSR): First Woman in Space" (June 16).

US OPEN (GOLF) CHAMPIONSHIP. June 18–21. Bethpage State Park (Black Course), Farmingdale, NY. For info: USGA, Golf House, Championship Dept, PO Box 708, Far Hills, NJ 07931. Phone: (908) 234-2300. Fax: (908) 234-9687. E-mail: usga@usga.org. Web: www.usga.org.

WAR OF 1812: DECLARATION ANNIVERSARY. June 18, 1812. After much debate in Congress between "hawks" such as Henry Clay and John Calhoun and "doves" such as John Randolph, Congress issued a declaration of war on Great Britain. The action was prompted primarily by Britain's violation of America's rights on the high seas and British incitement of Indian warfare on the frontier. War was seen by some as a way to acquire Florida and Canada. The hostilities ended with the signing of the Treaty of Ghent on Dec 24, 1814, at Ghent, Belgium.

June 2009

S	M	T	W	T	F	S
	1	2	3	4	5	6
7	8	9	10	11	12	13
14	15	16	17	18	19	20
21	22	23	24	25	26	27
28	29	30				

BIRTHDAYS TODAY

Lou Brock, 70, Hall of Fame baseball player, born El Dorado, AR, June 18, 1939.

Eddie Cibrian, 36, actor ("Third Watch"), born Burbank, CA, June 18, 1973.

Roger Ebert, 67, Pulitzer Prize–winning film critic, born Urbana, IL, June 18, 1942.

Carol Kane, 57, actress (*Hester Street, The Princess Bride,* "Taxi"), born Cleveland, OH, June 18, 1952.

Donald Keene, 87, literary critic, translator, educator, born New York, NY, June 18, 1922.

Paul McCartney, 67, singer, songwriter (The Beatles, Wings), born Liverpool, England, June 18, 1942.

Dr. James Peake, 65, US Secretary of Veteran's Affairs, born St. Louis, MO, June 18, 1944.

Richard Powers, 52, author (*The Echo Maker, Galatea 2.2*), born Evanston, IL, June 18, 1957.

John D. Rockefeller IV, 72, US Senator (D, West Virginia), born New York, NY, June 18, 1937.

Isabella Rossellini, 57, model, actress (*Blue Velvet, Cousins*), born Rome, Italy, June 18, 1952.

Tom Wicker, 83, journalist, author (*One of Us: Richard Nixon & the American Dream*), born Hamlet, NC, June 18, 1926.

June 19 — Friday

DAY 170 — 195 REMAINING

ANTIQUES BY THE BAY. June 19–20. St. Ignace, MI. 13th annual show for antique and classic original vehicles 25 years or older. Special tours and awards plus auto world celebrities. For info: Nostalgia Productions, Inc, 268 Hillcrest Blvd, St. Ignace, MI 49781. Phone: (906) 643-8087. Fax: (906) 643-9784. E-mail: ereavie@nostalgia-prod.com. Web: www.nostalgia-prod.com or www.auto-shows.com.

AVON HERITAGE DUCT TAPE FESTIVAL. June 19–21. Avon, OH. This three-day event celebrates duct tape, its enthusiasts and its wacky and fun uses. The festival also honors the history and heritage of the city that is proclaimed the Duct Tape Capital of the World. From sculptures and fashion to games and a parade, everything at the festival revolves around duct tape. A perfect celebration for Father's Day weekend, also includes a national "Duct Tape Dad of the Year" contest, and all the classic fair food, rides and live entertainment that make festivals such a great time. Est attendance: 50,000. For info: Avon Heritage Duct Tape Committee, PO Box 354, Avon, OH 44011. Phone: (866) 818-1116. E-mail: avonducttapefestival@hotmail.com. Web: www.avonducttapefestival.com.

BADGER STATE SUMMER GAMES. June 19–21 (also June 26–28). Madison, WI. 24th annual sports festival for Wisconsin residents of all ages and abilities, featuring 28 sports and opening ceremonies. Major sponsors: American Family Insurance, Wisconsin Milk Marketing Board and St. Joseph's Hospital. Est attendance: 20,000. For info: Badger State Games, PO Box 7788, Madison, WI 53707-7788. Phone: (608) 226-4780. Fax: (608) 226-9550. E-mail: info@SportsinWisconsin.com. Web: www.SportsinWisconsin.com.

BASCOM, EARL W.: BIRTH ANNIVERSARY. June 19, 1906. Rodeo showman and pioneer, Earl W. Bascom was born at Vernal, UT. During his career he developed the first side-delivery rodeo chute

(1916), the first hornless bronc saddle (1922) and the first one-handed bareback rigging (1924). He produced the first rodeo in Mississippi and also produced the first rodeo performed at night under electric lights (1935). Bascom died Aug 28, 1995, at Victorville, CA.

BATTLE OF PHILIPPINE SEA: 65th ANNIVERSARY. June 19–20, 1944. Determined to prevent any further advancement by the Allies in Japan's area of inner defense, Vice-Admiral Jisaburo Ozawa ordered the Imperial fleet to the Mariana Islands. Admiral Raymond Spruance, possibly the US's greatest and most successful naval commander, ordered a strike force against the Japanese fleet in the Philippine Sea. A furious battle developed in the skies between US carrier-borne aircraft and Japanese aircraft from their carriers and land bases on the Marianas. The Japanese lost three aircraft carriers (*Shokaku, Taiho* and *Hiyo*), two destroyers and one tanker. Three carriers, one battleship, three cruisers, one destroyer and three tankers were seriously damaged. The Japanese lost at least 400 aircraft, the Americans 130.

CANADA: NOVA SCOTIA MULTICULTURAL FESTIVAL. June 19–21. Dartmouth, NS. 25th annual. Cultural events include five tents housing exhibits, food booths, children's tent, performances and beer tent with live bands. Est attendance: 30,000. For info: Ifty Illyas, Exec Dir, Multicultural Assn of Nova Scotia, 1113 Marginal Rd, Halifax, NS, Canada B3H 4P7. Phone: (902) 423-6534. Fax: (902) 422-0881. E-mail: info@multifest.ca. Web: www.multifest.ca.

CHILTON COUNTY PEACH FESTIVAL. June 19–27. Downtown Clanton, AL. 62nd annual. This peach-oriented event features Miss Peach pageants including Little Miss, Young Miss, Junior Miss and Miss Peach; parades, cooking contests, antique car show, motorcycle show, 5k Peach Fun run, American Legion barbecue, a peach auction and much more. Est attendance: 10,000. For info: Pennie Broussard, Chilton County Chamber of Commerce, 500 5th Ave N, PO Box 66, Clanton, AL 35045. Phone: (205) 755-2400. Fax: (205) 755-8444. Web: www.chiltoncountychamber.com.

CICOTTE, EDDIE: 125th BIRTH ANNIVERSARY. June 19, 1884. Edward Victor (Eddie) Cicotte, baseball player, born at Detroit, MI. Pitching for the Chicago White Sox, Cicotte won 28 games in 1917 and 29 in 1919, using his knuckleball to great effectiveness. He was implicated in the Black Sox scandal of 1919 and banned from baseball for life. Died at Detroit, May 5, 1969.

DALESBURG MIDSUMMER FESTIVAL. June 19. Dalesburg Lutheran Church, rural Vermillion, SD. Celebration of Scandinavian and rural heritage. Programs, dances to raise the Midsummer Pole, a smorgasbord, arts and crafts area, band concert, children's activities and more. Est attendance: 900. For info: Ronald Johnson, Midsummer Committee, Dalesburg Midsummer Festival, 30595 University Rd, Vermillion, SD 57069-6507. Phone: (605) 253-2575. Web: www.angelfire.com/sd/dalesburg99/ or www.dalesburg.org.

DELMARVA CHICKEN FESTIVAL. June 19–20. Centreville, MD. 60th annual. A family event focusing on chicken, the leading agricultural enterprise on the Delmarva Peninsula. Food, entertainment and children's activities are featured. Est attendance: 25,000. For info: Connie Parvis, Delmarva Poultry Industry, Inc, 16686 County Seat Hwy, Georgetown, DE 19947-4881. Phone: (302) 856-9037. E-mail: dpi@dpichicken.com.

DENMARK: VIKING FESTIVAL. June 19–July 5. Frederiksund (about 25 miles northwest of Copenhagen). Famous outdoor plays based on Danish legends. Annually, the next-to-last Friday in June through the first Sunday in July.

EMANCIPATION DAY IN TEXAS. June 19, 1865. In honor of the emancipation of the slaves in Texas. See also: "Juneteenth" (June 19).

ENGLAND: EXETER FESTIVAL. June 19–July 4 (tentative). Various venues, Exeter, Devon. A broad ranging eclectic program of classical and contemporary performance in a variety of city venues, featuring the best of British and international arts and culture. Est attendance: 32,000. For info: David Whitelock, Exeter City Council, Paris Street, Exeter, England EX1 1JJ. Phone: (44) (139) 226-5200. Fax: (44) (139) 226-5366. E-mail: festival@exeter.gov.uk. Web: exeter.gov.uk/festival.

FIRST RUNNING OF THE BELMONT STAKES: ANNIVERSARY. June 19, 1867. The first running of the Belmont Stakes took place at Jerome Park, NY. The team of jockey J. Gilpatrick and his horse Ruthless finished in a time of 3:05. The Belmont Stakes continued at Jerome Park until 1889, then moved to Morris Park, NY, between 1890–1905, and in 1906 settled at Belmont Park, NY, where it has continued to the present day. The Belmont Stakes is the oldest event of horse racing's Triple Crown.

FORTAS, ABE: BIRTH ANNIVERSARY. June 19, 1910. Abe Fortas was born at Memphis, TN. He was appointed to the Supreme Court by President Lyndon Johnson in 1965. Prior to his appointment he was known as a civil libertarian, having argued cases for government employees and other individuals accused by Senator Joe McCarthy of having communist affiliations. He argued the 1963 landmark Supreme Court case of *Gideon v Wainwright*, which established the right of indigent defendants to free legal aid in criminal prosecutions. In 1968 he was nominated by Johnson to succeed Chief Justice Earl Warren, but his nomination was withdrawn after much conservative opposition in the Senate. In 1969 Fortas became the first Supreme Court Justice to be forced to resign after revelations about questionable financial dealings were made public. He died Apr 5, 1982, at Washington, DC.

FULTON COUNTY HISTORICAL POWER SHOW. June 19–21. Rochester, IN. This show features a different tractor each year. Power show will include antique tractors, hit 'n' miss engines, equipment and antique trucks. Also featuring vendors of swap parts, crafts, food, music and square dancing in the Round Barn and more. Contests held for exhibitors. Admission fee. Annually, third weekend in June. Est attendance: 6,000. For info: Fulton County Historical Power Assn, c/o Fulton County Historical Society, 37 E 375 N, Rochester, IN 46975. Phone: (574) 223-4436. E-mail: melinda@rtcol.com. Web: icss.net/~fchs.

GARFIELD: BIRTHDAY. June 19, 1978. America's favorite lasagna-loving cat celebrates his birthday. "Garfield," a modern classic comic strip created by Jim Davis, first appeared in 1978 and has brought laughter to millions. For info: Garfield Birthday. Web: www.garfield.com.

GEHRIG, LOU: BIRTH ANNIVERSARY. June 19, 1903. Baseball great Henry Louis Gehrig (lifetime batting average of .341), who played in seven World Series, was born at New York, NY, and died there June 2, 1941, from the degenerative muscle disease amyotropic lateral sclerosis, which has become known as Lou Gehrig's disease.

HERITAGE CRAFT AND DULCIMER MUSIC FESTIVAL. June 19–21. Roscoe Village, Coshocton, OH. Experience the rich canal heritage of Roscoe Village through the sights, sounds and traditional crafts of the 1800s. Listen to the blacksmith's anvil ring, watch the weaver spinning wool or see demonstrations of handmade crafts. The Mid-Eastern Regional Hammered and Mountain Dulcimer Championships will be featured. Guests can participate in workshops and contests all weekend. Annually, third weekend in June. Est attendance: 3,000. For info: Roscoe Village Foundation, 600 N Whitewoman St, Coshocton, OH 43812. Phone: (800) 877-1830 or (740) 622-9310. Fax: (740) 623-6555. E-mail: rvmarketing@roscoevillage.com. Web: www.roscoevillage.com.

HOWARD, MOE: BIRTH ANNIVERSARY. June 19, 1897. The head stooge in the Three Stooges, Moe Howard was born Moses Horwitz at Bensonhurst, NY. He died May 4, 1975, at Hollywood, CA. Howard began his show business career at age 12 by running errands at Vitagraph studios. He worked with Ted Healy in various comedy and singing acts, and together they teamed with Shemp Howard and Larry Fine in the mid-1920s for an early Stooges act.

In 1930 the Stooges made their film debut in *Soup to Nuts*. Although the members of the Three Stooges changed over the years, Moe Howard was one of the constants. Howard appeared in four feature films without the other Stooges, including *Doctor Death, Seeker of Souls*.

HUBBARD, ELBERT: BIRTH ANNIVERSARY. June 19, 1856. Born at Bloomington, IL, Elbert Green Hubbard, American author and craftsman, founded the Roycroft Press at East Aurora, NY. Best known of his writings were *A Message to Garcia* and a series of essays titled *Little Journeys*. He also became famous for his furniture designs. Hubbard lost his life with the sinking of the *Lusitania*, May 7, 1915.

HUCK FINN'S JUBILEE. June 19–21. Mojave Narrows Regional Park, Victorville, CA. A Huck Finn celebration with river raft building, country and bluegrass music, hayrides, old-time tent circus, crafts and food, plus Route 66 car show and the California State Arm Wrestling Championships. Annually, on Father's Day weekend. Est attendance: 16,000. For info: Don or Barbara Tucker, PO Box 56419, Riverside, CA 92517. Phone: (951) 780-8810. E-mail: huckfinn@huckfinn.com. Web: www.huckfinn.com.

"I'VE GOT A SECRET" TV PREMIERE: ANNIVERSARY. June 19, 1952. Celebrity panelists tried to guess the guests' secrets on this popular game show; celebrity guests also came on to baffle the panel. Guests whispered their secret to the host and the audience saw it on the screen. Garry Moore hosted the show, followed by Steve Allen and Bill Cullen. Allen Sherman ("My Son the Folk Singer") created the show and most of the celebrity "secrets." Celebrity panelists included Bill Cullen, Betsy Palmer, Henry Morgan, Bess Myerson, Steve Allen and Jayne Meadows.

JUNETEENTH. June 19. Celebrated in Texas to commemorate the day in 1865 when Union General Granger proclaimed the slaves of Texas free. Also proclaimed as Emancipation Day by the Florida legislature. Juneteenth has become an occasion for commemoration by African Americans in many parts of the US.

OLD TIME MUSIC OZARK HERITAGE FESTIVAL. June 19–20. Historic Court Square, West Plains, MO. Celebrate the unique culture of the Ozark Highlands. Old time music performances (with headliners), artisans in action, exhibits and activities. Jig dance competition, mule jumping competition, cooking and old-time gospel stage, Brush Arbor, Civil War reenactments and workshops. For info: Ozark Heritage Welcome Center, 2999 Porter Wagoner Blvd, West Plains, MO 65775. Phone: (888) 256-8835. Fax: (417) 255-1038. E-mail: toursomo@townsqr.com. Web: www.oldtimemusic.org.

OUTDOOR SUMMER THEATER. June 19–Aug 15. Farmington, NM. Performances are held in a natural sandstone amphitheater at the Lion's Wilderness park, with an optional southwest-style dinner served prior to each performance at 6:30 PM. Performances Thursday through Sunday at 8 PM. Est attendance: 4,000. For info: Farmington Conv and Visitors Bureau, 3041 E Main St, Farmington, NM 87402. Phone: (800) 448-1240 or (505) 326-7602. Fax: (505) 327-0577. E-mail: fmncvb@earthlink.net. Web: www.farmingtonnm.org.

PASCAL, BLAISE: BIRTH ANNIVERSARY. June 19, 1623. French philosopher, physicist and mathematician born at Clermont-Ferrand and died at Paris, Aug 19, 1662. It was Pascal who said, "Had Cleopatra's nose been shorter, the whole history of the world would have been different." And, in his *Provincial Letters*, he wrote, "I have made this letter longer than usual because I lack the time to make it short."

ROSENBERG EXECUTION: ANNIVERSARY. June 19, 1953. Anniversary of the electrocution of the only married couple ever executed together in the US. Julius (35) and Ethel (37) Rosenberg were executed for espionage at Sing Sing Prison, Ossining, NY. Time for the execution was advanced several hours to avoid conflict with the Jewish Sabbath. Their conviction has been a subject of controversy over the years.

SPACE MILESTONE: *ARIANE* (ESA). June 19, 1981. Launched from Kourou, French Guiana by the European Space Administration, *Ariane* carried two satellites into orbit: *Meteostat 2*, an ESA weather satellite, and *Apple*, a geostationary communications satellite for India, to be stationed over Sumatra.

URUGUAY: ARTIGAS DAY. June 19. National holiday. Commemorates the birth in 1764 of General José Gervasio Artigas, the father of Uruguayan independence.

"WAR IS HELL": ANNIVERSARY. June 19, 1879. Addressing the graduating class at Michigan Military Academy, General William Tecumseh Sherman uttered his famous words on war—more than a decade after the Civil War had ended. He said, "War is at best barbarism. . . . Its glory is all moonshine. It is only those who have neither fired a shot nor heard the shrieks and groans of the wounded who cry aloud for blood, more vengeance, more desolation. War is hell."

WORK@HOME FATHER'S DAY. June 19. One day each year to honor and celebrate those fathers who have elected to work from home—either as home-based entrepreneurs or teleworkers—to improve family interaction and professional satisfaction. Annually, the Friday before Father's Day. For info: Jeff Zbar, PO Box 8263, Coral Springs, FL 33075. Phone: (954) 346-4393. E-mail: jeff@chiefhomeofficer.com. Web: www.chiefhomeofficer.com.

WORLD SAUNTERING DAY. June 19. A day to revive the lost art of Victorian sauntering and to discourage jogging, lollygagging, sashaying, fast walking and trotting. (Originated by the late W.T. Rabe of Saulte Ste Marie, MI.)

BIRTHDAYS TODAY

Paula Abdul, 47, singer, dancer, choreographer, television personality ("American Idol"), born Los Angeles, CA, June 19, 1962.

Aung San Suu Kyi, 64, Nobel Peace Prize winner, born Rangoon, Burma (now Myanmar), June 19, 1945.

Charles Gwathmey, 71, architect, born Charlotte, NC, June 19, 1938.

Andy Lauer, 44, actor ("Caroline in the City," *I'll Be Home for Christmas*), born Santa Monica, CA, June 19, 1965.

Brian McBride, 37, soccer player, born Arlington Heights, IL, June 19, 1972.

Poppy Montgomery, 37, actress ("Without a Trace"), born Sydney, New South Wales, Australia, June 19, 1972.

Dirk Nowitzki, 31, basketball player, born Wurzburg, West Germany, June 19, 1978.

Phylicia Rashad, 61, actress ("The Cosby Show"), born Houston, TX, June 19, 1948.

Gena Rowlands, 79, actress ("Peyton Place," *A Woman Under the Influence*), born Cambria, WI, June 19, 1930 (some sources say 1936 or 1934).

Salman Rushdie, 62, author (*Satanic Verses, Midnight's Children*), born Bombay, India, June 19, 1947.

Kathleen Turner, 55, actress (*Body Heat, Peggy Sue Got Married, Romancing the Stone*), born Springfield, MO, June 19, 1954.

Ann Wilson, 58, musician, lead singer (Heart), born San Diego, CA, June 19, 1951.

June 2009

S	M	T	W	T	F	S
	1	2	3	4	5	6
7	8	9	10	11	12	13
14	15	16	17	18	19	20
21	22	23	24	25	26	27
28	29	30				

June 20 — Saturday

DAY 171 **194 REMAINING**

ARGENTINA: FLAG DAY. June 20. National holiday. Commemorates the death in 1820 of Manuel Belgrano, the designer of the Argentine flag.

BAYMEN'S SEAFOOD AND MUSIC FESTIVAL. June 20. Tuckerton Seaport, Tuckerton, NJ. Stroll the Tuckerton Seaport and sample delicious Jersey fresh clams, crabs and shrimp from the finest seafood purveyors. After you satisfy your appetite, move your feet to the beat of live, toe-tapping entertainment. Bring the family and your beach chairs and plan to spend the whole day. Est attendance: 1,600. For info: Renee Kennedy, Tuckerton Seaport, 120 W Main St, PO Box 52, Tuckerton, NJ 08087. Phone: (609) 296-8868. Fax: (609) 296-5810. E-mail: info@tuckertonseaport.org. Web: www.tuckertonseaport.org.

CHESNUTT, CHARLES W.: BIRTH ANNIVERSARY. June 20, 1858. Born at Cleveland, OH, Chesnutt was considered by many as the first important black novelist. His collections of short stories included *The Conjure Woman* (1899) and *The Wife of His Youth and Other Stories of the Color Line* (1899). *The Colonel's Dream* (1905) dealt with the struggles of the freed slave. His work has been compared to later writers such as William Faulkner, Richard Wright and James Baldwin. He died Nov 15, 1932, at Cleveland.

"THE ED SULLIVAN SHOW" ("TOAST OF THE TOWN") TV PREMIERE: ANNIVERSARY. June 20, 1948. "The Ed Sullivan Show" was officially titled "Toast of the Town" until 1955. It was the longest-running variety show (through 1971) and the most popular for decades. Ed Sullivan, the host, signed all types of acts, both well-known and new, trying to have something to please everyone. Thousands of performers appeared, many making their television debut, such as Irving Berlin, Victor Borge, Hedy Lamarr, Walt Disney, Fred Astaire and Jane Powell. Two acts attracted the largest audience of the time: Elvis Presley and the Beatles.

ENGLAND: CITY OF LONDON FESTIVAL. June 20–July 10. London. Annual multi-arts festival held in some of the city's most historically interesting buildings, including St. Paul's Cathedral and Mansion House. Est attendance: 130,000. For info: City of London Festival, 12–14 Mason's Ave, London, England EC2V 5BB. Phone: (44) (20) 7796 4949. E-mail: admin@colf.org. Web: www.colf.org.

FIRST BALLOON HONEYMOON: 100th ANNIVERSARY. June 20, 1909. Roger Burnham and Eleanor Waring took the first balloon honeymoon, ascending at 12:40 PM in the balloon *Pittsfield*. They began their trip at Woods Hole, Cape Cod, MA, and landed at 4:30 PM in an orchard at Holbrook, MA.

FIRST DOCTOR OF SCIENCE DEGREE EARNED BY A WOMAN: ANNIVERSARY. June 20, 1895. Caroline Willard Baldwin became the first woman to earn a doctor of science degree at Cornell University, Ithaca, NY.

FORT ABRAHAM LINCOLN FESTIVAL. June 20–21. Fort Abraham Lincoln State Park, Mandan, ND. Frontier Army reenactments of military life. Activities and demonstrations, as well as the Mandan Indian Nu-eta Corn Festival. Events will include noted speakers and authors presenting frontier military and Native American topics. Est attendance: 5,000. For info: Fort Abraham Lincoln State Park, 4480 Fort Lincoln Rd, Mandan, ND 58554. Phone: (701) 667-6350. Fax: (701) 667-6349. Web: www.fortlincoln.com.

HELLMAN, LILLIAN: BIRTH ANNIVERSARY. June 20, 1905. One of the 20th century's great playwrights, author of such works as *The Children's Hour* (1934), *The Little Foxes* (1939) and *Toys in the Attic* (1960). One of many artists blacklisted by Hollywood in the 1950s. Was the companion for 30 years of novelist Dashiell Hammett. Born at New Orleans, LA, Hellman died June 30, 1984, at Martha's Vineyard, MA.

***JAWS* FILM RELEASE: ANNIVERSARY.** June 20, 1975. With its tagline "Don't go in the water" and its ominous cello music, the Steven Spielberg–directed thriller shocked audiences on this date. Adapted from a Peter Benchley bestseller, *Jaws* showed a great white shark preying on the beachgoers of a New England town. It won three Oscars—best editing, best sound and best original score (by John Williams)—and was a blockbuster success.

KCQ COUNTRY MUSIC FEST. June 20. Saginaw, MI. 18th annual. Country music's hottest artists perform on stage on Ojibway Island. Also featuring a classic car show, art fair and great food, this is mid-Michigan's hottest summer attraction. Free admission. Est attendance: 80,000. For info: WKCQ, PO Box 1776, Saginaw, MI 48605. Phone: (989) 752-8161. Fax: (989) 752-8102. Web: www.98FMKCQ.com.

LAKESTRIDE HALF-MARATHON. June 20. Ludington, MI. Half-marathon race that begins at Lakeshore Drive and Tinkham (by the beach) takes runners along a scenic course through the wooded trails and sand dunes of Lake Michigan at Ludington State Park. Annually, the Saturday of Father's Day weekend. Est attendance: 10,000. For info: Ludington Area CVB, 5300 W US 10, Ludington, MI 49431. Phone: (800) 542-4600. Fax: (231) 845-6857. Web: www.ludington.org.

LIZZIE BORDEN VERDICT: ANNIVERSARY. June 20, 1893. Spectators at her trial cheered when the "not guilty" verdict was read by the jury foreman in the murder trial of Lizzy Borden on this date. Elizabeth Borden had been accused of and tried for the hacking deaths of her father and stepmother in their Fall River, MA, home, Aug 4, 1892.

LOCKPORT OLD CANAL DAYS. June 20–21. Lockport, IL. Festival in historic canal community. Crafts, parade, entertainment, food, carnival, contests, beer garden and more. Annually, the third weekend in June. Est attendance: 20,000. For info: Lockport Old Canal Days, PO Box 31, Lockport, IL 60441. Phone: (815) 838-4744. E-mail: northjoann@yahoo.com. Web: www.lockportcanaldays.com.

LONGEST DAM RACE. June 20. Fort Peck, MT. The run crosses 1.8 miles of Fort Peck Dam. At two miles into the 10k race, the course rises in elevation some 350 feet over a distance of approximately two miles. The 5k is flat. Both distances finish running downhill grade from the top of the dam. Included in the events is a 10-mile novice bike race. There are also 5k run/walks and a 1-mile run/walk. Annually, the third weekend in June. Est attendance: 400. For info: Glasgow Chamber of Commerce and Agriculture, Box 832, Glasgow, MT 59230. Phone: (406) 228-2222. Fax: (406) 228-2244. E-mail: chamber@glasgowmt.net. Web: www.glasgowmt.net.

MIDNIGHT SUN FESTIVAL. June 20–21. Nome, AK. A celebration of the summer solstice, which is when Nome experiences the midnight sun with more than 22 hours of direct sunlight. The festival usually includes a parade, raft race, folk fest and barbecue. Annually, on the Saturday and Sunday closest to the summer solstice. For info: Nome Conv & Visitors Bureau, PO Box 240, Nome, AK 99762. Phone: (907) 443-6624. Fax: (907) 443-5832. Web: www.nomealaska.org.

MISS ARIZONA PAGEANT. June 20. Gilbert, AZ. Part of the Miss America Organization. For info: Miss Arizona Scholarship Foundation, 2800 14th St, Douglas, AZ 85607-2627. Phone: (520) 364-5308. Fax: (520) 364-1137. Web: www.miss-arizona.org.

MURPHY, AUDIE: 85th BIRTH ANNIVERSARY. June 20, 1924. Born at Kingston, TX, Murphy was the most decorated soldier in WWII and later became an actor in Western and war movies. He died May 28, 1971, in a plane crash near Roanoke, VA.

NEW OXFORD OUTDOOR ANTIQUE SHOW. June 20. New Oxford, PA. Arts, crafts, antiques and flea market. Annually, the third Saturday in June. Est attendance: 30,000. For info: New Oxford Area Chamber of Commerce, PO Box 152, New Oxford, PA 17350. Phone: (717) 624-2800. E-mail: info@newoxford.org. Web: www.newoxford.org.

NORSKEDALEN'S MIDSUMMER FEST. June 20–21. Norskedalen Nature and Heritage Center, Coon Valley, WI. Celebrate the summer solstice and Sankt Hans Dag (Saint John's Day) in Scandinavian style. Pioneer crafts and demonstrations; children's activities, entertainment, food and raffle; nature hikes, animal presentations and horse-drawn wagon rides. Woodcarving show and competition, open air museum; artisans demonstrating and selling their works. Est attendance: 1,500. For info: Norskedalen Nature and Heritage Center, Inc, PO Box 235, Coon Valley, WI 54623. Phone: (608) 452-3424. Fax: (608) 452-3157. E-mail: info@norskedalen.org. Web: www.norskedalen.org.

OIL BOWL FOOTBALL CLASSIC. June 20. Memorial Stadium, Wichita Falls, TX. 70th annual. For more than 60 years, high school all-stars from Texas and Oklahoma tangle in Memorial Stadium, to benefit disadvantaged children. Annually, the third Saturday in June. Est attendance: 14,000. For info: Wichita Falls CVB, 1000 5th St, Wichita Falls, TX 76301. Phone: (940) 716-5500. Fax: (940) 716-5509. E-mail: mpec@wf.net. Web: www.wichitafalls.org.

POLAR BEAR SWIM. June 20. Nome, AK. 2 PM on the red sand beaches. More than 100 intrepid swimmers have plunged into the frigid Bering Sea on this day since 1975. The swim may be rescheduled if the ocean ice hasn't sufficiently broken up. For info: Leo B. Rasmussen, Nome Rotary Club, PO Box 2, Nome, AK 99762. Phone: (907) 443-2798 or (907) 443-6022. E-mail: leaknome@alaska.com.

PSFCA EAST WEST ALL-STAR GAME. June 20. Mansion Park, Altoona, PA. All-star football game featuring the finest college-bound athletes in Pennsylvania. Come see the "Beasts of the East" take on the "Best of the West" in a must-see, action-packed game. Annually, the last Saturday in June. Est attendance: 5,000. For info: Kathy Dodson, Allegheny Mountains CVB, One Convention Center Dr, Altoona, PA 16602. Phone: (814) 943-4183. Fax: (814) 943-8094. E-mail: info@amcvb.com. Web: www.eastwestgame.com.

ROCHESTERFEST. June 20–28. Rochester, MN. This community festival includes Midwestern lumberjack championships, children's and senior events, gigantic street parade, street vendors with exotic foods, country night, rock and roll night, street dance and breakfast on the farm. Est attendance: 150,000. For info: Carole Brown, Exec Dir, Box 007, Rochester, MN 55903. Phone: (507) 285-8769. Fax: (507) 285-8718. Web: www.rochesterfest.com.

SPANISH-AMERICAN WAR SURRENDER OF GUAM TO US: ANNIVERSARY. June 20, 1898. Not knowing that a war was in progress and having no ammunition on the island, the Spanish commander of Guam surrendered to Captain Glass of the USS *Charleston*.

SPIRIT OF THE WOODS FOLK FESTIVAL. June 20. Dickson Township Park, Brethren, MI. A one-day free outdoor festival of folk music, dance and handcrafts. Family friendly, this event features two stages, children's activities and good food. Annually, the third Saturday in June since 1978. For info: Spirit of the Woods Music Assn, 11171 Kerry Rd, Brethren, MI 49619. Phone: (231) 477-5381. E-mail: spiritmusic@jackpine.com. Web: www.spiritofthewoods.org.

TOAD HOLLOW DAY OF THANK YOU. June 20. A day to say or write a thank-you to the people who have helped us along the way. For info: Ralph Morrison, Director, Toad Hollow, PO Box 2132, Garden City, MI 48135. Phone: (800) 574-8623.

June 2009

S	M	T	W	T	F	S
	1	2	3	4	5	6
7	8	9	10	11	12	13
14	15	16	17	18	19	20
21	22	23	24	25	26	27
28	29	30				

UNITED NATIONS: WORLD REFUGEE DAY. June 20. A day to bring attention to the situation of refugees—their rights, as well as their suffering. First observed on June 20, 2001, the 50th anniversary of the 1951 Convention on the Status of Refugees. Date chosen to coincide with Africa Refugee Day. For info: United Nations, Dept of Public Info, New York, NY 10017. Web: www.un.org.

VINEGAR DAY. June 20. A day set aside to celebrate the virtues of vinegar. All over the world people will conduct vinegar tasting contests and host events connected with vinegar. There will be an International Vinegar Festival in Roslyn, SD, to commemorate. Annually, the third Saturday in June. For info: Lawrence Diggs, Vinegar Connoisseurs Intl, PO Box 41, Roslyn, SD 57261. Phone: (605) 486-4536. E-mail: vinegarday@vinegarman.com. Web: www.vinegarman.com.

WEST VIRGINIA: ADMISSION DAY: ANNIVERSARY. June 20, 1863. Became 35th state in 1863. Observed as a holiday in West Virginia. The state of West Virginia is a product of the Civil War. Originally part of Virginia, West Virginia became a separate state when Virginia seceded from the Union.

WOMAN RUNS THE HOUSE: ANNIVERSARY. June 20, 1921. Alice Robertson of Oklahoma became the first woman to preside in the US House of Representatives. Robertson presided for half an hour.

WORLD JUGGLING DAY. June 20. Juggling clubs all over the world hold local festivals to demonstrate, teach and celebrate their art. Annually, the Saturday on or closest to June 17. For info: Intl Jugglers' Assn, PO Box 7307, Austin, TX 78713-7307. E-mail: wjd@juggle.org. Web: www.juggle.org.

BIRTHDAYS TODAY

Danny Aiello, Jr, 76, actor ("Lady Blue," *Do the Right Thing*), born New York, NY, June 20, 1933.

LaVar Arrington, 31, football player, born Pittsburgh, PA, June 20, 1978.

Olympia Dukakis, 78, actress, theatrical director (Oscar for *Moonstruck; Steel Magnolias*), born Lowell, MA, June 20, 1931.

John Goodman, 57, actor ("Roseanne," *The Big Lebowski, The Flintstones*), born Afton, MO, June 20, 1952.

Nicole Kidman, 42, actress (Oscar for *The Hours*; *The Golden Compass, Cold Mountain, Moulin Rouge*), born Honolulu, HI, June 20, 1967.

Frank Lampard, 31, soccer player, born Romford, England, June 20, 1978.

Martin Landau, 78, actor (*Tucker: The Man and His Dream; Crimes and Misdemeanors*; Oscar for *Ed Wood*), born Brooklyn, NY, June 20, 1931.

Michael Landon, Jr, 45, actor ("Bonanza: The Return," "Bonanza: The Ghosts"), born Encino, CA, June 20, 1964.

Cyndi Lauper, 56, singer ("Girls Just Want to Have Fun"), born Brooklyn, NY, June 20, 1953.

John Mahoney, 69, actor ("Frasier"), born Manchester, England, June 20, 1940.

Anne Murray, 64, singer (*Country*, "Snowbird," "Could I Have This Dance"), born Springhill, NS, Canada, June 20, 1945.

Lionel Richie, 60, singer ("Truly"), songwriter, born Tuskegee, AL, June 20, 1949.

Robert Rodriguez, 41, director, screenwriter (*Sin City, Spy Kids, Desperado*), born San Antonio, TX, June 20, 1968.

James Tolkan, 78, actor (*Serpico, Back to the Future, Dick Tracy*), born Calumet, MI, June 20, 1931.

Bob Vila, 63, handyman, TV show host, born Miami, FL, June 20, 1946.

Abby Wambach, 29, soccer player, born June 20, 1980, in Pittsford, NY.

Andre Watts, 63, pianist, born Nuremburg, Germany, June 20, 1946.

Brian Wilson, 67, singer (The Beach Boys), songwriter, born Hawthorne, CA, June 20, 1942.

June 21 — Sunday

DAY 172 **193 REMAINING**

ANNE AND SAMANTHA DAY. June 21 (also Dec 21). Celebrated worldwide, this twice-yearly holiday is meant for reflection on Anne Frank and Samantha Smith's contributions to our world and to promote their candidacy as subjects worthy to be honored on official American postage stamps, as well as the stamps of all nations. Annually, on the solstice each June and December. For info: John O'Loughlin, 3124 Chisholm Trail, Irving, TX 75062. Phone: (972) 258-4996. E-mail: lldjohn@aol.com. Web: www.anneandsamantha.com.

BABY BOOMERS RECOGNITION DAY. June 21. As baby boomers, we'll never forget the Beatles, Vietnam War and other sixties events. However, many of us accomplished a great deal, becoming successful in business, education, medicine and other fields. This special day commemorates our contributions. Annually, June 21. For info: Dorothy Zjawin, 61 W Colfax Ave, Roselle Park, NJ 07204. Phone: (908) 241-6241.

BATTLE OF OKINAWA ENDS: ANNIVERSARY. June 21, 1945. With American grenades exploding in the background, inside the Japanese command cave at Mabuni the battle for Okinawa was ended when Major General Isamu Cho and Lieutenant General Mitsuru Ushijima killed themselves in the ceremonial rite of hara-kiri. In the long battle that had begun Apr 1, the American death toll reached enormous proportions by Pacific battle standards—7,613 died on land and 4,907 in the air or from kamikaze attacks. A total of 36 US warships were sunk. More than 70,000 Japanese and 80,000 civilian Okinawans died in the course of the battle.

BHUTTO, BENAZIR: BIRTH ANNIVERSARY. June 21, 1953. The first woman democratically elected to lead a Muslim nation, born at Karachi, Sindh, Pakistan. She served as that nation's prime minister from 1988–90 and then again from 1993–96, and she accomplished much national reform, especially on women's issues. However, during both of her terms, she was ejected from office under charges of corruption in Pakistan's turbulent and often violent political climate. She was assassinated by a suicide bomber as she tried to mount her third campaign for prime minister, Dec 27, 2007, at Rawalpindi, Punjab, Pakistan.

CANCER, THE CRAB. June 21–July 22. In the astronomical/astrological zodiac, which divides the sun's apparent orbit into 12 segments, the period June 21–July 22 is traditionally identified as the sun sign of Cancer, the Crab. The ruling planet is the moon.

CARPENTER ANT AWARENESS WEEK. June 21–27. Wood-destroying organisms cost Americans $5 billion in property damage annually. This week will focus attention on the identification, biology and habits of carpenter ants and provide consumers with information on the elimination of these costly pests. Annually, the last full week of June. For info: Chris Venuti, Marketing Mgr, or Jerry Batzner, Pres, Batzner Pest Management, Inc, 16948 W Victor Rd, New Berlin, WI 53151. Phone: (262) 797-4160. Fax: (262) 797-4166. E-mail: JerryB@batzner.com.

FAMILY AWARENESS DAY. June 21. A day to reflect on the important role of fathers in the American family. "Remembering always that every kid needs a Dad." A day and time to reestablish and reaffirm every man's place in our culture. Annually, the third Sunday in June. For info: Judith Natale, CEO & Founder, NCAC America-USA, PO Box 493703, Redding, CA 96049-3703. E-mail: childaware@aol.com.

✦ **FATHER'S DAY.** June 21. Presidential Proclamation issued for third Sunday in June in 1966 and annually since 1971. (PL 92–278 of Apr 24, 1972.)

FATHER'S DAY. June 21. Recognition of the third Sunday in June as Father's Day occurred first at the request of Mrs John B. Dodd of Spokane, WA, on June 19, 1910. It was proclaimed for that date by the mayor of Spokane and recognized by the governor of Washington. The idea was publicly supported by President Calvin Coolidge in 1924, but not presidentially proclaimed until 1966. It was assured of annual recognition by PL 92–278 of April 1972. Also celebrated on this day in Britain.

FATHER'S DAY CELEBRATION. June 21. Jenkinson's Aquarium, Point Pleasant Beach, NJ. Calling all kids! Bring your dad for a special day to learn about the roles of fathers in the marine environment. One father admitted free with each paid child's admission. Est attendance: 800. For info: Jenkinson's Aquarium, 300 Ocean Ave, Point Pleasant Beach, NJ 08742. Phone: (732) 899-1212. Fax: (732) 899-1717. E-mail: jenkinsonsaquarium@comcast.net. Web: www.jenkinsons.com.

GREENLAND: NATIONAL DAY. June 21. National holiday.

HIRSCHFELD, AL: BIRTH ANNIVERSARY. June 21, 1903. Caricature artist known for his inimitable sketches of Broadway and Hollywood stars, Al Hirschfeld was born at St. Louis, MO. His first cartoon appeared in 1926 in the now-defunct *New York Herald Tribune.* Later moving to *The New York Times,* his drawings appeared on the drama page for seven decades. He was known for hiding "Nina" (his daughter's name) somewhere in every caricature that he created after 1945. His art is found in many museums, including the Metropolitan Museum of Art in New York City. He died Jan 20, 2003, at New York, NY.

HURRICANE AGNES: ANNIVERSARY. June 21–26, 1972. Hurricane Agnes hit the eastern seaboard wreaking havoc across seven Atlantic Coast states. Casualties included 118 lives and 116,000 homes, leaving more than 200,000 homeless after Agnes dumped 28.1 trillion gallons of water over 5,000 square miles.

LONG BEACH BAYOU FESTIVAL. June 21–22. Rainbow Lagoon, Long Beach, CA. Celebrate Cajun/Creole cultures with food, live nonstop Cajun, Zydeco and blues music, arts and crafts, activities and a Mardi Gras Parade. Est attendance: 10,000. For info: Phone: (562) 427-3713. Web: www.LongBeachFestival.com.

MIDNIGHT SUN BASEBALL GAME. June 21. Fairbanks, AK. To celebrate the summer solstice. Game is played without artificial lights at 10:35 PM. Est attendance: 4,000. For info: Alaska Goldpanners, Box 71154, Fairbanks, AK 99707. Phone: (907) 451-0095. Web: www.goldpanners.com.

MIDSUMMER. June 21. One of the "Lesser Sabbats" during the Wiccan year, celebrating the peak of the Sun God in his annual cycle. Annually, on the summer solstice.

MIDSUMMER DAY/EVE CELEBRATIONS. June 21. Celebrates the beginning of summer with maypoles, music, dancing and bonfires. Observed mainly in northern Europe, including Finland, Latvia and Sweden. Day of observance is sometimes St. John's Day (June 24), with celebration on St. John's Eve (June 23) as well, or June 19. Time approximates the summer solstice. See also: "Summer" (June 21).

NEW HAMPSHIRE RATIFIES CONSTITUTION: ANNIVERSARY. June 21, 1788. By a vote of 57 to 47, New Hampshire became the ninth state to ratify the Constitution. With this ratification, the Constitution became effective for all ratifying states, as the approval of nine states was required for the Constitution to go into effect.

SARTRE, JEAN-PAUL: BIRTH ANNIVERSARY. June 21, 1905. French philosopher, "father of existentialism," born at Paris, France. In 1964 Sartre rejected the Nobel Prize for Literature when it was awarded to him. He died at Paris, Apr 15, 1980. In *Being and Nothingness*, he wrote: "Man can will nothing unless he has first understood that he must count on no one but himself; that he is alone, abandoned on earth in the midst of his infinite responsibilities, without help, with no other aim than the one he sets for himself, with no other destiny than the one he forges for himself on this earth."

SPACE MILESTONE: FIRST MANNED PRIVATE SPACEFLIGHT: 5th ANNIVERSARY. June 21, 2004. Michael Melvill, flying the privately financed SpaceShipOne, flew 62 miles in altitude on this date, leaving the Earth's atmosphere. The spacecraft was designed by Burt Rutan and was financed by Paul Allen, philanthropist and Microsoft cofounder. SpaceShipOne made the flight from Mojave Airport at Mojave, CA.

SUMMER. June 21–Sept 22. In the Northern Hemisphere summer begins today with the summer solstice, at 1:45 AM EDT. Note that in the Southern Hemisphere today is the beginning of winter. Anywhere between the Equator and the Arctic Circle, the sun rises and sets farthest north on the horizon for the year and length of daylight is maximum (12 hours, 8 minutes at equator, increasing to 24 hours at the Arctic Circle).

TANNER, HENRY OSSAWA: 150th BIRTH ANNIVERSARY. June 21, 1859. Henry Ossawa Tanner was one of the first black artists to be exhibited in galleries in the US. He was born at Pittsburgh, PA. He died May 25, 1937, at Paris.

TOMPKINS, DANIEL D.: BIRTH ANNIVERSARY. June 21, 1774. 6th vice president of the US (1817–25), born at Fox Meadows, NY. Died at Staten Island, NY, June 11, 1825.

WASHINGTON, MARTHA DANDRIDGE CUSTIS: BIRTH ANNIVERSARY. June 21, 1731. Wife of George Washington, first president of the US, born at New Kent County, VA. Died at Mount Vernon, VA, May 22, 1802.

WORLD HUMANIST DAY. June 21. World Humanist Day is celebrated annually on June 21 as a way to spread information—and combat misinformation—about the positive aspects of humanism as a philosophical life stance and means to effect change in the world. For info: Institute for Humanist Studies, 48 Howard St, Albany, NY 12207. Phone: (518) 432-7820. Fax: (518) 432-7821. E-mail: MCherry@HumanistStudies.org. Web: www.secularseasons.org.

BIRTHDAYS TODAY

Meredith Baxter, 62, actress ("Bridget Loves Bernie," "Family," "Family Ties"), born Los Angeles, CA, June 21, 1947.

Berke Breathed, 52, cartoonist ("Bloom County"), born Croatia, June 21, 1957.

Thomas Doane (Tom) Chambers, 50, former basketball player, born Ogden, UT, June 21, 1959.

Derrick D. Coleman, 42, former basketball player, born Mobile, AL, June 21, 1967.

Sammi Davis-Voss, 45, actress ("Homefront," *Hope and Glory*), born Kidderminster, Worcestershire, England, June 21, 1964.

Jim Douglas, 58, Governor of Vermont (R), born Springfield, MA, June 21, 1951.

Joe Flaherty, 69, writer, actor ("Second City TV," "SCTV Network 90"), born Pittsburgh, PA, June 21, 1940.

Michael Gross, 62, actor ("Family Ties"), born Chicago, IL, June 21, 1947.

Mariette Hartley, 68, actress ("Peyton Place," "The Rockford Files"), born New York, NY, June 21, 1941.

Richard Jefferson, 29, basketball player, born Los Angeles, CA, June 21, 1980.

Bernie Kopell, 76, actor ("Get Smart," "The Love Boat," "When Things Were Rotten"), born New York, NY, June 21, 1933.

Juliette Lewis, 36, actress (*The Other Sister, The Evening Star*), born Los Angeles, CA, June 21, 1973.

Nils Lofgren, 58, musician, singer, songwriter, born Chicago, IL, June 21, 1951.

Jane Russell, 88, actress (*The Outlaw, Gentlemen Prefer Blondes*), born Bemidji, MN, June 21, 1921.

Doug Savant, 45, actor ("Melrose Place," "Desperate Housewives"), born Burbank, CA, June 21, 1964.

Rick Sutcliffe, 53, former baseball player, born Independence, MO, June 21, 1956.

Larry Wachowski, 44, filmmaker with brother Andy Wachowski (*The Matrix*), born Chicago, IL, June 21, 1965.

Prince William (William Arthur Philip Louis), 27, son of Prince Charles and Princess Diana, born London, England, June 21, 1982.

June 2009	S	M	T	W	T	F	S
		1	2	3	4	5	6
	7	8	9	10	11	12	13
	14	15	16	17	18	19	20
	21	22	23	24	25	26	27
	28	29	30				

June 22 — Monday

DAY 173 | **192 REMAINING**

BLASS, BILL: BIRTH ANNIVERSARY. June 22, 1922. Born at Fort Wayne, IN, William Ralph Blass moved to New York at 17 to study fashion design. After service in WWII, he returned to New York and went to work for Anne Klein. By 1970 he had his own company and put American fashion on the map—favoring a sporty yet classy silhouette. His client list soon included Jacqueline Kennedy, Barbra Streisand and Gloria Vanderbilt, and he became one of the most successful fashion designers in history. He was known as a philanthropist in his later years and died soon after retirement at New Preston, CT, June 12, 2002.

BRADLEY, ED: BIRTH ANNIVERSARY. June 22, 1941. Television journalist Edward Rudolph Bradley, Jr, was born at Philadelphia, PA. His career began with battlefield reporting as he covered the fall of Saigon, and he was the first African-American television correspondent to cover the White House. He spent his entire career with CBS, and worked on the venerable "60 Minutes" for 26 years. Highly respected for his journalistic integrity, he earned 19 Emmy Awards and four George Peabody awards in the course of his career. He died at New York, NY, Nov 7, 2006.

BUTLER, OCTAVIA: BIRTH ANNIVERSARY. Oct 22, 1947. African-American science fiction author, born at Pasadena, CA. Significant works include *The Parable of the Sower* and the Patternist series, featuring *Wild Seed* and *Clay's Ark*. Winner of multiple Hugo and Nebula awards, in 1995, she became the first science fiction writer to be awarded a MacArthur Foundation fellowship, and in 2000 she received a PEN Award for lifetime achievement. She died Feb 24, 2006, at Seattle, WA.

CANADA: NEWFOUNDLAND DISCOVERY DAY. June 22. Commemorates the discovery of Newfoundland by John Cabot, June 24, 1497. Commemorated on the Monday nearest June 24.

***CHESAPEAKE-LEOPARD* AFFAIR: ANNIVERSARY.** June 22, 1807. One of the events leading to the War of 1812 occurred about 40 miles east of Chesapeake Bay. The US frigate *Chesapeake* was fired upon and boarded by the crew of the British man-of-war *Leopard*. The *Chesapeake*'s commander, James Barron, was court-martialed and convicted of not being prepared for action. Later Barron killed one of the judges (Stephen Decatur) in a duel fought at Bladensburg, MD, Mar 22, 1820.

CIRCUS TRAIN WRECK: ANNIVERSARY. June 22, 1918. A Michigan Central Railroad troop train, after several days shuttling soldiers to New York from Chicago, was deadheading back to the Midwest when it struck the rear of the Hagenbeck–Wallace Circus train. The circus train had stopped to have its brake box overhauled at Ivanhoe, IN. Fifty-three circus performers were killed. Of the circus animals not killed outright, many that were crippled and maimed had to be destroyed by police officers. The performers, of whom only three could be identified, were buried in a mass grave. The engineer, A.K. Sargent, who was accused of falling asleep at the throttle, was tried and acquitted.

CROATIA: ANTIFASCIST STRUGGLE DAY. June 22. National holiday. Commemorates uprising against fascist invaders in 1941.

ENGLAND: LAWN TENNIS CHAMPIONSHIPS AT WIMBLEDON. June 22–July 5. Wimbledon, London. World famous men's and women's singles and doubles championships for the most coveted titles in tennis. Tickets are allocated via public ballot. Send SASE for details between August 1 and December 15, 2008. For info: All England Lawn Tennis and Croquet Club, PO Box 98, Wimbledon, London, England SW19 5AE. Phone: (44) (20) 8971-2473. Fax: (44) (20) 8971-2528. Web: www.wimbledon.org.

JOE LOUIS v BRADDOCK/SCHMELING FIGHT ANNIVERSARIES. June 22, 1937/1938. At Chicago's Comiskey Park Joe Louis won the World Heavyweight Championship title by knocking out James J. Braddock (eighth round). Louis retained the title until his retirement in 1949. Exactly one year after the Braddock fight, on June 22, 1938, Louis met Germany's Max Schmeling, at New York City's Yankee Stadium. Louis knocked out Schmeling in the first round.

LINDBERGH, ANNE MORROW: BIRTH ANNIVERSARY. June 22, 1906. American author and aviator, born at Englewood, NJ. Wife of aviator Charles A. Lindbergh, she served as his copilot and navigator when he broke the transatlantic speed record in 1930. A prolific author and poet, in *Gift from the Sea* she wrote: "By and large, mothers and housewives are the only workers who do not have regular time off. They are the great vacationless class." She died Feb 7, 2001, at Passumpsic, VT.

MALTA: MNARJA. June 22–23. Buskett Gardens. A folk-cum-harvest festival. An all-night traditional Maltese "festa" with folk music, dancing and impromptu Maltese folk singing (ghana). This festival originated in the Middle Ages, and the word *Mnarja* is derived from *luminarja* because the countryside and the bastions around Mdina, Malta's ancient capital, used to be illuminated by "Fjakkoli" (torches made of sand mixed with oil and animal fat) on the eve of and on the feast day itself.

MOON PHASE: NEW MOON. June 22. Moon enters New Moon phase at 3:35 PM, EDT.

NATIONAL OLD-TIME FIDDLERS' CONTEST AND FESTIVAL®. June 22–27. Weiser, ID. 57th anniversary. Largest fiddling event in the world to help perpetuate the old-time fiddling. Annually, the third full week in June. Est attendance: 42,000. For info: National Old-Time Fiddlers' Contest, 115 West Idaho, Weiser, ID 83672. Phone: (800) 437-1280. E-mail: director@fiddlecontest.com. Web: www.fiddlecontest.com.

PAPP, JOSEPH: BIRTH ANNIVERSARY. June 22, 1921. Born Yosl Papirofsky at Brooklyn, NY, Joe Papp became one of the leading figures in American theater. At the helm of the New York Public Theatre, Papp produced a wide range of work from the classical to that of the newest American dramatists, including *Hair, Two Gentlemen of Verona, The Pirates of Penzance, The Mystery of Edwin Drood, That Championship Season* and *A Chorus Line*. He began in 1954 with the Shakespeare Theatre Workshop, taking touring productions around the city on a flatbed truck. When the truck broke down in Central Park, Papp turned his touring company into Shakespeare-in-the-Park. Producing and directing more than 400 productions, Papp garnered three Pulitzer Prizes, six New York Critics Circle Awards and 28 Tonys. He died Oct 31, 1991, at New York, NY.

PERIGEAN SPRING TIDES. June 22. Spring tides, the highest possible tides, occur when New Moon or Full Moon falls within 24 hours of the moment the moon is nearest Earth (perigee) in its monthly orbit. The word *spring* refers not to the season but comes from the German word, *springen*, "to rise up."

SOVIET UNION INVADED: ANNIVERSARY. June 22, 1941. German troops invaded the Soviet Union, beginning a conflict that left 27 million Soviet citizens dead. Ceremonies are held this day in Russia, Belarus and Ukraine, the areas of the former Soviet Union that bore the brunt of the initial invasion.

STUPID GUY THING DAY. June 22. Women are always talking about it, so here's the day to commemorate it! Women everywhere are to make a list of "stupid guy things" and pass it on! (©2006 by WH.) For info: Thomas & Ruth Roy, Wellcat Holidays, 2418 Long Ln, Lebanon, PA 17046. Phone: (717) 279-0184. E-mail: info@wellcat.com. Web: www.wellcat.com.

SWITZERLAND: MORAT BATTLE ANNIVERSARY. June 22, 1476. The little, walled town of Morat played a decisive part in Swiss history. There, the Confederates were victorious over Charles the Bold of Burgundy, laying the basis for French-speaking areas to become Swiss. Now an annual children's festival.

US DEPARTMENT OF JUSTICE: ANNIVERSARY. June 22, 1870. Established by an act of Congress, the Department of Justice is headed by the attorney general. Prior to 1870, the attorney general (whose office had been created Sept 24, 1789) had been a member of the president's cabinet but had not been the head of a department.

US WOMEN'S AMATEUR PUBLIC LINKS (GOLF) CHAMPIONSHIP. June 22–27. Red Tail Golf Club, Devens, MA. For info: USGA, Golf House, Championship Dept, PO Box 708, Far Hills, NJ 07931. Phone: (908) 234-2300. Fax: (908) 234-9687. E-mail: usga@usga.org. Web: www.usga.org.

VANCOUVER, GEORGE: BIRTH ANNIVERSARY. June 22, 1757. English navigator, explorer and author for whom Vancouver Island and the cities of Vancouver (British Columbia and Washington) are named was born at Norfolk, England, and joined the navy at the age of 13. He surveyed the coasts of Australia, New Zealand and western North America and sailed with Captain James Cook to the Arctic in 1780. Vancouver died at Petersham, Surrey, England, May 10, 1798, just as he was correcting the final pages of his *Journal*, which was published at London later that year.

V-MAIL DELIVERY: ANNIVERSARY. June 22, 1942. The first V-Mail (V for victory) was dispatched from New York on this date. The system was devised during WWII to conserve cargo space for war materials and supplies. Special paper was used for writing the letters. At post offices, the letters were opened, censored and photographed in reduced proportions. The film was then transported overseas. A complete roll of film contained 1,600 letters.

WILDER, BILLY: BIRTH ANNIVERSARY. June 22, 1906. One of the greatest directors of Hollywood's Golden Age was born Samuel Wilder at Sucha Beskidzka in the Austro-Hungarian Empire. After a short career in Berlin, Wilder fled Germany in 1933 and eventually landed in Hollywood, where he directed and cowrote some of the 20th century's greatest films. His classics include the film noir works *Double Indemnity* and *Sunset Boulevard*, the searing dramas *Stalag 17* and *The Lost Weekend* and the comic gem *Some Like It Hot*. He received six Oscars (out of 21 nominations), and Best Film Oscars went to *The Lost Weekend* and *The Apartment*. Wilder died at Los Angeles, CA, on Mar 27, 2002.

 BIRTHDAYS TODAY

Darrell Armstrong, 41, basketball player, born Gastonia, NC, June 22, 1968.

Klaus Maria Brandauer, 65, actor (*Out of Africa, White Fang*), born Altausse, Austria, June 22, 1944.

Amy Brenneman, 45, actress ("Judging Amy"), born Glastonbury, CT, June 22, 1964.

Dan Brown, 45, author (*The Da Vinci Code, Angels & Demons*), born Exeter, NH, June 22, 1964.

Carson Daly, 36, host ("MTV Live," "Last Call with Carson Daly"), born Santa Monica, CA, June 22, 1973.

Clyde Austin Drexler, 47, basketball coach and former player, born Houston, TX, June 22, 1962.

Dianne Feinstein, 76, US Senator (D, California), born San Francisco, CA, June 22, 1933.

Kris Kristofferson, 73, singer, actor (*Alice Doesn't Live Here Anymore, A Star Is Born*), born Brownsville, TX, June 22, 1936.

Michael Lerner, 68, actor (*The Candidate, Eight Men Out, Barton Fink*), born Brooklyn, NY, June 22, 1941.

Tracy Pollan, 49, actress ("Family Ties," *Bright Lights, Big City*), born New York, NY, June 22, 1960.

Todd Rundgren, 61, singer (*Something/Anything*), producer, born Upper Darby, PA, June 22, 1948.

Meryl Streep, 60, actress (*The Devil Wears Prada,* Oscars for *Kramer vs Kramer* and *Sophie's Choice*), born Summit, NJ, June 22, 1949.

Kurt Wagner, 38, football player, born Burlington, IA, June 22, 1971.

Lindsay Wagner, 60, actress ("The Bionic Woman," *The Paper Chase*), born Los Angeles, CA, June 22, 1949.

June 23 — Tuesday

DAY 174 | **191 REMAINING**

"THE BREAKFAST CLUB" RADIO PREMIERE: ANNIVERSARY. June 23, 1933. "The Breakfast Club with Don McNeil," which hit radio airwaves on this date, had a 35-year run. It was carried by 400 affiliates and tickets became as sought-after as those for a taping of "The Tonight Show" are today. The hour-long show included celebrities such as Fran Allison of "Kukla, Fran and Ollie" fame. Its popularity, however, stemmed mainly from regular features such as "Memory Time," when McNeil read poems and letters from listeners. During WWII "Prayer Time" was started. McNeil's "Call to Breakfast," which was announced every 15 minutes, invited listeners to get up and march around the breakfast table. McNeil died in 1996.

CASH, JUNE CARTER: 80th BIRTH ANNIVERSARY. June 23, 1929. Grammy-winning country-western star born Valerie June Carter at Maces Springs, VA. As a member of the Carter Family, a group that included her mother, sisters and various cousins, she toured as a performer from childhood. She met Johnny Cash on the road in 1961. She cowrote his hit song "Ring of Fire," and they began recording together. They married in 1968, and won two Grammys for their duets. She died May 15, 2004, at Nashville, TN.

June 2009	S	M	T	W	T	F	S
		1	2	3	4	5	6
	7	8	9	10	11	12	13
	14	15	16	17	18	19	20
	21	22	23	24	25	26	27
	28	29	30				

DENMARK: MIDSUMMER EVE. June 23. Celebrated all over the country with bonfires and merrymaking.

ESTONIA: VICTORY DAY. June 23. National holiday. Commemorates victory against Germany in 1919.

FIRST TYPEWRITER: ANNIVERSARY. June 23, 1868. First US typewriter was patented by Luther Sholes.

FOSSE, ROBERT LOUIS (BOB): BIRTH ANNIVERSARY. June 23, 1927. Bob Fosse was born at Chicago, IL. The son of a vaudeville singer, he began his show business career at the age of 13. He was the only director in history to win an Oscar, an Emmy and a Tony for his work. As a choreographer he was known for his unique dance style that focused on explosive angularity of the human body in its movement. His body of work included the plays *Pippin, Sweet Charity, Pajama Game, Chicago* and *Damn Yankees.* His films included *Cabaret, Lenny* and the autobiographical *All That Jazz.* Fosse died Sept 23, 1987, at Washington, DC.

KINSEY, ALFRED: BIRTH ANNIVERSARY. June 23, 1894. Born at Hoboken, NJ, Kinsey was a professor of zoology who moved into the study of human sexual behavior in the 1940s at Indiana University's Institute for Sex Research (later renamed after him). Kinsey published two controversial books based on his research: *Sexual Behavior in the Human Male* (1948) and *Sexual Behavior in the Human Female* (1953). Kinsey died Aug 25, 1956, at Bloomington, IN.

LAST FORMAL SURRENDER OF CONFEDERATE TROOPS: ANNIVERSARY. June 23, 1865. The last formal surrender of Confederate troops took place in the Oklahoma Territory. Cherokee leader and Confederate Brigadier General Waite surrendered his command of a battalion formed by Indians.

LET IT GO DAY. June 23. Whatever it is that's bugging you, drop it! It's only eating away at you and providing nothing positive. (©2006 by WH.) For info: Thomas & Ruth Roy, Wellcat Holidays, 2418 Long Ln, Lebanon, PA 17046-1708. Phone: (717) 279-0184. E-mail: info@wellcat.com. Web: www.wellcat.com.

LUXEMBOURG: NATIONAL HOLIDAY. June 23. Official birthday of His Royal Highness Grand Duke Jean in 1921. Also, Luxembourg's independence is celebrated June 23.

NATIONAL COLUMNIST'S DAY. June 23. Newspaper columnists, who bring you joy all year long, deserve to be celebrated by their readers at least once a year. Now you can send your favorite columnists, local or nationally syndicated, your own wishes for a Happy Columnist's Day and make them feel wonderful. Annually, the fourth Tuesday in June. For info: Jim Six, Columnist, *The Gloucester County Times*, 309 S Broad St, Woodbury, NJ 08096. Phone: (856) 845-3300. Fax: (856) 845-5480. E-mail: jimsix@sjnewsco.com.

RUDOLPH, WILMA: BIRTH ANNIVERSARY. June 23, 1940. Olympic gold medal sprinter, born at Bethlehem, TN. She won the 100 meters, the 200 meters and the 400-meter relay at the 1960 Rome games, thus becoming the first woman to win three gold medals at the same Olympics. She overcame polio as a child and went on to Tennessee State University to become an athlete. Rudolph won the Sullivan Award in 1961. Died at Brentwood, TN, Nov 12, 1994.

SWEDEN: MIDSUMMER. June 23–24. Celebrated throughout Sweden. Maypole dancing, games and folk music.

SWEDISH DAYS—A MIDSOMMAR FESTIVAL. June 23–28. Geneva, IL. Celebrating its 60th anniversary, this grandaddy of all Illinois festivals commemorates Swedish heritage. Six days of entertainment, music competitions, crafts, rosemaling displays, carnival, Kid's Day activities and a parade provide unlimited fun. Food stands throughout the downtown area tempt visitors with Swedish and American menus. Begins annually on the Tuesday after Father's Day. Est attendance: 250,000. For info: Geneva Chamber of Commerce, PO Box 481, 8 S Third St, Geneva, IL 60134. Phone: (630)

232-6060. Fax: (630) 232-6083. E-mail: chamberinfo@genevachamber.com. Web: www.genevachamber.com.

UNITED NATIONS: PUBLIC SERVICE DAY. June 23. The Assembly designated June 23 of each year as United Nations Public Service Day (Resolution 57/277). It encouraged member states to organize special events on that day to highlight the contribution of public service in the development process. For info: United Nations, Dept of Public Info, New York, NY 10017. Web: www.un.org.

WESTERN DAYS. June 23–27. Elgin, TX. Events include a parade, horseshoe contest, volleyball tournament, Miss Western Days contest, live music, arts and crafts, rodeo and carnival. Est attendance: 20,000. For info: Gena Carter, Elgin Chamber of Commerce, PO Box 408, Elgin, TX 78621. Phone: (512) 285-4515. Web: www.elgintx.com.

WINDJAMMER DAYS. June 23–24. Boothbay Harbor, ME. The premier maritime event along the coast of Maine. Parades, concerts, waterfront food, interactive children's activities, live music, fireworks, visiting military vessels, windjammers sailing into harbor under full sail and much more. Fun for the whole family. Est attendance: 20,000. For info: Boothbay Harbor Region Chamber of Commerce, PO Box 356, Boothbay Harbor, ME 04538. Phone: (207) 633-2353. Fax: (207) 633-7448. E-mail: seamaine@boothbayharbor.com. Web: www.boothbayharbor.com.

BIRTHDAYS TODAY

Bryan Brown, 62, actor (*A Town Like Alice, Breaker Morant, F/X*), born Sydney, Australia, June 23, 1947.

Randy Jackson, 53, musician, television personality ("American Idol"), born Baton Rouge, LA, June 23, 1956.

James Levine, 66, American conductor and pianist, Metropolitan Opera of New York City, born Cincinnati, OH, June 23, 1943.

Frances McDormand, 52, actress (Oscar for *Fargo; Mississippi Burning, Almost Famous*), born Chicago, IL, June 23, 1957.

Ted Shackelford, 63, actor ("Knots Landing," "Dallas"), born Oklahoma City, OK, June 23, 1946.

Clarence Thomas, 61, Supreme Court Associate Justice, born Pinpoint, GA, June 23, 1948.

LaDanian Tomlinson, 30, football player, born Waco, TX, June 23, 1979.

Louis Van Amstel, 37, professional dancer, television personality ("Dancing with the Stars"), born Amsterdam, Netherlands, June 23, 1972.

Zinedine Zidane, 37, former soccer player, born Marseille, France, June 23, 1972.

June 24 — Wednesday

DAY 175 — **190 REMAINING**

BEECHER, HENRY WARD: BIRTH ANNIVERSARY. June 24, 1813. Famous American clergyman and orator was born at Litchfield, CT. Died Mar 8, 1887, at Brooklyn, NY. His dying words were "Now comes the mystery."

BERLIN AIRLIFT: ANNIVERSARY. June 24, 1948. In the early days of the Cold War the Soviet Union challenged the West's right of access to Berlin. The Soviets created a blockade, and an airlift to supply some 2,250,000 people resulted. The airlift lasted a total of 321 days and brought into Berlin 1,592,787 tons of supplies. Joseph Stalin finally backed down and the blockade ended May 12, 1949.

CANADA: ST. JEAN-BAPTISTE DAY. June 24. Public holiday in Quebec.

CELEBRATION OF THE SENSES. June 24. Treat yourself to a stimulation of the five senses—taste, touch, scent, sight and sound—and you may experience the elevation known to many mystics as the elusive sixth sense. (©2006 by WH.) For info: Thomas & Ruth Roy, Wellcat Holidays, 2418 Long Ln, Lebanon, PA 17046. Phone: (717) 279-0184. E-mail: info@wellcat.com. Web: www.wellcat.com.

CHINA: MACAU DAY. June 24. Celebrates defeat of the Dutch invasion forces of 1622 and pays homage to patron saint of Macau, Saint John the Baptist. Macau is a former Portuguese colony that is now part of China.

CIARDI, JOHN: BIRTH ANNIVERSARY. June 24, 1916. American poet, critic, translator, teacher, etymologist and author of children's books, born at Boston, MA. John Anthony Ciardi's criticism and other writings were often described as honest and sometimes as harsh. Died at Edison, NJ, Mar 30, 1986.

DEMPSEY, JACK: BIRTH ANNIVERSARY. June 24, 1895. William Harrison Dempsey, known as "The Manassa Mauler," was world heavyweight boxing champion from 1919 to 1926. Following his boxing career Dempsey became a successful New York restaurant operator. Born at Manassa, CO, Dempsey died May 31, 1983, at New York, NY.

"HOPALONG CASSIDY" TV PREMIERE: 60th ANNIVERSARY. June 24, 1949. A western series starring William Boyd in the title role as a hero who wore black and rode a white horse. The original episodes were segments edited from 66 movie features of Hopalong Cassidy and his sidekick, Red Connors (Edgar Buchanan). The films were so popular that Boyd produced episodes especially for TV.

ITALY: CALCIO FIORENTINO. June 24–28. Florence. Revival of a 16th-century football match in medieval costumes. Fireworks also June 24.

LATVIA: JOHN'S DAY (MIDSUMMER NIGHT DAY). June 24. The festival of Jani, which commemorates the summer solstice and the name day of (Janis) John, is one of Latvia's most ancient as well as joyous rituals. This festival is traditionally celebrated in the countryside, as it emphasizes fertility and the beginning of summer. Festivities begin June 23.

LITTLE BIGHORN DAYS. June 24–28. Hardin, MT. To celebrate the history of the Old West. This annual celebration commemorates the anniversary of Custer's Last Stand. Activities include Custer's Last Stand reenactment (June 26–28), historical book fair, quilt show, arts and crafts, cowboy breakfast, street dance, parade, Grand Ball and Grand March. Est attendance: 5,000. For info: Hardin Area Chamber of Commerce, 10 E Railway St, Box #446, Hardin, MT 59034. Phone: (406) 665-1672 or (406) 665-3577. E-mail: hardinchamber@bhwi.net. Web: www.custerslaststand.org or hardinmtchamber.com.

ONIZUKA, ELLISON S.: BIRTH ANNIVERSARY. June 24, 1946. Lieutenant Colonel Ellison S. Onizuka, 39-year-old aerospace engineer, was mission specialist aboard the space shuttle *Challenger* when it exploded Jan 28, 1986 (killing all aboard). Onizuka was born at Kealakekua, Kona, HI. See also: "*Challenger* Space Shuttle Explosion Anniversary" (Jan 28).

PERU: COUNTRYMAN'S DAY. June 24. Half-day public holiday.

SAINT JOHN THE BAPTIST DAY. June 24. Celebrates the birth of the saint.

SCOTLAND: BANNOCKBURN DAY. June 24, 1314. Anniversary of the Battle of Bannockburn when Robert the Bruce won independence for Scotland.

SONOMA-MARIN FAIR. June 24–28. Petaluma Fairgrounds, Petaluma, CA. 70th annual county fair with livestock exhibitions, flowers, World's Ugliest Dog Contest, Lucha Libre wrestling, Destruction Derby, carnival and entertainment. Est attendance: 67,000. For info: Sonoma-Marin Fair, 175 Fairgrounds Dr, Petaluma, CA 94952. Phone: (707) 283-FAIR. Fax: (707) 283-3250. E-mail: info@sonoma-marinfair.org. Web: www.sonoma-marinfair.org.

THORNTON, MATTHEW: DEATH ANNIVERSARY. June 24, 1803. Signer of the Declaration of Independence. Born at Ireland about 1714, he died at Newburyport, MA.

VENEZUELA: BATTLE OF CARABOBO DAY. June 24. National holiday. Commemorates a victory in 1821 that assured Venezuelan independence from Spain.

BIRTHDAYS TODAY

Nancy Allen, 59, actress (*Carrie, Blow Out, Robocop*), born New York, NY, June 24, 1950.

Claude Chabrol, 79, filmmaker (*La Femme Infidèle, The Cousins*), born Sardent, France, June 24, 1930.

Mick Fleetwood, 67, musician (drummer with Fleetwood Mac, "Dreams," "Don't Stop"), born Cornwall, England, June 24, 1942.

Phyllis George, 60, former sportscaster, former Miss America, born Denton, TX, June 24, 1949.

Juli Inkster, 49, golfer, born Santa Cruz, CA, June 24, 1960.

Michele Lee, 67, actress ("Knots Landing"), born Los Angeles, CA, June 24, 1942.

Lionel Messi, 22, soccer player, born Rosario, Argentina, June 24, 1987.

Predrag (Preki) Radosavljevic, 46, soccer coach and former player, born Belgrade, Yugoslavia, June 24, 1963.

Sherry Stringfield, 42, actress ("NYPD Blue," "ER"), born Colorado Springs, CO, June 24, 1967.

Peter Weller, 62, actor (*Robocop, Naked Lunch*), born Stevens Point, WI, June 24, 1947.

June 25 — Thursday

DAY 176 — **189 REMAINING**

ARNOLD, HENRY H. "HAP": BIRTH ANNIVERSARY. June 25, 1886. US general and commander of the Army Air Force in all theaters throughout WWII, Arnold was born at Gladwyne, PA. Although no funds were made available, as early as 1938 Arnold was persuading the US aviation industry to step up manufacturing of airplanes. Production grew from 6,000 to 262,000 per year from 1940–44. He supervised pilot training and by 1944 Air Force personnel strength had grown to two million from a prewar high of 21,000. Made a full general in 1944, he became the US Air Force's first five-star general when the Air Force was made a separate military branch equal to the Army and Navy. Arnold died Jan 15, 1950, at Sonoma, CA.

BATTLE OF LITTLE BIGHORN: ANNIVERSARY. June 25, 1876. Lieutenant Colonel George Armstrong Custer, leading military forces of more than 200 men, attacked an encampment of Sioux Indians led by Chiefs Sitting Bull and Crazy Horse near Little Bighorn River, MT. Custer and all men in his immediate command were killed in the brief battle (about two hours) of Little Bighorn. One horse, named Comanche, is said to have been the only survivor among Custer's forces.

BHUTAN: NATIONAL DAY. June 25. National holiday observed.

CANADA'S FIRST WOMAN PRIME MINISTER: ANNIVERSARY. June 25, 1993. After winning the June 13 election to the leadership of the ruling Progressive-Conservative Party, Kim Campbell became Canada's 19th prime minister and its first woman prime minister. However, in the general election held Oct 25, 1993, the Liberal Party routed the Progressive-Conservatives in the worst defeat for a governing political party in Canada's 126-year history, reducing the former government's seats in the House of Commons from 154 to 2. Campbell was among those who lost their seats.

CBS SENDS FIRST COLOR TV BROADCAST OVER THE AIR: ANNIVERSARY. June 25, 1951. Columbia Broadcast System broadcast the first color television program. The four-hour program was carried by stations at New York City, Baltimore, Philadelphia, Boston and Washington, DC, although no color sets were owned by the public. At the time CBS itself owned fewer than 40 color receivers.

CENTRAL CHINA FLOOD: ANNIVERSARY. June 25, 1991. The Huai River flooded its banks and ravaged major portions of the central Chinese province of Anhui. The poor agricultural region was devastated and approximately 3,000 people were killed. The Anhui region sustained enormous damages when the government ordered dikes broken and sluice gates opened in the rural area to prevent flooding of economically important rivers farther downstream.

CIVIL WAR IN YUGOSLAVIA: ANNIVERSARY. June 25, 1991. In an Eastern Europe freed from the iron rule of communism and the USSR, separatist and nationalist tensions suppressed for decades rose to a violent boiling point. The republics of Croatia and Slovenia declared their independence, sparking a fractious and bitter war that spread throughout what was formerly Yugoslavia. Ethnic rivalries between Serbians and Croatians began the military conflicts that spread to Slovenia, and in 1992 fighting began in Bosnia-Herzegovina between Serbians and ethnic Muslims. Although the new republics were recognized by the UN and sanctions passed to stop the fighting, it raged on through 1995 despite the efforts of UN peacekeeping forces.

GILLARS, MILDRED "AXIS SALLY" E.: DEATH ANNIVERSARY. June 25, 1988. Mildred E. Gillars received the nickname "Axis Sally" during WWII, when she broadcast Nazi propaganda to US troops in Europe. An American citizen, born about 1900 at Portland, ME, she was arrested after the war, tried and convicted of treason. She was sentenced to 10 to 30 years in prison and fined $10,000. She was released after 12 years and later taught music in a convent school at Columbus, OH. She died June 25, 1988, at Columbus, OH.

HELEN KELLER FESTIVAL. June 25–28. Tuscumbia, AL. Commemorates the remarkable life of Helen Keller with stage shows for all ages, arts and crafts fair, free musical entertainment, races, historic tours of Helen Keller's birthplace and other beautiful homes and much more. *The Miracle Worker* play performed evenings during festival and for five weekends following. Annually, the last weekend in June. Est attendance: 105,000. For info: Debbie Wilson, Dir, Florence/Lauderdale Tourism, One Hightower Pl, Florence, AL 35630. Phone: (256) 740-4141 or (888) FLO-TOUR. Fax: (256) 740-4142. E-mail: Debbie@VisitFlorenceAl.com. Web: www.VisitFlorenceAl.com.

June 2009

S	M	T	W	T	F	S
	1	2	3	4	5	6
7	8	9	10	11	12	13
14	15	16	17	18	19	20
21	22	23	24	25	26	27
28	29	30				

KOREAN WAR BEGAN: ANNIVERSARY. June 25, 1950. Forces from northern Korea invaded southern Korea, beginning a civil war. US ground forces entered the conflict June 30. An armistice was signed at Panmunjom July 27, 1953, formally dividing the country in two—North Korea and South Korea.

MISS VIRGINIA PAGEANT. June 25–27. Roanoke Civic Center Auditorium, Roanoke, VA. Scholarship pageant held since 1953. Miss Virginia then appears in the Miss America pageant. Est attendance: 3,000. For info: The Miss Virginia Pageant, 102 N Mitchell Rd, Vinton, VA 24179. Phone: (540) 989-4531. Web: www.missva.com.

MONTSERRAT: VOLCANO ERUPTS: ANNIVERSARY. June 25, 1997. After lying dormant for 400 years, the Soufriere Hills volcano began to come to life in July 1995. It finally erupted, wiping out the capital city of Plymouth and two-thirds of the rest of this lush Carribean island on June 25, 1997. Two-thirds of the population relocated to other islands or to Great Britain.

MOZAMBIQUE: INDEPENDENCE DAY. June 25. National holiday. Commemorates independence from Portugal in 1975.

NATIONAL BOMB POP DAY. June 25. The Bomb Pop, invented in 1955 on Independence Avenue in Kansas City, MO, has roots in true Americana. This six-finned summertime treat is used to celebrate patriotism in conjunction with Fourth of July celebrations. As the anniversary of our country's independence draws near, celebrate with America's favorite red, white, and blue novelty. Annually, the last Thursday of June. For info: Wells' Dairy, Inc, One Blue Bunny Dr, Le Mars, IA 51031. Phone: (800) 942-3800. E-mail: webmaster@bluebunny.com. Web: www.bluebunny.com.

NATIONAL HANDSHAKE DAY. June 25. Get a grip on a professional handshake today! The handshake is an important part of corporate America, and can make or break a business deal, interview or other encounter. Take this day to perfect your own handshake and put it into practice. Annually, the last Thursday in June. For info: Miryam S. Roddy, BRODY Professional Development, 815 Greenwood Ave, Ste 8, Jenkintown, PA 19046. Phone: (215) 376-5082. Fax: (215) 886-1699. E-mail: mroddy@BrodyPro.com. Web: www.BrodyPro.com.

O'NEILL, ROSE CECIL: BIRTH ANNIVERSARY. June 25, 1874. Rose O'Neill was born at Wilkes-Barre, PA. Her career included work as an illustrator, author and doll designer, the latter gaining her commercial success with the Kewpie Doll. In 1910 *The Ladies Home Journal* devoted a full page to her Kewpie Doll designs, which were a marketing phenomenon for three decades. Died at Springfield, MO, Apr 6, 1944.

ORIGINS INTERNATIONAL GAME EXPO. June 25–28. Greater Columbus Convention Center, Columbus, OH. 35th annual. Enjoy board games, card games, role-playing, miniatures, classic games, and more. More than 200 vendors in the exhibit hall, art show featuring fantasy artists from around the world. Informative seminars on world history, game development, and games in education. With more than 4,000 events, it's one of North America's largest game conventions. Special programs for parents and other non-gaming family members. Kids nine and under are free with paid adult admission. Est attendance: 14,000. For info: Game Manufacturers Assn, 280 N High St, Ste 230, Columbus, OH 43215. Phone: (614) 255-4500. Fax: (614) 255-4499. E-mail: marketing@gama.org. Web: www.originsgames.com.

ORWELL, GEORGE: BIRTH ANNIVERSARY. June 25, 1903. English satirist, author of *Animal Farm, 1984* and other works, was born at Motihari, Bengal. George Orwell was the pseudonym of Eric Arthur Blair. Died at London, England, Jan 21, 1950.

REVERE, ANNE: BIRTH ANNIVERSARY. June 25, 1903. American actress Anne Revere was born at New York, NY. She won an Academy Award for her supporting role in *National Velvet* (1944) but was barred from films for 20 years after she refused to testify before the House Committee on Un-American Activities in the 1950s. In 1960 she won a Tony Award for her role in *Toys in the Attic*. Revere died Dec 18, 1990, at Locust Valley, NY.

SAINT IGNACE AUTO SHOW. June 25–27. St. Ignace, MI. 34th anniversary. Parade, cruise night and swap meet. Entries from 25 states and Canada. Est attendance: 80,000. For info: Edward K. Reavie, 268 Hillcrest Blvd, St. Ignace, MI 49781. Phone: (906) 643-8087. Fax: (906) 643-9784. E-mail: ereavie@nostalgia-prod.com. Web: www.nostalgia-prod.com or www.auto-shows.com.

SEVEN DAYS CAMPAIGN: ANNIVERSARY. June 25–July 1, 1862. In an effort to prevent an attack on Richmond, VA, Confederate General Robert E. Lee launched a series of engagements that became known as the Seven Days Campaign. Battles at Oak Grove, Gaine's Mills, Garnett's Farm, Golding's Farm, Savage's Station, White Oak Swamp and finally Malvern Hill left more than 35,000 casualties on both sides. Despite losing the final assault at Malvern Hill, the Confederates succeeded in preventing the Union army from taking Richmond.

SLOVENIA: NATIONAL DAY. June 25. Public holiday. Commemorates independence from the former Yugoslavia in 1991.

SUPREME COURT ABORTION NOTIFICATION RULING: ANNIVERSARY. June 25, 1990. The Supreme Court ruled, in a 5–4 decision, that it was unconstitutional for a state to require, without providing other options, that a minor notify both her parents before obtaining an abortion.

SUPREME COURT BANS SCHOOL PRAYER: ANNIVERSARY. June 25, 1962. The US Supreme Court ruled that a prayer read aloud in public schools violated the First Amendment's separation of church and state. The court again struck down a law pertaining to the First Amendment when it disallowed an Alabama law that permitted a daily one-minute period of silent meditation or prayer in public schools June 1, 1985. (Vote 6–3.)

SUPREME COURT UPHOLDS RIGHT TO DIE: ANNIVERSARY. June 25, 1990. In the case *Cruzan v Missouri*, the Supreme Court, in a 5–4 ruling, upheld the constitutional right of a person whose wishes are clearly known to refuse life-sustaining medical treatment.

TELLURIDE WINE FESTIVAL. June 25–28. Telluride, CO. 28th annual. This annual festival offers food and wine enthusiasts an unforgettable four-day event with a rare opportunity to meet winemakers, celebrity chefs, experts and authors. It's an unparalleled educational and epicurean experience. Single event tickets and four-day-weekend packages are available. Annually, the last weekend in June. Est attendance: 4,000. For info: Telluride Wine Festival, PO Box 1677, Telluride, CO 81435. Phone: (970) 728-3178. Fax: (970) 728-4865. E-mail: info@telluridewinefestival.com. Web: www.telluridewinefestival.com.

TWO YUGOSLAV REPUBLICS DECLARE INDEPENDENCE: ANNIVERSARY. June 25, 1991. The republics of Slovenia and Croatia formally declared independence from Yugoslavia. The two northwestern republics did not, however, secede outright.

VIRGINIA: RATIFICATION DAY. June 25. 10th state to ratify the Constitution in 1788.

WATERMELON THUMP (WITH WORLD CHAMPION SEED-SPITTING CONTEST). June 25–28. Luling, TX. Features World Champion Seed-Spitting Contest, street dance and concert each night, giant parade on Saturday, free live entertainment in the Beer Garden and Spitway, champion melon auction, arts and crafts exhibit and sales, food, games, fun run and rides. Annually, the last weekend in June (Thursday–Sunday). Est attendance: 45,000. For info: James Nickells, Sec, Luling Watermelon Thump Assn, Box 710, Luling, TX 78648. Phone: (830) 875-3214. Fax: (830) 875-2082. E-mail: jamie@watermelonthump.com. Web: www.watermelonthump.com.

BIRTHDAYS TODAY

Linda Cardellini, 34, actress (*Scooby-Doo, Legally Blonde*), born Redmond City, CA, June 25, 1975.

Carlos Delgado, 37, baseball player, born Mayaguez, Puerto Rico, June 25, 1972.

Ricky Gervais, 48, actor, comedian ("The Office" [UK version], "Extras"), born Reading, Berkshire, England, June 25, 1961.

June Lockhart, 84, actress ("Lassie," "Lost in Space"), born New York, NY, June 25, 1925.

Sidney Lumet, 85, director (*12 Angry Men, Serpico, Dog Day Afternoon, Network*), born Philadelphia, PA, June 25, 1924.

George Michael, 46, singer (Wham!, "Wake Me Up Before You Go-Go," "Faith"), born Radlett, England, June 25, 1963.

Dikembe Mutombo, 43, basketball player, born Kinshasa, Zaire, June 25, 1966.

Willis Reed, Jr, 67, Hall of Fame basketball player, basketball executive and former coach, born Hico, LA, June 25, 1942.

Carly Simon, 64, singer ("You're So Vain," "Nobody Does It Better"), songwriter, born New York, NY, June 25, 1945.

Billy Wagner, 38, baseball player, born Tannersville, VA, June 25, 1971.

Jimmie Walker, 61, actor, comedian ("Good Times," "B.A.D. Cats"), born New York, NY, June 25, 1948.

June 26 — Friday

DAY 177 **188 REMAINING**

BAR CODE INTRODUCED: 35th ANNIVERSARY. June 26, 1974. A committee formed in 1970 by US grocers and food manufacturers recommended in 1973 a Universal Product Code (i.e., a bar code) for supermarket items that would allow electronic scanning of prices. On this day in 1974 a pack of Wrigley's gum was swiped across the first checkout scanner at a supermarket in Troy, OH. Today bar codes are used to keep track of everything from freight cars to cattle.

BORDEN, SIR ROBERT LAIRD: BIRTH ANNIVERSARY. June 26, 1854. Canadian statesman and prime minister, born at Grand Pre, Nova Scotia. Died at Ottawa, June 10, 1937.

BUCK, PEARL SYDENSTRICKER: BIRTH ANNIVERSARY. June 26, 1892. American author (*The Good Earth*), noted authority on China and humanitarian. Nobel Prize winner. Born at Hillsboro, WV. Died Mar 6, 1973, at Danby, VT.

June 2009

S	M	T	W	T	F	S
	1	2	3	4	5	6
7	8	9	10	11	12	13
14	15	16	17	18	19	20
21	22	23	24	25	26	27
28	29	30				

CELTIC FLING. June 26–28. Mount Hope Estate and Winery, Manheim, PA. 'Tis but a wee journey to the Scottish Highlands or the Emerald Isle when you dance a jig through the gates of the Pennsylvania Renaissance Faire's annual "Celtic Fling." It's an official Highland Dance competition, Highland Games, an Irish Feis, 35 acres of authentic Celtic arts and crafts, music and dance, concerts by nationally acclaimed Celtic recording artists and, of course, beer and bagpipes. For info: Thomas Roy, PRF, 2775 Lebanon Rd, Manheim, PA 17545-8711. Phone: (717) 665-7021. Fax: (717) 664-3466. E-mail: tom@parenfaire.com. Web: www.parenfaire.com.

CLARKSON CZECH FESTIVAL. June 26–27. Main St, Clarkson, NE. Czech food, entertainment, music, polkas, cooking, demonstrations, carnival, arts and crafts. Annually, the fourth full weekend in June. Sponsor: Clarkson Commercial Club. Est attendance: 10,000. For info: Robert Brabec, 515 Elm St, Clarkson, NE 68629. Phone: (402) 892-3331 or (402) 892-3561. Fax: (402) 892-3318. E-mail: cphtvh@yahoo.com.

CLEARWATER CHAMBER OF COMMERCE RODEO. June 26–28. Clearwater, NE. 7:30 PM each day. Annually, the last full weekend of June. Est attendance: 6,000. For info: Clearwater Chamber of Commerce, Box 201, Clearwater, NE 68726.

CN TOWER OPENED: ANNIVERSARY. June 26, 1976. Birthday of the world's tallest building and freestanding structure, the CN Tower, 1,815 feet, 5 inches high, at Toronto, Ontario, Canada. For info: CN Tower, 301 Front St W, Toronto, ON, Canada M5V 2T6. Phone: (416) 360-8500. Fax: (416) 601-4713.

DOUBLEDAY, ABNER: BIRTH ANNIVERSARY. June 26, 1819. Abner Doubleday served in the US Army during the Mexican War and the Seminole War in Florida prior to his service in the American Civil War. His service found him at the battles of Second Bull Run, Antietam, Fredricksburg and as a major general commanding a division at Gettysburg. A commission set up to investigate the origins of baseball by sporting goods manufacturer Albert Spalding credited Doubleday with inventing the game in the year 1839. Subsequent research has debunked the commission's finding. Abner Doubleday was born at Ballston Spa, NY, and died at Mendham, NJ, Jan 26, 1893.

ENGLAND: GLASTONBURY FESTIVAL. June 26–28. Vale of Avalon, Glastonbury. The world's largest greenfield music and performing arts festival. The 1000 acres of the festival offer music, theatre, circus, cabaret, markets, children's activities and much more. For info: Dick Vernon, Manager, Glastonbury Festival, 28 Northload St, Glastonbury, Somerset, BA6 9JJ, England. Phone: (44) (871) 22-00-260. E-mail: office@glastonburyfestivals.co.uk. Web: www.glastonburyfestivals.co.uk.

FEDERAL CREDIT UNION ACT: 75th ANNIVERSARY. June 26, 1934. Commemorates signing by President Franklin Delano Roosevelt of the Federal Credit Union Act, thus enabling the formation of credit unions anywhere in the US.

GRANTSVILLE DAYS. June 26–28. Grantsville Park, Grantsville, MD. Three-day annual homecoming weekend. Free entertainment Friday 6:45 PM–Sunday 7 PM. Lion's chicken BBQ, local noncommercial food booths, children's games, horse- and tractor-pulling contests, gospel music, fireworks Friday and Saturday nights. Annually, the last weekend in June. Est attendance: 20,000. For info: Gerry Beachy, PO Box 189, 149 Main St, Grantsville, MD 21536. Fax: (301) 895-3623. E-mail: gbeachy@verizon.net. Web: www.grantsvilledays.com.

"GUIDING LIGHT" TV PREMIERE: ANNIVERSARY. June 26, 1952. "Guiding Light," previously on radio, holds the title of longest-lasting daytime show and longest-lasting series. Set in the fictional midwestern town of Springfield, this soap is still on the air.

HAYMARKET PARDON: ANNIVERSARY. June 26, 1893. Illinois Governor John Peter Altgeld pardoned Samuel Fielden, Michael Schwab and Oscar Neebe, three of the anarchists who had been convicted in the violence connected with the Haymarket Riot on May 4, 1886. At a protest meeting at Haymarket Square an unknown individual threw a bomb that caused the death of several policemen. Eight anarchists were tried and convicted of the bombing. Of those, one committed suicide the day before he was to be hanged;

three were hanged; and Fielden, Schwab and Neebe were imprisoned. In 1893 the newly elected Altgeld, at the urging of Clarence Darrow, reviewed the transcripts of the trial of these men and concluded that they had been railroaded. The pardon was widely criticized. It was an act of political suicide for Altgeld.

HUMAN GENOME MAPPED: ANNIVERSARY. June 26, 2000. Biologists J. Craig Venter and Francis S. Collins announced that their research groups had mapped the human genome, a strand of DNA with three billion parts that spells out our genetic code.

LOUISIANA PEACH FESTIVAL. June 26–28. Ruston, LA. The 59th annual Louisiana Peach Festival will feature rodeo, parade, concerts, cooking contests, sporting events, arts and crafts and more. Est attendance: 31,500. For info: Nancy Bergeron, Ruston-Lincoln Chamber of Commerce, 2205 N Trenton St, Ruston, LA 71270. Phone: (800) 392-9032. E-mail: peach@rustonlincoln.org. Web: www.louisianapeachfestival.org.

MADAGASCAR: INDEPENDENCE DAY. June 26. National holiday. Commemorates independence from France in 1960.

MIDDLETON, ARTHUR: BIRTH ANNIVERSARY. June 26, 1742. American Revolutionary leader and signer of the Declaration of Independence, born near Charleston, SC. Died at Goose Creek, SC, Jan 1, 1787.

NEWPORT FLOWER SHOW. June 26–28. Rosecliff, Newport, RI. New England's premier summertime flower and horticulture show includes judged flower arrangements, a horticultural tent brimming with plants and flowers, demonstrations, lectures and a spectacular garden marketplace in the elegant reception rooms and on the expansive oceanfront lawn of Rosecliff, a Gilded Age mansion. For info: The Preservation Society of Newport County, 424 Bellevue Ave, Newport, RI 02840. Phone: (401) 847-1000. Fax: (401) 841-1361. E-mail: events@newportmansions.org. Web: www.newportflowershow.org.

OREGON BACH FESTIVAL. June 26–July 12. Hult Center for the Performing Arts and the University of Oregon, Eugene, OR. Artistic director and conductor Helmuth Rilling leads an international gathering of musicians in choral-orchestral masterworks, intimate concerts and chamber music, informal free concerts and family events, adult education programs and master classes for conductors and composers. Emphasis is on J.S. Bach and his influence on succeeding generations of composers. Est attendance: 30,000. For info: George Evano, Oregon Bach Festival, 1257 University of Oregon, Eugene, OR 97403. Phone: (800) 457-1486 or (541) 346-5666. Fax: (541) 346-5669. E-mail: bachfest@uoregon.edu. Web: www.oregonbachfestival.com.

PARKER, "COLONEL" TOM: 100th BIRTH ANNIVERSARY. June 26, 1909. He was neither a colonel nor an American, but he guided the career of America's greatest superstar, Elvis Presley. Born at Breda, Netherlands, as Andreas Cornelis van Kuijk, he picked up the "colonel" and the alias when he came to America, where he became a music promoter. As agent/manager to Presley beginning in 1955, Parker rewrote the rules and made artist management big business—often to accusations of exploitation as he took up to 50% of Presley's earnings and pushed the rock idol into an unimpressive film career. Presley credited his superstardom to Parker and Parker was tireless in his promotion of "The King." He died Jan 21, 1997, at Las Vegas, NV.

PIZARRO, FRANCESCO: DEATH ANNIVERSARY. June 26, 1541. Spanish conqueror of Peru, born at Extremadura, Spain, ca 1471. Pizarro died at Lima, Peru.

SAINT LAWRENCE SEAWAY DEDICATION: 50th ANNIVERSARY. June 26, 1959. President Dwight D. Eisenhower and Queen Elizabeth II jointly dedicated the St. Lawrence Seaway in formal ceremonies held at St. Lambert, QC, Canada. A project undertaken jointly by Canada and the US, the waterway (which provides access between the Atlantic Ocean and the Great Lakes) had been opened to traffic Apr 25, 1959.

SCANDINAVIAN HJEMKOMST FESTIVAL. June 26–28. Moorhead, MN. 32nd annual. Featuring activities for all ages, including authentic Nordic entertainment, music and folk dancing, a marketplace, foods, exhibitions and demonstrations of arts, fine crafts and ethnic traditions from Denmark, Finland, Iceland, Norway, Sweden and Saami Land. Est attendance: 7,500. For info: Nordic Culture Clubs, PO Box 926, Fargo, ND 58107. Phone: (218) 299-5452. E-mail: fmshf@ci.moorhead.mn.us. Web: www.scandinavianhjemkomstfestival.org.

SOUTH ST. PAUL KAPOSIA DAYS. June 26–28. South St. Paul, MN. Family-oriented city festival including parades, pageant, children's activities, athletic competitions, craft and flea markets, musical entertainment and fireworks. Annually, the last full weekend in June. For info: South St. Paul Kaposia Days, PO Box 144, South St. Paul, MN 55075. Phone: (651) 451-2266. Fax: (651) 451-0846. E-mail: carol@riverheights.com. Web: www.kaposiadays.org.

STERNWHEELER DAYS. June 26–28. Port Marina Park, Cascade Locks, OR. Home of the sternwheeler *Columbia Gorge*. Mountain men encampment, parade, bingo, food, arts and crafts, live music. Est attendance: 6,000. For info: Columbia Gorge Lions, PO Box 522, Cascade Locks, OR 97014. Phone: (541) 374-2111. Web: www.cascadelocks.net.

TAKE YOUR DOG TO WORK DAY®. June 26. A day to celebrate the great companions dogs make and to encourage adoptions from animal shelters. Annually, the first Friday after Father's Day. For info: Pet Sitters Intl, 201 E King St, King, NC 27021. Phone: (336) 983-9222. Fax: (336) 983-5266. E-mail: dogday@petsit.com. Web: www.petsit.com or www.takeyourdog.com.

UNITED NATIONS CHARTER SIGNED: ANNIVERSARY. June 26, 1945. The UN Charter was signed at San Francisco by representatives of 50 nations.

UNITED NATIONS: INTERNATIONAL DAY AGAINST DRUG ABUSE AND ILLICIT TRAFFICKING. June 26. Following a recommendation of the 1987 International Conference on Drug Abuse and Illicit Trafficking, the United Nations General Assembly (Res 42/112) expressed its determination to strengthen action and cooperation for an international society free of drug abuse and proclaimed June 26 as an annual observance to raise public awareness. For info: UN, Dept of Public Info, Public Inquiries Unit, RM GA-57, New York, NY 10017. Phone: (212) 963-4475. E-mail: inquiries@un.org.

UNITED NATIONS: INTERNATIONAL DAY IN SUPPORT OF VICTIMS OF TORTURE. June 26. For info: United Nations, Dept of Public Info, New York, NY 10017. Web: www.un.org.

WORLD CHAMPIONSHIP ROTARY TILLER RACE AND PURPLEHULL PEA FESTIVAL. June 26–27. Emerson, AR. 20th annual festival. World Cup purplehull pea–shelling competition, rotary tiller race, domino tournaments, concessions, arts, crafts, entertainment, children's games, the Great Purplehull Peas and Cornbread Cook-off, Queen's pageant (various ages), 3-on-3 basketball. Est attendance: 10,000. For info: Publicity, Purplehull Pea Fest, PO Box 1, Emerson, AR 71740. Phone: (501) 315-7373. E-mail: purplehull@juno.com. Web: www.purplehull.com.

WORLD'S UGLIEST DOG CONTEST. June 26. Petaluma Fairgrounds, Petaluma, CA. 21st annual. Dogs from around the world compete for this title at the Sonoma-Marin Fair. Media coverage is extensive and dogs go on to fame and glory. Past competitions have been filmed by Animal Planet. It's a high-participation event for the audience, especially since the audience helps decide the winner in the final runoff round. To vote for candidates in the online pre-contest competition or learn how to enter your dog, visit www.sonoma-marinfair.org. For info: Sonoma-Marin Fair, 175 Fairgrounds Dr, Petaluma, CA 94952. Phone: (707) 283-FAIR. E-mail: info@sonoma-marinfair.org. Web: www.sonoma-marinfair.org.

ZAHARIAS, MILDRED "BABE" DIDRIKSON: 95th BIRTH ANNIVERSARY. June 26, 1914. Born Mildred Ella Didrikson at Port Arthur, TX, the great athlete was nicknamed "Babe" after legendary baseball player Babe Ruth. She was named to the women's All-America basketball team when she was 16. At the 1932 Olympic Games, she won two gold medals and also set world records in the javelin throw and the 80-meter high hurdles; only a technicality prevented her from obtaining the gold in the high jump. Didrikson married professional wrestler George Zaharias in 1938, six years after she began playing golf casually. In 1946 Babe won the US Women's Amateur tournament, and in 1947 she won 17 straight golf championships and became the first American winner of the British Ladies' Amateur tournament. Turning professional in 1948, she won the US Women's Open in 1950 and 1954, the same year she won the All-American Open. Babe also excelled in softball, baseball, swimming, figure skating, billiards—even football. In a 1950 Associated Press poll she was named the woman athlete of the first half of the 20th century. She died of cancer, Sept 27, 1956, at Galveston, TX.

BIRTHDAYS TODAY

Claudio Abbado, 76, conductor, born Milan, Italy, June 26, 1933.

Paul Thomas Anderson, 39, director, screenwriter (*Punch-Drunk Love, Magnolia, Boogie Nights*), born Studio City, CA, June 26, 1970.

Sean P. Hayes, 39, actor ("Will & Grace"), born Glen Ellyn, IL, June 26, 1970.

Chris Isaak, 53, singer, musician, actor ("The Chris Isaak Show"), born Stockton, CA, June 26, 1956.

Derek Jeter, 35, baseball player, born Pequannock, NJ, June 26, 1974.

Greg LeMond, 48, former cyclist, born Lakewood, CA, June 26, 1961.

Chris O'Donnell, 39, actor (*Scent of a Woman*), born Winnetka, IL, June 26, 1970.

Jason Schwartzman, 29, actor (*The Darjeeling Limited, Rushmore*), born Los Angeles, CA, June 26, 1980.

Gretchen Wilson, 36, country singer, born Granite City, IL, June 26, 1973.

Charlotte Zolotow, 94, author (*The Moon Was the Best, Peter and the Pigeons*), born Norfolk, VA, June 26, 1915.

June 27 — Saturday

DAY 178 — **187 REMAINING**

ARRL FIELD DAY. June 27–28. Weekend-long amateur radio event in which thousands of "hams" set up radio stations in remote and unusual places as they practice emergency operations such as were used in Hurricane Katrina. Sponsored by the ARRL, the national association for amateur radio. Annually, the fourth full weekend in June. Est attendance: 100,000. For info: Allen Pitts, ARRL, 225 Main St, Newington, CT 06111. Phone: (860) 594-0328. Fax: (860) 594-0259. E-mail: apitts@arrl.org. Web: www.arrl.org.

"CAPTAIN VIDEO AND HIS VIDEO RANGERS" TV PREMIERE: 60th ANNIVERSARY. June 2z7, 1949. "Captain Video" was the first of several TV space shows. The show was set in the 22nd century and starred Richard Coogan as Captain Video, a human who led a squad of agents (the Video Rangers) fighting villains from their own and other worlds. Al Hodge later replaced Coogan. Also featured were Ernest Borgnine, Jack Klugman and Tony Randall as guest villains.

COLORADO BREWERS' FESTIVAL. June 27–28. Fort Collins, CO. The kegs will be tapped once again for the annual festival in Old Town Square, Fort Collins, Colorado. Every year more than 30 Colorado breweries, including local favorites Odell's and New Belgium, come celebrate Colorado's rich brewing history and feature their best native beers. Annually, the last full weekend of June. Est attendance: 30,000. For info: Downtown Fort Collins Business Assoc, 19 Old Town Square #230, Fort Collins, CO 80524. Phone: (970) 484-6500. E-mail: info@downtownfortcollins.com. Web: www.downtownfortcollins.com.

"DARK SHADOWS" TV PREMIERE: ANNIVERSARY. June 27, 1966. This soap opera was completely different from all others because it featured vampires as main characters and had a dark, Gothic feel to it. The show focused on the Collins family living at Collinsport, ME, mainly Barnabas Collins (Jonathan Frid), a 200-year-old vampire. Other cast members included David Selby, Kate Jackson, Lara Parker and Jerry Lacy. Action shifted between the 1800s and the 1960s. This show was very popular with teenagers and was remade as a short-lived series in 1991.

DECIDE TO BE MARRIED DAY. June 27. To focus attention on the joy of couples deciding to get married. Based on the poem *Decide to Be Married*: "It's in the deciding to be united in love, to express your joyful oneness to every person you meet, and in every action you take and together a perfect marriage you'll make." For info: Barbara Gaughen-Muller, Pres, Gaughen Global Public Relations, 7456 Evergreen Dr, Santa Barbara, CA 93117. Phone: (805) 968-8567. Fax: (805) 968-5747. E-mail: Barbara@rain.org. Web: www.paradiseearthnow.com.

DJIBOUTI: INDEPENDENCE DAY. June 27. National day. Commemorates independence from France in 1977.

EASTERN MUSIC FESTIVAL. June 27–Aug 1 (tentative). Guilford College, Greensboro, NC. 48th annual summer festival of classical concerts and recitals performed by world-class guest artists, resident professionals and a corps of talented young students from the US and abroad. Est attendance: 63,000. For info: Eastern Music Festival, PO Box 22026, Greensboro, NC 27420. Phone: (336) 333-7450. Fax: (336) 333-7454. E-mail: info@easternmusicfestival.org. Web: www.easternmusicfestival.org.

GALESBURG RAILROAD DAYS. June 27–28. Galesburg, IL. Annual festival celebrating the city's railroad heritage that dates back to 1854. Carnival, street fair, railroad exhibits and displays, 5k run and concerts. Hobby train show with over 200 exhibitions and tables. Includes more than 40 events. Est attendance: 15,000. For info: Galesburg Area CVB, PO Box 60, Galesburg, IL 61402-0060. Phone: (309) 343-2485. Fax: (309) 343-2521. E-mail: visitors@visitgalesburg.com. Web: www.visitgalesburg.com.

GREAT AMERICAN BACKYARD CAMPOUT. June 27. 5th annual. The National Wildlife Federation encourages people of all ages to get outside and camp. Participants will register their campsites online at www.backyardcampout.org and receive exclusive information regarding activities, recipes, wildlife and more. More than 40,000 campers participated in 2007. Annually, the fourth Saturday in June. For info: Ashleigh Poff, National Wildlife Federation, 11100 Wildlife Center Dr, Reston, VA 20190. Phone: (703) 438-6515. E-mail: poffa@nwf.org. Web: www.nwf.org.

June 2009

S	M	T	W	T	F	S
	1	2	3	4	5	6
7	8	9	10	11	12	13
14	15	16	17	18	19	20
21	22	23	24	25	26	27
28	29	30				

HAPPY BIRTHDAY TO "HAPPY BIRTHDAY TO YOU": 150th ANNIVERSARY. June 27, 1859. The melody of probably the most often sung song in the world, "Happy Birthday to You," was composed by Mildred J. Hill, a schoolteacher born at Louisville, KY, on this date. Her younger sister, Patty Smith Hill, was the author of the lyrics, which were first published in 1893 as "Good Morning to All," a classroom greeting published in the book *Song Stories for the Sunday School*. The lyrics were amended in 1924 to include a stanza beginning "Happy Birthday to You." Now it is sung somewhere in the world every minute of the day. Although the authors are believed to have earned very little from the song, reportedly it later generated about $1 million a year for its copyright owner. The song is expected to enter public domain upon expiration of copyright in 2010. Mildred Hill died at Chicago, IL, June 5, 1916, without knowing that her melody would become the world's most popular song. See also: "Hill, Patty Smith: Birth Anniversary" (Mar 27).

HEARN, LAFCADIO: BIRTH ANNIVERSARY. June 27, 1850. Author, born on the Greek island of Santa Maura. Hearn, who had been a newspaper reporter at Cincinnati, OH, and at New Orleans, LA, went to Japan in 1890 as a magazine writer. Deeply attracted to the country and to the Japanese people, he stayed there as a writer and teacher until his death at Okubo, Japan, Sept 26, 1904. Though his writings are little remembered in America, he remains a popular figure in Japan, where his books are still used, especially in language classes. His home at Matsue is a tourist shrine.

INDUSTRIAL WORKERS OF THE WORLD FOUNDED: ANNIVERSARY. June 27, 1905. With the slogan "One Big Union for All" 43 labor groups merged together to found the IWW at Chicago, IL. Eventually known as the Wobblies, the IWW had a tremendous impact on US labor history.

KEESHAN, BOB: BIRTH ANNIVERSARY. June 27, 1927. Beloved to generations of American children as Captain Kangaroo, Robert J. Keeshan was born at Lynbrook, NJ. He made his acting debut at age 21 as the original Clarabell, the ever-silent clown, sidekick to Buffalo Bob Smith on "The Howdy Doody Show." He was eventually fired from the show, but his future as a children's entertainer was secure; on Oct 3, 1955, "Captain Kangaroo" premiered on CBS, and it remained on the air for 38 years. Captain Kangaroo was joined by characters Mr Green Jeans, Grandfather Clock, Bunny Rabbit and Mr Moose. His gentle, patient wisdom entertained and educated millions of children over the years. Keeshan died in Vermont on Jan 23, 2004.

KELLER, HELEN: BIRTH ANNIVERSARY. June 27, 1880. Born at Tuscumbia, AL, Helen Keller was left deaf and blind by a disease she contracted at 18 months of age. With the help of her teacher, Anne Sullivan, she graduated from college and had a career as an author and lecturer. She died June 1, 1968, at Westport, CT.

LADIES OF COUNTRY MUSIC SHOW. June 27. Waretown, NJ. Featuring Albert Music Hall's ladies of country and bluegrass. No alcoholic beverages or smoking allowed. For info: Albert Music Hall, PO Box 657, Waretown, NJ 08758. Phone: (609) 971-1593. Web:www.alberthall.org.

NATIONAL HIV TESTING DAY. June 27. A nationwide campaign encouraging education, voluntary HIV testing and counseling to people at risk for HIV. For info: Natl Assn of People with AIDS, 8401 Colesville Rd, Ste 505, Silver Spring, MD 20910. Phone: (240) 247-0880. Fax: (240) 247-0574. E-mail: info@napwa.org. Web: www.napwa.org.

NED KELLY'S LAST STAND: ANNIVERSARY. June 27–29, 1880. Australian folk hero and outlaw Ned Kelly, escaping with his gang from pursuing law officers, made a last stand at Glenrowan—rounding up the townspeople and holing up in a hotel. There he and his mates constructed 90-pound iron body armor. The armor hampered more than it helped, and Kelly's gang—including his brother Dan—were all killed. Kelly was captured and hung on Nov 11, 1880, at Melbourne. The Kelly Gang in their grim armor offered an antihero image that Australians have embraced in film and art.

PARNELL, CHARLES STEWART: BIRTH ANNIVERSARY. June 27, 1846. Irish nationalist leader and home-rule advocate born at Avondale, County Wicklow, Ireland. Politically ruined as a result of an affair with Katherine O'Shea, the estranged wife of a member of Parliament. O'Shea was divorced by her husband (who named Parnell corespondent), and on June 25, 1891, she married Parnell. Less than a month later Parnell was defeated in a by-election. He made his last public speech Sept 27, 1891, and died in the arms of his wife, at Brighton, Oct 6, 1891. Reportedly he was given "a magnificent funeral" by the city of Dublin, where he was buried. The anniversary of Parnell's death is observed by some as Ivy Day when a sprig of ivy is worn on the lapel to remember him. See also: "Ireland: Ivy Day" (Oct 6).

SMITH, JOSEPH, JR, AND HYRUM SMITH: DEATH ANNIVERSARY. June 27, 1844. The founding prophet of The Church of Jesus Christ of Latter-day Saints and his brother Hyrum were shot to death by an armed mob in Carthage, IL. At the time, Joseph Smith was the presidential candidate of the National Reform Party, the first US presidential candidate to be assassinated. Joseph Smith was born at Sharon, VT, Dec 23, 1805; Hyrum Smith was born at Tunbridge, VT, Feb 9, 1800.

SMITHSON, JAMES: DEATH ANNIVERSARY. June 27, 1829. Scientist and founder of the Smithsonian Institution, James Smithson was born at Paris, France, in 1765 (exact date unknown) and died at Genoa, Italy. His will, dated Oct 23, 1826, bequeathed his great wealth to a nation he had never visited, to found "at Washington under the name of the Smithsonian Institution, establishment for the increase and diffusion of knowledge among men." In spite of opposition, the Congress approved, on Aug 10, 1846, an act to establish the Smithsonian Institution. Most of Smithson's personal documents, books and collections were destroyed by fire in 1865. Smithson's remains were removed from Italy to Washington, DC, in 1904.

SNAKE HUNT. June 27–28. Cross Fork, PA. To raise funds for the fire company. Est attendance: 5,000. For info: Barry Gipe, Chmn, Kettle Creek Hose Co #1, 2605 Steward Hill Rd, Cross Fork, PA 17729. Phone: (570) 923-0848.

THURGOOD MARSHALL RESIGNS FROM SUPREME COURT: ANNIVERSARY. June 27, 1991. Signaling an end to the era of a liberal Supreme Court, Associate Justice Thurgood Marshall announced his resignation from the US Supreme Court, effective once his successor was confirmed by the US Senate. Marshall was a pioneering civil rights lawyer who helped lead the fight to end racial segregation and served as US Solicitor General prior to his appointment to the high court by President Lyndon Johnson in 1967 as the first black ever to sit on the Supreme Court. As an attorney for the NAACP, he successfully argued the case of *Brown v Board of Education* before the Supreme Court, ending the doctrine of "separate but equal." Marshall's 24-year tenure on the bench was marked by his strong liberal voice championing the rights of criminal defendants and defending abortion rights, his opposition to the death penalty and his commitment to civil rights. On July 1, 1991, President George Bush selected Clarence Thomas, a conservative black jurist, to succeed Marshall. See also: "Marshall, Thurgood: Birth Anniversary" (July 2).

BIRTHDAYS TODAY

J.J. Abrams, 43, television executive ("Lost," "Alias"), film director (*Mission Impossible III*), born New York, NY, June 27, 1966.

Isabelle Adjani, 54, actress (*The Story of Adele H., Camille Claudel*), born Paris, France, June 27, 1955.

Julia Duffy, 58, actress ("Newhart," "Designing Women"), born St. Paul, MN, June 27, 1951.

Shirley-Anne Field, 71, actress (*Alfie, My Beautiful Laundrette, Getting It Right*), born London, England, June 27, 1938.

Norma Kamali, 64, fashion designer, born New York, NY, June 27, 1945.

Svetlana Kuznetsova, 24, tennis player, born Leningrad, USSR (now St. Petersburg, Russia), June 27, 1985.

Tobey Maguire, 34, actor (*Spider-Man* films, *Seabiscuit, The Cider House Rules*), born Santa Monica, CA, June 27, 1975.

Jason Patric, 43, actor (*Speed 2, Sleepers*), born Queens, NY, June 27, 1966.

H. Ross Perot, 79, philanthropist, businessman, former presidential candidate, born Texarkana, TX, June 27, 1930.

Chuck Connors Person, 45, former basketball player, born Brantley, AL, June 27, 1964.

Ed Westwick, 22, actor ("Gossip Girl," *Son of Rambow*), born Stevenage, Hertfordshire, England, born June 27, 1987.

June 28 — Sunday

DAY 179 — 186 REMAINING

AMERICA'S KIDS DAY. June 28. A day set aside to reach out and teach our children in America the value of life, liberty and the pursuit of happiness. A time to help our kids to learn about the great nation that they live in and to help by demonstrating what it means to be an American. A time to teach them the historical value of their heritage as America's kids. Annually, the fourth Sunday in June. For info: Judith Natale, NCAC America-USA, PO Box 493703, Redding, CA 96049-3703. E-mail: childaware@aol.com.

"AMOS 'N' ANDY" TV PREMIERE: ANNIVERSARY. June 28, 1951. This show was based on the popular radio show about black characters played by white dialecticians Freeman Gosden and Charles Correll. In fact, it was the first dramatic series with an all-black cast. The cast included Tim Moore, Spencer Williams, Alvin Childress, Ernestine Wade, Amanda Randolph, Johnny Lee, Nick O'Demus and Jester Hairston. The series was widely syndicated until pressure from civil rights groups, who claimed the show was stereotypical and prejudicial, caused CBS to withdraw it from syndication.

BISCAYNE NATIONAL PARK ESTABLISHED: ANNIVERSARY. June 28, 1980. Including the coral reefs and waters of Biscayne Bay and the area of the Atlantic Ocean that surrounds the northernmost Florida Keys, Biscayne National Monument was authorized Oct 18, 1968. It became a national park in 1980.

COMECON AND WARSAW PACT DISBAND: ANNIVERSARY. June 28, 1991. The last vestiges of the Cold War–era Soviet bloc, the Council for Mutual Economic Assistance (COMECON) and the Warsaw Pact, formally disbanded on June 28 and July 1, 1991, respectively.

CYPRUS: SAINT PAUL'S FEAST. June 28–29. Kato Paphos, Cyprus. Religious festivities at Kato Paphos at which the archbishop officiates. Procession of the icon of Saint Paul through the streets.

June 2009

S	M	T	W	T	F	S
	1	2	3	4	5	6
7	8	9	10	11	12	13
14	15	16	17	18	19	20
21	22	23	24	25	26	27
28	29	30				

DESCENDANTS DAY. June 28. The day in each year when all the world's citizens take an accounting of their activities during the preceding year that will impact our descendants and our neighbors across time. Annually, the last Sunday in June. For info: Charles A. Howell, 4000 W End Ave, Nashville, TN 37205. Phone: (615) 297-7206. Fax: (615) 269-6268. E-mail: cahowell@comcast.net.

FREEDOM FROM FEAR OF SPEAKING WEEK. June 28–July 4. This week is dedicated to stamping out the fear monster of public speaking. For info: Priscilla Richardson, Pres, WriteSpeakforSuccess, PO Box 275, Cloverdale, VA 24077-0275. Phone: (540) 992-1279. E-mail: Guru@WriteSpeakforSuccess.com.

GAY AND LESBIAN PRIDE PARADE. June 28. Chicago, IL. Chicago's 40th annual parade begins at 12 PM. Est attendance: 450,000. For info: Gay and Lesbian Pride Parade, 3712 N Broadway, PMB #544, Chicago, IL 60613. Phone: (773) 348-8243. E-mail: pridechgo@aol.com. Web: www.chicagopridecalendar.org.

INDEPENDENCE SUNDAY IN IOWA. June 28. Sunday preceding July 4, by proclamation of the governor.

LEVITT PAVILION PERFORMING ARTS/MUSIC FESTIVAL. June 28–Aug 30. Levitt Pavilion, Westport, CT. 36th annual. Performing Arts/Music Festival conducts more than 50 nights of high-quality entertainment offered free to the general public. In addition, a few special concerts are presented with a nominal admission charged to underwrite the free nights of the festival. Est attendance: 60,000. For info: Freda Welsh, Exec Dir, Levitt Pavilion, 260 S Compo Rd, Westport, CT 06880. Phone: (203) 226-7600. Fax: (203) 226-2330. E-mail: levitt@westportct.gov. Web: www.levittpavilion.com.

LOG CABIN DAY. June 28. Commemorates log cabins with tours, open houses and special festivities throughout the state of Michigan. Est attendance: 4,000. For info: Virginia Handy, Sec/Treas, Log Cabin Society of Michigan, 3503 Rock Edwards Dr, Sodus, MI 49126. Phone: (269) 925-3836. E-mail: logcabincrafts@qtm.net. Web: www.qtm.net/logcabincrafts.

MAASS, CLARA: BIRTH ANNIVERSARY. June 28, 1876. Commemorates the birth in 1876 of Clara Louise Maass, the heroic nurse who gave her life in the yellow fever experiments of 1901. Maass died at Havana, Cuba, Aug 24, 1901.

MAYER, MARIA GOEPPERT: BIRTH ANNIVERSARY. June 28, 1906. German-American physicist Maria Goeppert Mayer was born at Kattowitz, Germany. A participant in the Manhattan Project, she worked on the separation of uranium isotopes for the atomic bomb. Mayer became the first American woman to win the Nobel Prize when she shared the 1963 prize for physics with J. Hans Daniel Jensen and Eugene P. Wigner for their explanation of the atomic nucleus, known as the nuclear shell theory. Mayer died Feb 20, 1972, at San Diego, CA.

MONDAY HOLIDAY LAW: ANNIVERSARY. June 28, 1968. President Lyndon B. Johnson approved PL 90–363, which amended section 6103(a) of title 5, United States Code, establishing Monday observance of Washington's Birthday, Memorial Day, Labor Day, Columbus Day and Veterans Day. The new holiday law took effect Jan 1, 1971. Veterans Day observance subsequently reverted to its former observance date, Nov 11. See individual holidays for further details.

NATIONAL PREVENTION OF EYE INJURIES AWARENESS WEEK. June 28–July 5. Information on fireworks safety is available at www.asotonline.org/downloads.html. For info: LoRetta Mann, US Eye Injury Registry, 1201 11th Ave S, Ste 300, Birmingham, AL 35205. Phone: (205) 933-0064. Fax: (205) 933-1341. E-mail: lorettamann@useironline.org. Web: www.useironline.org.

PUNXSUTAWNEY GROUNDHOG FESTIVAL. June 28–July 4. Punxsutawney, PA. Provides residents and visitors a festive week of free entertainment. Music, crafts, food, entertainers and contests. Est attendance: 16,000. For info: Roger Steele, Groundhog Festival Committee, PO Box 1001, Punxsutawney, PA 15767. Phone: (814) 938-2947. Web: www.groundhogfestival.com.

RADNER, GILDA: BIRTH ANNIVERSARY. June 28, 1946. Actress, comedienne ("Saturday Night Live," *Hanky Panky*), born at Detroit, MI. Died May 20, 1989, at Los Angeles, CA.

ROUSSEAU, JEAN-JACQUES: BIRTH ANNIVERSARY. June 28, 1712. Philosopher, born at Geneva, Switzerland. Died July 2, 1778, at Ermenonville, France. "Man is born free," he wrote in *The Social Contract*, "and everywhere he is in chains."

RUBENS, PETER PAUL: BIRTH ANNIVERSARY. June 28, 1577. Flemish painter and diplomat born at Siegen, Westphalia. Died of gout at Antwerp, Belgium, May 30, 1640.

SEAFAIR. June 28–Aug 2. Seattle, WA. The Northwest's largest summer festival. More than 35 events in all, highlighted by the Milk Carton Derby, Marathon, Triathlon Torchlight Run and Torchlight Parade and Air Show. Also dozens of community parades and events. Est attendance: 2,000,000. For info: Seafair, 2200 6th Ave, Ste 400, Seattle, WA 98121. Phone: (206) 728-0123. Fax: (206) 728-9506. E-mail: info@seafair.com. Web: www.seafair.com.

SINGING ON THE MOUNTAIN. June 28. Grandfather Mountain, Linville, NC. 85th annual sing. Modern and traditional gospel music featuring top groups and nationally known speakers. Annually, the fourth Sunday in June. Free admission. Est attendance: 7,000. For info: Grandfather Mountain, PO Box 129, Linville, NC 28646. Phone: (800) 468-7325. Web: www.grandfather.com.

SPECIAL RECREATION FOR DISABLED DAY. June 28. To focus attention on the recreation abilities, aspirations, needs and rights of people with disabilities. See "Special Recreation Week" (June 28–July 4). For info: John A. Nesbitt, EdD, SRDI—Special Recreation for disABLED Intl, 1 Oaknoll Ct, Iowa City, IA 52246. Phone: (319) 466-3192. E-mail: john-nesbitt@uiowa.edu. Web: www.globalvisionproject.org.

SPECIAL RECREATION WEEK. June 28–July 4. To focus attention on the recreation rights, needs, aspirations and abilities of people with disabilities—infants, children, youth, young adults, adults and seniors; living in the community, in residential services and in institutions; in 40 types of play, recreation and leisure pursuits. See "Special Recreation for Disabled Day" (June 28). For info: John A. Nesbitt, Pres/CEO, SRDI—Special Recreation for disABLED Intl, 1 Oaknoll Ct, Iowa City, IA 52246. Phone: (319) 466-3192. E-mail: john-nesbitt@uiowa.edu.

STONEWALL RIOT: 40th ANNIVERSARY. June 28, 1969. Early in the morning of June 28, 1969, the clientele of a gay bar, the Stonewall Inn at New York City, rioted after the club was raided by police. The riot was followed by several days of demonstrations. Stonewall is now recognized as the start of the gay liberation movement.

SUMMER FAIRY FUN DAY. June 28. A Fairy Fun Day is held once each season on the fourth Sunday. Summer Fairy Fun Day is where fairy friends dress up, enjoy picnics, fairy hunts, crafts events and just get together to sparkle, laugh, delight and appreciate fairies, children and Nature. Events take place worldwide—come join us! For info: Fairy Society Artist Community Network, 4128 Bye Way, Santa Cruz, CA 95060. Phone: (408) 564-5550. E-mail: michelle@elementaljoy.net. Web: http://thefairysociety.ning.com/.

TREATY OF VERSAILLES: 90th ANNIVERSARY. June 28, 1919. The signing of the Treaty of Versailles at Versailles, France, formally ended WWI.

TYSON BITES HOLYFIELD: ANNIVERSARY. June 28, 1997. In the third round of the WBA heavyweight championship at Las Vegas, NV, challenger and former title holder Mike Tyson twice bit the ears of defending champ Evander Holyfield. As the round ended, referee Mills Lane disqualified Tyson and Holyfield retained his title. Tyson lost his boxing license for a year and had to pay a $3 million fine for his conduct.

BIRTHDAYS TODAY

Kathy Bates, 61, actress (Oscar for *Misery*; *Fried Green Tomatoes, Delores Claiborne*, "Six Feet Under"), born Memphis, TN, June 28, 1948.

Donald Edward (Don) Baylor, 60, baseball manager, former player, born Austin, TX, June 28, 1949.

Danielle Brisebois, 40, actress ("All in the Family," "Knots Landing"), born Brooklyn, NY, June 28, 1969.

Mel Brooks, 81, actor, director (*The Producers, Blazing Saddles*), born Melvyn Kaminsky at New York, NY, June 28, 1928.

John Cusack, 43, actor (*High Fidelity, Say Anything, The Grifters, Bullets Over Broadway*), born Chicago, IL, June 28, 1966.

Bruce Davison, 63, actor (*Ulzana's Raid, Longtime Companion, Six Degrees of Separation*), born Philadelphia, PA, June 28, 1946.

John Albert Elway, 49, former football player, born Port Angeles, WA, June 28, 1960.

Mark Grace, 45, former baseball player, born Winston-Salem, NC, June 28, 1964.

Alice Krige, 55, actress (*Chariots of Fire, Barfly*), born Upington, South Africa, June 28, 1954.

Carl Levin, 75, US Senator (D, Michigan), born Detroit, MI, June 28, 1934.

Mary Stuart Masterson, 43, actress (*Fried Green Tomatoes, Benny & Joon*, "Law & Order: Special Victims Unit"), born New York, NY, June 28, 1966.

June 29 — Monday

DAY 180 — 185 REMAINING

DEATH PENALTY BANNED: ANNIVERSARY. June 29, 1972. In a decision that spared the lives of 600 individuals then sitting on death row, the US Supreme Court, in a 5–4 vote, found capital punishment a violation of the Eighth Amendment, which prohibits "cruel and unusual punishment." Later overruling themselves, the court determined on July 2, 1976, that the death penalty was not cruel and unusual punishment and on Oct 4, 1976, lifted the ban on the death penalty in murder cases. On Jan 15, 1977, Gary Gilmore became the first individual executed in the US in more than 10 years.

GOETHALS, GEORGE WASHINGTON: BIRTH ANNIVERSARY. June 29, 1858. American engineer and army officer, chief engineer of the Panama Canal and first civil governor of the Canal Zone, born at Brooklyn, NY. Died at New York, NY, Jan 21, 1928.

INTERSTATE HIGHWAY SYSTEM BORN: ANNIVERSARY. June 29, 1956. President Dwight Eisenhower signed a bill providing $33.5 billion for highway construction. It was the biggest public works program in history.

LATHROP, JULIA C.: BIRTH ANNIVERSARY. June 29, 1858. A pioneer in the battle to establish child-labor laws, Julia C. Lathrop was the first woman member of the Illinois State Board of Charities and in 1900 was instrumental in establishing the first juvenile court in the US. In 1912 President Taft named Lathrop chief of the newly created Children's Bureau, then part of the US Dept of Commerce and Labor. In 1925 she became a member of the Child Welfare Committee of the League of Nations. Born at Rockford, IL, she died there Apr 15, 1932.

MAYO, WILLIAM JAMES: BIRTH ANNIVERSARY. June 29, 1861. American surgeon, one of the Mayo brothers, establishers of the Mayo Foundation, born at LeSueur, MN. Died July 28, 1939, at Rochester, MN.

MOON PHASE: FIRST QUARTER. June 29. Moon enters First Quarter phase at 7:28 AM, EDT.

OLYMPIC NATIONAL PARK ESTABLISHED: ANNIVERSARY. June 29, 1938. Washington's Mount Olympus National Monument, proclaimed Mar 2, 1909, was transferred from the US Dept of Agriculture's Forest Service to the National Park Service Aug 10, 1933, then established as Olympic National Park five years later. For further park info: Olympic Natl Park, 600 E Park Ave, Port Angeles, WA 98362.

PLEASE TAKE MY CHILDREN TO WORK DAY. June 29. To recognize and celebrate the tough job that stay-at-home mothers do every day. *Please* Take My Children to Work Day lets busy moms laugh at themselves while getting a much-needed pat on the back. Annually, the last Monday in June. For info: Jen Singer, PO Box 117, Butler, NJ 07405. Phone: (973) 492-8780. E-mail: jensinger@MommaSaid.net. Web: www.MommaSaid.net.

SAINT PETER AND PAUL DAY. June 29. Feast day for Saint Peter and Saint Paul. Commemorates dual martyrdom of Christian apostles Peter (by crucifixion) and Paul (by beheading) during persecution by Roman Emperor Nero. Observed since third century.

SAINT PETER'S DAY. June 29. Antakya, Turkey. Peter first preached Christianity at this place. Ceremonies at Saint Peter's Grotto, early Christian cave near Antakya.

SEYCHELLES: INDEPENDENCE DAY. June 29. National holiday. Gained independence from Great Britain in 1976.

SPACE MILESTONE: *ATLANTIS* (US) AND *MIR* (USSR) DOCK. June 29, 1995. An American space shuttle docked with a Russian space station for the first time, resulting in the biggest craft ever assembled in space. The cooperation involved in this linkup was to serve as a stepping stone to building the International Space Station.

 **BIRTHDAYS TODAY**

Gary Busey, 65, actor (*Under Siege, The Buddy Holly Story*), musician, born Goose Creek, TX, June 29, 1944.

Theo Fleury, 41, former hockey player, born Oxbow, SK, Canada, June 29, 1968.

Fred Grandy, 61, former congressman (R, Iowa), former actor ("Love Boat"), born Sioux City, IA, June 29, 1948.

Joe Johnson, 28, basketball player, born Little Rock, AR, June 29, 1981.

Harmon Clayton Killebrew, 73, Hall of Fame baseball player, born Payette, ID, June 29, 1936.

Sharon Lawrence, 47, actress ("Fired Up," "NYPD Blue"), born Charlotte, NC, June 29, 1962.

June 2009

S	M	T	W	T	F	S
	1	2	3	4	5	6
7	8	9	10	11	12	13
14	15	16	17	18	19	20
21	22	23	24	25	26	27
28	29	30				

June 30 — Tuesday

DAY 181 **184 REMAINING**

BRITAIN CEDES CLAIM TO HONG KONG: ANNIVERSARY. June 30, 1997. The crested flag of the British Crown Colony was officially lowered at midnight and replaced by a new flag (marked by the bauhinia flower) representing China's sovereignty and the official transfer of power. Though Britain owned Hong Kong in perpetuity, the land areas surrounding the city were leased from China and the lease expired July 1, 1997. Rather than renegotiate a new lease, Britain ceded its claim to Hong Kong.

CHARLES BLONDIN'S CONQUEST OF NIAGARA FALLS: 150th ANNIVERSARY. June 30, 1859. Charles Blondin, a French acrobat and aerialist (whose real name was Jean François Gravelet), in view of a crowd estimated at more than 25,000 persons, walked across Niagara Falls on a tightrope. The walk required only about five minutes. On separate occasions he crossed blindfolded, pushing a wheelbarrow, carrying a man on his back and even on stilts. Blondin was born Feb 28, 1824, at St. Omer, France, and died at London, England, Feb 19, 1897.

CONGO (DEMOCRATIC REPUBLIC OF THE): INDEPENDENCE DAY. June 30. National holiday. Democratic Republic of the Congo was previously known as Zaire. Commemorates independence from Belgium in 1960.

GRAND TETON MUSIC FESTIVAL. June 30–Aug 15. Walk Festival Hall, Teton Village, WY. A seven-week summer celebration of classical music in the spectacular setting of Jackson Hole, WY. The festival features the world's finest artists in orchestral and chamber music concerts under the direction of Music Director Donald Runnicles. Est attendance: 25,000. For info: Grand Teton Music Festival, 4015 W Lake Creek Dr, #1, Wilson, WY 83014. Phone: (307) 733-1128. Fax: (307) 739-9043. E-mail: gtmf@gtmf.org. Web: www.gtmf.org.

GUATEMALA: ARMED FORCES DAY. June 30. Public holiday.

LEAP SECOND ADJUSTMENT TIME. June 30. June 30 is one of the times that has been favored for the addition or subtraction of a second from our clock time to coordinate atomic and astronomical time. The determination to adjust is made by the International Earth Rotation Service of the International Bureau of Weights and Measures, at Paris, France. See also: "Note about Leap Seconds" in appendices.

MISS SOUTH CAROLINA PAGEANT. June 30–July 2 and July 4. Spartanburg Memorial Auditorium, Spartanburg, SC. Part of the Miss America Organization. Televised competition. Est attendance: 3,500. For info: Miss South Carolina Organization, 124 W Main St, Liberty, SC 29657. Phone: (864) 843-9090. E-mail: socarpagt@aol.com. Web: www.misssouthcarolina.com.

MISS SOUTH CAROLINA TEEN COMPETITION. June 30–July 2 and July 4. Spartanburg Memorial Auditorium, Spartanburg, SC. Est attendance: 3,500. For info: Miss South Carolina Organization, 124 W Main St, Liberty, SC 29657. Phone: (864) 843-9090. E-mail: socarpagt@aol.com. Web: www.misssouthcarolina.com.

MONROE, ELIZABETH KORTRIGHT: BIRTH ANNIVERSARY. June 30, 1768. Wife of James Monroe, fifth president of the US, born at New York, NY. Died at their Oak Hill estate at Loudoun County, VA, Sept 23, 1830.

NOW FOUNDED: ANNIVERSARY. June 30, 1966. The National Organization for Women was founded at Washington, DC, by people attending the Third National Conference on the Commission on the Status of Women. NOW's purpose is to take action to bring women into full partnership in the mainstream of American society, exercising all privileges and responsibilities in equal partnership with men. For info: Natl Organization for Women, 1100 H St NW, 3rd Fl, Washington, DC 20005. Phone: (202) 628-8NOW. Fax: (202) 785-8576. E-mail: now@now.org. Web: www.now.org.

SIBERIAN EXPLOSION: ANNIVERSARY. June 30, 1908. Early in the morning, a spectacular explosion occurred over central Siberia. The seismic shock, firestorm, ensuing "black rain" and the illumination that was reportedly visible for hundreds of miles led to speculation that a meteorite was the cause. Said to have been the most powerful explosion in history.

SUDAN: REVOLUTION DAY. June 30. National holiday. Commemorates a bloodless coup in 1989.

WHEELER, WILLIAM ALMON: BIRTH ANNIVERSARY. June 30, 1819. 19th vice president of the US (1877–81), born at Malone, NY. Died there June 4, 1887.

BIRTHDAYS TODAY

Fantasia Barrino, 25, singer ("American Idol"), born High Point, NC, June 30, 1984.

Vincent D'Onofrio, 50, actor ("Law & Order: Criminal Intent," *Men in Black*), born Brooklyn, NY, June 30, 1959.

Nancy Dussault, 73, actress ("Too Close for Comfort," "The Ted Knight Show"), born Pensacola, FL, June 30, 1936.

Rupert Graves, 46, actor (*A Room with a View, Maurice*), born Weston-Super-Mare, England, June 30, 1963.

David Alan Grier, 54, actor (*A Soldier's Story, I'm Gonna Git You Sucka*), born Detroit, MI, June 30, 1955.

Lena Horne, 92, singer, actress (*Stormy Weather, Jamaica, Death of a Gunfighter, The Wiz*), born Brooklyn, NY, June 30, 1917.

Mitchell James (Mitch) Richmond, 44, former basketball player, born Ft Lauderdale, FL, June 30, 1965.

Patricia Schroeder, 69, president of the Association of American Publishers, former congresswoman (D, Colorado), born Portland, OR, June 30, 1940.

Michael Gerard (Mike) Tyson, 43, former heavyweight champion boxer, born New York, NY, June 30, 1966.

✦ July ✦

July 1 — Wednesday

DAY 182 **183 REMAINING**

ARAFAT RETURNS TO PALESTINE: 15th ANNIVERSARY. July 1, 1994. Yasser Arafat, head of the Palestine Liberation Organization (PLO), returned to Palestine for the first time in 33 years. Israel's control of Palestine had prevented his visiting the region because he was a sworn enemy of the State of Israel and was regarded by Israelis as a terrorist. The agreement between Israel and the PLO, signed in September 1993, made possible Arafat's return. He went first to Gaza City in the Gaza Strip, where he was welcomed by a crowd estimated at 200,000. Three days later he flew by helicopter to the city of Jericho. Both areas were granted Palestinian rule by the treaty.

ARTOWN. July 1–31. Reno, NV. 14th annual. More than 300 arts-related events including dance, plays, concerts, fine arts exhibits and demonstrations, hands-on programs for children and film. For info: Artown, PO Box 3058, Reno, NV 89505. Phone: (775) 322-1538. Fax: (775) 322-8777. Web: www.renoisartown.com.

BATTLE OF GETTYSBURG: ANNIVERSARY. July 1, 1863. After the Southern success at Chancellorsville, VA, Confederate general Robert E. Lee led his forces on an invasion of the North, initially targeting Harrisburg, PA. As Union forces moved to counter the invasion, the battle lines were eventually formed at Gettysburg, PA, in one of the Civil War's most crucial battles. On the climactic third day of the battle (July 3), Lee ordered an attack on the center of the Union line, later to be known as Pickett's Charge. The 15,000 rebels were repulsed, ending the Battle of Gettysburg. After the defeat, Lee's forces retreated back to Virginia, listing more than one-third of the troops as casualties in the failed invasion. Union general George Meade initially failed to pursue the retreating rebels, allowing Lee's army to escape across the rain-swollen Potomac River. With more than 50,000 casualties, this was the worst battle of the Civil War.

BEREAVED PARENTS AWARENESS MONTH. July 1–31. This month seeks to promote support for bereaved parents. Often people don't know what to say to or do for grieving parents. This observance encourages people to reach out to bereaved parents and their families by listening to them without advising them, giving them a shoulder to cry on and giving them a hug when appropriate and needed. Basically, this month seeks to inspire people to "be there" for the bereaved. For info: Peter and Deb Kulkkula, Coordinators, Bereaved Parents Awareness Month, 381 Billings Rd, Fitchburg, MA 01420-1407. Phone: (978) 343-4009. E-mail: info@BereavedParentsAwarenessMonth.com. Web: www.BereavedParentsAwarenessMonth.com.

"BIG TOP" TV PREMIERE: ANNIVERSARY. July 1, 1950. Charles Vanda produced this CBS kiddie circus program that broadcast weekly for seven years from Camden, NJ. Jack Sterling played ringmaster. The show also featured Dan Lurie and Ed McMahon (as a clown, in his first TV appearance).

BIOTERRORISM/DISASTER EDUCATION AND AWARENESS MONTH. July 1–31. To educate consumers, health care professionals, nonprofit organizations and health care facilities about being prepared for natural disasters, emergency care, bioterrorism and acts of God. For info: Fred Mayer, Pharmacists Planning Service, Inc, 101 Lucas Valley Rd, Ste 382, San Rafael, CA 94903. Phone: (415) 479-8628. Fax: (415) 479-8608. E-mail: ppsi@aol.com. Web: www.ppsinc.org.

BLERIOT, LOUIS: BIRTH ANNIVERSARY. July 1, 1872. Louis Bleriot, aviation pioneer and first man to fly an airplane across the English Channel (July 25, 1909), was born at Cambrai, France. He died at Paris, Aug 2, 1936.

BOTSWANA: SIR SERETSE KHAMA DAY. July 1. National holiday. Commemorates the birth in 1921 of the first president of Botswana.

BUREAU OF INTERNAL REVENUE ESTABLISHED: ANNIVERSARY. July 1, 1862. The Bureau of Internal Revenue was established by an act of Congress.

BURUNDI: INDEPENDENCE DAY. July 1. National holiday. Anniversary of establishment of independence from Belgian administration in 1962. Had been part of Ruanda-Urundi.

CANADA: CANADA DAY. July 1. Canada's national day, formerly known as Dominion Day. Observed on following day when July 1 is a Sunday. Commemorates the confederation of Upper and Lower Canada and some of the Maritime Provinces into the Dominion of Canada in 1867.

CANADA: CANADA DAY CELEBRATION. July 1. Ottawa, ON. Annual event celebrating Canada's anniversary. The heart of the capital comes alive with shows, street performers, concerts, games and activities for the whole family. In the evening a spectacular show featuring top Canadian performers is staged on Parliament Hill and culminates with a fireworks display. Est attendance: 350,000. For info: Natl Capital Commission, 202-40 Elgin St, Ottawa, ON, Canada K1P 1C7. Phone: (800) 465-1867 or (613) 239-5000. E-mail: info@ncc-ccn.ca. Web: www.canadascapital.gc.ca.

CANADA: CANADA DAY PARTY IN THE PARK. July 1. Bancroft, ON. Canada Day fireworks. Craft show, kids' games and local musicians. Est attendance: 5,000. For info: Bancroft and District Chamber of Commerce, PO Box 539, Bancroft, ON, Canada K0L 1C0. Phone: (613) 332-1513. Fax: (613) 332-2119. E-mail: chamber@commerce.bancroft.on.ca. Web: www.bancroftdistrict.com.

CANADA: MINERAL-COLLECTING FIELD TRIPS. July 1–Aug 30. Bancroft, ON. Geologist-led mineral-collecting field trips visit nearby rock dumps, abandoned mines and collecting sites. Participants are educated about mineral identification, collecting techniques and earth sciences. Annually, every Tuesday, Thursday and Saturday in July and August. Est attendance: 1,000. For info: Bancroft and District Chamber of Commerce, PO Box 539, Bancroft, ON, Canada K0L 1C0. Phone: (613) 332-1513. Fax: (613) 332-2119. E-mail: chamber@commerce.bancroft.on.ca. Web: www.bancroftdistrict.com.

July 2009

S	M	T	W	T	F	S
			1	2	3	4
5	6	7	8	9	10	11
12	13	14	15	16	17	18
19	20	21	22	23	24	25
26	27	28	29	30	31	

CANADA: THE NORTH AMERICAN TOURNAMENT. July 1–5. Spruce Meadows, Calgary, AB. Strong contingents from North America and Europe compete in this show-jumping tournament. The weekend features ATCO POWER Queen Elizabeth II Cup, the Sun Life Financial Reach for the Sun and the Chrysler Classic. The tournament will also feature a tribute to our Canadian military with exhibits for all to experience. Live entertainment Friday through Sunday on the Plaza. Est attendance: 100,000. For info: Spruce Meadows, RR 9, Calgary, AB, Canada T2J 5G5. Phone: (403) 974-4200. Web: www.sprucemeadows.com.

CANADA: ROYAL NOVA SCOTIA INTERNATIONAL TATTOO. July 1–8. Halifax, NS. The Tattoo combines more than 2,000 international military and civilian performers in bands, singing, dancing, marching, gymnastics and comedy. Est attendance: 22,000. For info: Royal Nova Scotia Intl Tattoo, 1586 Queen St, Halifax, NS, Canada B3J 2J1. Phone: (902) 420-1114 or (800) 563-1114. Fax: (902) 423-6629. E-mail: info@nstattoo.ca. Web: www.nstattoo.ca.

CANADA: YUKON GOLD PANNING CHAMPIONSHIPS. July 1. Dawson City, YT. Yukon residents compete for the honor of Territorial Champion Gold Panner. Dawson visitors can join in and compete for the Cheechako Award. Annually, July 1, Canada Day. Est attendance: 200. For info: Klondike Visitors Assn, PO Box 389, Dawson City, YT, Canada Y0B 1G0. Phone: (867) 993-5575. Fax: (867) 993-6415. E-mail: kva@dawson.net. Web: www.dawsoncity.ca.

CELL PHONE COURTESY MONTH. July 1–31. There are more than 219 million cell phone users in the US. This month is dedicated to encouraging the increasingly unmindful corps of cell phone users to be more respectful of their surroundings and those around them. Annually, the month of July. For info: Jacqueline Whitmore, Etiquette Expert, PO Box 3073, Palm Beach, FL 33480. Phone: (561) 586-9026. Fax: (561) 586-6689. E-mail: info@etiquetteexpert.com. Web: www.etiquetteexpert.com.

CHINA: HALF-YEAR DAY. July 1. National holiday in China. Midyear Day in Thailand.

CLEMSON, THOMAS GREEN: BIRTH ANNIVERSARY. July 1, 1807. The man for whom Clemson University was named was born at Philadelphia, PA. The mining engineer and agriculturist married John C. Calhoun's daughter, Anna. Clemson bequeathed the old Calhoun plantation to South Carolina, and Clemson Agricultural College (now Clemson University) was founded there in 1889. Clemson died at Clemson, SC, Apr 6, 1888.

CLEVELAND'S SECRET SURGERY: ANNIVERSARY. July 1, 1893. President Grover Cleveland boarded the yacht *Oneida* for surgery to be performed in secret on a cancerous growth in his mouth. As this was during the 1893 depression, secrecy was thought desirable to avoid further panic by the public. The whole left side of Cleveland's jaw was removed as well as a small portion of his soft palate. A second, less extensive operation was performed July 17. He was later fitted with a prosthesis of vulcanized rubber that he wore until his death on June 24, 1908. A single leak of the secret was plugged by Cleveland's secretary of war, Daniel Lamont, the only member of the administration to know about the surgery. The illness did not become public knowledge until an article appeared Sept 22, 1917, in the *Saturday Evening Post*, written by William W. Keen, who assisted in the surgery.

COURT TV DEBUT: ANNIVERSARY. July 1, 1991. The continuing evolution of entertainment brought on by the advent of cable television added another twist on July 1, 1991, with the debut of Court TV. Trials are broadcast in their entirety, with occasional commentary from the channel's anchor desk and switching between several trials in progress. Trials with immense popular interest, such as the Jeffrey Dahmer and O.J. Simpson trials, are broadcast along with lower profile cases.

DIANA, PRINCESS OF WALES: BIRTH ANNIVERSARY. July 1, 1961. Former wife of Charles, Prince of Wales, and mother of Prince William and Prince Harry. Born Lady Diana Spencer at Sandringham, England, she died in an automobile accident at Paris, France, Aug 31, 1997.

DIXON, WILLIE: BIRTH ANNIVERSARY. July 1, 1915. Blues legend Willie Dixon was born at Vicksburg, MI. He moved to Chicago in 1936 and began his career as a musician with the Big Three Trio. With the advent of instrument amplification Dixon migrated away from his acoustic upright bass into producing and songwriting with Chess Studios, where he became one of the primary architects of the classic Chicago sound in the 1950s. His songs were performed by Elvis Presley, the Everly Brothers, the Rolling Stones, Led Zeppelin, the Doors, Cream, the Yardbirds, Aerosmith, Jimi Hendrix and the Allman Brothers, among others. Dixon died Jan 29, 1992, at Burbank, CA.

DORSEY, THOMAS A.: BIRTH ANNIVERSARY. July 1, 1899. Thomas A. Dorsey, the father of gospel music, was born at Villa Rica, GA. Originally a blues composer, Dorsey eventually combined blues and sacred music to develop gospel music. It was Dorsey's composition "Take My Hand, Precious Lord" that Reverend Dr. Martin Luther King, Jr, had asked to have performed just moments before his assassination. Dorsey, who composed more than 1,000 gospel songs and hundreds of blues songs in his lifetime, died Jan 23, 1993, at Chicago, IL.

EASTPORT FOURTH OF JULY AND "OLD HOME WEEK" CELEBRATION. July 1–4. Eastport, ME. Event features a craft fair, theater, music, dance, parades, contests, games, fireworks display, public entertainment July 3–4, US naval ship in port and a variety of contests. Eastport, the easternmost city in the US, is bounded by the Atlantic Ocean on the Bay of Fundy and surrounded by Canadian islands. Canada Day, July 1, is celebrated every year. Est attendance: 10,000. For info: Eastport 4th of July Committee Inc, PO Box 187, Eastport, ME 04631. Phone: (207) 853-6076. E-mail: info@eastport4th.com. Web: www.eastport4th.com.

ENGLAND: HENLEY ROYAL REGATTA. July 1–5. Henley-on-Thames, Oxfordshire. International rowing event that is one of the big social events of the year. Annually since 1839. Est attendance: 245,000. For info: The Secretary, Henley Royal Regatta, Regatta Headquarters, Henley-on-Thames, Oxfordshire, England RG9 2LY. Phone: (44) (149) 157-2153. Fax: (44) (149) 157-5509. Web: www.hrr.co.uk.

FAMILY REUNION MONTH. July 1–31. July is the most popular month of the year for families to meet and celebrate their unique history. Trips back to family homesteads, tales of generations gone by and celebrations of generations yet to come are featured again and again as families meet around the country and around the globe. For info: Dina C. Carson, PO Box 999, Niwot, CO 80544. E-mail: info@reunionsolutions.com. Web: www.reunionsolutions.com.

FIRST PHOTOGRAPHS USED IN A NEWSPAPER REPORT: ANNIVERSARY. July 1, 1848. The first instance of photojournalism occurred during the Paris Riots of 1848, when an enterprising French photographer known only as Thibault scrambled to a rooftop to chronicle the events. Taken on June 25 and 26, the two resulting daguerreotypes show first a deserted street, the rue St. Maur, with barricades, then the same street with insurgents and the military in combat. Wood engravings were made of the daguerreotypes, and on July 1, 1848, the images appeared in the weekly newspaper *L'Illustration Journal Universel*. More than 3,000 Parisians lost their lives during the June revolt.

FIRST SCHEDULED TELEVISION BROADCAST: ANNIVERSARY. July 1, 1941. The National Broadcasting Company (NBC) began broadcasting from the Empire State Building on this day. The Federal Communications Commission had granted the first commercial TV licenses to 10 stations on May 2, 1941.

FIRST US POSTAGE STAMPS ISSUED: ANNIVERSARY. July 1, 1847. The first US postage stamps were issued by the US Postal Service, a 5-cent stamp picturing Benjamin Franklin and a 10-cent stamp honoring George Washington. Stamps had been issued by private postal services in the US prior to this date.

FIRST US ZOO: ANNIVERSARY. July 1, 1874. The Philadelphia Zoological Society, the first US zoo, opened. Three thousand visitors traveled by foot, horse and carriage and steamboat to visit the exhibits. Price of admission was 25 cents for adults and 10 cents for children. There were 1,000 animals in the zoo on opening day.

GHANA: REPUBLIC DAY. July 1. National holiday. Commemorates the inauguration of the Republic in 1960.

HERBAL/PRESCRIPTION INTERACTION AWARENESS MONTH. July 1–31. To educate health professionals and consumers on dietary supplements, herbs and nutritionals along with mixing those products with prescription drugs. There is a $15 charge for kit materials. For info: PPSI, c/o Pharmacy Council on Dietary Supplements, 101 Lucas Valley Rd, Ste 382, San Rafael, CA 94903. Phone: (415) 479-8628. Fax: (415) 479-8608. E-mail: ppsi@aol.com. Web: www.ppsinc.org.

INTERNATIONAL BLONDIE AND DEBORAH HARRY MONTH. July 1–31. Each July, this special month celebrates the Rock and Roll Hall of Fame band Blondie and its lead singer, Deborah Harry, and their contributions to popular music. For info: Allan Metz, 333 E Libby Dr, Springfield, MO 65803. E-mail: ametz@drury.edu. Web: www.blondiebook.com.

LAUDER, ESTÉE: BIRTH ANNIVERSARY. July 1, 1908 (some sources say 1906). The cosmetics magnate was born Josephine Esther Mentzer at Corona, Queens, NY. In high school, she took an interest in the work of her uncle, John Schotz, a Hungarian-born chemist who made beauty products for women. She began a business at her kitchen table in 1946 that has gone on to become one of the world's largest, most successful cosmetics companies. The introduction of her breakthrough formula for the bath oil Youth Dew in the 1950s led the way to a company currently worth more than $10 billion. At the time of her death on Apr 24, 2004, at New York, NY, Lauder was among the 500 richest women in the world.

"THE LIBERACE SHOW" TV PREMIERE: ANNIVERSARY. July 1, 1952. A pianist known for his outrageous style and a candelabra on his piano, Liberace hosted popular shows in the '50s and '60s. The first premiered on KLAC-TV in Los Angeles and went national in 1953. That did so well that he began a half-hour syndicated series that featured his brother George as violinist and orchestra leader. After a brief leave, he returned to TV in 1958 with a half-hour show. Liberace also hosted a British series and a summer series produced in London.

LINCOLN SIGNS INCOME TAX: ANNIVERSARY. July 1, 1862. President Abraham Lincoln signed into law a bill levying a 3 percent income tax on annual incomes of $600–$10,000 and 5 percent on incomes of more than $10,000. The revenues were to help pay for the Civil War. This tax law actually went into effect, unlike an earlier law passed Aug 5, 1861, making it the first income tax levied by the US. It was rescinded in 1872.

July 2009	S	M	T	W	T	F	S
				1	2	3	4
	5	6	7	8	9	10	11
	12	13	14	15	16	17	18
	19	20	21	22	23	24	25
	26	27	28	29	30	31	

"MAMA" TV PREMIERE: 60th ANNIVERSARY. July 1, 1949. One of TV's first popular sitcoms, "Mama" told the story of a Norwegian family living in San Francisco in 1917. The show aired live through 1956; after it was canceled, a second, filmed version lasted only 13 weeks. Cast members included Peggy Wood, Judson Laire, Rosemary Rice, Dick Van Patten, Iris Mann, Robin Morgan, Ruth Gates, Malcolm Keen, Carl Frank, Alice Frost, Patty McCormack and Kevin Coughlin. Toni Campbell replaced Robin Morgan in the revival.

MAMMOTH CAVE NATIONAL PARK ESTABLISHED: ANNIVERSARY. July 1, 1941. Area of central Kentucky, originally authorized May 25, 1926, was established as a national park. For more info: Mammoth Cave Natl Park, Mammoth Cave, KY 42259.

MEDICARE: ANNIVERSARY. July 1, 1968. Medicare, the US health insurance program for senior citizens, went into effect. The legislation authorizing the program had been signed by President Lyndon Johnson July 30, 1965. Former president Harry Truman received the first Medicare card.

MORRILL LAND GRANT ACT PASSED: ANNIVERSARY. July 1, 1862. This federal legislation led to the creation of the land grant universities and agricultural experiment stations in each state.

NATIONAL BLUEBERRIES MONTH. July 1–31. To make the public aware that this is the peak month for fresh blueberries. For info: North American Blueberry Council, PO Box 1036, Folsom, CA 95763. E-mail: info@nabcblues.org. Web: www.nabcblues.org.

NATIONAL CHILD-CENTERED DIVORCE MONTH. July 1–31. Dedicated to reminding parents to put the emotional, physical and spiritual needs of their children first when facing divorce or separation. Public lectures, seminars, workshops, picnics, film showings, concerts and other events are planned by individual therapists, mediators and divorce attorneys as well as their national professional associations, to build awareness of how children are affected by divorce—and what parents and the professional community can do on behalf of these innocent children. For info: Rosalind Sedacca, Child-Centered Divorce. Phone: (561) 742-3537. E-mail: rosalind@childcentereddivorce.com. Web: www.childcentereddivorce.com.

NATIONAL "DOGHOUSE REPAIRS" MONTH. July 1–31. Celebrate "Doghouse Repairs" Month by staying out of trouble with those you love and care about by doing something extra-special. For info: Heidi Richards, 7100 Pembroke Blvd, Miramar, FL 33023. Phone: (954) 981-5515. E-mail: heidi@successandthensome.com.

NATIONAL EDUCATION ASSOCIATION MEETING. July 1–6. San Diego, CA. Representative Assembly. For info: Natl Education Assn, 1201 16th St NW, Washington, DC 20036-3290. Phone: (202) 833-4000. Web: www.nea.org.

NATIONAL GRILLING MONTH. July 1–31. The sizzle, the smoke, and the mouth-watering aromas that come from a grill can be yours if you take the time out this month and enjoy the fun and ease of cooking on a grill—indoor or out! For info: Viking Culinary Arts Center/Viking Home Chef. Web: www.vikingculinary.com.

NATIONAL HORSERADISH MONTH. July 1–31. What 3,000-year-old plant has been used as a bitter herb for Passover Seders and a flavorful accompaniment for beef, chicken and seafood? If you guessed horseradish, you're right. This month, celebrate the healthful and hot horseradish, which has been praised for its numerous food uses for centuries. For info: Horseradish Information Council, 1100 Johnson Ferry Rd, Ste 300, Atlanta, GA 30342. Phone: (404) 252-3663. Fax: (404) 252-0774. E-mail: tgibson@kellencompany.com. Web: www.horseradish.org.

NATIONAL HOT DOG MONTH. July 1–31. Celebrates one of America's favorite and most patriotic foods with fun facts and new recipes. More than 3 billion hot dogs per year are consumed in the US. For info: Natl Hot Dog and Sausage Council, 1150 Connecticut Ave NW, 12th Fl, Washington, DC 20036. Phone: (202) 587-4200. Fax: (202) 587-4300. Web: www.hot-dog.org.

NATIONAL ICE CREAM MONTH. July 1–31. First designated by President Ronald Reagan in 1984, this month celebrates ice cream as a fun and nutritious food that is enjoyed by a full 90 percent of the nation's population. For info: Intl Dairy Foods Assn, 1250 H St

NW, Ste 900, Washington, DC 20005. Phone: (202) 737-4332. Web: www.idfa.org.

NATIONAL MAKE A DIFFERENCE TO CHILDREN MONTH. July 1–31. To remind us of the many ways adults can make a positive difference to children. Create opportunities for kids during this midsummer month when most children are not in school by doing three things: 1. Commit to do one special thing with a child in July—make some kind of positive difference for that child. 2. Support an organization that focuses on children—there are many to choose from. 3. Communicate with your elected leaders to make children a priority in policy and budget issues they address. For info: Kim Ratz, 3665 Woody Ln, Minnetonka, MN 55305. Phone: (952) 938-4472. E-mail: kimratz@aol.com. Web: www.kimratz.com.

NATIONAL RECREATION AND PARKS MONTH. July 1–31. To showcase and invite participation in healthy lifestyles for livable communities. For info: Natl Recreation and Park Assn, 22377 Belmont Ridge Rd, Ashburn, VA 20148. Phone: (703) 858-0784. Fax: (703) 858-0794. Web: www.nrpa.org.

NATIONAL SHARE A SUNSET WITH YOUR LOVER MONTH. July 1–31. 2nd annual. This month's purpose is to inspire your partner and you to share more romantic experiences with each other. Romance is essential to a happy love life. Even if you have been married to each other for over 40 years, you still need to be romantic with each other so you can increase the emotional closeness you share. For info: Melissa Chamberlin, PhD, 545 Eighth Ave, Ste 401, New York, NY 10018. Phone: (212) 613-6330.

NATIONAL TOM SAWYER DAYS (WITH FENCE PAINTING CONTEST). July 1–4. Hannibal, MO. 54th annual. Frog jumping, mud volleyball, Tom and Becky Contest, parade, Tomboy Sawyer Contest, 10k run, arts and crafts show and fireworks launched from the banks of the Mississippi River. Highlight is the National Fence Painting Contest. Sponsor: Hannibal Jaycees. Est attendance: 100,000. For info: Hannibal CVB, 505 N 3rd St, Hannibal, MO 63401. Phone: (573) 221-2477. Web: www.hannibaljaycees.org or www.visithannibal.com.

NATIONAL UNASSISTED HOMEBIRTH WEEK. July 1–7. Conferences and activities to create awareness and encouragement for couples who intentionally seek to give birth without a midwife or doctor. The third National Husband/Wife Homebirth Conference will be held in Liberty, MO, on July 4. For info: Lynn M. Griesemer, 4103 Plaza Ln, Fairfax, VA 22033. Phone: (703) 263-2468. E-mail: greeze@juno.com. Web: www.unassistedhomebirth.com.

NATIONAL WHEELCHAIR BEAUTIFICATION MONTH. July 1–31. Health care centers, hospitals and others participate in this project by using the power of a single flower to brighten the image of an ordinary wheelchair and spread smiles everywhere. Participants attach a florist's water tube with Velcro near the top of the chair. These tubes are perfect for living or artificial flowers and are available at florists for pennies. For info: Horace Knowles, Founder, Natl Wheelchair Beautification Project, 4367 Concord Blvd, Concord, CA 94521. Phone: (925) 708-5955. E-mail: horaceak@pacbell.net.

NICK AT NITE DEBUT: ANNIVERSARY. July 1, 1985. The first broadcast of Nick at Nite, the creation of the kids' network Nickelodeon, occurred. Owned and operated by MTV Networks, Nick at Nite presents many of the old classic television series.

RIVERFEST. July 1–5. Riverside Park, LaCrosse, WI. 27th annual Riverfest—the city's premier summer event! River activities, five stages to provide continuous entertainment, a children's area with games, face painting, etc. Also provided: a food pavilion featuring 16 different vendors, beverage tent, and an arts and crafts area. July 4th features a fireworks display. Est attendance: 40,000. For info: Riverfest, Inc, PO Box 1745, LaCrosse, WI 54602. Phone: (608) 782-6000. Fax: (608) 784-1580. E-mail: riverfest@centurytel.net. Web: www.riverfestlacrosse.com.

RWANDA: INDEPENDENCE DAY. July 1. National holiday. Commemorates independence from Belgium in 1962.

SAND, GEORGE: BIRTH ANNIVERSARY. July 1, 1804. French novelist, author of more than 100 volumes, whose real name was Amandine Aurore Lucile (Dupin) Dudevant, was born at Paris, France. Died at Nohant, France, June 8, 1876. She is better remembered for having been a liberated woman during a romantic epoch than for her literary works.

SANDWICH GENERATION MONTH. July 1–31. A national observance of the dedication and care exercised by those who are part of the Sandwich Generation: adults caring for their children as well as their own aging parents. For info: Phillip Silverstone, 717 Bethlehem Pike, Ste 300, Glenside, PA 19038. Phone: (215) 402-0200. E-mail: phillip@griswoldspecialcare.com. Web: www.sandwichgenerationmonth.com.

SECOND HALF OF THE NEW YEAR DAY. July 1. This day is a checkpoint for those who made New Year's resolutions. Celebrate your accomplishments, look at what you did not accomplish and why or set new resolutions. Stay on track to have a healthier, happier and more successful life. Annually, July 1. For info: Cindy Kubica, 414 Parish Pl, Franklin, TN 37067. Phone: (615) 771-3800. E-mail: cindy@cindykubica.com.

SMART IRRIGATION MONTH. July 1–31. Most home owners over-irrigate their lawns by 30 percent—not only wasting water but also washing nutrients into rivers and streams and away from the root zone where the plants can use them. Evaluate your irrigation system this month. For smart irrigation, consider adding a "smart" controller (one that uses weather, plant and soil data to determine when to water) or a rain-sensor shutoff device. To find out where your system might be wasting water, seek an irrigation system audit by a qualified irrigation auditor. For info: The Irrigation Assn, 6540 Arlington Blvd, Falls Church, VA 22042. Phone: (703) 536-7080. Fax: (703) 536-7019. E-mail: news@irrigation.org. Web: www.smartirrigationmonth.org.

SOCIAL WELLNESS MONTH. July 1–31. Improve your social and communication skills and learn to act appropriately in prominent situations. Create a positive and lasting first impression. Be distinguished, earn respect, and appear confident under public pressure. For info: Angela Brown Oberer, Words of Wellness, PO Box 49266, Charlotte, NC 28277. Phone: (704) 849-2900. E-mail: Angela@WordsofWellness.com. Web: www.WordsofWellness.com.

SOMALIA DEMOCRATIC REPUBLIC: NATIONAL DAY. July 1. Anniversary of the merger of newly independent British Somaliland and Italian Somaliland on July 1, 1960.

SPACE MILESTONE: *CASSINI-HUYGENS* REACHES SATURN: 5th ANNIVERSARY. July 1, 2004. Launched on Oct 15, 1997, the *Cassini-Huygens* spacecraft, a joint venture of NASA, the European Space Agency (ESA) and the Italian Space Agency (ISA), reached Saturn on this date and maneuvered into orbit. The ESA's *Huygens* probe touched down on Saturn's moon Titan on Jan 14, 2005. The purpose of the multibillion-dollar NASA/ESA/ISA mission is to explore the Saturnian system.

SPACE MILESTONE: *KOSMOS 1383* (USSR). July 1, 1982. First search-and-rescue satellite—equipped to hear distress calls from aircraft and ships—launched in cooperative project with the US and France.

SURINAME: LIBERATION DAY. July 1. National holiday. Commemorates the 1863 abolition of slavery in Dutch territory.

TWENTY-SIXTH AMENDMENT RATIFIED: ANNIVERSARY. July 1, 1971. The 26th Amendment to the Constitution granted the right to vote in all federal, state and local elections to all persons 18 years or older. On the date of ratification the US gained an additional 11 million voters. Up until this time, the minimum voting age was set by the states; in most states it was 21.

WOMEN'S MOTORCYCLE MONTH. July 1–31. This month is dedicated to honoring women who ride, coride, or wish they could ride motorcycles or their derivatives (sidecar rigs, trikes, etc). For info: Sylvia Henderson, Springboard Training, PO Box 588, Olney, MD 20830-0588. Phone: (301) 260-1538. E-mail: sylvia@springboardtraining.com. Web: www.springboardtraining.com.

ZIP CODES INAUGURATED: ANNIVERSARY. July 1, 1963. The US Postal Service introduced the five-digit zip code on this day.

BIRTHDAYS TODAY

Pamela Anderson, 42, model, actress ("V.I.P.," "Baywatch"), born Ladysmith, BC, Canada, July 1, 1967.

Dan Aykroyd, 57, actor (*Trading Places, The Blues Brothers,* "Saturday Night Live"), born Ottawa, ON, Canada, July 1, 1952.

Karen Black, 67, actress (*Five Easy Pieces, Nashville*), born Park Ridge, IL, July 1, 1942.

Andre Braugher, 47, actor ("Homicide," "Thief," *City of Angels*), born Chicago, IL, July 1, 1962.

Genevieve Bujold, 67, actress (*Choose Me, Trouble in Mind, Dead Ringers*), born Montreal, QC, Canada, July 1, 1942.

Hilarie Burton, 27, actress ("One Tree Hill"), host (MTV's "TRL"), born Sterling, VA, July 1, 1982.

Leslie Caron, 78, actress (*The L-Shaped Room, Gigi, Lili, An American in Paris*), dancer, born Paris, France, July 1, 1931.

Olivia de Havilland, 93, actress (Oscars for *To Each His Own, The Heiress*; *Gone with the Wind*), born Tokyo, Japan, July 1, 1916.

Missy Elliott, 38, singer, born Portsmouth, VA, July 1, 1971.

Jamie Farr, 75, actor ("M*A*S*H," *The Blackboard Jungle*), born Jameel Farah at Toledo, OH, July 1, 1934.

Debbie Harry, 64, lead singer (Blondie, "The Tide Is High"), born Miami, FL, July 1, 1945.

Frederick Carlton (Carl) Lewis, 48, Olympic gold medal track athlete, born Birmingham, AL, July 1, 1961.

Jean Marsh, 75, writer, actress ("Upstairs, Downstairs"), born Stoke Newington, England, July 1, 1934.

Alan Ruck, 53, actor ("Spin City," *Ferris Bueller's Day Off*), born Cleveland, OH, July 1, 1956.

Twyla Tharp, 68, dancer, choreographer (Tony for *Movin' Out*), born Portland, IN, July 1, 1941.

Liv Tyler, 32, actress (*Lord of the Rings* trilogy, *Armageddon*), born Portland, ME, July 1, 1977.

July 2009

S	M	T	W	T	F	S
			1	2	3	4
5	6	7	8	9	10	11
12	13	14	15	16	17	18
19	20	21	22	23	24	25
26	27	28	29	30	31	

July 2 — Thursday

DAY 183 **182 REMAINING**

AMELIA EARHART DISAPPEARS: ANNIVERSARY. July 2, 1937. In 1937, aviatrix Amelia Earhart planned an around-the-world trip via the equatorial route that would be the longest ever made. Having completed 22,000 miles of her journey, Earhart, accompanied by navigator Fred Noonan, took off on this date from Lae, New Guinea, for the final 7,000 miles over the Pacific. About 800 miles into their flight to tiny Howland Island, radio contact was lost with her craft. Despite a massive search by the US Navy and US Coast Guard, Earhart, Noonan and their plane were never found.

"THE ANDY WILLIAMS SHOW" TV PREMIERE: ANNIVERSARY. July 2, 1957. Singer Andy Williams hosted many variety shows, including "The Andy Williams–June Valli Show," "The Chevy Showroom" and "The Andy Williams Show." His shows featured Dick Van Dyke and the Bob Hamilton Trio, the New Christy Minstrels, the Osmond Brothers, Charlie Callas, Irwin Corey and Janos Prohaska. In 1976 Williams hosted "Andy," a syndicated show.

BELGIUM: OMMEGANG PAGEANT. July 2. Splendid historic festival of medieval pageantry at the illuminated Grand-Palace in Brussels. The annual event (first Thursday in July) re-creates an entertainment given in honor of Charles V and his court.

CIVIL RIGHTS ACT OF 1964: 45th ANNIVERSARY. July 2, 1964. President Lyndon Johnson signed the Voting Rights Act of 1964 into law, prohibiting discrimination on the basis of race in public accommodations, in publicly owned or operated facilities, in employment and union membership and in the registration of voters. The bill included Title VI, which allowed for the cutoff of federal funding in areas where discrimination persisted.

CONSTITUTION OF THE US TAKES EFFECT: ANNIVERSARY. July 2, 1788. Cyrus Griffin of Virginia, the president of the Congress, announced that the Constitution had been ratified by the required nine states (the ninth being New Hampshire June 21, 1788), and a committee was appointed to make preparations for the change of government.

CRANMER, THOMAS: BIRTH ANNIVERSARY. July 2, 1489. English clergyman, reformer and martyr, born at Aslacton, Nottinghamshire, England. One of the principal authors of *The English Book of Common Prayer.* Archbishop of Canterbury. Tried for treason and burned at the stake at Oxford, England, Mar 21, 1556.

DECLARATION OF INDEPENDENCE RESOLUTION: ANNIVERSARY. July 2, 1776. Anniversary of adoption by the Continental Congress, Philadelphia, PA, of a resolution introduced June 7, 1776, by Richard Henry Lee of Virginia: "Resolved, That these United Colonies are, and of right ought to be, free and independent States, that they are absolved from all allegiance to the British Crown, and that all political connection between them and the State of Great Britain is, and ought to be, totally dissolved. That it is expedient forthwith to take the most effectual measures for forming foreign Alliances. That a plan of confederation be prepared and transmitted to the respective Colonies for their consideration and approbation." This resolution prepared the way for adoption, July 4, 1776, of the Declaration of Independence. See also: "Declaration of Independence Approval and Signing: Anniversary" (July 4).

DENMARK: AALBORG AND REBILD FESTIVAL (AMERICAN INDEPENDENCE DAY CELEBRATION). July 2–5. Aalborg. This celebration of the American Independence Day, at the Rebild National Park, south of Aalborg, Denmark, is described as "the largest single gathering for this occasion in the world." Guest speakers and Danish and American entertainment. Est attendance: 10,000. For info: 4 July Committee, Visit Aalborg, Oesteragade 8, DK-9100 Aalborg, Denmark. Phone: (45) (99) 31-75-00. Fax: (45) (99) 31-75-19. E-mail: info@visitaalborg.com. Web: www.visitaalborg.com.

FIRST SOLO ROUND-THE-WORLD BALLOON FLIGHT: ANNIVERSARY. July 2, 2002. In his sixth attempt, Steve Fossett became the first person to circumnavigate the world nonstop and in a nonmotorized craft. In his "Spirit of Freedom" balloon, Fossett traveled 19,400 miles. He began his odyssey on June 18, 2002, from Northam, Australia, and arrived at his starting longitude (117° east) on July 2, 2002. (The first balloon flight around the world was accomplished by a two-man team in 1999. See also: "First Round-the-World Balloon Flight: Anniversary" [Mar 21].)

FREEDOM DAYS. July 2–5. Farmington, NM. Celebration with a variety of special events, including spectacular fireworks, food fair, auction, gem and mineral show, parade, triathlon. Est attendance: 70,000. For info: Farmington Conv and Visitors Bureau, 3041 E Main St, Farmington, NM 87402. Phone: (800) 448-1240 or (505) 326-7602. Fax: (505) 327-0577. E-mail: fmncvb@earthlink.net. Web: www.farmingtonnm.org.

GARFIELD, JAMES ABRAM: ASSASSINATION ANNIVERSARY. July 2, 1881. President James A. Garfield was shot as he entered the railway station at Washington, DC. He died Sept 19, 1881, never having recovered from the wound. The assassin, Charles J. Guiteau, was hanged June 30, 1882.

HALFWAY POINT OF 2009. July 2. At noon, July 2, 2009, 182½ days of the year will have elapsed and 182½ will remain before Jan 1, 2010.

I FORGOT DAY. July 2. A day to make up for all the birthdays, anniversaries, new births, graduations, etc, that you forgot to acknowledge with a greeting or gift. Annually, July 2. For info: Gaye Andersen, Davenport University, 8200 Georgia St, Merrillville, IN 46410. Phone: (219) 650-5218. Fax: (219) 756-8911. E-mail: gaye.andersen@davenport.edu.

ITALY: PALIO. July 2 (also Aug 16). Siena. Colorful medieval horse race, competing for the banner (Palio).

LACOSTE, RENE: BIRTH ANNIVERSARY. July 2, 1904. Jean Rene Lacoste, tennis player and clothier born at Paris, France. Lacoste, known as the Crocodile, was one-quarter of the great French tennis players in the 1920s known as the Four Musketeers. He won Wimbledon and the US championship twice each, won the French Open three times and was ranked number 1 in the world in 1926–27. He designed the first shirt specifically for tennis, a loose-fitting cotton polo shirt that soon became the standard. He adorned the Lacoste shirt with a small crocodile, the first apparel logo. Died at St. Jean-de-Luz, France, Oct 12, 1996.

"THE LAWRENCE WELK SHOW" TV PREMIERE: ANNIVERSARY. July 2, 1955. This musical series, hosted by accordionist and bandleader Lawrence Welk, lasted for almost three decades. In its early years it was known as "The Dodge Dancing Party." Regulars included the Lennon Sisters, Alice Lon, Norma Zimmer, Tanya Falan, Arthur Duncan, Joe Feeney, Guy Hovis, Jim Roberts, Ralna English, Larry Hooper, Jerry Burke and Bobby Burgess. During 1956–59, this show was on concurrently with either "Lawrence Welk's Top Tunes and New Talent" or "The Plymouth Show Starring Lawrence Welk (Lawrence Welk's Little Band)."

MARSHALL, THURGOOD: BIRTH ANNIVERSARY. July 2, 1908. Thurgood Marshall, the first African American on the US Supreme Court, was born at Baltimore, MD. For more than 20 years, he served as director-counsel of the NAACP Legal Defense and Educational Fund. He experienced his greatest legal victory May 17, 1954, when the Supreme Court decision on *Brown v Board of Education* declared an end to the "separate but equal" system of racial segregation in public schools in 21 states. Marshall argued 32 cases before the Supreme Court, winning 29 of them, before becoming a member of the high court himself. Nominated by President Lyndon Johnson, he began his 24-year career on the high court Oct 2, 1967, becoming a voice of dissent in an increasingly conservative court. Marshall announced his retirement June 27, 1991, and he died Jan 24, 1993, at Washington, DC.

SAINT LOUIS RACE RIOTS: ANNIVERSARY. July 2, 1917. Between 20 and 75 blacks were killed in a race riot in St. Louis, MO; hundreds more were injured. To protest this violence against blacks, W.E.B. DuBois and James Weldon Johnson of the NAACP led a silent march down Fifth Avenue at New York City.

VESEY, DENMARK: DEATH ANNIVERSARY. July 2, 1822. Planner of what would have been the biggest slave revolt in US history, Denmark Vesey was executed at Charleston, SC. He was born around 1767, probably in the West Indies, where he was sold at around age 14 to Joseph Vesey, captain of a slave ship. He purchased his freedom in 1800. In 1818 Vesey and others began to plot an uprising; he held secret meetings, collected disguises and firearms and chose a date in June 1822. But authorities were warned, and police and the military were out in full force. Over the next two months 130 blacks were taken into custody; 35, including Vesey, were hanged and 31 were exiled. As a result of the plot Southern legislatures passed more rigorous slave codes.

WESTMORELAND ARTS & HERITAGE FESTIVAL. July 2–5. Twin Lakes Park, Greensburg, PA. 35th annual festival celebrating more than three decades of arts and humanities. Multicultural celebration including food booths, children's area, crafts, fine art exhibition and continuous entertainment on five stages. Est attendance: 150,000. For info: WAHF, 252 Twin Lakes Rd, Latrobe, PA 15650. Phone: (724) 834-7474. E-mail: info@artsandheritage.com. Web: www.artsandheritage.com.

 BIRTHDAYS TODAY

José Canseco, Jr, 45, former baseball player, born Havana, Cuba, July 2, 1964.

Sean Casey, 35, baseball player, born Willingsboro, NJ, July 2, 1974.

Vicente Fox Quesada, 67, former president of Mexico, born Mexico City, July 2, 1942.

Polly Holliday, 72, actress ("Alice," "Home Improvement"), born Jasper, AL, July 2, 1937.

Lindsay Lohan, 23, actress (*Freaky Friday, Mean Girls*), born New York, NY, July 2, 1986.

Jimmy McNichol, 48, actor ("The Fitzpatricks," "California Fever"), born Los Angeles, CA, July 2, 1961.

Richard Petty, 72, race car driver, born Level Cross, NC, July 2, 1937.

Ron Silver, 63, actor, director (*Silkwood, Enemies: A Love Story*; stage: *Speed-the-Plow*), born New York, NY, July 2, 1946.

Ashley Tisdale, 24, actress, singer ("The Suite Life of Zach and Cody," *High School Musical*), born West Deal, NJ, July 2, 1985.

July 3 — Friday

DAY 184 — **181 REMAINING**

AIR CONDITIONING APPRECIATION DAYS. July 3–Aug 15. Northern Hemisphere. During Dog Days, the hottest time of the year in the Northern Hemisphere, to acknowledge the contribution of air conditioning to a better way of life. Annually, July 3–Aug 15. For info: Air-Conditioning and Refrig Institute, 4100 N Fairfax Dr, Ste 200, Arlington, VA 22203. Phone: (703) 524-8800. Fax: (703) 528-3816. E-mail: ari@ari.org. Web: www.ari.org.

BELARUS: INDEPENDENCE DAY. July 3. National holiday. Commemorates liberation of Minsk in 1944.

BENNETT, RICHARD BEDFORD: BIRTH ANNIVERSARY. July 3, 1870. Former Canadian prime minister, born at Hopewell Hill, NB. Died at Mickelham, England, June 26, 1947.

CANADA: ABBOTSFORD BERRY BEAT FESTIVAL. July 3–4. Abbotsford, BC. July heralds the height of the Raspberry Capital of Canada's berry season. Sample delicious local strawberry, raspberry and blueberry products. Linger to cheer the top musicians, magicians and clowns; play bingo or mini-golf. Enjoy the "berried" treasure hunt and sport and art activities. Browse through local craft and market-style food stands. Est attendance: 30,000. For info: Abbotsford Downtown Business Assn, 33728 Essendene Ave, Abbotsford, BC, Canada V2S 2G9. Phone: (604) 850-6547. Fax: (604) 859-6507. E-mail: adba@telus.net. Web: www.downtownabbotsford.com.

CANADA: CALGARY STAMPEDE. July 3–12. Calgary, AB. One of the world's largest rodeos, plus an agricultural fair, entertainment, parade and carnival. Annually since 1912. Est attendance: 1,218,000. For info: Calgary Exhibition and Stampede, 1410 Olympic Way SE, Calgary, AB, Canada T2P 2K8. Phone: (403) 261-0101. Web: www.calgarystampede.com.

COIN & STAMP EXPO. July 3–5. Elks Lodge, Pasadena, CA. Est attendance: 4,000. For info: Israel Bick, Exec Dir, Intl Stamp & Coin Collectors Society, Box 854, Van Nuys, CA 91408. Phone: (818) 997-6496. Fax: (818) 988-4337. E-mail: iibick@sbcglobal.net. Web: www.bick.net.

COMPLIMENT-YOUR-MIRROR DAY. July 3. Participation consists of complimenting your mirror on having such a wonderful owner and keeping track of whether other mirrors you meet during the day smile at you. For info: Bob Birch, Grand Punscorpion, Puns Corps, 3108 Dashiell Rd, Falls Church, VA 22042. Phone: (703) 533-3668.

DOG DAYS. July 3–Aug 11. Hottest days of the year in Northern Hemisphere. Usually about 40 days, but variously reckoned at 30–54 days. Popularly believed to be an evil time "when the sea boiled, wine turned sour, dogs grew mad, and all creatures became languid, causing to man burning fevers, hysterics and phrensies" (from Brady's *Clavis Calendarium*, 1813). Originally the days when Sirius, the Dog Star, rose just before or at about the same time as sunrise (no longer true owing to precession of the equinoxes). Ancients sacrificed a brown dog at the beginning of Dog Days to appease the rage of Sirius, believing that star was the cause of the hot, sultry weather.

EARTH AT APHELION. July 3. At approximately 10 PM, EDT, planet Earth will reach aphelion, that point in its orbit when it is farthest from the sun (about 94,510,000 miles). Earth's mean distance from the sun (mean radius of its orbit) is reached early in the months of April and October. Note that Earth is farthest from the sun during Northern Hemisphere summer. See also: "Earth at Perihelion" (Jan 4).

ENGLAND: CHELTENHAM MUSIC FESTIVAL. July 3–18. Cheltenham, Gloucestershire. The best of contemporary British music including symphony and chamber music, opera and late-night events. Est attendance: 30,000. For info: Miss Nia Clark, 109–111 Bath Rd, Cheltenham, Gloucestershire, England GL53 7LS. Phone: (44) (1242) 775-897. E-mail: music@cheltenham.gov.uk. Web: www.cheltenhamfestivals.co.uk.

ENNIS RODEO AND PARADE. July 3–4. Ennis, MT. Billed as the fastest two-day rodeo in Montana, this is a nonstop rodeo of excitement. Parade with clowns, bucking broncos and everything imaginable. Annually, July 3–4. Est attendance: 4,000. For info: Pat Hamilton, PR, Ennis Rodeo Club, PO Box 236, Ennis, MT 59729. Phone: (406) 682-4700.

FISHER, M.F.K.: BIRTH ANNIVERSARY. July 3, 1908. The prolific author Mary Frances Kennedy Fisher was born at Albion, MI. With the publication of her first book, *Serve It Forth* (1937), she essentially invented a new genre: essays about food. Her other titles include *The Gastronomical Me* (1943) and *With Bold Knife and Fork* (1969). Fisher died at Glen Ellen, CA, June 22, 1992.

July 2009	S	M	T	W	T	F	S
				1	2	3	4
	5	6	7	8	9	10	11
	12	13	14	15	16	17	18
	19	20	21	22	23	24	25
	26	27	28	29	30	31	

FOURTH OF JULY CELEBRATION. July 3–5. Hettinger, ND. Parade, free noon meal, events happening all week long and dances, food, booths and the largest fireworks display in SW North Dakota. Est attendance: 4,000. For info: Community Promotions Office, Box 1031, Hettinger, ND 58639. Phone: (701) 567-2531. Fax: (701) 567-2690. E-mail: adamschmbr@ndsupernet.com. Web: hettingernd.com.

HUNTINGTON, SAMUEL: BIRTH ANNIVERSARY. July 3, 1731. President of the Continental Congress, governor of Connecticut, signer of the Declaration of Independence, born at Windham, CT, and died at Norwich, CT, Jan 5, 1796.

IDAHO: ADMISSION DAY: ANNIVERSARY. July 3. Became 43rd state in 1890.

IRAN AIR FLIGHT 655 DISASTER: ANNIVERSARY. July 3, 1988. At 10:54 AM in the Persian Gulf, the US Navy warship *Vincennes* fired two surface-to-air missiles at Iran Air Flight 655, which destroyed the airbus, killing all 290 passengers aboard. The *Vincennes*, boasting the world's most sophisticated radar-detection equipment, reportedly misread radio signals of the airbus, mistaking it for a hostile F-14 fighter plane. A self-conducted military inquiry blamed human failure—stress on the tense crew rather than equipment malfunction—for the disaster. In the summer of 1992 the public learned that the ship had been in Iranian waters at the time in the course of an operation aimed at preventing Iranian boats from laying mines.

"MR PEEPERS" TV PREMIERE: ANNIVERSARY. July 3, 1952. This sitcom was broadcast live and focused on mild-mannered junior high school science teacher Robinson J. Peepers (Wally Cox). The cast also included Tony Randall, Georgann Johnson, Marion Lorne, Reta Shaw, Jack Warden and Ernest Truex. This half-hour series was a summer replacement, but it earned such positive reviews that it was brought back as a regular series. In 1954 *TV Guide* wrote that "'Mr Peepers' . . . comes close to being the perfect TV show."

MOUNT RUSHMORE INDEPENDENCE DAY CELEBRATION. July 3–4. Mount Rushmore National Memorial, SD. Fireworks July 3 and musical performances both days. Est attendance: 10,000. For info: Mount Rushmore Natl Memorial, 13000 Highway 244, Bldg 31, Ste 1, Keystone, SD 57751. Phone: (605) 574-2523. Fax: (605) 574-2307. Web: www.nps.gov/moru.

OLD-TIME FIDDLERS' JAMBOREE AND CRAFTS FESTIVAL. July 3–4. Smithville, TN. 32 categories of old-time bluegrass including clogging, buck dancing, old-time fiddle band, five-string banjo, dulcimer, dobro, flat-top guitar and fiddle-off to decide the Grand Champion Fiddler. Annually, the weekend nearest July 4. Est attendance: 135,000. For info: Smithville Fiddlers' Jamboree, PO Box 83, Smithville, TN 37166. Phone: (615) 597-8500. Web: www.dekalbtn.com or www.smithvillejamboree.com.

QUÉBEC FOUNDED: ANNIVERSARY. July 3, 1608. French explorer Samuel de Champlain founded a settlement called Québec, from the Algonquin word *kébec*, meaning "where the river narrows." Quebec City is thus one of the oldest settlements of European origin of North America.

RAID ON ENTEBBE: ANNIVERSARY. July 3, 1976. An Israeli commando unit staged a raid on the Entebbe airport in Uganda and rescued 103 hostages on a hijacked Air France airliner. Three of the hostages, seven hijackers and 20 Ugandan soldiers were killed in the raid. The plane had been en route from Tel Aviv to Paris when taken over by the pro-Palestinian guerrillas.

RED, WHITE & BOOM. July 3. Columbus, OH. Central Ohio's Independence Day celebration features one of the largest fireworks displays in the Midwest. Est attendance: 500,000. For info: Michael L. Collins, Exec Dir, Red, White & Boom, Inc, 929 Harrison Ave, Ste 303, Columbus, OH 43215. Phone: (614) 421-BOOM. Fax: (614) 291-9211. Web: www.redwhiteandboom.org.

STAY OUT OF THE SUN DAY. July 3. For health's sake, give your skin a break today. (©2006 by WH.) For info: Thomas & Ruth Roy, Wellcat Holidays, 2418 Long Ln, Lebanon, PA 17046. Phone: (717) 279-0184. E-mail: info@wellcat.com. Web: www.wellcat.com.

STOCK EXCHANGE HOLIDAY (INDEPENDENCE DAY). July 3 (observed). The holiday schedules for the various exchanges are subject to change if relevant rules, regulations or exchange policies are revised. If you have questions, contact: American Stock Exchange (866) 422-2639 (www.amex.com), Chicago Board of Trade (312) 435-3500 (www.cbot.com), Chicago Board Options Exchange (312) 786-5600 (www.cboe.com), NASDAQ Stock Market (646) 441-5200 (www.nasdaq.com), New York Stock Exchange (212) 656-3000 (www.nyse.com), Philadelphia Stock Exchange (800) THE-PHLX (www.phlx.com).

TEN THOUSAND CRESTONIANS. July 3–5. Downtown and McKinley Park, Creston, IA. Parade, fireworks, flea market, talent show, historical village, carnival and food. All to celebrate US founding. Est attendance: 10,000. For info: Creston Chamber of Commerce, PO Box 471, Creston, IA 50801. Phone: (641) 782-7021. E-mail: chamber@crestoniowachamber.com. Web: www.crestoniowachamber.com.

US VIRGIN ISLANDS: DANISH WEST INDIES EMANCIPATION DAY: ANNIVERSARY. July 3, 1848. Commemorates freeing of slaves in the Danish West Indies. Ceremony at Frederiksted, St. Croix, where actual proclamation was first read by Governor-General Peter Von Scholten.

VICKSBURG SURRENDERS: ANNIVERSARY. July 3, 1863. After weeks of immediate siege at the end of a yearlong campaign, Vicksburg, MS, surrendered to General Ulysses S. Grant. Formal surrender was consummated on July 4, and on July 8 the besieged city of Port Hudson also surrendered, giving the Union complete control of the Mississippi River. This cut off the western Confederacy from the rest of the South.

WASHINGTON TAKES COMMAND OF THE CONTINENTAL ARMY: ANNIVERSARY. July 3, 1775. George Washington took command of the Continental Army at Cambridge, MA.

BIRTHDAYS TODAY

Moises Alou, 43, baseball player, born Atlanta, GA, July 3, 1966.

Dave Barry, 62, humorist, author, born Brooklyn, NY, July 3, 1947.

Betty Buckley, 62, actress (*Cats, Sunset Boulevard*, "Eight Is Enough"), born Fort Worth, TX, July 3, 1947.

Tom Cruise, 47, actor (*Mission: Impossible* films, *Collateral, Jerry Maguire, Top Gun*), born Thomas Cruise Mapother IV, Syracuse, NY, July 3, 1962.

Pete Fountain, 79, jazz musician, born New Orleans, LA, July 3, 1930.

Thomas Gibson, 47, actor ("Criminal Minds," "Dharma & Greg"), born Charleston, SC, July 3, 1962.

Teemu Selanne, 39, hockey player, born Helsinki, Finland, July 3, 1970.

Kurtwood Smith, 67, actor ("That '70s Show," *Robocop*), born New Lisbon, WI, July 3, 1942.

Tom Stoppard, 72, playwright, screenwriter (Tony for *The Coast of Utopia; The Real Thing, Travesties, Rosencrantz and Guildenstern Are Dead*; Oscar for *Shakespeare in Love*), born Zlin, Czechoslovakia, July 3, 1937.

Montel Williams, 53, talk-show host ("The Montel Williams Show"), born Baltimore, MD, July 3, 1956.

July 4 — Saturday

DAY 185 — **180 REMAINING**

ADAMS, JOHN, AND JEFFERSON, THOMAS: DEATH ANNIVERSARY. July 4, 1826. Former US presidents John Adams and Thomas Jefferson died on the same day, July 4, 1826, the 50th anniversary of adoption of the Declaration of Independence. Adams had once written to Jefferson (1813): "You and I ought not to die before we have explained ourselves to each other." They thus began a spirited correspondence until their deaths. Adams's last words: "Thomas Jefferson still survives." Jefferson's last words: "This is the Fourth?"

"AMERICA THE BEAUTIFUL" PUBLISHED: ANNIVERSARY. July 4, 1895. The poem "America the Beautiful" by Katherine Lee Bates, a Wellesley College professor, was first published in the *Congregationalist*, a church publication.

"AMERICAN TOP 40" RADIO PREMIERE: ANNIVERSARY. July 4, 1970. Casey Kasem's hit-parade music countdown radio program, "American Top 40," was first broadcast on seven AM stations in the US on July 4, 1970. It is now heard in hundreds of markets around the world. For info: Pete Battistini, 6576 Lake Forest Dr, Avon, IN 46123. Phone: (317) 839-1421. E-mail: at40@aol.com. Web: www.at40book.com.

ANVIL MOUNTAIN RUN. July 4. Nome, AK. 31st annual running. At 8 AM the 17k run up 1,134-foot Anvil Mountain and return to the City of Nome starts the day's activities. Record time: 1 hour, 11 minutes, 23 seconds. Annually, July 4. Est attendance: 1,500. For info: Rasmussen's Music Mart, PO Box 2, Nome, AK 99762-0002. Phone: (907) 443-2798 or (907) 443-6022. Fax: (907) 443-5777.

ART ARMADA. July 4. Rotary Riverview Park, Sheboygan, WI. The most spectacular and hilarious races of somewhat seaworthy craft ever launched in Wisconsin. Person-powered one-of-a-kind boats compete in various classes for prizes. Awards for the most spirited team, the most beautiful boats, boats following a theme and the most spectacular sinking. Prizes for top finishers. Est attendance: 16,000. For info: John Michael Kohler Arts Center, 608 New York Ave, Sheboygan, WI 53081. Phone: (920) 458-6144. Fax: (920) 458-4473. Web: www.jmkac.org.

BOOM BOX PARADE. July 4. Willimantic, CT. Connecticut's unique people's parade. Anyone can march, enter a float or watch; only requirement—bring a radio. No "real" bands allowed. (Marching music broadcast on WILI-AM radio and played by "boom boxes" along the parade route.) 11 AM. Est attendance: 10,000. For info: Grand Marshall Wayne Norman, WILI-AM, 720 Main St, Willimantic, CT 06226. Phone: (860) 456-1111. Fax: (860) 456-9501. E-mail: wayne@wili.com. Web: www.wili.com/am.

BRISTOL CIVIC, MILITARY AND FIREMEN'S PARADE. July 4. Bristol, RI. The nation's oldest Fourth of July parade. Features floats, bands, veteran and patriotic organizations and military units. Patriotic exercises, a tradition dating to 1785, are held prior to the parade. Annually, July 4 except when July 4 is a Sunday, then the parade is held Monday, July 5. Est attendance: 175,000. For info: East Bay Chamber of Commerce, PO Box 588, Warren, RI 02885. Phone: (401) 245-0750. Fax: (401) 245-0110. Web: www.eastbayritourism.com or www.july4thbristolri.com.

CALITHUMPIAN PARADE. July 4. Biwabik, MN. Funny parade, clowns and bands; Biwabik's population of 1,000 jumps to more than 15,000 for a day. Annually, on the Fourth of July. Est attendance: 15,000. For info: 4th of July, Biwabik Area Civic Assn, Box 449, Biwabik, MN 55708. Phone: (218) 865-4183.

COKE ZERO 400 NASCAR SPRINT CUP SERIES RACE. July 4. Daytona International Speedway, Daytona Beach, FL. 51st running. Drivers battle for Independence Day glory under the lights. For info: Daytona International Speedway, PO Box 28014, Daytona Beach, FL 32120-2801. Phone: (800) PIT-SHOP. Web: www.daytonainternationalspeedway.com.

COOLIDGE, CALVIN: BIRTH ANNIVERSARY. July 4, 1872. The 30th president of the US was born John Calvin Coolidge at Plymouth, VT. He succeeded to the presidency Aug 3, 1923, following the death of Warren G. Harding. Coolidge was elected president once, in 1924, but did "not choose to run for president in 1928." Nicknamed Silent Cal, he is reported to have said, "If you don't say anything, you won't be called on to repeat it." Coolidge died at Northampton, MA, Jan 5, 1933.

THE DAM EXPERIENCE. July 4. Truman Dam, Warsaw, MO. Gigantic fireworks display viewed from land and boat. Est attendance: 15,000. For info: Warsaw Area Chamber of Commerce, PO Box 264, Warsaw, MO 65355. Phone: (800) WARSAW-4. E-mail: warsawcc@embarqmail.com. Web: www.warsawmo.org.

DECLARATION OF INDEPENDENCE APPROVAL AND SIGNING: ANNIVERSARY. July 4, 1776. The Declaration of Independence was approved by the Continental Congress: "Signed by Order and in Behalf of the Congress, John Hancock, President, Attest, Charles Thomson, Secretary." The official signing occurred Aug 2, 1776. The manuscript journals of the Congress for that date state: "The declaration of independence being engrossed and compared at the table was signed by the members."

FIRESTORM. July 4. Lakemont Park, Altoona, PA. The region's largest Fourth of July celebration with live entertainment on stage all day and a spectacular fireworks show. Est attendance: 20,000. For info: Lakemont Park, 700 Park Ave, Altoona, PA 16602. Phone: (814) 949-7275 or (800) 434-8006. Fax: (814) 949-9207. E-mail: lakemontparkfun@hotmail.com. Web: www.lakemontparkfun.com.

FIREWORKS CELEBRATION. July 4. Demopolis, AL. Each year the Demopolis Area Chamber of Commerce presents a spectacular array of fireworks in celebration of Independence Day. The fireworks celebration is held at the Demopolis City Landing and begins at 9 PM. Event also includes a children's patriotic parade. Est attendance: 10,000. For info: Kelley Smith, Demopolis Area Chamber of Commerce, Box 667, Demopolis, AL 36732. Phone: (334) 289-0270. Fax: (334) 289-1382. E-mail: dacc@westal.net. Web: www.demopolischamber.com.

FOSTER, STEPHEN: BIRTH ANNIVERSARY. July 4, 1826. Stephen Collins Foster, one of America's most famous and best-loved songwriters, was born at Lawrenceville, PA. Among his nearly 200 songs: "Oh! Susanna," "Camptown Races," "Old Folks at Home" ("Swanee River"), "Jeanie with the Light Brown Hair," "Old Black Joe" and "Beautiful Dreamer." Foster died in poverty at Bellevue Hospital at New York, NY, Jan 13, 1864.

FOURTH OF JULY PATRIOTIC CONCERT AND FIREWORKS. July 4. Aurora, IL. Annual patriotic concert and fireworks display. Concert begins at 8 PM and fireworks display begins at dusk. For info: City of Aurora, Mayor's Office of Special Events, 5 E Downer Pl, Ste A, Aurora, IL 60505. Phone: (630) 844-4731. Fax: (630) 844-4797.

FOURTH OF JULY SPECTACULAR. July 4. Aurora Municipal Center, Aurora, CO. In addition to having the largest fireworks display in the metro area, Aurora's Fourth of July Spectacular includes performances by the Aurora symphony, other live, interactive entertainment, food and festivities. Annually, the Fourth of July. Est attendance: 3,000. For info: Marie Addleman, City of Aurora, 1298 Peoria St, Aurora, CO 80011. Phone: (303) 326-8615. Fax: (303) 361-2954. Web: www.auroragov.org/events.

FRANCE: TOUR DE FRANCE. July 4–26. One of the great sporting events in the world. Cycling's best compete for more than 3,500 kilometers in 21 stages in the country of France. Stages are flat-terrain races, mountain races and time trials. For 2009, the Grand Dèpart will take place in Monaco, and, like every year from the beginning in 1903, the last stage will arrive in Paris at Champs Elysees. Est attendance: 5,000,000. For info: Amaury Sport Organisation, 2 rue Rouget de Lisle, 92137 Issy-les-Moulineaux cedex, France. Web: www.letour.fr.

FREEDOM FEST. July 4 (rain date July 5). Lake of the Woods, Mahomet, IL. Annual celebration of patriotism. Family activities capped off by a spectacular fireworks display. Admission charged. Est attendance: 5,000. For info: Champaign County Forest Preserve District, PO Box 1040, Mahomet, IL 61853. Phone: (217) 586-3360. Fax: (217) 586-5724. E-mail: hq@ccfpd.org. Web: www.ccfpd.org.

GOLDBERG, RUBE: BIRTH ANNIVERSARY. July 4, 1883. The cartoonist with an engineering degree who put his education to work inventing elaborate machines with involved steps to accomplish ludicrously simple tasks. He is best remembered for the creative inventions of his cartoon character Lucifer Gorgonzola Butts. Born at San Francisco, CA, Goldberg died Dec 7, 1970, at New York City.

GREAT SEAL OF THE US PROPOSED: ANNIVERSARY. July 4, 1776. The Continental Congress, meeting at Philadelphia, PA, after voting to adopt the Declaration of Independence, went on to approve the following: "Resolved, that Dr. Franklin, Mr J. Adams and Mr Jefferson, be a committee, to bring in a device for a seal for the United States of America," thus beginning the history of the Great Seal of the US on the first day of independence. The seal wasn't designed and used until 1782.

HAWTHORNE, NATHANIEL: BIRTH ANNIVERSARY. July 4, 1804. Novelist and short-story writer, born at Salem, MA. Works include *The Scarlet Letter*, *The House of the Seven Gables* and *The Blithedale Romance*. Hawthorne died at Plymouth, NH, May 19, 1864.

HOMETOWN FAMILY FOURTH. July 4. Hollywood, FL. Family event featuring evening popular music at the Hollywood Beach Theatre and a spectacular fireworks display offshore Hollywood Beach. Est attendance: 100,000. For info: Marketing, City of Hollywood, Dept of Parks, Recreation & Cultural Arts, 1405 S 28th Ave, Hollywood, FL 33020. Phone: (954) 921-3404.

ICE CREAM SOCIAL. July 4. Indianapolis, IN. Independence Day celebration. Music, lawn games and living history. Est attendance: 500. For info: President Benjamin Harrison Home, PR Dept, 1230 N Delaware St, Indianapolis, IN 46202. Phone: (317) 631-1888. Fax: (317) 632-5488. E-mail: harrison@presidentbenjaminharrison.org. Web: www.pbhh.org.

INDEPENDENCE DAY CELEBRATION. July 4. Mystic Seaport, Mystic, CT. Visitors can participate in a re-creation of an 1870s Fourth of July with costumed staff. There are patriotic ceremonies and a parade of the "Antiques and Horribles." Kids' old-fashioned spelling bee. Est attendance: 3,500. For info: Mystic Seaport, 75 Greenmanville Ave, Box 6000, Mystic, CT 06355. Phone: (860) 572-5315 or (888) 973-2767. Web: www.mysticseaport.org.

INDEPENDENCE DAY: THE FOURTH OF JULY. July 4, 1776. The US commemorates adoption of the Declaration of Independence by the Continental Congress. The nation's birthday. Legal holiday in all states and territories.

July 2009

S	M	T	W	T	F	S
			1	2	3	4
5	6	7	8	9	10	11
12	13	14	15	16	17	18
19	20	21	22	23	24	25
26	27	28	29	30	31	

INDEPENDENCE-FROM-MEAT DAY. July 4. Don't be a slave to tradition. Declare your freedom from flesh foods. Your fiery Fourth will be fantastic with a good-for-you vegetarian barbecue. Why not fix a freedom feast featuring veggie burgers and veggie dogs for your family and friends? It will be fun for you and your animal friends too! For info: Vegetarian Awareness Network, PO Box 3545, Washington, DC 20027-0045. Phone: (800) USA-VEGE.

INDIVISIBLE DAY. July 4. This holiday recognizes the necessity for the separation of church and state. For info: Matt Cherry, Institute for Humanist Studies, 48 Howard St, Albany, NY 12207. Phone: (518) 432-7820. Fax: (518) 432-7821. E-mail: MCherry@HumanistStudies.org. Web: HumanistStudies.org or www.secularseasons.org.

INTERNATIONAL CHERRY PIT SPITTING CHAMPIONSHIP. July 4. Tree-Mendus Fruit Farm, Eau Claire, MI. 36th annual. A nutritious sport—is there a better way to dispose of the pits once you have eaten the cherry? Entrants eat a cherry and then spit the pit as far as possible on a blacktop surface. The entrant who spits the pit the farthest including the roll is the champ. Annually, the first Saturday in July. Est attendance: 300. For info: Herb Teichman, Adv and Promo Mgr, Tree-Mendus Fruit Farm, 9351 E Eureka Rd, Eau Claire, MI 49111. Phone: (269) 782-7101. Fax: (269) 461-4187. E-mail: treemendus@qtm.net. Web: www.treemendus-fruit.com.

JULY FOURTH CELEBRATION AND ANVIL SHOOT. July 4. Museum of Appalacia, Clinton, TN. An old-fashioned celebration highlighted by the "shooting" of an anvil on July 4; also musicians and demonstrations of old-time activities such as sassafras tea brewing, spinning, sheep herding, rail splitting and more! For info: Elaine Meyer, Museum of Appalachia, 2819 Andersonville Hwy, Clinton, TN 37716. Phone: (865) 494-7680. E-mail: museum@museumofappalachia.org. Web: www.museumofappalachia.org.

JULY FOURTH FAMILY CELEBRATION. July 4. Fort Lauderdale, FL. Featuring live music, fireworks and food. Annually, July 4. For info: City of Fort Lauderdale. Phone: (954) 828-5363. Web: www.sunny.org.

KOKO THE GORILLA: BIRTHDAY. July 4, 1971. Koko, a lowland gorilla (full name: Hanabi-Ko, or "Fireworks Child" in Japanese), was born this day at the San Francisco Zoo. She is probably the most famous gorilla in the world due to her participation in the longest continuous experiment to teach language to animals. She was taught sign language beginning when she was about a year old, and she currently has a vocabulary of 1,000 signs.

LANDERS, ANN: BIRTH ANNIVERSARY. July 4, 1918. Born Esther Pauline Friedman at Sioux City, IA, the advice columnist was beloved worldwide. In 1955 she won a contest to be the new "Ann Landers" columnist for the *Chicago Sun-Times*. For 47 years, with spunky yet compassionate replies that were a refreshing change from prior columnists' styles, she helped everyday people overcome their problems. A trademark admonishment was "40 lashes with a wet noodle." (Her twin sister, Pauline Friedman, followed in her footsteps with a "Dear Abby" column.) By 2002 her column was carried in more than 1,200 newspapers worldwide and had a readership of 30 million. She died June 22, 2002, at Chicago, IL.

LEXINGTON'S FOURTH OF JULY BALLOON RALLY. July 4. Virginia Military Institute, Lexington, VA. Enjoy craft and food vendors, live entertainment, balloon glows, tethered balloon rides and actual balloon flights! Annually, July 4. For info: Sunrise Rotary Club, PO Box 63, Lexington, VA 24450. Phone: (877) 453-9822. E-mail: info@sunriserotarylexva.org. Web: www.sunriserotarylexva.org/balloon.htm.

LIBERTY CELEBRATION. July 4–5. Yorktown Victory Center, Yorktown, VA. Salute America by joining in military drills and learning about the sacrifices of our nation's founders, including those who signed the Declaration of Independence. For info: Jamestown-Yorktown Foundation, PO Box 1607, Williamsburg, VA 23187. Phone: (757) 253-4838 or (888) 593-4682. Fax: (757) 253-5299. Web: www.historyisfun.org.

MACKINAW CITY'S FOURTH OF JULY FIREWORKS. July 4. State Dock on South Huron Ave, Mackinaw City, MI. Starting at 1:30 PM on the marina lawn, there will be fun and games for all ages. One of the largest fireworks displays in the North will be shot off over the harbor at dusk. For info: Mackinaw City Chamber of Commerce, PO Box 856, Mackinaw City, MI 49701. Phone: (231) 436-5574 or (888) 455-8100. Web: www.mackinawchamber.com.

OLD VERMONT FOURTH. July 4. Woodstock, VT. A traditional Fourth of July with patriotic speeches and debates, making "1890" flags, a spelling bee for adults, ice cream making, sack race and more. Est attendance: 750. For info: Billings Farm and Museum, Rte 12 N, Woodstock, VT 05091. Phone: (802) 457-2355. Fax: (802) 457-4663. E-mail: info@billingsfarm.org. Web: www.billingsfarm.org.

PEACHTREE ROAD RACE. July 4. Atlanta, GA. 40th annual. The largest 10k run in the world. 55,000-runner limit; advance registration only. Send SASE by Mar 1, 2009. 45,000 entrants on first-come basis and 10,000 selected by lottery from other entries postmarked in March 2009. Est attendance: 150,000. For info: Atlanta Track Club, 3097 E Shadowlawn Ave, Atlanta, GA 30305. Phone: (404) 231-9064, ext 10. E-mail: atc@atlantatrackclub.org. Web: www.atlantatrackclub.org.

PHILIPPINES: FIL-AMERICAN FRIENDSHIP DAY. July 4. Formerly National Independence Day, when the Philippines were a colony of the US, now celebrated as Fil-American Friendship Day.

RED WINE AND BLUES FESTIVAL. July 4. Tuckerton, NJ. Team up with the Tuckerton Seaport for a perfect afternoon of wine tasting from New Jersey's finest wineries plus live blues entertainment, food, crafts and more. For info: Renee Kennedy, Tuckerton Seaport, 120 W Main St, PO Box 52, Tuckerton, NJ 08087. Phone: (609) 296-8868. Fax: (609) 296-5810. E-mail: info@tuckertonseaport.org. Web: www.tuckertonseaport.org.

"THE SOUPY SALES SHOW" TV PREMIERE: ANNIVERSARY. July 4, 1955. Soupy Sales hosted a number of national and local children's shows from 1955 to 1979. All of his programs included some of these features: jokes, puns, songs, sketches, puppets, silent films and pies in the face. Sales's humor occasionally went over the edge and got him in trouble; for example, in 1965 his show was suspended for a week because he asked his viewers to send him the green paper in their parents' wallets!

SPACE MILESTONE: *DEEP IMPACT* SMASHES INTO TEMPEL 1 (US). July 4, 2005. After a six-month journey and 83 million miles, the *Deep Impact* spacecraft smashed—as planned—into the comet Tempel 1. The purpose of the 820-pound, barrel-shaped craft's mission is to give scientists more information about comets.

SPACE MILESTONE: *MARS PATHFINDER* (US). July 4, 1997. Unmanned spacecraft landed on Mars after a seven-month flight. Carried *Sojourner*, a roving robotic explorer that sent back photographs of the landscape. One of its missions was to find if life ever existed on Mars. See also: "Space Milestone: *Mars Global Surveyor*" (Sept 11).

SPIRIT OF FREEDOM CELEBRATION. July 4. Florence, AL. Celebrate America's birthday on the banks of the beautiful Tennessee River at McFarland Park. Enjoy sunning, swimming, bicycling, golf and live music. Playground, picnic tables and campground available. Annually, on July 4. Est attendance: 60,000. For info: Florence/Lauderdale Tourism, One Hightower Pl, Florence, AL 35630. Phone: (256) 740-4141 or (888) FLO-TOUR. Fax: (256) 740-4142. E-mail: Debbie@VisitFlorenceAl.com. Web: www.VisitFlorenceAl.com.

TRADITIONAL SOUSA CONCERT. July 4. The American Club, Kohler, WI. Celebrate Independence Day on a great American note with a rousing Sousa concert performed by the award-winning Kiel

Municipal Band. This old-fashioned open-air social recalls the 1919 and 1925 Sousa concerts in Kohler's Ravine Park. Est attendance: 1,000. For info: The American Club, Highland Dr, Kohler, WI 53044. Phone: (800) 344-2838. Web: www.DestinationKohler.com.

TUSKEGEE INSTITUTE OPENING: ANNIVERSARY. July 4, 1881. Booker T. Washington's famed agricultural-industrial institution was built from the ground up by dedicated students seeking academic and vocational training. The institute started in a shanty before Washington purchased an abandoned plantation at Tuskegee, AL. The students built the dormitories, classrooms and chapel from bricks out of their own kiln.

UNITED NATIONS: INTERNATIONAL DAY OF COOPERATIVES. July 4. On Dec 16, 1992, the General Assembly proclaimed this observance for the first Saturday of July 1995 (Res 47/60). On Dec 23, 1994, recognizing that cooperatives were becoming an indispensable factor of economic and social development, the Assembly invited governments, international organizations, specialized agencies and national and international cooperative organizations to observe this day annually (Res 49/155). For info: United Nations, Dept of Public Info, New York, NY 10017. Web: www.un.org.

WORLD'S GREATEST LIZARD RACE. July 4. Chaparral Park, Lovington, NM. Participants and observers cheer as their lizards and iguanas race down a 16-ft ramp; winners are awarded trophies. Many other lizard events will be held throughout the day. Entertainment and other games are also featured. For info: Lovington Chamber of Commerce, 201 S Main St, Lovington, NM 88260. Phone: (505) 396-5311. Fax: (505) 396-2823. E-mail: jjohnson@lovingtoncoc.org. Web: www.lovingtoncoc.org.

BIRTHDAYS TODAY

Signy Coleman, 49, actress ("The Young and the Restless"), born Bolinas, CA, July 4, 1960.

Allen (Al) Davis, 80, Hall of Fame football player, executive, born Brockton, MA, July 4, 1929.

Horace Grant, 44, former basketball player, born Augusta, GA, July 4, 1965.

Gina Lollobrigida, 81, actress (*Belles de Nuit; Bread, Love and Dreams*), born Auviaco, Italy, July 4, 1928.

Becki Newton, 31, actress ("Ugly Betty"), born New Haven, CT, July 4, 1978.

Geraldo Rivera, 66, journalist, talk-show host ("Geraldo," *Exposing Myself*), born New York, NY, July 4, 1943.

Eva Marie Saint, 85, actress (Oscar for *On the Waterfront; North by Northwest, Exodus*), born Newark, NJ, July 4, 1924.

Pamela Howard (Pam) Shriver, 47, broadcaster and former tennis player, born Baltimore, MD, July 4, 1962.

Neil Simon, 82, playwright (*The Odd Couple, Barefoot in the Park*), born New York, NY, July 4, 1927.

George Michael Steinbrenner III, 79, baseball executive, born Rocky River, OH, July 4, 1930.

Abigail Van Buren, 91, advice columnist, born Pauline Esther Friedman at Sioux City, IA, July 4, 1918.

July 2009

S	M	T	W	T	F	S
			1	2	3	4
5	6	7	8	9	10	11
12	13	14	15	16	17	18
19	20	21	22	23	24	25
26	27	28	29	30	31	

July 5 — Sunday

DAY 186 **179 REMAINING**

ALGERIA: INDEPENDENCE DAY. July 5. National holiday. Commemorates the day in 1962 when Algeria gained independence from France.

BARNUM, PHINEAS TAYLOR: BIRTH ANNIVERSARY. July 5, 1810. Promoter of the bizarre and unusual. Barnum's American Museum opened in 1842, promoting unusual acts including the Feejee Mermaid, Chang and Eng (the original Siamese twins) and General Tom Thumb. In 1850 he began his promotion of Jenny Lind, "The Swedish Nightingale," and parlayed her singing talents into a major financial success. Barnum also cultivated a keen interest in politics. A founder of the newspaper *Herald of Freedom*, he wrote outspoken editorials that resulted not only in lawsuits but also in at least one jail sentence. In 1852 he declined the Democratic nomination for governor of Connecticut but did serve two terms in the Connecticut legislature beginning in 1865. He was defeated in a bid for US Congress in 1866 but served as mayor of Bridgeport, CT, from 1875 to 1876. In 1871 "The Greatest Show on Earth" opened at Brooklyn, NY; Barnum merged with his rival J.A. Bailey in 1881 to form the Barnum and Bailey Circus. P.T. Barnum was born at Bethel, CT, and died at Bridgeport, CT, Apr 7, 1891.

BE NICE TO NEW JERSEY WEEK. July 5–11. A time to recognize the assets of the state most maligned by American comedians. Annually, the first full week of July. For info: Lauren Barnett, Lone Star Publications of Humor, 8452 Fredericksburg Rd, PMB 103, San Antonio, TX 78229. E-mail: lspubs@aol.com. Web: members .aol.com/lspubs/lsindex.html.

BIKINI DEBUT: ANNIVERSARY. July 5, 1946. The skimpy two-piece bathing suit created by Louis Reard debuted at a fashion show in Paris. It was named after an atoll in the Pacific where the hydrogen bomb was first tested.

CALLAS'S LAST PERFORMANCE: ANNIVERSARY. July 5, 1965. Opera's preeminent soprano, Maria Callas, appeared on the operatic stage for the last time as Tosca at the Royal Opera House at Covent Garden, London. Months of health problems had forced Callas to cancel all but one scheduled performance in London—which was a charity gala with the royal family in attendance—and it turned out to be her last. Marshallng her strength, Callas delivered a performance that thrilled the audience, who asked for close to 15 curtain calls at the opera's conclusion.

CAPE VERDE: NATIONAL DAY. July 5. Public holiday. Commemorates independence from Portugal in 1975.

DUCKTONA 500. July 5. River Park, Sheboygan Falls, WI. Plastic duck race in the park river, dunk tank, car show, craft show, live music, games for children, pancake breakfast, burgers, brats, beverages. Annually, the first Sunday in July. Est attendance: 5,000. For info: Shirl Breunig, Program Coordinator, Sheboygan Falls Chamber Main St Office, 504 Broadway, Sheboygan Falls, WI 53085. Phone: (920) 467-6206. Fax: (920) 467-9571.

FARRAGUT, DAVID: BIRTH ANNIVERSARY. July 5, 1801. Born near Knoxville, TN, and died Aug 14, 1870, at Portsmouth, NH. Admiral in the American Civil War who was famous for his naval victories. At Mobile Bay, AL, in a disastrous attack on his entire fleet by the Confederates' Fort Morgan, Farragut proclaimed the famous cry, "Damn the torpedoes—full speed ahead!" They escaped the attack, and Mobile Bay surrendered.

LAVALLETTE INDEPENDENCE EXTRAVAGANZA WEEKEND. July 5. (Rain date is July 12.) Lavallette, NJ. 45-piece orchestra plays patriotic music during an outstanding fireworks display on the bay. Very suitable for boaters to watch from the water. Est attendance: 30,000. For info: Lavallette Heritage Committee, Inc, Ocean County Public Affairs, PO Box 2191, Toms River, NJ 08754. Phone: (732) 793-3652. Fax: (732) 793-1937. E-mail: zaccaria@optonline.net.

NATIONAL LABOR RELATIONS ACT (THE WAGNER ACT): ANNIVERSARY. July 5, 1935. This bill guaranteed workers the right to organize and bargain collectively with their employers. It also prohibited the formation of company unions. An enforcement agency, the National Labor Relations Board, was created by the Act.

RAFFLES, STAMFORD: BIRTH ANNIVERSARY. July 5, 1781. Sir Stamford Raffles, English colonial official, founder of Singapore, where he is supposed to have landed Jan 29, 1819, was born at sea, off Jamaica. He discovered with Joseph Arnold an East Indian fungus that is named after them, *Rafflesia Arnoldi*. Raffles died near London, England, on his birthday, July 5, 1826.

RHODES, CECIL JOHN: BIRTH ANNIVERSARY. July 5, 1853. English-born, South African millionaire politician. Said to have controlled at one time 90 percent of the world's diamond production. His will founded the Rhodes Scholarships at Oxford University for superior scholastic achievers. Rhodesia (now Zimbabwe) was named for him. Born at Bishop's Stortford, Hertfordshire, Rhodes died Mar 26, 1902, at Cape Town, South Africa.

SLOVAKIA: SAINT CYRIL AND METHODIUS DAY. July 5. This day is dedicated to the Greek priests and scholars from Thessaloniki, who were invited by Prince Rastislav of Great Moravia to introduce Christianity and the first Slavic alphabet to the pagan people of the kingdom in AD 863.

SPORTS CLICHÉ WEEK. July 5–11. This week honors the use of sports clichés by fans, athletes, sports announcers and sportswriters. Annually, the week of the Major League Baseball All-Star Game. For info: Don Powell, PhD (Dr. Cliché), 30445 Northwestern Hwy, Ste 350, Farmington Hills, MI 48334. Phone: (248) 539-1800. Fax: (248) 539-1808. E-mail: info@bestsportscliches.com. Web: www.bestsportscliches.com.

VENEZUELA: INDEPENDENCE DAY. July 5. National holiday. Commemorates Proclamation of Independence from Spain in 1811. Independence was not achieved until 1821.

ZETKIN, CLARA: BIRTH ANNIVERSARY. July 5, 1857. Women's rights advocate, born at Wiederau, Germany. Zetkin has been credited with being the initiator of International Women's Day, which has been observed on Mar 8 at least since 1910. She died at Arkhangelskoe, Russia, June 20, 1933. See also: "International (Working) Women's Day" (Mar 8).

BIRTHDAYS TODAY

Edie Falco, 46, actress ("The Sopranos"), born Brooklyn, NY, July 5, 1963.

Eliot Feld, 67, dancer, born Brooklyn, NY, July 5, 1942.

Richard Michael "Goose" Gossage, 58, Hall of Fame baseball player, born Colorado Springs, CO, July 5, 1951.

Chris Gratton, 34, hockey player, born Brantford, ON, Canada, July 5, 1975.

Katherine Helmond, 75, actress (stage: *The House of Blue Leaves*; "Soap," "Who's the Boss?"), born Galveston, TX, July 5, 1934.

Shirley Knight, 73, stage and screen actress (Tony for *Kennedy's Children*; *Sweet Bird of Youth, Petulia*), born Goessel, KS, July 5, 1936.

Huey Lewis, 59, singer (Huey Lewis and the News), born Hugh Anthony Cregg III at New York, NY, July 5, 1950.

James David Lofton, 53, former football player, born Fort Ord, CA, July 5, 1956.

Amélie Mauresmo, 30, tennis player, born Saint-Germain-en-Laye, France, July 5, 1979.

Robbie Robertson, 65, musician (guitarist with The Band), born Toronto, ON, Canada, July 5, 1944.

Janos Starker, 85, musician, born Budapest, Hungary, July 5, 1924.

Roger Wicker, 58, US Senator (R, Mississippi), born Pontotoc, MS, July 5, 1951.

July 6 — Monday

DAY 187 — **178 REMAINING**

BUSH, GEORGE W.: BIRTHDAY. July 6, 1946. 43rd president of the US (2001–). Born at New Haven, CT.

CANADA: KIMBERLEY INTERNATIONAL OLD-TIME ACCORDION CHAMPIONSHIPS. July 6–11. Kimberley, BC. World's old-time accordion competitions. Jam session, accordion and dance workshops, family dances, top-notch evening entertainment, pancake breakfasts, BBQ. Est attendance: 15,000. For info: Jean Irvin, PO Box 473, Kimberley, BC, Canada V1A 3B9. Phone: (888) 4-KIO-TAC. E-mail: info@kiotac.ca. Web: www.kiotac.ca.

CAPE MAY KIDS PLAYHOUSE. July 6–Aug 10. Cape May Convention Hall, Cape May, NJ. Welcoming kids and their families as jugglers, magicians, puppeteers, clowns and many others perform throughout the summer. At 10 AM and 7 PM on Mondays and Thursdays. Est attendance: 3,000. For info: Mid-Atlantic Center for the Arts, 1048 Washington St, Cape May, NJ 08204. Phone: (800) 275-4278. Fax: (609) 884-0574. E-mail: mac4arts@capemaymac.org. Web: www.capemaymac.org.

CARIBBEAN OR CARICOM DAY. July 6. The anniversary of the treaty establishing the Caribbean Community (also called the Treaty of Chaguaramas), signed by the prime ministers of Barbados, Guyana, Jamaica and Trinidad and Tobago July 4, 1973. Observed as a public holiday in Guyana and St. Vincent. Annually, the first Monday in July.

COMOROS: INDEPENDENCE DAY. July 6. Federal and Islamic Republic of Comoros commemorates declaration of independence from France in 1975.

CZECH REPUBLIC: COMMEMORATION DAY OF BURNING OF JOHN HUS. July 6. National holiday. In honor of Bohemian religious reformer John Hus, who was condemned as a heretic and burned at the stake July 6, 1415.

FIRST AIRSHIP CROSSING OF ATLANTIC: 90th ANNIVERSARY. July 6, 1919. The first airship crossing of the Atlantic was completed as a British dirigible landed at New York's Roosevelt Field.

FIRST BLACK US STATE'S ATTORNEY: ANNIVERSARY. July 6, 1961. Cecil Francis Poole became the first black US state's attorney when he was sworn in as US attorney for the Northern District of California. He served until his retirement on Feb 3, 1970.

FIRST SUCCESSFUL ANTIRABIES INOCULATION: ANNIVERSARY. July 6, 1885. Louis Pasteur gave the first successful antirabies inoculation to a boy who had been bitten by an infected dog.

GRIFFIN, MERV: BIRTH ANNIVERSARY. July 6, 1925. Born at San Mateo, CA, Mervyn Edward Griffin, Jr, began his career as a nightclub singer who happened by chance to land a film role that would launch a legendary career. He moved from film to television in 1958, working as a game show host, and in 1962 was given his own daytime talk show at NBC. "The Merv Griffin Show" ran for more than 21 years in syndication and won 11 Emmy Awards. He created and produced two of the most successful game shows in television history, "Jeopardy!" and "Wheel of Fortune," and also composed the iconic "Jeopardy!" theme music. He was a real estate mogul and at the time of his death was worth an estimated 1.6 billion dollars. He died at Los Angeles, CA, Aug 12, 2007.

ISLE OF MAN: TYNWALD DAY. July 6. For more than 1,000 years, the people of the Isle of Man have gathered at Tynwald Hill at St. John's to hear new laws read out, to present petitions and to swear in the island's four coroners. Tynwald (a word of Norse extraction) is the name of the Manx parliament, which is the world's oldest continually held parliament. Held annually on July 5, unless that date falls on a weekend, in which case the event occurs on the following Monday.

JONES, JOHN PAUL: BIRTH ANNIVERSARY. July 6, 1747. (Old Style date.) American naval officer born at Kirkbean, Scotland. Remembered for his victory in the battle of his ship, the *Bonhomme Richard*, with the British frigate *Serapis*, Sept 23, 1779. When Jones was queried: "Do you ask for quarter?" he made his famous reply: "I have not yet begun to fight!" Jones was victorious, but the *Bonhomme Richard*, badly damaged, sank two days later. Jones died at Paris, France, July 18, 1792.

KAHLO, FRIDA: BIRTH ANNIVERSARY. July 6, 1907. The great surrealist painter was born Magdalena Carmen Frida Kahlo Calderón at Coyoacán, Mexico. In 1925 she endured severe injuries in a bus accident that would plague her for the rest of her life (and become artistic subject matter). She turned to art at about this time, encouraged by the great muralist Diego Rivera, whom she married in 1929 (and 1941). She is known almost as much for her tumultuous life (she had an affair with Soviet exile Leon Trotsky and was active in leftist politics) as for her vibrant art works filled with symbols and the flora and fauna of her beloved Mexico. She was one of the first women painters to sell a work to the Louvre. She died at her Casa Azul family home in Coyoacán on July 13, 1954.

LEIGH, JANET: BIRTH ANNIVERSARY. July 6, 1927. Born Jeanette Helen Morrison at Merced, CA, Leigh was signed to a contract by MGM while still a teenager. She starred in *Touch of Evil* with Orson Wells (1958), *The Manchurian Candidate* with Frank Sinatra (1962) and *Bye Bye Birdie* (1963) with Dick Van Dyke. She is best remembered for the scene where she was attacked in the shower by Norman Bates, in Alfred Hitchcock's 1960 classic *Psycho.* She died Oct 3, 2004, at Los Angeles, CA.

LENNON MEETS MCCARTNEY: ANNIVERSARY. July 6, 1957. On this day in Liverpool, England, 15-year-old Paul McCartney watched a band called the Quarrymen led by the almost 17-year-old John Lennon. The two teens met later that day and before long created one of the most popular rock groups of the 20th century: the Beatles.

LITHUANIA: DAY OF STATEHOOD. July 6. National holiday. Commemorates the 1252 crowning of Mindaugas, who united Lithuania.

LUXEMBOURG: ETTELBRUCK REMEMBRANCE DAY. July 6. In honor of US General George Patton, Jr, liberator of the Grand-Duchy of Luxembourg in 1945, who is buried at the American Military Cemetery at Hamm, Germany, among 5,100 soldiers of his famous Third Army.

MAJOR LEAGUE BASEBALL HOLDS FIRST ALL-STAR GAME: ANNIVERSARY. July 6, 1933. The first midsummer All-Star Game was held at Comiskey Park, Chicago, IL. Babe Ruth led the American League with a home run, as they defeated the National League 4–2. Prior to the summer of 1933, All-Star contests consisted of pre- and postseason exhibitions that often found teams made up of a few stars playing beside journeymen and even minor leaguers.

MALAWI: REPUBLIC DAY. July 6. National holiday. Commemorates attainment of independence from Britain in 1964. Malawi was formerly known as Nyasaland.

"NAME THAT TUNE" TV PREMIERE: ANNIVERSARY. July 6, 1953. "Name That Tune" was a musical identification show that appeared in different formats in the '50s and the '70s. Red Benson was the host of the NBC series and Bill Cullen (and later George DeWitt) was the CBS host. Two contestants listened while an orchestra played a musical selection, and the first contestant who could identify it raced across the stage to ring a bell. The winner of the round then tried to identify a number of tunes within a specific time period. After 11 years, the show was brought back with Richard Hayes as host. In 1974 new network and syndicated versions appeared.

NUDE RECREATION WEEK. July 6–12. Looking for a way to relax this summer? Why not go barefoot all over? Give nude recreation a try this week by attending special events at a clothing-optional beach, campground or resort near you. For info: The Naturist Society, Box 132, Oshkosh, WI 54903. Phone: (920) 426-5009. Fax: (920) 426-5184. E-mail: naturist@naturistsociety.com. Web: www.naturistsociety.com.

OPERATION OVERCAST: ANNIVERSARY. July 6, 1945. As the end of the war approached, the US Army had begun to move German scientists and scientific equipment from the German territory designated for Russian occupation. On this date, the American Joint Chiefs of Staff authorized Operation Overcast, under which 350 German and Austrian scientists were transported to the US in a matter of months.

"THE QUIZ KIDS" TV PREMIERE: 60th ANNIVERSARY. July 6, 1949. This show began on radio and continued on TV with the original host, Joe Kelly, and later with Clifton Fadiman. The format was a panel of five child prodigies who answered questions sent in by viewers. Four were regulars, staying for weeks or months, while the fifth was a "guest child." The ages of the panelists varied from 6 to 16.

REPUBLICAN PARTY FORMED: ANNIVERSARY. July 6, 1854. The Republican Party originated at a convention at Ripon, WI, on Feb 28, 1854. A state convention meeting in Michigan formally adopted the name Republican on July 6.

SPACE MILESTONE: *SOYUZ 21* (USSR). July 6, 1976. Launched this date. Two cosmonauts, Colonel B. Volynov and Lieutenant Colonel V. Zholobov, traveled to *Salyut 5* space station (launched June 22, 1976) to study Earth's surface and conduct zoological-botanical experiments. Their stay was 48 days. Return landing on Aug 24.

SWITZERLAND: SEMPACH BATTLE COMMEMORATION. July 6. On the morning of the first Monday after July 4, the Lucerne government, military and student delegations and historical groups make their way in solemn procession to the battlefield of 1386. Commemorative address, battle report and solemn service in the chapel. Also an evening procession.

TAKE YOUR WEBMASTER TO LUNCH DAY. July 6. Keep the person running your website happy by making sure he or she is well fed. It makes your webmaster feel loved and gives him or her the energy to fix all the typos that you have on your site. (©2006 by WH.) For info: Thomas & Ruth Roy, Wellcat Holidays, 2418 Long Ln, Lebanon, PA 17046. Phone: (717) 279-0184. E-mail: info@wellcat.com. Web: www.wellcat.com.

ZAMBIA: HEROES DAY. July 6. First Monday in July is a Zambian national holiday—a memorial day for Zambians who died in the struggle for independence. Political rallies stress solidarity. See also "Zambia: Unity Day" (July 7).

BIRTHDAYS TODAY

Allyce Beasley, 55, actress ("Moonlighting"), born Brooklyn, NY, July 6, 1954.

Ned Beatty, 72, actor ("Homicide," *Hear My Song, Deliverance*), born Louisville, KY, July 6, 1937.

George W. Bush, 63, 43rd president of the US, former governor of Texas (R), born New Haven, CT, July 6, 1946.

Dalai Lama, 74, Tibet's spiritual leader and Nobel Peace Prize winner, born Taktser, China, July 6, 1935.

Pau Gasol, 29, basketball player, born Barcelona, Spain, July 6, 1980.

Grant Goodeve, 57, actor ("Eight Is Enough," "Dynasty"), born New Haven, CT, July 6, 1952.

July 2009

S	M	T	W	T	F	S
			1	2	3	4
5	6	7	8	9	10	11
12	13	14	15	16	17	18
19	20	21	22	23	24	25
26	27	28	29	30	31	

Nancy Davis Reagan, 88, former First Lady, wife of Ronald Reagan, 40th president of the US, born New York, NY, July 6, 1921.

Della Reese, 77, singer, actress ("Touched by an Angel"), born Deloreese Patricia Early at Detroit, MI, July 6, 1932.

Geoffrey Rush, 58, actor (*Pirates of the Caribbean, Quills*, Oscar for *Shine*), born Toowoomba, Queensland, Australia, July 6, 1951.

Sylvester Stallone, 63, actor (*Rocky* and *Rambo* films), director, born New York, NY, July 6, 1946.

Burt Ward, 64, actor ("Batman"), born Los Angeles, CA, July 6, 1945.

July 7 — Tuesday

DAY 188 — **177 REMAINING**

BONZA BOTTLER DAY™. July 7. To celebrate when the number of the day is the same as the number of the month. Bonza Bottler Day™ is an excuse to have a party at least once a month. For more information see Jan 1. For info: Gail M. Berger, 14 Fernwood Dr, Taylors, SC 29687. E-mail: bonza@bonzabottlerday.com. Web: www.bonzabottlerday.com.

BUCK MOON. July 7. So called by Native American tribes of New England and the Great Lakes because at this time of year the new antlers of buck deer begin to appear. Also called Thunder Moon for summer thunderstorms. The July Full Moon.

ENGLAND: HAMPTON COURT PALACE FLOWER SHOW. July 7–12. Hampton Court Palace, East Molesey, Surrey. A charity event that launches the world's largest flower show. Est attendance: 160,000. For info: Royal Horticultural Society, 80 Vincent Square, London SW1P 2PE, England. Phone: (44) (845) 3700-128. Fax: (44) (207) 6308-178. Web: www.rhs.org.uk/hamptoncourt.

FATHER-DAUGHTER TAKE A WALK TOGETHER DAY. July 7. A special time in the summer for fathers and daughters of all ages to spend time together in the beautiful weather. Annually, July 7. For info: Janet Dellaria, PO Box 39, Trout Creek, MI 49967. Phone: (906) 852-3539.

HAWAII ANNEXED BY US: ANNIVERSARY. July 7, 1898. President William McKinley signed a resolution annexing Hawaii. No change in government took place until 1900, when Congress passed an act making Hawaii an "incorporated" territory of the US. This act remained in effect until Hawaii became a state in 1959.

JAPAN: TANABATA (STAR FESTIVAL). July 7. As an offering to the stars, children set up bamboo branches to which colorful strips of paper bearing poems are tied.

JIMMY AND ROSALYNN CARTER WEDDING: ANNIVERSARY. July 7, 1946. Plains Methodist Church, Plains, GA. James Earl Carter, Jr, was 21 and Eleanor Rosalynn Smith was 18. They have four children: John William "Jack" Carter was born in 1947, James Carl "Chip" Carter, 1950, Donnell Jeffrey Carter, 1952, and Amy Lynn Carter, 1968.

KUNSTLER, WILLIAM: 90th BIRTH ANNIVERSARY. July 7, 1919. Radical attorney, defense lawyer for the Chicago Seven, born at New York, NY. Died Sept 4, 1995, at New York, NY.

LINCOLN ASSASSINATION CONSPIRATORS HANGING: ANNIVERSARY. July 7, 1865. Four persons convicted of complicity with John Wilkes Booth in the assassination of President Abraham Lincoln on Apr 14, 1865, were hanged at Washington, DC. The four: Mary E. Surratt, Lewis Payne, David E. Harold and George A. Atzerodt. Mary Surratt became the first woman executed for a crime in the US. Her conviction was and is a subject of controversy, as the only crime she appeared to have committed was to own the boardinghouse where John Wilkes Booth planned the assassination.

LONDON TERRORIST BOMBINGS: ANNIVERSARY. July 7, 2005. In the most violent attack on London since WWII, terrorists exploded four bombs in quick succession on three subway cars and one bus, killing more than 50 people and injuring 700. A splinter group of Al Qaeda claimed responsibility.

LUNAR ECLIPSE. July 7. Penumbral eclipse of the moon. Visible in continents North America, South America and Australia and the Pacific Ocean region.

MAJOR LEAGUE BASEBALL ALL-STAR GAME. July 7. Busch Stadium, St. Louis, MO. 80th annual All-Star Game. For info: Major League Baseball. E-mail: fanfeedback@website.mlb.com or tickets @website.mlb.com. Web: www.mlb.com.

MENOTTI, GIAN CARLO: BIRTH ANNIVERSARY. July 7, 1911. Composer, born at Cadegliano-Viconago, Italy, who wrote his first opera at age 11. He won two Pulitzer Prizes, for popular operas *The Consul* (1950) and *The Saint of Bleecker Street* (1955), and *Amahl and the Night Visitors* is a classic Christmas favorite. He died at Monte Carlo, Monaco, Feb 1, 2007.

MOON PHASE: FULL MOON. July 7. Moon enters Full Moon phase at 5:21 AM, EDT.

MOTHER FRANCES XAVIER CABRINI CANONIZED: ANNIVERSARY. July 7, 1946. Pope Pius XII presided over the canonization ceremonies for Mother Frances Xavier Cabrini as she became the first American to be canonized. She was the founder of the Missionary Sisters of the Sacred Heart of Jesus, and her principal shrine is at Mother Cabrini High School, New York, NY. Cabrini was born at Lombardy, Italy, July 15, 1850, and died at Chicago, IL, Dec 22, 1917. Her feast day is celebrated on Dec 22.

PAIGE, LEROY ROBERT (SATCHEL): BIRTH ANNIVERSARY. July 7, 1906. Baseball Hall of Fame pitcher born at Mobile, AL. Paige was the greatest attraction in the Negro Leagues and was also, at age 42, the first black pitcher in the American League. Inducted into the Hall of Fame in 1971. Died at Kansas City, MO, June 8, 1982.

"RYAN'S HOPE" TV PREMIERE: ANNIVERSARY. July 7, 1975. This ABC soap ran until 1989 and was set mostly at the fictional Ryan's Tavern or Riverside Hospital at New York City. The show depicted the lives of the ardently Irish Ryan family. The original cast included Faith Catlin, Justin Deas, Bernard Barrow, Helen Gallagher, Michael Hawkins, Ilene Kristen, Malcom Groome and Kate Mulgrew. Marg Helgenberger, Nell Carter, Yasmine Bleeth, Gloria DeHaven, Corbin Bernsen and Grant Show have been among the show's other regulars.

SOLOMON ISLANDS: INDEPENDENCE DAY: ANNIVERSARY. July 7. National holiday. Commemorates independence from Britain in 1978.

SPAIN: RUNNING OF THE BULLS. July 7–14. Pamplona, Spain. Event made famous by Hemingway in his novel *The Sun Also Rises*, in which young men run through the streets of Pamplona chased by bulls from the bull ring. Part of the festival of San Fermin.

TANZANIA: SABA SABA DAY. July 7. Tanzania's mainland ruling party, TANU, was formed on this day in 1954. Saba Saba means "Seven-Seven."

TELL THE TRUTH DAY. July 7. Today every American is challenged to go one whole day without telling a lie or saying anything misleading or dishonest. Annually, July 7. For info: Leslei Green, Teens Express, 9506 Silver Fox Turn, Clinton, MD 20735. Phone: (301) 877-0592. E-mail: programs@teensexpress.org.

WALES: LLANGOLLEN INTERNATIONAL MUSICAL EISTEDDFOD. July 7–12. Eisteddfod Field, Llangollen, Denbighshire, North Wales. 63rd annual. Thousands of singers and folk dancers from more than 50 countries take part in this annual international music festival. Friendly rivalry among amateur groups performing amid the Welsh rivers and mountains. Est attendance: 80,000. For info: Llangollen Intl Musical Eisteddfod, Llangollen, North Wales, UK LL20 8SW. Phone: (44) 1978 862-001. Fax: (44) (1978) 862-002. E-mail: info@international-eisteddfod.co.uk. Web: www.international-eisteddfod.co.uk.

ZAMBIA: UNITY DAY. July 7. Memorial day for Zambians who died in the struggle for independence. Political rallies stressing solidarity throughout country. Annually, the first Tuesday in July.

BIRTHDAYS TODAY

Billy Campbell, 50, actor ("The 4400," "Once and Again," *The Rocketeer*), born Charlottesville, VA, July 7, 1959.

Pierre Cardin, 87, fashion designer, born Venice, Italy, July 7, 1922.

Shelley Duvall, 60, actress (*Popeye, Nashville, Roxanne*), born Houston, TX, July 7, 1949.

Jorja Fox, 41, actress ("CSI," "ER"), born New York, NY, July 7, 1968.

Michelle Kwan, 29, figure skater, born Torrance, CA, July 7, 1980.

Lisa Leslie, 37, WNBA player, born Inglewood, CA, July 7, 1972.

Joe Sakic, 40, hockey player, born Burnaby, BC, Canada, July 7, 1969.

Ralph Lee Sampson, 49, former basketball player, born Harrisonburg, VA, July 7, 1960.

Doc Severinsen, 82, composer, conductor, musician (former bandleader on "The Tonight Show"), born Arlington, OR, July 7, 1927.

Ringo Starr, 69, singer, musician (The Beatles), born Richard Starkey at Liverpool, England, July 7, 1940.

July 8 — Wednesday

DAY 189 **176 REMAINING**

ASPINWALL CROSSES US ON HORSEBACK: ANNIVERSARY. July 8, 1911. Nan Jane Aspinwall rode into New York City carrying a letter to Mayor William Jay Gaynor from San Francisco mayor Patrick Henry McCarthy, becoming the first woman to cross the US on horseback. She began her trip in San Francisco on Sept 1, 1910, and covered 4,500 miles in 301 days.

DE SILHOUETTE, ETIENNE: 300th BIRTH ANNIVERSARY. July 8, 1709. Born in Limoges, de Silhouette would become briefly the French controller-general of finances in 1759 under Louis XV. A minor figure in history, de Silhouette was a wispy figure at the French court, thus lending his name to the black profile cut-outs that are today called silhouettes. He died in 1767.

DECLARATION OF INDEPENDENCE FIRST PUBLIC READING: ANNIVERSARY. July 8, 1776. Colonel John Nixon read the Declaration of Independence to the assembled residents at Philadelphia's Independence Square.

July 2009

S	M	T	W	T	F	S
			1	2	3	4
5	6	7	8	9	10	11
12	13	14	15	16	17	18
19	20	21	22	23	24	25
26	27	28	29	30	31	

DINOSAUR ROUNDUP RODEO. July 8–11. Vernal, UT. 59th annual presentation of one of the top PRCA rodeos, fun for the entire family. Est attendance: 10,000. For info: Vernal Rodeo, PO Box 1501, Vernal, UT 84078. Phone: (435) 790-1306. Web: www.vernalrodeo.com.

ECKSTINE, BILLY: 95th BIRTH ANNIVERSARY. July 8, 1914. Bandleader and bass-baritone singer Billy Eckstine was born William Clarence Eckstein at Pittsburgh, PA. After performing with the Earl Hines band for almost 20 years, Eckstine formed his own band in 1944. At one time or another the band's ranks included Charlie Parker, Dizzy Gillespie, Miles Davis, Fats Navarro, Dexter Gordon, Gene Ammons, Art Blakey and vocalist Sarah Vaughan—some of the greatest bebop musicians of all time. Among Eckstine's hits were "Fools Rush In," "Everything I Have Is Yours," "My Foolish Heart," "Blue Moon" and "Body and Soul." Billy Eckstine died Mar 8, 1993, at Pittsburgh, PA.

JOHNSON, PHILLIP: BIRTH ANNIVERSARY. July 8, 1906. Postmodern architect who promoted the International Style. He was director of the Department of Architecture of New York's Museum of Modern Art, worked with Mies van der Rohe on the Seagram Building at New York City and designed his own "Glass House" at New Canaan, CT. Born at Cleveland, OH, and died Jan 25, 2005, in his home at New Canaan.

JORDAN, LOUIS: BIRTH ANNIVERSARY. July 8, 1908. The "King of the Jukebox" was born at Brinkley, AR. The bandleader-vocalist-saxophonist performed from the mid-1920s through the 1950s and was a pioneer in American jazz. One of the most successful, influential African-American musicians of his era, *Rolling Stone* magazine proclaimed Jordan number 59 on their list of the "100 Greatest Artists of All Time." He died Feb 4, 1975, at Los Angeles, CA.

KIM IL SUNG: 15th DEATH ANNIVERSARY. July 8, 1994. President Kim Il Sung, the only leader in the history of North Korea, died just a few weeks before an historic summit with the president of South Korea was to take place, at Pyongyang, North Korea. A Stalinist-styled dictator, born at Man'gyandae, Korea, Apr 15, 1912, Kim had created a godlike personality cult surrounding himself and his son and presumed heir apparent, Kim Jong Il. His death came at a crucial time in world politics. North Korea and the US had recently cooled rhetoric regarding North Korea's nuclear program and had begun further talks just hours prior to the announcement of Kim's death. The North-South Summit and the US–North Korean talks were postponed.

MOULIN, JEAN: DEATH ANNIVERSARY. July 8, 1943. Jean Moulin, a Free French representative, born at Beziers, France, June 20, 1899, was parachuted into occupied France on Jan 1, 1942, with the task of uniting the underground resistance. Moulin had with him (in the false bottom of a matchbox) a personal message of admiration for the resistance from General Charles DeGaulle. On May 27, 1943, the underground agreed to the creation of a National Resistance Council with Moulin as president. A month later he was arrested at Lyon by the Gestapo. He was tortured for 11 days but betrayed no one. Moulin died on a train while being transferred by the Nazis to a concentration camp.

OLIVE BRANCH PETITION: ANNIVERSARY. July 8, 1775. Representatives of New Hampshire, Massachusetts Bay, Rhode Island, Providence, Connecticut, New York, New Jersey, Pennsylvania, Delaware, Maryland, Virginia, North Carolina and South Carolina signed a petition from the Congress to King George III, a final attempt by moderates in the Second Continental Congress to avoid a complete break with England.

ROCKEFELLER, NELSON ALDRICH: BIRTH ANNIVERSARY. July 8, 1908. Born at Bar Harbor, ME. Governor of New York (1958–73). Nominated as vice president by President Ford, Aug 20, 1974, under provisions of the 25th Amendment. Sworn in Dec 19, 1974, after confirmation by the Senate and served until Jan 20, 1977. Died at New York, NY, Jan 26, 1979. Rockefeller was the second person to become vice president without having been elected (Gerald R. Ford was the first).

SCUD DAY (SAVOR THE COMIC, UNPLUG THE DRAMA). July 8. A day to remind people of the benefits of spending more time in the Comic Zone and less in the Drama Zone. For info: Stephanie

West Allen, PO Box 9311, Denver, CO 80209. Phone: (303) 935-8866. E-mail: stephanie@westallen.com. Web: www.westallen.com.

WYANDOTTE STREET ART FAIR. July 8–11. Downtown Wyandotte, MI. More than 250 seasoned and emerging artists display and sell their wares. Also, music, street entertainers, Children's Emporium and sidewalk sales. Est attendance: 200,000. For info: Lisa Hooper, Executive Director, Downtown Development, 3131 Biddle Ave, Wyandotte, MI 48192. Phone: (734) 324-4506. Fax: (734) 324-4552.

***ZIEGFELD FOLLIES OF 1907*: ANNIVERSARY.** July 8, 1907. Theater impresario Florenz Ziegfeld staged the first of his extravagant musical revues in New York City. The show's slogan was "Glorifying the American Girl." The last *Follies* closed in 1957.

BIRTHDAYS TODAY

Kevin Bacon, 51, actor (*The Woodsman, Mystic River, Apollo 13, Footloose*), born Philadelphia, PA, July 8, 1958.

Sophia Bush, 27, actress ("One Tree Hill," *The Hitcher*), born Pasadena, CA, July 8, 1982.

Raffi Cavoukian, 61, children's singer and songwriter, born Cairo, Egypt, July 8, 1948.

Billy Crudup, 41, actor (Tony for *The Coast of Utopia: Voyage*; *Stage Beauty, Big Fish, Almost Famous*), born Manhasset, NY, July 8, 1968.

Kim Darby, 61, actress ("Rich Man, Poor Man," *True Grit*), born Los Angeles, CA, July 8, 1948.

Cynthia Gregory, 63, ballerina, born Los Angeles, CA, July 8, 1946.

Beck Hansen, 39, rock singer/songwriter, born Beck David Campbell at Los Angeles, CA, July 8, 1970.

Anjelica Huston, 58, actress (Oscar for *Prizzi's Honor*; *The Royal Tenenbaums, The Addams Family*), born Los Angeles, CA, July 8, 1951.

Toby Keith, 48, country singer, born Clinton, OK, July 8, 1961.

Steve Lawrence, 74, singer ("Party Doll," "Go Away Little Girl"), born Sidney Liebowitz at New York, NY, July 8, 1935.

Jeffrey Tambor, 65, actor ("Hill Street Blues," "The Larry Sanders Show," *City Slickers*), born San Francisco, CA, July 8, 1944.

Milo Ventimiglia, 32, actor ("Heroes," "Gilmore Girls"), born Anaheim, CA, July 8, 1977.

Alyce Faye Wattleton, 66, former executive director of Planned Parenthood Federation, born St. Louis, MO, July 8, 1943.

July 9 — Thursday

DAY 190 — **175 REMAINING**

ALASKA FLAG DAY CELEBRATION. July 9. This day celebrates the first time Alaska's flag was unfurled over the Jesse Lee Home at Seward, AK. In 1927 Territorial Governor George Parks announced a contest in which children all over Alaska in grades 7–12 were encouraged to design Alaska's flag. The winning flag was designed by John Ben (Benny) Benson, a resident of the Jesse Lee Home, an orphanage. He was the only child in US history to design a state flag. Each year this day is celebrated at Alaska Children's Services (formerly the Jesse Lee Home). Est attendance: 2,000. For info: Alaska Children's Services, 4600 Abbott Rd, Anchorage, AK 99507. Phone: (907) 346-2101. E-mail: akchild@ak.net. Web: www.acs.ak.org.

AMERICAN LIBRARY ASSOCIATION ANNUAL CONFERENCE. July 9–15. Chicago, IL. The American Library Association (ALA), the oldest and largest library association in the world, holds its annual conference each June. Its attendees include librarians, educators, writers, publishers, friends of libraries, trustees and special guests. More than 2,000 meetings, discussion groups, tours, special events and awards ceremonies (including the presentation of the Newbery and Caldecott medals) are spread throughout the weeklong conference. Est attendance: 25,000. For info: Public Information Office, American Library Assn, 50 E Huron St, Chicago, IL 60611. Phone: (312) 280-5044 or (800) 545-2433. Fax: (312) 944-8520. E-mail: pio@ala.org. Web: www.ala.org.

ARGENTINA: INDEPENDENCE DAY. July 9. Anniversary of establishment of independent republic, with the declaration of independence from Spain in 1816.

CANADA: CISCO OTTAWA BLUESFEST. July 9–19. Le Breton Flats, Ottawa, ON. 16th annual. Enjoy a spectacular explosion of blues, gospel, roots, world and popular music in the heart of Canada's national capital. The 11-day festival on multiple stages will offer more than 200 performances. Est attendance: 250,000. For info: Andre Sauve, Cisco Ottawa Bluesfest, 265 Catherine St, Ottawa, ON, Canada K1R 7S5. Phone: (613) 247-1188. Fax: (613) 247-2220. E-mail: ajsauve@ottawabluesfest.ca. Web: www.ottawabluesfest.ca.

EDWARDS, VINCE: BIRTH ANNIVERSARY. July 9, 1928. As Dr. Ben Casey on the 1961 television show "Ben Casey," Edwards's muscular, brooding charm made him an overnight sex symbol. Medical school enrollment increased while he was on the air. After conquering a gambling addiction, he became a real-life hero. Born at Brooklyn, NY, he died at Los Angeles, CA, Mar 11, 1996.

FAST OF TAMMUZ. July 9. Jewish holiday. Hebrew calendar date: Tammuz 17, 5769. Shiva Asar B'Tammuz begins at first light of day and commemorates the first-century Roman siege that breached the walls of Jerusalem. Begins a three-week time of mourning.

FIRST OPEN-HEART SURGERY: ANNIVERSARY. July 9, 1893. In Provident Hospital on Chicago's South Side, black surgeon Dr. Daniel Hale Williams performed the first successful open-heart surgery.

FOURTEENTH AMENDMENT TO US CONSTITUTION RATIFIED: ANNIVERSARY. July 9, 1868. The 14th Amendment defined US citizenship and provided that no state shall have the right to abridge the rights of any citizen without due process and equal protection under the law. Coming three years after the Civil War, the 14th Amendment also included provisions for barring individuals who assisted in any rebellion or insurrection against the US from holding public office, and releasing federal and state governments from any financial liability incurred in the assistance of rebellion or insurrection against the US.

HIGHEST TSUNAMI IN RECORDED HISTORY: ANNIVERSARY. July 9, 1958. An earthquake registering 8.3 on the Richter scale caused a massive landslide at the head of Lituya Bay, AK, which in turn created a tsunami of 1,700 feet—higher than the Sears Tower in Chicago (which is 1,450 feet). A 300-foot wave immediately followed, scouring bare about four to five square miles of land on both sides of the bay. Of three boats anchored at this remote spot, one was sunk with the loss of two lives; miraculously, the other two boats with their passengers survived the powerful waves.

HODAG COUNTRY FESTIVAL. July 9–12. Hodag "50" Track, Rhinelander, WI. 32nd annual country music festival, one of the oldest open-air festivals in the Midwest. Annually, the second full weekend in July. Est attendance: 70,000. For info: Hodag Country Fest, PO Box 1184, Rhinelander, WI 54501-1184. Phone: (715) 369-1300. Fax: (715) 362-3919. E-mail: hcf@hodag.com. Web: www.hodag.com.

HOT DOG NIGHT. July 9. Luverne, MN. More than 12,000 hot dogs are served free of charge, and free drink is also provided. Various demonstrations including wiener dog races. Est attendance: 5,000. For info: Jane Wildung, Exec Dir, Luverne Area Chamber of Commerce, 211 E Main, Luverne, MN 56156. Phone: (507) 283-4061. Fax: (507) 283-4061. E-mail: luvernechamber@iw.net. Web: www.luvernechamber.org.

HOWE, ELIAS: BIRTH ANNIVERSARY. July 9, 1819. American inventor of the sewing machine. Born at Spencer, MA, he died Oct 3, 1867, at Brooklyn, NY.

MARION COUNTY FAIR. July 9–12. State Fairgrounds, Salem, OR. Exceptional food and entertainment, carnival, talent show, commercial exhibits, 4-H/FFA exhibits, open class exhibits, longhorns and pygmy goat and llama shows. Est attendance: 25,000. For info: Marion County Fair, 5155 Silverton Rd NE, Salem, OR 97305. Phone: (503) 585-9998. Fax: (503) 588-7970. E-mail: marioncountyfair@co.marion.or.us. Web: www.mcfair.net.

MARTYRDOM OF THE BAB. July 9. Baha'i observance of the anniversary of the execution by a firing squad, July 9, 1850, at Tabriz, Persia, of the 30-year-old Siyyid Ali Muhammed, the Bab (prophet-herald of the Baha'i Faith). One of the nine days of the year when Baha'is suspend work. For info: Baha'is of the US, Office of Communications, 1233 Central St, Evanston, IL 60201. Phone: (847) 733-3559. Fax: (847) 733-3578. E-mail: ooc@usbnc.org. Web: www.bahai.us.

MISS OREGON SCHOLARSHIP PAGEANT. July 9–11. Seaside Civic and Convention Center, Seaside, OR. Part of the Miss America Organization. The Miss Oregon Scholarship Program is a not-for-profit corporation established solely to provide contestants with the opportunity to enhance their professional and educational goals and to achieve those pursuits with the assistance of monetary grants and awards. For info: Miss Oregon Scholarship Pageant, 217 Broadway, Seaside, OR 97138. E-mail: miss-or@seasurf.net. Web: www.missoregon.org.

MONTANA GOVERNOR'S CUP WALLEYE TOURNAMENT. July 9–11. Fort Peck, MT. Two-person team event, limited to 200 teams. $20,000 awarded in day money (based on a full field). There is an 80 percent payback of $400 entry fee. Kids' fishing event also. Est attendance: 2,000. For info: Glasgow Area Chamber of Commerce & Agriculture, Box 832, Glasgow, MT 59230. Phone: (406) 228-2222. Fax: (406) 228-2244. E-mail: chamber@glasgowmt.net. Web: www.mtgovcup.com.

MOROCCO: YOUTH DAY. July 9. National holiday. On the birthday in 1929 of King Hassan II.

OREGON TRAIL DAYS. July 9–12. Gering, NE. Oldest continuing celebration in state of Nebraska commemorating Oregon Trail. Parades, barbecues, street dances, International Food Fair, concert, Nebraska State CASI Chili Cookoff, musical plays and a Western art show highlight the annual celebration. Annually, the second full weekend in July. Est attendance: 30,000. For info: Event Coord, PO Box 334, Gering, NE 69341. Phone: (308) 436-4457. E-mail: info@oregontraildays.com. Web: www.oregontraildays.com.

RADCLIFFE, ANN WARD: BIRTH ANNIVERSARY. July 9, 1764. English novelist famous for her gothic novels (fiction works especially popular in the late 18th and early 19th centuries). Among her works are *The Romance of the Forest, The Mysteries of Udolpho* and *The Italian*. She was born at London, England, and died there Feb 7, 1823.

RESPIGHI, OTTORINO: BIRTH ANNIVERSARY. July 9, 1879. Italian composer (*The Fountains of Rome*) born at Bologna, Italy. He died at Rome, Apr 18, 1936.

RUSSELL-EINSTEIN MANIFESTO: ANNIVERSARY. July 9, 1955. Philosopher Bertrand Russell released this plea, signed by 11 prominent scientists, three months after Albert Einstein's death. Einstein had agreed to put his name to it in his final days. The manifesto urged nations to find peaceful ways to settle differences and to renounce the use of nuclear weapons, which only promised "universal death."

July 2009

S	M	T	W	T	F	S
			1	2	3	4
5	6	7	8	9	10	11
12	13	14	15	16	17	18
19	20	21	22	23	24	25
26	27	28	29	30	31	

TURKEY RAMA. July 9–11 (tentative). McMinnville, OR. This annual event at McMinnville, once known as the Turkey Capital of the World, continues to include Famous Turkey BBQ, Biggest Turkey contest, vendor street sales, 8k fun run, carnival, entertainment and street dance. Est attendance: 25,000. For info: McMinnville Area Chamber of Commerce, 417 NW Adams, McMinnville, OR 97128. Phone: (503) 472-6196. Fax: (503) 472-6198. E-mail: chamberinfo@mcminnville.org. Web: www.mcminnville.org/turkeyrama/.

US WOMEN'S OPEN CHAMPIONSHIP. July 9–12. Saucon Valley Country Club, Bethlehem, PA. For info: USGA, Golf House, Championship Dept, PO Box 708, Far Hills, NJ 07931-0708. Phone: (908) 234-2300. Fax: (908) 234-9687. E-mail: usga@usga.org. Web: www.usga.org.

WHITE CLOUD'S BIRTHDAY AND TATANKA FESTIVAL. July 9–12. National Buffalo Museum, Jamestown, ND. Annual celebration of the birth of the true albino buffalo, White Cloud, born in Michigan, ND, in July 1996. Included in the celebration are children's activities, a parade, cultural presentations, a street fair and a birthday cake. Est attendance: 1,000. For info: National Buffalo Museum, 500 17th St SE, Jamestown, ND 58401. Phone: (701) 252-8648. Fax: (701) 253-5803. E-mail: director@buffalomuseum.com. Web: www.nationalbuffalomuseum.com.

WILD HORSE STAMPEDE. July 9–11. Wolf Point, MT. The "Granddaddy" of all Montana rodeos features a wild-horse race, three rodeos, two parades and Native American culture. This is the oldest PRCA rodeo in Montana. Est attendance: 12,000. For info: Wolf Point Chamber of Commerce, 218 3rd Ave S, Ste B, Wolf Point, MT 59201. Phone: (406) 653-2012. E-mail: wpchmber@nemont.net.

BIRTHDAYS TODAY

Brian Dennehy, 71, actor (Tony for *Long Day's Journey into Night*), born Bridgeport, CT, July 9, 1938.

Margaret Gillis, 56, dancer, choreographer, born Montreal, QC, Canada, July 9, 1953.

Lindsey Graham, 54, US Senator (R, South Carolina), born Pickens County, SC, July 9, 1955.

Tom Hanks, 53, actor (*Saving Private Ryan, Cast Away*; Oscars for *Philadelphia, Forrest Gump*), born Concord, CA, July 9, 1956.

David Hockney, 72, artist, born Bradford, England, July 9, 1937.

Mathilde Krim, 83, geneticist, philanthropist, born Como, Italy, July 9, 1926.

Courtney Love, 44, singer, actress (*The People vs. Larry Flynt*), born San Francisco, CA, July 9, 1965.

Kelly McGillis, 52, actress (*Witness, Top Gun, The Accused*), born Newport Beach, CA, July 9, 1957.

Fred Savage, 33, actor ("The Wonder Years," "Working," *The Princess Bride*), born Highland Park, IL, July 9, 1976.

Orenthal James (O.J.) Simpson, 62, former sportscaster and actor, Hall of Fame football player, born San Francisco, CA, July 9, 1947.

Jimmy Smits, 54, actor (*Glitz*, "LA Law," "NYPD Blue"), born New York, NY, July 9, 1955.

John Tesh, 57, TV host ("Entertainment Tonight"), composer, born Garden City, NY, July 9, 1952.

July 10 — Friday

DAY 191 **174 REMAINING**

ALLIED INVASION OF SICILY: ANNIVERSARY. July 10, 1943. Operation Husky, the Allied infantry attack on Italy, began on the island of Sicily. The British entry into Syracuse was the first Allied success in Europe. General Dwight D. Eisenhower, the Allied commander in chief, described the invasion as "the first page in the liberation of the European Continent."

ASHE, ARTHUR: BIRTH ANNIVERSARY. July 10, 1943. Born at Richmond, VA, Arthur Ashe became a legend for his list of firsts as a black tennis player. Chosen for the US Davis Cup team in 1963, he became captain in 1980. He won the US men's singles championship and US Open in 1968 and in 1975 the men's singles at Wimbledon. Ashe won a total of 33 career titles. In 1985 he was inducted into the International Tennis Hall of Fame. He helped create inner-city tennis programs for youth and wrote the three-volume *A Hard Road to Glory: A History of the African-American Athlete.* Ashe announced Apr 8, 1992, that he had contracted HIV, probably through a transfusion during bypass surgery in 1983. In September 1992 he began a $5 million fund-raising effort on behalf of the Arthur Ashe Foundation for the Defeat of AIDS and campaigned for public awareness regarding the AIDS epidemic. He died at New York, NY, Feb 6, 1993, from pneumonia.

BAHAMAS: INDEPENDENCE DAY: ANNIVERSARY. July 10. Public holiday. At 12:01 AM in 1973 the Bahamas gained their independence after 250 years as a British Crown Colony.

"BASEBALL'S SAD LEXICON" PUBLISHED: ANNIVERSARY. July 10, 1910. Journalist Franklin P. Adams created the second best-known baseball poem (after "Casey at the Bat") for the *New York Evening Mail.* Adams extolled the double-play trio of Chicago Cubs Joe Tinker (shortstop), Johnny Evers (second base) and Frank Chance (first base): "These are the saddest of possible words/'Tinker to Evers to Chance.'/Trio of bear cubs, and fleeter than birds,/Tinker and Evers and Chance./Ruthlessly pricking our gonfalon bubble,/Making a Giant hit into a double—/Words that are heavy with nothing but trouble:/'Tinker to Evers to Chance.'" See also: "Mighty Casey Has Struck Out: Anniversary" (June 3) and "Tinker to Evers to Chance: First Double Play Anniversary" (Sept 15).

BETHUNE, MARY McLEOD: BIRTH ANNIVERSARY. July 10, 1875. Mary Jane McLeod Bethune was born at Mayesville, SC, the first in her family to be born free. Bethune became a teacher and in 1904 founded her own school in Florida, the Daytona Normal and Industrial School for Negro Girls. In 1931 the school merged with a local men's college, Cookman Institute, and was renamed Bethune-Cookman College. An adviser on minority affairs under President Franklin D. Roosevelt, she directed the Division of Negro Affairs of the National Youth Administration. She died May 18, 1955, at Daytona Beach, FL.

BORIS YELTSIN INAUGURATED AS RUSSIAN PRESIDENT: ANNIVERSARY. July 10, 1991. Boris Yeltsin took the oath of office as the first popularly elected president in Russia's 1,000-year history. He defeated the Communist Party candidate resoundingly, establishing himself as a powerful political counterpoint to Mikhail Gorbachev, the president of the Soviet Union, of which Russia was the largest republic. Yeltsin had been dismissed from the Politburo in 1987 and resigned from the Communist Party in 1989. His popularity forced Gorbachev to make concessions to the republics in the new union treaty forming the Confederation of Independent States. Suffering from poor health, Yeltsin resigned as president at the end of 1999.

BRINKLEY, DAVID: BIRTH ANNIVERSARY. July 10, 1920. Born at Wilmington, NC, David Brinkley was one of the most recognizable faces in American broadcast journalism for more than 50 years. He got his start as NBC's first White House correspondent, and his outstanding coverage of the 1956 Democratic and Republican national conventions landed him the anchor job on NBC's nightly TV newscast, paired with Chet Huntley until 1970. In 1981 Brinkley moved to ABC, creating a Sunday-morning interview show called "This Week with David Brinkley." His 1995 memoir was titled *David Brinkley: 11 Presidents, 4 Wars, 22 Political Conventions, 1 Moon Landing, 3 Assassinations, 2,000 Weeks of News and Other Stuff on Television, and 18 Years of Growing Up in North Carolina.* He died on June 12, 2003, at Houston, TX.

CALVIN, JOHN: 500th BIRTH ANNIVERSARY. July 10, 1509. Theologian, born at Noyon, France. Reformer and founder of Presbyterianism. Calvin died at Geneva, Switzerland, May 27, 1564.

CLERIHEW DAY. July 10. A day recognized in remembrance of Edmund Clerihew Bentley, journalist and author of the celebrated detective thriller *Trent's Last Case* (1912), but perhaps best known for his invention of a popular humorous verse form, the clerihew, consisting of two rhymed couplets of unequal length: Edmund's middle name was Clerihew/A name possessed by very few,/But verses by Mr Bentley/Succeeded eminently. Bentley was born at London, England, July 10, 1875, and died there, Mar 30, 1956.

DALLAS, GEORGE MIFFLIN: BIRTH ANNIVERSARY. July 10, 1792. 11th vice president of the US (1845–49), born at Philadelphia, PA. Died there, Dec 31, 1864.

DON'T STEP ON A BEE DAY. July 10. Wellcat Holidays reminds kids and grown-ups that now is the time of year when going barefoot can mean getting stung by a bee. If you get stung tell Mom. (©2006 by WH.) For info: Michael Roy, Wellcat Holidays, 2418 Long Ln, Lebanon, PA 17046. Phone: (717) 279-0184. E-mail: info@wellcat.com. Web: www.wellcat.com.

ENGLAND: WAYS WITH WORDS—A FESTIVAL OF WORDS AND IDEAS. July 10–19. Dartington Hall, Dartington, Devon. "The UK's most stylish literature festival." Some 200 writers give lectures, seminars, interviews, discussions and readings. On-site bar, restaurant. Bookshop and craft stalls. Est attendance: 15,000. For info: Kay Dunbar, Dir, Ways With Words, Droridge Farm, Dartington, Totnes, Devon, England TQ9 6JG. Phone: (44) (1803) 867-373. E-mail: admin@wayswithwords.co.uk. Web: www.waywithwords.co.uk.

GILBERT, JOHN: BIRTH ANNIVERSARY. July 10, 1897. Silent film star John Gilbert was born John Pringle at Logan, UT. In 1916 he had his billed screen debut in *Bullets and Brown Eyes.* In the early 1920s Gilbert had leading roles in several films, such as *The Merry Widow* and *The Big Parade.* Although he was a popular leading man, he was unable to succeed when sound came to movies and MGM released him from his contract in 1934. He died Jan 9, 1936, at Los Angeles, CA.

THE GREAT INTERNATIONAL CHICKEN WING SOCIETY COOK-OFF. July 10–12. Reno, NV. Festival where bars and restaurants compete to make the best chicken wings. Est attendance: 50,000. For info: Willie Davison, Great Intl Chicken Wing Society, PO Box 190, Sparks, NV 89431. Phone: (775) 358-8376. E-mail: mrdavison@aol.com.

GWYNNE, FREDERICK HUBBARD: BIRTH ANNIVERSARY. July 10, 1926. Stage, screen and TV actor, best known for the TV roles Herman Munster in "The Munsters" and Officer Muldoon in "Car 54, Where Are You?" Gwynne was born at New York, NY, and died at Taneytown, MD, July 2, 1993.

LAURA INGALLS WILDER PAGEANT. July 10–12 (also July 17–19 and 24–26). De Smet, SD. An outdoor pageant on the natural prairie stage depicting scenes historically based on Laura Ingalls Wilder's life and books. Est attendance: 10,000. For info: The Laura Ingalls Wilder Pageant, PO Box 154, De Smet, SD 57231. Phone: (800) 880-3383. Web: www.desmetpageant.org.

LITCHFIELD OPEN HOUSE TOUR. July 10–11. Litchfield, CT. Preview tour and cocktail reception on Friday. Open house tour features an assortment of homes as well as additional attractions of historical and architectural significance. Annually, the second weekend in July. Est attendance: 1,500. For info: Connecticut Junior Republic, PO Box 161, Goshen Rd, Litchfield, CT 06759. Phone: (860) 567-9423. Fax: (860) 567-8127. E-mail: info@ctjuniorrepublic.org. Web: www.ctjuniorrepublic.org and www.litchfieldct.com/cjr/tour.html.

NEWPORT MUSIC FESTIVAL. July 10–26. Newport, RI. Three, four and even five concerts held daily in Newport's fabled mansions featuring unique chamber music programs, American debuts, world-class artists and special events. Est attendance: 27,000. For info: Dr. Mark P. Malkovich III, Gen Dir, The Newport Music Festival, PO Box 3300, Newport, RI 02840-0992. Phone: (401) 846-1133. Box Office Phone: (401) 849-0700. Fax: (401) 849-1857. E-mail: staff@newportmusic.org. Web: www.newportmusic.org.

PORTLAND HISTORIC RACES. July 10–12. Portland International Raceway, Portland, OR. Featuring racing by some of the most celebrated vintage cars in history. Nearly 250 prestigious cars are divided into groups according to their age and horsepower to compete on the raceway's 1.95-mile track. Est attendance: 10,000. For info: Chris Crabb, Crabbsoup Public Relations, 4906 NE Siskiyou St, Portland, OR 97213. Phone: (503) 314-7583. E-mail: media@portlandhistorics.com. Web: www.portlandhistorics.com.

PROUST, MARCEL: BIRTH ANNIVERSARY. July 10, 1871. Famed author, born at Auteuil, France. He gained an international reputation for his 13-volume masterpiece, *A la Recherche du Temps Perdu* (*Remembrance of Things Past*). "Happiness," he wrote in *The Past Recaptured*, "is beneficial for the body but it is grief that develops the powers of the mind." Proust died Nov 19, 1922, at Paris.

***RAINBOW WARRIOR* SINKING: ANNIVERSARY.** July 10, 1985. The 160-ft ship, the *Rainbow Warrior*, operated by Greenpeace, an environmental organization, was sunk and a photographer aboard was killed while the ship was at Auckland, New Zealand. Reportedly a bomb was attached to the underside of the ship by saboteurs. The ship had been scheduled for use in a protest against nuclear tests in the South Pacific Ocean by the French government.

SAN FRANCISCO SILENT FILM FESTIVAL. July 10–12 (tentative). San Francisco, CA. 14th annual. A film festival devoted to the unique art form of the silent film. Est attendance: 9,500. For info: San Francisco Silent Film Festival, 833 Market St, Ste 812, San Francisco, CA 94103-1828. Phone: (415) 777-4908. Fax: (415) 777-4904. Web: www.silentfilm.org.

SLOW PITCH SOFTBALL TOURNAMENT. July 10–12. Elm Park, Williamsport, PA. 36th annual charitable tournament with 40 teams. Sponsor: Yuengling Mid-State Beverage Co. Est attendance: 8,500. For info: Don Phillips, 532 Sylvan Dr, South Williamsport, PA 17702. Phone: (570) 322-3331 or (570) 777-0165. E-mail: dphillips28@verizon.net.

SPACE MILESTONE: *TELSTAR* (US). July 10, 1962. First privately owned satellite (American Telephone and Telegraph Company) and first satellite to relay live TV pictures across the Atlantic was launched.

July 2009	S	M	T	W	T	F	S
				1	2	3	4
	5	6	7	8	9	10	11
	12	13	14	15	16	17	18
	19	20	21	22	23	24	25
	26	27	28	29	30	31	

US LIFTS SANCTIONS AGAINST SOUTH AFRICA: ANNIVERSARY. July 10, 1991. President George H.W. Bush lifted US trade and investment sanctions against South Africa. The sanctions had been imposed through the Comprehensive Anti-Apartheid Act of 1986, which Congress had passed to punish South Africa for policies of racial separation.

WAYNE CHICKEN SHOW. July 10–11. Wayne, NE. To allow humankind to pay tribute to chickenkind (without laying the proverbial egg). Parade, National Cluck-Off, Hard-Boiled Egg Eating Contest, food and craft vendors, games, contests and musical entertainment. Est attendance: 10,000. For info: Wayne Area Chamber of Commerce, 108 W 3rd St, Wayne, NE 68787. Phone: (402) 375-2240. E-mail: info@waedi.org. Web: www.chickenshow.com.

WHISTLER, JAMES ABBOTT McNEILL: 175th BIRTH ANNIVERSARY. July 10, 1834. American painter especially known for *Arrangement in Grey and Black: The Artist's Mother* (1871, also known as *Whistler's Mother*), born at Lowell, MA. Died at London, England, July 17, 1903. When a woman declared that a landscape reminded her of Whistler's paintings, he reportedly said, "Yes, madam, Nature is creeping up."

WYOMING: ADMISSION DAY: ANNIVERSARY. July 10. Became 44th state in 1890.

BIRTHDAYS TODAY

Andre Nolan Dawson, 55, former baseball player, born Miami, FL, July 10, 1954.

David Norman Dinkins, 82, former and first black mayor of New York City (D), born Trenton, NJ, July 10, 1927.

Ron Glass, 64, actor ("Barney Miller," voice on "Rugrats"), born Evansville, IN, July 10, 1945.

Arlo Guthrie, 62, singer ("The City of New Orleans," "Alice's Restaurant"), born Brooklyn, NY, July 10, 1947.

Brad Henry, 46, Governor of Oklahoma (D), born Shawnee, OK, July 10, 1963.

Jerry Herman, 76, composer, lyricist, born New York, NY, July 10, 1933.

Sue Lyon, 63, actress (*Lolita, The Flim Flam Man*), born Davenport, IA, July 10, 1946.

Lawrence Pressman, 70, actor ("Doogie Howser, MD," *The Hanoi Hilton*), born Cynthiana, KY, July 10, 1939.

Eunice Mary Kennedy Shriver, 88, founder of the Special Olympics, born Brookline, MA, July 10, 1921.

Jessica Simpson, 29, singer, actress (*Dukes of Hazzard*), born Abilene, TX, July 10, 1980.

Virginia Wade, 64, former tennis player, born Bournemouth, England, July 10, 1945.

July 11 — Saturday

DAY 192 — 173 REMAINING

ADAMS, JOHN QUINCY: BIRTH ANNIVERSARY. July 11, 1767. Sixth president of the US and the son of the second president, John Quincy Adams was born at Braintree, MA. After his single term as president, he served 17 years as a member of Congress from Plymouth, MA. He died Feb 23, 1848, at the House of Representatives (in the same room in which he had taken the presidential oath of office Mar 4, 1825). John Quincy Adams was the only president whose father had also been president of the US until George W. Bush became president in January 2001.

ART FAIR ON THE SQUARE. July 11–12. Madison, WI. This is one of the largest and most popular juried art fairs in the Midwest, with nearly 500 artists from around the country selling their works. The fair occupies eight blocks around Madison's state capitol and attracts large crowds. There's also entertainment and lots of food. For info: Art Fair Coordinator, Madison Museum of Contemporary Art, 227 State St, Madison, WI 53703. Phone: (608) 257-0158. E-mail: artfair@mmoca.org. Web: www.mmoca.org.

BABE RUTH'S DEBUT IN THE MAJORS: 95th ANNIVERSARY. July 11, 1914. Babe Ruth made his debut in major league baseball when he took the mound in Fenway Park for the Boston Red Sox against the Cleveland Indians. Ruth was relieved for the last two innings but was the winning pitcher in a 4–3 game.

BON ODORI "FESTIVAL OF THE LANTERNS." July 11. Midwest Buddhist Temple, Chicago, IL. One hundred performers, most clad in colorful kimonos, dance in celebration to music of different prefectures of Japan. The beat of the huge *taiko* (drum) helps keep tempo. Dances are performed outdoors, and public participation is encouraged. 8 PM. Est attendance: 750. For info: Midwest Buddhist Temple, 435 W Menomonee St, Chicago, IL 60614. Phone: (312) 943-7801. Fax: (312) 943-8069.

BOWDLER'S DAY. July 11. A day to remember the prudish medical doctor, Thomas Bowdler, born near Bath, England, on July 11, 1754. He gave up the practice of medicine and undertook the cleansing of the works of Shakespeare by removing all the words and expressions he considered to be indecent or impious. His *Family Shakespeare*, in 10 volumes, omitted all those words that "cannot with propriety be read aloud in a family." He also "purified" Edward Gibbon's *History of the Decline and Fall of the Roman Empire* and selections from the Old Testament. His name became synonymous with self-righteous expurgation, and the word *bowdlerize* has become part of the English language. Bowdler died at Rhyddings, in South Wales, Feb 24, 1825.

BURR-HAMILTON DUEL: ANNIVERSARY. July 11, 1804. US Vice President Aaron Burr shot and mortally wounded former secretary of the Treasury (and primary author of *The Federalist Papers*) Alexander Hamilton in a duel at Weehawken, NJ, on this date. Hamilton had insulted Burr and refused to make a public apology. Hamilton died the next day. Although Burr returned to Washington to execute his duties as vice president, the duel ended his political career.

CANADA: HARRISON FESTIVAL OF THE ARTS. July 11–19. Harrison Hot Springs, BC. A celebration of world music, dance, theater and visual art including a large outdoor art market. Various venues throughout the village. Variety of activities for the entire family. Est attendance: 12,000. For info: Ed Stenson, Gen Mgr, Harrison Fest, Box 399, Harrison Hot Springs, BC, Canada V0M 1K0. Phone: (604) 796-3664. Fax: (604) 796-3694. E-mail: info@harrisonfestival.com. Web: www.harrisonfestival.com.

CHILDREN'S DAY. July 11. Woodstock, VT. Traditional farm activities from corn shelling to sawing firewood—19th-century games, traditional spelling bee, ice cream and butter making, wagon rides. For info: Billings Farm and Museum, Rte 12 N, Woodstock, VT 05091. Phone: (802) 457-2355. Fax: (802) 457-4663. E-mail: info@billingsfarm.org. Web: www.billingsfarm.org.

CIRCUS CITY FESTIVAL. July 11–18. Peru, IN. Youth amateur circus performed by children 7 to 21 years of age helping to preserve the circus heritage of Miami County, IN. Circus parade, July 18, 10 AM. Annually, beginning the Saturday before and ending the Saturday after the third Wednesday of July. Est attendance: 75,000. For info: Circus City Festival Inc, 154 N Broadway, Peru, IN 46970. Phone: (765) 472-3918. Fax: (765) 472-2826. Web: www.perucircus.com.

CORN HILL ARTS FESTIVAL. July 11–12. Corn Hill neighborhood, Rochester, NY. Fine arts and crafts show organized by neighborhood residents for more than 40 years. Food and music from around the world, live entertainment, activities for children. All proceeds are reinvested in neighborhood projects. Est attendance: 200,000. For info: Corn Hill Arts Festival, 133 S Fitzhugh St, Rochester, NY 14608-2204. Phone: (585) 262-3142. Fax: (585) 546-4788. E-mail: chna@cornhill.org. Web: www.cornhill.org.

DAY OF THE FIVE BILLION: ANNIVERSARY. July 11, 1987. An eight-pound baby boy, Matej Gaspar, born at 1:35 AM, EST, at Zagreb, Yugoslavia, was proclaimed the five billionth inhabitant of Earth. The United Nations Fund for Population Activities, hoping to draw attention to population growth, proclaimed July 11 as "Day of the Five Billion," noting that 150 babies are born each minute. See also: "Day of the Six Billion: Anniversary" (Oct 12).

HIGHLIGHTS® FOUNDATION WRITER'S WORKSHOP. July 11–18. Chautauqua, NY. This annual workshop is designed for authors and artists interested in writing and illustrating for children. Writer workshops offered at beginner, intermediate and advanced levels. Classes offered include Children's Poetry, Book Promotion, Autobiographical Writing and much more. The Chautauqua experience includes powerful whole-group seminars, compelling small workshops, intensive one-on-one sessions and a host of informal activities to put writers in close touch with many mentors. Scholarships are available for first-time attendees. Request application by end of 2008. For info: Highlights Foundation, 814 Court St, Honesdale, PA 18431. Phone: (570) 253-1192. Fax: (570) 253-0179. E-mail: contact@highlightsfoundation.org. Web: www.highlightsfoundation.org.

MONGOLIA: NAADAM NATIONAL HOLIDAY. July 11. Public holiday. Commemorates overthrow of the feudal monarch in 1921.

NAPALM USED: ANNIVERSARY. July 11, 1945. The US dropped several thousand pounds of the recently developed weapon napalm on Japanese forces still holed up on Luzon in the Philippines. Napalm, which was later used heavily as a defoliant in Vietnam, was a thickener consisting of a mixture of aluminum soaps used to jell gasoline.

"THE NEWLYWED GAME" TV PREMIERE: ANNIVERSARY. July 11, 1966. Four newly married couples competed for prizes on this game show created by the inimitable Chuck Barris (mastermind of "The Gong Show"). The winners were determined by the couple that could best predict the responses of their respective spouses. Barris, Bob Eubanks and Paul Rodriguez have served as hosts.

NIAGARA MOVEMENT FOUNDED: ANNIVERSARY. July 11, 1905. Led by W.E.B. DuBois, 29 black intellectuals and activists founded the Niagara Movement at Niagara Falls, ON, Canada. The name of their movement alluded both to the location of their founding and to the "mighty current" of protest they hoped to undam. The movement disbanded in 1910, and the NAACP took over its goals.

SMITH, JAMES: DEATH ANNIVERSARY. July 11, 1806. Signer of the Declaration of Independence, born at Ireland about 1719 (exact date unknown). Died at York, PA.

SODBUSTER DAYS. July 11–12. Fort Ransom State Park, Fort Ransom, ND. Remember the way things were done in rural North Dakota during the early 1920s with shelling corn by hand, rope weaving, horse-drawn plowing and haying. Ladies' demonstrations, kids' games, live music. Located along the Sheyenne River Valley National Scenic Byway. Est attendance: 3,000. For info: Fort Ransom State Park, 5981 Walt Hjelle Pkwy, Ft Ransom, ND 58033-9712. Phone: (701) 973-4331. Fax: (701) 973-4151. E-mail: frsp@nd.gov. Web: www.parkrec.nd.gov.

SPACE MILESTONE: *SKYLAB* (US) FALLS TO EARTH: 30th ANNIVERSARY. July 11, 1979. The 82-ton spacecraft launched May 14, 1973, reentered Earth's atmosphere. Expectation was that 20–25 tons probably would survive to hit Earth, including one piece of about 5,000 pounds. This generated intense international public interest in where it would fall. The chance that some person would be hit by a piece of *Skylab* was calculated at one in 152. Targets were drawn and *Skylab* parties were held, but *Skylab* broke up and fell to Earth in a shower of pieces over the Indian Ocean and Australia, with no known casualties.

STERLING RENAISSANCE FESTIVAL. July 11–Aug 16 (Saturdays and Sundays only). Sterling, NY. 32nd annual re-creation of an English village set in the time period of Queen Elizabeth I. The festival features authentic jousting, more than 80 stage and street performances, music and dance of the period, beautiful arts and handcrafts, unique and delicious foods and drink and much more. For info: Festival Office, 15385 Farden Rd, Sterling, NY 13156. Phone: (800) 879-4446. E-mail: office@sterlingfestival.com. Web: sterlingfestival.com.

STONE HOUSE DAY. July 11. Hurley, NY. Tour six to nine privately owned, 250-plus-year-old stone houses, six within a 150-yard radius. Annually, the second Saturday in July. Est attendance: 750. For info: Stone House Day, Hurley Reformed Church, PO Box 328, Hurley, NY 12443. Phone: (845) 331-4121. Fax: (845) 331-4153. E-mail: info@StoneHouseDay.org. Web: www.StoneHouseDay.org.

***TO KILL A MOCKINGBIRD* PUBLISHED: ANNIVERSARY.** July 11, 1960. Harper Lee's evocative novel of tomboy Scout Finch coming of age in a Depression-era Alabama town was published this day by J.B. Lippincott. A bestseller almost immediately, it received a Pulitzer Prize on May 1, 1961. Librarians voted it the best novel of the 20th century.

UNITED NATIONS: WORLD POPULATION DAY. July 11. In June 1989 the Governing Council of the United Nations Development Programme recommended that July 11 be observed by the international community as World Population Day. An outgrowth of the Day of the Five Billion (July 11, 1987), this day seeks to focus public attention on the urgency and importance of population issues, particularly in the context of overall development plans and programs and the need to create solutions to these problems. For info: United Nations, Dept of Public Info, Public Inquiries Unit, RM GA-57, New York, NY 10017. Phone: (212) 963-4475. E-mail: inquiries@un.org.

WEST QUODDY HEAD LIGHT KEEPERS ASSOCIATION ANNIVERSARY CELEBRATION. July 11. Quoddy Head State Park, Lubec, ME. Live entertainment, local food vendors, raffle, museum, art gallery and special lighthouse tower climbing (supervised by the US Coast Guard). Est attendance: 750. For info: Manager, West Quoddy Head Light Keepers Assn & Visitor Center, PO Box 378, Lubec, ME 04652. Phone: (207) 733-2180. E-mail: info@westquoddy.com. Web: www.westquoddy.com.

WHITE, E.B.: BIRTH ANNIVERSARY. July 11, 1899. Versatile author of books for adults and children (*Charlotte's Web*) and *New Yorker* editor. Born at Mount Vernon, NY, White died at North Brooklyn, ME, Oct 1, 1985.

BIRTHDAYS TODAY

Giorgio Armani, 73, fashion designer, born Romagna, Italy, July 11, 1936.

Harold Bloom, 79, literary critic, born New York, NY, July 11, 1930.

Justin Chambers, 39, actor ("Grey's Anatomy," *The Wedding Planner*), born Springfield, OH, July 11, 1970.

Greg Grunberg, 43, actor ("Heroes," "Alias," "Felicity"), born Los Angeles, CA, July 11, 1966.

John Henson, 42, TV talk-show host ("Talk Soup"), born Stamford, CT, July 11, 1967.

Tab Hunter, 78, actor (*Damn Yankees*, "The Tab Hunter Show"), born Arthur Gelien at New York, NY, July 11, 1931.

Stephen Lang, 57, actor (*Last Exit to Brooklyn, Tombstone*), born Queens, NY, July 11, 1952.

Al MacInnis, 46, hockey executive and former player, born Inverness, NS, Canada, July 11, 1963.

Bonnie Pointer, 58, singer (Pointer Sisters, "Steam Heat"), born East Oakland, CA, July 11, 1951.

Michael Rosenbaum, 37, actor ("Smallville," *Sweet November*), born Oceanside, NJ, July 11, 1972.

Richie Sambora, 49, musician (Bon Jovi), born Amboy, NJ, July 11, 1960.

Leon Spinks, 56, former boxer, born St. Louis, MO, July 11, 1953.

Rod Strickland, 43, former basketball player, born the Bronx, NY, July 11, 1966.

Beverly Todd, 63, actress, director, producer (*Baby Boom, Clara's Heart*), born Chicago, IL, July 11, 1946.

Suzanne Vega, 50, singer, born Santa Monica, CA, July 11, 1959.

Sela Ward, 53, actress ("Sisters," "Once and Again"), born Meridian, MS, July 11, 1956.

July 2009

S	M	T	W	T	F	S
			1	2	3	4
5	6	7	8	9	10	11
12	13	14	15	16	17	18
19	20	21	22	23	24	25
26	27	28	29	30	31	

July 12 — Sunday

DAY 193 — **172 REMAINING**

BATTLE OF KURSK: ANNIVERSARY. July 12, 1943. The largest tank battle in history took place outside the small village of Prohorovka, Russia. Nine hundred Russian tanks attacked an equal number of German Panther and Porsche tanks. Though the German equipment was larger, that advantage was lost in a close-range battle where the tanks lacked maneuverability. When Hitler ordered a cease-fire, 300 German tanks remained strewn over the field.

BERLE, MILTON: BIRTH ANNIVERSARY. July 12, 1908. His nickname was "Mr Television," but Milton Berle had a long career as a vaudeville, film, radio and theater comedian as well. He was born Mendel Berlinger at Harlem, NY. He was popular before becoming the host of NBC's "Texaco Star Theater" in 1948, but that variety show made him a huge national star. Dressing in drag, rattling off corny jokes and drawing the day's biggest stars, "Uncle Miltie" made the show a television event until its end in 1953. He was one of the first seven inductees into the Academy of Television Arts and Sciences' TV Hall of Fame. Berle died Mar 27, 2002, at Los Angeles, CA.

De RITA, JOE: 100th BIRTH ANNIVERSARY. July 12, 1909. American comedian Curly Joe De Rita was the last surviving member of the Three Stooges comedy team. He joined the team in 1959 after Joe Besser left. He appeared in *Have Rocket, Will Travel* (1959), *Snow White and the Three Stooges* (1961) and *The Outlaw Is Coming* (1965). Born at Philadelphia, PA, De Rita died July 3, 1993, at Los Angeles, CA.

"EVENING AT POPS" TV PREMIERE: ANNIVERSARY. July 12, 1970. PBS's popular concert series premiered with conductor Arthur Fiedler heading the Boston Pops Orchestra. Conductor/composer John Williams took over the post upon Fiedler's death in 1979; Keith Lockhart is the current conductor.

FAMILY, CAREER AND COMMUNITY LEADERS OF AMERICA NATIONAL LEADERSHIP MEETING. July 12–16. Nashville, TN. This meeting is a unique opportunity to gain a national perspective on FCCLA activities and issues, elect officers, receive specialized leadership training and enhance chapter activities. Est attendance: 5,500. For info: Bana Yahnke, Family, Career and Community Leaders of America, Inc, 1910 Association Dr, Reston, VA 20191. Phone: (703) 476-4900. Fax: (703) 860-2713. E-mail: byahnke@fcclainc.org. Web: www.fcclainc.org.

"FAMILY FEUD" TV PREMIERE: ANNIVERSARY. July 12, 1976. From the production team of Mark Goodson and Bill Todman, this game show sets two families against each other to raise the greater number of points. The contestants have to predict the most common answers to a given survey question. Richard Dawson (TV's famous kissing host), the late Ray Combs, Louie Anderson and Richard Karn have been hosts.

FULLER, BUCKMINSTER: BIRTH ANNIVERSARY. July 12, 1895. Architect, inventor, engineer and philosopher, born Richard Buckminster Fuller at Milton, MA. His geodesic dome was one of the most important structural innovations of the 20th century. He died July 1, 1983, at Los Angeles, CA.

GERMANY ENDS MILITARY BAN: 15th ANNIVERSARY. July 12, 1994. Germany's Constitutional Court ended the ban on sending German troops to fight outside the country. The ban had been in effect since shortly after WWII, when Germany was disarmed. (Japan has a similar ban.) The ruling would allow German troops to join in peacekeeping missions of the United Nations or the North Atlantic Treaty Organization (NATO). As if to signal the change in status, German military units marched in the Bastille Day celebration at Paris on July 14, the first time German troops had appeared in France since the German occupation ended in 1945.

JONES WINS FIRST GRAND SLAM OF GOLF: ANNIVERSARY. July 12, 1930. Bobby Jones won the US Open Championship by two strokes over Macdonald Smith at the Interlachen Country Club at Hopkins, MN. Having already won the British Open, the British Amateur and the US Amateur, Jones became the only golfer to win the Grand Slam (the four major tournaments in one calendar year)—a usage that had to be invented by sportswriters, since no one had achieved that feat before.

KIRIBATI: INDEPENDENCE DAY: 30th ANNIVERSARY. July 12. Republic of Kiribati attained independence from Britain in 1979. Formerly known as the Gilbert Islands.

NATIONAL FARRIER'S WEEK. July 12–18. A salute from horse owners to the men and women who keep their horses shod and equine feet and legs in top-notch condition. Annually, the second or third week in July. For info: Frank Lessiter, American Farriers Journal, PO Box 624, Brookfield, WI 53008-0624. Phone: (262) 782-4480. Fax: (262) 782-1252. E-mail: lesspub@aol.com.

"NORTHERN EXPOSURE" TV PREMIERE: ANNIVERSARY. July 12, 1990. CBS's comedy-drama was essentially a fish-out-of-water (or rather a New Yorker out of Manhattan) series. Dr. Joel Fleischman (Rob Morrow) was forced to practice medicine in remote Cicely, AK, to pay off his student loans. He gradually accepted his lot with the help of the town's quirky citizens, who needed him because he was the only doctor in town. The show's cast featured Barry Corbin as Maurice Minnefield, a former NASA astronaut and Cicely's most prominent businessman; Janine Turner as bush pilot Maggie O'Connell; Elaine Miles as Joel's assistant Marilyn; Darren E. Burrows as Ed Chigliak, a half-Indian aspiring filmmaker; John Cullum as tavern owner Holling Vincoeur; Cynthia Geary as Holling's girlfriend and waitress Shelley Tambo; Peg Phillips as store proprietor Ruth-Anne and John Corbett as DJ Chris Stevens. The last episode aired in 1995.

NORTHERN IRELAND: ORANGEMEN'S DAY. July 12. National holiday commemorates Battle of Boyne, July 1 (OS), 1690, in which the forces of King William III of England, Prince of Orange, defeated those of James II, at Boyne River in Ireland. Ordinarily observed July 12. If July 12 is a Saturday or a Sunday, the holiday observance is on the following Monday.

SAO TOME AND PRINCIPE: INDEPENDENCE DAY. July 12. National holiday observed. Gained independence from Portugal in 1975.

SCOTLAND: THE OPEN CHAMPIONSHIP (BRITISH OPEN). July 12–19. Turnberry, Ayrshire. Est attendance: 200,000. For info: Ticket Office, The R&A, St. Andrews, Fife, Scotland KY16 9JD, United Kingdom. Phone: (44) (1334) 460-000. Fax: (44) (1334) 460-002. E-mail: tickets@randa.org.

SINCLAIR LEWIS DAYS. July 12–18. Sauk Centre, MN. Parade, kids' activities, dance, fireworks, Miss Sauk Centre pageant, flea market and craft sale in Sinclair Lewis's hometown. Est attendance: 10,000. For info: Sauk Centre Chamber of Commerce, PO Box 222, Sauk Centre, MN 56378. Phone: (320) 352-5201. Fax: (320) 352-5202. E-mail: chamber@saukcentrechamber.com. Web: www.saukcentrechamber.com.

SPACE MILESTONE: *PHOBOS 2* (USSR). July 12, 1988. Sent back the first close-up photos of Phobos, one of two small moons of Mars. Launched from Soviet space probe in central Asia on July 12, 1988.

THOREAU, HENRY DAVID: BIRTH ANNIVERSARY. July 12, 1817. American author and philosopher, born at Concord, MA. Died there May 6, 1862. In *Walden* he wrote, "I frequently tramped eight or ten miles through the deepest snow to keep an appointment with a beechtree, or a yellow birch, or an old acquaintance among the pines."

TURNER'S FRONTIER ADDRESS: ANNIVERSARY. July 12, 1893. Historian Frederick Jackson Turner delivered his paper "The Significance of the Frontier in American History" at a meeting of the American Historical Association at Chicago during the Columbian Exposition. Stating that the frontier was a spawning ground for many of the social and intellectual traits that made Americans different from Europeans, Turner saw the end of the frontier as a major break in the psychology of the nation. Turner's formalization of this idea came in part from his reading the *Extra Census Bulletin No 2: Distribution of Population According to Density: 1890*, which said, "Up to and including 1890 the country had a frontier of settlement, but at present the unsettled area has been so broken into by isolated bodies of settlement that there can hardly be said to be a frontier line."

WEDGWOOD, JOSIAH: BIRTH ANNIVERSARY. July 12, 1730. Famed pottery designer and manufacturer, born at Burslem, Staffordshire, England. Died at Etruria, Staffordshire, Jan 3, 1795.

BIRTHDAYS TODAY

Lisa Nicole Carson, 40, actress ("ER," "Ally McBeal"), born Brooklyn, NY, July 12, 1969.

Van Cliburn, 75, pianist, born Harvey Lavan Cliburn, Jr, at Shreveport, LA, July 12, 1934.

Bill Cosby, 71, comedian, actor (Emmys for "I Spy," "The Cosby Show"), born Philadelphia, PA, July 12, 1938.

Anna Friel, 33, actress ("Pushing Daisies," "Our Mutual Friend"), born Rochdale, Lancashire, England, July 12, 1976.

Paul Guilfoyle, 54, actor ("CSI"), born Boston, MA, July 12, 1955.

Mel Harris, 52, actress ("Something So Right," "thirtysomething"), born Bethlehem, PA, July 12, 1957.

Cheryl Ladd, 57, actress ("Charlie's Angels," "Grace Kelly"), born Huron, SD, July 12, 1952.

Christine McVie, 66, singer, musician (Fleetwood Mac), born Birmingham, England, July 12, 1943.

Denise Nicholas, 64, actress ("Room 222," "In the Heat of the Night," *Let's Do It Again*), born Detroit, MI, July 12, 1945.

Jamey Sheridan, 58, actor ("Law & Order: Criminal Intent," *The House on Carroll Street*), born Pasadena, CA, July 12, 1951.

Richard Simmons, 61, TV personality, weight loss guru, author, born New Orleans, LA, July 12, 1948.

Erik Per Sullivan, 18, actor ("Malcolm in the Middle," *The Cider House Rules*), born Worcester, MA, July 12, 1991.

Rolonda Watts, 50, talk-show host ("Rolonda"), born Winston-Salem, NC, July 12, 1959.

Kristi Tsuya Yamaguchi, 38, Olympic gold medal figure skater, born Hayward, CA, July 12, 1971.

July 13 — Monday

DAY 194 171 REMAINING

"BROTHERS" TV PREMIERE: 25th ANNIVERSARY. July 13, 1984. This sitcom was rejected by ABC and NBC before airing on Showtime, partly because one of its characters was openly gay. "Brothers" thus became the first original sitcom made for cable television. Robert Walden starred as Joe Waters, an ex-football player and restaurant owner; Brandon Maggart as eldest brother Lou, a conservative construction worker; and Paul Regina as youngest brother Clifford, who disclosed his orientation in the very first episode. Set in Philadelphia, the series dealt with sensitive topics such as gay-bashing, AIDS and male-to-male intimacy.

EMBRACE YOUR GEEKNESS DAY. July 13. Into dungeon games, comic books and vampire dress-up? Spend endless hours going strange places on the Internet? You're a geek, and this is the day to roar! (©2006 by WH.) For info: Thomas & Ruth Roy, Wellcat Holidays, 2418 Long Ln, Lebanon, PA 17046. Phone: (717) 279-0184. E-mail: info@wellcat.com. Web: www.wellcat.com.

FOLKMOOT USA: THE NORTH CAROLINA INTERNATIONAL FOLK FESTIVAL. July 13–26. Waynesville, NC. 26th annual. A festival of international folk dance featuring groups from 12 countries. Est attendance: 75,000. For info: Folkmoot USA, PO Box 658, Waynesville, NC 28786. Phone: (828) 452-2997 or (877) FOLK-USA. Fax: (828) 452-5762. Web: www.folkmootusa.org.

FORREST, NATHAN BEDFORD: BIRTH ANNIVERSARY. July 13, 1821. Confederate cavalry commander whose birthday is observed in schools in Tennessee, Forrest was also one of the founders of the short-lived original Ku Klux Klan. Forrest was born at Bedford County, TN, and died Oct 29, 1877, at Memphis, TN.

FRANCE: NIGHT WATCH (LA RETRAITE AUX FLAMBEAUX). July 13. France. Celebrates eve of the Bastille's fall. On the eve of Bastille Day, there are parades and fireworks.

GRUNTLED WORKERS DAY. July 13. There's so much news about disgruntled workers that today's the day for gruntled workers to unite! Drive to a fast-food restaurant and say, "Thanks. Your service is fast. Have a nice day." (©2006 by WH.) For info: Thomas & Ruth Roy, Wellcat Holidays, 2418 Long Ln, Lebanon, PA 17046. Phone: (717) 279-0184. E-mail: info@wellcat.com. Web: www.wellcat.com.

INTERNATIONAL TOWN CRIERS DAY. July 13. A day recognizing the ancient and honorable art and tradition of town crying and the significant contribution town criers make to promoting their respective towns and cities. Annually, the second Monday in July. For info: Doug Turvey, Official Town Crier, 784119 Rd 78, RR #5, Embro, ON, Canada N0J 1J0. Phone: (519) 475-4937. E-mail: zoringtowncrier@xplornet.com.

JAPAN: BON FESTIVAL (FEAST OF LANTERNS). July 13–15. Religious rites throughout Japan in memory of the dead, who, according to Buddhist belief, revisit Earth during this period. Lanterns are lighted for the souls. Spectacular bonfires in the shape of the character *dai* are burned on hillsides on the last day of the Bon (or O-Bon) Festival, bidding farewell to the spirits of the dead.

"LIVE AID" CONCERTS: ANNIVERSARY. July 13, 1985. Concerts at Philadelphia, PA, and London, England (Kennedy and Wembley stadiums), were seen by 162,000 attendees and an estimated 1.5 billion television viewers. Organized to raise funds for African famine relief; the musicians performed without a fee, and nearly $100 million was pledged toward aid to the hungry.

July 2009

S	M	T	W	T	F	S
			1	2	3	4
5	6	7	8	9	10	11
12	13	14	15	16	17	18
19	20	21	22	23	24	25
26	27	28	29	30	31	

NORTHWEST ORDINANCE: ANNIVERSARY. July 13, 1787. The Northwest Ordinance, providing for government of the territory north of the Ohio River, became law. The ordinance guaranteed freedom of worship and the right to trial by jury, and it prohibited slavery.

REPUBLIC OF MONTENEGRO: NATIONAL DAY. July 13.

US AMATEUR PUBLIC LINKS (GOLF) CHAMPIONSHIP. July 13–18. Jimmy Austin/University of Oklahoma Golf Club, Norman, OK. For info: USGA, Golf House, Championship Dept, PO Box 708, Far Hills, NJ 07931. Phone: (908) 234-2300. Fax: (908) 234-9687. E-mail: usga@usga.org. Web: www.usga.org.

WORLD CUP INAUGURATED: ANNIVERSARY. July 13, 1930. The first World Cup soccer competition was held at Montevideo, Uruguay, with 14 countries participating. On July 30, Uruguay defeated Argentina by a score of 4–2 to take the Cup.

BIRTHDAYS TODAY

Cameron Crowe, 52, director, screenwriter (*Fast Times at Ridgemont High, Jerry Maguire,* Oscar for *Almost Famous*), born Palm Springs, CA, July 13, 1957.

Harrison Ford, 67, actor (*Witness, The Fugitive,* the first Star Wars trilogy, the Indiana Jones films), born Chicago, IL, July 13, 1942.

Robert Forster, 68, actor ("Banyon," *Diamond Men, Jackie Brown*), born Rochester, NY, July 13, 1941.

Jane Hamilton, 52, author (*A Map of the World, The Book of Ruth*), born Oak Park, IL, July 13, 1957.

John French (Jack) Kemp, 74, former US Secretary of Housing and Urban Development, former football player, born Los Angeles, CA, July 13, 1935.

Louise Mandrell, 55, country western singer, born Corpus Christi, TX, July 13, 1954.

Cheech Marin, 63, writer, actor (Cheech and Chong films, "Nash Bridges"), born Los Angeles, CA, July 13, 1946.

Roger McGuinn, 67, musician (The Byrds), born James Joseph McGuinn at Chicago, IL, July 13, 1942.

Erno Rubik, 65, inventor of the Rubik's Cube, born in a hospital air raid shelter, Budapest, Hungary, July 13, 1944.

Wole Soyinka, 75, Nobel Prize–winning author (*The Lion and the Jewel, The Strong Breed*), born Abeokuta, Nigeria, July 13, 1934.

Michael Spinks, 53, former boxer, born St. Louis, MO, July 13, 1956.

Patrick Stewart, 69, actor ("Star Trek: The Next Generation," *X-Men* films, *A Christmas Carol, Excalibur*), born Mirfield, England, July 13, 1940.

David Storey, 76, author, playwright (*The Performance of Small Firms*), born Wakefield, England, July 13, 1933.

Anthony Jerome "Spud" Webb, 46, former basketball player, born Dallas, TX, July 13, 1963.

July 14 — Tuesday

DAY 195 **170 REMAINING**

ALPENFEST. July 14–18. Gaylord, MI. Swiss-inspired festival that has something for the whole family. Annual traditions include "The World's Largest Coffee Break," Lampion Parade, Burning of the Boogg and a Grand Parade. Free food and entertainment daily, 75 arts and crafts booths, free kids' games, contests and a carnival. Est attendance: 50,000. For info: Gayla Lamberies, Alpenfest, PO Box 513, Gaylord, MI 49734. Phone: (800) 345-8621. Fax: (989) 732-7990. E-mail: events@gaylordmichigan.com. Web: www.gaylordchamber.com.

BASCOM, FLORENCE: BIRTH ANNIVERSARY. July 14, 1862. After receiving her third bachelor's degree from the University of Wisconsin in 1884 and a master's degree in 1887, Florence Bascom entered Johns Hopkins University and received a doctorate in 1893. She taught at Ohio State and became a professor at Bryn Mawr. She also was the first woman appointed a geologist with the US Geological Survey, was associate editor of *American Geologist* (1890–1905) and became the first woman elected a Fellow of the Geological Society of America. Born at Williamstown, MA; died at Northampton, MA, June 18, 1945.

BERGMAN, INGMAR: BIRTH ANNIVERSARY. July 14, 1918. One of the most influential filmmakers of the 20th century, Bergman directed such classics as *Fanny and Alexander, Wild Strawberries* and *Cries and Whispers.* He wrote or directed 62 films and over 170 stage plays, mainly in his native Sweden, but was renowned all over the world and was nominated for nine Academy Awards. Born at Uppsala, Sweden, July 14, 1918, he died at Faro, Sweden, July 30, 2007.

CHANCELLOR, JOHN: BIRTH ANNIVERSARY. July 14, 1927. Television broadcast journalist John Chancellor was born at Chicago, IL. He rose through the ranks at the *Chicago Sun-Times,* from copyboy to feature writer. Chancellor spent more than four decades with the NBC network, beginning in 1950. During that time, he took a two-year respite from journalism to serve President Lyndon Johnson as director of the Voice of America. Chancellor retired in 1993, but his distinctive, familiar voice was still heard, such as when he narrated a PBS documentary in 1996. He died July 12, 1996, at Princeton, NJ.

CHILDREN'S PARTY AT GREEN ANIMALS. July 14. Green Animals Topiary Garden, Portsmouth, RI. Annual party for children and adults at Green Animals, a delightful topiary garden and children's toy museum. Party includes pony rides, games, clowns, refreshments, hot dogs, hamburgers and more. Annually, July 14. Est attendance: 1,500. For info: The Preservation Society of Newport County, 424 Bellevue Ave, Newport, RI 02840. Phone: (401) 847-1000. Web: www.NewportMansions.org.

EDWARDS, DOUGLAS: BIRTH ANNIVERSARY. July 14, 1917. American television journalist Douglas Edwards was born at Ada, OK. He began his career in radio, but in 1947 he became the first major announcer to move to television. He was anchor for CBS's first nightly news program, "Douglas Edwards with the News" (1948–62), where he gave memorable on-scene coverage of such events as the sinking of the *Andrea Doria* in 1956. Edwards worked for CBS until his retirement, two years before he died on Oct 13, 1990, at Sarasota, FL.

ENGLAND: BIRMINGHAM RIOT: ANNIVERSARY. July 14, 1791. Following a dinner celebrating the second anniversary of the fall of the Bastille, an angry mob rioted at Birmingham, England. The main target of their wrath was the home of scientist (discoverer of oxygen) Joseph Priestley, who was unpopular because of his religious views and his approval of the American and French revolutionary causes. The mob ruled Birmingham for three days, burning Priestley's home and laboratory as well as the homes of his friends. Priestley, in disguise, and his family narrowly escaped with their lives. They lived for a time at London before moving in 1794 to America. See also: "Priestley, Joseph: Birth Anniversary" (Mar 13).

FORD, GERALD RUDOLPH: BIRTH ANNIVERSARY. July 14, 1913. 38th president of the US (1974–77). Born Leslie King at Omaha, NE, Ford became 41st vice president of the US on Dec 6, 1973, by appointment, following the resignation of Spiro T. Agnew from that office on Oct 10, 1973. Ford became president on Aug 9, 1974, following the resignation from that office on that day of Richard M. Nixon. He was the first nonelected vice president and president of the US. He died at Rancho Mirage, CA, Dec 26, 2006.

FRANCE: BASTILLE DAY OR FETE NATIONAL. July 14. Public holiday commemorating the fall of the Bastille at the beginning of the French Revolution, July 14, 1789. Also celebrated or observed in many other countries.

GAGE COUNTY FAIR. July 14–19. Gage County Fair Grounds, Beatrice, NE. An annual event for more than 100 years. This award-winning fair has participants from the county and surrounding areas. Visitors and residents will enjoy the 4-H exhibits, livestock, midway rides, Grand Stand events and Beatrice Speedway Races with their annual Demolition Derby (held during fair week). If you're looking for traditional country flavor in a fair, this is the place to be! Annually, the third week of July. Est attendance: 100,000. For info: Gage County Fair and Expo, 1115 W Scott St, Beatrice, NE 68310. Phone: (402) 223-3247. E-mail: info@beatricechamber.com. Web: www.visitbeatrice.com.

GUTHRIE, WOODROW WILSON "WOODY": BIRTH ANNIVERSARY. July 14, 1912. American folksinger, songwriter ("This Land Is Your Land," "Union Maid," "Hard Traveling"), born at Okemah, OK. Traveled the country by freight train, singing and listening. Died Oct 3, 1967, at New York, NY. Father of Arlo Guthrie.

HANNA, WILLIAM: BIRTH ANNIVERSARY. July 14, 1910. Born at Melrose, NM, William Hanna was the cocreator of such popular animated characters as Tom and Jerry, Yogi Bear, Snagglepuss and Magilla Gorilla. With partner Joe Barbera, he won seven Academy Awards for his Tom and Jerry cartoon shorts, and eight other works were nominated. The Hanna-Barbera team created the first animated TV sitcom for adults, *The Flintstones* (1960), and such favorites as *The Jetsons* and *Scooby-Doo, Where Are You?* Hanna died at Los Angeles, CA, on Mar 22, 2001.

MISSION SAN ANTONIO DE PADUA: FOUNDING ANNIVERSARY. July 14. California. Mission to the Indians founded July 14, 1771.

MURRAY, KEN: BIRTH ANNIVERSARY. July 14, 1903. American comedian Ken Murray was born at New York, NY. He began in vaudeville, then moved to films and television. He died Oct 12, 1988, at Beverly Hills, CA.

SARTO, ANDREA DEL: BIRTH ANNIVERSARY. July 14, 1486. Celebrated Italian painter was born near Florence, Italy. "Sarto," a nickname referring to his father's trade as a tailor, was the name he chose during his lifetime, though the real surname was probably either Vanucchi or di Francesco. One of the most renowned artists of his time, his paintings hang in the great galleries of the world. He died at Florence, Jan 22, 1531.

SNAKE RIVER STAMPEDE. July 14–18. Nampa, ID. In its 94th year, this is one of the top 15 professional rodeo events in the nation, featuring the world's top cowboys and cowgirls in action. Events include bareback bronc riding, saddle bronc riding, bull riding, calf roping, team roping, steer wrestling and barrel racing. Est attendance: 45,000. For info: Jimmie Hurley, Snake River Stampede, PO Box 231, Nampa, ID 83653. Phone: (208) 466-8497. Fax: (208) 465-4438. E-mail: sstampede@earthlink.net.

BIRTHDAYS TODAY

Polly Bergen, 79, actress ("To Tell the Truth," *The Winds of War*), singer, born Knoxville, TN, July 14, 1930.

Matthew Fox, 43, actor ("Lost," "Party of Five"), born Crowheart, WY, July 14, 1966.

Missy Gold, 39, actress ("Benson"), born Great Falls, MT, July 14, 1970.

Roosevelt (Rosey) Grier, 77, actor, former football player, born Cuthbert, GA, July 14, 1932.

Jackie Earle Haley, 48, actor (*Breaking Away, The Bad News Bears, Little Children*), born Northridge, CA, July 14, 1961.

Joel Silver, 57, producer (*Lethal Weapon, Die Hard*), born South Orange, NJ, July 14, 1952.

Harry Dean Stanton, 83, actor (*Repo Man; Paris, Texas; Wild at Heart*), born West Irvine, KY, July 14, 1926.

Steve Stone, 62, sportscaster, former baseball player, born Euclid, OH, July 14, 1947.

Robin Ventura, 42, former baseball player, born Santa Maria, CA, July 14, 1967.

July 15 — Wednesday

DAY 196 **169 REMAINING**

BATTLE OF THE MARNE: ANNIVERSARY. July 15, 1918. General Erich Ludendorff launched Germany's fifth, and last, offensive to break through the Chateau-Thierry salient. This all-out effort involved three armies branching out from Rheims to cross the Marne River. The Germans were successful in crossing the Marne near Chateau-Thierry before American, British and Italian divisions stopped their progress. On July 18 General Foch, commander in chief of the Allied troops, launched a massive counteroffensive that resulted in a German retreat that continued for four months until Germany sued for peace in November.

CANADA: SAINT SWITHUN'S SOCIETY ANNUAL CELEBRATION. July 15. Toronto, ON. Goals include the promotion of feelings of goodwill, the encouragement of the celebration of St. Swithun's Day and the patterning of members' lives after the example of our patron. Affiliated with the Friends of Winchester Cathedral. Publishes "The Water Spout" newsletter, free upon request. Annually, July 15. Est attendance: 100. For info: Norman A. McMullen, KStG, Pres, St. Swithun's Society, 427 Lynett Crescent, Richmond Hill, ON, Canada L4C 2V6. Phone: (905) 883-0984. E-mail: nmcmullen@rogers.com.

CANADA: WINNIPEG FRINGE THEATRE FESTIVAL. July 15–26. Winnipeg, MB. Pushing the envelope in theatrical entertainment since 1988. A 12-day, noon-to-midnight, nonstop theatrical smorgasbord with more than 130 theater companies from around the world. Est attendance: 165,000. For info: The Winnipeg Fringe Festival, 174 Market Ave, Winnipeg, MB, Canada R3B 0P8. E-mail: info@winnipegfringe.com. Web: www.winnipegfringe.com.

DERRIDA, JACQUES: BIRTH ANNIVERSARY. July 15, 1930. Influential French philosopher; proponent of deconstruction. Born at El Biar, Algeria, Derrida died Oct 8, 2004, at Paris, France.

GEORGIA MOUNTAIN FAIR. July 15–26. Georgia Mountain Fairgrounds, Hiawassee, GA. Authentic mountain demonstrations including corn milling, board splitting, soap and hominy making in our Pioneer Village with one-room school, log cabin, barn, old store, corncrib and more. Nashville talent, clogging, midway, arts and crafts and much more. Est attendance: 80,000. For info: Georgia Mountain Fair, PO Box 444, Hiawassee, GA 30546. Phone: (706) 896-4191. Fax: (706) 896-4209. E-mail: gamtfair@alltel.net. Web: www.georgiamountainfairgrounds.com.

MOON PHASE: LAST QUARTER. July 15. Moon enters Last Quarter phase at 5:53 AM, EDT.

MOORE, CLEMENT CLARKE: BIRTH ANNIVERSARY. July 15, 1779. American author and teacher, best remembered for his popular verse "A Visit from Saint Nicholas" ("'Twas the Night Before Christmas"), which was first published anonymously and without Moore's knowledge in a newspaper, Dec 23, 1823. Moore was born at New York, NY, and died at Newport, RI, July 10, 1863. (In recent years, Moore's authorship of the poem has been challenged, with Henry Livingston, Jr, offered as the creator.)

NATIONAL RABBIT WEEK. July 15–21. To pay tribute to the rabbit for being a great companion to humans as a house pet. Recognition should also be given to any rabbit that has done something special to help mankind (e.g., saved someone's life, visited patients at a hospital, etc). The public should be informed during this week on the proper care of rabbits and the problems with buying an "Easter" rabbit. For info: Melvin Rabbit, CP 157, Place du Parc, Montreal, QC, Canada H2X 4A4. Phone: (514) 849-0888. E-mail: magician@total.net.

"ONE LIFE TO LIVE" TV PREMIERE: ANNIVERSARY. July 15, 1968. Set in a fictional Pennsylvania town, the show was created by Agnes Nixon to depict the class and ethnic struggles of the town's denizens. The initial cast featured many Jewish, Polish and African-American characters. The show departed from interethnic storytelling in the 1980s for more fantastic adventures set in locales such as heaven, the Old West and a futuristic mountain silo called Eternia. Since then, the show has returned to its strengths of traditional storytelling by featuring Latino and African-American actors as integral characters. Award-winning actress Erika Slezak heads the cast as the venerable Viki Lord Riley Buchanan Carpenter, the town's matron with five alternate personalities. Among those who have appeared on "OLTL" are Tom Berenger, Judith Light, Robert Desiderio, Tommy Lee Jones, Laurence Fishburne, Jameson Parker, Phylicia Rashad, Christine Ebersole, Richard Grieco, Blair Underwood, Joe Lando, Audrey Landers, Christian Slater and Yasmine Bleeth.

REMBRANDT: BIRTH ANNIVERSARY. July 15, 1606. Dutch painter and etcher, born Rembrandt Harmenszoon van Rijn at Leiden, Holland. One of the undisputed giants of Western art. Known for *The Night Watch* and many portraits and self-portraits. He died at Amsterdam, Holland, Oct 4, 1669.

SAINT FRANCES XAVIER CABRINI: BIRTH ANNIVERSARY. July 15, 1850. First American saint, founder of schools, orphanages, convents and hospitals, born at Lombardy, Italy. Died of malaria at Chicago, IL, Dec 22, 1917. Canonized July 7, 1946.

SAINT SWITHIN'S DAY. July 15. Swithun (Swithin), bishop of Winchester (AD 852–862), died July 2, 862. Little is known of his life, but his relics were transferred into Winchester Cathedral July 15, 971, a day on which there was a heavy rainfall. According to old English belief, it will rain for 40 days thereafter when it rains on this day. "St. Swithin's Day, if thou dost rain, for 40 days it will remain; St. Swithin's Day, if thou be fair, for 40 days, will rain nea mair."

July 2009

S	M	T	W	T	F	S
			1	2	3	4
5	6	7	8	9	10	11
12	13	14	15	16	17	18
19	20	21	22	23	24	25
26	27	28	29	30	31	

BIRTHDAYS TODAY

Willie Aames, 49, actor ("Eight Is Enough," "Charles in Charge"), born Newport Beach, CA, July 15, 1960.

Kim Alexis, 49, model, born Lockport, NY, July 15, 1960.

Julian Bream, 76, musician (classical guitar, lute), born London, England, July 15, 1933.

Jonathan Cheechoo, 29, hockey player, born Moose Factory, ON, Canada, July 15, 1980.

Lolita Davidovich, 48, actress (*Indictment, Cobb*), born London, ON, Canada, July 15, 1961.

Brian Austin Green, 36, actor ("Beverly Hills 90210"), singer, born Van Nuys, CA, July 15, 1973.

Arianna Huffington, 59, author, journalist ("The Huffington Post"), born Athens, Greece, July 15, 1950.

Irene Jacob, 43, actress (*Red, Othello*), born Paris, France, July 15, 1966.

Alex George Karras, 74, former football player, actor ("Webster," *Babe, Victor/Victoria*), born Gary, IN, July 15, 1935.

Ken Kercheval, 74, actor ("Dallas," "Search for Tomorrow"), born Wolcottville, IN, July 15, 1935.

Terry O'Quinn, 57, actor ("Lost," "The West Wing," "Alias"), born Newberry, MI, July 15, 1952.

Linda Ronstadt, 63, singer, songwriter, born Tucson, AZ, July 15, 1946.

Richard Russo, 60, author (*Empire Falls, Straight Man, Nobody's Fool*), born Johnstown, NY, July 15, 1949.

Adam Savage, 42, television personality, host ("MythBusters"), born New York, NY, July 15, 1967.

Jesse Ventura, 58, former professional wrestler, former Governor of Minnesota (I), born Minneapolis, MN, July 15, 1951.

Jan-Michael Vincent, 65, actor ("The Winds of War," "Airwolf"), born Denver, CO, July 15, 1944.

George V. Voinovich, 73, US Senator (R, Ohio), born Cleveland, OH, July 15, 1936.

Forest Whitaker, 48, actor ("The Shield," Oscar for *The Last King of Scotland; Bird, The Crying Game, Ghost Dog*), director (*Waiting to Exhale*), born Longview, TX, July 15, 1961.

July 16 — Thursday

DAY 197 — **168 REMAINING**

AMUNDSEN, ROALD: BIRTH ANNIVERSARY. July 16, 1872. Norwegian explorer born near Oslo, Roald Amundsen was the first man to sail from the Atlantic to the Pacific Ocean via the Northwest Passage (1903–05). He discovered the South Pole (Dec 14, 1911) and flew over the North Pole in a dirigible in 1926. He flew, with five companions, from Norway, June 18, 1928, in a daring effort to rescue survivors of an Italian Arctic expedition. No trace of the rescue party or the airplane was ever located. See also: "South Pole: Discovery Anniversary" (Dec 14).

ATOMIC BOMB TESTED: ANNIVERSARY. July 16, 1945. In the New Mexican desert at Alamogordo Air Base, 125 miles southeast of Albuquerque, the experimental atomic bomb was set off at 5:30 AM. Dubbed "Fat Boy" by its creator, the plutonium bomb vaporized the steel scaffolding holding it as the immense fireball rose 8,000 feet in a fraction of a second—ultimately creating a mushroom cloud to a height of 41,000 feet. At ground zero the bomb emitted heat three times the temperature of the interior of the sun. All plant and animal life for a mile around ceased to exist. When informed by President Truman at Potsdam of the successful experiment, Winston Churchill responded, "It's the Second Coming in wrath!"

BOLIVIA: LA PAZ DAY. July 16, 1548. Founding of city, now capital of Bolivia, on this day, 1548.

CANADA: JUST FOR LAUGHS: THE MONTREAL INTERNATIONAL COMEDY FESTIVAL. July 16–26. Montreal, QC. Make the trip to the worldwide capital of comedy! More than 1,000 artists from 19 countries play more than 2,000 shows and performances at indoor and outdoor venues that blanket the entire city. In the past, the Just for Laughs bilingual comedy marathon has featured some of the world's most impressive talent including Tim Allen, Jerry Seinfeld, Drew Carey, Kelsey Grammer, Rowan "Mr Bean" Atkinson, Jim Carrey and David Hyde Pierce, to name but a few. Est attendance: 1,700,000. For info: Just for Laughs Festival, 2101 St-Laurent Blvd, Montreal, QC, Canada H2X 2T5. Phone: (514) 845-3155 or (888) 244-3155. Fax: (514) 845-4140. E-mail: info@hahaha.com. Web: www.hahaha.com.

COMET CRASHES INTO JUPITER: 15th ANNIVERSARY. July 16, 1994. The first fragment of the comet Shoemaker-Levy crashed into the planet Jupiter, beginning a series of spectacular collisions, each unleashing more energy than the combined effect of an explosion of all our world's nuclear arsenal. Video imagery from earthbound telescopes as well as the Hubble telescope provided vivid records of the explosions and their aftereffects. In 1993 the comet had shattered into a series of about a dozen large chunks that resembled "pearls on a string" after its orbit brought it within the gravitational effects of our solar system's largest planet.

DISTRICT OF COLUMBIA ESTABLISHING LEGISLATION: ANNIVERSARY. July 16, 1790. George Washington signed legislation that selected the District of Columbia as the permanent capital of the US. Boundaries of the district were established in 1792. Plans called for the government to remain housed at Philadelphia, PA, until 1800, when the new national capital would be ready for occupancy.

EARTHQUAKE JOLTS PHILIPPINES: ANNIVERSARY. July 16, 1990. An earthquake measuring 7.7 on the Richter scale struck the Philippines, killing an estimated 1,621 persons and leaving approximately 1,000 missing. The quake struck in an area north of Manila, and heavy damage was reported at Cabanatuan, at Baguio and on Luzon island. The quake was the worst in the Philippines in 14 years.

EDDY, MARY BAKER: BIRTH ANNIVERSARY. July 16, 1821. Founder of Christian Science; born near Concord, NH, she died at Chestnut Hill, MA, Dec 3, 1910.

JAMBOREE IN THE HILLS. July 16–19. St. Clairsville, OH. 33rd year. Billed as the "Biggest Party of the Year," this festival is a four-day outdoor country music show featuring the top names in country music today. Annually, the third weekend in July. Est attendance: 110,000. For info: Shannon Wall, Publicity Director, Jamboree in the Hills, 1015 Main St, Wheeling, WV 26003. Phone: (800) 624-5456. Fax: (304) 233-0058. Web: www.jamboreeinthehills.com.

MISSION SAN DIEGO DE ALCALA: FOUNDING ANNIVERSARY. July 16, 1769. First of 21 California missions to the Indians.

REYNOLDS, JOSHUA: BIRTH ANNIVERSARY. July 16, 1723. (Old Style date.) English portrait painter whose paintings of 18th-century English notables are among the best of the time. Born at Plympton, Devon, England, Sir Joshua died at London, Feb 23, 1792, at age 68. "He who resolves never to ransack any mind but his own," Reynolds told students of the Royal Academy in 1774, "will be soon reduced, from mere barrenness, to the poorest of all imitations; he will be obliged to imitate himself, and to repeat what he has before often repeated."

ROGERS, GINGER: BIRTH ANNIVERSARY. July 16, 1911. Ginger Rogers is best remembered as Fred Astaire's dance partner in a series of romantic musicals. She appeared in 70 films during her six-decade career, winning an Oscar for her leading role in the 1940 film *Kitty Foyle*. Rogers was born at Independence, MO, and died Apr 25, 1995, at Rancho Mirage, CA.

SPACE MILESTONE: *APOLLO 11* (US): MAN SENT TO THE MOON: 40th ANNIVERSARY. July 16, 1969. This launch resulted in man's first moon landing, the first landing on any extraterrestrial body. See also: "Space Milestone: Moon Day" (July 20).

STANWYCK, BARBARA: BIRTH ANNIVERSARY. July 16, 1907. Actress Barbara Stanwyck was born Ruby Stevens at the Flatbush section of Brooklyn, NY. At the age of 18 she won a leading role in the Broadway melodrama *Noose*, appearing for the first time as Barbara Stanwyck. She appeared in 82 films including *Stella Dallas; Double Indemnity; Sorry, Wrong Number; The Lady Eve* and the television series "The Big Valley." In 1944 the government listed her as the nation's highest-paid woman, earning $400,000 per year. Stanwyck died at Santa Monica, CA, Jan 21, 1990.

VENTHAVEN VENTRILOQUIST CONVENTION. July 16–19. Fort Mitchell, KY. The world's oldest and largest continuing gathering of ventriloquists. It is *the* place to be if you want to better yourself as a ventriloquist or if you wish to learn more about the art of ventriloquism. For info: Daniel Robinson, VentHaven, 161 Republic Ave, Warren, OH 44483. Phone: (330) 219-4120. E-mail: danieljayrobinson@gmail.com. Web: www.venthaven.com.

VIRGINIA LAKE FESTIVAL. July 16–18. Clarksville, VA. Fun-filled weekend with Pig Pickin; opening ceremonies on Friday; arts and crafts show, hot-air balloons, live entertainment for children and adults and fireworks on Saturday. Annually, the third full weekend in July. Est attendance: 80,000. For info: Clarksville Lake Country Chamber of Commerce, 105 2nd St, Box 1017, Clarksville, VA 23927. Phone: (434) 374-2436 or (800) 557-5582. E-mail: clarksville@kerrlake.com. Web: www.clarksvilleva.com.

WELLS, IDA B.: BIRTH ANNIVERSARY. July 16, 1862. African-American journalist and antilynching crusader Ida B. Wells was born the daughter of slaves at Holly Springs, MS, and grew up as Jim Crow and lynching were becoming prevalent. Wells argued that lynchings occurred not to defend white women but because of whites' fear of economic competition from blacks. She traveled extensively, founding antilynching societies and black women's clubs. Wells's *Red Record* (1895) was one of the first accounts of lynchings in the South. She died Mar 25, 1931, at Chicago, IL.

BIRTHDAYS TODAY

Ruben Blades, 61, singer, actor (*Crossover Dreams, The Milagro Beanfield War*), born Panama City, Panama, July 16, 1948.

Phoebe Cates, 46, actress (*Fast Times at Ridgemont High, Gremlins*), born New York, NY, July 16, 1963.

Stewart Copeland, 57, composer, musician (The Police), born Alexandria, VA, July 16, 1952.

Will Farrell, 42, comedian, actor (*Semi-Pro, Blades of Glory, Stranger Than Fiction, Anchorman*), born Irvine, CA, July 16, 1967.

Corey Feldman, 38, actor (*Stand by Me, The Lost Boys*), born Reseda, CA, July 16, 1971.

Michael Flatley, 51, dancer (*Lord of the Dance, Feet of Flames*), born Chicago, IL, July 16, 1958.

Alexis Herman, 62, former Secretary of Labor (Clinton administration), born Mobile, AL, July 16, 1947.

Mark Indelicato, 15, actor ("Ugly Betty"), born Philadelphia, PA, July 16, 1994.

Bess Myerson, 85, former Miss America (1945), former government official, born New York, NY, July 16, 1924.

Barry Sanders, 41, former football player, born Wichita, KS, July 16, 1968.

Pinchas Zukerman, 61, violinist, born Tel Aviv, Israel, July 16, 1948.

July 2009	S	M	T	W	T	F	S
				1	2	3	4
	5	6	7	8	9	10	11
	12	13	14	15	16	17	18
	19	20	21	22	23	24	25
	26	27	28	29	30	31	

July 17 — Friday

DAY 198 — **167 REMAINING**

ABBOTT, BERENICE: BIRTH ANNIVERSARY. July 17, 1898. Berenice Abbott was born at Springfield, OH, and went on to become a pioneer of American photography. She is best remembered for her black-and-white photographs of New York City in the 1930s, many of which appeared in the book *Changing New York*. After publishing this collection she began photographing scientific experiments that illustrated the laws and processes of physics. She died at Monson, ME, Dec 11, 1991.

BIG SKY STATE GAMES. July 17–19. Billings, MT. An Olympic-style festival for Montana citizens. This statewide multisport program is designed to inspire people of all ages and skill levels to develop their physical and competitive abilities to the height of their potential through participation in fitness activities. There are 12,000 participants. Est attendance: 30,000. For info: Big Sky State Games, Box 7136, Billings, MT 59103-7136. Phone: (406) 254-7426. Fax: (406) 254-7439. E-mail: info@bigskygames.org. Web: www.bigskygames.org.

CANADA: VANCOUVER FOLK MUSIC FESTIVAL. July 17–19. Jericho Beach Park, Vancouver, BC. Come and join in the musical festival, which also features food booths, entertainment and much more. Est attendance: 30,000. For info: Vancouver Folk Music Festival, 468-411 Dunsmuir St, Vancouver, BC, Canada V6B 1X4. Phone: (604) 602-9798. Fax: (604) 602-9790. E-mail: inquiries@thefestival.bc.ca. Web: www.thefestival.bc.ca.

CHEYENNE FRONTIER DAYS. July 17–26. Frontier Park, Cheyenne, WY. Held annually since 1897, the world's largest outdoor rodeo is the "Daddy of 'em All" with nine rodeos, nine night shows, three free pancake breakfasts, four parades, chuckwagon racing, carnival midway and exhibitors. Annually, encompassing the last full week in July. Est attendance: 555,000. For info: Cheyenne Frontier Days, PO Box 2477, Cheyenne, WY 82003. Phone: (800) 227-6336 or (307) 778-7200. Web: www.cfdrodeo.com.

CZAR NICHOLAS II AND FAMILY EXECUTED: ANNIVERSARY. July 17, 1918. Russian czar Nicholas II; his wife, Alexandra; son and heir, Alexis; and daughters, Anastasia, Tatiana, Olga and Marie, were executed by firing squad on this date. The murder of the last of the 300-year-old Romanov dynasty occurred at Yekaterinburg, in the Ural Mountains of Siberia where Nicholas had been imprisoned since his abdication in 1917. Local Soviet officials, concerned about advancing promonarchist forces, executed the royal family rather than have them serve as a rallying point for the White Russians. In 1992 two of nine skeletons dug up the previous summer from a pit at Yekaterinburg were identified as the remains of the czar and czarina.

DECOY AND WILDLIFE ART SHOW. July 17–19. Clayton Recreation Park Arena, Clayton, NY. 41st annual juried show. World championship wildlife carvers, artists, taxidermists, collectors and dealers. Events include hunting decoy contest, gunning rig contest, contemporary painting contest and silent auction. Displays of handcrafted wildlife from wood, silver, gold and pewter. Annually, the third weekend in July. Est attendance: 3,000. For info: Thousand Islands Museum, PO Box 27, Clayton, NY 13624. Phone: (315) 686-5794. Fax: (315) 686-4867. E-mail: info@timuseum.org. Web: www.timuseum.org.

DISNEYLAND OPENED: ANNIVERSARY. July 17, 1955. Disneyland, America's first theme park, opened at Anaheim, CA.

GARDNER, ERLE STANLEY: BIRTH ANNIVERSARY. July 17, 1889. American author of detective fiction, born at Malden, MA. Best remembered for his series about lawyer-detective Perry Mason, Gardner also wrote novels under the pen name A.A. Fair. Gardner died at Temecula, CA, Mar 11, 1970.

GERRY, ELBRIDGE: BIRTH ANNIVERSARY. July 17, 1744. Fifth vice president of the US (1813–14), born at Marblehead, MA. Died at Washington, DC, Nov 23, 1814. His name became part of the language (gerrymander) after he signed a redistricting bill favoring his party while governor of Massachusetts in 1812.

THE GREAT WELLSVILLE BALLOON RALLY. July 17–19. Wellsville, NY. 34th annual. The Great Wellsville Balloon Rally is a great community and western New York state event that boasts four free mass hot-air balloon launches. More than 40 hot-air balloons launch, weather permitting, at 6 PM Friday and Saturday and 6 AM Saturday and Sunday. The weekend's festivities include a huge Wellsville Main Street Merchant Sidewalk Sale, free music, great food, fireworks and afterglow. Est attendance: 50,000. For info: Wellsville Area Chamber of Commerce. Phone: (585) 593-5080. Web: www.wellsvilleballoonrally.com.

KANSAS CITY HOTEL DISASTER: ANNIVERSARY. July 17, 1981. Anniversary of the collapse of aerial walkways at the Hyatt Regency Hotel at Kansas City, MO. About 1,500 people were attending the popular weekly tea dance when, at about 7 PM, two concrete and steel skywalks that were suspended from the ceiling of the hotel's atrium broke loose and fell on guests in the crowded lobby, killing 114 people. In 1986 a state board revoked the licenses of two engineers convicted of gross negligence for their part in designing the hotel.

KENTUCKY STATE CHAMPIONSHIP OLD-TIME FIDDLER'S CONTEST. July 17–18. Rough River Dam State Resort Park, Falls of Rough, KY. Old-time and bluegrass music competition; Governor's Cup trophy is awarded to the champion fiddler. More than $5,000 in prize money. Annually, the third Friday and Saturday in July. Est attendance: 4,000. For info: Brent L. Miller, PO Box 4042, Leitchfield, KY 42755. Phone: (270) 259-3578. Fax: (270) 259-0655. Web: www.kyfiddler.com.

KOREA: CONSTITUTION DAY. July 17. Legal national holiday. Commemorates the proclamation of the constitution of the Republic of Korea in 1948. Ceremonies at Seoul's capitol plaza and all major cities.

MINIMUM LEGAL DRINKING AGE AT 21: 25th ANNIVERSARY. July 17, 1984. Mothers Against Drunk Driving (MADD) helped pass the 21 Minimum Legal Drinking Age (MLDA) law because it makes sense and saves lives. President Ronald Reagan signed MLDA federal legislation making it illegal for anyone under 21 to purchase or publicly possess alcohol. An estimated 1,000 lives are saved each year as a result. For info: MADD. Phone: 800 GET-MADD. Web: www.madd.org.

NATCHITOCHES–NORTHWESTERN STATE UNIVERSITY FOLK FESTIVAL AND THE LOUISIANA STATE FIDDLE CHAMPIONSHIP. July 17–18. Prather Coliseum, Northwestern State University, Natchitoches, LA. The festival is a "purist" folk festival in that only folk artists who are reviving a traditional Louisiana folk art or still working a Louisiana tradition are invited. Music, food, crafts and narrative sessions. A four-time winner of the Top Twenty Events in the Southeast, as determined by the Southeast Tourism Society. Est attendance: 5,000. For info: Sheila Richmond, Louisiana Folklife Center, Natchitoches/NSU Folk Fest, NSU PO Box 3663, Natchitoches, LA 71497. Phone: (318) 357-4332 or (800) 259-1714. Fax: (318) 357-4331. E-mail: folklife@nsula.edu. Web: www.nsula.edu/folklife.

PUERTO RICO: MUÑOZ-RIVERA DAY. July 17. Public holiday on the anniversary of the birth of Luis Muñoz-Rivera. The Puerto Rican patriot, poet and journalist was born at Barranquitas, Puerto Rico, in 1859. He died at Santurce, a suburb of San Juan, Puerto Rico, Nov 15, 1916.

SHERWOOD ROBIN HOOD FESTIVAL. July 17–18. Sherwood, OR. Renaissance group; knighting ceremony; kids and family area; parade; world's only archery contest between Sherwood and Nottingham, England; flower and castle contest; teen dance; music; food and crafts vendors and much more! Annually, the third weekend in July. Est attendance: 18,000. For info: Robin Hood Festival Assn, PO Box 496, Sherwood, OR 97140. Phone: (503) 625-4233. Web: www.robinhoodfestival.com.

SHOW ME STATE GAMES. July 17–19 (also July 24–26 and July 31–Aug 2). Columbia, MO. An Olympic-style athletic festival for Missouri citizens. This statewide multisport program is designed to inspire Missourians of every age and skill level to develop their physical and competitive abilities to the height of their potential through participation in fitness activities. Est attendance: 55,000. For info: Show Me State Games, 1105 Carrie Francke Dr, Columbia, MO 65211. Phone: (573) 882-2105. Fax: (573) 884-4004. E-mail: unglesb@missouri.edu. Web: www.smsg.org.

SPACE MILESTONE: *APOLLO-SOYUZ* TEST PROJECT (US, USSR). July 17, 1975. After three years of planning, negotiation and preparation, the first US–USSR joint space project reached fruition with the linkup in space of *Apollo 18* (crew: T. Stafford, V. Brand, D. Slayton; landed in Pacific Ocean July 24, during 136th orbit) and *Soyuz 19* (crew: A.A. Leonov, V.N. Kubasov; landed July 21, after 96 orbits). *Apollo 18* and *Soyuz 19* were linked for 47 hours (July 17–19) while joint experiments and transfer of personnel and materials back and forth between crafts took place. Launch date was July 15, 1975.

SPACE MILESTONE: *SOYUZ T-12* (USSR): 25th ANNIVERSARY. July 17, 1984. Cosmonaut Svetlana Savitskaya became the first woman to walk in space (July 25) and the first woman to make more than one space voyage. Docked at *Salyut 7* July 18 and returned to Earth July 29.

STEALTH BOMBER FLIGHT: 20th ANNIVERSARY. July 17, 1989. The B-2 Stealth bomber airplane was flown successfully over the desert near Palmdale, CA, for almost two hours. A decade of work and $22 billion reportedly were spent on the project prior to the first flight. Designed to penetrate Soviet radar, the B-2 Stealth bomber was said to be capable of delivering up to 25 tons of nuclear or other bombs. Average cost of each of the 132 bombers requested by the Air Force was estimated to be $530 million. On this first test flight the plane flew at speeds of up to 180 knots (200 mph) and was put through several types of turns. Higher speeds and retraction of the landing gear were left for subsequent test flights.

TARGHEE FEST. July 17–19. Grand Targhee Mountain, Alta, WY. Folk arts festival with performances by artists like Emmy Lou Harris, Patty Griffin, Greg Brown, Taj Mahal, Keb Mo and many more! Incredible lineup at a beautiful mountain venue on the western slope of the Tetons. Great food, vendors, games and on-site activities are all a part of our summer music festival. Tent camping at Grand Targhee in our beautiful national forest is available during the weekend. Est attendance: 6,000. For info: Mandy Hood, Grand Targhee Resort, 3300 E Ski Hill Rd, Alta, WY 83414. Phone: (307) 353-2300. Fax: (307) 353-8148. E-mail: mhood@grandtarghee.com. Web: www.grandtarghee.com.

W.C. HANDY MUSIC FESTIVAL. July 17–26. Florence, AL. A week-long street-strutting, toe-tapping and hand-clapping celebration of the musical heritage of Florence native W.C. Handy ("the father of the blues") culminating in a spectacular Saturday-evening concert. Also includes athletic events. Est attendance: 150,000. For info: Nancy Gonce, Exec Dir, Music Preservation Society, PO Box 1827, Florence, AL 35631. Phone: (256) 766-7642. Fax: (256) 766-7549. Web: www.wchandymusicfestival.org.

WORLDFUTURE 2009. July 17–19. Chicago Hilton and Towers, Chicago, IL. Annual conference. For info: World Future Society, 7910 Woodmont Ave, Ste 450, Bethesda, MD 20814. Phone: (800) 989-8274 or (301) 656-8274. Fax: (301) 951-0394. E-mail: info@wfs.org. Web: www.wfs.org.

"WRONG WAY" CORRIGAN DAY: ANNIVERSARY. July 17, 1938. Douglas Groce Corrigan, an unemployed airplane mechanic, left Brooklyn, NY's Floyd Bennett Field, ostensibly headed for Los Angeles, CA, in a 1929 Curtiss Robin monoplane. He landed 28 hours, 13 minutes later at Dublin, Ireland's Baldonnell Airport after a 3,150-mile nonstop flight without radio or special navigation equipment and in violation of American and Irish flight regulations. Born at Galveston, TX, Jan 22, 1907, Corrigan received a hero's welcome home; he was nicknamed "Wrong Way" Corrigan because he claimed he accidentally followed the wrong end of his compass needle. Died at Santa Ana, CA, Dec 9, 1995.

YARMOUTH CLAM FESTIVAL. July 17–19. Yarmouth, ME. 44th annual. Family-oriented festival featuring clams and more. Annually, starts the third Friday in July. Est attendance: 120,000. For info: Yarmouth Chamber of Commerce, 162 Main St, Yarmouth, ME 04096. Phone: (207) 846-3984. Fax: (207) 846-5419. E-mail: info@clamfestival.com. Web: www.clamfestival.com.

 BIRTHDAYS TODAY

Lucie Arnaz, 58, actress ("Here's Lucy," "The Lucie Arnaz Show," *Lost in Yonkers*), born Los Angeles, CA, July 17, 1951.

Diahann Carroll, 74, singer, actress ("Julia," "Dynasty"), born Carol Diahann Johnson at New York, NY, July 17, 1935.

Phyllis Diller, 92, comedienne, actress (*Boy, Did I Get a Wrong Number!*), born Phyllis Driver at Lima, OH, July 17, 1917.

David Hasselhoff, 57, actor ("Knight Rider," "Baywatch"), born Baltimore, MD, July 17, 1952.

Jason Jennings, 31, baseball player, born Dallas, TX, July 17, 1978.

Aaron Lansky, 54, founder of National Yiddish Book Center, born New Bedford, MA, July 17, 1955.

Phoebe Snow, 57, singer ("Poetry Man"), born New York, NY, July 17, 1952.

Donald Sutherland, 74, actor (*M*A*S*H, Klute, Backdraft*), born St. John, NB, Canada, July 17, 1935.

Dawn Upshaw, 49, opera singer, born Nashville, TN, July 17, 1960.

Alex Winter, 44, actor (*Bill & Ted's Excellent Adventure*), born London, England, July 17, 1965.

July 2009	S	M	T	W	T	F	S
				1	2	3	4
	5	6	7	8	9	10	11
	12	13	14	15	16	17	18
	19	20	21	22	23	24	25
	26	27	28	29	30	31	

July 18 — Saturday

DAY 199 — **166 REMAINING**

BANNACK DAYS. July 18–19. Bannack, MT. Montana's first territorial capital, now a well-preserved ghost town, comes to life with a celebration of Montana's mining and pioneer history. Wagon rides, main street gunfights, old-time dancing, lots of music and fun are provided during this two-day celebration along Grasshopper Creek each year. Bannack State Park allows visitors to explore the old town and imagine what life was like in the mid-1800s. It is open year-round to the public. No admission fee. Est attendance: 4,000. For info: Dale Carlson, Park Manager, Montana Fish, Wildlife and Parks, 4200 Bannack Rd, Dillon, MT 59725. Phone: (406) 834-3413. E-mail: bannack@smtel.com.

CELEBRATION OF THE HORSE. July 18–19. Houston, TX. In honor of the human/equine bond and how horses affect people on an individual basis. Annually, the third weekend in July. For info: Tim Raisbeck, Charlotte's Saddlery, 11623A Katy Freeway, Houston, TX 77079. Phone: (281) 596-8225. Fax: (281) 596-8258. E-mail: csadd@charlottes-saddlery.com. Web: www.charlottes-saddlery.com.

CHICAGO GOLF CLUB: ANNIVERSARY. July 18, 1893. The first 18-hole golf course in America, laid out by Charles Blair MacDonald, was incorporated at Wheaton, IL. MacDonald was the architect of many of the early US courses, which he attempted to model on the best in Scotland and England. It was his belief that at each tee a golfer should face a hazard at the average distance of his or her shot.

COLTON COUNTRY DAY. July 18. Colton, NY. Annual flea market, live entertainment, museum exhibits. Special programs to be announced. Annually, the third weekend in July. Sponsor: Colton Historical Society. Est attendance: 1,500. For info: Dennis Eickhoff, Town Historian, 4846-1 State Hwy 56, Colton, NY 13625. Phone: (315) 262-2800. Fax: (315) 262-2182. E-mail: collib@nnyln.net.

EIGHTEENTH-CENTURY SUMMER MARKET FAIR. July 18–19. McLean, VA. Featuring 18th-century games, music, crafts, period food and drink, puppet show and militia drill. Est attendance: 3,500. For info: Claude Moore Colonial Farm at Turkey Run, 6310 Georgetown Pike, McLean, VA 22101. Phone: (703) 442-7557. Fax: (703) 442-0714. Web: www.1771.org.

EVANS, CHICK: BIRTH ANNIVERSARY. July 18, 1890. Charles (Chick) Evans, Jr, golfer born at Indianapolis, IN. Evans competed as an amateur against the best professionals in the early 20th century, winning the US Open in 1916. In the 1920s he established the Chick Evans Caddie Foundation, later called the Evans Scholarship Fund, which has helped send more than 4,000 people to college. Died at Chicago, IL, Nov 6, 1979.

FIRST PERFECT SCORE IN OLYMPIC HISTORY: ANNIVERSARY. July 18, 1976. At the Montreal Olympics, Romanian gymnast Nadia Comaneci scored the first "10" in Olympic history with her flawless performance of the compulsory exercise on the uneven bars. The scoreboard displayed a "1.00" because it couldn't go up to "10." Comaneci had seven total perfect scores and won five medals, including the gold for all-around performance. Four months previous to the Olympics, Comaneci had scored the first perfect score in international gymnastic competition history.

GROMYKO, ANDREI ANDREYEVICH: 100th BIRTH ANNIVERSARY. July 18, 1909. Soviet diplomat and statesman, born at Byelorussia, USSR. Gromyko played a leading role in Soviet history from World War II until the early days of Mikhail Gorbachev's reform programs. He entered diplomatic service in 1939 with a post in the Soviet Embassy in Washington, DC, and four years later was promoted to ambassador at the age of 34. He was instrumental in bringing the US, Britain and the USSR together for conferences in Yalta, Potsdam and Tehran. He became deputy foreign minister and permanent representative to the United Nations in 1946. Appointed foreign minister in February 1957, he became the voice of the Soviet Union in international debate. He was given the mostly ceremonial post of state president after Gorbachev's ascension in 1985 and retained that post until his death July 2, 1989, at Moscow.

HAYAKAWA, SAMUEL ICHIYE: BIRTH ANNIVERSARY. July 18, 1906. S.I. Hayakawa was born at Vancouver, BC, and came to the US in 1927. An academic, in 1968 he was appointed acting president of San Francisco State College. During student demonstrations on his first day in office he climbed atop a sound truck and disconnected the wires, silencing the demonstrators. His actions gained him enormous popularity among conservatives, and he was promoted to permanent president by Governor Ronald Reagan. As his popularity grew he switched from the Democratic to the Republican party and in 1976 was elected to the US Senate. He led the successful California initiative to declare English the state's official language in 1986. Hayakawa wrote nine textbooks on language and semantics. He died Feb 27, 1992, at Greenbrae, CA.

KIDSPREE. July 18–19. Bicentennial Park, Aurora, CO. The Denver metro area's only free outdoor festival for kids, featuring more than 50 hands-on activities ranging from educational and recreational to the arts, including local and national children's entertainment. Annually, the third weekend in July. Est attendance: 40,000. For info: Special Events Coordinator, City of Aurora, 1298 Peoria St, Aurora, CO 80011. Phone: (303) 326-8615. E-mail: maddlema@auroragov.org. Web: www.auroraevents.org/kidspree.

MANDELA, NELSON: BIRTHDAY. July 18, 1918. Former South African president Nelson Rolihlahla Mandela was born the son of a Tembu tribal chieftain at Qunu, near Umtata, in the Transkei territory of South Africa. Giving up his hereditary rights, Mandela chose to become a lawyer and earned his degree at the University of South Africa. He joined the African National Congress (ANC) in 1944, eventually becoming deputy national president in 1952. His activities in the struggle against apartheid resulted in his conviction for sabotage in 1964. During his 28 years in jail, Mandela remained a symbol of hope to South Africa's nonwhite majority, the demand for his release a rallying cry for civil rights activists. That release finally came Feb 11, 1990, as millions watched via satellite television. In 1994 Mandela was elected president of South Africa in the first all-race election there. See also: "Mandela, Nelson: Prison Release Anniversary" (Feb 11).

NATIONAL WOODIE WAGON DAY. July 18. The "woodie wagon," made famous in the 1940s and '50s, romanticized the American outing. From Route 66 to the surfer lifestyle, the woodie wagon was there. This national day will be celebrated in individual cities and towns across the US and will pay homage to this great American symbol of freedom and the casual lifestyle. Annually, the third Saturday in July. For info: Historic Preservations, Inc, PO Box 49241, Denver, CO 80249. Phone: (303) 949-5964. Fax: (720) 379-8271. E-mail: gregoryaraymer@yahoo.com.

NEW JERSEY STATE ICE CREAM FESTIVAL. July 18. Toms River, NJ. 7th annual. Features contestants from ice cream shops throughout the state vying for the title of NJ's best. Fun for the whole family, with rides, games, food and entertainment and best of all ice cream tasting (tasting kits available for a small fee). Est attendance: 10,000. For info: NJ State Ice Cream Festival, 218 Main St, Toms River, NJ 08753. Phone: (732) 341-8738. Web: www.downtowntomsriver.com.

ODETS, CLIFFORD: BIRTH ANNIVERSARY. July 18, 1906. Clifford Odets began his writing career as a poet before turning to acting. He helped found the Group Theatre in 1931. In 1935 he returned to writing with works for the Group Theatre such as *Waiting for Lefty, Awake and Sing!* and *Golden Boy.* His proletarian views helped make him a popular playwright during the Depression years. Odets was born at Philadelphia, PA, and died at Los Angeles, CA, Aug 15, 1963.

PRESIDENTIAL SUCCESSION ACT: ANNIVERSARY. July 18, 1947. President Harry S Truman signed an executive order determining the line of succession should the president be temporarily incapacitated or die in office. The speaker of the house and president pro tem of the Senate are next in succession after the vice president. This line of succession became the 25th Amendment to the Constitution, which was ratified Feb 10, 1967.

RESTLESS LEG SYNDROME (RLS) EDUCATION AND AWARENESS WEEK. July 18–25. Over 12 million Americans have severe leg pains called restless leg syndrome (RLS), and this education and awareness week, sponsored by the Pharmacy Council on Women's Health, is a means to educate and to call attention to various treatments and diagnoses to assist patients with this problem. There is a $15 charge for kit materials. For info: Fred Mayer, Pharmacists Planning Service, Inc, 101 Lucas Valley Rd, Ste 382, San Rafael, CA 94903. Phone: (415) 479-8628. Fax: (415) 479-8608. E-mail: ppsi@aol.com. Web: www.ppsinc.org.

RUTLEDGE, JOHN: DEATH ANNIVERSARY. July 18, 1800. American statesman, associate justice on the Supreme Court, born at Charleston, SC, in September 1739. Nominated second chief justice of US to succeed John Jay and served as acting chief justice until his confirmation was denied because of his opposition to the Jay Treaty. He died at Charleston, SC.

SPACE MILESTONE: *ROHINI 1* (INDIA). July 18, 1980. First successful launch from India, orbited 77-pound satellite.

SPAIN: CIVIL WAR BEGINS: ANNIVERSARY. July 18, 1936. General Francisco Franco led an uprising of army troops based in North Africa against the elected government of the Spanish Republic. Spain was quickly divided into a Nationalist and a Republican zone. Franco's Nationalists drew support from Fascist Italy and Nazi Germany. On Apr 1, 1939, the Nationalists won a complete victory when they entered Madrid. Franco ruled as dictator in Spain until his death in 1975.

THACKERAY, WILLIAM MAKEPEACE: BIRTH ANNIVERSARY. July 18, 1811. Author, best remembered for his novels *Pendennis* and *Vanity Fair*, was born at Calcutta, India, and died at London, England, Dec 23, 1863.

THOMPSON, HUNTER S.: 70th BIRTH ANNIVERSARY. July 18, 1939. Journalist and author born at Louisville, KY, Thompson was one of the first practitioners of "New," or "Gonzo," journalism, a style that featured first-person accounts and scathing criticism of contemporary American society. His most famous work, "Fear and Loathing in Las Vegas," published in *Rolling Stone* magazine in 1972, featured an alter-ego character in search of the American Dream via use of hallucinogenic drugs. Other works include *Hell's Angels, The Great Shark Hunt* and *The Proud Highway.* Long hailed as a hero of counterculture, Thompson committed suicide at his home in Woody Creek, CO, Feb 21, 2005.

TOSS AWAY THE "COULD HAVES" AND "SHOULD HAVES" DAY. July 18. On this day, people write down their "could haves" and "should haves" on a piece of paper, then throw that list in the trash. Then they make this resolution: "From this day forward, I choose not to live in the past—the past is history that I can't change. I can do something about the present—I choose to live in the present." Annually, the third Saturday in July. For info: Martha Ross-Rodgers, PO Box 99003, Norfolk, VA 23509-9003. Phone: (757) 558-4964. Fax: (757) 558-4965. E-mail: MRossrodge@aol.com. Web: www.jirehpublishers.com.

URUGUAY: CONSTITUTION DAY. July 18. National holiday. Commemorates the country's first constitution in 1830.

WHITE, GILBERT: BIRTH ANNIVERSARY. July 18, 1720. Born at Selborne, Hampshire, England, Gilbert White has been called the father of British naturalists. His book *The Natural History of Selborne*, published in 1788, enjoyed immediate success and is said never to have been out of print. White died near his birthplace, June 26, 1793. His home survives as a museum.

BIRTHDAYS TODAY

Kristin Bell, 29, actress ("Veronica Mars," *Reefer Madness: The Movie Musical*), born Detroit, MI, July 18, 1980.

James Brolin, 68, actor (Emmy for "Marcus Welby, MD"; "Hotel"), born Los Angeles, CA, July 18, 1941.

Richard Totten (Dick) Button, 80, sportscaster, Olympic gold medal figure skater, born Englewood, NJ, July 18, 1929.

Chace Crawford, 24, actor ("Gossip Girl"), born Lubbock, TX, born July 18, 1985.

Vin Diesel, 42, actor (*XXX, The Fast and the Furious, Pitch Black*), born Mark Vincent at New York, NY, July 18, 1967.

Dion DiMucci, 70, singer (Dion and the Belmonts), born the Bronx, NY, July 18, 1939.

Nick Faldo, 52, golfer, born Welwyn Garden City, England, July 18, 1957.

Steve Forbes, 62, publisher, chairman, Forbes Newspapers, born Morristown, NJ, July 18, 1947.

John Glenn, 88, astronaut, first American to orbit Earth, former US senator (D, Ohio), born Cambridge, OH, July 18, 1921.

Anfernee "Penny" Hardaway, 37, basketball player, born Memphis, TN, July 18, 1972.

Elizabeth McGovern, 48, actress (*Ordinary People, Racing with the Moon*), born Evanston, IL, July 18, 1961.

Calvin Peete, 66, golfer, born Detroit, MI, July 18, 1943.

Martha Reeves, 68, lead singer (Martha & the Vandellas, "Power of Love"), born Detroit, MI, July 18, 1941.

Ricky Skaggs, 55, musician (bluegrass guitar), singer ("I Don't Care"), born Cordell, KY, July 18, 1954.

Joe Torre, 69, baseball manager and former player, born New York, NY, July 18, 1940.

Yevgeny Yevtushenko, 76, poet, born Zima, USSR, July 18, 1933.

July 19 — Sunday

DAY 200 — 165 REMAINING

ANNE HUTCHINSON MEMORIAL DAY. July 19. Anne Hutchinson Memorial, Founders' Brook Park, Portsmouth, RI. An annual gathering to honor Anne Marbury Hutchinson (1591–1643), cofounder of Pocasset (Portsmouth), RI, in 1638. Wife, mother of 16, midwife, religious leader, she was a caretaker of and spiritual leader to women in Puritan Boston. Anne Hutchinson helped shape the tradition of free speech and religious tolerance that has become so important to modern Americans. Annually, on the Sunday near Anne Hutchinson's birth anniversary, July 20, 1591. For info: Valerie Debrule, Friends of Anne Hutchinson, 11 Cherry Creek Rd, Newport, RI 02840. Phone: (401) 846-8439. Fax: (401) 848-0373. E-mail: cherrycreek@efortress.com. Or Barbara Finelli. Phone: (401) 846-6101.

ATTACK ON FORT WAGNER: ANNIVERSARY. July 19, 1863. In a second attempt to capture Fort Wagner, outside Charleston, SC, federal troops were repulsed after losing 1,515 men as opposed to Southern losses of only 174. The attack was led by the 54th Massachusetts Colored Infantry, commanded by Colonel Robert Gould Shaw, who was killed in the action. This was the first use of black troops in the war. The film *Glory* was based on the Massachusetts 54th, and this was the attack featured in the film. Fort Wagner was never taken by the Union.

✦ CAPTIVE NATIONS WEEK. July 19–25. Presidential proclamation issued each year since 1959 for the third week of July. (PL86–90 of July 17, 1959.)

CONCOURS d'ELEGANCE. July 19. Forest Grove, OR. Set among the beauty of the Pacific University campus, this is one of the premier car shows on the West Coast with 300-plus beautifully restored vintage autos. A great family event. Annually, the third Sunday in July. Est attendance: 6,000. For info: Forest Grove Rotary Club, PO Box 387, Forest Grove, OR 97116. Phone: (503) 357-2300. Web: www.forestgroveconcours.org.

DEGAS, EDGAR: 175th BIRTH ANNIVERSARY. July 19, 1834. French impressionist painter, especially noted for his paintings of dancers in motion, was born at Paris, France, and died there Sept 26, 1917.

ELVIS PRESLEY'S FIRST SINGLE RELEASED: 55th ANNIVERSARY. July 19, 1954. "That's All Right (Mama)" backed by "Blue Moon of Kentucky" was released on this date by Sun Records of Memphis, TN. It was 19-year-old Elvis Presley's first professional record. Presley recorded it with guitarist Scotty Moore and bassist Bill Black. Memphis DJ Dewey Phillips previewed the single on July 7—literally two days after it was recorded—on his radio show and his listeners went crazy, demanding that Phillips play it again and again. See also "Elvis Presley's First Concert Appearance: Anniversary" (July 30).

FAIRBANKS SUMMER ARTS FESTIVAL. July 19–Aug 2. University of Alaska, Fairbanks, AK. A unique study-performance festival involving workshops and master classes in visual and performing arts with more than 90 prestigious guest artists. Performance opportunities in orchestra, jazz band, jazz, choral groups, dance, opera theater, creative writing, healing arts and ice skating. Est attendance: 1,200. For info: Jo Ryman Scott, Fairbanks Summer Arts Festival, Box 82510, Fairbanks, AK 99708. Phone: (907) 474-8869. Fax: (907) 479-4329. E-mail: festival@alaska.net. Web: www.fsaf.org.

FIRST UNASSISTED TRIPLE PLAY: 100th ANNIVERSARY. July 19, 1909. Cleveland Blues shortstop Neal Ball recorded the first unassisted triple play in American League history in a game against the Boston Pilgrims. Ball caught a line drive hit by Amby McConnell, stepped on second base to double off Heine Wagner and tagged Jake Stahl before he could get back to first base. Ball also hit a home run as Cleveland won, 6–1.

FIRST WOMAN VICE-PRESIDENTIAL CANDIDATE: 25th ANNIVERSARY. July 19, 1984. Congresswoman Geraldine Ferraro was nominated to run with presidential candidate Walter Mondale on the Democratic ticket. They were defeated by the Republican ticket headed by Ronald Reagan.

ISRA AL MI'RAJ: ASCENT OF THE PROPHET MUHAMMAD. July 19. Islamic calendar date: evening after Rajab 26, 1430. Commemorates the journey of the Prophet Muhammad from Mecca to Jerusalem, his ascension into the Seven Heavens and his return on the same night. Muslims believe that on that night Muhammad prayed together with Abraham, Moses and Jesus in the area of the Al-Aqsa Mosque in Jerusalem. The rock from which he is believed to have ascended to heaven to speak with God is the one inside the Dome of the Rock. Different methods for "anticipating" the visibility of the new moon crescent at Mecca are used by different Muslim groups. US date may vary.

July 2009

S	M	T	W	T	F	S
			1	2	3	4
5	6	7	8	9	10	11
12	13	14	15	16	17	18
19	20	21	22	23	24	25
26	27	28	29	30	31	

ITALY: FEAST OF THE REDEEMER. July 19. Venice. Procession of gondolas and other craft commemorating the end of the epidemic of 1575. Annually, the third Sunday in July.

***THE LORD OF THE RINGS*: FIRST PART PUBLISHED: 55th ANNIVERSARY.** July 19, 1954. *The Fellowship of the Ring*, the first part of J.R.R. Tolkien's epic *The Lord of the Rings*, was published on this date in London, England, by George Allen and Unwin. The publishers chose to publish the book in three parts because it was so long. *The Two Towers* was published on Nov 11, 1954, and *The Return of the King* was published on Oct 20, 1955.

LUXEMBOURG: BEER FESTIVAL. July 19. At Diekirch an annual beer festival is held on the third Sunday in July.

MARILYN MONROE'S FIRST SCREEN TEST: ANNIVERSARY. July 19, 1946. Marilyn Monroe was given her first screen test at Twentieth Century-Fox Studios. Even with no sound, this test was all they needed to sign her first contract. Beginning with *Scudda-Hoo! Scudda-Hay!* in 1948 and ending with *The Misfits* in 1961, Monroe made a total of 29 films during her short career.

MAYO, CHARLES HORACE: BIRTH ANNIVERSARY. July 19, 1865. American surgeon, one of the Mayo brothers, founders of the Mayo Clinic and Mayo Foundation, born at Rochester, MN. Died at Chicago, IL, May 26, 1939.

MERRIAM, EVE: BIRTH ANNIVERSARY. July 19, 1916. A poet, playwright and author of more than 50 books for both adults and children. Merriam's works, which often focused on feminism, include *It Doesn't Always Have to Rhyme, After Nora Slammed the Door: The Women's Unfinished Revolution, Mommies at Work* and a book of poems attacked by authorities as glamorizing crime, *The Urban Mother Goose.* Her play *Out of Our Father's House*, portraying the lives of American women, was presented on public television's "Great Performances" series. She also wrote the first documentary on women's rights for network TV, *We the Women.* Born at Philadelphia, PA, she died at New York, NY, Apr 11, 1992.

NATIONAL ICE CREAM DAY. July 19. To promote America's favorite dessert, ice cream, on "Sundae Sunday." Annually, the third Sunday in July.

NATIONAL INDEPENDENT RETAILERS WEEK. July 19–25. The week to celebrate and promote those who own and manage the thousands of independent retail businesses around the world. For info: Tom Shay, Profits Plus Seminars, PO Box 1577, St. Petersburg, FL 33731. Phone: (727) 464-2182. Fax: (727) 898-3179. E-mail: TomShay@profitsplus.org. Web: www.profitsplus.org.

NICARAGUA: NATIONAL LIBERATION DAY. July 19. Following the National Day of Joy (July 17—anniversary of date in 1979 when dictator Anastasio Somoza Debayle fled Nicaragua) is annual July 19 observance of National Liberation Day, anniversary of day the National Liberation Army claimed victory over the Somoza dictatorship.

RAGBRAI®—THE *REGISTER*'S ANNUAL GREAT BICYCLE RIDE ACROSS IOWA™. July 19–25 (tentative). A seven-day, leisurely tour from the western border of Iowa to the Mississippi River enjoying wonderful Iowa scenery and hospitality. RAGBRAI® is the oldest, largest and longest multiday bicycle ride in the United States. The *Des Moines Register* has coordinated this ride that attracts 10,000 riders from across the country (and around the world). Annually, the last full week of July. Est attendance: 10,000. For info: RAGBRAI, PO Box 622, Des Moines, IA 50303-0622. Phone: (800) 474-3342. E-mail: info@ragbrai.org. Web: www.ragbrai.org.

SAINT CYRIL'S PARISH FESTIVAL. July 19. Kiwanis Park, Sheboygan, WI. Outdoor dance, Slovenian foods, music, games and raffle, Polka Mass and bingo under the big top. Est attendance: 5,000. For info: St. Cyril & Methodius Parish, 822 New Jersey Ave, Sheboygan, WI 53081. Phone: (414) 457-7110.

SAINT VINCENT DE PAUL: OLD FEAST DAY. July 19. A day remembering the founder of the Vincentian Congregation and the Sisters of Charity, born at Pouy, France, Apr 24, 1581. He died Sept 27, 1660, at Paris, France. His feast day was formerly observed on July 19 but is now observed on the anniversary of his death, Sept 27.

SANTA FE CHAMBER MUSIC FESTIVAL. July 19–Aug 24. St. Francis Auditorium, Museum of Fine Arts and the Lensic Performing Arts Center, Santa Fe, NM. Highly acclaimed chamber music festival celebrates its 36th season. Draws on international talent, featuring works from the baroque, romantic and classical periods, as well as contemporary works, including world premiere performances. Est attendance: 15,000. For info: Santa Fe Chamber Music Festival, PO Box 2227, Santa Fe, NM 87504. Phone: (505) 983-2075. Fax: (505) 986-0251. E-mail: info@santafemusic.org. Web: www.santafemusic.org.

SWITZERLAND: DORNACH BATTLE COMMEMORATION. July 19. The victory at Dornach in 1499 is remembered on the battlefield and in the city of Solothurn on the Sunday nearest to July 22.

WOMEN'S RIGHTS CONVENTION AT SENECA FALLS: ANNIVERSARY. July 19, 1848. A convention concerning the rights of women, called by Lucretia Mott and Elizabeth Cady Stanton, was held at Seneca Falls, NY, July 19–20, 1848. The issues discussed included voting, property rights and divorce. The convention drafted a "Declaration of Sentiments" that paraphrased the Declaration of Independence, addressing man instead of King George, and called for women's "immediate admission to all the rights and privileges which belong to them as citizens of the United States." This convention was the beginning of an organized women's rights movement in the US. The most controversial issue was Stanton's demand for women's right to vote.

YALOW, ROSALYN: BIRTHDAY. July 19, 1921. Medical physicist Rosalyn Yalow was born at New York City. Along with Andrew V. Schally and Roger Guillemin, in 1977 Yalow was awarded the Nobel Prize in Physiology or Medicine. Through her research on medical applications of radioactive isotopes, Yalow developed RIA, a sensitive and simple technique used to measure minute concentrations of hormones and other substances in blood or other body fluids. First applied to the study of insulin concentration in the blood of diabetics, RIA was soon used in hundreds of other applications.

BIRTHDAYS TODAY

Anthony Edwards, 47, actor ("ER," *Fast Times at Ridgemont High, Top Gun*), born Santa Barbara, CA, July 19, 1962.

Topher Grace, 31, actor (*Spider-Man 3, In Good Company, Traffic,* "That 70s Show"), born New York, NY, July 19, 1978.

Clea Lewis, 44, actress ("Ellen," *The Rich Man's Wife*), born Cleveland Heights, OH, July 19, 1965.

George Stanley McGovern, 87, former US senator and 1972 Democratic presidential nominee, born Avon, SD, July 19, 1922.

Ilie Nastase, 63, former tennis player, born Bucharest, Romania, July 19, 1946.

Campbell Scott, 47, actor (*Roger Dodger, Singles*), born Westchester County, NY, July 19, 1962.

July 20 — Monday

DAY 201 **164 REMAINING**

"ARTHUR MURRAY PARTY" TV PREMIERE: ANNIVERSARY. July 20, 1950. This ballroom dancing show appeared on all four networks (ABC, DuMont, CBS and NBC) and was hosted by Kathryn Murray, wife of famed dance school founder Arthur Murray.

ATTEMPT ON HITLER'S LIFE: 65th ANNIVERSARY. July 20, 1944. During the daily staff meeting at German headquarters at Rastenburg, an attempt was made to assassinate Adolf Hitler. Count Claus Schenk von Stauffenberg, chosen from a group of German military and civil servants involved in the plot, left a briefcase containing a bomb only six feet from Hitler under the staff table in the briefing room. Four people were killed in the blast, but Hitler's life was saved, probably because Colonel Heinz Brandt (who was among those killed) found the briefcase in his way and moved it farther from the German dictator.

BASEBALL DECLARED NONESSENTIAL OCCUPATION: ANNIVERSARY. July 20, 1918. Secretary of War Newton D. Baker ruled that baseball was a nonessential occupation. He stated that all players of draft age should seek "employment to aid successful prosecution of the war or shoulder guns and fight." On July 26, Baker allowed baseball to continue until Sept 1. Nearly 250 ballplayers entered the armed services.

COLOMBIA: INDEPENDENCE DAY. July 20. National holiday. Commemorates the beginning of the independence movement with an uprising against Spanish officials in 1810 at Bogota. Colombia gained independence from Spain in 1819 when Simon Bolivar decisively defeated the Spanish.

GENEVA ACCORDS: 55th ANNIVERSARY. July 20, 1954. An agreement covering cessation of hostilities in Vietnam, signed at Geneva, Switzerland, on behalf of the commanders in chief of French forces at Vietnam and the People's Army of Vietnam. A further declaration of the Geneva Conference was released July 21, 1954. Partition, foreign troop withdrawal and elections for a unified government within two years were among provisions.

HILLARY, SIR EDMUND PERCIVAL: 90th BIRTH ANNIVERSARY. July 20, 1919. Explorer, mountaineer born at Auckland, New Zealand. With Tenzing Norgay, a Sherpa guide, became first to ascend summit of highest mountain in the world, Mt Everest (29,028 ft), at 11:30 AM, May 29, 1953. "We climbed because nobody climbed it before," he said. Hillary, who also listed his occupation as beekeeper, died Jan 11, 2008, at Auckland.

JAPAN: MARINE DAY. July 20. National holiday.

LOCUST PLAGUE OF 1874: ANNIVERSARY. July 20–30, 1874. The Rocky Mountain locust, long a pest in the American Midwest, became an even bigger threat in the summer of 1874. Beginning in late July, the largest recorded swarm of this insect descended on the Great Plains. It is estimated that 124 billion insects formed a swarm 1,800 miles long and 110 miles wide that ranged from Canada and the Dakotas down to Texas. Contemporary accounts said that the locusts blocked out the sun and devastated farms in mere minutes. The swarms continued in smaller size for the next several years and caused an estimated $200 million in crop destruction.

NATIONAL GET OUT OF THE DOGHOUSE DAY. July 20. In trouble with someone you know and care about? This is the day when anyone can "Get out of the doghouse!" Annually, the third Monday in July. For info: Heidi Richards, Success and Then Some, 10890 SW 27 Ct, Davie, FL 33328. Phone: (954) 981-5515. E-mail: heidi@successandthensome.com.

NATIONAL HUG YOUR KIDS DAY. July 20. A day set aside to encourage parents to hug their kids today and every day. Annually, the third Monday in July. For info: Michelle Nichols, PO Box 34432, Reno, NV 89533. Phone: (775) 303-8201. E-mail: hugs@HugYourKidsToday.com. Web: www.HugYourKidsToday.com.

RIOT ACT: ANNIVERSARY. July 20, 1715. To "read the riot act" now usually means telling children to be quiet or less boisterous, but in 18th-century England reading the riot act was a more serious matter. On July 20, 1715, the Riot Act took effect. By law in England, if 12 or more persons were unlawfully assembled to the disturbance of the public peace, an authority was required "with a loud voice" to command silence and read the riot act proclamation: "Our sovereign lord the king chargeth and commandeth all persons, being assembled, immediately to disperse themselves, and peaceably to depart to their habitations, or to their lawful business, upon the pains contained in the act made in the first year of King George, for preventing tumults and riotous assemblies. God save the king." Any persons who failed to obey within one hour were to be seized, apprehended and carried before a justice of the peace.

SPACE MILESTONE: MOON DAY: 40th ANNIVERSARY. July 20, 1969. Anniversary of man's first landing on the moon. Two US astronauts (Neil Alden Armstrong and Edwin Eugene Aldrin, Jr) landed lunar module *Eagle* at 4:17 PM EDT, and remained on the lunar surface 21 hours, 36 minutes and 16 seconds. The landing was made from the *Apollo XI*'s orbiting command-and-service module, code-named *Columbia*, whose pilot, Michael Collins, remained aboard. Armstrong was first to set foot on the moon. Armstrong and Aldrin were outside the spacecraft, walking on the moon's surface, approximately 2¼ hours. The astronauts returned to Earth July 24, bringing photographs and rock samples.

SPECIAL OLYMPICS: ANNIVERSARY. July 20. Official anniversary of the first ever International Special Olympics Competition, held in 1968 at Soldier Field, Chicago, IL. Special Olympics is an international year-round program of sports training and competition for individuals with mental retardation. More than one million athletes in over 150 countries train and compete in 26 Olympic-style summer and winter sports. Founded in 1968 by Eunice Kennedy Shriver, Special Olympics provides people with mental retardation continuing opportunities to develop fitness, demonstrate courage and experience joy as they participate in the sharing of gifts and friendship with other athletes, their families and the community. For info: Media Relations Mgr, Special Olympics, Inc, 1133 19th St NW, Washington, DC 20036. Phone: (202) 628-3630. Fax: (202) 824-0200. Web: www.specialolympics.org.

US GIRL'S JUNIOR (GOLF) CHAMPIONSHIP. July 20–25. Trump National Golf Club, Bedminster, NJ. For info: USGA, Golf House, Championship Dept, PO Box 708, Far Hills, NJ 07931. Phone: (908) 234-2300. Fax: (908) 234-9687. Web: www.usga.org.

US JUNIOR AMATEUR (GOLF) CHAMPIONSHIP. July 20–25. Trump National Golf Club, Bedminster, NJ. For info: USGA, Golf House, Championship Dept, PO Box 708, Far Hills, NJ 07931. Phone: (908) 234-2300. Fax: (908) 234-9687. E-mail: usga@usga.org. Web: www.usga.org.

BIRTHDAYS TODAY

Ray Allen, 34, basketball player, born Merced, CA, July 20, 1975.

Kim Carnes, 63, singer ("Bette Davis Eyes"), songwriter, born Hollywood, CA, July 20, 1946.

Judy Chicago, 70, artist, feminist, born Judy Cohen at Chicago, IL, July 20, 1939.

July 2009

S	M	T	W	T	F	S
			1	2	3	4
5	6	7	8	9	10	11
12	13	14	15	16	17	18
19	20	21	22	23	24	25
26	27	28	29	30	31	

Larry E. Craig, 64, US Senator (R, Idaho), born Council, ID, July 20, 1945.

John Daley, 24, actor ("Freaks and Geeks"), born New York, NY, July 20, 1985.

Charles Joseph (Chuck) Daly, 79, Hall of Fame basketball coach, sportscaster, born St. Mary's, PA, July 20, 1930.

Donna Dixon, 52, actress ("Bosom Buddies," *Dr. Detroit*), born Alexandria, VA, July 20, 1957.

Peter Forsberg, 36, hockey player, born Ornskoldvik, Sweden, July 20, 1973.

Josh Holloway, 40, actor ("Lost"), born at San Jose, CA, July 20, 1969.

Sally Ann Howes, 79, actress (*Dead of Night, The History of Mr Polly*), singer, born London, England, July 20, 1930.

Michael Ilitch, 80, sports executive, former minor league baseball player, born Detroit, MI, July 20, 1929.

Cormac McCarthy, 76, author (*The Road, No Country for Old Men, All the Pretty Horses*), born Providence, RI, July 20, 1933.

Barbara Ann Mikulski, 73, US Senator (D, Maryland), born Baltimore, MD, July 20, 1936.

Claudio Reyna, 36, former soccer player, born Livingston, NJ, July 20, 1973.

Diana Rigg, 71, actress (Tony for *Medea; King Lear, Bleak House*, "The Avengers"), born Doncaster, Yorkshire, England, July 20, 1938.

Carlos Santana, 62, musician, born Autlan, Mexico, July 20, 1947.

July 21 — Tuesday

DAY 202 **163 REMAINING**

BATTLE OF BULL RUN: ANNIVERSARY. July 21, 1861. Union general Irvin McDowell was defeated by Confederate troops led by General Joseph E. Johnston at the first Battle of Bull Run at Manassas, VA. It was the first major engagement of the war. It was during this battle that Confederate general T.J. Jackson won the nickname "Stonewall." In the second Battle of Bull Run, Aug 29–30, 1862, Union general John Pope was badly defeated by General Robert E. Lee.

BELGIUM: NATIONAL HOLIDAY. July 21. Marks accession of first Belgian king, Leopold I, in 1831, after independence from Netherlands.

CLEVELAND, FRANCES FOLSOM: BIRTH ANNIVERSARY. July 21, 1864. Wife of Grover Cleveland, 22nd and 24th president of the US, born at Buffalo, NY. She was the youngest first lady at age 22, and the first to marry a president in the White House. Died at Princeton, NJ, Oct 29, 1947.

EVERS, JOHNNY: BIRTH ANNIVERSARY. July 21, 1881. John Joseph (Johnny) Evers, Baseball Hall of Fame second baseman, born at Troy, NY. Evers was a member of the Tinker-to-Evers-to-Chance double-play combination for the Chicago Cubs that first took the field on Sept 13, 1902. Inducted into the Hall of Fame (with Tinker and Chance) in 1946. Evers died at Albany, NY, Mar 28, 1947.

FIRST ROBOT HOMICIDE: 25th ANNIVERSARY. July 21, 1984. The first reported killing of a human by a robot occurred at Jackson, MI. A robot turned and caught a 34-year-old worker between it and a safety bar, crushing him. He died of the injuries July 26, 1984. According to the National Institute for Occupational Safety and Health, it was "the first documented case of a robot-related fatality in the US."

GUAM: LIBERATION DAY. July 21. National holiday. Commemorates US forces' return to Guam in 1944, freeing the island from the Japanese.

HEMINGWAY BIRTHDAY CELEBRATION. July 21. Hemingway Museum, Oak Park, IL. Annual celebration of Ernest Hemingway's birth. Includes a lecture and reception. For info: The Ernest Hemingway Foundation of Oak Park, PO Box 2222, Oak Park, IL 60303-2222. Phone: (708) 848-2222. Fax: (708) 386-2952. E-mail: ehfop@sbcglobal.net. Web: www.ehfop.org.

HEMINGWAY, ERNEST: BIRTH ANNIVERSARY. July 21, 1899. American author born at Oak Park, IL. Made his name with such works as *The Sun Also Rises* (1926), *A Farewell to Arms* (1929), *For Whom the Bell Tolls* (1940) and *The Old Man and the Sea* (1952). He was awarded the Nobel Prize in 1954 and wrote little thereafter; he shot himself July 2, 1961, at Ketchum, ID, having been seriously ill for some time.

McLUHAN, MARSHALL: BIRTH ANNIVERSARY. July 21, 1911. (Herbert) Marshall McLuhan, university professor and author, called "the Canadian sage of the electronic age," was born at Edmonton, AB, Canada. *Understanding Media* and *The Medium Is the Massage* (not to be confused with his widely quoted aphorism: "The medium is the message"), among other books, were widely acclaimed for their fresh view of communication. McLuhan is reported to have said: "Most people are alive in an earlier time, but you must be alive in our own time." He died at Toronto, ON, Dec 31, 1980.

MOON PHASE: NEW MOON. July 21. Moon enters New Moon phase at 10:35 PM, EDT.

NATIONAL BABY FOOD FESTIVAL. July 21–25. Fremont, MI. 19th annual. Baby yourself at this festival in the hometown of Gerber Products. Adults face off in the baby-food-eating contest and tots crawl in races. Top entertainers, two parades and arts and crafts show round out the fun. Est attendance: 125,000. For info: Natl Baby Food Festival, 7 E Main St, Fremont, MI 49412. Phone: (800) 592-BABY. E-mail: nbff@fremontcommerce.com. Web: www.babyfoodfest.com.

NATIONAL WOMEN'S HALL OF FAME: 30th ANNIVERSARY. July 21, 1979. Seneca Falls, NY. Founded to honor American women whose contributions "have been of the greatest value in the development of their country" and located in the community known as the "birthplace of women's rights," where the first Women's Suffrage Movement convention was held in 1848, the Hall of Fame was dedicated with 23 inductees. Earlier National Women's Hall of Fame, honoring "Twenty Outstanding Women of the Twentieth Century," was dedicated at New York World's Fair, on May 27, 1965.

PERIGEAN SPRING TIDES. July 21. Spring tides, the highest possible tides, which occur when New Moon or Full Moon takes place within 24 hours of the moment the Moon is nearest Earth (perigee) in its monthly orbit at 11 PM, EDT. These tides are not named for the season of spring but for the German *springen*, "to leap up."

SOLAR ECLIPSE. July 21–22. Total eclipse of the sun. Visible in eastern Asia, the Pacific Ocean region and Hawaii.

 BIRTHDAYS TODAY

John Barrasso, 57, US Senator (R, Wyoming), born Casper, WY, July 21, 1952.

Brandi Chastain, 41, former soccer player, born San Jose, CA, July 21, 1968.

Lance Guest, 49, actor ("Lou Grant," *The Last Starfighter*), born Saratoga, CA, July 21, 1960.

Josh Hartnett, 31, actor (*Pearl Harbor, Halloween H2O*), born San Francisco, CA, July 21, 1978.

Edward Herrmann, 66, actor (*The Paper Chase, Eleanor and Franklin*, "Gilmore Girls"), born Washington, DC, July 21, 1943.

Norman Jewison, 83, producer, director (*Moonstruck, Fiddler on the Roof*), born Toronto, ON, Canada, July 21, 1926.

Jon Lovitz, 52, actor (*A League of Their Own*, "NewsRadio"), born Tarzana, CA, July 21, 1957.

Matt Mulhern, 49, actor ("Major Dad," *Biloxi Blues*), born Philadelphia, PA, July 21, 1960.

Janet Reno, 71, former US Attorney General (Clinton administration), born Miami, FL, July 21, 1938.

C.C. Sabathia, 29, baseball player, born Vallejo, CA, July 21, 1980.

Cat Stevens, 61, singer, songwriter, chosen Muslim name is Yusuf Islam, born Stephen Demetri Georgiou at London, England, July 21, 1948.

Garry Trudeau, 60, political cartoonist ("Doonesbury"), born New York, NY, July 21, 1949.

Robin Williams, 57, comedian, actor ("Mork and Mindy," *Mrs Doubtfire, Dead Poets Society, Good Will Hunting*), born Chicago, IL, July 21, 1952.

July 22 — Wednesday

DAY 203 162 REMAINING

ALLIES TAKE PALERMO: ANNIVERSARY. July 22, 1943. Two weeks after the July 10 Allied invasion of Sicily, the principal northern town of Palermo was captured. Americans had cut off 50,000 Italian troops in the west, but Germans were escaping to the northeastern corner of the island. After 39 days, on Aug 17, 1943, the entire island of Sicily was under the control of Allied forces. The official total of Germans and Italians captured was put at 130,000. The Germans, however, managed to transfer 60,000 of their 90,000 men back to the Italian mainland.

CALDER, ALEXANDER: BIRTH ANNIVERSARY. July 22, 1898. Internationally acclaimed American abstract artist who invented the mobile. Born at Lawnton, PA, Calder took a degree in mechanical engineering but was drawn into art in the 1920s. By the 1930s, he was the most famous American artist in the world. Calder created the mobile, a delicate hanging kinetic sculpture whose form changed continuously due to air currents or motors. His stationary abstract sculptures were termed "stabiles," and they influenced many generations of artists to turn to industrial materials and monumental scope for expression as he had (with works like *Flamingo* [1974]). Calder died Nov 11, 1976, at New York, NY.

DILLINGER, JOHN: 75th DEATH ANNIVERSARY. July 22, 1934. Bank robber, murderer, prison escapee and the first person to receive the FBI's appellation "Public Enemy Number 1" (July 1934). After nine years in prison (1924–33), Dillinger traveled through the Midwest, leaving a path of violent crimes. He was killed by FBI agents led by Melvin Purvis as he left Chicago's Biograph movie theater (where he had watched *Manhattan Melodrama*, starring Clark Gable and Myrna Loy), July 22, 1934. He was born at Indianapolis, IN, June 28, 1902.

July 2009	S	M	T	W	T	F	S
				1	2	3	4
	5	6	7	8	9	10	11
	12	13	14	15	16	17	18
	19	20	21	22	23	24	25
	26	27	28	29	30	31	

FAIRFEST. July 22–26. Adams County Fairgrounds, Hastings, NE. Annual county fair featuring midway; open-class competitions in culinary arts, needlework, floral culture, woodworking and the visual arts; Adams County 4-H competition, livestock show; strolling acts and live entertainment. Est attendance: 72,169. For info: Sandy Himmelberg, Genl Mgr, 947 S Baltimore, Hastings, NE 68901. Phone: (402) 462-3247. Fax: (402) 462-4731. Web: www.adamscountyfairgrounds.com.

HOOD RIVER COUNTY FAIR. July 22–25. Hood River, OR. From 4-H activities to the excitement of the carnival, this annual old-fashioned country fair is bustling with things to do! Est attendance: 25,000. For info: Hood River County Fair, Box 385, Odell, OR 97044. Phone: (541) 354-2865. Fax: (541) 354-2875.

MENDEL, GREGOR JOHANN: BIRTH ANNIVERSARY. July 22, 1822. Botanist Gregor Mendel was born of peasant parents at Heinzendorf, Austria. His pioneering work in genetics became the basis for the modern science of genetics and heredity. Around 1856 Mendel began experiments in his small monastery garden, crossing different varieties of the garden pea. The import of Mendel's work was not seen until many years after his death, Jan 6, 1884, at Brünn. In 1900 other European botanists discovered his papers and confirmed and extended his theories, which formed the basis of the study of heredity and genetics.

PIED PIPER OF HAMELIN: ANNIVERSARY—MAYBE. July 22, 1376. According to legend, the German town of Hamelin, plagued with rats, bargained with a piper who promised to, and did, pipe the rats out of town and into the Weser River. Refused payment for his work, the piper then piped the children out of town and into a hole in a hill, never to be seen again. More recent historians suggest that the event occurred in 1284 when young men of Hamelin left the city on colonizing adventures.

RAT-CATCHERS DAY. July 22. A day to recognize the rat-catchers who labor to exterminate members of the genus *Rattus*, disease-carrying rodents that infest most of the "civilized" world. Observed on the anniversary of the legendary feat of the Pied Piper of Hamelin on July 22, 1376 (according to 16th-century chronicler Richard Rowland Verstegen).

RILEY, JAMES WHITCOMB: DEATH ANNIVERSARY. July 22, 1916. American "Hoosier" poet, born at Greenfield, IN, Oct 7, probably in 1853, but possibly several years earlier. Riley died at Indianapolis, IN.

SPACE MILESTONE: *SOYUZ TM-3* (USSR). July 22, 1987. Two Soviet cosmonauts, Aleksandr Viktorenko and Aleksandr Aleksandrov, along with the first Syrian space traveler, Mohammed Faris, were launched on a projected 10-day mission. Launched from the Baikonur base in central Asia, the spacecraft orbited Earth for two days before linking with Soviet space station *Mir*. The *Soyuz TM-3* spacecraft was used as a shuttle to *Mir* into the 1990s.

SPOONER'S DAY (WILLIAM SPOONER BIRTH ANNIVERSARY). July 22. A day named for the Reverend William Archibald Spooner (born at London, England, July 22, 1844, warden of New College, Oxford, 1903–24, died at Oxford, England, Aug 29, 1930), whose frequent slips of the tongue led to coinage of the term *spoonerism* to describe them. A day to remember the scholarly man whose accidental transpositions gave us *blushing crow* (for crushing blow), *tons of soil* (for sons of toil), *queer old dean* (for dear old queen), *swell foop* (for fell swoop) and *half-warmed fish* (for half-formed wish).

VANDERBILT, AMY: BIRTH ANNIVERSARY. July 22, 1908. American journalist and etiquette expert born at New York, NY. Her *Amy Vanderbilt's Complete Book of Etiquette* (1952) became the bible for manners of courtesy and society. Vanderbilt also hosted the television program "It's in Good Taste" from 1954–60. She died at New York City on Dec 27, 1974.

BIRTHDAYS TODAY

Orson Bean, 81, actor ("To Tell the Truth," "Mary Hartman, Mary Hartman"), born Dallas Frederick Burroughs at Burlington, VT, July 22, 1928.

Irene Bedard, 42, actress ("Grand Avenue," "Crazy Horse"; voice of Pocahontas in the Disney film), born Anchorage, AK, July 22, 1967.

Albert Brooks, 62, comedian, director, actor (*Finding Nemo, Broadcast News, Mother*), born Albert Lawrence Einstein at Los Angeles, CA, July 22, 1947.

Willem Dafoe, 54, actor (*Platoon, Mississippi Burning, The Aviator, Spider-Man* movies), born Appleton, WI, July 22, 1955.

Oscar De La Renta, 77, fashion designer, born Santo Domingo, Dominican Republic, July 22, 1932.

Scott Dixon, 29, race car driver, born Brisbane, Australia, July 22, 1980.

Robert J. Dole, 86, former US senator (R, Kansas), born Russell, KS, July 22, 1923.

Rob Estes, 46, actor ("Melrose Place," "Silk Stalkings"), born Norfolk, VA, July 22, 1963.

Danny Glover, 62, actor (*Lethal Weapon, The Color Purple, To Sleep with Anger*), born San Francisco, CA, July 22, 1947.

Don Henley, 62, musician (The Eagles), songwriter, born Linden, TX, July 22, 1947.

Kay Bailey Hutchison, 66, US Senator (R, Texas), born Galveston, TX, July 22, 1943.

Rhys Ifans, 42, actor (*Notting Hill, Dancing at Lughnasa*), born Ruthin, Wales, July 22, 1967.

Keyshawn Johnson, 37, former football player, born Los Angeles, CA, July 22, 1972.

John Leguizamo, 45, actor ("ER," *Carlito's Way, Moulin Rouge!*, stage: *Mambo Mouth*), born Bogotá, Colombia, July 22, 1964.

Kristine Lilly, 38, soccer player, born New York, NY, July 22, 1971.

Alan Menken, 60, film score composer (*Pocahontas, Aladdin*), born New Rochelle, NY, July 22, 1949.

Bobby Sherman, 64, singer, actor, born Santa Monica, CA, July 22, 1945.

David Spade, 44, actor ("Saturday Night Live," "Just Shoot Me," "Rules of Engagement," *Black Sheep*), born Birmingham, MI, July 22, 1965.

Terence Stamp, 70, actor (*The Limey, Alien Nation, The Collector*), born London, England, July 22, 1939.

Keith Sweat, 48, R&B singer, born New York, NY, July 22, 1961.

Alex Trebek, 69, game-show host ("Concentration," "Jeopardy"), born Sudbury, ON, Canada, July 22, 1940.

July 23 — Thursday

DAY 204 — **161 REMAINING**

BIX BEIDERBECKE MEMORIAL JAZZ FESTIVAL. July 23–26. Davenport, IA. 38th annual. Four-day jazz festival honoring the memory of and perpetuating the music of world-renowned cornetist, pianist and composer Bix Beiderbecke. Includes concerts in four venues, food, etc. Est attendance: 12,000. For info: Bix Beiderbecke Memorial Society, PO Box 3688, Davenport, IA 52808. Phone: (563) 324-7170. Fax: (563) 326-1732. E-mail: info@bixsociety.org. Web: www.bixsociety.org or www.visitquadcities.com.

CANADA: CALGARY FOLK MUSIC FESTIVAL. July 23–26. Calgary, AB. Celebration of local, national and international folk music. Est attendance: 45,000. For info: Kerry Clarke, Artistic Director, Folk Festival Society of Calgary, PO Box 2897 Station M, Calgary, AB, Canada T2P 3C3. Phone: (403) 233-0904. E-mail: info@calgaryfolkfest.com. Web: www.calgaryfolkfest.com.

CHANDLER, RAYMOND: BIRTH ANNIVERSARY. July 23, 1888. The American master of postwar hard-boiled crime fiction didn't begin writing until he lost his management job at an oil company in 1933. After publishing short stories in *Black Mask* and other crime magazines, Chandler published his first novel, *The Big Sleep*, in 1939 to popular and critical acclaim. This and subsequent novels featured Philip Marlowe, a Los Angeles private eye who liked "liquor and women and chess and a few other things." Chandler was known for spare prose that featured gripping similes: "The wet air was as cold as the ashes of love" or "She had eyes like strange sins." Chandler also authored or coauthored three Hollywood screenplays, including the searing *Double Indemnity*. Born at Chicago, IL, Chandler died at La Jolla, CA, on Mar 26, 1959.

COMIC-CON INTERNATIONAL. July 23-26 (tentative). San Diego Convention Center, San Diego, CA. One of the largest showcases of comic art, artists, products and more. Some 9,000 exhibitors. Est attendance: 114,000. For info: Comic-Con International, PO Box 128458, San Diego, CA 92112. Fax: (619) 414-1022. E-mail: cci-info@comic-con.org. Web: www.comic-con.org/cci.

DELAWARE STATE FAIR. July 23–Aug 1. Harrington, DE. 90th annual fair will feature major concert and motor events, acres of carnival rides, livestock shows, petting zoos, commercial and competitive events, exotic food and free attractions throughout the grounds. Est attendance: 300,000. For info: Delaware State Fair, PO Box 28, Harrington, DE 19952. Phone: (302) 398-3269. Fax: (302) 398-5030. E-mail: info@delawarestatefair.com. Web: www.delawarestatefair.com.

DRYSDALE, DON: BIRTH ANNIVERSARY. July 23, 1936. Elected to the Baseball Hall of Fame in 1984, Don Drysdale was a pitcher for the Brooklyn and Los Angeles Dodgers from 1956 to 1969, compiling a won-lost record of 209–166 with a career ERA of 2.95. Following his playing career he became a successful and popular broadcast announcer for the Chicago White Sox and then for the Los Angeles Dodgers. He was born at Van Nuys, CA, and died at Montreal, QC, Canada, July 3, 1993.

EGYPT: REVOLUTION DAY. July 23. National holiday. Anniversary of the Revolution in 1952, which was launched by army officers and changed Egypt from a monarchy to a republic led by Nasser.

FIRST US SWIMMING SCHOOL OPENS: ANNIVERSARY. July 23, 1827. The first swimming school in the US opened at Boston, MA. Its pupils included John Quincy Adams and James Audubon.

"THE GENE AUTRY SHOW" TV PREMIERE: ANNIVERSARY. July 23, 1950. Popular CBS Western ran for six years starring movie actor Gene Autry. Along with sidekick Pat Buttram, Autry helped bring criminals to justice.

GORGEOUS GRANDMA DAY. July 23. A day honoring women who age, date and mate with style. For info: Alice Solomon, 7385 Cortes Lake Dr, Delray Beach, FL 33446. Phone: (561) 498-3543. Fax: (561) 499-4890. E-mail: GGalice@gorgeousgrandma.com. Web: www.gorgeousgrandma.com.

GREAT TEXAS MOSQUITO FESTIVAL. July 23–25. Clute, TX. More than 85 arts and crafts and food booths, headline entertainment, novelty games, carnival and a variety of contests for all ages during this fun-filled three-day family event. Meet "Willie Man Chew," a 26-foot inflatable mosquito complete with cowboy boots and hat. Annually, the last Thursday, Friday and Saturday in July. Est attendance: 17,000. For info: The Great Texas Mosquito Festival, City of Clute Parks and Rec Dept, PO Box 997, Clute, TX 77531. Phone: (979) 265-8392 or (800) 371-2971. Fax: (979) 265-8767. E-mail: buzz@mosquitofestival.com. Web: www.mosquitofestival.com.

HOT ENOUGH FOR YA DAY. July 23. We are permitted today to utter the words that suffice when nothing of intelligence comes to mind. "Is it hot enough for ya?" Annually, July 23. (©2006 by WH.) For info: Thomas & Ruth Roy, Wellcat Holidays, 2418 Long Ln, Lebanon, PA 17046-1708. Phone: (717) 279-0184. E-mail: info@wellcat.com. Web: www.wellcat.com.

JAPAN: SOMA NO UMAOI (WILD HORSE CHASING). July 23–25. Hibarigahara, Haramachi, Fukushima Prefecture, Japan. 1,000 horsemen clad in ancient armor compete for possession of three shrine flags shot aloft on Hibarigahara Plain, and men in white costumes attempt to catch wild horses corralled by the horsemen.

LEO, THE LION. July 23–Aug 22. In the astronomical/astrological zodiac, which divides the sun's apparent orbit into 12 segments, the period July 23–Aug 22 is traditionally identified as the sun sign of Leo, the Lion. The ruling celestial body is the sun.

LUMBERJACK WORLD CHAMPIONSHIPS. July 23–25. Hayward, WI. The "Olympics of the Forest" welcomes the world's best lumberjacks competing in a variety of competitions, including log rolling, tree climbing, cutting with saws and chainsaws and pole climbing. Annually, the last weekend in July. For info: Lumberjack World Championships, PO Box 666, Hayward, WI 54843. Phone: (715) 634-2484. E-mail: contact@lumberjackworldchampionships.com. Web: www.lumberjackworldchampionships.com.

MUSIC BY THE MILE. July 23–26. Central Mall, Wisconsin Sate Fair Grounds, West Allis, WI. Top notch music daily, fantastic food, child and family activities, retail vendors. Hosted by West Allis Charities, Inc. $5 admission (charity fundraiser). Est attendance: 50,000. For info: T.J. Meyers-Jansky, West Allis Charities, PO Box 14544, West Allis, WI 53214. Phone: (414) 520-2262. E-mail: westallischarities@yahoo.com. Web: www.westallischarities.org.

OREGON BREWERS FESTIVAL. July 23–26. Tom McCall Waterfront Park, Portland, OR. 72 microbreweries from across the country showcase their handcrafted brews to beer lovers. Annually, the last full weekend in July. Est attendance: 60,000. For info: Chris Crabb, Crabbsoup Public Relations, 4906 NE Siskiyou St, Portland, OR 97213. Phone: (503) 778-5917. E-mail: chrisc@oregonbrewfest.com. Web: www.oregonbrewfest.com.

"POORMAN'S PARADISE" GOLD PANNER CONTEST. July 23. Nome, AK. 109th anniversary. Open to all ages. Contestants pan a coffee can of beach material to free three small gold nuggets. All contestants are timed to determine the fastest gold panner. Trophies for first, second and third place overall; first place 12 years and younger; first place women. Held on the Red Sand Beaches of the Bering Sea. Est attendance: 500. For info: Rasmussen's Music Mart, PO Box 2, Nome, AK 99762. Phone: (907) 443-2798 or (907) 443-2919. Or, Gold Prospector's Assn of America, 43445 Business Park Dr, Ste 113, Temecula, CA 92590. Phone: (800) 551-9707.

REESE, HAROLD HENRY "PEE WEE": BIRTH ANNIVERSARY. July 23, 1918. Hall of Fame shortstop, born at Ekron, KY. Died Aug 14, 1999, at Louisville, KY.

SAINT APOLLINARIS: FEAST DAY. July 23. First bishop of Ravenna, and a martyr, of unknown date. Observed July 23.

July 2009	S	M	T	W	T	F	S
				1	2	3	4
	5	6	7	8	9	10	11
	12	13	14	15	16	17	18
	19	20	21	22	23	24	25
	26	27	28	29	30	31	

SHARM AL-SHEIKH BOMBINGS: ANNIVERSARY. July 23, 2005. In the worst act of terrorism of Egypt's recent history, the Red Sea resort city of Sharm al-Sheikh was the target of three bomb attacks that killed 88 people and injured more than 200. Various groups claimed responsibility for the attacks, which occurred on Egypt's Revolution Day.

SPACE MILESTONE: FIRST FEMALE COMMANDER: *COLUMBIA* (US): 10th ANNIVERSARY. July 23, 1999. Colonel Eileen Collins led a shuttle mission to deploy a $1.5 billion x-ray telescope, the Chandra observatory, into space. It is a sister satellite to the Hubble Space Telescope. The observatory is named after Nobel Prize winner Subrahamyar Chandrasekhar.

SPACE MILESTONE: *SOYUZ 37* (USSR). July 23, 1980. Cosmonauts Viktor Gorbatko and Lieutenant Colonel Pham Tuan, the first non-Caucasian in space (Vietnam), docked at *Salyut 6* July 24. Returned to Earth July 31.

BIRTHDAYS TODAY

Ronny Cox, 71, actor (*Deliverance, Bound for Glory, Total Recall*), born Cloudcroft, NM, July 23, 1938.

Gloria DeHaven, 84, actress (*Two Girls and a Sailor*, "Nakia"), born Los Angeles, CA, July 23, 1925.

Omar Epps, 36, actor ("House," *Love & Basketball*), born Brooklyn, NY, July 23, 1973.

Nicholas Gage, 70, journalist, film producer, writer (*Eleni*), born Lia, Greece, July 23, 1939.

Nomar Garciaparra, 36, baseball player, born Whittier, CA, July 23, 1973.

Woody Harrelson, 48, actor (Emmy for "Cheers"; *White Men Can't Jump, Natural Born Killers*), born Midland, TX, July 23, 1961.

Philip Seymour Hoffman, 42, stage and screen actor (Oscar for *Capote*; *Charlie Wilson's War, Mission: Impossible III*), born Fairport, NY, July 23, 1967.

Don Imus, 69, radio talk-show host, media icon and author, born Riverside, CA, July 23, 1940.

Arata Isozaki, 78, architect, born Oita, Japan, July 23, 1931.

Anthony M. Kennedy, 73, Supreme Court Associate Justice, born Sacramento, CA, July 23, 1936.

Eriq La Salle, 47, actor ("ER," *Coming to America*), born Hartford, CT, July 23, 1962.

Edie McClurg, 58, actress ("WKRP in Cincinnati," *Eating Raoul, A River Runs Through It*), born Kansas City, MO, July 23, 1951.

Belinda Montgomery, 59, actress ("Miami Vice," "Doogie Howser, MD"), born Winnipeg, MB, Canada, July 23, 1950.

Gary Dwayne Payton, 41, basketball player, born Oakland, CA, July 23, 1968.

Daniel Radcliffe, 20, actor (the Harry Potter films), born London, England, July 23, 1989.

Brandon Roy, 25, baseball player, born Seattle, WA, July 23, 1984.

Marlon Wayans, 37, actor ("In Living Color," *Scary Movie*), born New York, NY, July 23, 1972.

July 24 — Friday

DAY 205 **160 REMAINING**

ANTIQUE POWER EXHIBITION. July 24–26. Burton, OH. More than 100 old-time engines toot whistles and puff smoke as they demonstrate yesterday's feats such as wood sawing and grain threshing. Daily parades, slow races and tractor pulls. Est attendance: 2,600. For info: Century Village Museum, PO Box 153, Burton, OH 44021. Phone: (440) 834-1492. Fax: (440) 834-4012. Or Historical Engine Society, PO Box 945, Burton, OH 44021. Web: www.historicalengine.org.

ARCADIA DAZE. July 24–26. Arcadia, MI. The scenic village of Arcadia is the setting for this midsummer event. Activities include a parade on Sunday at 1:30 PM on Lake Street. An art fair, steak fry, fishing contest, games for the children, pancake breakfast, 5k running race on Saturday and a street dance on Friday and Saturday. Car show on Saturday. An old-fashioned good time for the whole family. Sponsor: Arcadia Lion Club. Est attendance: 2,500. For info: Wesley Hull, Arcadia Daze, 3269 Lake St, Arcadia, MI 49613. Phone: (231) 889-5555.

ARTS IN THE PARK. July 24–26. Kalispell, MT. Annual juried arts and crafts show and fair, food and entertainment. Est attendance: 12,000. For info: AIP Coordinator, Hockaday Museum of Art, 302 Second Ave E, Kalispell, MT 59901. Phone: (406) 755-5268. Fax: (406) 755-2023. E-mail: information@hockadaymuseum.org. Web: www.hockadaymuseum.org.

BELE CHERE. July 24–26. Asheville, NC. A community celebration featuring three food courts, six music stages, regional and national artists, children's area and events. The largest free outdoor street festival in the Southeast. Est attendance: 365,000. For info: Melissa Porter, Festival Coordinator, Asheville Parks & Rec/Festival Division, PO Box 7148, Asheville, NC 28802. Phone: (828) 259-5800. Fax: (704) 259-5606. Web: www.belecherefestival.com.

BOLÍVAR, SIMON: BIRTH ANNIVERSARY. July 24, 1783. "The Liberator," born at Caracas, Venezuela. Commemorated in Venezuela and other Latin American countries. Died Dec 17, 1830, at Santa Marta, Colombia. Bolivia is named after him.

CANADA: ANNUAL NOVA SCOTIA BLUEGRASS AND OLDTIME MUSIC FESTIVAL. July 24–26. Stewiacke, NS. 38th annual family event featuring acoustic music by groups from the US and Canada's Atlantic area. Annually, the last full weekend in July. Est attendance: 3,000. For info: Nova Scotia Bluegrass Oldtime Music Festival, 48 Boxwood Crescent, Lower Sackville, NS, Canada B4C 3Z1. E-mail: redhead1@eastlink.ca.

COUSINS DAY. July 24. A day to celebrate, honor and appreciate our cousins. For info: Claudia A. Evart, 30 Park Ave, #2P, New York, NY 10016-3833. Phone: (212) 779-2227. E-mail: cevart1@earthlink.net.

DETROIT FOUNDED: ANNIVERSARY. July 24, 1701. Anniversary of the landing at the site of Detroit by Antoine de la Mothe Cadillac in the service of Louis XIV of France. Fort Pontchartrain du Detroit was first settlement on site.

DODGE CITY DAYS. July 24–Aug 2. Dodge City, KS. Western heritage celebration with concerts, arts and crafts, parades, PRCA rodeo, street dances, cookouts, art show and classic car show. Est attendance: 90,000. For info: Dodge City Days/Dodge City Area COC, PO Box 939, 311 W Spruce, Dodge City, KS 67801. Phone: (620) 227-3119. Fax: (620) 227-2957. E-mail: dcdays@dodgechamber.com. Web: www.dodgecitydays.com.

DUMAS, ALEXANDRE: BIRTH ANNIVERSARY. July 24, 1802. French playwright and novelist, born at Villers-Cotterets, France. He is said to have written more than 300 volumes, including *The Count of Monte Cristo* and *The Three Musketeers*. Father of Alexandre Dumas (Dumas fils), also a novelist and playwright (1824–95). Dumas died near Dieppe, France, Dec 5, 1870.

EARHART, AMELIA: BIRTH ANNIVERSARY. July 24, 1897. American aviatrix lost on flight from New Guinea to Howland Island, in the Pacific Ocean, July 2, 1937. First woman to cross the Atlantic solo, second person to cross the Atlantic solo and first person to fly solo across the Pacific from Hawaii to California. Born at Atchison, KS.

GILROY GARLIC FESTIVAL. July 24–26. Gilroy, CA. 31st annual. Midsummer harvest celebration in the "Garlic Capital of the World." Great garlic recipe contest/cook-off. Ethnic foods, continuous entertainment on three stages, arts, crafts and children's area. Annually, the last full weekend of July, Friday through Sunday. Est attendance: 3,000,000. For info: Gilroy Garlic Festival Assn, PO Box 2311, Gilroy, CA 95021. Phone: (408) 842-1625. Fax: (408) 842-7337. E-mail: clove@gilroygarlicfestival.com. Web: www.gilroygarlicfestival.com.

GOLD DISCOVERY DAYS. July 24–26. Custer, SD. Parade, pancake breakfast, bed races, children's fair, fun run, volksmarch, arts and crafts festival, volleyball tournament and hot-air balloon rally. Est attendance: 7,000. For info: Gold Discovery Days Committee, PO Box 350, Custer, SD 57730. Phone: (605) 673-2244 or (800) 992-9818. E-mail: info@custersd.com. Web: www.custersd.com.

IOWA STORYTELLING FESTIVAL. July 24–25. City Park, Clear Lake, IA. This 21st annual storytelling event is held in a scenic lakeside setting. Friday evening "Stories After Dark." Two performances Saturday plus story exchange for novice tellers. Est attendance: 800. For info: Jean Casey, Dir, Clear Lake Public Library, 200 N 4th St, Clear Lake, IA 50428. Phone: (641) 357-6133. Fax: (641) 357-4645. E-mail: clplib@netins.net.

LOGGING MUSEUM FESTIVAL DAYS. July 24–25. Rangeley, ME. Bean-hole beans, Logger's Hall of Fame, Miss Woodchip Contest, parade, logging competition. Est attendance: 1,500. For info: Rangeley Logging Museum, Box 154, Rangeley, ME 04970. Phone: (207) 864-5595.

MONTANA STATE FAIR. July 24–Aug 2. Great Falls, MT. Mighty Thomas Carnival, night shows, PRCA rodeo, free acts, food fair, 4-H exhibits and much more. Est attendance: 150,000. For info: Montana State Fair, 400 3rd St NW, Great Falls, MT 59404. Phone: (406) 727-8900. Fax: (406) 452-8955. E-mail: info@goexpopark.com. Web: www.montanastatefair.com.

NATIONAL DRIVE-THRU DAY. July 24. After WWII, California sunshine and a love affair with automobiles spurred the growth of roadside businesses in the Golden State catering specifically to motorists. As America's first major drive-thru hamburger chain, Jack in the Box® restaurants (founded in 1951) helped pave the way for a delicious new dining experience. Annually, on July 24. For info: Brian Luscomb, Jack in the Box, 9330 Balboa Ave, San Diego, CA 92123. Phone: (858) 571-2121. Web: www.jackinthebox.com.

NATIONAL TELL AN OLD JOKE DAY. July 24. Keep traditional humor alive and well: tell someone an old joke! But keep it clean. Annually, July 24. For info (or old jokes): John Bohannon. E-mail: jazzwithjb@aol.com.

NESHOBA COUNTY FAIR. July 24–31. Philadelphia, MS. Billed as "Mississippi's Giant Houseparty," this is one of the nation's last Campground Fairs. At this 119th annual fair, harness racing, state and national political speaking, crafts, music and amusement are the order each day. Est attendance: 85,000. For info: Neshoba County Fair Assoc, 16800 Hwy 21 South, Philadelphia, MS 39350. Phone: (601) 656-8480. Fax: (601) 656-8461. Web: www.neshobacountyfair.org.

NORTH DAKOTA STATE FAIR. July 24–Aug 1. Minot, ND. The North Dakota State Fair features the best in big-name entertainment, farm and home exhibits, displays, the Midway and rodeo. Est attendance: 250,000. For info: North Dakota State Fair, Box 1796,

Minot, ND 58702. Phone: (701) 857-7620. Fax: (701) 857-7622. E-mail: ndsf@minot.com. Web: www.ndstatefair.com.

PIONEER DAY: ANNIVERSARY. July 24, 1847. Utah. State holiday. Commemorates the day when Brigham Young and his followers entered the Salt Lake Valley.

RAF JAMS NAZI RADAR IN OPERATION GOMORRAH: ANNIVERSARY. July 24, 1943. On the first of the Royal Air Force Operation Gomorrah raids on Hamburg, Germany, "windows" (bales of 10½-inch strips of aluminum foil) were pushed out of the bombers, causing the German radar screens to display a snowstorm of false echo "aircraft" on their screens. As a result only 12 of the 791 bombers sent on the mission were shot down.

BIRTHDAYS TODAY

Barry Bonds, 45, baseball player, born Riverside, CA, July 24, 1964.

Ruth Buzzi, 73, comedienne, actress ("Rowan & Martin's Laugh-In," "Sesame Street"), born Westerly, RI, July 24, 1936.

Rose Byrne, 30, actress ("Damages," *Wicker Park*), born Balmain, Sydney, New South Wales, Australia, July 24, 1979.

Lynda Carter, 58, actress ("Wonder Woman," "Partners in Crime"), former Miss World–USA, singer, born Phoenix, AZ, July 24, 1951.

Kristin Chenoweth, 41, actress, singer (stage: *Wicked;* Tony Award for *You're a Good Man, Charlie Brown*; "The West Wing"), born Broken Arrow, OK, Sept 22, 1968.

Charlie Crist, 53, Governor of Florida (R), born Altoona, PA, July 24, 1956.

Kadeem Hardison, 44, actor ("A Different World," "The Sixth Man"), born New York, NY, July 24, 1965.

Robert Hays, 62, actor (*Airplane!*, "Starman"), born Bethesda, MD, July 24, 1947.

Julie A. Krone, 46, former jockey, first woman in National Racing Hall of Fame, born Benton Harbor, MI, July 24, 1963.

Jennifer Lopez, 39, actress (*Maid in Manhattan, The Cell, Out of Sight*), singer, born the Bronx, NY, July 24, 1970.

Claire McCaskill, 56, US Senator (D, Missouri), born Rollo, MO, July 24, 1953.

Karl Malone, 46, former basketball player, born Summerfield, LA, July 24, 1963.

Pat Oliphant, 74, cartoonist, born Adelaide, Australia, July 24, 1935.

Anna Paquin, 27, actress (*X-Men* films, *The Piano, Fly Away Home*), born Winnipeg, MB, Canada, July 24, 1982.

Chris Sarandon, 67, actor (*Dog Day Afternoon, The Princess Bride*), born Beckley, WV, July 24, 1942.

Peter Serkin, 62, musician, born New York, NY, July 24, 1947.

Billy Taylor, 88, jazz musician, born Greenville, NC, July 24, 1921.

July 2009	S	M	T	W	T	F	S
				1	2	3	4
	5	6	7	8	9	10	11
	12	13	14	15	16	17	18
	19	20	21	22	23	24	25
	26	27	28	29	30	31	

July 25 — Saturday

DAY 206 **159 REMAINING**

ALL-AMERICAN SOAP BOX DERBY. July 25. Derby Downs, Akron, OH. 72nd annual derby. A weeklong festival culminating in world championship race by regional champs from US, Guam, New Zealand, Germany, Japan and Canada. Est attendance: 20,000. For info: Jeff Iula, General Manager, Intl Soap Box Derby, Inc, PO Box 7225, Derby Downs, Akron, OH 44306. Phone: (330) 733-8723. Fax: (330) 733-1370. E-mail: soapbox@aasbd.org. Web: www.aasbd.com.

ALLIES BREAK OUT OF NORMANDY BEACHHEAD: 65th ANNIVERSARY. July 25, 1944. Having made a spectacularly successful landing on D-Day (June 6), Allied forces then secured and extended their position by landing more than a million men and 60,000 tons of supplies. Despite early success with Operation *Overlord*, the Allies were pinned down, and a breakout was necessary if France was to be retaken. Sustained air bombardment (carpet bombing) created gaps in the German lines, and on this date Allied forces penetrated the lines and outflanked and bypassed the German units. The German forces were incredulous at the speed with which the Allies shook loose from them and advanced over the French countryside.

***ANDREA DORIA* SINKS: ANNIVERSARY.** July 25, 1956. The Italian luxury liner collided with the *Stockholm*, a Swedish liner, on its way to New York. Other ships in the area came to the rescue of the *Andrea Doria*. Some 1,634 people were rescued during the ordeal, including the captain and the crew.

ANTIQUE AND CLASSIC BOAT RENDEZVOUS. July 25–26. Mystic Seaport, Mystic, CT. Pre-1963 power and sailing yachts on view for Mystic Seaport visitors. Mystic River parade on Sunday. Est attendance: 4,000. For info: Mystic Seaport, 75 Greenmanville Ave, Box 6000, Mystic, CT 06355. Phone: (860) 527-0711 or (888) 973-2767. Web: www.mysticseaport.org.

ARTS AND CRAFTS FESTIVAL. July 25–26. Loveladies, NJ. 20th annual. Featuring juried arts and crafts displays, entertainment, food and more. For info: Long Beach Island Foundation of the Arts and Sciences, 120 Long Beach Blvd, Loveladies, NJ 08008. Phone: (609) 494-1241. Fax: (609) 494-0662. Web: www.lbifoundation.org.

COSTA RICA: GUANACASTE DAY. July 25. National holiday. Commemorates the 1814 transfer of the region of Guanacaste from Nicaragua to Costa Rica by Spain.

COW APPRECIATION DAY. July 25. Woodstock, VT. A "cowlege bowl" competition, dairy education programs, butter and ice cream making and more. Est attendance: 300. For info: Billings Farm and Museum, Rte 12 N, Woodstock, VT 05091. Phone: (802) 457-2355. Fax: (802) 457-4663. E-mail: info@billingsfarm.org. Web: www.billingsfarm.org.

FIRST AIRPLANE CROSSING OF ENGLISH CHANNEL: 100th ANNIVERSARY. July 25, 1909. Louis Bleriot, after asking from the cockpit, "Where is England?" took off from Les Baraques (near Calais), France, and landed on English soil at Northfall Meadow, near Dover, where he was greeted first by English police and customs officers. This, the world's first international overseas airplane flight, was accomplished in a 28-hp monoplane with a wingspan of 23 feet. See also: "Bleriot, Louis: Birth Anniversary" (July 1).

GENEVA ARTS FAIR. July 25–26. Geneva, IL. More than 140 artist booths welcome visitors to an open-air Fine Art Show held amid shady trees surrounding the historic Kane County Courthouse. Annually, the fourth Saturday and Sunday in July. Est attendance: 22,000. For info: Geneva Chamber of Commerce, PO Box 481, 8 S Third St, Geneva, IL 60134. Phone: (630) 232-6060. Fax: (630) 232-6083. E-mail: chamberinfo@genevachamber.com. Web: www.genevachamber.com.

GERMANY: WAGNER FESTSPIELE. July 25–Aug 28. Bayreuth. The works of Richard Wagner are performed daily at the Festival Theatre, which Wagner had built in 1872–76. For info: Bayreuther Festspiele, Pressebüro, Postfach 100262, Bayreuth, Germany D-95402.

GILFORD, JACK: BIRTH ANNIVERSARY. July 25, 1907. American actor Jack Gilford was born Jacob Gellman at New York, NY.

Though he was blacklisted for 10 years following refusal to answer questions before the House Un-American Activities Committee in the 1950s, he appeared in many films, stage productions and television programs including an Academy Award–nominated role opposite Jack Lemmon in *Save the Tiger* (1973) and his best-known role as Hysterium in the stage and film versions of *A Funny Thing Happened on the Way to the Forum*. He died June 4, 1990, at New York, NY.

HANOVER DUTCH FESTIVAL. July 25. Hanover, PA. Handmade crafts, ethnic foods, music, entertainment, children's carnival, antique car show. Annually, the last Saturday in July. Est attendance: 10,000. For info: Hanover Area Chamber of Commerce, 146 Carlisle St, Hanover, PA 17331. Phone: (717) 637-6130. Web: www.hanoverchamber.com.

HARRISON, ANNA SYMMES: BIRTH ANNIVERSARY. July 25, 1775. Wife of William Henry Harrison, ninth president of the US, born at Morristown, NJ. Died at North Bend, IN, Feb 25, 1864.

MUSSOLINI OUSTED: ANNIVERSARY. July 25, 1943. Two weeks after the Allied attack on Sicily began, the Fascist Grand Council met for the first time since December of 1939 and took a confidence vote resulting in Mussolini's being removed from office and placed under arrest. Italy's King Victor Emmanuel ordered Marshal Pietro Badoglio to form a new government.

NATIONAL DAY OF THE COWBOY. July 25. 5th annual. A day to pay homage to our cowboy and Western heritage, as well as to honor working cowboys and cowgirls, rodeo athletes, Western musicians, cowboy poets, Western artists, ranchers and all others who continue to contribute to the cowboy and Western culture in America today. Proclaimed by the US Senate in Resolution 138 for the first time for July 23, 2005. Now this day is set for the fourth Saturday in July. For info: National Day of the Cowboy, 162 N Railroad Ave, Willcox, AZ 85643. Phone: (520) 766-6362. E-mail: info@nationaldayofthecowboy.com. Web: www.nationaldayofthecowboy.com.

PUERTO RICO: CONSTITUTION DAY. July 25. Also called Commonwealth Day or Occupation Day. Commemorates proclamation of constitution in 1952.

PUERTO RICO: LOIZA ALDEA FIESTA. July 25–28. Best known of Puerto Rico's patron saint festivities. Villagers of Loiza Aldea, 20 miles east of San Juan, don devil masks and colorful costumes for a variety of traditional activities.

SPAIN: SAINT JAMES DAY. July 25. Holy day of the patron saint of Spain. When this day falls on a Sunday it is a holy year and pilgrims make the pilgrimage to Santiago de Compostela, the site of the saint's tomb. 2010 is the next holy year.

TAYLOR HORSEFEST. July 25. Taylor, ND. This annual celebration is highlighted by a parade of horses and horse-drawn equipment, ethnic food fest, craft vendors, exhibits, demonstrations, music and cowboy poetry. Horse-drawn taxis provide transportation throughout the town during the day. Est attendance: 2,000. For info: Taylor Horsefest, PO Box 7, Taylor, ND 58656. Phone: (701) 974-4210 or (877) 757-7545. Web: www.taylorhorsefest.com.

TEST-TUBE BABY: BIRTHDAY. July 25, 1978. Anniversary of the birth of Louise Brown at Oldham, England. First documented birth of a baby conceived outside the body of a woman. The attending physicians were Patrick Christopher Steptoe and Robert Geoffrey Edwards.

TIDEWATER ARCHAEOLOGY DIG. July 25–26. St. Mary's City, MD. Hands-on opportunity to explore at an archaeology site at Maryland's first capital. Special behind-the-scenes tours. Est attendance: 500. For info: Director of Marketing, Historic St. Mary's City, PO Box 39, St. Mary's City, MD 20686. Phone: (240) 895-4990 or (800) SMC-1634. Fax: (240) 895-4968. Web: www.stmaryscity.org.

TUNISIA: REPUBLIC DAY. July 25. National holiday. Commemorates the proclamation of the republic in 1957.

BIRTHDAYS TODAY

Midge Decter, 82, journalist, born St. Paul, MN, July 25, 1927.

Illeana Douglas, 44, actress (*Message in a Bottle, Grace of My Heart*), born Boston, MA, July 25, 1965.

Iman, 54, model, actress (*Star Trek VI*), born Iman Mohamed Abdulmajid at Mogadishu, Somalia, July 25, 1955.

James Lafferty, 24, actor ("One Tree Hill," *A Season on the Brink*), born Hemet, CA, July 25, 1985.

Matt LeBlanc, 42, actor ("Friends"), born Newton, MA, July 25, 1967.

Evgeni Nabokov, 34, hockey player, born Kamenogorsk, the former USSR, July 25, 1975.

Nathaniel (Nate) Thurmond, 68, Hall of Fame basketball player, born Akron, OH, July 25, 1941.

July 26 — Sunday

DAY 207 **158 REMAINING**

ADMINISTRATIVE PROFESSIONALS INTERNATIONAL ANNUAL CONVENTION AND EDUCATION FORUM. July 26–29. Minneapolis, MN. Est attendance: 2,000. For info: Intl Assn for Administrative Professionals, 10502 NW Ambassador Dr, PO Box 20404, Kansas City, MO 64195-0404. Phone: (816) 891-6600, ext 2223. Fax: (816) 891-9118. E-mail: meetings@iaap-hq.org. Web: www.iaap-hq.org.

AMERICANS WITH DISABILITIES ACT SIGNED: ANNIVERSARY. July 26, 1990. President George H.W. Bush signed the Americans with Disabilities Act, which went into effect two years later. It required that public facilities be made accessible to the disabled.

ARMED FORCES UNIFIED: ANNIVERSARY. July 26, 1947. President Truman signed legislation unifying the two branches of the armed forces into the Department of Defense. The branches merged were the War Department (Army) and the Navy. The Air Force was separated from the Army at the same time and made an independent force. Truman nominated James Forrestal to be the first secretary of defense. The legislation also provided for the National Security Council, the Central Intelligence Agency and the Joint Chiefs of Staff.

CANADA: MINERAL CAPITAL ROCK SHOW. July 26. Bancroft, ON. Mineral specimens from central Ontario and Quebec dealers, mineral exhibits, lapidary demonstrations, silent auctions and grand live auction. Est attendance: 1,500. For info: Attn: Events Coordinator, Bancroft and District Chamber of Commerce, PO Box 539, Bancroft, ON, Canada K0L 1C0. Phone: (613) 332-1513 or (888) 443-9999. E-mail: chamber@commerce.bancroft.on.ca. Web: www.bancroftdistrict.com.

CATLIN, GEORGE: BIRTH ANNIVERSARY. July 26, 1796. American artist famous for his paintings of Native American life, born at Wilkes-Barre, PA. In 1832 he toured North and South American tribes, recording their lives in his work. He died Dec 23, 1872, at Jersey City, NJ.

CLINTON, GEORGE: BIRTH ANNIVERSARY. July 26, 1739. (Old Style date.) Fourth vice president of the US (1805–12), born at Little Britain, NY. Died at Washington, DC, Apr 20, 1812.

CUBA: NATIONAL DAY: ANNIVERSARY OF REVOLUTION. July 26. Anniversary of the 1953 beginning of Fidel Castro's revolutionary "26th of July Movement." He launched a failed attack on the Moncada army barracks, and most involved were killed or captured. He was captured and given a trial, during which he made his famous speech, "History Will Absolve Me." Sentenced to 15 years, he was pardoned after just two.

CURAÇAO: CURAÇAO DAY. July 26. Traditional holiday commemorating Columbus companion Alonso de Ojeda's discovery of the island of Curaçao in 1499, when he sailed into Santa Ana Bay, the entrance of the harbor of Willemstad. Festivities on this day.

HUXLEY, ALDOUS: BIRTH ANNIVERSARY. July 26, 1894. English author, satirist, mystic and philosopher, Aldous Leonard Huxley was born at Godalming, Surrey, England. Best known of his works are *Brave New World* and *Point Counter Point.* Huxley died at Los Angeles, CA, Nov 22, 1963.

KUBRICK, STANLEY: BIRTH ANNIVERSARY. July 26, 1928. American filmmaker, born at the Bronx, NY. Kubrick started out in photography at the age of 16 with *Look* magazine. His first film, *Day of the Fight*, produced in 1950, was a documentary of his photo series about fighter Walter Cartier. His film credits include *Dr. Strangelove, Full Metal Jacket* and *2001: A Space Odyssey*. *Eyes Wide Shut,* Kubrick's final film, was released posthumously in the summer of 1999. He died at London, England, Mar 7, 1999.

LAVALLETTE HERITAGE ARTS AND CRAFTS SHOW. July 26 (rain date Aug 2). Lavallette, NJ. Juried arts and crafts. Only the best of the best welcome to exhibit. One of the best shows on the eastern seaboard. 9:30 AM to 5 PM. Ribbon and cash awards given in both categories. Annually, the last Sunday in July. Est attendance: 20,000. For info: Heritage Committee of Lavallette, 117 President Ave, Lavallette, NJ 08735. Phone: (732) 793-1936. Fax: (732) 793-1937. E-mail: zaccaria@optonline.net.

LIBERIA: INDEPENDENCE DAY. July 26. National holiday. Became republic in 1847, under aegis of the US societies for repatriating former slaves in Africa.

MALDIVES: INDEPENDENCE DAY. July 26. National holiday. Commemorates independence from Britain in 1965.

NEW YORK RATIFICATION DAY. July 26, 1788. 11th state to ratify Constitution in 1788.

ONE VOICE. July 26. A synchronized reading of the Universal Peace Covenant by people on all continents at 1 PM (CDT). In conjunction with the natural-time calendar year's "day out of time," the School of Metaphysics invites people all around the world to create one voice of peace by reading this document, penned in 1996 by more than two dozen spiritual teachers ages 20 to 70, from varied cultures and walks of life. The Universal Peace Covenant is available in several languages at www.peacedome.org, or you can write to have a copy sent to you. For info: Dr. Barbara Condron or Dr. Christine Madar, School of Metaphysics World HQ, 163 Moon Valley Rd, Windyville, MO 65783. Phone: (417) 345-8411. E-mail: peace@som.org.

✦ **PARENTS' DAY.** July 26. To pay tribute to the men and women across our country whose devotion as parents strengthens our society and forms the foundation for a bright future for America. Public Law 103-362. Annually, the fourth Sunday in July.

POTSDAM DECLARATION: ANNIVERSARY. July 26, 1945. As the Potsdam Conference came to a close in Germany, Churchill, Truman and China's representatives fashioned a communiqué to Japan offering it an opportunity to end the war. It demanded that Japan completely disarm, allowed it sovereignty to the four main islands and to minor islands to be determined by the Allies, and insisted that all Japanese citizens be given immediate and complete freedom of speech, religion and thought. The Japanese would be allowed to continue enough industry to maintain their economy. The communiqué concluded with a demand for unconditional surrender. Unaware these demands were backed up by an atomic bomb, on July 28 Japanese prime minister Admiral Kantaro Suzuki rejected the Potsdam Declaration.

ROBARDS, JASON: BIRTH ANNIVERSARY. July 26, 1922. A staple on the American stage and screen for six decades, Robards was born at Chicago, IL, and was a decorated WWII veteran. He won the Oscar for Best Supporting Actor two years in a row, for 1976's *All the President's Men* and 1977's *Julia.* His most famous stage roles were in the plays of Eugene O'Neill, including *The Iceman Cometh* and *Long Day's Journey into Night.* He won the Tony Award in 1959 for his portrayal of a fictionalized F. Scott Fitzgerald in *The Disenchanted.* He died at Bridgeport, CT, Dec 26, 2000.

SHAW, GEORGE BERNARD: BIRTH ANNIVERSARY. July 26, 1856. Irish playwright, essayist, vegetarian, socialist, antivivisectionist and, he said, "one of the hundred best playwrights in the world." His major works include *Arms and the Man, Man and Superman, Major Barbara* and *Pygmalion.* Born at Dublin, Ireland. Died at Ayot St. Lawrence, England, Nov 2, 1950.

SPACE MILESTONE: *APOLLO 15* (US). July 26, 1971. Launched this date. Astronauts David R. Scott and James B. Irwin landed on moon (lunar module *Falcon*) while Alfred M. Worden piloted command module *Endeavor. Rover 1,* a four-wheel vehicle, was used for further exploration. Departed moon Aug 2, after nearly three days. Pacific landing Aug 7.

US ARMY FIRST DESEGREGATION: 65th ANNIVERSARY. July 26, 1944. During WWII the US Army ordered desegregation of its training camp facilities. Later the same year black platoons were assigned to white companies in a tentative step toward integration of the battlefield. However, it was not until after the war—July 26, 1948—that President Harry Truman signed an order officially integrating the armed forces.

BIRTHDAYS TODAY

Kate Beckinsale, 36, actress (*Underworld, Pearl Harbor, Van Helsing*), born London, England, July 26, 1973.

Sandra Bullock, 45, actress (*Infamous, The Lake House, Crash, Speed*), born Arlington, VA, July 26, 1964.

Blake Edwards, 87, producer, writer, director (*Victor/Victoria, The Pink Panther*), born Tulsa, OK, July 26, 1922.

Susan George, 59, actress (*Straw Dogs*), born London, England, July 26, 1950.

Mick Jagger, 66, musician, lead singer (Rolling Stones), born Michael Philip Jagger at Dartford, England, July 26, 1943.

Helen Mirren, 63, actress (Oscar for *The Queen*; *Gosford Park*, "Prime Suspect," "Elizabeth I"), born London, England, July 26, 1946.

Taylor Momsen, 16, actress (*How the Grinch Stole Christmas, Paranoid Park,* "Gossip Girl"), born St. Louis, MO, July 26, 1993.

Jeremy Piven, 45, actor ("Entourage," "Ellen," *Grosse Pointe Blank*), born New York, NY, July 26, 1964.

Kevin Spacey, 50, actor (Oscars for *American Beauty* and *The Usual Suspects; L.A. Confidential*), born South Orange, NJ, July 26, 1959.

July 2009

S	M	T	W	T	F	S
			1	2	3	4
5	6	7	8	9	10	11
12	13	14	15	16	17	18
19	20	21	22	23	24	25
26	27	28	29	30	31	

July 27 — Monday

DAY 208 **157 REMAINING**

ATLANTIC TELEGRAPH CABLE LAID: ANNIVERSARY. July 27, 1866. Cable laying successfully completed.

BARBOSA, JOSÉ CELSO: BIRTH ANNIVERSARY. July 27, 1857. Puerto Rican physician and patriot, born at Bayamon, Puerto Rico. His birthday is a holiday in Puerto Rico. He died at San Juan, Puerto Rico, Sept 21, 1921.

DUMAS, ALEXANDRE (DUMAS FILS): BIRTH ANNIVERSARY. July 27, 1824. French novelist and playwright, as was his father. Author of *La Dame aux Camélias.* Dumas fils was born at Paris and died at Marly-le-Roi, France, Nov 27, 1895.

DUROCHER, LEO: BIRTH ANNIVERSARY. July 27, 1905. Leo Durocher was born at West Springfield, MA. He began his major league baseball career with the New York Yankees in 1925. He also played for the St. Louis Cardinals' "Gashouse Gang" and the Brooklyn Dodgers, where he first served as player-manager in 1939. On July 6, 1946, he used the phrase "Nice guys finish last," which would become his trademark. As a manager, he guided the New York Giants into two World Series. Following a five-year period away from baseball, he resurfaced as a coach with the Los Angeles Dodgers in 1961. In 1966 he signed with the Chicago Cubs as manager. After leaving the Cubs, he spent one season with the Houston Astros, then retired from baseball in 1973. He died Oct 7, 1991, at Palm Springs, CA.

EAA AIRVENTURE OSHKOSH. July 27–Aug 2. Wittman Regional Airport, Oshkosh, WI. World's largest sport aviation event. More than 10,000 airplanes annually fly in for this Experimental Aircraft Association event. Daily air shows, special programs, more than 500 forums, workshops and seminars. Est attendance: 500,000. For info: Dick Knapinski, Corporate Communications, Experimental Aircraft Assn, PO Box 3086, Oshkosh, WI 54903-3086. Phone: (920) 426-4800. E-mail: communications@eaa.org. Web: www.eaa.org.

INSULIN FIRST ISOLATED: ANNIVERSARY. July 27, 1921. Dr. Frederick Banting and his assistant at the University of Toronto Medical School, Charles Best, gave insulin to a dog whose pancreas had been removed. In 1922 insulin was first administered to a diabetic 14-year-old boy.

KOREAN WAR ARMISTICE: ANNIVERSARY. July 27, 1953. Armistice agreement ending war that had lasted three years and 32 days was signed at Panmunjom, Korea (July 26, US time), by US and North Korean delegates. Both sides claimed victory at conclusion of two years, 17 days of truce negotiations.

TAKE YOUR HOUSEPLANTS FOR A WALK DAY. July 27. Walking your plants around the neighborhood enables them to know their environment, thereby providing them with a sense of knowing, bringing on wellness. (©2006 by WH.) For info: Thomas & Ruth Roy, Wellcat Holidays, 2418 Long Ln, Lebanon, PA 17046. Phone: (717) 279-0184. E-mail: info@wellcat.com. Web: www.wellcat.com.

TINKER, JOE: BIRTH ANNIVERSARY. July 27, 1880. Born at Muscotah, KS, shortstop Joseph Bert Tinker was part of the Chicago Cubs' famous Tinker-to-Evers-to-Chance double-play combination that first took the field on Sept 13, 1902. For the next eight years this trio was the soul of the powerhouse Cubs—despite the fact that Tinker and Johnny Evers stopped speaking to each other in September 1905 (they continued the feud for 33 years). Tinker played with the Cincinnati Reds after the Cubs, played and managed in the Federal League and then managed the Cubs. Inducted into the Hall of Fame (with Evers and Chance) in 1946. Died at Orlando, FL, July 27, 1948. See also: "Tinker to Evers to Chance: First Double Play Anniversary" (Sept 15).

US DEPARTMENT OF STATE FOUNDED: ANNIVERSARY. July 27, 1789. The first presidential cabinet department, called the Department of Foreign Affairs, was established by the Congress. Later the name was changed to Department of State.

VIRGIN ISLANDS: HURRICANE SUPPLICATION DAY. July 27. Legal holiday. Population attends churches to pray for protection from hurricanes. Annually, the fourth Monday in July.

WALK ON STILTS DAY. July 27. A day to walk on stilts, providing a chance to develop self-confidence through mastery of balance and coordination. A chance to enjoy the challenge of childhood no matter your age. A celebration of daring accomplishments at homes, circuses and theme parks everywhere. For info: Bill "Stretch" Coleman, 930 S Decatur St, Denver, CO 80219. Phone: (303) 922-4655. E-mail: stretch@stiltwalker.com. Web: www.stiltwalker.com.

WORLD FOOTBAG CHAMPIONSHIPS. July 27–Aug 2. Portland, OR. 30th annual. Seven-day sports event spotlights competition of foot skills—the Super Bowl of footbag (also known as Hacky Sack®)! It attracts the world's top footbag competitors from the US and 10 other countries. Prize money exceeds $10,000. Sponsors: Sipa Sipa Footbags and Sandmaster Footbags. Est attendance: 5,000. For info: Bruce Guettich, Dir, World Footbag Assn, PO Box 775208, Steamboat Springs, CO 80477. Phone: (800) 878-8797. Fax: (970) 870-2846. E-mail: wfa@worldfootbag.com. Web: www.worldfootbag.com.

 BIRTHDAYS TODAY

Peggy Gale Fleming, 61, Olympic gold medal figure skater, sportscaster, born San Jose, CA, July 27, 1948.

Bobbie Gentry, 67, singer, songwriter ("Ode to Billie Joe"), born Roberta Streeter at Chicasaw County, MS, July 27, 1942.

Courtney Kupets, 23, gymnast, born Bedford, TX, July 27, 1986.

Norman Lear, 87, TV scriptwriter, producer ("All in the Family," "Maude"), born New Haven, CT, July 27, 1922.

Maureen McGovern, 60, singer ("The Morning After"), actress, born Youngstown, OH, July 27, 1949.

Julian McMahon, 41, actor ("Charmed," "Nip/Tuck"), born Sydney, New South Wales, Australia, July 27, 1968.

Michael Mukasey, 68, US Attorney General, born the Bronx, NY, July 28, 1941.

Jonathan Rhys-Meyers, 32, actor (*August Rush, Match Point, Elvis,* "The Tudors"), born County Dublin, Ireland, July 27, 1977.

Alex Rodriguez, 34, baseball player, born New York, NY, July 27, 1975.

Maya Rudolph, 37, actress, comedienne ("Saturday Night Live"), born Gainesville, FL, July 27, 1972.

Betty Thomas, 61, director, actress ("Hill Street Blues"), born St. Louis, MO, July 27, 1948.

Jerry Van Dyke, 78, actor ("Coach," "Teen Angel"), born Danville, IL, July 27, 1931.

James Victor, 70, actor (*Fuzz, Stand and Deliver*), born Santiago, Dominican Republic, July 27, 1939.

July 28 — Tuesday

DAY 209 | 156 REMAINING

AFRMA FANCY RAT & MOUSE DISPLAY. July 28–Aug 2 (tentative). Costa Mesa, CA. American Fancy Rat and Mouse Association exhibits rats and mice of "fancy" species that make good pets. For info: AFRMA, PO Box 2589, Winnetka, CA 91396-2589. Phone: (818) 992-5564 or (951) 685-2350 or (909) 238-5231. E-mail: afrma@afrma.org. Web: www.afrma.org.

FAROE ISLANDS: OLAI FESTIVAL. July 28–29. Torshavn. National festival held in honor of Saint Olav, the patron saint of these small islands of the Norwegian Sea that are part of the kingdom of Denmark. Begins the eve of St. Olav's Day (July 28), with a procession, sporting events, meetings and concerts. The festival continues on St. Olav's Day itself (July 29) with a ceremonial procession involving political, religious and community leaders to the parliament. After the prime minister's opening speech, the governmental year begins. Ceremonies end at midnight with community singing. Est attendance: 50,000.

FOX, TERRY: BIRTH ANNIVERSARY. July 28, 1958. With cancer requiring amputation of his right leg at age 18, Fox was determined to devote his life to a fight against the disease. His "Marathon of Hope," a planned 5,200-mile run westward across Canada, started Apr 12, 1980, at St. John's, NF, and continued 3,328 miles to Thunder Bay, ON, Sept 1, 1980, when he was forced to stop by spread of the disease. During the run (on an artificial leg) he raised $24 million for cancer research and inspired millions with his courage. Terry Fox was born at Winnipeg, MB, and died at New Westminster (near Vancouver), BC, Canada, June 28, 1981.

HAMBURG FIRESTORM: ANNIVERSARY. July 28, 1943. More than 42,000 civilians were killed when 2,326 tons of bombs, predominantly incendiaries, were dropped on Hamburg, Germany, by the Allies on this date. At the center of the firestorm the winds uprooted trees, and flames burned eight square miles in the eight hours the fire lasted. A firestorm occurs when the fires in a given area become so intense that they devour all the oxygen nearby and suck more into themselves, creating hurricane-force winds that feed the fires and move them at great speeds.

HEYWARD, THOMAS: BIRTH ANNIVERSARY. July 28, 1746. American Revolutionary soldier, signer of the Declaration of Independence. Died Mar 6, 1809.

MOON PHASE: FIRST QUARTER. July 28. Moon enters First Quarter phase at 6:00 PM, EDT.

ONASSIS, JACQUELINE LEE BOUVIER KENNEDY: 80th BIRTH ANNIVERSARY. July 28, 1929. Editor, widow of John Fitzgerald Kennedy (35th president of the US), born at Southampton, NY. Later married (Oct 20, 1968) Greek shipping magnate Aristotle Socrates Onassis, who died Mar 15, 1975. The widely admired and respected former first lady died May 19, 1994, at New York City.

PERU: INDEPENDENCE DAY. July 28. San Martin declared independence from Spain on this day in 1821. After the final defeat of Spanish troops by Simon Bolivar in 1824, Spanish rule ended.

POTTER, (HELEN) BEATRIX: BIRTH ANNIVERSARY. July 28, 1866. Author and illustrator of the Peter Rabbit stories for children, born at London, England. Died at Sawrey, Lancashire, England, Dec 22, 1943.

July 2009	S	M	T	W	T	F	S
				1	2	3	4
	5	6	7	8	9	10	11
	12	13	14	15	16	17	18
	19	20	21	22	23	24	25
	26	27	28	29	30	31	

SINGING TELEGRAM: ANNIVERSARY. July 28, 1933. Anniversary of the first singing telegram, said to have been delivered to singer Rudy Vallee on his 32nd birthday. Early singing telegrams often were delivered in person by uniformed messengers on bicycle. Later they were usually sung over the telephone.

SPACE MILESTONE: *SKYLAB 3* (US). July 28, 1973. Alan L. Bean, Owen K. Garriott and Jack R. Lousma started 59-day mission in the space station to test human space flight endurance. Pacific splashdown Sept 25.

VALLEE, RUDY: BIRTH ANNIVERSARY. July 28, 1901. American singer, saxophone player and radio idol of millions during the 1930s. Born Hubert Prior Vallee, at Island Pond, VT, the crooner used a megaphone to amplify his voice and introduced his performances with the salutation "Heigh-ho-everybody!" Vallee appeared in a number of movies, including *How to Succeed in Business Without Really Trying*. Among his best-remembered songs are "I'm Just a Vagabond Lover," "Say It Isn't So" and his signature song, "My Time Is Your Time." Vallee died at age 84 at North Hollywood, CA, July 3, 1986.

VETERANS BONUS ARMY EVICTION: ANNIVERSARY. July 28, 1932. Some 15,000 unemployed veterans of WWI marched on Washington, DC, in the summer of 1932, demanding payment of a war bonus. After two months' encampment in Washington's Anacostia Flats, eviction of the bonus marchers by the US Army was ordered by President Herbert Hoover. Under the leadership of General Douglas MacArthur, Major Dwight D. Eisenhower and Major George S. Patton, Jr (among others), cavalry, tanks and infantry attacked. Fixed bayonets, tear gas and the burning of the veterans' tents hastened the end of the confrontation. One death was reported.

WORLD WAR I BEGINS: 95th ANNIVERSARY. July 28, 1914. Archduke Francis Ferdinand of Austria-Hungary and his wife were assassinated at Sarajevo, Bosnia, by a Serbian nationalist June 28, 1914, touching off the conflict that became WWI. Austria-Hungary declared war on Serbia July 28, the formal beginning of the war. Within weeks, Germany entered the war on the side of Austria-Hungary and Russia, France and Great Britain on the side of Serbia.

BIRTHDAYS TODAY

William Warren (Bill) Bradley, 66, former US senator, Hall of Fame basketball player, born Crystal City, MO, July 28, 1943.

Jim Davis, 64, cartoonist ("Garfield"), born Marion, IN, July 28, 1945.

Manu Ginobili, 32, basketball player, born Bahai Blanca, Argentina, July 28, 1977.

Darryl Hickman, 78, actor ("The Americans," *The Tingler*), born Los Angeles, CA, July 28, 1931.

Linda Kelsey, 63, actress ("Lou Grant"), born Minneapolis, MN, July 28, 1946.

Lori Loughlin, 45, actress ("Full House," *Back to the Beach*), born Long Island, NY, July 28, 1964.

Jacques Piccard, 87, inventor, explorer, born Brussels, Belgium, July 28, 1922.

Sally Struthers, 61, actress ("All in the Family"), born Portland, OR, July 28, 1948.

Rick Wright, 64, singer, musician (keyboard player with Pink Floyd), born London, England, July 28, 1945.

July 29 — Wednesday

DAY 210 **155 REMAINING**

ADAMS COUNTY FAIR/RODEO. July 29–Aug 1. Hettinger, ND. 10th annual fair with booths, exhibits and special events. Est attendance: 2,500. For info: Community Promotions Office, PO Box 1031, Hettinger, ND 58639. Phone: (701) 567-2531. E-mail: adamschmbr@ndsupernet.com. Web: hettingernd.com.

CHINCOTEAGUE PONY PENNING. July 29–30. Chincoteague Island, VA. To round up the 150 wild ponies living on Assateague Island and swim them across the inlet to Chincoteague, where about 80–90 of them are sold. Annually, the last Wednesday and Thursday of July. Est attendance: 50,000. For info: Chincoteague Chamber of Commerce, Box 258, Chincoteague, VA 23336. Phone: (757) 336-6161. Fax: (757) 336-1242. E-mail: chincochamber@verizon.net. Web: www.chincoteaguechamber.com.

HIMES, CHESTER: 100th BIRTH ANNIVERSARY. July 29, 1909. Ground-breaking African-American author who accosted American racism in such novels as *If He Hollers Let Him Go* (1945). In the 1950s, after he relocated to a more friendly France, Himes created a series of hard-boiled mystery novels set in Harlem, including *Cotton Comes to Harlem* (1965), that featured black detectives "Coffin Ed" Johnson and "Grave Digger" Jones. Born at Jefferson City, MO, Himes died Nov 12, 1984, at Moraira, Spain.

***INDIANAPOLIS* SUNK: ANNIVERSARY.** July 29, 1945. After delivering the atomic bomb to Tinian Island, the American cruiser *Indianapolis* was headed for Okinawa to train for the invasion of Japan when it was torpedoed by a Japanese submarine. Of 1,196 crew members, more than 350 were immediately killed in the explosion or went down with the ship. There were no rescue ships nearby, and those fortunate enough to survive endured the next 84 hours in ocean waters. By the time they were spotted by air on Aug 2, only 318 sailors remained alive, the others having either drowned or been eaten by sharks. This is the US Navy's worst loss at sea.

JENNINGS, PETER: BIRTH ANNIVERSARY. July 29, 1938. Television news anchor, born at Toronto, ON, Canada, who had immense success as a journalist despite never graduating from high school or college. Highly respected for his calm delivery and known for his travels around the world, reporting the news wherever it happened. He received 16 Emmy Awards and two George Foster Peabody Awards, and served as chief anchor of ABC-TV's "World News Tonight" from 1983 until April 2005, when he announced during his broadcast that he had been diagnosed with lung cancer. He died on Aug 7, 2005, at New York, NY.

MAINE LOBSTER FESTIVAL. July 29–Aug 2. Rockland, ME. 62nd annual. Celebration and promotion of the lobster industry featuring lobster dinners, arts, crafts, exhibits, live entertainment, parade, contests and a road race. Est attendance: 100,000. For info: Maine Lobster Festival, PO Box 552, Rockland, ME 04841. Phone: (207) 596-0376 or (800) LOB-CLAW. Fax: (207) 596-6549. E-mail: info@mainelobsterfestival.com. Web: www.mainelobsterfestival.com.

MUSSOLINI, BENITO: BIRTH ANNIVERSARY. July 29, 1883. Italian Fascist leader, born at Dovia, Italy. Self-styled "Il Duce" (the leader), Mussolini governed Italy, first as prime minister and later as absolute dictator, 1922–43. It was Mussolini who said: "War alone . . . puts the stamp of nobility upon the peoples who have the courage to face it." But military defeat of Italy in WWII was Mussolini's downfall. Repudiated and arrested by the Italian government, he was temporarily rescued by German paratroops in 1943. Later, as they attempted to flee in disguise to Switzerland, he and his mistress, Clara Petacci, were killed by Italian partisans near Lake Como, Italy, Apr 28, 1945.

NASA ESTABLISHED: ANNIVERSARY. July 29, 1958. President Eisenhower signed a bill creating the National Aeronautics and Space Administration to direct US space policy.

NORWAY: OLSOK EVE. July 29. Commemorates Norway's Viking king St. Olav, who fell in battle at Stiklestad near Trondheim, Norway, July 29, 1030. Bonfires, historical pageants.

RAIN DAY AT WAYNESBURG, PENNSYLVANIA. July 29. Legend has it that rain will fall at Waynesburg, PA, on July 29 as it has most years for the last century, according to local records in this community, which was laid out in 1796 and incorporated in 1816.

ROOSEVELT, ALICE HATHAWAY LEE: BIRTH ANNIVERSARY. July 29, 1861. First wife of Theodore Roosevelt, 26th president of the US, whom she married in 1880. Born at Chestnut Hill, MA, she died at New York, NY, Feb 14, 1884.

SCOTLAND: ABERDEEN INTERNATIONAL YOUTH FESTIVAL. July 29–Aug 8. Aberdeen. Talented young people from all areas of the performing arts come from around the world to participate in this festival. Est attendance: 35,000. For info: Jennifer Phillips, Custom House, 35 Regent Quay, Aberdeen, Scotland AB11 5BE. Phone: (44) (1224) 213-800. Fax: (44) (1224) 213-833. E-mail: info@aiyf.org. Web: www.aiyf.org.

SPAIN: FIESTA DE SANTA MARTA DE RIBARTEME (FESTIVAL OF NEAR DEATH EXPERIENCES). July 29. As Neves, Pontevedra, Galicia. Religious festival honoring Santa Marta. Those who have been near death and survived are carried in open coffins or march in shrouds to the local church. Est attendance: 5,000.

TARKINGTON, BOOTH: BIRTH ANNIVERSARY. July 29, 1869. American novelist (*The Magnificent Ambersons*), born at Indianapolis, IN. Died there May 19, 1946.

TOCQUEVILLE, ALEXIS DE: BIRTH ANNIVERSARY. July 29, 1805. French politician and author whose 1831 trip to the US inspired *Democracy in America*, one of the most insightful books written on the US. "America is a land of wonders," he wrote, "in which everything is in constant motion and every change seems an improvement." Born at Verneuil, France, Tocqueville died at Cannes, France, on Apr 16, 1859.

 BIRTHDAYS TODAY

Debbie Black, 43, former basketball player, born Philadelphia, PA, July 29, 1966.

Ken Burns, 56, documentary filmmaker ("Civil War" series), born New York, NY, July 29, 1953.

Elizabeth Hanford Dole, 73, US Senator (R, North Carolina); former president, American Red Cross, former secretary of transportation and secretary of labor, born Salisbury, NC, July 29, 1936.

Fernando González, 29, tennis player, born Santiago, Chile, July 29, 1980.

Martina McBride, 43, country singer, born Sharon, KS, July 29, 1966.

Alexandra Paul, 46, actress ("Baywatch," *Dragnet*), born New York, NY, July 29, 1963.

Josh Radnor, 35, actor ("How I Met Your Mother"), born Columbus, OH, July 29, 1974.

Patty Scialfa, 53, singer, born Deal, NJ, July 29, 1956.

Paul Taylor, 79, dancer, choreographer, born Allegheny, NY, July 29, 1930.

David Warner, 68, actor ("Holocaust," *Tron*), born Manchester, England, July 29, 1941.

Wil Wheaton, 37, actor ("Star Trek: The Next Generation," *Stand by Me*), born Burbank, CA, July 29, 1972.

July 30 — Thursday

DAY 211 154 REMAINING

BRONTË, EMILY: BIRTH ANNIVERSARY. July 30, 1818. English novelist, one of the Brontë sisters, best known for *Wuthering Heights*. Born at Thornton, Yorkshire, England. Died Dec 19, 1848, at Haworth, Yorkshire.

CANADA: AGRIFAIR. July 30–Aug 3. Abbotsford, BC. Fun for everyone with attractions like draft horses, dairy, beef and poultry; milking display; Pride of the Valley trade show; antique farm display bursting with antique toys; midway; plus everything from national and international stage entertainment to a pro rodeo and fireworks. Est attendance: 45,000. For info: Pamela Brenner, Abbotsford Agrifair, PO Box 2334, Abbotsford, BC, Canada V2T 4X2. Phone: (604) 852-6674. Fax: (604) 852-6631. E-mail: agrifair@telus.net. Web: www.agrifair.ca.

CANADA: ROCKHOUND GEMBOREE. July 30–Aug 2. Bancroft, ON. Daily expeditions to prime mineral locations; dealers, demonstrations and displays, swapping. Est attendance: 16,000. For info: Bancroft and District Chamber of Commerce, PO Box 539, Bancroft, ON, Canada K0L 1C0. Phone: (613) 332-1513. Fax: (613) 332-2119. E-mail: chamber@commerce.bancroft.on.ca. Web: www.bancroftdistrict.com.

ELVIS PRESLEY'S FIRST CONCERT APPEARANCE: 55th ANNIVERSARY. July 30, 1954. Elvis Presley appeared in concert for the first time at Overton Park Orchestra Shell in Memphis, TN. He was billed third and country crooner Slim Whitman was the headliner. Presley, only 19 years old, nervously began gyrating his leg and a legend was born. See also: "Elvis Presley's First Single Released: Anniversary" (July 19).

FORD, HENRY: BIRTH ANNIVERSARY. July 30, 1863. Industrialist Henry Ford, whose assembly-line method of automobile production revolutionized the industry, was born at Wayne County, MI, on the family farm. His Model T made up half of the world's output of cars during its years of production. Ford built racing cars until in 1903 he and his partners formed the Ford Motor Company. In 1908 the company presented the Model T, which was produced until 1927, and in 1913 Ford introduced the assembly line and mass production. This innovation reduced the time it took to build each car from 12½ hours to only 1½. This enabled Ford to sell cars for $500, making automobile ownership a possibility for an unprecedented percentage of the population. He is also remembered for introducing a $5-a-day wage for automotive workers and for his statement "History is bunk." Died Apr 7, 1947, at age 83 at Dearborn, MI, where his manufacturing complex was located.

HOFFA, JAMES: DISAPPEARANCE: ANNIVERSARY. July 30, 1975. Former Teamsters Union leader, 62-year-old James Riddle Hoffa was last seen on this date outside a restaurant in Bloomfield Township, near Detroit, MI. His 13-year federal prison sentence had been commuted by President Richard M. Nixon in 1971. On Dec 8, 1982, seven years and 131 days after his disappearance, an Oakland County judge declared Hoffa officially dead as of July 30, 1982.

MOORE, HENRY: BIRTH ANNIVERSARY. July 30, 1898. English sculptor born at Castleford, Yorkshire, England. Died at Hertfordshire, Aug 31, 1986.

MOUNTAIN DANCE AND FOLK FESTIVAL. July 30–Aug 1. Asheville, NC. 82nd annual festival. More than 400 performers in this three-day fest, which celebrates the cultural heritage of the southern Appalachian Mountains. Includes dance teams, mountain fiddlers, banjo pickers, old-time string bands, storytellers, bluegrass bands and dulcimer sweepers. Oldest of its kind, founded in 1928 by Bascom Lamar Lunsford. Est attendance: 1,500. For info: Asheville Area Chamber of Commerce, Folk Heritage, PO Box 1010, Asheville, NC 28802. Phone: (828) 258-6101, ext 345. Web: www.folkheritage.org.

PAPERBACK BOOKS INTRODUCED: ANNIVERSARY. July 30, 1935. Although books bound in soft covers were first introduced in 1841 at Leipzig, Germany, by Christian Bernhard Tauchnitz, the modern paperback revolution dates to the publication of the first Penguin paperback by Sir Allen Lane at London, England, in 1935. Penguin Number 1 was *Ariel*, a life of Shelley by Andre Maurois.

QUILT ODYSSEY 2009. July 30–Aug 2. Hershey Lodge and Convention Center, Hershey, PA. Judged national quilt competition; antique and special quilt exhibits. Large merchants' mall. Classes and lectures by nationally known professional quilters. Est attendance: 7,000. For info: Quilt Odyssey, 15004 Burnt Mill Rd, Shippensburg, PA 17257. Phone: (717) 423-5148. E-mail: quiltodyssey@embarqmail.com.

SATCHMO SUMMERFEST. July 30–Aug 2. New Orleans, LA. The spirit of "Satchmo" lives with this annual birthday celebration of Louis "Satchmo" Armstrong's music, legacy and cultural contributions. The free event will include a jazz-filled music festival, children's activities, seminars and panels, photo exhibits and cultural displays, a jazz mass and Satchmo-inspired New Orleans cuisine. It's all part of New Orleans' ongoing tribute to the "International Ambassador of Jazz" in the birthplace of jazz. Est attendance: 45,000. For info: French Quarter Festivals, Inc, 400 N Peters St, #205, New Orleans, LA 70130. Phone: (800) 673-5725 or (504) 522-5730. E-mail: feedback@fqfi.org. Web: www.fqfi.org.

STENGEL, CHARLES DILLON (CASEY): BIRTH ANNIVERSARY. July 30, 1890. Baseball Hall of Fame outfielder and manager born at Kansas City, MO. His success as manager of the New York Yankees (10 pennants and 7 World Series titles in 12 years) made him one of the game's enduring stars. Inducted into the Hall of Fame in 1966. Died at Glendale, CA, Sept 29, 1975.

TISHA B'AV OR FAST OF AB. July 30. Hebrew calendar date: Ab 9, 5769. Commemorates and mourns the destruction of the first and second Temples in Jerusalem (586 BC and AD 70). Began at sundown July 29.

US SENIOR OPEN (GOLF) CHAMPIONSHIP. July 30–Aug 2. Crooked Stick Golf Club, Carmel, IN. For info: USGA, Golf House, Championship Dept, PO Box 708, Far Hills, NJ 07931. Phone: (908) 234-2300. Fax: (908) 234-9687. E-mail: usga@usga.org. Web: www.usga.org.

July 2009

S	M	T	W	T	F	S
			1	2	3	4
5	6	7	8	9	10	11
12	13	14	15	16	17	18
19	20	21	22	23	24	25
26	27	28	29	30	31	

VANUATU: INDEPENDENCE DAY. July 30. Vanuatu became an independent republic in 1980 (from France and the UK) and observes its national holiday.

VEBLEN, THORSTEIN: BIRTH ANNIVERSARY. July 30, 1857. American economist, born at Valders, WI, and died at Menlo Park, CA, Aug 3, 1929. "Conspicuous consumption," he wrote in *The Theory of the Leisure Class*, "of valuable goods is a means of reputability to the gentleman of leisure."

BIRTHDAYS TODAY

Lamar Alexander, 69, US Senator (R, Tennessee), born Maryville, TN, July 30, 1940.

Paul Anka, 68, singer, songwriter ("Diana," "My Way" for Frank Sinatra), born Ottawa, ON, Canada, July 30, 1941.

William Atherton, 62, actor (*The Day of the Locust, Ghostbusters, Die Hard, Die Hard 2*), born New Haven, CT, July 30, 1947.

Peter Bogdanovich, 70, producer, director, actor (*The Last Picture Show, Paper Moon,* "The Sopranos"), born Kingston, NY, July 30, 1939.

Alton Brown, 47, chef, television personality ("Good Eats," "Iron Chef America"), born Los Angeles, CA, July 30, 1962.

Delta Burke, 53, actress ("Designing Women"), former Miss Florida, born Orlando, FL, July 30, 1956.

Kate Bush, 51, singer ("The Man with the Child in His Eyes"), songwriter, born Lewisham, England, July 30, 1958.

Edd Byrnes, 76, actor ("77 Sunset Strip," *Darby's Rangers*), born New York, NY, July 30, 1933.

Laurence Fishburne, 48, actor (*Boyz N the Hood, What's Love Got to Do with It, The Matrix* movies, *Akeelah and the Bee*; Tony for *Two Trains Running*), born Augusta, GA, July 30, 1961.

Anita Faye Hill, 53, law professor, born on an Oklahoma farm, July 30, 1956.

Lisa Kudrow, 46, actress ("Friends," *Romy and Michele's High School Reunion*), born Encino, CA, July 30, 1963.

Christopher Paul (Chris) Mullin, 46, former basketball player, born New York, NY, July 30, 1963.

Ken Olin, 55, actor ("LA Doctors," "thirtysomething"), born Chicago, IL, July 30, 1954.

Jaime Pressly, 32, actress ("My Name Is Earl," *Not Another Teen Movie*), born Kinston, NC, July 30, 1977.

David Sanborn, 64, saxophonist, composer, born Tampa, FL, July 30, 1945.

Arnold Schwarzenegger, 62, Governor of California (R), bodybuilder, actor (*The Terminator, Twins, True Lies*), born Graz, Austria, July 30, 1947.

Allan Huber "Bud" Selig, 75, Commissioner of Baseball, born Milwaukee, WI, July 30, 1934.

Hope Solo, 28, soccer player, born Richland, WA, July 30, 1981.

Hilary Swank, 35, actress (Oscars for *Boys Don't Cry, Million Dollar Baby*), born Lincoln, NE, July 30, 1974.

July 31 — Friday

DAY 212 — **153 REMAINING**

BANGOR STATE FAIR. July 31–Aug 9. Bass Park Complex, Bangor, ME. For info: Bangor State Fair, 100 Dutton St, Bangor, ME 04401. Phone: (207) 947-5555. Fax: (207) 947-5105. E-mail: fair@bangormaine.gov. Web: www.bangorstatefair.com.

BOOM DAYS. July 31–Aug 2. Leadville, CO. The city's oldest annual celebration features a large parade, street races, mining events, pack burro race and arts and crafts. Fun for the whole family. Est attendance: 3,000. For info: Chamber of Commerce, PO Box 861, Leadville, CO 80461. Phone: (719) 486-3900 or (888) 532-3845. Fax: (719) 486-8478. E-mail: info@leadvilleboomdays.com. Web: www.leadvilleboomdays.com.

BURRO RACE. July 31–Aug 2. Leadville, CO. International Pack Burro Race leaves from Main Street up Mosquito Pass and back. Est attendance: 3,500. For info: Chamber of Commerce, Box 861, Leadville, CO 80461. Phone: (719) 486-3900 or (888) 532-3845. Fax: (719) 486-8478. E-mail: info@leadvilleboomdays.com. Web: www.leadvilleboomdays.com.

CANADA: CANADA'S NATIONAL UKRAINIAN FESTIVAL. July 31–Aug 2. Dauphin, MB. Experience the richness and flavors of Ukrainian culture. From the colorful, energized dancers to the powerful folk songs of Ukraine, there is something for everyone to enjoy. Est attendance: 5,000. For info: Canada's National Ukrainian Festival, Box 368, Dauphin, MB, Canada R7N 2V2. Phone: (204) 622-4600 or (877) 474-2683. Fax: (204) 622-4606. E-mail: cnuf@mts.net. Web: www.cnuf.ca.

FEAST OF SAINT IGNATIUS OF LOYOLA. July 31. 1491–1556. Founder of the Society of Jesus (Jesuits). Canonized in 1622.

FIRST INDIAN SAINT: ANNIVERSARY. July 31, 2002. In Mexico City, Mexico, Pope John Paul II canonized the Roman Catholic Church's first Indian saint, Juan Diego. In 1531 Diego claimed to have seen the Virgin of Guadalupe, whose rose-framed image later appeared on his cloak. See also: "Day of Our Lady of Guadalupe" (Dec 12).

FIRST US GOVERNMENT BUILDING: ANNIVERSARY. July 31, 1792. The cornerstone of the Philadelphia Mint, the first US government building, was laid on this day.

GIGGLEFEET DANCE FESTIVAL. July 31 and Aug 2. Ketchikan, AK. Two evening performances celebrating dance in the community, including jazz, tap, ballet, modern, hip-hop, Native Alaskan, breakdance and more. Annually, the first Friday and Sunday in August, part of the Blueberry Arts Festival. Est attendance: 1,000. For info: Ketchikan Area Arts & Humanities Council, 716 Totem Way, Ketchikan, AK 99901. Phone: (907) 225-2211. Fax: (907) 225-4330. E-mail: info@ketchikanarts.org.

KENNEDY INTERNATIONAL AIRPORT DEDICATION: ANNIVERSARY. July 31, 1948. New York's International Airport at Idlewild Field was dedicated by President Harry S Truman. It was later renamed John F. Kennedy International Airport.

***MOBY-DICK* MARATHON.** July 31–Aug 1. Mystic Seaport, Mystic, CT. Marathon reading of the classic *Moby-Dick* in celebration of Herman Melville's birthday. Reading takes place on deck of the nation's last wooden whaler, the *Charles W. Morgan*. Annually, 24-hour reading from noon July 31 to noon Aug 1. Est attendance: 6,000. For info: Mystic Seaport, 75 Greenmanville Ave, PO Box 6000, Mystic, CT 06355-0990. Phone: (860) 572-5315 or (888) 973-2767. Web: www.mysticseaport.org.

NATIONAL CZECH FESTIVAL. July 31–Aug 2. Wilber, NE. Festival to promote preservation of Czech culture, foods, traditions—accordion, polka and Czech band music, three parades, national queen contest, museum, art show, Czech dinners, programs, contests, fellowship, reunions. Annually, the first weekend in August. Sponsored by Nebraska Czechs of Wilber. Est attendance: 50,000. For info: National Czech Festival, PO Box 3, Wilber, NE 68465.

NEW JERSEY STATE FAIR/SUSSEX COUNTY FARM AND HORSE SHOW. July 31–Aug 9. Sussex County Fairgrounds, Augusta, NJ. The state's largest livestock and horse show also includes educational exhibits, amusements, commercial exhibits and entertainment. Est attendance: 200,000. For info: New Jersey State Fair, 37 Plains Rd, Branchville, NJ 07826. Phone: (973) 948-5500. Fax: (973) 948-0147. E-mail: thefair@njstatefair.org. Web: www.njstatefair.org.

SALVADOR, FRANCIS: DEATH ANNIVERSARY. July 31, 1776. The first Jew to die in the American Revolution, Salvador was also the first Jew elected to office in Colonial America. He was voted a member of the South Carolina Provincial Congress in January 1775.

"THE SHADOW" RADIO PREMIERE: ANNIVERSARY. July 31, 1930. "Who knows what evil lurks in the hearts of men? The Shadow knows!" This popular crime and suspense program premiered on CBS radio. Originally, the Shadow was just the narrator of the changing stories, but later he became a character with his own adventures—with the alter ego of Lamont Cranston. Orson Welles was the first Shadow.

US PATENT OFFICE OPENS: ANNIVERSARY. July 31, 1790. The first US Patent Office opened its doors, and the first US patent was issued to Samuel Hopkins of Vermont for a new method of making pearlash and potash. The patent was signed by George Washington and Thomas Jefferson.

 BIRTHDAYS TODAY

Dean Cain, 43, actor ("Lois & Clark: The New Adventures of Superman"), born Mount Clemens, MI, July 31, 1966.

Geraldine Chaplin, 65, actress (*Nashville, Roseland, Chaplin*), born Santa Monica, CA, July 31, 1944.

Susan Flannery, 66, actress ("The Bold & the Beautiful," "Dallas"), born Jersey City, NJ, July 31, 1943.

Evonne Goolagong, 58, former tennis player, born Griffith, Australia, July 31, 1951.

Gary Lewis, 63, singer ("This Diamond Ring"), born New York, NY, July 31, 1946.

Don Murray, 80, actor (*Bus Stop*, "Knots Landing"), born Hollywood, CA, July 31, 1929.

France Nuyen, 70, actress ("St. Elsewhere"), born Marseilles, France, July 31, 1939.

Jonathan Ogden, 35, football player, born Washington, DC, July 31, 1974.

Deval Patrick, 53, Governor of Massachusetts (D), born Chicago, IL, July 31, 1956.

J.K. Rowling, 44, author (the Harry Potter series), born Joanne Rowling at Bristol, England, July 31, 1965.

Wesley Snipes, 47, actor (*Blade, US Marshals, Jungle Fever, White Men Can't Jump*), born Orlando, FL, July 31, 1962.

August

August 1 — Saturday

DAY 213 **152 REMAINING**

AMERICAN ADVENTURES MONTH. Aug 1–31. This month celebrates vacationing in the Americas. Whether traveling in luxury or in primitive conditions, tourists are encouraged to explore South, Central and North America. Experiencing the Americas in a variety of ways unlocks new worlds for your family. Annually, the month of August. For info: Peter Kulkkula, American Adventurer, 381 Billings Rd, Fitchburg, MA 01420-1407. Phone: (978) 343-3333. E-mail: info@AmericanAdventures.info. Web: www.AmericanAdventures.info.

AMERICAN HISTORY ESSAY CONTEST. Aug 1–Dec 15. American History Committee activities are promoted throughout the year, with the essay contest conducted in grades 5–8 beginning in August. Essays are submitted for judging by Dec 15, with the winners announced in April at the Daughters of the American Revolution Continental Congress. Events vary but include programs, displays, spot announcements and recognition of essay writers. Essay topic can be obtained from DAR Headquarters. For info: Natl Society of Daughters of the American Revolution, Office of the Historian-General, Admin Bldg, 1776 D St NW, Washington, DC 20006-5392. Phone: (202) 628-1776. Web: www.dar.org.

BATTLE OF BUSHY RUN REENACTMENT. Aug 1–2. Harrison City, PA. This reenactment commemorates the decisive battle of Pontiac's War on Aug 5 and 6, 1763. Event includes a guided tour through the battle's historic camps and demonstrations of military crafts. Annually, the first weekend in August. Est attendance: 2,000. For info: Bushy Run Battlefield, PO Box 468, Harrison City, PA 15636-0468. Phone: (724) 527-5584.

BENIN: INDEPENDENCE DAY. Aug 1. Public holiday. Commemorates independence from France in 1960. Benin at that time was known as Dahomey.

BLACK BUSINESS MONTH. Aug 1–31. Six months after Black History Month, the focus on and awareness of black-owned and operated enterprises needs a boost. This month is dedicated to starting, maintaining, growing, buying from and committing to black-owned businesses and entrepreneurs. For info: Sylvia Henderson, Springboard Training, PO Box 588, Olney, MD 20830-0588. Phone: (301) 260-1538. E-mail: sylvia@springboardtraining.com. Web: www.springboardtraining.com.

BLUEBERRY ARTS FESTIVAL. Aug 1. State Office Building, Methodist Church and Mainstay Gallery, Ketchikan, AK. A street fair featuring arts and crafts, food, games and contests for all ages, performing arts events, and poetry and prose reading. Annually, the first Saturday in August. Est attendance: 7,000. For info: Ketchikan Area Arts and Humanities Council, 716 Totem Way, Ketchikan, AK 99901. Phone: (907) 225-2211. Fax: (907) 225-4330. E-mail: info@ketchikanarts.org.

BURK, MARTHA (CALAMITY JANE): DEATH ANNIVERSARY. Aug 1, 1903. Known as a frontierswoman and companion to Wild Bill Hickok, Calamity Jane Burk was born Martha Jane Cannary at Princeton, MO, in May 1852. As a young girl living in Montana, she became an excellent markswoman. She went to the Black Hills of South Dakota as a scout for a geologic expedition in 1875. Several opposing traditions account for her nickname, one springing from her kindness to people who were less fortunate, while another attributes it to the harsh warnings she would give men who offended her. She died at Terry, SD, and was buried at Deadwood, SD, next to Wild Bill Hickok.

CANADA: CANMORE FOLK MUSIC FESTIVAL. Aug 1–3. Centennial Park, Canmore, AB. 32nd annual. Alberta's longest-running folk festival. Featuring food and craft booths, entertainment, workshops and free pancake breakfast on Monday. Est attendance: 14,000. For info: Canmore Folk Music Festival, PO Box 8098, Canmore, AB, Canada T1W 2T8. Phone: (403) 678-2524. Fax: (403) 678-2524. E-mail: info@canmorefolkfestival.com. Web: www.canmorefolkfestival.com.

CATARACT AWARENESS MONTH. Aug 1–31. Cataracts are the leading cause of blindness in the world. There are close to 20.5 million Americans aged 40 and older with cataracts. More than half of all Americans will have cataracts by age 80. Prevent Blindness America® will offer tips about prevention and information about surgery. For info: Prevent Blindness America®, 211 W Wacker Dr, Ste 1700, Chicago, IL 60606. Phone: (800) 331-2020. E-mail: info@preventblindness.org. Web: www.preventblindness.org.

CHILDREN'S EYE HEALTH AND SAFETY MONTH. Aug 1–31. Prevent Blindness America® will provide information about amblyopia, a condition that can affect 2 to 3 percent of children and cause permanent vision loss. Additional information includes tips about preventing eye injuries in children, signs of possible eye problems and general eye health. For info: Prevent Blindness America®, 211 W Wacker Dr, Ste 1700, Chicago, IL 60606. Phone: (800) 331-2020. E-mail: info@preventblindness.org. Web: www.preventblindness.org.

CHILDREN'S VISION AND LEARNING MONTH. Aug 1–31. Researchers estimate that one out of four children has an undiagnosed vision problem that is interfering with the ability to read and learn. Since 80 percent of learning is dependent upon vision, it is vital that parents and educators ensure they understand the signs of vision problems. With children getting ready to go back to school, August is the perfect month for education. For info: College of Optometrists in Vision Development, 215 W Garfield Rd, Ste 210, Aurora, OH 44202. Phone: (330) 995-0718 or (888) 268-3770. Fax: (330) 995-0719. E-mail: info@covd.org. Web: www.covd.org.

CLARK, WILLIAM: BIRTH ANNIVERSARY. Aug 1, 1770. The soldier, explorer and public servant was born at Caroline County, VA. He served seven years in the US Army and then gained his lasting fame when Meriwether Lewis asked him to join an expedition exploring the Louisiana Territory (1803–06). Clark was an able leader and contributed detailed maps and animal illustrations on the journey. A grateful President Thomas Jefferson made Clark brigadier general of militia for the Louisiana Territory (1807–13) and superintendent of Indian Affairs (1807–38). Clark was also governor of the Missouri Territory (1813–20) and surveyor general for Illinois, Missouri and Arkansas (1824–25). Clark foresaw the tension between US interests and the native peoples of the western US, and he urged that the US treat western tribes with respect. Clark died at St. Louis, MO, on Sept 1, 1838.

COLORADO: ADMISSION DAY: ANNIVERSARY. Aug 1, 1876. Colorado admitted to the Union as the 38th state. The first Monday in August is celebrated as Colorado Day.

DIARY OF ANNE FRANK: THE LAST ENTRY: 65th ANNIVERSARY. Aug 1, 1944. To escape deportation to concentration camps, the Jewish family of Otto Frank hid for two years in the warehouse of his food products business at Amsterdam, Netherlands. Gentile friends smuggled in food and other supplies during their confinement. Thirteen-year-old Anne Frank, who kept a journal during the time of their hiding, penned her last entry in the diary Aug 1, 1944: "[I] keep on trying to find a way of becoming what I would like to be, and what I could be, if . . . there weren't any other people living in the world." Three days later (Aug 4, 1944), Grüne Polizei raided the "Secret Annex" where the Frank family was hidden. Anne and her sister were sent to Bergen-Belsen concentration camp, where Anne died at age 15, two months before the liberation of Holland. Young Anne's diary, later found in the family's hiding place, has been translated into 30 languages and has become a symbol of the indomitable strength of the human spirit. See also: "Frank, Anne: Birth Anniversary" (June 12).

EMANCIPATION OF 500: ANNIVERSARY. Aug 1, 1791. Virginia planter Robert Carter III confounded his family and friends by filing a deed of emancipation for his 500 slaves. One of the wealthiest men in the state, Carter owned 60,000 acres over 18 plantations. The deed included the following words: "I have for some time past been convinced that to retain them in Slavery is contrary to the true principles of Religion and Justice and therefore it is my duty to manumit them." The document established a schedule by which 15 slaves would be freed each Jan 1, over a 21-year period, plus slave children would be freed at age 18 for females and 21 for males. It is believed this was the largest act of emancipation in US history and predated the Emancipation Proclamation by 70 years.

ENGLAND: COWES WEEK. Aug 1–8. Cowes, Isle of Wight. Cowes Week is the largest, longest-running (since 1826) and most prestigious international sailing regatta in the world, with more than 1,000 boats across almost 40 classes of yacht racing. The event is a spectacle to behold. Est attendance: 100,000. For info: Cowes Week Ltd, 18 Bath Rd, Cowes, Isle of Wight, England PO31 7QN. Phone: 44 198 3295744. Fax: 44 198 3295329. E-mail: admin@cowesweek.co.uk. Web: www.cowesweek.co.uk.

FANCY FARM PICNIC. Aug 1. Downtown Fancy Farm, KY. Southern hospitality at its best. The small community volunteers its time to entertain with games, prizes and great fun. Raffle for a brand-new car. Bingo with wonderful prizes. Down-home country dinners including the famous Fancy Farm Picnic Barbecue. Annually, the first Saturday in August. Est attendance: 20,000. For info: Sharon Hayden, c/o Fancy Farm Picnic, 2759 Carrico Rd, Fancy Farm, KY 42039. Phone: (270) 623-6129. E-mail: toddhayden@wk.net.

FARM SANCTUARY HOEDOWN. Aug 1–2 (tentative). Farm Sanctuary, Watkins Glen, NY. America's premier shelter for farm animals hosts a fun and educational weekend of farm tours, hayrides, lectures, exhibits, music, food and more, all located on a beautiful 175-acre animal shelter with hundreds of cows, pigs, turkeys and other animals. Est attendance: 200. For registration info: Education Coordinator, Farm Sanctuary, PO Box 150, Watkins Glen, NY 14891. Phone: (607) 583-2225. Fax: (607) 583-2041. E-mail: info@farmsanctuary.org. Web: www.farmsanctuary.org.

FIRST US CENSUS: ANNIVERSARY. Aug 1, 1790. The first census revealed that there were 3,939,326 citizens in the 16 states and the Ohio Territory. The US has taken a census every 10 years since 1790. The next one will be in 2010.

GARCIA, JERRY: BIRTH ANNIVERSARY. Aug 1, 1942. Jerome John Garcia was born at San Francisco, CA. Country, bluegrass and folk musician, a guitar player of remarkable ability, Garcia was the leading force behind the legendary Grateful Dead, the band that sustained a veritable industry for its legion of followers. He died Aug 9, 1995, at Forest Knolls, CA, ending a musical career that spanned more than three decades.

GET READY FOR KINDERGARTEN MONTH. Aug 1–31. This is a celebration to support a happy entry into kindergarten for the almost 2 million children in the US. Going to kindergarten is a life-changing event not only for the child, but also for parents, siblings and educators. Tips are provided to help smooth the way for an easy transition. For info: Katie Davis, PO Box 551, Bedford Hills, NY 10507. Phone: (914) 244-8777. E-mail: office@getreadyforschool.com. Web: www.getreadyforkindergarten.com.

GIRLFRIEND'S DAY. Aug 1. Celebrate this special day by taking your girlfriend(s) shopping, to a play, to the movies, out to eat, to the spa and/or to the park. A fun slumber party is also recommended. Annually, Aug 1. For info: Thema Martin, 931 Monroe Dr NE, Ste A102, #226, Atlanta, GA 30308. Phone: (404) 849-1249. E-mail: tmartin@savionlife.com.

HAPPINESS HAPPENS MONTH. Aug 1–31. This 10th annual celebration is sponsored by the Secret Society of Happy People to encourage people to express happiness and discourage parade-raining. Visit our website to find out about activities. For info: Secret Society of Happy People, 425 Busher Dr, Lewisville, TX 75067. Phone: (972) 459-7031. E-mail: pamelagail@sohp.com. Web: www.sohp.com.

HAWAII VOLCANOES NATIONAL PARK ESTABLISHED: ANNIVERSARY. Aug 1, 1916. Area of Hawaii's Hawaii Island, including active volcanoes Kilauea and Mauna Loa, was established as Hawaii National Park in 1916, but its name was changed to Hawaii Volcanoes National Park in 1961. For park info: Hawaii Volcanoes National Park, Hawaii National Park, HI 96718.

HOT AUGUST NIGHTS. Aug 1–9. Reno and Sparks, NV. Celebration of the music and cars of the '50s and '60s features show and shine, parade, cruises, proms and concerts by the entertainers of the era. Est attendance: 800,000. For info: Hot August Nights, 1425 E Greg St, Sparks, NV 89431. Phone: (775) 356-1956. Web: www.hotaugustnights.net.

JAMAICA: ABOLITION OF SLAVERY. Aug 1, 1838. National day. Spanish settlers introduced the slave trade into Jamaica in 1509 and sugarcane in 1640. Slavery continued until Aug 1, 1834, when it was abolished by the British.

KEY, FRANCIS SCOTT: BIRTH ANNIVERSARY. Aug 1, 1779. American attorney, social worker, poet and author of the US national anthem. While on a legal mission, Key was detained on shipboard off Baltimore, MD, during the British bombardment of Fort McHenry on the night of Sept 13–14, 1814. Thrilled to see the American flag still flying over the fort at daybreak, Key wrote the poem "The Star-Spangled Banner." Printed in the *Baltimore American* Sept 21, 1814, it was soon popularly sung to the music of an old English tune, "Anacreon in Heaven." It did not become the official US national anthem until 117 years later when, on Mar 3, 1931, President Herbert Hoover signed into law an act for that purpose. Key was born at Frederick County, MD, and died at Baltimore, Jan 11, 1843.

LEAGUE OF NH CRAFTSMEN ANNUAL CRAFTSMEN'S FAIR. Aug 1–9. Mount Sunapee Resort, Newbury, NH. 76th annual. "America's oldest crafts fair." More than 200 crafts booths, Living with Crafts exhibit, CraftWear exhibit, sculpture garden, daily performing arts, children's activities and more. Est attendance: 40,000. For info: League of NH Craftsmen, 205 N Main St, Concord, NH 03301. Phone: (603) 224-3375. Fax: (603) 225-8452. Web: www.nhcrafts.org.

August 2009

S	M	T	W	T	F	S
						1
2	3	4	5	6	7	8
9	10	11	12	13	14	15
16	17	18	19	20	21	22
23	24	25	26	27	28	29
30	31					

LUGHNASADH. Aug 1. (Also called August Eve, Lammas Eve, Lady Day Eve and Feast of Bread.) One of the "Greater Sabbats" during the Wiccan year, Lughnasadh marks the first harvest. Annually, Aug 1.

MELVILLE, HERMAN: BIRTH ANNIVERSARY. Aug 1, 1819. American author and poet, best known for his epic novel, *Moby-Dick*. Its first sentence—"Call me Ishmael."—is one of the most famous in literature. In his Civil War poetry Melville wrote, "All wars are boyish, and are fought by boys." Born at New York, NY, Melville died there Sept 28, 1891.

MITCHELL, MARIA: BIRTH ANNIVERSARY. Aug 1, 1818. An interest in her father's hobby and an ability for mathematics resulted in Maria Mitchell's becoming the first female professional astronomer. In 1847, while assisting her father in a survey of the sky for the US Coast Guard, Mitchell discovered a new comet and determined its orbit. She received many honors because of this, including being elected to the American Academy of Arts and Sciences—its first woman. Mitchell joined the staff at Vassar Female College in 1865—the first US female professor of astronomy—and in 1873 was a cofounder of the Association for the Advancement of Women. Born at Nantucket, MA, Mitchell died June 28, 1889, at Lynn, MA.

MOTORSPORTS AWARENESS MONTH. Aug 1–31. National movement sponsored by the Motorsports Parts Manufacturer's Council, a SEMA Council, to promote motorsports. For info: James Skelly, Specialty Equipment Market Assn, 1575 S Valley Vista Dr, Diamond Bar, CA 91765. Phone: (909) 396-0289. E-mail: jimsk@sema.org.

MTV PREMIERE: ANNIVERSARY. Aug 1, 1981. The all-music-video channel debuted on this date. VH1, another music channel owned by MTV Networks that is aimed at older pop music fans, premiered in 1985.

NATIONAL IMMUNIZATION AWARENESS MONTH. Aug 1–31. Immunization is critical to maintaining health and preventing life-threatening diseases among people of all ages and cultures throughout the US. Each year in the US, tens of thousands of people die because of vaccine-preventable diseases or their complications, and even more experience pain, suffering and disability. This month calls attention to the importance of infant, child, adolescent and adult immunization and seeks to reduce disparities in vaccine use while maintaining public trust in its value and safety. National Immunization Awareness Month promotional materials are available. For info: Centers for Disease Control and Prevention, 1600 Clifton Rd, Atlanta, GA 30333. Phone: (800) CDC-INFO. Web: www.cdc.gov/vaccines/events/niam/default.htm.

NATIONAL INVENTORS' MONTH®. Aug 1–31. To educate the American public about the value of creativity and inventiveness and the importance of inventions and inventors to the quality of our lives. This will be accomplished by specially designed displays for libraries, an interactive website and the placement of media stories about living inventors in most of the top national, local and trade publications. Sponsored by the United Inventors Association of the USA (UIA-USA), the Academy of Applied Science and *Inventors' Digest*. For info: Inventors' Digest, PO Box 36761, Charlotte, NC 28236. Phone: (800) 838-8808. E-mail: info@inventorsdigest.com. Web: www.inventorsdigest.com.

NATIONAL MUSTARD DAY. Aug 1. Mustard lovers across the nation pay tribute to the king of condiments by slathering their favorite mustard on hot dogs, pretzels, circus peanuts and all things edible. The Mount Horeb Mustard Museum holds the world's largest collection of prepared mustards and mustard memorabilia. Activities include the mustard games, street music and lots of great food (with mustard, of course!). Join in the mustard college fight song with the "POUPON U" marching band. Annually, the first Saturday in August. Est attendance: 4,000. For info: Barry M. Levenson, Curator, The Mount Horeb Mustard Museum, 100 W Main St, Mount Horeb, WI 53572. Phone: (608) 437-3986. Fax: (608) 437-4018. E-mail: curator@mustardmuseum.com. Web: www.mustardmuseum.com.

NATIONAL PANINI MONTH. Aug 1–31. This August, Sargento salutes the *panino*, a sandwich made with a small loaf of bread, typically *ciabatta*, that is usually served hot or grilled. Known for its versatility, delicious flavors and variety of creative ingredients, the panino is a perfect catalyst to encourage the use of the many types of natural cheeses. Cheese is often a staple ingredient that serves the important and mouthwatering purpose of providing rich flavor while melding all other tastes together. There are countless ways to enjoy panini, and now there's a whole month to try them! For info: Carrie Becker, Sargento Food, Inc, 737 N Michigan Ave, Ste 2200, Chicago, IL 60611. Phone: (312) 755-6200. Fax: (312) 755-6201. E-mail: cbecker@wheatleytimmons.com. Web: www.sargentocheese.com.

NATIONAL WIN WITH CIVILITY MONTH. Aug 1–31. When we are civil to each other, we confirm our worth and acknowledge the worth of others. We can move in and out of all levels of society confident that we are always doing the "right thing." We gain recognition for civility, and we secure the respect of our fellow human beings. For info: Thomas Danaher, 211 S Maryland Pkwy, Las Vegas, NV 89101. Phone: (702) 384-7376. E-mail: thomasdanaher04@yahoo.com.

NEUROSURGERY OUTREACH MONTH. Aug 1–31. A month to help educate the public about the role of the neurosurgeon in treating a wide range of medical conditions and diseases. The American Association of Neurological Surgeons offers a large array of neurosurgical topics on its website. For info: AANS, 5550 Meadowbrook Dr, Rolling Meadows, IL 60008. Phone: (847) 378-0517. Fax: (847) 378-0617. Web: www.NeurosurgeryToday.org.

OAK RIDGE ATOMIC PLANT BEGUN: ANNIVERSARY. Aug 1, 1943. Ground was broken at Oak Ridge, TN, for the first plant built to manufacture the uranium 235 needed to build an atomic bomb. The plant was largely completed by July 1944 at a final cost of $280 million. By August 1945 the total cost for development of the A-bomb ran to $1 billion.

OLATHE SWEET CORN FESTIVAL. Aug 1. Olathe, CO. Fun family event featuring all the free "Olathe Sweet" sweet corn you can eat. Annually, the first Saturday in August. Est attendance: 18,000. For info: Bobbi Sale, Olathe Sweet Corn Festival, PO Box 87, 420 Horton Ave, Olathe, CO 81425. Phone: (970) 323-6006. Fax: (970) 323-6030. E-mail: ocornfest@olatheco.com. Web: www.olathesweetcornfest.com.

PASTIMES OF COLONIAL VIRGINIA. Aug 1–31. Jamestown Settlement, Williamsburg, VA; and Yorktown Victory Center, Yorktown, VA. Discover music, games, storytelling and other pastimes of 17th- and 18th-century Virginia through hands-on activities and interpretive programs. For info: Jamestown-Yorktown Foundation, PO Box 1607, Williamsburg, VA 23187. Phone: (757) 253-4838 or toll-free (888) 593-4682. Fax: (757) 253-5299. Web: www.historyisfun.org.

QUILT SHOW. Aug 1–Sept 20. Woodstock, VT. A juried showing of quilts made by Windsor County quilters, displayed with selected 19th-century Vermont quilts. Daily quilting demonstrations and activities. Est attendance: 9,700. For info: Billings Farm and Museum, Rte 12 N, Woodstock, VT 05091. Phone: (802) 457-2355. Fax: (802) 457-4663. E-mail: info@billingsfarm.org. Web: www.billingsfarm.org.

RESPECT FOR PARENTS DAY. Aug 1. A day set aside to think of the positive things parents contribute to society. Annually, Aug 1. For info: Marilyn Dalrymple, PO Box 1563, Lancaster, CA 93539. Web: members.tripod.com/MarilynDalrymple/index-4.html.

ROUNDS RESOUNDING DAY. Aug 1. To sing rounds, catches and canons in folk contrapuntal tradition. Motto: "As rounds re-sound and resound, all the world's joined in a circle of harmony." Annually, Aug 1. For info: Gloria T. Delamar, Founder, Rounds Resounding Society. E-mail: glo@delamar.org. Web: www.delamar.org/roundsresoundingsociety.htm.

"THE RUSH LIMBAUGH SHOW" NATIONAL RADIO PREMIERE: ANNIVERSARY. Aug 1, 1988. Conservative political commentator and radio personality Rush Limbaugh began his nationally syndicated show on this date with 56 stations. It quickly became the nation's top-rated show and rejuvenated the radio talk format. Today, more than 645 stations carry the program to an estimated 20 million listeners.

SPIDER-MAN DEBUTS: ANNIVERSARY. Aug 1, 1962. Stan Lee and Steve Ditko introduced a new superhero for Marvel Comics in issue #15 of *Amazing Fantasy* that hit newstands in August: Spider-Man. Nerdy teen Peter Parker is bitten by a radioactive spider and soon discovers that he has the proportionate strength and agility of the spider—as well as web-shooting talents and "spidey sense." The arachnid crime fighter got his own comic book in March 1963 and quickly became the center of a multimedia empire.

SPINAL MUSCULAR ATROPHY AWARENESS MONTH. Aug 1–31. To promote awareness of this congenital disease. For info: Families of Spinal Muscular Atrophy, PO Box 196, Libertyville, IL 60048-0196. Phone: (800) 886-1762. E-mail: info@fsma.org. Web: www.curesma.org or www.fsma.org.

SWITZERLAND: CONFEDERATION DAY. Aug 1. National holiday. Anniversary of the founding of the Swiss Confederation. Commemorates a pact made in 1291. Parades, patriotic gatherings, bonfires and fireworks. Young citizens' coming-of-age ceremonies. Observed since 600th anniversary of Swiss Confederation was celebrated in 1891.

TALL TIMBER DAYS FESTIVAL. Aug 1–2. Grand Rapids, MN. Festival features the Sheer Brothers Lumberjack Show, chainsaw carvers, arts and crafts and competitions. Families welcome. Annually, the first full weekend in August. Est attendance: 30,000. For info: Tall Timber Days, PO Box 134, Grand Rapids, MN 55744. Web: www.visitgrandrapids.com.

TRINIDAD AND TOBAGO: EMANCIPATION DAY. Aug 1. Public holiday. Slavery was abolished in all British colonies on this day in 1834. Also called Discovery Day.

US CUSTOMS: ANNIVERSARY. Aug 1, 1789. "The first US customs officers began to collect the revenue and enforce the Tariff Act of July 4, 1789, on this date. Since then, the customhouse and the customs officer have stood as symbols of national pride and sovereignty at ports of entry along the land and sea borders of our country." (From Presidential Proclamation 4306.)

WALES: NATIONAL EISTEDDFOD OF WALES. Aug 1–8. Pontcanna, Cardiff. In 1880 the National Eisteddfod association was formed and charged with the responsibility of staging an annual festival to be held in North and South Wales alternately, and with the exception of 1914 and 1940, this target has been successfully achieved. The National Eisteddfod of Wales is a cultural event with competitive festivals of music, drama, literature, art and crafts. All events conducted in Welsh with simultaneous translation into English available. Est attendance: 160,000. For info: Natl Eisteddfod of Wales, 40 Parc Ty Glas, Llanishen, Cardiff, Wales, UK CF14 5WU. Phone: (44) (2920) 763777. Fax: (44) (2920) 763737. Web: www.eisteddfod.org.uk.

WARSAW UPRISING: 65th ANNIVERSARY. Aug 1, 1944. Having received radio reports from Moscow promising aid from the Red Army, the Polish Home Army rose up against the Nazi oppressors. At 5 PM thousands of windows were thrown open and Polish patriots, 40,000 strong, began shooting at German soldiers in the streets. The Germans responded by throwing eight divisions into the battle. Despite appeals from the London-based Polish government-in-exile, no assistance was forthcoming from the Allies, and after two months of horrific fighting the rebellion was quashed.

WHAT WILL BE YOUR LEGACY MONTH. Aug 1–31. Many people do not realize how their actions affect others. They live their lives selfishly, not realizing the impact of their life choices on present and possibly future generations. What Will Be Your Legacy Month is a month for people to reflect on their past and present actions and vow to make positive changes that will affect generations. The seeds, whether positive or negative, that we plant in our children's lives will grow and reflect our teachings. For info: Martha J. Ross-Rodgers, 2442 Annie Circle, Chesapeake, VA 23323. Phone: (757) 558-4964. Fax: (757) 558-4965. E-mail: Mrossrodge@aol.com. Web: www.jirehpublishers.com.

WORLD BREASTFEEDING WEEK. Aug 1–7. Commemoration of signing of Innocenti Declaration. Includes a World Walk for Breastfeeding. Breastfeeding advocates, health care professionals and social service agencies focus attention on the importance and benefits of breastfeeding. Fairs, picnics, fund-raising and government proclamations highlight the week. Annually, the first seven days of August. For info: La Leche League Intl, 1400 N Meacham, Schaumburg, IL 60168-4079. Phone: (847) 519-7730. Fax: (847) 519-0035. E-mail: PRManager@llli.org or PRAssociate@llli.org. Web: www.lalecheleague.org or www.llli.org.

WORLD WIDE WEB: ANNIVERSARY. Aug 1, 1990. The creation of what would become the World Wide Web was suggested this month in 1990 by Tim Berners-Lee and Robert Cailliau at CERN, the European Laboratory for Particle Physics at Switzerland. By October they had designed a prototype Web browser. They also introduced HTML (hypertext markup language) and the URL (universal resource locator). Mosaic, the first graphical Web browser, was designed by Marc Andreessen and released in 1993. By early 1993 there were 50 Web servers worldwide.

August 2009	S	M	T	W	T	F	S
							1
	2	3	4	5	6	7	8
	9	10	11	12	13	14	15
	16	17	18	19	20	21	22
	23	24	25	26	27	28	29
	30	31					

Birthdays Today

Tempestt Bledsoe, 36, talk-show host, actress ("Tempestt," "The Cosby Show"), born Chicago, IL, Aug 1, 1973.

Robert Cray, 56, singer, guitarist, songwriter, born Columbus, GA, Aug 1, 1953.

Dom DeLuise, 76, comedian, actor (*Cannonball Run*), born Brooklyn, NY, Aug 1, 1933.

Giancarlo Giannini, 67, actor (*Swept Away . . . , Seven Beauties*), born La Spezia, Italy, Aug 1, 1942.

David James, 39, soccer player, born Welwyn Garden City, England, Aug 1, 1970.

Nwankwo Kanu, 33, soccer player, born Owerri, Nigeria, Aug 1, 1976.

Tom Wilson, 78, cartoonist ("Ziggy"), born Grant Town, WV, Aug 1, 1931.

August 2 — Sunday

DAY 214 **151 REMAINING**

ALBERT EINSTEIN'S ATOMIC BOMB LETTER: 70th ANNIVERSARY. Aug 2, 1939. Albert Einstein, world-famous scientist, a refugee from Nazi Germany, wrote a letter to US president Franklin D. Roosevelt, first mentioning a possible "new phenomenon . . . chain reactions . . . vast amounts of power." "A single bomb of this type," he wrote, "carried by boat and exploded in a port, might very well destroy the whole port together with some of the surrounding territory." Six years and four days later, Aug 6, 1945, the Japanese port of Hiroshima was destroyed by the first atomic bombing of a populated place.

AMERICAN FAMILY DAY IN ARIZONA. Aug 2. Observed in Arizona on the first Sunday in August. The observance date is designated by statute.

BALDWIN, JAMES: 85th BIRTH ANNIVERSARY. Aug 2, 1924. Black American author noted for descriptions of black life in the US. Born at New York, NY. His best-known work, *Go Tell It on the Mountain*, was published in 1953. Died at St. Paul-de-Vence, France, Nov 30, 1987.

COSTA RICA: FEAST OF OUR LADY OF ANGELS. Aug 2. National holiday. Celebrates Costa Rica's patron saint, the Virgin of Los Angeles.

DECLARATION OF INDEPENDENCE: OFFICIAL SIGNING: ANNIVERSARY. Aug 2, 1776. Contrary to widespread misconceptions, the 56 signers did not sign as a group and did not do so July 4, 1776. John Hancock and Charles Thomson signed only draft copies that day, the official day the Declaration was adopted by Congress. The signing of the official declaration occurred Aug 2, 1776, when 50 men probably took part. Later that year, five more apparently signed separately, and one added his name in a subsequent year. (From "Signers of the Declaration . . ." US Department of the Interior, 1975.) See also: "Declaration of Independence Approval and Signing: Anniversary" (July 4).

HUNT, LAMAR: BIRTH ANNIVERSARY. Aug 2, 1932. A legend in American professional sports, executive Hunt innovated the NFL, nurtured the growth of professional soccer in the US and cofounded the World Championship Tennis circuit. Hunt cofounded the AFL, which merged with the NFL. The AFL-NFL championship game was coined the "Super Bowl" by Hunt. He owned the Kansas City Chiefs and several soccer teams. Hunt also cofounded the NASL and Major League Soccer, and in recognition for that, America's oldest sporting tournament, the US Open Cup, was renamed for him. Hunt was a Hall of Famer in football, soccer and tennis. Born in El Dorado, AK, Hunt died in his longtime hometown of Dallas, TX, on Dec 13, 2006.

IRAQ INVADES KUWAIT: ANNIVERSARY. Aug 2, 1990. On orders of President Saddam Hussein, the Iraqi army invaded Kuwait. Hussein claimed that Kuwait presented a serious threat to Iraq's economic existence by overproducing oil and driving prices down on the world market. After conquering the capital, Kuwait City, Hussein installed a military government in Kuwait, prior to annexing it to Iraq on the claim that Kuwait was historically part of Iraq. This led to the 100-hour war against Iraq, Operation Desert Storm.

ITALY: JOUST OF THE QUINTANA. Aug 2. Ascoli/Piceno. The first Sunday in August is set aside for the Torneo della Quintana, a historical pageant with 15th-century costumes.

L'ENFANT, PIERRE CHARLES: BIRTH ANNIVERSARY. Aug 2, 1754. The architect, engineer and Revolutionary War officer who designed the plan for the city of Washington, DC, L'Enfant was born at Paris, France. He died at Prince Georges County, MD, June 14, 1825.

LOY, MYRNA: BIRTH ANNIVERSARY. Aug 2, 1905. America's favorite leading lady of the 1930s, Loy was born Myrna Adele Williams near Helena, MT. She soared to fame as the madcap New York sophisticate Nora Charles in the "Thin Man" movies with William Powell (Nick Charles). She also starred in the critically acclaimed *The Best Years of Our Lives* (1946). After a career spanning seven decades, she was awarded an honorary Oscar in 1991 and died at New York, NY, Dec 14, 1993.

MACEDONIA: NATIONAL DAY. Aug 2. Commemorates the nationalist uprising against the Ottoman Empire in 1903. Called Prophet Elias Day or Illinden. (See also: "Saint Elias Day (Illinden): Macedonian Uprising: Anniversary" below.)

O'CONNOR, CARROLL: 85th BIRTH ANNIVERSARY. Aug 2, 1924. Television, stage and screen actor born in New York, NY. He was best known for his portrayal of the bigoted, blue-collar Archie Bunker on "All in the Family." He played the role of Bunker from 1971 to 1979 and was nominated for eight Emmy Awards, winning four. He won a fifth Emmy in 1989 for "In the Heat of the Night." He was also inducted into the Television Hall of Fame in 1989. He died at Culver City, CA, on June 21, 2001.

SAINT ELIAS DAY (ILLINDEN): MACEDONIAN UPRISING: ANNIVERSARY. Aug 2, 1903. Most sacred, honored and celebrated day of the Macedonian people. Anniversary of the uprising of Macedonians against the Ottoman Empire. Turkish reprisals against the insurgents were ruthless, including the destruction of 105 villages and the execution of more than 1,700 noncombatants.

SINGLE WORKING WOMEN'S WEEK. Aug 2–8. Single working women today do it all. They bring home the bacon, fry it—and do the dishes. They earn the money, buy the groceries—and take out the garbage. They shop for, feed, nurture, and clean up after the pets. They pick out, buy and wrap gifts for and then attend everyone else's special occasions (showers, weddings, kids' birthdays). This week, it's their turn, and we celebrate the single women who make the modern world a better place—and who find the money, time and energy to lovingly support others. We celebrate Single Working Women every day this week: pick a day or two and buy your favorite single working woman a gift—or two! For info: Single Working Women's Affiliate Network (SWWAN). Phone: (773) 292-3294. Fax: (216) 472-8502. E-mail: info@swwan.org. Web: www.swwan.org.

SISTERS' DAY®. Aug 2. Celebrating the spirit of sisterhood: sisters nationwide show appreciation and give recognition to one another for the special relationship they share. Send a card; make a phone call; share memories, photos, flowers, candy, etc. Sisters may include biological sisters, sorority sisters, sisterly friends, etc. Annually, the first Sunday in August. Please call for a press kit. For info: Tricia Eleogram, 5112 Normandy Ave, Memphis, TN 38117. Phone: (901) 681-2145 or (901) 755-0751. Fax: (901) 754-9923.

SWISS VOLKSFEST. Aug 2. New Glarus, WI. Celebration of Swiss Independence Day. Annually, the first Sunday in August. Est attendance: 2,000. For info: Volksfest, 418 Railroad St, New Glarus, WI 53574. Phone: (608) 527-2095 or (800) 527-6838. E-mail: info@swisstown.com. Web: www.swisstown.com.

US VIRGIN ISLANDS NATIONAL PARK ESTABLISHED: ANNIVERSARY. Aug 2, 1956. The US Virgin Islands, including areas on St. John and St. Thomas, were established as a national park and preserve. On Oct 5, 1962, the Virgin Islands National Park was enlarged to encompass offshore areas, including coral reefs, shorelines and sea grass beds.

Birthdays Today

Joanna Cassidy, 65, actress ("Buffalo Bill," *Under Fire*), born Camden, NJ, Aug 2, 1944.

Wes Craven, 70, writer, director (*The Nightmare on Elm Street, Scream*), born Cleveland, OH, Aug 2, 1939.

James Fallows, 60, journalist, former editor (*US News & World Report*), born Philadelphia, PA, Aug 2, 1949.

Edward Furlong, 32, actor (*Before and After, Terminator 2*), born Glendale, CA, Aug 2, 1977.

Kathryn Harrold, 59, actress ("I'll Fly Away," "The Larry Sanders Show," *Modern Romance*), born Tazewell, VA, Aug 2, 1950.

Victoria Jackson, 50, actress ("Saturday Night Live," *I Love You to Death*), born Miami, FL, Aug 2, 1959.

Peter O'Toole, 76, actor (*Venus, Lawrence of Arabia, Becket*), born Connemara, Ireland, Aug 2, 1933.

Mary-Louise Parker, 45, actress (Tony Award for *Proof*; "Weeds," *Fried Green Tomatoes*), born Fort Jackson, SC, Aug 2, 1964.

Huston Street, 26, baseball player, born Austin, TX, Aug 2, 1983.

Michael Weiss, 33, figure skater, born Washington, DC, Aug 2, 1976.

August 3 — Monday

DAY 215 **150 REMAINING**

ANTIGUA AND BARBUDA: AUGUST MONDAY. Aug 3–4. The first Monday in August and the day following form the August Monday public holiday.

AUSTRALIA: PICNIC DAY. Aug 3. The first Monday in August is a bank holiday in New South Wales and Picnic Day in Northern Territory, Australia.

BAHAMAS: EMANCIPATION DAY. Aug 3. Public holiday in Bahamas. Annually, the first Monday in August. Commemorates the emancipation of slaves by the British in 1834.

CANADA: CIVIC HOLIDAY. Aug 3. The first Monday in August is observed as a holiday in seven of Canada's 10 provinces. Civic holiday in Manitoba, New Brunswick, Northwest Territories, Ontario and Saskatchewan; British Columbia Day in British Columbia, and Heritage Day in Alberta.

COLORADO DAY. Aug 3. Colorado. Annually, the first Monday in August. Commemorates Admission Day, Aug 1, 1876, when Colorado became the 38th state.

COLUMBUS SAILS FOR THE NEW WORLD: ANNIVERSARY. Aug 3, 1492. Christopher Columbus, "Admiral of the Ocean Sea," set sail half an hour before sunrise from Palos, Spain, Aug 3, 1492. With three ships, *Niña*, *Pinta* and *Santa Maria*, and a crew of 90, he sailed "for Cathay" but found instead a New World of the Americas, first landing at Guanahani (San Salvador Island in the Bahamas) Oct 12. See also: "Columbus Day" (Oct 12).

August 2009

S	M	T	W	T	F	S
						1
2	3	4	5	6	7	8
9	10	11	12	13	14	15
16	17	18	19	20	21	22
23	24	25	26	27	28	29
30	31					

EQUATORIAL GUINEA: ARMED FORCES DAY. Aug 3. National holiday.

EXHIBITOR APPRECIATION WEEK. Aug 3–7. An opportunity for trade/consumer show organizers to recognize and appreciate the thousands of exhibitors who make their events possible. For info: Susan Friedmann, CSP, The Tradeshow Coach, 2301 Saranac Ave, Lake Placid, NY 12946. Phone: (518) 523-1320. E-mail: susan@thetradeshowcoach.com. Web: www.thetradeshowcoach.com.

GRENADA: EMANCIPATION DAY. Aug 3. Grenada observes a public holiday annually on the first Monday in August. Commemorates the emancipation of slaves by the British in 1834.

GUINEA-BISSAU: COLONIZATION MARTYR'S DAY. Aug 3. National holiday. Also called Pidjiguiti Martyrs' Day.

ICELAND: AUGUST HOLIDAY. Aug 3. National holiday. The first Monday in August. Commemorates Iceland's constitution of 1874.

JAMAICA: INDEPENDENCE DAY. Aug 3. National holiday observing achievement of Jamaican independence from Britain Aug 6, 1962. Annually, the first Monday in August.

KUHN, MARGARET (MAGGIE): BIRTH ANNIVERSARY. Aug 3, 1905. When she was forced into retirement because she'd reached the age of 65, Maggie Kuhn founded the Gray Panthers organization to fight age discrimination. Subsequently she waged a battle that resulted in mandatory retirement's being banned. Born at Buffalo, NY, Kuhn died Apr 22, 1995, at Philadelphia, PA.

NIGER: INDEPENDENCE DAY. Aug 3. Niger gained its independence from France on this day in 1960.

OLD FIDDLERS' CONVENTION. Aug 3–8. Galax, VA. 74th annual. Event features dance, folk songs and old-time and bluegrass music competition. Est attendance: 35,000. For info: Thomas L. Jones Jr, Box 655, Galax, VA 24333. Phone: (276) 236-8541. Web: www.oldfiddlersconvention.com.

"PRIMETIME LIVE" TV PREMIERE: 20th ANNIVERSARY. Aug 3, 1989. Sam Donaldson and Diane Sawyer were the first hosts of this magazine show featuring investigative and consumer reports as well as human-interest stories.

PSYCHIC WEEK. Aug 3–7. To utilize the power of the psyche to bring peace, find lost individuals and concentrate "psychic power" on beneficial causes. Annually, the first week in August (Monday–Friday). (Created by the late Richard R. Falk.)

PYLE, ERNEST TAYLOR: BIRTH ANNIVERSARY. Aug 3, 1900. Ernie Pyle was born at Dana, IN, and began his career in journalism in 1923. After serving as managing editor of the *Washington Daily News*, he returned to his first journalistic love of working as a roving reporter in 1935. His column was syndicated by nearly 200 newspapers and often focused on figures behind the news. His reports of the bombing of London in 1940 and subsequent reports from Africa, Sicily, Italy and France earned him a Pulitzer Prize in 1944. He was killed by machine-gun fire at the Pacific island of Ie Shima, Apr 18, 1945.

SCOPES, JOHN T.: BIRTH ANNIVERSARY. Aug 3, 1900. Central figure in a cause célèbre (the "Scopes Trial" or the "Monkey Trial"), John Thomas Scopes was born at Paducah, KY. An obscure, 24-year-old schoolteacher at the Dayton, TN, high school in 1925, he became the focus of world attention. Scopes never uttered a word at his trial, which was a contest between two of America's best-known lawyers, William Jennings Bryan and Clarence Darrow. The trial, July 10–21, 1925, resulted in Scopes's conviction. He was fined $100 "for teaching evolution" in Tennessee. The verdict was upset on a technicality, and the statute he was accused of breaching was repealed in 1967. Scopes died at Shreveport, LA, Oct 21, 1970.

SCOTLAND: SUMMER BANK HOLIDAY. Aug 3. Bank and public holiday in Scotland. The first Monday in August.

STURGIS RALLY. Aug 3–9. Sturgis, SD. The granddaddy of all motorcycle rallies and races. For almost seven decades the small community of Sturgis has welcomed motorcycle enthusiasts from around the world to a week of varied cycle racing, tours of the beautiful Black Hills, trade shows and thousands of bikes on display. Annually, beginning the Monday after the first full weekend in August. Est attendance: 350,000. For info: Sturgis Bike Week Productions, PO Box 999, Sturgis, SD 57785. Phone: (605) 347-0200. Fax: (605) 347-8888. E-mail: jr@sbwproductions.com. Web: www.sturgisrallynews.com.

URIS, LEON: 85th BIRTH ANNIVERSARY. Aug 3, 1924. American novelist born to a family of Russian Jews at Baltimore, MD. His most successful novels were those that chronicled the Holocaust (1960's *Mila 18*) and the founding of Israel (1958's *Exodus*). His novels sold millions and were made into several feature films. Later titles included *QB VII*, a fictionalized account of his own trial for libel, and *Trinity*, which followed the life of three generations of an Irish family. Uris died June 21, 2003, at Shelter Island, NY.

US WOMEN'S AMATEUR (GOLF) CHAMPIONSHIP. Aug 3–9. Old Warson Country Club, St. Louis, MO. For info: USGA, Golf House, Championship Dept, PO Box 708, Far Hills, NJ 07931. Phone: (908) 234-2300. Fax: (908) 234-9687. E-mail: usga@usga.org. Web: www.usga.org.

ZAMBIA: YOUTH DAY. Aug 3. National holiday. Youth activities are the order of the day. The focal point is Lusaka's Independence Stadium. Annually, the first Monday in August.

Birthdays Today

Tony Bennett, 83, singer, born Anthony Dominick Benedetto at New York, NY, Aug 3, 1926.

Steven Berkoff, 72, actor, director, writer (*A Clockwork Orange, Beverly Hills Cop*), born London, England, Aug 3, 1937.

Tom Brady, 32, football player, born San Mateo, CA, Aug 3, 1977.

P.D. James, 89, mystery novelist, born Phyllis Dorothy James at Oxford, England, Aug 3, 1920.

Evangeline Lilly, 30, actress ("Lost"), born Fort Saskatchewan, AB, Canada, Aug 3, 1979.

John McGinley, 50, actor (*Platoon, Born on the Fourth of July*, "Scrubs"), born New York, NY, Aug 3, 1959.

Martin Sheen, 69, actor (*Apocalypse Now*, "The West Wing"), born Ramon Estevez at Dayton, OH, Aug 3, 1940.

Martha Stewart, 68, lifestyle consultant, TV personality, writer, born Nutley, NJ, Aug 3, 1941.

Isaiah Washington, 46, actor ("Grey's Anatomy," *Romeo Must Die, Exit Wounds*), born Houston, TX, Aug 3, 1963.

Blaine Wilson, 35, former gymnast, born Columbus, OH, Aug 3, 1974.

August 4 — Tuesday

DAY 216 — **149 REMAINING**

ARMSTRONG, LOUIS: BIRTH ANNIVERSARY. Aug 4, 1900 (or 1901). Jazz musician extraordinaire born at New Orleans, LA. Died at New York, NY, July 6, 1971. Armstrong often said he was born on the 4th of July, but documents in the Louis Armstrong Archives of Queens College, Flushing, NY, indicate that he was actually born Aug 4, 1900 or 1901. Asked to define jazz, Armstrong reportedly replied, "Man, if you gotta ask, you'll never know." The trumpet player was also known as Satchmo. He appeared in many films. Popular singles included "What a Wonderful World" and "Hello, Dolly" (with Barbra Streisand).

BURKINA FASO: REVOLUTION DAY. Aug 4. National holiday. Commemorates 1983 coup.

CIVIL RIGHTS WORKERS FOUND SLAIN: 45th ANNIVERSARY. Aug 4, 1964. After disappearing on June 21, three civil rights workers were found murdered and buried in an earthen dam outside Philadelphia, MS. The three young men were workers on the Mississippi Summer Project organized by the Student Nonviolent Coordinating Committee (SNCC) to increase black voter registration. Prior to their disappearance, James Chaney, Andrew Goodman and Michael Schwerner were detained by Neshoba County police on charges of speeding. When their car was found, burned, on June 23, President Lyndon Johnson ordered an FBI search for the men.

COAST GUARD DAY. Aug 4. Celebrates anniversary of founding of the Revenue Cutter Service in 1790, which merged with the Life Saving Service in 1915 to become the US Coast Guard.

CUNNINGHAM, GLENN: 100th BIRTH ANNIVERSARY. Aug 4, 1909. Glenn Clarence Cunningham, the "Kansas Ironman," American track athlete and 1934–37 world-record holder for the mile, member of the US Olympic teams in 1932 and 1936, was born at Atlanta, KS. On June 16, 1934, at Princeton, NJ, Cunningham set a world record for the mile (4:06.7) that stood for three years. After WWII, he and his wife opened a youth ranch and cared for more than 10,000 foster children plus 10 of their own. Cunningham died at Menifee, AR, Mar 10, 1988.

NATIONAL NIGHT OUT. Aug 4. Designed to heighten crime prevention awareness and to promote police-community partnerships. Annually, the first Tuesday in August. For info: Matt A. Peskin, Dir, Natl Assn of Town Watch, PO Box 303, Wynnewood, PA 19096. Phone: (610) 649-7055 or (800) 648-3688. Fax: (610) 649-5456. E-mail: info@natw.org. Web: www.nationalnightout.org.

QUEEN ELIZABETH, THE QUEEN MOTHER: BIRTH ANNIVERSARY. Aug 4, 1900. A beloved member of the English royal family, the Queen "Mum" saw England through some of its most trying times in the 20th century. She was born Elizabeth Angela Marguerite Bowes-Lyon at London, England, and married the then Duke of York in 1923. When her husband was unexpectedly crowned King George VI in 1936 (after the abdication of Edward VIII), she became his strong and guiding support. She won the undying gratitude of her subjects, moreover, when she refused to remove the royal family to the safety of the countryside during the German bombing of London in WWII. She died Mar 30, 2002.

RICHARD, MAURICE "ROCKET": BIRTH ANNIVERSARY. Aug 4, 1921. Hockey Hall of Fame right wing, born at Montreal, QC, Canada. Died May 27, 2000, at Montreal.

SCALIGER, JOSEPH JUSTUS: BIRTH ANNIVERSARY. Aug 4, 1540. (Old Style date.) French scholar who has been called the founder of scientific chronology. Born at Agen, France, the son of classical scholar Julius Caesar Scaliger. In 1582 he suggested a new system for measuring time and numbering years. His "Julian Period" (named for his father), which consisted of 7,980 consecutive years (beginning Jan 1, 4713 BC), is still in use by astronomers. He died at Leiden, Netherlands, Jan 21, 1609 (OS).

SCHUMAN, WILLIAM HOWARD: BIRTH ANNIVERSARY. Aug 4, 1910. American composer who won the first Pulitzer Prize for Composition and founded the Juilliard School of Music, born at New York City. His compositions include *American Festival Overture, New England Triptych*, the baseball opera *The Mighty Casey* and *On Freedom's Ground*, written for the centennial of the Statue of Liberty in 1986. He was instrumental in the conception of the Lincoln Center for the Performing Arts and served as its first president. In 1985 he was awarded a special Pulitzer Prize for his contributions. He also received a National Medal of Arts in 1985 and a Kennedy Center Honor in 1989. Schuman died at New York City, Feb 15, 1992.

SHELLEY, PERCY BYSSHE: BIRTH ANNIVERSARY. Aug 4, 1792. Poet Percy Bysshe Shelley, one of the leading English Romantic poets and embodiment of a free spirit, was born at Warnham, Sussex. He lived abroad in Italy until his death at sea off the coast of Viareggio, just a month before his 30th birthday, July 8, 1822. Shelley's important works include "Ozymandias," published in 1818; "Ode to the West Wind," "The Cloud," "To a Skylark" and *Prometheus Unbound* in 1819; and *Adonais* (an elegy for John Keats) in 1821.

 Birthdays Today

Richard Belzer, 65, comedian, actor ("Law & Order: SVU," "Homicide: Life on the Street"), born Bridgeport, CT, Aug 4, 1944.

Roger Clemens, 47, baseball player, born Dayton, OH, Aug 4, 1962.

Daniel Dae Kim, 41, actor ("Lost," "24"), born Pusan, South Korea, Aug 4, 1968.

Jeff Gordon, 38, race car driver, born Pittsboro, IN, Aug 4, 1971.

Barack Obama, 48, 2008 Democratic presidential candidate, US Senator (D, Illinois), born Honolulu, HI, Aug 4, 1961.

Ted Strickland, 68, Governor of Ohio (D), born Lucasville, OH, Aug 4, 1941.

Kristoffer Tabori, 57, actor ("Seventh Avenue," "Chicago Story"), born Los Angeles, CA, Aug 4, 1952.

Helen Thomas, 89, journalist (longtime White House correspondent), born Winchester, KY, Aug 4, 1920.

Billy Bob Thornton, 54, actor (*Bad News Bears, Friday Night Lights, Bad Santa*), director, screenwriter (Oscar for *Sling Blade*), born Hot Springs, AR, Aug 4, 1955.

August 5 — Wednesday

DAY 217 148 REMAINING

AIKEN, CONRAD: BIRTH ANNIVERSARY. Aug 5, 1899. American poet, short-story writer, critic and Pulitzer Prize winner (Poetry, 1930). He was born at Savannah, GA, and died there Aug 17, 1973.

"AMERICAN BANDSTAND" TV PREMIERE: ANNIVERSARY. Aug 5, 1957. "American Bandstand" and Dick Clark are synonymous; he hosted the show for more than 30 years. "AB" started out as a local show at Philadelphia, PA, in 1952. Clark, then a disk jockey, took over as host at the age of 26. The format was simple: teens dancing, performers doing their latest hits, Clark introducing songs and listing the top 10 songs each week. This hour-long show was not only TV's longest-running musical series but also the first one devoted exclusively to rock and roll. The show was canceled six months after Clark turned over the hosting duties to David Hirsch in 1989.

BATTLE OF MOBILE BAY: ANNIVERSARY. Aug 5, 1864. A Union fleet under Admiral David Farragut attempted to run past three Confederate forts into Mobile Bay, AL. After coming under fire, the Union fleet headed into a maze of underwater mines, known at that time as torpedoes. The ironclad *Tecumseh* was sunk by a torpedo, after which Farragut is said to have exclaimed, "Damn the torpedoes—full steam ahead!" The Union fleet was successful and Mobile Bay was secured.

August 2009

S	M	T	W	T	F	S
						1
2	3	4	5	6	7	8
9	10	11	12	13	14	15
16	17	18	19	20	21	22
23	24	25	26	27	28	29
30	31					

BURKINA FASO: REPUBLIC DAY. Aug 5. Burkina Faso (formerly Upper Volta) gained autonomy from France in 1960.

CANADA: CANADIAN OPEN OLD TIME FIDDLE CHAMPIONSHIP. Aug 5–9. Shelburne, ON. 59th annual. Est attendance: 13,000. For info: Shelburne Rotary Club, PO Box 27, Shelburne, ON, Canada L0N 1S0. Phone: (519) 925-2600, ext 238. E-mail: fiddleshelburne@yahoo.ca. Web: www.shelburnefiddlecontest.on.ca.

CROATIA: HOMELAND THANKSGIVING DAY. Aug 5. National holiday.

ELIOT, JOHN: BIRTH ANNIVERSARY. Aug 5, 1604. (Old Style date.) American "Apostle to the Indians," translator of the Bible into an Indian tongue (the first Bible to be printed in America), was born at Hertfordshire, England. He died at Roxbury, MA, May 21, 1690 (OS).

FIRST ENGLISH COLONY IN NORTH AMERICA: ANNIVERSARY. Aug 5, 1583. Sir Humphrey Gilbert, English navigator and explorer, aboard his sailing ship, the *Squirrel*, sighted the Newfoundland coast and took possession of the area around St. John's harbor in the name of Queen Elizabeth I, thus establishing the first English colony in North America. Gilbert was lost at sea, in a storm off the Azores, on his return trip to England.

HUSTON, JOHN: BIRTH ANNIVERSARY. Aug 5, 1906. This larger-than-life Hollywood figure, son of the actor Walter Huston, spent his whole life before or behind the camera as an actor, writer and director. His first film, 1941's masterpiece of detective-noir, *The Maltese Falcon*, catapulted Humphrey Bogart away from gangster roles into dark heroic roles. Huston and Bogart collaborated on other great films: *The Treasure of the Sierra Madre* (which featured Huston's father in a Best Supporting Actor role), *Key Largo*, *The African Queen* and *Beat the Devil*. Born at Nevada, MO, Huston died Aug 28, 1987, at Middletown, RI, not long after completing his final film, *The Dead* (1987).

IRELAND: BANK HOLIDAY. Aug 5. Bank holiday in the Republic of Ireland.

LUNAR ECLIPSE. Aug 5–6. Penumbral eclipse of the moon. Visible in North America, South America, Europe, Africa and western Asia.

LYNCH, THOMAS: BIRTH ANNIVERSARY. Aug 5, 1749. Signer, Declaration of Independence, born Prince George's Parish, SC. Died 1779 (lost at sea, exact date of death unknown).

MISS CRUSTACEAN USA BEAUTY PAGEANT AND OCEAN CITY CREEP. Aug 5. 6th St Beach, Ocean City, NJ. Participants are hermit tree crabs. To determine the most beautiful and fastest tree crab on Earth. Begins at 1 PM, EST. Est attendance: 500. For info: Mark Soifer, PR Dir, City of Ocean City, City Hall, Ocean City, NJ 08226. Phone: (609) 525-9300. Fax: (609) 399-0374. E-mail: msoifer@hotmail.com.

MONROE, MARILYN: DEATH ANNIVERSARY. Aug 5, 1962. The world fell in love with Monroe's unique combination of sensuality and approachability. She was the epitome of Hollywood glamour, making 29 films in her career. Her tragic death at age 36, at Los Angeles, CA, from an overdose of sleeping pills, is shrouded in controversy. She was born June 1, 1926, at Los Angeles.

MOON PHASE: FULL MOON. Aug 5. Moon enters Full Moon phase at 8:55 PM, EDT.

OHIO STATE FAIR. Aug 5–16. Columbus, OH. Family fun, amusement rides, games, food booths, parades, entertainment, agriculture exhibits and educational displays. Est attendance: 850,000. For info: Ohio State Fair, 717 E 17th Ave, Columbus, OH 43211. Phone: (614) 644-3247 or (888) OHO-EXPO. Fax: (614) 644-4031. Web: www.ohiostatefair.com.

OMARR, SYDNEY: BIRTH ANNIVERSARY. Aug 5, 1926. Born Sidney Kimmelman at Philadelphia, PA, this world-famous astrologer became fascinated by numerology and astrology and changed his name to "Sydney Omarr" at the age of 15. He began contributing to astrology magazines and eventually became well known in Hollywood. He wrote dozens of books, an average of 13 per year, which sold more than 50 million copies. His newspaper astrology column was syndicated in more than 200 newspapers. He died Jan 16, 2003, at Santa Monica, CA.

SEASHORE OPEN HOUSE TOUR. Aug 5. Loveladies, NJ. 43rd annual. Come and enjoy the fabulous shoreline houses. For info: Long Beach Island Foundation of the Arts and Sciences, 120 Long Beach Blvd, Loveladies, NJ 08008. Phone: (609) 494-1241. Fax: (609) 494-0662. Web: www.lbifoundation.org.

STURGEON MOON. Aug 5. So called by Native American tribes of New England and the Great Lakes because at this time of year, this important food fish was most abundant. The August Full Moon.

TEXAS COUNTY FAIR/OLD SETTLERS REUNION. Aug 5–8. Fair Grounds, Houston, MO. A fun festival with family night, cowboy night and health fair night. Featuring arts and crafts, carnival midway, music concerts, bluegrass and country bands, Big Country Idol contest, demolition derby, bull ride, and livestock exhibit and sale. Est attendance: 10,000. For info: Texas County Fair/Old Settlers Reunion, PO Box 374, Houston, MO 65483. Phone: (417) 967-2220. Fax: (417) 967-2178. E-mail: chamber004@centurytel.net.

WALLENBERG, RAOUL: BIRTH ANNIVERSARY. Aug 5, 1912. Swedish architect Raoul Gustaf Wallenberg was born at Stockholm, Sweden. He was the second person in history (Winston Churchill was the first) to be granted honorary American citizenship (US House of Representatives voted 396–2, Sept 22, 1981). He is credited with saving 100,000 Jews from almost certain death at the hands of the Nazis during WWII. Wallenberg was arrested by Soviet troops at Budapest, Hungary, Jan 17, 1945, and according to the official Soviet press agency, Tass, died in prison at Moscow, July 17, 1947.

WORLD'S FAIR OF MONEY. Aug 5–9. Los Angeles Convention Center, Los Angeles, CA. The greatest money show on earth, with more than 1,100 coin and paper money dealers, mints from around the world, exhibits, family activities and educational programs. For info: Jay Beeton, American Numismatic Assn, 818 N Cascade Ave, Colorado Springs, CO 80903. Phone: (719) 632-2646 or (800) 367-9723. E-mail: pr@money.org. Web: www.money.org.

Birthdays Today

Loni Anderson, 63, actress ("WKRP in Cincinnati," *The Jayne Mansfield Story*), born St. Paul, MN, Aug 5, 1946.

Neil Alden Armstrong, 79, former astronaut (first man to walk on moon), born Wapakoneta, OH, Aug 5, 1930.

Ja'net DuBois, 71, actress ("Good Times," "Beverly Hills 90210"), born Philadelphia, PA, Aug 5, 1938.

Patrick Aloysius Ewing, 47, former basketball player, born Kingston, Jamaica, Aug 5, 1962.

Lorrie Fair, 31, soccer player, born Los Altos, CA, Aug 5, 1978.

Eric Hinske, 32, baseball player, born Menasha, WI, Aug 5, 1977.

John Olerud, 41, baseball player, born Seattle, WA, Aug 5, 1968.

John Saxon, 73, actor ("Falcon Crest," *Enter the Dragon, Nightmare on Elm Street*), born Brooklyn, NY, Aug 5, 1936.

Jonathan Silverman, 43, actor ("The Single Guy," *Weekend at Bernie's*), born Los Angeles, CA, Aug 5, 1966.

Erika Slezak, 63, actress ("One Life to Live"), born Los Angeles, CA, Aug 5, 1946.

August 6 — Thursday

DAY 218 — **147 REMAINING**

AMERICAN PSYCHOLOGICAL ASSOCIATION CONVENTION. Aug 6–9. Toronto, ON, Canada. For info: Convention Office, American Psychological Assn, 750 First St NE, Washington, DC 20002-4242. Phone: (202) 336-6020. E-mail: convention.office@apa.org. Web: www.apa.org.

ATOMIC BOMB DROPPED ON HIROSHIMA: ANNIVERSARY. Aug 6, 1945. At 8:15 AM, local time, an American B-29 bomber, the *Enola Gay*, dropped an atomic bomb named "Little Boy" over the center of the city of Hiroshima, Japan. The bomb exploded about 1,800 feet above the ground, killing more than 105,000 civilians and destroying the city. It is estimated that another 100,000 persons were injured and died subsequently as a direct result of the bomb and the radiation it produced. This was the first time in history that such a devastating weapon had been used by any nation.

BALL, LUCILLE: BIRTH ANNIVERSARY. Aug 6, 1911. Film and television pioneer and comedienne born at Jamestown, NY. In addition to her many film and television credits, Lucille Ball will always be remembered for her role in the 1950's CBS sitcom "I Love Lucy." As Lucy Ricardo, the wife of bandleader Ricky Ricardo (her real-life husband, Desi Arnaz), she exhibited a comedic style that became a trademark of early television comedy. She died Apr 26, 1989, at Los Angeles, CA.

BOLIVIA: INDEPENDENCE DAY. Aug 6. National holiday. Gained freedom from Spain in 1825. Named after Simón Bolivar.

CANADA: EDMONTON FOLK MUSIC FESTIVAL. Aug 6–9. Gallagher Park, Edmonton, AB. Folk music and fun for the entire family highlighting blues, country, Celtic, traditional folk and bluegrass music, arts and crafts displays and a food fair. Est attendance: 85,000. For info: Edmonton Folk Music Festival Society, PO Box 4130, Edmonton, AB, Canada T6E 4T2. Phone: (780) 429-1899. E-mail: fadmin@efmf.ab.ca. Web: www.edmontonfolkfest.org.

ELECTROCUTION FIRST USED TO CARRY OUT DEATH PENALTY: ANNIVERSARY. Aug 6, 1890. At Auburn Prison, Auburn, NY, William Kemmler of Buffalo, NY, became the first man to be executed by electrocution. He had been convicted of the hatchet murder of his common-law wife, Matilde Ziegler, on Mar 28, 1889. This first attempt at using electrocution to carry out the death penalty was a botched affair. As reported by George Westinghouse, Jr, "It has been a brutal affair. They could have done better with an axe."

FESTIVAL AT SANDPOINT. Aug 6–9 (also Aug 13–16). Sandpoint, ID. Summer concert series featuring classical, country, jazz, pop, world, blues and folk. Est attendance: 20,000. For info: Dyno Wahl, Exec Dir, Festival at Sandpoint, PO Box 695, Sandpoint, ID 83864. Phone: (888) 265-4554. Fax: (208) 263-6858. E-mail: festival@sandpoint.net. Web: www.festivalatsandpoint.com.

FIRST WOMAN SWIMS THE ENGLISH CHANNEL: ANNIVERSARY. Aug 6, 1926. The first woman to swim the English Channel was 19-year-old Gertrude Ederle of New York, NY. Her swim was completed in 14 hours and 31 minutes.

FLEMING, ALEXANDER: BIRTH ANNIVERSARY. Aug 6, 1881. Sir Alexander Fleming, Scottish bacteriologist, discoverer of penicillin and 1945 Nobel Prize recipient, was born at Lochfield, Scotland. He died at London, England, Mar 11, 1955.

HIROSHIMA DAY: ANNIVERSARY. Aug 6. Memorial observances in many places for victims of the first atomic bombing of a populated place, which occurred at Hiroshima, Japan, in 1945, when an American B-29 bomber dropped an atomic bomb over the center of the city. More than 205,000 civilians died either immediately in the explosion or subsequently of radiation.

HOPE WATERMELON FESTIVAL. Aug 6–8. Hope, AR. An event in which the entire family can participate while promoting the city of Hope and having fun. Hope is the birthplace of the 42nd president of the US, Bill Clinton. Est attendance: 40,000. For info: Hope–Hempstead County Chamber of Commerce, PO Box 250, Hope, AR

71802-0250. Phone: (870) 777-3640. Fax: (870) 722-6154. E-mail: hopemelonfest@yahoo.com. Web: www.hopemelonfest.com.

JAPAN: PEACE FESTIVAL. Aug 6. Hiroshima. The festival held annually at Peace Memorial Park is observed in memory of the victims of the Aug 6, 1945, atomic bomb explosion there.

JUDGE CRATER DISAPPEARANCE: ANNIVERSARY. Aug 6, 1930. Anniversary of mysterious disappearance at age 41 of Joseph Force Crater, justice of the New York State Supreme Court. Never seen or heard from after disappearance on this date. Declared legally dead in 1939.

"LIL" MARGARET'S BLUEGRASS AND OLD-TIME MUSIC FESTIVAL. Aug 6–8. Leonardtown, MD. Bluegrass music, crafts, old-time cars and tractors, plenty of home-cooked meals and lots of fun. Annually, the second weekend in August. Est attendance: 1,000. For info: Joseph H. Goddard, Lil Margaret's Bluegrass, 20529 White Point Rd, Leonardtown, MD 20650. Phone: (301) 475-8191. Web: www.bluegrassville.com/lilmarg or www.lilmargaretsbluegrass.com.

MITCHUM, ROBERT: BIRTH ANNIVERSARY. Aug 6, 1917. Film actor (*The Night of the Hunter, The Story of GI Joe*), born at Bridgeport, CT. Died July 1, 1997, at Santa Barbara County, CA.

NATIONAL BLUEBERRY FESTIVAL. Aug 6–9. South Haven, MI. 46th annual. At the World's Highbush Blueberry Capital, enjoy events such as concerts, a parade, pie-eating contests, craft fair, children's fun and much more on the shores of Lake Michigan. Est attendance: 50,000. For info: South Haven Chamber of Commerce, 606 Philips St, South Haven, MI 49090. Phone: (269) 637-5171. Web: www.blueberryfestival.com.

NATIONAL FRESH BREATH DAY. Aug 6. This is an educational awareness day designed to bring attention to the importance of fresh breath as an integral part of your overall health and wellness. Bad breath is one of life's most personal problems. The goal of the day is to make people confident about their breath and teach them how to achieve and maintain a "Golden Fresh Breath Smile." For info: Linda J. Golden, The Golden Dental Wellness Center, 444 Community Dr, Ste 204, Manhasset, NY 11030. Phone: (516) 627-8400. Fax: (516) 627-9047. Web: www.goldensmile.com.

NATIONAL HOBO CONVENTION. Aug 6–9. Britt, IA. Held since 1900, the National Hobo Convention celebrates current and retired hoboes and the independent lifestyle they lead. Events include the crowning of the Hobo King and Queen, storytelling, flea market, carnival, parade, live entertainment, antique and classic car show, and consumption of the traditional mulligan stew. For info: Britt Chamber of Commerce, PO Box 63, Britt, IA 50423. Phone: (641) 843-3867. E-mail: brittcoc@WCTAtel.net. Web: www.hobo.com/convention.htm.

O'CONNELL, DANIEL: BIRTH ANNIVERSARY. Aug 6, 1775. Irish Catholic political leader Daniel O'Connell, known as "the Liberator" for his role in achieving the right of Catholics to sit in parliament, was born near Cahirciveen, County Kerry. He died at age 81, May 15, 1847, at Genoa, Italy.

PARSONS, LOUELLA: BIRTH ANNIVERSARY. Aug 6, 1881. A legendary Hollywood gossip columnist, the first of her kind, Parsons was born at Freeport, IL. At the height of her popularity and power—from the 1930s to the 1950s—her column appeared in more than 400 newspapers and was read by approximately 20 million people. She gloried in her power and occasionally used her column in spite, making her a woman feared by many in Hollywood whose careers depended on their reputations and positive publicity. Parsons retired in 1965 and died Dec 9, 1972, at Santa Monica, CA.

August 2009	S	M	T	W	T	F	S
							1
	2	3	4	5	6	7	8
	9	10	11	12	13	14	15
	16	17	18	19	20	21	22
	23	24	25	26	27	28	29
	30	31					

RIBFEST. Aug 6–8. Kalamazoo, MI. Features the smell of sizzling ribs as rib-burners from throughout the US tantalize the taste buds of West Michigan. Festival will feature live entertainment, family-oriented events, food booths and the "Best Ribs in Kalamazoo" cook-off. Annually, the first full weekend in August (including Thursday). Est attendance: 30,000. For info: Deborah Droppers, Community Advocates for Persons with Developmental Disabilities, 814 S Westnedge St, Kalamazoo, MI 49008-1162. Phone: (269) 388-2830. E-mail: eventkzoo@chartermi.net. Web: www.ribfestkalamazoo.com.

ROOSEVELT, EDITH KERMIT CAROW: BIRTH ANNIVERSARY. Aug 6, 1861. Second wife of Theodore Roosevelt, 26th president of the US, whom she married in 1886. Born at Norwich, CT, she died at Long Island, NY, Sept 30, 1948.

SPACE MILESTONE: *VOSTOK 2* (USSR). Aug 6, 1961. Launched on Aug 6, 1961, Gherman Titov orbited Earth 17 times over a period of 25 hours, 18 minutes. Titov broadcast messages in passage over countries, controlled spaceship manually for two hours.

TENNYSON, ALFRED, LORD: 200th BIRTH ANNIVERSARY. Aug 6, 1809. English poet born at Somersby, Lincolnshire, England. His celebrated works include the poems "The Lady of Shalott" and "Ulysses" and the verse novelettes *Maud, Enoch Arden, In Memoriam, Locksley Hall Sixty Years After* and *The Idylls of the King*. Appointed English poet laureate in 1850 in succession to William Wordsworth and made a peer in 1884. Died at Aldworth, England, Oct 6, 1892.

VOTING RIGHTS ACT OF 1965 SIGNED: ANNIVERSARY. Aug 6, 1965. Signed into law by President Lyndon Johnson, the Voting Rights Act of 1965 was designed to thwart attempts to discriminate against minorities at the polls. The act suspended literacy and other disqualifying tests, authorized appointment of federal voting examiners and provided for judicial relief on the federal level to bar discriminatory poll taxes. Congress voted to extend the Act in 1975, 1984 and 1991.

WARHOL, ANDY: BIRTH ANNIVERSARY. Aug 6, 1928. The artist, filmmaker and provocateur was born Andrew Warhola to Czech immigrant parents at Forest City, PA. (Some sources cite his birth year as 1927.) A leader of the pop art movement, Warhol challenged the definitions of art. After a stint as a commercial artist, Warhol gained attention in 1962 with paintings of ordinary commercial products—most famously, Campbell's Soup cans—and pop culture figures. He moved on to silk-screen portraits (of subjects such as Marilyn Monroe, Elvis Presley and Mao Tse-tung) and experimental film projects (*Empire* [1964] was a static depiction of the Empire State Building that ran more than eight hours). Warhol was the center of New York's celebrity scene, and in 1968 it was he who claimed, "In the future everyone will be world-famous for fifteen minutes." Warhol died Feb 22, 1987, at New York, NY.

WISCONSIN STATE FAIR. Aug 6–16. State Fair Park, Milwaukee, WI. Wisconsin celebrates its rural heritage at the state's most popular and most historic annual event. Features numerous midway rides, 28 free stages of entertainment, hundreds of animals, wide variety of food and beverages and top-name entertainment. (Call 24-hour recorded information line at 1-800-884-FAIR for up-to-date information.) Est attendance: 910,000. For info: PR Dept, Wisconsin State Fair Park, PO Box 14990, West Allis, WI 53214-0990. Phone: (414) 266-7000. Fax: (414) 266-7007. E-mail: wsfp@sfp.state.wi.us. Web: www.wistatefair.com.

Birthdays Today

Peter Bonerz, 71, actor ("The Bob Newhart Show," "9 to 5"), director, born Portsmouth, NH, Aug 6, 1938.

Soleil Moon Frye, 33, actress ("Punky Brewster"), born Glendora, CA, Aug 6, 1976.

Romola Garai, 27, actress (*I Capture the Castle, Atonement*), born Hong Kong, Aug 6, 1982.

Melissa George, 33, actress ("Alias"), born Perth, Western Australia, Australia, Aug 6, 1976.

Dorian Harewood, 59, actor (*The Falcon and the Snowman, Full Metal Jacket*), born Dayton, OH, Aug 6, 1950.

Catherine Hicks, 58, actress (*Peggy Sue Got Married, Turbulence,* "Seventh Heaven"), born Scottsdale, AZ, Aug 6, 1951.

Shirley Ann Jackson, 63, first woman to chair US Nuclear Regulatory Commission, born Washington, DC, Aug 6, 1946.

David Robinson, 44, former basketball player, born Key West, FL, Aug 6, 1965.

M. Night Shyamalan, 39, filmmaker (*Lady in the Water, Signs, The Sixth Sense*), born Pondicherry, India, Aug 6, 1970.

Michelle Yeoh, 47, actress (*Crouching Tiger, Hidden Dragon; Tomorrow Never Dies*), born Yang Zi Chong at Ipoh, Perak, Malaysia, Aug 6, 1962.

August 7 — Friday

DAY 219 **146 REMAINING**

BLUEBERRY FESTIVAL. Aug 7–8. Library Lawn and Village Green, Montrose, PA. 30th annual fund-raiser for the Susquehanna County Library and Historical Society. Two days filled with food, fun and festivity. Raffles, book sale, children's games, silent auction, hand-stitched quilt, commemorative items and more. Annually, the first Friday and Saturday in August. Est attendance: 5,000. For info: Hilary Caws-Elwitt, Susquehanna County Library, 2 Monument Sq, Montrose, PA 18801. Phone: (570) 278-1881. Fax: (570) 278-9336. E-mail: info@susqcolibrary.org. Web: www.susqcolibrary.org/bluefest.

BLUEGRASS FESTIVAL. Aug 7–9. Grand Targhee Resort, Alta, WY. 22nd annual. Set in a beautiful outdoor venue on a pristine mountainside on the gorgeous western slopes of the Grand Teton Mountains, this festival is three days of incredible bluegrass music featuring national, regional and local talent such as Alison Krauss, Del McCoury Band, Peter Rowan and David Grisman. Also, arts and crafts, food and beverages. Est attendance: 7,000. For info: Mandy Hood, Grand Targhee Resort, 3300 E Ski Hill Rd, Alta, WY 83414. Phone: (800) TAR-GHEE. Fax: (307) 353-8148. E-mail: info@grandtarghee.com. Web: www.grandtarghee.com.

BONDS BREAKS AARON'S CAREER HOME RUN RECORD: ANNIVERSARY. Aug 7, 2007. Barry Bonds of the San Francisco Giants hit his 756th home run to pass Hank Aaron's career record of 755.

BRAHAM PIE DAY. Aug 7. Freedom Park, Braham, MN. Celebrate Braham's status as "Homemade Pie Capital of Minnesota" during this one-day festival. Visitors will find homemade pies, craft displays, pie-eating contests, a pie auction, a pie art show, a pie trivia contest, the "Pie-alluia" chorus and performing artists in Braham's main street park. Est attendance: 4,000. For info: Braham Pie Day, 2nd St SW, PO Box 383, Braham, MN 55006. Phone: (320) 396-4956. E-mail: varrow2@ecenet.com. Web: www.braham.com or www.pieday.com.

BUNCHE, RALPH JOHNSON: BIRTH ANNIVERSARY. Aug 7, 1904. American statesman, UN official, Nobel Peace Prize recipient (the first black to win the award), born at Detroit, MI. Died Dec 9, 1971, at New York, NY. See also: "Ralph Bunche Awarded Nobel Peace Prize: Anniversary" (Dec 10).

CANADA: ABBOTSFORD INTERNATIONAL AIRSHOW. Aug 7–9. Abbotsford Airport, Abbotsford, BC. "Canada's National Airshow," 47th annual. Leading air show in North America attracts the world's top aeronautical performers. Thrill to the grace of the Canadian Snowbirds, the raw power of the international air demonstration squadrons, dramatic teams of daring performers and soloists. Static displays and food booths. Open daily 8–6; aerial show 10–5. Airshow camping facilities. Est attendance: 160,000. For info: Abbotsford Intl Airshow, 1276 Tower St, Unit #4, Abbotsford, BC, Canada V2T 6H5. E-mail: info@abbotsfordairshow.com. Web: www.abbotsfordairshow.com.

CANADA: HALIFAX INTERNATIONAL BUSKER FESTIVAL. Aug 7–15. Halifax, NS. Street performers and artists from around the world, vaudeville nights and entertainment tent. Annually, beginning the first Friday after Natal Day (first Monday in August). Est attendance: 450,000. For info: Halifax Intl Busker Fest, c/o Pickford & Black, 1869 Upper Water St, 5th Fl, Halifax, NS, Canada B3J 1S9. Phone: (902) 429-1068. Fax: (902) 429-7554. E-mail: jessica@espproductions.ca. Web: www.buskers.ca.

COLOMBIA: BATTLE OF BOYACÁ DAY. Aug 7. National holiday. Commemorates victory over Spanish forces in 1819.

CÔTE D'IVOIRE: NATIONAL DAY. Aug 7. Commemorates the independence of the Ivory Coast from France in 1960.

CRAFTSMEN'S CLASSIC ARTS & CRAFTS FESTIVAL. Aug 7–9. Myrtle Beach Convention Center, Myrtle Beach, SC. 27th annual. Features work from more than 260 talented artists and craftspeople. All juried exhibitors' work has been handmade by the exhibitors and must be their own original design and creation. See the creative process in action with several exhibitors demonstrating throughout the weekend. Something for every style, taste and budget with items from the most contemporary to the most traditional. Est attendance: 15,000. For info: Gilmore Enterprises, Inc, 3514-A Drawbridge Pkwy, Greensboro, NC 27410-8584. Phone: (336) 282-5550. E-mail: contact@gilmoreshows.com. Web: www.CraftShow.com or www.gilmoreshows.com.

DESERT SHIELD: ANNIVERSARY. Aug 7, 1990. Five days after the Iraqi invasion of Kuwait, US president George H.W. Bush ordered the military buildup that would become known as Desert Shield to prevent further Iraqi advances.

GINZA HOLIDAY: JAPANESE CULTURAL FESTIVAL. Aug 7–9. Midwest Buddhist Temple, Chicago, IL. Experience the Waza (National Treasures tradition) by viewing 300 years of Edo craft tradition and seeing it come alive as master craftspeople from Tokyo demonstrate their arts. Japanese folk and classical dancing, martial arts, *taiko* (drums), flower arrangements and cultural displays. Chicken teriyaki, sushi, *udon*, shaved ice, corn on the cob and refreshments. Annually, the second weekend in August. Est attendance: 15,000. For info: Office Secretary, Midwest Buddhist Temple, 435 W Menomonee St, Chicago, IL 60614. Phone: (312) 943-7801. Fax: (312) 943-8069.

GREAT RIVER TUG FEST. Aug 7–8. Port Byron, IL, and LeClaire, IA. 23rd annual. The Tug is the only tug-of-war across the mighty Mississippi River or any other moving body of water in the world. For two hours barge traffic, pleasure boats and gambling and paddle boats yield the right of way to a 400-foot, 680-pound rope that stretches between Illinois and Iowa. At 1 PM Saturday, the first team of 20 tuggers grip the rope, the crowd counts down and dirt starts flying! Festivals on both sides of the river Friday and Saturday. Fireworks Friday evening. Annually, the second weekend in August. For info: Great River Tug Fest. Phone: (563) 289-3946 or (309) 523-

3734. Web: www.tugfest.com. For info on the Quad Cities: Quad Cities CVB. Phone: (800) 747-7800. Web: www.visitquadcities.com.

GREENE, NATHANIEL: BIRTH ANNIVERSARY. Aug 7, 1742. (Old Style date.) Born at Patowomut, RI, American Revolutionary War general Nathaniel Greene was described as the "ablest military officer of the Revolution under Washington." Greene died at Savannah, GA, June 19, 1786.

GULF OF TONKIN RESOLUTION: 45th ANNIVERSARY. Aug 7, 1964. Congress approved the "Gulf of Tonkin Resolution," pertaining to the war in Vietnam, which gave President Lyndon Johnson authority "to take all necessary measures to repel any armed attack against the forces of the United States and to prevent further aggression."

HATFIELD-McCOY FEUD ERUPTS: ANNIVERSARY. Aug 7–9, 1882. The long-simmering tension between two Appalachian families who lived by Tug Fork on the Kentucky–West Virginia border erupted into full-scale violence on Election Day 1882. Brothers Tolbert, Pharmer and Randolph McCoy knifed and shot Ellison Hatfield. The Hatfield family captured the three McCoys. When Ellison Hatfield died on Aug 9, the Hatfields executed the brothers. The feud continued with much loss of life. In 1888, when Kentucky authorities sought to detain feud murder suspects and West Virginia authorities complained, the dispute went all the way to the US Supreme Court, which decided in Kentucky's favor. The feud sputtered out by the end of the century.

INDIANA STATE FAIR. Aug 7–23. Indiana State Fairgrounds, Indianapolis, IN. Top-rated livestock exhibition, world-class harness racing, top music and entertainment, giant midway and Pioneer Village. Est attendance: 850,000. For info: Andy Klotz, Public Relations Dir, Indiana State Fair, 1202 E 38th St, Indianapolis, IN 46205-2869. Phone: (317) 927-7524. Fax: (317) 927-7578. Web: www.indianastatefair.com.

ISING, RUDOLF C.: BIRTH ANNIVERSARY. Aug 7, 1903. Rudolf C. Ising, cocreator with Hugh Harmon of "Looney Tunes" and "Merrie Melodies," was born at Kansas City, MO. Ising and Harmon's initial production, "Bosko the Talk-Ink Kid" (1929), was the first talkie cartoon synchronizing dialogue on the soundtrack with the action on screen. Ising received an Academy Award in 1940 for *Milky Way*, a cartoon about three kittens. During WWII he headed the animation division for the Army Air Corps movie unit developing training films. Rudolf Ising died July 18, 1992, at Newport Beach, CA.

LOVE CANAL DECLARED DISASTER AREA: ANNIVERSARY. Aug 7, 1978. President Jimmy Carter declared Love Canal, a section of Niagara Falls, NY, to be a disaster area. Residents had begun evacuation Aug 4. A nearby chemical company had dumped toxic waste into the canal between 1947 and 1952.

MATA HARI: BIRTH ANNIVERSARY. Aug 7, 1876. Mata Hari (child of the dawn) was born Margaret Gertrude Zelle at Leeuwarden, Netherlands. Her spectacular career as a dancer, courtesan and spy made her known around the world. Probably an ineffective double agent, she nevertheless fascinated royalty and high officials of several countries. Arrested as a German spy (Agent H-21) in a Paris hotel, Feb 13, 1917, she was tried, convicted and sentenced to death. The greatest of her many roles was the final one—when she refused a blindfold and threw a kiss to the firing squad at Vincennes, France, Oct 15, 1917.

MONTANAFAIR. Aug 7–15. MetraPark, Billings, MT. Montana's biggest event featuring exhibits, livestock events, carnival, rodeo and entertainment. Est attendance: 240,000. For info: MetraPark, PO Box 2514, Billings, MT 59103. Phone: (406) 256-2400. Web: www.metrapark.com or www.montanafair.com.

August 2009

S	M	T	W	T	F	S
						1
2	3	4	5	6	7	8
9	10	11	12	13	14	15
16	17	18	19	20	21	22
23	24	25	26	27	28	29
30	31					

MONTGOMERY COUNTY AGRICULTURAL FAIR. Aug 7–15. Gaithersburg, MD. 61st annual. Maryland's largest county fair, family-oriented entertainment, farm animals, arts and crafts exhibits of all types, many contests, carnival rides, grandstand entertainment to include demolition derby, horse events and musical performances. Est attendance: 250,000. For info: Montgomery County Agricultural Fair, 16 Chestnut St, Gaithersburg, MD 20877. Phone: (301) 926-3100. Fax: (301) 926-1532. Web: www.mcagfair.com.

MUSIKFEST. Aug 7–16. Bethlehem, PA. Entertainment, ethnic foods and music—more than 300 performers on 14 indoor and outdoor stages. Est attendance: 1,000,000. For info: ArtsQuest, 25 W Third St, Bethlehem, PA 18015-1238. Phone: (610) 332-1300. Fax: (610) 861-2644. E-mail: info@fest.org. Web: www.musikfest.org.

PARTICULARLY PREPOSTEROUS PACKAGING DAY. Aug 7. Buy anything lately? Did you succeed in getting the durn thing open? What do older people do when even mainstream society can't open a simple bottle of aspirin, let alone a milk carton? Annually, Aug 7. (©2006 by WH.) For info: Thomas & Ruth Roy, Wellcat Holidays, 2418 Long Ln, Lebanon, PA 17046. Phone: (717) 279-0184. E-mail: info@wellcat.com. Web: www.wellcat.com.

PROFESSIONAL SPEAKERS DAY. Aug 7. A day celebrating the consummate professionals who help people through their oratorical skills. For info: Jim Barber, 1101 Marcano Blvd, Plantation, FL 33322. Phone: (954) 476-9252. Fax: (954) 424-0309. E-mail: pro.speaker.day@thebarbershop.com. Web: www.professionalspeakersday.com.

PURPLE HEART: ANNIVERSARY. Aug 7, 1782. At Newburgh, NY, General George Washington ordered the creation of a Badge of Military Merit. The badge consisted of a purple cloth heart with silver braided edge. Only three are known to have been awarded during the Revolutionary War. The award was reinstituted on the bicentennial of Washington's birth, Feb 22, 1932, and recognizes those wounded in action.

SCOTLAND: EDINBURGH FESTIVAL FRINGE. Aug 7–31. Edinburgh. The largest arts gathering in the world. Three weeks of nonstop entertainment with more than 1,800 different events in 250 venues around the city, including theater, comedy, dance, music and children's shows. Est attendance: 750,000. For info: Edinburgh Festival Fringe, 180 High St, Edinburgh, Scotland EH1 1QS. Phone: (44) (131) 226-0026. Fax: (44) (131) 226-0016. E-mail: admin@edfringe.com. Web: www.edfringe.com.

SCOTLAND: EDINBURGH MILITARY TATTOO: THE MAIN EVENT. Aug 7–29. Edinburgh Castle, Edinburgh, Lothian. Display of military color and pageantry held at night on the floodlit esplanade of Edinburgh Castle. A unique blend of music, ceremony, entertainment and theater. Est attendance: 217,000. For info: The Edinburgh Military Tattoo, The Tattoo Office, 32 Market St, Edinburgh, Scotland EH1 1QB. Phone: (44) (131) 225-1188. Fax: (44) (131) 225-8627. E-mail: tickets@edintattoo.co.uk. Web: www.edintattoo.co.uk.

SPACE MILESTONE: FIRST PICTURE OF EARTH FROM SPACE: 50th ANNIVERSARY. Aug 7, 1959. US satellite *Explorer VI* transmitted the first picture of Earth from space. For the first time we had a likeness of our planet based on more than projections and conjectures.

TETONKAHA RENDEZVOUS. Aug 7–9. Hole in the Mountain County Park, Lake Benton, MN. Presents the fur-trading atmosphere of the 1840s. Muzzle-loader contest, tomahawk and knife throw, log sawing, canoe races, kids' games. Est attendance: 300. For info: Dave Huebner, Brookings Renegade Muzzle Loaders, 47826 Main St, Bushnell, SD 57276. Phone: (605) 693-4589.

TWINS DAY FESTIVAL. Aug 7–9. Twinsburg, OH. 34th festival. According to *Guinness Book of World Records*, this is the world's largest gathering of twins. Annually, the first full weekend in August. For info: Twins Day Festival Committee, 9825 Ravenna Rd, Twinsburg, OH 44087. Phone: (330) 425-3652. E-mail: info@twinsdays.org. Web: www.twinsdays.org.

US WAR DEPARTMENT ESTABLISHED: ANNIVERSARY. Aug 7, 1789. The second presidential cabinet department, the War Department, was established by Congress.

Birthdays Today

Sidney Crosby, 22, hockey player, born Cole Harbour, NS, Canada, Aug 7, 1987.

David Duchovny, 49, actor ("The X-Files," "Californication"), born New York, NY, Aug 7, 1960.

Stan Freberg, 83, satirist, born Pasadena, CA, Aug 7, 1926.

John Glover, 65, actor (stage: *Great God Brown; Julia, Melvin and Howard*), born Salisbury, MD, Aug 7, 1944.

Garrison Keillor, 67, humorist, producer, host ("The Prairie Home Companion"), author (*Lake Wobegon Days*), born Anoka, MN, Aug 7, 1942.

DeLane Matthews, 48, actress ("Dave's World"), born Rockledge, FL, Aug 7, 1961.

Harold Parrineau, 46, actor ("Lost," "Oz"), born Brooklyn, NY, Aug 7, 1963.

Alberto Salazar, 52, marathon runner, born Havana, Cuba, Aug 7, 1957.

Charlize Theron, 34, actress (Oscar for *Monster*; *In the Valley of Elah, Aeon Flux, The Italian Job*), born Benoni, South Africa, Aug 7, 1975.

Billy Joe (B.J.) Thomas, 67, singer ("Raindrops Keep Falling on My Head"), born Houston, TX, Aug 7, 1942.

August 8 — Saturday

DAY 220 145 REMAINING

ANTIQUE SHOW. Aug 8. Somerset, PA. 39th annual. More than 100 vendors dealing in quality antiques and collectibles. Est attendance: 5,000. For info: Sandy Berkebile, Somerset County Chamber of Commerce, 601 N Center Ave, Somerset, PA 15501. Phone: (814) 445-6431. E-mail: info@somersetcountychamber.com.

BONZA BOTTLER DAY™. Aug 8. To celebrate when the number of the day is the same as the number of the month. Bonza Bottler Day™ is an excuse to have a party at least once a month. For more information see Jan 1. For info: Gail M. Berger, 14 Fernwood Dr, Taylors, SC 29687. E-mail: bonza@bonzabottlerday.com. Web: www.bonzabottlerday.com.

BUD BILLIKEN PARADE. Aug 8. Chicago, IL. 80th annual parade especially for children begun in 1929 by Robert S. Abbott. The second-largest parade in the US, it features bands, floats, drill teams and celebrities. There are 65,000 participants and 1.5 million spectators—plus another 25 million watching on TV. Annually, the second Saturday in August. Est attendance: 1,500,000. For info: Chicago Defender Charities, 700 E Oakwood Blvd, 5th Fl, Chicago, IL 60616. Phone: (773) 536-3710. Fax: (773) 536-3718. E-mail: budbillikenparade@sbcglobal.net. Web: budbillikenparade.com.

COUPEVILLE ARTS AND CRAFTS FESTIVAL. Aug 8–9. Coupeville, WA. 46th annual. One of the longest-running arts festivals in the Pacific Northwest. Features handcrafted items from carefully selected artisans, fine arts, live entertainment, activities for the kids and food. Proceeds are donated to the community in the form of grants and scholarships. Located on the historic waterfront of Coupeville. Est attendance: 20,000. For info: Coupeville Arts and Crafts Festival, PO Box 611, Coupeville, WA 98239. Phone: (360) 678-5116. E-mail: info@coupevilleartsandcraftsfestival.org. Web: www.coupevilleartsandcraftsfestival.org.

CRATER LAKE RIM RUNS AND MARATHON. Aug 8. Crater Lake National Park, OR. 34th annual. One of the toughest and most spectacular races you'll ever run! Race routes are around Crater Lake, the deepest lake in the US. Included are a 6.7-mile walk and 6.7-mile run and a 13-mile run (half marathon) and a full marathon. The field is limited to 500 competitors. Annually, the second Saturday in August. For info: Crater Lake Rim Runs, 5830 Mack Ave, Klamath Falls, OR 97603. Phone: (541) 884-6939. E-mail: rimruns@aol.com or info@craterlakerimruns.com. Web: www.craterlakerimruns.com.

THE DATE TO CREATE. Aug 8. A day to increase awareness of individual and organizational potential to solve problems and make things happen. All of us have this potential but may not realize it. Learn your innovative capacity and plan activities that increase it. Rediscover your creative spark. Annually, Aug 8. For info: Diane Decker. Phone: (847) 394-0994. E-mail: dcdecker@msn.com. Web: www.qualitytransitions.com.

ELEANOR ROOSEVELT DAY. Aug 8–10. Raymond, WA. Sponsored by the Willapa Chapter of DAWN (Domestic Abuse Women's Net) and the Northwest Carriage Museum. Three days celebrating a great woman's life. Annually, the long weekend ending in the second Monday in August. Established in 1995 by the National Grange. For info: Exec Dir Patricia Martin, Willapa DAWN, PO Box 878, Raymond, WA 98577-0878. Phone: (360) 942-9761. E-mail: execdir@willapachapterdawn.org. Web: www.willapadawn.net.

ELVIS WEEK. Aug 8–16. Memphis, TN. Each year Elvis fans from around the world visit Memphis to celebrate the King of Rock and Roll® at his beloved home, Graceland Mansion. Events occur throughout the city with special events sponsored by Graceland. A commemoration of the music, magic and memories associated with the legacy of Elvis Presley. Est attendance: 75,000. For info: Graceland, 3734 Elvis Presley Blvd, Memphis, TN 38116. Phone: (800) 238-2000 or (901) 332-3322. Web: www.elvisweek.com.

HAPPINESS HAPPENS DAY. Aug 8. This day celebrates the 11th birthday of the Secret Society of Happy People by encouraging the expression of happiness and discouraging parade-raining. Suggested celebration activities are available on our website. For info: Secret Society of Happy People, 425 Busher Dr, Lewisville, TX 75067. Phone: (972) 459-7031. E-mail: pamelagail@sohp.com. Web: www.sohp.com.

HENSON, MATTHEW A.: BIRTH ANNIVERSARY. Aug 8, 1866. African-American explorer, born at Charles County, MD. He met Robert E. Peary while working in a Washington, DC, store in 1888 and was hired to be Peary's valet. He accompanied Peary on his seven subsequent Arctic expeditions. During the successful 1908–09 expedition to the North Pole, Henson and two of the four Eskimo guides reached their destination Apr 6, 1909. Peary arrived minutes later and verified the location. Henson's account of the expedition, *A Negro Explorer at the North Pole*, was published in 1912. In addition to the Congressional Medal awarded all members of the North Pole expedition, Henson received the Gold Medal of the Geographical Society of Chicago and, at 81, was made an honorary member of the Explorers Club at New York, NY. Died Mar 9, 1955, at New York.

INTER-STATE FAIR AND RODEO. Aug 8–15. Coffeyville, KS. "Largest outdoor fair and rodeo event in southeast Kansas and northeast Oklahoma." Includes truck and tractor pull, concerts, demo derby, four nights of PRCA rodeo and livestock shows. Est attendance: 75,000. For info: Montgomery County Fair Assn, Box 457, Coffeyville, KS 67337. Phone: (620) 251-2550. Fax: (620) 251-5448. E-mail: fairandrodeo@coffeyville.com. Web: www.fairandrodeo.com.

JOURS DE FÊTE (DAYS OF CELEBRATION). Aug 8–9. Ste. Genevieve, MO. Celebration of town's French heritage. Tours of historic homes dating to the 1700s that exemplify some of the finest French Creole architecture. Also more than 600 arts and crafts booths and colonial crafts demonstrations by authentically costumed crafters. Annually, the second full weekend of August. Est attendance: 40,000. For info: Ste. Genevieve Tourist Info Center, 66 S Main, Ste. Genevieve, MO 63670. Phone: (573) 883-7097 or (800) 373-7007. E-mail: sgtourism@brick.net.

MARCH, FREDRIC: BIRTH ANNIVERSARY. Aug 8, 1897. Award-winning actor born Frederick McIntyre Bickel at Racine, WI. Over the course of his long and distinguished career, March performed on both the stage and screen. He made more than 65 movies and was nominated for five Academy Awards, winning in 1932 for his role in *Dr. Jekyll and Mr Hyde* and in 1947 for *The Best Years of Our Lives*. In 1956 he appeared on stage in the world premiere of Eugene O'Neill's *Long Day's Journey into Night*. He received the Tony Award for that performance. He died Apr 14, 1975, at Los Angeles, CA.

MARKERT, RUSSELL: BIRTH ANNIVERSARY. Aug 8, 1899. American choreographer Russell Markert was born at Jersey City, NJ. He founded the Radio City Music Hall Rockettes and directed them from 1932 to 1971. He died Dec 1, 1990, at Waterbury, CT.

MORRIS, ESTHER HOBART McQUIGG: BIRTH ANNIVERSARY. Aug 8, 1814. Esther Hobart McQuigg Morris was born at Tioga County, NY, but eventually moved to the Wyoming Territory, where she worked in the women's rights movement and had a key role in getting a women's suffrage bill passed. Morris became justice of the peace of South Pass City, WY, in 1870, one of the first times a woman held public office in the US. She represented Wyoming at the national suffrage convention in 1895. She died Apr 2, 1902, at Cheyenne, WY.

NATIONAL GARAGE SALE DAY. Aug 8. A day to turn the nation into a giant shopping mall! Annually, the second Saturday in August. (Copyright © 2001.) For info: C. Daniel Rhodes, 1900 Crossvine Rd, Hoover, AL 35244. Phone: (205) 908-6781. E-mail: rhodan@charter.net.

ODIE: BIRTHDAY. Aug 8, 1978. Commemorates the birthday of Odie, Garfield's sidekick, who first appeared in the "Garfield" comic strip Aug 8, 1978. For info: Odie's Birthday. Web: www.garfield.com.

PENNSYLVANIA RENAISSANCE FAIRE. Aug 8–Oct 24 (Saturdays, Sundays, Labor Day). Manheim, PA. Re-creation of 16th-century Elizabethan village. Lords and ladies, mongers, merchants, jousting, human chess match, medieval foods and crafts. Est attendance: 200,000. For info: Thomas Roy, Mount Hope Estate and Winery, 2775 Lebanon Rd, Manheim, PA 17545-8711. Phone: (717) 665-7021. Fax: (717) 664-3466. E-mail: Tom@parenfaire.com. Web: www.parenfaire.com.

RAWLINGS, MARJORIE KINNAN: BIRTH ANNIVERSARY. Aug 8, 1896. American short-story writer and novelist (*The Yearling*), born at Washington, DC. Rawlings died at St. Augustine, FL, Dec 14, 1953.

SECOND BATTLE OF AMIENS: ANNIVERSARY. Aug 8, 1918. Two days after the Battle of Marne ended, the British Fourth Army mounted an offensive at Amiens with the objective of freeing the Amiens-Paris railway from bombardment by the German Second and Eighteenth Armies. More than 16,000 German prisoners were taken in two hours of fighting the first day. The German forces were forced back to the Hindenburg line by Sept 3. This battle is considered a turning point by many historians because of its impact on the psyche of Germany. Aug 8 was described by General Erich Ludendorff as a "Black Day" for Germany.

SHILTS, RANDY: BIRTH ANNIVERSARY. Aug 8, 1951. Journalist known for his reporting on the AIDS epidemic. One of the first openly homosexual journalists to work for a mainstream newspaper and the author of *And the Band Played On: Politics, People and the AIDS Epidemic*. Born at Davenport, IA, and died at Guerneville, CA, Feb 17, 1994.

SNEAK SOME ZUCCHINI ONTO YOUR NEIGHBORS' PORCH NIGHT. Aug 8. Due to overzealous planting of zucchini, citizens are asked to drop off baskets of the squash on neighbors' doorsteps. Annually, Aug 8. (©2006 by WH.) For info: Thomas & Ruth Roy, Wellcat Holidays, 2418 Long Ln, Lebanon, PA 17046. Phone: (717) 279-0184. E-mail: info@wellcat.com. Web: www.wellcat.com.

SPACE MILESTONE: *GENESIS* (US). Aug 8, 2001. The robotic explorer *Genesis* was launched on a mission to gather tiny particles of the sun. Its three-year, 20-million-mile round-trip mission was to shed light on the origin of the solar system. It traveled to a spot where the gravitational pulls of the sun and Earth are equal and gathered atoms from the solar wind hurtling by. But on Sept 8, 2004, the *Genesis* return capsule crashed in a western US desert and most of its solar samples were destroyed.

SPACE MILESTONE: *PIONEER VENUS MULTIPROBE* (US). Aug 8, 1978. Launch of second craft in Pioneer Venus program. Split into five and probed Venus atmosphere Dec 9.

STREETSCENE. Aug 8. Covington, VA. Car show, open to all types of vehicles. Entertainment throughout the day. Annually, the second Saturday in August. Est attendance: 8,000. For info: Kars Unlimited, Inc, PO Box 851, Covington, VA 24426. Phone: (540) 962-3642.

TANZANIA: FARMERS' DAY. Aug 8. National holiday. Also called "Nane Nane" (8–8).

WATERMELON FESTIVAL. Aug 8. Rush Springs, OK. Beginning with watermelon judging and ending with the crowning of the festival queen, the celebration is highlighted by the serving of 50,000 pounds of free watermelon at Jeff Davis Park. Annually, the second Saturday in August. Est attendance: 20,000. For info: Rush Springs Lions Club, PO Box 1137, Rush Springs, OK 73082. Phone: (580) 476-3519 or (580) 476-3255.

WYOMING STATE FAIR AND RODEO. Aug 8–15. Douglas, WY. 97th annual. Recognizing the products, achievements and cultural heritage of the people of Wyoming. Bringing together rural and urban citizens for an inexpensive, entertaining and educational experience. Features Livestock Shows for beef, goats, swine, sheep and horses; Junior Livestock Shows for beef, swine, sheep, horses, goats, dogs, poultry and rabbits; competitions and displays for culinary arts, needlework, visual arts, and floriculture; 4-H and FFA County/Chapters State qualification competitions; Demo Derby, live entertainment, carnival, PRCA Rodeo, Ranch Rodeo and an Antique Tractor Pull. Est attendance: 47,000. For info: Wyoming State Fair, PO Drawer 10, Douglas, WY 82633. Phone: (307) 358-2398. Fax: (307) 358-6030. E-mail: wsf@netcommander.com. Web: www.wystatefair.com.

August 2009

S	M	T	W	T	F	S
						1
2	3	4	5	6	7	8
9	10	11	12	13	14	15
16	17	18	19	20	21	22
23	24	25	26	27	28	29
30	31					

Birthdays Today

Keith Carradine, 59, actor (*Nashville, Will Rogers Follies,* "Deadwood"), singer, born San Mateo, CA, Aug 8, 1950.

Dino De Laurentiis, 90, producer, born Torre Annunziata, Italy, Aug 8, 1919.

The Edge, 48, musician (U2), born David Evans at East London, England, Aug 8, 1961.

Roger Federer, 28, tennis player, born Basel, Switzerland, Aug 8, 1981.

Dustin Hoffman, 72, actor (Oscars for *Rain Man* and *Kramer vs. Kramer; The Graduate, Midnight Cowboy, Outbreak*), born Los Angeles, CA, Aug 8, 1937.

Drew Lachey, 33, singer (98 Degrees), television personality ("Dancing with the Stars"), born Cincinatti, OH, Aug 8, 1976.

Deborah Norville, 51, TV host ("Inside Edition"), born Dalton, GA, Aug 8, 1958.

Roberta Cooper Ramo, 67, first woman president of the American Bar Association, born Denver, CO, Aug 8, 1942.

Ed Schafer, 63, US Secretary of Agriculture, born Bismarck, ND, Aug 8, 1946.

Connie Stevens, 71, actress ("Hawaiian Eye"), born Brooklyn, NY, Aug 8, 1938.

Mel Tillis, 77, singer, songwriter, born Pahokee, FL, Aug 8, 1932.

Michael Urie, 29, actor ("Ugly Betty"), born Dallas, TX, Aug 8, 1980.

Esther Williams, 86, swimmer, actress (*Take Me Out to the Ball Game, Dangerous When Wet*), born Los Angeles, CA, Aug 8, 1923.

August 9 — Sunday

DAY 221 — **144 REMAINING**

ASSISTANCE DOG WEEK. Aug 9–15. Assistance dogs transform the lives of their human partners with debilitating physical and mental disabilities by serving as a companion, helper, aide, best friend and close member of the family. Assistance dogs include service dogs, guide dogs, hearing alert dogs and alert/seizure response dogs. They can be from a variety of breeds including, but not limited to, Labrador retrievers, golden retrievers and standard poodles, as well as shelter dogs. Please celebrate the selfless love and devotion these dogs so humbly provide to their disabled partners by observing Assistance Dog Week. Annually, the second full week in August. For info: Marcie Davis, 59 Wildflower Way, Santa Fe, NM 87506. Phone: (505) 424-6631. Fax: (505) 424-6632. E-mail: mdavis@workinglikedogs.com. Web: www.workinglikedogs.com.

ATOMIC BOMB DROPPED ON NAGASAKI: ANNIVERSARY. Aug 9, 1945. Three days after the atomic bombing of Hiroshima, an American B-29 bomber named *Bock's Car* left its base on Tinian Island carrying a plutonium bomb nicknamed "Fat Man." Its target was the Japanese city of Kokura, but because of clouds and poor visibility, the bomber headed for a secondary target, Nagasaki, where at 11:02 AM, local time, it dropped the bomb, killing an estimated 70,000 persons and destroying about half the city. Memorial services are held annually at Nagasaki and also at Kokura, where those who were spared because of the bad weather also grieve for those at Nagasaki who suffered in their stead.

COCHRAN, JACQUELINE: DEATH ANNIVERSARY. Aug 9, 1980. American pilot Jacqueline Cochran was born at Pensacola, FL, about 1910. She began flying in 1932 and by the time of her death, she had set more distance, speed and altitude records than any other pilot, male or female. She was founder and head of the WASPs (Women's Air Force Service Pilots) during WWII; she won the Distinguished Service Medal in 1945 and the US Air Force Distinguished Flying Cross in 1969. She died at Indio, CA.

HERBERT HOOVER DAY. Aug 9. Iowa. Annually, the Sunday nearest Aug 10, the birthday of Herbert Hoover.

ITALY: PALIO DEL GOLFO. Aug 9. La Spezia. A rowing contest over a 2,000-meter course is held on the second Sunday in August.

JAPAN: MOMENT OF SILENCE. Aug 9. Nagasaki. Memorial observance held at Peace Memorial Park for victims of second atomic bomb, which was dropped on Nagasaki by an American bomber Aug 9, 1945.

LASSEN VOLCANIC NATIONAL PARK ESTABLISHED: ANNIVERSARY. Aug 9, 1916. California's Lassen Peak and Cinder Cone National Monument, proclaimed May 6, 1907, and other wilderness land were combined and established as a national park. For further park info: Lassen Volcanic Natl Park, Mineral, CA 96063.

NATIONAL RESURRECT ROMANCE WEEK. Aug 9–15. Event focuses on celebrating creative romance. Encourages men and women to find ways to be romantic every day this week by using their hearts. For info: Michael Webb, The Romantic, PO Box 1567, Cary, NC 27512. Phone: (919) 859-9123. E-mail: michael@theromantic.com.

NIXON RESIGNS: 35th ANNIVERSARY. Aug 9, 1974. The resignation from the presidency of the US by Richard Milhous Nixon, which had been announced in a speech to the American people the night before, became effective at noon. Nixon, under threat of impeachment as a result of the Watergate scandal, became the first US president to resign.

PERSEID METEOR SHOWERS. Aug 9–13. Among the best-known and most spectacular meteor showers are the Perseids, peaking about Aug 10–12. As many as 50–100 may be seen in a single night. Wish upon a "falling star"!

ROBERT GRAY BECOMES FIRST AMERICAN TO CIRCUMNAVIGATE EARTH: ANNIVERSARY. Aug 9, 1790. When Robert Gray docked the *Columbia* at Boston Harbor, he became the first American to circumnavigate Earth. He sailed from Boston, MA, in September 1787, to trade with Indians of the Pacific Northwest. From there he sailed to China and then continued around the world. His 42,000-mile journey opened trade between New England and the Pacific Northwest and helped the US establish claims to the Oregon Territory.

SHEEP HERDING WITH BORDER COLLIES. Aug 9. Billings Farm and Museum, Woodstock, VT. This daylong event focuses on the many aspects of wool production, including sheep herding, and features many hands-on activities for all ages to enjoy. Border collie demonstrations will show how these natural shepherds efficiently round up sheep, drive them from one area to another and corral them. Est attendance: 700. For info: Billings Farm and Museum, Rte 12 N, Woodstock, VT 05091. Phone: (802) 457-2355. Fax: (802) 457-4663. E-mail: info@billingsfarm.org. Web: www.billingsfarm.org.

SINGAPORE: NATIONAL DAY. Aug 9, 1965. Most festivals in Singapore are Chinese, Indian or Malay, but celebration of National Day is shared by all to commemorate the withdrawal of Singapore from Malaysia and its becoming an independent state in 1965. Music, parades, dancing.

SOUTH AFRICA: NATIONAL WOMEN'S DAY. Aug 9. National holiday. Commemorates the march of women in Pretoria to protest the pass laws in 1956.

TRAVIS, WILLIAM BARRET: 200th BIRTH ANNIVERSARY. Aug 9, 1809. Born at Saluda County, SC, Travis was one of many young American men who sought fortune in the Mexican territory of Texas. Swept up in the burgeoning revolutionary activities by American settlers to secede from Mexico, Travis found himself at the age of 26 commander of a small band of volunteer troops at the Alamo at San Antonio, TX. Mexican troops, commanded by General Santa Anna, overwhelmed the small force on Mar 6, 1836, and all Texans were killed.

UNITED NATIONS: INTERNATIONAL DAY OF THE WORLD'S INDIGENOUS PEOPLE. Aug 9. On Dec 23, 1994, the General Assembly decided that the International Day of the World's Indigenous People be observed Aug 9 every year during the International Decade of the World's Indigenous People (1994–2004) (Resolution 49/214). On Dec 20, 2004, the assembly proclaimed the Second International Decade of the World's Indigenous People (2005–14); it also decided to continue observing the day every year during the Second Decade (Resolution 59/1740). For info: United Nations, Dept of Public Info, Public Inquiries Unit, Rm GA-57, New York, NY 10017. Phone: (212) 963-4475. E-mail: inquiries@un.org.

VEEP DAY. Aug 9. Commemorates the day in 1974 when Richard Nixon's resignation let Gerald Ford succeed to the presidency of the US. This was the first time the new Constitutional provisions for presidential succession took effect. For info: Bob Birch, The Puns Corps, 3108 Dashiell Rd, Falls Church, VA 22042. Phone: (703) 533-3668.

WALTON, IZAAK: BIRTH ANNIVERSARY. Aug 9, 1593. (Old Style date.) English author of classic treatise on fishing, *The Compleat Angler*, published in 1653, was born at Stafford, England. Died at Winchester, England, Dec 15, 1683 (OS). "Angling," Walton wrote, "may be said to be so like the mathematics that it can never be fully learnt."

WEBSTER-ASHBURTON TREATY SIGNED: ANNIVERSARY. Aug 9, 1842. The treaty delimiting the eastern section of the Canadian-American border was negotiated by the US secretary of state, Daniel Webster, and Alexander Baring, president of the British Board of Trade. The treaty established the boundaries between the St. Croix and Connecticut rivers, between Lake Superior and the Lake of the Woods and between Lakes Huron and Superior. The treaty was signed at Washington, DC.

Birthdays Today

Gillian Anderson, 41, actress ("The X-Files," *The House of Mirth*, "Bleak House"), born Chicago, IL, Aug 9, 1968.

Eric Bana, 41, actor (*Hulk, Munich*), born Melbourne, Australia, Aug 9, 1968.

Amanda Bearse, 51, actress ("Married . . . With Children"), born Winter Park, FL, Aug 9, 1958.

Robert Joseph (Bob) Cousy, 81, Hall of Fame basketball player, former coach, born New York, NY, Aug 9, 1928.

Sam Elliott, 65, actor ("Mission Impossible," *Gettysburg*), born Sacramento, CA, Aug 9, 1944.

Melanie Griffith, 52, actress (*Working Girl, Something Wild, Milk Money*), born New York, NY, Aug 9, 1957.

Chamique Holdsclaw, 32, former basketball player, born Astoria, NY, Aug 9, 1977.

Whitney Houston, 46, singer, actress (*Waiting to Exhale*), born Newark, NJ, Aug 9, 1963.

Brett Hull, 45, hockey player, born Belleville, ON, Canada, Aug 9, 1964.

Rodney George (Rod) Laver, 71, former tennis player, born Rockhampton, Australia, Aug 9, 1938.

Kenneth Howard (Ken) Norton, Sr, 64, former boxer, born Jacksonville, IL, Aug 9, 1945.

Deion Sanders, 42, former football player, former baseball player, born Fort Myers, FL, Aug 9, 1967.

David Steinberg, 67, comedian ("The David Steinberg Show"), born Winnipeg, MB, Canada, Aug 9, 1942.

Audrey Tautou, 33, actress (*Amélie, The Da Vinci Code*), born Beaumont, Puy-de-Dôme, France, Aug 9, 1976.

August 2009

S	M	T	W	T	F	S
						1
2	3	4	5	6	7	8
9	10	11	12	13	14	15
16	17	18	19	20	21	22
23	24	25	26	27	28	29
30	31					

August 10 — Monday

DAY 222 — 143 REMAINING

"CANDID CAMERA" TV PREMIERE: ANNIVERSARY. Aug 10, 1948. This show—which appeared at various times on the big three networks and in syndication—was created and hosted by Allen Funt. The show was initially an Armed Forces Radio program based on Funt's success in recording and broadcasting soldiers' gripes. The show's modus operandi was to catch people unawares on camera—either as part of a practical joke or just being themselves. It spawned numerous imitators.

ECUADOR: INDEPENDENCE DAY. Aug 10. National holiday. Celebrates declaration of independence in 1809. Freedom from Spain was attained May 24, 1822.

HOOVER, HERBERT CLARK: BIRTH ANNIVERSARY. Aug 10, 1874. The 31st president of the US (1929–33) was born at West Branch, IA. Hoover was the first president born west of the Mississippi River and the first to have a telephone on his desk (installed Mar 27, 1929). "Older men declare war. But it is youth that must fight and die," he said at Chicago, IL, at the Republican National Convention, June 27, 1944. Hoover died at New York, NY, Oct 20, 1964. The Sunday nearest Aug 10 is observed in Iowa as Herbert Hoover Day.

JAPAN'S UNCONDITIONAL SURRENDER: ANNIVERSARY. Aug 10, 1945. A gathering to discuss surrender terms took place in Emperor Hirohito's bomb shelter; the participants were stalemated. Hirohito settled the question, believing continuation of the war would only result in further loss of Japanese lives. A message was transmitted to Japanese ambassadors in Switzerland and Sweden to accept the terms issued at Potsdam July 26, 1945, except that the Japanese emperor's sovereignty must be maintained. The Allies devised a plan in which the emperor and the Japanese government would administer under the rule of the Supreme Commander of the Allied Powers, and the Japanese surrendered.

MISSOURI: ADMISSION DAY: ANNIVERSARY. Aug 10. Became 24th state in 1821.

PGA CHAMPIONSHIP. Aug 10–16. Hazeltine National Golf Club, Chaska, MN. The 91st championship conducted by the Professional Golfers' Association of America. Est attendance: 150,000. For info: PGA of America, 100 Ave of the Champions, Palm Beach Gardens, FL 33418. Phone: (561) 624-8495. Fax: (561) 624-8429. Web: www.pga.com.

SMITHSONIAN INSTITUTION FOUNDED: ANNIVERSARY. Aug 10, 1846. Founding of the Smithsonian Institution at Washington, DC. For info: Smithsonian Institution, 900 Jefferson Dr SW, Washington, DC 20560. Phone: (202) 357-2700.

VICTORY DAY. Aug 10. Rhode Island. State holiday commemorating President Harry Truman's announcement of the surrender of the Japanese to the Allies on Aug 14, 1945. Annually, the second Monday in August.

Birthdays Today

Ian Anderson, 62, musician, lead singer (Jethro Tull), born Blackpool, England, Aug 10, 1947.

Rosanna Arquette, 50, actress (*Desperately Seeking Susan, New York Stories*), born New York, NY, Aug 10, 1959.

Antonio Banderas, 49, actor (*Spy Kids, The Mask of Zorro, Desperado*), born Malaga, Spain, Aug 10, 1960.

Riddick Bowe, 42, boxer, born Brooklyn, NY, Aug 10, 1967.

Jimmy Dean, 81, singer ("Big Bad John," "P.T. 109"), born Seth Ward at Plainview, TX, Aug 10, 1928.

Eddie Fisher, 81, singer, born Philadelphia, PA, Aug 10, 1928.

Angie Harmon, 37, actress ("Law & Order," "Baywatch Nights"), born Dallas, TX, Aug 10, 1972.

Betsey Johnson, 67, fashion designer, born Wethersfield, CT, Aug 10, 1942.

August 11 — Tuesday

DAY 223 | **142 REMAINING**

ATCHISON, DAVID R.: BIRTH ANNIVERSARY. Aug 11, 1807. Missouri legislator who was president of the US for one day. Born at Frogtown, KY. Atchison's strong proslavery opinions made his name prominent in legislative debates. He served as president pro tempore of the Senate a number of times, and he became president of the US for one day—Sunday, Mar 4, 1849—pending the swearing in of President-elect Zachary Taylor on Monday, Mar 5, 1849. The city of Atchison, KS, and the county of Atchison, MO, are named for him. He died at Gower, MO, Jan 26, 1886.

BAHAMAS: FOX HILL DAY. Aug 11. Nassau. Annually, the second Tuesday in August.

BOND, CARRIE JACOBS: BIRTH ANNIVERSARY. Aug 11, 1862. American composer of well-known songs, including "I Love You Truly" and "A Perfect Day," and of scores for motion pictures, Carrie Jacobs Bond was born at Janesville, WI. She died at Hollywood, CA, at age 84, Dec 28, 1946.

CHAD: INDEPENDENCE DAY. Aug 11. National holiday. Commemorates independence from France in 1960.

DOUGLAS, MIKE: BIRTH ANNIVERSARY. Aug 11, 1925. This pioneer of daytime talk shows was born Michael Delaney Dowd, Jr, at Chicago, IL. Douglas hosted his first afternoon talk show in Cleveland in 1961 and within five years was a household name. His nationally syndicated show featured celebrity interviews and topics and remained on the air until 1981. The show received the first Emmy Award for Individual Achievement in Daytime Television, and memorable guests included first-time performances by Aretha Franklin, Barbra Streisand and Bill Cosby. Tiger Woods appeared at the age of two alongside avid golfer Bob Hope. Douglas died Aug 11, 2006, at North Palm Beach, FL.

FIRST FOREIGN-BORN OFFICER APPOINTED CHAIR OF JOINT CHIEFS: ANNIVERSARY. Aug 11, 1993. President Bill Clinton appointed Army General John Shalikashvili to succeed Colin Powell as chairman of the Joint Chiefs of Staff. Shalikashvili was born at Poland, but his family fled to Germany in 1944 to escape advancing Soviet troops. After moving to the US, his family lived at Peoria, IL. "General Shali" has a distinguished military record and is a Vietnam War veteran.

HALEY, ALEX PALMER: BIRTH ANNIVERSARY. Aug 11, 1921. Born at Ithaca, NY, Alex Palmer Haley was raised by his grandmother at Henning, TN. In 1939 he entered the US Coast Guard and served as a cook, but eventually he became a writer and college professor. His interview with Malcolm X for *Playboy* led to his first book, *The Autobiography of Malcolm X*, which sold six million copies and was translated into eight languages. *Roots*, his Pulitzer Prize–winning novel published in 1976, sold millions, was translated into 37 languages and was made into an eight-part TV miniseries in 1977. The story generated an enormous interest in family ancestry. Haley died at Seattle, WA, Feb 13, 1992.

INGERSOLL DAY. Aug 11. Ingersoll Day is an annual celebration on or around Aug 11, the birthday of Robert Green Ingersoll, to celebrate the life and works of one of the most popular freethinkers in US history. For info: Matt Cherry, Institute for Humanist Studies, 48 Howard St, Albany, NY 12207. Phone: (518) 432-7820. Fax: (518) 432-7821. E-mail: MCherry@HumanistStudies.org. Web: HumanistStudies.org or www.secularseasons.org.

PRESIDENTIAL JOKE DAY: 25th ANNIVERSARY. Aug 11, 1984. Anniversary of President Ronald Reagan's voice-test joke. In preparation for a radio broadcast, during a thought-to-be-off-the-record voice level test, instead of counting "one, two, three . . ." the president said: "My fellow Americans, I am pleased to tell you I just signed legislation which outlaws Russia forever. The bombing begins in five minutes." The statement was picked up by live television cameras and was heard by millions worldwide. The incident provoked national and international reactions, including a news network proposal of new ground rules concerning the use of "off-the-record" remarks.

SAINT CLARE OF ASSISI: FEAST DAY. Aug 11, 1253. Chiara Favorone di Offreduccio, a religious leader inspired by St. Francis of Assisi, was the first woman to write her own religious order rule. Born at Assisi, Italy, July 16, 1194, she died there Aug 11, 1253. A "Privilege of Poverty" freed her order from any constraint to accept material security, making the "Poor Clares" totally dependent on God.

SIOUX EMPIRE FAIR. Aug 11–16. W.H. Lyon Fairgrounds, Sioux Falls, SD. 70th annual. Grandstand concerts, free entertainment, livestock exhibits, 4-H activities, flower and vegetable displays and craft exhibits. Camping available, with full hook-ups. Est attendance: 261,000. For info: Sioux Empire Fair, W.H. Lyon Fairgrounds, 4000 W 12th St, Sioux Falls, SD 57107. Phone: (605) 367-7178. Fax: (605) 367-7886. E-mail: info@siouxempirefair.com. Web: www.siouxempirefair.com.

SPACE MILESTONE: *VOSTOK 3* (USSR). Aug 11, 1962. Launched on this date, Andrian Nikolayev orbited Earth 64 times over a period of 94 hours, 25 minutes, covering a distance of 1,242,500 miles. Achieved radio communication with *Vostok 4* and telecast from spacecraft.

WATTS RIOT: ANNIVERSARY. Aug 11, 1965. A minor clash between the California Highway Patrol and two young blacks set off six days of riots in the Watts area of Los Angeles. Thirty-four deaths were reported and more than 3,000 people were arrested. Damage to property was listed at $40 million. The less-immediate cause of the disturbance and the others that followed was racial tension between whites and blacks in American society.

ZIMBABWE: HEROES' DAY. Aug 11. National holiday. Followed by Defense Forces Day on Aug 12.

Birthdays Today

Joanna Coles, 65, children's author, born Newark, NJ, Aug 11, 1944.

Arlene Dahl, 81, actress ("One Life to Live," "Fantasy Island"), born Minneapolis, MN, Aug 11, 1928.

Will Friedle, 33, actor ("Boy Meets World"), born Hartford, CT, Aug 11, 1976.

Hulk Hogan, 56, wrestler, actor, born Terry Gene Bollea at Augusta, GA, Aug 11, 1953.

Joe Jackson, 54, musician, songwriter, born Burton-on-Trent, England, Aug 11, 1955.

Ashley Jensen, 40, actress ("Ugly Betty," "Extras"), born Annan, Dumfries & Galloway, Scotland, Aug 11, 1969.

Anna Massey, 72, actress (*Bunny Lake Is Missing, A Doll's House*), born Thankeham, England, Aug 11, 1937.

Marilyn vos Savant, 63, columnist ("Ask Marilyn"), claims world's highest IQ, born St. Louis, MO, Aug 11, 1946.

Stephen Wozniak, 59, Apple computer cofounder, born Sunnyvale, CA, Aug 11, 1950.

August 12 — Wednesday

DAY 224 — 141 REMAINING

BEWICK, THOMAS: BIRTH ANNIVERSARY. Aug 12, 1753. English artist, wood engraver and author, remembered especially for his book illustrations in *General History of Quadrupeds, A History of British Birds* and *Aesop's Fables.* Born at Cherryburn, Northumberland, and died at Gateshead, Durham, England, Nov 8, 1828.

CANTINFLAS: BIRTH ANNIVERSARY. Aug 12, 1911. Mexico's most famous comic actor, Cantinflas, was born at Mexico City as Mario Moreno Reyes. Particularly popular with the poor people of Mexico because he most often portrayed the underdog, Cantinflas got his start in Mexico City *carpas*, the equivalent of vaudeville. He became internationally known for his role in *Around the World in 80 Days.* The name Cantinflas was invented by the comic to prevent his parents from learning he was in show business, which they considered a shameful endeavor. Died Apr 20, 1993, at Mexico City.

DeMILLE, CECIL B.: BIRTH ANNIVERSARY. Aug 12, 1881. Born at Ashfield, MA, Cecil Blount DeMille was a film showman extraordinaire known for lavish screen spectacles. He produced more than 70 major films, which were noted more for their large scale than for their subtle artistry, including *Cleopatra, The Plainsman, Reap the Wild Wind* and *The Ten Commandments* (in 1923 and 1956). DeMille was awarded an Oscar for *The Greatest Show on Earth* in 1953. He died Jan 21, 1959, at Hollywood, CA.

HOME SEWING MACHINE PATENTED: ANNIVERSARY. Aug 12, 1851. Isaac Singer developed the sewing machine for use in homes.

IBM PERSONAL COMPUTER INTRODUCED: ANNIVERSARY. Aug 12, 1981. IBM's first personal computer was released. The computer cost the equivalent of $3,000 in today's currency. Although IBM was one of the pioneers in making mainframe and other large computers, this was the company's first foray into the desktop computer market. Eventually, more IBM-compatible computers were manufactured by IBM's competitors than by IBM itself.

KIDD, MICHAEL: BIRTH ANNIVERSARY. Aug 12, 1915. Dancer and choreographer born Milton Greenwald at New York, NY. He was responsible for some of the most memorable Broadway productions of all time, including *Finian's Rainbow, Guys and Dolls* and *Can-Can.* His film choreography included *Seven Brides for Seven Brothers* and *Hello, Dolly!* He won five Tony Awards for his Broadway productions and an honorary Oscar for "service to the art of dance" in feature films. He died at Los Angeles, CA, Dec 23, 2007.

KING PHILIP ASSASSINATION: ANNIVERSARY. Aug 12, 1676. Philip, a son of Massasoit, chief of the Wampanog tribe, was killed near Mt Hope, RI, by a member of his own tribe, bringing to an end the first and bloodiest war between American Indians and white settlers of New England, a war that had raged for nearly two years and was known as King Philip's War.

MATHEWSON, CHRISTY: BIRTH ANNIVERSARY. Aug 12, 1880. Famed American baseball player Christopher (Christy) Mathewson, one of the first players named to Baseball's Hall of Fame, was born at Factoryville, PA. Died at Saranac Lake, NY, Oct 7, 1925. He pitched three complete games during the 1905 World Series without allowing opponents to score a run. In 17 years he won 372 games while losing 188 and striking out 2,499 players.

MOUNT OGURA PLANE CRASH: ANNIVERSARY. Aug 12, 1985. A Japan Airlines plane crashed into the side of Mount Ogura, Japan, claiming 520 lives. The worst air disaster involving a single plane. See also: "Canary Islands Plane Disaster: Anniversary" (Mar 27).

OWENS, BUCK: 80th BIRTH ANNIVERSARY. Aug 12, 1929. Country-and-western star, creator of the "Bakersfield sound" in the 1960s, Alvis Edgar "Buck" Owens was born to a sharecropper outside Sherman, TX. His family moved west with Dust Bowl refugees during the Great Depression, and Owens became a honky-tonk performer in California. He had 19 consecutive number-one singles from 1963 to 1967, and his success led him to a cohosting gig on the popular TV variety show "Hee Haw" (1969–86). Inducted into the Country Music Hall of Fame in 1996, Owens died at Bakersfield, CA, Mar 25, 2006.

SPACE MILESTONE: *ECHO I* (US). Aug 12, 1960. First successful communications satellite in Earth's orbit to relay voice and TV signals from one ground station to another was launched.

SPACE MILESTONE: *ENTERPRISE* (US). Aug 12, 1977. Reusable orbiting vehicle (space shuttle) makes first successful flight on its own within Earth's atmosphere. Launched from Boeing 747 on Aug 12, 1977.

SWEDEN: CRAYFISH PREMIERE. Aug 12. Crayfish may be sold and served in restaurants the following day after the season opens. Annually, the second Wednesday in August.

SWITZERLAND: LUCERNE FESTIVAL IN SUMMER. Aug 12–Sept 19. Lucerne. Featuring 100 events and directed by Michael Haefliger since 1999, the summer festival has been restructured and now intensively focuses on specific festival topics. Important artistic accents are set by each year's "artistes étoile," composers-in-residence and orchestras-in-residence as well as the concert cycles "Moderne," "Debut" and "Children's Corner." For info: Lucerne Festival, PO Box CH-6002, Lucerne, Switzerland. Phone: (41) 226-4400. Fax: (41) 226-4460. E-mail: info@lucernefestival.ch. Web: www.lucernefestival.ch.

August 2009

S	M	T	W	T	F	S
						1
2	3	4	5	6	7	8
9	10	11	12	13	14	15
16	17	18	19	20	21	22
23	24	25	26	27	28	29
30	31					

THAILAND: BIRTHDAY OF THE QUEEN. Aug 12. The entire kingdom of Thailand celebrates the birthday of Queen Sirikit.

UNITED NATIONS: INTERNATIONAL YOUTH DAY. Aug 12. Day to increase public awareness of the World Programme of Action for Youth to the Year 2000 and Beyond, which calls for action in 10 priority areas: education, employment, hunger and poverty, health, environment, drug abuse, juvenile delinquency, leisure-time activities, girls and young women, and full and effective participation of youths (15 to 24 years old) in the life of society and in decision making. For info: United Nations, Dept of Public Info, New York, NY 10017. Web: www.un.org.

VINYL RECORD DAY. Aug 12. We all need a reminder sometimes that life is good, regardless of national news and daily challenges. Favorite songs can bring back fond memories, and Vinyl Record Day encourages celebrating these music memories with family and friends. The day also seeks to recognize the tremendous cultural influence that vinyl records and album covers have had for more than 60 years and the need to preserve that audio history. Annually, on Aug 12—the day Thomas Edison invented the phonograph in 1877. For info: Gary Freiberg, 1107 11th St, Los Osos, CA 93402. Phone: (888) 644-4567. Fax: (805) 528-1365. E-mail: gary@VinylRecordDay.org. Web: www.VinylRecordDay.org.

WYATT, JANE: BIRTH ANNIVERSARY. Aug 12, 1910. Born at Bergen County, NJ, this Hollywood actress had her big break starring in Frank Capra's *Lost Horizon* in 1937. Other classic performances included her role opposite Gregory Peck in 1947's *Gentlemen's Agreement*. Wyatt's film career suffered when she criticized Senator Joseph McCarthy in the 1950s. She is best remembered for the television show "Father Knows Best," for which she won three consecutive Emmy Awards for her portrayal of Margaret Anderson (1958–61). Wyatt died Aug 20, 2006, at Bel Air, CA.

Birthdays Today

Casey Affleck, 34, actor (*The Assassination of Jesse James by the Coward Robert Ford, Gone Baby Gone*), born Falmouth, MA, Aug 12, 1975.

William Goldman, 78, writer (*The Princess Bride, Marathon Man*), born Chicago, IL, Aug 12, 1931.

George Hamilton, 70, actor (*Love at First Bite, Act One*, "The Survivors"), born Memphis, TN, Aug 12, 1939.

Sam J. Jones, 55, actor (*Flash Gordon, 10*), born Chicago, IL, Aug 12, 1954.

Peter Krause, 44, actor ("Dirty Sexy Money," "Six Feet Under," "Sports Night"), born Minneapolis, MN, Aug 12, 1965.

Ann M. Martin, 54, author (The Baby-Sitter's Club series), born Princeton, NJ, Aug 12, 1955.

Pat Metheny, 55, jazz guitarist, born Lee's Summit, MO, Aug 12, 1954.

Pete Sampras, 38, former tennis player, born Washington, DC, Aug 12, 1971.

George Soros, 79, billionaire, financier, philanthropist, born Budapest, Hungary, Aug 12, 1930.

Antoine Walker, 33, basketball player, born Chicago, IL, Aug 12, 1976.

August 13 — Thursday

DAY 225 — **140 REMAINING**

BERLIN WALL ERECTED: ANNIVERSARY. Aug 13, 1961. Early in the morning, the East German government closed the border between east and west sectors of Berlin with barbed wire to discourage further population movement to the west. Telephone and postal services were interrupted, and later in the week, a concrete wall was built to strengthen the barrier between official crossing points. The dismantling of the wall began Nov 9, 1989. See also: "Berlin Wall Opened: Anniversary" (Nov 9).

CANADA: EDMONTON INTERNATIONAL FRINGE THEATRE FESTIVAL. Aug 13–23. Edmonton, AB. A 10-day extravaganza of new plays, old plays, dance, music, mime and street entertainment. More than 1,000 performances of 140 productions in 28 indoor and outdoor theaters. Performers from around the world. Regarded as the largest and most exciting festival of alternative theater in North America. Est attendance: 500,000. For info: Fringe Theatre Adventures, 10330-84 Ave, Edmonton, AB, Canada T6E 2G9. Phone: (780) 448-9000. Web: www.fringetheatreadventures.ca.

CAXTON, WILLIAM: BIRTH ANNIVERSARY. Aug 13, 1422. First English printer, born at Kent, England. Died at London, England, 1491. Caxton produced his first book printed in English (while he was at Bruges), the *Recuyell of the Histories of Troy*, in 1476, and in the autumn of that year set up a print shop at Westminster, becoming the first printer in England.

CENTRAL AFRICAN REPUBLIC: INDEPENDENCE DAY. Aug 13. Commemorates Proclamation of Independence from France in 1960.

CHANNEL ISLANDS: JERSEY BATTLE OF FLOWERS. Aug 13–14. St. Helier, Jersey, Channel Islands. Colorful parade of floats decorated with hundreds of flowers. First held in 1902 to mark the coronation of Edward VII and Queen Alexandra. Annually, the second Thursday and Friday in August. Est attendance: 27,500. For info: The Jersey Battle of Flowers Assn, Meadow Bank, St. Lawrence, Jersey, Channel Islands, England JE3 1EE. Phone: (44) (153) 463-9000. E-mail: battle@battleofflowers.com. Web: www.battleofflowers.com.

HITCHCOCK, ALFRED (JOSEPH): BIRTH ANNIVERSARY. Aug 13, 1899. English film director and master of suspense born at London, England. Hitchcock's career as a filmmaker dates back to the silent film era when he made *The Lodger* in 1926, based on the tale of Jack the Ripper. American audiences were introduced to the Hitchcock style in 1935 with *The Thirty-Nine Steps* and *The Lady Vanishes* in 1938, after which he went to Hollywood. There he produced a string of classics including *Rebecca, Suspicion, Notorious, Rear Window, To Catch a Thief, The Birds, Psycho* and *Frenzy*, in addition to his TV series, "Alfred Hitchcock Presents." He died Apr 29, 1980, at Beverly Hills, CA.

HOGAN, BEN: BIRTH ANNIVERSARY. Aug 13, 1912. Golfer born at Dublin, TX. Hogan was one of only four players to win all four major professional championships, and his 63 career victories rank him third after Sam Snead and Jack Nicklaus. Died at Fort Worth, TX, July 25, 1997.

IOWA STATE FAIR. Aug 13–23. Iowa State Fairgrounds, Des Moines, IA. One of America's oldest and largest state fairs. A grand showcase of Iowa agriculture, talent and tradition. The fair boasts one of the world's largest livestock shows, 10-acre carnival, superstar grandstand stage shows, track events and spectacular free entertainment. 160-acre campgrounds. Est attendance: 1,002,464. For info: Lori Chappell, Mktg Dir, Iowa State Fair, PO Box 57130, Des Moines, IA 50317-0003. Phone: (515) 262-3111, ext 204. Fax: (515) 262-6906. E-mail: info@iowastatefair.org. Web: www.iowastatefair.org.

KRUPP, ALFRIED von BOHLEN und HALBACH: BIRTH ANNIVERSARY. Aug 13, 1907. As sole owner of the massive Krupp industries, Alfried Krupp took over the factories of German-occupied countries and used them for the Nazi war machine. Sometimes he had complete facilities dismantled and reassembled inside Germany. He used prisoners of war, civilians from occupied countries and inmates of concentration camps as forced labor in his factories. Found guilty as a war criminal by the military court at Nuremberg in 1948, he regained his property after serving 3 years of a 12-year sentence. He was named Alfried von Bohlen und Halbach at birth, but the family was authorized by Emperor Wilhelm II to add the mother's maiden name of Krupp to their own. Born at Essen, Germany, he died there July 30, 1967.

MILWAUKEE IRISH FEST. Aug 13–16. Milwaukee, WI. 29th annual. World's largest Irish music and cultural event, with the best of Irish and Irish American music, dance and theater on 15 stages. Activities include a cultural village, sports, contests, parades, displays, food, marketplace and children's activities. Weeklong summer school (open to the public) precedes the festival. Annually, the third weekend in August. Est attendance: 130,000. For info: Milwaukee Irish Fest, 1532 Wauwatosa Ave, Milwaukee, WI 53213. Phone: (414) 476-3378. E-mail: info@irishfest.com. Web: www.irishfest.com.

MISSOURI STATE FAIR. Aug 13–23. Sedalia, MO. Livestock shows, commercial and competitive exhibits, horse show, car races, tractor pulls, carnival and headline musical entertainment. Economical family entertainment. Est attendance: 375,000. For info: Missouri State Fair, 2503 W 16th, Sedalia, MO 65301. Phone: (660) 827-8150 or (800) 422-FAIR. Fax: (660) 827-8160. Web: www.mostatefair.com.

MOON PHASE: LAST QUARTER. Aug 13. Moon enters Last Quarter phase at 2:55 PM, EDT.

OAKLEY, ANNIE: BIRTH ANNIVERSARY. Aug 13, 1860. Annie Oakley was born at Darke County, OH. She developed an eye as a markswoman early as a child, becoming so proficient that she was able to pay off the mortgage on her family farm by selling the game she killed. A few years after defeating vaudeville marksman Frank Butler in a shooting match, she married him and they toured as a team until joining Buffalo Bill's Wild West Show in 1885. She was one of the star attractions for 17 years. She died Nov 3, 1926, at Greenville, OH.

SKOWHEGAN STATE FAIR. Aug 13–22. Skowhegan, ME. 191st annual. Huge fair with horse pulling, tractor pulls, harness racing, carnival midway, exhibits, flower show, grandstand shows, coliseum events, truck pulls, demolition derby and much more. Annually, beginning three weeks before Labor Day. Est attendance: 75,000. For info: Skowhegan State Fair Assn, PO Box 39, Skowhegan, ME 04976. Phone: (207) 474-2947. E-mail: skowfair@beeline-online.net. Web: www.skowheganstatefair.com.

SPACE MILESTONE: *HELIOS* SOLAR WING. Aug 13, 2001. The solar-powered plane *Helios* broke the altitude records for propeller-driven aircraft and nonrocket planes on this date, soaring higher than 96,500 feet. The plane has a wingspan longer than a Boeing 747 and uses solar-powered motors to power 14 propellers, flying at speeds as high as 170 mph. NASA plans to develop similar craft for unmanned flights on Mars.

STONE, LUCY: BIRTH ANNIVERSARY. Aug 13, 1818. American women's rights pioneer, born near West Brookfield, MA, Lucy Stone dedicated her life to the abolition of slavery and the emancipation of women. Although she graduated from Oberlin College, she had to finance her education by teaching for nine years, because her father did not favor college education for women. An eloquent speaker for her causes, she headed the list of 89 men and women who signed the call to the first national Woman's Rights Convention, held at Worcester, MA, October 1850. On May 1, 1855, she married Henry Blackwell. She and her husband aided in the founding of the American Suffrage Association, taking part in numerous referendum campaigns to win suffrage amendments to state constitutions. She died Oct 18, 1893, at Dorchester, MA.

TUNISIA: WOMEN'S DAY. Aug 13. General holiday. Celebration of independence of women.

August 2009

S	M	T	W	T	F	S
						1
2	3	4	5	6	7	8
9	10	11	12	13	14	15
16	17	18	19	20	21	22
23	24	25	26	27	28	29
30	31					

Birthdays Today

Kathleen Battle, 61, opera soprano, born Portsmouth, OH, Aug 13, 1948.

Danny Bonaduce, 50, radio personality, actor ("The Partridge Family"), born Broomall, PA, Aug 13, 1959.

Fidel Castro, 82, former president of Cuba (1959–2008), born Mayari, Oriente Province, Cuba, Aug 13, 1927.

Quinn Cummings, 42, actress (*The Goodbye Girl,* "Family"), born Los Angeles, CA, Aug 13, 1967.

Pat Harrington, Jr, 80, actor, comedian ("The Jack Paar Show," "One Day at a Time"), born New York, NY, Aug 13, 1929.

Kevin Tighe, 65, actor ("Emergency," *The Graduate, What's Eating Gilbert Grape?*), born Los Angeles, CA, Aug 13, 1944.

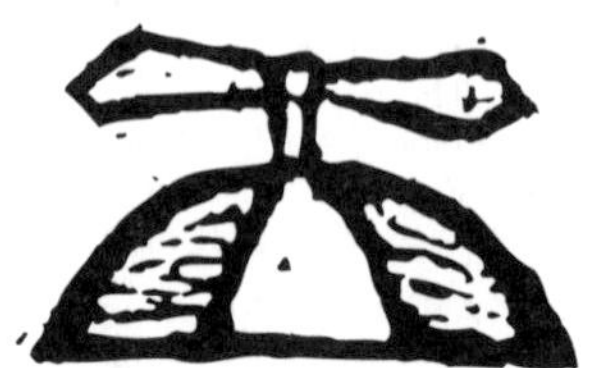

August 14 — Friday

DAY 226 | **139 REMAINING**

ATLANTIC CHARTER SIGNING: ANNIVERSARY. Aug 14, 1941. The eight-point agreement was signed by US president Franklin D. Roosevelt and British prime minister Winston S. Churchill. The charter grew out of a three-day conference aboard ship in the Atlantic Ocean, off the Newfoundland coast, and stated policies and hopes for the future agreed to by the two nations.

CHENEY, LYNNE: BIRTHDAY. Aug 14, 1941. Wife of Vice President Richard (Dick) Cheney, born at Casper, WY. Former chair of the National Endowment for the Humanities (1986–93).

COLOGNE CATHEDRAL COMPLETION: ANNIVERSARY. Aug 14, 1880. The largest Gothic church in northern Europe, the Cologne Cathedral at Cologne, Germany, was completed on this date, 632 years after rebuilding began on Aug 14, 1248. In fact, there had been a church on its site since 873, but a fire in 1248 made rebuilding necessary. The cathedral was again damaged, by bombing, during WWII.

FESTIVAL OF THE LITTLE HILLS. Aug 14–16. Frontier Park and Historic Main, St. Charles, MO. The largest festival of the year. Includes more than 350 craft booths, live music, and food and beverage booths. Annually, the third weekend in August. Est attendance: 300,000. For info: Greater St. Charles CVB, 230 S Main St, St. Charles, MO 63301-2855. Phone: (800) 366-2427 or (636) 946-7776. Web: www.festivalofthelittlehills.com.

ILLINOIS STATE FAIR. Aug 14–23. Springfield, IL. Amusement rides, food booths, parade, various types of entertainment, and tractor pulls. Est attendance: 700,000. For info: Illinois State Fair, PO Box 19427, Springfield, IL 62794. Phone: (217) 782-6661. Fax: (217) 782-9115. Web: www.illinoisstatefair.info.

INDIA: KRISHNA JANMASHTAMI. Aug 14. Hindu holiday. Birth anniversary of Lord Vishnu in his human incarnation as Krishna. Because there is no one universally accepted Hindu calendar, this holiday may be celebrated on a different date in some parts of India, but it always falls in August or September.

JUST, ERNEST E.: BIRTH ANNIVERSARY. Aug 14, 1883. American marine biologist Ernest E. Just was born at Charleston, SC. He was the first recipient of the NAACP's Spingarn Medal and was a professor at Howard University from 1907 to 1941, where he was head of physiology at the medical school (1912–20) and head of zoology (1912–41). He died Oct 27, 1941, at Washington, DC.

KOOL-AID DAYS. Aug 14–16. Hastings, NE. Family festival in the town where Kool-Aid was invented. Large inflatable games, live entertainment, festival foods, commemoratives, parade, free celebrity concert, sports tournaments, games for kids. Purchase a mug and receive free Kool-Aid all day from the world's largest Kool-Aid stand where we pour more than a gallon a minute of 22 flavors. Annually, the second weekend in August. Est attendance: 20,000. For info: Kool-Aid Days, Nebraska's Official Soft Drink Heritage Foundation, 301 S Burlington Ave, Ste 122, Hastings, NE 68901. Phone: (800) 967-2189. E-mail: info@kool-aiddays.com. Web: www.kool-aiddays.com.

MAE WEST BIRTHDAY GALA. Aug 14–17. New York, NY. To commemorate the stage career of legendary Brooklyn-born entertainer Mae West, several Mae-themed events are scheduled in Manhattan. Events—including song recitals, exhibitions and archival installations—always kick off by or before Aug 17, the date of West's birth in 1893. The Mae West Gala has been featured on The Biography Channel, on Bloomberg Radio and in the print media. Est attendance: 5,000. For info: Conrad Bradford, 24 Fifth Ave, Box 611, New York, NY 10011. Phone: (917) 403-0980. Fax: (212) 533-4073. E-mail: comeupseeMAE@aol.com. Web: MaeWest.blogspot.com.

MUDDY FROGWATER COUNTRY CLASSIC FESTIVAL. Aug 14–16. Yantis Park, Milton-Freewater, OR. Arts, crafts, food, country music, frog-jumping contest, book sale, fun run, square dancing, firefighters' water fight, 3-on-3 basketball tournament, barbecue chicken dinner, corn roast, watermelon feed and softball tournament. Annually, the third weekend in August. Est attendance: 8,000. For info: Milton-Freewater Area Chamber of Commerce, 157 S Columbia, Milton-Freewater, OR 97862. Phone: (541) 938-5563. Fax: (541) 938-5564. E-mail: mfmdfrog@oregontrail.net. Web: www.muddyfrogwatercountry.com.

NAVAJO NATION: NAVAJO CODE TALKERS DAY. Aug 14. The Navajo Nation Council has established Aug 14 of each year as a tribal holiday recognizing and honoring the distinguished record of the Code Talkers during WWII. The Code Talkers transmitted military messages in the Navajo language during the war, and Axis powers were unable to break the code. For info: Office of the Speaker, Navajo Nation Council, PO Box 3390, Window Rock, AZ 86515. Phone: (928) 871-7160. Fax: (928) 871-7255. Web: www.navajonationcouncil.org.

NORTHEASTERN WISCONSIN ANTIQUE POWER AND MACHINERY SHOW THRESHEREE. Aug 14–16. Sturgeon Bay, WI. Continuous display of operating antique machinery, antique tractor pull, barefoot horse pull, crafts, games for kids, food and refreshments. Annually, the third weekend in August. Est attendance: 3,500. For info: Bernie Geisel. Phone: (920) 743-4859. Or Josie Bochek. Phone: (920) 743-5251. E-mail: coldcomfortfarms@hotmail.com.

PAKISTAN: INDEPENDENCE DAY. Aug 14, 1947. Gained independence from Britain in 1947.

SCOTLAND: EDINBURGH INTERNATIONAL FESTIVAL. Aug 14–Sept 6 (tentative). Edinburgh, Lothian. The festival is one of the most exciting places in the world to experience opera, dance, theater, classical music and visual arts. It offers the chance to see and hear some of the world's greatest companies and performers. Est attendance: 420,000. For info: Edinburgh Intl Festival, The Hub, Castlehill, Edinburgh, Scotland EH1 2NE. Phone: (44) (131) 473 2000. Fax: (44) (131) 473 2002. Web: www.eif.co.uk.

SHANTY DAYS: CELEBRATION OF THE LAKE. Aug 14–16. Legion Park, Algoma, WI. Three-day festival to celebrate lakeshore heritage. Entertainment, ethnic food, arts and crafts, street fair, 5k walk/run, fishing contest, kids' area, book sale, community parade, photo contest and fireworks finale. Est attendance: 23,000. For info: Pam Ritchie, Algoma Area Chamber of Commerce, 1226 Lake St, Algoma, WI 54201. Phone: (920) 487-2041 or (800) 498-4888. Fax: (920) 487-5519. E-mail: chamber@itol.com. Web: www.algoma.org.

SOCIAL SECURITY ACT: ANNIVERSARY. Aug 14, 1935. President Franklin D. Roosevelt signed the Social Security Act, which contained provisions for the establishment of a Social Security Board to administer federal old-age and survivors' insurance in the US. By signing the bill into law, Roosevelt was fulfilling a 1932 campaign promise.

THAYER, ERNEST LAWRENCE: BIRTH ANNIVERSARY. Aug 14, 1863. The man who wrote the famous comic baseball ballad "Casey at the Bat" was born at Lawrence, MA. He wrote a series of comic poems for the *San Francisco Examiner*, of which "Casey at the Bat" was the last. It was published Sunday, June 3, 1888, and Thayer received $5 in payment for it. Thayer, who regarded the poem's fame as a nuisance and whose other writings are largely forgotten, died at Santa Barbara, CA, Aug 21, 1940.

365-INNING SOFTBALL GAME: ANNIVERSARY. Aug 14–15, 1976. The Gager's Diner softball team played the Bend'n Elbow Tavern in a 365-inning softball game. Starting at 10 AM Aug 14, the game was called because of rain and fog at 4 PM, Aug 15. The 70 players, including 20 women, raised $4,000 for construction of a new softball field and for the Monticello, NY, Community General Hospital. The Gagers beat the Elbows 491–467. To date, this remains the longest softball game on record.

TOPPENISH WESTERN ART SHOW. Aug 14–16. Railroad Park, Toppenish, WA. Western art show featuring more than 30 Northwest artists. Also included: auction, quick draw, and "kids-n-art." Annually, the third weekend of August. Est attendance: 3,000. For info: Sara J. Frederiksen, Dir, Toppenish Chamber of Commerce, PO Box 28, Toppenish, WA 98948. Phone: (509) 865-3262. E-mail: chamber@toppenish.net.

V-J DAY: ANNIVERSARY. Aug 14, 1945. Anniversary of President Harry Truman's announcement that Japan had surrendered to the Allies, setting off celebrations across the nation. Official ratification of surrender occurred aboard the USS *Missouri* at Tokyo Bay, Sept 2 (Far Eastern time).

WEST VIRGINIA STATE FAIR. Aug 14–22. Lewisburg, WV. For info: The State Fair of West Virginia, PO Drawer 986, Lewisburg, WV 24901. Phone: (304) 645-1090. E-mail: publicrelations@statefairofwv.com. Web: www.statefairofwv.com.

WESTERN IDAHO FAIR. Aug 14–23. Boise, ID. 112th annual. Largest fair in the state, including four stages of entertainment on the grounds with local and regional talent, three nights of grandstand concerts, carnival midway and 70 food booths. Est attendance: 254,000. For info: Bob Batista, Mgr, Western Idaho Fair, 5610 Glenwood, Boise, ID 83714. Phone: (208) 287-5650. Fax: (208) 375-9972. Web: www.idahofair.com.

Birthdays Today

Russell Baker, 84, journalist, author, TV host ("Masterpiece Theatre"), born Loudoun County, VA, Aug 14, 1925.

Catherine Bell, 41, actress ("JAG"), born London, England, Aug 14, 1968.

Halle Berry, 41, actress (*Die Another Day, X-Men*, Oscar for *Monster's Ball*), born Cleveland, OH, Aug 14, 1968.

Lynne Cheney, 68, wife of Dick Cheney, 46th vice president of the US, born Casper, WY, Aug 14, 1941.

David Crosby, 68, singer (Crosby, Stills & Nash), songwriter, born Los Angeles, CA, Aug 14, 1941.

Antonio Fargas, 63, actor (*Shaft, I'm Gonna Git You Sucka, Car Wash*), born the Bronx, NY, Aug 14, 1946.

Buddy Greco, 83, singer ("Mr Lonely"), composer, musician, born Philadelphia, PA, Aug 14, 1926.

Marcia Gay Harden, 50, actress (Oscar for *Pollock; Space Cowboys, Mystic River*), born La Jolla, CA, Aug 14, 1959.

Terin Humphrey, 23, gymnast, born St. Louis, MO, Aug 14, 1986.

Earvin "Magic" Johnson, Jr, 50, Hall of Fame basketball player, born Lansing, MI, Aug 14, 1959.

Mila Kunis, 26, actress ("That 70s Show," "Family Guy"), born Kiev, Ukraine, Aug 14, 1983.

Arthur Betz Laffer, 69, economist (the Laffer curve), born Youngstown, OH, Aug 14, 1940.

Gary Larson, 59, cartoonist ("The Far Side"), born Tacoma, WA, Aug 14, 1950.

Jay Manuel, 37, photographer, makeup artist, television personality ("America's Next Top Model"), born Toronto, ON, Canada, Aug 14, 1972.

Steve Martin, 64, comedian, actor (*Shopgirl, LA Story, Roxanne, Parenthood*), novelist, born Waco, TX, Aug 14, 1945.

Susan Saint James, 63, actress ("MacMillan and Wife," "Kate and Allie"), born Long Beach, CA, Aug 14, 1946.

Danielle Steel, 62, author (*Vanished, Wanderlust*), born New York, NY, Aug 14, 1947.

Rusty Wallace, 53, auto racer, born St. Louis, MO, Aug 14, 1956.

August 15 — Saturday

DAY 227 — 138 REMAINING

ALLIED LANDINGS IN SOUTH OF FRANCE: 65th ANNIVERSARY. Aug 15, 1944. After several postponements, Allied forces began Operation Dragoon, the landing on the south coast of France. More than 2,000 transports and landing craft transported 94,000 men to an area between Toulon and Cannes, with only 183 Allied losses. They encountered minimal opposition, and by the end of August, the French coast from the mouth of the Rhône to Nice was in Allied hands.

AMERICAN SOCIETY OF ASSOCIATION EXECUTIVES ANNUAL MEETING AND EXPOSITION. Aug 15–18. Toronto, ON, Canada. Major meeting for ASAE members, nonmembers and suppliers including education sessions, trade show, speakers and networking events. Est attendance: 5,000. For info: American Society of Assn Executives, 1575 I St NW, Washington, DC 20005. Phone: (202) 626-2723. Fax: (202) 371-8825. E-mail: pr@asaenet.org. Web: www.asaenet.org or www.asaeannualmeeting.org.

ANTIQUE MARINE ENGINE EXPOSITION. Aug 15–16. Mystic Seaport, Mystic, CT. Collectors from across the US and Canada gather for an annual exposition of preWWII marine engines and engine models. For info: Mystic Seaport, 75 Greenmanville Ave, PO Box 6000, Mystic, CT 06355-0990. Phone: (860) 572-5315 or (888) 973-2767. Web: www.mysticseaport.org.

ASSUMPTION OF THE VIRGIN MARY. Aug 15. Greek and Roman Catholic churches celebrate Mary's ascent to heaven. In Orthodox churches, called the Dormition of Theotokos and commemorated on Aug 15 or 28. A holiday in many Christian countries.

BARRYMORE, ETHEL: BIRTH ANNIVERSARY. Aug 15, 1879. Celebrated award-winning actress of stage, screen and television, born Ethel Blythe at Philadelphia, PA. Sister of John and Lionel Barrymore. Died at Beverly Hills, CA, June 18, 1959.

August 2009	S	M	T	W	T	F	S
							1
	2	3	4	5	6	7	8
	9	10	11	12	13	14	15
	16	17	18	19	20	21	22
	23	24	25	26	27	28	29
	30	31					

BATTLE OF BLUE LICKS CELEBRATION. Aug 15–16. Blue Licks Battlefield State Park, Mount Olivet, KY. Commemorates the anniversary of Revolutionary War Battle of Blue Licks (which involved Daniel Boone). Living-history demonstrations, arts, crafts, games, competitions and battle reenactment. Annually, the third weekend in August. Est attendance: 5,000. For info: Park Naturalist, Blue Licks Battlefield State Resort Park, PO Box 66, Mt Olivet, KY 41064-0066. Phone: (859) 289-5507. Fax: (859) 289-5409. Web: parks.ky.gov.

BEST FRIEND'S DAY. Aug 15. Celebrate this special day by doing something fun with your best friend. Go shopping, go to the movies, go to a park or restaurant, play a game, or just hang out and be together. For info: Thema Martin, 931 Monroe Dr NE, Ste A102, #226, Atlanta, GA 30308. Phone: (404) 849-1249. E-mail: tmartin@savionlife.com.

BIKE VAN BUREN. Aug 15–16. Van Buren County, IA. A laid-back bicycle tour of the villages, landmarks and landscape of this rural Iowa county. The "red carpet of hospitality" is rolled out for the bikers as they pass through. Annually, the third weekend in August. Est attendance: 500. For info: Villages of Van Buren, Inc, PO Box 9, Keosauqua, IA 52565. Phone: (800) 868-7822. Fax: (319) 293-7116. E-mail: info@villagesofvanburen.com. Web: www.villagesofvanburen.com.

BOHEMIAN NIGHTS AT NEW WEST FEST. Aug 15–16. Fort Collins, CO. More than 300 artists showcase their creations during this festival, also featuring a carnival, kids' activities, food booths, beer gardens, and eight stages of local bands, singers and dancers in "Old Town" Fort Collins. For info: Downtown Fort Collins Business Assn, 19 Old Town Square #230, Fort Collins, CO 80524. Phone: (970) 484-6500. E-mail: info@DowntownFortCollins.com. Web: www.DowntownFortCollins.com.

BONAPARTE, NAPOLEON: BIRTH ANNIVERSARY. Aug 15, 1769. Anniversary (240th) of the birth of French emperor Napoleon Bonaparte on the island of Corsica. He died in exile at 5:49 PM, May 5, 1821, on the island of St. Helena. Public holiday at Corsica, France.

CHAUVIN DAY. Aug 15. A day named for Nicholas Chauvin, French soldier from Rochefort, France, who idolized Napoleon and who eventually became a subject of ridicule because of his blind loyalty and dedication to anything French. Originally referring to bellicose patriotism, *chauvinism* has come to mean blind or absurdly intense attachment to any cause. Observed on Napoleon's birth anniversary because Chauvin's birth date is unknown.

CHILD, JULIA: BIRTH ANNIVERSARY. Aug 15, 1912. America's beloved food authority, who didn't take a cooking lesson until she was in her 30s, was born at Pasadena, CA. Child's cookbooks and television shows (most famously, "The French Chef") encouraged Americans to cook and eat well and to be skeptical of food fads and diet strictures. "Cooking is not a chore; it is a joy," Child believed. She died at Santa Barbara, CA, Aug 13, 2004.

COEUR D'ALENE INDIAN PILGRIMAGE. Aug 15. Coeur d'Alene's Old Mission State Park, Cataldo, ID. The annual Feast of the Assumption pilgrimage by the Coeur d'Alene Indians. Annually, Aug 15. Est attendance: 1,800. For info: Park Mgr, Coeur d'Alene's Old Mission State Park, PO Box 30, Cataldo, ID 83810-0030. Phone: (208) 682-3814. Fax: (208) 682-4032. E-mail: old@idpr.state.id.us. Web: www.visitidaho.org or www.idahoparks.org.

COMISKEY, CHARLES: 150th BIRTH ANNIVERSARY. Aug 15, 1859. Charles Albert Comiskey, Baseball Hall of Fame first baseman, manager and executive, born at Chicago, IL. Comiskey's career spanned 50 years, 30 of them as founding owner of the Chicago White Sox. But before that, he was an outstanding and innovative player and a tough, successful manager. Inducted into the Hall of Fame in 1939. Died at Eagle River, WI, Oct 26, 1931.

CONGO (BRAZZAVILLE): NATIONAL DAY. Aug 15. National day of the People's Republic of the Congo. Commemorates independence from France in 1960.

DORMITION OF THEOTOKOS. Aug 15. Orthodox observance. According to New Calendar (Gregorian), the Dormition Fast is observed Aug 1–14, followed by Dormition of Theotokos Aug 15.

EQUATORIAL GUINEA: CONSTITUTION DAY. Aug 15. National holiday. Commemorates the 1982 revision of the original constitution of 1968.

FERBER, EDNA: BIRTH ANNIVERSARY. Aug 15, 1887. Edna Ferber was born at Kalamazoo, MI. She wrote her first novel, *Dawn O'Hara*, in 1911 and became a prolific writer, producing many popular magazine stories. Her novel *So Big* brought her commercial success in 1924 as well as a Pulitzer Prize. Her other novels include *Show Boat, Cimarron, Saratoga Trunk, Giant* and *Ice Palace*, all of which were made into successful films. Ferber collaborated with George Kaufman in writing for the stage on *The Royal Family, Dinner at Eight, Stage Door* and *Bravo*. Ferber died at New York, NY, Apr 16, 1968.

HARDING, FLORENCE KLING DeWOLFE: BIRTH ANNIVERSARY. Aug 15, 1860. Wife of Warren Gamaliel Harding, 29th president of the US, born at Marion, OH. Died there Nov 21, 1924.

INDIA: INDEPENDENCE DAY. Aug 15. National holiday. Anniversary of Indian independence from Britain in 1947.

KOREA: INDEPENDENCE DAY. Aug 15. National holiday commemorates acceptance by Japan of Allied terms of surrender in 1945, thereby freeing Korea from 36 years of Japanese domination. Also marks formal proclamation of Republic of Korea in 1948. Military parades and ceremonies throughout country.

LIECHTENSTEIN: NATIONAL DAY. Aug 15. Public holiday on Assumption Day.

MAINE HIGHLAND GAMES. Aug 15. Thomas Point Beach, Brunswick, ME. 31st annual. Presented by the Saint Andrew's Society of Maine. Bagpipe bands; Highland and Scottish dancing; Scottish arts and crafts fair; folksingers; Scottish fiddling; children's games; adult athletics including tossing of the caber, wheat sheaf toss and putting of the stone; border collie herding demonstrations; Highland cattle and individual piping contests. American and Scottish foods galore. The only Scottish event of its kind held in Maine! Scots and non-Scots will enjoy the color, pageantry and friendly atmosphere. Est attendance: 8,000. For info: Thomas Point Beach, 29 Meadow Rd, Brunswick, ME 04011. Phone: (207) 725-6009. Web: www.thomaspointbeach.com.

MINNESOTA RENAISSANCE FESTIVAL. Aug 15–Sept 27 (weekends; Labor Day). Shakopee, MN. A celebration of 16th-century Renaissance Europe with entertainment on 12 lively stages, food, arts and crafts, games and live jousting. Est attendance: 300,000. For info: Minnesota Renaissance Festival, 1244 S Canterbury Rd, Ste 306, Shakopee, MN 55379. Phone: (800) 966-8215 or (952) 445-7361. Fax: (952) 445-7380. Web: www.renaissancefest.com.

NATIONAL HOMELESS ANIMALS DAY® AND CANDLELIGHT VIGILS. Aug 15. A day to call attention to the fact that millions of healthy dogs and cats are killed each year in the US in animal shelters because of overpopulation—a problem that has a solution: spay/neuter! It stops the killing! The vigils memorialize the animals killed in the preceding year and sympathize with the caring shelter personnel who must take the lives of the animals. Vigils will be held throughout the US and beyond. For info: Intl Society for Animal Rights, Inc, Susan Dapsis, Pres, 965 Griffin Pond Rd, Clarks Summit, PA 18411-9214. Phone: (570) 586-2200. Fax: (570) 586-9580. E-mail: contact@ISARonline.org.

NATIONAL RELAXATION DAY. Aug 15. Hold the phones, call in sick, or just take a nap. Today is the perfect excuse to reduce stress and improve your lifestyle by relaxing. Spend a few minutes learning or sharing the art of relaxation with family, friends and coworkers. Annually, Aug 15. For info: Sean M. Moeller, PO Box 593, Jenison, MI 49429-0593.

PANAMA CANAL OPENS: 95th ANNIVERSARY. Aug 15, 1914. After 10 years of construction and much multination diplomacy, the Panama Canal opened for operation. A self-propelled crane boat made the first passage through the canal, a 50-mile waterway connecting the Atlantic and Pacific Oceans, on Jan 7, 1914. The first ocean steamer, the SS *Ancon*, passed through Aug 3, 1914, and the canal officially opened Aug 15, 1914.

PANAMA: PANAMA CITY FOUNDATION DAY. Aug 15. Traditional annual cultural observance recognizes foundation of Panama City.

PETERSON, OSCAR: BIRTH ANNIVERSARY. Aug 15, 1925. Jazz musician born at Montreal, QC, Canada. Also a composer and vocalist, he was considered one of the greatest pianists ever to perform and record in the genre. His recordings won seven Grammy Awards, and he is a member of several music halls of fame. He died at Mississauga, ON, Canada, Dec 23, 2007.

SANDCASTLE & SCULPTURE DAY. Aug 15. Jetties Beach, Nantucket, MA. 36th annual. Islanders and visitors create masterpiece sandcastles and sand sculptures on the beach. Ribbons will be awarded in various categories. For info: Nantucket Chamber of Commerce, Zero Main St, Nantucket, MA 02554. Phone: (508) 228-1700. E-mail: info@nantucketchamber.org. Web: www.nantucketchamber.org.

SCOTT, SIR WALTER: BIRTH ANNIVERSARY. Aug 15, 1771. Born at Edinburgh, Scotland. Famed poet and novelist. "But no one shall find me rowing against the stream," he wrote in the introduction to *The Fortunes of Nigel*. "I care not who knows it—I write for the general amusement." Died at Abbotsford, Scotland, Sept 21, 1832.

TRANSCONTINENTAL US RAILWAY COMPLETION: ANNIVERSARY. Aug 15, 1870. The Golden Spike ceremony at Promontory Point, UT, May 10, 1869, was long regarded as the final link in a transcontinental railroad track reaching from an Atlantic port to a Pacific port. In fact, that link occurred unceremoniously on another date in another state. Diaries of engineers working at the site establish "the completion of a transcontinental track at a point 928 feet east of today's milepost 602, or 3,812 feet east of the present Union Pacific depot building at Strasburg (formerly Comanche)," CO. The final link was made at 2:53 PM, Aug 15, 1870. Annual celebration at Strasburg, CO, on a weekend in August. See also: "Golden Spike Driving: Anniversary" (May 10).

WOODSTOCK: 40th ANNIVERSARY. Aug 15, 1969. The Woodstock Music and Art Fair opened on this day on an alfalfa field on or near Yasgur's Farm at Bethel, NY. The three-day rock concert featured 24 bands and drew a crowd of more than 400,000 people.

XTERRA WHEELER CANYON XDURO. Aug 15. Pineview Reservoir, Ogden, UT. The XTERRA Trail Run Series boasts more than 50 events across the country with runs ranging from 5k to 25k. These extreme, off-road trail runs give runners the chance to prove their skills against a variety of terrain. From calf-burning hills to slippery, mud-covered paths athletes will face the ultimate test of endurance. This race features an off-road half-marathon distance trail run. For info: Ann Mickey, XTERRA/TEAM Unlimited, 720 Iwilei Rd #290, Honolulu, HI 96817. Phone: (877) 751-8880. E-mail: info@xterraplanet.com. Web: www.xterratrailrun.com.

 Birthdays Today

Ben Affleck, 37, actor (*Hollywoodland, The Sum of All Fears, Pearl Harbor*), director (*Gone Baby Gone*), born Berkeley, CA, Aug 15, 1972.

Princess Anne, 59, Princess Royal of the UK, horsewoman, born London, England, Aug 15, 1950.

Stephen G. Breyer, 71, US Supreme Court justice, born San Francisco, CA, Aug 15, 1938.

Mike Connors, 84, actor ("Mannix"), born Krekor Ohanian at Fresno, CA, Aug 15, 1925.

Linda Ellerbee, 65, journalist, born Bryan, TX, Aug 15, 1944.

Zeljko Ivanek, 52, actor ("Damages," "24," *Donnie Brasco*), born Ljubljana, Slovenia, Aug 15, 1957.

Joe Jonas, 20, singer (The Jonas Brothers), actor (*Camp Rock*), born Casa Grande, AZ, Aug 15, 1989.

Vernon Jordan, Jr, 74, civil rights leader, born Atlanta, GA, Aug 15, 1935.

Debra Messing, 41, actress ("Will & Grace"), born Brooklyn, NY, Aug 15, 1968.

Phyllis Stewart Schlafly, 85, conservative spokeswoman, author, born St. Louis, MO, Aug 15, 1924.

Kathryn Whitmire, 63, first woman mayor of Houston, Texas, born Houston, TX, Aug 15, 1946.

August 16 — Sunday

DAY 228 | **137 REMAINING**

BATTLE OF CAMDEN: ANNIVERSARY. Aug 16, 1780. Revolutionary War battle fought near Camden, SC. American troops led by General Horatio Gates suffered disastrous losses. Nearly 1,000 Americans killed and another 1,000 captured by the British. British losses about 325. One of America's worst defeats in the war.

BEGIN, MENACHEM: BIRTH ANNIVERSARY. Aug 16, 1913. Born at Brest Litovsk, Poland. A militant Zionist and anticommunist, he fled to Russia in 1939 ahead of the advancing Nazis; he was soon arrested and sent to Siberia. Freed in 1941, he went to Palestine and became a leader in the Jewish underground, fighting for Israel's independence; by 1943 he headed the national military organization. Elected prime minister of Israel in 1977, he signed the historic peace treaty between Israel and Egypt with President Anwar el Sadat of Egypt and US president Jimmy Carter at Camp David in 1979. He died Mar 9, 1992, at Tel Aviv, Israel.

BENNINGTON BATTLE DAY: ANNIVERSARY. Aug 16, 1777. Anniversary of battle is legal holiday in Vermont.

August 2009

S	M	T	W	T	F	S
						1
2	3	4	5	6	7	8
9	10	11	12	13	14	15
16	17	18	19	20	21	22
23	24	25	26	27	28	29
30	31					

DOMINICAN REPUBLIC: RESTORATION OF THE REPUBLIC. Aug 16. The anniversary of the restoration of the Republic in 1863 is celebrated as an official public holiday.

HARMONIC CONVERGENCE: ANNIVERSARY. Aug 16, 1987. At about 20 designated "sacred sites" around the world (including Lake Titicaca, Bolivia; Boulder, CO; Niagara Falls and the Grand Canyon) believers gathered to meditate about peace and to ward off any impending doom. The harmonic convergence, projected from ancient Mayan and Aztec calendars to begin on this date, was said to signal the beginning of a period of cleansing that would last until 1992, in preparation for alien intelligence to be confronted in the next century.

JOE MILLER'S JOKE DAY. Aug 16. A day to tell a joke in honor of the English comic actor Joseph (or Josias) Miller, who was born in 1684 (exact date unknown). Miller acted at the Drury Lane Theatre at London, England, and was a popular favorite. He died at London, Aug 16, 1738. A book with which Miller had no direct connection, *Joe Miller's Jests*, was compiled by John Mottley and first published in 1739. It contained 247 jokes. Revised and expanded hundreds of times, it contained more than 1,500 jokes in the ensuing two centuries. From *Joe Miller's Jests*, London, 1739: "A melting Sermon being preached in a country Church, all fell a weeping but one Man, who being asked, why he did not weep with the rest? O! said he. I belong to another Parish."

KLONDIKE GOLD DISCOVERY: ANNIVERSARY. Aug 16, 1896. According to the oral tradition of the Tagish First Nations People, Skookum Jim, Dawson Charlie and George Carmack found gold in Rabbit Creek, a tributary of the Klondike River, lying "thick between the flaky slabs like cheese sandwiches." This event, which led to the great Klondike Gold Rush, is celebrated in the Yukon each year with a public holiday, Discovery Day, observed on the nearest Monday.

LAWRENCE (OF ARABIA), T.E.: BIRTH ANNIVERSARY. Aug 16, 1888. British soldier, archaeologist and writer, born at Tremadoc, North Wales. During WWI, led the Arab revolt against the Turks and served as a spy for the British. His book, *Seven Pillars of Wisdom*, is a personal account of the Arab revolt. He was killed in a motorcycle accident at Dorset, England, May 19, 1935.

MacFADDEN, BERNARR: BIRTH ANNIVERSARY. Aug 16, 1868. Physical culture enthusiast and publisher, born at Mill Springs, MO. He was publisher of *Physical Culture, True Story, True Romances, True Detective Mystery Magazine* and many others. MacFadden made parachute jumps on his 81st, 83rd and 84th birthdays. He died at Jersey City, NJ, of jaundice, following a three-day fast, Oct 12, 1955.

MEANY, GEORGE: BIRTH ANNIVERSARY. Aug 16, 1894. American labor leader George Meany was born at New York, NY. A plumber by trade, he became president of the AFL (American Federation of Labor) in 1952, and when he merged the AFL with the CIO (Congress of Industrial Organizations), he became the leading labor spokesperson in the US. In 1957 he expelled Jimmy Hoffa's Teamsters Union from the AFL-CIO, and he lost the United Auto Workers in 1967. His tenure as president lasted until 1979. He died Jan 10, 1980, at Washington, DC.

NATIONAL AVIATION WEEK. Aug 16–22. A celebration of flight designed to increase public awareness, knowledge and appreciation of aviation. Annually, the week of Orville Wright's birthday, Aug 19. For info: Lafayette Natural History Museum and Planetarium, 433 Jefferson St, Lafayette, LA 70501. Phone: (337) 291-5547. Fax: (337) 291-5464. Web: www.lnhmpmuseum.org.

PRESLEY, ELVIS: DEATH ANNIVERSARY. Aug 16, 1977. One of America's most popular singers, Elvis Presley was pronounced dead at the Memphis Baptist Hospital at 3:30 PM, Aug 16, 1977, at age 42. The anniversary of his death is an occasion for pilgrimages by admirers to Graceland, his home and gravesite at Memphis, TN. See also: "Presley, Elvis: Birth Anniversary" (Jan 8).

RUTH, BABE: DEATH ANNIVERSARY. Aug 16, 1948. Baseball fans of all ages and all walks of life mourned when the great "Bambino" died of cancer at New York City at the age of 53. Born Feb 6, 1895, at Baltimore, MD, the left-handed pitcher and "Sultan of Swat" hit 714 home runs in 22 major league seasons of play and played in 10 World Series. His body lay in state at the main entrance of Yankee Stadium, where people waited in line for hours to march past the coffin. On Aug 19 countless people surrounded St. Patrick's Cathedral for the funeral mass and lined the streets along the route to the cemetery as America bade farewell to one of baseball's greatest legends.

STAGG, AMOS ALONZO: BIRTH ANNIVERSARY. Aug 16, 1862. Amos Alonzo Stagg, football player and coach born at West Orange, NJ. Stagg played baseball and football at Yale and then forsook the ministry for physical education. He built the football program at the University of Chicago as an integral part of William Rainey Harper's plan to build a great university. Over 40 years at Chicago, he became the game's greatest innovator and master strategist. When Chicago deemphasized football, he moved to the College of the Pacific, finishing his career with a record of 314–181–15. Died at Stockton, CA, Mar 17, 1965.

WILL ROGERS & WILEY POST FLY-IN. Aug 16. Oologah, OK. Celebrating the life and death of these two famous Oklahomans who perished in an Aug 15, 1935, plane crash just south of Barrows, AK. Pilots can land on a 2,000-foot airstrip adjacent to the birthplace home of Will Rogers. For info: Will Rogers Memorial Museum, 1720 W Will Rogers Blvd, Claremore, OK 74017. Phone: (800) 324-9455. Web: www.willrogers.com.

Birthdays Today

Angela Bassett, 51, actress (*Malcolm X, What's Love Got to Do with It, Waiting to Exhale*), born New York, NY, Aug 16, 1958.

James Cameron, 55, director (Oscar for *Titanic; True Lies*), born Kapuskasing, ON, Canada, Aug 16, 1954.

Steve Carell, 46, actor, comedian ("The Office," "The Daily Show," *Get Smart, The 40-Year-Old Virgin*), born Acton, MA, Aug 16, 1963.

Robert Culp, 79, actor ("I Spy," *Bob and Carol and Ted and Alice*), born Berkeley, CA, Aug 16, 1930.

Frank Newton Gifford, 79, sportscaster, Hall of Fame football player, born Santa Monica, CA, Aug 16, 1930.

Kathie Lee Gifford, 56, TV personality, singer, born Paris, France, Aug 16, 1953.

Eydie Gorme, 77, singer ("Blame It on the Bossa Nova"), born Edith Gormezano at New York, NY, Aug 16, 1932.

Timothy Hutton, 49, actor (*Sunshine State*, Oscar for *Ordinary People*), born Malibu, CA, Aug 16, 1960.

Laura Innes, 49, actress ("ER," "Wings"), born Pontiac, MI, Aug 16, 1960.

Madonna, 51, singer, actress (*Desperately Seeking Susan, Evita*), born Madonna Louise Veronica Ciccone at Bay City, MI, Aug 16, 1958.

Julie Newmar, 74, actress (Cat Woman on TV's "Batman," *Li'l Abner*), born Hollywood, CA, Aug 16, 1935.

Fess Parker, 82, actor ("Daniel Boone," *Davy Crockett*), born Fort Worth, TX, Aug 16, 1927.

Jeff Perry, 54, actor ("Nash Bridges"), founder of Chicago's Steppenwolf Theater, born Highland Park, IL, Aug 16, 1955.

Seth Peterson, 39, actor ("Providence"), born the Bronx, NY, Aug 16, 1970.

Reginald VelJohnson, 57, actor (*Ghostbusters, Die Hard, Die Hard 2*), born Queens, NY, Aug 16, 1952.

Lesley Ann Warren, 63, actress (*Victor/Victoria, Choose Me*, "Cinderella"), born New York, NY, Aug 16, 1946.

August 17 — Monday

DAY 229 | **136 REMAINING**

ALLIES TAKE SICILY: ANNIVERSARY. Aug 17, 1943. After only 39 days, the entire island of Sicily was under the control of Allied forces. The official total of Germans and Italians captured was put at 130,000. The Germans, however, managed to transfer 60,000 of their 90,000 men back to the Italian mainland.

ARGENTINA: DEATH ANNIVERSARY OF SAN MARTÍN. Aug 17. National holiday. Commemorates the death in 1850 of the hero of the struggle for independence.

BALLOON CROSSING OF ATLANTIC OCEAN: ANNIVERSARY. Aug 17, 1978. Three Americans—Maxie Anderson, 44, Ben Abruzzo, 48, and Larry Newman, 31—all of Albuquerque, NM, became first to complete a transatlantic trip in a balloon. Starting from Presque Isle, ME, Aug 11, they traveled some 3,200 miles in 137 hours, 18 minutes, landing at Miserey, France (about 60 miles west of Paris), in their craft, named the *Double Eagle II*.

CANADA: YUKON DISCOVERY DAY. Aug 17. In the Klondike region of the Yukon, at Bonanza Creek (formerly known as Rabbit Creek), George Washington Carmack discovered gold Aug 16 or 17, 1896. During the following year, more than 30,000 people joined the gold rush to the area. Anniversary is celebrated as a holiday (Discovery Day) in the Yukon, on nearest Monday.

CHASE, HARRISON V.: BIRTH ANNIVERSARY. Aug 17, 1913. Cofounder and coeditor of *Chase's Annual Events*, professor at Florida State University, born at Big Rapids, MI. Died Feb 6, 2000, at Tallahassee, FL.

CLINTON'S "MEANING OF 'IS' IS": ANNIVERSARY. Aug 17, 1998. During grand jury hearings that sought to clarify President Bill Clinton's relationship with Monica Lewinsky, Clinton engaged in some semantic fine-tuning: "It depends on what your meaning of 'is' is. If 'is' means 'is and never has been,' that's one thing—if it means 'there is none,' that was a completely true statement." Clinton also parsed the meanings of "alone," "sexual relations" and "sex." His testimony was later televised to the nation on Sept 21.

CROCKETT, DAVID (DAVY): BIRTH ANNIVERSARY. Aug 17, 1786. American frontiersman, adventurer and soldier, born at Hawkins County, TN. Died during final heroic defense of the Alamo, Mar 6, 1836, at San Antonio, TX. In his *Autobiography* (1834), Crockett wrote, "I leave this rule for others when I'm dead, Be always sure you're right—then go ahead."

FORT SUMTER SHELLED BY NORTHERN FORCES: ANNIVERSARY. Aug 17, 1863. In what would become a long siege, Union forces began shelling Fort Sumter at Charleston, SC. The site of the first shots fired during the Civil War on Apr 12, 1861, Sumter endured the siege for a year and a half before being returned to Union hands.

FULTON SAILS STEAMBOAT: ANNIVERSARY. Aug 17, 1807. Robert Fulton began the first American steamboat trip between Albany and New York, NY, on a boat later called the *Clermont*. After years of promoting submarine warfare, Fulton engaged in a partnership with Robert R. Livingston, the US minister to France, allowing Fulton to design and construct a steamboat. His first success came in August 1803 when he launched a steam-powered vessel on the Seine. That same year the US Congress granted Livingston and Fulton exclusive rights to operate steamboats on New York waters during the next 20 years. The first Albany-to-New York trip took 32 hours to travel the 150-mile course. Although his efforts were labeled "Fulton's Folly" by his detractors, his success allowed the partnership to begin commercial service the next year, Sept 4, 1808.

GABON: INDEPENDENCE DAY. Aug 17. National holiday. Commemorates independence from France in 1960.

INDONESIA: INDEPENDENCE DAY. Aug 17. National holiday. Republic proclaimed in 1945. It was only after several years of fighting, however, that Indonesia was formally granted its independence by the Netherlands, Dec 27, 1949.

POWERS, FRANCIS GARY: 80th BIRTH ANNIVERSARY. Aug 17, 1929. One of America's most famous aviators, Francis Gary Powers was born at Jenkins, KY. The CIA agent, pilot of a U-2 overflight across the Soviet Union, was shot down May 1, 1960, near Sverdlovsk, USSR. He was tried, convicted and sentenced to 10 years' imprisonment, at Moscow, USSR, in August 1960. Returned to the US in 1962, in exchange for an imprisoned Soviet spy (Colonel Rudolf Abel), he found an unwelcoming homeland. Powers died in a helicopter crash near Los Angeles, CA, Aug 2, 1977.

TURKISH EARTHQUAKE: 10th ANNIVERSARY. Aug 17, 1999. A quake with a magnitude of 7.4 struck northwestern Turkey where 45 percent of the population lives. More than 17,000 died and thousands more remained missing. Many of the deaths were due to the shoddy construction of apartment houses. Aftershocks in the region through September 1999 resulted in more deaths. On Nov 12, 1999, a magnitude 7.2 earthquake struck Turkey, killing more than 800 people. Also in 1999 there were earthquakes in Greece (139 dead) and Taiwan (2,200 dead and many missing).

WEIRD CONTEST WEEK. Aug 17–21. Music Pier, Ocean City, NJ. One contest daily. Contests include artistic pie eating (chewing something meaningful out of a TastyKake Pie), saltwater taffy sculpting, french fry sculpting, wet T-shirt throwing, Little Miss and Little Mister Chaos, and Miss Miscellaneous Contest. 11 AM. Annually, the third week in August. Sponsors: The City of Ocean City, TastyKake Baking Company, Shriver's Saltwater Taffy, The Promenade. Est attendance: 4,500. For info: Mark Soifer, PR Dir, City of Ocean City, City Hall, 9th Asbury Ave, Ocean City, NJ 08226. Phone: (609) 525-9300. Fax: (609) 399-0374. E-mail: msoifer@hotmail.com.

WEST, MAE: BIRTH ANNIVERSARY. Aug 17, 1893 (some sources say 1892). The stage and screen siren, famous for her naughty wisecracks, was born Mary Jane West at Brooklyn, NY. She acted in vaudeville from the age of five and made her Hollywood debut in 1932. Unique among stars in that she wrote her own plays and film scripts—mostly concerning the joys of men and sex. Her Broadway play *Sex* resulted in her conviction for public obscenity in 1927 and she served time for eight days. Master of the risqué bon mot, West said in *I'm No Angel* (1933), "When I'm good, I'm very, very good, but when I'm bad, I'm better." She died Nov 22, 1980, at Los Angeles, CA.

Birthdays Today

Belinda Carlisle, 51, singer (The Go-Go's, "Mad About You"), born Hollywood, CA, Aug 17, 1958.

Norm Coleman, 60, US Senator (R, Minnesota), born Brooklyn, NY, Aug 17, 1949.

Robert De Niro, 66, actor (Oscars for *Raging Bull, The Godfather Part II; Taxi Driver*), born New York, NY, Aug 17, 1943.

W. Mark Felt, 96, former associate director of the Federal Bureau of Investigation (Nixon administration), "Deep Throat," born at Twin Falls, ID, Aug 17, 1913.

Jonathan Franzen, 50, author (*The Corrections*), born Western Springs, IL, Aug 17, 1959.

Thierry Henry, 32, soccer player, born Paris, France, Aug 17, 1977.

Robert Joy, 58, actor (*Atlantic City, Longtime Companion*), born Montreal, QC, Canada, Aug 17, 1951.

Christian Laettner, 40, former basketball player, born Angola, NY, Aug 17, 1969.

Maureen O'Hara, 89, actress (*Miracle on 34th Street, The Hunchback of Notre Dame*), born Dublin, Ireland, Aug 17, 1920.

August 2009

S	M	T	W	T	F	S
						1
2	3	4	5	6	7	8
9	10	11	12	13	14	15
16	17	18	19	20	21	22
23	24	25	26	27	28	29
30	31					

Sean Penn, 49, actor (Oscar for *Mystic River; Dead Man Walking*), born Santa Monica, CA, Aug 17, 1960.

Nelson Piquet, 57, former auto racer, born Brasilia, Brazil, Aug 17, 1952.

Guillermo Vilas, 57, former tennis player, born Mar del Plata, Argentina, Aug 17, 1952.

Donnie Wahlberg, 40, actor ("Band of Brothers"), former singer (New Kids on the Block), born Boston, MA, Aug 17, 1969.

August 18 — Tuesday

DAY 230 **135 REMAINING**

AMERICAN NEUTRALITY APPEAL: 95th ANNIVERSARY. Aug 18, 1914. President Woodrow Wilson followed his Aug 4 Proclamation of Neutrality with an appeal to the American people to remain impartial in thought and deed with respect to the war that was raging in Europe (WWI).

BAD POETRY DAY. Aug 18. After all the "good" poetry you were forced to study in school, here's a chance for a payback. Invite some friends over, compose some really rotten verse and send it to your old high school English teacher. (©2006 by WH.) For info: Thomas & Ruth Roy, Wellcat Holidays, 2418 Long Ln, Lebanon, PA 17046. Phone: (717) 279-0184. E-mail: info@wellcat.com. Web: www.wellcat.com.

BIRTH CONTROL PILLS SOLD: ANNIVERSARY. Aug 18, 1960. The first commercially produced oral contraceptives were marketed by the G.D. Searle Company of Illinois. The pill, developed by Gregory Pincus, had been undergoing clinical trials since 1954.

CLEMENTE, ROBERTO: 75th BIRTH ANNIVERSARY. Aug 18, 1934. National League baseball player, born at Carolina, Puerto Rico. Drafted by the Pittsburgh Pirates in 1954, he played his entire major league career with them. Clemente died in a plane crash Dec 31, 1972, while on a mission of mercy to Nicaragua to deliver supplies he had collected for survivors of an earthquake. He was elected to the Baseball Hall of Fame in 1973.

DARE, VIRGINIA: BIRTH ANNIVERSARY. Aug 18, 1587. (Old Style date.) Virginia Dare, the first child of English parents to be born in the New World, was born to Ellinor and Ananias Dare, at Roanoke Island, NC, on this date. When a ship arrived to replenish their supplies in 1591, the settlers (including Virginia Dare) had vanished, without leaving a trace of the settlement.

LEWIS, MERIWETHER: BIRTH ANNIVERSARY. Aug 18, 1774. American explorer (of Lewis and Clark expedition), born at Albemarle County, VA. Died Oct 11, 1809, near Nashville, TN.

MAIL-ORDER CATALOG: ANNIVERSARY. Aug 18, 1872. The first mail-order catalog was published by Montgomery Ward. It was only a single sheet of paper. By 1904 the Montgomery Ward catalog weighed four pounds. In 1985 Montgomery Ward closed its catalog operation; in 2000 it announced the closing of its retail stores.

NINETEENTH AMENDMENT TO US CONSTITUTION RATIFIED: ANNIVERSARY. Aug 18, 1920. The 19th Amendment extended the right to vote to women.

PENN STATE'S AG PROGRESS DAYS. Aug 18–20. The Larson Agricultural Research Center, Rock Springs, PA. 33rd annual. To provide the public with the latest information on agricultural industries and developments Penn State has made in the field of agriculture. More than 350 commercial exhibitors. Est attendance:

50,000. For info: Robert Oberheim, Penn State Univ, 420 Agricultural Admin Bldg, University Park, PA 16802. Phone: (814) 865-2081. Fax: (814) 865-1677. E-mail: agprogressdays@psu.edu. Web: apd.cas.psu.edu.

SOUTH MOUNTAIN FAIR. Aug 18–22. South Mountain Fair Grounds, Arendtsville, PA. Display of agricultural products, arts, crafts, and industrial and agricultural exhibits. Est attendance: 12,500. For info: South Mountain Fair Grounds, PO Box 58, Arendtsville, PA 17303. Phone: (717) 677-9663. Web: www.southmountainfair.com.

Birthdays Today

Elayne Boosler, 57, comedienne, born Brooklyn, NY, Aug 18, 1952.

Felipe Calderón Hinojosa, 47, President of Mexico, born Morelia, Michoacán, Mexico, Aug 18, 1962.

Eleanor Rosalynn Smith Carter, 82, former First Lady, wife of Jimmy Carter, 38th president of the US, born Plains, GA, Aug 18, 1927.

Bobby Higginson, 39, former baseball player, born Philadelphia, PA, Aug 18, 1970.

Luc Montagnier, 77, virologist, discovered the AIDS virus in 1983, born Chabris, France, Aug 18, 1932.

Martin Mull, 66, actor, comedian ("Sabrina, the Teenage Witch," "Roseanne"), born Chicago, IL, Aug 18, 1943.

Edward Norton, 40, actor (*The Incredible Hulk, 25th Hour, Primal Fear*), born Boston, MA, Aug 18, 1969.

Roman Polanski, 76, filmmaker (*Rosemary's Baby, Macbeth, Chinatown*), born Paris, France, Aug 18, 1933.

Robert Redford, 72, actor (*Butch Cassidy and the Sundance Kid, The Sting, The Natural*), director (Oscar for *Ordinary People*), born Santa Monica, CA, Aug 18, 1937.

Christian Slater, 40, actor (*Heathers, Broken Arrow, Pump Up the Volume*), born New York, NY, Aug 18, 1969.

Madeleine Stowe, 51, actress (*The Last of the Mohicans, Short Cuts*), born Los Angeles, CA, Aug 18, 1958.

Patrick Swayze, 55, dancer, actor ("North and South," *Dirty Dancing*), born Houston, TX, Aug 18, 1954.

Malcolm-Jamal Warner, 39, actor ("The Cosby Show"), born Jersey City, NJ, Aug 18, 1970.

August 19 — Wednesday

DAY 231 — **134 REMAINING**

AFGHANISTAN: INDEPENDENCE DAY. Aug 19. National day. Gained independence from British control, Treaty of Rawalpindi in 1919.

ARTISTS IN THE PARK. Aug 19. Cate Park, Wolfeboro, NH. 30th annual. Juried exhibit and sale including 41 artists and craftspeople, demonstrations throughout the day and family entertainment. Held rain or shine, 10 AM–5 PM. Sponsor: Governor Wentworth Arts Council. Est attendance: 4,000. For info: Deborah Hopkins, Chair, PO Box 1322, Wolfeboro, NH 03894. Phone: (603) 569-4994.

"BLACK COW" ROOT BEER FLOAT CREATED: ANNIVERSARY. Aug 19, 1893. Frank J. Wisner, owner of Cripple Creek Brewing, served the first root beer float in Cripple Creek, CO. Inspired by the moonlit view of snowcapped Cow Mountain, he added a scoop of ice cream to his Myers Avenue Red root beer and began serving it as the "Black Cow Mountain." Kids loved it and shortened the name to "Black Cow." Cripple Creek Brewing still sells beverages based on the original formulas. For info: Michael Lynn, Cripple Creek Brewing, 23244 Rebecca Ct, Naperville, IL 60564. Phone: (630) 904-0022. E-mail: lbartl6415@aol.com. Web: www.cripplecreekbrewing.com.

CHANEL, COCO: BIRTH ANNIVERSARY. Aug 19, 1883. The most important fashion designer of the 20th century was born Gabrielle Chanel in rural Saumur, France. After starting out in a millinery shop, she began a fashion revolution upon moving on to couture fashion in the late teens: using men's clothing (pants) for women's wear; creating simple, comfortable clothing that was nonetheless elegant; making dramatic use of costume jewelry (especially ropes of pearls); and popularizing the "little black dress" and sportswear. She was the first couturier to put her name on a signature perfume: Chanel No. 5 (created in 1921, it was an immediate sensation and today sells every 30 seconds around the world). After closing her shop with the outbreak of WWII, Chanel reopened it in 1954 and introduced her signature suit of collarless, bias-trimmed jacket with skirt. "Elegance does not consist in putting on a new dress," she once stated. The fashion icon died on Jan 10, 1971, at Paris, France.

CLINTON, WILLIAM JEFFERSON (BILL): BIRTHDAY. Aug 19, 1946. The 42nd US president (1993–2001), born at Hope, AR.

FARNSWORTH, PHILO: BIRTH ANNIVERSARY. Aug 19, 1906. Farnsworth was a television pioneer who conceived of the idea of television broadcasting while still in high school and realized his dream at 21. His first transmitted image was of a dollar sign. Farnsworth was born at Beaver, UT, and died on Mar 11, 1971, at Salt Lake City, UT.

FORBES, MALCOLM: 90th BIRTH ANNIVERSARY. Aug 19, 1919. Publisher, born at New York, NY. Malcolm Forbes was an unabashed proponent of capitalism, and his beliefs led to his colorful and successful climb to the top of the magazine-publishing industry. Known as much for his lavish lifestyle as his publishing acumen, Forbes was also an avid motorcyclist and hot-air balloonist. He died Feb 24, 1990, at Far Hills, NJ.

GERMAN PLEBISCITE: 75th ANNIVERSARY. Aug 19, 1934. In a plebiscite, 89.9 percent of German voters approved giving Chancellor Adolf Hitler the additional office of president, placing the Führer in uncontestable supreme command of that country's destiny.

HO, DON: BIRTH ANNIVERSARY. Aug 19, 1930. The man who introduced Hawaiian music to the American public was born at Honolulu, HI. A Waikiki nightclub musician who began performing in Hollywood and Las Vegas, he had an unlikely Top 40 hit with "Tiny Bubbles" in 1966. In the 1970s he was a minor television celebrity, hosting his own variety show, but he was always most comfortable playing for the tourists at various nightclubs in Waikiki. For many years no vacation to Hawaii was complete without a stop for a mai tai at a Don Ho performance, and he continued to entertain until his death at Honolulu on Apr 14, 2007.

LARDNER, RING, JR: BIRTH ANNIVERSARY. Aug 19, 1915. Born at Chicago, IL, son of fabled baseball writer and humorist Ring Lardner. Lardner, Jr, was an Academy Award–winning screenwriter (Oscar for *Woman of the Year; M*A*S*H*), and he also wrote for television. He was a member of the Hollywood Ten, a group of film industry executives sent to federal prison in 1950 for their refusal to tell the House Un-American Activities Committee if they were members of the Communist Party. He served nine months and was blacklisted for many years. Died at New York, NY, Oct 31, 2000.

NASH, OGDEN: BIRTH ANNIVERSARY. Aug 19, 1902. American writer, best remembered for his humorous verse. Born at Rye, NY; died May 19, 1971, at Baltimore, MD.

✦ **NATIONAL AVIATION DAY.** Aug 19. Presidential Proclamation 2343, of July 25, 1939, covers all succeeding years. Always Aug 19 of each year since 1939. Observed annually on birth anniversary of Orville Wright, who piloted "first self-powered flight in history," Dec 17, 1903. First proclaimed by President Franklin D. Roosevelt.

RODDENBERRY, GENE: BIRTH ANNIVERSARY. Aug 19, 1921. The creator of the popular TV series "Star Trek," Gene Roddenberry was born at El Paso, TX. Turning from his first career as an airline pilot to writing, he created one of the most successful TV science fiction series ever. The original series, which ended its run in 1969, lives on in reruns and led to other popular spin-off series. Ten films also have been spawned from the original concept. Roddenberry died Oct 24, 1991, at Santa Monica, CA.

SPACE MILESTONE: *SOYUZ T-7* (USSR). Aug 19, 1982. Launched from Tyuratam, USSR, with second woman in space (test pilot Svetlana Savitskaya) and two other cosmonauts. Docked at *Salyut 7* and visited the cosmonauts who had been in residence there for the three previous months before returning to Earth on Aug 27 in the *Soyuz T-5* vehicle, which had been docked there. The *Soyuz T-7* returned to Earth Dec 10.

SPACE MILESTONE: *SPUTNIK 5* (USSR). Aug 19, 1960. Space menagerie satellite with dogs Belka and Strelka, mice, rats, houseflies and plants launched. These passengers became the first living organisms recovered from orbit when the satellite returned safely to Earth the next day.

WRIGHT, ORVILLE: BIRTH ANNIVERSARY. Aug 19, 1871. Aviation pioneer born at Dayton, OH, and died there Jan 30, 1948. See also: "Wright Brothers First Powered Flight: Anniversary" (Dec 17).

Birthdays Today

Adam Arkin, 53, actor ("Chicago Hope," "Northern Exposure"), born Brooklyn, NY, Aug 19, 1956.

William Jefferson Clinton, 63, 42nd president of the US, born Hope, AK, Aug 19, 1946.

Kevin Dillon, 44, actor ("Entourage"), born Mamaroneck, NY, Aug 19, 1965.

Peter Gallagher, 54, actor (*sex, lies and videotape*; *Short Cuts*, "The O.C."), born New York, NY, Aug 19, 1955.

Tipper Gore, 61, wife of Al Gore, 45th vice president of the US, advocate for the homeless, mental health and children's causes, born Mary Elizabeth Aitcheson at Washington, DC, Aug 19, 1948.

Frank McCourt, 78, author (*Angela's Ashes*, *'Tis*), born Brooklyn, NY, Aug 19, 1931.

Gerald McRaney, 61, actor ("Simon & Simon," "Major Dad"), born Collins, MS, Aug 19, 1948.

Jennifer Morrison, 30, actress ("House"), born Chicago, IL, Aug 19, 1979.

Diana Muldaur, 71, actress ("Star Trek: The Next Generation," "LA Law," *The Swimmer*), born New York, NY, Aug 19, 1938.

(Franklin) Story Musgrave, 74, former astronaut, born Boston, MA, Aug 19, 1935.

Cindy Nelson, 54, former alpine skier, born Lutsen, MN, Aug 19, 1955.

Matthew Perry, 40, actor ("Friends," *Fools Rush In*), born Williamstown, MA, Aug 19, 1969.

Jill St. John, 69, actress (*Diamonds Are Forever*), born Jill Oppenheim at Los Angeles, CA, Aug 19, 1940.

Kyra Sedgwick, 44, actress ("The Closer," *Phenomenon*, *Born on the Fourth of July*), born New York, NY, Aug 19, 1965.

John Stamos, 46, actor ("ER," "Full House"), born Los Angeles, CA, Aug 19, 1963.

Fred Thompson, 67, former US Senator (R, Tennessee), actor ("Law & Order," *In the Line of Fire*), born Sheffield, AL, Aug 19, 1942.

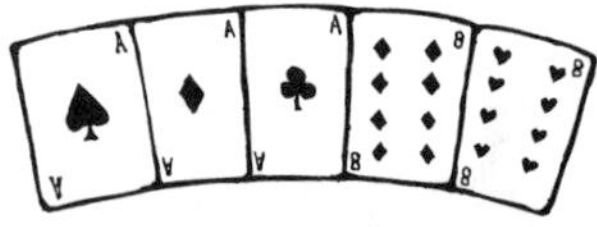

August 2009	S	M	T	W	T	F	S
							1
	2	3	4	5	6	7	8
	9	10	11	12	13	14	15
	16	17	18	19	20	21	22
	23	24	25	26	27	28	29
	30	31					

August 20 — Thursday

DAY 232 **133 REMAINING**

CANADA: OTTAWA FOLK FESTIVAL. Aug 20–23. Britannia Park, Ottawa, ON. A four-day celebration of acoustic music on the banks of the Ottawa River, featuring North America's finest folk performers. Est attendance: 23,000. For info: Ottawa Folk Festival, 100-858 Bank St, Ottawa, ON, Canada K1S 3W3. Phone: (613) 230-8234. E-mail: festival@ottawafolk.org. Web: www.ottawafolk.org.

GUEST, EDGAR ALBERT: BIRTH ANNIVERSARY. Aug 20, 1881. Newspaperman and author of folksy, homespun verse that enjoyed great popularity and was syndicated in more than 100 newspapers. Born at Birmingham, England; died at Detroit, MI, Aug 5, 1959. "Eddie Guest Day" usually proclaimed on birth anniversary in Detroit.

HARRISON, BENJAMIN: BIRTH ANNIVERSARY. Aug 20, 1833. The 23rd president of the US, born at North Bend, OH. He was the grandson of William Henry Harrison, 9th president of the US. His term of office, Mar 4, 1889–Mar 3, 1893, was preceded and followed by the presidential terms of Grover Cleveland (who thus became the 22nd and 24th president of the US). Harrison died at Indianapolis, IN, Mar 13, 1901.

HUNGARY: SAINT STEPHEN'S DAY. Aug 20. National holiday. Commemorates the canonization of Saint Stephen, king and founder of the state, in 1083. Under the Communists, commemorated as Constitution Day.

KENTUCKY STATE FAIR (WITH WORLD'S CHAMPIONSHIP HORSE SHOW). Aug 20–30. Kentucky Fair and Expo Center, Louisville, KY. Midway, concerts by nationally known artists and the World's Championship Horse Show. Since 1904. Est attendance: 650,000. For info: Media Office, KY Fair and Expo Ctr, Box 37130, Louisville, KY 40233. Phone: (502) 367-5000 or (502) 367-5180. Web: www.kyexpo.org.

LOVECRAFT, H.P.: BIRTH ANNIVERSARY. Aug 20, 1890. Howard Phillips Lovecraft, American author of horror tales of the supernatural, a pioneering science fiction writer and a notable epistoler, was born at Providence, RI, and died there Mar 15, 1937.

MOON PHASE: NEW MOON. Aug 20. Moon enters New Moon phase at 6:02 AM, EDT.

MOROCCO: REVOLUTION OF THE KING AND THE PEOPLE: ANNIVERSARY. Aug 20. National holiday. Commemorates the response of the people to Sultan (later King) Sidi Muhammed's being sent into exile in 1953 by the French.

O'HIGGINS, BERNARDO: BIRTH ANNIVERSARY. Aug 20, 1778. First ruler of Chile after its declaration of independence. Called the "Liberator of Chile." Born at Chillan, Chile. Died at Lima, Peru, Oct 24, 1842.

PLUTONIUM FIRST WEIGHED: ANNIVERSARY. Aug 20, 1942. University of Chicago scientist Glen Seaborg and his colleagues first weighed plutonium, the first man-made element.

PRESIDENT BENJAMIN HARRISON'S BIRTHDAY CELEBRATION. Aug 20. Indianapolis, IN, Harrison's hometown. Also free tours of his Victorian mansion. Est attendance: 300. For info: PR Dept, President Benjamin Harrison Home, 1230 N Delaware St, Indianapolis, IN 46202. Phone: (317) 631-1888. Fax: (317) 632-5488. E-mail: harrison@pbhh.org. Web: www.pbhh.org.

REEVES, JIM: 85th BIRTH ANNIVERSARY. Aug 20, 1924. Country music star Jim Reeves was born at Galloway, Panola County, TX, and died at Nashville, TN, July 31, 1964, when the single-engine plane in which he was traveling crashed in a dense fog. Reeves's biggest hit was "He'll Have to Go" (1959), and he was inducted into the Country Music Hall of Fame in 1967.

SAARINEN, EERO: BIRTH ANNIVERSARY. Aug 20, 1910. Born at Kirkkonummi, Finland, but raised in the United States by his architect father, Eliel, and sculptor mother, Saarinen was a leading postwar architect and furniture designer whose sculptural designs were in contrast to the reigning International Style. Saarinen died Sept 1, 1961, at Ann Arbor, MI.

SAARINEN, ELIEL: BIRTH ANNIVERSARY. Aug 20, 1873. Famed architect. Born at Helsinki, Finland. Died at Bloomfield Hills, MI, July 1, 1950.

SHELDON OLD SETTLERS' PICNIC. Aug 20–22. Sheldon, MO. An annual homecoming event held in a beautiful city park. The three-day festival features many events, including a tractor pull, softball tournament, live entertainment, horse pull and parade. Annually, the third Thursday, Friday and Saturday in August. For info: Travis Denney, Sheldon Picnic, PO Box 163, Sheldon, MO 64784. Phone: (417) 667-1440. E-mail: sheldonpicnic@yahoo.com. Web: www.geocities.com/sheldonpicnic/missouri.

SOLDIERS' REUNION CELEBRATION. Aug 20. Newton, NC. Parade climaxes the 120th annual soldiers' reunion celebration—"oldest patriotic event of its kind in the US, honoring all veterans." Annually, the third Thursday in August. Concerts, arts, crafts, food and games. Est attendance: 33,500. For info: Soldiers' Reunion Committee, Box 267, Newton, NC 28658. Phone: (828) 464-2383.

SPACE MILESTONE: *VIKING 1* AND 2 (US). Aug 20 and Sept 9, 1975. Sister ships launched toward Mars from Cape Canaveral, FL, on Aug 20 and Sept 9, 1975. *Viking 1*'s lander touched down on Mars July 20, 1976, and *Viking 2*'s lander on Sept 3, 1976. Sent back to Earth high-quality photographs, analysis of atmosphere, weather information and results of sophisticated experiments intended to determine whether life may be present on Mars.

SPACE MILESTONE: *VOYAGER 2* (US). Aug 20, 1977. This unmanned spacecraft journeyed past Jupiter in 1979, Saturn in 1981, Uranus in 1986 and Neptune in 1989, sending photographs and data back to scientists on Earth.

SUN PRAIRIE'S SWEET CORN FESTIVAL. Aug 20–23. Sun Prairie, WI. Family-oriented fun. Carnival, midget auto races, parade, beer, brats, food, exhibits, entertainment, craft fair and tons of hot, buttered sweet corn. Est attendance: 100,000. For info: Sun Prairie Chamber of Commerce, 109 E Main St, Sun Prairie, WI 53590. Phone: (608) 837-4547. Fax: (608) 837-8765. E-mail: spchamber@verizon.net. Web: www.sunprairiechamber.com.

SWEDEN: SOUR HERRING PREMIERE. Aug 20. By ordinance, the year's supply of sour herring may begin to be sold on the third Thursday in August.

VIRTUAL WORLDS DAY. Aug 20. An annual celebration of virtual worlds. For info: Edita Kaye, iVinnie LLC, 200 Executive Way, Ste 206, Ponte Vedra Beach, FL 32082. Phone: (954) 734-5000. E-mail: edita@ivinnie.com. Web: www.ivinnie.com.

Birthdays Today

Amy Adams, 34, actress (*Enchanted, Junebug*), born Vicenza, Italy, Aug 20, 1975.

Joan Allen, 53, actress (*Searching for Bobby Fischer, Nixon, The Contender, The Bourne Ultimatum*), born Rochelle, IL, Aug 20, 1956.

Andy Benes, 42, former baseball player, born Evansville, IN, Aug 20, 1967.

Connie Chung, 63, journalist, born Constance Yu-Hwa at Washington, DC, Aug 20, 1946.

Tara Dakides, 34, snowboarder, born Mission Viejo, CA, Aug 20, 1975.

Todd Helton, 36, baseball player, born Knoxville, TN, Aug 20, 1973.

Donald (Don) King, 78, boxing promoter, born Cleveland, OH, Aug 20, 1931.

Mark Edward Langston, 49, former baseball player, born San Diego, CA, Aug 20, 1960.

Robert Plant, 61, singer, born Bromwich, England, Aug 20, 1948.

Al Roker, 55, television personality ("Today Show"), born Brooklyn, NY, Aug 20, 1954.

Theresa Saldana, 54, actress ("The Commish"), born Brooklyn, NY, Aug 20, 1955.

August 21 — Friday

DAY 233 | **132 REMAINING**

AMERICAN BAR ASSOCIATION FOUNDING: ANNIVERSARY. Aug 21, 1878. Organized at Saratoga, NY.

AQUINO, BENIGNO: ASSASSINATION ANNIVERSARY. Aug 21, 1983. Filipino opposition leader Benigno S. Aquino, Jr, was shot and killed at the Manila airport on his return to the Philippines on Aug 21, 1983. The killing precipitated greater anti-Marcos feeling and figured significantly in the Feb 7, 1986, election that brought about the collapse of the government administration of Ferdinand E. Marcos and the inauguration of Corazon C. Aquino, widow of the slain man, as president.

BEARDSLEY, AUBREY VINCENT: BIRTH ANNIVERSARY. Aug 21, 1872. English artist and illustrator born at Brighton, England. Died at Menton, France, Mar 16, 1898.

CALIFORNIA STATE FAIR. Aug 21–Sept 7 (tentative). Sacramento, CA. Top-name entertainment, fireworks, California counties exhibits, livestock nursery, culinary delights, carnival rides and award-winning wines and microbrews. For info: California State Fair, PO Box 15649, Sacramento, CA 95852. Phone: (916) 263-FAIR. Web: www.bigfun.org.

CANADA: MORDEN CORN AND APPLE FESTIVAL. Aug 21–23. Morden, MB. It's fun and it's free! Est attendance: 70,000. For info: Morden Chamber of Commerce, 311 N Railway St, Morden, MB, Canada R6M 1S9. Phone: (204) 822-5630. Fax: (204) 822-2041. E-mail: chamber@mordenmb.com. Web: www.cornandapple.com.

CHAMBERLAIN, WILT: BIRTH ANNIVERSARY. Aug 21, 1936. Basketball Hall of Fame center, born at Philadelphia, PA. Died Oct 12, 1999, at Los Angeles, CA.

COBBLESTONE FESTIVAL. Aug 21–23. Falls City, NE. Includes games, sporting events, contests, dodgeball competition, bull riding, carnival rides, flea market, food concessions, fishing contest, parade, craft demos and more. Est attendance: 5,000. For info: Falls City Chamber of Commerce, 1705 Stone St, Falls City, NE 68355. Phone: (402) 245-4228. Fax: (402) 245-4228. E-mail: fcchamber@sentco.net.

ELWOOD GLASS FESTIVAL. Aug 21–23. Elwood, IN. Glass factory tours, parade, craft market, flea market, quilt show, entertainment, carnival, kids' activities and more. Est attendance: 20,000. For info: Chamber of Commerce, 108 S Anderson St, Elwood, IN 46036. Phone: (765) 552-0180. E-mail: elwoodchamber@sbcglobal.net. Web: www.elwoodchamber.org.

FIESTA LA BALLONA. Aug 21–23 (tentative). Veterans Park, Culver City, CA. A Culver City community celebration since 1951. The Fiesta La Ballona features carnival rides, arts and crafts booths, nonprofit booths, local business booths and more. Culver City is known as the "Heart of Screenland" and is the historical site of the MGM and Hal Roach studios. Annually, the weekend before Labor Day weekend. Est attendance: 12,000. For info: Pam Robinson, Culver City Park, Recreation & Community Services Dept, 4117 Overland Ave, Culver City, CA 90230-3733. Phone: (310) 253-6632. Fax: (310) 253-6629. E-mail: pam.robinson@culvercity.org. Web: fiestalaballona.org.

HAWAII ADMISSION DAY HOLIDAY. Aug 21. The third Friday in August is observed as a state holiday each year, recognizing the anniversary of Hawaii's statehood. Hawaii became the 50th state Aug 21, 1959.

HAWAII: ADMISSION DAY: 50th ANNIVERSARY. Aug 21, 1959. President Dwight Eisenhower signed a proclamation admitting Hawaii to the Union. The statehood bill had passed the previous March with a stipulation that statehood should be approved by a vote of Hawaiian residents. The referendum passed by a huge margin in June, and Eisenhower proclaimed Hawaii the 50th state on Aug 21.

ITALY: STRESA FESTIVAL. Aug 21–Sept 5. Stresa. 48th annual. International festival includes concerts by symphonic orchestras, chamber music and recitals. Since 2006 the Stresa Music Academy has organized master classes given by important musicians during the festival period, followed by a couple of concerts held by the best students. For info: Settimane Musicali di Stresa del Lago Maggiore, Via Carducci, 38, 28838 Stresa (VB), Italy. Phone: (39) (0323) 31095. Fax: (39) (0323) 33006. E-mail: info@stresafestival.eu. Web: www.stresafestival.eu.

LINCOLN-DOUGLAS DEBATES: ANNIVERSARY. Aug 21–Oct 15, 1858. At Ottawa, IL, Abraham Lincoln began a series of debates throughout Illinois with Stephen A. Douglas that would propel him to national notoriety. Republican Lincoln was challenging Democrat Douglas's bid for reelection to the US Senate. The two men conducted seven spirited public debates that often wrestled with the question of slavery in US territories. Although Douglas won reelection, Lincoln's eloquence gained him acclaim and he was chosen to be the Republican Party's candidate for president in the 1860 elections. In 1860 Lincoln defeated Douglas to become president.

LITTLE LEAGUE BASEBALL WORLD SERIES. Aug 21–30. Williamsport, PA. Sixteen teams from the US and foreign countries compete for the World Championship. Est attendance: 300,000. For info: Little League International, Box 3485, Williamsport, PA 17701. Phone: (570) 326-1921. Web: www.LittleLeague.org.

MACHIAS WILD BLUEBERRY FESTIVAL. Aug 21–23. Machias, ME. Harvest festival includes crafts sale, lobster boil, five-mile race, entertainment, children's parade, blueberry foods and a wild blueberry pie–eating contest. Annually, the third weekend in August. Est attendance: 22,000. For info: Machias Wild Blueberry Festival, PO Box 265, Machias, ME 04654. Phone: (207) 255-6665. Web: www.machiasblueberry.com.

August 2009

S	M	T	W	T	F	S
						1
2	3	4	5	6	7	8
9	10	11	12	13	14	15
16	17	18	19	20	21	22
23	24	25	26	27	28	29
30	31					

MEXICAN FIESTA INTERNACIONAL. Aug 21–23. Milwaukee, WI. Mexican Fiesta brings the sound and taste of Mexico to Milwaukee's lakefront. Three days of fun, food, mariachi and fiesta for everyone. Plus the traditional jalapeño-eating contest, national and international entertainment, and the best Mexican cuisine. Est attendance: 70,000. For info: Mexican Fiesta, 1220 W Windlake Ave, Milwaukee, WI 53215. Phone: (414) 383-7066. Fax: (414) 383-6677. E-mail: fiestamilw@aol.com. Web: www.mexicanfiesta.org.

NATIONAL MEN'S GROOMING DAY. Aug 21. Participating salons and barbershops will host a day of grooming events for men. The day was founded and is sponsored by American Crew, the leading maker of men's grooming products carried in salons and barbershops nationwide. Annually, the third Friday in August. For info: Megan Cantrell, Colomer Salon Division, 1515 Wazee St, Ste 200, Denver, CO 80202. Phone: (303) 928-2090. Fax: (303) 292-4851. E-mail: media@americancrew.com. Web: www.americancrew.com.

POET'S DAY. Aug 21. A day for all poets to celebrate their special talents and the vision that makes them so wonderful and dear. Poet's Day is a time to share special thoughts about poets and poetry. (©2001 C. Daniel Rhodes.) For info: C. Daniel Rhodes or Natalie Danielle Rhodes, 1900 Crossvine Rd, Hoover, AL 35244. Phone: (205) 908-6781. E-mail: rhodan@charter.net.

QUANTRILL'S RAID ON LAWRENCE, KANSAS: ANNIVERSARY. Aug 21, 1863. Confederate raider William Clarke Quantrill launched a predawn terrorist raid on Lawrence, KS, leaving 150 civilians dead and much of the town ruined. Quantrill had been denied a commission in the Southern army for his barbaric approach to war.

SEMINOLE TRIBE OF FLORIDA LEGALLY ESTABLISHED: ANNIVERSARY. Aug 21, 1957. In 1953 Congress adopted a proposal to terminate assistance to nonrecognized Indian tribes. Seminole leaders and tribal members began to fight the proposal by drafting a constitution and charter for the Seminole Tribe. These were later approved by the secretary of the interior. On this date a majority of tribal members voted to establish the Seminole Tribe of Florida. Today, 2,200 Seminoles live on five reservations in Florida.

SPACE MILESTONE: *GEMINI 5* (US). Aug 21, 1965. Launched on this date, this craft carrying astronauts Lieutenant Colonel Cooper and Lieutenant Commander Conrad orbited Earth 128 times for new international record of eight days.

Birthdays Today

Steve Case, 51, founder of America Online, born Oahu, HI, Aug 21, 1958.

Kim Cattrall, 53, actress ("Sex and the City," *Mannequin*), born Liverpool, England, Aug 21, 1956.

Jackie DeShannon, 65, singer, songwriter ("Put a Little Love in Your Heart"), born Hazel, KY, Aug 21, 1944.

Brody Jenner, 26, television personality, born Los Angeles, CA, Aug 21, 1983.

James Robert (Jim) McMahon, 50, former football player, born Jersey City, NJ, Aug 21, 1959.

Hayden Panettiere, 20, actress ("Heroes," "Guiding Light"), born Palisades, NY, Aug 21, 1989.

Kenny Rogers, 71, singer ("Lucille," "Lady"), born Houston, TX, Aug 21, 1938.

Jon Tester, 53, US Senator (D, Montana), born Havre, MT, Aug 21, 1956.

Melvin Van Peebles, 77, actor, director, playwright (*Ain't Supposed to Die a Natural Death*), born Chicago, IL, Aug 21, 1932.

Peter Weir, 65, director (*Dead Poets Society, Gallipoli, The Truman Show*), born Sydney, Australia, Aug 21, 1944.

Clarence Williams III, 70, actor ("The Mod Squad," *Purple Rain*), born New York, NY, Aug 21, 1939.

Alicia Witt, 34, actress ("Cybill"), born Worcester, MA, Aug 21, 1975.

August 22 — Saturday

DAY 234 131 REMAINING

BATTLE OF STALINGRAD BEGINS: ANNIVERSARY. Aug 22, 1942. Having captured Sevastopol on the Crimea on July 2, after an eight-month seige, the Germans began an offensive to capture Stalingrad. During this five-month-long battle, the city of 500,000 people dwindled to a population of 1,515. In the fighting, Russia lost 750,000 troops, the Germans 400,000, the Romanians nearly 200,000 and the Italians 130,000—a total of 1,480,000. The last German strongholds at Stalingrad surrendered to the Russian army on Feb 2, 1943.

BE AN ANGEL DAY. Aug 22. A day to do "one small act of service for someone. Be a blessing in someone's life." Annually, Aug 22. For info: Angel Heights Healing Center, Rev Jayne M. Howard Feldman, PO Box 95, Upperco, MD 21155. Phone: (410) 833-6912. E-mail: earthangel4peace@aol.com. Web: earthangel4peace.com.

CAMEROON: VOLCANIC ERUPTION: ANNIVERSARY. Aug 22, 1986. Deadly fumes from a presumed volcanic eruption under Lake Nios at Cameroon killed more than 1,500 persons. A similar occurrence two years earlier had killed 37 persons.

CARTIER-BRESSON, HENRI: BIRTH ANNIVERSARY. Aug 22, 1908. Pioneering photojournalist who cofounded the Magnum photo agency. Probably the most respected 20th-century photographer. Famous for looking for "the decisive moment." Born at Chanteloup, France, he died Aug 2, 2004, at l'Ile-sur-Sorgue, France.

COUNTRY FEST AND AUCTION. Aug 22. Garrett County Fairgrounds, Deep Creek Lake, McHenry, MD. Family-oriented activities, demonstrations, crafts, baked goods, horse-and-buggy and pony rides, farm animal petting zoo, gospel music, chicken barbecue and an auction featuring handcrafted wood items, locally made quilts and much more. Hours 8 AM to 5 PM. Event sponsored by the Bittinger Mennonite Church. Annually, the fourth Saturday in August. Est attendance: 2,500. For info: Country Fest & Auction, 1705 Foy Rd, Accident, MD 21520. Phone: (301) 245-4564 or (301) 245-4326. E-mail: lmaust@juno.com. Web: www.countryfest.org.

DEBUSSY, CLAUDE: BIRTH ANNIVERSARY. Aug 22, 1862. (Achille) Claude Debussy, French musician and composer, especially remembered for his impressionistic "tone poems," was born at St. Germain-en-Laye, France. He died at Paris, France, Mar 25, 1918.

HERRIMAN, GEORGE: BIRTH ANNIVERSARY. Aug 22, 1880. In 1910 when George Herriman introduced a cat and mouse as subplot characters to his comic strip "The Dingbat Family," their non-sequitur dialogue gained enough attention to result in a spin-off strip of their own. The superbly drafted "Krazy Kat and Ignatz" had as its central theme unrequited love. Kat loved Ignatz, but the malevolent mouse took every opportunity to throw bricks at the devoted cat. "Krazy Kat" was popular with a mass audience as well as artists and intellectuals, and it remained enormously popular after Herriman's death. Born at New Orleans, LA, he died at Hollywood, CA, Apr 25, 1944.

INTERNATIONAL YACHT RACE: ANNIVERSARY. Aug 22, 1851. A silver trophy (then known as the "Hundred Guinea Cup" and offered by the Royal Yacht Squadron) was won in a race around the Isle of Wight by the US yacht *America*. The trophy, later turned over to the New York Yacht Club, became known as the America's Cup.

LANGLEY, SAMUEL PIERPONT: 175th BIRTH ANNIVERSARY. Aug 22, 1834. American astronomer, physicist and aviation pioneer for whom Langley Air Force Base, VA, is named. Born at Roxbury, MA, Langley died at Aiken, SC, Feb 27, 1906.

MORMON CHOIR FIRST PERFORMANCE: ANNIVERSARY. Aug 22, 1847. What would later become the world-famous Mormon Tabernacle Choir gave its first public performance at Salt Lake City, UT, for an outdoor meeting of The Church of Jesus Christ of Latter-day Saints. Widely known for its concert tours, recordings and weekly radio and television broadcasts from Temple Square, the choir's radio program "Music and the Spoken Word" is the longest continuously running radio program in network history, dating back to 1929.

RAMADAN: THE ISLAMIC MONTH OF FASTING. Aug 22–Sept 20. Begins on Islamic lunar calendar date Ramadan 1, 1430. Ramadan, the ninth month of the Islamic calendar, is holy because it was during this month that the Holy Qur'an (Koran) was revealed. All adults of sound body and mind fast from dawn (before sunrise) until sunset to achieve spiritual and physical purification and self-discipline, abstaining from food, drink and intimate relations. It is a time for feeling a common bond with people who are poor and needy, a time of piety and prayer. Different methods for "anticipating" the visibility of the new moon crescent at Mecca are used by different Muslim groups. US date may vary. Began at sunset the preceding day.

RIEFENSTAHL, LENI: BIRTH ANNIVERSARY. Aug 22, 1902. Controversial actress and filmmaker who directed the infamous Nazi propaganda films *Triumph of the Will* (1934) and *Olympia* (1936). Both films are noted for innovative filming techniques. Born at Berlin, Germany, Riefenstahl died at Pöcking, Germany, on September 8, 2003.

SIDEWALK ART FESTIVAL. Aug 22. Portland, ME. Sponsored by WCSH 6, this 44th annual festival is Maine's largest and oldest one-day art show. More than 300 artists from around the Northeast with works for sale. On Congress St, from Park St to Elm St (closed to vehicular traffic). Annually, the fourth Saturday in August. For info: Community Relations, WCSH 6, One Congress Sq, Portland, ME 04101. Phone: (207) 828-6666. Fax: (207) 828-6620. E-mail: communityrelations@WCSH6.com. Web: WCSH6.com.

SOUTHERN HEMISPHERE HOODIE-HOO DAY. Aug 22. Long awaited by our Southern-half friends, this is the day to go outdoors at high noon and yell "Hoodie-Hoo" to chase winter and make ready for spring, only one month away. (©2006 by WH.) For info: Thomas & Ruth Roy, Wellcat Holidays, 2418 Long Ln, Lebanon, PA 17046. Phone: (717) 279-0184. E-mail: info@wellcat.com. Web: www.wellcat.com.

VIETNAM CONFLICT BEGINS: ANNIVERSARY. Aug 22, 1945. Less than a week after the Japanese surrender ended WWII, a team of Free French parachuted into southern Indochina in response to a successful coup by a Communist guerrilla named Ho Chi Minh in the French colony.

WILLARD, ARCHIBALD M.: BIRTH ANNIVERSARY. Aug 22, 1836. American artist, best known for his painting *The Spirit of '76*, was born at Bedford, OH. Willard died at Cleveland, OH, Oct 11, 1918.

Birthdays Today

Adewale Akinnuoye-Agbaje, 42, actor ("Lost," "Oz"), born London, England, Aug 22, 1967.

Tori Amos, 46, musician, singer, songwriter, born Newton, NC, Aug 22, 1963.

Ray Bradbury, 89, author (*The Toynbee Convector, Fahrenheit 451*), born Waukegan, IL, Aug 22, 1920.

Gerald Paul Carr, 77, former astronaut, born Denver, CO, Aug 22, 1932.

Giada De Laurentiis, 39, chef, cookbook author, television personality ("Everyday Italian"), born Rome, Italy, Aug 22, 1970.

Valerie Harper, 68, actress ("The Mary Tyler Moore Show," "Rhoda"), born Suffern, NY, Aug 22, 1941.

Steve Kroft, 64, television journalist, editor ("60 Minutes"), born Kokomo, IN, Aug 22, 1945.

Paul Leo Molitor, 53, former baseball player, born St. Paul, MN, Aug 22, 1956.

Duane Charles (Bill) Parcells, 68, football coach, born Englewood, NJ, Aug 22, 1941.

E. Annie Proulx, 74, author (*The Shipping News, Accordian Crimes*), born Norwich, CT, Aug 22, 1935.

Norman H. Schwarzkopf, 75, retired army general, born Trenton, NJ, Aug 22, 1934.

Cindy Williams, 61, actress (*American Graffiti*, "Laverne & Shirley"), born Van Nuys, CA, Aug 22, 1948.

Carl Michael Yastrzemski, 70, Hall of Fame baseball player, born Southampton, NY, Aug 22, 1939.

August 23 — Sunday

DAY 235 **130 REMAINING**

FIRST MAN-POWERED FLIGHT: ANNIVERSARY. Aug 23, 1977. At Schafter, CA, Bryan Allen pedaled the 70-pound *Gossamer Condor* for a mile at a "minimal altitude of two pylons" in a flight certified by the Royal Aeronautical Society of Britain, winning a £50,000 prize offered by British industrialist Henry Kremer. See also: "First Man-Powered Flight Across English Channel: Anniversary" (June 12).

ITALY: INTERNATIONAL FEDERATION OF LIBRARY ASSOCIATIONS ANNUAL CONFERENCE. Aug 23–27. Milan. The theme for the 75th annual conference is "Libraries Create Futures: Building on Cultural Heritage." For info: Intl Federation of Library Assns Conference Secretariat, 4B, 50 Spiers Wharf, Port Dundas, Glasgow G4 9TH, Scotland. Phone: (44) (141) 331 0123. E-mail: ifla2009@congrex.com. Web: www.congrex.com.

August 2009	S	M	T	W	T	F	S
							1
	2	3	4	5	6	7	8
	9	10	11	12	13	14	15
	16	17	18	19	20	21	22
	23	24	25	26	27	28	29
	30	31					

KELLY, GENE: BIRTH ANNIVERSARY. Aug 23, 1912. Actor, dancer, director, choreographer born at Pittsburgh, PA. His movies included the musicals *Singin' in the Rain* and *An American in Paris.* Kelly died at Beverly Hills, CA, Feb 2, 1996.

LUXEMBOURG: SCHUEBERMESS SHEPHERD'S FAIR. Aug 23–Sept 5. Fair dates from 1340. (Two weeks beginning on the next-to-last Sunday in August.)

MASTERS, EDGAR LEE: BIRTH ANNIVERSARY. Aug 23, 1869. American poet, author of the *Spoon River Anthology*, was born at Garnett, KS. He died at Melrose Park, PA, Mar 5, 1950.

PERRY, OLIVER HAZARD: BIRTH ANNIVERSARY. Aug 23, 1785. American naval hero, born at South Kingston, RI. Died Aug 23, 1819, at sea. Best remembered is his announcement of victory at the Battle of Lake Erie, Sept 10, 1813: "We have met the enemy, and they are ours."

PITTSBURGH RENAISSANCE FESTIVAL. Aug 23–24. (also Aug 30–Sept 1, Sept 6–7, 13–14, 20–21 and 27–28). West Newton, PA. A re-creation of a 16th-century marketplace where the king and queen come on holiday. Featured are more than 100 craft shops, six themed stages, games, food and armored contact jousting. Est attendance: 100,000. For info: Lori Hughes, Pittsburgh Renaissance Festival, 112 Renaissance Ln, West Newton, PA 15089. Phone: (724) 872-1670. E-mail: info@pgh-renfest.com.

ROMANIA SURRENDER TO USSR: 65th ANNIVERSARY. Aug 23, 1944. Romanian king Michael I removed pro-German premier Jon Antonescue from his position, dismissed his entire government and broadcast to the people of Romania that all hostilities had ceased and that he had accepted all peace terms demanded by the Allies. Most important, the Ploesti oil fields would be secured by the Allies.

SACCO-VANZETTI MEMORIAL DAY: ANNIVERSARY. Aug 23, 1927. Nicola Sacco and Bartolomeo Vanzetti were electrocuted at the Charlestown, MA, prison on this date. Convicted of a shoe factory payroll robbery during which a guard had been killed, Sacco and Vanzetti maintained their innocence to the end. Six years of appeals marked this American cause célèbre during which substantial evidence was presented to show that both men were elsewhere at the time of the crime. On the 50th anniversary of their execution, Massachusetts governor Michael S. Dukakis proclaimed Aug 23, 1977, a memorial day, noting that the 1921 trial had been "permeated by prejudice."

SPACE MILESTONE: *INTELSAT-4 F-7* (US). Aug 23, 1973. International Communications Satellite Consortium's *Intelsat* launched Aug 23, 1973, to relay communications from North and South America to Europe and Africa.

"STOCKHOLM SYNDROME" BANK ROBBERY: ANNIVERSARY. Aug 23–28, 1973. In a botched bank robbery at Stockholm, Sweden, Jan Erik Olsson took four hostages and barricaded himself with them and a friend, Clark Olofsson, in the vault. After a six-day siege, the police piped in gas and the hostages were freed. Afterward, it emerged that the hostages were more afraid of the police than of their captors, and Swedish professor Nils Bejerot coined the term "Stockholm syndrome" to explain the phenomenom of hostages identifying and sympathizing with their captors.

UNITED NATIONS: INTERNATIONAL DAY FOR THE REMEMBRANCE OF THE SLAVE TRADE AND ITS ABOLITION. Aug 23. For info: United Nations, Dept of Public Info, New York, NY 10017. Web: www.un.org.

VALENTINO MEMORIAL SERVICE. Aug 23. Hollywood Cathedral Mausoleum, Hollywood Forever Cemetery, Los Angeles, CA. Since 1927 annual memorial service celebrating the life of the silent screen's biggest male star, Rudolph Valentino. Held each year on the anniversary of his 1926 death at 12:10 PM—the time he died (in New York City). Attendees include the "Lady in Black." For info: Hollywood Forever Cemetery, 6000 Santa Monica Blvd, Los Angeles, CA, 90038.

VIRGO, THE VIRGIN. Aug 23–Sept 22. In the astronomical/astrological zodiac, which divides the sun's apparent orbit into 12 segments, the period Aug 23–Sept 22 is traditionally identified as the sun sign of Virgo, the Virgin. The ruling planet is Mercury.

Birthdays Today

Tony Bill, 69, actor (*You're a Big Boy Now*), director (*My Bodyguard*), born San Diego, CA, Aug 23, 1940.

Kobe Bryant, 31, basketball player, born Philadelphia, PA, Aug 23, 1978.

Barbara Eden, 75, actress ("I Dream of Jeannie," *Harper Valley P.T.A.*), born Barbara Huffman at Tucson, AZ, Aug 23, 1934.

Sonny Jurgensen, 75, Hall of Fame football player, born Wilmington, NC, Aug 23, 1934.

Cortez Kennedy, 41, former football player, born Osceola, AR, Aug 23, 1968.

Shelley Long, 60, actress ("Cheers," *Irreconcilable Differences*), born Fort Wayne, IN, Aug 23, 1949.

Patricia McBride, 67, dancer, born Teaneck, NJ, Aug 23, 1942.

Vera Miles, 79, actress (*The Wrong Man, Psycho*), born Boise City, OK, Aug 23, 1930.

Jay Mohr, 39, actor (*Jerry Maguire, Picture Perfect*, "Action"), comedian, born Verona, NJ, Aug 23, 1970.

Antonia Novello, 65, first woman and first Hispanic US Surgeon General (1990–93), born Fajardo, Puerto Rico, Aug 23, 1944.

Mark Russell, 77, political comedian, born Mark Ruslander at Buffalo, NY, Aug 23, 1932.

Richard Sanders, 69, actor ("WKRP in Cincinnati," "Berrengers"), born Harrisburg, PA, Aug 23, 1940.

Rik Smits, 43, former basketball player, born Eindhoven, Netherlands, Aug 23, 1966.

Rick Springfield, 60, singer, actor, born Sydney, Australia, Aug 23, 1949.

August 24 — Monday

DAY 236 | **129 REMAINING**

ARAFAT, YASSER: 80th BIRTH ANNIVERSARY. Aug 24, 1929. Controversial Middle Eastern leader who for almost 50 years was the face of the Palestinian cause. Reviled by some as a terrorist (as leader of Al-Fatah and the PLO) and cheered by others as a freedom fighter, Arafat shared the 1994 Nobel Peace Prize with Shimon Peres and Yitzhak Rabin. Born Muhammad Abdul Raouf Arafat al-Qudwa al-Husseini at Cairo, Egypt (some sources say Jerusalem or Gaza), Arafat died Nov 11, 2004, in a hospital near Paris, France.

BORGES, JORGE LUIS: BIRTH ANNIVERSARY. Aug 24, 1899. Argentinean author, critic and poet who created intellectually fantastical tales (collected in *Ficciones* and *The Aleph and Other Stories*). "There are so many futures," he said, "[all] quite different from each other." Born at Buenos Aires, Argentina, Borges died June 14, 1986, at Geneva, Switzerland.

"THE FACTS OF LIFE" TV PREMIERE: 30th ANNIVERSARY. Aug 24, 1979. This NBC sitcom was spun off from "Diff'rent Strokes" with Drummond family housekeeper Edna Garrett (Charlotte Rae) moving to Peekskill, NY, to take over as housemother at Eastland, a boarding school for girls. During the first season, the cast included John Lawlor as Headmaster Steven Bradley, Jenny O'Hara as Miss Mahoney, Lisa Whelchel as Blair Warner, Mindy Cohn as Natalie Green, Kim Fields as Dorothy "Tootie" Ramsey, Felice Schachter as Nancy Olson, Julie Piekarski as Sue Ann Weaver, Julie Anne Haddock as Cindy Webster and Molly Ringwald as Molly Parker. The last episode aired in 1986.

JARVIS, GREGORY B.: 65th BIRTH ANNIVERSARY. Aug 24, 1944. Gregory B. Jarvis, a civilian engineer with Hughes Aircraft Company, was born at Detroit, MI. He was the 41-year-old payload specialist who perished with other crew members and Christa McAuliffe in the space shuttle *Challenger* explosion on Jan 28, 1986. See also: "*Challenger* Space Shuttle Explosion: Anniversary" (Jan 28).

KAHANAMOKU, DUKE: BIRTH ANNIVERSARY. Aug 24, 1890. Duke Paoa Kahanamoku, Olympic-gold-medal swimmer and "father of international surfing," born at Honolulu, HI. Kahanamoku won gold medals in the 100-meter freestyle at the 1912 Olympics and at the 1920 Olympics. In total, he won five medals in four Olympics. Credited with inventing the flutter kick, he enjoyed a long career, not retiring from competition until age 42. Kahanamoku was also Hawaii's ambassador of surfing, popularizing the sport around the world. In 1917, on a 16-foot, 114-pound board, he rode a wave off Waikiki for 1.75 miles. The "Duke" acted in movies and served as sheriff of Honolulu, running alternately on the Republican and Democratic tickets. Died at Honolulu, Jan 22, 1968. Hawaii has honored him with a statue on Waikiki Beach, on which fans place leis.

LIBERIA: FLAG DAY. Aug 24. National holiday.

NATIONAL SAFE AT HOME WEEK. Aug 24–28. More people are injured in and around home than at work. This week promotes and emphasizes safety in and around the home to eliminate senseless home-related injuries. Annually, the last Monday through Friday in August. For info: Randy DeVaul, Safe at Home, Intl, 7573 E Rte 20, Westfield, NY 14787. Phone: (716) 326-6262. Fax: (716) 299-2040. E-mail: safetypro@roadrunner.com. Web: www.safeathomeonline.com.

PLUTO DEMOTED: ANNIVERSARY. Aug 24, 2006. On the last day of the annual International Astronomical Union meeting at Prague, Czech Republic, 424 astronomers voted to demote Pluto from planet status. They determined that Pluto is instead a dwarf planet.

SAINT BARTHOLOMEW'S DAY MASSACRE: ANNIVERSARY. Aug 24, 1572. Anniversary of the massacre in Paris and throughout France of thousands of Protestant Huguenots. The massacre began when the church bells tolled at dawn on Saint Bartholomew's Day, Aug 24, 1572, and continued for several days. Pope Gregory XIII ordered a medal struck to commemorate the event, but Protestant countries abhorred the killings, estimated at 2,000 to 70,000.

SOUTHERN CYCLONE: ANNIVERSARY. Aug 24, 1893. A hurricane hit Savannah, GA, and Charleston, SC, killing between 1,000 and 2,000 people.

SPACE MILESTONE: *VOYAGER 2* (US) REACHES NEPTUNE: 20th ANNIVERSARY. Aug 24, 1989. Launched in 1977, *Voyager 2* had its first close encounter with Neptune.

UKRAINE: INDEPENDENCE DAY. Aug 24. National day. Commemorates independence from the former Soviet Union in 1991.

US AMATEUR (GOLF) CHAMPIONSHIP. Aug 24–30. Southern Hills Country Club, Tulsa, OK. For info: USGA, Golf House, Championship Dept, PO Box 708, Far Hills, NJ 07931. Phone: (908) 234-2300. Fax: (908) 234-9687. E-mail: usga@usga.org. Web: www.usga.org.

VESUVIUS DAY. Aug 24, AD 79. Anniversary of the eruption of Vesuvius, an active volcano in southern Italy, which destroyed the cities of Pompeii, Stabiae and Herculaneum. Pliny the Younger, who escaped the disaster, wrote of it to the historian Tacitus: "[B]lack and horrible clouds, broken by sinuous shapes of flaming winds, were opening with long tongues of fire. . . ."

WARNER WEATHER QUOTATION: ANNIVERSARY. Aug 24, 1897. Charles Dudley Warner, American newspaper editor for the *Hartford Courant*, published this now-famous and oft-quoted sentence: "Everybody talks about the weather, but nobody does anything about it." The quotation is often mistakenly attributed to his friend and colleague Mark Twain. Warner and Twain were part of the most notable American literary circle during the late 19th century. Warner was a journalist, essayist, novelist, biographer and author who collaborated with Twain in writing *The Gilded Age* in 1873.

WASHINGTON, DC: INVASION ANNIVERSARY. Aug 24–25, 1814. British forces briefly invaded and raided Washington, DC, burning the Capitol, the president's house and most other public buildings. President James Madison and other high US government officials fled to safety until British troops (not knowing the strength of their position) departed the city two days later.

Birthdays Today

Gerry Cooney, 53, former boxer, born New York, NY, Aug 24, 1956.

Bob Corker, 57, US Senator (R, Tennessee), born Orangeburg, SC, Aug 24, 1952.

Stephen Fry, 52, actor (*Gosford Park, Wilde*, "Jeeves and Wooster"), novelist, born Hampstead, London, England, Aug 24, 1957.

Rafael Furcal, 31, baseball player, born Loma de Cabrera, Dominican Republic, Aug 24, 1978.

Rupert Grint, 21, actor (*Harry Potter* films), born Hertfordshire, England, Aug 24, 1988.

Steve Guttenberg, 51, actor ("Billy," *Three Men and a Baby*), born Brooklyn, NY, Aug 24, 1958.

Oscar Hijuelos, 58, author (*Mambo Kings Play Songs of Love*), born New York, NY, Aug 24, 1951.

Mike Huckabee, 54, former Governor of Arkansas, born Hope, AR, Aug 24, 1955.

Craig Kilborn, 47, TV personality, born Hastings, MN, Aug 24, 1962.

Joe Manchin III, 62, Governor of West Virginia (D), born Farmington, WV, Aug 24, 1947.

Marlee Matlin, 44, actress (Oscar for *Children of a Lesser God*, "The West Wing," "The L Word"), born Morton Grove, IL, Aug 24, 1965.

Reginald Wayne (Reggie) Miller, 44, basketball player, born Riverside, CA, Aug 24, 1965.

Chad Michael Murray, 28, actor ("One Tree Hill," "Dawson's Creek," *House of Wax*), born Buffalo, NY, Aug 24, 1981.

Michael Richards, 59, actor ("Seinfeld," *Trial and Error*), born Culver City, CA, Aug 24, 1950.

Calvin Edward (Cal) Ripken, Jr, 49, former baseball player, born Havre de Grace, MD, Aug 24, 1960.

Mason Williams, 71, composer, born Abilene, TX, Aug 24, 1938.

August 2009

S	M	T	W	T	F	S
						1
2	3	4	5	6	7	8
9	10	11	12	13	14	15
16	17	18	19	20	21	22
23	24	25	26	27	28	29
30	31					

August 25 — Tuesday

DAY 237 — 128 REMAINING

BE KIND TO HUMANKIND WEEK. Aug 25–31. 21st annual. All of the negative news that you read and hear about in the media is disheartening—but the truth is the positive stories outweigh the negative stories by a long shot! We just don't hear about them as often. Take heart—most people are caring individuals. Show you care by being kind. Daily affirmations: Motorist Consideration Monday, Touch a Heart Tuesday, Willing to Lend a Hand Wednesday, Thoughtful Thursday, Forgive Your Foe Friday, Speak Kind Words Saturday, Sacrifice Our Wants for Others' Needs Sunday. For info: Lorraine Jara, PO Box 131397, Ann Arbor, MI 48113. E-mail: Lorraine@bekindweek.org. Web: www.bekindweek.org.

BERNSTEIN, LEONARD: BIRTH ANNIVERSARY. Aug 25, 1918. American conductor and composer Leonard Bernstein was born at Lawrence, MA. One of the greatest conductors in American music history, he first conducted the New York Philharmonic Orchestra at age 25 and was its director from 1959 to 1969. His musicals include *West Side Story* and *On the Town*, and his operas and operettas include *Candide*. He died five days after his retirement, Oct 14, 1990, at New York, NY.

GIBSON, ALTHEA: BIRTH ANNIVERSARY. Aug 25, 1927. Born at Silver, SC, Althea Gibson learned paddle tennis by chance as a child when her block of W 143rd St in New York was designated as a Police Athletic League play street. She overcame great financial and social adversity and eventually won 10 consecutive national titles in the American Tennis Association, a league for black players. On Aug 28, 1950, she became the first black player to compete in the national tennis championship at Forest Hills, NY. A few years later, she became the first black woman to win the singles championship at Wimbledon. In her prime, she was ranked as high as seventh in the United States, winning titles at the French Open, Wimbledon and US Nationals at Forest Hills. She died at East Orange, NJ, Sept 28, 2003.

HARTE, BRET: BIRTH ANNIVERSARY. Aug 25, 1836. Francis Bret(t) Harte, journalist, poet, printer, teacher and novelist, especially remembered for his early stories of California ("The Luck of Roaring Camp," "The Outcasts of Poker Flat" and "How Santa Claus Came to Simpson's Bar"), was born at Albany, NY. He died at London, England, May 5, 1902.

KELLY, WALT: BIRTH ANNIVERSARY. Aug 25, 1913. American cartoonist and creator of the comic strip "Pogo" was born at Philadelphia, PA. It was Kelly's character Pogo who paraphrased Oliver Hazard Perry to say, "We has met the enemy, and it is us." Kelly died at Hollywood, CA, Oct 18, 1973. See also: "Perry, Oliver Hazard: Birth Anniversary" (Aug 23).

KISS-AND-MAKE-UP DAY. Aug 25. A day to make amends and for relationships that need mending. For info: Jacqueline V. Milgate, 121 Little Tree Ln, Hilton, NY 14468.

NATIONAL SECONDHAND WARDROBE DAY. Aug 25. A secondhand wardrobe can help people feel great about their appearance, their finances and their impact on the planet. The purpose of this day is to remove the stigma of previously owned clothing by educating everyone on the benefits of creating a wardrobe out of secondhand finds. For info: Cheryl Gorn, PO Box 1746, Latham, NY 12110.

PARIS LIBERATED: 65th ANNIVERSARY. Aug 25, 1944. As dawn broke, the men of the Second French Armored Division entered Paris, France, ending the long German occupation of the City of Light. That afternoon General Charles de Gaulle led a parade down the Champs Elysées. Though Hitler had ordered the destruction of Paris, German occupying-officer General Dietrich von Choltitz refused that order and instead surrendered to French major general Jacques Le Clerc.

PINKERTON, ALLAN: BIRTH ANNIVERSARY. Aug 25, 1819. Scottish-born American detective, founder of detective agency at Chicago, IL, in 1850, first chief of US Army's secret service, remembered now because of his strikebreaking and his lack of sympathy for working people. Pinkerton was born at Glasgow, Scotland, and died at Chicago, July 1, 1884.

URUGUAY: INDEPENDENCE DAY. Aug 25. National holiday. Declared independence from Brazil in 1825. Independence granted in 1828.

***THE WIZARD OF OZ* RELEASED: 70th ANNIVERSARY.** Aug 25, 1939. This motion-picture classic directed by Victor Fleming was a musical adaptation of the L. Frank Baum children's book with both black-and-white and color sequences. It starred Judy Garland as Dorothy as well as Frank Morgan as the Wizard (and four other characters), Ray Bolger as the Scarecrow, Bert Lahr as the Lion, Jack Haley as the Tin Man and Margaret Hamilton as the Wicked Witch of the West. Nominated for six Academy Awards, it won two for best original music score and best song, "Over the Rainbow" (Harold Arlen music and E.Y. Harburg lyrics).

Birthdays Today

Martin Amis, 60, author (*The Information, London Fields*), critic, born Oxford, England, Aug 25, 1949.

Anne Archer, 62, actress ("Falcon Crest"; stage: *A Couple of White Chicks Sitting Around Talking*), born Los Angeles, CA, Aug 25, 1947.

Albert Belle, 43, former baseball player, born Shreveport, LA, Aug 25, 1966.

Cornelius O'Landa Bennett, 43, former football player, born Birmingham, AL, Aug 25, 1966.

Rachel Bilson, 28, actress ("The OC"), born Los Angeles, CA, Aug 25, 1981.

Tim Burton, 51, director (*Edward Scissorhands, The Nightmare Before Christmas*), born Burbank, CA, Aug 25, 1958.

Sean Connery, 79, actor (James Bond movies; *The Man Who Would Be King*), born Edinburgh, Scotland, Aug 25, 1930.

Elvis Costello, 55, singer, songwriter born Declan McManus at Paddington, London, England, Aug 25, 1954.

Billy Ray Cyrus, 48, country singer ("Achy Breaky Heart"), actor ("Hannah Montana"), born Flatwoods, KY, Aug 25, 1961.

Frederick Forsyth, 71, author (*The Day of the Jackal*), born Ashford, Kent, England, Aug 25, 1938.

Monty Hall, 86, former TV host ("Let's Make a Deal"), born Winnipeg, MB, Canada, Aug 25, 1923.

Anthony Heald, 65, actor (*The Silence of the Lambs, Searching for Bobby Fischer*), born New Rochelle, NY, Aug 25, 1944.

Blake Lively, 22, actress (*Sisterhood of the Traveling Pants,* "Gossip Girl"), born Tarzana, CA, Aug 25, 1987.

Regis Philbin, 76, TV show host ("Live with Regis & Kelly," "Who Wants to Be a Millionaire?"), born New York, NY, Aug 25, 1933.

Rachael Ray, 41, chef, cookbook author, television personality ("30 Minute Meals," "$40 a Day"), born Cape Cod, MA, Aug 25, 1968.

John Savage, 60, actor ("Carnivàle," "Dark Angel," *The Deer Hunter, Hair*), born Long Island, NY, Aug 25, 1949.

Claudia Schiffer, 39, model, born Rheinberg, Germany, Aug 25, 1970.

Wayne Shorter, 76, jazz musician ("High Life"), born Newark, NJ, Aug 25, 1933.

Gene Simmons, 60, cofounder of KISS, actor, born Chaim Witz at Haifa, Israel, Aug 25, 1949.

Tom Skerritt, 76, actor ("Brothers & Sisters," "Picket Fences," *Steel Magnolias*), born Detroit, MI, Aug 25, 1933.

Blair Underwood, 45, actor ("One Life to Live," "LA Law"), born Tacoma, WA, Aug 25, 1964.

Ally Walker, 48, actress ("The Profiler"), born Tullahoma, TN, Aug 25, 1961.

Joanne Whalley, 45, actress ("The Singing Detective"; stage: *What the Butler Saw*), born Manchester, England, Aug 25, 1964.

August 26 — Wednesday

DAY 238 — **127 REMAINING**

CHINA: DOUBLE SEVEN FESTIVAL. Aug 26. Also called Chinese Valentine's Day. Observed on seventh day of seventh lunar month. From a folktale in which two lovers (a cowherd and a weaver) are separated by the Milky Way. They are able to meet once a year when all the world's magpies form a bridge for the lovers.

CORN PALACE FESTIVAL. Aug 26–30. Mitchell, SD. Celebration of the harvest and the annual redecoration of the world's only Corn Palace (with ears of corn). Midway and carnival rides, games, specialty vendors, food and top-name entertainment on the stage of the Corn Palace. Est attendance: 40,000. For info: Corn Palace, 612 N Main, Mitchell, SD 57301. Phone: (605) 995-8427. Fax: (605) 995-8443. E-mail: mschilling@midco.net. Web: www.cornpalacefestival.com.

De FOREST, LEE: BIRTH ANNIVERSARY. Aug 26, 1873. American inventor of the electron tube, the radio knife for surgery and the photoelectric cell and a pioneer in the creation of talking pictures and television. Born at Council Bluffs, IA, De Forest was holder of hundreds of patents but is perhaps best remembered by the moniker he gave himself in the title of his autobiography, *Father of Radio*, published in 1950. So unbelievable was the idea of wireless radio broadcasting that De Forest was accused of fraud and arrested for selling stock to underwrite the invention that later was to become an essential part of daily life. De Forest died at Hollywood, CA, June 30, 1961.

FIRST BASEBALL GAMES TELEVISED: 70th ANNIVERSARY. Aug 26, 1939. WXBS television, at New York City, broadcast the first major league baseball games—a doubleheader between the Cincinnati Reds and the Brooklyn Dodgers at Ebbets Field. Announcer Red Barber interviewed Leo Durocher, manager of the Dodgers, and William McKechnie, manager of the Reds, between games.

GOSPEL FEST. Aug 26. Central City, KY. Featuring the Crabb Family and friends. Est attendance: 2,500. For info: Central City Music Festival, 208 N First St, Central City, KY 42330. Phone: (270) 754-9603. Fax: (270) 754-9067. E-mail: cctourism@muhlon.com. Web: www.centralcitykytourism.com.

ISHERWOOD, CHRISTOPHER: BIRTH ANNIVERSARY. Aug 26, 1904. Author of short stories, plays and novels, Christopher William Isherwood was born at High Lane, Cheshire, England. The play and motion picture *I Am a Camera* and the musical *Cabaret* were based on the short story "Sally Bowles" in his collection from the 1930s titled *Goodbye to Berlin*, which contained the line "I am a camera with its shutter open, quite passive, recording, not thinking." Isherwood died at Santa Monica, CA, Jan 4, 1986.

KRAKATOA ERUPTION: ANNIVERSARY. Aug 26, 1883. Anniversary of the biggest explosion in historic times. The eruption of the Indonesian volcanic island Krakatoa (Krakatau) was heard 3,000 miles away, created tidal waves 120 feet high (killing 36,000 persons), hurled five cubic miles of Earth fragments into the air (some to a height of 50 miles) and affected the oceans and the atmosphere for years.

MONTGOLFIER, JOSEPH MICHEL: BIRTH ANNIVERSARY. Aug 26, 1740. French merchant and inventor, born at Vidalonlez-Annonay, France, who, with his brother Jacques Etienne in November 1782, conducted experiments with paper and fabric bags filled with smoke and hot air, which led to invention of the hot-air balloon and man's first flight. Died at Balaruc-les-Bains, France, June 26, 1810. See also: "Montgolfier, Jacques Etienne: Birth Anniversary" (Jan 7), "First Balloon Flight: Anniversary" (June 5) and "Aviation History Month" (Nov 1).

NAMIBIA: HEROES' DAY. Aug 26. National holiday. Commemorates beginning of struggle for independence in 1966.

NATIONAL DOG DAY. Aug 26. More people have dogs for pets than any other animal in the country. Why? Because they are loving and loyal companions. They treat us better than we treat each other. Here is one day to recognize and honor them for their love, loyalty and lifesaving skills. Annually, Aug 26. For info: Animal Miracle Foundation, PO Box 2061, Kingston, WA 98346. Phone: (877) 205-0871. E-mail: info@nationaldogday.com. Web: www.nationaldogday.com.

NEVADA STATE FAIR. Aug 26–30. Reno Livestock Events Center, Reno, NV. 135th annual. State entertainment and carnival, with creative living, agriculture and commercial exhibits. Est attendance: 60,000. For info: Nevada State Fair, 1350-A N Wells Ave, Reno, NV 89512. Phone: (775) 688-5767. Fax: (775) 335-8942. E-mail: info@nvstatefair.com. Web: www.nvstatefair.com.

SABIN, ALBERT BRUCE: BIRTH ANNIVERSARY. Aug 26, 1906. American medical researcher Albert Bruce Sabin was born at Bialystok, Poland. He is most noted for his oral vaccine for polio, which replaced Jonas Salk's injected vaccine because Sabin's provided lifetime protection. He was awarded the US National Medal of Science in 1971. Sabin died Mar 3, 1993, at Washington, DC.

SPACE MILESTONE: *SOYUZ 31* (USSR). Aug 26, 1978. Launched on Aug 26, Valery Bykovsky and Sigmund Jaehn docked at *Salyut 6* on Aug 27, stayed for a week, and then returned to Earth in *Soyuz 29* vehicle, leaving their *Soyuz 31* docked at space station. Earth landing on Sept 3.

SPAIN: LA TOMATINA. Aug 26. Buñol (near Valencia). The world's biggest food fight takes place today as 35,000 revelers hurl 120 tons of tomatoes at each other (and the town) for two hours. La Tomatina ("Tomato Festival") occurs annually the last Wednesday of August. Festivities kick off with a competition to see who can reach a ham at the top of a greased pole. With the ham secured, the trucks arrive with tomatoes.

TENNESSEE WALKING HORSE NATIONAL CELEBRATION. Aug 26–Sept 5. Celebration Grounds, Shelbyville, TN. More than 5,000 entries compete for more than $650,000 in prizes and awards—and the World Grand Championship titles. An 11-day festival for the whole family, plus trade show. Est attendance: 235,000. For info: Chip Walters, Dir Public & Media Relations, Tennessee Walking Horse Natl Celebration, Calhoun and Evans, PO Box 1010, Shelbyville, TN 37162. Phone: (931) 684-5915. Fax: (931) 684-5949. E-mail: twhnc@twhnc.com. Web: www.twhnc.com.

✦ **WOMEN'S EQUALITY DAY.** Aug 26. Presidential Proclamation issued in 1973 and 1974 at request and since 1975 without request.

WOMEN'S EQUALITY DAY. Aug 26. Anniversary of certification as part of US Constitution, in 1920, of the 19th Amendment, prohibiting discrimination on the basis of sex with regard to voting. Congresswoman Bella Abzug's bill to designate Aug 26 of each year as "Women's Equality Day" in August 1974 became Public Law 93–382.

Birthdays Today

Benjamin Crowninshield Bradlee, 88, journalist, editor, born Boston, MA, Aug 26, 1921.

Christopher Burke, 44, actor ("Life Goes On"), born New York, NY, Aug 26, 1965.

Macaulay Culkin, 29, actor (*Home Alone, My Girl*), born New York, NY, Aug 26, 1980.

Geraldine Ferraro, 74, first woman vice-presidential candidate, born Newburgh, NY, Aug 26, 1935.

Irving R. Levine, 87, broadcast journalist, born Pawtucket, RI, Aug 26, 1922.

Branford Marsalis, 49, musician, born Beaux Bridge, LA, Aug 26, 1960.

August 2009

S	M	T	W	T	F	S
						1
2	3	4	5	6	7	8
9	10	11	12	13	14	15
16	17	18	19	20	21	22
23	24	25	26	27	28	29
30	31					

August 27 — Thursday

DAY 239 — 126 REMAINING

ACTON FAIR. Aug 27–30. Acton, ME. A country fair featuring horse and ox pulls; antique tractor pull; firemen's muster; 4-H projects; flowers; arts and crafts; draft horse, pony and mule show; beef and dairy shows;, full midway; stage shows; and handicrafts. Vendors call Douglas Roberts at (207) 324-1250 (after 6 PM). Est attendance: 15,000. For info: Lista C. Staples, Secy, 178 Nason Rd, Shapleigh, ME 04076. Phone: (207) 636-2026.

ALASKA STATE FAIR. Aug 27–Sept 7. Palmer, AK. Cows and critters, music and dancing, rides, excitement and family fun at the state's largest summer extravaganza. See 100-lb cabbages, native art, more than 500 events including demonstrations, high-caliber entertainment, rodeos, horse shows, crafts and agricultural exhibits. Est attendance: 300,000. For info: Alaska State Fair, Inc, 2075 Glenn Hwy, Palmer, AK 99645. Phone: (907) 745-4827 or (800) 850-FAIR. Fax: (907) 746-2699. E-mail: info@alaskastatefair.org. Web: www.alaskastatefair.org.

DAWES, CHARLES GATES: BIRTH ANNIVERSARY. Aug 27, 1865. 30th vice president of the US (1925–29), born at Marietta, OH. Won the Nobel Peace Prize in 1925 for the Dawes Plan for German reparations. Died at Evanston, IL, Apr 23, 1951.

DREISER, THEODORE: BIRTH ANNIVERSARY. Aug 27, 1871. American novelist Theodore Dreiser was born at Terre Haute, IN. He was an exponent of American naturalism in literature. His first novel, *Sister Carrie* (1900), was suppressed by his publisher on moral grounds. Dreiser's finest achievement is widely considered to be his novel *An American Tragedy* (1925). He died Dec 28, 1945, at Hollywood, CA.

"THE DUCHESS" WHO WASN'T DAY. Aug 27. At least once on Aug 27 repeat the following now-famous quotation from the novel *Molly Bawn*: "Beauty is in the eye of the beholder." Margaret Wolfe Hungerford often wrote under the pseudonym "The Duchess," which was the title of her most popular novel—hence the name of this event. A popular romance novelist with about 40 books published, Hungerford was born at Rosscarbery, County Cork, Ireland, on Aug 27, 1850; she died at Bandon, County Cork, in 1897. (Originated by the late Peggy Shirley.)

FIRST COMMERCIAL OIL WELL: 150th ANNIVERSARY. Aug 27, 1859. W.A. "Uncle Billy" Smith discovered oil in a shaft being sunk by Colonel E.L. Drake at Titusville, in western Pennsylvania. Drilling had reached 69 feet, 6 inches, when Smith saw a dark film floating on the water below the derrick floor. Soon 20 barrels of crude were being pumped each day. The first oil was refined to make kerosene for lighting, replacing whale oil. Later it was refined to make gasoline for cars. The first gas station opened in 1907.

FIRST PLAY PRESENTED IN NORTH AMERICAN COLONIES: ANNIVERSARY. Aug 27, 1655. Acomac, VA, was the site of the first play presented in the North American colonies. The play was *Ye Bare and Ye Cubb*, by Phillip Alexander Bruce. Three local residents were arrested and fined for acting in the play. At the time, most colonies had laws prohibiting public performances; Virginia, however, had no such ordinance.

"GOOD SEX! WITH DR. RUTH WESTHEIMER" TV PREMIERE: 25th ANNIVERSARY. Aug 27, 1984. This program premiered on the Lifetime Cable Channel with sex therapist Ruth Westheimer counseling actors appearing as her patients. The show's format later changed to include celebrity and physician interviews and call-ins.

HAMLIN, HANNIBAL: 200th BIRTH ANNIVERSARY. Aug 27, 1809. 15th vice president of the US (1861–65), born at Paris, ME. Died at Bangor, ME, July 4, 1891.

HOTTER 'N HELL HUNDRED BIKE RACE. Aug 27–30. Wichita Falls, TX. 28th annual. Cyclists of all ages participate in the largest sanctioned century ride in the US. Treks of 100, 50 or 25 miles. Est attendance: 15,000. For info: Hotter 'N Hell Hundred, PO Box 2096, Wichita Falls, TX 76307. Phone: (940) 322-3223. Fax: (940) 322-1118. E-mail: info@hh100.org. Web: www.hh100.org.

JOHNSON, LYNDON BAINES: BIRTH ANNIVERSARY. Aug 27, 1908. The 36th president of the US succeeded to the presidency following the assassination of John F. Kennedy. Johnson's term of office: Nov 22, 1963–Jan 20, 1969. In 1964 he said: "The challenge of the next half century is whether we have the wisdom to use [our] wealth to enrich and elevate our national life—and to advance the quality of American civilization." Johnson was born near Stonewall, TX, and died at San Antonio, TX, Jan 22, 1973. His birthday is observed as a holiday in Texas.

MINNESOTA STATE FAIR. Aug 27–Sept 7. St. Paul, MN. Twelve days of fun ending on Labor Day. Major entertainers, agricultural displays, arts, crafts, food, carnival rides, animal judging and performances. Est attendance: 1,700,000. For info: Minnesota State Fair, 1265 Snelling Ave N, St. Paul, MN 55108-3099. Phone: (651) 288-4400. E-mail: fairinfo@mnstatefair.org. Web: www.mnstatefair.org.

MOLDOVA: INDEPENDENCE DAY. Aug 27. Republic of Moldova. Moldova declared its independence from the Soviet Union in 1991.

MOON PHASE: FIRST QUARTER. Aug 27. Moon enters First Quarter phase at 7:42 AM, EDT.

MOTHER TERESA: BIRTH ANNIVERSARY. Aug 27, 1910. Albanian Roman Catholic nun born Agnes Gonxha Bojaxhiu at Skopje, Macedonia. She founded the Order of the Missionaries of Charity, which cares for the destitute people of Calcutta, India, and other places. She won the Nobel Peace Prize in 1979. She died at Calcutta, Sept 5, 1997.

MOUNTBATTEN, LOUIS: 30th ASSASSINATION ANNIVERSARY. Aug 27, 1979. Lord Mountbatten (Louis Francis Albert Victor Nicholas Mountbatten), celebrated British war hero, cousin of Queen Elizabeth II, last viceroy of India, was killed by bomb, along with his 14-year-old grandson and two others, while on his yacht in Donegal Bay off the coast of Ireland, on Aug 27, 1979. Provisional Irish Republican Army claimed responsibility for the explosion and for the killing of 18 British soldiers later the same day, deepening the crisis and conflict between Protestants and Catholics and between England and Ireland. Lord Mountbatten was born at Windsor, England, June 25, 1900.

NEW YORK STATE FAIR. Aug 27–Sept 7. Syracuse, NY. Agricultural and livestock competitions, top-name entertainment, the International Horse Show, business and industrial exhibits, the midway and ethnic presentations. Est attendance: 1,000,000. For info: Frederic Pierce, Public Relations Dir, NY State Fair, 581 State Fair Blvd, Syracuse, NY 13209. Phone: (315) 487-7711, ext 1240. Fax: (315) 487-9260.

RAYE, MARTHA: BIRTH ANNIVERSARY. Aug 27, 1916. Born at Butte, MT, Martha Raye began singing when she was three. Raye performed for American servicemen during three wars and received the Jean Hersholt Humanitarian Award from the Academy of Motion Picture Arts and Sciences (1969) for that service. She appeared in her first film, *Rhythm on the Range*, in 1936. She had several TV shows, including "The Martha Raye Show" (1955–56). In 1993 Raye was awarded the Presidential Medal of Freedom. Martha Raye died Oct 19, 1994, at Los Angeles, CA.

Birthdays Today

Sarah Chalke, 33, actress ("Roseanne," "Scrubs"), born Ottawa, ON, Canada, Aug 27, 1976.

Daryl Dragon, 67, musician (Captain and Tennille), songwriter, born Studio City, CA, Aug 27, 1942.

Carlos Moya, 33, tennis player, born Palma, Majorca, Spain, Aug 27, 1976.

Paul Reubens, 57, actor, writer ("Pee-wee's Playhouse," *Pee-wee's Big Adventure*), born Peekskill, NY, Aug 27, 1952.

Tommy Sands, 72, singer ("Teen-Age Crush," "Goin' Steady"), born Chicago, IL, Aug 27, 1937.

Jim Thome, 39, baseball player, born Peoria, IL, Aug 27, 1970.

Tuesday Weld, 66, actress ("The Many Loves of Dobie Gillis," *Looking for Mr Goodbar*), born Susan Kerr at New York, NY, Aug 27, 1943.

Chandra Wilson, 40, actress ("Grey's Anatomy"), born Houston, TX, Aug 27, 1969.

August 28 — Friday

DAY 240 125 REMAINING

BOYER, CHARLES: BIRTH ANNIVERSARY. Aug 28, 1889. Film star (*Mayerling, Gaslight*), born at Figeac, France. Died at Scottsdale, AZ, Aug 26, 1978.

CANADA: CLASSIC BOAT FESTIVAL. Aug 28–30. Victoria, BC. Classic sail and power vessels from all over the west coast of the US, Canada and beyond gather in Victoria's Inner Harbour. View these lovingly restored and maintained boats with their polished brass fittings and rich teak and oak decks and hulls. Schooner races, sail-past, steamboat parade. Sponsored by Victoria Real Estate Board and Black Press. For info: Classic Boat Festival, 3035 Nanaimo St, Victoria, BC, Canada V8T 4W2. Phone: (604) 385-7766. Fax: (604) 385-8773. E-mail: classicboat@vreb.org. Web: www.classicboatfestival.ca.

CORVETTE CROSSROADS AUTO SHOW. Aug 28–29. Mackinaw City, MI. Boat cruise on Friday; show and visitor viewing, awards and parade across the Mackinaw Bridge on Saturday at 7 PM. Est attendance: 4,000. For info: Corvette Show, PO Box 856, Mackinaw City, MI 49701. Phone: (231) 436-5574 or (888) 455-8100. Web: www.mackinawchamber.com.

DREAM DAY QUEST AND JUBILEE. Aug 28. The anniversary of the 1963 Dream March on Washington led by Reverend Dr. Martin Luther King, Jr. One of the three Days of Respect. Dream Day visually affirms spiritual and moral principles and provides practice in peoplehood. See also: "Humanitarian Day" (Jan 15) and "Victims of Violence Wholly Day" (Apr 4). For info: EvAngel Mamadee YHWHnewBN, Global Committee Commemorating King Days of Respect, PO Box 21050, Chicago, IL 60621. Phone: (888) 399-9494. E-mail: YHWHnewBN@aol.com.

FEAST OF SAINT AUGUSTINE. Aug 28. Bishop of Hippo, author of *Confessions* and *The City of God*, born Nov 13, 354 AD, at Tagaste, in what is now Algeria. Died Aug 28, 430, at Hippo, also in North Africa.

GOETHE, JOHANN WOLFGANG von: BIRTH ANNIVERSARY. Aug 28, 1749. German author, poet, dramatist and philosopher, born at Frankfurt, Germany. Died Mar 22, 1832, at Weimar, Germany. Best known for the novels *The Sorrows of Young Werther* and *Wilheim Meister* and the play *Faust.*

HAYES, LUCY WARE WEBB: BIRTH ANNIVERSARY. Aug 28, 1831. The wife of Rutherford Birchard Hayes, 19th president of the US, born at Chillicothe, OH. Died at Fremont, OH, June 25, 1889. She was nicknamed "Lemonade Lucy" because she and the president, both teetotalers, served no alcoholic beverages at White House receptions.

MARCH ON WASHINGTON: ANNIVERSARY. Aug 28, 1963. More than 250,000 people attended this Civil Rights rally at Washington, DC, at which Reverend Dr. Martin Luther King, Jr, made his famous "I Have a Dream" speech.

MARYLAND STATE FAIR. Aug 28–Sept 7. Timonium, MD. Home arts, agricultural and livestock presentations, midway rides, live entertainment and thoroughbred horse racing. Est attendance: 500,000. For info: Maryland State Fair, Publicity Dept, State Fairgrounds, PO Box 188, Timonium, MD 21094. Phone: (410) 252-0200. E-mail: msfair@msn.com. Web: www.marylandstatefair.com.

MICHIGAN STATE FAIR. Aug 28–Sept 7 (tentative). State Fairgrounds, Detroit, MI. Est attendance: 350,000. For info: State Fairgrounds, Eight Mile Road and Woodward Ave, Detroit, MI 48203. Phone: (313) 369-8250. Fax: (313) 369-8410. Web: www.michigan statefair.com.

NEBRASKA STATE FAIR. Aug 28–Sept 7. Lincoln, NE. Showcasing Nebraska pride, people and products. Food booths, variety of entertainment, amusement rides, concerts, livestock shows, tractor pulls, car racing and demo derby. Est attendance: 300,000. For info: Nebraska State Fair, PO Box 81223, Lincoln, NE 68501. Phone: (402) 474-5371. Fax: (402) 473-4114. E-mail: nestatefair@statefair .org. Web: www.statefair.org.

O'CONNOR, DONALD: BIRTH ANNIVERSARY. Aug 28, 1925. Singer, dancer and vaudeville performer Donald O'Connor was born into a family of circus performers at Chicago, IL, Aug 28, 1925. He joined the family's vaudeville act at a very young age and was soon under contract with Universal Studios. He starred opposite Francis the Mule in a string of very successful film comedies throughout the 1950s but is best remembered for his role opposite Gene Kelly and Debbie Reynolds in 1952's *Singin' in the Rain.* His solo number "Make 'Em Laugh" is considered one of Hollywood's finest moments. O'Connor died Sept 28, 2003, at Woodland Hills, CA.

OREGON STATE FAIR. Aug 28–Sept 7. Salem, OR. Exhibits, products and displays illustrate Oregon's role as one of the nation's major agricultural and recreational states. Floral gardens, sports and recreation activities, sustainable energy displays, carnival, entertainment, horse show and food. Est attendance: 360,000. For info: Oregon State Fair, 2330 17th St NE, Salem, OR 97303-3201. Phone: (503) 947-3247. Web: www.oregonstatefair.org.

PETERSON, ROGER TORY: BIRTH ANNIVERSARY. Aug 28, 1908. Naturalist, author of *A Field Guide to Birds*, born at Jamestown, NY. Peterson died at Old Lyme, CT, July 28, 1996.

PORT ROYAL HURRICANE: ANNIVERSARY. Aug 28, 1722. The hapless Jamaican town of Port Royal was devastated twice within a 30-year span by two natural disasters—an earthquake in 1692 and a hurricane in 1722. The hurricane killed 400 townspeople and sank 26 merchant ships.

PRAIRIE VILLAGE JAMBOREE. Aug 28–30. Prairie Village, Madison, SD. Come and join the fun with 40 restored buildings, parades, tractor pulls, threshing, plowing, wagon trains, flea market, train and carousel rides, entertainment and much more. Est attendance: 15,000. For info: Prairie Village Jamboree, PO Box 256, Madison, SD 57042. Phone: (800) 693-3644. E-mail: prairiev@rapidnet.com. Web: www.prairievillage.org.

RACE YOUR MOUSE AROUND THE ICONS DAY. Aug 28. While you're waiting for any number of endless items to finally come up on your screen, don't just sit there. Race your mouse in and around the icons. You'll feel peppy for doing it. (©2006 by WH.) For info: Thomas & Ruth Roy, Wellcat Holidays, 2418 Long Ln, Lebanon, PA 17046. Phone: (717) 279-0184. E-mail: info@wellcat.com. Web: www.wellcat.com.

August 2009	S	M	T	W	T	F	S
							1
	2	3	4	5	6	7	8
	9	10	11	12	13	14	15
	16	17	18	19	20	21	22
	23	24	25	26	27	28	29
	30	31					

RADIO COMMERCIALS: ANNIVERSARY. Aug 28, 1922. Broadcasters realized radio could earn profits from the sale of advertising time. WEAF in New York ran a commercial "spot," which was sponsored by the Queensboro Realty Corporation of Jackson Heights to promote Hawthorne Court, a group of apartment buildings at Queens. The commercial rate was $100 for 10 minutes.

TILL, EMMETT: DEATH ANNIVERSARY. Aug 28, 1955. Emmett Till, a 14-year-old African-American teenager from Chicago visiting relatives in Money, MS, was murdered on this date by a group of white men angry at Till's reported flirtation with a white woman. The Till murder and the acquittal of two of the men involved brought the nation's attention to racial tensions in the South and helped spark civil rights protests later that year—most famously, Rosa Parks's refusal to give up her seat to a white man on a municipal bus in Montgomery, AL, in December of that year.

WISCONSIN STATE COW-CHIP THROW. Aug 28–29. Prairie du Sac, WI. Cow-Chip Throw, 5k and 10k runs, arts and crafts fair, live music and parade. Annually, the Friday night and Saturday of Labor Day weekend. Est attendance: 50,000. For info: Wisconsin State Cow-Chip Throw, PO Box 3, Prairie du Sac, WI 53578. Phone: (608) 643-4317. Fax: (608) 643-5421. E-mail: marietta@toolsof marketing.com.

Birthdays Today

Mamadou Diallo, 38, soccer player, born Dakar, Senegal, Aug 28, 1971.

Ben Gazzara, 79, actor (*Anatomy of a Murder*, "Run for Your Life"), born New York, NY, Aug 28, 1930.

Ronald Ames (Ron) Guidry, 59, former baseball player, born Lafayette, LA, Aug 28, 1950.

Scott Hamilton, 51, Olympic gold medal figure skater, born Toledo, OH, Aug 28, 1958.

Paul Martin, 71, 21st prime minister of Canada (2003–06), born Windsor, ON, Canada, Aug 28, 1938.

Lou Piniella, 66, baseball manager and former player, born Tampa, FL, Aug 28, 1943.

Jason Priestley, 40, actor ("Beverly Hills 90210," *Tombstone*), born Vancouver, BC, Canada, Aug 28, 1969.

Carlos Quentin, 27, baseball player, born Bellflower, CA, Aug 28, 1982.

LeAnn Rimes, 27, country-and-western singer, born Jackson, MS, Aug 28, 1982.

Rick Rossovich, 52, actor (*The Terminator, Roxanne*), born Palo Alto, CA, Aug 28, 1957.

Emma Samms, 49, actress ("General Hospital," "Dynasty"), born Emma Samuelson at London, England, Aug 28, 1960.

David Soul, 63, actor ("Starsky and Hutch," *Salem's Lot*), born Chicago, IL, Aug 28, 1946.

Daniel Stern, 52, actor (*City Slickers, Home Alone*), born Bethesda, MD, Aug 28, 1957.

Shania Twain, 44, country singer, born Eileen Twain at Windsor, ON, Canada, Aug 28, 1965.

August 29 — Saturday

DAY 241 **124 REMAINING**

"ACCORDING TO HOYLE" DAY (EDMOND HOYLE DEATH ANNIVERSARY). Aug 29, 1769. A day to remember Edmond Hoyle and a day for fun and games *according to the rules.* He is believed to have studied law. For many years he lived at London, England, and gave instructions in the playing of games. His "Short Treatise" on the game of whist (published in 1742) became a model guide to the rules of the game. Hoyle's name became synonymous with the idea of correct play according to the rules, and the phrase "according to Hoyle" became a part of the English language. Hoyle was born at London about 1672 and died there.

***AMISTAD* SEIZED: ANNIVERSARY.** Aug 29, 1839. In January 1839, 53 Africans were seized near modern-day Sierra Leone, taken to Cuba and sold as slaves. While being transferred to another part of the island on the ship *Amistad*, led by the African Cinque, they seized control of the ship, telling the crew to take them back to Africa. However, the crew secretly changed course, and the ship landed at Long Island, NY, where it and its "cargo" were seized as salvage. The *Amistad* was towed to New Haven, CT, where the Africans were imprisoned and a lengthy legal battle began to determine if they were property to be returned to Cuba or free men. John Quincy Adams took their case all the way to the Supreme Court, where on Mar 9, 1841, it was determined that they were free and could return to Africa.

BERGMAN, INGRID: BIRTH ANNIVERSARY. Aug 29, 1915. One of cinema's greatest actresses. Bergman was born at Stockholm, Sweden, and died at London, England, on her 67th birthday, Aug 29, 1982. Three-time Academy Award winner for *Gaslight, Anastasia* and *Murder on the Orient Express.* Controversy over her personal life made her and her films unpopular to American audiences during an interval of several years between periods of awards and adulation.

CHAMPLAIN VALLEY FAIR. Aug 29–Sept 7. Essex Junction, VT. Vermont's largest fair. Agricultural exhibits and competitions, variety of entertainment, arts and crafts, midway rides, commercial exhibits, great food and much more. Est attendance: 300,000. For info: Chris Ashby, Dir of Sales and Mktg, Champlain Valley Fair, PO Box 209, Essex Junction, VT 05453. Phone: (802) 878-5545. Fax: (802) 879-5404. E-mail: info@cvexpo.org. Web: www.cvexpo.org.

COLORADO STATE FAIR. Aug 29–Sept 7. State Fairgrounds, Pueblo, CO. One of the nation's oldest Western fairs, it is also Colorado's largest single event. Family fun, top-name entertainment, lots of food and festivities. Est attendance: 485,000. For info: Colorado State Fair, 1001 Beulah Ave, Pueblo, CO 81004. Phone: (719) 561-8484. E-mail: info@coloradostatefair.com. Web: www.coloradostatefair.com.

DENMARK: HO SHEEP MARKET. Aug 29. The village of Ho, near Esbjerg, holds its annual sheep market on the last Saturday in August, when some 50,000 people visit the fair.

HOLMES, OLIVER WENDELL: 200th BIRTH ANNIVERSARY. Aug 29, 1809. Physician and author, father of Supreme Court Justice Oliver Wendell Holmes, born at Cambridge, MA. Died at Boston, MA, Oct 7, 1894. "A moment's insight," he wrote, "is sometimes worth a life's experience."

HURRICANE KATRINA STRIKES GULF COAST: ANNIVERSARY. Aug 29, 2005. After hitting the southern Florida coast on Aug 25, Hurricane Katrina moved into the Gulf of Mexico and grew into one of the most devastating hurricanes in US history. On this date, as a Category 3 storm, it struck Buras, LA, and surrounding areas, destroying communities up and down the Gulf Coast. Levees in New Orleans were breached, and within two days more than 80 percent of the city lay underwater, trapping tens of thousands of people. The death toll in Louisiana, Mississippi, Alabama and Florida was more than 1,300, with more than 1,000 fatalities coming in Louisiana. Thousands remained missing at the end of 2005. The estimated one million people evacuated before and after the storm accounted for the largest movement of people in the US since the Great Depression and the Civil War. And with $100 billion to $200 billion in damage over 90,000 square miles, Hurricane Katrina was the most expensive natural disaster in US history.

LOCKE, JOHN: BIRTH ANNIVERSARY. Aug 29, 1632. (Old Style date.) English philosopher, founder of philosophical liberalism, born at Wrington, England. His ideas influenced the American colonists and were enshrined in the Constitution. Locke died at Essex, England, Oct 28, 1704 (OS).

MARYLAND RENAISSANCE FESTIVAL. Aug 29–Oct 25 (Saturdays, Sundays and Labor Day). Annapolis, MD. A 16th-century English festival with Henry VIII, sword swallowers, magicians, authentic jousting, juggling, music, theater, games, food and crafts. Est attendance: 298,000. For info: Jules Smith, Maryland Renaissance Festival, PO Box 315, Crownsville, MD 21032. Phone: (410) 266-7304. Fax: (410) 573-1508. E-mail: info@rennfest.com. Web: www.rennfest.com.

MORE HERBS, LESS SALT DAY. Aug 29. It's healthier, zestier and lustier! (©2006 by WH.) For info: Thomas & Ruth Roy, Wellcat Holidays, 2418 Long Ln, Lebanon, PA 17046. Phone: (717) 279-0184. E-mail: info@wellcat.com. Web: www.wellcat.com.

NATIONAL SARCOIDOSIS AWARENESS DAY. Aug 29. To focus national attention on sarcoidosis with appropriate programs, activities and education. Annually, Aug 29. For info: Foundation for Sarcoidosis Research, 122 S Michigan Ave, Ste 1700, Chicago, IL 60603. Phone: (312) 341-0500. Fax: (312) 322-9808. Web: www.stopsarcoidosis.org.

PARKER, CHARLIE: BIRTH ANNIVERSARY. Aug 29, 1920. Jazz saxophonist Charlie Parker was born at Kansas City, KS. He earned the nickname "Yardbird" (later "Bird") from his habit of sitting in the backyard of speakeasies, fingering his saxophone. His career as a jazz saxophonist took him from jam sessions in Kansas City to New York, where he met Dizzy Gillespie and others who were creating a style of music that would become known as bop or bebop. Although Parker's musical genius was unquestioned, his addiction to heroin haunted his life. He died at Rochester, NY, Mar 12, 1955, at the age of 34.

ROCKY MOUNTAIN BALLOON FESTIVAL. Aug 29–30. Chatfield State Park, Denver, CO. Hot-air balloon festival and outdoor celebration. Fun family event with dawn balloon ascensions and Saturday sunset "Lites in the Nite" mass balloon illumination. Annually, the weekend before Labor Day weekend. Est attendance: 50,000. For info: Rocky Mountain Balloon Festival. Phone: (303) 697-1039. E-mail: info@rockymountainballoonfestival.com. Web: www.rockymountainballoonfestival.com.

***ROYAL GEORGE* SINKS: ANNIVERSARY.** Aug 29, 1792. Prized British battleship *Royal George* sank due to fatal human error in one of the worst maritime disasters in history. While the ship was being repaired at Spithead, the port side was tilted too close to the waterline. A gust of wind lowered the ship even farther, allowing tons of water to flood into its open gunports. The ship sank within minutes before many of the 1,300 on board realized what was happening, and more than 900 people drowned.

SHAYS'S REBELLION: ANNIVERSARY. Aug 29, 1786. Daniel Shays, veteran of the battles of Lexington, Bunker Hill, Ticonderoga and Saratoga, was one of the leaders of more than 1,000 rebels who sought redress of grievances during the depression days of 1786–87. They prevented general court sessions, and on Sept 26 they prevented Supreme Court sessions at Springfield, MA. On Jan 25, 1787, they attacked the federal arsenal at Springfield; Feb 2, Shays's troops were routed and fled. Shays was sentenced to death but pardoned June 13, 1788. Later he received a small pension for services in the American Revolution.

SLOVAKIA: NATIONAL UPRISING DAY. Aug 29. National holiday. Commemorates resistance to Nazi occupation in 1944.

SOVIET COMMUNIST PARTY SUSPENDED: ANNIVERSARY. Aug 29, 1991. The Supreme Soviet, the parliament of the USSR, suspended all activities of the Communist Party, seizing its property and bringing to an end the institution that ruled the Soviet Union for nearly 75 years. The action followed an unsuccessful coup Aug 19–21 that sought to overthrow the government of Soviet president Mikhail Gorbachev but instead prompted a sweeping wave of democratic change. Gorbachev quit as party leader Aug 24.

Birthdays Today

Sir Richard Attenborough, 86, filmmaker (*In Which We Serve, The Great Escape*), born Cambridge, England, Aug 29, 1923.

Rebecca De Mornay, 47, actress (*Risky Business, The Hand That Rocks the Cradle*), born Santa Rosa, CA, Aug 29, 1962.

William Friedkin, 70, filmmaker (Oscar for *The French Connection*; *The Exorcist*), born Chicago, IL, Aug 29, 1939.

Richard Gere, 60, actor (*Chicago, An Officer and a Gentleman, Pretty Woman*), born Philadelphia, PA, Aug 29, 1949.

Elliott Gould, 71, actor (*M*A*S*H, The Long Goodbye*), born Elliott Goldstein at Brooklyn, NY, Aug 29, 1938.

Michael Jackson, 51, singer, songwriter, born Gary, IN, Aug 29, 1958.

Robin Leach, 68, TV host ("Lifestyles of the Rich and Famous"), born London, England, Aug 29, 1941.

Pablo Mastrioeni, 33, soccer player, born Mendoza, Argentina, Aug 29, 1976.

John Sidney McCain III, 73, 2008 Republican presidential candidate, US Senator (R, Arizona), born Panama Canal Zone, Aug 29, 1936.

Mark Morris, 53, choreographer, dancer, born Seattle, WA, Aug 29, 1956.

Roy Oswalt, 32, baseball player, born Kosciusko, MS, Aug 29, 1977.

William Edward (Will) Perdue III, 44, former basketball player, born Melbourne, FL, Aug 29, 1965.

Pierre Turgeon, 40, hockey player, born Rouyn, QC, Canada, Aug 29, 1969.

August 30 — Sunday

DAY 242 — **123 REMAINING**

ARTHUR, ELLEN LEWIS HERNDON: BIRTH ANNIVERSARY. Aug 30, 1837. Wife of Chester Alan Arthur, 21st president of the US, born at Fredericksburg, VA. Died at New York, Jan 12, 1880.

BOOTH, SHIRLEY: BIRTH ANNIVERSARY. Aug 30, 1898. American actress Shirley Booth was born Thelma Booth Ford at New York, NY. She won a Tony Award and an Oscar for her roles in the stage (1950) and film (1952) productions of *Come Back, Little Sheba*, but she is best known for her title role in the television program "Hazel" (1961–66). She died at Chatham, MS, Oct 16, 1992.

FAMILY DAY IN TENNESSEE. Aug 30. Observed annually on the last Sunday in August.

FIRST WHITE HOUSE PRESIDENTIAL BABY: BIRTH ANNIVERSARY. Aug 30, 1893. Frances Folsom Cleveland (Mrs Grover Cleveland) was the first presidential wife to have a baby at the White House when she gave birth to a baby girl (Esther). The first child ever born in the White House was a grandson to Thomas Jefferson in 1806.

HUEY P. LONG DAY. Aug 30. A legal holiday in Louisiana.

MacMURRAY, FRED: BIRTH ANNIVERSARY. Aug 30, 1908. Fred MacMurray was born at Kankakee, IL. His film and television career included a wide variety of roles, ranging from comedy (*The Absent-Minded Professor, Son of Flubber, The Shaggy Dog, The Happiest Millionaire*) to serious drama (*The Caine Mutiny, Fair Wind to Java, Double Indemnity*). During 1960–72 he portrayed the father on "My Three Sons," which was second only to "Ozzie and Harriet" as network TV's longest-running family sitcom. He died Nov 5, 1991, at Santa Monica, CA.

✦ **MINORITY ENTERPRISE DEVELOPMENT WEEK.** Aug 30–Sept 5 (tentative). Presidential Proclamation issued without request since 1983.

NATIONAL HOLISTIC PET DAY. Aug 30. A day to celebrate the growing interest in natural/holistic medicine and the animals that are treated holistically. For info: Shawn Messonnier, 2145 W Park, Plano, TX 75075. Phone: (972) 867-8800. Fax: (972) 985-9216. E-mail: shawnvet@sbcglobal.net.

PERU: SAINT ROSE OF LIMA DAY. Aug 30. Saint Rose of Lima was the first saint of the Western Hemisphere. She lived at the time of the colonization by Spain in the 16th century. Patron saint of the Americas and the Philippines. Public holiday in Peru.

PHILIPPINES: NATIONAL HEROES' DAY. Aug 30. National holiday. The last Sunday in August. Commemorates the Aug 26, 1896, beginning of the Philippine fight for independence from Spain.

PONY EXPRESS FESTIVAL. Aug 30. Hollenberg Pony Express Station, State Historic Site, Hanover, KS. Reenactment of Pony Express ride with mochila exchange, pioneer living-history demonstrations, 1860s historic-dress group, circuit-rider church service and a noon meal on the grounds. Annually, the last Sunday in August. Sponsor: Kansas State Historical Society, Friends of Hollenberg Station. Est attendance: 2,000. For info: Duane Durst, Curator, Hollenberg Pony Express Station, State Historic Site, RR1, 2889 23rd Rd, Hanover, KS 66945. Phone: (785) 337-2635. Fax: (785) 337-2309. E-mail: hollenberg@kshs.org.

RUTHERFORD, ERNEST: BIRTH ANNIVERSARY. Aug 30, 1871. Physicist, born at Nelson, New Zealand. He established the nuclear nature of the atom and the electrical structure of matter and achieved the transmutation of elements, research that later resulted in the atomic bomb. Rutherford died at Cambridge, England, Oct 19, 1937.

SHELLEY, MARY WOLLSTONECRAFT: BIRTH ANNIVERSARY. Aug 30, 1797. English novelist Mary Shelley, daughter of the philosopher William Godwin and the feminist Mary Wollstonecraft and wife of the poet Percy Bysshe Shelley, was born at London, England, and died there Feb 1, 1851. In addition to being the author of the famous novel *Frankenstein*, Shelley is important in literary history for her work in the editing and publishing of her husband's unpublished work after his early death.

SPACE MILESTONE: *CHALLENGER STS-8* (US). Aug 30, 1983. Shuttle *Challenger* with five astronauts (Richard Truly, Daniel Brandenstein, Guion Bluford, Jr, Dale Garner and William Thornton) was launched from Kennedy Space Center, FL, on this date. Return landing six days later on Sept 5 at Edwards Air Force Base, CA.

SPACE MILESTONE: *DISCOVERY* (US): 25th ANNIVERSARY. Aug 30, 1984. Space shuttle *Discovery* was launched from Kennedy Space Center, FL, for its maiden flight with a six-member crew. During the flight, the crew deployed three satellites and used a robot arm before landing at Edwards Air Force Base, CA, Sept 5.

August 2009

S	M	T	W	T	F	S
						1
2	3	4	5	6	7	8
9	10	11	12	13	14	15
16	17	18	19	20	21	22
23	24	25	26	27	28	29
30	31					

STRAITH, CLAIRE, MD: BIRTH ANNIVERSARY. Aug 30, 1891. Innovator in plastic and cosmetic surgery, born at Southfield, MI. After attending an international meeting at Paris, France, at the end of WWI to share information regarding reconstructive surgical techniques used on the battlefield, Straith dedicated his career to the new field of plastic surgery. He developed many of the techniques used in plastic and cosmetic surgery, designed new surgical instruments and led a campaign that persuaded automakers, in 1930, to use safety glass and remove dangerous projections from the interior of cars. Straith died July 13, 1958.

TURKEY: VICTORY DAY. Aug 30. Commemorates victory in War of Independence in 1922. Military parades, performing of the Mehtar band (the world's oldest military band), fireworks.

WILKINS, ROY: BIRTH ANNIVERSARY. Aug 30, 1901. Roy Wilkins, grandson of a Mississippi slave, civil rights leader, active in the National Association for the Advancement of Colored People (NAACP), retired as its executive director in 1977. Born at St. Louis, MO. Died at New York, NY, Sept 8, 1981.

WILLIAMS, TED: BIRTH ANNIVERSARY. Aug 30, 1918. Born Theodore Samuel Williams at San Diego, CA, Ted Williams played his first major league baseball game for the Boston Red Sox on Apr 22, 1939. In the years that followed, he became known as perhaps the best hitter ever to play the game. His career batting average was .344, and his record average of .406 set during the 1941 season stands unsurpassed. He played 19 seasons for the Red Sox, but during the prime of his career, he missed three full seasons while serving as a navy pilot in WWII and most of two seasons serving as a marine pilot in the Korean War. He was elected to the Baseball Hall of Fame in 1966. He died July 5, 2002, at Inverness, FL.

Birthdays Today

Elizabeth Ashley, 70, actress (*Agnes of God, Cat on a Hot Tin Roof,* "Evening Shade"), born Elizabeth Ann Cole at Ocala, FL, Aug 30, 1939.

Lewis Black, 61, comedian ("The Daily Show"), born Silver Springs, MD, Aug 30, 1948.

Timothy Bottoms, 58, actor (*The Last Picture Show, The Paper Chase*), born Santa Barbara, CA, Aug 30, 1951.

Michael Chiklis, 46, actor (Emmy and Golden Globe for "The Shield"), born Lowell, MA, Aug 30, 1963.

Cameron Diaz, 37, actress (*Charlie's Angels, My Best Friend's Wedding, There's Something About Mary*), born San Diego, CA, Aug 30, 1972.

Jean-Claude Killy, 66, Olympic gold medal alpine skier, born Saint Cloud, France, Aug 30, 1943.

Peggy Lipton, 62, actress ("The Mod Squad," "Twin Peaks"), born New York, NY, Aug 30, 1947.

Michael Michele, 43, actress ("Homicide: Life on the Street," "ER"), born Evansville, IN, Aug 30, 1966.

Robert Lee Parish, 56, former basketball player, born Shreveport, LA, Aug 30, 1953.

David Paymer, 55, actor (*City Slickers, Mr Saturday Night*), born Long Island, NY, Aug 30, 1954.

Andy Roddick, 27, tennis player, born Omaha, NE, Aug 30, 1982.

Kitty Wells, 90, singer ("Jealousy"), born Muriel Deason at Nashville, TN, Aug 30, 1919.

August 31 — Monday

DAY 243 **122 REMAINING**

"ALICE" TV PREMIERE: ANNIVERSARY. Aug 31, 1976. Linda Lavin played the title role in this CBS comedy that was based on the 1975 film *Alice Doesn't Live Here Anymore.* Alice Hyatt had dreams of making it big as a singer—while trying to make ends meet by waitressing at a diner. Lavin's costars included Vic Tayback as diner owner Mel Sharples; Philip McKeon as Alice's son, Tommy; Beth Howland as waitress Vera Gorman; and Polly Holliday as sassy waitress Flo Castleberry. The last telecast aired on July 2, 1985.

BAGHDAD STAMPEDE: ANNIVERSARY. Aug 31, 2005. Close to 1,000 Shiite Muslims died when rumors of a suicide bomber sparked a panicked stampede among nearly one million participants in a religious procession in Baghdad, Iraq. Trapped on a bridge with one closed gate, most were trampled or suffocated. The bridge then collapsed into the Tigris River, drowning many. More than 800 were injured.

CHARLESTON EARTHQUAKE: ANNIVERSARY. Aug 31, 1886. Charleston, SC. The first major earthquake in the recorded history of the eastern US occurred on this date. It is believed that about 100 persons perished in the quake, centered near Charleston but felt up to 800 miles away. Though a number of smaller eastern US quakes had been described and recorded since 1638, this affected persons living in an area of some two million square miles.

COBURN, JAMES: BIRTH ANNIVERSARY. Aug 31, 1928. Academy Award–winning actor born at Laurel, NE. He rose to fame as the knife thrower in *The Magnificent Seven* and became known for his tough-guy roles in films such as *The Great Escape* and *Our Man Flint.* He received an Oscar for his supporting role in 1999's *Affliction.* He died at Los Angeles, CA, Nov 18, 2002.

"CRANKSHAFT": ANNIVERSARY. Aug 31, 1987. Celebrating the anniversary of the nationally syndicated comic strip that premiered Aug 31, 1987. For info: Tom Batiuk, 2750 Substation Rd, Medina, OH 44256. Phone: (330) 722-8755.

DIANA, PRINCESS OF WALES: DEATH ANNIVERSARY. Aug 31, 1997. Diana, Princess of Wales, died in a car crash with her companion, Dodi Fayed, on this date, at Paris, France. Although press photographers had been pursuing her car, French courts determined that the paparazzi were not responsible for the crash but rather a driver operating under the influence of alcohol. Diana, a very popular British royal who worked on behalf of many charities, was mourned the world over.

HONG KONG: LIBERATION DAY. Aug 31. Public holiday to celebrate liberation from the Japanese in 1945. Annually, the last Monday in August.

KAZAKHSTAN: CONSTITUTION DAY. Aug 31. National holiday. Commemorates the constitution of 1995.

KLONDIKE ELDORADO GOLD DISCOVERY: ANNIVERSARY. Aug 31, 1896. Two weeks after the Rabbit/Bonanza Creek claim was filed, gold was discovered on Eldorado Creek, a tributary of Bonanza. More than $30 million worth of gold (worth some $600–$700 million in today's dollars) was mined from the Eldorado Claim in 1896.

KYRGYZSTAN: INDEPENDENCE DAY. Aug 31. National holiday. Commemorates independence from the former Soviet Union in 1991.

LOVE LITIGATING LAWYERS DAY. Aug 31. Lawyer jokes abound, but when push comes to shove, these are the folks who can end up saving the day. (©2006 by WH.) For info: Thomas & Ruth Roy, Wellcat Holidays, 2418 Long Ln, Lebanon, PA 17046. Phone: (717) 279-0184. E-mail: info@wellcat.com. Web: www.wellcat.com.

MALAYSIA: FREEDOM DAY. Aug 31. National holiday. Commemorates independence from Britain in 1957.

MOLDOVA: NATIONAL LANGUAGE DAY. Aug 31. National holiday. Also called Mother Tongue Day. Commemorates the replacement of the Cyrillic alphabet with the Latin alphabet in 1991.

MONTESSORI, MARIA: BIRTH ANNIVERSARY. Aug 31, 1870. Italian physician and educator, born at Chiaraville, Italy. Founder of the Montessori method of teaching children. Montessori died at Noordwijk, Holland, May 6, 1952.

NATIONAL OLD-TIME COUNTRY MUSIC CONTEST, FESTIVAL & EXPO. Aug 31–Sept 6. Plymouth County Fairgrounds, Le Mars, IA. Country music fans come from around the world to hear their favorites. Also many arts and crafts displays, other musical entertainment and food booths. Est attendance: 50,000. For info: Natl Old-Time Country Music Contest, Festival & Expo, PO Box 492, Anita, IA 50020. Phone: (712) 762-4363. E-mail: bobeverhart@yahoo.com. Web: www.oldtimemusic.tipzu.com.

POLAND: SOLIDARITY FOUNDED: ANNIVERSARY. Aug 31, 1980. The Polish trade union Solidarity was formed at the Baltic Sea port of Gdansk, Poland. It was outlawed by the government, and many of its leaders were arrested. Led by Lech Walesa, Solidarity persisted in its opposition to the Communist-controlled government, and Aug 19, 1989, Polish president Wojciech Jaruzelski astonished the world by nominating for the post of prime minister Tadeusz Mazowiecki, a deputy in the Polish Assembly, 1961–72, and editor in chief of Solidarity's weekly newspaper, bringing to an end 42 years of Communist Party domination.

SAROYAN, WILLIAM: BIRTH ANNIVERSARY. Aug 31, 1908. American writer of Armenian descent, author of *The Human Comedy* and of the Pulitzer Prize–winning play *The Time of Your Life*, was born at Fresno, CA, and died there May 18, 1981. In April 1981 he gave reporters a final statement for publication after his death: "Everybody has got to die, but I have always believed an exception would be made in my case. Now what?"

SHAWN, WILLIAM: BIRTH ANNIVERSARY. Aug 31, 1907. William Shawn, editor of *The New Yorker* for 35 years, was born at Chicago, IL. He was virtual dictator of editorial policy for the magazine, which in turn had an impact on the literary and reportorial styles of writers throughout the country. Nonfiction pieces in *The New Yorker* contributed to public opinion on important issues during Shawn's tenure. Shawn died Dec 8, 1992, at New York, NY.

TRINIDAD AND TOBAGO: INDEPENDENCE DAY. Aug 31. National holiday. Became an independent nation within the British Commonwealth on this day in 1962. Trinidad became a republic, Sept 24, 1976.

UNITED KINGDOM: SUMMER BANK HOLIDAY. Aug 31. Bank and public holiday in England, Wales and Northern Ireland. (Scotland not included.) Annually, the last Monday in August.

WHITECHAPEL MURDERS BEGIN: ANNIVERSARY. Aug 31, 1888. At 3:40 AM, the body of Mary Ann Nichols was found in the impoverished Whitechapel district of London, England. This was (debatably) the first in a series of brutal murders that autumn that claimed the lives of at least five women, perhaps more, by a serial killer who has come to be known as "Jack the Ripper" because of the mutilations he inflicted on his victims. The ferocity of the Whitechapel killings created an "Autumn of Terror" in which the entire populace of London was terrified and where mobs frequently tried to mete out justice to suspects they picked. Mary Kelly, found Nov 9, is considered the last victim. No suspect was ever tried for the murders. See also: "'Jack the Ripper' Letter: Anniversary" (Sept 27).

Birthdays Today

Jennifer Azzi, 41, basketball player, born Oak Ridge, TN, Aug 31, 1968.

Debbie Gibson, 39, singer ("Only in My Dreams," "Foolish Beat"), born Brooklyn, NY, Aug 31, 1970.

Van Morrison, 64, singer, songwriter ("Brown Eyed Girl," "Domino"), born Belfast, Northern Ireland, Aug 31, 1945.

Edwin Corley Moses, 54, Olympic gold medal track athlete, born Dayton, OH, Aug 31, 1955.

Hideo Nomo, 41, former baseball player, born Osaka, Japan, Aug 31, 1968.

Itzhak Perlman, 64, violinist, born Tel Aviv, Israel, Aug 31, 1945.

Pepe Reina, 27, soccer player, born Madrid, Spain, Aug 31, 1982.

Frank Robinson, 74, Hall of Fame baseball player, former baseball executive and manager, born Beaumont, TX, Aug 31, 1935.

Daniel Schorr, 93, journalist, born New York, NY, Aug 31, 1916.

G.D. Spradlin, 89, actor (*The Godfather Part II, North Dallas Forty, The War of the Roses*), born Garvin County, OK, Aug 31, 1920.

Jack Thompson, 69, actor (*The Chant of Jimmie Blacksmith, Breaker Morant*), born Sydney, Australia, Aug 31, 1940.

Glenn Tilbrook, 52, singer, musician, born London, England, Aug 31, 1957.

Chris Tucker, 37, actor (*Rush Hour, The Fifth Element*), born Decatur, GA, Aug 31, 1972.

✦ September ✦

September 1 — Tuesday

DAY 244 **121 REMAINING**

"ART LINKLETTER'S HOUSE PARTY" TV PREMIERE: ANNIVERSARY. Sept 1, 1952. Television's longest-running daytime variety show was hosted by Art Linkletter. This blend of talk and audience participation started on radio. In 1968 the show was renamed "The Linkletter Show" and moved from the afternoon to a morning slot. The series was well known for its daily interview with four schoolchildren.

ATRIAL FIBRILLATION MONTH. Sept 1–30. To raise awareness of how to manage and treat the most common irregular heartbeat, atrial fibrillation. For info: Mellanie True Hills, StopAfib.org, PO Box 541, Greenwood, TX 76246. Phone: (940) 466-9898. E-mail: mhills@stopafib.org. Web: www.StopAfib.org.

ATTENTION DEFICIT HYPERACTIVITY DISORDER MONTH. Sept 1–30. To educate healthcare groups, children and family organizations, teachers, parents and others interested in childhood health issues by providing information on effective treatments for ADHD. Some treatments have been scientifically validated, tested and proven to reduce the severity of ADHD symptoms and thereby reduce adverse consequences in the child's current and future life. There is a $15 charge for kit materials. For info: PPSI, c/o Pharmacy Council on Children's Health, 101 Lucas Valley Rd, Ste 382, San Rafael, CA 94903. Phone: (415) 479-8628. Fax: (415) 479-8608. E-mail: ppsi@aol.com. Web: www.ppsinc.org.

BACKPACK SAFETY AMERICA MONTH. Sept 1–30. Millions of school-age children are straining in pain under backpacks that are too heavy for their growing bodies. This month is set aside to remind students, parents and teachers about the safe and proper ways to choose, pack, lift and carry a backpack. Annually, the month of September. For info: John Carroll, PO Box 2430, Mt Pleasant, SC 29465. Phone: (800) 672-4277. Fax: (843) 881-6746. E-mail: info@backpacksafe.com. Web: www.backpacksafe.com.

BE KIND TO EDITORS AND WRITERS MONTH. Sept 1–30. A time for editors and writers to show uncommon courtesy toward each other. For info: Lauren Barnett, Lone Star Publications of Humor, 8452 Fredericksburg Rd, PMB 103, San Antonio, TX 78229. E-mail: lspubs@aol.com. Web: members.aol.com/lspubs/lsindex.html.

BRAZIL: INDEPENDENCE WEEK. Sept 1–7. The independence of Brazil from Portugal in 1822 is commemorated with civic and cultural ceremonies promoted by federal, state and municipal authorities. On Sept 7, a grand military parade takes place and the National Defense League organizes the Running Race in Honor of the Symbolic Torch of the Brazilian Nation.

BUILDING AND CODE STAFF APPRECIATION DAY. Sept 1. In appreciation for the hard work and dedication of building and code staff who work to ensure public health, life safety and welfare in the built environment. For info: Denice Ward, 2 Commerce Blvd, Palm Coast, FL 32164. Phone: (386) 986-3768. Fax: (386) 986-3781. E-mail: dward@ci.palm-coast.fl.us.

BURROUGHS, EDGAR RICE: BIRTH ANNIVERSARY. Sept 1, 1875. US novelist (*Tarzan of the Apes*), born at Chicago, IL. Correspondent for the *Los Angeles Times*, died at Encino, CA, Mar 19, 1950.

CARTIER, JACQUES: DEATH ANNIVERSARY. Sept 1, 1557. French navigator and explorer who sailed from St. Malo, France, Apr 20, 1534, in search of a northwest passage to the Orient. Instead, he discovered the St. Lawrence River, explored Canada's coastal regions and took possession of the country for France. Cartier was born at St. Malo, about 1491 (exact date unknown) and died there.

CHICKEN BOY'S BIRTHDAY. Sept 1. Chicken Boy is a 22-foot statue of a boy with a chicken's head, holding a bucket of chicken. Formerly the mascot for the restaurant for which he is named, he was rescued from destruction when the restaurant went out of business by Future Studio of Los Angeles, a graphic design studio. Chicken Boy has since become a pop culture icon, and has recently been installed on a rooftop in Los Angeles, so he is once again viewable by the public. For info: Amy Inouye, Future Studio, PO Box 292000, Los Angeles, CA 90029. Phone: (323) 254-4565. E-mail: futurestudio@sbcglobal.net. Web: www.chickenboy.com.

CHILDREN'S GOOD MANNERS MONTH ™. Sept 1–30. With children returning to school, September is the perfect month to remind them to treat others with respect and kindness by using good manners. For info: Fleming Allaire, PhD, 35 Eastfield St, Manchester, CT 06042. Phone: (860) 916-3428. E-mail: flemingallaire@gmail.com.

CHILE: NATIONAL MONTH. Sept 1–30. A month of special significance in Chile: arrival of spring, a Day of Unity on the first Monday in September, Independence of Chile anniversary (proclaimed Sept 18, 1810) and celebration of the 1980 Constitution and Army Day, Sept 19.

COLLEGE SAVINGS MONTH. Sept 1–30. Encourages families to plan ahead for the cost of college attendance. College savings programs make it easy and affordable for the average family to save and are available in most states. The programs offer affordable, flexible and tax-advantaged savings options that deliver the dream of education to our most precious resources—the children of America. Sponsored by the College Savings Plan Network of the National Association of State Treasurers. For info: College Savings Plan Network, PO Box 11910, Lexington, KY 40578-1910. Phone: (859) 244-8175. Fax: (859) 244-8053. E-mail: cspn@csg.org. Web: www.collegesavings.org.

EMMA M. NUTT DAY. Sept 1. A day to honor the first woman telephone operator, Emma M. Nutt, who reportedly began her professional career at Boston, MA, Sept 1, 1878, and continued working as a telephone operator for some 33 years.

FALL HAT MONTH. Sept 1–30. A month of celebration during which the straw hat is put aside in favor of the felt or fabric hat by both men and women. Local businesses and the media are encouraged to plan hat-related activities. Widely observed in the fashion industry. Originally sponsored by the Headwear Information Bureau.

FALL ON NANTUCKET. Sept 1–Nov 30. Nantucket Island, MA. Includes the Nantucket Arts Festival, Chowder Contest, Nantucket Restaurant Week, Harvest Fair and more. Est attendance: 2,000. For info: Nantucket Island Chamber of Commerce, Zero Main St, Nantucket, MA 02554-3595. Phone: (508) 228-1700. Web: www.nantucketchamber.org.

GERMANY: CAPITAL RETURNS TO BERLIN: 10th ANNIVERSARY. Sept 1, 1999. In July the monthlong process of moving the German government from Bonn to Berlin began, eight years after Parliament had voted to return to its prewar seat. Berlin officially became the capital of Germany on Sept 1, 1999, and Parliament reconvened at the newly restored Reichstag on Sept 7, 1999.

GO WILD DURING CALIFORNIA WILD RICE MONTH. Sept 1–30. To promote greater appreciation and use of cultivated wild rice. California wild rice growers want America to know that wild rice is no longer simply hiding inside a holiday turkey. This versatile grain can add a gourmet touch to meals year-round. Stuff it inside pork chop pockets and chicken breasts or toss it into soups, salads, stir-frys and even pancake and muffin batters. Let your imagination run wild! Annually, the month of September. For info: California Wild Rice Advisory Board. Phone: (916) 863-0312. Web: www.cawildrice.com.

GREAT AMERICAN LOW-CHOLESTEROL, LOW-FAT PIZZA BAKE. Sept 1–30. Pizza parlors, restaurants and volunteer agencies nationwide create healthy pizza recipes to increase the public's awareness of the benefits of controlling high cholesterol levels through diet. For info: Fred Mayer, Cholesterol Council of America, c/o Pharmacists Planning Service, Inc, 101 Lucas Valley Rd, Ste 382, San Rafael, CA 94903. Phone: (415) 479-8628. Fax: (415) 479-8608. E-mail: ppsi@aol.com. Web: www.ppsinc.org.

GYNECOLOGIC CANCER AWARENESS MONTH. Sept 1–30. During September, women are encouraged to learn more about gynecologic cancers—how they can be detected and prevented before they become fatal. For more information, please visit the Gynecologic Cancer Foundation at www.thegcf.org or the Women's Cancer Network at www.wcn.org. For info: Gynecologic Cancer Foundation, 230 W Monroe, Ste 2528, Chicago, IL 60606. Phone: (312) 578-1439. Fax: (312) 578-9769. E-mail: info@thegcf.org. Web: www.thegcf.org.

INTERNATIONAL ENTHUSIASM WEEK. Sept 1–7. Display genuine enthusiasm to every person, every project, every possibility that comes your way. It will change your week, your month, your year, your life. For info: Carolyn Stein, PO Box 630034, Miami, FL 33163. Phone: (877) 771-0772. Fax: (305) 682-1416. E-mail: carolyn@carolynstein.com. Web: www.carolynstein.com.

INTERNATIONAL PEOPLE SKILLS MONTH. Sept 1–30. Get a better job, improve the office atmosphere and increase rapport with your family. How? By refining your people skills and learning how to "de-puzzle" human behavior. More information is available on resolving conflicts, gaining influence and encouraging others. For info: Karla Brandau, People Skills International, 4985 Chartley Circle, Lilburn, GA 30047. Phone: (770) 923-0883. Fax: (770) 931-2530. E-mail: karla@karlaspeaks.com.

INTERNATIONAL SELF-AWARENESS MONTH. Sept 1–30. Cathcart Institute Inc of Lake Sherwood, CA, hosts this month each year to draw attention to the value of knowing oneself. Taking Socrates' advice "Know thyself," this effort is targeted to identify, highlight and explore all the various means and models people use for improved understanding. For info: Jim Cathcart, Cathcart Institute Inc, 2324 Crombie Ct, Lake Sherwood, CA 91361-5322. Phone: (800) 222-4883. E-mail: info@cathcart.com. Web: www.cathcart.com.

September 2009

S	M	T	W	T	F	S
		1	2	3	4	5
6	7	8	9	10	11	12
13	14	15	16	17	18	19
20	21	22	23	24	25	26
27	28	29	30			

INTERNATIONAL STRATEGIC THINKING MONTH. Sept 1–30. A monthlong effort to bring awareness of the universal need to improve thinking skills. The International Center for Strategic Planning hosts this month each year to draw attention to the value of proactively seeking to expand individual views of the world and to remove thought barriers that prevent professional achievement, personal fulfillment, cultural awareness and tolerance. For info: Sherrin Ross Ingram, Intl Center for Strategic Planning, 3 Grant Sq, #101, Hinsdale, IL 60521. Phone: (800) 962-4750. E-mail: info@icfsp.com. Web: www.icfsp.com.

JAPAN: KANTO EARTHQUAKE MEMORIAL DAY. Sept 1. A day to remember the 57,000 people who died during Japan's greatest earthquake in 1923.

KOREAN AIR LINES FLIGHT 007 DISASTER: ANNIVERSARY. Sept 1, 1983. Korean Air Lines Flight 007, en route from New York, NY, to Seoul, Korea, reportedly strayed more than 100 miles off course, flying over secret Soviet military installations on the Kamchatka Peninsula and Sakhalin Island. Two and one half hours after it was said to have entered Soviet airspace, a Soviet interceptor plane destroyed the Boeing 747 with 269 persons on board which then crashed in the Sea of Japan. There were no survivors. President Reagan, in Proclamation 5093, named Sunday, Sept 11, 1983, as a National Day of Mourning as "homage to the memory of those who died."

LIBRARY CARD SIGN-UP MONTH. Sept 1–30. This observance was launched in 1987 to meet the challenge of then Secretary of Education William J. Bennett who said, "Let's have a national campaign. . . . every child should obtain a library card—and use it." Since then, thousands of public and school libraries join each fall in a national effort to ensure every child does just that. Annually, the month of September. For info: American Library Assn, Public Information Office, 50 E Huron St, Chicago, IL 60611. Phone: (312) 280-5043 or (312) 280-5042. E-mail: pio@ala.org. Web: www.ala.org.

LIBYA: REVOLUTION DAY. Sept 1. Commemorates the revolution in 1969 when King Idris I was overthrown by Colonel Qaddafi. National holiday.

MARCIANO, ROCKY: BIRTH ANNIVERSARY. Sept 1, 1923. Rocky Marciano, boxer born Rocco Francis Marchegiano at Brockton, MA. Marciano used superb conditioning to fashion an impressive record that propelled him to fight against Jersey Joe Walcott for the heavyweight title on Sept 23, 1952. Marciano knocked Walcott out and in 1956 he retired as the only undefeated heavyweight champion. Died in a plane crash at Newton, IA, Aug 31, 1969. The film *Somebody Up There Likes Me* recounts his life story.

MEXICO: PRESIDENT'S STATE OF THE UNION ADDRESS. Sept 1. National holiday.

MILLION MINUTE FAMILY CHALLENGE™. Sept 1–Dec 31. 9th annual. A national effort to bring family, friends and neighbors together through board games. Goal is one million minutes of game playing. Add your minutes to the running total at www.millionminute.com. Special teacher material and media information available, including press kits, interviews, etc. Annually, September through December. For info: Beth Muehlenkamp, Million Minute Family Challenge, 1400 E Inman Pkwy, Beloit, WI 53511. Phone: (800) 524-4263. Fax: (608) 362-8178. E-mail: bethm@patchproducts.com. Web: www.millionminute.com.

MISSION SAN LUIS OBISPO DE TOLOSA: FOUNDING ANNIVERSARY. Sept 1, 1772. California mission to the Indians.

MOLD AWARENESS MONTH. Sept 1–30. Mold growth indoors and its negative impact on human health, especially on children and the elderly, is something only recently understood and widely accepted. As we begin to close our doors and our windows for the winter months ahead, take this time to become more aware about mold growth indoors, its causes, cures and prevention. For info: Jason Earle, MoldFacts.org, 66 Witherspoon St, Ste 378, Princeton, NJ 08542. E-mail: info@MoldFacts.org. Web: www.MoldFacts.org.

NATIONAL ALCOHOL AND DRUG ADDICTION RECOVERY MONTH. Sept 1–30. An initiative of the US Department of Health and Human Services and Substance Abuse and Mental Health Services Administration. Celebrated in local communities throughout the nation, this celebration highlights the benefits of substance abuse treatment and recovery, lauds the contributions of drug and alcohol abuse treatment providers and promotes the message that recovery from drug and alcohol use in all its forms is possible. For info: Consumer Affairs, Natl Alcohol and Drug Addiction Recovery Month, 1 Choke Cherry Rd, Rockville, MD 20857. Phone: (240) 276-2750. Fax: (240) 276-1670. Web: www.recoverymonth.gov.

NATIONAL CHICKEN MONTH. Sept 1–30. Focuses food shoppers' and restaurant customers' attention on chicken as the most healthy, convenient, economical and versatile food available; in short, "America's favorite." For info: Bill Roenigk, Sr VP, Natl Chicken Council, 1015 15th St NW, Ste 930, Washington, DC 20005. Phone: (202) 296-2622. Fax: (202) 293-4005. E-mail: WRoenigk@chickenUSA.org. Web: www.eatchicken.com or www.nationalchickencouncil.com.

NATIONAL COUPON MONTH. Sept 1–30. Sponsored by the Coupon Council of the Promotional Marketing Association and celebrates the nearly three billion dollar savings American consumers receive each year by redeeming coupons for their favorite brands. Contests and fun activities are planned on a national level to raise the awareness of coupons and their redemption value. For info: Charles K. Brown, NCH Marketing Services, Inc, 155 Pfingsten Rd, Ste 200, Deerfield, IL 60015. Phone: (847) 317-5588. Fax: (847) 317-5628. E-mail: cbrown@nchmarketing.com. Web: www.couponmonth.com.

NATIONAL HONEY MONTH. Sept 1–30. To honor the US's 212,000 beekeepers and 2.41 million colonies of honeybees, which produce more than 200 million pounds of honey each year. For info: Natl Honey Board, 11409 Business Park Circle, Ste 210, Firestone, CO 80504. Phone: (303) 776-2337. Web: www.honey.com.

NATIONAL MUSHROOM MONTH. Sept 1–30. To promote the greater appreciation and use of fresh mushrooms. For info: The Mushroom Council, 2880 Zanker Rd, Ste 203, San Jose, CA 95134. Phone: (408) 432-7210. Fax: (408) 432-7213. E-mail: info@mushroomcouncil.com. Web: mushroomcouncil.com.

NATIONAL ORGANIC HARVEST MONTH. Sept 1–30. National celebration to educate all ages about organic agriculture and products sponsored by Organic Trade Association. Local and regional events organized by retailers, manufacturers, distributors and consumer groups include food fairs, tastings, farm tours, cooking demonstrations and meet-the-farmer days. Annually, the month of September. For info: Holly Givens, Organic Trade Assn, PO Box 547, Greenfield, MA 01302. Phone: (413) 774-7511. Fax: (413) 774-6432. E-mail: info@ota.com. Web: www.theorganicreport.org.

NATIONAL OSTEOPATHIC MEDICINE MONTH. Sept 1–30. Celebrated by the American Osteopathic Association to raise public awareness of osteopathic medicine. Activities may include a health fair, blood drive, public advertising campaigns and more. For info: American Osteopathic Assn, 142 E Ontario St, Chicago, IL 60611. Phone: (312) 202-8000. Fax: (312) 202-8200. Web: www.osteopathic.org.

✦ **NATIONAL OVARIAN CANCER AWARENESS MONTH.** Sept 1–30.

NATIONAL PEDICULOSIS PREVENTION MONTH. Sept 1–30. To promote awareness of how to prevent pediculosis and protect against unnecessary and potentially harmful pesticide treatments for head lice. For info: Natl Pediculosis Assn, PO Box 610189, Newton, MA 02461. Phone: (781) 449-NITS. Fax: (401) 823-4557. E-mail: npa@headlice.org. Web: www.headlice.org or www.licemeister.org.

NATIONAL PIANO MONTH. Sept 1–30. Recognizes America's most popular instrument and its more than 20 million players; also encourages piano study by people of all ages. For info: Donald W. Dillon, Exec Dir, Natl Piano Foundation, 5960 W Parker Rd, Ste 278, Plano, TX 75093-7792. Phone: (972) 625-0110. E-mail: don@dondillon.com. Web: www.pianonet.com.

NATIONAL PREPAREDNESS MONTH. Sept 1–30. A nationwide coordinated effort held each September to promote emergency preparedness in the home, workplace, school and community. The US Department of Homeland Security and a wide variety of public and private sector organizations will participate in events and activities to highlight the importance of emergency preparedness. For info: US Department of Homeland Security, Office of Public Affairs, Washington, DC 20528. Phone: (202) 282-8010. Web: www.ready.gov/america.

NATIONAL PRIME BEEF MONTH. Sept 1–30. To celebrate and enjoy America's best beef, USDA Prime, the beef the US Department of Agriculture calls "the ultimate in tenderness, juiciness and flavor." Just one to two percent of all beef is good enough to be receive the coveted Prime grade. Sponsored by Allen Brothers, the nation's leading source of USDA Prime aged beef. For info: Todd Hatoff, Allen Brothers, 3737 South Halsted St, Chicago, IL 60609. Phone: (800) 548-7777. Fax: (773) 890-9377. E-mail: thatoff@allenbrothers.com. Web: www.allenbrothers.com.

NATIONAL RICE MONTH. Sept 1–30. To focus attention on the importance of rice to the American diet and to salute the US rice industry. For info: USA Rice Federation, 4301 N Fairfax Dr, Ste 425, Arlington, VA 22203. Phone: (703) 236-2300. E-mail: riceinfo@usarice.com. Web: www.usarice.com.

NATIONAL SICKLE CELL AWARENESS MONTH. Sept 1–30. For info: Sickle Cell Disease Assn of America, Inc, 231 E Baltimore St, Ste 800, Baltimore, MD 21202. Phone: (410) 528-1555. Web: www.SickleCellDisease.org.

NATIONAL SKIN CARE AWARENESS MONTH. Sept 1–30. Learn how to achieve healthy, glowing beautiful skin! Topics include protecting your skin from the dangers of the sun, how diet and lifestyle affect your skin, developing a proper skin care routine and myths and facts about skin care products. All important knowledge for great-looking skin. For info: Renee Rouleau Skin Care, 4025 Preston Rd, Ste 606, Plano, TX 75093. Phone: (972) 378-6655. Web: www.reneerouleau.com.

ONE-ON-ONE MONTH. Sept 1–30. This is a month to get to know your co-workers, family members and friends better by meeting one on one. When people spend time together one on one, they are more likely to talk about their lives in a meaningful way. It is easier for them to express their hopes, dreams, ideas, and share their interests in ways that they would never do in a group or even a threesome. Annually every September. For info: Harriet Meyerson, The Confidence Center. Phone: (214) 373-0080. Fax: (469) 854-2957. E-mail: Harriet@ConfidenceCenter.com. Web: www.ConfidenceCenter.com.

OVARIAN CANCER AWARENESS MONTH. Sept 1–30. For info: Natl Ovarian Cancer Coalition, 5205 N O'Connor Blvd, Ste 300, Irving, TX 75039. Phone: (469) 587-3826. E-mail: nocc@ovarian.org. Web: www.ovarian.org.

PEDIATRIC CANCER AWARENESS MONTH. Sept 1–30. Bear Necessities Pediatric Cancer Foundation is dedicated to eliminating pediatric cancer and to providing hope and support to those touched by it. Pediatric cancer is the number one cause of death by disease in children. For info: Bear Necessities Pediatric Cancer Foundation, 23 W Hubbard St, 3rd Fl, Chicago, IL 60610. Phone: (312) 836-BEAR. Fax: (312) 836-1284. E-mail: office@bearnecessities.org. Web: www.bearnecessities.org.

PHILLIS WHEATLEY'S POETRY COLLECTION PUBLISHED: ANNIVERSARY. Sept 1, 1773. On this date in 1773, the first book of poetry composed by an African American was published. Phillis Wheatley's *Poems on Various Subjects, Religious and Moral* was published at London, England. This publication came only 12 years after her arrival in America as a child slave from Senegal. In those 12 years, she learned to read and write English and studied literature in English and Latin. Feted in America and England, Wheatley eventually gained her freedom but died in poverty. See also: "Wheatley, Phillis: Death Anniversary" (Dec 5).

PICATINNY PEAK FALL HAWKWATCH. Sept 1–Nov 30. Picatinny Arsenal, Dover, NJ. Fall hawkwatch to count migrating raptors. Between 9,000 and 12,000 raptors per year are counted. Member site of Hawk Migration Association of North America (HMANA). For info: John J. Reed, 31 Croft Rd, Lake Hopatcong, NJ 07849-1023. Phone: (973) 663-2443. E-mail: hawkgawkers@verizon.net.

PLEASURE YOUR MATE MONTH. Sept 1–30. To promote love and show appreciation to your mate. Look for new ways to create happiness together. Use this event to establish a lifelong habit of sharing pleasure. Annually, the month of September. For info: Donald Etkes, PhD, 11693 San Vincente Blvd, #491, Los Angeles, CA 90049. Phone: (310) 979-0245. E-mail: drdonetkes@aol.com.

REUNION PLANNING MONTH. Sept 1–30. September is the month when family, class, military, association and corporate reunion committees meet to start planning their upcoming reunions. This is the month to start locating members of your reunion group, organizing your committee, finding a place to meet and designing a reunion that your members will remember for years to come. For info: Dina Carson, PO Box 999, Niwot, CO 80544. E-mail: info@reunionsolutions.com. Web: www.reunionsolutions.com.

REUTHER, WALTER PHILIP: BIRTH ANNIVERSARY. Sept 1, 1907. American labor leader who began work in a steel factory at age 16 and later became president of the United Automobile Workers (UAW) and the Congress of Industrial Organizations (CIO). Born at Wheeling, WV, Reuther worked for two years in a Russian automobile factory. Often at the center of controversy, he was the target of an assassin in 1948. Reuther and his wife died in an airplane crash May 9, 1970, at Black Lake, MI. The UAW Family Education Center, a project which he had cherished, was later named for Walter and May Reuther.

SCHOOLHOUSE TRIANGLE PROJECT MONTH. Sept 1–30. Promote excellence in our public schools through focus on the TRIANGLE: student, parents and teachers—all working together. Honor and encourage responsible, respectful and resourceful TRIANGLES everywhere! Education works when we focus together on the mission of excellence. For info: Miriam Freedman, PO Box 960515, Boston, MA 02196. Phone: (617) 510-0248. Fax: (617) 556-8989. E-mail: miriamkfreedman@gmail.com. Web: schoollawpro.com.

SEA CADET MONTH. Sept 1–30. Nationwide year-round youth program for boys and girls 11–17 teaches leadership and self-discipline with emphasis on nautically oriented training without military obligation. Various events will take place during each month, nationwide. Est attendance: 10,000. For info: US Naval Sea Cadet Corps, 2300 Wilson Blvd, Ste 200, Arlington, VA 22201. Phone: (703) 243-6910. Fax: (703) 243-3985. E-mail: mford@NAVYLEAGUE.org. Web: www.seacadets.org.

SELF-UNIVERSITY WEEK. Sept 1–7. Since 1989. Reminds adults (in or out of school) that each of us has a responsibility to help shape the future by pursuing lifelong learning. Committed to self-education as the lifeblood of democracy and the key to living life to its fullest. Dedicated to furthering education not as something you get but as something you take. We assert that America's greatest treasures are found not in our shopping malls but in our libraries. Annually, the first seven days of September. For info: Charles Hayes, Publisher, Autodidactic Press, PO Box 872749, Wasilla, AK 99687. Phone: (907) 376-2932. Fax: (907) 376-2932. E-mail: info@autodidactic.com. Web: www.autodidactic.com.

SEPTEMBER IS HEALTHY AGING® MONTH. Sept 1–30. Annual health observance designed to focus national attention on the positive aspects of growing older. This month is part of the Healthy Aging® Campaign, a national, ongoing health promotion designed to broaden awareness of the positive aspects of aging and to provide inspiration for adults, ages 50+, to improve their physical, mental, social and financial health. The Campaign is developed and produced by Educational Television Network, Inc. (ETNET), a nonprofit corporation based in Pennsylvania. For info: The Healthy Aging® Campaign, PO Box 442, Unionville, PA 19375. Phone: (610) 793-0979. E-mail: info@healthyaging.net. Web: www.healthyaging.net.

SHAMELESS PROMOTION MONTH. Sept 1–30. This is the month for you to go out and promote yourself, your business, your book or your product shamelessly. For outrageous tips, visit our website. For info: Marisa D'Vari, 25 Columbus Circle, Apt ST-55E, New York, NY 10019. E-mail: mdvari@deg.com. Web: www.buildingbuzz.com.

SLOVAKIA: CONSTITUTION DAY. Sept 1. Anniversary of the adoption of the Constitution of the Slovak Republic in 1992.

SPORTS AND HOME EYE SAFETY MONTH. Sept 1–30. There are thousands of eye injuries each year related to sports and hazards around the house. Tips on how to protect yourself and your children from such eye injuries will be discussed. For info: Prevent Blindness America®, 211 W Wacker Dr, Ste 1700, Chicago, IL 60606. Phone: (800) 331-2020. E-mail: info@preventblindness.com. Web: www.preventblindness.org.

SUBLIMINAL COMMUNICATIONS MONTH. Sept 1–30. Not getting the results you want? Make a change for the positive and learn how to maximize your effectiveness. Learn how to put to use your entrepreneurial thinking to achieve your goals and increase your visibility socially or in the corporate world. Recognize and apply prosperity-building opportunities for increasing your networking, marketing and publicity goals through the use of color, scents and language. Finish the last quarter of the year successfully by using the powerful resources you already possess. It's your choice! For tips and suggestions send $2.50 to Lorrie Walters Marsiglio, Lorimar Communications, PO Box 284-CC, Wasco, IL 60183-0284. Phone: (630) 584-9368.

***TITANIC* DISCOVERED: ANNIVERSARY.** Sept 1, 1985. Almost 75 years after the *Titanic* sank in the North Atlantic after striking an iceberg, a joint American-French expedition force led by marine geologist Dr. Robert Ballard located the wreck. The luxury liner was resting on the ocean floor 12,500 feet down—about 350 miles southeast from Newfoundland, Canada. In July 1986 Ballard returned in an expedition aboard the *Atlantis II* to explore the ship with underwater robots. Two memorial bronze plaques were left on the deck. See also: "Sinking of the *Titanic*: Anniversary" (Apr 15).

TOY TIPS EXECUTIVE TOY TEST. Sept 1. New York, NY. Annual event where senior corporate executives test toys and learn how to use creativity in the workplace. For info: Toy Tips, Inc. Phone: (414) 421-9668. Fax: (414) 421-9778. E-mail: marianne@toytips.com. Web: www.toytips.com.

September 2009

S	M	T	W	T	F	S
		1	2	3	4	5
6	7	8	9	10	11	12
13	14	15	16	17	18	19
20	21	22	23	24	25	26
27	28	29	30			

TWITTY, CONWAY: BIRTH ANNIVERSARY. Sept 1, 1933. Country and western music star who began his career as a rock and roll performer in the style of Elvis Presley, born at Friars Point, MS. Died June 5, 1993, at Springfield, MO.

UPDATE YOUR RESUME MONTH. Sept 1–30. This month encourages employed individuals to update and maintain their resumes. For info: Laura DeCarlo, Career Directors International, 1665 Clover Circle, Melbourne, FL 32935. Phone: (888) 867-7972. Fax: (801) 752-7517. E-mail: info@careerdirectors.com.

UZBEKISTAN: INDEPENDENCE DAY. Sept 1. National holiday. Commemorates independence upon the dissolution of the Soviet Union in 1991.

WAIKIKI ROUGHWATER SWIM. Sept 1. Waikiki Beach, Honolulu, HI. The 40th annual swim is 2.4 miles from Sans Souci Beach to Duke Kahanamoku Beach. "The World's Most Prestigious Open Water Swimming Event." Preregistration is required. Online registration at www.active.com. Est attendance: 1,000. For info: Waikiki Roughwater Swim Committee, PO Box 2847, Waikulu, HI 96793. Web: www.WaikikiRoughwaterSwim.com.

WORLD ANIMAL REMEMBRANCE MONTH. Sept 1–30. A worldwide observance to remember, respect and honor the memory of all animals—a month to pay tribute to companion animal family members; animal victims of abuse, cruelty and neglect; animals lost in natural disasters and animals killed in the line of duty. Annually, the month of September. For info: PALS Foundation, PO Box 1271, San Luis Obispo, CA 93406. Phone: (805) 544-0984. Web: www.PALS.R8.org.

WORLD WAR II BEGINS: GERMANY INVADES POLAND: 70th ANNIVERSARY. Sept 1, 1939. After securing a nonagression pact with the USSR (which secretly allowed for the partition of Poland by the Soviet Union and Germany) on Aug 23, Germany invaded Poland without a declaration of war at 4:45 AM. Two days later, Britain and France declared war, with Canada, Australia, New Zealand and South Africa soon following with their own declarations. Poland, overwhelmed by German air and land power, was in German and Soviet hands before the month concluded.

Birthdays Today

Alan Dershowitz, 71, attorney, author, born Brooklyn, NY, Sept 1, 1938.

Gloria Estefan, 52, singer, born Havana, Cuba, Sept 1, 1957.

Barry Gibb, 63, singer (with the Bee Gees, "Staying Alive"), songwriter, born Manchester, England, Sept 1, 1946.

Timothy Duane (Tim) Hardaway, 43, former basketball player, born Chicago, IL, Sept 1, 1966.

Dr. Phil McGraw, 59, psychologist, author, television personality ("The Oprah Winfrey Show," "Dr. Phil"), born Vinita, OK, Sept 1, 1950.

Seiji Ozawa, 74, conductor, born Hoten, Japan, Sept 1, 1935.

Don Stroud, 72, actor ("Mike Hammer," *The Buddy Holly Story, License to Kill*), born Honolulu, HI, Sept 1, 1937.

Lily Tomlin, 70, actress, comedienne, born Detroit, MI, Sept 1, 1939.

September 2 — Wednesday

DAY 245 — **120 REMAINING**

BISON-TEN-YELL DAY. Sept 2. Honoring the "bicentennial" of the birth of Bison-Ten-Yell, imaginary inventor of a set of ten battle yells as signals, based on the traditional memory aid system eventually adopted by football players. For info: Bob Birch, Grand Punscorpion, Puns Corps, 3108 Dashiell Rd, Falls Church, VA 22042. Phone: (703) 533-3668.

CALENDAR ADJUSTMENT DAY: ANNIVERSARY. Sept 2. Pursuant to the British Calendar Act of 1751, Britain (and the American colonies) made the "Gregorian Correction" in 1752. The Act proclaimed that the day following Wednesday, Sept 2, should become Thursday, Sept 14, 1752. There was rioting in the streets by those who felt cheated and who demanded the 11 days back. The Act also provided that New Year's Day (and the change of year number) should fall Jan 1 (instead of Mar 25) in 1752 and every year thereafter. As a result, 1751 only had 282 days. See also: "Gregorian Calendar Adjustment: Anniversary" (Feb 24, Oct 4).

COLUMBIA COUNTY FAIR. Sept 2–7. Chatham, NY. Midway and agricultural exhibits for the family to enjoy. For info: Columbia County Tourism Dept, 401 State St, Hudson, NY 12534. Phone: (800) 724-1846. Web: www.columbiacountyny.org or www.columbiafair.com.

FORTEN, JAMES: BIRTH ANNIVERSARY. Sept 2, 1766. James Forten was born of free black parents at Philadelphia, PA. As a powder boy on an American Revolutionary warship, he escaped being sold as a slave when his ship was captured due to the intervention of the son of the British commander. While in England he became involved with abolitionists. On his return to Philadelphia, he became an apprentice to a sailmaker and eventually purchased the company for which he worked. He was active in the abolition movement, and in 1816 his support was sought by the American Colonization Society for the plan to settle American blacks at Liberia. He rejected their ideas and their plans to make him the ruler of the colony. From the large profits of his successful sailmaking company, he contributed heavily to the abolitionist movement and was a supporter of William Lloyd Garrison's antislavery journal, *The Liberator*. Died at Philadelphia, PA, Mar 4, 1842.

GREAT FIRE OF LONDON: ANNIVERSARY. Sept 2–5, 1666. (Old Style date.) The fire generally credited with bringing about our system of fire insurance started Sept 2, 1666 (OS), in the wooden house of a baker named Farryner, at London's Pudding Lane, near the Tower. During the ensuing three days more than 13,000 houses were destroyed, though it is believed that only six lives were lost in the fire.

HISTORIC MARATHON RUNS: ANNIVERSARY. Sept 2–9, 490 BC. Anniversary of the event during the Persian Wars from which the marathon race is derived. Phidippides, "an Athenian and by profession and practice a trained runner," according to Herodotus, was dispatched from Marathon to Sparta (26 miles), Sept 2 to seek help in repelling the invading Persian army. Help being unavailable by religious law until after the next full moon, Phidippides ran the 26 miles back to Marathon Sept 4. Without Spartan aid, the Athenians defeated the Persians at the Battle of Marathon Sept 9. According to legend Phidippides carried the news of the battle to Athens and died as he spoke the words, "Rejoice, we are victorious." The marathon race was revived at the 1896 Olympic Games at Athens. Course distance, since 1924, is 26 miles, 385 yards. See also: "Battle of Marathon: Anniversary" (Sept 9).

McAULIFFE, CHRISTA: BIRTH ANNIVERSARY. Sept 2, 1948. Christa McAuliffe, a 37-year-old Concord, NH, high school teacher, was to have been the first "ordinary citizen" in space. Born Sharon Christa Corrigan at Boston, MA, she perished with six crew members in the Space Shuttle *Challenger* explosion Jan 28, 1986. See also: "Challenger Space Shuttle Explosion: Anniversary" (Jan 28).

NUGGET BEST IN THE WEST RIB COOK-OFF. Sept 2–7. Victorian Square, Sparks, NV. 21st annual. Rib cookers from across the country compete for the title of Nugget Best in the West Rib Cooker.

Competing cookers sell ribs to the crowd over the Labor Day weekend. Free concerts nightly feature groups like BTO, War and Terri Clark. Other music groups presented throughout the day—all free. Hundreds of craft booths and activities for the whole family. Est attendance: 500,000. For info: John Ascuaga's Nugget, 1100 Nugget Ave, Sparks, NV 89431. Phone: (800) 648-1177. Web: www.nuggetribcookoff.com.

SHERMAN ENTERS ATLANTA: ANNIVERSARY. Sept 2, 1864. After a four-week siege, Union General William Tecumseh Sherman entered Atlanta, GA. The city had been evacuated on the previous day by Confederate troops under General John B. Hood. Hood had mistakenly assumed Sherman was ending the siege Aug 27, when actually Sherman was beginning the final stages of his attack. Hood then sent troops to attack the Union forces at Jonesboro. Hood's troops were defeated, opening the way for the capture of Atlanta.

US TREASURY DEPARTMENT: ANNIVERSARY. Sept 2, 1789. The third presidential cabinet department, the Treasury Department, was established by Congress.

VIETNAM: INDEPENDENCE DAY. Sept 2. Ho Chi Minh formally proclaimed the independence of Vietnam from France and the establishment of the Democratic Republic of Vietnam on this day in 1945. National holiday.

V-J DAY: ANNIVERSARY. Sept 2, 1945. Official ratification of Japanese surrender to the Allies occurred aboard the USS *Missouri* at Tokyo Bay Sept 2 (Far Eastern time) in 1945, thus prompting President Truman's declaration of this day as Victory-over-Japan Day. Japan's initial, informal agreement of surrender was announced by Truman and celebrated in the US Aug 14.

Birthdays Today

Nathaniel "Tiny" Archibald, 61, Hall of Fame basketball player, born New York, NY, Sept 2, 1948.

Terry Paxton Bradshaw, 61, sportscaster, Hall of Fame football player, born Shreveport, LA, Sept 2, 1948.

Marge Champion, 86, dancer, actress ("Marge and Gower Champion Show," *Show Boat*), born Los Angeles, CA, Sept 2, 1923.

Jimmy Connors, 57, former tennis player, born East St. Louis, IL, Sept 2, 1952.

Jim DeMint, 58, US Senator (R, South Carolina), born Greenville, SC, Sept 2, 1951.

Eric Dickerson, 49, Hall of Fame football player, broadcaster, born Sealy, TX, Sept 2, 1960.

Mark Harmon, 58, actor ("NCIS," "St. Elsewhere," "Chicago Hope"), born Burbank, CA, Sept 2, 1951.

Salma Hayek, 43, actress (*Ask the Dust, Bandidas, Frida*), born Veracruz, Mexico, Sept 2, 1966.

Linda Purl, 54, actress ("Matlock"), born Greenwich, CT, Sept 2, 1955.

Keanu Reeves, 45, actor (*The Matrix, Speed*), born Beirut, Lebanon, Sept 2, 1964.

John Thompson, 68, college basketball coach, former player, born Washington, DC, Sept 2, 1941.

Peter Victor Ueberroth, 72, former commissioner of baseball and Olympic organizer, born Evanston, IL, Sept 2, 1937.

Carlos Valderrama, 48, former soccer player, born Santa Marta, Colombia, Sept 2, 1961.

Cynthia Watros, 41, actress ("Lost," "The Drew Carey Show," "Guiding Light"), born Lake Orion, MI, Sept 2, 1968.

September 2009

S	M	T	W	T	F	S
		1	2	3	4	5
6	7	8	9	10	11	12
13	14	15	16	17	18	19
20	21	22	23	24	25	26
27	28	29	30			

September 3 — Thursday

DAY 246 **119 REMAINING**

BEGINNING OF THE PENNY PRESS: ANNIVERSARY. Sept 3, 1833. Benjamin H. Day launched the *New York Sun*, the first truly successful penny newspaper in the US, on this date. The *Sun* was sold on sidewalks by newspaper boys. By 1836 the paper was the largest seller in the country with a circulation of 30,000. It was possibly Day's concentration on human interest stories and sensationalism that made his publication a success while efforts at penny papers at Philadelphia and Boston had failed.

BLUE HILL FAIR. Sept 3–7. Blue Hill, ME. A "down-to-earth" country fair. Annually, Labor Day weekend. Est attendance: 35,000. For info: Blue Hill Fair, PO Box 390, Blue Hill, ME 04614. Phone: (207) 374-3701. Fax: (207) 374-3702. Web: www.bluehillfair.com.

BRITAIN DECLARES WAR ON GERMANY: 70th ANNIVERSARY. Sept 3, 1939. British ultimatum to Germany, demanding halt to invasion of Poland (which had started at dawn on Sept 1), expired at 11 AM, GMT, Sept 3, 1939. At 11:15 AM, in a radio broadcast, Prime Minister Neville Chamberlain announced the declaration of war against Germany. France, Canada, Australia, New Zealand and South Africa quickly issued separate declarations of war. Winston Churchill was named First Lord of the Admiralty. See also: "World War II Begins: Germany Invades Poland" (Sept 1).

CANADA: TORONTO INTERNATIONAL FILM FESTIVAL. Sept 3–12. Toronto, ON. 34th annual. A 10-day festival of contemporary Canadian and international cinema at various downtown theatres. Call or write for info or to be put on mailing list. Est attendance: 250,000. For info: Toronto Intl Film Festival, 2 Carlton St, Ste 1600, Toronto, ON, Canada M5B 1J3. Phone: (416) 968-FILM. Fax: (416) 967-9477. E-mail: tiffg@tiffg.ca. Web: www.tiffg.ca.

CHINA: FESTIVAL OF HUNGRY GHOSTS. Sept 3. Important Chinese festival, also known as the Chung Yuan Festival. According to Chinese legend, during the seventh lunar month the souls of the dead are released from purgatory to roam the Earth. Joss sticks are burned in homes; prayers, food and "ghost money" are offered to appease the ghosts. Market stallholders join together to hold celebrations to ensure that their businesses will prosper in the coming year. Wayang (Chinese street opera) and puppet shows are performed, and fruit and Chinese delicacies are offered to the spirits of the dead. Chung Yuan is observed on the 15th day of the seventh lunar month. Date in other countries will differ from China's.

CRANDALL, PRUDENCE: BIRTH ANNIVERSARY. Sept 3, 1803. Born to a Quaker family at Hopkinton, RI, this American schoolteacher sparked controversy in the 1830s with her efforts to educate black girls. When her private academy for girls was boycotted because she admitted a black girl, she started a school for "young ladies and misses of colour." Died Jan 28, 1890, at Elk Falls, KS.

DOUGLASS'S ESCAPE TO FREEDOM: ANNIVERSARY. Sept 3, 1838. Dressed as a sailor and carrying identification papers borrowed from a retired merchant seaman, Frederick Douglass boarded a train at Baltimore, MD, a slave state, and rode to Wilmington, DE, where he caught a steamboat to the free city of Philadelphia. He then transferred to a train headed for New York City where he entered the protection of the Underground Railway network. Douglass later became a great orator and one of the leaders of the antislavery struggle.

ENGLAND: THE LAND ROVER BURGHLEY HORSE TRIALS. Sept 3–6. Burghley Park, Stamford, Lincolnshire, England. Major four-star event: dressage, cross country, show jumping, etc. Est attendance: 160,000. For info: Burghley Horse Trials, Stamford, Lincolnshire, PE9 2LH England. Phone: (44) (1780) 752-131. Fax: (44) (1780) 752-982. E-mail: info@burghley-horse.co.uk. Web: www.burghley-horse.co.uk.

FILENE, EDWARD ALBERT: BIRTH ANNIVERSARY. Sept 3, 1860. American merchant and philanthropist, born at Salem, MA, who established the US credit union movement in 1921. Died at Paris, France, Sept 26, 1937.

FIRST SECRET SERVICE AGENT TO DIE IN THE LINE OF DUTY: ANNIVERSARY. Sept 3, 1902. While on duty protecting President Theodore Roosevelt, William Craig was killed when a streetcar collided with the carriage carrying the president (who suffered some cuts). The United States Secret Service was founded in 1865 as a branch of the Treasury Department entrusted with foiling counterfeiting, but was given the additional role of protecting the US president upon the assassination of William McKinley. Craig, born in Glasgow, Scotland, in 1855, was also a bodyguard for Queen Victoria before moving to Chicago. Roosevelt affectionately called Craig his "shadow."

HOPKINTON STATE FAIR. Sept 3–7. Contoocook, NH. 94th fair. "A Labor Day Weekend Tradition." For info: Hopkinton State Fair, PO Box 700, Contoocook, NH 03229-0700. Phone: (603) 746-4191. Fax: (603) 746-3037. E-mail: hsfinfo@tds.net. Web: www.hsfair.org.

ITALY SURRENDERS: ANNIVERSARY. Sept 3, 1943. General Giuseppe Castellano signed three copies of the "short armistice," effectively surrendering "unconditionally" for the Italian government. That same day the British Eighth Army, commanded by General Bernard Montgomery, invaded the Italian mainland.

LOUISIANA SHRIMP AND PETROLEUM FESTIVAL AND FAIR. Sept 3–7. Morgan City, LA. Free admission to this event that recognizes and celebrates the importance of the shrimp and petroleum industries to the area. Arts, crafts, water and street parades, Cajun culinary classic, music in the park, unique children's village (a magical adventureland), gospel tent, coronation pageant and ball, carnival, blessing of the fleet. Chosen as the American Bus Association's "Festival of the Year" for the past four years. Est attendance: 150,000. For info: Louisiana Shrimp and Petroleum Festival and Fair Assn, Box 103, Morgan City, LA 70381. Phone: (504) 385-0703. Fax: (504) 384-4628. E-mail: info@shrimp-petrofest.org.

NATIONAL SWEETCORN FESTIVAL. Sept 3–7. McFerron Park, Hoopeston, IL. Annual festival includes 29 tons of free corn on the cob, nationally sanctioned beauty pageant, carnival, flea market, horse show, demolition derby, bands and talent shows. Est attendance: 50,000. For info: Jeanie Cooke, Exec Dir, Danville Area Conv/Visitors Bureau, PO Box 992, Danville, IL 61834. Phone: (217) 442-2096. E-mail: dacvb@danvilleareainfo.com.

OLD THRESHERS REUNION. Sept 3–7. McMillan Park, Mount Pleasant, IA. The reunion began in 1950. Old Threshers is a celebration of our rich agricultural heritage. Attractions range from displays of steam engines and agricultural exhibits to turn-of-the-century living and antique cars, tractors and gas engines. There are also steam trains, trolleys, crafts, museums, music and camping. Annually, five days ending on Labor Day. Est attendance: 60,000. For info: Midwest Old Threshers, 405 E Threshers Rd., Mt Pleasant, IA 52641. Phone: (319) 385-8937. Fax: (319) 385-0563. E-mail: info@oldthreshers.com. Web: www.oldthreshers.com.

QATAR: INDEPENDENCE DAY. Sept 3. National holiday. Commemorates the severing in 1971 of treaty with Britain, which had handled Qatar's foreign relations.

SAN MARINO: NATIONAL DAY. Sept 3. Public holiday. Honors St. Marinus, the traditional founder of San Marino.

"SEARCH FOR TOMORROW" TV PREMIERE: ANNIVERSARY. Sept 3, 1951. This soap lasted for 35 years. It began as a 15-minute program and expanded to 30 minutes in 1968, when performances began to be videotaped instead of airing live. "Search" was set in the town of Henderson, and its central character was Joanne Gardner Barron Tate Vincente Tourneur (played by Mary Stuart). Other notable cast members have included: Don Knotts, Robert Mandan, Ken Kercheval, Jill Clayburgh, Natalie Schafer, Susan Sarandon, Robert Loggia, Hal Linden, Morgan Fairchild, Joe Morton, Robby Benson, Kevin Kline, Cynthia Gibb and Olympia Dukakis.

SOUTH DAKOTA STATE FAIR. Sept 3–7. Huron, SD. Grandstand entertainment nightly, two free stages with multiple shows daily, hundreds of commercial exhibits and thousands of livestock exhibits. One of the largest agricultural fairs in the US. Est attendance: 151,000. For info: South Dakota State Fair, 890 3rd St SW, Huron, SD 57350-1275. Phone: (605) 353-7340 or (800) 529-0900. Fax: (605) 353-7348. Web: www.sdstatefair.com.

SULLIVAN, LOUIS: BIRTH ANNIVERSARY. Sept 3, 1856. An American architect responsible for the modern, steel-framed skyscraper, his designs are characterized by rich ornamentation, plain outer surfaces and cubic forms. His famous motto was, "form follows function." Frank Lloyd Wright was a student of Sullivan's before the two quarreled. Born at Boston, MA, Sullivan died Apr 14, 1924, at Chicago, IL.

THOMAS POINT BEACH BLUEGRASS FESTIVAL. Sept 3–6. Brunswick, ME. 31st annual. Featuring world-class bluegrass musicians on the southern coast of Maine. Swimming, playground, picnic area, snack bar, free camping, Sunday morning worship service on the beach. Fun for the whole family. Enjoy an end-of-summer family outing and terrific bluegrass music. Est attendance: 4,000. For tickets and info: Thomas Point Beach, 29 Meadow Rd, Brunswick, ME 04011. Phone: (207) 725-6009 or (877) TPB-4321. E-mail: summer@thomaspointbeach.com. Web: www.thomaspointbeach.com.

TREATY OF PARIS ENDS AMERICAN REVOLUTION: ANNIVERSARY. Sept 3, 1783. Treaty between Britain and the US, ending the Revolutionary War, signed at Paris, France. American signatories: John Adams, Benjamin Franklin and John Jay.

Birthdays Today

Eileen Brennan, 72, actress ("Seventh Heaven," "Will & Grace," *The Last Picture Show, Private Benjamin*), born Los Angeles, CA, Sept 3, 1937.

Pauline Collins, 69, stage and screen actress (Olivier and Tony awards for *Shirley Valentine*; "Upstairs, Downstairs"), born Exmouth, England, Sept 3, 1940.

Kiran Desai, 38, author (*The Inheritance of Loss, Hullabaloo in the Guava Orchard*), born New Delhi, India, Sept 3, 1971.

Anne Jackson, 83, actress (*Lovers and Other Strangers*), born Allegheny, PA, Sept 3, 1926.

Alison Lurie, 83, author (*Foreign Affairs, The War Between the Tates*), born Chicago, IL, Sept 3, 1926.

Valerie Perrine, 66, actress (*Lenny, W.C. Fields and Me*), born Galveston, TX, Sept 3, 1943.

Charlie Sheen, 44, actor ("Two and a Half Men," *Wall Street, Platoon*), born Carlos Irwin Estevez at New York, NY, Sept 3, 1965.

Damon Stoudamire, 36, basketball player, born Portland, OR, Sept 3, 1973.

Mort Walker, 86, cartoonist ("Beetle Bailey"), born Addison Morton Walker at El Dorado, KS, Sept 3, 1923.

September 4 — Friday

DAY 247 **118 REMAINING**

BENTON NEIGHBOR DAY. Sept 4–5. Benton, MO. Large festival that includes exhibits, greased pole climb, amusement park, Little Mr and Miss Contest, Queen Contest, Junior Miss Contest, lawn mower races, live bands, antique car show, horseshoe tournament, parade and talent show. Antique tractor pull, outdoor games for kids and adults. Annually, the Friday and Saturday before Labor Day. Est attendance: 3,000. For info: Benton Chamber of Commerce, PO Box 477, Benton, MO 63736. Phone: (573) 545-3125.

BRITT DRAFT HORSE SHOW. Sept 4–6. Hancock County Fairgrounds, Britt, IA. One of the largest draft horse hitch shows in North America, featuring 18 six-horse hitches from the US and Canada representing the very best of the Belgian, Percheron and Clydesdale performance horses. Annually, Labor Day weekend. Est attendance: 10,000. For info: Randel or Melodie Hiscocks, Britt Draft Horse Assn, PO Box 312, Britt, IA 50423. Phone: (641) 843-4181.

BRUCKNER, ANTON: BIRTH ANNIVERSARY. Sept 4, 1824. Austrian composer born at Ansfelden, Austria. Died at Vienna, Austria, Oct 11, 1896.

BURNHAM, DANIEL: BIRTH ANNIVERSARY. Sept 4, 1846. American architect and city planner born at Henderson, NY. Daniel Hudson Burnham was an advocate of tall, fireproof buildings, probably the first to be called "sky-scrapers." In 1909 he proposed a long-range city plan for Chicago, IL, that was a key factor in the "forever open, clear and free" policy which resulted in Chicago having the most beautiful lakefront of any major city in the US. Died June 1, 1912, at Heidelberg, Germany.

"CAPTAIN MIDNIGHT" TV PREMIERE: 55th ANNIVERSARY. Sept 4, 1954. A children's show starring Richard Webb as Captain Midnight, a WWI flying ace who battled crime as part of the Secret Squadron. Webb was joined by Sid Melton as Ichabod (Ikky) Mudd, his assistant, and Olan Soule as Tut, an eccentric scientist. "Captain Midnight" moved to TV from radio, where it was sponsored by Ovaltine. In reruns the name was changed to "Jet Jackson, Flying Commando" because Ovaltine owned the rights to the Captain Midnight name.

CHATEAUBRIAND, FRANCOIS RENE DE: BIRTH ANNIVERSARY. Sept 4, 1768. French poet, novelist, historian, explorer and statesman, witness to the French Revolution. Born at St. Malo, France, he died at Paris, France, July 4, 1848.

COIN & STAMP EXPO. Sept 4–6. Radisson Hotel, Anaheim, CA. Est attendance: 4,000. For info: Israel Bick, Exec Dir, Intl Stamp & Coin Collectors Society, PO Box 854, Van Nuys, CA 91408. Phone: (818) 997-6496. Fax: (818) 988-4337. E-mail: iibick@sbcglobal.net. Web: www.bick.net.

September 2009	S	M	T	W	T	F	S
			1	2	3	4	5
	6	7	8	9	10	11	12
	13	14	15	16	17	18	19
	20	21	22	23	24	25	26
	27	28	29	30			

CURAÇAO: ANIMALS' DAY. Sept 4. In Curaçao the Association for the Protection of Animals organizes an animal show for this day and the best-kept animals are awarded prizes.

DANIEL BOONE PIONEER FESTIVAL. Sept 4–6. Winchester, KY. Take yourself back to the days of Daniel Boone and the pioneers. Features street dance, fireworks, 5k run, arts and crafts displays and food booths. A nationally known country music entertainer will perform in concert. Est attendance: 35,000. For info: Daniel Boone Pioneer Festival, 2 S Maple St, Winchester, KY 40391. Phone: (859) 744-0556. Fax: (859) 744-9229. E-mail: info@tourwinchester.com.

ENGLAND: BLACKPOOL ILLUMINATIONS. Sept 4–Nov 1. The Promenade, Blackpool, Lancashire. "A five-mile spectacle of lighting." Est attendance: 3,000,000. For info: Blackpool Tourism, 1 Clifton St, Blackpool, Lancashire, England FY1 1LY. Phone: (44) 1253 478222. Fax: (44) 1253 478210. E-mail: tourism@blackpool.gov.uk. Web: www.visitblackpool.com.

FESTIVAL OF CHILDREN. Sept 4–30 (weekends). South Coast Plaza, Costa Mesa, CA. The festival includes more than 65 local charities and Southern California organizations hosting live performances, free workshops, activities and special guest appearances. Est attendance: 2,000,000. For info: Festival of Children, South Coast Plaza, 3333 Bristol St, Costa Mesa, CA 92626. Phone: (714) 438-3286. Web: www.festivalofchildren.org.

FIRST ELECTRIC LIGHTING: ANNIVERSARY. Sept 4, 1882. Four hundred electric lights came on in offices on Spruce, Wall, Nassau and Pearl streets in lower Manhattan as Thomas Edison hooked up light bulbs to an underground cable carrying direct current electrical power. Edison had demonstrated his first incandescent light bulb in 1879. See also: "Incandescent Lamp Demonstrated: Anniversary" (Oct 21).

FORT BRIDGER RENDEZVOUS. Sept 4–7. Fort Bridger, WY. Come and join in the family fun with entertainment, food booths, merchandise exhibits and much more. Est attendance: 30,000. For info: Traci Hardy, Fort Bridger Rendezvous Assn, PO Box 9, Woodruff, UT 84086. Phone: (435) 793-4570 or (435) 213-5133. E-mail: fbrainc@hotmail.com. Web: www.fortbridgerrendezvous.net.

HARVEST MOON. Sept 4. So called because the full moon nearest the autumnal equinox extends the hours of light into the evening and helps the harvester with his long day's work.

HOG CAPITAL OF THE WORLD FESTIVAL. Sept 4–7. Kewanee, IL. World's largest pork chop BBQ. Also features professional entertainment, carnival, flea market, Model T races, parade, four-mile run (Hog Stampede) and the Hogatta Regatta. Annually, Labor Day weekend. Est attendance: 60,000. For info: Mark Mikenas, Exec VP, Kewanee Chamber of Commerce, 113 E 2nd St, Kewanee, IL 61443. Phone: (309) 852-2175. Fax: (309) 852-2176. E-mail: chamber@kewanee-il.com. Web: www.kewanee-il.com or www.kewaneehogdays.com.

HOISINGTON CELEBRATION. Sept 4–7. Bicentennial Park, Hoisington, KS. Annual event includes dances, demolition derby, parade, car show, carnival, kiddie events, baby contest, float contest. Annually, Labor Day weekend. Est attendance: 25,000. For info: Hoisington Labor Day Committee, 123 N Main, Hoisington, KS 67544. Phone: (620) 653-4311. E-mail: hoisingtoncofc@embarqmail.com.

JOHNSON CITY FIELD DAYS. Sept 4–7. Northside Park, Johnson City, NY. Amusement rides, game booths, live entertainment, food concessions, area's largest fireworks display. The annual celebration benefits many nonprofit organizations in Johnson City. Annually, Labor Day weekend. For info: Johnson City Celebration Committee, 243 Main St, Johnson City, NY 13790. Phone: (607) 798-7861 or (607) 797-9098. Fax: (607) 798-7865. E-mail: jcplanning-secretary@stny.rr.com.

LIFELIGHT OUTDOOR MUSIC FESTIVAL. Sept 4–6. Sioux Falls, SD. Outdoor Christian music festival, featuring more than 100 bands on six stages, children's activities, seminars, waterpark, camping and extreme sports. Annually, Labor Day weekend. Est attendance: 300,000. For info: LifeLight Fest, 2601 S Western Ave, Sioux Falls, SD 57105. Phone: (605) 338-2847. Fax: (605) 336-1056. E-mail: office@lifelight.org. Web: www.lifelight.org.

LITTLE ROCK NINE: ANNIVERSARY. Sept 4–25, 1957. Governor Orval Faubus called out the Arkansas National Guard to turn away nine black students who had been trying to attend Central High School in Little Rock. President Eisenhower sent in the 101st Army Airborne to enforce the law allowing the students to integrate the school, and on Sept 25, national troops escorted the nine into the school.

LOS ANGELES, CALIFORNIA, FOUNDED: ANNIVERSARY. Sept 4, 1781. Los Angeles founded by decree and called "El Pueblo de Nuestra Señora La Reina de Los Angeles de Porciuncula." The City of Los Angeles was incorporated on Apr 4, 1850.

MOON PHASE: FULL MOON. Sept 4. Moon enters Full Moon phase at 12:03 PM, EDT.

NATIONAL CHAMPIONSHIP CHUCKWAGON RACES. Sept 4–6. Clinton, AR. 24th annual. Five divisions of chuckwagon races, bronc fanning, Snowy River race, live entertainment, trail rides, barn dance, Western show, Western art, saddles, tack-clothing vendors. Annually, Labor Day weekend. Est attendance: 25,000. For info: Dan Eoff, 2848 Shake Rag Rd, Clinton, AR 72031. Phone: (501) 745-8407. Fax: (501) 745-8473. E-mail: chuckwag@artelco.com. Web: www.chuckwagonraces.com.

NATIONAL HARD CRAB DERBY AND FAIR. Sept 4–6. Somers Cover Marina grounds, Crisfield, MD. 62nd annual. An annual Labor Day Weekend tradition celebrating Chesapeake Bay's favorite crustacean. Features the famous crab races, crab feast, Miss Crustacean beauty contest, fishing contest, crab picking contest, boat parades, great food and lots more. For info: Crisfield Chamber of Commerce, 906 W Main St, PO Box 292, Crisfield, MD 21817. Phone: (410) 968-2500 or (800) 782-3913. Fax: (410) 968-0524. Web: www.crisfieldchamber.com/crabderby.htm.

NEW MEXICO STATE FAIR. Sept 4–20. Albuquerque, NM. Nationally known recording artists perform at Tingley Coliseum. PRCA rodeo competitions. Thoroughbred and Quarterhorse racing. Villa Hispana, Native American Village and African-American Pavilion. Free entertainment. Est attendance: 738,664. For info: New Mexico State Fair, PO Box 8546, Albuquerque, NM 87198. Phone: (505) 265-EXPO. Fax: (505) 266-7784. Web: www.exponm.com.

NEWSPAPER CARRIER DAY. Sept 4. Anniversary of the hiring of the first "newsboy" in the US, 10-year-old Barney Flaherty, who is said to have answered the following classified advertisement, which appeared in *The New York Sun* in 1833: "To the Unemployed—a number of steady men can find employment by vending this paper. A liberal discount is allowed to those who buy to sell again."

OATMEAL FESTIVAL. Sept 4–5. Bertram/Oatmeal, TX. Annual festival to honor Oatmeal, the community and the cereal, and to have a weekend of family fun, good food and a whole lot of foolishness. Annually, Friday and Saturday before Labor Day. Est attendance: 7,000. For info: Oatmeal Fest, PO Box 70, Bertram/Oatmeal, TX 78605. Phone: (512) 355-2197 or (512) 355-2549. Fax: (512) 355-3182. Web: www.bertramtx.com.

ODYSSEY—A GREEK FESTIVAL. Sept 4–7. Orange, CT. An indoor/outdoor festival celebrating Greek culture, featuring authentic Greek cuisine, live music and marketplace. Est attendance: 15,000. For info: St. Barbara Greek Orthodox Church, 480 Racebrook Rd, Orange, CT 06477. Phone: (203) 795-1347. Web: www.saintbarbara.org. Or: Greater New Haven Conv & Visitors Bureau, One Long Wharf Dr, New Haven, CT, 06511. Phone: (203) 777-8550 or (800) 332-STAY. Fax: (203) 782-7755.

ON THE WATERFRONT. Sept 4–6. Rockford, IL. Illinois's largest music festival. Six music stages, more than 130 performers, more than 50 specialty foods, and dozens of special events. Annually, the Thursday through Sunday of Labor Day weekend. Est attendance: 300,000. For info: On the Waterfront, Inc, 308 W State St, Ste 115, Rockford, IL 61101. Phone: (815) 964-4388 or (815) 963-4FUN. E-mail: 4fun@onthewaterfront.com. Web: www.onthewaterfront.com.

OREGON TRAIL RODEO. Sept 4–6. Hastings, NE. PRCA-sponsored rodeo. Annually, Friday–Sunday of Labor Day weekend. Est attendance: 9,400. For info: Sandy Himmelberg, Genl Mgr, Oregon Trail Rodeo, 947 S Baltimore, Hastings, NE 68901. Phone: (402) 462-3247. Fax: (402) 462-4731. Web: www.adamscountyfairgrounds.com.

PAYSON GOLDEN ONION DAYS. Sept 4–7. Payson, UT. This unique festival includes amusement rides, fireworks, a parade, arts and crafts displays, entertainment, food booths and much more. Annually, Labor Day weekend. Est attendance: 13,000. For info: Payson Community Services Dir, 439 W Utah Ave, Payson, UT 84651. Phone: (801) 465-5217. Fax: (801) 465-5208. E-mail: debbieb@payson.org. Web: www.payson.org.

PENNSYLVANIA ARTS & CRAFTS COLONIAL FESTIVAL. Sept 4–7. Westmoreland Fairgrounds, Greensburg, PA. Step back to colonial times with more than 220 exhibits of handcrafted furniture, floral arrangements, ceramics, tole, decorative paintings and wrought iron. Historical encampment, fife and drum music and food booths. Est attendance: 21,000. For info: Debbie & Dave Stoner, Family Festivals Assn, Inc, PO Box 166, Irwin, PA 15642. Phone: (724) 863-4577. Fax: (724) 863-5427. E-mail: familyfestivals@hotmail.com. Web: www.familyfestivals.com.

POLK, SARAH CHILDRESS: BIRTH ANNIVERSARY. Sept 4, 1803. Wife of James Knox Polk, 11th president of the US. Born at Murfreesboro, TN, and died at Nashville, TN, Aug 14, 1891.

SANTA-CALI-GON DAYS FESTIVAL. Sept 4–7. Historic Square, Independence, MO. Regional celebration for the three trails—Santa Fe, California, Oregon—which all started in Independence. Huge arts and crafts show, live Nashville performers, large carnival midway and free admission. Largest Labor Day weekend event in Kansas City metropolitan area. Est attendance: 225,000. For info: Santa-Cali-Gon Days, 210 W Truman Rd, Independence, MO 64051. Phone: (816) 252-4745. Web: www.santacaligon.com.

A TASTE OF COLORADO. Sept 4–7. Denver, CO. The Rocky Mountain region's largest free outdoor festival, this four-day food and entertainment extravaganza over Labor Day weekend features 50 Colorado area restaurants. Musical entertainment on six outdoor stages, gourmet cooking demonstrations, 280 arts and crafts vendors and children's music and activities. Est attendance: 500,000. For info: Susan Rogers Kark, Event Mgr, Downtown Denver Partnership, Inc, 511 16th St, Ste 200, Denver, CO 80202. Phone: (303) 534-6161 or (303) 478-7878 (Hotline). Fax: (303) 534-2803. E-mail: susan@downtowndenver.com. Web: www.atasteofcolorado.com.

TENNESSEE STATE FAIR. Sept 4–13. Nashville, TN. A huge variety of exhibits, carnival midway, animal and variety shows, live stage presentations, livestock, agricultural and craft competitions and food and game booths. Annually, beginning the first Friday after Labor Day. Est attendance: 240,000. For info: Tennessee Fair Office, PO Box 40208, Melrose Station, Nashville, TN 37204. Phone: (615) 862-8980. Fax: (615) 862-8992. E-mail: tsf@nashville.gov. Web: www.tennesseestatefair.org.

VERMONT STATE FAIR. Sept 4–13. Fairgrounds, Rutland, VT. Est attendance: 100,000. For info: Vermont State Fair, 175 S Main St, Rutland, VT 05701. Phone: (802) 775-5200. E-mail: vtstfair@comcast.net. Web: www.vermontstatefair.net.

WEST VIRGINIA ITALIAN HERITAGE FESTIVAL. Sept 4–6. Clarksburg, WV. Includes pasta cook-off (participants cook a pasta dish to compete for prizes), homemade wine contest, live entertainment, parade and more. All free to the public. Est attendance: 150,000. For info: West Virginia Italian Heritage Festival Office, Box 1632, Clarksburg, WV 26302. Phone: (304) 622-7314. Fax: (304) 622-5727. E-mail: benvenuto79@wvihf.com. Web: www.wvihf.com.

WESTFEST. Sept 4–6. West, TX. West celebrates its Czech heritage with folk dances, Czech pastries, sausage, polka music, arts and crafts, children's area, 5k run, parade. Est attendance: 35,000. For info: Westfest, Box 65, West, TX 76691. Phone: (254) 826-5058. Web: www.westfest.com.

WOODSTOCK FAIR. Sept 4–7. Woodstock, CT. Annually, Labor Day weekend. Est attendance: 250,000. For info: Woodstock Fair, PO Box 1, South Woodstock, CT 06267. Phone: (860) 928-3246. Web: www.woodstockfair.com.

WRIGHT, RICHARD: BIRTH ANNIVERSARY. Sept 4, 1908. Novelist and short story writer whose works included *Native Son, Uncle Tom's Children* and *Black Boy*, born at Natchez, MS. Wright died at Paris, France, Nov 28, 1960.

Birthdays Today

Mitzi Gaynor, 78, singer, dancer, actress (*South Pacific*), born Franchesca Mitzi Marlene de Charney von Gerber at Chicago, IL, Sept 4, 1931.

Paul Harvey, 91, broadcaster, commentator ("The Rest of the Story"), born Tulsa, OK, Sept 4, 1918.

Judith Ivey, 58, actress (*Compromising Positions, Brighton Beach Memoirs*; stage: *Steaming*), born El Paso, TX, Sept 4, 1951.

Beyoncé Knowles, 28, singer, actress (*Dreamgirls, Austin Powers in Goldmember*), born Houston, TX, Sept 4, 1981.

Michael Joseph (Mike) Piazza, 41, former baseball player, born Norristown, PA, Sept 4, 1968.

Jennifer Salt, 65, actress ("Soap"), born Los Angeles, CA, Sept 4, 1944.

Ione Skye, 39, actress (*Say Anything . . .; Gas, Food, Lodging*), born Hertfordshire, England, Sept 4, 1970.

Thomas Sturges (Tom) Watson, 60, golfer, born Kansas City, MO, Sept 4, 1949.

Damon Wayans, 49, actor, comedian ("In Living Color"), born New York, NY, Sept 4, 1960.

September 5 — Saturday

DAY 248 **117 REMAINING**

ALBANY RIVERFRONT JAZZ FESTIVAL. Sept 5. Riverfront Amphitheater, Albany, NY. A daylong celebration of traditional and smooth jazz music. Great food and beverages, as well as children's activities, make for a great free festival. Est attendance: 15,000. For info: Albany Special Events, City Hall, 4th Fl, Eagle St, Albany, NY 12207. Phone: (518) 434-2032. Fax: (518) 426-0759. E-mail: info@albanyevents.org. Web: www.albanyevents.org.

BABE RUTH'S FIRST PRO HOMER: 95th ANNIVERSARY. Sept 5, 1914. Babe Ruth hit his first home run as a professional while playing for Providence in the International League, a type of minor league affiliate of the Boston Red Sox. He pitched a one-hit shutout against Toronto.

BE LATE FOR SOMETHING DAY. Sept 5. To create a release from the stresses and strains resulting from a consistent need to be on time. For info: Les Waas, Pres, Procrastinators' Club of America, Inc, Box 712, Bryn Athyn, PA 19009. Phone: (215) 947-9020. Fax: (215) 947-7210. E-mail: procrastinators_club_of_america@yahoo.com. Web: www.geocities.com/procrastinators_club_of_america.

September 2009

S	M	T	W	T	F	S
		1	2	3	4	5
6	7	8	9	10	11	12
13	14	15	16	17	18	19
20	21	22	23	24	25	26
27	28	29	30			

BUMBERSHOOT: SEATTLE'S MUSIC & ARTS FESTIVAL. Sept 5–7. Seattle Center, Seattle, WA. Celebrates the arts in every genre; includes kids' activities. Annually, Labor Day weekend. Est attendance: 150,000. For info: One Reel, PO Box 9750, Seattle, WA 98109. Phone: (206) 281-7788. E-mail: info@onereel.org. Web: www.bumbershoot.org.

CAGE, JOHN: BIRTH ANNIVERSARY. Sept 5, 1912. Avant-garde American composer John Cage was born at Los Angeles, CA. He pioneered the experimental music and performance art schools. He used nontraditional instruments such as flower pots and cowbells in innovative situations, such as performances governed by chance, in which the *I Ching* was consulted to determine the direction of the performance. In 1978 he was elected to the American Academy of Arts and Sciences, and in 1982 was awarded France's highest honor for cultural contributions, *Commandeur de l'Ordre des Arts et des Lettres*. He died Aug 12, 1992, at New York, NY.

CARNOVSKY, MORRIS: BIRTH ANNIVERSARY. Sept 5, 1897. American actor Morris Carnovsky was born at St. Louis, MO. In 1931 with actor Lee Strasberg and others he founded the Group Theater at New York, NY. He was blacklisted in the 1950s by the House Un-American Activities Committee, but was still asked by John Houseman to perform in the American Shakespeare Festival in 1956 and began a successful Shakespearean career. He was elected to the Theater Hall of Fame in 1979. Carnovsky died Sept 1, 1992, at Easton, CT.

CLASSIC BOAT SHOW. Sept 5–6. Tuckerton, NJ. Join the Tuckerton Seaport and the Philadelphia Chapter of the Antique and Classic Boat Society for two splendid days of classic wood and glass boat exhibitors, demonstrations, and entertainment. Watch the parent/child boat building contest or take a cruise up Tuckerton Creek. The Classic Boat Show is fun for the whole family. Est attendance: 2,500. For info: Renee Kennedy, Tuckerton Seaport, 120 W Main St, PO Box 52, Tuckerton, NJ 08087. Phone: (609) 296-8868. Fax: (609) 296-5810. E-mail: info@tuckertonseaport.org. Web: www.tuckertonseaport.org.

CLEVELAND NATIONAL AIR SHOW. Sept 5–7. Burke Lakefront Airport, Cleveland, OH. Country's oldest air show, featuring extensive military and foreign aircraft participation. Est attendance: 80,000. For info: Cleveland Natl Air Show, Burke Lakefront Airport, Cleveland, OH 44114. Phone: (216) 781-0747. Fax: (216) 781-7810. E-mail: info@clevelandairshow.com. Web: www.clevelandairshow.com.

CLOTHESLINE FAIR. Sept 5–7. Prairie Grove Battlefield State Park, Prairie Grove, AR. 58th annual fair with more than 200 arts and crafts exhibitors; parade; folk, bluegrass, gospel and country music; square-dancing exhibitions and competitions; living history programs and tours. Annually, Labor Day weekend. Est attendance: 50,000. For info: Art Center of the Ozarks, PO Box 725, Springdale, AR 72765. Phone: (479) 751-5441. E-mail: acozarks@swbell.net. Web: www.artscenteroftheozarks.org.

COMMONWHEEL LABOR DAY WEEKEND ARTS AND CRAFTS FESTIVAL. Sept 5–7. Memorial Park, Manitou Springs, CO. 35th annual juried arts and crafts festival, featuring 120 fine artists and craftsmen and a variety of foods with continuous live entertainment ranging from Celtic harp music to jazz, including original acoustic songwriters. Est attendance: 30,000. For info: Commonwheel Artists Fair, PO Box 42, Manitou Springs, CO 80829. Phone: (719) 577-7700. E-mail: festival@commonwheel.com.

EASTERN IDAHO STATE FAIR. Sept 5–12. Blackfoot, ID. Family fun, amusement rides, food booths, entertainment, tractor pulls and more. Est attendance: 212,000. For info: Manager, Eastern

Idaho State Fair, PO Box 250, Blackfoot, ID 83221. Phone: (208) 785-2480. Fax: (208) 785-2483. E-mail: theFair@idaho-state-fair.com. Web: www.idaho-state-fair.com.

EVERLY BROTHERS/CENTRAL CITY ROCK 'N' ROLL CRUISE-IN & CONCERT. Sept 5. Central City, KY. Cruise the "famous Central City Strip" in your street rod or muscle car and enjoy the concert! Lots of concessions, booths and fun. Est attendance: 3,000. For info: Central City Music Festival, 208 N First St, Central City, KY 42330. Phone: (270) 754-9603. Fax: (270) 754-9067. E-mail: cctourism@muhlon.com. Web: www.centralcitykytourism.com.

FIRST CONTINENTAL CONGRESS ASSEMBLY: ANNIVERSARY. Sept 5, 1774. The first assembly of this forerunner of the US Congress took place at Philadelphia, PA. Peyton Randolph, delegate from Virginia, was elected president.

FIRST LABOR DAY OBSERVANCE: ANNIVERSARY. Sept 5, 1882. On this day in New York City, the first observance of Labor Day was held. It was organized by the Central Labor Union. Historians debate whether the inspiration came from Peter McGuire, general secretary of the Brotherhood of Carpenters and Joiners, or Matthew Maguire, secretary of the Central Labor Union. By 1884, other cities were honoring working people. In 1894, it became a federal holiday.

GERALD FORD: ASSASSINATION ATTEMPT: ANNIVERSARY. Sept 5, 1975. Lynette A. "Squeaky" Fromme, a follower of convicted murderer Charles Manson, attempted to shoot President Gerald Ford. On Sept 22 of the same year, another attempt on Ford's life occurred when Sara Jane Moore shot at him.

HANG AROUND VICTOR DAY. Sept 5. Victor, NY. 33rd annual festival with artists, craftsmen, antique dealers, civic and social organizations, family entertainment, pet parade and pet contest, cloggers, magicians, clowns and food vendors. Est attendance: 25,000. For info: Victor Chamber of Commerce, 37 E Main St, Victor, NY 14564. Phone: (585) 742-1476. Fax: (585) 742-1501.

IROQUOIS ARTS FESTIVAL. Sept 5–7. Iroquois Indian Museum, Howes Cave, NY. 28th annual celebration of Iroquois arts. Demonstrations of Iroquois arts and crafts, including beadwork, cornhusk dolls, pottery and more. Many items for sale by the artists. Children's activities. Iroquois social dancing and nature walks. Annually, Labor Day weekend. Est attendance: 2,000. For info: Iroquois Indian Museum, PO Box 7, Howes Cave, NY 12092. Phone: (518) 296-8949. Fax: (518) 296-8955. E-mail: info@iroquoismuseum.org. Web: www.iroquoismuseum.org.

ISRAELI OLYMPIAD MASSACRE: ANNIVERSARY. Sept 5–6, 1972. Eleven members of the Israeli Olympic Team were killed in an attack on the Olympic Village at Munich and attempted kidnapping of team members. Four of seven guerrillas, members of the Black September faction of the Palestinian Liberation Army, were also killed. In retaliation, Israeli jets bombed Palestinian positions at Lebanon and Syria on Sept 8, 1972.

JAMES, JESSE: BIRTH ANNIVERSARY. Sept 5, 1847. Western legend and bandit Jesse Woodson James was born at Centerville (now Kearney), MO. His criminal exploits were glorified and romanticized by writers for Eastern readers looking for stories of Western adventure and heroism. After the Civil War, James and his brother, Frank, formed a group of eight outlaws who robbed banks, stagecoaches and stores. In 1873 the James gang began holding up trains. The original James gang was put out of business Sept 7, 1876, while attempting to rob a bank at Northfield, MN. Every member of the gang except for the James brothers was killed or captured. The brothers formed a new gang and resumed their criminal careers in 1879. Two years later, the governor of Missouri offered a $10,000 reward for their capture, dead or alive. On Apr 3, 1882, at St. Joseph, MO, Robert Ford, a member of the gang, shot 34-year-old Jesse in the back of the head and claimed the reward.

JAPANESE FESTIVAL. Sept 5–7. Missouri Botanical Garden, St. Louis, MO. Japanese cultural activities including taiko (drumming), bon odori festival dancing, bonsai demonstrations, martial arts, tea ceremonies, cooking demonstrations, craft demos, ikebana, karaoke, kimono fashion show and much more. For info: Missouri Botanical Garden, 4344 Shaw Blvd, St. Louis, MO 63110. Phone: (314) 577-9400 or (800) 642-8842. Web: www.mobot.org.

JUBILEE DAYS FESTIVAL. Sept 5–7. Zion, IL. 61st annual. Communitywide festival features arts and crafts, Queen's Pageant, Illinois's largest Labor Day parade and fireworks. Annually, Labor Day weekend. Est attendance: 10,000. For info: Richard Walker, Exec Dir, Jubilee Days Fest, Inc, PO Box 23, Zion, IL 60099. Phone: (847) 746-5500.

KOESTLER, ARTHUR: BIRTH ANNIVERSARY. Sept 5, 1905. Born at Budapest, Hungary, Koestler is best known for his novel about his disillusionment with Communism, *Darkness at Noon*, and for *The God That Failed*. Died at London, England, Mar 3, 1983.

"THE MacNEIL-LEHRER NEWSHOUR" TV PREMIERE: ANNIVERSARY. Sept 5, 1983. Originally, this PBS news show was called "The MacNeil-Lehrer Report" and was on every weeknight for a half hour starting in 1976. Robert MacNeil and Jim Lehrer were joined by Charlayne Hunter-Gault and Judy Woodruff. In 1983 the show was expanded to an hour and became TV's first regularly scheduled daily hour news show. The show has been praised for its depth and objectivity. In 1995 Robert MacNeil retired and the show was retitled "The Newshour with Jim Lehrer."

MICHIGAN'S GREAT FIRE OF 1881: ANNIVERSARY. Sept 5, 1881. According to the Michigan Historical Commission, "Small fires were burning in the forests of the 'Thumb area of Michigan,' tinder-dry after a long, hot summer, when a gale swept in from the southwest on Sept 5, 1881. Fanned into an inferno, the fire raged for three days. A million acres were devastated in Sanilac and Huron counties alone. At least 125 persons died, and thousands more were left destitute. The new American Red Cross won support for its prompt aid to the fire victims. This was the first disaster relief furnished by this great organization."

NIELSEN, ARTHUR CHARLES: BIRTH ANNIVERSARY. Sept 5, 1897. Marketing research engineer, founder of AC Nielsen Company, in 1923, known for radio and TV audience surveys, was born at Chicago, IL, and died there June 1, 1980.

SCOTLAND: BRAEMAR ROYAL HIGHLAND GATHERING. Sept 5. Princess Royal and Duke of Fife Memorial Park, Braemar, Grampian. Kilted clansmen from all over the world gather. Traditional activities including tossing cabers, dancing and playing bagpipes. Est attendance: 18,000. For info: Mr W.A. Meston, Secretary, Coilacriech, Ballater, Aberdeenshire, Scotland AB35 5UH. Phone: (44) (133) 975-5377. E-mail: info@braemargathering.org.

SIDEWALK ARTS FESTIVAL. Sept 5. Sioux Falls, SD. Live entertainment, music, great food, cultural activities and more than 250 booths featuring the area's best art and folk displays. Est attendance: 60,000. For info: Visual Arts Center at the Washington Pavilion, 301 S Main Ave, Sioux Falls, SD 57104. Phone: (605) 367-7397. Fax: (605) 367-7399. E-mail: info@washingtonpavilion.org. Web: www.washingtonpavilion.org.

SPACE MILESTONE: *VOYAGER 1* (US). Sept 5, 1977. Twin of *Voyager 2*, which was launched Aug 20. On Feb 18, 1998, *Voyager 1* set a new distance record when after more than 20 years in space it reached 6.5 billion miles from Earth.

STA-BIL NATIONALS CHAMPIONSHIP LAWN MOWER RACE. Sept 5–6. Delaware, OH. Five classes of races for winners of regional races held across the US. Mowers will travel at speeds ranging from 10 mph to more than 50 mph. Est attendance: 2,000. For info: US Lawn Mower Racing Assn, 1812 Glenview Rd, Glenview, IL 60025. Phone: (847) 729-7363. E-mail: letsmow@aol.com. Web: www.letsmow.com.

SWITZERLAND: SAINT GOTTHARD AUTOMOBILE TUNNEL OPENING: ANNIVERSARY. Sept 5, 1980. The longest underground motorway in the world, the St. Gotthard Auto Tunnel in Switzerland, was opened to traffic. More than 10 miles long, requiring $417,000,000 and 10 years for construction, it became the most direct route from Switzerland to the southern regions of the continent. The St. Gotthard Pass, the main passage since the Middle Ages, was closed much of every year by massive snow drifts.

TASTE OF MADISON. Sept 5–6 (tentative). Capitol Square, Madison, WI. Food and entertainment festival, including booths from more than 80 restaurants, four stages, waiters' race and Kiddie Korner. Est attendance: 250,000. For info: Keith Peterson, Events Manager, Madison Festivals, Inc, c/o ASG, 2981 Cahill Main, Ste 2, Madison, WI 53711. Phone: (608) 276-9797. Fax: (608) 276-9780. E-mail: event@madisonfestivals.com. Web: www.madisonfestivals.com.

TOOLS AND SKILLS THAT BUILT THE COLONY. Sept 5. Wormsloe Historic Site, Savannah, GA. Living history demonstrations relating to the tools and skills that were used to build the colony. These will include woodworking, blacksmithing, spinning, candlemaking and more. Museum, film and trails. 11 AM to 4 PM. Annually, the Saturday before Labor Day. Est attendance: 500. For info: Wormsloe State Historic Site, 7601 Skidaway Rd, Savannah, GA 31406. Phone: (912) 353-3023. E-mail: wormsloe@bellsouth.net. Web: www.wormsloe.org.

TOTAH FESTIVAL. Sept 5–6. Farmington, NM. Native American arts and crafts show and marketplace—highlighted by an Indian rug auction. Annually, the Saturday and Sunday of Labor Day weekend. Est attendance: 13,000. For info: Farmington CVB, 3041 E Main St, Farmington, NM 87402. Phone: (800) 448-1240 or (505) 326-7602. Fax: (505) 327-0577. E-mail: fmncvb@earthlink.net. Web: www.farmingtonnm.org.

WORLD CHAMPIONSHIP BARBECUE GOAT COOK-OFF AND ARTS AND CRAFTS FAIR. Sept 5. Richards Park, Brady, TX. 36th annual cook-off to promote Brady/McCulloch County and the sheep and goat industry. Arts and crafts fair featuring local and statewide artists. Annually, the Saturday of Labor Day weekend. Est attendance: 30,000. For info: Brady/McCulloch County Chamber of Commerce, 101 E First St, Brady, TX 76825. Phone: (325) 597-3491. Fax: (325) 792-9181. E-mail: chamber@bradytx.us. Web: www.bradytx.com.

ZANUCK, DARRYL F.: BIRTH ANNIVERSARY. Sept 5, 1902. Born at Wahoo, NE, Darryl F. Zanuck became a celebrated—and controversial—movie producer. He was also a cofounder of Twentieth Century Studios, which later merged with Fox. His film credits include *The Jazz Singer* (the first sound picture), *Forever Amber, The Snake Pit* and *The Grapes of Wrath*. He died Dec 21, 1979, at Palm Springs, CA.

Birthdays Today

Kristian Alfonso, 45, actress ("Days of Our Lives," "Melrose Place"), born Brockton, MA, Sept 5, 1964.

William Devane, 70, actor ("24," "Knots Landing"), born Albany, NY, Sept 5, 1939.

Dennis Dugan, 63, actor, director (*Big Daddy, Problem Child*), born Wheaton, IL, Sept 5, 1946.

Cathy Lee Guisewite, 59, cartoonist ("Cathy"), born Dayton, OH, Sept 5, 1950.

Carol Lawrence, 74, singer, actress (*West Side Story*), born Carol Maria Laraia at Melrose Park, IL, Sept 5, 1935.

Rose McGowan, 36, actress (*Jawbreaker*, "Charmed"), born Florence, Italy, Sept 5, 1973.

Bob Newhart, 80, comedian ("The Bob Newhart Show," "Newhart"), born Chicago, IL, Sept 5, 1929.

Brian Schweitzer, 54, Governor of Montana (D), born Havre, MT, Sept 5, 1955.

Raquel Welch, 67, actress (*The Three Musketeers, Woman of the Year*), model, born Chicago, IL, Sept 5, 1942.

Dweezil Zappa, 40, singer, actor ("Normal Life"), born Hollywood, CA, Sept 5, 1969.

September 2009

S	M	T	W	T	F	S
		1	2	3	4	5
6	7	8	9	10	11	12
13	14	15	16	17	18	19
20	21	22	23	24	25	26
27	28	29	30			

September 6 — Sunday

DAY 249 **116 REMAINING**

ADDAMS, JANE: BIRTH ANNIVERSARY. Sept 6, 1860. American worker for peace, social welfare, rights of women, founder of Hull House (Chicago), cowinner of Nobel Prize, 1931. Born at Cedarville, IL, she died May 21, 1935, at Chicago, IL.

BALTIC STATES' INDEPENDENCE RECOGNIZED: ANNIVERSARY. Sept 6, 1991. The Soviet government recognized the independence of the Baltic states—Latvia, Estonia and Lithuania. The action came 51 years after the Baltic states were annexed by the Soviet Union. All three Baltic states had earlier declared their independence, and many nations had already recognized them diplomatically, including the US, Sept 2, 1991.

BEECHER, CATHARINE ESTHER: BIRTH ANNIVERSARY. Sept 6, 1800. Catharine Esther Beecher was born at East Hampton, NY. In addition to teaching herself mathematics, philosophy and Latin, Beecher had been formally educated in art and music. An early advocate for equal education for women, she founded the Hartford Female Seminary, which was widely recognized for its advanced curriculum. She was also instrumental in the founding of women's colleges in Iowa, Illinois and Wisconsin. Beecher died May 12, 1878, at Elmira, NY.

BELGIUM: HISTORICAL PROCESSION. Sept 6. Tournai. Traditional cultural observance. Annually, the Sunday closest to Sept 8.

BULGARIA: UNIFICATION DAY. Sept 6. National holiday. Commemorates the anniversary of the reunification of the southern part of Bulgaria with the rest of the country in 1885.

DALTON, JOHN: BIRTH ANNIVERSARY. Sept 6, 1766. English chemist, physicist, teacher and developer of atomic theory, was born at Eaglesfield, near Cockermouth, England. Dalton died at Manchester, England, July 27, 1844.

FIRST RADIO BROADCAST OF A PRIZEFIGHT: ANNIVERSARY. Sept 6, 1920. In the first boxing match broadcast on radio, Jack Dempsey knocked out Billy Miske in the third round of a scheduled 10-round fight.

HARVEST WINE CELEBRATION. Sept 6–7. Livermore, CA. The Harvest Wine Celebration is an open-house event offering the public an opportunity to visit more than 43 wineries, sample wines, learn more about this historic wine region, enjoy entertainment and shop for arts and crafts. Shuttle bus service is available between the wineries. Annually, Labor Day weekend. Est attendance: 13,000. For info: Livermore Valley Winegrowers Assn, 3585 Greenville Rd, Ste 4, Livermore, CA 94550. Phone: (925) 447-9463. Fax: (925) 447-0433. E-mail: lvwa@livermorewine.com. Web: www.livermorewine.com.

ITALY: HISTORICAL REGATTA. Sept 6. Venice. Traditional competition among two-oar racing gondolas, preceded by a procession of Venetian ceremonial boats of the epoch of the Venetian Republic. Annually, the first Sunday in September.

ITALY: JOUST OF THE SARACEN. Sept 6. Arezzo. The first Sunday in September is set aside for the Giostra del Saracino, a tilting contest of the 13th century, with knights in armor.

JERRY LEWIS MUSCULAR DYSTROPHY ASSOCIATION TELETHON. Sept 6–7. The annual Labor Day TV broadcast to raise money for 40 neuromuscular diseases. For info: Muscular Dystrophy Assn, 3300 E Sunrise Dr, Tucson, AZ 85718. Phone: (800) 572-1717. Web: www.mda.org.

LAFAYETTE, MARQUIS DE: BIRTH ANNIVERSARY. Sept 6, 1757. The French general and aristocrat, whose full name was Marie-Joseph-Paul-Yves-Roch-Gilbert du Motier, came to America to assist in the revolutionary cause. Lafayette, who had convinced Louis XVI to send 6,000 French soldiers to assist the Americans, was given command of an army at Virginia and was instrumental in forcing the surrender of Lord Cornwallis at Yorktown. He was called "The Hero of Two Worlds" and was appointed a brigadier general on his return to France in 1782. He became a leader of the liberal aristocrats during the early days of the French revolution. As the commander of the newly formed national guard of Paris, he rescued Louis XVI and Marie-Antoinette from a crowd that stormed Versailles Oct 6, 1789. His popularity waned after his guards opened fire on angry demonstrators demanding abdication of the king in 1791. He fled to Austria with the overthrow of the monarchy in 1792, returning when Napoleon Bonaparte came to power. Born at Chavaniac, he died at Paris, May 20, 1834.

NATIONAL WAFFLE WEEK. Sept 6–12. A celebration of the wonderful, crispy breakfast orb and its contributions to American society. Annually, the first week of September. For info: Waffle House, PO Box 6450, Norcross, GA 30091. Phone: (770) 729-5884. Fax: (770) 729-5999. Web: www.wafflehouse.com.

PAKISTAN: DEFENSE OF PAKISTAN DAY. Sept 6. National holiday. Commemorates the Indo-Pakistan War of 1965.

ROSE, BILLY: BIRTH ANNIVERSARY. Sept 6, 1899. The American theatrical producer, author, songwriter and husband of Fanny Brice was born William S. Rosenberg at New York, NY. His songs include: "That Old Gang of Mine," "Me and My Shadow," "Without a Song," "It's Only a Paper Moon" and hundreds of others. Rose died at Montego Bay, Jamaica, Feb 10, 1966.

SAINT PETERSBURG NAME RESTORED: ANNIVERSARY. Sept 6, 1991. Russian legislators voted to restore the name Saint Petersburg to the nation's second largest city. The city had been known as Leningrad for 67 years in honor of the Soviet Union's founder, Vladimir I. Lenin. The city, founded in 1703 by Peter the Great, had three names in the 20th century with Russian leaders changing its German-sounding name to Petrograd at the beginning of WWI in 1914 and Soviet Communist leaders changing its name to Leningrad in 1924 following their leader's death.

SCANDINAVIAN FEST. Sept 6. Vasa Park, Budd Lake, NJ. Celebrate and sample the cultures, traditions and contemporary life of the Nordic countries: Denmark, Estonia, Finland, Iceland, Norway and Sweden through food, entertainment, music, dancing, handicrafts and lectures. Annually, the Sunday before Labor Day. Est attendance: 6,000. For info: Carl Anderson, PO Box 5103, Bethlehem, PA 18015. Phone: (610) 417-1483. E-mail: info@ScanFest.org. Web: www.ScanFest.org.

SWAZILAND: INDEPENDENCE DAY. Sept 6. National holiday. Commemorates attainment of independence from Britain in 1968. Also called Somhlolo Day in honor of the great 19th-century Swazi leader.

UNITED NATIONS: MILLENNIUM SUMMIT: ANNIVERSARY. Sept 6–8, 2000. More than 150 world leaders met at the United Nations in New York City, the largest gathering of such leaders in history. Among the kings, prime ministers, presidents and generals attending were US President Bill Clinton, Fidel Castro and Yasser Arafat. These leaders adopted a declaration that committed them to promote democracy, strengthen respect for human rights, reverse the spread of AIDS, cut poverty, protect the planet and improve the ability of the UN to keep the peace.

"WYATT EARP" TV PREMIERE: ANNIVERSARY. Sept 6, 1955. Officially titled "The Life and Legend of Wyatt Earp," this half-hour series marked the beginning of the trend toward "adult Westerns." It was loosely based on fact, with Hugh O'Brian as Earp, marshall of Dodge City, KS, and later of Tombstone, AZ.

Birthdays Today

Jane Curtin, 62, actress ("Saturday Night Live," "3rd Rock from the Sun"), comedienne, born Cambridge, MA, Sept 6, 1947.

Jeff Foxworthy, 51, comedian, actor ("The Jeff Foxworthy Show"), author (*No Shirt, No Shoes . . . No Problem*), born Atlanta, GA, Sept 6, 1958.

Tim Henman, 35, tennis player, born Oxford, England, Sept 6, 1974.

Swoosie Kurtz, 65, actress ("Sisters," *The World According to Garp*; Tony for *The House of Blue Leaves*), born Omaha, NE, Sept 6, 1944.

Rosie Perez, 45, actress (*King of the Jungle, White Men Can't Jump*), born Brooklyn, NY, Sept 6, 1964.

Bill Ritter, 53, Governor of Colorado (D), born Denver, CO, Sept 6, 1956.

Sarah Strange, 35, actress ("Men in Trees," "Da Vinci's Inquest"), born Vancouver, BC, Canada, Sept 6, 1974.

Elizabeth Vargas, 47, television journalist, born Paterson, NJ, Sept 6, 1962.

Justin Whalin, 35, actor ("Charles in Charge," "Lois & Clark"), born San Francisco, CA, Sept 6, 1974.

Jo Anne Worley, 72, comedienne, actress ("Rowan & Martin's Laugh-In"), born Lowell, IA, Sept 6, 1937.

September 7 — Monday

DAY 250 **115 REMAINING**

AUTUMN'S COLORS AT LONGWOOD GARDENS. Sept 7–Nov 22. Kennett Square, PA. Longwood celebrates September beauty and bounty with harvest displays, flower shows, thousands of chrysanthemums, gardening demonstrations, family entertainment, a miniature garden railway and giant pumpkins. Est attendance: 50,000. For info: Longwood Gardens, PO Box 501, Kennett Square, PA 19348-0501. Phone: (610) 388-1000. Web: www.longwoodgar dens.org.

BRAZIL: INDEPENDENCE DAY. Sept 7. Declared independence from Portugal in 1822. National holiday.

CANADA: LABOR DAY. Sept 7. Annually, the first Monday in September.

COLUMBIA RIVER CROSS CHANNEL SWIM. Sept 7. Hood River, OR. 67th annual. The annual swim across the mighty Columbia River draws 550 contestants each year to swim the approximately one-mile distance for fun. Annually, on Labor Day. Est attendance: 1,000. For info: Columbia River Cross Channel Swim, Hood River County Chamber of Commerce, 720 E Port Marina Dr, Hood River, OR 97031. Phone: (800) 366-3530. E-mail: hrccc@hoodriver.org. Web: www.hoodriver.org.

CORBETT-SULLIVAN PRIZE FIGHT: ANNIVERSARY. Sept 7, 1892. John L. Sullivan was knocked out by James J. Corbett in the 21st round of a prize fight at New Orleans, LA. It was the first major fight under the Marquess of Queensberry Rules.

"THE FLYING NUN" TV PREMIERE: ANNIVERSARY. Sept 7, 1967. This sitcom about a nun at a convent in Puerto Rico who discovers that she can fly starred Sally Field as Elsie Ethrington (Sister Bertrille) and featured Madeleine Sherwood, Marge Redmond, Shelley Morrison, Alejandro Rey and Vito Scotti.

GOOGLE FOUNDED: ANNIVERSARY. Sept 7, 1998. Sergey Brin and Larry Page incorporated the Internet search engine company Google on this date at Menlo Park, CA. Although still in beta, Google.com was receiving 10,000 queries a day at that time. Within a year, the company was doing 3 million searches a day. Before long, Google entered the pop culture zeitgeist by becoming a verb for Internet searching.

GRANDMA MOSES DAY. Sept 7. Anna Mary (Robertson) Moses, modern primitive American painter born at Greenwich, NY, Sept 7, 1860. Started painting at the age of 78. Her 100th birthday was proclaimed Grandma Moses Day in New York state. Died at Hoosick Falls, NY, Dec 13, 1961.

GREAT BATHTUB RACE. Sept 7. Nome, AK. 32nd annual. Bathtubs mounted on wheels are raced down Front Street. Each team has five members, one in the tub, with bubbles apparent in the bath water. Tub must be full of water at beginning and have at least 10 gallons at the finish line. The other four team members must wear large-brim hats and suspenders and carry either a bar of soap, washcloth, towel or bath mat for the entire race. Winning team claims trophy: a statue of Miss Piggy and Kermit taking a bath, which is handed down from year to year. Annually, at noon on Labor Day. Est attendance: 1,500. For info: Rasmussen's Music Mart, PO Box 2, Nome, AK 99762-0002. Phone: (907) 443-2798 or (907) 443-2919. Fax: (907) 443-5777.

HOLLY, BUDDY: BIRTH ANNIVERSARY. Sept 7, 1936. American popular music performer, composer and bandleader. Called one of the most innovative and influential musicians of his time, he was a pioneer of rock 'n' roll. His hits included "That'll Be the Day" and "Peggy Sue." Born Charles Harden Holley, at Lubbock, TX, he died at age 22 in an airplane crash near Mason City, IA, Feb 3, 1959.

KAZAN, ELIA: 100th BIRTH ANNIVERSARY. Sept 7, 1909. Born Elia Kazanjoglou at Constantinople, Turkey, Elia Kazan was one of the most influential directors in history of American stage and film. He directed the Broadway premieres of Arthur Miller's *Death of a Salesman* and Tennessee Williams's *A Streetcar Named Desire* as well as many other Williams plays. He won directing Oscars for the films *On the Waterfront* and *Gentleman's Agreement.* He discovered and promoted actors such as Marlon Brando, Warren Beatty and James Dean, whom he directed in *East of Eden*. In 1952 he angered much of Hollywood by testifying before the House Un-American Activities Committee, naming persons he thought to be members of the Communist Party. Kazan died at New York, NY, Sept 7, 2003.

September 2009

S	M	T	W	T	F	S
		1	2	3	4	5
6	7	8	9	10	11	12
13	14	15	16	17	18	19
20	21	22	23	24	25	26
27	28	29	30			

LABOR DAY. Sept 7. Legal public holiday. Public Law 90–363 sets Labor Day on the first Monday in September. Observed in all states. First observance was a parade on Tuesday, Sept 5, 1882, at New York, NY, probably organized by Peter J. McGuire, a Carpenters and Joiners Union secretary. In 1883 a union resolution declared "the first Monday in September of each year a Labor Day." By 1893 more than half of the states were observing Labor Day on one or another day and a bill to establish Labor Day as a federal holiday was introduced in Congress. On June 28, 1894, President Grover Cleveland signed into law an act making the first Monday in September a legal holiday for federal employees and the District of Columbia. Canada also celebrates Labor Day on the first Monday in September. In most other countries, Labor Day is observed May 1. See also "First Labor Day Observance: Anniversary" (Sept 5).

LAWRENCE, JACOB: BIRTH ANNIVERSARY. Sept 7, 1917. African American painter, born at Atlantic City, NJ. Lawrence was best known for his series of historical paintings on John Brown and on the migration of African Americans out of the South. A recipient of the NAACP's Spingarn Medal, he won many other awards during his lifetime. Lawrence died June 9, 2000, at Seattle, WA.

MACKINAC BRIDGE WALK. Sept 7. St. Ignace, MI. 52nd annual event. This is the only day of the year pedestrians are permitted to walk across the five-mile-long span, one of the world's longest suspension bridges, connecting Michigan's two peninsulas. Walk is from St. Ignace to Mackinaw City. Est attendance: 50,000. For info: Mackinac Bridge Authority, N-415 Interstate 75, St. Ignace, MI 49781. Phone: (906) 643-7600. Fax: (906) 643-7668. Web: www.mackinacbridge.org.

NATIONAL PAYROLL WEEK. Sept 7–11. Founded in 1996 by the American Payroll Association to recognize the important partnership of America's workers and the payroll professionals who pay them on time and accurately. Provides an annual opportunity to proudly proclaim "America Works Because We're Working for America!" For info: Mark Coindreau, American Payroll Assn, 660 N Main Ave, Ste 100, San Antonio, TX 78205. Phone: (210) 226-4600. Fax: (210) 224-2028. E-mail: mcoindreau@americanpayroll.org. Web: www.nationalpayrollweek.com.

NATIONAL STEARMAN FLY-IN DAYS. Sept 7–13. Galesburg, IL. The largest gathering of Stearman airplanes—the biplane trainers that gave wings to more military pilots than any other series of aircraft in the world. Est attendance: 7,500. For info: Galesburg Area CVB, PO Box 60, Galesburg, IL 61402-0060. Phone: (309) 343-2485. Fax: (309) 343-2521. E-mail: visitors@visitgalesburg.com. Web: www.visitgalesburg.com.

NATIONAL SUICIDE PREVENTION WEEK. Sept 7–12. Annually, the week that includes National Suicide Prevention Day on Sept 10. For info: American Assn of Suicidology, 5221 Wisconsin Ave NW, Second Fl, Washington, DC 20015. Phone: (202) 237-2280. Fax: (202) 237-2282. E-mail: info@suicidology.org. Web: www.suicidology.org.

"NEITHER SNOW NOR RAIN" DAY: 95th ANNIVERSARY. Sept 7, 1914. Anniversary of the opening to the public on Labor Day 1914 of the New York Post Office Building at Eighth Avenue between 31st and 33rd streets. On the front of this building was an inscription supplied by William M. Kendall of the architectural firm that planned the building. The inscription, a free translation from Herodotus, reads: "Neither snow nor rain nor heat nor gloom of night stays these couriers from the swift completion of their appointed rounds." This has long been believed to be the motto of the US Post Office and Postal Service. They have, in fact, no motto—but the legend remains.

QUEEN ELIZABETH I: BIRTH ANNIVERSARY. Sept 7, 1533. Queen of England, daughter of Henry VIII and Anne Boleyn, after whom the Elizabethan era was named, was born at Greenwich Palace. She ascended the throne in 1558 at the age of 25. During her reign, the British defeated the Spanish Armada in July 1588, the Anglican Church was essentially established and England became a world power. She died at Richmond, England, Mar 24, 1603.

SNAKE RIVER DUCK RACE. Sept 7. Nome, AK. Since 1992 thousands of plastic ducks have negotiated the historic Snake River to Nome's power plant. 2 PM. For info: Leo B. Rasmussen, Nome

Rotary Club, PO Box 2, Nome, AK 99762. Phone: (907) 443-2798 or (907) 443-6022. E-mail: leaknome@alaska.com.

STOCK EXCHANGE HOLIDAY (LABOR DAY). Sept 7. The holiday schedules for the various exchanges are subject to change if relevant rules, regulations or exchange policies are revised. If you have questions, contact: American Stock Exchange (866) 422-2639 (www.amex.com), Chicago Board of Trade (312) 435-3500 (www.cbot.com), Chicago Board Options Exchange (312) 786-5600 (www.cboe.com), NASDAQ Stock Market (646) 441-5200 (www.nasdaq.com), New York Stock Exchange (212) 656-3000 (www.nyse.com), Philadelphia Stock Exchange (800) THE-PHLX (www.phlx.com).

"TRUTH OR CONSEQUENCES" TV PREMIERE: ANNIVERSARY. Sept 7, 1950. This game show lasted for many years on both radio and TV. The half-hour show was based on a parlor game: contestants who failed to answer a question before the buzzer (nicknamed Beulah) went off had to perform stunts (i.e., pay the consequences). Ralph Edwards created and hosted the show until 1954, then it became a prime-time show hosted by Jack Bailey. Bob Barker succeeded him in 1966 and hosted it through its syndicated run. In 1977 the show was revived as "The New Truth or Consequences" with Bob Hilton as host.

Birthdays Today

Corbin Bernsen, 55, actor ("LA Law," "Ryan's Hope," *Major League*), born North Hollywood, CA, Sept 7, 1954.

Susan Blakely, 59, actress (*The Way We Were, The Lords of Flatbush, Shampoo*), born Frankfurt, Germany, Sept 7, 1950.

Michael Feinstein, 53, singer, pianist, born Columbus, OH, Sept 7, 1956.

Arthur Ferrante, 88, pianist (Ferrante and Teicher), composer, born New York, NY, Sept 7, 1921.

Chrissie Hynde, 58, singer, songwriter (Pretenders), born Akron, OH, Sept 7, 1951.

Daniel Ken Inouye, 85, US Senator (D, Hawaii), born Honolulu, HI, Sept 7, 1924.

Julie Kavner, 58, actress (*Radio Days*, "Rhoda," Marge Simpson's voice on "The Simpsons"), born Los Angeles, CA, Sept 7, 1951.

Richard Roundtree, 67, actor (*Shaft, Q, Once upon a Time When We Were Colored*), born New Rochelle, NY, Sept 7, 1942 (some sources say 1939).

Devon Sawa, 31, actor (*Wild America, The Boy's Club*), born Vancouver, BC, Canada, Sept 7, 1978.

Briana Scurry, 38, soccer player, born Minneapolis, MN, Sept 7, 1971.

Evan Rachel Wood, 22, actress (*Thirteen, The Upside of Anger, Across the Universe,* "Once and Again"), born Raleigh, NC, Sept 7, 1987.

September 8 — Tuesday

DAY 251 — **114 REMAINING**

ANDORRA: NATIONAL HOLIDAY. Sept 8. Honors our Lady of Meritxell.

ANOTHER LOOK UNLIMITED DAY. Sept 8. Your house, garage, barn, shed, attic or yard. Encourages everyone to look over their possessions and give surplus to charity or reuse in other projects. Lessen the flow to landfills. Annually, the day after Labor Day. For info: ENVIRA MYNYTL, PO Box 220, Holts Summit, MO 65043. E-mail: envira-myntyl@cal-a-co.com.

CLINE, PATSY: BIRTH ANNIVERSARY. Sept 8, 1932. Country and western singer, born Virginia Patterson Hensley at Winchester, VA. Patsy Cline got her big break in 1957 when she won an Arthur Godfrey Talent Scout show, singing "Walking After Midnight." Her career took off and she became a featured singer at the Grand Ole Opry, attaining the rank of top female country singer. She died in a plane crash Mar 5, 1963, at Camden, TN, along with singers Hawkshaw Hawkins and Cowboy Copas.

CONCORDIA FALL FESTIVAL. Sept 8–12. Concordia, MO. Held annually in September the week following the Labor Day holiday to celebrate the agricultural and German roots of the area. Daily attractions include carnival games and rides, exhibits, parades, bands, food and a German-style beer garden. For info: Concordia Fall Festival, PO Box 586, Concordia, MO 64020. E-mail: info@concordiafallfestival.com. Web: www.concordiafallfestival.com.

GALVESTON HURRICANE: ANNIVERSARY. Sept 8, 1900. The worst national disaster in US history in terms of lives lost. More than 6,000 people were killed when a hurricane struck Galveston, TX, with winds of more than 120 mph, followed by a huge tidal wave. More than 2,500 buildings were destroyed.

MACEDONIA: INDEPENDENCE DAY. Sept 8. National holiday. Commemorates independence from the Yugoslav Union in 1991.

MALTA: SIEGE BROKEN: ANNIVERSARY. Sept 8. "Two Sieges and Regatta Day" festivities now commemorate victory over the Turks, Sept 8, 1565, when the siege that began in May 1565 was broken by the Maltese and the Knights of St. John after a loss of nearly 10,000 lives. Also commemorated is survival of the 1943 siege by the Axis Powers. Parades, fireworks, boat races, etc, especially at the capital, Valleta, and the Grand Harbour.

McGWIRE BREAKS HOME RUN RECORD: ANNIVERSARY. Sept 8, 1998. Mark McGwire of the St. Louis Cardinals hit his 62nd home run, breaking Roger Maris's 1961 record for the most home runs in a single season. McGwire hit his homer at Busch Stadium at St. Louis against pitcher Steve Trachsel of the Chicago Cubs as the Cardinals won, 6–3. McGwire finished the season with 70 home runs. On Oct 5, 2001, Barry Bonds hit his 71st home run, breaking McGwire's record. Bonds finished the season with 73 homers.

MISS AMERICA FIRST CROWNED: ANNIVERSARY. Sept 8, 1921. Margaret Gorman of Washington, DC, was crowned the first Miss America at the end of a two-day pageant at Atlantic City, NJ.

MISSION SAN GABRIEL ARCHANGEL: FOUNDING ANNIVERSARY. Sept 8, 1771. California mission to the Indians founded on this date.

NIXON PARDONED: 35th ANNIVERSARY. Sept 8, 1974. Anniversary of the "full, free, and absolute pardon unto Richard Nixon, for all offenses against the United States which he, Richard Nixon, has committed or may have committed or taken part in during the period from January 20, 1969, through August 9, 1974." (Presidential Proclamation 4311, Sept 8, 1974, by Gerald R. Ford.)

NORTHERN PACIFIC RAILROAD COMPLETED: ANNIVERSARY. Sept 8, 1883. After 19 years of construction, the Northern Pacific Railroad became the second railroad to link the two coasts. The Union Pacific and Central Pacific lines met at Utah in 1869.

"THE OPRAH WINFREY SHOW" TV PREMIERE: ANNIVERSARY. Sept 8, 1986. This daytime talk show was the top-rated talk show for years and also has the distinction of being the first talk show hosted by an African American woman, Oprah Winfrey. Her show is taped in front of a studio audience who are solicited for their questions and feedback. In the mid-1990s, fed up with the plethora of trashy talk shows that had sprung up everywhere, Winfrey decided to upgrade the quality of topics that her show presented. Her book club feature has been a popular element of her show, and chosen books usually become bestsellers.

PEPPER, CLAUDE DENSON: BIRTH ANNIVERSARY. Sept 8, 1900. US Representative and Senator, born near Dudleyville, AL. Pepper's career in politics spanned 53 years and 10 presidents, and he became the champion for America's senior citizens. He was elected to the US Senate in 1936, where he was a principal architect of many of the nation's "safety net" social programs including Social Security, the minimum wage and medical assistance for the elderly and for handicapped children. After a 14-year career in the Senate, he returned to Congress in the House of Representatives where he served 14 terms. He served as chairman of the House Select Committee on Aging, drafted legislation banning forced retirement and fought against cutting Social Security benefits. Pepper died at Washington, DC, May 30, 1989.

PLAY DAYS. Sept 8–12. 32nd annual. In a world filled with downsizing, rightsizing and shaftsizing, we need humor to reaffirm our humanity and sanity. In the week after Labor Day, the HUMOR Project will playfully spread the word on 1,001 ways to add humor to your life and work. Jest for success—humor works—the funny line and bottom line intersect! Annually, the Tuesday through Saturday after Labor Day. For info: The HUMOR Project, 480 Broadway, Ste 210-C, Saratoga Springs, NY 12866-2288. Phone: (518) 587-8770. E-mail: chase@HumorProject.com. Web: www.HumorProject.com.

SELLERS, PETER: BIRTH ANNIVERSARY. Sept 8, 1925. Award-winning British comedian and film star, born Richard Henry Sellers at Southsea, Hampshire, England. Sellers is remembered for his multiple roles in *Dr. Strangelove*, his Oscar-nominated role as Chance the Gardener in *Being There* and for his role as the bumbling Inspector Clouseau in the *Pink Panther* films. Died at London, England, July 24, 1980.

"STAR TREK" TV PREMIERE: ANNIVERSARY. Sept 8, 1966. The first of 79 episodes of the TV series "Star Trek" was aired on the NBC network. Although the science fiction show set in the future only lasted a few seasons, it has remained enormously popular through syndication reruns. It has been given new life through many motion pictures, a cartoon TV series and popular spin-off TV series such as "Star Trek: The Next Generation," "Enterprise" and others. It has consistently ranked among the biggest titles in the motion picture, television, home video and licensing divisions of Paramount Pictures.

"TARZAN" TV PREMIERE: ANNIVERSARY. Sept 8, 1966. This hour adventure series was based on Edgar Rice Burroughs's character, who appeared for the first time on TV. Tarzan, an English lord who preferred the jungle, was played by Ron Ely. Manuel Padilla, Jr, was Jai, a jungle orphan, Alan Caillou was Jason Flood, Jai's tutor, and Rockne Tarkington was Rao, a veterinarian. There was no Jane.

"THAT GIRL" TV PREMIERE: ANNIVERSARY. Sept 8, 1966. "That Girl" was a half-hour sitcom starring Marlo Thomas as Ann Marie, an independent aspiring actress in New York City. Ted Bessell also starred as her boyfriend Don Hollinger. They were finally engaged in 1970. Also featured were Lew Parker, Rosemary De Camp and Bonnie Scott. Well-known performers who appeared on the show include Dabney Coleman, George Carlin and Bernie Kopell.

UNITED NATIONS: INTERNATIONAL LITERACY DAY. Sept 8. An international day observed by the organizations of the United Nations system. For info: United Nations, Dept of Public Info, New York, NY 10017. Web: www.un.org.

September 2009

S	M	T	W	T	F	S
		1	2	3	4	5
6	7	8	9	10	11	12
13	14	15	16	17	18	19
20	21	22	23	24	25	26
27	28	29	30			

Birthdays Today

David Arquette, 38, actor (*Scream, Muppets from Space*), born Winchester, VA, Sept 8, 1971.

Sid Caesar, 87, comedian, actor ("Your Show of Shows"), born Yonkers, NY, Sept 8, 1922.

Alan Feinstein, 68, actor ("Edge of Night," "Love of Life," "Search for Tomorrow"), born New York, NY, Sept 8, 1941.

Pink, 30, singer, born Alecia Moore at Doylestown, PA, Sept 8, 1979.

Bernie Sanders, 68, US Senator (I, Vermont), born Brooklyn, NY, Sept 8, 1941.

Latrell Sprewell, 39, basketball player, born Milwaukee, WI, Sept 8, 1970.

Henry Thomas, 38, actor (*All the Pretty Horses, E.T. The Extra-Terrestrial*), born San Antonio, TX, Sept 8, 1971.

Jonathan Taylor Thomas, 28, actor ("Home Improvement"), born Bethlehem, PA, Sept 8, 1981.

Rogatien (Rogie) Vachon, 64, former hockey executive and player, born Palmarolle, QC, Canada, Sept 8, 1945.

September 9 — Wednesday

DAY 252 — 113 REMAINING

BATTLE OF MARATHON: ANNIVERSARY. Sept 9. On the day of the ninth month's full moon in the year 490 BC, the numerically superior invading army of Persia was met and defeated on the Plain of Marathon by the Athenian army, led by Miltiades. More than 6,000 men died in the day's battle, which drove the Persians to the sea. The mound of earth covering the dead is still visible at the site. This date is in dispute. See also: "Historic Marathon Runs: Anniversary" (Sept 2) for the legendary running of Phidippides and the origin of the marathon race.

BATTLE OF SALERNO: ANNIVERSARY. Sept 9–16, 1943. US General Mark Clark's Fifth Army made an amphibious assault on Salerno, Italy (Operation Avalanche), at 3:30 AM. The British 1st Airborne Division seized the southern Italian port of Taranto (Operation Slapstick) without opposition. Initial gains along the western coast of Italy were checked by strong German forces by Sept 12. In some places the Allied forces were pushed back to within two miles of the coast. On Sept 15 US 82nd Airborne and British 7th Armoured counter-attacked and on Sept 16 units of the American 5th Army and the British 8th Army joined up near Vallo di Lucania.

BONZA BOTTLER DAY™. Sept 9. To celebrate when the number of the day is the same as the number of the month. Bonza Bottler Day™ is an excuse to have a party at least once a month. For more information see Jan 1. For info: Gail M. Berger, 14 Fernwood Dr, Taylors, SC 29687. E-mail: bonza@bonzabottlerday.com. Web: www.bonzabottlerday.com.

CALIFORNIA: ADMISSION DAY: ANNIVERSARY. Sept 9. Became 31st state in 1850.

CANADA: THE MASTERS. Sept 9–13. Spruce Meadows, Calgary, AB. International show jumping competition, along with Equi-Fair, TELUS Battle of the Breeds and the BP Festival of Nations, CN Images of Canada Exhibit and Emergo's Age of Exploration Exhibit. Featured events are the EnCana Cup, the ATCO Electric Circuit "Six-Bar," the BMO Financial Group Nations' Cup and the CN

International. Est attendance: 180,000. For info: Spruce Meadows, RR 9, Calgary, AB, Canada T2J 5G5. Phone: (403) 974-4200. Fax: (403) 974-4270. E-mail: information@sprucemeadows.com. Web: www.sprucemeadows.com.

DEFEAT OF JESSE JAMES DAYS. Sept 9–13. Northfield, MN. Bank raid reenactment, 5k and 15k runs, arts, crafts, bike race, parade and professional rodeo. Est attendance: 100,000. For info: Northfield Chamber of Commerce, PO Box 198, Northfield, MN 55057. Phone: (507) 645-5604. Fax: (507) 663-7782. Web: www.defeatofjessejamesdays.org.

FARMERS AND THRESHERMENS JUBILEE. Sept 9–13. New Centerville, PA. Held since 1953. Many steam engines, threshing demonstrations using manpower, horses and steam, quilt show, crafts, truck and tractor pulls. Live entertainment, good food. Est attendance: 25,000. For info: Farmers & Threshermens Jubilee, 1428 Casselman Rd, Rockwood, PA 15557. Phone: (814) 926-3142.

"FAT ALBERT AND THE COSBY KIDS" TV PREMIERE: ANNIVERSARY. Sept 9, 1972. This cartoon series was hosted by Bill Cosby, with characters based on his childhood friends at Philadelphia. Its central characters—Fat Albert, Weird Harold, Mush Mouth and Donald—were weird-looking but very human. The show sent messages of tolerance and harmony. In 1979 the show was renamed "The New Fat Albert Show."

JAPAN: CHRYSANTHEMUM DAY. Sept 9. Traditional chrysanthemum festival.

KOREA, DEMOCRATIC PEOPLE'S REPUBLIC OF: NATIONAL DAY. Sept 9. National holiday in the Democratic People's Republic of [North] Korea.

LUXEMBOURG: LIBERATION CEREMONY. Sept 9. Petange. Commemoration of liberation of Grand-Duchy by the Allied forces in 1944. Ceremony at monument of the American soldier.

MAO TSE-TUNG: DEATH ANNIVERSARY. Sept 9, 1976. People's Republic of China pays tribute to memory of the Chinese revolutionary leader, who died at Beijing. Memorial Hall, where his flag-draped body lies encased in crystal, was opened at Tiananmen Square at Beijing on the first anniversary of his death. Mao was born Dec 26, 1893, at Hunan Province, China.

MORTON PUMPKIN FESTIVAL. Sept 9–12. Morton, IL. Carnival, parade, entertainment and fantastic food to celebrate the pumpkin in the "Pumpkin Capital of the World." Est attendance: 70,000. For info: Morton Chamber of Commerce, 415 W Jefferson St, Morton, IL 61550. Phone: (888) 765-6588. Fax: (309) 263-2401. E-mail: chamber@mtco.com. Web: www.pumpkincapital.com.

"RHODA" TV PREMIERE: 35th ANNIVERSARY. Sept 9, 1974. This spin-off from "The Mary Tyler Moore Show" starred Valerie Harper as Rhoda Morgenstern, who returns to New York, finds a job and gets married (she also gets separated and divorced). The last episode aired in 1978.

SANDERS, COLONEL HARLAND DAVID: BIRTH ANNIVERSARY. Sept 9, 1890. Founder of Kentucky Fried Chicken, born near Henryville, IN. Died Dec 16, 1980, at Shelbyville, KY.

TAJIKISTAN: INDEPENDENCE DAY. Sept 9. National holiday commemorating independence from the Soviet Union in 1991.

TOLSTOY, LEO: BIRTH ANNIVERSARY. Sept 9, 1828. Russian novelist and moral philosopher, born at Tula Province, Russia. Best known for his novels (*War and Peace, Anna Karenina*), Tolstoy also wrote short stories, plays and essays. A member of the nobility, in his moral and religious writings he condemned private property and championed nonviolent protest. Died Nov 20, 1910, at Astapovo, Russia.

"WELCOME BACK, KOTTER" TV PREMIERE: ANNIVERSARY. Sept 9, 1975. In this half-hour sitcom, Gabe Kotter (Gabe Kaplan) returned to James Buchanan High School, his alma mater, to teach the "sweathogs," a group of hopeless underachievers. Other cast members included Marcia Strassman, John Travolta, Robert Hegyes, Ron Palillo, Lawrence Hilton-Jacobs and John Sylvester White. The theme song, "Welcome Back," was sung by John Sebastian. The last telecast was Aug 10, 1979.

WILLIAM, THE CONQUEROR: DEATH ANNIVERSARY. Sept 9, 1087. William I, The Conqueror, King of England and Duke of Normandy, whose image is portrayed in the Bayeux Tapestry, was born about 1028 at Falaise, Normandy. Victorious over Harold at the Battle of Hastings (the Norman Conquest) in 1066, William was crowned King of England at Westminster Abbey on Christmas Day of that year. Later, while waging war in France, William met his death at Rouen, Sept 9, 1087.

WONDERFUL WEIRDOS DAY. Sept 9. All of us are blessed with one or two wonderful weirdos in our lives. These are the folks who remind us to think outside the box, to be a little more true to ourselves. Today's the day to thank them. So give them a hug, and say "I love you, you weirdo!" (©2006 by WH.) For info: Thomas & Ruth Roy, Wellcat Holidays, 2418 Long Lane, Lebanon, PA 17046. Phone: (717) 279-0184. E-mail: info@wellcat.com. Web: www.wellcat.com.

Birthdays Today

Benjamin Roy (BJ) Armstrong, 42, former basketball player, born Detroit, MI, Sept 9, 1967.

Mario Batali, 49, chef, author, television personality ("Molto Mario"), born Seattle, WA, Sept 9, 1960.

Shane Battier, 31, basketball player, born Birmingham, MI, Sept 9, 1978.

Michael Bublé, 34, singer, born Burnaby, BC, Canada, born Sept 9, 1975.

Angela Cartwright, 57, actress ("Lost in Space," *The Sound of Music*), born Cheshire, England, Sept 9, 1952.

Hugh Grant, 49, actor (*Notting Hill, About a Boy, Four Weddings and a Funeral*), born London, England, Sept 9, 1960.

Mike Hampton, 37, baseball player, born Brooksville, FL, Sept 9, 1972.

Rachel Hunter, 40, model, born New Zealand, Sept 9, 1969.

Kazuhiro Ishii, 36, baseball player, born Chiba, Japan, Sept 9, 1973.

Michael Keaton, 58, actor (*Batman, Beetlejuice, My Life*), born Michael Douglas at Pittsburgh, PA, Sept 9, 1951.

Daniel Lewis (Dan) Majerle, 44, former basketball player, born Traverse City, MI, Sept 9, 1965.

Sylvia Miles, 75, actress (*Midnight Cowboy*; *Farewell, My Lovely*), born New York, NY, Sept 9, 1934.

Cliff Robertson, 84, actor ("Falcon Crest," *Brainstorm, Charly, PT-109*), born La Jolla, CA, Sept 9, 1925.

Adam Sandler, 43, actor, comedian ("Saturday Night Live," *The Wedding Singer*), born Brooklyn, NY, Sept 9, 1966.

Joseph Robert (Joe) Theisman, 60, sportscaster, Hall of Fame football player, born New Brunswick, NJ, Sept 9, 1949.

Goran Visnjic, 37, actor ("ER," *The Deep End*), born Sibenik, Croatia, Sept 9, 1972.

Michelle Williams, 29, actress (*Brokeback Mountain*, "Dawson's Creek"), born Kalispell, MT, Sept 9, 1980.

Tom Wopat, 58, actor ("The Dukes of Hazzard," "Cybill," *Annie Get Your Gun*), born Lodi, WI, Sept 9, 1951.

September 10 — Thursday

DAY 253 112 REMAINING

BELIZE: SAINT GEORGE'S CAYE DAY. Sept 10. Public holiday celebrated in honor of the 1798 battle between the European Baymen Settlers and the Spaniards for the territory of Belize.

BRAXTON, CARTER: BIRTH ANNIVERSARY. Sept 10, 1736. American revolutionary statesman and signer of the Declaration of Independence. Born at Newington, VA, he died Oct 10, 1797, at Richmond, VA.

CARRY NATION FESTIVAL. Sept 10–13. Downtown Holly, MI. 35th annual festival re-creates the historical visit of Carry Nation, the Kansas City saloon smasher. Includes pageant, parade, entertainment tent, carnival, street dance and craft show. Annually, the weekend after Labor Day. Est attendance: 25,000. For info: Holly Chamber of Commerce, PO Box 214, Holly, MI 48442. Phone: (248) 215-7099. Fax: (248) 215-7106. Web: www.carrynation.org.

"GENTLE BEN" TV PREMIERE: ANNIVERSARY. Sept 10, 1967. This show was about the adventures of a boy, Mark Wedloe (Clint Howard) and his pet bear, Ben. Also featured were Dennis Weaver as his father Tom, a game warden, Beth Brickell as his mother Ellen, Jack Worley as Tom's friend Spencer and Angelo Rutherford as his friend Willie. It was filmed on location in Florida.

GOULD, STEPHEN JAY: BIRTH ANNIVERSARY. Sept 10, 1941. Evolutionary biologist and influential writer for academic and lay audiences. With colleague Niles Eldredge, he proposed the theory of punctuated equilibrium to explain sudden changes (and lack of changes) in fossil records. He died in his birthplace city, New York, NY, on May 20, 2002.

"GUNSMOKE" TV PREMIERE: ANNIVERSARY. Sept 10, 1955. "Gunsmoke" was TV's longest-running Western, moving from radio to TV. John Wayne turned down the role of Marshall Matt Dillon but recommended James Arness, who got the role. Other regulars included Amanda Blake as Kitty Russell, saloon-owner; Dennis Weaver as Chester B. Goode, Dillon's deputy; and Milburn Stone as Doc Adams. In 1962 a fifth character was added—the "rugged male." Burt Reynolds played Quint Asper, followed by Roger Ewing as Thad Greenwood, and Buck Taylor as Newly O'Brien. In 1964 Ken Curtis was added as funnyman Festus Haggen, the new deputy. "Gunsmoke" was the number-one rated series for four seasons, and a top ten hit for six seasons. The last telecast was Sept 1, 1975.

KURALT, CHARLES: 75th BIRTH ANNIVERSARY. Sept 10, 1934. TV journalist ("On the Road with Charles Kuralt") born at Wilmington, NC. Died at New York, NY, July 4, 1997.

LONGS PEAK SCOTTISH/IRISH HIGHLAND FESTIVAL. Sept 10–13. Estes Park, CO. 33rd annual Scottish-Irish celebration festival with pipe bands, Highland and Irish dancing, jousting and gathering of the clans. Featuring professional Scottish and Irish entertainers, "Dogs of the British Isles" dog competition, professional Scottish athletes and vendors with imported and handcrafted merchandise. Annually, the first weekend after Labor Day. Est attendance: 70,000. For info: Longs Peak Scottish/Irish Highland Festival, Inc, PO Box 1820, Estes Park, CO 80517. Phone: (800) 903-7837. Fax: (970) 586-5328. E-mail: info@scotfest.com. Web: www.scotfest.com.

MARION POPCORN FESTIVAL. Sept 10–12. Marion, OH. Performances by nationally known entertainers every evening; parade, athletic and popcorn cooking competitions, arts and crafts. Est attendance: 350,000. For info: Marion Popcorn Festival, PO Box 1101, Marion, OH 43301-1101. Phone: (740) 387-3378. Web: www.popcornfestival.com.

MARIS, ROGER: 75th BIRTH ANNIVERSARY. Sept 10, 1934. Baseball player born Roger Eugene Maras at Hibbing, MN. In 1961 Maris surpassed the mark set by Babe Ruth in 1927, hitting 61 home runs, a record which wasn't broken until 1998. He won the American League MVP award in 1960 and 1961 and finished his career with the St. Louis Cardinals. Died at Houston, TX, Dec 14, 1985.

SCHIAPARELLI, ELSA: BIRTH ANNIVERSARY. Sept 10, 1890. Born in Rome, Italy, Elsa Schiaparelli was one of the world's leading fashion designers from the late 1920s through the 1950s. Based in Paris, France, Schiaparelli created striking, often surrealistic designs in collaboration with such artists as Salvador Dali and Jean Cocteau. She introduced the shoulder pad to women's fashion, named "shocking pink" (hot pink) and worked with man-made materials. A white evening dress bedecked with a lobster and a hat that appeared to be a giant shoe were some of her avant-garde looks. "If you define fashion as time moving . . ." she wrote, "then you are not fully alive unless you are moving with it." Schiaparelli died at Paris on Nov 13, 1973.

SWAP IDEAS DAY. Sept 10. To encourage people to explore ways in which their ideas can be put to work for the benefit of humanity, and to encourage development of incentives that will encourage use of creative imagination. For info: Robert L. Birch, Puns Corps, 3108 Dashiell Rd, Falls Church, VA 22042. Phone: (703) 533-3668.

UTAH STATE FAIR. Sept 10–20. Utah State FairPark, Salt Lake City, UT. Exhibits, livestock, family contests, cook-offs, concerts and entertainment. Annually, beginning the first Thursday after Labor Day. Est attendance: 277,000. For info: Utah State FairPark, 155 N 1000 W, Salt Lake City, UT 84116. Phone: (801) 538-8400. Fax: (801) 538-8455. E-mail: utstfair@fiber.net. Web: www.utah-state-fair.com.

WERFEL, FRANZ: BIRTH ANNIVERSARY. Sept 10, 1890. Austrian author (*The Song of Bernadette, The Forty Days of Musa Dagh*), born at Prague, Czechoslovakia. Died at Hollywood, CA, Aug 26, 1945.

"THE X-FILES" TV PREMIERE: ANNIVERSARY. Sept 10, 1993. "The Truth Is Out There" was the mantra of FOX's scary and brainy sci-fi drama. Special FBI agents Fox Mulder (David Duchovny) and Dana Scully (Gillian Anderson) solved the cases too weird for the Bureau and also uncovered a vast conspiracy involving aliens and human-alien hybrids. *TV Guide* named "The X-Files" one of the greatest TV shows of all time. Two feature-length films were created as well. The series ended in 2002.

YELLOW DAISY FESTIVAL. Sept 10–13. Stone Mountain Park, Stone Mountain, GA. 41st annual. Arts and crafts festival with more than 500 exhibitors. Continuous entertainment and foods. Annually, the weekend after Labor Day. Est attendance: 225,000. For info: Special Events Office, Stone Mountain Park, PO Box 778, Stone Mountain, GA 30086. Phone: (770) 498-5633. Fax: (770) 413-5059. E-mail: jmcdonald@stonemountainpark.com. Web: www.stonemountainpark.com.

September 2009

S	M	T	W	T	F	S
		1	2	3	4	5
6	7	8	9	10	11	12
13	14	15	16	17	18	19
20	21	22	23	24	25	26
27	28	29	30			

Birthdays Today

José Feliciano, 64, singer, musician ("Light My Fire"), born Lares, Puerto Rico, Sept 10, 1945.

Colin Firth, 49, actor (*Bridget Jones's Diary, Valmont,* "Pride and Prejudice"), born Grayshott, Hampshire, England, Sept 10, 1960.

Judy Geeson, 61, actress (*To Sir with Love, The Eagle Has Landed*), born Arundel, Sussex, England, Sept 10, 1948.

Matt Geiger, 40, former basketball player, born Salem, MA, Sept 10, 1969.

Amy Irving, 56, actress (*Carrie, Crossing Delancey,* "Alias"), born Palo Alto, CA, Sept 10, 1953.

Clark Johnson, 45, actor ("Homicide"), born Philadelphia, PA, Sept 10, 1964.

Randy Johnson, 46, baseball player, born Walnut Creek, CA, Sept 10, 1963.

Karl Lagerfeld, 71, fashion designer, born Hamburg, Germany, Sept 10, 1938.

Joe Nieuwendyk, 43, hockey player, born Oshawa, ON, Canada, Sept 10, 1966.

Arnold Palmer, 80, golfer, born Latrobe, PA, Sept 10, 1929.

Yma Sumac, 81, singer, born Ichocan, Peru, Sept 10, 1928.

John Sununu, 45, US Senator (R, New Hampshire), born Boston, MA, Sept 10, 1964.

September 11 — Friday

DAY 254 **111 REMAINING**

ARCOLA BROOM CORN FESTIVAL. Sept 11–13. Arcola, IL. 39th annual. The town invites one and all to help celebrate. Free entertainment, arts and crafts, flea markets, food and large parade featuring the Lawn Ranger. Est attendance: 60,000. For info: Arcola Chamber of Commerce, PO Box 274, Arcola, IL 61910. Phone: (800) 336-5456. Web: www.arcolachamber.com.

ATTACK ON AMERICA: ANNIVERSARY. Sept 11, 2001. Terrorists hijacked four planes, piloting two of them into the World Trade Center's twin towers in New York City and one into the Pentagon in Washington, DC. Passengers on the fourth plane appear to have attempted to overcome the hijackers, causing the plane to crash in western Pennsylvania instead of reaching its target in Washington. The twin towers at the WTC collapsed about an hour after being hit. More than 3,000 people died as a result of the attacks. The hijackers were agents of the Al Qaeda terrorist group led by Islamic extremist Osama bin Laden, who was headquartered in Afghanistan. In response, the US began unprecedented internal security measures and launched a war on terrorism with the support of many nations. See also: "The Fall of Kabul: Anniversary" (Nov 13) and "World Trade Center Recovery and Cleanup Ends: Anniversary" (May 30).

BATTLE OF BRANDYWINE: ANNIVERSARY. Sept 11, 1777. The largest engagement of the American Revolution, between the Continental Army led by General George Washington and British troops led by General William Howe. General Howe was marching to take Philadelphia when Washington chose to try and stop the British advance at the Brandywine River near Chadds Ford, PA. The American forces were defeated and the British went on to take Philadelphia Sept 26. They spent the winter in the city while Washington's troops suffered at their encampment at Valley Forge, PA.

"THE CAROL BURNETT SHOW" TV PREMIERE: ANNIVERSARY. Sept 11, 1967. This popular comedy/variety show starred comedienne Carol Burnett, who started the show by taking questions from the audience and ended with an ear tug. Sketches and spoofs included recurring characters like "The Family" (later to be spun off as "Mama's Family") and "As the Stomach Turns." Regular cast members included Harvey Korman, Lyle Waggoner and Vicki Lawrence. Later, Tim Conway joined the cast. Dick Van Dyke briefly joined after Korman left in 1977.

CLINTON COUNTY CORN FESTIVAL. Sept 11–13. Clinton County Fairgrounds, Wilmington, OH. 32nd annual. Help us celebrate our agricultural heritage as we honor one of the area's biggest industries. The festival features antique farm machinery, a parade (Saturday at 10 AM), games, all types of food made from corn, a quilt show, music, antiques, crafts and the Corn Olympics. This is an event not to miss in Clinton County! For info: Clinton County CVB, 13 N South St, Wilmington, OH 45177. Phone: (877) 428-4748. Fax: (937) 382-1738. E-mail: info@clintoncountyohio.com. Web: www.clintoncountyohio.com.

ETHIOPIA: NEW YEAR'S DAY. Sept 11. In the year 2009, this day will start the year 2003 on the Ethiopian Orthodox calendar. On the Coptic Orthodox calendar, it begins the year 1726.

FESTIVAL OF THE VINE. Sept 11–13. Geneva, IL. Flavors of fall are celebrated with music, wine tasting, antique carriage rides, arts and crafts, entertainment and specialties of Geneva's fine restaurants. Est attendance: 75,000. For info: Geneva Chamber of Commerce, 8 S Third St, PO Box 481, Geneva, IL 60134. Phone: (630) 232-6060. Fax: (630) 232-6083. E-mail: chamberinfo@genevachamber.com. Web: www.genevachamber.com.

FOOD STAMPS AUTHORIZED: 50th ANNIVERSARY. Sept 11, 1959. Congress passed a bill authorizing food stamps for low-income Americans.

KANSAS STATE FAIR. Sept 11–20. Hutchinson, KS. Commercial and competitive exhibits, entertainment, carnival, car racing and other special attractions. Annually, beginning the first Friday after Labor Day. Est attendance: 350,000. For info: Denny Stoecklein, Gen Mgr, Kansas State Fair, 2000 N Poplar St, Hutchinson, KS 67502. Phone: (620) 669-3600. E-mail: info@kansasstatefair.com. Web: www.kansasstatefair.com.

KETTLE MORAINE JAZZ FESTIVAL. Sept 11–12. Riverside Park, West Bend, WI. Features nationally recognized jazz musicians and vocalists. Past performers have included Richard Elliott, Chris Botti and Rick Braun. Est attendance: 5,500. For info: Dave Amoroso, Ron Sonntag Public Relations, 9406 N 107th St, Milwaukee, WI 53224. Phone: (877) 271-6903. Fax: (414) 354-5317. E-mail: info@kmjazz.com. Web: www.kmjazz.com.

LAWRENCE, DAVID HERBERT: BIRTH ANNIVERSARY. Sept 11, 1885. English novelist, author of *Lady Chatterley's Lover.* Born at Eastwood, Nottinghamshire, England, D.H. Lawrence died Mar 2, 1930, at Vence, France.

LIBRARIES REMEMBER. Sept 11. Libraries represent the sum of all human knowledge. They also represent equal access to that knowledge as well as freedom of expression, celebration of diversity, preservation of heritage and commitment to the future. Libraries represent everything that is antithetical to the fanaticism responsible for the terrorist events of Sept 11, 2001. Libraries Remember encourages libraries across the United States to remain open for the entire 24 hours of Sept 11 as remarkable symbols of freedom, tolerance and hope. For info: Bill Erbes, Bensenville Community Public Library, 200 S Church Rd, Bensenville, IL 60106. Phone: (630) 766-4642. Fax: (630) 595-9171. E-mail: billerbes@aol.com. Web: www.bensenville.lib.il.us.

LIGONIER HIGHLAND GAMES. Sept 11–12. Ligonier, PA. Scottish bagpipe bands on parade, Highland dancers and athletes in daylong performances. Clan gatherings, dog show. Offers imported woolens, china, jewelry, records and foods. Mail SASE for schedule of events. Est attendance: 10,000. For info: David L. Peet, Ligonier Highland Games, PO Box 884, Bethel Park, PA 15102-0884. Phone: (412) 851-9900. E-mail: ligdir@verizon.net. Web: www.ligoniergames.org.

LIND, JENNY: US PREMIERE: ANNIVERSARY. Sept 11, 1850. Jenny Lind, the "Swedish Nightingale," gave her first American performance in the Castle Garden Theatre, New York, NY, on this day.

"LITTLE HOUSE ON THE PRAIRIE" TV PREMIERE: 35th ANNIVERSARY. Sept 11, 1974. This hour-long family drama was based on books by Laura Ingalls Wilder. It focused on the Ingalls family and their neighbors living at Walnut Grove, MN: Michael Landon as Charles (Pa), Karen Grassle as Caroline (Ma), Melissa Sue Anderson as daughter Mary, Melissa Gilbert as daughter Laura, from whose point of view the stories were told, Lindsay and Sidney Greenbush as daughter Carrie and Wendi and Brenda Turnbaugh as daughter Grace. In its last season (1982), the show's name was changed to "Little House: A New Beginning." Landon appeared less often and the show centered around Laura and her husband.

MARCOS, FERDINAND EDRALIN: BIRTH ANNIVERSARY. Sept 11, 1917. Former ruler of the Philippines, born at Sarrat, Philippines. Ferdinand Marcos served as head of state from 1966 until his ouster in 1986. His authoritarian regime was marred by widespread corruption and suppression of democratic processes. Marcos died in exile Sept 28, 1989, at Honolulu, HI.

MARIGOLD FESTIVAL. Sept 11–13. Pekin, IL. Parade, arts, crafts, golf, carnival, Festive Foods and other family-oriented activities. Est attendance: 100,000. For info: Pekin Chamber of Commerce, PO Box 636, Pekin, IL 61555-0636. Phone: (309) 346-2106. Fax: (309) 346-2104. E-mail: chamber@pekin.net.

MOON PHASE: LAST QUARTER. Sept 11. Moon enters Last Quarter phase at 10:16 PM, EDT.

MOUNTAIN MEADOWS MASSACRE: ANNIVERSARY. Sept 11, 1857. As tensions grew between the US government and Governor Brigham Young of the Utah Territory, a wagon train of 140 emigrants bound for California from Arkansas was attacked. On this date, the emigrants surrendered to local Mormon leader John Doyle Lee but were then massacred. Seventeen small children were parceled out to Mormon families. Despite the ensuing national uproar, federal prosecution didn't happen until 1875. Lee was executed in 1877.

NORDICFEST. Sept 11–13. Libby, MT. Scandinavian festival with food booths, dinners, cultural exhibits, craft shows, quilt show, art show, folk dance performances, entertainment and the international fjord horse show. Parade showcases a contingent of Norwegian fjord horses plus a variety of floats. Est attendance: 10,000. For info: Libby Nordicfest, Inc, Box 791, Libby, MT 59923. Phone: (800) 785-6541. E-mail: libbynordicfest@yahoo.com. Web: www.libbynordicfest.org.

NORWALK SEAPORT OYSTER FESTIVAL. Sept 11–13. Norwalk, CT. Huge festival with vintage ships on display, 225 juried crafters, main stage entertainment, oyster shucking and slurping contests and Kids' Cove (children's entertainment). Annually, the weekend following Labor Day. Est attendance: 82,000. For info: Norwalk Seaport Assn, 132 Water St, Norwalk, CT 06854. Phone: (203) 838-9444. Fax: (203) 855-1017. E-mail: info@seaport.org. Web: www.seaport.org.

O. HENRY (WILLIAM S. PORTER): BIRTH ANNIVERSARY. Sept 11, 1862. William Sydney Porter, American author, who wrote under the pen name O. Henry. Best known for his short stories, including "Gift of the Magi." Born at Greensboro, NC, he died at New York, NY, June 5, 1910.

OHIO RIVER STERNWHEEL FESTIVAL. Sept 11–13. Ohio River Levee, Marietta, OH. A three-day riverfront extravaganza. More than two dozen sternwheelers line the Ohio River shore in Marietta, OH. Continuous musical entertainment for all ages, food concessions, queen coronation, sternwheel races, fireworks. Annually, the weekend following Labor Day. Est attendance: 85,000. For info: Ohio River Sternwheel Festival Committee, 316 Third St, Marietta, OH 45750. Phone: (740) 373-5178 or (800) 288-2577. Fax: (740) 374-4959. E-mail: info@mariettaohio.org. Web: www.ohioriversternwheelfestival.org.

OKTOBERFEST. Sept 11–13. MainStrasse Village, Covington, KY. Celebration of the German "storybook wedding reception" kicks off with a beer-tapping ceremony. Features include German and American food, live Bavarian music and dancing, arts and crafts, children's rides and much more. Est attendance: 150,000. For info: Donna Kremer, Administrative Coordinator, MainStrasse Village, 406 W 6th St, Ste 201, Covington, KY 41011. Phone: (859) 491-0458. Fax: (859) 655-7932. E-mail: dkremer@mainstrasse.org. Web: www.mainstrasse.org.

ONE ARM DOVE HUNT. Sept 11–12. Olney, TX. 38th annual. Held since 1972, the One Arm Dove Hunt is Texas's most unusual event and the only one of its kind on Earth. Every person with the loss of use of an arm or hand or who is an arm or hand amputee is invited to Olney for fellowship, fun activities and to hunt dove. Events include Glove Swap, One Arm Jokes and Tales, One Arm Golf Tournament, Cow Chip Chunk'n (Amputee vs Politician), musical entertainment, auction and the famous 10 cents a finger breakfast. Annually, the Friday and Saturday after Labor Day. For info: Jack Northrup, One Arm Dove Hunt, PO Box 582, Olney, TX 76374. Web: www.onearmdovehunt.com.

PAKISTAN: FOUNDER'S DEATH ANNIVERSARY. Sept 11. Pakistan observes the death anniversary in 1948 of Qaid-e-Azam Mohammed Ali Jinnah (founder of Pakistan) as a national holiday. His birth date of Dec 25 is also a national holiday.

PATRIOT DAY. Sept 11. On Dec 18, 2001, a joint resolution of Congress amended Title 36, Chapter 1, Sec. 144 of the US Code to permit the president to declare Sept 11 of each year as Patriot Day, in commemoration of the terrorist attacks on the United States on Sept 11, 2001. The resolution requests that all state and local governments observe this day "with appropriate programs and activities," that the flag be displayed at half-staff from sunrise till sundown, and that a moment of silence be observed in honor of those who lost their lives in the attacks.

PUYALLUP FAIR. Sept 11–27. Puyallup, WA. The 109th fair. Entertainment, rodeo, animals, rides, displays and food. Est attendance: 1,100,000. For info: Puyallup Fair, 110 Ninth Ave SW, Puyallup, WA 98371. Phone: (253) 841-5045. Fax: (253) 841-5390. E-mail: info@thefair.com. Web: www.thefair.com.

"THE ROOKIES" TV PREMIERE: ANNIVERSARY. Sept 11, 1972. This hour-long crime show focused on three young police recruits: Michael Ontkean as Willie Gates, Georg Stanford Brown as Terry Webster and Sam Melville as Mike Danko. Also featured were Gerald S. O'Loughlin as Lieutenant Ed Ryker; Kate Jackson as nurse Jill Danko, Mike's wife, and Bruce Fairbairn as Chris Owens. The show was produced by Aaron Spelling and Leonard Goldberg.

1786 ANNAPOLIS CONVENTION: ANNIVERSARY. Sept 11–14, 1786. Twelve delegates from New York, New Jersey, Delaware, Pennsylvania and Virginia met at Annapolis, MD, to discuss commercial matters of mutual interest. The delegates voted, on Sept 14, to adopt a resolution prepared by Alexander Hamilton asking all states to send representatives to a convention at Philadelphia, PA, in May 1787 "to render the constitution of the Federal Government adequate to the exigencies of the Union."

SPACE MILESTONE: *MARS GLOBAL SURVEYOR* (US). Sept 11, 1997. Launched Nov 7, 1996, this unmanned vehicle was put into orbit around Mars. It was designed to compile global maps of Mars by taking high-resolution photos. This mission inaugurated a new series of Mars expeditions in which NASA launched pairs of orbiters and landers to Mars. *Mars Global Surveyor* was paired with the lander *Mars Pathfinder*. See also: "Space Milestone: *Mars Pathfinder*" (July 4).

September 2009

S	M	T	W	T	F	S
		1	2	3	4	5
6	7	8	9	10	11	12
13	14	15	16	17	18	19
20	21	22	23	24	25	26
27	28	29	30			

SUGARLOAF CRAFTS FESTIVAL. Sept 11–13. Prince William County Fairgrounds, Manassas, VA. This show, now in its 29th year, features 200 nationally recognized craft designers and fine artists displaying and selling their original creations. Craft demonstrations, live music, food, children's entertainment, hourly gift certificate drawings and more. Est attendance: 13,000. For info: Sugarloaf Mountain Works, 200 Orchard Ridge Dr, #215, Gaithersburg, MD 20878. Phone: (800) 210-9900. Fax: (301) 253-9620. Web: www.sugarloafcrafts.com.

TYLER'S CABINET RESIGNS: ANNIVERSARY. Sept 11, 1841. In protest of President John Tyler's veto of the Banking Bill all of his cabinet except Secretary of State Daniel Webster resigned on this day.

Birthdays Today

Daniel K. Akaka, 85, US Senator (D, Hawaii), born Honolulu, HI, Sept 11, 1924.

Franz Beckenbauer, 64, soccer executive and Hall of Fame player, born Munich, Germany, Sept 11, 1945.

Harry Connick, Jr, 42, singer, pianist, stage and screen actor, born New Orleans, LA, Sept 11, 1967.

Brian De Palma, 69, filmmaker (*Mission: Impossible, The Untouchables, Carrie*), born Newark, NJ, Sept 11, 1940.

Lola Falana, 66, actress ("The New Bill Cosby Show," "Ben Vereen—Comin' at Ya"), born Camden, NJ, Sept 11, 1943.

Donna Lopiano, 63, women's sports executive and former softball player, born Stamford, CT, Sept 11, 1946.

Amy Madigan, 58, actress (*Places in the Heart, Field of Dreams, Uncle Buck*), born Chicago, IL, Sept 11, 1951.

Virginia Madsen, 46, actress (*Sideways, Dune*), born Winnetka, IL, Sept 11, 1963.

Kristy McNichol, 47, actress ("Empty Nest," *Little Darlings, Summer of My German Soldier,* Emmys for "Family"), born Los Angeles, CA, Sept 11, 1962.

Moby, 44, rock singer/songwriter, born Richard Melville Hall at New York, NY, Sept 11, 1965.

September 12 — Saturday

DAY 255 | **110 REMAINING**

AUTUMN ARTS FESTIVAL. Sept 12–13 (tentative). Jonathan Hager House, City Park, Hagerstown, MD. Featuring more than 50 demonstrating craftsmen, great Appalachian-style music and great food. (Formerly Jonathan Hager Frontier Craft Days.) Est attendance: 7,500. For info: John Bryan, Jonathan Hager House and Museum, 110 Key St, Hagerstown, MD 21740. Phone: (301) 739-8393. E-mail: hagerhouse@hagerstownmd.org.

BATTLE OF SAINT-MIHIEL: ANNIVERSARY. Sept 12, 1918. Under the command of General John J. Pershing, the 1st US Army attacked the Germans at the Saint-Mihiel salient. This was the first major US offensive of WWI. Sixteen army divisions, coupled with French II Colonial Corps tanks and artillery support, forced back the Germans after 36 hours of heavy fighting and reclaimed 200 square miles of French territory that had been in the hands of the Germans since 1914. The 1st US Army lost about 7,000 soldiers in the Battle of Saint-Mihiel.

BIG MAC SHORELINE FALL SCENIC BIKE TOUR & RIDE ACROSS THE MACKINAC BRIDGE. Sept 12–13. Mackinaw City Public School, Mackinaw City, MI. A one-of-a-kind bike tour that has become a tradition for many bikers in Michigan and surrounding states. On Saturday, more than 600 participants ride 25-, 50-, 75- or 100-mile bike tours along the shores of Lake Michigan. The routes are clearly marked and a number of rest areas dot the course. SAG Safety Wagons also circle the route to ensure safety for riders. For those who participate on Saturday, there is a beautiful ride across Mackinac Bridge on Sunday at 7 AM. Est attendance: 600. For info: Kelly Vieau, Mackinaw Chamber of Commerce, PO Box 856, Mackinaw City, MI 49701. Phone: (231) 436-5574. Fax: (231) 436-7989. E-mail: info@mackinawchamber.com. Web: www.mackinawchamber.com.

BOONESBOROUGH DAYS. Sept 12–13. Shafer Memorial Park, Boonsboro, MD. Crafts, antiques, living history, demonstrations, food. Boonesborough was the original spelling of the town's name. Est attendance: 10,000. For info: Boonsboro Historical Society, PO Box 213, Boonsboro, MD 21713. Phone: (301) 432-5889.

BULLS SIGN MICHAEL JORDAN: 25th ANNIVERSARY. Sept 12, 1984. The Chicago Bulls signed their No. 1 draft choice, Michael Jordan, a guard from the University of North Carolina. Jordan was the No. 3 choice overall behind Akeem (later Hakeem) Olajuwon, taken by Houston, and Sam Bowie, selected by Portland.

CANYONLANDS NATIONAL PARK ESTABLISHED: 45th ANNIVERSARY. Sept 12, 1964. Area of southeastern Utah established as a national park. For further park info: Canyonlands Natl Park, 125 W—2000 S, Moab, UT 84532.

CHADDS FORD DAYS. Sept 12–13. Chadds Ford, PA. Open-air Brandywine celebration with 18th-century craft demonstrations, Brandywine Valley art, live music, kids korner, colonial and contemporary crafts for sale, good food. Est attendance: 8,000. For info: Chadds Ford Historical Society, PO Box 27, Chadds Ford, PA 19317. Phone: (610) 388-7376. Fax: (610) 388-7480. E-mail: info@chaddsfordhistory.org. Web: www.chaddsfordhistory.org.

CHARLES LEROUX'S LAST JUMP: ANNIVERSARY. Sept 12, 1889. American aeronaut of French extraction, born in New York, NY, about 1857, achieved world fame as a parachutist. After his first public performance (Philadelphia, PA, 1887) he toured European cities, where his parachute jumps attracted wide attention. Credited with 238 successful jumps. On Sept 12, 1889, he jumped from a balloon over Tallinn, Estonia, and perished in the Bay of Reval.

CHILDREN'S DAY AT JAMESTOWN. Sept 12. Jamestown Settlement, Williamsburg, VA. A festive day of children's 17th-century games, music, juggling, stilt walking, puppet shows, storytelling and hands-on crafts. For info: Jamestown-Yorktown Foundation, PO Box 1607, Williamsburg, VA 23187. Phone: (757) 253-4838 or (888) 593-4682. Fax: (757) 253-5299. Web: www.historyisfun.org.

DEFENDERS DAY. Sept 12. Maryland. Public holiday. Annual reenactment of bombardment of Fort McHenry in 1814 that inspired Francis Scott Key to write the "Star-Spangled Banner."

FLAX SCUTCHING FESTIVAL. Sept 12–13. Stahlstown, PA. Demonstrations of the art of making linen from the flax plant. Second oldest continuous complete flax demonstration festival in the world. Annually, the second full weekend in September. Est attendance: 15,000. For info: Marilee Pletcher, Flax Scutching Festival, 4158 Main St, Stahlstown, PA 15687. Phone: (724) 593-7813.

GUINEA-BISSAU: NATIONAL HOLIDAY. Sept 12. Amilcar Cabral's birthday, Sept 12, is observed as a national holiday.

HERITAGE DAY FESTIVAL. Sept 12 (rain date Sept 13). Lavallette, NJ. Clowns, antique cars, four live bands, games, food, children's games and rides and finale with a string band performing. 10 AM–dusk. Annually, the first Saturday after Labor Day. Est attendance: 30,000. For info: Heritage Committee Inc, 117 President Ave, Lavallette, NJ 08735. Phone: (732) 793-1936. Fax: (732) 793-1937. E-mail: zaccaria@optonline.net.

ISRAEL COMPLETES GAZA PULLOUT: ANNIVERSARY. Sept 12, 2005. In the early hours of Sept 12, the last of Israel's troops left Gaza, and the withdrawal of settlers and military begun in August

2005 was finished. Israel had occupied Gaza for 38 years. The Palestinian Authority assumed control of Gaza.

"LASSIE" TV PREMIERE: 55th ANNIVERSARY. Sept 12, 1954. This long-running series was originally about a boy and his courageous and intelligent dog, Lassie (played by more than six different dogs, all male). For the first few seasons, Lassie lived on the Miller farm. The family included Jeff (Tommy Rettig), his widowed mother Ellen (Jan Clayton) and George Cleveland as Gramps. Throughout the years there were many format and cast changes, as Lassie was exchanged from one family to another in order to have a variety of new perils and escapades. Other featured performers included Cloris Leachman, June Lockhart and Larry Wilcox.

LITTLE FALLS ARTS AND CRAFTS FAIR. Sept 12–13. Little Falls, MN. 650 artists, craftspeople and hobbyists displaying and selling their items. Est attendance: 80,000. For info: Chamber of Commerce, 200 NW First St, Little Falls, MN 56345. Phone: (320) 632-5155. Fax: (320) 632-2122. E-mail: artsandcrafts@littlefallsmnchamber.com. Web: www.littlefallsmnchamber.com.

"MAUDE" TV PREMIERE: ANNIVERSARY. Sept 12, 1972. Bea Arthur's character, Maude Findlay, was first introduced as Edith Bunker's cousin on "All in the Family." She was a loud, opinionated liberal, living with her fourth husband Walter (Bill Macy). Other characters on the show were her divorced daughter by a previous marriage, Carol Trainer (Adrienne Barbeau), Conrad Bain as Dr. Arthur Harmon, Rue McClanahan as Arthur's wife Vivian, Esther Rolle as Florida Evans, Maude's maid, and John Amos as her husband, Henry. This was one of the first shows to tackle the controversial issue of abortion.

MENCKEN, HENRY LOUIS: BIRTH ANNIVERSARY. Sept 12, 1880. American newspaperman, lexicographer and critic, "the Sage of Baltimore" was born at Baltimore, MD, and died there Jan 29, 1956. "If, after I depart this vale," he wrote in 1921 (Epitaph, *Smart Set*), "you ever remember me and have thought to please my ghost, forgive some sinner and wink your eye at some homely girl."

"THE MONKEES" TV PREMIERE: ANNIVERSARY. Sept 12, 1966. Featuring a rock group that was supposed to be an American version of the Beatles, this half-hour show featured a blend of comedy and music. Four young actors were chosen from more than 400 to play the group members: Micky Dolenz, Davy Jones, Mike Nesmith and Peter Tork. Dolenz and Jones had previous acting experience and Tork and Nesmith had previous musical experience. The music that they performed on the show proved to be immensely popular; at first they sang with a studio band but later insisted on writing and performing their own music. They released several albums and toured several times. In 1986, the Monkees, except for Nesmith, were reunited for a 20th Anniversary tour and the show was broadcast in reruns on MTV. The Monkees sans Nesmith also toured in 1996 for the 30th reunion celebration.

MUSHROOM FESTIVAL. Sept 12–13. Downtown Kennett Square, PA. Weekend of fun, food and fungi in the Mushroom Capital of the World! Help taste and judge the soup cook-off, attend cooking or growing demos. Also mushroom judging, car show, WineFest, Street Festival with entertainment and mushroom farm tours. Est attendance: 100,000. For info: The Mushroom Festival, PO Box 1000, 114 W State St, Kennett Square, PA 19348. Phone: (888) 440-9920. E-mail: info@mushroomfestival.org. Web: www.mushroomfestival.org.

NANTICOKE INDIAN POWWOW. Sept 12–13. Millsboro, DE. Annual gathering of Native Americans during which Native American dances, music and storytelling are presented and Native American foods and arts and crafts are sold. 40 different tribes participate. Dance sessions: Saturday, noon–5 PM, Sunday, 2–5 PM. Sunday worship service, 10 AM. Annually, the weekend after Labor Day. Est attendance: 40,000. For info: Nanticoke Indian Assn, 27073 John J. William Hwy, Millsboro, DE 19966. Phone: (302) 945-3400. E-mail: nanticok@verizon.net.

OWENS, JESSE: BIRTH ANNIVERSARY. Sept 12, 1913. James Cleveland (Jesse) Owens, American athlete, winner of four gold medals at the 1936 Olympic Games at Berlin, Germany, was born at Oakville, AL. Owens set 11 world records in track and field. During one track meet, at Ann Arbor, MI, May 23, 1935, Owens, representing Ohio State University, broke three world records and tied a fourth in the space of 45 minutes. Died at Tucson, AZ, Mar 31, 1980.

PENDLETON ROUND-UP. Sept 12–19. Pendleton, OR. America's classic rodeo. A 99-year-old Western tradition, with participating Indian tribes from the Pacific Northwest. Plus historical Happy Canyon, an outdoor pageant each evening. Kickoff parade and concert plus professional bull riding events early in the week. Est attendance: 48,000. For info: Pendleton Round-Up Assn, Box 609, Pendleton, OR 97801. Phone: (800) 457-6336. Web: www.pendletonroundup.com.

SODBUSTER DAYS—THE HARVEST. Sept 12–13. Sunne Farm, Fort Ransom State Park, Fort Ransom, ND. Demonstrations of life on a small family farm of the 1920s during the fall harvest. Activities include threshing, fall field work, gathering prairie hay, ladies' demonstrations, kids games, food, music. Most farm machinery is horse drawn. Annually, the weekend after Labor Day. Located along the Sheyenne River Valley National Scenic Byway. Est attendance: 2,000. For info: Fort Ransom State Park, 5981 Walt Hjelle Pkwy, Fort Ransom, ND 58033-9712. Phone: (701) 973-4331. Fax: (701) 973-4151. E-mail: frsp@nd.gov. Web: www.parkrec.nd.gov.

SOUTHEAST MISSOURI DISTRICT FAIR. Sept 12–19. Arena Park Fairgrounds, Cape Girardeau, MO. Oldest outdoor fair in the state. Celebrating its 154th year with beauty pageants, livestock exhibition, horse show, entertainment, carnival, food and 4-H and FFA displays. Annually, starts the Saturday after Labor Day and continues to the next Saturday. Est attendance: 100,000. For info: SEMO District Fair Assn, 410 Kiwanis Dr, Ste 200, Cape Girardeau, MO 63701. Phone: (800) 455-FAIR or (573) 334-9250. E-mail: info@semofair.com. Web: www.semofair.com.

SPACE MILESTONE: *LUNA 2* (USSR): 50th ANNIVERSARY. Sept 12, 1959. First spacecraft to land on moon was launched.

USGA SENIOR AMATEUR (GOLF) CHAMPIONSHIP. Sept 12–17. The Beverly Country Club, Chicago, IL. For info: USGA, Golf House, Championship Dept, PO Box 708, Far Hills, NJ 07931. Phone: (908) 234-2300. Fax: (908) 234-9687. E-mail: usga@usga.org. Web: www.usga.org.

US SENIOR WOMEN'S AMATEUR (GOLF) CHAMPIONSHIP. Sept 12–17. The Homestead, Hot Springs, VA. For info: USGA, Golf House, Championship Dept, PO Box 708, Far Hills, NJ 07931. Phone: (908) 234-2300. Fax: (908) 234-9687. E-mail: usga@usga.org. Web: www.usga.org.

VALPARAISO POPCORN FESTIVAL. Sept 12. Valparaiso, IN. Celebration of popcorn with a parade, the Popcorn Panic and Little Kernel Puff running races, arts, crafts, food booths, music and entertainment, kids' inflatables area and a hot-air balloon show. Annually, the first Saturday after Labor Day. Est attendance: 65,000. For info: Tina St. Aubin, Events Dir, 162 W Lincolnway, Valparaiso, IN 46383. Phone: (219) 464-8332. Fax: (219) 464-2343. E-mail: popcorn@popcornfest.org. Web: www.popcornfest.org.

September 2009

S	M	T	W	T	F	S
		1	2	3	4	5
6	7	8	9	10	11	12
13	14	15	16	17	18	19
20	21	22	23	24	25	26
27	28	29	30			

VIDEO GAMES DAY. Sept 12. A day for kids who love video games to celebrate the fun they have playing them and to thank their parents for all the cartridges and quarters they have provided to indulge this enthusiasm.

WALKER CUP. Sept 12–13. Merion Golf Club, Ardmore, PA. Biennial golf competition between amateur teams from the US and UK. For info: USGA, Golf House, Championship Dept, PO Box 708, Far Hills, NJ 07931. Phone: (908) 234-2300. Fax: (908) 234-9687. E-mail: usga@usga.org. Web: www.usga.org.

WARNER, CHARLES DUDLEY: BIRTH ANNIVERSARY. Sept 12, 1829. American newspaperman, born at Plainfield, MA, authored many works, but is perhaps best remembered for a single sentence (in an editorial, *Hartford Courant*, Aug 24, 1897): "Everybody talks about the weather, but nobody does anything about it." The quotation is often mistakenly attributed to his friend, Mark Twain. Died at Hartford, CT, Oct 20, 1900.

WHIPPOORWILL MORGAN HORSE VERSATILITY EVENT. Sept 12. Old Lyme, CT. Morgan horses in performance. Carriage, dressage, reining, bareback riders—a day of free fun for the whole family. Est attendance: 700. For info: McCulloch Farm, Whippoorwill Morgan, 100 Whippoorwill Rd, Old Lyme, CT 06371. Phone: (860) 434-7355.

WOODLAND INDIAN DISCOVERY DAY. Sept 12. St. Mary's City, MD. Explore the lifeways of the Yaocomaco Indian people at the Woodland Indian Hamlet. Hands-on demonstrations, storytelling and more. Est attendance: 800. For info: Director of Marketing, Historic St. Mary's City, PO Box 39, St. Mary's City, MD 20686. Phone: (240) 895-4990 or (800) SMC-1634. Fax: (240) 895-4968. Web: www.stmaryscity.org.

Birthdays Today

Sam Brownback, 53, US Senator (R, Kansas), born Garnett, KS, Sept 12, 1956.

Irene Dailey, 89, actress ("Another World"), born New York, NY, Sept 12, 1920.

Linda Gray, 68, actress ("Dallas," "Melrose Place"), born Santa Monica, CA, Sept 12, 1941.

Ian Holm, 78, actor (*The Sweet Hereafter*, Oscar for *Chariots of Fire*), born Goodmayes, England, Sept 12, 1931.

Jennifer Hudson, 28, singer, actress ("American Idol," Oscar for *Dreamgirls; Sex and the City*), born Chicago, IL, Sept 12, 1981.

George Jones, 78, singer, born Saratoga, TX, Sept 12, 1931.

Benjamin McKenzie, 31, actor ("The O.C.," *Junebug*), born Austin, TX, Sept 12, 1978.

Yao Ming, 29, basketball player, born Shanghai, China, Sept 12, 1980.

Maria Muldaur, 66, singer ("Midnight at the Oasis," "I'm a Woman"), born New York, NY, Sept 12, 1943.

Joe Pantoliano, 55, actor (*Risky Business, The Fugitive*; "The Sopranos," stage: *Orphans*), born Jersey City, NJ, Sept 12, 1954.

Emmy Rossum, 23, actress (*The Day After Tomorrow, The Phantom of the Opera*), born New York, NY, Sept 12, 1986.

Peter Scolari, 55, actor ("Bosom Buddies," "Newhart"), born New Rochelle, NY, Sept 12, 1954.

Rachel Ward, 52, actress ("The Thorn Birds," *Against All Odds*), born London, England, Sept 12, 1957.

Amy Yasbeck, 46, actress (*The Mask*, "Wings"), born Cincinnati, OH, Sept 12, 1963.

September 13 — Sunday

DAY 256 | **109 REMAINING**

ANDERSON, SHERWOOD: BIRTH ANNIVERSARY. Sept 13, 1876. American author and newspaper publisher, born at Camden, OH. His best remembered book is *Winesburg, Ohio*. Anderson died at Colon, Panama, Mar 8, 1941.

ART IN THE GARDEN. Sept 13. Washington, PA. Est attendance: 600. For info: Joyce Mullen, Washington County Historical Society, 49 E Maiden St, Washington, PA 15301. Phone: (724) 225-6740. Fax: (724) 225-8495. E-mail: info@wchspa.org. Web: www.wchspa.org.

BALANCE AWARENESS WEEK. Sept 13–19. To develop public awareness of balance and disorders of balance system (vestibular disorders); to unite professionals, educators, support groups, medical facilities in a week-long effort to focus attention of the public and the media. Annually, the third full week in Sept. For info: Vestibular Disorders Assn, PO Box 13305, Portland, OR 97213. Phone: (800) 837-8428. Fax: (503) 229-8064. E-mail: info@vestibular.org. Web: www.vestibular.org.

BARRY, JOHN: DEATH ANNIVERSARY. Sept 13, 1803. Revolutionary War hero John Barry, first American to hold the rank of commodore, died at Philadelphia, PA. He was born at Tacumshane, County Wexford, Ireland, in 1745. He has been called the "Father of the American Navy."

COLBERT, CLAUDETTE: BIRTH ANNIVERSARY. Sept 13, 1903. Actress and comedienne Colbert, born Lily Claudette Chauchoin at Paris, France, was a beloved movie star of the '30s. She was best known for her films *Midnight, Cleopatra* and *It Happened One Night,* for which she won an Oscar in 1934. In addition to more than 60 movies, she appeared in Broadway shows and won a Golden Globe Award for her role in the 1986 miniseries "The Two Mrs Grenvilles." She also received a Life Achievement Award from the Kennedy Center for Performing Arts in 1989. She died July 30, 1996, at Bridgetown, Barbados.

DAHL, ROALD: BIRTH ANNIVERSARY. Sept 13, 1916. Author (*Charlie and the Chocolate Factory, James and the Giant Peach*), born at Llandaff, South Wales, Great Britain. Died Nov 23, 1990, at Oxford, England.

ITALY: GIOSTRA DELLA QUINTANA. Sept 13. Foligno. A revival of a 17th-century joust of the Quintana, featuring 600 knights in full costume. Annually, the second Sunday in September.

"LAW & ORDER" TV PREMIERE: ANNIVERSARY. Sept 13, 1990. Filmed on location at New York City, "Law & Order" shows the interaction between the police and the district attorney's office in dealing with a crime. Almost the entire cast has changed over the life of this program and has included Michael Moriarty (Assistant District Attorney Benjamin Stone), Sam Waterston (ADA Jack McCoy), Jerry Orbach (Detective Lennie Briscoe), Christopher Noth (Detective Mike Logan), Jesse L. Martin (Detective Edward Green) and many others. "Law & Order" has spun off two other series: "Law & Order: Special Victims Unit" and "Law & Order: Criminal Intent."

"THE MUPPET SHOW" TV PREMIERE: ANNIVERSARY. Sept 13, 1976. This comedy-variety show was hosted by Kermit the Frog of "Sesame Street." The new Jim Henson puppet characters included Miss Piggy, Fozzie Bear and The Great Gonzo. Many celebrities appeared as guests on the show, which was broadcast in more than 100 countries. The show ran until 1981. "Muppet Babies" was a Saturday morning cartoon that ran from 1984 until 1992. *The Muppet Movie* (1979) was the first of five films based on "The Muppet Show." In 1996 a new show, "Muppets Tonight!," was created.

NATIONAL ASSISTED LIVING WEEK. Sept 13–19. A weeklong observance designed to raise awareness of the role assisted living plays in serving the nation's elderly. Annually, Grandparents' Day through the following Saturday. For info: Natl Center for Assisted Living, 1201 L St NW, Washington, DC 20005. Phone: (202) 842-4444. Fax: (202) 842-3860.

NATIONAL CELIAC AWARENESS DAY. Sept 13. For info: Celiac Sprue Assn/USA, PO Box 31700, Omaha, NE 68131-0700. Phone: (402) 643-4101 or (877) CSA-4CSA. Fax: (402) 643-4108. E-mail: celiacs@csaceliacs.org. Web: www.csaceliacs.org.

NATIONAL CONSTITUTION CENTER CONSTITUTION WEEK. Sept 13–19. To celebrate and commemorate the signing of the US Constitution Sept 17, 1787. The National Constitution Center hosts special events and activities. Est attendance: 50,000. For info: Natl Constitution Center, 525 Arch St, Independence Mall, Philadelphia, PA 19106. Phone: (215) 409-6600. Web: www.constitutioncenter.org.

NATIONAL GRANDPARENTS' DAY. Sept 13. To honor grandparents, to give grandparents an opportunity to show love for their children's children and to help children become aware of the strength, information and guidance older people can offer. Annually, the first Sunday after Labor Day.

✦ **NATIONAL HISTORICALLY BLACK COLLEGES AND UNIVERSITIES WEEK.** Sept 13–19 (tentative).

NATIONAL URBAN EDEN DAY. Sept 13. A holiday dedicated to bringing Eden into the city. A day to increase awareness of the human-friendly and dog-friendly use of urban spaces and to encourage the inclusion of nature in all aspects of urban life. Annually, the second Sunday of September. For info: Ami Moore, National Urban Eden Day, 910 W Van Buren #242, Chicago, IL 60607. Phone: (847) 284-7760. E-mail: doggiedoright911@yahoo.com. Web: www.dogdoright.com/urban-eden-day.htm.

NORTHEAST MISSOURI TRIATHLON. Sept 13. Thousand Hills State Park, Kirksville, MO. Swim 3/4 mile, bike 18 miles, run 5 miles. USA Triathlon sanctioned. Qualifier for International Course Nationals. Annually, the Sunday after Labor Day. Est attendance: 350. For info: ATSU-TCC, 210 S Osteopathy, Kirksville, MO 63501. Phone: (660) 626-2213. Fax: (660) 626-2071. E-mail: lcrossgrove@atsu.edu. Web: www.nemotriathlon.org.

PEDDLER'S VILLAGE SCARECROW CONTEST AND OUTDOOR DISPLAY. Sept 13–Oct 25. Peddler's Village, Lahaska, PA. Contestants compete for $4,900 in cash prizes. Categories include: "A Scarecrow Whirligig": a scarecrow that makes noise and moves with the wind, "An Extraordinary Contemporary Scarecrow": an imaginative piece created to give a good scare in the garden, "A Traditional Scarecrow": an outstanding example of the American Scarecrow and "The Amateur Scarecrow": for those who haven't won previously. Free registration. Est attendance: 650,000. For info: Peddler's Village, Routes 202 and 263, Lahaska, PA 18931. Phone: (215) 794-4000. Fax: (215) 794-4001. Web: www.peddlersvillage.com.

PERSHING, JOHN J.: BIRTH ANNIVERSARY. Sept 13, 1860. US Army general who commanded the American Expeditionary Force (AEF) during WWI, Pershing was born at Laclede, MO. The AEF, as part of the inter-Allied offensive, successfully assaulted the Saint-Mihiel salient in September 1918 and later that month quickly regrouped for the Meuse-Argonne operation that led to the Armistice of Nov 11, 1918. Pershing died July 15, 1948, at Washington, DC.

REED, WALTER: BIRTH ANNIVERSARY. Sept 13, 1851. American army physician, especially known for his Yellow Fever research. Born at Gloucester County, VA, he served as an army surgeon for more than 20 years and as a professor at the Army Medical College. He died at Washington, DC, Nov 22, 1902. The US Army's general hospital at Washington, DC, is named in his honor.

"SCOOBY-DOO, WHERE ARE YOU?" TV PREMIERE: 40th ANNIVERSARY. Sept 13, 1969. A tremendously popular Saturday morning cartoon, Hanna-Barbera's show featured four wacky kids and lovable Great Dane Scooby-Doo solving spooky (and often hilarious) mysteries. Fred, Daphne and Velma usually do the work, while Shaggy (originally voiced by radio personality Casey Kasem) and Scooby-Doo look for something to eat. A live-action feature film was released in 2002 starring Freddie Prinze, Jr, Sarah Michelle Gellar, Matthew Lillard, Linda Cardellini and a digital Scooby.

"SOAP" TV PREMIERE: ANNIVERSARY. Sept 13, 1977. "Soap" was a prime-time comedy that parodied soap operas. It had plots that were funny (e.g., Corinne's baby is possessed by the devil), controversial (e.g., Billy joins a cult) and downright bizarre (e.g., Burt is abducted by aliens). The show focused on two families, the wealthy Tates and the middle-class Campbells. It starred Katherine Helmond, Robert Mandan, Jennifer Salt, Diana Canova, Jimmy Baio, Robert Guillaume, Cathryn Damon, Richard Mulligan, Ted Wass, Billy Crystal, Richard Libertini, Kathryn Reynolds, Robert Urich, Arthur Peterson, Roscoe Lee Browne and Jay Johnson. Rod Roddy was the announcer who recapped what had happened on the previous episode.

"STAR-SPANGLED BANNER" INSPIRED: ANNIVERSARY. Sept 13–14, 1814. On the night of Sept 13, Francis Scott Key was aboard a ship that was delayed in Baltimore harbor by the British attack there on Fort McHenry. Key had no choice but to anxiously watch the battle. That experience and seeing the American flag still flying over the fort the next morning inspired him to pen the verses that, coupled with the tune of a popular drinking song, became our official national anthem in 1931, 117 years after the words were written.

UNITED KINGDOM: BATTLE OF BRITAIN WEEK. Sept 13–19. Annually, the week of September containing Battle of Britain Day (Sept 15).

US CAPITAL ESTABLISHED AT NEW YORK CITY: ANNIVERSARY. Sept 13, 1788. Congress picked New York, NY, as the location of the new US government in place of Philadelphia, which had served as the capital up until this time. In 1790 the capital moved back to Philadelphia for ten years, before moving permanently to Washington, DC.

Birthdays Today

Fiona Apple, 32, singer, born New York, NY, Sept 13, 1977.

Jacqueline Bisset, 65, actress (*Rich & Famous, The Deep*), born Weybridge, England, Sept 13, 1944.

Peter Cetera, 65, singer (former lead singer of Chicago), songwriter, born Chicago, IL, Sept 13, 1944.

Robert Indiana, 81, artist (*As I Opened Fire*), born New Castle, IA, Sept 13, 1928.

Michael Johnson, 42, track athlete, born Dallas, TX, Sept 13, 1967.

Richard Kiel, 70, actor (*The Longest Yard, Silver Streak, The Spy Who Loved Me*), born Detroit, MI, Sept 13, 1939.

Judith Martin, 71, author, journalist ("Miss Manners"), born Washington, DC, Sept 13, 1938.

Daisuke Matsuzake, 29, baseball player, born Tokyo, Japan, Sept 13, 1980.

Stella McCartney, 38, fashion designer, born London, England, Sept 13, 1971.

Ben Savage, 29, actor ("Boy Meets World"), born Chicago, IL, Sept 13, 1980.

Fred Silverman, 72, TV producer, born New York, NY, Sept 13, 1937.

Jean Smart, 50, stage and screen actress ("24," "Designing Women"), born Seattle, WA, Sept 13, 1959.

Bernabe (Bernie) Williams, 41, baseball player, born San Juan, Puerto Rico, Sept 13, 1968.

September 2009

S	M	T	W	T	F	S
		1	2	3	4	5
6	7	8	9	10	11	12
13	14	15	16	17	18	19
20	21	22	23	24	25	26
27	28	29	30			

September 14 — Monday

DAY 257 **108 REMAINING**

DANTE ALIGHIERI: DEATH ANNIVERSARY. Sept 14, 1321. Italian poet, author of the *Divine Comedy*, died at Ravenna, Italy. He was born in May 1265 (exact date unknown) at Florence, Italy.

"THE GOLDEN GIRLS" TV PREMIERE: ANNIVERSARY. Sept 14, 1985. This comedy starred Bea Arthur, Betty White, Rue McClanahan and Estelle Getty as four divorced/widowed women sharing a house in Florida during their golden years. The last episode aired Sept 14, 1992, but the show remains popular in syndication.

"HAVE GUN WILL TRAVEL" TV PREMIERE: ANNIVERSARY. Sept 14, 1957. "Have Gun, Will Travel . . ." So read the business card of Paladin (Richard Boone), a loner whose professional services were available for a price. This half-hour Western also featured Kam Tong as his servant, Hey Boy. The show was extremely popular and ranked in the top five for most of its run.

"IRONSIDE" TV PREMIERE: ANNIVERSARY. Sept 14, 1967. This crime series starred Raymond Burr as Robert T. Ironside, Chief of Detectives for the San Francisco Police Department (he was in a wheelchair, paralyzed from an assassination attempt). Also featured were Don Galloway as his assistant, Detective Sergeant Ed Brown; Barbara Anderson as Officer Eve Whitfield; Don Mitchell as Mark Sanger, Ironside's personal assistant; Gene Lyons as Commissioner Dennis Randall; Elizabeth Baur as Officer Fran Belding; and Joan Pringle as Diana, Mark's wife.

LINE DANCE WEEK. Sept 14–19. A week to celebrate the line dance! Line dance is a great way to exercise and to meet people. Annually, the second Monday in September through the second Saturday. For info: Shirley Mitchell, 19769 Murray Hill, Detroit, MI 48235. Phone: (313) 272-9832. Fax: (313) 273-6337. E-mail: smitc87213@aol.com.

McKINLEY, WILLIAM: DEATH ANNIVERSARY. Sept 14, 1901. President William McKinley was shot at Buffalo, NY, Sept 6, 1901. He died eight days later. Assassin Leon Czolgosz was executed Oct 29, 1901.

NATIONAL BOSS/EMPLOYEE EXCHANGE DAY. Sept 14. To help bosses and employees appreciate each other by sharing each other's point of view for a day. Annually, the first Monday after Labor Day. For info: A.C. Vierow, Box 71, Clio, MI 48420-0071.

NATIONAL INVISIBLE CHRONIC ILLNESS AWARENESS WEEK. Sept 14–20. San Diego, CA. Activities include online events and outreach to communities and churches, encouraging them to participate in calling attention to reaching out to those with chronic illness. For info: Lisa Copen, PO Box 502928, San Diego, CA 92150. Phone: (888) 751-7378. Fax: (800) 933-1078. E-mail: rest@restministries.org. Web: www.invisibleillness.com.

NICARAGUA: BATTLE OF SAN JACINTO DAY. Sept 14. National holiday. Commemorates the 1856 defeat of US invader William Walker.

PENNSYLVANIA RV & CAMPING SHOW. Sept 14–20. Hersheypark® Entertainment Complex, Hershey, PA. 41st annual. America's largest RV show, with more than 1,300 RVs on display. The equivalent of 26 football fields of RVs! Sept 14–15 are for the trade only; show is open to the public Sept 16–20. Est attendance: 40,000. For info: PRVCA, 4000 Trindle Rd, Camp Hill, PA 17011. Phone: (888) 303-2887. Fax: (717) 303-0297. E-mail: rvcamping@prvca.org. Web: www.largestRVShow.com.

SANGER, MARGARET (HIGGINS): BIRTH ANNIVERSARY. Sept 14, 1879. Feminist, nurse and founder of the birth control movement in the US. Born at Corning, NY. (Note: birth year not entirely certain because, apparently, Sanger often used a later date when obliged to divulge her birthday. Best evidence now points to Sept 14, 1879, rather than the frequently used 1883 date.) She died at Tucson, AZ, Sept 6, 1966.

SETON, ELIZABETH ANN: CANONIZATION: ANNIVERSARY. Sept 14, 1975. Elizabeth Ann Seton became the first native-born American to be canonized. She was declared a saint in 1974 by Pope Paul VI.

SOLO TRANSATLANTIC BALLOON CROSSING: 25th ANNIVERSARY. Sept 14–18, 1984. Joe W. Kittinger, 56-year-old balloonist, left Caribou, ME, in a 10-story-tall helium-filled balloon named *Rosie O'Grady's Balloon of Peace* Sept 14, 1984, crossed the Atlantic Ocean and reached the French coast, above the town of Capbreton, in bad weather Sept 17 at 4:29 PM, EDT. He crash-landed amid wind and rain near Savone, Italy, at 8:08 AM, EDT, Sept 18. Kittinger suffered a broken ankle when he was thrown from the balloon's gondola during the landing. His nearly 84-hour flight, covering about 3,535 miles, was the first solo balloon crossing of the Atlantic Ocean and a record distance for a solo balloon flight.

SUBSTITUTE TEACHER APPRECIATION WEEK. Sept 14–19. Although substitute teachers get no sick days or respect, they teach when the regular teacher cannot and continually adjust to different classroom situations. Annually, the third week of September. For info: Dorothy Zjawin, Dir, 61 W Colfax Ave, Roselle Park, NJ 07204. Phone: (908) 241-6241.

"THE WALTONS" TV PREMIERE: ANNIVERSARY. Sept 14, 1972. This epitome of the family drama spawned nearly a dozen knockoffs during its nine-year run on CBS. The drama was based on creator/writer Earl Hamner Jr's experiences growing up during the Depression in rural Virginia. It began as the TV movie "The Homecoming," which was turned into a weekly series covering the years 1933–43. The cast went through numerous changes through the years; the principals were: Michael Learned as Olivia Walton, mother of the clan; Ralph Waite as John Walton, father; Richard Thomas as John-Boy, eldest son; Jon Walmsley as son Jason; Judy Norton-Taylor as daughter Mary Ellen; Eric Scott as son Ben; Mary Beth McDonough as daughter Erin; David W. Harper as son Jim-Bob and Kami Cotler as daughter Elizabeth. The Walton grandparents were played by Ellen Corby and Will Geer. The last telecast aired Aug 20, 1981.

WILSON, JAMES: BIRTH ANNIVERSARY. Sept 14, 1742. Signer of the Declaration of Independence and one of the first associate justices of the US Supreme Court. Born at Fifeshire, Scotland, he died Aug 21, 1798, at Edenton, NC.

Birthdays Today

Zoe Caldwell, 76, actress (*Medea, The Prime of Miss Jean Brodie*), born Melbourne, Australia, Sept 14, 1933.

Dan Cortese, 42, actor ("Veronica's Closet," *Public Enemies*), born Sewickley, PA, Sept 14, 1967.

Mary Crosby, 50, actress ("Dallas," *Tapeheads*), born Los Angeles, CA, Sept 14, 1959.

Faith Ford, 45, actress ("Hope & Faith," "Murphy Brown"), born Alexandria, LA, Sept 14, 1964.

Joey Heatherton, 65, actress (*Cry Baby, Bluebeard*), born Rockville Centre, NY, Sept 14, 1944.

Walter Koenig, 73, actor, writer, director, producer ("Star Trek" and *Star Trek* movies), born Chicago, IL, Sept 14, 1936.

Dmitry Medvedev, 44, president of Russia, born Leningrad, USSR, Sept 14, 1965.

Kate Millett, 75, feminist, writer (*Sexual Politics, Flying*), born St. Paul, MN, Sept 14, 1934.

Sam Neill, 62, actor (*My Brilliant Career, Jurassic Park, The Piano*), born Northern Ireland, Sept 14, 1947.

Nicol Williamson, 71, actor (*Robin and Marian, Excalibur*), born Hamilton, Scotland, Sept 14, 1938.

Amy Winehouse, 26, singer, born London, England, Sept 14, 1983.

September 15 — Tuesday

DAY 258 **107 REMAINING**

ACUFF, ROY: BIRTH ANNIVERSARY. Sept 15, 1903. Grand Ole Opry "King of Country Music" Roy Acuff was born at Maynardville, TN. Singer and fiddler Acuff (who was cofounder of Acuff-Rose Publishing Company, the leading publisher of country music) was a regular host on weekly Grand Ole Opry broadcasts. He frequently appeared at the Opry with his group, the Smoky Mountain Boys. In December of 1991 Acuff became the first living member elected to the Country Music Hall of Fame. Some of his more famous songs were "The Wabash Cannonball" (his theme song), "Pins and Needles (In My Heart)" and "Night Train to Memphis." Roy Acuff died Nov 23, 1992, at Nashville, TN.

"BACHELOR FATHER" TV PREMIERE: ANNIVERSARY. Sept 15, 1957. John Forsythe (Bentley Gregg) and Noreen Corcoran (Kelly Gregg) starred in this sitcom about a bachelor attorney's life turning upside-down after his orphaned niece moves in with him. The last episode aired Sept 25, 1962. Supporting players included: Sammee Tong as Peter Tong, the butler, and Jimmy Boyd as Kelly's boyfriend, Howard Meechim.

"CHiPS" TV PREMIERE: ANNIVERSARY. Sept 15, 1977. A popular action-packed NBC police series depicting cases and chases of the motorcycle-riding California Highway Patrol. The show starred Erik Estrada as Francis "Ponch" Poncherello and Larry Wilcox as Jon Baker, two quick-witted cops. Wilcox left the show, and Estrada's new partner, Bobby "Hot Dog" Nelson, was played by Tom Reilly. The last telecast aired July 17, 1983.

CHRISTIE, AGATHA: BIRTH ANNIVERSARY. Sept 15, 1890. English author of nearly a hundred books (mysteries, drama, poetry and nonfiction), born at Torquay, England. Died at Wallingford, England, Jan 12, 1976. "Every murderer," she wrote, in *The Mysterious Affair at Styles*, "is probably somebody's old friend."

"COLUMBO" TV PREMIERE: ANNIVERSARY. Sept 15, 1971. "Columbo," based on a 1968 made-for-TV movie, entered the lineup of NBC's "Mystery Movie" series on this date. Peter Falk starred as one of TV's great characters, Lieutenant Columbo, the crime-solving policeman dressed in rumpled raincoat and bearing a chewed-up cigar. In almost every episode, Columbo latches himself onto the main suspect, usually a polished sophisticate in comparison to Columbo's seeming simpleness, and nags him or her to death with questions and comments such as "But one thing bothers me, sir." The series ended in 1978, but reemerged in the form of periodic movies beginning in 1989.

September 2009

S	M	T	W	T	F	S
		1	2	3	4	5
6	7	8	9	10	11	12
13	14	15	16	17	18	19
20	21	22	23	24	25	26
27	28	29	30			

COOPER, JAMES FENIMORE: BIRTH ANNIVERSARY. Sept 15, 1789. American novelist, historian and social critic, born at Burlington, NJ, James Fenimore Cooper was one of the earliest American writers to develop a native American literary tradition. His most popular works are the five novels comprising *The Leatherstocking Tales,* featuring the exploits of one of the truly unique American fictional characters, Natty Bumppo. These novels, *The Deerslayer, The Last of the Mohicans, The Pathfinder, The Pioneers* and *The Prairie,* chronicle Natty Bumppo's continuing flight away from the rapid settlement of America. Other works, including *The Monikins* and *Satanstoe,* reveal him as an astute critic of American life. He died Sept 14, 1851, at Cooperstown, NY, the town founded by his father.

COSTA RICA: INDEPENDENCE DAY. Sept 15. National holiday. Gained independence from Spain in 1821.

EL SALVADOR: INDEPENDENCE DAY. Sept 15. National holiday. Gained independence from Spain in 1821.

FIRST NATIONAL CONVENTION FOR BLACKS: ANNIVERSARY. Sept 15, 1830. The first national convention for blacks was held at Bethel Church, Philadelphia, PA. The convention was called to find ways to better the condition of black people and was attended by delegates from seven states. Bishop Richard Allen was elected as the first convention president.

GREENPEACE FOUNDED: ANNIVERSARY. Sept 15, 1971. The environmental organization Greenpeace, committed to a green and peaceful world, was founded by 12 members of the Don't Make a Wave committee of Vancouver, BC, Canada, when the boat *Phyllis Cormack* sailed to Amchitka, AK, to protest US nuclear testing. Greenpeace's basic principle is "that determined individuals can alter the actions and purposes of even the overwhelmingly powerful by 'bearing witness'—drawing attention to an environmental abuse through their mere unwavering presence, whatever the risk."

GUATEMALA: INDEPENDENCE DAY. Sept 15. National holiday. Gained independence from Spain in 1821.

HONDURAS: INDEPENDENCE DAY. Sept 15. National holiday. Gained independence from Spain in 1821.

HUSKER HARVEST DAYS. Sept 15–17. Grand Island, NE. The largest irrigated working agricultural show on a permanent site in the United States. 80 acres of exhibits, 700 acres of field demonstrations and more. Annually, the Tuesday–Thursday of the second full week of September. Est attendance: 50,000. For info: Renee Seifert, Grand Island/Hall County CVB, 2424 S Locust St, Ste C, Grand Island, NE 68801. Phone: (308) 382-4400. Fax: (308) 382-4908. E-mail: info@visitgrandisland.com. Web: www.visitgrand island.com.

"I SPY" TV PREMIERE: ANNIVERSARY. Sept 15, 1965. Bill Cosby made television history as the first African American actor starring in a major dramatic role in this spy series. Cosby played Alexander "Scotty" Scott, an intellectual spy with a cover as a tennis trainer. Robert Culp played Kelly Robinson, the "tennis pro" and Scotty's partner in espionage. The series was notable for filming worldwide.

KENTUCKY BOURBON FESTIVAL. Sept 15–20. Bardstown, KY. Visit the "Bourbon Capital of the World" and celebrate the history and making of Kentucky's finest product, Kentucky bourbon. Enjoy tours, displays, music, food, competitions and much more. Est attendance: 55,000. For info: Pamela Gover, Kentucky Bourbon Festival, One Court Square, Bardstown, KY 40004. Phone: (502) 348-3623. Fax: (502) 348-3403. E-mail: info@kybourbonfestival .com. Web: www.kybourbonfestival.com.

"THE LONE RANGER" TV PREMIERE: 60th ANNIVERSARY. Sept 15, 1949. This character was created for a radio serial in 1933 by George W. Trendle. The famous masked man was the alter ego of John Reid, a Texas Ranger who was the only survivor of an ambush. He was nursed back to health by his Native American friend, Tonto. Both men traveled around the West on their trusty steeds, Silver and Scout, fighting injustice. Clayton Moore played the Lone Ranger/John Reid and Jay Silverheels costarred as Tonto. The theme music was Rossini's "William Tell Overture." The last episode aired Sept 12, 1957.

✦ **NATIONAL HISPANIC HERITAGE MONTH.** Sept 15–Oct 15. Presidential Proclamation. Beginning in 1989, always issued for Sept 15–Oct 15 of each year (PL100–402 of Aug 17, 1988). Previously issued each year for the week including Sept 15 and 16 since 1968 at request (PL90–498 of Sept 17, 1968).

NETHERLANDS: PRINSJESDAG. Sept 15. Official opening of parliament at The Hague. The queen of the Netherlands, by tradition, rides in a golden coach to the hall of knights for the annual opening of parliament. Annually, on the third Tuesday in September.

NICARAGUA: INDEPENDENCE DAY. Sept 15. National holiday. Gained independence from Spain in 1821.

QUARTERLY ESTIMATED FEDERAL INCOME TAX PAYERS' DUE DATE. Sept 15. For those individuals whose fiscal year is the calendar year and who make quarterly estimated federal income tax payments, today is one of the due dates. (Jan 15, Apr 15, June 15 and Sept 15, 2009.)

16th STREET BAPTIST CHURCH BOMBING: ANNIVERSARY. Sept 15, 1963. In a horrific episode of the civil rights struggle, a bomb blast in the basement of the 16th Street Baptist Church in Birmingham, AL, killed four girls preparing for church: Denise McNair, Carole Robertson, Cynthia Wesley and Addie Mae Collins. Previously, the church had been the center for marches led by Dr. Martin Luther King, Jr. Three suspects were brought to trial in 1977, 2001 and 2002 and found guilty.

SPACE MILESTONE: *ARIANE-3* (ESA). Sept 15, 1987. European Space Agency rocket carrying two (Australian and European) communications satellites into Earth's orbit marked the re-entry of western nations into commercial space projects. Launched this date from Kourou, French Guiana, with Arianespace, a private company operating the rocket for the 13-nation European Space Agency.

TAFT, WILLIAM HOWARD: BIRTH ANNIVERSARY. Sept 15, 1857. The 27th president of the US was born at Cincinnati, OH. His term of office was Mar 4, 1909–Mar 3, 1913. Following his presidency he became a law professor at Yale University until his appointment as Chief Justice of the US Supreme Court in 1921. Died at Washington, DC, Mar 8, 1930, and was buried at Arlington National Cemetery.

TINKER TO EVERS TO CHANCE: FIRST DOUBLE PLAY ANNIVERSARY. Sept 15, 1902. Chicago Cubs' shortstop Joe Tinker, second baseman Johnny Evers and first baseman Frank Chance recorded their first double play together on this date. This was two days after they took the field for the first time in this configuration, and the Cubs went on to beat the Cincinnati Reds, 6–3. The threesome were later immortalized in Franklin Adams's poem "Baseball's Sad Lexicon." Tinker, Evers and Chance were inducted together into the Baseball Hall of Fame in 1946. See also: "'Baseball's Sad Lexicon' Published: Anniversary" (July 10).

UNITED KINGDOM: BATTLE OF BRITAIN DAY. Sept 15. Commemorates end of biggest daylight bombing raid of Britain by German Luftwaffe, in 1940. Said to have been the turning point against Hitler's siege of Britain in WWII.

UNITED NATIONS: OPENING DAY OF GENERAL ASSEMBLY. Sept 15. The 61st session. Annually, the third Tuesday in September. For info: United Nations, Dept of Public Info, New York, NY 10017. Web: www.un.org.

US TROOPS ENTER GERMANY: 65th ANNIVERSARY. Sept 15, 1944. US troops of the VII and V Corps reached the southwestern frontier of Germany. The war had finally moved into the Third Reich's backyard.

***USA TODAY* FIRST PUBLISHED: ANNIVERSARY.** Sept 15, 1982. Media corporation Gannett published a new kind of daily—the "Nation's Newspaper"—that featured general interest articles for a national audience on this date.

WRAY, FAY: BIRTH ANNIVERSARY. Sept 15, 1907. Hollywood's "Scream Queen" was born in Alberta, Canada, on this day. The star of numerous silent films (notably Erich von Stroheim's *The Wedding March*), Wray made her mark in 1930s thrillers—and then became a pop culture icon through her role as Ann Darrow, the giant ape's obsession in the 1933 film *King Kong*. Wray died at New York City, Aug 8, 2004. See also: "*King Kong* Film Premiere: Anniversary" (Mar 2).

Birthdays Today

Dave Annable, 30, actor ("Brothers & Sisters"), born Suffern, NY, Sept 15, 1979.

Jackie Cooper, 87, actor (*Our Gang* shorts, "The People's Choice"), producer, born Los Angeles, CA, Sept 15, 1922.

Norm Crosby, 82, comedian, born Boston, MA, Sept 15, 1927.

Sherman Douglas, 43, former basketball player, born Washington, DC, Sept 15, 1966.

Prince Harry (Henry Charles Albert David), 25, second son of Prince Charles and Princess Diana, born London, England, Sept 15, 1984.

Tommy Lee Jones, 63, actor (Oscar for *The Fugitive*; *Coal Miner's Daughter, Men in Black, No Country for Old Men*), born San Saba, TX, Sept 15, 1946.

Daniel Constantine (Dan) Marino, Jr, 48, former football player, born Pittsburgh, PA, Sept 15, 1961.

Carmen Maura, 64, actress (*Women on the Verge of a Nervous Breakdown*), born Madrid, Spain, Sept 15, 1945.

Heidi Montag, 23, television personality ("The Hills," "Laguna Beach"), born Crested Butte, CO, Sept 15, 1986.

Jessye Norman, 64, soprano, opera singer, born Augusta, GA, Sept 15, 1945.

Merlin Jay Olsen, 69, Hall of Fame football player, sportscaster, actor ("Little House on the Prairie"), born Logan, UT, Sept 15, 1940.

Gaylord Jackson Perry, 71, Hall of Fame baseball player, born Williamston, NC, Sept 15, 1938.

Oliver Stone, 63, director (*Platoon, JFK, Wall Street*), screenwriter, born New York, NY, Sept 15, 1946.

September 16 — Wednesday

DAY 259 — **106 REMAINING**

ANNE BRADSTREET DAY. Sept 16. An official date proclaimed by the governor of the Commonwealth of Massachusetts to honor Anne Bradstreet, America's first poet, who is also recognized as the first published woman poet in the English language. Anne Bradstreet was born in 1612 in England and came to America in 1630. Unbeknownst to Anne, her brother-in-law took some of her poetry back to England where it was published in 1650 as *The Tenth Muse Lately Sprung Up in America.* Subsequent editions were also published in Boston. She died at Old Andover, MA, Sept 16, 1672. For info: Director, Stevens Memorial Library, 345 Main St, PO Box 8, North Andover, MA 01845. Phone: (978) 688-9505. Fax: (978) 688-9507. E-mail: mquinn@mvlc.org.

CHEROKEE STRIP DAY: ANNIVERSARY. Sept 16, 1893. Optional school holiday, Oklahoma. Greatest "run" for Oklahoma land in 1893.

"FRASIER" TV PREMIERE: ANNIVERSARY. Sept 16, 1993. In this acclaimed spin-off of "Cheers," psychiatrist Dr. Frasier Crane (Kelsey Grammer) has moved to Seattle, where he dispenses advice on the radio, produced by Roz Doyle (Peri Gilpin). He lives with his ex-cop father Martin (John Mahoney) and Martin's physical therapist Daphne Moon (Jane Leeves). His brother, Dr. Niles Crane (David Hyde Pierce), frequently asks for Frasier's advice about his love life. The show, which was a five-time Emmy winner for Outstanding Comedy Series (not to mention numerous Emmys for cast and crew), finished its run in 2004.

GENERAL MOTORS: FOUNDING ANNIVERSARY. Sept 16, 1908. The giant automobile manufacturing company was founded by William Crapo "Billy" Durant, a Flint, MI, entrepreneur.

GOLDEN ASPEN MOTORCYCLE RALLY. Sept 16–20. Ruidoso, NM. Trade show, bike shows, riding tours, skill events, parade, awards banquet, stunt shows and thousands in prizes. Est attendance: 35,000. For info: Golden Aspen Rally Assn, PO Box 1467, Ruidoso, NM 88355. Phone: (800) 452-8045. E-mail: info@motorcyclerally.com. Web: www.motorcyclerally.com.

GREAT SEAL OF THE US: ANNIVERSARY. Sept 16, 1782. On this date the Great Seal of the United States was, for the first time, impressed upon an official document. That document authorized George Washington to negotiate a prisoner of war agreement with the British. See also: "Great Seal of the United States: Anniversary" (Jan 28 and July 4).

"MANNIX" TV PREMIERE: ANNIVERSARY. Sept 16, 1967. Mike Connors starred as Joe Mannix, a Los Angeles private investigator working for the computer organization Intertect, in this long-running CBS crime series. Joseph Campanella played his boss, Lou Wickersham, during the first season. The show then changed format with Mannix setting up his own agency. The new cast members were Gail Fisher as Peggy Fair, his secretary, Robert Reed as Lieutenant Adam Tobias and Ward Wood as Lieutenant Art Malcolm.

MAYFLOWER DAY: ANNIVERSARY. Sept 16, 1620. Anniversary of the departure of the *Mayflower* from Plymouth, England, with 102 passengers and a small crew. Vicious storms were encountered en route, which caused serious doubt about the wisdom of continuing, but the ship reached Provincetown, MA, Nov 21, and discharged the Pilgrims at Plymouth, MA, Dec 26, 1620.

MEXICO: INDEPENDENCE DAY. Sept 16. National Day. The official celebration begins at 11 PM, Sept 15 and continues through Sept 16. On the night of the 15th, the president of Mexico steps onto the balcony of the National Palace at Mexico City and voices the same "El Grito" (Cry for Freedom) that Father Hidalgo gave on the night of Sept 15, 1810, that began Mexico's rebellion from Spain.

MIDDLEMARK, MARVIN: 90th BIRTH ANNIVERSARY. Sept 16, 1919. Marvin Middlemark was born at Long Island, NY. His passion for inventing and tinkering led to many inventions, most of which enjoyed little commercial success, like the water-driven automatic potato peeler. But it was as the inventor of a device to improve TV reception, known as "rabbit ears," that he became successful. He died Sept 14, 1989, at Old Westbury, NY.

NATIONAL CHAMPIONSHIP AIR RACES. Sept 16–20. Reno, NV. 46th annual. Six classes of races—Unlimited, Sport, Jet, Formula One, T-6 and Biplane—compete. The event includes thrilling aerobatics and displays of military, vintage and contemporary aircraft. Est attendance: 223,000. For info: National Championship Air Races, 14501 Mt Anderson St, Reno, NV 89506. Phone: (775) 972-6663. Web: www.airrace.org.

September 2009

S	M	T	W	T	F	S
		1	2	3	4	5
6	7	8	9	10	11	12
13	14	15	16	17	18	19
20	21	22	23	24	25	26
27	28	29	30			

NATIONAL GUITAR FLAT-PICKING CHAMPIONSHIPS AND WALNUT VALLEY FESTIVAL. Sept 16–20. Cowley County Fairgrounds, Winfield, KS. The Walnut River is the site of this 38th annual family event featuring four stages with eight contests, at least 14 workshops and many first-class concerts. The Walnut Valley Arts and Crafts Festival features handmade instruments and a large variety of arts and crafts items, both ornamental and functional. All-weather facilities. Est attendance: 45,000. For info: Walnut Valley Assn, Bob Redford, PO Box 245, Winfield, KS 67156. Phone: (620) 221-3250. Fax: (620) 221-3109. E-mail: hq@wvfest.com. Web: www.wvfest.com.

OLD IRONSIDES SAVED BY POEM: ANNIVERSARY. Sept 16, 1830. Alarmed by a newspaper report that Congress was to have the USS *Constitution* (popularly known as "Old Ironsides") sent to a scrap yard, law student Oliver Wendell Holmes dashed off a poem in protest. The poem began "Ay, tear her tattered ensign down!/Long has it waved on high,/And many an eye has danced to see/That banner in the sky." "Old Ironsides," published anonymously this day in the *Boston Daily Advertisor*, was to stir up national outrage as newspaper after newspaper reprinted it. Congress instead appropriated money for the frigate's reconstruction, and Old Ironsides still floats today. (Some historians think that Holmes never actually saw the ship he saved.) See also: "Old Ironsides Launched: Anniversary" (Oct 21).

PALESTINIAN MASSACRE: ANNIVERSARY. Sept 16, 1982. Christian militiamen (the Phalangists) entered Sabra and Shatila, two Palestinian refugee camps in West Beirut. They began open shooting and by Sept 18 hundreds of Palestinians, including elderly men, women and children, were dead. Phalangists had demanded the blood of Palestinians since the assassination of their president, Bashir Gemayel, on Sept 14. Survivors of the massacre said they had not seen Israeli forces inside the camp; however, they claimed Israelis sealed off boundaries to the camps and allowed Christian militiamen to enter.

PANIZZI, ANTHONY: BIRTH ANNIVERSARY. Sept 16, 1797. Sir Anthony Panizzi, the only librarian ever hanged in effigy, was born Antonio Genesio Maria Panizzi at Brescello, Italy. As a young man he joined a forbidden Italian patriotic society that advocated the overthrow of the oppressive Austrians who then controlled most of northern Italy. Tried in absentia by an Austrian court in 1820, he was sentenced to death and all his property was confiscated. He fled to England in 1823, learned the language and by 1831 was employed in the British Museum where, in 1856, he was named principal librarian. Later described as the "prince of librarians," Panizzi died at London, England, Apr 8, 1879.

PAPUA NEW GUINEA: INDEPENDENCE DAY. Sept 16. National holiday. Commemorates independence from Australian administration in 1975.

PARKMAN, FRANCIS: BIRTH ANNIVERSARY. Sept 16, 1823. American historian, author of *The Oregon Trail*, was born at Boston, MA, and died there Nov 8, 1893.

TORQUEMADA, TOMAS DE: DEATH ANNIVERSARY. Sept 16, 1498. One of history's most malevolent persons, feared and hated by millions. As Inquisitor-General of Spain, he ordered burning at the stake for more than 10,000 persons and burning in effigy for another 7,000 (according to 18th-century estimates). Torquemada persuaded Ferdinand and Isabella to rid Spain of the Jews. More than a million families were driven from the country and Spain suffered a commercial decline from which it never recovered. Torquemada was born at Valladolid, Spain, in 1420 (exact date unknown) and died at Avila, Spain.

UNITED NATIONS: INTERNATIONAL DAY FOR THE PRESERVATION OF THE OZONE LAYER. Sept 16. On Dec 19, 1994, the General Assembly proclaimed this day to commemorate the date in 1987 on which Montreal Protocol on Substances that Deplete the Ozone Layer was signed (Res 49/114). States are invited to devote the Day to promote, at the national level, activities in accordance with the objectives of the Protocol. The ozone layer filters sunlight and prevents the adverse effects of ultraviolet radiation from reaching the Earth's surface, thereby preserving life on the planet. For info: United Nations, Dept of Public Info, Public Inquiries Unit, Rm GA-57, New York, NY 10017. Phone: (212) 963-4475. E-mail: inquiries@un.org. Web: www.un.org.

Birthdays Today

Marc Anthony, 40, singer, actor (*Bringing Out the Dead*), born New York, NY, Sept 16, 1969.

Lauren Bacall, 85, actress (*Applause, Woman of the Year, Key Largo*), born Betty Joan Perske at New York, NY, Sept 16, 1924.

Elgin Gay Baylor, 75, Hall of Fame basketball player, former coach, born Washington, DC, Sept 16, 1934.

Ed Begley, Jr, 60, actor ("St. Elsewhere," "Seventh Heaven," "Six Feet Under," *A Mighty Wind*), born Los Angeles, CA, Sept 16, 1949.

Alexis Bledel, 27, actress (*The Sisterhood of the Traveling Pants,* "Gilmore Girls"), born Houston, TX, Sept 16, 1982.

Sabrina Bryan, 25, singer, actress ("The Cheetah Girls," "Dancing with the Stars"), born Yorba Linda, CA, Sept 16, 1984.

David Copperfield, 53, illusionist, born David Kotkin at Metuchen, NJ, Sept 16, 1956.

Peter Falk, 82, actor (*Wings of Desire, The In-Laws,* "Columbo"), born New York, NY, Sept 16, 1927.

Anne Francis, 77, actress (*Bad Day at Black Rock, Blackboard Jungle, Forbidden Planet*), born Ossining, NY, Sept 16, 1932.

Henry Louis Gates, Jr, 59, scholar of African American studies, author, editor, born Keyser, WV, Sept 16, 1950.

Orel Leonard Hershiser IV, 51, former baseball player, born Buffalo, NY, Sept 16, 1958.

Nick Jonas, 17, singer (The Jonas Brothers), actor (*Camp Rock*), born Dallas, TX, Sept 16, 1992.

B.B. King, 84, singer ("Rock Me Baby," "The Thrill Is Gone"), born Itta Bena, MS, Sept 16, 1925.

Richard Marx, 46, singer, born Chicago, IL, Sept 16, 1963.

Mark McEwen, 55, weatherman, music editor, born San Antonio, TX, Sept 16, 1954.

Janis Paige, 86, singer, actress (stage: *The Pajama Game, Silk Stockings*), born Tacoma, WA, Sept 16, 1923.

Amy Poehler, 38, actress, comedienne (*Baby Mama, Blades of Glory,* "Saturday Night Live"), born Burlington, MA, Sept 16, 1971.

Tim Raines, 50, former baseball player, born Sanford, FL, Sept 16, 1959.

Mickey Rourke, 53, actor (*Sin City, 9½ Weeks, Diner*), born Schenectady, NY, Sept 16, 1956.

Susan Ruttan, 59, actress ("LA Law"), born Oregon City, OR, Sept 16, 1950.

Molly Shannon, 45, actress ("Saturday Night Live"), born Shaker Heights, OH, Sept 16, 1964.

Jennifer Tilly, 48, actress (*Johnny Be Good, Made in America*), born Los Angeles, CA, Sept 16, 1961.

Robin R. Yount, 54, Hall of Fame baseball player, born Danville, IL, Sept 16, 1955.

September 17 — Thursday

DAY 260 — **105 REMAINING**

ANGOLA: DAY OF THE NATIONAL HERO. Sept 17. National holiday.

BATTLE OF ANTIETAM: ANNIVERSARY. Sept 17, 1862. This date has been called America's bloodiest day in recognition of the high casualties suffered in the Civil War battle between General Robert E. Lee's Confederate forces and General George McClellan's Union army. Estimates vary, but more than 25,000 Union and Confederate soldiers were killed or wounded in this battle on the banks of the Potomac River at Maryland.

"BEWITCHED" TV PREMIERE: 45th ANNIVERSARY. Sept 17, 1964. This sitcom centered around blonde-haired witch Samantha Stephens (Elizabeth Montgomery). Although she promises not to use her witchcraft in her daily life, Samantha finds herself twitching her nose in many situations. Her husband, Darrin Stephens, was played by Dick York and Dick Sargent, and her daughter, Tabitha Stephens, was played by Erin and Diane Murphy. The last episode aired July 1, 1972. Other cast members included Agnes Moorehead, David White, Alice Ghostley, Bernard Fox and Paul Lynde.

BURGER, WARREN E.: BIRTH ANNIVERSARY. Sept 17, 1907. Former Chief Justice of the US Supreme Court, Warren E. Burger was born at St. Paul, MN. A conservative on criminal matters, but a progressive on social issues, he had the longest tenure (1969–86) of any chief justice in the 20th century. Appointed by President Nixon, he voted in the majority on *Roe v Wade* (1973), which upheld a woman's right to an abortion, and on *US v Nixon* (1974), which forced Nixon to surrender audiotapes to the Watergate special prosecutor. He died June 25, 1995, at Washington, DC.

✦ **CITIZENSHIP DAY.** Sept 17. Presidential Proclamation always issued for Sept 17 at request (PL82–261 of Feb 29, 1952). Customarily issued as "Citizenship Day and Constitution Week." Replaces Constitution Day.

CONNOLLY, MAUREEN: 75th BIRTH ANNIVERSARY. Sept 17, 1934. Maureen ("Little Mo") Catherine Connolly Brinker, tennis player born at San Diego, CA. Connolly became the second-youngest woman to win the US National championship at Forest Hills, NY, when she captured that title in 1951. She repeated in 1952 and won Wimbledon as well. In 1953 she became the first woman to win the Grand Slam, taking the US, French, Australian and Wimbledon championships. After winning a second straight French title and a third straight Wimbledon, she suffered a crushed leg in a horseback riding accident and never competed again. Died at Dallas, TX, June 21, 1969.

CONSTITUTION COMMEMORATION DAY IN ARIZONA. Sept 17. Arizona. This state holiday commemorates the signing of the US Constitution on Sept 17, 1787.

CONSTITUTION DAY/PLEDGE ACROSS AMERICA. Sept 17. Every school is invited to join a synchronized recitation of the Pledge of Allegiance coast to coast, 8 AM Hawaiian time to 2 PM Eastern time. Supported by the US Department of Education, this event enables our nation's youth to unite during regular school hours for a patriotic observance. Senator Robert Byrd drafted legislation—passed by Congress—requiring public schools to provide an exercise about the US Constitution on Constitution Day. Resources for schools available, including a free CD with musical renditions of the Pledge, Preamble, Constitution and Bill of Rights. Annually, Sept 17. For info: Paula Burton, President, Celebration USA, 17853 Santiago Blvd, Ste 107, Villa Park, CA 92861. Phone: (714) 283-1892. E-mail: pbcusa@sbcglobal.net. Web: www.celebrationusa.org.

CONSTITUTION OF THE US: ANNIVERSARY. Sept 17, 1787. Delegations from 12 states (Rhode Island did not send a delegate) at the Constitutional Convention at Philadelphia, PA, voted unanimously to approve the proposed document. Thirty-nine of the 42 delegates present signed it and the Convention adjourned, after drafting a letter of transmittal to the Congress. The proposed constitution stipulated that it would take effect when ratified by nine states. This day is a legal holiday in Florida.

✦ **CONSTITUTION WEEK.** Sept 17–23. Presidential Proclamation always issued for the period of Sept 17–23 each year since 1955 (PL84–915 of Aug 2, 1956).

FOSTER, ANDREW (RUBE): BIRTH ANNIVERSARY. Sept 17, 1879. Rube Foster's efforts in baseball earned him the title of "The Father of Negro Baseball." He was a manager and star pitcher, pitching 51 victories in one year. In 1919, he called a meeting of black baseball owners and organized the first black baseball league, the Negro National League. He served as its president until his death in 1930. Foster was born at Calvert, TX, the son of a minister. He died Dec 9, 1930, at Kankakee, IL.

"THE FUGITIVE" TV PREMIERE: ANNIVERSARY. Sept 17, 1963. A nail-biting adventure series on ABC. Dr. Richard Kimble (David Janssen) was wrongly convicted and sentenced to death for his wife's murder, but escaped from his captors in a train wreck. This popular program aired for four years detailing Kimble's search for the one-armed man (Bill Raisch) who had killed his wife, Helen (Diane Brewster). In the meantime Kimble himself was being pursued by Lieutenant Philip Gerard (Barry Morse). The final episode aired Aug 29, 1967, and featured Kimble extracting a confession from the one-armed man as they struggled from the heights of a water tower in a deserted amusement park. That single episode was the highest-rated show ever broadcast until 1976. The TV series generated a hit movie in 1993 with Harrison Ford as Kimble and Oscar-winner Tommy Lee Jones as Gerard.

HENDRICKS, THOMAS ANDREWS: BIRTH ANNIVERSARY. Sept 17, 1819. Twenty-first vice president of the US (1885) born at Muskingum County, OH. Died at Indianapolis, IN, Nov 25, 1885.

HERZOG, CHAIM: BIRTH ANNIVERSARY. Sept 17, 1918. President of Israel, an ex-general and chief delegate to the UN, author, lawyer, born at Belfast, Northern Ireland. He was a British army officer in WWII. Died at Tel Aviv, Israel, Apr 17, 1997.

"HOME IMPROVEMENT" TV PREMIERE: ANNIVERSARY. Sept 17, 1991. This comedy was a TV program about a TV program. Tim Taylor, played by Tim Allen, was host of the popular fix-it show "Tool Time." His wife Jill, played by Patricia Richardson, was a housewife going back to school to get a degree in psychology. The couple's three sons were played by Zachery Ty Bryan, Jonathan Taylor Thomas and Taran Noah Smith. Other cast members included Richard Karn as Tim's TV assistant, and Earl Hindman, Debbe Dunning and Pamela Anderson. The last episode aired May 25, 1999.

HUMMER/BIRD CELEBRATION. Sept 17–20. Rockport and Fulton, TX. To celebrate the spectacular fall migration of the ruby-throated hummingbird and other birds from their summer nesting grounds in the north along the eastern Gulf Coast on the way to their winter grounds in Mexico and Central America, and the hummerbirds' 500-mile journey across the Gulf. There are programs, workshops, booths, concessions, bus and boat tours. Est attendance: 6,000. For info: Rockport Fulton Area Chamber of Commerce, Hummer/Bird Celebration, 404 Broadway, Rockport, TX 78382. Phone: (800) 242-0071 or (361) 729-6445. Fax: (361) 729-7681. E-mail: tourism@1rockport.org. Web: www.rockporthummingbird.com.

"M*A*S*H" TV PREMIERE: ANNIVERSARY. Sept 17, 1972. This popular award-winning CBS series was based on the 1970 Robert Altman movie and a book by Richard Hooker. Set during the Korean War, the show aired for 11 years (lasting longer than the war). It followed the lives of doctors and nurses on the war front with both humor and pathos. The cast included: Alan Alda as Captain Benjamin Franklin "Hawkeye" Pierce, Wayne Rogers as Captain John "Trapper John" McIntyre, McLean Stevenson as Lieutenant Colonel Henry Blake, Loretta Swit as Major Margaret "Hot Lips" Houlihan, Larry Linville as Major Frank Burns, Gary Burghoff as Corporal Walter "Radar" O'Reilly, William Christopher as Father Francis Mulcahy, Jamie Farr as Corporal Max Klinger, Harry Morgan as Colonel Sherman Potter and Mike Farrell as Captain B.J. Hunnicut. Its final episode, "Goodbye, Farewell and Amen" was the highest-rated program of all time, topping the "Who Shot J.R.?" revelation on "Dallas." See also: "M*A*S*H: The Final Episode: Anniversary" (Feb 28). The show generated two spin-offs: "Trapper John, MD" and "After M*A*S*H."

"MISSION: IMPOSSIBLE" TV PREMIERE: ANNIVERSARY. Sept 17, 1966. This action-adventure espionage series was produced by Bruce Geller, appearing on CBS for seven years. The premise of the show was simple: each week the IMF (Impossible Missions Force) leader would receive instructions on a super-secret mission to be carried out by the crew. Steven Hill played the first IMF leader, Dan Briggs. He was replaced by Peter Graves, who played Jim Phelps. The crew included: Martin Landau as Rollin Hand, master of disguise; Barbara Bain, real-life wife of Landau, as Cinnamon Carter; Greg Morris as Barney Collier, technical expert; Peter Lupus as Willy Armitage, tough guy; Leonard Nimoy as Hand's replacement, Paris; Lesley Ann Warren as Dana Lambert; Sam Elliott as Doug; Lynda Day George as Lisa Casey and Barbara Anderson as Mimi Davis. The show was remade for ABC in 1988; it lasted two seasons.

NATIONAL FOOTBALL LEAGUE FORMED: ANNIVERSARY. Sept 17, 1920. The National Football League was formed at Canton, OH.

NEWPORT INTERNATIONAL BOAT SHOW. Sept 17–20. Newport, RI. More than 650 new sail and power boats in the water and displays of accessories, equipment and services. New product information, TrawlerPort program, seminars, etc. Est attendance: 42,000. For info: Newport Exhibition Group, PO Box 698, Newport, RI 02840. Phone: (401) 846-1115. Web: www.newportboatshow.com.

OKLAHOMA STATE FAIR. Sept 17–27. State Fair Park, Oklahoma City, Oklahoma. One of the top state fairs in North America includes six buildings of commercial exhibits, ten barns for livestock and horse competitions, Disney On Ice, PRCA championship rodeo, live entertainment and motor sports events. Est attendance: 1,000,000. For info: Oklahoma State Fair, PO Box 74943, Oklahoma City, OK 73147. Phone: (405) 948-6700. Fax: (405) 948-6828. E-mail: mail@oklahomastatefair.com. Web: www.oklahomastatefair.com.

SELFRIDGE, THOMAS E.: DEATH ANNIVERSARY. Sept 17, 1908. Lieutenant Thomas E. Selfridge, 26-year-old passenger in 740-lb biplane piloted by Orville Wright, was killed when, after four minutes in the air, the plane fell from a height of 75 feet. Nearly 2,000 spectators witnessed the crash at Fort Myer, VA. The plane was being tested for possible military use by the Army Signal Corps. Orville Wright was seriously injured in the crash. Selfridge Air Force Base, MI, was named after the young lieutenant, a West Point graduate, who was the first fatality of powered airplane travel.

SPACE MILESTONE: *PEGASUS 1* (US). Sept 17, 1978. 23,000-pound research satellite broke up over Africa and fell to Earth. Major pieces are believed to have fallen into Atlantic Ocean off the coast of Angola. The satellite had been orbiting Earth for more than 13 years since being launched Feb 16, 1965.

VFW LADIES AUXILIARY ORGANIZED: 95th ANNIVERSARY. Sept 17, 1914. This organization is loyal to the issues and actions affecting America's heroes. Its members offer assistance in addition to supporting veterans' issues in Congress. Part of the organization's mission, according to its charter, is "to assist the Posts and members thereof . . . to foster true patriotism; and to preserve and defend the United States from all her enemies, whomsoever." For info: Veterans of Foreign Wars of the US, Women's Auxiliary, 406 W 34th St, Kansas City, MO 64111. Phone: (816) 561-8655. Fax: (816) 931-4753. Web: www.ladiesauxvfw.com.

September 2009

S	M	T	W	T	F	S
		1	2	3	4	5
6	7	8	9	10	11	12
13	14	15	16	17	18	19
20	21	22	23	24	25	26
27	28	29	30			

VON STEUBEN, BARON FRIEDRICH: BIRTH ANNIVERSARY. Sept 17, 1730. Prussian-born general who volunteered to serve in the American Revolution. He died at Remsen, NY, Nov 28, 1794. Von Steuben Day is commemorated on this day, on the following Saturday or on the 4th Sunday in September.

WILLIAMS, HANK, SR: BIRTH ANNIVERSARY. Sept 17, 1923. Hiram King Williams, country and western singer, born at Georgia, AL. He achieved his first hit with "Lovesick Blues," which brought him a contract with the Grand Ole Opry. His string of hits included "Cold, Cold Heart," "Honky Tonk Blues," "Jambalaya," "Your Cheatin' Heart," "Take These Chains from My Heart" and "I'll Never Get Out of This World Alive," which was released prior to his death Jan 1, 1953, at Oak Hill, VA.

Birthdays Today

Paul Benedict, 71, actor ("The Jeffersons"), born Silver City, NM, Sept 17, 1938.

George Blanda, 82, Hall of Fame football player, born Youngwood, PA, Sept 17, 1927.

Mark Brunell, 39, football player, born Los Angeles, CA, Sept 17, 1970.

Kyle Chandler, 44, actor ("Friday Night Lights," "Homefront," *King Kong*), born Buffalo, NY, Sept 17, 1965.

Charles Grassley, 76, US Senator (R, Iowa), born New Hartford, IA, Sept 17, 1933.

Philip D. (Phil) Jackson, 64, basketball coach, former player, born Deer Lodge, MT, Sept 17, 1945.

Cassandra Peterson, 58, actress (movie hostess Elvira), born Manhattan, KS, Sept 17, 1951.

Rita Rudner, 53, comedienne, actress (*Peter's Friends*), born Miami, FL, Sept 17, 1956.

David H. Souter, 70, Associate Justice of the US Supreme Court, born Melrose, MA, Sept 17, 1939.

Rasheed Wallace, 35, basketball player, born Philadelphia, PA, Sept 17, 1974.

September 18 — Friday

DAY 261 | 104 REMAINING

"THE ADDAMS FAMILY" TV PREMIERE: 45th ANNIVERSARY. Sept 18, 1964. Charles Addams's quirky *New Yorker* cartoon creations were brought to life in this ABC sitcom about a family full of oddballs. John Astin played lawyer Gomez Addams; with Carolyn Jones as his morbid wife Morticia; Ken Weatherwax as son Pugsley; Lisa Loring as daughter Wednesday; Jackie Coogan as Uncle Fester; Ted Cassidy as both Lurch, the butler, and Thing, a disembodied hand; Blossom Rock as Grandmama and Felix Silla as Cousin Itt. The last episode aired Sept 2, 1966. In 1991, *The Addams Family* movie was released, followed by a sequel. Both starred Anjelica Huston as Morticia, Raul Julia as Gomez, Christopher Lloyd as Uncle Fester, Jimmy Workman as Pugsley and Christina Ricci as Wednesday.

APPLEJACK FESTIVAL. Sept 18–20. Nebraska City, NE. Celebrate the 41st annual apple harvest. Nebraska City is home to three apple orchards—which have expanded to include peaches, cherries, vineyards and more. Citywide events include All-You-Can-Eat Waffle Feed, Applejack Fun Run and Walk, Fire House Grill Lunch, annual parade and marching band competition, car show, Spaghetti Feed, AppleJam Fest—A Children's Paradise, specialty shopping deals, live music and much more. Est attendance: 45,000. For info: Nebraska City Tourism & Commerce, 806 1st Ave, Nebraska City, NE 68410. Phone: (800) 514-9113. Fax: (402) 873-6701. E-mail: tourism@nebraskacity.com. Web: www.nebraskacity.com.

BENNINGTON CAR SHOW. Sept 18–20. Green Mountain Racetrack, Pownal, VT. Classic cars, Woodies and muscle cars. A display and demonstration of antique motorcycles, tractor and farm machinery are also featured. Live entertainment and flea market as well. Annually, the second weekend after Labor Day. Est attendance: 10,000. For info: Bennington Area Chamber of Commerce, 100 Veterans Memorial Dr, Bennington, VT 05201. Phone: (802) 447-3311. Fax: (802) 447-1163. E-mail: chamber@bennington.com. Web: www.bennington.com.

THE BIG E. Sept 18–Oct 4. West Springfield, MA. New England's autumn tradition and one of the nation's largest fairs. Each September, The Big E features all free entertainment including top-name talent, a big-top circus and horse show. Also children's attractions, daily parade with custom-built Mardi Gras floats, historic village, Avenue of States, Better Living Center and much more. Annually, beginning the second Friday after Labor Day. Est attendance: 1,250,000. For info: Eastern States Exposition, 1305 Memorial Ave, West Springfield, MA 01089. Phone: (413) 737-2443. Fax: (413) 787-0127. E-mail: info@thebige.com. Web: www.thebige.com.

BRAZZI, ROSSANO: BIRTH ANNIVERSARY. Sept 18, 1916. Hollywood actor Rossano Brazzi was born at Bologna, Italy. A leading romantic figure in the 1950s and 1960s, he appeared in more than 200 films (*South Pacific, Summertime*). He died Dec 24, 1994, at Rome, Italy.

CHILE: INDEPENDENCE DAY. Sept 18. National holiday. Declared independence from Spain in 1810. Sept 19 is commemorated as Armed Forces Day in Chile.

COLUMBUS'S LAST VOYAGE TO THE NEW WORLD: ANNIVERSARY. Sept 18, 1502. Columbus landed at Costa Rica on his fourth and last voyage to the New World. He returned to Spain in 1504 and died there in 1506.

DeMILLE, AGNES: BIRTH ANNIVERSARY. Sept 18, 1905. Dancer, choreographer for ballet and Broadway shows such as *Oklahoma*, born at New York, NY. DeMille died at New York, NY, Oct 7, 1993.

DIEFENBAKER, JOHN: BIRTH ANNIVERSARY. Sept 18, 1895. Canadian lawyer, statesman and Conservative prime minister (1957–63). Born at Normandy Township, ON, Canada, he died at Ottawa, ON, Aug 16, 1979. Diefenbaker was a member of the Canadian Parliament from 1940 until his death.

ENGLAND: HARROGATE AUTUMN FLOWER SHOW. Sept 18–20. Great Yorkshire Showground, Harrogate, North Yorkshire. See Britain's finest blooms and talk to the experts. More than 90 nurseries plus plant societies and vegetable championships. Est attendance: 37,000. For info: Mary Bond, North of England Horticultural Society, 4A South Park Rd, Harrogate, North Yorkshire, England HG1 5QU. Phone: (44) (1423) 561049. Fax: (44) (1423) 536880. E-mail: info@flowershow.org.uk. Web: www.flowershow.org.uk.

FRIENDS OF LAKE FOREST LIBRARY ANNUAL BOOK SALE. Sept 18–20. West Park, Lake Forest, IL. A three-day sale of used books in excellent condition set up in 30 categories. Est attendance: 5,000. For info: Kaye Grabbe, Lake Forest Library, 360 E Deerpath, Lake Forest, IL 60045. Phone: (847) 234-0636. Fax: (847) 234-1453. E-mail: kgrabbe@lfl.alibrary.com. Web: www.lakeforestlibrary.org/FOLFLnew.html.

GARBO, GRETA: BIRTH ANNIVERSARY. Sept 18, 1905. International film actress Greta Garbo was born Greta Lovisa Gustafsson at Stockholm, Sweden. A famous recluse, she retired temporarily, then permanently, from films after 19 years and 27 films, which spanned the late silent era and beginning of sound movies. Her on-screen roles were characterized by an image of a seductress involved in tragic love affairs. She died Apr 15, 1990, at New York, NY.

"GET SMART" TV PREMIERE: ANNIVERSARY. Sept 18, 1965. A spy-thriller spoof appearing on both NBC (1965–69) and CBS (1969–70). Don Adams starred as bumbling CONTROL Agent 86, Maxwell Smart. His mission was to thwart the evildoings of the KAOS organization. Agent Smart was usually successful with the help of his friends: Barbara Feldon as Agent 99 (whom Smart eventually married), Edward Platt as The Chief, Robert Karvelas as Agent Larrabee, Dick Gautier as Hymie the Robot and David Ketchum as Agent 13.

HULL HOUSE OPENS: ANNIVERSARY. Sept 18, 1889. This settlement house was founded in Chicago by Jane Addams and Ellen Gates Starr. It soon became the heart of one of the country's most influential social reform movements, offering a mix of cultural and education programs to new immigrants. See also: "Addams, Jane: Birth Anniversary" (Sept 6).

IRON HORSE OUTRACED BY HORSE: ANNIVERSARY. Sept 18, 1830. In a widely celebrated race, the first locomotive built in America, the Tom Thumb, lost to a horse. Mechanical difficulties plagued the steam engine over the nine-mile course between Riley's Tavern and Baltimore, MD, and a boiler leak prevented the locomotive from finishing the race. In the early days of trains, engines were nicknamed "Iron Horses."

JOHNSON, SAMUEL: 300th BIRTH ANNIVERSARY. Sept 18, 1709. (Old Style date.) English lexicographer and literary lion, creator of the first great dictionary of the English language (1755) and author of poems, novels and essays. Johnson was born at Lichfield, Staffordshire, England, and died at London, England, Dec 13, 1784. Johnson, master of the quip, stated, "Patriotism is the last refuge of a scoundrel."

"LOVE IS A MANY SPLENDORED THING" TV PREMIERE: ANNIVERSARY. Sept 18, 1967. A soap opera created by veteran writer Irna Phillips, airing on CBS for five years. It was based on the 1955 film starring William Holden and Jennifer Jones. Irna Phillips left the show after the network nixed interracial romance in favor of political storylines. David Birney, Bibi Besch and Donna Mills appeared on the show.

MID-SOUTH FAIR. Sept 18–27. Fairgrounds, Memphis, TN. Regional fair featuring concerts, free entertainment, midway, livestock, exhibits and special events. Est attendance: 500,000. For info: Mid-South Fair, 940 Early Maxwell Blvd, Memphis, TN 38104. Phone: (901) 274-8800. Fax: (901) 274-8804. E-mail: info@midsouthfair.org. Web: www.midsouthfair.org.

MONTEREY JAZZ FESTIVAL. Sept 18–20. Monterey, CA. Celebrating its 52nd year, the country's oldest continuous jazz festival features the sounds of some of the world's finest jazz musicians. Est attendance: 40,000. For info: Monterey Jazz Festival, PO Box Jazz, Monterey, CA 93942. Phone: (925) 275-9255 (tickets and info) or (831) 373-3366 (corporate offices). E-mail: jazzinfo@montereyjazzfestival.org. Web: www.montereyjazzfestival.org.

MOON PHASE: NEW MOON. Sept 18. Moon enters New Moon phase at 2:44 PM, EDT.

✦ **NATIONAL POW/MIA RECOGNITION DAY.** Sept 18. Annually, the third Friday of September.

September 2009	S	M	T	W	T	F	S
			1	2	3	4	5
	6	7	8	9	10	11	12
	13	14	15	16	17	18	19
	20	21	22	23	24	25	26
	27	28	29	30			

NATIONAL RESPECT DAY. Sept 18. Family Violence Prevention Fund is encouraging the nation to Give Respect on this day and thereafter as part of the RESPECT! Campaign, a national effort to build safer, healthier communities for future generations. The goal of the RESPECT! Campaign is to prevent dating and domestic violence, sexual assault and child abuse nationwide by engaging individuals everywhere in a conversation about one of the most compelling and simple ways to prevent violence—RESPECT. Annually, the third Friday in September. For info: Family Violence Prevention Fund, 383 Rhode Island, San Francisco, CA 94103. Phone: (415) 252-8900. Fax: (415) 252-8991. E-mail: mindy@endabuse.org. Web: www.endabuse.org.

NEW HAMPSHIRE HIGHLAND GAMES. Sept 18–20 (tentative). Loon Mountain, Lincoln, NH. From the tossing of the caber to the lilting melodies of the clarsach plus massed pipe bands on parade, there's something for everyone at New Hampshire's Highland Games: a three-day Scottish festival crammed with music, dance, crafts, athletic events, Scottish food and more. For those of Scottish heritage, there's also a chance to look up one's clan connection, as more than 60 Scottish clans and societies have tents with displays. Admission charged. Est attendance: 42,000. For info: New Hampshire Highland Games, PO Box 4197, Concord, NH 03302-4197. Phone: (603) 229-1975. Fax: (603) 223-6678. E-mail: info@nhscot.org. Web: www.nhscot.org.

THE *NEW YORK TIMES* FIRST PUBLISHED: ANNIVERSARY. Sept 18, 1851. The *Times* debuted as *The New-York Daily Times*. The name was changed to the current one in 1857.

ON THE WATERFRONT SWAP MEET AND CAR SHOW. Sept 18–20. Downtown St. Ignace, MI. 19th anniversary. Car show, toy show, truck display and swap meet. Est attendance: 8,000. For info: Nostalgia Prod, Inc, 268 Hillcrest Blvd, St. Ignace, MI 49781. Phone: (906) 643-8087. Fax: (906) 643-9784. E-mail: ereavie@nostalgia-prod.com. Web: www.nostalgia-prod.com or www.auto-shows.com.

ORPHAN TRAIN HERITAGE SOCIETY OF AMERICA: ANNUAL REUNION. Sept 18–19. Concordia, KS. Between 1854 and 1929, more than 150,000 homeless children and poor families were transported out of New York City, Boston and Chicago aboard trains accompanied by "agents" for the New York Children's Aid Society who arranged for midwestern families to take the children under a contract agreement. Infants placed by the New York Foundling Hospital were indentured. The national reunion, plus regional reunions in Oklahoma, Missouri, Kansas, Texas, Iowa, Illinois, Indiana, California, Louisiana, Nebraska and Minnesota bring together survivors of the Orphan Trains era, their descendants and interested persons. All gatherings are open to the public, with a small registration fee charged at each. Books containing stories of the Orphan Train Riders are available at each reunion. Est attendance: 250. For info: OTHSA, PO Box 322, Concordia, KS 66901. Phone: (785) 243-4471. E-mail: othsa@msn.com. Web: www.orphantraindepot.com.

READ, GEORGE: BIRTH ANNIVERSARY. Sept 18, 1733. Lawyer and signer of the Declaration of Independence, born at Cecil County, MD. Died Sept 21, 1798, at New Castle, DE.

RICHARD CRANE MEMORIAL TRUCK SHOW. Sept 18–20. St. Ignace, MI. 14th annual show featuring 18-wheeler competition. $2,000 cash Best of Show. Parade of Lights across the Mackinac Bridge. Est attendance: 10,000. For info: Nostalgia Productions, Inc, 268 Hillcrest Blvd, St. Ignace, MI 49781. Phone: (906) 643-8087. Fax: (906) 643-9784. E-mail: ereavie@nostalgia-prod.com. Web: www.nostalgia-prod.com or www.auto-shows.com.

ROSH HASHANAH BEGINS AT SUNDOWN. Sept 18. Jewish New Year. See also: "Rosh Hashanah" (Sept 19).

SEVEN SWEETS AND SOURS FESTIVAL. Sept 18–19. Intercourse, PA. 35th annual. The biggest time of the year is when we put up our fruits and vegetables for the long winter. The whole village is invaded with wonderful end-of-the-garden creations. Don't miss the pumpkin bowling! Annually, the third Friday and Saturday in September. Est attendance: 30,000. For info: Kitchen Kettle Village, Box 380, Intercourse, PA 17534. Phone: (800) 732-3538 or (717) 768-8261. Web: www.kitchenkettle.com.

"SHIRLEY TEMPLE THEATRE" TV PREMIERE: ANNIVERSARY. Sept 18, 1960. An NBC children's anthology of specials appearing on Sundays, hosted by Shirley Temple. Reruns were broadcast on ABC on the following Mondays. "Beauty and the Beast," "Rumplestiltskin," "Rapunzel," "Mother Goose," "The Land of Oz" and "Babes in Toyland" were among the stories presented.

STORY, JOSEPH: BIRTH ANNIVERSARY. Sept 18, 1779. Associate justice of the US Supreme Court (1811–45) was born at Marblehead, MA. "It is astonishing," he wrote a few months before his death, "how easily men satisfy themselves that the Constitution is exactly what they wish it to be." Story died Sept 10, 1845, at Cambridge, MA, having served 33 years on the Supreme Court bench.

STREET MACHINE FALL NATIONALS. Sept 18–20. Springfield, MO. Car and truck show with Family Fun Zone and Performance Market Place. For info: Missouri Entertainment & Event Center, 3001 N Grant, Springfield, MO 65803. Phone: (417) 833-2660. Fax: (417) 833-3769. Web: www.entertainmo.com.

SUMMERSET FESTIVAL. Sept 18–20. Clement Park, Littleton, CO. A family-oriented event, held for the purpose of saying good-bye to summer. There is something for everyone: car show, arts and crafts, business and nonprofit exhibitors, fishing derby, food concessions, kids areas, softball tournament, entertainment and loads of family fun! Est attendance: 40,000. For info: Lora Knowlton, Summerset Festival, PO Box 621788, Littleton, CO 80162-1788. Phone: (303) 973-1209. Fax: (303) 948-5550. E-mail: summersetfest@aol.com. Web: www.summersetfest.com.

TELLURIDE BLUES & BREWS FESTIVAL. Sept 18–20. Telluride, CO. Three-day blues festival with 20 nationally touring bands and 3-hour grand tasting with 50 microbreweries on the Saturday of the festival. Includes Rainbow Kids area, late-night juke joints and free acoustic concerts. Est attendance: 8,000. For info: Telluride Blues & Brews Festival, PO Box 2966, Telluride, CO 81435. Phone: (970) 728-8037. Fax: (970) 728-1350. E-mail: info@tellurideblues.com. Web: www.tellurideblues.com.

US AIR FORCE ESTABLISHED: ANNIVERSARY. Sept 18, 1947. Although its heritage dates back to 1907 when the Army first established military aviation, the US Air Force became a separate military service on this date. Responsible for providing an Air Force that is capable, in conjunction with the other armed forces, of preserving the peace and security of the US, the department is separately organized under the Secretary of the Air Force and operates under the authority, direction and control of the Secretary of Defense.

US CAPITOL CORNERSTONE LAID: ANNIVERSARY. Sept 18, 1793. President George Washington laid the Capitol cornerstone at Washington, DC, in a Masonic ceremony. That event was the first and last recorded occasion at which the stone with its engraved silver plate was seen. In 1958, during the extension of the east front of the Capitol, an unsuccessful effort was made to find it.

US TAKES OUT ITS FIRST LOAN: ANNIVERSARY. Sept 18, 1789. The first loan taken out by the US was negotiated and secured by Alexander Hamilton on Feb 17, 1790. After beginning negotiations with the Bank of New York and the Bank of North America on Sept 18, 1789, Hamilton obtained the sum of $191,608.81 from the two banks in what became known as the Temporary Loan of 1789. The loan was obtained without authority of law and was used to pay the salaries of the president, senators, representatives and officers of the first Congress. Repayment was completed on June 8, 1790.

"WAGON TRAIN" TV PREMIERE: ANNIVERSARY. Sept 18, 1957. "Wagon Train" was a popular western on NBC and ABC, airing for eight years with its last telecast Sept 5, 1965. Each week travelers on a journey along the wagon trail from Missouri to California encountered new surroundings and interacted with different guest stars. Ward Bond played wagonmaster Major Seth Adams until his death in 1960. He was replaced by John McIntire as Chris Hale. Other regulars were: Robert Horton (scout Flint McCullough), Frank McGrath (cook Charlie Wooster), Terry Wilson (Bill Hawks), Denny (Scott) Miller (scout Duke Shannon), Michael Burns (Barnaby West) and Robert Fuller as scout Cooper.

WHITE WOMAN MADE AMERICAN INDIAN CHIEF: ANNIVERSARY. Sept 18, 1891. Harriet Maxwell Converse was made a chief of the Six Nations Tribe at the Tonawanda Reservation, NY. She was given the name Ga-is-wa-noh, which means "The Watcher." She had been adopted as a member of the Seneca tribe in 1884 in appreciation of her efforts on behalf of the tribe.

WO-ZHA-WA DAYS FALL FESTIVAL. Sept 18–20. Wisconsin Dells, WI. Celebrates the beginning of the fall season. Arts, crafts, 100-unit parade, Maxwell Street Days, Wo-Zha-Wa Run and antique flea market. Est attendance: 100,000. For info: Wisconsin Dells Visitors Bureau, PO Box 390, Wisconsin Dells, WI 53965. Phone: (800) 223-3557. E-mail: info@wisdells.com. Web: www.wisdells.com.

Birthdays Today

Lance Armstrong, 38, cyclist, national and world champion, two-time Olympian, seven-time winner of the Tour de France, born Plano, TX, Sept 18, 1971.

Frankie Avalon, 70, singer, actor (*Beach Blanket Bingo*), born Philadelphia, PA, Sept 18, 1939.

Robert F. Bennett, 76, US Senator (R, Utah), born Salt Lake City, UT, Sept 18, 1933.

Robert Blake, 71, actor ("Baretta," *In Cold Blood, Little Rascals*), born Michael Gubitosi at Nutley, NJ, Sept 18, 1938.

Scotty Bowman, 76, Hall of Fame hockey coach, born Montreal, QC, Canada, Sept 18, 1933.

James Gandolfini, 48, actor ("The Sopranos"), born Westwood, NJ, Sept 18, 1961.

Jada Pinkett Smith, 38, actress (*The Nutty Professor, Menace II Society*), born Baltimore, MD, Sept 18, 1971.

Ryne Sandberg, 50, Hall of Fame baseball player, born Spokane, WA, Sept 18, 1959.

Aisha Tyler, 39, television host, actress ("Talk Soup," "24," "CSI"), born San Francisco, CA, Sept 18, 1970.

September 19 — Saturday

DAY 262 103 REMAINING

AEROSPACE WALK OF HONOR. Sept 19. Lancaster, CA. In the tradition of the aerospace industry of the Antelope Valley, the City of Lancaster Aerospace Walk of Honor attracts visitors to Lancaster Boulevard for the unveiling of granite monuments honoring Edwards Air Force Base test pilots whose aviation careers are marked by significant achievements. Honorees such as Neil Armstrong, Chuck Yeager and William "Pete" Knight are selected because they have soared above the rest. Est attendance: 400. For info: City of Lancaster, 44933 Fern Ave, Lancaster, CA 93534. Phone: (661) 723-6077. Fax: (661) 723-5913. Web: www.cityoflancasterca.org.

BIG WHOPPER LIAR'S CONTEST. Sept 19. Thrall's Opera House, New Harmony, IN. Twenty "storytellers" compete to see who can tell the BIGGEST whopper. Annually, the third Saturday in September. Est attendance: 250. For info: Jeff Fleming, PO Box 598, Olney, IL 62450. Phone: (618) 395-8491. Fax: (618) 392-3174.

BOYS AND GIRLS CLUBS DAY FOR KIDS. Sept 19. A day to celebrate and honor children by spending meaningful time with them. Annually, the third Saturday in September. For info: Boys & Girls Clubs of America, 1275 Peachtree St NE, Atlanta, GA 30309-3506. Phone: (404) 487-5700. Fax: (404) 487-5787. E-mail: dayforkids@bgca.org. Web: www.bgca.org or www.dayforkids.org.

BRIGGS & AL'S RUN+WALK FOR CHILDREN'S HOSPITAL. Sept 19. Milwaukee, WI. Choose from an 8k run, 5-mile walk or 3-mile walk along the lake and through the streets. Benefit fundraiser for Children's Hospital of Wisconsin. Finish line party on Summerfest grounds with free entertainment and fitness expo. Est attendance: 17,000. For info: Children's Hospital Foundation, PO Box 1997 MS#3050, Milwaukee, WI 53201. Phone: (414) 266-6320. Fax: (414) 266-6139. Web: www.alsrun.com.

BROUGHAM, HENRY PETER: BIRTH ANNIVERSARY. Sept 19, 1778. Scottish jurist and orator born at Edinburgh, Scotland. Died at Cannes, France, May 7, 1868. The Brougham carriage was named after him. "Education," he said, "makes a people easy to lead, but difficult to drive; easy to govern, but impossible to enslave."

CARROLL, CHARLES: BIRTH ANNIVERSARY. Sept 19, 1737. (Old Style date.) American Revolutionary leader and signer of the Declaration of Independence, born at Annapolis, MD. The last surviving signer of the Declaration, he died Nov 14, 1832, at Baltimore, MD.

CHEROKEE STRIP CELEBRATION. Sept 19. Perry, OK. To commemorate the opening of the Cherokee Strip to settlement on Sept 16, 1893. Annually, the Saturday or weekend nearest Sept 16. Est attendance: 8,000. For info: Carolyn Briegge, Chamber of Commerce, Box 426, Perry, OK 73077. Phone: (580) 336-4684. Fax: (580) 336-3522. E-mail: information@perrychamber.org.

COVERED BRIDGE FESTIVAL. Sept 19–20. Washington and Greene County, PA. Arts and crafts, entertainment and lots of homestyle food at each of ten covered bridges. Annually, the third weekend in September. Est attendance: 110,000. For info: Washington Co Tourism, 273 S Main St, Washington, PA 15301. Phone: (800) 531-4114 or (724) 228-5520. E-mail: info@washwow.com. Web: www.washwow.com.

EISENHOWER WORLD WAR II WEEKEND. Sept 19–20. Eisenhower National Historic Site, Gettysburg, PA. A living history encampment featuring Allied soldiers, German prisoners of war, tanks and military vehicles of that time. Annually, the third weekend in September. Est attendance: 2,500. For info: Gettysburg CVB, PO Box 4117, Gettysburg, PA 17325. Phone: (717) 334-6274. Fax: (717) 334-1166. E-mail: info@gettysburg.travel. Web: www.gettysburg.travel or www.nps.gov/eise.

"ER" TV PREMIERE: 15th ANNIVERSARY. Sept 19, 1994. This medical drama takes place in the emergency room of the fictional County General Hospital in Chicago. Doctors and nurses care for life-and-death cases while experiencing their personal traumas as well. Cast has included Anthony Edwards, George Clooney, Sherry Stringfield, Noah Wyle, Laura Innes, Gloria Reuben, Eriq La Salle, Maura Tierney, Goran Visnjic and Alex Kingston. On Dec 6, 2007, the 300th episode aired.

FALL FEST. Sept 19. Monett, MO. Street festival in historic downtown featuring live entertainment, including line dancing, cloggers, storytelling, and pancake breakfast, pork steak barbecue, car show with antique and classic vehicles from four states, food and craft booths, full carnival, children's rides, carriage rides, ARTExpo display, karaoke, Little Miss and Mr Oktoberfest, best downtown window display contest and more. Annually, on the third Saturday of September. Est attendance: 5,000. For info: Monett Chamber of Commerce, 705 E Broadway, Monett, MO 65708. Phone: (417) 235-7919 or (417) 235-3349.

FESTIVAL OF ADVENTURES. Sept 19–20. Aitkin, MN. This annual festival celebrates the area's fur-trading history. Rendezvous at the City Park with trappers, traders, ethnic dancers, music and food. Est attendance: 5,000. For info: Aitkin Area Chamber of Commerce, PO Box 127, Aitkin, MN 56431. Phone: (218) 927-2316 or (800) 526-8342. Fax: (218) 927-4494. E-mail: upnorth@aitkin.com. Web: www.aitkin.com.

FESTIVAL OF THE SEA. Sept 19 (rain date Sept 20). Point Pleasant Beach, NJ. Come join the fun with arts, crafts, food, games for the kids, pony rides, antiques, nonprofit and commercial exhibits. Free admission. Est attendance: 55,000. For info: Point Pleasant Beach Chamber of Commerce, 517A Arnold Ave, Point Pleasant Beach, NJ 08742. Phone: (732) 899-2424. Fax: (732) 899-0103. E-mail: info@pointpleasantbeachnj.com. Web: www.pointpleasantbeachnj.org.

FESTIVAL 2009: FESTIVAL OF FINE ARTS AND FINE CRAFTS. Sept 19–20. Dalton, GA. 46th annual. Fine arts and fine crafts festival includes outdoor artist booths, food vendors, children's arts festival, entertainment for adults and children, cash awards. Est attendance: 7,000. For info: Creative Arts Guild, Box 1485, Dalton, GA 30722-1485. Phone: (706) 278-0168. Fax: (706) 278-6996. E-mail: cagarts@creativeartsguild.org.

"FLIPPER" TV PREMIERE: 45th ANNIVERSARY. Sept 19, 1964. An adventure series starring Flipper, the intelligent, communicative and helpful dolphin. The human cast members included Brian Kelly as Chief Ranger Porter Ricks, Luke Halpin as his son Sandy, Tommy Norden as his son Bud and Ulla Strömstedt as biochemist Ulla Norstrand. The last telecast of this series was Sept 1, 1968. The series was briefly re-created under the same title in the '90s.

GETTYSBURG OUTDOOR ANTIQUE SHOW. Sept 19. Gettysburg, PA. More than 150 dealers displaying their wares on the sidewalk. Est attendance: 25,000. For info: Gettysburg CVB, PO Box 4117, Gettysburg, PA 17325. Phone: (717) 334-6274. Fax: (717) 334-1166. E-mail: info@gettysburg.travel. Web: www.gettysburg.travel.

GOLDING, SIR WILLIAM: BIRTH ANNIVERSARY. Sept 19, 1911. Born at Columb Minor at Cornwall, England, this celebrated author was recognized for his contributions to literature with a Nobel Prize in 1983. His first and most popular novel was *Lord of the Flies.* He died June 19, 1993, near Truro, Cornwall.

"ICEMAN" MUMMY DISCOVERED: ANNIVERSARY. Sept 19, 1991. At 10,531 feet in the Austrian-Italian Alps, two hikers discovered a 5,300-year-old frozen mummy from late Neolithic times. The man carried rough bow and arrows as well as a copper axe, and wore a grass cloak for warmth. His shoes were made from bearskin, deer hide and tree bark. He now rests as a frozen exhibit at the South Tyrol Museum of Archaeology at Bolzano, Italy. The "Iceman" was gently thawed in September 2000 in order for scientists to conduct valuable DNA analysis and determine his last meal.

INTERNATIONAL COASTAL CLEANUP. Sept 19. A million volunteers remove and tabulate 12 million pieces of trash on 21,000 miles of beaches as well as below the water in 100 countries. Annually, the third Saturday in September. For info: The Ocean Conservancy, 2029 K St NW, Washington, DC 20006. Phone: (202) 429-5609. E-mail: cleanup@oceanconservancyva.org. Web: www.oceanconservancy.org or www.coastalcleanup.org.

September 2009

S	M	T	W	T	F	S
		1	2	3	4	5
6	7	8	9	10	11	12
13	14	15	16	17	18	19
20	21	22	23	24	25	26
27	28	29	30			

INTERNATIONAL EAT AN APPLE DAY. Sept 19. To promote the beginning of fall with its vivid color and crispness, celebrate by eating an apple, the fruit of the fall season. Annually, the third Saturday in September. For info: Apple Berry Farm Market, 360 LaHave St, Bridgewater, NS, Canada B4V 2T7. Phone: (902) 543-6622. Fax: (902) 527-1470. Web: www.appleberrymarket.ca.

INTERNATIONAL TALK LIKE A PIRATE DAY. Sept 19. A day when people everywhere can swash their buckles and add a touch of larceny to their dialogue by talking like pirates: for example, "Arr, matey, it be a fine day." While it's inherently a guy thing, women have been known to enjoy the day because they have to be addressed as "me beauty." Celebrated by millions on all seven continents. Arr! Annually, Sept 19. For info: Mark "Cap'n Slappy" Summers, 925 First Ave E, Albany, OR 97321. Phone: (541) 791-8281. E-mail: capnslappy@talklikeapirate.com. Web: www.talklikeapirate.com.

JAMESTOWN BURNED BY BACON'S REBELLION: ANNIVERSARY. Sept 19, 1676. Virginia governor Sir William Berkeley, supporting Charles II's efforts to exploit the colony, adopted new laws allowing only property holders to vote, raising taxes and raising the cost of shipping while lowering the price for tobacco. The resulting discontent exploded when the frontier of the colony was attacked by local tribes and the governor refused to defend the settlers. Nathaniel Bacon, a colonist on the governor's council, led frontier farmers and successfully defeated the tribes. Denounced by Berkeley as rebels, Bacon and his men occupied Jamestown, forcing the governor to call an election, the first in 15 years. The Berkeley laws were repealed and election and tax reforms were instituted. While Bacon and his troops were gone on a raiding party against the Indians, Berkeley again denounced them. They returned and attacked Berkeley's forces, defeating them and burning Jamestown on Sept 19, 1676. Berkeley fled and Bacon became ruler of Virginia. When he died suddenly a short time later, the rebellion collapsed. Berkeley returned to power and Bacon's followers were hunted down, some executed and their property confiscated. Berkeley was replaced the next year and peace was restored.

JOHNNY APPLESEED FESTIVAL. Sept 19–20. Fort Wayne, IN. Amble through two parks at the actual site of John Chapman's grave marker. Chapman, known as "Johnny Appleseed," planted hundreds of apple orchards along the early Indiana frontier. This festival celebrates his life with reenactments of pioneer life, old-fashioned food, educational demonstrations, handicrafts, roving entertainers, children's games, dancing and music. Free admission. Annually, the third full weekend in September. Est attendance: 300,000. For info: Johnny Appleseed Festival, Inc, 1502 Harry Baals Dr, Fort Wayne, IN 46805-1453. Phone: (260) 427-6003. Web: www.johnnyappleseedfest.com.

KING TURKEY DAYS (WITH TURKEY RACE). Sept 19. Worthington, MN. Community celebration that includes live turkey race between Paycheck, Worthington, MN, and Ruby Begonia, Cuero, TX. Also included are a grand parade, live entertainment, beer garden, free pancake breakfast and family activities. Est attendance: 15,000. For info: King Turkey Days, Inc, 1121 Third Ave, Worthington, MN 56187. Phone: (800) 279-2919 or (507) 372-2919. Fax: (507) 372-2827. E-mail: wcofc@frontiernet.net.

LUYTS, JAN: BIRTH ANNIVERSARY. Sept 19, 1655. Dutch scholar, physicist, mathematician and astronomer, Jan Luyts was born at Hoorn in western Netherlands. Little remembered except for his books: *Astronomica Institutio . . .* (1689) and *Introductio ad Geographiam . . .* (1690).

"THE MARY TYLER MOORE SHOW" TV PREMIERE: ANNIVERSARY. Sept 19, 1970. This show—one of the most popular sitcoms of the '70s—combined good writing, an effective supporting cast and contemporary attitudes. The show centered around the two most important places in Mary Richards's (Mary Tyler Moore) life—the WJM-TV newsroom and her apartment at Minneapolis. At home she shared the ups and downs of life with her friend Rhoda Morgenstern (Valerie Harper) and the manager of her apartment building, Phyllis Lindstrom (Cloris Leachman). At work, as the associate producer (later producer) of "The Six O'Clock News," Mary struggled to function in a man's world. Figuring in her professional life were her irascible boss Lou Grant (Ed Asner), levelheaded and softhearted news writer Murray Slaughter (Gavin MacLeod) and narcissistic anchorman Ted Baxter (Ted Knight). In the last of 168 episodes (Mar 19, 1977), the unthinkable happened: everyone in the WJM newsroom except the inept Ted was fired.

MEXICO CITY EARTHQUAKE: ANNIVERSARY. Sept 19–20, 1985. Nearly 10,000 persons perished in the earthquakes (8.1 and 7.5 respectively, on the Richter scale) that devastated Mexico City. Damage to buildings was estimated at more than $1 billion, and 100,000 homes were destroyed or severely damaged.

OSAGE RIVER MOUNTAIN MAN FESTIVAL AND BLACK POWDER SHOOT. Sept 19–20. Lake Ozark, MO. 22nd annual. Mountain men, Indians, musicians, storytellers in authentic attire gather to reenact a pre-1840s wilderness rendezvous. Est attendance: 6,000. For info: Lake Area Chamber of Commerce, PO Box 1570, Lake Ozark, MO 65049. Phone: (800) 451-4117 or (573) 964-1008. Fax: (573) 964-1010. E-mail: kkopis@lakeareachamber.com or mcook@lakeareachamber.com. Web: lakeareachamber.com.

OZARK HAM & TURKEY FESTIVAL. Sept 19. California, MO. Fun for the whole family with more than 100 food and craft vendors, 5k race, car show, carriage rides, barbecue contest and much more. Annually, the third Saturday in September. Est attendance: 15,000. For info: California Area Chamber of Commerce, PO Box 85,California, MO 65018. Web: www.calmo.com

PEDDLER'S VILLAGE SCARECROW FESTIVAL. Sept 19–20. Peddler's Village, Lahaska, PA. Weekend festival includes scarecrow making, pumpkin-painting workshops, musical entertainment and scarecrow competition display. Free admission and free live entertainment, charge for workshops. Est attendance: 16,000. For info: Peddler's Village, Routes 202 and 263, Lahaska, PA 18931. Phone: (215) 794-4000. Fax: (215) 794-4001. Web: www.peddlersvillage.com.

POWELL, LEWIS F., JR: BIRTH ANNIVERSARY. Sept 19, 1907. Former associate justice of the Supreme Court of the US, nominated by President Nixon Oct 21, 1971. (Took office Jan 7, 1972.) Justice Powell was born at Suffolk, VA. In 1987, he announced his retirement from the Court. He died Aug 25, 1998, at Richmond, VA.

ROAD CHURCH FIRST CONGREGATIONAL COUNTRY FAIR. Sept 19. Road Congregational Church, Pequot Trail, Stonington, CT. Harvest table, bake table and crafts. Famous Barnes's Chowder Luncheon at noon (served in Civil War kettles). Est attendance: 300. For info: Libby Kennedy, 21 Roosevelt Ave, Mystic, CT 06355. Phone: (860) 536-1514. E-mail: roadchurch@juno.com. Web: www.roadchurch.org.

ROSH HASHANAH or JEWISH NEW YEAR. Sept 19–20. Jewish holy day observed on two consecutive days. Hebrew calendar date: Tishri 1–2, 5770. Rosh Hashanah (literally "Head of the Year") is the beginning of ten days of repentance and spiritual renewal. (Began at sundown Sept 18.)

ROYKO, MIKE: BIRTH ANNIVERSARY. Sept 19, 1932. Syndicated columnist to more than 600 newspapers nationwide, Pulitzer Prize–winner and author (*Boss, Slats Grobnick*). Born at Chicago, IL, he died there, Apr 29, 1997.

SAINT CHRISTOPHER (SAINT KITTS) AND NEVIS: INDEPENDENCE DAY. Sept 19. National holiday. Commemorates independence from Britain in 1983.

SAINT JANUARIUS (GENNARO): FEAST DAY. Sept 19. Fourth-century bishop of Benevento, martyred near Naples, Italy, whose relics in the Naples Cathedral are particularly famous because on his feast days the blood in a glass vial is said to liquefy in response to prayers of the faithful. In September 1979, the Associated Press reported that some 5,000 persons gathered at the cathedral at dawn, and that "the blood liquefied after 63 minutes of prayers." This phenomenon is said to occur also on the first Saturday in May.

SANDY SPRINGS FESTIVAL. Sept 19–20. Heritage Green, Sandy Springs, GA. Now in its 24th year, Sandy Springs Festival has grown from a small, picnic-style gathering to an event drawing more than 20,000. This neighborhood event welcomes new families and friends. Celebrating community and tradition, there is something for everyone! Annually, the third weekend of September. Est attendance: 20,000. For info: Sandy Springs Festival, 135 Hilderbrand Dr, Sandy Springs, GA 30328. Phone: (404) 851-9111. Fax: (404) 851-9807. E-mail: info@sandyspringsfestival.com. Web: www.sandyspringsfestival.com.

SUNTRUST BIG LICK BLUES FESTIVAL. Sept 19. Roanoke, VA. Est attendance: 5,000. For info: Suntrust Big Lick Blues Fest, PO Box 8276, Roanoke, VA 24014. Phone: (540) 342-2640, ext 247. E-mail: erin@eventzone.org. Web: www.eventzone.org.

TITAN II MISSILE EXPLOSION: ANNIVERSARY. Sept 19, 1980. The third major accident involving America's most powerful single weapon occurred near Damascus, AR. The explosion, at 3 AM, came nearly 11 hours after a fire had started in the missile silo. The multimegaton nuclear warhead (a hydrogen bomb) reportedly was briefly airborne, but came to rest a few hundred feet away. One dead, 21 injured in accident. Previous major Titan Missile accidents: Aug 9, 1965, near Searcy, AR (53 dead); and Aug 24, 1978, near Rock, KS (2 dead, 29 injured).

TRAIL OF COURAGE LIVING-HISTORY FESTIVAL. Sept 19–20. Rochester, IN. Portrayal of life in frontier Indiana when it was Indian territory. Historic skits, two stages with music and dancing, historic encampments for Revolutionary War, French and Indian War, Voyageurs, Western Fur Trade and Plains Indians; re-created 1832 Chippeway Village, also Woodland Indian Village, pioneer foods and crafts, muzzle-loading and tomahawk contests, canoe rides. Museum, round barn and Living History Village on grounds. Special honored Potawatomi family from Indiana's history each year. Est attendance: 18,000. For info: Fulton County Historical Society, 37 E 375N, Rochester, IN 46975. Phone: (574) 223-4436. E-mail: fchs@rtcol.com. Web: www.icss.net/~fchs.

"THE VIRGINIAN" TV PREMIERE: ANNIVERSARY. Sept 19, 1962. TV's first 90-minute Western starred James Drury as the Virginian, a foreman trying to come to terms with the westward expansion of civilization. It was set on the Shiloh Ranch, in Wyoming. Key players included Doug McClure (with Drury, the only cast member to stay for the entire run), Lee J. Cobb, Roberta Shore, Pippa Scott, Gary Clarke, David Hartman and Tim Matheson. In the last season, the title was changed to "The Men from Shiloh," and Stewart Granger and Lee Majors joined the cast.

September 2009

S	M	T	W	T	F	S
		1	2	3	4	5
6	7	8	9	10	11	12
13	14	15	16	17	18	19
20	21	22	23	24	25	26
27	28	29	30			

WIFE APPRECIATION DAY. Sept 19. Husbands, show your wives how much you love and appreciate them. Communicate the difference your wife makes in your life. Annually, the third Saturday in September. For info: Brooke Espinoza, PO Box 6158, Folsom, CA 95763. E-mail: keptbythepowerofgod@yahoo.com.

WINGS 'N' WATER FESTIVAL. Sept 19–20. Wetlands Institute, Stone Harbor, NJ. 27th annual. Coastal arts celebration of the environment throughout seaside towns of Stone Harbor and Avalon. This award-winning festival features Wildlife, Duck Stamp, Maritime and Landscape art. Plus bird and fish carvings, decoys, photography, crafts, quilts, music, retriever demos, live animals, boat cruises, kayaking, seafood and more. Est attendance: 5,000. For info: Nancy Morrow, Wetlands Institute, 1075 Stone Harbor Blvd, Stone Harbor, NJ 08247-1424. Phone: (609) 368-1211. Fax: (609) 368-3871. Web: www.wetlandsinstitute.org.

 Birthdays Today

James Anthony (Jim) Abbott, 42, former baseball player, born Flint, MI, Sept 19, 1967.

Jimmy Fallon, 35, comedian, actor ("Saturday Night Live," *Fever Pitch*), born Brooklyn, NY, Sept 19, 1974.

Kevin Hooks, 51, actor, director ("The White Shadow," *Sounder*), born Philadelphia, PA, Sept 19, 1958.

Jeremy Irons, 61, actor (Oscar for *Reversal of Fortune*; *Lolita, Dead Ringers*), born Cowes, Isle of Wight, England, Sept 19, 1948.

Nick Johnson, 31, baseball player, born Sacramento, CA, Sept 19, 1978.

Joan Lunden, 58, broadcast journalist, born Sacramento, CA, Sept 19, 1951.

Randolph Mantooth, 64, actor ("Emergency"), born Sacramento, CA, Sept 19, 1945.

David McCallum, 76, actor ("NCIS," "The Man from U.N.C.L.E.," *The Great Escape*), born Glasgow, Scotland, Sept 19, 1933.

Joe Morgan, 66, broadcaster, Hall of Fame baseball player, born Bonham, TX, Sept 19, 1943.

Soledad O'Brien, 43, television journalist, born St. James, NY, Sept 19, 1966.

Twiggy, 60, actress (*The Boy Friend, The Blues Brothers*), model, born Leslie Hornby at London, England, Sept 19, 1949.

Adam West, 81, actor ("Batman," "The Last Precinct"), born Walla Walla, WA, Sept 19, 1928 (some sources say 1929 or 1930).

Paul Williams, 69, singer, composer (Oscar for "Evergreen" from *A Star Is Born*), born Omaha, NE, Sept 19, 1940.

Trisha Yearwood, 45, singer, born Monticello, GA, Sept 19, 1964.

September 20 — Sunday

DAY 263 **102 REMAINING**

ARTS/QUINCY RIVERFEST. Sept 20. Quincy, IL. Celebration of the arts and the Mississippi River in the riverfront parks. Fine arts and crafts and a children's area featuring hands-on activities and performances. Annually, the third Sunday in September. Est attendance: 5,000. For info: Quincy Society of Fine Arts, 300 Civic Center Plaza, Ste 244, Quincy, IL 62301-4162. Phone: (217) 222-3432. Fax: (217) 228-2787. E-mail: art@artsqcy.org. Web: www.artsqcy.org.

AUERBACH, RED: BIRTH ANNIVERSARY. Sept 20, 1917. Basketball coach Arnold Jacob Auerbach was born at Brooklyn, NY. As coach of the Boston Celtics from 1950 to 1966, he won nine NBA titles, including eight straight from 1959 to 1966. After retiring from coaching, Auerbach was either general manager or president of the Celtics from 1966 until 1997. He was team president from 2001 until his death at Washington, DC, on Oct 28, 2006. In 1980 he was named the greatest coach in NBA history by the Professional Basketball Writers Association, and is widely considered to be the best sports executive in history.

BILLIE JEAN KING WINS THE "BATTLE OF THE SEXES": ANNIVERSARY. Sept 20, 1973. Billie Jean King defeated Bobby Riggs in the nationally televised "Battle of the Sexes" tennis match in three straight sets.

BUILD A BETTER IMAGE WEEK. Sept 20–26. In order to be a success, you need to look like one. This week is set aside for people to evaluate their professional image and take the steps necessary to improve on it. For "10 Steps to a Better Image" tip sheet, send #10 SASE. Annually, the third full week of September. For info: Marlys K. Arnold, ImageSpecialist, PO Box 901808, Kansas City, MO 64190-1808. Phone: (816) 746-7888. E-mail: marnold@imagespecialist.com. Web: www.imagespecialist.com.

"THE COSBY SHOW" TV PREMIERE: 25th ANNIVERSARY. Sept 20, 1984. This Emmy Award–winning comedy set in New York City revolved around the members of the Huxtable family. Father Dr. Heathcliff Huxtable was played by Bill Cosby; his wife Clair, an attorney, was played by Phylicia Rashad. Their four daughters were played by Sabrina Le Beauf (Sondra), Lisa Bonet (Denise), Tempestt Bledsoe (Vanessa) and Keshia Knight Pulliam (Rudy); Malcolm-Jamal Warner played son Theo. By the end of the series in 1992, the two oldest daughters had finished college and were married. "A Different World" was a spin-off set at historically black Hillman College where Denise was a student.

COUNCIL OF SUPPLY CHAIN MANAGEMENT PROFESSIONALS ANNUAL CONFERENCE. Sept 20–23. Chicago, IL. Professional development and dialogue. Est attendance: 3,000. For info: Council of Supply Chain Management Professionals, 333 E Butterfield Rd, Ste 140, Lombard, IL 60148. Phone: (630) 574-0985. Fax: (630) 574-0989. E-mail: membership@cscmp.org. Web: www.cscmp.org.

DEAF AWARENESS WEEK. Sept 20–26. Nationwide celebration to promote deaf culture, American Sign Language and deaf heritage. Activities might include library displays, interpreted story hours, open houses in residential schools and mainstream programs, exhibit booths in shopping malls with "Five Minute Sign Language Lessons," material distribution. Annually, the last full week of September. For info: Natl Assn of the Deaf, 8630 Fenton St, Ste 820, Silver Spring, MD 20910-3819. Fax: (301) 587-1791. E-mail: nadinfo@nad.org. Web: www.nad.org.

EQUAL RIGHTS PARTY FOUNDING: 125th ANNIVERSARY. Sept 20, 1884. The Equal Rights Party was formed at San Francisco, CA. Its candidate for president, nominated in convention, was Mrs Belva Lockwood. The vice presidential candidate was Marietta Stow.

FINANCIAL PANIC OF 1873: ANNIVERSARY. Sept 20, 1873. For the first time in its history, the New York Stock Exchange was forced to close because of a banking crisis. Although the worst of the panic and crisis was over within a week, the psychological effect on businessmen, investors and the nation at large was more lasting.

HOLLYWOOD BEACH LATIN FESTIVAL. Sept 20. Hollywood, FL. 16th annual. Festival features Latin entertainment, arts and crafts, food and health court. Est attendance: 35,000. For info: Marketing, City of Hollywood, Dept of Parks, Recreation & Cultural Arts, 1405 S 28th St, Hollywood, FL 33020. Phone: (954) 921-3404.

LIBERACE PIANO COMPETITION. Sept 20. The Liberace Museum, Las Vegas, NV. Open to all competitors in Showmanship and Classical categories, live auditions for this contest began in August and the Competitor's Showcase took place on Sept 13. The competition finals take place today. Est attendance: 1,000. For info: The Liberace Museum, 1775 E Tropicana Ave, Las Vegas, NV 89119. Phone: (702) 798-5595. E-mail: info@liberace.org. Web: www.liberace.org.

MORTON, FERDINAND "JELLY ROLL": BIRTH ANNIVERSARY. Sept 20, 1885. American jazz pianist, composer and orchestra leader, was born at New Orleans, LA (some scholars believe in 1890). Morton, subject of a biography titled *Mr Jelly Roll* by Alan Lomax, died July 10, 1941, at Los Angeles, CA.

NATIONAL ADULT IMMUNIZATION AWARENESS WEEK. Sept 20–26 (tentative). Thousands of deaths occur each year—deaths which could be easily prevented by today's available vaccines. NAIAW emphasizes the importance of appropriately vaccinating adults against measles, mumps, rubella, hepatitis A, hepatitis B, tetanus, diphtheria, influenza, pneumococcal disease and varicella. A campaign kit of materials is available. For info: Natl Coalition for Adult Immunization, 4733 Bethesda Ave, Ste 750, Bethesda, MD 20814-5278. Phone: (301) 656-0003. Fax: (301) 907-0878. E-mail: ncai@nfid.org. Web: www.NFID.org.

NATIONAL CLEAN HANDS WEEK. Sept 20–26. Established by the Clean Hands Coalition, a unified alliance of public and private partners, working together to create and support coordinated, sustained initiatives to significantly improve health and save lives through clean hands. Activities will be held nationwide to raise awareness about the importance of good hand hygiene. Annually, the third full week in September. For info: Clean Hands Coalition. E-mail: nbock@cleaning101.com. Web: www.cleaning101.com.

✦ **NATIONAL FARM SAFETY AND HEALTH WEEK.** Sept 20–26. Presidential Proclamation issued since 1982 for the third week in September. Previously, from 1944, for one of the last two weeks in July.

NATIONAL KEEP KIDS CREATIVE WEEK. Sept 20–26. More than ever before, kids today need encouragement to be imaginative. Their busy, task-oriented schedules in home and school give children little room for creative play. Set aside time this week to celebrate the inventive minds of kids. Encourage a child to make up a story, draw, even look for animals in cloud shapes—let their imaginations soar. Annually, the last week in September. For info: Bruce Van Patter, Let's Get Creative! Phone: (570) 524-9770. Web: www.brucevanpatter.com/keepkidscreative.html.

NATIONAL REHABILITATION AWARENESS CELEBRATION. Sept 20–26. The observance salutes the determination of the more than 50 million Americans with disabilities. It is a time to applaud the efforts of rehab professionals, provide a forum for education and offer an occasion to call upon our citizens to find new ways to fulfill needs that still exist. Annually, the third full week in Sept. For info: Natl Rehabilitation Awareness Foundation, 100 Abington Executive Park, Clarks Summit, PA 18411. Phone: (570) 341-4637 or (800) 943-6723. Fax: (570) 341-4331. Web: www.nraf-rehabnet.org.

NATIONAL RESEARCH COUNCIL: FIRST MEETING: ANNIVERSARY. Sept 20, 1916. Anniversary of first meeting of National Research Council, at New York, NY. Formed at request of President Woodrow Wilson for "encouraging the investigation of natural phenomena" for American business and national security.

NATIONAL SINGLES WEEK. Sept 20–26. To celebrate single life and to recognize singles and their contributions to society. For info: Rich Gosse, Chairman, American Singles, 205 Mark Twain Ave, San Rafael, CA 94903. Phone: (415) 479-3800. E-mail: rich@richgosse.com.

PERKINS, MAXWELL: 125th BIRTH ANNIVERSARY. Sept 20, 1884. The most powerful and influential book editor of the early 20th century, Perkins discovered, nurtured, cajoled, guided and edited such authors as F. Scott Fitzgerald, Ernest Hemingway, Thomas Wolfe and others at Charles Scribners' Sons. Born at New York, NY, Perkins died June 17, 1947, at Stamford, CT.

"THE PHIL SILVERS SHOW" TV PREMIERE: ANNIVERSARY. Sept 20, 1955. This popular half-hour sitcom starred Phil Silvers as Sergeant Ernie Bilko, a scheming but good-natured con man whose schemes rarely worked out. Guest stars included Fred Gwynne, Margaret Hamilton, Dick Van Dyke and Alan Alda in his first major TV role.

PROSTATE CANCER AWARENESS WEEK. Sept 20–26. Free or low-cost prostate cancer screenings for all men over the age of 40 and men in high-risk groups such as African American men and Hispanics over age 35. Annually, the third week in September. For info: Prostate Cancer Education Council, 7009 S Potomac St, Ste 125, Centennial, CO 80112. Phone: (303) 316-4685. Web: www.pcaw.com.

ROCK OF CHICKAMAUGA: ANNIVERSARY. Sept 20, 1863. After disastrous moves by Union General William Starke Rosecrans, Confederate forces appeared to be carrying the day at the Battle of Chickamauga in Tennessee. With Rosecrans in flight to Chattanooga, Union General Henry Thomas and his men maintained their position and repeatedly turned back Southern attacks until they were reinforced. Thomas's actions saved the Union forces from a complete rout and earned him the nickname "Rock of Chickamauga." Rosecrans was relieved of his command.

SINCLAIR, UPTON BEALL: BIRTH ANNIVERSARY. Sept 20, 1878. American novelist and politician born at Baltimore, MD. He worked for political and social reforms, and his best-known novel, *The Jungle*, prompted one of the nation's first pure food laws. Died at Bound Brook, NJ, Nov 25, 1968.

TOLKIEN WEEK. Sept 20–26. To promote appreciation and enjoyment of the works of J.R.R. Tolkien. Annually, the week that includes Hobbit Day (Sept 22). For info: American Tolkien Society, PO Box 97, Highland, MI 48357-0097. E-mail: americantolkiensociety@yahoo.com. Web: www.americantolkiensociety.org.

WOMEN'S FRIENDSHIP DAY. Sept 20. Every woman has special friends she can't live without; those women to whom she tells everything, friends who will always listen and who know just what to say. Women's Friendship Day provides the perfect opportunity for women to acknowledge the special women in their lives. Annually, the third Sunday in September. For info: Attn Heidi Roy, Kappa Delta Sorority, 3205 Players Ln, Memphis, TN 38125. Phone: (901) 748-1897. Fax: (901) 748-0949. E-mail: dircomm@kappadelta.org. Web: www.kappadelta.org.

 Birthdays Today

Joyce Brothers, 81, psychologist, author, born New York, NY, Sept 20, 1928.

Donald A. Hall, 81, former US poet laureate, born New Haven, CT, Sept 20, 1928.

Kristen Johnston, 42, actress ("3rd Rock from the Sun"), born Washington, DC, Sept 20, 1967.

Guy Damien LaFleur, 58, Hall of Fame hockey player, born Thurso, QC, Canada, Sept 20, 1951.

Sophia Loren, 75, actress (*Black Orchid, Marriage Italian Style*, "Brief Encounter," Oscar for *Two Women*), born Sofia Scicoloni at Rome, Italy, Sept 20, 1934.

Anne Meara, 80, actress ("Fame"), comedienne (Stiller and Meara), born New York, NY, Sept 20, 1929.

September 2009

S	M	T	W	T	F	S
		1	2	3	4	5
6	7	8	9	10	11	12
13	14	15	16	17	18	19
20	21	22	23	24	25	26
27	28	29	30			

September 21 — Monday

DAY 264 **101 REMAINING**

ARMENIA: INDEPENDENCE DAY. Sept 21. Public holiday. Commemorates independence from Soviet Union in 1991.

BELIZE: INDEPENDENCE DAY. Sept 21. National holiday. Commemorates independence of the former British Honduras from Britain in 1981.

FAST OF GEDALYA. Sept 21. Jewish holiday. Hebrew calendar date: Tishri 3, 5770. Tzom Gedalya begins at first light of day and commemorates the sixth-century BC assassination of Gedalya Ben Achikam.

EID-AL-FITR: CELEBRATING THE FAST. Sept 21. Islamic calendar date: Shawwal 1, 1430. This feast/festival celebrates the completion of the Ramadan fasting and usually lasts for several days. Everyone wears new clothes; children receive gifts from parents and relatives; children are allowed to stay up late and participate in games, folktales, plays, puppet shows and trips to amusement parks. This holiday is known as Seker Bayram in Turkey and Hari Raya Puasa in Southeast Asia. Different methods for "anticipating" the visibility of the new moon crescent at Mecca are used by different Muslim groups. US date may vary. Began at sunset the preceding day.

HOPKINSON, FRANCIS: BIRTH ANNIVERSARY. Sept 21, 1737. Signer of the Declaration of Independence. Born at Philadelphia, PA, he died there May 9, 1791.

HURRICANE HUGO HITS AMERICAN COAST: 20th ANNIVERSARY. Sept 21, 1989. After ravaging the Virgin Islands, Hurricane Hugo hit the American coast at Charleston, SC. In its wake, Hugo left destruction totaling at least $8 billion.

INTERNATIONAL WOMEN'S ECOMMERCE DAYS. Sept 21–23. This event will celebrate women around the globe and their economic impact and purchasing power. The schedule of events (subject to change) includes encouraging women around the world to make an online purchase today, sending information to the media on all continents, coordinating with more than 240 partnering organizations (made up of 250,000 members) to spread the word and culminating in a World Congress to be held in Miami, FL. For info: Heidi Richards, WeChamber, 10890 SW 27 Ct, Davie, FL 33328. Phone: (945) 981-5515. E-mail: heidi@wechamber.org. Web: www.wechamber.org.

JAPAN: RESPECT FOR THE AGED DAY. Sept 21. National holiday to honor Japan's senior citizens—especially those who are centenarians. Annually, the third Monday of September.

JONES, CHUCK: BIRTH ANNIVERSARY. Sept 21, 1912. Born at Spokane, WA, Chuck Jones worked as a child extra in Hollywood in the 1920s. After attending art school, he landed a job washing animation cels for famed Disney animator Ub Iwerks. He learned the craft, and by 1962 he headed his own unit at Warner Bros. Animation. He created the characters Road Runner and Wile E. Coyote, Marvin the Martian and Pepe le Pew. He worked on the development of Bugs Bunny, Elmer Fudd, Daffy Duck and Porky Pig, and also produced, directed and wrote the screenplay for the animated 1966 television classic "Dr. Seuss' How the Grinch Stole Christmas." He won several Academy Awards for his work, and his cartoon "What's Opera, Doc?" is in the National Film Registry. He died on Feb 22, 2002, at Corona del Mar, CA.

JOSEPH, CHIEF: DEATH ANNIVERSARY. Sept 21, 1904. Admirable Nez Percé chief, whose Indian name was In-Mut-Too-Yah-Lat-Lat, was born about 1840 at Wallowa Valley, Oregon Territory, and died on the Colville Reservation at Washington. Faced with war or resettlement to a reservation, Chief Joseph led a dramatic attempt to escape to Canada. After three months and more than 1,000 miles, he and his people were surrounded 40 miles from Canada and sent to a reservation at Oklahoma. Though the few survivors were later allowed to relocate to another reservation at Washington, they never regained their ancestral lands.

MALTA: INDEPENDENCE DAY: 45th ANNIVERSARY. Sept 21. National Day. Commemorates independence from Britain in 1964.

"MONDAY NIGHT FOOTBALL" TV PREMIERE: ANNIVERSARY. Sept 21, 1970. Following the complete merger of the American Football League and the National Football League, ABC joined CBS and NBC in televising weekly games with the debut of "Monday Night Football." The show began as an experiment but soon became an institution. Announcers Howard Cosell, Keith Jackson and Don Meredith called the first game, a 31–21 victory by the Cleveland Browns over the New York Jets. On Dec 26, 2005, "Monday Night Football" made its final telecast on ABC. In 2006, it moved to the cable channel ESPN.

NATIONAL LOVE YOUR FILES WEEK. Sept 21–25. A good filing system can be a powerful asset. Filing gets a bad rap because people do it the hard way. If a filing system is set up correctly, it's easy to maintain and a pleasure to use. Annually, the third full week (Monday through Friday) in September. For info: Jan Jasper. Phone: (212) 465-7472. E-mail: JanJasper52@hotmail.com. Web: www.janjasper.com.

NATIONAL WOMAN ROAD WARRIOR DAY. Sept 21. A day to honor the nation's traveling businesswomen. Woman Road Warriors are accountants and artists, techies and team builders, entrepreneurs and educators. They cover millions of miles each year to maintain that all-important in-person presence in the often impersonal and increasingly global business world. Simultaneously, many are also moms, coaches, wives and homework advisors, keeping busy households nurtured and on schedule, even from the other side of the world. This is a day to salute their persistence, flexibility, stamina and style. Annually, the third Monday in September. For info: Kathleen Ameche, 1040 W Montana St, Ste 100, Chicago, IL 60610. Phone: (312) 202-0034. Fax: (312) 642-6483. E-mail: kameche@amechegroup.com. Web: www.womanroadwarrior.com.

"NYPD BLUE" TV PREMIERE: ANNIVERSARY. Sept 21, 1993. This gritty New York City police drama had a large and changing cast. The central characters were partners Detective Bobby Simone (who later died), played by Jimmy Smits, and Detective Andy Sipowicz, played by Dennis Franz. Other cast members included Kim Delaney as Detective Diane Russell, James McDaniel as Lieutenant Arthur Fancy, Gordon Clapp as Detective Gregory Medavoy, Rick Schroder as Detective Danny Sorenson, Nicholas Turturro as Detective James Martinez, Mark-Paul Gosselaar as Detective John Clark and Esai Morales as Lieutenant Tony Rodriguez. The series ended in 2005.

"PERRY MASON" TV PREMIERE: ANNIVERSARY. Sept 21, 1957. Raymond Burr will forever be associated with the character of Perry Mason, a criminal lawyer who won the great majority of his cases. Episodes followed a similar format: the action took place in the first half, with the killer's identity unknown, and the courtroom drama took place in the latter half. Mason was particularly adept at eliciting confessions from the guilty parties. Regulars and semi-regulars included Barbara Hale, William Hopper, William Talman and Ray Collins. Following the series' end, with the last telecast on Jan 27, 1974, a number of successful "Perry Mason" TV movies aired and the show remains popular in reruns.

TAYLOR, MARGARET SMITH: BIRTH ANNIVERSARY. Sept 21, 1788. Wife of Zachary Taylor, 12th president of the US, born at Calvert County, MD. Died Aug 18, 1852.

"THE TEXACO STAR THEATER" TV PREMIERE: ANNIVERSARY. Sept 21, 1948. Also known as "The Milton Berle Show" and sponsored by Texaco until 1953, this popular variety show was a good sign for the fledgling TV industry. Milton Berle became a superstar. The show featured singing and comedy, especially sight gags and outrageous costumes, and guest stars. Changes were made in the fourth season: Berle cut back his appearances, new writers and a new director were added and the format was changed to a show-within-a-show. Ruth Gilbert, Fred Clark and Arnold Stang were featured, along with the new pitchman, ventriloquist Jimmy Nelson and his dummy Danny O'Day.

UNITED NATIONS: INTERNATIONAL DAY OF PEACE. Sept 21. The General Assembly proclaimed the International Day of Peace in 1981, "devoted to commemorating and strengthening the ideals of peace both within and among all nations and peoples." In 2001, the Assembly decided that, beginning in 2002, the International Day of Peace would be observed on Sept 21 each year (Resolution 55/282) as a day of global ceasefire and nonviolence, an invitation to all nations and people to honor a cessation of hostilities throughout the day. For info: United Nations, Dept of Public Info, New York, NY 10017. Web: www.un.org.

WELLS, HERBERT GEORGE: BIRTH ANNIVERSARY. Sept 21, 1866. English novelist and historian, born at Bromley, Kent, England. Among his books: *The Time Machine, The Invisible Man, The War of the Worlds* and *The Outline of History*. H.G. Wells died at London, Aug 13, 1946. "Human history," he wrote, "becomes more and more a race between education and catastrophe."

 Birthdays Today

Ethan Coen, 52, writer, producer (*Fargo*), born Minneapolis, MN, Sept 21, 1957.

Leonard Cohen, 75, singer, songwriter, born Montreal, QC, Canada, Sept 21, 1934.

David James Elliott, 49, actor ("JAG"), born Toronto, ON, Canada, Sept 21, 1960.

Cecil Grant Fielder, 46, former baseball player, born Los Angeles, CA, Sept 21, 1963.

Fannie Flagg, 65, actress, author (*Fried Green Tomatoes*), born Birmingham, AL, Sept 21, 1944.

Henry Gibson, 74, comedian ("Rowan and Martin's Laugh-In"), actor (*Nashville*, "Boston Legal"), born Germantown, PA, Sept 21, 1935.

Artis Gilmore, 60, former basketball player, born Chipley, FL, Sept 21, 1949.

Larry Hagman, 78, actor ("I Dream of Jeannie," "Dallas"), born Fort Worth,TX, Sept 21, 1931.

Faith Hill, 42, country singer, born Jackson, MS, Sept 21, 1967.

Stephen King, 62, author (*Christine, Pet Sematary, The Shining, Misery, The Stand*), born Portland, ME, Sept 21, 1947.

Bill Kurtis, 69, TV journalist, born Pensacola, FL, Sept 21, 1940.

Ricki Lake, 41, talk-show host, actress (*Hairspray, Serial Mom*), born New York, NY, Sept 21, 1968.

Rob Morrow, 47, actor ("Numb3rs," "Northern Exposure," *Quiz Show*), born New Rochelle, NY, Sept 21, 1962.

Bill Murray, 59, comedian, actor (*Lost in Translation, Groundhog Day, Caddyshack*), born Evanston, IL, Sept 21, 1950.

Nicole Richie, 28, television personality ("The Simple Life"), born Berkeley, CA, Sept 21, 1981.

Kay Ryan, 64, US Poet Laureate, born San Jose, CA, Sept 21, 1945.

Nancy Travis, 48, actress ("Becker," *Three Men and a Baby*), born New York, NY, Sept 21, 1961.

Luke Wilson, 38, actor (*Old School, The Royal Tenenbaums, Legally Blonde*), born Dallas, TX, Sept 21, 1971.

September 22 — Tuesday

DAY 265 100 REMAINING

AMERICAN BUSINESS WOMEN'S DAY. Sept 22. A day set forth by Congress on which all Americans can recognize the important contributions more than 57 million American working women have made and are continuing to make to this nation. Annually, Sept 22. For info: American Business Women's Assn, 9100 Ward Pkwy, Kansas City, MO 64114. Phone: (800) 228-0007. Fax: (816) 361-4991. E-mail: abwa@abwa.org. Web: www.abwa.org.

AUTUMN. Sept 22–Dec 21. In the Northern Hemisphere, autumn begins today with the autumnal equinox, at 5:18 PM, EDT. Note that in the Southern Hemisphere today is the beginning of spring. Everywhere on Earth (except near the poles) the sun rises due east and sets due west and daylight length is nearly identical—about 12 hours, 8 minutes.

"CHARLIE'S ANGELS" TV PREMIERE: ANNIVERSARY. Sept 22, 1976. This extremely popular show of the '70s featured three attractive women solving crimes. Sabrina Duncan (Kate Jackson), Jill Munroe (Farrah Fawcett-Majors) and Kelly Garrett (Jaclyn Smith) signed on with detective agency Charles Townsend Associates. Their boss was never seen, only heard (the voice of John Forsythe); messages were communicated to the women by his associate John Bosley (David Doyle). During the course of the series, Cheryl Ladd replaced Fawcett, Shelley Hack and Tanya Roberts succeeded Kate Jackson. The show went off the air in 1981 but feature films were made in 2000 and 2003.

DEAR DIARY DAY. Sept 22. Put it on paper. You'll feel better. No need to be a professional writer. (©2006 by WH.) For info: Thomas & Ruth Roy, Wellcat Holidays, 2418 Long Ln, Lebanon, PA 17046. Phone: (717) 279-0184. E-mail: info@wellcat.com. Web: www.wellcat.com.

ELEPHANT APPRECIATION DAY. Sept 22. Celebrate the earth's largest, most interesting and most noble endangered land animal. Free info kit from: Wayne Hepburn, Mission Media, Inc, PO Box 50095, Sarasota, FL 34232. Phone: (941) 355-4552. Fax: (941) 355-6592. Web: www.himandus.net/elephanteria.

EMANCIPATION PROCLAMATION: ANNIVERSARY. Sept 22, 1862. One of the most important presidential proclamations of American history is that of Sept 22, 1862, in which Abraham Lincoln, by executive proclamation, freed the slaves in the rebelling states. "That on . . . [Jan 1, 1863] . . . all persons held as slaves within any state or designated part of a state, the people whereof shall then be in rebellion against the United States, shall be then, thenceforward, and forever, free." See also: "13th Amendment Anniversary" (Dec 18) for abolition of slavery in all states.

"FAMILY TIES" TV PREMIERE: ANNIVERSARY. Sept 22, 1982. This popular '80s sitcom was set at Columbus, OH, and focused on the Keaton family: Ex-hippies Elyse (Meredith Baxter-Birney), an architect, and Steven (Michael Gross), a station manager of the local public TV station, Alex (Michael J. Fox), their smart, conservative and financially driven son, Mallory (Justine Bateman), their materialistic, ditzy daughter and Jennifer (Tina Yothers), their tomboy youngest daughter. Later in the series Elyse gave birth to Andrew (Brian Bonsall). Marc Price played Irwin "Skippy" Handleman, the nerdy next-door neighbor who adored the Keatons, and Mallory in particular. The last episode aired Sept 17, 1989.

September 2009	S	M	T	W	T	F	S
			1	2	3	4	5
	6	7	8	9	10	11	12
	13	14	15	16	17	18	19
	20	21	22	23	24	25	26
	27	28	29	30			

FARADAY, MICHAEL: BIRTH ANNIVERSARY. Sept 22, 1791. English scientist and early experimenter with electricity, born at Newington, Surrey, England. Died at Hampton Court, Aug 25, 1867.

FIRST ALL-WOMAN JURY EMPANELED IN COLONIES: ANNIVERSARY. Sept 22, 1656. The General Provincial Court at Patuxent, MD, empaneled the first all-woman jury in the colonies to hear the case of Judith Catchpole, accused of murdering her child. The defendant claimed she had never even been pregnant, and after all the evidence was heard, the jury acquitted her.

"FRIENDS" TV PREMIERE: 15th ANNIVERSARY. Sept 22, 1994. This hugely popular NBC comedy brought together six single friends and the issues in their personal lives, ranging from their jobs to their romances. The cast was Courteney Cox Arquette, Lisa Kudrow, Jennifer Aniston, Matthew Perry, David Schwimmer and Matt Le Blanc. The show concluded its run in 2004, with a finale in which 51.1 million viewers tuned in, making its finale the fourth most-watched TV program in history.

HOBBIT DAY. Sept 22. To commemorate the birthdays of Frodo and Bilbo Baggins and their creator J.R.R. Tolkien. For info: Secretary, American Tolkien Society, PO Box 97, Highland, MI 48357-0097. E-mail: americantolkiensociety@yahoo.com. Web: www.americantolkiensociety.org.

HOUSEMAN, JOHN: BIRTH ANNIVERSARY. Sept 22, 1902. American actor and producer John Houseman was born Jacques Haussmann at Bucharest. He is best known for his collaboration with Orson Welles on the 1938 radio production of *War of the Worlds* and for his role as Professor Kingsfield in the film and television version of *The Paper Chase*. He won an Oscar for that film role in 1974 and helped establish the Juilliard drama school and the Acting Company repertory group. He died Oct 30, 1988, at Malibu, CA.

ICE CREAM CONE: ANNIVERSARY. Sept 22, 1903. Italo Marchiony emigrated from Italy in the late 1800s and soon thereafter went into business at New York, NY, with a pushcart dispensing lemon ice. Success soon led to a small fleet of pushcarts, and the inventive Marchiony was inspired to develop a cone, first made of paper, later of pastry, to hold the tasty delicacy. On Sept 22, 1903, his application for a patent for his new mold was filed, and US Patent No 746971 was issued to him Dec 15, 1903.

INTERNATIONAL DAY OF RADIANT PEACE. Sept 22. Observed since 1999, this day celebrates and commemorates Radiant Peace, peace that starts with each one of us. Commemorations of the International Day of Radiant Peace range from Walks for Radiant Peace to citywide and statewide proclamations recognizing the International Day of Radiant Peace, special Radiant Peace projects with children, ringing bells for Radiant Peace, and Radiant Peace Picnics. Observed annually on Sept 22. For info: The Radiant Peace Foundation Intl, Inc, PO Box 40822, St. Petersburg, FL 33743. Phone: (727) 343-8212. E-mail: RadiantPeaceIntl@gmail.com. Web: www.radiantpeace.org.

IRAN-IRAQ WAR: ANNIVERSARY. Sept 22, 1980. Iraq invaded western Iran on this date, starting an eight-year war. This deadly war saw one million casualties, the use of chemical weapons and extensive damage to each nation's economy.

JACKSON COUNTY APPLE FESTIVAL. Sept 22–26. Jackson County, OH. Mountains of apples and barrels of cider. Homemade apple butter, apple pies and candy apples. Est attendance: 225,000. For info: Jackson County Apple Festival, Inc, PO Box 8, Jackson, OH 45640-0008. Phone: (740) 286-1339. Web: www.jacksonapplefestival.com.

JAPAN: AUTUMNAL EQUINOX DAY. Sept 22. National holiday in Japan.

LONG COUNT DAY: ANNIVERSARY. Sept 22, 1927. Anniversary of world championship boxing match between Jack Dempsey and Gene Tunney, at Soldier Field, Chicago, IL. It was the largest fight purse ($990,446) in the history of boxing to that time. Nearly half the population of the US is believed to have listened to the radio broadcast of this fight. In the seventh round of the 10-round fight, Tunney was knocked down. Following the rules, Referee Dave Barry interrupted the count when Dempsey failed to go to the farthest corner. The count was resumed and Tunney got to his feet at the count of nine. Stopwatch records of those present claimed the total elapsed time from the beginning of the count until Tunney got to his feet at 12–15 seconds. Tunney, awarded seven of the 10 rounds, won the fight and claimed the world championship. Dempsey's appeal was denied and he never fought again. Tunney retired the following year after one more (successful) fight.

MABON. Sept 22. (Also called Alban Elfed.) One of the "Lesser Sabbats" during the Wiccan year, Mabon marks the second harvest as Nature prepares for the coming of winter. Annually, on the autumnal equinox.

MALI: INDEPENDENCE DAY. Sept 22. National holiday commemorating independence from France in 1960. Mali, in West Africa, was known as the French Sudan while a colony.

"MAVERICK" TV PREMIERE: ANNIVERSARY. Sept 22, 1957. This popular Western starred James Garner as Bret Maverick, a clever man who preferred card playing to fighting. A second Maverick was introduced when production was behind schedule—Jack Kelly played his brother Bart. Garner and Kelly played most episodes separately, and when Garner left in 1961, Kelly was in almost all the episodes. Other performers included Roger Moore, Robert Colbert and Diane Brewster. This Western distinguished itself by its light touch and parody of other Westerns.

STANHOPE, PHILIP DORMER: BIRTH ANNIVERSARY. Sept 22, 1694. (Old Style date.) Philip Dormer Stanhope, the 4th Earl of Chesterfield, was born at London, England. He was a brilliant politician and orator. On Feb 20, 1751, he brought a bill into the House of Lords that caused the "New Style" Gregorian calendar to replace the "Old Style" Julian calendar in 1752. His influential political career was eclipsed by the fame of the letters he wrote to his son Philip, giving shrewd counsel on manners, morals and the ways of the world. Published less than a year after his own death at London, Mar 24, 1773, the *Letters* became immensely popular, were translated and republished in many editions. The Chesterfield, a kind of sofa, is said to be named for him.

US POSTMASTER GENERAL ESTABLISHED: ANNIVERSARY. Sept 22, 1789. Congress established office of Postmaster General, following the Departments of State, War and Treasury.

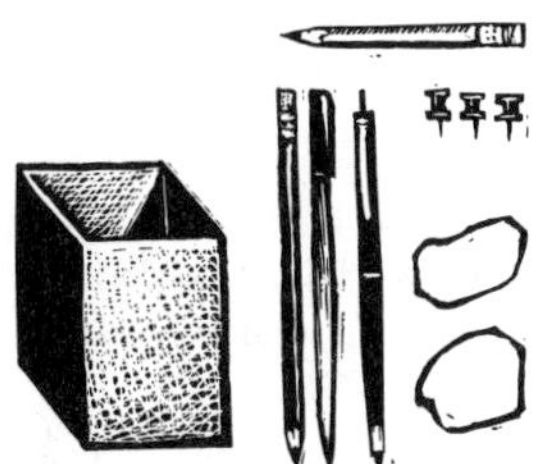

Birthdays Today

Scott Baio, 48, actor ("Happy Days," "Diagnosis Murder," "Charles in Charge"), born Brooklyn, NY, Sept 22, 1961.

Shari Belafonte-Harper, 55, model, actress, born New York, NY, Sept 22, 1954.

Debbie Boone, 53, singer ("You Light Up My Life," "Baby, I'm Yours"), born Hackensack, NJ, Sept 22, 1956.

Bonnie Hunt, 45, actress (*Jerry Maguire, Jumanji*), born Chicago, IL, Sept 22, 1964.

Joan Jett, 49, singer ("I Love Rock 'n' Roll"), born Philadelphia, PA, Sept 22, 1960.

Thomas Charles (Tommy) Lasorda, 82, Hall of Fame baseball manager and former player, born Norristown, PA, Sept 22, 1927.

Paul Le Mat, 64, actor (*American Graffiti, Melvin and Howard*), born Rahway, NY, Sept 22, 1945.

Catherine Oxenberg, 48, actress ("Dynasty"), born New York, NY, Sept 22, 1961.

Mike Richter, 43, former hockey player, born Philadelphia, PA, Sept 22, 1966.

Ronaldo, 33, soccer player, born Ronaldo Luiz Nazario de Lima at Rio de Janeiro, Brazil, Sept 22, 1976.

Arthur O. Sulzberger, 58, publisher (*The New York Times*), born Mount Kisco, NY, Sept 22, 1951.

Junko Tabei, 70, mountaineer (first woman to climb Mount Everest), born Fukushima Prefecture, Japan, Sept 22, 1939.

September 23 — Wednesday

DAY 266 — **99 REMAINING**

AMERICAN MASSAGE THERAPY ASSOCIATION® NATIONAL CONVENTION. Sept 23–26. Rosen Shingle Creek Resort, Orlando, FL. Annual meeting and convention of the American Massage Therapy Association (AMTA). The AMTA is a nonprofit, professional association with more than 57,000 members from throughout the US. Includes continuing education classes, association governance and current massage research. Exhibit area of products and services pertinent to the profession. Est attendance: 1,000. For info: American Massage Therapy Assn, 500 Davis St, Evanston, IL 60201. Phone: (877) 905-2700. E-mail: media@amtamassage.org. Web: www.amtamassage.org.

BASEBALL'S GREATEST DISPUTE: ANNIVERSARY. Sept 23, 1908. In the decisive game between the Chicago Cubs and the New York Giants, the National League pennant race erupted in controversy during the bottom of the ninth with the score tied 1–1, at the Polo Grounds, New York, NY. New York was at bat with two men on. The batter hit safely to center field, scoring the winning run. Chicago claimed that the runner on first, Fred Merkle, seeing the winning run scored, headed toward the dugout without advancing to second base, thus invalidating the play. The Chicago second baseman, Johnny Evers, attempted to get the ball and tag Merkle out, but was prevented by the fans streaming onto the field. Days later Harry C. Pulliam, head of the National Commission of Organized Baseball, decided to call the game a tie. The teams were forced to play a postseason play-off game, which the Cubs won 4–2. Fans invented the terms "boner" and "bonehead" in reference to the play and it has gone down in baseball history as "Merkle's Boner."

BLACK WALNUT FESTIVAL. Sept 23–26. Stockton, MO. 48th annual. Tours of the largest black walnut processing plant in the world. Also included are a parade, craft demonstrations, queen contest, carnival and musical entertainment. Est attendance: 30,000. For info: Stockton Area Chamber of Commerce, PO Box 410, Stockton, MO 65785. Phone: (417) 276-5213. E-mail: stocktonchamber@windstream.net. Web: www.stocktonmochamber.com.

CHARLES, RAY: BIRTH ANNIVERSARY. Sept 23, 1930. Born at Albany, GA, Ray Charles Robinson began losing his sight at age 5. He began formal music training at the St. Augustine School for the Deaf and Blind, and by age 15 was earning a living as a musician. He went on to become one of the most influential performers of all time. As a pianist, singer, songwriter, band leader and producer, he played country, jazz, rock, gospel and standards. His renditions of "Georgia on My Mind," "I Can't Stop Loving You" and "America the Beautiful" are considered true American classics. He died at Beverly Hills, CA, June 10, 2004.

CHECKERS DAY: ANNIVERSARY. Sept 23. Anniversary of the nationally televised "Checkers Speech" by then vice presidential candidate Richard M. Nixon, on Sept 23, 1952. Nixon was found "clean as a hound's tooth" in connection with a private fund for political expenses, and he declared he would never give back the cocker spaniel, Checkers, which had been a gift to his daughters. Other dogs prominent in American politics: Abraham Lincoln's dog, Fido; Franklin D. Roosevelt's much-traveled terrier, Fala; Harry S. Truman's dogs, Mike and Feller; Dwight D. Eisenhower's dog, Heidi; Lyndon Johnson's beagles, Him and Her; Ronald Reagan's dogs, Lucky and Rex; George H.W. Bush's dog, Millie; Bill Clinton's dog, Buddy; and George Bush's scottie, Barney.

COMAL COUNTY FAIR. Sept 23–27. Comal County Fairgrounds, New Braunfels, TX. 116th annual fair. Local and surrounding community festival with exhibits of livestock, arts and crafts, antiques, agricultural products, poultry, handwork, baked goods and horticulture. Est attendance: 80,000. For info: Comal County Fair Assn, PO Box 310223, New Braunfels, TX 78131. Phone: (830) 625-1505 or (830) 609-2860. Web: www.comalcountyfair.org.

INNERGIZE DAY. Sept 23. A day set aside for anyone who has said "I don't have time to do the personal things I want to do for myself." Today is the day to set time aside for yourself to do anything you want to do. Annually, the day after the autumnal equinox. For info: Michelle Porchia, inner dimensions, 4 Daniels Farm Rd, Ste 137, Trumbull, CT 06611. Phone: (203) 924-1012. E-mail: michelle .porchia@gmail.com. Web: www.michelleporchia.com.

"THE JETSONS" TV PREMIERE: ANNIVERSARY. Sept 23, 1962. "Meet George Jetson. His boy Elroy. Daughter Judy. Jane, his wife." These words introduced us to the Jetsons, a cartoon family living in the twenty-first century, the Flintstones of the Space Age. We followed the exploits of George and his family, as well as his work relationship with his greedy, ruthless boss Cosmo Spacely. Voices were provided by George O'Hanlon as George, Penny Singleton as Jane, Janet Waldo as Judy, Daws Butler as Elroy, Don Messick as Astro, the family dog, and Mel Blanc as Spacely. New episodes were created in 1985 which also introduced a new pet, Orbity.

LEWIS & CLARK EXPEDITION RETURNS: ANNIVERSARY. Sept 23, 1806. After more than two years in the American West, the Corps of Discovery returned to St. Louis amid much fanfare. They had traveled—with the assistance of guides Toussaint Charbonneau and his wife Sacagawea (a member of the Shoshone tribe)—to what is now North Dakota and Montana, over the Continental Divide and to the Columbia River, which took them to the Pacific (November 1805). They lost only one man from the 33-member group. Their valuable findings on western tribes, geography, plants and animals dispelled many longstanding myths about the region. (See also Jan 18 and May 14.)

LIBRA, THE BALANCE. Sept 23–Oct 22. In the astronomical/astrological zodiac that divides the sun's apparent orbit into 12 segments, the period Sept 23–Oct 22 is identified traditionally as the sun sign of Libra, the Balance. The ruling planet is Venus.

LIPPMANN, WALTER: BIRTH ANNIVERSARY. Sept 23, 1889. American journalist, political philosopher and author. Born at New York, NY, he died there Dec 14, 1974. As a syndicated newspaper columnist he was the foremost and perhaps the most influential commentator in the nation. "Without criticism," he said in an address to the International Press Institute in 1965, "and reliable and intelligent reporting, the government cannot govern."

McGUFFEY, WILLIAM HOLMES: BIRTH ANNIVERSARY. Sept 23, 1800. American educator and author of the famous *McGuffey Readers*, born at Washington County, PA. Died at Charlottesville, VA, May 4, 1873.

September 2009

S	M	T	W	T	F	S
		1	2	3	4	5
6	7	8	9	10	11	12
13	14	15	16	17	18	19
20	21	22	23	24	25	26
27	28	29	30			

PAULUS, FRIEDRICH: BIRTH ANNIVERSARY. Sept 23, 1890. The German commander of the Sixth Army who led the advance on Stalingrad in 1942, Friedrich von Paulus was born at Breitenau, Germany. Paulus's troops succeeded in taking most of Stalingrad in November 1942, but eventually became trapped within the city they had captured. Paulus surrendered to the Russians Jan 31, 1943, the same day that Hitler promoted him to field marshal. He appeared as a key witness for the Soviet prosecution at the Nuremberg trials. Paulus died Feb 1, 1957, at Dresden, East Germany.

PETIT JEAN FALL ANTIQUE AUTO SWAP MEET. Sept 23–26. Petit Jean Mountain, Morrilton, AR. 10th annual antique auto swap meet, car corral, flea market and arts and crafts. Military vehicle show Friday and Saturday. More than 1,400 vendor spaces. Est attendance: 20,000. For info: Alan Hoelzeman, Museum of Automobiles, 8 Jones Ln, Morrilton, AR 72110. Phone: (501) 727-5427. Fax: (501) 727-6482. E-mail: moa@ipa.net. Web: museumofautos .com.

PIDGEON, WALTER: BIRTH ANNIVERSARY. Sept 23, 1897. Actor Walter Pidgeon was born at East St. John, NB, Canada. He died at age 87, Sept 25, 1984, at Santa Monica, CA. He made his film debut in 1925 in *Mannequin*. Among his films are *Saratoga* and *Mrs Miniver*.

PLANET NEPTUNE DISCOVERY: ANNIVERSARY. Sept 23, 1846. Neptune is 2,796,700,000 miles from the sun (about 30 times as far from the sun as Earth). Eighth planet from the sun, Neptune takes 164.8 years to revolve around the sun. Diameter is about 31,000 miles compared to Earth at 7,927 miles. Discovered by German astronomer Johann Galle.

SAUDI ARABIA: KINGDOM UNIFICATION. Sept 23. National holiday. Commemorates unification in 1932.

WOODHULL, VICTORIA CHAFLIN: BIRTH ANNIVERSARY. Sept 23, 1838. American feminist, reformer and first female candidate for the presidency of the US. Born at Homer, OH, she died at Norton Park, Bremmons, Worcestershire, England, June 10, 1927.

Birthdays Today

Jason Alexander, 50, actor ("Seinfeld," *Pretty Woman*; *Bye, Bye, Birdy*; stage: *Jerome Robbins' Broadway*), born Newark, NJ, Sept 23, 1959.

Ani DiFranco, 39, folk-punk singer and songwriter, born Buffalo, NY, Sept 23, 1970.

Julio Iglesias, 66, singer, songwriter, born Madrid, Spain, Sept 23, 1943.

Tony Joseph Mandarich, 43, former football player, born Oakville, ON, Canada, Sept 23, 1966.

Larry Hogan Mize, 51, golfer, born Augusta, GA, Sept 23, 1958.

Elizabeth Peña, 48, actress (*Rush Hour, Lone Star, Jacob's Ladder*), born Elizabeth, NJ, Sept 23, 1961.

Paul Petersen, 64, actor ("The Donna Reed Show," *Houseboat*), born Glendale, CA, Sept 23, 1945.

Mary Kay Place, 62, writer, actress ("Mary Hartman, Mary Hartman," *The Big Chill*), born Tulsa, OK, Sept 23, 1947.

Mickey Rooney, 89, actor (*Andy Hardy* movies, *The Black Stallion*), born Joe Yule, Jr, at Brooklyn, NY, Sept 23, 1920.

Bruce Springsteen, 60, singer, songwriter, born Freehold, NJ, Sept 23, 1949.

September 24 — Thursday

DAY 267 **98 REMAINING**

BARNESVILLE PUMPKIN FESTIVAL. Sept 24–27. Downtown Barnesville, OH. This 46th annual festival features King Pumpkin contest, Queen Pageant, Giant Pumpkin Parade, classic car show, banjo and fiddle contest and more. Annually, the last full weekend of September. Est attendance: 100,000. For info: Tom Michelli, President, Barnesville Pumpkin Festival, Inc, PO Box 5, Barnesville, OH 43713. Phone: (740) 425-2593. Fax: (740) 425-1042. E-mail: michelli@zippytech.com. Web: www.barnesvillepumpkinfestival.com.

CAMBODIA: CONSTITUTIONAL DECLARATION DAY. Sept 24. National holiday. Commemorates the new constitution of 1993.

"DANIEL BOONE" TV PREMIERE: 45th ANNIVERSARY. Sept 24, 1964. A successful show based loosely on the life of pioneer Daniel Boone, who helped settle Kentucky in the 1770s. Fess Parker starred as the American hero. Ed Ames played Mingo, Boone's friend, an educated Cherokee, and Pat Blair played his wife, Rebecca. Also featured were Albert Salmi, Jimmy Dean, Roosevelt Grier, Darby Hinton, Veronica Cartwright and Dallas McKennon.

FAIRMOUNT MUSEUM DAYS/REMEMBERING JAMES DEAN FESTIVAL. Sept 24–27. Fairmount, IN. The town where James Dean grew up honors Dean and other celebrated former citizens such as Jim Davis, creator of Garfield, journalist Phil Jones and Robert Sheets, retired director of the National Hurricane Center. The Fairmount Museum boasts "the Authentic James Dean Exhibit" of memorabilia and personal items of Dean's and it sponsors the festival that also includes a parade, James Dean Look-Alike Contest, custom car show featuring the James Dean Run for pre-1972 autos, Garfield Cat Photo and Art Contest, Garfield Great Run, carnival, booths, live '50s entertainment and more. Annually, the last full weekend in September. Est attendance: 40,000. For info: Fairmount Historical Museum, Inc, 203 E Washington St, PO Box 92, Fairmount, IN 46928. Phone: (765) 948-4555. Web: www.jamesdeanartifacts.com.

FANEUIL HALL OPENED TO THE PUBLIC: ANNIVERSARY. Sept 24, 1742. On this date Faneuil Hall at Boston, MA, opened to the public. Designed by painter John Smibiert, it was enlarged in 1805 according to plans by Charles Bulfinch. Today it is on the Freedom Trail, as part of the Boston Historical Park administered by the National Park Service.

THE 59 MINUTE 37 SECOND ANVIL MOUNTAIN CHALLENGE. Sept 24. Nome, AK. 14th annual running event that starts at the base of Anvil Mountain, where runners must run 834 feet up the face of the mountain and return in less than 59 minutes and 37 seconds or be disqualified from the competition. Trophies awarded for first–third finishers, first woman finisher and first finisher 16 years of age and under. Record time is 25 minutes 37 seconds. Est attendance: 1,000. For info: Rasmussen's Music Mart, PO Box 2, Nome, AK 99762-0002. Phone: (907) 443-2798 or (907) 443-2919. Fax: (907) 443-5777.

FITZGERALD, F. SCOTT: BIRTH ANNIVERSARY. Sept 24, 1896. American short story writer and novelist; author of *This Side of Paradise, The Great Gatsby* and *Tender Is the Night.* Born Francis Scott Key Fitzgerald, at St. Paul, MN, he died at Hollywood, CA, Dec 21, 1940.

GREAT AMERICAN BEER FESTIVAL. Sept 24–26. Denver, CO. Annual festival holds the Guinness World Record for most beers tapped in one location with 1,884 beers on tap. More than 408 US breweries will be found on the festival floor. Also featuring live music and Beer Garden and Food Marketplace. In the cooking demonstration area you can learn to cook with beer and pair a beer style with a particular food. Est attendance: 46,000. For info: Cindy Jones, Brewers Assn, 736 Pearl St, Boulder, CO 80302. Phone: (303) 447-0816. Fax: (303) 447-2825. E-mail: cindy@brewersassociation.org. Web: www.GreatAmericanBeerFestival.com.

GUINEA-BISSAU: INDEPENDENCE DAY. Sept 24. National holiday. Commemorates declaration of independence from Portugal in 1973.

HENSON, JIM: BIRTH ANNIVERSARY. Sept 24, 1936. Puppeteer, born at Greenville, MS. Jim Henson created a unique family of puppets known as the Muppets. Kermit the Frog, Big Bird, Rowlf, Bert and Ernie, Gonzo, Animal, Miss Piggy and Oscar the Grouch are a few of the puppets that captured the hearts of children and adults alike in television and film productions including "Sesame Street," "The Jimmy Dean Show," "The Muppet Show," *The Muppet Movie, The Muppets Take Manhattan, The Great Muppet Caper* and *The Dark Crystal.* Henson began his career in 1954 as producer of the TV show "Sam and Friends" at Washington, DC. He introduced the Muppets in 1956. His creativity was rewarded with 18 Emmy Awards, seven Grammy Awards, four Peabody Awards and five ACE Awards from the National Cable Television Association. Henson died unexpectedly May 16, 1990, at New York, NY.

"THE LOVE BOAT" TV PREMIERE: ANNIVERSARY. Sept 24, 1977. This one-hour comedy-drama featured guest stars aboard a cruise ship, the *Pacific Princess.* All stories had to do with finding or losing love.The ship's crew were the only regulars: Gavin MacLeod as Captain Merrill Stubing, Bernie Kopell as Doctor Adam Bricker, Fred Grandy as assistant purser Burl "Gopher" Smith, Ted Lange as bartender Isaac Washington and Lauren Tewes as cruise director Julie McCoy. The series ended with the last telecast on Sept 5, 1986, but special TV movies were broadcast in later years.

"LOVE OF LIFE" TV PREMIERE: ANNIVERSARY. Sept 24, 1951. This serial, which began as a 15-minute show, ran for 28 years. The story lines shifted from a focus on two sisters to a larger number of characters. The diverse cast included such notables as Christopher Reeve, Karen Grassle, Roy Scheider, Dana Delaney, John Aniston, Marsha Mason, Bert Convy, Warren Beatty and Barnard Hughes. The final airdate was Feb 1, 1980.

MARSHALL, JOHN: BIRTH ANNIVERSARY. Sept 24, 1755. Fourth Chief Justice of Supreme Court, born at Germantown, VA. Served in House of Representatives and as secretary of state under John Adams. Appointed by President Adams to the position of chief justice in January 1801, he became known as "The Great Chief Justice." Marshall's court was largely responsible for defining the role of the Supreme Court and basic organizing principles of government in the early years after adoption of the Constitution in such cases as *Marbury v Madison, McCulloch v Maryland, Cohens v Virginia* and *Gibbons v Ogden.* He died at Philadelphia, PA, July 6, 1835.

MOZAMBIQUE: ARMED FORCES DAY. Sept 24. National holiday. Commemorates the beginning of the war for independence in 1964.

"THE MUNSTERS" TV PREMIERE: 45th ANNIVERSARY. Sept 24, 1964. "The Munsters" was a half-hour sitcom about an unusual family who thought they were ordinary. Each family member resembled a different type of monster: Herman Munster (Fred Gwynne) was Frankenstein's monster; Lily, his wife (Yvonne DeCarlo), and Grandpa, her father (Al Lewis), were vampires and his son Eddie (Butch Patrick) was a werewolf. Only their niece, Marilyn (Beverly Owen and Pat Priest), looked normal, and they considered her the unattractive family member. Most of the show's laughs came from the family's interactions with outsiders. The last telecast was on Sept 1, 1966.

NATIONAL PUNCTUATION DAY. Sept 24. A celebration of the lowly comma, the correctly used quote, and other proper uses of periods, semicolons, and the ever-mysterious ellipsis. For info: Jeff Rubin, Founder, 1517 Buckeye Court, Pinole, CA 94564. Phone: (510) 724-9507 or (877) 588-1212. Fax: (510) 741-8698. E-mail: jeff@nationalpunctuationday.com. Web: www.nationalpunctuationday.com.

PRESTON COUNTY BUCKWHEAT FESTIVAL. Sept 24–27. Kingwood, WV. 68th annual. Celebrating the fall harvest, with coronations, parades, exhibits, arts and crafts, antique cars, livestock, carnival, country music and Buckwheat Cake Dinners. Annually, beginning the last Thursday in September. Est attendance: 100,000. For info: Darla Kuhn, Fest Secy, Kingwood Volunteer Fire Dept, PO Box 74, Kingwood, WV 26537. Phone: (304) 379-2203. Fax: (304) 329-0021. Web: www.buckwheatfest.com.

SCHWENKFELDER THANKSGIVING. Sept 24. On this day in 1734 members of the Schwenkfelder Society gave thanks for their deliverance from Old World persecution as they prepared to take up new lives in the Pennsylvania-Dutch counties of Pennsylvania. Still celebrated.

"60 MINUTES" TV PREMIERE: ANNIVERSARY. Sept 24, 1968. TV's longest-running prime-time program, TV's first newsmagazine offering in-depth investigative reports and profiles, was originally hosted by Harry Reasoner and Mike Wallace. The show's correspondents have included Ed Bradley, Steve Kroft, Lesley Stahl, Morley Safer, Andy Rooney, Scott Pelley, Dan Rather, Diane Sawyer and Bob Simon. Tough interviewer Mike Wallace announced his retirement from the show in 2006.

SOUTH AFRICA: HERITAGE DAY. Sept 24. A celebration of South African nationhood, commemorating the multicultural heritage of this rainbow nation.

STATE FAIR OF VIRGINIA. Sept 24–Oct 4. Meadow Event Park, Doswell, VA. It's the Big Red Barn, racing pigs, the State Fair Animal Nursery, the famous State Fair Duck Slide and more! Get up close and personal with more than 5,000 farm animals in Virginia's largest outdoor classroom. Enjoy 11 days of rides, thrills and fun for the whole family with blue ribbon competitions, exhibits, midway rides and shows. There's daily entertainment on the MusicFest Stage and in the Classic Amphitheatre. It's a Virginia tradition and the only place to get that delicious State Fair food. Est attendance: 350,000. For info: Mike Fritzsche, Fair Mgr, PO Box 26805, Richmond, VA 23261-6805. Phone: (804) 569-3200. Fax: (804) 569-3252. Web: www.statefair.com or www.statefairva.org.

Birthdays Today

Gordon Clapp, 61, actor ("NYPD Blue"), born North Conway, NH, Sept 24, 1948.

Alan Colmes, 59, journalist, talk show host ("Hannity & Colmes"), born New York, NY, Sept 24, 1950.

Morgan Hamm, 27, gymnast, born Ashland, WI, Sept 24, 1982.

Paul Hamm, 27, gymnast, born Ashland, WI, Sept 24, 1982.

Sheila MacRae, 86, singer, actress, born London, England, Sept 24, 1923.

Rafael Corrales Palmeiro, 45, former baseball player, born Havana, Cuba, Sept 24, 1964.

Kevin Sorbo, 51, actor ("Hercules"), born Mound, MN, Sept 24, 1958.

Nia Vardalos, 47, screenwriter, actress (*My Big Fat Greek Wedding*), born Winnipeg, MB, Canada, Sept 24, 1962.

September 2009

S	M	T	W	T	F	S
		1	2	3	4	5
6	7	8	9	10	11	12
13	14	15	16	17	18	19
20	21	22	23	24	25	26
27	28	29	30			

September 25 — Friday

DAY 268 — **97 REMAINING**

BALTIMORE BOOK FESTIVAL. Sept 25–27. Baltimore, MD. The mid-Atlantic's premier celebration of literary arts features authors, poetry readings, cooking and home and garden demonstrations and more than 125 exhibitors and booksellers. Many special programs for children. For info: Baltimore Book Festival, 7 E Redwood St, Ste 500, Baltimore, MD 21202. Phone: (410) 752-8632. Fax: (410) 385-0361. Web: www.baltimorebookfestival.com.

BAYFEST. Sept 25–27. Corpus Christi, TX. Plenty of fun at this waterfront festival. Includes amusement rides, games, arts and crafts displays, musical entertainment, food booths, merchandise exhibitors and much more. Est attendance: 150,000. For info: Bayfest, PO Box 1858, Corpus Christi, TX 78403. Phone: (361) 887-0868. Fax: (361) 887-9773. Web: www.bayfesttexas.com.

"BEAUTY AND THE BEAST" TV PREMIERE: ANNIVERSARY. Sept 25, 1987. This updated version of the fairy tale was a romantic hit and acquired a cult following. It followed the experiences of Catherine Chandler (Linda Hamilton), a Manhattan lawyer who is beaten and abandoned and subsequently found and cared for by Vincent (Ron Perlman), a man-beast living under the city. Other cast members included Roy Dotrice, Jay Acovone, Ren Woods, Cory Danziger and David Greenlee. Hamilton left the series at the beginning of the third season; the series ended shortly thereafter.

CELTIC CLASSIC HIGHLAND GAMES & FESTIVAL. Sept 25–27. Bethlehem, PA. America's largest highland games and festival, celebrating Celtic culture with three free days of Celtic music, Irish dance, world-class Highland athletic competitions, Border Collie exhibitions, pipe band and drum major competitions, art and history workshops, foods, crafts, entertainment and much more. Annually, the weekend beginning on the last Friday in September. For info: Celtic Cultural Alliance, Celtic Classic, 532 Main St, Bethlehem, PA 18018. Phone: (610) 868-9599. Fax: (610) 868-9730. E-mail: info@celticculturalalliance.org. Web: www.celticcultural alliance.org.

CHILI COOK-OFF AND FALL FESTIVAL OF THE ARTS AND CRAFTS. Sept 25–27. Washington, MO. Thirty teams compete for awards for best chili. Juried festival featuring the creative talents of two- and three-dimensional artists and crafters. Free children's area, beer area, specialty foods, music and live entertainment. Admission includes a commemorative chili mug (Fall Festival is free). For info: Downtown Washington, Inc, PO Box 144, Washington, MO 63090. Phone: (636) 239-1743. Fax: (636) 239-4832. E-mail: events @downtownwashmo.org. Web: downtownwashmo.org.

COMMON GROUND COUNTRY FAIR. Sept 25–27. MOFGA's Common Ground, Unity, ME. Old-time country fair celebrating rural life with the revival of forgotten skills and demonstrations of technology appropriate for the future. Features Maine-produced food, crafts, entertainment, farming demonstrations and talks, a very special children's area with daily and ongoing participatory activities. Annually, the third weekend after Labor Day. Sponsor: Maine Organic Farmers and Gardeners Assn. Est attendance: 60,000. For info: Jim Ahearne, Fair Dir, Common Ground Country Fair, PO Box 170, Unity, ME 04988. Phone: (207) 568-4142. Fax: (207) 568-4141. E-mail: cgcf@mofga.org. Web: www.mofga.org.

FABULOUS 1890s WEEKEND. Sept 25–26. Mansfield, PA. Night football in America began in 1892 with a game between Mansfield University and Wyoming Seminary. Annually, Mansfield celebrates a "Fabulous 1890s Weekend" to commemorate the event. Motorless parade, period exhibits, crafts and other events, including the re-creation of the first night football game. Sponsors: Mansfield University of Pennsylvania and Greater Area Mansfield Chamber of Commerce. Est attendance: 10,000. For info: Dennis Miller, Dir PR, Mansfield University, Beecher House, Mansfield, PA 16933. Phone: (570) 662-4293. Fax: (570) 662-4965. E-mail: dmiller@ mansfield.edu. Web: www.1890sweekend.com.

FAULKNER, WILLIAM CUTHBERT: BIRTH ANNIVERSARY. Sept 25, 1897. American novelist and short story writer William Faulkner (born Falkner) was born at New Albany, MS. A Nobel Prize–winner who changed the style and structure of the American novel, he died at Byhalia, MS, on July 6, 1962. Faulkner's first novel, *Soldiers' Pay*, was published in 1926. His best-known book, *The Sound and the Fury*, appeared in 1929. Shunning literary circles, Faulkner moved to a pre–Civil War house on the outskirts of Oxford, MS, in 1930. From 1930 until the onset of WWII he published an incredible body of work. In June 1962 Faulkner published his last novel, *The Reivers*.

FIRST AMERICAN NEWSPAPER PUBLISHED: ANNIVERSARY. Sept 25, 1690. The first (and only) edition of *Publick Occurrences Both Foreign and Domestick* was published by Benjamin Harris, at the London-Coffee-House, Boston, MA. Authorities considered this first newspaper published in the US offensive and ordered immediate suppression.

FIRST WOMAN SUPREME COURT JUSTICE: ANNIVERSARY. Sept 25, 1981. Sandra Day O'Connor was sworn in as the first woman associate justice on the US Supreme Court on this date. She had been nominated by President Ronald Reagan in July 1981.

GREENWICH MEAN TIME BEGINS: ANNIVERSARY. Sept 25, 1676. (Old Style date.) Two very accurate clocks were set in motion at the Royal Observatory at Greenwich, England. Greenwich Mean Time (now known as Universal Time) became the standard for England; in 1884 it became the standard for the world.

LIBERTY FALL FESTIVAL. Sept 25–27. Liberty, MO. Arts and crafts booth, food booths, children's activities, a carnival, a parade, car show, entertainment provided throughout the three-day festival. Annually, the fourth weekend in September. Est attendance: 35,000. For info: Liberty Area Chamber of Commerce, 9 S Leonard St, Liberty, MO 64068. Phone: (816) 781-5200. Fax: (816) 781-4901. E-mail: info@libertyfallfestival.com. Web: www.libertyfallfestival.com.

LOVE NOTE DAY. Sept 25. Words of love—powerful and poignant—expressed on paper. Who doesn't like to receive a love note? When it is so easy to get caught up in the "busy-ness" of life, here's a day to remember what is truly important in our life: our love partner. Send a love note today. Annually, the fourth Friday in September. For info: Leona Hamel, Love Note Day, 782 Annick St, Granby, QC, Canada J2J 2Z9. Phone: (450) 375-9566. E-mail: leona@romanceunlimited.com.

MAJOR LEAGUE BASEBALL'S FIRST DOUBLEHEADER: ANNIVERSARY. Sept 25, 1882. The first major league baseball doubleheader was played between the Providence and Worcester teams.

MOUNT PLEASANT GLASS & ETHNIC FESTIVAL. Sept 25–27. Mount Pleasant, PA. Large outdoor street festival featuring glass blowing demos, ethnic foods, arts and crafts, giant parade, national and regional entertainment, Old Town Mount Pleasant area and a nightly dancing light show to music. Free entertainment on three stages, fireworks, a carnival and unique activities. Est attendance: 45,000. For info: Jeff Landy, Mount Pleasant Glass and Ethnic Festival, Municipal Bldg, 1 Etze Ave, Mt Pleasant, PA 15666. Phone: (724) 830-7544. Fax: (724) 547-0115. Web: www.mtpleasantglassandethnicfestival.com.

NATIONAL ONE-HIT WONDER DAY. Sept 25. Honors the one-hit wonders of rock'n' roll. Anyone who ever had a hit single deserves eternal remembrance. For info: Steven Rosen, 2906 Utopia Pl, Cincinnati, OH 45208. Phone: (513) 321-1018. E-mail: srosenone@aol.com.

NEW YORK FILM FESTIVAL. Sept 25–Oct 11. Lincoln Center, New York City. The 47th annual film festival presented by the Film Society of Lincoln Center. 17-day showcase of the newest and most important films from around the world. Most features are US premieres, and more than 20 nations are represented. For info: New York Film Festival, Film Society of Lincoln Center, 165 W 65th St, New York, NY 10023-6595. E-mail: marketing@filmlinc.com. Web: www.filmlinc.com.

PACIFIC OCEAN DISCOVERED: ANNIVERSARY. Sept 25, 1513. Vasco Núñez de Balboa, a Spanish conquistador, stood high atop a peak in the Darien, in present-day Panama, becoming the first European to look upon the Pacific Ocean, claiming it as the South Sea in the name of the King of Spain.

PROWSE, JULIET: BIRTH ANNIVERSARY. Sept 25, 1936. Dancer, actress, born Bombay, India. Died Sept 14, 1996.

RAMEAU, JEAN PHILLIPPE: BAPTISM ANNIVERSARY. Sept 25, 1683. French composer Jean Phillippe Rameau was baptised today at Dijon, France (his birth date is unknown). Called by some the greatest French composer and musical theorist of the 18th century, Rameau died at Paris, France, Sept 12, 1764.

REEVE, CHRISTOPHER: BIRTH ANNIVERSARY. Sept 25, 1952. Born at New York, NY, this actor was best known for his portrayal of the title character in *Superman* (1978) and three sequels during the 1980s. After being paralyzed in a horseback riding accident, he was confined to a wheelchair and became an activist for spinal-cord research and awareness. He died at Mount Kisco, NY, Oct 10, 2004.

RIZZUTO, PHIL: BIRTH ANNIVERSARY. Sept 25, 1917. Hall of Fame baseball player who spent his entire career with the New York Yankees, born at Brooklyn, NY. He played shortstop from 1941–1956, winning the league MVP in 1950, and played in nine World Series, winning seven. After his playing career, he became the radio (and later television) broadcaster for the Yankees, and remained on the air for more than 40 years. His home run call of "Holy Cow!" is considered legendary. He died at West Orange, NJ, Aug 13, 2007.

RWANDA: REPUBLIC DAY. Sept 25. National holiday. Marks the 1961 abolition of the monarchy.

SEQUOIA AND KINGS CANYON NATIONAL PARK ESTABLISHED: ANNIVERSARY. Sept 25, 1890. Area in central California established as a national park. For further park info: Sequoia Natl Park, Three Rivers, CA 93271.

SHOSTAKOVICH, DMITRI: BIRTH ANNIVERSARY. Sept 25, 1906. Russian composer born at St. Petersburg, Russia. Died at Moscow, USSR, Aug 9, 1975.

SMITH, WALTER WESLEY "RED": BIRTH ANNIVERSARY. Sept 25, 1905. Pulitzer Prize–winning sports columnist and newspaperman for 54 years, Walter Wesley (Red) Smith was born at Green Bay, WI. Called the "nation's most respected sportswriter," Smith's columns appeared in some 500 newspapers. He died at Stamford, CT, Jan 15, 1982.

STATE FAIR OF TEXAS. Sept 25–Oct 18. Fair Park, Dallas, TX. Features a Broadway musical, college football games, new car show, concerts, livestock shows and traditional events and entertainment including exhibits, creative arts and parades. Est attendance: 3,000,000. For info: Public Relations, State Fair of Texas, PO Box 150009, Dallas, TX 75315. Phone: (214) 421-8715. Fax: (214) 421-8710. E-mail: pr@bigtex.com. Web: www.bigtex.com.

TACA FALL CRAFT FAIR. Sept 25–27. Centennial Park, Nashville, TN. 31st annual fair. The state's premier outdoor showcase for American fine crafts featuring 190 selected American craft artists from across the nation.TACA's Fall Craft Fair offers shoppers the opportunity to meet and talk with exhibiting artists, enjoy children's activities, visit special exhibits and demonstrations and purchase a wide variety of unique handcrafted works. Annually, the last weekend in September. Est attendance: 45,000. For info: Tennessee Assn of Craft Artists, PO Box 120066, Nashville, TN 37212. Phone: (615) 385-1904. Fax: (615) 385-1909. E-mail: taca@tennesseecrafts.org. Web: www.tennesseecrafts.org.

VIRGINIA PEANUT FESTIVAL. Sept 25–27. Emporia, VA. Annual celebration promoting peanuts and harvesting. Features musical concerts, arts and crafts, parade, corporate village, carnival, car show and fireworks. Sponsored by Emporia-Greensville Chamber of Commerce. Est attendance: 15,000. For info: Virginia Peanut Festival, Attn: Lisa Council, PO Box 956, Emporia, VA 23847. Phone: (434) 634-5405. E-mail: cor@ci.emporia.va.us.

WARRENS CRANBERRY FESTIVAL. Sept 25–27. Warrens, WI. 37th annual. A community celebration of the ruby-red fruit at the "Cranberry Capital of Wisconsin." During this "Cranfest," you can ride guided tour bus of a cranberry marsh to see how cranberries are raised and harvested. Also featured are more than 1300 booths of arts, crafts, antiques and flea market items, and mouth-watering fall produce including flavored honey, candy, Amish noodles, apples, and of course a variety of cranberry items. Est attendance: 110,000. For info: Warrens Cranberry Festival, Inc, PO Box 146, Warrens, WI 54666. Phone: (608) 378-4200. Fax: (608) 378-4250. E-mail: cranfest@cranfest.com. Web: www.cranfest.com.

 Birthdays Today

Chauncey Billups, 33, basketball player, born Denver, CO, Sept 25, 1976.

Tate Donovan, 46, actor ("Damages," *Love Potion No. 9*), born New York, NY, Sept 25, 1963.

Michael Douglas, 65, actor (Oscar for *Wall Street*; *Traffic, Wonder Boys, Fatal Attraction*), director, producer, born New York, NY, Sept 25, 1944.

Robert Gates, 66, US Secretary of Defense, born Wichita, KS, Sept 25, 1943.

Mark Hamill, 58, actor ("General Hospital," *Star Wars*), born Oakland, CA, Sept 25, 1951.

Heather Locklear, 48, actress ("Spin City," "Melrose Place," "Dynasty"), born Los Angeles, CA, Sept 25, 1961.

Michael Madsen, 50, actor (*Species, Reservoir Dogs, Kill Bill* films), born Chicago, IL, Sept 25, 1959.

Lee Norris, 28, actor ("One Tree Hill," "Boy Meets World"), born Greenville, NC, Sept 25, 1981.

Jamie Hyneman, 53, television personality, host ("MythBusters"), born Marshall, MI, Sept 25, 1956.

Scottie Pippen, 44, former basketball player, born Hamburg, AR, Sept 25, 1965.

Will Smith, 41, actor (*I Am Legend, Ali, Men in Black, Independence Day*), singer, born Philadelphia, PA, Sept 25, 1968.

Robert Walden, 66, actor ("Lou Grant," *All the King's Men*), born New York, NY, Sept 25, 1943.

Barbara Walters, 78, TV journalist, interviewer, born Boston, MA, Sept 25, 1931.

Catherine Zeta-Jones, 40, actress (Oscar for *Chicago*; *Traffic, The Mask of Zorro*), born Swansea, Glamorgan, Wales, Sept 25, 1969.

September 2009

S	M	T	W	T	F	S
		1	2	3	4	5
6	7	8	9	10	11	12
13	14	15	16	17	18	19
20	21	22	23	24	25	26
27	28	29	30			

September 26 — Saturday

DAY 269 **96 REMAINING**

APPLE SATURDAYS. Sept 26 (also Oct 3 and 10). Sabbathday Lake Shaker Village, New Gloucester, ME. Guided tours of the Shaker orchard exhibit and special events. For info: Leonard Brooks, Sabbathday Lake Shaker Village, 707 Shaker Rd, New Gloucester, ME 04260. Phone: (207) 926-4597. E-mail: usshakers@aol.com. Web: www.shaker.lib.me.us.

APPLESEED, JOHNNY: BIRTH ANNIVERSARY. Sept 26, 1774. John Chapman, better known as Johnny Appleseed, believed to have been born at Leominster, MA. Died at Allen County, IN, Mar 11, 1845. Planter of orchards and friend of wild animals, he was regarded as a great medicine man by the Indians.

BATTLE OF MEUSE–ARGONNE FOREST: ANNIVERSARY. Sept 26, 1918. As part of four major efforts to break the Hindenburg line, a Franco-American offensive began on this date, with the US First Army striking between the Meuse River and the Argonne Forest and the French Fourth Army to their west. After four taxing weeks of attack, the Germans were gradually pushed back. By Oct 31, the Americans had advanced 10 miles, the French had reached the Aisne River 20 miles away and the Argonne Forest was rid of the Central Power forces. This was the final great battle of WWI.

"THE BEVERLY HILLBILLIES" TV PREMIERE: ANNIVERSARY. Sept 26, 1962. This half-hour comedy was one of the most successful "rural" comedies on TV; in addition, according to Nielsen, the eight most-watched half-hour shows are episodes of this series. "The Beverly Hillbillies" was about an Appalachian man, Jed Clampett (Buddy Ebsen), who found oil on his property, so he moved his family to a better life in Beverly Hills, CA. Most of its jokes were based on its fish-out-of-water premise. Also in the cast were Irene Ryan as Granny, Jed's mother-in-law; Donna Douglas as his daughter Elly May; Max Baer, Jr, as his nephew Jethro Bodine; Raymond Bailey as neurotic Milburn Drysdale, Jed's neighbor; Nancy Kulp as Jane Hathaway, Drysdale's secretary; and Harriet MacGibbon as Margaret Drysdale, Milburn's wife.

"THE BRADY BUNCH" TV PREMIERE: 40th ANNIVERSARY. Sept 26, 1969. This popular sitcom starred Robert Reed as widower Mike Brady who has three sons and is married to Carol (played by Florence Henderson), who has three daughters. Housekeeper Alice was played by Ann B. Davis. Sons Greg (Barry Williams), Peter (Christopher Knight) and Bobby (Mike Lookinland) and daughters Marcia (Maureen McCormick), Jan (Eve Plumb) and Cindy (Susan Olsen) experienced the typical crises of youth. The program steered clear of social issues and portrayed childhood as a time of innocence. The last episode was telecast on Aug 30, 1974. The program continues to be popular in reruns, and there were also many spin-offs: a cartoon, a variety series, a sitcom, a short-lived dramatic series and films.

BUFFALO ROUNDUP ARTS FESTIVAL. Sept 26–28. Custer, SD. 16th annual. South Dakota artists and craftsmen display and sell their arts and crafts. Also Western and Native American entertainment, pancake feeds, chili cook-off and much more. Est attendance: 15,000. For info: Craig Pugsley, Visitor Services Coord, Custer State Park, 13329 US Highway 16A, Custer, SD 57730. Phone: (605) 255-4515. Fax: (605) 255-4460. E-mail: craig.pugsley@state.sd.us. Web: www.custerstatepark.info.

BY LAND AND BY SEA. Sept 26–27. Mystic Seaport, Mystic, CT. Get up close and personal with vehicles that industry relied on at the turn of the century. A dazzling display of authentic cars, trucks and motorcycles followed by a classic parade. For info: Mystic Seaport, 75 Greenmanville Ave, Mystic, CT 06355. Phone: (860) 572-5315 or (888) 973-2767. Web: www.mysticseaport.org.

DONIZETTI'S *LUCIA DI LAMMERMOOR* PREMIERE: ANNIVERSARY. Sept 26, 1835. *Lucia di Lammermoor*, one of opera's greatest tragic love stories, premiered in Naples, Italy. The opera was composed by Gaetano Donizetti with a libretto by Salvatore Cammarano. The plot was based on Sir Walter Scott's *The Bride of Lammermoor* and takes place in 17th-century Scotland. Lucia, thwarted by a blood feud from marrying the man she loves, kills her husband and then herself.

ELIOT, T.S.: BIRTH ANNIVERSARY. Sept 26, 1888. Thomas Stearns Eliot, Nobel Prize winner, poet, playwright and critic, was born at St. Louis, MO. "There never was a time," he believed, "when those that read at all, read so many more books by living authors than books by dead authors; there never was a time so completely parochial, so shut off from the past." Eliot died at London, England, Jan 4, 1965.

EVERYBODY'S DAY FESTIVAL. Sept 26. Thomasville, NC. A downtown street festival for "everybody." Crafts, food vendors and live entertainment. Annually, the last Saturday in Sept. Est attendance: 82,000. For info: Thomasville Area Chamber of Commerce, Box 1400, Thomasville, NC 27361. Phone: (336) 475-6134. Fax: (336) 475-4802. E-mail: tvillecoc@northstate.net. Web: www.everybodysday.com.

FALLASBURG FALL FESTIVAL. Sept 26–27. Fallasburg Park, Lowell, MI. Unique event with 85 artists displaying and selling their work. Historical setting, arts, entertainment, kids activities and food. Annually, the last full weekend in September. For info: Lowell Area Arts Council, 149 S Hudson, PO Box 53, Lowell, MI 49331. Phone: (616) 897-8545. Fax: (616) 897-3061. E-mail: info@lowellartscouncil.org. Web: www.lowellartscouncil.org.

FAMILY HEALTH AND FITNESS DAY—USA. Sept 26. 13th annual national event promoting family health and fitness. Families across the country will be involved in locally organized health promotion activities at hundreds of locations all on the same day. Always held the last Saturday in September. Est attendance: 25,000. For info: Carrie Farella, Program Mgr, Health Info Resource Center, 1850 Winchester Rd, Ste 213, Libertyville, IL 60048. Phone: (800) 828-8225. Fax: (847) 816-8662. E-mail: info@fitnessday.com. Web: www.fitnessday.com.

FESTIFALL. Sept 26–27. Friendship Hill National Historic Site, Point Marion, PA. To celebrate the 19th-century arts, crafts and music of the Allegheny Plateau. Historic foods are available for purchase. Annually, the last Saturday and Sunday in September. Est attendance: 4,000. For info: Friendship Hill Natl Historic Site, 223 New Geneva Rd, Point Marion, PA 15474. Phone: (724) 725-9190. Fax: (724) 725-1999. Web: www.nps.gov/frhi.

FIRST TELEVISED PRESIDENTIAL DEBATE: ANNIVERSARY. Sept 26, 1960. The debate between presidential candidates John F. Kennedy and Richard Nixon was televised from WBBM-TV, a Chicago TV studio. Howard K. Smith was the moderator.

FISH AMNESTY DAY. Sept 26. Give animals a break by not fishing. Fish are intelligent animals who feel pain just like the dogs and cats who share our homes. Annually, the fourth Saturday in September. For info: Lindsay Rajt, 501 Front St, Norfolk, VA 23510. Phone: (757) 622-7382.

FRANCE, BILL: 100th BIRTH ANNIVERSARY. Sept 26, 1909. William Henry Getty (Bill) France, Sr, stock car racing executive, born at Washington, DC. While running a service station at Daytona Beach, FL, France took an interest in the auto races contested on the beach. He got involved in race promotion and organization and founded NASCAR in 1948. He remained at the helm long enough to see the once-primitive sport evolve into a series of fantastic spectator events. Died at Ormond Beach, FL, June 7, 1992.

GENEVA AREA GRAPE JAMBOREE. Sept 26–27. Geneva, OH. 46th annual. Grape harvest and products. Annually, the last full weekend in September. Est attendance: 250,000. For info: Geneva Grape Jamboree, Box 92, Geneva, OH 44041. Phone: (440) 466-5262. Web: www.grapejamboree.com.

GERSHWIN, GEORGE: BIRTH ANNIVERSARY. Sept 26, 1898. American composer remembered for his many enduring songs and melodies, including: "The Man I Love," "Strike Up the Band," "Funny Face," "I Got Rhythm" and the opera *Porgy and Bess*. Many of his works were in collaboration with his brother, Ira. Born at Brooklyn, NY, he died of a brain tumor at Beverly Hills, CA, July 11, 1937. See also: "Gershwin, Ira: Birth Anniversary" (Dec 6).

"GILLIGAN'S ISLAND" TV PREMIERE: 45th ANNIVERSARY. Sept 26, 1964. Seven people set sail aboard the *Minnow* for a three-hour tour and became stranded on an island. They used the resources on the island for food, shelter and entertainment. The cast included Bob Denver as Gilligan, Alan Hale, Jr, as the Skipper, Jim Backus as Thurston Howell III, Natalie Schafer as Mrs "Lovey" Howell, Russell Johnson as the Professor, Dawn Wells as Mary Ann and Tina Louise as Ginger Grant, the movie star. The last telecast aired on Sept 4, 1967.

"HAWAII FIVE-O" TV PREMIERE: ANNIVERSARY. Sept 26, 1968. "Book 'em, Dano" became a national catchphrase after this CBS crime series began airing. It starred the granite-jawed Jack Lord as Steve McGarrett, leader of a special Hawaiian state police force that only answered to the governor. His officers included Danny "Dano" Williams (James MacArthur), Chin Ho Kelly (Kam Fong), Duke Lukela (Herman Wedemeyer) and others. Filmed on location at Oahu, HI, and featuring a popular theme song by the Ventures, the show was a huge hit until it concluded in 1980.

"KNIGHT RIDER" TV PREMIERE: ANNIVERSARY. Sept 26, 1982. David Hasselhoff starred in this one-hour adventure series about a cop who was nearly killed, then brought back to life with a new identity (Michael Knight) by a mysterious millionaire. Together with a car that talked, a Pontiac Trans Am called KITT (Knight Industries Two Thousand), Knight had various adventures. Other cast members included: Edward Mulhare as Devon Miles, aide to the deceased millionaire, Patricia McPherson as mechanic Bonnie Barstow, Rebecca Holden as April Curtis, William Daniels as the voice of KITT and Peter Parros as Reginald Cornelius III, truck driver/chauffeur for KITT.

MARION COUNTY COUNTRY HAM DAYS. Sept 26–27. Lebanon, KY. Country ham breakfast served under a tent in downtown Lebanon. Pokey pig 5k run, PIGasus parade, more than 100 arts and crafts booths and free entertainment. Est attendance: 40,000. For info: Kathy Browning, Lebanon-Marion County Chamber of Commerce, 239 N Spalding Ave, Ste 201, Lebanon, KY 40033. Phone: (270) 692-9594. Fax: (270) 692-2661. E-mail: info@hamdays.com. Web: www.hamdays.com.

MEDIEVAL FESTIVAL. Sept 26. Oatland Island Wildlife Center, Savannah, GA. Travel back to the time of knights and royalty. With the help of the Society for Creative Anachronism experience living in the Middle Ages. Featuring demonstrations of skills from the time period including sword fighting, crossbow demonstrations, storytelling, dancing and lots more. Also children's games and crafts, pony rides, face painting and other activities. For info: Oatland Island Wildlife Center, 711 Sandtown Rd, Savannah, GA 31410. Phone: (912) 898-3980. Web: www.oatlandisland.org.

MOON PHASE: FIRST QUARTER. Sept 26. Moon enters First Quarter phase at 12:50 AM, EDT.

✦ **NATIONAL HUNTING AND FISHING DAY.** Sept 26. Presidential Proclamation 4682, of Sept 11, 1979, covers all succeeding years. Annually, the fourth Saturday of September.

NATIONAL PUBLIC LANDS DAY. Sept 26. 16th annual. The nation's largest hands-on volunteer effort to improve and enhance the public lands that Americans enjoy. Each year, more than 90,000 volunteers take part in all 50 states, the District of Columbia and Puerto Rico. They build trails and bridges, plant trees and plants, remove trash and pull out invasive plants. Sponsored by Toyota. Annually, the last Saturday in September. Est attendance: 1,000,000. For info: National Environmental Education and Training Foundation, National Public Lands Day, 4301 Connecticut Ave NW, Ste 160, Washington, DC 20008. Phone: (202) 833-2933. Fax: (202) 261-6464. Web: www.neetf.org or www.publiclandsday.org.

NORSKEDALEN'S THRESHING BEE. Sept 26. Norskedalen Nature and Heritage Center, Coon Valley, WI. Antique engines and pioneer demonstrations, such as winnowing, threshing, corn shredding, shelling and grinding; cream separating and butter-making; horse-drawn wagon rides, rope braiding, sawmill, quilt show and farm tool displays. Threshers' meal served, reservations required. Est attendance: 500. For info: Norskedalen Nature and Heritage Center, Inc, PO Box 235, Coon Valley, WI 54623. Phone: (608) 452-3424. Fax: (608) 452-3157.

NORTHEAST MONTANA THRESHING BEE AND ANTIQUE SHOW. Sept 26–27. Culbertson, MT. See how Grandma and Grandpa worked and lived at the threshing grounds one mile southeast of town. Annually, the fourth full weekend in September. Est attendance: 2,000. For info: Rodney Iverson or David Krogedal, Northeast Montana Threshing Bee/Antique Show, Culbertson, MT 59218. Phone: (406) 787-5265 or (406) 963-2360. E-mail: dmkranch@yahoo.com.

OCEAN COUNTY DECOY AND GUNNING SHOW. Sept 26–27. Pinelands High School, Tip Seaman County Park and Tuckerton Seaport, Tuckerton, NJ. 27th annual. Gathering to celebrate the local waterfowling heritage. Emphasizes traditional skills such as decoy carving, working decoy rigs, sneakbox building, gunning, retrieving and goose- and duck-calling contests. Wildlife art and crafts, outdoor clothing and gear, hunting and fishing supplies. More than 400 vendors. Free. Rain or shine. Est attendance: 20,000. For info: Wells Mills Co Park. Phone: (609) 971-3085. Web: www.oceancountyparks.org.

POPE PAUL VI: BIRTH ANNIVERSARY. Sept 26, 1897. Giovanni Battista Montini, 262nd pope of the Roman Catholic Church, born at Concesio, Italy. Elected pope June 21, 1963. Died at Castel Gandolfo, near Rome, Italy, Aug 6, 1978.

R.E.A.D. IN AMERICA DAY. Sept 26. National Mall, Washington, DC. R.E.A.D. stands for "Reading helps Everyone Accomplish Dreams." An annual event, R.E.A.D. in America Day is sponsored by the CheeREADing program. The day's motto is "Anything is possible if you read." It is through the power of reading that goals are set and dreams are realized. The day's purpose is to raise awareness about youth literacy and to encourage the power of daily reading for our youth. The day's activities will include: a rally for reading (with local heroes and celebrities stopping by to read a book and share how reading has changed their lives), local bookstore "Power of One Hour" reading sessions and local school events. Annually, the fourth Saturday in September. For info: Ashley Anderson, CheeREADing, 5230 Norborne Ln, Houston, TX 77069. Phone: (281) 583-8440. E-mail: bkanderson1@sbcglobal.net.

SHAMU'S BIRTHDAY. Sept 26, 1985. Shamu was born at Sea World at Orlando, FL, and is the first killer whale born in captivity to survive. Shamu is now living at Sea World's Texas park.

SHEYENNE VALLEY ARTS & CRAFTS FESTIVAL. Sept 26–27. Fort Ransom, ND. This 42nd annual festival is one of the oldest and best in the area. Artists and crafters from several states join local people in offering 200 displays, church bazaar and dinner, turkey barbecue—all in a rustic historic atmosphere. Annually, the last full weekend in September. Sponsor: Sheyenne Valley Arts and Crafts Assn, Inc, a nonprofit organization. Est attendance: 10,000. For info: SVACA, PO Box 21, Fort Ransom, ND 58033. Phone: (701) 973-4461. E-mail: svaca@drtel.net.

TASTE OF MORGAN HILL. Sept 26–27. Downtown Morgan Hill, CA. 20th annual family festival featuring fine arts and quality crafts, entertainment, wine and beer garden, local restaurants and food booths, custom and classic car show and kids zone. Est attendance: 50,000. For info: Patti DeLaRosa, Morgan Hill Chamber of Commerce, PO Box 786, Morgan Hill, CA 95038. Phone: (408) 779-9444. Fax: (408) 779-5405. E-mail: mhcc@morganhill.org. Web: www.morganhill.org.

TRI-STATE BAND FESTIVAL. Sept 26. Luverne, MN. 59th annual festival with more than 2,500 high school students from Minnesota, South Dakota and Iowa; trophies awarded in four classes. Annually, the last Saturday in September. Est attendance: 8,000. For info: Jane Wildung, Exec Dir, Luverne Area Chamber of Commerce, 211 E Main, Luverne, MN 56156. Phone: (507) 283-4061. Fax: (507) 283-4061. E-mail: luvernechamber@iw.net. Web: www.luvernechamber.org.

***WEST SIDE STORY* PREMIERE: ANNIVERSARY.** Sept 26, 1957. Composer Leonard Bernstein's updated Romeo and Juliet musical premiered on Broadway and ran until 1960. Stephen Sondheim wrote the lyrics, Arthur Laurents wrote the book and Jerome Robbins created the choreography.

WILD WEST SHOW AND BULLWHACKER DAYS. Sept 26–27. Mahaffie Stagecoach Stop and Farm, Olathe, KS. A multicultural celebration of Olathe's Santa Fe Trail heritage with 1800s-period demonstrations, Mexican and American music, children's games and stagecoach rides. The Mahaffie Stagecoach Stop and Farm on the Santa Fe and Oregon Trails served warm meals for travelers as a stagecoach stop from 1863 to 1869. "Bullwhackers" were the men who drove teams of oxen. Annually, the last full weekend in September. Est attendance: 6,000. For info: Mahaffie Stagecoach Stop, 1200 Kansas City Rd, Olathe, KS 66061. Phone: (913) 971-5111. Web: www.olatheks.org/visitors/mahaffie.

XTERRA NATIONAL TRAIL RUNNING CHAMPIONSHIP. Sept 26. Bend, OR. The XTERRA Trail Run Series boasts over 50 events across the country with runs ranging from 5k to 25k. These extreme, off-road trail runs give runners the chance to prove their skills against a variety of terrain. From calf-burning hills to slippery, mud-covered paths athletes will face the ultimate test of endurance. This race is the championship for the ten XTERRA Trail Run series races that have taken place around the country, featuring off-road 5k, 10k and half-marathon distance trail runs. For info: XTERRA/TEAM Unlimited, 720 Iwilei Road #290, Honolulu, HI 96817. Phone: (877) 751-8880. E-mail: info@xterraplanet.com. Web: www.xterraplanet.com.

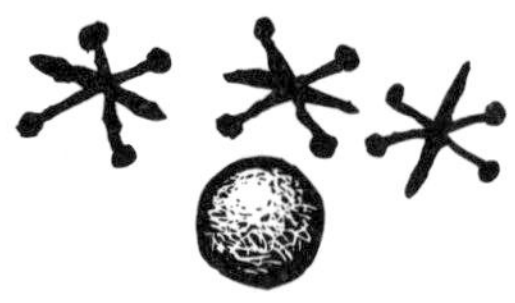

Birthdays Today

Lynn Anderson, 62, singer ("Rose Garden"), born Grand Forks, ND, Sept 26, 1947.

Melissa Sue Anderson, 47, actress ("Little House on the Prairie"), born Berkeley, CA, Sept 26, 1962.

Michael Ballack, 33, soccer player, born Gorlitz, Germany, Sept 26, 1976.

Bryan Ferry, 64, singer, songwriter, born Durham, England, Sept 26, 1945.

Linda Hamilton, 52, actress (*Terminator, Terminator 2;* "Beauty and the Beast"), born Salisbury, MD, Sept 26, 1957.

Mary Beth Hurt, 61, actress (*The World According to Garp, Six Degrees of Separation*), born Marshalltown, IA, Sept 26, 1948.

Olivia Newton-John, 61, singer ("Physical"), actress (*Grease*), born Cambridge, England, Sept 26, 1948.

Jane Smiley, 60, author (*A Thousand Acres, Moo*), born Los Angeles, CA, Sept 26, 1949.

Christine T. Whitman, 63, former administrator of the Environmental Protection Agency, former Governor of New Jersey (R), born New York, NY, Sept 26, 1946.

Serena Williams, 28, tennis player, born Saginaw, MI, Sept 26, 1981.

September 2009

S	M	T	W	T	F	S
		1	2	3	4	5
6	7	8	9	10	11	12
13	14	15	16	17	18	19
20	21	22	23	24	25	26
27	28	29	30			

September 27 — Sunday

DAY 270 **95 REMAINING**

ADAMS, SAMUEL: BIRTH ANNIVERSARY. Sept 27, 1722. Revolutionary leader and Massachusetts state politician Samuel Adams, cousin to President John Adams (1797–1801), was born at Boston. He died there Oct 2, 1803. As a delegate to the First and Second Continental Congresses Adams urged a vigorous stand against England. He signed the Declaration of Independence and the Articles of Confederation and supported the war for independence. Adams served as lieutenant governor of Massachusetts under John Hancock from 1789 to 1793 and then as governor until 1797.

ANCESTOR APPRECIATION DAY. Sept 27. A day to learn about and appreciate one's forebears. For info: AAD Assn, 2460 Devonshire Rd, Ann Arbor, MI 48104-2706.

AUTUMN FAIRY FUN DAY. Sept 27. A Fairy Fun Day is held once each season on the fourth Sunday. Autumn Fairy Fun Day is where fairy friends dress up, enjoy picnics, fairy hunts, arts and crafts and just get together to sparkle, laugh, delight and appreciate fairies, children and Nature. Events organized worldwide—join us to organize an event in your area! For info: Fairy Society Artist Community Network, 4128 Bye Way, Santa Cruz, CA 95060. Phone: (408) 564-5550. E-mail: michelle@elementaljoy.net. Web: http://thefairysociety.ning.com/.

BATTLE OF CAMBRAI–SAINT QUENTIN: ANNIVERSARY. Sept 27, 1918. British General Sir Douglas Haig moved his armies toward Cambrai and St. Quentin as part of four major efforts to break the Hindenburg line in the German salient that extended from Verdun to the sea. To the south the New Zealand and Canadian divisions smashed through the Hindenburg line on Oct 6. German General Erich Ludendorff resigned Oct 16, and the line was taken between Oct 18 and 20.

CRUIKSHANK, GEORGE: BIRTH ANNIVERSARY. Sept 27, 1792. English illustrator, especially known for caricatures and for illustration of Charles Dickens's books. Born at London, England, and died there Feb 1, 1878.

ETHIOPIA: TRUE CROSS DAY. Sept 27. National holiday. Commemorates the finding of the true cross (*Maskal*). Also a holiday in Eritrea.

GERMANY: real,- BERLIN MARATHON. Sept 27. Berlin. 36th annual. Awarded a road race Gold Label by the International Association of Athletics Federations. The real,- Berlin Marathon—with 40,000 participants—offers fantastic atmosphere with the final meters of the course going through the Brandenburg Gate. For info: Berlin Marathon, SCC-RUNNING Events GmbH, Glockenturmstrasse 23, 14055 Berlin, Germany. Phone: (49) 30-30-12-88-12. Fax: (49) 30-30-12-88-20. E-mail: office@berlin-marathon.com. Web: www.real-berlin-marathon.com or www.scc-events.com.

✦ **GOLD STAR MOTHER'S DAY.** Sept 27. Presidential Proclamation always for last Sunday of each September since 1936. Proclamation 2424 of Sept 14, 1940, covers all succeeding years.

"JACK THE RIPPER" LETTER: ANNIVERSARY. Sept 27, 1888. In the midst of the "Autumn of Terror" in which London, England, was convulsed over the crimes of a brutal serial killer, the city's Central News Agency received a letter written in red ink purporting to be written by the killer. He dubbed himself "Jack the Ripper" and threatened more killings. Police at the time and most historians today believe(d) the letter to be a hoax by an irresponsible journalist, but the name took hold in the public imagination and is forever associated with the Whitechapel murders of 1888. See also: "Whitechapel Murders Begin: Anniversary" (Aug 31).

NAST, THOMAS: BIRTH ANNIVERSARY. Sept 27, 1840. American political cartoonist born at Landau, Germany, best known for his cartoons attacking New York's Tweed ring. Died Dec 7, 1902, at Guayaquil, Ecuador.

NATIONAL CHIMNEY SAFETY WEEK. Sept 27–Oct 3. Each year CSIA Certified Chimney Sweeps work to raise awareness of chimney safety. For a list of Certified Chimney Sweeps in your state, call CSIA at (800) 536-0118. Annually, the week prior to National Fire Prevention Week. For info: CSIA, 2155 Commercial Dr, Plainfield, IN 46168. Phone: (317) 837-5362. Fax: (317) 837-5365. E-mail: office@csia.org. Web: www.csia.org.

REMEMBER TO REGISTER TO VOTE WEEK (US GENERAL ELECTIONS). Sept 27–Oct 3. This is the last week that every state in the nation still allows US citizens to register to vote for the November general elections. After this week, different states' deadlines will pass each day. One easy way to register to vote is at the free website Congress.org, where you can fill out an application, print, sign and mail it to the appropriate address. Annually, the seven days ending the 5th Saturday before the general election (which is the first Tuesday after the first Monday in November). For info: Lara Perkins, Capitol Advantage, 2751 Prosperity Ave, 6th Fl, Fairfax, VA 22031. Phone: (703) 289-4670. Fax: (703) 289-4678. E-mail: lperkins@capitoladvantage.com. Web: www.capitoladvantage.com.

SAINT VINCENT DE PAUL: FEAST DAY. Sept 27. French priest, patron of charitable organizations, and cofounder of the Sisters of Charity. Canonized 1737 (lived 1581?–1660).

SEMMES, RAPHAEL: 200th BIRTH ANNIVERSARY. Sept 27, 1809. Born at St. Charles County, MD, and died Aug 30, 1877, at Mobile, AL. Daring Confederate naval officer, best known for his incredible raids on Union merchant ships during the middle two years of the Civil War. As commander of the *Alabama*, he captured, sank or burned 82 Union ships valued at more than $6,000,000.

SPACE MILESTONE: *SOYUZ 12* (USSR). Sept 27, 1973. Because of the death of the crew of *Soyuz 11* upon reentry, it was decided that cosmonauts must wear pressurized space suits on takeoff and landing. Thus there was no longer room for three cosmonauts on a flight. Two Soviet cosmonauts (V.G. Lazarev and O.G. Makarov) made the two-day flight launched on this date.

"THE TONIGHT SHOW" TV PREMIERE: 55th ANNIVERSARY. Sept 27, 1954. "The Tonight Show" has gone through numerous changes over the years, yet it has remained a top-rated show that set the standards for all variety/talk shows to come. Steve Allen served as host from 1954–57. He introduced the format of the show with an opening monologue, games or segments for the studio audience, and then the interview on a simple desk and couch set. Jack Paar hosted from 1957–62 and Johnny Carson reigned as the king of comedy from 1962–92. Comedian Jay Leno serves as its current host.

WARREN COMMISSION REPORT: 45th ANNIVERSARY. Sept 27, 1964. On this day, the Warren Commission issued a report stating that Lee Harvey Oswald acted alone in the assassination of President John F. Kennedy on Nov 22, 1963. Congress reopened the investigation and in 1979 the House Select Committee on Assassinations issued a report stating a conspiracy was most likely involved. See also: "Committee on Assassinations Report: Anniversary" (Mar 29).

WORLD TOURISM DAY. Sept 27. Observed on the anniversary of the adoption of the World Tourism Organization Statutes in 1970. Annually, Sept 27. For info: World Tourism Organization, Calle Capitán Haya 42, 28020 Madrid, Spain. Phone: (34) 91-567-81-00. Fax: (34) 91-571-37-33. Web: www.world-tourism.org.

YOM KIPPUR BEGINS AT SUNDOWN. Sept 27. Jewish Day of Atonement. See "Yom Kippur" (Sept 28).

 Birthdays Today

Wilford Brimley, 75, actor (*Cocoon*, "Our House"), born Salt Lake City, UT, Sept 27, 1934.

Shaun Cassidy, 50, television producer, singer, actor ("The Hardy Boys"), born Los Angeles, CA, Sept 27, 1959.

Claude Jarman, Jr, 75, actor (*The Yearling, Rio Grande*), born Nashville, TN, Sept 27, 1934.

Steve Kerr, 44, former basketball player, born Beirut, Lebanon, Sept 27, 1965.

Jayne Meadows, 85, actress ("I've Got a Secret," "The Steve Allen Show," *Lady in the Lake*), born Chang, China, Sept 27, 1924.

Meat Loaf, 62, singer, musician (*The Rocky Horror Picture Show*), born Marvin Lee Aday at Dallas, TX, Sept 27, 1947.

Bello Nock, 41, circus clown, born Demetrius Nock at Sarasota, FL, Sept 27, 1968.

Arthur Heller Penn, 87, filmmaker (*Bonnie and Clyde, The Miracle Worker*), born Philadephia, PA, Sept 27, 1922.

Michael Jack (Mike) Schmidt, 60, Hall of Fame baseball player, born Dayton, OH, Sept 27, 1949.

Delores Taylor, 70, actress, writer, producer (*Billy Jack, The Trial of Billy Jack*), born Winner, SD, Sept 27, 1939.

Sada Thompson, 80, actress (*Twigs*, "Family"), born Des Moines, IA, Sept 27, 1929.

Francesco Totti, 33, soccer player, born Rome, Italy, Sept 27, 1976.

September 28 — Monday

DAY 271 — 94 REMAINING

BUFFALO ROUNDUP. Sept 28. Custer, SD. 44th annual. To round up, brand and separate 1,500 buffalo before auction in November. Est attendance: 11,500. For info: Craig Pugsley, Custer State Park, 13329 US Highway 16A, Custer, SD 57730. Phone: (605) 255-4515. Fax: (605) 255-4460. E-mail: craig.pugsley@state.sd.us. Web: www.custerstatepark.info.

CABRILLO DAY: ANNIVERSARY OF DISCOVERY OF CALIFORNIA. Sept 28, 1542. California. Commemorates discovery of California by Portuguese navigator Juan Rodr'guez Cabrillo, who reached San Diego Bay. Cabrillo died at San Miguel Island, CA, Jan 3, 1543. His birth date is unknown. The Cabrillo National Monument marks his landfall and Cabrillo Day is still observed in California (in some areas on the Saturday nearest Sept 28).

CAPP, AL: 100th BIRTH ANNIVERSARY. Sept 28, 1909. The creator of the fictitious village of Dogpatch, KY, Al Capp was born Alfred Gerald Caplin at New Haven, CT. The comic strip "Li'l Abner" appeared in daily newspapers from 1934 until its final episode was published Nov 13, 1977. Along with the misadventures of Abner Yokum, Capp lampooned famous public figures. The minor American institution of "Sadie Hawkins Day" made its debut in "Li'l Abner." Al Capp died Nov 5, 1979, at Cambridge, MA.

FAMILY DAY—A DAY TO EAT DINNER WITH YOUR CHILDREN™. Sept 28. A national movement to encourage parents to frequently eat dinner with their kids and be involved in their children's lives. Research by The National Center on Addiction and Substance Abuse (CASA) at Columbia University has shown that the more often children eat dinner with their families, the less likely they are to smoke, drink or use illegal drugs. Materials available on the benefits of frequent family dinners and how to address tough issues. Annually, the fourth Monday of September. For info: Family Day, CASA, 633 Third Ave, 19th Fl, New York, NY 10017. Phone: (212) 841-5200. Fax: (212) 956-8020. E-mail: familyday@casacolumbia.org. Web: www.casafamilyday.org.

FIRST NIGHT FOOTBALL GAME: ANNIVERSARY. Sept 28, 1892. The first night football game in America was played between Mansfield State Normal School (now Mansfield University) and Wyoming Seminary.

"HAZEL" TV PREMIERE: ANNIVERSARY. Sept 28, 1961. "Hazel" was based on a comic strip of the same name about a maid working for the Baxter family who gets into everyone's business. Hazel was played by Shirley Booth, and the Baxters were played by Don DeFore, Whitney Blake and Bobby Buntrock. "Hazel" moved from NBC to CBS after the third season and Hazel switched families from George to younger brother Steve Baxter. These Baxters were played by Ray Fulmer, Lynn Borden and Julia Benjamin. This successful series also featured Mala Powers and Ann Jillian.

INDIA: DASARA (VIJAYA DASAMI). Sept 28. Hindu holiday. Marks the triumph of Lord Rama over the demon king, Ravana, or the victory of good over evil. Effigies of Ravana are burned. Because there is no one universally accepted Hindu calendar, this holiday may be celebrated on a different date in some parts of India, but it always occurs in September or October.

MASTROIANNI, MARCELLO: 85th BIRTH ANNIVERSARY. Sept 28, 1924. One of the great international stars of cinema, born at Fontana Liri, Italy. Mastroianni worked with the master directors of the mid-20th century, among them Federico Fellini and Luchino Visconti. Two of his most famous roles were the world-weary journalist of *La Dolce Vita* (1960) and the in-crisis movie director of *8½* (1963)—both films directed by Fellini. He was nominated for Oscars three times and twice won the Best Actor Award at the Cannes Film Festival. Died at Paris, France, Dec 19, 1996.

NORTHEAST KINGDOM FALL FOLIAGE FESTIVAL. Sept 28–Oct 4. Walden, Cabot, Plainfield, Peacham, Barnet, Groton and St. Johnsbury, VT. Seven towns welcome visitors during Vermont's famous fall foliage season. Enjoy local food, music, arts and crafts, culture, historical demonstrations and more. Est attendance: 3,500. For info: Northeast Kingdom Chamber of Commerce, Fall Festival, 51 Depot Square, Ste 3, St. Johnsbury, VT 05819. Phone: (802) 748-3678 or (800) 639-6379. E-mail: nekinfo@nekchamber.com. Web: www.nekchamber.com.

SCHMELING, MAX: BIRTH ANNIVERSARY. Sept 28, 1905. First European boxer to hold the world heavyweight boxing title (1930–32). Best known for fighting American great Joe Louis twice: the first time defeating him; the second time losing. The Nazi government tried to use Schmeling—to his dismay—as a propaganda tool to demonstrate the superiority of the Aryan race. Schmeling rejected that role, never joined the Nazi party and was punished by being given dangerous WWII combat duties. Schmeling saved two Jewish boys during the November 1938 Kristallnacht terrors. Schmeling and Louis developed a strong friendship outside the ring and Schmeling paid for Louis's funeral. Born at Klein Luckow, Germany, Schmeling died Feb 2, 2005, at Hollenstedt, Germany.

SULLIVAN, ED: BIRTH ANNIVERSARY. Sept 28, 1901. Known as the "King of TV Variety," born at New York, NY. Sullivan started his media career in 1932 as a sportswriter for the *Daily News* in New York. His popular variety show, "The Ed Sullivan Show" ("Toast of the Town"), ran from 1948 until 1971. It included such sensational acts as Elvis Presley and the Beatles. He died at New York, NY, Oct 13, 1974.

September 2009

S	M	T	W	T	F	S
		1	2	3	4	5
6	7	8	9	10	11	12
13	14	15	16	17	18	19
20	21	22	23	24	25	26
27	28	29	30			

TAIWAN: CONFUCIUS'S BIRTHDAY AND TEACHERS' DAY. Sept 28. National holiday, designated as Teachers' Day. Confucius is the Latinized name of Kung-futzu, born at Shantung province on the 27th day of the tenth moon (lunar calendar) in the 22nd year of Kuke Hsiang of Lu (551 BC). He died at age 72, having spent some 40 years as a teacher. Teachers' Day is observed annually on Sept 28.

UNITED NATIONS: WORLD MARITIME DAY. Sept 28. This date varies by nation, but always takes place during the last week in September. A day to stress the importance of shipping safety and the maritime environment. For info: United Nations, Dept of Public Info, New York, NY 10017. Web: www.un.org.

WIGGIN, KATE DOUGLAS: BIRTH ANNIVERSARY. Sept 28, 1856. Kate Wiggin was born Kate Douglas Smith at Philadelphia, PA. She helped organize the first free kindergarten on the West Coast in 1878 at San Francisco and in 1880 she and her sister established the California Kindergarten Training School. After moving back east she devoted herself to writing, producing a number of children's books including *The Birds' Christmas Carol, Polly Oliver's Problem* and *Rebecca of Sunnybrook Farm*. She died at Harrow, England, Aug 24, 1923.

WILLARD, FRANCES ELIZABETH CAROLINE: BIRTH ANNIVERSARY. Sept 28, 1839. American educator and reformer, president of the Women's Christian Temperance Union, 1879–98, and women's suffrage leader, born at Churchville, NY. Died at New York, NY, Feb 18, 1898.

YOM KIPPUR or DAY OF ATONEMENT. Sept 28. Holiest Jewish observance. A day for fasting, repentance and seeking forgiveness. Hebrew calendar date: Tishri 10, 5770. Began at sundown on Sept 27.

Birthdays Today

Brigitte Bardot, 75, actress (*And God Created Woman, Viva Maria*), animal rights activist, born Camille Javal at Paris, France, Sept 28, 1934.

Hilary Duff, 22, actress (*A Cinderella Story,* "Lizzie McGuire"), born Houston, TX, Sept 28, 1987.

Janeane Garofalo, 45, actress (*Reality Bites, The Truth About Cats and Dogs*), born Newton, NJ, Sept 28, 1964.

Jeffrey Jones, 62, actor (*Beetlejuice, Stay Tuned*), born Buffalo, NY, Sept 28, 1947.

Ben E. King, 71, singer, musician ("There Goes My Baby"), born Henderson, NC, Sept 28, 1938.

Steve M. Largent, 55, Hall of Fame football player, born Tulsa, OK, Sept 28, 1954.

Emeka Okafor, 27, basketball player, born Houston, TX, Sept 28, 1982.

Se Ri Pak, 32, golfer, born Daejeon, South Korea, Sept 28, 1977.

Gwyneth Paltrow, 36, actress (Oscar for *Shakespeare in Love*; *Proof, The Talented Mr Ripley*), born Los Angeles, CA, Sept 28, 1973.

Brian Rafalski, 36, hockey player, born Dearborn, MI, Sept 28, 1973.

Suzanne Whang, 47, comedian, television personality ("House Hunters"), actress ("Las Vegas"), born Arlington, VA, Sept 28, 1962.

William Windom, 86, actor ("Murder She Wrote," Emmy for "My World and Welcome to It"), born New York, NY, Sept 28, 1923.

September 29 — Tuesday

DAY 272 — **93 REMAINING**

ANTONIONI, MICHELANGELO: BIRTH ANNIVERSARY. Sept 29, 1912. Groundbreaking Italian filmmaker, born at Ferrara, Italy. His films are known for their experiments with color, cinemetography, pacing and narrative structure. He was nominated for two Academy Awards for *Blowup* (1966) and was granted a Lifetime Achievement Oscar in 1996. He died at Rome, Italy, July 30, 2007.

AUTRY, GENE: BIRTH ANNIVERSARY. Sept 29, 1907. Born at Tioga, TX, Autry was arguably America's favorite singing cowboy in a career that spanned almost seven decades. He began performing on local radio in his late teens before signing with Columbia Records in 1931 and appearing for a time on the "National Barn Dance" radio show. His film career began soon after, and he starred in nearly 100 films, almost all of which were B-westerns in which his singing featured prominently. After retiring from acting, Autry became a baseball sports executive. He died at Los Angeles, CA, on Oct 2, 1998.

FERMI, ENRICO: BIRTH ANNIVERSARY. Sept 29, 1901. Nuclear physicist, born at Rome, Italy. Played a prominent role in the splitting of the atom and the construction of the first American nuclear reactor. Died at Chicago, IL, Nov 28, 1954.

HOWARD, TREVOR: BIRTH ANNIVERSARY. Sept 29, 1916. British actor Trevor Howard was born at Cliftonville, England. He appeared in more than 70 films including *The Third Man* (1950) and *Mutiny on the Bounty* (1962). He died Jan 7, 1988, at Bushey, England.

"MAKE ROOM FOR DADDY" TV PREMIERE: ANNIVERSARY. Sept 29, 1953. Danny Thomas starred as Danny Williams, a nightclub singer and comedian, in this family sitcom. The series was renamed "The Danny Thomas Show" in 1956 after Jean Hagen (who played his wife, Margaret) left the show. Thomas's costars were: Sherry Jackson and Penney Parker as Danny's daughter Terry and Angela Cartwright as daughter Linda; Rusty Hamer as son Rusty; Amanda Randolph as housekeeper Louise; Horace McMahon as Danny's agent, Phil Arnold; Jesse White as agent Jesse Leeds; Sid Melton as Charlie Halper, owner of the Copa Club; Ben Lessy as Danny's pianist, Ben; Mary Wickes as his publicist, Liz O'Neal; Hans Conried as Uncle Tonoose; Nan Bryant as Danny's mother-in-law and Marjorie Lord as his new wife Kathy. Many cast members returned for the show's sequel, "Make Room for Granddaddy," in 1970.

MICHAELMAS. Sept 29. The feast of St. Michael and All Angels in the Greek and Roman Catholic Churches.

NELSON, HORATIO: BIRTH ANNIVERSARY. Sept 29, 1758. English naval hero of the Battle of Trafalgar, born at Burnham Thorpe, Norfolk, England. Died during a battle at sea off Cape Trafalgar, Spain, Oct 21, 1805.

PARAGUAY: BOQUERÓN DAY. Sept 29. National holiday. Commemorates a victorious battle over Bolivia during the 1932 Chaco War.

SCOTLAND YARD FIRST APPEARANCE: ANNIVERSARY. Sept 29, 1829. The first public appearance of Greater London's Metropolitan Police occurred amid jeering and abuse from disapproving political opponents. Public sentiment turned to confidence and respect in the ensuing years. The Metropolitan Police had been established by an act of Parliament in June 1829, at the request of Home Secretary Sir Robert Peel, after whom the London police officers became more affectionately known as "bobbies." Scotland Yard, the site of their first headquarters near Charing Cross, soon became the official name of the force.

SPACE MILESTONE: *DISCOVERY* (US). Sept 29, 1988. Space Shuttle *Discovery*, after numerous reschedulings, launched from Kennedy Space Center, FL, with a five-member crew on board, and landed Oct 3 at Edwards Air Force Base, CA. It marked the first American manned flight since the *Challenger* tragedy in 1986. See also: "*Challenger*, Space Shuttle Explosion: Anniversary" (Jan 28).

SPACE MILESTONE: *SALYUT 6* (USSR). Sept 29, 1977. Soviet space station launched this date. *Salyut* stayed in space for four years, during which 31 spacecraft docked with the space station. Burned up when it reentered Earth's atmosphere after nearly five years on July 29, 1982.

"THIRTYSOMETHING" TV PREMIERE: ANNIVERSARY. Sept 29, 1987. This ABC drama series about a group of seven baby boomers was created by Ed Zwick and Marshall Herskovitz. It depicted the struggles of the show's characters—such as the death of a parent, illness, singlehood, marriage, divorce, career setbacks and the birth of a child. The cast featured Ken Olin as Michael Steadman; Mel Harris as his wife, Hope; Timothy Busfield as Michael's business partner, Elliot Weston; Patricia Wettig as Elliot's wife, Nancy; Polly Draper as Hope's friend Ellyn Warren; Melanie Mayron as Michael's cousin, Melissa Steadman; and Peter Horton as family friend Gary Shepherd. The last telecast was Sept 3, 1991.

VETERANS OF FOREIGN WARS ESTABLISHED: ANNIVERSARY. Sept 29, 1899. This organization is loyal to the issues and actions affecting America's heroes. Its members offer assistance in addition to supporting veterans issues in Congress. Part of the organization's mission, according to its charter, is "to preserve and strengthen comradeship among its members; to foster true patriotism; and to preserve and defend the United States from all her enemies, whomsoever." For info: Veterans of Foreign Wars of the United States, 406 W 34th St, Kansas City, MO 64111. Phone: (816) 756-3390. Fax: (816) 968-1149. E-mail: info@vfw.org. Web: www.vfw.org.

WORLD DAIRY EXPO. Sept 29–Oct 3. Madison, WI. World's largest dairy cattle exhibition and trade show features more than 680 commercial exhibitors and 2,500 head of cattle in seven breed shows at the Alliant Energy Center. About 200 animals offered for sale in five cattle breed sales. Educational forum. Open to the public. Est attendance: 65,000. For info: World Dairy Expo, 3310 Latham Dr, Madison, WI 53713. Phone: (608) 224-6455. Fax: (608) 224-0300. E-mail: wde@wdexpo.com. Web: www.world-dairy-expo.com.

Birthdays Today

Anita Ekberg, 78, actress (*La Dolce Vita*), born Malmo, Sweden, Sept 29, 1931.

Bryant Gumbel, 61, TV journalist, host, born New Orleans, LA, Sept 29, 1948.

Hersey R. Hawkins, Jr, 43, former basketball player, born Chicago, IL, Sept 29, 1966.

Patricia Hodge, 63, actress ("Rumpole of the Bailey," *The Elephant Man, Betrayal*), born Cleethorpes, Lincolnshire, England, Sept 29, 1946.

Jerry Lee Lewis, 74, singer, musician ("Whole Lot of Shakin' Goin' On," "Great Balls of Fire"), born Ferriday, LA, Sept 29, 1935.

Emily Lloyd, 39, actress (*Wish You Were Here, In Country, A River Runs Through It*), born North London, England, Sept 29, 1970.

Ian McShane, 67, actor ("Deadwood," "Lovejoy," *Sexy Beast*; stage: *The Homecoming*), born Blackburn, England, Sept 29, 1942.

Bill Nelson, 67, US Senator (D, Florida), born Miami, FL, Sept 29, 1942.

John Paxson, 49, former basketball player, born Dayton, OH, Sept 29, 1960.

Andriy Shevchenko, 33, soccer player, born Kiev, Ukraine, Sept 29, 1976.

Lech Walesa, 66, Polish statesman, Solidarity founder, born Popowo, Poland, Sept 29, 1943.

Dave Wilcox, 67, Hall of Fame football player, born Ontario, OR, Sept 29, 1942.

September 2009

S	M	T	W	T	F	S
		1	2	3	4	5
6	7	8	9	10	11	12
13	14	15	16	17	18	19
20	21	22	23	24	25	26
27	28	29	30			

September 30 — Wednesday

DAY 273 — **92 REMAINING**

AMERICAN DENTAL ASSOCIATION ANNUAL SESSION. Sept 30–Oct 4. Honolulu, HI. Est attendance: 50,000. For info: James P. Donovan, American Dental Assn, 211 E Chicago Ave, Ste 200, Chicago, IL 60611. Fax: (312) 440-2707. E-mail: annualsession@ada.org. Web: www.ada.org.

BABE RUTH SETS HOME RUN RECORD: ANNIVERSARY. Sept 30, 1927. George Herman "Babe" Ruth hit his 60th home run of the season off Tom Zachary, of the Washington Senators. Ruth's record for the most homers in a single season stood for 34 years—until Roger Maris hit 61 in 1961. Maris's record was broken in 1998 by Mark McGwire with 62 home runs. Barry Bonds broke McGwire's record on Oct 5, 2001.

BABE RUTH'S LAST GAME AS YANKEE: 75th ANNIVERSARY. Sept 30, 1934. On this date Babe Ruth played his last game for the New York Yankees. Soon after, while watching the fifth game of the World Series (between the St. Louis Cardinals and Detroit Tigers) and angry that he was not to be named Yankees manager, Ruth told Joe Williams, sports editor of the Scripp-Howard newspapers, that after 15 seasons he would no longer be playing for the Yankees.

BOTSWANA: INDEPENDENCE DAY. Sept 30. National holiday. The former Bechuanaland Protectorate (British Colony) became the independent Republic of Botswana in 1966.

CAPOTE, TRUMAN: 85th BIRTH ANNIVERSARY. Sept 30, 1924. American novelist and literary celebrity, was born Truman Streckfus Persons at New Orleans, LA. He later took the name of his stepfather to become Truman Capote. Among his best-remembered books: *Other Voices, Other Rooms; Breakfast at Tiffany's* and *In Cold Blood.* He was working on a new novel, *Answered Prayers*, at the time of his death at Los Angeles, CA, Aug 25, 1984.

"CHEERS" TV PREMIERE: ANNIVERSARY. Sept 30, 1982. NBC sitcom revolving around the owner, employees and patrons of a Beacon Street bar at Boston. Original cast: Ted Danson as owner Sam Malone, Shelley Long and Rhea Perlman as waitresses Diane Chambers and Carla Tortelli, Nicholas Colasanto as bartender Ernie "Coach" Pantusso, John Ratzenberger as mailman Cliff Clavin and George Wendt as accountant Norm Peterson. Later cast members: Woody Harrelson as bartender Woody Boyd, Kelsey Grammer as Dr. Frasier Crane, Kirstie Alley as Rebecca Howe and Bebe Neuwirth as Dr. Lilith Sternin Crane. The theme song "Where Everybody Knows Your Name," was sung by Gary Portnoy. The last episode aired Aug 19, 1993.

DAVIDSON FELLOWS AWARD RECEPTION. Sept 30. Library of Congress, Washington, DC. Each year, the Davidson Institute for Talent Development honors our nation's brightest young minds, students under the age of 18, who have completed prodigious works in science, mathematics, technology, music, literature, philosophy or outside the box. These students are recognized as Davidson Fellows Award recipients and receive up to a $50,000 scholarship to attend an accredited institute of learning. The Davidson Institute is a national nonprofit foundation dedicated to supporting America's most intelligent young people. Annually, the last Wednesday in September. For info: Tacie Moessner, Davidson Institute, 9665 Gateway Dr, Ste B, Reno, NV 89521. Phone: (775) 852-3483, ext 423. Fax: (775) 852-2184. E-mail: davidsonfellows@ditd.org. Web: www.davidsonfellows.org.

DEAN, JAMES: DEATH ANNIVERSARY. Sept 30, 1955. Rising young film star James Dean died in an auto accident near Cholame, CA, two hours after getting a speeding ticket. He was 24 years old. His final films, *Rebel Without a Cause* and *Giant*, were released posthumously in 1956. See also "Dean, James: Birth Anniversary" (Feb 8).

FEAST OF SAINT JEROME. Sept 30. Patron saint of scholars and librarians.

FIRST ANNUAL FAIR IN AMERICA: ANNIVERSARY. Sept 30, 1641. According to the Laws and Ordinances of New Netherlands (now New York and New Jersey), on Sept 30, 1641, authorities declared that "henceforth there shall be held annually at Fort Amsterdam" a Cattle Fair (Oct 15) and a Hog Fair (Nov 1), and that "whosoever hath any things to sell or buy can regulate himself accordingly."

FIRST CRIMINAL EXECUTION IN AMERICAN COLONIES: ANNIVERSARY. Sept 30, 1630. John Billington, one of the first Pilgrims to land in America, was hanged for murder, becoming the first criminal to be executed in the American colonies.

"THE FLINTSTONES" TV PREMIERE: ANNIVERSARY. Sept 30, 1960. This Hanna Barbera cartoon comedy was set in prehistoric times. Characters included two Stone Age families, Fred and Wilma Flintstone and neighbors Barney and Betty Rubble. In 1994 *The Flintstones* movie was released, starring John Goodman, Rick Moranis and Rosie O'Donnell.

GUADALUPE MOUNTAINS NATIONAL PARK ESTABLISHED: ANNIVERSARY. Sept 30, 1972. Area in western Texas along Texas–New Mexico border, originally authorized Oct 15, 1966, was established as a national park. For further park info: Guadalupe Mountains Natl Park, HC 60, Box 400, Salt Flat, TX 79847-9400.

GUTENBERG BIBLE PUBLISHED: ANNIVERSARY. Sept 30, 1452. The first section of the Gutenberg Bible, the first book printed from movable type, was published at Mainz, Germany. Johann Gutenberg was the printer. The book was completed by 1456.

HALEAKALA NATIONAL PARK ESTABLISHED: ANNIVERSARY. Sept 30, 1960. Summit of a volcano on Maui in the Hawaiian Islands was authorized as a part of Hawaii National Park on Aug 1, 1916. In 1960 Haleakala was established as a separate national park. The park was expanded in 1969 to include the Kipahulu Valley. For further park info: Haleakala Natl Park, PO Box 369, Makawao, HI 96768.

KERR, DEBORAH: BIRTH ANNIVERSARY. Sept 30, 1921. Film actress born at Helensburgh, Dunbartonshire, Scotland, she starred in such classics as *The King and I, From Here to Eternity* and *An Affair to Remember.* She was nominated for six Oscars, holding the record for most nominations without a win, but did receive a Lifetime Achievement Award in 1994. She died at Suffolk, England, Oct 16, 2007.

***LITTLE WOMEN* PUBLICATION ANNIVERSARY.** Sept 30, 1868. Louisa May Alcott's beloved Civil War–era novel of Jo, Meg, Beth and Amy was published today to great immediate success.

MEREDITH ENROLLS AT OLE MISS: ANNIVERSARY. Sept 30, 1962. Rioting broke out when James Meredith became the first black to enroll in the all-white University of Mississippi. President Kennedy sent US troops to the area to force compliance with the law. Three people died in the fighting and 50 were injured. On June 6, 1966, Meredith was shot while participating in a civil rights march at Mississippi. On June 25 Meredith, barely recovered, rejoined the marchers near Jackson, MS.

"MURDER, SHE WROTE" TV PREMIERE: 25th ANNIVERSARY. Sept 30, 1984. Angela Lansbury starred as crime novelist Jessica Fletcher from Cabot Cove, Maine, who traveled the country solving murders. This top-rated detective show also featured Tom Bosley as Sheriff Amos Tupper and William Windom as Dr. Seth Hazlett. The program aired for 12 years and is still in syndication.

NATIONAL WOMEN'S HEALTH AND FITNESS DAY. Sept 30. 8th annual event to promote the value of health and fitness for women of all ages. More than 700 local women's health events will be held across the country on the same day. Call the toll-free number for further info and a list of local events. Annually, the last Wednesday in September. Est attendance: 70,000. For info: Tina Godin, Program Mgr, Health Information Resource Center, 1850 W Winchester Rd #213, Libertyville, IL 60048. Phone: (800) 828-8225. Fax: (847) 816-8662. E-mail: info@fitnessday.com. Web: www.fitnessday.com.

"THE RED SKELTON SHOW" TV PREMIERE: ANNIVERSARY. Sept 30, 1951. Vaudevillian and radio performer Red Skelton hosted several popular variety shows on NBC and CBS in a career that spanned 20 years. He was a gifted comedian, famous for his loony characters, sight gags, pantomimes and ad-libs. His show was also notable for introducing Johnny Carson and the Rolling Stones to a national audience.

Birthdays Today

Deborah Allen, 56, singer, songwriter, born Memphis, TN, Sept 30, 1953.

Crystal Bernard, 45, actress ("Wings"), born Garland, TX, Sept 30, 1964.

Marion Cotillard, 34, actress (Oscar for *La Vie en Rose*; *Big Fish*), born Paris, France, Sept 30, 1975.

Angie Dickinson, 78, actress (Emmy for "Police Woman"; *Dressed to Kill*), born Angeline Brown at Kulm, ND, Sept 30, 1931.

Fran Drescher, 52, actress ("The Nanny," *Jack*), born Flushing, NY, Sept 30, 1957.

Jenna Elfman, 38, actress ("Dharma & Greg," "Townies"), born Los Angeles, CA, Sept 30, 1971.

Martina Hingis, 29, tennis player, born Kosice, Slovakia, Sept 30, 1980.

Blanche Lambert Lincoln, 49, US Senator (D, Arkansas), born Helena, MT, Sept 30, 1960.

Johnny Mathis, 74, singer ("Chances Are"), born Gilmer, TX, Sept 30, 1935.

Marilyn McCoo, 66, singer (Fifth Dimension, "Up, Up and Away"), actress, born Jersey City, NJ, Sept 30, 1943.

Dominique Moceanu, 28, Olympic gold medal gymnast, born Hollywood, CA, Sept 30, 1981.

Eric Stoltz, 48, actor (*Fast Times at Ridgemont High, Pulp Fiction, House of Mirth*), born Los Angeles, CA, Sept 30, 1961.

Victoria Tennant, 56, actress ("Winds of War," *All of Me, LA Story*), born London, England, Sept 30, 1953.

Elie Wiesel, 81, author, human rights activist, Nobel Peace Prize recipient, founder of the Elie Wiesel Foundation for Humanity, born Sighet, Romania, Sept 30, 1928.

✦ October ✦

October 1 — Thursday

DAY 274 — **91 REMAINING**

ADOPT-A-SHELTER-DOG MONTH. Oct 1–31. To promote the adoption of dogs from local shelters, the ASPCA sponsors this important observance. "Make Pet Adoption Your First Option®" is a message the organization promotes throughout the year in an effort to end the euthanasia of all adoptable animals. For info: ASPCA Media & Communications Dept, New York, NY. Phone: (212) 876-7700, ext 4565. E-mail: shonalib@aspca.org. Web: www.aspca.org.

ANTIDEPRESSANT DEATH AWARENESS MONTH. Oct 1–31. A month to remember those who have been injured or who have died as a result of taking antidepressants or at the hands of someone who was on antidepressants. Any adverse reactions or death while taking any drug should be reported to the Food and Drug Administration at www.FDA.com under the "Contact the FDA" section. For info: Ernest and Catherine Ryan, 9138 Legacy Ct, Temperance, MI 48182. Phone: (734) 847-2282.

BABE RUTH CALLS HIS SHOT?: ANNIVERSARY. Oct 1, 1932. In the fifth inning of game three of the World Series, with a count of two balls and two strikes and with hostile Cubs fans shouting epithets at him, Babe Ruth pointed to the center field bleachers in Chicago's Wrigley Field and followed up by hitting a soaring home run high above the very spot to which he had just gestured. With that homer Ruth squashed the Chicago Cubs' hopes of winning the game, and the Yankees went on to sweep the Series with four straight victories. For more than half a century the question has remained: Did Ruth actually call his shot that day? Even eyewitnesses disagree. Joe Williams of the *New York Times* wrote, "In no mistaken motions, the Babe notified the crowd that the nature of his retaliation would be a wallop right out of the confines of the park." But Cubs pitcher Charlie Root said, "Ruth did *not* point at the fence before he swung. If he'd made a gesture like that, I'd have put one in his ear and knocked him on his ass." Ruth's daughter has said that he denied it. But the Babe himself also claimed he did it.

BRAZIL: FESTIVAL OF PENHA. Oct 1–31. Rio de Janeiro. Pilgrimages, especially on Saturdays during October, to the Church of Our Lady of Penha, which is built on top of a rock, requiring a climb of 365 steps (representing the days of the year), or a ride in a car on an inclined plane (for children, invalids and aged), for those troubled and sick who seek hope or cure.

CARTER, JIMMY: 85th BIRTHDAY. Oct 1, 1924. 39th president of US (1977–81), Nobel Peace Prize recipient, born James Earl Carter, Jr, at Plains, GA.

October 2009	S	M	T	W	T	F	S
					1	2	3
	4	5	6	7	8	9	10
	11	12	13	14	15	16	17
	18	19	20	21	22	23	24
	25	26	27	28	29	30	31

CELEBRATING THE BILINGUAL CHILD MONTH. Oct 1–31. A month to recognize the many children who speak two or more languages and understand multiple cultures. These children connect our communities and can play a big part in improving global communications. For info: Anneke Forzani, Language Lizard, PO Box 421, Basking Ridge, NJ 07920. Phone: (888) 554-9273. Fax: (908) 613-3639. E-mail: info@LanguageLizard.com. Web: www.LanguageLizard.com.

CELIAC DISEASE AWARENESS MONTH. Oct 1–31. For info: Celiac Sprue Assn/USA, PO Box 31700, Omaha, NE 68131-0700. Phone: (402) 643-4101 or (877) CSA-4CSA. Fax: (402) 643-4108. E-mail: celiacs@csaceliacs.org. Web: www.csaceliacs.org.

CHILDREN'S MAGAZINE MONTH. Oct 1–31. Nationwide literacy initiative to raise awareness and create interest in children's magazines. For info: Children's Magazine Month, 66 Witherspoon St, #207, Princeton, NJ 08542. E-mail: contact@childmagmonth.org. Web: www.childmagmonth.org.

CHINA, PEOPLE'S REPUBLIC OF: NATIONAL DAY. Oct 1. Commemorates the founding of the People's Republic of China in 1949.

CHRISTMAS SEAL CAMPAIGN®. Oct 1–Dec 31. An American tradition dating back to 1907 when the first Christmas Seals® were made available in the US, the annual campaign is a major support of American Lung Association programs dedicated to fighting lung diseases such as asthma, emphysema, tuberculosis and lung cancer, as well as their causes. For info: American Lung Assn, 61 Broadway, 6th Fl, New York, NY 10006. Phone: (800) LUNG-USA. Web: www.lungusa.org or www.christmasseals.org.

CHURCH LIBRARY MONTH. Oct 1–31. To encourage churches to begin libraries/media centers and to encourage people of all ages to use their church libraries. For info: Evangelical Church Library Assn, PO Box 353, Glen Ellyn, IL 60138-0353. Phone: (630) 375-7865. E-mail: info@eclalibraries.org. Web: www.eclalibraries.org.

CHURCH SAFETY AND SECURITY MONTH. Oct 1–31. A yearly reminder to churches that there are easy and inexpensive ways to protect themselves from intruders, accidents, injuries and other tragedies that could impact the church's vitality. The GuideOne Center for Risk Management provides churches across the country free tips, materials and resources to help protect faithful congregations. Topics addressed include playground safety, transportation safety, fire prevention and protection, food safety in church kitchens, how to deal effectively with crisis situations and general building security. For info: The GuideOne Center for Risk Management, 1111 Ashworth Rd, West Des Moines, IA 50265. Phone: (515) 267-5709. Fax: (515) 267-2250. E-mail: eabbas@guideone.com. Web: www.guideonecenter.com.

CLASS REUNION MONTH. Oct 1–31. Every October, classmates from around the country and the world gather to reconnect, reminisce and remember those carefree days of youth. For info: Dina C. Carson, PO Box 999, Niwot, CO 80544. E-mail: info@reunionsolutions.com. Web: www.reunionsolutions.com.

COLLINS, ALBERT: BIRTH ANNIVERSARY. Oct 1, 1932. Blues guitarist Albert Collins was born at Leona, TX. An exciting, improvisational musician, he won a Grammy for *Showdown!* (1985), which was recorded with blues guitarists Robert Cray and Johnny Copeland. He was inducted into the Blues Hall of Fame in 1989. He died Nov 24, 1993, at Las Vegas, NV.

CO-OP AWARENESS MONTH. Oct 1–31. Co-Op Awareness Month reminds advertisers to take advantage of the vast amounts of co-op funding made available by manufacturers to help subsidize the cost of local advertising. Most funds are designd to expire on Dec 31, so advertisers not taking advantage may be throwing money away! For info: Christine Hunt, Sales Development Services, Inc, 600 N Cleveland Ave, Ste 600, Westerville, OH 43082. Phone: (800) 667-3237. Fax: (800) 548-4223. E-mail: christine@salesdevelopment.com. Web: www.admall.com.

COWBOY HALL OF FAME CEREMONY AND BANQUET. Oct 1. Willcox Community Center, Willcox, AZ. The Cowboy Hall of Fame events lead into the Rex Allen Days celebration (Oct 2–4). Open house 6 PM; dinner 7 PM. Includes Cowboy Hall of Fame induction ceremony, favorite son/daughter award. Est attendance: 340. For info: Willcox Chamber of Commerce. Phone: (520) 384-2272 or (800) 200-2272. Web: www.willcoxchamber.com.

"CYBERSPACE" COINED: 25th *NEUROMANCER* PUBLICATION ANNIVERSARY. Oct 1, 1984. The groundbreaking science fiction novel *Neuromancer*, by William Gibson, was published on this day and featured a word now commonplace in popular culture: "cyberspace." The novel was a winner of the Hugo, Nebula and Philip K. Dick awards.

CYPRUS: INDEPENDENCE DAY. Oct 1. National holiday. Commemorates independence from Britain in 1960.

DISNEY WORLD OPENED: ANNIVERSARY. Oct 1, 1971. Disney's second theme park opened at Orlando, FL. See also "Disneyland Opened: Anniversary" (July 17).

DOMESTIC VIOLENCE AWARENESS MONTH. Oct 1–31. Commemorated since 1987, this month attempts to raise awareness of efforts to end violence against women and their children. The Domestic Violence Awareness Month Project is a collaborative effort of the National Resource Center on Domestic Violence, Family Violence Prevention Fund, National Coalition Against Domestic Violence, National Domestic Violence Hotline and the National Network to End Domestic Violence. For info: NCADV, 1120 Lincoln St, Ste 1603, Denver, CO 80203. Phone: (303) 839-1852. Web: www.ncadv.org.

DYSLEXIA AWARENESS MONTH. Oct 1–31. The 47 branches of the International Dyslexia Association host Dyslexia Awareness Month during October. State branches host workshops, lectures and fund-raisers with the goal of raising public awareness of the signs of dyslexia in adults and children. For info: Michael Hayes, Intl Dyslexia Assn, 40 York Rd, Ste 400, Baltimore, MD 21204-5202. Phone: (410) 296-0232. Fax: (410) 321-5069. E-mail: mhayes@interdys.org. Web: www.interdys.org.

EAST TEXAS POULTRY FESTIVAL. Oct 1–3. Shelby County Courthouse Square, Center, TX. County fair–style festival featuring carnival rides, food booths run by local charities, art and craft exhibits, live entertainment, chicken clucking contest, street dance, 4-H broiler show and auction. Annually, the first Thursday, Friday and Saturday of October. Est attendance: 15,000. For info: Shelby County Chamber of Commerce, 100 Courthouse Square, A-101, Center, TX 75935. Phone: (936) 598-3682. Fax: (936) 598-8163. E-mail: info@shelbycountychamber.com. Web: www.shelbycountychamber.com.

EAT BETTER, EAT TOGETHER MONTH. Oct 1–31. Time to encourage families to eat together. Research indicates that children who eat with their families not only have better nutrition, but also do better in school and have fewer behavior problems. A tool kit has been created to show how family meals can be simple, easy and nutritious. Call for the top 10 ways to eat better, eat together. For info: Nutrition Education Network of Washington State, Cooperative Extention, Washington State University, 7612 Pioneer Way E, Puyallup, WA 98371-4998. Phone: (253) 445-4553. Web: nutrition.wsu.edu/ebet.

EMOTIONAL INTELLIGENCE AWARENESS MONTH. Oct 1–31. Since 2006, a month to increase awareness of this important behavioral initiative. *Emotional intelligence*, a term introduced by psychologist Daniel Goleman, describes the ability to understand and manage emotions in order to think and communicate in a more healthful manner. Annually, the month of October. For info: Emotional Intelligence Institute, PO Box 2238, New Springfield, OH 44443. Phone: (330) 549-9577. E-mail: info@e-ii.org. Web: www.e-ii.org.

EMOTIONAL WELLNESS MONTH. Oct 1–31. Get more out of every day with laughter and enjoyment. This is a time to reduce stress and seek moderation in mood swings. Balance your activities to support your emotional state, and keep your positive attitude in check. Take an anger management course to learn how to control explosive tempers. Seek the help of a therapist. Distance yourself from drama and chaos. Create a humor file with clipped columns and cartoons, and watch comedy on TV and film. Lighten up and learn to laugh at yourself. For info: Angela Brown Oberer, Words of Wellness, PO Box 49266, Charlotte, NC 28277. Phone: (704) 849-2900. E-mail: angela@wordsofwellness.com. Web: www.wordsofwellness.com.

ENERGY MANAGEMENT IS A FAMILY AFFAIR—IMPROVE YOUR HOME. Oct 1–Mar 31, 2010. Replace energy-consuming units with new efficient home conveniences and remodel to prevent heating and cooling loss. Editorial package includes approximately 50 camera-ready stories and photos free to editors. Also available on website. For info: James A. Stewart, Jr, Home Improvement Time, Inc, PO Box 247, Oakdale, PA 15071-0247. Phone: (412) 787-2881. Fax: (412) 787-3233. Web: www.homeimprovementtime.com.

FIREPUP'S® BIRTHDAY. Oct 1. Firepup spends his time teaching fire and burn prevention and life safety awareness to children and their parents in a fun-filled and nonthreatening manner. Materials are available through local fire departments. For info: Natl Fire Safety Council, Inc, PO Box 378, Michigan Center, MI 49254-0378. Phone: (517) 764-2811. E-mail: tlusby@nfcd.org.

GAY AND LESBIAN HISTORY MONTH. Oct 1–31. October was selected to commemorate the first two lesbian and gay marches on Washington in October 1979 and 1987.

GERMAN-AMERICAN HERITAGE MONTH. Oct 1–31. A month celebrating America's German heritage. Numerous historical programs, museum and library exhibits, cultural events, genealogical workshops and more planned. For info: Dr. Don Heinrich Tolzmann, German-American Citizens League, 6829 Westin Ridge, Cleves, OH 45002. Phone: (513) 574-1741. E-mail: dhtolzmann@yahoo.com. Web: www.gacl.org.

GLOBAL DIVERSITY AWARENESS MONTH. Oct 1–31. Celebrating, promoting and appreciating the global diversity of our society. Also, a month to foster and further our understanding of the inherent value of all races, genders, nationalities, age groups, religions, sexual orientations, classes and physical disabilities. Annually, in October. For info: Carole Copeland Thomas, C. Thomas & Assoc, 400 W Cummings Park, Ste 1725-154, Woburn, MA 01801. Phone: (508) 947-5755. Fax: (508) 947-3903. E-mail: Carole@TellCarole.com. Web: www.TellCarole.com.

GO HOG WILD—EAT COUNTRY HAM MONTH. Oct 1–31. Suuueee! It's not just a word; it's a state of mind. For more than 200 years, Americans have been curing and eating country ham. The custom of curing that began in the state of Virginia during the mid-1700s continues today from Georgia to Missouri and points in between. Discover the difference between "city ham" and "country ham" and get some great recipes to boot during Eat Country Ham Month. For info: Natl Country Ham Assn, PO Box 948, Conover, NC 28613. Phone: (800) 820-4HAM. E-mail: eatham@countryham.org. Web: www.countryham.org.

HALLOWEEN SAFETY MONTH. Oct 1–31. There are steps you can take to create a safe Halloween for children and teens. Information about the dangers of cosmetic contact lenses will be included, as the use of these lenses increases during this holiday. For info: Prevent Blindness America®, 211 W Wacker Dr, Ste 1700, Chicago, IL 60606. Phone: (800) 331-2020. E-mail: info@preventblindness.org. Web: www.preventblindness.org.

HARRIS, RICHARD: BIRTH ANNIVERSARY. Oct 1, 1930. Born at Limerick, Ireland, Richard Harris became known as a stage actor on the London theater scene in the 1950s. Although his first love was the stage, it was in films that he earned his highest degree of success. He was unforgettable as King Arthur in the film version of *Camelot* (1967) and was twice nominated for Best Actor Oscars: for 1963's *This Sporting Life* and 1991's *The Field.* He portrayed headmaster Albus Dumbledore in the first two Harry Potter films in 2001 and 2002. He died Oct 25, 2002, at London, England.

HARRISON, CAROLINE LAVINIA SCOTT: BIRTH ANNIVERSARY. Oct 1, 1832. First wife of Benjamin Harrison, 23rd president of the US, born at Oxford, OH. Died at Washington, DC, Oct 25, 1892. She was the second first lady to die in the White House.

HEALTH LITERACY MONTH. Oct 1–31. Now in its 11th year, Health Literacy Month is a time when advocates worldwide promote the importance of understandable health information. For info: Health Literacy Consulting, 31 Highland St, Ste 201, Natick, MA 01760. Phone: (508) 653-1199. E-mail: helen@healthliteracy.com. Web: www.healthliteracymonth.org.

HOROWITZ, VLADIMIR: BIRTH ANNIVERSARY. Oct 1, 1904. Virtuoso pianist, born at Berdichev, Russia. Horowitz was widely hailed as one of the world's greatest pianists, renowned for his masterful technique. His debut was at Kiev in 1920, and at the age of 20 he played a series of 23 recitals at Leningrad, performing a total of more than 200 works with no duplications. He made his US debut in 1928 with the New York Philharmonic. He settled in the US in 1940 and became a citizen in 1944. His career swung full circle Apr 20, 1986, when he performed his first concert in his native Russia after a self-imposed absence of 60 years. He died Nov 5, 1989, at New York, NY.

IG® NOBEL PRIZE CEREMONY. Oct 1 (tentative). Sanders Theatre, Harvard University, Cambridge, MA. The "Nineteenth 1st Annual." Honors achievements that make people laugh and then make them think. Prizes awarded by Nobel laureates. Sponsored by the science humor magazine *Annals of Improbable Research.* Annually, first Thursday in October, pending theater availability. For info: Marc Abrahams, Annals of Improbable Research, PO Box 380853, Cambridge, MA 02238. Phone: (617) 491-4437. E-mail: marca@chem2.harvard.edu. Web: www.improbable.com.

INTERNATIONAL STARMAN MONTH. Oct 1–31. Celebrates the TV series "Starman," which first aired in 1986 and inspired many people around the world to change their lives in positive ways. Spotlight Starman International is a group of people who appreciate the quality, consciousness and themes of the show and continue to gather annually to celebrate that spirit while raising funds for environmental, social and/or educational causes. (The organization is open to all without membership dues.) For info: Vicki Werkley, Spotlight Starman Intl, 16563 Ellen Springs Rd, Lower Lake, CA 95457-9477. Phone: (707) 995-1228. E-mail: spotlight_starman@bigfoot.com (put "Starman" in subject line). Web: www.starmanet.com.

October 2009	S	M	T	W	T	F	S
					1	2	3
	4	5	6	7	8	9	10
	11	12	13	14	15	16	17
	18	19	20	21	22	23	24
	25	26	27	28	29	30	31

INTERNATIONAL STRATEGIC PLANNING MONTH. Oct 1–31. The start of the final quarter of the year provides a great opportunity for businesses and individuals to review the results of their efforts to date, make adjustments to meet this year's goals, and begin thinking about next year's goals. Strategic planning is a systematic and continuous process of evaluation, decision, implementation and measuring. For info: Sherrin Ross Ingram, Intl Center for Strategic Planning, 3 Grant Sq, #101, Hinsdale, IL 60521. Phone: (800) 962-4750. E-mail: info@icfsp.com. Web: www.icfsp.com.

***THE JOY OF SEX*: PUBLICATION ANNIVERSARY.** Oct 1, 1972. English publisher Mitchell Beazely released Dr. Alex Comfort's landmark book this month in 1972. Published in the midst of the Western world's sexual revolution, *The Joy of Sex* was an immediate bestseller and to date has sold almost 10 million copies.

"KUNG FU" TV PREMIERE: ANNIVERSARY. Oct 1, 1972. David Carradine starred in this unusual ABC western as Kwai Chang Caine, a half-Chinese martial arts master and drifter who was exiled from China. Appearing in flashback were: Keye Luke as Master Po, Philip Ahn as Master Kan and Radames Pera as the younger Caine. The show ran for three years. "Kung Fu" returned as a 1986 TV movie introducing the late Brandon Lee as Caine's son. A sequel series currently appears in syndication starring a much older Carradine.

LAWRENCE, JAMES: BIRTH ANNIVERSARY. Oct 1, 1781. Brilliant American naval officer, whose last battle was a defeat, but whose dying words became a most honored naval motto. Lawrence, born at Burlington, NJ, was captain of the *Chesapeake* when it engaged in a naval duel with HMS *Shannon* off Boston, June 1, 1813. The *Chesapeake* was captured and towed to Halifax as a British prize. Lawrence was mortally wounded by a musket ball during the engagement and uttered his famous last words, "Don't give up the ship," as he was being carried off the ship's deck.

LONG TERM CARE PLANNING MONTH. Oct 1–31. As life spans increase and family structures change, this month promotes discussion of the variety of ways to plan for future long-term care and encourages everyone to make this planning part of their personal retirement plan. Long Term Care Planning Month asks, "What is *your* long-term care plan?" Annually, the month of October. For info: Marilee Driscoll, Long Term Care Learning Institute, PO Box 956, Plymouth, MA 02362. Phone: (508) 830-9975. Fax: (508) 830-9976. E-mail: info@LTCmonth.com. Web: www.LTCmonth.com.

MADISON COUNTY FAIR. Oct 1–3. Wanda Priest Park, Fredericktown, MO. 8th annual (after a 53-year absence). Madison County Fair has a farming and livestock heritage but also provides entertainment, games, food, crafts and activities. The fair also includes the fall festival. Annually, the first weekend in October. Est attendance: 5,000. For info: Madison County Fair, PO Box 296, Fredericktown, MO 63645. Phone: (573) 783-3303. E-mail: madisoncountyfair@yahoo.com.

MARIS BREAKS RUTH HOME RUN RECORD: ANNIVERSARY. Oct 1, 1961. Roger Maris of the New York Yankees hit his 61st home run, breaking Babe Ruth's record for the most home runs in a season. Maris hit his homer against pitcher Tracy Stallard of the Boston Red Sox as the Yankees won, 1–0. Controversy over the record arose because the American League had adopted a 162-game schedule in 1961, and Maris played in 161 games. In 1927, when Ruth set his record, the schedule called for 154 games, and Ruth played in 151. On Sept 8, 1998, Mark McGwire of the St. Louis Cardinals hit his 62nd home run, breaking Maris's record. On Oct 5, 2001, Barry Bonds of the San Francisco Giants broke McGwire's record.

MATTHAU, WALTER: BIRTH ANNIVERSARY. Oct 1, 1920. Actor (*The Odd Couple, Grumpy Old Men*), born at New York, NY. Died July 1, 2000, at Santa Monica, CA.

"THE MERV GRIFFIN SHOW" TV PREMIERE: ANNIVERSARY. Oct 1, 1962. Singer and game show king Merv Griffin's first effort as an afternoon talk-show host premiered on NBC but was later dropped for syndication. The afternoon show continued until 1969, when Griffin was tapped to host a late-night program on CBS to compete with "The Tonight Show with Johnny Carson."

MODEL T INTRODUCED: ANNIVERSARY. Oct 1, 1908. Ford introduced the Model T at a price of $850, but by 1924 the basic model sold for as little as $260. Between 1908 and 1927 Ford sold 15,007,033 Model Ts in the US. Although the first Model Ts were not built on an assembly line, the demand for the cars was so high that Ford developed a system where workers remained at their stations and cars came to them. This enabled Ford to turn out a Model T every 10 seconds.

MONTH OF FREETHOUGHT. Oct 1–31. The Month of Freethought was inspired by the work done in Texas to commemorate the many German Freethinkers that emigrated to this area, and several others across the US, during the 19th century. For info: Matt Cherry, Institute for Humanist Studies, 48 Howard St, Albany, NY 12207. Phone: (518) 432-7820. Fax: (518) 432-7821. E-mail: MCherry@HumanistStudies.org. Web: HumanistStudies.org or www.secularseasons.org.

NATIONAL ANIMAL SAFETY AND PROTECTION MONTH. Oct 1–31. Observance to promote the appropriate ways to protect and care for domestic and wild animals and help people strengthen skills for staying safe around animals. For info: PALS Foundation, PO Box 1271, San Luis Obispo, CA 93406. Phone: (805) 544-0984. Fax: (805) 544-2027. Web: www.PALS.R8.org.

NATIONAL BAKE AND DECORATE MONTH. Oct 1–31. This month kicks off the fall and holiday baking season with recipes and baking and decorating tips for all types of tasty, fun foods. For info: Diana Rodriguez, Wilton Enterprises, 2240 W 75th St, Woodridge, IL 60517. Phone: (630) 963-7100. E-mail: drodriguez@wilton.com. Web: www.wilton.com.

✦ **NATIONAL BREAST CANCER AWARENESS MONTH.** Oct 1–31.

NATIONAL BREAST CANCER AWARENESS MONTH. Oct 1–31. Now in its second decade of public and professional education and awareness. This month is promoted by 15 major national nonprofit cancer organizations working in partnership to raise awareness of breast cancer and to provide access to screening services. The third Friday in October (Oct 16 in 2009) is National Mammography Day. For info: call the American Cancer Society toll-free at (800) 227-2345 or the National Cancer Institute toll-free at (800) 4-CANCER. Web: www.nbcam.org.

NATIONAL CHILI MONTH. Oct 1–31. National observance and celebration of chili, one of the most historical and traditional American dishes. For info: Williams Foods, Inc, 13301 W 99th St, Lenexa, KS 66215. E-mail: 2chilicooks@williamsfoods.com.

NATIONAL CHIROPRACTIC MONTH. Oct 1–31. For info: American Chiropractic Assn, 1701 Clarendon Blvd, Arlington, VA 22209. Phone: (800) 986-4636. Web: www.acatoday.org.

NATIONAL CRIME PREVENTION MONTH. Oct 1–31. During Crime Prevention Month, individuals can commit to working on at least one of three levels—family, neighborhood or community—to drive violence and drugs from our world. It is also a time to honor individuals who have accepted personal responsibility for their neighborhoods and groups who work for the community's common good. Annually, every October. For info: Natl Crime Prevention Council, 2345 Crystal Dr, Ste 500, Arlington, VA 22202-4801. Phone: (202) 466-6272. Fax: (202) 296-1356. Web: www.ncpc.org.

NATIONAL CYBER SECURITY AWARENESS MONTH. Oct 1–31. A national campaign focused on educating the American public, businesses, schools and government agencies about ways to secure their part of cyber space, computers and our nation's critical infrastructure. The goal is to educate everyday Internet users on how to "Protect Yourself Before You Connect Yourself," by taking simple and effective steps to safeguard one's computer from the latest online threats, offer ways to respond to potential cyber-crime incidents and link how each person's cyber security affects securing our nation's critical infrastructure. For info: Natl Cyber Security Alliance, 1101 Pennsylvania Ave NW, Ste 600, Washington, DC 20004. Phone: (202) 756-2284. E-mail: ncsaalyssa@aol.com. Web: www.staysafeonline.org.

NATIONAL DENTAL HYGIENE MONTH. Oct 1–31. To increase public awareness of the importance of preventive oral health care and the dental hygienist's role as the preventive professional. Annually, during the month of October. For info: Public Relations, American Dental Hygienists' Assn, 444 N Michigan Ave, Ste 3400, Chicago, IL 60611. Phone: (312) 440-8900 or (800) 243-ADHA. Fax: (312) 440-1702. E-mail: media@adha.net. Web: www.adha.org.

NATIONAL DEPRESSION EDUCATION AND AWARENESS MONTH. Oct 1–31. A nonprofit campaign to educate patients, the elderly and professionals about depression disorders. Kit of materials available for $15. Annually, the month of October. For info: PPSI, c/o Pharmacy Council on Depression Education, 101 Lucas Valley Rd, Ste 382, San Rafael, CA 94903. Phone: (415) 479-8628. Fax: (415) 479-8608. E-mail: ppsi@aol.com. Web: www.ppsinc.org.

✦ **NATIONAL DISABILITY EMPLOYMENT AWARENESS MONTH.** Oct 1–31. Presidential Proclamation issued for the month of October (PL100–630, Title III, Sec 301a of Nov 7, 1988). Previously issued as "National Employ the Handicapped Week" for a week beginning during the first week in October since 1945.

NATIONAL DISABILITY EMPLOYMENT AWARENESS MONTH. Oct 1–31. To foster the full integration of people with disabilities into the workforce. For info: US Dept of Labor, Office of Disability Employment Policy, 200 Constitution Ave NW, Rm S1303, Washington, DC 20210-0002. Phone: (202) 693-7880. Fax: (202) 693-7888. E-mail: infoODEP@dol.gov. Web: www.dol.gov/odep.

✦ **NATIONAL DOMESTIC VIOLENCE AWARENESS MONTH.** Oct 1–31.

NATIONAL DOWN SYNDROME AWARENESS MONTH. Oct 1–31. To promote better understanding of Down Syndrome. For info: Natl Down Syndrome Congress, 1370 Center Dr, Ste 102, Atlanta, GA 30338. Phone: (800) 232-NDSC. E-mail: info@ndsccenter.org. Web: www.ndsccenter.org.

NATIONAL FAMILY SEXUALITY EDUCATION MONTH/LET'S TALK! Oct 1–31. A national coalition effort to support parents as the first and primary sexuality educators of their children by providing information for parents and young people. For info: Planned Parenthood Federation of America, Education Dept, 434 W 33rd St, New York, NY 10001. Phone: (212) 261-4627. Fax: (212) 247-6269. E-mail: education@ppfa.org. Web: www.plannedparenthood.org.

NATIONAL "GAIN THE INSIDE ADVANTAGE" MONTH. Oct 1–31. Gaining the "Inside Advantage" is how ordinary people accomplish extraordinary things. It refers to taking control of your life from the inside out. It means learning how to live deeply, joyfully and successfully. For info: Cathy W. Lauro. Phone: (813) 727-9859. E-mail: mind@CWLauro.com. Web: www.CWLauro.com.

NATIONAL GO ON A FIELD TRIP MONTH. Oct 1–31. A month to highlight the importance of the field trip as a way to help children learn. Studies show that children learn 85 percent more when a lesson is reinforced outside the classroom, and the field trip is a great way to teach valuable life skills and career education. For info: Field Trip Factory, 2211 N Elston, Ste 304, Chicago, IL 60614. Phone: (800) 987-6409. Web: www.fieldtripfactory.com.

NATIONAL LIVER AWARENESS MONTH. Oct 1–31. To increase understanding of the importance of liver functions, to promote healthful practices and to encourage research into the causes and cures of liver diseases, including hepatitis. Annually, the month of October. For info: Marketing & Communications Dept, American Liver Foundation, 75 Maiden Ln, Ste 603, New York, NY 10038. E-mail: info@liverfoundation.org. Web: www.liverfoundation.org.

NATIONAL MEDICAL LIBRARIANS MONTH. Oct 1–31. Recognizes and celebrates the importance and the achievements of health sciences information professionals. Medical librarians offer efficient access to quality print and online medical and health-related information within a wide variety of health care settings. Librarians representing 23 specialty groups and 14 regional chapters of the Medical Library Association (MLA) sponsor several events and educational opportunities throughout the month of October. For info: Medical Library Assn, 65 E Wacker Pl, Ste 1900, Chicago, IL 60601. Phone: (312) 419-9094. Fax: (312) 419-8950. E-mail: info@mlahg.org. Web: www.mlanet.org.

NATIONAL ORTHODONTIC HEALTH MONTH. Oct 1–31. A beautiful, healthy smile is only the most obvious benefit of orthodontic treatment. Orthodontic care plays an important role in dental health, overall physical health and emotional well-being. National Orthodontic Health Month is sponsored by the American Association of Orthodontists (AAO), the oldest and largest dental specialty organization in the world, established in 1900. The AAO supports research and education leading to quality patient care, as well as increased public awareness of the need for and benefits of orthodontic treatment. For info: Pam Paladin, American Assn of Orthodontists, 401 N Lindbergh Blvd, St. Louis, MO 63141-7816. Phone: (314) 993-1700. E-mail: ppaladin@aaortho.org. Web: www.braces.org.

NATIONAL PHYSICAL THERAPY MONTH. Oct 1–31. To increase awareness of the role of physical therapy in health care, thousands of physical therapists nationwide celebrate by hosting special activities such as fitness clinics, open houses, hotlines, athletic events, health seminars and exhibits. Annually, the month of October. For info: The American Physical Therapy Assn, 1111 N Fairfax St, Alexandria, VA 22314-1488. Phone: (800) 999-2782 or (703) 684-2782. Web: www.apta.org/consumer.

NATIONAL POPCORN POPPIN' MONTH. Oct 1–31. To celebrate the wholesome, economical, natural food value of popcorn, America's native snack. For info: The Popcorn Board, 401 N Michigan Ave, Chicago, IL 60611-4267. Phone: (312) 644-6610. Web: www.popcorn.org.

NATIONAL READING GROUP MONTH. Oct 1–31. Reading group members celebrate the joy of a book shared and inspire individuals who do not belong to a reading group to join one or start their own. Organizations, bookstores and libraries are encouraged to sponsor reading group events during this month. For info: Jill A. Tardiff, Women's Natl Book Assn, 625 Madison St, Ste 2, Hoboken, NJ 07030. E-mail: jtardiff-wnbanational@att.net. Alternate contact: Laurie Beckelman. Email: lbeckelman@aol.com. Web: www.wnba-books.org.

NATIONAL ROLLER SKATING MONTH. Oct 1–31. A monthlong celebration recognizing the health benefits and recreational enjoyment of this long-loved pastime. Also includes in-line skating and an emphasis on safe skating. For info: Roller Skating Assn, 6905 Corporate Dr, Indianapolis, IN 46278. Phone: (317) 347-2626. Fax: (317) 347-2636. E-mail: rsa@rollerskating.com. Web: www.rollerskating.com or www.rollerskating.org.

NATIONAL RSV AWARENESS MONTH. Oct 1–31. Most babies get respiratory synctial virus (RSV) before they turn two, and it generally has symptoms much like a common cold. However, other children who get RSV, especially those born early or with ongoing lung problems, may develop serious complications associated with it, such as pneumonia or bronchiolitis. Each year, 125,000 babies are hospitalized because of complications with RSV, and some of these babies die. Parents and health care providers can help reduce the risk of RSV in preemies through infection-control techniques and preventive medication. A free booklet on RSV is available. For info: PreemieCare, c/o MOST (Mothers of Supertwins), PO Box 306, East Islip, NY 11730-0306. Phone: (631) 859-1110. E-mail: info@PreemieCare.org. Web: www.PreemieCare.org.

October 2009	S	M	T	W	T	F	S
					1	2	3
	4	5	6	7	8	9	10
	11	12	13	14	15	16	17
	18	19	20	21	22	23	24
	25	26	27	28	29	30	31

NATIONAL SARCASTICS AWARENESS MONTH. Oct 1–31. To help people everywhere understand the positive and negative aspects of sarcasm. For info: Dr. Virginia Tooper, Dir of Barbs, Sarcastics Anonymous, 100 Bay Pl, #2112, Oakland, CA 94610. Phone: (510) 891-8479. E-mail: vtooper@aol.com

NATIONAL SPINA BIFIDA AWARENESS MONTH. Oct 1–31. Promoting public awareness of current scientific, medical and educational issues related to spina bifida—the most frequently occuring permanently disabling birth defect. For info: Natl Resource Center, Natl Spina Bifida Assn of America, 4590 MacArthur Blvd NW, Ste 250, Washington, DC 20007-4226. Phone: (202) 944-3285 or (800) 621-3141. E-mail: sbaa@sbaa.org. Web: www.sbaa.org.

NATIONAL STAMP COLLECTING MONTH. Oct 1–31. Since 1981 the US Postal Service has designated the month of October as National Stamp Collecting Month (NSCM). Developed to introduce children aged 8–12 to this popular and educational hobby, the NSCM program is also intended to raise awareness about the recreational benefits of stamp collecting among all age groups. The Postal Service traditionally kicks off NSCM by issuing new commemorative stamps in late September or early October. For info and educational kits: US Postal Service. Web: www.usps.com/communications/community/nscm.htm.

NATIONAL WORK AND FAMILY MONTH. Oct 1–31. On Sept 5, 2003, US Senate Resolution 210 was passed designating October as National Work and Family Month. The resolution expressed "the sense of the Senate that supporting a balance between work and personal life is in the best interest of national worker productivity" and that reducing any conflict between the two "should be a national priority."

NIGERIA: INDEPENDENCE DAY. Oct 1. National holiday. Became independent of Great Britain in 1960 and a republic in 1963.

***NIGHT OF THE LIVING DEAD* RELEASED: ANNIVERSARY.** Oct 1, 1968. George A. Romero's low-budget horror film of rampaging cannibalistic zombies was released on this date. It quickly became a cult favorite and influenced many other horror filmmakers.

NORWAY: PAGEANTRY IN OSLO. Oct 1. The Storting (Norway's parliament) convenes on the first weekday in October, when it decides the date for the ceremonial opening of the Storting—usually the following weekday—and the parliamentary session is then opened by King Harald V in the presence of Corps Diplomatique, preceded and followed by a military procession between the Royal Palace and the Storting.

ORGANIZE YOUR MEDICAL INFORMATION MONTH. Oct 1–31. This month is dedicated to learning how to acquire, understand, utilize and store pertinent medical information and knowledge, enabling each of us to become a more informed and active participant in our own medical care. This organization leads to fewer medical errors, shorter hospital stays, increased positive outcomes, the motivation to seek preventive care and the skills to negotiate the health care system. For info: Lynda Shrager. Phone/fax: (518) 475-1792. E-mail: LShrager@otherwisehealthy.com. Web: www.otherwisehealthy.com.

PHOTOGRAPHER APPRECIATION MONTH. Oct 1–31. A month to acknowledge and appreciate the good work done by photographers everywhere to preserve family history, current events, the beauty of nature—in short, everything we all see yet tend to forget. Annually, the month of October. For info: Hud Andrews, 652 N Trezevant St, Memphis, TN 38112. Phone: (901) 452-4700. Fax: (901) 843-3093. E-mail: andrewsh@rhodes.edu.

POLISH-AMERICAN HERITAGE MONTH. Oct 1–31. A national celebration of Polish history, culture and pride, in cooperation with the Polish-American Congress and Polonia Across America. For info: Michael Blichasz, Chair, Polish American Cultural Center, Natl HQ, 308 Walnut St, Philadelphia, PA 19106. Phone: (215) 922-1700. Fax: (215) 922-1518. E-mail: mail@polishamericancenter.org. Web: www.polishamericancenter.org.

POSITIVE ATTITUDE MONTH. Oct 1–31. Sometimes it just comes down to attitude! Zig Ziglar says that attitude, more than aptitude, affects altitude. Keith Harrell says attitude is everything. *Atta-tude* is a self-reflection of who you think you are. This month is dedicated to establishing, boosting or forcing ourselves to adopt positive attitudes and discovering and/or creating positive self-images. For info: Sylvia Henderson, Springboard Training, PO Box 588, Olney, MD 20830-0588. Phone: (301) 260-1538. E-mail: sylvia@springboardtraining.com. Web: www.springboardtraining.com.

RAPTOR MONTH. Oct 1–31. An invitation to schools, nature organizations and environmental groups to take time in October to celebrate our fall migrating birds of prey. Raptor Month is an annual initiative of The Avian Promise, a nonprofit organization dedicated to the education and awareness of wild bird habits, characteristics and needs. For info: Marsha Pearson, The Avian Promise, 8785 Duveen Dr, Wyndmoor, PA 19038. Phone: (215) 657-0400. E-mail: info@theavianpromise.org. Web: www.raptormonth.org.

REHNQUIST, WILLIAM HUBBS: BIRTH ANNIVERSARY. Oct 1, 1924. Born at Milwaukee, WI, William Hubbs Rehnquist earned master's degrees in political science and government before finishing Stanford Law School in 1952. He was serving as counsel in the Nixon White House when he was nominated to the US Supreme Court as associate justice in 1971. As the most conservative member of the court, he was a staunch supporter of states' rights and wrote a dissent to 1973's *Roe v Wade* decision. President Reagan nominated him as chief justice upon the retirement of Warren Burger, and he assumed that position on Sept 26, 1986. He presided over the impeachment hearing of President Clinton and ruled on 2000's *Bush v Gore* case, which awarded the presidential election to George W. Bush following controversial ballot miscounting in Florida. Rehnquist died Sept 3, 2005, at Arlington, VA.

"REMINGTON STEELE" TV PREMIERE: ANNIVERSARY. Oct 1, 1982. Laura Holt (Stephanie Zimbalist), an imaginative private detective, could not get a case of her own—until she made up a partner, Remington Steele, who was conveniently out of the office when clients came calling. Then she met the suave stranger (Pierce Brosnan) who called himself Remington Steele. They began a working partnership . . . which ended in marriage. The show aired on NBC, with the last telecast on Mar 9, 1987, and costarred James Read, Janet DeMay and Doris Roberts. Henry Mancini composed the theme song.

RETT SYNDROME AWARENESS MONTH. Oct 1–31. To promote awareness of this neurological disease. For info: Intl Rett Syndrome Assn, 9121 Piscataway Rd, Ste 2B, Clinton, MD 20735. Phone: (301) 856-3334 or (800) 818-RETT. E-mail: admin@rettsyndrome.org. Web: www.rettsyndrome.org.

RIGHT-BRAINERS RULE MONTH. Oct 1–31. Right-brainers are often ridiculed and reprimanded for their unorthodox and creative ways of doing things. The month of October is a chance to show how the right-brained person can survive and thrive in a very left-brained world. For info: Lee Silber, Creative Lee Speaking, 822 Redondo Ct, San Diego, CA 92109. Phone: (858) 488-4249. E-mail: leesilber@earthlink.net. Web: www.creativelee.com.

SELF-PROMOTION MONTH. Oct 1–31. Learn how to toot your own horn and promote your business to another level of success. Discover insightful and low-cost marketing strategies. For info: Debbie Allen, Allen & Assoc Consulting, Inc, PO Box 27946, Scottsdale, AZ 85255-0149. Phone: (800) 359-4544. Web: www.debbieallen.com.

SOUTH KOREA: ARMED FORCES DAY. Oct 1. Marked by many colorful military parades, aerial acrobatics and honor guard ceremonies, held around the reviewing plaza at Yoido, an island in the Han River.

SPINACH LOVERS MONTH. Oct 1–31. Spinach has finally become "the darling of vegetables": from its delectable taste to the breaking news on its lutein content for the prevention of macular degeneration. "Spinach—it's not just for breakfast anymore!" For info: Burgundy L. Olivier, "The Spinach Lady," 211 S Parkerson St, Rayne, LA 70578. Phone: (337) 334-6994. E-mail: email@ilovespinach.com. Web: www.ilovespinach.com.

SQUIRREL AWARENESS MONTH. Oct 1–31. Set aside to honor one of our friendliest forms of wildlife: squirrels. Annually, the month of October. For info: Gregg Bassett, The Squirrel Lover's Club, 318 W Fremont Ave, Elmhurst, IL 60126. Phone: (630) 833-1117. E-mail: sqrlman@thesquirrelloversclub.com. Web: www.thesquirrelloversclub.com.

STOCKTON, RICHARD: BIRTH ANNIVERSARY. Oct 1, 1730. Lawyer and signer of the Declaration of Independence, born at Princeton, NJ. Died there, Feb 8, 1781.

TALK ABOUT PRESCRIPTIONS MONTH. Oct 1–31. For info: Natl Council on Patient Information and Education, 4915 Saint Elmo Ave, Ste 505, Bethesda, MD 20814-6082. Phone: (301) 656-8565. Fax: (301) 656-4464. E-mail: ncpie@ncpie.info. Web: www.talkaboutrx.org, www.bemedwise.org or mustforseniors.org.

"THIS IS YOUR LIFE" TV PREMIERE: ANNIVERSARY. Oct 1, 1952. Ralph Edwards hosted this program that lured unsuspecting guests onto the show and surprised them by detailing their lives and achievements with their family and friends. It began as a radio show in 1948.

"TOM CORBETT, SPACE CADET" TV PREMIERE: ANNIVERSARY. Oct 1, 1950. This space show was set in the 2350s at the Space Academy and starred Frankie Thomas in the title role as an eager cadet. "Tom Corbett" was one of the few shows to be aired on all four major networks, including running on two networks (NBC and ABC) at the same time.

TUVALU: NATIONAL HOLIDAY. Oct 1. Gained independence from Britain on this day in 1978.

UNITED NATIONS: INTERNATIONAL DAY OF OLDER PERSONS. Oct 1. Designated by the General Assembly on Dec 14, 1990 (originally "International Day for the Elderly," the name was changed later on Dec 21, 1995). A day to encourage all societies to better integrate aging issues into the larger context of development. States are encouraged to do everything in their power to enable all men and women to age with security and dignity. For info: United Nations, Dept of Public Info, Public Inquiries Unit, Rm GA-57, New York, NY 10017. Phone: (212) 963-4475. E-mail: inquiries@un.org. Web: www.un.org.

UNIVERSITY OF CHICAGO FIRST DAY OF CLASSES: ANNIVERSARY. Oct 1, 1892. The University of Chicago opened with an enrollment of 594 and a faculty of 103, including eight former college presidents.

US 2010 FEDERAL FISCAL YEAR BEGINS. Oct 1, 2009–Sept 30, 2010.

VEGETARIAN MONTH. Oct 1–31. This educational event advances awareness of the many surprising ethical, environmental, economic, health, humanitarian and other benefits of the increasingly popular vegetarian lifestyle. (Formerly Vegetarian Awareness Month.) For info: Vegetarian Awareness Network, PO Box 3545, Washington, DC 20027-0045. Phone: (800) USA-VEGE.

WOMEN'S SMALL BUSINESS MONTH. Oct 1–31. National events celebrate women's small businesses. Seminars, award ceremonies and prize giveaways annually every October. For info: Linda Hollander, 4214 Glencoe Ave, Marina Del Rey, CA 90292. Phone: (310) 337-1430. Fax: (310) 641-5823. E-mail: info@womenssmallbusinessexpo.com. Web: www.womenssmallbusinessexpo.com.

WORKPLACE POLITICS AWARENESS MONTH. Oct 1–31. Workplace politics often seem to be a moral morass and a colossal waste of time. Many of us try to avoid participating, but too often, we seem to be inevitably drawn in. This month, we try to increase awareness that trying to avoid workplace politics is futile—instead we can learn to deal with it. For info: Richard Brenner, Chaco Canyon Consulting, 700 Huron Ave, Ste 11J, Cambridge, MA 02138. Phone: (617) 491-6289. Fax: (617) 395-2628. E-mail: rbrenner@ChacoCanyon.com. Web: www.ChacoCanyon.com.

WORLD VEGETARIAN DAY. Oct 1. Celebration of vegetarianism's benefits to humans, animals and our planet. In addition to individuals, participants include libraries, schools, colleges, restaurants, food services, health care centers, health food stores, workplaces and many more. For info: North American Vegetarian Society, PO Box 72, Dolgeville, NY 13329. Phone: (518) 568-7970. Fax: (518) 568-7979. E-mail: navs@telenet.net. Web: www.worldvegetarianday.org.

YOSEMITE NATIONAL PARK ESTABLISHED: ANNIVERSARY. Oct 1, 1890. Yosemite Valley and Mariposa Big Tree Grove, granted to the State of California June 30, 1864, were combined and established as a national park. For further park info: Yosemite Natl Park, PO Box 577, Yosemite Natl Park, CA 95389.

Birthdays Today

Julie Andrews, 74, actress, singer (Emmy for "The Julie Andrews Hour"; Oscar for *Mary Poppins*), born Julia Wells at Walton-on-Thames, England, Oct 1, 1935.

Tom Bosley, 82, actor ("Happy Days," "Father Dowling Mysteries"), born Chicago, IL, Oct 1, 1927.

Rodney Cline (Rod) Carew, 64, Hall of Fame baseball player, born Gatun, Panama Canal Zone, Oct 1, 1945.

Jimmy Carter, 85, 39th president of the US, born James Earl Carter, Jr, at Plains, GA, Oct 1, 1924.

Stephen Collins, 62, actor ("7th Heaven," *All the President's Men*), born Des Moines, IA, Oct 1, 1947.

Mark McGwire, 46, former baseball player, born Pomona, CA, Oct 1, 1963.

October 2009	S	M	T	W	T	F	S
					1	2	3
	4	5	6	7	8	9	10
	11	12	13	14	15	16	17
	18	19	20	21	22	23	24
	25	26	27	28	29	30	31

Esai Morales, 47, actor ("American Family," "NYPD Blue"), born Brooklyn, NY, Oct 1, 1962.

Tim O'Brien, 63, author (*In the Lake of the Woods, Going After Cacciato*), born Austin, MN, Oct 1, 1946.

Randy Quaid, 59, actor (*Brokeback Mountain, Independence Day, The Last Picture Show*), born Houston, TX, Oct 1, 1950.

Stella Stevens, 73, actress ("Ben Casey," "Flamingo Road"), born Hot Coffee, MS, Oct 1, 1936.

Grete Waitz, 56, marathoner, born Oslo, Norway, Oct 1, 1953.

October 2 — Friday

DAY 275 — 90 REMAINING

"ALFRED HITCHCOCK PRESENTS" TV PREMIERE: ANNIVERSARY. Oct 2, 1955. Alfred Hitchcock was already an acclaimed director when he began hosting this mystery anthology series that aired on CBS and NBC for 10 years. Each episode began with an introduction by Hitchcock, the man with the world's most recognized profile. Hitchcock directed about 22 episodes of the series; Robert Altman also directed. Among the many stars who appeared on the show were: Barbara Bel Geddes, Brian Keith, Gena Rowlands, Dick York, Cloris Leachman, Joanne Woodward, Steve McQueen, Peter Lorre, Dick Van Dyke, Robert Redford and Katherine Ross.

COHOCTON FALL FOLIAGE FESTIVAL. Oct 2–4. Cohocton, NY. 42nd annual. World-famous tree-sitting contest. Parade, more than 200 food, antiques, arts and crafts booths. Annually, the first weekend in October. Est attendance: 50,000. For info: Tom Cox, PO Box 204, Cohocton, NY 14826-0204. Phone: (585) 384-5287. Web: www.fallfoliagefestival.com.

COIN & STAMP EXPO. Oct 2–4. Radisson Hotel, Anaheim, CA. Est attendance: 4,000. For info: Israel Bick, Exec Dir, Intl Stamp & Coin Collectors Society, PO Box 854, Van Nuys, CA 91408. Phone: (818) 997-6496. Fax: (818) 988-4337. E-mail: iibick@sbcglobal.net. Web: www.bick.net.

COME AND TAKE IT FESTIVAL. Oct 2–4. Gonzales, TX. This celebration commemorating the first shot fired for Texas independence in 1835 is named for the defiant battle cry of the colonists when the Mexican military demanded the return of a cannon. Est attendance: 20,000. For info: Chamber of Commerce, 414 St. Lawrence, Gonzales, TX 78629. Phone: (830) 672-6532. Fax: (830) 672-6533. E-mail: info@gonzalestexas.com. Web: www.gonzalestexas.com.

DALTON DEFENDERS DAY. Oct 2–3 (tentative). Coffeyville, KS. Event to honor citizens killed during Dalton Gang's robbery of two banks on Oct 5, 1892. Est attendance: 5,000. For info: Coffeyville Area Chamber of Commerce, PO Box 457, Coffeyville, KS 67337. Phone: (620) 251-2550 or (800) 626-3357. Fax: (620) 251-5448. E-mail: chamber@coffeyville.com.

GANDHI, MOHANDAS KARAMCHAND (MAHATMA): BIRTH ANNIVERSARY. Oct 2, 1869. The Indian political and spiritual leader who achieved world honor and fame for his advocacy of nonviolent resistance as a weapon against tyranny was born at Porbandar, India. He was assassinated in the garden of his home at New Delhi, Jan 30, 1948. On the anniversary of Gandhi's birth (Gandhi Jayanti) thousands gather at the park on the Jumna River at Delhi where Gandhi's body was cremated. Hymns are sung; verses from the Gita, the Koran and the Bible are recited; and cotton thread is spun on small spinning wheels (one of Gandhi's favorite activities). Other observances held at his birthplace and throughout India on this public holiday.

"THE GEORGE GOBEL SHOW" TV PREMIERE: 55th ANNIVERSARY. Oct 2, 1954. George Gobel hosted this comedy-variety show for five years on NBC. Chanteuse Peggy King and Jeff Donnell were also on the show, with Eddie Fisher as "permanent guest star." In 1959 Gobel switched networks to CBS and appeared for a year with Joe Flynn, Anita Bryant and Harry Von Zell.

GREENE, GRAHAM: BIRTH ANNIVERSARY. Oct 2, 1904. British author Graham Greene was born at Berkhamsted, Hertfordshire, England. He centered his works around characters facing salvation and damnation in a world of chaos, often with complex Catholic settings. His works include *The Power and the Glory* (1940) and *The Third Man* (1950). He died Apr 3, 1991, at Vevey, Switzerland.

GUARDIAN ANGELS DAY. Oct 2. We all have guardian angels. Now's the time to give them recognition and thanks for being in our lives with their own special day. Take the time today to find out how they've played a special role in our lives, in various cultures, religions, even foods. Celebrate today by doing something special to recognize their special qualities. Annually, Oct 2. For info: Lorrie Walters Marsiglio, PO Box 284-CC, Wasco, IL 60183-0284.

GUINEA: INDEPENDENCE DAY. Oct 2. National day. Guinea gained independence from France in 1958.

GUNN, MOSES: 80th BIRTH ANNIVERSARY. Oct 2, 1929. The 1981 winner of the NAACP Image Award for his performance as Booker T. Washington in the film *Ragtime* was born at St. Louis, MO. His appearances on stage ranged from the title role in *Othello* to Jean Genet's *The Blacks*. He received an Emmy nomination for his role in *Roots* and was awarded several Obies for off-Broadway performances. On film he appeared in *Shaft* and *The Great White Hope*. He died Dec 17, 1993, at Guilford, CT.

HULL, CORDELL: BIRTH ANNIVERSARY. Oct 2, 1871. American statesman who served in both houses of the Congress and as secretary of state was born at Pickett County, TN. Noted for his contributions to the "Good Neighbor" policies of the US with regard to countries of the Americas and to the establishment of the United Nations. Hull died at Bethesda, MD, July 23, 1955.

"THE JIMMY DURANTE SHOW" TV PREMIERE: 55th ANNIVERSARY. Oct 2, 1954. Affectionately known as "the Schnozz," Durante hosted a Saturday-night variety show with his former vaudeville partner, Eddie Jackson. It alternated with "The Donald O'Connor Show" on NBC and aired for two years.

KENTUCKY APPLE FESTIVAL. Oct 2–3. Paintsville, KY. Apple blossom beauty pageants, country music show, arts and crafts, flea market, antique car show, Corvette show, Apple Bowl, Terrapin Trot, amusement rides, food booths, clogging and square dancing. Annually, the first Friday and Saturday in October. Est attendance: 50,000. For info: Kentucky Apple Festival, Inc, PO Box 1245, Paintsville, KY 41240-5245. Phone: (606) 789-4355 or (800) 542-5790. Web: www.kyapplefest.org.

LEE NATIONAL DENIM DAY®. Oct 2. Lee Jeans invites companies, groups, teams and individuals to participate by wearing denim on Denim Day in exchange for a $5 donation to the Women's Cancer Programs of EIF. Since 1996, this program has raised more than $70 million for the breast cancer research and treatment programs. For info: Nancy White, Lee Jeans, One Lee Dr, Merriam, KS 66202. Phone: (800) 521-5533. Fax: (913) 789-0106. E-mail: denimday@vfc.com. Web: www.denimday.com.

MARSHALL, THURGOOD, SWORN IN TO SUPREME COURT: ANNIVERSARY. Oct 2, 1967. Thurgood Marshall was sworn in as the first black associate justice to the US Supreme Court. On June 27, 1991, he announced his resignation, effective upon the confirmation of his successor. See also: "Marshall, Thurgood: Birth Anniversary" (July 2).

MARX, GROUCHO: BIRTH ANNIVERSARY. Oct 2, 1890. Born Julius Henry Marx at New York, NY. Comedian who along with his brothers constituted the famous Marx Brothers. The Marx Brothers began as a singing group and then acted in such movies as *Duck Soup* and *Animal Crackers*. During the '40s and '50s, Groucho was the host of the television and radio show "You Bet Your Life." Died at Los Angeles, CA, Aug 19, 1977.

McFARLAND, GEORGE (SPANKY): BIRTH ANNIVERSARY. Oct 2, 1928. Chubby child star of the "Our Gang" comedy film shorts. Born at Dallas, TX, and died at Grapevine, TX, June 30, 1993.

MISSISSINEWA 1812. Oct 2–4. Marion, IN. Largest War of 1812 living-history event in US includes reenactment of battle. Military, trappers, woodland tribes, settlers, food purveyors and musicians, living as they did 200 years ago. Est attendance: 30,000. For info: Mississinewa Battlefield Society, PO Box 1812, Marion, IN 46952. Phone: (800) 822-1812. Fax: (765) 662-1809. E-mail: war1812@aol.com. Web: www.mississinewa1812.com.

NATIONAL CUSTODIAL WORKERS DAY. Oct 2. A day to honor all janitorial and custodial workers—those who clean up after us. For info: Bette Tadajewski, Saint John the Baptist Church, 2425 Frederick, Alpena, MI 49707. Phone: (989) 354-3019.

NATIONAL DIVERSITY DAY. Oct 2. A day to celebrate and embrace who we are, despite our differences, no matter what race, religion, gender, sexual orientation, age, nationality or disability. A day to reflect on and learn about different cultures and ideologies. A day to vow acceptance and tolerance. A day to consciously address these areas at educational and religious institutions, as well as in the workplace and at home. Our slogan: "Embrace diversity, embrace our world." Annually, the first Friday in October. For info: Leo Parvis. E-mail: drparvis@gmail.com. Web: www.nationaldiversityday.com.

NATIONAL STORYTELLING FESTIVAL. Oct 2–4. Jonesborough, TN. Tennessee's oldest town plays host to the most dynamic storytelling event dedicated to the oral tradition. This three-day celebration showcases storytellers, stories and traditions from across America and around the world. Annually, the first full weekend in October. Est attendance: 10,000. For info: Intl Storytelling Center, 116 W Main, Jonesborough, TN 37659. Phone: (800) 952-8392. Fax: (423) 913-8219. E-mail: info@storytellingcenter.net. Web: www.storytellingcenter.net.

NO SALT WEEK. Oct 2–9. Give no-salt cooking and food preparation a try! This celebration will help with recipes and combinations. For ideas send a large SASE. For info: Make It Tasty Spice Co, Box 416, Denver, CO 80201. Phone: (303) 575-5676. E-mail: starsuccess@excite.com.

NORTH CASCADES NATIONAL PARK ESTABLISHED: ANNIVERSARY. Oct 2, 1968. Located in Washington state.

OKTOBERFEST. Oct 2–3 (also Oct 9–10). New Ulm, MN. Celebrating New Ulm's German heritage, with musical entertainment, food and dancing. Est attendance: 6,000. For info: New Ulm Chamber of Commerce, Box 384, New Ulm, MN 56073. Phone: (507) 233-4300 or (888) 463-9856. E-mail: nuchamber@newulmtel.net. Web: www.newulmoktoberfest.com.

OZARK FALL FARMFEST. Oct 2–4. Ozark Empire Fairgrounds, Springfield, MO. The largest agricultural trade show in the Ozarks. Exhibits fill the grounds and all buildings. Free admission and free parking. For info: Ozark Empire Fair, 3001 N Grant, Springfield, MO 65803. Phone: (417) 833-2660. Fax: (417) 833-3769. Web: www.ozarkempirefair.com.

"PEANUTS" DEBUTS: ANNIVERSARY. Oct 2, 1950. This comic strip by Charles Schulz featured Charlie Brown, Lucy, Linus, Sally and Charlie's dog, Snoopy. The last new "Peanuts" strip was published Feb 13, 2000.

PHILEAS FOGG'S WAGER DAY: ANNIVERSARY. Oct 2, 1872. Anniversary, from Jules Verne's *Around the World in Eighty Days*, of the famous wager upon which the book is based: "I will bet twenty thousand pounds against anyone who wishes, that I will make the tour of the world in eighty days or less." Then, consulting a pocket almanac, Phileas Fogg said: "As today is Wednesday, the second of October, I shall be due in London, in this very room of the Reform Club, on Saturday, the twenty-first of December, at a quarter before nine PM; or else the twenty thousand pounds . . . will belong to you." See also: "Phileas Fogg Wins a Wager Day" (Dec 21).

RAYMOND, ALEX: 100th BIRTH ANNIVERSARY. Oct 2, 1909. This influential comic strip artist, born at New Rochelle, NY, was the creator in 1934 of the science fiction strip "Flash Gordon." The strip's huge popularity led to Hollywood serials starring Buster Crabbe a few years later. Raymond also created "Secret Agent X-9" and "Rip Kirby," but his career was cut short by a fatal automobile accident on Sept 6, 1956, at Westport, CT.

REDWOOD NATIONAL PARK ESTABLISHED: ANNIVERSARY. Oct 2, 1968. California's Redwood National Park was established. For further park info: Redwood Natl Park, 1111 Second St, Crescent City, CA 95531.

REX ALLEN DAYS. Oct 2–4. Willcox, AZ. Annual celebration honors hometown boy the late Rex Allen, who gained fame as a singer, cowboy movie star and narrator for Walt Disney Productions. Celebration also honors Rex Allen, Jr, famed singer, who appeared on TNN's "Yesteryears" and "Statler Brothers' Show." Activities include golf tournament, parade, country fair, rodeo, General Willcox Turtle Race, arts and crafts, country and western concert, carnival, softball tournament, cowboy dances. Est attendance: 20,000. For info: Rex Allen Museum, 150 N Railroad Ave, Willcox, AZ 85643. Phone: (520) 384-4583 or (877) 234-4111. Web: www.rexallenmuseum.org or www.willcoxchamber.com.

SPRINGS FOLK FESTIVAL. Oct 2–3. Springs, PA. 51st annual festival during the peak of fall foliage in Amish country. Features 140 craftsmen, Dutch food and continuous live music. Est attendance: 15,000. For info: Springs Folk Festival, PO Box 293, Springs, PA 15562. Phone: (814) 662-4158. Web: www.springspa.org.

STREETER, RUTH CHENEY: BIRTH ANNIVERSARY. Oct 2, 1895. Born at Brookline, MA, Ruth Cheney Streeter was the first director of the US Marine Corps Women's Reserve. She was active in unemployment relief, public health, welfare and old-age assistance in New Jersey during the 1930s. A student of aeronautics, she learned to fly while serving as an adjutant of a flight group in the Civil Air Patrol during the early years of WWII. She died Sept 30, 1990, at Morristown, NJ.

SUGARLOAF CRAFTS FESTIVAL. Oct 2–4. Maryland State Fairgrounds, Timonium, MD. This show, now in its 33rd year, features more than 350 nationally recognized fine artists and craft designers displaying and selling their original creations. Includes craft demonstrations, live music, specialty food, children's entertainment, hourly gift certificate drawings and more. Est attendance: 17,000. For info: Sugarloaf Mountain Works, 200 Orchard Ridge Dr, #215, Gaithersburg, MD 20878. Phone: (800) 210-9900. Fax: (301) 253-9620. Web: www.sugarloafcrafts.com.

SUKKOT BEGINS AT SUNDOWN. Oct 2. Jewish Feast of Tabernacles. See "Sukkot" (Oct 3).

SWAPPIN' MEETIN'. Oct 2–3. Southeast Community and Technical College, Cumberland, KY. 45th annual. A celebration of the rich heritage of the mountain people. Handmade goods such as quilts and woodwork are displayed; demonstrations include lye soap making, sorghum molasses making and folksinging. Est attendance: 6,000. For info: Michael Corriston, Facility Dir, Appalachian Center, 700 College Rd, Cumberland, KY 40823. Phone: (606) 589-3137. Fax: (606) 589-3181. E-mail: michael.corriston@kctcs.edu. Web: www.state.ky.us.

TENNESSEE VALLEY OLD-TIME FIDDLERS CONVENTION. Oct 2–3. Athens State University, Athens, AL. This convention annually attracts thousands of old-time music fans and brings some 200 contestants to the grounds of historic Athens State University. More than $11,000 in cash prizes is awarded, and the fiddle champion takes home $1,000 plus a trophy. There is competition in 16 categories at this, the "Granddaddy of Mid-South Fiddlers Conventions." Annually, the first full weekend in October. Est attendance: 20,000. For info: Rick Mould, Athens State University, 300 N Beaty St, Athens, AL 35611. Phone: (256) 233-8215. Fax: (256) 230-2565. E-mail: mouldrl@athens.edu. Web: www.athens.edu.

"THE TWILIGHT ZONE" TV PREMIERE: 50th ANNIVERSARY. Oct 2, 1959. "The Twilight Zone" went on the air with these now-familiar words: "There is a fifth dimension, beyond that which is known to man. It is a dimension as vast as space and as timeless as infinity. It is the middle ground between light and shadow, between science and superstition, and it lies between the pit of man's fear and the summit of his knowledge. This is the dimension of imagination. It is an area which we call The Twilight Zone." The anthology program ran five seasons for 154 installments, with a one-year hiatus between the third and fourth seasons. Created and hosted by Rod Serling, it is now considered to have been one of the best dramas to appear on television. The last original episode was telecast June 15, 1964.

WORLD FARM ANIMALS DAY. Oct 2. Celebrated on Gandhi's birthday. To expose and memorialize the needless suffering and death of billions of innocent, sentient animals in factories, farms and slaughterhouses. Local actions include memorial services, vigils, street theater, picketing, leafletting and information tables. For info: Farm Animal Reform Movement, 10101 Ashburton Ln, Bethesda, MD 20817. Phone: (301) 530-1737. Fax: (301) 530-5747. E-mail: info@wfad.org. Web: www.wfad.org.

WORLD SMILE DAY. Oct 2. A day dedicated to good works and good cheer throughout the world. The official theme for the day is "Do an act of kindness. Help one person smile." The symbol for the day is the world-famous "smiley face" icon, created in 1963 by Harvey Ball of Worcester, MA. This icon is now the international symbol of happiness and goodwill. Annually, the first Friday in October. For info: Charles P. Ball, President, World Smile Corp, 22 Front St, PO Box 171, Worcester, MA 01614. Web: www.worldsmileday.com.

October 2009	S	M	T	W	T	F	S
					1	2	3
	4	5	6	7	8	9	10
	11	12	13	14	15	16	17
	18	19	20	21	22	23	24
	25	26	27	28	29	30	31

 Birthdays Today

Lorraine Bracco, 54, actress ("The Sopranos," *Goodfellas*), born Brooklyn, NY, Oct 2, 1955.

Clay S. Felker, 81, journalist, editor, publisher (founder of *New York* magazine), born St. Louis, MO, Oct 2, 1928.

Donna Karan, 61, fashion designer, born Forest Hills, NY, Oct 2, 1948.

Don McLean, 64, singer, songwriter ("American Pie"), born New Rochelle, NY, Oct 2, 1945.

Rex Reed, 70, movie critic, born Fort Worth, TX, Oct 2, 1939.

Kelly Ripa, 39, actress ("Hope & Faith," "All My Children"), TV host ("Live with Regis & Kelly"), born Stratford, NJ, Oct 2, 1970.

Sting, 58, singer, songwriter, actor (*Dune*), born Gordon Sumner at London, England, Oct 2, 1951.

Paul Teutul, Jr, 35, motorcycle designer, television personality ("American Chopper"), born Oct 2, 1974.

October 3 — Saturday

DAY 276 89 REMAINING

ALBUQUERQUE INTERNATIONAL BALLOON FIESTA. Oct 3–11. Balloon Fiesta Park, Albuquerque, NM. Held since 1972, the largest hot-air balloon gathering in the world features more than 700 hot-air and gas balloons, mass ascensions, balloon glows and specially shaped balloons. The 10-day event includes entries from more than 20 countries. Annually, the first through second weekends in October. For info: Albuquerque International Balloon Fiesta, Inc, 4401 Alameda NE, Albuquerque, NM 87113. Phone: (505) 821-1000 or (888) 422-7277. Fax: (505) 828-2887. E-mail: balloons@balloon fiesta.com. Web: www.balloonfiesta.com.

"THE ANDY GRIFFITH SHOW" TV PREMIERE: ANNIVERSARY. Oct 3, 1960. Marks the airing of the first of 249 episodes. Set in rural Mayberry, NC, the show starred Griffith as Sheriff Andy Taylor, Ron Howard as his son, Opie, Frances Bavier as Aunt Bee Taylor and Don Knotts as Deputy Barney Fife. Although the last telecast aired Sept 16, 1968, more than 12,000 members of "The Andy Griffith Show" Rerun Watchers Club and others celebrate this day with festivities every year.

BANCROFT, GEORGE: BIRTH ANNIVERSARY. Oct 3, 1800. American historian, known as the "Father of American History," born at Worcester, MA. Died at Washington, DC, Jan 27, 1891.

BATTLE OF GERMANTOWN REENACTMENT. Oct 3. Philadelphia, PA. Annual reenactment of the Oct 4, 1777, Battle of Germantown. Featured are more than 300 authentically costumed troops re-creating the original battle at noon and at 3 PM. Single admission to eight other nearby historical sites with the Revolutionary Germantown Passport. Annually, the first Saturday in October. Est attendance: 4,000. For info: Public Relations, Cliveden of the National Trust, 6401 Germantown Ave, Philadelphia, PA 19144. Phone: (215) 848-1777. Fax: (215) 438-2892. E-mail: info@cliveden .org. Web: www.cliveden.org.

CABRILLO FESTIVAL. Oct 3–4. San Diego, CA. Colorful pageant reenacts the historic landing of explorer Juan Rodríguez Cabrillo, who sailed into San Diego Bay on Sept 28, 1542. Kumeyaay basket-weaving, acorn grinding and flint knapping demonstrations. Knot-tying exhibition. Reenactment of Spanish soldier encampment. Portuguese, Spanish, Native American and Mexican dances and food. Pageant takes place annually on the Sunday on or following Sept 28. A commemorative ceremony takes place annually on the Saturday before the pageant. Est attendance: 5,000. For info: Cabrillo Natl Monument, 1800 Cabrillo Memorial Dr, San Diego, CA 92106. Phone: (619) 557-5450. Fax: (619) 226-6311. Web: www .nps.gov/cabr or www.cabrillofestival.org.

"CAPTAIN KANGAROO" TV PREMIERE: ANNIVERSARY. Oct 3, 1955. On the air until 1985, this was the longest-running children's TV show until it was surpassed by "Sesame Street." Starring Bob Keeshan as Captain Kangaroo, it was broadcast on CBS and PBS. Other characters included Mr Green Jeans, Grandfather Clock, Bunny Rabbit, Mr Moose and Dancing Bear. Keeshan was an advocate for excellence in children's programming and even supervised which commercials would appear on the program. In 1997 "The All New Captain Kangaroo" debuted, starring John McDonough.

CHINA: MOON FESTIVAL (OR MID-AUTUMN FESTIVAL). Oct 3. According to folk legend this day is the birthday of the earth god T'u-ti Kung. The festival indicates the year's hard work in the fields will soon end with the harvest. People express gratitude to heaven as represented by the moon and to earth as symbolized by the earth god for all good things from the preceding year. Special harvest foods are eaten, especially "moon cakes." Observed on the 15th day of the eighth month of the Chinese lunar calendar, this festival is called by different names in different places, but is widely recognized throughout the Far East, including Taiwan, Korea, Singapore and Hong Kong. Date here is for China; date in other countries will differ.

CHOWDERFEST. Oct 3–4. Bay Village, Beach Haven, NJ. Fans of both Manhattan and New England–style chowders vote for their favorite recipes after sampling the entries of nearly 20 participating restaurants. The suspense is intense as each chef hopes to hit a grand slam home run and capture the trophy and bragging rights. Live music, a Merchants Mart featuring blow-out bargains and an outdoor food court top off the festivities. For info: Linda Morris, Chowderfest, 265 W 9th St, Ship Bottom, NJ 08008. Phone: (800) 292-6372. E-mail: event@discoversouthernocean.com. Web: www .chowderfest.com.

"THE DICK VAN DYKE SHOW" TV PREMIERE: ANNIVERSARY. Oct 3, 1961. This Carl Reiner–created sitcom wasn't an immediate success but soon became a hit. It starred Dick Van Dyke as Rob Petrie, a TV show writer, and Mary Tyler Moore as his wife, Laura, a former dancer. This was one of the first shows revolving around the goings-on at a TV series. Other cast members included: Morey Amsterdam, Rose Marie, Richard Deacon, Carl Reiner, Jerry Paris, Ann Morgan Guilbert and Larry Matthews. The last episode aired Sept 7, 1966, but the show remains popular in reruns.

FALL CITYWIDE GARAGE SALE. Oct 3. Electra, TX. Sales throughout the Electra area. Chamber of Commerce will provide free coffee and maps at 7 AM. The Chamber of Commerce office will close at 8 AM so that staff, too, may enjoy all of the bargains. Est attendance: 500. For info: Sherry Strange, Electra Chamber of Commerce, 112 W Cleveland, Electra, TX 76360. Phone: (940) 495-3577. E-mail: electracoc@electratel.net. Web: www.electratexas.org.

FELL'S POINT FUN FESTIVAL. Oct 3–4. Fell's Point National Historic District, Baltimore, MD. 43rd annual popular outdoor street festival held in Baltimore's original seaport. 400+ arts and crafts vendors, antique market, carnival rides, Hispanic area, five stages featuring rock and roll, bluegrass, jazz, blues, folk, gospel, dancing, etc, family and children's area, three beer gardens, international bazaar retail area, 40+ food vendors in three food courts and much more. Annually, the first full weekend in October. Sponsor: The Preservation Society. Est attendance: 700,000. For info: Fell's Point Fun Festival, 812 S Ann St, Baltimore, MD 21231. Phone: (410) 675-6756. Fax: (410) 675-6769. Web: www.preservationsociety.com.

FIRST WOMAN US SENATOR: ANNIVERSARY. Oct 3, 1922. Mrs W.H. (Rebecca) Felton, 87, of Cartersville, GA, was appointed on Oct 3, 1922, by Governor Thomas Hardwick of Georgia to the Senate seat vacated by the death of Thomas E. Watson. It was a two-day ad interim appointment.

GERMAN REUNIFICATION: ANNIVERSARY. Oct 3, 1990. After 45 years of division, East and West Germany reunited just four days short of East Germany's 41st founding anniversary (Oct 7, 1949). The new united Germany took the name the Federal Republic of Germany, the formal name of the former West Germany, and adopted the constitution of the former West Germany. Today is a national holiday in Germany, Tag der Deutschen Einheit (Day of German Unity).

GORGAS, WILLIAM CRAWFORD: BIRTH ANNIVERSARY. Oct 3, 1854. Physician and sanitary engineer, born at Toulminville, AL. He eradicated yellow fever from Havana and the Panama Canal, allowing the completion of the canal. Gorgas died at London, England, July 4, 1920.

HERRIOT, JAMES: BIRTH ANNIVERSARY. Oct 3, 1916. Author and veterinarian born James Alfred Wight at Glasgow, Scotland. Under the pen name Herriot he wrote more than 12 books chronicling his life as a veterinarian in northern England. His *All Creatures Great and Small* (1974) was made into a TV series that was an international hit. He was made a member of the Order of the British Empire in 1979. Herriot died Feb 23, 1995, at Yorkshire, England.

HONDURAS: FRANCISCO MORAZÁN HOLIDAY. Oct 3. Public holiday in honor of Francisco Morazán, national hero, who was born in 1799.

ISSAQUAH SALMON DAYS FESTIVAL. Oct 3–4. Issaquah, WA. To celebrate the return of the spawning salmon to the hatchery with more than 300 arts and crafts vendors, sporting events, food and more. Annually, the first full weekend in October. Est attendance: 150,000. For info: Issaquah Salmon Days Festival, 155 NW Gilman Blvd, Issaquah, WA 98027. Phone: (425) 392-0661. Fax: (425) 392-8101. E-mail: info@salmondays.org. Web: www.salmondays.org.

JOHNNY APPLESEED DAYS. Oct 3–4. Lake City, MN. Apple pie, arts and crafts fair, basket raffles, chili cook-off, kid pedal tractor pull, scarecrow contest, pancake breakfast and more. Annually, the first full weekend in October. Est attendance: 6,500. For info: Lake City Area Chamber of Commerce, 101 W Center St, Lake City, MN 55041. Phone: (800) 369-4123. E-mail: chamberevents@lakecity.org.

KNOX COUNTY SCENIC DRIVE. Oct 3–4 (also Oct 10–11). Knox County, IL. A self-conducted 100-mile driving tour through rural Spoon River Valley resplendent with fall colors. Different attractions at every stop feature food, crafts, art, antiques, fresh produce, old skills demonstrations, flea markets or games. Est attendance: 75,000. For info: Galesburg Area CVB, PO Box 60, Galesburg, IL 61402-0060. Phone: (309) 343-2485. Fax: (309) 343-2521. E-mail: visitors @visitgalesburg.com. Web: www.visitgalesburg.com.

KOREA: CHUSOK. Oct 3. Gala celebration by Koreans everywhere. Autumn harvest thanksgiving moon festival. Observed on 15th day of eighth lunar month (eighth full moon of lunar calendar) each year. Koreans pay homage to ancestors and express gratitude to guarding spirits for another year of rich crops. A time to visit tombs, leave food and prepare for the coming winter season. Traditional food is the "moon cake," made on the eve of Chusok, with rice, chestnuts and jujube fruits. Games, dancing and gift exchanges. Observed since Silla Dynasty (beginning of First Millennium).

KOREA: NATIONAL FOUNDATION DAY. Oct 3. National holiday also called Tangun Day, as it commemorates day when legendary founder of the Korean nation, Tangun, established his kingdom of Chosun in 2333 BC.

KURTZMAN, HARVEY: BIRTH ANNIVERSARY. Oct 3, 1902. Cartoonist and founder of *Mad* magazine, Harvey Kurtzman was born at Brooklyn, NY. At 14 he had his first cartoon published, and he began his career in comic books in 1943. His career led him to EC (Educational Comics), and with the support of William Gaines, he created *Mad* magazine, which first appeared in 1952. He died Feb 21, 1993, at Mount Vernon, NY.

"LA LAW" TV PREMIERE: ANNIVERSARY. Oct 3, 1986. Set in the Los Angeles law firm of McKenzie, Brackman, Chaney and Kuzak, this drama had a large cast. Divorce lawyer Arnie Becker was played by Corbin Bernsen, public defender Victor Sifuentes by Jimmy Smits and managing partner Douglas Brackman by Alan Rachins. Other cast members included Harry Hamlin as Michael Kuzak, Richard Dysart as Leland McKenzie, Susan Dey as Grace Van Owen, Jill Eikenberry as Ann Kelsey, Michael Tucker as Stuart Markowitz and Susan Ruttan as Roxanne Melman. The last telecast was May 19, 1994.

LONG BEACH ISLAND CHOWDER COOK-OFF. Oct 3–4. Bayfront Park, Beach Haven, NJ. Weekend-long festival featuring unlimited tasting of up to 30 different red/white clam chowders prepared by area restaurants. Entertainment; other food/beverages available. Annually, the weekend before Columbus Day weekend. Est attendance: 24,000. For info: Southern Ocean County Chamber of Commerce, 265 W 9th St, Ship Bottom, NJ 08008. Phone: (800) 292-6372 or (609) 494-7211. Fax: (609) 494-5807. E-mail: event@ discoversouthernocean.com. Web: www.chowderfest.com.

October 2009	S	M	T	W	T	F	S
					1	2	3
	4	5	6	7	8	9	10
	11	12	13	14	15	16	17
	18	19	20	21	22	23	24
	25	26	27	28	29	30	31

MANSON, PATRICK: BIRTH ANNIVERSARY. Oct 3, 1844. British parasitologist and surgeon sometimes called the father of tropical medicine. Manson's research into insects as carriers of parasites was instrumental in later understanding of mosquitoes as transmitters of malaria. Born at Aberdeen, Scotland, Manson died Apr 9, 1922, at London, England.

"MICKEY MOUSE CLUB" TV PREMIERE: ANNIVERSARY. Oct 3, 1955. This afternoon show for children was on ABC. Among its young cast members were Mouseketeers Annette Funicello and Shelley Fabares. A later version, "The New Mickey Mouse Club," starred Keri Russell, Christina Aguilera and Britney Spears.

MORRO BAY HARBOR FESTIVAL. Oct 3–4. Morro Bay, CA. Celebrates a working waterfront at play. Showcases seafood, fishing industry and diversity of marine life and coastal lifestyles. Features California Seafood Faire, wine and premium beer tasting and a flotilla of family-oriented attractions. Annually, the first full weekend in October. Phone in California: (800) 366-6043. Est attendance: 25,000. For info: Exhibits Coord, Morro Bay Harbor Festival, Inc, 895 Napa St, Ste A-3, Morro Bay, CA 93442. Phone: (805) 772-1155. Fax: (805) 772-2107. E-mail: exhibits@mbhf.com. Web: www.mbhf.com.

NATIONAL APPLE HARVEST FESTIVAL. Oct 3–4 (also Oct 10–11). South Mountain Fairgrounds, Gettysburg, PA. 45th annual. Celebration includes tours of orchards, apple-butter boiling and antique cider press. Est attendance: 100,000. For info: Gettysburg CVB, PO Box 4117, Gettysburg, PA 17325. Phone: (717) 334-6274. Fax: (717) 334-1166. E-mail: info@gettysburg.travel. Web: www.gettysburg .travel or www.appleharvest.com.

NETHERLANDS: RELIEF OF LEIDEN DAY. Oct 3. Celebration of the liberation of Leiden in 1574.

"OUR MISS BROOKS" TV PREMIERE: ANNIVERSARY. Oct 3, 1952. This half-hour sitcom began on the radio, and unlike with many radio programs that moved to TV, most of the original radio cast was retained. It was about a favorite high school English teacher named Connie Brooks (played by Eve Arden). Also featured were Gale Gordon, Richard Crenna, Gloria McMillan and Jane Morgan.

"OZZIE AND HARRIET" TV PREMIERE: ANNIVERSARY. Oct 3, 1952. "Ozzie and Harriet" was TV's longest-running sitcom. The successful radio-turned-TV show about the Nelson family starred the real-life Nelsons—Ozzie; his wife, Harriet, and their sons, David and Ricky. Officially titled "The Adventures of Ozzie and Harriet," this show was set in the family's home. The boys were one reason the show was successful, and Ricky used the advantage to become a pop star. David and Rick's real-life wives—June Blair and Kris Nelson—also joined the cast. The show was canceled at the end of the 1965–66 season after 435 episodes, 409 of which were in black and white and 26 in color. The last episode aired Sept 3, 1966.

"THE PAT BOONE SHOW" TV PREMIERE: ANNIVERSARY. Oct 3, 1957. Clean-cut singer Pat Boone hosted three shows between 1957 and 1969. The first was a prime-time variety series with the McGuire Sisters and the Mort Lindsey Orchestra as regulars. The second show featured the Paul Smith Orchestra and was a daytime variety and talk show. "Pat Boone in Hollywood" was the title of the third, a 90-minute talk show.

PUMPKIN AND APPLE CELEBRATION. Oct 3–4. Woodstock, VT. Hands-on activities and educational programs highlight these two versatile fall crops. Events include apple and pumpkin displays, apple tasting, trivia contest, cider pressing, apple scavenger hunt, pumpkin races, apples-on-a-string, making pumpkin ice cream, cooking apple butter in the farmhouse and the annual pumpkin sale. For info: Billings Farm and Museum, Rte 12 N, Woodstock, VT 05091. Phone: (802) 457-2355. Fax: (802) 457-4663. E-mail: info@billingsfarm.org. Web: www.billingsfarm.org.

"QUINCY" TV PREMIERE: ANNIVERSARY. Oct 3, 1976. This medically oriented crime show starred Jack Klugman as Dr. Raymond Quincy, a medical examiner for the Los Angeles coroner's office. Quincy's curiosity about his cases led to investigative work that often solved them. Later in the series, the show focused on social issues that were unrelated to forensic medicine. The last telecast aired on Sept 5, 1983.

"THE REAL McCOYS" TV PREMIERE: ANNIVERSARY. Oct 3, 1957. This first successful rural comedy program was one of the most popular, predating similar shows such as "The Beverly Hillbillies" by many seasons. It was set in rural California and featured the McCoys, played by Walter Brennan, Richard Crenna, Kathleen Nolan, Michael Winkelman and Lydia Reed.

ROBINSON NAMED BASEBALL'S FIRST BLACK MAJOR LEAGUE MANAGER: 35th ANNIVERSARY. Oct 3, 1974. The only major league player selected Most Valuable Player in both the American and National leagues, Frank Robinson was hired by the Cleveland Indians as baseball's first black major league manager. During his playing career Robinson represented the American League in four World Series playing for the Baltimore Orioles, led the Cincinnati Reds to a National League pennant and hit 586 home runs in 21 years of play.

"SCARECROW AND MRS KING" TV PREMIERE: ANNIVERSARY. Oct 3, 1983. A one-hour adventure series starring Bruce Boxleitner as Lee Stetson (code name "Scarecrow"), a government agent working with Mrs Amanda King (Kate Jackson), a housewife-turned-agent. Mr King, played by Sam Melville, appeared once, but he was out of the picture when Mrs King and Scarecrow were married in the final season.

SCARECROW FESTIVAL. Oct 3. Beech Springs Farm Market, Winchester, KY. Design your own scarecrow at this fun fall festival. Entries are accepted in several categories including traditional, celebrity and whimsical. The scarecrow is then auctioned off at our annual festival and all proceeds are given to charity. The festival includes many children's games and activities. It's a day for the entire family. Annually, the first Saturday in October. For info: Nancy Turner, Tour Winchester, 2 S Maple St, Winchester, KY 40391. Phone: (859) 744-0556. Fax: (859) 744-9226. E-mail: info@tourwinchester.com. Web: www.tourwinchester.com.

SPOON RIVER VALLEY SCENIC DRIVE. Oct 3–4 (also Oct 10–11). Fulton County, IL. Fall festival in 15 villages with fall foliage, arts and crafts, antiques and collectibles, demonstrations, exhibits, food and the beauty of the 100-mile-long Spoon River Valley. Performance of *Spoon River Anthology* in Lewistown. Annually, the first two full weekends in October. Est attendance: 100,000. For info: Spoon River Valley Scenic Drive, PO Box 525, Canton, IL 61520. Phone: (309) 647-8980. Web: www.spoonriverdrive.org.

SUKKOT, SUCCOTH or FEAST OF TABERNACLES, FIRST DAY. Oct 3–11. Hebrew calendar date: Tishri 15, 5770, begins nine-day festival in commemoration of Jewish people's 40 years of wandering in the desert and thanksgiving for the fall harvest. This high-holiday season closes with Shemini Atzeret (see entry on Oct 10) and Simchat Torah (see entry on Oct 11). Began at sundown Oct 2.

US MID-AMATEUR (GOLF) CHAMPIONSHIP. Oct 3–8. Kiawah Island Golf Resort, Charleston, SC. For info: USGA, Golf House, Championship Dept, PO Box 708, Far Hills, NJ 07931. Phone: (908) 234-2300. Fax: (908) 234-9687. Web: www.usga.org.

US WOMEN'S MID-AMATEUR (GOLF) CHAMPIONSHIP. Oct 3–8. Golden Hills Club, Ocala, FL. For info: USGA, Golf House, Championship Dept, PO Box 708, Far Hills, NJ 07931. Phone: (908) 234-2300. E-mail: usga@usga.org. Web: www.usga.org.

WINFIELD ART-IN-THE-PARK FESTIVAL. Oct 3. Scenic Island Park, Winfield, KS. More than 100 artists and craftspersons display and sell their wares. Entertainment; food services available. $2 contribution for those over 12 years of age. Annually, the first Saturday in October. Est attendance: 6,000. For info: Winfield Arts and Humanities Council, 700 Gary, Ste A, Winfield, KS 67156-3731. Phone: (620) 221-2161. Fax: (620) 221-0587. E-mail: info@winfieldarts.com.

WOOFSTOCK. Oct 3. Wichita, KS. An annual celebration of peace, love and pets, Woofstock invites canines and their owners to participate in activities catered exclusively to them, including a one-mile mutt strut, two-mile fun run, contests for dogs and much more. Silent auction, more than 80 pet-friendly vendors, demonstrations of dog agility, canine search and rescue, water retrieval and sheep herding. All proceeds benefit the Kansas Humane Society and the 16,000 animals it receives each year. Est attendance: 15,000. For info: Kansas Humane Society, PO Box 945, Wichita, KS 67201. Phone: (316) 524-1590. Fax: (316) 554-0356. Web: www.kshumane.org.

WORLD CARD MAKING DAY. Oct 3. *Paper Crafts* magazine celebrates the connections handmade cards create and kicks off the holiday card-making season. This day is set aside to offer card makers fun and inspiring environments in which to create by providing card ideas, tips, sweepstakes and ways to connect through store events, classes, group activities and/or individual card making. For info: Stacy Croninger, *Paper Crafts*, 14850 Pony Express Rd, Bluffdale, UT 84065. Phone: (801) 816-8336. E-mail: scroninger@ckmedia.com. Web: www.WorldCardMakingDay.com.

XTERRA NEVADA TRAIL RUN. Oct 3. Incline Village, NV. The XTERRA Trail Run Series boasts over 50 events across the country with runs ranging from 5k to 25k. These extreme, off-road trail runs give runners the chance to prove their skills against a variety of terrain. From calf-burning hills to slippery, mud-covered paths athletes will face the ultimate test of endurance. This race features off-road 5k and 10k trail runs. For info: Ann Mickey, XTERRA/TEAM Unlimited, 720 Iwilei Rd #290, Honolulu, HI 96817. Phone: (877) 751-8880. E-mail: info@xterraplanet.com. Web: www.xterratrailrun.com.

Birthdays Today

Jeff Bingaman, 66, US Senator (D, New Mexico), born El Paso, TX, Oct 3, 1943.

Lindsey Buckingham, 62, singer, songwriter (with Fleetwood Mac, "Go Your Own Way"), born Palo Alto, CA, Oct 3, 1947.

Neve Campbell, 36, actress ("Party of Five," *Scream*), born Guelph, ON, Canada, Oct 3, 1973.

Chubby Checker, 68, musician, singer ("The Twist"), born Ernest Evans at Philadelphia, PA, Oct 3, 1941.

Fred Couples, 50, golfer, born Seattle, WA, Oct 3, 1959.

Dennis Lee Eckersley, 55, former baseball player, born Oakland, CA, Oct 3, 1954.

Janel Maloney, 40, actress ("From the Earth to the Moon," "The West Wing"), born Woodland Hills, CA, Oct 3, 1969.

Clive Owen, 45, actor (*Children of Men, Elizabeth: The Golden Age, Closer, Sin City*), born Keresley, Coventry, Warwickshire, England, Oct 3, 1964.

Bob Riley, 65, Governor of Alabama (R), born Ashland, AL, Oct 3, 1944.

Gwen Stefani, 40, singer (No Doubt), born Anaheim, CA, Oct 3, 1969.

Gore Vidal, 84, author (*Burr, Myra Breckinridge*), born West Point, NY, Oct 3, 1925.

Jack P. Wagner, 50, actor ("Melrose Place," "General Hospital"), born Washington, MO, Oct 3, 1959.

David Mark (Dave) Winfield, 58, Hall of Fame baseball player, born St. Paul, MN, Oct 3, 1951.

October 4 — Sunday

DAY 277 88 REMAINING

"THE ALVIN SHOW" TV PREMIERE: ANNIVERSARY. Oct 4, 1961. This prime-time cartoon was based on Ross Bagdasarian's novelty group the Chipmunks, which began as recordings with speeded-up vocals. In the series, the three chipmunks, Alvin, Simon and Theodore, sang and had adventures along with their songwriter-manager, David Seville. Bagdasarian supplied the voices. "Alvin" was more successful as a Saturday-morning cartoon. It returned in reruns in 1979 and also prompted a sequel, "Alvin and the Chipmunks," in 1983.

APPLE FESTIVAL. Oct 4. Old Prairie Town at Ward-Meade Historic Site, Topeka, KS. Celebration of harvest and heritage of Kansas located in 5½-acre historical park. Ethnic foods, live entertainment, special shows, turn-of-the-century town square activities, nearly 65 craft booths. Annually, the first Sunday in October. Est attendance: 5,000. For info: Gena Brooks, Old Prairie Town at Ward-Meade Historic Site, 1st & Clay, Topeka, KS 66606. Phone: (785) 368-2439. Fax: (785) 368-3890.

BLESSING OF THE FISHING FLEET. Oct 4. Church of Saints Peter and Paul and Fisherman's Wharf, San Francisco, CA. Annually, the first Sunday in October.

CATTUS ISLAND NATURE FESTIVAL. Oct 4. Cattus Island County Park, Toms River, NJ. 29th annual environmental organizations fair with natural history programs throughout the day, including boat and van tours, canoe floats, children's games, nature walks and more. Est attendance: 1,500. For info: Cattus Island Park, 1170 Cattus Island Blvd, Toms River, NJ 08753. Phone: (732) 270-6960. E-mail: jkline@co.ocean.nj.us.

CORSICA LIBERATED: ANNIVERSARY. Oct 4, 1943. The island of Corsica became the first French territory in Europe freed from Nazi control when Free French troops entered the city of Bastia, the culmination of a French uprising that had begun on the island on Sept 19.

COUNTRY INN, BED-AND-BREAKFAST DAY. Oct 4. Across America and Canada country inns and bed-and-breakfasts will welcome visitors with information, special events and fellowship. The weekend will also introduce people to the world of inns and B&Bs. Annually, the first Sunday of October. For info: Tina Czarnota. Web: www.tinaczarnota.com.

DICK TRACY DEBUTS: ANNIVERSARY. Oct 4, 1931. Square-jawed detective Dick Tracy made his comic strip debut in the *Detroit Daily Mirror* in "Plainclothes Tracy."

October 2009	S	M	T	W	T	F	S
					1	2	3
	4	5	6	7	8	9	10
	11	12	13	14	15	16	17
	18	19	20	21	22	23	24
	25	26	27	28	29	30	31

✦ **FIRE PREVENTION WEEK.** Oct 4–10. Presidential Proclamation issued annually for the first or second week in October since 1925. For many years prior to 1925, National Fire Prevention Day was observed in October. Sponsored by the National Fire Protection Association. Annually, the Sunday-through-Saturday period during which the Oct 9 anniversary date falls.

FIRE PREVENTION WEEK. Oct 4–10. To increase awareness of the dangers of fire and to educate the public on how to stay safe from fire. For info: Natl Fire Protection Assn, One Batterymarch Park, Quincy, MA 02169. Phone: (617) 770-3000. E-mail: publicaffairs@nfpa.org. Web: www.nfpa.org and www.firepreventionweek.org.

FRANCE: PRIX DE L'ARC DE TRIOMPHE. Oct 4. Longchamp Racecourse, Paris. One of the world's greatest horse races has been held on the first Sunday in October since 1920. Up to 20 of the best entire horses and fillies aged three and above line up each year for the mile-and-a-half contest. Since 2008 and the signature of a five-year partnership with the Qatar Racing and Equestrian Club, the "Arc" has become the richest thoroughbred race in the world with a total purse of 4 million euros. For info: French Racing and Breeding Committee, 46 Place Abel Gance, 92655 Boulogne Cedex, France. E-mail: info@frbc.net. Web: www.france-galop.com.

FRYEBURG FAIR. Oct 4–11. Rte 5, Fryeburg, ME. Agricultural exposition, draft horse competitions, oxen and horse pulling, midway, nightly shows, harness racing, Woodsmen's Day (always Monday), tractor pulling, baking contests, Forestry Resource Center, Fireman's Muster, sheepdog trials and juried crafts show. Annually, the week that includes the first Wednesday in October. Est attendance: 350,000. For info: Secretary, Fryeburg Fair, PO Box 78, Fryeburg, ME 04037. Phone: (207) 935-3268. Fax: (207) 935-3662. E-mail: info@fryeburgfair.org.

GERMANY: ERNTEDANKFEST. Oct 4. A harvest thanksgiving festival, or potato harvest festival, Erntedankfest (or Erntedanktag) is generally observed on the first Sunday in October.

GREGORIAN CALENDAR ADJUSTMENT: ANNIVERSARY. Oct 4, 1582. Pope Gregory XIII issued a bulletin that decreed that the day following Thursday, Oct 4, 1582, should be Friday, Oct 15, 1582, thus correcting the Julian Calendar, then 10 days out of date relative to the seasons. This reform was effective in most Catholic countries; the Julian Calendar continued in use in Britain and the American colonies until 1752, in Russia until 1918 and in Greece until 1923. See also: "Gregorian Calendar Adjustment: Anniversary" (Feb 24) and "Calendar Adjustment Day: Anniversary" (Sept 2).

HAYES, RUTHERFORD BIRCHARD: BIRTH ANNIVERSARY. Oct 4, 1822. Rutherford Birchard Hayes, 19th president of the US (Mar 4, 1877–Mar 3, 1881), was born at Delaware, OH. In his inaugural address, Hayes said: "He serves his party best who serves the country best." He died at Fremont, OH, Jan 17, 1893.

HUNTER'S MOON. Oct 4. The full moon following Harvest Moon. So called because the moon's light in evening extends day's length for hunters. The October Full Moon.

INTERGENERATION DAY. Oct 4. Connecting generations through communication, celebration and education. Annually, the first Sunday in October begins Intergeneration Week. For info: Intergeneration Foundation, 430 N Tejon St, Ste 300, Colorado Springs, CO 80903. Phone: (719) 471-3691. Fax: (719) 471-3696. E-mail: information@intergenerationday.org. Web: www.intergenerationday.org.

JOHNSON, ELIZA McCARDLE: BIRTH ANNIVERSARY. Oct 4, 1810. Wife of Andrew Johnson, 17th president of the US, born at Leesburg, TN. Died at Greeneville, TN, Jan 15, 1876.

KEATON, BUSTER: BIRTH ANNIVERSARY. Oct 4, 1895. Born Joseph Francis Keaton at Piqua, KS, Buster Keaton (supposedly nicknamed by Harry Houdini) was one of America's greatest filmmakers. He became a star on the vaudeville stage by age 6 in a family show with his parents, but moved on to films at age 21, costarring in several comic shorts with Roscoe "Fatty" Arbuckle and then starring in, writing, directing and producing his own shorts—which featured improbable stunts and physical gags along with Keaton's deadpan expression. His full-length silent films are regarded as masterpieces of American comedy, especially *Sherlock, Jr* (1924) and the Civil War epic *The General* (1927)—both of which are on the Library of Congress's National Film Registry. Alcoholism and troubled relations with the MGM studio sidelined his career in the 1930s and '40s, but he later began a quieter career writing gags, making comic cameos in such films as *Around the World in Eighty Days*, appearing on TV's "Candid Camera" and even performing as a clown in Paris's Cirque Medrano. Keaton died on Feb 1, 1966, at Los Angeles, CA.

"LEAVE IT TO BEAVER" TV PREMIERE: ANNIVERSARY. Oct 4, 1957. This family sitcom was a stereotypical portrayal of American family life. It focused on Theodore "Beaver" Cleaver (Jerry Mathers) and his family: his patient, understanding and all-knowing father, Ward (Hugh Beaumont); impeccably dressed housewife and mother, June (Barbara Billingsley) and Wally (Tony Dow), Beaver's good-natured, all-American brother. The "perfectness" of the Cleaver family was balanced by other, less-than-perfect characters played by Ken Osmond, Frank Bank, Richard Deacon, Diane Brewster, Sue Randall, Rusty Stevens and Madge Blake. The last episode aired Sept 12, 1963. "Leave It to Beaver" remained popular in reruns.

LESOTHO: INDEPENDENCE DAY. Oct 4. National holiday. Commemorates independence from Britain in 1966. Formerly Basutoland.

MENTAL ILLNESS AWARENESS WEEK. Oct 4–10. To increase public awareness of the causes of, symptoms of and treatments for mental illnesses. Annually, the first full week in October. For info: Div of Public Affairs, American Psychiatric Assn, 1000 Wilson Blvd, Ste 1825, Arlington, VA 22209-3901. Phone: (703) 907-7300. E-mail: apa@psych.org. Web: www.psych.org.

MOON PHASE: FULL MOON. Oct 4. Moon enters Full Moon phase at 2:10 AM, EDT.

MYSTERY SERIES WEEK. Oct 4–10. A celebration of continuing characters in mystery fiction. Two-thirds of all new mysteries each year feature a series detective. The series tradition has been alive and well for more than 100 years. Series readers today can choose from more than 20,000 adult mysteries featuring more than 4,000 continuing characters from living writers. Mystery Series Week celebrates fictional cops, private eyes and amateur sleuths from all walks of life—solving crimes from 55 BC to the 22nd century. Annually, the first full week in October. For info: Purple Moon Press, 3319 Greenfield Rd, #317, Dearborn, MI 48120-1212. Phone: (313) 593-1033. E-mail: info@purplemoonpress.com. Web: www.mysteryseriesweek.com.

NATIONAL CARRY A TUNE WEEK. Oct 4–10. This week calls for people to celebrate favorite tunes from the past by performing them in a concert, at school, at church or at home. The purpose is to remember tunes from America's past and keep them alive. Annually, the week nearest the birthday of William Billings (born Oct 7, 1746), America's first important tune composer ("Chester"). Sponsor: Tune Lovers Society. For info: Pine Tree Productions, 235 Prospect St, Stoughton, MA 02072. Phone: (781) 344-6954. E-mail: pinetreemusic@aol.com. Web: www.americanmusicpreservation.com/announcements.htm.

NATIONAL METRIC WEEK. Oct 4–10. To maintain an awareness of the importance of the metric system as the primary system of measurement for the US. Annually, the week of the 10th month containing the 10th day of the month. For info: US Metric Assn, 10245 Andasol Ave, Northridge, CA 91325-1504. Phone: (818) 363-5606. Web: www.metric.org.

NATIONAL NEWSPAPER WEEK. Oct 4–10. To emphasize the importance of newspapers to the public. Annually, the first full week in October. For info: Newspaper Assn Managers, Inc, 70 Washington St, Ste 214, Salem, MA 01970. Phone: (978) 744-8940. Fax: (978) 744-0333. E-mail: mlp@nenews.org. Web: www.nammanagers.com.

NATIONAL WORK FROM HOME WEEK. Oct 4–10. A week to celebrate the trends, technology and tactics that allow millions of Americans to work from home as entrepreneurs, corporate teleworkers and heads of households handling family finances and affairs. For info: Jeff Zbar, PO Box 8263, Coral Springs, FL 33075-8263. Phone: (954) 346-4393. E-mail: jeff@chiefhomeofficer.com. Web: www.chiefhomeofficer.com.

PULASKI DAY PARADE. Oct 4. Philadelphia, PA. Parade honoring the Polish patriot known as the "Father of the American Cavalry." Begins at 20th and Benjamin Franklin Pkwy and ends at 19th and Benjamin Franklin Pkwy. For info: Polish American Congress, Eastern Pennsylvania District, 308 Walnut St, Philadelphia, PA 19106. Phone: (215) 739-3408. Fax: (215) 922-1518. Web: www.polishamericancongress.com.

REMINGTON, FREDERIC S.: BIRTH ANNIVERSARY. Oct 4, 1861. Born at Canton, NY. Artist and writer Frederic Remington was devoted to the outdoors of New York's North Country and the rugged characters and landscapes of the Old West. He began as an illustrator for popular magazines and worked to become a fine artist and sculptor, capturing images of Native Americans, Buffalo Soldiers, cowboys, horses and Western adventure. Died Dec 26, 1909, at age 48, at Ridgefield, CT, following an appendectomy. Illustrations, watercolors, oil paintings, sketches, bronzes on display at the Frederic Remington Art Museum. For museum info: Frederic Remington Art Museum, 303 Washington St, Ogdensburg, NY 13669. Phone: (315) 393-2425. E-mail: info@fredericremington.org. Web: www.fredericremington.org.

RUNYAN, DAMON: 125th BIRTH ANNIVERSARY. Oct 4, 1884. American newspaperman and author, born at Manhattan, KS, and died at New York, NY, Dec 10, 1946. The musical *Guys and Dolls* was based on one of his short stories. "Always try to rub up against money," he wrote, "for if you rub up against money long enough, some of it may rub off on you."

SAINT FRANCIS OF ASSISI: FEAST DAY. Oct 4. Giovanni Francesco Bernardone, religious leader, founder of the Friars Minor (Franciscan Order), born at Assisi, Umbria, Italy, in 1181. Died at Porziuncula, Oct 3, 1226.

SPACE MILESTONE: *LUNA 3* (USSR): 50th ANNIVERSARY. Oct 4, 1959. First satellite to photograph moon's distant side was launched on this date.

SPACE MILESTONE: *SPUTNIK* (USSR). Oct 4, 1957. Anniversary of launching of first successful man-made Earth satellite. *Sputnik I* ("satellite"), weighing 184 pounds, was fired into orbit from the USSR's Tyuratam launch site. Transmitted radio signal for 21 days, decayed Jan 4, 1958. Beginning of Space Age and man's exploration beyond Earth. This first-in-space triumph by the Soviets resulted in a stepped-up emphasis on the teaching of science in American classrooms.

STRATEMEYER, EDWARD L.: BIRTH ANNIVERSARY. Oct 4, 1862. American author of children's books, Stratemeyer was born at Elizabeth, NJ. He created numerous series of popular children's books including The Bobbsey Twins, The Hardy Boys, Nancy Drew and Tom Swift. He and his Stratemeyer Syndicate, using 60 or more pen names, produced more than 800 books. More than four million copies were in print in 1987. Stratemeyer died at Newark, NJ, May 10, 1930.

TEN-FOUR DAY. Oct 4. The fourth day of the tenth month is a day of recognition for radio operators, whose code words, "Ten-Four," signal an affirmative reply.

UNITED NATIONS: WORLD SPACE WEEK. Oct 4–10. To celebrate the contributions of space science and technology to the betterment of the human condition. The dates recall the launch, on Oct 4, 1957, of the first artificial satellite, *Sputnik*, and the entry into force, on Oct 10, 1967, of the Treaty on Principles Governing the Activities of States in the Exploration and Use of Outer Space. For info: United Nations, Dept of Public Info, New York, NY 10017. Web: www.un.org.

WORLD COMMUNION SUNDAY. Oct 4. Communion is celebrated by Christians all over the world. Annually, the first Sunday in October.

Birthdays Today

Armand Assante, 60, actor (*Belizaire the Cajun, The Mambo Kings, Fatal Instinct*), born New York, NY, Oct 4, 1949.

Abraham Benrubi, 40, actor ("ER," "Men in Trees"), born Indianapolis, IN, Oct 4, 1969.

Jackie Collins, 68, author (*Lucky*), born London, England, Oct 4, 1941.

Rachael Leigh Cook, 30, actress (*She's All That*, "The Baby-Sitter's Club"), born Minneapolis, MN, Oct 4, 1979.

Clifton Davis, 64, singer, actor ("That's My Mama," "Amen"), composer, born Chicago, IL, Oct 4, 1945.

Anita L. DeFrantz, 57, Olympics executive and former rower, born Philadelphia, PA, Oct 4, 1952.

Charles (Chuck) Hagel, 63, US Senator (R, Nebraska), born North Platte, NE, Oct 4, 1946.

Tony La Russa, Jr, 65, baseball manager and former player, born Tampa, FL, Oct 4, 1944.

Anne Rice, 68, novelist (*Interview with the Vampire*), born New Orleans, LA, Oct 4, 1941.

Susan Sarandon, 63, actress (Oscar for *Dead Man Walking*; *Thelma and Louise*), born Susan Tomaling at New York, NY, Oct 4, 1946.

Alicia Silverstone, 33, actress (*Clueless, Batman & Robin*), born San Francisco, CA, Oct 4, 1976.

Alvin Toffler, 81, author (*Future Shock, Power Shift*), born New York, NY, Oct 4, 1928.

Jimy Williams, 66, baseball manager and former player, born Santa Maria, CA, Oct 4, 1943.

October 5 — Monday

DAY 278 — 87 REMAINING

ARTHUR, CHESTER ALAN: BIRTH ANNIVERSARY. Oct 5, 1829. The 21st president of the US, Chester Alan Arthur, was born at Fairfield, VT, and succeeded to the presidency following the death of James A. Garfield. Term of office: Sept 20, 1881–Mar 3, 1885. Arthur was not successful in obtaining the Republican Party's nomination for the following term. He died at New York, NY, Nov 18, 1886.

BONDS BREAKS SEASON HOME RUN RECORD: ANNIVERSARY. Oct 5, 2001. Barry Bonds of the San Francisco Giants broke Mark McGwire's 1998 season home run record when he hit his 71st homer of the season in a game against the Los Angeles Dodgers at Pacific Bell Park. Later in the game he hit another homer. The Dodgers beat the Giants, 11–10, eliminating them from the playoffs. On Oct 7 Bonds hit one more homer to finish the season with 73. He also broke Babe Ruth's slugging record of .847 with .863. On Aug 7, 2007, Bonds passed Hank Aaron on the all-time homer list by slugging number 756.

CALIFORNIA RIDESHARE WEEK. Oct 5–9. Reduce pollution and traffic by forming a car pool to take to work, or try public transportation. Annually, the first full business week in October. For info: Donna Blanchard, Metro, One Gateway Pl, Los Angeles, CA 90012. Phone: (213) 922-5614. Fax: (213) 922-5640. E-mail: blanchardd@metro.net. Web: www.metro.net.

CHASE'S CALENDAR OF EVENTS 2010 PUBLISHED. Oct 5. The 2010 *Chase's* is now available. Buy a copy through your book retailer or on our website at www.chases.com.

CHIEF JOSEPH SURRENDER: ANNIVERSARY. Oct 5, 1877. After a 1,700-mile retreat, Chief Joseph and the Nez Percé Indians surrendered to US Cavalry troops at Bear's Paw near Chinook, MT, Oct 5, 1877. Chief Joseph made his famous speech of surrender, "From where the sun now stands, I will fight no more forever."

✦ **CHILD HEALTH DAY.** Oct 5. Presidential Proclamation always issued for the first Monday of October. Proclamation has been issued since 1928. In 1959 Congress changed celebration day from May 1 to the present observance (Pub Res No 46 of May 18, 1928, and PL86–352 of Sept 22, 1959).

CIVIL WAR "SUBMARINE" ATTACK: ANNIVERSARY. Oct 5, 1863. In an attempt to disrupt the Union blockade of Charleston Harbor, the Confederate semisubmersible *David* rammed the Federal ironclad *New Ironsides* with a spar torpedo. This was the first successful Southern attack using a submersible craft. Although both sides experimented with submarine warfare during the Civil War, the results were far from encouraging as the submarines caused more fatalities to their own crews than to the opposing side.

EDWARDS, JONATHAN: BIRTH ANNIVERSARY. Oct 5, 1703. (Old Style date.) The great theologian and leader of the "Great Awakening," the religious revival in the Colonies, was born at East Windsor, CT. His "Sinners in the Hands of an Angry God" is the most famous sermon in American history. He later became president of the College of New Jersey (now Princeton University). Edwards died at Princeton, NJ, Mar 22, 1758, when he contracted smallpox from an inoculation.

ENRICO FERMI ATOMIC POWER PLANT ACCIDENT: ANNIVERSARY. Oct 5, 1966. A radiation alarm and Class I alert at 3:09 PM, EST, signaled a problem at the Enrico Fermi Atomic Power Plant, Lagoona Beach, near Monroe, MI. The accident was contained, but nearly a decade was required to complete the decommissioning and disassembly of the plant.

FINANCIAL PLANNING WEEK. Oct 5–11. Everyone is entitled to objective advice from a competent, ethical financial planner to make smart financial decisions. Financial Planning Week is designed to help the public discover the value of financial planning and advance the financial planning profession. Many of the FPA's 100 chapters hold free events in their communities to promote financial literacy and provide resources for the public. More than 20 states have declared the first full week of October (Monday through Sunday) to be Financial Planning Week each year. For info: Ryanne Enyeart, The Financial Planning Assn, 4100 E Mississippi Ave, Ste 400, Denver, CO 80246. Phone: (303) 759-4900, ext 7151. Fax: (303) 759-0749. E-mail: fpa@fpanet.org. Web: www.financialplanningweek.org.

FINE, LARRY: BIRTH ANNIVERSARY. Oct 5, 1902. The fuzzy-haired Stooge, many times a victim of the mean-tempered Moe, was born Louis Fienberg at Philadelphia, PA. He started his show business career in vaudeville with a joke-and-violin act (he was an accomplished musician). Fine was an orginal member of the Three Stooges, formed in 1925. Fine died Jan 24, 1975, at Woodland Hills, CA.

October 2009

S	M	T	W	T	F	S
				1	2	3
4	5	6	7	8	9	10
11	12	13	14	15	16	17
18	19	20	21	22	23	24
25	26	27	28	29	30	31

GODDARD, ROBERT HUTCHINGS: BIRTH ANNIVERSARY. Oct 5, 1882. The "father of the Space Age," born at Worcester, MA. Largely ignored or ridiculed during his lifetime because of his dreams of rocket travel, including travel to other planets. Launched a liquid-fuel-powered rocket Mar 16, 1926, at Auburn, MA. Died Aug 10, 1945, at Baltimore, MD. See also: "Goddard Day" (Mar 16).

IMPROVE YOUR HOME OFFICE DAY. Oct 5. Spend the day improving the way you work from home—find the best place to work, equip your office with the right technology, make your home office fit your work style. For info: Lisa Kanarek, HomeOffice Life.com, 660 Preston Forest Center, #120, Dallas, TX 75230. Phone: (214) 361-0556. E-mail: info@homeofficelife.com. Web: www.home officelife.com.

KIDS' GOAL-SETTING WEEK. Oct 5–10. Encourages parents, teachers and coaches to foster goal-setting habits in children's lives so that the children can make their dreams come true. For info: Gary Ryan Blair, The GoalsGuy, 36181 E Lake Rd, Ste 139, Palm Harbor, FL 34685. Phone: (877) GOALS-GUY. Fax: (813) 435-2022. E-mail: info@goalsguy.com. Web: www.goalsguy.com.

LUMIÈRE, LOUIS: BIRTH ANNIVERSARY. Oct 5, 1864. Born at Besançon, France, Louis Lumière with brother Auguste were film pioneers who created the first movie, "Workers Leaving the Lumière Factory" (1895). He died at Bandol, France, on June 6, 1948.

"MONTY PYTHON'S FLYING CIRCUS" TV PREMIERE: 40th ANNIVERSARY. Oct 5, 1969. This wacky comedy series debuted on BBC-1 in Great Britain and aired until 1974. The cast was made up of Graham Chapman, John Cleese, Eric Idle, Terry Jones, Michael Palin and American Terry Gilliam. John Philip Sousa's "Liberty Bell March" got the show started, and viewers were treated to surreal animation and such skits as "The Spanish Inquisition" and "The Ministry of Silly Walks." On Oct 6, 1974, "Monty Python's Flying Circus" began airing in the US. The cast members also made four films together.

NUCLEAR MEDICINE WEEK. Oct 5–11. Dedicated to recognizing the professionals devoted to using nuclear medicine as an integral part of patient care. This is the perfect time to promote the value and safety of nuclear medicine to patients, referring physicians and your community. Promotional items will be available through SNM. For info: SNM. Phone: (703) 708-9000. Web: www.snm.org.

PORTUGAL: REPUBLIC DAY. Oct 5. National holiday. Commemorates establishment of the republic in 1910.

SPACE MILESTONE: *CHALLENGER STS 41-G*: 25th ANNIVERSARY. Oct 5, 1984. Space shuttle *Challenger*'s sixth mission with crew of seven, including two women. Launched from Kennedy Space Center, FL, on this date and landed there on Oct 13, 1984. Kathryn D. Sullivan became the first American woman to walk in space.

SPINNING AND WEAVING WEEK. Oct 5–11. To celebrate the timeless craft of weaving and spinning and to honor craftspeople past and present who perpetuate a legacy of fine handmade textiles. Annually, the first full week in October, Monday–Sunday. For info: Handweavers Guild of America, Inc, 1255 Buford Hwy, Ste 211, Suwanee, GA 30024. Phone: (678) 730-0010. E-mail: hga@weavespindye.org. Web: www.weavespindye.org.

STONE, THOMAS: DEATH ANNIVERSARY. Oct 5, 1787. Signer of the Declaration of Independence, born 1743 (exact date unknown) at Charles County, MD. Died at Alexandria, VA.

SUPREME COURT 2009–2010 TERM BEGINS. Oct 5. Traditionally, the Supreme Court's annual term begins on the first Monday in October and continues with seven two-week sessions of oral arguments. Between the sessions are six recesses during which the opinions are written by the justices. Ordinarily, all cases are decided by the following June or July.

TECUMSEH: DEATH ANNIVERSARY. Oct 5, 1813. Shawnee Indian chief and orator, born at Old Piqua near Springfield, OH, in March 1768. Tecumseh was one of the greatest of Native American leaders. He came to prominence between the years 1799 and 1804 as a powerful orator, defending his people against whites. He denounced as invalid all treaties by which tribes ceded their lands and condemned the chieftains who had entered into such agreements. With his brother Tenskwatawa, the Prophet, he established a town on the Tippecanoe River near Lafayette, IN, and then embarked on a mission to organize an Indian confederation to stop white encroachment. Although he advocated peaceful methods and negotiation, he did not rule out war as a last resort as he visited tribes throughout the country. While he was away, William Henry Harrison defeated the Prophet at the Battle of Tippecanoe Nov 7, 1811, and burned the town. Tecumseh organized a large force of Indian warriors and assisted the British in the War of 1812. Tecumseh was defeated and killed at the Battle of the Thames, Oct 5, 1813.

UNITED NATIONS: WORLD HABITAT DAY. Oct 5. The United Nations General Assembly, by a resolution of Dec 17, 1985, has designated the first Monday of October each year as World Habitat Day—a day to reflect on the living conditions of human beings and for actions to be taken to address the shortcomings of those conditions. The first observance of this day, Oct 5, 1986, marked the 10th anniversary of the first international conference on the subject. For info: United Nations, Dept of Public Info, Public Inquiries Unit, Rm GA-57, New York, NY 10017. Phone: (212) 963-4475. E-mail: inquiries@un.org. Web: www.un.org.

UNITED NATIONS: WORLD TEACHERS' DAY. Oct 5. A day to honor teachers and their contributions to learning. For info: United Nations, Dept of Public Info, New York, NY 10017. Web: www.un.org.

"YOU BET YOUR LIFE" TV PREMIERE: ANNIVERSARY. Oct 5, 1950. This funny game show began on radio in 1947 and moved to TV with Groucho Marx as host and George Fenneman as announcer and scorekeeper. Players tried to answer questions in the category of their choice, but Groucho's improvised interviews stole the show. Many guests appeared, including Phyllis Diller and Candice Bergen, who later became famous. Players could also win money by uttering the secret word, an everyday word suspended above the stage on a duck that dropped when the word was spoken. This was one of the few shows to be filmed, because the interviews needed to be edited. Two short-lived revivals of the series aired, with Buddy Hackett as host in 1980, and with Bill Cosby in 1992.

"ZANE GREY THEATER" TV PREMIERE: ANNIVERSARY. Oct 5, 1956. Officially titled "Dick Powell's Zane Grey Theater," this Western anthology series was hosted by Powell and featured both stories by Grey and original telecasts. Powell occasionally starred in an episode. Guest stars included Hedy Lamarr (in her only dramatic TV role), Ginger Rogers, Claudette Colbert and Esther Williams.

Birthdays Today

Karen Allen, 58, actress (*The Wanderers, Raiders of the Lost Ark, Starman*), born Carrollton, IL, Oct 5, 1951.

Michael Andretti, 47, race car driver, son of Mario Andretti, born Bethlehem, PA, Oct 5, 1962.

Raymond Lester "Trace" Armstrong, 44, former football player, born Bethesda, MD, Oct 5, 1965.

Clive Barker, 57, author, born Liverpool, England, Oct 5, 1952.

Josie Bissett, 39, actress ("Melrose Place"), born Seattle, WA, Oct 5, 1970.

Ben Cardin, 66, US Senator (D, Maryland), born Baltimore, MD, Oct 5, 1943.

Jeff Conaway, 59, actor ("Taxi," *Grease*), born New York, NY, Oct 5, 1950.

Bill Dana, 85, actor, comedian, born Quincy, MA, Oct 5, 1924.

Laura Davies, 46, golfer, 1994 LPGA Championship winner, born Coventry, England, Oct 5, 1963.

Bob Geldof, 58, singer (Boomtown Rats), social activist, born Dublin, Ireland, Oct 5, 1951.

Václav Havel, 73, dramatist, former president of the Czech Republic, born Prague, Czechoslovakia, Oct 5, 1936.

Grant Hill, 37, basketball player, born Dallas, TX, Oct 5, 1972.

Glynis Johns, 86, actress (*Mary Poppins, The Ref, A Little Night Music*), born Pretoria, South Africa, Oct 5, 1923.

Bil Keane, 87, cartoonist ("Family Circus"), born Philadelphia, PA, Oct 5, 1922.

Mario Lemieux, 44, Hall of Fame hockey player, hockey executive, born Montreal, QC, Canada, Oct 5, 1965.

Steve Miller, 66, musician, singer (Steve Miller Band), born Dallas, TX, Oct 5, 1943.

Parminder K. Nagra, 34, actress (*Bend It Like Beckham,* "ER"), born Leicester, Leicestershire, England, Oct 5, 1975.

Patrick Roy, 44, former hockey player, born Quebec City, QC, Canada, Oct 5, 1965.

Kate Winslet, 34, actress (*Finding Neverland, Little Children, Titanic*), born Reading, England, Oct 5, 1975.

October 6 — Tuesday

DAY 279 **86 REMAINING**

AMERICAN LIBRARY ASSOCIATION FOUNDING: ANNIVERSARY. Oct 6, 1876. Founded at Philadelphia, PA, by 103 librarians attending the Centennial Exposition.

"CSI: CRIME SCENE INVESTIGATION" TV PREMIERE: ANNIVERSARY. Oct 6, 2000. CBS's consistently top-rated mystery drama focuses on the Las Vegas Police forensics team led by preternaturally calm Gil Grissom (William Petersen). "CSI" brings science to the foreground, with close-up looks at technology and lab techniques. The 100th episode aired Nov 18, 2004. The show spawned equally successful spin-offs: "CSI: Miami" and "CSI: New York."

EGYPT: ARMED FORCES DAY. Oct 6. The Egyptian army celebrates crossing into Sinai in 1973.

EL-SADAT, ANWAR: ASSASSINATION ANNIVERSARY. Oct 6, 1981. Egyptian president and Nobel Peace Prize recipient Anwar el-Sadat was killed by assassins at Cairo while he was reviewing a military parade commemorating the 1973 Egyptian-Israeli War. At least eight other persons were reported killed in the attack on Sadat. Anwar el-Sadat was born Dec 25, 1918, at Mit Abu Al-Kom, a village near the Nile River delta.

GAYNOR, JANET: BIRTH ANNIVERSARY. Oct 6, 1906. Born Laura Gainor at Philadelphia, PA, in 1929 she became the first winner of the Academy Award for Best Actress for her cumulative work in two 1927 films, *Sunrise* and *Seventh Heaven*, and for 1928's *Street Angel*. Gaynor died Sept 14, 1984, at Palm Springs, CA.

HEYERDAHL, THOR: 95th BIRTH ANNIVERSARY. Oct 6, 1914. The anthropologist and explorer was born at Larvik, Norway. Seeking to prove the plausibility of South American peoples' having settled Polynesia, he embarked on an epic raft ride with five companions in 1947. The "Kon-Tiki" made the 4,300-mile voyage from Peru to Raroia in 101 days. Heyerdahl's book chronicling the adventure became an international bestseller. He continued his travels (including a solo 1970 trip in a reed boat from North Africa to Barbados) and writing until his death. He died at Italy on Apr 18, 2002.

IRELAND: IVY DAY. Oct 6. The anniversary of the death of Irish nationalist leader and Home Rule advocate Charles Stewart Parnell is observed, especially in Ireland, as Ivy Day. A sprig of ivy is worn on the lapel to remember Parnell. James Joyce's short story "Ivy Day in the Committee Room," published in the collection titled *Dubliners*, addresses this event. See also: "Parnell, Charles Stewart: Birth Anniversary" (June 27).

JACKIE MAYER REHAB DAY. Oct 6. Sandusky, OH. Known as Sandusky's "favorite daughter," Jacquelyn Jeanne Mayer, Miss America 1963 and stroke survivor since 1970, is honored on Oct 6, the anniversary of the 1997 renaming of Providence Hospital's rehab and nursing facility as the Jackie Mayer Rehab Center. After seven years of self-directed rehab to regain her speech and mobility, Jackie Mayer has been a motivational speaker and tireless advocate on behalf of stroke survivors across the US and Canada. For info: Dr. Nancy Linenkugel, OSF, Chatfield College, 20918 State Rte 251, St. Martin, OH 45118-9705. Phone: (513) 875-3344. Fax: (513) 875-3912. Web: www.jackiemayer.com. To contact Ms Mayer, phone (419) 357-1510.

LIND, JENNY: BIRTH ANNIVERSARY. Oct 6, 1820. Opera singer known as the "Swedish Nightingale," born at Stockholm, Sweden. She died at Malvern, England, Nov 2, 1887.

MOODY, HELEN WILLS: BIRTH ANNIVERSARY. Oct 6, 1905. One of the greatest tennis players of the 20th century was born at Centreville, CA. Moody, 1921's US national junior champion, had a phenomenal professional career: with a .919 winning average, she won 52 out of 92 tournaments between 1919 and 1938. She won Wimbledon eight out of nine tries, the US Open seven times and the French Open four times. Amazingly, from 1927 to 1932, she did not lose one single set in any singles competition. A 1924 Olympic gold medal winner for singles and doubles, Moody also became in 1928 the first player to win a grand slam. "Little Miss Poker Face" (as she was nicknamed for her no-nonsense style) was inducted into the International Tennis Hall of Fame in 1969. She died Jan 1, 1998, at Carmel, CA.

✦ **NATIONAL GERMAN-AMERICAN DAY.** Oct 6. Celebration of German heritage and contributions German Americans have made to the building of the nation. A Presidential Proclamation has been issued each year since 1987. Annually, Oct 6.

NATIONAL GERMAN-AMERICAN DAY. Oct 6. Annual day celebrated since the 19th century that honors the contributions of German immigrants to US culture and history. Celebrated on the day in 1683 when 13 Mennonite families disembarked near Philadelphia, PA, from Krefeld. These families later founded Germantown, PA. The day is celebrated by all those who are culturally German from all parts of Europe. This special day had a boost in popularity when President Ronald Reagan became the first US president to proclaim it in 1987.

NATIONAL PHYSICIAN ASSISTANTS (PA) WEEK. Oct 6–12. To acknowledge the unique contribution of physician assistants in providing access to medical care on the anniversary of the graduation of the first class of PAs from Duke University. For info: American Academy of Physician Assistants, 950 N Washington St, Alexandria, VA 22314-1534. Phone: (703) 836-2272. Fax: (703) 684-1924. E-mail: aapa@aapa.org. Web: www.aapa.org.

NOBEL CONFERENCE 45. Oct 6–7. Gustavus Adolphus College, St. Peter, MN. Annual two-day scientific symposium (45th year), and the first one sanctioned by the Nobel Foundation, Stockholm.

October 2009

S	M	T	W	T	F	S
				1	2	3
4	5	6	7	8	9	10
11	12	13	14	15	16	17
18	19	20	21	22	23	24
25	26	27	28	29	30	31

Annually, the first Tuesday and Wednesday in October. Est attendance: 6,000. For info: Dean Wahlund, Dir of Special Events, Gustavus Adolphus College, 800 W College Ave, St. Peter, MN 56082-1498. Phone: (507) 933-7520. E-mail: dwahlund@gac.edu. Web: www.gustavus.edu/nobelconference.

SEIBERT, FLORENCE: BIRTH ANNIVERSARY. Oct 6, 1897. American physician Florence B. Seibert was born at Easton, PA. She developed the test for tuberculosis that was adopted by the US and used worldwide by the World Health Organization. She died Aug 23, 1991, at St. Petersburg, FL.

SZYMANOWSKI, KAROL: BIRTH ANNIVERSARY. Oct 6, 1882. Birthday of one of Poland's outstanding composers, whose art played a role in Polish 20th-century music. Born at Timoshovka, Ukraine. Died Mar 29, 1937, at Lausanne, Switzerland.

WESTINGHOUSE, GEORGE: BIRTH ANNIVERSARY. Oct 6, 1846. Engineer and inventor of the air brake for trains, born at Central Bridge, NY. He was the first employer to give his employees paid vacations. Westinghouse died at New York, NY, Mar 12, 1914.

YOM KIPPUR WAR: ANNIVERSARY. Oct 6–25, 1973. A surprise attack by Egypt and Syria pushed Israeli forces several miles behind the 1967 cease-fire lines. Israel was caught off guard, partly because the attack came on the holiest Jewish religious day. After 18 days of fighting, hostilities were halted by the UN Oct 25. Israel partially recovered from the initial setback but failed to regain all the land lost in the fighting.

Birthdays Today

Britt Ekland, 67, actress (*The Night They Raided Minsky's*), born Stockholm, Sweden, Oct 6, 1942.

Rebecca Lobo, 36, basketball player, born Southwick, MA, Oct 6, 1973.

Elisabeth Shue, 46, actress (*Adventures in Babysitting, Leaving Las Vegas*), born Wilmington, DE, Oct 6, 1963.

Jeremy Sisto, 35, actor ("Six Feet Under," "Law & Order"), born Green Valley, CA, Oct 6, 1974.

Fred Travalena, 67, actor ("Keep on Truckin'," "ABC Comedy Hour"), born New York, NY, Oct 6, 1942.

Stephanie Zimbalist, 53, actress ("Remington Steele"), born Encino, CA, Oct 6, 1956.

David Zucker, 62, writer, producer (*Naked Gun* movies, *Airplane!*), born Milwaukee, WI, Oct 6, 1947.

October 7 — Wednesday

DAY 280 — **85 REMAINING**

BALLOONS AROUND THE WORLD. Oct 7. 10th annual. Balloon twisting and sculpting artists donate an hour or more to a charity of their choice in their community. Annually, the first Wednesday in October. For info: Jeff Brown, 214 Dixon St, Juneau, AK 99801. Phone: (907) 586-1670. E-mail: jbrown@alaska.net. Web: www.balloonsaroundtheworld.com.

***CATS* PREMIERE: ANNIVERSARY.** Oct 7, 1982. The second longest-running production in Broadway history (after *Phantom of the Opera*) opened this day. *Cats* was based on a book of poetry by T.S. Eliot and had a score by Andrew Lloyd Webber. More than 10 million theatergoers saw the New York City production, which closed Sept 10, 2000, after 7,485 performances. *Cats* was also produced in 30 other countries.

DOW JONES INDUSTRIAL AVERAGE: ANNIVERSARY. Oct 7, 1896. Dow Jones began reporting an average of the prices of 12 industrial stocks in the *Wall Street Journal* on this day. In the early years these were largely railroad stocks. In 1928 Mr Dow expanded the number of stocks to 30, where it remains today. Today, the large, frequently traded stocks in the DJIA represent about a fifth of the market value of all US stocks.

ENGLAND: NOTTINGHAM GOOSE FAIR. Oct 7–11. Forest Recreation Ground, Nottingham. Held annually since 1284 (except during the Great Plague in 1665 and the two World Wars), the fair formerly lasted three weeks and boasted as many as 20,000 geese on display. Now lasting five days, the Nottingham Goose Fair always operates in early October. A traditional fair with modern amusements. Est attendance: 500,000. For info: Nottingham Tourism Centre, 1-4 Smithy Row, Nottingham, England NG1 2BY. E-mail: tourist.information@nottinghamcity.gov.uk. Web: www.nottinghamgoosefair.co.uk.

MISSISSIPPI STATE FAIR. Oct 7–18. Jackson, MS. Features nightly professional entertainment, livestock show, midway carnival, domestic art exhibits. Begins on the first Wednesday of October. Est attendance: 620,000. For info: Mississippi Fair Commission, PO Box 892, Jackson, MS 39205. Phone: (601) 961-4000. Fax: (601) 354-6545.

RODNEY, CAESAR: BIRTH ANNIVERSARY. Oct 7, 1728. (Old Style date.) Signer of the Declaration of Independence who cast a tie-breaking vote. Born near Dover, DE, he died June 26, 1784. Rodney is on the Delaware quarter issued by the US Mint in 1999, the first in a series of quarters that commemorate each of the 50 states.

TENNESSEE FALL HOMECOMING. Oct 7–11. Museum of Appalachia, Norris, TN. A celebration of the culture and heritage of Appalachian, pioneer, mountain and rural life. Four stages provide continuous musical performances by more than 400 old-time musicians and legendary greats. Scores of traditional mountain activities such as molasses making, sheep herding, rail splitting, soap making and sawmilling are demonstrated to help preserve the old ways in an interesting and educational manner. For info: John Rice Irwin or Elaine Irwin Meyer, Museum of Appalachia, PO Box 1189, Norris, TN 37828. Phone: (865) 494-0514 or (865) 494-7680. Web: www.museumofappalachia.com.

WALLACE, HENRY AGARD: BIRTH ANNIVERSARY. Oct 7, 1888. Thirty-third vice president of the US (1941–45), born at Adair County, IA. Died at Danbury, CT, Nov 18, 1965.

WISE, THOMAS J.: 150th BIRTH ANNIVERSARY. Oct 7, 1859. English bibliophile and literary forger, born at Gravesend, England. One of England's most distinguished bibliographic experts, he was revealed, in 1934, to have forged dozens of "first editions" and "unique" publications over a period of more than 20 years. Many of them had been sold at high prices to collectors and libraries. The forgeries in some cases purported to predate the real first editions. Wise died at Hampstead, England, May 13, 1937.

"YOUR HIT PARADE" TV PREMIERE: ANNIVERSARY. Oct 7, 1950. "Your Hit Parade" began as a radio show in 1935. When it finally made it to TV, the format was simple: the show's cast performed the week's top musical hits. To sustain interest, since many of the same songs appeared weekly, eye-catching production sequences were created. "YHP" was the starting point for many famous choreographers and dancers, including Peter Gennaro and Bob Fosse. Regulars included Dorothy Collins, Eileen Wilson, Snooky Lanson and Sue Bennett. The show was overhauled many times and switched networks before leaving the air in 1959. A summer revival in 1974 was short-lived. See also: "'Your Hit Parade' Radio Premiere: Anniversary" (Apr 12).

Birthdays Today

Amiri Baraka, 75, poet, dramatist, born Everett LeRoi Jones at Newark, NJ, Oct 7, 1934.

Joy Behar, 66, comedienne, television personality, born Brooklyn, NY, Oct 7, 1943.

Toni Braxton, 42, singer, born Severn, MD, Oct 7, 1967.

Simon Cowell, 50, television producer, personality ("American Idol"), born Brighton, East Sussex, England, Oct 7, 1959.

Charles Dutoit, 73, conductor, born Lausanne, Switzerland, Oct 7, 1936.

Thomas Keneally, 74, novelist (*Schindler's List*), born New South Wales, Australia, Oct 7, 1935.

Yo-Yo Ma, 54, cellist, born Paris, France, Oct 7, 1955.

Al Martino, 82, actor, singer (*Hello Dolly, Phantom of the Opera*), born Alfred Cini at Philadelphia, PA, Oct 7, 1927.

John Mellencamp, 58, singer, songwriter, born Seymour, IN, Oct 7, 1951.

Oliver Laurence North, 66, US Marine Corps Lieutenant Colonel (retired), born San Antonio, TX, Oct 7, 1943.

Vladimir Putin, 57, former Russian president, born St. Petersburg, Russia, Oct 7, 1952.

Desmond Tutu, 78, South African archbishop, Nobel Peace Prize recipient, born Klerksdorp, South Africa, Oct 7, 1931.

October 8 — Thursday

DAY 281 — 84 REMAINING

ALVIN C. YORK DAY. Oct 8, 1918. Sergeant Alvin C. York (while in the Argonne Forest, France, and separated from his patrol) killed 20 enemy soldiers and captured a hill, 132 enemy soldiers and 35 machine guns. He was awarded the US Medal of Honor and French Croix de Guerre. Ironically, York had petitioned for exemption from the draft as a conscientious objector, but was turned down by his local draft board.

CHICAGO INTERNATIONAL FILM FESTIVAL. Oct 8–21 (tentative). Chicago, IL. 45th annual. North America's oldest competitive film festival. Some of cinema's greatest filmmakers have been introduced at this festival. Gold and Silver Hugos awarded at its conclusion. For info: Chicago Intl Film Fest, 30 E Adams St, Ste 800, Chicago, IL 60603. Phone: (312) 683-0121. E-mail: info@chicagofilmfestival.com. Web: www.chicagofilmfestival.com.

COSAC ANNUAL CONFERENCE: ISSUES IN AUTISM. Oct 8–10. Atlantic City, NJ. The NJ Center for Outreach and Services for the Autism Community (COSAC) holds its annual autism conference—one of the largest in the nation—featuring educational workshops, exhibitions and an awards reception. Est attendance: 1,300. For info: COSAC, 1450 Parkside Ave, Ste 22, Ewing, NJ 08638. Phone: (609) 883-8100. Fax: (609) 883-5509. E-mail: information@njcosac.org. Web: www.njcosac.org.

October 2009

S	M	T	W	T	F	S
				1	2	3
4	5	6	7	8	9	10
11	12	13	14	15	16	17
18	19	20	21	22	23	24
25	26	27	28	29	30	31

CROATIA: STATEHOOD DAY. Oct 8. Croatia's national day. Public holiday.

GEORGIA NATIONAL FAIR. Oct 8–18. Georgia National Fairgrounds, Perry, GA. Traditional state agricultural fair features thousands of entries in horse, livestock, horticultural, youth, home and fine arts categories. Family entertainment, education and fun. Sponsored by the State of Georgia. Est attendance: 443,351. For info: Georgia Natl Fair, PO Box 1367, Perry, GA 31069. Phone: (478) 987-3247. Fax: (478) 987-7218. E-mail: thawk@gnfa.com. Web: www.georgianationalfair.com.

GREAT CHICAGO FIRE: ANNIVERSARY. Oct 8, 1871. Great fire of Chicago began, according to legend, when Mrs O'Leary's cow kicked over the lantern in her barn on DeKoven Street. The fire leveled 3½ square miles, destroying 17,450 buildings and leaving 98,500 people homeless and about 250 people dead. Financially, the loss was $200 million. On the same day a fire destroyed the entire town of Peshtigo, WI, killing more than 1,100 people.

NATIONAL DEPRESSION SCREENING DAY. Oct 8 (tentative). Offers free, anonymous education and screening for depression, bipolar disorder, generalized anxiety disorder and post-traumatic stress disorder. The screenings connect people in need with treatment and provide support and resources for friends and family members. For info: Screening for Mental Health, One Washington St, Ste 304, Wellesley Hills, MA 02481-1706. Phone: (781) 239-0071. Fax: (781) 431-7447. E-mail: NDSD@MentalHealthScreening.org. Web: www.MentalHealthScreening.org.

OZZIE AND HARRIET RADIO DEBUT: 65th ANNIVERSARY. Oct 8, 1944. Ozzie and Harriet Nelson made their CBS Radio debut in "The Adventures of Ozzie and Harriet." Although their sons, David and Ricky, were referred to frequently on air and eventually played by others, it was not until Feb 20, 1949, that David (age 12) and Rick (age 8) first appeared playing themselves on the show. "The Adventures of Ozzie and Harriet" hit television airwaves Oct 3, 1952, on ABC.

PESHTIGO FOREST FIRE: ANNIVERSARY. Oct 8, 1871. One of the most disastrous forest fires in history began at Peshtigo, WI, the same day the Great Chicago Fire began. The Wisconsin fire burned across six counties, killing more than 1,100 people.

RICKENBACKER, EDWARD V.: BIRTH ANNIVERSARY. Oct 8, 1890. American auto racer, war hero and airline executive (Eastern Airlines). Dubbed "America's Ace of Aces" for his victories as a pilot in the 94th Aero Squadron during WWI. Recipient of the Congressional Medal of Honor, the Distinguished Service Medal and the French Croix de Guerre. Born at Columbus, OH, Rickenbacker died July 23, 1973, at Zurich, Switzerland.

SCHUTZ, HEINRICH: BIRTH ANNIVERSARY. Oct 8, 1585. German musician and composer sometimes called the father of German music. Born at Kostritz, Saxony, Schutz died at Dresden, Germany, Nov 6, 1672. His works enjoyed renewed attention on the occasions of the bicentennials (1885) and tricentennials (1985) of two of his most devoted followers: George Frederick Handel and Johann Sebastian Bach.

Birthdays Today

Rona Barrett, 73, gossip columnist, born New York, NY, Oct 8, 1936.

Chevy Chase, 66, comedian, actor, born Cornelius Crane at New York, NY, Oct 8, 1943.

Clodagh, 72, designer, born Clodagh Aubry at Galway, Ireland, Oct 8, 1937.

Matt Damon, 39, actor (*Ocean's Eleven, The Bourne Identity, Good Will Hunting*), born Cambridge, MA, Oct 8, 1970.

Bill Elliott, 54, race car driver, born Dawsonville, GA, Oct 8, 1955.

Darrell Hammond, 49, comedian, actor ("Saturday Night Live"), born Melbourne, FL, Oct 8, 1960.

Paul Hogan, 70, actor, writer (*Crocodile Dundee*), born Lightning Ridge, Australia, Oct 8, 1939.

Jesse Jackson, 68, clergyman, civil rights leader, born Greenville, NC, Oct 8, 1941.

Sarah Purcell, 61, TV personality ("Real People"), born Richmond, IN, Oct 8, 1948.

Faith Ringgold, 79, artist, writer (*Tar Beach, My Dream of Martin Luther King*), born New York, NY, Oct 8, 1930.

Rashaan Salaam, 35, former football player, born San Diego, CA, Oct 8, 1974.

R.L. Stine, 66, author (Goosebumps series), born Columbus, OH, Oct 8, 1943.

Sigourney Weaver, 60, actress (*Ghostbusters, Gorillas in the Mist, Aliens*), born New York, NY, Oct 8, 1949.

October 9 — Friday

DAY 282 | **83 REMAINING**

ALABAMA NATIONAL FAIR. Oct 9–18. Garrett Coliseum/Fairgrounds, Montgomery, AL. A midway filled with exciting rides and games, arts and crafts, exhibits, livestock shows, racing pigs, a circus, a petting zoo, food and entertainment. Est attendance: 225,000. For info: Russell Melton, Alabama National Fair, PO Box 3304, Montgomery, AL 36109-0304. Phone: (334) 272-6831. Fax: (334) 272-6835. E-mail: anf@alnationalfair.org. Web: www.alnationalfair.org.

ALGONQUIN MILL FALL FESTIVAL. Oct 9–11. Four miles south of Carrollton, OH. Presented by the Carroll County Historical Society. An 1800s pioneer festival featuring steam-powered gristmill and sawmill in operation. Also featured are antique tools and farm museum; antique cars and tractors; quilting, spinning, dyeing and weaving demonstrations; four log buildings (including a two-story home); musical entertainment and quality craftspeople selling their products. A one-room school and a railroad station are on exhibit. Est attendance: 35,000. For info: Carroll County CVB. Phone: (877) 727-0103. Web: www.carrollcountyohio.com/history.

APPLE BUTTER MAKIN' DAYS. Oct 9–11. Mt Vernon, MO. A huge festival highlighting the making of apple butter in large copper kettles on the courthouse lawn. Also, 375 crafters displaying and selling handmade goods, free entertainment all three days, apple pie eating contest, hairy legs contest, log sawing contest, bubble gum blowing contest, nail driving contest, pet parade and terrapin race. Annually, the second full weekend in October. Est attendance: 60,000. For info: Chamber of Commerce, PO Box 373, Mt Vernon, MO 65712. Phone: (417) 466-7654.

ARIZONA STATE FAIR. Oct 9–Nov 1 (tentative). Phoenix, AZ. Festival, concerts, entertainment and food. Closed Mondays. For info: Arizona State Fair, 1826 W McDowell Rd, Phoenix, AZ 85007. Phone: (602) 252-6771. Fax: (602) 495-1302. E-mail: info@azstatefair.com. Web: www.azstatefair.com.

ARKANSAS STATE FAIR AND LIVESTOCK SHOW. Oct 9–18. Barton Coliseum and State Fairground, Little Rock, AR. Est attendance: 400,000. For info: Arkansas State Fair, 2600 Howard St, Little Rock, AR 72206. Phone: (501) 372-8341. Fax: (501) 372-4197. Web: www.arkansasstatefair.com.

CANADA: KITCHENER-WATERLOO OKTOBERFEST. Oct 9–17. Kitchener and Waterloo, ON. The second-largest Oktoberfest in the world. More than 70 events and festhalls, including one of the premier parades in Canada on Canadian Thanksgiving morning. Est attendance: 700,000. For info: K-W Oktoberfest Inc, 17 Benton St, Kitchener, ON, Canada N2G 3G9. Phone: (519) 570-4267 or (888) 294-HANS. E-mail: info@oktoberfest.ca. Web: www.oktoberfest.ca.

COLUMBUS DAY FESTIVAL AND HOT AIR BALLOON REGATTA. Oct 9–11. Columbus, KS. Regatta starts with Balloon Glow on Friday evening; prizes are awarded for both Saturday and Sunday races. Also, car show, arts and crafts fair, entertainment, children's festival and more. Est attendance: 15,000. For info: Jean Pritchett, Mgr, Columbus Chamber of Commerce, 320 E Maple, Columbus, KS 66725. Phone/fax: (620) 429-1492. E-mail: columbuschamber@columbus-ks.com. Web: www.columbus-ks.com/chamber.

CRAFTSMEN'S CLASSIC ARTS & CRAFTS FESTIVAL. Oct 9–11. Roanoke Civic Center, Roanoke, VA. 22nd annual. Features work from more than 250 talented artists and craftspeople. All juried exhibitors' work has been handmade by the exhibitors and must be their own original design and creation. See the creative process in action, with several exhibitors demonstrating throughout the weekend. Something for every style, taste, and budget with items from the most contemporary to the most traditional. Est attendance: 20,000. For info: Gilmore Enterprises, 3514-A Drawbridge Pkwy, Greensboro, NC 27410-8584. Phone: (336) 282-5550. E-mail: contact@gilmoreshows.com. Web: www.CraftShow.com or www.gilmoreshows.com.

DREYFUS, ALFRED: 150th BIRTH ANNIVERSARY. Oct 9, 1859. This French army officer, born at Mulhouse, France, was the center of a military scandal from 1894 to 1906. From when he was accused of treason (forged documents were used to convict him) in 1894 and sentenced to life in 1895 at Devil's Island, the Dreyfus affair was a lightning rod for rival factions in France and exposed the virulent anti-Semitism in the country (Dreyfus was Jewish). The case was notable for the involvement of France's major literary figures in his defense, most famously Emile Zola, who published "J'Accuse" in 1898 in a periodical and accused the French army of a massive cover-up. Public outrage insured two more trials for Dreyfus. He was still found guilty, but was pardoned at his last trial in 1899. A 1906 civilian court finally cleared Dreyfus, who eventually returned to the military. He died July 12, 1935, at Paris, France.

FORT LIGONIER DAYS. Oct 9–11. Ligonier, PA. Commemorates the Battle of Ligonier. Reenactments, parade, outdoor entertainment, craft booths and food booths. For info: Rachel Roehrig, Ligonier Chamber of Commerce, 120 E Main St, Ligonier, PA 15658. Phone: (724) 238-4200. Fax: (724) 238-4610. E-mail: thechamber@ligonier.com.

GUMBO FESTIVAL. Oct 9–11. Bridge City, LA. To promote Cajun-French culture and provide the opportunity for people from everywhere to enjoy continuous Cajun entertainment on an outdoor stage and cuisine. Gumbo cooking contests and 5k Bridge Run. Annually, the second full weekend in October. Est attendance: 150,000. For info: Rev Msgr J. Anthony Luminais, Pastor, Holy Guardian Angels Church, Box 9069, Bridge City, LA 70096. Phone: (504) 436-4712. Fax: (504) 436-4070. E-mail: gumbofestival@aol.com. Web: www.hgaparish.org/gumbofestival.htm.

ICELAND: LEIF ERIKSON DAY. Oct 9. Celebrates discovery of North America in the year 1000 by Norse explorer.

KOREA: ALPHABET DAY (HANGUL). Oct 9. Celebrates anniversary of promulgation of Hangul (24-letter phonetic alphabet) by King Sejong of the Yi dynasty in 1446.

✦ **LEIF ERIKSON DAY.** Oct 9. Presidential Proclamation always issued for Oct 9 since 1964 (PL88-566 of Sept 2, 1964) at request.

LENNON, JOHN: BIRTH ANNIVERSARY. Oct 9, 1940. John Winston Lennon, English composer, musician and member of the Beatles, the sensationally popular group of musical performers who captivated audiences first in England and Germany, and later throughout the world. A fervent activist for peace. Born at Liverpool, England, Lennon was murdered at New York City, Dec 8, 1980.

MEDFORD JAZZ JUBILEE. Oct 9–11. Medford, OR. Seventeen nationally known bands will play in downtown Medford locations. More than 100 performances along with fun, food and music for all ages. Est attendance: 6,000. For info: Medford Jazz Jubilee, PMB 201, 221 N Central, Medford, OR 97501. Phone: (541) 770-6972 or (800) 599-0039. E-mail: info@medfordjazz.org. Web: www.medfordjazz.org.

MISSION DELORES FOUNDING: ANNIVERSARY. Oct 9, 1776. The oldest building at San Francisco, CA. Formerly known as Mission San Francisco de Asis, the mission survived the great earthquake and fire of 1906.

OCEAN COUNTY COLUMBUS DAY PARADE AND ITALIAN FESTIVAL. Oct 9–11. Seaside Heights, NJ. Parade features bands, floats, groups, organizations, antique cars and special performers from Italy. The festival features ethnic and traditional foods, entertainment, exhibits and performances from special guests. Est attendance: 80,000. For info: Ocean County Columbus Day Parade Committee, PO Box 1492, 500 Christopher Columbus Blvd, Seaside Heights, NJ 08751. Phone: (732) 477-6507. Web: www.oceancountytourism.com/columbus.

OZ FEST. Oct 9–11. Liberal, KS. A three-day festival that will have you remembering the classic 1939 movie *The Wizard of Oz* (a few of the original cast members attend each year). Royal Procession, look-alike contests, games and dinner with Munchkins, Glinda, Toto, the Wicked Witch, Auntie Em and of course Dorothy. Follow the yellow brick road to Oz Fest! Annually, the second weekend in October. Est attendance: 3,000. For info: JoAnne Mansell, Coronado Museum, Dorothy's House & The Land of Oz, 567 E Cedar, Liberal, KS 67901. Phone: (620) 624-7624. E-mail: schs@swko.net. Web: www.sewardcountymuseum.com.

PARKE COUNTY COVERED BRIDGE FESTIVAL. Oct 9–18. Rockville, IN. Covered bridge capital of the world, 31 historic covered bridges. Headquarters: Courthouse Lawn, Rockville. Guided bus tours on covered bridge routes. Hundreds of booths of arts, crafts, demonstrations and old-fashioned homemade foods. Annually, beginning on the second Friday in October. Est attendance: 2,000,000. For info: Covered Bridge Capital, PO Box 165, Rockville, IN 47872-0165. Phone: (765) 569-5226. Fax: (765) 569-3900. E-mail: pci@ticz.com. Web: www.coveredbridges.com.

PERU: DAY OF NATIONAL HONOR. Oct 9. Public holiday. Commemorates nationalization of the oil fields in 1968.

ROCKPORT SEAFAIR. Oct 9–11. Ski Basin area, Rockport, TX. Features fresh-from-the-bay seafood, gumbo cook-off, ongoing live musical entertainment, crab races, arts and crafts booths and land parade on Saturday. Annually, Columbus Day weekend. Est attendance: 20,000. For info: Rockport Seafair, 404 Broadway, Rockport, TX 78382. Phone: (800) 242-0071 or (361) 729-6445. E-mail: tourism@1rockport.org. Web: www.rockportseafair.org.

ST. CHARLES SCARECROW FESTIVAL. Oct 9–10. St. Charles, IL. More than 100 handcrafted scarecrows invade St. Charles along with live musical entertainment, carnival, children's activities, great food, huge craft show and much more. Est attendance: 80,000. For info: St. Charles CVB, 311 N Second St, Ste 100, St. Charles, IL 60174. Phone: (800) 777-4373. Fax: (630) 513-0566. Web: www.scarecrowfest.com.

SHAPING BLACK CULTURE IN THE DIASPORA. Oct 9–12. Nate Holden Performing Arts Center, Los Angeles, CA. A conference to address the urban culture core and its creative sector's "best practices" for the health and long-term sustainability of black cultural expression of the African Diaspora locally, nationally and internationally. The conference, sponsored by the Ebony Repertory Theatre (ERT), Heritage Empowered Arts Legacy (HEAL), and the City of Los Angeles Department of Cultural Affairs, will offer panels, speakers, conference planning sessions and closing night festivities for participants and attendees. International African Diaspora Day on Oct 11 is a key observance. Annually, Columbus Day weekend. Est attendance: 1,500. For info: Ernest Dillihay, PO Box 936, Los Angeles, CA 91031. Phone: (323) 257-2196. E-mail: ernest.dillihay@lacity.org.

SOUTHERN FESTIVAL OF BOOKS: A CELEBRATION OF THE WRITTEN WORD. Oct 9–11. War Memorial Plaza, Nashville, TN. The festival annually welcomes more than 200 authors from throughout the nation and in every genre for readings, panel discussions and book signings. The festival hosts popular book exhibitors and programs and features three performance stages throughout the event. Special events for children are planned throughout the weekend. Annually, the second full weekend in October. Est attendance: 20,000. For info: Southern Festival of Books, Humanities Tennessee, 306 Gay St, Ste 306, Nashville, TN 37201. Phone: (615) 770-0006. Fax: (615) 770-0007. E-mail: serenity@humanitiestennessee.org. Web: www.humanitiestennessee.org.

SUGARLOAF CRAFTS FESTIVAL. Oct 9–11. Montgomery County Fairgrounds, Gaithersburg, MD. This show, now in its ninth year, features more than 400 nationally recognized craft designers and fine artists displaying and selling their original creations. Includes craft demonstrations, live music, specialty food, children's entertainment, hourly gift certificate drawings and more. Est attendance: 20,000. For info: Sugarloaf Mountain Works, 200 Orchard Ridge Dr, #215, Gaithersburg, MD 20878. Phone: (800) 210-9900. Fax: (310) 253-9620. Web: www.sugarloafcrafts.com.

TATI, JACQUES: 100th BIRTH ANNIVERSARY. Oct 9, 1909. Born at Le Pecq, France, Tati was a filmmaker and performer who made internationally beloved comic masterpieces—often combining the best of silent comedy in films that depicted the Average Joe's misalliance with modern industrialized society. Tati's filmic alter ego was the pipe-smoking, rumpled hat-wearing Monsieur Hulot, who was always out of step wherever he was. Tati's six films included *Mr. Hulot's Holiday* (1953), *Mon oncle* (*My Uncle* 1958) and *Playtime* (1967). Tati died Nov 5, 1982, at Paris, France.

UGANDA: INDEPENDENCE DAY. Oct 9. National holiday commemorating achievement of autonomy from Britain in 1962.

UNITED NATIONS: WORLD POST DAY. Oct 9. An annual special observance of Postal Administrations of the Universal Postal Union (UPU). For info: United Nations, Dept of Public Info, Public Inquiries Unit, Rm GA-57, New York, NY 10017. Phone: (212) 963-4475. E-mail: inquiries@un.org. Web: www.un.org.

Birthdays Today

Scott Bakula, 55, actor ("Enterprise," "Quantum Leap"), born St. Louis, MO, Oct 9, 1954.

Jackson Browne, 59, singer, songwriter, born Heidelberg, Germany, Oct 9, 1950.

Zachery Ty Bryan, 28, actor ("Home Improvement"), born Aurora, CO, Oct 9, 1981.

Russell Myers, 71, cartoonist ("Broom Hilda"), born Pittsburg, KS, Oct 9, 1938.

Michael Pare, 50, actor (*Streets of Fire, The Philadelphia Experiment*), born Brooklyn, NY, Oct 9, 1959.

Joseph Anthony (Joe) Pepitone, 69, former baseball player, born New York, NY, Oct 9, 1940.

October 2009

S	M	T	W	T	F	S
				1	2	3
4	5	6	7	8	9	10
11	12	13	14	15	16	17
18	19	20	21	22	23	24
25	26	27	28	29	30	31

Brandon Routh, 30, actor ("One Life to Live," *Superman Returns*), born Des Moines, IA, Oct 9, 1979.

Tony Shalhoub, 56, actor ("Monk," "Wings," *Big Night*), born Green Bay, WI, Oct 9, 1953.

Donald Sinden, 86, actor (*The Day of the Jackal*), born Plymouth, England, Oct 9, 1923.

Michael (Mike) Singletary, 51, Hall of Fame football player, born Houston, TX, Oct 9, 1958.

Annika Sorenstam, 39, former golfer, born Stockholm, Sweden, Oct 9, 1970.

Robert Wuhl, 58, writer, actor (*Bull Durham, Cobb*), born Union, NJ, Oct 9, 1951.

October 10 — Saturday

DAY 283 **82 REMAINING**

AGNEW RESIGNATION: ANNIVERSARY. Oct 10, 1973. Spiro Theodore Agnew became the second person to resign the office of vice president of the US. Agnew entered a plea of no contest to a charge of income tax evasion (on contract kickbacks received while he was governor of Maryland and after he became vice president). He was sentenced to pay a $10,000 fine and serve three years' probation. Agnew was elected vice president twice, serving under President Richard M. Nixon. See also "Agnew, Spiro: Birth Anniversary" (Nov 9).

APPLE BUTTER FESTIVAL. Oct 10–11. Berkeley Springs, WV. Fall festival with spicy apple butter simmering in copper kettles in the town square. A parade, two days of mountain music and old-fashioned contests. Fine crafts, farmer's market, down-home cooking and fall foliage. Annually, Columbus Day weekend. Est attendance: 40,000. For info: Apple Butter Festival, 127 Fairfax St, Berkeley Springs, WV 25411. Phone: (304) 258-3738. Web: www.berkeleysprings.com.

"THE BOB NEWHART SHOW" TV PREMIERE: ANNIVERSARY. Oct 10, 1962. This half-hour variety series was hosted by Bob Newhart, a successful stand-up comedian famous for his trademark "telephone conversation" monologues. The show was critically acclaimed, winning both an Emmy and a Peabody in its short time on the air. Newhart later starred in situation comedies. In "The Bob Newhart Show," which aired 1972–78, he played a psychologist. See also: "'Newhart' TV Premiere: Anniversary" (Oct 25).

BONZA BOTTLER DAY™. Oct 10. To celebrate when the number of the day is the same as the number of the month. Bonza Bottler Day™ is an excuse to have a party at least once a month. For more information see Jan 1. For info: Gail M. Berger, 14 Fernwood Dr, Taylors, SC 29687. E-mail: bonza@bonzabottlerday.com. Web: www.bonzabottlerday.com.

CANADA: WINDSOR PUMPKIN REGATTA. Oct 10. Windsor, NS, Canada. Held since 1999, the regatta is a unique event in which intrepid competitors race giant pumpkin boats (500 to 800 pounds) across Lake Pezaquid. There are three racing divisions: Motor, Paddling and Experimental. The pumpkin boats are referred to as PVCs (personal vegetable crafts). A parade and decoration contest add to the festivities. Annually, the second Sunday in October. Est attendance: 5,000. For info: The Windsor-West Hants Pumpkin Festival Society, PO Box 623, Windsor, NS, Canada B0N 2T0. Phone: (902) 798-9440. E-mail: windsorpumpkins@netscape.net. Web: www.worldsbiggestpumpkins.com or www.pumpkinregatta.

CATOCTIN COLORFEST ARTS AND CRAFTS SHOW. Oct 10–11. Thurmont, MD. 46th annual. Live music, food, 350 arts and crafts booths featuring artists from Maryland, Virginia, West Virginia and Pennsylvania. Annually, the second weekend in October. Est attendance: 100,000. For info send a SASE to: Catoctin ColorFest, Inc, Box 33, Thurmont, MD 21788. Phone: (301) 271-4432. E-mail: info@colorfest.org. Web: www.colorfest.org.

CHOWDERFEST. Oct 10–12. Mystic Seaport, Mystic, CT. Columbus Day weekend. A riverfront festival of New England chowders. Est attendance: 9,000. For info: Mystic Seaport, 75 Greenmanville Ave, PO Box 6000, Mystic, CT 06355-0990. Phone: (860) 572-5315 or (888) 973-2767. Web: www.mysticseaport.org.

CUBA: BEGINNING OF INDEPENDENCE WARS DAY. Oct 10. National holiday. Commemorates the beginning of struggle against Spain in 1868.

DOUBLE TENTH DAY: ANNIVERSARY. Oct 10, 1911. Tenth day of 10th month, Double Tenth Day, is observed by many Chinese as the anniversary of the outbreak of the revolution against the imperial Manchu dynasty, Oct 10, 1911. Sun Yat-sen and Huan Hsing were among the revolutionary leaders. This is a holiday in Taiwan.

ELDON TURKEY FESTIVAL. Oct 10. Eldon, MO. A celebration of Miller County's state and national ranking as a top producer of wild and domestic turkeys. Event includes more than 200 crafters and exhibitors, turkey events, food, quilt show and old-time machinery show. Annually, the second Saturday in October. Est attendance: 12,000. For info: Eldon Chamber of Commerce, PO Box 209, Eldon, MO 65026. Phone: (573) 392-3752. Fax: (573) 392-0634. Web: www.eldonchamber.com.

FEAST OF THE HUNTERS' MOON. Oct 10–11. Fort Ouiatenon Historic Park, Lafayette, IN. Re-creation of French and Native American life at mid-1700s fur-trading outpost. 8,000 participants. Est attendance: 45,000. For info: Tippecanoe County Historical Assn, 1001 South St, Lafayette, IN 47901. Phone: (765) 476-8411. Fax: (765) 476-8414. E-mail: info@tcha.mus.in.us. Web: www.tcha.mus.in.us.

FIJI: INDEPENDENCE DAY. Oct 10. National holiday. Commemorates independence from Britain in 1970. Observed on the second Monday of October (Oct 12).

FIREANT FESTIVAL. Oct 10. Marshall, TX. Arts and crafts, chili cook-off, Tour de FireAnt bike ride, 5k run, fireant calling contest, fireant roundup, rubber chicken chunking, gurning contest (ugly face), Diaper Derby Contest (crawling), parade, men's crazy leg contest and gospelfest. Annually, the second Saturday in October. Est attendance: 5,000. For info: Marshall Chamber of Commerce, PO Box 520, Marshall, TX 75671. Phone: (903) 935-7868. Fax: (903) 935-9982. E-mail: chambermfi@hotmail.com. Web: www.marshalltxchamber.com.

HARVEST WEEKEND. Oct 10–11. Woodstock, VT. Traditional celebration of the harvest featuring a husking bee and barn dance. Also, farm harvest activities including food preservation, shelling corn and cider pressing. Est attendance: 1,600. For info: Billings Farm and Museum, Rte 12 N, Woodstock, VT 05091. Phone: (802) 457-2355. Fax: (802) 457-4663. E-mail: info@billingsfarm.org. Web: www.billingsfarm.org.

HAYES, HELEN: BIRTH ANNIVERSARY. Oct 10, 1900. Actress Helen Hayes, often called the First Lady of the American Theater, was born at Washington, DC. Hayes's greatest stage triumph was her role as the long-lived British monarch Queen Victoria in the play *Victoria Regina*. Her first great success was in *Coquette* (1927). She won an Academy Award for Best Actress for her first major film role in *The Sin of Madelon Claudet* (1931) and won Best Supporting Actress for her role in *Airport* (1971). Helen Hayes died Mar 17, 1993, at Nyack, NY.

INTERNATIONAL NEWSPAPER CARRIER DAY. Oct 10. Each year one day is set aside to recognize the accomplishments of carriers who work hard to get the newspaper in the hands of readers. Today, honor the hardworking people who bring us the information we look forward to each day. For info: Newspaper Association of America, 1921 Gallows Rd, Ste 600, Vienna, VA 22182. Phone: (703) 902-1600. Web: www.naa.org.

THE JACK-O-LAUNCH. Oct 10. DeLaney Farm, Aurora, CO. Aurora's award-winning fall festival, featuring the Jack-o-Launch, family entertainment and practically every activity you can think of having to do with pumpkins. Annually, the second Saturday of October. Est attendance: 26,000. For info: Jack-o-Launch, 1298 Peoria St, Aurora, CO 80011. Phone: (303) 326-8615. Fax: (303) 361-2954. E-mail: maddlema@auroragov.org. Web: www.auroragov.org/pumpkinfest.

LONG BEACH ISLAND SURF FISHING TOURNAMENT. Oct 10–Nov 22. Long Beach Island, NJ. 55th annual LBI Surf Fishing Tournament. Thousands of dollars in daily, weekly and grand prizes for bluefish and striped bass. Always starts the Saturday of Columbus Day weekend. For info: Southern Ocean County Chamber of Commerce, 265 W 9th St, Ship Bottom, NJ 08008. Phone: (800) 292-6372. Fax: (609) 494-5807. E-mail: socccmanager@comcast.net. Web: www.LBIFT.com.

LOUISIANA ART & FOLK FESTIVAL. Oct 10. Columbia, LA. Festival that centers on the rich folklife of Louisiana as well as on the fine arts. Wonderful music all day, craft booths, children's art, petting zoo, as well as food to please everyone. Est attendance: 2,500. For info: Caldwell Parish Chamber of Commerce, PO Box 726, Columbia, LA 71418. Phone: (318) 649-0726.

MONSTER MYTHS BY MOONLIGHT. Oct 10. Milford State Park, Milford, KS. Learn the truth about spiders, snakes, bats, vultures, owls and other Halloween "monsters." Meet the real creatures as you walk the nature trail and learn the truth about them from witches, snake charmers and Little Red Riding Hood. Wear costumes. Cookies and cider served by Mother Nature. Sponsored by Friends of Milford Nature Center and State Park. Est attendance: 650. For info: Milford Nature Center, 3415 Hatchery Dr, Junction City, KS 66441. Phone: (785) 238-5323. Fax: (785) 238-5775.

MOUNTAIN GLORY FESTIVAL. Oct 10. Marion, NC. 26th annual. A celebration of mountain heritage in western North Carolina. Arts, crafts, children's area and continuous entertainment. Annually, the second Saturday in October. Est attendance: 20,000. For info: Mountain Glory Festival, PO Drawer 700, Marion, NC 28752. Phone: (828) 652-3551. Fax: (828) 652-1983. E-mail: info@mtngloryfestival.com. Web: www.mtngloryfestival.com.

NATCHITOCHES HISTORIC PILGRIMAGE. Oct 10–11. Natchitoches, LA. Tour of homes in the National Historic Landmark District and plantation homes in Cane River Country. Est attendance: 5,000. For info: Natchitoches Parish Tourist Commission, 781 Front St, Natchitoches, LA 71457. Phone: (318) 352-8072 or 800-259-1714. Fax: (318) 352-2415. Web: www.natchitoches.net.

October 2009

S	M	T	W	T	F	S
				1	2	3
4	5	6	7	8	9	10
11	12	13	14	15	16	17
18	19	20	21	22	23	24
25	26	27	28	29	30	31

NATIONAL CAKE DECORATING DAY. Oct 10. A day to encourage Americans to try cake decorating. Decorating adds to the enjoyment of cakes, cookies, cupcakes and other foods shared with family and friends. For info: Diana Rodriguez, Wilton Enterprises, 2240 W 75th St, Woodridge, IL 60517. Phone: (630) 963-7100. E-mail: drodriguez@wilton.com. Web: www.wilton.com.

NORTHEAST MARBLE MEET. Oct 10–11. Marriott Courtyard, Marlborough, MA. Auction, exhibits; dealers and collectors buy, sell and trade marbles. Est attendance: 1,000. For info: Bert Cohen, 455 Clinton Rd, Brookline, MA 02446. Phone/fax: (617) 487-5808. E-mail: marblebert@aol.com. Web: www.marblebert.com.

NORTHERN INTERNATIONAL LIVESTOCK EXPOSITION. Oct 10–17. MetraPark, Billings, MT. PRCA rodeo, trade show exhibits, horse clinics and cattle, sheep, swine and horse sales. Est attendance: 25,000. For info: Justin Mills, Gen Mgr, NILE Office, PO Box 1981, Billings, MT 59103. Phone: (406) 256-2495. Fax: (406) 256-2494. E-mail: info@thenile.org. Web: www.thenile.org.

OKLAHOMA HISTORICAL DAY. Oct 10. Oklahoma.

OYSTER FESTIVAL. Oct 10. Chincoteague Island, VA. Oysters fixed every way possible—all you can eat. Annually, Saturday of Columbus Day weekend. Tickets can be obtained in advance by contacting Chincoteague Chamber of Commerce. Est attendance: 2,700. For info: Chincoteague Chamber of Commerce, 6733 Maddox Blvd, Chincoteague Island, VA 23336. Phone: (757) 336-6161. Fax: (757) 336-1242. E-mail: chincochamber@verizon.net. Web: www.chincoteaguechamber.com.

PEARL, DANIEL: BIRTH ANNIVERSARY. Oct 10, 1963. Born at Princeton, NJ, Daniel Pearl was a foreign correspondent for the *Wall Street Journal* when he was assassinated by a terrorist group in Pakistan. His body was found in Karachi, Pakistan, where he had been researching terrorist threats against America. British-born Islamic militant Ahmed Omar Sheikh, a leader of the National Movement for the Restoration of Pakistani Sovereignty, was convicted of Pearl's kidnapping and murder. Pearl was 38 at the time he was kidnapped, on Jan 23, 2002.

PINE BARRENS JAMBOREE. Oct 10. Wells Mills County Park, Waretown, NJ. Celebrate the culture and natural history of the New Jersey Pinelands. Live folk and country music, crafts, wood-carvers, live demonstrations, nature walks, canoeing, children's activities, animals, food and more. Includes exhibits featuring traditional industries of the Pinelands. Free; rain or shine. Est attendance: 2,000. For info: Amanda Truhan, Coordinator, Wells Mills County Park, 905 Wells Mills Rd, Waretown, NJ 08758. Phone: (609) 971-3085. Fax: (609) 971-9540. Web: www.oceancountyparks.org.

PRATER'S MILL COUNTRY FAIR. Oct 10–11. Dalton, GA. A Southern festival of artists, craftsmen, music and food. Est attendance: 15,000. For info: Prater's Mill Foundation, Inc, PO Drawer H, Varnell, GA 30756. Phone: (706) 694-MILL. Fax: (706) 694-8413. E-mail: pratersmill@PratersMill.org. Web: PratersMill.org.

QUADRANGLE FESTIVAL. Oct 10–11. Downtown Texarkana, TX and AR. 28th annual festival features 5k BiState Race on the Texas-Arkansas state line. Also, three stages of entertainment, more than 150 artists and craftsmen, cheerleading competition, Miss Quadrangle Pageant, battle of the bands, antique autos, pet shows; country/rock, traditional and contemporary music; street dancing and food vendors. Est attendance: 35,000. For info: Texarkana Museums System, PO Box 2343, Texarkana, TX 75504. Phone: (903) 793-4831. Fax: (903) 793-7108.

SCENIC DRIVE FESTIVAL. Oct 10–11. Van Buren County, IA. Scenic landscapes, historic architecture, flea market, arts festival, crafts and more. Annually, the second full weekend in October. Est attendance: 18,000. For info: Villages of Van Buren, Inc, PO Box 9, Keosauqua, IA 52565. Phone: (800) 868-7822. Fax: (319) 293-7116. E-mail: info@villagesofvanburen.com. Web: www.villagesofvanburen.com.

SEDONA ARTS FESTIVAL. Oct 10–11. Sedona, AZ. Annual celebration of visual, performing and culinary arts. Creative artisans present a unique collection of fine arts, foods and continuous live entertainment, surrounded by the scenic grandeur of towering red rocks. Application deadline: Apr 15. Proceeds will benefit student art programs and scholarships. Rated one of the best festivals in the country. Est attendance: 6,000. For info: Sedona Arts Festival, PO Box 2729, Sedona, AZ 86339-2729. Phone: (928) 204-9456. Fax: (928) 204-9456. E-mail: info@sedonaartsfestival.org. Web: www.sedonaartsfestival.org.

SHEMINI ATZERET. Oct 10. Hebrew calendar date: Tishri 22, 5770. The eighth day of Solemn Assembly, part of the Sukkot Festival (see entry on Oct 3), with memorial services and cycle of Biblical readings in the synagogue. Began at sundown on Oct 9.

TAIWAN: DOUBLE TENTH DAY. Oct 10. Commemorates the proclamation of the Chinese Republic in 1911.

TUXEDO CREATED: ANNIVERSARY. Oct 10, 1886. Griswold Lorillard of Tuxedo Park, NY, fashioned the first tuxedo for men by cutting the tails off a tailcoat.

UNITED NATIONS: WORLD MENTAL HEALTH DAY. Oct 10. For info: United Nations, Dept of Public Info, New York, NY 10017. Web: www.un.org.

UNIVERSAL MUSIC DAY. Oct 10. This day advocates, celebrates and encourages profound gratitude for music, musicians, music teachers and music making. Observers dedicate themselves to creating a synergistic network to support this sacred work of sound and vibration. Annually, the second Saturday in October. For info: Susan Patricia Golden, PO Box 557, Dundedin, FL 34698. Phone: (727) 804-4908. Fax: (727) 841-1040. E-mail: info@UniversalMusicDay.org. Web: www.UniversalMusicDay.org.

"UPSTAIRS, DOWNSTAIRS" TV PREMIERE: ANNIVERSARY. Oct 10, 1971. The 52 episodes of this "Masterpiece Theatre" series covered the years 1903 to 1930 in the life of a wealthy London family ("Upstairs") and their many servants ("Downstairs"). Produced by London Weekend Television. Cast members included Angela Baddeley, Pauline Collins, Gordon Jackson and Jean Marsh. Won a Golden Globe for Best Drama TV Show in 1975 and an Emmy for Outstanding Limited Series in 1976. The last episode aired May 1, 1977, though the series has been rerun several times on PBS.

US NAVAL ACADEMY FOUNDED: ANNIVERSARY. Oct 10, 1845. A college to train officers for the navy was established at Annapolis, MD. Women were admitted in 1976. The Academy's motto is "Honor, Courage, Commitment." For more info: www.usna.edu.

VERDI, GIUSEPPI: BIRTH ANNIVERSARY. Oct 10, 1813. Italian composer, born at Le Roncole, Italy. His 26 operas, including *Rigoletto*, *Il Trovatore*, *La Traviata* and *Aida*, are among the most popular of all operatic music today. Died at Milan, Italy, Jan 27, 1901.

WHIPPOORWILL MORGAN HORSE OPEN BARN. Oct 10–12. Old Lyme, CT. Visitors can pet newborn foals and watch stallions and mares perform. There will also be an informative and informal introduction to the Morgan horse. No admission fee. Est attendance: 900. For info: McCulloch Farm, Whippoorwill Morgan, 100 Whippoorwill Rd, Old Lyme, CT 06371. Phone: (860) 434-7355.

Birthdays Today

Bob Burnquist, 33, skateboarder, born Rio de Janiero, Brazil, Oct 10, 1976.

Charles Dance, 63, actor (*The Jewel in the Crown, White Mischief*), born Worcestershire, England, Oct 10, 1946.

Dale Earnhardt, Jr, 35, race car driver, born Concord, NC, Oct 10, 1974.

Brett Favre, 40, football player, born Gulfport, MS, Oct 10, 1969.

Adrian Grenier, 33, actor ("Entourage"), born Brooklyn, NY, July 10, 1976.

Jessica Harper, 60, actress (*Stardust Memories, Pennies from Heaven, My Favorite Year*), born Chicago, IL, Oct 10, 1949.

Mario Lopez, 36, actor ("Saved by the Bell," "Pacific Blue"), born San Diego, CA, Oct 10, 1973.

Harold Pinter, 79, playwright (*Betrayal, The Birthday Party*), actor, born London, England, Oct 10, 1930.

Chris Pronger, 35, hockey player, born Dryden, ON, Canada, Oct 10, 1974.

Nora Roberts, 59, author (*Birthright, Hidden Riches, Rising Tides*), born Silver Springs, MD, Oct 10, 1950.

David Lee Roth, 54, singer (Van Halen), born Bloomington, IN, Oct 10, 1955.

Tanya Tucker, 51, singer ("Delta Dawn"), born Seminole, TX, Oct 10, 1958.

Ben Vereen, 63, actor, singer, dancer (Tony for *Pippin*; *Roots, All That Jazz*, "Webster"), born Miami, FL, Oct 10, 1946.

October 11 — Sunday

DAY 284 — **81 REMAINING**

BANK OF AMERICA CHICAGO MARATHON. Oct 11 (tentative). Grant Park, Chicago, IL. Flat, fast 26.2-mile course attracts everyone from elite athletes to novice marathon runners from all 50 states and more than 120 foreign countries. Est attendance: 850,000. For info: Bank of America Chicago Marathon, PO Box 2784, Chicago, IL 60690-2784. Phone: (312) 904-9800. Fax: (312) 904-9820. E-mail: marathon.office@abnamro.com. Web: www.chicagomarathon.com.

BLAKEY, ART: 90th BIRTH ANNIVERSARY. Oct 11, 1919. Born at Pittsburgh, PA, jazz musician Blakey recorded many albums with his group, the Jazz Messengers. Died at New York, NY, Oct 16, 1990.

BRAZIL: CIRIO DE NAZARE. Oct 11–24. Greatest festival of northern Brazil, the Feast of Cirio starts on the second Sunday of October in the city of Belem (St. Mary of Bethlehem), capital of the state of Para. Festival lasts two weeks.

BUILD YOUR BUSINESS WITH BUSINESS CARDS WEEK. Oct 11–17. Celebrate the power of the world's most portable, affordable and versatile marketing tool—the business card. An excellent reason to contact previous customers and cultivate new relationships. Event ideas and materials available. Annually, the week beginning with the second Sunday in October. For info: Diana Ratliff. E-mail: diana@dianaratliff.com. Web: www.businesscardweek.com.

BURGOO FESTIVAL. Oct 11. Downtown, North Utica, IL. Only the "Burgoomeister" knows the secret recipe for this pioneer stew, burgoo, served outdoors at this annual Utica festival. Other events include arts and crafts, antiques, food and music. Free admission. Annually, the Sunday of Columbus Day weekend. Est attendance: 30,000. For info: Burgoo Chairman, LaSalle County Historical Museum, PO Box 278, Utica, IL 61373. Phone: (815) 667-4861. E-mail: LCHSMuseum@gmail.com. Web: www.lasallecountymuseum.org.

EMERGENCY NURSES WEEK. Oct 11–17. Sponsored by the Emergency Nurses Association (ENA) since 1989, this is a weeklong celebration recognizing emergency nurses for their dedication, service and commitment to their patients and communities. Special focus is given on Wednesday, which is Emergency Nurses Day (Oct 14), to honor nursing professionals who provide care to those whose lives have been touched by life's tragedies. For info: Emergency Nurses Assn Headquarters, 915 Lee St, Des Plaines, IL 60016-6569. Phone: (800) 900-9659. E-mail: pr@ena.org. Web: www.ena.org.

✦ **GENERAL PULASKI MEMORIAL DAY.** Oct 11. Presidential Proclamation always issued for Oct 11 since 1929. Requested by Congressional Resolution each year, 1929–1946. (Since 1947 has been issued by custom.) Note: Proclamation 4869, of Oct 5, 1981, covers all succeeding years.

GETTING THE WORLD TO BEAT A PATH TO YOUR DOOR WEEK. Oct 11–17. To focus attention on improving "public relationships" in order to create success for companies, products and individuals. Free self-evaluation available. Annually, the third week in October. For info: Gaughen Global Public Relations, 7456 Evergreen Dr, Santa Barbara, CA 93117. Phone: (805) 968-8567. Fax: (805) 968-5747. E-mail: bgaughenmu@aol.com. Web: www.robertmuller.org.

GRANDMOTHER'S DAY IN FLORIDA. Oct 11. A ceremonial day on the second Sunday in October.

HOME-BASED BUSINESS WEEK. Oct 11–17. To celebrate, recognize and promote the home-based entrepreneur. Annually, the week including the second Tuesday of October. For info: Beverley Williams, The Home Business Advocate. E-mail: bevspeaks@earthlink.net. Web: www.beverleywilliams.com.

INTERNATIONAL AFRICAN DIASPORA DAY. Oct 11. Nate Holden Performing Arts Center, Los Angeles, CA. A component of the "Shaping Black Culture in the Diaspora: An Ark for the 21st Century" conference, which is held each year to address the urban cultural core. Focuses on the creative sector's best practices for the health and long-term sustainability of black cultural expression in African Diaspora, locally, nationally and internationally. Est attendance: 1,500. For info: Ernest Dillahay, PO Box 926, Los Angeles, CA 91031. Phone: (323) 257-2196. E-mail: ernest.dillihay@lacity.org.

INTERNATIONAL CREDIT UNION WEEK. Oct 11–17. Worldwide observance to recognize the contribution of credit unions to the development and practice of democracy. For info: Public Relations, Credit Union Natl Assn, PO Box 431, Madison, WI 53701-0431. Phone: (800) 356-9655. Web: www.cuna.org.

LEIF ERICSON DAY CELEBRATION. Oct 11. Statue of Thorfin Karlsefne, Philadelphia, PA. Celebration honoring the first European to set foot on the North American continent. Event also seeks to promote knowledge about and a realistic historic image of the Viking people as merchants, navigators, shipbuilders, artists, explorers and warriors. Sponsored by the Leif Ericson Viking Ship, Inc, and the Leif Ericson Society. Annually, the Sunday nearest Oct 9. For info: Leif Ericson Viking Ship, Inc, PO Box 393, Swarthmore, PA 19081-0393. Phone/fax: (410) 275-8516. E-mail: info@vikingship.org. Web: www.vikingship.org.

MOON PHASE: LAST QUARTER. Oct 11. Moon enters Last Quarter phase at 4:56 AM, EDT.

NATIONAL CHESTNUT WEEK. Oct 11–17. A celebration of the chestnut throughout the US. Events to include farm visits, chestnut roasts, grower displays and more. Annually, the second full week of October. For info: Ray Young, PO Box 841, Ridgefield, WA 98642. Phone: (360) 887-3669. E-mail: Ray@ChestnutsOnLine.com. Web: www.wcga.net.

NATIONAL COMING OUT DAY. Oct 11. A project of the Human Rights Campaign since 1988. Every Oct 11, thousands of gay, lesbian, bisexual and transgender (GLBT) individuals and their supportive allies celebrate National Coming Out Day, which encourages GLBT individuals to come out and be honest about themselves. Every year, workshops, speak-outs, rallies and other kinds of events are held—all aimed at showing the public that GLBT people are everywhere. For info: Natl Coming Out Project, 1640 Rhode Island Ave NW, Washington, DC 20036. Phone: (800) 866-6263. Fax: (202) 347-5323. E-mail: comingout@hrc.org. Web: www.hrc.org/comingout.

NATIONAL FOOD BANK WEEK. Oct 11–17. Educates and recognizes efforts of food banks, their donors and volunteers to alleviate hunger in the US. Observed at local food banks around the country. Annually, the week encompassing World Food Day (Oct 16). For info on activities in your area, go to Second Harvest's website at www.secondharvest.org and do a zip code search.

October 2009

S	M	T	W	T	F	S
				1	2	3
4	5	6	7	8	9	10
11	12	13	14	15	16	17
18	19	20	21	22	23	24
25	26	27	28	29	30	31

PATENT ISSUED FOR FIRST ADDING MACHINE: ANNIVERSARY. Oct 11, 1887. A patent was granted to Dorr Eugene Felt for the Comptometer, which was the first adding machine known to be absolutely accurate at all times.

REVSON, CHARLES: BIRTH ANNIVERSARY. Oct 11, 1906. Revson, born at Boston, MA, was the colorful and hard-driving force behind Revlon cosmetics, a company he created in 1932. Revson was fond of saying, "Creative people are like a wet towel. You wring them out and pick up another one." By the time of his death, Aug 24, 1975, Revson had an estate valued at $100 million and a cosmetics empire.

ROBBINS, JEROME: BIRTH ANNIVERSARY. Oct 11, 1918. Choreographer and ballet dancer, born at New York, NY. Robbins choreographed several Broadway musicals including *Fiddler on the Roof, The King and I* and *On the Town*. He died at New York, NY, July 29, 1998.

ROBINSON, ROSCOE, JR: BIRTH ANNIVERSARY. Oct 11, 1928. The first black American to achieve the army rank of four-star general. Born at St. Louis, MO, and died at Washington, DC, July 22, 1993.

ROOSEVELT, ANNA ELEANOR: 125th BIRTH ANNIVERSARY. Oct 11, 1884. Wife of Franklin Delano Roosevelt, 32nd president of the US, was born at New York, NY. She led an active and independent life and was the first wife of a president to give her own news conference in the White House (1933). Widely known throughout the world, she was affectionately called "the first lady of the world." She served as US delegate to the United Nations General Assembly for a number of years before her death at New York, NY, Nov 7, 1962. A prolific writer, she wrote in *This Is My Story*, "No one can make you feel inferior without your consent."

SAMOA AND AMERICAN SAMOA: WHITE SUNDAY. Oct 11. The second Sunday in October. For the children of Samoa and American Samoa, this is the biggest day of the year. Traditional roles are reversed, as children lead church services, are served special foods and receive gifts of new church clothes and other special items. All the children dress in white. The following Monday is an official holiday.

"SATURDAY NIGHT LIVE" TV PREMIERE: ANNIVERSARY. Oct 11, 1975. Originally titled "NBC's Saturday Night," this live show features skits, commercial parodies and news satires, with a different guest host and musical guest performing. Its first guest host was comedian George Carlin. Notable cast members have included Chevy Chase, Dan Aykroyd, John Belushi, Jane Curtin, Garrett Morris, Laraine Newman, Gilda Radner, Bill Murray, Joe Piscopo, Eddie Murphy, Billy Crystal, Martin Short, Christopher Guest, Harry Shearer, Joan Cusack, Robert Downey, Jr, Nora Dunn, Jon Lovitz, Dana Carvey, Phil Hartman, Jan Hooks, Dennis Miller, Chris Farley, Mike Myers, Adam Sandler, Will Ferrell, Molly Shannon, Tina Fey and Amy Poehler.

SIMCHAT TORAH. Oct 11. Hebrew calendar date: Tishri 23, 5770. Rejoicing in the Torah concludes the nine-day Sukkot Festival (see entry on Oct 3). Public reading of the Pentateuch is completed and begun again, symbolizing the need for ever-continuing study. Began at sundown on Oct 10.

SPACE MILESTONE: *DISCOVERY STS-92*: 100th SHUTTLE FLIGHT. Oct 11, 2000. *Discovery* was launched on its 28th flight. This marked the shuttle program's 100th mission. On this flight, *Discovery* headed to the International Space Station, where it docked on Oct 13. On earlier flights, the shuttles *Columbia, Challenger, Endeavour, Atlantis* and *Discovery* had launched the Hubble Space Telescope and Chandra X-Ray Observatory, docked with the *Mir* space station and supported scientific research. The first shuttle flight took place in 1981. Since the first mission, space shuttles have carried 261 individuals and nearly three million pounds of payload, logging an estimated 350 million miles. See: "Space Milestone: *Columbia STS-1*" (Apr 12).

STONE, HARLAN FISKE: BIRTH ANNIVERSARY. Oct 11, 1872. Former associate justice and later chief justice of the US who wrote more than 600 opinions and dissents for that court, Stone was born at Chesterfield, NH. He served on the Supreme Court from 1925 until his death, at Washington, DC, Apr 22, 1946.

VATICAN COUNCIL II: ANNIVERSARY. Oct 11, 1962. The 21st ecumenical council of the Roman Catholic Church was convened by Pope John XXIII. It met in four annual sessions, concluding Dec 8, 1965. It dealt with the renewal of the Church and introduced sweeping changes, such as the use of the vernacular rather than Latin in the Mass.

WEEMS, PARSON (MASON LOCKE): 250th BIRTH ANNIVERSARY. Oct 11, 1759. Mason Locke Weems was born at Anne Arundel County, MD. An Episcopal clergyman and traveling bookseller, Weems is remembered for the fictitious stories he presented as historical fact. Best known of his "fables" is the story describing George Washington cutting down his father's cherry tree with a hatchet. Weems's fictionalized histories, however, delighted many readers who accepted them as true. They became immensely popular and were bestsellers for many years. Weems died May 23, 1825, at Beaufort, SC.

WEST, DOTTIE: BIRTH ANNIVERSARY. Oct 11, 1932. American singer Dottie West was born at McMinnville, TN. In 1964 she won the first Grammy ever by a country vocalist for "Here Comes My Baby." She died Sept 4, 1991, at Nashville, TN.

WILLIAM AND HILLARY CLINTON WEDDING: ANNIVERSARY. Oct 11, 1975. William Jefferson (Blythe) Clinton was 29 and Hillary Rodham was 27 when they wed on this date at Fayetteville, AR. They have one child, Chelsea Victoria Clinton, born in 1980.

Birthdays Today

Joan Cusack, 47, actress (*Working Girl, In & Out*), born Evanston, IL, Oct 11, 1962.

Emily Deschanel, 33, actress ("Bones"), born Los Angeles, CA, Oct 11, 1976.

Robert Gale, 64, physician, cofounder of the International Bone Marrow Registry, born Brooklyn Heights, NY, Oct 11, 1945.

Daryl Hall, 61, singer, musician (Hall and Oates), born Pottstown, PA, Oct 11, 1948.

Orlando "El Duque" Hernandez, 40, baseball player, born Villa Clara, Cuba, Oct 11, 1969.

Jane Krakowski, 41, actress ("Ally McBeal," "30 Rock," Tony Award for *Nine*), born Parsippany, NJ, Oct 11, 1968.

Ron Leibman, 72, stage and screen actor (*Norma Rae*; Tony for *Angels in America*), born New York, NY, Oct 11, 1937.

Elmore Leonard, 84, writer (*Glitz, Get Shorty*), born New Orleans, LA, Oct 11, 1925.

David Morse, 56, actor ("St. Elsewhere," *Proof of Life*), born Beverly, MA, Oct 11, 1953.

Patty Murray, 59, US Senator (D, Washington), born Seattle, WA, Oct 11, 1950.

Luke Perry, 43, actor ("Beverly Hills 90210," *Buffy the Vampire Slayer*), born Fredricktown, MO, Oct 11, 1966.

Steve Young, 48, former football player, born Salt Lake City, UT, Oct 11, 1961.

October 12 — Monday

DAY 285 — **80 REMAINING**

AMERICAN INDIAN HERITAGE DAY (ALABAMA). Oct 12. First declared in 2000, this state holiday is also observed as Columbus Day in Alabama. Annually, the second Monday in October.

BAHAMAS: DISCOVERY DAY. Oct 12. Commemorates the landing of Columbus in the Bahamas in 1492.

BALI TERRORIST BOMBING: ANNIVERSARY. Oct 12, 2002. Two bombs detonated in Kuta on the Indonesian island of Bali killed more than 200 people and injured hundreds. The bombs were placed at bars where vacationing tourists were known to gather. Although the terrorist group Al Qaeda claimed responsibility, suspects who later confessed to the crime stated that they were working independently.

BELIZE: COLUMBUS DAY. Oct 12. Public holiday.

"THE BOB HOPE SHOW" TV PREMIERE: ANNIVERSARY. Oct 12, 1953. Premier funnyman, well-known and well-loved Bob Hope made monthly appearances on TV in the 1950s. During the first season he hosted "The Colgate Comedy Hour," and during the later seasons his show was seen replacing and then alternating with Milton Berle (and in 1955–56 with Martha Raye and Dinah Shore). Leo Robin and Ralph Rainger wrote Hope's trademark show-closing song, "Thanks for the Memory."

BOER WAR: ANNIVERSARY. Oct 12, 1899. The Boers of the Transvaal and Orange Free State in southern Africa declared war on the British. The Boer states were annexed by Britain in 1900 but guerrilla warfare on the part of the Boers caused the war to drag on. It was finally ended May 31, 1902, by the Treaty of Vereeniging.

"THE BURNS AND ALLEN SHOW" TV PREMIERE: ANNIVERSARY. Oct 12, 1950. The comedic husband-and-wife duo of George Burns and Gracie Allen starred as themselves in this comedy series in which Burns was the straight man and Allen was known for her ditziness. The show employed the technique of speaking directly to the camera ("breaking the fourth wall"); Burns often commented on the plot, told jokes or tried to make sense of Allen's actions and statements. Also on the show were their real-life son, Ronnie Burns; Bea Benaderet; Hal March; John Brown (until blacklisted by McCarthyites in the "red scare"); Fred Clark; Larry Keating; Bill Goodwin and Harry Von Zell. The show was done live for the first two seasons and included vaudeville scenes at the end of each episode.

CANADA: THANKSGIVING DAY. Oct 12. Observed on second Monday in October each year.

✦ **COLUMBUS DAY.** Oct 12. Presidential Proclamation always the second Monday in October. Observed on Oct 12 from 1934 to 1970 (Pub Res No 21 of Apr 30, 1934). PL90–363 of June 28, 1968, required that beginning in 1971 it would be observed on the second Monday in October.

COLUMBUS DAY (TRADITIONAL). Oct 12. Public holiday in most countries in the Americas and in most Spanish-speaking countries. Observed under different names (Dia de la Raza or Day of the Race) and on different dates (most often, as in US, on the second Monday in October). Anniversary of Christopher Columbus's arrival, Oct 12, 1492, after a dangerous voyage across "shoreless Seas," at the Bahamas (probably the island of Guanahani), which he renamed El Salvador and claimed in the name of the Spanish crown. See also: "Columbus Day Observance" (Oct 12).

COLUMBUS DAY OBSERVANCE. Oct 12. Public Law 90–363 sets observance of Columbus Day on the second Monday in October. Applicable to federal employees and to the District of Columbia, but observed also in most states. Commemorates the landfall of Columbus in the New World, Oct 12, 1492. See also: "Columbus Day (Traditional)" (Oct 12).

DAY OF THE SIX BILLION: 10th ANNIVERSARY. Oct 12, 1999. According to the United Nations, the population of the world reached six billion on this date. More than one-third of the world's people live in China and India. It wasn't until 1804 that the world's population reached one billion; now a billion people are added to the population about every 12 years. See also: "Day of the Five Billion" (July 11).

DISCOVERERS' DAY IN HAWAII. Oct 12. Honors all discoverers, including Pacific and Polynesian navigators. Second Monday in October.

EQUATORIAL GUINEA: INDEPENDENCE DAY. Oct 12. National holiday. Gained independence from Spain in 1968.

FREETHOUGHT DAY. Oct 12. During the Month of Freethought, Freethought "Coming Out" Day is an annual day of celebration which gives those freethinkers who have been unable to proudly declare themselves a platform from which to do so. Held on Oct 12, newly declared freethinkers can gain strength and support from fellow "open" freethinkers. For info: Matt Cherry, Institute for Humanist Studies, 48 Howard St, Albany, NY 12207. Phone: (518) 432-7820. Fax: (518) 432-7821. E-mail: MCherry@HumanistStudies.org. Web: HumanistStudies.org or www.secularseasons.org.

GORDONE, CHARLES: BIRTH ANNIVERSARY. Oct 12, 1925. First black playwright to win the Pulitzer Prize for Drama, for his play *No Place to Be Somebody.* Born at Cleveland, OH. Died Nov 17, 1995, at College Station, TX.

INTERNATIONAL MOMENT OF FRUSTRATION SCREAM DAY. Oct 12. To share any or all of our frustrations, all citizens of the world will go outdoors at 1200 hours Greenwich time and scream for 30 seconds. We will all feel better or Earth will go off its orbit. Annually, Oct 12. (©2006 by WH.) For info: Thomas & Ruth Roy, Wellcat Holidays, 2418 Long Ln, Lebanon, PA 17046. Phone: (717) 279-0184. E-mail: info@wellcat.com. Web: www.wellcat.com.

JAPAN: HEALTH-SPORTS DAY. Oct 12. National holiday to encourage physical activity for building sound body and mind. Created in 1966 to commemorate the day of the opening of the 18th Olympic Games at Tokyo, Oct 10, 1964. Annually, the second Monday in October.

MacDONALD, ANNE THOMPSON: DEATH ANNIVERSARY. Oct 12, 1993. Born in 1896, MacDonald founded a nonprofit organization, Recording for the Blind, that produces audiotapes of books to benefit blind and learning-disabled people. MacDonald founded the organization in 1948; its library currently contains more than 80,000 titles. She died at Huntington, NY.

McNAIR, RONALD E.: BIRTH ANNIVERSARY. Oct 12, 1950. Ronald E. McNair, a 35-year-old physicist, was the second black American astronaut in space (February 1984). He was born at Lake City, SC. As mission specialist for the crew, he perished in the space shuttle *Challenger* explosion Jan 28, 1986. See also: "Challenger Space Shuttle Explosion: Anniversary" (Jan 28).

MEXICO: DIA DE LA RAZA. Oct 12. Columbus Day is observed as the "Day of the Race," a fiesta time to commemorate the discovery of America as well as the common interests and cultural heritage of the Spanish and Indian peoples and the Hispanic nations.

October 2009	S	M	T	W	T	F	S
					1	2	3
	4	5	6	7	8	9	10
	11	12	13	14	15	16	17
	18	19	20	21	22	23	24
	25	26	27	28	29	30	31

NATIONAL KICK-BUTT DAY. Oct 12. On this day we commit to kicking ourselves in the butt to take action on goals we've set and not achieved, actions we've committed to and not taken, promises we've made and not kept, excuses we've created that have us stalled and difficulties we've faced and not overcome. This is the day we get our butts in gear and move forward in our lives. No butts about it! Annually, the second Monday of October. For info: Sylvia Henderson, Springboard Training, PO Box 588, Olney, MD 20830-0588. Phone: (301) 260-1538. E-mail: sylvia@springboardtraining.com. Web: www.springboardtraining.com.

NATIONAL SALESPERSON'S DAY. Oct 12. Salespeople are essential resources for customers today. The talented salesperson filters the vast amount of information that is available to customers and helps businesspeople make the best purchasing decisions. Salespeople also help consumers make better, quicker decisions with the counsel they offer. With the impact of new technologies, the role of the salesperson continually evolves. For info: Maura Schreier-Fleming, Best@Selling, 7028 Judi, Dallas, TX 75252. Phone: (972) 380-0200. Fax: (972) 733-0126. E-mail: Maura@BestAtSelling.com. Web: www.BestAtSelling.com.

NATIONAL SCHOOL LUNCH WEEK. Oct 12–16. To celebrate good nutrition and healthy, safe school lunches. Created in 1962 by President John F. Kennedy. Annually, the second full week in October. For info: School Nutrition Assn, 700 S Washington St, Ste 300, Alexandria, VA 22314-4287. Phone: (703) 739-3900. Fax: (703) 739-3915. E-mail: servicecenter@schoolnutrition.org. Web: www.schoolnutrition.org.

NATIVE AMERICANS' DAY (SOUTH DAKOTA). Oct 12. Observed in the state of South Dakota as a legal holiday, dedicated to the remembrance of the great Native American leaders who contributed so much to the history of South Dakota. Annually, the second Monday in October.

PAVAROTTI, LUCIANO: BIRTH ANNIVERSARY. Oct 12, 1935. Born at Modena, Italy, Pavarotti made opera accessible for a wide audience. The most popular tenor of his time, he was known for his perfect tone, especially in the highest ranges. A regular performer at the Metropolitan Opera House in New York for decades, he brought his music to a wider audience in the 1980s and '90s by performing as one of the Three Tenors. He, along with Plácido Domingo and José Carreras, crossed into mainstream pop music with television appearances and nationwide tours and sold millions of records. Pavarotti was a philanthropist and was active in raising funding and awareness for many humanitarian causes. Widely considered to be the best *bel canto* singer of the 20th century, he died at Modena Sept 6, 2007.

"SNEAK PREVIEWS" TV PREMIERE: ANNIVERSARY. Oct 12, 1978. This show with film critics Gene Siskel and Roger Ebert got its start on public television in Chicago in 1975. In 1978 it went national on PBS. In 1981 the program moved to network TV and the name was changed to "At the Movies." After Siskel's death in 1999, a rotating panel of critics joined Ebert and in 2000 journalist Richard Roeper was named the permanent cohost. The title was changed to "Ebert & Roeper and the Movies."

SPAIN: NATIONAL HOLIDAY. Oct 12. Called Hispanity Day or Day of Spanish Consciousness. Honors Christopher Columbus and the Spanish conquerors of Latin America.

TRUMBULL, JONATHAN: BIRTH ANNIVERSARY. Oct 12, 1710. American patriot, counselor and friend of George Washington, governor of Connecticut Colony, born at Lebanon, CT. Died there, Aug 17, 1785.

VAUGHAN WILLIAMS, RALPH: BIRTH ANNIVERSARY. Oct 12, 1872. English composer and conductor Ralph Vaughan Williams was born at Down Ampney, Gloucestershire. He is considered England's first great truly national composer, having rooted "modern" composition techniques in traditional English folk and Tudor music and themes to create a uniquely English style. Among his many works are nine symphonies, church and choral music, film and stage music and several operas. His major compositions include the *Mass in G Minor* and the opera *The Pilgrim's Progress.* He died Aug 26, 1958, at London.

VIRGIN ISLANDS–PUERTO RICO FRIENDSHIP DAY. Oct 12. Columbus Day (second Monday in October) also celebrates historical friendship between peoples of Virgin Islands and Puerto Rico.

WORLD RAINFOREST WEEK. Oct 12–18. Rainforest activists worldwide will sponsor events to increase public awareness of rainforest destruction and motivate people to protect the earth's rainforests and support the rights of their inhabitants. The global rate of destruction of rainforests is 2.4 acres per second—equivalent to two US football fields. For info: Grassroots Coord, Rainforest Action Network, 221 Pine St, 5th Fl, San Francisco, CA 94104. Phone: (415) 398-4404. Fax: (415) 398-2732. E-mail: activism@ran.org. Web: www.ran.org.

YORKTOWN VICTORY DAY. Oct 12. Observed as a holiday in Virginia. Annually, the second Monday in October. Commemorates the Revolutionary War battle fought in 1781.

Birthdays Today

Susan Anton, 59, singer, actress (*Goldengirl*), born Yucaipa, CA, Oct 12, 1950.

Carlos Bernard, 47, actor ("24"), born Evanston, IL, Oct 12, 1962.

Kirk Cameron, 39, actor ("Growing Pains," "Kirk"), born Panorama City, CA, Oct 12, 1970.

Chris Chandler, 44, former football player, born Everett, WA, Oct 12, 1965.

Dave Freudenthal, 59, Governor of Wyoming (D), born Thermopolis, WY, Oct 12, 1950.

Dick Gregory, 77, comedian, author, activist, born St. Louis, MO, Oct 12, 1932.

Hugh Jackman, 41, actor (*The Prestige, X-Men, X2*), born Sydney, Australia, Oct 12, 1968.

Marion Jones, 34, former track runner, born Los Angeles, CA, Oct 12, 1975.

Anthony Christopher (Tony) Kubek, 73, sportscaster, former baseball player, born Milwaukee, WI, Oct 12, 1936.

Jean Nidetch, 86, founder of Weight Watchers, born Brooklyn, NY, Oct 12, 1923.

Adam Rich, 41, actor ("Eight Is Enough"), born Brooklyn, NY, Oct 12, 1968.

Chris Wallace, 62, broadcaster ("Dateline"), White House correspondent, born Chicago, IL, Oct 12, 1947.

October 13 — Tuesday

DAY 286 — **79 REMAINING**

BROWN, JESSE LEROY: BIRTH ANNIVERSARY. Oct 13, 1926. Jesse Leroy Brown was the first black American naval aviator and also the first black naval officer to lose his life in combat when he was shot down over Korea, Dec 4, 1950. On Mar 18, 1972, USS *Jesse L. Brown* was launched as the first ship to be named in honor of a black naval officer. Brown was born at Hattiesburg, MS.

BRUCE, LENNY: BIRTH ANNIVERSARY. Oct 13, 1925. Born Leonard Alfred Schneider at New York, NY, Lenny Bruce was an innovative, hip and searing stand-up comedian whose material touched on adult themes. His satiric and sometimes shocking routines gained him the wrath of public officials, and he was arrested multiple times on obscenity charges. His trials became celebrated calls to arms to protect First Amendment rights. By the time of his death by morphine overdose on Aug 3, 1966, at Hollywood Hills, CA, Bruce was banned in many US cities, Australia and England, and from comedy clubs that feared legal action.

BURUNDI: ASSASSINATION OF THE HERO OF THE NATION DAY. Oct 13. National holiday. Commemorates the assassination of Prince Louis Rwagasore in 1961.

MONTAND, YVES: BIRTH ANNIVERSARY. Oct 13, 1921. French actor Yves Montand was born Ivo Livi at Monsummano Alto, Italy. His career was successful in both France and America, including more than 50 films. He died Nov 9, 1991, at Senlis, France.

NATIONAL FACE YOUR FEARS DAY. Oct 13. This unique day helps people face and overcome their fears—whether seeking a better job or pursuing a new relationship. National Face Your Fears Day is all about going for it. Annually, the second Tuesday in October. For info: Steve Hughes, 412 Luther Ct, St. Louis, MO 63122. Phone: (314) 821-8700. E-mail: info@hityourstride.com. Web: www.FaceYourFearsToday.com.

NAVY BIRTHDAY. Oct 13. Since 1972 a Navywide celebration (for members of the active forces and reserves, as well as retirees and dependents) recognizing the authorization of the Continental Navy on this date in 1775. The celebration is meant "to enhance a greater appreciation of [the] Navy heritage and to provide a positive influence toward pride and professionalism in the naval service." See also: "US Navy: Authorization Anniversary" (Oct 13). For info: www.history.navy.mil.

PITCHER, MOLLY: BIRTH ANNIVERSARY. Oct 13, 1754. "Molly Pitcher," heroine of the American Revolution, was a water carrier at the Battle of Monmouth (Sunday, June 28, 1778), where she distinguished herself by loading and firing a cannon after her husband, William Hays, was wounded. Affectionately known as "Sergeant Molly" after General Washington issued her a warrant as a noncommissioned officer. Her real name was Mary Hays McCauley (née Ludwig). Born near Trenton, NJ, she died at Carlisle, PA, Jan 22, 1832.

SAINT EDWARD, THE CONFESSOR: FEAST DAY. Oct 13. King of England, 1042–66, Edward was the son of King Ethelred the Unready. Born at Islip, England, in 1003, he died Jan 5, 1066, at London. On Oct 13, 1163, his remains were transported in a ceremony that was of national interest. Since then Oct 13 has been observed as his principal feast day.

THATCHER, MARGARET HILDA ROBERTS: BIRTHDAY. Oct 13, 1925. First woman prime minister in 700 years of English parliamentary history. Election of May 3, 1979, gave the Conservative Party victory, and Thatcher accepted Queen Elizabeth's appointment as prime minister on May 4. She held the office until forced to resign on Nov 22, 1990. She was given a life peerage as Baroness Thatcher of Kesteven, June 5, 1992, a position that entitles her to a seat in the House of Lords, where she remains an active Tory voice. Thatcher was born at Grantham, Lincolnshire, England.

US NATIONAL COMMISSION ON SPACE: 25th ANNIVERSARY. Oct 13, 1984. President Reagan signed executive order creating a

National Commission on Space to prepare 20-year agenda for civilian space program.

US NAVY: AUTHORIZATION ANNIVERSARY. Oct 13, 1775. Commemorates legislation passed by Second Continental Congress authorizing the acquisition of ships and establishment of a navy.

VIRCHOW, RUDOLF: BIRTH ANNIVERSARY. Oct 13, 1821. German political leader, scientist, teacher and author. Called "the founder of cellular pathology." Born at Schivelbein, Prussia; died at Berlin, Germany, Sept 5, 1902.

WHITE HOUSE CORNERSTONE LAID: ANNIVERSARY. Oct 13, 1792. The presidential residence at 1600 Pennsylvania Ave NW, Washington, DC, designed by James Hoban (q.v.), observes its birthday Oct 13. The cornerstone was laid; the first presidential family to occupy it was that of John Adams, in November 1800. With three stories and more than 100 rooms, the White House is the oldest building at Washington. First described as the "presidential palace," it acquired the name "White House" about 10 years after construction was completed. Burned by British troops in 1814, it was reconstructed, refurbished and reoccupied by 1817.

Birthdays Today

Ashanti, 29, singer, actress (*The Muppets' Wizard of Oz*), born Ashanti Sequoiah Douglas at Long Island, NY, Oct 13, 1980.

Maria Cantwell, 51, US Senator (D, Washington), born Indianapolis, IN, Oct 13, 1958.

Chris Carter, 52, creator of "The X-Files," born Bellflower, CA, Oct 13, 1957.

Sasha Baron Cohen, 38, comedian, actor ("Da Ali G Show," *Borat*), born London, England, Oct 13, 1971.

Melinda Dillon, 70, actress (*Close Encounters of the Third Kind, A Christmas Story*), born Hope, AR, Oct 13, 1939.

Sammy Hagar, 60, singer, musician, born Monterrey, CA, Oct 13, 1949.

Nancy Kerrigan, 40, former figure skater, born Woburn, MA, Oct 13, 1969.

Jermaine O'Neal, 31, basketball player, born Columbia, SC, Oct 13, 1978.

Marie Osmond, 50, actress, singer, born Ogden, UT, Oct 13, 1959.

Paul Pierce, 32, basketball player, born Oakland, CA, Oct 13, 1977.

Kelly Preston, 47, actress (*Christine, Twins*), born Honolulu, HI, Oct 13, 1962.

Jerry Lee Rice, 47, former football player, born Starkville, MS, Oct 13, 1962.

Glenn Anton "Doc" Rivers, 48, basketball coach and former player, born Maywood, IL, Oct 13, 1961.

Paul Simon, 68, singer (Simon and Garfunkel), musician, born Newark, NJ, Oct 13, 1941.

Margaret Hilda Roberts Thatcher, 84, former Prime Minister of England, born Grantham, England, Oct 13, 1925.

Pamela Tiffin, 67, actress (*Harper*; stage: *Dinner at Eight*), born Oklahoma City, OK, Oct 13, 1942.

Kate Walsh, 42, actress ("Grey's Anatomy," "The Drew Carey Show"), born San Jose, CA, Oct 13, 1967.

October 2009	S	M	T	W	T	F	S
					1	2	3
	4	5	6	7	8	9	10
	11	12	13	14	15	16	17
	18	19	20	21	22	23	24
	25	26	27	28	29	30	31

October 14 — Wednesday

DAY 287 — 78 REMAINING

"THE ADVENTURES OF ELLERY QUEEN" TV PREMIERE: ANNIVERSARY. Oct 14, 1950. The first of many series to portray fictional detective Ellery Queen, it began on the DuMont network and later moved to ABC. Queen was played by Richard Hart. In the next four series, he would also be played by Lee Bowman, Hugh Marlowe, George Nadar, Lee Philips, Peter Lawford and Jim Hutton. In each series Queen talked to the home audience at the show's climax to see if they were able to identify the killer. Future series were titled "Ellery Queen" and "The Further Adventures of Ellery Queen." The last telecast aired on Sept 5, 1976.

BATTLE OF HASTINGS: ANNIVERSARY. Oct 14, 1066. The Anglo-Saxon age came to an end with the death of King Harold Godwinson and the defeat of English forces by Norman invaders at Hastings on this day. William, Duke of Normandy, led the daring invasion and was crowned King of England Dec 25 of that year.

BE BALD AND BE FREE DAY. Oct 14. For those who are bald and who either do wear or do not wear a wig or toupee, this is the day to go "shiny" and be proud. Annually, Oct 14. (©2006 by WH.) For info: Thomas & Ruth Roy, Wellcat Holidays, 2418 Long Ln, Lebanon, PA 17046. Phone: (717) 279-0184. E-mail: info@wellcat.com. Web: www.wellcat.com.

DE VALERA, EAMON: BIRTH ANNIVERSARY. Oct 14, 1882. Irish statesman, born at New York, NY. A revolutionary who survived the Easter Rising in 1916, De Valera went on to found the Fianna Fáil political party, which came to power in 1932 and by 1937 was successful in declaring the Free State of Ireland. As leader of Fianna Fáil, De Valera served as Ireland's prime minister three times and as president from 1959 to 1973. He died Aug 29, 1975, at Dublin, Ireland.

EAST TEXAS YAMBOREE. Oct 14–17. Gilmer, TX. Est attendance: 100,000. For info: Joan Small, Exec Dir, Gilmer Area Chamber of Commerce, Box 854, Gilmer, TX 75644. Phone: (903) 843-2413 or (903) 843-3981. Fax: (903) 843-3759. E-mail: upchamber@aol.com. Web: www.yamboree.com.

EISENHOWER, DWIGHT DAVID: BIRTH ANNIVERSARY. Oct 14, 1890. The 34th president of the US, Dwight David Eisenhower, was born at Denison, TX. Serving two terms as president, Jan 20, 1953–Jan 20, 1961, Eisenhower was the first president to be baptized after taking office (Sunday, Feb 1, 1953). Nicknamed "Ike," he held the rank of five-star general of the army (resigned in 1952, and restored by act of Congress in 1961). He served as supreme commander of the Allied forces in western Europe during WWII. In his Farewell Address (Jan 17, 1961), speaking about the "conjunction of an immense military establishment and a large arms industry," he warned: "In the councils of government, we must guard against the acquisition of unwarranted influence, whether sought or unsought, by the military-industrial complex. The potential for the disastrous rise of misplaced power exists and will persist." An American hero, Eisenhower died at Washington, DC, Mar 28, 1969.

EMERGENCY NURSES DAY. Oct 14. Sponsored by the Emergency Nurses Association (ENA) since 1989, this day serves to recognize emergency nurses for their dedication, service and commitment to their patients and communities. It honors nursing professionals who provide care to those whose lives have been touched by life's tragedies. For info: Emergency Nurses Assn Headquarters, 915 Lee St, Des Plaines, IL 60016-6569. Phone: (800) 900-9659. E-mail: pr@ena.org. Web: www.ena.org.

FODOR, EUGENE: BIRTH ANNIVERSARY. Oct 14, 1905. Travel writer Eugene Fodor was born at Leva, Hungary. His first travel book was published in 1936, after which he published more than 140, bringing to them a human element previously lacking in travel books. He died Feb 18, 1991, at Torrington, CT.

GERMANY: FRANKFURT BOOK FAIR. Oct 14–18. Fairgrounds, Frankfurt. World's largest international book fair; also important event for electronic media. Best place for international rights and licenses. Open to trade for three days and to the public for two. Est attendance: 285,000. For info: Frankfurt Book Fair, Reineckstr. 3, D-60529 Frankfurt am Main, Germany. Phone: (49) 69-2102-266. Fax: (49) 69-2102-227. E-mail: info@book-fair.com. Web: www.book-fair.com.

GISH, LILLIAN: BIRTH ANNIVERSARY. Oct 14, 1893. American actress Lillian Diana Gish was born at Springfield, OH. Her film and stage career spanned more than 85 years, 100 films, the silent and sound eras of film and numerous stage productions. She was awarded an honorary Oscar in 1970 and made her last film appearance in *The Whales of August* (1987). She died Feb 27, 1993, at New York, NY.

INTERNATIONAL TOP SPINNING DAY. Oct 14. 7th annual. A worldwide top celebration. The world is a large top, spinning on its axis. Spin a top or tops wherever you are in the world today to recognize this fun and scientific fact. Sponsored by the Spinning Top & Yo-Yo Museum. Annually, the second Wednesday of October. For info: Spinning Top & Yo-Yo Museum, 533 Milwaukee Ave (Hwy 36), Burlington, WI 53105. Phone: (262) 763-3946. E-mail: thetopmuseum@hotmail.com. Web: www.topmuseum.org.

JAPAN: MEGA KENKA MATSURI or ROUGHHOUSE FESTIVAL. Oct 14–15. Himeji. Palanquin bearers jostle one another to demonstrate their skill and balance in handling their burdens.

KING AWARDED NOBEL PEACE PRIZE: 45th ANNIVERSARY. Oct 14, 1964. Martin Luther King, Jr, became the youngest recipient of the Nobel Peace Prize when awarded the honor. King donated the entire $54,000 prize money to furthering the causes of the civil rights movement.

LEE, FRANCIS LIGHTFOOT: 275th BIRTH ANNIVERSARY. Oct 14, 1734. Signer of the Declaration of Independence. Born at Westmoreland County, VA, he died Jan 11, 1797, at Richmond County, VA.

NATIONAL BRING YOUR TEDDY BEAR TO WORK DAY. Oct 14. A celebration and observation of the help, stress relief and joy that teddy bears bring into the lives of people of all ages and stages. Annually, the second Wednesday in October. For info: Susan E. Schwartz, Teddies Are the Answer, 454 26th Ave, San Mateo, CA 94403. Phone: (650) 345-4944. E-mail: suwho2@rcn.com.

PENN, WILLIAM: BIRTH ANNIVERSARY. Oct 14, 1644. Founder of Pennsylvania, born at London, England. Penn died July 30, 1718, at Buckinghamshire, England. Presidential Proclamation 5284 of Nov 28, 1984, conferred honorary citizenship of the US upon William Penn and his second wife, Hannah Callowhill Penn. They were the third and fourth persons to receive honorary US citizenship (following Winston Churchill and Raoul Wallenberg).

SOUND BARRIER BROKEN: ANNIVERSARY. Oct 14, 1947. Flying a Bell X-1 at Muroc Dry Lake Bed, CA, Air Force pilot Chuck Yeager broke the sound barrier, ushering in the era of supersonic flight.

SOUTH CAROLINA STATE FAIR. Oct 14–25 (tentative). Columbia, SC. Conklin shows, rides, musical entertainment, food booths and children's activities. Est attendance: 576,000. For info: South Carolina State Fair, PO Box 393, Columbia, SC 29202. Phone: (803) 799-3387. Fax: (803) 799-1760. E-mail: geninfo@scstatefair.org. Web: www.scstatefair.org.

UNITED NATIONS: INTERNATIONAL DAY FOR NATURAL DISASTER REDUCTION. Oct 14. The General Assembly made this designation for the second Wednesday of October each year as part of its efforts to foster international cooperation in reducing the loss of life, property damage and social and economic disruption caused by natural disasters. For info: United Nations, Dept of Public Info, New York, NY 10017. Web: www.un.org.

 Birthdays Today

Harry Anderson, 57, actor ("Night Court," "Dave's World"), born Newport, RI, Oct 14, 1952.

Beth Daniel, 53, Hall of Fame golfer, born Charleston, SC, Oct 14, 1956.

John Dean, 71, lawyer (White House counsel during Watergate), born Akron, OH, Oct 14, 1938.

Greg Evigan, 56, actor ("B.J. and the Bear," "Masquerade"), born South Amboy, NJ, Oct 14, 1953.

Gary Graffman, 81, pianist, born New York, NY, Oct 14, 1928.

Charles Everett Koop, 93, former US Surgeon General, born Brooklyn, NY, Oct 14, 1916.

Ralph Lauren, 70, designer, born Ralph Lipschitz at the Bronx, NY, Oct 14, 1939.

Natalie Maines, 35, country singer (Dixie Chicks), born Lubbock, TX, Oct 14, 1974.

Roger Moore, 81, actor (James Bond movies, "The Saint"), born London, England, Oct 14, 1928.

Usher, 31, singer, actor ("Moesha"), born Usher Raymond IV at Chattanooga, TN, Oct 14, 1978.

October 15 — Thursday

DAY 288 | **77 REMAINING**

BIKETOBERFEST®. Oct 15–18. Daytona Beach, FL. Bikers return to Daytona Beach for that last chance to ride before winter. Rides, concerts and shows highlight the long weekend. Est attendance: 150,000. For info: Daytona Beach Area CVB, 126 E Orange Ave, Daytona Beach, FL 32114. Phone: (866) 296-8970. Fax: (386) 255-5478. E-mail: info@daytonabeach.com. Web: www.biketoberfest.org.

CANADA: TORONTO SKI, SNOWBOARD AND TRAVEL SHOW. Oct 15–18. Exhibition Place, Toronto, ON. Ski manufacturers (equipment, fashions, accessories), retailers, ski resorts, hotels, travel agencies, tourist bureaus, ski clinics and demonstrations, ski clubs, associations, movies and live entertainment. Catering to all ski disciplines—Alpine, cross-country and snowboarding. Est attendance: 35,000. For info: Canadian Natl Sportsmen's Shows, 30 Village Centre Pl, Mississauga, ON, Canada L4Z 1V9. Phone: (905) 361-2677. Fax: (905) 361-2679. Web: www.torontoskishow.com or www.snowboardshow.ca.

CHINA: BIRTHDAY OF CONFUCIUS. Oct 15. Observed on 27th day of eighth lunar month.

CHINA: CANTON AUTUMN TRADE FAIR. Oct 15–Nov 15. The Guangzhou (Canton) Autumn Trade Fair is held during the same dates each year.

CROW RESERVATION OPENED FOR SETTLEMENT: ANNIVERSARY. Oct 15, 1892. By presidential proclamation, 1.8 million acres of Crow reservation were opened to settlers. The government had induced the Crow to give up a portion of their land in the mountainous western area in the state of Montana, for which they received 50 cents per acre.

FALL CYCLE SCENE MOTORCYCLE RACES. Oct 15–18. Daytona International Speedway, Daytona Beach, FL. For info: Daytona International Speedway, PO Box 2801, Daytona Beach, FL 32120-2801. Phone: (800) PIT-SHOP. Web: www.daytonainternationalspeedway.com.

FIRST MANNED FLIGHT: ANNIVERSARY. Oct 15, 1783. Jean Francois Pilatre de Rozier and Francois Laurent, Marquis d'Arlandes, became the first people to fly when they ascended in a Montgolfier hot-air balloon at Paris, France, less than three months after the first public balloon flight demonstration (June 5, 1783), and only a year after the first experiments with small paper and fabric balloons by the Montgolfier brothers, Joseph and Jacques, in November 1782. The first manned free flight lasted about 4 minutes and carried the passengers at a height of about 84 feet. On Nov 21, 1783, they soared 3,000 feet over Paris for 25 minutes.

GALBRAITH, JOHN KENNETH: BIRTH ANNIVERSARY. Oct 15, 1908. Influential liberal economist, professor, author, diplomat and adviser to presidents Roosevelt, Kennedy and Johnson. Galbraith helped Lyndon Johnson create his Great Society programs. Galbraith's most famous book (out of 33 penned) was *The Affluent Society* (1958), in which he criticized a myopic US consumer culture that ignored community values. Born at Dunwich Township, ON, Canada, Galbraith died Apr 29, 2006, at Cambridge, MA.

GET SMART ABOUT CREDIT DAY. Oct 15. Thousands of bankers visit high schools across America today to teach youth the importance of establishing and maintaining good credit. Annually, the third Thursday of October. For info: American Bankers Assn, 1120 Connecticut Ave NW, Washington, DC 20036. Phone: (800) BANKERS. E-mail: EduFoun@aba.com. Web: www.aba.com.

"I LOVE LUCY" TV PREMIERE: ANNIVERSARY. Oct 15, 1951. This enormously popular sitcom, TV's first smash hit, starred the real-life husband-and-wife team of Cuban actor/bandleader Desi Arnaz and talented redheaded actress/comedienne Lucille Ball. They played Ricky and Lucy Ricardo, a New York bandleader and his aspiring actress/homemaker wife who was always scheming to get on stage. Costarring were William Frawley and Vivian Vance as Fred and Ethel Mertz, the Ricardos' landlords and good friends, who participated in the escapades and dealt with the consequences of Lucy's often well-intentioned plans. Famous actors guest-starred on the show, including Harpo Marx, Rock Hudson, William Holden, Hedda Hopper and John Wayne. This was the first sitcom to be filmed live before a studio audience, and it did extremely well in the ratings both the first time around and in reruns. The last telecast ran Sept 24, 1961.

INTERNATIONAL CREDIT UNION DAY. Oct 15. On Jan 17, 1927, the Credit Union League of Massachusetts celebrated the first official holiday for credit union members and staff on the birthday of Benjamin Franklin, America's apostle of thrift. In 1948, the 100th anniversary of the credit union movement, the Credit Union National Association (CUNA) set aside the third Thursday in October as the day of observance. More than 43,000 credit unions, representing 136 million people in 91 countries, celebrate the credit union difference on this day and during International Credit Union Week (Oct 12–18). For info: CUNA and Affiliates, PO Box 431, Madison, WI 53701. Phone: (800) 356-9655. Web: www.cuna.org.

JAPAN: NEWSPAPER WEEK. Oct 15–20. The Nihon Shinbun Kyokai (NSK), or The Japan Newspaper Publishers and Editors Association, sponsors this week to increase public awareness of the significance of "free and responsible newspapers" and, at the same time, to stimulate a sense of responsibility within the press. Originated in 1948. Annually, Oct 15–20. For info: NSK. Web: www.pressnet.or.jp.

MANN, MARTY: BIRTH ANNIVERSARY. Oct 15, 1904. American social activist and author was born at Chicago, IL. She was founder in 1944 of the National Committee for Education on Alcoholism and author of *A New Primer on Alcoholism*. She died at Bridgeport, CT, July 22, 1980.

MATA HARI: EXECUTION ANNIVERSARY. Oct 15, 1917. Possibly history's most famous spy, Mata Hari refused a blindfold and threw a kiss to the firing squad at her execution. See also: "Mata Hari: Birth Anniversary" (Aug 7).

NATIONAL GROUCH DAY. Oct 15. Honor a grouch; all grouches deserve a day to be recognized. Annually, Oct 15. For info: Alan R. Miller, Carter Middle School, 300 Upland Dr, Room 207, Clio, MI 48420. Phone: (810) 591-0503.

NIETZSCHE, FRIEDRICH WILHELM: BIRTH ANNIVERSARY. Oct 15, 1844. Influential German philosopher born at Rocken, Germany. Especially remembered among his philosophical beliefs are contempt for the weak and expected ultimate triumph of a superman. Nietzsche died at Weimar, Germany, Aug 25, 1900, a decade after suffering a mental breakdown.

SPACE MILESTONE: *CASSINI* (US). Oct 15, 1997. The plutonium-powered spacecraft was launched to arrive at Saturn in July 2004. It arrived on schedule, passing between the rings of the planet on June 30, 2004, and sending back photographs of the moons. It orbits the planet, continues to take pictures of its 18 known moons and dispatched a probe to Titan, the largest of these moons.

SULLIVAN, JOHN L.: BIRTH ANNIVERSARY. Oct 15, 1858. Boxer, born at Roxbury, MA. "The Great John L." was one of America's first sports heroes. He captured the world's bare-knuckle heavyweight championship on Feb 7, 1882, and went six years without defending the title. He won the last bare-knuckle fight in 1889 and then lost the title to James J. Corbett in 1892. This was the first fight in which the boxers used gloves and were governed by the Marquess of Queensberry rules. Died at Abingdon, MA, Feb 2, 1918.

✦ **WHITE CANE SAFETY DAY.** Oct 15. Presidential Proclamation always issued for Oct 15 since 1964 (PL88–628 of Oct 6, 1964).

WILSON, EDITH BOLLING GALT: BIRTH ANNIVERSARY. Oct 15, 1872. Second wife of Woodrow Wilson, 28th president of the US, born at Wytheville, VA. Died at Washington, DC, Dec 28, 1961.

WISHBONES FOR PETS. Oct 15–Nov 30. This is a voluntary program designed for professional pet sitters to host a pet goods or fund drive in their community around Thanksgiving with all proceeds going to their favorite local pet-related charity. For info: Janet Depathy, Wishbones for Pets, PO Box 777, Plymouth, MA 02362. Phone: (508) 747-4259. E-mail: icpets@comcast.net. Web: www.wishbonesforpets.com.

WODEHOUSE, PELHAM GRENVILLE: BIRTH ANNIVERSARY. Oct 15, 1881. English author, lyricist ("Bill"), humorist, creator of Bertie Wooster and Jeeves. Born at Guildford, Surrey, England, P.G. Wodehouse died at Southampton, Long Island, NY, Feb 14, 1975.

Birthdays Today

Victor Banerjee, 63, actor (*A Passage to India, The Home and the World*), born Calcutta, India, Oct 15, 1946.

Paige Davis, 40, actress, television personality ("Trading Spaces"), born Philadelphia, PA, Oct 15, 1969.

Sarah Ferguson, 50, Duchess of York (former wife of Prince Andrew), born London, England, Oct 15, 1959.

Lee Iacocca, 85, former automobile executive (Ford and Chrysler), born Allentown, PA, Oct 15, 1924.

Tito Jackson, 56, singer, musician (Jackson 5), born Toriano Adaryll Jackson at Gary, IN, Oct 15, 1953.

Linda Lavin, 70, actress (Tony for *Broadway Bound*; "Alice"), born Portland, ME, Oct 15, 1939.

Penny Marshall, 67, director (*Big, A League of Their Own*), actress ("Laverne & Shirley"), born New York, NY, Oct 15, 1942.

James Alvin (Jim) Palmer, 64, Hall of Fame baseball player, sportscaster, born New York, NY, Oct 15, 1945.

October 2009

S	M	T	W	T	F	S
				1	2	3
4	5	6	7	8	9	10
11	12	13	14	15	16	17
18	19	20	21	22	23	24
25	26	27	28	29	30	31

October 16 — Friday

DAY 289 — 76 REMAINING

AMERICA'S FIRST DEPARTMENT STORE: ANNIVERSARY. Oct 16, 1868. Salt Lake City, UT. America's first department store, "ZCMI" (Zion's Co-Operative Mercantile Institution), is still operating at Salt Lake City (although under a new name and new ownership). It was founded under the direction of Brigham Young.

APPLE BUTTER STIRRIN'. Oct 16–18. Coshocton, OH. With more than 100 crafters, this invitational craft festival celebrates the sights, sounds and scents of autumn. Smell the fresh apple butter simmering over an open fire; cooking demonstrations as you stroll through the street to the tunes of bluegrass and old-time music. Cooking demonstrations, craft auction, hog calling contest, quilt raffle, living history tours, canal boat rides, children's activities and more. Annually, the third weekend of October. Est attendance: 37,000. For info: Roscoe Village Foundation, 600 N Whitewoman St, Coshocton, OH 43812. Phone: (800) 877-1830 or (740) 622-9310. Fax: (740) 623-6555. E-mail: rvmarketing@roscoevillage.com. Web: www.roscoevillage.com.

BEN-GURION, DAVID: BIRTH ANNIVERSARY. Oct 16, 1886. First prime minister of the state of Israel. Born at Plonsk, Poland; died at Tel Aviv, Israel, Dec 1, 1973.

CRAFTSMEN'S CLASSIC ARTS & CRAFTS FESTIVAL. Oct 16–18. Dulles Expo and Convention Center, Chantilly, VA. 14th annual. Features work from more than 400 talented artists and craftspeople. All juried exhibitors' work has been handmade by the exhibitors and must be their own original design and creation. See the creative process in action, with several exhibitors demonstrating throughout the weekend. Something for every style, taste, and budget with items from the most contemporary to the most traditional. Est attendance: 30,000. For info: Gilmore Enterprises, Inc, 3514-A Drawbridge Pkwy, Greensboro, NC 27410-8584. Phone: (336) 282-5550. E-mail: contact@gilmoreshows.com. Web: www.CraftShow.com or www.gilmoreshows.com.

CRIMEAN WAR: ANNIVERSARY. Oct 16, 1853. The Ottoman Empire declared war on Russia on this day to stem Russian expansionist policies in the empire. Britain, France and parts of Italy allied themselves with the Turks against Russia. A battle in this war was immortalized in Tennyson's poem "The Charge of the Light Brigade." Health conditions for soldiers were scandalous, leading Florence Nightingale to work in the British hospital at Istanbul. This was the first war to be observed firsthand by newspaper reporters and photographers.

DICTIONARY DAY. Oct 16. The birthday of Noah Webster, American teacher and lexicographer, is occasion to encourage every person to acquire at least one dictionary—and to use it regularly.

DOUGLAS, WILLIAM ORVILLE: BIRTH ANNIVERSARY. Oct 16, 1898. American jurist, world traveler, conservationist, outdoorsman and author. Born at Maine, MN, he served as justice of the US Supreme Court longer than any other (36 years). Died at Washington, DC, Jan 19, 1980.

FALL FESTIVAL OF LEAVES. Oct 16–18. Bainbridge, Ross County, OH. Celebrating the beauty of the season and region. Folk arts, crafts, music, antique car show, log sawing contest, flea markets and parades. To obtain a map of self-guided scenic tours send SASE to sponsor. For info: Fall Festival of Leaves, Box 571, Bainbridge, Ross County, OH 45612. Phone: (740) 634-3173. Web: www.fallfestivalofleaves.com.

FIRST BIRTH CONTROL CLINIC OPENED: ANNIVERSARY. Oct 16, 1916. Margaret Sanger, Fania Mindell and Ethel Burne opened the first birth control clinic in the US at 46 Amboy St, Brooklyn, NY. Sanger believed that the poor should be able to control the size of their families.

GHOST TALES OF THE CIVIL WAR. Oct 16–17 (also Oct 23–24). President Benjamin Harrison Home, Indianapolis, IN. Tour the home of the 23rd president and experience the spirits from the battlefields of the Civil War. Est attendance: 600. For info: President Benjamin Harrison Home, 1230 N Delaware St, Indianapolis, IN 46202. Phone: (317) 631-1888. Fax: (317) 632-5488. E-mail: harrison@presidentbenjaminharrison.org. Web: www.pbhh.org.

JOHN BROWN'S RAID: 150th ANNIVERSARY. Oct 16, 1859. White abolitionist John Brown, with a band of about 20 men, seized the US Arsenal at Harpers Ferry, WV. Brown was captured and the insurrection put down by Oct 19. Brown was hanged at Charles Town, WV, Dec 2, 1859.

MARIE ANTOINETTE: EXECUTION ANNIVERSARY. Oct 16, 1793. Queen Marie Antoinette, whose extravagance and "let them eat cake" attitude toward the starving French underclass made her a target of the French Revolution, was beheaded on this date.

MILLION MAN MARCH: ANNIVERSARY. Oct 16, 1995. Hundreds of thousands of black men met at Washington, DC, for a "holy day of atonement and reconciliation" organized by Louis Farrakhan, leader of the Nation of Islam. Marchers pledged to take responsibility for themselves, their families and their communities.

NATIONAL MAMMOGRAPHY DAY. Oct 16. On this day, or throughout the month of October, radiologists provide discounted or free screening mammograms. Annually, the third Friday of October. For info: Web: www.nbcam.org.

NORTH CAROLINA STATE FAIR. Oct 16–25. State Fairgrounds, Raleigh, NC. Agricultural fair with livestock, arts and crafts, home arts, entertainment and carnival. Est attendance: 750,000. For info: North Carolina State Fair, 1025 Blue Ridge Blvd, Raleigh, NC 27607. Phone: (919) 821-7400. Fax: (919) 733-5079. Web: www.ncstatefair.org.

NORTHERN IRELAND: BELFAST FESTIVAL AT QUEEN'S. Oct 16–31. Queen's University, Belfast, County Antrim. International festival of the arts that includes theater, dance, opera and all types of music from folk to rock and pop to classical. Est attendance: 70,000. For info: Belfast Fest at Queen's, Queen's University, University Rd, Belfast, Northern Ireland BT7 1NN. Phone: 44289066 7687. Fax: 442890663733. Web: www.qub.ac.uk/festival or www.belfastfestival.com.

O'NEILL, EUGENE GLADSTONE: BIRTH ANNIVERSARY. Oct 16, 1888. American playwright (*Long Day's Journey into Night, The Iceman Cometh, Ah! Wilderness*), recipient of Pulitzer and Nobel prizes. Born at New York, NY, he died at Boston, MA, Nov 27, 1953.

PENNSYLVANIA ARTS & CRAFTS CHRISTMAS FESTIVAL. Oct 16–18 (also Oct 24–25). Washington County Fairgrounds, Washington, PA. More than 200 exhibits of handcrafted furniture, gift items, children's toys, dolls, dried floral arrangements and clothing. Holiday food and entertainment. Est attendance: 18,000. For info: Debbie & Dave Stoner, Family Festivals Assn, Inc, PO Box 166, Irwin, PA 15642. Phone: (724) 863-4577. Fax: (724) 863-5427. E-mail: familyfestivals@hotmail.com. Web: www.familyfestivals.com.

SUWANNEE RIVER QUILT SHOW AND SALE. Oct 16–18. Stephen Foster Folk Culture Center State Park, White Springs, FL. More than 200 quilts will be exhibited including traditional bed quilts, art quilts, children's quilts and antique quilts as quilters gather to share their work. Workshops, keynote speakers and demonstrations are part of the fun. For info: Kelly Green, Stephen Foster Folk Culture Center State Park, PO Drawer G, White Springs, FL 32096. Phone: (386) 397-4478. Fax: (386) 397-4262. E-mail: kelly.green@dep.state.fl.us. Web: www.floridastateparks.org/stephenfoster.

UNITED NATIONS: WORLD FOOD DAY. Oct 16. Annual observance to heighten public awareness of the world food problem and to strengthen solidarity in the struggle against hunger, malnutrition and poverty. Date of observance is anniversary of founding of Food and Agriculture Organization (FAO), Oct 16, 1945, at Quebec, Canada. For info: United Nations, Dept of Public Info, New York, NY 10017. Web: www.un.org.

WAR CRIMINALS (GERMAN) EXECUTION: ANNIVERSARY. Oct 16, 1946. The War Crimes Trials of Berlin and Nuremberg had sentenced 12 of the 22 defendants to death by hanging. They were: Hermann Goering, Joachim von Ribbentrop, Wilhelm Keitel, Ernst Kaltenbrunner, Alfred Rosenberg, Hans Frank, Wilhelm Frick, Julius Streicher, Fritz Sauckel, Alfred Jodl, Martin Bormann and Arthur von Seyss-Inquart. Goering committed suicide a few hours before his scheduled execution, and Martin Bormann had not been found (he was tried in absentia). The remaining 10 were hanged at Nuremberg Prison on this date.

WEBSTER, NOAH: BIRTH ANNIVERSARY. Oct 16, 1758. American teacher and journalist whose name became synonymous with the word *dictionary* after his compilations of the earliest American dictionaries of the English language. Born at West Hartford, CT, he died at New Haven, CT, May 28, 1843.

WILDE, OSCAR: BIRTH ANNIVERSARY. Oct 16, 1854. Irish wit, poet and playwright Oscar Fingal O'Flahertie Wills Wilde was born at Dublin, Ireland. At the height of his career he was imprisoned for two years on a morals offense, during which time he wrote "A Ballad of Reading Gaol." Best known of his plays is *The Importance of Being Earnest.* "We are all in the gutter," he wrote in *Lady Windermere's Fan*, "but some of us are looking at the stars." Wilde died at Paris, France, Nov 30, 1900.

WORLD FOOD DAY. Oct 16. To increase awareness, understanding and informed action on hunger. Annually, on the founding date of the UN Food and Agriculture Organization. For info: Patricia Young, Natl Coordinator, US Natl Committee for World Food Day, 2175 K St NW, Washington, DC 20437. Phone: (202) 653-2404. Web: www.worldfooddayusa.org.

YALE UNIVERSITY FOUNDED: ANNIVERSARY. Oct 16, 1701. (Old Style date.) The Collegiate School was founded at Branford, CT, by Congregationalists dissatisfied with the growing liberalism at Harvard. In 1716, the school was moved to New Haven, CT, where it became Yale College, named after Elihu Yale, a governor of the East India Company. The first degrees were awarded in 1716. Yale became a university in 1887. Founded as a school for men, Yale began admitting women undergraduates in 1969.

Birthdays Today

Melissa Louise Belote, 53, Olympic gold medal swimmer, born Washington, DC, Oct 16, 1956.

Manute Bol, 47, former basketball player, born Gogrial, Sudan, Oct 16, 1962.

Barry Corbin, 69, actor ("Northern Exposure," *Stir Crazy, Any Which Way You Can*), born Dawson County, TX, Oct 16, 1940.

Juan Gonzalez, 40, baseball player, born Vaga Baja, Puerto Rico, Oct 16, 1969.

Gunter Grass, 82, author (*The Tin Drum, Dog Years*), born Danzig, Germany, Oct 16, 1927.

Paul Kariya, 35, hockey player, born Vancouver, BC, Canada, Oct 16, 1974.

Angela Lansbury, 84, actress ("Murder She Wrote," *National Velvet*; Tony for *Sweeney Todd*), born London, England, Oct 16, 1925.

Kellie Martin, 34, actress ("Life Goes On," "ER"), born Riverside, CA, Oct 16, 1975.

John Mayer, 32, singer, born Bridgeport, CT, Oct 16, 1977.

Tim Robbins, 51, actor (Oscar for *Mystic River*; *The Player*), director, born West Covina, CA, Oct 16, 1958.

Suzanne Somers, 63, actress ("Three's Company," "Step by Step," *American Graffiti*), born San Bruno, CA, Oct 16, 1946.

Kordell Stewart, 37, football player, born New Orleans, LA, Oct 16, 1972.

Bob Weir, 62, musician (The Grateful Dead), born San Francisco, CA, Oct 16, 1947.

October 2009

S	M	T	W	T	F	S
				1	2	3
4	5	6	7	8	9	10
11	12	13	14	15	16	17
18	19	20	21	22	23	24
25	26	27	28	29	30	31

October 17 — Saturday

DAY 290 — 75 REMAINING

AMERICAN DIETETIC ASSOCIATION FOOD & NUTRITION CONFERENCE & EXPO. Oct 17–20. Denver, CO. Est attendance: 10,000. For info: Public Relations, American Dietetic Assn, 120 S Riverside Plaza, Ste 2000, Chicago, IL 60606-6995. Phone: (312) 899-0040. Fax: (312) 899-0008. E-mail: mtgsinfo@eatright.org. Web: www.eatright.org.

APPLE DAY AT STONEWALL JACKSON HOUSE. Oct 17. Stonewall Jackson House, Lexington, VA. Families can enjoy watching apple cider being made from a hand-cranked press, make crafts, play old-fashioned games and enjoy music popular in the nineteenth century. Est attendance: 500. For info: Stonewall Jackson House, 8 E Washington St, Lexington, VA 24450. Phone: (540) 463-2552. E-mail: development@stonewalljackson.org. Web: www.stonewalljackson.org.

ARTHUR, JEAN: BIRTH ANNIVERSARY. Oct 17, 1900. American actress Jean Arthur was born Gladys Georgianna Greene at Plattsburg, NY. Her films included *Mr Deeds Goes to Town* (1936), *Mr Smith Goes to Washington* (1939) and *Shane* (1953). She died June 19, 1991, at Carmel, CA.

BRIDGE DAY. Oct 17. New River Gorge Bridge, Fayetteville, WV. 30th annual. World's biggest extreme sports event and West Virginia's largest festival. Up to 500 BASE jumpers leap off North America's longest single span bridge at a height of 876 feet. Annually, the third Saturday in October. Est attendance: 100,000. For info: Fayette County Chamber of Commerce, 310 Oyler Av, Oak Hill, WV 25901. Phone: (800) 927-0263 or (304) 465-5617. Web: www.newrivercvb.com or www.officialbridgeday.com.

COMMUNITY AFFAIR. Oct 17. Menomonee Falls High School, Menomonee Falls, WI. Community League's 27th annual fair features timeless treasures and today's trends. More than 100 exhibitors; Country Luncheon of homemade food and desserts; quilt raffle; "Pastries 'n' More" and silent auction. Admission charged. Est attendance: 4,000. For info: Jeanne Verbsky, Community League, Inc, Publicity—ACA, PO Box 973, Menomonee Falls, WI 53052. Phone: (414) 297-9446. E-mail: cleague@communityleague.com. Web: www.communityleague.com.

DEUTSCH COUNTRY DAYS. Oct 17–18. Luxenhaus Farm, Marthasville, MO. 28th annual. An authentic re-creation of early German life in Missouri as 80 costumed artisans demonstrate log hewing, *kloppolei*, beekeeping, broom making, wood turning, quilting and more. Period music, meals, a sorghum press driven by Missouri mules and a steam-powered sawmill add to the festivities. Est attendance: 9,000. For info: Deutsch Country Days, Historic Luxenhaus Farm, 18055 State Hwy O, Marthasville, MO 63357. Phone: (636) 433-5669. E-mail: info@deutschcountrydays.org. Web: www.deutschcountrydays.org.

EIGHTEENTH-CENTURY AUTUMN MARKET FAIR. Oct 17–18. McLean, VA. Crafts, games, music and dancing. Period food and wares. Est attendance: 3,500. For info: Claude Moore Colonial Farm at Turkey Run, 6310 Georgetown Pike, McLean, VA 22101. Phone: (703) 442-7557. Fax: (703) 442-0714. Web: www.1771.org.

EWING, BUCK: 150th BIRTH ANNIVERSARY. Oct 17, 1859. William Buckingham (Buck) Ewing, Baseball Hall of Fame catcher, born at Hoagland, OH. Ewing was one of the best catchers of the 19th century and is credited by some with being the first to crouch immediately under the batter. Inducted into the Hall of Fame in 1939. Died at Cincinnati, OH, Oct 20, 1906.

FOOD AND DRUG INTERACTION EDUCATION AND AWARENESS WEEK. Oct 17–24. This campaign has been designed to help educate health professionals, patients and consumers about the problems of certain foods mixed with prescription drugs, over-the-counter drugs and herbal/alternative medicines. There is a $15 charge for kit materials. For info: Fred Mayer, Pharmacists Planning Service, Inc, 101 Lucas Valley Rd, Ste 382, San Rafael, CA 94903. Phone: (415) 479-8628. Fax: (415) 479-8608. E-mail: ppsi@aol.com. Web: www.ppsinc.org.

GRAND MILITIA MUSTER. Oct 17. St. Mary's City, MD. Seventeenth-century military reenactment gathering. Tacticals, contests of skill and camp-life demonstrations. Est attendance: 500. For info: Historic St. Mary's City, PO Box 39, St. Mary's City, MD 20686. Phone: (240) 895-4990 or (800) SMC-1634. Fax: (240) 895-4968. Web: www.stmaryscity.org.

HAMMON, JUPITER: BIRTH ANNIVERSARY. Oct 17, 1711. America's first published black poet, whose birth anniversary is celebrated annually as Black Poetry Day, was born into slavery, probably at Long Island, NY. He was taught to read, however, and as a trusted servant was allowed to use his master's library. On Dec 25, 1760, Jupiter Hammon, then 49, published the 88-line broadside poem "An Evening Thought," and thus became the first black in America to publish poetry. Hammon died around 1806. The exact date and place of his death are unknown.

HASSAM, CHILDE: 150th BIRTH ANNIVERSARY. Oct 17, 1859. Artist who brought French impressionism to America. Born at Boston, MA, Hassam's luminous works featured scenes of New York City. He died Aug 17, 1935, at East Hampton, NY.

"THE HOLLYWOOD SQUARES" TV PREMIERE: ANNIVERSARY. Oct 17, 1966. On this game show, nine celebrities sat in a giant grid. Two contestants played tic-tac-toe by determining if an answer given by a celebrity was correct. Peter Marshall hosted the show for many years with panelists Paul Lynde, Rose Marie, Cliff Arquette, Wally Cox, John Davidson and George Gobel among others. John Davidson took over as host in 1986 for a new version of the game show with Joan Rivers and, later, Shadoe Stevens at center square. In 1998 "Hollywood Squares" appeared again with Tom Bergeron as host and Whoopi Goldberg as the center square.

INDIA: DIWALI (DEEPAVALI). Oct 17. Diwali, the five-day festival of lights that begins today, is the prettiest of all Indian festivals. It celebrates the return of Lord Rama to Ayodhya after a 14-year exile. Thousands of flickering lights illuminate houses and transform urban landscapes while fireworks add color and noise. The goddess of wealth, Lakshmi, is worshipped in Hindu homes on Diwali. Houses are whitewashed and cleaned and elaborate designs drawn on thresholds with colored powder to welcome the fastidious goddess. Because there is no one universally accepted Hindu calendar, this holiday may be celebrated on a different date in some parts of India, but it always falls in the months of October or November.

JOHNSON, RICHARD MENTOR: BIRTH ANNIVERSARY. Oct 17, 1780. Ninth vice president of the US (1837–41). Born at Floyd's Station, KY. Died at Frankfort, KY, Nov 19, 1850.

MILLER, ARTHUR: BIRTH ANNIVERSARY. Oct 17, 1915. Born at New York, NY, Miller began writing plays in college and also published several novels and collections of short stories. He won the Pulitzer Prize in 1949 for *Death of a Salesman*, one of the most significant works in American literature. The play won the Tony Award twice: once in 1949, and again in 1999 when it won for Best Revival. Miller also received a Tony for *The Crucible*, a drama about the Salem witch trials, and a lifetime achievement award in 1999. He was married to actress Marilyn Monroe in the 1950s and wrote the 1963 play *After the Fall* about their relationship. Miller died at Roxbury, CT, Feb 11, 2005.

MISSOURI DAY FESTIVAL. Oct 17–18. North Central Missouri Fairgrounds, Trenton, MO. Annual festival in conjunction with high school marching band competitions. Features a parade, car show, baby show, quilt show, craft booths, flea market, food vendors and entertainment of all kinds. Est attendance: 20,000. For info: Missouri Day Festival, Trenton Chamber of Commerce, 617 Main, Trenton, MO 64683. Phone: (660) 359-4324. E-mail: trentonchamber@grundyec.net.

MULLIGAN DAY. Oct 17. A day for giving yourself or another a second chance; a day for a "do-over." For info: C. Daniel Rhodes, 1900 Crossvine Rd, Hoover, AL 65244. Phone: (205) 908-6781. E-mail: rhodan@charter.net.

POPE JOHN PAUL I: BIRTH ANNIVERSARY. Oct 17, 1912. Albino Luciani, 263rd pope of the Roman Catholic Church. Born at Forno di Canale, Italy, he was elected pope Aug 26, 1978. Died at Rome, 34 days after his election, Sept 28, 1978. Shortest papacy since Pope Leo XI (Apr 1–27, 1605).

QUINCY PRESERVES FALL ARCHITECTURAL TOUR. Oct 17. Quincy, IL. Tour historic homes decked out in their finest. Homes range in size from Quincy's grandest mansions to quaint cottages. Inside each home, ticket holders are awed by the architectural splendors. 10AM–4PM. Annually, the third Saturday in October. Est attendance: 1,000. For info: Fran Cook, Quincy Preserves, 310 S 16th St, Quincy, IL 62301. Phone: (217) 224-2587.

ROMP IN THE SWAMP FUN WALK. Oct 17. Gordon Bubolz Nature Preserve, Appleton, WI. Choose to hike ¼-, 1½-, 2½- or 4-mile distances on the preserve's beautiful trail system. Food and activities at rest stops along the way. Est attendance: 600. For info: Cindy Mueller, Program Coordinator, Gordon Bubolz Nature Preserve, 4815 N Lynndale Dr, Appleton, WI 54913. Phone: (920) 731-6041. Fax: (920) 731-9593. E-mail: info@bubolzpreserve.org.

SAINT MARY'S COUNTY OYSTER FESTIVAL. Oct 17–18. Fairgrounds, Leonardtown, MD. Oysters served every style, national oyster-shucking contest and national oyster cook-off. Est attendance: 18,000. For info: David L. Taylor, Admin, Oyster Fest Office, Box 766, California, MD 20619-0766. Phone: (301) 863-5015. Fax: (301) 863-7789. Web: www.usoysterfest.com.

SAN FRANCISCO 1989 EARTHQUAKE: 20th ANNIVERSARY. Oct 17, 1989. The San Francisco Bay area was rocked by an earthquake registering 7.1 on the Richter scale at 5:04 PM, EDT, just as the nation's baseball fans settled in to watch the 1989 World Series at Candlestick Park. A large audience was tuned in to the pregame coverage when the quake hit and knocked the broadcast off the air. The quake caused damage estimated at $10 billion and killed 67 people, many of whom were caught in the collapse of the double-decked Interstate 80, at Oakland, CA.

SWEETEST DAY. Oct 17. Around 1922, a candy company employee named Herbert Birch Kingston decided that it would be a wonderful thing to distribute candy to the sick, shut-ins and orphans of Cleveland, OH. Thus, Sweetest Day was born. Do something nice for someone today, something that will make him or her say, "Oh, that's so sweet!" Annually, the third Saturday in October.

300 MILLIONTH AMERICAN BORN: ANNIVERSARY. Oct 17, 2006. The US Census Bureau reported that the 300 millionth American would be born in the early hours of Oct 17, 2006. A baby girl born in Chicago, IL, at 5:58 AM was probably that American—although there was a margin of error of a few hours. The US population now increases by one every 11 seconds. The 200 millionth American was born Nov 20, 1967.

TRAIL OF HISTORY. Oct 17–18. Glacial Park, Ringwood, IL. Experience what life was like in the Northwest Territory from 1670 to 1850. Each step takes you back in time as more than 100 period re-enactors and encampments greet you at each stop along the Trail. Walk the Trail of History and experience traces of the past with live entertainment, jugglers, military demonstrations and hands-on activities. Annually, the third weekend in October. Est attendance: 10,000. For info: McHenry County Conservation District, 18410 US Hwy 14, Woodstock, IL 60098. Phone: (815) 338-6223. E-mail: mccd@MCCDistrict.org. Web: www.MCCDistrict.org.

UNITED NATIONS: INTERNATIONAL DAY FOR THE ERADICATION OF POVERTY. Oct 17. The General Assembly proclaimed this observance (Res 47/196) to promote public awareness of the need to eradicate poverty and destitution in all countries, particularly the developing nations. For info: United Nations, Dept of Public Info, New York, NY 10017. Web: www.un.org.

WISCONSIN DELLS AUTUMN HARVEST FEST. Oct 17–18. Wisconsin Dells, WI. Celebrate the 12th annual event with activities including scarecrow stuffing, pumpkin decorating, an arts and crafts fair, farmer's market, hay and pony rides, live entertainment, microbrew tasting and more. Est attendance: 25,000. For info: Wisconsin Dells Visitor & Convention Bureau, PO Box 390, Wisconsin Dells, WI 53965. Phone: (800) 223-3557. E-mail: info@wisdells.com. Web: www.wisdells.com.

WOOLLY WORM FESTIVAL. Oct 17–18. Banner Elk, NC. Annual woolly worm races, mountain entertainment, crafts and food. Third full weekend in October. Est attendance: 25,000. For info: Chamber of Commerce, PO Box 335, Banner Elk, NC 28604. Phone: (828) 898-5605. Fax: (828) 898-8287. E-mail: chamber@averycounty.com. Web: www.averycounty.com.

YORKTOWN VICTORY CELEBRATION. Oct 17–18. Yorktown Victory Center, Yorktown, VA. Military life and artillery demonstrators mark the 228th anniversary of America's climactic victory at Yorktown. To experience Continental Army life firsthand, visitors may enroll in "A School for the Soldier," where they can try on uniforms, drill with wooden muskets and join in other hands-on military activities. Special programs also are held at Yorktown Battlefield, administered by the National Park Service. For info: Jamestown-Yorktown Foundation, PO Box 1607, Williamsburg, VA 23187. Phone: (757) 253-4838 or toll-free (888) 593-4682. Fax: (757) 253-5299. Web: www.historyisfun.org.

October 2009	S	M	T	W	T	F	S
					1	2	3
	4	5	6	7	8	9	10
	11	12	13	14	15	16	17
	18	19	20	21	22	23	24
	25	26	27	28	29	30	31

Birthdays Today

Ernie Els, 40, golfer, born Johannesburg, South Africa, Oct 17, 1969.

Eminem, 37, musician, rapper, actor, born Marshall Bruce Mathers III at Kansas City, MO, Oct 17, 1972.

Beverly Garland, 83, actress ("My Three Sons," "Port Charles"), born Beverly Fessenden at Santa Cruz, CA, Oct 17, 1926.

Mae Jemison, 53, scientist, astronaut, born Decatur, AL, Oct 17, 1956.

Margot Kidder, 61, actress (Lois Lane in *Superman* movies), born Yellowknife, NT, Canada, Oct 17, 1948.

Norm Macdonald, 46, comedian, actor ("Saturday Night Live," "Norm"), born Quebec City, QC, Canada, Oct 17, 1963.

Michael McKean, 62, actor ("Laverne & Shirley," *This Is Spinal Tap*), born New York, NY, Oct 17, 1947.

Richard Roeper, 50, newspaper columnist, film reviewer ("Ebert & Roeper and the Movies"), born Chicago, IL, Oct 17, 1959.

George Wendt, 61, actor ("Cheers," "The Naked Truth"), born Chicago, IL, Oct 17, 1948.

October 18 — Sunday

DAY 291 — 74 REMAINING

AIDS WALK ATLANTA. Oct 18. Piedmont Park, Atlanta, GA. AIDS Walk Atlanta is a 10-kilometer fundraising walkathon benefiting AID Atlanta and other AIDS service and education providers around metro Atlanta. Annually, the third Sunday in October. Est attendance: 15,000. For info: AIDS Walk Atlanta, 1605 Peachtree St NE, Atlanta, GA 30309. Phone: (404) 876-9255. Fax: (404) 870-7739. E-mail: kristenp@aidswalkatlanta.com. Web: www.aidswalkatlanta.com.

ANDREE, SALOMON AUGUSTE: BIRTH ANNIVERSARY. Oct 18, 1854. Swedish explorer and balloonist born at Grenna, Sweden. His North Pole expedition of 1897 attracted world attention but ended tragically. With two companions, Andree left Spitzbergen, July 11, 1897, in a balloon, hoping to place the Swedish flag at the North Pole. The last message from Andree, borne by carrier pigeons, was dated noon, July 13, 1897. The frozen bodies of the explorers were found 33 years later by another polar expedition in the summer of 1930. Diaries, maps and exposed photographic negatives also were found. The photos were developed successfully, providing a pictorial record of the ill-fated expedition.

AZERBAIJAN: INDEPENDENCE DAY. Oct 18. National holiday. Commemorates declaration of independence from the Soviet Union in 1991.

BERGSON, HENRI: 150th BIRTH ANNIVERSARY. Oct 18, 1859. French philosopher, Nobel Prize winner and author of *Creative Evolution*, born at Paris, France. Died there Jan 4, 1941.

BROOKS, JAMES DAVID: BIRTH ANNIVERSARY. Oct 18, 1906. Born at St. Louis, MO, during the Depression Brooks worked as a muralist in the Federal Art Project of the Works Progress Administration. His best-known work of that period was "Flight," a mural on the rotunda of the Marine Air Terminal at La Guardia National Airport in New York. It was painted over during the 1950s but restored in 1980. Brooks served with the US Army from 1942 to 1945. When he returned to New York, his interest shifted to abstract expressionism. His paintings were exhibited in the historic "Ninth

Street Exhibition" as a part of the Museum of Modern Art's exhibits "Twelve Americans" and "New American Painting," among others. He died Mar 8, 1992, at Brookhaven, NY.

CANADA: PERSONS DAY. Oct 18. A day to commemorate the anniversary of the 1929 ruling that declared women to be persons in Canada. Prior to this ruling English common law prevailed ("Women are persons in matters of pains and penalties, but are not persons in matters of rights and privileges"). The celebrated cause, popularly known as the "Persons Case," was brought by five women of Alberta, Canada; leader of the courageous "Famous Five" was Emily Murphy (1868–1933). This ruling by the Judicial Committee of England's Privy Council, Oct 18, 1929, overturned a 1928 decision of the Supreme Court of Canada. Fifty years after the Persons Case decision, in 1979, the Governor General's Awards in Commemoration of the Persons Case were established to recognize deserving persons who have made outstanding contributions to the quality of life of women in Canada.

CANALETTO, GIOVANNI ANTONIO: BIRTH ANNIVERSARY. Oct 18, 1697. Italian painter Giovanni Antonio Canaletto (born Canale), who is best known for his detailed landscapes of Venice and London, was born at Venice and died there at age 70, Apr 20, 1768. He was known for his accurate use of perspective, shadow and light. He went to England in 1746 and expanded his range of subjects to include English landscapes and country homes.

FIRST NEWSPAPER COMIC STRIP: ANNIVERSARY. Oct 18, 1896. Although cartoons had appeared in newspapers for many years, the comic strip—a narrative told in cartoons over several panels—took its main form with the appearance of "The Yellow Kid Takes a Hand at Golf" in the *New York Journal*'s weekly supplement *American Humorist*. The creator was Richard Fenton Outcault. In March 1897 the *Yellow Kid Magazine* gathered the strips and became the first published collection of a comic strip—setting the stage for the first comic books in the late 1920s. See also: "Outcault, Richard Fenton: Birth Anniversary" (Jan 14).

FREEDOM FROM BULLIES WEEK. Oct 18–24. A time for courage, support, inspiration and peace for people suffering health-endangering bullying and for others who witness the mistreatment. For info: Workplace Bullying Institute, PO Box 29915, Bellingham, WA 98228. Phone: (360) 656-6630. E-mail: help@bullyinginstitute.org. Web: www.bullyinginstitute.org or www.workplacebullyinglaw.org.

LIEBLING, A.J.: BIRTH ANNIVERSARY. Oct 18, 1904. American journalist and author who said, "Freedom of the press belongs to those who own one." Abbott Joseph Liebling was born at New York, NY, and died there Dec 28, 1963.

MERCOURI, MELINA: BIRTH ANNIVERSARY. Oct 18, 1920. Greek actress and politician Melina Mercouri was born Maria Amalia Mercouri at Athens, Greece, Oct 18, 1920 or 1925 (both reported). Of her more than 70 films and plays she is best known for her role in *Never on Sunday* (1960). In 1977 she was elected to Greece's parliament and became the first woman in Greece's senior cabinet when appointed by Premier Andreas Papandreou to the position of minister of culture in 1981. She died Mar 6, 1994, at New York, NY.

MOON PHASE: NEW MOON. Oct 18. Moon enters New Moon phase at 1:33 AM, EDT.

✦ **NATIONAL CHARACTER COUNTS WEEK.** Oct 18–24. One of the greatest building blocks of character is citizen service. The future belongs to those who have the strength of character to live a life of service to others.

NATIONAL CHEMISTRY WEEK. Oct 18–24. To celebrate the contributions of chemistry to modern life and to help the public understand that chemistry affects every part of our lives. The American Chemical Society provides activities including open houses, contests, workshops, exhibits and classroom visits around the US and Puerto Rico. 2009 theme: "Chemistry—It's Elemental." 10 million participants nationwide. For info: Office of Community Activities, American Chemical Society, 1155 16th St NW, Washington, DC 20036. Phone: (800) 227-5558, ext 6097. Fax: (202) 872-4353. E-mail: ncw@acs.org. Web: www.acs.org/ncw.

✦ **NATIONAL FOREST PRODUCTS WEEK.** Oct 18–24. Presidential Proclamation always issued for the week beginning with the third Sunday in October since 1960 (PL86–753 of Sept 13, 1960).

NATIONAL SCHOOL BUS SAFETY WEEK. Oct 18–24. This week is set aside to focus attention on school bus safety—from the standpoint of the bus drivers, students and the motoring public. Annually, the third full week of October, starting on Sunday. For info: Natl Assn for Pupil Transportation, 1840 Western Ave, Albany, NY 12203. Phone: (800) 989-6278. E-mail: sbsw@napt.org. Web: www.napt.org.

"ROSEANNE" TV PREMIERE: ANNIVERSARY. Oct 18, 1988. This comedy showed the blue-collar Conner family trying to make ends meet. Rosanne played wise-cracking Roseanne Conner, John Goodman played her husband, Dan, and Laurie Metcalf played her sister, Jackie. The Conner children were played by Sara Gilbert (Darlene), Alicia Goranson and Sarah Chalke (Becky) and Michael Fishman (D.J.). The last episode aired Nov 14, 1997, but it remains popular in reruns.

SAINT LUKE: FEAST DAY. Oct 18. Patron saint of doctors and artists, himself a physician and painter; authorship of the third Gospel and Acts of the Apostles is attributed to him. Died about AD 68. Legend says that he painted portraits of Mary and Jesus.

SILVERSTEIN, SHEL: BIRTH ANNIVERSARY. Oct 18, 1932. Cartoonist and children's author, best remembered for his poetry that included *A Light in the Attic* and *The Giving Tree*. Silverstein won the Michigan Young Reader's Award for *Where the Sidewalk Ends*. Also a songwriter, he wrote "The Unicorn Song" and "A Boy Named Sue." Born at Chicago, IL, he died at Key West, FL, May 9, 1999.

TEEN READ WEEK™. Oct 18–24. The teen years are a time when many young adults reject reading as being just another dreary assignment. The goal of Teen Read Week is to encourage young adults to read for the fun of it and to remind parents, teachers, booksellers and others that reading for fun is important for teens. This week also seeks to increase awareness of the many library resources available. Thousands of school and public libraries across the US participate each year. For info: Young Adult Library Services Assn, American Library Assn, 50 E Huron St, Chicago, IL 60611. Phone: (800) 545-2433, ext 4390. E-mail: yalsa@ala.org. Web: www.ala.org/teenread.

TRUDEAU, PIERRE ELLIOTT: 90th BIRTH ANNIVERSARY. Oct 18, 1919. Prime minister of Canada 1968–79, 1980–84, born at Montreal, QC, Canada, on Oct 18, 1919, he died there Sept 28, 2000.

WATER POLLUTION CONTROL ACT: ANNIVERSARY. Oct 18, 1972. Overriding President Nixon's veto, Congress passed a $25 billion Water Pollution Control Act.

WORLD MENOPAUSE DAY. Oct 18. The World Menopause Day challenge calls on every nation to make menopausal health a principal issue in their research and public health agendas in order to help women prevent unpleasant symptoms that can affect productivity and quality of life, as well as reduce rates of osteoporosis, heart disease, colon cancer and other aging- and hormone-related diseases. For info: Intl Menopause Society, PO Box 687, Wray, Lancaster, LA2 8WY United Kingdom. Phone: (44) (1524) 221-190. Web: www.imsociety.org.

YWCA WEEK WITHOUT VIOLENCE. Oct 18–24. Celebrated the third full week in October, this annual campaign seeks to make people aware of the violence in their communities and suggest alternatives to it. For info: YWCA USA, 1015 18th St NW, Ste 1100, Washington, DC 20036. Phone: (202) 467-0801. Fax: (202) 467-0802. Web: www.ywca.org.

Birthdays Today

Chuck Berry, 83, singer, songwriter ("Johnny B. Goode," "Roll Over Beethoven"), musician, born Charles Edward Anderson at St. Louis, MO, Oct 18, 1926.

Pam Dawber, 58, actress ("Mork & Mindy," "My Sister Sam"), born Farmington, MI, Oct 18, 1951.

Mike Ditka, 70, Hall of Fame football player, former coach, sportscaster, born Carnegie, PA, Oct 18, 1939.

Zac Efron, 22, actor (*High School Musical, Hairspray*), born San Luis Obispoo, CA, Oct 18, 1987.

Wynton Marsalis, 48, jazz musician, born New Orleans, LA, Oct 18, 1961.

Terry McMillan, 58, author (*How Stella Got Her Groove Back, Waiting to Exhale*), born Port Huron, MI, Oct 18, 1951.

Erin Moran, 48, actress ("Happy Days," "Joanie Loves Chachi"), born Burbank, CA, Oct 18, 1961.

Joe Morton, 62, actor (*The Brother from Another Planet, Trouble in Mind, City of Hope*), born New York, NY, Oct 18, 1947.

Martina Navratilova, 53, former tennis player, born Martina Subertova at Prague, Czechoslovakia, Oct 18, 1956.

Ntozake Shange, 61, dramatist, poet, born Paulette L. Williams at Trenton, NJ, Oct 18, 1948.

Vincent Spano, 47, actor (*Baby, It's You; Rumblefish*), born New York, NY, Oct 18, 1962.

Jean-Claude Van Damme, 49, actor (*Kickboxer*), born Brussels, Belgium, Oct 18, 1960.

October 19 — Monday

DAY 292 | **73 REMAINING**

ALASKA DAY. Oct 19. Alaska. Anniversary of transfer of Alaska on Oct 18, 1867, from Russia to the US. The transfer became official on Sitka's Castle Hill. This is a holiday in Alaska; when it falls on a weekend it is observed on the following Monday.

BROWNE, THOMAS: BIRTH ANNIVERSARY. Oct 19, 1605. (Old Style date.) Physician, scholar and author, Thomas Browne was born at London, England. At age 55 he wrote: "The long habit of living indisposeth us for dying." His most famous work, *Religio Medici*, was published in 1642. Browne died at Norwich, England, Oct 19, 1682 (OS).

DOW JONES BIGGEST DROP: ANNIVERSARY. Oct 19, 1987. The Dow Jones Industrial Average plunged 508 points, or 22.6 percent, after frenzied selling, the largest percentage drop in history.

EVALUATE YOUR LIFE DAY. Oct 19. To encourage everyone to check and see if they're really headed where they want to be. (©2006 by WH.) For info: Thomas & Ruth Roy, Wellcat Holidays, 2418 Long Ln, Lebanon, PA 17042-0774. Phone: (717) 279-0184. E-mail: info@wellcat.com. Web: www.wellcat.com.

October 2009

S	M	T	W	T	F	S
				1	2	3
4	5	6	7	8	9	10
11	12	13	14	15	16	17
18	19	20	21	22	23	24
25	26	27	28	29	30	31

JAMAICA: NATIONAL HEROES DAY. Oct 19. National holiday established in 1969. Always observed on third Monday of October.

JEFFERSON, MARTHA WAYLES SKELTON: BIRTH ANNIVERSARY. Oct 19, 1748. Wife of Thomas Jefferson, third president of the US. Born at Charles City County, VA, she died at Monticello, VA, Sept 6, 1782.

LUMIÈRE, AUGUSTE: BIRTH ANNIVERSARY. Oct 19, 1862. Born at Besançon, France, Auguste Lumière with brother Louis were film pioneers who created the first movie, "Workers Leaving the Lumière Factory" (1895). He died at Lyon, France, on Apr 10, 1954.

NATIONAL BUSINESS WOMEN'S WEEK. Oct 19–25. Since 1928, this week celebrates the contributions of working women to American society, the economy and the family. It is commemorated nationwide by special activities. Annually, starting the third Monday in October. For info: Business and Professional Women/USA, 1620 Eye St NW, Ste 210, Washington, DC 20006. Phone: (202) 293-1100. Fax: (202) 861-0298. E-mail: editor@bpwusa.org. Web: www.bpwusa.org.

PECK, ANNIE S.: BIRTH ANNIVERSARY. Oct 19, 1850. World-renowned mountain climber Annie S. Peck won an international following in 1895 when she climbed the Matterhorn in the Swiss Alps. Peck climbed the Peruvian peak Huascaran (21,812 feet), giving her the record for the highest peak climbed in the Western Hemisphere by an American man or woman, and at age 61 she climbed Mount Coropuna in Peru (21,250 feet) and placed a "Votes for Women" banner at its pinnacle. Annie Peck died July 18, 1935, at New York City.

VIRGIN ISLANDS: HURRICANE THANKSGIVING DAY. Oct 19. Third Monday of October is a legal holiday celebrating the end of hurricane season.

YORKTOWN DAY. Oct 19. Yorktown, VA. Representatives of the US, France and other nations involved in the American Revolution gather to celebrate the anniversary of the victory (Oct 19, 1781) that assured American independence. Parade and commemorative ceremonies. Annually, Oct 19. Est attendance: 5,000. For info: Public Affairs Officer, Colonial Natl Historical Park, PO Box 210, Yorktown, VA 23690. Phone: (757) 898-2410. Web: www.nps.gov/colo.

YORKTOWN DAY: ANNIVERSARY. Oct 19, 1781. More than 7,000 English and Hessian troops, led by British general Lord Cornwallis, surrendered to General George Washington at Yorktown, VA, effectively ending the war between Britain and its American colonies. There were no more major battles, but the provisional treaty of peace was not signed until Nov 30, 1782, and the final Treaty of Paris, Sept 3, 1783.

Birthdays Today

Michael Gambon, 69, actor ("The Singing Detective," *The Cook, The Thief, His Wife & Her Lover*), born Dublin, Ireland, Oct 19, 1940.

Evander Holyfield, 47, boxer, born Atlanta, GA, Oct 19, 1962.

Patricia Ireland, 64, feminist, social activist, born Oak Park, IL, Oct 19, 1945.

John LeCarré, 78, author (*The Spy Who Came in from the Cold, The Constant Gardener*), born David John Moore Cornwell at Poole, Dorset, England, Oct 19, 1931.

John Lithgow, 64, actor (*Don Quixote, Harry & the Hendersons*, "3rd Rock from the Sun"), born Rochester, NY, Oct 19, 1945.

Peter Max, 72, artist, designer, born Berlin, Germany, Oct 19, 1937.

Ty Pennington, 44, carpenter, television personality ("Trading Spaces," "Extreme Makeover: Home Edition"), born Atlanta, GA, Oct 19, 1965.

Simon Ward, 68, actor (*The Three Musketeers, The Four Musketeers*), born London, England, Oct 19, 1941.

Michael Young, 33, baseball player, born Covina, CA, Oct 19, 1976.

October 20 — Tuesday

DAY 293 — 72 REMAINING

BIRTH OF THE BAB: ANNIVERSARY. Oct 20, 1819. Baha'i observance of anniversary of the birth in Shiraz, Persia, of Siyyid Ali Muhammad, who later took the title "the Bab"; the Bab was the prophet-herald of the Baha'i Faith. One of the nine days of the year when Baha'is suspend work. For info: Baha'is of the US, Office of Communications, 1233 Central St, Evanston, IL 60201. Phone: (847) 733-3559. Fax: (847) 733-3578. E-mail: ooc@usbnc.org. Web: www.bahai.us.

DEWEY, JOHN: 150th BIRTH ANNIVERSARY. Oct 20, 1859. American psychologist, philosopher and educational reformer born at Burlington, VT. His philosophical views of education have been termed pragmatism, instrumentalism and experimentalism. Died at New York, NY, June 1, 1952.

GUATEMALA: REVOLUTION DAY. Oct 20. Public holiday. Commemorates the overthrow of dictator Jorge Ubico Castañada in 1944.

KENYA: KENYATTA DAY. Oct 20. Public holiday.

LUGOSI, BELA: BIRTH ANNIVERSARY. Oct 20, 1882. Born Bela Ferenc Denzso Blasko at Lugos, Hungary. Known best for his role as Count Dracula in *Dracula*. Lugosi died of a heart attack at Los Angeles, CA, Aug 16, 1956.

MacARTHUR RETURNS: US LANDINGS ON LEYTE, PHILIPPINES: 65th ANNIVERSARY. Oct 20, 1944. In mid-September of 1944 American military leaders made the decision to begin the invasion of the Philippines on Leyte, a small island north of the Surigao Strait. With General Douglas MacArthur in overall command, US aircraft dropped hundreds of tons of bombs in the area of Dulag. Four divisions were landed on the east coast, and after a few hours General MacArthur set foot on Philippine soil for the first time since he was ordered to Australia Mar 11, 1942, thus fulfilling his promise, "I shall return."

MANN, JAMES ROBERT: BIRTH ANNIVERSARY. Oct 20, 1856. American lawyer and legislator, born near Bloomington, IL, Republican member of Congress from Illinois from 1896 until his death, Nov 30, 1922, at Washington, DC. Mann was the author and sponsor of the "White Slave Traffic Act," also known as the "Mann Act," passed by Congress on June 25, 1910. The act prohibited, under heavy penalties, the interstate transportation of women for immoral purposes.

MANTLE, MICKEY: BIRTH ANNIVERSARY. Oct 20, 1931. Baseball Hall of Famer, born at Spavinaw, OK. Died Aug 13, 1995, at Dallas, TX.

MISS AMERICAN ROSE DAY. Oct 20. Miss American Rose is a pageant devoted to high achievement and community service for girls and women of all ages. On this day, treat the women in your life like beautiful American roses, and/or perform a community service project. For info: Lynanne White, Miss American Rose Pageants, 19689 7th Av, PMB 323, Poulsbo, WA 98370. E-mail: miss@americanrose.com. Web: www.americanrose.com.

MOSCOW SOCCER TRAGEDY: ANNIVERSARY. Oct 20, 1982. The world's worst soccer disaster occurred at Moscow when 340 sports fans were killed during a game between Soviet and Dutch players. Details of the event, blaming police for the tragedy in which spectators were crushed to death in an open staircase, were not published until nearly seven years later (July 1989) in *Sovietsky Sport*.

ORBACH, JERRY: BIRTH ANNIVERSARY. Oct 20, 1935. Actor born at the Bronx, NY, he starred in the original Broadway productions of *The Fantasticks, 42nd Street* and *Chicago*. He won a Best Actor Tony Award for *Promises, Promises* in 1969. Films include *Dirty Dancing* and the voice of Lumiere in Disney's *Beauty and the Beast*. His most popular role was that of wisecracking homicide detective Lennie Briscoe on television's "Law & Order," a role he played from 1998 until his death at New York, NY, on Dec 28, 2004.

SATURDAY NIGHT MASSACRE: ANNIVERSARY. Oct 20, 1973. Anniversary of dramatic turning point in the Watergate affair. On Oct 20, 1973, the White House announced at 8:24 PM, EDT, that President Richard M. Nixon had discharged Archibald Cox (special Watergate prosecutor) and William B. Ruckelshaus (deputy attorney general) and that Attorney General Elliot L. Richardson had resigned. Immediate and widespread demands for impeachment of the president ensued and were not stilled until President Nixon resigned, Aug 9, 1974.

"THE SIX MILLION DOLLAR MAN" TV PREMIERE: ANNIVERSARY. Oct 20, 1973. This action-adventure series based on the novel *Cyborg* was a monthly feature on "The ABC Suspense Movie" before becoming a regular series in 1974. Lee Majors starred as astronaut Steve Austin, who, after an accident, was "rebuilt" with bionic legs, arms and an eye. He worked for the Office of Strategic Information (OSI) carrying out sensitive missions. Also in the cast were Richard Anderson, Alan Oppenheimer and Martin E. Brooks. "The Bionic Woman," starring Lindsay Wagner, was a spin-off from this show, and the two main characters were paired for several made-for-TV sequels.

SYDNEY OPERA HOUSE OPENS: ANNIVERSARY. Oct 20, 1973. One of the most iconic and dramatic man-made structures of the 20th century, the Sydney Opera House, was opened by Queen Elizabeth II at Sydney, Australia, on this date. Designed by Danish architect Jørn Utzon, the theater is perched on Sydney Harbor and appears to be a ship in full sail. It took 14 years to build, and its roof is covered with more than one million tiles.

WREN, CHRISTOPHER: BIRTH ANNIVERSARY. Oct 20, 1632. (Old Style date.) Sir Christopher Wren, English architect, astronomer and mathematician, was born at East Knoyle, Wiltshire, England. Died Feb 25, 1723 (OS), at London. His epitaph, written by his son, is inscribed over the interior of the north door at St. Paul's Cathedral, London: "Si monumentum requiris, circumspice." ("If you would see his monument, look about you.")

Birthdays Today

William Christopher, 77, actor ("M*A*S*H," *With Six You Get Eggroll*), born Evanston, IL, Oct 20, 1932.

Keith Hernandez, 56, former baseball player, born San Francisco, CA, Oct 20, 1953.

Eddie Jones, 38, basketball player, born Pompano Beach, FL, Oct 20, 1971.

John Krasinski, 30, actor ("The Office," *Leatherheads*), born Newton, MA, Oct 20, 1979.

Melanie Mayron, 57, actress (Emmy for "thirtysomething"; *Car Wash, My Blue Heaven*), born Philadelphia, PA, Oct 20, 1952.

Viggo Mortensen, 51, actor (*Eastern Promises, A History of Violence, The Lord of the Rings* trilogy), born New York, NY, Oct 20, 1958.

Tom Petty, 56, singer, songwriter, born Gainesville, FL, Oct 20, 1953.

Sheldon Whitehouse, 54, US Senator (D, Rhode Island), born New York, NY, Oct 20, 1955.

October 21 — Wednesday

DAY 294 71 REMAINING

BATTLE OF TRAFALGAR: ANNIVERSARY. Oct 21, 1805. This famous naval action between the British Royal Navy and the combined French and Spanish fleets removed the threat of Napoleon's invasion of England. The British victory, off Trafalgar on the coast of Spain, guaranteed the fame of Viscount Horatio Nelson, who died in the battle.

CARLETON, WILL: BIRTH ANNIVERSARY. Oct 21, 1845. Anniversary of the birth of poet Will Carleton, observed (by 1919 statute) in Michigan schools, where poems of Carleton must be read on this day. Best known of his poems: "Over the Hill to the Poorhouse." Carleton died in 1912.

CIRCLEVILLE PUMPKIN SHOW. Oct 21–24. Circleville, OH. More than 100,000 pounds of pumpkins, squash and gourds. Est attendance: 300,000. For info: Pumpkin Show Inc, 159 E Franklin St, Circleville, OH 43113. Phone: (740) 474-7000. Fax: (740) 474-6611. Web: www.pumpkinshow.com.

COLERIDGE, SAMUEL TAYLOR: BIRTH ANNIVERSARY. Oct 21, 1772. English poet ("The Rime of the Ancient Mariner") and essayist born at Ottery St. Mary, Devonshire, England. Died at Highgate, England, July 25, 1834. In *Table Talk*, he wrote: "I wish our clever young poets would remember my homely definitions of prose and poetry; that is, prose = words in their best order; poetry = the *best* words in the best order."

CRUZ, CELIA: 85th BIRTH ANNIVERSARY. Oct 21, 1924. The Grammy Award–winning singer was dubbed the "Queen of Salsa" by her adoring fans. Born as Celia de la Caridad Cruz Alonso at Havana, Cuba (some sources cite her birth year as 1925 or 1929), Cruz had a career spanning six decades and recorded some 70 albums. Her energetic performances were punctuated by her call of "Azucar!" ("Sugar!") and flamboyant costumes. President Bill Clinton awarded her the National Medal of Arts in 1994. Cruz died at New York, NY, on July 16, 2003.

FILLMORE, CAROLINE CARMICHAEL McINTOSH: BIRTH ANNIVERSARY. Oct 21, 1813. Second wife of Millard Fillmore, 13th president of the US, born at Morristown, NJ. Died at New York, Aug 11, 1881.

GILLESPIE, JOHN BIRKS "DIZZY": BIRTH ANNIVERSARY. Oct 21, 1917. Dizzy Gillespie, trumpet player, composer, bandleader and one of the founding fathers of modern jazz, was born at Cheraw, SC. In the early 1940s Gillespie and alto saxophonist Charlie (Yardbird) Parker created bebop. In the late '40s he created a second music revolution by incorporating Afro-Cuban music into jazz. In 1953 someone fell on Gillespie's trumpet and bent it. Finding he could hear the sound better, he kept it that way; his puffed cheeks and bent trumpet became his trademarks. He won a Grammy in 1975 for *Oscar Peterson and Dizzy Gillespie* and again in 1991 for *Live at the Royal Festival Hall.* He died Jan 6, 1993, at Englewood, NJ.

October 2009	S	M	T	W	T	F	S
					1	2	3
	4	5	6	7	8	9	10
	11	12	13	14	15	16	17
	18	19	20	21	22	23	24
	25	26	27	28	29	30	31

INCANDESCENT LAMP DEMONSTRATED: ANNIVERSARY. Oct 21, 1879. Thomas A. Edison demonstrated the first incandescent lamp that could be used economically for domestic purposes. This prototype, developed at his Menlo Park, NJ, laboratory, could burn for 13½ hours.

MISSOURI DAY. Oct 21. Observed by teachers and pupils in schools with appropriate exercises throughout state of Missouri. Annually, the third Wednesday of October.

NATIONAL SUPPORT YOUR LOCAL CHAMBER OF COMMERCE DAY. Oct 21. A day to honor the local chamber of commerce. If your company is a COC member, make a donation, upgrade your membership, recruit a new member or buy a sponsorship of a chamber ad. Join a local chamber if your company is not yet a member. Send flowers or chocolates to your local chamber office. Annually, the third Wednesday in October. For info: Joy McCarthy-Sessing, Warsaw Kosciusko Chamber of Commerce, 313 S Buffalo St, Warsaw, IN 46580. Phone: (800) 776-6311. Fax: (574) 267-7762. E-mail: jmccarthy-sessing@wkchamber.com. Web: www.wkchamber.com.

NOBEL, ALFRED BERNHARD: BIRTH ANNIVERSARY. Oct 21, 1833. Chemist and engineer who invented dynamite was born at Stockholm, Sweden, and died at San Remo, Italy, Dec 10, 1896. His will established the Nobel Prize.

OLD IRONSIDES LAUNCHED: ANNIVERSARY. Oct 21, 1797. The USS *Constitution* was launched and christened by Captain James Sever on this date at Boston, MA, making this frigate the oldest commissioned warship afloat in the world. Congress had commissioned *Constitution* and five other ships in 1794. The *Constitution* earned its nickname and place in America's heart through valiant service in the War of 1812: in a fight with Britain's HMS *Guerriere* on Aug 19, 1812, sailors reported a British shot repelled by the side of the ship and declared that its sides were made of iron. No enemy ever boarded the ship in its days of active service. It now rests at Boston Harbor. See also: "Old Ironsides Saved by Poem: Anniversary" (Sept 16).

SHAWN, TED: BIRTH ANNIVERSARY. Oct 21, 1891. Named Edwin Myers Shawn at birth, Ted Shawn was born at Kansas City, MO. Partially paralyzed by diphtheria, Shawn was introduced to ballet for therapeutic purposes and became a professional dancer by the age of 21. The Denishawn School of Dancing was established with the help of his wife, Ruth St. Denis, and became the epicenter of much innovation in 20th-century dance and choreography. Among his many achievements is Jacob's Pillow Dance Festival, which he inaugurated and directed for the remainder of his years, and such modern ballets as *Osage-Pawnee*, *Labor Symphony* and *John Brown.* He died Jan 9, 1972.

SOLTI, GEORG: BIRTH ANNIVERSARY. Oct 21, 1912. Conductor born at Budapest, Hungary. Sir Georg conducted orchestras at London (for which he was knighted), Paris and Chicago. He died at Antibes, France, Sept 5, 1997.

TACOMA HOLIDAY FOOD AND GIFT FESTIVAL. Oct 21–25. Tacoma Dome, Tacoma, WA. Arts and crafts, gifts, gourmet foods, entertainment and dining, all under the Tacoma Dome. Est attendance: 40,000. For info: Showcase Events, Inc, PO Box 2815, Kirkland, WA 98083. Phone: (425) 889-9494 or (800) 521-7469. Fax: (425) 889-8165. E-mail: tacoma@showcaseevents.org. Web: www.showcaseevents.org.

TAIWAN: OVERSEAS CHINESE DAY. Oct 21. Thousands of overseas Chinese come to Taiwan for this and other occasions that make October a particularly memorable month.

VIETNAM WAR PROTESTERS STORM PENTAGON: ANNIVERSARY. Oct 21, 1967. Some 250 protesters were arrested when thousands of the 50,000 participants in a rally against the Vietnam War at Washington, DC, crossed the Potomac River and stormed the Pentagon. No shots were fired, but many demonstrators were struck with nightsticks and rifle butts.

Birthdays Today

Elvin Bishop, 67, musician, born Glendale, CA, Oct 21, 1942.

Carrie Fisher, 53, actress (*Star Wars, Shampoo*), novelist (*Postcards from the Edge*), born Beverly Hills, CA, Oct 21, 1956.

Frances Fitzgerald, 69, journalist, author (*The Fire in the Lake*), born New York, NY, Oct 21, 1940.

Edward Charles "Whitey" Ford, 81, Hall of Fame baseball player, born New York, NY, Oct 21, 1928.

Ursula K. LeGuin, 80, author (*The Wind's Twelve Quarters, A Wizard of Earthsea*), born Berkeley, CA, Oct 21, 1929.

Ken Watanabe, 50, actor (*The Last Samurai*), born Kansaku Watanabe at Koide, Niigata, Japan, Oct 21, 1959.

October 22 — Thursday

DAY 295 | **70 REMAINING**

BEADLE, GEORGE: BIRTH ANNIVERSARY. Oct 22, 1903. Born on a farm near Wahoo, NE, Beadle began his professional career as a professor of genetics at Harvard, eventually becoming president of the University of Chicago. Dr. Beadle won many international prizes, including the Nobel Prize in Medicine in 1958 for his work in genetic research, as well as the National Award of the American Cancer Society in 1959 and the Kimber Genetica Award of the National Academy of Science in 1960. Beadle demonstrated how the genes control the basic chemistry of the living cell. Because of his work, he has been described as "the man who did most to put modern genetics on its chemical basis." Beadle died June 9, 1989, at Pomona, CA.

CAPA, ROBERT: BIRTH ANNIVERSARY. Oct 22, 1913. Born Andrei Friedmann at Budapest, Hungary, Capa was one of the great photojournalists in the 20th century, best known for his gritty, close-up battle photography from the five wars he covered in his brief life—most notably the Spanish Civil War, WWII and the early Vietnam War. His handful of images from the midst of the D-Day invasion are legendary, as is his shot of a Spanish loyalist soldier who has just been killed in 1936. Cofounder of the elite Magnum Photos agency, Capa was killed by a land mine on May 25, 1954, at Thai Binh, Vietnam.

CUBAN MISSILE CRISIS: ANNIVERSARY. Oct 22, 1962. President John F. Kennedy, in a nationwide television address Oct 22, 1962, demanded the removal from Cuba of Soviet missiles, launched equipment and bombers and imposed a naval "quarantine" to prevent further weaponry from reaching Cuba. On Oct 28, the USSR announced it would remove the weapons in question. In return, the US removed missiles from Turkey that were aimed at the USSR.

HOWARD, CURLY: BIRTH ANNIVERSARY. October 22, 1903. Howard, born Jerome Lester Horwitz at Brooklyn, NY, was the brother of Stooges Moe and Shemp. The two older brothers groomed Curly for a life in show business, and he got his big break in 1932 when brother Shemp left the Stooges. Curly took his place, and his manic style of slapstick comedy (with trademark "n'yuk-n'yuks") quickly made him popular. On May 6, 1946, while shooting his 97th Three Stooges film, Howard suffered a stroke and subsequently retired. He died Jan 18, 1952, at San Gabriel, CA.

INTERNATIONAL STUTTERING AWARENESS DAY. Oct 22. For info: National Stuttering Assn, 119 W 40th St, 14th Fl, New York, NY 10018. Phone: (800) 364-1677 or (800) WE-STUTTER. E-mail: info@WeStutter.org. Web: www.westutter.org or www.stutteringhomepage.com.

LEARY, TIMOTHY: BIRTH ANNIVERSARY. Oct 22, 1920. Timothy Francis Leary was born at Springfield, MA. Prominent psychologist and professor at Harvard, Leary became an icon of the countercultural movement in the 1960s. He lost his professorship after giving a hallucinogenic drug, psilocybin, to students. Leary was arrested numerous times, and on one occasion, while being held at a California prison, he was forced to submit to a personality test that he had designed himself several years earlier. He continued to advocate the use of LSD in the pursuit of spiritual and political freedom and simply for the fun of it, until his death, of prostate cancer, May 31, 1996, at Beverly Hills, CA.

LISZT, FRANZ: BIRTH ANNIVERSARY. Oct 22, 1811. Hungarian pianist and composer (*Hungarian Rhapsodies*). Born at Raiding, Hungary. Died July 31, 1886, at Bayreuth, Germany.

LOUISIANA YAMBILEE FESTIVAL. Oct 22–25. Evangeline Downs Racetrack and Casino, Opelousas, LA. 64th annual. Come out and support the city of Opelousas at the third oldest agricultural festival in the state of Louisiana. Fun for the entire family: sweet potato shows, cooked foods show, "yam-i-mal" contest, live music, carnival, games, junior pageants and the crowning of the 64th Louisiana Yambilee Queen. Est attendance: 15,000. For info: Brandi Smith Zeringue, Louisiana Yambilee, Inc, 1939 W Landry St, #103, Opelousas, LA 70570-2010. Phone: (337) 948-8848. Fax: (337) 948-4331. E-mail: info@yambilee.com. Web: www.yambilee.com.

METROPOLITAN OPERA HOUSE OPENING: ANNIVERSARY. Oct 22, 1883. Grand opening of the original New York Metropolitan Opera House was celebrated with a performance of Gounod's *Faust*.

RANDOLPH, PEYTON: DEATH ANNIVERSARY. Oct 22, 1775. First president of the Continental Congress, died at Philadelphia, PA. Born about 1721 (exact date unknown), at Williamsburg, VA.

STATE FAIR OF LOUISIANA. Oct 22–Nov 8. Fairgrounds, Shreveport, LA. Educational, agricultural, commercial exhibits; entertainment. Est attendance: 400,000. For info: Chris Giordano, President, Louisiana State Fairgrounds, 3701 Hudson St, Shreveport, LA 71109. Phone: (318) 635-1361. Fax: (318) 631-4909. E-mail: info@statefairoflouisiana.com. Web: www.statefairoflouisiana.com.

WORLD'S END DAY: ANNIVERSARY. Oct 22, 1844. Anniversary of the day set as the one on which the world would end by followers of William Miller, religious leader and creator of a movement known as Millerism. Stories about followers disposing of all earthly possessions and climbing to high places on that date are believed to be apocryphal. (Miller was born at Pittsfield, MA, Feb 15, 1782. Died at Low Hampton, NY, Dec 20, 1849.)

Birthdays Today

Haley Barbour, 62, Governor of Mississippi (R), born Yazoo County, MS, Oct 22, 1947.

Brian Anthony Boitano, 46, Olympic gold medal figure skater, born Mountain View, CA, Oct 22, 1963.

Jan De Bont, 66, director (*Speed, Twister*), born Amsterdam, the Netherlands, Oct 22, 1943.

Catherine Deneuve, 66, actress (*Repulsion, Indochine*), born Catherine Dorleac at Paris, France, Oct 22, 1943.

Annette Funicello, 67, singer, actress ("Mickey Mouse Club," Beach Party movies), born Utica, NY, Oct 22, 1942.

Jeff Goldblum, 57, actor (*The Big Chill, The Fly, Jurassic Park*), born Pittsburgh, PA, Oct 22, 1952.

Valeria Golino, 43, actress (*Big Top Pee-wee, Hot Shots!*), born Naples, Italy, Oct 22, 1966.

Derek Jacobi, 71, actor ("I Claudius," *The Day of the Jackal*), born London, England, Oct 22, 1938.

Christopher Lloyd, 71, actor ("Taxi," *Back to the Future* films), born Stamford, CT, Oct 22, 1938.

Tony Roberts, 70, actor (*Victor/Victoria, Annie Hall*), born New York, NY, Oct 22, 1939.

Ichiro Suzuki, 36, baseball player, born Kasugai, Japan, Oct 22, 1973.

October 23 — Friday

DAY 296 69 REMAINING

APPERT, NICOLAS: BIRTH ANNIVERSARY. Oct 23, 1752. Also known as "Canning Day," this is the anniversary of the birth of French chef, chemist, confectioner, inventor and author Nicolas Appert, at Chalons-Sur-Marne. Appert, who also invented the bouillon tablet, is best remembered for devising a system of heating foods and sealing them in airtight containers. Known as the "father of canning," Appert won a prize of 12,000 francs from the French government in 1809, and the title "Benefactor of Humanity" in 1812, for his inventions, which revolutionized our previously seasonal diet. Appert died at Massy, France, June 3, 1841.

BATTLE OF LEYTE GULF: 65th ANNIVERSARY. Oct 23–26, 1944. In response to the Allied invasion of the Philippines at Leyte, the Japanese initiated Sho-Go ("Operation Victory"), an attempt to counter the Allies' next invasion by heavy air attacks. Four carriers were sent south from Japanese waters to lure the US aircraft carriers away from Leyte Gulf. At the same time, Japanese naval forces from Singapore were sent to Brunei Bay, split up into two groups and converged on Leyte Gulf from the north and southwest. The group in the north, under Vice Admiral Kurita Takeo, was to enter the Pacific through the San Bernardino Strait between the Philippine islands of Samar and Luzon. On Oct 23 Kurita lost two of his heavy cruisers to US submarine attack, and one of Japan's greatest battleships, the *Musashi*, was sunk in an aerial attack the next day, but Kurita made his way unopposed through the San Bernardino Strait on Oct 25. The southern group commanded by Vice Admiral Nishimura Teiji was detected on its way to the Surigao Strait and was practically annihilated by the US 7th Fleet as it entered the Leyte Gulf on Oct 25. Kurita, as a result, was forced to turn back from his planned rendezvous with Nishimura. Japan's Sho-Go, rather than inflicting damage on the Americans, resulted in serious losses for the Japanese.

BEIRUT TERRORIST ATTACK: ANNIVERSARY. Oct 23, 1983. A suicidal terrorist attack on American forces at Beirut, Lebanon, killed 240 US personnel when a truck loaded with TNT was driven into and exploded at US headquarters there. A similar attack on French forces killed scores more.

CAMBODIA: PEACE TREATY DAY. Oct 23. National holiday. Commemorates peace treaty of 1991.

CARSON, JOHNNY: BIRTH ANNIVERSARY. Oct 23, 1925. Television talk show host, born in Corning, IA. He worked for various radio and television shows, including "Who Do You Trust?" He first appeared on "The Tonight Show" in 1958, and was named the permanent host in 1962 with the resignation of Jack Paar. He remained on the air for more than 30 years, and along with sidekick Ed McMahon and bandleader Doc Severinsen, basically invented the TV talk show format as we know it today. When he retired from television in 1992, he was regarded as a national institution. Carson died at Los Angeles, CA, Jan 23, 2005.

October 2009	S	M	T	W	T	F	S
					1	2	3
	4	5	6	7	8	9	10
	11	12	13	14	15	16	17
	18	19	20	21	22	23	24
	25	26	27	28	29	30	31

EDERLE, GERTRUDE: BIRTH ANNIVERSARY. Oct 23, 1906. American swimming champion, born at New York City, Gertrude Caroline Ederle was the first woman to swim the English Channel (from Cape Gris-nez, France, to Dover, England). At age 19 she broke the previous world record by swimming the 35-mile distance in 14 hours, 31 minutes, on Aug 6, 1926. During her swimming career she broke many other records and was a gold medal winner at the 1924 Olympic Games. She died at Wyckoff, NJ, Nov 30, 2003.

FANTASY FEST. Oct 23–Nov 1. Key West, FL. Ten-day adult costume festival with street parties, masked balls and nighttime grand parade. Est attendance: 75,000. For info: Fantasy Fest, Linda O'Brien, Box 230, Key West, FL 33041. Phone: (305) 296-1817. Fax: (305) 294-3335. Web: www.fantasyfest.net.

GHOSTLY GATHERING. Oct 23–24. Heritage Green, Sandy Springs, GA. Spooky storytellers, enchanting magicians, and costume contests set the stage for Ghostly Gathering. Young children enjoy the frightful fun of the Magician, Bubbling Brook and Ghostly Walk, and older children get thrills from the Fortune Teller and spine-chilling Witch. For info: Heritage Sandy Springs, 135 Hilderbrand Dr, Sandy Springs, GA 30328. Phone: (404) 851-9111. Fax: (404) 851-9807. E-mail: events@heritagesandysprings.org. Web: www.heritagesandysprings.org.

HALLOWEEN HIKE. Oct 23–24. Savannah, GA. Take a hike with your little "trick-or-treater" in the Friendly Forest. Children will collect treats and meet some lovable, huggable critters along the way. This is a fun, safe, not-so-scary event, and children are encouraged to wear costumes and comfortable walking shoes. Treat bags will be provided. Other activities include crafts, face painting, pony rides and hayrides. Est attendance: 1,400. For info: Oatland Island Wildlife Center, 711 Sandtown Rd, Savannah, GA 31410. Phone: (912) 898-3980. Web: www.oatlandisland.org.

HUNGARY: ANNIVERSARY OF 1956 REVOLUTION. Oct 23. National holiday. Also called Uprising Day of Remembrance. Commemorates revolt against Soviet domination, which was crushed on Nov 4, 1956.

HUNGARY DECLARES INDEPENDENCE: 20th ANNIVERSARY. Oct 23, 1989. Hungary declared itself an independent republic, 33 years after Russian troops crushed a popular revolt against Soviet rule. The announcement followed a weeklong purge by parliament of the Stalinist elements from Hungary's 1949 constitution, which defined the country as a socialist people's republic. Acting head of state Matyas Szuros made the declaration in front of tens of thousands of Hungarians at Parliament Square, speaking from the same balcony from which Imre Nagy addressed rebels 33 years earlier. Nagy was hanged for treason after Soviet intervention. Free elections held in March 1990 removed the Communist party to the ranks of the opposition for the first time in four decades.

HUNGARY: REPUBLIC DAY. Oct 23. Public holiday observing Hungary's creation as an independent republic in 1989.

IPOD UNVEILED: ANNIVERSARY. Oct 23, 2001. The Apple company unveiled its portable MP3 music player to the press on this date. The iPod officially went on sale on Nov 10, 2001, for $399. Critics at the time complained about the cost, but the iPod became incredibly popular. On Apr 9, 2007, Apple announced that it had sold its 100 millionth iPod.

NATIONAL MOLE DAY. Oct 23. Celebrated on Oct 23 each year from 6:02 AM to 6:02 PM in observance of the "mole." For 2009 the Mole Day theme is "Molar Express." The "mole" is a way of counting the Avogadro number, 6.02 × 10 to the 23rd power of anything (just like a "dozen" is a way of counting 12 of anything). Mole Day owes its existence to an early-19th-century Italian physics professor named Amedeo Avogadro. He discovered that the number of molecules in a mole is the same for all substances. Because of this, chemists are able to precisely measure quantities of chemicals in the laboratory. Mole Day is celebrated to help all persons, especially chemistry students, become enthused about chemistry, which is the central science. Individual teachers develop their own ways of observing Mole Day. For info: Tom Tweedle, Executive Director, National Mole Day Foundation, PO Box 602, Millersport, OH 43046. E-mail: mole@avolve.net. Web: moleday.org.

ROBIE HOUSE SECRETS & SHADOWS TOUR. Oct 23–24. Fredrick C. Robie House, Chicago, IL. Frank Lloyd Wright's Robie House opens its doors after dark for a unique seasonal tour. The Robie House's nearly century-old history will be explored under a veil of darkness as guides from Preservation Trust lead the special tours by flashlight. Stories and myths surrounding Robie House and its previous inhabitants will be shared, as well as exclusive access to areas rarely open to the public. For info: Frank Lloyd Wright Preservation Trust, 931 Chicago Ave, Oak Park, IL 60302. Phone: (708) 848-1976. Fax: (708) 848-1248. E-mail: info@gowright.org. Web: www.gowright.org.

SAINT JOHN OF CAPISTRANO: DEATH ANNIVERSARY. Oct 23, 1456. Giovanni da Capistrano, Franciscan lawyer, educator and preacher, was born at Capistrano, Italy, in 1386, and died of plague on Oct 23, 1456. Feast Day is Mar 28.

SCORPIO, THE SCORPION. Oct 23–Nov 22. In the astronomical/astrological zodiac that divides the sun's apparent orbit into 12 segments, the period Oct 23–Nov 22 is traditionally identified as the sun sign of Scorpio, the Scorpion. The ruling planet is Pluto or Mars.

STEVENSON, ADLAI EWING: BIRTH ANNIVERSARY. Oct 23, 1835. Twenty-third vice president of the US (1893–97), born at Christian County, KY. Died at Chicago, IL, June 14, 1914. He was grandfather of Adlai E. Stevenson, the Democratic candidate for president in 1952 and 1956. See also: "Stevenson, Adlai Ewing: Birth Anniversary" (Feb 5).

SUGARLOAF ART FAIR. Oct 23–25. Rock Financial Showplace, Novi, MI. This show, now in its 15th year, features more than 200 nationally recognized craft designers and fine artists displaying and selling their original creations. Includes craft demonstrations, live music, children's entertainment, specialty foods, hourly gift certificate drawings and more. Est attendance: 17,000. For info: Sugarloaf Mountain Works, 200 Orchard Ridge Dr, #215, Gaithersburg, MD 20878. Phone: (800) 210-9900. Fax: (310) 253-9620. Web: www.sugarloafcrafts.com.

SWALLOWS DEPART FROM SAN JUAN CAPISTRANO. Oct 23. Traditional date for swallows to depart for the winter from old mission of San Juan Capistrano, CA. See also: "Swallows Return to San Juan Capistrano" (Mar 19).

THAILAND: CHULALONGKORN DAY. Oct 23. Annual commemoration of the death of King Chulalongkorn the Great, who died Oct 23, 1910, after a 42-year reign. King Chulalongkorn abolished slavery at Thailand. Special ceremonies with floral tributes and incense at the foot of his equestrian statue in front of Bangkok's National Assembly Hall.

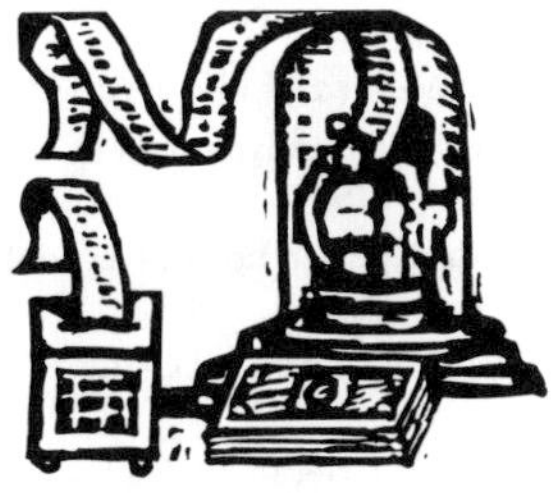

Birthdays Today

Jim Bunning, 78, US Senator (R, Kentucky), born Southgate, KY, Oct 23, 1931.

Michael Crichton, 67, writer (*Jurassic Park, Rising Sun*), born Chicago, IL, Oct 23, 1942.

Douglas Richard (Doug) Flutie, 47, sportscaster, former football player, born Manchester, MD, Oct 23, 1962.

Nancy Grace, 51, talk show host, born Macon, GA, Oct 23, 1958.

Ang Lee, 55, director (Oscars for *Brokeback Mountain* and *Crouching Tiger, Hidden Dragon*), born Taiwan, Oct 23, 1954.

Melquiades (Mel) R. Martinez, 63, US Senator (R, Florida), former US Secretary of Housing and Urban Development, born Sagua la Grande, Cuba, Oct 23, 1946.

Tiffeny Milbrett, 37, former soccer player, born Portland, OR, Oct 23, 1972.

Pelé, 69, former soccer player, born Edson Arantes do Nascimento at Tres Coracoes, Brazil, Oct 23, 1940.

Juan "Chi-Chi" Rodriguez, 75, former golfer, born Rio Piedras, Puerto Rico, Oct 23, 1934.

Michael John (Mike) Tomczak, 47, former football player, born Calumet City, IL, Oct 23, 1962.

Keith Van Horn, 34, basketball player, born Fullerton, CA, Oct 23, 1975.

Alfred Matthew "Weird Al" Yankovic, 50, singer, satirist, born Lynwood, CA, Oct 23, 1959.

Dwight Yoakam, 53, country singer, actor (*Sling Blade*), born Pikeville, KY, Oct 23, 1956.

October 24 — Saturday

DAY 297 — **68 REMAINING**

ALABAMA RENAISSANCE FAIRE. Oct 24–25. Florence, AL. Celebration in grand 16th-century style with music, arts and crafts, costumes, theater and dance. Listen to minstrels, dulcimers and autoharps and watch as knights in shining armor transform Wilson Park into "Fountain-on-the-Green," the scene of a 16th-century faire. Est attendance: 30,000. For info: Debbie Wilson, Dir, Florence/Lauderdale Tourism, One Hightower Pl, Florence, AL 35630. Phone: (256) 740-4141 or (800) 888-FLO-TOUR. Fax: (256) 740-4142. E-mail: debbie@visitflorenceal.com. Web: www.visitflorenceal.com.

BATTLE OF VITTORIO VENETO: ANNIVERSARY. Oct 24–Nov 3, 1918. Italian forces, commanded by General Armando Diaz, began the last offensive against Austrian troops in upper Italy on this date. The battle began north of the Piave River, and on Oct 30 the Austrian headquarters at Vittorio Veneto was taken. By Nov 1 Austrian troops were breaking up into deserting mobs. A truce was signed at Villa Giusti on Nov 3, which provided for fighting to end the next day. This Allied victory led to the collapse of the Austro-Hungarian Empire.

BLUE RIDGE FOLKLIFE FESTIVAL. Oct 24. Ferrum College/Blue Ridge Institute and Museum, Ferrum, VA. The largest celebration of authentic folkways in Virginia featuring food, crafts, music and exhibits. Annually, the fourth Saturday in October. Est attendance: 20,000. For info: Roddy Moore, BRI Dir, Ferrum College/BRI, PO Box 1000, Rte 40 W, Ferrum, VA 24088. Phone: (540) 365-4412. Fax: (540) 365-4419. E-mail: bri@ferrum.edu. Web: www.blueridgeinstitute.org.

FIRST BARREL JUMP OVER NIAGARA FALLS: ANNIVERSARY. Oct 24, 1901. The spectacle of Niagara Falls attracted no end of daredevils through the centuries, but the first one to go over the falls and survive in any kind of contraption was the unlikely Annie Edson Taylor, a 63-year-old former dance teacher who was down on her luck and hoping for fame and fortune. On this date, she accomplished this feat in a 160-pound barrel. No one repeated her stunt until 1911.

HOGEYE FESTIVAL. Oct 24. Elgin, TX. Day's events include Road Hog Car Show, barbecue pork cook-off, crowning of King Hog or Queen Sowpreme, handmade arts and crafts, kids' activities and Elgin's famous hot sausage and live music. Annually, the fourth Saturday in October. Est attendance: 20,000. For info: Hogeye Festival, PO Box 591, Elgin, TX 78621. Phone: (512) 281-5724. Fax: (512) 285-5962. E-mail: hogeye@ci.elgin.tx.us. Web: www.elgintx.com.

LOCKWOOD, BELVA A. BENNETT: BIRTH ANNIVERSARY. Oct 24, 1830. Belva Lockwood, an educator, lawyer and advocate for women's rights, was born at Royalton, NY. In 1879 she was admitted to practice before the US Supreme Court—the first woman to do so. While practicing law at Washington, DC, she secured equal property rights for women. By adding amendments to statehood bills, Lockwood helped to provide voting rights for women in Oklahoma, New Mexico and Arizona. In 1884 she was the first woman formally nominated for the US presidency. Died May 19, 1917, at Washington, DC.

MAKE A DIFFERENCE DAY. Oct 24. This national day of community service is sponsored by *USA Weekend* magazine. Volunteer projects are judged by well-known celebrities. Selected projects receive $10,000 charitable awards to further their good work. Key projects are honored in April during National Volunteer Week. More than three million people nationwide participate. For info: Make a Difference Day, *USA Weekend*, 7950 Jones Branch Dr, McLean, VA 22107. Phone: (800) 416-3824. E-mail: diffday@usaweekend.com. Web: www.makeadifferenceday.com.

PRESCRIPTION ERRORS EDUCATION AND AWARENESS WEEK. Oct 24–31. According to a Harvard study, more than 107,000 Americans take their prescription medications incorrectly, resulting in hospitalization or death. This week focuses on educating patients and consumers about serious drug interactions, adverse drug events, allergies and the mixing of prescription drugs with herbals and over-the-counter medications. There is a $15 charge for kit materials. For info: Fred Mayer, Pharmacists Planning Service, Inc, 101 Lucas Valley Rd, Ste 382, San Rafael, CA 94903. Phone: (415) 479-8628. Fax: (415) 479-8608. E-mail: ppsi@aol.com. Web: www.ppsinc.org.

SEA WITCH HALLOWEEN & FIDDLERS FESTIVAL. Oct 24–25. Rehoboth Beach/Dewey Beach, DE. Fiddlers Festival, costume parade and contest, Sea Witch Hunt, horse show on the beach, best costumed pet contest, spook shows, horse-drawn hayrides and entertainment. Annually, the last full weekend in October. Est attendance: 150,000. For info: Elizabeth Beck, Festival Dir, PO Box 216, Rehoboth Beach, DE 19971. Phone: (800) 441-1329, ext 12. Fax: (302) 227-8351. E-mail: rehoboth@beach-fun.com. Web: www.beach-fun.com.

SHERMAN, JAMES SCHOOLCRAFT: BIRTH ANNIVERSARY. Oct 24, 1855. Twenty-seventh vice president of the US (1909–12), born at Utica, NY. Died there Oct 30, 1912.

STOCK MARKET PANIC: 80th ANNIVERSARY. Oct 24, 1929. After several weeks of a downward trend in stock prices, investors began panic selling on Black Thursday, Oct 24, 1929. More than 13 million shares were dumped. Desperate attempts to support the market brought a brief rally. See also: "Stock Market Crash of 1929: Anniversary" (Oct 29).

✦ **UNITED NATIONS DAY.** Oct 24. Presidential Proclamation. Always issued for Oct 24 since 1948. (By unanimous request of the UN General Assembly.)

UNITED NATIONS DAY: ANNIVERSARY OF FOUNDING. Oct 24, 1945. Official United Nations holiday commemorates founding of the United Nations and effective date of the United Nations Charter. In 1971 the General Assembly recommended this day be observed as a public holiday by UN member states (Res 2782/xxvi). For info: United Nations, Dept of Public Info, Public Inquiries Unit, Rm GA-57, New York, NY 10017. Phone: (212) 963-4475. Fax: (212) 963-0071. E-mail: inquiries@un.org. Web: www.un.org.

UNITED NATIONS: DISARMAMENT WEEK. Oct 24–30. In 1978 the General Assembly called on member states to highlight the danger of the arms race, propagate the need for its cessation and increase public understanding of the urgent task of disarmament. Observed annually, beginning on the anniversary of the founding of the UN. For info: United Nations, Dept of Public Info, New York, NY 10017. Web: www.un.org.

UNITED NATIONS: WORLD DEVELOPMENT INFORMATION DAY. Oct 24. Anniversary of 1970 adoption by United Nations General Assembly of the International Development Strategy for the Second United Nations Development Decade. Object is to "draw the attention of the world public opinion each year to development problems and the necessity of strengthening international cooperation to solve them." For info: United Nations, Dept of Public Info, New York, NY 10017. Web: www.un.org.

XTERRA MAKENA BEACH TRAIL RUN. Oct 24. Makena, Maui, HI. The XTERRA Trail Run Series boasts over 50 events across the country with runs ranging from 5k to 25k. These extreme, off-road trail runs give runners the chance to prove their skills against a variety of terrain. From calf-burning hills to slippery, mud-covered paths athletes will face the ultimate test of endurance. This race features off-road 5k and 10k trail runs. For info: XTERRA/TEAM Unlimited, 720 Iwilei Rd #290, Honolulu, HI 96817. Phone: (877) 751-8880. E-mail: info@xterraplanet.com. Web: www.xterratrailrun.com.

ZAMBIA: INDEPENDENCE DAY. Oct 24. Zambia. National holiday commemorates the independence of what was then Northern Rhodesia from Britain in 1964. Celebrations in all cities, but main parades of military, labor and youth organizations are at the capital, Lusaka. Observed on the fourth Monday in October (Oct 26).

Birthdays Today

F. Murray Abraham, 69, actor (Oscar for *Amadeus*), born El Paso, TX, Oct 24, 1940.

Kevin Kline, 62, actor (Oscar for *A Fish Called Wanda*; *Wild Wild West, Dave*), born St. Louis, MO, Oct 24, 1947.

Kweisi Mfume, 61, former NAACP president, born Baltimore, MD, Oct 24, 1948.

Monica, 29, singer, born Monica Arnold at Atlanta, GA, Oct 24, 1980.

David Nelson, 73, actor ("The Adventures of Ozzie and Harriet"), born New York, NY, Oct 24, 1936.

Wayne Rooney, 24, soccer player, born Liverpool, England, Oct 24, 1985.

Mike Rounds, 55, Governor of South Dakota (R), born Huron, SD, Oct 24, 1954.

Yelberton Abraham (Y.A.) Tittle, Jr, 83, Hall of Fame football player, born Marshall, TX, Oct 24, 1926.

Bill Wyman, 73, musician (Rolling Stones), born William Perks at London, England, Oct 24, 1936.

October 2009

S	M	T	W	T	F	S
				1	2	3
4	5	6	7	8	9	10
11	12	13	14	15	16	17
18	19	20	21	22	23	24
25	26	27	28	29	30	31

October 25 — Sunday

DAY 298 **67 REMAINING**

CHAUCER, GEOFFREY: DEATH ANNIVERSARY. Oct 25, 1400. The best-known English writer and poet of the Middle Ages, Chaucer was born at London, England, probably about 1340. His greatest work, *Canterbury Tales,* consists of some 17,000 poetic lines. Unfinished at his death, it tells the stories of 23 pilgrims. Among his lesser-known prose writings was a treatise on the astrolabe titled *Brede and Milke for Children* (1387), written for "little Lewis, my son." Chaucer died at London and is buried at Westminster Abbey.

A FAMILY HALLOWEEN. Oct 25. Billings Farm and Museum, Woodstock, VT. Mystery stories, doughnuts on a string, pumpkin carving, costume parades, plus wagon rides. Children in costume accompanied by an adult admitted free. For info: Billings Farm and Museum, Rte 12 N, Woodstock, VT 05091. Phone: (802) 457-2355. Fax: (802) 457-4663. E-mail: info@billingsfarm.org. Web: www.billingsfarm.org.

FIRST FEMALE FBI AGENTS: ANNIVERSARY. Oct 25, 1972. The first women to become FBI agents completed training at Quantico, VA. The new agents, Susan Lynn Roley and Joanne E. Pierce, graduated from the 14-week course with a group of 45 men.

GRENADA INVADED BY US: ANNIVERSARY. Oct 25, 1983. Some 2,000 US Marines and Army Rangers invaded the Caribbean island of Grenada, taking control after a political coup the previous week had made the island a "Soviet-Cuban colony," according to President Reagan. Commemorated as Thanksgiving Day in Grenada, a public holiday.

HAUTE DOG CHARITY HOWL'OWEEN PARADE. Oct 25. Belmont Shore, Long Beach, CA. Just about every breed from boxer to poodle will take over Belmont Shore for the annual Haute Dog Howl'oween Parade. The event has raised thousands of dollars for animal shelters and rescue organizations. About 600 pooches—colorfully costumed for Halloween—are expected to pack Livingston Park for a Yappy Hour before beginning their parade down Second Street. Prizes awarded for the best canine costumes. Annually, the Sunday before Halloween. Est attendance: 3,000. For info: Justin Rudd. Phone: (562) 439-3316. E-mail: justin@justinrudd.com. Web: www.hautedogs.org.

INTERNATIONAL MAGIC WEEK. Oct 25–31. A week to celebrate the world of magic and the magicians who create it. Annually, Oct 25–31—culminating on Oct 31, the anniversary of Harry Houdini's death and Magic Day. For info: Sir Nemo Turner, The Protocol Institute, CP 157, Place du Parc, Montreal, QC, H2X 4A4 Canada. Phone: (514) 849-0888. E-mail: magician@total.net.

MACAULAY, THOMAS BABINGTON: BIRTH ANNIVERSARY. Oct 25, 1800. English essayist and historian, born at Rothley Temple, Leicestershire, England. Died at Campden Hill, London, Dec 28, 1859. "Nothing," he wrote, "is so useless as a general maxim."

MOON PHASE: FIRST QUARTER. Oct 25. Moon enters First Quarter phase at 8:42 PM, EDT.

MOTHER-IN-LAW DAY. Oct 25. Traditionally, the fourth Sunday in October is occasion to honor mothers-in-law for their contribution to the success of families and for their good humor in enduring bad jokes.

"NEWHART" TV PREMIERE: ANNIVERSARY. Oct 25, 1982. Bob Newhart starred in this sitcom as Dick Loudon, an author of how-to books who moved with his wife, Joanna (Mary Frann), to Vermont to take over the Stratford Inn. Regulars included Tom Poston as George Utley, inn caretaker; Julia Duffy as Stephanie Vanderkellen, the reluctant maid; Peter Scolari as Michael Harris, producer of Dick's talk show and Stephanie's squeeze; and, as the owners of the Minute Man Café, William Sanderson as Larry and Tony Papenfuss and John Volstad as his silent brothers, both named Darryl. The last telecast was Sept 8, 1990.

PASTORAL CARE WEEK. Oct 25–31. Honors clergy of all faiths who provide pastoral care in congregations and in such specialized settings as hospitals, correctional facilities, mental health systems, the military and counseling centers. For info: Pastoral Care Week. Web: www.pastoralcareweek.org.

PEARL, MINNIE: BIRTH ANNIVERSARY. Oct 25, 1912. Comedian, Grand Ole Opry star born at Centerville, TN. Pearl died at Nashville, TN, Mar 4, 1996.

PICASSO, PABLO RUIZ: BIRTH ANNIVERSARY. Oct 25, 1881. Called by many the greatest artist of the 20th century, Pablo Picasso excelled as a painter, sculptor and engraver. He is said to have commented once: "I am only a public entertainer who has understood his time." Born at Málaga, Spain, he died Apr 8, 1973, at Mougins, France.

REFORMATION SUNDAY. Oct 25. Many Protestant churches commemorate Reformation Day (Oct 31—anniversary of the day on which Martin Luther nailed his 95 theses to the door of Wittenberg's Palace church, protesting the sale of papal indulgences, in 1517) each year on the Sunday preceding Oct 31, or on the 31st, if a Sunday.

SAINT CRISPIN'S DAY. Oct 25. Martyr in the reign of Diocletian. Saint Crispin's Day is famous as the day in 1415 when King Henry V defeated the superior forces of France at the Battle of Agincourt. A passage in Shakespeare's *Henry V* notes this.

SOUREST DAY. Oct 25. To emphasize the balance of things in nature. A day for sour (Sauer) people. For info: Richard Ankli, Allen Creek Hydro, Inc, 100 S 4th Ave #608, Ann Arbor, MI 48104.

SOUTHERN CALIFORNIA FIRESTORMS: 15th ANNIVERSARY. Oct 25, 1993. The Southern California fire season began viciously when fires swept from the celebrity-studded beachfront homes of Malibu to the Mexican border. Blown out of the desert by the fierce Santa Anna winds, the fires destroyed suburban enclaves south of Los Angeles at Laguna Beach and northeast of Los Angeles at Altadena. As winds died down, firefighters appeared to gain control as the flames reached the Santa Monica Mountains, but the winds roared again, spreading the fire into Malibu—often jumping the Pacific Coast Highway to destroy the beachfront homes of the wealthy celebrities who lived there. Damage from the fires was estimated at more than $1 billion.

TAIWAN EXPELLED FROM UN: ANNIVERSARY. Oct 25, 1971. The United Nations General Assembly voted to admit mainland China and expel Taiwan. This was after many years of debate about which government was the "official" government of China. In 1979 the US accorded diplomatic recognition to mainland China.

TAIWAN: RETROCESSION DAY. Oct 25. Commemorates restoration of Taiwan to Chinese rule in 1945, after half a century of Japanese occupation.

XTERRA WORLD CHAMPIONSHIP. Oct 25. Makena, Maui, HI. Heralded as the hot new king of multisport, the XTERRA World Championship is the culmination of more than 100 events held across the globe. Includes 1.5k rough-water swim, 30k mountain bike race and 11k cross-country run. $130,000 pro purse. Est attendance: 10,000. For info: TEAM Unlimited, 720 Iwilei Rd #290, Honolulu, HI 96817. Phone: (808) 521-4322. Fax: (808) 538-0314. E-mail: info@xterraplanet.com. Web: www.xterraplanet.com.

 **Birthdays Today**

Brian Kerwin, 60, actor ("Lobo," "The Blue and the Gray"), born Chicago, IL, Oct 25, 1949.

Robert Montgomery (Bobby) Knight, 69, college basketball coach and former player, born Orrville, OH, Oct 25, 1940.

Pedro Martinez, 38, baseball player, born Manoguyabo, Dominican Republic, Oct 25, 1971.

Midori, 38, violinist, born Osaka, Japan, Oct 25, 1971.

Helen Reddy, 67, singer, songwriter ("I Am Woman"), born Melbourne, Australia, Oct 25, 1942.

Marion Ross, 73, actress ("Happy Days," *The Evening Star*), born Albert Lea, MN, Oct 25, 1936.

Anne Tyler, 68, author (*The Accidental Tourist, Breathing Lessons*), born Minneapolis, MN, Oct 25, 1941.

October 26 — Monday

DAY 299 **66 REMAINING**

AUSTRIA: NATIONAL DAY. Oct 26. National holiday. Commemorates the withdrawal of Soviet troops in 1955.

CHINA: CHUNG YEUNG FESTIVAL (OR DOUBLE NINE FESTIVAL). Oct 26. This festival relates to the old story of the Han dynasty, when a soothsayer advised a man to take his family to a high place on the ninth day of the ninth moon for 24 hours in order to avoid disaster. The man obeyed and found, on returning home, that all living things had died a sudden death in his absence. Part of the celebration is climbing to high places. Date in other countries will differ from China's.

DANTON, GEORGES: 250th BIRTH ANNIVERSARY. Oct 26, 1759. Born at Arcis-sur-Aube, Danton was a lawyer who gradually emerged as a leader in the French Revolution. Despite his charisma, though, he was unable to rein in the murderous factions swirling in the movement. On Mar 29, 1794, Danton and his moderate followers were arrested. His last words before his execution by guillotine at Paris, France, on Apr 5 were: "Show my head to the people. It is worth the trouble."

ERIE CANAL: ANNIVERSARY. Oct 26, 1825. The Erie Canal, first US major man-made waterway, was opened, providing a water route from Lake Erie to the Hudson River. Construction started July 4, 1817, and the canal cost $7,602,000. Cannons fired and celebrations were held all along the route for the opening.

GIVE WILDLIFE A BRAKE! WEEK. Oct 26–Nov 1. As daylight saving time ends, it's time to Give Wildlife a Brake! At this time of year, many of us are now driving to and from work in near darkness, just as large animals such as deer are entering mating season, and others are active in preparing for the long winter ahead. Scan the road as you drive, watching the edges for wildlife about to cross. Not only will this help you avoid killing harmless wildlife, but it will also make you aware of other hazards such as bicyclists, children at play and slow-moving vehicles. Be alert! For info: Humane Society of the US, 2100 L St NW, Washington, DC 20037. Phone: (202) 452-1100. E-mail: wildlife@hsus.org. Web: www.hsus.org.

GUNFIGHT AT THE O.K. CORRAL: ANNIVERSARY. Oct 26, 1881. At 2:30 PM, the Earp brothers and gambler/dentist Doc Holliday confronted the Clanton and McLaury brothers at a vacant lot behind the O.K. Corral in Tombstone, AZ. After 30 seconds of gunfire, three deaths and decades of romanticizing, the incident would become the most notorious of the Old West. Marshal Virgil Earp and Deputy Marshals Wyatt and Morgan Earp attempted to disarm the Clanton faction, when gunfire erupted, although some witnesses claimed that the Clantons and McLaurys threw up their hands when ordered to. Billy Clanton and Frank and Thomas McLaury died. Virgil and Morgan Earp were wounded. After a 30-day murder trial, the presiding judge dismissed the charges stating that the Earps and Holliday had acted in self-defense.

HANSOM, JOSEPH: BIRTH ANNIVERSARY. Oct 26, 1803. English architect and inventor Joseph Aloysius Hansom registered his "Patent Safety Cab" in 1834. The two-wheeled, one-horse, enclosed cab, with driver seated above and behind the passengers, quickly became a familiar and favorite vehicle for public transportation. Hansom was born at York, England, and died at London, June 29, 1882.

IRELAND: OCTOBER BANK HOLIDAY. Oct 26. Bank holiday in the Republic of Ireland. Annually, the last Monday in October. Also called Halloween Holiday.

JACKSON, MAHALIA: BIRTH ANNIVERSARY. Oct 26, 1911. Born at New Orleans, LA, Jackson was the most famous gospel singer of her time. After moving to Chicago, IL, in 1928, Jackson sang with the Johnson Gospel Singers. Thomas A. Dorsey, the father of gospel music, was her adviser and accompanist from 1937 to 1946. By the 1950s, Jackson could be heard in concert halls around the world. She sang at the inauguration of President John F. Kennedy and at the 1963 March on Washington rally. Dr. Martin Luther King, Jr, described her voice as "one heard once in a millennium." She died at Chicago, on Jan 27, 1972, and was buried in New Orleans, LA, where her funeral procession was thronged with mourners.

MULE DAY. Oct 26. Anniversary of the first importation of Spanish jacks to the US, a gift from King Charles III of Spain. Mules are said to have been bred first in this country by George Washington from this pair of jacks delivered at Boston, Oct 26, 1785.

NEW ZEALAND: LABOR DAY. Oct 26. National holiday on the fourth Monday in October.

ROCKEFELLER, ABBY GREENE ALDRICH: BIRTH ANNIVERSARY. Oct 26, 1874. A philanthropist and art patron, Abby Rockefeller was one of the three founders of the New York Museum of Modern Art in 1929. Born at Providence, RI, she died Apr 5, 1948, at New York City.

"ST. ELSEWHERE" TV PREMIERE: ANNIVERSARY. Oct 26, 1982. A popular one-hour medical drama set in St. Eligius Hospital at Boston. Among its large and changing cast were Ed Flanders; William Daniels; Ed Begley, Jr; David Morse; Howie Mandel; Christina Pickles; Denzel Washington; Norman Lloyd; David Birney; G.W. Bailey; Kavi Raz; Stephen Furst; Mark Harmon and Alfre Woodard. The last episode of the series aired on Aug 10, 1988.

SCARLATTI, DOMENICO: BIRTH ANNIVERSARY. Oct 26, 1685. Italian keyboard composer, born at Naples, Italy. Died July 23, 1757, at Madrid, Spain.

SPACE MILESTONE: *SOYUZ 3* (USSR). Oct 26, 1968. After the crash of *Soyuz 1* and the death of its cosmonaut, *Soyuz 3* was launched this date with Colonel Georgi Beregovoy. It orbited Earth 64 times, rendezvousing but not docking with unmanned *Soyuz 2*, which had been launched the day before. Both vehicles returned to Earth under ground control. *Soyuz* means "union."

October 2009

S	M	T	W	T	F	S
				1	2	3
4	5	6	7	8	9	10
11	12	13	14	15	16	17
18	19	20	21	22	23	24
25	26	27	28	29	30	31

Birthdays Today

Tom Cavanagh, 41, actor ("Ed"), born Ottawa, ON, Canada, Oct 26, 1968.

Hillary Rodham Clinton, 62, US Senator (D, New York), former First Lady, wife of Bill Clinton, 42nd president of the US, born Park Ridge, IL, Oct 26, 1947.

Sasha Cohen, 25, figure skater, born Westwood, CA, Oct 26, 1984.

Nick Collison, 29, basketball player, born Orange City, IA, Oct 26, 1980.

Pat Conroy, 64, writer (*The Prince of Tides, The Lords of Discipline*), born Atlanta, GA, Oct 26, 1945.

Cary Elwes, 47, actor (*Saw, Glory, The Princess Bride*), born London, England, Oct 26, 1962.

Bob Hoskins, 67, actor (*Mona Lisa, Who Framed Roger Rabbit?*), born Bury St. Edmonds, Suffolk, England, Oct 26, 1942.

Dylan McDermott, 47, actor ("The Practice"), born Waterbury, CT, Oct 26, 1962.

Natalie Merchant, 46, singer, born Jamestown, NY, Oct 26, 1963.

James Pickens, Jr, 55, actor ("Grey's Anatomy," "The X-Files," "The Practice"), born Cleveland, OH, Oct 26, 1954.

Jeff Probst, 47, television personality ("Survivor"), born Wichita, KS, Oct 26, 1962.

Ivan Reitman, 63, filmmaker (*Dave, Ghost Busters*), born Komarno, Czechoslovakia, Oct 26, 1946.

Pat Sajak, 63, game show host ("Wheel of Fortune"), born Chicago, IL, Oct 26, 1946.

Jaclyn Smith, 62, actress ("Charlie's Angels"), former Breck Girl, born Houston, TX, Oct 26, 1947.

Keith Urban, 40, country singer, born Whangarei, New Zealand, Oct 26, 1969.

October 27 — Tuesday

DAY 300 **65 REMAINING**

COOK, JAMES: BIRTH ANNIVERSARY. Oct 27, 1728. (Old Style date.) English sea captain of the ship *Endeavour* and explorer who brought Australia and New Zealand into the British Empire. Born at Marton-in-Cleveland, Yorkshire, England, he was killed Feb 14, 1779, at the Hawaiian Islands, which he discovered.

CRANKY COWORKERS DAY. Oct 27. Because all of us have bad days (some more than others), here's a day when crankiness at work is actually encouraged. (©2006 by WH.) For info: Thomas & Ruth Roy, Wellcat Holidays, 2418 Long Ln, Lebanon, PA 17046. Phone: (717) 279-0184. E-mail: info@wellcat.com. Web: www.wellcat.com.

***FEDERALIST PAPERS*: ANNIVERSARY.** Oct 27, 1787. The first of the 85 "Federalist" papers appeared in print in a New York City newspaper, Oct 27, 1787. These essays, written by Alexander Hamilton, James Madison and John Jay, argued in favor of adoption of the new Constitution and the new form of federal government. The last of the essays was completed Apr 4, 1788.

HURRICANE MITCH: ANNIVERSARY. Oct 27, 1998. More than 7,000 people were killed at Honduras by flooding caused by Hurricane Mitch. Thousands more were killed in other Central American countries, especially Nicaragua.

LICHTENSTEIN, ROY: BIRTH ANNIVERSARY. Oct 27, 1923. Pop artist who used comic strips and other elements of pop culture in his paintings. Born at New York City, he died there Sept 29, 1997.

NATIONAL SCHOLARSHIP PROVIDERS ASSOCIATION ANNUAL CONFERENCE. Oct 27–30. New Orleans, LA. Bringing together scholarship providers to network, share best practices and take advantage of professional development opportunities. The mission of the NSPA is to advance the collective impact of scholarship providers, and the scholarships they award, through exchanging best practices, offering professional development opportunities and promoting student access and success in higher education. For info: Amy Weinstein, NSPA, 101 Monroe St, Denver, CO 80206. Phone: (720) 941-4498. Fax: (720) 941-4492. E-mail: aweinstein@scholarshipproviders.org. Web: www.scholarshipproviders.org.

NAVY DAY. Oct 27. Established in 1922 to honor the "past and present services" of the US Navy to the nation. Also honored Theodore Roosevelt, whose birth date is Oct 27 (and who had been assistant secretary of the Navy early in his public career). Not a national holiday, it was last observed in 1949.

NEW YORK CITY SUBWAY: ANNIVERSARY. Oct 27, 1904. Running from City Hall to W 145th St, the New York City subway began operation. It was privately operated by the Interborough Rapid Transit Company and later became part of the system operated by the New York City Transit Authority.

PAGANINI, NICOLO: BIRTH ANNIVERSARY. Oct 27, 1782. Hailed as the greatest violin virtuoso of all time, Paganini was born at Genoa, Italy. Unusually long arms contributed to his legendary Mephistophelian appearance—and probably to his unique skills as a performer. His immensely popular concerts brought him great wealth, but his compulsive gambling repeatedly humbled the genius. Paganini died at Nice, France, May 27, 1840.

ROOSEVELT, THEODORE: BIRTH ANNIVERSARY. Oct 27, 1858. Twenty-sixth president of the US, succeeded to the presidency on the death of William McKinley. His term of office: Sept 14, 1901–Mar 3, 1909. Roosevelt was the first president to ride in an automobile (1902), to submerge in a submarine (1905) and to fly in an airplane (1910). Although his best-remembered quote was perhaps "Speak softly and carry a big stick," he also said: "The first requisite of a good citizen in this Republic of ours is that he shall be able and willing to pull his weight." Born at New York, NY, Roosevelt died at Oyster Bay, NY, Jan 6, 1919. His last words: "Put out the light."

SAINT VINCENT AND THE GRENADINES: INDEPENDENCE DAY: 30th ANNIVERSARY. Oct 27. National day commemorating independence from Britain in 1979.

THOMAS, DYLAN MARLAIS: 95th BIRTH ANNIVERSARY. Oct 27, 1914. Welsh poet, memoirist and playwright, born at Swansea, Wales. One of his most famous poems was "Do Not Go Gentle into That Good Night" (1951). Died at New York, NY, Nov 9, 1953.

TURKMENISTAN: INDEPENDENCE DAY. Oct 27. National holiday. Commemorates independence from the Soviet Union in 1991.

"WALT DISNEY" TV PREMIERE: 55th ANNIVERSARY. Oct 27, 1954. This highly successful and long-running show appeared on different networks under different names but was essentially the same show. It was the first ABC series to break the Nielsen's top 20 and the first prime-time anthology series for kids. "Walt Disney" was originally titled "Disneyland" to promote the park and upcoming Disney releases. When it switched networks, it was called "Walt Disney's Wonderful World of Color" to highlight its being broadcast in color. Presentations featured edited versions of previously released Disney films and original productions (including natural history documentaries, behind-the-scenes peeks at Disney shows and dramatic shows, such as the popular Davy Crockett segments, which were the first TV miniseries). The show went off the air in December 1980 after 25 years, making it the longest-running series in prime-time TV history. In 1997 ABC revived the series as "Wonderful World of Disney."

Birthdays Today

Roberto Benigni, 57, actor, director (Oscar for *Life Is Beautiful*), born Arezzo, Italy, Oct 27, 1952.

John Cleese, 70, actor, writer ("Monty Python's Flying Circus," *A Fish Called Wanda*), born Weston-Super-Mare, England, Oct 27, 1939.

Ruby Dee, 85, actress ("Ossie and Ruby," *Zora Is My Name, Do the Right Thing*), born Cleveland, OH, Oct 27, 1924.

Nanette Fabray, 89, actress (Emmy for "Caesar's Hour"; "One Day at a Time," *Our Gang* comedies), born San Diego, CA, Oct 27, 1920.

Simon LeBon, 51, singer (Duran Duran), born Bushey, England, Oct 27, 1958.

Fran Lebowitz, 59, essayist, humorist (*Social Studies*), born Morristown, NJ, Oct 27, 1950.

Marla Maples, 46, model, actress, born Dalton, GA, Oct 27, 1963.

Zadie Smith, 34, author (*On Beauty, White Teeth*), born Sadie Smith at Brent, London, England, Oct 27, 1975.

October 28 — Wednesday

DAY 301 — 64 REMAINING

CZECH REPUBLIC: INDEPENDENCE DAY. Oct 28. National day, anniversary of the bloodless revolution at Prague in 1918 resulting in independence from the Austro-Hungarian Empire, after which the Czechs and Slovaks united to form Czechoslovakia (a union they dissolved without bloodshed in 1993).

DAY OF NATIONAL CONCERN ABOUT YOUNG PEOPLE AND GUN VIOLENCE. Oct 28 (tentative). Students across America are asked to voluntarily sign a "Student Pledge Against Gun Violence," a solemn promise never to bring a gun to school, never to use a gun to settle a personal problem or dispute, and to discourage their friends from using guns inappropriately. Formerly issued as a presidential proclamation. Since 1996, more than 10 million students have participated. For info: Student Pledge Against Gun Violence, 112 Nevada St, Northfield, MN 55057. Phone: (507) 645-5378. Web: www.pledge.org.

DONNER PARTY FAMINE: ANNIVERSARY. Oct 28, 1846–Apr 21, 1847. The pioneering Donner party, a group of 90 people consisting of immigrants, families and businessmen led by George and Jacob Donner and James F. Reed, headed toward California in 1846 from Springfield, IL, in hopes of beginning a new life. They experienced the normal travails of caravan travel until their trip took several sensational twists. Indian attacks and winter weather, which forced them to interrupt their journey, led to famine and outright cannibalism, which took their toll on members of the party, whose numbers dwindled to 48 by journey's end.

October 2009	S	M	T	W	T	F	S
					1	2	3
	4	5	6	7	8	9	10
	11	12	13	14	15	16	17
	18	19	20	21	22	23	24
	25	26	27	28	29	30	31

ERASMUS, DESIDERIUS: BIRTH ANNIVERSARY. Oct 28, 1467. Dutch author and scholar Desiderius Erasmus was born at Rotterdam, Netherlands, probably Oct 28, 1467. Best known of his writings is *Encomium Moriae* (*In Praise of Folly*). Erasmus died at Basel, Switzerland, July 12, 1536.

ESCOFFIER, GEORGES AUGUSTE: BIRTH ANNIVERSARY. Oct 28, 1846. Celebrated French chef and author, inventor of the peche Melba (honoring the operatic singer Dame Nellie Melba), Escoffier became known as the "king of chefs and the chef of kings." Born at Villeneuve-Loubet, France. He was awarded the Legion d'Honneur in recognition of his contribution to the international reputation of French cuisine, and his service at the Savoy and Carlton hotels at London, England, brought him world fame. He died at Monte Carlo, Monaco, Feb 12, 1935.

FIRST WOMAN US AMBASSADOR APPOINTED: 60th ANNIVERSARY. Oct 28, 1949. Helen Eugenie Moore Anderson became the first woman to hold the post of US ambassador when she was sworn in by President Harry S Truman on this date. She served as ambassador to Denmark.

GERMAN REVOLUTION OF 1918: ANNIVERSARY. Oct 28, 1918. On this date in the final days of WWI, crews of six German battleships protested a series of planned cruiser raids. A mutiny broke out in the fleet at Kiel. All but one of the ships remaining in port ran up the red flag of revolution, 600 sailors were arrested and imprisoned on shore. The uprising spread to Hamburg, Bremen and Lubeck. On Nov 9 a general strike at Berlin brought the administration to a halt. The abdication of Kaiser Wilhelm began to be seen as the only way to avoid a full-scale revolution.

GREECE: "OCHI DAY." Oct 28. National holiday commemorating Greek resistance and refusal to open its borders when Mussolini's Italian troops attacked Greece, Oct 28, 1940. *Ochi* means "no." Celebrated with military parades, especially at Athens and Thessaloniki.

HANSON, HOWARD: BIRTH ANNIVERSARY. Oct 28, 1896. Born at Wahoo, NE, Howard Hanson in 1921 became the first American to win the Prix de Rome. In 1924 he became head of the Eastman School of Music at the University of Rochester, NY, where he served for 40 years. Best known for the music he composed, Hanson was awarded the Pulitzer Prize as outstanding contemporary composer in 1944 for his composition *Symphony No 4*, the George Foster Peabody Award in 1946, the Laurel Leaf of the American Composers Alliance in 1957 and the Huntington Hartford Foundation Award in 1959. He died at Rochester, Feb 26, 1981.

HARVARD UNIVERSITY FOUNDED: ANNIVERSARY. Oct 28, 1636. (Old Style date.) Harvard University founded at Cambridge, MA, when the Massachusetts General Court voted to provide £400 for a "schoale or colledge."

"THE JACK BENNY PROGRAM" TV PREMIERE: ANNIVERSARY. Oct 28, 1950. One of radio's favorite comedians, Jack Benny made the transition to favorite TV personality with this situation comedy–variety show in 1950. Regulars included Eddie Anderson, Don Wilson, Dennis Day, Mel Blanc, Mary Livingstone (Benny's real-life wife) and Frank Nelson. Benny also had guest stars, including Ken Murray, Frank Sinatra, Claudette Colbert, Basil Rathbone and TV newcomers Johnny Carson, Marilyn Monroe and Humphrey Bogart. Famous for his cheapness, Benny had a guard for his vaults, which created many laughs.

SAINT JUDE'S DAY. Oct 28. St. Jude, the saint of hopeless causes, was martyred along with St. Simon at Persia, and their feast is celebrated jointly. St. Jude was supposedly the brother of Jesus and, like his brother, a carpenter by trade. He is most popular with those who attempt the impossible and with students, who often ask for his help on exams.

SALK, JONAS: 95th BIRTH ANNIVERSARY. Oct 28, 1914. Dr. Jonas Salk, developer of the Salk polio vaccine, was born at New York, NY. Salk announced his development of a successful vaccine in 1953, the year after a polio epidemic claimed some 3,300 lives in the US. Polio deaths were reduced by 95 percent after the introduction of the vaccine. Salk spent the last 10 years of his life doing AIDS research. He died June 23, 1995, at La Jolla, CA.

SPACE MILESTONE: INTERNATIONAL SPACE RESCUE AGREEMENT. Oct 28, 1970. US and USSR officials agreed upon space rescue cooperation.

STATUE OF LIBERTY: DEDICATION ANNIVERSARY. Oct 28, 1886. Frederic Auguste Bartholdi's famous sculpture, the statue of *Liberty Enlightening the World*, on Bedloe's Island in New York Harbor, was dedicated. Ground breaking for the structure was in April 1883. A sonnet by Emma Lazarus, inside the pedestal of the statue, contains the words: "Give me your tired, your poor, your huddled masses yearning to breathe free, the wretched refuse of your teeming shore. Send these, the homeless, tempest-tossed, to me: I lift my lamp beside the golden door."

WORLD RELIGIOUS TRAVEL EXPO. Oct 28–31 (tentative). Nashville, TN. Annual gathering of the religious travel industry including sellers and consumers. For info: Kevin J. Wright, President, World Religious Travel Assn, 8156-E South Wadsworth Blvd, #338, Littleton, CO 80128. Phone: (303) 933-8705. E-mail: kwright@religioustravelassociation.com. Web: www.religioustravelexpo.com.

Birthdays Today

Jane Alexander, 70, actress (*The Great White Hope, Kramer vs Kramer*), former chair of the National Endowment for the Arts, born Jane Quigley at Boston, MA, Oct 28, 1939.

Charlie Daniels, 73, musician, singer, songwriter ("Devil Went Down to Georgia"), born Wilmington, NC, Oct 28, 1936.

Jeremy Davies, 40, actor (*Saving Private Ryan*), born Rockford, IA, Oct 28, 1969.

Terrell Davis, 37, football player, born San Diego, CA, Oct 28, 1972.

Dennis Franz, 65, actor ("Hill Street Blues," "NYPD Blue"), born Maywood, IL, Oct 28, 1944.

Bill Gates, 54, former computer software executive (Microsoft), philanthropist, born Seattle, WA, Oct 28, 1955.

Jami Gertz, 44, actress ("Still Standing," *Twister*), born Chicago, IL, Oct 28, 1965.

Lauren Holly, 46, actress (*Dumb & Dumber*, "Picket Fences"), born Geneva, NY, Oct 28, 1963.

Telma Hopkins, 61, singer, actress ("Family Matters"), born Louisville, KY, Oct 28, 1948.

William Bruce Jenner, 60, sportscaster, Olympic gold medal decathlete, born Mount Kisco, NY, Oct 28, 1949.

Brad Paisley, 37, country singer, born Glen Dale, WV, Oct 28, 1972.

Annie Potts, 57, actress ("Designing Women," *Ghostbusters, Pretty in Pink*), born Nashville, TN, Oct 28, 1952.

Andy Richter, 43, actor, former cohost ("Late Night with Conan O'Brien"), born Grand Rapids, MI, Oct 28, 1966.

Julia Roberts, 42, actress (Oscar for *Erin Brockovich*; *Ocean's Eleven, My Best Friend's Wedding*), born Smyrna, GA, Oct 28, 1967.

October 29 — Thursday

DAY 302 — 63 REMAINING

BOSWELL, JAMES: BIRTH ANNIVERSARY. Oct 29, 1740. (Old Style date.) Scottish biographer, born at Edinburgh, Scotland. Died at London, England, May 19, 1795. "I think," he wrote in his monumental biography, *Life of Samuel Johnson*, "no innocent species of wit or pleasantry should be suppressed: and that a good pun may be admitted among the smaller excellencies of lively conversation."

EBBETS, CHARLES: 150th BIRTH ANNIVERSARY. Oct 29, 1859. Charles Hercules Ebbets, baseball executive, born at New York, NY. Ebbets bought into the Brooklyn baseball club in 1890 and became controlling owner in 1898. He sold 50 percent of the team to build Ebbets Field, the park whose enduring reputation has been the model for the new, old-fashioned parks constructed in recent years. Died at New York, Apr 18, 1925.

EMMETT, DANIEL DECATUR: BIRTH ANNIVERSARY. Oct 29, 1815. Creator of words and music for the song "Dixie's Land" ("Dixie"), which became a fighting song for Confederate troops and unofficial anthem of the South. Emmett was born at Mount Vernon, OH, and died there June 28, 1904.

FORT LAUDERDALE INTERNATIONAL BOAT SHOW. Oct 29–Nov 2. Fort Lauderdale, FL. Everything from small boats to mega-yachts to boating equipment. Visitors attend from all over the world. For info: Greater Fort Lauderdale CVB, 100 E Broward Blvd, Ste 200, Fort Lauderdale, FL 33301. Phone: (954) 765-4466. Web: www.sunny.org or www.showmanagement.com.

GOEBBELS, PAUL JOSEF: BIRTH ANNIVERSARY. Oct 29, 1897. German Nazi leader, born at Rheydt, Germany, who became Hitler's minister of propaganda, having earlier been rejected by the military because of a limp caused by infantile paralysis. Killed himself and his wife and children May 1, 1945, in Hitler's bunker in Berlin as Russian forces advanced into the city.

INTERNET CREATED: 40th ANNIVERSARY. Oct 29, 1969. The first connection on what would become the Internet was made on this day when bits of data flowed between computers at UCLA and the Stanford Research Institute. This was the beginning of ARPANET, the precurser to the Internet developed by the Department of Defense. By the end of 1969 four sites were connected: UCLA, the Stanford Research Institute, the University of California at Santa Barbara and the University of Utah. By the next year there were 10 sites, and soon there were applications like e-mail and file transfer utilities. The @ symbol was adopted in 1972 and a year later 75 percent of ARPANET traffic was e-mail. ARPANET was decommissioned in 1990, and the National Science Foundation's NSFnet took over the role of backbone of the Internet.

SPACE MILESTONE: OLDEST MAN IN SPACE: *DISCOVERY* (US). Oct 29, 1998. Former astronaut and senator John Glenn became the oldest man in space when he traveled on the space shuttle *Discovery* at the age of 77. In 1962 on *Friendship 7* Glenn had been the first American to orbit Earth. See "Space Milestone: *Friendship 7*" (Feb 20).

STOCK MARKET CRASH OF 1929: 80th ANNIVERSARY. Oct 29, 1929. Prices on the New York Stock Exchange plummeted and virtually collapsed four days after President Herbert Hoover had declared, "The fundamental business of the country . . . is on a sound and prosperous basis." More than 16 million shares were dumped, and billions of dollars were lost. The boom was over, and the nation faced nearly a decade of depression. Some analysts had warned that the buying spree, with prices 15 to 150 times above earnings, had to stop at some point. Frightened investors ordered their brokers to sell at whatever price. The resulting Great Depression, which lasted until about 1939, involved North America, Europe and other industrialized countries. In 1932 one out of four US workers was unemployed.

TURKEY: REPUBLIC DAY. Oct 29. Anniversary of the founding of the republic in 1923.

 Birthdays Today

Richard Dreyfuss, 62, actor (*Mr Holland's Opus, Jaws*; Oscar for *The Goodbye Girl*), born Brooklyn, NY, Oct 29, 1947.

Joely Fisher, 44, actress ("Ellen"), born Los Angeles, CA, Oct 29, 1965.

Finola Hughes, 49, actress ("Blossom," "General Hospital"), born London, England, Oct 29, 1960.

Kate Jackson, 61, actress ("Charlie's Angels," "Scarecrow and Mrs King"), born Birmingham, AL, Oct 29, 1948.

Randy Jackson, 48, singer (Jackson 5), born Steven Randall Jackson at Gary, IN, Oct 29, 1961.

Dirk Kempthorne, 58, US Secretary of the Interior, former Governor of Idaho (R), born San Diego, CA, Oct 29, 1951.

Melba Moore, 64, singer, actress, born New York, NY, Oct 29, 1945.

Winona Ryder, 38, actress (*Girl, Interrupted*; *Little Women*), born Winona Horowitz at Winona, MN, Oct 29, 1971.

Gabrielle Union, 37, actress (*Bring It On, The Honeymooners*), born Omaha, NE, Oct 29, 1972.

October 30 — Friday

DAY 303 — **62 REMAINING**

ADAMS, JOHN: BIRTH ANNIVERSARY. Oct 30, 1735. Second president of the US (term of office: Mar 4, 1797–Mar 3, 1801). Adams had been George Washington's vice president and was the father of John Quincy Adams (sixth president of the US). Born at Braintree, MA, he once wrote in a letter to his wife, Abigail: "I must study politics and war that my sons may have liberty to study mathematics and philosophy." Adams and Thomas Jefferson died on the same day, July 4, 1826. Adams died at Quincy, MA. See also: "Adams, John, and Jefferson, Thomas: Death Anniversary" (July 4).

ATLAS, CHARLES: BIRTH ANNIVERSARY. Oct 30, 1893. Charles Atlas (ex-97-pound weakling), whose original name was Angelo Siciliano, was born at Acri, Calabria, Italy. A bodybuilder and physical culturist, he created a popular mail-order bodybuilding course. The legendary sand-kicking episode used later in advertising for his course occurred at Coney Island when a lifeguard kicked sand in Atlas's face and stole his girlfriend. Three generations of comic book fans read his advertisements. He died Dec 24, 1972, at Long Beach, NY.

CLOSING OF COLUMBIAN EXPOSITION: ANNIVERSARY. Oct 30, 1893. After a rousing success, the Columbian Exposition held "American Cities Day" Oct 28, and Chicago mayor Carter Harrison gave a speech before the visiting mayors. After he arrived home, Harrison's doorbell rang. When the mayor answered the door he was shot and killed by Patrick Eugene Pendergast. Instead of the elaborate ceremony that had been planned to close the exposition on Oct 30, a single speech was given and the flags were lowered to half-mast.

October 2009

S	M	T	W	T	F	S
				1	2	3
4	5	6	7	8	9	10
11	12	13	14	15	16	17
18	19	20	21	22	23	24
25	26	27	28	29	30	31

CREATE A GREAT FUNERAL DAY. Oct 30. A day to remind people of all the benefits of creating their own unique funerals or memorial services, regardless of age or state of health. For info: Stephanie West Allen, PO Box 9311, Denver, CO 80209. Phone: (303) 935-8866. E-mail: stephanie@westallen.com. Web: www.westallen.com.

DEVIL'S NIGHT. Oct 30. Formerly a "Mischief Night" on the evening before Halloween and an occasion for harmless pranks, chiefly observed by children. However, in some areas of the US, the destruction of property and endangering of lives has led to the imposition of dusk-to-dawn curfews during the last two or three days of October. Not to be confused with "Trick or Treat," or "Beggar's Night," usually observed on Halloween. See also: "Hallowe'en" (Oct 31).

EDGAR ALLAN POE EVERMORE. Oct 30–Nov 15. Mount Hope Estate, Manheim, PA. Friday, Saturday and Sunday evenings. Nights of suspense featuring the spine-chilling short stories of Edgar Allan Poe. Professionals from the Pennsylvania Renaissance Faire Actors Conservatory perform, wine served. Est attendance: 10,000. For info: Thomas Roy, Mount Hope Estate and Winery, 2775 Lebanon Rd, Manheim, PA 17545. Phone: (717) 665-7021. Fax: (717) 664-3466. E-mail: Tom@parenfaire.com. Web: www.parenfaire.com.

FRANKENSTEIN FRIDAY. Oct 30. This holiday has been designed to honor and celebrate the "mother" and "father" of Frankenstein, Mary Shelley and Boris Karloff. Every year a different venue will be used to celebrate this occasion. In years past it has included a torch-lighting ceremony, film festival and awarding of THE FRANKY. For info: Ron MacCloskey. E-mail: ronmac55@optonline.net.

HALSEY, WILLIAM "BULL" FREDERICK: BIRTH ANNIVERSARY. Oct 30, 1882. American admiral and fleet commander who played a leading role in the defeat of the Japanese in the Pacific naval battles of WWII, William Halsey was born at Elizabeth, NJ. In April 1942, aircraft carriers under his command ferried Jimmy Doolittle's B-25s to within several hundred miles of Japan's coast. From that location the aircraft were launched from the decks of the carriers for a raid on Tokyo. In October 1942, as commander of all the South Pacific area, Halsey led naval forces in the defeat of Japan at Guadalcanal, and in November 1943 he directed the capture of Bougainville. He supported the landings in the Philippines in June 1944. In the great naval battle of Leyte Gulf (Oct 23–26, 1944) he assisted in an overwhelming defeat of the Japanese. On Sept 2, 1945, Japan's final instrument of surrender was signed in Tokyo Bay aboard Halsey's flagship, the USS *Missouri*. Halsey died at Fishers Island, NY, Aug 16, 1959.

HAUNTED REFRIGERATOR NIGHT. Oct 30. Who knows what evil lurks in the refrigerators of men and women? It's time to be afraid, very afraid. Gather friends, open the refrigerator door and venture unto the realm of the lower shelf, rear. That "thing" inside that container is much more horrifying than any haunted hayride. Annually, Oct 30. (©2006 by WH.) For info: Thomas & Ruth Roy, Wellcat Holidays, 2418 Long Ln, Lebanon, PA 17046. Phone: (717) 279-0184. E-mail: info@wellcat.com. Web: www.wellcat.com.

MALLE, LOUIS: BIRTH ANNIVERSARY. Oct 30, 1932. Born at Thumeries, France, film director Louis Malle was known for his experimental approach to filmmaking and his investigation of controversial topics. *Le Souffle Au Coeur* (1971), *Lancombe, Lucien* (1974) and *Pretty Baby* (1978), for instance, dealt with the issues of incest, the collaboration of France with its Nazi occupiers and child prostitution, respectively. Of all his films, Malle wished most to be remembered for *Au Revoir, Les Enfants* (1987). Died Nov 23, 1995, at Beverly Hills, CA.

POST, EMILY: BIRTH ANNIVERSARY. Oct 30, 1872. Emily Post was born at Baltimore, MD. Published in 1922, her book *Etiquette: The Blue Book of Social Usage* instantly became the American bible of manners and social behavior and established Post as the household name in matters of etiquette. It was in its 10th edition at the time of her death Sept 25, 1960, at New York, NY. *Etiquette* inspired a great many letters asking Post for advice on manners in specific situations. She used these letters as the basis for her radio show and her syndicated newspaper column, which eventually appeared in more than 200 papers.

POUND, EZRA LOOMIS: BIRTH ANNIVERSARY. Oct 30, 1885. Modernist poet, editor and critic, born at Hailey, ID. His success as a poet began in 1909 with the publication of *Personae*. In 1912 Pound initiated the Imagist movement, edited its first anthology in 1914 and collaborated with James Joyce and T.S. Eliot. He moved to Italy in 1924. As a result of his pro-Fascist radio broadcasts from Italy, Pound was indicted for treason July 26, 1943, and arrested near Genoa by the US Army. He was confined to St. Elizabeth's Hospital, Washington, DC, from 1946 to 1958. Considered mentally unable to stand trial, he was never tried for treason. Pound died at Venice, Italy, Nov 1, 1972.

RE/MAX BALLUNAR LIFTOFF FESTIVAL. Oct 30–Nov 1. NASA/Johnson Space Center, Clear Lake Area, Houston, TX. Featuring more than 100 hot-air balloons, skydiving competitions, arts and crafts, midway game area, food, music and other entertainment. Sponsored by NASA/Johnson Space Center, Clear Lake Area Chamber of Commerce, Re/Max and Space Center Houston. Est attendance: 30,000. For info: Ballunar Liftoff Festival, 1201 NASA Rd One, Houston, TX 77058. Phone: (281) 488-7676. Fax: (281) 488-8981.

SHERIDAN, RICHARD BRINSLEY: BIRTH ANNIVERSARY. Oct 30, 1751. Dramatist, born at Dublin, Ireland. Died at London, England, July 7, 1816. Sheridan is said to have extended the following invitation to a young lady: "Won't you come into the garden? I would like my roses to see you."

SISLEY, ALFRED: BIRTH ANNIVERSARY. Oct 30, 1839. French impressionist painter, born at Paris, France. One of the most influential artists of his time, he died near Fontainbleau, Jan 29, 1899.

SUGARLOAF CRAFTS FESTIVAL. Oct 30–Nov 1. Garden State Exhibit Center, Somerset, NJ. This show, now in its 15th year, features more than 300 nationally recognized craft designers and fine artists displaying and selling their original creations. Includes craft demonstrations, live music, children's entertainment, specialty foods, hourly gift certificate drawings and more. Est attendance: 15,000. For info: Sugarloaf Mountain Works, 200 Orchard Ridge Dr, #215, Gaithersburg, MD 20878. Phone: (800) 210-9900. Fax: (301) 253-9620. Web: www.sugarloafcrafts.com.

"WAR OF THE WORLDS": BROADCAST ANNIVERSARY. Oct 30, 1938. As part of a series of radio dramas based on famous novels, Orson Welles with the Mercury Players produced H.G. Wells's *War of the Worlds*. Near panic resulted when listeners believed the simulated news bulletins, which described a Martian invasion of New Jersey, to be real.

Birthdays Today

Robert A. Caro, 74, author (three-volume biography of Lyndon B. Johnson), born New York, NY, Oct 30, 1935.

Dick Gautier, 72, actor (*Bye Bye Birdie*, "Here We Go Again"), born Los Angeles, CA, Oct 30, 1937.

Harry Hamlin, 58, actor ("LA Law," "Studs Lonigan"), born Pasadena, CA, Oct 30, 1951.

Ed Lauter, 69, actor (*The Longest Yard, Fat Man and Little Boy*), born Long Beach, NY, Oct 30, 1940.

Diego Armando Maradona, 49, former soccer player, born Lanus, Argentina, Oct 30, 1960.

Andrea Mitchell, 63, news correspondent, born New York, NY, Oct 30, 1946.

Kevin Pollak, 51, actor (*A Few Good Men, Grumpy Old Men*), born San Francisco, CA, Oct 30, 1958.

Grace Slick, 70, singer (Jefferson Airplane, "White Rabbit"), born Chicago, IL, Oct 30, 1939.

Charles Martin Smith, 56, actor (*American Graffiti, The Untouchables*), director, born Los Angeles, CA, Oct 30, 1953.

Dick Vermeil, 73, football coach, born Calistoga, CA, Oct 30, 1936.

Henry Winkler, 64, actor ("Happy Days"), director, children's author, born New York, NY, Oct 30, 1945.

October 31 — Saturday

DAY 304 | 61 REMAINING

BOOKS FOR TREATS DAY. Oct 31. San Jose, CA. The Books for Treats cause gives gently read children's books at Halloween instead of candy. "Feed kids' minds, not their cavities. Give them brain candy." Supported by the city of San Jose and numerous community institutions. For info: Rebecca Morgan, Books for Treats, 1440 Newport Ave, San Jose, CA 95125. Phone: (408) 998-7977. E-mail: rebecca@rebeccamorgan.com. Web: www.BooksForTreats.org.

CANADA: BANFF MOUNTAIN FILM AND BOOK FESTIVAL. Oct 31–Nov 8. Banff, AB. The 34th annual festival brings the best films and videos on mountain subjects to the town of Banff. The weekend's activities, which take place at The Banff Centre, include continuous film screenings, guest speakers, literary lunches, a climbing wall, trade fair, mountain art and craft sale and more. Film festival is presented by National Geographic and New Balance; book festival is presented by Canadian Mountain Holidays and National Geographic. Est attendance: 12,000. For info: Nicky Lynch, Marketing Officer, Mountain Film Festival, PO Box 1020, Station 38, Banff, AB, Canada T1L 1H5. Phone: (403) 762-7594. Fax: (403) 762-6277. E-mail: mountainculture@banffcentre.ca. Web: www.banffmountainfestivals.ca.

CANDY, JOHN: BIRTH ANNIVERSARY. Oct 31, 1950. Comedic actor who got his start in Second City improvisation at Toronto and graduated to film stardom (*Uncle Buck, Home Alone*). Born at Toronto, ON, Canada; died Mar 4, 1994, while on location for a film at Chupederos, Mexico.

"CAR TALK" NATIONAL RADIO PREMIERE: ANNIVERSARY. Oct 31, 1987. "Car Talk," the irreverent talk show that diagnoses auto ills, premiered nationally on National Public Radio on this date. Hosted by brothers Ray and Tom Magliozzi (also known as "Click and Clack, the Tappet Brothers"), "Car Talk" originally debuted in Boston in 1977. Today, almost 4.4 million listeners tune in to the Peabody Award–winning show on 588 NPR stations.

CHIANG KAI-SHEK: BIRTH ANNIVERSARY. Oct 31, 1887. Chinese soldier and statesman, born at Chekiang, China. Educated at the Wampoa Military Academy, Chiang led the KMT (nationalist) forces in the struggle against the Communist army led by Mao Tse-Tung and eventually had to flee mainlaind China. He died at Taipei, Taiwan, Apr 5, 1975.

EMMA CRAWFORD FESTIVAL AND MEMORIAL COFFIN RACE. Oct 31. Manitou Springs, CO. Fun-filled day of artistically created coffins, Emma's costumes and coffin racing. Est attendance: 5,000. For info: Manitou Springs Chamber of Commerce, 354 Manitou Ave, Manitou Springs, CO 80829. Phone: (800) 642-2567. Fax: (719) 685-0355. Web: www.manitousprings.org.

FIRST BLACK PLAYS IN NBA GAME: ANNIVERSARY. Oct 31, 1950. Earl Lloyd became the first black ever to play in an NBA game when he took the floor for the Washington Capitols at Rochester, NY. Lloyd was actually one of three blacks to become an NBA player in the 1950 season, the others being Nat "Sweetwater" Clifton, who was signed by the New York Knicks, and Chuck Cooper, who was drafted by the Boston Celtics (and debuted the night after Lloyd).

HALLOWE'EN or ALL HALLOW'S EVE. Oct 31. An ancient celebration combining Druid autumn festival and Christian customs. Hallowe'en (All Hallow's Eve) is the beginning of Hallowtide, a season that embraces the Feast of All Saints (Nov 1) and the Feast of

All Souls (Nov 2). The observance, dating from the sixth or seventh century, has long been associated with thoughts of the dead, spirits, witches, ghosts and devils. In fact, the ancient Celtic Feast of Samhain, the festival that marked the beginning of winter and of the New Year, was observed Nov 1. See also: "Trick or Treat or Beggar's Night" (Oct 31).

HALLOWEEN PARADE. Oct 31. Toms River, NJ. Reported as the second-largest Halloween parade in the nation, with 8,000 participants, 118 prizes and 100,000 spectators. Parade covers a one-mile route. Est attendance: 100,000. For info: Carl Weingroff, c/o Toms River Fire Company 1, PO Box 1035, Toms River, NJ 08754. Phone: (732) 349-0144. Fax: (732) 349-5024. E-mail: trfd25no1@aol.com.

HOUDINI, HARRY: DEATH ANNIVERSARY. Oct 31, 1926. Harry Houdini (whose real name was Ehrich Weisz), magician, illusionist and escape artist, died at Grace Hospital, Detroit, MI, of peritonitis following an Oct 19 blow to the abdomen. Houdini's death anniversary, on Halloween, is occasion for meetings of magicians. See also: "Houdini, Harry: Birth Anniversary" (Mar 24).

KEATS, JOHN: BIRTH ANNIVERSARY. Oct 31, 1795. One of England's greatest poets, born at London, England. Keats wrote to Fanny Brawne (in 1820): "If I should die . . . I have left no immortal work behind me—nothing to make my friends proud of my memory—but I have loved the principle of beauty in all things, and if I had had time I would have made myself remembered." Died at the age of 25 at Rome, Italy, Feb 23, 1821.

LANDON, MICHAEL: BIRTH ANNIVERSARY. Oct 31, 1936. American actor, born Eugene Maurice Orowitz, at Forest Hills, NY. He is best known for his roles in the television series "Bonanza" (1959–73), "Little House on the Prairie" (1974–83) and "Highway to Heaven" (1984–89). He died July 1, 1991, at Malibu, CA.

LOW, JULIET GORDON: BIRTH ANNIVERSARY. Oct 31, 1860. Founded Girl Scouts of the USA Mar 12, 1912, at Savannah, GA. Born at Savannah, Low died there Jan 17, 1927.

MAGIC DAY. Oct 31. Traditionally observed on the anniversary of the death of Harry Houdini in 1926.

MOUNT RUSHMORE COMPLETION: ANNIVERSARY. Oct 31, 1941. The Mount Rushmore National Memorial was completed after 14 years of work. First suggested by Jonah Robinson of the South Dakota State Historical Society, the memorial was dedicated in 1925, and work began in 1927. The memorial contains sculptures of the heads of presidents George Washington, Thomas Jefferson, Abraham Lincoln and Theodore Roosevelt. The 60-foot-tall sculptures represent, respectively, the nation's founding, political philosophy, preservation and expansion and conservation.

NATIONAL KNOCK-KNOCK DAY. Oct 31. Celebrated in tandem with Halloween, National Knock-Knock Day answers the age-old question "Who's there?" A day for kids of all ages to try out their best knock-knock jokes (eg, Knock Knock/Who's there?/Weirdo/Weirdo who?/Weirdo you keep all your Halloween candy? I'm starving!). For a list of Halloween Knock-Knock Jokes, contact children's joke book authors Matt Rissinger and Philip Yates. Annually, on October 31. For info: Matt Rissinger/Philip Yates. Phone: (610) 650-9136. E-mail: mrissinger@aol.com or laugharoni@msn.com. Web: www.laugh-a-roni.com.

✦ **NATIONAL UNICEF DAY.** Oct 31. Presidential Proclamation 3817, of Oct 27, 1967, covers all succeeding years. Annually, Oct 31.

NEVADA: ADMISSION DAY: ANNIVERSARY. Oct 31, 1864. Became 36th state in 1864. Observed as a holiday in Nevada.

PACA, WILLIAM: BIRTH ANNIVERSARY. Oct 31, 1740. Signer of the Declaration of Independence and governor of Maryland. Born near Abingdon, MD, he died Oct 13, 1799, at Talbot County, MD.

October 2009

S	M	T	W	T	F	S
				1	2	3
4	5	6	7	8	9	10
11	12	13	14	15	16	17
18	19	20	21	22	23	24
25	26	27	28	29	30	31

PRESIDENT'S ENVIRONMENTAL YOUTH AWARD NATIONAL COMPETITION DEADLINE. Oct 31. Young people in all 50 states are invited to participate in the President's Environmental Youth Awards program, which offers them, individually and collectively, an opportunity to be recognized for environmental efforts in their community. The program encourages individuals, school classes, schools, summer camps and youth organizations to promote local environmental awareness and positive community involvement. The annual deadline is always Oct 31, and applications should be returned to EPA regional offices. Regional contacts can be found at www.epa.gov/enviroed. For additional info: Office of Children's Health, Protection and Environmental Education, US Environmental Protection Agency, 1200 Pennsylvania Ave NW (MC 1704A), Washington, DC 20460. Phone: (202) 564-0443. Fax: (202) 564-2754. Web: www.epa.gov/enviroed.

REFORMATION DAY: ANNIVERSARY. Oct 31, 1517. Anniversary of the day on which Martin Luther nailed his 95 theses to the door of Wittenberg's Palace church, denouncing the selling of papal indulgences—the beginning of the Reformation in Germany. Observed by many Protestant churches on Reformation Sunday, on this day if it is a Sunday or on the Sunday before Oct 31.

SAMHAIN. Oct 31. (Also called November Eve, Hallowmas, Hallowe'en, All Hallow's Eve, Feast of Souls, Feast of the Dead, Feast of Apples and Calan Gaeaf.) One of the "Greater Sabbats" during the Wiccan year, Samhain, or "Summer's end," marks the death of the Sun-God, who then awaits his rebirth from the Mother Goddess at Yule (Dec 21 in 2009). In the Celtic tradition, the feast of Samhain was also celebrated as New Year's Eve, as their new year began on Nov 1. Annually, Oct 31.

SCARED SILLY: HALLOWEEN IN PROSPECT PARK. Oct 31. Prospect Park, Brooklyn, NY. Celebrate Halloween with a haunted walk through the Ravine and a full carnival on the Nethermead. Hear scary stories at Lefferts Historic House—even ride a haunted carousel. Est attendance: 10,000. For info: Public Info Office, Prospect Park Alliance, 95 Prospect Park W, Brooklyn, NY 11215. Phone: (718) 965-8999. Web: www.prospectpark.org.

SLEIDANUS, JOHANNES: DEATH ANNIVERSARY. Oct 31, 1556. German historian, born at Schleiden in 1506. His *Famous Chronicle of Oure Time*, called *Sleidanes Comentaires*, was first translated into English in 1560. The translator spoke thus to the book: "Go forth my painful Boke, Thou art no longer mine. Eche man may on thee loke, The Shame or praise is thine." He died at Strasbourg, Oct 31, 1556.

SWEDEN: ALL SAINTS' DAY. Oct 31. Honors the memory of deceased friends and relatives. Annually, the Saturday following Oct 30.

TAIWAN: CHIANG KAI-SHEK DAY. Oct 31. National holiday to honor the memory of Generalissimo Chiang Kai-Shek, the first constitutional president of the Republic of China, born Oct 31, 1887.

TEXAS BOOK FESTIVAL. Oct 31–Nov 1. State Capitol and Capitol Extension, Austin, TX. 14th annual fair benefiting the public libraries of Texas. More than 150 authors will give readings, participate in panel discussions and sign books. Outdoor book fair with displays by publishers and booksellers. Free. For info: Texas Book Festival, 610 Brazos St, Ste 200, Austin, TX 78701. Phone: (512) 477-4055. Fax: (512) 322-0722. Web: www.texasbookfestival.org.

TRICK OR TREAT or BEGGAR'S NIGHT. Oct 31. A popular custom on Hallowe'en, in which children wearing costumes visit neighbors' homes, calling out "Trick or treat" and "begging" for candies or gifts to place in their beggars' bags. In recent years there has been increased participation by adults, often parading in elaborate or outrageous costumes and also requesting candy.

WATERS, ETHEL: BIRTH ANNIVERSARY. Oct 31, 1896. Married when she was 13, Ethel Waters began her singing career at the urging of friends. At age 17 she was singing at Baltimore, MD, billing herself as Sweet Mama Stringbean. Her career took her to New York, where she divided her work between the stage, nightclubs and films. She made her Broadway debut in 1927 in the revue *Africana*, and her other stage credits include *Blackbirds* and *Thousands Cheer*. Her memorable stage roles in *Cabin in the Sky* and *A Member of the Wedding* (for which she won the Drama Critics' Award) were re-created for film. Born at Chester, PA, she died Sept 9, 1977, at Chatsworth, GA.

WMAS 94.7 FM HALLOWEEN COSTUME BALL. Oct 31. Springfield, MA. Our annual listener-appreciation ball, where listeners come dressed in their wildest and most creative costumes. Lots of prize categories in which people can win trips, VCRs, TVs, jewelry and more. Est attendance: 2,500. For info: Promotions Dept, WMAS 94.7 FM, PO Box 9500, Springfield, MA 01102. Phone: (413) 737-1414. Fax: (413) 737-1488.

Birthdays Today

Michael Collins, 78, former astronaut, born Rome, Italy, Oct 31, 1931.

Deidre Hall, 61, actress ("Our House," "Days of Our Lives"), born Lake Worth, FL, Oct 31, 1948.

Peter Jackson, 48, director (*The Lord of the Rings* trilogy, *King Kong*), born Pukerua Bay, North Island, New Zealand, Oct 31, 1961.

Frederick Stanley (Fred) McGriff, 46, former baseball player, born Tampa, FL, Oct 31, 1963.

Larry Mullen, 48, musician (drummer with U2), born Dublin, Ireland, Oct 31, 1961.

Dermot Mulroney, 46, actor (*About Schmidt, My Best Friend's Wedding*), born Alexandria, VA, Oct 31, 1963.

Jane Pauley, 59, television personality, born Indianapolis, IN, Oct 31, 1950.

Dan Rather, 78, journalist (former anchor "CBS Evening News"), born Wharton, TX, Oct 31, 1931.

Stephen Rea, 66, actor (*The Crying Game, Michael Collins*), born Belfast, Northern Ireland, Oct 31, 1943.

Ron Rifkin, 70, stage and screen actor (Tony for *Caberet*; Drama Desk and Obie awards for *The Substance of Fire*; "Alias"), born New York, NY, Oct 31, 1939.

Rob Schneider, 46, actor (*Deuce Bigalow: Male Gigolo*, "Saturday Night Live"), born San Francisco, CA, Oct 31, 1963.

David Ogden Stiers, 67, actor ("M*A*S*H," *North and South*), born Peoria, IL, Oct 31, 1942.

Vanilla Ice, 42, rapper, actor, born Robert Van Winkle at Miami, FL, Oct 31, 1967.

November

November 1 — Sunday

DAY 305 60 REMAINING

ALGERIA: REVOLUTION DAY. Nov 1. National holiday. Commemorates beginning of revolt against France in 1954.

ALL HALLOWS or ALL SAINTS' DAY. Nov 1. Roman Catholic Holy Day of Obligation. Commemorates the blessed, especially those who have no special feast days. Observed on Nov 1 since Pope Gregory IV set the date of recognition in AD 835. All Saints' Day is a legal holiday in Louisiana. Halloween is the evening before All Hallows Day.

AMERICAN DIABETES MONTH. Nov 1–30. American Diabetes Month is designed to communicate the seriousness of diabetes and the importance of proper diabetes control and treatment to those diagnosed with the disease and their families. Throughout the month, the American Diabetes Association holds special events and programs on a variety of topics related to diabetes care and treatment. For info: American Diabetes Assn. Phone: (800) DIABETES. Web: www.diabetes.org.

ANTIGUA AND BARBUDA: INDEPENDENCE DAY. Nov 1. National holiday. Commemorates independence from Britain in 1981.

AVIATION HISTORY MONTH. Nov 1–30. Anniversary of aeronautical experiments in November 1782 (exact dates unknown) by Joseph Michel Montgolfier and Jacques Etienne Montgolfier, brothers living at Annonay, France. Inspired by Joseph Priestley's book *Experiments Relating to the Different Kinds of Air*, the brothers experimented with filling paper and fabric bags with smoke and hot air, leading to the invention of the hot-air balloon, man's first flight and the entire science of aviation and flight.

CRANE, STEPHEN: BIRTH ANNIVERSARY. Nov 1, 1871. American author (*The Red Badge of Courage*), born at Newark, NJ. Died June 5, 1900, at Badenweiler, Germany.

DAYLIGHT SAVING TIME ENDS; STANDARD TIME RESUMES. Nov 1–Mar 7, 2010. Standard time resumes at 2 AM on the first Sunday in November in each time zone, as provided by the Uniform Time Act of 1966 (as amended in 1986 by Public Law 99–359). The Energy Policy Act of 2005 extended the period of daylight saving time beginning in 2007. Many people use the popular rule "Spring forward, fall back" to remember which way to turn their clocks. See also: "Daylight Saving Time" (Mar 8).

DIABETIC EYE DISEASE MONTH. Nov 1–30. Can people with diabetes prevent the onset of diabetic eye disease? During this observance, Prevent Blindness America® will offer information to help the 5.3 million Americans aged 18 and older who suffer from diabetic eye disease. For info: Prevent Blindness America®, 211 W Wacker Dr, Ste 1700, Chicago, IL 60606. Phone: (800) 331-2020. E-mail: info@preventblindness.org. Web: www.preventblindness.org.

***EBONY* MAGAZINE: ANNIVERSARY.** Nov 1, 1945. Black publishing entrepreneur John H. Johnson launched *Ebony* on this date—three years to the day after his first successful African-American lifestyle magazine, *Negro Digest* (1942). By 1946 *Ebony* had a circulation of more than 300,000 copies. On Nov 1, 1951, Johnson launched the equally successful publication *Jet*.

ENGLAND: LONDON TO BRIGHTON VETERAN CAR RUN. Nov 1. London. A 60-mile run for approximately 500 veteran cars, along the A23 road from Hyde Park, London, to Madeira Drive, Brighton. Only cars (three wheels or more) built before Dec 31, 1904, are eligible to participate. Celebrates the November 1896 English law raising the speed limit of "light locomotives" from 4 mph to 14 mph. Annually, the first Sunday in November. For info: LBVCR, Motion Works UK Ltd, Silverstone Innovation Centre, Silverstone, Northamptonshire, NN12 8GX England. Phone: (44) (1327) 856-024. Fax: (44) (1327) 856-025. E-mail: lbvcr@motion-works.co.uk. Web: www.LBVCR.com.

EPILEPSY AWARENESS MONTH. Nov 1–30. To increase public awareness that despite dramatic gains in treatment, epilepsy is a serious and chronic health condition for which there is no cure. Annually, the month of November. For info: PR Dept, Epilepsy Foundation, 8301 Professional Pl, Landover, MD 20785. Phone: (800) 332-1000. Web: www.epilepsyfoundation.org.

EUROPEAN UNION ESTABLISHED: ANNIVERSARY. Nov 1, 1993. The Maastricht Treaty went into effect on this day, formally establishing the European Union. The treaty was drafted in 1991. By 1993, 12 nations had ratified it. In 1995 three more nations ratified the treaty. The European Union grew out of the European Economic Community (also known as the Common Market), which was established in 1958.

FAMILY STORIES MONTH. Nov 1–30. November starts out with crisper weather and ends with the gathering of family and friends around the table, which makes it the perfect month to start telling and saving family stories. For info: Joanna Campbell Slan, 12033 Dorsett Rd, Maryland Heights, MO 63043. E-mail: savetales@aol.com. Web: www.scrapbookstorytelling.com.

GLUTEN-FREE DIET AWARENESS MONTH. Nov 1–30. To promote awareness of the gluten-free diet and celebrate the abundance of food products and cuisine available for enjoying a healthy, delicious and satisfying gluten-free lifestyle. For info: GF Culinary Productions, Inc. Phone: (303) 368-9990. E-mail: info@prchefs.com. Web: www.theglutenfreelifestyle.com.

GUATEMALA: KITE FESTIVAL OF SANTIAGO SACATEPEQUEZ. Nov 1. Long ago, when evil spirits disturbed the good spirits in the local cemetery, a magician told the townspeople a secret way to get rid of the evil spirits—by flying kites (because the evil spirits were frightened by the noise of wind against paper). Since then, the kite festival has been held at the cemetery each year on Nov 1 or Nov 2, and it is said that "to this day no one knows of bad spirits roaming the streets or the cemetery of Santiago Sacatepequez," a village about 20 miles from Guatemala City. Nowadays, the youths of the village work for many weeks to make the giant, elaborate kites to fly on All Saints' Day (Nov 1) or All Souls' Day (Nov 2).

HOCKEY MASK INVENTED: 50th ANNIVERSARY. Nov 1, 1959. Tired of stopping hockey pucks with his face, Montreal Canadiens goalie Jacques Plante, having received another wound, reemerged from the locker room with seven new stitches—and a face mask he had made from fiberglass and resin. Cliff Benedict had tried a leather mask back in the '20s, but the idea didn't catch on until Plante wore his. Then goalies throughout the NHL began wearing protective plastic face shields.

THE ING NEW YORK CITY MARATHON. Nov 1. New York, NY. About 38,000 runners from all over the world gather to compete, with more than 2.5 million spectators watching from the sidelines. Annually, the first Sunday in November. Est attendance: 2,000,000. For info: NY Road Runners. Phone: (212) 423-2249. Web: www.ingnycmarathon.org.

November 2009

S	M	T	W	T	F	S
1	2	3	4	5	6	7
8	9	10	11	12	13	14
15	16	17	18	19	20	21
22	23	24	25	26	27	28
29	30					

LISBON EARTHQUAKE: ANNIVERSARY. Nov 1, 1755. A powerful earthquake struck Lisbon, Portugal, on this day in 1755. The earthquake probably had a Richter scale magnitude of 9 and caused a tsunami to sweep over the capital. In the resulting deluge and fires, more than 75 percent of Lisbon was destroyed. Some 90,000 people died in Portugal, and an additional 10,000 people died in other parts of the Mediterranean.

LUNG CANCER AWARENESS MONTH. Nov 1–30. LCAM is a national campaign dedicated to increasing attention to lung cancer issues—early detection, increased research funding and increased support for those living with lung cancer. The Lung Cancer Allliance is the leading organization dedicated to helping people at risk for and living with lung cancer. Support and education resources are available free of charge by phone, mail or Internet. For info: The Lung Cancer Alliance, 888 16th St NW, Washington, DC 20006. Phone: (202) 463-2080. E-mail: info@lungcanceralliance.org. Web: www.lungcanceralliance.org.

MEDICAL SCHOOL FOR WOMEN OPENED AT BOSTON: ANNIVERSARY. Nov 1, 1848. Founded in Boston, MA, by Samuel Gregory, a pioneer in medical education for women, the Boston Female Medical School opened as the first medical school exclusively for women. The original enrollment was 12 students. In 1874 the school merged with the Boston University School of Medicine and formed one of the first coed medical schools in the world.

MEXICO: DAY OF THE DEAD. Nov 1–2. Observance begins during last days of October when "dead men's bread" is sold in bakeries—round loaves, decorated with sugar skulls. Departed souls are remembered not in mourning but with a spirit of friendliness and good humor. Cemeteries are visited, and graves are decorated.

MISSION SAN JUAN CAPISTRANO: FOUNDING ANNIVERSARY. Nov 1, 1776. California mission founded on this date, collapsed during the 1812 earthquake. The swallows of Capistrano nest in the ruins of the old mission church, departing each year on Oct 23 and returning the following year on or near St. Joseph's Day (Mar 19).

MONTH OF THE MILITARY FAMILY. Nov 1–30. All military posts. A special month to celebrate the military family, including their challenges and successes, and volunteering together! For info: Danielle Hamilton, 246 Creek Nation Dr, Auburn, AL 36830. Phone: (334) 332-5333. E-mail: danielle.hamilton@us.army.mil.

✦ **NATIONAL ADOPTION MONTH.** Nov 1–30.

NATIONAL ADOPTION MONTH. Nov 1–30. To commemorate the success of three kinds of adoption—infant, special needs and intercountry—through a variety of special events. For info: Natl Council for Adoption, 225 N Washington St, Alexandria, VA 22314-2561. Phone: (703) 299-6633. Fax: (703) 299-6004. E-mail: ncfa@adoptioncouncil.org. Web: www.adoptioncouncil.org.

NATIONAL AIDS AWARENESS MONTH. Nov 1–30. To educate consumers, patients, students and professionals on the prevention of AIDS and sexually transmitted diseases. Kit of materials available for $15. For info: Fred Mayer, Pharmacists Planning Service, Inc, 101 Lucas Valley Rd, Ste 382, San Rafael, CA 94903. Phone: (415) 479-8628. Fax: (415) 479-8608. E-mail: ppsi@aol.com. Web: www.ppsinc.org.

NATIONAL ALZHEIMER'S DISEASE MONTH. Nov 1–30. To increase awareness of Alzheimer's disease and what the Alzheimer's Association is doing to advance research and help patients, their families and their caregivers. For info: Alzheimer's Assn, 225 N Michigan Ave, Ste 1700, Chicago, IL 60601. Phone: (312) 335-8700. E-mail: info@alz.org. Web: www.alz.org.

✦ **NATIONAL AMERICAN INDIAN HERITAGE MONTH.** Nov 1–30.

NATIONAL ANIMAL SHELTER APPRECIATION WEEK. Nov 1–7. This is a week to focus on and recognize the indispensable role that animal shelters play in maintaining the safety and health of a community, for all of its residents. Through celebration and promotion of the week, animal shelters and other humane organizations can educate the public about the important services they provide. It's also a great opportunity for individuals or groups to volunteer their time or resources to help the animal shelter care for the community's homeless and abused animals. For info: Humane Society of the US, 2100 L St NW, Washington, DC 20037. Web: www.hsus.org or www.AnimalSheltering.org.

NATIONAL AUTHORS' DAY. Nov 1. This observance was adopted by the General Federation of Women's Clubs in 1929 and in 1949 was given a place on the list of special days, weeks and months prepared by the US Department of Commerce. The resolution states in part: "By celebrating an Authors' Day as a nation, we would not only show patriotism, loyalty, and appreciation of the men and women who have made American literature possible, but would also encourage and inspire others to give of themselves in making a better America." It was also resolved "that we commemorate an Authors' Day to be observed on November First each year."

✦ **NATIONAL DIABETES MONTH.** Nov 1–30.

✦ **NATIONAL FAMILY CAREGIVERS MONTH.** Nov 1–30. To honor family members who care for aging relatives or those with disabilities.

NATIONAL FAMILY CAREGIVERS MONTH. Nov 1–30. A nationwide month of recognition for the millions of family caregivers. For info: Natl Family Caregivers Assn, 10400 Connecticut Ave, Ste 500, Kensington, MD 20895-3944. Phone: (800) 896-3650. Fax: (301) 942-2302. E-mail: info@thefamilycaregiver.org. Web: www.thefamilycaregiver.org.

NATIONAL FAMILY LITERACY DAY®. Nov 1. Celebrated all over the country with special activities and events that showcase the importance of family literacy programs. Family literacy programs bring parents and children together in the classroom to learn and support each other in efforts to further their education and improve their life skills. Sponsored by the National Center for Family Literacy and Toyota. Annually, Nov 1. For info: Natl Center for Family Literacy, 325 W Main St, Ste 300, Louisville, KY 40202. Phone: (502) 584-1133 or (877) FAM-LIT1. Fax: (502) 584-0172. E-mail: ncfl@famlit.org. Web: www.famlit.org.

NATIONAL FIG WEEK. Nov 1–7. To celebrate the completion of the California fig harvest and encourage consumers to use California figs as part of their diet for the taste, high fiber and nutritional value. For info: California Fig Advisory Board, 7395 N Palm Bluffs Ave, Ste 106, Fresno, CA 93711. Phone: (800) 588-2344. Fax: (559) 438-5405. E-mail: info@californiafigs.com. Web: www.californiafigs.com.

NATIONAL GEORGIA PECAN MONTH. Nov 1–30. To herald the Georgia pecan harvest and recognize Georgia's status as the nation's top pecan-producing state, providing 50 percent of the nation's supply. For info: Marcia Crowley, Georgia Agricultural Commodity Commission for Pecans (GACCP), Commodities Promotion Div, Georgia Dept of Agriculture, 328 Agriculture Bldg, Capitol Sq, Atlanta, GA 30334. Phone: (404) 656-3678. Fax: (404) 656-9380.

NATIONAL INSPIRATIONAL ROLE MODELS MONTH. Nov 1–30. To acknowledge the impact contemporary and historic role models have on our lives. Individuals chosen for recognition may include celebrities, historic figures, relatives, friends, colleagues, associates, etc. Celebrate with creative projects and activities featuring historic role models and by spending time with contemporary role models. For info: Darlene House, House of Communications, PO Box 23598, Detroit, MI 48223. Phone: (313) 778-1550. Web: www.nirmm.com.

NATIONAL LIFEWRITING MONTH. Nov 1–30. An opportunity to celebrate ourselves and our families by committing our life stories to writing. Preserving our autobiographies in writing allows us to know ourselves better and to share our stories with future generations. For info: Soleil Lifestory Network, 95 Gould Rd, #33, Lisbon Falls, ME 04252. Phone: (207) 353-5454. E-mail: lifewritingmonth@turningmemories.com.

NATIONAL LONG-TERM CARE AWARENESS MONTH. Nov 1–30. Annual event organized by the American Association for Long-Term Care Insurance (AALTCI) and supported by association members and leading industry organizations. The goal is to create heightened awareness of the need for long-term care and the importance of planning options available to Americans and their families. For info: Jesse Slome, Exec Dir, American Assn for Long-Term Care Insurance, 3835 E Thousand Oaks Blvd, Ste 336, Westlake Village, CA 91362. Phone: (818) 597-3227. Web: www.AALTCI.org.

NATIONAL PATIENT ACCESSIBILITY WEEK. Nov 1–7. The purpose of this week is to increase awareness that physicians need, and are obligated to have, accessible health-care facilities for patients who are older, obese or disabled in order to provide the requisite level of quality care. We support the relationship between physicians and patients to create an examination environment that is accessible and barrier-free. Annually, Nov 1–7. For info: Susan Kaiser, Public Relations, Midmark, 60 Vista Dr, Versailles, OH 45380. Phone: (937) 526-8785. Fax: (937) 526-7426. E-mail: skaiser@midmark.com. Web: www.midmark.com.

NATIONAL PET CANCER AWARENESS MONTH. Nov 1–30. Sponsored by Veterinary Pet Insurance to encourage awareness of cancer in pets. For info: Brian Iannessa, 3060 Saturn St, Brea, CA 92821. Phone: (714) 989-5652. Fax: (714) 989-0533. E-mail: biannessa@petinsurance.com. Web: www.petinsurance.com.

NATIONAL POMEGRANATE MONTH. Nov 1–30. Fresh pomegranates are one of the few fruits that are seasonal—and their season coincides with the festive season. Grown in California, pomegranates are available only from October through January. This month, celebrate them in eating, snacking and decorating. For info: Corporate Communications, POM Wonderful, LLC, 11444 W Olympic Blvd, Los Angeles, CA 90064. Phone: (310) 966-5800. E-mail: pr@pomwonderful.com. Web: www.pomwonderful.com.

NATIONAL ROASTING MONTH. Nov 1–30. From roasted leg of lamb to perfectly cooked roast beef, learn this tried-and-true method of cooking in your own oven. For info: Viking Culinary Arts Center/Viking Home Chef. Web: www.vikingculinary.com.

NATIONAL SCHOLARSHIP MONTH. Nov 1–30. To increase awareness of the need and importance of scholarships as well as to acknowledge and celebrate the positive impact of private-sector scholarships on access, choice and success in higher education. (Formerly observed in May.) For info: National Scholarship Providers Assn, 101 Monroe St, Denver, CO 80206. Phone: (720) 941-4498. Fax: (720) 941-4492. E-mail: aweinstein@scholarshipproviders.org. Web: www.scholarshipproviders.org.

OZARK MOUNTAIN CHRISTMAS/BRANSON FESTIVAL OF LIGHTS. Nov 1–Dec 31. Branson, MO. More than 1.4 million visitors relish the opportunity to celebrate the season by combining a traditional Christmas ambiance with a dash of dazzle as only Branson can offer. The area is illuminated in twinkling lights, with special holiday events and shows galore. For info: Branson Area CVB, PO Box 1897, Branson, MO 65615. Phone: (888) 886-3637. Fax: (417) 334-4139. E-mail: info@bransoncvb.com. Web: www.explorebranson.com.

PEANUT BUTTER LOVERS' MONTH. Nov 1–30. Celebration of America's favorite food and number one sandwich. For info: Peanut Advisory Board, 1025 Sugar Pike Way, Canton, GA 30115. Web: www.peanutbutterlovers.com.

PREMATURITY AWARENESS MONTH. Nov 1–30. Sponsored by the March of Dimes to alert Americans to the common, serious and costly problem of premature birth (before 37 weeks). One in eight babies is born prematurely in this country, many without warning and with no known cause. Prematurity is the leading cause of newborn death (before the first month in life), and babies who do survive often face chronic health and developmental disabilities for the rest of their lives. For info: March of Dimes, 1275 Mamaroneck Ave, White Plains, NY 10605. Phone: (914) 428-7100. Fax: (914) 428-8203. Web: www.marchofdimes.com.

PRESIDENT OCCUPIES THE WHITE HOUSE: ANNIVERSARY. Nov 1, 1800. Philadelphia had served as the nation's capital from 1790 to 1800. On Nov 1, 1800, President John Adams and his family moved into the newly completed White House, as Washington, DC, became the new capital.

PRIME MERIDIAN SET: 125th ANNIVERSARY. Nov 1, 1884. Delegates from 25 nations met in October at Washington, DC, at the International Meridian Conference to set up time zones for the world. On this day the treaty adopted by the conference took effect, making Greenwich, England, the Prime Meridian (i.e., zero° longitude) and setting the International Date Line at 180° longitude in the Pacific. Every 15° of longitude equals one hour, and there are 24 meridians. While some countries do not strictly observe this system (for example, while China stretches over five time zones, it is the same time everywhere in China), it has brought predictability and logic to time throughout the world.

SEABISCUIT DEFEATS WAR ADMIRAL: ANNIVERSARY. Nov 1, 1938. In a special match race at Pimlico in Laurel, MD, Seabiscuit, ridden by George Wolff, defeated favored War Admiral before a crowd of 40,000. Seabiscuit captured the winner-take-all purse of $15,000.

US VIRGIN ISLANDS: LIBERTY DAY. Nov 1. Officially "D. Hamilton Jackson Memorial Day," commemorating establishment of the first press in the Virgin Islands in 1915.

VEGAN MONTH. Nov 1–30. This outreach event encourages everyone to GO VEGAN! Vegans choose to neither eat nor use any animal products (eg, meat, poultry, seafood, dairy products, eggs, gelatin, leather, fur). A growing number of caring, compassionate people are adopting this conscientious lifestyle. Primarily ethical reasons, but also health and environmental concerns, motivate them to GO VEGAN. For info: VEGANET, PO Box 3545, Washington, DC 20027-0045. Phone: (877) GO-VEGAN.

ZERO-TASKING DAY. Nov 1. Today is the day daylight saving time ends—when we turn our clocks back and "gain" an hour. Instead of filling that extra 60 minutes with more work and stress, use that hour to do nothing but take a breath, relax, reenergize, refresh and deload (opposite of overload). For info: Nancy Christie, PO Box 4505, Austintown, OH 44515. Phone: (330) 793-3675. E-mail: nancy@communityofchange.com.

BIRTHDAYS TODAY

Penn Bagdley, 23, actor ("The Bedford Diaries," "Gossip Girl"), born Baltimore, MD, Nov 1, 1986.

Toni Collette, 37, actress (*The Sixth Sense, About a Boy, Muriel's Wedding*), born Sidney, New South Wales, Australia, Nov 1, 1972.

Larry Claxton Flynt, 67, publisher, born Magoffin County, KY, Nov 1, 1942.

November 2009

S	M	T	W	T	F	S
1	2	3	4	5	6	7
8	9	10	11	12	13	14
15	16	17	18	19	20	21
22	23	24	25	26	27	28
29	30					

James Jackson Kilpatrick, 89, journalist ("60 Minutes"), born Oklahoma City, OK, Nov 1, 1920.

Lyle Lovett, 52, singer ("My Baby Don't Tolerate"), born Klein, TX, Nov 1, 1957.

Jenny McCarthy, 37, model, actress (*Scary Movie 3*), born Chicago, IL, Nov 1, 1972.

Betsy Palmer, 83, actress ("I've Got a Secret," "Knots Landing," "Today"), born Patricia Bromek at East Chicago, IN, Nov 1, 1926.

Tim Pawlenty, 49, Governor of Minnesota (R), born St. Paul, MN, Nov 1, 1960.

Gary Jim Player, 74, former golfer, born Johannesburg, South Africa, Nov 1, 1935.

Rachel Ticotin, 51, actress (*Total Recall, Natural Born Killers*), born the Bronx, NY, Nov 1, 1958.

Fernando Anguamea Valenzuela, 49, former baseball player, born Navojoa, Sonora, Mexico, Nov 1, 1960.

November 2 — Monday

DAY 306 | 59 REMAINING

ALL SOULS' DAY. Nov 2. Commemorates the faithful departed. Catholic observance.

AUSTRALIA: RECREATION DAY. Nov 2. The first Monday in November is observed as Recreation Day at Northern Tasmania, Australia.

BEAVER MOON. Nov 2. So called by Native American tribes of New England and the Great Lakes because at this time of year, beavers are industriously preparing themselves for the coming winter. The November Full Moon.

BOONE, DANIEL: 275th BIRTH ANNIVERSARY. Nov 2, 1734. (New Style date.) American frontiersman, explorer and militia officer, born at Berks County, near Reading, PA. In February 1778 he was captured at Blue Licks, KY, by Shawnee Indians, under Chief Blackfish, who adopted Boone when he was inducted into the tribe as "Big Turtle." Boone escaped after five months and in 1781 was captured briefly by the British. He experienced a series of personal and financial disasters during his life but continued a rugged existence, hunting until his 80s. Boone died at St. Charles County, MO, Sept 26, 1820. The bodies of Daniel Boone and his wife, Rebecca, were moved to Frankfort, KY, in 1845.

FIRST SCHEDULED RADIO BROADCAST: ANNIVERSARY. Nov 2, 1920. Station KDKA at Pittsburgh, PA, broadcast the results of the presidential election. The station got its license to broadcast Nov 7, 1921. By 1922 there were about 400 licensed radio stations in the US.

HARDING, WARREN GAMALIEL: BIRTH ANNIVERSARY. Nov 2, 1865. The 29th president of the US was born at Corsica, OH. His term of office: Mar 4, 1921–Aug 2, 1923 (died in office). His undistinguished administration was tainted by the Teapot Dome scandal, and his sudden death in San Francisco, CA, while on a western speaking tour prompted many rumors.

INDIA: GURU NANAK'S BIRTH ANNIVERSARY. Nov 2. According to the Hindu solar calendar, this is the birth anniversary of Guru Nanak, the founder of Sikhism.

LANCASTER, BURT: BIRTH ANNIVERSARY. Nov 2, 1913. Distinguished American actor, born Burton Stephen Lancaster, who began his career in show business as a circus acrobat. In a career spanning 45 years, he appeared in nearly 80 films. Some of his more memorable roles are in *From Here to Eternity* (1953), *The Bird Man of Alcatraz* (1962) and *The Leopard* (1963); he received an Academy Award for his performance in the title role of *Elmer Gantry* (1961). His later popular movies include *Atlantic City* (1981), *Local Hero* (1983) and *Field of Dreams* (1989). Born at New York City, he died Oct 20, 1994, at Los Angeles, CA.

MOON PHASE: FULL MOON. Nov 2. Moon enters Full Moon phase at 2:14 PM, EST.

NATIONAL TRAFFIC DIRECTORS DAY. Nov 2. A day honoring radio and TV traffic departments, which schedule programs and announcements on the nation's broadcast stations. Annually, Nov 2 (observed on following Monday if Nov 2 falls on a Saturday or Sunday). For info: Traffic Directors Guild of America, 26000 Avenida Aeropuerto, Ste 114, San Juan Capistrano, CA 92675. Phone: (949) 429-7063. Fax: (949) 429-7083. E-mail: tdga@cox.net. Web: www.tdga.org.

NEW YORK SUBWAY ACCIDENT: ANNIVERSARY. Nov 2, 1918. The Brighton Beach Express, exceeding its speed limit five times over (going 30 mph) while approaching the station near the Malbone Street tunnel at Brooklyn, jumped the tracks, killing 97 people and injuring 100. The supervisor-engineer, taking the place of a striking motorman of the Brotherhood of Locomotive Engineers, was tried and acquitted of charges of negligence.

NORTH DAKOTA: ADMISSION DAY: ANNIVERSARY. Nov 2. Became 39th state in 1889.

PLAN YOUR EPITAPH DAY. Nov 2. Dedicated to the proposition that a forgettable gravestone is a fate worse than death and that everyone can be in the same league with William Shakespeare and W.C. Fields. Annually, coincides with the Day of the Dead. For info: Lance Hardie, Dead or Alive, PO Box 4595, Arcata, CA 95518. Phone: (707) 822-6924. E-mail: sunrise@hardiehouse.org. Web: www.hardiehouse.org/epitaph.

POLK, JAMES KNOX: BIRTH ANNIVERSARY. Nov 2, 1795. The 11th president of the US was born at Mecklenburg County, NC. His term of office: Mar 4, 1845–Mar 3, 1849. A compromise candidate at the 1844 Democratic Party convention, Polk was awarded the nomination on the ninth ballot. He declined to be a candidate for a second term and declared himself to be "exceedingly relieved" at the completion of his presidency. He died shortly thereafter at Nashville, TN, June 15, 1849.

SENECA FALLS CONVENTION SURVIVOR VOTES: ANNIVERSARY. Nov 2, 1920. The only woman who attended the historic Seneca Falls Women's Rights Convention in 1848 who lived long enough to exercise her right to vote under the 19th Amendment, Charlotte Woodward voted at Philadelphia, PA, in the general election on Nov 2, 1920.

SOUTH DAKOTA: ADMISSION DAY: ANNIVERSARY. Nov 2. Became 40th state in 1889.

SPACE MILESTONE: INTERNATIONAL SPACE STATION INHABITED. Nov 2, 2000. On Oct 31, 2000, a *Soyuz* shuttle left with the first crew to live in the International Space Station, consisting of American commander Bill Shepherd and two Russian cosmonauts. The flight left from the same site in central Asia where *Sputnik* was launched in 1957, beginning the Space Age. The astronauts stayed on board the International Space Station (ISS) until March 2001, when they were replaced by a crew that arrived on the shuttle *Discovery*. Sixteen nations are participating in the ISS project. The construction of the station will be complete in 2010.

SPRUCE GOOSE FLIGHT: ANNIVERSARY. Nov 2, 1947. The mammoth flying boat *Hercules*, then the world's largest airplane, was designed, built and flown (once) by Howard Hughes. Its first and only flight was about one mile and at an altitude of 70 feet over Long Beach Harbor, CA. The $25 million, 200-ton plywood craft was nicknamed the "Spruce Goose." It is now displayed at the Evergreen Aviation Museum in McMinnville, OR.

BIRTHDAYS TODAY

Patrick Buchanan, 71, political commentator, born Washington, DC, Nov 2, 1938.

Shere Hite, 67, researcher on sexual behavior, author (*The Hite Report, Women and Love*), born St. Joseph, MO, Nov 2, 1942.

k.d. lang, 48, singer, born Kathryn Dawn Lang at Consort, AB, Canada, Nov 2, 1961.

Stefanie Powers, 67, actress ("Hart to Hart"), born Hollywood, CA, Nov 2, 1942.

David Knapp (Dave) Stockton, 68, golfer, born San Bernardino, CA, Nov 2, 1941.

November 3 — Tuesday

DAY 307 — 58 REMAINING

AUSTIN, STEPHEN FULLER: BIRTH ANNIVERSARY. Nov 3, 1793. A principal founder of Texas, for whom its capital city was named, Austin was born at Wythe County, VA. He first visited Texas in 1821 and established a settlement there the following year, continuing a colonization project started by his father, Moses Austin. Thrown in prison when he advocated formation of a separate state (Texas still belonged to Mexico), he was freed in 1835, lost a campaign for the presidency (of the Republic of Texas) to Sam Houston in 1836 and died (while serving as Texas secretary of state) at Austin, TX, Dec 27, 1836.

AUSTRALIA: MELBOURNE CUP. Nov 3. Flemington Racecourse, Melbourne. First run in 1861, the Cup is one of the world's great horse races—celebrated throughout Australia and a public holiday in Melbourne. The handicapped race is 3,200 meters with prize money of AU$5.1 million. Famous winners include Phar Lap (1930) and Makybe Diva (2003, 2004, 2005). Annually, the first Tuesday in November. For info: Victoria Racing Club, 448 Epsom Rd, Flemington Victoria 3031, Australia. E-mail: customerservice@vrc.net.au. Web: www.vrc.net.au.

BRONSON, CHARLES: BIRTH ANNIVERSARY. Nov 3, 1921. Movie tough-guy Charles Bronson was born Charles Buchinsky at Ehrenfeld, PA. One of 15 children, he was raised in poverty and was working in the coal mines by age 16. He discovered acting after a stint in the army and was soon making low-budget films, usually violent. His best-known films include *The Magnificent Seven* (1960), *The Great Escape* (1963), *Death Wish* (1974) and four *Death Wish* sequels. He died at Los Angeles, CA, Sept 6, 2003.

BRYANT, WILLIAM CULLEN: BIRTH ANNIVERSARY. Nov 3, 1794. American poet ("Thanatopsis"), born at Cummington, MA. Died at New York, NY, June 12, 1878.

November 2009

S	M	T	W	T	F	S
1	2	3	4	5	6	7
8	9	10	11	12	13	14
15	16	17	18	19	20	21
22	23	24	25	26	27	28
29	30					

CANADA: NEW INUIT TERRITORY APPROVED: ANNIVERSARY. Nov 3, 1992. Canada's Inuit people voted to accept a federal land-claim package granting them control over a new territory, Nunavut, to be carved out of the existing Northwest Territories by 1999. The voting on Nov 3–5, 1992, indicated that 69 percent of the 9,648 eligible Inuit voters accepted the settlement. In exchange for the new territory, approximately 135,000 square miles, the Inuits gave up their rights to a territory of 775,000 square miles. See also: "Canada: Nunavut Independence" (Apr 1).

CLICHÉ DAY. Nov 3. Use clichés as much as possible today. Hey, why not? Give it a shot! Win some, lose some. You'll never know 'til you try it. Annually, Nov 3. (©2006 by WH.) For info: Thomas & Ruth Roy, Wellcat Holidays, 2418 Long Ln, Lebanon, PA 17046-1708. Phone: (717) 279-0184. E-mail: info@wellcat.com. Web: www.wellcat.com.

"DEWEY DEFEATS TRUMAN" HEADLINE: ANNIVERSARY. Nov 3, 1948. This headline in the *Chicago Tribune* notwithstanding, Harry Truman defeated Republican candidate Thomas E. Dewey for the US presidency.

DOMINICA: NATIONAL DAY. Nov 3. National holiday. Commemorates independence from Britain in 1978.

GENERAL ELECTION DAY. Nov 3. Annually, the Tuesday after the first Monday in November. Many state and local government elections are held on this day, as well as presidential and congressional elections in the appropriate years. All US congressional seats and one-third of US senatorial seats are up for election in even-numbered years. Presidential elections are held in even-numbered years that can be divided equally by four. This day is a state holiday in 12 states.

JAPAN: CULTURE DAY. Nov 3. National holiday.

MICRONESIA, FEDERATED STATES OF: INDEPENDENCE DAY. Nov 3. National holiday commemorating independence from US in 1980.

NAGURSKI, BRONKO: BIRTH ANNIVERSARY. Nov 3, 1908. Bronislau ("Bronko") Nagurski, College Football Hall of Famer and charter member of the Pro Football Hall of Fame. Born at Rainy River, ON, Canada, he played football at the University of Minnesota, earning All-American honors at both tackle and fullback, and for the Chicago Bears. After retiring from football, Nagurski wrestled professionally. He died at International Falls, MN, Jan 7, 1990.

PANAMA: INDEPENDENCE DAY. Nov 3. Panama declared itself independent of Colombia in 1903.

PUBLIC TELEVISION DEBUTS: 40th ANNIVERSARY. Nov 3, 1969. A string of local educational TV channels united on this day under the Public Broadcasting System banner. Today there are more than 350 PBS stations.

SANDWICH DAY: BIRTH ANNIVERSARY OF JOHN MONTAGUE. Nov 3, 1718. A day to recognize the inventor of the sandwich, John Montague, Fourth Earl of Sandwich, born at London, England. England's first lord of the admiralty, secretary of state for the northern department, postmaster general and the man after whom Captain James Cook named the Sandwich Islands in 1778. A rake and a gambler, he is said to have invented the sandwich as a time-saving nourishment while engaged in a 24-hour-long gambling session in 1762. He died at London, Apr 30, 1792.

SOS ADOPTED: ANNIVERSARY. Nov 3, 1906. On this date the Second International Radio Telegraphic Conference at Berlin, Germany, proposed a new wireless distress signal: SOS. After its use during the sinking of the *Titanic* in 1912, SOS became the standard distress signal at sea.

SPACE MILESTONE: *SPUTNIK 2* (USSR). Nov 3, 1957. A dog named Laika became the first animal sent into space. Total weight of craft and dog was 1,121 pounds. The satellite was not capable of returning the dog to Earth, and she died when her air supply was gone. Nicknamed "Muttnik" by the American press.

WHITE, EDWARD DOUGLASS: BIRTH ANNIVERSARY. Nov 3, 1845. Ninth chief justice of the US, born at Lafourche Parish, LA.

During the Civil War he served in the Confederate army after which he returned to New Orleans to practice law. Elected to the US Senate in 1891, he was appointed to the Supreme Court by President Grover Cleveland in 1894. He became chief justice under President William Taft in 1910 and served until 1921. He died at Washington, DC, May 19, 1921.

BIRTHDAYS TODAY

Adam Ant, 55, singer, born Stewart Goddard at London, England, Nov 3, 1954.

Ken Berry, 76, actor ("F Troop," "Mayberry RFD," "Mama's Family"), singer, dancer, born Moline, IL, Nov 3, 1933.

Kate Capshaw, 56, actress (*The Love Letter, How to Make an American Quilt*), born Fort Worth, TX, Nov 3, 1953.

Michael S. Dukakis, 76, former Governor of Massachusetts (D), 1988 presidential candidate, born Brookline, MA, Nov 3, 1933.

Robert William Andrew (Bob) Feller, 91, Hall of Fame baseball player, born Van Meter, IA, Nov 3, 1918.

Kathy Kinney, 55, actress ("The Drew Carey Show"), born Stevens Point, WI, Nov 3, 1954.

Steve Landesberg, 64, actor ("Barney Miller"), born the Bronx, NY, Nov 3, 1945.

Dolph Lundgren, 50, actor (*A View to a Kill, Rocky IV*), born Stockholm, Sweden, Nov 3, 1959.

Dennis Miller, 56, comedian, actor ("Saturday Night Live," "The Dennis Miller Show"), born Pittsburgh, PA, Nov 3, 1953.

Evgeny Plushenko, 27, figure skater, born Vologograd, Russia, Nov 3, 1982.

Roseanne, 56, comedienne, actress ("Roseanne," *She-Devil*), born Roseanne Barr at Salt Lake City, UT, Nov 3, 1953.

Philip (Phil) Simms, 53, sportscaster, former football player, born Lebanon, KY, Nov 3, 1956.

Monica Vitti, 76, actress (*The Red Desert*), born Monica Luisa Ceciarelli at Rome, Italy, Nov 3, 1933.

November 4 — Wednesday

DAY 308 — **57 REMAINING**

BUSH, LAURA: BIRTHDAY. Nov 4, 1946. First Lady, wife of President George W. Bush, born Laura Welch at Midland, TX.

CARNEY, ART: BIRTH ANNIVERSARY. Nov 4, 1918. Born at Mt Vernon, NY, this comedian and actor got his start on the vaudeville circuit. He appeared in dozens of Broadway shows and feature films, winning the Oscar for *Harry and Tonto* in 1974, but will always be best remembered for his role of sewer worker Ed Norton on the television classic "The Honeymooners." He played Jackie Gleason's upstairs neighbor on this show for many years, winning six Emmys. He died at Chester, CT, Nov 9, 2003.

DOUGLAS, BOB: 125th BIRTH ANNIVERSARY. Nov 4, 1884. Robert L. (Bob) Douglas, Basketball Hall of Fame executive, born at St. Kitts, British West Indies. Douglas came to the US in 1888 and played basketball before founding the New York Renaissance, one of the game's greatest teams, in 1922. The Rens got their name from the Harlem Renaissance ballroom, where they played their home games, but they barnstormed extensively as well. Over 22 years, they won 2,381 games, including the 1931 World Professional Championship. The Rens were inducted into the Hall of Fame as a team in 1963. Douglas followed as an individual contributor in 1971. Died at New York, NY, July 16, 1979.

ITALY: VICTORY DAY. Nov 4. Commemorates the signing of a WWI treaty by Austria in 1918, which resulted in the transfer of Trentino and Trieste from Austria to Italy.

KING TUT TOMB DISCOVERY: ANNIVERSARY. Nov 4, 1922. In 1922 one of the most important archaeological discoveries of modern times occurred at Luxor, Egypt. It was the tomb of Egypt's child-king, Tutankhamen, who became pharaoh at the age of nine and died, probably in the year 1352 BC, when he was 19. Perhaps the only ancient Egyptian royal tomb to have escaped plundering by grave robbers, it was discovered more than 3,000 years after Tutankhamen's death by English archaeologist Howard Carter, leader of an expedition financed by Lord Carnarvon. The priceless relics yielded by King Tut's tomb were placed in Egypt's National Museum at Cairo.

MAPPLETHORPE, ROBERT: BIRTH ANNIVERSARY. Nov 4, 1946. Born at Floral Park, NY, Mapplethorpe was one of photography's most controversial artists, known initially for his photographs of sadomasochistic rituals and later for his still lifes, nudes and portraits. Mapplethorpe died at Boston, MA, Mar 9, 1989. Exhibits of his work sparked controversy in 1989 and 1990, leading to intense political debate about the funding practices of the National Endowment for the Arts when its charter was up for renewal by Congress. An exhibition of his work in Cincinnati, OH, led to the arrest of the museum's curator, causing an additional uproar over First Amendment freedoms and obscenity issues.

MISCHIEF NIGHT. Nov 4. Observed in England, Australia and New Zealand. Nov 4, the eve of Guy Fawkes Day, is an occasion for bonfires and firecrackers to commemorate failure of the plot to blow up the Houses of Parliament Nov 5, 1605. See also: "England: Guy Fawkes Day" (Nov 5).

NATIONAL CHICKEN LADY DAY. Nov 4. Miami, FL. The Chicken Lady has helped thousands to learn the art of public speaking through her nonprofit organization The Professional Speakers Network, Inc. Each year as a thank-you, people come out and have a celebration to show their appreciation for what she has done to help them. Seventy-five of them, thanks to the Chicken Lady, have published their own books. For info: Dr. Marthenia "Tina" Dupree, The Chicken Lady, PO Box 9906, Fort Lauderdale, FL 33310. Phone: (866) SPEAK-2U or (954) 485-5100. E-mail: chickenlady@prodigy.net. Web: www.thechickenlady.com.

PANAMA: FLAG DAY. Nov 4. Public holiday.

ROGERS, WILL: BIRTH ANNIVERSARY. Nov 4, 1879. William Penn Adair Rogers, American writer, actor, humorist and grassroots philosopher, born at Oologah, Indian Territory (now Oklahoma). With aviator Wiley Post, he was killed in an airplane crash near Point Barrow, AK, Aug 15, 1935. "My forefathers," he said, "didn't come over on the *Mayflower*, but they met the boat."

SEIZURE OF US EMBASSY IN TEHRAN: 30th ANNIVERSARY. Nov 4, 1979. About 500 Iranians seized the US Embassy in Tehran, taking some 90 hostages, of whom 66 were Americans. They vowed to hold the hostages until the former shah, Mohammad Reza Pahlavi (in the US for medical treatments), was returned to Iran for trial. The shah died July 27, 1980, in an Egyptian military hospital near Cairo. Fourteen Americans were released in 1979 and 1980, but the remaining 52 hostages weren't released until Jan 20, 1981, after 444 days of captivity. The release occurred on America's Presidential Inauguration Day, during the hour in which the American presidency was transferred from Jimmy Carter to Ronald Reagan.

UNESCO: ANNIVERSARY. Nov 4, 1946. The United Nations Educational, Scientific and Cultural Organization was formed.

USE YOUR COMMON SENSE DAY. Nov 4. A day celebrating common sense in business and in life—on Will Rogers's birthday. Rogers said, "Common sense ain't all that common." On this day, don't ignore your common sense—use it. Do at least one thing your common sense tells you to do: stop smoking for a day, have a talk with your children, begin an exercise program, etc. For info: Bud Bilanich, The Common Sense Guy, 875 S Colorado Blvd, Ste 773, Denver, CO 80246. Phone: (303) 393-0446. Fax: (303) 393-0081. E-mail: Bud@BudBilanich.com. Web: www.SuccessCommonSense.com.

WILL ROGERS DAY. Nov 4. Oklahoma.

WILL ROGERS DAYS. Nov 4–7. Claremore and Oologah, OK. Festival celebrating the birth and life of the famed Oklahoma humorist with a variety of events and activities at the Will Rogers Birthplace Ranch at Oologah and at the Will Rogers Memorial Museum in Claremore. Includes a birthday party (at ranch), parade in downtown Claremore and wreath-laying ceremony at the museum. For info: Will Rogers Memorial Museum, 1720 W Will Rogers Blvd, Claremore, OK 74017. Phone: (800) 324-9455. Web: www.willrogers.com.

BIRTHDAYS TODAY

Laura Bush, 63, First Lady, wife of George W. Bush, 43rd president of the US, born Midland, TX, Nov 4, 1946.

Sean "Diddy" Combs, 39, rapper, music and fashion executive, actor, born New York, NY, Nov 4, 1970.

Walter Leland Cronkite, Jr, 93, journalist (former anchor for "CBS Evening News"), born St. Joseph, MO, Nov 4, 1916.

Kathy Griffin, 43, comedienne, actress ("Suddenly Susan"), born Chicago, IL, Nov 4, 1966.

Carlos Gutierrez, 56, US Secretary of Commerce, born Havana, Cuba, Nov 4, 1953.

Devin Hester, 27, football player, born Riviera Beach, FL, Nov 4, 1982.

Ralph Macchio, 47, actor (*The Karate Kid*), born Huntington, NY, Nov 4, 1962.

Andrea McArdle, 46, singer, Tony Award–winning stage actress (*Annie*), born Philadelphia, PA, Nov 4, 1963.

Matthew McConaughey, 40, actor (*Failure to Launch, Sahara, A Time to Kill*), born Uvalde, TX, Nov 4, 1969.

Orlando Pace, 34, football player, born Sandusky, OH, Nov 4, 1975.

Markie Post, 59, actress ("Night Court," "Hearts Afire"), born Palo Alto, CA, Nov 4, 1950.

Doris Roberts, 79, actress ("Everybody Loves Raymond," "Remington Steele"), born St. Louis, MO, Nov 4, 1930.

Loretta Swit, 72, actress ("M*A*S*H"), born Passaic, NJ, Nov 4, 1937.

November 2009

S	M	T	W	T	F	S
1	2	3	4	5	6	7
8	9	10	11	12	13	14
15	16	17	18	19	20	21
22	23	24	25	26	27	28
29	30					

November 5 — Thursday

DAY 309 — 56 REMAINING

BRANSON VETERANS HOMECOMING WEEK. Nov 5–11. Branson, MO. An areawide celebration honoring America's veterans. Annually, the seven days in November ending with the 11th. Est attendance: 50,000. For info: Bill Groninger, Branson Veterans Task Force, PO Box 128, Branson, MO 65615. Phone: (417) 337-8387. E-mail: bvtf1@suddenlinkmail.com. Web: www.bransonveterans.com.

DEBS, EUGENE VICTOR: BIRTH ANNIVERSARY. Nov 5, 1855. American politician, first president of the American Railway Union, founder of the Social Democratic Party of America, and Socialist Party candidate for president of the US in 1904, 1908, 1912 and 1920; sentenced to 10-year prison term in 1918 (for sedition) and pardoned by President Warren Harding in 1921. Debs was born at Terre Haute, IN, and died at Elmhurst, IL, Oct 20, 1926.

DURANT, WILL: BIRTH ANNIVERSARY. Nov 5, 1885. American author and popularizer of history and philosophy. Among his books: *The Story of Philosophy* and *The Story of Civilization* (a 10-volume series of which the last four were coauthored by his wife, Ariel). Born at North Adams, MA, and died Nov 7, 1981, at Los Angeles, CA.

EL SALVADOR: DAY OF THE FIRST SHOUT FOR INDEPENDENCE. Nov 5. National holiday. Commemorates the first Central American battle for independence in 1811.

ENGLAND: GUY FAWKES DAY. Nov 5. United Kingdom. Anniversary of the "Gunpowder Plot." Conspirators planned to blow up the Houses of Parliament and King James I, Nov 5, 1605 (OS). Twenty barrels of gunpowder, which they had secreted in a cellar under Parliament, were discovered on the night of Nov 4, the very eve of the intended explosion, and the conspirators were arrested. They were tried and convicted, and Jan 31, 1606, eight (including Guy Fawkes) were beheaded and their heads displayed on pikes at London Bridge. Though there were at least 11 conspirators, Guy Fawkes is most remembered. In 1606 the parliament, which was to have been annihilated, enacted a law establishing Nov 5 as a day of public thanksgiving. It is still observed, and on the night of Nov 5, "the whole country lights up with bonfires and celebration." "Guys" are burned in effigy and the old verses repeated: "Remember, remember the fifth of November,/Gunpowder treason and plot;/I see no reason why Gunpowder Treason/Should ever be forgot."

FIRST SHATTERED BACKBOARD: ANNIVERSARY. Nov 5, 1946. Chuck Connors of the Boston Celtics became the first NBA player to shatter a backboard, doing so during the pregame warm-up in Boston Garden. Connors also played major league baseball with the Brooklyn Dodgers and the Chicago Cubs and gained fame as star of the television series "The Rifleman."

GEORGE W. AND LAURA BUSH WEDDING: ANNIVERSARY. Nov 5, 1977. George W. Bush and Laura Welch were married at Midland, TX. They have twin daughters, Barbara Pierce Bush and Jenna Welch Bush, born in 1981.

LOEWY, RAYMOND: BIRTH ANNIVERSARY. Nov 5, 1893. Raymond Fernand Loewy, the "father of streamlining," an inventor, engineer and industrial designer whose ideas changed the look of 20th-century life, was born at Paris, France. His designs are evident in almost every area of modern life—the US Postal Service logo; the president's airplane, *Air Force One*; and in streamlined automobiles, trains, refrigerators and pens. "Between two products equal in price, function and quality," he said, "the better looking will outsell the other." Loewy died at Monte Carlo, Monaco, July 14, 1986.

MAXWELL, ROBERT: DEATH ANNIVERSARY. Nov 5, 1991. Born Jan Ludwig Hoch in 1923 to a poor farm family in the Carpathian Mountains of Czechoslovakia, Maxwell became a billionaire with a media empire that included TV stations in France, the Macmillan Publishing Company in the US, newspapers in Hungary and the former East Germany, MTV Europe, the only official English-language newspaper in China and two of the biggest tabloids in the English-speaking world: New York's *Daily News* and London's *Daily*

Mirror. After a brief career as a member of parliament, he began his rise as a media baron. Maxwell died after falling overboard from his yacht near the Canary Islands. After his death, his empire was found to be in significant financial disrepair.

McCREA, JOEL: BIRTH ANNIVERSARY. Nov 5, 1905. American actor Joel McCrea was born at South Pasadena, CA. His more than 80 films include *Wells Fargo* (1937), *Union Pacific* (1939), *Sullivan's Travels* (1941) and *Foreign Correspondent* (1940). He died Oct 20, 1990, at Los Angeles, CA.

"THE NAT KING COLE SHOW" TV PREMIERE: ANNIVERSARY. Nov 5, 1956. Popular African-American pianist and singer Cole hosted his own variety show for NBC. The Nelson Riddle Orchestra and the Randy Van Horne Singers also appeared as regulars on the show. It began as a 15-minute program, which was expanded to half an hour. Sponsors wouldn't back the show, however, and many affiliates declined to carry it. As a result, it was canceled.

NATIONAL ASSOCIATION FOR GIFTED CHILDREN CONVENTION. Nov 5–8. Est. attendance: 4000. St. Louis, MO. Educational sessions for administrators, counselors, coordinators, teachers and parents. For info: Natl Assn for Gifted Children, 1707 L St NW, Ste 550, Washington, DC 20036. Phone: (202) 785-4268. Fax: (202) 785-4248. E-mail: nagc@nagc.org. Web: www.nagc.org.

NATIONAL MEN MAKE DINNER DAY. Nov 5. One day set aside for "Non-Cooking Men Only" in the kitchen. Give wives a break, and let the men whip up some culinary delight with no help from family members. In the true spirit of Men Make Dinner Day, barbecues are not allowed. For info: Sandy Sharkey, 939 BOB-FM Radio, 87 George St, Ottawa, ON, Canada K1N 9H7. Phone: (613) 738-2372. Fax: (613) 739-4040. E-mail: ssharkey@939bobfm.com. Web: www.menmakedinnerday.com.

***NEW YORK WEEKLY JOURNAL* FIRST ISSUE: ANNIVERSARY.** Nov 5, 1733. John Peter Zenger, colonial American printer and journalist, published the first issue of the *New York Weekly Journal* newspaper. He was arrested and imprisoned on Nov 17, 1734, for libel. The trial remains an important landmark in the history of the struggle for freedom of the press. See also: "Zenger, John Peter: Arrest Anniversary" (Nov 17).

RETURN DAY. Nov 5. Georgetown, DE. The day when officially tabulated election returns are read from the balcony of Georgetown's redbrick, Greek Revival courthouse to the throngs of voters assembled below. Always the second day after a general election. An official "half-holiday" in Sussex County.

ROGERS, ROY: BIRTH ANNIVERSARY. Nov 5, 1912. Known as the "King of the Cowboys," Rogers was born Leonard Slye at Cincinnati, OH. His many songs included "Don't Fence Me In" and "Happy Trails to You." He made his acting debut in *Under Western Stars* in 1935 and later hosted his own TV show, "The Roy Rogers Show," in 1951. Rogers died at Apple Valley, CA, July 6, 1998. See also: "'The Roy Rogers Show' TV Premiere: Anniversary" (Dec 30).

TARBELL, IDA M.: BIRTH ANNIVERSARY. Nov 5, 1857. American writer born at Erie County, PA. She edited the muckraking journal *McClure's Magazine*, which exposed the political and industrial corruption of the day and emphasized the need for reform. Died at Bethel, CT, Jan 6, 1944.

VIRGINIA CHRISTMAS SHOW. Nov 5–8. Showplace Exhibition Center and Annex, Richmond, VA. 24th annual. Show features 450 artisans and crafters, Christmas gourmet food shops, boutiques, Christmas Holiday Theatre, entertainment, legendary "Sgt Santa." Est attendance: 40,000. For info: Virginia Show Productions Inc, PO Box 305, Chase City, VA 23924. Phone: (434) 372-3996. Fax: (434) 372-3410. E-mail: vashowsinc@aol.com. Web: www.vashowsinc.com.

BIRTHDAYS TODAY

Bryan Adams, 50, singer, songwriter, born Vancouver, BC, Canada, Nov 5, 1959.

Arthur (Art) Garfunkel, 68, singer (Simon and Garfunkel), actor (*Carnal Knowledge*), born Forest Hills, NY, Nov 5, 1941.

Kevin Jonas, 22, singer (The Jonas Brothers), actor (*Camp Rock*), born Teaneck, NJ, Nov 5, 1987.

Ted Kulongoski, 69, Governor of Oregon (D), born in rural Missouri, Nov 5, 1940.

Javy Lopez, 39, baseball player, born Ponce, Puerto Rico, Nov 5, 1970.

Corin Nemec, 38, actor ("Stargate SG-1," "Parker Lewis Can't Lose"), born Little Rock, AR, Nov 5, 1971.

Tatum O'Neal, 46, actress (Oscar for *Paper Moon*; *Bad News Bears*), born Los Angeles, CA, Nov 5, 1963.

Sam Shepard, 66, dramatist, actor (*Buried Child, The Right Stuff*), born Samuel Shepard Rogers at Fort Sheridan, IL, Nov 5, 1943.

Elke Sommer, 68, actress (*A Shot in the Dark, The Prize*), born Elke Schletze at Berlin, Germany, Nov 5, 1941.

Jerry Stackhouse, 35, basketball player, born Kinston, NC, Nov 5, 1974.

Tilda Swinton, 49, actress (*Michael Clayton, The Deep End*), born London, England, Nov 5, 1960.

Bill Walton, 57, broadcaster, Hall of Fame basketball player, born Mesa, CA, Nov 5, 1952.

Geoffrey Wolff, 72, author (*The Duke of Deception, The Age of Consent*), born Los Angeles, CA, Nov 5, 1937.

November 6 — Friday

DAY 310 **55 REMAINING**

BREEDERS' CUP WORLD CHAMPIONSHIPS. Nov 6–7. Santa Anita Park, Arcadia, CA. Since 1982, the Breeders' Cup World Championships has brought together the world's best horses to compete in 14 sensational races. The Breeders' Cup culminates the racing season and crowns the fleetest sprinters, the most promising two-year-olds, the best turf horses. The right to be called the best of the best belongs to the winner of the weekend's final and richest race: the $5 million Breeders' Cup Classic. For info: Breeders' Cup Limited, PO Box 4230, Lexington, KY 40544-4230. Phone: (859) 223-5444. Fax: (859) 223-3945. E-mail: bcracing@breederscup.com. Web: www.breederscup.com.

COLORADO COUNTRY CHRISTMAS GIFT SHOW. Nov 6–8. Denver Merchandise Mart, Denver, CO. More than 400 booths of holiday gifts. Exhibitors from 25 states participate. Free parking. Est attendance: 25,000. For info: Kym Billings, Showcase Events, PO Box 2815, Kirkland, WA 98083. Phone: (800) 521-7469. Fax: (425) 889-8165. E-mail: denver@showcaseevents.org. Web: www.showcaseevents.org.

CRAFTSMEN'S CHRISTMAS CLASSIC ARTS & CRAFTS FESTIVAL. Nov 6–8. Richmond Raceway Complex, Richmond, VA. 30th annual. Features work from more than 500 talented artists and craftspeople. All juried exhibitors' work has been handmade by the exhibitors and must be their own original design and creation. See the creative process in action with several exhibitors demonstrating throughout the weekend. Visit Christmas Tree Village to view the uniquely decorated Christmas trees by some of our exhibitors. Something for every style, taste and budget with items from the most contemporary to the most traditional. Est attendance: 35,000. For info: Gilmore Enterprises, Inc, 3514-A Drawbridge Pkwy, Greensboro, NC 27410-8584. Phone: (336) 282-5550. E-mail: contact@gilmoreshows.com. Web: www.CraftShow.com or www.gilmoreshows.com.

"GOOD MORNING AMERICA" TV PREMIERE: ANNIVERSARY. Nov 6, 1975. This ABC morning program, set in a living room, is a mixture of news reports, features and interviews with news makers and people of interest. It was the first program to compete with NBC's "Today" show and initially aired as "A.M. America." Hosts have included David Hartman, Nancy Dussault, Sandy Hill, Charles Gibson, Joan Lunden, Lisa McRee, Kevin Newman and Diane Sawyer.

HOLIDAY MARKET. Nov 6–8. Greensboro Coliseum Complex Special Events Center, Greensboro, NC. 20th annual. Commercial holiday gift show that is a true feast for all the senses. Of course there is shopping with a capital SHOP! Enjoy the singing of the Victorian-costumed strolling carolers, and let the children visit with Santa. You'll come away with ideas, recipes, samples, beauty makeovers and lots of holiday gifts and ideas. Est attendance: 25,000. For info: Gilmore Enterprises, 3514-A Drawbridge Pkwy, Greensboro, NC 27410. Phone: (336) 274-5550. E-mail: contact@gilmoreshows.com. Web: www.gilmoreshows.com or www.CraftShow.com.

"MEET THE PRESS" TV PREMIERE: ANNIVERSARY. Nov 6, 1947. "Meet the Press" holds the distinction of being the oldest program on TV. It originally debuted on radio in 1945. The show has changed its format little since it began: a well-known guest (usually a politician) is questioned on current, relevant issues by a panel of journalists. The moderators throughout the years have included Martha Rountree, Lawrence E. Spivak, Ned Brooks, Bill Monroe, Marvin Kalb, Chris Wallace, Garrick Utley, Tim Russert and Tom Brokaw.

MOROCCO: ANNIVERSARY OF THE GREEN MARCH. Nov 6. National holiday. Commemorates the march into the Spanish Sahara in 1975 to claim the land for Morocco.

NAISMITH, JAMES: BIRTH ANNIVERSARY. Nov 6, 1861. Inventor of the game of basketball was born at Almonte, ON, Canada. Died at Lawrence, KS, Nov 28, 1939. Inducted into the Basketball Hall of Fame in 1959. Basketball became an Olympic sport in 1936.

NATIONAL FARM TOY SHOW. Nov 6–8. Beckman HS, National Farm Toy Museum and The Commercial Club Park, Dyersville, IA. This "granddaddy" of farm toy shows features tours of farm toy manufacturers, an auction, craft bazaar, pedal pull and more than 400 vendors dealing in farm toys and implements. Annually, the first full weekend in November. Est attendance: 15,000. For info: Dyersville Area Chamber of Commerce, 1100 16th Ave Ct SE, Dyersville, IA 52040. Phone: (563) 875-2311. Fax: (563) 875-8391. E-mail: dyersvillechamber@dyersville.org. Web: www.dyersville.org.

NATIONAL MEDICAL SCIENCE LIAISON (MSL) AWARENESS AND APPRECIATION DAY. Nov 6. Created to educate the public on the role of medical science liaisons and what they do across the pharmaceutical and biotechnology industries. For info: Dr. Erin Albert, Pharm LLC, PO Box 335, Fishers, IN 46037. Phone: (317) 722-1671. Fax: (317) 863-0962. E-mail: erin@pharmllc.com. Web: www.pharmllc.com.

NEVADAPEX COIN AND STAMP EXPO. Nov 6–8. River Palms Casino, Laughlin, NV. Est attendance: 5,000. For info: Israel Bick, Exec Dir, Intl Stamp & Coin Collectors Society, PO Box 854, Van Nuys, CA 91408. Phone: (818) 997-6496. Fax: (818) 988-4337. E-mail: iibick@sbcglobal.net. Web: www.bick.net.

PADEREWSKI, IGNACY JAN: BIRTH ANNIVERSARY. Nov 6, 1860. Polish composer, pianist, patriot born at Kurylowka, Podolia, Poland. He died at New York, NY, June 29, 1941. When Poland fell into the hands of the Soviets after WWII, his family decided he would remain buried in Arlington National Cemetery. In May 1963 President John F. Kennedy dedicated a plaque to Paderewski's memory and declared that the pianist would rest in Arlington until Poland was free. Paderewski's remains were returned to his native country on June 29, 1992, the 51st anniversary of his death, after Poland held its first parliamentary election following its independence from the Soviet Union.

"THE PHIL DONAHUE SHOW" TV PREMIERE: ANNIVERSARY. Nov 6, 1967. The first talk show with audience participation went on the air on this date at Dayton, OH. The first guest interviewed by host Phil Donahue was atheist Madalyn Murray O'Hair. In 1970 the program went national; it moved to Chicago in 1974 and to New York in 1985. In later years the program was titled "Donahue." After winning 19 Emmy Awards, the show left daytime TV in 1996. Phil Donahue briefly aired a show on the MSNBC cable network, but it was canceled after six months on Feb 25, 2003.

SAMOA: ARBOR DAY. Nov 6. The first Friday in November is observed as Arbor Day in Samoa (formerly Western Samoa).

SAXOPHONE DAY (ADOLPHE SAX BIRTH ANNIVERSARY). Nov 6. A day to recognize the birth anniversary of Adolphe Sax, Belgian musician and inventor of the saxophone and the saxotromba. Born at Dinant, Belgium, in 1814, Antoine Joseph Sax, later known as Adolphe, was the eldest of 11 children of a musical instrument builder. Sax contributed an entire family of brass wind instruments for band and orchestra use. He was accorded fame and great wealth, but business misfortunes led to bankruptcy. Sax died in poverty at Paris, France, Feb 7, 1894.

SOUSA, JOHN PHILIP: BIRTH ANNIVERSARY. Nov 6, 1854. American composer and band conductor, remembered for stirring marches such as "The Stars and Stripes Forever," "Semper Fidelis" and "El Capitan," born at Washington, DC. Died at Reading, PA, Mar 6, 1932. See also: "'The Stars and Stripes Forever' Day: Anniversary" (May 14).

SWEDEN: GUSTAVUS ADOLPHUS DAY. Nov 6. Honors Sweden's king and military leader killed in 1632.

UNITED NATIONS: INTERNATIONAL DAY FOR PREVENTING THE EXPLOITATION OF THE ENVIRONMENT IN WAR AND ARMED CONFLICT. Nov 6. A day calling attention to the irreparable damage to ecosystems and natural resources caused by armed conflict. For info: United Nations, Dept of Public Info, New York, NY 10017. Web: www.un.org.

WORLD CHAMPIONSHIP PUNKIN CHUNKIN. Nov 6–8. Bridgeville, DE. 24th annual. Adult and youth teams vie for the distinction of throwing an 8- to 10-pound pumpkin the farthest. The different classes include catapult, trebuchet, human power and theatrical, among others. Orange attire welcomed. Annually, the full weekend that includes the first Saturday in November. For info: World Championship Punkin Chunkin Assn, PO Box 217, Nassau, DE 19969. E-mail: punkassoc@gmail.com. Web: www.punkinchunkin.com.

BIRTHDAYS TODAY

Sally Field, 63, actress (Oscars for *Norma Rae, Places in the Heart*; Emmy for *Sybil*), born Pasadena, CA, Nov 6, 1946.

Glenn Frey, 61, musician, songwriter, singer ("The Heat Is On"), born Detroit, MI, Nov 6, 1948.

Nigel Havers, 60, actor (*Chariots of Fire, Empire of the Sun*), born London, England, Nov 6, 1949.

Ethan Hawke, 39, actor (*Training Day, Dead Poets Society*), novelist, born Austin, TX, Nov 6, 1970.

Lance Kerwin, 49, actor ("James at 15"), born Newport Beach, CA, Nov 6, 1960.

Thandie Newton, 37, actress (*Crash, Mission Impossible II, Beloved*), born in Zambia, Nov 6, 1972.

November 2009

S	M	T	W	T	F	S
1	2	3	4	5	6	7
8	9	10	11	12	13	14
15	16	17	18	19	20	21
22	23	24	25	26	27	28
29	30					

Mike Nichols, 78, film and stage director and producer (Oscar for *The Graduate*), born Michael Igor Peschkowsky at Berlin, Germany, Nov 6, 1931.

Rebecca Romijn, 37, model, actress (*X-Men, Femme Fatale,* "Ugly Betty"), born Berkeley, CA, Nov 6, 1972.

Kelly Rutherford, 41, actress ("Melrose Place," "Gossip Girl"), born Elizabethtown, KY, Nov 6, 1968.

Maria Owings Shriver, 54, First Lady of California, broadcast journalist, born Chicago, IL, Nov 6, 1955.

November 7 — Saturday

DAY 311 **54 REMAINING**

APPLE FESTIVAL. Nov 7–8. Peddler's Village, Lahaska, PA. Craftspeople gather to show their wares and demonstrate their skills. Enjoy country apple butter, cider, fritters and dumplings. Live entertainment and pie-eating contests add to the festivities of this traditional fall celebration. Free admission. For info: Peddler's Village, Rtes 202 & 263, PO Box 218, Lahaska, PA 18931. Phone: (215) 794-4000. Fax: (215) 794-4001. Web: www.peddlersvillage.com.

BANGLADESH: SOLIDARITY DAY. Nov 7. National holiday. Commemorates a coup in 1975.

CAMUS, ALBERT: BIRTH ANNIVERSARY. Nov 7, 1913. French writer and philosopher, winner of the Nobel Prize for Literature in 1957, was born at Mondavi, Algeria. "The struggle to reach the top is itself enough to fulfill the heart of man. One must believe that Sisyphus is happy," he wrote, in *Le Mythe de Sisyphe*. Camus was killed in an automobile accident in France, Jan 4, 1960.

CANADIAN PACIFIC RAILWAY: TRANSCONTINENTAL COMPLETION ANNIVERSARY. Nov 7, 1885. At 9:30 AM the last spike was driven at Craigellachie, British Columbia, completing the Canadian Pacific Railway's 2,980-mile transcontinental railroad track between Montreal, Quebec, in the east and Port Moody, British Columbia, in the west.

CONTINENT-SIZED WINDSTORMS DISCOVERED: ANNIVERSARY. Nov 7, 1991. A satellite that had been launched from the space shuttle *Discovery* on Sept 15, 1991, discovered large windstorms in Earth's upper atmosphere. The satellite's 10 instruments became functional on Nov 7 and detected the continent-sized windstorms, which measured velocities of up to 200 mph in areas that are 600 to 6,000 miles wide in the mesosphere. The largest storm was discovered in the Southern Hemisphere and reached from western Australia eastward to points halfway across the Atlantic Ocean.

CURIE, MARIE SKLODOWSKA: BIRTH ANNIVERSARY. Nov 7, 1867. Polish chemist and physicist, born at Warsaw, Poland. In 1903 she was awarded, with her husband, the Nobel Prize in Physics for their discovery of the element radium. Died near Sallanches, France, July 4, 1934.

DOWNTOWN FESTIVAL AND ART SHOW. Nov 7–8. Downtown Gainesville, FL. 28th annual. See 250 fine artists display one-of-a-kind art for purchase. Two full days of live entertainment on three stages, with children's activity area and food vendors. Est attendance: 115,000. For info: Linda Piper, City of Gainesville, Division of Cultural Affairs, PO Box 490, Gainesville, FL 32602. Phone: (352) 334-5064. Fax: (352) 334-2249. E-mail: piperLr@cityofgainesville.org. Web: www.gvlculturalaffairs.org.

"FACE THE NATION" TV PREMIERE: 55th ANNIVERSARY. Nov 7, 1954. The CBS counterpart to NBC's "Meet the Press," this show employed a similar format: panelists interviewed a well-known guest. In 1983 the panel was changed to include experts in addition to journalists. Though usually produced at Washington, DC, the show occasionally interviewed people elsewhere (such as Khrushchev in Moscow in 1957).

FALA DAY. Nov 7. Little White House State Historic Site, Warm Springs, GA. Annual tribute to Franklin Delano Roosevelt's faithful dog Fala. Includes parades, bagpipes and storytelling. Leashed Scotties are welcome. Annually, the first Saturday in November. For info: FDR's Little White House, 401 Little White House Rd, Warm Springs, GA 31830. Phone: (706) 655-5870. Fax: (706) 655-5872. Web: www.gastateparks.org.

FALL COUNTRY JAMBOREE. Nov 7–8. Pioneer Settlement for the Creative Arts, Barberville, FL. A celebration of pioneer life and food. More than 100 demonstrating crafters and tradespeople, along with five continuous musical stages featuring more than 150 noted artists. Historical displays include Indian and Cracker camps. Also, model railroaders. Annually, the first Saturday and Sunday in November. Est attendance: 12,000. For info: Pioneer Settlement for the Creative Arts, PO Box 6, Barberville, FL 32105. Phone: (386) 749-2959. E-mail: events@pioneersettlement.org. Web: www.pioneersettlement.org.

FIRST BLACK GOVERNOR ELECTED: 20th ANNIVERSARY. Nov 7, 1989. L. Douglas Wilder was elected governor of Virginia, becoming the first elected black governor in US history. Wilder had previously served as lieutenant governor of Virginia, becoming the first black elected to statewide office in the South since Reconstruction.

GREAT OCTOBER SOCIALIST REVOLUTION: ANNIVERSARY. Nov 7, 1917. This holiday in the old Soviet Union was observed for two days with parades, military displays and appearances by Soviet leaders. In the mid-1990s, President Yeltsin issued a decree renaming the holiday the "Day of National Reconciliation and Agreement." According to the old Russian calendar, the revolution took place Oct 25, 1917. Soviet calendar reform causes observance to fall Nov 7 (Gregorian). The Bolshevik Revolution began at Petrograd, Russia, on the evening of Nov 6 (Gregorian), 1917. A new government headed by Lenin took office the following day under the name Council of People's Commissars. Leon Trotsky was commissar for foreign affairs, and Joseph Stalin became commissar of national minorities.

INTERNATIONAL TONGUE TWISTER CONTEST. Nov 7. Burlington, WI. 9th annual. Come to watch or try. Competitors say as many tongue twisters as they can before their tongues twist. Laughter and a gift promised for all. Prizes include a portion of a peck of pickled peppers. A unique family evening out. For info: Logic Puzzle Museum, 533 Milwaukee Ave (Hwy 36), Burlington, WI 53105. Phone: (262) 763-3946. E-mail: logicpuzzlemuseum@hotmail.com. Web: www.logicpuzzlemuseum.org.

JAGGER, DEAN: BIRTH ANNIVERSARY. Nov 7, 1903. American actor Dean Jagger was born at Columbus Grove, OH. Predominantly a character actor, he appeared in more than 120 films, including *Twelve O'Clock High* (1950), for which he won an Oscar for best supporting actor. He died Feb 5, 1991, at Santa Monica, CA.

LOVINGTON FALL ARTS AND CRAFTS FESTIVAL. Nov 7–8. Lea County Fairgrounds, Lovington, NM. 32nd annual. Displays from more than 100 local and regional crafters. Annually, the first weekend in November. Est attendance: 10,000. For info: Lovington Chamber of Commerce, 201 S Main St, Lovington, NM 88260. Phone: (505) 396-5311. Fax: (505) 396-2823. E-mail: jjohnson@lovingtoncoc.org. Web: www.lovingtoncoc.org.

NIXON'S "LAST" PRESS CONFERENCE: ANNIVERSARY. Nov 7, 1962. Richard M. Nixon, having been narrowly defeated in his bid for the presidency by John F. Kennedy in the 1960 election, returned to politics two years later as a candidate for governor of California in the election of Nov 6, 1962. Defeated again (this time by incumbent governor Edmund G. Brown), Nixon held his "last" press conference with assembled reporters in Los Angeles at midmorning the next day, at which he said: "Just think how much you're going to be missing. You won't have Nixon to kick around anymore, because, gentlemen, this is my last press conference."

REPUBLICAN SYMBOL: ANNIVERSARY. Nov 7, 1874. Thomas Nast used an elephant to represent the Republican Party in a satirical cartoon in *Harper's Weekly*. Today, the elephant is still a well-recognized symbol for the Republican Party in political cartoons.

ROOSEVELT ELECTED TO FOURTH TERM: 65th ANNIVERSARY. Nov 7, 1944. Defeating Thomas Dewey, Franklin D. Roosevelt became the first, and only, person elected to four terms as president of the US. Roosevelt was inaugurated the following Jan 20 but died in office Apr 12, 1945, serving only 53 days of his fourth term.

RUSSIA: OCTOBER REVOLUTION. Nov 7. National holiday in Russia and Ukraine. Commemorates the Great Socialist Revolution, which occurred in October 1917 under the Old Style calendar. In 1997 the holiday was renamed the "Day of National Reconciliation and Agreement."

SADIE HAWKINS DAY. Nov 7. Widely observed in US, usually on the first Saturday in November. Tradition established in "Li'l Abner" comic strip in 1930s by cartoonist Al Capp. A popular occasion when women and girls are encouraged to take the initiative in inviting the man or boy of their choice for a date. A similar tradition is associated with Feb 29 in leap years.

STEEPLECHASE AT CALLAWAY GARDENS. Nov 7. Pine Mountain, GA. A six-race steeplechase "meet" where riders match their horses for speed and split-second timing over brush jumps. Box seating and infield tailgating spaces available. Est attendance: 10,000. For info: The Steeplechase at Callaway Gardens, PO Box 2311, Columbus, GA 31902. Phone: (706) 324-6252. Fax: (706) 324-3651. Web: www.steeplechaseatcallaway.org.

VERBOORT SAUSAGE AND KRAUT DINNER. Nov 7. Visitation Parish, Forest Grove, OR. 75th annual event features crafts, Bingo, raffles, beer garden, local produce, home-baked goods and, of course, famous Verboort sausage and kraut. Annually, the first Saturday in November. Est attendance: 8,000. For info: Visitation Parish, 4189 NW Visitation Rd, Forest Grove, OR 97116. Phone: (503) 357-6990. Web: www.verboort.org/dinner.

BIRTHDAYS TODAY

Rio Ferdinand, 31, soccer player, born Peckham, England, Nov 7, 1978.

Billy Graham, 91, evangelist, born William Franklin Graham at Charlotte, NC, Nov 7, 1918.

Keith Lockhart, 50, Boston Pops conductor, born Poughkeepsie, NY, Nov 7, 1959.

Jeremy London, 37, actor ("I'll Fly Away," "Party of Five"), born San Diego, CA, Nov 7, 1972.

Joni Mitchell, 66, singer, songwriter ("Woodstock"), born Roberta Joan Anderson at McLeod, AB, Canada, Nov 7, 1943.

Barry Newman, 71, actor ("Petrocelli," *Vanishing Point*), born Boston, MA, Nov 7, 1938.

Johnny Rivers, 67, singer ("Poor Side of Town," "Secret Agent Man"), born John Ramistella at New York, NY, Nov 7, 1942.

Joan Sutherland, 83, opera singer, born Sydney, Australia, Nov 7, 1926.

Mary Travers, 72, singer (Peter, Paul and Mary), born Louisville, KY, Nov 7, 1937.

November 2009

S	M	T	W	T	F	S
1	2	3	4	5	6	7
8	9	10	11	12	13	14
15	16	17	18	19	20	21
22	23	24	25	26	27	28
29	30					

November 8 — Sunday

DAY 312 — **53 REMAINING**

ABET AND AID PUNSTERS DAY. Nov 8. Laugh instead of groan at incredibly dreadful puns. All-time greatest triple pun: "Though he's not very humble, there's no police like Holmes," from the register of worst puns of Punsters Unlimited. (Originated by Earl Harris, retired, and the late William Rabe.)

BARNARD, CHRISTIAAN: BIRTH ANNIVERSARY. Nov 8, 1922. Pioneering heart surgeon, born at Beaufort West, South Africa. Barnard performed the first human heart transplant on Dec 3, 1967, after years of practicing the procedure, mainly on dogs. The patient, Louis Washkansky, lived for 18 days before dying from an infection. Today, heart transplants are performed regularly and with good success. Barnard died at Paphos, Cyprus, Sept 2, 2001, of heart failure.

COOK SOMETHING BOLD AND PUNGENT DAY. Nov 8. Especially for those of us who have tightly closed up the house against chilly weather for the next six months. Now is the time to create the heavenly, homey odor of pungently bold cooking. Don't forget the sauerkraut and garlic! (©2006 by WH.) For info: Thomas & Ruth Roy, Wellcat Holidays, 2418 Long Ln, Lebanon, PA 17046. Phone: (717) 279-0184. E-mail: info@wellcat.com. Web: www.wellcat.com.

CORTÉS CONQUERS MEXICO: ANNIVERSARY. Nov 8, 1519. After landing on the Yucatán peninsula in April, Spaniard Hernán Cortés and his troops marched into the interior of Mexico to the Aztec capital and took the Aztec emperor Montezuma hostage.

"DAYS OF OUR LIVES" TV PREMIERE: ANNIVERSARY. Nov 8, 1965. This popular daytime serial, like many others, has gone through many changes throughout its run. It expanded from 30 minutes to an hour; it went to number one in the ratings and slipped to nine out of 12 in the 1980s; and it dropped or deemphasized older characters, which angered its audience. The soap is set in Salem and centers around the Horton and Brady families. Notable cast members have included Mary Frann, Joan Van Ark, Susan Oliver, Mike Farrell, Kristian Alfonso, Garry Marshall, John Aniston, Josh Taylor, Wayne Northrop, John DeLancie, Andrea Barber, Deidre Hall, Thaao Penghlis, Jason Bernard, Marilyn McCoo, Charles Shaughnessy, Peter Reckell, Francis Reid, Patsy Pease and Genie Francis.

DEAR SANTA LETTER WEEK. Nov 8–13. Consumer advocate Bob O'Brien answers "Dear Santa" letters for the holiday season. For info: Bob O'Brien, Consumer Advocate, 1061 Koelle Blvd, Secaucus, NJ 07094. Phone: (646) 233-6610. E-mail: robtfobrien@aol.com.

ENGLAND: REMEMBRANCE SUNDAY. Nov 8. Cenotaph, Whitehall, London. Wreath-laying ceremony to commemorate the dead of both world wars by Her Majesty the Queen, members of the royal family, government and service organizations. Annually, the Sunday closest to Nov 11. For info: Public Info Office, HQ London District Military, Horse Guards, Whitehall, London, England SW1A 2AX.

GELLHORN, MARTHA: BIRTH ANNIVERSARY. Nov 8, 1908. Pioneering female war correspondent who covered more than a dozen wars, from the Spanish Civil War to Vietnam. She was the author of numerous nonfiction and fiction works. She was married to Ernest Hemingway from 1940 to 1945 when both were covering WWII. Born at St. Louis, MO, Gellhorn died at London, England, Feb 15, 1998.

HALLEY, EDMUND: BIRTH ANNIVERSARY. Nov 8, 1656. (Old Style date.) Astronomer and mathematician born at London, England. Astronomer Royal, 1721–42. Died at Greenwich, England, Jan 14, 1742 (OS). He observed the great comet of 1682 (now named for him), first conceived its periodicity and wrote in his *Synopsis of Comet Astronomy*: "I may venture to foretell that this Comet will return again in the year 1758." It did, and Edmund Halley's memory is kept alive by the once-every-generation appearance of Halley's Comet. There have been 28 recorded appearances of this comet since 240 BC. Average time between appearances is 76 years. Halley's Comet is next expected to be visible in 2061.

MITCHELL, MARGARET: BIRTH ANNIVERSARY. Nov 8, 1900. American novelist who won a Pulitzer Prize (1937) for her only book, *Gone with the Wind*, a romantic novel about the Civil War and Reconstruction. *Gone with the Wind* sold about 10 million copies and was translated into 30 languages. Born at Atlanta, GA, Mitchell died there after being struck by an automobile Aug 16, 1949.

MONTANA: ADMISSION DAY: ANNIVERSARY. Nov 8. Became 41st state in 1889.

MOUNT HOLYOKE COLLEGE FOUNDED: ANNIVERSARY. Nov 8, 1837. The first college for women in the US was founded as Mount Holyoke Seminary in 1837 at South Hadley, MA. While many colleges for women became coeducational institutions in the 1970s and 1980s, Mount Holyoke remains a women's college.

NATIONAL PARENTS AS TEACHERS DAY. Nov 8. To pay tribute to the more than 3,000 organizations offering Parents as Teachers services across the country and around the world. These programs give all parents of young children support and information on their developing child so all children will learn, grow and develop to realize their full potential. For info: Parents as Teachers National Center, 2228 Ball Dr, St. Louis, MO 63146. Phone: (866) PAT-4YOU. Fax: (314) 432-8963. E-mail: info@ParentsAsTeachers.org. Web: www.ParentsAsTeachers.org.

RORSCHACH, HERMANN: 125th BIRTH ANNIVERSARY. Nov 8, 1884. Psychiatrist born at Zürich, Switzerland, who used his youthful interest in art and sketching to create the unusual and controversial inkblot test that now bears his name. In 1918 Rorschach began showing his patients inkblots on cards—created at random—and asked for their interpretations to gain insight into their unconscious. Rorschach, a psychoanalyst, continued his experimentation before publishing a comprehensive volume of his findings in 1921. He died Apr 2, 1922.

TUNISIA: TREE FESTIVAL. Nov 8. National agricultural festival. Annually, the second Sunday in November.

X-RAY DISCOVERY DAY: ANNIVERSARY. Nov 8, 1895. On this day, physicist Wilhelm Conrad Röntgen (1845–1923) discovered X-rays, beginning a new era in physics and medicine. Although X-rays had been observed previously, it was Röentgen, a professor at the University of Wurzburg (Germany), who successfully repeated X-ray experimentation and who is credited with the discovery.

BIRTHDAYS TODAY

Edgardo Alfonzo, 36, baseball player, born St. Teresa, Venezuela, Nov 8, 1973.

Mary Hart, 58, TV host, born Madison, SD, Nov 8, 1951.

June Havoc, 93, actress (*Gentleman's Agreement, Brewster's Millions*), born Vancouver, BC, Canada, Nov 8, 1916.

Christie Hefner, 57, business executive (*Playboy*), born Chicago, IL, Nov 8, 1952.

Ricki Lee Jones, 55, singer, musician ("Chuck E.'s in Love"), born Chicago, IL, Nov 8, 1954.

Virna Lisi, 72, actress (*How to Murder Your Wife, The Secret of Santa Vittoria*), born Ancona, Italy, Nov 8, 1937.

Patti Page, 82, singer ("The Doggie in the Window," "Allegheny Moon"), born Clara Ann Fowler at Clarence, OK, Nov 8, 1927.

Parker Posey, 41, actress (*Personal Velocity, Best in Show, The House of Yes*), born Baltimore, MD, Nov 8, 1968.

Bonnie Raitt, 60, singer ("Sweet Forgiveness"), born Los Angeles, CA, Nov 8, 1949.

Gordon Ramsay, 43, chef, television personality ("Hell's Kitchen," "The F Word"), born Glasgow, Scotland, Nov 8, 1966.

Tara Reid, 34, actress (*American Pie, Josie & the Pussycats*), born Wyckoff, NJ, Nov 8, 1975.

Morley Safer, 78, journalist ("60 Minutes"), born Toronto, ON, Canada, Nov 8, 1931.

Courtney Thorne-Smith, 42, actress ("According to Jim," "Ally McBeal"), born San Francisco, CA, Nov 8, 1967.

Alfre Woodard, 56, actress (*Cross Creek, Miss Evers' Boys, How to Make an American Quilt*), born Tulsa, OK, Nov 8, 1953.

November 9 — Monday

DAY 313 — 52 REMAINING

AGNEW, SPIRO THEODORE: BIRTH ANNIVERSARY. Nov 9, 1918. 39th vice president of the US, born at Baltimore, MD. Twice elected vice president (1968 and 1972), Agnew became the second person to resign that office, Oct 10, 1973. Agnew entered a plea of no contest to a charge of income tax evasion (on contract kickbacks received while he was governor of Maryland and after he became vice president). He died Sept 17, 1996, at Berlin, MD. See also: "Vice Presidential Resignation: Anniversary" (Dec 28) and "Calhoun, John Caldwell: Birth Anniversary" (Mar 18).

BANNEKER, BENJAMIN: BIRTH ANNIVERSARY. Nov 9, 1731. American astronomer, mathematician, clock maker, surveyor and almanac author, called "first black man of science." Took part in original survey of Washington, DC. Banneker's *Almanac* was published 1792–97. Born at Elliott's Mills, MD, he died at Baltimore, MD, Oct 9, 1806. A fire that started during his funeral destroyed his home, library, notebooks, almanac calculations, clocks and virtually all belongings and documents related to his life.

BERLIN WALL OPENED: 20th ANNIVERSARY. Nov 9, 1989. After 28 years as a symbol of the Cold War, the Berlin Wall was opened on this evening, and citizens of both sides walked freely through an opening in the barrier as others danced atop the structure to celebrate the end of a historic era. Coming amid the celebration of East Germany's 40-year anniversary, prodemocracy demonstrations led to the resignation of Erich Honecker, East Germany's head of state and party chief. It was Honecker who had supervised the construction of the 27.9-mile wall across the city during the night of Aug 13, 1961, because US President John F. Kennedy had ordered a troop buildup in response to the blockade of West Berlin by the Soviets.

BOSTON FIRE: ANNIVERSARY. Nov 9, 1872. Though Boston, MA, had experienced several damaging fires, the worst one started on this Saturday evening in a dry-goods warehouse. Spreading rapidly in windy weather, it devastated several blocks of the business district, destroying nearly 800 buildings. Damage was estimated at more than $75 million. It was said that the fire caused a bright red glare in the sky that could be seen from nearly 100 miles away. The Boston fire came one year, one month and one day after the Great Chicago Fire of Oct 8, 1871.

CAMBODIA: INDEPENDENCE DAY: 60th ANNIVERSARY. Nov 9. National Day. Declared independence from France in 1949.

DANDRIDGE, DOROTHY: BIRTH ANNIVERSARY. Nov 9, 1923. Actress and singer Dandridge was a child star, born at Cleveland, OH, who toured with her sisters, Vivian and Etta Jones, as the Dandridge Sisters. They played at the Cotton Club, sharing the stage with artists such as Cab Calloway and W.C. Handy. Dandridge went solo in 1941 to perform in Hollywood movies and on stage with the Desi Arnaz Band. Her big break came with the lead role in Otto Preminger's musical *Carmen Jones*. Dandridge received an Oscar nomination for her performance. Unfortunately, she could not overcome Hollywood's racism and tendency to typecast, and her career foundered. She died at West Hollywood, CA, Sept 8, 1965.

EAST COAST BLACKOUT: ANNIVERSARY. Nov 9, 1965. Massive electric power failure starting in western New York state at 5:16 PM cut electric power to much of northeastern US and Ontario and Quebec in Canada. More than 30 million people in an area of 80,000 square miles were affected. The experience provoked studies of the vulnerability of 20th-century technology.

FULBRIGHT, J. WILLIAM: BIRTH ANNIVERSARY. Nov 9, 1905. US senator, born at Sumner, MO. He sponsored the legislation that created the Fulbright scholarships for international study for graduate students, faculty and researchers. Died Feb 9, 1995.

KRISTALLNACHT (CRYSTAL NIGHT): ANNIVERSARY. Nov 9–10, 1938. During the evening of Nov 9 and into the morning of Nov 10, 1938, mobs in Germany destroyed thousands of shops and homes carrying out a pogrom against Jews. Synagogues were burned down or demolished. There were bonfires in every Jewish neighborhood, fueled by Jewish prayer books, Torah scrolls and volumes of philosophy, history and poetry. More than 30,000 Jews were arrested and 91 killed. The night got its name from the smashing of glass store windows.

THE LINKS, INC: ANNIVERSARY. Nov 9, 1946. In Philadelphia, PA, Margaret Roselle Hawkins and Sarah Strickland Scott founded a nonpartisan, volunteer organization called The Links, "linking" their friendship and resources in an effort to better the lives of disadvantaged African Americans after WWII. From a first group of nine, The Links grew to an incorporated organization of 8,000 women in 240 local chapters in 40 states plus the District of Columbia and two foreign countries. The Links promotes educational, cultural and community activities through a variety of projects here and in Africa. In May of 1985 The Links became an official nongovernmental organization of the UN.

LOVEJOY, ELIJAH P.: BIRTH ANNIVERSARY. Nov 9, 1802. American newspaper publisher and abolitionist born at Albion, ME. Died Nov 7, 1837, at Alton, IL, in a fire started by a mob angry about his antislavery views.

MOON PHASE: LAST QUARTER. Nov 9. Moon enters Last Quarter phase at 10:56 AM, EST.

NATIONAL CHILD SAFETY COUNCIL FOUNDED: ANNIVERSARY. Nov 9, 1955. The National Child Safety Council (NCSC) at Jackson, MI, is the oldest and largest nonprofit organization in the US dedicated solely to child safety. Distributes comprehensive safety education materials to children and adults through local law enforcement and the council's mascot, Safetypup®. For info: NCSC, Box 1368, Jackson, MI 49204-1368. Phone: (517) 764-6070. E-mail: tlusby@nfcd.org.

"OMNIBUS" TV PREMIERE: ANNIVERSARY. Nov 9, 1952. This eclectic series deserved its name, offering a variety of presentations, including dramas, documentaries and musicals, for more than 10 years. Alistair Cooke hosted the program, which was the first major TV project to be underwritten by the Ford Foundation. Notable presentations included James Agee's "Mr Lincoln"; *Die Fledermaus*, with Eugene Ormandy conducting the Metropolitan Opera Orchestra; Agnes DeMille's ballet *Three Virgins and the Devil* (presented as *Three Maidens and the Devil*); and documentaries from underwater explorer Jacques Cousteau.

SAGAN, CARL: 75th BIRTH ANNIVERSARY. Nov 9, 1934. Astronomer, biologist, author (*Broca's Brain, Cosmos*), born at New York, NY. Died at Seattle, WA, Dec 20, 1996.

VIETNAM VETERANS MEMORIAL STATUE UNVEILING: 25th ANNIVERSARY. Nov 9, 1984. The Vietnam Veterans Memorial was completed by the addition of a statue, *Three Servicemen* (sculpted by Frederick Hart), which was unveiled on this date. The statue faces the black granite wall on which are inscribed the names of more than 58,000 Americans who were killed or missing in action in the Vietnam War.

WHITE, STANFORD: BIRTH ANNIVERSARY. Nov 9, 1853. American architect who designed the old Madison Square Garden, the Washington Square Arch, and the Players Club, Century and Metropolitan Club at New York City. Stanford White was born at New York City and was shot to death on the roof of Madison Square Garden by Harry Thaw, June 25, 1906.

WILHELM II ABDICATES: ANNIVERSARY. Nov 9, 1918. As WWI was coming to a close and it became clear their cause was lost, a revolt broke out in Germany. The kaiser was advised by his military staff that the loyalty of the army could not be guaranteed. On Nov 9, 1918, it was announced in Berlin that Kaiser Wilhelm II had abdicated his throne. The former leader then fled to Holland. Philipp Scheidemann, a Socialist leader, proclaimed a German Republic and became its first chancellor.

WORLD ORPHANS DAY. Nov 9. To facilitate public awareness of orphans and street children's social issues, to highlight the current year's statistics on the AIDS orphans pandemic and to engage community support for the causes. Annually, the second Monday in November. For info: Cheryl Robeson Clemmons, The Stars Foundation. Phone: (704) 649-3132. E-mail: cherylclemmons11@yahoo.com. Web: www.thestarsfoundation.com.

BIRTHDAYS TODAY

Nikki Blonsky, 21, actress (*Hairspray*), born Great Neck, NY, Nov 9, 1988.

Sherrod Brown, 57, US Senator (D, Ohio), born Mansfield, OH, Nov 9, 1952.

Adam Dunn, 30, baseball player, born Houston, TX, Nov 9, 1979.

David Duval, 38, golfer, born Jacksonville, FL, Nov 9, 1971.

Lou Ferrigno, 58, actor (*Pumping Iron*, "The Incredible Hulk"), former bodybuilder, born Brooklyn, NY, Nov 9, 1951.

Robert (Bob) Gibson, 74, Hall of Fame baseball player, born Omaha, NE, Nov 9, 1935.

Nick Lachey, 36, singer, television personality ("Newlyweds: Nick & Jessica"), born Harlan, KY, Nov 9, 1973.

Thomas Quasthoff, 50, opera singer, born Hanover, Germany, Nov 9, 1959.

Thomas Daniel (Tom) Weiskopf, 67, broadcaster, former golfer, born Massillon, OH, Nov 9, 1942.

November 10 — Tuesday

DAY 314 — **51 REMAINING**

AREA CODES INTRODUCED: ANNIVERSARY. Nov 10, 1951. The 10-digit North American Numbering Plan, which provides area codes for Canada, the US and many Caribbean nations, was devised in 1947 by AT&T and Bell Labs. Eighty-four area codes were assigned. However, all long-distance calls at that time were operator-assisted. On this date in 1951, the mayor of Englewood, NJ (area code 201), direct-dialed the mayor of Alameda, CA. By 1960 all telephone customers could dial long-distance calls. The system is administered by the North American Numbering Plan Administration. For info: www.nanpa.com.

BADLANDS NATIONAL PARK ESTABLISHED: ANNIVERSARY. Nov 10, 1978. South Dakota's Badlands National Monument, authorized Mar 4, 1929, was established as a national park and preserve.

November 2009

S	M	T	W	T	F	S
1	2	3	4	5	6	7
8	9	10	11	12	13	14
15	16	17	18	19	20	21
22	23	24	25	26	27	28
29	30					

BURTON, RICHARD: BIRTH ANNIVERSARY. Nov 10, 1925. Welsh-born stage and film actor who led an intense and tempestuous personal life and career. Richard Burton was never knighted and never won an Oscar, but he was generally regarded as one of the great acting talents of his time. Born Richard Jenkins at Pontrhydyfen, South Wales, the son of a coal miner, he later took the name of his guardian, schoolmaster Philip Burton. Burton played King Arthur in the original production of *Camelot.* His films include *Cleopatra, Becket, Who's Afraid of Virginia Woolf?, Anne of the Thousand Days* and *Equus*. Burton died at Geneva, Switzerland, Aug 5, 1984.

***EDMUND FITZGERALD* MEMORIAL BEACON LIGHTING.** Nov 10. Noon–6 PM, Split Rock Lighthouse, Two Harbors, MN. Includes information on the *Edmund Fitzgerald* and other shipwrecks on Lake Superior; beacon lighting at dusk in memory of the 29 men lost on the *Edmund Fitzgerald* on Nov 10, 1975, and of all those who lost their lives in other Great Lakes shipwrecks. Lighthouse open. Est attendance: 500. For info: Lee Radzak, 3713 Split Rock Lighthouse Rd, Two Harbors, MN 55616. Phone: (218) 226-6372. E-mail: splitrock@mnhs.org.

***EDMUND FITZGERALD* SINKING: ANNIVERSARY.** Nov 10, 1975. The ore carrier *Edmund Fitzgerald* broke in two during a heavy storm in Lake Superior (near Whitefish Point). There were no survivors of this, the worst Great Lakes ship disaster of the decade, which took the lives of 29 crew members.

GOLDSMITH, OLIVER: BIRTH ANNIVERSARY. Nov 10, 1728. Irish writer, author of the play *She Stoops to Conquer*. Born at Pallas, County Longford, Ireland, he died Apr 4, 1774, at London, England. "A book may be amusing with numerous errors," he wrote (Advertisement to *The Vicar of Wakefield*), "or it may be very dull without a single absurdity."

HOGARTH, WILLIAM: BIRTH ANNIVERSARY. Nov 10, 1697. English painter and engraver, famed for his satiric series of engravings (*A Harlot's Progress, A Rake's Progress, Four Stages of Cruelty*, etc). Born at London, England, he died there, Oct 26, 1764.

LUTHER, MARTIN: BIRTH ANNIVERSARY. Nov 10, 1483. The Augustinian monk who was a founder and leader of the Protestant Reformation was born at Eisleben, Saxony. Luther tacked his 95 Theses "On the Power of Indulgences" on the door of Wittenberg's castle church, on Oct 31, 1517, the eve of All Saints' Day. Luther asserted that the Bible was the sole authority of the church, called for reformation of abuses by the Roman Catholic Church and denied the supremacy of the pope. Tried for heresy by the Roman Church, threatened with excommunication and finally banned by a papal bull (Jan 2, 1521), he responded by burning the bull. In 1525 he married Katherine von Bora, one of nine nuns who had left the convent due to his teaching. Luther died near his birthplace, at Eisleben, Feb 18, 1546.

MARINE CORPS BIRTHDAY: ANNIVERSARY. Nov 10, 1775. Commemorates the Marine Corps's establishment in 1775. Originally part of the navy, it became a separate unit July 11, 1789.

MICROSOFT RELEASES WINDOWS: ANNIVERSARY. Nov 10, 1983. In 1980 Microsoft signed a contract with IBM to design an operating system, MS-DOS, for a personal computer that IBM was developing. On Nov 10, 1983, Microsoft released Windows, an extension of MS-DOS with a graphical user interface.

NATIONAL YOUNG READER'S DAY. Nov 10. Pizza Hut and the Center for the Book in the Library of Congress established National Young Reader's Day to remind Americans of the joys and importance of reading for young people. Schools, libraries, families and communities nationwide use this day to celebrate youths reading in a variety of creative and educational ways. Ideas on ways you can celebrate this special day available. Annually, the second Tuesday in November. For info: The BOOK IT! Program, PO Box 2999, Wichita, KS 67201. Phone: (800) 426-6548. Fax: (316) 685-0977. Web: www.bookitprogram.com.

PANAMA: FIRST SHOUT OF INDEPENDENCE. Nov 10. National holiday. Commemorates Panama's first battle for independence from Spain in 1821.

"SESAME STREET" TV PREMIERE: 40th ANNIVERSARY. Nov 10, 1969. An important, successful, long-running children's show, "Sesame Street" educates children while they have fun. It takes place along a city street, featuring a diverse cast of humans and puppets. Through singing, puppetry, film clips and skits, children are taught letters, numbers, concepts and other lessons. Shows are "sponsored" by letters and numbers. Human cast members have included Loretta Long, Matt Robinson, Roscoe Orman, Bob McGrath, Linda Bove, Buffy Sainte-Marie, Ruth Buzzi, Will Lee, Northern J. Calloway, Emilio Delgado and Sonia Manzano. Favorite Jim Henson Muppets include Ernie, Bert, Grover, Oscar the Grouch, the Cookie Monster, Big Bird and Mr Snuffleupagus.

STANLEY FINDS LIVINGSTONE: ANNIVERSARY. Nov 10, 1871. Having begun his search the previous March for the then two-years-missing explorer-missionary David Livingstone, explorer Henry M. Stanley found him on this day at Ujiji (Africa) and uttered those now immortal words, "Dr. Livingstone, I presume?"

VON SCHILLER, FRIEDRICH: 250th BIRTH ANNIVERSARY. Nov 10, 1759. Born at Marbach, Württemberg, von Schiller was the leading German dramatist of his age. His works include *Don Carlos* (1787), the Wallenstein trilogy (1798–1801) and *Wilhelm Tell* (1804). His "An die Freude" ("Ode to Joy") was used by Beethoven in the choral finale to his Symphony no. 9 in D Minor. Died May 9, 1805, at Weimer, Germany.

BIRTHDAYS TODAY

Vanessa Angel, 46, actress (*Spies Like Us, Kingpin*), born London, England, Nov 10, 1963.

Isaac Bruce, 37, football player, born Ft Lauderdale, FL, Nov 10, 1972.

Saxby Chambliss, 66, US Senator (R, Georgia), born Warrenton, NC, Nov 10, 1943.

Roland Emmerich, 54, director, producer (*The Day After Tomorrow, Independence Day*), born Stuttgart, Germany, Nov 10, 1955.

Donna Fargo, 60, singer ("Funny Face"), songwriter, born Yvonne Vaughan at Mount Airy, NC, Nov 10, 1949.

Neil Gaiman, 49, author, comic book writer (the Sandman series), born Porchester, England, Nov 10, 1960.

Russell Charles Means, 69, Native American rights activist, born Pine Ridge, SD, Nov 10, 1940.

Tracy Morgan, 41, comedian, actor ("Saturday Night Live," "30 Rock"), born the Bronx, NY, Nov 10, 1968.

Brittany Murphy, 32, actress (*Sin City, 8 Mile, Clueless*), born Atlanta, GA, Nov 10, 1977.

Mackenzie Phillips, 50, actress ("One Day at a Time," *American Graffiti*), born Alexandria, VA, Nov 10, 1959.

Ellen Pompeo, 40, actress ("Grey's Anatomy," *Moonlight Mile*), born Everett, MA, Nov 10, 1969.

Ann Reinking, 60, Tony Award–winning performer, director and choreographer (*Chicago*), born Seattle, WA, Nov 10, 1949.

Tim Rice, 65, Tony Award–winning lyricist (*Aida, Evita, Jesus Christ Superstar*), born Amersham, England, Nov 10, 1944.

Sinbad, 53, comedian, actor (*Jingle All the Way*, "A Different World"), born David Adkins at Benton Harbor, MI, Nov 10, 1956.

November 11 — Wednesday

DAY 315 | 50 REMAINING

ANGOLA: INDEPENDENCE DAY. Nov 11. National holiday. Angola gained its independence from Portugal in 1975.

BONZA BOTTLER DAY™. Nov 11. To celebrate when the number of the day is the same as the number of the month. Bonza Bottler Day™ is an excuse to have a party at least once a month. For more information see Jan 1. For info: Gail M. Berger, 14 Fernwood Dr, Taylors, SC 29687. E-mail: bonza@bonzabottlerday.com. Web: www.bonzabottlerday.com.

CANADA: REMEMBRANCE DAY. Nov 11. Honors those who died in WWI and WWII. Public holiday.

CHURCH OF ENGLAND VOTES TO ALLOW WOMEN PRIESTS: ANNIVERSARY. Nov 11, 1992. The Church of England, one of 28 national churches within the international Anglican Communion, voted Nov 11, 1992, to allow women to become priests.

COLOMBIA: CARTAGENA INDEPENDENCE DAY. Nov 11. National holiday. Commemorates declaration of independence from Spain of the city of Cartagena in 1811.

DEATH/DUTY DAY. Nov 11. Honoring soldiers on both sides who died on Nov 11, 1918, the day of the armistice that ended the fighting in WWI, 1914–18. The order was to stop fighting at 11 AM, rather than on receipt of the order. For info: Bob Birch, Punscorpion, The Puns Corps, 3108 Dashiell Rd, Falls Church, VA 22042. Phone: (703) 533-3668.

DOSTOYEVSKY, FYODOR MIKHAYLOVICH: BIRTH ANNIVERSARY. Nov 11, 1821. Russian novelist, author of *The Brothers Karamazov, Crime and Punishment* and *The Idiot*, was born at Moscow, Russia, and died at St. Petersburg, Russia, Feb 9, 1881. A political revolutionary, he was arrested, tried, convicted and sentenced to death, but instead of execution he served a sentence in a Siberian prison and later served in the army there.

"GOD BLESS AMERICA" FIRST PERFORMED: ANNIVERSARY. Nov 11, 1938. Irving Berlin wrote this song especially for Kate Smith. She first sang it during her regular radio broadcast. It quickly became a great patriotic favorite of the nation and one of Smith's most requested songs.

MALDIVES: REPUBLIC DAY. Nov 11. National holiday. Commemorates the abolition of the sultanate in 1968.

MARTINMAS. Nov 11. The Feast Day of Saint Martin of Tours, who lived about AD 316–397. A bishop, he became one of the most popular saints of the Middle Ages. The period of warm weather often occurring about the time of his feast day is sometimes called Saint Martin's Summer (especially in England).

PATTON, GEORGE S., JR: BIRTH ANNIVERSARY. Nov 11, 1885. American military officer, graduate of West Point (1909), George Smith Patton, Jr, was born at San Gabriel, CA. Ambitious and flamboyant, he lived for combat. He served in the punitive expedition into Mexico (1916), in Europe in WWI, and in North Africa and Europe in WWII. He received world attention and official censure in 1943 for slapping a hospitalized shell-shocked soldier. While a full general, owing to his critical public statements, he was relieved of his command in 1945. He died at Heidelberg, Germany, Dec 21, 1945, of injuries received in an automobile accident.

POLAND: INDEPENDENCE DAY. Nov 11. Poland regained independence in 1918, after having been partitioned among Austria, Prussia and Russia for more than 120 years.

SPACE MILESTONE: *COLUMBIA STS-5* (US). Nov 11, 1982. Shuttle *Columbia* launched from Kennedy Space Center, FL, with four astronauts: Vance Brand, Robert Overmyer, William Lenoir and Joseph Allen. "First operational mission" delivered two satellites into orbit for commercial customers. *Columbia* landed at Edwards Air Force Base, CA, Nov 16, 1982.

SPACE MILESTONE: *GEMINI 12* (US). Nov 11, 1966. Last Project Gemini manned Earth orbit launched. Buzz Aldrin spent five hours on a space walk, setting a new record.

SWEDEN: SAINT MARTIN'S DAY. Nov 11. Originally in memory of Saint Martin of Tours; also associated with Martin Luther, who is celebrated the day before. Marks the end of the autumn's work and the beginning of winter activities.

SWITZERLAND: MARTINMAS GOOSE (MARTINIGIANS). Nov 11. Sursee, Canton Lucerne. At 3 PM on Martinmas (the day on which interest is due), the "Gansabhauet" is staged in front of Town Hall. Blindfolded participants try to bring down, with a single sword stroke, a dead goose suspended on a wire.

✦ **VETERANS DAY.** Nov 11. Presidential Proclamation. Formerly called Armistice Day and proclaimed each year since 1926 for Nov 11. PL 83–380 of June 1, 1954, changed the name to Veterans Day. PL 90–363 of June 28, 1968, required that, beginning in 1971, it would be observed the fourth Monday in October. PL 94–97 of Sept 18, 1975, required that, effective Jan 1, 1978, the observance would revert to Nov 11.

VETERANS DAY. Nov 11. Veterans Day was observed on Nov 11 from 1919 through 1970. Public Law 90–363, the "Monday Holiday Law," provided that, beginning in 1971, Veterans Day would be observed on the fourth Monday in October. This movable observance date, which separated Veterans Day from the Nov 11 anniversary of WWI armistice, proved unpopular. State after state moved its observance back to the traditional Nov 11 date, and finally Public Law 94–97 of Sept 18, 1975, required that, effective Jan 1, 1978, the observance of Veterans Day revert to Nov 11. As Armistice Day this is a holiday in Belgium, France and other European countries. At the eleventh hour of the eleventh day of the eleventh month fighting ceased in WWI.

VICTOR EMMANUEL III: BIRTH ANNIVERSARY. Nov 11, 1869. Last king of Italy Victor Emmanuel III was born at Naples, Italy, and became king upon the assassination of his father in July 1900. For the first 20 years of his reign, Victor Emmanuel followed Italy's constitutional custom of selecting a prime minister based on the parliamentary majority, but with parliament in disarray after WWI, he named Benito Mussolini to form a cabinet and then failed to prevent Mussolini and the Fascists from seizing power. The king became little more than a figurehead. In 1946 Victor Emmanuel abdicated the throne, and he and the crown prince went into exile. He died at Alexandria, Egypt, Dec 28, 1947.

VIETNAM WOMEN'S MEMORIAL DEDICATION: ANNIVERSARY. Nov 11, 1993. In recognition of the 11,500 women who served in the Vietnam War, the bronze sculpture erected at Washington, DC, was dedicated this day.

November 2009

S	M	T	W	T	F	S
1	2	3	4	5	6	7
8	9	10	11	12	13	14
15	16	17	18	19	20	21
22	23	24	25	26	27	28
29	30					

VONNEGUT, KURT, JR: BIRTH ANNIVERSARY. Nov 11, 1922. Novelist and playwright, born at Indianapolis, IN. His idiosyncratic, semiautobiographical, blackly comic works were campus favorites in the Vietnam-roiled 1960s and '70s, especially *Cat's Cradle* (1963), *Slaughterhouse-Five* (1969) and *Breakfast of Champions* (1973). *Slaughterhouse-Five*, part of which was based on his WWII experience as a German prisoner of war, is frequently cited as one of the 100 best novels of the 20th century. Vonnegut died Apr 11, 2007, at New York, NY.

WASHINGTON: ADMISSION DAY: ANNIVERSARY. Nov 11. Became 42nd state in 1889.

WORLD WAR I ARMISTICE: ANNIVERSARY. Nov 11, 1918. Anniversary of armistice between Allied and Central Powers ending WWI, signed at 5 AM, Nov 11, 1918, in Marshal Foch's railway car in the forest of Compiègne, France. Hostilities ceased at 11 AM. Recognized in many countries as Armistice Day, Remembrance Day, Veterans Day, Victory Day or WWI Memorial Day. Many places observe silent memorial at the 11th hour of the 11th day of the 11th month each year. See also: "Veterans Day" (Nov 11).

BIRTHDAYS TODAY

Bibi Andersson, 74, actress (*Story of a Woman, Persona*), born Birgitta Anderson at Stockholm, Sweden, Nov 11, 1935.

Barbara Boxer, 69, US Senator (D, California), born Brooklyn, NY, Nov 11, 1940.

Leonardo DiCaprio, 35, actor (*Blood Diamond, The Departed, The Aviator, Titanic*), born Hollywood, CA, Nov 11, 1974.

Calista Flockhart, 45, actress ("Ally McBeal," "Brothers & Sisters"), born Freeport, IL, Nov 11, 1964.

Demi Moore, 47, actress (*Charlie's Angels: Full Throttle, GI Jane, Ghost*), born Roswell, NM, Nov 11, 1962.

Reynaldo Ordonez, 37, baseball player, born Havana, Cuba, Nov 11, 1972.

Jonathan Winters, 84, comedian, actor ("The Jonathan Winters Show," *Viva Max!*), born Dayton, OH, Nov 11, 1925.

Frank Urban "Fuzzy" Zoeller, 58, golfer, born New Albany, IN, Nov 11, 1951.

November 12 — Thursday

DAY 316 — **49 REMAINING**

BIRTH OF BAHA'U'LLAH: ANNIVERSARY. Nov 12, 1817. Baha'i observance of the anniversary of the birth of Baha'u'llah (born Mirza Husayn Ali) at Nur, Persia. Baha'u'llah was prophet-founder of the Baha'i Faith. One of the nine days of the year when Baha'is suspend work. For info: Baha'is of the US, Office of Communications, 1233 Central St, Evanston, IL 60201. Phone: (847) 733-3559. Fax: (847) 733-3578. E-mail: ooc@usbnc.org. Web: www.bahai.us.

BLACKMUN, HARRY A.: BIRTH ANNIVERSARY. Nov 12, 1908. Former associate justice of the US Supreme Court, nominated by President Richard Nixon Apr 14, 1970. He retired from the Court Aug 3, 1994. Justice Blackmun was born at Nashville, IL, and died at Arlington, VA, Mar 4, 1999.

KELLY, GRACE PATRICIA: 80th BIRTH ANNIVERSARY. Nov 12, 1929. American award-winning actress (Oscar for *The Country Girl*; *Rear Window, To Catch a Thief*) who became Princess Grace of Monaco when she married that country's ruler, Prince Rainier III, in 1956. Born at Philadelphia, PA, she died of injuries sustained in an automobile accident, Sept 14, 1982, at Monte Carlo, Monaco.

MEXICO: POSTMAN'S DAY. Nov 12. Every year on "Día del cartero," Mexicans show their appreciation for their postal carriers by leaving a little something in their mailboxes.

RODIN, AUGUSTE: BIRTH ANNIVERSARY. Nov 12, 1840. French sculptor (*The Kiss, The Thinker*), born at Paris, France. Died Nov 17, 1917, near Paris.

SPACE MILESTONE: *COLUMBIA STS-2* (US). Nov 12, 1981. Shuttle *Columbia*, launched from Kennedy Space Center, FL, with Joe Engle and Richard Truly on board, became the first spacecraft launched from Earth for a second orbiting mission. Landed at Edwards Air Force Base, CA, Nov 14, 1981.

STANTON, ELIZABETH CADY: BIRTH ANNIVERSARY. Nov 12, 1815. Women's suffragist and reformer, Elizabeth Cady Stanton was born at Johnstown, NY. "We hold these truths to be self-evident," she said at the first Women's Rights Convention, in 1848, "that all men and women are created equal." She died at New York, NY, Oct 26, 1902.

SUN YAT-SEN: BIRTH ANNIVERSARY (TRADITIONAL). Nov 12. Although his actual birth date in 1866 is not known, Dr. Sun Yat-sen's traditional birthday commemoration is held Nov 12. Heroic leader of China's 1911 revolution, he died at Beijing, China, Mar 12, 1925. A holiday in Taiwan. His death anniversary is also widely observed. See also: "Sun Yat-sen: Death Anniversary" (Mar 12).

TRIPLE CROWN OF SURFING. Nov 12–Dec 20. Oahu, HI. 27th annual. The Triple Crown includes three professional big-wave surf meets on Oahu's North Shore that mark the conclusion of the year-long Association of Surfing Professionals (ASP) world tour. Following the Triple Crown, the ASP Men's and Women's Champions are crowned. Est attendance: 30,000. For info: Randy Rarick, 59-063-A Hoalua St, Haleiwa, HI 96712. Phone: (808) 638-7266. Fax: (808) 638-7764. E-mail: surfpro@hawaii.rr.com. Web: www.triplecrownofsurfing.com.

TYLER, LETITIA CHRISTIAN: BIRTH ANNIVERSARY. Nov 12, 1790. First wife of John Tyler, 10th president of the US, born at New Kent County, VA. Died at Washington, DC, Sept 10, 1842.

BIRTHDAYS TODAY

Nadia Comaneci, 48, Olympic gold medal gymnast, born Onesti, Romania, Nov 12, 1961.

Ryan Gosling, 29, actor (*The Notebook, Lars and the Real Girl*), born London, ON, Canada, Nov 12, 1980.

Tonya Harding, 39, former figure skater, born Portland, OR, Nov 12, 1970.

Norman Mineta, 78, former US Secretary of Transportation, born San Jose, CA, Nov 12, 1931.

Megan Mullally, 51, actress ("Will & Grace"), born Los Angeles, CA, Nov 12, 1958.

Jack Reed, 60, US Senator (D, Rhode Island), born Providence, RI, Nov 12, 1949.

David Schwimmer, 43, actor ("Friends"), director, born Queens, NY, Nov 12, 1966.

Sammy Sosa, 41, baseball player, born San Pedro de Macoris, Dominican Republic, Nov 12, 1968.

Neil Young, 64, singer (Buffalo Springfield and Crosby, Stills, Nash & Young), songwriter, born Toronto, ON, Canada, Nov 12, 1945.

November 13 — Friday

DAY 317 **48 REMAINING**

BOOTH, EDWIN (THOMAS): BIRTH ANNIVERSARY. Nov 13, 1833. Famed American actor and founder of the Players Club, born near Bel Air, MD. His brother, John Wilkes Booth, assassinated President Abraham Lincoln. Died at New York, NY, June 7, 1893.

BRANDEIS, LOUIS DEMBITZ: BIRTH ANNIVERSARY. Nov 13, 1856. American jurist, associate justice of US Supreme Court (1916–39), born at Louisville, KY. Died at Washington, DC, Oct 5, 1941.

CHRISTKINDL MARKT. Nov 13–15. Cultural Center for the Arts, Canton, OH. 38th annual. Fine arts and crafts show and sale. Sponsored by the Canton Fine Arts Associates to benefit the Canton Museum of Art. Est attendance: 5,000. For info: Christkindl Markt, 1001 Market Ave N, Canton, OH 44702. Phone: (330) 453-7666. Fax: (330) 453-1034. Web: www.cantonchristkindl.org.

COIN & STAMP EXPO: AMERICA. Nov 13–15. Radisson Hotel, Anaheim, CA. Est attendance: 4,000. For info: Israel Bick, Exec Dir, Intl Stamp & Coin Collectors Society, PO Box 854, Van Nuys, CA 91408. Phone: (818) 997-6496. Fax: (818) 988-4337. E-mail: iibick@sbcglobal.net. Web: www.bick.net.

COIN & STAMP EXPO: CALIFORNIA. Nov 13–15. Pasadena Convention Center, Pasadena, CA. Est attendance: 4,000. For info: Israel Bick, Exec Dir, Intl Stamp & Coin Collectors Society, PO Box 854, Van Nuys, CA 91408. Phone: (818) 997-6496. Fax: (818) 988-4337. E-mail: iibick@sbcglobal.net. Web: www.bick.net.

FALL OF KABUL: ANNIVERSARY. Nov 13, 2001. Northern Alliance troops opposing the Islamic extremist regime of the Taliban moved into the capital of Afghanistan on this date—the first major victory in the war on terrorism prompted by the Sept 11, 2001, attacks on America. After fleeing Kabul (which they had controlled since 1996), the Taliban regime quickly collapsed. The US had demanded that the Taliban regime give up Al Qaeda terrorists and their leader, Osama bin Laden, or face reprisals. Upon the Taliban's prevarication, the US led a multinational force in support of the Northern Alliance that began with a bombardment and was followed by ground warfare in Afghanistan. The fall of Kabul was the first major step to destroying Al Qaeda's Afghanistan stronghold. See also "Attack on America: Anniversary" (Sept 11).

FOUR CORNER STATES BLUEGRASS FESTIVAL. Nov 13–15. Wickenburg, AZ. 29th annual old-time fiddle, banjo, mandolin, flat-pick guitar championships. Includes gospel music. Special entertainment by nationally known bands as well as 13 competitive events. Est attendance: 5,000. For info: J. Brooks, Exec Dir, Chamber of Commerce, 216 N Frontier St, Wickenburg, AZ 85390. Phone: (928) 684-5479 or (928) 684-0977. Fax: (928) 684-5470. E-mail: events@wickenburgchamber.com. Web: www.wickenburgchamber.com.

GUINNESS WORLD RECORDS' DAY. Nov 13 (tentative). Annual day celebrating ordinary people around the world doing extraordinary things. Also a day to encourage everyone to reach into their imaginations and attempt to break their own Guinness World Record. Sponsored by Guinness World Records, the universally recognized authority on record-breaking achievement. The *Guinness World Records* book, published since 1955, reached its own milestone in 2004 when it sold its 100 millionth copy. For more information on this special day, contact a regional Guinness World Records office. For info: Laura Plunkett, Guinness World Records, 230 Park Ave South, 13th Fl, New York, NY 10003. Phone: (212) 463-9623. Fax: (212) 463-9626. Web: www.guinnessworldrecords.com.

HOLLAND TUNNEL: ANNIVERSARY. Nov 13, 1927. The Holland Tunnel, running under the Hudson River between New York, NY, and Jersey City, NJ, was opened to traffic. The tunnel was built and operated by the New York–New Jersey Bridge and Tunnel Commission. Comprising two tubes, each large enough for two lanes of traffic, the Holland was the first underwater tunnel built in the US.

MAXWELL, JAMES CLERK: BIRTH ANNIVERSARY. Nov 13, 1831. British physicist noted for his work in the field of electricity and magnetism. Born at Edinburgh, Scotland, he died of cancer Nov 5, 1879, at Cambridge, England.

NATIONAL DONOR SABBATH. Nov 13–15. To increase awareness about the dire need for organs and tissues for transplantation and to dispel fears that tissue and organ donation is incompatible with religion. Annually, the Friday, Saturday and Sunday two weekends before Thanksgiving. For info: Health Resources and Services Admin, US Dept of Health and Human Services. Phone: (301) 443-7577. Web: www.organdonor.gov.

SALT LAKE'S FAMILY CHRISTMAS GIFT SHOW. Nov 13–15. Sandy, UT. A delightful holiday experience. Shoppers will find gifts and decorations from vendors across the nation. A festive shopping atmosphere with music, entertainment, Santa Claus and a specialty food area for all to enjoy. Est attendance: 25,000. For info: Showcase Events, Inc, PO Box 2815, Kirkland, WA 98083. Phone: (800) 521-SHOW. E-mail: anna@showcaseevents.org. Web: www.showcaseevents.org.

STEVENSON, ROBERT LOUIS: BIRTH ANNIVERSARY. Nov 13, 1850. Scottish author, born at Edinburgh, Scotland, known for his *Child's Garden of Verses* and novels such as *Treasure Island* and *Kidnapped.* Died at Samoa, Dec 3, 1894.

STOKES BECOMES FIRST BLACK MAYOR IN US: ANNIVERSARY. Nov 13, 1967. Carl Burton Stokes became the first black in the US elected mayor when he won the Cleveland, OH, mayoral election Nov 13, 1967. Died Apr 3, 1996.

SUGARLOAF CRAFTS FESTIVAL. Nov 13–15. Connecticut Expo Center, Hartford, CT. Now in its sixth year, this show features 300 nationally recognized craft designers and fine artists displaying and selling their original creations. Includes craft demonstrations, live music, specialty foods, children's entertainment, hourly gift certificate drawings and more. Est attendance: 16,000. For info: Sugarloaf Mountain Works, 200 Orchard Ridge Dr, #215, Gaithersburg, MD 20878. Phone: (800) 210-9900. Fax: (301) 253-9620. Web: www.sugarloafcrafts.com.

TRELAWNEY, EDWARD JOHN: BIRTH ANNIVERSARY. Nov 13, 1792. English traveler and author, friend of Shelley and Byron, born at London, England. He died at Sompting, Sussex, England, Aug 13, 1881, and was buried at Rome, Italy, next to Shelley.

WATERFOWL FESTIVAL. Nov 13–15. Easton, MD. The ultimate weekend for the sophisticated sports enthusiast or art lover. Twelve venues throughout the city feature world-class wildlife paintings, carvings, photography, sculpture, collectible decoys and sporting gear. Scheduled events include world-championship calling contests; decoy auctions; shooting; retriever, stunt dog and fly-fishing demonstrations; and evening concerts. The wine-tasting pavilion is not to be missed. Annually, the second full weekend in November. Proceeds contributed to wildlife conservation. Est attendance: 15,000. For info: Waterfowl Festival, PO Box 929, Easton, MD 21601. Phone: (410) 822-4567. Fax: (410) 820-9286. E-mail: facts@waterfowlfestival.org. Web: www.waterfowlfestival.org.

November 2009

S	M	T	W	T	F	S
1	2	3	4	5	6	7
8	9	10	11	12	13	14
15	16	17	18	19	20	21
22	23	24	25	26	27	28
29	30					

WORLD KINDNESS DAY. Nov 13. The Kindness Movement has gone global! The World Kindness Movement grew out of a series of Kindness Conferences convened by the Japanese Small Kindness Movement in 1996. The Random Acts of Kindness Foundation, USA, has been a part of these conferences along with representatives from Japan, Singapore, Australia, Canada, Thailand and England. This day represents the pledge of each of these countries to join together to build a kinder and more compassionate world. For info: Random Acts of Kindness Foundation, 1727 Tremont Pl, Denver, CO 80202. Phone: (800) 660-2811. E-mail: rakinfo@actsofkindness.org. Web: www.actsofkindness.org.

BIRTHDAYS TODAY

Gerard Butler, 40, actor (*P.S. I Love You, 300, The Phantom of the Opera*), born Glasgow, Scotland, Nov 13, 1969.

Monique Coleman, 19, actress (*High School Musical*), born Orangeburg, SC, Nov 13, 1980.

Sheila E. Frazier, 61, actress (*Super Fly*), born the Bronx, NY, Nov 13, 1948.

Whoopi Goldberg, 60, comedienne, actress (Oscar for *Ghost*; *Sister Act, The Color Purple*), born Caryn Elaine Johnson at New York, NY, Nov 13, 1949.

Jimmy Kimmel, 42, late night talk-show host, comedian ("The Man Show," "Jimmy Kimmel Live"), born Brooklyn, NY, Nov 13, 1967.

Joe Mantegna, 62, actor (stage: Tony for *Glengarry Glen Ross*; *House of Games, Things Change*), born Chicago, IL, Nov 13, 1947.

Garry Marshall, 75, producer, director (*Beaches, Pretty Woman*), actor ("Murphy Brown"), born New York, NY, Nov 13, 1934.

Chris Noth, 52, actor ("Sex and the City," "Law & Order"), born Madison, WI, Nov 13, 1957.

Tracy Scoggins, 50, actress ("Babylon 5"), born Galveston, TX, Nov 13, 1959.

Madeline Sherwood, 87, actress ("The Flying Nun"), born Montreal, QC, Canada, Nov 13, 1922.

Vincent Frank (Vinny) Testaverde, 46, football player, born New York, NY, Nov 13, 1963.

Steve Zahn, 41, actor (*Rescue Dawn, National Security, Sahara*), born Marshall, MN, Nov 13, 1968.

November 14 — Saturday

DAY 318 — **47 REMAINING**

BROOKS, LOUISE: BIRTH ANNIVERSARY. Nov 14, 1906. Born at Cherryvale, KS, Brooks started out as a dancer before finding fame as an actress in the 1920s' cinema. She is best known for her performances in two 1929 German films: *Pandora's Box* (as Lulu) and *Diary of a Lost Girl*. Would-be flappers the world over copied her trademark hairstyle: a sleek, helmetlike bob. Brooks wrote a well-received book of reminiscences, *Lulu in Hollywood* (1982), before her death on Aug 8, 1985, at Rochester, NY.

CANE GRINDING AND HARVEST FESTIVAL. Nov 14. Savannah, GA. Join us for this popular preholiday event. Enjoy some old-time fun amid the sounds and aromas of an old-fashioned cane grinding. Entertainment, hayrides, pony rides. Cane syrup, and other fun festival foods will be available. Annually, the second Saturday in November. Est attendance: 2,500. For info: Oatland Island Wildlife Center, 711 Sandtown Rd, Savannah, GA 31410. Phone: (912) 898-3980. Fax: (912) 898-3983. Web: www.oatlandisland.org.

COPLAND, AARON: BIRTH ANNIVERSARY. Nov 14, 1900. American composer Aaron Copland was born at Brooklyn, NY. Incorporating American folk music and, later, the 12-tone system, he strove to create an American music style that was both popular and artistic. He composed ballets, film scores and orchestral works including *Fanfare for the Common Man* (1942), *Appalachian Spring* (1944) (for which he won the Pulitzer Prize) and the score for *The Heiress* (1948) (for which he won an Oscar). He died Dec 2, 1990, at North Tarrytown, NY.

DOW JONES TOPS 1,000: ANNIVERSARY. Nov 14, 1972. The Dow Jones Index of 30 major industrial stocks topped the 1,000 mark for the first time.

EISENHOWER, MAMIE DOUD: BIRTH ANNIVERSARY. Nov 14, 1896. Wife of Dwight David Eisenhower, 34th president of the US, born at Boone, IA. Died Nov 1, 1979, at Gettysburg, PA.

ENGLAND: LORD MAYOR'S SHOW. Nov 14. The City of London. Each year a colorful parade steps off at 11 AM from the Guildhall to the Royal Courts of Justice to mark the inauguration of the new lord mayor, who pledges allegiance to the Crown. Annually, the second Saturday in November. Est attendance: 500,000. For info: Pageantmaster, The Lord Mayor's Show, The Barge, Hindringham Rd, Great Walsingham, Norfolk, England NR22 6DR. Phone: (44) (1328) 824-420. Fax: (44) (1328) 824-422. E-mail: show@reidandreid.com. Web: www.lordmayorshow.org.

ESSENCE OF MOTOWN LITERARY JAM. Nov 14. Detroit, MI. Literary celebration for readers, writers, poets and authors. Annually, the second Saturday in November. For info: Sylvia Hubbard, Essence of Motown, PO Box 27310, Detroit, MI 48227. Phone: (313) 289-8614. E-mail: motownwriters@yahoo.com. Web: EssenceofMotown.com.

FULTON, ROBERT: BIRTH ANNIVERSARY. Nov 14, 1765. Inventor of the steamboat, born at Little Britain, PA. Died Feb 24, 1815, at New York, NY.

GUINEA-BISSAU: READJUSTMENT MOVEMENT'S DAY. Nov 14. National holiday.

INDIA: CHILDREN'S DAY. Nov 14. Holiday observed throughout India.

JORDAN: KING HUSSEIN: BIRTH ANNIVERSARY. Nov 14. H.M. King Hussein's birthday is honored each year on the anniversary of his birth in 1935. He died at Jordan Feb 7, 1999.

LOOSEN UP, LIGHTEN UP DAY. Nov 14. A day to remind people of all the benefits of joy and laughter. For info: Stephanie West Allen, PO Box 9311, Denver, CO 80209. Phone: (303) 935-8866. E-mail: stephanie@westallen.com. Web: www.westallen.com.

McCARTHY, JOSEPH: BIRTH ANNIVERSARY. Nov 14, 1908. Controversial politician born near Appleton, WI. As a Republican senator, McCarthy became a household name when he began making sweeping statements about the prevalence of secret Communists in the US. In this period of postwar uncertainty and fear of the Soviets, Americans responded to his claims with fear and indignation. He soon spread his attacks, accusing politicians, State Department employees, journalists and members of the armed forces of being secret Communists. He held congressional hearings to uncover "traitors," using sensational methods that uncovered nothing of substance. After failing to prove any of his allegations, he soon fell out of favor and was censured by Congress for unbecoming conduct in December 1954. He died at Bethesda, MD, May 2, 1957.

MONET, CLAUDE: BIRTH ANNIVERSARY. Nov 14, 1840. French Impressionist painter (*Water Lillies*), born at Paris, France. Died at Giverny, France, Dec 5, 1926.

"MURPHY BROWN" TV PREMIERE: ANNIVERSARY. Nov 14, 1988. This intelligent, often acerbic sitcom set in Washington, DC, starred Candice Bergen as an egotistical, seasoned journalist working for the fictitious TV news show "FYI." Featured were Grant Shaud as the show's high-strung producer, Miles Silverberg (later replaced by Lily Tomlin); Faith Ford as the former Miss America–turned–anchor, Corky Sherwood; Joe Regalbuto as neurotic reporter Frank Fontana; Charles Kimbrough as uptight anchorman Jim Dial; Pat Corley as Phil, owner of the local watering hole; and

Robert Pastorelli as Eldin Bernecky, perfectionist housepainter and aspiring artist. The series ended with the May 31, 1998, episode.

NEHRU, JAWAHARLAL: BIRTH ANNIVERSARY. Nov 14, 1889. Indian leader and first prime minister after independence. Born at Allahabad, India, he died May 27, 1964, at New Delhi, India.

SALISBURY, HARRISON: BIRTH ANNIVERSARY. Nov 14, 1908. American journalist Harrison Evans Salisbury was born at Minneapolis, MN. *New York Times* Moscow correspondent from 1949 to 1954. Salisbury won the Pulitzer Prize in 1955 for a series of articles on the Soviet Union. He died July 5, 1993, at Providence, RI.

SPACE MILESTONE: *APOLLO 12* (US): 40th ANNIVERSARY. Nov 14, 1969. Launched this date. This was the second manned lunar landing—in Ocean of Storms. First pinpoint landing. Astronauts Pete Conrad, Alan Bean and Richard Gordon visited *Surveyor 3* and took samples. Earth splashdown Nov 24.

SPIRIT OF NSA DAY. Nov 14. The National Speakers Association (NSA) has designated today as a national day of advocacy encouraging professional speakers to support one another. NSA members are encouraged to focus on giving back, providing genuine support to speaking colleagues and taking time to connect, help, mentor or refer business to other members without any expectation of reciprocation. For info: Stacy Tetschner, NSA, 1500 S Priest Dr, Tempe, AZ 85281. Phone: (480) 968-2552. Fax: (480) 968-0911. E-mail: stacy@nsaspeaker.org. Web: www.nsaspeaker.org.

STEIG, WILLIAM: BIRTH ANNIVERSARY. Nov 14, 1907. Prolific cartoonist, satirist and illustrator, William Steig was born at Brooklyn, NY. *The New Yorker* published more than 1,600 of his drawings, including 117 covers, and he wrote more than 25 books for children. He won the Caldecott Medal in 1970 for *Sylvester and the Magic Pebble* and received two Newbery Honors, for *Abel's Island* and *Dr. De Soto.* Other favorites include *The Amazing Bone, Brave Irene, CDB* and *Shrek*, the basis for a series of animated films. Steig died at Boston, MA, Oct 3, 2003.

UNITED NATIONS: WORLD DIABETES DAY. Nov 14. Welcoming the fact that the International Diabetes Federation has been observing World Diabetes Day globally since 1991, with cosponsorship of the World Health Organization, the UN General Assembly on Dec 20, 2006, designated this day as a United Nations Day, to be observed every year beginning in 2007 (Resolution 61/225). For info: United Nations, Dept of Public Info, New York, NY 10017. Web: www.un.org.

BIRTHDAYS TODAY

Boutros Boutros-Ghali, 87, former Secretary-General of the UN, born Cairo, Egypt, Nov 14, 1922.

Prince Charles, 61, Prince of Wales, heir to the British throne, born London, England, Nov 14, 1948.

Condoleezza Rice, 55, US Secretary of State, former US National Security Adviser, born Birmingham, AL, Nov 14, 1954.

Laura San Giacomo, 47, actress (*sex, lies and videotape*, "Just Shoot Me"), born Hoboken, NJ, Nov 14, 1962.

Curt Schilling, 43, baseball player, born Anchorage, AK, Nov 14, 1966.

Joseph "Run" Simmons, 45, rapper (Run DMC), born Queens, NY, Nov 14, 1964.

D.B. Sweeney, 48, actor (*Spawn, The Cutting Edge*), born Shoreham, Long Island, NY, Nov 14, 1961.

Yanni, 55, New Age composer, born Yanni Chrysomalis at Kalamata, Greece, Nov 14, 1954.

November 2009

S	M	T	W	T	F	S
1	2	3	4	5	6	7
8	9	10	11	12	13	14
15	16	17	18	19	20	21
22	23	24	25	26	27	28
29	30					

November 15 — Sunday

DAY 319 **46 REMAINING**

✦ **AMERICA RECYCLES DAY.** Nov 15.

AMERICA RECYCLES DAY. Nov 15. To promote recycling and buying recycled products. Annually, every Nov 15. For info: Natl Program Mgr, America Recycles Day, 805 15th St NW, Ste 425, Washington, DC 20005. Phone: (202) 789-1430, ext 14. Web: www.americarecyclesday.org.

AMERICAN EDUCATION WEEK. Nov 15–21. Focuses attention on the importance of education and all that it stands for. Annually, the week preceding the week of Thanksgiving. For info: Natl Education Assn (NEA), 1201 16th St NW, Washington, DC 20036. Phone: (202) 833-4000. Web: www.nea.org.

BELGIUM: DYNASTY DAY. Nov 15. National holiday in honor of Belgian monarchy.

BRAZIL: REPUBLIC DAY. Nov 15. Commemorates the proclamation of the republic in 1889. Celebrated on the Monday nearest Nov 15.

GEORGE SPELVIN DAY. Nov 15. Believed to be the anniversary of George Spelvin's theatrical birth—in Charles A. Gardiner's play *Karl the Peddler* on Nov 15, 1886, in a production at New York, NY. The name (or equivalent—Georgina, Georgetta, etc) is used in play programs to conceal the fact that an actor is performing in more than one role. The fictitious Spelvin is said to have appeared in more than 10,000 Broadway performances. See also: "England: Walter Plinge Day" (Dec 2) for British equivalent.

GERMANY: VOLKSTRAUERTAG. Nov 15. Memorial Day and national day of mourning in all German states for victims of National Socialism and the dead of both world wars. Observed on the Sunday before Totensonntag. See also: "Germany: Totensonntag" (Nov 22).

GYPSY CONDEMNATION ORDER: ANNIVERSARY. Nov 15, 1943. An order was issued by Heinrich Himmler for nomadic Gypsies and part-Gypsies to be placed in concentration camps. In cases of doubt, it was up to local heads of police to determine who was a Gypsy. Some estimates put the number of Gypsies killed in the Holocaust as high as half a million.

I LOVE TO WRITE DAY. Nov 15. New York City, Los Angeles, Boston, Chicago, Philadelphia and other major cities across the US. I Love to Write Day encourages people of all ages to write something: a poem, a short story or a letter to the editor, or to start or finish a novel—the possibilities are endless! Special writing events and activities take place in more than 15,000 schools, libraries, bookstores and community centers all across the US. Annually, Nov 15. For info: John Riddle, 6 Basset Pl, Bear, DE 19701. Phone: (302) 834-4910. E-mail: johnriddle@sprintmail.com. Web: www.ilovetowriteday.org.

JAPAN: SHICHI-GO-SAN. Nov 15. Annual children's festival. The *Shichi-Go-San* (Seven-Five-Three) rite is "the most picturesque event in the autumn season." Parents take their three-year-old children of either sex, five-year-old boys and seven-year-old girls to the parish shrines dressed in their best clothes. There the guardian spirits are thanked for the healthy growth of the children, and prayers are offered for their further development.

NATIONAL BUNDT DAY. Nov 15. A day for everyone young and old to pull the Bundt pans from the cupboards and get ready for baking delicious masterpiece cakes for the upcoming holiday season.The Bundt pan has stood the test of time for more than 50 years and is a fixture in nearly every home in America. The Bundt is the quintessential kitchenware icon. Bake a cake in the traditional design or choose one of the more than 40 Bundt shapes for your own special creation to share with family and friends. For info: Dana Norsten, Nordicware, 5005 Hwy 7, Minneapolis, MN 55416. Phone: (952) 924-8601. Fax: (952) 924-9668. E-mail: dananorsten @nordicware.com. Web: www.nordicware.com.

O'KEEFFE, GEORGIA: BIRTH ANNIVERSARY. Nov 15, 1887. Described as one of the greatest American artists of the 20th century, Georgia O'Keeffe was born at Sun Prairie, WI. In 1924 she married the famous photographer Alfred Stieglitz. His more than 500 photographs of her have been called "the greatest love poem in the history of photography." She painted desert landscapes and flower studies. She died at Santa Fe, NM, Mar 6, 1986.

ROMMEL, ERWIN: BIRTH ANNIVERSARY. Nov 15, 1891. Field marshal and commander of the German Afrika Korps in WWII, Erwin Rommel was born at Heidenheim, in Württemberg, Germany. Rommel commanded the Seventh Panzer Division in the Battle of France. He was considered an excellent commander, and his early success in Africa made him a legend as the "Desert Fox," but in early 1943 he was outmaneuvered by Field Marshal Bernard Montgomery, and Germany surrendered Tunis in May of that year. Implicated in July 1944 in an attempted assassination of Hitler, he was given the choice of suicide or a trial and chose the former. Rommel died by his own hand at age 52, Oct 14, 1944, near Ulm, Germany.

SPACE MILESTONE: *BURAN* (USSR). Nov 15, 1988. The Soviet Union's first reusable space plane, *Buran*, landed on this date, completing a smooth, unmanned mission at approximately 1:25 AM, EST, after orbiting Earth twice in 3 hours, 25 minutes. Launched at Baikonur, Soviet central Asia. The importance of this mission was in its computer-controlled liftoff and return.

UNITED NATIONS: WORLD DAY OF REMEMBRANCE FOR ROAD TRAFFIC VICTIMS. Nov 15. On Oct 26, 2005, the UN General Assembly invited member states and the international community to annually recognize the third Sunday in November as the World Day of Remembrance for Road Traffic Victims, as acknowledgment for victims of road traffic crashes and their families (Resolution 60/5). For info: United Nations, Dept of Public Info, New York, NY 10017. Web: www.un.org.

BIRTHDAYS TODAY

Ed Asner, 80, actor ("The Mary Tyler Moore Show," "Lou Grant," *Roots*), born Kansas City, MO, Nov 15, 1929.

Daniel Barenboim, 67, musician, conductor, born Buenos Aires, Argentina, Nov 15, 1942.

Joanna Barnes, 75, actress (*The Parent Trap*), born Boston, MA, Nov 15, 1934.

Petula Clark, 77, singer ("Downtown"), actress, born Ewell, Surrey, England, Nov 15, 1932.

Beverly D'Angelo, 55, actress (*Hair, Coal Miner's Daughter*), born Columbus, OH, Nov 15, 1954.

Kevin Eubanks, 52, "The Tonight Show" bandleader, born Philadelphia, PA, Nov 15, 1957.

Yaphet Kotto, 72, actor ("Homicide," *Midnight Run, Blue Collar, Live and Let Die*), born New York, NY, Nov 15, 1937.

Jonny Lee Miller, 37, actor (*Byron, Mansfield Park, Trainspotting*), born Kingston, England, Nov 15, 1972.

Bill Richardson, 62, Governor of New Mexico (D), born Pasadena, CA, Nov 15, 1947.

Joseph Wapner, 90, television personality ("People's Court"), retired judge, born Los Angeles, CA, Nov 15, 1919.

Sam Waterston, 69, actor ("Law & Order," "I'll Fly Away," *The Killing Fields, The Great Gatbsy*), born Cambridge, MA, Nov 15, 1940.

November 16 — Monday

DAY 320 — 45 REMAINING

ESTONIA: DAY OF NATIONAL REBIRTH: ANNIVERSARY. Nov 16. National holiday. Commemorates the 1988 Declaration of Sovereignty. Became independent from the Soviet Union in 1991.

HANDY, WILLIAM CHRISTOPHER: BIRTH ANNIVERSARY. Nov 16, 1873. American composer, bandleader, "father of the blues," W.C. Handy was born at Florence, AL. He died at New York, NY, Mar 28, 1958.

LEWIS AND CLARK EXPEDITION REACHES PACIFIC OCEAN: ANNIVERSARY. Nov 16, 1805. Lewis and Clark's Corps of Discovery reached the Pacific Ocean on this date. They had glimpsed it on Nov 7, moving Clark to write in his journal: "Great joy in camp! We are in view of the Ocean, this great Pacific Ocean which we have been so anxious to see. And the roaring or noise of the waves breaking on the rocky shores . . . may be heard distinctly."

MEREDITH, BURGESS: BIRTH ANNIVERSARY. Nov 16, 1907. Actor (*Of Mice and Men, Rocky*) born at Cleveland, OH. Some sources give his year of birth as 1908 or 1909. Died at Malibu, CA, Sept 9, 1997.

MOON PHASE: NEW MOON. Nov 16. Moon enters New Moon phase at 2:14 PM, EST.

OKLAHOMA: ADMISSION DAY: ANNIVERSARY. Nov 16. Became 46th state in 1907.

RIEL, LOUIS: HANGING ANNIVERSARY. Nov 16, 1885. Born at St. Boniface, MB, Canada, Oct 23, 1844, Louis Riel, leader of the Metis (French/Indian mixed ancestry), was elected to Canada's House of Commons in 1873 and 1874 but never seated. Having been confined to asylums for madness (feigned or falsely charged, some said), Riel became a US citizen in 1883. In 1885 he returned to western Canada to lead the North West Rebellion. Defeated, he surrendered and was tried for treason, convicted and hanged, at Regina, Canada. Seen as a patriot and protector of French culture in Canada, Riel became a legend and a symbol of the problems between French and English Canadians.

ROMAN CATHOLICS ISSUE NEW CATECHISM: ANNIVERSARY. Nov 16, 1992. For the first time since 1563, the Roman Catholic Church issued a new universal catechism, which addressed modern-day issues.

SAINT EUSTATIUS, WEST INDIES: STATIA AND AMERICA DAY. Nov 16, 1776. St. Eustatius, Leeward Islands. To commemorate the first salute to an American flag by a foreign government, from Fort Oranje in 1776. Festivities include sports events and dancing. During the American Revolution, St. Eustatius was an important trading center and a supply base for the colonies.

SPACE MILESTONE: *SKYLAB 4* (US). Nov 16, 1973. The 30th manned US space flight was launched with three astronauts, Gerald P. Carr, William R. Page and Edward G. Gibson, who spent 84 days on the space station. Space walks totaled 22 hours. Returned to Earth on Feb 8, 1974.

SPACE MILESTONE: *VENERA 3* (USSR). Nov 16, 1965. Launched this date, this unmanned space probe crashed into Venus, Mar 1, 1966. First man-made object on another planet.

UNITED NATIONS: INTERNATIONAL DAY FOR TOLERANCE. Nov 16. On Dec 12, 1996, the General Assembly established the International Day for Tolerance, to commemorate the adoption by UNESCO member states of the Declaration of Principles on Tolerance in 1995. For info: United Nations, Dept of Public Info, New York, NY 10017. Web: www.un.org.

BIRTHDAYS TODAY

Oksana Baiul, 32, Olympic gold medal figure skater, born Dniepropetrovsk, Ukraine, Nov 16, 1977.

Lisa Bonet, 42, actress ("The Cosby Show," "A Different World," *Angel Heart*), born San Francisco, CA, Nov 16, 1967.

Susanna Clarke, 50, author (*Jonathan Strange & Mr. Norrell*), born Nottingham, England, Nov 16, 1959.

Elizabeth Drew, 74, journalist, born Cincinnati, OH, Nov 16, 1935.

Dwight Eugene Gooden, 45, former baseball player, born Tampa, FL, Nov 16, 1964.

Maggie Gyllenhall, 32, actress (*Mona Lisa Smile, Secretary, Donnie Darko*), born New York, NY, Nov 16, 1977.

Marg Helgenberger, 51, actress ("CSI," "China Beach"), born Fremont, NE, Nov 16, 1958.

Diana Krall, 45, jazz singer, born Nanaimo, BC, Canada, Nov 16, 1964.

Martha Plimpton, 39, stage and screen actress (*Top Girls, The Coast of Utopia*), born New York, NY, Nov 16, 1970.

Paul Scholes, 35, soccer player, born Salford, England, Nov 16, 1974.

Amare Stoudemire, 27, basketball player, born Lake Wales, FL, Nov 16, 1982.

November 17 — Tuesday

DAY 321 | **44 REMAINING**

HOMEMADE BREAD DAY. Nov 17. A day for the family to remember and enjoy the making, baking and eating of nutritious homemade bread. For info: Homemade Bread Day Committee, 2460 Devonshire Rd, Ann Arbor, MI 48104-2706.

HONDA, SOICHIRO: BIRTH ANNIVERSARY. Nov 17, 1906. Born at Hamamatsu, Japan, Honda was the enterprising auto racer turned businessman who founded the Honda Motor Company, a great part of Japan's postwar emergence as an economic power. Honda retired in 1973 and died Aug 5, 1991, at Tokyo, Japan.

MÖBIUS, AUGUST: BIRTH ANNIVERSARY. Nov 17, 1790. German astronomer, mathematician, teacher and author, August Ferdinand Möbius was born at Schulpforte, Germany. Möbius was a pioneer in the field of topology and first described the Möbius net and the Möbius strip. He died at Leipzig, Germany, Sept 26, 1868.

November 2009	S	M	T	W	T	F	S
	1	2	3	4	5	6	7
	8	9	10	11	12	13	14
	15	16	17	18	19	20	21
	22	23	24	25	26	27	28
	29	30					

MONTGOMERY, BERNARD LAW: BIRTH ANNIVERSARY. Nov 17, 1887. Bernard Law Montgomery, who commanded the British Eighth Army to victory at El Alamein in North Africa in 1943, was born at St. Mark's Vicarage, Kennington Oval, London, England. He also led the Eighth Army in the Sicilian and Italian campaigns and commanded all ground forces in the 1944 Normandy landing. Montgomery died Mar 24, 1976, at Alton, Hampshire, England.

QUEEN ELIZABETH I: ACCESSION: ANNIVERSARY. Nov 17, 1558. Anniversary of accession of Elizabeth I to English throne; celebrated as a holiday in England for more than a century after her death in 1603.

SUEZ CANAL: ANNIVERSARY. Nov 17, 1869. Formal opening of the Suez Canal. It had taken 1.5 million men a decade to dig the 100-mile canal. It shortened the sea route from Europe to India by 6,000 miles. An Anglo-French commission ran the canal until 1956, when Egypt's president, Gamal Abdel Nasser, seized it.

ZENGER, JOHN PETER: 275th ARREST ANNIVERSARY. Nov 17, 1734. Colonial printer and journalist who established the *New York Weekly Journal* (first issue, Nov 5, 1733). Zenger was arrested Nov 17, 1734, for libel against the colonial governor but continued to edit his newspaper from jail. Trial was held during August 1735. Zenger's acquittal was an important early step toward freedom of the press in America. Zenger was born at Germany in 1697, came to the US in 1710 and died July 28, 1746, at New York, NY.

BIRTHDAYS TODAY

Howard Dean, 61, Chairman of the Democratic National Committee, former Governor of Vermont (D), born East Hampton, NY, Nov 17, 1948.

Danny DeVito, 65, actor ("Taxi," *Twins*), director (*Throw Mama from the Train*), born Neptune, NJ, Nov 17, 1944.

Daisy Fuentes, 43, actress, TV personality, born Havana, Cuba, Nov 17, 1966.

Isaac Hanson, 29, singer (Hanson), born Tulsa, OK, Nov 17, 1980.

Lauren Hutton, 65, model, actress (*American Gigolo*), born Charleston, SC, Nov 17, 1944.

James M. Inhofe, 75, US Senator (R, Oklahoma), born Des Moines, IA, Nov 17, 1934.

Gordon Lightfoot, 71, singer, songwriter ("Early Morning Rain"), born Orilla, ON, Canada, Nov 17, 1938.

Sophie Marceau, 43, actress (*The World Is Not Enough, Braveheart*), born Paris, France, Nov 17, 1966.

Mary Elizabeth Mastrantonio, 51, actress (*Robin Hood: Prince of Thieves, The Color of Money, Scarface*), born Oak Park, IL, Nov 17, 1958.

Lorne Michaels, 65, producer ("Saturday Night Live"), born Toronto, ON, Canada, Nov 17, 1944.

RuPaul, 49, model, actor, born RuPaul Andre Charles at San Diego, CA, Nov 17, 1960.

Martin Scorsese, 67, director (*Mean Streets, The Color of Money, Raging Bull, Goodfellas*), born Flushing, NY, Nov 17, 1942.

George Thomas (Tom) Seaver, 65, Hall of Fame baseball player, broadcaster, born Fresno, CA, Nov 17, 1944.

Matthew Settle, 40, actor ("Brothers & Sisters," "Gossip Girl"), born Hickory, NC, Nov 17, 1969.

Dylan Walsh, 46, actor ("Nip/Tuck"), born Los Angeles, CA, Nov 17, 1963.

November 18 — Wednesday

DAY 322 43 REMAINING

DAGUERRE, LOUIS JACQUES MANDÉ: BIRTH ANNIVERSARY. Nov 18, 1789. French tax collector, theater scene-painter, physicist and inventor, born at Cormeilles-en-Parisis, France. He is remembered for his invention of the daguerreotype photographic process—one of the earliest to permit a photographic image to be chemically fixed to provide a permanent picture. The process was presented to the French Academy of Science Jan 7, 1839. Daguerre died near Paris, France, July 10, 1851.

GATEWAY FARM EXPO. Nov 18–19. Buffalo County Fairgrounds, Kearney, NE. Est attendance: 8,000. For info: Kearney Area Chamber of Commerce, PO Box 607, Kearney, NE 68848. Phone: (877) 720-4885. E-mail: mmeyer@kearneycoc.org. Web: www.gatewayfarmexpo.org.

GERMANY: BUSS UND BETTAG. Nov 18. Buss und Bettag (Repentance Day) is observed on the Wednesday before the last Sunday of the church year. A legal public holiday in all German states except Bavaria (where it is observed only in communities with predominantly Protestant populations).

GILBERT, SIR WILLIAM SCHWENCK: BIRTH ANNIVERSARY. Nov 18, 1836. English author of librettos for the famed Gilbert and Sullivan comic operas, born at London, England. Died May 29, 1911, at Harrow Weald, Middlesex, England, as a result of a heart attack experienced while saving a woman from drowning.

GRAY, ASA: BIRTH ANNIVERSARY. Nov 18, 1810. Botanist and natural history professor at Harvard, born at Paris, NY. Gray was known as a pioneer in the field of plant geography and a chief advocate of Darwin. Died at Cambridge, MA, Jan 30, 1888.

HAITI: ARMY DAY. Nov 18. Commemorates the Battle of Vertiéres, Nov 18, 1803, in which Haitians defeated the French.

"HOWARD STERN SHOW" RADIO PREMIERE: ANNIVERSARY. Nov 18, 1985. Radio's pioneering shock jock, Howard Stern, began broadcasting with sidekick Robin Quivers on New York radio station WXRK-FM. With outrageous humor and a gleeful disregard for taste, Stern quickly became popular nationally, but many remain outraged at his show elements. The FCC frequently fined his broadcasting company. Radio listeners today number around 25 million. On Dec 16, 2005, Stern ended his show on regular radio and moved it to satellite radio.

JONESTOWN MASSACRE: ANNIVERSARY. Nov 18, 1978. On this date Indiana-born, 47-year-old Reverend Jim Jones, leader of the "People's Temple," was reported to have directed the suicides of more than 900 persons at Jonestown, Guyana. US Representative Leo J. Ryan of California and four members of his party were killed in an ambush at Port Kaituma airstrip on Nov 18, 1978, when they attempted to leave after an investigative visit to the remote jungle location of the religious cult. On the following day Jones and his mistress killed themselves after watching the administration of Kool-Aid laced with the deadly poison cyanide to members of the cult. At least 912 persons died in the biggest murder-suicide in history.

LATVIA: INDEPENDENCE DAY. Nov 18. National holiday. Commemorates the declaration of an independent Latvia from Germany and Russia in 1918.

LOMBROSO, CESARE: BIRTH ANNIVERSARY. Nov 18, 1836. Italian founder of criminology, born at Verona, Italy. A professor of psychiatry, Lombroso believed that criminality could be identified with certain physical types of people. He died at Turin, Italy, Oct 19, 1909.

MARRIED TO A SCORPIO SUPPORT DAY. Nov 18. A worldwide day of remembrance to honor all those married to Scorpios and who suffer greatly. Assert yourself today! Hide their household flowcharts. Annually, Nov 18. (©2006 by WH.) For info: Thomas & Ruth Roy, Wellcat Holidays, 2418 Long Ln, Lebanon, PA 17046. Phone: (717) 279-0184. E-mail: info@wellcat.com. Web: www.wellcat.com.

MERCER, JOHN HERNDON (JOHNNY): 100th BIRTH ANNIVERSARY. Nov 18, 1909. American songwriter, singer, radio performer and actor, born at Savannah, GA. Johnny Mercer wrote lyrics (and often the music) for some of the great American popular music from the 1930s through the 1960s, including "Autumn Leaves," "One for My Baby," "Satin Doll," "On the Achison, Topeka, and the Santa Fe," "You Must Have Been a Beautiful Baby," "Come Rain or Come Shine," "Hooray for Hollywood" and "Jeepers Creepers." Mercer died June 25, 1976, at Bel Air, CA.

MICKEY MOUSE'S BIRTHDAY. Nov 18. The comical activities of squeaky-voiced Mickey Mouse first appeared in 1928, on the screen of the Colony Theatre at New York City. The film, Walt Disney's "Steamboat Willie," was the first animated cartoon talking picture.

NATIONAL EDUCATIONAL SUPPORT PROFESSIONALS DAY. Nov 18. A mandate of the delegates to the 1987 National Education Association Representative Assembly called for a special day during American Education Week to honor the contributions of school support employees. Local associations and school districts salute support staff on this 21st-annual observance, the Wednesday of American Education Week. For info: Natl Education Assn (NEA), 1201 16th St NW, Washington, DC 20036. Phone: (202) 833-4000. Fax: (202) 822-7974. Web: www.nea.org.

OMAN: NATIONAL HOLIDAY. Nov 18. Sultanate of Oman celebrates its national day, the birthday in 1942 of Sultan Qaboos bin Said.

PUSH-BUTTON PHONE DEBUTS: ANNIVERSARY. Nov 18, 1963. Push-button telephones went into service as an alternative to rotary-dial phones. Touch-tone service was available as an option at an extra charge. This option was available only in two Pennsylvania cities.

"SEE IT NOW" TV PREMIERE: ANNIVERSARY. Nov 18, 1951. "See It Now" was a high-quality and significant public affairs show of the 1950s. Known for using its own film footage, unrehearsed interviews and no dubbing, "See It Now" covered many relevant and newsworthy stories of its time, including desegregation, lung cancer and anticommunist fervor. One of the most notable programs focused on Senator Joseph McCarthy, leading to McCarthy's appearance on the show—an appearance that damaged his credibility. "See It Now" was hosted by Edward R. Murrow, who also produced it jointly with Fred W. Friendly. Its premiere was the first live commercial coast-to-coast broadcast. The show had premiered on radio the year before as "Hear It Now."

SHEPARD, ALAN: BIRTH ANNIVERSARY. Nov 18, 1923. Former astronaut and the first American in space (in 1961), Shepard was born at East Derry, NH. He was one of only 12 Americans who have walked on the moon and was America's only lunar golfer, practicing his drive in space with a six iron. He was awarded the Medal of Honor in 1979. Shepard died near Monterey, CA, July 21, 1998.

SOUTH AFRICA ADOPTS NEW CONSTITUTION: ANNIVERSARY. Nov 18, 1993. After more than 300 years of white majority rule, basic civil rights were finally granted to blacks in South Africa. The constitution providing such rights was approved by representatives of the ruling party, as well as members of 20 other political parties.

US UNIFORM TIME ZONE PLAN: ANNIVERSARY. Nov 18, 1883. Charles Ferdinand Dowd, a college professor and one of the early advocates of uniform time, proposed a time zone plan of the US (four zones of 15 degrees), which he and others persuaded the railroads to adopt and place in operation on this date. Because it didn't involve the enactment of any law, some localities didn't change their clocks. A year later, an international conference applied the same procedure to create time zones for the entire world. US time zones weren't nationally legalized until 1918, with the passage of the Standard Time Act. See also: "Prime Meridian Set: Anniversary" (Nov 1) and "US Standard Time Act: Anniversary" (Mar 19).

WEBER, CARL MARIA VON: BIRTH ANNIVERSARY. Nov 18, 1786. Composer, founder of the German romantic school, was born at Eutin, Germany. Member of a musical family, he is remembered mainly for his operas, especially the immensely popular *Der Freischutz* (1821). He died at London, England, June 5, 1826, at age 39.

BIRTHDAYS TODAY

Margaret Eleanor Atwood, 70, author (*Cat's Eye, The Handmaid's Tale*), born Ottawa, ON, Canada, Nov 18, 1939.

Dante Bichette, 46, former baseball player, born West Palm Beach, FL, Nov 18, 1963.

Linda Evans, 67, actress ("Dynasty," "Big Valley"), born Hartford, CT, Nov 18, 1942.

Wilma Mankiller, 64, Chief of the Cherokee Nation 1985–95, born Tahlequah, OK, Nov 18, 1945.

Andrea Marcovicci, 61, actress ("Trapper John, MD"), singer, born New York, NY, Nov 18, 1948.

Harold Warren Moon, 53, former football player, born Los Angeles, CA, Nov 18, 1956.

Kevin Nealon, 56, comedic actor ("Champs," "Saturday Night Live"), born St. Louis, MO, Nov 18, 1953.

Jameson Parker, 62, actor ("Simon and Simon," *A Small Circle of Friends*), born Baltimore, MD, Nov 18, 1947.

Elizabeth Perkins, 49, actress (*About Last Night . . ., Big, The Flintstones*), born Queens, NY, Nov 18, 1960.

Katey Sagal, 53, actress ("Married . . . With Children," "8 Simple Rules," "Futurama"), born Los Angeles, CA, Nov 18, 1956.

Gary Sheffield, 41, baseball player, born Tampa, FL, Nov 18, 1968.

Ted Stevens, 86, US Senator (R, Alaska), born Indianapolis, IN, Nov 18, 1923.

Susan Sullivan, 65, actress ("Falcon Crest," "Dharma & Greg"), born New York, NY, Nov 18, 1944.

Brenda Vaccaro, 70, stage and film actress (*The Goodbye People*), born Brooklyn, NY, Nov 18, 1939.

Owen Wilson, 41, actor (*Wedding Crashers, Starsky & Hutch, The Royal Tenenbaums*), screenwriter, born Dallas, TX, Nov 18, 1968.

November 2009

S	M	T	W	T	F	S
1	2	3	4	5	6	7
8	9	10	11	12	13	14
15	16	17	18	19	20	21
22	23	24	25	26	27	28
29	30					

November 19 — Thursday

DAY 323 — **42 REMAINING**

AMERICAN SPEECH-LANGUAGE-HEARING ASSOCIATION CONVENTION. Nov 19–21. New Orleans, LA. Scientific sessions held on language, speech disorders, hearing science and hearing disorders and matters of professional interest to speech-language pathologists and audiologists. Est attendance: 15,000. For info: American Speech-Language-Hearing Assn, 10801 Rockville Pike, Rockville, MD 20852-3279. Phone: (301) 897-5700. E-mail: convention@asha.org. Web: www.asha.org.

BELIZE: GARIFUNA DAY. Nov 19. Public holiday celebrating the first arrival of black Caribs from St. Vincent and Rotan to southern Belize in 1823.

CAMPANELLA, ROY: BIRTH ANNIVERSARY. Nov 19, 1921. Roy Campanella, one of the first black major leaguers and a star of one of baseball's greatest teams, the Brooklyn Dodgers' "Boys of Summer," was born at Philadelphia, PA. He was named the National League MVP three times in his 10 years of play, in 1951, 1953 and 1955. Campanella had his highest batting average in 1951 (.325), and in 1953 he established three single-season records for a catcher—most putouts (807), most home runs (41) and most runs batted in (142)—as well as having a batting average of .312. His career was cut short on Jan 28, 1958, when an automobile accident left him paralyzed. Campanella gained even more fame after his accident as an inspiration and spokesman for people with disabilities. He was named to the Baseball Hall of Fame in 1969. Roy Campanella died June 26, 1993, at Woodland Hills, CA.

COLD WAR FORMALLY ENDED: ANNIVERSARY. Nov 19–21, 1990. A summit was held at Paris, France, with the leaders of the Conference on Security and Cooperation in Europe (CSCE). The highlight of the summit was the signing of a treaty to dramatically reduce conventional weapons in Europe, thereby ending the Cold War.

DRUCKER, PETER: 100th BIRTH ANNIVERSARY. Nov 19, 1909. Born at Vienna, Austria, Drucker was an economist, theorist, consultant, journalist, professor and author. Arriving in America in 1937 (after leaving his Nazi-overrun homeland), Drucker grew to be one of the most important business thinkers of the century, practically inventing the idea of management as a profession. In 1954 he published his most famous work, *The Practice of Management*—one of almost 40 works. In his long career, he moved from thinking of the corporation as a community builder to being a critical gadfly in the wake of business scandals at the end of the century. He died Nov 11, 2005, at his home in Claremont, CA.

FIRST AUTOMATIC TOLL COLLECTION MACHINE: 55th ANNIVERSARY. Nov 19, 1954. At the Union Toll Plaza on New Jersey's Garden State Parkway, motorists dropped 25¢ into a wire mesh hopper and a green light would flash. The first modern toll road was the Pennsylvania Turnpike, which opened in 1940.

FIRST PRESIDENTIAL LIBRARY: 70th ANNIVERSARY. Nov 19, 1939. President Franklin D. Roosevelt laid the cornerstone for his presidential library at Hyde Park, NY. He donated the land, but public donations provided funds for the building, which was dedicated on June 30, 1941.

GARFIELD, JAMES ABRAM: BIRTH ANNIVERSARY. Nov 19, 1831. The 20th president of the US (and the first left-handed president) was born at Orange, OH. Term of office: Mar 4–Sept 19, 1881. While walking into the Washington, DC, railway station on the morning of July 2, 1881, Garfield was shot by disappointed office seeker Charles J. Guiteau. He survived, in very weak condition, until Sept 19, 1881, when he succumbed to blood poisoning at Elberon, NJ (where he had been taken for recuperation). Guiteau was tried, convicted and hanged at the jail at Washington, June 30, 1882.

GETTYSBURG ADDRESS MEMORIAL CEREMONY. Nov 19. Gettysburg, PA. The 146th anniversary of Lincoln's Gettysburg Address is celebrated with brief memorial services at the Soldiers' National Monument in Gettysburg National Cemetery. Est attendance: 2,000. For info: Gettysburg CVB, PO Box 4117, Gettysburg, PA 17325.

Phone: (717) 334-6274. Fax: (717) 334-1166. E-mail: info@gettysburg.travel. Web: www.gettysburg.travel.

GREAT AMERICAN SMOKEOUT. Nov 19. A day observed annually to celebrate smoke-free environments. Annually, the third Thursday in November. For info: American Cancer Society. Phone: (800) ACS-2345. Web: www.cancer.org.

"HAVE A BAD DAY" DAY. Nov 19. For those who are filled with revulsion at being told endlessly to "have a nice day," this day is a brief respite. Store and business owners are to ask workers to tell customers to "have a bad day." Annually, Nov 19. (©2006 by WH.) For info: Thomas & Ruth Roy, Wellcat Holidays, 2418 Long Ln, Lebanon, PA 17046. Phone: (717) 279-0184. E-mail: info@wellcat.com. Web: www.wellcat.com.

LINCOLN'S GETTYSBURG ADDRESS: ANNIVERSARY. Nov 19, 1863. In 1863, 17 acres of the battlefield at Gettysburg, PA, were dedicated as a national cemetery. Noted orator Edward Everett spoke for two hours; the address that Lincoln delivered in less than two minutes was later recognized as one of the most eloquent of the English language. Five manuscript copies in Lincoln's hand survive, including the rough draft begun in ink at the executive mansion at Washington and concluded in pencil at Gettysburg on the morning of the dedication (kept at the Library of Congress).

MEXICO CITY EXPLOSION: 25th ANNIVERSARY. Nov 19, 1984. More than 300 people were killed when a gas truck explosion set off a series of explosions at a butane and liquefied gas storage facility in the Mexico City suburb Tlalnepantla. An area of approximately 60 acres was razed by the blasts and resulting fires. The four storage tanks involved held more than three million gallons of liquefied gas.

MONACO: NATIONAL HOLIDAY. Nov 19.

✦ **NATIONAL GREAT AMERICAN SMOKEOUT DAY.** Nov 19.

PELÉ SCORES 1,000th GOAL: 40th ANNIVERSARY. Nov 19, 1969. Playing for the Santos team, legendary Brazilian soccer player Pelé scored his 1,000th goal in competition on a penalty kick against the team Vasco de Gama. Pelé dedicated this emotional and tremendous feat to Brazil's poor children and its elderly and suffering people. By the time Pelé retired in 1977, he had scored an astounding 1,281 goals in 1,363 matches—a world record that still stands.

PUERTO RICO: DISCOVERY DAY. Nov 19. Public holiday. Columbus discovered Puerto Rico in 1493 on his second voyage to the New World.

"ROCKY AND HIS FRIENDS" TV PREMIERE: 50th ANNIVERSARY. Nov 19, 1959. This popular cartoon featured the adventures of a talking squirrel, Rocky (Rocket J. Squirrel), and his friend Bullwinkle, a flaky moose. The tongue-in-cheek dialogue contrasted with the simple plots in which Rocky and Bullwinkle tangled with Russian bad guys Boris Badenov and Natasha (who worked for Mr Big). Other popular segments on the show included "Fractured Fairy Tales," "Bullwinkle's Corner" and the adventures of Sherman and Mr Peabody (an intelligent talking dog). In 1961 the show was renamed "The Bullwinkle Show," but the cast of characters remained the same.

SOUTH TEXAS WILDLIFE AND BIRDING FESTIVAL. Nov 19–22. Kingsville, TX. Birding and wildlife tours, speakers, demonstrations and a nature marketplace. Est attendance: 3,000. For info: Kingsville CVB, 1501 N Hwy 77, Kingsville, TX 78363. Phone: (800) 333-5032. Fax: (361) 592-3227. E-mail: visitors@kingsvilletexas.com. Web: www.kingsvilletexas.com.

SUFFRAGISTS' VOTING ATTEMPT: ANNIVERSARY. Nov 19, 1868. Testing the wording of the 14th Amendment that says "no State shall make or enforce any law which shall abridge the privileges or immunities of citizens of the United States," 172 New Jersey suffragists, including four black women, attempted to vote in the presidential election. Denied, they cast their votes instead into a women's ballot box overseen by 84-year-old Quaker Margaret Pryer.

SUNDAY, BILLY: BIRTH ANNIVERSARY. Nov 19, 1862. Born William Ashley Sunday at Ames, IA, Sunday rose from poverty to become a professional baseball player with the Chicago White Stockings in 1883. He quit baseball in 1891 to devote himself to evangelism after hearing gospel singers at a Chicago mission. Sunday's fiery, athletic sermons—especially against demon rum—made him a star in the early 1900s, and at each revival he attracted around 100,000 listeners. At a typical revival in Detroit, MI, Sunday exhorted, "Help me, Jesus, help me save all in Detroit who are rushing to hell so fast that you can't see them for the dust." Sunday died Nov 6, 1935, at Chicago, IL.

WOMEN'S CHRISTIAN TEMPERANCE UNION ORGANIZED: ANNIVERSARY. Nov 19, 1874. Developed out of the Women's Temperance Crusade of 1873, the Women's Christian Temperance Union was organized at Cleveland, OH. The crusade had swept through 23 states with women going into saloons to sing hymns, pray and ask saloonkeepers to stop selling liquor. Today, the temperance group, headquartered at Evanston, IL, includes more than a million members with chapters in 72 countries and continues to be concerned with educating people on the potential dangers of the use of alcohol, narcotics and tobacco.

ZION NATIONAL PARK ESTABLISHED: 90th ANNIVERSARY. Nov 19, 1919. Utah's Mukuntuweap National Monument, proclaimed July 31, 1909, and later incorporated in Zion National Monument by proclamation Mar 18, 1918, was established as Zion National Park in 1919.

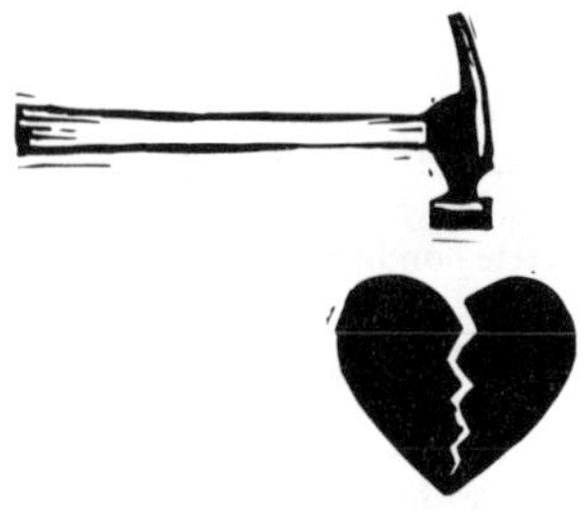

BIRTHDAYS TODAY

Dick Cavett, 73, TV pundit ("The Dick Cavett Show"), born Gibbon, NE, Nov 19, 1936.

Eileen Collins, 53, first female space shuttle commander, Lieutenant Colonel USAF retired, born Elmira, NY, Nov 19, 1956.

Ann Curry, 53, television journalist, born at Guam, Nov 19, 1956.

Gail Devers, 43, Olympic gold medal sprinter, born Seattle, WA, Nov 19, 1966.

Terry Farrell, 46, actress ("Star Trek: Deep Space Nine," "Becker"), born Cedar Rapids, IA, Nov 19, 1963.

Jodie Foster, 47, actress (Oscars for *The Accused, The Silence of the Lambs; Taxi Driver*), director (*Home for the Holidays*), born Los Angeles, CA, Nov 19, 1962.

Savion Glover, 36, dancer, choreographer (*Bring in 'Da Noise, Bring in 'Da Funk*), born Newark, NJ, Nov 19, 1973.

Thomas R. Harkin, 70, US Senator (D, Iowa), born Cumming, IA, Nov 19, 1939.

Ryan Howard, 30, baseball player, born St. Louis, MO, Nov 19, 1979.

Scott Jacoby, 53, actor (*The Little Girl Who Lives Down the Lane, Return to Horror High*), born Chicago, IL, Nov 19, 1956.

Allison Janney, 49, actress (*American Beauty*, "The West Wing"), born Dayton, OH, Nov 19, 1960.

Larry King, 76, talk-show host ("Larry King Live"), born Brooklyn, NY, Nov 19, 1933.

Calvin Klein, 67, fashion designer, born New York, NY, Nov 19, 1942.

Glynnis O'Connor, 54, actress (*Ode to Billy Joe*), born New York, NY, Nov 19, 1955.

Kathleen Quinlan, 55, actress (*Breakdown, Apollo 13*), born Pasadena, CA, Nov 19, 1954.

Ahmad Rashad, 60, sportscaster, former football player, born Bobby Moore at Portland, OR, Nov 19, 1949.

Meg Ryan, 48, actress (*When Harry Met Sally . . ., Sleepless in Seattle*), born Fairfield, CT, Nov 19, 1961.

Kerri Strug, 32, Olympic gymnast, born Tucson, AZ, Nov 19, 1977.

Ted Turner, 71, baseball, basketball and cable TV executive, born Cincinnati, OH, Nov 19, 1938.

Garrick Utley, 70, journalist, born Chicago, IL, Nov 19, 1939.

Jack Welch, 74, ex-chairman of GE, born Peabody, MA, Nov 19, 1935.

November 20 — Friday

DAY 324 — **41 REMAINING**

BATTLE OF TARAWA-MAKIN: ANNIVERSARY. Nov 20, 1943. The US began its offensive against Japan in the Central Pacific (Operation Galvanic) by attacking the Gilbert Islands, particularly the islets of Betio and Makin. The Japanese had heavily fortified the Tarawa chain of atolls, especially Tarawa, with pillboxes, blockhouses and ferroconcrete bombproofs. In the eight days it took the 5th Amphibious Corps, 2nd Marine Division and 27th Infantry Division to take the Tarawa and Makin Islands, 1,000 US soldiers were killed and 2,311 wounded. The Japanese loss was tallied at 4,700 men killed, 17 wounded and captured, and 129 Koreans surrendered. The US public, who through censorship previously had been kept in the dark about the human cost of the war, was appalled by casualty figures and photographs from this battle.

BILL OF RIGHTS: ANNIVERSARY OF FIRST STATE RATIFICATION. Nov 20, 1789. New Jersey became the first state to ratify 10 of the 12 amendments to the US Constitution proposed by Congress Sept 25. These 10 amendments came to be known as the Bill of Rights.

CANADA: RALLY OF THE TALL PINES. Nov 20–21. Bancroft, ON. Combining winter road surfaces with the scenic, winding back roads of the Canadian Shield makes this event of the Canadian Rally Car Race Circuit one of the most popular. For info: Bancroft & District Chamber of Commerce, Box 539, Bancroft, ON, K0L 1C0, Canada. Phone: (613) 332-1513. Fax: (613) 332-2119. E-mail: chamber@commerce.bancroft.on.ca. Web: www.BancroftDistrict.com.

CFA INTERNATIONAL CAT SHOW. Nov 20–22. Site TBA. 21st annual. The most prestigious cat competition in the world, with more than 700 cats representing 41 breeds. Cats come from the US, Asia, Canada, Europe and South America. For info: The Cat Fanciers' Assn, Inc, PO Box 1005, Manasquan, NJ 08736-0805. Phone: (732) 528-9797. Fax: (732) 528-7391. E-mail: cfa@cfa.org. Web: www.cfa.org.

CHATTERTON, THOMAS: BIRTH ANNIVERSARY. Nov 20, 1752. English poet Thomas Chatterton was born at Bristol, England, and killed himself at age 17 by taking arsenic at his London garret, Aug 24, 1770. A gifted but lonely child, before he reached his teens Chatterton had created a fantasy poet-priest, Thomas Rowley, who lived in the 16th century. With his own pen, Chatterton created enough verses "by" Rowley to fill more than 600 printed pages. Chatterton's fantasy-forgery poems attracted little attention during his short life, but they were later admired by Wordsworth, Coleridge, Shelley, Keats and Byron. In addition, he became the subject of at least one play, an opera and a novel.

COLORADO RIVER CROSSING BALLOON FESTIVAL. Nov 20–22. Cibola High School, Yuma, AZ. 19th annual. 55 balloons. Sunrise balloon liftoffs on Saturday and Sunday at Cibola High School. Sunset balloon glow and fireworks on Saturday evening at Ray Kroc Complex/Desert Sun Stadium. Entertainment, food, vendors. Free admission. Est attendance: 17,000. For info: Caballeros de Yuma, Inc, PO Box 5987, Yuma, AZ 85366. Phone: (928) 343-1715. Fax: (928) 783-1609. E-mail: caballeros@beamspeed.net. Web: www.caballeros.org.

COOKE, ALISTAIR: BIRTH ANNIVERSARY. Nov 20, 1908. Broadcast journalist and author Alfred Alistair Cooke was born at Salford, England. He came to the US in the 1930s and eventually became an American citizen. His program "Letter from America" was broadcast in more than 50 countries by BBC Radio for an astonishing 58 years. He was the chief American correspondent for *The Guardian* for 26 years, and he hosted PBS's "Masterpiece Theatre" for more than 20 years. Highly regarded for his sophisticated grace and style in both writing and broadcasting, he continued to broadcast "Letter from America" until his death at New York, NY, Mar 30, 2004.

GOULD, CHESTER: BIRTH ANNIVERSARY. Nov 20, 1900. In 1931 Chester Gould created comic strip character Dick Tracy, the clean-cut, square-jawed, plainclothed detective who represented the code that "crime doesn't pay." The strip first appeared Oct 4, 1931, in the *Detroit Daily Mirror* and later was syndicated in nearly 1,000 newspapers worldwide. "Dick Tracy" (originally called "Plainclothes Tracy") featured Tess Trueheart (later Mrs Tracy) and a host of bad guys with ugly names and faces to match their ugly ways—Mole, Pruneface, Flat Top, B-B Eyes, Mumbles and others. Closely following actual police methods of crime prevention, it included a "Crimestopper Notebook" with tips on self-protection. More violent than most comic strips, "Dick Tracy" was a combination of realism and science fiction. Chester Gould was born at Pawnee, OK, and died May 11, 1985, at Woodstock, IL.

GRAND ILLUMINATION. Nov 20. Lahaska, PA. Santa switches on the village's outdoor light display on Friday at 6:15 PM to kick off the holiday season. Free cider and toasted marshmallows. Preview of new gift ideas in shops. Free admission. Est attendance: 5,000. For info: Peddler's Village, Rtes 202 and 263, Lahaska, PA 18931. Phone: (215) 794-4000. Fax: (215) 794-4001. Web: www.peddlersvillage.com.

GREATER PITTSBURGH ARTS & CRAFTS HOLIDAY SPECTACULAR. Nov 20–22. Monroeville Expomart, Monroeville, PA. Approximately 200 booths including pottery, jewelry, quilts, furniture, tole and decorative painting, leather, toys and much more. Find that perfect gift for the holidays. Est attendance: 13,000. For info: Debbie & Dave Stoner, PO Box 166, Irwin, PA 15642. Phone: (724) 863-4577. E-mail: familyfestivals@hotmail.com. Web: www.familyfestivals.com.

HOLIDAY FOLK FAIR INTERNATIONAL. Nov 20–22. Wisconsin State Fair Park, Milwaukee, WI. International festival featuring costumes, dancing, entertainment, exhibits, workshops, folk wares and cuisine from 65 cultures. Also children's activities. Annually, the weekend before Thanksgiving. Est attendance: 50,000. For info: Holiday Folk Fair International, Intl Institute of Wisconsin, 1110 N Old World Third St, Ste 420, Milwaukee, WI 53203. Phone: (414) 225-6220. Fax: (414) 225-6235. E-mail: folkfair@execpc.com.

HUBBLE, EDWIN POWELL: BIRTH ANNIVERSARY. Nov 20, 1889. American astronomer Edwin Hubble was born at Marshfield, MO. His discovery and development of the concept of an expanding universe has been described as the "most spectacular astronomical discovery" of the 20th century. As a tribute, the Hubble Space Telescope, deployed Apr 25, 1990, from US space shuttle *Discovery*, was named for him. The Hubble Space Telescope, with a 240-centimeter mirror, was to allow astronomers to see farther into space than they had ever seen from telescopes on Earth. Hubble died at San Marino, CA, Sept 28, 1953.

November 2009

S	M	T	W	T	F	S
1	2	3	4	5	6	7
8	9	10	11	12	13	14
15	16	17	18	19	20	21
22	23	24	25	26	27	28
29	30					

KENNEDY, ROBERT FRANCIS: BIRTH ANNIVERSARY. Nov 20, 1925. US senator and younger brother of John F. Kennedy (35th president) was born at Brookline, MA. An assassin shot him at Los Angeles, CA, June 5, 1968, while he was campaigning for the presidential nomination. He died the next day. Sirhan Sirhan was convicted of his murder.

LAGERLOF, SELMA: BIRTH ANNIVERSARY. Nov 20, 1858. Swedish author, member of the Swedish Academy and the first woman to receive the Nobel Prize for Literature (1909) was born at Sweden's Varmland Province. She died there Mar 16, 1940.

LANDIS, KENESAW MOUNTAIN: BIRTH ANNIVERSARY. Nov 20, 1866. Baseball Hall of Fame executive born at Millville, OH. Landis, a federal judge, was named the first commissioner of baseball in 1920. He ruled with an absolutely firm hand and imposed his view of how baseball should operate upon owners and players alike. Inducted into the Hall of Fame in 1944. Died at Chicago, IL, Nov 25, 1944.

LAURIER, SIR WILFRED: BIRTH ANNIVERSARY. Nov 20, 1841. Canadian statesman (premier, 1896–1911), born at St. Lin, QC, Canada. Died Feb 17, 1919, at Ottawa, ON, Canada.

MARRIAGE OF ELIZABETH AND PHILIP: ANNIVERSARY. Nov 20, 1947. The Princess Elizabeth Alexandra Mary was wed to Philip Mountbatten on Nov 20, 1947. Elizabeth was the first child of King George VI and Queen Elizabeth. Philip, the former Prince Philip of Greece, had become a British subject nine months earlier and the title Duke of Edinburgh was bestowed on him. The bride later became Elizabeth II, Queen of the United Kingdom of Great Britain and Northern Ireland and Head of the Commonwealth, upon the death of her father on Feb 6, 1952, her coronation taking place at Westminster Abbey on June 2, 1953.

MEXICO: REVOLUTION DAY. Nov 20. Anniversary of the social revolution launched by Francisco I. Madero in 1910. National holiday.

NAME YOUR PC DAY. Nov 20. Hey, why not? People name their boats! There are a lot more PCs than boats these days. "Binky" is already taken. Annually, Nov 20. (©2006 by WH.) For info: Thomas & Ruth Roy, Wellcat Holidays, 2418 Long Ln, Lebanon, PA 17046. Phone: (717) 279-0184. E-mail: info@wellcat.com. Web: www.wellcat.com.

✦ **NATIONAL FARM-CITY WEEK.** Nov 20–26. Presidential Proclamation issued for a week in November since 1956, customarily for the week ending with Thanksgiving Day. Requested by congressional resolutions 1956–58; since 1959 issued annually without request.

NCAA DIVISION I FIELD HOCKEY CHAMPIONSHIP. Nov 20 and 22. Trager Stadium, Louisville, KY. Est attendance: 1,000. For info: NCAA, 700 W Washington St, PO Box 6222, Indianapolis, IN 46206-6222. Phone: (317) 917-6222. Web: www.NCAAsports.com.

NUREMBERG WAR CRIMES TRIALS: ANNIVERSARY. Nov 20, 1945. The first session of the German war crimes trials started at Berlin with indictments against 24 former Nazi leaders. Later sessions were held at Nuremberg, Germany, starting Nov 20, 1945. One defendant committed suicide during his trial, and another was excused because of his physical and mental condition. The trials lasted more than 10 months, and delivery of the judgment was completed on Oct 1, 1946. Twelve were sentenced to death by hanging, three to life imprisonment, four to lesser prison terms, and three were acquitted.

PEDDLER'S VILLAGE GINGERBREAD HOUSE COMPETITION & DISPLAY. Nov 20–Jan 7, 2010. Lahaska, PA. More than 100 gingerbread house entries compete for more than $3,400 in cash prizes in such categories as traditional, authentic reproduction of a significant building, amateur, incredibly unusual three-dimensional and children's (12 and under; 13–18). The creative masterpieces are displayed throughout the holiday season in the village gazebo. Free admission. Est attendance: 850,000. For info: Peddler's Village, Rtes 202 and 263, Lahaska, PA 18931. Phone: (215) 794-4000. Fax: (215) 794-4001. Web: www.peddlersvillage.com.

***THE SHEIK* FILM RELEASE: ANNIVERSARY.** Nov 20, 1921. The silent film that catapulted Rudolph Valentino into stardom was given a general release on this date after premieres in New York and Los Angeles. The romantic melodrama, about a prince of the desert's obsession with an Englishwoman, was a hit that actually had women fainting in theaters. The film was scandalously frank for the times about sexual desire. "Sheik" even became slang for a man women couldn't resist. While the film made Valentino a reluctant sex symbol, it also typecast him—to his frustration. A sequel, *The Son of the Sheik*, was released in September 1926 a few weeks after Valentino's sudden death.

SILVER BELLS IN THE CITY. Nov 20. Lansing, MI. 25th annual. Michigan's capital city sparkles with hospitality on the streets of downtown Lansing's business district for this celebration of lights, music and holiday cheer including an electric light parade, lighting of the official State of Michigan Christmas Tree and a fireworks display (weather permitting) over the state capitol dome. Annually, the Friday before Thanksgiving. Coordinated by Arts Council of Greater Lansing, Inc. Est attendance: 120,000. For info: Arts Council of Greater Lansing, Inc, Center for the Arts, 425 S Grand Ave, Lansing, MI 48933. Phone: (517) 372-4636. Fax: (517) 484-2564. E-mail: info@lansingarts.org. Web: www.lansingarts.org or www.silverbellsinthecity.org.

SUGARLOAF CRAFTS FESTIVAL. Nov 20–22. Montgomery County Fairgrounds, Gaithersburg, MD. This show, now in its 34th year, features more than 500 nationally recognized craft designers and fine artists displaying and selling their original creations. Includes craft demonstrations, live music, children's entertainment, specialty foods, hourly gift certificate drawings and more. Est attendance: 25,000. For info: Sugarloaf Mountain Works, 200 Orchard Ridge Dr, #215, Gaithersburg, MD 20878. Phone: (800) 210-9900. Fax: (301) 253-9620. Web: www.sugarloafcrafts.com.

TIERNEY, GENE: BIRTH ANNIVERSARY. Nov 20, 1920. Known best for the title role in the film *Laura*, actress Gene Tierney was born at Brooklyn, NY. Her other films include *Heaven Can Wait, A Bell for Adano, Advise and Consent* and her last film, *The Pleasure Seekers*. She died Nov 6, 1991, at Houston, TX.

UNITED NATIONS: AFRICA INDUSTRIALIZATION DAY. Nov 20. The General Assembly proclaimed this day for the purpose of mobilizing the commitment of the international community to the industrialization of the continent (Resolution 44/237, Dec 22, 1989). For info: United Nations, Dept of Public Info, New York, NY 10017. Web: www.un.org.

UNITED NATIONS: UNIVERSAL CHILDREN'S DAY. Nov 20. Designated by the United Nations General Assembly as Universal Children's Day. First observance was in 1953. A time to honor children with special ceremonies and festivals and to make children's needs known to governments. Observed on different days and in different ways in more than 120 nations. For info: United Nations, Dept of Public Info, New York, NY 10017. Web: www.un.org.

WOLCOTT, OLIVER: BIRTH ANNIVERSARY. Nov 20, 1726. Signer of the Declaration of Independence, governor of Connecticut, born at Windsor, CT. Died Dec 1, 1797, at Litchfield, CT.

YORK INTERNATIONAL POSTCARD FAIR. Nov 20–21. York Fairgrounds, York, PA. Est attendance: 1,000. For info: Mary Martin Ltd, 4899 Pulaski Hwy, Rte 40, Perryville, MD 21903. Phone: (410) 642-3581. Fax: (410) 642-2053. E-mail: marymartinpostcards@prodigy.net.

BIRTHDAYS TODAY

Joseph (Joe) Robinette Biden, Jr, 67, US Senator (D, Delaware), born Scranton, PA, Nov 20, 1942.

Matt Blunt, 39, Governor of Missouri (R), born Strafford, MO, Nov 20, 1970.

Carlos Boozer, 28, basketball player, born Juneau, AK, Nov 20, 1981.

Robert C. Byrd, 92, US Senator (D, West Virginia), born North Wilkesboro, NC, Nov 20, 1917.

Steve Dahl, 55, Chicago radio personality, born La Canada, CA, Nov 20, 1954.

Richard Dawson, 77, actor, game show host ("Hogan's Heroes"; Emmy for "Family Feud"), born Gosport, England, Nov 20, 1932.

Don DeLillo, 73, author (*White Noise, Underworld*), born New York, NY, Nov 20, 1936.

Bo Derek, 53, actress (*10, Bolero, Tarzan, A Change of Seasons*), born Cathleen Collins at Long Beach, CA, Nov 20, 1956.

Nadine Gordimer, 86, Nobel Laureate, author (*The Pickup, July's People*), born Springs, South Africa, Nov 20, 1923.

Veronica Hamel, 66, actress ("Hill Street Blues"), born Philadelphia, PA, Nov 20, 1943.

Sabrina Lloyd, 39, actress (*Sports Night, Sliders*), born Mount Dora, FL, Nov 20, 1970.

Richard Masur, 61, actor ("One Day at a Time," *Heartburn*), born New York, NY, Nov 20, 1948.

Ricardo Montalban, 89, actor ("Fantasy Island," *Star Trek II: The Wrath of Khan*), born Mexico City, Mexico, Nov 20, 1920.

Estelle Parsons, 82, stage and screen actress (*Miss Margarida's Way*), born Marblehead, MA, Nov 20, 1927.

Dick Smothers, 70, comedian, folksinger (with brother Tom, "The Smothers Brothers Comedy Hour"), born New York, NY, Nov 20, 1939.

Ming-Na Wen, 42, actress ("ER," *One Night Stand*), born Macau, China, Nov 20, 1967.

Judy Woodruff, 63, journalist, author, born Tulsa, OK, Nov 20, 1946.

Sean Young, 50, actress (*Blade Runner, No Way Out*), born Louisville, KY, Nov 20, 1959.

November 21 — Saturday

DAY 325 — **40 REMAINING**

ALASCATTALO DAY. Nov 21. Anchorage, AK. To honor humor in general and Alaskan humor in particular. Event is named after "alascattalo," said to be the genetic cross between a moose and a walrus. For info: Steven C. Levi, Parsnackle Press, PO Box 241467, Anchorage, AK 99524. Phone/fax: (907) 337-2021. E-mail: scl@parsnackle.com.

BARTLETT, JOSIAH: BIRTH ANNIVERSARY. Nov 21, 1729. Signer of the Declaration of Independence. Born at Amesbury, MA, he died at Kingston, NH, May 19, 1795.

BEAUMONT, WILLIAM: BIRTH ANNIVERSARY. Nov 21, 1785. US Army surgeon whose contribution to classic medical literature and world fame resulted from another man's shotgun wound. When Canadian fur trapper Alexis St. Martin received a wound June 6, 1822—a nearly point-blank blast to the abdomen—Beaumont began observing his stomach and digestive processes through an opening in his abdominal wall. His findings were published in 1833 in *Experiments and Observations on the Gastric Juice and the Physiology of Digestion*. St. Martin returned to Canada in 1834 and resisted Beaumont's efforts to have him return for further study. He outlived his doctor by 20 years and was buried at a depth of eight feet to discourage any attempt at posthumous examination. Beaumont, born at Lebanon, CT, died Apr 25, 1853, at St. Louis, MO.

CONGRESS FIRST MEETS AT WASHINGTON: ANNIVERSARY. Nov 21, 1800. Congress met at Philadelphia from 1790 to 1800, when the north wing of the new Capitol at Washington, DC, was completed. The House and the Senate had been scheduled to meet in the new building Nov 17, 1800, but a quorum wasn't achieved until Nov 21, 1800.

CUSTER STATE PARK BUFFALO AUCTION. Nov 21. Custer, SD. A live sale at 10 AM, MST, of 200–300 surplus buffalo (calves, yearlings, mature cows and two-year-old bulls). Est attendance: 400. For info: Gary Brundige, Custer State Park, 13329 US Hwy 16A, Custer, SD 57730. Phone: (605) 255-4515. Fax: (605) 255-4460. E-mail: gary.brundige@state.sd.us.

DOW JONES TOPS 5,000: ANNIVERSARY. Nov 21, 1995. The Dow Jones Index of 30 major industrial stocks topped the 5,000 mark for the first time.

ELLA FITZGERALD WINS APOLLO AMATEUR NIGHT: 75th ANNIVERSARY. Nov 21, 1934. A shy, impoverished teenager, dressed in borrowed clothes and men's shoes, stepped on the stage of Harlem, NY's Apollo Theater for Amateur Night on this date. Ella Fitzgerald, in her stage debut, was so nervous that she fumbled her first song, but prompted to restart, she sang "Object of My Affection" and "Judy" to a crowd that exploded with applause. She won the contest. Bandleader Benny Carter, whose orchestra was backing the amateurs that night, helped Fitzgerald make music industry connections, and in 1935 she began to find success as a singer.

FAMILY VOLUNTEER DAY. Nov 21. To encourage and mobilize families in community-oriented projects. Designed to showcase the benefits of families working together, support organizations and businesses engaging family volunteers and encourage those who haven't yet made the commitment to volunteer with their family to begin doing so. Strategically occurring the Saturday before Thanksgiving Day, Family Volunteer Day is the perfect way for families and those who work with them to kick off a caring and giving holiday season. For info: Points of Light Foundation, 1400 I St NW, Ste 800, Wahington, DC 20005. Phone: (202) 729-8000. Fax: (202) 729-8100. E-mail: YouthandFamily@PointsofLight.org. Web: www.FamilyCares.org or www.PointsofLight.org.

FRENCHMAN ROWS ACROSS PACIFIC: ANNIVERSARY. Nov 21, 1991. Gerard d'Aboville completed a four-month solo journey across the Pacific Ocean on this date. D'Aboville began rowing across the Pacific on July 11 when he left Choshi, Japan. His journey ended at Ilwaco, WA.

GREEN, HETTY: BIRTH ANNIVERSARY. Nov 21, 1835. Henrietta Howland Robinson Green, better known as Hetty Green, reported to have been the richest woman in America, was born at New Bedford, MA. She was an able financier who managed her own wealth, which was estimated to have been in excess of $100 million. Died at New York, NY, July 3, 1916.

HOLIDAYS IN THE CITY GRAND ILLUMINATION PARADE. Nov 21. Norfolk, VA. A cherished tradition, the buildings of downtown

November 2009	S	M	T	W	T	F	S
	1	2	3	4	5	6	7
	8	9	10	11	12	13	14
	15	16	17	18	19	20	21
	22	23	24	25	26	27	28
	29	30					

Norfolk and Olde Towne Portsmouth illuminate their profiles to create a picture-postcard skyline. On the first evening of the illumination, a downtown lighted street parade kicks off the celebration of the season. All of the floats, bands and entries in this nighttime parade are lighted. Annually, the Saturday before Thanksgiving. Est attendance: 100,000. For info: Parade Mgr, Downtown Norfolk Council, 201 Granby St, Ste 101, Norfolk, VA 23510. Phone: (757) 623-1757. Fax: (757) 623-1756. E-mail: dnc@downtownnorfolk.org. Web: www.downtownnorfolk.org.

NAIA MEN'S AND WOMEN'S CROSS-COUNTRY NATIONAL CHAMPIONSHIPS. Nov 21. Site TBD. Men compete on an 8k course and women compete on a 5k course with the top 25 individual finishers in each championship receiving All-America honors. 54th men's championship; 30th women's. For info: Natl Assn of Intercollegiate Athletics, 1200 Grand Blvd, Kansas City, MO 64106. E-mail: rstein@naia.org. Web: www.naia.org.

NAIA WOMEN'S NATIONAL VOLLEYBALL CHAMPIONSHIP. Nov 21, Dec 1–5. Tyson Event Center, Sioux City, IA (for final). 36 teams qualify. 24 teams play in opening-round pairings at campus sites. 12 winners join 12 byes at final site for 24-team pool-play tournament to determine the national champion. 30th annual. Est attendance: 3,000. For info: Natl Assn of Intercollegiate Athletics, 1200 Grand Blvd, Kansas City, MO 64106. E-mail: rstein@naia.org. Web: www.naia.org.

NATCHITOCHES FESTIVAL OF LIGHTS. Nov 21–Jan 5, 2010. Natchitoches, LA. 82nd annual. A fairyland of multicolored lights, created by 350,000 Christmas bulbs strung along city streets and incorporated into 72 unique set pieces along Cane River Lake. Est attendance: 500,000. For info: Natchitoches Parish Tourist Commission, Calendar of Events, 781 Front St, Natchitoches, LA 71457. Phone: (318) 352-8072 or (800) 259-1714. Fax: (318) 352-2415. Web: www.natchitoches.net or www.christmasfestival.com.

NORTH CAROLINA: RATIFICATION DAY. Nov 21. 12th state to ratify Constitution in 1789.

POPE BENEDICT XV: BIRTH ANNIVERSARY. Nov 21, 1854. Giacomo dela Chiesa, 258th pope of the Roman Catholic Church, born at Pegli, Italy, and elected pope Sept 3, 1914. Died at Rome, Italy, Jan 22, 1922.

PURCELL, HENRY: DEATH ANNIVERSARY. Nov 21, 1695. (Old Style date.) The great English composer of the early Baroque period, born in 1659 at London, England, had a tragically short life yet was a prolific composer. His fame rests on the proto-operas *Dido and Aeneas* (1689) and *The Fairy Queen* (1692, based on Shakespeare's *Midsummer Night's Dream*), ceremonial odes for the court of King Charles II and more than 100 songs. The holder of various court musical positions, Purcell died at London.

RANCH HAND BREAKFAST. Nov 21. King Ranch, Kingsville, TX. A breakfast cooked and served outdoors at the world-famous King Ranch. See longhorn cattle and real cowboys on horseback. Annually, the Saturday before Thanksgiving. Est attendance: 7,000. For info: Kingsville Convention & Visitors Bureau, 1501 N Hwy 77, Kingsville, TX 78364-1562. Phone: (800) 333-5032. Fax: (361) 592-3227. E-mail: visitors@kingsvilletexas.com. Web: www.kingsvilletexas.com.

REMEMBRANCE DAY. Nov 21. Gettysburg, PA. An annual event held in conjunction with the Lincoln Observance, with a parade of Civil War troops to the High Water Mark and then to the Albert Woolson Monument for a wreath-laying ceremony. Civil War Ball held in the evening at Eisenhower Inn and Conference Center. Sponsored by the Sons of Union Veterans. Est attendance: 5,000. For info: Gettysburg CVB, PO Box 4117, Gettysburg, PA 17325. Phone: (717) 334-6274. Fax: (717) 334-1166. E-mail: info@gettysburg.travel. Web: www.gettysburg.travel.

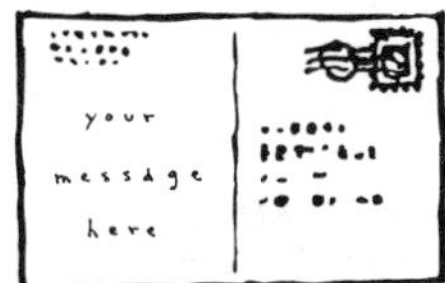

THAILAND: ELEPHANT ROUNDUP AT SURIN. Nov 21. Elephant demonstrations in morning, elephant races and tug-of-war between 100 men and one elephant. Observed since 1961 on third Saturday in November. Special trains from Bangkok on previous day.

UNITED NATIONS: WORLD TELEVISION DAY. Nov 21. On Dec 17, 1996, the General Assembly proclaimed this day as World Television Day, commemorating the date in 1996 on which the first World Television Forum was held at the UN. For info: United Nations, Dept of Public Info, New York, NY 10017. Web: www.un.org.

VOLTAIRE, JEAN FRANÇOIS MARIE: BIRTH ANNIVERSARY. Nov 21, 1694. French author and philosopher to whom is attributed (perhaps erroneously) the statement: "I disapprove of what you say, but I will defend to the death your right to say it." His most famous work is the novel *Candide.* Born at Paris, France, he died there May 30, 1778.

WORLD HELLO DAY. Nov 21. 37th annual. Everyone who participates greets 10 people. People in 180 countries have participated in this annual activity for advancing peace through personal communication. Heads of state of 114 countries have expressed approval of the event. For info: The McCormacks, PO Box 15592, Beverly Hills, CA 90209. Web: www.worldhelloday.org.

BIRTHDAYS TODAY

Troy Aikman, 43, sportscaster, former football player, born West Covina, CA, Nov 21, 1966.

Bjork, 44, singer, actress, born Björk Godmundsdóttir at Reykjavik, Iceland, Nov 21, 1965.

Phil Bredesen, 66, Governor of Tennessee (D), born Shortsville, NY, Nov 21, 1943.

Marcy Carsey, 65, television producer, born South Weymouth, MA, Nov 21, 1944.

James DePreist, 73, conductor, born Philadelphia, PA, Nov 21, 1936.

Richard J. Durbin, 65, US Senator (D, Illinois), born East St. Louis, IL, Nov 21, 1944.

George Kenneth (Ken) Griffey, Jr, 40, baseball player, born Donora, PA, Nov 21, 1969.

Goldie Hawn, 64, actress (*The Banger Sisters, Private Benjamin*; Oscar for *Cactus Flower*), born Washington, DC, Nov 21, 1945.

Laurence Luckinbill, 75, actor (*Star Trek V*), born Fort Smith, AR, Nov 21, 1934.

Lorna Luft, 57, singer, actress, born Los Angeles, CA, Nov 21, 1952.

Juliet Mills, 68, actress ("Nanny and the Professor," "Passions," *So Well Remembered, Carry on Jack*), born London, England, Nov 21, 1941.

Stanley Frank "Stan the Man" Musial, 89, Hall of Fame baseball player, born Donora, PA, Nov 21, 1920.

Harold Ramis, 65, actor, director, writer, producer (*Groundhog Day, Ghost Busters*), born Chicago, IL, Nov 21, 1944.

Cynthia Rhodes, 53, actress, dancer (*Flashdance, Dirty Dancing*), born Nashville, TN, Nov 21, 1956.

Tasha Schwikert, 25, gymnast, born Las Vegas, NV, Nov 21, 1984.

Nicollette Sheridan, 46, actress ("Desperate Housewives," "Knots Landing"), born Worthing, Sussex, England, Nov 21, 1963.

Marlo Thomas, 71, actress ("That Girl"), author (*Free to Be . . . You and Me*), born Detroit, MI, Nov 21, 1938.

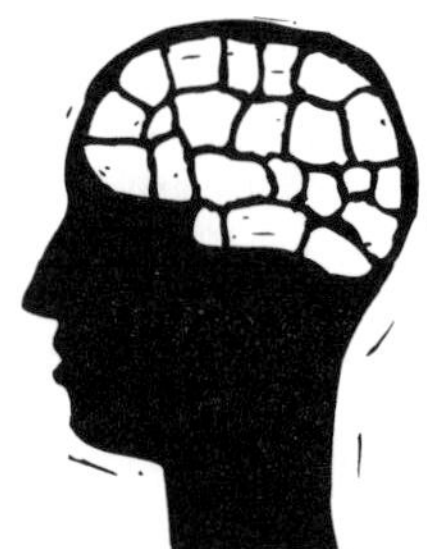

November 22 — Sunday

DAY 326 39 REMAINING

ADAMS, ABIGAIL SMITH: BIRTH ANNIVERSARY. Nov 22, 1744. Wife of John Adams, second president of the US, and mother of John Quincy Adams, sixth president of the US. An intelligent woman interested in politics and current affairs, she was a prodigious letter writer and an influence on her husband. Abigail Adams argued to her husband that Congress "should remember the ladies" as the new American government took form. Born at Weymouth, MA, she died Oct 28, 1818, at Quincy, MA.

BRITTEN, EDWARD BENJAMIN: BIRTH ANNIVERSARY. Nov 22, 1913. English composer born at Lowestoft, Suffolk, England. Lord Britten, Baron Britten of Aldeburgh, died at Aldeburgh, Dec 4, 1976.

CARMICHAEL, HOAGIE: BIRTH ANNIVERSARY. Nov 22, 1899. Hoagland Howard Carmichael, an attorney who gave up the practice of law to become an actor and songwriter, was born at Bloomington, IN. Among his many popular songs: "Stardust," "Lazybones," "Two Sleepy People" and "Skylark." Carmichael died at Rancho Mirage, CA, Dec 27, 1981.

***CHINA CLIPPER*: ANNIVERSARY.** Nov 22, 1935. A Pan American Martin 130 "flying boat" called the *China Clipper* began regular transpacific mail service on Nov 22, 1935. The plane, powered by four Pratt and Whitney Twin Wasp engines, took off from San Francisco, CA. It reached Manila, Philippines, 59 hours and 48 minutes later. About 20,000 persons watched the historic takeoff. Commercial passenger service was established the following year (Oct 21, 1936).

De GAULLE, CHARLES ANDRÉ MARIE: BIRTH ANNIVERSARY. Nov 22, 1890. President of France from December 1958 until his resignation in April 1969, Charles de Gaulle was born at Lille, France. A military leader, he wrote *The Army of the Future* (1934), in which he predicted just the type of armored warfare that was used against his country by Nazi Germany in WWII. After France's defeat at the hands of the Germans, he declared the existence of "Free France" and made himself head of that organization. When the French Vichy government began to collaborate openly with the Germans, the French citizenry looked to de Gaulle for leadership. His greatest moment of triumph was when he entered liberated Paris on Aug 26, 1944. De Gaulle died at Colombey-les-Deux-Eglises, France, Nov 19, 1970.

ELIOT, GEORGE: BIRTH ANNIVERSARY. Nov 22, 1819. English novelist George Eliot, whose real name was Mary Ann Evans, was born at Chilvers Coton, Warwickshire, England. Her works include *Silas Marner* and *Middlemarch*. She died at Chelsea, England, Dec 22, 1880.

GARNER, JOHN NANCE: BIRTH ANNIVERSARY. Nov 22, 1868. The 32nd vice president of the US (1933–41). Garner was a congressional representative from 1903 to 1933 and speaker of the House for two years (1931–33). Garner worked closely with President Franklin D. Roosevelt on New Deal legislation, but eventually split with the president over Roosevelt's plan to reorganize the Supreme Court. Garner was born at Red River County, TX; died at Uvalde, TX, Nov 7, 1967.

GERMANY: TOTENSONNTAG. Nov 22. In Germany, Totensonntag is the Protestant population's day for remembrance of the dead. It is celebrated on the last Sunday of the church year (the Sunday before Advent).

THE HUMANE SOCIETY OF THE UNITED STATES: ANNIVERSARY. Nov 22, 1954. When the Humane Society of the United States (HSUS) was founded by a handful of dedicated visionaries, the modern concept of "animal welfare" barely existed. A half century later, the HSUS has become the nation's largest animal protection organization, with a constituency of millions, and a leader in the parallel rise of the modern animal welfare movement. The HSUS mission is to create a humane and sustainable world for all animals, including people, through education, advocacy and the promotion of respect and compassion. For info: Humane Society of the US, 2100 L St NW, Washington, DC 20037. Phone: (202) 452-1100. Web: www.hsus.org.

KENNEDY, JOHN F.: ASSASSINATION ANNIVERSARY. Nov 22, 1963. President John F. Kennedy was slain by a sniper while riding in an open automobile at Dallas, TX. Accused assassin Lee Harvey Oswald was killed by Jack Ruby while in police custody awaiting trial.

LEBANON: INDEPENDENCE DAY. Nov 22. National Day. Gained independence from France in 1943.

MOTHER GOOSE PARADE. Nov 22. El Cajon, CA. 63rd annual. "A celebration of children." Floats depict Mother Goose rhymes and fairy tales and/or annual theme. Bands, equestrians and clowns. Traditionally, the Sunday before Thanksgiving. Est attendance: 250,000. For info: Mother Goose Parade Assn, 480 N Magnolia Ave, Ste 106, El Cajon, CA 92020. Phone: (619) 444-8712. Fax: (619) 444-3971. E-mail: info@mothergooseparade.org. Web: www.mothergooseparade.org.

NATIONAL BIBLE WEEK. Nov 22–29. An interfaith campaign to promote reading of the Bible. Free resources available. Governors and mayors across the country proclaim National Bible Week observance to their constituencies. Annually, from the Sunday preceding Thanksgiving to the following Sunday. For info: Rose Ann M. Beni, Exec Asst, Natl Bible Assn, 405 Lexington Ave, New York, NY 10174. Phone: (212) 907-6427. Fax: (212) 898-1147. E-mail: rbeni@nationalbible.org. Web: www.nationalbible.org.

✦ **NATIONAL FAMILY WEEK.** Nov 22–28.

NATIONAL GAME & PUZZLE WEEK™. Nov 22–28. 15th annual event to increase appreciation of board games and puzzles while preserving the tradition of investing time with family and friends. Part of The Million Minute Family Challenge™, conducted Sept 1–Dec 31. Special teacher materials and media information available, including press kits, interviews, etc. Annually, the Sunday through Saturday of Thanksgiving week. For info: Beth Muehlenkamp, National Game & Puzzle Week, 1400 E Inman Pkwy, Beloit, WI 53511. Phone: (800) 524-4263. Fax: (608) 362-8178. E-mail: bethm@patchproducts.com. Web: www.millionminute.com.

NATIONAL TEENS DON'T TEXT AND DRIVE WEEK. Nov 22–28. The Etiquette & Leadership Institute sponsors this event annually during the heavily traveled Thanksgiving week. The goal is to teach teens across America about the importance of driving safely: not just during Thanksgiving week, but every week. The Teens Don't Text & Drive Survey, a first-of-its-kind national poll examining current teen driving behavior, will also take place. Annually, the Sunday through Saturday that includes Thanksgiving Day. For info: Debra Lassiter, Etiquette & Leadership Institute, 2 S Main St, Town Center North, PO Box 1455, Watkinsville, GA 30677. Phone: (888) 769-5150. E-mail: eli@etiquetteleadership.com. Web: www.etiquetteleadership.com.

NETHERLANDS: PAN AMSTERDAM: THE ART AND ANTIQUES FAIR OF THE LOW COUNTRIES. Nov 22–29. RAI Parkhal, Ams-

November 2009

S	M	T	W	T	F	S
1	2	3	4	5	6	7
8	9	10	11	12	13	14
15	16	17	18	19	20	21
22	23	24	25	26	27	28
29	30					

terdam, the Netherlands. The fair presents an impressive selection of antique and modern silver and glassware, jewelry, textile, furniture and clocks, 16th-century to contemporary paintings and sculptures, art nouveau and art deco objects, prints and manuscripts, icons and photography. More than 80 experts vet every object for quality, condition and authenticity. Est attendance: 32,000. For info: Pan Amsterdam, TEFAF Maastricht, Broekwal 64, 5268 HD Helvoirt, The Netherlands. Phone: (31) (41) 164-50-90. E-mail: press @tefaf.com. Web: www.pan-amsterdam.nl.

***ON THE ORIGIN OF SPECIES* PUBLISHED: 150th ANNIVERSARY.** Nov 22, 1859. Charles Darwin's monumental work, *On the Origin of Species by Means of Natural Selection, or the Preservation of Favoured Races in the Struggle for Life*, was published on this date by London publisher John Murray. The print run of 1,250 (priced at 15 shillings) sold out the same day. A second print run of 3,000 in December also sold quickly. The book immediately generated a firestorm of public and private discussion. The word *evolution* did not appear until the 1872 (last) edition of *Origin*.

POST, WILEY: BIRTH ANNIVERSARY. Nov 22, 1898. Barnstorming aviator, stunt parachutist and adventurer, Wiley Post was born at Grand Plain, TX. Post, who taught himself to fly, and his plane, the *Winnie Mae*, were the center of world attention in the 1930s. He was coauthor (with his navigator, Harold Gatty) of *Around the World in Eight Days*. In 1935 Post and friend Will Rogers started on a flight to Asia. Their plane crashed near Point Barrow, AK, Aug 15, 1935; both were killed.

SAGITTARIUS, THE ARCHER. Nov 22–Dec 21. In the astronomical/astrological zodiac that divides the sun's apparent orbit into 12 segments, the period Nov 22–Dec 21 is traditionally identified as the sun sign of Sagittarius, the Archer. The ruling planet is Jupiter.

SAINT CECILIA: FEAST DAY. Nov 22. Roman virgin, Christian martyr and patron of music and musicians lived during the second or third century. Survived sentence of suffocation by steam but succumbed to sentence of beheading. Subject of poetry and musical compositions, and her feast day is still an occasion for musical events.

BIRTHDAYS TODAY

Boris Becker, 42, former tennis player, born Leimen, Germany, Nov 22, 1967.

Guion S. Bluford, Jr, 67, first black astronaut in space, born West Philadelphia, PA, Nov 22, 1942.

Tom Conti, 68, stage and screen actor (Tony Award for *Whose Life Is It Anyway?*), born Paisley, Scotland, Nov 22, 1941.

Jamie Lee Curtis, 51, actress (*True Lies, Halloween, A Fish Called Wanda*), born Los Angeles, CA, Nov 22, 1958.

Harry Edwards, 67, sports sociologist, born St. Louis, MO, Nov 22, 1942.

Terry Gilliam, 69, actor, writer ("Monty Python's Flying Circus," *Life of Brian*), director (*Brazil*), born Minneapolis, MN, Nov 22, 1940.

Mariel Hemingway, 48, actress (*Manhattan, Personal Best, Superman IV*), born Ketchum, ID, Nov 22, 1961.

Scarlett Johansson, 25, actress (*The Other Boleyn Girl, Match Point, Lost in Translation*), born New York, NY, Nov 22, 1984.

Richard Kind, 52, actor ("Spin City," "Mad About You"), born Trenton, NJ, Nov 22, 1957.

Billie Jean King, 66, former tennis player, born Long Beach, CA, Nov 22, 1943.

Robert Vaughn, 77, actor ("The Man From U.N.C.L.E.," *The Magnificent Seven*), born New York, NY, Nov 22, 1932.

November 23 — Monday

DAY 327 — **38 REMAINING**

ASHFORD, EMMETT LITTLETON: 95th BIRTH ANNIVERSARY. Nov 23, 1914. Emmett Littleton Ashford, born at Los Angeles, CA, was the first black to officiate at a major league baseball game. Ashford began his pro career calling games in the minors in 1951 and went to the majors in 1966. He was noted for his flamboyant style when calling strikes and outs as well as for his dapper dress, which included cuff links with his uniform. He died Mar 1, 1980, at Marina del Rey, CA.

BETTER CONVERSATION WEEK. Nov 23–29. 9th annual. This special week can strengthen personal bonds through meaningful, enjoyable talk among friends and family members. Check the website for articles and a free weekly newsletter on conversation skills. For info: Dr. Loren Ekroth. Phone: (702) 214-6782. E-mail: loren @conversation-matters.com. Web: www.conversation-matters.com.

BILLY THE KID: 150th BIRTH ANNIVERSARY. Nov 23, 1859. Legendary outlaw of western US. Probably named Henry McCarty at birth (New York, NY), he was better known as William H. Bonney. Ruthless killer, a failure at everything legal, he escaped from jail at age 21 while under sentence of hanging. Recaptured at Stinking Springs, NM, and returned to jail, he again escaped, only to be shot through the heart by pursuing Lincoln County sheriff Pat Garrett at Fort Sumner, NM, during the night of July 14, 1881. His last words, answered by two shots, reportedly were, "Who is there?"

CANADA: CANADIAN WESTERN AGRIBITION. Nov 23–28. IPSCO Place, Regina, SK. Canada's premier agricultural show and marketplace featuring more than 4,200 head of livestock including 13 purebred cattle breeds, commercial cattle, light and heavy horses, bison, dairy cattle, sheep and goats, as well as specialized livestock displays. The show is also known for its extensive trade show, the Canadian Cowboy's Association Finals Rodeo and western entertainment and attractions. Est attendance: 140,000. For info: Canadian Western Agribition, Box 3535, Regina, SK, Canada S4P 3J8. Phone: (306) 565-0565. Fax: (306) 757-9963. E-mail: info@agribition.com. Web: www.agribition.com.

"DOCTOR WHO" TV PREMIERE: ANNIVERSARY. Nov 23, 1963. The first episode of "Doctor Who" premiered on British TV with William Hartnell as the first doctor. Traveling through time and space in the TARDIS (an acronym for Time and Relative Dimensions in Space), the doctor and his companions found themselves in mortal combat with creatures such as the Daleks. The series aired until 1989, with a special film in 1996. "Doctor Who" didn't air in the US until Sept 29, 1975. A new version of the series began in 2005, with Christopher Eccleston and David Tennant as the ninth and tenth Doctors.

FIRST PLAY-BY-PLAY FOOTBALL GAME BROADCAST: 90th ANNIVERSARY. Nov 23, 1919. The first play-by-play football game radio broadcast in the US took place on this day. Texas A&M blanked the University of Texas 7–0.

GILBERT ISLANDS TAKEN: ANNIVERSARY. Nov 23, 1943. The US Second Marine Division took control of the Gilbert Islands after fierce fighting on the heavily fortified Tarawa Atoll. In the 76-hour battle the marines beat back a "death charge" in which the Japanese ran directly at the American guns. American troops sustained 3,500 killed and wounded. The Japanese suffered 5,000 killed and 17 wounded and captured. (The Gilbert Islands are the westernmost of the Polynesians, midway between Australia and Hawaii, and today are part of the nation of Kiribati.)

JAPAN: LABOR THANKSGIVING DAY. Nov 23. National holiday.

KARLOFF, BORIS: BIRTH ANNIVERSARY. Nov 23, 1887. Born William Henry Pratt at London, England. An actor known for his portrayal of ghoulish figures, his movies included *Frankenstein, The Body Snatcher* and *The Bride of Frankenstein*. Karloff died Feb 2, 1969, at Sussex, England.

***LIFE* MAGAZINE DEBUTS: ANNIVERSARY.** Nov 23, 1936. The illustrated magazine *Life* debuted on this day. The first cover featured a dramatic photograph by Margaret Bourke-White of Fort Peck Dam.

MARX, HARPO: BIRTH ANNIVERSARY. Nov 23, 1893. Harpo (Adolph Arthur) Marx was born at New York, NY. He was the second born of the famed Marx brothers, who were a popular comedy team of stage, screen and radio for 30 years. The silent brother, Harpo wore a red curly wig and communicated by honking a taxi horn at the most inopportune moments. He was a self-taught and expert player of the harp. Marx died Sept 28, 1964, at Hollywood, CA. Other family members who participated in the comedy team were Groucho (Julius), Chico (Leonard) and, briefly, Zeppo (Herbert) and Gummo (Milton).

PIERCE, FRANKLIN: BIRTH ANNIVERSARY. Nov 23, 1804. The 14th president of the US was born at Hillsboro, NH. Term of office: Mar 4, 1853–Mar 3, 1857. Not nominated until the 49th ballot at the Democratic Party convention in 1852, he was refused his party's nomination in 1856 for a second term. Pierce died at Concord, NH, Oct 8, 1869.

RUTLEDGE, EDWARD: BIRTH ANNIVERSARY. Nov 23, 1749. Signer of the Declaration of Independence, governor of South Carolina, born at Charleston, SC. Died there Jan 23, 1800.

SWITZERLAND: LUCERNE FESTIVAL AT THE PIANO. Nov 23–29. Lucerne. This piano festival focusing on keyboards is unique in Europe for the range of piano music it offers, ranging from classical to jazz music, performed on modern and historical instruments. Exhibitions, workshops, films and more on the topic of keyboard instruments will additionally expand the range of events. Piano Off-Stage!, a festival of bar-piano music, will take place simultaneously in the beautiful restaurants, hotels and bars of Lucerne. For info: Lucerne Festival, PO Box CH-6002, Lucerne, Switzerland. Phone: (41) 226-44-00. Fax: (41) 226-44-60. E-mail: info@lucernefestival.ch. Web: www.lucernefestival.ch.

SWITZERLAND: ONION MARKET (ZIBELEMARIT). Nov 23. Berne. Best known and most popular of Switzerland's many autumn markets. Great heaps of onions in front of Federal Palace. Fourth Monday in November commemorates granting of market right to people after great fire of Berne in 1405.

BIRTHDAYS TODAY

Susan Anspach, 64, actress (*Five Easy Pieces, Play It Again Sam, Montenegro*), born New York, NY, Nov 23, 1945.

Vin Baker, 38, basketball player, born Lake Wales, FL, Nov 23, 1971.

Jerry Bock, 81, composer, lyricist (Tonys for *Fiddler on the Roof, Fiorello!*), born New Haven, CT, Nov 23, 1928.

Miley Cyrus, 17, actress, singer ("Hannah Montana"), born Destiny Hope Cyrus at Franklin, TN, Nov 23, 1992.

Jim Doyle, 64, Governor of Wisconsin (D), born Madison, WI, Nov 23, 1945.

Lucas Grabeel, 25, actor (*High School Musical*), born Springfield, MO, Nov 23, 1984.

Steve Harvey, 53, comedian, actor (*The Original Kings of Comedy*, "The Steve Harvey Show"), born Welch, WV, Nov 23, 1956.

Mary L. Landrieu, 54, US Senator (D, Louisiana), born Arlington, VA, Nov 23, 1955.

Krzysztof Penderecki, 76, composer, born Debica, Poland, Nov 23, 1933.

Charles E. Schumer, 59, US Senator (D, New York), born Brooklyn, NY, Nov 23, 1950.

November 2009	S	M	T	W	T	F	S
	1	2	3	4	5	6	7
	8	9	10	11	12	13	14
	15	16	17	18	19	20	21
	22	23	24	25	26	27	28
	29	30					

November 24 — Tuesday

DAY 328 — **37 REMAINING**

BARKLEY, ALBEN WILLIAM: BIRTH ANNIVERSARY. Nov 24, 1877. The 35th vice president of the US (1949–53) was born at Graves County, KY. Died at Lexington, VA, Apr 30, 1956.

BATTLE OF CHATTANOOGA: ANNIVERSARY. Nov 24, 1863. After reinforcing the besieged Union army at Chattanooga, TN, General Ulysses S. Grant launched the Battle of Chattanooga on this date. Falsely secure in the knowledge that his troops were in an impregnable position on Lookout Mountain, Confederate general Braxton Bragg and his army were overrun by the Union forces, Bragg himself barely escaping capture. The battle is famous for the Union army's spectacular advance up a heavily fortified slope into the teeth of the enemy guns.

BUCKLEY, WILLIAM F., JR: BIRTH ANNIVERSARY. Nov 24, 1925. Entertaining and influential postwar conservative standard-bearer as well as author, editor, talk show host and master of polysyllabic parlance. Founded the *National Review* in 1955. Born at New York, NY, Buckley died Feb 24, 2008, at Stamford, CT.

CARNEGIE, DALE: BIRTH ANNIVERSARY. Nov 24, 1888. American inspirational lecturer and author, Dale Carnegie was born at Maryville, MO. His best-known book, *How to Win Friends and Influence People*, published in 1936, sold nearly five million copies and was translated into 29 languages. Carnegie died at New York, NY, Nov 1, 1955.

CARRS/SAFEWAY GREAT ALASKA SHOOTOUT. Nov 24–28. Sullivan Arena, Anchorage, AK. Top NCAA basketball action as eight men's and four women's Division I teams from around the country compete. Est attendance: 48,000. For info: University of Alaska–Anchorage, Athletic Dept, 3211 Providence Dr, Anchorage, AK 99508. Phone: (907) 786-1250. Fax: (907) 563-4565. E-mail: tim@uaa.alaska.edu. Web: www.goseawolves.com.

CELEBRATE YOUR UNIQUE TALENT DAY. Nov 24. We all have at least one extraordinary—and many times weird—ability. Now's the time to get out there and indulge in yours. Sponsored by the record holder for the football-throwing game at ESPN Zone! For info: Shannon Hurd, 10556 Graymont Ln, #22C, Highlands Ranch, CO 80126. Phone: (720) 936-3326. Fax: (720) 920-9256. E-mail: writersmh@hotmail.com.

CHURCH/STATE SEPARATION WEEK. Nov 24. A holiday inspired by the invaluable work of organizations such as Americans United for the Separation of Church and State, the Institute for First Amendment Studies and many others, Church/State Separation Week offers concerned and active citizens an opportunity to educate others about the importance of this subject. For info: Institute for Humanist Studies, 48 Howard St, Albany, NY 12207. Phone: (518) 432-7820. Fax: (518) 432-7821. E-mail: MCherry@HumanistStudies.org. Web: www.secularseasons.org.

"D.B. COOPER" HIJACKING: ANNIVERSARY. Nov 24–25, 1971. A middle-aged man whose plane ticket was made out to "D.B. Cooper" parachuted from a Northwest Airlines 727 jetliner on Nov 25, 1971, carrying $200,000, which he had collected from the airline as ransom for the plane and passengers as a result of threats made during his Nov 24 flight from Portland, OR, to Seattle, WA. He jumped from the plane over an area of wilderness south of Seattle and was never apprehended. Several thousand dollars of the marked ransom money turned up in February 1980, along the Columbia River, near Vancouver, WA.

DUFF, HOWARD: BIRTH ANNIVERSARY. Nov 24, 1913. American actor Howard Duff was born at Bremerton, WA. He played detective Sam Spade on radio in the 1940s and then went on to films and television ("Knots Landing"). He died July 8, 1990, at Santa Barbara, CA.

JOPLIN, SCOTT: BIRTH ANNIVERSARY. Nov 24, 1868. American musician and composer famed for his piano rags, born at Texarkana, TX. Died at New York, NY, Apr 1, 1917.

MANSTEIN, ERICH VON: BIRTH ANNIVERSARY. Nov 24, 1887. Considered by many to be the greatest strategist of WWII, Erich von Manstein was born at Berlin, Germany. His plan for the invasion of France in 1940 was a complete success. He was dismissed by Hitler in March 1944. Manstein died at Irschenhausen, Germany, June 10, 1973.

MOON PHASE: FIRST QUARTER. Nov 24. Moon enters First Quarter phase at 4:39 PM, EST.

SPINOZA, BARUCH: BIRTH ANNIVERSARY. Nov 24, 1632. (Old Style date.) Dutch philosopher, born at Amsterdam, Netherlands. Died at The Hague, Netherlands, Feb 21, 1677 (OS). "Peace is not an absence of war," wrote Spinoza, in 1670, "it is a virtue, a state of mind, a disposition for benevolence, confidence, justice."

STERNE, LAURENCE: BIRTH ANNIVERSARY. Nov 24, 1713. Novelist, born at Clonmel, Ireland. Died at London, England, Mar 18, 1768. In his dedication to *Tristram Shandy*, Sterne wrote: "I live in a constant endeavour to fence against the infirmities of ill health, and other evils of life, by mirth; being firmly persuaded that every time a man smiles—but much more so, when he laughs, that it adds something to this Fragment of Life."

TAYLOR, ZACHARY: 225th BIRTH ANNIVERSARY. Nov 24, 1784. The Mexican War hero and career soldier who became 12th president of the US was born at Orange County, VA. Term of office: Mar 4, 1849–July 9, 1850. He was nominated at the Whig Party convention in 1848, but the story goes he did not accept the letter notifying him of his nomination because it had postage due. He cast his first vote in 1846, when he was 62 years old. Becoming ill July 4, 1850, he died at the White House, July 9. His last words: "I am sorry that I am about to leave my friends."

TOULOUSE-LAUTREC, HENRI DE: BIRTH ANNIVERSARY. Nov 24, 1864. French painter and designer of posters. Born at Albi, France, he died Sept 9, 1901, at Bordeaux, France.

US MILITARY LEAVES PHILIPPINES: ANNIVERSARY. Nov 24, 1992. The Philippines became a US colony at the turn of the last century when it was taken over from Spain after the Spanish-American War. Though President Franklin D. Roosevelt signed a bill Mar 24, 1934, granting the Philippines independence to be effective July 4, 1946, before that date Manila and Washington signed a treaty allowing the US to lease military bases on the island. In 1991 the Philippine Senate voted to reject a renewal of that lease, and on Nov 24, 1992, after almost 100 years of military presence on the island, the last contingent of US marines left Subic Base.

BIRTHDAYS TODAY

Katherine Heigl, 31, actress ("Grey's Anatomy," *27 Dresses, Knocked Up*), born Washington, DC, Nov 24, 1978.

Stanley Livingston, 59, actor ("My Three Sons"), born Los Angeles, CA, Nov 24, 1950.

Keith Primeau, 38, hockey player, born Toronto, ON, Canada, Nov 24, 1971.

Oscar Palmer Robertson, 71, Hall of Fame basketball player, born Charlotte, TN, Nov 24, 1938.

Dwight Schultz, 62, actor ("Star Trek: The Next Generation," *Fat Man and Little Boy*), born Baltimore, MD, Nov 24, 1947.

Brad Sherwood, 45, comedian, actor ("Whose Line Is It Anyway?"), born Chicago, IL, Nov 24, 1964.

Rudolph (Rudy) Tomjanovich, 61, basketball coach and former player, born Hamtramck, MI, Nov 24, 1948.

November 25 — Wednesday

DAY 329 — 36 REMAINING

AUTOMOBILE SPEED REDUCTION: ANNIVERSARY. Nov 25, 1973. Anniversary of the presidential order requiring a cutback from the 70-mph speed limit. The 55-mph National Maximum Speed Limit (NMSL) was established by Congress in January 1974 (PL 93–643). The National Highway Traffic Safety Administration reported that "analysis of available data shows that the 55 mph NMSL forestalled 48,310 fatalities through 1980. There were also reductions in crash-related injuries and property damage." Motor fuel savings were estimated at 2.4 billion gallons per year. Notwithstanding, in 1987 Congress permitted states to increase speed limits on rural interstate highways to 65 mph.

BOSNIA AND HERZEGOVINA: NATIONAL DAY. Nov 25. National holiday. Commemorates the declaration of statehood within the federation of Yugoslavia in 1943.

CARNEGIE, ANDREW: BIRTH ANNIVERSARY. Nov 25, 1835. American financier, philanthropist and benefactor of more than 2,500 libraries, born at Dunfermline, Scotland. Carnegie Hall, the Carnegie Foundation and the Carnegie Endowment for International Peace are among his gifts. Carnegie wrote in 1889, "Surplus wealth is a sacred trust which its possessor is bound to administer in his lifetime for the good of the community. . . . The man who dies . . . rich dies disgraced." Carnegie died at his summer estate, Shadowbrook, MA, Aug 11, 1919.

DiMAGGIO, JOSEPH PAUL (JOE): 95th BIRTH ANNIVERSARY. Nov 25, 1914. Baseball Hall of Fame outfielder, born at Martinez, CA. In 1941 he was on "the streak," getting a hit in 56 consecutive games. He was the American League MVP for three years, was the batting champion in 1939 and led the league in RBIs in both 1941 and 1948. DiMaggio was married to actress Marilyn Monroe in 1954, but they later divorced. He died at Harbour Island, FL, Mar 8, 1999.

GERMANY: FRANKFURT CHRISTMAS MARKET. Nov 25–Dec 23. "Weinachtsmarkt auf dem Romerberg," the Christmas market in Frankfurt, is one of Germany's best. Bells are rung simultaneously from nine downtown churches. Glockenspiels are sounded by hand and trumpets are blown from the old St. Nicolas Church.

KENNEDY, JOHN F., JR: BIRTH ANNIVERSARY. Nov 25, 1960. Lawyer, editor (*George* magazine), born at Washington, DC. Son of John F. Kennedy (35th president of the US) and Jacqueline Bouvier Kennedy. He died along with his wife, Carolyn, and his sister-in-law, Lauren Bessette, when the plane he was piloting crashed off of Cape Cod, MA, July 16, 1999.

MIRABEL SISTERS MURDERED: ANNIVERSARY. Nov 25, 1960. On this date Maria, Teresa and Minerva Mirabel, political activists in the Dominican Republic, were assassinated on orders of dictator Rafael Trujillo. The anniversary of their deaths is now observed by the United Nations as International Day for the Elimination of Violence Against Women.

NATION, CARRY AMELIA MOORE: BIRTH ANNIVERSARY. Nov 25, 1846. American temperance leader, famed as hatchet-wielding smasher of saloons, born at Garrard County, KY. Died at Leavenworth, KS, June 9, 1911.

POPE JOHN XXIII: BIRTH ANNIVERSARY. Nov 25, 1881. Angelo Roncalli, 261st pope of the Roman Catholic Church, born at Sotte il Monte, Italy. Elected pope, Oct 28, 1958. Died June 3, 1963, at Rome, Italy.

SAINT CATHERINE'S DAY. Nov 25. Patron saint of maidens, mechanics and philosophers, as well as of all who work with wheels.

SCOTLAND: SCOTTISH INTERNATIONAL BADMINTON CHAMPIONSHIP. Nov 25–28. Kelvin Hall International Sports Arena, Glasgow. A European Badminton Union Grand Prix Tournament. Est attendance: 7,000. For info: Badminton Scotland, Cockburn Centre, 40 Bogmoor Pl, Glasgow, Scotland G51 4TQ. Phone: (44) (141) 445-1218. Fax: (44) (141) 425-1218. E-mail: enquiries@badmintonscotland.org.uk. Web: www.badmintonscotland.org.uk.

SHOPPING REMINDER DAY. Nov 25. One month before Christmas, a reminder to shoppers that after today there are only 28 more shopping days (excluding Thanksgiving and Christmas Eve) until Christmas.

SURINAME: INDEPENDENCE DAY. Nov 25. Holiday. Gained independence from the Netherlands in 1975.

TIE ONE ON DAY. Nov 25. Tie One On and celebrate the humble apron and the spirit of women of earlier generations who donned this universal symbol of home, family and mothering as the uniform of their daily wardrobe and helped make America the great country it is today. On the eve of Thanksgiving, wrap a loaf of bread in an apron and tuck a prayer or note of encouragement in the pocket. Tie One On—an apron, of course—and deliver the wrapped bread to someone without your bounty and in need of spiritual or physical sustenance. For info: EllynAnne Geisel, 605 W 17th St, Pueblo, CO 81003. Phone: (877) 9-APRONS. Fax: (719) 542-3947. E-mail: ellynanne@apronmemories.com. Web: www.apronmemories.com.

UNITED NATIONS: INTERNATIONAL DAY FOR THE ELIMINATION OF VIOLENCE AGAINST WOMEN. Nov 25. Observed by the United Nations since 1993 on the anniversary of the 1960 murders of the Mirabel sisters in the Dominican Republic. In 2004 UN Secretary-General Kofi Annan said, "Let us be encouraged that there is a growing understanding of the problem. But let us also pledge to do our utmost to protect women, banish such violence and build a world in which women enjoy their rights and freedoms on an equal basis with men." Annually, Nov 25. For more info: www.un.org.

WONDERLAND OF LIGHTS. Nov 25–Dec 30. Marshall, TX. More than 10 million tiny white lights cover the city. Features JC's lighted Christmas parade, candlelight home tours. Outdoor ice-skating on the square and live entertainment on the square Tuesdays, Thursdays, Fridays and Saturdays. First Saturday (Dec 5) Cowboy Christmas Celebration with breakfast, entertainment, stick-horse races, mule rides, carriage rides, bus tours and Santa Claus. Est attendance: 500,000. For info: Geraldine Mauthe, Director, Greater Marshall Chamber of Commerce, PO Box 520, Marshall, TX 75671. Phone: (903) 935-7868. Fax: (903) 935-9982. E-mail: chambermfi@hotmail.com. Web: www.marshalltxchamber.com.

BIRTHDAYS TODAY

Christina Applegate, 38, actress (*Anchorman*, "Samantha Who?," "Married . . . With Children"), born Hollywood, CA, Nov 25, 1971.

Cris Carter, 44, former football player, born Troy, OH, Nov 25, 1965.

Bucky Dent, 58, former baseball player and manager, born Russell Earl O'Dey at Savannah, GA, Nov 25, 1951.

Jerry Ferrara, 30, actor ("Entourage"), born Brooklyn, NY, Nov 25, 1979.

Joe Jackson Gibbs, 69, Hall of Fame football coach, sportscaster, born Mocksville, NC, Nov 25, 1940.

Amy Grant, 49, singer ("Baby, Baby"), born Augusta, GA, Nov 25, 1960.

Jill Hennessy, 40, actress ("Crossing Jordan," "Law & Order"), born Edmonton, AB, Canada, Nov 25, 1969.

Bernie Joseph Kosar, Jr, 46, former football player, born Boardman, OH, Nov 25, 1963.

John Larroquette, 62, actor (Emmy for "Night Court"), born New Orleans, LA, Nov 25, 1947.

John Lynch, 57, Governor of New Hampshire (D), born Waltham, MA, Nov 25, 1952.

Lenny Moore, 76, Hall of Fame football player, born Reading, PA, Nov 25, 1933.

Eddie Steeples, 36, actor ("My Name Is Earl"), born in Texas, Nov 25, 1973.

Ben Stein, 65, actor, journalist, former speechwriter, born Washington, DC, Nov 25, 1944.

November 2009	S	M	T	W	T	F	S
	1	2	3	4	5	6	7
	8	9	10	11	12	13	14
	15	16	17	18	19	20	21
	22	23	24	25	26	27	28
	29	30					

November 26 — Thursday

DAY 330 — 35 REMAINING

***ALICE'S ADVENTURES IN WONDERLAND* PUBLISHED: ANNIVERSARY.** Nov 26, 1865. Lewis Carroll's fun-house novel was published on this date. *Through the Looking-Glass, and What Alice Found There* followed in 1871. Lewis Carroll was the pen name of Oxford lecturer in mathematics Charles L. Dodgson.

AMERICA'S THANKSGIVING DAY PARADE®. Nov 26. Detroit, MI. One of Michigan's largest events, the parade has been a beloved Thanksgiving tradition since 1924. The streets of downtown Detroit come alive with bands, floats and more for all ages. Est attendance: 1,000,000. For info: The Parade Company, 9500 Mt Elliott, Studio A, Detroit, MI 48211. Phone: (313) 923-7400. Fax: (313) 923-2920. Web: www.theparade.org/parade.

***CASABLANCA* PREMIERE: ANNIVERSARY.** Nov 26, 1942. Because of the landing of the Allies in North Africa on Nov 8, the premiere and release of the film were moved up from June 1943 to Nov 26, 1942, when it premiered at New York City on Thanksgiving Day. The general nationwide release followed on Jan 23, 1943, during the Roosevelt-Churchill conferences in Casablanca.

DALLAS YMCA TURKEY TROT. Nov 26. Dallas, TX. 42nd annual. The Turkey Trot is the largest Thanksgiving Day event of its kind in the country. Starting from humble beginnings 40 years ago at White Rock Lake, it has grown into the undisputed "Way to Begin Thanksgiving Day" for thousands of locals as well as those who travel to share in our great event. The 8-mile race begins at 9 AM; the 3-mile Fun Run/Walk begins at 9:15 AM. Friendly dogs welcome on leash. Sponsored by Capital One. Annually, Thanksgiving Day. Est attendance: 40,000. For info: Dallas YMCA Turkey Trot, YMCA of Metropolitan Dallas, 601 N Akard, Dallas, TX 75201. Phone: (214) 954-0500. Fax: (214) 953-0632. E-mail: susancasey@ymcadallas.org or joec@ymcadallas.org. Web: www.thetrot.com.

DAYTONA TURKEY RUN. Nov 26–29. Daytona International Speedway, Daytona Beach, FL. 36th annual car show of all makes of 1980 and older collector vehicles. Show includes display of classics, street rods, muscle cars, race cars, customs and special trucks on the speedway infield, with a large swap meet (4,400 vendors) of auto parts and accessories and car sales corral. Also a craft sale. Annually, Thanksgiving weekend. Est attendance: 150,000. For info: Ron Baynton, Mgr of Show Operations, Daytona Beach Racing and Recreational Facilities District, PO Box 1958, Daytona Beach, FL 32115-1958. Phone: (386) 255-7355. Fax: (386) 255-5755. Web: www.turkeyrun.com or www.daytonabeachcarshows.com.

FIRST US HOLIDAY BY PRESIDENTIAL PROCLAMATION: ANNIVERSARY. Nov 26, 1789. President George Washington proclaimed Nov 26, 1789, to be Thanksgiving Day. Both houses of Congress, by their joint committee, had requested him to recommend "a day of public thanksgiving and prayer, to be observed by acknowledging with grateful hearts the many and signal favors of Almighty God, especially by affording them an opportunity to peaceably establish a form of government for their safety and happiness." Proclamation issued Oct 3, 1789. Next proclaimed by President Abraham Lincoln in 1863 for the last Thursday in November. In 1939 President Franklin D. Roosevelt moved Thanksgiving to the fourth Thursday in November.

FOODS & FEASTS OF COLONIAL VIRGINIA. Nov 26–28. Jamestown Settlement, Williamsburg, VA; and Yorktown Victory Center, Yorktown, VA. Explore the 17th- and 18th-century culinary practices of Virginia at this three-day event starting on Thanksgiving Day. At Jamestown Settlement, learn how food was gathered, preserved and prepared on land and at sea by Virginia's English colonists and Powhatan Indians. At Yorktown Victory Center, learn about typical soldiers' fare during the American Revolution and trace the bounty of a 1780s farm from field to kitchen. For info: Jamestown-Yorktown Foundation, PO Box 1607, Williamsburg, VA 23187. Phone: (757) 253-4838 or toll-free (888) 593-4682. Fax: (757) 253-5299. Web: www.historyisfun.org.

GARDEN OF LIGHTS. Nov 26–Dec 31. Honor Heights Park, Muskogee, OK. A winter celebration that includes a drive-through display of more than one million shimmering lights. The lights are strung carefully to enhance the natural beauty of the park, gardens, trees, gazebo, waterfalls and ponds. Displays also include a giant entrance tunnel of lights and a wide variety of animated wildlife depicting the creatures that make their home in the park. Free admission but donations are accepted. Gift shop on site. Est attendance: 280,000. For info: Muskogee Chamber of Commerce. Phone: (866) 381-6543. Web: www.muskogeechamber.org.

GOMEZ, LEFTY: BIRTH ANNIVERSARY. Nov 26, 1908. Vernon Louis ("Lefty") Gomez, Baseball Hall of Fame pitcher, born at Rodeo, CA. Gomez was a star pitcher with the New York Yankees from 1930 to 1942. He won six World Series games without a defeat and was the winning pitcher in the first All-Star game. Inducted into the Hall of Fame in 1972. Died at Greenbrae, CA, Feb 17, 1989.

GRIMKE, SARAH MOORE: BIRTH ANNIVERSARY. Nov 26, 1792. American antislavery and women's rights advocate along with her sister Angelina. Born at Charleston, SC, and died Dec 23, 1873, at Hyde Park, MA.

HARVARD, JOHN: BIRTH ANNIVERSARY. Nov 26, 1607. English clergyman and scholar. Born in England, he died Sept 24, 1638, in the Massachusetts Bay Colony. Harvard bequeathed part of his estate to a local college, which renamed itself Harvard in his honor.

HOLIDAY LIGHTS ON THE LAKE. Nov 26–Jan 3, 2010. Lakemont Park, Altoona, PA. Drive-through displays of more than 51 acres of animated holiday lights, plus a holiday gift shop, food, model train displays and visits from Santa Claus. Annually, from Thanksgiving Day through the Sunday after New Year's Day. Est attendance: 75,000. For info: Lakemont Park, 700 Park Ave, Altoona, PA 16602. Phone: (814) 949-7275 or (800) 434-8006. Fax: (814) 949-9207. E-mail: lakemontparkfun@hotmail.com. Web: www.lakemontparkfun.com.

JAPAN AGREES TO END USE OF DRIFT NETS: ANNIVERSARY. Nov 26, 1991. Japan agreed to comply with a 1989 United Nations moratorium on the use of huge fishing nets in the northern Pacific Ocean. The large nets extend up to 40 miles and have been criticized as "walls of death," causing widespread destruction of marine life, including whales, turtles, birds and many varieties of fish. Japan agreed to end half of its drift-net fishing by the June 30, 1992, deadline, and the remainder by the end of 1992.

LONGWOOD GARDENS CHRISTMAS DISPLAY. Nov 26–Jan 10, 2010. Kennett Square, PA. Indoor conservatory display of thousands of poinsettias and decorated trees. Outdoors, more than 500,000 lights, ice skating and holiday fountain displays. Est attendance: 200,000. For info: Longwood Gardens, PO Box 501, Kennett Square, PA 19348-0501. Phone: (610) 388-1000. Web: www.longwoodgardens.org.

MACY'S THANKSGIVING DAY PARADE. Nov 26. New York, NY. 83rd annual. Starts at 9 AM, EST, at Central Park West. A part of everyone's Thanksgiving, the parade grows bigger and better each year. Featuring floats, giant balloons, marching bands and famous stars, the parade is televised for the whole country. For info: New York CVB, 810 7th Ave, 3rd Fl, New York, NY 10019. Phone: (212) 484-1222. Web: www.nycvisit.com or macysparade.com.

MONGOLIA: REPUBLIC DAY. Nov 26. National holiday. Commemorates the declaration of the republic in 1924.

LA POSADA de KINGSVILLE: A CELEBRATION OF LIGHTS. Nov 26–Dec 31. Kingsville, TX. While a celebration of lights recaptures the joy and spirit of Christmas, businesses and neighborhoods twinkle with lights from the weekend before Thanksgiving. Many holiday events with a south Texas flavor are scheduled: special activities for children, nighttime parade with lighted floats and holiday music and much more. Call for dates of specific events. Est attendance: 50,000. For info: Kingsville CVB, 1501 N Hwy 77, Kingsville, TX 78364-1562. Phone: (800) 333-5032. Fax: (361) 592-3227. Web: www.kingsvilletexas.com.

"THE PRICE IS RIGHT" TV PREMIERE: ANNIVERSARY. Nov 26, 1956. This popular show is also TV's longest-running daily game show, surviving changes in format, networks, time slots and hosts. It began in 1956 with Bill Cullen as host, Don Pardo as announcer; four contestants had to bid on an item, and the one who bid closest to the manufacturer's suggested price without going over won the item. In 1972, after a seven-year hiatus, "The Price Is Right" came back in two versions. Bob Barker was the host of the network version until 2007. Johnny Olsen was the announcer until his death in 1985; Rod Roddy took his place. Also on the show are attractive women who model the prizes to be won and help set up the price-guessing games. "Price" contestants are drawn from the studio audience.

QUEEN ELIZABETH II AGREES TO PAY TAXES: ANNIVERSARY. Nov 26, 1992. Prime Minister John Major announced that Britain's monarch, Queen Elizabeth, had decided to begin paying taxes on her personal income.

SCHULZ, CHARLES: BIRTH ANNIVERSARY. Nov 26, 1922. Cartoonist, born at Minneapolis, MN. Created the "Peanuts" comic strip that debuted on Oct 2, 1950. The strip included Charlie Brown; his sister, Sally; his dog, Snoopy; friends Linus and Lucy; and a variety of other characters. Schulz's last daily strip was published Jan 3, 2000, and his last Sunday strip was published Feb 13, 2000. The strip ran in more than 2,500 newspapers in many countries. Schulz won the Reuben Award in both 1955 and 1964 and was named International Cartoonist of the Year in 1978. Several TV specials were spin-offs of the strip including, "It's the Great Pumpkin Charlie Brown" and "You're a Good Man, Charlie Brown." Schulz died at Santa Rosa, CA, Feb 12, 2000. See also "'Peanuts' Debuts: Anniversary" (Oct 2).

SEVAREID, ERIC: BIRTH ANNIVERSARY. Nov 26, 1912. American journalist Eric (Arnold) Sevareid was born at Velva, ND. He worked for CBS News as a radio reporter during WWII, appeared regularly on "The CBS News with Walter Cronkite" from 1964 to 1977, won the Peabody Award for news interpretations (1950, 1964 and 1967) and earned two Emmys in 1973. He died July 9, 1992, at Washington, DC.

STOCK EXCHANGE HOLIDAY (THANKSGIVING DAY). Nov 26. The holiday schedules for the various exchanges are subject to change if relevant rules, regulations or exchange policies are revised. If you have questions, contact: American Stock Exchange (866) 422-2639 (www.amex.com), Chicago Board of Trade (312) 435-3500 (www.cbot.com), Chicago Board Options Exchange (312) 786-5600 (www.cboe.com), NASDAQ Stock Market (646) 441-5200 (www.nasdaq.com), New York Stock Exchange (212) 656-3000 (www.nyse.com), Philadelphia Stock Exchange (800) THE-PHLX (www.phlx.com).

TERRITORIAL CHRISTMAS CELEBRATION. Nov 26–Dec 23. Guthrie, OK. Take a step back in time and celebrate Christmas in grand Victorian style. Enjoy the Pollard's production of "A Territorial Christmas Carol," the Victorian Walk, Bed & Breakfast Home Tour, Christmas light tour on the trolley, street carolers, peanut vendors, Christmas tree auction and reception and election of the territorial governor. Est attendance: 13,000. For info: Guthrie CVB, PO Box 995, Guthrie, OK 73044-0995. Phone: (800) 299-1889 or (405) 282-1947. Fax: (405) 282-0061. E-mail: info@guthrieok.com. Web: www.guthrieok.com.

✦ **THANKSGIVING DAY.** Nov 26. Presidential Proclamation. Always issued for the fourth Thursday in November. See also: "First US Holiday by Presidential Proclamation: Anniversary" (Nov 26).

THANKSGIVING DAY. Nov 26. Legal public holiday. (Public Law 90–363 sets Thanksgiving Day on the fourth Thursday in November.) Observed in all states. In most states, the Friday after Thanksgiving is also a holiday; in Nevada it is called Family Day.

TRUTH, SOJOURNER: DEATH ANNIVERSARY. Nov 26, 1883. A former slave who had been sold four times, Sojourner Truth became an evangelist who argued for abolition and women's rights. After a troubled early life, she began her evangelical career in 1843, traveling through New England until she discovered the utopian colony called the Northampton Association of Education and Industry. It was there she was exposed to, and became an advocate for, the cause of abolition, working with Frederick Douglass, Wendell Phillips, William Lloyd Garrison and others. In 1850 she befriended Lucretia Mott, Elizabeth Cady Stanton and other feminist leaders and actively began supporting calls for women's rights. In 1870 she attempted to petition Congress to create a "Negro State" on public lands in the West. Born at Ulster County, NY, about 1790, with the name Isabella Van Wagener, she died Nov 26, 1883, at Battle Creek, MI.

TURKEY-FREE THANKSGIVING. Nov 26. This is a time for you to take turkey off your table, forgoing flesh foods "cold turkey" and having a harvest of health. Why not carve a compassionate celebration centerpiece—a tasty mock turkey made from tofu, tempeh or *seitan*? The turkeys will thank you for having a humane holiday. For info: Vegetarian Awareness Network, PO Box 3545, Washington, DC 20027-0045. Phone: (800) USA-VEGE.

"TWENTY QUESTIONS" TV PREMIERE: 60th ANNIVERSARY. Nov 26, 1949. This game show was based on the old guessing game. A celebrity panel had to guess the identity of an object (at the start they were told only if it was animal, vegetable or mineral) by asking up to 20 questions. Bill Slater hosted two network versions of the show on NBC and Dumont. Jay Jackson took over when it switched from NBC to ABC. "Twenty Questions" first began on radio. Regular panelists included Fred Van Deventer, Florence Rinard, Herb Polesie and Johnny McPhee.

WALKER, MARY EDWARDS: BIRTH ANNIVERSARY. Nov 26, 1832. American physician and women's rights leader, born at Oswego, NY. First female surgeon in US Army (Civil War). Spent four months in Confederate prison. First and only woman ever to receive Medal of Honor (Nov 11, 1865). Two years before her death, on June 3, 1916, a government review board asked that her award be revoked. She continued to wear it, in spite of official revocation, until her death, Feb 21, 1919, at Oswego. On June 11, 1977, the secretary of the army posthumously restored the Medal of Honor to Dr. Walker.

November 2009

S	M	T	W	T	F	S
1	2	3	4	5	6	7
8	9	10	11	12	13	14
15	16	17	18	19	20	21
22	23	24	25	26	27	28
29	30					

THE WEATHER CHANNEL ATLANTA MARATHON AND HALF MARATHON. Nov 26. Atlanta, GA. 26.2-mile and 13.1-mile races (USATF certified). Advance registration only; entry forms available in July; please send SASE. Est attendance: 8,000. For info: Atlanta Track Club, Atlanta Marathon, 3097 E Shadowlawn Ave, Atlanta, GA 30305. Phone: (404) 231-9064, ext 10. Fax: (404) 364-0708. E-mail: atc@atlantatrackclub.org. Web: www.atlantatrackclub.org.

BIRTHDAYS TODAY

Garcelle Beauvais-Nilon, 43, actress ("NYPD Blue," *Bad Company*), born St. Marc, Haiti, Nov 26, 1966.

Samuel Bodman, 71, US Secretary of Energy, born Chicago, IL, Nov 26, 1938.

Shannon Dunn, 37, Olympic snowboarder, born Arlington Heights, IL, Nov 26, 1972.

Dale Jarrett, 53, race car driver, born Conover, NC, Nov 26, 1956.

Shawn Kemp, 40, former basketball player, born Elkhart, IN, Nov 26, 1969.

Richard (Rich) Caruthers Little, 71, impressionist, born Ottawa, ON, Canada, Nov 26, 1938.

Tina Turner, 71, singer ("What's Love Got to Do with It"), born Nutbush, TN, Nov 26, 1938.

November 27 — Friday

DAY 331 | **34 REMAINING**

AGEE, JAMES: 100th BIRTH ANNIVERSARY. Nov 27, 1909. Poet, critic, novelist (*A Death in the Family*), social historian (*Let Us Now Praise Famous Men*), scriptwriter, born at Knoxville, TN. Died at New York, NY, May 16, 1955.

AT&T HOLIDAY TREE LIGHTING AT ANCHORAGE. Nov 27. Town Square, Anchorage, AK. Join Santa and a live team of nine reindeer to celebrate the holiday season and the lighting of the Holiday Tree. Free cookies and cocoa. Est attendance: 2,000. For info: Anchorage Downtown Partnership, Ltd, 333 W 4th Ave, Ste 317, Anchorage, AK 99501. Phone: (907) 279-5650. Fax: (907) 279-5651. E-mail: cspink@anchoragedowntown.org. Web: www.anchoragedowntown.org.

BANK BAILOUT BILL: ANNIVERSARY. Nov 27, 1991. Both houses of Congress approved legislation authorizing $70 billion in additional borrowing authority for the Federal Deposit Insurance Corporation (FDIC) because of the record number of savings and loan failures.

BEARD, CHARLES A.: BIRTH ANNIVERSARY. Nov 27, 1874. American historian Charles Austin Beard, who wrote many books in collaboration with his wife, Mary R. Beard, was born near Knightstown, IN. He died at New Haven, CT, Sept 1, 1948.

BELSNICKEL CRAFT SHOW. Nov 27–28. Boyertown, PA. Sale of juried fine crafts. Annually, the first Friday and Saturday after Thanksgiving. Est attendance: 5,000. For info: Lindsay Dieroff, Collection Dir, Boyertown Area Historical Society, 43 S Chestnut St, Boyertown, PA 19512. Phone: (610) 367-5255. E-mail: boyertown history@dejazzd.com or mdmarkley@aol.com.

BLACK FRIDAY. Nov 27. The traditional beginning of the Christmas shopping season on the Friday after Thanksgiving. Called "Black Friday" because traditionally retailers were in the "black" by this day of the year.

BUY NOTHING DAY. Nov 27. A 24-hour moratorium on consumer spending. A celebration of simplicity, about getting our runaway consumer culture back onto a sustainable path. Annually, on the first shopping day after Thanksgiving. For info: The Media Foundation, 1243 W 7th Ave, Vancouver, BC, Canada V6H 1B7. Phone: (800) 663-1243 or (604) 736-9401. Fax: (604) 737-6021. E-mail: bnd@adbusters.org. Web: www.adbusters.org.

CHRISTKINDLMARKT. Nov 27–Dec 31. Bethlehem, PA. Handmade crafts by the nation's finest artisans, live holiday music and food from around the world. Est attendance: 65,000. For info: ArtsQuest, 25 W Third St, Bethlehem, PA 18015-1238. Phone: (610) 332-1300. Fax: (610) 861-2644. E-mail: info@fest.org. Web: www.christmas city.org.

CHRISTMAS CANDLELIGHT TOUR. Nov 27–28 (also Dec 4–5 and Dec 11–12). My Old Kentucky Home State Park, Bardstown, KY. Christmas in the style and flavor of the 1800s. Annually, the first three weekends after Thanksgiving. Est attendance: 10,000. For info: My Old Kentucky Home State Park, PO Box 323, Hwy 150, Bardstown, KY 40004. Phone: (800) 323-7803 or (502) 348-3502. Fax: (502) 349-0054. Web: www.kystateparks.com.

CRAFTSMEN'S CHRISTMAS CLASSIC ARTS & CRAFTS FESTIVAL. Nov 27–29. Greensboro Coliseum Complex Special Events Center, Greensboro, NC. 36th annual. Features work from more than 500 talented artists and craftspeople. All juried exhibitors' work has been handmade by the exhibitors and must be their own original design and creation. See the creative process in action as many exhibitors demonstrate throughout the weekend. Visit Christmas Tree Village to view the uniquely decorated Christmas trees by some of our exhibitors. Something for every style, taste and budget with items from the most contemporary to the most traditional. Est attendance: 35,000. For info: Gilmore Enterprises, 3514-A Drawbridge Pkwy, Greensboro, NC 27410. Phone: (336) 282-5550. E-mail: contact@gilmoreshows.com. Web: www.CraftShow.com or www.gilmoreshows.com.

DICKENS OF A CHRISTMAS AT MOUNT HOPE MANSION. Nov 27–Dec 23 (Fridays, Saturdays, Sundays). Mount Hope Estate and Winery, Manheim, PA. It's wine, merriment and carols by the huge Victorian fireplace as Dickens favorites such as Tiny Tim, Oliver Twist and Ebenezer Scrooge present "A Christmas Carol" and other yuletide favorites. Est attendance: 10,000. For info: Thomas Roy, Mgr, Mount Hope Estate and Winery, 2775 Lebanon Rd, Manheim, PA 17545. Phone: (717) 665-7021, ext 127. Fax: (717) 664-3466. E-mail: tom@parenfaire.com. Web: www.parenfaire.com.

"THE DINAH SHORE SHOW" TV PREMIERE: ANNIVERSARY. Nov 27, 1951. Dinah Shore hosted a successful 15-minute musical show until 1957 and then an hour variety show from 1957 to 1962, one of the few women to have done so. The music show was sponsored by Chevrolet (and was officially known as "The Dinah Shore Chevy Show") and featured a backup group called the Skylarks. Shore also starred in specials and hosted a variety series, with a guest host filling in for her every fourth week. She later moved on to hosting a talk show.

DUBCEK, ALEXANDER: BIRTH ANNIVERSARY. Nov 27, 1921. The man who attempted to give his country "socialism with a human face," Alexander Dubcek was born at Uhrocev, a village in western Slovakia. As first secretary of the Czechoslovak Communist Party during the "Prague Spring" of 1968, he moved to achieve the "widest possible democratization" and to loosen the dominant influence of the Soviet Union. As a result, Czechoslovakia was invaded by armed forces of the Warsaw Pact on Aug 21, 1968. Dubcek died Nov 7, 1992, at Prague.

FAMILY DAY IN NEVADA. Nov 27. Observed annually on the Friday following the fourth Thursday in November.

FIELD DAYS. Nov 27–28. Mystic Seaport, Mystic, CT. Families enjoy special Thanksgiving weekend activities including wagon rides, food, entertainment and outdoor games on the green. Est attendance: 3,000. For info: Mystic Seaport, 75 Greenmanville Ave, PO Box 6000, Mystic, CT 06355-0990. Phone: (860) 572-5315 or (888) 973-2767. Web: www.mysticseaport.org.

HEARTH AND HOME IN EARLY MARYLAND. Nov 27–28. St. Mary's City, MD. From everyday meals to feasts, join us as we examine the colonial table. Demonstrations of food preservation and hearth cooking. 10 AM–5 PM. Est attendance: 500. For info: Director of Marketing, Historic St. Mary's City, PO Box 39, St. Mary's City, MD 20686. Phone: (240) 895-4990 or (800) SMC-1634. Fax: (240) 895-4968. Web: www.stmaryscity.org.

HENDRIX, JIMI: BIRTH ANNIVERSARY. Nov 27, 1942. American musician and songwriter Jimi Hendrix was born at Seattle, WA. One of the greatest rock guitarists in history, he revolutionized the guitar sound with heavy use of feedback and incredible fretwork. His success first came in England, and then in the US after his appearance at the Monterey Pop Festival (1967). His albums included *Are You Experienced?*, *Electric Ladyland* and *Band of Gypsys*. He died Sept 18, 1970, at London, England.

HOLIDAY MAGIC. Nov 27. Galena Blvd in downtown Aurora, IL. Annual celebration as Santa Claus arrives in the Parade of Lights, followed by the lighting of the city Christmas tree and fireworks. Begins at 6 PM, EST. For info: City of Aurora, Mayor's Office of Special Events, 5 E Downer Pl, Ste A, Aurora, IL 60507. Phone: (630) 844-4731. Fax: (630) 844-4797. Web: www.aurora-il.org.

JULE FEST. Nov 27–29. Elk Horn, IA. Danish Christmas festival. Est attendance: 3,000. For info: Lisa Riggs, Danish Windmill, PO Box 245, Elk Horn, IA 51531. Phone: (712) 764-7472 or (800) 451-7960. Fax: (712) 764-7475. E-mail: info@danishwindmill.com. Web: www .danishwindmill.com.

KEMBLE, FANNY: 200th BIRTH ANNIVERSARY. Nov 27, 1809. Frances Anne Kemble, English actress, born at London, England, and died there Jan 15, 1893.

LEE, BRUCE: BIRTH ANNIVERSARY. Nov 27, 1940. The actor and martial artist was born at San Francisco, CA, but raised in Hong Kong. In 1959 he returned to the US to teach martial arts, opening schools in Seattle, WA, and Oakland, CA. Spotted at a competition by a TV producer, Lee was cast as Kato in TV's *The Green Hornet* in 1966. He moved on to film, where he displayed an intense charisma that would make him a star. Before he could enjoy this new success, Lee died of a cerebral edema on July 20, 1973, in Hong Kong. His films included *Fists of Fury* (1972) and *Enter the Dragon* (1973).

LIVINGSTON, ROBERT R.: BIRTH ANNIVERSARY. Nov 27, 1746. (Old Style date.) Member of the Continental Congress, farmer, diplomat and jurist, born at New York, NY. It was Livingston who administered the oath of office to President George Washington in 1789. He died at Clermont, NY, Feb 26, 1813.

MAIZE DAY. Nov 27. Celebrating the First Nations of the Americas and the central role of corn in these cultures and cuisines. Almost every day, people throughout the Western Hemisphere enjoy foods cultivated by the indigenous people of North, Central and South America. On this day Americans celebrate living indigenous cultures, as well as cultures of the past. Families and friends gather to remember and talk about the cultures and to feast on the foods Native Americans have contributed to our amalgamated cultures. For info: Corinne Lightweaver, PO Box 66153, Los Angeles, CA 90066. Phone: (310) 391-5827. E-mail: editor.corlight@verizon.net. Web: www.maizeday.com.

MASTERSON, BAT: BIRTH ANNIVERSARY. Nov 27, 1853. Old American West gambler, saloon keeper, lawman and newswriter/editor. Born at Henryville, QC, Canada; died Oct 25, 1921, at New York, NY.

NATIONAL FLOSSING DAY. Nov 27. Americans are encouraged to consider the role flossing has played in their lives and make plans to help spread "Peace of Mouth" in their own lives and the lives of others around them, in ways with and without floss. On this day our children should also be made aware of the richness and health that flossing can bring to life. For info: National Flossing Council, 533 4th St SE, Washington, DC 20003. Phone: (202) 544-0711. E-mail: nfd@flossing.org. Web: www.flossing.org.

REVEREND FRANCIS GASTRELL'S EJECTMENT: 250th ANNIVERSARY. Nov 27, 1759. The Stratford-upon-Avon town corporation gave orders to bring an "action of Ejectment" against the Reverend Francis Gastrell, vicar of Frodsham, who lived in William Shakespeare's home. Gastrell had cut down the 150-year-old mulberry tree that had been planted by Shakespeare. Gastrell maliciously felled the tree because he was annoyed by the many Shakespeare enthusiasts who came to look at it. He sold the tree for firewood, but it was recovered by a jeweler-woodcarver, Thomas Sharp, who fashioned hundreds of relics from it. Gastrell was ejected from Stratford "amid the ragings and cursings of its people, a citizen well lost"—for one of "the meanest petty infamies in our annals."

SINKIE DAY. Nov 27. "Sinkies" (people who occasionally dine over the kitchen sink and elsewhere) are encouraged to celebrate this time-honored, casual-yet-tasteful cuisine culture. This is a particularly appropriate day to become acquainted with the sinkie style of dining. Christmas shopping and Thanksgiving leftovers provide the perfect reasons to enjoy a quick meal. Also the day the annual list of "Six Prominent Suspected Closet-Sinkies" is announced. Annually, the day after Thanksgiving. If it has anything to do with having a quick bite, it has everything to do with being a sinkie. For info: Norm Hankoff, Founder, Intl Assn of People Who Dine over the Kitchen Sink, PO Box 221413, Sacramento, CA 95822. E-mail: normh@sinkie.com. Web: www.sinkie.com.

VICTORIAN CHRISTMAS CELEBRATION. Nov 27–Dec 31. Gordon-Roberts House, Cumberland, MD. Victorian Christmas tea and candlelight tours with musical entertainment. Various workshops and children's programs. Theme decorating in an 1867 Victorian mansion museum. Est attendance: 1,500. For info: Sharon Nealis, Admin, Gordon-Roberts House, 218 Washington St, Cumberland, MD 21502. Phone: (301) 777-8678. Web: www.historyhouse.allconet.org.

WEIZMANN, CHAIM: BIRTH ANNIVERSARY. Nov 27, 1874. Israeli statesman born near Pinsk, Byelorussia. He played an important role in bringing about the British government's Balfour Declaration, calling for the establishment of a national home for Jews at Palestine. He died at Tel Aviv, Israel, Nov 9, 1952.

WORLD FAMOUS FISH HOUSE PARADE. Nov 27. Aitkin, MN. 19th annual special parade of uniquely and humorously decorated fish houses used for ice fishing during the winter. Annually, the Friday after Thanksgiving. Est attendance: 6,000. For info: Sue Marxen, Executive Director, Aitkin Area Chamber of Commerce, PO Box 127, Aitkin, MN 56431. Phone: (800) 526-8342. Fax: (218) 927-4494. E-mail: upnorth@aitkin.com. Web: www.aitkin.com.

November 2009	S	M	T	W	T	F	S
	1	2	3	4	5	6	7
	8	9	10	11	12	13	14
	15	16	17	18	19	20	21
	22	23	24	25	26	27	28
	29	30					

WORLD'S CHAMPIONSHIP DUCK-CALLING CONTEST AND WINGS OVER THE PRAIRIE FESTIVAL. Nov 27–28. Stuttgart, AR. Annually, Thanksgiving weekend. Duck-calling contests, duck gumbo cook-off, carnival, 10k race, arts and crafts, beauty pageant, concessions, sporting collectibles, Sportsman's Party, commercial exhibitors, fun shoot. Est attendance: 65,000. For info: Stuttgart Chamber of Commerce, 507 S Main, Stuttgart, AR 72160. Phone: (870) 673-1602. Fax: (870) 673-1604. Web: www.stuttgartarkansas.com.

YAWM ARAFAT: THE STANDING AT ARAFAT. Nov 27. Islamic calendar date: Dhu-Hijjah 9, 1430. The day when people on the hajj (pilgrimage to Mecca) assemble for "the Standing" at the plain of Arafat at Mina, Saudi Arabia, near Mecca. This gathering is a foreshadowing of the Day of Judgment. Different methods for "anticipating" the visibility of the new moon crescent at Mecca are used by different Muslim groups. US date may vary. Began at sunset the preceding day.

YOU'RE WELCOMEGIVING DAY. Nov 27. The day after Thanksgiving, to create a four-day weekend. For info: Richard Ankli, Allen Creek Hydro, Inc, 100 S 4th Ave, #608, Ann Arbor, MI 48104.

BIRTHDAYS TODAY

Robin Givens, 45, actress ("Head of the Class," *A Rage in Harlem*), born New York, NY, Nov 27, 1964.

Samantha Harris, 36, television personality ("Dancing with the Stars," "E! News"), born Hopkins, MN, Nov 27, 1973.

Jimmy Rollins, 31, baseball player, born Oakland, CA, Nov 27, 1978.

Gail Henion Sheehy, 72, author (*Passages*), born Mamaroneck, NY, Nov 27, 1937.

Fisher Stevens, 46, actor (*The Brother from Another Planet, Bob Roberts*), born Chicago, IL, Nov 27, 1963.

Nick Van Exel, 38, basketball player, born Kenosha, WI, Nov 27, 1971.

Jaleel White, 33, actor ("Family Matters"), born Los Angeles, CA, Nov 27, 1976.

November 28 — Saturday

DAY 332 — **33 REMAINING**

ALBANIA: INDEPENDENCE DAY. Nov 28. Commemorates independence from the Ottoman Empire in 1912.

ALSTON, CHARLES H.: BIRTH ANNIVERSARY. Nov 28, 1907. African-American painter and sculptor born at Charlotte, NC, and died at New York, NY, Apr 27, 1977. Throughout his career, Alston experimented with styles ranging from realism to abstraction. His realistic WPA murals at Harlem Hospital depict a narrative in the style of Diego Rivera. The Cubist painting *The Family* (1955) is an excellent example of Alston's early work, influenced by Italian artist Amedeo Modigliani. *Black Man, Black Woman USA* has a decidedly Egyptian style of portraiture. *Walking* (1958), which depicts a silent crowd, almost prophesied the turmoil and social agitation of the Civil Rights movement.

BLAKE, WILLIAM: BIRTH ANNIVERSARY. Nov 28, 1757. English visionary poet and artist born at London, England. Composed "The Tyger," which begins memorably, "Tyger! Tyger! burning bright/In the forests of the night,/What immortal hand or eye/Could frame thy fearful symmetry?" Blake died in poverty at London on Aug 12, 1827.

BUNYAN, JOHN: BIRTH ANNIVERSARY. Nov 28, 1628. (Old Style date.) English cleric and author of *A Pilgrim's Progress*, born at Elstow, Bedfordshire, England. Died at London, England, Aug 31, 1688 (OS).

CHAD: REPUBLIC DAY. Nov 28. National holiday. Commemorates proclamation of the republic in 1958.

EID-AL-ADHA: FEAST OF THE SACRIFICE. Nov 28. Islamic calendar date: Dhu-Hijjah 10, 1430. Commemorates Abraham's willingness to sacrifice his son Ishmael in obedience to God. It is part of the hajj (pilgrimage to Mecca). The day begins with the sacrifice of an animal in remembrance of the Angel Gabriel's substitution of a lamb as Abraham's offering. One-third of the meat is given to poor people and the rest is shared with friends and family. Celebrated with gifts and general merrymaking, the festival usually continues for several days. It is celebrated as Tabaski in Benin, Burkina Faso, Guinea, Guinea-Bissau, Ivory Coast, Mali, Niger and Senegal; as Hari Raya Hajj in Southeast Asia, and as Kurban Bayram in Turkey and Bosnia. Different methods for "anticipating" the visibility of the moon crescent at Mecca are used by different Muslim groups. US date may vary. Began at sunset the preceding day.

GETTYSBURG HOLIDAY FESTIVAL. Nov 28–Dec 27, Dec 31 (weekends). Gettysburg, PA. Tours of decorated historic homes, live nativity scene, caroling and handbell choirs, Christmas parade, community concerts, tuba fest, candlelight walking tour and Adams County New Year's Eve Bash with fireworks. Annually, weekends in November–December and New Year's Eve. Est attendance: 10,000. For info: Gettysburg CVB, PO Box 4117, Gettysburg, PA 17325. Phone: (717) 334-6274. Fax: (717) 334-1166. E-mail: info@gettysburg.travel. Web: www.gettysburg.travel.

INTERNATIONAL AURA AWARENESS DAY. Nov 28. A day to increase awareness of the human energy body, or aura. Annually, the fourth Saturday in November. For info: Cynthia Larson, PO Box 7393, Berkeley, CA 94707. Phone: (510) 528-2044. E-mail: cynthia@realityshifters.com. Web: realityshifters.com/pages/auraday.html.

"THE LIGHT OF THE WORLD" CHRISTMAS PAGEANT. Nov 28–29 (also Dec 6). Courthouse square, Minden, NE. 64th annual. Pageant presented on two sides of the courthouse square with approximately 115 local citizens performing in beautiful costumes. At the climax some 12,000 Christmas lights are turned on around the downtown square. 7 PM; free admission. Annually, the first Saturday after Thanksgiving and the next two Sundays. Est attendance: 1,000. For info: Marcy Brandt, Mgr, Minden Chamber of Commerce, PO Box 375, Minden, NE 68959. Phone: (308) 832-1811. E-mail: mindenchamber@gtmc.net. Web: www.mindenne.org.

LULLY, JEAN BAPTISTE: BIRTH ANNIVERSARY. Nov 28, 1632. Versatile musician and composer, born at Florence, Italy, who chose France for his homeland. Noted for his quick temper, it is said that he struck his own foot with a baton while in a rage. The resulting wound led to blood poisoning, from which he died, at Paris, France, Mar 22, 1687.

MAURITANIA: INDEPENDENCE DAY. Nov 28. National holiday. Attained sovereignty from France in 1960.

MEXICO: GUADALAJARA INTERNATIONAL BOOK FAIR. Nov 28–Dec 6. Latin America's largest book fair with exhibitors from all over the Spanish-speaking world. Est attendance: 550,000. For info: David Unger, Guadalajara Book Fair—US Office, Div of Hum, NAC 5225, City College, New York, NY 10031. Phone: (212) 650-7925. Fax: (212) 650-7912. E-mail: filny@aol.com.

PANAMA: INDEPENDENCE FROM SPAIN. Nov 28. Public holiday. Commemorates the independence of Panama (which at the time was part of Colombia) from Spain in 1821.

SMITH, ANNA NICOLE: BIRTH ANNIVERSARY. Nov 28, 1967. Born Vickie Lynn Hogan at Houston, TX, this model and actress earned a certain degree of fame for appearing in *Playboy* and marrying an 89-year-old billionaire. Her life was one of publicity, scandal and drug abuse, and her death from a lethal drug interaction at Hollywood, FL, on Feb 8, 2007, sparked an unexpected media frenzy. The cause of her death, paternity of and custody of her infant daughter, and the disposition of her estate were all subjects of intense interest by the tabloid and mainstream media.

SPACE MILESTONE: *MARINER 4* (US): 45th ANNIVERSARY. Nov 28, 1964. The first successful mission to Mars. Approached within 6,118 miles of Mars on July 14, 1965. Took photographs and instrument readings.

SPIRITS IN HARMONY. Nov 28. New Harmony, IN. Held in New Harmony's historic buildings, Spirits in Harmony is a wine- and cider-tasting event with food and music. Annually, the Saturday after Thanksgiving. For info: Jan Kahle, Spirits in Harmony, PO Box 579, New Harmony, IN 47631. Phone: (812) 682-4488. Fax: (812) 682-4313. E-mail: jkahle@usi.edu. Web: www.newharmony.org.

TEHRAN CONFERENCE: ANNIVERSARY. Nov 28–Dec 1, 1943. President Franklin D. Roosevelt, British prime minister Winston Churchill and Soviet premier Joseph Stalin met at Tehran, Iran, to formulate a plan for an Allied assault, a second front, in Western Europe. The resulting plan was "Operation Overlord," which commenced with the landing on Normandy's beaches on June 6, 1944 ("D-day").

BIRTHDAYS TODAY

Michael Chertoff, 56, US Secretary of Homeland Security, born Elizabeth, NJ, Nov 28, 1953.

Berry Gordy, Jr, 80, record and motion picture executive (cofounder of Motown), born Detroit, MI, Nov 28, 1929.

Ed Harris, 59, actor (*The Hours, Pollock, The Right Stuff*), born Englewood, NJ, Nov 28, 1950.

Gary Hart, 71, former senator, former presidential candidate, born Gary Hartpence at Ottawa, KS, Nov 28, 1938.

S. Epatha Merkerson, 57, actress ("Law & Order," *Lackawanna Blues*), born Detroit, MI, Nov 28, 1952.

Judd Nelson, 50, actor (*The Breakfast Club, St. Elmo's Fire*, "Suddenly Susan"), born Portland, ME, Nov 28, 1959.

Randy Newman, 66, singer, songwriter ("Short People"), composer (film scores for *Ragtime, The Natural*), born New Orleans, LA, Nov 28, 1943.

Paul Shaffer, 60, bandleader ("Late Night with David Letterman"), comedian, born Thunder Bay, ON, Canada, Nov 28, 1949.

Jon Stewart, 47, writer, comedian ("The Daily Show"), born Jonathan Stuart Leibowitz at New York, NY, Nov 28, 1962.

Matt Williams, 44, former baseball player, born Bishop, CA, Nov 28, 1965.

November 29 — Sunday

DAY 333 — 32 REMAINING

ADVENT, FIRST SUNDAY. Nov 29. Advent includes the four Sundays before Christmas, Nov 29, Dec 6, Dec 13 and Dec 20 in 2009.

ALCOTT, LOUISA MAY: BIRTH ANNIVERSARY. Nov 29, 1832. American author, born at Philadelphia, PA. Died at Boston, MA, Mar 6, 1888. Her most famous novel was *Little Women*, the classic story of Meg, Jo, Beth and Amy.

BERKELEY, BUSBY: BIRTH ANNIVERSARY. Nov 29, 1895. William Berkeley Enos was born at Los Angeles, CA. After serving in WWI as an entertainment officer, he changed his name to Busby Berkeley and began a career as an actor. He turned to directing in 1921, and his lavish Broadway and Hollywood creations include *Forty-Second Street, Gold Diggers of 1933, Footlight Parade, Stage Struck, Babes in Arms, Strike Up the Band, Girl Crazy* and *Take Me Out to the Ball Game*. He retired in 1962 and returned to Broadway in 1970 to supervise a revival of *No, No, Nanette*. He died Mar 14, 1976, at Palm Springs, CA.

CHRISTMAS ON THE RIVER. Nov 29–Dec 5. Demopolis, AL. Fun with arts and crafts, children's parade, Alabama State Barbecue Cook-Off and a riverboat parade. Annually, the week concluding with the first Saturday of December. Est attendance: 40,000. For info: Kelley Smith, Demopolis Area Chamber of Commerce, Box 667, Demopolis, AL 36732. Phone: (334) 289-0270. Fax: (334) 289-1382. E-mail: dacc@westal.net. Web: www.demopolischamber.com.

CHRISTMAS TRADITIONS. Nov 29–Dec 20. St. Charles, MO. Holiday festivities include caroling, chestnut roasting and authentically costumed Santas from around the world. Enjoy old-fashioned holiday shopping on Wednesdays, Fridays and Saturdays. "Las Posadas," a traditional reenactment of Mary and Joseph seeking shelter, is Saturday, Dec 5. Annually, after Thanksgiving until Christmas. Est attendance: 50,000. For info: St. Charles CVB, 230 S Main St, St. Charles, MO 63301. Phone: (800) 366-2427. Web: www.stcharleschristmas.com.

CZECHOSLOVAKIA ENDS COMMUNIST RULE: 20th ANNIVERSARY. Nov 29, 1989. Czechoslovakia ended 41 years of one-party Communist rule when the Czechoslovak parliament voted unanimously to repeal the constitutional clauses giving the Communist Party a guaranteed leading role in the country and promoting Marxism-Leninism as the state ideology. The vote came at the end of a 12-day revolution sparked by the beating of protestors Nov 17. Although the Communist Party remained in power, the tide of reform led to its ouster by the Civic Forum, headed by playwright Václav Havel. The Civic Forum demanded free elections with equal rights for all parties, a mixed economy and support for foreign investment. In the first free elections in Czechoslovakia since WWII, Václav Havel was elected president.

ELECTRONIC GREETINGS DAY. Nov 29. Save a letter carrier, save a tree, save a stamp! Today's the day to send your greetings the free, electronic way, via the Internet. (©2006 by WH.) For info: Thomas & Ruth Roy, Wellcat Holidays, 2418 Long Ln, Lebanon, PA 17046. Phone: (717) 279-0184. E-mail: info@wellcat.com. Web: www.wellcat.com.

FIRST ARMY-NAVY GAME: ANNIVERSARY. Nov 29, 1890. Army played Navy for the first time in football, and Navy won, 24–0. Red Emrich scored four touchdowns (worth four points each) and kicked two field goals (worth two points each), and Moulton Johnson added the other touchdown to account for all the scoring.

HANDEL'S MESSIAH SING-ALONG. Nov 29. Richard Nixon Library and Birthplace, Yorba Linda, CA. Audience members are invited to join in singing the choruses of this beloved oratorio in the beautiful East Room of the Nixon Library. Performers include a master choir, orchestra and soloists. Seventeenth-century costumes are encouraged. Free. Annually, the Sunday of Thanksgiving weekend. For info: Yorba Linda Arts Alliance, PO Box 1037, Yorba Linda, CA 92885. Phone: (714) 996-1960. Fax: (714) 996-0920. E-mail: messiahsing@aol.com. Web: www.messiahsing.org.

JOHN F. KENNEDY DAY IN MASSACHUSETTS. Nov 29. Annually, the last Sunday in November.

"KUKLA, FRAN AND OLLIE" TV PREMIERE: ANNIVERSARY. Nov 29, 1948. This popular children's show featured puppets created and handled by Burr Tillstrom and was equally popular with adults. Fran Allison was the only human on the show. Tillstrom's lively and eclectic cast of characters, called the "Kuklapolitans," included the bald, high-voiced Kukla, the big-toothed Oliver J. Dragon (Ollie), Fletcher Rabbit, Cecil Bill, Buelah the Witch, Colonel Crackie, Madame Ooglepuss and Dolores Dragon. Most shows were performed without scripts.

November 2009	S	M	T	W	T	F	S
	1	2	3	4	5	6	7
	8	9	10	11	12	13	14
	15	16	17	18	19	20	21
	22	23	24	25	26	27	28
	29	30					

LEWIS, C.S. (CLIVE STAPLES): BIRTH ANNIVERSARY. Nov 29, 1898. British scholar, novelist and author (*The Screwtape Letters*, *Chronicles of Narnia*), born at Belfast, Ireland, died at Oxford, England, Nov 22, 1963.

NETHERLANDS: MIDWINTER HORN BLOWING. Nov 29–Jan 6, 2010. Twente and several other areas in the Netherlands. Midwinter horn blowing, folkloric custom of announcing the birth of Christ, begins with Advent and continues until Epiphany (Jan 6) of the following year.

RADIOLOGICAL SOCIETY OF NORTH AMERICA SCIENTIFIC ASSEMBLY AND ANNUAL MEETING. Nov 29–Dec 4. McCormick Place, Chicago, IL. 95th annual. Est attendance: 62,000. For info: Radiological Society of North America, 820 Jorie Blvd, Oak Brook, IL 60523-2251. Phone: (630) 571-2670. Fax: (630) 571-7837. Web: www.rsna.org.

ROSS, NELLIE TAYLOE: BIRTH ANNIVERSARY. Nov 29, 1876. Nellie Tayloe Ross became the first female governor in the US when she was chosen to serve out the last month and two days of her husband's term as governor of Wyoming after he died in office. She was elected in her own right in the Nov 4, 1924, election but lost the 1927 race. Ross was appointed vice chairman of the Democratic National Committee in 1926 and named director of the US Mint by President Franklin D. Roosevelt in 1933. She served in that capacity for 20 years. Born at St. Joseph, MO, she died Dec 20, 1977, at Washington, DC.

THOMSON, CHARLES: BIRTH ANNIVERSARY. Nov 29, 1729. America's first official record keeper. Chosen secretary of the First Continental Congress Sept 5, 1774, Thomson recorded proceedings for 15 years and delivered his journals together with tens of thousands of records to the federal government in 1789. Born in Ireland, he died Aug 16, 1824. It was Thomson who notified George Washington of his election as president.

TRAVELERS WITH DISABILITIES AWARENESS WEEK. Nov 29–Dec 5. To promote the economic well-being of Americans with disabilities who travel and to create an environment free of obstacles throughout the tourism and travel industry for Americans with disabilities. Annually, the week following Thanksgiving. For info: Society for Accessible Travel and Hospitality, 347 Fifth Ave, Ste 605, New York, NY 10016. Phone: (212) 447-7284. E-mail: sathtravel@aol.com. Web: www.sath.org.

UNITED NATIONS: INTERNATIONAL DAY OF SOLIDARITY WITH THE PALESTINIAN PEOPLE. Nov 29. Annual observance proclaimed by UN General Assembly in 1977. At request of the assembly, observance is organized by secretary-general in consultation with Committee on the Exercise of the Inalienable Rights of the Palestinian People. Recommendations include a plan for return of the Palestinians to their homes and the establishment of an "independent Palestinian entity." For info: United Nations, Dept of Public Info, New York, NY 10017. Web: www.un.org.

WAITE, MORRISON R.: BIRTH ANNIVERSARY. Nov 29, 1816. Seventh chief justice of the US, born at Lyme, CT. Appointed chief justice by President Ulysses S. Grant Jan 19, 1874. The Waite Court is remembered for its controversial rulings that did much to rehabilitate the idea of states' rights after the Civil War and early Reconstruction years. Waite died at Washington, DC, Mar 23, 1888.

BIRTHDAYS TODAY

Don Cheadle, 45, actor (*Talk to Me, Hotel Rwanda, Crash, Ocean's Eleven*), born Kansas City, MO, Nov 29, 1964.

Jacques Rene Chirac, 77, former president of France, born Paris, France, Nov 29, 1932.

Joel Coen, 55, producer, screenwriter (*Fargo*), born Minneapolis, MN, Nov 29, 1954.

Kim Delaney, 48, actress ("NYPD Blue"), born Philadelphia, PA, Nov 29, 1961.

Ryan Giggs, 36, soccer player, born Cardiff, Wales, Nov 29, 1973.

Kasey Keller, 40, soccer player, born Olympia, WA, Nov 29, 1969.

Diane Ladd, 77, actress (*Alice Doesn't Live Here Anymore, Ramblin' Rose, The Cemetery Club*), born Rose Diane Ladner at Meridian, MS, Nov 29, 1932.

Howie Mandel, 54, comedian, game show host ("Deal or No Deal"), actor ("St. Elsewhere"), born Toronto, ON, Canada, Nov 29, 1955.

Chuck Mangione, 69, musician, composer (Grammy for "Bellavia"), born Rochester, NY, Nov 29, 1940.

John Mayall, 76, musician, bandleader (The Bluesbreakers), born Manchester, England, Nov 29, 1933.

Andrew McCarthy, 47, actor (*Pretty in Pink, Weekend at Bernie's*), born Westfield, NJ, Nov 29, 1962.

Cathy Moriarty, 49, actress (*Raging Bull, The Mambo Kings*), born the Bronx, NY, Nov 29, 1960.

Janet Napolitano, 52, Governor of Arizona (D), born Pittsburgh, PA, Nov 29, 1957.

Mariano Rivera, 40, baseball player, born Panama City, Panama, Nov 29, 1969.

Vincent Edward (Vin) Scully, 82, sportscaster, born New York, NY, Nov 29, 1927.

Garry Shandling, 60, comedian ("The Larry Sanders Show"), born Chicago, IL, Nov 29, 1949.

November 30 — Monday

DAY 334 — **31 REMAINING**

ARTICLES OF PEACE BETWEEN GREAT BRITAIN AND THE US: ANNIVERSARY. Nov 30, 1782. These provisional articles of peace, which were to end America's War of Independence, were signed at Paris, France. The refined and definitive treaty of peace between Great Britain and the US was signed at Paris on Sept 3, 1783. In it "His Britannic Majesty acknowledges the said United States . . . to be free, sovereign and independent states; that he treats them as such; and for himself, his heirs and successors, relinquishes all claims to the government, propriety and territorial rights of the same, and every part thereof. . . ."

BARBADOS: INDEPENDENCE DAY. Nov 30. National holiday. Gained independence from Great Britain in 1966.

CHISHOLM, SHIRLEY: 85th BIRTH ANNIVERSARY. Nov 30, 1924. Born at Brooklyn, NY, Shirley St. Hill Chishom was an educator, author and politician who was the first African-American woman elected to the US House of Representatives. A liberal Democrat, she was known for her strong opinions and outspoken nature as she represented the Bedford-Stuyvesant neighborhood of New York City in Congress during 1974–82. She fought against poverty and discrimination and ran for the 1972 Democratic nomination for president just to prove that she could. She retired from politics in the 1980s and died at Ormond Beach, FL, Jan 1, 2005.

CHURCHILL, WINSTON: BIRTH ANNIVERSARY. Nov 30, 1874. Winston Leonard Spencer Churchill, British statesman and the first man to be made an honorary citizen of the US (by an act of Congress, Apr 9, 1963), was born at Blenheim Palace, Oxfordshire, England. Died Jan 24, 1965, at London, England. Dedicated to Britain and total victory over Germany, Churchill as minister of defense and prime minister was a strong leader during WWII. A stirring public speaker, Churchill said upon becoming prime minister in 1940, "I have nothing to offer but blood, toil, tears and sweat."

CLEMENS, SAMUEL LANGHORNE (MARK TWAIN): BIRTH ANNIVERSARY. Nov 30, 1835. Celebrated American author, whose books include: *The Adventures of Tom Sawyer, The Adventures of Huckleberry Finn* and *The Prince and the Pauper*. Born at Florida, MO, Twain is quoted as saying, "I came in with Halley's Comet in 1835. It is coming again next year, and I expect to go out with it." He did. Twain died at Redding, CT, Apr 21, 1910 (just one day after Halley's Comet perihelion).

COMPUTER SECURITY DAY. Nov 30. The use of computers and the concern for security increases daily. This annual observance reminds people to protect their computers, programs and data at home and at work. More than 1,500 companies participate worldwide. For info: Assn for Computer Security Day, 5014 Rodman Rd, Bethesda, MD 20816. Phone: (301) 229-2346. E-mail: computer_security_day@acm.org. Web: www.computersecurityday.com or www.geocities.com/a4csd.

CYBER MONDAY. Nov 30. Traditional beginning of the online Christmas shopping season—when consumers return to work and start etailing. The Monday after Thanksgiving.

HOFFMAN, ABBOT (ABBIE): BIRTH ANNIVERSARY. Nov 30, 1936. Political activist, born at Worcester, MA, Abbie Hoffman rose to prominence during the 1968 Democratic National Convention at Chicago, IL, and at his subsequent trial as a member of the Chicago Seven, a group of radicals accused of conspiring to disrupt the convention. Combining politics and street theater was a Hoffman trait. During the 1967 march on the Pentagon, he sought a permit to allow 1,200 demonstrators to encircle and levitate the military headquarters in an attempt to end the war in Vietnam. He, Jerry Rubin and Paul Krassner conceived the Yippie movement as a youth festival of life to run concurrently with the 1968 convention. Hoffman fled underground in 1974 to avoid trial on cocaine-possession charges and remained a fugitive for nearly seven years. Surrendering to authorities in 1980, he served his sentence in a work-release program. Hoffman died Apr 12, 1989, at New Hope, PA.

***THE JOY OF COOKING*: PUBLICATION ANNIVERSARY.** Nov 30, 1931. America's favorite all-purpose cookbook was self-published on this date by Irma Rombauer (1877–1962). Rombauer was a comforting voice for cooks during the Depression, and the book grew into an institution. The first commercial edition of the book appeared in 1936, and it offered a revolutionary "action format" (chronologically ordered ingredients followed by instructions) now commonplace in cookbooks. The numerous editions overseen by Rombauer and later her daughter and grandson sold more than 14 million copies.

NAIA MEN'S SOCCER NATIONAL CHAMPIONSHIP. Nov 30–Dec 5. Fresno, CA. Twenty-team field competes for national championship. 51st annual. For info: Natl Assn of Intercollegiate Athletics, 1200 Grand Blvd, Kansas City, MO 64106. E-mail: smcclure@naia.org. Web: www.naia.org.

NAIA WOMEN'S SOCCER NATIONAL CHAMPIONSHIP. Nov 30–Dec 5. Site TBD. Twenty-team field competes for national championship. 26th annual. For info: Natl Assn of Intercollegiate Athletics, 1200 Grand Blvd, Kansas City, MO 64106. E-mail: balmeida@naia.org. Web: www.naia.org.

PARKS, GORDON: BIRTH ANNIVERSARY. Nov 30, 1912. Award-winning and groundbreaking photojournalist and filmmaker, Parks was born the youngest of 15 children to a poor family at Fort Scott, KS. His photography career encompassed glamorous fashion shoots for *Vogue*, portraits of world leaders and searing photo essays for *Life*, where he was that magazine's first black staff photographer. Parks became the first major black Hollywood film director, with such important works as *The Learning Tree* and *Shaft*. He died Mar 7, 2006, at New York, NY.

PHILIPPINES: BONIFACIO DAY. Nov 30. Also known as National Heroes' Day. Commemorates birth of Andres Bonifacio, leader of the 1896 revolt against Spain. Bonifacio was born in 1863.

SAINT ANDREW'S DAY. Nov 30. Feast day of the apostle and martyr Andrew, who died about AD 60. Patron saint of Scotland.

SIDNEY, PHILIP: BIRTH ANNIVERSARY. Nov 30, 1554. English poet, statesman and soldier born at Penshurst, Kent, England. Best known of his poems is *Arcadia* (1580). Mortally wounded as he led an English detachment aiding the Dutch near Zutphen, Netherlands, Sept 22, 1586, Sidney gave his water bottle to another dying soldier with the words, "Thy necessity is yet greater than mine." He died at Arnhem, Oct 17, 1586, and all England mourned his death.

STATUE OF RAMSES II UNEARTHED: ANNIVERSARY. Nov 30, 1991. Egyptian construction workers in the ancient provincial town of Akhimim, 300 miles south of Cairo, unearthed a statue of Ramses II. Akhimim was an important provincial district that included the city of Ipu, a mecca for worshippers of the fertility god Min. The statue was uncovered during an excavation to prepare a foundation for a post office. An additional statue was uncovered 33 feet away, but the identity of its subject was unknown.

STAY HOME BECAUSE YOU'RE WELL DAY. Nov 30. So we can call in "well," instead of faking illness, and stay home from work. (©2006 by WH.) For info: Thomas & Ruth Roy, Wellcat Holidays, 2418 Long Ln, Lebanon, PA 17046. Phone: (717) 279-0184. E-mail: info@wellcat.com. Web: www.wellcat.com.

SWIFT, JONATHAN: BIRTH ANNIVERSARY. Nov 30, 1667. (Old Style date.) Clergyman and satirist born at Dublin, Ireland. Died there Oct 19, 1745 (OS). Author of *Gulliver's Travels.* "I never saw, heard, nor read," Swift wrote in *Thoughts on Religion*, "that the clergy were beloved in any nation where Christianity was the religion of the country. Nothing can render them popular but some degree of persecution."

 BIRTHDAYS TODAY

Richard Burr, 54, US Senator (R, North Carolina), born Charlottesville, VA, Nov 30, 1955.

Dick Clark, 80, longtime host of "American Bandstand," entertainer, producer, born Mount Vernon, NY, Nov 30, 1929.

Joan Ganz Cooney, 80, founder of the Children's Television Workshop and creator of "Sesame Street," born Phoenix, AZ, Nov 30, 1929.

Elisha Cuthbert, 27, actress ("24," *The Girl Next Door*), born Calgary, AB, Canada, Nov 30, 1982.

Des'ree, 39, singer (*I Ain't Movin'*), born London, England, Nov 30, 1970.

Robert Guillaume, 82, actor ("Soap," "Benson"), born St. Louis, MO, Nov 30, 1927.

Billy Idol, 54, singer, songwriter, born William Michael Albert Broad, Surrey, England, Nov 30, 1955.

Vincent Edward "Bo" Jackson, 47, former baseball player, former football player, born Bessemer, AL, Nov 30, 1962.

G. Gordon Liddy, 79, convicted Watergate coconspirator, radio talk-show host, born New York, NY, Nov 30, 1930.

David Mamet, 62, dramatist (*American Buffalo, Oleanna, Things Change*), born Chicago, IL, Nov 30, 1947.

Colin Mochrie, 52, comedian, actor ("Whose Line Is It Anyway?"), born Ayrshire, Scotland, Nov 30, 1957.

Sandra Oh, 39, actress (*Under the Tuscan Sun, Sideways*, "Grey's Anatomy"), born Nepean, ON, Canada, Nov 30, 1970.

Mandy Patinkin, 57, actor (Tony for *Evita; Sunday in the Park with George*, "Chicago Hope"), born Chicago, IL, Nov 30, 1952.

Ivan "Pudge" Rodriguez, 38, baseball player, born Vega Baja, Puerto Rico, Nov 30, 1971.

Amy Ryan, 40, actress ("The Wire," *Gone Baby Gone*), born Queens, NY, Nov 30, 1969.

Ridley Scott, 72, director (*Alien, Blade Runner, Gladiator*), born Northumberland, England, Nov 30, 1937.

Margaret Spellings, 52, US Secretary of Education, born in Michigan, Nov 30, 1957.

Ben Stiller, 44, actor, director (*Starsky and Hutch, Meet the Parents, Reality Bites*), born New York, NY, Nov 30, 1965.

Noel Paul Stookey, 72, singer, songwriter (Peter, Paul and Mary), born Baltimore, MD, Nov 30, 1937.

Efrem Zimbalist, Jr, 86, actor ("The F.B.I.," *Airport*), born New York, NY, Nov 30, 1923.

✦ December ✦

December 1 — Tuesday

DAY 335 **30 REMAINING**

BASKETBALL CREATED: ANNIVERSARY. Dec 1, 1891. James Naismith was a teacher of physical education at the International YMCA Training School at Springfield, MA. To create an indoor sport that could be played during the winter months, he nailed up peach baskets at opposite ends of the gym and gave students soccer balls to toss into them. Thus was born the game of basketball.

BIFOCALS AT THE MONITOR LIBERATION DAY. Dec 1. Our hearts fill with compassion today for coworkers stuck wearing bifocals at the PC. Shed a tear as their heads bob up and down, in and out, trying to read the monitor, trying to decide which set of lenses to use. Annually, Dec 1. (©2006 by WH.) For info: Thomas & Ruth Roy, Wellcat Holidays, 2418 Long Ln, Lebanon, PA 17046. Phone: (717) 279-0184. E-mail: info@wellcat.com. Web: www.wellcat.com.

BINGO'S BIRTHDAY MONTH. Dec 1–31. To celebrate the innovation and manufacture of the game of Bingo in 1929 by Edwin S. Lowe. Bingo has grown into a five-billion-dollar-a-year charitable fund-raiser. For info: Tara Snowden, Pres, Bingo Bugle, Inc, Box 527, Vashon, WA 98070. Phone: (800) 327-6437 or (206) 463-5656. E-mail: tara@bingobugle.com.

CANADA: YUKON ORDER OF PIONEERS: ANNIVERSARY. Dec 1, 1894. The Yukon Order of Pioneers held its founding meeting on this date at Fortymile, Yukon. It began as a vigilante police force to deter claim jumping and later inaugurated Discovery Day (Aug 17), a statutory Yukon holiday commemorating the discovery of gold on Bonanza Creek in 1896.

CHRISTMAS NEW ORLEANS STYLE. Dec 1–31. New Orleans, LA. Cathedral Christmas concerts, caroling in Jackson Square, holiday parades with Papa Noel, cooking demonstrations, Celebration in the Oaks, Christmas Day Concert, tours of 19th-century houses in holiday dress, Reveillon dinners and Papa Noel hotel rates. For info: French Quarter Festivals, Inc, 400 N Peters St, #205, New Orleans, LA 70130. Phone: (800) 673-5725 or (504) 522-5730. E-mail: feedback@fqfi.org. Web: www.fqfi.org.

CIVIL AIR PATROL FOUNDED: ANNIVERSARY. Dec 1, 1941. The Director of Civilian Defense, former New York Mayor Fiorello H. LaGuardia, signed a formal order creating the Civil Air Patrol, a US Air Force Auxiliary. The CAP has a three-part mission: to provide an aerospace education program, a CAP cadet program and an emergency services program. For info: Civil Air Patrol, 105 S Hansell St, Maxwell AFB, AL 36112-6332. Phone: (205) 953-5463.

A COLONIAL CHRISTMAS. Dec 1–Jan 3, 2010. Jamestown Settlement, Williamsburg, VA, and Yorktown Victory Center, Yorktown, VA. Experience 17th- and 18th-century holiday traditions. At Jamestown Settlement, a film and special guided tours compare and contrast English Christmas customs of the period with how the season may have been observed in the difficult early years of the Jamestown colony. At the Yorktown Victory Center, hear accounts of Christmas and winter in military encampments during the American Revolution and glimpse holiday preparations on a 1780s Virginia farm. For info: Jamestown-Yorktown Foundation, PO Box 1607, Williamsburg, VA 23187. Phone: (757) 253-4838 or (888) 593-4682. Fax: (757) 253-5299. Web: www.historyisfun.org.

COLORECTAL CANCER EDUCATION AND AWARENESS MONTH. Dec 1–31. To educate consumers, patients and professionals regarding the need for early diagnosis and treatment of colorectal cancer. For info: PPSI, c/o Pharmacy Council on Colorectal Cancer Education, 101 Lucas Valley Rd, Ste 382, San Rafael, CA 94903. Phone: (415) 479-8628. Fax: (415) 479-8608. E-mail: ppsi@aol.com. Web: www.ppsinc.org.

COOKIE CUTTER WEEK. Dec 1–7. The Cookie Cutter Collectors Club celebrates a special time of baking cookies and collecting cutters. And what better time than the first week of December—baking season? For info: Paula W. Mullins, 207 Ash, Box 8, Lawrenceburg, KY 40342. Phone: (502) 598-1901.

DAY WITH(OUT) ART. Dec 1. An annual observance about the impact of AIDS on the visual arts. Events to increase public awareness through the visual arts and direct services to artists living with HIV/AIDS. For info: Visual AIDS, 526 W 26th St, #510, New York, NY 10001. Phone: (212) 627-9855. Fax: (212) 627-9815. E-mail: info@visualaids.org. Web: www.visualaids.org.

ICELAND: UNIVERSITY STUDENTS' CELEBRATION: ANNIVERSARY. Dec 1, 1918. Marks the day in 1918 when Iceland became an independent state from Denmark (but still remained under the king of Denmark).

MARTIN, MARY: BIRTH ANNIVERSARY. Dec 1, 1913. American stage star was born Mary Virginia Martin at Weatherford, TX. She is best known for her title role in the Broadway and television productions of *Peter Pan*. She won Tony awards for her starring roles in *South Pacific* and *Peter Pan*. She died Nov 3, 1990, at Rancho Mirage, CA.

MOORE, JULIA A. DAVIS: BIRTH ANNIVERSARY. Dec 1, 1847. Julia Moore, known as the "Sweet Singer of Michigan," was born in a log cabin at Plainfield, MI. A writer of homely verse and ballads, Moore enjoyed remarkable popularity and gave many public readings before realizing that her public appearances were occasions for laughter and ridicule. Her poems were said to be "so bad, her subjects so morbid and her naïveté so genuine" that they were actually gems of humorous genius. At her final public appearance she told her audience: "You people paid 50 cents to see a fool, but I got 50 dollars to look at a house full of fools." Moore died June 17, 1920, near Manton, MI.

✦ **NATIONAL DRUNK AND DRUGGED DRIVING PREVENTION MONTH.** Dec 1–31.

NATIONAL TIE MONTH. Dec 1–31. Annually in December. Twenty percent of all ties sold are bought as Christmas gifts. Celebrate the tie, and promote its proper use this month. For info: Sir Nemo Turner, The Protocol Institute, CP 157, Place du Parc, Montreal, QC, H2X 4A4, Canada. Phone: (514) 849-0888. E-mail: magician@total.net.

NATIONAL WRITE A BUSINESS PLAN MONTH. Dec 1–31. Time to get out of your cubicle and turn your business ideas into reality! Use the last month of the year to craft a business plan—and get a great start in the new year to come. For info: Jocelyn Saccuci, 4898 S Fresno St, Chandler, AZ 85249. E-mail: jocelyn@ezbizplans.com.

OPERATION SANTA PAWS. Dec 1–19. During the holiday season extra help is needed for abused and abandoned animals in the care of local animal shelters. One grassroots organization, "Operation Santa Paws," is helping by spearheading a canine/feline toy/treat drive to benefit less-fortunate pets this season. Justin Rudd, organizer of this holiday effort, is encouraging animal lovers to purchase a new dog or cat toy, treat or supply that will be delivered in time for Christmas to local shelters and rescue organizations. For info: Justin Rudd. Phone: (562) 439-3316. E-mail: justin@justinrudd.com. Web: www.santapaws.info.

***PLAYBOY* FIRST PUBLISHED: ANNIVERSARY.** Dec 1, 1953. *Playboy* magazine was launched at Chicago, IL, by publisher Hugh Hefner.

PORTUGAL: INDEPENDENCE DAY. Dec 1. Public holiday. Became independent of Spain in 1640.

PRYOR, RICHARD: BIRTH ANNIVERSARY. Dec 1, 1940. African-American comedian and actor, born at Peoria, IL, who began performing at age seven. He was known for his use of profanity, and his humor was frequently based on racial stereotypes. Extremely successful as a stand-up, Pryor won five Grammy Awards for his comedy albums, and he also wrote or starred in any number of classic comedy films, including *Stir Crazy, Silver Streak* and *Car Wash*. His drug problems were well documented in his comedy act, and he struggled with multiple sclerosis late in his life. He died at Encino, CA, Dec 10, 2005.

RAWLS, LOU: BIRTH ANNIVERSARY. Dec 1, 1933. Born at Chicago, IL, Rawls was the popular singer with the unmistakably smooth voice—"sweet as sugar, soft as velvet, strong as steel, smooth as butter"—at home equally in gospel, blues, jazz, soul and pop. The recipient of three Grammys (with 13 nominations) and the creator of 60 albums, later in life Rawls became an indefatigable supporter of humanitarian causes, most famously the United Negro College Fund. Rawls died Jan 6, 2006, at Los Angeles, CA.

RECIPE GREETINGS FOR THE HOLIDAYS. Dec 1–8. A week in which to send recipes as great greetings. Create your own or send a large SASE for ideas. For info: Recipe Greetings Update, PO Box 416, Denver, CO 80201. Phone: (303) 575-5676. E-mail: mail@contentprovidermedia.com.

RISING STAR MONTH. Dec 1–31. A month urging people to reach for the stars by designing a personal life plan. It takes place in December because that is the month that everyone can review the past year and design, revise or redesign their life plan for the next year. Remember to reach for the stars by designing your life plan! For info: Deborah and Peter Kulkkula, 381 Billings Rd, Fitchburg, MA 01420. Phone: (967) 343-3333. E-mail: info@RisingStarMonth.info. Web: www.RisingStarMonth.info.

ROCKEFELLER CENTER CHRISTMAS TREE: ANNUAL LIGHTING. Dec 1 (tentative). New York, NY. Lighting of the huge Christmas tree in Rockefeller Center signals the opening of the holiday season at New York City. More than 30,000 lights are strung on five miles of electric wire. In 1933 the first formal tree lighting ceremony took place with 700 lights. Date is usually the Tuesday or Wednesday after Thanksgiving.

ROMANIA: NATIONAL DAY. Dec 1. National holiday. Marks unification of Romania and Transylvania in 1918 and the overthrow of the communist regime in 1989.

ROSA PARKS DAY: ANNIVERSARY OF ARREST. Dec 1, 1955. Anniversary of the arrest of Rosa Parks, at Montgomery, AL, for refusing to give up her seat and move to the back of a municipal bus. Her arrest triggered a yearlong boycott of the city bus system and led to legal actions that ended racial segregation on municipal buses throughout the southern US. The event has been called the birth of the modern civil rights movement. Rosa McCauley Parks was born at Tuskegee, AL, Feb 4, 1913.

SAFE TOYS AND GIFTS MONTH. Dec 1–31. What are the most dangerous types of toys to children's eyesight? Tips on how to choose age-appropriate, safe toys will be distributed. For info: Prevent Blindness America®, 211 W Wacker Dr, Ste 1700, Chicago, IL 60606. Phone: (800) 331-2020. E-mail: info@preventblindness.org. Web: www.preventblindness.org.

SPIRITUAL LITERACY MONTH. Dec 1–31. Promoting respect for and among the world's religions by engaging people in exploring the sacred texts of humankind. Discussions are held at libraries, community centers, civic clubs, coffee houses, houses of worship and private homes. Participants are invited to download free booklets containing selections from the text under study and open-ended questions derived from the text to encourage dialogue. Separate leader's guides are also available to assist those facilitating a discussion. Sponsored by the One River Foundation, a not-for-profit educational organization devoted to the study of the world's religions. For info: Rabbi Rami Shapiro, One River Foundation, 2441-Q Old Fort Parkway, Ste 412, Murfreesboro, TN 37128. Phone: (615) 653-5041. E-mail: rabbirami@earthlink.net. Web: www.oneriver.org.

UNITED NATIONS: WORLD AIDS DAY. Dec 1. In 1988 the World Health Organization of the UN declared Dec 1 as World AIDS Day, an international day of awareness and education about AIDS. The WHO is the leader in global direction and coordination of AIDS prevention, control, research and education. A program called UNAIDS was created to bring together the skills and expertise of the World Bank, UNDP, UNESCO, UNICEF, UNFPA and the WHO to strengthen and expand national capacities to respond to the pandemic. For info: United Nations, Dept of Public Info, New York, NY 10017. Web: www.un.org.

✦ **WORLD AIDS DAY.** Dec 1.

BIRTHDAYS TODAY

Woody Allen, 74, filmmaker (Oscar for *Annie Hall; Manhattan, Hannah and Her Sisters*), actor, born Allen Stewart Konigsberg at Brooklyn, NY, Dec 1, 1935.

Carol Alt, 49, model, born New York, NY, Dec 1, 1960.

Nestor Carbonell, 42, actor ("Suddenly Susan"), born New York, NY, Dec 1, 1967.

Bette Midler, 64, singer ("You Are the Wind Beneath My Wings"), actress (*Beaches, For the Boys, Down and Out in Beverly Hills*), born Paterson, NJ, Dec 1, 1945.

Reggie Sanders, 42, baseball player, born Florence, SC, Dec 1, 1967.

Lee Buck Trevino, 70, golfer, born Dallas, TX, Dec 1, 1939.

Larry Walker, 43, former baseball player, born Maple Ridge, BC, Canada, Dec 1, 1966.

Treat Williams, 57, actor (*Hair, Smooth Talk*), born Rowayton, CT, Dec 1, 1952.

December 2 — Wednesday

DAY 336 — 29 REMAINING

ARTIFICIAL HEART TRANSPLANT: ANNIVERSARY. Dec 2, 1982. Barney C. Clark, 61, became the first recipient of a permanent artificial heart. The operation was performed at the University of Utah Medical Center at Salt Lake City. Near death at the time of the operation, Clark survived almost 112 days after the implantation. He died Mar 23, 1983.

BROWN, JOHN: 150th EXECUTION ANNIVERSARY. Dec 2, 1859. Abolitionist leader who is remembered for his raid on the US Arsenal at Harper's Ferry was hanged for treason at Charles Town, WV.

CALLAS, MARIA: BIRTH ANNIVERSARY. Dec 2, 1923. American opera singer born at New York, NY. Died at Paris, Sept 16, 1977.

December 2009

S	M	T	W	T	F	S
		1	2	3	4	5
6	7	8	9	10	11	12
13	14	15	16	17	18	19
20	21	22	23	24	25	26
27	28	29	30	31		

COLD MOON. Dec 2. So called by Native American tribes of New England and the Great Lakes because the nights have become long at this time of year. Also called the Long Nights Moon. The December Full Moon.

ENGLAND: WALTER PLINGE DAY. Dec 2. A day to recognize Walter Plinge, said to have been a London pub landlord in 1900. His generosity to actors led to the use of his name as an actor in play programs to conceal the fact that an actor was playing more than one role. See also: "George Spelvin Day" (Nov 15) for US equivalent.

ENRON FILES FOR BANKRUPTCY: ANNIVERSARY. Dec 2, 2001. The once high-flying Houston, TX, energy services company filed for bankruptcy on this date. Subsequent investigations revealed questionable accounting practices and unethical dealings, to the extent that "Enron" became the buzzword for corporate malfeasance of the late 1990s and into the 21st century. Many other corporations were found to have questionable financial statements after the Enron scandal (in which thousands of employees lost their jobs and retirement savings), and investor confidence in the US stock market was shaken. Federal Reserve chairman Alan Greenspan, in a July 16, 2002, report to the Senate Banking Committee, indicted such corporate misbehavior: "An infectious greed seemed to grip much of our business community [in the 1990s]."

FIRST SELF-SUSTAINING NUCLEAR CHAIN REACTION: ANNIVERSARY. Dec 2, 1942. Physicist Enrico Fermi led a team of scientists at the University of Chicago in producing the first controlled, self-sustaining nuclear chain reaction. Their first simple nuclear reactor was built under the stands of the University's football stadium.

"IMUS IN THE MORNING" RADIO PREMIERE: ANNIVERSARY. Dec 2, 1971. Award-winning radio broadcaster Don Imus signed on to New York City's WNBC on this date. The show offered cantankerous takes on current affairs. On Apr 12, 2007, CBS dropped the show due to racial slurs made by Imus.

LAOS: NATIONAL DAY. Dec 2. National holiday commemorating declaration of the republic in 1975.

McCARTHY SILENCED BY SENATE: 55th ANNIVERSARY. Dec 2, 1954. On Feb 9, 1950, Joseph McCarthy, a relatively obscure senator from Wisconsin, announced during a speech in Wheeling, WV, that he had a list of Communists in the State Department. Over the next two years he made increasingly sensational charges and in 1953 McCarthyism reached its height as he held Senate hearings in which he bullied defendants. In 1954 McCarthy's tyranny was exposed in televised hearings during which he took on the Army and on Dec 2, 1954, the Senate voted to censure him. McCarthy died May 2, 1957.

MONROE DOCTRINE: ANNIVERSARY. Dec 2, 1823. President James Monroe, in his annual message to Congress, enunciated the doctrine that bears his name and that was long hailed as a statement of US policy. ". . . in the wars of the European powers in matters relating to themselves we have never taken any part. . . . We should consider any attempt on their part to extend their system to any portion of this hemisphere as dangerous to our peace and safety. . . ."

MOON PHASE: FULL MOON. Dec 2. Moon enters Full Moon phase at 2:30 AM, EST.

NATIONAL PARKS ESTABLISHED IN ALASKA: ANNIVERSARY. Dec 2, 1980. Eight national parks were established in Alaska on this date. Mount McKinley National Park, which was established Feb 26, 1917, and Denali National Monument, which was proclaimed Dec 1, 1978, were combined as Denali National Park and Preserve. Gates of the Arctic National Monument, proclaimed Dec 1, 1978; Glacier Bay National Monument, proclaimed Feb 25, 1925; and Katmai National Monument, proclaimed Sept 24, 1918, were established as national parks and preserves. Kenai Fjords National Monument, proclaimed Dec 1, 1978, and Kobuk Valley National Monument, proclaimed Dec 1, 1978, were established as national parks. Lake Clark National Monument, proclaimed Dec 1, 1978, and Wrangell–St. Elias National Monument, proclaimed Dec 1, 1978, were established as national parks and preserves. For info: www.nps.gov.

SAFETY RAZOR PATENTED: ANNIVERSARY. Dec 2, 1901. American King Camp Gillette designed the first razor with disposable blades. Up until this time, men shaved with a straight-edge razor that they sharpened on a leather strap.

SEURAT, GEORGES: 150th BIRTH ANNIVERSARY. Dec 2, 1859. French Neo-Impressionist painter born at Paris, France. Died there Mar 29, 1891. Seurat is known for his style of painting with small spots of color, called *pointillism*, as in *Sunday Afternoon on the Island of Grand Jatte*.

SPECIAL EDUCATION DAY. Dec 2. Celebrate the anniversary of the first US special education law—Dec 2, 1975. A time to reflect and move forward. Where were we when President Ford signed the groundbreaking legislation? Where are we now? And where do we need to be tomorrow? A day to honor progress, dialogue about challenges we face, and consider reforms for the future of educating all children. For info: Special Education Day Committee (SPEDCO). E-mail: info@specialeducationday.com. Web: www.specialeducationday.com.

SPECIAL KIDS DAY. Dec 2. Elmhurst, IL. A day to honor children who are developmentally delayed or physically challenged with a community-wide party. Established in 1990. this event builds on UN Resolution #47/3, which sets aside a day to promote integrating the disabled into society. This free, all-volunteer party features a family photo session with Santa, food and gifts for all special needs children and their siblings. Est attendance: 400. For info: Rich Rosenberg, Special Kids Day, 111 Linden, Elmhurst, IL 60126. Phone: (630) 530-8000. Fax: (630) 530-8800. E-mail: info@specialkidsday.org. Web: www.specialkidsday.org.

UNITED ARAB EMIRATES: NATIONAL DAY. Dec 2. Anniversary of the day in 1971 when a federation of seven sheikdoms known as the Trucial States declared independence from the UK and became known as the United Arab Emirates.

UNITED NATIONS: INTERNATIONAL DAY FOR THE ABOLITION OF SLAVERY. Dec 2. Recalls the date of adoption by the General Assembly in 1949 of the Convention for the Suppression of the Traffic in Persons and the Exploitation of Others. For info: United Nations, Dept of Public Info, New York, NY 10017. Web: www.un.org.

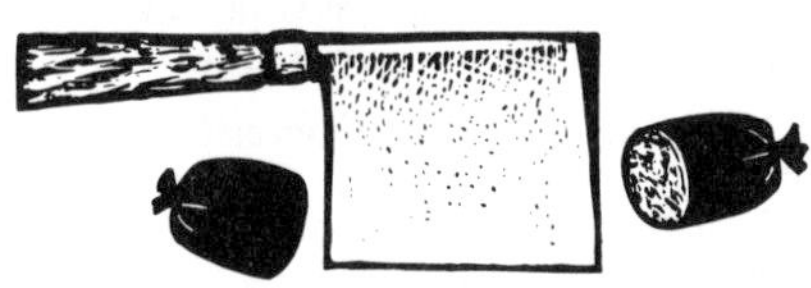

BIRTHDAYS TODAY

Wayne Allard, 66, US Senator (R, Colorado), born Fort Collins, CO, Dec 2, 1943.

T. Coraghessan Boyle, 61, author (*Riven Rock, The Tortilla Curtain*), born Peekskill, NY, Dec 2, 1948.

Dan Butler, 55, actor ("Frasier"), born Huntington, IN, Dec 2, 1954.

Dennis Christopher, 54, actor (*Sweet Dreams, Breaking Away*), born Philadelphia, PA, Dec 2, 1955.

Cathy Lee Crosby, 61, actress ("That's Incredible," *Coach*), born Los Angeles, CA, Dec 2, 1948.

Nelly Furtado, 31, singer, born Victoria, BC, Canada, Dec 2, 1978.

Randy Gardner, 51, former figure skater, choreographer, born Marina del Rey, CA, Dec 2, 1958.

Julie Harris, 84, actress (winner of six Tony awards; "Knots Landing," *I Am a Camera, The Member of the Wedding*), born Grosse Pointe, MI, Dec 2, 1925.

Lucy Liu, 42, actress (*Lucky Number Slevin, Charlie's Angels*, "Ally McBeal"), born Queens, NY, Dec 2, 1967.

Stone Phillips, 55, anchor ("Dateline," "20/20"), born Texas City, TX, Dec 2, 1954.

Harry Reid, 70, US Senator (D, Nevada), born Searchlight, NV, Dec 2, 1939.

Monica Seles, 36, tennis player, born Novi Sad, Yugoslavia, Dec 2, 1973.

Britney Spears, 28, singer, born Kentwood, LA, Dec 2, 1981.

William Wegman, 66, artist, photographer, born Holyoke, MA, Dec 2, 1943.

December 3 — Thursday

DAY 337 — 28 REMAINING

BELGIUM: LOVER'S FAIR. Dec 3. Arlon, Belgium. Traditional cultural observance. Annually, the first Thursday in December.

BHOPAL POISON GAS DISASTER: 25th ANNIVERSARY. Dec 3, 1984. At Bhopal, India, a leak of deadly gas (methyl isocyanate) at a Union Carbide Corp plant killed more than 4,000 persons and injured more than 200,000 in the world's worst industrial accident.

CONRAD, JOSEPH: BIRTH ANNIVERSARY. Dec 3, 1857. English novelist, born Józef Korzeniowski to Polish parents at Berdichev in the Ukraine. He learned English as a sailor on British ships. Author of *Lord Jim* and *Heart of Darkness*, among others. Died Aug 3, 1924, at Bishopsbourne, Kent, England.

FIRST HEART TRANSPLANT: ANNIVERSARY. Dec 3, 1967. Dr. Christiaan Barnard, a South African surgeon, performed the world's first successful heart transplantation at Cape Town, South Africa. See also: "Barnard, Christiaan Neethling: Birthday" (Nov 8).

HOLIDAY ALE FESTIVAL. Dec 3–6. Pioneer Courthouse Square, Portland, OR. The only beer festival in the Northwest to be held outdoors in the dark, cold and often wet month of December, the Holiday Ale Festival is truly distinctive. Despite chilly temperatures and often-inclement weather outside, attendees stay warm and dry under a large clear tent that covers the venue while allowing for views of the city lights. More than 40 Northwest winter ales are featured at the event. Est attendance: 15,000. For info: Chris Crabb, Crabbsoup Public Relations, 4906 NE Siskiyou St, Portland, OR 97213. Phone: (503) 314-7583. E-mail: crabbsoup@comcast.net. Web: www.holidayale.com.

ILLINOIS: ADMISSION DAY: ANNIVERSARY. Dec 3. Became 21st state in 1818.

LANTERN LIGHT TOURS. Dec 3–20 (tentative). Mystic, CT. Step into Christmas past. You may find yourself riding in a horse-drawn omnibus, kicking up your heels with revelers in the tavern or spying on silver-haired St. Nick. Est attendance: 7,000. For info: Mystic Seaport, 75 Greenmanville Ave, Box 6000, Mystic, CT 06355. Phone: (860) 572-5315 or (888) 973-2767. Web: www.mysticseaport.org.

December 2009

S	M	T	W	T	F	S
		1	2	3	4	5
6	7	8	9	10	11	12
13	14	15	16	17	18	19
20	21	22	23	24	25	26
27	28	29	30	31		

MONTOYA, CARLOS: BIRTH ANNIVERSARY. Dec 3, 1903. Guitarist and composer renowned for popularizing flamenco guitar music. His solo performances of the Spanish folk form lifted flamenco from its traditional accompaniment role. Montoya never learned to read music and relied on the traditional improvisational nature of flamenco rooted in the Andalusian Gypsy form of music that stressed rhythms and harmonic patterns. He was born at Madrid, Spain, and died Mar 3, 1993, at Wainscott, NY.

NORTH STAR CLASSIC. Dec 3–6. Valley City, ND. Four-day livestock show and sale featuring 11 breeds of cattle shows and 5 breed sales, plus a junior livestock show and a Bull Preview Day. Also a commercial exhibit area that features only items and equipment related to livestock production. Est attendance: 15,000. For info: North Star Classic, PO Box 846, Valley City, ND 58072. Phone: (701) 845-1401 or (800) 437-0218. Fax: (701) 845-3914. E-mail: ndws@northdakotawintershow.com. Web: www.northdakotawintershow.com.

SAINT OLAF CHRISTMAS FESTIVAL. Dec 3–6. St. Olaf College, Northfield, MN. Annually since 1912. This celebration of the Christmas season brings together approximately 600 student musicians (a 90-piece symphony orchestra and 500 singers) to perform sacred and folk songs from around the world. Annually, the weekend after Thanksgiving, Thurs–Sun. Est attendance: 12,000. For info: Bob Johnson, St. Olaf College, 1520 St. Olaf Ave, Northfield, MN 55057-1098. Phone: (507) 786-3179. E-mail: musicman@stolaf.edu. Web: www.stolaf.edu.

***A STREETCAR NAMED DESIRE* BROADWAY OPENING: ANNIVERSARY.** Dec 3, 1947. Tennessee Williams's drama opened on Broadway at the Ethel Barrymore Theatre with Jessica Tandy (as Blanche Du Bois) and newcomer Marlon Brando (as Stanley Kowalski). Williams was already a Broadway star with his first play, *Glass Menagerie*, and *Streetcar* was to be equally successful: it ran for two years and won the Pulitzer Prize for Drama. Marlon Brando's performance, using his Method style, was a sensation to audience members and critics. Tandy won the Tony Award for Best Actress in a Play.

STUART, GILBERT CHARLES: BIRTH ANNIVERSARY. Dec 3, 1755. American portrait painter whose most famous painting is that of George Washington. He also painted portraits of Madison, Monroe, Jefferson and other important Americans. Stuart was born near Narragansett, RI, and died July 9, 1828, at Boston, MA.

UNITED NATIONS: INTERNATIONAL DAY OF PERSONS WITH DISABILITIES. Dec 3. On Oct 14, 1992 (Res 47/3), at the end of the Decade of Disabled Persons, the General Assembly proclaimed Dec 3 to be an annual observance to promote the continuation of integrating the disabled into general society. Formerly called the International Day of Disabled Persons. For info: United Nations, Dept of Public Info, New York, NY 10017. Web: www.un.org.

VICTORIAN SLEIGH BELL PARADE & OLD CHRISTMAS WEEKEND. Dec 3–6. Manistee, MI. Re-creation of Manistee history. No motorized vehicles, no amplification. Horse-drawn entries, walking entries, singers, animals and St. Nick. Est attendance: 10,000. For info: Manistee Area Chamber of Commerce, 11 Cypress St, Manistee, MI 49660. Phone: (231) 723-2575 or (800) 288-2286. E-mail: chamber@manistee.com. Web: www.manisteecountychamber.com.

 BIRTHDAYS TODAY

Bruno Campos, 35, actor ("Nip/Tuck"), born Rio de Janeiro, Brazil, Dec 3, 1974.

Holly Marie Combs, 36, actress ("Picket Fences," "Charmed"), born San Diego, CA, Dec 3, 1973.

Michael Essien, 27, soccer player, born Accra, Ghana, Dec 3, 1982.

Brendan Fraser, 41, actor (*Mummy, The Quiet American*), born Indianapolis, IN, Dec 3, 1968.

Jean Luc Godard, 79, filmmaker (*Breathless, Weekend*), born Paris, France, Dec 3, 1930.

Daryl Hannah, 48, actress (*Splash, Grumpy Old Men*), born Chicago, IL, Dec 3, 1961.

Ferlin Husky, 82, singer ("Gone," "On the Wings of a Dove"), born Flat River, MO, Dec 3, 1927.

Bucky Lasek, 37, skateboarder, born Baltimore, MD, Dec 3, 1972.

Rick Ravon Mears, 58, former auto racer, born Wichita, KS, Dec 3, 1951.

Julianne Moore, 48, actress (*Children of Men, The Hours, Far from Heaven*), born Fort Bragg, Fayetteville, NC, Dec 3, 1961.

Jaye P. Morgan, 77, singer ("That's All I Want from You," "The Longest Walk"), born Mancos, CO, Dec 3, 1932.

Ozzy Osbourne, 61, singer, songwriter (originally lead singer for Black Sabbath), born Birmingham, England, Dec 3, 1948.

Andy Williams, 79, singer (platinum album *Love Story*, 13 gold albums), born Wall Lake, IA, Dec 3, 1930.

Katarina Witt, 44, Olympic figure skater, born Karl-Marx-Stadt, East Germany, Dec 3, 1965.

December 4 — Friday

DAY 338 **27 REMAINING**

BUTLER, SAMUEL: BIRTH ANNIVERSARY. Dec 4, 1835. English author (*Erewhon, The Way of All Flesh*), born at Bingham, Nottinghamshire, England. Died at London, June 18, 1902.

CARLYLE, THOMAS: BIRTH ANNIVERSARY. Dec 4, 1795. Scottish essayist and historian, born at Ecclefechan, Scotland. Died at London, Feb 4, 1881. "A well-written Life is almost as rare as a well-spent one," Carlyle wrote in his *Critical and Miscellaneous Essays*.

CHASE'S CALENDAR OF EVENTS: BIRTHDAY. Dec 4, 1957. Today in 1957 the first copies of the first edition of *Chase's Calendar of Annual Events* (for the year 1958) were delivered by the printer at Flint, MI. Two thousand copies, consisting of 32 pages and listing 364 events, were printed. Now annual editions are more than 700 pages long and list more than 12,000 events. It has several offspring, including *The Teacher's Calendar*, which debuted in 1999.

CHRISTMAS STROLL WEEKEND. Dec 4–6. Nantucket Island, MA. Christmas trees, costumed carolers, theatrical performances. Santa arrives via Coast Guard boat and is driven up Main Street in a horse-drawn carriage. Est attendance: 8,000. For info: Nantucket Island Chamber of Commerce, Zero Main St, Nantucket, MA 02554-3595. Phone: (508) 228-1700. Web: www.nantucketchamber.org.

CHRISTMAS WALK AND HOUSE TOUR. Dec 4–5. Geneva, IL. A special holiday tradition emphasizing the warmth and hospitality of our town. Spend the day touring charming homes aglow with holiday decorations. In the evening Santa Lucia, the Swedish symbol of the season, arrives, and Santa Claus opens his house for children's visits. Merchants graciously serve traditional holiday refreshments, including roasted chestnuts, as carolers fill the air with the sounds of the season. Est attendance: 35,000. For info: Geneva Chamber of Commerce, PO Box 481, 8 S Third St, Geneva, IL 60134. Phone: (630) 232-6060. Fax: (630) 232-6083. E-mail: chamberinfo@genevachamber.com. Web: www.genevachamber.com.

DICKENS FESTIVAL. Dec 4–5 (also Dec 11–12 and 18–19). Holly, MI. Circa 1850 comes to life in downtown Holly. Bah humbug with Scrooge, encourage Tiny Tim, sing with the carolers, banter with the street vendors. Enjoy delicacies such as roasted chestnuts, open-flame baked potatoes and plum pudding. Entertainment on the hour. Est attendance: 55,000. For info: Village of Holly Downtown Development Authority, 202 S Saginaw St, Holly, MI 48442. Phone: (248) 634-9571. Fax: (248) 634-4211. Web: www.dickensfestivalholly.org.

"FALCON CREST" TV PREMIERE: ANNIVERSARY. Dec 4, 1981. This nighttime serial was set in California wine country and originally focused on Angela Channing's determined efforts to gain control of the Falcon Crest vineyard and winery; later in the nine-year run the emphasis turned to crime. Famous actors who were a part of the cast at one time or another include: Jane Wyman, Lorenzo Lamas, Billy R. Moses, Cliff Robertson, Lana Turner, Gina Lollobrigida, Parker Stevenson, Anne Archer, Apollonia, Cesar Romero, Morgan Fairchild, Ken Olin and Mary Ann Mobley. In the season finale, Angela received Falcon Crest and everyone was happy.

GHANA: NATIONAL FARMERS' DAY. Dec 4. Public holiday. Honors and celebrates the farmers of Ghana. Observed the first Friday in December.

LAST AMERICAN HOSTAGE RELEASED IN LEBANON: ANNIVERSARY. Dec 4, 1991. A sad chapter of US history came to a close when Terry Anderson, an Associated Press correspondent, became the final American hostage held in Lebanon to be freed. Anderson had been held since Mar 16, 1985, one of 15 Americans who were held hostage for from two months to as long as six years and eight months. Three of the hostages, William Buckley, Peter Kilburn and Lieutenant Colonel William Higgins, were killed during their captivity. The other hostages, released previously one or two at a time, were Jeremy Levin, Benjamin Weir, the Reverend Lawrence Martin Jenco, David Jacobsen, Thomas Sutherland, Frank Herbert Reed, Joseph Cicippio, Edward Austin Tracy, Alan Steen, Jesse Turner and Robert Polhill.

MISSION SANTA BARBARA: FOUNDING ANNIVERSARY. Dec 4, 1786. Franciscan Mission to the Indians founded at Santa Barbara, CA. Present structure is the fourth to stand on same site. Last one destroyed by 1812 earthquake.

NATIONAL DICE DAY. Dec 4. A day for everyone to enjoy playing the game of dice. The goal of the game is to get to 10,000 points. Each player rolls 5 dice. If you roll a 5, it counts for 500 points. If you roll a 1, it counts for 100 points. If you roll neither, you lose your turn. If you roll 3-of-a-kind, it will count for the number x 100. If you roll 4-of-a-kind, double the number; 5-of-a-kind, double the number. If you roll a straight 12345 or 23456, you earn 1,500 points. Once someone reaches 10,000 points, they have to make every die count; once they do that everyone else has a chance to beat their score. For info: Julia Chase, 2681 Balmoral Ct, Ann Arbor, MI 48103.

NATIONAL GRANGE FOUNDING: ANNIVERSARY. Dec 4, 1786. The anniversary of the National Grange, the first organized agricultural movement in the US.

NCAA DIVISION I WOMEN'S SOCCER CHAMPIONSHIP—THE COLLEGE CUP. Dec 4 & 6. College Station, TX. Est attendance: 14,000. For info: NCAA, 700 W Washington St, PO Box 6222, Indianapolis, IN 46206-6222. Phone: (317) 917-6222. Web: www.NCAAsports.com.

RUSSELL, LILLIAN: BIRTH ANNIVERSARY. Dec 4, 1861. American singer and actress who in 1881 gained fame in the comic opera *The Great Mogul*. Born Helen Louise Leonard at Clinton, IA, she died June 6, 1922, at Pittsburgh, PA.

SAINT BARBARA'S DAY. Dec 4. On this day, traditionally the feast day of St. Barbara, a young girl places a twig from a cherry tree in a glass of water. If it blooms by Christmas Eve, she is certain to marry the following year. Because the narratives of her life and martyrdom are legendary, St. Barbara was dropped from the Roman Catholic Calendar of Saints in 1970.

SPACE MILESTONE: INTERNATIONAL SPACE STATION LAUNCH (US). Dec 4, 1998. The shuttle *Endeavour* took a US component of the space station named *Unity* into orbit 220 miles from Earth where spacewalking astronauts fastened it to a component launched by the Russians Nov 20, 1998. On July 25, 2000, the Russian service module *Zvezda* docked with the station. Projected completion date for the space station is 2010. When finished, it will be 356′ across and 290′ long and will support a crew of up to seven. On Oct 31, 2000, NASA launched the first expedition with a three-man crew to stay aloft for four months.

VICTORIAN CHRISTMAS HOME TOUR AND MINER'S BALL. Dec 4–6. Leadville, CO. 27th annual. Highlight of the holiday season—annual showing off of Leadville's historic homes and buildings bedecked in Christmas trimmings. Locals and guests alike dress in period fashions. Activities include the Victorian Afternoon Tea, parade of lights, dinner. Annually, the first weekend in Dec. Est attendance: 350. For info: Chamber of Commerce, Box 861, Leadville, CO 80461. Phone: (719) 486-3900 or (888) 532-3845. Fax: (719) 486-8478. E-mail: leadville@leadvilleusa.com. Web: www.leadvilleusa.com.

WINTERFEST. Dec 4–6. Luverne, MN. Christmas Light Parade, Parade of Homes, craft show, historical tours, dinner theater. For info: Jane Wildung, Exec Dir, Luverne Area Chamber of Commerce, 211 E Main, Luverne, MN 56156. Phone: (507) 283-4061. Fax: (507) 283-4061. E-mail: luvernechamber@iw.net. Web: www.luvernechamber.org.

WOLF POINT'S ANNUAL CHRISTMAS PARADE. Dec 4. Wolf Point, MT. The city comes alive with the Christmas spirit in this magical and enchanting evening, which features a parade in which all the floats are illuminated with lights, Santa is the master of ceremonies and awards for floats are given in three categories. This event will make you remember what Christmas looks like through the eyes of a child. Est attendance: 1,000. For info: Wolf Point Chamber of Commerce, 218 3rd Ave S, Ste B, Wolf Point, MT 59201. Phone: (406) 653-2012. E-mail: wpchmber@nemont.net.

BIRTHDAYS TODAY

Max Baer, Jr, 72, actor ("The Beverly Hillbillies"), producer (*Ode to Billy Joe*), born Oakland, CA, Dec 4, 1937.

Tyra Banks, 36, model, actress, talk show host ("America's Next Top Model"), born Los Angeles, CA, Dec 4, 1973.

Jeff Bridges, 60, actor (*The Contender, Starman, The Last Picture Show*), born Los Angeles, CA, Dec 4, 1949.

Helen M. Chase, 85, retired chronicler of contemporary civilization as coeditor of *Chase's Annual Events*, born Whitehall, MI, Dec 4, 1924.

Deanna Durbin, 88, actress (*It Started with Eve, Can't Help Singing*), born Winnipeg, MB, Canada, Dec 4, 1921.

Chris Hillman, 67, musician (the Byrds, the Desert Rose Band), born Los Angeles, CA, Dec 4, 1942.

Stewart Rawlings Mott, 72, philanthropist, born Flint, MI, Dec 4, 1937.

Mary E. Peters, 61, US Secretary of Transportation, born Phoenix, AZ, Dec 4, 1948.

Marisa Tomei, 45, actress (*In the Bedroom*, Oscar for *My Cousin Vinny*), born Brooklyn, NY, Dec 4, 1964.

Patricia Wettig, 58, actress ("St. Elsewhere," *City Slickers*; Emmys for "thirtysomething"), born Cincinnati, OH, Dec 4, 1951.

Cassandra Wilson, 54, jazz singer, born Jackson, MS, Dec 4, 1955.

December 2009

S	M	T	W	T	F	S
		1	2	3	4	5
6	7	8	9	10	11	12
13	14	15	16	17	18	19
20	21	22	23	24	25	26
27	28	29	30	31		

December 5 — Saturday

DAY 339 **26 REMAINING**

"THE ABBOTT AND COSTELLO SHOW" TV PREMIERE: ANNIVERSARY. Dec 5, 1952. Bud Abbott and Lou Costello made 52 half-hour films for television incorporating many of their best burlesque routines. The show ran for two seasons, until 1954. Costello was born at Paterson, NJ, Mar 6, 1906, and died at East Los Angeles, CA, Mar 3, 1959. In 1966 Hanna-Barbera Productions produced an animated cartoon based on the characters of Abbott and Costello. Abbott supplied his own voice while Stan Irwin imitated Costello. Bud Abbott was born at Asbury Park, NJ, Oct 2, 1895, and died at Woodland Hills, CA, Apr 24, 1974.

AFL-CIO FOUNDED: ANNIVERSARY. Dec 5, 1955. The American Federation of Labor and the Congress of Industrial Organizations joined together in 1955, following 20 years of rivalry, to become the nation's leading advocate for trade unions.

AUSTRIA: KRAMPUSLAUF. Dec 5. Salzburg region. On the eve of St. Nicholas's Day, Austrians celebrate the Krampuslauf (Krampus Run). In folklore, the Krampus is a devilish companion of St. Nicholas who punishes bad children just as St. Nicholas rewards good ones. The Krampus, represented by costumed revelers, is usually depicted as a dark, hairy, cloven-hooved beast with red horns, a leering mouth, chains and a switch. Children are invited to throw snowballs at the Krampus. Also known as Krampus Day.

BATHTUB PARTY DAY. Dec 5. Almost everyone nowadays takes showers, so here's a day to recall some of the warm-water luxury of days gone by. Invite a few friends. (©2006 by WH.) For info: Thomas & Ruth Roy, Wellcat Holidays, 2418 Long Ln, Lebanon, PA 17046. Phone: (717) 279-0184. E-mail: info@wellcat.com. Web: www.wellcat.com.

CALDWELL COUNTRY CHRISTMAS PARADE & FIREWORKS. Dec 5. Columbia, LA. Lighted nighttime parade will roll down Main St and through Historic Downtown Columbia. This parade is the highlight of the Christmas season with several bands from the area. Fireworks on the river follow the parade. Est attendance: 8,000. For info: Caldwell Parish Chamber of Commerce, PO Box 726, Columbia, LA 71418. Phone: (318) 649-0726. Or contact: Columbia Main Street, PO Box 10, Columbia, LA 71418. Phone: (318) 649-2138.

CAMBRIDGE COUNTRY CHRISTMAS. Dec 5–6. Cambridge, WI. The Dickens-inspired festival offers carriage rides, roasted chestnuts, hot apple cider, strolling carolers, live nativity scene and a beautifully decorated village to truly enjoy the season. Est attendance: 3,500. For info: Cambridge Chamber of Commerce, PO Box 572, Cambridge, WI 53523. Phone: (608) 423-3780. Web: www.cambridgewi.com.

CHESTER GREENWOOD DAY PARADE. Dec 5. Farmington, ME. Celebration of Farmington's famous inventor of the earmuff. An earmuff-themed parade with flag raising. Annually, the first Saturday in December. Est attendance: 2,500. For info: Franklin County Chamber of Commerce, 407 Wilton Rd, Ste 1, Farmington, ME 04938. Phone: (207) 778-4215.

CHRISTMAS CANDLELIGHT HOUSE TOURS. Dec 5 (also Dec 12 and 19). Throughout Cape May, NJ. 36th annual. More than 20 bed and breakfast inns, guesthouses, hotels and churches open their festively decorated doors to reveal the charm, holiday cheer and Victorian interiors that make Christmas in Cape May truly special. These self-guided tours are from 5:30 to 8:30 PM and cost $24 for adults, $19 for children ages 3–12; advance reservations strongly recommended. Est attendance: 6,000. For info: Mid-Atlantic Center for the Arts, 1048 Washington St, Cape May, NJ 08204. Phone: (800) 275-4278. Fax: (609) 884-0574. E-mail: mac4arts@capemaymac.org. Web: www.capemaymac.org.

CHRISTMAS CANDLELIGHTINGS. Dec 5 (also Dec 12 and 19). Roscoe Village, Coshocton, OH. On the first three Saturdays of December, Roscoe Village cheers on the holiday season with its Christmas Candlelightings. Share in the tradition of lighting the Christmas tree and light your own candle as "Silent Night" is sung. Throughout the day, guests enjoy art with Santa Claus, strolling carolers, live reindeer, roaster chestnuts, candlelight tours, complimentary hot-mulled cider and cookies and many other holiday festivities. Est attendance: 7,000. For info: Roscoe Village Foundation, 600 N Whitewoman St, Coshocton, OH 43812. Phone: (740) 622-9310 or (800) 877-1830. Fax: (740) 623-6555. E-mail: rvmarketing@roscoevillage.com. Web: www.roscoevillage.com.

CHRISTMAS FESTIVAL OF LIGHTS. Dec 5. Natchitoches, LA. 83rd annual. Featuring a parade, fireworks, food, entertainment, a fun run/walk and Christmas lighting. Listed as one of the "Top 100 Events in North America" by the American Bus Association. Est attendance: 150,000. For info: Natchitoches Parish Tourist Commission, 781 Front St, Natchitoches, LA 71457. Phone: (318) 352-8072 or (800) 259-1714. Fax: (318) 352-2415. Web: www.natchitoches.net or www.christmasfestival.com.

CHRISTMAS IN THE VILLAGES. Dec 5–6. Van Buren County, IA. Event features tour of homes, English high tea, cookie walk, Festival of Trees, horse-drawn carriage rides, bake sales, lighting contests and displays, soup suppers and the natural beauty of the season that is found throughout the county. Est attendance: 5,000. For info: Villages of Van Buren, Inc, PO Box 9, Keosauqua, IA 52565. Phone: (800) 868-7822. Fax: (319) 293-7116. E-mail: info@villagesofvanburen.com. Web: www.villagesofvanburen.com.

CHRISTMAS ON THE PRAIRIE. Dec 5–6. Saunders County Museum, Wahoo, NE. Old-fashioned Christmas featuring entertainment by local groups, lots of period costumes, special postal cancellation, children's activities common to the 1800s and demonstrations in the historical village decorated in the 1800s style. Annually, the first weekend of December. Sponsor: Christmas on the Prairie Steering Committee. Est attendance: 3,000. For info: Curator, Saunders County Museum, 240 N Walnut, Wahoo, NE 68066-1858. Phone: (402) 443-3090. E-mail: saunderscomuseum@hotmail.com. Web: www.visitsaunderscounty.org/attractions/museum.

CHRISTMAS PARADE. Dec 5. El Centro, CA. 64th annual. Annually, the first Saturday in December. Est attendance: 10,000. For info: El Centro Chamber of Commerce, Box 3006, El Centro, CA 92244. Phone: (760) 352-3681. Fax: (760) 352-3246. Web: www.elcentrochamber.com.

CHRISTMAS REMEMBERED AT STONEWALL JACKSON HOUSE. Dec 5. Stonewall Jackson House, Lexington, VA. Free tours by costumed docents, music, hot cider and home-made cookies. Children's crafts are part of the holiday fun. Est attendance: 500. For info: Stonewall Jackson House, 8 E Washington St, Lexington, VA 24450. Phone: (540) 463-2552. E-mail: development@stonewalljackson.org. Web: www.stonewalljackson.org.

COATS AND TOYS FOR KIDS DAY. Dec 5. Charity drive and live television broadcast from seven locations across Maine. More than 12,000 new and gently used children's winter coats and new, unwrapped toys are collected in a giant one-day pep rally. The holiday campaign collects more than 40,000 coats annually. For info: Community Relations, WCSH 6, One Congress Square, Portland, ME 04101. Phone: (207) 828-6666. Fax: (207) 828-6620. E-mail: communityrelations@WCSH6.com. Web: WCSH6.com.

DICKENS ON THE STRAND. Dec 5–6. Galveston, TX. Victorian Christmas celebration focuses on the 19th-century architecture of Galveston's Strand National Historic Landmark District and ties to Charles Dickens's 19th-century London. Annually, the first weekend in December. Est attendance: 35,000. For info: Galveston Historical Foundation, 502 20th St, Galveston, TX 77550. Phone: (409) 765-7834. Fax: (409) 765-7851. E-mail: foundation@galvestonhistory.org. Web: www.dickensonthestrand.org or www.galvestonhistory.org.

DISNEY, WALT: BIRTH ANNIVERSARY. Dec 5, 1901. Animator, filmmaker, theme park developer, born at Chicago, IL. Disney died at Los Angeles, CA, Dec 15, 1966.

GRANT'S SPEECH OF APOLOGY: ANNIVERSARY. Dec 5, 1876. President Ulysses S. Grant delivered his speech of apology to Congress claiming mistakes he made while he was president were due to his inexperience. His errors, he said, were "errors of judgment, not intent." While Grant's personal integrity was never formally questioned, he was closely associated with many government scandals, which became public during his presidency. He unwittingly aided Jay Gould in an attempt to corner the gold market during his first term. During the second, the Credit Mobilier affair involving many of the president's friends aired, while significant fraud was discovered in the Treasury Department and Indian Service.

HAITI: DISCOVERY DAY. Dec 5. Commemorates the discovery of Haiti by Christopher Columbus in 1492. Public holiday.

HOLIDAY HAPPINESS. Dec 5. Upper Arlington Public Library, Upper Arlington, OH. Holiday crafts, music and activities, including a visit from Santa Claus, for the whole family to enjoy. Annually, the first Saturday of December. For info: Upper Arlington Public Library, 2800 Tremont Rd, Upper Arlington, OH 43221. Phone: (614) 486-9621. Web: www.ualibrary.org.

HOLLYWOOD BEACH CANDY CANE PARADE. Dec 5. Hollywood, FL. More than 200 floats and marching units line the Hollywood Beach Boardwalk during this popular evening event. Est attendance: 50,000. For info: Marketing, City of Hollywood, Dept of Parks, Recreation & Cultural Arts, 1405 S 28th Ave, Hollywood, FL 33020. Phone: (954) 921-3404.

"IRRATIONAL EXUBERANCE" ENTERS LEXICON: ANNIVERSARY. Dec 5, 1996. In a speech to the Washington, DC–based American Enterprise Institute for Policy Research, Federal Reserve Chairman Alan Greenspan uttered a new catchphrase that the media quickly saw as a warning about the high-flying 1990s stock market. He asked, "How do we know when irrational exuberance has unduly escalated asset values. . . . And how do we factor that assessment into monetary policy?" Those two words, buried in an academic speech, nonetheless sparked panic in markets fearing the Fed would raise interest rates. The Tokyo, Hong Kong, Frankfurt, London and US markets dropped 2–4 percent after his speech. Most economists thought Greenspan was simply suggesting that markets needed to slow down a bit. But "irrational exuberance" lives on as Greenspan's most famous quote.

MARTIN VAN BUREN WREATH-LAYING. Dec 5. Martin Van Buren National Historic Site, Kinderhook, NY. Annual ceremony honoring Van Buren on his birth anniversary. Organized by the Village of Kinderhook. Participants include the mayor of Kinderhook, mayor of Valatie, a representative from the White House, the president of Friends of Lindenwald, the superintendent of Martin Van Buren NHS, local historians and local schoolchildren. For info: Chief Ranger, Martin Van Buren National Historic Site, 1013 Old Post Rd, Kinderhook, NY 12106-3605. Web: www.nps.gov/mava.

MONTGOMERY BUS BOYCOTT BEGINS: ANNIVERSARY. Dec 5, 1955. Rosa Parks was arrested at Montgomery, AL, for refusing to give up her seat on a bus to a white man. In support of Parks, and to protest the arrest, the black community of Montgomery organized a boycott of the bus system. The boycott lasted from Dec 5, 1955, to Dec 20, 1956, when a US Supreme Court ruling was implemented at Montgomery, integrating the public transportation system.

NORSKEDALEN'S OLD-FASHIONED CHRISTMAS. Dec 5–6. Coon Valley, WI. Celebrate an old-fashioned Christmas with decorated pioneer log homes to view, entertainment, à la carte ethnic foods, raffle, horse-drawn wagon/sleigh rides and outdoor activities. Fun for all ages. 10 AM–4 PM. Est attendance: 500. For info: Norskedalen Nature and Heritage Center, Inc, PO Box 235, Coon Valley, WI 54623. Phone: (608) 452-3424. Fax: (608) 452-3157. E-mail: info@norskedalen.org. Web: www.norskedalen.org.

PARADE OF LIGHTS. Dec 5. Kingsville, TX. Breakfast with Santa kicks off a fun-filled day of holiday activities for children ending with an illuminated nighttime parade for children of all ages in historic downtown Kingsville. Est attendance: 8,000. For info: Kingsville CVB, 1501 N Hwy 77, Kingsville, TX 78363. Phone: (800) 333-5032. Fax: (361) 592-3227. E-mail: visitors@kingsvilletexas.com. Web: www.kingsvilletexas.com.

PICKETT, BILL: BIRTH ANNIVERSARY. Dec 5, 1870. American rodeo cowboy, born at Williamson County, TX; died Apr 21, 1932, at Tulsa, OK. Inventor of bulldogging, the modern rodeo event that involves wrestling a running steer to the ground.

ROSSETTI, CHRISTINA: BIRTH ANNIVERSARY. Dec 5, 1830. Great English poet of beautiful yet melancholy verses who is best known for her lyrical fable "Goblin Market." Born at London, where she died on Dec 29, 1894.

SHAKER CHRISTMAS FAIR. Dec 5. Sabbathday Lake Shaker Village, New Gloucester, ME. Traditional holiday church fair featuring home-baked foods. Nine rooms of the 1816 Trustee's Office are filled with holiday items for all ages. For info: Leonard Brooks, Sabbathday Lake Shaker Village, 707 Shaker Rd, New Gloucester, ME 04260. Phone: (207) 926-4597. E-mail: usshakers@aol.com. Web: www.shaker.lib.me.us.

TAMALE FIESTA. Dec 5. Bucklin Park, El Centro, CA. 8th annual. Taste tamales from local vendors while enjoying the various arts and crafts tables and live entertainment. Annually, the first Saturday in December. Est attendance: 5,000. For info: El Centro Chamber of Commerce, PO Box 3006, El Centro, CA 92244. Phone: (760) 352-3681. Fax: (760) 352-3246. E-mail: generalinfo@elcentrochamber.com. Web: www.elcentrochamber.com.

THAILAND: KING'S BIRTHDAY AND NATIONAL DAY. Dec 5. Celebrated throughout the kingdom with colorful pageantry. Stores and houses decorated with spectacular illuminations at night. Public holiday.

December 2009	S	M	T	W	T	F	S
			1	2	3	4	5
	6	7	8	9	10	11	12
	13	14	15	16	17	18	19
	20	21	22	23	24	25	26
	27	28	29	30	31		

THURMOND, STROM: BIRTH ANNIVERSARY. Dec 5, 1902. One of the longest-serving senators in American history, James Strom Thurmond was born at Edgefield, SC. The only senator ever elected by a write-in vote, he joined the US Senate in 1954. He was elected as both a Democrat and a Republican and is remembered for his record-breaking filibuster protesting pending civil rights legislation. He did not yield the floor for 24 hours, 18 minutes over Aug 28–29, 1957, although the legislation did pass less than two hours later. He served in the Senate until Nov 19, 2002, just a few weeks shy of his 100th birthday. He died at Edgefield on June 26, 2003.

TWENTY-FIRST AMENDMENT TO THE US CONSTITUTION RATIFIED: ANNIVERSARY. Dec 5, 1933. Prohibition ended with the repeal of the 18th Amendment, as the 21st Amendment was ratified. Congress proposed repeal of Amendment XVIII (" . . . the manufacture, sale, or transportation of intoxicating liquors, within, the importation thereof into, or the exportation thereof from the United States and all territory subject to the jurisdiction thereof, for beverage purposes is hereby prohibited. . . .") Feb 20, 1933. By Dec 5, 1933, the repeal amendment had been ratified by the required 36 states and went into effect immediately as Amendment XXI to the US Constitution.

UNITED NATIONS: INTERNATIONAL VOLUNTEER DAY FOR ECONOMIC AND SOCIAL DEVELOPMENT. Dec 5. In a resolution of Dec 17, 1985, the United Nations General Assembly recognized the desirability of encouraging the work of all volunteers. It invited governments to observe annually on Dec 5 the "International Volunteer Day for Economic and Social Development, urging them to take measures to heighten awareness of the important contribution of volunteer service." A day commemorating the establishment in December 1970 of the UN Volunteers program and inviting world recognition of volunteerism in the international development movement. For info: United Nations, Dept of Public Info, Public Inquiries Unit, Rm GA-57, New York, NY 10017. Phone: (212) 963-4475. E-mail: inquiries@un.org. Web: www.un.org.

VAN BUREN, MARTIN: BIRTH ANNIVERSARY. Dec 5, 1782. The eighth president of the US (term of office: Mar 4, 1837–Mar 3, 1841) was the first to have been born a citizen of the US. He was a widower for nearly two decades before he entered the White House. His daughter-in-law, Angelica, served as White House hostess during an administration troubled by bank and business failures, depression and unemployment. Van Buren was born at Kinderhook, NY, and died there July 24, 1862.

WHEATLEY, PHILLIS: 225th DEATH ANNIVERSARY. Dec 5, 1784. Born at Senegal, West Africa, about 1753 or 1754, Phillis Wheatley was brought to the US in 1761 and purchased as a slave by a Boston tailor named John Wheatley. She was allotted unusual privileges for a slave, including being allowed to learn to read and write. She wrote her first poetry at age 14, and her first work was published in 1770. Wheatley's fame as a poet spread throughout Europe as well as the US after her *Poems on Various Subjects, Religious and Moral* was published at England in 1773. She was invited to visit George Washington's army headquarters after he read a poem she had written about him in 1776. Phillis Wheatley died at about age 30, at Boston, MA.

 BIRTHDAYS TODAY

Morgan Brittany, 59, actress ("Dallas," "Glitter"), born Suzanne Cupito at Hollywood, CA, Dec 5, 1950.

José Carreras, 63, opera singer, one of the "Three Tenors," born Barcelona, Spain, Dec 5, 1946.

Margaret Cho, 41, actress, comedienne, born San Francisco, CA, Dec 5, 1968.

Joan Didion, 75, author, journalist (*The Year of Magical Thinking, The White Album*), born Sacramento, CA, Dec 5, 1934.

Jeroen Krabbe, 65, actor (*A World Apart, King of the Hill, The Fugitive*), born Amsterdam, the Netherlands, Dec 5, 1944.

Little Richard, 74, singer ("Tutti Frutti," "Long Tall Sally"), songwriter, born Richard Penniman at Macon, GA, Dec 5, 1935.

Jim Messina, 62, singer ("Your Mama Don't Dance"), songwriter, born Maywood, CA, Dec 5, 1947.

Chad Mitchell, 73, lead singer (Chad Mitchell trio, "Lizzie Borden"), born Spokane, WA, Dec 5, 1936.

Art Monk, 52, former football player, born White Plains, NY, Dec 5, 1957.

Frankie Muniz, 24, actor ("Malcolm in the Middle," *My Dog Skip*), born Ridgewood, NJ, Dec 5, 1985.

Calvin Trillin, 74, author (*American Stories, Remembering Denny*), born Kansas City, MO, Dec 5, 1935.

December 6 — Sunday

DAY 340 **25 REMAINING**

ADORATION PARADE. Dec 6. Branson, MO. The 61st annual Adoration Parade will present a celebration of Christmas—the traditional values of faith, family and friendliness. Annually, the first Sunday in December. For info: Branson Area CVB, PO Box 1897, Branson, MO 65615. Phone: (888) 886-3637. Fax: (417) 334-4139. E-mail: info@bransoncvb.com. Web: www.explorebranson.com.

ALTAMONT CONCERT: 40th ANNIVERSARY. Dec 6, 1969. A free concert featuring performances by the Rolling Stones; Jefferson Airplane; Santana; Crosby, Stills, Nash and Young and the Flying Burrito Brothers turned into tragedy. The "thank-you" concert for 300,000 fans was marred by overcrowding, drug overdoses and the fatal stabbing of a spectator by a member of the Hell's Angels motorcycle gang, who had been hired as security guards for the event. The concert was held at the Altamont Speedway, Livermore, CA.

BCHS CHRISTMAS OPEN HOUSE AND GINGERBREAD CONTEST. Dec 6. Ainsworth, NE. Displays, gingerbread houses, refreshments, sing-along at 2 PM. Annually, the first Sunday in December. Est attendance: 125. For info: Carol Larson, Brown County Historical Society, HC 65 Box 158, Ainsworth, NE 69210. E-mail: Carolarson10@hotmail.com.

CHRISTMAS IN OLD APPALACHIA. Dec 6–24. Museum of Appalachia, Clinton, TN. The spirit, memories and warmth of an old-time Christmas will be revived, recalling a time of simple gifts, handmade decorations and family gatherings. Pioneer cabins are decorated in austere frontier fashion. In the gaily decorated turn-of-the-century Homestead House, old-time musicians play and sing the songs of yore; and the old log schoolhouse is decorated with ornaments made by local schoolchildren. For info: Museum of Appalachia, 2819 Andersonville Hwy, Clinton, TN 37716. Phone: (865) 494-7680. Fax: (865) 494-8957. E-mail: museum@museumofappalachia.org. Web: www.museumofappalachia.org.

CHRISTMAS TO REMEMBER. Dec 6. Laurel, MT. To officially open the Christmas season in Laurel, this daylong celebration includes the arrival of Santa, a community bazaar, children's craft activities, musical entertainment, lighting ceremony, parade of lights and fireworks. Annually, the first Sunday of December. Est attendance: 5,000. For info: Christmas to Remember Committee, Jean Carroll Thompson, PO Box 463, Laurel, MT 59044. Phone: (406) 248-8557.

CLERC-GALLAUDET WEEK. Dec 6–12. Week in which to celebrate the birth anniversaries of Laurent Clerc (Dec 26, 1785) and Thomas Hopkins Gallaudet (Dec 10, 1787). Clerc and Gallaudet pioneered education for the deaf in the US. Library activities will include a lecture on Clerc and Gallaudet and their contemporaries, storytelling for all ages and a display of books, videos, magazines, newspapers and posters. For info: National Literary Society of the Deaf, 2930 Craiglawn Rd, Silver Spring, MD 20904-1816. Web: www.folda.net/nlsd.

ECUADOR: DAY OF QUITO: 475th FOUNDING ANNIVERSARY. Dec 6. Commemorates founding of city of Quito by Spaniards in 1534.

EISENSTAEDT, ALFRED: BIRTH ANNIVERSARY. Dec 6, 1898. American photojournalist Alfred Eisenstaedt was born at Dirschau, Prussia. One of the greatest photojournalists in US history, he is best known for his 86 photos that were used on covers of *Life* magazine, including the iconic image of a sailor kissing a nurse in New York's Times Square at the end of WWII. He died Aug 23, 1995, at Martha's Vineyard, MA.

EVERGLADES NATIONAL PARK ESTABLISHED: ANNIVERSARY. Dec 6, 1947. Part of vast marshland area on southern Florida peninsula, originally authorized May 30, 1934, was established as a national park.

FINLAND: INDEPENDENCE DAY. Dec 6. National holiday. Declaration of independence from Russia in 1917.

GERALD FORD SWEARING-IN AS VICE PRESIDENT: ANNIVERSARY. Dec 6, 1973. Gerald Ford was sworn in as vice president under Richard Nixon, following the resignation of Spiro Agnew who pled no contest to a charge of income tax evasion. See also "Agnew, Spiro Theodore: Birth Anniversary" (Nov 9) and "Ford, Gerald Rudolph: Birth Anniversary" (July 14).

GERSHWIN, IRA: BIRTH ANNIVERSARY. Dec 6, 1896. Pulitzer Prize–winning American lyricist and author who collaborated with his brother, George, and with many other composers. Among his Broadway successes: *Lady Be Good, Funny Face, Strike Up the Band* and such songs as "The Man I Love," "Someone to Watch Over Me" and "I Got Rhythm." Born at New York, NY, he died at Beverly Hills, CA, Aug 17, 1983.

HALIFAX, NOVA SCOTIA, DESTROYED: ANNIVERSARY. Dec 6, 1917. More than 1,650 people were killed at Halifax when the Norwegian ship *Imo* plowed into the French munitions ship *Mont Blanc. Mont Blanc* was loaded with 4,000 tons of TNT, 2,300 tons of picric acid, 61 tons of other explosives and a deck of highly flammable benzene, which ignited and touched off an explosion. In addition to those killed, 1,028 were injured. A tidal wave caused by the explosion washed much of the city out to sea.

KILMER, JOYCE (ALFRED): BIRTH ANNIVERSARY. Dec 6, 1886. American poet most famous for his poem "Trees," which was published in 1913, was born at New Brunswick, NJ. Kilmer was killed in action near Ourcy, France, in WWI, July 30, 1918. The Army's Camp Kilmer in New Jersey was named for him.

LEVINE, CHARLES A.: DEATH ANNIVERSARY. Dec 6, 1991. Charles A. Levine, whose efforts to beat Charles Lindbergh across the Atlantic by plane were stymied by a lawsuit, nevertheless became the first air passenger to cross the Atlantic Ocean. Levine's 225-horsepower plane, *The Columbia*, was grounded when one of his copilots filed a suit hours after Lindbergh took off from Roosevelt Field. Not to be overshadowed by Lindbergh's success, Levine announced that his flight, leaving June 4, 1927, would fly beyond Paris to Berlin, with himself as a passenger. Piloted by Clarence Chamberlin, the plane exhausted its fuel and landed at Eisleben, Germany, June 6, 100 miles short of his goal. The flight set a new record of 3,911 miles in 43 hours of nonstop flight, besting Lindbergh by approximately 300 miles. Levine was born at North Adams, MA, in 1897, and died at Washington, DC.

MINER'S DAY. Dec 6. In appreciation, honor and remembrance of the accomplishments and sacrifices of miners in the state of West Virginia. To provide a sober reminder of the risks that miners are routinely exposed to in their work and to set aside some time on this day for quiet contemplation to honor those brave miners who have perished in our mines. A resolution designating Dec 6 annually as Miner's Day was adopted by both the House of Delegates and the Senate of the State of West Virginia in 2006. For info: Creed Holden, 301 Nuzum Place, Fairmont, WV 26554. Phone: (304) 366-0008. E-mail: creed.holden@gmail.com. Web: www.minersday.org.

MISSOURI EARTHQUAKES: ANNIVERSARY. Dec 6, 1811. New Madrid, MO. Most prolonged series of earthquakes in US history occurred not in California, but in the Midwest. Lasted until Feb 12, 1812. There were few deaths because of the sparse population. These were the most severe earthquakes in the contiguous US; those higher on the Richter scale have all occurred in Alaska.

NATIONAL PAWNBROKERS DAY. Dec 6. Celebrated on St. Nicholas Day, the patron saint of pawnbroking. Designed to acknowledge the valuable lending and retail services the pawnbroker provides his or her clientele. For info: Michael Goldstein, Empire Loan, 1130 Washington St, Boston, MA 02118. Phone: (617) 423-9366.

ROBERT-HOUDIN, JEAN EUGÈNE: ANNIVERSARY. Dec 6, 1805. The founder of modern magic who was the first to use electricity in his illusions. Robert-Houdin also popularized wearing evening attire (instead of wizard's robes) on stage. He inspired scores of younger magicians, including Harry Houdini, whose stage name saluted Robert-Houdin's name. Born at Blois, France, Robert-Houdin died at St. Gervais, France, on June 13, 1871.

SAINT NICHOLAS DAY. Dec 6. One of the most venerated saints of both Eastern and Western Christian churches, of whose life little is known, except that he was Bishop of Myra (in what is today's Turkey) in the fourth century, and that from early times he has been especially noted for his charity. Santa Claus and the presentation of gifts is said to derive from St. Nicholas.

SPAIN: CONSTITUTION DAY. Dec 6. National holiday. Commemorates the voters' approval of a new constitution in 1978.

"TALENT SCOUTS" TV PREMIERE: ANNIVERSARY. Dec 6, 1948. Officially titled "Arthur Godfrey's Talent Scouts," this TV show was created when host Arthur Godfrey took his radio show to TV in 1948. On this talent show, celebrity guests introduced amateur and young professional acts. It was a weekly show until 1958. For several years beginning in 1960 it was a summer replacement series called "Celebrity Talent Scouts" and "Hollywood Talent Scouts." Hosts included Sam Levenson, Jim Backus, Merv Griffin and Art Linkletter. Pat Boone, Shari Lewis and the McGuire Sisters got their start here.

THIRTEENTH AMENDMENT TO THE US CONSTITUTION RATIFIED: ANNIVERSARY. Dec 6, 1865. The 13th Amendment to the Constitution was ratified, abolishing slavery in the US. "Neither slavery nor involuntary servitude, save as a punishment for crime whereof the party shall have been duly convicted, shall exist within the United States, or any place subject to their jurisdiction." This amendment was proclaimed Dec 18, 1865. The 13th, 14th and 15th amendments are considered the Civil War Amendments. See also: "Emancipation Proclamation: Anniversary" (Jan 1) for Lincoln's proclamation freeing slaves in the rebelling states.

XTERRA TRAIL RUNNING WORLD CHAMPIONSHIP. Dec 6. Kualoa Ranch, Oahu, HI. The XTERRA Trail Run Series boasts over 50 events across the country with runs ranging from 5k to 25k. These extreme, off-road trail runs give runners the chance to prove their skills against a variety of terrains. From calf-burning hills to slippery, mud-covered paths athletes will face the ultimate test of endurance. This race features off-road 5k, 10k and half-marathon distance trail runs on the beautiful island of Oahu. For info: Ann Mickey, XTERRA Trail Run, 720 Iwilei Rd #290, Honolulu, HI 96817. Phone: (877) 751-8880. E-mail: info@xterraplanet.com. Web: www.xterratrailrun.com.

December 2009

S	M	T	W	T	F	S
		1	2	3	4	5
6	7	8	9	10	11	12
13	14	15	16	17	18	19
20	21	22	23	24	25	26
27	28	29	30	31		

BIRTHDAYS TODAY

Dave Brubeck, 89, jazz musician, born Concord, CA, Dec 6, 1920.

Macy Gray, 40, singer, born Canton, OH, Dec 6, 1969.

Thomas Hulce, 56, actor (*Amadeus, Parenthood*), born Plymouth, MI, Dec 6, 1953.

James Naughton, 64, actor (*The Paper Chase, The Good Mother*; stage: *Long Day's Journey into Night*), born Middletown, CT, Dec 6, 1945.

Craig Newmark, 57, founder of craigslist, born Morristown, NJ, Dec 6, 1952.

Janine Turner, 47, actress ("Northern Exposure," *Cliffhanger*), born Lincoln, NE, Dec 6, 1962.

JoBeth Williams, 56, actress (*The Ponder Heart, The Big Chill*), born Houston, TX, Dec 6, 1953.

Steven Wright, 54, comedian, born New York, NY, Dec 6, 1955.

December 7 — Monday

DAY 341 — **24 REMAINING**

ARMENIAN EARTHQUAKE OF 1988: ANNIVERSARY. Dec 7, 1988. An earthquake measuring 6.9 on the Richter scale rocked the Soviet province of Armenia killing upward of 60,000 people. Many of the deaths were blamed on poor construction practices as many homes had been made of adobe, mud or stones; had unreinforced masonry or were prefabricated structures made of loosely connected concrete slabs. In the quake's aftermath, Soviet President Mikhail Gorbachev cut short his trip to the US to fly home and head the massive worldwide relief efforts.

CATHER, WILLA SIBERT: BIRTH ANNIVERSARY. Dec 7, 1873. American author born at Winchester, VA. Died at New York, NY, Apr 24, 1947. Best known for her novels about the development of early 20th-century American life, such as *O Pioneers!* and *My Ántonia*. She won a Pulitzer Prize in 1922 for her book *One of Ours*.

CENTRAL AFRICAN REPUBLIC: NATIONAL DAY OBSERVED. Dec 7. Commemorates Proclamation of the Republic Dec 1, 1958. Usually observed on the first Monday in December.

CHAPIN, HARRY: BIRTH ANNIVERSARY. Dec 7, 1942. Folksinger/songwriter Harry Chapin was one of only five songwriters to receive the Special Congressional Gold Medal for his devotion to the issue of hunger throughout the world. Born at New York, NY, he was killed in a car accident July 16, 1981, at Long Island, NY.

CÔTE D'IVOIRE: COMMEMORATION DAY. Dec 7. National holiday. Commemorates the death of the first president, Félix Houphouët-Boigny, in 1993.

DELAWARE RATIFIES CONSTITUTION: ANNIVERSARY. Dec 7, 1787. Delaware became the first state to ratify the proposed Constitution. It did so by unanimous vote.

ELECTRIC LIGHT PARADE. Dec 7. Downtown Lovington, NM. Christmas shines in Lovington with more than 60 entries including floats, motor homes, cars and motorcycles decorated with Christmas lights. Annually, early December. Est attendance: 2,000. For info: Lovington Chamber of Commerce, 201 S Main St, Lovington, NM 88260. Phone: (505) 396-5311. E-mail: jjohnson@lovingtoncoc.org. Web: www.lovingtoncoc.org.

NATIONAL FIRE SAFETY COUNCIL: 30th FOUNDING ANNIVERSARY. Dec 7, 1979. Founded to promote fire and burn prevention and life safety awareness. Council distributes comprehensive material to children and adults through local fire departments and the Council's mascot, Firepup®. For info: Natl Fire Safety Council Inc, PO Box 378, Michigan Center, MI 49254-0378. Phone: (517) 764-2811. E-mail: tlusby@nfcd.org.

✦ **NATIONAL PEARL HARBOR REMEMBRANCE DAY.** Dec 7.

PEARL HARBOR DAY: ANNIVERSARY. Dec 7, 1941. At 7:55 AM (local time) Dec 7, 1941, "a date that will live in infamy," nearly 200 Japanese aircraft attacked Pearl Harbor, Hawaii, long considered the US "Gibraltar of the Pacific." The raid, which lasted little more than one hour, left nearly 3,000 dead. Nearly the entire US Pacific Fleet was at anchor there and few ships escaped damage. Several were sunk or disabled, while 200 US aircraft on the ground were destroyed. The attack on Pearl Harbor brought about immediate US entry into WWII, a declaration of war being requested by President Franklin D. Roosevelt and approved by the Congress Dec 8, 1941.

SPACE MILESTONE: *APOLLO 17* (US). Dec 7, 1972. Launched this date with three-man crew—Eugene A. Cernan, Harrison H. Schmidt, Ronald E. Evans—who explored the moon, Dec 11–14. Lunar landing module named *Challenger*. Pacific splashdown, Dec 19. This was the last manned mission to the moon.

SPACE MILESTONE: *GALILEO* (US). Dec 7, 1995. Launched Oct 18, 1989, by the space shuttle *Atlantis*, the spacecraft *Galileo* entered the orbit of Jupiter after a six-year journey. It has been orbiting Jupiter ever since, sending out probes to study three of its moons. Organic compounds, the ingredients of life, were found on them. On May 25, 2001, it passed within 86 miles of Callisto, one of Jupiter's moons.

TUSSAUD, MARIE GROSHOLTZ: BIRTH ANNIVERSARY. Dec 7, 1761. Creator of Madame Tussaud's waxwork museum, born at Strasbourg, France. Some of the wax figures she created are still on view at Madame Tussaud's at London. She died at London, Apr 15, 1850.

UNITED NATIONS: INTERNATIONAL CIVIL AVIATION DAY. Dec 7. On Dec 6, 1996, the General Assembly proclaimed Dec 7 as International Civil Aviation Day. On Dec 7, 1944, the Convention on International Civil Aviation, which established the International Civil Aviation Organization, was signed. For info: United Nations, Dept of Public Info, New York, NY 10017. Web: www.un.org.

BIRTHDAYS TODAY

Johnny Lee Bench, 62, Hall of Fame baseball player, born Oklahoma City, OK, Dec 7, 1947.

Larry Joe Bird, 53, Hall of Fame basketball player, former coach, born West Baden, IN, Dec 7, 1956.

Ellen Burstyn, 77, actress (Oscar for *Alice Doesn't Live Here Anymore; Same Time, Next Year; Requiem for a Dream*), born Edna Rae Gilhooley at Detroit, MI, Dec 7, 1932.

Thad Cochran, 72, US Senator (R, Mississippi), born Pontotoc, MS, Dec 7, 1937.

Susan M. Collins, 57, US Senator (R, Maine), born Caribou, ME, Dec 7, 1952.

Edd Hall, 51, announcer ("The Tonight Show with Jay Leno"), born Boston, MA, Dec 7, 1958.

C. Thomas Howell, 43, actor ("Two Marriages," *Soul Man, Tank*), born Los Angeles, CA, Dec 7, 1966.

Tino Martinez, 42, former baseball player, born Tampa, FL, Dec 7, 1967.

John Terry, 29, soccer player, born Barking, England, Dec 7, 1980.

Tom Waits, 60, singer, songwriter ("I Never Talk to Strangers"), actor (*Down by Law, Short Cuts*), born Pomona, CA, Dec 7, 1949.

Eli Wallach, 94, actor (*The Tiger Makes Out*; Emmy for "The Poppy Is Also a Flower"), born New York, NY, Dec 7, 1915.

December 8 — Tuesday

DAY 342 | **23 REMAINING**

AMERICA ENTERS WORLD WAR II: ANNIVERSARY. Dec 8, 1941. One day after the surprise Japanese attack on Pearl Harbor, Congress declared war against Japan and the US entered WWII.

AMERICAN FEDERATION OF LABOR (AFL) FOUNDED: ANNIVERSARY. Dec 8, 1886. Originally founded at Pittsburgh, PA, as the Federation of Organized Trades and Labor Unions of the United States and Canada in 1881, the union was reorganized in 1886 under the name American Federation of Labor (AFL). The AFL was dissolved as a separate entity in 1955 when it merged with the Congress of Industrial Organizations to form the AFL-CIO. See also: "AFL-CIO Founded: Anniversary (Dec 5)."

CHINESE NATIONALISTS MOVE TO FORMOSA: 60th ANNIVERSARY. Dec 8, 1949. The government of Chiang Kai-Shek moved to Formosa (Taiwan) after being driven out of Mainland China by the Communists led by Mao Tse-Tung.

CLUTE'S CHRISTMAS IN THE PARK. Dec 8–11. Clute Municipal Park, Clute, TX. A Christmas event with nightly entertainment, Santa's Land, a beautifully decorated Christmas tree forest and a marshmallow roasting pit. Food and crafts. Great family fun for all ages; from 6:00–8:30 PM. Est attendance: 4,500. For info: Clute Parks and Recreation, PO Box 997, Clute, TX 77531. Phone: (800) 371-2971 or (979) 265-8392. Fax: (979) 265-8767. E-mail: buzz@mosquitofestival.com.

DAVIS, SAMMY, JR: BIRTH ANNIVERSARY. Dec 8, 1925. Born at New York, NY, Sammy Davis, Jr, was the son of vaudevillians and first appeared on the stage at the age of four. He made his first film appearance in *Rufus Jones for President* in 1931. He joined the Will Mastin Trio, a song-and-dance team popular on the night club circuit; as Davis matured, his singing, dancing and impersonations became the center of the act. Davis began performing on his own in the 1950s, headlining club engagements, appearing on television variety shows and making numerous records. His Broadway debut came in 1956 in the hit musical *Mr Wonderful*, and in the late '50s and early '60s he starred in a number of films, including a series with Frank Sinatra and the Rat Pack. Davis died at Los Angeles, CA, May 16, 1990.

DURANT, WILLIAM CRAPO: BIRTH ANNIVERSARY. Dec 8, 1861. "Billy" Durant, a leading producer of carriages at Flint, MI; promoter of the Buick car; cofounder of Chevrolet and founder, in 1908, of General Motors. He lost, regained and again lost control of GM, after which he founded Durant Motors, went bankrupt in the Depression and operated a Flint bowling alley in his last working years. Durant was born at Boston, MA, and died at New York, NY, Mar 18, 1947.

FEAST OF THE IMMACULATE CONCEPTION. Dec 8. Roman Catholic Holy Day of Obligation. A public holiday in Nicaragua.

FIRST STEP TOWARD A NUCLEAR-FREE WORLD: ANNIVERSARY. Dec 8, 1987. The former Soviet Union and the US signed a treaty at Washington eliminating medium-range and shorter-range missiles. This was the first treaty completely eliminating two entire classes of nuclear arms. These missiles, with a range of 500 to 5,500 kilometers, were to be scrapped under strict supervision within three years of the signing.

GUAM: LADY OF CAMARIN DAY. Dec 8. Declared a legal holiday by Guam legislature, Mar 2, 1971.

HOBAN, JAMES: DEATH ANNIVERSARY. Dec 8, 1831. Irish-born architect who designed the US President's Executive Mansion, later known as the White House. He was born at Callan, County Kilkenny, Ireland, in 1762 (exact date unknown) and died at Washington, DC. The cornerstone for the White House, Washington's oldest public building, was laid in 1792.

JOHN LENNON SHOT: ANNIVERSARY. Dec 8, 1980. On this date deranged gunman Mark David Chapman shot and killed rock star John Lennon outside his apartment building as he returned from a recording session. The death of the former Beatle, who was an international peace activist, shocked the world. His widow, Yoko Ono, asked for 10 minutes of silence at 2 PM, EST on the following Sunday, Dec 14, and many US and international radio stations observed it. See also: "Lennon, John: Birth Anniversary" (Oct 9).

MOON PHASE: LAST QUARTER. Dec 8. Moon enters Last Quarter phase at 7:13 PM, EST.

MORRISON, JIM: BIRTH ANNIVERSARY. Dec 8, 1943. Songwriter, poet, lead singer of The Doors, Jim Morrison is considered to be one of the fathers of contemporary rock. The bacchic Morrison, known as "The Lizard King," brought avant-garde theatrics to his musical performances and mystical influences to his songs. Born at Melbourne, FL, and died at Paris, France, July 3, 1971.

NAFTA SIGNED: ANNIVERSARY. Dec 8, 1993. President Clinton signed the North American Free Trade Agreement, which cut tariffs and eliminated other trade barriers among the US, Canada and Mexico. The agreement went into effect Jan 1, 1994.

RIVERA, DIEGO: BIRTH ANNIVERSARY. Dec 8, 1886. Mexican painter whose murals became center of political controversy, born at Guanajuato, Mexico. Died in his studio at San Angel, near Mexico City, Nov 25, 1957.

SEGAR, ELZIE CRISLER: BIRTH ANNIVERSARY. Dec 8, 1894. Popeye creator Elzie Crisler Segar was born at Chester, IL. Originally called *Thimble Theater*, the comic strip that came to be known as *Popeye* had the unusual format of a one-act play in cartoon form. Centered on the Oyl family, especially daughter Olive, the strip introduced a new central character in 1929. A one-eyed sailor with bulging muscles, Popeye became the strip's star attraction almost immediately. Popeye made it to the silver screen in animated form and in 1980 became a movie with Robin Williams playing the lead. Segar died Oct 13, 1938, at Santa Monica, CA.

SOVIET UNION DISSOLVED: ANNIVERSARY. Dec 8, 1991. The Union of Soviet Socialist Republics (USSR) ceased to exist, as the republics of Russia, Byelorussia and Ukraine signed an agreement at Minsk, Byelorussia, creating the Commonwealth of Independent States. The remaining republics, with the exception of Georgia, joined in the new commonwealth as it began the slow and arduous process of removing the yoke of Communism and dealing with strong separatist and nationalistic movements within the various republics.

December 2009	S	M	T	W	T	F	S
			1	2	3	4	5
	6	7	8	9	10	11	12
	13	14	15	16	17	18	19
	20	21	22	23	24	25	26
	27	28	29	30	31		

TAKE A NEW YEAR'S RESOLUTION TO STOP SMOKING (TANYRSS). Dec 8–Feb 10, 2010. 21st annual. To educate consumers/patients, health care professionals to take a New Year's resolution to stop smoking. Kit materials available for $15. For info: Fred Mayer, Pharmacists Planning Service, Inc, c/o Pharmacy Council on Tobacco Dependence (PCTD), 101 Lucas Valley Rd, Ste 382, San Rafael, CA 94903. E-mail: ppsi@aol.com. Web: www.ppsinc.org.

THURBER, JAMES: BIRTH ANNIVERSARY. Dec 8, 1894. James Grover Thurber, American humorist and artist, long-time contributor to the *New Yorker*, born at Columbus, OH. Died at New York, NY, Nov 2, 1961.

UZBEKISTAN: CONSTITUTION DAY. Dec 8. National holiday. Commemorates the constitution of 1991.

WHITNEY, ELI: BIRTH ANNIVERSARY. Dec 8, 1765. Inventor of the cotton gin, born at Westboro, MA. Died at New Haven, CT, Jan 8, 1825.

BIRTHDAYS TODAY

Gregg Allman, 62, singer ("Ramblin' Man"), actor (*Rush*), born Nashville, TN, Dec 8, 1947.

Kim Basinger, 56, actress (Oscar for *L.A. Confidential*; *Batman, The Natural*), born Athens, GA, Dec 8, 1953.

Gordon Arthur "Red" Berenson, 68, former hockey player and coach, born Regina, SK, Canada, Dec 8, 1941.

David Carradine, 69, actor (*Kill Bill*, "Kung Fu"), born Hollywood, CA, Dec 8, 1940.

Ann Coulter, 48, political commentator, author (*Slander: Liberal Lies About the American Right*), born New Canaan, CT, Dec 8, 1961.

James Galway, 70, flutist, born Belfast, Northern Ireland, Dec 8, 1939.

Jeff George, 42, former football player, born Indianapolis, IN, Dec 8, 1967.

Teri Hatcher, 45, actress ("Desperate Housewives," "Lois & Clark"), born Sunnyvale, CA, Dec 8, 1964.

Dwight Howard, 24, basketball player, born Atlanta, GA, Dec 8, 1985.

James MacArthur, 72, actor ("Hawaii Five-O"), born Los Angeles, CA, Dec 8, 1937.

Dominic Monaghan, 33, actor (*The Lord of the Rings* trilogy, "Lost"), born Berlin, Germany, Dec 8, 1976.

Mike Mussina, 41, baseball player, born Williamsport, PA, Dec 8, 1968.

Sinead O'Connor, 43, singer, songwriter, born Dublin, Ireland, Dec 8, 1966.

Maximilian Schell, 79, actor (*Deep Impact, Topkapi, Judgment at Nuremberg*), producer, born Vienna, Austria, Dec 8, 1930.

Ian Somerhalder, 31, actor ("Lost," "Smallville"), born Covington, LA, Dec 8, 1978.

Mary Woronov, 63, actress (*Rock 'n' Roll High School, Eating Raoul*), born Brooklyn, NY, Dec 8, 1946.

December 9 — Wednesday

DAY 343 — 22 REMAINING

AMERICA'S FIRST FORMAL CREMATION: ANNIVERSARY. Dec 9, 1792. The first formal cremation of a human body in America took place near Charleston, SC. Henry Laurens, Colonial statesman and signer of the Treaty of Paris ending the Revolutionary War, in his will provided: "I do solemnly enjoin it on my son, as an indispensable duty, that as soon as he conveniently can, after my decease, he cause my body to be wrapped in twelve yards of tow cloth and burned until it be entirely consumed, and then, collecting my bones, deposit them wherever he may think proper." Laurens died Dec 8, 1792, at his plantation and was cremated there.

BIRDSEYE, CLARENCE: BIRTH ANNIVERSARY. Dec 9, 1886. American industrialist who developed a way of deep-freezing foods. He was marketing frozen fish by 1925 and was one of the founders of General Foods Corporation. Born at Brooklyn, NY, he died at New York City, Oct 7, 1956.

FOXX, REDD: BIRTH ANNIVERSARY. Dec 9, 1922. Born John Elroy Sanford at St. Louis, MO, Redd Foxx plied his comedic trade on vaudeville stages, in nightclubs, on television, in films and on record albums. His talents reached a national audience with the TV sitcom "Sanford and Son." He died after collapsing during a rehearsal for a new TV sitcom, "The Royal Family," at Los Angeles, CA, Oct 11, 1991.

GENOCIDE CONVENTION: ANNIVERSARY. Dec 9, 1948. The United Nations General Assembly unanimously approved the Convention on Prevention and Punishment of the Crime of Genocide on Dec 9, 1948. It took effect Jan 12, 1951, when ratification by 20 nations had been completed. President Truman sent it to the US Senate for approval on June 16, 1949; it was supported by presidents Kennedy, Johnson, Nixon, Ford, Carter and Reagan. Thirty-seven years after its submission, and after approval by more than 90 nations, the Senate approved it, Feb 19, 1986, by a vote of 83–11.

HARRIS, JOEL CHANDLER: BIRTH ANNIVERSARY. Dec 9, 1848. American author, creator of the "Uncle Remus" stories, born at Eatonton, GA. Died July 3, 1908, at Atlanta, GA.

HOLIDAY TOUR OF HOMES. Dec 9 (also Dec 11–12, 16, 18–19). Natchitoches, LA. Come join us for the magic and the beauty of Christmas in historic Natchitoches. Christmas will be brought to life this holiday season during the Christmas by Candlelight tour. Each tour day will have three homes on tour. Come join us for this wonderful experience. Admission charge. Est attendance: 2,500. For info: Natchitoches Parish Tourist Commission. Phone: (800) 259-1714. Web: www.natchitoches.net.

HOPPER, GRACE: BIRTH ANNIVERSARY. Dec 9, 1906. Born at New York, NY. When she retired from the US Navy at the age of 79, she was the oldest naval officer ever on active duty. She attained the rank of rear admiral and was a leader in the computer revolution, having developed the computer language COBOL. Grace Hopper died Jan 1, 1992, at Arlington, WV.

KELLY, EMMETT: BIRTH ANNIVERSARY. Dec 9, 1898. American circus clown and entertainer, born at Sedan, KS. Kelly was best known for "Weary Willie," a clown dressed in tattered clothes, with a beard and large nose. Died at Sarasota, FL, Mar 28, 1979.

MILTON, JOHN: BIRTH ANNIVERSARY. Dec 9, 1608. English poet, historian, civil servant and defender of freedom of the press born at Bread Street, Cheapside, London. Considered one of the greatest poets of the English language, second only to William Shakespeare. Author of the great verse epics *Paradise Lost* (1667) and *Paradise Regained* (1671). Died from gout, Nov 8, 1674, at London, England. "No man who knows aught," he wrote, "can be so stupid to deny that all men naturally were born free."

PETRIFIED FOREST NATIONAL PARK ESTABLISHED: ANNIVERSARY. Dec 9, 1962. Arizona's Petrified Forest National Monument, proclaimed Dec 8, 1906, was established as a national park. For further park info: Petrified Forest Natl Park, Petrified Forest Natl Park, AZ 86028.

SANDYS, EDWIN: BIRTH ANNIVERSARY. Dec 9, 1561. Sir Edwin Sandys, English statesman and one of the founders of the Virginia Colony (treasurer, the Virginia Company, 1619–20), born at Worcestershire, England. Died at Kent, England, in October 1629 (exact date unknown).

TANZANIA: INDEPENDENCE AND REPUBLIC DAY. Dec 9. Tanganyika became independent of Britain in 1961. The republics of Tanganyika and Zanzibar joined to become one state (Apr 27, 1964), renamed (Oct 29, 1964) the United Republic of Tanzania.

BIRTHDAYS TODAY

Joan Armatrading, 59, singer, songwriter (*Me, Myself, I*), born Saint Kitts, West Indies, Dec 9, 1950.

Reiko Aylesworth, 37, actress ("24," "One Life to Live"), born Chicago, IL, Dec 9, 1972.

Beau Bridges, 68, actor ("James Brady Story," *The Fabulous Baker Boys*), born Los Angeles, CA, Dec 9, 1941.

Richard Marvin (Dick) Butkus, 67, Hall of Fame football player, sportscaster, actor, born Chicago, IL, Dec 9, 1942.

Thomas Daschle, 62, former US Senator (D, South Dakota), born Aberdeen, SD, Dec 9, 1947.

Judi Dench, 75, actress (*Mrs Brown, Iris*; Oscar for *Shakespeare in Love*), born York, England, Dec 9, 1934.

Kirk Douglas, 93, actor (*Champion, Lust for Life*), author, born Issur Danielovitch Demsky at Amsterdam, NY, Dec 9, 1916.

David Anthony Higgins, 48, actor ("Ellen," "Malcolm in the Middle"), born Des Moines, IA, Dec 9, 1961.

Felicity Huffman, 47, actress (*Transamerica*, "Desperate Housewives," "Sports Night"), born Bedford, NY, Dec 9, 1962.

Thomas O. Kite, Jr, 60, golfer, born Austin, TX, Dec 9, 1949.

Joe Lando, 48, actor ("Dr. Quinn, Medicine Woman"), born Chicago, IL, Dec 9, 1961.

John Malkovich, 56, actor (*Eragon, Ripley's Game, The Killing Fields*), filmmaker, born Christopher, IL, Dec 9, 1953.

Dina Merrill, 84, actress (*Desk Set, Operation Petticoat*), born New York, NY, Dec 9, 1925.

Jesse Metcalfe, 31, actor ("Desperate Housewives," "Passions"), born Waterford, CT, Dec 9, 1978.

Michael Nouri, 64, actor ("Search for Tomorrow," *Flashdance*), born Washington, DC, Dec 9, 1945.

Donny Osmond, 52, actor, singer, born Ogden, UT, Dec 9, 1957.

Dick Van Patten, 81, actor ("Eight Is Enough," "Mama"), born Richmond Hill, NY, Dec 9, 1928.

December 10 — Thursday

DAY 344 — 21 REMAINING

DEWEY, MELVIL: BIRTH ANNIVERSARY. Dec 10, 1851. American librarian and inventor of the Dewey decimal book classification system was born at Adams Center, NY. Born Melville Louis Kossuth Dewey, he was an advocate of spelling reform, urged use of the metric system and was interested in many other education reforms. Dewey died at Highlands County, FL, Dec 26, 1931.

DICKINSON, EMILY: BIRTH ANNIVERSARY. Dec 10, 1830. One of America's greatest poets, Emily Dickinson was born at Amherst, MA. She was reclusive, mysterious and frail in health. Seven of her poems were published during her life, but after her death her sister, Lavinia, discovered almost 2,000 more poems written on the backs of envelopes and other scraps of paper locked in her bureau. They were published gradually, over 50 years, beginning in 1890. She died May 15, 1886, at Amherst, MA. The little-known Emily Dickinson who was born, lived and died at Amherst now is recognized as one of the most original poets of the English-speaking world.

FIRST GRAND OLE OPRY BROADCAST: ANNIVERSARY. Dec 10, 1927. Grand Ole Opry made its first radio broadcast from Nashville, TN.

FIRST US HEAVYWEIGHT CHAMP DEFEATED IN ENGLAND: ANNIVERSARY. Dec 10, 1810. Tom Molineaux, the first unofficial heavyweight champion of the US, was a freed slave from Virginia. He was beaten in the 40th round by Tom Cribb, the English champion, in a boxing match at Copthall Common at London.

FIRST US SCIENTIST RECEIVES NOBEL PRIZE: ANNIVERSARY. Dec 10, 1907. University of Chicago professor Albert Michelson, eminent physicist known for his research on the speed of light and optics became the first US scientist to receive the Nobel Prize.

GALLAUDET, THOMAS HOPKINS: BIRTH ANNIVERSARY. Dec 10, 1787. A hearing educator who, with Laurent Clerc, founded the first public school for deaf people, Connecticut Asylum for the Education and Instruction of Deaf and Dumb Persons (now the American School for the Deaf), at Hartford, CT, Apr 15, 1817. Gallaudet was born at Philadelphia, PA, and died Sept 9, 1851, at Hartford, CT.

✦ **HUMAN RIGHTS DAY.** Dec 10. Presidential Proclamation 2866, of Dec 6, 1949, covers all succeeding years. Customarily issued as "Bill of Rights Day, Human Rights Day and Week."

✦ **HUMAN RIGHTS WEEK.** Dec 10–17. Presidential Proclamation issued since 1958 for the week of Dec 10–17, except in 1986. See also: "Human Rights Day" (Dec 10) and "Bill of Rights Day" (Dec 15).

JANE ADDAMS DAY IN ILLINOIS. Dec 10. A day set aside to celebrate Jane Addams' life by the state of Illinois—on the anniversary of Addams receiving the first Nobel Peace Prize ever awarded to an American woman. Illinois honors Jane Addams' memory with a commemorative holiday to observe her lifelong commitment to making the city of Chicago, the state of Illinois and the entire world a better place. Annually, Dec 10. For info: For info: Jane Addams Hull-House Museum, 800 S Halsted St, Chicago, IL 60607. Phone: (312) 413-5353. Fax: (312) 413-2092. Web: www.janeaddamsday.org or www.hullhousemuseum.org.

LAMOUR, DOROTHY: 95th BIRTH ANNIVERSARY. Dec 10, 1914. Singer, actress (*The Hurricane, Road to Singapore*), born New Orleans, LA. Died Sept 22, 1996, at Los Angeles, CA.

"THE MIGHTY MOUSE PLAYHOUSE" TV PREMIERE: ANNIVERSARY. Dec 10, 1955. An all-time favorite of the Saturday-morning crowd (including adults). CBS had a hit with their pint-sized cartoon character Mighty Mouse, who was a tongue-in-cheek version of Superman. The show had other feature cartoons such as "The Adventures of Gandy Goose."

MISSISSIPPI: ADMISSION DAY: ANNIVERSARY. Dec 10. Became 20th state in 1817.

NOBEL PRIZE AWARDS CEREMONIES. Dec 10. Oslo, Norway and Stockholm, Sweden. Alfred Nobel, Swedish chemist and inventor of dynamite who died in 1896, provided in his will that income from his $9 million estate should be used for annual prizes—to be awarded to people who are judged to have made the most valuable contributions to the good of humanity. The Nobel Peace Prize is awarded by a committee of the Norwegian parliament and the presentation is made at the Oslo City Hall. Five other prizes, for physics, chemistry, medicine, literature and economics, are presented in a ceremony at Stockholm, Sweden. Both ceremonies traditionally are held on the anniversary of the death of Alfred Nobel. First awarded in 1901, the current value of each prize is about $1,000,000. See also "Nobel, Alfred Bernhard: Birth Anniversary" (Oct 21).

NORTON, MARY: BIRTH ANNIVERSARY. Dec 10, 1903. British author Mary Norton was born at London, England. An author of children's books, she is best known for *Bedknob and Broomstick* (1957). She died Aug 29, 1992, at Hartland, England.

RALPH BUNCHE AWARDED NOBEL PEACE PRIZE: ANNIVERSARY. Dec 10, 1950. Dr. Ralph Johnson Bunche became the first black man awarded the Nobel Peace Prize. Bunche was awarded the prize for his efforts in mediation between Israel and neighboring Arab states in 1949.

RED CLOUD: 100th DEATH ANNIVERSARY. Dec 10, 1909. Sioux Indian chief Red Cloud was born in 1822 (exact date unknown), near North Platte, NE. A courageous leader and defender of Indian rights, Red Cloud was the son of Lone Man and Walks as She Thinks. His unrelenting determination caused US abandonment of the Bozeman trail and of three forts that interfered with Indian hunting grounds. Red Cloud died at Pine Ridge, SD.

SPACE MILESTONE: *SOYUZ 26* (USSR). Dec 10, 1977. Launched this date with cosmonauts Yuri Romanenko and Georgi Grechko who linked it with *Salyut 6* space station on Dec 11, after the unsuccessful attempt by *Soyuz 25* earlier that year. Returned to Earth in *Soyuz 27*, Mar 16, 1978, after record-setting 96 days in space.

THAILAND: CONSTITUTION DAY. Dec 10. National holiday. Commemorates the constitution of 1932, the nation's first.

THOMASVILLE'S VICTORIAN CHRISTMAS. Dec 10–11. Thomasville, GA. Downtown Thomasville relives Christmas past as it celebrates the Victorian era of the late 1800s. Costumed strollers and carolers, horse-drawn carriages and colorful characters from the past fill the streets of downtown. Victorian-clad merchants welcome shoppers with hot cider and confections and street vendors offer Christmas delicacies. Free—wonderful family event. Est attendance: 30,000. For info: Thomasville Victorian Christmas, Thomasville Main Street, PO Box 1540, Thomasville, GA 31799. Phone: (229) 227-7020. E-mail: felicia@thomasville.org. Web: www.downtownthomasville.com.

TREATY OF PARIS ENDS SPANISH-AMERICAN WAR: ANNIVERSARY. Dec 10, 1898. Following the conclusion of the Spanish-American War in 1898, American and Spanish ambassadors met at Paris, France, to negotiate a treaty. Under the terms of this treaty, Spain granted the US the Philippine Islands and the islands of Guam and Puerto Rico and agreed to withdraw from Cuba. Senatorial debate over the treaty centered on the US's move toward imperialism by acquiring the Philippines. A vote was taken Feb 6, 1899, and the treaty passed by a one-vote margin. President William McKinley signed the treaty Feb 10, 1899.

UNITED NATIONS: HUMAN RIGHTS DAY. Dec 10. Official United Nations observance day. Date is the anniversary of adoption of the "Universal Declaration of Human Rights" in 1948. The Declaration sets forth basic rights and fundamental freedoms to which all men and women everywhere in the world are entitled. For info: United Nations, Dept of Public Info, New York, NY 10017. E-mail: inquiries@un.org. Web: www.un.org.

December 2009

S	M	T	W	T	F	S
		1	2	3	4	5
6	7	8	9	10	11	12
13	14	15	16	17	18	19
20	21	22	23	24	25	26
27	28	29	30	31		

 BIRTHDAYS TODAY

Rod Blagojevich, 53, Governor of Illinois (D), born Chicago, IL, Dec 10, 1956.

Kenneth Branagh, 49, actor (*Shackleton*), director (*Hamlet, Henry V*), born Belfast, Northern Ireland, Dec 10, 1960.

Susan Dey, 57, model, actress ("The Partridge Family," "LA Law,"), born Pekin, IL, Dec 10, 1952.

Harold Gould, 86, actor (*Freaky Friday, The Sting*), born Schenectady, NY, Dec 10, 1923.

Gloria Loring, 63, singer, actress ("Days of Our Lives"), born New York, NY, Dec 10, 1946.

December 11 — Friday

DAY 345 **20 REMAINING**

BUELL, MARJORIE H.: BIRTH ANNIVERSARY. Dec 11, 1904. Cartoonist, creator of comic strip character Little Lulu, Marjorie Buell was considered a pioneer for creating a female character who outsmarted the neighborhood boys. She was born at Philadelphia, PA, and died May 30, 1993, at Elyria, OH.

BURKINA FASO: NATIONAL DAY. Dec 11. Gained independence within the French community, 1958.

CANNON, ANNIE JUMP: BIRTH ANNIVERSARY. Dec 11, 1863. American astronomer and discoverer of five stars, was born at Dover, DE. Author and winner of the National Academy of Science Draper Medal, she died at Cambridge, MA, Apr 13, 1941.

EDWARD VIII ABDICATION: ANNIVERSARY. Dec 11, 1936. Christened Edward Albert Christian George Andrew Patrick David, King Edward VIII was born at Richmond Park, England, on June 12, 1894, and became Prince of Wales in July 1911. He ascended to the English throne upon the death of his father, George V, on Jan 20, 1936, but coronation never took place. He abdicated on Dec 11, 1936, in order to marry "the woman I love," twice-divorced American Wallis Warfield Simpson. They were married in France, June 3, 1937. Edward was named Duke of Windsor by his brother-successor, George VI. The duke died at Paris, May 28, 1972, but was buried in England, near Windsor Castle.

INDIANA: ADMISSION DAY: ANNIVERSARY. Dec 11. Became 19th state in 1816.

LA GUARDIA, FIORELLO HENRY: BIRTH ANNIVERSARY. Dec 11, 1882. Popularly known as the "Little Flower," Fiorello H. La Guardia was not too busy as mayor of New York City to read the "funnies" to radio listeners during the New York newspaper strike. He said of himself: "When I make a mistake it's a beaut!" La Guardia was born at New York, NY, and died there Sept 20, 1947.

"MAGNUM, PI" TV PREMIERE: ANNIVERSARY. Dec 11, 1980. Premiered on CBS television network, starring Tom Selleck, John Hillerman, Roger E. Mosley and Larry Manetti. Each year on this anniversary, "Magnum" fans turn to the international fan organization "Magnum Memorabilia by David Romas" as the center of observances worldwide. For info: David Romas, Magnum Memorabilia, 438 Leroy St, Ferndale, MI 48220. E-mail: ac2942@wayne.edu.

NCAA DIVISION I MEN'S SOCCER CHAMPIONSHIP—THE COLLEGE CUP. Dec 11 & 13. Cary, NC. For info: NCAA, 700 W Washington St, PO Box 6222, Indianapolis, IN 46206-6222. Phone: (317) 917-6222. Web: www.NCAAsports.com.

SUGARLOAF CRAFTS FESTIVAL. Dec 11–13. Dulles Expo Center, Chantilly, VA. This show, now in its fourth year, features more than 350 nationally recognized craft designers and fine artists displaying and selling their original creations. Includes craft demonstrations, live music, specialty foods, children's entertainment, hourly gift certificate drawings, and more. Est attendance: 17,000. For info: Sugarloaf Mountain Works, 200 Orchard Ridge Dr, #215, Gaithersburg, MD 20878. Phone: (800) 210-9900. Fax: (301) 253-9620. Web: www.sugarloafcrafts.com.

UNITED NATIONS: INTERNATIONAL MOUNTAIN DAY. Dec 11. With mountains covering one-quarter of the Earth's land surface and home to 12 percent of the world's population, mountain people are affected by conflict out of all proportion to their numbers and the land they occupy. The UN General Assembly declared Dec 11 International Mountain Day as a result of the successful observance of the UN International Year of Mountains in 2002, which increased global awareness of the importance of mountains, stimulated the establishment of national committees in 78 countries and strengthened alliances through promoting the creation of the Mountain Partnership. For info: United Nations, Dept of Public Info, New York, NY 10017. Web: www.un.org or www.mountainpartnership.org.

UNITED NATIONS: UNICEF ESTABLISHED: ANNIVERSARY. Dec 11, 1946. Anniversary of the establishment by the United Nations General Assembly of the United Nations International Children's Emergency Fund (UNICEF). For info: United Nations, Dept of Public Info, New York, NY 10017. Web: www.unicef.org.

WASSAIL CELEBRATION. Dec 11–13. Woodstock, VT. Activities include a horse rider and carriage parade, Santa comes to town, house tours, concert by The Ten Men's Vocal Choir, caroling, burning the yule log on the Village Green and additional events each year. Est attendance: 5,000. For info: Marketing Director, Woodstock Area Chamber of Commerce, 29 Central St, PO Box 486, Woodstock, VT 05091. Phone: (802) 457-3555 or (888) 496-6378. E-mail: info@woodstockvt.com. Web: www.woodstockvt.com.

 BIRTHDAYS TODAY

Max Baucus, 68, US Senator (D, Montana), born Helena, MT, Dec 11, 1941.

Jay Bell, 44, former baseball player, born Pensacola, FL, Dec 11, 1965.

Mos Def, 36, rapper, actor (*16 Blocks, The Italian Job*), born Dante Terrell Smith at Brooklyn, NY, Dec 11, 1973.

Gary Dourdan, 43, actor ("CSI," *Alien: Resurrection*), born Philadelphia, PA, Dec 11, 1966.

Teri Garr, 60, actress (*Young Frankenstein, Tootsie, The Black Stallion*), born Lakewood, OH, Dec 11, 1949.

David Gates, 69, singer, songwriter, born Tulsa, OK, Dec 11, 1940.

Tom Hayden, 69, journalist, activist, politician, born Royal Oak, MI, Dec 11, 1940.

Jermaine Jackson, 55, singer, musician (Jackson 5), born Gary, IN, Dec 11, 1954.

John F. Kerry, 66, US Senator (D, Massachusetts), born Denver, CO, Dec 11, 1943.

Brenda Lee, 65, singer ("I'm Sorry," "All Alone Am I"), born Brenda Mae Tarpley at Atlanta, GA, Dec 11, 1944.

Donna Mills, 66, actress ("Knots Landing," "Melrose Place"), born Chicago, IL, Dec 11, 1943.

Rita Moreno, 78, singer, actress (Oscar for *West Side Story*; Tony for *The Ritz*), born Hunacao, Puerto Rico, Dec 11, 1931.

Susan Seidelman, 57, filmmaker (*Desperately Seeking Susan, Making Mr Right*), born Philadelphia, PA, Dec 11, 1952.

Rider Strong, 30, actor ("Boy Meets World"), born San Francisco, CA, Dec 11, 1979.

Ken Wahl, 56, actor ("Wiseguy," *The Wanderers, Fort Apache: The Bronx*), born Chicago, IL, Dec 11, 1953.

Curtis Williams, 47, musician, singer (Penguins, "Earth Angel"), born Buffalo, NY, Dec 11, 1962.

December 12 — Saturday

DAY 346 | **19 REMAINING**

AKC/EUKANUBA NATIONAL CHAMPIONSHIP. Dec 12–13. Long Beach Convention Center, Long Beach, CA. At the AKC/Eukanuba National Championship, the top dogs from around the globe compete for the biggest cash prizes offered in the sport. Intense competition, unique awards for breeders and special events for spectators make this the most exciting event in the dog world. For info: American Kennel Club, 260 Madison Ave, New York, NY 10016. Phone: (212) 696-8200. E-mail: invitational@akc.org. Web: www.akc.org.

BONZA BOTTLER DAY™. Dec 12. To celebrate when the number of the day is the same as the number of the month. Bonza Bottler Day™ is an excuse to have a party at least once a month. For more information see Jan 1. For info: Gail M. Berger, 14 Fernwood Dr, Taylors, SC 29687. E-mail: bonza@bonzabottlerday.com. Web: www.bonzabottlerday.com.

CHANUKAH. Dec 12–19. Feast of Lights or Feast of Dedication. Festival lasting eight days commemorates victory of Maccabees over Syrians (165 BC) and rededication of Temple of Jerusalem. Begins on Hebrew calendar date Kislev 25, 5770. Began at sundown on Dec 11.

DAY OF OUR LADY OF GUADALUPE. Dec 12. The legend of Guadalupe tells how in December 1531, an Indian, Juan Diego, saw the Virgin Mother on a hill near Mexico City, who instructed him to go to the bishop and have him build a shrine to her on the site of the vision. After his request was initially rebuffed, the Virgin Mother appeared to Juan Diego three days later. She instructed him to pick roses growing on a stony and barren hillside nearby and take them to the bishop as proof. Although flowers do not normally bloom in December, Juan Diego found the roses and took them to the bishop. As he opened his mantle to drop the roses on the floor, an image of the Virgin Mary appeared among them. The bishop built the sanctuary as instructed. Our Lady of Guadalupe became the patroness of Mexico City and by 1746 was the patron saint of all New Spain and by 1910 of all Latin America.

FIRST BLACK SERVES IN US HOUSE OF REPRESENTATIVES: ANNIVERSARY. Dec 12, 1870. Joseph Hayne Rainey of Georgetown, SC, was sworn in as the first black to serve in the US House of Representatives. Rainey filled the seat of Benjamin Franklin Whittemore, which had been declared vacant by the House. He served until Mar 3, 1879.

December 2009	S	M	T	W	T	F	S
			1	2	3	4	5
	6	7	8	9	10	11	12
	13	14	15	16	17	18	19
	20	21	22	23	24	25	26
	27	28	29	30	31		

FLAUBERT, GUSTAVE: BIRTH ANNIVERSARY. Dec 12, 1821. French author whose works include one of the greatest French novels, *Madame Bovary*, was born at Rouen. Flaubert died at Croisset, France, May 8, 1880.

GARRISON, WILLIAM LLOYD: BIRTH ANNIVERSARY. Dec 12, 1805. American antislavery leader, poet and journalist, was born at Newburyport, MA. Garrison died at New York, NY, May 24, 1879.

INTERNATIONAL SHAREWARE DAY. Dec 12. A day to take the time to reward the efforts of thousands of computer programmers who trust that if we try their programs and like them, we will pay for them. Unfortunately, very few payments are received, thus stifling the programmers' efforts. This observance is meant to prompt each of us to inventory our PCs and Macs, see if we are using any shareware and then take the time in the holiday spirit to write payment checks to the authors. Hopefully this will keep shareware coming. Annually, the second Saturday in December. For info: David Lawrence, Online Today, Net Music Countdown, 145 S Glenoaks Blvd, Ste 336, Burbank, CA 91501. Phone: (818) 563-3123. E-mail: david@onlinetonight.net. Web: onlinetonight.net.

JAY, JOHN: BIRTH ANNIVERSARY. Dec 12, 1745. (Old Style date.) American statesman, diplomat and first chief justice of the US (1789–95), coauthor (with Alexander Hamilton and James Madison) of the influential *Federalist* papers, was born at New York, NY. Jay died at Bedford, NY, May 17, 1829.

KENYA: JAMHURI DAY. Dec 12. Jamhuri Day (Independence Day) is Kenya's official National Day, commemorating proclamation of the republic and independence from Britain in 1963.

LIVE: FAMILY CHRISTMAS AT THE BENJAMIN HARRISON HOME. Dec 12. Indianapolis, IN. Guided tour of the 23rd president's home decorated in seasonal Victorian style. For info: President Benjamin Harrison Home, 1230 N Delaware St, Indianapolis, IN 46202-2531. Phone: (317) 631-1888. Fax: (317) 632-5488. E-mail: harrison@pbhh.org. Web: www.pbhh.org.

MEXICO: GUADALUPE DAY. Dec 12. One of Mexico's major celebrations. Honors the "Dark Virgin of Guadalupe," the republic's patron saint. Parties and pilgrimages, with special ceremonies at the Shrine of Our Lady of Guadalupe at Mexico City.

NATIONAL DAY OF THE HORSE. Dec 12. The horse is a living link to the heritage and history of our nation and represents a common bond among all peoples who led the way in building our country. Today, the horse industry contributes more than $112 billion annually to the American economy. Therefore, the California State Legislature (as well as the US Senate) has declared the second Saturday of December to be the Day of the Horse in honor of these magnificent creatures.

PENNSYLVANIA RATIFIES CONSTITUTION: ANNIVERSARY. Dec 12, 1787. Pennsylvania became the second state to ratify the US Constitution, by a vote of 46 to 23, in 1787.

POINSETTIA DAY (JOEL ROBERTS POINSETT: DEATH ANNIVERSARY). Dec 12. A day to enjoy poinsettias and to honor Dr. Joel Roberts Poinsett, the American diplomat who introduced the Central American plant which is named for him into the US. Poinsett was born at Charleston, SC, Mar 2, 1799. He also served as a member of Congress and as secretary of war. He died near Statesburg, SC, Dec 12, 1851. The poinsettia has become a favorite Christmas-season plant.

POLISH CHRISTMAS OPEN HOUSE. Dec 12. Polish American Cultural Center Museum, Philadelphia, PA. Sw. Mikolaj (Polish St. Nicholas) will greet everyone with gifts for the children. Polish Christmas Tree and entertainment. Free admission. For info: Polish American Cultural Center Museum, 308 Walnut St, Philadelphia, PA 19106. Phone: (215) 922-1700. Fax: (215) 922-1518. E-mail: mail@polishamericancenter.org. Web: www.polishamericancenter.org.

PUERTO RICO: LAS MAÑANITAS. Dec 12. Ponce, Puerto Rico. Procession at 5 AM honoring our patron saint, Virgen de la Guadalupe.

Mass with music from a mariachi band; free breakfast afterward. Annually, on Dec 12. For info: Vangie Rivera, Director, Culture and Tourism Office, PO Box 331709, Ponce, PR 00733-1709. Phone: (787) 841-8044 or (787) 284-4141. Fax: (787) 259-1316. E-mail: cultponce@hotmail.com. Web: www.visitponce.com.

RUSSIA: CONSTITUTION DAY. Dec 12. National holiday commemorating the adoption of a new constitution in 1993.

SINATRA, FRANK: BIRTH ANNIVERSARY. Dec 12, 1915. Born at Hoboken, NJ, Frank Sinatra matured from a teen idol to the premier singer of American popular music. Known as the "Chairman of the Board" to his fans, he made more than 200 albums. His signature songs included "All the Way," "New York, New York" and "My Way." His film career included musicals (*On the Town* and *Pal Joey*) and two gritty films: *From Here to Eternity* (Oscar for Best Supporting Actor) and *The Man with the Golden Arm* (Oscar nomination). Died May 14, 1998, at Los Angeles, CA.

SUPREME COURT RULES FOR BUSH: ANNIVERSARY. Dec 12, 2000. The Supreme Court ruled by a vote of 5 to 4 that there could be no further counting of Florida's disputed presidential votes, ending deliberations over the 2000 presidential election. After five weeks of conflict over this pivotal vote count in Florida, Democratic candidate Al Gore conceded the election to George W. Bush. While Bush won the electoral vote to become the nation's 43rd president, Gore won the popular vote. Bush was only the fourth president in American history to be elected without winning the popular vote.

TURKMENISTAN: NEUTRALITY DAY. Dec 12. National holiday. Commemorates the UN's recognition of Turkmenistan's neutrality in 1995.

VICTORIAN CHRISTMAS TOURS AT FRANK LLOYD WRIGHT HOME. Dec 12 (also Dec 19). Oak Park, IL. A wonderful Christmas tradition, the Frank Lloyd Wright Preservation Trust presents free Victorian Christmas tours of Wright's home in Oak Park. These tours feature stories of how the Wright family celebrated the holidays at the turn of the 20th century and are led by Junior Interpreters: specially trained middle and high school students who bring a new perspective to the tour experience. Annually, the second and third Saturdays of Dec. For info: Frank Lloyd Wright Preservation Trust, 931 Chicago Ave, Oak Park, IL 60302. Phone: (708) 848-1976. E-mail: info@gowright.org. Web: www.gowright.org.

WATIE, STAND: BIRTH ANNIVERSARY. Dec 12, 1806. Born at Rome, GA, and died there Sept 9, 1871. Cherokee chief who, by signing the treaty of New Echota, surrendered his people's land in Georgia, forcing relocation to Oklahoma. Though the three other signers were murdered, Watie escaped and went on to initiate the first volunteer Cherokee regiment for the Confederates in the Civil War. Promoted to brigadier general, he was active in destroying the property of other Native Americans who supported the Union.

WINTERFEST BOAT PARADE. Dec 12. More than 100 decorated yachts sail up Fort Lauderdale's Intracoastal Waterway starting at New River to Pompano Beach. Est attendance: 1,000,000. For info: Winterfest, 512 NE 3rd Ave, Fort Lauderdale, FL 33301. Phone: (954) 767-0686. Fax: (954) 767-0665. E-mail: info@winterfestparade.com. Web: www.winterfestparade.com.

BIRTHDAYS TODAY

Tracy Ann Austin, 47, former tennis player, born Rolling Hills Estates, CA, Dec 12, 1962.

Bob Barker, 86, television personality, game show host (Emmy for "The Price Is Right"), born Darrington, WA, Dec 12, 1923.

Mayim Bialik, 34, actress ("Blossom"), born San Diego, CA, Dec 12, 1975.

Jennifer Connelly, 39, actress (*Reservation Road, Blood Diamond,* Oscar for *A Beautiful Mind*), born Catskill Mountains, NY, Dec 12, 1970.

Sheila E, 50, singer, musician ("The Glamorous Life"), born Sheila Escoveda at San Francisco, CA, Dec 12, 1959.

Connie Francis, 71, singer ("Where the Boys Are"), born Constance Franconero at Newark, NJ, Dec 12, 1938.

Edward Irwin Koch, 85, former mayor of New York City, born New York, NY, Dec 12, 1924.

Robert Lindsay, 60, actor (*Me and My Girl* [Olivier, Tony, Theatre World and Drama Desk Awards]), born Derbyshire, England, Dec 12, 1949.

Rey Mysterio, Jr, 35, professional wrestler, born Óscar Gutiérrez Rubio at Washington, DC, Dec 12, 1974.

Robert Lee (Bob) Pettit, Jr, 77, Hall of Fame basketball player, born Baton Rouge, LA, Dec 12, 1932.

Cathy Rigby, 57, former Olympic gymnast, born Long Beach, CA, Dec 12, 1952.

Dionne Warwick, 68, singer ("I Say a Little Prayer for You," "This Girl's in Love with You"), born East Orange, NJ, Dec 12, 1941.

Tom Wilkinson, 61, actor (*In the Bedroom, The Full Monty, Michael Clayton*), born Leeds, West Yorkshire, England, Dec 12, 1948.

December 13 — Sunday

DAY 347 **18 REMAINING**

BROOKS, PHILLIPS: BIRTH ANNIVERSARY. Dec 13, 1835. American clergyman and composer born at Boston, MA. Best remembered for his lyrics for the Christmas carol "O Little Town of Bethlehem." Brooks died at Boston, Jan 23, 1893.

COLONIAL CHRISTMAS AT WORMSLOE. Dec 13. Wormsloe Historic Site, Savannah, GA. Join us for caroling, burning of the Yule log and other holiday observances of the Colonial Period, including games and refreshments. For info: Wormsloe Historic Site, 7601 Skidaway Rd, Savannah, GA 31406. Phone: (912) 353-3023. E-mail: wormsloe@bellsouth.net. Web: www.wormsloe.org.

THE COMPASSIONATE FRIENDS WORLDWIDE CANDLE LIGHTING. Dec 13. A day to remember the more than 79,000 children who die in the US every year. Annually, the second Sunday in December. For info: The Compassionate Friends, PO Box 3696, Oak Brook, IL 60522-3696. Phone: (877) 969-0010. E-mail: nationaloffice@compassionatefriends.org. Web: www.compassionatefriends.org.

EIGHTEENTH-CENTURY CHRISTMAS WASSAIL. Dec 13. McLean, VA. Greet the winter solstice and Christmas season with a toast to the apple trees. Caroling and warm refreshments. Bring pots or other noisemakers to frighten off evil spirits threatening next year's apple crop. Est attendance: 800. For info: Claude Moore Colonial Farm at Turkey Run, 6310 Georgetown Pike, McLean, VA 22101. Phone: (703) 442-7557. Fax: (703) 442-0714. Web: www.1771.org.

GLUTEN-FREE BAKING WEEK. Dec 13–19. Baking without wheat and gluten can be challenging, particularly during the holidays. This campaign provides consumers with expert advice on gluten-free baking from top chefs and cookbook authors around the country. The week focuses on using the wide variety of gluten-free flours and mixes available to replace the wheat flour in traditional baking with an emphasis on solid, gluten-free baking techniques and delicious recipes. For info: GF Culinary Productions, Inc. Phone: (303) 368-9990. E-mail: info@prchefs.com. Web: www.theglutenfreelifestyle.com.

HEINE, HEINRICH: BIRTH ANNIVERSARY. Dec 13, 1797. German poet and critic, born at Dusseldorf. Died at Paris, France, Feb 17, 1856.

LINCOLN, MARY TODD: BIRTH ANNIVERSARY. Dec 13, 1818. Wife of Abraham Lincoln, 16th president of the US, born at Lexington, KY. Died at Springfield, IL, July 16, 1882.

MALTA: REPUBLIC DAY. Dec 13. National holiday. Malta became a republic in 1974.

MOORE, ARCHIE: BIRTH ANNIVERSARY. Dec 13, 1913. Born Archibald Lee Wright at Benoit, MS. One of the most colorful fighters ever, Moore boxed from the mid-1930s to 1963, holding the light-heavyweight title for a record nine years. For much of his career, he fought an average of once a month. Moore let an aura of celebrity surround him: he lied about his age, ate an unusual diet, married five times and spoke out on a variety of political and social issues. Died at San Diego, CA, Dec 9, 1998.

NEW ZEALAND FIRST SIGHTED BY EUROPEANS: ANNIVERSARY. Dec 13, 1642. Captain Abel Tasman of the Dutch East India Company first sighted New Zealand but was kept from landing by Maori warriors. In 1769 Captain James Cook landed and claimed formal possession for Great Britain.

NORTH AND SOUTH KOREA END WAR: ANNIVERSARY. Dec 13, 1991. North and South Korea signed a treaty of reconciliation and nonaggression, formally ending the Korean War—38 years after fighting ceased in 1953. This agreement was not hailed as a peace treaty, and the armistice that was signed July 27, 1953, between the UN and North Korea, was to remain in effect until it could be transformed into a formal peace.

QUINCY PRESERVES CHRISTMAS CANDLELIGHT TOUR. Dec 13. Quincy, IL. Tour historic homes decked out in their Christmas finest. Each year this walking tour features a different neighborhood. Homes range in size from grand mansions to quaint cottages. Annually, the second Sunday in December. Est attendance: 1,000. For info: Fran Cook, Quincy Preserves, 310 S 16th St, Quincy, IL 62301. Phone: (217) 224-2587.

SWEDEN: SANTA LUCIA DAY. Dec 13. Nationwide celebration of festival of light, honoring St. Lucia. Many hotels have their own Lucia, a young girl attired in a long, flowing white gown, who serves guests coffee and lussekatter (saffron buns) in the early morning.

WSBA/WARM 103/WSOX 96.1 CHRISTMAS CRAFT SHOW. Dec 13. York Fairgrounds, York, PA. More than 250 craft displays, from country to contemporary, Victorian and southwestern, handcrafted furniture, wood carvings, dolls, jewelry, pottery, collectibles, quilts, baskets, fine arts and much more. Admission fee. Est attendance: 3,500. For info: Joe Alfano, Special Events, 5989 Susquehanna Plaza Dr, York, PA 17406. Phone: (717) 764-1155. Fax: (717) 252-4807. E-mail: joe.alfano@cumulus.com. Web: www.warm103.com.

BIRTHDAYS TODAY

Steve Buscemi, 51, actor (*Ghost World, Fargo, Reservoir Dogs*), born Brooklyn, NY, Dec 13, 1958.

John Davidson, 68, singer, actor, former TV host, born Pittsburgh, PA, Dec 13, 1941.

Sergei Fedorov, 40, hockey player, born Pskov, Russia, Dec 13, 1969.

Jamie Foxx, 42, actor (Oscar for *Ray*; *Jarhead, Collateral*), born Dallas, TX, Dec 13, 1967.

Wendie Malick, 59, actress ("Just Shoot Me"), born Buffalo, NY, Dec 13, 1950.

Ted Nugent, 60, singer ("Cat Scratch Fever"), born Detroit, MI, Dec 13, 1949.

Christopher Plummer, 80, actor (Emmy for "The Moneychangers"; *The Sound of Music, Dolores Claiborne*), born Toronto, ON, Canada, Dec 13, 1929.

Robert Prosky, 79, actor ("Hill Street Blues," "Veronica's Closet"), born Philadelphia, PA, Dec 13, 1930.

Taylor Swift, 20, country singer, born Reading, PA, Dec 13, 1989.

Dick Van Dyke, 84, comedian, actor (*Mary Poppins*, "The Dick Van Dyke Show," "Diagnosis Murder"), born West Plains, MO, Dec 13, 1925.

December 2009

S	M	T	W	T	F	S
		1	2	3	4	5
6	7	8	9	10	11	12
13	14	15	16	17	18	19
20	21	22	23	24	25	26
27	28	29	30	31		

December 14 — Monday

DAY 348 **17 REMAINING**

ALABAMA: ADMISSION DAY: ANNIVERSARY. Dec 14. Became 22nd state in 1819.

DOOLITTLE, JAMES HAROLD: BIRTH ANNIVERSARY. Dec 14, 1896. American aviator and WWII hero General James Doolittle was born at Alameda, CA. A lieutenant general in the US Army Air Force, he was the first person to fly across North America in less than a day. On Apr 18, 1942, Doolittle led a squadron of 16 B-25 bombers, launched from aircraft carriers, on the first US aerial raid on Japan of WWII. He was awarded the Congressional Medal of Honor for this accomplishment. Doolittle also headed the Eighth Air Force during the Normandy invasion. He died Sept 27, 1993, at Pebble Beach, CA.

HALCYON DAYS. Dec 14–28. Traditionally, the seven days before and the seven days after the winter solstice. To the ancients a time when fabled bird (called the halcyon—pronounced hal-cee-on) calmed the wind and waves—a time of calm and tranquility.

NOSTRADAMUS: BIRTH ANNIVERSARY. Dec 14, 1503. French physician, best remembered for his astrological predictions (written in rhymed quatrains), was born Michel de Notredame, at St. Rémy, Provence, France. Many believed that his book of prophecies actually foretold the future. Nostradamus died at Salon, France, July 2, 1566.

REMICK, LEE: BIRTH ANNIVERSARY. Dec 14, 1935. American actress Lee Remick was born at Quincy, MA. Her films include *A Face in the Crowd* (1957), *Anatomy of a Murder* (1959) and *Days of Wine and Roses* (1963). She died July 2, 1991, at Los Angeles, CA.

SMITH, MARGARET CHASE: BIRTH ANNIVERSARY. Dec 14, 1897. American politician Margaret Madeline Chase Smith was born at Skowhegan, ME. As the first woman to be elected to both houses of Congress (1941 to the House and 1949 to the Senate), she was also one of seven Republican senators to issue a "declaration of conscience" to denounce Senator Joseph R. McCarthy's communist witch hunt. She died May 29, 1995, at Skowhegan.

SOUTH POLE DISCOVERY: ANNIVERSARY. Dec 14, 1911. The elusive object of many expeditions dating from the seventeenth century, the South Pole was located and visited by Roald Amundsen with four companions and 52 sled dogs. All five men and 12 of the dogs returned to base camp safely. Next to visit the South Pole, Jan 17, 1912, was a party of five led by Captain Robert F. Scott, all of whom perished during the return trip. A search party found their frozen bodies 11 months later. See also: "Amundsen, Roald: Birth Anniversary" (July 16).

WASHINGTON, GEORGE: DEATH ANNIVERSARY. Dec 14, 1799. The first president of the US died at his home at Mount Vernon,

VA, shortly before midnight. He had battled a sudden acute respiratory infection and been bled four times. "I die hard, but I am not afraid to go" were his famous near-dying words. After he confirmed his own burial plans, Washington's actual last words were, "'Tis well." He was mourned throughout the US but also in Europe.

BIRTHDAYS TODAY

Craig Biggio, 44, former baseball player, born Smithtown, NY, Dec 14, 1965.

Jane Birkin, 63, actress (*Blow-Up, Death on the Nile, Evil Under the Sun*), born London, England, Dec 14, 1946.

Leonardo Boff, 71, Catholic theologian, born Concordia, Brazil, Dec 14, 1938.

William Joseph (Bill) Buckner, 60, former baseball player, born Vallejo, CA, Dec 14, 1949.

Patty Duke, 63, actress (Oscar for *The Miracle Worker*; Emmy for *My Sweet Charlie*), born New York, NY, Dec 14, 1946.

Don Hewitt, 87, TV news producer ("60 Minutes"), born New York, NY, Dec 14, 1922.

Vanessa Hudgens, 21, actress (*High School Musical*), born Salinas, CA, Dec 14, 1988.

Michael Owen, 30, soccer player, born Chester, England, Dec 14, 1979.

Dee Wallace Stone, 61, actress (*10, E.T. The Extra-Terrestrial*), born Kansas City, MO, Dec 14, 1948.

December 15 — Tuesday

DAY 349 — **16 REMAINING**

BATTLE OF SAN PIETRO: ANNIVERSARY. Dec 15, 1943. A German panzer battalion inflicted heavy casualties on American forces trying to take the 700-year-old Italian village of San Pietro, before withdrawing from the town. San Pietro was reduced almost entirely to rubble. The American movie director John Huston, serving as an Army lieutenant, filmed the battle for the military. So graphic was the film that it was described as antiwar by the military brass at the War Department. The film was cut from five to three reels before censors allowed it to be released in 1944. It was later re-edited for the television series "The Big Picture."

BILL OF RIGHTS: ANNIVERSARY. Dec 15, 1791. The first 10 amendments to the US Constitution, known as the Bill of Rights, became effective following ratification by Virginia. The anniversary of ratification and of effect is observed as Bill of Rights Day.

✦ **BILL OF RIGHTS DAY.** Dec 15. Presidential Proclamation. Has been proclaimed each year since 1962, but was omitted in 1967 and 1968. (Issued in 1941 and 1946 at Congressional request and in 1947 without request.) Since 1968 has been included in Human Rights Day and Week Proclamation.

CAT HERDERS DAY. Dec 15. If you can say that your job—or even your life—is like trying to herd cats, then this day is for you—with our sympathy. (©2006 by WH.) For info: Thomas & Ruth Roy, Wellcat Holidays, 2418 Long Ln, Lebanon, PA 17046. Phone: (717) 279-0184. E-mail: wellcat@comcast.net. Web: www.wellcat.com.

CURAÇAO: KINGDOM DAY AND ANTILLEAN FLAG DAY. Dec 15. This day commemorates the Charter of Kingdom, signed in 1954 at the Knight's Hall at The Hague, granting the Netherlands Antilles complete autonomy. The Antillean flag was hoisted for the first time on this day in 1959.

"DAVY CROCKETT" TV PREMIERE: 55th ANNIVERSARY. Dec 15, 1954. This show, a series of five segments, can be considered TV's first miniseries. Shown on Walt Disney's "Disneyland" show, it starred Fess Parker as American western hero Davy Crockett and was immensely popular. The show spawned Crockett paraphernalia, including the famous coonskin cap (even after we found out that Crockett never wore a coonskin cap).

EIFFEL, ALEXANDRE GUSTAVE: BIRTH ANNIVERSARY. Dec 15, 1832. Eiffel, the French engineer who designed the 1,000-ft-high, million-dollar, open-lattice wrought-iron Eiffel Tower and who participated in designing the Statue of Liberty, was born at Dijon, France. The Eiffel Tower, weighing more than 7,000 tons, was built for the Paris International Exposition of 1889. Eiffel died at Paris, France, Dec 23, 1923.

GAL, UZI: BIRTH ANNIVERSARY. Dec 15, 1923. Inventor of the 9-millimeter submachine gun that bears his name, Uziel Gal was born in Germany but spent most of his life in Israel. A mechanical engineer, he fought in the 1948 Arab-Israeli war, to which he brought a homemade submachine gun. He went on to design the Uzi, and by 1956 it was being manufactured by Israeli Military Industries, whose management named it for him against his own wishes. The gun itself revolutionized automatic weaponry and is currently found in the arsenals of armies, secret-service organizations, bodyguards, etc, worldwide. Gal died at Philadelphia, PA, on Sept 2, 2002.

***GONE WITH THE WIND* FILM PREMIERE: 70th ANNIVERSARY.** Dec 15, 1939. One of the 20th century's biggest film blockbusters premiered on this date in Atlanta, GA. Based on Margaret Mitchell's bestselling and Pulitzer Prize–winning novel of Civil War passions, the film starred Vivian Leigh and Clark Gable and was produced by the dynamic David O. Selznick. It won an unprecedented eight Academy Awards, including best picture. Hattie McDaniel won a best supporting actress Oscar—the first time an African-American actor had won or been nominated. No film would touch its Oscar achievement or monetary grosses for decades. At the chilly Atlanta premiere, more than 300,000 people lined the streets to catch sight of the film's stars arriving at the Loew's Grand Theater. See also "Gone with the Wind Published: Anniversary" (May 19).

MILITARY DICTATORSHIP ENDED IN CHILE: 20th ANNIVERSARY. Dec 15, 1989. In an election on this date, Patricio Aylwin defeated General Augusto Pinochet's former finance minister, Hernan Buchi, bringing the military dictatorship of Pinochet to an end. Fourteen months previously, Pinochet suffered defeat in a national plebiscite on eight more years of his rule. This defeat prompted democratic elections and crippled the Pinochet regime. Pinochet came to power when the military overthrew a democratically elected government and killed Marxist president Salvador Allende in a 1973 coup. Patricio Aylwin avoided a two-candidate runoff by achieving 55.2 percent of the vote. He was inaugurated on Mar 11, 1990.

PUERTO RICO: NAVIDADES. Dec 15–Jan 6. Traditional Christmas season begins mid-December and ends on Three Kings Day. Elaborate nativity scenes, carolers, special Christmas foods and trees from Canada and US. Gifts on Christmas Day and on Three Kings Day.

SITTING BULL: DEATH ANNIVERSARY. Dec 15, 1890. Famous Sioux Indian leader, medicine man and warrior of the Hunkpapa Teton band. Known also by his native name, Tatanka-yatanka, Sitting Bull was born on the Grand River, SD. He first accompanied his father on the warpath at the age of 14 against the Crow and thereafter rapidly gained influence within his tribe. In 1866 he led a raid on Fort Buford. His steadfast refusal to go to a reservation led General Phillip Sheridan to initiate a campaign against him, which led to the massacre of Lieutenant Colonel George Custer's men at the Little Bighorn, after which Sitting Bull fled to Canada, remaining there until 1881. Although many in his tribe surrendered on their return, Sitting Bull remained hostile until his death in a skirmish with the US soldiers along the Grand River.

SPACE MILESTONE: *VEGA 1* (USSR): 25th ANNIVERSARY. Dec 15, 1984. Craft launched this date to rendezvous with Halley's Comet in March 1986. *Vega 2*, launched Dec 21, 1984, was part of same mission, which, in cooperation with the US, carried US-built "comet-dust" detection equipment.

US FORCES LAND IN MINDORO, PHILIPPINES: 65th ANNIVERSARY. Dec 15, 1944. After the usual barrage from naval guns, the US 24th Division landed on Mindoro, the largest of the islands immediately south of Luzon (the most important island of the Philippines). American soldiers easily advanced eight miles inland, took the perimeter of their beachhead and started construction of an airfield. Japanese kamikaze counterattacks, however, sank two motor torpedo boats and damaged the escort carrier *Marcus Island*, two destroyers and a third motor torpedo boat, making Mindoro a more costly conquest than the island of Leyte had been.

BIRTHDAYS TODAY

Adam Brody, 30, actor ("The O.C.," *Growing Up Brady*), born San Diego, CA, Dec 15, 1979.

Nicholas (Nick) Buoniconti, 69, former football player, born Springfield, MA, Dec 15, 1940.

Dave Clark, 67, musician (leader of the Dave Clark Five, "I Like It Like That"), born London, England, Dec 15, 1942.

Tim Conway, 76, comedian, actor ("McHale's Navy," "The Carol Burnett Show"), born Willoughby, OH, Dec 15, 1933.

Don Johnson, 60, actor ("Miami Vice," "Nash Bridges"), born Flatt Creek, MO, Dec 15, 1949.

Edna O'Brien, 78, author (*Country Girls Trilogy, Time and Tide*), born Tuamgraney, Ireland, Dec 15, 1931.

Helen Slater, 46, actress (*City Slickers, The Secret of My Success*), born Long Island, NY, Dec 15, 1963.

Alexandra Stevenson, 29, tennis player, born San Diego, CA, Dec 15, 1980.

Garrett Wang, 41, actor ("Star Trek: Voyager"), born Riverside, CA, Dec 15, 1968.

Mark Warner, 55, former governor of Virginia (D), born Indianapolis, IN, Dec 15, 1954.

December 16 — Wednesday

DAY 350 — **15 REMAINING**

AUSTEN, JANE: BIRTH ANNIVERSARY. Dec 16, 1775. English novelist (*Pride and Prejudice, Sense and Sensibility*), born at Steventon, Hampshire, England. Died July 18, 1817, at Winchester, England.

BAHRAIN: INDEPENDENCE DAY. Dec 16. National holiday. Commemorates independence from British protection in 1971.

BANGLADESH: VICTORY DAY. Dec 16. National holiday. Commemorates victory over Pakistan in 1971. The former East Pakistan became Bangladesh.

December 2009

S	M	T	W	T	F	S
		1	2	3	4	5
6	7	8	9	10	11	12
13	14	15	16	17	18	19
20	21	22	23	24	25	26
27	28	29	30	31		

BARBIE AND BARNEY BACKLASH DAY. Dec 16. If we have to explain this to you, you don't have kids. It's one day each year when Mom and Dad can tell the kids that Barbie and Barney don't exist. (©2006 by WH.) For info: Thomas & Ruth Roy, Wellcat Holidays, 2418 Long Ln, Lebanon, PA 17046. Phone: (717) 279-0184. E-mail: info@wellcat.com. Web: www.wellcat.com.

BATTLE OF NASHVILLE: ANNIVERSARY. Dec 16, 1864. On the second day of battle at Nashville, Union troops defeated Confederate forces under General John B. Hood, essentially knocking the Confederate Army of Tennessee out of the war.

BATTLE OF THE BULGE: 65th ANNIVERSARY. Dec 16, 1944. A German offensive was launched in the Belgian Ardennes Forest, where Hitler had managed to concentrate 250,000 men. The Nazi commanders, hoping to minimize any aerial counterattack by the Allies, chose a time when foggy, rainy weather prevailed and the initial attack by eight armored divisions along a 75-mile front took the Allies by surprise, the Fifth Panzer Army penetrating to within 20 miles of crossings on the Meuse River. US troops were able to hold fast at bottlenecks in the Ardennes, but by the end of December the German push had penetrated 65 miles into the Allied lines (though their line had narrowed from the initial 75 miles to 20 miles). By that time the Allies began to respond and the Germans were stopped by Montgomery on the Meuse and by Patton at Bastogne. The weather then cleared and Allied aircraft began to bomb the German forces and supply lines by Dec 26. The Allies reestablished their original line by Jan 21, 1945.

BEETHOVEN, LUDWIG VAN: BIRTH ANNIVERSARY. Dec 16, 1770. Regarded by many as the greatest orchestral composer of all time, Ludwig van Beethoven was born at Bonn, Germany. Impairment of his hearing began before he was 30, but even total deafness did not halt his composing and conducting. His last appearance on the concert stage was to conduct the premiere of his *Ninth Symphony*, at Vienna, May 7, 1824. He was unable to hear either the orchestra or the applause. Often in love, he never married. Of a stormy temperament, he is said to have died during a violent thunderstorm Mar 26, 1827, at Vienna.

BOSTON TEA PARTY: ANNIVERSARY. Dec 16, 1773. Anniversary of Boston patriots' boarding of British vessel at anchor at Boston Harbor. Contents of nearly 350 chests of tea were dumped into the harbor.

CALABRIA EARTHQUAKE: ANNIVERSARY. Dec 16, 1857. Calabria—an especially quake-prone region near Naples, Italy—experienced a devastating earthquake of great magnitude that left more than 10,000 people dead and entire villages destroyed. Between 1783 (the last big quake) and 1857, about 111,000 people lost their lives in the unstable region.

CLARKE, ARTHUR C.: BIRTH ANNIVERSARY. Dec 16, 1917. Born at Minehead, England, Clarke was a popular writer of science fiction in the twentieth century. His short story "The Sentinel" (1951) was the inspiration for the successful film classic *2001: A Space Odyssey* (1968). Clarke, who was knighted in 2000, worked on sequels to the *2001* story and died Mar 19, 2008, at Colombo, Sri Lanka.

COWARD, NOËL: BIRTH ANNIVERSARY. Dec 16, 1899. English playwright, actor and wit known for his sophisticated comedies *Private Lives* (1930), *Design for Living* (1933), *Blithe Spirit* (1941) and others—many of which were later filmed. He is also known for such songs as "Mad Dogs and Englishmen." He advised actors: "Learn the lines and don't bump into the furniture." Born at Teddington, England, Coward died at St. Mary, Jamaica, on Mar 26, 1973.

"DRAGNET" TV PREMIERE: ANNIVERSARY. Dec 16, 1951. This famous crime show stressed authenticity, and episodes were supposedly based on real cases. It starred Jack Webb as stoic and determined Sergeant Joe Friday, a man whose life was his investigative police work and who was recognized by his recurring line, "Just the facts, ma'am." Friday had many partners: Barton Yarborough played Sergeant Ben Romero for three episodes; for the rest of the season Barney Phillips played Sergeant Ed Jacobs and Ben Alexander played his comedic sidekick, Officer Frank Smith. A new version appeared in 1967 with Webb and his new partner, Officer Bill Gannon (Harry Morgan). "Dragnet" is also known for its theme music and its narrative epilogue describing the fate of the bad guys.

KAZAKHSTAN: INDEPENDENCE DAY. Dec 16. National Day. Commemorates independence from the Soviet Union in 1991.

MEAD, MARGARET: BIRTH ANNIVERSARY. Dec 16, 1901. American anthropologist and author, especially known for her studies of peoples of the southwest Pacific area, and for her forthright manner in speaking and writing. Born at Philadelphia, PA, Mead died at New York, NY, Nov 15, 1978.

MEXICO: POSADAS. Dec 16–24. A nine-day annual celebration throughout Mexico. Processions of "pilgrims" knock at doors asking for posada (shelter), commemorating the search by Joseph and Mary for a shelter in which the infant Jesus might be born. Pilgrims are invited inside, and fun and merrymaking ensue with blindfolded guests trying to break a piñata filled with gifts and goodies suspended from the ceiling. Once the piñata is broken, the gifts are distributed and celebration continues.

MOON PHASE: NEW MOON. Dec 16. Moon enters New Moon phase at 7:02 AM, EST.

NEW WORLD SYMPHONY PREMIERE: ANNIVERSARY. Dec 16, 1893. Antonín Dvořák's *New World Symphony* premiered at the newly erected Carnegie Hall with the New York Philharmonic playing. The composer attended and enjoyed enthusiastic applause from the audience. The symphony contains snatches from black spirituals and American folk music. Dvorák, a Bohemian, had been in the US only a year when he composed it as a greeting to his friends in Europe.

"ONE DAY AT A TIME" TV PREMIERE: ANNIVERSARY. Dec 16, 1975. This sitcom about a divorced mother raising two girls in Indianapolis starred Bonnie Franklin as Ann Romano, Mackenzie Phillips and Valerie Bertinelli as daughters Julie and Barbara Cooper. Other regulars included: Pat Harrington, Jr, as tool-belt-wearing maintenance man Dwayne Schneider; Richard Masur as David Kane, Ann's boyfriend; and Nanette Fabray as Ann's mother. All three female leads got married and Ann opened her own ad agency before the series ended in 1984.

PHILIPPINES: PHILIPPINE CHRISTMAS OBSERVANCE. Dec 16–Jan 6. Philippine Islands. Said to be the world's longest Christmas celebration.

PHILIPPINES: SIMBANG GABI. Dec 16–25. Nationwide. A nine-day novena of predawn masses, also called "Misa de Gallo." One of the traditional Filipino celebrations of the holiday season.

SANTAYANA, GEORGE: BIRTH ANNIVERSARY. Dec 16, 1863. Philosopher and author born at Madrid, Spain. At the age of nine he emigrated to the US where he attended and later taught at Harvard University. In 1912 he returned to Europe and traveled extensively. It was Santayana who said, "Those who cannot remember the past are condemned to repeat it." He died at Rome, Italy, Sept 26, 1952.

SOUTH AFRICA: RECONCILIATION DAY. Dec 16. National holiday. Celebrates the spirit of reconciliation, national unity and peace among all citizens.

UNITED NATIONS REVOKES RESOLUTION ON ZIONISM: ANNIVERSARY. Dec 16, 1991. The United Nations voted 111 to 25 to revoke Resolution 3379, which equated Zionism with racism. Resolution 3379 was approved Nov 10, 1975, with 72 countries voting in favor, 35 against and 32 abstentions. The largest block of changed votes came from the former Soviet Union and Eastern Europe.

BIRTHDAYS TODAY

Bruce N. Ames, 81, biochemist, cancer researcher, born New York, NY, Dec 16, 1928.

Steven Bochco, 66, TV writer, producer ("Hill Street Blues," "NYPD Blue"), born New York, NY, Dec 16, 1943.

Benjamin Bratt, 46, actor (*Traffic, Miss Congeniality*, "Law & Order"), born San Francisco, CA, Dec 16, 1963.

Donald Carcieri, 67, Governor of Rhode Island (R), born East Greenwich, RI, Dec 16, 1942.

James Gibbons, 65, Governor of Nevada (R), born Sparks, NV, Dec 16, 1944.

Alison La Placa, 50, actress ("The John Laroquette Show"), born Lincolnshire, IL, Dec 16, 1959.

William "The Refrigerator" Perry, 47, former football player, born Aiken, SC, Dec 16, 1962.

Clifford (Cliff) Ralph Robinson, 43, basketball player, born Buffalo, NY, Dec 16, 1966.

Lesley Stahl, 68, journalist ("60 Minutes," former White House correspondent), born Lynn, MA, Dec 16, 1941.

Jon Tenney, 48, actor ("Brooklyn South," "The Closer"), born Princeton, NJ, Dec 16, 1961.

Liv Johanne Ullmann, 70, actress (*The Immigrants, Scenes from a Marriage*), born Tokyo, Japan, Dec 16, 1939.

December 17 — Thursday

DAY 351 | **14 REMAINING**

AZTEC CALENDAR STONE DISCOVERY: ANNIVERSARY. Dec 17, 1790. One of the wonders of the western hemisphere—the Aztec Calendar or Solar Stone—was found beneath the ground by workmen repairing Mexico City's Central Plaza. The centuries-old, intricately carved stone—11 ft, 8 inches in diameter and weighing nearly 25 tons—proved to be a highly developed calendar monument to the sun. Believed to have been carved in the year 1479, this extraordinary time-counting basalt tablet originally stood in the Great Temple of the Aztecs. Buried along with other Aztec idols soon after the Spanish conquest in 1521, it remained hidden until 1790. Its 52-year cycle had regulated many Aztec ceremonies, including grisly human sacrifices, to save the world from destruction by the gods.

BOLÍVAR, SIMÓN: DEATH ANNIVERSARY. Dec 17, 1830. Commemorated in Venezuela and other Latin American countries. Bolívar, called "The Liberator," was born July 24, 1783, at Caracas, Venezuela, and died Dec 17, 1830, at Santa Marta, Colombia.

***A CHRISTMAS CAROL* PUBLISHED: ANNIVERSARY.** Dec 17, 1843. This holiday classic by Charles Dickens was published in a print run of 6,000 copies that sold out in one week. By Jan 6, 1844, another 2,000 were sold. The reformation of Ebenezer Scrooge ("Bah humbug!") has remained immensely popular.

CLEAN AIR ACT PASSED BY CONGRESS: ANNIVERSARY. Dec 17, 1967. A sweeping set of laws passed to protect the nation from air pollution. This was the first legislation to place pollution controls on the automobile industry.

FIRST FLIGHT ANNIVERSARY CELEBRATION. Dec 17. Kill Devil Hills, NC. Each year since 1928, on the anniversary of the Wright brothers' first successful heavier-than-air flight at Kitty Hawk, NC, Dec 17, 1903, a celebration has been held at the Wright Brothers

National Memorial, with wreaths, flyover and other observances—regardless of weather.

FLOYD, WILLIAM: 275th BIRTH ANNIVERSARY. Dec 17, 1734. Signer of the Declaration of Independence, member of Congress, born at Brookhaven, Long Island. Died at Westernville, NY, Aug 4, 1821.

HENRY, JOSEPH: BIRTH ANNIVERSARY. Dec 17, 1797. Scientist Joseph Henry was born at Albany, NY. One of his great discoveries was the principle of self-induction; the unit used in the measure of electrical inductance was named "the henry" in his honor. In 1831 Henry constructed the first model of an electric telegraph with an audible signal. This formed the basis of nearly all later work on commercial wire telegraphy. In 1832 Henry was named professor of natural philosophy at the College of New Jersey, now Princeton University. Henry was involved in the planning of the Smithsonian Institution and became its first secretary in 1846. President Lincoln named Henry as one of the original 50 scientists to make up the National Academy of Sciences in 1863. He served as that organization's president from 1868 until his death May 13, 1878, at Washington, DC.

KING, W.L. MACKENZIE: BIRTH ANNIVERSARY. Dec 17, 1874. Former Canadian prime minister, born at Berlin, ON. Served 21 years, the longest term of any prime minister in the English-speaking world. Died at Kingsmere, July 22, 1950.

LIBBY, WILLARD FRANK: BIRTH ANNIVERSARY. Dec 17, 1908. American educator, chemist, atomic scientist and Nobel Prize winner was born at Grand Valley, CO. He was the inventor of the carbon-14 "atomic clock" method for dating ancient and prehistoric plant and animal remains and minerals. Died at Los Angeles, CA, Sept 8, 1980.

NATIONAL REGIFTING DAY. Dec 17. Regifters reveal coworkers as one of the most likely recipients of their regifts. Therefore, National Regifting Day was created in honor of holiday office parties and the "unique" gifts exchanged there. Bring a gift out of the supply closet and turn your office gift exchange into a regifting party. Rest assured that most people (60%) think that regifting is becoming more accepted. Annually, the Thursday before Christmas Eve and Christmas. For info: Kim McGrigg, 9009 W Loop S, 7th Fl, Houston, TX 77096. Phone: (866) 889-9347. Fax: (713) 394-3209. E-mail: kimmcgrigg@moneymanagement.org. Web: www.nationalregiftingday.com.

SAMPSON, DEBORAH: BIRTH ANNIVERSARY. Dec 17, 1760. Born at Plympton, MA, Deborah Sampson spent her childhood as an indentured servant. In 1782, wishing to participate in the Revolutionary War, she disguised herself as a man and enlisted in the Continental Army's Fourth Massachusetts Regiment under the name Robert Shurtleff. Her identity was unmasked, and she was dismissed from the army in 1783. In 1802 Sampson became perhaps the first woman to lecture professionally in the US when she began giving public speeches on her experiences. Deborah Sampson died Apr 29, 1827, at Sharon, MA. Full military pension was provided for her heirs by an act of Congress in 1838.

SATURNALIA. Dec 17–23. Ancient Roman festival honoring Saturnus, the god of agriculture. It was a time of merriment at the end of harvesting and wine making. Presents were exchanged, sacrifices offered, and masters served their slaves. Approximates the winter solstice. Some say that the date for the observance of the nativity of Jesus was selected by the early Christian church leaders to fall on Dec 25 partly to counteract the popular but disapproved-of pre-Christian Roman festival of Saturnalia.

"THE SIMPSONS" TV PREMIERE: 20th ANNIVERSARY. Dec 17, 1989. TV's hottest animated family, "The Simpsons," premiered on this date. The originator of Homer, Marge, Bart, Lisa and Maggie is cartoonist Matt Groening. The show's 300th episode, "Barting Over," aired Feb 16, 2003. The 400th episode, "You Kent Always Say What You Want," aired May 20, 2007.

TINY TIM WEDS MISS VICKI ON "THE TONIGHT SHOW": 40th ANNIVERSARY. Dec 17, 1969. In the highest-rated show in "The Tonight Show" history, 45 million viewers saw ukulele-playing eccentric Tiny Tim marry Miss Vicki (née Budinger), his 17-year-old girlfriend. The live ceremony was accented by thousands of tulips, since Tiny Tim's claim to fame was his falsetto revival of the song "Tiptoe through the Tulips."

WHITTIER, JOHN GREENLEAF: BIRTH ANNIVERSARY. Dec 17, 1807. Poet and abolitionist, born at Haverhill, Essex County, MA. Whittier's books of poetry include *Legends of New England* and *Snowbound*. Died at Hampton Falls, NH, Sept 7, 1892.

✦ **WRIGHT BROTHERS DAY.** Dec 17. Presidential Proclamation always issued for Dec 17 since 1963 (PL88–209 of Dec 17, 1963). Issued twice earlier at Congressional request in 1959 and 1961.

WRIGHT BROTHERS FIRST POWERED FLIGHT: ANNIVERSARY. Dec 17, 1903. Orville and Wilbur Wright, brothers, bicycle shop operators, inventors and aviation pioneers, after three years of experimentation with kites and gliders, achieved the first documented successful powered and controlled flights of an airplane. The flights, near Kitty Hawk, NC, piloted first by Orville then by Wilbur Wright, were sustained for less than one minute but represented man's first powered airplane flight and the beginning of a new form of transportation. Orville Wright was born at Dayton, OH, Aug 19, 1871, and died there Jan 30, 1948. Wilbur Wright was born at Millville, IN, Apr 16, 1867, and died at Dayton, OH, May 30, 1912.

BIRTHDAYS TODAY

Christopher Cazenove, 64, actor (*Zulu Dawn, Eye of the Needle*), born Winchester, England, Dec 17, 1945.

Bob Guccione, 79, publisher, born Brooklyn, NY, Dec 17, 1930.

Bernard Hill, 65, actor (*The Lord of the Rings: Return of the King, Great Expectations, Titanic*), born Manchester, England, Dec 17, 1944.

Ernie Hudson, 64, actor (*Ghostbusters, The Hand That Rocks the Cradle*), born Benton Harbor, MI, Dec 17, 1945.

Eugene Levy, 63, comedian, actor (*American Pie, Best in Show*, "Second City TV"), born Hamilton, ON, Canada, Dec 17, 1946.

Bill Pullman, 55, actor (*Independence Day, While You Were Sleeping*), born Delphi, NY, Dec 17, 1954.

William Safire, 80, author, journalist (*Coming to Terms, Words of Wisdom*), born New York, NY, Dec 17, 1929.

Tommy Steele, 73, actor (*The Happiest Millionaire, Half a Sixpence*), born London, England, Dec 17, 1936.

Sean Patrick Thomas, 39, actor (*Save the Last Dance*, "The District"), born Wilmington, DE, Dec 17, 1970.

Chase Utley, 31, baseball player, born Pasadena, CA, Dec 17, 1978.

December 2009

S	M	T	W	T	F	S
		1	2	3	4	5
6	7	8	9	10	11	12
13	14	15	16	17	18	19
20	21	22	23	24	25	26
27	28	29	30	31		

December 18 — Friday

DAY 352 13 REMAINING

BRANDT, WILLY: BIRTH ANNIVERSARY. Dec 18, 1913. Former West German chancellor Willy Brandt was born Herbert Ernst Karl Frahm at Lubeck, Germany. An anti-Nazi exile during WWII, he won the Nobel Peace Prize in 1971 for seeking better East-West relations. He died Oct 8, 1992, at Unkel, Germany.

CAPITOL REEF NATIONAL PARK ESTABLISHED: ANNIVERSARY. Dec 18, 1971. Area of outstanding geological features, colorful canyons, prehistoric Fremont petroglyphs and Mormon historic fruit orchards and buildings in south central Utah, originally proclaimed a national monument Aug 2, 1937, was established as a national park. For further park info: Capitol Reef Natl Park, Box 15, Torrey, UT 84775. E-mail: care-interpretation@nps.gov. Web: www.nps.gov/care.

COBB, TYRUS RAYMOND "TY": BIRTH ANNIVERSARY. Dec 18, 1886. Famed American baseball player born at Narrows, GA. Died at Atlanta, GA, July 17, 1961. Lifetime batting average of .367 compiled over 24 years during which he played in more than 3,000 games. Cobb was among the first five players inducted into the National Baseball Hall of Fame in 1936.

DAVIS, BENJAMIN O., JR: BIRTH ANNIVERSARY. Dec 18, 1912. The WWII hero was born at Washington, DC, to the Army's first black general. Davis had a distinguished career serving the US: he was the first African American to graduate from West Point in the 20th century; he led the first all-black air unit, the 99th Pursuit Squadron (the Tuskegee Airmen), in WWII; he helped plan the integration of the US Air Force in 1948–49 and he was the Air Force's first black general (1954). He died at Washington, DC, on July 4, 2002. See also "Tuskegee Airmen Activated: Anniversary" (Mar 22).

DAVIS, OSSIE: BIRTH ANNIVERSARY. Dec 18, 1917. Born at Cogdell, GA, Davis began his career as an actor with the Rose McClendon Players in Harlem, NY, in the 1940s. He became involved with civil rights, counting among his friends W.E.B. DuBois, Richard Wright and Langston Hughes, and worked to promote African Americans in the entertainment industry throughout his life. Often sharing the stage or screen with wife Ruby Dee, he was featured in dozens of stage productions and feature films. He died at Miami Beach, FL, Feb 4, 2005.

GRIMALDI, JOSEPH: BIRTH ANNIVERSARY. Dec 18, 1778. Known as the "greatest clown in history" and the "king of pantomime," Joseph Grimaldi began his stage career at age two. He was an accomplished singer, dancer and acrobat. Born at London, England, he is best remembered as the original "Joey the Clown" and for the innovative humor he brought to the clown's role in theater. Illness forced his early retirement in 1823, and he died at London, May 31, 1837.

ISLAMIC NEW YEAR. Dec 18. Islamic calendar date: Muharram 1, 1431. The first day of the first month of the Islamic calendar. Different methods for "anticipating" the visibility of the new moon crescent at Mecca are used by different groups. US date may vary. Began at sunset the preceding day.

MEXICO: FEAST OF OUR LADY OF SOLITUDE. Dec 18. Oaxaca. Pilgrims venerate the patron of the lonely.

NEW JERSEY RATIFICATION DAY: ANNIVERSARY. Dec 18, 1787. New Jersey became the third state to ratify the Constitution (following Delaware and Pennsylvania). It did so unanimously.

NIGER: REPUBLIC DAY. Dec 18. National holiday. Gained autonomy within the French community in 1958.

STRADIVARI, ANTONIO: DEATH ANNIVERSARY. Dec 18, 1737. Celebrated Italian violin maker was born probably in the year 1644, and died at Cremona, at about age 93.

"TO TELL THE TRUTH" TV PREMIERE: ANNIVERSARY. Dec 18, 1956. This long-running, popular game show was a production of the Mark Goodson–Bill Todman team. A celebrity panel (and the home audience) tried to guess which of three guests claiming to be the same person was telling the truth. Panelists took turns questioning the guests, and, at the conclusion, the identity of the person was revealed. Hosts have included Bud Collyer, Garry Moore, Joe Garagiola, Robin Ward, Gordon Elliott and Alex Trebek. Celebrity panelists included Dick Van Dyke, Tom Poston, Peggy Cass, Kitty Carlisle and Bill Cullen.

UNDERDOG DAY. Dec 18. To salute, before the year's end, all of the underdogs and unsung heroes—the Number Two people who contribute so much to the Number One people we read about. (Sherlock Holmes's Dr. Watson and Robinson Crusoe's Friday are examples.) Observed annually on the third Friday in December since its founding in 1976 by the late Peter Moeller, THE Chief Underdog. For info: A.C. Vierow, Underdogs Intl, Box 71, Clio, MI 48420-0071.

UNITED NATIONS: INTERNATIONAL MIGRANTS DAY. Dec 18. Recognizes the contributions that millions of migrant workers make to the global economy and seeks to draw attention to the precarious state of their rights. For info: United Nations, Dept of Public Info, New York, NY 10017. Web: www.un.org.

 BIRTHDAYS TODAY

Christina Aguilera, 29, singer, born Staten Island, NY, Dec 18, 1980.

Rachel Griffiths, 41, actress ("Six Feet Under," "Brothers & Sisters," *Hilary and Jackie, The Rookie*), born Melbourne, Australia, Dec 18, 1968.

Katie Holmes, 31, actress (*Batman Begins, Pieces of April,* "Dawson's Creek"), born Toledo, OH, Dec 18, 1978.

Ray Liotta, 54, actor (*Unforgettable, Goodfellas, Field of Dreams, Something Wild*), born Newark, NJ, Dec 18, 1955.

Leonard Maltin, 59, movie critic, author (*Maltin's Guide*), born New York, NY, Dec 18, 1950.

Charles Oakley, 46, former basketball player, born Cleveland, OH, Dec 18, 1963.

Brad Pitt, 45, actor (*The Assassination of Jesse James by the Coward Robert Ford, Babel, Ocean's Eleven*), born Shawnee, OK, Dec 18, 1964.

Keith Richards, 66, musician, singer (Rolling Stones), born Dartford, England, Dec 18, 1943.

Steven Spielberg, 62, producer, director (*E.T. The Extra-Terrestrial, Indiana Jones* movies, *Close Encounters of the Third Kind, Jurassic Park, The Color Purple*; Oscars for *Schindler's List, Saving Private Ryan*), born Cincinnati, OH, Dec 18, 1947.

December 19 — Saturday

DAY 353 **12 REMAINING**

BREZHNEV, LEONID: BIRTH ANNIVERSARY. Dec 19, 1906. Leader of the Soviet Union after the overthrow of Nikita Khrushchev in 1964 (which he had a part in). He expanded and modernized Soviet military and nuclear power at the cost of the country's economic health. Born at Kamenskoye, Ukraine, Brezhnev died at Moscow, Russia, Nov 10, 1982.

FISKE, MINNIE MADDERN: BIRTH ANNIVERSARY. Dec 19, 1865. American theater actress with a long, distinguished career. First stage appearance at the age of three as "Little Minnie Maddern." Born at New Orleans, LA, she died Feb 15, 1932, at Hollis, NY.

LIVERMORE, MARY ASHTON: BIRTH ANNIVERSARY. Dec 19, 1821. American reformer and women's suffrage leader, born at Boston, MA. Died May 23, 1905, at Melrose, MA.

***THE MUSIC MAN* PREMIERE: ANNIVERSARY.** Dec 19, 1957. Meredith Willson's musical premiered on Broadway today and ran until 1961. It received five Tony Awards, including Best Musical (beating out *West Side Story*) and Best Actor for star Robert Preston.

NAIA FOOTBALL NATIONAL CHAMPIONSHIP GAME. Dec 19. Rome, GA. 16-team field competes, ending with the final two teams vying for the national championship. 54th annual. For info: Natl Assn of Intercollegiate Athletics, 1200 Grand Blvd, Kansas City, MO 64106. E-mail: dgreen@naia.org. Web: www.naia.org.

PARRY, WILLIAM: BIRTH ANNIVERSARY. Dec 19, 1790. British explorer Sir William Edward Parry was born at Bath, England. Remembered for his Arctic expeditions and for his search for a Northwest Passage, Parry died at Ems, Germany, July 8, 1855.

SPACE MILESTONE: FIRST RADIO BROADCAST FROM SPACE. Dec 19, 1958. At 3:15 PM, EST, the US Earth satellite *Atlas* transmitted the first radio voice broadcast from space, a 58-word recorded Christmas greeting from President Dwight D. Eisenhower: "to all mankind America's wish for peace on earth and good will toward men everywhere." The satellite had been launched from Cape Canaveral Dec 18.

SPACE MILESTONE: *INTELSAT 4 F-3* (US). Dec 19, 1971. Communications satellite launched by NASA on contract with COMSAT. Mission involved intercontinental relay phone and TV communications.

SUSSKIND, DAVID: BIRTH ANNIVERSARY. Dec 19, 1920. American television producer David (Howard) Susskind was born at New York, NY. In 1952 he started his own television production company and soon was producing more live programs than the three networks combined. He began to host talk shows in 1958 and was widely respected for focusing on serious matters. He died Feb 22, 1987, at New York, NY.

December 2009

S	M	T	W	T	F	S
		1	2	3	4	5
6	7	8	9	10	11	12
13	14	15	16	17	18	19
20	21	22	23	24	25	26
27	28	29	30	31		

34th STREET EXPRESS. Dec 19. Chartered Amtrak train leaves from Boston, MA. Christmas shopping special to New York City also takes in the Radio City Christmas Spectacular. Annually, the second Saturday in December. Est attendance: 300. For info: Mystic Valley Railway Society, Inc, PO Box 365486, Hyde Park, MA 02136-0009. Phone: (617) 361-4445. Fax: (617) 361-4445*51 (dial all as one number). Web: www.mysticvalleyrs.org.

***TITANIC* RELEASED: ANNIVERSARY.** Dec 19, 1997. The most expensive film made (up to that time) at $200 million was released in theaters on this date. *Titanic*, written and directed by James Cameron, featured the drama of star-crossed lovers (Leonardo DiCaprio and Kate Winslet) paired with the amazing special effects re-creation of the doomed 1912 ocean liner's first and last voyage. The film won 11 Academy Awards, including best picture, which tied it with 1959's *Ben-Hur*. It is widely considered one of the most successful films ever made.

UNITED NATIONS: DAY FOR SOUTH-SOUTH COOPERATION. Dec 19. On Dec 23, 2004, the UN General Assembly declared this day each year as the United Nations Day for South-South Cooperation (Resolution 58/220). This marks the date, in 1978, when the General Assembly endorsed the Buenos Aires Plan of Action for Promoting and Implementing Technical Cooperation among Developing Countries (Resolution 33/134). For info: United Nations, Dept of Public Info, New York, NY 10017. Web: www.un.org.

WOODSON, CARTER GODWIN: BIRTH ANNIVERSARY. Dec 19, 1875. Historian who introduced black studies to colleges and universities, born at New Canton, VA. His scholarly works included *The Negro in Our History, The Education of the Negro Prior to 1861.* Known as the father of Black history, he inaugurated Negro History Week. Woodson was working on a six-volume *Encyclopaedia Africana* when he died at Washington, DC, Apr 3, 1950.

BIRTHDAYS TODAY

Jennifer Beals, 46, actress ("The L Word," *Flashdance*), born Chicago, IL, Dec 19, 1963.

Janie Fricke, 57, country singer ("It Ain't Easy"), born Whitney, IN, Dec 19, 1952.

Tom Gugliotta, 40, former basketball player, born Huntington Station, NY, Dec 19, 1969.

Jake Gyllenhall, 29, actor (*Brokeback Mountain, Jarhead, Donnie Darko*), born Los Angeles, CA, Dec 19, 1980.

Richard E. Leakey, 65, anthropologist, born Nairobi, Kenya, Dec 19, 1944.

Kevin Edward McHale, 52, Hall of Fame basketball player, born Hibbing, MN, Dec 19, 1957.

Alyssa Milano, 37, actress ("Charmed," "Melrose Place"), born Brooklyn, NY, Dec 19, 1972.

Tim Reid, 65, actor ("Frank's Place," "WKRP in Cincinnati"), born Norfolk, VA, Dec 19, 1944.

Kristy Swanson, 40, actress (*Buffy the Vampire Slayer*), born Mission Viejo, CA, Dec 19, 1969.

Cicely Tyson, 70, actress (Emmy for *The Autobiography of Miss Jane Pittman*; *Sounder*), born New York, NY, Dec 19, 1939.

December 20 — Sunday

DAY 354 11 REMAINING

AMERICAN POET LAUREATE ESTABLISHMENT: ANNIVERSARY. Dec 20, 1985. A bill empowering the Librarian of Congress to name, annually, a poet laureate/consultant in poetry was signed into law by President Ronald Reagan. In return for a stipend as poet laureate and a salary as the consultant in poetry, the person named will present at least one major work of poetry and will appear at selected national ceremonies. The first poet laureate of the US was Robert Penn Warren, appointed to that position by the Librarian of Congress Feb 26, 1986. See also: "Warren, Robert Penn: Birth Anniversary" (Apr 24).

CATHODE-RAY TUBE PATENTED: ANNIVERSARY. Dec 20, 1938. The kinescope, today known as the cathode-ray tube, was patented by Russian immigrant Vladimir Zworykin. It is still used today in computer monitors and television sets.

CLINTON IMPEACHMENT PROCEEDINGS: ANNIVERSARY. Dec 20, 1998. President William Clinton was impeached by a House of Representatives that was divided along party lines. He was convicted of perjury and obstruction of justice stemming from a sexual relationship with a White House intern. He was then tried by the Senate in January 1999. On Feb 12, 1999, the Senate acquitted him on both charges. Clinton was only the second US president to undergo impeachment proceedings. Andrew Johnson was impeached by the House in 1868, but the Senate voted against impeachment and he finished his term of office. See also: "Johnson Impeachment Proceedings" (Feb 24).

COMMUNITY CAROL SING. Dec 20. Mystic, CT. Lift up your voice in song to celebrate the season. Museum admission is free when you bring a canned good to be donated to charity. A brass quartet and the Mystic Seaport carolers lead an afternoon of joyous musical cheer. Est attendance: 3,000. For info: Mystic Seaport, 75 Greenmanville Ave, Box 6000, Mystic, CT 06355. Phone: (860) 572-5315 or (888) 973-2767. Web: www.mysticseaport.org.

"THE DATING GAME" TV PREMIERE: ANNIVERSARY. Dec 20, 1965. Another game show developed by Chuck Barris, it typically featured a "bachelorette" who questioned three men who were hidden from her view and decided, based on their answers, which guy appealed to her the most. The couple was then sent on a date, courtesy of the show. Occasionally, a bachelor would question three women. Jim Lange was the host of the network series and two syndicated ones. Elaine Joyce and Jeff MacGregor hosted one season each on the retitled "The New Dating Game."

FIRESTONE, HARVEY S.: BIRTH ANNIVERSARY. Dec 20, 1868. American industrialist, businessman and founder of the Firestone Tire and Rubber Company, Harvey Samuel Firestone was born at Columbiana County, OH. A close friend of Henry Ford, Thomas Edison and John Burroughs, Firestone died at Miami Beach, FL, Feb 7, 1938.

***IT'S A WONDERFUL LIFE* FILM PREMIERE: ANNIVERSARY.** Dec 20, 1946. America's favorite Christmas drama premiered on this date at New York, NY. Directed by Frank Capra and starring James Stewart (George Bailey), Donna Reed (Mary Bailey), Henry Travers (as Clarence Oddbody, trying to earn his angel wings) and Lionel Barrymore (as villainous Mr Potter), the film was nominated for five Academy Awards.

LANGER, SUSANNE K.: BIRTH ANNIVERSARY. Dec 20, 1895. Susanne Langer, a leading American philosopher, author of *Philosophy in a New Key: A Study in the Symbolism of Reason, Rite, and Art*, was born at New York, NY. Her studies of aesthetics and art exerted a profound influence on thinking in the fields of psychology, philosophy and the social sciences. She died at Old Lyme, CT, July 17, 1985.

MACAU REVERTS TO CHINESE CONTROL: 10th ANNIVERSARY. Dec 20, 1999. Macau, a tiny province on the southeast coast of China, reverted to Chinese rule. It had been a Portuguese colony since 1557.

MENZIES, ROBERT GORDON: BIRTH ANNIVERSARY. Dec 20, 1894. Australian statesman and conservative leader, born at Jeparit, Victoria, Australia, Sir Robert died at Melbourne, Australia, May 14, 1978, at age 83.

MONTGOMERY BUS BOYCOTT ENDS: ANNIVERSARY. Dec 20, 1956. The US Supreme Court ruling of Nov 13, 1956, calling for integration of the Montgomery, AL, public bus system was implemented. Since Dec 5, 1955, the black community of Montgomery had refused to ride on the segregated buses. The boycott was in reaction to the Dec 1, 1955, arrest of Rosa Parks for refusing to relinquish her seat on a Montgomery bus to a white man.

MUDD DAY: ANNIVERSARY. Dec 20, 1833. A day to remember Dr. Samuel A. Mudd (born near Bryantown, MD, Dec 20, 1833), sentenced to life imprisonment for giving medical aid to disguised John Wilkes Booth, fleeing assassin of Abraham Lincoln. Imprisoned four years before being pardoned by President Andrew Johnson. Died on Jan 10, 1883.

RICKEY, BRANCH: BIRTH ANNIVERSARY. Dec 20, 1881. Wesley Branch Rickey, Baseball Hall of Fame player, manager and executive born at Lucasville, OH. Rickey was baseball's most innovative general manager. He invented the farm system, instituted unique training and teaching methods and, most prominently, signed Jackie Robinson to play major league baseball with the Brooklyn Dodgers. Inducted into the Hall of Fame in 1967. Died at Columbia, MO, Dec 9, 1965.

SACAGAWEA: DEATH ANNIVERSARY. Dec 20, 1812. As a young Shoshone Indian woman, Sacagawea in 1805 (with her two-month-old son strapped to her back) traveled with the Lewis and Clark expedition, serving as an interpreter. It is said that the expedition could not have succeeded without her aid. She was born about 1787 and died at Fort Manuel on the Missouri River, Dec 20, 1812. Few other women have been so often honored. There are statues, fountains and memorials of her, and her name has been given to a mountain peak. In 2000 the US Mint issued a $1 coin honoring her.

SOUTH CAROLINA: SECESSION ANNIVERSARY. Dec 20, 1860. South Carolina's legislature voted to secede from the US, the first state to do so. Within six weeks, five more states seceded. On Feb 4, 1861, representatives from the six states met at Montgomery, AL, to establish a government and on Feb 9 Jefferson Davis was elected president of the Confederate States of America. By June 1861, 11 states had seceded.

UNITED NATIONS: INTERNATIONAL HUMAN SOLIDARITY DAY. Dec 20. In connection with its observance of first UN Decade for the Eradication of Poverty (1997–2006), the UN General Assembly, on Dec 22, 2005, declared this date each year as International Human Solidarity Day (Resolution 60/209). In taking that action, it recalled that the Millennium Declaration identified solidarity as one of the fundamental and universal values that should underlie relations between peoples in the twenty-first century. For info: United Nations, Dept of Public Info, New York, NY 10017. Web: www.un.org.

US INVASION OF PANAMA: 20th ANNIVERSARY. Dec 20, 1989. The US launched operation "Just Cause," invading Panama in an attempt to seize Manuel Noriega and bring him to justice for narcotics trafficking. Seven months after Noriega had ruled unfavorable election results null and void, the US toppled the Noriega government and oversaw the installation of Guillermo Endara as president. Although the initial military action was declared a success, Noriega eluded capture. He surrendered to US troops on Jan 4, 1990, and was tried, convicted and imprisoned in the US.

VIRGINIA COMPANY EXPEDITION TO AMERICA: ANNIVERSARY. Dec 20, 1606. Three small ships, the *Susan Constant*, the *Godspeed* and the *Discovery*, commanded by Captain Christopher Newport, departed London, England, bound for America, where the royally chartered Virginia Company's approximately 120 persons established the first permanent English settlement in what is now the United States at Jamestown, VA, May 14, 1607.

BIRTHDAYS TODAY

Jenny Agutter, 57, actress (Emmy for "The Snow Goose"), born London, England, Dec 20, 1952.

David Cook, 27, singer, television personality ("American Idol"), born Houston, TX, Dec 20, 1982.

Uri Geller, 63, psychic, clairvoyant, born Tel Aviv, Israel, Dec 20, 1946.

John Hillerman, 77, actor ("Magnum, PI"), born Denison, TX, Dec 20, 1932.

David Levine, 83, artist, caricaturist (*New York Review of Books*), born Brooklyn, NY, Dec 20, 1926.

Sonny Perdue, 63, Governor of Georgia (R), born Perry, GA, Dec 20, 1946.

William Julius Wilson, 74, sociologist, educator, writer (*When Work Disappears*), born Derry Township, PA, Dec 20, 1935.

December 21 — Monday

DAY 355 — 10 REMAINING

BELGIUM: NUTS FAIR. Dec 21. Bastogne. Traditional cultural observance. Annually, the third Monday in December.

BÖLL, HEINRICH: BIRTH ANNIVERSARY. Dec 21, 1917. German novelist, winner of the 1972 Nobel Prize for Literature, author of some 20 books including *Billiards at Half-Past Nine, The Clown* and *Group Portrait with Lady*, was born at Cologne, Germany. He died near Bonn, Germany, July 16, 1985.

DISRAELI, BENJAMIN: BIRTH ANNIVERSARY. Dec 21, 1804. British novelist and statesman, born at London and died there Apr 19, 1881. "No government," he wrote, "can be long secure without a formidable opposition."

ELVIS PRESLEY MEETS PRESIDENT NIXON: ANNIVERSARY. Dec 21, 1970. After writing President Richard M. Nixon offering to be a "Federal Agent-at-Large" to fight drug abuse and the drug culture, Elvis Presley met with Nixon at the White House on this date. Presley was not made a federal agent, but the two men had a cordial meeting. The photograph of them shaking hands is the most requested reproduction from the National Archives (more than the Bill of Rights or the US Constitution).

December 2009

S	M	T	W	T	F	S
		1	2	3	4	5
6	7	8	9	10	11	12
13	14	15	16	17	18	19
20	21	22	23	24	25	26
27	28	29	30	31		

FIRST CROSSWORD PUZZLE: ANNIVERSARY. Dec 21, 1913. The first crossword puzzle was compiled by Arthur Wynne and published in a supplement to the *New York World*.

FOREFATHERS' DAY. Dec 21. Observed mainly in New England in commemoration of landing at Plymouth Rock on this day in 1620.

GIBSON, JOSH: BIRTH ANNIVERSARY. Dec 21, 1912. Joshua (Josh) Gibson, Baseball Hall of Fame catcher born at Buena Vista, GA, is regarded as the greatest slugger to play in the Negro Leagues and perhaps the greatest ballplayer ever. Gibson starred with the Pittsburgh Crawfords. His long home runs are the stuff of legend. Inducted into the Hall of Fame in 1972. Died at Pittsburgh, PA, Jan 20, 1947.

HUMBUG DAY. Dec 21. Allows all those preparing for Christmas to vent their frustrations. Twelve "humbugs" allowed. (©2006 by WH.) For info: Thomas & Ruth Roy, Wellcat Holidays, 2418 Long Ln, Lebanon, PA 17046. Phone: (717) 279-0184. E-mail: info@wellcat.com. Web: www.wellcat.com.

NATIONAL HAIKU POETRY DAY. Dec 21. A day to celebrate the popular Japanese poetry form called haiku. Public libraries, literary groups, school libraries, etc, can observe the day with haiku readings, artwork and other events. Haiku are traditionally about the seasons, so this day is celebrated annually on the winter solstice. For info: Sari Grandstaff. E-mail: imabluestocking@yahoo.com. Web: www.rainpuddlejumper.com.

PAN AMERICAN FLIGHT 103 EXPLOSION: ANNIVERSARY. Dec 21, 1988. Pan Am World Airways Flight 103 exploded in midair and crashed into the heart of Lockerbie, Scotland, the result of a terrorist bombing. The 259 passengers and crew members and 11 persons on the ground were killed in the disaster. The tragedy raised questions about security and the notification of passengers in the event of threatened flights. In the resultant investigation it was revealed that government agencies and the airline had known that the flight was possibly the target of a terrorist attack.

PARKINSON, JAMES: DEATH ANNIVERSARY. Dec 21, 1824. The remarkable English physician and paleontologist who first described the "shaking palsy" later had it named for him—Parkinson's disease. He was the author of numerous books and articles on a variety of subjects. His *Organic Remains of a Former World* is called the first attempt to give a scientific account of fossils. Under oath, Parkinson declared that he was a member of the group that hatched the "Pop-gun Plot" to assassinate King George III in a theater, using a poisoned dart for the deed. Parkinson was born at London about 1755, and died there, Dec 21, 1824.

PHILEAS FOGG WINS A WAGER DAY. Dec 21. Anniversary, from Jules Verne's *Around the World in Eighty Days*, of the winning of Phileas Fogg's wager, on Dec 21, 1872, when Fogg walked into the saloon of the Reform Club at London, announcing "Here I am, gentlemen!" exactly 79 days, 23 hours, 59 minutes and 59 seconds after starting his trip "around the world in 80 days," to win his £20,000 wager. See also: "Phileas Fogg's Wager Day" (Oct 2).

PILGRIM LANDING: ANNIVERSARY. Dec 21, 1620. According to Governor William Bradford's *History of Plymouth Plantation*, "On Munday," [Dec 21, 1620, New Style] the Pilgrims, aboard the *Mayflower*, reached Plymouth, MA, "sounded ye harbor, and founde it fitt for shipping; and marched into ye land, & founde diverse cornfields, and ye best they could find, and ye season & their presente necessitie made them glad to accepte of it. . . . And after wards tooke better view of ye place, and resolved wher to pitch their dwelling; and them and their goods." Plymouth Rock, the legendary place of landing since it first was "identified" in 1769, nearly 150 years after the landing, has been a historic shrine since. The landing anniversary is observed in much of New England as Forefathers' Day. See also: "Forefathers' Day" (Dec 21).

SHERMAN TAKES SAVANNAH: ANNIVERSARY. Dec 21, 1864. Despite efforts by Confederate General William Hardee to defend the city of Savannah, GA, Southern troops were forced to pull out of the city, and on this date Union forces under William Tecumseh Sherman captured the town. By marching from Atlanta to the coast at Savannah, Sherman had cut the lower South off from the center.

***SNOW WHITE AND THE SEVEN DWARFS* FILM PREMIERE: ANNIVERSARY.** Dec 21, 1937. America's first full-length animated feature film (and also the first Technicolor feature) premiered on this date at the Carthay Circle Theater, Hollywood, CA. The labor of love from Walt Disney—who for years wanted to create a feature-length cartoon—involved more than 750 artists and 1,500 colors in four years of development. The film features the classic songs "Some Day My Prince Will Come" and "Whistle While You Work." Walt Disney received a special Oscar for *Snow White*—along with seven miniature Oscars.

SPACE MILESTONE: *APOLLO 8* (US). Dec 21, 1968. First moon voyage launched, manned by Colonel Frank Borman, Captain James A. Lovell, Jr and Major William A. Anders. Orbited moon Dec 24, returned to Earth Dec 27. First men to orbit the moon and see the side of the moon away from Earth.

STALIN, JOSEPH: BIRTH ANNIVERSARY. Dec 21, 1879. Russian dictator whose family name was Dzhugashvili, was born at Gori, Georgia. One of the most powerful and most feared men of the 20th century, Stalin died (of a stroke) at the Kremlin, at Moscow, Mar 5, 1953.

SZOLD, HENRIETTA: BIRTH ANNIVERSARY. Dec 21, 1860. Teacher, writer, social worker, organizer and pioneer Zionist, Henrietta Szold is best remembered as founder and first president of Hadassah, the Women's Zionist Organization of America. Born at Baltimore, MD, she was influenced by her father Rabbi Benjamin Szold, an active and vocal abolitionist. She established the first "night school" at Baltimore, focused on teaching English and job skills to immigrants. Her trip to Palestine in 1910 sparked the genesis of Hadassah. While there, Szold was alarmed by the lack of social, medical and educational services and returned with the idea that a national women's Zionist organization must be formed to carry out practical projects. The "Mother of Social Service in Palestine," Szold died at Jerusalem, Feb 13, 1945. See also: "Hadassah: Anniversary" (Feb 24).

UNITED KINGDOM ALLOWS SAME-SEX CIVIL PARTNERSHIPS: ANNIVERSARY. Dec 21, 2005. On this date a new law took effect legally recognizing same-sex civil unions in the United Kingdom. The law took effect on Dec 19 in Northern Ireland, but on Dec 20 in Scotland and then Dec 21 in England and Wales. Pop star Elton John and his partner filmmaker David Furnish were among the first celebrities to wed on the 21st.

WINTER. Dec 21–Mar 20, 2010. In the Northern Hemisphere winter begins today with the winter solstice, at 12:47 PM, EST. Note that in the Southern Hemisphere today is the beginning of summer. Between Equator and Arctic Circle the sunrise and sunset points on the horizon are farthest south for the year and daylight length is minimum (ranging from 12 hours, 8 minutes, at the equator to zero at the Arctic Circle).

YALDA. Dec 21. Yalda, the longest night of the year, is celebrated by Iranians. The ceremony has an Indo-Iranian origin, where Light and Good were considered to struggle against Darkness and Evil. With fires burning and lights lit, family and friends gather to stay up through the night helping the sun in its battle against darkness. They recite poetry, tell stories and eat special fruits and nuts until the sun, triumphant, reappears in the morning.

YULE. Dec 21. (Also called Alban Arthan.) One of the "Lesser Sabbats" during the Wiccan year, Yule marks the death of the Sun-God and his rebirth from the Earth Goddess. Annually, on the winter solstice.

ZAPPA, FRANK: BIRTH ANNIVERSARY. Dec 21, 1940. Rock musician and composer, Zappa was noted for his satire and as a leading advocate against censorship of contemporary music. He formed the group Mothers of Invention. Born at Baltimore, MD, he died Dec 4, 1993, at Los Angeles, CA, at age 52.

BIRTHDAYS TODAY

Tina Brown, 56, former *New Yorker* editor, born London, England, Dec 21, 1953.

Andy Dick, 44, actor ("NewsRadio"), born Charleston, SC, Dec 21, 1965.

Phil Donahue, 74, former TV talk-show host ("Donahue"), born Cleveland, OH, Dec 21, 1935.

Christine Marie (Chris) Evert, 55, sportscaster, former tennis player, born Ft Lauderdale, FL, Dec 21, 1954.

Jane Fonda, 72, actress (Oscars for *Klute, Coming Home*; *Julia, On Golden Pond*), born New York, NY, Dec 21, 1937.

Samuel L. Jackson, 61, actor (*SWAT, Shaft, Pulp Fiction*), born Washington, DC, Dec 21, 1948.

Jane Kaczmarek, 54, actress ("Malcolm in the Middle"), born Milwaukee, WI, Dec 21, 1955.

Joe Paterno, 83, college football coach, born Brooklyn, NY, Dec 21, 1926.

Ray Romano, 52, comedian, actor ("Everybody Loves Raymond"), born Queens, NY, Dec 21, 1957.

Kiefer Sutherland, 43, actor ("24," *Flatliners, A Few Good Men*), born London, England, Dec 21, 1966.

Michael Tilson Thomas, 65, conductor, pianist, organist, born Hollywood, CA, Dec 21, 1944.

Andrew James (Andy) Van Slyke, 49, former baseball player, born Utica, NY, Dec 21, 1960.

Karrie Webb, 35, golfer, born Ayr, Queensland, Australia, Dec 21, 1974.

December 22 — Tuesday

DAY 356 | **9 REMAINING**

ASHCROFT, PEGGY: BIRTH ANNIVERSARY. Dec 22, 1907. British actress Dame Edith Margaret Emily Ashcroft was born at Croyden, England. In addition to her many accolades on the British stage, she won an Oscar for her supporting role in *Passage to India* (1985) and a special British Olivier Award for lifetime achievement in 1991. She died June 14, 1991, at London, England.

CAPRICORN, THE GOAT. Dec 22–Jan 19. In the astronomical and astrological zodiac that divides the sun's apparent orbit into 12 segments, the period Dec 22–Jan 19 is traditionally identified as the sun sign of Capricorn, the goat. The ruling planet is Saturn.

"DING DONG SCHOOL" TV PREMIERE: ANNIVERSARY. Dec 22, 1952. Named by a three-year-old after watching a test broadcast of the opening sequence (a hand ringing a bell), "Ding Dong School" was one of the first children's educational series. Miss Frances (Dr. Frances Horwich, head of Roosevelt College's education department at Chicago) was the host of this weekday show.

ELLERY, WILLIAM: BIRTH ANNIVERSARY. Dec 22, 1727. Signer of the Declaration of Independence, born at Newport, RI, and died there Feb 15, 1820.

FIRST GORILLA BORN IN CAPTIVITY: ANNIVERSARY. Dec 22, 1956. "Colo" was born at the Columbus, OH, zoo, weighing in at 3¼ pounds, the first gorilla born in captivity.

JOHNSON, CLAUDIA TAYLOR (LADY BIRD): BIRTH ANNIVERSARY. Dec 22, 1912. Former First Lady, born Claudia Alta Taylor at Karnack, TX, this daughter of an East Texas cotton grower married young politician Lyndon Baines Johnson in 1934. She ran his congressional office during his navy stint in WWII and was at his side as his career ran its course from Texas congressman to 36th president of the US. Her personal causes included highway beautification and she founded the National Wildflower Research Center in Austin, TX, in 1995 (later renamed for her). She died at Austin, July 11, 2007.

OGLETHORPE, JAMES EDWARD: BIRTH ANNIVERSARY. Dec 22, 1696. English general, author and colonizer of Georgia. Founder of the city of Savannah. Oglethorpe was born at London. He died June 30, 1785, at Cranham Hall, Essex, England.

PUCCINI, GIACOMO: BIRTH ANNIVERSARY. Dec 22, 1858. Italian composer of such operas as *La Boheme*, *Tosca* and *Madama Butterfly*. Born at Lucca, Tuscany, Italy, he died Nov 29, 1924, at Brussels, Belgium.

ROBINSON, EDWIN ARLINGTON: BIRTH ANNIVERSARY. Dec 22, 1869. Three-time Pulitzer Prize winner best known for his short dramatic poems, including "Richard Cory" and "Miniver Cheevy." Born at Head Tide, ME, and died at Los Angeles, CA, Apr 6, 1935.

 BIRTHDAYS TODAY

Barbara Billingsley, 87, actress ("Leave It to Beaver," *Airplane!*), born Los Angeles, CA, Dec 22, 1922.

Steven Norman (Steve) Carlton, 65, Hall of Fame baseball player, born Miami, FL, Dec 22, 1944.

Hector Elizondo, 73, actor (*Pretty Woman, Frankie and Johnny*, "Chicago Hope"), born New York, NY, Dec 22, 1936.

Ralph Fiennes, 47, actor (*Harry Potter* films, *Schindler's List, The English Patient*), born Suffolk, England, Dec 22, 1962.

Steve Garvey, 61, former baseball player, born Tampa, FL, Dec 22, 1948.

Robin Gibb, 60, singer, musician (The Bee Gees), born Manchester, England, Dec 22, 1949.

Diane K. Sawyer, 63, journalist ("60 Minutes," "Prime Time Live"), born Glasgow, KY, Dec 22, 1946.

Jan Stephenson, 58, golfer, born Sydney, Australia, Dec 22, 1951.

December 2009

S	M	T	W	T	F	S
		1	2	3	4	5
6	7	8	9	10	11	12
13	14	15	16	17	18	19
20	21	22	23	24	25	26
27	28	29	30	31		

December 23 — Wednesday

DAY 357 — 8 REMAINING

FEDERAL RESERVE SYSTEM: ANNIVERSARY. Dec 23, 1913. Established pursuant to authority contained in the Federal Reserve Act of Dec 23, 1913, the system serves as the nation's central bank, with the responsibility for execution of monetary policy. It is called on to contribute to the strength and vitality of the US economy, in part by influencing the lending and investing activities of commercial banks and the cost and availability of money and credit.

FIRST NONSTOP FLIGHT AROUND THE WORLD WITHOUT REFUELING: ANNIVERSARY. Dec 23, 1987. Dick Rutan and Jeana Yeager set a new world record of 216 hours of continuous flight, breaking their own record of 111 hours set July 15, 1986. The aircraft *Voyager* departed from Edwards Air Force Base in California, Dec 14, 1987, and landed Dec 23, 1987. The journey covered 24,986 miles at an official speed of 115 miles per hour.

HUMANLIGHT CELEBRATION. Dec 23. HumanLight is a celebration of humanist values: tolerance, compassion, empathy, honesty, free inquiry, reason and rationality and more. The event began in New Jersey by the New Jersey Humanist Network in 2001. The event provides an excellent alternative to Christmas celebrations. For info: Institute for Humanist Studies, 48 Howard St, Albany, NY 12207. Phone: (518) 432-7820. Fax: (518) 432-7821. E-mail: MCherry@HumanistStudies.org. Web: www.secularseasons.org.

JAPAN: BIRTHDAY OF THE EMPEROR. Dec 23. National Day. Holiday honoring Emperor Akihito, born in 1933.

METRIC CONVERSION ACT: ANNIVERSARY. Dec 23, 1975. The Congress of the US passed Public Law 94–168, known as the Metric Conversion Act of 1975. This act declares that the SI (International System of Units) will be this country's basic system of measurement and establishes the United States Metric Board, which is responsible for the planning, coordination and implementation of the nation's voluntary conversion to SI. (Congress had authorized the metric system as a legal system of measurement in the US by an act passed July 28, 1866. In 1875, the US became one of the original signers of the Treaty of the Metre, which established an international metric system.)

MEXICO: FEAST OF THE RADISHES. Dec 23. Oaxaca. Figurines of people and animals cleverly carved out of radishes are sold during festivities.

MONROE, HARRIET: BIRTH ANNIVERSARY. Dec 23, 1860. American poet, editor and founder of *Poetry* magazine. Born at Chicago, IL. Died Sept 26, 1936, at Arequipa, Peru.

SMITH, JOSEPH, JR: BIRTH ANNIVERSARY. Dec 23, 1805. The founding prophet of The Church of Jesus Christ of Latter-day Saints was born at Sharon, VT. He was assassinated by an armed mob on June 27, 1844, at Carthage, IL. See also: "Smith, Joseph, Jr, and Hyrum: Death Anniversary" (June 27).

TOJO HIDEKI EXECUTION: ANNIVERSARY. Dec 23, 1948. Tojo Hideki, prime minister of Japan from Oct 16, 1941, until his resignation July 19, 1944. After Japan's surrender in August 1945, Tojo was arrested as a war criminal, tried by a military tribunal and sentenced to death Nov 12, 1948. Born at Tokyo, Japan, Dec 30, 1884, Tojo was hanged (with six other Japanese wartime military leaders) at Sugamo Prison, Tokyo, Dec 23, 1948, the sentence being carried out by the US 8th Army.

TRANSISTOR UNVEILED: ANNIVERSARY. Dec 23, 1947. John Bardeen, Walter Brattain and William Shockley of Bell Laboratories shared the 1956 Nobel Prize for their invention of the transistor, which led to a revolution in communications and electronics. It was smaller, lighter, more durable, more reliable and generated less heat than the vacuum tube that had been used up to that time.

BIRTHDAYS TODAY

Akihito, 76, Emperor of Japan, born Tokyo, Japan, Dec 23, 1933.

Robert Bly, 83, poet, author (*Iron John, What Have I Ever Lost by Dying?*), born Madison, MN, Dec 23, 1926.

Scott Gomez, 30, hockey player, born Anchorage, AK, Dec 23, 1979.

Corey Haim, 38, actor (*Murphy's Romance, The Lost Boys*), born Toronto, ON, Canada, Dec 23, 1971.

James Joseph (Jim) Harbaugh, 46, former football player, born Toledo, OH, Dec 23, 1963.

Susan Lucci, 60, actress ("All My Children," *Mafia Princess*), born Westchester, NY, Dec 23, 1949.

Gerald O'Loughlin, 88, actor ("The Rookies," "Our House"), born New York, NY, Dec 23, 1921.

Hanley Ramirez, 26, baseball player, born Samana, Dominican Republic, Dec 23, 1983.

December 24 — Thursday

DAY 358 **7 REMAINING**

***AIDA* PREMIERE: ANNIVERSARY.** Dec 24, 1871. Giuseppe Verdi's opera *Aida* premiered at Cairo. It was commissioned by the Khedive of Egypt to celebrate the opening of the Suez Canal.

ARNOLD, MATTHEW: BIRTH ANNIVERSARY. Dec 24, 1822. English poet and essayist, born at Laleham, England. Died Apr 15, 1888, at Liverpool, England. "One has often wondered," he wrote in *Culture and Anarchy*, "whether upon the whole earth there is anything so unintelligent, so unapt to perceive how the world is really going, as an ordinary young Englishman of our upper class."

AUSTRIA: "SILENT NIGHT, HOLY NIGHT" CELEBRATIONS. Dec 24. Oberndorf, Hallein and Wagrain, Salzburg, Austria. Commemorating the creation of the Christmas carol here in 1818.

CARSON, CHRISTOPHER "KIT": 200th BIRTH ANNIVERSARY. Dec 24, 1809. American frontiersman, soldier, trapper, guide and Indian agent best known as Kit Carson. Born at Madison County, KY, he died at Fort Lyon, CO, May 23, 1868.

CHRISTMAS BELLS RING AGAIN IN ST. BASIL'S: ANNIVERSARY. Dec 24, 1990. For the first time since the death of Lenin in 1924, the bells of St. Basil's Cathedral, on Red Square in Moscow, rang to celebrate Christmas.

CHRISTMAS EVE. Dec 24. Family gift-giving occasion in many Christian countries.

CHRISTMAS EVE TORCHLIGHT PARADE. Dec 24. Winter Park Resort, Winter Park, CO. One of Winter Park Resort's most beloved traditions, highlighted by Santa Claus leading a procession of torch-bearing skiers down Lower Hughes trail under a spectacular fireworks display. Est attendance: 1,500. For info: Winter Park Resort, PO Box 36, Winter Park, CO 80482. Phone: (970) 726-1564. Fax: (970) 726-1572. E-mail: wpinfo@skiwinterpark.com. Web: winterparkresort.com.

FIRST SURFACE-TO-SURFACE GUIDED MISSILE: ANNIVERSARY. Dec 24, 1942. German rocket engineer Wernher von Braun launched the first surface-to-surface guided missile. Buzz bombs, a form of guided missile, were used by Germany against Great Britain starting Sept 8, 1944. On Feb 24, 1949, the first rocket to reach outer space (an altitude of 25 miles) was fired. The two-stage rocket, a Wac Corporal set in the nose of a German V-2, was launched from the White Sands Proving Grounds, NM, by a team of scientists headed by von Braun.

GARDNER, AVA: BIRTH ANNIVERSARY. Dec 24, 1922. Actress and leading sex symbol of the 1940s and '50s, Ava Lavinnia Gardner was born at Smithfield, NC. Among Gardner's numerous movies are *The Barefoot Contessa, Bhowani Junction, The Sun Also Rises* and *The Life and Times of Judge Roy Bean*. Gardner was married to Mickey Rooney (1942–43), Artie Shaw (1945–46) and Frank Sinatra (1951–57). Died at London, England, Jan 25, 1990.

HUGHES, HOWARD ROBARD: BIRTH ANNIVERSARY. Dec 24, 1905. Wealthy American industrialist, aviator and movie producer who spent his latter years as a recluse. Born at Houston, TX, he died in airplane en route from Acapulco, Mexico, to Houston, Apr 5, 1976.

JOULE, JAMES PRESCOTT: BIRTH ANNIVERSARY. Dec 24, 1818. English physicist and inventor after whom Joule's Law (the first law of thermodynamics) was named was born at Salford, Lancashire, England. The unit of measurement of the mechnical equivalent of heat is known as the joule. He died at Cheshire, England, Oct 11, 1889.

LIBYA: INDEPENDENCE DAY. Dec 24. Libya gained its independence from Italy in 1951.

MOON PHASE: FIRST QUARTER. Dec 24. Moon enters First Quarter phase at 12:36 PM, EST.

"THE PERRY COMO SHOW" TV PREMIERE: ANNIVERSARY. Dec 24, 1948. Singer Perry Como hosted "The Chesterfield Supper Club" when it came to TV from radio. Also featured were the Mitchell Ayres Orchestra and the Fontane Sisters. The show was retitled "The Perry Como Show" during 1955–59 and then "The Kraft Music Hall" during 1959–63. The Ray Charles Singers and the Louis DaPron Dancers were featured. Como's theme song was "Dream Along with Me."

BIRTHDAYS TODAY

Diedrich Bader, 43, actor ("The Drew Carey Show"), born Alexandria, VA, Dec 24, 1966.

Mary Higgins Clark, 78, author (*Where Are the Children?, Silent Night*), born New York, NY, Dec 24, 1931.

Ricky Martin, 38, singer, actor ("General Hospital"), born Enrique José Martín, San Juan, Puerto Rico, Dec 24, 1971.

Ryan Seacrest, 35, television host ("American Idol"), radio personality ("America's Top 40"), born Atlanta, GA, Dec 24, 1974.

Jeff Sessions, 63, US Senator (R, Alabama), born Hybart, AL, Dec 24, 1946.

December 25 — Friday

DAY 359 **6 REMAINING**

A'PHABET DAY. Dec 25. Also known as "No-L" Day, this celebration is for people who do not want to send Christmas cards but who want to greet their friends; so they send out cards listing the letters of the alphabet in order, but with a gap where L would be. For info: Bob Birch, The Puns Corps, 3108 Dashiell Rd, Falls Church, VA 22042. Phone: (703) 533-3668.

BARTON, CLARA: BIRTH ANNIVERSARY. Dec 25, 1821. Clarissa Harlowe Barton, American nurse and philanthropist, founder of the American Red Cross, was born at Oxford, MA. In 1881, she became first president of the American Red Cross (founded May 21, 1881). She died at Glen Echo, MD, Apr 12, 1912.

BOGART, HUMPHREY: BIRTH ANNIVERSARY. Dec 25, 1899. American stage and screen actor, Humphrey DeForest Bogart was born at New York, NY. Among his best-remembered films are: *The African Queen, The Maltese Falcon, Casablanca* and *To Have and Have Not.* Bogart died Jan 14, 1957, at Hollywood, CA.

BOOTH, EVANGELINE CORY: BIRTH ANNIVERSARY. Dec 25, 1865. Salvation Army general, active in England, Canada and the US. Author and composer of songs, Booth was born at London, England. She died at Hartsdale, NY, July 17, 1950.

CALLOWAY, CAB: BIRTH ANNIVERSARY. Dec 25, 1907. American singer and bandleader Cabell Calloway was born at Rochester, NY. George Gershwin modeled the part of Sportin' Life in *Porgy and Bess* (1935) after this jazz singer who also played the role across the US until 1956. He is best known for his song "Minnie the Moocher" (1931). He died Nov 18, 1994, at Hockessin, DE.

CEAUSESCU, NICOLAE: 20th DEATH ANNIVERSARY. Dec 25, 1989. On Christmas evening a broadcast of a Christmas symphony on state-run television was interrupted with the report that Romanian president Nicolae Ceausescu and his wife had been executed, bringing to an end the last hard-line regime in the Soviet bloc. Ceausescu's downfall began when he ordered members of his black-shirted state police, the Securitate, to use force to quell a disturbance in the town of Timisorara. The brutal crackdown led to estimates of as many as 4,500 killed. Ceausescu's rule was marked by corruption, deprivation and terror.

CHRISTMAS. Dec 25. Christian festival commemorating the birth of Jesus of Nazareth. Most popular of Christian observances, Christmas as a Feast of the Nativity dates from the fourth century. Although Jesus's birth date is not known, the Western church selected Dec 25 for the feast, possibly to counteract the non-Christian festivals of that approximate date. Many customs from non-Christian festivals (Roman Saturnalia, Mithraic sun's birthday, Teutonic yule, Druidic and other winter solstice rites) have been adopted as part of the Christmas celebration (lights, mistletoe, holly and ivy, holiday tree, wassailing and gift giving, for example). Some Orthodox churches celebrate Christmas Jan 7 based on the "old calendar" (Julian). Theophany (recognition of the divinity of Jesus) is observed on this date and also on Jan 6, especially by the Eastern Orthodox Church.

CUBA: CHRISTMAS RETURNS: ANNIVERSARY. Dec 25, 1998. Christmas was celebrated in Cuba after Fidel Castro's government announced that it was again a regular holiday in the Cuban calendar. In 1997 the government had granted a Christmas holiday in deference to Pope John Paul II who was visiting the island the next month. Christmas had been abolished as a holiday in Cuba in 1969.

FARLEY, CAL: BIRTH ANNIVERSARY. Dec 25, 1895. Cal Farley, known as "America's Greatest Foster Father," started Cal Farley's Boys Ranch in 1939 with nine boys. The ranch has grown into a modern community of 441 boys (and girls since 1992), which has housed and educated more than 4,000 boys and girls over the years. Cal Farley was born at Saxton, IA; he died Feb 19, 1967, at Boys Ranch, TX.

December 2009

S	M	T	W	T	F	S
		1	2	3	4	5
6	7	8	9	10	11	12
13	14	15	16	17	18	19
20	21	22	23	24	25	26
27	28	29	30	31		

FIRST INDOOR BASEBALL GAME: ANNIVERSARY. Dec 25, 1888. Long before the domed stadiums of the late 20th century, a large building at the state fairgrounds in Philadelphia, PA, was the site of the first indoor baseball game. Two thousand spectators watched the Downtowners beat the Uptowners, 6–1.

IT'S ABOUT TIME WEEK!. Dec 25–31. Innovative week dedicated to time-to-give, time-to-live and time-to-remember. Encourages creativity applied to problems and honors pioneers and partnerships in research, ideas and services for "ABetterWay; ABetterWorld." Awards to pioneers and partnerships. Send nominations by October. For info: The ForGoodnessSake! Center, 427 E 7th St, Michigan City, IN 46360. E-mail: ForGood@adsnet.com.

JINNAH, MOHAMMED ALI (QAID-E-AZAM): BIRTH ANNIVERSARY. Dec 25, 1876. The founder of the Islamic Republic of Pakistan, Mohammed Ali Jinnah was born at Karachi, then part of India. When Pakistan became an independent political entity (Aug 15, 1947), Jinnah became its first governor general. He was given the title Qaid-e-Azam (Great Leader) in 1947. He died at Karachi, Sept 11, 1948. Jinnah's birth anniversary is a holiday in Pakistan.

"METROPOLITAN OPERA RADIO BROADCASTS" PREMIERE: ANNIVERSARY. Dec 25, 1931. On Christmas Day 1931, the Metropolitan Opera of New York City broadcast an entire opera, *Hansel and Gretel*, on the NBC radio network—the first time this had ever been done. This broadcast was the first of an ongoing radio series of Saturday matinees. On Dec 7, 1940, Texaco (now ChevronTexaco) became a sponsor and began the longest continuous sponsorship in broadcast history—a sponsorship that ended after the 2003–2004 season. For decades, the Metropolitan Opera radio broadcasts have introduced opera to new fans far from New York. Today, the broadcasts are heard internationally in 42 countries and are currently sponsored by Toll Brothers.

"THE STEVE ALLEN SHOW" TV PREMIERE: ANNIVERSARY. Dec 25, 1950. Talented actor, comedian, singer and musician, Steve Allen hosted a number of variety shows from 1950 to 1969 (with a few breaks in between to host specials and "The Tonight Show"). For two years, his television show was similar to his radio show and featured singer Peggy Lee, announcer Bern Bennett and Llemuel the llama. His next show competed with Ed Sullivan's show, though Allen's stressed comedy. Some of his "funnymen" were Don Knots; Tom Poston; Louis Nye; Gabe Dell; Pat Harrington, Jr; Dayton Allen and Bill Dana. His other shows included a talk show, a game show, a comedy show, an educational music show and a flashback-comedy show.

STOCK EXCHANGE HOLIDAY (CHRISTMAS DAY). Dec 25. The holiday schedules for the various exchanges are subject to change if relevant rules, regulations or exchange policies are revised. If you have questions, contact: American Stock Exchange (866) 422-2639 (www.amex.com), Chicago Board of Trade (312) 435-3500 (www.cbot.com), Chicago Board Options Exchange (312) 786-5600 (www.cboe.com), NASDAQ Stock Market (646) 441-5200 (www.nasdaq.com), New York Stock Exchange (212) 656-3000 (www.nyse.com), Philadelphia Stock Exchange (800) THE-PHLX (www.phlx.com).

TAIWAN: CONSTITUTION DAY. Dec 25. National holiday. Commemorates the adoption of the 1946 constitution.

UNITED KINGDOM: CHRISTMAS HOLIDAY. Dec 25. Bank and public holiday in England, Wales, Scotland and Northern Ireland.

WASHINGTON CROSSES THE DELAWARE: ANNIVERSARY. Dec 25, 1776. One of the most famous events of the American Revolution happened on a bleak Christmas night, during driving snow. General George Washington led 2,400 men across the Delaware River at McConkey's Ferry, Bucks County, PA, to conduct a surprise attack on Hessian troops at Trenton, NJ. Local fishermen conducted the troops across the river, finally assembling at 3:00 AM on the other side. Washington achieved victory at Trenton, a key event that changed the course of the war to the rebelling colonists' favor.

WEST, REBECCA: BIRTH ANNIVERSARY. Dec 25, 1892. English author, literary critic, prizewinning journalist and noted feminist, Dame Rebecca West was born Cicily Isabel Fairfield at London, England. She died there Mar 15, 1983.

BIRTHDAYS TODAY

Jimmy Buffett, 63, singer ("Margaritaville"), songwriter, born Pascagoula, MS, Dec 25, 1946.

Lawrence Richard (Larry) Csonka, 63, Hall of Fame football player, born Stow, OH, Dec 25, 1946.

Rickey Henley Henderson, 51, former baseball player, born Chicago, IL, Dec 25, 1958.

Annie Lennox, 55, singer (Eurythmics, "Sweet Dreams Are Made of This"), born Aberdeen, Scotland, Dec 25, 1954.

Barbara Mandrell, 61, singer ("I Was Country When Country Wasn't Cool"), born Houston, TX, Dec 25, 1948.

Karl Rove, 59, political consultant and presidential advisor, born Denver, CO, Dec 25, 1950.

Gary Sandy, 64, actor ("All That Glitters," "WKRP in Cincinnati"), born Dayton, OH, Dec 25, 1945.

Hanna Schygulla, 66, actress (*The Marriage of Maria Braun, Berlin Alexanderplatz*), born Kattowitz, Germany, Dec 25, 1943.

Mary Elizabeth (Sissy) Spacek, 60, actress (*In the Bedroom, Crimes of the Heart, Carrie*; Oscar for *Coal Miner's Daughter*), born Quitman, TX, Dec 25, 1949.

December 26 — Saturday

DAY 360 | **5 REMAINING**

ALLEN, STEVE: BIRTH ANNIVERSARY. Dec 26, 1921. American entertainer and TV pioneer, Steve Allen created the original "Tonight" show for NBC in 1953. Also known as a composer and the author of more than 40 books, he was born at New York, NY, Dec 26, 1921. He died at Encino, CA, Oct 30, 2000.

BABBAGE, CHARLES: BIRTH ANNIVERSARY. Dec 26, 1792. English mathematician, born at Teignmouth, England. He developed the principles on which modern computers are designed. Babbage died at London, England, Oct 18, 1871.

BAHAMAS: JUNKANOO. Dec 26. Kaleidoscope of sound and spectacle combining a bit of Mardi Gras, mummers' parade and ancient African tribal rituals. Revelers in colorful costumes parade through the streets to sounds of cowbells, goat skin drums and many other homemade instruments. Always on Boxing Day.

BOXING DAY. Dec 26. Ordinarily observed on the first day after Christmas. A legal holiday in Canada, the United Kingdom and many other countries. Formerly (according to Robert Chambers) a day when Christmas gift boxes were "regularly expected by a postman, the lamplighter, the dustman and generally by all those functionaries who render services to the public at large, without receiving payment therefore from any individual." When Boxing Day falls on a Saturday or Sunday, the Monday or Tuesday immediately following may be proclaimed or observed as a bank or public holiday.

BOXING DAY AT THE HEMINGWAY BIRTHPLACE. Dec 26. Hemingway Birthplace, Oak Park, IL. The Hemingway family celebrated Boxing Day with extended family, eating special foods and sharing literary works and poetry. The Ernest Hemingway Foundation of Oak Park will re-create this holiday celebration with English tea, music and dramatic readings of Christmas tales. For info: The Ernest Hemingway Foundation, PO Box 2222, Oak Park, IL 60303-2222. Phone: (708) 848-2222. Fax: (708) 386-2952. E-mail: ehfop@sbcglobal.net. Web: www.ehfop.org.

CLERC, LAURENT: BIRTH ANNIVERSARY. Dec 26, 1785. The first deaf teacher in America, Laurent Clerc assisted Thomas Hopkins Gallaudet in establishing the first public school for the deaf, Connecticut Asylum for the Education and Instruction of Deaf and Dumb Persons (now the American School for the Deaf), at Hartford, CT, in 1817. For 41 years Clerc trained new teachers in the use of sign language and in methods of teaching the deaf. Clerc was born at LaBalme, France, and died July 18, 1869.

FIRST BLACK HEAVYWEIGHT CHAMPION: ANNIVERSARY. Dec 26, 1908. Jack Johnson became the first black man to win the heavyweight boxing championship when he knocked out Tommy Burns in the 14th round of a fight at Sydney, Australia.

HOLIDAY MAGIC. Dec 26–Jan 4, 2010. Mystic, CT. Everyone pays reduced admission and enjoys a full day of crafts, entertainment and the lore of the sea. Est attendance: 3,000. For info: Mystic Seaport, 75 Greenmanville Ave, Box 6000, Mystic, CT 06355. Phone: (860) 572-5315 or (888) 973-2767. Web: www.mysticseaport.org.

IRELAND: DAY OF THE WREN. Dec 26. Dingle Peninsula. Masked revelers and musicians go from door to door asking for money. Traditional day and night of public merrymaking.

KWANZAA. Dec 26–Jan 1, 2010. American black family observance created in 1966 by Dr. Maulana Karenga in recognition of traditional African harvest festivals. This seven-day festival stresses unity of the black family, with a harvest feast (karamu) on the first day and a day of meditation on the final one. Kwanzaa means "first fruit" in Swahili.

LOVERA, JUAN: BIRTH ANNIVERSARY. Dec 26, 1778. Venezuelan "Artist of Independence," whose best-known canvases commemorate the independence dates of Apr 19, 1810, and July 5, 1811. Known as the founder of historical painting in Venezuela. Died in 1841 (exact date unknown).

LUXEMBOURG: BLESSING OF THE WINE. Dec 26. Greiveldange, Luxembourg. Winemakers parade to the church, where a barrel of wine is blessed.

MAO TSE-TUNG: BIRTH ANNIVERSARY. Dec 26, 1893. Chinese librarian, teacher, communist revolutionist and "founding father" of the People's Republic of China, born at Hunan Province, China. Died at Beijing, Sept 9, 1976.

MILLER, HENRY (VALENTINE): BIRTH ANNIVERSARY. Dec 26, 1891. Controversial American novelist (*Tropic of Cancer*), born at New York, NY. Died at Pacific Palisades, CA, June 7, 1980.

NATIONAL THANK YOU NOTE DAY. Dec 26. The presents have been unwrapped and put away. It's official: the holidays are winding down. Now it's time to write those thank you notes. National Thank You Note Day recognizes the importance of showing gratitude toward loved ones. Annually, Dec 26. For info: Elizabeth Sulock, PO Box 4955, Middletown, RI 02842. E-mail: thankyou@thankyoutips.com. Web: www.thankyoutips.com.

NATIONAL WHINER'S DAY™. Dec 26. A day dedicated to whiners, especially those who return Christmas gifts and need lots of attention. People are encouraged to be happy about what they do have, rather than unhappy about what they don't have. The most famous whiner(s) of the year will be announced. Nominations accepted through Dec 15. For more info, please send SASE to: Kevin C. Zaborney, 2023 Vickory Rd, Caro, MI 48723. Phone: (989) 673-6696. E-mail: kevin@nationalhuggingday.com. Web: www.nationalhuggingday.com.

NELSON, THOMAS: BIRTH ANNIVERSARY. Dec 26, 1738. Merchant and signer of the Declaration of Independence, born at Yorktown, VA. Died at Hanover County, VA, Jan 4, 1789.

RADIUM DISCOVERED: ANNIVERSARY. Dec 26, 1898. French scientists Pierre and Marie Curie discovered the element radium, for which they later won the Nobel Prize for Physics.

SAINT STEPHEN'S DAY. Dec 26. One of the seven deacons named by the apostles to distribute alms. Died during first century. Feast Day is Dec 26 and is observed as a public holiday in Austria and the Republic of Ireland.

SECOND DAY OF CHRISTMAS. Dec 26. Observed as holiday in many countries.

SHENANDOAH NATIONAL PARK ESTABLISHED: ANNIVERSARY. Dec 26, 1935. Area of Blue Ridge Mountains of Virginia, originally authorized May 22, 1926, was established as a national park. For further park info: Shenandoah Natl Park, Rte 4, Box 348, Luray, VA 22835.

SLOVENIA: INDEPENDENCE DAY. Dec 26. National holiday. Commemorates 1990 announcement of separation from the Yugoslav Union.

SOUTH AFRICA: DAY OF GOODWILL. Dec 26. National holiday. Replaces Boxing Day.

SUMATRAN-ANDAMAN EARTHQUAKE AND TSUNAMIS: 5th ANNIVERSARY. Dec 26, 2004. One of the strongest and most lethal earthquakes of modern history unleashed tsunami waves that devastated coasts all around the Indian Ocean, where it was centered. An estimated 250,000 people died, with thousands missing and millions displaced. With a magnitude in the range of 9.3, this was the second-strongest earthquake of all time. The power was the equivalent of a 100 gigaton bomb, and its action vibrated the entire planet. The Earth spun faster and the day was fractionally shortened as a result. This was also the longest-lasting earthquake recorded, with a length of about 10 minutes as opposed to the more typical few seconds.

UNITED KINGDOM: BOXING DAY BANK HOLIDAY. Dec 26. Bank and public holiday in England, Wales, Scotland and Northern Ireland.

BIRTHDAYS TODAY

Evan Bayh, 54, US Senator (D, Indiana), born Shirkleville, IN, Dec 26, 1955.

Carlton Ernest Fisk, 62, Hall of Fame baseball player, born Bellows Falls, VT, Dec 26, 1947.

Marcelo Rios, 34, tennis player, born Santiago, Chile, Dec 26, 1975.

Osborne Earl (Ozzie) Smith, 55, Hall of Fame baseball player, born Mobile, AL, Dec 26, 1954.

Phil Spector, 69, music producer, born New York, NY, Dec 26, 1940.

December 2009	S	M	T	W	T	F	S
			1	2	3	4	5
	6	7	8	9	10	11	12
	13	14	15	16	17	18	19
	20	21	22	23	24	25	26
	27	28	29	30	31		

December 27 — Sunday

DAY 361 — **4 REMAINING**

ASARAH B'TEVET. Dec 27. Hebrew calendar date: Tevet 10, 5770. The Fast of the 10th of Tevet begins at first morning light and commemorates the beginning of the Babylonian siege of Jerusalem in the sixth century BC. Began at sundown on Dec 26.

ASHURA: TENTH DAY. Dec 27. Islamic calendar date: Muharram 10, 1431. Different methods for "anticipating" the visibility of the new moon crescent at Mecca are used by different groups. US date may vary. Began at sunset the preceding day.

CAYLEY, GEORGE: BIRTH ANNIVERSARY. Dec 27, 1773. Aviation pioneer Sir George Cayley, English scientist and inventor, was a theoretician who designed airplanes, helicopters and gliders. He is credited as the father of aerodynamics and he was the pilot of the world's first manned glider flight. Born at Scarborough, Yorkshire, England, he died at Brompton Hall, Yorkshire, Dec 15, 1857.

DIETRICH, MARLENE: BIRTH ANNIVERSARY. Dec 27, 1901. Born at Berlin, Germany, Dietrich enrolled in Max Reinhardt's drama school. Her first big break was in 1930 when Josef Von Sternberg cast her in *The Blue Angel*, the first talkie made in Germany. A year later, she and Sternberg moved to Hollywood and began a string of six films together with *Morocco*, the only film for which she received an Academy Award nomination. Some of her other films were *Destry Rides Again, Around the World in 80 Days, Touch of Evil, Judgment at Nuremberg* and *Witness for the Prosecution*. During the 1950s she was a cabaret singer in a stage revue that toured the globe. Dietrich died May 6, 1992, at Paris, France.

"HOWDY DOODY" TV PREMIERE: ANNIVERSARY. Dec 27, 1947. The first popular children's show was brought to TV by Bob Smith and was one of the first regular NBC shows to be shown in color. It was set in the circus town of Doodyville. Children sat in the bleachers' "Peanut Gallery" and participated in activities such as songs and stories. Human characters were Buffalo Bob (Bob Smith), the silent clown Clarabell (Bob Keeshan, Bobby Nicholson and Lew Anderson), storekeeper Cornelius Cobb (Nicholson), Chief Thunderthud (Bill LeCornec), Princess Summerfall Winterspring (Judy Tyler and Linda Marsh), Bison Bill (Ted Brown) and wrestler Ugly Sam (Dayton Allen). Puppet costars included Howdy Doody, Phineas T. Bluster, Dilly Dally, Flub-a-Dub, Captain Scuttlebutt, Double Doody and Heidi Doody. The filmed adventures of Gumby were also featured. In the final episode, Clarabell broke his long silence to say, "Goodbye, kids."

KEPLER, JOHANNES: BIRTH ANNIVERSARY. Dec 27, 1571. One of the world's greatest astronomers, called "the father of modern astronomy," German mathematician Johannes Kepler was born at Württemberg, Germany; he died at Regensburg, Germany, Nov 15, 1630.

PASTEUR, LOUIS: BIRTH ANNIVERSARY. Dec 27, 1822. French chemist-bacteriologist born at Dole, Jura, France. Died at Villeneuve l'Etang, France, Sept 28, 1895. Discoverer of prophylactic inoculation against rabies. Pasteurization process named for him.

RADIO CITY MUSIC HALL: ANNIVERSARY. Dec 27, 1932. Radio City Music Hall, at New York City, opened on this date. Among the opening-night performers were the "Radio Roxyettes."

SAINT JOHN, APOSTLE-EVANGELIST: FEAST DAY. Dec 27. Son of Zebedee, Galilean fisherman, and Salome. Died about AD 100. Roman Rite Feast Day is Dec 27. (Observed May 8 by Byzantine Rite.)

SALK, LEE: BIRTH ANNIVERSARY. Dec 27, 1926. American child psychologist Lee Salk was born at New York, NY. He became well known for proving the calming effect of a mother's heartbeat on a newborn infant. Salk's warning during the 1970s that women should not abandon full-time child rearing was met with wide opposition, especially from working mothers. He died May 2, 1992, at New York, NY.

WINTER FAIRY FUN DAY. Dec 27. A Fairy Fun Day is held once each season on the fourth Sunday. Winter Fairy Fun Day is where fairy friends dress up, attend a "Mad Fairy Tea Party," arts and crafts and just get together to sparkle, laugh, delight and appreciate fairies, children and Nature. Events organized worldwide—join us to attend an event in your area! For info: Fairy Society Artist Community Network, 4128 Bye Way, Santa Cruz, CA 95060. Phone: (408) 564-5550. E-mail: michelle@elementaljoy.net. Web: http://thefairysociety.ning.com/.

BIRTHDAYS TODAY

Gerard Depardieu, 61, actor (*The Return of Martin Guerre, Cyrano de Bergerac*), born Chateauroux, France, Dec 27, 1948.

Tovah Feldshuh, 57, actress (*Holocaust*), born New York, NY, Dec 27, 1952.

Masi Oka, 35, actor ("Heroes," "Scrubs"), born Tokyo, Japan, Dec 27, 1974.

Carson Palmer, 30, football player, born Fresno, CA, Dec 27, 1979.

Cokie Roberts, 66, news correspondent, born New Orleans, LA, Dec 27, 1943.

December 28 — Monday

DAY 362 **3 REMAINING**

AUSTRALIA: PROCLAMATION DAY. Dec 28. Observed in South Australia.

ENDANGERED SPECIES ACT: ANNIVERSARY. Dec 28, 1973. President Richard Nixon signed the Endangered Species Act into law.

HOLY INNOCENTS DAY (CHILDERMAS). Dec 28. Commemoration of the massacre of children at Bethlehem, ordered by King Herod who wanted to destroy, among them, the infant Savior. Early and medieval accounts claimed as many as 144,000 victims, but more recent writers, noting that Bethlehem was a very small town, have revised the estimates of the number of children killed to between 6 and 20.

IOWA: ADMISSION DAY: ANNIVERSARY. Dec 28. Became 29th state in 1846.

MESSINA EARTHQUAKE: ANNIVERSARY. Dec 28, 1908. Messina, Sicily. The ancient town of Messina was struck by an earthquake. Nearly 80,000 persons died in the disaster, and half of the town's buildings were destroyed.

MOLSON, JOHN: BIRTH ANNIVERSARY. Dec 28, 1763. John Molson, an orphan, left his home at Lincolnshire, England, to settle in Montreal in 1782. He soon acquired a brewery and became patriarch of the Molson brewery family. Born at Lincolnshire, he died at Montreal, QC, Canada, Jan 11, 1836.

PLEDGE OF ALLEGIANCE RECOGNIZED: ANNIVERSARY. Dec 28, 1945. The US Congress officially recognized the Pledge of Allegiance and urged its frequent recitation in America's schools. The pledge was composed in 1892 by Francis Bellamy, a Baptist minister. At the time, Bellamy was chairman of a committee of state school superintendents of education, and several public schools adopted his pledge as part of the Columbus Day quadricentennial celebration that year. In 1954 the Knights of Columbus persuaded Congress to add the words "under God" to the pledge. In 2002 a federal appeals court found the pledge unconstitutional for use in public schools due to the "under God" phrase.

***POOR RICHARD'S ALMANACK*: ANNIVERSARY.** Dec 28, 1732. The *Pennsylvania Gazette* carried the first-known advertisement for the first issue of *Poor Richard's Almanack* by Richard Saunders (Benjamin Franklin) for the year 1733. The advertisement promised "many pleasant and witty verses, jests and sayings . . . new fashions, games for kisses . . . men and melons . . . breakfast in bed, &c." America's most famous almanac, *Poor Richard's* was published through the year 1758 and has been imitated many times since.

VICE PRESIDENTIAL RESIGNATION: ANNIVERSARY. Dec 28, 1832. John C. Calhoun, who had served as vice president of the US under two presidents (John Quincy Adams and Andrew Jackson), Mar 4, 1825–Dec 28, 1832, finding himself in growing disagreement with President Jackson, resigned the office of vice president, the first to do so. He spent most of his subsequent political life as a US senator from South Carolina.

WILSON, WOODROW: BIRTH ANNIVERSARY. Dec 28, 1856. The 28th president of the US was born Thomas Woodrow Wilson at Staunton, VA. Twice elected president (1912 and 1916), it was Wilson who said, "The world must be made safe for democracy," as he asked the Congress to declare war on Germany, Apr 2, 1917. His first wife, Ellen, died Aug 6, 1914, and he married Edith Bolling Galt, Dec 18, 1915. He suffered a paralytic stroke, Sept 16, 1919, never regaining his health. There were many speculations about who (possibly Mrs Wilson?) was running the government during his illness. His second term of office ended Mar 3, 1921, and he died at Washington, DC, Feb 3, 1924.

BIRTHDAYS TODAY

David Archuleta, 19, singer, television personality ("American Idol"), born Miami, FL, Dec 28, 1990.

Michael Beebe, 63, Governor of Arkansas (D), born Amagon, AR, Dec 28, 1946.

James Blake, 30, tennis player, born Yonkers, NY, Dec 28, 1979.

Ray Bourque, 49, former hockey player, born Montreal, QC, Canada, Dec 28, 1960.

Malcolm Gets, 45, actor ("Caroline in the City"), born near Gainesville, FL, Dec 28, 1964.

Hubert Myatt (Hubie) Green III, 63, golfer, born Birmingham, AL, Dec 28, 1946.

Johnny Isakson, 65, US Senator (R, Georgia), born Atlanta, GA, Dec 28, 1944.

Lou Jacobi, 96, actor (*Irma La Douce*), born Toronto, ON, Canada, Dec 28, 1913.

Tim Johnson, 63, US Senator (D, South Dakota), born Canton, SD, Dec 28, 1946.

John Legend, 31, R&B singer, born John Stephens at Springfield, OH, Dec 28, 1978.

Sienna Miller, 28, actress (*Factory Girl, Interview*), born New York, NY, Dec 28, 1981.

Patrick Rafter, 37, tennis player, born Mount Isa, Queensland, Australia, Dec 28, 1972.

Todd Richards, 40, Olympic snowboarder, born Worchester, MA, Dec 28, 1969.

Maggie Smith, 75, actress (Oscars for *The Prime of Miss Jean Brodie* and *California Suite*; Tony for *Lettice & Lovage; Harry Potter* films), born Ilford, England, Dec 28, 1934.

Denzel Washington, 55, actor (*The Hurricane, Malcolm X*; Oscars for *Training Day* and *Glory*), born Mount Vernon, NY, Dec 28, 1954.

Edgar Winter, 63, singer, musician (*Edgar Winter's White Trash, They Only Come Out at Night*), born Beaumont, TX, Dec 28, 1946.

December 29 — Tuesday

DAY 363 **2 REMAINING**

CASALS, PABLO: BIRTH ANNIVERSARY. Dec 29, 1876. Famed cellist Pablo Carlos Salvador Defillio de Casals was born at Venrell, Spain, and died at Rio Pedros, Puerto Rico, Oct 22, 1973.

GLADSTONE, WILLIAM EWART: 200th BIRTH ANNIVERSARY. Dec 29, 1809. English statesman and author for whom the Gladstone (luggage) bag was named. Inspiring orator, eccentric individual, intensely loved or hated by all who knew him (cheered from the streets and jeered from the balconies), Gladstone is said to have left more writings (letters, diaries, journals, books) than any other major English politician. However, his preoccupation with the charitable rehabilitation of prostitutes was perhaps easily misunderstood. Born at Liverpool, England, he was four times Britain's prime minister. Gladstone died at Hawarden, Wales, May 19, 1898.

JOHNSON, ANDREW: BIRTH ANNIVERSARY. Dec 29, 1808. Seventeenth president of the US, Andrew Johnson, proprietor of a tailor shop at Laurens, SC, before he entered politics, was born at Raleigh, NC. Upon Abraham Lincoln's assassination Johnson became president. He was the first president to be impeached by the House and was acquitted Mar 26, 1868, by the Senate. After his term of office as president (Apr 15, 1865–Mar 3, 1869) he made several unsuccessful attempts to win public office. Finally he was elected to the US Senate from Tennessee and served in the Senate from Mar 4, 1875, until his death at Carter's Station, TN, July 31, 1875.

RASPUTIN, GRIGORY YEFIMOVICH: ASSASSINATION ANNIVERSARY. Dec 29, 1916. Russian monk and mystic, born Grigory Yefimovich Novjkh, about 1871, at Siberia. Rasputin gained great influence with Russian emperor Nicholas II and the empress Alexandra, urging severe measures in dealing with the peasant masses, virtually dictating government policy. Notoriously dissolute and corrupt, Rasputin was said to have possessed hypnotic powers. He claimed divine inspiration and the ability to perform miracles. His name became synonymous with corruption and evil, and he was called the "plague pot" of Russia. In fact, Rasputin was a nickname from the Russian word *rasputny*, meaning debauched, profligate, licentious. When an attempt to poison him failed, he was shot to death and his body dropped through a hole in the ice into the Neva River. It was recovered three days later and buried in a silver casket at Tsarkoe Selo. The imperial government was crushed by the 1917 Revolution within a year of his death.

SAINT THOMAS OF CANTERBURY: FEAST DAY. Dec 29. Thomas, Archbishop of Canterbury, was born at London in 1118 and was murdered at the Canterbury Cathedral on this date in 1170.

TEXAS: ADMISSION DAY: ANNIVERSARY. Dec 29. Became 28th state in 1845.

TICK TOCK DAY. Dec 29. Time runs out! All those dreams you've had, all those fantasies? It's time, friend. Do it! Annually, Dec 29. (©2006 by WH.) For info: Thomas & Ruth Roy, Wellcat Holidays, 2418 Long Ln, Lebanon, PA 17046. Phone: (717) 279-0184. E-mail: info@wellcat.com. Web: www.wellcat.com.

December 2009	S	M	T	W	T	F	S
			1	2	3	4	5
	6	7	8	9	10	11	12
	13	14	15	16	17	18	19
	20	21	22	23	24	25	26
	27	28	29	30	31		

WOUNDED KNEE MASSACRE: ANNIVERSARY. Dec 29, 1890. Anniversary of the massacre of more than 200 Native American men, women and children by the US Seventh Cavalry at Wounded Knee Creek, SD. Government efforts to suppress a ceremonial religious practice, the Ghost Dance (which called for a messiah who would restore the bison to the plains, make the white men disappear and bring back the old Native American way of life), had resulted in the death of Sitting Bull, Dec 15, 1890, which further inflamed the disgruntled Native Americans and culminated in the slaughter at Wounded Knee, Dec 29.

YMCA ORGANIZED: ANNIVERSARY. Dec 29, 1851. The first US branch of the Young Men's Christian Association was organized at Boston. It was modeled on an organization begun at London in 1844.

BIRTHDAYS TODAY

Patricia Clarkson, 50, actress (*Married Life, Lars and the Real Girl, The Station Agent, Far from Heaven*), born New Orleans, LA, Dec 29, 1959.

Ted Danson, 62, actor ("Cheers," "Becker," *Three Men and a Baby*), born San Diego, CA, Dec 29, 1947.

Marianne Faithfull, 63, singer ("As Tears Go By," "Summer Nights"), actress, born London, England, Dec 29, 1946.

Thomas Edwin Jarriel, 75, broadcast journalist, born LaGrange, GA, Dec 29, 1934.

Jason Kreis, 37, soccer coach and former player, born Omaha, NE, Dec 29, 1972.

Jude Law, 37, actor (*Closer, Cold Mountain, The Talented Mr Ripley*), born London, England, Dec 29, 1972.

Mary Tyler Moore, 73, actress (two Emmys for "The Dick Van Dyke Show"; three Emmys for "The Mary Tyler Moore Show"; *Ordinary People*), born Brooklyn, NY, Dec 29, 1936.

Jon Polito, 59, actor ("Homicide"), born Philadelphia, PA, Dec 29, 1950.

Paula Poundstone, 50, comedienne, born Sudbury, MA, Dec 29, 1959.

Jon Voight, 71, actor (*Midnight Cowboy, Deliverance*), born Yonkers, NY, Dec 29, 1938.

Andy Wachowski, 42, filmmaker with brother Larry Wachowski (*The Matrix*), born Chicago, IL, Dec 29, 1967.

December 30 — Wednesday

DAY 364 **1 REMAINING**

FALLING NEEDLES FAMILY FEST. Dec 30. Now that the yuletide tree's been up for weeks and hasn't been watered since a couple of days before Christmas, gather the gang around and watch the needles gently fall one by one. Live it up! Dance barefoot! (©2006 by WH.) For info: Thomas & Ruth Roy, Wellcat Holidays, 2418 Long Ln, Lebanon, PA 17046. Phone: (717) 279-0184. E-mail: info@wellcat.com. Web: www.wellcat.com.

GUGGENHEIM, SIMON: BIRTH ANNIVERSARY. Dec 30, 1867. American capitalist and philanthropist, born at Philadelphia, PA. He established, in memory of his son, the John Simon Guggenheim Memorial Foundation, in 1925. Died Nov 2, 1941, at New York, NY.

KIPLING, RUDYARD: BIRTH ANNIVERSARY. Dec 30, 1865. English poet, novelist and short story writer, Nobel Prize laureate, Kipling was born at Bombay, India. After working as a journalist at India, he traveled around the world. He married an American and lived in Vermont for several years. Kipling is best known for his children's stories, such as *The Jungle Book* and *Just So Stories* and poems such as "The Ballad of East and West" and "If." He died at London, England, Jan 18, 1936.

LEACOCK, STEPHEN: BIRTH ANNIVERSARY. Dec 30, 1869. Canadian economist and humorist, born at Swanmore, Hampshire, England. Died Mar 28, 1944, at Toronto, Canada. "Lord Ronald. . .," he wrote in *Nonsense Novels*, "flung himself upon his horse and rode madly off in all directions."

"LET'S MAKE A DEAL" TV PREMIERE: ANNIVERSARY. Dec 30, 1963. Monty Hall hosted this outrageous and no-skill-required game show. Audience members, many of whom wore costumes, were selected to sit in the trading area, and some were picked to "make a deal" with Hall by trading something of their own for something they were offered. Sometimes prizes were worthless ("zonks"). At the end of the show, the two people who had won the most were given the option to trade their winnings for a chance at the "Big Deal," hidden behind one of three doors. The most recent revival (1990–91) was hosted by Bob Hilton.

***MONITOR* SINKS: ANNIVERSARY.** Dec 30, 1862. The Union ironclad ship USS *Monitor* (which achieved fame after its battle with the *Merrimac*) sank off Cape Hatteras during a storm. Sixteen of its crew were lost. See also: "Battle of the *Monitor* and the *Merrimac*: Anniversary" (Mar 9).

PARKS, BERT: 95th BIRTH ANNIVERSARY. Dec 30, 1914. Bert Parks was born at Atlanta, GA. An actor whose career spanned radio, film, television and Broadway, his name became synonymous with the Miss America pageant, which he emceed for 25 years, ending in 1980. Parks made a special return appearance for the 1990 pageant, once again singing his signature song "There She Is." He died Feb 2, 1992, at La Jolla, CA.

PHILIPPINES: RIZAL DAY. Dec 30. National holiday. Commemorates martyrdom of Dr. Jose Rizal in 1896.

"THE ROY ROGERS SHOW" TV PREMIERE: ANNIVERSARY. Dec 30, 1951. This very popular TV western starred Roy Rogers and his wife, Dale Evans, as themselves. It also featured Pat Brady as Rogers's sidekick who rode a jeep named Nellybelle, the singing group Sons of the Pioneers, Rogers's horse Trigger, Evans's horse Buttermilk and a German shepherd named Bullet. This half-hour show was especially popular with young viewers.

USSR ESTABLISHED: ANNIVERSARY. Dec 30, 1922. After the Russian revolution of 1917 and the subsequent three-year civil war, the Union of Soviet Socialist Republics (or Soviet Union) was founded, a confederation of Russia, Byelorussia, the Ukraine and the Transcaucasian Federation. It was the first state in the world to be based on Marxist communism. The Soviet Union was dissolved Dec 8, 1991. See also: "Soviet Union Dissolved" (Dec 8).

BIRTHDAYS TODAY

Joseph Bologna, 71, actor, writer (*The Big Bus, My Favorite Year, Blame It on Rio*), born Brooklyn, NY, Dec 30, 1938.

James Burrows, 69, director ("Cheers," "Taxi"), born Los Angeles, CA, Dec 30, 1940.

Eliza Dushku, 29, actress ("Buffy the Vampire Slayer," "Angel"), born Boston, MA, Dec 30, 1980.

Sean Hannity, 48, journalist, talk show host ("Hannity & Colmes"), born New York, NY, Dec 30, 1981.

LeBron James, 25, basketball player, born Akron, OH, Dec 30, 1984.

Davy Jones, 63, actor, singer (The Monkees, "Daydream Believer"), born Manchester, England, Dec 30, 1946.

Sanford (Sandy) Koufax, 74, Hall of Fame baseball player, former sportscaster, born Brooklyn, NY, Dec 30, 1935.

Kristin Kreuk, 27, actress ("Smallville"), born Vancouver, BC, Canada, Dec 30, 1982.

Matt Lauer, 52, news anchor ("Today"), born New York, NY, Dec 30, 1957.

Kenyon Martin, 32, basketball player, born Saginaw, MI, Dec 30, 1977.

Michael Nesmith, 67, singer, songwriter (The Monkees), director, born Houston, TX, Dec 30, 1942.

Patti Smith, 63, singer ("Because the Night"), born Chicago, IL, Dec 30, 1946.

Russ Tamblyn, 74, actor ("Twin Peaks," *Peyton Place, West Side Story*), born Los Angeles, CA, Dec 30, 1935.

Concetta Tomei, 64, actress ("Providence," "China Beach"), born Kenosha, WI, Dec 30, 1945.

Tracey Ullman, 50, actress, singer ("The Tracey Ullman Show," *I Love You to Death*), born Buckinghamshire, England, Dec 30, 1959.

Meredith Vieira, 58, television journalist, cohost ("Today Show"), born Providence, RI, Dec 30, 1951.

Eldrick "Tiger" Woods, 34, golfer, born Cypress, CA, Dec 30, 1975.

December 31 — Thursday

DAY 365 **0 REMAINING**

BLUE MOON. Dec 31. When two full moons fall within the same month, the second is called the "Blue Moon."

CANADA: FIRST NIGHTS. Dec 31. These Canadian cities have First Night celebrations: Banff, Drayton Valley, Edmonton and Red Deer, AB; Kamloops and Whistler, BC; Yellowknife, NT; and Chatham-Kent, Hamilton, Kingston, Peterborough and Toronto, ON. For info: First Night Intl, 84 Court St, Ste 507, Binghamton, NY 13901. Phone: (607) 772-3597. Fax: (607) 772-6305. Web: www.firstnight.com.

DENVER, JOHN: BIRTH ANNIVERSARY. Dec 31, 1943. Born Henry John Deutschendorf at Roswell, NM, this singer-songwriter ("Rocky Mountain High," "Sunshine on My Shoulder") died in a plane crash off the coast of California, Oct 12, 1997.

FIRE AND ICE NEW YEAR'S EVE CELEBRATION. Dec 31. Town Square, Downtown Anchorage, AK. Celebrate the New Year Alaska style—outdoors in the cold! Event features live outdoor music, ice skating, fire jugglers, ice carving, dance and more. Sponsored by NECA/IBEW. Est attendance: 4,000. For info: Anchorage Downtown Partnership, Ltd, 333 W 4th Ave, Ste 317, Anchorage, AK 99501. Phone: (907) 279-5650. Fax: (907) 279-5651. E-mail: cspink@anchoragedowntown.org. Web: www.anchoragedowntown.org.

FIRST BANK OPENS IN US: ANNIVERSARY. Dec 31, 1781. The first modern bank in the US, the Bank of North America, was organized by Robert Morris and received its charter from the Confederation Congress. It began operations Jan 7, 1782, at Philadelphia, PA.

FIRST NIGHT BOSTON. Dec 31. Boston, MA. The largest New Year's arts festival in North America, First Night Boston has grown to be a highly anticipated tradition. The festival features more than 1,000 artists in 250 performances and exhibitions in 40 venues throughout downtown Boston, a Mardi Gras-style Grand Procession, large-scale ice sculptures, music, dance, theater, family entertainment, fireworks at midnight and much more! Boston was the site of the first First Night in 1976. Est attendance: 1,000,000. For info: First Night, Inc, 31 Saint James Ave, Ste 949, Boston, MA 02116. Phone: (617) 542-1399. Fax: (617) 426-9531. E-mail: info@firstnight.org. Web: www.firstnight.org.

FIRST NIGHTS. Dec 31. The following US cities have First Night celebrations: Mobile, AL; Fayetteville, AR; Bakersfield, Escondido, Fullerton, Martinez, Monterey, San Diego, San Luis Obispo, Santa Barbara, Santa Cruz, Santa Fe Springs, Santa Rosa, Stockton and Whittier, CA; Fort Collins and Pikes Peak, CO; Cheshire, Danbury, Hartford, Torrington and Westport/Weston, CT; Dover and Wilmington, DE; Delray Beach, Dunedin, Fort Walton Beach, Miami Beach and St. Petersburg, FL; Athens, Gainesville, Golden Isles, Macon and Savannah, GA; Boise and Idaho Falls, ID; Aurora, Bloomington/Normal, Centralia, Evanston, Pontiac, River Bend, Rockford and Springfield, IL; Evansville, IN; Owensboro, KY; Annapolis, Frederick, Montgomery County and Talbot, MD; Beverly, Boston, Chatham, Fall River, Martha's Vineyard, New Bedford, Northampton, Pittsfield, Quincy, Sharon, Sturbridge, Twin Cities and Worcester, MA; Jackson, MS; Cadillac and Birmingham, MI; St. Paul, MN; Columbia and Springfield, MO; Flathead and Missoula, MT; Asheville, NC; Portsmouth and Wolfeboro, NH; Bridgewater/Raritan/Somerville, Flemington, Haddonfield, Manasquan, Maplewood/South Orange, Montclair, Moorestown, Morris County, Mount Holly, Newark, Ocean City, Ocean County, Red Bank, Ridgewood, Summit, Teaneck and Westfield, NJ; Albany, Binghamton, Buffalo, Gloversville/Johnstown, Greenport, Middletown, New York City, Nyack, Oneonta, Saratoga, Sayville, Staten Island, Syracuse and Watertown, NY; Asheville and Raleigh, NC; Grand Forks, ND; Akron, Canfield, Columbus, Toledo and Youngstown, OH; Eugene and Salem, OR; Bethlehem, Bloomsburg, Bradford, Bristol, Carlisle, Doylestown, Erie, Hanover, Newtown, Norwin, Oil City, Philipsburg, Pittsburgh, Scranton, State College, Warren and York, PA; Providence and Westerly, RI; Charleston and Varnville, SC; Yankton, SD; Kingsport, TN; The Woodlands, TX; Ogden, Provo, Salt Lake City and St. George, UT; Bennington, Burlington, Montpelier, Rutland and St. Johnsbury, VT; Augusta, Blacksburg, Charlottesville, Fredericksburg, Harrisonburg, Leesburg, Warrenton, Williamsburg and Winchester, VA; Tacoma and Tri-Cities, WA; and Morgantown, WV. For info: First Night Intl, 84 Court St, Ste 507, Binghamton, NY 13901. Phone: (607) 772-3597. Fax: (607) 772-6305. Web: www.firstnight.com.

JAPAN: NAMAHAGE. Dec 31. Oga Peninsula, Akita Prefecture, Japan. In the evening, groups of "Namahage" men disguised as devils make door-to-door visits, growling, "Any good-for-nothing fellow hereabout?" The object of this annual event is to give sluggards an opportunity to change their minds and become diligent. Otherwise, according to legend, they will be punished by devils.

LEAP SECOND ADJUSTMENT TIME. Dec 31. One of the times that have been favored for the addition or subtraction of a second from clock time (to coordinate atomic and astronomical time). The determination to adjust is made by the International Earth Rotation Service of the International Bureau of Weights and Measures, at Paris, France. See also: "Leap Seconds" (see Contents).

December 2009

S	M	T	W	T	F	S
		1	2	3	4	5
6	7	8	9	10	11	12
13	14	15	16	17	18	19
20	21	22	23	24	25	26
27	28	29	30	31		

LUNAR ECLIPSE. Dec 31. Partial eclipse of the moon. Visible in Europe, Africa, Asia and Australia.

MAKE UP YOUR MIND DAY. Dec 31. A day for all those people who have a hard time making up their minds. Make a decision today and follow through with it! Annually, Dec 31. For info: A.C. Vierow and M.A. Dufour, Box 71, Clio, MI 48420-0071.

MARSHALL, GEORGE CATLETT: BIRTH ANNIVERSARY. Dec 31, 1880. Chairman of the newly formed Joint Chiefs of Staff Committee throughout the US's involvement in WWII, General George Marshall was born at Uniontown, PA. He accompanied Roosevelt or represented the US at most Allied war conferences. He served as secretary of state and was designer of the Marshall Plan after the war. Died Oct 16, 1959, at Washington, DC.

MATISSE, HENRI: BIRTH ANNIVERSARY. Dec 31, 1869. Painter born at Le Cateau, France. Matisse also designed textiles and stained-glass windows. Died at Nice, France, Nov 3, 1954.

MOON PHASE: FULL MOON. Dec 31. Moon enters Full Moon phase at 2:13 PM, EST.

NEW YEAR'S EVE. Dec 31. The last evening of the Gregorian calendar year, traditionally a night for merrymaking to welcome in the new year.

NEW YEAR'S FEST. Dec 31. Bronson Park, Kalamazoo, MI. Kalamazoo comes alive as families, teens and seniors come downtown to welcome the New Year. Featuring more than 28 different artists, performances are hosted in 9 different indoor sites throughout downtown Kalamazoo. The cultural celebration offers music, theater, puppetry, dance, mime and storytelling. Artists come from throughout the Midwest to join in this nonalcoholic celebration. Est attendance: 6,500. For info: Deborah Droppers, New Year's Fest, Inc, 346 W Michigan Ave, Kalamazoo, MI 49007. Phone: (269) 388-2830. E-mail: EventKzoo@chartermi.net. Web: www.newyearsfest.com.

NIXON, JOHN: DEATH ANNIVERSARY. Dec 31, 1808. Revolutionary patriot and businessman, Commander of the Philadelphia City Guard, born 1733 (exact date unknown). Appointed to conduct the first public reading of the Declaration of Independence, July 8, 1776. Died at Philadelphia, PA.

NO INTERRUPTIONS DAY. Dec 31. On this day—the last business day of the year—there shall be no interruptions! At work we will minimize or eliminate interruptions to our thought processes or tasks we are performing. At home we will silence and shut down all devices that interrupt us so we can devote ourselves to our families or to ourselves. This is a day for quiet and/or focus. It is a day to renew our energies to prepare ourselves for the new calendar year ahead. For info: Sylvia Henderson, Springboard Training, PO Box 588, Olney, MD 20830-0588. Phone: (301) 260-1538. E-mail: sylvia@springboardtraining.com. Web: www.springboardtraining.com.

PANAMA: ASSUMES CONTROL OF CANAL: 10th ANNIVERSARY. Dec 31, 1999. With the expiration of the Panama Canal Treaty of 1979 at noon, the Republic of Panama assumed full responsibility for the canal and the US Panama Canal Commission ceased to exist.

SAINT SYLVESTER'S DAY. Dec 31. Observed in Belgium, Germany, France, Switzerland. Commemorates death of Pope Sylvester I in AD 335. Feasting, particularly upon "St. Sylvester's Carp."

SAMOA: SAMOAN FIRE DANCE. Dec 31. New Year's Eve is occasion for Samoan bamboo fireworks, singing and traditional performances such as the Samoan Fire Dance.

SCOTLAND: HOGMANAY. Dec 31. The Scottish New Year celebrations date from ancient pagan times. Hogmanay (no one is sure the origin of the name) traditions include fireworks and torch-lit processions in the cities and bonfires in the rural areas. "First footing" is still observed: it is believed to be good luck for the first foot over the threshold to be that of a dark-haired stranger bearing a piece of coal, shortbread or whiskey. After the midnight chimes, everyone sings "Auld Lang Syne."

SUN BOWL. Dec 31. Sun Bowl Stadium, El Paso, TX. 76th annual. For info: Sun Bowl Assn, 4150 Pinnacle St, Ste 100, El Paso, TX 79902. Phone: (800) 915-BOWL. Web: www.sunbowl.org.

UNIVERSAL HOUR OF PEACE. Dec 31. Begins at 11:30 PM on Dec 31, 2009, and ends at 12:30 AM on Jan 1, 2010. An hour dedicated to creating peace throughout our planet. Every man, woman and child is asked to spend the hour in meditation, prayer, conversation, listening to beautiful music or whatever helps them concentrate on peace. The simple truth is "living peaceably begins by thinking peacefully." To add your name to the "Millions for Peace" list, e-mail your name, city, state/country to peace@som.org. An hourlong cassette tape of the Universal Peace Covenant voiced in seven languages is available at no charge by contacting SOM. One hour of peace, a world of difference. For info: Dr. Barbara Condron, Intl Coordinator, School of Metaphysics World HQ, 163 Moon Valley Rd, Windyville, MO 65783. Phone: (417) 345-8411. Fax: (417) 345-6668. E-mail: peace@som.org. Web: www.peacedome.org.

WIESENTHAL, SIMON: BIRTH ANNIVERSARY. Dec 31, 1908. Born at Buczacz, Austria-Hungary (now the Ukraine), Wiesenthal was a Holocaust survivor who dedicated his postwar life to fighting anti-Semitism and speaking out against racism. For more than 50 years, his Jewish Documentation Center in Vienna compiled data about war criminals not yet apprehended as well as information about the 6 million victims of Nazi persecution. In all, he helped to bring almost 1,100 Nazi war criminals to trial—most famously Adolf Eichmann. In 1977, The Simon Wiesenthal Center, an internationally renowned organization dedicated to remembering the Holocaust, was established in Los Angeles, CA. Wiesenthal died at Vienna, Sept 20, 2005.

WORLD PEACE MEDITATION. Dec 31. An opportunity for people around the world to focus their thoughts and energy on peace. The event is observed internationally, beginning at noon Greenwich Mean Time (GMT) and lasting one hour (7 AM–8 AM, EST). For info: Quartus Foundation, PO Box 1768, Boerne, TX 78006. Phone: (830) 249-3985. Fax: (830) 249-3318. E-mail: quartus@quartus.org. Web: www.quartus.org.

BIRTHDAYS TODAY

Sir Anthony Hopkins, 72, actor (Oscar for *The Silence of the Lambs; The Human Stain, Proof*), born Port Talbot, South Wales, UK, Dec 31, 1937.

Val Kilmer, 50, actor (*Batman Forever, The Doors, Heat*), born Los Angeles, CA, Dec 31, 1959.

Ben Kingsley, 66, actor (Oscar for *Gandhi*; *Sexy Beast, Schindler's List*), born Krishna Bhanji at Yorkshire, England, Dec 31, 1943.

Tim Matheson, 61, actor (*Animal House*, "The Virginian," "Bonanza"), born Los Angeles, CA, Dec 31, 1948.

Sarah Miles, 68, actress (*The Servant, Blow-Up, Hope and Glory*), born Ingatestone, England, Dec 31, 1941.

Bebe Neuwirth, 51, actress ("Cheers," "Frasier"; stage: *Chicago*), born Newark, NJ, Dec 31, 1958.

Odetta, 79, folksinger, musician, born Odetta Homes Felious Gordon at Birmingham, AL, Dec 31, 1930.

James Remar, 56, actor (*48 Hrs, Drugstore Cowboy*), born Boston, MA, Dec 31, 1953.

Donna Summer, 61, singer ("Bad Girls"), born LaDonna Andrea Gaines at Boston, MA, Dec 31, 1948.

Andy Summers, 67, musician (The Police), born Poulton-le-Fylde, England, Dec 31, 1942.

Diane Halfin von Furstenberg, 64, fashion designer, author, born Brussels, Belgium, Dec 31, 1945.

Calendar Information for the Year 2009

Time shown is Eastern Standard Time. All dates are given in terms of the Gregorian calendar.

(Based in part on information prepared by the Nautical Almanac Office, US Naval Observatory.)

ERAS	YEAR	BEGINS
Byzantine	7518	Sept 14
Jewish*	5770	Sept 19
Chinese (Year of the Ox)	4707	Jan 26
Roman (AUC)	2762	Jan 14
Nabonassar	2758	Apr 23
Japanese (Heisei)	21	Jan 1
Grecian (Seleucidae)	2321	Sept 14 (or Oct 14)
Indian (Saka)	1931	Mar 22
Diocletian	1726	Sept 11
Islamic (Hegira)**	1431	Dec 18

**Year begins the previous day at sunset.*

***Year begins the previous evening at moon crescent.*

RELIGIOUS CALENDARS

Epiphany .... Jan 6
Shrove Tuesday .... Feb 24
Ash Wednesday .... Feb 25
Lent .... Feb 25–Apr 11
Palm Sunday .... Apr 5
Good Friday .... Apr 10
Easter Day .... Apr 12
Ascension Day .... May 21
Whit Sunday (Pentecost) .... May 31
Trinity Sunday .... June 7
First Sunday in Advent .... Nov 29
Christmas Day (Thursday) .... Dec 25

Eastern Orthodox Church Observances

Great Lent begins .... Mar 2
Pascha (Easter) .... Apr 19
Ascension .... May 28
Pentecost .... June 7

Jewish Holy Days*

Purim .... Mar 10
Passover (1st day) .... Apr 9
Shavuot .... May 29–30
Tisha B'av .... July 30
Rosh Hashanah (New Year) .... Sept 19–20
Yom Kippur .... Sept 28
Succoth .... Oct 3–11
Chanukah .... Dec 12–19

**All Jewish holy days begin the previous day at sundown.*

Islamic Holy Days**

First Day of Ramadan (1430) .... Aug 22
Eid-Al-Fitr (1430) .... Sept 21
Islamic New Year (1431) .... Dec 18

***All Islamic holy days begin the previous evening at moon crescent.*

CIVIL CALENDAR—USA—2009

New Year's Day .... Jan 1
Martin Luther King's Birthday (obsvd) .... Jan 19
Lincoln's Birthday .... Feb 12
Washington's Birthday (obsvd)/Presidents' Day .... Feb 16
Memorial Day (obsvd) .... May 25
Independence Day .... July 4
Labor Day .... Sept 7
Columbus Day (obsvd) .... Oct 12
General Election Day .... Nov 3
Veterans Day .... Nov 11
Thanksgiving Day .... Nov 26

Other Days Widely Observed in US—2009

Groundhog Day (Candlemas) .... Feb 2
St. Valentine's Day .... Feb 14
St. Patrick's Day .... Mar 17
Mother's Day .... May 10
Flag Day .... June 14
Father's Day .... June 21
National Grandparents Day .... Sept 13
Hallowe'en .... Oct 31

CIVIL CALENDAR—CANADA—2009

Victoria Day .... May 18
Canada Day .... July 1
Labor Day .... Sept 7
Thanksgiving Day .... Oct 12
Remembrance Day .... Nov 11
Boxing Day .... Dec 26

CIVIL CALENDAR—MEXICO—2009

New Year's Day .... Jan 1
Constitution Day .... Feb 5
Benito Juarez Birthday .... Mar 21
Labor Day .... May 1
Battle of Puebla Day (Cinco de Mayo) .... May 5
Independence Day* .... Sept 16
Dia de La Raza .... Oct 12
Mexican Revolution Day .... Nov 20
Guadalupe Day .... Dec 12

*Celebration begins Sept 15 at 11:00 P.M.

CIVIL CALENDAR—UNITED KINGDOM—2009

Accession of Queen Elizabeth II .... Feb 6
St. David (Wales) .... Mar 1
Commonwealth Day .... Mar 9
St. Patrick (Ireland) .... Mar 17
Birthday of Queen Elizabeth II .... Apr 21
St. George (England) .... Apr 23
Coronation Day .... June 2
The Queen's Official Birthday (tentative) .... June 13
Birthday of Prince Philip, Duke of Edinburgh .... June 10
Remembrance Sunday .... Nov 8
Birthday of the Prince of Wales .... Nov 14
St. Andrew (Scotland) .... Nov 30

BANK AND PUBLIC HOLIDAYS—UNITED KINGDOM—2009

Observed during 2009 in England and Wales, Scotland and Northern Ireland unless otherwise indicated

New Year .... Jan 1
Bank Holiday (Scotland) .... Jan 2
St. Patrick's Day (Northern Ireland) .... Mar 17
Good Friday .... Apr 10
Easter Monday (except Scotland) .... Apr 13
May Day Bank Holiday .... May 4
Spring Bank Holiday .... May 25
Orangeman's Day (Battle of the Boyne) (Northern Ireland) .... July 12
Bank Holiday (Scotland) .... Aug 3
Summer Bank Holiday (except Scotland) .... Aug 31
Christmas Day Holiday .... Dec 25
Boxing Day Holiday .... Dec 26

SEASONS

Spring (Vernal Equinox) .... Mar 20, 7:44 AM, EDT
Summer (Summer Solstice) .... June 21, 1:45 PM, EDT
Autumn (Autumnal Equinox) .... Sept 22, 5:18 PM, EDT
Winter (Winter Solstice) .... Dec 21, 12:47 PM, EST

DAYLIGHT SAVING TIME SCHEDULE—2009*

Sunday, Mar 8, 2:00 AM–Sunday, Nov 1, 2:00 AM—in all time zones.

**Extended per the Energy Policy Act of 2005.*

CHRONOLOGICAL CYCLES

Dominical Letter .... D
Epact 3
Golden Number (Lunar Cycle) XV
Julian Period (year of) 6722
Roman Indiction 2
Solar Cycle 2

Calendar Information for the Year 2010

Time shown is Eastern Standard Time. All dates are given in terms of the Gregorian calendar.

(Based in part on information prepared by the Nautical Almanac Office, US Naval Observatory.)

ERAS	YEAR	BEGINS
Byzantine	7519	Sept 14
Jewish*	5771	Sept 9
Chinese (Year of the Tiger)	4708	Feb 14
Roman (AUC)	2763	Jan 14
Nabonassar	2759	Apr 23
Japanese (Heisei)	22	Jan 1
Grecian (Seleucidae)	2322	Sept 14 (or Oct 14)
Indian (Saka)	1932	Mar 22
Diocletian	1727	Sept 11
Islamic (Hegira)**	1432	Dec 7

**Year begins the previous day at sunset.*

***Year begins the previous evening at moon crescent.*

RELIGIOUS CALENDARS

Epiphany ... Jan 6
Shrove Tuesday ... Feb 16
Ash Wednesday ... Feb 17
Lent ... Feb 17–Apr 3
Palm Sunday ... Mar 28
Good Friday ... Apr 2
Easter Day ... Apr 4
Ascension Day ... May 13
Whit Sunday (Pentecost) ... May 23
Trinity Sunday ... May 30
First Sunday in Advent ... Nov 28
Christmas Day (Thursday) ... Dec 25

Eastern Orthodox Church Observances

Great Lent begins ... Feb 15
Pascha (Easter) ... Apr 4
Ascension ... May 13
Pentecost ... May 23

Jewish Holy Days*

Purim ... Feb 28
Passover (1st day) ... Mar 30
Shavuot ... May 19–20
Tisha B'av ... July 20
Rosh Hashanah (New Year) ... Sept 9–10
Yom Kippur ... Sept 18
Succoth ... Sept 23–Oct 1
Chanukah ... Dec 2–9

**All Jewish holy days begin the previous day at sundown.*

Islamic Holy Days**

First Day of Ramadan (1431) ... Aug 11
Eid-Al-Fitr (1431) ... Sept 9
Islamic New Year (1432) ... Dec 7

***All Islamic holy days begin the previous evening at moon crescent.*

CIVIL CALENDAR—USA—2010

New Year's Day ... Jan 1
Martin Luther King's Birthday (obsvd) ... Jan 18
Lincoln's Birthday ... Feb 12
Washington's Birthday (obsvd)/Presidents' Day ... Feb 15
Memorial Day (obsvd) ... May 31
Independence Day ... July 4
Labor Day ... Sept 6
Columbus Day (obsvd) ... Oct 11
General Election Day ... Nov 2
Veterans Day ... Nov 11
Thanksgiving Day ... Nov 25

Other Days Widely Observed in US—2010

Groundhog Day (Candlemas) ... Feb 2
St. Valentine's Day ... Feb 14
St. Patrick's Day ... Mar 17
Mother's Day ... May 9
Flag Day ... June 14
Father's Day ... June 20
National Grandparents Day ... Sept 12
Hallowe'en ... Oct 31

CIVIL CALENDAR—CANADA—2010

Victoria Day ... May 24
Canada Day ... July 1
Labor Day ... Sept 6
Thanksgiving Day ... Oct 11
Remembrance Day ... Nov 11
Boxing Day ... Dec 26

CIVIL CALENDAR—MEXICO—2010

New Year's Day ... Jan 1
Constitution Day ... Feb 5
Benito Juarez Birthday ... Mar 21
Labor Day ... May 1
Battle of Puebla Day (Cinco de Mayo) ... May 5
Independence Day* ... Sept 16
Dia de La Raza ... Oct 12
Mexican Revolution Day ... Nov 20
Guadalupe Day ... Dec 12

*Celebration begins Sept 15 at 11:00 P.M.

CIVIL CALENDAR—UNITED KINGDOM—2010

Accession of Queen Elizabeth II ... Feb 6
St. David (Wales) ... Mar 1
Commonwealth Day ... Mar 8
St. Patrick (Ireland) ... Mar 17
Birthday of Queen Elizabeth II ... Apr 21
St. George (England) ... Apr 23
Coronation Day ... June 2
The Queen's Official Birthday (tentative) ... June 12
Birthday of Prince Philip, Duke of Edinburgh ... June 10
Remembrance Sunday ... Nov 14
Birthday of the Prince of Wales ... Nov 14
St. Andrew (Scotland) ... Nov 30

BANK AND PUBLIC HOLIDAYS—UNITED KINGDOM—2010

Observed during 2010 in England and Wales, Scotland and Northern Ireland unless otherwise indicated

New Year ... Jan 1
Bank Holiday (Scotland) ... Jan 4
St. Patrick's Day (Northern Ireland) ... Mar 17
Good Friday ... Apr 2
Easter Monday (except Scotland) ... Apr 5
May Day Bank Holiday ... May 3
Spring Bank Holiday ... May 31
Orangeman's Day (Battle of the Boyne) (Northern Ireland) ... July 12
Bank Holiday (Scotland) ... Aug 2
Summer Bank Holiday (except Scotland) ... Aug 30
Christmas Day Holiday ... Dec 25
Boxing Day Holiday ... Dec 26

SEASONS

Spring (Vernal Equinox) ... Mar 20, 1:32 PM, EDT
Summer (Summer Solstice) ... June 21, 7:28 AM, EDT
Autumn (Autumnal Equinox) ... Sept 22, 11:09 PM, EDT
Winter (Winter Solstice) ... Dec 21, 6:38 PM, EST

DAYLIGHT SAVING TIME SCHEDULE—2010*

Sunday, Mar 14, 2:00 AM–Sunday, Nov 7, 2:00 AM—in all time zones.

**Extended per the Energy Policy Act of 2005.*

CHRONOLOGICAL CYCLES

Dominical Letter ... C
Epact ... 14
Golden Number (Lunar Cycle) ... XVI
Julian Period (year of) ... 6723
Roman Indiction ... 3
Solar Cycle ... 3

Calendar Information for the Year 2011

Time shown is Eastern Standard Time. All dates are given in terms of the Gregorian calendar.

(Based in part on information prepared by the Nautical Almanac Office, US Naval Observatory.)

ERAS	YEAR	BEGINS
Byzantine	7520	Sept 14
Jewish*	5772	Sept 29
Chinese (Year of the Rabbit)	4709	Feb 3
Roman (AUC)	2764	Jan 14
Nabonassar	2760	Apr 23
Japanese (Heisei)	23	Jan 1
Grecian (Seleucidae)	2323	Sept 14 (or Oct 14)
Indian (Saka)	1933	Mar 22
Diocletian	1728	Sept 11
Islamic (Hegira)**	1433	Nov 27

**Year begins the previous day at sunset.*

***Year begins the previous evening at moon crescent.*

RELIGIOUS CALENDARS

Epiphany .... Jan 6
Shrove Tuesday .... Mar 8
Ash Wednesday .... Mar 9
Lent .... Mar 9–Apr 23
Palm Sunday .... Apr 17
Good Friday .... Apr 22
Easter Day .... Apr 24
Ascension Day .... June 2
Whit Sunday (Pentecost) .... June 12
Trinity Sunday .... June 19
First Sunday in Advent .... Nov 27
Christmas Day (Thursday) .... Dec 25

Eastern Orthodox Church Observances

Great Lent begins .... Mar 7
Pascha (Easter) .... Apr 24
Ascension .... June 2
Pentecost .... June 12

Jewish Holy Days*

Purim .... Mar 20
Passover (1st day) .... Apr 19
Shavuot .... June 8–9
Tisha B'av .... Aug 9
Rosh Hashanah (New Year) .... Sept 29–30
Yom Kippur .... Oct 8
Succoth .... Oct 13–21
Chanukah .... Dec 21–28

**All Jewish holy days begin the previous day at sundown.*

Islamic Holy Days**

First Day of Ramadan (1432) .... Aug 1
Eid-Al-Fitr (1432) .... Aug 31
Islamic New Year (1433) .... Nov 27

***All Islamic holy days begin the previous evening at moon crescent.*

CIVIL CALENDAR—USA—2011

New Year's Day .... Jan 1
Martin Luther King's Birthday (obsvd) .... Jan 17
Lincoln's Birthday .... Feb 12
Washington's Birthday (obsvd)/Presidents' Day .... Feb 21
Memorial Day (obsvd) .... May 30
Independence Day .... July 4
Labor Day .... Sept 5
Columbus Day (obsvd) .... Oct 10
General Election Day .... Nov 8
Veterans Day .... Nov 11
Thanksgiving Day .... Nov 24

Other Days Widely Observed in US—2011

Groundhog Day (Candlemas) .... Feb 2
St. Valentine's Day .... Feb 14
St. Patrick's Day .... Mar 17
Mother's Day .... May 8
Flag Day .... June 14
Father's Day .... June 19
National Grandparents Day .... Sept 11
Hallowe'en .... Oct 31

CIVIL CALENDAR—CANADA—2011

Victoria Day .... May 23
Canada Day .... July 1
Labor Day .... Sept 5
Thanksgiving Day .... Oct 10
Remembrance Day .... Nov 11
Boxing Day .... Dec 26

CIVIL CALENDAR—MEXICO—2011

New Year's Day .... Jan 1
Constitution Day .... Feb 5
Benito Juarez Birthday .... Mar 21
Labor Day .... May 1
Battle of Puebla Day (Cinco de Mayo) .... May 5
Independence Day* .... Sept 16
Dia de La Raza .... Oct 12
Mexican Revolution Day .... Nov 20
Guadalupe Day .... Dec 12

*Celebration begins Sept 15 at 11:00 P.M.

CIVIL CALENDAR—UNITED KINGDOM—2011

Accession of Queen Elizabeth II .... Feb 6
St. David (Wales) .... Mar 1
Commonwealth Day .... Mar 14
St. Patrick (Ireland) .... Mar 17
Birthday of Queen Elizabeth II .... Apr 21
St. George (England) .... Apr 23
Coronation Day .... June 2
The Queen's Official Birthday (tentative) .... June 11
Birthday of Prince Philip, Duke of Edinburgh .... June 10
Remembrance Sunday .... Nov 13
Birthday of the Prince of Wales .... Nov 14
St. Andrew (Scotland) .... Nov 30

BANK AND PUBLIC HOLIDAYS—UNITED KINGDOM—2011

Observed during 2011 in England and Wales, Scotland and Northern Ireland unless otherwise indicated

New Year .... Jan 1
Bank Holiday (Scotland) .... Jan 3
St. Patrick's Day (Northern Ireland) .... Mar 17
Good Friday .... Apr 22
Easter Monday (except Scotland) .... Apr 25
May Day Bank Holiday .... May 2
Spring Bank Holiday .... May 30
Orangeman's Day (Battle of the Boyne) (Northern Ireland) .... July 12
Bank Holiday (Scotland) .... Aug 1
Summer Bank Holiday (except Scotland) .... Aug 29
Christmas Day Holiday .... Dec 25
Boxing Day Holiday .... Dec 26

SEASONS

Spring (Vernal Equinox) .... Mar 20, 7:21 PM, EDT
Summer (Summer Solstice) .... June 21, 1:16 PM, EDT
Autumn (Autumnal Equinox) .... Sept 23, 5:04 AM, EDT
Winter (Winter Solstice) .... Dec 22, 12:30 AM, EST

DAYLIGHT SAVING TIME SCHEDULE—2011*

Sunday, Mar 13, 2:00 AM–Sunday, Nov 6, 2:00 AM—in all time zones.

**Extended per the Energy Policy Act of 2005.*

CHRONOLOGICAL CYCLES

Dominical Letter .... B
Epact 25
Golden Number (Lunar Cycle) XVII
Julian Period (year of) 6724
Roman Indiction 4
Solar Cycle 4

Looking Forward

2010
FIFA World Cup, South Africa
Games of the XXI Winter Olympiad, Vancouver, British Columbia, Canada
Spain: Holy Year
South Carolina secession, 150th anniversary
First radio broadcast, 100th anniversary
Boy Scouts of America founding, 100th anniversary
Camp Fire Girls (now Camp Fire USA) founding, 100th anniversary
To Kill a Mockingbird published, 50th anniversary

2011
FIFA Women's World Cup
Rugby World Cup, New Zealand
Kansas Statehood Sesquicentennial
King James Bible published, 400th anniversary
New Madrid earthquakes, 200th anniversary
American Civil War begins, 150th anniversary
South Pole reached, 100th anniversary
Ronald Reagan's birth, 100th anniversary
Indianapolis 500, 100th anniversary
Berlin Wall erected, 50th anniversary

2012
Games of the XXX Olympiad, London, England
Transit of Venus—the last of the 21st century
US presidential election
Louisiana Statehood Bicentennial
Arizona Statehood Centennial
New Mexico Statehood Centennial
Joan of Arc's birth, 600th anniversary
Jean-Jacques Rousseau birth, 300th anniversary
War of 1812, 200th anniversary
Charles Dickens' birth, 200th anniversary
Woody Guthrie's birth, 100th anniversary
Titanic sinking, 100th anniversary
Girl Scouts of the USA founding, 100th anniversary
Cuban Missile Crisis, 50th anniversary

2013
First US Income Tax, 100th anniversary
The zipper patented, 100th anniversary
First crossword puzzle published, 100th anniversary
Gerald Ford's birth, 100th anniversary
Richard Nixon's birth, 100th anniversary
Jesse Owens' birth, 100th anniversary
Rosa Parks' birth, 100th anniversary

2014
"Star-Spangled Banner" composed, 200th anniversary
World War I begins, 100th anniversary
Panama Canal opens, 100th anniversary

2015
Magna Carta, 800th anniversary
Battle of Waterloo, 200th anniversary
Billie Holiday's birth, 100th anniversary
Saul Bellow's birth, 100th anniversary

2016
Games of the XXXI Olympiad
US presidential election
Indiana Statehood Bicentennial
First birth control clinic opened, 100th anniversary
James Herriot's birth, 100th anniversary

2017
Mexican Constitution, 100th anniversary
Mississippi Statehood Bicentennial
John Quincy Adams' birth, 250th anniversary
Andrew Jackson's birth, 250th anniversary
Frank Lloyd Wright's birth, 150th anniversary
John F. Kennedy's birth, 100th anniversary
Byron White's birth, 100th anniversary

2018
Illinois Statehood Bicentennial
US Standard Time Act, 100th anniversary
Czar Nicholas II executed, 100th anniversary

2019
Alabama Statehood Bicentennial
Apollo 11 astronauts walk on the moon, 50th anniversary

2020
US presidential election
Maine Statehood Bicentennial

2050
World population predicted to be 9 billion

2061
Halley's Comet returns

Perpetual Calendar, 1753–2100

A perpetual calendar lets you find the day of the week for any date in any year. Since January 1 may fall on any of the seven days of the week, and may be a leap or non-leap year, 14 different calendars are possible. The number next to each year corresponds to one of the 14 calendars. Calendar 5 will be used in 2009; calendar 6 will be used in 2010; calendar 7 will be used in 2011.

YEAR/NO	YEAR/NO	YEAR/NO	YEAR/NO	YEAR/NO	YEAR/NO	YEAR/NO	YEAR/NO	YEAR/NO	YEAR/NO	YEAR/NO	YEAR/NO
1753 2	1782 3	1811 3	1840 11	1869 6	1898 7	1927 7	1956 8	1985 3	2014 4	2043 5	2072 13
1754 3	1783 4	1812 11	1841 6	1870 7	1899 1	1928 8	1957 3	1986 4	2015 5	2044 13	2073 1
1755 4	1784 12	1813 6	1842 7	1871 1	1900 2	1929 3	1958 4	1987 5	2016 13	2045 1	2074 2
1756 12	1785 7	1814 7	1843 1	1872 9	1901 3	1930 4	1959 5	1988 13	2017 1	2046 2	2075 3
1757 7	1786 1	1815 1	1844 9	1873 4	1902 4	1931 5	1960 13	1989 1	2018 2	2047 3	2076 11
1758 1	1787 2	1816 9	1845 4	1874 5	1903 5	1932 13	1961 1	1990 2	2019 3	2048 11	2077 6
1759 2	1788 10	1817 4	1846 5	1875 6	1904 13	1933 1	1962 2	1991 3	2020 11	2049 6	2078 7
1760 10	1789 5	1818 5	1847 6	1876 14	1905 1	1934 2	1963 3	1992 11	2021 6	2050 7	2079 1
1761 5	1790 6	1819 6	1848 14	1877 2	1906 2	1935 3	1964 11	1993 6	2022 7	2051 1	2080 9
1762 6	1791 7	1820 14	1849 2	1878 3	1907 3	1936 11	1965 6	1994 7	2023 1	2052 9	2081 4
1763 7	1792 8	1821 2	1850 3	1879 4	1908 11	1937 6	1966 7	1995 1	2024 9	2053 4	2082 5
1764 8	1793 3	1822 3	1851 4	1880 12	1909 6	1938 7	1967 1	1996 9	2025 4	2054 5	2083 6
1765 3	1794 4	1823 4	1852 12	1881 7	1910 7	1939 1	1968 9	1997 4	2026 5	2055 6	2084 14
1766 4	1795 5	1824 12	1853 7	1882 1	1911 1	1940 9	1969 4	1998 5	2027 6	2056 14	2085 2
1767 5	1796 13	1825 7	1854 1	1883 2	1912 9	1941 4	1970 5	1999 6	2028 14	2057 2	2086 3
1768 13	1797 1	1826 1	1855 2	1884 10	1913 4	1942 5	1971 6	2000 14	2029 2	2058 3	2087 4
1769 1	1798 2	1827 2	1856 10	1885 5	1914 5	1943 6	1972 14	2001 2	2030 3	2059 4	2088 12
1770 2	1799 3	1828 10	1857 5	1886 6	1915 6	1944 14	1973 2	2002 3	2031 4	2060 12	2089 7
1771 3	1800 4	1829 5	1858 6	1887 7	1916 14	1945 2	1974 3	2003 4	2032 12	2061 7	2090 1
1772 11	1801 5	1830 6	1859 7	1888 8	1917 2	1946 3	1975 4	2004 12	2033 7	2062 1	2091 2
1773 6	1802 6	1831 7	1860 8	1889 3	1918 3	1947 4	1976 12	2005 7	2034 1	2063 2	2092 10
1774 7	1803 7	1832 8	1861 3	1890 4	1919 4	1948 12	1977 7	2006 1	2035 2	2064 10	2093 5
1775 1	1804 8	1833 3	1862 4	1891 5	1920 12	1949 7	1978 1	2007 2	2036 10	2065 5	2094 6
1776 9	1805 3	1834 4	1863 5	1892 13	1921 7	1950 1	1979 2	2008 10	2037 5	2066 6	2095 7
1777 4	1806 4	1835 5	1864 13	1893 1	1922 1	1951 2	1980 10	2009 5	2038 6	2067 7	2096 8
1778 5	1807 5	1836 13	1865 1	1894 2	1923 2	1952 10	1981 5	2010 6	2039 7	2068 8	2097 3
1779 6	1808 13	1837 1	1866 2	1895 3	1924 10	1953 5	1982 6	2011 7	2040 8	2069 3	2098 4
1780 14	1809 1	1838 2	1867 3	1896 11	1925 5	1954 6	1983 7	2012 8	2041 3	2070 4	2099 5
1781 2	1810 2	1839 3	1868 11	1897 6	1926 6	1955 7	1984 8	2013 3	2042 4	2071 5	2100 6

1

JAN	S	M	T	W	T	F	S
	1	2	3	4	5	6	7
	8	9	10	11	12	13	14
	15	16	17	18	19	20	21
	22	23	24	25	26	27	28
	29	30	31				

FEB	S	M	T	W	T	F	S
				1	2	3	4
	5	6	7	8	9	10	11
	12	13	14	15	16	17	18
	19	20	21	22	23	24	25
	26	27	28				

MAR	S	M	T	W	T	F	S
				1	2	3	4
	5	6	7	8	9	10	11
	12	13	14	15	16	17	18
	19	20	21	22	23	24	25
	26	27	28	29	30	31	

APR	S	M	T	W	T	F	S
							1
	2	3	4	5	6	7	8
	9	10	11	12	13	14	15
	16	17	18	19	20	21	22
	23	24	25	26	27	28	29
	30						

MAY	S	M	T	W	T	F	S
		1	2	3	4	5	6
	7	8	9	10	11	12	13
	14	15	16	17	18	19	20
	21	22	23	24	25	26	27
	28	29	30	31			

JUNE	S	M	T	W	T	F	S
					1	2	3
	4	5	6	7	8	9	10
	11	12	13	14	15	16	17
	18	19	20	21	22	23	24
	25	26	27	28	29	30	

JULY	S	M	T	W	T	F	S
							1
	2	3	4	5	6	7	8
	9	10	11	12	13	14	15
	16	17	18	19	20	21	22
	23	24	25	26	27	28	29
	30	31					

AUG	S	M	T	W	T	F	S
			1	2	3	4	5
	6	7	8	9	10	11	12
	13	14	15	16	17	18	19
	20	21	22	23	24	25	26
	27	28	29	30	31		

SEPT	S	M	T	W	T	F	S
						1	2
	3	4	5	6	7	8	9
	10	11	12	13	14	15	16
	17	18	19	20	21	22	23
	24	25	26	27	28	29	30

OCT	S	M	T	W	T	F	S
	1	2	3	4	5	6	7
	8	9	10	11	12	13	14
	15	16	17	18	19	20	21
	22	23	24	25	26	27	28
	29	30	31				

NOV	S	M	T	W	T	F	S
				1	2	3	4
	5	6	7	8	9	10	11
	12	13	14	15	16	17	18
	19	20	21	22	23	24	25
	26	27	28	29	30		

DEC	S	M	T	W	T	F	S
						1	2
	3	4	5	6	7	8	9
	10	11	12	13	14	15	16
	17	18	19	20	21	22	23
	24	25	26	27	28	29	30
	31						

2

JAN	S	M	T	W	T	F	S
		1	2	3	4	5	6
	7	8	9	10	11	12	13
	14	15	16	17	18	19	20
	21	22	23	24	25	26	27
	28	29	30	31			

FEB	S	M	T	W	T	F	S
					1	2	3
	4	5	6	7	8	9	10
	11	12	13	14	15	16	17
	18	19	20	21	22	23	24
	25	26	27	28			

MAR	S	M	T	W	T	F	S
					1	2	3
	4	5	6	7	8	9	10
	11	12	13	14	15	16	17
	18	19	20	21	22	23	24
	25	26	27	28	29	30	31

APR	S	M	T	W	T	F	S
	1	2	3	4	5	6	7
	8	9	10	11	12	13	14
	15	16	17	18	19	20	21
	22	23	24	25	26	27	28
	29	30					

MAY	S	M	T	W	T	F	S
			1	2	3	4	5
	6	7	8	9	10	11	12
	13	14	15	16	17	18	19
	20	21	22	23	24	25	26
	27	28	29	30	31		

JUNE	S	M	T	W	T	F	S
						1	2
	3	4	5	6	7	8	9
	10	11	12	13	14	15	16
	17	18	19	20	21	22	23
	24	25	26	27	28	29	30

JULY	S	M	T	W	T	F	S
	1	2	3	4	5	6	7
	8	9	10	11	12	13	14
	15	16	17	18	19	20	21
	22	23	24	25	26	27	28
	29	30	31				

AUG	S	M	T	W	T	F	S
				1	2	3	4
	5	6	7	8	9	10	11
	12	13	14	15	16	17	18
	19	20	21	22	23	24	25
	26	27	28	29	30	31	

SEPT	S	M	T	W	T	F	S
							1
	2	3	4	5	6	7	8
	9	10	11	12	13	14	15
	16	17	18	19	20	21	22
	23	24	25	26	27	28	29
	30						

OCT	S	M	T	W	T	F	S
		1	2	3	4	5	6
	7	8	9	10	11	12	13
	14	15	16	17	18	19	20
	21	22	23	24	25	26	27
	28	29	30	31			

DEC	S	M	T	W	T	F	S
					1	2	3
	4	5	6	7	8	9	10
	11	12	13	14	15	16	17
	18	19	20	21	22	23	24
	25	26	27	28	29	30	

DEC	S	M	T	W	T	F	S
							1
	2	3	4	5	6	7	8
	9	10	11	12	13	14	15
	16	17	18	19	20	21	22
	23	24	25	26	27	28	29
	30	31					

3

JAN	S	M	T	W	T	F	S
			1	2	3	4	5
	6	7	8	9	10	11	12
	13	14	15	16	17	18	19
	20	21	22	23	24	25	26
	27	28	29	30	31		

FEB	S	M	T	W	T	F	S
						1	2
	3	4	5	6	7	8	9
	10	11	12	13	14	15	16
	17	18	19	20	21	22	23
	24	25	26	27	28		

MAR	S	M	T	W	T	F	S
						1	2
	3	4	5	6	7	8	9
	10	11	12	13	14	15	16
	17	18	19	20	21	22	23
	24	25	26	27	28	29	30
	31						

APR	S	M	T	W	T	F	S
		1	2	3	4	5	6
	7	8	9	10	11	12	13
	14	15	16	17	18	19	20
	21	22	23	24	25	26	27
	28	29	30				

MAY	S	M	T	W	T	F	S
				1	2	3	4
	5	6	7	8	9	10	11
	12	13	14	15	16	17	18
	19	20	21	22	23	24	25
	26	27	28	29	30	31	

JUNE	S	M	T	W	T	F	S
							1
	2	3	4	5	6	7	8
	9	10	11	12	13	14	15
	16	17	18	19	20	21	22
	23	24	25	26	27	28	29
	30						

JULY	S	M	T	W	T	F	S
		1	2	3	4	5	6
	7	8	9	10	11	12	13
	14	15	16	17	18	19	20
	21	22	23	24	25	26	27
	28	29	30	31			

AUG	S	M	T	W	T	F	S
					1	2	3
	4	5	6	7	8	9	10
	11	12	13	14	15	16	17
	18	19	20	21	22	23	24
	25	26	27	28	29	30	31

SEPT	S	M	T	W	T	F	S
	1	2	3	4	5	6	7
	8	9	10	11	12	13	14
	15	16	17	18	19	20	21
	22	23	24	25	26	27	28
	29	30					

OCT	S	M	T	W	T	F	S
			1	2	3	4	5
	6	7	8	9	10	11	12
	13	14	15	16	17	18	19
	20	21	22	23	24	25	26
	27	28	29	30	31		

NOV	S	M	T	W	T	F	S
						1	2
	3	4	5	6	7	8	9
	10	11	12	13	14	15	16
	17	18	19	20	21	22	23
	24	25	26	27	28	29	30

DEC	S	M	T	W	T	F	S
	1	2	3	4	5	6	7
	8	9	10	11	12	13	14
	15	16	17	18	19	20	21
	22	23	24	25	26	27	28
	29	30	31				

4

JAN	S	M	T	W	T	F	S
				1	2	3	4
	5	6	7	8	9	10	11
	12	13	14	15	16	17	18
	19	20	21	22	23	24	25
	26	27	28	29	30	31	

FEB	S	M	T	W	T	F	S
							1
	2	3	4	5	6	7	8
	9	10	11	12	13	14	15
	16	17	18	19	20	21	22
	23	24	25	26	27	28	

MAR	S	M	T	W	T	F	S
							1
	2	3	4	5	6	7	8
	9	10	11	12	13	14	15
	16	17	18	19	20	21	22
	23	24	25	26	27	28	29
	30	31					

APR	S	M	T	W	T	F	S
			1	2	3	4	5
	6	7	8	9	10	11	12
	13	14	15	16	17	18	19
	20	21	22	23	24	25	26
	27	28	29	30			

MAY	S	M	T	W	T	F	S
					1	2	3
	4	5	6	7	8	9	10
	11	12	13	14	15	16	17
	18	19	20	21	22	23	24
	25	26	27	28	29	30	31

JUNE	S	M	T	W	T	F	S
	1	2	3	4	5	6	7
	8	9	10	11	12	13	14
	15	16	17	18	19	20	21
	22	23	24	25	26	27	28
	29	30					

JULY	S	M	T	W	T	F	S
			1	2	3	4	5
	6	7	8	9	10	11	12
	13	14	15	16	17	18	19
	20	21	22	23	24	25	26
	27	28	29	30	31		

AUG	S	M	T	W	T	F	S
						1	2
	3	4	5	6	7	8	9
	10	11	12	13	14	15	16
	17	18	19	20	21	22	23
	24	25	26	27	28	29	30
	31						

SEPT	S	M	T	W	T	F	S
		1	2	3	4	5	6
	7	8	9	10	11	12	13
	14	15	16	17	18	19	20
	21	22	23	24	25	26	27
	28	29	30				

OCT	S	M	T	W	T	F	S
				1	2	3	4
	5	6	7	8	9	10	11
	12	13	14	15	16	17	18
	19	20	21	22	23	24	25
	26	27	28	29	30	31	

NOV	S	M	T	W	T	F	S
							1
	2	3	4	5	6	7	8
	9	10	11	12	13	14	15
	16	17	18	19	20	21	22
	23	24	25	26	27	28	29
	30						

DEC	S	M	T	W	T	F	S
		1	2	3	4	5	6
	7	8	9	10	11	12	13
	14	15	16	17	18	19	20
	21	22	23	24	25	26	27
	28	29	30	31			

5

2009

JAN	S	M	T	W	T	F	S
					1	2	3
	4	5	6	7	8	9	10
	11	12	13	14	15	16	17
	18	19	20	21	22	23	24
	25	26	27	28	29	30	31

FEB	S	M	T	W	T	F	S
	1	2	3	4	5	6	7
	8	9	10	11	12	13	14
	15	16	17	18	19	20	21
	22	23	24	25	26	27	28

MAR	S	M	T	W	T	F	S
	1	2	3	4	5	6	7
	8	9	10	11	12	13	14
	15	16	17	18	19	20	21
	22	23	24	25	26	27	28
	29	30	31				

APR	S	M	T	W	T	F	S
				1	2	3	4
	5	6	7	8	9	10	11
	12	13	14	15	16	17	18
	19	20	21	22	23	24	25
	26	27	28	29	30		

MAY	S	M	T	W	T	F	S
						1	2
	3	4	5	6	7	8	9
	10	11	12	13	14	15	16
	17	18	19	20	21	22	23
	24	25	26	27	28	29	30
	31						

JUNE	S	M	T	W	T	F	S
		1	2	3	4	5	6
	7	8	9	10	11	12	13
	14	15	16	17	18	19	20
	21	22	23	24	25	26	27
	28	29	30				

JULY	S	M	T	W	T	F	S
				1	2	3	4
	5	6	7	8	9	10	11
	12	13	14	15	16	17	18
	19	20	21	22	23	24	25
	26	27	28	29	30	31	

AUG	S	M	T	W	T	F	S
							1
	2	3	4	5	6	7	8
	9	10	11	12	13	14	15
	16	17	18	19	20	21	22
	23	24	25	26	27	28	29
	30	31					

SEPT	S	M	T	W	T	F	S
			1	2	3	4	5
	6	7	8	9	10	11	12
	13	14	15	16	17	18	19
	20	21	22	23	24	25	26
	27	28	29	30			

OCT	S	M	T	W	T	F	S
					1	2	3
	4	5	6	7	8	9	10
	11	12	13	14	15	16	17
	18	19	20	21	22	23	24
	25	26	27	28	29	30	31

NOV	S	M	T	W	T	F	S
	1	2	3	4	5	6	7
	8	9	10	11	12	13	14
	15	16	17	18	19	20	21
	22	23	24	25	26	27	28
	29	30					

DEC	S	M	T	W	T	F	S
			1	2	3	4	5
	6	7	8	9	10	11	12
	13	14	15	16	17	18	19
	20	21	22	23	24	25	26
	27	28	29	30	31		

6

2010

JAN	S	M	T	W	T	F	S
						1	2
	3	4	5	6	7	8	9
	10	11	12	13	14	15	16
	17	18	19	20	21	22	23
	24	25	26	27	28	29	30
	31						

FEB	S	M	T	W	T	F	S
		1	2	3	4	5	6
	7	8	9	10	11	12	13
	14	15	16	17	18	19	20
	21	22	23	24	25	26	27
	28						

MAR	S	M	T	W	T	F	S
		1	2	3	4	5	6
	7	8	9	10	11	12	13
	14	15	16	17	18	19	20
	21	22	23	24	25	26	27
	28	29	30	31			

APR	S	M	T	W	T	F	S
					1	2	3
	4	5	6	7	8	9	10
	11	12	13	14	15	16	17
	18	19	20	21	22	23	24
	25	26	27	28	29	30	

MAY	S	M	T	W	T	F	S
							1
	2	3	4	5	6	7	8
	9	10	11	12	13	14	15
	16	17	18	19	20	21	22
	23	24	25	26	27	28	29
	30	31					

JUNE	S	M	T	W	T	F	S
			1	2	3	4	5
	6	7	8	9	10	11	12
	13	14	15	16	17	18	19
	20	21	22	23	24	25	26
	27	28	29	30			

JULY	S	M	T	W	T	F	S
					1	2	3
	4	5	6	7	8	9	10
	11	12	13	14	15	16	17
	18	19	20	21	22	23	24
	25	26	27	28	29	30	31

AUG	S	M	T	W	T	F	S
	1	2	3	4	5	6	7
	8	9	10	11	12	13	14
	15	16	17	18	19	20	21
	22	23	24	25	26	27	28
	29	30	31				

SEPT	S	M	T	W	T	F	S
				1	2	3	4
	5	6	7	8	9	10	11
	12	13	14	15	16	17	18
	19	20	21	22	23	24	25
	26	27	28	29	30		

OCT	S	M	T	W	T	F	S
						1	2
	3	4	5	6	7	8	9
	10	11	12	13	14	15	16
	17	18	19	20	21	22	23
	24	25	26	27	28	29	30
	31						

NOV	S	M	T	W	T	F	S
		1	2	3	4	5	6
	7	8	9	10	11	12	13
	14	15	16	17	18	19	20
	21	22	23	24	25	26	27
	28	29	30				

DEC	S	M	T	W	T	F	S
				1	2	3	4
	5	6	7	8	9	10	11
	12	13	14	15	16	17	18
	19	20	21	22	23	24	25
	26	27	28	29	30	31	

7

2011

JAN

S	M	T	W	T	F	S
						1
2	3	4	5	6	7	8
9	10	11	12	13	14	15
16	17	18	19	20	21	22
23	24	25	26	27	28	29
30	31					

FEB

S	M	T	W	T	F	S
		1	2	3	4	5
6	7	8	9	10	11	12
13	14	15	16	17	18	19
20	21	22	23	24	25	26
27	28					

MAR

S	M	T	W	T	F	S
		1	2	3	4	5
6	7	8	9	10	11	12
13	14	15	16	17	18	19
20	21	22	23	24	25	26
27	28	29	30	31		

APR

S	M	T	W	T	F	S
					1	2
3	4	5	6	7	8	9
10	11	12	13	14	15	16
17	18	19	20	21	22	23
24	25	26	27	28	29	30

MAY

S	M	T	W	T	F	S
1	2	3	4	5	6	7
8	9	10	11	12	13	14
15	16	17	18	19	20	21
22	23	24	25	26	27	28
29	30	31				

JUNE

S	M	T	W	T	F	S
			1	2	3	4
5	6	7	8	9	10	11
12	13	14	15	16	17	18
19	20	21	22	23	24	25
26	27	28	29	30		

JULY

S	M	T	W	T	F	S
					1	2
3	4	5	6	7	8	9
10	11	12	13	14	15	16
17	18	19	20	21	22	23
24	25	26	27	28	29	30
31						

AUG

S	M	T	W	T	F	S
	1	2	3	4	5	6
7	8	9	10	11	12	13
14	15	16	17	18	19	20
21	22	23	24	25	26	27
28	29	30	31			

SEPT

S	M	T	W	T	F	S
				1	2	3
4	5	6	7	8	9	10
11	12	13	14	15	16	17
18	19	20	21	22	23	24
25	26	27	28	29	30	

OCT

S	M	T	W	T	F	S
						1
2	3	4	5	6	7	8
9	10	11	12	13	14	15
16	17	18	19	20	21	22
23	24	25	26	27	28	29
30	31					

NOV

S	M	T	W	T	F	S
		1	2	3	4	5
6	7	8	9	10	11	12
13	14	15	16	17	18	19
20	21	22	23	24	25	26
27	28	29	30			

DEC

S	M	T	W	T	F	S
				1	2	3
4	5	6	7	8	9	10
11	12	13	14	15	16	17
18	19	20	21	22	23	24
25	26	27	28	29	30	31

8

JAN

S	M	T	W	T	F	S
1	2	3	4	5	6	7
8	9	10	11	12	13	14
15	16	17	18	19	20	21
22	23	24	25	26	27	28
29	30	31				

FEB

S	M	T	W	T	F	S
			1	2	3	4
5	6	7	8	9	10	11
12	13	14	15	16	17	18
19	20	21	22	23	24	25
26	27	28	29			

MAR

S	M	T	W	T	F	S
				1	2	3
4	5	6	7	8	9	10
11	12	13	14	15	16	17
18	19	20	21	22	23	24
25	26	27	28	29	30	31

APR

S	M	T	W	T	F	S
1	2	3	4	5	6	7
8	9	10	11	12	13	14
15	16	17	18	19	20	21
22	23	24	25	26	27	28
29	30					

MAY

S	M	T	W	T	F	S
		1	2	3	4	5
6	7	8	9	10	11	12
13	14	15	16	17	18	19
20	21	22	23	24	25	26
27	28	29	30	31		

JUNE

S	M	T	W	T	F	S
					1	2
3	4	5	6	7	8	9
10	11	12	13	14	15	16
17	18	19	20	21	22	23
24	25	26	27	28	29	30

JULY

S	M	T	W	T	F	S
1	2	3	4	5	6	7
8	9	10	11	12	13	14
15	16	17	18	19	20	21
22	23	24	25	26	27	28
29	30	31				

AUG

S	M	T	W	T	F	S
			1	2	3	4
5	6	7	8	9	10	11
12	13	14	15	16	17	18
19	20	21	22	23	24	25
26	27	28	29	30	31	

SEPT

S	M	T	W	T	F	S
						1
2	3	4	5	6	7	8
9	10	11	12	13	14	15
16	17	18	19	20	21	22
23	24	25	26	27	28	29
30						

OCT

S	M	T	W	T	F	S
	1	2	3	4	5	6
7	8	9	10	11	12	13
14	15	16	17	18	19	20
21	22	23	24	25	26	27
28	29	30	31			

NOV

S	M	T	W	T	F	S
				1	2	3
4	5	6	7	8	9	10
11	12	13	14	15	16	17
18	19	20	21	22	23	24
25	26	27	28	29	30	

DEC

S	M	T	W	T	F	S
						1
2	3	4	5	6	7	8
9	10	11	12	13	14	15
16	17	18	19	20	21	22
23	24	25	26	27	28	29
30	31					

9

JAN

S	M	T	W	T	F	S
	1	2	3	4	5	6
7	8	9	10	11	12	13
14	15	16	17	18	19	20
21	22	23	24	25	26	27
28	29	30	31			

FEB

S	M	T	W	T	F	S
				1	2	3
4	5	6	7	8	9	10
11	12	13	14	15	16	17
18	19	20	21	22	23	24
25	26	27	28	29		

MAR

S	M	T	W	T	F	S
					1	2
3	4	5	6	7	8	9
10	11	12	13	14	15	16
17	18	19	20	21	22	23
24	25	26	27	28	29	30
31						

APR

S	M	T	W	T	F	S
	1	2	3	4	5	6
7	8	9	10	11	12	13
14	15	16	17	18	19	20
21	22	23	24	25	26	27
28	29	30				

MAY

S	M	T	W	T	F	S
			1	2	3	4
5	6	7	8	9	10	11
12	13	14	15	16	17	18
19	20	21	22	23	24	25
26	27	28	29	30	31	

JUNE

S	M	T	W	T	F	S
						1
2	3	4	5	6	7	8
9	10	11	12	13	14	15
16	17	18	19	20	21	22
23	24	25	26	27	28	29
30						

JULY

S	M	T	W	T	F	S
	1	2	3	4	5	6
7	8	9	10	11	12	13
14	15	16	17	18	19	20
21	22	23	24	25	26	27
28	29	30	31			

AUG

S	M	T	W	T	F	S
				1	2	3
4	5	6	7	8	9	10
11	12	13	14	15	16	17
18	19	20	21	22	23	24
25	26	27	28	29	30	31

SEPT

S	M	T	W	T	F	S
1	2	3	4	5	6	7
8	9	10	11	12	13	14
15	16	17	18	19	20	21
22	23	24	25	26	27	28
29	30					

OCT

S	M	T	W	T	F	S
		1	2	3	4	5
6	7	8	9	10	11	12
13	14	15	16	17	18	19
20	21	22	23	24	25	26
27	28	29	30	31		

NOV

S	M	T	W	T	F	S
					1	2
3	4	5	6	7	8	9
10	11	12	13	14	15	16
17	18	19	20	21	22	23
24	25	26	27	28	29	30

DEC

S	M	T	W	T	F	S
1	2	3	4	5	6	7
8	9	10	11	12	13	14
15	16	17	18	19	20	21
22	23	24	25	26	27	28
29	30	31				

10

JAN

S	M	T	W	T	F	S
		1	2	3	4	5
6	7	8	9	10	11	12
13	14	15	16	17	18	19
20	21	22	23	24	25	26
27	28	29	30	31		

FEB

S	M	T	W	T	F	S
					1	2
3	4	5	6	7	8	9
10	11	12	13	14	15	16
17	18	19	20	21	22	23
24	25	26	27	28	29	

MAR

S	M	T	W	T	F	S
						1
2	3	4	5	6	7	8
9	10	11	12	13	14	15
16	17	18	19	20	21	22
23	24	25	26	27	28	29
30	31					

APR

S	M	T	W	T	F	S
		1	2	3	4	5
6	7	8	9	10	11	12
13	14	15	16	17	18	19
20	21	22	23	24	25	26
27	28	29	30			

MAY

S	M	T	W	T	F	S
				1	2	3
4	5	6	7	8	9	10
11	12	13	14	15	16	17
18	19	20	21	22	23	24
25	26	27	28	29	30	31

JUNE

S	M	T	W	T	F	S
1	2	3	4	5	6	7
8	9	10	11	12	13	14
15	16	17	18	19	20	21
22	23	24	25	26	27	28
29	30					

JULY

S	M	T	W	T	F	S
		1	2	3	4	5
6	7	8	9	10	11	12
13	14	15	16	17	18	19
20	21	22	23	24	25	26
27	28	29	30	31		

AUG

S	M	T	W	T	F	S
					1	2
3	4	5	6	7	8	9
10	11	12	13	14	15	16
17	18	19	20	21	22	23
24	25	26	27	28	29	30
31						

SEPT

S	M	T	W	T	F	S
	1	2	3	4	5	6
7	8	9	10	11	12	13
14	15	16	17	18	19	20
21	22	23	24	25	26	27
28	29	30				

OCT

S	M	T	W	T	F	S
			1	2	3	4
5	6	7	8	9	10	11
12	13	14	15	16	17	18
19	20	21	22	23	24	25
26	27	28	29	30	31	

NOV

S	M	T	W	T	F	S
						1
2	3	4	5	6	7	8
9	10	11	12	13	14	15
16	17	18	19	20	21	22
23	24	25	26	27	28	29
30						

DEC

S	M	T	W	T	F	S
	1	2	3	4	5	6
7	8	9	10	11	12	13
14	15	16	17	18	19	20
21	22	23	24	25	26	27
28	29	30	31			

11

JAN

S	M	T	W	T	F	S
			1	2	3	4
5	6	7	8	9	10	11
12	13	14	15	16	17	18
19	20	21	22	23	24	25
26	27	28	29	30	31	

FEB

S	M	T	W	T	F	S
						1
2	3	4	5	6	7	8
9	10	11	12	13	14	15
16	17	18	19	20	21	22
23	24	25	26	27	28	29

MAR

S	M	T	W	T	F	S
1	2	3	4	5	6	7
8	9	10	11	12	13	14
15	16	17	18	19	20	21
22	23	24	25	26	27	28
29	30	31				

APR

S	M	T	W	T	F	S
			1	2	3	4
5	6	7	8	9	10	11
12	13	14	15	16	17	18
19	20	21	22	23	24	25
26	27	28	29	30		

MAY

S	M	T	W	T	F	S
					1	2
3	4	5	6	7	8	9
10	11	12	13	14	15	16
17	18	19	20	21	22	23
24	25	26	27	28	29	30
31						

JUNE

S	M	T	W	T	F	S
	1	2	3	4	5	6
7	8	9	10	11	12	13
14	15	16	17	18	19	20
21	22	23	24	25	26	27
28	29	30				

JULY

S	M	T	W	T	F	S
			1	2	3	4
5	6	7	8	9	10	11
12	13	14	15	16	17	18
19	20	21	22	23	24	25
26	27	28	29	30	31	

AUG

S	M	T	W	T	F	S
						1
2	3	4	5	6	7	8
9	10	11	12	13	14	15
16	17	18	19	20	21	22
23	24	25	26	27	28	29
30	31					

SEPT

S	M	T	W	T	F	S
		1	2	3	4	5
6	7	8	9	10	11	12
13	14	15	16	17	18	19
20	21	22	23	24	25	26
27	28	29	30			

OCT

S	M	T	W	T	F	S
				1	2	3
4	5	6	7	8	9	10
11	12	13	14	15	16	17
18	19	20	21	22	23	24
25	26	27	28	29	30	31

NOV

S	M	T	W	T	F	S
1	2	3	4	5	6	7
8	9	10	11	12	13	14
15	16	17	18	19	20	21
22	23	24	25	26	27	28
29	30					

DEC

S	M	T	W	T	F	S
		1	2	3	4	5
6	7	8	9	10	11	12
13	14	15	16	17	18	19
20	21	22	23	24	25	26
27	28	29	30	31		

12

JAN

S	M	T	W	T	F	S
				1	2	3
4	5	6	7	8	9	10
11	12	13	14	15	16	17
18	19	20	21	22	23	24
25	26	27	28	29	30	31

FEB

S	M	T	W	T	F	S
1	2	3	4	5	6	7
8	9	10	11	12	13	14
15	16	17	18	19	20	21
22	23	24	25	26	27	28
29						

MAR

S	M	T	W	T	F	S
	1	2	3	4	5	6
7	8	9	10	11	12	13
14	15	16	17	18	19	20
21	22	23	24	25	26	27
28	29	30	31			

APR

S	M	T	W	T	F	S
				1	2	3
4	5	6	7	8	9	10
11	12	13	14	15	16	17
18	19	20	21	22	23	24
25	26	27	28	29	30	

MAY

S	M	T	W	T	F	S
						1
2	3	4	5	6	7	8
9	10	11	12	13	14	15
16	17	18	19	20	21	22
23	24	25	26	27	28	29
30	31					

JUNE

S	M	T	W	T	F	S
		1	2	3	4	5
6	7	8	9	10	11	12
13	14	15	16	17	18	19
20	21	22	23	24	25	26
27	28	29	30			

JULY

S	M	T	W	T	F	S
				1	2	3
4	5	6	7	8	9	10
11	12	13	14	15	16	17
18	19	20	21	22	23	24
25	26	27	28	29	30	31

AUG

S	M	T	W	T	F	S
1	2	3	4	5	6	7
8	9	10	11	12	13	14
15	16	17	18	19	20	21
22	23	24	25	26	27	28
29	30	31				

SEPT

S	M	T	W	T	F	S
			1	2	3	4
5	6	7	8	9	10	11
12	13	14	15	16	17	18
19	20	21	22	23	24	25
26	27	28	29	30		

OCT

S	M	T	W	T	F	S
					1	2
3	4	5	6	7	8	9
10	11	12	13	14	15	16
17	18	19	20	21	22	23
24	25	26	27	28	29	30
31						

NOV

S	M	T	W	T	F	S
	1	2	3	4	5	6
7	8	9	10	11	12	13
14	15	16	17	18	19	20
21	22	23	24	25	26	27
28	29	30				

DEC

S	M	T	W	T	F	S
			1	2	3	4
5	6	7	8	9	10	11
12	13	14	15	16	17	18
19	20	21	22	23	24	25
26	27	28	29	30	31	

13

JAN

S	M	T	W	T	F	S
					1	2
3	4	5	6	7	8	9
10	11	12	13	14	15	16
17	18	19	20	21	22	23
24	25	26	27	28	29	30
31						

FEB

S	M	T	W	T	F	S
	1	2	3	4	5	6
7	8	9	10	11	12	13
14	15	16	17	18	19	20
21	22	23	24	25	26	27
28	29					

MAR

S	M	T	W	T	F	S
		1	2	3	4	5
6	7	8	9	10	11	12
13	14	15	16	17	18	19
20	21	22	23	24	25	26
27	28	29	30	31		

APR

S	M	T	W	T	F	S
					1	2
3	4	5	6	7	8	9
10	11	12	13	14	15	16
17	18	19	20	21	22	23
24	25	26	27	28	29	30

MAY

S	M	T	W	T	F	S
1	2	3	4	5	6	7
8	9	10	11	12	13	14
15	16	17	18	19	20	21
22	23	24	25	26	27	28
29	30	31				

JUNE

S	M	T	W	T	F	S
			1	2	3	4
5	6	7	8	9	10	11
12	13	14	15	16	17	18
19	20	21	22	23	24	25
26	27	28	29	30		

JULY

S	M	T	W	T	F	S
					1	2
3	4	5	6	7	8	9
10	11	12	13	14	15	16
17	18	19	20	21	22	23
24	25	26	27	28	29	30
31						

AUG

S	M	T	W	T	F	S
	1	2	3	4	5	6
7	8	9	10	11	12	13
14	15	16	17	18	19	20
21	22	23	24	25	26	27
28	29	30	31			

SEPT

S	M	T	W	T	F	S
				1	2	3
4	5	6	7	8	9	10
11	12	13	14	15	16	17
18	19	20	21	22	23	24
25	26	27	28	29	30	

OCT

S	M	T	W	T	F	S
						1
2	3	4	5	6	7	8
9	10	11	12	13	14	15
16	17	18	19	20	21	22
23	24	25	26	27	28	29
30	31					

NOV

S	M	T	W	T	F	S
		1	2	3	4	5
6	7	8	9	10	11	12
13	14	15	16	17	18	19
20	21	22	23	24	25	26
27	28	29	30			

DEC

S	M	T	W	T	F	S
				1	2	3
4	5	6	7	8	9	10
11	12	13	14	15	16	17
18	19	20	21	22	23	24
25	26	27	28	29	30	31

14

JAN

S	M	T	W	T	F	S
						1
2	3	4	5	6	7	8
9	10	11	12	13	14	15
16	17	18	19	20	21	22
23	24	25	26	27	28	29
30	31					

FEB

S	M	T	W	T	F	S
		1	2	3	4	5
6	7	8	9	10	11	12
13	14	15	16	17	18	19
20	21	22	23	24	25	26
27	28	29				

MAR

S	M	T	W	T	F	S
			1	2	3	4
5	6	7	8	9	10	11
12	13	14	15	16	17	18
19	20	21	22	23	24	25
26	27	28	29	30	31	

APR

S	M	T	W	T	F	S
						1
2	3	4	5	6	7	8
9	10	11	12	13	14	15
16	17	18	19	20	21	22
23	24	25	26	27	28	29
30						

MAY

S	M	T	W	T	F	S
	1	2	3	4	5	6
7	8	9	10	11	12	13
14	15	16	17	18	19	20
21	22	23	24	25	26	27
28	29	30	31			

JUNE

S	M	T	W	T	F	S
				1	2	3
4	5	6	7	8	9	10
11	12	13	14	15	16	17
18	19	20	21	22	23	24
25	26	27	28	29	30	

JULY

S	M	T	W	T	F	S
						1
2	3	4	5	6	7	8
9	10	11	12	13	14	15
16	17	18	19	20	21	22
23	24	25	26	27	28	29
30	31					

AUG

S	M	T	W	T	F	S
		1	2	3	4	5
6	7	8	9	10	11	12
13	14	15	16	17	18	19
20	21	22	23	24	25	26
27	28	29	30	31		

SEPT

S	M	T	W	T	F	S
					1	2
3	4	5	6	7	8	9
10	11	12	13	14	15	16
17	18	19	20	21	22	23
24	25	26	27	28	29	30

OCT

S	M	T	W	T	F	S
1	2	3	4	5	6	7
8	9	10	11	12	13	14
15	16	17	18	19	20	21
22	23	24	25	26	27	28
29	30	31				

NOV

S	M	T	W	T	F	S
			1	2	3	4
5	6	7	8	9	10	11
12	13	14	15	16	17	18
19	20	21	22	23	24	25
26	27	28	29	30		

DEC

S	M	T	W	T	F	S
					1	2
3	4	5	6	7	8	9
10	11	12	13	14	15	16
17	18	19	20	21	22	23
24	25	26	27	28	29	30
31						

National Days of the World for 2009

(Compiled from publications of the U.S. Department of State, the United Nations and from information received from the countries listed.)

Most nations set aside one or more days each year as national public holidays, often recognizing the anniversary of the attainment of independence, or the birthday of the country's ruler. Below, the national days are listed alphabetically. It should be noted that in some countries the Gregorian Calendar date of observance varies from year to year. See the Index and the main chronology for further details of observance, and for numerous holidays in addition to the national days listed here.

Afghanistan . . . . Aug 19
Albania . . . . Nov 28
Algeria . . . . Nov 1
Andorra . . . . Sept 8
Angola . . . . Nov 11
Antigua and Barbuda . . . . Nov 1
Argentina . . . . May 25
Armenia . . . . Sept 21
Australia . . . . Jan 26
Austria . . . . Oct 26
Azerbaijan . . . . May 28
Bahamas . . . . July 10
Bahrain . . . . Dec 16
Bangladesh . . . . Mar 26
Barbados . . . . Nov 30
Belarus . . . . July 3
Belgium . . . . July 21
Belize . . . . Sept 21
Benin . . . . Aug 1
Bhutan . . . . Dec 17
Bolivia . . . . Aug 6
Bosnia and Herzegovina . . . . Mar 1
Botswana . . . . Sept 30
Brazil . . . . Sept 7
Brunei Darussalam . . . . Feb 23
Bulgaria . . . . Mar 3
Burkina Faso . . . . Dec 11
Burundi . . . . July 1
Cambodia . . . . Nov 9
Cameroon . . . . May 20
Canada . . . . July 1
Cape Verde . . . . July 5
Central African Republic . . . . Dec 1
Chad . . . . Aug 11
Chile . . . . Sept 18
China . . . . Oct 1
Colombia . . . . July 20
Comoros . . . . July 6
Congo . . . . Aug 15
Congo, Democratic Republic of . . . . June 30
Costa Rica . . . . Sept 15
Cote D'Ivoire . . . . Aug 7
Croatia . . . . Oct 8
Cuba . . . . Jan 1
Cyprus . . . . Oct 1
Czech Republic . . . . Oct 28
Denmark . . . . June 5
Djibouti . . . . June 27
Dominica . . . . Nov 3
Dominican Republic . . . . Feb 27
East Timor . . . . Nov 28
Ecuador . . . . Aug 10
Egypt . . . . July 23
El Salvador . . . . Sept 15
Equatorial Guinea . . . . Oct 12
Eritrea . . . . May 24
Estonia . . . . Feb 24
Ethiopia . . . . May 28
Fiji . . . . Oct 10
Finland . . . . Dec 6
France . . . . July 14
Gabon . . . . Aug 17
Gambia . . . . Feb 18
Georgia . . . . May 26
Germany . . . . Oct 3
Ghana . . . . Mar 6
Greece . . . . Mar 25
Grenada . . . . Feb 7
Guatemala . . . . Sept 15
Guinea . . . . Oct 2
Guinea-Bissau . . . . Sept 24
Guyana . . . . Feb 23
Haiti . . . . Jan 1
Holy See . . . . Oct 22
Honduras . . . . Sept 15
Hungary . . . . Aug 20
Iceland . . . . June 17
India . . . . Jan 26
Indonesia . . . . Aug 17
Iran . . . . Apr 1
Iraq . . . . Apr 9
Ireland . . . . Mar 17
Israel . . . . Apr 30
Italy . . . . June 2
Jamaica . . . . Aug 6
Japan . . . . Dec 23
Jordan . . . . May 25
Kazakhstan . . . . Dec 16
Kenya . . . . Dec 12
Kiribati . . . . July 12
Korea, Democratic People's Republic of . . . . Sept 9
Korea, Republic of . . . . Aug 15
Kuwait . . . . Feb 25
Kyrgyzstan . . . . Aug 31
Lao People's Democratic Republic . . . Dec 2
Latvia . . . . Nov 18
Lebanon . . . . Nov 22
Lesotho . . . . Oct 4
Liberia . . . . July 26
Libya . . . . Sept 1
Liechtenstein . . . . Aug 15
Lithuania . . . . Feb 16
Luxembourg . . . . June 23
Macedonia . . . . Aug 2
Madagascar . . . . June 26
Malawi . . . . July 6
Malaysia . . . . Aug 31
Maldives . . . . July 26
Mali . . . . Sept 22
Malta . . . . Sept 21
Marshall Islands . . . . May 1
Mauritania . . . . Nov 28
Mauritius . . . . Mar 12
Mexico . . . . Sept 16
Micronesia (Federated States of) . . . May 10
Moldova, Republic of . . . . Aug 27
Monaco . . . . Nov 19
Mongolia . . . . July 11
Montenegro, Republic of . . . . July 13
Morocco . . . . Mar 3
Mozambique . . . . June 25
Myanmar . . . . Jan 4
Namibia, Republic of . . . . Mar 21
Nauru . . . . Jan 31
Nepal . . . . *
Netherlands . . . . Apr 30
New Zealand . . . . Feb 6
Nicaragua . . . . Sept 15
Niger . . . . Dec 18
Nigeria . . . . Oct 1
Norway . . . . May 17
Oman . . . . Nov 18
Pakistan . . . . Mar 23
Panama . . . . Nov 3
Papua New Guinea . . . . Sept 16
Paraguay . . . . May 15
Peru . . . . July 28
Philippines . . . . June 12
Poland . . . . May 3
Portugal . . . . June 10
Qatar . . . . Sept 3
Romania . . . . Dec 1
Russian Federation . . . . June 12
Rwanda . . . . July 1
Saint Christopher (St Kitts) and Nevis . . . . Sept 19
Saint Lucia . . . . Feb 22
Saint Vincent and the Grenadines . . . Oct 27
Samoa . . . . June 1
San Marino . . . . Sept 3
Sao Tome and Principe . . . . July 12
Saudi Arabia . . . . Sept 23
Senegal . . . . Apr 4
Serbia . . . . Feb 15
Seychelles . . . . June 18
Sierra Leone . . . . Apr 27
Singapore . . . . Aug 9
Slovakia . . . . Sept 1
Slovenia . . . . June 25
Solomon Islands . . . . July 7
Somalia . . . . July 1
South Africa . . . . Apr 27
Spain . . . . Oct 12
Sri Lanka . . . . Feb 4
Sudan . . . . Jan 1
Suriname . . . . Nov 25
Swaziland . . . . Sept 6
Sweden . . . . June 6
Switzerland . . . . Aug 1
Syria . . . . Apr 17
Taiwan . . . . Oct 10
Tajikistan . . . . Sept 9
Tanzania, United Republic of . . . . Apr 26
Thailand . . . . Dec 5
Togo . . . . Apr 27
Tonga . . . . June 4
Trinidad and Tobago . . . . Aug 31
Tunisia . . . . Mar 20
Turkey . . . . Oct 29
Turkmenistan . . . . Oct 27
Tuvalu . . . . Oct 1
Uganda . . . . Oct 9
Ukraine . . . . Aug 24
United Arab Emirates . . . . Dec 2
United Kingdom** . . . . June 13
United States of America . . . . July 4
Uruguay . . . . Aug 25
Uzbekistan . . . . Sept 1
Vanuatu . . . . July 30
Venezuela . . . . July 5
Vietnam . . . . Sept 2
Yemen . . . . May 22
Zambia . . . . Oct 24
Zimbabwe . . . . Apr 18

**Nepal abolished its national day in 2006 and has not yet set a new one.*

***Trooping the Colour—Queen's official birthday.*

Selected Special Years: 1990–2011

As sponsored by the United Nations

Intl Literacy Year: 1990
US Decade of the Brain: 1990-99
Intl Space Year: 1992
Intl Year for World's Indigenous Peoples: 1993
Intl Year of the Family: 1994
Year for Tolerance: 1995
Intl Year for Eradication of Poverty: 1996
Intl Year of the Ocean: 1998
Intl Year of Older Persons: 1999
Intl Year for the Culture of Peace: 2000
Intl Year of Thanksgiving: 2000
Intl Year of Volunteers: 2001
Year of Dialogue Among Civilizations: 2001
Intl Decade for a Culture of Peace: 2001–10
Intl Year of Mobilization Against Racism: 2001
Intl Year of Mountains: 2002
Intl Year of Ecotourism: 2002
Intl Year of Freshwater: 2003
Intl Year of Microcredit: 2005
Intl Year of Human Rights Learning: 2008–2009
Intl Year of Languages: 2008
Intl Year of the Potato: 2008
Intl Year of Planet Earth: 2008
Intl Year of Sanitation: 2008
Intl Year of Astronomy: 2009
Intl Year of Natural Fibers: 2009
Intl Year of Reconciliation: 2009
Intl Year for the Rapproachment of Cultures: 2010
Intl Year of Biodiversity: 2010
Intl Year of Forests: 2011

Chinese Calendar

The Chinese lunar year is divided into 12 months of 29 or 30 days. The calendar is adjusted to the length of the solar year by the addition of extra months at regular intervals. The years are arranged in major cycles of 60 years. Each successive year is named after one of 12 animals. These 12-year cycles are continuously repeated.

2005 .... Rooster
2006 .... Dog
2007 .... Boar (Pig)
2008 .... Rat
2009 .... Ox
2010 .... Tiger
2011 .... Hare
2012 .... Dragon
2013 .... Snake
2014 .... Horse
2015 .... Sheep (Goat)
2016 .... Monkey

Wedding Anniversary Gifts

1st .... paper, plastics, clocks
2nd .... cotton, china, calico
3rd .... leather, crystal, glass
4th .... books, electrical appliances, silk, fruit, flowers
5th .... wood, silverware
6th .... sugar, candy, wood, iron
7th .... wool, copper, desk sets
8th .... bronze, pottery, linens, laces, electrical appliances
9th .... pottery, willow, leather
10th .... tin, aluminum, diamond jewelry
11th .... steel, fashion jewelry, accessories
12th .... silk, linen, pearls, colored gems
13th .... lace, textiles, furs
14th .... ivory, gold jewelry
15th .... crystal, watches, glass
16th .... silver hollowware
17th .... furniture
18th .... porcelain
19th .... bronze
20th .... china, platinum
21st .... brass, nickel
22nd .... copper
23rd .... silver plate
24th .... musical instruments
25th .... silver
26th .... original pictures
27th .... sculpture
28th .... orchids
29th .... new furniture
30th .... pearl, diamond
31st .... time pieces
32nd .... conveyances (including automobiles)
33rd .... amethyst
34th .... opal
35th .... coral, jade
36th .... bone china
37th .... alabaster
38th .... beryl, tourmaline
39th .... lace
40th .... ruby
41st .... land
42nd .... improved real estate
43rd .... trips
44th .... groceries
45th .... sapphire
46th .... original poetry tributes
47th .... books
48th .... optical (spectacles, microscopes, telescopes)
49th .... luxuries of any kind
50th .... gold
55th .... emerald
60th .... diamond
75th .... diamond

World Map of Time Zones

Reprinted courtesy of Her Majesty's Nautical Almanac Office and the UK Hydrographic Office.

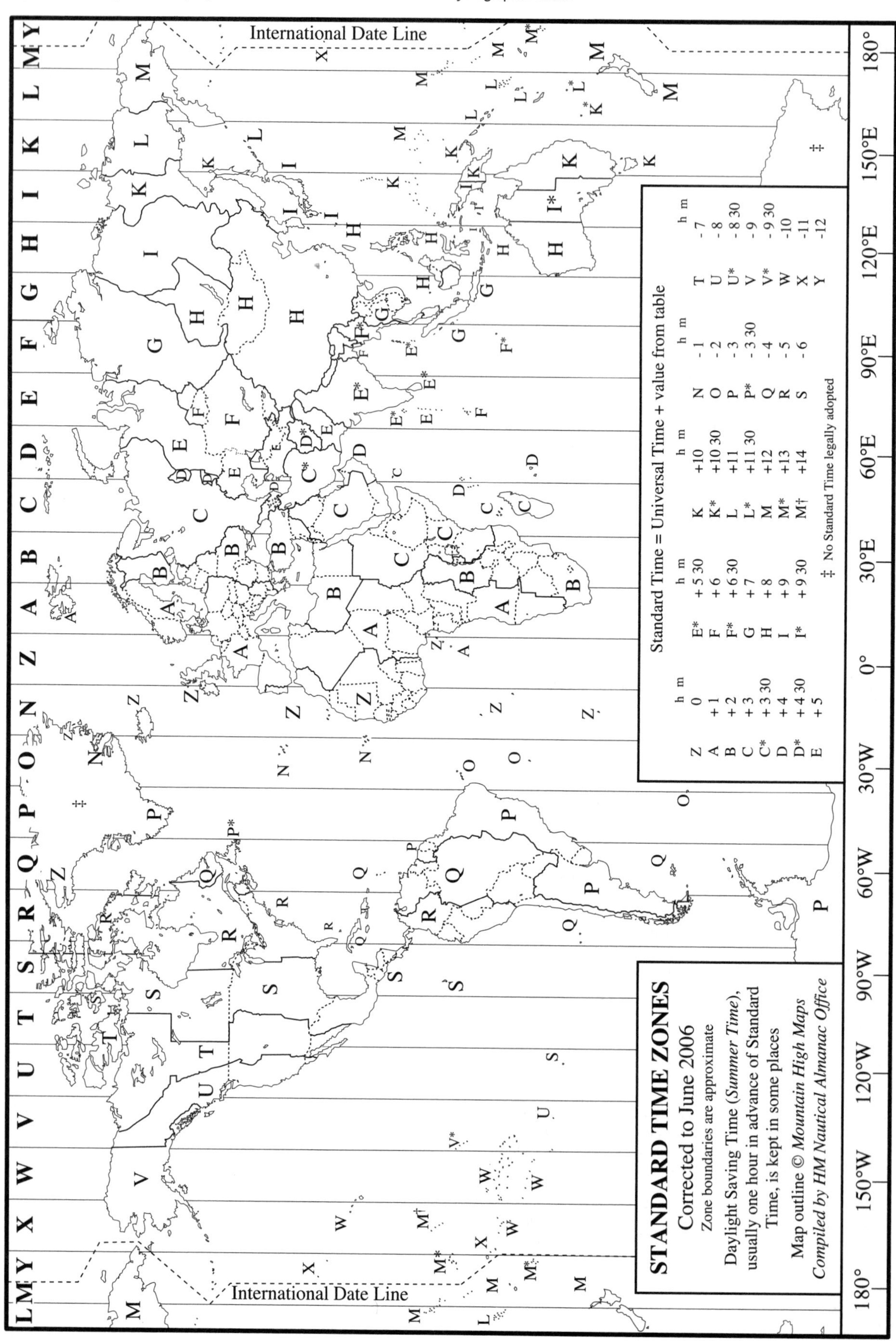

Universal, Standard and Daylight Times

Universal Time (UT) is also known as Greenwich Mean Time (GMT) and is the standard time of the Greenwich meridian (0° of longitude). A time given in UT may be converted to local mean time by the addition of east longitude (or the subtraction of west longitude), where the longitude of the place is expressed in time-measure at the rate of one hour for every 15°. Local clock times may differ from standard times, especially in summer when clocks are often advanced by one hour ("daylight saving" or "summer" time).

The time used in this book is Eastern Standard Time. The following table provides conversion between Universal Time and all Time Zones in the United States. An asterisk denotes that the time is on the preceding day.

UNIVERSAL TIME	EASTERN DAYLIGHT TIME	EASTERN STANDARD TIME AND CENTRAL DAYLIGHT TIME	CENTRAL STANDARD TIME MOUNTAIN DAYLIGHT TIME	MOUNTAIN STANDARD TIME PACIFIC DAYLIGHT TIME	PACIFIC STANDARD TIME
0^h	*8 P.M.	*7 P.M.	*6 P.M.	*5 P.M.	*4 P.M.
1	*9	*8	*7	*6	*5
2	*10	*9	*8	*7	*6
3	*11 P.M.	*10	*9	*8	*7
4	0 MIDNIGHT	*11 P.M.	*10	*9	*8
5	1 A.M.	0 MIDNIGHT	*11 P.M.	*10	*9
6	2	1 A.M.	0 MIDNIGHT	*11 P.M.	*10
7	3	2	1 A.M.	0 MIDNIGHT	*11 P.M.
8	4	3	2	1 A.M.	0 MIDNIGHT
9	5	4	3	2	1 A.M.
10	6	5	4	3	2
11	7	6	5	4	3
12	8	7	6	5	4
13	9	8	7	6	5
14	10	9	8	7	6
15	11 A.M.	10	9	8	7
16	12 NOON	11 A.M.	10	9	8
17	1 P.M.	12 NOON	11 A.M.	10	9
18	2	1.P.M.	12 NOON	11 A.M.	10
19	3	2	1 P.M.	12 NOON	11 A.M.
20	4	3	2	1 P.M.	12 NOON
21	5	4	3	2	1 P.M.
22	6	5	4	3	2
23	7 P.M.	6 P.M.	5 P.M.	4 P.M.	3 P.M.

The longitudes of the standard meridians for the standard time zones are:
Eastern . . . . . 75° West   Central . . . . . 90° West   Mountain . . . . . 105° West   Pacific . . . . . 120° West

Leap Seconds

The information below is developed by the editors from data supplied by the US Naval Observatory.

Because of Earth's slightly erratic rotation and the need for greater precision in time measurement it has become necessary to add a "leap second" from time to time to man's clocks to coordinate them with astronomical time. Rotation of the Earth has been slowing since 1900, making an astronomical second longer than an atomic second. Since 1972, by international agreement, adjustments have been made to keep astronomical and atomic clocks within 0.9 second of each other. The determination to add (or subtract) seconds is made by the Central Bureau of the International Earth Rotation Service, in Paris. Preferred times for adjustment have been June 30 and December 31, but any time may be designated by the International Earth Rotation Service. The first such adjustment was made in 1972, and as of July 2007, a total of 23 leap seconds had been added. The additions have been made at 23:59:60 UTC (Coordinated Universal Time) = 6:59:60 EST (Eastern Standard Time). Leap seconds have been inserted into the UTC time scale on the following dates:

June 30, 1972
Dec 31, 1972
Dec 31, 1973
Dec 31, 1974
Dec 31, 1975
Dec 31, 1976
Dec 31, 1977
Dec 31, 1978
Dec 31, 1979
June 30, 1981
June 30, 1982
June 30, 1983
June 30, 1985
Dec 31, 1987
Dec 31, 1989
Dec 31, 1990
June 30, 1992
June 30, 1993
June 30, 1994
Dec 31, 1995
June 30, 1997
Dec 31, 1998
Dec 31, 2005
Dec 31, 2008

Astronomical Phenomena for the Years 2009–2011

All dates are given in terms of Eastern Standard or Daylight Time and the Gregorian calendar.

(Based in part on information prepared by the Nautical Almanac Office, US Naval Observatory.)

2009

PRINCIPAL PHENOMENA, EARTH

Perihelion	Jan 4
Aphelion	July 3
Equinoxes	Mar 20, Sept 22
Solstices	June 21, Dec 21

PHASES OF THE MOON

● New Moon	☽ First Quarter	○ Full Moon	☾ Last Quarter
	Jan 4	Jan 10	Jan 17
Jan 26	Feb 2	Feb 9	Feb 16
Feb 24	Mar 4	Mar 10	Mar 18
Mar 26	Apr 2	Apr 9	Apr 17
Apr 24	May 1	May 9	May 17
May 24	May 30	June 7	June 15
June 22	June 29	July 7	July 15
July 21	July 28	Aug 5	Aug 13
Aug 20	Aug 27	Sept 4	Sept 11
Sept 18	Sept 26	Oct 4	Oct 11
Oct 18	Oct 25	Nov 2	Nov 9
Nov 16	Nov 24	Dec 2	Dec 8
Dec 16	Dec 24	Dec 31	

ECLIPSES

Annular eclipse of the Sun	Jan 26
Penumbral eclipse of the Moon	Feb 9
Penumbral eclipse of the Moon	July 7
Total eclipse of the Sun	July 22
Penumbral eclipse of the Moon	Aug 6
Partial eclipse of the Moon	Dec 31

VISIBILITY OF PLANETS IN MORNING AND EVENING TWILIGHT

	Morning	Evening
Venus	Apr–Oct	Jan–Mar
Mars	Mar–Dec	———
Jupiter	Feb–Aug	Aug–Dec
Saturn	Jan–Mar, Oct–Dec	Mar–Aug

2010

PRINCIPAL PHENOMENA, EARTH

Perihelion	Jan 2
Aphelion	July 6
Equinoxes	Mar 20, Sept 22
Solstices	June 21, Dec 21

PHASES OF THE MOON

● New Moon	☽ First Quarter	○ Full Moon	☾ Last Quarter
			Jan 7
Jan 15	Jan 23	Jan 30	Feb 5
Feb 13	Feb 21	Feb 28	Mar 7
Mar 15	Mar 23	Mar 29	Apr 6
Apr 14	Apr 21	Apr 28	May 6
May 13	May 20	May 27	June 4
June 12	June 19	June 26	July 4
July 11	July 18	July 25	Aug 3
Aug 9	Aug 16	Aug 24	Sept 1
Sept 8	Sept 15	Sept 23	Sept 30
Oct 7	Oct 14	Oct 22	Oct 30
Nov 6	Nov 13	Nov 21	Nov 28
Dec 5	Dec 13	Dec 21	Dec 27

ECLIPSES

Annular eclipse of the Sun	Jan 15
Partial eclipse of the Moon	June 26
Total eclipse of the Sun	July 11
Total eclipse of the Moon	Dec 21

2011

PRINCIPAL PHENOMENA, EARTH

Perihelion	Jan 3
Aphelion	July 4
Equinoxes	Mar 20, Sept 23
Solstices	June 21, Dec 22

PHASES OF THE MOON

● New Moon	☽ First Quarter	○ Full Moon	☾ Last Quarter
Jan 4	Jan 12	Jan 19	Jan 26
Feb 2	Feb 11	Feb 18	Feb 24
Mar 4	Mar 12	Mar 19	Mar 26
Apr 3	Apr 11	Apr 17	Apr 24
May 3	May 10	May 17	May 24
June 1	June 8	June 15	June 23
July 1	July 8	July 15	July 23
July 30	Aug 6	Aug 13	Aug 21
Aug 28	Sept 4	Sept 12	Sept 20
Sept 27	Oct 3	Oct 11	Oct 19
Oct 26	Nov 2	Nov 10	Nov 18
Nov 25	Dec 2	Dec 10	Dec 17
Dec 24			

ECLIPSES

Partial eclipse of the Sun	Jan 4
Partial eclipse of the Sun	June 1
Total eclipse of the Moon	June 15
Total eclipse of the Sun	July 1
Partial eclipse of the Sun	Nov 25
Total eclipse of the Moon	Dec 10

The Naming of Hurricanes

(Compiled from information issued by the US Department of Commerce, National Oceanic and Atmospheric Administration.)

Why are hurricanes named? Experience shows that the use of short, distinctive names greatly reduces confusion when two or more tropical storms occur at the same time. The use of easily remembered names in written and spoken communication is quicker and less subject to error than the older, more cumbersome latitude-longitude identification methods, advantages which are especially important in exchanging detailed storm information between hundreds of widely scattered stations, airports, coastal bases and ships at sea.

The practice of naming hurricanes began hundreds of years ago, but only relatively recently did they begin to be named solely for women. During World War II forecasters and meteorologists began using female names for storms in weather map discussions, and in 1953 the US weather services adopted the practice, creating a new international phonetic alphabet of women's names from A–W to name hurricanes. In 1978 men's names were also introduced into the storm lists.

Because hurricanes affect other nations and are tracked by their weather services, the lists have an international flavor. Names are agreed upon during international meetings of the World Meteorological Organization by the nations involved, and can be retired and replaced with new names in the event of particularly severe storms.

The National Hurricane Center near Miami, FL, keeps a constant watch on oceanic storm-breeding areas for tropical disturbances that may herald the formation of a hurricane. If a disturbance intensifies into a tropical storm—with rotary circulation and wind speeds above 39 miles per hour—the Center will give the storm a name from one of six lists. The Atlantic and Eastern Pacific lists are rotated year by year so that the 2009 set, for example, will be used again to name storms in 2015.

The lists of names for Central Pacific and Western Pacific hurricanes (tropical cyclones) are not rotated on a yearly basis. Meteorologists follow each list until all those names have been used, then go on to the next list. The name of a particularly severe storm is retired and replaced. For example, Iniki—the name of the hurricane that devastated Hawaii—has been replaced with Iolana on List 2.

ATLANTIC HURRICANE NAMES

2009	2010	2011
Ana	Alex	Arlene
Bill	Bonnie	Bret
Claudette	Colin	Cindy
Danny	Danielle	Don
Erika	Earl	Emily
Fred	Fiona	Franklin
Grace	Gaston	Gert
Henri	Hermine	Harvey
Ida	Igor	Irene
Joaquin	Julia	Jose
Kate	Karl	Katia
Larry	Lisa	Lee
Mindy	Matthew	Maria
Nicholas	Nicole	Nate
Odette	Otto	Ophelia
Peter	Paula	Philippe
Rose	Richard	Rina
Sam	Shary	Sean
Teresa	Tomas	Tammy
Victor	Virginie	Vince
Wanda	Walter	Whitney

EASTERN PACIFIC HURRICANE NAMES

2009	2010	2011
Andres	Agatha	Adrian
Blanca	Blas	Beatriz
Carlos	Celia	Calvin
Dolores	Darby	Dora
Enrique	Estelle	Eugene
Felicia	Frank	Fernanda
Guillermo	Georgette	Greg
Hilda	Howard	Hilary
Ignacio	Isis	Irwin
Jimena	Javier	Jova
Kevin	Kay	Kenneth
Linda	Lester	Lidia
Marty	Madeline	Max
Nora	Newton	Norma
Olaf	Orlene	Otis
Patricia	Paine	Pilar
Rick	Roslyn	Ramon
Sandra	Seymour	Selma
Terry	Tina	Todd
Vivian	Virgil	Veronica
Waldo	Winifred	Wiley
Xina	Xavier	Xina
York	Yolanda	York
Zelda	Zeke	Zelda

If more than 24 tropical cyclones occur in a year, then the Greek alphabet will be used following Zelda or Zeke.

CENTRAL PACIFIC TROPICAL CYCLONE NAMES

LIST 1	LIST 2	LIST 3
Akoni (ah-KOH-nee)	Aka (AH-kah)	Alika (ah-LEE-kah)
Ema (EH-ma)	Ekeka (eh-KEH-kah)	Ele (EH-leh)
Hana (HAH-nah)	Hali (HAH-lee)	Huko (HOO-koh)
Io (EE-oo)	Iolana (ee-OH-lah-nah)	Ioke (ee-OH-keh)
Keli (KEH-lee)	Keoni (keh-OH-nee)	Kika (KEE-kah)
Lala (LAH-lah)	Li (LEE)	Kika (KEE-kah)
Moke (MOH-keh)	Mele (MEH-leh)	Maka (MAH-kah)
Nele (NEH-leh)	Nona (NOH-nah)	Neki (NEH-kee)
Oka (OH-kah)	Oliwa (oh-LEE-vah)	Oleka (oh-LEH-kah)
Peke (PEH-keh)	Paka (PAH-hak)	Peni (PEH-nee)
Uleki (oo-LEH-kee)	Upana (oo-PAH-nah)	Ulia (oo-LEE-ah)
Wila (VEE-lah)	Wene (WEH-neh)	Wali (WAH-lee)

LIST 4

Ana (AH-nah)	Kimo (KEE-moh)	Oko (OH-koh)
Ela (EH-lah)	Loke (LOH-keh)	Pali (PAH-lee)
Halola (hah-LOH-lah)	Malia (mah-LEE-ah)	Ulika (oo-LEE-kah)
Iune (ee-OO-neh)	Niala (nee-AH-lah)	Walaka (wah-LAH-kah)

In Hawaiian, all letters are pronounced, including double or triple vowels.

WESTERN PACIFIC TROPICAL CYCLONE NAMES

LIST 1	LIST 2	LIST 3	LIST 4	LIST 5
Damrey	Kong-rey	Nakri	Krovanh	Sarika
Longwang	Yutu	Fengshen	Dujuan	Haima
Kirogi	Toraji	Kalmaegi	Maemi	Meari
Kai-Tak	Man-yi	Fung-wong	Choi-wan	Ma-on
Tenbin	Usagi	Kanmuri	Koppu	Tokage
Bolaven	Pabuk	Phanfone	Ketsana	Nock-ten
Chanchu	Wutip	Vongfong	Parma	Muifa
Jelawat	Sepat	Rusa	Melor	Merbok
Ewinlar	Fitow	Sinlaku	Nepartak	Nanmadol
Bilis	Danas	Hagupit	Lupit	Talas
Gaemi	Nari	Changmi	Sudal	Noru
Prapiroon	Vipa	Megkhla	Nida	Kularb
Maria	Francisco	Higos	Omais	Roke
Saomai	Lekima	Bavi	Conson	Sonca
Bopha	Krosa	Maysak	Chanthu	Nesat
Wukong	Haiyan	Haishen	Dianmu	Haitang
Sonamu	Podul	Pongsona	Mindule	Nalgae
Shanshan	Lingling	Yanyan	Tingting	Banyan
Yagi	Kaziki	Kuzira	Kompasu	Washi
Xangsane	Faxai	Chan-hom	Namtheun	Matsa
Bebinca	Vamei	Linfa	Malou	Sanvu
Rumbia	Tapah	Nangka	Meranti	Mawar
Soulik	Mitag	Soudelor	Rananin	Guchol
Cimaron	Hagibis	Imbudo	Malakas	Talim
Chebi	Noguri	Koni	Megi	Nabi
Durian	Ramasoon	Hanuman	Chaba	Khanun
Utor	Chataan	Etau	Kodo	Vicete
Trami	Halong	Vamco	Songda	Saola

Some Facts About the US Presidents

	NAME	BIRTHDATE, PLACE	PARTY	TENURE	DIED	FIRST LADY	VICE PRESIDENT
1.	George Washington	2/22/1732, Westmoreland Cnty, VA	Federalist	1789–1797	12/14/1799	Martha Dandridge Custis	John Adams
2.	John Adams	10/30/1735, Braintree (Quincy), MA	Federalist	1797–1801	7/4/1826	Abigail Smith	Thomas Jefferson
3.	Thomas Jefferson	4/13/1743, Shadwell, VA	Democratic-Republican	1801–1809	7/4/1826	Martha Wayles Skelton	Aaron Burr, 1801–05 George Clinton, 1805–09
4.	James Madison	3/16/1751, Port Conway, VA	Democratic-Republican	1809–1817	6/28/1836	Dolley Payne Todd	George Clinton, 1809–12 Elbridge Gerry, 1813–14
5.	James Monroe	4/28/1758, Westmoreland Cnty, VA	Democratic-Republican	1817–1825	7/4/1831	Elizabeth Kortright	Daniel D. Tompkins
6.	John Q. Adams	7/11/1767, Braintree (Quincy), MA	Democratic-Republican	1825–1829	2/23/1848	Louisa Catherine Johnson	John C. Calhoun
7.	Andrew Jackson	3/15/1767, Waxhaw Settlement, SC	Democrat	1829–1837	6/8/1845	Mrs. Rachel Donelson Robards	John C. Calhoun, 1829–32 Martin Van Buren, 1833–37
8.	Martin Van Buren	12/5/1782, Kinderhook, NY	Democrat	1837–1841	7/24/1862	Hannah Hoes	Richard M. Johnson
9.	William H. Harrison	2/9/1773, Charles City Cnty, VA	Whig	1841	4/4/1841†	Anna Symmes	John Tyler
10.	John Tyler	3/29/1790, Charles City Cnty, VA	Whig	1841–1845	1/18/1862	Letitia Christian Julia Gardiner	
11.	James K. Polk	11/2/1795, near Pineville, NC	Democrat	1845–1849	6/15/1849	Sarah Childress	George M. Dallas
12.	Zachary Taylor	11/24/1784, Barboursville, VA	Whig	1849–1850	7/9/1850†	Margaret Mackall Smith	Millard Fillmore
13.	Millard Fillmore	1/7/1800, Locke, NY	Whig	1850–1853	3/8/1874	Abigail Powers Mrs. Caroline Carmichael McIntosh	
14.	Franklin Pierce	11/23/1804, Hillsboro, NH	Democrat	1853–1857	10/8/1869	Jane Means Appleton	William R. D. King
15.	James Buchanan	4/23/1791, near Mercersburg, PA	Democrat	1857–1861	6/1/1868		John C. Breckinridge
16.	Abraham Lincoln	2/12/1809, near Hodgenville, KY	Republican	1861–1865	4/15/1865*	Mary Todd	Hannibal Hamlin, 1861–65 Andrew Johnson, 1865
17.	Andrew Johnson	12/29/1808, Raleigh, NC	Democrat	1865–1869	7/31/1875	Eliza McCardle	
18.	Ulysses S. Grant	4/27/1822, Point Pleasant, OH	Republican	1869–1877	7/23/1885	Julia Boggs Dent	Schuyler Colfax, 1869–73 Henry Wilson, 1873–75
19.	Rutherford B. Hayes	10/4/1822, Delaware, OH	Republican	1877–1881	1/17/1893	Lucy Ware Webb	William A. Wheeler
20.	James A. Garfield	11/19/1831, Orange, OH	Republican	1881	9/19/1881*	Lucretia Rudolph	Chester A. Arthur
21.	Chester A. Arthur	10/5/1829, Fairfield, VT	Republican	1881–1885	11/18/1886	Ellen Lewis Herndon	
22.	Grover Cleveland	3/18/1837, Caldwell, NJ	Democrat	1885–1889	6/24/1908	Frances Folsom	Thomas A. Hendricks, 1885
23.	Benjamin Harrison	8/20/1833, North Bend, OH	Republican	1889–1893	3/13/1901	Caroline Lavinia Scott Mrs. Mary Dimmick	Levi P. Morton
24.	Grover Cleveland	3/18/1837, Caldwell, NJ	Democrat	1893–1897	6/24/1908	Frances Folsom	Adlai Stevenson, 1893–97
25.	William McKinley	1/29/1843, Niles, OH	Republican	1897–1901	9/14/1901*	Ida Saxton	Garret A. Hobart, 1897–99 Theodore Roosevelt, 1901
26.	Theodore Roosevelt	10/27/1858, New York, NY	Republican	1901–1909	1/6/1919	Alice Hathaway Lee Edith Kermit Carow	Charles W. Fairbanks
27.	William H. Taft	9/15/1857, Cincinnati, OH	Republican	1909–1913	3/8/1930	Helen Herron	James S. Sherman

	NAME	BIRTHDATE, PLACE	PARTY	TENURE	DIED	FIRST LADY	VICE PRESIDENT
28.	**Woodrow Wilson**	12/28/1856, Staunton, VA	Democrat	1913–1921	2/3/1924	Ellen Louise Axson Edith Bolling Galt	Thomas R. Marshall
29.	**Warren G. Harding**	11/2/1865, near Corsica, OH	Republican	1921–1923	8/2/1923†	Florence Kling DeWolfe	Calvin Coolidge
30.	**Calvin Coolidge**	7/4/1872, Plymouth Notch, VT	Republican	1923–1929	1/5/1933	Grace Anna Goodhue	Charles G. Dawes
31.	**Herbert C. Hoover**	8/10/1874, West Branch, IA	Republican	1929–1933	10/20/1964	Lou Henry	Charles Curtis
32.	**Franklin D. Roosevelt**	1/30/1882, Hyde Park, NY	Democrat	1933–1945	4/12/1945†	Eleanor Roosevelt	John N. Garner, 1933–41 Henry A. Wallace, 1941–45 Harry S. Truman, 1945
33.	**Harry S. Truman**	5/8/1884, Lamar, MO	Democrat	1945–1953	12/26/1972	Elizabeth Virginia (Bess) Wallace	Alben W. Barkley
34.	**Dwight D. Eisenhower**	10/14/1890, Denison, TX	Republican	1953–1961	3/28/1969	Mamie Geneva Doud	Richard M. Nixon
35.	**John F. Kennedy**	5/29/1917, Brookline, MA	Democrat	1961–1963	11/22/1963*	Jacqueline Lee Bouvier	Lyndon B. Johnson
36.	**Lyndon B. Johnson**	8/27/1908, near Stonewall, TX	Democrat	1963–1969	1/22/1973	Claudia Alta (Lady Bird) Taylor	Hubert H. Humphrey
37.	**Richard M. Nixon**	1/9/1913, Yorba Linda, CA	Republican	1969–1974**	4/22/1994	Thelma Catherine (Pat) Ryan	Spiro T. Agnew, 1969–73 Gerald R. Ford, 1973–74
38.	**Gerald R. Ford**	7/14/1913, Omaha, NE	Republican	1974–1977	12/26/2006	Elizabeth (Betty) Bloomer	Nelson A. Rockefeller
39.	**James E. Carter, Jr**	10/1/1924, Plains, GA	Democrat	1977–1981		Rosalynn Smith	Walter F. Mondale
40.	**Ronald W. Reagan**	2/6/1911, Tampico, IL	Republican	1981–1989	6/5/2004	Nancy Davis	George H. W. Bush
41.	**George H. W. Bush**	6/12/1924, Milton, MA	Republican	1989–1993		Barbara Pierce	J. Danforth Quayle
42.	**William J. Clinton**	8/19/1946, Hope, AR	Democrat	1993–2001		Hillary Rodham	Albert Gore Jr.
43.	**George W. Bush**	7/6/1946, New Haven, CT	Republican	2001–2009		Laura Welch	Richard Cheney

** assassinated while in office*
*** resigned Aug 9, 1974*
† died while in office—nonviolently

Presidental Proclamations Issued, January 1, 2007–June 15, 2008

NO.	TITLE, OBSERVANCE DATES (DATE OF SIGNING)
2007	
8099	Martin Luther King, Jr, Federal Holiday, 2007: Jan 15, 2007 (Jan 11, 2007)
8100	Religious Freedom Day, 2007: Jan 16, 2007 (Jan 11, 2007)
8101	National Sanctity of Human Life Day, 2007: Jan 21, 2007 (Jan 18, 2007)
8102	Fifth Anniversary of USA Freedom Corps, 2007: Jan 29, 2007 (Jan 25, 2007)
8103	National African American History Month, 2007: February (Jan 26, 2007)
8104	American Heart Month, 2007: February (Feb 1, 2007)
8105	National Consumer Protection Week, 2007: Feb 4–10, 2007 (Feb 2, 2007)
810	275th Anniversary of the Birth of George Washington: Feb 22, 2007 (Feb 16, 2007)
8107	Irish American Heritage Month, 2007: March (Feb 26, 2007)
8108	American Red Cross Month, 2007: March (Feb 27, 2007)
8109	Women's History Month, 2007: March (Feb 27, 2007)
8110	Save Your Vision Week, 2007: Mar 4–10, 2007 (Feb 28, 2007)
8111	Implementation of the Dominican Republic-Central America-United States Free Trade Agreement with Respect to the Dominican Republic and for Other Purposes (Feb 28, 2007)
8112	Amending Proclamation 8031 of June 15, 2006, to read, "Establishment of the Papahanaumokuakea Marine National Monument" (Feb 28, 2007)
8113	National Poison Prevention Week, 2007: Mar 18–28, 2007 (Mar 16, 2007)
8114	To Implement Modifications to the Caribbean Basin Economic Recovery Act and the African Growth and Opportunity Act and for Other Purposes (Mar 19, 2007)
8115	Greek Independence Day: A National Day of Celebration of Greek and American Democracy, 2007: Mar 25, 2007 (Mar 21, 2007)
8116	Education and Sharing Day, U.S.A., 2007: Mar 30, 2007 (Mar 26, 2007)
8117	National Child Abuse Prevention Month, 2007: April (Mar 27, 2007)
8118	National Donate Life Month, 2007: April (Mar 28, 2007)
8119	Cancer Control Month, 2007: April (Mar 29, 2007)
8120	Pan American Day and Pan American Week, 2007: Apr 14, 2007 and Apr 8–14, 2007 (Apr 5, 2007)
8121	National Former Prisoner of War Recognition Day, 2007: Apr 9, 2007 (Apr 5, 2007)
8122	400th Anniversary of Jamestown (Apr 6, 2007)
8123	National D.A.R.E. (Drug Abuse Resistance Education) Day, 2007: Apr 12, 2007 (Apr 11, 2007)
8124	Thomas Jefferson Day, 2007: Apr 13, 2007 (Apr 11, 2007)
8125	National Volunteer Week, 2007: Apr 15–21, 2007 (Apr 11, 2007)
8126	Honoring the Victims of the Tragedy at Virginia Tech (Apr 17, 2007)
8127	Small Business Week, 2007: Apr 22–28, 2007 (Apr 19, 2007)
8128	Dutch-American Friendship Day, 2007: Apr 19, 2007 (Apr 19, 2007)
8129	National Day of Prayer, 2007: May 3, 2007 (Apr 20, 2007)
8130	National Crime Victim's Rights Week, 2007: Apr 22–28, 2007 (Apr 20, 2007)
8131	National Park Week, 2007: Apr 22–29, 2007 (Apr 20, 2007)
8132	Malaria Awareness Day, 2007: Apr 25, 2007 (Apr 24, 2007)
8133	Asian/Pacific American Heritage Month, 2007: May (Apr 26, 2007)
8134	National Charter Schools Week, 2007: Apr 29–May 5, 2007 (Apr 27, 2007)
8135	Law Day, U.S.A., 2007: May 1, 2007 (Apr 27, 2007)
8136	Jewish-American Heritage Month, 2007: May (Apr 30, 2007)
8137	Loyalty Day, 2007: May 1, 2007 (Apr 30, 2007)
8138	National Physical Fitness and Sports Month, 2007: May (May 1, 2007)
8139	Older Americans Month, 2007: May (May 1, 2007)
8140	Mother's Day, 2007: May 13, 2007 (May 7, 2007)
8141	Military Spouse Day, 2007: May 11, 2007 (May 9, 2007)
8142	National Defense Transportation Day and National Transportation Week, 2007: May 18, 2007 and May 13–19, 2007 (May 10, 2007)
8143	National Safe Boating Week, 2007: May 19–25, 2007 (May 10, 2007)
8144	Peace Officers Memorial Day and Police Week, 2007: May 15, 2007 and May 13–19, 2007 (May 11, 2007)
8145	Prayer for Peace, Memorial Day, 2007: May 28, 2007 (May 15, 2007)
8146	National Hurricane Preparedness Week, 2007: May 20–26, 2007 (May 18, 2007)
8147	World Trade Week, 2007: May 20–26, 2007 (May 18, 2007)
8148	National Maritime Day, 2007: May 22, 2007 (May 18, 2007)
8149	Great Outdoors Month, 2007: June (May 25, 2007)
8150	National Oceans Month, 2007: June (May 30, 2007)
8151	Black Music Month, 2007: June (May 31, 2007)
8152	National Child's Day, 2007: June 3, 2007 (May 31, 2007)
8153	Caribbean-American Heritage Month, 2007: June (June 1, 2007)
8154	National Homeownership Month, 2007: June (June 1, 2007)
8155	Flag Day and National Flag Week, 2007: June 14, 2007 and June 10–16, 2007 (June 5, 2007)
8156	Father's Day, 2007: June 17, 2007 (June 11, 2007)
8157	To Modify Duty-Free Treatment Under the Generalized System of Preferences, Take Certain Actions Under the African Growth and Opportunity Act and for Other Purposes (June 28, 2007)
8158	Suspension of Entry as Immigrants and Nonimmigrants of Persons Responsible for Policies and Actions That Threaten Lebanon's Sovereignty and Democracy (June 28, 2007)
8159	Grant of Executive Clemency for Lewis "Scooter" Libby (July 2, 2007)
8160	Captive Nations Week, 2007: July 15–21, 2007 (July 10, 2007)
8161	Parent's Day, 2007: July 22, 2007 (July 12, 2007)
8162	Death of Lady Bird Johnson (July 12, 2007)
8163	Anniversary of the Americans with Disabilities Act: July 26, 2007 (July 24, 2007)
8164	Women's Equality Day, 2007: Aug 26, 2007 (Aug 6, 2007)
8165	National Ovarian Cancer Awareness Month, 2007: September (Aug 20, 2007)
8166	National Prostate Cancer Awareness Month, 2007: September (Aug 20, 2007)
8167	National Alcohol and Drug Addiction Recovery Month, 2007: September (Aug 20, 2007)
8168	Citizenship Day and Constitution Week, 2007: Sept 17, 2007 and Sept 17–23, 2007 (Aug 21, 2007)
8169	Minority Enterprise Development Week, 2007: Sept 9–15, 2007 (Aug 28, 2007)
8170	National Preparedness Month, 2007: September (Aug 30, 2007)
8171	National Employer Support of the Guard and Reserve Week, 2007: Sept 9–15, 2007 (Aug 30, 2007)
8172	National Historically Black Colleges and Universities Week, 2007: Sept 9–15, 2007 (Sept 4, 2007)
8173	National Days of Prayer and Remembrance, 2007: Sept 7–9, 2007 (Sept 4, 2007)
8174	Patriot Day, 2007: Sept 11, 2007 (Sept 4, 2007)
8175	National Hispanic Heritage Month, 2007: Sept 15–Oct 15, 2007 (Sept 12, 2007)
8176	National Farm Safety and Health Week, 2007: Sept 16–22, 2007 (Sept 12, 2007)
8177	National POW/MIA Recognition Day, 2007: Sept 21, 2007 (Sept 20, 2007)
8178	Family Day, 2007: Sept 24, 2007 (Sept 20, 2007)
8179	Gold Star Mother's Day, 2007: Sept 30, 2007 (Sept 21, 2007)
8180	Duty Elimination for Certain Goods of Mexico Under the North American Free Trade Agreement (Sept 28, 2007)
8181	National Breast Cancer Awareness Month, 2007: October (Sept 28, 2007)
8182	National Disability Employment Awareness Month, 2007: October (Sept 28, 2007)

NO.	TITLE, OBSERVANCE DATES (DATE OF SIGNING)
8183	National Domestic Violence Awareness Month, 2007: October (Oct 1, 2007)
8184	Child Health Day, 2007: Oct 1, 2007 (Oct 1, 2007)
8185	German-American Day, 2007: Oct 6, 2007 (Oct 3, 2007)
8186	Columbus Day, 2007: Oct 8, 2007 (Oct 4, 2007)
8187	Leif Erikson Day, 2007: Oct 9, 2007 (Oct 4, 2007)
8188	Fire Prevention Week, 2007: Oct 7–13, 2007 (Oct 4, 2007)
8189	General Pulaski Memorial Day, 2007: Oct 11, 2007 (Oct 10, 2007)
8190	National School Lunch Week, 2007: Oct 14–20, 2007 (Oct 12, 2007)
8191	White Cane Safety Day, 2007: Oct 15, 2007 (Oct 12, 2007)
8192	National Character Counts Week, 2007: Oct 21–27, 2007 (Oct 19, 2007)
8193	National Forest Products Week, 2007: Oct 21–27, 2007 (Oct 19, 2007)
8194	United Nations Day, 2007: Oct 24, 2007 (Oct 23, 2007)
8195	National Adoption Month, 2007: November (Oct 31, 2007)
8196	National American Indian Heritage Month, 2007: November (Oct 31, 2007)
8197	National Family Caregivers Month, 2007: November (Oct 31, 2007)
8198	National Hospice Month, 2007: November (Oct 31, 2007)
8199	Veteran's Day and National Veteran's Awareness Week, 2007: Nov 11, 2007 and Nov 11–17, 2007 (Oct 31, 2007)
8200	National Alzheimer's Disease Awareness Month, 2007: November (Oct 31, 2007)
8201	National Diabetes Month, 2007: November (Oct 31, 2007)
8202	World Freedom Day, 2007: Nov 9, 2007 (Nov 8, 2007)
8203	America Recycles Day, 2007: Nov 15, 2007 (Nov 15, 2007)
8204	Thanksgiving Day, 2007: Nov 15, 2007 (Nov 15, 2007)
8205	National Farm-City Week, 2007: Nov 16–22, 2007 (Nov 16, 2007)
8206	National Family Week, 2007: Nov 18–24, 2007 (Nov 16, 2007)
8207	World AIDS Day, 2007: Dec 1, 2007 (Nov 29, 2007)
8208	National Drunk and Drugged Driving Prevention Month, 2007: December (Nov 30, 2007)
8209	National Pearl Harbor Remembrance Day, 2007: Dec 7, 2007 (Dec 4, 2007)
8210	Human Rights Day, Bill of Rights Day and Human Rights Week, 2007: Dec 10, Dec 15 and Dec 10–17, 2007 (Dec 6, 2007)
8211	Wright Brothers Day, 2007: Dec 17, 2007 (Dec 11, 2007)
8212	National Mentoring Month, 2008: January (Dec 19, 2007)
8213	To Implement an Amendment to the Dominican Republic-Central America-United States Free Trade Agreement (Dec 20, 2007)
8214	Proclamation to Adjust the Rules of Origin Under the United States–Chile Free Trade Agreement and the United States–Singapore Free Trade Agreement (Dec 27, 2007)

2008

NO.	TITLE, OBSERVANCE DATES (DATE OF SIGNING)
8215	Religious Freedom Day, 2008: Jan 16, 2008 (Jan 14, 2008)
8216	Martin Luther King, Jr, Federal Holiday, 2008: Jan 21, 2008 (Jan 14, 2008)
8217	National Sanctity of Human Life Day, 2008: Jan 20, 2008 (Jan 18, 2008)
8218	National African American History Month, 2008: February (Jan 28, 2008)
8219	Sixth Anniversary of USA Freedom Corps, 2008: Jan 29, 2008 (Jan 28, 2008)
8220	American Heart Month, 2008, and National Go Red Day, 2008: February and Feb 1, 2008 (Feb 1, 2008)
8221	American Red Cross Month, 2008: March (Feb 28, 2008)
8222	Save Your Vision Week, 2008: Mar 2–8, 2008 (Feb 28, 2008)
8223	Irish American Heritage Month, 2008: March (Feb 29, 2008)
8224	National Consumer Protection Week, 2008: Mar 2–8, 2008 (Feb 29, 2008)
8225	Women's History Month, 2008: March (Mar 10, 2008)
8226	National Poison Prevention Week, 2008: Mar 16–22, 2008 (Mar 14, 2008)
8227	Greek Independence Day: A National Day of Celebration of Greek and American Democracy, 2008: Mar 25, 2008 (Mar 20, 2008)
8228	To Modify the Harmonized Tariff Schedule of the United States and for Other Purposes (Mar 28, 2008)
8229	Cancer Control Month, 2008: April (Apr 1, 2008)
8230	National Child Abuse Prevention Month, 2008: April (Apr 1, 2008)
8231	National Donate Life Month, 2008: April (Apr 1, 2008)
8232	National Fair Housing Month, 2008: April (Apr 1, 2008)
8233	National Tartan Day, 2008: Apr 6, 2008 (Apr 4, 2008)
8234	National Former Prisoner of War Recognition Day, 2008: Apr 9, 2008 (Apr 8, 2008)
8235	National D.A.R.E. (Drug Abuse Resistance Education) Day, 2008: Apr 10, 2008 (Apr 9, 2008)
8236	Pan American Day and Pan American Week, 2008: Apr 14, 2008 and Apr 13–19, 2008 (Apr 10, 2008)
8237	National Crime Victim's Rights Week, 2008: Apr 13–19, 2008 (Apr 11, 2008)
8238	Education and Sharing Day, U.S.A., 2008: Apr 16, 2008 (Apr 15, 2008)
8239	National Park Week, 2008: Apr 19–27, 2008 (Apr 15, 2008)
8240	To Take Certain Actions Under the African Growth and Opportunity Act and the Generalized System of Preferences (Apr 17)
8241	Small Business Week, 2008: Apr 20–26, 2008 (Apr 17, 2008)
8242	National Day of Prayer, 2008: May 1, 2008 (Apr 21, 2008)
8243	Older Americans Month, 2008: May (Apr 22, 2008)
8244	National Volunteer Week, 2008: Apr 27–May 3, 2008 (Apr 22, 2008)
8245	Loyalty Day, 2008: May 1, 2008 (Apr 22, 2008)
8246	Malaria Awareness Day, 2008: Apr 25, 2008 (Apr 25, 2008)
8247	Asian/Pacific American Heritage Month, 2008: May (Apr 29, 2008)
8248	Jewish-American Heritage Month, 2008: May (Apr 29, 2008)
8249	National Physical Fitness and Sports Month, 2008: May (Apr 29, 2008)
8250	Law Day, U.S.A., 2008: May 1, 2008 (Apr 30, 2008)
8251	National Charter Schools Week, 2008: May 4–10, 2008 (May 2, 2008)
8252	Military Spouse Day, 2008: May 9, 2008 (May 5, 2008)
8253	Mother's Day, 2008: May 11, 2008 (May 8, 2008)
8254	National Defense Transportation Day and National Transportation Week, 2008: May 16, 2008 and May 11–17, 2008 (May 9, 2008)
8255	Peace Officers Memorial Day and Police Week, 2008: May 15, 2008 and May 11–17, 2008 (May 9, 2008)
8256	National Safe Boating Week, 2008: May 17–23, 2008 (May 15, 2008)
8257	World Trade Week, 2008: May 18–24, 2008 (May 15, 2008)
8258	A Day of Solidarity with the Cuban People, 2008: May 21, 2008 (May 20, 2008)
8259	National Maritime Day, 2008: May 22, 2008 (May 21, 2008)
8260	Prayer for Peace, Memorial Day, 2008: May 26, 2008 (May 22, 2008)
8261	National Hurricane Preparedness Week, 2008: May 25–31, 2008 (May 23, 2008)
8262	Caribbean-American Heritage Month, 2008: June (May 29, 2008)
8263	National Homeownership Month, 2008: June (May 29, 2008)
8264	Black Music Month, 2008: June (May 30, 2008)
8265	Great Outdoors Month, 2008: June (May 30, 2008)
8266	Italian Independence Day, 2008: June 2, 2008 (May 30, 2008)
8267	National Child's Day, 2008: June 1, 2008 (May 30, 2008)
8268	National Oceans Month, 2008: June (May 30, 2008)
8269	Flag Day and National Flag Week, 2008: June 14, 2008 and June 8–14, 2008 (June 6, 2008)
8270	Father's Day, 2008: June 15, 2008 (June 12, 2008)

Some Facts About the United States

STATE	CAPITAL	POPULAR NAME	AREA (SQ. MI.)	STATE BIRD	STATE FLOWER	STATE TREE	ADMITTED TO THE UNION	ORDER OF ADMISSION
Alabama	Montgomery	Cotton or Yellowhammer State; or Heart of Dixie	51,609	Yellowhammer	Camellia	Southern pine (Longleaf pine)	1819	22
Alaska	Juneau	Last Frontier	591,004	Willow ptarmigan	Forget-me-not	Sitka spruce	1959	49
Arizona	Phoenix	Grand Canyon State	114,000	Cactus wren	Saguaro (giant cactus)	Palo Verde	1912	48
Arkansas	Little Rock	The Natural State	53,187	Mockingbird	Apple blossom	Pine	1836	25
California	Sacramento	Golden State	158,706	California valley quail	Golden poppy	California redwood	1850	31
Colorado	Denver	Centennial State	104,091	Lark bunting	Rocky Mountain columbine	Blue spruce	1876	38
Connecticut	Hartford	Constitution State	5,018	Robin	Mountain laurel	White oak	1788	5
Delaware	Dover	First State	2,044	Blue hen chicken	Peach blossom	American holly	1787	1
Florida	Tallahassee	Sunshine State	58,664	Mockingbird	Orange blossom	Cabbage (sabal) palm	1845	27
Georgia	Atlanta	Empire State of the South	58,910	Brown thrasher	Cherokee rose	Live oak	1788	4
Hawaii	Honolulu	Aloha State	6,471	Nene (Hawaiian goose)	Hibiscus	Kukui	1959	50
Idaho	Boise	Gem State	83,564	Mountain bluebird	Syringa (mock orange)	Western white pine	1890	43
Illinois	Springfield	Prairie State	56,345	Cardinal	Native violet	White oak	1818	21
Indiana	Indianapolis	Hoosier State	36,185	Cardinal	Peony	Tulip tree or yellow poplar	1816	19
Iowa	Des Moines	Hawkeye State	56,275	Eastern goldfinch	Wild rose	Oak	1846	29
Kansas	Topeka	Sunflower State	82,277	Western meadowlark	Sunflower	Cottonwood	1861	34
Kentucky	Frankfort	Bluegrass State	40,409	Kentucky cardinal	Goldenrod	Kentucky coffeetree	1792	15
Louisiana	Baton Rouge	Pelican State	47,752	Pelican	Magnolia	Bald cypress	1812	18
Maine	Augusta	Pine Tree State	33,265	Chickadee	White pine cone and tassel	White pine	1820	23
Maryland	Annapolis	Old Line State	10,577	Baltimore oriole	Black-eyed Susan	White oak	1788	7
Massachusetts	Boston	Bay State	8,284	Chickadee	Mayflower	American elm	1788	6
Michigan	Lansing	Wolverine State	58,527	Robin	Apple blossom	White pine	1837	26
Minnesota	St. Paul	North Star State	84,402	Common loon	Pink and white lady's-slipper	Norway, or red, pine	1858	32
Mississippi	Jackson	Magnolia State	47,689	Mockingbird	Magnolia	Magnolia	1817	20
Missouri	Jefferson City	Show Me State	69,697	Bluebird	Hawthorn	Flowering dogwood	1821	24
Montana	Helena	Treasure State	147,046	Western meadowlark	Bitterroot	Ponderosa pine	1889	41

STATE	CAPITAL	POPULAR NAME	AREA (SQ. MI.)	STATE BIRD	STATE FLOWER	STATE TREE	ADMITTED TO THE UNION	ORDER OF ADMISSION
Nebraska	Lincoln	Cornhusker State	77,355	Western meadowlark	Goldenrod	Cottonwood	1867	37
Nevada	Carson City	Silver State	110,540	Mountain bluebird	Sagebrush	Single-leaf piñon	1864	36
New Hampshire	Concord	Granite State	9,304	Purple finch	Purple lilac	White birch	1788	9
New Jersey	Trenton	Garden State	7,787	Eastern goldfinch	Purple violet	Red oak	1787	3
New Mexico	Santa Fe	Land of Enchantment	121,593	Roadrunner	Yucca flower	Piñon, or nut pine	1912	47
New York	Albany	Empire State	49,108	Bluebird	Rose	Sugar maple	1788	11
North Carolina	Raleigh	Tar Heel State or Old North State	52,669	Cardinal	Dogwood	Pine	1789	12
North Dakota	Bismarck	Peace Garden State	70,702	Western meadowlark	Wild prairie rose	American elm	1889	39
Ohio	Columbus	Buckeye State	41,330	Cardinal	Scarlet carnation	Buckeye	1803	17
Oklahoma	Oklahoma City	Sooner State	69,956	Scissortail flycatcher	Mistletoe	Redbud	1907	46
Oregon	Salem	Beaver State	97,073	Western meadowlark	Oregon grape	Douglas fir	1859	33
Pennsylvania	Harrisburg	Keystone State	45,308	Ruffed grouse	Mountain laurel	Hemlock	1787	2
Rhode Island	Providence	Ocean State	1,212	Rhode Island Red	Violet	Red maple	1790	13
South Carolina	Columbia	Palmetto State	31,113	Carolina wren	Carolina jessamine	Palmetto	1788	8
South Dakota	Pierre	Sunshine State	77,116	Ring-necked pheasant	American pasqueflower	Black Hills spruce	1889	40
Tennessee	Nashville	Volunteer State	42,114	Mockingbird	Iris	Tulip poplar	1796	16
Texas	Austin	Lone Star State	266,807	Mockingbird	Bluebonnet	Pecan	1845	28
Utah	Salt Lake City	Beehive State	84,899	Sea Gull	Sego lily	Blue spruce	1896	45
Vermont	Montpelier	Green Mountain State	9,614	Hermit thrush	Red clover	Sugar maple	1791	14
Virginia	Richmond	Old Dominion	40,767	Cardinal	Dogwood	Dogwood	1788	10
Washington	Olympia	Evergreen State	68,139	Willow goldfinch	Coast rhododendron	Western hemlock	1889	42
West Virginia	Charleston	Mountain State	24,231	Cardinal	Rhododendron	Sugar maple	1863	35
Wisconsin	Madison	Badger State	56,153	Robin	Wood violet	Sugar maple	1848	30
Wyoming	Cheyenne	Equality State	97,809	Meadowlark	Indian paintbrush	Cottonwood	1890	44

STATE & TERRITORY ABBREVIATIONS: UNITED STATES

Alabama . . . . . AL
Alaska . . . . . AK
Arizona . . . . . AZ
Arkansas . . . . . AR
American Samoa . . . . . AS
California . . . . . CA
Colorado . . . . . CO
Connecticut . . . . . CT
Delaware . . . . . DE
District of Columbia . . . . . DC
Florida . . . . . FL
Georgia . . . . . GA
Guam . . . . . GU
Hawaii . . . . . HI
Idaho . . . . . ID
Illinois IL
Indiana . . . . . IN
Iowa . . . . . IA
Kansas . . . . . KS
Kentucky . . . . . KY
Louisiana . . . . . LA
Maine . . . . . ME
Maryland . . . . . MD
Massachusetts . . . . . MA
Michigan . . . . . MI
Minnesota . . . . . MN
Mississippi . . . . . MS
Missouri . . . . . MO
Montana . . . . . MT
Nebraska . . . . . NE
Nevada . . . . . NV
New Hampshire . . . . . NH
New Jersey . . . . . NJ
New Mexico . . . . . NM
New York . . . . . NY
North Carolina . . . . . NC
North Dakota . . . . . ND
Ohio . . . . . OH
Oklahoma . . . . . OK
Oregon . . . . . OR
Pennsylvania . . . . . PA
Puerto Rico . . . . . PR
Rhode Island . . . . . RI
South Carolina . . . . . SC
South Dakota . . . . . SD
Tennessee . . . . . TN
Texas . . . . . TX
Utah . . . . . UT
Vermont . . . . . VT
Virginia . . . . . VA
Virgin Islands VI
Washington . . . . . WA
West Virginia . . . . . WV
Wisconsin . . . . . WI
Wyoming . . . . . WY

STATE GOVERNORS/US SENATORS/US SUPREME COURT

GOVERNORS
Name (Party, State)

Bob Riley (R, AL)
Sarah Palin (R, AK)
Janet Napolitano (D, AZ)
Michael Beebe (D, AR)
Arnold Schwarzenegger (R, CA)
Bill Ritter (D, CO)
M. Jodi Rell (R, CT)
Ruth Ann Minner (D, DE)*
Charlie Crist (R, FL)
Sonny Perdue (R, GA)
Linda Lingle (R, HI)
Butch Otter (R, ID)
Rod Blagojevich (D, IL)
Mitchell Daniels (R, IN)*
Chet Culver (D, IA)
Kathleen Sebelius (D, KS)
Steve Beshear (D, KY)
Bobby Jindal (R, LA)
John Baldacci (D, ME)
Martin O'Malley (D, MD)
Deval Patrick (D, MA)
Jennifer Granholm (D, MI)
Tim Pawlenty (R, MN)
Haley Barbour (R, MS)
Matt Blunt (R, MO)*
Brian Schweitzer (D, MT)*
David Heineman (R, NE)
James Gibbons (R, NV)
John Lynch (D, NH)*
Jon Corzine (D, NJ)
Bill Richardson (D, NM)
David Paterson (D, NY)
Mike Easley (D, NC)*
John Hoeven (R, ND)*
Ted Strickland (D, OH)
Brad Henry (D, OK)
Ted Kulongoski (D, OR)
Ed Rendell (D, PA)
Donald Carcieri (R, RI)
Mark Sanford (R, SC)
Mike Rounds (R, SD)
Phil Bredesen (D, TN)
Rick Perry (R, TX)
Jon Huntsman Jr (R, UT)*
Jim Douglas (R, VT)*
Tim Kaine (D, VA)
Christine Gregoire (D, WA)*
Joe Manchin III (D, WV)*
Jim Doyle (D, WI)
Dave Freudenthal (D, WY)

*Office holders were current as of July 2008. Elections will take place in November 2008 for those seats marked with a *.*

† At press time, Senators Obama and McCain are campaigning for office of president of the United States. Please see www.senate.gov for information regarding the replacement for the winning candidate.

SENATORS
Name (Party, State)

Jeff Sessions (R, AL)*
Richard C. Shelby (R, AL)
Ted Stevens (R, AK)*
Lisa Murkowski (R, AK)
Jon Kyl (R, AZ)
John McCain (R, AZ)†
Blanche Lambert Lincoln (D, AR)
Mark Pryor (D, AR)*
Dianne Feinstein (D, CA)
Barbara Boxer (D, CA)
Wayne Allard (R, CO)*
Ken Salazar (D, CO)
Christopher J. Dodd (D, CT)
Joseph I. Lieberman (I, CT)
Thomas Carper (D, DE)
Joseph R. Biden Jr (D, DE)*
Mel Martinez (R, FL)
Bill Nelson (D, FL)
Saxby Chambliss (R, GA)*
Johnny Isakson (R, GA)
Daniel K. Inouye (D, HI)
Daniel K. Akaka (D, HI)
Larry E. Craig (R, ID)*
Michael Crapo (R, ID)
Richard J. Durbin (D, IL)*
Barack Obama (D, IL)†
Richard G. Lugar (R, IN)
Evan Bayh (D, IN)
Charles E. Grassley (R, IA)
Tom Harkin (D, IA)*
Sam Brownback (R, KS)
Pat Roberts (R, KS)*
Jim Bunning (R, KY)
Mitch McConnell (R, KY)*
Mary L. Landrieu (D, LA)*
David Vitter (R, LA)
Susan M. Collins (R, ME)*
Olympia J. Snowe (R, ME)
Benjamin Cardin (D, MD)
Barbara A. Mikulski (D, MD)
Edward M. Kennedy (D, MA)
John F. Kerry (D, MA)*
Debbie Stabenow (D, MI)
Carl Levin (D, MI)*
Amy Klobuchar (D, MN)
Norm Coleman (R, MN)*
Thad Cochran (R, MS)*
Roger Wicker (R, MS)*
Claire McCaskill (D, MO)
Christopher S. Bond (R, MO)
Max S. Baucus (D, MT)*
Jon Tester (D, MT)
Chuck Hagel (R, NE)*
Ben Nelson (D, NE)
Harry M. Reid (D, NV)
John Ensign (R, NV)
John Sununu (R, NH)*
Judd Gregg (R, NH)
Frank Lautenberg (D, NJ)*
Robert Menendez (D, NJ)
Pete V. Domenici (R, NM)*
Jeff Bingaman (D, NM)
Hillary Rodham Clinton (D, NY)
Charles E. Schumer (D, NY)
Elizabeth Dole (R, NC)*
Richard Burr (R, NC)
Kent Conrad (D, ND)
Byron L. Dorgan (D, ND)
George Voinovich (R, OH)
Sherrod Brown (D, OH)
James M. Inhofe (R, OK)*
Tom Coburn (R, OK)
Gordon Smith (R, OR)*
Ron Wyden (D, OR)
Arlen Specter (R, PA)
Robert P. Casey Jr (D, PA)
Jack Reed (D, RI)*
Sheldon Whitehouse (D, RI)
Lindsey Graham (R, SC)*
Jim DeMint (R, SC)
Tim Johnson (D, SD)*
John R. Thune (R, SD)
Bob Corker (R, TN)
Lamar Alexander (R, TN)*
John Cornyn (R, TX)*
Kay Bailey Hutchison (R, TX)
Orrin G. Hatch (R, UT)
Robert F. Bennett (R, UT)
Patrick J. Leahy (D, VT)
Bernard Sanders (I, VT)
John W. Warner (R, VA)*
Jim Webb (D, VA)
Maria Cantwell (D, WA)
Patty Murray (D, WA)
Robert C. Byrd (D, WV)
John D. Rockefeller IV (D, WV)*
Herbert H. Kohl (D, WI)
Russell D. Feingold (D, WI)
Michael B. Enzi (R, WY)*
John Barrasso (R, WY)*

SUPREME COURT JUSTICES
Name (Appointed by, Year)

John G. Roberts Jr, Chief Justice (G.W. Bush, 2005)
John P. Stevens (Ford, 1975)
Antonin Scalia (Reagan, 1986)
Anthony M. Kennedy (Reagan, 1988)
David H. Souter (G.H.W. Bush, 1990)
Clarence Thomas (G.H.W. Bush, 1991)
Ruth Bader Ginsburg (Clinton, 1993)
Stephen G. Breyer (Clinton, 1994)
Samuel A. Alito Jr, (G.W. Bush, 2006)

SOME FACTS ABOUT CANADA

PROVINCE/TERRITORY	CAPITAL	POPULATION*	FLOWER	LAND/FRESH WATER (SQ. MI.)	TOTAL AREA
Alberta	Edmonton	3,290,350	Wild Rose	248,000/7,541	255,541
British Columbia	Victoria	4,113,487	Pacific dogwood	357,216/7,548	364,764
Manitoba	Winnipeg	1,148,401	Prairie crocus	213,729/36,387	250,116
New Brunswick	Fredericton	729,997	Purple violet	27,587/563	28,150
Newfoundland & Labrador	St. John's	505,469	Pitcher plant	144,343/12,100	156,543
Northwest Territories	Yellowknife	41,464	Mountain avens	456,791/62,943	519,734
Nova Scotia	Halifax	913,462	Mayflower	20,593/752	21,345
Nunavut	Iqaluit	29,474	Purple saxifrage	747,537/60,648	808,185
Ontario	Toronto	12,160,282	White trillium	354,341/61,256	415,599
Prince Edward Island	Charlottetown	135,851	Lady's-slipper	2,185/0	2,185
Quebec	Quebec City	7,546,131	White garden lily	527,079/68,313	595,391
Saskatchewan	Regina	968,157	Western red lily	228,445/22,921	251,366
Yukon Territory	Whitehorse	30,372	Fireweed	183,163/3,109	186,272

**Based on the 2006 Canadian Census*

PROVINCE & TERRITORY ABBREVIATIONS: CANADA

Alberta . . . . AB
British Columbia . . . . BC
Manitoba . . . . MB
New Brunswick . . . . NB
Newfoundland & Labrador . . . . NF
Northwest Territories . . . . NT
Nova Scotia . . . . NS
Nunavut . . . . NU
Ontario . . . . ON
Prince Edward Island . . . . PE
Quebec . . . . QC
Saskatchewan . . . . SK
Yukon Territory . . . . YT

SOME FACTS ABOUT MEXICO

STATE	ABBREVIATION	CAPITAL	POPULATION*	AREA (SQ. MI.)
Aguascalientes	Ags.	Aguascalientes	1,051,000	2,156
Baja California	B.C.	Mexicali	2,842,000	27,655
Baja California Sur	B.C.S.	La Paz	517,000	27,979
Campeche	Camp.	Campeche	751,000	19,672
Chiapas	Chis.	Tuxtla Gutiérrez	4,256,000	28,732
Chihuahua	Chih.	Chihuahua	3,238,000	94,831
Coahuila	Coah.	Saltillo	2,475,000	58,067
Colima	Col.	Colima	562,000	2010
Distrito Federal	D.F.	Mexico City	8,670,000	573
Durango	Dgo.	Durango	1,489,000	47,691
Guanajuato	Gto.	Guanajuato	4,893,000	11,805
Guerrero	Gro.	Chilpancingo	3,116,000	24,887
Hidalgo	Hgo.	Pachuca	2,334,000	8058
Jalisco	Jal.	Guadalajara	6,652,000	31,152
México	Mex.	Toluca	14,161,000	8,268
Michoacán	Mich.	Morelia	3,988,000	23,202
Morelos	Mor.	Cuernavaca	1,605,000	1,917
Nayarit	Nay.	Tepic	943,000	10,547
Nuevo León	N.L.	Monterrey	4,164,000	25,136
Oaxaca	Oax.	Oaxaca	3,522,000	36,375
Puebla	Pue.	Puebla	5,391,000	13,126
Querétaro	Qro.	Querétaro	1,593,000	4,432
Quintana Roo	Q.R.	Chetumal	1,134,000	19,630
San Luis Potosí	S.L.P.	San Luis Potosí	2,412,000	24,417
Sinaloa	Sin.	Culiacán	2,610,000	22,582
Sonora	Son.	Hermosillo	2,384,000	70,484
Tabasco	Tab.	Villahermosa	2,013,000	9,783
Tamaulipas	Tamps.	Ciudad Victoria	3,020,000	30,734
Tlaxcala	Tlax.	Tlaxcala	1,061,000	1,555
Veracruz	Ver.	Jalapa	7,081,000	27,759
Yucatán	Yuc.	Mérida	1,803,000	14,868
Zacatecas	Zac.	Zacatecas	1,357,000	28,125

**Based on the 2005 Mexican Census*

2009 Special Months

For more information on these special months, see the listing on the first day of the month (unless specified otherwise).

January

Be On-Purpose Month, Natl
Book Blitz Month
California Dried Plum Digestive Health Month
Celebration of Life Month
Cervical Cancer Screening Month
Change Your Stars Month, Intl
Clean Up Your Computer Month, Natl
Creativity Month, Intl
Family Fit Lifestyle Month
Financial Wellness Month
Get Organized Month
Glaucoma Awareness Month, Natl
Hot Tea Month, Natl
Mailorder Gardening Month, Natl
Mentoring Month, Natl
New Years' Resolutions Month for Businesses, Intl
Oatmeal Month
Personal Self-Defense Awareness Month, Natl
Poverty in America Awareness Month, Natl
Quality of Life Month, Intl
Radon Action Month, Natl
Skating Month, Natl
Wayfinding Month, Intl
Wealth Mentality Month, Intl

February

AMD/Low Vision Awareness Month
American Heart Month
Bake for Family Fun Month
Bird Feeding Months, Natl
Black History Month, Natl
Boost Self-Esteem Month, Natl
Care About Your Indoor Air Month, Natl
Cherry Month, Natl
Children's Dental Health Month, Natl
February Is Fabulous Florida Strawberry Month
Laugh-Friendly Month, Natl
Library Lovers' Month
Marfan Syndrome Awareness Month
Mend a Broken Heart Month, Natl
Parent Leadership Month, Natl
Pet Dental Health Month, Natl
Plant the Seeds of Greatness Month
Relationship Wellness Month
Return Shopping Carts to the Supermarket Month
Senior Independence Month, Natl
Spunky Old Broads Month
Sweet Potato Month
Time Management Month, Natl
Weddings Month, Natl
Wise Health Care Consumer Month
Youth Leadership Month

March

Caffeine Awareness Month, Natl
Chronic Fatigue Syndrome Awareness Month, Natl
Clean Up Your IRS Act Month, Natl
Colorectal Cancer Awareness Month, Natl
Craft Month, Natl
Ethics Awareness Month, Natl
Employee Spirit Month
Expanding Girls' Horizons in Science and Engineering Month
Expect Success Month, Intl
Eye Donor Month, Natl
Frozen Food Month, Natl
Honor Society Awareness Month
Humorists Are Artists Month
Ideas Month, Intl
Irish-American Heritage Month
Kidney Month, Natl
Listening Awareness Month, Intl
March into Literacy Month, Natl
Mirth Month, Intl
Multiple Sclerosis Education and Awareness Month, Natl
Music in Our Schools Month
Nutrition Month®, Natl
On-Hold Month, Natl
Optimism Month
Play-the-Recorder Month
Poison Prevention Awareness Month
Red Cross Month
Save Your Vision Month
Small Press Month
Social Work Month, Natl
Spiritual Wellness Month
Umbrella Month, Natl
Women's History Month, Natl
Workplace Eye Health and Safety Month
Youth Art Month

March–April

Deaf History Month (Mar 13–Apr 15)

April

African-American Women's Fitness Month, Natl
Alcohol Awareness Month
Cancer Control Month
Car Care Months
Card and Letter Writing Month, Natl
Celebrate Diversity Month
Child Abuse Prevention Month, Natl
Couple Appreciation Month
Customer Loyalty Month, Intl
Decorating Month, Natl
DNA, Genomics and Stem Cell Educational and Awareness Month, Natl
Donate Life Month, Natl
Emotional Overeating Awareness Month
Fresh Florida Tomato Month
Grange Month
Holy Humor Month
Humor Month, Natl
Informed Woman Month
Jazz Appreciation Month
Kite Month, Natl
Knuckles Down Month, Natl
Landscape Architecture Month, Natl
Lawn Care Month, Natl
Month of the Military Child
Month of the Young Child®
Occupational Therapy Month, Natl
Parkinson Awareness Month, Natl
Pecan Month, Natl
Pet First Aid Awareness Month, Natl
Pharmacists War on Diabetes
Physical Wellness Month
Poetry Month, Natl
Prevent Lyme in Dogs Month
Prevention of Animal Cruelty Month
Rosacea Awareness Month
School Library Media Month
Sexual Assault Awareness and Prevention Month, Natl
Sexually Transmitted Diseases (STDs) Education and Awareness Month, Natl
Southern Belles Month
Straw Hat Month
Stress Awareness Month
Twit Award Month, Intl
Women's Eye Health and Safety Month
Workplace Conflict Awareness Month
World Habitat Awareness Month
Youth Sports Safety Month, Natl

May

Allergy/Asthma Awareness Month, Natl
Arthritis Month, Natl
Asian/Pacific American Heritage Month
Awareness of Medical Orphans Month
Barbecue Month, Natl
Better Hearing and Speech Month
Bike Month, Natl
Business Image Improvement Month, Intl
Creative Beginnings Month
Egg Month, Natl
Family Wellness Month
Fibromyalgia Education and Awareness Month
Freedom Shrine Month
Get Caught Reading Month
Gifts from the Garden Month
Good Car-Keeping Month, Natl
Haitian Heritage Month
Hamburger Month, Natl
Heal the Children Month
Healthy Vision Month
Hepatitis Awareness Month, Natl
Huntington's Disease Awareness Month
Internal Audit Awareness Month, Intl
Jewish American Heritage Month
Latino Books Month
Meditation Month, Natl
Melanoma/Skin Cancer Detection and Prevention Month
Mental Health Month, Natl
Military Appreciation Month, Natl
Motorcycle Safety Month
Moving Month, Natl
Older Americans Month
Osteoporosis Awareness and Prevention Month, Natl
Personal History Month
Photo Month, Natl
Physical Fitness and Sports Month, Natl
Preservation Month, Natl
REACT Month
Revise Your Work Schedule Month
Salad Month, Natl
Salsa Month, Natl
Smile Month, Natl
Strike Out Strokes Month
Stroke Awareness Month, Natl
Sweet Vidalia® Onion Month, Natl
Teen Self-Esteem Month
Tennis Month
Ultraviolet Awareness Month
Victorious Woman Month, Intl
Vinegar Month, Natl
Women's Health Care Month
Young Achievers/Leaders of Tomorrow Month

May–June

Family Month, Natl (May 10–June 21)
Prepare Tomorrow's Parents Month (May 10–June 21)

June

Accordion Awareness Month, Natl
Adopt-a-Shelter-Cat Month

Aphasia Awareness Month, Natl
Cancer from the Sun Month
Candy Month, Natl
Celibacy Awareness Month
Child Vision Awareness Month
Childhood Cancer Campaign Month, Intl
Children's Awareness Month
Dairy Alternatives Month
Effective Communications Month
Entrepreneurs "Do It Yourself" Marketing Month
Fireworks Safety Months
Gay and Lesbian Pride Month
GLBT Book Month, Natl
Great Outdoors Month
Iced Tea Month, Natl
June Dairy Month
June Is Perennial Gardening Month
June Is Turkey Lovers' Month
Men's Month, Intl
Pharmacists Declare War on Alcoholism
Potty Training Awareness Month
Professional Wellness Month
Rebuild Your Life Month
Rivers Month, Natl
Rose Month, Natl
Safety Month, Natl
Soul Food Month, Natl
Sports America Kids Month
Steakhouse Month, Natl
Student Safety Month
Vision Research Month

July
Bereaved Parents Awareness Month
Bioterrorism/Disaster Education and Awareness Month
Blondie and Deborah Harry Month, Intl
Blueberries Month, Natl
Cell Phone Courtesy Month
Child-Centered Divorce Month, Natl
"Doghouse Repairs" Month, Natl
Family Reunion Month
Grilling Month, Natl
Herbal/Prescription Awareness Month
Horseradish Month, Natl
Hot Dog Month, Natl
Ice Cream Month, Natl
Make a Difference to Children Month, Natl
Recreation and Parks Month, Natl
Sandwich Generation Month
Share a Sunset with Your Lover Month
Smart Irrigation Month
Social Wellness Month
Wheelchair Beautification Month, Natl
Women's Motorcycle Month

August
American Adventures Month
Black Business Month
Cataract Awareness Month
Children's Eye Health and Safety Month
Children's Vision and Learning Month
Get Ready for Kindergarten Month
Happiness Happens Month
Immunization Awareness Month, Natl
Inventors' Month®, Natl
Motorsports Awareness Month
Neurosurgery Outreach Month
Panini Month, Natl
Spinal Muscular Atrophy Awareness Month
What Will Be Your Legacy Month
Win with Civility Month, Natl

September
Alcohol and Drug Addiction Recovery Month, Natl
Animal Remembrance Month, World
Atrial Fibrillation Month
Attention Deficit Hyperactivity Disorder Month
Backpack Safety America Month
Be Kind to Editors and Writers Month
Chicken Month, Natl
Children's Good Manners Month
College Savings Month
Coupon Month, Natl
Fall Hat Month
Go Wild During California Wild Rice Month
Gynecologic Cancer Awareness Month
Honey Month, Natl
Library Card Sign-Up Month
Mold Awareness Month
Mushroom Month, Natl
One-on-One Month
Organic Harvest Month, Natl
Osteopathic Medicine Month, Natl
Ovarian Cancer Awareness Month, Natl
Pediatric Cancer Awareness Month
Pediculosis Prevention Month, Natl
People Skills Month, Intl
Piano Month, Natl
Pleasure Your Mate Month
Prime Beef Month, Natl
Reunion Planning Month
Rice Month, Natl
Schoolhouse Triangle Project Month
Sea Cadet Month
Self-Awareness Month, Intl
September Is Healthy Aging® Month
Shameless Promotion Month
Sickle Cell Awareness Month, Natl
Skin Care Awareness Month, Natl
Sports and Home Eye Safety Month
Strategic Thinking Month, Intl
Subliminal Communications Month
Update Your Resume Month

September–October
Hispanic Heritage Month, Natl (Sept 15–Oct 15)

October
Adopt-a-Shelter-Dog Month
Animal Safety and Protection Month, Natl
Antidepressant Death Awareness Month
Bake and Decorate Month, Natl
Breast Cancer Awareness Month, Natl
Celebrating the Bilingual Child Month
Celiac Disease Awareness Month
Children's Magazine Month
Chili Month, Natl
Chiropractic Month, Natl
Church Library Month
Church Safety and Security Month
Class Reunion Month
Co-op Awareness Month
Crime Prevention Month, Natl
Cyber Security Awareness Month, Natl
Dental Hygiene Month, Natl
Depression Education and Awareness Month, Natl
Disability Employment Awareness Month, Natl
Domestic Violence Awareness Month
Down Syndrome Awareness Month, Natl
Dyslexia Awareness Month
Eat Better, Eat Together Month
Emotional Intelligence Awareness Month
Emotional Wellness Month
Family Sexuality Education Month, Natl
"Gain the Inside Advantage" Month, Natl
Gay and Lesbian History Month
German-American Heritage Month
Global Diversity Awareness Month
Go Hog Wild—Eat Country Ham Month
Go on a Field Trip Month, Natl
Halloween Safety Month
Health Literacy Month
Liver Awareness Month, Natl
Long-Term Care Planning Month
Medical Librarians Month, Natl
Month of Freethought
Organize Your Medical Information Month
Orthodontic Health Month, Natl
Photographer Appreciation Month
Physical Therapy Month, Natl
Polish-American Heritage Month
Popcorn Poppin' Month, Natl
Positive Attitude Month
Raptor Month
Reading Group Month, Natl
Rett Syndrome Awareness Month
Right-Brainers Rule Month
Roller Skating Month, Natl
RSV Awareness Month, Natl
Sarcastics Awareness Month, Natl
Self-Promotion Month
Spina Bifida Awareness Month, Natl
Spinach Lovers Month
Squirrel Awareness Month
Stamp Collecting Month, Natl
Starman Month, Intl
Strategic Planning Month, Intl
Talk About Prescriptions Month
Vegetarian Month
Women's Small Business Month
Work and Family Month, Natl
Workplace Politics Awareness Month

November
Adoption Month, Natl
AIDS Awareness Month, Natl
Alzheimer's Disease Month, Natl
American Diabetes Month
American Indian Heritage Month, Natl
Aviation History Month
Diabetic Eye Disease Month
Epilepsy Awareness Month
Family Caregivers Month, Natl
Family Stories Month
Georgia Pecan Month, Natl
Gluten-Free Diet Awareness Month
Inspirational Role Models Month, Natl
Lifewriting Month, Natl
Long-Term Care Awareness Month, Natl
Lung Cancer Awareness Month
Month of the Military Family
Peanut Butter Lovers' Month
Pet Cancer Awareness Month
Pomegranate Month, Natl
Prematurity Awareness Month
Roasting Month, Natl
Scholarship Month, Natl
Vegan Month

December
Bingo's Birthday Month
Colorectal Cancer Education and Awareness Month
Drunk and Drugged Driving Prevention Month, Natl
Rising Star Month
Safe Toys and Gifts Month
Spiritual Literacy Month
Tie Month, Natl
Write a Business Plan Month, Natl

Major Awards Presented in 2007–2008

AWARDS FOR STAGE, FILM AND TELEVISION

TONY AWARDS

62nd Annual, for 2007–2008 Achievement

Play: *August: Osage County*
Musical: *In the Heights*
Book of a Musical: Stew, *Passing Strange*
Original Musical Score: Lin-Mañuel Miranda, *In the Heights*
Revival of a Play: *Boeing-Boeing*
Revival of a Musical: *South Pacific*
Director of a Play: Anna D. Shapiro, *August: Osage County*
Director of a Musical: Bartlett Sher, *South Pacific*
Leading Actor in a Play: Mark Rylance, *Boeing-Boeing*
Leading Actress in a Play: Deanna Dunagan, *August: Osage County*
Leading Actor in a Musical: Paulo Szot, *South Pacific*
Leading Actress in a Musical: Patti LuPone, *Gypsy*
Featured Actor in a Play: Jim Norton, *The Seafarer*
Featured Actress in a Play: Rondi Reed, *August: Osage County*
Featured Actor in a Musical: Boyd Gaines, *Gypsy*
Featured Actress in a Musical: Laura Benanti, *Gypsy*
Scenic Design of a Play: Todd Rosenthal, *August: Osage County*
Scenic Design of a Musical: Michael Yeargan, *South Pacific*
Costume Design of a Play: Katrina Lindsay, *Les Liaisons Dangereuses*
Costume Design of a Musical: Catherine Zuber, *South Pacific*
Lighting Design of a Play: Kevin Adams, *The 39 Steps*
Lighting Design of a Musical: Donald Holder, *South Pacific*
Sound Design of a Play: Mic Pool, *The 39 Steps*
Sound Design of a Musical: Scott Lehrer, *South Pacific*
Choreography: Andy Blankenbuehler, *In the Heights*
Orchestration: Alex Lacamoire and Bill Sherman, *In the Heights*
Special Award for Regional Theater: Chicago Shakespeare Theater, Chicago, IL
Special Award for Lifetime Achievement: Stephen Sondheim

2008 ACADEMY AWARDS

80th Annual, for 2007 Achievement

Picture: *No Country for Old Men*
Director: Joel Coen and Ethan Coen, *No Country for Old Men*
Actor: Daniel Day-Lewis, *There Will Be Blood*
Actress: Marion Cotillard, *La Vie en Rose*
Supporting Actor: Javier Bardem, *No Country for Old Men*
Supporting Actress: Tilda Swinton, *Michael Clayton*
Original Screenplay: Diablo Cody, *Juno*
Adapted Screenplay: Joel Coen and Ethan Coen, *No Country for Old Men*
Foreign Language Film: *The Counterfeiters* (Austria)
Animated Feature: *Ratatouille*
Animated Short Film: "Peter & the Wolf"
Live Action Short Film: "Le Mozart des Pickpockets (The Mozart of Pickpockets)"
Documentary Feature: *Taxi to the Dark Side*
Documentary Short Subject: "Freeheld"

Film Editing: Christopher Rouse, *The Bourne Ultimatum*
Costume Design: Alexandra Byrne, *Elizabeth: The Golden Age*
Cinematography: Robert Elswit, *There Will Be Blood*
Art Direction: Dante Ferretti (Art Direction), Francesco Lo Schiavo (Set Decoration), *Sweeney Todd: The Demon Barber of Fleet Street*
Visual Effects: Michael Fink, Bill Westenhofer, Ben Morris and Trevor Wood, *The Golden Compass*
Makeup: Didier Lavergne and Jan Archibald, *La Vie en Rose*
Sound Mixing: Scott Millan, David Parker and Kirk Francis, *The Bourne Ultimatum*
Sound Editing: Karen Baker Landers and Per Hallberg, *The Bourne Ultimatum*
Original Score: Dario Marianelli, *Atonement*
Original Song: Glen Hansard and Marketa Irglova, "Falling Slowly" from *Once*

2008 SUNDANCE FILM FESTIVAL AWARDS

26th Annual

Dramatic Grand Jury Prize: *Frozen River*
Documentary Grand Jury Prize: *Trouble the Water*
Dramatic Audience Award: *The Wackness*
Documentary Audience Award: *Fields of Fuel*
World Cinema Dramatic Grand Jury Prize: *King of Ping Pong*
World Cinema Documentary Grand Jury Prize: *Man on Wire*
World Cinema Audience Award, Dramatic: *Captain Abu Raed*
World Cinema Audience Award, Documentary: *Man on Wire*
Directing Award, Dramatic: Lance Hammer, *Ballast*
Directing Award, Documentary: Nanette Burstein, *American Teen*
World Cinema Directing Award, Dramatic: Anna Melikyan, *Mermaid*
World Cinema Directing Award, Documentary: Nino Kirtadze, *Durakovo: Village of Fools*
Cinematography Award, Dramatic: Lol Crawley, *Ballast*
Cinematography Award, Documentary: Phillip Hunt and Steven Sebring, *Patti Smith: Dream of Life*
World Cinematography Award, Dramatic: Askild Vik Edvardsen, *King of Ping Pong*
World Cinematography Award, Documentary: al Massad, *Recycle*
Editing Award, Documentary: Joe Bini, *Roman Polanski: Wanted and Desired*
World Cinema Editing Award, Documentary: Irena Dol, *The Art Star and the Sudanese Twins*
Waldo Salt Screenwriting Award: Alex Rivera and David Riker, *Sleep Dealer*
World Cinema Screenwriting Award: Samuel Benchetrit, *I Always Wanted to Be a Gangster*
Special Jury Prize, Documentary: Lisa F. Jackson, *The Greatest Silence: Rape in the Congo*
Special Jury Prize, Dramatic, The Spirit of Independence: Chusy Haney-Jardin, *Anywhere, USA*
Special Jury Prize, Dramatic, Work by an Ensemble Cast: Sam Rockwell, Anjelica Huston, Kelly MacDonald, Brad Henke, *Choke*
Special Jury Prize, World Cinema Dramatic: Ernesto Contreras, *Párpados Azules (Blue Eyelids)*
Jury Prizes in Short Filmmaking: "My Olympic Summer" and "Sikumi (On the Ice)"
Jury Prize in International Short Filmmaking: "Soft"
Alfred P. Sloan Prize: *Sleep Dealer*

2008 CANNES FILM FESTIVAL

61st Annual

Palme d'Or (Golden Palm): *The Class (Entre les murs)*
Grand Prix: *Gomorra*
Jury Prize: *Il Divo*
Best Actress: Sandra Corveloni, *Linha de Passe*
Best Actor: Benicio del Toro, *Che*
Best Director: Nuri Bilge Ceylan, *Three Monkeys*
Best Screenplay: Jean-Pierre and Luc Dardenne, *Lorna's Silence*

2008 GOLDEN GLOBE AWARDS

65th Annual, for 2007 Achievement

MOVIES

Drama: *Atonement*
Musical or Comedy: *Sweeney Todd: The Demon Barber of Fleet Street*
Director: Julian Schnabel, *The Diving Bell and the Butterfly*
Actor, Drama: Daniel Day-Lewis, *There Will Be Blood*
Actress, Drama: Julie Christie, *Away from Her*
Actor, Musical or Comedy: Johnny Depp, *Sweeney Todd: The Demon Barber of Fleet Street*
Actress, Musical or Comedy: Marion Cotillard, *La Vie en Rose*
Supporting Actor: Javier Bardem, *No Country for Old Men*
Supporting Actress: Cate Blanchett, *I'm Not There*
Screenplay: Ethan Coen and Joel Coen, *No Country for Old Men*
Animated Film: *Ratatouille*
Foreign Language Film: *The Diving Bell and the Butterfly*, France, USA
Original Score: Dario Marianelli, *Atonement*
Original Song: Eddie Vedder, "Guaranteed," *Into the Wild*

TELEVISION

Series, Drama: "Mad Men"
Series, Musical or Comedy: "Extras"
Miniseries or TV Movie: *Longford*
Actor, Series, Drama: Jon Hamm, "Mad Men"
Actress, Series, Drama: Glenn Close, "Damages"
Actor, Series, Musical or Comedy: David Duchovny, "Californication"
Actress, Series, Musical or Comedy: Tina Fey, "30 Rock"
Actor, Miniseries or TV Movie: Jim Broadbent, *Longford*
Actress, Miniseries or TV Movie: Queen Latifah, *Life Support*
Actor, Supporting Role: Jeremy Piven, "Entourage"
Actress, Supporting Role: Samantha Morton, *Longford*

2007 PRIME TIME EMMY AWARDS

Major Categories—59th Annual

Drama: "The Sopranos," HBO
Comedy: "30 Rock," NBC
Miniseries: *Broken Trail*, AMC
Made-for-Television Movie: *Bury My Heart at Wounded Knee*, HBO
Variety, Music or Comedy Series: "The Daily Show with Jon Stewart," Comedy Central
Variety, Music or Comedy Special: "Tony Bennett: An American Classic," NBC
Children's Program: "Nick News with Linda Ellerbee: Private Worlds: Kids and Autism," Nickelodeon
Animated Program (Less than One Hour): "South Park: Make Love, Not Warcraft," Comedy Central
Animated Program (One Hour or More): "Where's Laszo? (Camp Lazlo)," Cartoon Network
Reality Program: "Kathy Griffin: My Life on the D-List," Bravo
Reality/Competition Program: "The Amazing Race," CBS
Nonfiction Program (Special Class): "The 60th Annual Tony Awards," CBS
Nonfiction Series: "Planet Earth," Discovery Channel
Nonfiction Special: "Ghosts of Abu Ghraib," HBO
Lead Actress in a Drama Series: Sally Field, "Brothers & Sisters," ABC
Lead Actor in a Drama Series: James Spader, "Boston Legal," ABC
Lead Actress in a Comedy Series: America Ferrera, "Ugly Betty," ABC
Lead Actor in a Comedy Series: Ricky Gervais, "Extras," HBO
Lead Actress in a Miniseries or TV Movie: Helen Mirren, *Prime Suspect: The Final Act (Masterpiece Theatre)*, PBS
Lead Actor in a Miniseries or TV Movie: Robert Duvall, *Broken Trail*, AMC
Supporting Actress in a Drama Series: Katherine Heigl, "Grey's Anatomy," ABC
Supporting Actor in a Drama Series: Terry O'Quinn, "Lost," ABC
Supporting Actress in a Comedy Series: Jaime Pressly, "My Name Is Earl," NBC
Supporting Actor in a Comedy Series: Jeremy Piven, "Entourage," HBO
Supporting Actress in a Miniseries or TV Movie: Judy Davis, *The Starter Wife*, USA
Supporting Actor in a Miniseries or TV Movie: Thomas Haden Church, *Broken Trail*, AMC
Guest Actor in a Drama Series: John Goodman, "Studio 60 on the Sunset Strip," NBC
Guest Actress in a Drama Series: Leslie Caron, "Law & Order: Special Victims Unit," NBC
Guest Actor in a Comedy Series: Stanley Tucci, "Monk," USA
Guest Actress in a Comedy Series: Elaine Stritch, "30 Rock," NBC
Performance in a Variety, Music or Comedy Program: Tony Bennett, "Tony Bennett: An American Classic," NBC
Drama Series Directing: Alan Taylor, "The Sopranos: Kennedy and Heidi," HBO
Comedy Series Directing: Richard Shepard, "Ugly Betty: Pilot," ABC
Variety, Music or Comedy Program Directing: Rob Marshall, "Tony Bennett: An American Classic," NBC
Miniseries or TV Movie Directing: Philip Martin, *Prime Suspect: The Final Act (Masterpiece Theatre)*, PBS
Nonfiction Directing: Spike Lee, "When the Levees Broke: A Requiem in Four Acts," HBO
Drama Series Writing: David Chase, "The Sopranos: Made in America," HBO
Comedy Series Writing: Greg Daniels, "The Office: Gay Witch Hunt," NBC
Variety, Music or Comedy Program Writing: Mike Sweeney, Conan O'Brien, et al, "Late Night with Conan O'Brien," NBC
Miniseries or TV Movie Writing: Frank Deasy, *Prime Suspect: The Final Act (Masterpiece Theatre)*, PBS
Nonfiction Writing: James Sanders and Ric Burns, "American Masters: Andy Warhol: A Documentary Film," PBS

2008 DAYTIME EMMY AWARDS

35th Annual

Drama: "General Hospital," ABC
Lead Actress in a Drama Series: Jeanne Cooper, "The Young and the Restless," CBS
Lead Actor in a Drama Series: Anthony Geary, "General Hospital," ABC
Supporting Actress in a Drama Series: Gina Tognoni, "Guiding Light," CBS
Supporting Actor in a Drama Series: Kristoff St. John, "The Young and the Restless," CBS
Younger Actress in a Drama Series: Jennifer Landon, "As the World Turns," CBS
Younger Actor in a Drama Series: Tom Pelphrey, "Guiding Light," CBS
Drama Series Writing Team: "One Life to Live," ABC
Drama Series Directing Team: "One Life to Live," ABC
Preschool Children's Series: "Sesame Street," PBS
Children's Series: **TIE:** "Greatest Inventions with Bill Nye," Discovery Channel, and "Jack Hanna's Into the Wild," syndicated
Performer in a Children's Series: Bindi Irwin, "Bindi the Jungle Girl," Discovery Kids
Children's Series Writing Team: "Between the Lions," PBS
Children's Series Directing: Dorothy Dickie, "Design Squad," PBS
Children's Animated Program: "Curious George," PBS
Performer in an Animated Program: Eartha Kitt, "Disney's The Emperor's New School," Disney
Special Class Animated Program: "The Backyardigans," Nick Jr.
Morning Program: "Good Morning America," ABC

Special Class Series: "Made," MTV
Special Class Special: "America's Invisible Children," CW TV
Special Class Writing Team: "The View," ABC
Special Class Directing: Ron de Moraes, "Walt Disney World Christmas Day Parade 2007," ABC
Talk Show/Entertainment: "Rachael Ray," syndicated
Talk Show/Informative: "The Tyra Banks Show," syndicated
Talk Show Host: Ellen DeGeneres, "The Ellen DeGeneres Show," syndicated
Talk Show Directing: Barry Glazer and Manny Rodriguez, "The Ellen DeGeneres Show," syndicated
Game Show: "Cash Cab," Discovery Channel
Game Show Host: Alex Trebek, "Jeopardy!" syndicated
Lifestyle Program: "Everyday Italian," Food Network
Lifestyle Program Host: Giada de Laurentiis, "Everyday Italian," Food Network
Lifestyle Program Directing: Juliet D'Annibale, "Everyday Italian," Food Network

AWARDS FOR ARTS, HUMANITIES AND JOURNALISM

2007 NATIONAL ENDOWMENT AWARDS
Awarded November 14, 2007

2007 National Medal of Arts:
Morten Lauridsen, composer
N. Scott Momaday, author, essayist, poet, professor, painter
Roy R. Neuberger, arts patron
R. Craig Noel, Old Globe Theatre director
Les Paul, guitarist, inventor
Henry Steinway, arts patron
George Tooker, painter
University of Idaho Lionel Hampton International Jazz Festival, music competition and festival, Moscow, ID
Andrew Wyeth, painter

2007 National Medal of Humanities:
Stephen H. Balch, scholar and advocate
Russell Freedman, author
Victor Davis Hanson, military historian and author
Roger Hertog, philanthropist
Cynthia Ozick, author
Richard Pipes, author and historian
Pauline L. Schultz, curator and author
Henry Leonard Snyder, scholar and innovator
Ruth R. Wisse, scholar and author
Monuments Men Foundation for the Preservation of Art

NOBEL PRIZES
Highly prestigious international awards given yearly since 1901. Details can be found at www.nobel.se.

2007 Recipients:
Peace: Intergovernmental Panel on Climate Change (IPCC) and Albert Arnold (Al) Gore Jr
Physics: Albert Fert and Peter Grünberg
Chemistry: Gerhard Ertl
Physiology or Medicine: Mario R. Capecchi, Sir Martin J. Evans and Oliver Smithies
Literature: Doris Lessing
Economics: Leonid Hurwicz, Eric S. Maskin and Roger B. Myerson

2007 PULITZER PRIZES

THE ARTS
Fiction: *The Brief Wondrous Life of Oscar Wao,* Junot Diaz
Drama: *August: Osage County,* Tracy Letts
History: *What Hath God Wrought,* Daniel Walker Howe
Biography: *Eden's Outcasts,* John Matteson
Poetry: *Time and Materials,* Robert Hass, and *Failure,* Philip Schultz
General Nonfiction: *The Years of Extermination,* Saul Friedlander
Music: *The Little Match Girl Passion,* David Lang
Special Citation: Bob Dylan

JOURNALISM
Public Service: *Washington Post*
Breaking News Reporting: Staff, *Washington Post*
Investigative Reporting: Staff, *Chicago Tribune,* and Walt Bogdanich and Jake Hooker, *New York Times*
Explanatory Reporting: Amy Harmon, *New York Times*
Local Reporting: David Umhoefer, *Milwaukee Journal-Sentinel*
National Reporting: Jo Becker and Barton Gellman, *Washington Post*
International Reporting: Steve Fainaru, *Washington Post*
Feature Writing: Gene Weingarten, *Washington Post*
Commentary: Steven Pearlstein, *Washington Post*
Criticism: Mark Feeney, *Boston Globe*
Editorial Cartooning: Michael Ramirez, *Investor's Business Daily*
Breaking News Photography: Andrees Latif, Reuters
Feature Photography: Preston Gannaway, *Concord Monitor*

2007 GEORGE POLK AWARDS
Awarded for special achievement in journalism.
Consumer Reporting: Staff, *Chicago Tribune*
Economic Reporting: Staff, *Charlotte Observer*
Environmental Reporting: Shai Oster, *Wall Street Journal*
Financial Reporting: Edward Chancellor, *Institutional Investor*
Foreign Reporting: Leila Fadel, McClatchy Company
Legal Reporting: Joshua Micah Marshall, Talking Points Memo (blog)
Local Reporting: Chauncey W. Bailey Jr, *Oakland Post,* Oakland, CA
Medical Reporting: Charles A. Duhigg, *New York Times*
Magazine Reporting: Joshua A. Kors, *Nation*
Political Reporting: Barton D. Gellman and Jo Becker, *Washington Post*
State Reporting: Jerry W. Mitchell, *Clarion-Ledger,* Jackson, MS
Television Reporting: Jim Sciutto, Angus Hines and Tom Murphy, "ABC World News with Charles Gibson"
Book Award: Jeremy Scahill, *Blackwater: The Rise of the World's Most Powerful Mercenary Army*
Career Award: John McPhee

2007 PEABODY AWARDS
67th Annual
"30 Rock," Universal Media Studios
"Art: 21—Art in the 21st Century," PBS
"Speaking of Faith: The Ecstatic Faith of Rumi," American Public Media
"Bob Woodruff Reporting: Wounds of War—The Long Road Home of Our Nation's Veterans," ABC News
"Money for Nothing," "The Buried and the Dead," "Television Justice" and "Kinder Prison," WFAA-TV (Dallas)
"Judgment Day: Intelligent Design on Trial," NOVA/WGBH Educational Foundation (Boston)
"Whole Lotta Shakin'," Texas Heritage Music Foundation
"White Horse," BBC World News America, BBC America, BBC World
"Just Words," The Center for Emerging Media
"CNN Presents: God's Warriors," CNN
"Dexter," Showtime
"Planet Earth," Discovery Channel, BBC
"CBS News Sunday Morning: The Way Home," CBS News
"Fight for Open Records," WTAE-TV (Pittsburgh, PA)
"To Die in Jerusalem," HBO Documentary Films
"Design Squad," WGBH Educational Foundation (Boston)
"Craft in America: Memory, Landscape and Community," Craft in America Inc.
"Univision's Ya Es Hora," Univision Communications
"NATURE: Silence of the Bees," Partisan Pictures, Inc, Thirteen/WNET New York

"A Journey Across Afghanistan: Opium and Roses," Balkan News Corporation—bTV
"The MTT Files," American Public Media, San Francisco Symphony
"Project Runway," Bravo
Taxi to the Dark Side, Jigsaw Pictures
"Security Risks at Sky Harbor," KNXV-TV (Phoenix, AZ)
"Wait, Wait. . . Don't Tell Me!" National Public Radio, Chicago Public Radio
"Independent Lens: Sisters in Law," Vixen Films, Independent Television Service (ITVS)
"Virginia Tech Shooting: The First 48 Hours," WSLS-TV (Roanoke, VA)
"The Brian Lehrer Show: Radio That Builds Community Rather than Divides," WNYC Radio
"Nimrod Nation," Sundance Channel
"FRONTLINE: Cheney's Law," FRONTLINE, Kirk Documentary Group, Ltd, WGBH-Boston
"mtvU: Half of Us," mtvU
"Independent Lens: Billy Strayhorn—Lush Life," Robert Levi Films, Independent Television Service (ITVS), Washington Square Films
"CBS News/60 Minutes: The Killings in Haditha," CBS News, 60 Minutes
"Mad Men," AMC, Lionsgate Pictures Television
"The Colbert Report," Hello Doggie Inc, Busboy Productions and Spartina Productions

AWARDS FOR LITERATURE

NATIONAL BOOK AWARDS 2007

Given annually by the National Book Foundation.

Fiction: *Tree of Smoke,* Denis Johnson
Nonfiction: *Legacy of Ashes: The History of the CIA,* Tim Weiner
Poetry: *Time and Materials,* Robert Hass
Young People's Literature: *The Absolutely True Story of a Part-Time Indian,* Sherman Alexie

THE NATIONAL BOOK CRITICS CIRCLE AWARDS 2007

Fiction: *The Brief Wondrous Life of Oscar Wao,* Junot Diaz
General Nonfiction: *Medical Apartheid,* Harriet Washington
Biography: *Stanley: The Impossible Life of Africa's Greatest Explorer,* Tim Jeal
Autobiography: *Brother, I'm Dying,* Edwidge Danticat
Poetry: *Elegy,* Mary Jo Bang
Criticism: *The Rest Is Noise,* Alex Ross

PEN/FAULKNER AWARD FOR FICTION 2008

An award given by an organization of writers to honor its peers.

Kate Christensen, *The Great Man*
Finalists
Annie Dillard, *The Maytrees*
David Leavitt, *The Indian Clerk*
T.M. McNally, *The Gateway: Stories*
Ron Rash, *Chemistry and Other Stories*

THE BOOK SENSE BOOK OF THE YEAR 2008

Given annually by the American Booksellers Association.

Adult Fiction: *A Thousand Splendid Suns,* Khaled Hosseini
Adult Nonfiction: *Animal, Vegetable, Miracle: A Year of Food Life,* Barbara Kingsolver
Children's Illustrated: *Knuffle Bunny Too: A Case of Mistaken Identity,* Mo Willems
Children's Literature: *The Invention of Hugo Cabret,* Brian Selznick

2008 AMERICAN LIBRARY ASSOCIATION AWARDS FOR CHILDREN'S BOOKS

NEWBERY MEDAL

For most distinguished contribution to American literature for children published in 2007:

Laura Amy Schlitz, author, *Good Masters! Sweet Ladies! Voices from a Medieval Village*
Honor Books
Christopher Paul Curtis, author, *Elijah of Buxton*
Gary D. Schmidt, author, *The Wednesday Wars*
Jacqueline Woodson, author, *Feathers*

CALDECOTT MEDAL

For most distinguished American picture book for children published in 2007:

Brian Selznick, illustrator and author, *The Invention of Hugo Cabret*
Honor Books
Kadir Nelson, illustrator, *Henry's Freedom Box: A True Story from the Underground Railroad*, written by Ellen Levine
Laura Vaccaro Seeger, illustrator and author, *First the Egg*
Peter Sis, illustrator and author, *The Wall: Growing Up Behind the Iron Curtain*
Mo Willems, illustrator and author, *Knuffle Bunny Too: A Case of Mistaken Identity*

CORETTA SCOTT KING AWARD

For outstanding books by African American authors and illustrators:

Christopher Paul Curtis, author, *Elijah of Buxton*
Ashley Bryan, illustrator and author, *Let It Shine: Three Favorite Spirituals*
Honor Books—Authors
Sharon M. Draper, author, *November Blues*
Charles R. Smith, Jr, author, *Twelve Rounds to Glory: The Story of Muhammad Ali*
Honor Books—Illustrators
Nancy Devard, illustrator, *The Secret Olivia Told Me*, written by N. Joy
Leo and Diane Dillon, illustrators and authors, *Jazz on a Saturday Night*
John Steptoe New Talent Author Award
Sundee T. Frazier, author, *Brendan Buckley's Universe and Everything in It*

MICHAEL L. PRINTZ AWARD

For excellence in writing literature for young adults:

Geraldine McCaughrean, author, *The White Darkness*
Honor Books
Elizabeth Knox, author, *Dreamquake: Book Two of the Dreamhunter Duet*
Judith Clarke, author, *One Whole and Perfect Day*
A.M. Jenkins, author, *Repossessed*
Stephanie Hemphill, author, *Your Own, Sylvia: A Verse Portrait of Sylvia Plath*

ROBERT F. SIBERT AWARD

For most distinguished informational book for children published in 2007:

Peter Sis, illustrator and author, *The Wall: Growing Up Behind the Iron Curtain*

Honor Books

Brian Floca, illustrator and author, *Lightship*

Nic Bishop, illustrator and author, *Nic Bishop Spiders*

PURA BELPRÉ AWARDS

For the Latino author whose work best portrays, celebrates and affirms Latino culture in a children's book:

Margarita Engle, author, *The Poet Slave of Cuba: A Biography of Juan Francisco Manzano*

Honor Books—Authors

Carmen T. Bernier-Grand, author, *Frida: ¡Viva la vida! Long Live Life!*

Carmen Agra Deedy, author, *Martina the Beautiful Cockroach: A Cuban Folktale,* illustrated by Michael Austin

Marisa Montes, author, *Los Gatos Black on Halloween,* illustrated by Yuyi Morales

For the Latino illustrator whose work best portrays, celebrates and affirms Latino culture in a children's book:

Yuyi Moralez, illustrator, *Los Gatos Black on Halloween*

Honor Books—Illustrators

Raúl Colón, illustrator, *My Name Is Gabito: The Life of Gabriel García Márquez/Me llamo Gabito: la vida de Gabriel García Márquez,* written by Monica Brown

Maya Christina Gonzales, illustrator and author, *My Colors, My World/Mis colores, mi mundo*

THEODOR SEUSS GEISEL MEDAL

For the author and illustrator of the most distinguished contribution to the body of American children's literature known as beginning reader books published in 2007:

Mo Willems, author and illustrator, *There Is a Bird on Your Head!*

Honor Books can be found at www.ala.org

MILDRED L. BATCHELDER AWARD

For the best children's book in English translation (first published in a foreign country) published in the US:

VIZ Media, publisher, *Brave Story,* written by Miyuki Miyabe, translated from the Japanese by Alexander O. Smith

Honor Books can be found at www.ala.org

ANDREW CARNEGIE MEDAL FOR EXCELLENCE IN CHILDREN'S VIDEO

Kevin Lafferty, producer, *Jump In: Freestyle Edition*

MAY HILL ARBUTHNOT LECTURE AWARD

Walter Dean Myers, recipient

MARGARET A. EDWARDS AWARD

For lifetime achievement in writing books for young adults:

Orson Scott Card, recipient

THE MAN BOOKER PRIZE

Given annually to the best full-length novel written in English by a citizen of the UK, the Commonwealth, Eire, Pakistan, or South Africa.

The Gathering, Anne Enright

Shortlisted titles

Darkmans, Nicola Barker

The Reluctant Fundamentalist, Mohsin Hamid

Mister Pip, Lloyd Jones

On Chesil Beach, Ian McEwan

Animal's People, Indra Sinha

COSTA/WHITBREAD BOOK AWARDS 2007

An award given to celebrate the most enjoyable British writing of the year.

Novel: *Day,* A.L. Kennedy

First Novel: *What Was Lost,* Catherine O'Flynn

Poetry: *Tilt,* Jean Sprackland

Biography: *Young Stalin,* Simon Sebag Montefiore

Children's Book: *The Bower Bird,* Ann Kelley

Book of the Year: *Day,* A.L. Kennedy

2007 ORANGE PRIZE FOR FICTION

A British award celebrating the excellence of women's writing.

The Road Home, Rose Tremain

THE EDGAR AWARDS 2008

The Mystery Writers of America honor the best in mystery writing produced in the previous year. Named in honor of Edgar Allan Poe.

Best Novel: *Down River,* John Hart

Best First Novel by an American Author: *In the Woods,* Tana French

Best Paperback Original: *Queenpin,* Megan Abbott

Best Critical/Biographical Work: *Arthur Conan Doyle: A Life in Letters,* Jon Lellenberg, Daniel Stashower and Charles Foley

Best Fact Crime: *Reclaiming History: The Assassination of President John F. Kennedy,* Vincent Bugliosi

Best Short Story: "The Golden Gopher" in *Los Angeles Noir,* Susan Straight

Best Young Adult: *Rat Life,* Tedd Arnold

Best Juvenile: *The Night Tourist,* Katherine Marsh

Best Play: *Panic,* Joseph Goodrich

Best Television Episode Teleplay: "Pilot," *Burn Notice,* Matt Nix

Best Motion Picture Screenplay: *Michael Clayton,* Tony Gilroy

Grand Master: Bill Pronzini

Robert L. Fish Award: "The Catch," Mark Ammons

Raven Award: Kate's Mystery Books, North Cambridge, MA (Kate Mattes, owner); Library of Congress, Center for the Book

Mary Higgins Clark Award: *Wild Indigo,* Sandi Ault

THE HUGO AWARDS 2007

Also known as the Science Fiction Achievement Award, given annually by the World Science Fiction Society. 53rd annual awards.

Best Novel: *Rainbows End,* Vernor Vinge

Best Novella: "A Billion Eyes," Robert Reed

Best Novelette: "The Djinn's Wife," Ian McDonald

Best Related Nonfiction Book: *James Tiptree Jr: The Double Life of Alice B Sheldon,* Julie Phillips

Best Short Story: "Impossible Dreams," Tim Pratt

THE NEBULA AWARDS 2007

43rd annual awards given by Science Fiction and Fantasy Writers of America, Inc.

Novel: *The Yiddish Policemen's Union,* Michael Chabon

Novella: "Fountain of Age," Nancy Kress

Novelette: "The Merchant and the Alchemist's Gate," Ted Chiang

Script: *Pan's Labyrinth,* Guillermo del Toro

Short Story: "Always," Karen Joy Fowler

THE LAMBDA LITERARY AWARDS

20th annual, to recognize excellence in lesbian/gay/bisexual/transgender (LGBT) literature, for works published in 2007.

Men's Fiction: *Call Me by Your Name,* Andre Aciman
Men's Romance: *Changing Tides,* Michael Thomas Ford
Men's Mystery: *Murder in the Rue Chartres,* Greg Herren
Men's Memoir/Biography: *Mississippi Sissy,* Kevin Sessums
Women's Fiction: *The IHOP Papers,* Ali Liebegott
Women's Romance: *Out of Love,* K.G. MacGregor
Women's Mystery: *Wall of Silence,* Gabrielle Goldsby
Women's Memoir/Biography: *And Now We Are Going to Have a Party,* Nicola Griffith
LGBT Anthology: *First Person Queer,* edited by Richard Labonte and Lawrence Schimel
LGBT Arts and Culture: *The View from Here,* Matthew Hays
LGBT Children/Young Adult: *Hero,* Perry Moore
LGBT Drama/Theater: *Return to the Caffe Cino,* edited by Steve Susoyev and George Birimisa
LGBT Erotica: *Homosex: 60 Years of Gay Erotica,* Simon Sheppard
LGBT Nonfiction: *Gay Artists in Modern American Culture,* Michael S. Sherry
LGBT Poetry: *Blackbird and Wolf,* Henri Cole
LGBT Science Fiction/Fantasy/Horror: *The Dust of Wonderland,* Lee Thomas
LGBT Studies: *Between Women,* Sharon Marcus
Bisexual: *Split Screen,* Brent Hartinger
Transgender: *Transparent,* Cris Beam
Debut Gay Fiction: *A Push and a Shove,* Christopher Kelly
Debut Lesbian Fiction: *Among Other Things, I've Taken Up Smoking,* Aoibheann Sweeney

THE JAMES BEARD FOUNDATION/KITCHENAID BOOK AWARDS 2007

Given annually to the best original, English-language books on culinary topics published in the previous year.

Asian Cooking: *My Bombay Kitchen: Traditional and Modern Parsi Home Cooking,* Niloufer Ichaporia King
Baking & Dessert: *Peter Reinhart's Whole Grain Breads: New Techniques, Extraordinary Flavor,* Peter Reinhart
Cooking from a Professional Point of View: *The Fundamental Techniques of Classic Cuisine,* The French Culinary Institute with Judith Choate
Entertaining and Special Occasions: *Dish Entertains,* Trish Magwood
Food of the Americas: *A Love Affair with Southern Cooking,* Jean Anderson
General: *Cooking,* James Peterson
Healthy Focus: *The EatingWell Diet,* Jean Harvey-Berino with Joyce Hendley and the editors of *EatingWell* magazine
International: *The Country Cooking of France,* Anne Willan
Photography: France Ruffenach, photographer, *The Country Cooking of France,* Anne Willan
Reference: *A Geography of Oysters: The Connoisseur's Guide to Oyster Eating in North America,* Rowan Jacobsen
Single Subject: *The River Cottage Meat Book,* Hugh Fearnley-Whittingstall
Wines and Spirits: *Imbibe!: From Absinthe Cocktail to Whiskey Smash, a Salute in Stories and Drinks to "Professor" Jerry Thomas, Pioneer of the American Bar,* David Wondrich
Writing on Food: *Animal, Vegetable, Miracle: A Year of Food Life,* Barbara Kingsolver
Kitchenaid Cookbook Hall of Fame: *Couscous and Other Good Food from Morocco,* Paula Wolfert
Kitchenaid Cookbook of the Year: *The River Cottage Meat Book,* Hugh Fearnley-Whittingstall

AWARDS FOR MUSIC

2007 AMERICAN MUSIC AWARDS

35th Annual Awards

Pop/Rock

Male Artist: Justin Timberlake
Female Artist: Fergie
Band, Duo or Group: Nickelback
Album: *Daughtry,* Daughtry

Soul/Rhythm & Blues

Male Artist: Akon
Female Artist: Rihanna
Album: *FutureSex/LoveSounds,* Justin Timberlake

Country

Male Artist: Tim McGraw
Female Artist: Carrie Underwood
Band, Duo or Group: Rascal Flatts
Album: *Some Hearts,* Carrie Underwood

Rap/Hip-Hop

Male Artist: T.I.
Band, Duo or Group: Bone Thugs-n-Harmony
Album: *T.T. vs. T.I.P.,* T.I.

Adult Contemporary

Artist: Daughtry

Alternative Music

Artist: Linkin Park

Latin

Artist: Jennifer Lopez

Contemporary Inspirational

Artist: Casting Crowns

Breakthrough

Artist: Daughtry

2007 COUNTRY MUSIC AWARDS

41st Annual Awards

Entertainer of the Year: Kenny Chesney
Male Vocalist of the Year: Brad Paisley
Female Vocalist of the Year: Carrie Underwood
Horizon Award: Taylor Swift
Vocal Group of the Year: Rascal Flatts
Vocal Duo of the Year: Sugarland
Single of the Year: "Before He Cheats," Carrie Underwood; Mark Bright, producer
Album of the Year: *It Just Comes Natural,* George Strait; Tony Brown and George Strait, producers
Song of the Year: "Give It Away," Bill Anderson, Buddy Cannon and Jamey Johnson
Musical Event of the Year: Tracy Lawrence featuring Tim McGraw and Kenny Chesney: "Find Out Who Your Friends Are"
Music Video of the Year: "Online," Brad Paisley; Jason Alexander, director
Musician of the Year: Jerry Douglas—dobro

2008 DOVE AWARDS

39th Annual Awards, Presented by the Gospel Music Association

Song of the Year: "East to West," Mark Hall and Bernie Herms
Songwriter of the Year: Cindy Morgan
Male Vocalist of the Year: Chris Tomlin
Female Vocalist of the Year: Natalie Grant
Group of the Year: Casting Crowns
Artist of the Year: tobyMac
New Artist of the Year: Brandon Heath
Producer of the Year: Ian Eskelin
Rap/Hip Hop Recorded Song: "Name Droppin'," T-Bone
Rap/Hip Hop Album: *Group 1 Crew,* Group 1 Crew
Rock Recorded Song: "Comatose," Skillet
Rock Album: *Scars Remain,* Disciple
Rock/Contemporary Recorded Song: "Everything Glorious," David Crowder*Band
Rock/Contemporary Album: *Portable Sounds,* tobyMac
Pop/Contemporary Recorded Song: "East to West," Casting Crowns
Pop/Contemporary Album: *The Altar and the Door,* Casting Crowns
Inspirational Recorded Song: "By His Wounds," Steven Curtis Chapman
Inspirational Album: *I Love to Tell the Story, a Hymns Collection;* Mark Lowry
Southern Gospel Recorded Song: "Get Away, Jordan"; Ernie Haase & Signature Sound
Southern Gospel Album: *Get Away, Jordan;* Ernie Haase & Signature Sound
Bluegrass Recorded Song: "He's in Control," Austins Bridge
Bluegrass Album: *Salt of the Earth,* Ricky Skaggs & The Whites
Country Recorded Song: "How You Live (Turn Up the Music)," Point of Grace
Country Album: *Big Sky,* The Isaacs
Urban Recorded Song: "Listen," Trin-I-Tee 5:7
Urban Album: *T57,* Trin-I-Tee 5:7
Traditional Gospel Recorded Song: "Ready for a Miracle," LeAnn Rimes
Traditional Gospel Album: *Past and Present,* Lillie Knauls
Contemporary Gospel Recorded Song: "Say So," Israel & New Breed
Contemporary Gospel Album: *A Deeper Level,* Israel & New Breed
Worship Song: "How Great Is Our God," Chris Tomlin, Jesse Reeves and Ed Cash
Worship Album: *Remedy,* David Crowder*Band
Instrumental Album: *Amazing Grace (Original Score),* David Arnold
Christmas Album: *It's a Wonderful Christmas,* Michael W. Smith
Children's Music Album: *VeggieTales Christian Hit Music,* VeggieTales
Spanish Language Album: *De Corazon a Corazon,* Seth Condrey
Special Event Album: *Glory Revealed,* various artists
Musical: *Amazing Grace—My Chains Are Gone,* Dennis & Nan Allen
Youth/Children's Musical: *Praise Rocks,* Gina Boe, Barb Dorn, Sue C. Smith and Brian Green
Recorded Music Packaging: *Remedy,* David Crowther*Band
Short Form Music Video: "Boomin'," tobyMac
Long Form Music Video: *Live from Hawaii,* Audio Adrenaline

2008 GRAMMY AWARDS

Record of the Year: "Rehab," Amy Winehouse
Album of the Year: *River: The Joni Letters,* Herbie Hancock
Song of the Year: "Rehab," Amy Winehouse, songwriter (Amy Winehouse)
Best New Artist: Amy Winehouse
Best Female Pop Vocal Performance: "Rehab," Amy Winehouse
Best Male Pop Vocal Performance: "What Goes Around . . . Comes Around," Justin Timberlake
Best Pop Performance by a Duo or Group with Vocals: "Makes Me Wonder," Maroon 5
Best Pop Collaboration with Vocals: "Gone Gone Gone (Done Moved On)," Robert Plant and Alison Krauss
Best Pop Instrumental Performance: "One Week Last Summer," Joni Mitchell
Best Pop Instrumental Album: *The Mix-Up,* Beastie Boys
Best Pop Vocal Album: *Back to Black,* Amy Winehouse
Best Dance Recording: "LoveStoned/I Think She Knows," Justin Timberlake and Timbaland
Best Electronic/Dance Album: *We Are the Night,* The Chemical Brother
Best Traditional Pop Vocal Album: *Call Me Irresponsible,* Michael Buble
Best Solo Rock Vocal Performance: "Radio Nowhere," Bruce Springsteen
Best Rock Performance by a Duo or Group with Vocals: "Icky Thump," The White Stripes
Best Hard Rock Performance: "The Pretender," Foo Fighters
Best Metal Performance: "Final Six," Slayer
Best Rock Instrumental Performance: "Once Upon a Time in the West," Bruce Springsteen
Best Rock Song: "Radio Nowhere," Bruce Springsteen, songwriter (Bruce Springsteen)
Best Rock Album: *Echoes, Silence, Patience & Grace,* Foo Fighters
Best Alternative Music Album: *Icky Thump,* The White Stripes
Best Female R&B Vocal Performance: "No One," Alicia Keys
Best Male R&B Vocal Performance: "Future Baby Mama," Prince
Best R&B Performance by a Duo or Group with Vocals: "Disrepectful," Chaka Khan featuring Mary J. Blige
Best Traditional R&B Vocal Performance: "In My Songs," Gerald Levert
Best Urban/Alternative Performance: "Daydreamin'," Lupe Fiasco featuring Jill Scott
Best R&B Song: "No One," Dirty Harry, Kerry Brothers and Alicia Keys, songwriters (Alicia Keys)
Best R&B Album: *Funk This,* Chaka Khan
Best Contemporary R&B Album: *Because of You,* Ne-Yo
Best Rap Solo Performance: "Stronger," Kanye West
Best Rap Performance by a Duo or Group: "Southside," Common featuring Kanye West
Best Rap/Sung Collaboration: "Umbrella," Rihanna featuring Jay-Z
Best Rap Song: "Good Life," Aldrin Davis, Mike Dean, Faheem Najm and Kanye West, songwriters (Kanye West featuring T-Pain)
Best Rap Album: *Graduation,* Kanye West
Best Female Country Vocal Performance: "Before He Cheats," Carrie Underwood
Best Male Country Vocal Performance: "Stupid Boy," Keith Urban

Best Country Performance by a Duo or Group with Vocals: "How Long," Eagles
Best Country Collaboration with Vocals: "Lost Highway," Willie Nelson and Ray Price
Best Country Instrumental Performance: "Throttleneck," Brad Paisley
Best Country Song: "Before He Cheats," Josh Kear and Chris Tompkins, songwriters (Carrie Underwood)
Best Country Album: *These Days,* Vince Gill
Best Traditional Blues Album: *Last of the Great Mississippi Delta Bluesmen: Live in Dallas,* Henry James Townsend, Joe Willie "Pinetop" Perkins, Robert Lockwood Jr and David "Honeyboy" Edwards
Best Contemporary Blues Album: *The Road to Escondido,* J.J. Cale and Eric Clapton
Best Bluegrass Album: *The Bluegrass Diaries,* Jim Lauderdale
Best New Age Album: *Crestone,* Paul Winter Consort
Best Contemporary Jazz Album: *River: The Joni Letters,* Herbie Hancock
Best Jazz Vocal Album: *Avant Gershwin,* Patti Austin
Best Jazz Instrumental Solo: "Anagram," Michael Brecker, soloist
Best Jazz Instrumental Album, Individual or Group: *Pilgrimage,* Michael Brecker
Best Large Jazz Ensemble Album: *A Tale of God's Will (A Requiem for Katrina),* Terence Blanchard
Best Latin Jazz Album: *Funk Tango,* Paquito D'Rivera Quintet
Best Latin Pop Album: *El Tren de los Momentos,* Alejandro Sanz
Best Latin Rock or Alternative Album: *No Hay Espacio,* Black:Guayaba
Best Latin Urban Album: *Residente o Visitante,* Calle 13
Best Tropical Latin Album: *La Llave de Mi Corazon,* Juan Luis Guerra
Best Mexican/Mexican-American Album: *100 (Percent) Mexicano,* Pepe Aguilar
Best Tejano Album: *Before the Next Teardrop Falls,* Little Joe & La Familia
Best Norteño Album: *Detalles y Emociones,* Los Tigres del Norte
Best Banda Album: *Te Va a Gustar,* El Chapo
Best Traditional Folk Album: *Dirt Farmer,* Levon Helm
Best Contemporary Folk/Americana Album: *Washington Square Serenade,* Steve Earle
Best Native American Music Album: *Totemic Flute Chants,* Johnny Whitehorse
Best Hawaiian Music Album: *Treasures of Hawaiian Slack Key Guitar,* various artists
Best Zydeco or Cajun Music Album: *Live! Worldwide,* Terrance Simien & The Zydeco Experience
Best Reggae Album: *Mind Control,* Stephen Marley
Best Traditional World Music Album: *African Spirit,* Soweto Gospel Choir
Best Contemporary World Music Album: *Djin Djin,* Angelique Kidjo
Best Polka Album: *Come Share the Wine,* Jimmy Sturr and His Orchestra
Best Gospel Performance: **TIE:** "Blessed & Highly Favored," The Clark Sisters; and "Never Gonna Break My Faith," Aretha Franklin and Mary J. Blige (featuring the Harlem Boys Choir)
Best Gospel Song: "Blessed & Highly Favored," Karen Clark-Sheard, songwriter (The Clark Sisters)
Best Rock or Rap Gospel Album: *Before the Daylight's Shot,* Ashley Cleveland
Best Pop/Contemporary Gospel Album: *A Deeper Level,* Israel and New Breed
Best Southern, Country or Bluegrass Gospel Album: *Salt of the Earth,* Ricky Skaggs & The Whites
Best Traditional Gospel Album: *Live—One Last Time,* The Clark Sisters
Best Contemporary R&B Gospel Album: *Free to Worship,* Fred Hammond
Best Musical Album for Children: *A Green and Red Christmas,* The Muppets
Best Spoken Word Album for Children: *Harry Potter and the Deathly Hallows,* Jim Dale
Best Spoken Word Album: *The Audacity of Hope: Thoughts on Reclaiming the American Dream,* Barack Obama
Best Comedy Album: *The Distant Future,* Flight of the Conchords
Best Musical Show Album: *Spring Awakening*
Best Compilation Soundtrack Album for a Motion Picture, Television or Other Visual Media: *Love,* The Beatles
Best Score Soundtrack Album for a Motion Picture, Television or Other Visual Media: *Ratatouille,* Michael Giacchino, composer
Best Song Written for a Motion Picture, Television or Other Visual Media: "Love You I Do" (from *Dreamgirls*), Siedah Garrett and Henry Krieger, songwriters (Jennifer Hudson)
Best Instrumental Composition: "Cerulean Skies," Maria Schneider, composer (Maria Schneider Orchestra)
Best Instrumental Arrangement: "In a Silent Way," Vince Mendoza, arranger (Joe Zawinul)
Best Instrumental Arrangement with Accompanying Vocalist(s): "I'm Gonna Live Till I Die," John Clayton, arranger (Queen Latifah)
Best Engineered Album, Nonclassical: *Beauty & Crime,* Tchad Blake, Cameron Craig, Emery Dobyns and Jimmy Hogarth, engineers (Suzanne Vega)
Producer of the Year, Nonclassical: Mark Ronson
Best Remixed Recording, Nonclassical: *Bring the Noise (Benny Benassi Sfaction Remix),* Benny Benassi, remixer (Public Enemy)
Best Surround Sound Album: *Love,* Paul Hicks and Tim Young, engineers (The Beatles)
Best Engineered Album, Classical: *Grechaninov: Passion Week,* John Newton, engineer (Charles Bruffy, Phoenix Bach Choir and Kansas City Chorale)
Producer of the Year, Classical: Judith Sherman
Best Classical Album: *Tower: Made in America,* Leonard Slatkin, conductor; Tim Handley, producer (Nashville Symphony)
Best Orchestral Performance: *Tower: Made in America,* Leonard Slatkin, conductor (Nashville Symphony)
Best Opera Recording: *Humperdinck: Hansel & Gretel,* Sir Charles Mackerras, conductor; Rebecca Evans, Jane Henschel and Jennifer Larmore; Brian Couzens, producer (Sarah Coppen, Diana Montague and Sarah Tynan; New London Children's Choir; Philharmonia Orchestra)
Best Choral Performance: *Brahms: Ein Deutsches Requiem,* Simon Rattle, conductor; Simon Halsey, chorus master (Thomas Quasthoff and Dorothea Roschmann; Rundfunkchor Berlin; Berliner Philharmoniker)
Best Instrumental Soloist(s) Performance (with Orchestra): *Barber/Korngold/Walton: Violin Concertos,* Bramwell Tovey, conductor; James Ehnes (Vancouver Symphony Orchestra)
Best Instrumental Soloist Performance (Without Orchestra): *Beethoven Sonatas, Vol. 3,* Garrick Ohlsson
Best Chamber Music Performance: *Strange Imaginary Animals,* Eighth Blackbird
Best Small Ensemble Album Performance: *Stravinsky: Apollo, Concerto in D; Prokofiev: 20 Visions Fugutives,* Yuri Bashmet, conductor; Moscow Soloists
Best Classical Vocal Performance: *Lorraine Hunt Lieberson Sings Peter Lieberson: Neruda Songs,* Lorraine Hunt Lieberson, soloist
Best Classical Contemporary Composition: *Made in America,* Joan Tower, composer
Best Classical Crossover Album: *A Love Supreme: The Legacy of John Coltrane,* Turtle Island Quartet
Best Music Video, Short Form: *God's Gonna Cut You Down,* Johnny Cash
Best Music Video, Long Form: *The Confessions Tour,* Madonna
Best Recording Package: *Cassadaga,* Zachary Nipper, art director (Bright Eyes)
Best Boxed or Special Limited Edition Recording Package: *What It Is!: Funky Soul and Rare Grooves (1967–1977),* Masaki Koike, art director (various artists)
Best Album Notes: *John Work III: Recording Black Culture,* Bruce Nemerov, album notes writer (various artists)
Best Historical Album: *The Live Wire—Woody Guthrie in Performance 1949,* Nora Guthrie and Jorge Arevalo Mateus, compilation producers; Jamie Howarth, Steve Rosenthal, Warren Russell-Smith and Dr. Kevin Short, mastering engineers (Woody Guthrie)

THE NATIONAL FILM REGISTRY

Under the terms of the National Film Preservation Act, each year the Librarian of Congress names 25 "culturally, historically or aesthetically" significant motion pictures to the Registry. The list is designed to reflect the full breadth and diversity of America's film heritage, thus increasing public awareness of the richness of American cinema and the need for its preservation. A film must be at least ten years old to be considered. These are the 2007 additions to the archive; the full list can be found at www.loc.gov/film/titles.html.

Back to the Future (1985)
Bullitt (1968)
Close Encounters of the Third Kind (1977)
Dance, Girl, Dance (1940)
Dances with Wolves (1990)
Days of Heaven (1978)
Glimpse of the Garden (1957)
Grand Hotel (1932)
"The House I Live In" (1945)
In a Lonely Place (1950)
The Man Who Shot Liberty Valance (1962)
"Mighty Like a Moose" (1926)
The Naked City (1948)
Now, Voyager (1942)
Oklahoma! (1955)
"Our Day" (1938)
Peege (1972)
"The Sex Life of the Polyp" (1940)
The Strong Man (1926)
"Three Little Pigs" (1933)
Tol'able David (1921)
Tom, Tom the Piper's Son (1969–71)
12 Angry Men (1957)
The Women (1939)
Wuthering Heights (1939)

THE NATIONAL RECORDING REGISTRY

Founded in 2002 by the National Recording Preservation Board at the Library of Congress, the National Recording Registry maintains and preserves sound recordings and collections of sound recordings that are culturally, historically or aesthetically significant. These are the 2007 additions to the archive; the full list can be found at www.loc.gov/rr/record/nrpb.

The First Trans-Atlantic Broadcast (March 14, 1925)
"Allons a Lafayette," performed by Joseph Falcon (1928)
"Casta Diva," from Bellini's *Norma*, performed by Rosa Ponselle, accompanied by the Metropolitan Opera Orchestra and Chorus, conducted by Giulio Setti (Dec 31, 1928, and Jan 30, 1929)
"If I Could Hear My Mother Pray Again," performed by Thomas A. Dorsey (1934)
"Sweet Lorraine," performed by Art Tatum (Feb 22, 1940)
Fibber's Closet Opens for the First Time, "Fibber McGee and Molly" radio program (March 4, 1940)
"Wings Over Jordan" television broadcast, performed by Wings Over Jordan (1941)
Fiorello LaGuardia reading the comics (1945)
"Call It Stormy Monday but Tuesday Is Just as Bad," performed by T-Bone Walker (1947)
Harry S Truman speech at the 1948 Democratic National Convention (July 15, 1948)
"The Jazz Scene," performed by various artists, produced by Norman Granz (1949)
"It Wasn't God Who Made Honky Tonk Angels," performed by Kitty Wells (May 30, 1952)
"My Fair Lady," performed by the original Broadway cast (1956)
Navajo Shootingway Ceremony Field Recordings, recorded by David McAllester (1957–58)
"'Freight Train,' and Other North Carolina Folk Songs and Tunes," performed by Elizabeth Cotten (1959)
Marine Band Concert Album to Help Benefit the National Cultural Center (1963)
"Oh, Pretty Woman," performed by Roy Orbison (1964)
"Tracks of My Tears," performed by Smokey Robinson and the Miracles (1965)
"You'll Sing a Song and I'll Sing a Song," performed by Ella Jenkins (1966)
Music from the "Morning of the World," performed by various artists; recorded by David Lewiston (1966)
"For the Roses," performed by Joni Mitchell (1972)
"Headhunters," performed by Herbie Hancock (1973)
Ronald Reagan radio broadcasts (1976–79)
"The Sounds of Earth," disc prepared for the *Voyager* spacecraft (1977)
"Thriller," performed by Michael Jackson (1982)

Index

A
Aames, Willie: Birth, Jul 15
Aaron, Hank: Birth, Feb 5
Aaron, Hank: Home Run Record: Anniv, Apr 8
Abbado, Claudio: Birth, Jun 26
Abbott and Costello Show TV Premiere: Anniv, Dec 5
Abbott, Berenice: Birth Anniv, Jul 17
Abbott, Jim: Birth, Sep 19
Abdul, Paula: Birth, Jun 19
Abdul-Jabbar, Kareem: Birth, Apr 16
Aberdeen Intl Youth Fest (Aberdeen, Scotland), Jul 29
Abolition Society Founded, First American: Anniv, Apr 14
Abortion Counseling, Supreme Court Upholds Ban: Anniv, May 23
Abortion First Legalized: Anniv, Apr 25
Abortion: Roe v Wade Supreme Court Decision: Anniv, Jan 22
Abraham, F. Murray: Birth, Oct 24
Abrams, J.J.: Birth, Jun 27
Abuse: Day of Hope, Natl, Apr 1
Abuse: Heal the Children Month, May 1
Abuse: Mend a Heart Broken Month, Natl, Feb 1
Abuse: Respect Day, Natl, Sep 18
Abused Women and Children's Awareness Day, Jun 14
Academy Awards Presentation, Feb 22
Academy Awards, First: Anniv, May 16
Acadia Natl Park Established: Anniv, Jan 1
According to Hoyle Day, Aug 29
Accordion Awareness Month, Natl, Jun 1
Accordion Chmpshps, Kimberley Intl Old-time (Kimberley, BC, Canada), Jul 6
Ace, Goodman: Birth Anniv, Jan 15
Acevedo Vila, Anibal: Birth, Feb 13
Achelis, Elisabeth: Birth Anniv, Jan 24
Ackland, Joss: Birth, Feb 29
Act Happy Week, Mar 16
Acuff, Roy: Birth Anniv, Sep 15
Adams County Fair/Rodeo (Hettinger, ND), Jul 29
Adams, Abigail: Birth Anniv, Nov 22
Adams, Amy: Birth, Aug 20
Adams, Ansel: Birth Anniv, Feb 20
Adams, Brooke: Birth, Feb 8
Adams, Bryan: Birth, Nov 5
Adams, Edie: Birth, Apr 16
Adams, Joey Lauren: Birth, Jan 6
Adams, John Quincy: Birth Anniv, Jul 11
Adams, John Quincy: Returns to Congress: Anniv, Mar 4
Adams, John, and Jefferson, Thomas: Death Anniv, Jul 4
Adams, John: Birth Anniv, Oct 30
Adams, Louisa Catherine Johnson: Birth Anniv, Feb 12
Adams, Maud: Birth, Feb 12
Adams, Samuel: Birth Anniv, Sep 27
Adams, Scott: Birth, Jun 8
Addai, Joseph: Birth, May 3
Addams Family TV Premiere: Anniv, Sep 18
Addams, Charles: Birth Anniv, Jan 7
Addams, Jane: Birth Anniv, Sep 6
Adding Machine, Patent Issued for First: Anniv, Oct 11
Addison, Joseph: Birth Anniv, May 1
Adjani, Isabelle: Birth, Jun 27
Administrative Professionals Day, Apr 22
Administrative Professionals Intl Conv (Minneapolis, MN), Jul 26
Administrative Professionals Week, Apr 19
Adolfo: Birth, Feb 15
Adopt-a-Shelter-Cat Month, Jun 1
Adopt-a-Shelter-Dog Month, Oct 1
Adoption Month, Natl, Nov 1
Adult Immunization Awareness Week, Natl, Sep 20
Advent, First Sunday, Nov 29
Adventures of Ellery Queen TV Premiere: Anniv, Oct 14
Advertising: Co-Op Awareness Month, Oct 1
Advertising: Mobius Awards (Los Angeles, CA), Feb 7
Affleck, Ben: Birth, Aug 15
Affleck, Casey: Birth, Aug 12
Afghanistan
  Fall of Kabul: Anniv, Nov 13
  Independence Day, Aug 19
  Soviet Troop Withdrawal Deadline, Feb 15
AFL Founded: Anniv, Dec 8
AFL-CIO Founded: Anniv, Dec 5
Africa Industrialization Day (UN), Nov 20
African American
  African American History Month, Natl, Feb 1
  African Burial Ground Natl Monument Established: Anniv, Feb 27
  African Methodist Episcopal Church Organized: Anniv, Apr 9
  African-American Coaches Day, Feb 3
  African-American Women's Fitness Month, Natl, Apr 1
  Alpha Kappa Alpha Sorority Founded: Anniv, Jan 15
  Amistad Seized: Anniv, Aug 29
  Anderson, Marian: Easter Concert: Anniv, Apr 9
  Attack on Fort Wagner: Anniv, Jul 19
  Black Business Month, Aug 1
  Black History Month, Natl, Feb 1
  Black Page Appointed to US House: Anniv, Apr 9
  Black Press Day: Anniv of First Black Newspaper in US, Mar 16
  Black Senate Page Appointed: Anniv, Apr 8
  Black Single Parents' Week, May 31
  Blacks Ruled Eligible to Vote: Anniv, Apr 3
  Chisholm, Shirley: Birth Anniv, Nov 30
  Civil Rights Act of 1964: Anniv, Jul 2
  Civil Rights Bill of 1866: Anniv, Apr 9
  Civil Rights Workers Found Slain: Anniv, Aug 4
  Desegregation, US Army First: Anniv, Jul 26
  Dream Day Quest and Jubilee, Aug 28
  Dred Scott Decision: Anniv, Mar 6
  Ebony Magazine: Anniv, Nov 1
  Emancipation of 500: Anniv, Aug 1
  Escape to Freedom (F. Douglass): Anniv, Sep 3
  First American Abolition Society Founded: Anniv, Apr 14
  First Black Governor Elected: Anniv, Nov 7
  First Black Heavyweight Champion: Anniv, Dec 26
  First Black Plays in NBA Game: Anniv, Oct 31
  First Black Receives Congressional Medal: Anniv, May 23
  First Black Serves in US House of Representatives: Anniv, Dec 12
  First Black US Cabinet Member: Anniv, Jan 18
  First Black US State's Attorney: Anniv, Jul 6
  First Natl Convention for Blacks: Anniv, Sep 15
  Freedom Riders: Anniv, May 4
  From Africa to Virginia Month (Williamsburg, VA), Feb 1
  Greensboro Sit-In: Anniv, Feb 1
  Harlem Globetrotters Play First Game: Anniv, Jan 7
  Historically Black Colleges and Universities Week, Natl (Pres Proc), Sep 13
  Jackie Robinson Breaks Baseball Color Line: Anniv, Apr 15
  Johnson, John H.: Birth Anniv, Jan 19
  Juneteenth, Jun 19
  King Awarded Nobel Peace Prize: Anniv, Oct 14
  Kwanzaa Fest, Dec 26
  Links, Inc: Anniv, Nov 9
  Little Rock Nine: Anniv, Sep 4
  Malcolm X Assassinated: Anniv, Feb 21
  Malcolm X: Birth Anniv, May 19
  Marshall, Thurgood: Birth Anniv, Jul 2
  Marshall, Thurgood: Resigns from Supreme Court: Anniv, Jun 27
  Marshall, Thurgood: Sworn in to Supreme Court: Anniv, Oct 2
  Medgar Evers Assassinated: Anniv, Jun 13
  Meredith (James) Enrolls at Ole Miss: Anniv, Sep 30
  Million Man March: Anniv, Oct 16
  Minority Enterprise Development Week (Pres Proc), Aug 30
  Montgomery Boycott Arrests: Anniv, Feb 22
  Montgomery Bus Boycott Begins: Anniv, Dec 5
  Montgomery Bus Boycott Ends: Anniv, Dec 20
  NAACP Founded: Anniv, Feb 12
  New York Slave Revolt: Anniv, Apr 7
  Niagara Movement Founded: Anniv, Jul 11
  Parks, Rosa: Birth Anniv, Feb 4
  Ralph Bunche Awarded Nobel Peace Prize: Anniv, Dec 10
  Robinson Named Baseball's First Black Manager: Anniv, Oct 3
  Rosa Parks Day, Dec 1
  Saint Louis Race Riots: Anniv, Jul 2
  Scottsboro Trial: Anniv, Apr 6
  Shaping Black Culture in the Diaspora (Los Angeles, CA), Oct 9
  16th Street Baptist Church Bombing: Anniv, Sep 15

Soul Food Month, Natl, Jun 1
Spelman College Established: Anniv, Apr 11
Stokes Becomes First Black Mayor in US: Anniv, Nov 13
Truth, Sojourner: Death Anniv, Nov 26
Tubman, Harriet: Death Anniv, Mar 10
Tuskegee Airmen Activated: Anniv, Mar 22
Tuskegee Institute Opening: Anniv, Jul 4
Wheatley, Phillis: Poetry Collection Published: Anniv, Sep 1
Zora Neale Hurston Fest (Eatonville, FL), Jan 20
African Diaspora Day, Intl (Los Angeles, CA), Oct 11
African Natl Congress Ban Lifted, Feb 2
Agassi, Andre: Birth, Apr 29
Agassiz, Louis: Birth Anniv, May 28
Agee, James: Birth Anniv, Nov 27
Aggie Muster, Apr 21
Agnew Resignation: Anniv, Oct 10
Agnew, Spiro: Birth Anniv, Nov 9
Agriculture (including state and county fairs)
Acton Fair (Acton, ME), Aug 27
Agriculture Day, Natl, Mar 20
Agriculture Week, Natl, Mar 15
Agrifair (Abbotsford, BC, Canada), Jul 30
Alabama Natl Fair (Montgomery, AL), Oct 9
Alaska State Fair (Palmer, AK), Aug 27
Arizona State Fair (Phoenix, AZ), Oct 9
Arkansas State Fair (Little Rock, AR), Oct 9
Bangor State Fair (Bangor, ME), Jul 31
Beef Empire Days (Garden City, KS), May 27
Big E (West Springfield, MA), Sep 18
Blue Hill Fair (Blue Hill, ME), Sep 3
Calgary Stampede (Calgary, AB, Canada), Jul 3
California State Fair (Sacramento, CA), Aug 21
Canadian Western Agribition (Regina, SK, Canada), Nov 23
Central Florida Fair (Orlando, FL), Apr 16
Champlain Valley Fair (Essex Junction, VT), Aug 29
Clinton County Corn Fest (Wilmington, OH), Sep 11
Colorado State Fair (Pueblo, CO), Aug 29
Columbia County Fair (Chatham, NY), Sep 2
Comal County Fair (New Braunfels, TX), Sep 23
Common Ground Country Fair (Unity, ME), Sep 25
Corn Palace Fest (Mitchell, SD), Aug 26
Dairy Expo, World (Madison, WI), Sep 29
Delaware State Fair (Harrington, DE), Jul 23
Delmarva Chicken Fest (Centreville, MD), Jun 19
Eastern Idaho State Fair (Blackfoot, ID), Sep 5
Fairfest (Hastings, NE), Jul 22
Farm Safety Week, Natl (Pres Proc), Sep 20
Farm Sanctuary Hoedown (Watkins Glen, NY), Aug 1
Farm Toy Show & Auction (Sauk Centre, MN), Feb 14
Farm-City Week, Natl (Pres Proc), Nov 20
Florida State Fair (Tampa, FL), Feb 5
Fryeburg Fair (Fryeburg, ME), Oct 4
Gage County Fair (Beatrice, NE), Jul 14
Gateway Farm Expo (Kearney, NE), Nov 18
Georgia National Fair (Perry, GA), Oct 8
Grange Month, Apr 1
Harvard Milk Days Fest (Harvard, IL), Jun 5
Hood River County Fair (Hood River, OR), Jul 22
Hoof-Care Summit, Intl (Cincinnati, OH), Feb 3
Hopkinton State Fair (Contoocook, NH), Sep 3
Husker Harvest Days (Grand Island, NE), Sep 15
Illinois State Fair (Springfield, IL), Aug 14
Indiana State Fair (Indianapolis, IN), Aug 7
Iowa State Fair (Des Moines, IA), Aug 13
Kansas State Fair (Hutchinson, KS), Sep 11
Kentucky State Fair (Louisville, KY), Aug 20
Livestock Show, Rio Grande Valley (Mercedes, TX), Mar 13
Louisiana, State Fair of (Shreveport, LA), Oct 22
Madison County Fair (Fredericktown, MO), Oct 1
Marion County Fair (Salem, OR), Jul 9
Maryland State Fair (Timonium, MD), Aug 28
Michigan State Fair (Detroit, MI), Aug 28
Mid-South Fair (Memphis, TN), Sep 18
Minnesota State Fair (St. Paul, MN), Aug 27
Mississippi State Fair (Jackson, MS), Oct 7
Missouri State Fair (Sedalia, MO), Aug 13
Montana State Fair (Great Falls, MT), Jul 24
Montana Winter Fair (Lewistown, MT), Jan 22
MontanaFair (Billings, MT), Aug 7
Montgomery County Agricultural Fair (Gaithersburg, MD), Aug 7
Morrill Land Grant Act Passed: Anniv, Jul 1
Nebraska State Fair (Lincoln, NE), Aug 28
Nevada State Fair (Reno, NV), Aug 26
New Jersey State Fair/Sussex Farm and Horse Show (Augusta, NJ), Jul 31
New Mexico State Fair (Albuquerque, NM), Sep 4
New York State Fair (Syracuse, NY), Aug 27
North Carolina State Fair (Raleigh, NC), Oct 16
North Dakota State Fair (Minot, ND), Jul 24
North Star Classic (Valley City, ND), Dec 3
Northeast Montana Threshing Bee/Antique Show (Culbertson, MT), Sep 26
Northeastern Wisconsin Antique Power and Machinery Show Thresheree (Sturgeon Bay, WI), Aug 14
Northern Intl Livestock Expo (Billings, MT), Oct 10
No-Tillage Conference, Natl (Indianapolis, IN), Jan 14
Nottingham Goose Fair (Nottingham, England), Oct 7
Ohio State Fair (Columbus, OH), Aug 5
Oklahoma State Fair (Oklahoma City, OK), Sep 17
Oregon State Fair (Salem, OR), Aug 28
Organic Harvest Month, Natl, Sep 1
Ozark Fall Farmfest (Springfield, MO), Oct 2
Penn State's Ag Progress Days (Rock Springs, PA), Aug 18
Pennsylvania Farm Show (Harrisburg, PA), Jan 10
Puyallup Fair (Puyallup, WA), Sep 11
Rice Month, Natl, Sep 1
Rotary Tiller Race, World Chmpshp/Purplehull Pea Fest (Emerson, AR), Jun 26
Ruffin, Edmund: Birth Anniv, Jan 5
Rural Life Sunday, May 17
Sheep to Shawl Fest (Savannah, GA), Mar 28
Sioux Empire Fair (Sioux Falls, SD), Aug 11
Sioux Empire Farm Show (Sioux Falls, SD), Jan 27
Sodbuster Days (Fort Ransom, ND), Jul 11
Sodbuster Days—Harvest (Fort Ransom, ND), Sep 12
Sonoma-Marin Fair (Petaluma, CA), Jun 24
South Carolina State Fair (Columbia, SC), Oct 14
South Dakota State Fair (Huron, SD), Sep 3
South Mountain Fair (Arendtsville, PA), Aug 18
Southeast Missouri District Fair (Cape Girardeau, MO), Sep 12
Southwestern Expo Livestock Show/Rodeo (Fort Worth, TX), Jan 16
State Fair of Texas (Dallas, TX), Sep 25
Tennessee State Fair (Nashville, TN), Sep 4
Traditional Plowing Match (Woodstock, VT), May 3
Utah State Fair (Salt Lake City, UT), Sep 10
Vermont State Fair (Rutland, VT), Sep 4
Virginia, State Fair of (Richmond, VA), Sep 24
Wayne Chicken Show (Wayne, NE), Jul 10
West Virginia State Fair (Lewisburg, WV), Aug 14
Western Idaho Fair (Boise, ID), Aug 14
Winter Show (Valley City, ND), Mar 3
Wisconsin State Fair (Milwaukee, WI), Aug 6
Women in Blue Jeans Days, Jan 15
World Ag Expo (Tulare, CA), Feb 10
World Farm Animals Day, Oct 2
Wyoming State Fair & Rodeo (Douglas, WY), Aug 8
Aguilera, Christina: Birth, Dec 18
Agutter, Jenny: Birth, Dec 20
Aida Premieres: Anniv, Dec 24
AIDS
Awareness Month, Natl, Nov 1
Condom Week, Natl, Feb 14
First Noted: Anniv, Jun 5
World AIDS Day (Pres Proc), Dec 1
World AIDS Day (UN), Dec 1
Aiello, Danny, Jr: Birth, Jun 20
Aiken, Conrad: Birth Anniv, Aug 5
Aikman, Troy: Birth, Nov 21
Ailey, Alvin: Birth Anniv, Jan 5
Aimee, Anouk: Birth, Apr 27
Ainge, Danny: Birth, Mar 17
Air Conditioning Appreciation Days, Jul 3

Air Force Academy, US, Established: Anniv, Apr 1
Ajaye, Franklyn: Birth, May 13
Akaka, Daniel K.: Birth, Sep 11
AKC/Eukanuba Natl Chmpshp (Long Beach, CA), Dec 12
Akers, Michelle: Birth, Feb 1
Akihito: Birth, Dec 23
Akinnuoye-Agbaje, Adewale: Birth, Aug 22
Al Qaeda
Attack on America: Anniv, Sep 11
Fall of Kabul: Anniv, Nov 13
London Terrorist Bombings: Anniv, Jul 7
Madrid Train Bombings: Anniv, Mar 11
Alabama
Admission Day, Dec 14
Alabama Renaissance Faire (Florence), Oct 24
American Indian Heritage Day, Oct 12
Battle of Mobile Bay: Anniv, Aug 5
Chilton County Peach Fest (Clanton), Jun 19
Christmas on the River (Demopolis), Nov 29
Confederate Memorial Day, Apr 27
Fireworks Celebration (Demopolis), Jul 4
Helen Keller Fest (Tuscumbia), Jun 25
Interstate Mullet Toss (Orange Beach), Apr 24
Joe Cain Procession (Mobile), Feb 22
NAIA Men's & Women's Tennis Natl Chmpshps (Mobile), May 11
Natl Fair (Montgomery), Oct 9
Panoply (Huntsville), Apr 24
Riley, Bob: Birth, Oct 3
Senior Bowl Football Game (Mobile), Jan 24
Sessions, Jeff: Birth, Dec 24
Shelby, Richard C.: Birth, May 6
Southern Appalachian Dulcimer Fest (McCalla), May 2
Spirit of Freedom Celebration (Florence), Jul 4
Stevenson Depot Days (Stevenson), Jun 8
Tennessee Valley Old Time Fiddlers Conv (Athens), Oct 2
W.C. Handy Music Fest (Florence), Jul 17
XTERRA Oak Mountain Xduro (Pelham), Jun 6
Alamo: Anniv of the Fall, Mar 6
Alaska
Admission Day, Jan 3
Alascattalo Day (Anchorage), Nov 21
Alaska Day, Oct 19
Alaska Flag Day Celebration, Jul 9
Anvil Mountain Run (Nome), Jul 4
Blueberry Arts Fest (Ketchikan), Aug 1
Carrs/Safeway Great Alaska Shootout (Anchorage), Nov 24
Earthquake Strikes Alaska: Anniv, Mar 27
Fairbanks Summer Arts Fest (Fairbanks), Jul 19
Fest of the North (Ketchikan), Feb 1
59 Min 37 Sec Anvil Mountain Challenge (Nome), Sep 24
Fire and Ice New Year's Eve Celebration (Anchorage), Dec 31
Gigglefeet Dance Fest (Ketchikan), Jul 31
Great Bathtub Race (Nome), Sep 7
Holiday Tree Lighting (Anchorage), Nov 27
Iditarod Trail Sled Dog Race (Anchorage), Mar 7
Kodiak Crab Fest (Kodiak), May 21
Midnight Sun Baseball Game (Fairbanks), Jun 21
Midnight Sun Fest (Nome), Jun 20
Murkowski, Lisa: Birth, May 22
National Parks Established: Anniv, Dec 2
Nenana Tripod Raising Fest (Nenana), Mar 7
Palin, Sarah: Birth, Feb 11
Polar Bear Swim (Nome), Jun 20
Poorman's Paradise Gold Panner Contest (Nome), Jul 23
Seward's Day, Mar 30
Sled Dogs Save Nome: Anniv, Feb 2
Snake River Duck Race (Nome), Sep 7
State Fair (Palmer), Aug 27
Stevens, Ted: Birth, Nov 18
Summer Music Fest (Sitka), Jun 5
Tsunami, Highest in Recorded History: Anniv, Jul 9
Yukon Quest Intl 1,000-Mile Sled Dog Race (Fairbanks), Feb 14
Alba, Jessica: Birth, Apr 28
Albania: Independence Day, Nov 28
Albany Riverfront Jazz Fest (Albany, NY), Sep 5
Albee, Edward: Birth, Mar 12
Alberghetti, Anna Maria: Birth, May 15
Albert, Marv: Birth, Jun 12
Albom, Mitch: Birth, May 23
Albright, Madeleine: Birth, May 15
Albuquerque Intl Balloon Fiesta (Albuquerque, NM), Oct 3
Alcohol, Alcoholism
Alcohol and Drug Addiction Recovery Month, Natl, Sep 1
Alcohol-Free Weekend, Apr 3
Alcoholics Anonymous: Founding Anniv, Jun 10
Awareness Month, Apr 1
Pharmacists Declare War on Alcoholism, Jun 1
Screening Day, Natl, Apr 9
Women's Christian Temperance Union Organized: Anniv, Nov 19
Alcott, Amy Strum: Birth, Feb 22
Alcott, Louisa May: Birth Anniv, Nov 29
Alcott, Louisa May: Little Women Publication Anniv, Sep 30
Alda, Alan: Birth, Jan 28
Aldrin, Edwin "Buzz": Birth, Jan 20
Aleichem, Sholem: Birth Anniv, Feb 18
Alexander, Jane: Birth, Oct 28
Alexander, Jason: Birth, Sep 23
Alexander, Lamar: Birth, Jul 30
Alexis, Kim: Birth, Jul 15
Alfonso, Kristian: Birth, Sep 5
Alfonzo, Edgardo: Birth, Nov 8
Alfred Hitchcock Presents TV Premiere: Anniv, Oct 2
Alger, Horatio, Jr: Birth Anniv, Jan 13
Algeria
Independence Day, Jul 5
Revolution Day, Nov 1
Algonquin Mill Fall Fest (Carrollton, OH), Oct 9
Ali, Muhammad: Birth, Jan 17
Ali, Muhammad: Clay Becomes Heavyweight Champ: Anniv, Feb 25
Ali, Muhammad: Stripped of Title: Anniv, Apr 30
Alice TV Premiere: Anniv, Aug 31
Alice's Adventures in Wonderland Published: Anniv, Nov 26
Alito, Samuel A., Jr: Birth, Apr 1
All Fools' Day, Apr 1
All Hallows, Nov 1
All Hallow's Eve, Oct 31
All in the Family TV Premiere: Anniv, Jan 12
All My Children TV Premiere: Anniv, Jan 5
All Saints' Day, Nov 1
All Souls' Day, Nov 2
All the News That's Fit to Print: Anniv, Feb 10
Allard, Wayne: Birth, Dec 2
Allen, Byron: Birth, Apr 22
Allen, Chad: Birth, Jun 5
Allen, Debbie: Birth, Jan 16
Allen, Deborah: Birth, Sep 30
Allen, Ethan: Birth Anniv, Jan 21
Allen, Joan: Birth, Aug 20
Allen, Karen: Birth, Oct 5
Allen, Marcus: Birth, Mar 26
Allen, Nancy: Birth, Jun 24
Allen, Ray: Birth, Jul 20
Allen, Rex, Days (Willcox, AZ), Oct 2
Allen, Steve: Birth Anniv, Dec 26
Allen, Tim: Birth, Jun 13
Allen, Woody: Birth, Dec 1
Allergy/Asthma Awareness Month, Natl, May 1
Alley, Kirstie: Birth, Jan 12
Allilueva, Svetlana: Birth, Feb 28
Allman, Gregg: Birth, Dec 8
All-Star Game, First Major League Baseball: Anniv, Jul 6
Allstate Sugar Bowl (New Orleans, LA), Jan 2
Almanack, Poor Richard's: Anniv, Dec 28
Alomar, Roberto: Birth, Feb 5
Alopecia Day: Children with Alopecia Day, Apr 14
Alou, Moises: Birth, Jul 3
Alpert, Herb: Birth, Mar 31
Alpha Kappa Alpha Sorority Founded: Anniv, Jan 15
Alphabet Day (Korea), Oct 9
Alston, Charles H.: Birth Anniv, Nov 28
Alt, Carol: Birth, Dec 1
Altamont Concert: Anniv, Dec 6
Altman, Robert: Birth Anniv, Feb 20
Alvin Show TV Premiere: Anniv, Oct 4
Alzheimer, Alois: Birth Anniv, Jun 14
Alzheimer's Disease Month, Natl, Nov 1
AMA Founded: Anniv, May 5
Amateur Radio Day, Intl, Apr 18
AMD/Low Vision Awareness Month, Feb 1
Ameche, Don: Birth Anniv, May 31
America Recycles Day, Nov 15
America Recycles Day (Pres Proc), Nov 15
America the Beautiful Published: Anniv, Jul 4
American Adventures Month, Aug 1
American Bandstand TV Premiere: Anniv, Aug 5
American Bandstand: Dick Clark Retires: Anniv, Mar 23
American Council on Education Annual Mtg (Washington, DC), Feb 7
American Dental Assn Annual Session (Honolulu, HI), Sep 30
American Dietetic Assn Food & Nutrition Conf & Expo (Denver, CO), Oct 17
American Education Week, Nov 15
American Federation of Labor Founded: Anniv, Dec 8
American Flight Crashes at O'Hare: Anniv, May 25
American Historical Assn Annual Mtg (New York, NY), Jan 2
American History Essay Contest, Aug 1
American Idol TV Premiere: Anniv, Jun 11

American Indian Heritage Day (AL), Oct 12
American Indian Heritage Month, Natl, Nov 1
American Library Assn Founding: Anniv, Oct 6
American Psychological Assn Conv (Toronto, CA), Aug 6
American Red Cross Founded: Anniv, May 21
American Samoa: White Sunday, Oct 11
Americans with Disabilities Act: Anniv, Jul 26
America's Cup: Intl Yacht Race: Anniv, Aug 22
America's First Department Store: Anniv, Oct 16
America's Kids Day, Jun 28
America's Most Wanted TV Premiere: Anniv, Feb 7
America's Thanksgiving Day Parade (Detroit, MI), Nov 26
Ames, Bruce N.: Birth, Dec 16
Amis, Kingsley: Birth Anniv, Apr 16
Amis, Martin: Birth, Aug 25
Amistad Seized: Anniv, Aug 29
Amnesty for Polygamists: Anniv, Jan 4
Amnesty International Founded: Anniv, May 28
Amos 'n' Andy TV Premiere: Anniv, Jun 28
Amos, Tori: Birth, Aug 22
Ampere, Andre: Birth Anniv, Jan 22
Amtrak: Anniv, May 1
Amundsen, Roald: Birth Anniv, Jul 16
Ancestor Appreciation Day, Sep 27
Andersen, Hans Christian: Birth Anniv, Apr 2
Anderson, Dame Judith: Birth Anniv, Feb 10
Anderson, George Lee "Sparky": Birth, Feb 22
Anderson, Gillian: Birth, Aug 9
Anderson, Harry: Birth, Oct 14
Anderson, Helen E.M.: First Woman US Ambassador Appointed: Anniv, Oct 28
Anderson, Ian: Birth, Aug 10
Anderson, Kevin: Birth, Jan 13
Anderson, Loni: Birth, Aug 5
Anderson, Louie: Birth, Mar 23
Anderson, Lynn: Birth, Sep 26
Anderson, Marian: Birth Anniv, Feb 27
Anderson, Marian: Easter Concert: Anniv, Apr 9
Anderson, Marian: Performs with Metropolitan Opera: Anniv, Jan 7
Anderson, Melissa Sue: Birth, Sep 26
Anderson, Pamela: Birth, Jul 1
Anderson, Paul Thomas: Birth, Jun 26
Anderson, Richard Dean: Birth, Jan 23
Anderson, Sherwood: Birth Anniv, Sep 13
Anderson, Wes: Birth, May 1
Andersson, Bibi: Birth, Nov 11
Andorra: National Holiday, Sep 8
Andrea Doria Sinks: Anniv, Jul 25
Andree, Salomon A.: Birth Anniv, Oct 18
Andress, Ursula: Birth, Mar 19
Andretti, Mario: Birth, Feb 28
Andretti, Michael: Birth, Oct 5
Andrew, Prince: Birth, Feb 19
Andrews, Julie: Birth, Oct 1
Andrews, Julie: Sound of Music Film Premiere: Anniv, Mar 2
Andrews, Naveen, Jan 17
Andy Griffith Show TV Premiere: Anniv, Oct 3
Andy Williams Show TV Premiere: Anniv, Jul 2
Anesthetic First Used in Surgery: Anniv, Mar 30
Angel Day, Be an, Aug 22
Angel, Vanessa: Birth, Nov 10
Angelou, Maya: Birth, Apr 4
Angels: Guardian Angels Day, Oct 2
Anglund, Joan Walsh: Birth, Jan 3
Angola
  Armed Struggle Day, Feb 4
  Day of the National Hero, Sep 17
  Independence Day, Nov 11
Animals. See also Birds; Cats; Dogs; Horses; Pets; Rats
  AFRMA Display at America's Family Pet Expo (Costa Mesa, CA), Apr 10
  Animal Poison Prevention Week, Natl, Mar 15
  Animal Safety and Protection Month, Natl, Oct 1
  Animal Shelter Appreciation Week, Natl, Nov 1
  Answer Your Cat's Question Day, Jan 22
  Bark in the Park (Chicago, IL), May 2
  Be Kind to Animals Week, May 3
  Blessing of Animals at the Cathedral (Mexico), Jan 17
  Buffalo Auction (Custer, SD), Nov 21
  Buffalo Roundup (Custer, SD), Sep 28
  Burro Race (Leadville, CO), Jul 31
  Cloning of an Adult Animal, First: Anniv, Feb 23
  Cow Appreciation Day (Woodstock, VT), Jul 25
  Cow Milked While Flying: Anniv, Feb 18
  Crufts Dog Show (Birmingham, England), Mar 5
  Day of the Seal Celebration, Intl (Point Pleasant Beach, NJ), Mar 14
  Dog Day, Natl, Aug 26
  Elephant Appreciation Day, Sep 22
  Elephant Roundup at Surin (Thailand), Nov 21
  Fancy Rat & Mouse Display, AFRMA (Costa Mesa, CA), Jul 28
  Fancy Rat and Mouse Annual Show (Riverside, CA), Jan 24
  Farm Sanctuary Hoedown (Watkins Glen, NY), Aug 1
  Field Trial Chmpshp, Natl (Bird Dogs) (Grand Junction, TN), Feb 9
  First US Zoo: Anniv (Philadelphia, PA), Jul 1
  Fish Amnesty Day, Sep 26
  Give Wildlife a Brake! Week, Oct 26
  Go Fetch! Natl Food Drive for Homeless Animals, May 1
  Gorilla Born in Captivity, First: Anniv, Dec 22
  Hairball Awareness Day, Natl, Apr 24
  Happy Mew Year for Cats Day, Jan 2
  Hedgehog Day, Feb 2
  Ho Sheep Market (Denmark), Aug 29
  Holistic Pet Day, Natl, Aug 30
  Homeless Animals Day, Natl/Candlelight Vigils, Aug 15
  Hoof-Care Summit, Intl (Cincinnati, OH), Feb 3
  Hug Your Cat Day, May 29
  Humane Society of the US: Anniv, Nov 22
  Jumbo the Elephant Arrives in America: Anniv, Apr 9
  Jumping Frog Jubilee/Calaveras Fair (Angel Camp, CA), May 13
  King Turkey Days (Worthington, MN), Sep 19
  Koko the Gorilla: Birthday, Jul 4
  Lizard Race, World's Greatest (Lovington, NM), Jul 4
  Miss Crustacean/Ocean City Creep (Ocean City, NJ), Aug 5
  Moth-er Day, Mar 14
  Mule Day, Oct 26
  Mule Day (Columbia, TN), Apr 2
  Operation Santa Paws, Dec 1
  Pet Dental Health Month, Natl, Feb 1
  Pet First Aid Awareness Month, Intl, Apr 1
  Pet Owners Independence Day, Apr 18
  Pet Week, Natl, May 3
  Pig Day, Natl, Mar 1
  Positively Penguins (Point Pleasant Beach, NJ), Jan 10
  Prevention of Animal Cruelty Month, Apr 1
  Professional Pet Sitters Week, Mar 1
  Rabbit Week, Natl, Jul 15
  Rattlesnake Derby (Mangum, OK), Apr 24
  Save the Florida Panther Day, Mar 21
  Seal, Intl Day of the, Mar 22
  Shamu's Birthday, Sep 26
  Sheep Herding with Border Collies (Woodstock, VT), Aug 9
  Snake Hunt (Cross Fork, PA), Jun 27
  Spay Day USA, Feb 24
  Squirrel Awareness Month, Oct 1
  Toad Suck Daze (Conway, AR), May 1
  Turkey Vultures Return to the Living Sign (Canisteo, NY), Mar 11
  Turtle Races (Danville, IL), Jun 13
  What If Cats and Dogs Had Opposable Thumbs Day, Mar 3
  White Cloud Days (Jamestown, ND), Jul 9
  Wild Horse Chasing (Japan), Jul 23
  Wildlife Week, Natl, Apr 18
  Wishbones for Pets, Oct 15
  Woolly Worm Fest (Banner Elk, NC), Oct 17
  World Animal Remembrance Month, Sep 1
  World Farm Animals Day, Oct 2
  World Habitat Awareness Month, Apr 1
  World Turtle Day, May 23
  World's Largest Rattlesnake Roundup (Sweetwater, TX), Mar 13
Animation: Bugs Bunny's Debut: Anniv, Apr 30
Aniston, Jennifer: Birth, Feb 11
Anka, Paul: Birth, Jul 30
Annable, Dave: Birth, Sep 15
Annan, Kofi: Birth, Apr 8
Annapolis Convention: Anniv, Sep 11
Anne and Samantha Day, Jun 21
Anne, Princess: Birth, Aug 15
Annenberg, Walter: Birth Anniv, Mar 13
Ann-Margret: Birth, Apr 28
Annunciation, Feast of, Mar 25
Another Look Unlimited Day, Sep 8
Another World TV Premiere: Anniv, May 4
Anson, Cap: Birth Anniv, Apr 17
Anspach, Susan: Birth, Nov 23
Answer Your Cat's Question Day, Jan 22
Ant, Adam: Birth, Nov 3
Antarctica: Shackleton, Ernest: Birth Anniv, Feb 15
Anthem Day, Natl, Mar 3
Anthony, Carmelo: Birth, May 29
Anthony, Marc: Birth, Sep 16
Anthony, Susan B.: Day, Feb 15
Anthony, Susan B.: Fined for Voting: Anniv, Jun 6

Antidepressant Death Awareness Month, Oct 1
Antietam, Battle of: Anniv, Sep 17
Antigua and Barbuda
August Monday, Aug 3
Independence Day, Nov 1
Antique Power Exhibition (Burton, OH), Jul 24
Antiques
Antique Marine Engine Exposition (Mystic, CT), Aug 15
Antique Show (Somerset, PA), Aug 8
Antiques at Memorial Day (Cape May, NJ), May 24
Antiques on the Diamond (Ligonier, PA), Jun 13
Arizona Antique Show/Sale (Yuma, AZ), Jan 3
Charleston Intl Antiques Show (Charleston, SC), Mar 20
Cherish an Antique Day, Natl, Apr 9
Cotton Pickin' Fair (Gay, GA), May 2
Gettysburg Outdoor Antique Show (Gettysburg, PA), Sep 19
Gettysburg Outdoor Antique Show (Gettysburg, PA), May 16
Lucky May Show and Sale (Chapel Hill, NC), May 2
New Oxford Outdoor Antique Show (New Oxford, PA), Jun 20
Pan Amsterdam (Amsterdam, Netherlands), Nov 22
Pec Thing (Pecatonica, IL), May 16
Vegaspex (Las Vegas, NV), Jan 23
Anti-Saloon League Founded: Anniv, May 24
Anton, Susan: Birth, Oct 12
Antonioni, Michelangelo: Birth Anniv, Sep 29
Anwar, Gabrielle: Birth, Feb 4
Anxiety and Depression Awareness Week, Natl, May 3
ANZAC Day, Apr 25
Apache Wars Began: Anniv, Feb 4
Apartheid Law, South Africa Repeals Last: Anniv, Jun 17
Apgar, Virginia: Birth Anniv, Jun 7
A'phabet Day, Dec 25
Aphasia Awareness Month, Natl, Jun 1
Aphelion, Earth at, Jul 3
Apollo I: Spacecraft Fire: Anniv, Jan 27
Appert, Nicolas: Birth Anniv, Oct 23
Apple Blossom Fest (Annapolis Valley, NS, Canada), May 27
Apple Blossom Fest (Gettysburg, PA), May 2
Apple Blossom Fest, Washington State (Wenatchee, WA), Apr 23
Apple Butter Makin' Days (Mount Vernon, MO), Oct 9
Apple Butter Stirrin' (Coshocton, OH), Oct 16
Apple Fest (Topeka, KS), Oct 4
Apple Fest, Jackson County (Jackson, OH), Sep 22
Apple Fest, Kentucky (Paintsville, KY), Oct 2
Apple Harvest Fest, Natl (Gettysburg, PA), Oct 3
Apple II Computer Released: Anniv, Jun 5
Apple, Fiona: Birth, Sep 13
Applegate, Christina: Birth, Nov 25
Applejack Fest (Nebraska City, NE), Sep 18
Apples: Eat an Apple Day, Intl, Sep 19
Appleseed Days, Johnny (Lake City, MN), Oct 3
Appleseed, Johnny: Birth Anniv, Sep 26
Appleseed: Johnny Appleseed Day, Mar 11
April Fools' Day, Apr 1
Aprons: Tie One On Day, Nov 25
Aquarius Begins, Jan 20
Aquino, Benigno: Assassination Anniv, Aug 21
Aquino, Corazon: Birth, Jan 25
Arab Oil Embargo Lifted: Anniv, Mar 13
Arab-Israeli War (Yom Kippur War): Anniv, Oct 6
Arafat Returns to Palestine: Anniv, Jul 1
Arafat, Yasser: Birth Anniv, Aug 24
Arbor Day (Florida), Jan 16
Arbor Day Fest (Nebraska City, NE), Apr 24
Arbor Day in Arizona, Apr 24
Arbor Day, Natl, Apr 24
Archeology
Aztec Calendar Stone Discovery: Anniv, Dec 17
Iceman Mummy Discovered: Anniv, Sep 19
King Tut Tomb Discovery: Anniv, Nov 4
Statue of Ramses II Unearthed: Anniv, Nov 30
Sutton Hoo Ship Burial Discovered: Anniv, May 11
Archer, Anne: Birth, Aug 25
Archibald, Nate: Birth, Sep 2
Architecture: First Skyscraper: Anniv, May 1
Archuleta, David: Birth, Dec 28
Area Codes Introduced: Anniv, Nov 10
Arenas, Gilbert: Birth, Jan 6
Argentina
Dakar Rally, Jan 3
Day of Memory for Truth and Justice, Natl, Mar 24
Death Anniversary of San Martin, Aug 17
Falkland Islands War: Anniv, Apr 2
Flag Day, Jun 20
Independence Day, Jul 9
Malvinas Day, Apr 2
Revolution Day, May 25
Aries Begins, Mar 21
Arizona
Admission Day, Feb 14
American Family Day, Aug 2
Americana Indian and Western Art Show/Sale (Yuma), Jan 30
Apache Wars Began: Anniv, Feb 4
Arbor Day, Apr 24
Arizona Antique Show/Sale (Yuma), Jan 3
Arizona Musicfest (Carefree), Feb 4
Arizona Renaissance Fest (Apache Junction), Feb 7
Coin & Stamp Expo Arizona (Mesa), Jan 2
Colorado River Crossing Balloon Festival (Yuma), Nov 20
Constitution Commemoration Day, Sep 17
Cowboy Hall of Fame Ceremony (Willcox), Oct 1
Doll Show (Yuma), Feb 7
Fest of the West, Natl, and Log Home Show (Scottsdale), Mar 19
Fiesta de los Vaqueros (Tucson), Feb 21
Four Corner States Bluegrass Fest (Wickenburg), Nov 13
Gold Rush Days (Wickenburg), Feb 13
Grand Canyon Natl Park Established: Anniv, Feb 26
Kyl, Jon: Birth, Apr 25
Lost Dutchman Days (Apache Junction), Feb 20
McCain, John Sidney, III: Birth, Aug 29
Midnight at the Oasis (Yuma), Mar 6
Miss Arizona Pageant (Gilbert), Jun 20
Napolitano, Janet: Birth, Nov 29
NBA All-Star Game (Phoenix), Feb 15
Petrified Forest Natl Park Established: Anniv, Dec 9
Rex Allen Days (Willcox), Oct 2
Scottsdale Culinary Fest (Scottsdale), Apr 14
Sedona Arts Fest (Sedona), Oct 10
State Fair (Phoenix), Oct 9
Tempe Spring Fest of Arts (Tempe), Mar 27
Tucson Intl Mariachi Conf (Tucson), Apr 20
Wings Over Willcox—Sandhill Crane Celebration (Willcox), Jan 15
Winterfest (Flagstaff), Feb 1
Yuma Home & Garden Show (Yuma), Jan 16
Yuma Square and Round Dance Fest (Yuma), Feb 13
Arkansas
Admission Day, Jun 15
Beebe, Michael: Birth, Dec 28
Bluegrass Fest (Hope), May 9
Chicken and Egg Fest (Prescott), Jun 5
Chuckwagon Races, Natl Chmpshp (Clinton), Sep 4
Clothesline Fair (Prairie Grove), Sep 5
Dermott's Annual Crawfish Fest (Dermott), May 15
Duck-Calling Contest/Wings over Prairie Fest (Stuttgart), Nov 27
Eagles Et Cetera Fest (Bismarck), Jan 30
Homefest (Bald Knob), May 7
Hope Watermelon Fest (Hope), Aug 6
Hot Springs Natl Park Established: Anniv, Mar 4
Huckabee, Mike: Birth, Aug 24
Lincoln, Blanche Lambert: Birth, Sep 30
Ozark UFO Conf (Eureka Springs), Apr 10
Petit Jean Antique Auto Show/Swap Meet (Morrilton), Jun 16
Petit Jean Fall Antique Auto Swap Meet (Morrilton), Sep 23
Pryor, Mark: Birth, Jan 10
Quadrangle Fest (Texarkana), Oct 10
Riverfest (Little Rock), May 22
Rotary Tiller Race, World Chmpshp/Purplehull Pea Fest (Emerson), Jun 26
State Fair and Livestock Show (Little Rock), Oct 9
Toad Suck Daze (Conway), May 1
Arkin, Adam: Birth, Aug 19
Arkin, Alan: Birth, Mar 26
Arlen, Harold: Birth Anniv, Feb 15
Armani, Giorgio: Birth, Jul 11
Armatrading, Joan: Birth, Dec 9
Armed Forces Day (Egypt), Oct 6
Armed Forces Day (Pres Proc), May 17
Armed Forces Unified: Anniv, Jul 26
Armenia
Armenian Church Christmas, Jan 6
Armenian Martyrs Day, Apr 24
Earthquake of 1988: Anniv, Dec 7
Independence Day, Sep 21
Armistice Day, Nov 11
Armistice Day: See Veterans Day, Nov 11
Armstrong, BJ: Birth, Sep 9
Armstrong, Darrell: Birth, Jun 22
Armstrong, Lance: Birth, Sep 18
Armstrong, Louis: Birth Anniv, Aug 4

Armstrong, Neil: Birth, Aug 5
Armstrong, Trace: Birth, Oct 5
Armstrong-Jones, Anthony: Birth, Mar 7
Army, US: Established: Anniv, Jun 14
Army, US: First Desegregation: Anniv, Jul 26
Army-Navy Game, First: Anniv, Nov 29
Arnaz, Desi, Jr: Birth, Jan 19
Arnaz, Desi: Birth Anniv, Mar 2
Arnaz, Lucie: Birth, Jul 17
Arness, James: Birth, May 26
Arnold, Benedict: Birth Anniv, Jan 14
Arnold, Henry "Hap": Birth Anniv, Jun 25
Arnold, Matthew: Birth Anniv, Dec 24
Arnold, Tom: Birth, Mar 6
Arquette, Courteney Cox: Birth, Jun 15
Arquette, David: Birth, Sep 8
Arquette, Patricia: Birth, Apr 8
Arquette, Rosanna: Birth, Aug 10
Arrington, LaVar: Birth, Jun 20
Arsenio Hall Show TV Premiere: Anniv, Jan 3
Art Car Parade (Houston, TX), May 9
Art Deco Weekend (Miami Beach, FL), Jan 16
Art Linkletter's House Party TV Premiere: Anniv, Sep 1
Arthritis Month, Natl, May 1
Arthur Murray Party TV Premiere: Anniv, Jul 20
Arthur, Beatrice: Birth, May 13
Arthur, Chester A.: Birth Anniv, Oct 5
Arthur, Ellen: Birth Anniv, Aug 30
Arthur, Jean: Birth Anniv, Oct 17
Articles of Confederation: Ratification Anniv, Mar 1
Articles of Peace: Anniv, Nov 30
Arts and Crafts. See also Quilt
- Alpenfest (Gaylord, MI), Jul 14
- Amcore Bank Faire on the Square Art & Craft Fair (Baraboo, WI), May 16
- Artists in the Park (Wolfeboro, NH), Aug 19
- Arts & Crafts Fest (Loveladies, NJ), Jul 25
- Autumn Arts Fest (Hagerstown, MD), Sep 12
- Belsnickel Craft Show (Boyertown, PA), Nov 27
- Blue Ridge Folklife Fest (Ferrum, VA), Oct 24
- Cambridge Pottery Fest and US Pottery Games (Cambridge, WI), Jun 13
- Capitol Hill People's Fair (Denver, CO), Jun 6
- Card Making Day, World, Oct 3
- Catoctin ColorFest Arts/Crafts (Thurmont, MD), Oct 10
- Christkindl Markt (Canton, OH), Nov 13
- Christmas Craft Show (York, PA), Dec 13
- Clothesline Fair (Prairie Grove, AR), Sep 5
- Commonwheel Arts and Crafts Fest (Manitou Springs, CO), Sep 5
- Corn Hill Arts Fest (Rochester, NY), Jul 11
- Country Fest and Auction (Deep Creek Lake, MD), Aug 22
- Coupeville Arts & Crafts Fest (Coupeville, WA), Aug 8
- Craft & Hobby Assn Winter Conv & Trade Show (Anaheim, CA), Jan 25
- Craft Month, Natl, Mar 1
- Craftsmen's Christmas Classic Arts & Crafts Fest (Greensboro, NC), Nov 27
- Craftsmen's Christmas Classic Arts & Crafts Fest (Richmond, VA), Nov 6
- Craftsmen's Classic Arts & Crafts Fest (Chantilly, VA), Mar 27
- Craftsmen's Classic Arts & Crafts Fest (Chantilly, VA), Oct 16
- Craftsmen's Classic Arts & Crafts Fest (Columbia, SC), Mar 6
- Craftsmen's Classic Arts & Crafts Fest (Myrtle Beach, SC), Aug 7
- Craftsmen's Classic Arts & Crafts Fest (Richmond, VA), Mar 13
- Craftsmen's Classic Arts & Crafts Fest (Roanoke, VA), Oct 9
- Easter Craft Show (York, PA), Mar 22
- Fall Country Jamboree (Barberville, FL), Nov 7
- Fallasburg Fall Fest (Lowell, MI), Sep 26
- Fest of the Little Hills (St. Charles, MO), Aug 14
- Festival 2009: Fest of Fine Arts and Fine Crafts (Dalton, GA), Sep 19
- Greater Pittsburgh Arts & Crafts Holiday Spectacular (Monroeville, PA), Nov 20
- Heritage Days Fest (Cumberland, MD), Jun 13
- Jours de Fete (Ste. Genevieve, MO), Aug 8
- Lavallette Heritage Arts & Crafts Show (Lavallette, NJ), Jul 26
- League of NH Craftsmen Annual Craftsmen's Fair (Newbury, NH), Aug 1
- Little Falls Arts/Crafts (Little Falls, MN), Sep 12
- Louisiana Art & Folk Fest (Columbia, LA), Oct 10
- Lovington Fall Arts/Crafts Fest (Lovington, NM), Nov 7
- Maritime Gig Fest (Gig Harbor, WA), Jun 6
- Meet the Artists and Artisans Show (Milford Green, CT), May 9
- Melrose Plantation Arts/Crafts Fest (Melrose, LA), Jun 13
- Mossy Creek Barnyard Fest (Warner Robins, GA), Apr 18
- Mount Pleasant Glass & Ethnic Fest (Mount Pleasant, PA), Sep 25
- Original Raggedy Ann & Andy Fest (Arcola, IL), Jun 13
- Peddler's Village Scarecrow Contest and Outdoor Display (Lahaska, PA), Sep 13
- Pennsylvania Arts & Crafts Christmas Fest (Washington, PA), Oct 16
- Pennsylvania Arts & Crafts Colonial Fest (Greensburg, PA), Sep 4
- Pittsburgh Arts & Crafts Spring Fever Fest (Greensburg, PA), Mar 27
- Quilting Day, Natl, Mar 21
- Sedona Arts Fest (Sedona, AZ), Oct 10
- SFCC Spring Arts Fest (Gainesville, FL), Mar 28
- Sheep to Shawl Fest (Savannah, GA), Mar 28
- Sheyenne Valley Arts/Crafts (Fort Ransom, ND), Sep 26
- Sidewalk Arts Fest (Sioux Falls, SD), Sep 5
- Spinning and Weaving Week, Oct 5
- Springs Folk Fest (Springs, PA), Oct 2
- Sugarloaf Art Fair (Novi, MI), Apr 17
- Sugarloaf Art Fair (Novi, MI), Oct 23
- Sugarloaf Crafts Fest (Chantilly, VA), Jan 30
- Sugarloaf Crafts Fest (Chantilly, VA), May 1
- Sugarloaf Crafts Fest (Chantilly, VA), Dec 11
- Sugarloaf Crafts Fest (Gaithersburg, MD), Apr 3
- Sugarloaf Crafts Fest (Gaithersburg, MD), Oct 9
- Sugarloaf Crafts Fest (Gaithersburg, MD), Nov 20
- Sugarloaf Crafts Fest (Hartford, CT), Mar 27
- Sugarloaf Crafts Fest (Hartford, CT), Nov 13
- Sugarloaf Crafts Fest (Manassas, VA), Sep 11
- Sugarloaf Crafts Fest (Somerset, NJ), Mar 13
- Sugarloaf Crafts Fest (Somerset, NJ), Oct 30
- Sugarloaf Crafts Fest (Timonium, MD), Apr 24
- Sugarloaf Crafts Fest (Timonium, MD), Oct 2
- TACA Fall Craft Fair (Nashville, TN), Sep 25
- Tempe Spring Fest of Arts (Tempe, AZ), Mar 27
- Totah Fest (Farmington, NM), Sep 5
- Virginia Spring Show (Richmond, VA), Mar 13
- Winfield Art-in-the-Park Fest (Winfield, KS), Oct 3
- Wyandotte Street Art Fair (Wyandotte, MI), Jul 8

Arts, Fine and Performing; Art Shows
- Americana Indian and Western Art Show/Sale (Yuma, AZ), Jan 30
- Art Deco Weekend (Miami Beach, FL), Jan 16
- Art Fair and Winefest (Washington, MO), May 15
- Art Fair on the Square (Madison, WI), Jul 11
- Art in the Garden (Washington, PA), Sep 13
- Artown (Reno, NV), Jul 1
- Arts in the Park (Kalispell, MT), Jul 24
- Arts/Quincy Riverfest (Quincy, IL), Sep 20
- Ballet Introduced to the US: Anniv, Feb 7
- Belfast Fest at Queen's (Belfast, Northern Ireland), Oct 16
- Buffalo Roundup Arts Fest (Custer, SD), Sep 26
- Bumbershoot: Seattle's Music & Arts Fest (Seattle, WA), Sep 5
- Cartoonists Day, May 5
- Cellular South Gum Tree Fest (Tupelo, MS), May 9
- City of London Fest (London, England), Jun 20
- Day With(out) Art, Dec 1
- Decoy and Wildlife Art Show (Clayton, NY), Jul 17
- Downtown Fest/Art Show (Gainesville, FL), Nov 7
- European Fine Art Fair (Maastricht, Netherlands), Mar 13
- Fairbanks Summer Arts Fest (Fairbanks, AK), Jul 19
- Fest of the North (Ketchikan, AK), Feb 1
- Festival 2009: Fest of Fine Arts and Fine Crafts (Dalton, GA), Sep 19
- Florida Manatee Fest (Crystal River, FL), Jan 10
- Geneva Arts Fair (Geneva, IL), Jul 25
- Grant Wood Art Fest (Anamosa, IA), Jun 14
- History Meets the Arts (Gettysburg, PA), Apr 17
- Inspire Your Heart with the Arts Day, Jan 31
- Meet the Artists and Artisans Show (Milford Green, CT), May 9

Mural-in-a-Day (Toppenish, WA), Jun 6
Northwest Folklife Fest (Seattle, WA), May 22
Panoply (Huntsville, AL), Apr 24
Peddler's Village Fine Art & Crafts Show (Lahaska, PA), Jun 6
Riverfest (Little Rock, AR), May 22
Sidewalk Art Fest (Portland, ME), Aug 22
Toppenish Western Art Show (Toppenish, WA), Aug 14
Westmoreland Arts & Heritage Fest (Greensburg, PA), Jul 2
Youth Art Month, Mar 1
Aruba: Flag Day, Mar 18
As the World Turns TV Premiere: Anniv, Apr 2
As Young as You Feel Day, Mar 22
Asarah B'Tevet, Jan 6
Asarah B'Tevet, Dec 27
Ascension Day, May 21
Ascension of Baha'u'llah, May 29
Ash Wednesday, Feb 25
Ashanti: Birth, Oct 13
Ashcroft, Peggy: Birth Anniv, Dec 22
Ashe, Arthur: Birth Anniv, Jul 10
Ashford, Emmett: Birth Anniv, Nov 23
Ashford, Evelyn: Birth, Apr 15
Ashford, Nickolas: Birth, May 4
Ashley, Elizabeth: Birth, Aug 30
Ashura: Tenth Day (1430), Jan 7
Ashura: Tenth Day (1431), Dec 27
Asian/Pacific American Heritage Month (Pres Proc), May 1
Asimov, Isaac: Birth Anniv, Jan 2
Asner, Ed: Birth, Nov 15
Aspinwall Crosses US on Horseback: Anniv, Jul 8
Assante, Armand: Birth, Oct 4
Assassination Attempt: Pope John Paul II: Anniv, May 13
Assassinations Report, Committee on: Anniv, Mar 29
Assisted Living Week, Natl, Sep 13
Assumption of the Virgin Mary, Aug 15
Astaire, Fred: Birth Anniv, May 10
Astin, John: Birth, Mar 30
Astin, MacKenzie: Birth, May 12
Astin, Sean: Birth, Feb 25
Astor Place Riot: Anniv, May 10
Astrology
Aquarius, Jan 20
Aries, Mar 21
Cancer, Jun 21
Capricorn, Dec 22
Gemini, May 21
Leo, Jul 23
Libra, Sep 23
Pisces, Feb 20
Sagittarius, Nov 22
Scorpio, Oct 23
Taurus, Apr 20
Virgo, Aug 23
Astronomers Find New Solar System: Anniv, Apr 15
Astronomy Day, May 2
Astronomy Week, Apr 27
Astronomy, Intl Year of (UN), Jan 1
AT&T Divestiture: Anniv, Jan 8
Ataturk, Mustafa Kemal: Birth Anniv, Mar 12
Atchison, David R.: Birth Anniv, Aug 11
Atherton, William: Birth, Jul 30
Atkins, Christopher: Birth, Feb 21
Atkinson, Rowan: Birth, Jan 6
Atlantic Charter Signing: Anniv, Aug 14
Atlantic Telegraph Cable Laid: Anniv, Jul 27
Atlas, Charles: Birth Anniv, Oct 30
Atler, Vanessa: Birth, Feb 17
Atomic Bomb Dropped on Hiroshima: Anniv, Aug 6
Atomic Bomb Dropped on Nagasaki: Anniv, Aug 9
Atomic Bomb Tested: Anniv, Jul 16
Atomic Plant Begun, Oak Ridge: Anniv, Aug 1
Atrial Fibrillation Month, Sep 1
Attack on America: Anniv, Sep 11
Attacks Against America: Libraries Remember, Sep 11
Attenborough, David: Birth, May 8
Attenborough, Sir Richard: Birth, Aug 29
Attention Deficit Hyperactivity Disorder Month, Sep 1
Attlee, Clement Richard: Birth Anniv, Jan 3
Attucks, Crispus: Day, Mar 5
Atwood, Margaret: Birth, Nov 18
Auberjonois, Rene: Birth, Jun 1
Auctioneers Day, Natl, Apr 18
Auden, W.H.: Birth Anniv, Feb 21
Audubon, John J.: Birth Anniv, Apr 26
Auerbach, Red: Birth Anniv, Sep 20
Augusta Futurity (Augusta, GA), Jan 15
Aung San Suu Kyi: Birth, Jun 19
Aura Awareness Day, Intl, Nov 28
Auschwitz Liberated: Anniv, Jan 27
Austen, Jane: Birth Anniv, Dec 16
Austin, Stephen F.: Birth Anniv, Nov 3
Austin, Tracy: Birth, Dec 12
Autism: Adult Autism Awareness Day, Apr 18
Australia
ANZAC Day, Apr 25
Australia Day, Jan 26
Canberra Day, Mar 16
Commonwealth Formed: Anniv, Jan 1
Eight Hour Day (Labor Day), Mar 2
Melbourne Cup (Melbourne), Nov 3
Ned Kelly's Last Stand: Anniv, Jun 27
Picnic Day, Aug 3
Proclamation Day, Dec 28
Recreation Day, Nov 2
Sorry Day, May 26
Sydney Opera House Opens: Anniv, Oct 20
Austria
Fasching, Feb 23
Fasching Sunday, Feb 22
Invaded by Nazi Germany: Anniv, Mar 12
Krampuslauf, Dec 5
National Day, Oct 26
Saint Stephen's Day, Dec 26
Silent Night, Holy Night Celebrations, Dec 24
Authors' Day, Natl, Nov 1
Autism: COSAC Annual Conference (Atlantic City, NJ), Oct 8
Automatic Toll Collection Machine, First: Anniv, Nov 19
Automobile Production Halted, Civilian: Anniv, Feb 10
Automobile Speed Reduction: Anniv, Nov 25
Automobiles (including shows, races, etc)
AMA Grand Natl Singles Chmpnshp Dirt Track Race (Daytona Beach, FL), Mar 4
Antiques by the Bay (St. Ignace, MI), Jun 19
Automotion (Wisconsin Dells, WI), May 16
Automotive Service Professionals Week, Natl, Jun 8
Bennington Car Show (Bennington, VT), Sep 18
By Land and by Sea (Mystic, CT), Sep 26
Camping World 300 Presented by Chevy NASCAR Nationwide Series Race (Daytona Beach, FL), Feb 14
Car Care Month, Apr 1
Coke Zero 400 NASCAR Sprint Cup Series Race (Daytona, FL), Jul 4
Concours d'Elegance (Forest Grove, OR), Jul 19
Corvette and High Performance Meet (Puyallup, WA), Feb 7
Corvette Show (Mackinaw City, MI), Aug 28
Cruisin' Downtown (Toms River, NJ), May 13
Dakar Rally (Argentina and Chile), Jan 3
Daytona 200 by Honda Qualifying Day (Daytona Beach, FL), Mar 5
Daytona 500 (Daytona Beach, FL), Feb 15
Daytona 500 Pole Day (Daytona Beach, FL), Feb 8
Daytona Turkey Run (Daytona Beach, FL), Nov 26
Drowsy Driver Awareness Day, Apr 6
55-mph Speed Limit: Anniv, Jan 2
First Car Insurance: Anniv, Feb 1
Ford Mustang Day, Intl, Apr 17
Gatorade Duel Qualifying Races (Daytona Beach, FL), Feb 12
Good Car-Keeping Month, Natl, May 1
Grand Prix de Monaco (Monte Carlo, Monaco), May 21
Hot August Nights (Reno and Sparks, NV), Aug 1
Houston Art Car Parade (Houston, TX), May 9
Indianapolis 500: Anniv, May 30
Indy 500-Mile Race (Indianapolis, IN), May 24
Interstate Highway System Born: Anniv, Jun 29
London/Brighton Veteran Car Run (London, England), Nov 1
Lost in the '50s (Sandpoint, ID), May 14
Magic Dragon Street Meet Nationals and Extreme Car Shows (Lake Ozark, MO), May 1
Midnight at the Oasis (Yuma, AZ), Mar 6
Model T Introduced: Anniv, Oct 1
Motorsports Awareness Month, Aug 1
NASCAR Craftsman Truck Series 250 (Daytona Beach, FL), Feb 13
North American Intl Auto Show (Detroit, MI), Jan 11
On the Waterfront Swap Meet/Car Show (St. Ignace, MI), Sep 18
Petit Jean Antique Auto Show/Swap Meet (Morrilton, AR), Jun 16
Petit Jean Fall Antique Auto Swap Meet (Morrilton, AR), Sep 23
Portland Historic Races (Portland, OR), Jul 10
Rally of the Tall Pines (Bancroft, ON, Canada), Nov 20
Richard Crane Memorial Truck Show (St. Ignace, MI), Sep 18
Rolex 24 at Daytona (Daytona, FL), Jan 24
Shootout at Daytona Sprint Cup Series Race (Daytona Beach, FL), Feb 7
St. Ignace Auto Show (St. Ignace, MI), Jun 25
Street Machine Fall Nationals (Springfield, MO), Sep 18
Streetscene (Covington, VA), Aug 8

24 Hours of Le Mans (Le Mans), Jun 13
Woodie Wagon Day, Natl, Jul 18
Autry, Gene: Birth Anniv, Sep 29
Autumn Begins, Sep 22
Autumn Fairy Fun Day, Sep 27
Autumn Market Fair, Eighteenth-Century (McLean, VA), Oct 17
Avalon, Frankie: Birth, Sep 18
Avedon, Richard: Birth Anniv, May 15
Aviation; Aviation History; Air Shows; Airplane Fly-ins
Abbotsford Intl Airshow (Abbotsford, BC, Canada), Aug 7
Amelia Earhart Atlantic Crossing: Anniv, May 20
Amelia Earhart Disappears: Anniv, Jul 2
American Flight Crashes at O'Hare: Anniv, May 25
Aviation Day, Natl (Pres Proc), Aug 19
Aviation History Month, Nov 1
Aviation in America: Anniv, Jan 9
Aviation Week, Natl, Aug 16
Balloon Crossing of Atlantic: Anniv, Aug 17
Berlin Airlift: Anniv, Jun 24
Campbell Becomes First American Air Ace: Anniv, Apr 14
Canary Islands Plane Disaster: Anniv, Mar 27
Cayley, George: Birth Anniv, Dec 27
China Clipper: Anniv, Nov 22
Chmpshp Air Races, Natl (Reno, NV), Sep 16
Civil Air Patrol Founded: Anniv, Dec 1
Civil Aviation Day, Intl (UN), Dec 7
Cleveland Natl Air Show (Cleveland, OH), Sep 5
Coleman, Bessie: Birth Anniv, Jan 26
EAA Airventure Oshkosh (Oshkosh, WI), Jul 27
Earhart, Amelia: Birth Anniv, Jul 24
First Airplane Crossing of English Channel: Anniv, Jul 25
First Airship Crossing of Atlantic: Anniv, Jul 6
First Balloon Flight: Anniv, Jun 5
First Balloon Flight Across English Channel: Anniv, Jan 7
First Concorde Flight: Anniv, Jan 21
First Fatal Aviation Accident: Anniv, Jun 15
First Flight Anniv Celebration (Kill Devil Hills, NC), Dec 17
First Flight Attendant: Anniv, May 15
First Flight into the Stratosphere: Anniv, May 27
First Free Flight by a Woman: Anniv, Jun 4
First Manned Flight: Anniv, Oct 15
First Man-Powered Flight: Anniv, Aug 23
First Man-Powered Flight Across English Channel: Anniv, Jun 12
First Nonstop Flight of World/No Refueling: Anniv, Dec 23
First Nonstop Transatlantic Flight: Anniv, Jun 14
First Round-the-World Balloon Flight: Anniv, Mar 21
First Scheduled Transcontinental Flight: Anniv, Jan 25
First Solo Round-the-World Balloon Flight: Anniv, Jul 2
Hindenburg Disaster: Anniv, May 6
Iran Air Flight 655 Disaster: Anniv, Jul 3
Johnson, Amy: Flight Anniv, May 5
Kennedy Intl Airport Dedication: Anniv, Jul 31
Lady Be Good Lost: Anniv, Apr 4
Levine, Charles A.: Death Anniv, Dec 6
Lindbergh Flight: Anniv, May 20
Lindbergh, Charles A.: Birth Anniv, Feb 4
Montgolfier, Jacques: Birth Anniv, Jan 7
Pan Am Circles Earth: Anniv, Jan 6
Pan Am Flight 103 Explosion: Anniv, Dec 21
Post, Wiley: Birth Anniv, Nov 22
Quad City Air Show (Davenport, IA), Jun 13
Sikorsky, Igor: Birth Anniv, May 25
Solo Transatlantic Balloon Crossing: Anniv, Sep 14
Sound Barrier Broken: Anniv, Oct 14
Spruce Goose Flight: Anniv, Nov 2
Stearman Fly-In Days, Natl (Galesburg, IL), Sep 7
Streeter, Ruth Cheney: Birth Anniv, Oct 2
Tuskegee Airmen Activated: Anniv, Mar 22
US Air Force Academy Established: Anniv, Apr 1
US Air Force Established: Anniv, Sep 18
Will Rogers & Wiley Post Fly-In (Oologah, OK), Aug 16
Wright Brothers Day (Pres Proc), Dec 17
Wright Brothers First Powered Flight: Anniv, Dec 17
Wrong Way Corrigan Day, Jul 17
Awkward Moments Day, Mar 18
Aykroyd, Dan: Birth, Jul 1
Aylesworth, Reiko: Birth, Dec 9
Aylwin, Patricio: Military Dictatorship Ended, Dec 15
Azalea Fest (Muskogee, OK), Apr 1
Azalea Fest, Brookings-Harbor (Brookings, OR), May 22
Azaria, Hank: Birth, Apr 25
Azerbaijan
Day of the Republic, May 28
Independence Day, Oct 18
Martyrs' Day, Jan 20
Aznavour, Charles: Birth, May 22
Aztec Calendar Stone Discovery: Anniv, Dec 17
Azzi, Jennifer: Birth, Aug 31

B
Bab, Birth of the (Baha'i): Anniv, Oct 20
Babbage, Charles: Birth Anniv, Dec 26
Babenco, Hector: Birth, Feb 7
Baby Boomer Born, First: Anniv, Jan 1
Baby Boomers Recognition Day, Jun 21
Baby Food Fest, Natl (Fremont, MI), Jul 21
Baby Massage Day, Apr 11
Babysitters Day, Natl, May 9
Bacall, Lauren: Birth, Sep 16
Bach Fest (Leipzig, Germany), Jun 11
Bach, Catherine: Birth, Mar 1
Bach, Johann Sebastian: Birth Anniv, Mar 21
Bacharach, Burt: Birth, May 12
Bachelor Father TV Premiere: Anniv, Sep 15
Backpack Safety America Month, Sep 1
Backus, Jim: Birth Anniv, Feb 25
Backyard Games Week, Natl, May 18
Bacon, Francis: Birth Anniv, Jan 22
Bacon, Kevin: Birth, Jul 8
Bacon's Rebellion, Jamestown Burned by: Anniv, Sep 19
Bad Day Day, Have a, Nov 19
Bad Poetry Day, Aug 18
Baden-Powell, Robert: Birth Anniv, Feb 22
Bader, Diedrich: Birth, Dec 24
Badlands Natl Park Established: Anniv, Nov 10
Badminton Horse Trials (Badminton, England), May 7
Badminton: Scottish Intl Chmpshp (Edinburgh, Scotland), Nov 25
Badu, Erykah: Birth, Feb 26
Baer, Max: Birth Anniv, Feb 11
Baer, Max, Jr: Birth, Dec 4
Baez, Joan: Birth, Jan 9
Bagdley, Penn: Birth, Nov 1
Baghdad Stampede: Anniv, Aug 31
Bagwell, Jeff: Birth, May 27
Baha'i
American Baha'i Community: Anniv, Jun 5
Ascension of Baha'u'llah, May 29
Baha'i New Year's Day: Naw-Ruz, Mar 21
Birth of Baha'u'llah, Nov 12
Birth of the Bab: Anniv, Oct 20
Declaration of the Bab, May 23
Fest of Ridvan, Apr 21
Martyrdom of the Bab, Jul 9
Race Unity Day, Jun 14
Bahamas
Discovery Day, Oct 12
Emancipation Day, Aug 3
Fox Hill Day (Nassau), Aug 11
Independence Day, Jul 10
Junkanoo, Dec 26
Labor Day, Jun 5
Bahrain: Independence Day, Dec 16
Bailey, F. Lee: Birth, Jun 10
Bailey, Pearl Mae: Birth Anniv, Mar 29
Baines, Harold: Birth, Mar 15
Baio, Scott: Birth, Sep 22
Baiul, Oksana: Birth, Nov 16
Bake and Decorate Month, Natl, Oct 1
Bake for Family Fun Month, Feb 1
Baker, Anita: Birth, Jan 26
Baker, Carroll: Birth, May 28
Baker, Diane: Birth, Feb 25
Baker, Joe Don: Birth, Feb 12
Baker, Josephine: Birth Anniv, Jun 3
Baker, Kathy: Birth, Jun 8
Baker, Russell: Birth, Aug 14
Baker, Vin: Birth, Nov 23
Baking: Gluten-Free Baking Week, Dec 13
Bakker, Jim: Birth, Jan 2
Bakula, Scott: Birth, Oct 9
Balance Awareness Week, Sep 13
Balanchine, George: Birth Anniv, Jan 22
Balboa: Pacific Ocean Discovered: Anniv, Sep 25
Bald and Be Free Day, Be, Oct 14
Bald Eagle Appreciation Days (Keokuk, IA), Jan 16
Baldacci, John: Birth, Jan 30
Baldwin, Adam: Birth, Feb 27
Baldwin, Alec: Birth, Apr 3
Baldwin, Caroline: First Woman Dr. Science: Anniv, Jun 20
Baldwin, James: Birth Anniv, Aug 2
Baldwin, Roger Nash: Birth Anniv, Jan 21
Baldwin, Stephen: Birth, May 12
Baldwin, William: Birth, Feb 21
Bale, Christian: Birth, Jan 30
Balfour, Eric: Birth, Apr 24
Bali Terrorist Bombing: Anniv, Oct 12
Ball, Lucille: Birth Anniv, Aug 6
Ballack, Michael: Birth, Sep 26
Ballesteros, Seve: Birth, Apr 9
Ballet Introduced to the US: Anniv, Feb 7
Ballet: Rite of Spring Premiere and Riot: Anniv, May 29

Balloons, Hot-Air
Albuquerque Intl Balloon Fiesta (Albuquerque, NM), Oct 3
Aviation in America: Anniv, Jan 9
Balloon Crossing of Atlantic: Anniv, Aug 17
Balloons Around the World, Oct 7
Colorado River Crossing Balloon Festival (Yuma, AZ), Nov 20
Columbus Fest/Hot Air Balloon Regatta (Columbus, KS), Oct 9
Farmington Invitational Balloon Fest (Farmington, NM), May 22
First Balloon Flight Across English Channel: Anniv, Jan 7
First Balloon Flight: Anniv, Jun 5
First Balloon Honeymoon: Anniv, Jun 20
First Flight into the Stratosphere: Anniv, May 27
First Manned Flight: Anniv, Oct 15
First Round-the-World Balloon Flight: Anniv, Mar 21
First Solo Round-the-World Balloon Flight: Anniv, Jul 2
Great Wellsville Balloon Rally (Wellsville, NY), Jul 17
Lexington's 4th of July Balloon Rally (Lexington, VA), Jul 4
Re/Max Ballunar Liftoff Fest (Houston, TX), Oct 30
Rocky Mountain Balloon Fest (Denver, CO), Aug 29
Solo Transatlantic Balloon Crossing: Anniv, Sep 14
Telluride Balloon Fest (Telluride, CO), Jun 5
Ballpoint Pen Patented: Anniv, Jun 10
Baltimore Book Fest (Baltimore, MD), Sep 25
Balzac, Honore de: Birth Anniv, May 20
Bamber, Jamie: Birth, Apr 3
Ban Ki-Moon: Birth, Jun 13
Bana, Eric: Birth, Aug 9
Banana Split Fest (Wilmington, OH), Jun 12
Bancroft, George: Birth Anniv, Oct 3
Band Fest, Great American Brass (Danville, KY), Jun 11
Banderas, Antonio: Birth, Aug 10
Banerjee, Victor: Birth, Oct 15
Bangladesh
Independence Day, Mar 26
Martyrs Day, Feb 21
Solidarity Day, Nov 7
Victory Day, Dec 16
Bank Holiday, Spring (United Kingdom), May 25
Bank Holiday, Summer (Scotland), Aug 3
Bank Holiday, Summer (United Kingdom), Aug 31
Bank Opens in US, First: Anniv, Dec 31
Banks, Ernie: Birth, Jan 31
Banks, Tyra: Birth, Dec 4
Banneker, Benjamin: Birth Anniv, Nov 9
Bannister Breaks Four-Minute Mile: Anniv, May 6
Bannister, Dr. Roger: Birth, Mar 23
Bar Assn, American, Founding: Anniv, Aug 21
Bar Code Introduced: Anniv, Jun 26
Barak, Ehud: Birth, Feb 12
Baraka, Amiri: Birth, Oct 7
Baranski, Christine: Birth, May 2
Barbados: Independence Day, Nov 30
Barbeau, Adrienne: Birth, Jun 11
Barbecue Month, Natl, May 1
Barbed Wire Swap/Sell (La Crosse, KS), May 1
Barber, Frances: Birth, May 13
Barber, Red: Birth Anniv, Feb 17
Barber, Red: First Baseball Games Televised: Anniv, Aug 26
Barbera, Joe: Birth Anniv, Mar 24
Barbershop Ballad Contest, All-Northwest (Forest Grove, OR), Feb 27
Barbershop Quartet Day, Apr 11
Barbie and Barney Backlash Day, Dec 16
Barbie Debuts: Anniv, Mar 9
Barbosa, Jose Celso: Birth Anniv, Jul 27
Barbour, Haley: Birth, Oct 22
Bardem, Javier: Birth, Mar 1
Bardot, Brigitte: Birth, Sep 28
Barenboim, Daniel: Birth, Nov 15
Barker, Bob: Birth, Dec 12
Barker, Clive: Birth, Oct 5
Barkin, Ellen: Birth, Apr 16
Barkley, Alben: Birth Anniv, Nov 24
Barkley, Charles: Birth, Feb 20
Barnaby Jones TV Premiere: Anniv, Jan 28
Barnard, Christiaan: Birth Anniv, Nov 8
Barnard, Christiaan: First Heart Transplant: Anniv, Dec 3
Barnes, Clive: Birth, May 13
Barnes, Joanna: Birth, Nov 15
Barnesville Pumpkin Fest (Barnesville, OH), Sep 24
Barney & Friends TV Premiere: Anniv, Apr 6
Barney Miller TV Premiere: Anniv, Jan 23
Barnum, Phineas Taylor: Birth Anniv, Jul 5
Baron Bliss Day (Belize), Mar 9
Barrasso, John: Birth, Jul 21
Barrett, Rona: Birth, Oct 8
Barrie, Barbara: Birth, May 23
Barrino, Fantasia: Birth, Jun 30
Barris, Chuck: Birth, Jun 3
Barrow, Clyde: Bonnie and Clyde: Death Anniv, May 23
Barry, Dave: Birth, Jul 3
Barry, Gene: Birth, Jun 14
Barry, John: Death Anniv, Sep 13
Barrymore, Drew: Birth, Feb 22
Barrymore, Ethel: Birth Anniv, Aug 15
Barrymore, John: Birth Anniv, Feb 15
Barrymore, Lionel: Birth Anniv, Apr 28
Barth, John: Birth, May 27
Bartholdi, Frederic A.: Birth Anniv, Apr 2
Bartholomew, Freddie: Birth Anniv, Mar 28
Bartlett, John: Birth Anniv, Jun 14
Bartlett, Josiah: Birth Anniv, Nov 21
Bartok, Bela: Birth Anniv, Mar 25
Bartoli, Cecilia: Birth, Jun 4
Barton, Clara: American Red Cross Founded: Anniv, May 21
Barton, Clara: Birth Anniv, Dec 25
Barton, Mischa: Birth, Jan 24
Baryshnikov, Mikhail: Birth, Jan 27
Bascom, Earl W.: Birth Anniv, Jun 19
Bascom, Florence: Birth Anniv, Jul 14
Bascom, George N.: Birth Anniv, Apr 24
Bascom, Texas Rose: Birth Anniv, Feb 25
Baseball. See also Softball
Ashford, Emmett: Birth Anniv, Nov 23
Babe Didrikson Pitches for Athletics: Anniv, Mar 21
Babe Ruth Calls His Shot?: Anniv, Oct 1
Babe Ruth's First Major League Home Run: Anniv, May 6
Babe Ruth's First Pro Homer: Anniv, Sep 5
Baseball Declared Nonessential: Anniv, Jul 20
Baseball First Played Under Lights: Anniv, May 24
Baseball Hall of Fame Dedicated, Natl: Anniv, Jun 12
Baseball's Greatest Dispute: Anniv, Sep 23
Baseball's Sad Lexicon Published: Anniv, Jul 10
Bell, James: Birth Anniv, May 17
Big Ten Tourn, May 20
Bonds Breaks Aaron's Career Home Run Record: Anniv, Aug 7
Bonds Breaks Season Home Run Record, Oct 5
Caray, Harry: Birth Anniv, Mar 1
Cobb, Ty: Birth Anniv, Dec 18
Designated Hitter Rule Adopted: Anniv, Jan 11
Doubleday, Abner: Birth Anniv, Jun 26
Evers, Johnny: Birth Anniv, Jul 21
First Baseball Games Televised: Anniv, Aug 26
First Baseball Strike Ends: Anniv, Apr 13
First Indoor Game: Anniv, Dec 25
First Perfect Game: Anniv, Jun 12
First Unassisted Triple Play, Anniv, Jul 19
Gehrig, Lou: Birth Anniv, Jun 19
Gibson, Josh: Birth Anniv, Dec 21
Greenberg, Hank: Birth Anniv, Jan 1
Hall of Fame's Charter Members: Anniv, Feb 2
Home Run Record: Anniv, Apr 8
Jackie Robinson Breaks Baseball Color Line: Anniv, Apr 15
Ladies' Day Initiated in Baseball: Anniv, Jun 16
Little League World Series (Williamsport, PA), Aug 21
Major League Baseball First All-Star Game: Anniv, Jul 6
Major League's First Double Header, Sep 25
Maris Breaks Ruth Home Run Record: Anniv, Oct 1
Martin, Billy: Birth Anniv, May 16
McGwire Breaks Home Run Record: Anniv, Sep 8
Midnight Sun Baseball Game (Fairbanks, AK), Jun 21
Mighty Casey Has Struck Out: Anniv, Jun 3
MLB All-Star Game (St. Louis, MO), Jul 7
NAIA World Series (Lewiston, ID), May 22
NCAA Div I Men's College World Series (Omaha, NE), Jun 13
President Taft Opens Baseball Season: Anniv, Apr 14
Ripken Streak Begins: Anniv, May 30
Robinson Named First Black Manager: Anniv, Oct 3
Tinker to Evers to Chance: First Double Play Anniv, Sep 15
Tinker, Joe: Birth Anniv, Jul 27
Young, Cy: Birth Anniv, Mar 29
Bashoff, Blake: Birth, May 30
Basinger, Kim: Birth, Dec 8
Basketball
Basketball Created: Anniv, Dec 1
Big Ten Men's Basketball Tourn (Indianapolis, IN), Mar 12
Big Ten Women's Basketball Tourn (Indianapolis, IN), Mar 5
Bulls Sign Michael Jordan: Anniv, Sep 12
Carrs/Safeway Great Alaska Shootout (Anchorage, AK), Nov 24

Chicago Bulls Third Straight Title for the Second Time, Jun 14
First Black Plays in NBA Game: Anniv, Oct 31
First Shattered Backboard: Anniv, Nov 5
First Women's Collegiate Basketball Game: Anniv, Mar 22
Harlem Globetrotters Play First Game: Anniv, Jan 7
NAIA Div I Men's Chmpshp (Kansas City, MO), Mar 18
NAIA Div I Women's Chmpshp (Jackson, TN), Mar 18
NAIA Div II Men's Chmpshp (Point Lookout, MO), Mar 11
NAIA Div II Women's Chmpshp (Sioux City, IA), Mar 11
NBA All-Star Game (Phoenix, AZ), Feb 15
NCAA Div I Men's Chmpshp (Detroit, MI), Apr 4
NCAA Div I Women's Chmpshp (St. Louis, MO), Apr 5
NJCAA Div II Men's Natl Basketball Finals (Danville, IL), Mar 18
Bassett, Angela: Birth, Aug 16
Bassey, Shirley: Birth, Jan 8
Bastille Day (France), Jul 14
Bataan Death March: Anniv, Apr 10
Bataan Death March: Araw ng Kagitingan (Philippines), Apr 9
Batali, Mario: Birth, Sep 9
Bateman, Jason: Birth, Jan 14
Bateman, Justine: Birth, Feb 19
Bates, Kathy: Birth, Jun 28
Bathtub Day, Read in the, Feb 9
Bathtub Party Day, Dec 5
Bathtub Race, Great (Nome, AK), Sep 7
Batman Debuts: Anniv, May 1
Batman TV Premiere: Anniv, Jan 12
Battier, Shane: Birth, Sep 9
Battle of Brandywine: Anniv, Sep 11
Battle of Britain Day (United Kingdom), Sep 15
Battle of Britain Week (United Kingdom), Sep 13
Battle of Bushy Run Reenactment (Harrison City, PA), Aug 1
Battle of Hastings: Anniv, Oct 14
Battle of Kursk: Anniv, Jul 12
Battle of Lexington and Concord: Anniv, Apr 19
Battle of Little Bighorn: Anniv, Jun 25
Battle of Midway: Anniv, Jun 4
Battle of Spotsylvania: Anniv, May 12
Battle, Kathleen: Birth, Aug 13
Baucus, Max: Birth, Dec 11
Baum, L. Frank: Birth Anniv, May 15
Baxter, Meredith: Birth, Jun 21
Bay of Pigs Invasion Launched: Anniv, Apr 17
Bay to Breakers Race, Ing (San Francisco, CA), May 17
Bayfest (Corpus Christi, TX), Sep 25
Bayh, Evan: Birth, Dec 26
Baylor, Don: Birth, Jun 28
Baylor, Elgin Gay: Birth, Sep 16
Baywatch TV Premiere: Anniv, Apr 23
BCS Natl Chmpshp Game (Miami, FL), Jan 8
Be Bald and Be Free Day, Oct 14
Be Electrific Day, Feb 11
Be Kind to Animals Week, May 3
Be Kind to Humankind Week, Aug 25
Be Late for Something Day, Sep 5
Be Nice to New Jersey Week, Jul 5
Beadle, George: Birth Anniv, Oct 22
Beals, Jennifer: Birth, Dec 19
Bean, Alan: Birth, Mar 15
Bean, Andy: Birth, Mar 13
Bean, Orson: Birth, Jul 22
Bean, Sean: Birth, Apr 17
Bean-Throwing Fest (Japan), Feb 3
Beard, Charles: Birth Anniv, Nov 27
Beard, James: Birth Anniv, May 5
Beardsley, Aubrey V.: Birth Anniv, Aug 21
Bearse, Amanda: Birth, Aug 9
Beasley, Allyce: Birth, Jul 6
Beasley, DaMarcus: Birth, May 24
Beat the Clock TV Premiere: Anniv, Mar 23
Beatles, The
Appear on The Ed Sullivan Show: Anniv, Feb 9
Bed-in for Peace: Anniv, Mar 25
Break Up: Anniv, Apr 10
Harrison, George: Birth Anniv, Feb 25
John Lennon Shot: Anniv, Dec 8
Last Concert: Anniv, Jan 30
Lennon Meets McCartney: Anniv, Jul 6
Lennon, John: Birth Anniv, Oct 9
McCartney, Paul: Birth, Jun 18
Sgt Pepper's Lonely Hearts Club Band Released: Anniv, Jun 1
Starr, Ringo: Birth, Jul 7
Take Over Music Charts: Anniv, Apr 4
Beatrix, Queen: Birth, Jan 31
Beatty, Ned: Birth, Jul 6
Beatty, Warren: Birth, Mar 30
Beaufort Scale Day, May 7
Beaumont, William: Birth Anniv, Nov 21
Beauregard, Genl: Battle of Shiloh: Anniv, Apr 6
Beauty and the Beast TV Premiere: Anniv, Sep 25
Beauty Contests, Pageants
First Miss America: Anniv, Sep 8
Miss American Rose Day, Oct 20
Miss Arizona Pageant (Gilbert, AZ), Jun 20
Miss Ohio Pageant (Mansfield, OH), Jun 12
Miss Oregon Scholarship Pageant (Seaside, OR), Jul 9
Miss South Carolina Pageant (Spartanburg, SC), Jun 30
Miss South Carolina Teen Competition (Spartanburg, SC), Jun 30
Miss Tennessee Pageant (Jackson, TN), Jun 17
Miss Virginia Pageant (Roanoke, VA), Jun 25
Beauty: Turn Beauty Inside Out Day, May 20
Beauvais-Nilon, Garcelle: Birth, Nov 26
Beauvoir, Simone de: Birth Anniv, Jan 9
Beaver Moon, Nov 2
Beavers, Louise: Birth Anniv, Mar 8
Beck, John: Birth, Jan 28
Beckenbauer, Franz: Birth, Sep 11
Becker, Boris: Birth, Nov 22
Beckett, Samuel: Birth Anniv, Apr 13
Beckham, David: Birth, May 2
Beckham, Victoria Adams: Birth, Apr 17
Beckinsale, Kate: Birth, Jul 26
Bed-and-Breakfast: Country Inn, Bed-and-Breakfast Day, Oct 4
Bedard, Irene: Birth, Jul 22
Bedelia, Bonnie: Birth, Mar 25
Bed-in for Peace: Anniv, Mar 25
Bednarik, Chuck: Birth, May 1
Beebe, Michael: Birth, Dec 28
Beecher, Catharine Esther: Birth Anniv, Sep 6
Beecher, Henry W.: Birth Anniv, Jun 24
Beef Empire Days (Garden City, KS), May 27
Beer; Beer-related Events
Beer Day (Iceland), Mar 1
Beer Fest (Luxembourg), Jul 19
Brewers Fest, Oregon (Portland, OR), Jul 23
Craft Brewers Conf & BrewExpo America (Boston, MA), Apr 21
Great American Beer Fest (Denver, CO), Sep 24
Telluride Blues & Brews Fest (Telluride, CO), Sep 18
Beethoven, Ludwig van: Birth Anniv, Dec 16
Beethoven's Ninth Symphony Premiere: Anniv, May 7
Beggar's Night, Oct 31
Begin, Menachem: Birth Anniv, Aug 16
Begley, Ed, Jr: Birth, Sep 16
Behan, Brendan: Birth Anniv, Feb 9
Behar, Joy: Birth, Oct 7
Beirut Terrorist Attack: Anniv, Oct 23
Belafonte, Harry: Birth, Mar 1
Belafonte-Harper, Shari: Birth, Sep 22
Belarus
Constitution Day, Mar 15
Independence Day, Jul 3
Bele Chere (Asheville, NC), Jul 24
Belfour, Ed: Birth, Apr 21
Belgium
Dynasty Day, Nov 15
Historical Procession (Tournai), Sep 6
Lover's Fair, Dec 3
Military Music Fest, Jun 14
National Holiday, Jul 21
Nuts Fair (Bastogne), Dec 21
Ommegang Pageant, Jul 2
Play of St. Evermaar, May 1
Procession of Golden Chariot (Mons), Jun 2
Procession of the Holy Blood, May 21
Believe It or Not TV Premiere: Anniv, Mar 1
Belize
Baron Bliss Day, Mar 9
Columbus Day, Oct 12
Commonwealth Day, May 24
Garifuna Day, Nov 19
Independence Day, Sep 21
Saint George's Caye Day, Sep 10
Bell, Alexander Graham: Birth Anniv, Mar 3
Bell, Catherine: Birth, Aug 14
Bell, James: Birth Anniv, May 17
Bell, Jay: Birth, Dec 11
Bell, Kristin: Birth, Jul 18
Bellamy, Ralph: Birth Anniv, Jun 17
Belle, Albert: Birth, Aug 25
Bellow, Saul: Birth Anniv, Jun 10
Belly Laugh Day, Jan 24
Belmont Stakes (Belmont Park, NY), Jun 6
Belote, Melissa: Birth, Oct 16
Beltane, Apr 30
Belushi, Jim: Birth, Jun 15
Belushi, John: Birth Anniv, Jan 24
Belzer, Richard: Birth, Aug 4
Benatar, Pat: Birth, Jan 10
Bench, Johnny: Birth, Dec 7
Benedict XVI, Pope: Birth, Apr 16
Benedict, Paul: Birth, Sep 17
Benes, Andy: Birth, Aug 20
Benet, William Rose: Birth Anniv, Feb 2
Ben-Gurion, David: Birth Anniv, Oct 16
Benigni, Roberto: Birth, Oct 27

Benin: Independence Day, Aug 1
Bening, Annette: Birth, May 29
Benjamin, Andre: Birth, May 27
Benjamin, Richard: Birth, May 22
Bennett, Arnold: Birth Anniv, May 27
Bennett, Cornelius: Birth, Aug 25
Bennett, Joan: Birth Anniv, Feb 27
Bennett, Richard Bedford: Birth Anniv, Jul 3
Bennett, Robert F.: Birth, Sep 18
Bennett, Tony: Birth, Aug 3
Bennington Battle Day: Anniv, Aug 16
Benny, Jack: Birth Anniv, Feb 14
Benrubi, Abraham: Birth, Oct 4
Benson, George: Birth, Mar 22
Benson, Robby: Birth, Jan 21
Bentley, Edmund Clerihew: Clerihew Day, Jul 10
Benton, Thomas Hart: Birth Anniv, Apr 15
Bereaved Parents Awareness Month, Jul 1
Berenger, Tom: Birth, May 31
Berenson, Marisa: Birth, Feb 15
Berenson, Red: Birth, Dec 8
Bergen, Candice: Birth, May 9
Bergen, Edgar: Birth Anniv, Feb 16
Bergen, Polly: Birth, Jul 14
Bergeron, Tom: Birth, May 6
Bergin, Michael: Birth, Mar 19
Bergl, Emily: Birth, Apr 25
Bergman, Ingmar: Birth Anniv, Jul 14
Bergman, Ingrid: Birth Anniv, Aug 29
Bergman, Peter: Birth, Jun 11
Bergson, Henri: Birth Anniv, Oct 18
Berkeley, Busby: Birth Anniv, Nov 29
Berkoff, Steven: Birth, Aug 3
Berle, Milton: Birth Anniv, Jul 12
Berlin Airlift: Anniv, Jun 24
Berlin Intl Film Fest (Berlin, Germany), Feb 5
Berlin Marathon (Berlin, Germany), Sep 27
Berlin Wall Erected: Anniv, Aug 13
Berlin Wall Opened: Anniv, Nov 9
Berlin Wall: Tear Down This Wall Speech: Anniv, Jun 12
Berlin, Irving: Birth Anniv, May 11
Berman, Shelley: Birth, Feb 3
Bermuda Colonized by English: Anniv, Mar 12
Bermuda: Peppercorn Ceremony, Apr 23
Bernard, Carlos: Birth, Oct 12
Bernard, Crystal: Birth, Sep 30
Berners-Lee, Tim: Birth, Jun 8
Bernhard, Sandra: Birth, Jun 6
Bernsen, Corbin: Birth, Sep 7
Bernstein, Carl: Birth, Feb 14
Bernstein, Leonard: Birth Anniv, Aug 25
Bernstein, Leonard: West Side Story Premiere: Anniv, Sep 26
Berra, Yogi: Birth, May 12
Berridge, Elizabeth: Birth, May 2
Berry, Chuck: Birth, Oct 18
Berry, Halle: Birth, Aug 14
Berry, Ken: Birth, Nov 3
Bertinelli, Valerie: Birth, Apr 23
Bertolucci, Bernardo: Birth, Mar 16
Beshear, Steve: Birth, Sept 21
Best Friend's Day, Aug 15
Best, George: Birth Anniv, May 22
Bethune, Mary McLeod: Birth Anniv, Jul 10
Bethune, Norman: Birth Anniv, Mar 3
Bettis, Jerome: Birth, Feb 16
Beverly Hillbillies TV Premiere: Anniv, Sep 26
Bewick, Thomas: Birth Anniv, Aug 12
Bewitched TV Premiere: Anniv, Sep 17
Bezos, Jeff: Birth, Jan 12
Bhopal Poison Gas Disaster: Anniv, Dec 3
Bhutan
  Coronation Day, Jun 2
  Natl Day, Jun 25
Bhutto, Benazir: Birth Anniv, Jun 21
Bialik, Mayim: Birth, Dec 12
Bibby, Mike: Birth, May 13
Bible Week, Natl, Nov 22
Bichette, Dante: Birth, Nov 18
Bicycles
  Big Mac Shoreline Fall Scenic Bike Tour (Mackinaw City, MI), Sep 12
  Big Mac Spring Scenic Bike Tour (Mackinaw City, MI), Jun 13
  Bike Month, Natl, May 1
  Bike to Work Day, Natl, May 15
  Bike Van Buren (Van Buren County, IA), Aug 15
  Five Boro Bike Tour (New York, NY), May 3
  Hotter 'n Hell Hundred Bike Race (Wichita Falls, TX), Aug 27
  Perry's "BRR" (Bike Ride to Rippey) (Perry, IA), Feb 7
  RAGBRAI—Register's Bicycle Ride Across Iowa (Des Moines, IA), Jul 19
  Tour de France, Jul 4
  Tour of Somerville (Somerville, NJ), May 25
Biddle, Nicholas: Birth Anniv, Jan 8
Biden, Joe: Birth, Nov 20
Biel, Jessica: Birth, Mar 3
Bifocals at the Monitor Liberation Day, Dec 1
Big Bend Natl Park Established: Anniv, Jun 12
Big Bertha Paris Gun: Anniv, Mar 23
Big E, The (West Springfield, MA), Sep 18
Big Mac Spring Scenic Bike Tour (Mackinaw City, MI), Jun 13
Big Sky State Games (Billings, MT), Jul 17
Big Top TV Premiere: Anniv, Jul 1
Big Wind: Anniv, Apr 12
Biggio, Craig: Birth, Dec 14
Biggs, Jason: Birth, May 12
Bike to Work Day, Natl, May 15
Bikel, Theodore: Birth, May 2
Bikini Debut: Anniv, Jul 5
Bill of Rights Proposed: Anniv, Jun 8
Bill of Rights: Anniv, Dec 15
Bill of Rights: Anniv of First State Ratification, Nov 20
Bill of Rights: Day (Pres Proc), Dec 15
Bill, Tony: Birth, Aug 23
Billingsley, Barbara: Birth, Dec 22
Billington, James Hadley: Birth, Jun 1
Billups, Chauncey: Birth, Sep 25
Billy the Kid: Birth Anniv, Nov 23
Bilson, Rachel: Birth, Aug 25
Bingaman, Jeff: Birth, Oct 3
Bingo's Birthday Month, Dec 1
Binoche, Juliette: Birth, Mar 9
Biodiesel Day, Natl (Rudolph Diesel Birth Anniv), Mar 18
Biographers Day, May 16
Biological Clock Gene Discovered: Anniv, Apr 28
Biological Diversity, Intl Day for (UN), May 22
Bioterrorism/Disaster Education and Awareness Month, Jul 1
Bird, Larry: Birth, Dec 7
Birds
  Bald Eagle Appreciation Days (Keokuk, IA), Jan 16
  Bird Feeding Months, Natl, Feb 1
  Crane Watch (Kearney, NE), Mar 1
  Curlew Day, Mar 16
  Down East Spring Birding Fest (Eastport, Whiting, Lubec, ME), May 22
  Duck-Calling Contest/Wings over Prairie Fest (Stuttgart, AR), Nov 27
  Eagle Day at the Lake (Kansas City, KS), Jan 17
  Eagle Days (Junction City, KS), Jan 17
  Eagle Days in Springfield (Springfield, MO), Jan 17
  Eagles Et Cetera Fest (Bismarck, AR), Jan 30
  Fest of Owls, Intl (Houston, MN), Mar 6
  Great Backyard Bird Count, Feb 13
  Hummer/Bird Celebration (Rockport, Fulton, TX), Sep 17
  Migratory Bird Celebration, Intl (Chincoteague, VA), May 9
  Migratory Bird Day, Intl, May 9
  Nestbox Week, Natl, Feb 14
  Picatinny Peak Fall Hawkwatch (Dover, NJ), Sep 1
  Raptor Month, Oct 1
  Respect for Chickens Day, Intl, May 4
  South Texas Wildlife and Birding Fest (Kingsville, TX), Nov 19
  Swallows Depart from San Juan Capistrano (CA), Oct 23
  Swallows Return to San Juan Capistrano (CA), Mar 19
  Waterfowl Fest (Easton, MD), Nov 13
  Wings over the Platte Spring Migration Celebration (Grand Island, NE), Feb 14
  Wings over Willcox—Sandhill Crane Celebration (Willcox, AZ), Jan 15
Birdseye, Clarence: Birth Anniv, Dec 9
Birkebeiner, American (Cable to Hayward, WI), Feb 19
Birkebeinerrennet (Rena and Lillehammer, Norway), Mar 21
Birkin, Jane: Birth, Dec 14
Birmingham (AL) Resistance: Anniv, Apr 3
Birmingham Riot: Anniv (England), Jul 14
Birney, David: Birth, Apr 23
Birth Control Clinic Opened, First: Anniv, Oct 16
Birth Control Pills Sold: Anniv, Aug 18
Birthday of Mother's Whistler, May 18
Biscayne Natl Park Established: Anniv, Jun 28
Bishop, Elvin: Birth, Oct 21
Bison-Ten-Yell Day, Sep 2
Bisset, Jacqueline: Birth, Sep 13
Bissett, Josie: Birth, Oct 5
Bjork: Birth, Nov 21
Black Cow Created: Anniv, Aug 19
Black Dahlia Murder: Anniv, Jan 15
Black Friday, Nov 27
Black Hills Stock Show and Rodeo (Rapid City, SD), Jan 30
Black History Month, Natl, Feb 1
Black Nazarene Fiesta (Philippines), Jan 1
Black Nazarene, Feast of the (Philippines), Jan 9
Black Press Day: Anniv of the First Black Newspaper, Mar 16
Black Single Parents' Week, May 31
Black Walnut Fest (Stockton, MO), Sep 23
Black, Clint: Birth, Feb 4
Black, Debbie: Birth, Jul 29
Black, Karen: Birth, Jul 1
Black, Lewis: Birth, Aug 30
Black, Shirley Temple: Birth, Apr 23
Blackmun, Harry A.: Birth Anniv, Nov 12
Blackout, East Coast: Anniv, Nov 9

Blackstone, William: Birth Anniv, Mar 5
Blackwell, Elizabeth, Awarded MD: Anniv, Jan 23
Blackwell, Elizabeth: Birth Anniv, Feb 3
Blades, Ruben: Birth, Jul 16
Blagojevich, Rod: Birth, Dec 10
Blah Blah Blah Day, Apr 17
Blaine, David: Birth, Apr 4
Blair, Bonnie: Birth, Mar 18
Blair, Linda: Birth, Jan 22
Blair, Tony: Birth, May 6
Blake, Eubie: Birth Anniv, Feb 7
Blake, James: Birth, Dec 28
Blake, Robert: Birth, Sep 18
Blake, William: Birth Anniv, Nov 28
Blakely, Susan: Birth, Sep 7
Blakey, Art: Birth Anniv, Oct 11
Blame Someone Else Day, Feb 13
Blanc, Mel: Birth Anniv, May 30
Blanchett, Cate: Birth, May 14
Blanco, Cuauhtemoc: Birth, Jan 17
Blanda, George: Birth, Sep 17
Blass, Bill: Birth Anniv, Jun 22
Blatty, William: Birth, Jan 7
Bledel, Alexis: Birth, Sep 16
Bledsoe, Drew: Birth, Feb 14
Bledsoe, Tempestt: Birth, Aug 1
Bleeth, Yasmine: Birth, Jun 14
Bleriot, Louis: Birth Anniv, Jul 1
Blessing of Animals at the Cathedral (Mexico), Jan 17
Blethyn, Brenda: Birth, Feb 20
Bleu, Corbin: Birth, Feb 21
Blige, Mary J.: Birth, Jan 11
Bliss, Lizzie: Birth Anniv, Apr 11
Blizzard, Great of '88: Anniv, Mar 12
Blondie and Deborah Harry Month, Intl, Jul 1
Blondin, Charles: Birth Anniv, Feb 28
Blondin, Charles: Conquest of Niagara Falls: Anniv, Jun 30
Blonsky, Nikki: Birth, Nov 9
Bloodworth-Thomason, Linda: Birth, Apr 15
Bloody Sunday (Northern Ireland): Anniv, Jan 30
Bloom, Claire: Birth, Feb 15
Bloom, Harold: Birth, Jul 11
Bloom, Orlando: Birth, Jan 13
Bloomberg, Michael: Birth, Feb 14
Bloomer, Amelia Jenks: Birth Anniv, May 27
Bloomsday: Anniv, Jun 16
Blue Hill Fair (Blue Hill, ME), Sep 3
Blue Moon, Dec 31
Blue Ribbon Week, Natl (Child Abuse), Apr 5
Blue Ridge Folklife Fest (Ferrum, VA), Oct 24
Blueberries Month, Natl, Jul 1
Blueberry Arts Fest (Ketchikan, AK), Aug 1
Blueberry Fest (Montrose, PA), Aug 7
Blueberry Fest, Natl (South Haven, MI), Aug 6
Bluegrass. See also Fiddlers
- Bluegrass Fest (Alta, WY), Aug 7
- Bluegrass Fest (Hope, AR), May 9
- Four Corner States Bluegrass Fest (Wickenburg, AZ), Nov 13
- Kentucky State Chmpshp Fiddler's Contest (Falls of Rough, KY), Jul 17
- Ladies of Country Music Show (Waretown, NJ), Jun 27
- Lil Margaret's Bluegrass and Old-Time Music Fest (Leonardtown, MD), Aug 6
- Nova Scotia Oldtime Music Fest (Stewiacke, NS), Jul 24
- Ocean County Bluegrass Fest (Waretown, NJ), Feb 8
- Old Fiddlers' Conv (Galax, VA), Aug 3
- Old-Time Fiddlers' Jamboree (Smithville, TN), Jul 3
- Polk County Ramp Tramp Fest (Benton, TN), Apr 24
- Red, White & Bluegrass (Hollywood, FL), May 15
- Targhee Fest (Alta, WY), Jul 17
- Thomas Point Beach Bluegrass Fest (Brunswick, ME), Sep 3

Bluford, Guion S., Jr: Birth, Nov 22
Blume, Judy: Birth, Feb 12
Blunt, Emily: Birth, Feb 23
Blunt, James: Birth, Feb 22
Blunt, Matt: Birth, Nov 20
Bly, Nellie: Around the World in 72 Days: Anniv, Jan 25
Bly, Nellie: Birth Anniv, May 5
Bly, Robert: Birth, Dec 23
Boats, Ships, Things That Float. See also Rowing
- Antique/Classic Boat Rendezvous (Mystic, CT), Jul 25
- Art Armada (Sheboygan, WI), Jul 4
- Big Ten Women's Rowing Chmpshps (Columbus, OH), May 2
- Burlington Steamboat Days/Music Fest (Burlington, IA), Jun 16
- Calgary Boat/Sportsmen's Show (Calgary, AB, Canada), Feb 12
- Civil War Submarine Attack: Anniv, Oct 5
- Classic Boat Fest (Victoria, BC, Canada), Aug 28
- Classic Boat Show (Tuckerton, NJ), Sep 5
- Cowes Week (Isle of Wight, England), Aug 1
- Devizes/Westminster Intl Canoe Race (Devizes, England), Apr 10
- Edmund Fitzgerald Sinking: Anniv, Nov 10
- First American to Circumnavigate Earth: Anniv, Aug 9
- Fort Lauderdale Intl Boat Show (Fort Lauderdale, FL), Oct 29
- Frenchman Rows Across Pacific: Anniv, Nov 21
- Fulton Sails Steamboat: Anniv, Aug 17
- Grand Rapids Boat Show (Grand Rapids, MI), Feb 18
- Head of the River Race (London, England), Mar 21
- Henley Royal Regatta (Henley-on-Thames, England), Jul 1
- Historical Regatta (Venice, Italy), Sep 6
- London Boat Show (London, England), Jan 9
- Lousiana Sportsmen's Show and Fest (Gonzales, LA), Mar 5
- Merrimac Destroyed: Anniv, May 11
- Miami Intl Boat/Sailboat Show (Miami Beach, FL), Feb 12
- Milwaukee Boat Show (Milwaukee, WI), Jan 16
- Monitor Sinking: Anniv, Dec 30
- New Orleans Boat Show (New Orleans, LA), Jan 7
- Newport Intl Boat Show (Newport, RI), Sep 17
- Newport Spring Boat Show (Newport, RI), May 15
- Ohio River Sternwheel Fest (Marietta, OH), Sep 11
- Ottawa Boat/Sportsmen Show (Ottawa, ON, Canada), Feb 26
- Palio del Golfo (La Spezia, Italy), Aug 9
- Providence Boat Show (Providence, RI), Jan 29
- Pumpkin Regatta, Windsor (Windsor, NS, Canada), Oct 10
- Queen Mary, RMS: Maiden Voyage: Anniv, May 27
- Remember the Maine Day: Anniv, Feb 15
- Royal George Sinks: Anniv, Aug 29
- Safe Boating Week, Natl, May 16
- Safe Boating Week, Natl (Pres Proc), May 16
- San Diego Boat Show (San Diego, CA), Jan 8
- Sea Music Fest (Mystic, CT), Jun 12
- SOS Adopted: Anniv, Nov 3
- Spanish War/Maine Memorial Day (MA), Feb 15
- Sternwheeler Days (Cascade Locks, OR), Jun 26
- Toms River Canoe and Kayak Race (Toms River, NJ), May 17
- Tybee 500 (Hollywood, FL; and Tybee Island, GA), May 10
- Ultimate Fishing Show (Novi, MI), Jan 8
- Vancouver Intl Boat Show (Vancouver, BC, Canada), Feb 4
- Washington Boat Show (Washington, DC), Feb 19
- Windjammer Days (Boothbay Harbor, ME), Jun 23
- Winterfest Boat Parade (Fort Lauderdale, FL), Dec 12
- Yacht Race, Intl: Anniv, Aug 22

Bob Hope Show TV Premiere: Anniv, Oct 12
Bob Newhart Show TV Premiere: Anniv, Oct 10
Bochco, Steven: Birth, Dec 16
Bock, Jerry: Birth, Nov 23
Bocuse, Paul: Birth, Feb 11
Bodman, Samuel: Birth, Nov 26
Boer War: Anniv, Oct 12
Boff, Leonardo: Birth, Dec 14
Bogart, Humphrey: Birth Anniv, Dec 25
Bogdanovich, Peter: Birth, Jul 30
Boggs, Wade: Birth, Jun 15
Bogosian, Eric: Birth, Apr 24
Bogues, Muggsy: Birth, Jan 9
Boi, Big: Birth, Feb 1
Boitano, Brian: Birth, Oct 22
Bol, Manute: Birth, Oct 16
Bold and the Beautiful TV Premiere: Anniv, Mar 23
Boleyn, Anne: Execution Anniv, May 19
Bolin, Jane M.: Birth Anniv, Apr 11
Bolivar, Simon: Birth Anniv, Jul 24
Bolivar, Simon: Death Anniv, Dec 17
Bolivia
- Alacitis Fair, Jan 24
- Independence Day, Aug 6
- La Paz Day, Jul 16

Boll, Heinrich: Birth Anniv, Dec 21
Bollingen Prize Award: Anniv, Feb 19
Bologna, Joseph: Birth, Dec 30
Bolton, Michael: Birth, Feb 27
Bomb Pop Day, Natl, Jun 25
Bombeck, Erma: Birth Anniv, Feb 21
Bombing, Oklahoma City: Anniv, Apr 19
Bombing, World Trade Center: Anniv, Feb 26
Bon Fest (Feast of Lanterns) (Japan), Jul 13
Bon Jovi, Jon: Birth, Mar 2
Bonaduce, Danny: Birth, Aug 13

Bonaparte, Napoleon: Birth Anniv, Aug 15
Bond, Carrie Jacobs: Birth Anniv, Aug 11
Bond, Christopher S.: Birth, Mar 6
Bond, Julian: Birth, Jan 14
Bonds Breaks Aaron's Career Home Run Record: Anniv, Aug 7
Bonds Breaks Season Home Run Record: Anniv, Oct 5
Bonds, Barry: Birth, Jul 24
Bonds, Gary U.S.: Birth, Jun 6
Bonerz, Peter: Birth, Aug 6
Bonet, Lisa: Birth, Nov 16
Bonham Carter, Helena: Birth, May 26
Bonheur, Rosa: Birth Anniv, Mar 16
Bonilla, Bobby: Birth, Feb 23
Bonnie and Clyde: Death Anniv, May 23
Bonnie Blue Natl Horse Show (Lexington, VA), May 14
Bono: Birth, May 10
Bonza Bottler Day, Jan 1
Bonza Bottler Day, Feb 2
Bonza Bottler Day, Mar 3
Bonza Bottler Day, Apr 4
Bonza Bottler Day, May 5
Bonza Bottler Day, Jun 6
Bonza Bottler Day, Jul 7
Bonza Bottler Day, Aug 8
Bonza Bottler Day, Sep 9
Bonza Bottler Day, Oct 10
Bonza Bottler Day, Nov 11
Bonza Bottler Day, Dec 12
Book and Copyright Day, World (UN), Apr 23
Books for Treats Day (San Jose, CA), Oct 31
Books. See also Library/Librarians
Alice's Adventures in Wonderland Published: Anniv, Nov 26
Appreciate a Dragon Day, Jan 16
Authors' Day, Natl, Nov 1
Baltimore Book Fest (Baltimore, MD), Sep 25
Bible Week, Natl, Nov 22
Biographers Day, May 16
Book Blitz Month, Jan 1
Book Day (Spain), Apr 23
BookExpo America (New York, NY), May 28
Children's Authors & Illustrators Week, Feb 1
Children's Book Day, Intl, Apr 2
Children's Book Week, Natl, May 11
Christmas Carol Published: Anniv, Dec 17
Copyright Law Passed: Anniv, May 31
Copyright Revision Law: Anniv, Jan 1
Cyberspace Coined: Neuromancer Publication Anniv, Oct 1
Dictionary Day, Oct 16
Essence of Motown Literary Jam (Detroit, MI), Nov 14
First Dictionary of American English Published: Anniv, Apr 14
Folk Tales and Fables Week, World, Mar 1
Frankfurt Book Fair (Frankfurt, Germany), Oct 14
Get Caught Reading Month, May 1
Ghostwriters Week, Natl, Mar 1
GLBT Book Month, Natl, Jun 1
Gone with the Wind Published: Anniv, May 19
Grapes of Wrath Published: Anniv, Apr 14
Guadalajara Intl Book Fair (Guadalajara, Mexico), Nov 28
Gutenberg Bible Published: Anniv, Sep 30
Joy of Cooking: Publication Anniv, Nov 30
Joy of Sex Published: Anniv, Oct 1
King James Bible Published: Anniv, May 2
Latino Books Month, May 1
Little Women Publication Anniv, Sep 30
London Book Fair (England), Apr 20
Lord of the Rings, First Part Published: Anniv, Jul 19
Maltese Falcon: Publication Anniv, Feb 14
Melville (Moby-Dick) Marathon (Mystic, CT), Jul 31
Mirror of the World Translation, Caxton's: Anniv, Mar 8
On the Origin of Species Published: Anniv, Nov 22
Paperback Books Introduced: Anniv, Jul 30
Profiles in Courage Published: Anniv, Jan 1
R.E.A.D. in America Day (Washington, DC), Sep 26
Read an E-Book Week, Mar 8
Reading Group Month, Natl, Oct 1
Reading Is Fun Week, May 10
Return the Borrowed Books Week, Mar 1
Romance Reader's Luncheon (Portland, OR), Apr 25
Small Press Month, Mar 1
Southern Fest of Books (Nashville, TN), Oct 9
Teen Read Week, Oct 18
To Kill a Mockingbird Published: Anniv, Jul 11
Young Reader's Day, Natl, Nov 10
Boom Box Parade (Willimantic, CT), Jul 4
Boom Days (Leadville, CO), Jul 31
Boomer Bonus Day, Apr 1
Boone, Bret: Birth, Apr 6
Boone, Daniel: Battle of Blue Licks Celebration (Mount Olivet, KY), Aug 15
Boone, Daniel: Birth Anniv, Nov 2
Boone, Daniel: Boone Day, Jun 7
Boone, Debbie: Birth, Sep 22
Boone, Pat: Birth, Jun 1
Boonesborough Days (Boonsboro, MD), Sep 12
Boorman, John: Birth, Jan 18
Boosler, Elayne: Birth, Aug 18
Booth, Edwin: Birth Anniv, Nov 13
Booth, Evangeline: Birth Anniv, Dec 25
Booth, John Wilkes, Escape Route Tour (Clinton, MD), Apr 11
Booth, Shirley: Birth Anniv, Aug 30
Booth, William: Birth Anniv, Apr 10
Boozer, Carlos: Birth, Nov 20
Borden, Lizzie, Verdict: Anniv, Jun 20
Borden, Sir Robert Laird: Birth Anniv, Jun 26
Boreanaz, David: Birth, May 16
Borg, Bjorn: Birth, Jun 6
Borges, Jorge Luis: Birth Anniv, Aug 24
Borglum, Gutzon: Birth Anniv, Mar 25
Borgnine, Ernest: Birth, Jan 24
Borman, Frank: Birth, Mar 14
Bosh, Chris: Birth, Mar 24
Bosley, Tom: Birth, Oct 1
Bosnia and Herzegovina
Independence Day, Mar 1
National Day, Nov 25
Boss/Employee Exchange Day, Natl, Sep 14
Boston Fire: Anniv, Nov 9
Boston Marathon (Boston, MA), Apr 20
Boston Massacre: Anniv, Mar 5
Boston Public Library: Anniv, Apr 3
Boston Tea Party: Anniv, Dec 16
Bostwick, Barry: Birth, Feb 24
Boswell, James: Birth Anniv, Oct 29
Bosworth, Kate: Birth, Jan 2
Botswana
Independence Day, Sep 30
Sir Seretse Khama Day, Jul 1
Bottoms, Timothy: Birth, Aug 30
Boucher, Brian: Birth, Jan 2
Boulez, Pierre: Birth, Mar 26
Bounty, Mutiny on the: Anniv, Apr 28
Bourke-White, Margaret: Birth Anniv, Jun 14
Bourque, Ray: Birth, Dec 28
Boutros-Ghali, Boutros: Birth, Nov 14
Bowditch, Nathaniel: Birth Anniv, Mar 26
Bowdler's Day, Jul 11
Bowe, Riddick: Birth, Aug 10
Bowen, Julie: Birth, Mar 3
Bowie, David: Birth, Jan 8
Bowman, Scotty: Birth, Sep 18
Boxer, Barbara: Birth, Nov 11
Boxing
Braddock, James: Birth Anniv, Jun 7
Clay Becomes Heavyweight Champ: Anniv, Feb 25
Corbett-Fitzsimmons Title Fight: Anniv, Mar 17
Corbett-Sullivan Prize Fight: Anniv, Sep 7
First Black Heavyweight Champion: Anniv, Dec 26
First US Heavyweight Champ Defeated: Anniv, Dec 10
Johnson, John (Jack) Arthur: Birth Anniv, Mar 31
Long Count Day, Sep 22
Louis v Braddock/Schmeling Fight Anniv, Jun 22
Louis, Joe: Birth Anniv, May 13
Moore, Archie: Birth Anniv, Dec 13
Muhammad Ali Stripped of Title: Anniv, Apr 30
Patterson, Floyd: Birth Anniv, Jan 4
Robinson, Sugar Ray: Birth Anniv, May 3
Schmeling, Max: Birth Anniv, Sep 28
Tyson Bites Holyfield: Anniv, Jun 28
Boxing Day (United Kingdom), Dec 26
Boxing Day Bank Holiday (United Kingdom), Dec 26
Boxleitner, Bruce: Birth, May 12
Boy George: Birth, Jun 14
Boy Scouts of America Founded: Anniv, Feb 8
Boy Scouts: Baden-Powell, Robert: Birth Anniv, Feb 22
Boycott, Charles C.: Birth Anniv, Mar 12
Boyd, Belle: Birth Anniv, May 9
Boyd, William: Birth Anniv, Jun 5
Boyer, Charles: Birth Anniv, Aug 28
Boyle, Lara Flynn: Birth, Mar 24
Boyle, Robert: Birth Anniv, Jan 25
Boyle, T. Coraghessan: Birth, Dec 2
Boys' Clubs Founded: Anniv, May 19
Bracco, Lorraine: Birth, Oct 2
Brackett Day, Joseph, May 6
Bradbury, Ray: Birth, Aug 22
Braddock, James: Birth Anniv, Jun 7
Bradford, Barbara Taylor: Birth, May 10
Bradford, William: Birth Anniv, Mar 19
Bradlee, Benjamin: Birth, Aug 26
Bradley, Bill: Birth, Jul 28
Bradley, Ed: Birth Anniv, Jun 22
Bradshaw, Terry: Birth, Sep 2
Bradstreet: Anne Bradstreet Day, Sep 16
Brady Bunch TV Premiere: Anniv, Sep 26
Brady, Mathew: First Presidential Photograph: Anniv, Feb 14
Brady, Sarah: Birth, Feb 6
Brady, Tom: Birth, Aug 3

Braemar Royal Highland Gathering (Braemar, Scotland), Sep 5
Braff, Zach: Birth, Apr 6
Braga, Sonia: Birth, Jun 16
Brahms Requiem Premiere: Anniv, Apr 10
Brahms, Johannes: Birth Anniv, May 7
Braille, Louis: Birth Anniv, Jan 4
Brain Awareness Week, Intl, Mar 16
Branagh, Kenneth: Birth, Dec 10
Branch Davidian Fire at Waco: Anniv, Apr 19
Brand, Elton: Birth, Mar 11
Brand, Oscar: Birth, Feb 7
Brandauer, Klaus Maria: Birth, Jun 22
Brandeis, Louis D.: Birth Anniv, Nov 13
Brando, Marlon: Birth Anniv, Apr 3
Brando, Marlon: Godfather Film Premiere: Anniv, Mar 15
Brandt, Willy: Birth Anniv, Dec 18
Brandy: Birth, Feb 11
Branson Veterans Homecoming (Branson, MO), Nov 5
Brasilia Inaugurated: Anniv, Apr 21
Bratt, Benjamin: Birth, Dec 16
Braugher, Andre: Birth, Jul 1
Braxton, Carter: Birth Anniv, Sep 10
Braxton, Toni: Birth, Oct 7
Brazil
  Brasilia Inaugurated: Anniv, Apr 21
  Carnival, Feb 21
  Cirio de Nazare, Oct 11
  Discovery of Brazil Day, Apr 22
  Fest of Penha (Rio de Janeiro), Oct 1
  Independence Day, Sep 7
  Independence Week, Sep 1
  Nosso Senhor Do Bonfim Fest, Jan 20
  Republic Day, Nov 15
  San Sebastian's Day, Jan 20
  Tiradentes Day, Apr 21
Brazleton, T. Berry: Birth, May 10
Brazzi, Rossano: Birth Anniv, Sep 18
Breach of Promise Suit, First US: Anniv, Jun 14
Bread Day, Homemade, Nov 17
Bread Pudding Recipe Exchange, May 1
Breakfast Club Radio Premiere: Anniv, Jun 23
Bream, Julian: Birth, Jul 15
Breast Cancer Awareness Month, Natl, Oct 1
Breast Cancer Awareness Month, Natl (Pres Proc), Oct 1
Breastfeeding Week, World, Aug 1
Breathed, Berke: Birth, Jun 21
Brecht, Bertolt: Birth Anniv, Feb 10
Breckinridge, John Cabell: Birth Anniv, Jan 21
Bredesen, Phil: Birth, Nov 21
Breeders' Cup (Arcadia, CA), Nov 6
Brees, Drew: Birth, Jan 15
Brennan, Eileen: Birth, Sep 3
Brennan, William: Birth Anniv, Apr 25
Brenneman, Amy: Birth, Jun 22
Brenner, David: Birth, Feb 4
Brent, Margaret: Demands a Political Voice: Anniv, Jan 21
Breslin, Abigail: Birth, Apr 14
Brett, George: Birth, May 15
Brewers Fest, Oregon (Portland, OR), Jul 23
Breyer, Stephen G.: Birth, Aug 15
Brezhnev, Leonid: Birth Anniv, Dec 19
Brickell, Edie: Birth, Mar 10
Brickhouse, Jack: Birth Anniv, Jan 24
Bridge Day (Fayetteville, WV), Oct 17
Bridge Fest, Covered (Washington County, PA), Sep 19
Bridge Fest, Parke County Covered (Rockville, IN), Oct 9
Bridge over the Neponset: Anniv, Apr 1
Bridger, Jim: Birth Anniv, Mar 17
Bridges, Beau: Birth, Dec 9
Bridges, Jeff: Birth, Dec 4
Bridges, Todd: Birth, May 27
Brimley, Wilford: Birth, Sep 27
Brinkley, Christie: Birth, Feb 2
Brinkley, David: Birth Anniv, Jul 10
Brisebois, Danielle: Birth, Jun 28
Britain Declares War on Germany: Anniv, Sep 3
British and World Marbles Chmpshp, Apr 10
British Museum: Anniv, Jan 15
British North America Act: Anniv, Mar 29
British Open (Open Chmpshp) (Turnberry, Scotland), Jul 12
Brittany, Morgan: Birth, Dec 5
Britten, (Edward) Benjamin: Birth Anniv, Nov 22
Britton, Connie: Birth, Mar 6
Broadbent, Jim: Birth, May 24
Brock, Lou: Birth, Jun 18
Broderick, Matthew: Birth, Mar 21
Brodeur, Martin: Birth, May 6
Brody, Adam: Birth, Dec 15
Brody, Adrien: Birth, Apr 14
Brokaw, Tom: Birth, Feb 6
Brolin, James: Birth, Jul 18
Brolin, Josh: Birth, Feb 12
Bronson, Charles: Birth Anniv, Nov 3
Bronte, Charlotte: Birth Anniv, Apr 21
Bronte, Emily: Birth Anniv, Jul 30
Brook, Peter: Birth, Mar 21
Brooklyn Bridge Opened: Anniv, May 24
Brooks, Albert: Birth, Jul 22
Brooks, Garth: Birth, Feb 7
Brooks, James David: Birth Anniv, Oct 18
Brooks, James L.: Birth, May 9
Brooks, Jason: Birth, May 10
Brooks, Louise: Birth Anniv, Nov 14
Brooks, Mel: Birth, Jun 28
Brooks, Phillips: Birth Anniv, Dec 13
Brosnan, Pierce: Birth, May 16
Brother's Day, May 24
Brothers TV Premiere: Anniv, Jul 13
Brothers, Joyce: Birth, Sep 20
Brothers: Siblings Day, Natl, Apr 10
Brougham, Henry P.: Birth Anniv, Sep 19
Brown v Board of Education: Anniv, May 17
Brown, Alton, Jul 30
Brown, Bobby: Birth, Feb 5
Brown, Bryan: Birth, Jun 23
Brown, Curtis, Jr: Birth, Mar 11
Brown, Dan: Birth, Jun 22
Brown, Gordon: Birth, Feb 20
Brown, Helen Gurley: Birth, Feb 18
Brown, James: Birth Anniv, May 3
Brown, Jesse Leroy: Birth Anniv, Oct 13
Brown, Jim: Birth, Feb 17
Brown, John: Birth Anniv, May 9
Brown, John: Execution Anniv, Dec 2
Brown, John: Raid Anniv, Oct 16
Brown, Sherrod: Birth, Nov 9
Brown, Tina: Birth, Dec 21
Brown, Tony: Birth, Apr 11
Brownback, Sam: Birth, Sep 12
Browne, Jackson: Birth, Oct 9
Browne, Thomas: Birth Anniv, Oct 19
Browning, Elizabeth Barrett: Birth Anniv, Mar 6
Browning, John Moses: Birth Anniv, Jan 21
Browning, Robert: Birth Anniv, May 7
Brownmiller, Susan: Birth, Feb 15
Broz, Josip "Tito": Birth Anniv, May 25
Brubeck, Dave: Birth, Dec 6
Bruce, Isaac: Birth, Nov 10
Bruce, Lenny: Birth Anniv, Oct 13
Bruckner, Anton: Birth Anniv, Sep 4
Brummell, Beau: Birth Anniv, Jun 7
Brunei: National Day, Feb 23
Brunell, Mark: Birth, Sep 17
Brutus Day, Mar 15
Bryan, Sabrina: Birth, Sep 16
Bryan, William Jennings: Birth Anniv, Mar 19
Bryan, Zachery Ty: Birth, Oct 9
Bryant, Anita: Birth, Mar 25
Bryant, Kobe: Birth, Aug 23
Bryant, William C.: Birth Anniv, Nov 3
Bryce Canyon Natl Park Established: Anniv, Jan 1
Bryson, Peabo: Birth, Apr 13
Bubba Day, Natl, Jun 2
Bubble Gum Day, Feb 6
Bubble Week, Natl, Mar 20
Bubble Wrap Appreciation Day, Jan 26
Bublé, Michael: Birth, Sep 9
Buchanan, James: Birth Anniv, Apr 23
Buchanan, Patrick: Birth, Nov 2
Buchenwald, Liberation of: Anniv, Apr 11
Buck Moon, Jul 7
Buck Rogers TV Premiere: Anniv, Apr 15
Buck, Pearl S.: Birth Anniv, Jun 26
Buckingham, Lindsey: Birth, Oct 3
Buckley, Betty: Birth, Jul 3
Buckley, William F.: Birth Anniv, Nov 24
Buckner, Bill: Birth, Dec 14
Buckwheat Fest, Preston County (Kingwood, WV), Sep 24
Buddha: Birth Anniv, Apr 8
Buddha: Birthday (China), May 2
Buell, Marjorie H.: Birth Anniv, Dec 11
Buffalo Auction (Custer, SD), Nov 21
Buffalo Bill (William F. Cody): Birth Anniv, Feb 26
Buffalo Days Celebration (Luverne, MN), Jun 5
Buffalo Roundup (Custer, SD), Sep 28
Buffett, Jimmy: Birth, Dec 25
Buffy the Vampire Slayer TV Premiere: Anniv, Mar 10
Bugs Bunny's Debut: Anniv, Apr 30
Bujold, Genevieve: Birth, Jul 1
Bulgaria
  Babin Den (Day of the Midwives), Jan 23
  Culture Day, May 24
  Hristo Botev Day, Jun 2
  Liberation Day, Mar 3
  Saint Lasarus's Day, Apr 1
  Unification Day, Sep 6
  Viticulturists' Day, Feb 14
Bulldogs Are Beautiful Day, Natl, Apr 25
Bullfinch Exchange Fest (Japan), Jan 7
Bullock, Sandra: Birth, Jul 26
Bullwinkle Show: Rocky and His Friends TV Premiere: Anniv, Nov 19
Bullying: Freedom from Bullies Week, Oct 18
Bumbershoot: Seattle's Music & Arts Fest (Seattle, WA), Sep 5
Bun Day (Iceland), Feb 23
Bunche, Ralph: Awarded Nobel Peace Prize: Anniv, Dec 10
Bunche, Ralph: Birth Anniv, Aug 7
Bundt Day, Natl, Nov 15
Bunker Hill Day (Suffolk County, MA), Jun 17
Bunning, Jim: Birth, Oct 23

Bunsen Burner Day, Mar 31
Bunsen, Robert: Birth, Mar 31
Bunyan, John: Birth Anniv, Nov 28
Buonarroti, Michelangelo: Birth Anniv, Mar 6
Buoniconti, Nick: Birth, Dec 15
Burbank, Luther: Birth Anniv, Mar 7
Bure, Candace Cameron: Birth, Apr 6
Bure, Pavel: Birth, Mar 31
Bureau of Indian Affairs Established, Mar 11
Bureau of Internal Revenue Established: Anniv, Jul 1
Burger, Warren E.: Birth Anniv, Sep 17
Burgess, Anthony: Birth Anniv, Feb 25
Burghoff, Gary: Birth, May 24
Burgoo Fest (Utica, IL), Oct 11
Burk, Martha (Calamity Jane): Death Anniv, Aug 1
Burke, Cheryl: Birth, May 12
Burke, Christopher: Birth, Aug 26
Burke, Delta: Birth, Jul 30
Burke, Edmund: Birth Anniv, Jan 12
Burkina Faso
  National Day, Dec 11
  Republic Day, Aug 5
  Revolution Day, Aug 4
Burnett, Carol: Birth, Apr 26
Burnham, Daniel: Birth Anniv, Sep 4
Burnquist, Bob: Birth, Oct 10
Burns and Allen Show TV Premiere: Anniv, Oct 12
Burns, George: Birth Anniv, Jan 20
Burns, Ken: Birth, Jul 29
Burns, Robert: Birth Anniv, Jan 25
Burr, Aaron: Birth Anniv, Feb 6
Burr, Aaron: Duel with Alexander Hamilton: Anniv, Jul 11
Burr, Raymond: Birth Anniv, May 21
Burr, Richard: Birth, Nov 30
Burro Race (Leadville, CO), Jul 31
Burroughs, Edgar Rice: Birth Anniv, Sep 1
Burroughs, John: Birth Anniv, Apr 3
Burrows, James: Birth, Dec 30
Bursting Day (Iceland), Feb 24
Burstyn, Ellen: Birth, Dec 7
Burton, Hilarie: Birth, Jul 1
Burton, LeVar: Birth, Feb 16
Burton, Richard: Birth Anniv, Nov 10
Burton, Tim: Birth, Aug 25
Burundi
  Assassination of the Hero of the Nation Day, Oct 13
  Independence Day, Jul 1
Buscemi, Steve: Birth, Dec 13
Busey, Gary: Birth, Jun 29
Busfield, Timothy: Birth, Jun 12
Bush, Barbara Pierce: Birth, Jun 8
Bush, George H.W. and Barbara, Wedding: Anniv, Jan 6
Bush, George Herbert Walker: Birthday, Jun 12
Bush, George W. and Laura, Wedding: Anniv, Nov 5
Bush, George W.: Birthday, Jul 6
Bush, George W.: Supreme Court Rules for Bush: Anniv, Dec 12
Bush, Kate: Birth, Jul 30
Bush, Laura: Birthday, Nov 4
Bush, Reggie: Birth, Mar 2
Bush, Sophia: Birth, Jul 8
Business (including business history, skills, workplace life, types of). See also Careers
  American Business Women's Day, Sep 22
  America's First Department Store: Anniv, Oct 16
  AT&T Divestiture: Anniv, Jan 8
  Be Heard Day, Natl, Mar 7
  Better Business Communication Day, Jan 26
  Black Business Month, Aug 1
  Boss/Employee Exchange Day, Natl, Sep 14
  Bring Your Teddy Bear to Work Day, Natl, Oct 14
  Build a Better Trade Show Image Week, Feb 15
  Build Your Business with Business Cards Week, Oct 11
  Business Etiquette Week, Jun 7
  Business Image Improvement Month, Intl, May 1
  Business of America Quotation: Anniv, Jan 17
  Business Women's Week, Natl, Oct 19
  Clean-Off-Your-Desk Day, Natl, Jan 12
  Companies That Care Day, Mar 19
  Computer Security Day, Nov 30
  Co-Op Awareness Month, Oct 1
  Craft Brewers Conf & BrewExpo America (Boston, MA), Apr 21
  Credit Union Week, Intl, Oct 11
  Customer Loyalty Month, Intl, Apr 1
  Cyber Monday, Nov 30
  Employee Legal Awareness Day, Feb 13
  Employee Spirit Month, Mar 1
  Enron Files for Bankruptcy: Anniv, Dec 2
  Entrepreneurs "Do It Yourself" Marketing Month, Jun 1
  Ethics Awareness Month, Natl, Mar 1
  Fair Trade Day, World, May 9
  Federal Government Seizure of Steel Mills: Anniv, Apr 8
  First US Chamber of Commerce Founded: Anniv, Apr 5
  Five-Dollar-a-Day Minimum Wage: Anniv, Jan 5
  Fun at Work Day, Jan 30
  Fun at Work Day, Natl, Apr 1
  Get to Know Your Customer Day, Jan 15
  Getting the World to Beat a Path to Your Door Week, Oct 11
  Google Founded: Anniv, Sep 7
  Handshake Day, Natl, Jun 25
  Home Office Day, Improve Your, Oct 5
  Home-Based Business Week, Oct 11
  Independent Retailers Week, Natl, Jul 19
  Internal Audit Awareness Month, Intl, May 1
  Irrational Exuberance Enters Lexicon: Anniv, Dec 5
  Just Say No to PowerPoint Week, Feb 9
  Laugh and Get Rich Day, Feb 8
  Laugh at Work Week, Apr 1
  Laugh-Friendly Month, Natl, Feb 1
  Leave the Office Earlier Day, Natl, Jun 2
  Ludlow Mine Incident: Anniv, Apr 20
  Mail-Order Catalog: Anniv, Aug 18
  Mom and Pop Business Owners Day, Natl, Mar 29
  Montgomery Ward Seized: Anniv, Apr 26
  Napping Day, Natl, Mar 9
  Networking Week, Intl, Feb 2
  Networking Week, Natl, Apr 6
  New Years' Resolutions Month for Businesses, Intl, Jan 1
  New York Stock Exchange Established: Anniv, May 17
  On-Hold Month, Natl, Mar 1
  Payroll Week, Natl, Sep 7
  Printing Week, Intl, Jan 11
  Professional Wellness Month, Jun 1
  Publicity for Profit Week, Feb 1
  Recess at Work Day, Jun 18
  Record Store Day, Apr 18
  Return to Work Week, Natl, May 10
  Revise Your Work Schedule Month, May 1
  Scrapbooking Industry Day, Intl, Mar 4
  Self-Promotion Month, Oct 1
  Shameless Promotion Month, Sep 1
  Smith, Adam: Birth Anniv, Jun 5
  Stay Home Because You're Well Day, Nov 30
  Stock Market Crash of 1893: Anniv, May 5
  Stock Market Crash of 1929: Anniv, Oct 29
  Strategic Planning Month, Intl, Oct 1
  Subliminal Communications Month, Sep 1
  Support Your Local Chamber of Commerce Day, Natl, Oct 21
  Take Our Daughters and Sons to Work Day, Apr 23
  Take Your Dog to Work Day, Jun 26
  Telecommuter Appreciation Week, Mar 1
  Tourism Week, Natl, May 9
  Triangle Shirtwaist Fire: Anniv, Mar 25
  Wear Your Pajamas to Work Day, Natl, Apr 16
  Women's Ecommerce Day, Intl, Sep 21
  Women's Small Business Month, Oct 1
  Work and Family Month, Natl, Oct 1
  Work from Home Week, Natl, Oct 4
  Workplace Conflict Awareness Month, Apr 1
  Workplace Eye Health and Safety Month, Mar 1
  Workplace Politics Awareness Month, Oct 1
  Write a Business Plan Month, Natl, Dec 1
Butkus, Dick: Birth, Dec 9
Butler, Benjamin: Farragut Captures New Orleans: Anniv, Apr 25
Butler, Brett: Birth, Jan 30
Butler, Caron: Birth, Mar 13
Butler, Dan: Birth, Dec 2
Butler, Gerard: Birth, Nov 13
Butler, Octavia: Birth Anniv, Jun 22
Butler, Samuel: Birth Anniv, Dec 4
Button, Dick: Birth, Jul 18
Butts, Alfred M.: Birth Anniv, Apr 13
Buy Nothing Day, Nov 27
Buzzi, Ruth: Birth, Jul 24
Bynes, Amanda: Birth, Apr 3
Byrd, Robert C.: Birth, Nov 20
Byrne, David: Birth, May 14
Byrne, Gabriel: Birth, May 12
Byrne, Rose: Birth, Jul 24
Byrnes, Edd: Birth, Jul 30
Byron, George Gordon: Birth Anniv, Jan 22

C

Caan, James: Birth, Mar 26
Cabinet, US: Perkins, Frances (First Woman Appointed), Mar 4
Cable Car Patent: Anniv, Jan 17
Cabrillo Day (CA), Sep 28
Cabrillo Fest (San Diego, CA), Oct 3
Cabrini, Mother Frances Xavier: Canonization Anniv, Jul 7
Caesar, Sid: Birth, Sep 8
Caesarean Section, First: Anniv, Jan 14
Caffeine Awareness Month, Natl, Mar 1
Cage, John: Birth Anniv, Sep 5
Cage, Nicolas: Birth, Jan 7
Cagney & Lacey TV Premiere: Anniv, Mar 25

Cahn, Sammy: Birth Anniv, Jun 18
Cain, Dean: Birth, Jul 31
Caine, Michael: Birth, Mar 14
Cake Decorating Day, Natl, Oct 10
Calabro, Thomas: Birth, Feb 3
Calamity Jane (Martha Burk): Death Anniv, Aug 1
Calder, Alexander: Birth Anniv, Jul 22
Calderon, Felipe: Birth, Aug 18
Caldwell, Zoe: Birth, Sep 14
Calendar Adjustment Day: Anniv, Sep 2
Calendar Day, Gregorian, Feb 24
Calendar Stone, Aztec, Discovery: Anniv, Dec 17
Calhoun, John C.: Birth Anniv, Mar 18
Calhoun, John C.: VP Resignation: Anniv, Dec 28
California
Admission Day, Sep 9
Aerospace Walk of Honor (Lancaster), Sep 19
African Diaspora Day, Intl (Los Angeles), Oct 11
AFRMA Display at America's Family Pet Expo (Costa Mesa), Apr 10
AKC/Eukanuba Natl Chmpshp (Long Beach), Dec 12
Blessing of the Fishing Fleet (San Francisco), Oct 4
Bob Hope Chrysler Classic (Palm Springs), Jan 19
Books for Treats Day (San Jose), Oct 31
Boxer, Barbara: Birth, Nov 11
Breeders' Cup (Arcadia), Nov 6
Cabrillo Day, Sep 28
Cabrillo Fest (San Diego), Oct 3
Calaveras Fair/Jumping Frog Jubilee (Angel Camp), May 13
California Artichoke Fest (Castroville), May 16
California Gold Discovery: Anniv, Jan 24
California Poppy Fest (Lancaster), Apr 25
California State Fair (Sacramento), Aug 21
CAMEX (Anaheim), Mar 13
Carlsbad Marathon (Carlsbad), Jan 25
Catholic Educational Assn Conv/Expo, Natl (Anaheim), Apr 14
Cesar Chavez Day, Mar 31
Channel Islands Natl Park Established: Anniv, Mar 5
Chinese New Year Fest & Parade (San Francisco), Jan 24
Chinese New Year Parade (San Francisco), Feb 7
Christmas Parade (El Centro), Dec 5
Clam Chowder Cook-off (Santa Cruz), Feb 21
Coin & Stamp Expo (Anaheim), May 1
Coin & Stamp Expo (Anaheim), Sep 4
Coin & Stamp Expo (Anaheim), Oct 2
Coin & Stamp Expo (Los Angeles), Mar 27
Coin & Stamp Expo (Pasadena), Feb 13
Coin & Stamp Expo (Pasadena), May 22
Coin & Stamp Expo (Pasadena), Jul 3
Coin & Stamp Expo (Sherman Oaks), Jun 12
Coin & Stamp Expo: America (Anaheim), Nov 13
Coin & Stamp Expo: California (Pasadena), Nov 13
Comic-Con Intl (San Diego), Jul 23
Craft & Hobby Assn Winter Conv & Trade Show (Anaheim), Jan 25
Date Fest, Natl (Indio), Feb 13
Disneyland Opened: Anniv, Jul 17
Education Assn Meeting, Natl (San Diego), Jul 1
Fancy Rat & Mouse Display, AFRMA (Costa Mesa), Jul 28
Feinstein, Dianne: Birth, Jun 22
Festival of Children (Costa Mesa), Sep 4
Fiesta la Ballona (Culver City), Aug 21
Gilroy Garlic Fest (Gilroy), Jul 24
Go Wild During California Wild Rice Month, Sep 1
Golden Gate Bridge Opened: Anniv, May 27
Grubstake Days (Yucca Valley), May 23
Handel's Messiah Sing-Along (Yorba Linda), Nov 29
Harvest Wine Celebration (Livermore), Sep 6
Haute Dog Charity Easter Parade (Long Beach), Apr 12
Haute Dog Charity Howl'oween Parade (Long Beach), Oct 25
Huck Finn's Jubilee (Victorville), Jun 19
Ing Bay to Breakers Race (San Francisco), May 17
Invisible Chronic Illness Awareness Week, Natl (San Diego), Sep 14
Kraft Nabisco Chmpshp (Rancho Mirage), Mar 30
Lassen Volcanic Natl Park Established: Anniv, Aug 9
Long Beach Bayou Fest (Long Beach), Jun 21
Los Angeles Founded: Anniv, Sep 4
Los Angeles Riots: Anniv, Apr 29
Mainly Mozart Fest (San Diego), Jun 8
Mission San Carlos Borromeo de Carmelo: Founding Anniv, Jun 3
Mobius Awards (Los Angeles), Feb 7
Monterey Jazz Fest (Monterey), Sep 18
Morro Bay Harbor Fest (Morro Bay), Oct 3
Mother Goose Parade (El Cajon), Nov 22
NAIA Men's Soccer Natl Chmpshp (Fresno), Nov 30
NAPNAP Annual Conf (San Diego), Mar 19
Newspaper Assn of America Conv (San Diego), Apr 5
Nixon Birthday Holiday (Yorba Linda), Jan 9
Pasadena Doo Dah Parade (Pasadena), Jan 18
Pelosi, Nancy: Birth, Mar 26
Proposition 13: Anniv, Jun 6
Rat and Mouse Annual Show, Fancy (Riverside), Jan 24
Redwood Natl Park Established: Anniv, Oct 2
Rideshare Week, Oct 5
Rose Bowl Game (Pasadena), Jan 1
Sacramento Jazz Jubilee (Sacramento), May 22
San Diego Boat Show (San Diego), Jan 8
San Francisco Silent Film Fest (San Francisco), Jul 10
Schwarzenegger, Arnold: Birth, Jul 30
Sequoia and Kings Canyon Natl Park Established: Anniv, Sep 25
Shaping Black Culture in the Diaspora (Los Angeles), Oct 9
Snowbirds Pancake Breakfast (El Centro), Jan 10
Sonoma-Marin Fair (Petaluma), Jun 24
Southern California Firestorms: Anniv, Oct 25
Swallows Depart from San Juan Capistrano, Oct 23
Swallows Return to San Juan Capistrano, Mar 19
Tamale Fiesta (El Centro), Dec 5
Taste of Morgan Hill (Morgan Hill), Sep 26
Tournament of Roses Parade (Pasadena), Jan 1
US Intl Film/Video Awards (Los Angeles), Jun 5
World Ag Expo (Tulare), Feb 10
World's Fair of Money (Los Angeles), Aug 5
World's Ugliest Dog Contest (Petaluma), Jun 26
XTERRA Vail Lake Xduro (Temecula), May 16
Yosemite Natl Park Established: Anniv, Oct 1
Callas, Maria: Birth Anniv, Dec 2
Callas, Maria: Last Performance: Anniv, Jul 5
Callis, James: Birth, Jun 4
Callow, Simon: Birth, Jun 15
Calloway, Cab: Birth Anniv, Dec 25
Calvin, John: Birth Anniv, Jul 10
Cambodia
Constitutional Declaration Day, Sep 24
Falls to the Khmer Rouge: Anniv, Apr 17
Independence Day, Nov 9
Invaded by US: Anniv, Apr 30
Peace Treaty Day, Oct 23
Pol Pot Overthrown: Anniv, Jan 7
Camcorder Developed: Anniv, Jan 20
Camden, Battle of: Anniv, Aug 16
Cameron, James: Birth, Aug 16
Cameron, James: Titanic Released: Anniv, Dec 19
Cameron, Kirk: Birth, Oct 12
Cameroon
Natl Holiday, May 20
Volcanic Eruption: Anniv, Aug 22
Youth Day, Feb 11
CAMEX (Anaheim, CA), Mar 13
Camp David Accord Signed: Anniv, Mar 26
Camp Fire Birthday Week, Mar 16
Camp Fire Founders Day, Mar 17
Camp, Walter: Birth Anniv, Apr 7
Campanella, Roy: Birth Anniv, Nov 19
Campbell, Billy: Birth, Jul 7
Campbell, Christian: Birth, May 12
Campbell, Douglas: Becomes First American Air Ace: Anniv, Apr 14
Campbell, Earl: Birth, Mar 29
Campbell, Glen: Birth, Apr 22
Campbell, Kim: Birth, Mar 10
Campbell, Kim: Canada's First Woman Prime Minister: Anniv, Jun 25
Campbell, Malcolm: Birth Anniv, Mar 11
Campbell, Naomi: Birth, May 22
Campbell, Neve: Birth, Oct 3
Camping: Great American Backyard Campout, Jun 27
Campion, Jane: Birth, Apr 30
Campos, Bruno: Birth, Dec 3
Camus, Albert: Birth Anniv, Nov 7
Canada
Abbotsford Berry Beat Fest (Abbotsford, BC), Jul 3
Abbotsford Intl Airshow (Abbotsford, BC), Aug 7
Agrifair (Abbotsford, BC), Jul 30
American Psychological Assn Conv (Toronto, ON), Aug 6

American Society of Association Executives Mtg/Expo (Toronto, ON), Aug 15
Apple Blossom Fest (Annapolis Valley, NS), May 27
Banff Mountain Film & Book Fest (Banff, AB), Oct 31
British North America Act: Anniv, Mar 29
Calgary Boat/Sportsmen's Show (Calgary, AB), Feb 12
Calgary Folk Music Fest (Calgary, AB), Jul 23
Calgary Stampede (Calgary, AB), Jul 3
Canada Day, Jul 1
Canada Day Celebration (Ottawa, ON), Jul 1
Canada Day Party in the Park (Bancroft, ON), Jul 1
Canada's Natl Ukrainian Fest (Dauphin, MB), Jul 31
Canadian Open Old Time Fiddle Chmpshp (Shelburne, ON), Aug 5
Canadian Tulip Fest (Ottawa, ON), May 1
Canadian Western Agribition (Regina, SK), Nov 23
Canmore Folk Music Fest (Canmore, AB), Aug 1
Cisco Ottawa Bluesfest (Ottawa, ON), Jul 9
Civic Holiday, Aug 3
Classic Boat Fest (Victoria, BC), Aug 28
CN Tower: Anniv, Jun 26
Constitution Act: Anniv, Apr 18
Edmonton Folk Music Fest (Edmonton, AB), Aug 6
Edmonton Intl Fringe Theatre Fest (Edmonton, AB), Aug 13
Elmira Maple Syrup Fest (Elmira, ON), Apr 4
Family Day in Alberta, Feb 16
First Nights, Dec 31
First Woman Prime Minister: Anniv, Jun 25
Halifax Intl Busker Fest (Halifax, NS), Aug 7
Halifax, Nova Scotia, Destroyed: Anniv, Dec 6
Harrison Fest of Arts (Harrison Hot Springs, BC), Jul 11
Immigrants' Day, May 22
Just For Laughs Fest (Montreal, QC), Jul 16
Kimberley Intl Old-time Accordion Chmpshps (Kimberley, BC), Jul 6
Kitchener-Waterloo Oktoberfest (Kitchener/Waterloo, ON), Oct 9
Klondike Eldorado Gold Discovery: Anniv, Aug 31
Klondike Gold Discovery: Anniv, Aug 16
Labor Day, Sep 7
Maple Fest of Nova Scotia (Northern Nova Scotia), Mar 14
Maple Leaf Flag Adopted: Anniv, Feb 15
Masters (Calgary, AB), Sep 9
Mineral Capital Rock Show (Bancroft, ON), Jul 26
Mineral Collecting Field Trips (Bancroft, ON), Jul 1
Montreal Hunting, Fishing & Camping Show (Montreal, QC), Feb 26
Morden Corn/Apple Fest (Morden, MB), Aug 21
Mourning, Natl Day of, Apr 28
Multicultural Fest (Dartmouth, NS), Jun 19
Natl Tourn (Calgary, AB), Jun 3
New Inuit Territory Approved: Anniv, Nov 3
Newfoundland Discovery Day, Jun 22
Newfoundland: Saint George's Day, Apr 20
North American Tournament (Calgary, AB), Jul 1
Nova Scotia Bluegrass/Oldtime Music Fest (Stewiacke, NS), Jul 24
Nunavut Independence: Anniv, Apr 1
Ontario Winter Carnival Bon Soo (Sault Ste. Marie, ON), Feb 6
Ottawa Boat/Sportsmen Show (Ottawa, ON), Feb 26
Ottawa Folk Fest (Ottawa, ON), Aug 20
Persons Day, Oct 18
Quebec City Hunting, Fishing, Camping, & Boat Show (Quebec City, QC), Mar 12
Quebec Founded: Anniv, Jul 3
Rally of the Tall Pines (Bancroft, ON), Nov 20
Remembrance Day, Nov 11
Rockhound Gemboree (Bancroft, ON), Jul 30
Royal Nova Scotia Intl Tattoo (Halifax, NS), Jul 1
Saint Jean-Baptiste Day (Quebec, QC), Jun 24
Saint Swithun's Celebration (Toronto, ON), Jul 15
Sam Steele Days (Cranbrook, BC), Jun 18
Shelburne County Lobster Fest (Shelburne County, NS), Jun 4
Thanksgiving Day, Oct 12
Toronto Intl Film Fest (Toronto, ON), Sep 3
Toronto Ski, Snowboard and Travel Show (Toronto, ON), Oct 15
Toronto Sportsmen's Show (Toronto, ON), Mar 18
Upper Canada Village (Morrisburg, ON), May 16
Vancouver Folk Music Fest (Vancouver, BC), Jul 17
Vancouver Intl Boat Show (Vancouver, BC), Feb 4
Victoria Day, May 18
Windsor Pumpkin Regatta (Windsor, NS), Oct 10
Winnipeg Fringe Theatre Fest (Winnipeg, MB), Jul 15
Winnipeg Intl Children's Fest (Winnipeg, MB), Jun 4
Winterlude (Ottawa, ON), Feb 6
Yukon Discovery Day, Aug 17
Yukon Gold Panning Chmpshps (Dawson City, YT), Jul 1
Yukon Order of Pioneers: Anniv, Dec 1
Yukon Quest Intl 1,000-Mile Sled Dog Race (Whitehorse, YT), Feb 14
Yukon Sourdough Rendezvous (Whitehorse, YT), Feb 20
Canadian Pacific RR: Transcontinental Completion Anniv, Nov 7
Canaletto, Giovanni Antonio: Birth Anniv, Oct 18
Canary Islands Plane Disaster: Anniv, Mar 27
Cancer (Zodiac) Begins, Jun 21
Cancer Campaign Month, Intl Childhood, Jun 1
Cancer Control Month (Pres Proc), Apr 1
Cancer from the Sun Month, Jun 1
Cancer Survivors Day, Natl, Jun 7
Candid Camera TV Premiere: Anniv, Aug 10
Candlemas Day (Presentation of the Lord), Feb 2
Candy Month, Natl, Jun 1
Candy, John: Birth Anniv, Oct 31
Caniff, Milton: Birth Anniv, Feb 28
Cannes Film Fest (Cannes, France), May 13
Canning: Appert, Nicolas: Birth Anniv, Oct 23
Cannon, Annie Jump: Birth Anniv, Dec 11
Cannon, Dyan: Birth, Jan 4
Canova, Diana: Birth, Jun 2
Canseco, Jose, Jr: Birth, Jul 2
Cantinflas: Birth Anniv, Aug 12
Cantwell, Maria: Birth, Oct 13
Canyonlands Natl Park Established: Anniv, Sep 12
Capa, Robert: Birth Anniv, Oct 22
Cape Verde: National Day, Jul 5
Capek, Karel: Robot Enters World Lexicon: Anniv, Jan 25
Capital One Bowl (Orlando, FL), Jan 1
Capitol Cornerstone Laid, US: Anniv, Sep 18
Capitol Reef Natl Park Established: Anniv, Dec 18
Capone, Al: Birth Anniv, Jan 17
Capote, Truman: Birth Anniv, Sep 30
Capp, Al: Birth Anniv, Sep 28
Capra, Francis: Birth, Apr 22
Capra, Frank: Birth Anniv, May 18
Capra, Frank: It Happened One Night Film Release: Anniv, Feb 22
Capra, Frank: It's a Wonderful Life Film Premiere: Anniv, Dec 20
Capriati, Jennifer: Birth, Mar 29
Capricorn Begins, Dec 22
Capshaw, Kate: Birth, Nov 3
Captain Kangaroo TV Premiere: Anniv, Oct 3
Captain Kangaroo: Keeshan, Bob: Birth Anniv, Jun 27
Captain Midnight TV Premiere: Anniv, Sep 4
Captain Video and His Video Rangers TV Premiere: Anniv, Jun 27
Captive Nations Week (Pres Proc), Jul 19
Car Care Month, Apr 1
Car Talk Natl Radio Premiere: Anniv, Oct 31
Cara, Irene: Birth, Mar 18
Carabao Fest (Philippines), May 14
Caraway, Hattie Wyatt: Birth Anniv, Feb 1
Caraway, Hattie Wyatt: First Elected Woman Senator: Anniv, Jan 12
Caray, Harry: Birth Anniv, Mar 1
Carbon-14 Dating Inventor (Libby): Birth Anniv, Dec 17
Carbonell, Nestor: Birth, Dec 1
Carcieri, Donald: Birth, Dec 16
Card and Letter Writing Month, Natl, Apr 1
Card Making Day, World, Oct 3
Cardellini, Linda: Birth, Jun 25
Cardin, Ben: Birth, Oct 5
Cardin, Pierre: Birth, Jul 7
Care Sunday (England), Mar 29
Careers (employment, employees, occupations, professions). See also Business, Labor
Administrative Professionals Day, Apr 22
Administrative Professionals Intl Conv (Minneapolis, MN), Jul 26
Administrative Professionals Week, Apr 19

American Society of Association Executives Mtg/Expo (Toronto, Canada), Aug 15
Auctioneers Day, Natl, Apr 18
Automotive Service Professionals Week, Natl, Jun 8
Be Kind to Editors and Writers Month, Sep 1
Be Kind to Lawyers Day, Natl, Apr 14
Building & Code Staff Appreciation Day, Sep 1
Columnist's Day, Natl, Jun 23
Companies That Care Day, Mar 19
Cranky Coworkers Day, Oct 27
Custodial Workers Day, Natl, Oct 2
Disability Employment Awareness Month, Natl, Oct 1
Emergency Nurses Day, Oct 14
Emergency Nurses Week, Oct 11
Employee Spirit Month, Mar 1
Engineers Week, Natl, Feb 15
Executive Coaching Day, May 1
Exhibitor Appreciation Week, Aug 3
Expanding Girls' Horizons in Science & Engineering Month, Mar 1
Explore Your Career Options Week, Apr 5
First Flight Attendant: Anniv, May 15
First Labor Day Observance: Anniv, Sep 5
Flexible Work Arrangements Week, May 3
Freedom from Bullies Week, Oct 18
Freelance Writers Appreciation Week, Feb 8
Goodwill Industries Week, May 3
Groundhog Job Shadow Day, Feb 2
Gruntled Workers Day, Jul 13
Hairstylist Day, Apr 30
Hospital Admitting Clerks Day, Apr 3
Labor Day, May 1
Labor Day, Sep 7
Legal Assistants Day, Mar 26
Miner's Day in West Virginia, Dec 6
Mom and Pop Business Owners Day, Natl, Mar 29
Newspaper Carrier Day, Intl, Oct 10
Nightshift Workers Day, Natl, May 13
Nurse Anesthetists Week, Natl, Jan 25
Nurses Week, Natl, May 6
Nursing Assistants Day and Week, Natl, Jun 11
Occupational Therapy Month, Natl, Apr 1
Pastoral Care Week, Oct 25
Pawnbrokers Day, Natl, Dec 6
Peace Officer Memorial Day, Natl, May 15
Physician Assistants Day, Natl, Oct 6
Police Week, Natl, May 10
Professional Pet Sitters Week, Mar 1
Protocol Officers Week, Natl, Mar 23
Receptionists Day, Natl, May 13
Return to Work Week, Natl, May 10
Salesperson's Day, Natl, Oct 12
Single Working Women's Week, Aug 2
Substitute Teacher Appreciation Week, Sep 14
Sword Swallowers Awareness Day, Intl, Feb 28
Tailors Day, Natl, Jun 3
Take Our Daughters and Sons to Work Day, Apr 23
Third Shift Workers Day, Natl, May 13
Update Your References Week, May 3
Update Your Resume Month, Sep 1
Virtual Assistants Day, Intl, May 15
Waitstaff Day, Natl, May 21
Weatherman's Day, Feb 5
Woman Road Warrior Day, Natl, Sep 21
Work at Home Moms Week, May 18
Workers Memorial Day, Apr 28
Working Women's Day, Intl, Mar 8
Wound Ostomy and Continence Nurse Week, Apr 19
Carell, Steve: Birth, Aug 16
Carew, Rod: Birth, Oct 1
Carey, Drew: Birth, May 23
Carey, Mariah: Birth, Mar 27
Caribbean or Caricom Day, Jul 6
Caricom or Caribbean Day, Jul 6
Carillon Fest, Intl (Springfield, IL), May 31
Car-Keeping Month, Natl Good, May 1
Carleton, Will: Birth Anniv, Oct 21
Carlisle, Belinda: Birth, Aug 17
Carlsbad Caverns Natl Park Established: Anniv, May 14
Carlton, Steve: Birth, Dec 22
Carlyle, Robert: Birth, Apr 14
Carlyle, Thomas: Birth Anniv, Dec 4
Carmichael, Hoagie: Birth Anniv, Nov 22
Carnegie, Andrew: Birth Anniv, Nov 25
Carnegie, Dale: Birth Anniv, Nov 24
Carnes, Kim: Birth, Jul 20
Carney, Art: Birth Anniv, Nov 4
Carney, William: First Black Receives Congressional Medal: Anniv, May 23
Carnival, Feb 23
Carnival (Malta), Feb 21
Carnival (Port of Spain, Trinidad and Tobago), Feb 23
Carnival de Ponce (Ponce, PR), Feb 18
Carnival Season, Jan 6
Carnival Week (Milan, Italy), Feb 22
Carnovsky, Morris: Birth Anniv, Sep 5
Caro, Robert A.: Birth, Oct 30
Carol Burnett Show TV Premiere: Anniv, Sep 11
Caroline, Princess: Birth, Jan 23
Caron, Leslie: Birth, Jul 1
Carpenter Ant Awareness Week, Jun 21
Carpenter, John: Birth, Jan 16
Carpenter, Mary Chapin: Birth, Feb 21
Carper, Tom: Birth, Jan 23
Carr, Gerald Paul: Birth, Aug 22
Carradine, David: Birth, Dec 8
Carradine, John: Birth Anniv, Feb 5
Carradine, Keith: Birth, Aug 8
Carreras, Jose: Birth, Dec 5
Carrere, Tia: Birth, Jan 2
Carrey, Jim: Birth, Jan 17
Carroll, Charles: Birth Anniv, Sep 19
Carroll, Diahann: Birth, Jul 17
Carroll, Lewis: Alice's Adventures in Wonderland Published: Anniv, Nov 26
Carroll, Lewis: Birth Anniv. See Dodgson, Charles, Jan 27
Carroll, Pat: Birth, May 5
Carry a Tune Week, Natl, Oct 4
Carsey, Marcy: Birth, Nov 21
Carson, Johnny: Birth Anniv, Oct 23
Carson, Johnny: Final Show: Anniv, May 22
Carson, Kit: Birth Anniv, Dec 24
Carson, Lisa Nicole: Birth, Jul 12
Carson, Rachel: Birth Anniv, May 27
Carson, Rachel: Silent Spring Publication: Anniv, Apr 13
Carter, Chris: Birth, Oct 13
Carter, Cris: Birth, Nov 25
Carter, Dixie: Birth, May 25
Carter, Gary: Birth, Apr 8
Carter, Hodding, III: Birth, Apr 7
Carter, Jimmy and Rosalynn, Wedding Anniv, Jul 7
Carter, Jimmy: Birthday, Oct 1
Carter, Lynda: Birth, Jul 24
Carter, Maybelle: Birth Anniv, May 10
Carter, Robert III: Emancipation of 500: Anniv, Aug 1
Carter, Rosalynn: Birth, Aug 18
Carter, Vince: Birth, Jan 25
Cartier, Jacques: Death Anniv, Sep 1
Cartier-Bresson, Henri: Birth Anniv, Aug 22
Cartoonists Day, May 5
Cartoons: Bugs Bunny's Debut: Anniv, Apr 30
Cartwright, Angela: Birth, Sep 9
Cartwright, Edmund: Birth Anniv, Apr 24
Caruso, David: Birth, Jan 7
Caruso, Enrico: Birth Anniv, Feb 25
Carver, George Washington: Death Anniv, Jan 5
Carver, Raymond: Birth Anniv, May 25
Carvey, Dana: Birth, Jun 2
Casablanca Premiere: Anniv, Nov 26
Casady, Jack: Birth, Apr 13
Casals, Pablo: Birth Anniv, Dec 29
Casanova, Giovanni: Birth Anniv, Apr 2
Case, Steve: Birth, Aug 21
Casey at the Bat: Mighty Casey Has Struck Out: Anniv, Jun 3
Casey, Bernie: Birth, Jun 8
Casey, Robert: Birth, Apr 13
Casey, Sean: Birth, Jul 2
Cash, Johnny: Birth Anniv, Feb 26
Cash, Johnny: Plays at Folsom Prison: Anniv, Jan 13
Cash, June Carter: Birth Anniv, Jun 23
Cash, Pat: Birth, May 27
Casillas, Iker: Birth, May 20
Cassatt, Mary: Birth Anniv, May 22
Cassel, Seymour: Birth, Jan 22
Cassidy, Butch (Robert Leroy Parker): Birth Anniv, Apr 13
Cassidy, David: Birth, Apr 12
Cassidy, Joanna: Birth, Aug 2
Cassidy, Shaun: Birth, Sep 27
Cassini-Huygens Reaches Saturn, Jul 1
Castro, Fidel: Birth, Aug 13
Castro, Raul: Birth, Jun 3
Cat Herders Day, Dec 15
Cataract Awareness Month, Aug 1
Cates, Phoebe: Birth, Jul 16
Cathedral: Cologne Cathedral Completion: Anniv, Aug 14
Cather, Willa: Birth Anniv, Dec 7
Cathode-Ray Tube Patented: Anniv, Dec 20
Catholic Educational Assn Conv/Expo, Natl (Anaheim, CA), Apr 14
Catholic Hour TV Premiere: Anniv, Jan 4
Catholic Schools Week, Jan 25
Catlin, George: Birth Anniv, Jul 26
Cats Premiere: Anniv, Oct 7
Cats. See also Animals
Adopt-a-Shelter-Cat Month, Jun 1
CFA Intl Cat Show, Nov 20
Hairball Awareness Day, Natl, Apr 24
Hug Your Cat Day, May 29
Catt, Carrie Lane Chapman: Birth Anniv, Jan 9
Cattrall, Kim: Birth, Aug 21
Cauthen, Steve: Birth, May 1
Cavalcade of Stars TV Premiere: Anniv, Jun 4
Cavallari, Kristin: Birth, Jan 14
Cavanagh, Tom: Birth, Oct 26
Cavett, Dick: Birth, Nov 19
Cavill, Henry: Birth, May 5
Cavoukian, Raffi: Birth, Jul 8
Caxton, William: Birth Anniv, Aug 13
Caxton's "Mirror of the World" Translation: Anniv, Mar 8

Cayley, George: Birth Anniv, Dec 27
Cazenove, Christopher: Birth, Dec 17
CBS Evening News TV Premiere: Anniv, May 3
Ceausescu, Nicolae: Death Anniv, Dec 25
Ceccato, Aldo: Birth, Feb 18
Cedric the Entertainer: Birth, Apr 24
Celebrate Your Name Week, Mar 1
Celebrating the Bilingual Child Month, Oct 1
Celebration of Life Day, Jan 22
Celebration of Life Month, Jan 1
Celebration of the Senses, Jun 24
Celiac Awareness Day, Natl, Sep 13
Celiac Disease Awareness Month, Oct 1
Celibacy Awareness Month, Jun 1
Cell Phone Courtesy Month, Jul 1
Cellophane Tape Patented: Anniv, May 27
Celtic Fest, Southern Maryland (St. Leonard, MD), Apr 25
Cena, John: Birth, Apr 23
Census, First US: Anniv, Aug 1
Central African Republic
  Boganda Day, Mar 29
  Independence Day, Aug 13
  National Day, Dec 7
Cermak, Anton J.: Assassination Anniv, Feb 15
Cervantes Saavedra, Miguel de: Death Anniv, Apr 23
Cervical Cancer Screening Month, Jan 1
Cetera, Peter: Birth, Sep 13
Cezanne, Paul: Birth Anniv, Jan 19
Chabrol, Claude: Birth, Jun 24
Chad
  African Freedom Day, May 25
  Independence Day, Aug 11
  Republic Day, Nov 28
Chadds Ford Days (Chadds Ford, PA), Sep 12
Chalke, Sarah: Birth, Aug 27
Challenger Space Shuttle Explosion: Anniv, Jan 28
Chamber of Commerce Founded, First US: Anniv, Apr 5
Chamberlain, Richard: Birth, Mar 31
Chamberlain, Wilt: Birth Anniv, Aug 21
Chambers, Justin: Birth, Jul 11
Chambers, Tom: Birth, Jun 21
Chambliss, Saxby: Birth, Nov 10
Champion, Marge: Birth, Sep 2
Chan, Jackie: Birth, Apr 7
Chance, Frank: Baseball's Sad Lexicon Published: Anniv, Jul 10
Chancellor, John: Birth Anniv, Jul 14
Chandler, Chris: Birth, Oct 12
Chandler, Kyle: Birth, Sep 17
Chandler, Raymond: Birth Anniv, Jul 23
Chanel, Coco: Birth Anniv, Aug 19
Chaney, Goodman, Schwerner: Civil Rights Workers Found Slain: Anniv, Aug 4
Chaney, Lon: Birth Anniv, Apr 1
Chang, Michael: Birth, Feb 22
Change Your Stars Month, Intl, Jan 1
Channel Islands Natl Park Established: Anniv, Mar 5
Channel Islands: Jersey Battle of Flowers (St. Lawrence), Aug 13
Channing, Carol: Birth, Jan 31
Channing, Stockard: Birth, Feb 13
Channing, William Ellery: Birth Anniv, Apr 7
Chanukah, Dec 12
Chao, Elaine: Birth, Mar 26
Chapin, Harry: Birth Anniv, Dec 7
Chaplin, Charles: Birth Anniv, Apr 16
Chaplin, Charles: Tramp Debuts: Anniv, Feb 7
Chaplin, Geraldine: Birth, Jul 31
Chapman, John (Johnny Appleseed): Birth Anniv, Sep 26
Chapman, John: Death Anniv: Johnny Appleseed Day, Mar 11
Chapman, John: Johnny Appleseed Fest (Fort Wayne, IN), Sep 19
Chapman, Tracy: Birth, Mar 30
Character Counts Week, Natl (Pres Proc), Oct 18
Charles I: Execution Anniv, Jan 30
Charles II: Restoration and Birth Anniv, May 29
Charles, Prince: Birth, Nov 14
Charles, Ray: Birth Anniv, Sep 23
Charleston Earthquake: Anniv, Aug 31
Charlie the Tuna: Sorry Charlie Day, Apr 1
Charlie's Angels TV Premiere: Anniv, Sep 22
Charo: Birth, Mar 13
Charro Days Fiesta (Brownsville, TX; Matamoros, Mexico), Feb 26
Charvet, David: Birth, May 15
Chase, Chevy: Birth, Oct 8
Chase, Harrison, V.: Birth Anniv, Aug 17
Chase, Helen M.: Birth, Dec 4
Chase, Salmon Portland: Birth Anniv, Jan 13
Chase, Samuel: Birth Anniv, Apr 17
Chase, Sylvia: Birth, Feb 23
Chase, William D.: Birth, Apr 8
Chase's Calendar Deadline Approaching, Mar 2
Chase's Calendar of Events 2010 Published, Oct 5
Chase's Calendar of Events: Birthday, Dec 4
Chastain, Brandi: Birth, Jul 21
Chateaubriand, Francois Rene de: Birth Anniv, Sep 4
Chatterton, Thomas: Birth Anniv, Nov 20
Chaucer, Geoffrey: Death Anniv, Oct 25
Chauvin Day, Aug 15
Chavez, Cesar Estrada: Birth Anniv, Mar 31
Cheadle, Don: Birth, Nov 29
Check Your Batteries Day, Mar 8
Checker, Chubby: Birth, Oct 3
Checkers Day, Sep 23
Cheechoo, Jonathan: Birth, Jul 15
Cheer Coach Day, Jun 6
Cheerleading Week, Natl, Mar 2
Cheers TV Premiere: Anniv, Sep 30
Cheese Fest, Great Wisconsin (Little Chute, WI), Jun 5
Cheese Rolling, Gloucestershire (Cotswolds, England), May 25
Chekhov, Anton Pavlovich: Birth Anniv, Jan 29
Chelios, Chris: Birth, Jan 25
Chemistry Week, Natl, Oct 18
Chemists Celebrate Earth Day, Apr 22
Chen, Joan: Birth, Apr 26
Cheney, Lynne: Birthday, Aug 14
Cheney, Richard (Dick): Birthday, Jan 30
Cheng Huang: Birth Anniv Celebration (Taiwan), Jun 5
Chenoweth, Kristin: Birth, Jul 24
Cher: Birth, May 20
Chernobyl Nuclear Reactor Disaster: Anniv, Apr 26
Cherokee Strip Celebration (Perry, OK), Sep 19
Cherokee Strip Day (OK), Sep 16
Cherry Blossom Fest (Washington, DC), Mar 28
Cherry Blossom Fest, Intl (Macon, GA), Mar 20
Cherry Month, Natl, Feb 1
Cherry Pit Spitting Chmpshp, Intl (Eau Claire, MI), Jul 4
Chertoff, Michael: Birth, Nov 28
Chesapeake-Leopard Affair: Anniv, Jun 22
Chesney, Kenny: Birth, Mar 26
Chesnut, Mary Boykin Miller: Birth Anniv, Mar 31
Chesnutt, Charles W.: Birth Anniv, Jun 20
Chess: First Computer Victory: Anniv, Feb 10
Chesterton, Gilbert: Birth Anniv, May 29
Chestnut Week, Natl, Oct 11
Chiang Kai-Shek Day (Taiwan), Oct 31
Chiang Kai-Shek: Birth Anniv, Oct 31
Chicago Blues Fest (Chicago, IL), Jun 11
Chicago Bulls Third Straight Title for the Second Time, Jun 14
Chicago Cubs: Baseball's Sad Lexicon Published: Anniv, Jul 10
Chicago Cubs: Tinker to Evers to Chance: First Double Play Anniv, Sep 15
Chicago Fire, Great: Anniv, Oct 8
Chicago Flag Exhibit Controversy: Anniv, Feb 17
Chicago Flood, Great: Anniv, Apr 13
Chicago Marathon, Bank of America (Chicago, IL), Oct 11
Chicago Sketch Comedy Fest (Chicago, IL), Jan 8
Chicago, Judy: Birth, Jul 20
Chicago, Univ of, First Day Classes: Anniv, Oct 1
Chicago: Incorporated as City: Anniv, Mar 4
Chicken and Egg Fest (Prescott, AR), Jun 5
Chicken Boy's Birthday, Sep 1
Chicken Days, Wayne (Wayne, NE), Jul 10
Chicken Lady Day, Natl, Nov 4
Chicken Month, Natl, Sep 1
Chicken Wing Society Cook-off, Great Intl (Reno, NV), Jul 10
Chickens: Respect for Chickens Day, Intl, May 4
Chief Joseph Surrender: Anniv, Oct 5
Chiklis, Michael: Birth, Aug 30
Child Abuse Prevention Month, Apr 1
Child Abuse Prevention Month, Natl, Apr 1
Child, Julia: Birth Anniv, Aug 15
Child, Julia: French Chef TV Premiere: Anniv, Feb 11
Child, Lydia Maria: Birth Anniv, Feb 11
Childermas, Dec 28
Children
  Absolutely Incredible Kid Day, Mar 19
  Abused Women and Children's Awareness Day, Jun 14
  Adoption Month, Natl, Nov 1
  America's Kids Day, Jun 28
  Appreciate a Dragon Day, Jan 16
  Attention Deficit Hyperactivity Disorder Month, Sep 1
  Australia: Sorry Day, May 26
  Babysitters Day, Natl, May 9
  Backpack Safety America Month, Sep 1
  Blue Ribbon Week, Natl (Child Abuse), Apr 5
  Boy Scouts of America Founded: Anniv, Feb 8
  Bud Billiken Parade (Chicago, IL), Aug 8
  Camp Fire Founders Day, Mar 17
  Celebrating the Bilingual Child Month, Oct 1
  Child Abuse Prevention Month, Apr 1

Child Abuse Prevention Month, Natl, Apr 1
Child Abuse Prevention Month, Natl (Pres Proc), Apr 1
Child Health Day (Pres Proc), Oct 5
Child Safety Council Founded, Natl: Anniv, Nov 9
Child Vision Awareness Month, Jun 1
Child-Centered Divorce Month, Natl, Jul 1
Childhood Cancer Campaign Month, Intl, Jun 1
Childhood Depression Awareness Day, May 5
Children with Alopecia Day, Apr 14
Children's Awareness Memorial Day, Jun 7
Children's Awareness Month, Jun 1
Children's Book Day, Intl, Apr 2
Children's Book Week, Natl, May 11
Children's Day (FL), Apr 14
Children's Day (Japan), May 5
Children's Day (MA), Jun 14
Children's Day (South Korea), May 5
Children's Day (Woodstock, VT), Jul 11
Children's Day, Intl (China), Jun 1
Children's Day/Natl Sovereignty (Turkey), Apr 23
Children's Dental Health Month, Natl, Feb 1
Children's Eye Health and Safety Month, Aug 1
Children's Good Manners Month, Sep 1
Children's Magazine Month, Oct 1
Children's Party at Green Animals (Newport, RI), Jul 14
Children's Sunday, Jun 14
Children's Vision and Learning Month, Aug 1
Circus City Fest (Peru, IN), Jul 11
Compassionate Friends Worldwide Candle Lighting, Dec 13
Davidson Fellows Award Reception (Washington, DC), Sep 30
Day of Hope, Natl, Apr 1
Day of Natl Concern about Young People and Gun Violence, Oct 28
Family Day—A Day to Eat Dinner with Your Children, Sep 28
Family Month, Natl, May 10
Festival of Children (Costa Mesa, CA), Sep 4
Firepup's Birthday, Oct 1
Get Ready For Kindergarten Month, Aug 1
Gifted Children Conv, Natl Assn for (Tampa, FL), Nov 5
Girl Scouts Founding: Anniv, Mar 12
Heal the Children Month, May 1
Innocent Children Victims of Aggression, Intl Day of, Jun 4
Keep Kids Alive—Drive 25 Day, May 1
Keep Kids Creative Week, Natl, Sep 20
Kid Inventors' Day, Jan 17
Kids' Goal Setting Week, Oct 5
KidsDay, Natl, Sep 19
KidSpree (Aurora, CO), Jul 18
Library Card Sign-up Month, Sep 1
Little League Baseball World Series (Williamsport, PA), Aug 21
Love Our Children Day, Natl, Apr 4
Make a Difference to Children Month, Natl, Jul 1
March into Literacy Month, Natl, Mar 1
Mend a Broken Heart Month, Natl, Feb 1
Military Child, Month of the, Apr 1
Missing Children's Day, Natl, May 25
Mother Goose Day, May 1
Multicultural American Child Awareness Day, Jun 14
Music in Our Schools Month, Mar 1
No Homework Day, May 6
Pediatric Cancer Awareness Month, Sep 1
Pediatric Nurse Practitioner Week, Mar 15
Playground Safety Week, Natl, Apr 19
Potty Training Awareness Month, Jun 1
President's Environmental Youth Award Natl Competition, Oct 31
R.E.A.D. in America Day (Washington, DC), Sep 26
Read Across America Day, Mar 2
Read Me Week (TN), Feb 23
RSV Awareness Month, Natl, Oct 1
Safe Toys and Gifts Month, Dec 1
School Lunch Week, Natl, Oct 12
Sea Cadet Month, Sep 1
Spank Out Day USA, Apr 30
Sports America Kids Month, Jun 1
Student Safety Month, Jun 1
Summer Reading Club (El Paso, TX), Jun 6
Teach Children to Save Day, Natl, Apr 21
Texas Love the Children Day, Mar 29
Tooth Fairy Day, Natl, Feb 28
Universal Children's Day (UN), Nov 20
Vegetarian Resource Group's Essay Contest for Kids, May 1
Video Games Day, Sep 12
White Sunday (Samoa, American Samoa), Oct 11
Winnipeg Intl Children's Fest (Winnipeg, MB, Canada), Jun 4
World Orphans Day, Nov 9
Young Achievers/Leaders of Tomorrow Month, May 1
Young Child, Month of the (MI), Apr 1
Young Child, Week of the, Apr 19
Young Reader's Day, Natl, Nov 10
Youth Art Month, Mar 1
Youth Day (Cameroon), Feb 11
Youth Day (Taiwan), Mar 29
Youth Day (Zambia), Aug 3
Youth Leadership Month, Feb 1
Youth Service Day, Global, Apr 24

Children's Authors & Illustrators Week, Feb 1
Chile
Battle of Iquique, May 21
Dakar Rally, Jan 3
Independence Day, Sep 18
Military Dictatorship Ended: Anniv, Dec 15
National Month, Sep 1
Strongest Earthquake of the 20th Century: Anniv, May 22
Chili Cook-Off, State Chmpshp (Roanoke, VA), May 2
Chili Day, Natl, Feb 26
Chili Month, Natl, Oct 1
Chimborazo Day, Jun 3
Chimney Safety Week, Natl, Sep 27
China Beach TV Premiere: Anniv, Apr 26
China Clipper: Anniv, Nov 22
China, People's Republic of
Birthday of Confucius (Observance), Oct 15
Birthday of Lord Buddha, May 2
Canton Autumn Trade Fair, Oct 15
Canton Spring Trade Fair, Apr 15
Central China Flood: Anniv, Jun 25
Chung Yeung Fest (or Double Nine Fest), Oct 26
Double Seven Fest, Aug 26
Double Tenth Day, Oct 10
Dragon Boat Fest, May 28
Fest of Hungry Ghosts, Sep 3
Half-Year Day, Jul 1
International Children's Day, Jun 1
Lantern Fest, Feb 9
Macau Day, Jun 24
Macau Reverts to Chinese Control: Anniv, Dec 20
Moon Fest (Mid-Autumn Fest), Oct 3
National Day, Oct 1
Qing Ming Fest or Tomb Sweeping Day, Apr 4
Shanghai Communique: Anniv, Feb 27
Sun Yat-sen: Birth Anniv, Nov 12
Taiwan Expelled from UN: Anniv, Oct 25
Tiananmen Square Massacre: Anniv, Jun 4
Youth Day, May 4

Chinese Nationalists Move to Formosa: Anniv, Dec 8
Chinese New Year, Jan 26
Chinese New Year Fest & Parade (San Francisco, CA), Jan 24
Chipotle Day, Totally, May 5
CHiPs TV Premiere: Anniv, Sep 15
Chirac, Jacques: Birth, Nov 29
Chiropractic Month, Natl, Oct 1
Chisholm, Shirley: Birth Anniv, Nov 30
Cho, Margaret: Birth, Dec 5
Chocolate Fest (Galesburg, IL), Feb 14
Chokachi, David: Birth, Jan 16
Chong, Tommy: Birth, May 24
Chou En-Lai: Death Anniv, Jan 8
Chow Yun-Fat: Birth, May 18
Chretien, Jean: Birth, Jan 11
Christ, Circumcision of, Jan 1
Christensen, Hayden: Birth, Apr 19
Christian Unity, Week of, Jan 18
Christianity Week, Consider, Mar 29
Christie, Agatha: Birth Anniv, Sep 15
Christie, Julie: Birth, Apr 14
Christie, Lou: Birth, Feb 19
Christmas
Adoration Parade (Branson, MO), Dec 6
Armenian Christmas, Jan 6
BCHS Christmas Open House (Ainsworth, NE), Dec 6
Black Friday, Nov 27
Boxing Day at the Hemingway Birthplace (Oak Park, IL), Dec 26
Caldwell Country Christmas Parade & Fireworks (Columbia, LA), Dec 5
Christkindlmarkt (Bethlehem, PA), Nov 27
Christmas, Dec 25
Christmas Bells Ring Again (CIS): Anniv, Dec 24
Christmas Candlelight House Tours (Cape May, NJ), Dec 5
Christmas Candlelight Tour (Bardstown, KY), Nov 27
Christmas Candlelightings (Coshocton, OH), Dec 5
Christmas Craft Show (York, PA), Dec 13
Christmas Eve, Dec 24
Christmas Eve Torchlight Parade (Winter Park, CO), Dec 24
Christmas Fest of Lights (Natchitoches, LA), Dec 5
Christmas in Old Appalachia (Clinton, TN), Dec 6
Christmas in the Villages (Van Buren County, IA), Dec 5
Christmas New Orleans Style (New Orleans, LA), Dec 1

Christmas on the Prairie (Wahoo, NE), Dec 5
Christmas on the River (Demopolis, AL), Nov 29
Christmas Parade (El Centro, CA), Dec 5
Christmas Seal Campaign, Oct 1
Christmas Stroll Weekend (Nantucket Island, MA), Dec 4
Christmas to Remember (Laurel, MT), Dec 6
Christmas Traditions (St. Charles, MO), Nov 29
Christmas Walk and House Tour (Geneva, IL), Dec 4
Clute's Christmas in the Park (Clute, TX), Dec 8
Colonial Christmas (Williamsburg, VA), Dec 1
Colonial Christmas at Wormsloe (Savannah, GA), Dec 13
Colorado Country Christmas Gift Show (Denver, CO), Nov 6
Community Carol Singing (Mystic, CT), Dec 20
Country Christmas (Cambridge, WI), Dec 5
Craftsmen's Christmas Classic Arts & Crafts Fest (Greensboro, NC), Nov 27
Craftsmen's Christmas Classic Arts & Crafts Fest (Richmond, VA), Nov 6
Cuba: Christmas Returns: Anniv, Dec 25
Dear Santa Letter Week, Nov 8
Dickens' Christmas Extravaganza (Cape May, NJ), Dec 6
Dickens Fest (Holly, MI), Dec 4
Dickens of a Christmas at Mount Hope Mansion (Manheim, PA), Nov 27
Eighteenth-Century Christmas Wassail (McLean, VA), Dec 13
Electric Light Parade (Lovington, NM), Dec 7
Falling Needles Family Fest, Dec 30
Family Christmas at Benjamin Harrison Home (Indianapolis, IN), Dec 12
First Radio Broadcast from Space: Anniv, Dec 19
Frankfurt Christmas Market (Frankfurt, Germany), Nov 25
Garden of Lights (Muskogee, OK), Nov 26
Gettysburg Holiday Fest (Gettysburg, PA), Nov 28
Grand Illumination (Lahaska, PA), Nov 20
Holiday Happiness (Upper Arlington, OH), Dec 5
Holiday Lights on the Lake (Altoona, PA), Nov 26
Holiday Magic (Aurora, IL), Nov 27
Holiday Market (Greensboro, NC), Nov 6
Holiday Tour of Homes (Natchitoches, LA), Dec 9
Holidays in the City Grand Illumination Parade (Norfolk, VA), Nov 21
Hollywood Beach Candy Cane Parade (Hollywood, FL), Dec 5
Humbug Day, Dec 21
Jule Fest (Elk Horn, IA), Nov 27
Lantern Light Tours (Mystic, CT), Dec 3
Light of the World Christmas Pageant (Minden, NE), Nov 28
Longwood Gardens Christmas Display (Kennett Square, PA), Nov 26
Natchitoches Fest of Lights (Natchitoches, LA), Nov 21
Navidades (Puerto Rico), Dec 15
Norskedalen's Old-Fashioned Christmas (Coon Valley, WI), Dec 5
Operation Santa Paws, Dec 1
Ozark Mountain Christmas/Branson Fest of Lights (Branson, MO), Nov 1
Parade of Lights (Kingsville, TX), Dec 5
Pennsylvania Arts & Crafts Christmas Fest (Washington, PA), Oct 16
Philippines: Christmas Observance, Dec 16
Polish Christmas Open House (Philadelphia, PA), Dec 12
Posada de Kingsville (Kingsville, TX), Nov 26
Quincy Preserves Christmas Candlelight Tour (Quincy, IL), Dec 13
Recipe Greetings for the Holidays, Dec 1
Regifting Day, Natl, Dec 17
Rockefeller Center Christmas Tree Lighting (New York, NY), Dec 1
Russia: Christmas Day, Jan 7
Saint Nicholas Day, Dec 6
Saint Olaf Christmas Fest (Northfield, MN), Dec 3
Salt Lake's Family Christmas Gift Show (Sandy, UT), Nov 13
Shaker Christmas Fair (New Gloucester, ME), Dec 5
Shopping Reminder Day, Nov 25
Silent Night, Holy Night Celebrations (Austria), Dec 24
Territorial Christmas Celebration (Guthrie, OK), Nov 26
Thank You Note Day, Natl, Dec 26
34th St Express (Boston, MA), Dec 19
Thomasville's Victorian Christmas (Thomasville, GA), Dec 10
Three Kings Day, Jan 6
Victorian Christmas Celebration (Cumberland, MD), Nov 27
Victorian Christmas Home Tour (Leadville, CO), Dec 4
Victorian Christmas Sleigh Bell Parade (Manistee, MI), Dec 3
Victorian Christmas Tours at Frank Lloyd Wright Home (Oak Park, IL), Dec 12
Virginia Christmas Show (Richmond, VA), Nov 5
Wassail Celebration (Woodstock, VT), Dec 11
Whiner's Day, Natl, Dec 26
Winterfest (Luverne, MN), Dec 4
Winterfest Boat Parade (Fort Lauderdale, FL), Dec 12
Wolf Point's Annual Christmas Parade (Wolf Point, MT), Dec 4
Wonderland of Lights (Marshall, TX), Nov 25

Christmas Carol Published: Anniv, Dec 17
Christo: Birth, Jun 13
Christopher, Dennis: Birth, Dec 2
Christopher, William: Birth, Oct 20
Chronic Fatigue Syndrome Awareness Month, Natl, Mar 1
Chuckwagon Races, Natl Chmpshp (Clinton, AR), Sep 4
Chung Yeung Fest (China), Oct 26
Chung Yuan Fest (China), Sep 3
Chung, Connie: Birth, Aug 20
Church Library Month, Oct 1
Church of England Allows Women Priests: Anniv, Nov 11
Church of England Ordains Women Priests: Anniv, Mar 12
Church of Jesus Christ of Latter-day Saints: Anniv, Apr 6
Church Safety and Security Month, Oct 1
Church, Charlotte: Birth, Feb 21
Church, Thomas Haden: Birth, Jun 17
Church/State Separation Week, Nov 24
Churchill, Randolph Henry Spencer: Birth Anniv, Feb 13
Churchill, Winston: Birth Anniv, Nov 30
Churchill, Winston: Day, Apr 9
Chusok, Oct 3
CIA Agent Arrested as Spy: Anniv, Feb 21
Ciardi, John: Birth Anniv, Jun 24
Cibrian, Eddie: Birth, Jun 18
Cicotte, Eddie: Birth Anniv, Jun 19
Cigarette Advertising Banned: Anniv, Apr 1
Cigarettes Reported Hazardous: Anniv, Jan 11
Cimarron Territory Celebration and World Cow Chip-Throwing Chmpshp (Beaver, OK), Apr 11
Cinco de Mayo (Mexico), May 5
Circumcision of Christ, Jan 1
Circus
Circus City Fest (Peru, IN), Jul 11
Circus Train Wreck: Anniv, Jun 22
Emmett Kelly Clown Fest (Houston, MO), May 1
Greatest Show on Earth: Anniv, Mar 28
Jumbo the Elephant Arrives in America: Anniv, Apr 9
Citizen Kane Film Premiere: Anniv, May 1
Citizenship Day (Pres Proc), Sep 17
Civil Air Patrol Founded: Anniv, Dec 1
Civil Aviation Day, Intl (UN), Dec 7
Civil Rights
Birmingham Resistance: Anniv, Apr 3
Blacks Ruled Eligible to Vote: Anniv, Apr 3
Brown v Board of Education: Anniv, May 17
Civil Rights Act of 1964: Anniv, Jul 2
Civil Rights Act of 1968: Anniv, Apr 11
Civil Rights Bill of 1866: Anniv, Apr 9
Civil Rights Workers Found Slain: Anniv, Aug 4
Dred Scott Decision: Anniv, Mar 6
15th Amendment Ratified (Voting Rights), Feb 3
Freedom Riders: Anniv, May 4
Greensboro Sit-In: Anniv, Feb 1
Little Rock Nine: Anniv, Sep 4
March on Washington: Anniv, Aug 28
Meredith (James) Enrolls at Ole Miss: Anniv, Sep 30
Montgomery Bus Boycott: Anniv, Dec 5
Montgomery Bus Boycott Ends: Anniv, Dec 20
Parks, Rosa: Birth Anniv, Feb 4
Poll Tax Outlawed: Anniv, Apr 8
Rosa Parks Day, Dec 1
Selma Civil Rights March: Anniv, Mar 21
16th Street Baptist Church Bombing: Anniv, Sep 15
24th Amendment (Eliminated Poll Taxes), Jan 23
Civil Service Created: Anniv, Jan 16
Civil War, American
Amnesty Issued for Southern Rebels: Anniv, May 29
Attack on Fort Sumter: Anniv, Apr 12
Attack on Fort Wagner: Anniv, Jul 19
Battle of Antietam: Anniv, Sep 17
Battle of Bull Run: Anniv, Jul 21
Battle of Chattanooga: Anniv, Nov 24
Battle of Cold Harbor: Anniv, Jun 3
Battle of Gettysburg: Anniv, Jul 1
Battle of La Glorietta Pass: Anniv, Mar 28
Battle of Mobile Bay: Anniv, Aug 5

Battle of Nashville: Anniv, Dec 16
Battle of Shiloh: Anniv, Apr 6
Battle of Spotsylvania: Anniv, May 12
Battle of the Wilderness: Anniv, May 5
Civil War Ending: Anniv, Apr 9
Civil War Peace Talks: Anniv, Feb 3
Civil War Reenactment (Keokuk, IA), Apr 24
Civil War Submarine Attack: Anniv, Oct 5
Davis, Jefferson: Inauguration: Anniv, Feb 18
Defeat at Five Forks: Anniv, Apr 1
Doubleday, Abner: Birth Anniv, Jun 26
Fall of Richmond: Anniv, Apr 3
Farragut Captures New Orleans: Anniv, Apr 25
First Black Receives Congressional Medal: Anniv, May 23
Fort Sumter Returned to Union Control: Anniv, Feb 17
Fort Sumter Shelled by North: Anniv, Aug 17
Gettysburg Address Memorial Ceremony (Gettysburg, PA), Nov 19
Grant Commissioned Commander: Anniv, Mar 9
Hunter Frees the Slaves: Anniv, May 9
John Wilkes Booth Escape Route Tour (Clinton, MD), Apr 11
Last Formal Surrender of Confederate Troops: Anniv, Jun 23
Lincoln Approves 13th Amendment (Freedom Day), Feb 1
Lincoln Assassination Anniv, Apr 14
Lincoln Assassination Conspirators Hanging: Anniv, Jul 7
Lincoln Signs Income Tax: Anniv, Jul 1
Lincoln's Gettysburg Address: Anniv, Nov 19
Massacre at Fort Pillow: Anniv, Apr 12
Memorial Day Ceremonies (Andersonville, GA), May 24
Merrimac Destroyed: Anniv, May 11
Monitor Sinking: Anniv, Dec 30
Natural Bridge Battle (Tallahassee, FL), Mar 6
Peninsula Campaign Intensified: Anniv, May 9
Quantrill's Raid on Lawrence, KS: Anniv, Aug 21
Raid on Richmond: Anniv, Mar 1
Remembrance Day (Gettysburg, PA), Nov 21
Rock of Chickamauga: Anniv, Sep 20
Ruffin, Edmund: Birth Anniv, Jan 5
Seven Days Campaign: Anniv, Jun 25
Sherman Enters Atlanta: Anniv, Sep 2
Sherman Takes Savannah: Anniv, Dec 21
South Carolina: Secession Anniv, Dec 20
Sultana Explosion: Anniv, Apr 27
Surrender at Durham Station: Anniv, Apr 18
Surrender of Fort Donelson: Anniv, Feb 16
Union Officers Escape Libby Prison: Anniv, Feb 9
Vicksburg Surrenders: Anniv, Jul 3
Wade-Davis Reconstruction Bill: Anniv, May 4
Civility Month, Natl Win with, Aug 1
Clam Chowder Cook-off (Santa Cruz, CA), Feb 21
Clancy, Tom: Birth, Apr 12
Clapp, Gordon: Birth, Sep 24
Clapton, Eric: Birth, Mar 30
Clark, Abraham: Birth Anniv, Feb 15
Clark, Barney: Artificial Heart Transplant: Anniv, Dec 2
Clark, Barney: Death Anniv, Mar 23
Clark, Dave: Birth, Dec 15
Clark, Dick: American Bandstand TV Premiere: Anniv, Aug 5
Clark, Dick: Birth, Nov 30
Clark, Dick: Retires from American Bandstand: Anniv, Mar 23
Clark, Mark: Birth Anniv, May 1
Clark, Mary Higgins: Birth, Dec 24
Clark, Petula: Birth, Nov 15
Clark, Roy: Birth, Apr 15
Clark, Susan: Birth, Mar 8
Clark, William: Birth Anniv, Aug 1
Clarke, Arthur C.: Birth Anniv, Dec 16
Clarke, Susanna: Birth, Nov 16
Clarkson, Kelly: Birth, Apr 24
Clarkson, Patricia: Birth, Dec 29
Class Reunion Month, Oct 1
Clay (Muhammad Ali) Becomes Heavyweight Champ: Anniv, Feb 25
Clay, Cassius, Jr (Muhammad Ali): Birth, Jan 17
Clay, Henry: Birth Anniv, Apr 12
Clayburgh, Jill: Birth, Apr 30
Clayton, Adam: Birth, Mar 13
Clean Air Act Passed by Congress: Anniv, Dec 17
Clean Hands Week, Natl, Sep 20
Clean Up Your Computer Month, Natl, Jan 1
Cleaning Week, Natl, Mar 22
Clean-Off-Your-Desk Day, Natl, Jan 12
Cleary, Beverly: Birth, Apr 12
Cleese, John: Birth, Oct 27
Clemens, Roger: Birth, Aug 4
Clemens, Samuel (Mark Twain): Birth Anniv, Nov 30
Clemente, Roberto: Birth Anniv, Aug 18
Clements, George Harold: Birth, Jan 26
Clemons, Clarence: Birth, Jan 11
Clemson, Thomas: Birth Anniv, Jul 1
Clerc, Laurent: Birth Anniv, Dec 26
Clerc-Gallaudet Week, Dec 6
Clergy: Pastoral Care Week, Oct 25
Clerihew Day (Edmund Bentley Clerihew Birth Anniv), Jul 10
Cleveland Natl Air Show (Cleveland, OH), Sep 5
Cleveland, Esther: First White House Presidential Baby, Aug 30
Cleveland, Frances: Birth Anniv, Jul 21
Cleveland, Grover: Birth Anniv, Mar 18
Cleveland, Grover: Cleveland's Secret Surgery: Anniv, Jul 1
Cleveland, Grover: Second Inauguration: Anniv, Mar 4
Cliburn, Van, Conquers Moscow: Anniv, Apr 14
Cliburn, Van: Birth, Jul 12
Cliburn, Van: Intl Piano Competition (Fort Worth, TX), May 22
Cliche Day, Nov 3
Cliche Week, Sports, Jul 5
Clijsters, Kim: Birth, Jun 8
Cline, Patsy: Birth Anniv, Sep 8
Clinton, George: Birth Anniv, Jul 26
Clinton, Hillary Rodham: Birth, Oct 26
Clinton, William
Birthday, Aug 19
and Hillary, Wedding: Anniv, Oct 11
Impeachment Proceedings: Anniv, Dec 20
"Meaning of 'Is' Is": Anniv, Aug 17
Senate Acquits: Anniv, Feb 12
Clodagh: Birth, Oct 8
Cloning of an Adult Animal, First: Anniv, Feb 23
Clooney, George: Birth, May 6
Clooney, Rosemary: Birth Anniv, May 23
Close, Glenn: Birth, Mar 19
Clothesline Fair (Prairie Grove, AR), Sep 5
Clothesline Week, Intl, Jun 6
Clowns: Grimaldi, Joseph: Birth Anniv, Dec 18
Clowns: Kelly, Emmett: Birth Anniv, Dec 9
Clute's Christmas in the Park (Clute, TX), Dec 8
Clymer, George: Birth Anniv, Mar 16
CN Tower: Anniv, Jun 26
CNN Debut: Anniv, Jun 1
Coaching; Coaching Events
African-American Coaches Day, Feb 3
Cheer Coach Day, Jun 6
Coaching Week, Intl, Feb 1
Dating and Life Coach Recognition Week, May 4
Executive Coaching Day, May 1
Natl Soccer Coaches Assn of America Natl Conv (St. Louis, MO), Jan 14
Coal Miner Days (Novinger, MO), May 24
Coast Guard Day, Aug 4
Coastal Cleanup, Intl, Sep 19
Coats & Toys for Kids Day (ME), Dec 5
Cobb, Tyrus "Ty": Birth Anniv, Dec 18
Cobblestone Fest (Falls City, NE), Aug 21
Coburn, James: Birth Anniv, Aug 31
Coburn, Tom: Birth, Mar 14
Cochise: Death Anniv, Jun 8
Cochran, Jacqueline: Death Anniv, Aug 9
Cochran, Thad: Birth, Dec 7
Cocker, Joe: Birth, May 20
Cody, William F. "Buffalo Bill": Birth Anniv, Feb 26
Coen, Ethan: Birth, Sep 21
Coen, Joel: Birth, Nov 29
Cohen, Leonard: Birth, Sep 21
Cohen, Rob: Birth, Mar 12
Cohen, Sasha Baron: Birth, Oct 13
Cohen, Sasha: Birth, Oct 26
Cohocton Fall Foliage Fest (Cohocton, NY), Oct 2
Coin Week, Natl, Apr 19
Coins Stamped "In God We Trust": Anniv, Apr 22
Colantoni, Enrico: Birth, Feb 14
Colbert, Claudette: Birth Anniv, Sep 13
Colbert, Claudette: It Happened One Night Film Release: Anniv, Feb 22
Colbert, Stephen: Birth, May 13
Cold Moon, Dec 2
Cold War: Treaty Signed to Mark End: Anniv, Nov 19
Cole, Nat "King": Birth Anniv, Mar 17
Cole, Natalie: Birth, Feb 6
Coleman, Bessie: Birth Anniv, Jan 26
Coleman, Dabney: Birth, Jan 3
Coleman, Derrick: Birth, Jun 21
Coleman, Gary: Birth, Feb 8
Coleman, Jack: Birth, Feb 21
Coleman, Monique: Birth, Nov 13
Coleman, Norm: Birth, Aug 17
Coleman, Ornette: Birth, Mar 19
Coleman, Signy: Birth, Jul 4
Coleridge, Samuel: Birth Anniv, Oct 21
Coles, Joanna: Birth, Aug 11
Colfax, Schuyler: Birth Anniv, Mar 23
College Bowl TV Premiere: Anniv, Jan 4
College Cup (NCAA Div I Women's Soccer Chmpshp) (College Station, TX), Dec 4
College Savings Month, Sep 1
Collette, Toni: Birth, Nov 1

Collins, Albert: Birth Anniv, Oct 1
Collins, Eileen: Birth, Nov 19
Collins, Gary: Birth, Apr 30
Collins, Jackie: Birth, Oct 4
Collins, Joan: Birth, May 23
Collins, Judy: Birth, May 1
Collins, Michael: Birth, Oct 31
Collins, Pauline: Birth, Sep 3
Collins, Phil: Birth, Jan 30
Collins, Stephen: Birth, Oct 1
Collins, Susan M.: Birth, Dec 7
Collins, Wilkie: Birth Anniv, Jan 8
Collinsworth, Cris: Birth, Jan 27
Collison, Nick: Birth, Oct 26
Colmes, Alan: Birth, Sep 24
Cologne Cathedral Completion: Anniv, Aug 14
Colombia
Battle of Boyaca Day, Aug 7
Cartagena Independence Day, Nov 11
Independence Day, Jul 20
Colonial Christmas (Williamsburg, VA), Dec 1
Color TV Broadcast, First: Anniv, Jun 25
Colorado
Abortion First Legalized: Anniv, Apr 25
Admission Day: Anniv, Aug 1
Allard, Wayne: Birth, Dec 2
American Dietetic Assn Food & Nutrition Conf & Expo (Denver), Oct 17
Bohemian Nights at New West Fest (Fort Collins), Aug 15
Bolder Boulder 10k (Boulder), May 25
Boom Days (Leadville), Jul 31
Burro Race (Leadville), Jul 31
Capitol Hill People's Fair (Denver), Jun 6
Christmas Eve Torchlight Parade (Winter Park), Dec 24
Coca-Cola Spring Splash (Winter Park), Apr 12
Colorado Brewers' Fest (Fort Collins), Jun 27
Colorado Country Christmas Gift Show (Denver), Nov 6
Colorado Day, Aug 3
Commonwheel Arts and Crafts Fest (Manitou Springs), Sep 5
Emma Crawford Fest and Memorial Coffin Race (Manitou Springs), Oct 31
Fourth of July Spectacular (Aurora), Jul 4
Great American Beer Fest (Denver), Sep 24
Great Fruitcake Toss (Manitou Springs), Jan 3
Jack-o-Launch (Aurora), Oct 10
KidSpree (Aurora), Jul 18
Longs Peak Scottish/Irish Highland Fest (Estes Park), Sep 10
Olathe Sweet Corn Fest (Olathe), Aug 1
Ritter, Bill: Birth, Sep 6
Rocky Mountain Balloon Fest (Denver), Aug 29
Rocky Mountain Natl Park Established: Anniv, Jan 26
Salazar, Ken: Birth, Mar 2
State Fair (Pueblo), Aug 29
Summerset Fest (Littleton), Sep 18
Taste of Colorado (Denver), Sep 4
Telluride Balloon Fest (Telluride), Jun 5
Telluride Blues & Brews Fest (Telluride), Sep 18
Telluride Wine Fest (Telluride), Jun 25
Victorian Christmas Home Tour (Leadville), Dec 4
Wells Fargo Golden Bunny Egg Hunt and Race (Winter Park), Apr 12
Western Stock Show and Rodeo, Natl (Denver), Jan 10
Colorado River Crossing Balloon Festival (Yuma, AZ), Nov 20
Colorectal Cancer Awareness Month, Natl, Mar 1
Colorectal Cancer Education/Awareness Month, Dec 1
Colter, Jessi: Birth, May 25
Coltrane, Robbie: Birth, Mar 30
Columbia Space Shuttle Disaster: Anniv, Feb 1
Columbian Exposition Closing: Anniv, Oct 30
Columbian Exposition Opening: Anniv, May 1
Columbine High School Killings: Anniv, Apr 20
Columbo TV Premiere: Anniv, Sep 15
Columbus Day Parade and Italian Fest, Ocean County (Seaside Heights, NJ), Oct 9
Columbus, Christopher
Columbus Day (Observed), Oct 12
Columbus Day (Traditional), Oct 12
Columbus Day, Natl (Pres Proc), Oct 12
Columbus Sails for New World: Anniv, Aug 3
Columbus's Last Voyage to New World: Anniv, Sep 18
Discovery of Jamaica by: Anniv, May 4
Columnist's Day, Natl, Jun 23
Comaneci, Nadia: Birth, Nov 12
Comaneci, Nadia: First Perfect Score in Olympic History: Anniv, Jul 18
Combs, Holly Marie: Birth, Dec 3
Combs, Sean "Diddy": Birth, Nov 4
Come and Take It Fest (Gonzales, TX), Oct 2
COMECON and Warsaw Pact Disband: Anniv, Jun 28
Comet, Closest Approach to Earth: Anniv, Feb 20
Comic-Con Intl (San Diego, CA), Jul 23
Comics (Newspaper and Comic Books)
Batman Debuts: Anniv, May 1
Caniff, Milton: Birth Anniv, Feb 28
Capp, Al: Birth Anniv, Sep 28
Cartoonists Day, May 5
Crankshaft: Anniv, Aug 31
Dick Tracy Debuts: Anniv, Oct 4
Eisner, Will: Birth Anniv, Mar 6
First Newspaper Comic Strip: Anniv, Oct 18
Funky Winkerbean: Anniv, Mar 27
Garfield: Birthday, Jun 19
Gould, Chester: Birth Anniv, Nov 20
Gray, Harold Lincoln: Birth Anniv, Jan 20
Herriman, George: Birth Anniv, Aug 22
Kelly, Walt: Birth Anniv, Aug 25
King, Frank: Birth Anniv, Apr 9
Messick, Dale: Birth Anniv, Apr 11
Mutt and Jeff Debut: Anniv, Mar 29
New York Comic Con (New York, NY), Feb 6
Odie: Birthday, Aug 8
Outcault, Richard Felton: Birth Anniv, Jan 14
Peanuts Debuts: Anniv, Oct 2
Popeye Debuts: Anniv, Jan 17
Schulz, Charles: Birth Anniv, Nov 26
Spider-Man Debuts: Anniv, Aug 1
Superman Debuts: Anniv, Jun 1
Wallet, Skeezix: Birthday, Feb 14
Young, Chic: Birth Anniv, Jan 9
Coming Out Day, Natl, Oct 11
Comiskey, Charles: Birth Anniv, Aug 15
Commercial Bank, First US: Anniv, Jan 7
Commodore Perry Day, Apr 10
Common Prayer Day (Denmark), May 8
Common Sense Day, Use Your, Nov 4
Common Sense Published: Anniv, Jan 10
Commoner, Barry: Birth, May 28
Commonwealth Day (Belize), May 24
Commonwealth Day (United Kingdom), Mar 9
Communications
Better Conversation Week, Nov 23
Card and Letter Writing Month, Natl, Apr 1
Communication Day, Better Business, Jan 26
Communications Month, Effective, Jun 1
Freedom from Fear of Speaking Week, Jun 28
Networking Week, Natl, Apr 6
Speak Up and Succeed Day, Natl, Jan 27
Subliminal Communications Month, Sep 1
Telecommunication Day, World (UN), May 17
Communist Manifesto Published: Anniv, Feb 26
Communist Party Suspended, Soviet: Anniv, Aug 29
Community Spirit Days, Apr 1
Comoros: Independence Day, Jul 6
Companies That Care Day, Mar 19
Compliment Day, Natl, Jan 24
Compliment-Your-Mirror Day, Jul 3
Computer
Apple II Computer Released: Anniv, Jun 5
Babbage, Charles: Birth Anniv, Dec 26
Bifocals at the Monitor Liberation Day, Dec 1
Cathode-Ray Tube Patented: Anniv, Dec 20
Clean Up Your Computer Month, Natl, Jan 1
Computer Security Day, Nov 30
Cyber Security Awareness Month, Natl, Oct 1
Eckert, J. Presper, Jr: Birth Anniv, Apr 9
ENIAC Introduced: Anniv, Feb 14
First Computer Chess Victory: Anniv, Feb 10
Google Founded: Anniv, Sep 7
IBM PC Introduced: Anniv, Aug 12
Internet Created: Anniv, Oct 29
Lotus 1-2-3 Released: Anniv, Jan 26
Macintosh Debuts: Anniv, Jan 25
Microsoft Releases Windows: Anniv, Nov 10
Name Your PC Day, Nov 20
Race Your Mouse Around the Icons Day, Aug 28
Read an E-Book Week, Mar 8
Shareware Day, Intl, Dec 12
Take Your Webmaster to Lunch Day, Jul 6
World Wide Web: Anniv, Aug 1
Conaway, Jeff: Birth, Oct 5
Concorde Flight, First: Anniv, Jan 21
Concordia Fall Fest (Concordia, MO), Sep 8
Concours d'Elegance (Forest Grove, OR), Jul 19
Condom Week, Natl, Feb 14
Cone, David: Birth, Jan 2
Confederate Decoration Day (TN), Jun 3
Confederate Heroes Day (TX), Jan 19
Confederate Memorial Day (AL), Apr 27
Confederate Memorial Day (FL, GA), Apr 26

Confederate Memorial Day (KY, LA, TN), Jun 3
Confederate Memorial Day (MS), Apr 27
Confederate Memorial Day (NC, SC), May 10
Confederation, Articles of: Ratification Anniv, Mar 1
Confucius: Birthday and Teacher's Day (Taiwan), Sep 28
Confucius: Birthday Observance (China), Oct 15
Congenital Heart Defect Awareness Week, Feb 7
Congo (Brazzaville)
Day of Natl Reconciliation, Jun 10
National Holiday, Aug 15
Congo (Dem Rep of the)
Independence Day, Jun 30
Congress, US
Adams, John Quincy: Returns to Congress: Anniv, Mar 4
Assembles (US), Jan 5
Brawl in US House of Representatives, First: Anniv, Jan 30
Congressional Page, First Female: Anniv, Jan 3
First Black Serves in US House of Representatives: Anniv, Dec 12
First Meeting Under Constitution: Anniv, Mar 4
First Meets at Washington: Anniv, Nov 21
House of Representatives, First Quorum: Anniv, Apr 1
Sumner Attacked in the Senate: Anniv, May 22
Woman Runs the US House of Representatives: Anniv, Jun 20
Connecticut
Antique Marine Engine Exposition (Mystic), Aug 15
Antique/Classic Boat Rendezvous (Mystic), Jul 25
Boom Box Parade (Willimantic), Jul 4
By Land and By Sea (Mystic), Sep 26
Chowderfest (Mystic), Oct 10
Community Carol Singing (Mystic), Dec 20
Constitution Ratification: Anniv, Jan 9
Dodd, Christopher J.: Birth, May 27
Field Days (Mystic), Nov 27
Holiday Magic (Mystic), Dec 26
Lantern Light Tours (Mystic), Dec 3
Levitt Pavilion Performing Arts/Music Fest (Westport), Jun 28
Lieberman, Joseph: Birth, Feb 24
Litchfield Open House Tour (Litchfield), Jul 10
Lobster Days (Mystic), May 23
Meet the Artists and Artisans Show (Milford Green), May 9
Melville (Moby-Dick) Marathon (Mystic), Jul 31
Mystic Seaport Independence Day Celebration (Mystic), Jul 4
Norwalk Seaport Oyster Fest (Norwalk), Sep 11
Odyssey—A Greek Fest (Orange), Sep 4
Rell, M. Jodi: Birth, Jun 16
Road Church First Congregational Country Fair (Stonington), Sep 19
Sea Music Fest (Mystic), Jun 12
Sugarloaf Crafts Fest (Hartford), Mar 27
Sugarloaf Crafts Fest (Hartford), Nov 13
Supreme Court Strikes Down Law Banning Contraception: Anniv, Jun 7
Whippoorwill Morgan Horse Open Barn (Old Lyme), Oct 10
Whippoorwill Morgan Horse Versatility Event (Old Lyme), Sep 12
Woodstock Fair (Woodstock), Sep 4
Connelly, Jennifer: Birth, Dec 12
Connery, Sean: Birth, Aug 25
Connick, Harry, Jr: Birth, Sep 11
Connolly, Kevin: Birth, Mar 5
Connolly, Maureen: Birth Anniv, Sep 17
Connors, Chuck: Birth Anniv, Apr 10
Connors, Chuck: First Shattered Backboard: Anniv, Nov 5
Connors, Jimmy: Birth, Sep 2
Connors, Mike: Birth, Aug 15
Conrad, Joseph: Birth Anniv, Dec 3
Conrad, Kent: Birth, Mar 12
Conrad, Lauren: Birth, Feb 1
Conrad, Robert: Birth, Mar 1
Conroy, Pat: Birth, Oct 26
Constable, John: Birth Anniv, Jun 11
Constantinople Falls to the Turks: Anniv, May 29
Constitution Day/Pledge Across America, Sep 17
Constitution, US
11th Amendment Ratified (States' Sov), Feb 7
12th Amendment Ratified (Electoral College Modified), Jun 15
13th Amendment Ratified (Abolished Slavery), Dec 6
14th Amendment Ratified (Citizenship), Jul 9
15th Amendment Ratified (Voting Rights), Feb 3
16th Amendment Ratified (Income Tax), Feb 3
17th Amendment Ratified (Direct Election of Senators), Apr 8
18th Amendment Ratified (Prohibition), Jan 16
19th Amendment Ratified (Women's Right to Vote), Aug 18
20th Amendment Ratified (Inaugural, Congress Opening Dates), Jan 23
21st Amendment Ratified (Prohibition Repealed), Dec 5
22nd Amendment Ratified (Two-Term Limit), Feb 27
23rd Amendment Ratified (DC Residents Right to Vote), Mar 29
24th Amendment Ratified (Eliminated Poll Taxes), Jan 23
25th Amendment Ratified (Pres Succession, Disability), Feb 10
26th Amendment Ratified (Voting Age to 18), Jul 1
27th Amendment Ratified (No Midterm Congressional Pay Raises), May 7
Bill of Rights: Anniv of First State Ratification, Nov 20
Constitution of the US: Anniv, Sep 17
Constitution Week (Pres Proc), Sep 17
Constitution Week, Natl, Sep 13
Constitutional Convention: Anniv, May 25
Equal Rights Amendment Sent to States for Ratification, Mar 22
Federalist Papers: Anniv, Oct 27
Presidential Succession Act: Anniv, Jul 18
Religious Freedom Day, Jan 16
Takes Effect: Anniv, Jul 2
Women's Suffrage Amendment Introduced: Anniv, Jan 10
Consumer Awareness Week, Apr 19
Consumer Electronics Show, Intl (Las Vegas, NV), Jan 8
Consumer Protection Week, Natl (Pres Proc), Mar 1
Consumerism: Buy Nothing Day, Nov 27
Conti, Bill: Birth, Apr 13
Conti, Tom: Birth, Nov 22
Continental Congress Assembly, First: Anniv, Sep 5
Conversation Week, Better, Nov 23
Converse, Frank: Birth, May 22
Converse, Harriet: White Woman Made Indian Chief: Anniv, Sep 18
Conway, Gary: Birth, Feb 4
Conway, Kevin: Birth, May 29
Conway, Tim: Birth, Dec 15
Coogan, Keith: Birth, Jan 13
Cook Something Bold and Pungent Day, Nov 8
Cook, Dane: Birth, Mar 18
Cook, David: Birth, Dec 20
Cook, James: Birth Anniv, Oct 27
Cook, Rachael Leigh: Birth, Oct 4
Cooke, Alistair: Birth Anniv, Nov 20
Cooke, Alistair: Letter from America Radio Premiere: Anniv, Mar 24
Cookie Cutter Week, Dec 1
Cooking: Joy of Cooking: Publication Anniv, Nov 30
Coolidge, Calvin: Birth Anniv, Jul 4
Coolidge, Calvin: Business of America Quotation: Anniv, Jan 17
Coolidge, Grace: Birth Anniv, Jan 3
Coolidge, Rita: Birth, May 1
Cooney, Gerry: Birth, Aug 24
Cooney, Joan Ganz: Birth, Nov 30
Co-Op Awareness Month, Oct 1
Cooper, Alice: Birth, Feb 4
Cooper, Anderson: Birth, Jun 3
Cooper, Bradley: Birth, Jan 5
Cooper, Cynthia: Birth, Apr 14
Cooper, D.B. Hijacking: Anniv, Nov 24
Cooper, Gary: Birth Anniv, May 7
Cooper, Jackie: Birth, Sep 15
Cooper, James Fenimore: Birth Anniv, Sep 15
Cooperatives, Intl Day of (UN), Jul 4
Copeland, Stewart: Birth, Jul 16
Copernicus, Nicolaus: Birth Anniv, Feb 19
Copland, Aaron: Birth Anniv, Nov 14
Copperfield, David: Birth, Sep 16
Coppola, Francis Ford: Birth, Apr 7
Coppola, Francis Ford: Godfather Film Premiere: Anniv, Mar 15
Cops TV Premiere: Anniv, Mar 11
Copyright Law Passed: Anniv, May 31
Copyright Revision Law: Anniv, Jan 1
Coral Sea, Battle of the: Anniv, May 8
Coray, Melissa Burton: Birth Anniv, Mar 2
Corbett-Fitzsimmons Title Fight: Anniv, Mar 17
Corbett-Sullivan Prize Fight: Anniv, Sep 7
Corbin, Barry: Birth, Oct 16
Corddry, Rob: Birth, Feb 4
Corea, Chick: Birth, Jun 12
Corelli, Arcangelo: Birth Anniv, Feb 17
Corker, Bob: Birth, Aug 24
Corman, Roger: Birth, Apr 5
Corn Palace Fest (Mitchell, SD), Aug 26
Cornwall: Saint Piran's Day, Mar 5
Cornwell, Patricia: Birth, Jun 9
Cornyn, John: Birth, Feb 2
Corpus Christi, Jun 11
Corpus Christi (US): Observance, Jun 14
Corrigan, Mairead: Birth, Jan 27
Corrigan, Wrong Way Day, Jul 17

Cort, Bud: Birth, Mar 29
Cortes Conquers Mexico: Anniv, Nov 8
Cortese, Dan: Birth, Sep 14
Corvette and High Performance Meet (Puyallup, WA), Feb 7
Corvette Show (Mackinaw City, MI), Aug 28
Corzine, Jon: Birth, Jan 1
Cosby Show TV Premiere: Anniv, Sep 20
Cosby, Bill: Birth, Jul 12
Cosell, Howard: Birth Anniv, Mar 25
Cosmographiae Introductio: Publication Anniv, Apr 25
Costa Rica
Feast of Our Lady of Angels, Aug 2
Guanacaste Day, Jul 25
Independence Day, Sep 15
Juan Santamaria Day, Apr 11
Costas, Bob: Birth, Mar 22
Costello, Elvis: Birth, Aug 25
Costello, Lou: Birth Anniv, Mar 6
Costner, Kevin: Birth, Jan 18
Cote D'Ivoire
Commemoration Day, Dec 7
Natl Day, Aug 7
Cotillard, Marion: Birth, Sep 30
Cotten, Joseph: Birth Anniv, May 15
Cotton Bowl Classic (Dallas, TX), Jan 2
Cotton Pickin' Fair (Gay, GA), May 2
Coulter, Ann: Birth, Dec 8
Council of Nicaea I: Anniv, May 20
Country-Western
Acuff, Roy: Birth Anniv, Sep 15
Cash, Johnny: Birth Anniv, Feb 26
Cash, June Carter: Birth Anniv, Jun 23
Johnny Cash at Folsom Prison: Anniv, Jan 13
Ladies of Country Music Show (Waretown, NJ), Jun 27
Twitty, Conway: Birth Anniv, Sep 1
Williams, Hank, Sr: Birth Anniv, Sep 17
Wills, Bob: Birth Anniv, Mar 6
Couple Appreciation Month, Apr 1
Couples, Fred: Birth, Oct 3
Coupon Month, Natl, Sep 1
Courage: Face Your Fears Day, Natl, Oct 13
Courageous Follower Day, Mar 4
Couric, Katie: Birth, Jan 7
Court TV Debut: Anniv, Jul 1
Courtenay, Tom: Birth, Feb 25
Courtesy Day, Natl Common, Mar 21
Cousins Day, Jul 24
Cousteau, Jacques: Birth Anniv, Jun 11
Cousy, Bob: Birth, Aug 9
Covered Bridge Fest (Washington County, PA), Sep 19
Cow Chip-Throwing Chmpshp, World (Beaver, OK), Apr 11
Coward, Noel: Birth Anniv, Dec 16
Cowboy Hall of Fame Ceremony (Willcox, AZ), Oct 1
Cowboy, Natl Day of the, Jul 25
Cowboys, Frontier, Old West
Bannack Days (Bannack, MT), Jul 18
Bascom, Texas Rose: Birth Anniv, Feb 25
Calamity Jane (Martha Burk): Death Anniv, Aug 1
Cherokee Strip Celebration (Perry, OK), Sep 19
Come and Take It Fest (Gonzales, TX), Oct 2
Cowboy Hall of Fame Ceremony (Willcox, AZ), Oct 1
Cowboy Poetry Gathering, Natl (Elko, NV), Jan 24
Cowboy Poetry Gathering, Texas (Alpine, TX), Feb 27
Day of the Cowboy, Natl, Jul 25
Defeat of Jesse James Days (Northfield, MN), Sep 9
Dodge City Days (Dodge City, KS), Jul 24
Fiesta Bullwhacker/Wild West Show (Olathe, KS), Sep 26
Fort Abraham Lincoln Fest (Mandan, ND), Jun 20
Gold Rush Days (Wickenburg, AZ), Feb 13
Gunfight at the O.K. Corral: Anniv, Oct 26
Little Bighorn Days (Hardin, MT), Jun 24
Oakley, Annie: Birth Anniv, Aug 13
Oregon Trail Days (Gering, NE), Jul 9
Pendleton Round-Up (Pendleton, OR), Sep 12
Pony Express Fest (Hanover, KS), Aug 30
Reenactment of Cowtown's Last Gunfight (Fort Worth, TX), Feb 8
Russell, Charles M.: Birth Anniv, Mar 19
Santa-Cali-Gon Days Fest (Independence, MO), Sep 4
Western Days (Elgin, TX), Jun 23
Cow-Chip Throw, Wisconsin (Prairie du Sac, WI), Aug 28
Cowell, Simon: Birth, Oct 7
Cowher, Bill: Birth, May 8
Cox, Bobby: Birth, May 21
Cox, Ronny: Birth, Jul 23
Crabbe, Buster: Birth Anniv, Feb 17
Craft & Hobby Assn Winter Conv & Trade Show (Anaheim, CA), Jan 25
Craig, Daniel: Birth, Mar 2
Craig, Larry E.: Birth, Jul 20
Cramer, Jim: Birth, Feb 10
Crandall, Prudence: Birth Anniv, Sep 3
Crane Watch (Kearney, NE), Mar 1
Crane, Stephen: Birth Anniv, Nov 1
Crankshaft: Anniv, Aug 31
Cranky Coworkers Day, Oct 27
Cranmer, Thomas: Birth Anniv, Jul 2
Cranston, Bryan: Birth, Mar 7
Crapo, Michael: Birth, May 20
Crapper, Thomas: Death Anniv, Jan 27
Crater Lake Natl Park Established: Anniv, May 22
Crater Lake Rim Runs and Marathon (Klamath Falls, OR), Aug 8
Crater, Judge Joseph F.: Disappearance Anniv, Aug 6
Craven, Wes: Birth, Aug 2
Crawfish Fest, Clear Lake (Seabrook, TX), Apr 3
Crawfish Fest, Dermott's Annual (Dermott, AR), May 15
Crawford, Chace: Birth, Jul 18
Crawford, Cindy: Birth, Feb 20
Crawford, Joan: Birth Anniv, Mar 23
Crawford, Michael: Birth, Jan 19
Crawford, Wahoo Sam: Birth Anniv, Apr 18
Crawfordsville Strawberry Fest (Crawfordsville, IN), Jun 12
Cray, Robert: Birth, Aug 1
Crayfish Premiere (Sweden), Aug 12
Creative Beginnings Month, May 1
Creativity Month, Intl, Jan 1
Creativity: Date to Create, The, Aug 8
Creativity: Swap Ideas Day, Sep 10
Crede, Joe: Birth, Apr 26
Credit Union Act: Anniv, Jun 26
Credit Union Day, Intl, Oct 15
Credit Union Week, Intl, Oct 11
Credit: Get Smart About Credit Day, Oct 15
Creeley, Robert: Birth, May 21
Cremation, America's First: Anniv, Dec 9
Crenshaw, Ben: Birth, Jan 11
Cribb, Tom: First US Heavyweight Defeated: Anniv, Dec 10
Crichton, Michael: Birth, Oct 23
Crick, Francis: Birth Anniv, Jun 8
Crime
Billy the Kid: Birth Anniv, Nov 23
Black Dahlia Murder: Anniv, Jan 15
Bonnie and Clyde: Death Anniv, May 23
Borden, Lizzie, Verdict: Anniv, Jun 20
Capone, Al: Birth Anniv, Jan 17
Columbine High School Killings: Anniv, Apr 20
Crime Prevention Month, Natl, Oct 1
Crime Victims' Rights Week, Natl (Pres Proc), Apr 19
D.B. Cooper Hijacking: Anniv, Nov 24
Dillinger, John: Death Anniv, Jul 22
Electrocution for Death Penalty, First: Anniv, Aug 6
Jack the Ripper Letter: Anniv, Sep 27
Miranda Decision: Anniv, Jun 13
Ned Kelly's Last Stand: Anniv, Jun 27
Saint Valentine's Day Massacre: Anniv, Feb 14
Siegel, Bugsy: Birth Anniv, Feb 28
Stockholm Syndrome Bank Robbery: Anniv, Aug 23
Ten Most Wanted List Debuts: Anniv, Mar 14
Virginia Tech Shootings: Anniv, Apr 16
Whitechapel Murders Begin: Anniv, Aug 31
Crimean War: Anniv, Oct 16
Crispus Attucks Day, Mar 5
Crist, Charlie: Birth, Jul 24
Crist, Judith: Birth, May 22
Croatia
Antifascist Struggle Day, Jun 22
Homeland Thanksgiving Day, Aug 5
Statehood Day, Oct 8
Crockett, David: Birth Anniv, Aug 17
Cromwell, James: Birth, Jan 27
Cronenberg, David: Birth, May 15
Cronkite, Walter: Birth, Nov 4
Croquet, Wicket World of (Indianapolis, IN), Jun 13
Crosby, Cathy Lee: Birth, Dec 2
Crosby, David: Birth, Aug 14
Crosby, Harry L. "Bing": Birth Anniv, May 3
Crosby, Mary: Birth, Sep 14
Crosby, Norm: Birth, Sep 15
Crosby, Sidney: Birth, Aug 7
Cross, Marcia: Birth, Mar 25
Crossword Puzzle Tourn, American (Brooklyn, NY), Feb 27
Crossword Puzzle, First: Anniv, Dec 21
Crouch, Peter: Birth, Jan 30
Crouse, Lindsay: Birth, May 12
Crow, Sheryl: Birth, Feb 11
Crowded Nest Awareness Day, Jun 12
Crowe, Cameron: Birth, Jul 13
Crowe, Russell: Birth, Apr 7
Crudup, Billy: Birth, Jul 8
Cruelty Month, Prevention of Animal, Apr 1
Crufts Dog Show (Birmingham, England), Mar 5
Cruikshank, George: Birth Anniv, Sep 27
Cruise, Tom: Birth, Jul 3
Cruyff, Johan: Birth, Apr 25
Cruz, Celia: Birth Anniv, Oct 21
Cruz, Penelope: Birth, Apr 28
Cryer, Jon: Birth, Apr 16

Crystal, Billy: Birth, Mar 14
CSI: Crime Scene Investigation TV Premiere: Anniv, Oct 6
Csonka, Larry: Birth, Dec 25
Cuba
Anniv of the Revolution, Jan 1
Bay of Pigs Invasion Launched: Anniv, Apr 17
Beginning of Independence Wars Day, Oct 10
Christmas Returns: Anniv, Dec 25
Cuban Missile Crisis: Anniv, Oct 22
Liberation Day, Jan 1
Marti, Jose Julian: Birth Anniv, Jan 28
National Day, Jul 26
Cuckoo Dancing Week, Jan 11
Culkin, Macaulay: Birth, Aug 26
Cullen, Countee: Birth Anniv, May 30
Culligan, Emmett J.: Birth Anniv, Mar 5
Cullum, John: Birth, Mar 2
Culp, Robert: Birth, Aug 16
Cultural Diversity for Dialogue and Development, World Day for (UN), May 21
Culver, Chet: Birth, Jan 1
Cumming, Alan: Birth, Jan 27
Cummings, Quinn: Birth, Aug 13
Cummings, Robert: Birth Anniv, Jun 9
Cummings, Terry: Birth, Mar 15
Cunningham, Glenn: Birth Anniv, Aug 4
Cunningham, Merce: Birth, Apr 16
Cunningham, Randall: Birth, Mar 27
Curacao
Animals' Day, Sep 4
Curacao Day, Jul 26
Kingdom Day and Antillean Flag Day, Dec 15
Memorial Day, May 4
Curie, Marie: Birth Anniv, Nov 7
Curie, Pierre: Birth Anniv, May 15
Curlew Day, Mar 16
Curling Is Cool Day, Feb 23
Curry, Ann: Birth, Nov 19
Curry, Mark: Birth, Jun 1
Curry, Tim: Birth, Apr 19
Curtin, Jane: Birth, Sep 6
Curtis, Charles: Birth Anniv, Jan 25
Curtis, Jamie Lee: Birth, Nov 22
Curtis, Tony: Birth, Jun 3
Curtiss, Glenn: Birth Anniv, May 21
Curwood Fest (Owosso, MI), Jun 4
Cusack, Joan: Birth, Oct 11
Cusack, John: Birth, Jun 28
Custer, George: Battle of Little Bighorn: Anniv, Jun 25
Custodial Workers Day, Natl, Oct 2
Customer Day, Get To Know Your, Jan 15
Customer Loyalty Month, Intl, Apr 1
Cuthbert, Elisha: Birth, Nov 30
Cyber Monday, Nov 30
Cyber Security Awareness Month, Natl, Oct 1
Cyberspace Coined: Anniv, Oct 1
Cyprus
Independence Day, Oct 1
Procession of Icon of Saint Lazarus, Apr 11
Saint Paul's Feast, Jun 28
Cyrus, Billy Ray: Birth, Aug 25
Cyrus, Miley: Birth, Nov 23
Czar Nicholas II and Family Executed: Anniv, Jul 17
Czech
Clarkson Czech Fest (Clarkson, NE), Jun 26
Czech Days (Tabor, SD), Jun 18
Czech Fest, Natl (Wilber, NE), Jul 31
Czech Republic
Commemoration Day, Jul 6
Independence Day, Oct 28
Liberation Day, May 8
Teachers' Day, Mar 28
Czechoslovakia
Czechoslovakia Ends Communist Rule: Anniv, Nov 29
Czech-Slovak Divorce: Anniv, Jan 1
Rape of Lidice: Anniv, Jun 10

D

D.A.R.E. Day, Natl (Pres Proc), Apr 9
D'Abo, Olivia: Birth, Jan 22
Daffodil Fest Weekend (Nantucket Island, MA), Apr 24
Dafoe, Willem: Birth, Jul 22
Daguerre, Louis: Birth Anniv, Nov 18
Dahl, Arlene: Birth, Aug 11
Dahl, Roald: Birth Anniv, Sep 13
Dahl, Steve: Birth, Nov 20
Dailey, Irene: Birth, Sep 12
Dailey, Janet: Birth, May 21
Dairy Alternatives Month, Jun 1
Dairy Expo, World (Madison, WI), Sep 29
Dairy Month, June, Jun 1
Dakar Rally (Argentina and Chile), Jan 3
Dakides, Tara: Birth, Aug 20
Dalai Lama Flees Tibet: Anniv, Mar 31
Dalai Lama: Birth, Jul 6
Dale, Alan: Birth, May 6
Daley, John: Birth, Jul 20
Daley, Richard M.: Birth, Apr 24
Dali, Salvador: Birth Anniv, May 11
Dallas Cup (Frisco, TX), Apr 5
Dallas TV Premiere: Anniv, Apr 2
Dallas, George: Birth Anniv, Jul 10
Dalton Defenders Day (Coffeyville, KS), Oct 2
Dalton, John: Birth Anniv, Sep 6
Dalton, Timothy: Birth, Mar 21
Daltrey, Roger: Birth, Mar 1
Daly, Carson: Birth, Jun 22
Daly, Chuck: Birth, Jul 20
Daly, John: Birth, Apr 28
Daly, Timothy: Birth, Mar 1
Daly, Tyne: Birth, Feb 21
Damian, Michael: Birth, Apr 26
Damon, Matt: Birth, Oct 8
Damone, Vic: Birth, Jun 12
Dana, Bill: Birth, Oct 5
Dance
Ailey, Alvin: Birth Anniv, Jan 5
Balanchine, George: Birth Anniv, Jan 22
Ballet Introduced to the US: Anniv, Feb 7
Dance Day, Natl, Apr 29
Duncan, Isadora: Birth Anniv, May 27
English Riviera Dance Fest (Torquay, England), May 29
Folkmoot USA (Waynesville, NC), Jul 13
Fonteyn, Margot: Birth Anniv, May 18
Fosse, Bob: Birth Anniv, Jun 23
Gigglefeet Dance Fest (Ketchikan, AK), Jul 31
Graham, Martha: Birth Anniv, May 11
Line Dance Week, Sep 14
Merrie Monarch Fest & Hula Competition (Hilo, HI), Apr 12
Robinson, Bill "Bojangles": Birth Anniv, May 25
Tap Dance Day, Natl, May 25
Yuma Square and Round Dance Fest (Yuma, AZ), Feb 13
Dance, Charles: Birth, Oct 10
Dandridge, Dorothy: Birth Anniv, Nov 9
Danes, Claire: Birth, Apr 12
D'Angelo, Beverly: Birth, Nov 15
Daniel Boone Pioneer Fest (Winchester, KY), Sep 4
Daniel Boone TV Premiere: Anniv, Sep 24
Daniel, Beth: Birth, Oct 14
Daniels, Charlie: Birth, Oct 28
Daniels, Jeff: Birth, Feb 19
Daniels, Mitchell: Birth, Apr 7
Daniels, William: Birth, Mar 31
Danner, Blythe: Birth, Feb 3
Danson, Ted: Birth, Dec 29
Dante Alighieri: Death Anniv, Sep 14
Danton, Georges: Birth Anniv, Oct 26
Danza, Tony: Birth, Apr 21
Darby, Kim: Birth, Jul 8
Dare, Virginia: Birth Anniv, Aug 18
Dark Day in New England: Anniv, May 19
Dark Shadows TV Premiere: Anniv, Jun 27
Darren, James: Birth, Jun 8
Darrow, Clarence: Birth Anniv, Apr 18
Darrow, Clarence: Death Commemoration (Chicago, IL), Mar 13
Darts: Blueberry Hill Open Dart Tourn (St. Louis, MO), May 8
Darwin Day, Feb 12
Darwin, Charles Robert: Birth Anniv, Feb 12
Darwin, Charles: On the Origin of Species Published: Anniv, Nov 22
Dasara (India), Sep 28
Daschle, Thomas: Birth, Dec 9
Date Fest, Natl (Indio, CA), Feb 13
Dating Game TV Premiere: Anniv, Dec 20
Daumier, Honore: Birth Anniv, Feb 26
Davenport, Lindsay: Birth, Jun 8
David, Keith: Birth, Jun 4
Davidovich, Lolita: Birth, Jul 15
Davidson, John: Birth, Dec 13
Davies, Jeremy: Birth, Oct 28
Davies, Laura: Birth, Oct 5
Davies, Marion: Birth Anniv, Jan 3
Davis, Al: Birth, Jul 4
Davis, Angela: Birth, Jan 26
Davis, Baron: Birth, Apr 13
Davis, Benjamin O., Jr: Birth Anniv, Dec 18
Davis, Bette: Birth Anniv, Apr 5
Davis, Clifton: Birth, Oct 4
Davis, Eric: Birth, May 29
Davis, Geena: Birth, Jan 21
Davis, Jefferson: Birth Anniv, Jun 3
Davis, Jefferson: Inauguration: Anniv, Feb 18
Davis, Jim: Birth, Jul 28
Davis, Judy: Birth, Apr 23
Davis, Mac: Birth, Jan 21
Davis, Miles: Birth Anniv, May 25
Davis, Ossie: Birth Anniv, Dec 18
Davis, Paige: Birth, Oct 15
Davis, Sammy, Jr: Birth Anniv, Dec 8
Davis, Terrell: Birth, Oct 28
Davison, Bruce: Birth, Jun 28
Davis-Voss, Sammi: Birth, Jun 21
Davy Crockett TV Premiere: Anniv, Dec 15
Davydenko, Nikolay: Birth, Jun 2
Dawber, Pam: Birth, Oct 18
Dawes, Charles: Birth Anniv, Aug 27
Dawson, Andre: Birth, Jul 10
Dawson, Dermontti: Birth, Jun 17
Dawson, Richard: Birth, Nov 20
Dawson, Rosario: Birth, May 9
Day of Hope, Natl, Apr 1
Day of Radiant Peace, Intl, Sep 22
Day of Reason, Natl, May 7
Day of the Five Billion: Anniv, Jul 11

Day of the Race: See Columbus Day, Oct 12
Day of the Six Billion: Anniv, Oct 12
Day With(out) Art, Dec 1
Day, Doris: Birth, Apr 3
Day-Lewis, Daniel: Birth, Apr 29
Daylight Saving Time Begins (US), Mar 8
Daylight Saving Time Ends (US), Nov 1
Daylight Saving Time: Napping Day, Natl, Mar 9
Dayne, Taylor: Birth, Mar 7
Days of Our Lives TV Premiere: Anniv, Nov 8
Daytona 500 (Daytona Beach, FL), Feb 15
D-Day: Anniv, Jun 6
De Bont, Jan: Birth, Oct 22
De Forest, Lee: Birth Anniv, Aug 26
De Gaulle, Charles: Birth Anniv, Nov 22
de Havilland, Olivia: Birth, Jul 1
de Klerk, Frederik Willem: Birth, Mar 18
De La Hoya, Oscar: Birth, Feb 4
De La Renta, Oscar: Birth, Jul 22
De Laurentiis, Dino: Birth, Aug 8
De Laurentiis, Giada: Birth, Aug 22
de Matteo, Drea: Birth, Jan 19
De Mornay, Rebecca: Birth, Aug 29
De Niro, Robert: Birth, Aug 17
De Palma, Brian: Birth, Sep 11
De Rita, Joe: Birth Anniv, Jul 12
De Rosario, Dwayne: Birth, May 15
de Rossi, Portia: Birth, Jan 31
De Sade, Donatien: Birth Anniv, Jun 2
De Silhouette, Etienne: Birth Anniv, Jul 8
De Valera, Eamon: Birth Anniv, Oct 14
De Young, Cliff: Birth, Feb 12
Deaf Awareness Week, Sep 20
Deaf Day, Mother, Father, Apr 26
Deaf History Month, Mar 13
Deaf, First School for: Anniv, Apr 15
Dean, Dizzy: Birth Anniv, Jan 16
Dean, Howard: Birth, Nov 17
Dean, James: Birth Anniv, Feb 8
Dean, James: Birthday Celebration (Fairmount, IN), Feb 7
Dean, James: Death Anniv, Sep 30
Dean, James: Fairmount Fest/Remembering (Fairmount, IN), Sep 24
Dean, Jimmy: Birth, Aug 10
Dean, John: Birth, Oct 14
Dear Santa Letter Week, Nov 8
Death of a Salesman Premiere: Anniv, Feb 10
Death Penalty Banned: Anniv, Jun 29
Death/Duty Day, Nov 11
Death: Plan Your Epitaph Day, Nov 2
DeBarge, Eldra: Birth, Jun 4
Debs, Eugene V.: Birth Anniv, Nov 5
Debussy, Claude: Birth Anniv, Aug 22
Decatur, Stephen: Birth Anniv, Jan 5
Decency, Rally for: Anniv, Mar 23
Decisions: Make Up Your Mind Day, Dec 31
Declaration of Independence
  Approval and Signing: Anniv, Jul 4
  First Public Reading: Anniv, Jul 8
  Official Signing: Anniv, Aug 2
  Resolution: Anniv, Jul 2
Declaration of the Bab, May 23
Decorating Month, Natl, Apr 1
Decoration Day (Memorial Day), May 25
Decoy and Wildlife Art Show (Clayton, NY), Jul 17
Decoys: Ward World Chmpshp Waterfowl Carving Competition (Ocean City, MD), Apr 24
Decter, Midge: Birth, Jul 25
Dee, Ruby: Birth, Oct 27
Deep Impact Smashes into Tempel 1, Jul 4
Deepavali (India), Oct 17
Dees, Rick: Birth, Mar 14
Def, Mos: Birth, Dec 11
Defenders Day, Sep 12
Defense Transportation Day, Natl (Pres Proc), May 15
DeFrantz, Anita L.: Birth, Oct 4
Degas, Edgar: Birth Anniv, Jul 19
DeGeneres, Ellen: Birth, Jan 26
DeHaven, Gloria: Birth, Jul 23
Del Toro, Benicio: Birth, Feb 19
Delaney, Kim: Birth, Nov 29
Delano, Jane: Birth Anniv, Mar 26
Delany, Dana: Birth, Mar 13
Delaware
  Biden, Joe: Birth, Nov 20
  Carper, Tom: Birth, Jan 23
  Delaware State Fair (Harrington), Jul 23
  Minner, Ruth Ann: Birth, Jan 17
  Nanticoke Indian Powwow (Millsboro), Sep 12
  Ratification Day, Dec 7
  Return Day (Georgetown), Nov 5
  Sea Witch Halloween & Fiddlers Fest (Rehoboth Beach/Dewey Beach), Oct 24
  World Chmpshp Punkin Chunkin (Bridgeville), Nov 6
Delgado, Carlos: Birth, Jun 25
DeLillo, Don: Birth, Nov 20
Delmonico, Lorenzo: Birth Anniv, Mar 13
DeLuise, Dom: Birth, Aug 1
DeMille, Agnes: Birth Anniv, Sep 18
DeMille, Cecil B.: Birth Anniv, Aug 12
DeMint, Jim: Birth, Sep 2
Demme, Jonathan: Birth, Feb 22
Dempsey, Jack: Birth Anniv, Jun 24
Dempsey, Jack: Long Count Day, Sep 22
Dempsey, Patrick: Birth, Jan 13
DeMunn, Jeffrey: Birth, Apr 25
Denali Natl Park: Anniv, Dec 2
Dench, Judi: Birth, Dec 9
Deneuve, Catherine: Birth, Oct 22
Deng, Luol: Birth, Apr 16
Denim Day, Lee Natl, Oct 2
Denmark
  Aalborg and Rebild Fest (Aalborg and Rebild), Jul 2
  Common Prayer Day, May 8
  Constitution Day, Jun 5
  Ho Sheep Market, Aug 29
  Midsummer Eve, Jun 23
  Observation of 1945 Liberation, May 5
  Observation of Nazi Occupation, Apr 9
  Queen Margrethe's Birthday, Apr 16
  Tivoli Gardens Season (Copenhagen), May 1
  Viking Fest (Frederiksund), Jun 19
Dennehy, Brian: Birth, Jul 9
Dennis, Sandy: Birth Anniv, Apr 27
Dent, Bucky: Birth, Nov 25
Dental Drill Patent: Anniv, Jan 26
Dental Health Month, Natl Children's, Feb 1
Dental Hygiene Month, Natl, Oct 1
Dental: Flossing Day, Natl, Nov 27
Dentistry: Root Canal Appreciation Day, May 13
Denton, James: Birth, Jan 20
Denver, Bob: Birth Anniv, Jan 9
Denver, John: Birth Anniv, Dec 31
Depardieu, Gerard: Birth, Dec 27
Depp, Johnny: Birth, Jun 9
DePreist, James: Birth, Nov 21
Depression Awareness Day, Childhood, May 5
Depression Education and Awareness Month, Natl, Oct 1
Depression Screening Day, Natl, Oct 8
Derek, Bo: Birth, Nov 20
Dern, Bruce: Birth, Jun 4
Dern, Laura: Birth, Feb 10
Derrida, Jacques: Birth Anniv, Jul 15
Dershowitz, Alan: Birth, Sep 1
Desai, Kiran: Birth, Sep 3
Descartes, Rene: Birth, Mar 31
Descendants Day, Jun 28
Deschanel, Emily: Birth, Oct 11
Desegregation, US Army First: Anniv, Jul 26
Desert Shield: Anniv, Aug 7
Desert Storm: Ground War Begins: Anniv, Feb 23
Desert Storm: Gulf War Begins: Anniv, Jan 16
Desert Storm: Kuwait Liberated: Anniv, Feb 27
DeShannon, Jackie: Birth, Aug 21
Designated Hitter Rule Adopted: Anniv, Jan 11
Des'ree: Birth, Nov 30
Detroit Auto Show: North American Intl Auto Show (Detroit, MI), Jan 11
Detroit Founded: Anniv, Jul 24
Devane, William: Birth, Sep 5
Development Information Day, World (UN), Oct 24
Devers, Gail: Birth, Nov 19
Devil's Night, Oct 30
DeVito, Danny: Birth, Nov 17
Devlin, Bernadette: Birth, Apr 23
DeVoe, Ronald: Birth, Feb 17
Dewey Defeats Truman Headline: Anniv, Nov 3
Dewey, John: Birth Anniv, Oct 20
Dewey, Melvil: Birth Anniv, Dec 10
Dewhurst, Colleen: Birth Anniv, Jun 3
Dewitt, Joyce: Birth, Apr 23
Dey, Susan: Birth, Dec 10
Dia de la Raza (Mexico), Oct 12
Dia de la Raza: See Columbus Day, Oct 12
Diabetes Assn Alert Day, American, Mar 24
Diabetes Day, World, Nov 14
Diabetes Month, American, Nov 1
Diabetes Month, Natl (Pres Proc), Nov 1
Diabetic Eye Disease Month, Nov 1
Diallo, Mamadou: Birth, Aug 28
Diamond, Dustin: Birth, Jan 7
Diamond, Neil: Birth, Jan 24
Diana, Princess of Wales: Birth Anniv, Jul 1
Diana, Princess of Wales: Death Anniv, Aug 31
Diary Day, Dear, Sep 22
Diaz, Cameron: Birth, Aug 30
DiCaprio, Leonardo: Birth, Nov 11
Dice Day, Natl, Dec 4
Dicing for Bibles (Huntingdonshire, England), Jun 1
Dick Cavett Show TV Premiere: Anniv, Mar 4
Dick Tracy Debuts: Anniv, Oct 4
Dick Van Dyke Show TV Premiere: Anniv, Oct 3
Dick, Andy: Birth, Dec 21
Dickens' Christmas Extravaganza (Cape May, NJ), Dec 6
Dickens on the Strand (Galveston, TX), Dec 5
Dickens, Charles: Birth Anniv, Feb 7
Dickens, Charles: Christmas Carol Published: Anniv, Dec 17
Dickerson, Eric: Birth, Sep 2

Dickinson, Angie: Birth, Sep 30
Dickinson, Emily: Birth Anniv, Dec 10
Dictionary Day, Oct 16
Dictionary of American English Published, First: Anniv, Apr 14
Didion, Joan: Birth, Dec 5
Didrikson Pitches for Athletics: Anniv, Mar 21
Didrikson, Babe: See under Zaharias, Jun 26
Diefenbaker, John: Birth Anniv, Sep 18
Diego, Jose de: Birth Anniv, Apr 16
Dien Bien Phu Falls: Anniv, May 7
Diesel Engine Patented: Anniv, Feb 23
Diesel, Rudolph: Natl Biodiesel Day, Mar 18
Diesel, Vin: Birth, Jul 18
Dietrich, Marlene: Birth Anniv, Dec 27
Diets, Dieting (including weight loss and weight issues). See also Health
  Diet Resolution Week, Jan 1
  Family Fit Lifestyle Month, Jan 1
  Healthy Weight Week, Jan 18
  No Diet Day, May 6
  Rid the World of Fad Diets/Gimmicks Day, Jan 20
  Women's Healthy Weight Day, Jan 22
Difference Day, Make a, Oct 24
DiFranco, Ani: Birth, Sep 23
Diggs, Taye: Birth, Jan 2
Diller, Phyllis: Birth, Jul 17
Dillinger, John: Death Anniv, Jul 22
Dillon, Kevin: Birth, Aug 19
Dillon, Matt: Birth, Feb 18
Dillon, Melinda: Birth, Oct 13
DiMaggio, Joe: Birth Anniv, Nov 25
Dimpled Chad Day, Jan 4
DiMucci, Dion: Birth, Jul 18
Dinah Shore Show TV Premiere: Anniv, Nov 27
Ding Dong School TV Premiere: Anniv, Dec 22
Ding Ling: Death Anniv, Mar 4
Dinkins, David: Birth, Jul 10
Dinosaur Roundup Rodeo (Vernal, UT), Jul 8
Dion, Celine: Birth, Mar 30
Dionne Quintuplets: Birthday, May 28
Dior, Christian: Birth Anniv, Jan 21
Disabled
  Americans with Disabilities Act: Anniv, Jul 26
  Bell, Alexander Graham: Birth Anniv, Mar 3
  Clerc-Gallaudet Week, Dec 6
  Deaf Awareness Week, Sep 20
  Deaf History Month, Mar 13
  Disability Employment Awareness Month, Natl, Oct 1
  Disability Employment Awareness Month, Natl (Pres Proc), Oct 1
  First School for Deaf: Anniv, Apr 15
  Fishing Has No Boundaries (Hayward, WI), May 15
  Fishing Has No Boundaries (Monticello, IN), May 16
  Goodwill Industries Week, May 3
  Helen Keller's Miracle: Anniv, Apr 5
  Mother, Father Deaf Day, Apr 26
  One Arm Dove Hunt (Olney, TX), Sep 11
  Persons with Disabilities, Intl Day of (UN), Dec 3
  Rehabilitation Awareness Celebration, Natl, Sep 20
  Seeing Eye Established: Anniv, Jan 29
  Special Olympics Day, Jul 20
  Special Recreation Day, Jun 28
  Special Recreation Week, Jun 28
  Travelers with Disabilities Awareness Week, Nov 29
Disarmament Week (UN), Oct 24
Discoverers' Day (Hawaii), Oct 12
Discovery Launches Satellite: Anniv, Nov 7
Dishonor List, New Year's, Jan 1
Disney World Opened: Anniv, Oct 1
Disney, Walt: Birth Anniv, Dec 5
Disneyland Opened: Anniv, Jul 17
Disraeli, Benjamin: Birth Anniv, Dec 21
Distinguished Service Medal: Anniv, Mar 7
Ditka, Mike: Birth, Oct 18
Divac, Vlade: Birth, Feb 3
Diversity Awareness Month, Global, Oct 1
Diversity Day, Natl, Oct 2
Diversity Month, Celebrate, Apr 1
Diversity: Two Different Colored Shoes Day, Natl, May 3
Divorce: Child-Centered Divorce Month, Natl, Jul 1
Diwali (India), Oct 17
Dix, Dorothea L.: Birth Anniv, Apr 4
Dixie, Holiday in (Shreveport and Bossier City, LA), Apr 17
Dixon, Donna: Birth, Jul 20
Dixon, Scott: Birth, Jul 22
Dixon, Willie: Birth Anniv, Jul 1
Djibouti: Independence Day, Jun 27
DNA, Genomics & Stem Cell Education and Awareness Month, Natl, Apr 1
Dobson, Kevin: Birth, Mar 18
Doctor Who TV Premiere: Anniv, Nov 23
Doctorow, E.L.: Birth, Jan 6
Doctor-Patient Trust Week, Mar 22
Doctors' Day, Mar 30
Doctors TV Premiere: Anniv, Apr 1
Dodd, Christopher J.: Birth, May 27
Dodgson, Charles Lutwidge: Birth Anniv, Jan 27
Dog Days, Jul 3
Doghouse Day, Natl Get Out of the, Jul 20
Doghouse Repairs Month, Natl, Jul 1
Dogs. See also Sled Dogs
  Adopt-a-Shelter-Dog Month, Oct 1
  AKC/Eukanuba Natl Chmpshp (Long Beach, CA), Dec 12
  Assistance Dog Week, Aug 9
  Bark in the Park (Chicago, IL), May 2
  Bulldogs Are Beautiful Day, Natl, Apr 25
  Crufts Dog Show (Birmingham, England), Mar 5
  Dog Bite Prevention Week, Natl, May 17
  Dog Day, Natl, Aug 26
  Fala Day (Warm Springs, GA), Nov 7
  Field Trial Chmpshp, Natl (Bird Dogs) (Grand Junction, TN), Feb 9
  Haute Dog Charity Easter Parade (Long Beach, CA), Apr 12
  Haute Dog Charity Howl'oween Parade (Long Beach, CA), Oct 25
  Laika: Sputnik 2, Nov 3
  Prevent Lyme in Dogs Month, Apr 1
  Puppy Day, Natl, Mar 23
  Scoop the Poop Week, Natl, Apr 24
  Seeing Eye Established: Anniv, Jan 29
  Sled Dogs Save Nome: Anniv, Feb 2
  Take Your Dog to Work Day, Jun 26
  Westminster Kennel Club Dog Show (New York, NY), Feb 9
  What if Cats and Dogs Had Opposable Thumbs Day, Mar 3
  Woofstock (Wichita, KS), Oct 3
  World's Ugliest Dog Contest (Petaluma, CA), Jun 26
Doherty, Shannen: Birth, Apr 12
Dohring, Jason: Birth, Mar 30
Dolby, Ray: Birth, Jan 18
Dole, Elizabeth: Birth, Jul 29
Dole, Robert J.: Birth, Jul 22
Dolenz, Micky: Birth, Mar 8
Doll Fest (Japan), Mar 3
Doll Show (Yuma, AZ), Feb 7
Doll, Kewpie: Rose C. O'Neill: Birth Anniv, Jun 25
Domenici, Pete V.: Birth, May 7
Domestic Violence Awareness Month, Oct 1
Domestic Violence Awareness Month, Natl (Pres Proc), Oct 1
Domingo, Placido: Birth, Jan 21
Dominica: National Day, Nov 3
Dominican Republic
  Independence Day, Feb 27
  National Holiday, Jan 26
  Restoration of the Republic, Aug 16
Domino, Fats: Birth, Feb 26
Donahue, Elinor: Birth, Apr 19
Donahue, Phil: Birth, Dec 21
Donald Duck: Birthday, Jun 9
Donaldson, Sam: Birth, Mar 11
Donate Life Month, Natl, Apr 1
Donate Life Month, Natl (Pres Proc), Apr 1
Donizetti's Lucia Di Lammermoor Premiere: Anniv, Sep 26
Donna Reed Performing Arts Fest (Denison, IA), Jun 15
Donner Party Famine: Anniv, Oct 28
Donny and Marie TV Premiere: Anniv, Jan 16
D'Onofrio, Vincent: Birth, Jun 30
Donor Sabbath, Natl, Nov 13
Donovan, Landon: Birth, Mar 4
Donovan, Tate: Birth, Sep 25
Donovan: Birth, Feb 10
Don't Step on a Bee Day, Jul 10
Dooley, Paul: Birth, Feb 22
Doolittle, Eliza: Day, May 20
Doolittle, James Harold: Birth Anniv, Dec 14
Dorgan, Byron L.: Birth, May 14
Dormer, Natalie: Birth, Feb 11
Dormition of Theotokos, Aug 15
Dorsett, Tony: Birth, Apr 7
Dorsey, Thomas A.: Birth Anniv, Jul 1
Dostoyevsky, Fyodor M.: Birth Anniv, Nov 11
Double Nine Fest (China), Oct 26
Double Seven Fest (China), Aug 26
Double Tenth Day (China), Oct 10
Doubleday, Abner: Birth Anniv, Jun 26
Douglas, Bob: Birth Anniv, Nov 4
Douglas, Illeana: Birth, Jul 25
Douglas, Jim: Birth, Jun 21
Douglas, Kirk: Birth, Dec 9
Douglas, Michael: Birth, Sep 25
Douglas, Mike: Birth Anniv, Aug 11
Douglas, Sherman: Birth, Sep 15
Douglas, Virginia O'Hanlon: Death Anniv, May 13
Douglas, William O.: Birth Anniv, Oct 16
Douglass, Frederick
  Death Anniv, Feb 20
  Escape to Freedom: Anniv, Sep 3
Dourdan, Gary: Birth, Dec 11
Dourif, Brad: Birth, Mar 18
Dow Jones Biggest Drop: Anniv, Oct 19
Dow Jones Industrial Average: Anniv, Oct 7
Dow Jones Tops 1,000: Anniv, Nov 14
Dow Jones Tops 3,000: Anniv, Apr 17
Dow Jones Tops 5,000: Anniv, Nov 21
Dow Jones Tops 10,000: Anniv, Mar 29

Dow Jones Tops 11,000: Anniv, May 3
Dow, Tony: Birth, Apr 13
Dowie, John: Birth Anniv, May 25
Down Syndrome Awareness Month, Natl, Oct 1
Down, Lesley-Anne: Birth, Mar 17
Downey, Robert, Jr: Birth, Apr 4
Downey, Roma: Birth, May 6
Downs, Hugh: Birth, Feb 14
Doyle, Jim: Birth, Nov 23
Doyle, Sir Arthur Conan: Birth Anniv, May 22
Drabble, Margaret: Birth, Jun 5
Dracula Premiere: Anniv, Feb 12
Dragnet TV Premiere: Anniv, Dec 16
Dragon Boat Fest (China), May 28
Dragon, Daryl: Birth, Aug 27
Dragons: Appreciate a Dragon Day, Jan 16
Dream 2009 Day, Mar 11
Dream Day Quest and Jubilee, Aug 28
Dream Hotline, Natl, Apr 24
Dred Scott Decision: Anniv, Mar 6
Dreiser, Theodore: Birth Anniv, Aug 27
Drescher, Fran: Birth, Sep 30
Dresden Firebombing: Anniv, Feb 13
Drew, Charles: Birth Anniv, Jun 3
Drew, Elizabeth: Birth, Nov 16
Drexler, Clyde Austin: Birth, Jun 22
Dreyfus, Alfred: Birth Anniv, Oct 9
Dreyfuss, Richard: Birth, Oct 29
Drinking Age: Minimum Legal at 21: Anniv, Jul 17
Drinking Straw Patented: Anniv, Jan 3
Drive-In Movie Opens, First: Anniv, Jun 6
Driver, Minnie: Birth, Jan 31
Drive-Thru Day, Natl, Jul 24
Drogba, Didier: Birth, Mar 11
Drowsy Driver Awareness Day, Apr 6
Drucker, Peter: Birth Anniv, Nov 19
Drug Abuse/Illicit Trafficking, Intl Day Against (UN), Jun 26
Drugs: Just Pray No: Worldwide Weekend Prayer, Apr 18
Drunk and Drugged Driving Prevention Month, Natl (Pres Proc), Dec 1
Drysdale, Don: Birth Anniv, Jul 23
Du Bois, W.E.B.: Niagara Movement Founded: Anniv, Jul 11
Dubai Desert (Golf) Classic (Dubai, UAE), Jan 26
Dubcek, Alexander: Birth Anniv, Nov 27
DuBois, Ja'net: Birth, Aug 5
DuBois, W.E.B.: Birth Anniv, Feb 23
Duchovny, David: Birth, Aug 7
Duck-Calling Contest, World's Chmpshp (Stuttgart, AR), Nov 27
Duct Tape Fest (Avon, OH), Jun 19
Duff, Haylie: Birth, Feb 19
Duff, Hilary: Birth, Sep 28
Duff, Howard: Birth Anniv, Nov 24
Duffy, Julia: Birth, Jun 27
Duffy, Patrick: Birth, Mar 17
Dugan, Dennis: Birth, Sep 5
Dukakis, Michael: Birth, Nov 3
Dukakis, Olympia: Birth, Jun 20
Duke, Patty: Birth, Dec 14
Dukes of Hazzard TV Premiere: Anniv, Jan 26
Dulcimer Fest, Southern Appalachian (McCalla, AL), May 2
Dullea, Keir: Birth, May 30
Dumars, Joe: Birth, May 24
Dumas, Alexandre (Fils): Birth Anniv, Jul 27
Dumas, Alexandre: Birth Anniv, Jul 24
Dumb Week (Greece), Apr 5
Dump Your "Significant Jerk" Week, Feb 7
Dunant, Jean-Henri: Birth Anniv, May 8
Dunaway, Faye: Birth, Jan 14
Duncan, Isadora: Birth Anniv, May 27
Duncan, Sandy: Birth, Feb 20
Duncan, Tim: Birth, Apr 25
Dunkirk Evacuated: Anniv, May 26
Dunn, Adam: Birth, Nov 9
Dunn, Nora: Birth, Apr 29
Dunn, Shannon: Birth, Nov 26
Dunn, Warrick: Birth, Jan 5
Dunne, Griffin: Birth, Jun 8
Dunne, Philip: Birth Anniv, Feb 11
Dunst, Kirsten: Birth, Apr 30
Duran, Roberto: Birth, Jun 16
Durang, Christopher: Birth, Jan 2
Durant, Will: Birth Anniv, Nov 5
Durant, William: Birth Anniv, Dec 8
Durante, Jimmy: Birth Anniv, Feb 10
Durbin, Deanna: Birth, Dec 4
Durbin, Richard J.: Birth, Nov 21
Durer, Albrecht: Birth Anniv, May 21
Durning, Charles: Birth, Feb 28
Durocher, Leo: Birth Anniv, Jul 27
Dushku, Eliza: Birth, Dec 30
Dussault, Nancy: Birth, Jun 30
Duston, Hannah: American Heroine Rewarded: Anniv, Jun 8
Dutoit, Charles: Birth, Oct 7
Dutton, Charles S.: Birth, Jan 30
Duval, David: Birth, Nov 9
Duvall, Robert: Birth, Jan 5
Duvall, Shelley: Birth, Jul 7
Dvorak, Anton: New World Symphony Premiere: Anniv, Dec 16
Dykstra, Lenny: Birth, Feb 10
Dylan, Bob: Birth, May 24
Dynasty TV Premiere: Anniv, Jan 12
Dysart, Richard: Birth, Mar 30
Dyslexia Awareness Month, Oct 1

E

E, Sheila: Birth, Dec 12
Eads, George: Birth, Mar 1
Eagle Days in Springfield (Springfield, MO), Jan 17
Eagles Et Cetera Fest (Bismarck, AR), Jan 30
Earhart, Amelia, Atlantic Crossing: Anniv, May 20
Earhart, Amelia: Birth Anniv, Jul 24
Earhart, Amelia: Disappears: Anniv, Jul 2
Earmuffs Patented: Anniv, Mar 13
Earnhardt, Dale, Jr: Birth, Oct 10
Earnhardt, Dale: Birth Anniv, Apr 29
Earp Brothers (Wyatt, Morgan, Virgil): Gunfight at the O.K. Corral: Anniv, Oct 26
Earp, Wyatt: Birth Anniv, Mar 19
Earth at Aphelion, Jul 3
Earth at Perihelion, Jan 4
Earth Day, Apr 22
Earth Day, Chemists Celebrate, Apr 22
Earthquakes
- Calabria (Italy) Earthquake: Anniv, Dec 16
- Earthquake Jolts Philippines: Anniv, Jul 16
- Earthquake of 1988, Armenian: Anniv, Dec 7
- Earthquake Strikes Alaska: Anniv, Mar 27
- Indian Earthquake: Anniv, Jan 26
- Japan Suffers Major Quake: Anniv, Jan 17
- Lisbon: Anniv, Nov 1
- Mexico City Earthquake: Anniv, Sep 19
- Missouri Earthquakes: Anniv, Dec 6
- Plymouth Plantation: Anniv, Jun 1
- Richter Scale Day, Apr 26
- San Francisco 1906 Earthquake: Anniv, Apr 18
- San Francisco 1989 Earthquake: Anniv, Oct 17
- Southern California: Anniv, Jan 17
- Strongest Earthquake of the 20th Century: Anniv, May 22
- Sumatran-Andaman Earthquake and Tsunamis: Anniv, Dec 26
- Turkish Earthquake: Anniv, Aug 17

Earth's Rotation Proved: Anniv, Jan 8
Easley, Mike: Birth, Mar 23
East Coast Blackout: Anniv, Nov 9
East Texas Poultry Fest (Center, TX), Oct 1
East Timor: Independence: Anniv, May 20
Easter
- Chincoteague Easter Decoy Show (Chincoteague Island, VA), Apr 10
- Easter Even, Apr 11
- Easter Monday, Apr 13
- Easter Monday Bank Holiday (United Kingdom), Apr 13
- Easter Sunday, Apr 12
- Easter Sundays Through the Year 2011, Apr 12
- First White House Easter Egg Roll: Anniv, Apr 2
- Haute Dog Charity Easter Parade (Long Beach, CA), Apr 12
- Holy Humor Month, Apr 1
- Holy Week, Apr 5
- Longwood Gardens Easter Celebration (Kennett Square, PA), Apr 11
- Lucerne Fest at Easter (Lucerne, Switzerland), Mar 28
- Marksville Easter Egg Knocking Contest (Marksville, LA), Apr 12
- Moravian Easter Sunrise Service (Winston-Salem, NC), Apr 12
- Orthodox Easter Sunday, Apr 19
- Passion Week, Mar 29
- Passiontide, Mar 29
- Wells Fargo Golden Bunny Egg Hunt and Race (Winter Park, CO), Apr 12
- White House Easter Egg Roll (Washington, DC), Apr 13

Easter Rising (Ireland), Apr 24
Easton, Sheena: Birth, Apr 27
Eastport "Old Home Week" Celebration (Eastport, ME), Jul 1
Eastwood, Clint: Birth, May 31
Eat Better, Eat Together Month, Oct 1
Eat What You Want Day, May 11
Eating Disorders Awareness Week, Natl, Feb 22
Ebersole, Christine: Birth, Feb 21
Ebert, Roger: Birth, Jun 18
Ebert, Roger: Film Fest (Champaign, IL), Apr 22
Ebony Magazine: Anniv, Nov 1
Ebsen, Buddy: Birth Anniv, Apr 2
Eccleston, Christopher: Birth, Feb 16
Eckersley, Dennis: Birth, Oct 3
Eckert, J. Presper, Jr: Birth Anniv, Apr 9
Eckhart, Aaron: Birth, Mar 12
Eckstine, Billy: Birth Anniv, Jul 8
Eclipses
- Annular Solar Eclipse, Jan 26
- Lunar Eclipse, Aug 5
- Lunar Eclipse, Dec 31
- Partial Lunar Eclipse, Jul 7
- Penumbral Lunar Eclipse, Feb 9
- Total Solar Eclipse, Jul 21

Eco, Umberto: Birth, Jan 5

Ecommerce Day, Intl Women's, Sep 21
Ecuador
Battle of Pichincha, May 24
Day of Quito, Dec 6
Independence Day, Aug 10
Ed Sullivan Show TV Premiere: Anniv, Jun 20
Ed Sullivan Show: The Beatles Appear: Anniv, Feb 9
Eddy, Duane: Birth, Apr 26
Eddy, Mary Baker: Birth Anniv, Jul 16
Edelman, Marian Wright: Birth, Jun 6
Edelstein, Lisa: Birth, May 21
Eden, Barbara: Birth, Aug 23
Ederle, Gertrude: Birth Anniv, Oct 23
Ederle, Gertrude: Swims English Channel: Anniv, Aug 6
Edge of Night TV Premiere: Anniv, Apr 2
Edge, The: Birth, Aug 8
Edinburgh Fest Fringe (Scotland), Aug 7
Edinburgh Intl Fest (Edinburgh, Scotland), Aug 14
Edinburgh Military Tattoo (Edinburgh, Scotland), Aug 7
Edison, Thomas
Birth Anniv, Feb 11
Black Maria Studio: Anniv, Feb 1
First Electric Lighting: Anniv, Sep 4
Incandescent Lamp Demonstrated: Anniv, Oct 21
Record of a Sneeze: Anniv, Feb 2
Edison, Thomas: Be Electrific Day, Feb 11
Editors and Writers Month, Be Kind to, Sep 1
Edmonds, Kenneth "Babyface": Birth, Apr 10
Edmonton Intl Fringe Theatre Fest (Edmonton, AB, Canada), Aug 13
Edmund Fitzgerald Beacon Lighting (Two Harbors, MN), Nov 10
Edmund Fitzgerald Sinking: Anniv, Nov 10
Education and Sharing Day (Pres Proc), Mar 27
Education, Learning, Schools
American Council on Education Annual Mtg (Washington, DC), Feb 7
American Education Week, Nov 15
CAMEX (Anaheim, CA), Mar 13
Catholic Educational Assn Conv/Expo, Natl (Anaheim, CA), Apr 14
Catholic Schools Week, Jan 25
Chemistry Week, Natl, Oct 18
Children's Book Day, Intl, Apr 2
College Savings Month, Sep 1
Education Assn Meeting, Natl (San Diego, CA), Jul 1
Educational Support Personnel Day, Natl, Nov 18
Eliza Doolittle Day, May 20
Expanding Girls' Horizons in Science & Engineering Month, Mar 1
Family Literacy Day, Natl, Nov 1
Froebel, Friedrich: Birth Anniv, Apr 21
Geographic Bee Finals, Natl (Washington, DC), May 19
Geographic Bee, School Level, Natl, Jan 2
Geographic Bee, State Level, Natl, Apr 3
Get Ready for Kindergarten Month, Aug 1
Get Smart About Credit Day, Oct 15
Gifted Children Conv, Natl Assn for (Tampa, FL), Nov 5
Go on a Field Trip Month, Natl, Oct 1
Groundhog Job Shadow Day, Feb 2
Harvard Univ Founded: Anniv, Oct 28
Historically Black Colleges and Universities Week, Natl (Pres Proc), Sep 13
Honor Society Awareness Month, Mar 1
Kindergarten Day, Apr 21
Learning Disabilities Assn Intl Conf (Salt Lake City, UT), Feb 25
Library Week, Natl, Apr 12
Literacy Day, Intl (UN), Sep 8
Mentoring Month, Natl, Jan 1
Metric Week, Natl, Oct 4
MiAEYC Early Childhood Conf (Grand Rapids, MI), Mar 26
Mole Day, Natl, Oct 23
Morrill Land Grant Act Passed: Anniv, Jul 1
Mount Holyoke College Founded, Nov 8
Museum Day, Intl, May 18
Music in Our Schools Month, Mar 1
Newspaper in Education Week, Mar 2
Paraprofessional Appreciation Day, Apr 1
Parents as Teachers Day, Natl, Nov 8
Peabody, Elizabeth Palmer: Birth Anniv, May 16
PTA Founders' Day, Natl, Feb 17
Public School, First in America: Anniv, Apr 23
Read Across America Day, Mar 2
Read Me Week (TN), Feb 23
Reading Is Fun Week, May 10
Scholarship Month, Natl, Nov 1
Scholarship Providers Assn Conf, Natl (New Orleans, LA), Oct 27
School Bus Safety Week, Natl, Oct 18
School for Deaf Founded, First: Anniv, Apr 15
School Library Media Month, Apr 1
School Lunch Week, Natl, Oct 12
School Nurse Day, Natl, May 6
School Principals' Day, May 1
School Spirit Season, Intl, Apr 30
Schoolhouse Triangle Project Month, Sep 1
Self-University Week, Sep 1
Special Education Day, Dec 2
Spelling Bee Finals, Scripps Natl, May 27
Spelman College Established: Anniv, Apr 11
Student Government Day (MA), Apr 3
Substitute Teacher Appreciation Week, Sep 14
Sullivan, Anne: Birth Anniv, Apr 14
Teacher Appreciation Week, May 3
Teacher Day, Natl, May 5
Teachers' Day (Czech Republic), Mar 28
Truancy Law: Anniv, Apr 12
Tuskegee Institute Opening: Anniv, Jul 4
Univ of Chicago First Day of Classes, Oct 1
World Teachers' Day (UN), Oct 5
Yale Univ Founded: Anniv, Oct 16
Young Child, Week of the, Apr 19
Young Reader's Day, Natl, Nov 10
Edward VIII: Abdication Anniv, Dec 11
Edward, Jonathan: Birth Anniv, Oct 5
Edward, Prince: Birth, Mar 10
Edwards, Anthony: Birth, Jul 19
Edwards, Blake: Birth, Jul 26
Edwards, Douglas: Birth Anniv, Jul 14
Edwards, Harry: Birth, Nov 22
Edwards, John: Birth, Jun 10
Edwards, Vince: Birth Anniv, Jul 9
Effectiveness Week, Natl, May 18
Efron, Zac: Birth, Oct 18
Egg Month, Natl, May 1
Egg Races (Switzerland), Apr 13
Egg Roll, First White House Easter: Anniv, Apr 2
Egg Salad Week, Apr 13
Eggar, Samantha: Birth, Mar 5
Eggert, Nicole: Birth, Jan 13
Eggsibit (Phillipsburg, NJ), Mar 28
Egypt
Armed Forces Day, Oct 6
Camp David Accord Signed: Anniv, Mar 26
Evacuation Day, Jun 18
Revolution Day, Jul 23
Sharm al-Sheikh Bombings: Anniv, Jul 23
Sinai Day, Apr 25
Statue of Ramses II Unearthed: Anniv, Nov 30
Suez Canal Formal Opening: Anniv, Nov 17
Suez Canal Opens: Anniv, Mar 7
Ehrlich, Paul: Birth, May 29
Eichhorn, Lisa: Birth, Feb 4
Eid-al-Adha: Feast of the Sacrifice (Muslim), Nov 28
Eid-al-Fitr: Celebrating the Fast (Muslim), Sep 21
Eiffel Tower: Anniv (Paris, France), Mar 31
Eiffel, Alexandre Gustave: Birth Anniv, Dec 15
Eight Is Enough TV Premiere: Anniv, Mar 15
Eikenberry, Jill: Birth, Jan 21
Einstein, Albert: Atomic Bomb Letter: Anniv, Aug 2
Einstein, Albert: Birth Anniv, Mar 14
Einstein, Albert: Russell-Einstein Manifesto: Anniv, Jul 9
Eisenhower Assumes Command: Anniv, Jan 16
Eisenhower World War II Weekend (Gettysburg, PA), Sep 19
Eisenhower, David: Birth, Apr 1
Eisenhower, Dwight: Birth Anniv, Oct 14
Eisenhower, Dwight: Ike's Farewell (military-industrial warning): Anniv, Jan 17
Eisenhower, Mamie Doud: Birth Anniv, Nov 14
Eisenhower: Interstate Highway System Born: Anniv, Jun 29
Eisenstaedt, Alfred: Birth Anniv, Dec 6
Eisner, Michael: Birth, Mar 7
Eisner, Will: Birth Anniv, Mar 6
Ekberg, Anita: Birth, Sep 29
Ekland, Britt: Birth, Oct 6
El Salvador
Day of the First Shout for Independence, Nov 5
Day of the Soldier, May 7
Independence Day, Sep 15
Natl Day of Peace, Jan 16
Eldard, Ron: Birth, Feb 20
Eldon Turkey Fest (Eldon, MO), Oct 10
Eleanor Roosevelt Day (Raymond, WA), Aug 8
Elections, Caucuses, Political Conventions
Dimpled Chad Day, Jan 4
General Election Day, US, Nov 3
Last Week to Register to Vote in US General Elections, Sep 27
Return Day (Georgetown, DE), Nov 5
Supreme Court Rules for Bush: Anniv, Dec 12
Electra, Carmen: Birth, Apr 20
Electric Lighting, First: Anniv, Sep 4
Electricity: Incandescent Lamp Demonstrated: Anniv, Oct 21

Electrocution for Death Penalty, First: Anniv, Aug 6
Electronic Greetings Day, Nov 29
Elephant Appreciation Day, Sep 22
Elephant Roundup at Surin (Thailand), Nov 21
Elephants: Jumbo Arrives in America: Anniv, Apr 9
Elfman, Jenna: Birth, Sep 30
Eliot, George: Birth Anniv, Nov 22
Eliot, John: Birth Anniv, Aug 5
Eliot, T.S.: Birth Anniv, Sep 26
Elizabeth I, Queen: Accession Anniv, Nov 17
Elizabeth I, Queen: Birth Anniv, Sep 7
Elizabeth II, Queen: Accession Anniv, Feb 6
Elizabeth II, Queen: Agrees to Pay Taxes, Nov 26
Elizabeth II, Queen: Birth, Apr 21
Elizabeth II: Marriage of Elizabeth and Philip: Anniv, Nov 20
Elizabeth, the Queen Mother: Birth Anniv, Aug 4
Elizondo, Hector: Birth, Dec 22
Elkin, Stanley: Birth Anniv, May 11
Ellerbee, Linda: Birth, Aug 15
Ellery, William: Birth Anniv, Dec 22
Ellington, Duke: Birth Anniv, Apr 29
Elliott, Bill: Birth, Oct 8
Elliott, Chris: Birth, May 31
Elliott, David James: Birth, Sep 21
Elliott, Missy: Birth, Jul 1
Elliott, Sam: Birth, Aug 9
Elliott, Sean: Birth, Feb 2
Ellis Island Family History Day, Apr 17
Ellis Island Opened: Anniv, Jan 1
Ellison, Ralph Waldo: Birth Anniv, Mar 1
Ellsberg, Daniel: Birth, Apr 7
Ellsworth, Oliver: Birth Anniv, Apr 29
Els, Ernie: Birth, Oct 17
Elvis Week (Memphis, TN), Aug 8
Elway, John: Birth, Jun 28
Elwes, Cary: Birth, Oct 26
Emaishen (Luxembourg), Apr 13
Emancipation Day (Texas), Jun 19
Emancipation of 500: Anniv, Aug 1
Emancipation Proclamation Takes Effect: Anniv, Jan 1
Emancipation Proclamation: Anniv, Sep 22
Embassy Seizure, US, in Tehran: Anniv, Nov 4
Embrace Your Geekness Day, Jul 13
Emergency Nurses Day, Oct 14
Emergency Nurses Week, Oct 11
Emergency TV Premiere: Anniv, Jan 22
Emerson, Ralph Waldo: Birth Anniv, May 25
Eminem: Birth, Oct 17
Emmerich, Roland: Birth, Nov 10
Emmett Kelly Clown Fest (Houston, MO), May 1
Emmett, Daniel D.: Birth Anniv, Oct 29
Emotional Intelligence Awareness Month, Oct 1
Emotional Overeating Awareness Month, Apr 1
Emotional Wellness Month, Oct 1
Employee Legal Awareness Day, Feb 13
Employee Spirit Month, Mar 1
Empowerment Week, Women's Self-, Jan 5
Enberg, Dick: Birth, Jan 9
Endangered Species Act: Anniv, Dec 28
Energy Management Is a Family Affair, Oct 1
Energy: Cut Your Energy Costs Day, Natl, Jan 10
Engineering: Introduce a Girl to Day, Feb 19
Engineers Week, Natl, Feb 15
England
- Badminton Horse Trials (Badminton), May 7
- Battle of Hastings: Anniv, Oct 14
- Birmingham Riot: Anniv, Jul 14
- Blackpool Illuminations (Blackpool, Lancashire), Sep 4
- British Air Raid on Berlin: Anniv, Jan 16
- British and World Marbles Chmpshp, Apr 10
- British Museum: Anniv, Jan 15
- Care Sunday, Mar 29
- Charles II: Restoration and Birth Anniv, May 29
- Chelsea Flower Show (London), May 19
- Cheltenham Hunt Fest (Prestbury), Mar 10
- Cheltenham Music Fest (Cheltenham), Jul 3
- Christmas Holiday, Dec 25
- City of London Fest (London), Jun 20
- Cowes Week (Isle of Wight), Aug 1
- Crufts Dog Show (Birmingham), Mar 5
- Derby, The, Jun 6
- Devizes/Westminster Intl Canoe Race (Devizes), Apr 10
- Dicing for Bibles, Jun 1
- English Riviera Dance Fest (Torquay), May 29
- Exeter Fest (Exeter), Jun 19
- George VI's Coronation: Anniv, May 12
- Glastonbury Fest (Glastonbury), Jun 26
- Gloucestershire Cheese Rolling (Cotswolds), May 25
- Grand National (Liverpool), Apr 2
- Great Britain Formed: Anniv, May 1
- Great Fire of London: Anniv, Sep 2
- Guy Fawkes Day, Nov 5
- Hallaton Bottle Kicking (Hallaton), Apr 13
- Hampton Court Palace Flower Show (East Molesey, Surrey), Jul 7
- Harrogate Autumn Flower Show (Harrogate, North Yorkshire), Sep 18
- Harrogate Spring Flower Show (Harrogate), Apr 23
- Head of the River Race (London), Mar 21
- Helston Furry Dance (Helston, Cornwall), May 8
- Henley Royal Regatta (Henley-on-Thames), Jul 1
- Land Rover Burghley Horse Trials (Stamford), Sep 3
- Lawn Tennis Chmpshps at Wimbledon (London), Jun 22
- London Boat Show (London), Jan 9
- London Book Fair (London), Apr 20
- London Marathon (London), Apr 26
- London Terrorist Bombings: Anniv, Jul 7
- London/Brighton Veteran Car Run (London), Nov 1
- Lord Mayor's Show (London), Nov 14
- Marriage of Elizabeth and Philip: Anniv, Nov 20
- Mothering Sunday, Mar 22
- New Year's Day Parade (London), Jan 1
- Nottingham Goose Fair (Nottingham), Oct 7
- Plough Monday, Jan 12
- Queen Elizabeth I: Birth Anniv, Sep 7
- RAF Bombs Hitler Celebration: Anniv, Jan 30
- Remembrance Sunday (London), Nov 8
- Royal Ascot, Jun 16
- Royal George Sinks: Anniv, Aug 29
- Royal Windsor Horse Show (Windsor), May 14
- Saint George: Feast Day, Apr 23
- Scotland Yard First Appearance Anniv, Sep 29
- Shrovetide Pancake Race (Olney, Buckinghamshire), Feb 24
- Slave Trade Abolished: Anniv, Mar 25
- Trooping Colours/Queen's Official Birthday, Jun 13
- Walter Plinge Day, Dec 2
- Ways With Words (Dartington), Jul 10
- Words by the Water: A Cumbrian Literature Fest (Lake District), Feb 27

English Channel, First Airplane Crossing: Anniv, Jul 25
English Channel, First Man-Powered Flight Across: Anniv, Jun 12
English Colony in North America, First: Anniv, Aug 5
English Language: Words Matter Week, Natl, Mar 1
ENIAC Computer Introduced: Anniv, Feb 14
Enigma Machine, British Capture of: Anniv, May 9
Eno, Brian: Birth, May 15
Enrico Fermi Atomic Power Plant: Accident Anniv, Oct 5
Enron Files for Bankruptcy: Anniv, Dec 2
Ensign, John: Birth, Mar 25
Entebbe, Raid on: Anniv, Jul 3
Enthusiasm Week, Intl, Sep 1
Entrepreneurs "Do It Yourself" Marketing Month, Jun 1
Environment Day, World (UN), Jun 5
Environmental
- Aldo Leopold Weekend (WI), Mar 6
- America Recycles Day, Nov 15
- Arbor Day, Natl, Apr 24
- Bike to Work Day, Natl, May 15
- Biodiesel Day, Natl (Rudolph Diesel Birth Anniv), Mar 18
- Biological Diversity, Intl Day for (UN), May 22
- Care About Your Indoor Air Month, Natl, Feb 1
- Cattus Island Nature Fest (Toms River, NJ), Oct 4
- Chemists Celebrate Earth Day, Apr 22
- Chernobyl Reactor Disaster: Anniv, Apr 26
- Clean Air Act Passed by Congress: Anniv, Dec 17
- Clothesline Week, Intl, Jun 6
- Coastal Cleanup, Intl, Sep 19
- Day for Preventing the Exploitation of the Environment in War and Armed Conflict, Intl (UN), Nov 6
- Earth Day, Apr 22
- Earth Day Community Fest (St. Louis, MO), Apr 26
- Endangered Species Act: Anniv, Dec 28
- Environmental Policy Act, Natl: Anniv, Jan 1
- Exxon Valdez Oil Spill: Anniv, Mar 24
- Greenpeace Founded: Anniv, Sep 15
- Hanging Out Day, Natl, Apr 19
- Intl Day for Preservation of the Ozone Layer (UN), Sep 16
- Japan Agrees to End Use of Drift Nets: Anniv, Nov 26
- Keep Norfolk Beautiful Day (Norfolk, VA), Mar 28

Love Canal Declared Disaster Area: Anniv, Aug 7
Mother Ocean Day, May 9
Natural Disaster Reduction, Intl Day for (UN), Oct 14
Paperboard Packaging Week, Natl, Apr 20
President's Environmental Youth Award Natl Competition, Oct 31
Public Lands Day, Natl, Sep 26
Rainbow Warrior Sinking: Anniv, Jul 10
Rainforest Week, World, Oct 12
Respect Your Mother (Point Pleasant Beach, NJ), Apr 18
Rivers Month, Natl, Jun 1
Rural Life Sunday, May 17
Sierra Club Founded: Anniv, May 28
Silent Spring Publication: Anniv, Apr 13
Smart Irrigation Month, Jul 1
Trails Day, Natl, Jun 6
Urban Eden Day, Natl, Sep 13
Water Pollution Control Act: Anniv, Oct 18
Water, World Day for (UN), Mar 22
Week of Ocean Fest Sea-Son, Natl (Fort Lauderdale, FL), Mar 5
Week of the Ocean, Natl, Apr 5
Wildlife Week, Natl, Apr 18
World Day to Combat Desertification and Drought (UN), Jun 17
World Environment Day (UN), Jun 5
Year of Natural Fibers, Intl (UN), Jan 1
Enzi, Michael B.: Birth, Feb 1
Ephron, Nora: Birth, May 19
Epilepsy Awareness Month, Nov 1
Epiphany (Twelfth Day), Jan 6
Episcopal Bishop, First Woman: Anniv, Feb 11
Epitaph Day, Plan Your, Nov 2
Epps, Omar: Birth, Jul 23
Equal Rights Party Founding: Anniv, Sep 20
Equatorial Guinea
Armed Forces Day, Aug 3
Constitution Day, Aug 15
Independence Day, Oct 12
Equinox, Autumn, Sep 22
Equinox, Spring, Mar 20
ER TV Premiere: Anniv, Sep 19
Erasmus, Desiderius: Birth Anniv, Oct 28
Erdrich, Louise: Birth, Jun 7
Erie Canal: Anniv, Oct 26
Erikson, Leif: Day (Iceland), Oct 9
Erikson, Leif: Day (Pres Proc), Oct 9
Eritrea: Independence Day, May 24
Eritrea: Timket (Epiphany), Jan 19
Ermey, R. Lee: Birth, Mar 24
Ernie Kovacs TV Premiere: Anniv, May 14
Erving, Julius: Birth, Feb 22
Escoffier, Georges: Birth Anniv, Oct 28
Esiason, Boomer: Birth, Apr 17
Esposito, Giancarlo: Birth, Apr 26
Esposito, Phil: Birth, Feb 20
Essay Contest, American History, Aug 1
Essence of Motown Literary Jam (Detroit, MI), Nov 14
Essien, Michael: Birth, Dec 3
Estefan, Emilio: Birth, Mar 4
Estefan, Gloria: Birth, Sep 1
Estes, Rob: Birth, Jul 22
Estevez, Emilio: Birth, May 12
Estonia
Baltic States' Independence Recognized: Anniv, Sep 6
Day of National Rebirth, Nov 16
Independence Day, Feb 24
Victory Day, Jun 23
Estrada, Erik: Birth, Mar 16
Etheridge, Melissa: Birth, May 29
Ethics Awareness Month, Natl, Mar 1
Ethiopia
Adwa Day, Mar 2
National Day, May 28
New Year's Day, Sep 11
Patriots Victory Day, May 5
Timket (Epiphany), Jan 19
True Cross Day, Sep 27
Ethnic Awareness Programs (Macon, GA), Apr 17
Ethnic Observances. See also nationality names
Asian/Pacific American Heritage Month (Pres Proc), May 1
Czech Days (Tabor, SD), Jun 18
German-American Day, Natl (Pres Proc), Oct 6
German-American Heritage Month, Oct 1
Haitian Heritage Month, May 1
Herrinfesta Italiana (Herrin, IL), May 21
Hispanic Heritage Month, Sep 15
Holiday Folk Fair Intl (Milwaukee, WI), Nov 20
Irish-American Heritage Month, Mar 1
Italian Fest and Columbus Day Parade, Ocean County (Seaside Heights, NJ), Oct 9
Midsummer Day/Eve Celebrations, Jun 21
Polish-American Heritage Month, Oct 1
Pulaski Day Parade (Philadelphia, PA), Oct 4
Saint Piran's Day (Cornish) Celebration (Kansas City, MO), Mar 7
Scandinavian Fest (Budd Lake, NJ), Sep 6
Westfest (Czech) (West, TX), Sep 4
Etiquette
Business Etiquette Week, Jun 7
Cell Phone Courtesy Month, Jul 1
Children's Good Manners Month, Sep 1
Civility Month, Natl Win with, Aug 1
Common Courtesy Day, Natl, Mar 21
Etiquette Week, Natl, May 11
Fresh Breath Day, Natl, Aug 6
I Forgot Day, Jul 2
On-Hold Month, Natl, Mar 1
Protocol Officers Week, Natl, Mar 23
Thank You Note Day, Natl, Dec 26
Toad Hollow Day of Thank You, Jun 20
Write a Letter of Appreciation Week, Natl, Mar 1
Eubanks, Bob: Birth, Jan 8
Eubanks, Kevin: Birth, Nov 15
Euro Introduced: Anniv, Jan 1
Europe: Summer Daylight-Saving Time, Mar 29
European Union Established: Anniv, Nov 1
European Union: Schuman Plan Anniv, May 9
Evacuation Day (Boston, MA), Mar 17
Evacuation Day (Egypt), Jun 18
Evaluate Your Life Day, Oct 19
Evangelista, Linda: Birth, Jun 10
Evans, Bob: Birth, May 30
Evans, Chick: Birth Anniv, Jul 18
Evans, Heloise Cruse: Birth, Apr 15
Evans, Linda: Birth, Nov 18
Evans, Sara: Birth, Feb 5
Evening at Pops TV Premiere: Anniv, Jul 12
Everest Summit Reached: Anniv, May 29
Everest: First Woman to Climb: Anniv, May 16
Everett, Chad: Birth, Jun 11
Everett, Rupert: Birth, May 29
Everglades Natl Park Established: Anniv, Dec 6
Everly, Don: Birth, Feb 1
Everly, Phil: Birth, Jan 19
Evers, Johnny: Baseball's Sad Lexicon Published: Anniv, Jul 10
Evers, Johnny: Birth Anniv, Jul 21
Evers, Medgar, Assassinated: Anniv, Jun 13
Evert, Chris: Birth, Dec 21
Everybody's Day Fest (Thomasville, NC), Sep 26
Evigan, Greg: Birth, Oct 14
Ewell, Tom: Birth Anniv, Apr 29
Ewing, Buck: Birth Anniv, Oct 17
Ewing, Patrick: Birth, Aug 5
Exchange Club Birthday, Natl, Mar 27
Exchange Club: Freedom Shrine Month, May 1
Execution: First Criminal in American Colonies: Anniv, Sep 30
Executive Coaching Day, May 1
Exhibitor Appreciation Week, Aug 3
Expanding Girls' Horizons in Science & Engineering Month, Mar 1
Explore Your Career Options Week, Apr 5
Explosion of the Cart (Florence, Italy), Apr 12
Explosion: Halifax, Nova Scotia, Destroyed: Anniv, Dec 6
Explosion: Mexico City: Anniv, Nov 19
Explosion: Texas City Disaster: Anniv, Apr 16
Extraterrestrial Culture Day (New Mexico), Feb 12
Extreme Sports (parachuting, etc.)
Bridge Day (Fayetteville, WV), Oct 17
Dakar Rally (Argentina and Chile), Jan 3
XTERRA Makena Beach Trail Run (Makena, HI), Oct 24
XTERRA Nevada Trail Run (Incline Village, NV), Oct 3
XTERRA Oak Mountain Xduro (Pelham, AL), Jun 6
XTERRA Richmond Xduro and James River Scramble (Richmond, VA), Jun 13
XTERRA Trail Running Chmpshp, Natl (Bend, OR), Sep 26
XTERRA Trail Running World Chmpshp (Oahu, HI), Dec 6
XTERRA Vail Lake Xduro (Temecula, CA), May 16
XTERRA Wheeler Canyon Xduro (Ogden, UT), Aug 15
XTERRA World Chmpshp (Maui, HI), Oct 25
Exxon Valdez Oil Spill: Anniv, Mar 24
Eye Donor Month, Natl, Mar 1
Eye Health and Safety Month, Children's, Aug 1
Eye Health and Safety Month, Women's, Apr 1
Eyes: Healthy Vision Month, May 1

F

Fabares, Shelley: Birth, Jan 19
Faberge, Carl: Birth Anniv, May 30
Fabian: Birth, Feb 6
Fabio: Birth, Mar 15
Fabray, Nanette: Birth, Oct 27
Fabregas, Cesc: Birth, May 4
Face the Nation TV Premiere: Anniv, Nov 7
Face Your Fears Day, Natl, Oct 13
Facts of Life TV Premiere: Anniv, Aug 24
Fahrenheit, Gabriel D.: Birth Anniv, May 14
Fain, Sammy: Birth Anniv, Jun 17
Fair, First Annual, in America: Anniv, Sep 30

Fair, Lorrie: Birth, Aug 5
Fair Trade Day, World, May 9
Fairbanks, Charles W.: Birth Anniv, May 11
Fairbanks, Douglas: Birth Anniv, May 23
Fairchild, David G.: Birth Anniv, Apr 7
Fairchild, Morgan: Birth, Feb 3
Fairy
Autumn Fairy Fun Day, Sep 27
Fairie Fest, May Day (Glen Rock, PA), May 1
Spring Fairy Fun Day, Mar 22
Summer Fairy Fun Day, Jun 28
Winter Fairy Fun Day, Dec 27
Faithfull, Marianne: Birth, Dec 29
Fake Howard Hughes Biography: Anniv, Jan 9
Fala Day (Warm Springs, GA), Nov 7
Falana, Lola: Birth, Sep 11
Falco, Edie: Birth, Jul 5
Falcon Crest TV Premiere: Anniv, Dec 4
Faldo, Nick: Birth, Jul 18
Falk, Peter: Birth, Sep 16
Falkland Islands War: Anniv, Apr 2
Fall Fest of Leaves (Ross County, OH), Oct 16
Fall Fest, Wo-Zha-Wa (Wisconsin Dells, WI), Sep 18
Fall of Kabul: Anniv, Nov 13
Fall of the Alamo: Anniv, Mar 6
Fall on Nantucket (Nantucket Island, MA), Sep 1
Falling Needles Family Fest, Dec 30
Fallon, Jimmy: Birth, Sep 19
Fallows, James: Birth, Aug 2
Fame TV Premiere: Anniv, Jan 7
Family Feud TV Premiere: Anniv, Jul 12
Family Ties TV Premiere: Anniv, Sep 22
Family. See also Romance
Absolutely Incredible Kid Day, Mar 19
Adoption Month, Natl, Nov 1
American Family Day, Aug 2
Ancestor Appreciation Day, Sep 27
Bake for Family Fun Month, Feb 1
Bereaved Parents Awareness Month, Jul 1
Black Single Parents' Week, May 31
Brother's Day, May 24
Canada: Family Day in Alberta, Feb 16
Child Abuse Prevention Month, Apr 1
Child-Centered Divorce Month, Natl, Jul 1
Cousins Day, Jul 24
Crowded Nest Awareness Day, Jun 12
Descendants Day, Jun 28
Eat Better, Eat Together Month, Oct 1
Ellis Island Family History Day, Apr 17
Energy Management Is a Family Affair, Oct 1
Families, Intl Day of (UN), May 15
Family Awareness Day, Jun 21
Family Caregivers Month, Natl, Nov 1
Family Caregivers Month, Natl (Pres Proc), Nov 1
Family Day (TN), Aug 30
Family Day in Nevada, Nov 27
Family Day—A Day to Eat Dinner with Your Children, Sep 28
Family Fit Lifestyle Month, Jan 1
Family Health and Fitness Days—USA, Sep 26
Family History Day, Jun 14
Family Literacy Day, Natl, Nov 1
Family Month, Natl, May 10
Family Reunion Month, Jul 1
Family Sexuality Education Month, Natl, Oct 1
Family Stories Month, Nov 1
Family Volunteer Day, Nov 21
Family Week, Natl, May 3
Family Week, Natl (Pres Proc), Nov 22
Family Wellness Month, May 1
Family, Career and Community Leaders of America Natl Leadership Mtg (Nashville, TN), Jul 12
Family-Leave Bill: Anniv, Feb 5
Father-Daughter Take a Walk Together Day, Jul 7
Father's Day, Jun 21
Father's Day (Pres Proc), Jun 21
Forgive Mom & Dad Day, Mar 18
Game & Puzzle Week, Natl, Nov 22
Genealogy Day, Mar 7
Grandparents' Day, Natl, Sep 13
Hug Your Kids Day, Natl, Jul 20
Hugging Day, Natl, Jan 21
Husband Caregiver Day, Jun 15
Intergeneration Day, Oct 4
KidsDay, Natl, Sep 19
Lifewriting Month, Natl, Nov 1
Love Our Children Day, Natl, Apr 4
Married to a Scorpio Support Day, Nov 18
Men Make Dinner Day, Natl, Nov 5
Million Minute Family Challenge™, Sep 1
Mother-in-Law Day, Oct 25
Mother's Day, May 10
Moving Month, Natl, May 1
Orlando Family Spring Break (Orlando, FL), Mar 1
Parent Leadership Month, Natl, Feb 1
Parents as Teachers Day, Natl, Nov 8
Parents' Day (Pres Proc), Jul 26
Personal History Month, May 1
Please Take My Children to Work Day, Jun 29
Prepare Tomorrow's Parents Month, May 10
Respect for Parents Day, Aug 1
Salute to 35+ Moms Week, May 10
Sandwich Generation Month, Jul 1
Siblings Day, Natl, Apr 10
Sisters' Day, Aug 2
Take Our Daughters and Sons to Work Day, Apr 23
Unassisted Homebirth Week, Natl, Jul 1
Visit Your Relatives Day, May 18
Weddings Month, Natl, Feb 1
Wife Appreciation Day, Sep 19
Work and Family Month, Natl, Oct 1
Work@Home Father's Day, Jun 19
World Marriage Day, Feb 8
Write to Your Father Day, Jun 7
Faneuil Hall Opened to the Public: Anniv, Sep 24
Fanny Pack Day, Intl, Mar 14
Fantasia: Birth, Jun 30
Fantasy Fest (Key West, FL), Oct 23
Fantasy Island TV Premiere: Anniv, Jan 28
Faraday, Michael: Birth Anniv, Sep 22
Farentino, James: Birth, Feb 24
Fargas, Antonio: Birth, Aug 14
Fargo, Donna: Birth, Nov 10
Farina, Dennis: Birth, Feb 29
Farley, Cal: Birth Anniv, Dec 25
Farm Animals Day, World, Oct 2
Farm Safety Week, Natl (Pres Proc), Sep 20
Farm-City Week, Natl (Pres Proc), Nov 20
Farmer, James: Birth Anniv, Jan 12
Farmer, Philip Jose: Birth, Jan 26
Farmers & Threshermens Jubilee (New Centerville, PA), Sep 9
Farmington Country Days (Farmington, MO), Jun 5
Farnsworth, Philo: Birth Anniv, Aug 19
Faroe Islands: Olai Fest (Torshavn), Jul 28
Farr, Jamie: Birth, Jul 1
Farragut, David: Battle of Mobile Bay: Anniv, Aug 5
Farragut, David: Birth Anniv, Jul 5
Farragut, David: Farragut Captures New Orleans: Anniv, Apr 25
Farrakhan, Louis: Birth, May 11
Farrell, Colin: Birth, May 31
Farrell, James T.: Birth Anniv, Feb 27
Farrell, Mike: Birth, Feb 6
Farrell, Terry: Birth, Nov 19
Farrell, Will: Birth, Jul 16
Farrier's Week, Natl, Jul 12
Farrow, Mia: Birth, Feb 9
Fasching (Germany, Austria), Feb 23
Fasching Sunday (Germany, Austria), Feb 22
Fashion; Fashion Shows
Adolfo: Birth, Feb 15
Bikini Debut: Anniv, Jul 5
Blass, Bill: Birth Anniv, Jun 22
Cardin, Pierre: Birth, Jul 7
Chanel, Coco: Birth Anniv, Aug 19
Dior, Christian: Birth Anniv, Jan 21
Fall Hat Month, Sep 1
Fanny Pack Day, Intl, Mar 14
Givenchy, Hubert de: Birth, Feb 21
Intimate Apparel Market Week, Feb 2
Kamali, Norma: Birth, Jun 27
Karan, Donna: Birth, Oct 2
Lacroix, Christian: Birth, May 17
Lagerfeld, Karl: Birth, Sep 10
Schiaparelli, Elsa: Birth Anniv, Sep 10
Secondhand Wardrobe Day, Natl, Aug 25
Straw Hat Month, Apr 1
Tie Month, Natl, Dec 1
Tuxedo Created: Anniv, Oct 10
Wear Red Day, Natl, Feb 6
Wig Out Day, Natl, May 22
Fast of Esther: Ta'anit Esther, Mar 9
Fast of Gedalya, Sep 21
Fat Albert and the Cosby Kids TV Premiere: Anniv, Sep 9
Father-Daughter Take a Walk Together Day, Jul 7
Father's Day, Jun 21
Father's Day (Pres Proc), Jun 21
Fatima, Pilgrimage to (Portugal), May 12
Faulk, Marshall: Birth, Feb 26
Faulkner, William: Birth Anniv, Sep 25
Fauset, Jessie Redmon: Birth Anniv, Apr 26
Faustino, David: Birth, Mar 3
Favre, Brett: Birth, Oct 10
Fawcett, Farrah: Birth, Feb 2
Fawkes, Guy: Day (England), Nov 5
FBI: First Female FBI Agents: Anniv, Oct 25
FBI: Hoover, J. Edgar: Birth Anniv, Jan 1
FBI: 10 Most Wanted List Debuts: Anniv, Mar 14
FDA Approves Botox: Anniv, Apr 15
FDA Approves Viagra: Anniv, Mar 27
Feast of Lanterns (Bon Fest) (Japan), Jul 13
Feast of St. Paul's Shipwreck (Valletta, Malta), Feb 10
Feast of the Immaculate Conception, Dec 8
Feast of the Incappucciati (Gradoli, Italy), Feb 19
Feast of the Redeemer (Venice, Italy), Jul 19
Federal Communications Commission Created: Anniv, Feb 26
Federal Credit Union Act: Anniv, Jun 26
Federal Reserve System: Anniv, Dec 23
Federalist Papers: Anniv, Oct 27
Federer, Roger: Birth, Aug 8
Federline, Kevin: Birth, Mar 21

FedEx Orange Bowl (Miami, FL), Jan 1
Fedorov, Sergei: Birth, Dec 13
Feiffer, Jules: Birth, Jan 26
Feingold, Russell D.: Birth, Mar 2
Feinstein, Alan: Birth, Sep 8
Feinstein, Dianne: Birth, Jun 22
Feinstein, Michael: Birth, Sep 7
Feld, Eliot: Birth, Jul 5
Feldman, Corey: Birth, Jul 16
Feldon, Barbara: Birth, Mar 12
Feldshuh, Tovah: Birth, Dec 27
Feliciano, Jose: Birth, Sep 10
Felker, Clay S.: Birth, Oct 2
Feller, Bob: Birth, Nov 3
Fellini, Federico: Birth Anniv, Jan 20
Fell's Point Fun Fest (Baltimore, MD), Oct 3
Felt, W. Mark: Birth, Aug 17
Felton, Mrs W.H.: First Woman US Senator: Anniv, Oct 3
Feltsman, Vladimir: Birth, Jan 8
Feminine Mystique Published: Anniv, Feb 19
Fender, Freddy: Birth Anniv, Jun 4
Fenn, Sherilyn: Birth, Feb 1
Fenwick, Millicent: Birth Anniv, Feb 25
Ferber, Edna: Birth Anniv, Aug 15
Ferdinand, Rio: Birth, Nov 7
Fergie: Birth, Mar 27
Ferguson, Craig: Birth, May 17
Ferlinghetti, Lawrence: Birth, Mar 24
Fermi, Enrico: Birth Anniv, Sep 29
Fernandez, Giselle: Birth, May 15
Ferrante, Arthur: Birth, Sep 7
Ferrara, Jerry: Birth, Nov 25
Ferraro, Geraldine: Birth, Aug 26
Ferrell, Conchata: Birth, Mar 28
Ferrer, Jose: Birth Anniv, Jan 8
Ferrer, Miguel: Birth, Feb 7
Ferrera, America: Birth, Apr 18
Ferrigno, Lou: Birth, Nov 9
Ferris Wheel Day, Feb 14
Ferry, Bryan: Birth, Sep 26
Fes Festival of World Sacred Music (Fes, Morocco), Jun 5
Fest of the Sea (Point Pleasant Beach, NJ), Sep 19
Fest of the West, Natl, and Log Home Show (Scottsdale, AZ), Mar 19
Fey, Tina: Birth, May 18
Fibromyalgia Education and Awareness Month, May 1
Fiddlers. See also Bluegrass
  Canadian Open Old-Time Fiddle Chmpshp (Shelburne, ON, Canada), Aug 5
  Kentucky State Fiddler's Chmpshp (Falls of Rough, KY), Jul 17
  Louisiana State Fiddle Chmpshp (Natchitoches, LA), Jul 17
  Old Fiddlers' Conv (Galax, VA), Aug 3
  Old-Time Fiddlers' Contest and Fest, Natl (Weiser, ID), Jun 22
  Sea Witch Halloween & Fiddlers Fest (Rehoboth Beach/Dewey Beach, DE), Oct 24
  Tennessee Valley Old Time Fiddlers Conv (Athens, AL), Oct 2
Field Trial Chmpshp (Bird Dogs), Natl (Grand Junction, TN), Feb 9
Field, Sally: Birth, Nov 6
Field, Shirley-Anne: Birth, Jun 27
Fielder, Cecil: Birth, Sep 21
Fields, Kim: Birth, May 12
Fields, W.C.: Birth Anniv, Jan 29
Fiennes, Joseph: Birth, May 27
Fiennes, Ralph: Birth, Dec 22
Fierstein, Harvey: Birth, Jun 6
Fiesta La Ballona (Culver City, CA), Aug 21
Fiesta San Antonio (San Antonio, TX), Apr 17
Fig Week, Natl, Nov 1
Figure Skating: Skating Month, Natl, Jan 1
Fiji: Independence Day, Oct 10
Filene, Edward Albert: Birth Anniv, Sep 3
Files Week, Natl Love Your, Sep 21
Fillion, Nathan: Birth, Mar 27
Fillmore, Abigail P.: Birth Anniv, Mar 13
Fillmore, Caroline: Birth Anniv, Oct 21
Fillmore, Millard: Birth Anniv, Jan 7
Film
  Academy Awards Presentation, Feb 22
  Academy Awards, First: Anniv, May 16
  Ann Arbor Film Fest (Ann Arbor, MI), Mar 24
  Banff Mountain Film & Book Fest (Banff, AB, Canada), Oct 31
  Berlin Intl Film Fest (Berlin, Germany), Feb 5
  Black Maria Studio: Anniv, Feb 1
  Bugs Bunny's Debut: Anniv, Apr 30
  Cannes Film Fest (Cannes, France), May 13
  Casablanca Premiere: Anniv, Nov 26
  Chaplin's Tramp Debuts: Anniv, Feb 7
  Chicago Intl Film Fest (Chicago, IL), Oct 8
  Citizen Kane Premiere: Anniv, May 1
  Dracula Premiere: Anniv, Feb 12
  First Drive-In Movie Opens: Anniv, Jun 6
  First Movie Theater Opens: Anniv, Apr 23
  Godfather Film Premiere: Anniv, Mar 15
  Golden Globe Awards, Jan 11
  Gone with the Wind Premiere: Anniv, Dec 15
  It Happened One Night Release: Anniv, Feb 22
  It's a Wonderful Life Premiere: Anniv, Dec 20
  Jaws Release: Anniv, Jun 20
  KidFilm® Fest (Dallas, TX), Jan 12
  King Kong Premiere: Anniv, Mar 2
  Lumiere, Auguste: Birth Anniv, Oct 19
  Lumiere, Louis: Birth Anniv, Oct 5
  Marilyn Monroe's First Screen Test: Anniv, Jul 19
  New York Film Fest (New York, NY), Sep 25
  Night of the Living Dead Released: Anniv, Oct 1
  Psycho Premiere: Anniv, Jun 16
  Record of a Sneeze: Anniv, Feb 2
  Roger Ebert's Film Fest (Champaign, IL), Apr 22
  San Francisco Silent Film Fest (San Francisco, CA), Jul 10
  Sheik Film Release: Anniv, Nov 20
  Singin' in the Rain Premiere: Anniv, Mar 27
  Slamdance (Park City, UT), Jan 15
  Snow White and the Seven Dwarfs Film Premiere: Anniv, Dec 21
  Sound of Music Premiere: Anniv, Mar 2
  Star Wars Released: Anniv, May 25
  Sundance Film Fest (Park City, UT), Jan 15
  Titanic Released: Anniv, Dec 19
  Toronto Intl Film Fest (Toronto, ON, Canada), Sep 3
  2001: A Space Odyssey Premiere: Anniv, Apr 3
  US Intl Film/Video Awards (Los Angeles, CA), Jun 5
  USA Film Fest (Dallas, TX), Apr 29
  Valentino (Rudolph) Memorial Service, Aug 23
  Wildlife Film Fest, Intl (Missoula, MT), May 9
  Wizard of Oz Released: Anniv, Aug 25
Final Four: NCAA Div I Men's Basketball Chmpshp (Detroit, MI), Apr 4
Financial Panic of 1873: Anniv, Sep 20
Financial Planning Week, Oct 5
Financial Wellness Month, Jan 1
Fine, Larry: Birth Anniv, Oct 5
Finland
  Flag Day, Jun 4
  Independence Day: Anniv, Dec 6
Finney, Albert: Birth, May 9
Fiorentino, Linda: Birth, Mar 9
Fire
  Apollo Spacecraft Fire: Anniv, Jan 27
  Fire Prevention Week, Oct 4
  Fire Prevention Week (Pres Proc), Oct 4
  Great Chicago Fire: Anniv, Oct 8
  Great Fire of London: Anniv, Sep 2
  Great Michigan Fire of 1881: Anniv, Sep 5
  Peshtigo Forest Fire: Anniv, Oct 8
  Southern California Firestorms: Anniv, Oct 25
  Texas City Disaster: Anniv, Apr 16
  Triangle Shirtwaist Fire: Anniv, Mar 25
Fire Safety Council, Natl: Anniv, Dec 7
Fireant Fest (Marshall, TX), Oct 10
Firepup's Birthday, Oct 1
Fireside Chat, FDR's First: Anniv, Mar 12
Fireside Theatre TV Premiere: Anniv, Apr 5
Firestone, Harvey: Birth Anniv, Dec 20
Fireworks Safety Months, Jun 1
First American to Orbit Earth: Anniv, Feb 20
First Baby Boomer Born: Anniv, Jan 1
First Barrel Jump over Niagara Falls: Anniv, Oct 24
First Baseball Strike Ends: Anniv, Apr 13
First Car Insurance: Anniv, Feb 1
First Elected Woman Senator: Anniv, Jan 12
First Indoor Baseball Game: Anniv, Dec 25
First Labor Day Observance: Anniv, Sep 5
First Man in Space: Anniv, Apr 12
First Manned Private Spaceflight: Anniv, Jun 21
First Moon Landing: Anniv, Jul 20
First Nights, Dec 31
First Perfect Game: Anniv, Jun 12
First Perfect Score in Olympic History: Anniv, Jul 18
First Roller Coaster Opens: Anniv, Jun 13
First Round-the-World Balloon Flight: Anniv, Mar 21
First Scheduled Radio Broadcast: Anniv, Nov 2
First Scheduled Television Broadcast: Anniv, Jul 1
First Secret Service Agent to Die in the Line of Duty: Anniv, Sep 3
First Session of Supreme Court: Anniv, Feb 1
First Solo Round-the-World Balloon Flight: Anniv, Jul 2
First Tourist in Space, Apr 28
First UN General Assembly: Anniv, Jan 10
First Woman British Prime Minister: Anniv, May 4
First Woman in Space: Anniv, Jun 16
First Woman to Climb Mount Everest: Anniv, May 16

First Women's Collegiate Basketball Game: Anniv, Mar 22
Firth, Colin: Birth, Sep 10
Fiscal Year, US Federal, Oct 1
Fischer, Jenna: Birth, Mar 7
Fishburne, Laurence: Birth, Jul 30
Fisher, Carrie: Birth, Oct 21
Fisher, Eddie: Birth, Aug 10
Fisher, Isla: Birth, Feb 3
Fisher, Joely: Birth, Oct 29
Fisher, M.F.K.: Birth Anniv, Jul 3
Fishing
Blessing of the Fishing Fleet (San Francisco, CA), Oct 4
Fish Amnesty Day, Sep 26
Fishing Contest (Lakewood, NJ), May 2
Fishing Has No Boundaries (Hayward, WI), May 15
Fishing Has No Boundaries (Monticello, IN), May 16
Hunting and Fishing Day, Natl (Pres Proc), Sep 26
Ice Fishing Derby (Fort Peck, MT), Feb 21
Long Beach Island Surf Fishing Tourn (Long Beach Island, NJ), Oct 10
Montana Governor's Cup Walleye Tourn (Fort Peck, MT), Jul 9
Montreal Hunting, Fishing & Camping Show (Montreal, QC, Canada), Feb 26
Morro Bay Harbor Fest (Morro Bay, CA), Oct 3
Ottawa Boat/Sportsmen Show (Ottawa, ON, Canada), Feb 26
Ouachita River Big Bass Fishing Tourn (West Monroe, LA), May 16
Palmetto Sportsmen's Classic (Columbia, SC), Mar 27
Ultimate Fishing Show (Novi, MI), Jan 8
Ultimate Sport Show (Grand Rapids, MI), Mar 19
World Famous Fish House Parade (Aitkin, MN), Nov 27
Fisk, Carlton: Birth, Dec 26
Fiske, Minnie M.: Birth Anniv, Dec 19
Fitness, Physical, and Sports Month, Natl, May 1
Fitness: African-American Women's Fitness Month, Natl, Apr 1
Fitzgerald, Edward: Birth Anniv, Mar 31
Fitzgerald, Ella: Birth Anniv, Apr 25
Fitzgerald, Ella: Wins Apollo Amateur Night: Anniv, Nov 21
Fitzgerald, F. Scott: Birth Anniv, Sep 24
Fitzgerald, Frances: Birth, Oct 21
Five Billion, Day of the: Anniv, Jul 11
Five Boro Bike Tour (New York, NY), May 3
Flack, Roberta: Birth, Feb 10
Flag Act of 1818: Anniv, Apr 4
Flag Day (Pres Proc), Jun 14
Flag Day USA, Pause for Pledge, Natl, Jun 14
Flag Day: Anniv of the Stars and Stripes, Jun 14
Flag Exhibit Controversy, Chicago: Anniv, Feb 17
Flag Week, Natl (Pres Proc), Jun 14
Flagg, Fannie: Birth, Sep 21
Flaherty, Joe: Birth, Jun 21
Flaherty, Robert J.: Birth Anniv, Feb 16
Flair, Ric: Birth, Feb 25
Flannery, Susan: Birth, Jul 31
Flatley, Michael: Birth, Jul 16
Flaubert, Gustave: Birth Anniv, Dec 12
Flax Scutching Fest (Stahlstown, PA), Sep 12
Fleetwood, Mick: Birth, Jun 24
Fleming, Alexander: Birth Anniv, Aug 6
Fleming, Ian: Birth Anniv, May 28
Fleming, Peggy: Birth, Jul 27
Fleury, Theo: Birth, Jun 29
Flexible Work Arrangements Week, May 3
Flight Attendant, First: Anniv, May 15
Flight. See Aviation
Flintstones TV Premiere: Anniv, Sep 30
Flipper TV Premiere: Anniv, Sep 19
Flirting Week, Intl, Feb 9
Flockhart, Calista: Birth, Nov 11
Flood, Curt: Birth Anniv, Jan 18
Flood, Great Chicago: Anniv, Apr 13
Flood, Johnstown: Anniv, May 31
Floral Design Day, Feb 28
Florida
Acquired by US: Anniv, Feb 22
Admission Day, Mar 3
AHRMA Vintage Motorcycle Races (Daytona Beach), Mar 2
AMA Grand Natl Singles Chmpnshp Dirt Track Race (Daytona Beach), Mar 4
American Massage Therapy Assn, Natl Conv (Orlando), Sep 23
Arbor Day, Jan 16
Art Deco Weekend (Miami Beach), Jan 16
BCS Natl Chmpshp Game (Miami), Jan 8
Biketoberfest (Daytona Beach), Oct 15
Biscayne Natl Park Established: Anniv, Jun 28
Camping World 300 Presented by Chevy NASCAR Nationwide Series Race (Daytona Beach), Feb 14
Capital One Bowl (Orlando), Jan 1
Central Florida Fair (Orlando), Apr 16
Children's Day, Apr 14
Coke Zero 400 NASCAR Sprint Cup Series Race (Daytona), Jul 4
Confederate Memorial Day, Apr 26
Crist, Charlie: Birth, Jul 24
Daytona 200 by Honda Classic (Daytona Beach), Mar 7
Daytona 200 by Honda Qualifying Day (Daytona Beach), Mar 5
Daytona 500 (Daytona Beach), Feb 15
Daytona 500 Pole Day (Daytona Beach), Feb 8
Daytona Supercross by Honda (Daytona Beach), Mar 6
Daytona Turkey Run (Daytona Beach), Nov 26
Disney World Opened: Anniv, Oct 1
Downtown Fest/Art Show (Gainesville), Nov 7
Dr. Martin Luther King, Jr, Celebration (Hollywood), Jan 16
Easter Beach Run (Daytona Beach), Apr 11
Everglades Natl Park Established: Anniv, Dec 6
Fall Country Jamboree (Barberville), Nov 7
Fall Cycle Scene Motorcycle Races (Daytona Beach), Oct 15
Fantasy Fest (Key West), Oct 23
February Is Fabulous Florida Strawberry Month, Feb 1
FedEx Orange Bowl (Miami), Jan 1
Floral City Strawberry Fest (Floral City), Mar 7
Florida Folk Fest (White Springs), May 22
Fort Lauderdale Intl Boat Show (Fort Lauderdale), Oct 29
Gasparilla Extravaganza and Pirate Fest (Tampa), Jan 24
Gator Knap-In (White Springs), Jan 30
Gatorade Duel Qualifying Races (Daytona Beach), Feb 12
Gifted Children Conv, Natl Assn for (Tampa), Nov 5
Grandmother's Day, Oct 11
Hatsume Fair (Delray Beach), Feb 21
Hoggetowne Medieval Faire (Gainesville), Jan 24
Hollywood Beach Candy Cane Parade (Hollywood), Dec 5
Hollywood Beach Latin Fest (Hollywood), Sep 20
Hometown Family Fourth (Hollywood), Jul 4
Interstate Mullet Toss (Pensacola), Apr 24
Isle of Eight Flags Shrimp Fest (Fernandina Beach), May 1
July 4th Family Celebration (Fort Lauderdale), Jul 4
Law Enforcement Appreciation Month, May 1
Manatee Fest (Crystal River), Jan 10
Mardi Gras Fiesta Tropicale (Hollywood), Feb 21
Maroone Hispanicfest (Hollywood), Mar 28
Martinez, Mel: Birth, Oct 23
Miami Intl Boat/Sailboat Show (Miami Beach), Feb 12
NASCAR Craftsman Truck Series 250 (Daytona Beach), Feb 13
Natural Bridge Battle (Tallahassee), Mar 6
Nelson, Bill: Birth, Sep 29
Orlando Family Spring Break (Orlando), Mar 1
Outback Bowl (Tampa), Jan 1
Pan-American Day, Apr 14
Pascua Florida Day, Apr 2
Patriots' Day, Apr 19
Poetry Day, May 25
Ponce de Leon Discovers Florida: Anniv, Apr 2
Red, White & Bluegrass (Hollywood), May 15
Reenactment of the Battle of Olustee (Olustee), Feb 13
Rolex 24 at Daytona (Daytona Beach), Jan 24
Save the Florida Panther Day, Mar 21
Seminole Tribe of Florida Legally Established: Anniv, Aug 21
SFCC Spring Arts Fest (Gainesville), Mar 28
Shootout at Daytona Sprint Cup Series Race (Daytona Beach), Feb 7
South Florida Senior Games (Hollywood), Jan 21
State Fair (Tampa), Feb 5
Stephen Foster Day (White Springs), Jan 11
Strawberry Fest (Plant City), Feb 26
SunFest (West Palm Beach), Apr 29
Super Bowl (Tampa Bay), Feb 1
Suwannee River Quilt Show and Sale (White Springs), Oct 16
Tarpon Springs Fine Arts Fest (Tarpon Springs), Mar 28
Teacher's Day, May 15
Tybee 500 (Hollywood and Tybee Island, GA), May 10
US Women's Mid-Amateur Chmpshp (Ocala), Oct 3
Week of Ocean Fest Sea-Son, Natl (Fort Lauderdale), Mar 5
Wild Azalea Fest (White Springs), Mar 21

Winterfest Boat Parade (Fort Lauderdale), Dec 12
World Golf Chmpshps-CA Chmpshp (Miami), Mar 9
Zora Neale Hurston Fest (Eatonville), Jan 20
Flossing Day, Natl, Nov 27
Flower Moon, May 9
Flowers, Flower Shows
Albany Tulip Fest (Albany, NY), May 8
Azalea Fest (Muskogee, OK), Apr 1
California Poppy Fest (Lancaster, CA), Apr 25
Canadian Tulip Fest (Ottawa, ON, Canada), May 1
Chelsea Flower Show (London, England), May 19
Cherry Blossom Fest (Washington, DC), Mar 28
Cherry Blossom Fest, Intl (Macon, GA), Mar 20
Daffodil Fest Weekend (Nantucket Island, MA), Apr 24
Fest of Camellias (Fort Valley, GA), Feb 1
Floral Design Day, Feb 28
Flower Fest (Japan), Apr 8
Hampton Court Palace Flower Show (East Molesey, Surrey, England), Jul 7
Harrogate Autumn Flower Show (Harrogate, England), Sep 18
Harrogate Spring Flower Show (Harrogate, England), Apr 23
Holland Tulip Time Fest (Holland, MI), May 2
Indiana Flower and Patio Show (Indianapolis, IN), Mar 14
Jersey Battle of Flowers (St. Lawrence, Channel Islands), Aug 13
Lei Day (Hawaii), May 1
Lilac Fest (Mackinac Island, MI), Jun 5
Lilac Fest (Rochester, NY), May 8
Longwood Gardens Christmas Display (Kennett Square, PA), Nov 26
Longwood Gardens Orchid Extravaganza (Kennett Square, PA), Jan 24
Longwood Gardens Spring Blooms (Kennett Square, PA), Apr 1
Marigold Fest (Pekin, IL), Sep 11
Maryland Home and Garden Show (Baltimore, MD), Mar 6
Mother's Day Annual Rhododendron Show (Portland, OR), May 9
Newport Flower Show (Newport, RI), Jun 26
Orangeburg Fest of Roses (Orangeburg, SC), May 1
Orchid Show (St. Louis, MO), Jan 31
Philadelphia Flower Show (Philadelphia, PA), Mar 1
Poinsettia Day, Dec 12
Portland Rose Fest (Portland, OR), May 28
Rhododendron Fest (Florence, OR), May 15
Rose Month, Natl, Jun 1
Seed Swap Day, Natl, Jan 31
Skagit Valley Tulip Fest (Burlington, WA), Apr 1
South Carolina Fest of Flowers (Greenwood, SC), Jun 5
Sumter Iris Fest (Sumter, SC), May 22
Take Your Houseplants for a Walk Day, Jul 27
Tournament of Roses Parade (Pasadena, CA), Jan 1
Washington Home, Garden & Flower Show (Washington, DC), Mar 19
Wild Azalea Fest (White Springs, FL), Mar 21
Wildflower Week, Natl, May 4
Yellow Daisy Fest (Stone Mountain, GA), Sep 10
Floyd, William: Birth Anniv, Dec 17
Flutie, Doug: Birth, Oct 23
Flying Nun TV Premiere: Anniv, Sep 7
Flynt, Larry: Birth, Nov 1
Foch, Nina: Birth, Apr 20
Fodor, Eugene: Birth Anniv, Oct 14
Fogg, Phileas: Wager Day: Anniv, Oct 2
Fogg, Phileas: Wins a Wager Day, Dec 21
Foley, Dave: Birth, Jan 4
Folger, Henry C.: Birth Anniv, Jun 18
Foliage Fest, Northeast Kingdom Fall (Walden, VT), Sep 28
Folk Fair Intl, Holiday (Milwaukee, WI), Nov 20
Folk Fest, Florida (White Springs, FL), May 22
Folk Tales and Fables Week, World, Mar 1
Folklife Fest, Texas (San Antonio, TX), Jun 12
Folkmoot USA: The NC Intl Folk Fest (Waynesville, NC), Jul 13
Follett, Ken: Birth, Jun 5
Fonda, Bridget: Birth, Jan 27
Fonda, Henry: Birth Anniv, May 16
Fonda, Jane: Birth, Dec 21
Fonda, Peter: Birth, Feb 23
Fonteyn, Margot: Birth Anniv, May 18
Food and Beverage-Related Events and Observances
Abbotsford Berry Beat Fest (Abbotsford, BC, Canada), Jul 3
American Dietetic Assn Food & Nutrition Conf & Expo (Denver, CO), Oct 17
Anti-Saloon League Founded: Anniv, May 24
Appert, Nicolas: Birth Anniv, Oct 23
Apple Butter Fest (Berkeley Springs, WV), Oct 10
Apple Butter Makin' Days (Mount Vernon, MO), Oct 9
Apple Butter Stirrin' (Coshocton, OH), Oct 16
Apple Fest (Lahaska, PA), Nov 7
Apple Fest (Topeka, KS), Oct 4
Apple Fest, Kentucky (Paintsville, KY), Oct 2
Apple Harvest Fest, Natl (Gettysburg, PA), Oct 3
Apple Saturdays (New Gloucester, ME), Sep 26
Applejack Fest (Nebraska City, NE), Sep 18
Art Fair and Winefest (Washington, MO), May 15
Baby Food Fest, Natl (Fremont, MI), Jul 21
Bake and Decorate Month, Natl, Oct 1
Bake for Family Fun Month, Feb 1
Banana Split Fest (Wilmington, OH), Jun 12
Barbecue Month, Natl, May 1
Beer Day (Iceland), Mar 1
Black Cow Created: Anniv, Aug 19
Black Walnut Fest (Stockton, MO), Sep 23
Blueberries Month, Natl, Jul 1
Blueberry Arts Fest (Ketchikan, AK), Aug 1
Blueberry Fest (Montrose, PA), Aug 7
Blueberry Fest, Natl (South Haven, MI), Aug 6
Bomb Pop Day, Natl, Jun 25
Braham Pie Day (Braham, MN), Aug 7
Bread Pudding Recipe Exchange, May 1
Brewers Fest, Oregon (Portland, OR), Jul 23
Bubble Gum Day, Feb 6
Bun Day (Iceland), Feb 23
Bundt Day, Natl, Nov 15
Burgoo Fest (Utica, IL), Oct 11
Caffeine Awareness Month, Natl, Mar 1
Cake Decorating Day, Natl, Oct 10
California Artichoke Fest (Castroville, CA), May 16
California Dried Plum Digestive Health Month, Jan 1
Candy Month, Natl, Jun 1
Cane Grinding and Harvest Fest (Savannah, GA), Nov 14
Cheese Fest, Great Wisconsin (Little Chute, WI), Jun 5
Cherry Month, Natl, Feb 1
Cherry Pit Spitting Chmpshp, Intl (Eau Claire, MI), Jul 4
Chestnut Week, Natl, Oct 11
Chicken Fest, Delmarva (Centreville, MD), Jun 19
Chicken Month, Natl, Sep 1
Chili Cook-Off, State Chmpshp (Roanoke, VA), May 2
Chili Day, Natl, Feb 26
Chili Month, Natl, Oct 1
Chilton County Peach Fest (Clanton, AL), Jun 19
Chocolate Fest (Galesburg, IL), Feb 14
Chowderfest (Beach Haven, NJ), Oct 3
Chowderfest (Mystic, CT), Oct 10
Clam Chowder Cook-off (Santa Cruz, CA), Feb 21
Clam Fest, Yarmouth (Yarmouth, ME), Jul 17
Clear Lake Crawfish Fest (Seabrook, TX), Apr 3
Clinton County Corn Fest (Wilmington, OH), Sep 11
Colorado Brewers' Fest (Fort Collins, CO), Jun 27
Cook Something Bold and Pungent Day, Nov 8
Cookie Cutter Week, Dec 1
Country Ham Days, Marion County (Lebanon, KY), Sep 26
Crawfish Fest, Dermott's Annual (Dermott, AR), May 15
Crawfordsville Strawberry Fest (Crawfordsville, IN), Jun 12
Crayfish Premiere (Sweden), Aug 12
Dairy Alternatives Month, Jun 1
Dairy Month, June, Jun 1
Dandelion May Fest (Dover, OH), May 1
Date Fest, Natl (Indio, CA), Feb 13
Diet Resolution Week, Jan 1
Drive-Thru Day, Natl, Jul 24
Eat an Apple Day, Intl, Sep 19
Eat What You Want Day, May 11
Egg Month, Natl, May 1
Egg Salad Week, Apr 13
Eldon Turkey Fest (Eldon, MO), Oct 10
Electra Goat BBQ Cook-Off (Electra, TX), May 8
Elmira Maple Syrup Fest (Elmira, ON, Canada), Apr 4
Emotional Overeating Awareness Month, Apr 1

Fall on Nantucket (Nantucket Island, MA), Sep 1
February Is Fabulous Florida Strawberry Month, Feb 1
Festival of the Sugar Maples (Marengo, IL), Mar 7
Fig Week, Natl, Nov 1
First McDonald's Opens: Anniv, Apr 15
Floral City Strawberry Fest (Floral City, FL), Mar 7
Florida Strawberry Fest (Plant City, FL), Feb 26
Food Bank Week, Natl, Oct 11
Foods/Feasts of Colonial Virginia (Williamsburg, VA), Nov 26
French Chef TV Premiere: Anniv, Feb 11
Fresh Squeezed Juice Week, Natl, Jan 18
Frozen Food Month, Natl, Mar 1
Georgia Pecan Month, Natl, Nov 1
Gilroy Garlic Fest (Gilroy, CA), Jul 24
Gloucestershire Cheese Rolling (Cotswolds, England), May 25
Gluten-Free Baking Week, Dec 13
Gluten-Free Diet Awareness Month, Nov 1
Go Hog Wild—Eat Country Ham Month, Oct 1
Go Wild During California Wild Rice Month, Sep 1
Grape Jamboree, Geneva Area (Geneva, OH), Sep 26
Great American Beer Fest (Denver, CO), Sep 24
Great American Low-Cholesterol, Low-Fat Pizza Bake, Sep 1
Great American Meatout, Mar 20
Great Fruitcake Toss (Manitou Springs, CO), Jan 3
Great Intl Chicken Wing Society Cook-off (Reno, NV), Jul 10
Grilling Month, Natl, Jul 1
Gumbo Fest (Bridge City, LA), Oct 9
Hamburger Month, Natl, May 1
Hard Crab Derby and Fair, Natl (Crisfield, MD), Sep 4
Harvest Wine Celebration (Livermore, CA), Sep 6
Hearth and Home in Early Maryland (St. Mary's City, MD), Nov 27
Herb Fest (Mattoon, IL), Apr 25
Herrinfesta Italiana (Herrin, IL), May 21
Highland County Maple Fest (Highland County, VA), Mar 14
Hog Capital of the World Fest (Kewanee, IL), Sep 4
Homebrew Day, Natl, May 2
Homemade Bread Day, Nov 17
Honey Month, Natl, Sep 1
Hope Watermelon Fest (Hope, AR), Aug 6
Horseradish Fest (Collinsville, IL), Jun 13
Horseradish Month, Natl, Jul 1
Hot Dog Month, Natl, Jul 1
Hot Dog Night (Luverne, MN), Jul 9
Hot Heads Chili Cook-off (Ruston, LA), Jan 17
Hot Tea Month, Natl, Jan 1
Ice Cream Cone: Anniv, Sep 22
Ice Cream Day, Natl, Jul 19
Ice Cream Fest, Old-Fashioned (Utica, OH), May 23
Iced Tea Month, Natl, Jun 1
Isle of Eight Flags Shrimp Fest (Fernandina Beach, FL), May 1
Jackson County Apple Fest (Jackson, OH), Sep 22
Jell-O Week, Feb 8
June Is Turkey Lovers' Month, Jun 1
Kentucky Bourbon Fest (Bardstown, KY), Sep 15
Kodiak Crab Fest (Kodiak, AK), May 21
Kool-Aid Days (Hastings, NE), Aug 14
La Tomatina (Spain), Aug 26
Licorice Day, Natl, Apr 12
Lobster Days (Mystic, CT), May 23
Lobster Fest, Maine (Rockland, ME), Jul 29
Long Beach Island Chowder Cook-Off (Beach Haven, NJ), Oct 3
Louisiana Peach Fest (Ruston, LA), Jun 26
Machias Wild Blueberry Fest (Machias, ME), Aug 21
Maize Day, Nov 27
Maple Fair, Parke County (Rockville, IN), Feb 21
Maple Fest of Nova Scotia (Northern Nova Scotia, Canada), Mar 14
Maple Syrup Saturday (Appleton, WI), Mar 21
Mardi Gras Fiesta Tropicale (Hollywood, FL), Feb 21
Marion Popcorn Fest (Marion, OH), Sep 10
Men Make Dinner Day, Natl, Nov 5
Morden Corn/Apple Fest (Morden, MB, Canada), Aug 21
More Herbs, Less Salt Day, Aug 29
Morel Mushroom Fest (Muscoda, WI), May 16
Morton Pumpkin Fest (Morton, IL), Sep 9
Mudbug Madness (Shreveport, LA), May 21
Mushroom Fest (Kennett Square, PA), Sep 12
Mushroom Month, Natl, Sep 1
Mustard Day, Natl, Aug 1
Natl Sweet Vidalia Onion Month, May 1
Newport Seafood and Wine Fest (Newport, OR), Feb 20
NJ State Chili & Salsa Cook-Off (Toms River, NJ), May 16
NJ State Ice Cream Fest (Toms River, NJ), Jul 18
No Salt Week, Oct 2
Norwalk Seaport Oyster Fest (Norwalk, CT), Sep 11
Nugget Best in the West Rib Cook-Off (Sparks, NV), Sep 2
Nuts Fair (Bastogne, Belgium), Dec 21
Oatmeal Month, Jan 1
Olathe Sweet Corn Fest (Olathe, CO), Aug 1
Onion Market (Zibelemarit, Switzerland), Nov 23
Open That Bottle Night, Feb 28
Organic Harvest Month, Natl, Sep 1
Oyster Fest (Chincoteague Island, VA), Oct 10
Oyster Fest, St. Mary's County (Leonardtown, MD), Oct 17
Pancake Day, Intl (Liberal, KS), Feb 24
Pancake Week, Natl, Feb 22
Panini Month, Natl, Aug 1
Payson Golden Onion Days (Payson, UT), Sep 4
Peanut Butter Lovers' Month, Nov 1
Pecan Day, Mar 25
Pecan Month, Natl, Apr 1
Personal Chef Day, Natl, Feb 23
Pizza Party Day, Natl, May 15
Polk County Ramp Tramp Fest (Benton, TN), Apr 24
Pomegranate Month, Natl, Nov 1
Popcorn Fest (Valparaiso, IN), Sep 12
Popcorn Poppin' Month, Natl, Oct 1
Poteet Strawberry Fest (Poteet, TX), Apr 3
Prairie Dog Chili Cook-off/Quail-Egg Eat (Grand Prairie, TX), Apr 4
Prime Beef Month, Natl, Sep 1
Pumpkin Show, Circleville (Circleville, OH), Oct 21
Ranch Hand Breakfast (Kingsville, TX), Nov 21
Recipe Greetings for the Holidays, Dec 1
Return Shopping Carts to the Supermarket Month, Feb 1
Rhubarb Fest (Intercourse, PA), May 15
Ribfest (Kalamazoo, MI), Aug 6
Rice God, Day of the (Chiyoda, Japan), Jun 7
Rice Month, Natl, Sep 1
Rice Planting Fest (Osaka, Japan), Jun 14
Roasting Month, Natl, Nov 1
Rockport Seafair (Rockport, TX), Oct 9
Salad Month, Natl, May 1
Salsa Month, Natl, May 1
Sandwich Day, Nov 3
Schmeckfest (Freeman, SD), Mar 27
School Breakfast Week, Natl, Mar 2
Scottsdale Culinary Fest (Scottsdale, AZ), Apr 14
Seven Sweets & Sours Fest (Intercourse, PA), Sep 18
Shelburne County Lobster Fest (Shelburne County, NS, Canada), Jun 4
Shrimp and Petroleum Fest, Louisiana (Morgan City, LA), Sep 3
Shrimp Fest, Low Country (McClellanville, SC), May 2
Sinkie Day, Nov 27
Sneak Some Zucchini onto Your Neighbors' Porch Night, Aug 8
Solo Diners Eat Out Week, Feb 1
Soul Food Month, Natl, Jun 1
Sour Herring Premiere (Sweden), Aug 20
Spinach Lovers Month, Oct 1
Steakhouse Month, Natl, Jun 1
Strawberry Fest (Lahaska, PA), May 2
Sun Prairie's Sweet Corn Fest (Sun Prairie, WI), Aug 20
Sweet Potato Month, Feb 1
Sweetcorn Fest, Natl (Hoopeston, IL), Sep 3
Tacoma Holiday Food and Gift Fest (Tacoma, WA), Oct 21
Tamale Fiesta (El Centro, CA), Dec 5
Taste of Cincinnati (Cincinnati, OH), May 23
Taste of Colorado (Denver, CO), Sep 4
Taste of Madison (Madison, WI), Sep 5
Taste of Morgan Hill (Morgan Hill, CA), Sep 26
Telluride Wine Fest (Telluride, CO), Jun 25
Texas Hill Country Wine & Food Fest (Austin, TX), Apr 16
Tomato Month, Fresh Florida, Apr 1
Totally Chipotle Day, May 5
Turkey Rama (McMinnville, OR), Jul 9
Turkey-Free Thanksgiving, Nov 26
Vegan Month, Nov 1
Vegetarian Day, World, Oct 1
Vegetarian Month, Oct 1
Verboort Sausage and Kraut Dinner (Forest Grove, OR), Nov 7
Vermont Maple Fest (St. Albans, VT), Apr 24
Vinegar Day, Jun 20
Vinegar Month, Natl, May 1

Virginia Peanut Fest (Emporia,VA), Sep 25
Waffle Week, Natl, Sep 6
Warrens Cranberry Fest (Warrens, WI), Sep 25
Washington State Apple Blossom Fest (Wenatchee, WA), Apr 23
Watermelon Fest (Rush Springs, OK), Aug 8
Watermelon Thump (Luling, TX), Jun 25
World Chmpshp BBQ Goat Cook-off (Brady, TX), Sep 5
World Food Day, Oct 16
World Food Day (UN), Oct 16
World's Biggest Fish Fry (Paris, TN), Apr 20
World's Largest Breakfast Table (Battle Creek, MI), Jun 13
Yambilee Fest, Louisiana (Opelousas, LA), Oct 22
Food and Drug Interaction Education and Awareness Week, Oct 17
Food Drive: Letter Carriers "Stamp Out Humor" Food Drive, May 9
Food Fight, World's Largest: La Tomatina (Spain), Aug 26
Food Stamps Authorized: Anniv, Sep 11
Footbag Chmpshps, World (Portland, OR), Jul 27
Football
Allstate Sugar Bowl (New Orleans, LA), Jan 2
AT&T Cotton Bowl Classic (Dallas, TX), Jan 2
BCS Natl Chmpshp Game (Miami, FL), Jan 8
Capital One Bowl (Orlando, FL), Jan 1
Colts Sneak Out of Baltimore: Anniv, Mar 28
Fabulous 1890s Weekend (Mansfield, PA), Sep 25
FedEx Orange Bowl (Miami, FL), Jan 1
First Army-Navy Game: Anniv, Nov 29
First Night Football Game (Mansfield, PA), Sep 28
First Play-by-Play Football Game Broadcast: Anniv, Nov 23
First Super Bowl: Anniv, Jan 15
Football League, Natl, Formed: Anniv, Sep 17
Monday Night Football TV Premiere: Anniv, Sep 21
NAIA Natl Chmpshp (Rome, GA), Dec 19
Oil Bowl Football Classic (Wichita Falls, TX), Jun 20
Outback Bowl (Tampa, FL), Jan 1
PSFCA East West All-Star Game (Altoona, PA), Jun 20
Rose Bowl Game (Pasadena, CA), Jan 1
Senior Bowl Football Game (Mobile, AL), Jan 24
Sun Bowl (El Paso, TX), Dec 31
Super Bowl (Tampa Bay, FL), Feb 1
For Pete's Sake Day, Feb 26
Forbes, Malcolm: Birth Anniv, Aug 19
Forbes, Michelle: Birth, Feb 17
Forbes, Steve: Birth, Jul 18
Ford, Eileen: Birth, Mar 25
Ford, Elizabeth (Betty): Birth, Apr 8
Ford, Faith: Birth, Sep 14
Ford, Gerald
Assassination Attempts: Anniv, Sep 5
Birth Anniv, Jul 14
Veep Day, Aug 9
Vice Presidential Swearing In: Anniv, Dec 6
Ford, Glenn: Birth Anniv, May 1
Ford, Harrison: Birth, Jul 13
Ford, Henry: Birth Anniv, Jul 30
Ford, John: Birth Anniv, Feb 1
Ford, Richard: Birth, Feb 16
Ford, Whitey: Birth, Oct 21
Forefathers' Day, Dec 21
Foreman, George: Birth, Jan 10
Forest Products Week, Natl (Pres Proc), Oct 18
Forgive Mom & Dad Day, Mar 18
Forman, Milos: Birth, Feb 18
Former Prisoner of War Recognition Day, Natl (Pres Proc), Apr 9
Forrest, Nathan Bedford: Birth Anniv, Jul 13
Forsberg, Peter: Birth, Jul 20
Forster, E.M.: Birth Anniv, Jan 1
Forster, Robert: Birth, Jul 13
Forsyth, Frederick: Birth, Aug 25
Forsythe, John: Birth, Jan 29
Fort Ligonier Days (Ligonier, PA), Oct 9
Fort Moore Established: Anniv, Apr 24
Fort Sumter Shelled by North: Anniv, Aug 17
Fort Union Trading Post Rendezvous (Williston, ND), Jun 18
Fortas, Abe: Birth Anniv, Jun 19
Forten, James: Birth Anniv, Sep 2
48 Hours TV Premiere: Anniv, Jan 19
Fosse, Bob: Birth Anniv, Jun 23
Fossey, Dian: Birth Anniv, Jan 16
Foster, Andrew "Rube": Birth Anniv, Sep 17
Foster, Jodie: Birth, Nov 19
Foster, Meg: Birth, May 14
Foster, Stephen, Day (White Springs, FL), Jan 11
Foster, Stephen: Birth Anniv, Jul 4
Foucault, Jean: Earth's Rotation Proved: Anniv, Jan 8
Foudy, Julie: Birth, Jan 27
Foundation Day, Natl (Japan), Feb 11
Founders' Day (Toms River, NJ), Jun 6
Fountain, Pete: Birth, Jul 3
Fountains, Longwood Gardens Fest of (Kennett Square, PA), May 23
Four Chaplains Memorial Day, Feb 3
Fox, Bernard: Birth, May 11
Fox, James: Birth, May 19
Fox, Jorja: Birth, Jul 7
Fox, Matthew: Birth, Jul 14
Fox, Michael J.: Birth, Jun 9
Fox, Terry: Birth Anniv, Jul 28
Fox, Vicente: Birth, Jul 2
Foxfield Races (Charlottesville, VA), Apr 25
Foxworthy, Jeff: Birth, Sep 6
Foxx, Jamie: Birth, Dec 13
Foxx, Redd: Birth Anniv, Dec 9
Foxx, Redd: Sanford and Son TV Premiere: Anniv, Jan 14
Foyt, A.J.: Birth, Jan 16
Frampton, Peter: Birth, Apr 22
France
Bastille Day, Jul 14
Cannes Film Fest (Cannes), May 13
Eiffel Tower: Anniv (Paris), Mar 31
Nice Carnival, Feb 13
Night Watch (La Retraite aux Flambeaux), Jul 13
Prix de l'Arc de Triomphe (Paris), Oct 4
Sarkozy, Nicolas: Birth, Jan 28
Tour de France, Jul 4
24 Hours of Le Mans (Le Mans), Jun 13
Victory Day, May 8
Francis, Anne: Birth, Sep 16
Francis, Connie: Birth, Dec 12
Francis, Genie: Birth, May 26
Francis, Ron: Birth, Mar 1
Franco, James: Birth, Apr 19
Francoeur, Jeff: Birth, Jan 8
Frank, Anne, Diary: Last Entry: Anniv, Aug 1
Frank, Anne: Birth Anniv, Jun 12
Frankel, Max: Birth, Apr 3
Franken, Al: Birth, May 21
Frankenstein Friday, Oct 30
Frankfurt Book Fair (Frankfurt, Germany), Oct 14
Franklin Day, Joe, Mar 9
Franklin Prefers Turkey: Anniv, Jan 26
Franklin, Aretha: Birth, Mar 25
Franklin, Benjamin: Birth Anniv, Jan 17
Franklin, Benjamin: Poor Richard's Almanack: Anniv, Dec 28
Franklin, Bonnie: Birth, Jan 6
Franklin, Pamela: Birth, Feb 4
Franks, Tommy: Birth, Jun 17
Franz, Arthur: Birth, Feb 29
Franz, Dennis: Birth, Oct 28
Franzen, Jonathan: Birth, Aug 17
Fraser, Brendan: Birth, Dec 3
Frasier TV Premiere: Anniv, Sep 16
Frazier, Joe: Birth, Jan 12
Frazier, Sheila E.: Birth, Nov 13
Freberg, Stan: Birth, Aug 7
Fred Waring Show TV Premiere: Anniv, Apr 17
Freedom Day: Anniv, Feb 1
Freedom of Information Day, Mar 16
Freedom Riders: Anniv, May 4
Freedom Shrine Month, May 1
Freelance Writers Appreciation Week, Feb 8
Freeman, Al, Jr: Birth, Mar 21
Freeman, Morgan: Birth, Jun 1
Freer, Charles L.: Birth Anniv, Feb 25
Freethinker's Day, Jan 29
Freethought Day, Oct 12
Frelich, Phyllis: Birth, Feb 29
French and Indian War, Treaty of Paris Ends: Anniv, Feb 10
French Chef TV Premiere: Anniv, Feb 11
French Quarter Fest (New Orleans, LA), Apr 17
French West Indies
Carnival (Martinique), Feb 21
French, Daniel C.: Birth Anniv, Apr 20
Frenchman Rows Across Pacific: Anniv, Nov 21
Fresh Breath Day, Natl, Aug 6
Fresh Squeezed Juice Week, Natl, Jan 18
Freud, Sigmund: Birth Anniv, May 6
Freudenthal, Dave: Birth, Oct 12
Frey, Glenn: Birth, Nov 6
Fricke, Janie: Birth, Dec 19
Fricker, Brenda: Birth, Feb 17
Friday the Thirteenth, Feb 13
Friedan, Betty: Birth Anniv, Feb 4
Friedel, Brad: Birth, May 18
Friedkin, William: Birth, Aug 29
Friedlander, Judah: Birth, Mar 16
Friedle, Will: Birth, Aug 11
Friel, Anna: Birth, Jul 12
Friends TV Premiere: Anniv, Sep 22
Friendship Day, Women's, Sep 20
Friendship: Best Friend's Day, Aug 15
Friendship: Girlfriend's Day, Aug 1
Friendship: New Friends, Old Friends Week, Intl, May 17
Frisch, Max: Birth Anniv, May 15
Froebel, Friedrich: Birth Anniv, Apr 21
Frog Jumping Jubilee/Calaveras Fair (Angel Camp, CA), May 13

Frontier Address, Turner's: Anniv, Jul 12
Frontline TV Premiere: Anniv, Jan 17
Frost, David: Birth, Apr 7
Frost, Robert: Birth Anniv, Mar 26
Frozen Food Month, Natl, Mar 1
Frozen Four: NCAA Div I Men's Ice Hockey Chmpshp (Washington, DC), Apr 9
Fruitcake Toss, Great (Manitou Springs, CO), Jan 3
Fry, Elizabeth: Birth Anniv, May 21
Fry, Stephen: Birth, Aug 24
Frye, Soleil Moon: Birth, Aug 6
Fuentes, Daisy: Birth, Nov 17
Fugitive TV Premiere: Anniv, Sep 17
Fukudome, Kosuke: Birth, Apr 26
Fulbright, J. William: Birth Anniv, Nov 9
Fuller, Alfred Carl: Birth Anniv, Jan 13
Fuller, Buckminster: Birth Anniv, Jul 12
Fuller, Margaret: Birth Anniv, May 23
Fuller, Melville Weston: Birth Anniv, Feb 11
Fulton, Robert: Birth Anniv, Nov 14
Fulton, Robert: Sails Steamboat: Anniv, Aug 17
Fun at Work Day, Jan 30
Fun at Work Day, Natl, Apr 1
Fun Day, Natl, Apr 1
Fun Facts About Names Day, Mar 2
Funeral Day, Create a Great, Oct 30
Funicello, Annette: Birth, Oct 22
Funky Winkerbean: Anniv, Mar 27
Fur Trade, Voyageurs
  Fest of Adventures (Aitkin, MN), Sep 19
  Fort Union Trading Post Rendezvous (Williston, ND), Jun 18
  Prairie Villa Rendezvous (Prairie du Chien, WI), Jun 18
  Tetonkaha Rendezvous (Lake Benton, MN), Aug 7
Furcal, Rafael: Birth, Aug 24
Furlong, Edward: Birth, Aug 2
Furnishings Market, Intl Home (High Point, NC), Apr 27
Furtado, Nelly: Birth, Dec 2

G
G, Kenny: Birth, Jun 6
G.I. Joe Introduced: Anniv, Feb 1
Gable, Clark: Birth Anniv, Feb 1
Gable, Clark: Gone with the Wind Film Premiere: Anniv, Dec 15
Gable, Clark: It Happened One Night Film Release: Anniv, Feb 22
Gabon: Independence Day, Aug 17
Gabon: National Day, Mar 12
Gabor, Zsa Zsa: Birth, Feb 6
Gabriel, Peter: Birth, Feb 13
Gagarin, Yuri A.: Birth Anniv, Mar 9
Gage, Nicholas: Birth, Jul 23
Gagne, Eric: Birth, Jan 7
Gagne, Simon: Birth, Feb 29
Gail, Max: Birth, Apr 5
Gaiman, Neil: Birth, Nov 10
Gain the Inside Advantage Month, Natl, Oct 1
Gaines, Ernest J.: Birth, Jan 15
Gaines, William M.: Birth Anniv, Mar 1
Gainsborough, Thomas: Birth Anniv, May 14
Gal, Uzi: Birth Anniv, Dec 15
Galbraith, John Kenneth: Birth Anniv, Oct 15
Gale, Robert: Birth, Oct 11
Galecki, Johnny: Birth, Apr 30
Galeotti, Bethany Joy: Birth, Apr 2
Galilei, Galileo: Birth Anniv, Feb 15
Gallagher, Peter: Birth, Aug 19
Gallaudet, Thomas Hopkins: Birth Anniv, Dec 10
Galligan, Zach: Birth, Feb 14
Gallo, Frank: Birth, Jan 13
Gallo, Julio: Anniv, Mar 21
Galveston Historic Homes Tour (Galveston Island, TX), May 2
Galveston, TX, Hurricane: Anniv, Sep 8
Galway, James: Birth, Dec 8
Gambia: Independence Day, Feb 18
Gambill, Jan-Michael: Birth, Jun 3
Gambon, Michael: Birth, Oct 19
Game & Puzzle Week, Natl, Nov 22
Games, Multisport Competitions
  Backyard Games Week, Natl, May 18
  Badger State Summer Games (Madison, WI), Jun 19
  Big Sky State Games (Billings, MT), Jul 17
  Dice Day, Natl, Dec 4
  Show Me State Games (Columbia, MO), Jul 17
  Simplot Games (Pocatello, ID), Feb 19
  Special Olympics World Winter Games (Boise, ID), Feb 6
  Tongue Twister Contest, Intl (Burlington, WI), Nov 7
  Wicket World of Croquet (Indianapolis, IN), Jun 13
  Winter Games of Idaho (ID), Jan 30
Gandhi, Mohandas, Assassinated: Anniv, Jan 30
Gandhi, Mohandas: Birth Anniv, Oct 2
Gandhi, Mohandas: Makes Salt: Anniv, Apr 6
Gandhi, Rajiv, Assassinated: Anniv, May 21
Gandolfini, James: Birth, Sep 18
Ganz, Bruno: Birth, Mar 22
Garage Sale Day, Natl, Aug 8
Garagiola, Joe: Birth, Feb 12
Garai, Romola: Birth, Aug 6
Garber, Victor: Birth, Mar 16
Garbo, Greta: Birth Anniv, Sep 18
Garcia, Andy: Birth, Apr 12
Garcia, Jeff: Birth, Feb 24
Garcia, Jerry: Birth Anniv, Aug 1
Garcia, Jorge: Birth, Apr 28
Garcia, Sergio: Birth, Jan 9
Garcia-Marquez, Gabriel: Birth, Mar 6
Garciaparra, Nomar: Birth, Jul 23
Garden
  Everything Autumn at Longwood Gardens (Kennett Square, PA), Sep 7
  Garden Meditation Day, May 3
  Gifts from the Garden Month, May 1
  Historic Garden Week (VA), Apr 18
  June Is Perennial Gardening Month, Jun 1
  Landscape Architecture Month, Natl, Apr 1
  Mailorder Gardening Month, Natl, Jan 1
  Michigan Home & Garden Show at Ford Field (Detroit, MI), Mar 13
  Savannah Tour of Homes and Gardens (Savannah, GA), Mar 26
  Seed Swap Day, Natl, Jan 31
  Washington Home, Garden & Flower Show (Washington, DC), Mar 19
Gardenia, Vincent: Birth Anniv, Jan 7
Gardner, Ava: Birth Anniv, Dec 24
Gardner, Erle Stanley: Birth Anniv, Jul 17
Gardner, Randy: Birth, Dec 2
Garfield, James A.: Birth Anniv, Nov 19
Garfield, James: Assassination Anniv, Jul 2
Garfield, Lucretia R.: Birth Anniv, Apr 19
Garfield: Birthday, Jun 19
Garfunkel, Art: Birth, Nov 5
Garland, Beverly: Birth, Oct 17
Garland, Judy: Birth Anniv, Jun 10
Garland, Judy: Wizard of Oz Released: Anniv, Aug 25
Garner, James: Birth, Apr 7
Garner, Jennifer: Birth, Apr 17
Garner, John Nance: Birth Anniv, Nov 22
Garnett, Kevin: Birth, May 19
Garofalo, Janeane: Birth, Sep 28
Garr, Teri: Birth, Dec 11
Garrett, Brad: Birth, Apr 14
Garrick, David: Birth Anniv, Feb 19
Garrison, William Lloyd: Birth Anniv, Dec 12
Garten, Ina: Birth, Feb 2
Garth, Jennie: Birth, Apr 3
Garvey, Steve: Birth, Dec 22
Gasol, Pau: Birth, Jul 6
Gasoline Alley Creator: King, Frank: Birth Anniv, Apr 9
Gastrell, Francis: Ejectment Anniv, Nov 27
Gates of the Arctic Natl Park: Anniv, Dec 2
Gates, Bill: Birth, Oct 28
Gates, David: Birth, Dec 11
Gates, Henry Louis, Jr: Birth, Sep 16
Gates, Robert: Birth, Sep 25
Gatlin, Justin: Birth, Feb 10
Gatlin, Larry: Birth, May 2
Gator Knap-In (White Springs, FL), Jan 30
Gauguin, Paul: Birth Anniv, Jun 7
Gautier, Dick: Birth, Oct 30
Gay & Lesbian
  Coming Out Day, Natl, Oct 11
  First US Same-Sex Marriages: Anniv, May 17
  Gay and Lesbian History Month, Oct 1
  Gay and Lesbian Pride Month, Jun 1
  Gay and Lesbian Pride Parade (Chicago, IL), Jun 28
  GLBT Book Month, Natl, Jun 1
  Military Ban on Homosexuals Eased: Anniv, Jan 29
  Stonewall Riot: Anniv, Jun 28
  UK Allows Same-Sex Civil Partnerships: Anniv, Dec 21
Gayle, Crystal: Birth, Jan 9
Gaynor, Janet: Birth Anniv, Oct 6
Gaynor, Mitzi: Birth, Sep 4
Gaza: Israel Completes Pullout: Anniv, Sep 12
Gazzara, Ben: Birth, Aug 28
Geary, Anthony: Birth, May 29
Gedalya, Fast of, Sep 21
Geeson, Judy: Birth, Sep 10
Geffen, David: Birth, Feb 21
Gehrig, Lou: Birth Anniv, Jun 19
Gehry, Frank: Birth, Feb 28
Geiger, Matt: Birth, Sep 10
Geisel, Theodor "Dr. Seuss": Birth Anniv, Mar 2
Gelbart, Larry: Birth, Feb 25
Geldof, Bob: Birth, Oct 5
Gellar, Sarah Michelle: Birth, Apr 14
Geller, Uri: Birth, Dec 20
Gellhorn, Martha: Birth Anniv, Nov 8
Gemini Begins, May 21
Gene Autry Show TV Premiere: Anniv, Jul 23
Genealogy Day, Mar 7
Genealogy: Ellis Island Family History Day, Apr 17
Genealogy: Personal History Month, May 1
General Election Day (US), Nov 3
General Electric Theater TV Premiere: Anniv, Feb 1

General Hospital TV Premiere: Anniv, Apr 1
General Motors: Founding Anniv, Sep 16
Geneva Accords: Anniv, Jul 20
Genocide Convention: Anniv, Dec 9
Gentle Ben TV Premiere: Anniv, Sep 10
Gentry, Bobbie: Birth, Jul 27
Geographers Annual Mtg, Assn of American (Las Vegas, NV), Mar 22
Geographic Bee Finals, Natl (Washington, DC), May 19
Geographic Bee, School Level, Natl, Jan 2
Geographic Bee, State Level, Natl, Apr 3
George Gobel Show TV Premiere: Anniv, Oct 2
George III: Birth Anniv, Jun 4
George Spelvin Day, Nov 15
George VI's Coronation: Anniv, May 12
George, Jeff: Birth, Dec 8
George, Melissa: Birth, Aug 6
George, Phyllis: Birth, Jun 24
George, Susan: Birth, Jul 26
Georgia
AIDS Walk Atlanta (Atlanta), Oct 18
Atlanta Marathon and Half Marathon, Weather Channel (Atlanta), Nov 26
Augusta Futurity (Augusta), Jan 15
Cane Grinding and Harvest Fest (Savannah), Nov 14
Chambliss, Saxby: Birth, Nov 10
Cherry Blossom Fest, Intl (Macon), Mar 20
Colonial Christmas at Wormsloe (Savannah), Dec 13
Colonial Faire and Muster (Savannah), Feb 7
Confederate Memorial Day, Apr 26
Cotton Pickin' Fair (Gay), May 2
Ethnic Awareness Programs (Macon), Apr 17
Fala Day (Warm Springs), Nov 7
FDR Commemorative Ceremony (Warm Springs), Apr 12
Fest of Camellias (Fort Valley), Feb 1
Festival 2009: Fest of Fine Arts and Fine Crafts (Dalton), Sep 19
Georgia National Fair (Perry), Oct 8
Georgia Pecan Month, Natl, Nov 1
Georgia Renaissance Spring Fest (Atlanta), Apr 18
Ghostly Gathering (Sandy Springs), Oct 23
Halloween Hike (Savannah), Oct 23
Heritage Green Concerts by the Springs (Sandy Springs), May 3
Isakson, Johnny: Birth, Dec 28
Medieval Fest (Savannah), Sep 26
Memorial Day Ceremonies (Andersonville), May 24
Mossy Creek Barnyard Fest (Warner Robins), Apr 18
Mountain Fair (Hiawassee), Jul 15
NAIA Natl Football Chmpshp (Rome), Dec 19
Peachtree Road Race (Atlanta), Jul 4
Perdue, Sonny: Birth, Dec 20
Prater's Mill Country Fair (Dalton), Oct 10
Ratification Day, Jan 2
Sandy Springs Fest (Atlanta), Sep 19
Savannah Tour of Homes and Gardens (Savannah), Mar 26
Sheep to Shawl Fest (Savannah), Mar 28
Sherman Enters Atlanta: Anniv, Sep 2
Sherman Takes Savannah: Anniv, Dec 21
Southern Cyclone: Anniv, Aug 24
Steeplechase at Callaway Gardens (Pine Mountain), Nov 7
Thomasville's Victorian Christmas (Thomasville), Dec 10
Tools and Skills That Built the Colony (Savannah), Sep 5
Tybee 500 (Tybee Island), May 10
War of Jenkin's Ear: Living History (Savannah), May 23
Yellow Daisy Fest (Stone Mountain), Sep 10
Georgia (Europe): Independence Day, May 26
Georgia (Europe): Soviet Georgia Votes Independence, Mar 31
Gerard, Gil: Birth, Jan 23
Gere, Richard: Birth, Aug 29
German. See also Octoberfest; Oktoberfest
Deutsch Country Days (Marthaville, MO), Oct 17
German-American Day, Natl (Pres Proc), Oct 6
German-American Heritage Month, Oct 1
Hanover Dutch Fest (Hanover, PA), Jul 25
Oktoberfest (New Ulm, MN), Oct 2
Schmeckfest (Freeman, SD), Mar 27
German-American Day, Natl, Oct 6
Germantown Reenactment, Battle of (Philadelphia, PA), Oct 3
Germany
Bach Fest (Leipzig), Jun 11
Berlin Airlift: Anniv, Jun 24
Berlin Intl Film Fest (Berlin), Feb 5
Berlin Marathon (Berlin), Sep 27
Berlin Wall Opened: Anniv, Nov 9
Buss und Bettag, Nov 18
Capital Returns to Berlin: Anniv, Sep 1
Day of Remembrance for Victims of Nazism, Jan 27
Dresden Firebombing: Anniv, Feb 13
Erntedankfest, Oct 4
Fasching, Feb 23
Fasching Sunday, Feb 22
Frankfurt Book Fair (Frankfurt), Oct 14
Frankfurt Christmas Market (Frankfurt), Nov 25
German Plebiscite: Anniv, Aug 19
German Surrender at Stalingrad: Anniv, Feb 2
Germany Ends Military Ban: Anniv, Jul 12
Hamburg Harbor Birthday, May 7
Invades Poland: Anniv, Sep 1
Kristallnacht: Anniv, Nov 9
Munich Fasching Carnival, Jan 7
Nuremberg War Crimes Trials: Anniv, Nov 20
Red Army Departs Berlin: Anniv, Jun 11
Reunification: Anniv, Oct 3
Totensonntag, Nov 22
Volkstrauertag, Nov 15
Wagner Festspiele (Bayreuth), Jul 25
Waldchestag (Frankfurt), Jun 2
Wilhelm II Abdicates: Anniv, Nov 9
Geronimo: Death Anniv, Feb 17
Gerrard, Steven: Birth, May 30
Gerry, Elbridge: Birth Anniv, Jul 17
Gershwin, George: Birth Anniv, Sep 26
Gershwin, Ira: Birth Anniv, Dec 6
Gertz, Jami: Birth, Oct 28
Gervais, Ricky: Birth, Jun 25
Get Smart TV Premiere: Anniv, Sep 18
Gets, Malcolm: Birth, Dec 28
Getty, Balthazar: Birth, Jan 22
Gettysburg Address Memorial Ceremony (Gettysburg, PA), Nov 19
Gettysburg Address, Lincoln's: Anniv, Nov 19
Gettysburg Outdoor Antique Show (Gettysburg, PA), May 16
Getz, Stan: Birth Anniv, Feb 2
Ghana
Farmers' Day, Natl, Dec 4
Independence Day, Mar 6
Republic Day, Jul 1
Ghosts, Fest of Hungry (China), Sep 3
Ghostwriters Week, Natl, Mar 1
Giamatti, Bartlett: Birth Anniv, Apr 4
Giamatti, Paul: Birth, Jun 6
Giambi, Jason: Birth, Jan 8
Giannini, Giancarlo: Birth, Aug 1
Gibb, Barry: Birth, Sep 1
Gibb, Robin: Birth, Dec 22
Gibbon, Edward: Birth Anniv, Apr 27
Gibbons, James: Birth, Dec 16
Gibbons, Leeza: Birth, Mar 26
Gibbs, Joe Jackson: Birth, Nov 25
Gibbs, Marla: Birth, Jun 14
Gibbs, Mifflin Wister: Birth Anniv, Apr 28
Gibran, Kahlil: Birth Anniv, Jan 6
Gibson, Althea: Birth Anniv, Aug 25
Gibson, Bob: Birth, Nov 9
Gibson, Debbie: Birth, Aug 31
Gibson, Henry: Birth, Sep 21
Gibson, Josh: Birth Anniv, Dec 21
Gibson, Kirk: Birth, May 28
Gibson, Mel: Birth, Jan 3
Gibson, Thomas: Birth, Jul 3
Gibson, William: Cyberspace Coined: Anniv, Oct 1
Gielgud, Sir John: Birth Anniv, Apr 14
Gifford, Frank: Birth, Aug 16
Gifford, Kathie Lee: Birth, Aug 16
Giggs, Ryan: Birth, Nov 29
Giguere, Jean-Sebastien: Birth, May 16
Gilbert, John: Birth Anniv, Jul 10
Gilbert, Melissa: Birth, May 8
Gilbert, Sara: Birth, Jan 29
Gilbert, Sir William: Birth Anniv, Nov 18
Gilford, Jack: Birth Anniv, Jul 25
Gillars, Mildred E.: Death Anniv, Jun 25
Gillespie, Dizzy: Birth Anniv, Oct 21
Gilley, Mickey: Birth, Mar 9
Gilliam, Armon: Birth, May 28
Gilliam, Terry: Birth, Nov 22
Gilligan's Island TV Premiere: Anniv, Sep 26
Gillis, Margaret: Birth, Jul 9
Gilmore, Artis: Birth, Sep 21
Gilmour, Dave: Birth, Mar 6
Gilpin, Peri: Birth, May 27
Gilroy Garlic Fest (Gilroy, CA), Jul 24
Gingerbread House Competition & Display, Peddler's Village (Lahaska, PA), Nov 20
Ginobili, Manu: Birth, Jul 28
Ginsberg, Allen: Birth Anniv, Jun 3
Ginsburg, Ruth Bader: Birth, Mar 15
Girl Scouts Founding: Anniv, Mar 12
Girlfriend's Day, Aug 1
Girls and Women in Sports Day, Natl, Feb 4
Girls Write Now Day, Mar 8
Gish, Lillian: Birth Anniv, Oct 14
Giuliani, Rudolph: Birth, May 28
Give Wildlife a Brake! Week, Oct 26
Givenchy, Hubert de: Birth, Feb 21
Givens, Robin: Birth, Nov 27
Giving: Tangible Karma Day, Apr 4
Glacier Bay Natl Park: Anniv, Dec 2
Glacier Natl Park: Anniv, May 11
Gladstone, William: Birth Anniv, Dec 29
Glaser, Paul Michael: Birth, Mar 25

Glass Fest, Elwood (Elwood, IN), Aug 21
Glass, Ira: Birth, Mar 3
Glass, Philip: Birth, Jan 31
Glass, Ron: Birth, Jul 10
Glastonbury Fest (Glastonbury, England), Jun 26
Glaucoma Awareness Month, Natl, Jan 1
Glavine, Tom: Birth, Mar 25
Gleason, Jackie: Birth Anniv, Feb 26
Glenn, John: Birth, Jul 18
Glenn, Scott: Birth, Jan 26
Gless, Sharon: Birth, May 31
Glover, Crispin: Birth, Apr 20
Glover, Danny: Birth, Jul 22
Glover, John: Birth, Aug 7
Glover, Savion: Birth, Nov 19
Gluten-Free Baking Week, Dec 13
Gluten-Free Diet Awareness Month, Nov 1
Go Barefoot Day, Natl, Jun 1
Go Fetch! Natl Food Drive for Homeless Animals, May 1
Go Hog Wild—Eat Country Ham Month, Oct 1
Go on a Field Trip Month, Natl, Oct 1
Goals, Goal Setting (personal and professional growth)
- Be On-Purpose Month, Natl, Jan 1
- Build a Better Image Week, Sep 20
- Effectiveness Week, Natl, May 18
- Evaluate Your Life Day, Oct 19
- Expect Success Month, Intl, Mar 1
- Gain the Inside Advantage Month, Natl, Oct 1
- Guinness World Records' Day, Nov 13
- Kick-Butt Day, Natl, Oct 12
- Kids' Goal Setting Week, Oct 5
- March Forth—Do Something Day, Mar 4
- New Years' Resolutions Month for Businesses, Intl, Jan 1
- New Year's Resolutions Week, Jan 4
- No Interruptions Day, Dec 31
- Plant the Seeds of Greatness Month, Feb 1
- Rising Star Month, Dec 1
- Second Half of the New Year Day, Jul 1
- Single-Tasking Day, Feb 21
- Take a New Year's Resolution to Stop Smoking, Dec 8
- Tick Tock Day, Dec 29
- Time Management Month, Natl, Feb 1
- Toss Away the "Could Haves" and "Should Haves" Day, Jul 18

Goat Cook-off, World Chmpshp BBQ/Crafts Fair (Brady, TX), Sep 5
God Bless America First Performed: Anniv, Nov 11
Godard, Jean Luc: Birth, Dec 3
Goddard Day: Anniv, Mar 16
Goddard, Robert H.: Birth Anniv, Oct 5
Godfather Film Premiere: Anniv, Mar 15
Godwin, Mary. See Wollstonecraft, Mary: Birth Anniv, Apr 27
Goebbels, Paul Josef: Birth Anniv, Oct 29
Goethals, George W.: Birth Anniv, Jun 29
Goethe, Johann W.: Birth Anniv, Aug 28
Gogol, Nikolai: Birth Anniv, Mar 31
Gold Discovery Days (Custer, SD), Jul 24
Gold Discovery, California: Anniv, Jan 24
Gold Discovery, Klondike Eldorado: Anniv, Aug 31
Gold Discovery, Klondike: Anniv, Aug 16
Gold Panner Contest, Poorman's Paradise (Nome, AK), Jul 23
Gold Rush Days (Wickenburg, AZ), Feb 13
Gold Star Mother's Day (Pres Proc), Sep 27
Gold, Missy: Birth, Jul 14
Gold, Tracey: Birth, May 16
Goldberg, Rube: Birth Anniv, Jul 4
Goldberg, Whoopi: Birth, Nov 13
Goldbergs TV Premiere: Anniv, Jan 17
Goldblum, Jeff: Birth, Oct 22
Golden Aspen Motorcycle Rally (Ruidoso, NM), Sep 16
Golden Gate Bridge Opened: Anniv, May 27
Golden Girls TV Premiere: Anniv, Sep 14
Golden Globe Awards, Jan 11
Golden Spike Driving: Anniv, May 10
Golding, Sir William: Birth Anniv, Sep 19
Goldman, William: Birth, Aug 12
Goldsmith, Oliver: Birth Anniv, Nov 10
Goldwyn, Samuel: Birth Anniv, Jan 31
Goldwyn, Tony: Birth, May 20
Golf
- Big Ten Men's Chmpshps (University Park, PA), May 1
- Big Ten Women's Chmpshps (West Lafayette, IN), Apr 24
- Bob Hope Chrysler Classic (Palm Springs, CA), Jan 19
- Chicago Golf Club: Anniv, Jul 18
- Dubai Desert Classic (Dubai, UAE), Jan 26
- First PGA Chmpshp: Anniv, Apr 10
- Hogan, Ben: Birth Anniv, Aug 13
- Jones Wins First Grand Slam: Anniv, Jul 12
- Jones, Bobby: Birth Anniv, Mar 17
- Kraft Nabisco Chmpshp (Rancho Mirage, CA), Mar 30
- Miniature Golf Day, Natl, May 9
- NAIA Men's Natl Chmpshps (Moline, IL), May 19
- NAIA Women's Natl Chmpshps (Rapid City, SD), May 12
- NCAA Div I Men's Chmpshps (Toledo, OH), May 27
- NCAA Div I Women's Chmpshps (Owings Mills, MD), May 19
- Open Chmpshp (British Open) (Turnberry, Scotland), Jul 12
- Ouimet, Francis DeSales: Birth Anniv, May 8
- PGA Chmpshp (Bloomfield Township, MI), Aug 10
- PGA Founded: Anniv, Jan 17
- PGA Seniors' Chmpshp (Beechwood, OH), May 21
- Sarazen, Gene: Birth Anniv, Feb 27
- Snead, Sam: Birth Anniv, May 27
- US Amateur Chmpshp (Tulsa, OK), Aug 24
- US Amateur Public Links Chmpshp (Norman, OK), Jul 13
- US Girl's Junior Chmpshp (Bedminster, NJ), Jul 20
- US Junior Amateur Chmpshp (Bedminster, NJ), Jul 20
- US Mid-Amateur Chmpshp (Charleston, SC), Oct 3
- US Open Chmpshp (Farmingdale, NY), Jun 18
- US Senior Open Chmpshp (Carmel, IN), Jul 30
- US Senior Women's Amateur Chmpshp (Hot Springs, VA), Sep 12
- US Women's Amateur Chmpshp (St. Louis, MO), Aug 3
- US Women's Amateur Public Links Chmpshp (Devens, MA), Jun 22
- US Women's Mid-Amateur Chmpshp (Ocala, FL), Oct 3
- US Women's Open Chmpshp (Bethlehem, PA), Jul 9
- USGA Senior Amateur Chmpshp (Chicago, IL), Sep 12
- Walker Cup (Ardmore, PA), Sep 12
- WGC-CA Chmpshp (Miami, FL), Mar 9
- Zaharias, Mildred Babe Didrikson: Birth Anniv, Jun 26

Golino, Valeria: Birth, Oct 22
Gomez, Lefty: Birth Anniv, Nov 26
Gomez, Scott: Birth, Dec 23
Gompers, Samuel: Birth Anniv, Jan 27
Gone with the Wind Film Premiere: Anniv, Dec 15
Gone with the Wind Published: Anniv, May 19
Gong Show TV Premiere: Anniv, Jun 14
González, Fernando: Birth, Jul 29
Gonzales, Pancho: Birth Anniv, May 9
Gonzalez, Juan: Birth, Oct 16
Good Friday, Apr 10
Good Friday Bank Holiday (United Kingdom), Apr 10
Good Friday Peace Agreement in Northern Ireland: Anniv, Apr 10
Good Morning America TV Premiere: Anniv, Nov 6
Good Samaritan Involvement Day, Mar 13
Good Sex! with Dr. Ruth Westheimer TV Premiere: Anniv, Aug 27
Good Times TV Premiere: Anniv, Feb 1
Goodall, Jane: Birth, Apr 3
Gooden, Dwight: Birth, Nov 16
Goodeve, Grant: Birth, Jul 6
Gooding, Cuba, Jr: Birth, Jan 2
Goodman, Benny: Birth Anniv, May 30
Goodman, Ellen: Birth, Apr 11
Goodman, John: Birth, Jun 20
Goodson, Mark: Birth Anniv, Jan 24
Goodwill Industries Week, May 3
Goodwill: Helms, Edgar J.: Birth Anniv, Jan 19
Goof-Off Day, Intl, Mar 22
Google Founded: Anniv, Sep 7
Goolagong, Evonne: Birth, Jul 31
Goorjian, Michael: Birth, Feb 4
Gorbachev, Mikhail: Birth, Mar 2
Gordimer, Nadine: Birth, Nov 20
Gordon, Jeff: Birth, Aug 4
Gordon, Keith: Birth, Feb 3
Gordone, Charles: Birth Anniv, Oct 12
Gordon-Levitt, Joseph: Birth, Feb 17
Gordy, Berry, Jr: Birth, Nov 28
Gore, Al: Birth, Mar 31
Gore, Lesley: Birth, May 2
Gore, Tipper: Birth, Aug 19
Gorgas, William Crawford: Birth Anniv, Oct 3
Gorilla Born in Captivity, First: Anniv, Dec 22
Gorillas: Koko: Birthday, Jul 4
Gorme, Eydie: Birth, Aug 16
Gosling, Ryan: Birth, Nov 12
Gospel. See also Music
- Dorsey, Thomas A.: Birth Anniv, Jul 1
- Gospel Fest (Central City, KY), Aug 26
- Jackson, Mahalia: Birth Anniv, Oct 26
- LifeLight Outdoor Music Fest (Sioux Falls, SD), Sep 4
- Singing on the Mountain (Linville, NC), Jun 28

Gossage, Goose: Birth, Jul 5
Gosselaar, Mark-Paul: Birth, Mar 1
Gossett, Louis, Jr: Birth, May 27
Gottlieb, Robert: Birth, Apr 29
Gottschalk, Louis Moreau: Birth Anniv, May 8
Gould, Chester: Birth Anniv, Nov 20

Gould, Elliott: Birth, Aug 29
Gould, Harold: Birth, Dec 10
Gould, Stephen Jay: Birth Anniv, Sep 10
Goya, Francisco Jose de: Birth Anniv, Mar 30
Grabeel, Lucas: Birth, Nov 23
Grace, Mark: Birth, Jun 28
Grace, Nancy: Birth, Oct 23
Grace, Topher: Birth, Jul 19
Grady, Don: Birth, Jun 8
Graf, Steffi: Birth, Jun 14
Graffman, Gary: Birth, Oct 14
Grafton, Sue: Birth, Apr 24
Graham, Billy: Birth, Nov 7
Graham, Calvin "Baby Vet": Birth Anniv, Apr 3
Graham, Heather: Birth, Jan 29
Graham, Lauren: Birth, Mar 16
Graham, Lindsey: Birth, Jul 9
Graham, Martha: Birth Anniv, May 11
Grahame, Kenneth: Birth Anniv, Mar 8
Grammar Day, Natl, Mar 4
Grammer, Kelsey: Birth, Feb 21
Grammy Awards, Feb 8
Granato, Cammi: Birth, Mar 25
Grand Canyon Natl Park Established: Anniv, Feb 26
Grand Militia Muster (St. Mary's City, MD), Oct 17
Grand Ole Opry Broadcast, First: Anniv, Dec 10
Grand Prix de Monaco (Monte Carlo, Monaco), May 21
Grand Teton Music Fest (Teton Village, WY), Jun 30
Grand Teton Natl Park Established: Anniv, Feb 26
Grandma Day, Gorgeous, Jul 23
Grandmother's Day in Florida, Oct 11
Grandparents' Day, Natl, Sep 13
Grandy, Fred: Birth, Jun 29
Grange Founding, Natl: Anniv, Dec 4
Grange Month, Apr 1
Grange, Red: Birth Anniv, Jun 13
Granholm, Jennifer: Birth, Feb 5
Grant, Amy: Birth, Nov 25
Grant, Cary: Birth Anniv, Jan 18
Grant, Horace: Birth, Jul 4
Grant, Hugh: Birth, Sep 9
Grant, Jennifer: Birth, Feb 26
Grant, Julia Dent: Birth Anniv, Jan 26
Grant, Richard E.: Birth, May 5
Grant, Ulysses S.
  Battle of Chattanooga: Anniv, Nov 24
  Battle of Cold Harbor: Anniv, Jun 3
  Battle of Shiloh: Anniv, Apr 6
  Battle of the Wilderness: Anniv, May 5
  Birth Anniv, Apr 27
  Commissioned Commander: Anniv, Mar 9
  Speech of Apology: Anniv, Dec 5
  Surrender of Fort Donelson: Anniv, Feb 16
  Vicksburg Surrenders: Anniv, Jul 3
Grantsville Days (Grantsville, MD), Jun 26
Grape Jamboree, Geneva Area (Geneva, OH), Sep 26
Grapes of Wrath Published: Anniv, Apr 14
Grass Is Always Browner on the Other Side of the Fence Day, Mar 30
Grass, Gunter: Birth, Oct 16
Grassle, Karen: Birth, Feb 25
Grassley, Charles: Birth, Sep 17
Gratton, Chris: Birth, Jul 5
Graves, Peter: Birth, Mar 18
Graves, Rupert: Birth, Jun 30
Gray, Asa: Birth Anniv, Nov 18
Gray, Erin: Birth, Jan 7
Gray, Harold Lincoln: Birth Anniv, Jan 20
Gray, Linda: Birth, Sep 12
Gray, Macy: Birth, Dec 6
Gray, Robert, Circumnavigates Earth: Anniv, Aug 9
Grayson, Kathryn: Birth, Feb 9
Great (Holy) Week, Apr 5
Great American Backyard Campout, Jun 27
Great American Smokeout, Nov 19
Great American Smokeout Day, Natl (Pres Proc), Nov 19
Great Backyard Bird Count, Feb 13
Great Britain Formed: Anniv, May 1
Great Smoky Mountains Natl Park Established: Anniv, Jun 15
Great Wellsville Balloon Rally (Wellsville, NY), Jul 17
Greatest Show on Earth Formed: Anniv, Mar 28
Greco, Buddy: Birth, Aug 14
Greece
  Dumb Week, Apr 5
  Independence Day, Mar 25
  Midwife's Day or Women's Day, Jan 8
  Ochi Day, Oct 28
Greek Culture Event: Odyssey—A Greek Fest (Orange, CT), Sep 4
Greek Independence Day (Pres Proc), Mar 25
Greeley, Father Andrew: Birth, Feb 5
Greeley, Horace: Birth Anniv, Feb 3
Green. See Environmental.
Green, Al: Birth, Apr 13
Green, Brian: Birth, Jul 15
Green, Hetty: Birth Anniv, Nov 21
Green, Hubie: Birth, Dec 28
Green, Seth: Birth, Feb 8
Green Monday, Mar 2
Greenberg, Hank: Birth Anniv, Jan 1
Greene, Bob: Birth, Mar 10
Greene, Graham: Birth Anniv, Oct 2
Greene, Nathaniel: Birth Anniv, Aug 7
Greene, Shecky: Birth, Apr 8
Greenfield, Jeff: Birth, Jun 10
Greenland: National Day, Jun 21
Greenpeace Founded: Anniv, Sep 15
Greenpeace: Rainbow Warrior Sinking: Anniv, Jul 10
Greensboro Sit-In: Anniv, Feb 1
Greenspan, Alan: Birth, Mar 6
Greenspan, Alan: Irrational Exuberance Enters Lexicon: Anniv, Dec 5
Greenwich Mean Time Begins: Anniv, Sep 25
Greer, Germaine: Birth, Jan 29
Gregg, Judd: Birth, Feb 14
Gregoire, Christine: Birth, Mar 24
Gregorian Calendar Adjustment: Anniv, Oct 4
Gregorian Calendar Day, Feb 24
Gregory, Bettina: Birth, Jun 4
Gregory, Cynthia: Birth, Jul 8
Gregory, Dick: Birth, Oct 12
Greist, Kim: Birth, May 12
Grenada
  Emancipation Day, Aug 3
  Independence Day, Feb 7
  Invasion by US: Anniv, Oct 25
Grenadines and Saint Vincent: Independence Day, Oct 27
Grenier, Adrian: Birth, Oct 10
Gretzky, Wayne: Birth, Jan 26
Grey, Jennifer: Birth, Mar 26
Grey, Joel: Birth, Apr 11
Grey, Zane: Birth Anniv, Jan 31
Grieco, Richard: Birth, Mar 23
Grieg, Edvard: Birth Anniv, Jun 15
Grieg, Edvard: Birth Anniv Celebration (Norway), Jun 15
Grier, David Alan: Birth, Jun 30
Grier, Pam: Birth, May 26
Grier, Roosevelt (Rosey): Birth, Jul 14
Griese, Bob: Birth, Feb 3
Grieve, Ben: Birth, May 4
Griffey, Ken: Birth, Nov 21
Griffin, John H.: Birth Anniv, Jun 16
Griffin, Kathy: Birth, Nov 4
Griffin, Merv: Birth Anniv, Jul 6
Griffith, Andy, Show TV Premiere: Anniv, Oct 3
Griffith, Andy: Birth, Jun 1
Griffith, D.W.: Birth Anniv, Jan 22
Griffith, Melanie: Birth, Aug 9
Griffith, Yolanda: Birth, Mar 1
Griffiths, Rachel: Birth, Dec 18
Grilling Month, Natl, Jul 1
Grimaldi, Joseph: Birth Anniv, Dec 18
Grimes, Gary: Birth, Jun 2
Grimke, Sarah: Birth Anniv, Nov 26
Grimm, Jacob: Birth Anniv, Jan 4
Grimm, Wilhelm: Birth Anniv, Feb 24
Grint, Rupert: Birth, Aug 24
Grisham, John: Birth, Feb 8
Groban, Josh: Birth, Feb 27
Grodin, Charles: Birth, Apr 21
Groening, Matt: Birth, Feb 15
Gromyko, Andrei Andreyevich: Birth Anniv, Jul 18
Gross, Mary: Birth, Mar 25
Gross, Michael: Birth, Jun 21
Grotius, Hugo: Birth Anniv, Apr 10
Grouch Day, Natl, Oct 15
Ground Zero Recovery and Cleanup Ends: Anniv, May 30
Groundhog Day, Feb 2
Groundhog Day (Punxsutawney, PA), Feb 2
Groundhog Day Celebration and Prognostication (Sun Prairie, WI), Jan 31
Groundhog Days (Woodstock, IL), Jan 29
Groundhog Fest (Punxsutawney, PA), Jun 28
Groundhog Job Shadow Day, Feb 2
Groundhog Run (Kansas City, MO), Jan 25
Grubstake Days (Yucca Valley, CA), May 23
Grump Out, Great American, May 6
Grunberg, Greg: Birth, Jul 11
Gruntled Workers Day, Jul 13
Grylls, Bear: Birth, Jun 7
Guadalajara Intl Book Fair (Guadalajara, Mexico), Nov 28
Guadalcanal, Allies Retake: Anniv, Feb 9
Guadalupe Hidalgo, Treaty of: Anniv, Feb 2
Guadalupe Natl Park Established: Anniv, Sep 30
Guadalupe, Day of Our Lady of, Dec 12
Guam
  Discovery Day, Mar 2
  Lady of Camarin Day, Dec 8
  Liberation Day, Jul 21
  Magellan Day, Mar 2
  Spanish-American War: Surrender, to US: Anniv, Jun 20
Guardian Angels Day, Oct 2
Guatemala
  Armed Forces Day, Jun 30
  Independence Day, Sep 15
  Kite Fest of Santiago Sacatepequez, Nov 1
  Revolution Day, Oct 20
Guccione, Bob: Birth, Dec 17
Guernica Massacre: Anniv, Apr 26

Guerrero, Vladimir: Birth, Feb 9
Guess: Take a Wild Guess Day, Natl, Apr 15
Guest, Christopher: Birth, Feb 5
Guest, Edgar A.: Birth Anniv, Aug 20
Guest, Lance: Birth, Jul 21
Guggenheim, Simon: Birth Anniv, Dec 30
Gugliotta, Tom: Birth, Dec 19
Guiding Light TV Premiere: Anniv, Jun 26
Guidry, Ron: Birth, Aug 28
Guilfoyle, Paul: Birth, Jul 12
Guillaume, Robert: Birth, Nov 30
Guillotin, Joseph: Birth Anniv, May 28
Guinea: Anniversary of the Second Republic, Apr 3
Guinea: Independence Day, Oct 2
Guinea-Bissau
Colonization Martyr's Day, Aug 3
Independence Day, Sep 24
National Holiday, Sep 12
Natl Heroes Day, Jan 20
Readjustment Movement's Day, Nov 14
Guinness World Records' Day, Nov 13
Guinness, Sir Alec: Birth Anniv, Apr 2
Guisewite, Cathy Lee: Birth, Sep 5
Guitar Flat-Picking Chmpshps, Natl (Winfield, KS), Sep 16
Gulf of Tonkin Resolution: Anniv, Aug 7
Gumbel, Bryant: Birth, Sep 29
Gumbel, Greg: Birth, May 3
Gumbo Fest (Bridge City, LA), Oct 9
Gumby Show TV Premiere: Anniv, Mar 16
Gun Shows, Sales, Competition
Ocean County Decoy/Gun Show (Tuckerton, NJ), Sep 26
Gunn, Moses: Birth Anniv, Oct 2
Guns: Day of Natl Concern About Young People and Gun Violence, Oct 28
Gunsmoke TV Premiere: Anniv, Sep 10
Gutenberg Bible Published: Anniv, Sep 30
Guterson, David: Birth, May 4
Guth, Alan: Birth, Feb 27
Guthrie, Arlo: Birth, Jul 10
Guthrie, Janet: Birth, Mar 7
Guthrie, Woody: Birth Anniv, Jul 14
Gutierrez, Carlos: Birth, Nov 4
Guttenberg, Steve: Birth, Aug 24
Guy, Jasmine: Birth, Mar 10
Guyana: National Day, Feb 23
Gwathmey, Charles: Birth, Jun 19
Gwinnett, Button: Death Anniv, May 16
Gwynn, Tony: Birth, May 9
Gwynne, Fred: Birth Anniv, Jul 10
Gyllenhall, Jake: Birth, Dec 19
Gyllenhall, Maggie: Birth, Nov 16
Gymnastics (competitions, championships, etc)
Big Ten Men's Chmpshps (Ann Arbor, MI), Apr 3
Big Ten Women's Chmpshps (Champaign-Urbana, IL), Mar 21
Natl Collegiate Women's Gymnastics (Lincoln, NE), Apr 16
Gynecologic Cancer Awareness Month, Sep 1
Gypsy Rose Lee (Rose L. Hovick): Birth Anniv, Feb 9

H
Haas, Lukas: Birth, Apr 16
Habitat Day, World (UN), Oct 5
Hackman, Gene: Birth, Jan 30
Hadassah Founded: Anniv, Feb 24
Haden, Pat: Birth, Jan 23
Hagar, Sammy: Birth, Oct 13
Hagel, Chuck: Birth, Oct 4
Hagerty, Julie: Birth, Jun 15
Haggard, Merle: Birth, Apr 6
Hagler, Marvelous Marvin: Birth, May 23
Hagman, Larry: Birth, Sep 21
Haid, Charles: Birth, Jun 2
Haiku Poetry Day, Natl, Dec 21
Haim, Corey: Birth, Dec 23
Hair Broadway Opening: Anniv, Mar 28
Hairball Awareness Day, Natl, Apr 24
Hairstylist Day, Apr 30
Haiti
Ancestors' Day, Jan 2
Army Day, Nov 18
Discovery Day: Anniv, Dec 5
Flag and University Day, May 18
Independence Day, Jan 1
Haitian Heritage Month, May 1
HAL (computer): Birth, Jan 12
Halas, George: Birth Anniv, Feb 2
Halcyon Days, Dec 14
Hale, Barbara: Birth, Apr 18
Hale, Nathan: Birth Anniv, Jun 6
Haleakala Natl Park Established: Anniv, Sep 30
Haley, Alex Palmer: Birth Anniv, Aug 11
Haley, Jackie Earle: Birth, Jul 14
Halfway Point of 2009, Jul 2
Halifax Busker Fest, Intl (Halifax, NS, Canada), Aug 7
Halifax Independence Day (NC), Apr 12
Halifax, Nova Scotia, Destroyed: Anniv, Dec 6
Hall, Anthony Michael: Birth, Apr 14
Hall, Arsenio: Birth, Feb 12
Hall, Daryl: Birth, Oct 11
Hall, Deidre: Birth, Oct 31
Hall, Donald A.: Birth, Sep 20
Hall, Edd: Birth, Dec 7
Hall, Lyman: Birth Anniv, Apr 12
Hall, Michael C.: Birth, Feb 1
Hall, Monty: Birth, Aug 25
Hall, Tom T.: Birth, May 25
Halladay, Roy: Birth, May 14
Halley, Edmund: Birth Anniv, Nov 8
Hallmark Hall of Fame TV Premiere: Anniv, Jan 6
Halloween
Books for Treats Day (San Jose, CA), Oct 31
Devil's Night, Oct 30
Emma Crawford Fest and Memorial Coffin Race (Manitou Springs, CO), Oct 31
Family Halloween (Woodstock, VT), Oct 25
Fantasy Fest (Key West, FL), Oct 23
Frankenstein Friday, Oct 30
Ghostly Gathering (Sandy Springs, GA), Oct 23
Halloween Hike (Savannah, GA), Oct 23
Hallowe'en or All Hallow's Eve, Oct 31
Halloween Parade (Toms River, NJ), Oct 31
Halloween Safety Month, Oct 1
Haunted Refrigerator Night, Oct 30
Haute Dog Charity Howl'oween Parade (Long Beach, CA), Oct 25
Knock-Knock Day, Natl, Oct 31
Magic Day, Oct 31
Monster Myths by Moonlight (Milford, KS), Oct 10
Samhain, Oct 31
Scared Silly: Halloween in Prospect Park (Brooklyn, NY), Oct 31
Sea Witch Halloween & Fiddlers Fest (Rehoboth Beach/Dewey Beach, DE), Oct 24
Trick or Treat or Beggar's Night, Oct 31
WMAS Annual Halloween Ball (Springfield, MA), Oct 31
Halsey, William "Bull": Birth Anniv, Oct 30
Ham: Go Hog Wild—Eat Country Ham Month, Oct 1
Hamburger Hill, Battle of: Anniversary, May 11
Hamburger Month, Natl, May 1
Hamel, Veronica: Birth, Nov 20
Hamill, Mark: Birth, Sep 25
Hamilton, Alexander: Birth Anniv, Jan 11
Hamilton, Alexander: Duel with Aaron Burr: Anniv, Jul 11
Hamilton, Alice: Birth Anniv, Feb 27
Hamilton, George: Birth, Aug 12
Hamilton, Jane: Birth, Jul 13
Hamilton, Josh: Birth, May 21
Hamilton, Linda: Birth, Sep 26
Hamilton, Richard: Birth, Feb 14
Hamilton, Scott: Birth, Aug 28
Hamlin, Hannibal: Birth Anniv, Aug 27
Hamlin, Harry: Birth, Oct 30
Hamlisch, Marvin: Birth, Jun 2
Hamm, Jon: Birth, Mar 10
Hamm, Mia: Birth, May 17
Hamm, Morgan: Birth, Sep 24
Hamm, Paul: Birth, Sep 24
Hammer, Armand: Birth Anniv, May 21
Hammer, M.C.: Birth, Mar 30
Hammerstein II, Oscar: Oklahoma! Broadway Premiere: Anniv, Mar 31
Hammett, Dashiell: Birth Anniv, May 27
Hammett, Dashiell: Maltese Falcon: Publication Anniv, Feb 14
Hammon, Jupiter: Birth Anniv, Oct 17
Hammond, Darrell: Birth, Oct 8
Hampton, Lionel: Birth Anniv, Apr 20
Hampton, Mike: Birth, Sep 9
Hancock, Herbie: Birth, Apr 12
Hancock, John: Birth Anniv, Jan 23
Hancock, Winfield Scott: Birth Anniv, Feb 14
Handel, George Frederick: Birth Anniv, Feb 23
Handel, George Frederick: Premiere of Messiah: Anniv, Apr 13
Handshake Day, Natl, Jun 25
Handwriting Day, Natl, Jan 23
Handy, W.C., Music Fest (Florence, AL), Jul 17
Handy, William C.: Birth Anniv, Nov 16
Hang Around Victor Day (Victor, NY), Sep 5
Hanging Out Day, Natl, Apr 19
Hangul (Korea), Oct 9
Hanks, Tom: Birth, Jul 9
Hanna, William: Birth Anniv, Jul 14
Hannah, Daryl: Birth, Dec 3
Hannigan, Alyson: Birth, May 24
Hannity, Sean: Birth, Dec 30
Hannukah: See Chanukah, Dec 12
Hansberry, Lorraine: Birth Anniv, May 19
Hansen, Beck: Birth, Jul 8
Hansom, Joseph: Birth Anniv, Oct 26
Hanson, Howard: Birth Anniv, Oct 28
Hanson, Isaac: Birth, Nov 17
Happiness Happens Day, Aug 8
Happiness Happens Month, Aug 1
Happiness: Hunt for Happiness Week, Jan 18
Happy Birthday to "Happy Birthday to You," Jun 27

Happy Days TV Premiere: Anniv, Jan 15
Happy Mew Year for Cats Day, Jan 2
Harbaugh, Jim: Birth, Dec 23
Hard Crab Derby and Fair, Natl (Crisfield, MD), Sep 4
Hardaway, Penny: Birth, Jul 18
Hardaway, Tim: Birth, Sep 1
Harden, Marcia Gay: Birth, Aug 14
Harding, Florence: Birth Anniv, Aug 15
Harding, Tonya: Birth, Nov 12
Harding, Warren G.: Birth Anniv, Nov 2
Harding, Warren G.: First Radio Broadcast, Jun 14
Hardison, Kadeem: Birth, Jul 24
Hardy, Oliver: Birth Anniv, Jan 18
Harewood, Dorian: Birth, Aug 6
Hargitay, Mariska: Birth, Jan 23
Hari, Mata: Execution Anniv, Oct 15
Harkin, Thomas R.: Birth, Nov 19
Harlem Globetrotters Play First Game: Anniv, Jan 7
Harmon, Angie: Birth, Aug 10
Harmon, Mark: Birth, Sep 2
Harmonic Convergence: Anniv, Aug 16
Harper, Jessica: Birth, Oct 10
Harper, Stephen: Birth, Apr 30
Harper, Valerie: Birth, Aug 22
Harrelson, Woody: Birth, Jul 23
Harrington, Pat, Jr: Birth, Aug 13
Harris, Ed: Birth, Nov 28
Harris, Emmylou: Birth, Apr 2
Harris, Franco: Birth, Mar 7
Harris, Joel Chandler: Birth Anniv, Dec 9
Harris, Julie: Birth, Dec 2
Harris, Mel: Birth, Jul 12
Harris, Neil Patrick: Birth, Jun 15
Harris, Patricia Roberts: Birth Anniv, May 31
Harris, Richard: Birth Anniv, Oct 1
Harris, Roy: Birth Anniv, Feb 12
Harris, Samantha: Birth, Nov 27
Harrison, Anna: Birth Anniv, Jul 25
Harrison, Benjamin
  Benjamin Harrison Day (Indianapolis, IN), Mar 4
  Birth Anniv, Aug 20
  Birthday Celebration (Indianapolis, IN), Aug 20
  Family Christmas at Benjamin Harrison Home (Indianapolis, IN), Dec 12
Harrison, Caroline L.S.: Birth Anniv, Oct 1
Harrison, George: Birth Anniv, Feb 25
Harrison, Gregory: Birth, May 31
Harrison, Mary: Birth Anniv, Apr 30
Harrison, Rex: Birth Anniv, Mar 5
Harrison, William Henry: Birth Anniv, Feb 9
Harrold, Kathryn: Birth, Aug 2
Harry, Debbie: Birth, Jul 1
Harry, Deborah, and Blondie Month, Intl, Jul 1
Harry, Prince: Birth, Sep 15
Hart, Charles: Birth, Jun 3
Hart, Gary: Birth, Nov 28
Hart, John: Death Anniv, May 11
Hart, Mary: Birth, Nov 8
Hart, Melissa Joan: Birth, Apr 18
Harte, Bret: Birth Anniv, Aug 25
Hartley, Mariette: Birth, Jun 21
Hartman Black, Lisa: Birth, Jun 1
Hartman, David: Birth, May 19
Hartnett, Josh: Birth, Jul 21
Haru-No-Yabuiri (Japan), Jan 16
Harvard Univ Founded: Anniv, Oct 28
Harvard, John: Birth Anniv, Nov 26
Harvest Moon, Sep 4
Harvey, Paul: Birth, Sep 4
Harvey, Steve: Birth, Nov 23
Harvey, William: Birth Anniv, Apr 1
Harwell, Ernie: Birth, Jan 25
Hasek, Dominik: Birth, Jan 29
Hassam, Childe: Birth Anniv, Oct 17
Hasselhoff, David: Birth, Jul 17
Hastert, Dennis: Birth, Jan 2
Hat Month, Fall, Sep 1
Hat Month, Straw, Apr 1
Hatch, Orrin: Birth, Mar 22
Hatcher, Teri: Birth, Dec 8
Hate Week, Apr 4
Hatfield-McCoy Feud Erupts: Anniv, Aug 7
Hatsume Fair (Delray Beach, FL), Feb 21
Hauer, Rutger: Birth, Jan 23
Haunted Refrigerator Night, Oct 30
Hauptmann Execution: Anniv, Apr 3
Have a Bad Day Day, Nov 19
Have Gun Will Travel TV Premiere: Anniv, Sep 14
Havel, Vaclav: Birth, Oct 5
Havers, Nigel: Birth, Nov 6
Havlicek, John: Birth, Apr 8
Havoc, June: Birth, Nov 8
Hawaii
  Admission Day Holiday, Aug 21
  Akaka, Daniel K.: Birth, Sep 11
  American Dental Assn Annual Session (Honolulu), Sep 30
  Annexed by US: Anniv, Jul 7
  Discoverers' Day, Oct 12
  Haleakala Natl Park Established: Anniv, Sep 30
  Hawaii Statehood: Anniv, Aug 21
  Hawaii Volcanoes Natl Park Established: Anniv, Aug 1
  Inouye, Daniel: Birth, Sep 7
  King Kamehameha I Day, Jun 11
  Lei Day, May 1
  Lingle, Linda: Birth, Jun 4
  Merrie Monarch Fest (Hilo), Apr 12
  Prince Jonah Kuhio Kalanianole Day, Mar 26
  Queen Liliuokalani Deposed: Anniv, Jan 17
  Triple Crown of Surfing (Oahu), Nov 12
  Waikiki Roughwater Swim (Honolulu), Sep 1
  XTERRA Makena Beach Trail Run (Makena, Maui), Oct 24
  XTERRA Trail Running World Chmpshp (Oahu), Dec 6
  XTERRA World Chmpshp (Maui), Oct 25
Hawaii Five-O TV Premiere: Anniv, Sep 26
Hawk, Tony: Birth, May 12
Hawke, Ethan: Birth, Nov 6
Hawking, Stephen: Birth, Jan 8
Hawkins, Hersey: Birth, Sep 29
Hawn, Goldie: Birth, Nov 21
Haworth, Cheryl Ann: Birth, Apr 18
Hawthorne, Nathaniel: Birth Anniv, Jul 4
Hayakawa, Samuel: Birth Anniv, Jul 18
Hayden, Tom: Birth, Dec 11
Haydn, Franz Joseph: Birth Anniv, Mar 31
Hayek, Salma: Birth, Sep 2
Hayes, Helen: Birth Anniv, Oct 10
Hayes, Ira Hamilton: Birth Anniv, Jan 12
Hayes, Lucy: Birth Anniv, Aug 28
Hayes, Rutherford B.: Birth Anniv, Oct 4
Hayes, Sean P.: Birth, Jun 26
Haymarket Pardon: Anniv, Jun 26
Haymarket Square Riot: Anniv, May 4
Hay-on-Wye Fest of Literature (Hay-on-Wye, Wales), May 21
Hays, Robert: Birth, Jul 24
Haysbert, Dennis: Birth, Jun 2
Hazel TV Premiere: Anniv, Sep 28
Headache Awareness Week, Natl, Jun 7
Headly, Glenne: Birth, Mar 13
Heald, Anthony: Birth, Aug 25
Health and Welfare
  Act Happy Week, Mar 16
  Adoption Month, Natl, Nov 1
  Adult Immunization Awareness Week, Natl, Sep 20
  African-American Women's Fitness Month, Natl, Apr 1
  AIDS Awareness Month, Natl, Nov 1
  AIDS First Noted: Anniv, Jun 5
  AIDS Walk Atlanta (Atlanta, GA), Oct 18
  Alcohol and Drug Addiction Recovery Month, Natl, Sep 1
  Alcohol Awareness Month, Apr 1
  Alcohol Screening Day, Natl, Apr 9
  Alcohol-Free Weekend, Apr 3
  Allergy/Asthma Awareness Month, Natl, May 1
  Alzheimer's Disease Month, Natl, Nov 1
  AMA Founded: Anniv, May 5
  AMD/Low Vision Awareness Month, Feb 1
  American Dental Assn Annual Session (Honolulu, HI), Sep 30
  American Massage Therapy Assn, Natl Conv (Orlando, FL), Sep 23
  American Red Cross Founded: Anniv, May 21
  Anesthetic First Used in Surgery: Anniv, Mar 30
  Antidepressant Death Awareness Month, Oct 1
  Anxiety and Depression Awareness Week, Natl, May 3
  Aphasia Awareness Month, Natl, Jun 1
  Arthritis Month, Natl, May 1
  Artificial Heart Transplant: Anniv, Dec 2
  Assisted Living Week, Natl, Sep 13
  Atrial Fibrillation Month, Sep 1
  Attention Deficit Hyperactivity Disorder Month, Sep 1
  Awareness of Medical Orphans Month, May 1
  Baby Massage Day, Apr 11
  Backpack Safety America Month, Sep 1
  Balance Awareness Week, Sep 13
  Better Hearing and Speech Month, May 1
  Birth Control Clinic Opened, First: Anniv, Oct 16
  Birth Control Pills Sold: Anniv, Aug 18
  Brain Awareness Week, Intl, Mar 16
  Breast Cancer Awareness Month, Natl, Oct 1
  Breast Cancer Awareness Month, Natl (Pres Proc), Oct 1
  Caesarean Section, First: Anniv, Jan 14
  Caffeine Awareness Month, Natl, Mar 1
  California Dried Plum Digestive Health Month, Jan 1
  Cancer Control Month (Pres Proc), Apr 1
  Cancer from the Sun Month, Jun 1
  Cancer Survivors Day, Natl, Jun 7
  Cataract Awareness Month, Aug 1
  Celiac Awareness Day, Natl, Sep 13
  Celiac Disease Awareness Month, Oct 1
  Cervical Cancer Screening Month, Jan 1
  Child Health Day (Pres Proc), Oct 5
  Child Vision Awareness Month, Jun 1
  Childhood Cancer Campaign Month, Intl, Jun 1
  Childhood Depression Awareness Day, May 5

Children with Alopecia Day, Apr 14
Children's Dental Health Month, Natl, Feb 1
Children's Eye Health and Safety Month, Aug 1
Children's Vision and Learning Month, Aug 1
Chiropractic Month, Natl, Oct 1
Christmas Seal Campaign, Oct 1
Chronic Fatigue Syndrome Awareness Month, Natl, Mar 1
Cigarettes Reported Hazardous: Anniv, Jan 11
Clean Hands Week, Natl, Sep 20
Colorectal Cancer Awareness Month, Natl, Mar 1
Colorectal Cancer Education/Awareness Month, Dec 1
Condom Week, Natl, Feb 14
Congenital Heart Defect Awareness Week, Feb 7
COSAC Annual Conference (Atlantic City, NJ), Oct 8
Dairy Alternatives Month, Jun 1
Deaf History Month, Mar 13
Dental Hygiene Month, Natl, Oct 1
Depression Education and Awareness Month, Natl, Oct 1
Depression Screening Day, Natl, Oct 8
Diabetes Assn Alert Day, American, Mar 24
Diabetes Day, World, Nov 14
Diabetes Month, American, Nov 1
Diabetes Month, Natl (Pres Proc), Nov 1
Diabetic Eye Disease Month, Nov 1
Diet Resolution Week, Jan 1
DNA, Genomics & Stem Cell Education and Awareness Month, Natl, Apr 1
Doctor-Patient Trust Week, Mar 22
Doctors' Day, Mar 30
Donate Life Month, Natl, Apr 1
Donate Life Month, Natl (Pres Proc), Apr 1
Donor Sabbath, Natl, Nov 13
Down Syndrome Awareness Month, Natl, Oct 1
Eat Better, Eat Together Month, Oct 1
Eating Disorders Awareness Week, Natl, Feb 22
Emotional Intelligence Awareness Month, Oct 1
Emotional Wellness Month, Oct 1
Epilepsy Awareness Month, Nov 1
Eye Donor Month, Natl, Mar 1
Family Fit Lifestyle Month, Jan 1
Family Health and Fitness Days—USA, Sep 26
Family Sexuality Education Month, Natl, Oct 1
FDA Approves Botox: Anniv, Apr 15
FDA Approves Viagra: Anniv, Mar 27
Fibromyalgia Education and Awareness Month, May 1
Flossing Day, Natl, Nov 27
Food and Drug Interaction Education and Awareness Week, Oct 17
Fresh Breath Day, Natl, Aug 6
Glaucoma Awareness Month, Natl, Jan 1
Goof-Off Day, Intl, Mar 22
Great American Low-Cholesterol, Low-Fat Pizza Bake, Sep 1
Great American Smokeout, Nov 19
Great American Smokeout Day, Natl (Pres Proc), Nov 19
Gynecologic Cancer Awareness Month, Sep 1
Have-a-Heart Day, Natl, Feb 14
Headache Awareness Week, Natl, Jun 7
Health Literacy Month, Oct 1
Healthy Vision Month, May 1
Healthy Weight Week, Jan 18
Heart Month, American, Feb 1
Heart Month, American (Pres Proc), Feb 1
Heart Transplant, First: Anniv, Dec 3
Hepatitis Awareness Month, Natl, May 1
Herbal/Prescription Interaction Awareness Month, Jul 1
HIV Testing Day, Natl, Jun 27
Huntington's Disease Awareness Month, May 1
Immunization Awareness Month, Natl, Aug 1
Infertility Survival Day, Natl, May 3
Insulin First Isolated: Anniv, Jul 27
Invisible Chronic Illness Awareness Week, Natl (San Diego, CA), Sep 14
Jackie Mayer Rehab Day (OH), Oct 6
Jerry Lewis Muscular Dystrophy Association Telethon, Sep 6
Kidney Day, World, Mar 12
Kidney Month, Natl, Mar 1
Lee Natl Denim Day, Oct 2
Lister, Joseph: Birth Anniv, Apr 5
Liver Awareness Month, Natl, Oct 1
Long-Term Care Planning Month, Oct 1
Long-Term Care Awareness Month, Natl, Nov 1
Lung Cancer Awareness Month, Nov 1
Malaria Awareness Day (Pres Proc), Apr 25
Malaria Day, World, Apr 25
Mammography Day, Natl, Oct 16
Marfan Syndrome Awareness Month, Feb 1
Medical Group Practice Week, Natl, Jan 19
Medical Science Liaison (MSL) Awareness and Appreciation Day, Natl, Nov 6
Medicare: Anniv, Jul 1
Medication Safety Week, Apr 1
Melanoma Monday, May 4
Melanoma/Skin Cancer Detection and Prevention Month, May 1
Men's Grooming Day, Natl, Aug 21
Mental Health Month, Natl, May 1
Mental Illness Awareness Week, Oct 4
Mold Awareness Month, Sep 1
More Herbs, Less Salt Day, Aug 29
Multiple Sclerosis Awareness Week, Mar 2
Multiple Sclerosis Education & Awareness Month, Natl, Mar 1
Neurosurgery Outreach Month, Aug 1
No Diet Day, May 6
Nuclear Medicine Week, Oct 5
Nurse Anesthetists Week, Natl, Jan 25
Nurses Week, Natl, May 6
Nursing Assistants Day and Week, Natl, Jun 11
Nursing Home Week, Natl, May 10
Nutrition Month, Natl, Mar 1
Occupational Therapy Month, Natl, Apr 1
Open-Heart Surgery, First: Anniv, Jul 9
Organize Your Medical Information Month, Oct 1
Orthodonic Health Month, Natl, Oct 1
Osteopathic Medicine Month, Natl, Sep 1
Osteoporosis Awareness and Prevention Month, Natl, May 1
Ovarian Cancer Awareness Month, Sep 1
Ovarian Cancer Awareness Month, Natl (Pres Proc), Sep 1
Pandemic of 1918 Hits US: Anniv, Mar 11
Parkinson Awareness Month, Natl, Apr 1
Patient Accessibility Week, Natl, Nov 1
Patient Recognition Week, Natl, Feb 1
Pediatric Cancer Awareness Month, Sep 1
Pediatric Nurse Practitioner Week, Mar 15
Pediculosis Prevention Month, Natl, Sep 1
Personal Training Week, Natl, Apr 12
Pharmacists Declare War on Alcoholism, Jun 1
Pharmacists' War on Diabetes, Apr 1
Physical Fitness and Sports Month, Natl, May 1
Physical Therapy Month, Natl, Oct 1
Physical Wellness Month, Apr 1
Poison Prevention Awareness Month, Mar 1
Poison Prevention Week, Natl, Mar 15
Polio Vaccine: Anniv, Apr 12
Prematurity Awareness Day, Nov 1
Prescription Errors Education & Awareness Week, Oct 24
Prostate Cancer Awareness Week, Sep 20
Radon Action Month, Natl, Jan 1
Rebuild Your Life Month, Jun 1
Red Cross Month, Mar 1
Red Cross Month, American (Pres Proc), Mar 1
Registered Dietitian Day, Mar 11
Rehabilitation Awareness Celebration, Natl, Sep 20
Relaxation Day, Natl, Aug 15
Restless Leg Syndrome (RLS) Education and Awareness Week, Jul 18
Rett Syndrome Awareness Month, Oct 1
Rid the World of Fad Diets/Gimmicks Day, Jan 20
Root Canal Appreciation Day, May 13
Rosacea Awareness Month, Apr 1
RSV Awareness Month, Natl, Oct 1
Sarcoidosis Awareness Day, Natl, Aug 29
Save Your Vision Month, Mar 1
Save Your Vision Week (Pres Proc), Mar 1
School Breakfast Week, Natl, Mar 2
Senior Health and Fitness Day, Natl, May 27
September Is Healthy Aging Month, Sep 1
Sexually Transmitted Diseases (STDs) Awareness Month, Natl, Apr 1
Sickle Cell Awareness Month, Natl, Sep 1
Skin Care Awareness Month, Natl, Sep 1
Sleep Awareness Week, Natl, Mar 1
Smallpox Vaccine Discovered: Anniv, May 14
Smile Month, Natl, May 1
Social Security Act: Anniv, Aug 14
Social Work Month, Natl, Mar 1
Special Recreation Week, Jun 28
Speech-Language-Hearing Conv, American (New Orleans, LA), Nov 19
Spina Bifida Awareness Month, Natl, Oct 1
Spinal Muscular Atrophy Awareness Month, Aug 1
Sports & Home Eye Safety Month, Sep 1
Stay Out of the Sun Day, Jul 3
Stress Awareness Day, Natl, Apr 16
Stress Awareness Month, Apr 1
Strike Out Strokes Month, May 1
Stroke Awareness Month, Natl, May 1
Stuttering Awareness Day, Intl, Oct 22
Stuttering Awareness Week, Natl, May 11
Successful Antirabies Inoculation, First: Anniv, Jul 6
Suicide Prevention Week, Natl, Sep 7
Tai Chi and Qigong Day, World, Apr 25
Take a New Year's Resolution to Stop Smoking, Dec 8

Talk About Prescriptions Month, Oct 1
Testicular Cancer Awareness Week, Apr 1
Test-Tube Baby: Birthday, Jul 25
Ultraviolet Awareness Month, May 1
Vegetarian Day, World, Oct 1
Vegetarian Month, Oct 1
Vision Research Month, Jun 1
Vitamin C Isolated: Anniv, Apr 4
Wear Red Day, Natl, Feb 6
Wheelchair Beautification Month, Natl, Jul 1
White Cane Safety Day (Pres Proc), Oct 15
Wise Health Care Consumer Month, Feb 1
Women's Eye Health and Safety Month, Apr 1
Women's Health and Fitness Day, Natl, Sep 30
Women's Health Care Month, May 1
Women's Healthy Weight Day, Jan 22
Women's Heart Week, Feb 1
Women's Nutrition Week, Natl, Apr 5
Workplace Eye Health and Safety Month, Mar 1
World AIDS Day (Pres Proc), Dec 1
World AIDS Day (UN), Dec 1
World Breastfeeding Week, Aug 1
World Food Day (UN), Oct 16
World Health Day (UN), Apr 7
World Lupus Day, May 10
World Mental Health Day (UN), Oct 10
World No-Tobacco Day (UN), May 31
World Red Cross Day, May 8
Young Child, Month of the (MI), Apr 1
Youth Sports Safety Month, Natl, Apr 1
Heard, John: Birth, Mar 7
Hearing and Speech Month, Better, May 1
Hearn, Lafcadio: Birth Anniv, Jun 27
Hearst, William R.: Birth Anniv, Apr 29
Heart Day, Natl Have-a-, Feb 14
Heart Month, American, Feb 1
Heart Month, American (Pres Proc), Feb 1
Heart: Atrial Fibrillation Month, Sep 1
Heart: Congenital Heart Defect Awareness Week, Feb 7
Heatherton, Joey: Birth, Sep 14
Heaton, Patricia: Birth, Mar 4
Hebron Massacre: Anniv, Feb 25
Heche, Anne: Birth, May 25
Hecht, Ben: Birth Anniv, Feb 28
Heckerling, Amy: Birth, May 7
Hedgehog Day, Feb 2
Hee Haw TV Premiere: Anniv, Jun 15
Hefner, Christie: Birth, Nov 8
Hefner, Hugh: Birth, Apr 9
Heiden, Eric: Birth, Jun 14
Heigl, Katherine: Birth, Nov 24
Heimlich Maneuver Introduced: Anniv, Jun 1
Heine, Heinrich: Birth Anniv, Dec 13
Heineman, Dave: Birth, May 12
Hejduk, Milan: Birth, Feb 14
Helfer, Tricia: Birth, Apr 11
Helgenberger, Marg: Birth, Nov 16
Hellman, Lillian: Birth Anniv, Jun 20
Hello Day, World, Nov 21
Hell's Angels: Altamont Concert: Anniv, Dec 6
Helmond, Katherine: Birth, Jul 5
Helms, Ed: Birth, Jan 24
Helms, Edgar J.: Birth Anniv, Jan 19
Heloise: Birth, Apr 15
Helston Furry Dance (Helston, Cornwall, England), May 8
Helton, Todd: Birth, Aug 20
Hemingway Birthday Celebration (Oak Park, IL), Jul 21
Hemingway, Ernest: Birth Anniv, Jul 21
Hemingway, Ernest: Boxing Day at Birthplace (Oak Park, IL), Dec 26
Hemingway, Mariel: Birth, Nov 22
Hemsley, Sherman: Birth, Feb 1
Henderson, Florence: Birth, Feb 14
Henderson, Rickey: Birth, Dec 25
Hendricks, Thomas A: Birth Anniv, Sep 17
Hendrix, Jimi: Birth Anniv, Nov 27
Henie, Sonja: Birth Anniv, Apr 8
Henin, Justine: Birth, Jun 1
Henley, Don: Birth, Jul 22
Henman, Tim: Birth, Sep 6
Henner, Marilu: Birth, Apr 6
Hennessy, Jill: Birth, Nov 25
Henried, Paul: Birth Anniv, Jan 10
Henriksen, Lance: Birth, May 5
Henry, Brad: Birth, Jul 10
Henry, Joseph: Birth Anniv, Dec 17
Henry, Justin: Birth, May 25
Henry, O. (William S. Porter): Birth Anniv, Sep 11
Henry, Patrick: Birth Anniv, May 29
Henry, Thierry: Birth, Aug 17
Henson, Jim: Birth Anniv, Sep 24
Henson, John: Birth, Jul 11
Henson, Matthew A.: Birth Anniv, Aug 8
Hentoff, Nat: Birth, Jun 10
Hepatitis Awareness Month, Natl, May 1
Hepburn, Audrey: Birth Anniv, May 4
Hepburn, Katharine: Birth Anniv, May 12
Herb Fest (Mattoon, IL), Apr 25
Herbal/Prescription Interaction Awareness Month, Jul 1
Herbert, Victor: Birth Anniv, Feb 1
Heritage Day Fest (Lavallette, NJ), Sep 12
Heritage Week (New Harmony, IN), Apr 21
Herman, Alexis: Birth, Jul 16
Herman, Jerry: Birth, Jul 10
Hermit, Robert the: Death Anniv, Apr 1
Hernandez, Keith: Birth, Oct 20
Hernandez, Orlando: Birth, Oct 11
Heroes: Inspirational Role Models Month, Natl, Nov 1
Herriman, George: Birth Anniv, Aug 22
Herriot, James: Birth Anniv, Oct 3
Herrmann, Edward: Birth, Jul 21
Hersey, John: Birth Anniv, Jun 17
Hersh, Seymour: Birth, Apr 8
Hershey, Barbara: Birth, Feb 5
Hershiser, Orel: Birth, Sep 16
Herzl, Theodor: Birth Anniv, May 20
Herzog, Chaim: Birth Anniv, Sep 17
Hess, Rudolf: Birth Anniv, Apr 26
Hesseman, Howard: Birth, Feb 27
Hester, Devin: Birth, Nov 4
Hewes, Joseph: Birth Anniv, Jan 23
Hewitt, Don: Birth, Dec 14
Hewitt, Jennifer Love: Birth, Feb 21
Hewitt, Lleyton: Birth, Feb 24
Heyerdahl, Thor: Birth Anniv, Oct 6
Heyward, Thomas: Birth Anniv, Jul 28
Hickman, Darryl: Birth, Jul 28
Hickman, Dwayne: Birth, May 18
Hickok, Wild Bill: Birth Anniv, May 27
Hicks, Catherine: Birth, Aug 6
Higgins, David Anthony: Birth, Dec 9
Higginson, Bobby: Birth, Aug 18
High Five Day, Natl, Apr 16
Highlights Foundation Writer's Workshop (Chautauqua, NY), Jul 11
Hightower, Jim: Birth, Jan 11
Highway Numbers Introduced: Anniv, Mar 2
Hijuelos, Oscar: Birth, Aug 24
Hill Street Blues TV Premiere: Anniv, Jan 15
Hill, Anita: Birth, Jul 30
Hill, Bernard: Birth, Dec 17
Hill, Dule: Birth, May 3
Hill, Faith: Birth, Sep 21
Hill, Grant: Birth, Oct 5
Hill, Lauryn: Birth, May 25
Hill, Mildred J.: Happy Birthday to "Happy Birthday to You," Jun 27
Hill, Patty Smith: Birth Anniv, Mar 27
Hill, Steven: Birth, Feb 24
Hillary, Sir Edmund: Birth Anniv, Jul 20
Hillary, Sir Edmund: Everest Summit Reached: Anniv, May 29
Hillerman, John: Birth, Dec 20
Hillman, Chris: Birth, Dec 4
Hilton, Paris: Birth, Feb 17
Hilton, Perez: Birth, Mar 23
Himes, Chester: Birth Anniv, Jul 29
Hinamatsuri (Japan), Mar 3
Hindenburg Disaster: Anniv, May 6
Hindu: Dasara (Vijaya Dasami), Sep 28
Hindu: Diwali, Oct 17
Hindu: Holi, Mar 11
Hindu: Krishna Janmashtami, Aug 14
Hines, Gregory: Birth Anniv, Feb 14
Hingis, Martina: Birth, Sep 30
Hinske, Eric: Birth, Aug 5
Hirohito, Emperor: Birth Anniv, Apr 29
Hirohito, Emperor: Death Anniv, Jan 7
Hiroshima Day, Aug 6
Hirsch, Emile: Birth, Mar 13
Hirsch, Judd: Birth, Mar 15
Hirschfeld, Al: Birth Anniv, Jun 21
Hispanic
Cabrillo Fest (San Diego, CA), Oct 3
Charro Days Fiesta (Brownsville, TX; Matamoros, Mexico), Feb 26
Cinco de Mayo (Mexico), May 5
Hispanic Heritage Month, Natl (Pres Proc), Sep 15
Latino Books Month, May 1
League of United Latin American Citizens (LULAC) Founded: Anniv, Feb 17
Maroone Hispanicfest (Hollywood, FL), Mar 28
Mexican Fiesta Internacional (Milwaukee, WI), Aug 21
Tucson Intl Mariachi Conf (Tucson, AZ), Apr 20
Zoot Suit Riots: Anniv, Jun 3
Historical Fest, Fort Sisseton (Lake City, SD), Jun 5
Historically Black Colleges and Universities Week, Natl (Pres Proc), Sep 13
Hitchcock, Alfred: Birth Anniv, Aug 13
Hitchcock, Alfred: Psycho Film Premiere: Anniv, Jun 16
Hite, Shere: Birth, Nov 2
Hitler Celebration, RAF Bombs: Anniv, Jan 30
Hitler Youth Deployed: Anniv, Jan 26
Hitler, Adolf: Birth Anniv, Apr 20
Hitler, Adolf: German Plebiscite: Anniv, Aug 19
Hitler, Adolf: Gersdorff Assassination Attempt: Anniv, Mar 21
Hitler, Adolf: Operation Flash: Anniv, Mar 13
HIV Testing Day, Natl, Jun 27
Ho Chi Minh: Birth Anniv, May 19
Ho, Don: Birth Anniv, Aug 19
Hoban, James: Death Anniv, Dec 8
Hobart, Garret A.: Birth Anniv, Jun 3

Hobbit Day, Sep 22
Hobo Convention, Natl (Britt, IA), Aug 6
Hockey (field, ice)
Hockey Mask Invented: Anniv, Nov 1
Miracle on Ice: US Team Defeats USSR: Anniv, Feb 22
NCAA Div I Field Hockey Chmpshp (Louisville, KY), Nov 20
NCAA Div I Men's Chmpshp (Washington, DC), Apr 9
Hockney, David: Birth, Jul 9
Hodge, Patricia: Birth, Sep 29
Hoeven, John: Birth, Mar 13
Hoffa, James: Disappearance Anniv, Jul 30
Hoffman, Abbie: Birth Anniv, Nov 30
Hoffman, Alice: Birth, Mar 16
Hoffman, Dustin: Birth, Aug 8
Hoffman, Mat: Birth, Jan 9
Hoffman, Philip Seymour: Birth, Jul 23
Hog Capital of the World Fest (Kewanee, IL), Sep 4
Hogan, Ben: Birth Anniv, Aug 13
Hogan, Hulk: Birth, Aug 11
Hogan, Paul: Birth, Oct 8
Hogarth, William: Birth Anniv, Nov 10
Hogeye Fest (Elgin, TX), Oct 24
Hogmanay (Scottish New Year), Dec 31
Hoiby, Lee: Birth, Feb 17
Holbrook, Hal: Birth, Feb 17
Holden, William: Birth Anniv, Apr 17
Holdsclaw, Chamique: Birth, Aug 9
Holi (India), Mar 11
Holiday Day, Make Up Your Own, Mar 26
Holiday, Billie: Birth Anniv, Apr 7
Holiday, First US by Pres Proc: Anniv, Nov 26
Holistic Pet Day, Natl, Aug 30
Holland Tunnel: Anniv, Nov 13
Holliday, Doc: Gunfight at the O.K. Corral: Anniv, Oct 26
Holliday, Polly: Birth, Jul 2
Holliger, Heinz: Birth, May 21
Hollings, Ernest F.: Birth, Jan 1
Holloway, Josh: Birth, Jul 20
Holly, Buddy. See Day the Music Died: Anniv, Feb 3
Holly, Buddy: Birth Anniv, Sep 7
Holly, Lauren: Birth, Oct 28
Hollyhock Fest (Kyoto, Japan), May 15
Hollywood Squares TV Premiere: Anniv, Oct 17
Holm, Celeste: Birth, Apr 29
Holm, Ian: Birth, Sep 12
Holmes, Katie: Birth, Dec 18
Holmes, Oliver W.: Birth Anniv, Aug 29
Holmes, Oliver Wendell: Old Ironsides Saved by Poem: Anniv, Sep 16
Holmes, Rupert: Birth, Feb 24
Holmgren, Mike: Birth, Jun 15
Holocaust Day (Israel), Apr 21
Holtz, Lou: Birth, Jan 6
Holy Humor Month, Apr 1
Holy Innocents Day, Dec 28
Holy See: National Holiday, Apr 24
Holy Thursday, Apr 9
Holy Week, Apr 5
Holyfield, Evander: Birth, Oct 19
Holyfield, Evander: Tyson Bites Holyfield: Anniv, Jun 28
Home Improvement Time, Apr 1
Home Improvement TV Premiere: Anniv, Sep 17
Home Office
Improve Your Home Office Day, Oct 5
Organize Your Home Office Day, Mar 10
Safety and Security Week, Jan 5
Work from Home Week, Natl, Oct 4
Home Owner's Day, New, May 1
Home Owners Loan Act: Anniv, Jun 13
Home Run Record: Anniv, Apr 8
Home Sewing Machine Patented: Anniv, Aug 12
Home Shows and Tours
Fest of Houses and Gardens (Charleston, SC), Mar 19
Galveston Historic Homes Tour (Galveston Island, TX), May 2
Holiday Tour of Homes (Natchitoches, LA), Dec 9
Home Furnishings Market, Intl (High Point, NC), Apr 27
Litchfield Open House Tour (Litchfield, CT), Jul 10
Maryland Home and Garden Show (Baltimore, MD), Mar 6
Natchez Spring Pilgrimage (Natchez, MS), Mar 7
Natchitoches Historic Pilgrimage (Natchitoches, LA), Oct 10
Original Massachusetts Home & Garden Show (West Springfield, MA), Mar 26
Quincy Preserves Fall Architectural Tour (Quincy, IL), Oct 17
Robie House Secrets & Shadows Tour (Chicago, IL), Oct 23
Savannah Tour of Homes and Gardens (Savannah, GA), Mar 26
Seashore Open House Tour (Loveladies, NJ), Aug 5
Spring Fest (Cape May, NJ), Apr 24
Stone House Day (Hurley, NY), Jul 11
Victorian Christmas Home Tour (Leadville, CO), Dec 4
Wright, Frank Lloyd: Wright Plus (Oak Park, IL), May 16
Yuma Home & Garden Show (Yuma, AZ), Jan 16
Home: Decorating Month, Natl, Apr 1
Home: Organize Your Home Day, Jan 12
Home-Based Business Week, Oct 11
Homebirth Week, Natl Unassisted, Jul 1
Homebrew Day, Natl, May 2
Homefest (Bald Knob, AR), May 7
Homeless Animals Day, Natl, Aug 15
Homer, Louise Dilworth: Birth Anniv, Apr 28
Homer, Winslow: Birth Anniv, Feb 24
Homestead Act: Anniv, May 20
Homestead Days (Beatrice, NE), Jun 16
Honda, Soichiro: Birth Anniv, Nov 17
Honduras
Dia De Las Americas, Apr 14
Francisco Morazan Holiday, Oct 3
Hurricane Mitch: Anniv, Oct 27
Independence Day, Sep 15
Honest Abe Awards: Natl Honesty Day, Apr 30
Honesty Day, Natl, Apr 30
Honey Month, Natl, Sep 1
Honeymoon, First Balloon: Anniv, Jun 20
Hong Kong
Britain Cedes Claim to: Anniv, Jun 30
Lease Anniv, Jun 9
Liberation Day, Aug 31
Honor Society Awareness Month, Mar 1
Hoodie-Hoo Day, Northern Hemisphere, Feb 20
Hooks, Jan: Birth, Apr 23
Hooks, Kevin: Birth, Sep 19
Hooks, Robert: Birth, Apr 18
Hooper, William: Birth Anniv, Jun 17
Hoover, Herbert: Birth Anniv, Aug 10
Hoover, Herbert: Day (IA), Aug 9
Hoover, J. Edgar: Birth Anniv, Jan 1
Hoover, Lou H.: Birth Anniv, Mar 29
Hopalong Cassidy TV Premiere: Anniv, Jun 24
Hope, Bob: Birth Anniv, May 29
Hope, Bob: Chrysler Golf Classic (Palm Springs, CA), Jan 19
Hope, Leslie: Birth, May 6
Hopkins, Bo: Birth, Feb 2
Hopkins, Sir Anthony: Birth, Dec 31
Hopkins, Stephen: Birth Anniv, Mar 7
Hopkins, Telma: Birth, Oct 28
Hopkinson, Francis: Birth Anniv, Sep 21
Hopkinton State Fair (Contoocook, NH), Sep 3
Hopper, Dennis: Birth, May 17
Hopper, Grace: Birth Anniv, Dec 9
Horn, Paul: Birth, Mar 17
Hornacek, John: Birth, May 3
Horne, Lena: Birth, Jun 30
Horne, Marilyn: Birth, Jan 16
Horowitz, Vladimir: Birth Anniv, Oct 1
Horrocks, Jane: Birth, Jan 18
Horseradish Month, Natl, Jul 1
Horses
Augusta Futurity (Augusta, GA), Jan 15
Badminton Horse Trials (Badminton, England), May 7
Belmont Stakes (Belmont Park, NY), Jun 6
Belmont Stakes, First Running of: Anniv, Jun 19
Bonnie Blue Natl Horse Show (Lexington, VA), May 14
Breeders' Cup (Arcadia, CA), Nov 6
Britt Draft Horse Show (Britt, IA), Sep 4
Celebration of the Horse (Houston, TX), Jul 18
Cheltenham Hunt Fest (Prestbury, England), Mar 10
Chincoteague Pony Penning (Chincoteague Island, VA), Jul 29
Day of the Horse, Natl, Dec 12
Derby, The (Epsom Downs, England), Jun 6
Farrier's Week, Natl, Jul 12
First Kentucky Derby: Anniv, May 17
Foxfield Races (Charlottesville, VA), Apr 25
Grand National (Liverpool, England), Apr 2
Iron Horse Outraced by Horse: Anniv, Sep 18
Kentucky Derby (Louisville, KY), May 2
Kentucky Derby Fest (Louisville, KY), Apr 17
Kentucky State Fair (Louisville, KY), Aug 20
Land Rover Burghley Horse Trials (Stamford, England), Sep 3
Masters (Calgary, AB, Canada), Sep 9
Melbourne Cup (Melbourne, Australia), Nov 3
Miles City Bucking Horse Sale (Miles City, MT), May 14
Missouri State Chmpshp Racking Horse Show (Dexter, MO), Jun 6
Natl Tourn (Calgary, AB, Canada), Jun 3
New Jersey State Fair/Sussex Farm and Horse Show (Augusta, NJ), Jul 31
North American Tournament (Calgary, AB, Canada), Jul 1
Palio (Siena, Italy), Jul 2
Pony Express, Inauguration of: Anniv, Apr 3

Preakness Stakes (Baltimore, MD), May 16
Preakness Stakes: Anniv, May 27
Prix de l'Arc de Triomphe (Paris, France), Oct 4
Royal Ascot (Ascot, Berkshire, England), Jun 16
Royal Windsor Horse Show (Windsor, England), May 14
Seabiscuit Defeats War Admiral: Anniv, Nov 1
Steeplechase at Callaway Gardens (Pine Mountain, GA), Nov 7
Strawberry Hill Races (Richmond, VA), Apr 11
Taylor Horsefest (Taylor, ND), Jul 25
Tennessee Walking Horse Natl Celebration (Shelbyville, TN), Aug 26
Virginia Gold Cup (Warrenton, VA), May 2
Whippoorwill Morgan Horse Open Barn (Old Lyme, CT), Oct 10
Whippoorwill Morgan Horse Versatility Event (Old Lyme, CT), Sep 12
Horseshoe Tourn, Head-of-the-Mon-River (Fairmont, WV), May 23
Horsley, Lee: Birth, May 15
Hoskins, Bob: Birth, Oct 26
Hospital Admitting Clerks Day, Apr 3
Hossa, Marian: Birth, Jan 12
Hostage Released, Last American: Anniv, Dec 4
Hostos, Eugenio Maria: Birth Anniv, Jan 11
Hot Dog Month, Natl, Jul 1
Hot Enough for Ya Day, Jul 23
Hot Springs Natl Park Established: Anniv, Mar 4
Hotter 'n Hell Hundred Bike Race (Wichita Falls, TX), Aug 27
Houdini, Harry: Birth Anniv, Mar 24
Houdini, Harry: Death Anniv, Oct 31
Houdini, Harry: Magic Day, Oct 31
Hounsou, Djimon: Birth, Apr 24
House Divided Speech: Anniv, Jun 16
House of Representatives, First Black Serves in: Anniv, Dec 12
House of Representatives, First Brawl: Anniv, Jan 30
House of Representatives, First Quorum: Anniv, Apr 1
Houseman, John: Birth Anniv, Sep 22
Houseplants: Take Your Houseplants for a Walk Day, Jul 27
Housework Day, No, Apr 7
Houston Marathon (Houston, TX), Jan 18
Houston, Sam: Birth Anniv, Mar 2
Houston, Whitney: Birth, Aug 9
Hovick, Rose L. (Gypsy Rose Lee): Birth Anniv, Feb 9
Howard, Curly: Birth Anniv, Oct 22
Howard, Dwight: Birth, Dec 8
Howard, Juwan: Birth, Feb 7
Howard, Ken: Birth, Mar 28
Howard, Leslie: Birth Anniv, Apr 3
Howard, Moe: Birth Anniv, Jun 19
Howard, Robert: Birth Anniv, Jan 22
Howard, Ron: Birth, Mar 1
Howard, Ryan: Birth, Nov 19
Howard, Shemp: Birth Anniv, Mar 17
Howard, Susan: Birth, Jan 28
Howard, Terrence: Birth, Mar 11
Howard, Traylor: Birth, Jun 14
Howard, Trevor: Birth Anniv, Sep 29
Howdy Doody TV Premiere: Anniv, Dec 27
Howe, Elias: Birth Anniv, Jul 9
Howe, Gordie: Birth, Mar 31
Howell, C. Thomas: Birth, Dec 7
Howes, Sally Ann: Birth, Jul 20
Hoyle, Edmond: Death Anniv, Aug 29
Hu, Kelly: Birth, Feb 13
Hubbard, Elbert: Birth Anniv, Jun 19
Hubbard, L. Ron: Birth Anniv, Mar 13
Hubble Space Telescope Deployed: Anniv, Apr 25
Hubble, Edwin Powell: Birth Anniv, Nov 20
Huck Finn's Jubilee (Victorville, CA), Jun 19
Huckabee, Mike: Birth, Aug 24
Hudgens, Vanessa: Birth, Dec 14
Hudson, Ernie: Birth, Dec 17
Hudson, Jennifer: Birth, Sep 12
Hudson, Kate: Birth, Apr 19
Huerta, Dolores: Birth, Apr 10
Huffington, Arianna: Birth, Jul 15
Huffman, Felicity: Birth, Dec 9
Hug an Australian Day, Apr 26
Hug Holiday Week, Natl, May 3
Hug Your Kids Day, Natl, Jul 20
Hugging Day, Natl, Jan 21
Hughes, Charles E.: Birth Anniv, Apr 11
Hughes, Finola: Birth, Oct 29
Hughes, Howard: Birth Anniv, Dec 24
Hughes, John: Birth, Feb 18
Hughes, Langston: Birth Anniv, Feb 1
Hughes, Sarah: Birth, May 2
Hughley, D.L.: Birth, Mar 6
Hugo, Victor: Birth Anniv, Feb 26
Hula Dancing: Merrie Monarch Fest & Hula Competition (Hilo, HI), Apr 12
Hula in the Coola Day, Feb 1
Hulce, Thomas: Birth, Dec 6
Hull House Opens: Anniv, Sep 18
Hull, Bobby: Birth, Jan 3
Hull, Brett: Birth, Aug 9
Hull, Cordell: Birth Anniv, Oct 2
Hull, John: First Mint in America: Anniv, Jun 10
Human Genome Mapped: Anniv, Jun 26
Human Relations. See also Romance
American Red Cross Founded: Anniv, May 21
Amnesty International Founded: Anniv, May 28
Awkward Moments Day, Mar 18
Be an Angel Day, Aug 22
Be Kind to Humankind Week, Aug 25
Black History Month, Natl, Feb 1
Blame Someone Else Day, Feb 13
Celebration of Life Day, Jan 22
Celibacy Awareness Month, Jun 1
Change Your Stars Month, Intl, Jan 1
Coaching Week, Intl, Feb 1
Compliment Day, Natl, Jan 24
Diversity Awareness Month, Global, Oct 1
Diversity Day, Natl, Oct 2
Diversity Month, Celebrate, Apr 1
Doghouse Repairs Month, Natl, Jul 1
Dyslexia Awareness Month, Oct 1
Emancipation Proclamation: Anniv, Sep 22
Eradication of Poverty, Intl Day for (UN), Oct 17
Ethics Awareness Month, Natl, Mar 1
First Natl Convention for Blacks: Anniv, Sep 15
First US Breach of Promise Suit: Anniv, Jun 14
Fourteen Points Proposed: Anniv, Jan 8
Get Out of the Doghouse Day, Natl, Jul 20
Good Samaritan Involvement Day, Mar 13
Great American Grump Out, May 6
High Five Day, Natl, Apr 16
Honesty Day, Natl, Apr 30
Hug Holiday Week, Natl, May 3
Human Rights Day (Pres Proc), Dec 10
Human Rights Day (UN), Dec 10
Human Rights Week (Pres Proc), Dec 10
I Want You to Be Happy Day, Mar 3
Joygerm Day, Natl, Jan 8
Kindness Day, World, Nov 13
Kiss-and-Make-Up Day, Aug 25
League of Nations: Anniv, Jan 10
Lumpy Rug Day, May 3
Moment of Laughter Day, Intl, Apr 14
Networking Week, Intl, Feb 2
New Friends, Old Friends Week, Intl, May 17
One-on-One Month, Sep 1
Peace Corps Founded: Anniv, Mar 1
People Skills Month, Intl, Sep 1
Positive Attitude Month, Oct 1
Poverty in America Awareness Month, Natl, Jan 1
Quality of Life Month, Intl, Jan 1
Race Relations Day, Feb 14
Race Unity Day, Jun 14
Ralph Bunche Awarded Nobel Peace Prize: Anniv, Dec 10
Reconciliation Day, Apr 2
Red Cross Day, World, May 8
Religion Day, World, Jan 18
Right-Brainers Rule Month, Oct 1
Salvation Army Founder's Day, Apr 10
Salvation Army in US: Anniv, Mar 10
Senior Independence Month, Natl, Feb 1
Social Justice, World Day for (UN), Feb 20
Spring Fever Week, Natl, Mar 16
Swap Ideas Day, Sep 10
Sweetest Day, Oct 17
Teen Self-Esteem Month, May 1
Toad Hollow Day of Encouragement, Jan 26
Toad Hollow Week, Natl, Mar 14
Turn Beauty Inside Out Day, May 20
Universal Hour of Peace, Dec 31
World Day of Prayer, Mar 6
World Hello Day, Nov 21
World Smile Day, Oct 2
Worldwide Renaissance of the Heart Month, Feb 1
Write a Letter of Appreciation Week, Natl, Mar 1
Year of Human Rights Learning, Intl (UN), Jan 1
Human Spirit Day, World, Feb 17
Humane Society of the US: Anniv, Nov 22
Humanist Day, World, Jun 21
Humanitarian Day, Jan 15
HumanLight Celebration, Dec 23
Humbug Day, Dec 21
Hummel, Sister Maria Innocentia: Birth Anniv, May 21
Humor, Comedy
Abet and Aid Punsters Day, Nov 8
Alascattalo Day (Anchorage, AK), Nov 21
A'phabet Day, Dec 25
Belly Laugh Day, Jan 24
Bubba Day, Natl, Jun 2
Chicago Sketch Comedy Fest (Chicago, IL), Jan 8
Fun Day, Natl, Apr 1
Gaines, William M.: Birth Anniv, Mar 1
Holy Humor Month, Apr 1
Humor Month, Natl, Apr 1
Humorists Are Artists Month (HAAM), Mar 1
Just for Laughs Fest (Montreal, QC, Canada), Jul 16

Kurtzman, Harvey: Birth Anniv, Oct 3
Laugh at Work Week, Apr 1
Laugh-Friendly Month, Natl, Feb 1
Loosen Up, Lighten Up Day, Nov 14
Love May Make World Go 'Round, but Laughter Keeps Us from Getting Dizzy Week, Feb 8
Mirth Month, Intl, Mar 1
Moment of Laughter Day, Intl, Apr 14
O. Henry Museum Pun-Off (Austin, TX), May 16
Play Days, Sep 8
SCUD Day, Jul 8
Someday We'll Laugh About This Week, Jan 2
Tell an Old Joke Day, Natl, Jul 24
TWIT Award Month, Intl, Apr 1
Humperdinck, Engelbert: Birth, May 3
Humphrey, Hubert: Birth Anniv, May 27
Humphrey, Terin: Birth, Aug 14
Humphries, Barry: Birth, Feb 17
Hungary
Anniv of 1848 Revolution, Mar 15
Anniv of 1956 Revolution, Oct 23
Declares Independence: Anniv, Oct 23
Republic Day, Oct 23
Saint Stephen's Day, Aug 20
Hunger: Food Bank Week, Natl, Oct 11
Hungerford, Margaret Wolfe: The Duchess Who Wasn't Day, Aug 27
Hunnicutt, Gayle: Birth, Feb 6
Hunt, Bonnie: Birth, Sep 22
Hunt, Helen: Birth, Jun 15
Hunt, Lamar: Birth Anniv, Aug 2
Hunt, Linda: Birth, Apr 2
Hunter, Catfish: Birth Anniv, Apr 8
Hunter, David: Hunter Frees the Slaves: Anniv, May 9
Hunter, Holly: Birth, Mar 20
Hunter, Rachel: Birth, Sep 9
Hunter, Tab: Birth, Jul 11
Hunter-Gault, Charlayne: Birth, Feb 27
Hunter's Moon, Oct 4
Hunters' Moon, Feast of (Lafayette, IN), Oct 10
Hunting and Fishing Day, Natl (Pres Proc), Sep 26
Hunting: Cheltenham Hunt Fest (Prestbury, England), Mar 10
Hunting: One Arm Dove Hunt (Olney, TX), Sep 11
Huntington, Samuel: Birth Anniv, Jul 3
Huntington's Disease Awareness Month, May 1
Huntsman, John, Jr: Birth, Mar 26
Huppert, Isabelle: Birth, Mar 16
Hurley, Elizabeth: Birth, Jun 10
Hurricanes, Tornados, Cyclones, Typhoons
Atlantic, Caribbean and Gulf Hurricane Season, Jun 1
Central Pacific Hurricane Season, Jun 1
Eastern Pacific Hurricane Season, May 15
Galveston, TX: Anniv, Sep 8
Hurricane Agnes: Anniv, Jun 21
Hurricane Hugo Hits American Coast: Anniv, Sep 21
Hurricane Mitch: Anniv, Oct 27
Hurricane Supplication Day (Virgin Islands), Jul 27
Hurricane Thanksgiving Day (Virgin Islands), Oct 19
Katrina Strikes Gulf Coast: Anniv, Aug 29
Port Royal (Jamaica) Hurricane: Anniv, Aug 28
Southern Cyclone: Anniv, Aug 24
Texas Panhandle Tornado: Anniv, Apr 9
Western Pacific Hurricane Season, Jan 1
Hurston, Zora Neale: Birth Anniv, Jan 7
Hurston, Zora: Zora Neale Hurston Fest (Eatonville, FL), Jan 20
Hurt, John: Birth, Jan 22
Hurt, Mary Beth: Birth, Sep 26
Hurt, William: Birth, Mar 20
Hus, John: Commemoration Day (Czech Republic), Jul 6
Husband Caregiver Day, Jun 15
Husky, Ferlin: Birth, Dec 3
Hussein, King of Jordan: Birth Anniv, Nov 14
Hussein, Saddam: Birth Anniv, Apr 28
Hussein, Saddam: Operation Iraqi Freedom: Anniv, Mar 19
Hussey, Olivia: Birth, Apr 17
Huston, Anjelica: Birth, Jul 8
Huston, John: Birth Anniv, Aug 5
Hutchins, Robert Maynard: Birth Anniv, Jan 17
Hutchinson, Anne: Memorial Day (Portsmouth, RI), Jul 19
Hutchison, Kay Bailey: Birth, Jul 22
Hutton, Lauren: Birth, Nov 17
Hutton, Timothy: Birth, Aug 16
Huxley, Aldous: Birth Anniv, Jul 26
Huygens, Christiaan: Birth Anniv, Apr 14
Hynde, Chrissie: Birth, Sep 7
Hyneman, Jamie: Birth, Sep 25
Hypnotism Day, World, Jan 4

I

I Love Lucy TV Premiere: Anniv, Oct 15
I Need a Patch for That Day, May 21
I Spy TV Premiere: Anniv, Sep 15
I Want You to Be Happy Day, Mar 3
Iacocca, Lee: Birth, Oct 15
IBM PC Introduced: Anniv, Aug 12
Ibsen, Henrik: Birth Anniv, Mar 20
Ice Cream Cone: Anniv, Sep 22
Ice Cream Day, Natl, Jul 19
Ice Cream Fest, Old-Fashioned (Utica, OH), May 23
Ice Cream Social (Indianapolis, IN), Jul 4
Ice Fest (Ligonier, PA), Jan 24
Ice Fishing Derby (Fort Peck, MT), Feb 21
Ice T: Birth, Feb 16
Iced Tea Month, Natl, Jun 1
Iceland
August Holiday, Aug 3
Beer Day, Mar 1
Bun Day, Feb 23
Bursting Day, Feb 24
First Day of Summer, Apr 23
Independence Day, Jun 17
Laki Volcano Eruption: Anniv, Jun 8
Leif Erikson Day, Oct 9
University Students' Celebration, Dec 1
Iceman Mummy Discovered: Anniv, Sep 19
Idaho
Admission Day, Jul 3
Coeur d'Alene Indian Pilgrimage (Cataldo), Aug 15
Craig, Larry E.: Birth, Jul 20
Crapo, Michael: Birth, May 20
Eastern Idaho State Fair (Blackfoot), Sep 5
Fest at Sandpoint (Sandpoint), Aug 6
Lionel Hampton Jazz Fest (Moscow), Feb 25
Lost in the '50s (Sandpoint), May 14
NAIA Baseball World Series (Lewiston), May 22
Old-Time Fiddlers' Contest and Fest, Natl (Weiser), Jun 22
Otter, Butch: Birth, May 3
Simplot Games (Pocatello), Feb 19
Snake River Stampede (Nampa), Jul 14
Special Olympics World Winter Games (Boise), Feb 6
Western Idaho Fair (Boise), Aug 14
Winter Games of Idaho, Jan 30
Ideas Month, Intl, Mar 1
Ides of March, Mar 15
Iditarod Trail Sled Dog Race (Anchorage, AK), Mar 7
Idle, Eric: Birth, Mar 29
Idol, Billy: Birth, Nov 30
Ifans, Rhys: Birth, Jul 22
Ig Nobel Prize Ceremony (Cambridge, MA), Oct 1
Iglesias, Enrique: Birth, May 8
Iglesias, Julio: Birth, Sep 23
Ilitch, Mike: Birth, Jul 20
Illinden: Saint Elias Day: Macedonian Uprising: Anniv, Aug 2
Illinois
Admission Day, Dec 3
American Assn for the Advancement of Science Mtg (Chicago), Feb 12
American Library Assn Conf (Chicago), Jul 9
Arcola Broom Corn Fest (Arcola), Sep 11
Arts/Quincy Riverfest (Quincy), Sep 20
Bank of America Chicago Marathon (Chicago), Oct 11
Bark in the Park (Chicago), May 2
Blagojevich, Rod: Birth, Dec 10
Blues on the Fox (Aurora), Jun 12
Bon Odori Fest of Lanterns (Chicago), Jul 11
Boxing Day at the Hemingway Birthplace (Oak Park), Dec 26
Bud Billiken Parade (Chicago), Aug 8
Burgoo Fest (Utica), Oct 11
Carillon Fest, Intl (Springfield), May 31
Chicago Blues Fest (Chicago), Jun 11
Chicago Golf Club: Anniv, Jul 18
Chicago Intl Film Fest (Chicago), Oct 8
Chicago Sketch Comedy Fest (Chicago), Jan 8
Chocolate Fest (Galesburg), Feb 14
Christmas Walk and House Tour (Geneva), Dec 4
City of Chicago Incorporated: Anniv, Mar 4
Clarence Darrow Death Commemoration (Chicago), Mar 13
Columbian Exposition Opening: Anniv, May 1
Council of Supply Chain Mgmt Professionals Annual Conf (Chicago), Sep 20
Durbin, Richard J.: Birth, Nov 21
Ethnic Fest (Oak Park), May 2
Fest of the Vine (Geneva), Sep 11
Festival of the Sugar Maples (Marengo), Mar 7
Fourth of July Patriotic Concert & Fireworks (Aurora), Jul 4
Freedom Fest (Mahomet), Jul 4
Friends of Lake Forest Library Book Sale (Lake Forest), Sep 18
Galesburg Railroad Days (Galesburg), Jun 27
Gay and Lesbian Pride Parade (Chicago), Jun 28
Geneva Arts Fair (Geneva), Jul 25
Ginza Holiday: Japanese Cultural Fest (Chicago), Aug 7
Great Chicago Flood: Anniv, Apr 13

Great River Tug Fest (Port Byron), Aug 7
Groundhog Days (Woodstock), Jan 29
Gymnastics Chmpshps, Big Ten Women's (Champaign-Urbana), Mar 21
Harold Washington Elected Chicago's First Black Mayor: Anniv, Apr 11
Harvard Milk Days Fest (Harvard), Jun 5
Haymarket Pardon: Anniv, Jun 26
Haymarket Square Riot: Anniv, May 4
Hemingway Birthday Celebration (Oak Park), Jul 21
Herb Fest (Mattoon), Apr 25
Herrinfesta Italiana (Herrin), May 21
Hog Capital of the World Fest (Kewanee), Sep 4
Holiday Magic (Aurora), Nov 27
Horseradish Fest (Collinsville), Jun 13
Illinois Snow Sculpting Competition (Rockford), Jan 21
Illinois State Fair (Springfield), Aug 14
Jane Addams Day, Dec 10
Jubilee Days Fest (Zion), Sep 5
Knox County Scenic Drive (Galesburg), Oct 3
Lincoln-Douglas Debates: Anniv, Aug 21
Lockport Old Canal Days (Lockport), Jun 20
Marigold Fest (Pekin), Sep 11
Memorial Day Parade (Aurora), May 25
Morton Pumpkin Fest (Morton), Sep 9
NAIA Men's Golf Natl Chmpshps (Moline), May 19
NJCAA Div II Men's Natl Basketball Finals (Danville), Mar 18
Obama, Barack: Birth, Aug 4
On the Waterfront (Rockford), Sep 4
Original Raggedy Ann & Andy Fest (Arcola), Jun 13
Pec Thing (Pecatonica), May 16
Quincy Preserves Christmas Candlelight Tour (Quincy), Dec 13
Quincy Preserves Fall Architectural Tour (Quincy), Oct 17
Radiological Soc of North America Scientific Assembly and Annual Mtg (Chicago), Nov 29
Robie House Secrets & Shadows Tour (Chicago), Oct 23
Roger Ebert's Film Fest (Champaign), Apr 22
Scarecrow Fest (St. Charles), Oct 9
Special Kids Day (Elmhurst), Dec 2
Spoon River Valley Scenic Drive (Lewistown), Oct 3
Stearman Fly-In Days, Natl (Galesburg), Sep 7
Superman Celebration (Metropolis), Jun 11
Swedish Days (Geneva), Jun 23
Sweetcorn Fest, Natl (Hoopeston), Sep 3
Trail of History (Ringwood), Oct 17
Turtle Races (Danville), Jun 13
USGA Senior Amateur (Golf) Chmpshp (Chicago), Sep 12
Victorian Christmas Tours at Frank Lloyd Wright Home (Oak Park), Dec 12
World Chmpshp Old-Time Piano Playing Contest (Peoria), May 22
WorldFuture 2009 (Chicago), Jul 17
Wright, Frank Lloyd: Wright Plus (Oak Park), May 16
I'm Not Going to Take It Anymore Day, Jan 7
Image Week, Build a Better, Sep 20
Iman: Birth, Jul 25
Imbolc, Feb 2
Immaculate Conception, Feast of, Dec 8
Immigrants' Day (Canada), May 22
Immigration: Ellis Island Opened: Anniv, Jan 1
Immunization Awareness Month, Natl, Aug 1
Impeachment: Clinton Proceedings: Anniv, Dec 20
Impeachment: Johnson Proceedings: Anniv, Feb 24
Impeachment: Senate Acquits Clinton: Anniv, Feb 12
Imperioli, Michael: Birth, Jan 1
Imus, Don: Birth, Jul 23
Imus, Don: Imus in the Morning Radio Premiere: Anniv, Dec 2
In Living Color TV Premiere: Anniv, Apr 15
Inaba, Carrie Ann: Birth, Jan 5
Inane Answering Message Day, Jan 30
Inauguration Day, Jan 20
Inauguration Day Public Holiday Observance, Jan 20
Inauguration Day, Old, Mar 4
Incandescent Lamp Demonstarted: Anniv, Oct 21
Income Tax Birthday, Feb 3
Income Tax Due Date, Quarterly Estimated Federal, Jan 15
Income Tax Due Date, Quarterly Estimated Federal, Apr 15
Income Tax Due Date, Quarterly Estimated Federal, Jun 15
Income Tax Due Date, Quarterly Estimated Federal, Sep 15
Income Tax Pay Day, Apr 15
Income Tax: Anniv, Mar 8
Inconvenience Yourself Day, Feb 25
Incredible Hulk TV Premiere: Anniv, Mar 10
Indelicato, Mark: Birth, Jul 16
Independence Day (Russia), Jun 12
Independence Day, US (Fourth of July)
Aalborg and Rebild Fest (Aalborg and Rebild, Denmark), Jul 2
Boom Box Parade (Willimantic, CT), Jul 4
Bristol Civic, Military/Firemen's Parade (Bristol, RI), Jul 4
Calithumpian Parade (Biwabik, MN), Jul 4
Dam Experience (Warsaw, MO), Jul 4
Declaration of Independence Approval and Signing: Anniv, Jul 4
Firestorm (Altoona, PA), Jul 4
Fireworks Celebration (Demopolis, AL), Jul 4
Fourth of July Celebration (Hettinger, ND), Jul 3
Fourth of July Fireworks (Mackinaw City, MI), Jul 4
Fourth of July Patriotic Concert & Fireworks (Aurora, IL), Jul 4
Freedom Days (Farmington, NM), Jul 2
Freedom Fest (Mahomet, IL), Jul 4
Hometown Family Fourth (Hollywood, FL), Jul 4
Independence Extravaganza Weekend (Lavallette, NJ), Jul 5
July Fourth Celebration & Anvil Shoot (Clinton, TN), Jul 4
Liberty Celebration (Yorktown, VA), Jul 4
Mount Rushmore Independence Day Celebration (Mount Rushmore, SD), Jul 3
Mystic Seaport Independence Day Celebration (Mystic, CT), Jul 4
Old Vermont Fourth (Woodstock, VT), Jul 4
Red, White & Boom (Columbus, OH), Jul 3
Independence Sunday (IA), Jun 28
Independence-from-Meat Day, Jul 4
India
Bhopal Poison Gas Disaster: Anniv, Dec 3
Children's Day, Nov 14
Dasara (Vijaya Dasami), Sep 28
Deepavali (Diwali), Oct 17
Gandhi, Mohandas: Assassination Anniv, Jan 30
Gandhi, Mohandas: Birth Anniv, Oct 2
Gandhi, Mohandas: Makes Salt: Anniv, Apr 6
Guru Nanak's Birth Anniv, Nov 2
Holi, Mar 11
Independence Day, Aug 15
Indian Earthquake: Anniv, Jan 26
Krishna Janmashtami, Aug 14
New Year's Day, Mar 22
Rajiv Gandhi Assassinated: Anniv, May 21
Republic Day, Jan 26
Vaisakhi, Apr 13
Indian Ocean Earthquake and Tsunamis: Anniv, Dec 26
Indian Saint, First: Anniv, Jul 31
Indiana
Admission Day, Dec 11
Bayh, Evan: Birth, Dec 26
Benjamin Harrison Day (Indianapolis), Mar 4
Benjamin Harrison's Birthday Celebration (Indianapolis), Aug 20
Big Ten Men's Basketball Tourn (Indianapolis), Mar 12
Big Ten Men's Swimming/Diving Chmpshps (West Lafayette), Feb 26
Big Ten Women's Basketball Tourn (Indianapolis), Mar 5
Big Ten Women's Golf Chmpshps (West Lafayette), Apr 24
Big Ten Women's Indoor Track/Field Chmpshps (Bloomington), Feb 28
Big Whopper Liar's Contest (New Harmony), Sep 19
Circus City Fest (Peru), Jul 11
Crawfordsville Strawberry Fest (Crawfordsville), Jun 12
Daniels, Mitchell: Birth, Apr 7
Elwood Glass Fest (Elwood), Aug 21
Fairmount Fest/Remembering James Dean (Fairmount), Sep 24
Family Christmas at Benjamin Harrison Home (Indianapolis), Dec 12
Feast of the Hunters' Moon (Lafayette), Oct 10
Fishing Has No Boundaries (Monticello), May 16
Fulton County Historical Power Show (Rochester), Jun 19
Ghost Tales of the Civil War (Indianapolis), Oct 16
Heritage Week (New Harmony), Apr 21
Ice Cream Social (Indianapolis), Jul 4
Indiana Flower and Patio Show (Indianapolis), Mar 14
Indy 500-Mile Race (Indianapolis), May 24
James Dean Birthday Celebration (Fairmount), Feb 7
Johnny Appleseed Fest (Fort Wayne), Sep 19
Lugar, Richard G.: Birth, Apr 4
Mississinewa 1812 (Marion), Oct 2

No-Tillage Conference, Natl (Indianapolis), Jan 14
Parke County Covered Bridge Fest (Rockville), Oct 9
Parke County Maple Fair (Rockville), Feb 21
Popcorn Fest (Valparaiso), Sep 12
Presidents' Day: Live from Delaware St (Indianapolis), Feb 16
Primary Day: Live from Delaware St (Indianapolis), May 5
Redbud Trail Rendezvous (Rochester), Apr 25
Spirits in HarmonIE (New Harmony), Nov 28
State Fair (Indianapolis), Aug 7
Trail of Courage Living-History Fest (Rochester), Sep 19
US Senior Open (Golf) Chmpshp (Carmel), Jul 30
Wicket World of Croquet (Indianapolis), Jun 13
Indiana, Robert: Birth, Sep 13
Indianapolis 500: Anniv, May 30
Indianapolis Sunk: Anniv, Jul 29
Indivisible Day, Jul 4
Indonesia
Independence Day, Aug 17
Kartini Day, Apr 21
Indoor Air: Care About Your Indoor Air Month, Natl, Feb 1
Industrial Workers of the World (IWW) Founded: Anniv, Jun 27
Infertility Survival Day, Natl, May 3
Informed Woman Month, Apr 1
Ingels, Marty: Birth, Mar 9
Ingersoll Day (Robert Green Ingersoll), Aug 11
Ingram, James: Birth, Feb 16
Inhofe, James M.: Birth, Nov 17
Inkster, Juli: Birth, Jun 24
Inn: Country Inn, Bed-and-Breakfast Day, Oct 4
Innergize Day, Sep 23
Innes, Laura: Birth, Aug 16
Inouye, Daniel: Birth, Sep 7
Insects: Carpenter Ant Awareness Week, Jun 21
Inspirational News Week, Natl, Apr 19
Inspire Your Heart with the Arts Day, Jan 31
Insulin First Isolated: Anniv, Jul 27
Intergeneration Day, Oct 4
Internal Audit Awareness Month, Intl, May 1
Internet Created: Anniv, Oct 29
Interstate Highway System Born: Anniv, Jun 29
Interstate Mullet Toss (Orange Beach, AL; Pensacola, FL), Apr 24
Intimate Apparel Market Week, Feb 2
Invention: Kid Inventors' Day, Jan 17
Inventors Congress, Minnesota (Redwood Falls, MN), Jun 12
Inventors Hall of Fame, Woman Inducted into: Anniv, May 18
Inventors' Month, Natl, Aug 1
Iowa
Admission Day, Dec 28
Bald Eagle Appreciation Days (Keokuk), Jan 16
Bell Tower Fest (Jefferson), Jun 12
Big Ten Men's and Women's Outdoor Track/Field Chmpshps (Iowa City), May 15
Bike Van Buren (Van Buren County), Aug 15
Bix Beiderbecke Memorial Jazz Fest (Davenport), Jul 23
Britt Draft Horse Show (Britt), Sep 4
Burlington Steamboat Days/Music Fest (Burlington), Jun 16
Christmas in the Villages (Van Buren County), Dec 5
Civil War Reenactment (Keokuk), Apr 24
Culver, Chet: Birth, Jan 1
Donna Reed Performing Arts Fest (Denison), Jun 15
Farm Toy Show, Natl (Dyersville), Nov 6
Glenn Miller Birthplace Society Fest (Clarinda), Jun 11
Grant Wood Art Fest (Anamosa), Jun 14
Grassley, Charles: Birth, Sep 17
Great River Tug Fest (LeClaire), Aug 7
Harkin, Thomas R.: Birth, Nov 19
Herbert Hoover Day, Aug 9
Hobo Convention, Natl (Britt), Aug 6
Independence Sunday, Jun 28
Iowa Storytelling Fest (Clear Lake), Jul 24
Jule Fest (Elk Horn), Nov 27
NAIA Div II Women's Basketball Chmpshp (Sioux City), Mar 11
NAIA Women's Natl Volleyball Chmpshp (Sioux City), Nov 21
NAIA Wrestling Chmpshps (Sioux City), Mar 5
Old Threshers Reunion (Mount Pleasant), Sep 3
Old-Time Country Music Contest, Fest & Expo, Natl (Le Mars), Aug 31
Perry's "BRR" (Bike Ride to Rippey) (Perry), Feb 7
Quad City Air Show (Davenport), Jun 13
RAGBRAI—Register's Bicycle Ride Across Iowa (Des Moines), Jul 19
Scenic Drive Fest (Van Buren County), Oct 10
State Fair, Iowa (Des Moines), Aug 13
Summer Farm Toy Show (Dyersville), Jun 5
Ten Thousand Crestonians (Creston), Jul 3
Tivoli Fest (Elk Horn), May 23
Iowa, Explosion on USS: Anniv, Apr 19
iPod Unveiled: Anniv, Oct 23
Iran
Fifteenth of Khordad, Jun 5
Iran Air Flight 655 Disaster: Anniv, Jul 3
Iran-Iraq War: Anniv, Sep 22
Islamic Republic Day, Apr 1
Khomeini: Death Anniv, Jun 3
Natl Day of Oil, Mar 19
New Year (Noruz), Mar 21
Seizure of US Embassy: Anniv, Nov 4
Tehran Conference: Anniv, Nov 28
Victory of Islamic Revolution, Feb 11
Yalda, Dec 21
Iran Hostages: US Attempt to Free: Anniv, Apr 24
Iraq
Baghdad Stampede: Anniv, Aug 31
Congress Authorized Force Against Iraq: Anniv, Jan 12
Desert Shield: Anniv, Aug 7
Ground War Against Iraq Begins: Anniv, Feb 23
Gulf War Begins: Anniv, Jan 16
Iran-Iraq War: Anniv, Sep 22
Iraq Invades Kuwait: Anniv, Aug 2
National Day, Apr 9
Operation Iraqi Freedom: Anniv, Mar 19
Ireland
Bank Holiday, Aug 5
Bank Holiday, Jun 3
Bloomsday: Anniv, Jun 16
Day of the Wren, Dec 26
Easter Rising, Apr 24
Ivy Day, Oct 6
May Day Bank Holiday, May 4
National Day, Mar 17
October Bank Holiday, Oct 26
Saint Stephen's Day, Dec 26
Ireland, Kathy: Birth, Mar 8
Ireland, Patricia: Birth, Oct 19
Irish-American Heritage Month, Mar 1
Iron Curtain Speech: Anniv, Mar 5
Irons, Jeremy: Birth, Sep 19
Ironside TV Premiere: Anniv, Sep 14
Iroquois Arts Fest (Howes Cave, NY), Sep 5
Irrational Exuberance Enters Lexicon: Anniv, Dec 5
Irrigation: Smart Irrigation Month, Jul 1
Irving, Amy: Birth, Sep 10
Irving, Clifford: Fake Howard Hughes Biography: Anniv, Jan 9
Irving, John: Birth, Mar 2
Irving, Washington: Birth Anniv, Apr 3
Irwin Earns First Medal of Honor: Anniv, Feb 13
Irwin, Bill: Birth, Apr 11
Irwin, Hale S.: Birth, Jun 3
Isaak, Chris: Birth, Jun 26
Isakson, Johnny: Birth, Dec 28
Isherwood, Christopher: Birth Anniv, Aug 26
Ishii, Kazuhiro: Birth, Sep 9
Ising, Rudolf C.: Birth Anniv, Aug 7
Isle of Man: Tourist Trophy, May 30
Isle of Man: Tynwald Day, Jul 6
Isle Royale Natl Park Established: Anniv, Apr 3
Isozaki, Arata: Birth, Jul 23
Isra al Mi'raj: Ascent of Prophet Muhammad, Jul 19
Israel
Arafat Returns to Palestine: Anniv, Jul 1
Camp David Accord Signed: Anniv, Mar 26
Completes Gaza Pullout: Anniv, Sep 12
Hashoah/Holocaust Day, Apr 21
Hebron Massacre: Anniv, Feb 25
Independence Day (Yom Ha'atzma'ut), Apr 29
Israeli Siege of Suez City Ends: Anniv, Jan 28
Jerusalem Day (Yom Yerushalayim), May 22
Remembrance Day (Yom Ha'zikkaron), Apr 28
Israeli Olympiad Massacre: Anniv, Sep 5
Issaquah Salmon Days Fest (Issaquah, WA), Oct 3
It Happened One Night Film Release: Anniv, Feb 22
It Takes a Thief TV Premiere: Anniv, Jan 9
Italian Heritage Fest, West Virginia (Clarksburg, WV), Sep 4
Italy
Battle of San Pietro Anniv, Dec 15
Calabria Earthquake: Anniv, Dec 16
Calcio Fiorentino (Florence), Jun 24
Carnival Week (Milan), Feb 22
Epiphany Fair (Rome), Jan 5
Explosion of the Cart (Florence), Apr 12
Feast of the Incappucciati (Gradoli), Feb 19
Feast of the Redeemer (Venice), Jul 19
Federation of Library Assns Annual Conf, Intl (Milan), Aug 23

Fest of St. Efisio (Cagliari), May 1
Gioco Del Ponte (Pisa), Jun 7
Giostra della Quintana (Foligno), Sep 13
Historical Regatta (Venice), Sep 6
Joust of the Quintana (Ascoli/Piceno), Aug 2
Joust of the Saracen (Arezzo), Sep 6
La Befana, Jan 6
Liberation Day, Apr 25
Monte Cassino Bombed: Anniv, Feb 15
Mussolini Ousted: Anniv, Jul 25
Palio (Siena), Jul 2
Palio Dei Balestrieri (Gubbio), May 31
Palio del Golfo (La Spezia), Aug 9
Procession of Addolorata and Mysteries (Taranto), Apr 9
Purgatory Banquet (Gradoli), Feb 25
Republic Day, Jun 2
Stresa Fest (Stresa), Aug 21
Victory Day, Nov 4
Wedding of the Sea (Venice), May 24
It's a Wonderful Life Film Premiere: Anniv, Dec 20
It's About Time Week, Dec 25
Ivanek, Zeljko: Birth, Aug 15
I've Got a Secret TV Premiere: Anniv, Jun 19
Iverson, Allen: Birth, Jun 7
Iverson, Johnathan Lee: Birth, Jan 30
Ives, Burl: Birth Anniv, Jun 14
Ivey, Judith: Birth, Sep 4
Ivy Day (Ireland), Oct 6
Iwo Jima Day: Anniv, Feb 23
Izzard, Eddie: Birth, Feb 7

J

Jack Benny Program TV Premiere: Anniv, Oct 28
Jack the Ripper Letter: Anniv, Sep 27
Jackie Mayer Rehab Day (Sandusky, OH), Oct 6
Jackman, Hugh: Birth, Oct 12
Jackson, Andrew: Battle of New Orleans: Anniv, Jan 8
Jackson, Andrew: Birth Anniv, Mar 15
Jackson, Anne: Birth, Sep 3
Jackson, Bo: Birth, Nov 30
Jackson, Glenda: Birth, May 9
Jackson, Jackie: Birth, May 4
Jackson, Janet: Birth, May 16
Jackson, Jermaine: Birth, Dec 11
Jackson, Jesse: Birth, Oct 8
Jackson, Joe: Birth, Aug 11
Jackson, Jonathan: Birth, May 11
Jackson, Joshua: Birth, Jun 11
Jackson, Kate: Birth, Oct 29
Jackson, Mahalia: Birth Anniv, Oct 26
Jackson, Marlon: Birth, Mar 12
Jackson, Michael: Birth, Aug 29
Jackson, Peter: Birth, Oct 31
Jackson, Phil: Birth, Sep 17
Jackson, Rachel D.: Birth Anniv, Jun 15
Jackson, Randy: Birth, Jun 23
Jackson, Randy: Birth, Oct 29
Jackson, Reggie: Birth, May 18
Jackson, Samuel L.: Birth, Dec 21
Jackson, Shirley Ann: Birth, Aug 6
Jackson, Stonewall: Birthday Celebration, Jan 21
Jackson, Stonewall: Lee-Jackson Day, Jan 16
Jackson, Thomas J. "Stonewall": Birth Anniv, Jan 21
Jackson, Tito: Birth, Oct 15
Jackson, Victoria: Birth, Aug 2
Jacob, Irene: Birth, Jul 15
Jacobi, Derek: Birth, Oct 22
Jacobi, Lou: Birth, Dec 28
Jacoby, Scott: Birth, Nov 19
Jaeger, Andrea: Birth, Jun 4
Jagger, Bianca: Birth, May 2
Jagger, Dean: Birth Anniv, Nov 7
Jagger, Mick: Birth, Jul 26
Jagr, Jaromir: Birth, Feb 15
Jahn, Helmut: Birth, Jan 1
Jakes, John: Birth, Mar 31
Jamaica
Abolition of Slavery, Aug 1
Discovery by Columbus: Anniv, May 4
Independence Day, Aug 3
Maroon Fest, Jan 6
Natl Heroes Day, Oct 19
Port Royal Hurricane: Anniv, Aug 28
Jamboree in the Hills (St. Clairsville, OH), Jul 16
James, David: Birth, Aug 1
James, Henry: Birth Anniv, Apr 15
James, Jesse: Birth Anniv, Sep 5
James, John: Birth, Apr 18
James, Kevin: Birth, Apr 26
James, LeBron: Birth, Dec 30
James, P.D.: Birth, Aug 3
James, Sonny: Birth, May 1
James, William: Birth Anniv, Jan 11
Jamestown and Bermuda (Williamsburg, VA), Mar 1
Jamestown Burned by Bacon's Rebellion: Anniv, Sep 19
Jamestown Day (Williamsburg, VA), May 16
Jamestown, VA: Founding Anniv, May 14
Jamieson, Bob: Birth, Feb 1
Jane Addams Day in Illinois, Dec 10
Janis, Byron: Birth, Mar 24
Janković, Jelena: Birth, Feb 28
Janney, Allison: Birth, Nov 19
Jansen, Dan: Birth, Jun 17
Japan
Autumnal Equinox Day, Sep 22
Battle of Bismarck Sea: Anniv, Mar 2
Bean-Throwing Fest (Setsubun), Feb 3
Birthday of the Emperor, Dec 23
Bon Fest (Feast of Lanterns), Jul 13
Children's Day, May 5
Chrysanthemum Day, Sep 9
Coming-of-Age Day, Jan 12
Constitution Memorial Day, May 3
Cormorant Fishing Fest, May 11
Culture Day, Nov 3
Day of the Rice God (Chiyoda), Jun 7
Doll Fest (Hinamatsuri), Mar 3
Flower Fest (Hana Matsuri), Apr 8
Foundation Day, Natl, Feb 11
Golden Week Holidays, Apr 29
Greenery Day, May 4
Ha-Ri-Ku-Yo (Needle Mass), Feb 8
Haru-No-Yabuiri, Jan 16
Health-Sports Day, Oct 12
Hiroshima Day, Aug 6
Hollyhock Fest (Kyoto), May 15
Japan Agrees to End Use of Drift Nets: Anniv, Nov 26
Japan Bombed: Anniv, Apr 18
Japanese Era New Year, Jan 1
Kakizome, Jan 2
Kanto Earthquake Memorial Day, Sep 1
Labor Thanksgiving Day, Nov 23
Marine Day, Jul 20
Mega Kenka Matsuri, Oct 14
Moment of Silence (Nagasaki), Aug 9
Mount Ogura Plane Crash: Anniv, Aug 12
Namahage, Dec 31
Nanakusa, Jan 7
Newspaper Week, Oct 15
Peace Fest (Hiroshima), Aug 6
Respect for the Aged Day, Sep 21
Rice Planting Fest (Osaka), Jun 14
Roughhouse Fest, Oct 14
Shichi-Go-San, Nov 15
Showa Day, Apr 29
Snow Fest, Feb 8
Soma No Umaoi (Wild Horse Chasing), Jul 23
Suffers Major Earthquake: Anniv, Jan 17
Tanabata (Star Fest), Jul 7
Usokae (Bullfinch Exchange Fest), Jan 7
Vernal Equinox Day, Mar 20
Water-Drawing Fest, Mar 1
Japanese
Bon Odori Fest of Lanterns (Chicago, IL), Jul 11
Ginza Holiday (Chicago, IL), Aug 7
Hatsume Fair (Delray Beach, FL), Feb 21
Japanese Fest (St. Louis, MO), Sep 5
Japanese Attack US Mainland: Anniv, Feb 23
Japanese Internment (WWII): Anniv, Feb 19
Jarman, Claude, Jr: Birth, Sep 27
Jarreau, Al: Birth, Mar 12
Jarrett, Dale: Birth, Nov 26
Jarriel, Thomas Edwin: Birth, Dec 29
Jarvik, Robert: Birth, May 11
Jarvis, Gregory B.: Birth Anniv, Aug 24
Jaws Film Release: Anniv, Jun 20
Jay, John: Birth Anniv, Dec 12
Jazz and Blues
Albany Riverfront Jazz Fest (Albany, NY), Sep 5
Appreciation Month, Apr 1
Big Band/Swing Dance Weekend (Asheville, NC), Jan 23
Bix Beiderbecke Memorial Jazz Fest (Davenport, IA), Jul 23
Blues on the Fox (Aurora, IL), Jun 12
Chicago Blues Fest (Chicago, IL), Jun 11
Davis, Miles: Birth Anniv, May 25
Jazz Day, Intl, May 23
Kettle Moraine Jazz Fest (West Bend, WI), Sep 11
Lionel Hampton Jazz Fest (Moscow, ID), Feb 25
Medford Jazz Jubilee (Medford, OR), Oct 9
Monterey Jazz Fest (Monterey, CA), Sep 18
Natchitoches Jazz Fest (Natchitoches, LA), Apr 17
New Orleans Jazz/Heritage Fest (New Orleans, LA), Apr 24
Parker, Charlie: Birth Anniv, Aug 29
Ra, Sun: Birth Anniv, May 22
Red Wine and Blues Fest (Tuckerton, NJ), Jul 4
Sacramento Jazz Jubilee (Sacramento, CA), May 22
Satchmo Summerfest (New Orleans, LA), Jul 30
SunFest (West Palm Beach, FL), Apr 29
Suntrust Big Lick Blues Fest (Roanoke, VA), Sep 19
Jeffers, Robinson: Birth Anniv, Jan 10
Jefferson Davis Day (Confederate Memorial Day, KY), Jun 3
Jefferson, Joseph: Birth Anniv, Feb 20
Jefferson, Martha: Birth Anniv, Oct 19
Jefferson, Richard: Birth, Jun 21
Jefferson, Thomas, and Adams, John: Death Anniv, Jul 4
Jefferson, Thomas: Birth Anniv, Apr 13

Jefferson, Thomas: Day (Pres Proc), Apr 13
Jeffersons TV Premiere: Anniv, Jan 18
Jeffries, John: Weatherman's Day, Feb 5
Jelly Bean Day, Natl, Apr 22
Jemison, Mae: Birth, Oct 17
Jenkins's Ear Day, Apr 9
Jenks, Bobby: Birth, Mar 14
Jenner, Brody: Birth, Aug 21
Jenner, Bruce: Birth, Oct 28
Jenner, Edward: Birth Anniv, May 17
Jennings, Jason: Birth, Jul 17
Jennings, Peter: Birth Anniv, Jul 29
Jensen, Ashley: Birth, Aug 11
Jeopardy TV Premiere: Anniv, Mar 30
Jerry Lewis Muscular Dystrophy Association Telethon, Sep 6
Jeter, Derek: Birth, Jun 26
Jetsons TV Premiere: Anniv, Sep 23
Jett, Joan: Birth, Sep 22
Jewel: Birth, May 23
Jewish American Heritage Month (Pres Proc), May 1
Jewish Observances
- Asarah B'Tevet (5769), Jan 6
- Asarah B'Tevet (5770), Dec 27
- Chanukah, Dec 12
- Fast of Gedalya, Sep 21
- Fast of Tammuz, Jul 9
- Hadassah Founded: Anniv, Feb 24
- Lag B'Omer, May 12
- Passover Begins, Apr 8
- Pesach (Passover), Apr 9
- Purim, Mar 10
- Rosh Hashanah (New Year), Sep 19
- Rosh Hashanah Begins, Sep 18
- Shabbat Across America/Canada, Mar 20
- Shavuot, May 29
- Shavuot Begins, May 28
- Shemini Atzeret, Oct 10
- Simchat Torah, Oct 11
- Sukkot Begins, Oct 2
- Sukkot/Succoth/Feast of Tabernacles, Oct 3
- Ta'anit Esther (Fast of Esther), Mar 9
- Tisha B'Av (Fast of Ab), Jul 30
- Tu B'Shvat, Feb 9
- Yom Kippur, Sep 28
- Yom Kippur Begins, Sep 27

Jewison, Norman: Birth, Jul 21
Jillette, Penn: Birth, Mar 5
Jillian, Ann: Birth, Jan 29
Jimmy Durante Show TV Premiere: Anniv, Oct 2
Jindal, Bobby: Birth, Jun 10
Jinnah, Mohammed Ali: Birth Anniv, Dec 25
Joan of Arc: Birth Anniv, Jan 6
Jobs, Steven: Birth, Feb 24
Joe Cain Procession (Mobile, AL), Feb 22
Joel, Billy: Birth, May 9
Johansson, Scarlett: Birth, Nov 22
John Parker Day, Apr 19
John, Elton: Birth, Mar 25
John, Tommy: Birth, May 22
Johnny Appleseed Day, Mar 11
Johnny Appleseed Days (Lake City, MN), Oct 3
Johnny Appleseed Fest (Fort Wayne, IN), Sep 19
Johns, Glynis: Birth, Oct 5
Johns, Jasper: Birth, May 15
Johnson, Amy: Flight Anniv, May 5
Johnson, Andrew: Birth Anniv, Dec 29
Johnson, Andrew: Impeachment Proceedings: Anniv, Feb 24
Johnson, Arte: Birth, Jan 20
Johnson, Avery: Birth, Mar 25
Johnson, Ban: Birth Anniv, Jan 6
Johnson, Betsey: Birth, Aug 10
Johnson, Clark: Birth, Sep 10
Johnson, Davey: Birth, Jan 30
Johnson, Don: Birth, Dec 15
Johnson, Eliza M.: Birth Anniv, Oct 4
Johnson, Jimmy: Birth, Mar 31
Johnson, Joe: Birth, Jun 29
Johnson, John (Jack) Arthur: Birth Anniv, Mar 31
Johnson, John H.: Birth Anniv, Jan 19
Johnson, John H.: Ebony Magazine: Anniv, Nov 1
Johnson, Kevin: Birth, Mar 4
Johnson, Keyshawn: Birth, Jul 22
Johnson, Lady Bird: Birth Anniv, Dec 22
Johnson, Lyndon B.: Birth Anniv, Aug 27
Johnson, Lyndon B.: Civil Rights Act of 1968: Anniv, Apr 11
Johnson, Lyndon B.: Monday Holiday Law: Anniv, Jun 28
Johnson, Magic: Birth, Aug 14
Johnson, Michael: Birth, Sep 13
Johnson, Nick: Birth, Sep 19
Johnson, Phillip: Birth Anniv, Jul 8
Johnson, Randy: Birth, Sep 10
Johnson, Richard M.: Birth Anniv, Oct 17
Johnson, Robert: Birth Anniv, May 8
Johnson, Samuel: Birth Anniv, Sep 18
Johnson, Tim: Birth, Dec 28
Johnson, William H.: Birth Anniv, Mar 18
Johnston, Joseph: Birth Anniv, Feb 3
Johnston, Joseph: Surrender at Durham Station: Anniv, Apr 18
Johnston, Kristen: Birth, Sep 20
Johnstown Flood: Anniv, May 31
Join Hands Day, May 2
Joke Day, Presidential, Aug 11
Jokes: Tell an Old Joke Day, Natl, Jul 24
Jolie, Angelina: Birth, Jun 4
Jolson, Al: Birth Anniv, May 26
Jonas, Frankie: Birth, Sep 28
Jonas, Joe: Birth, Aug 15
Jonas, Kevin: Birth, Nov 5
Jonas, Nick: Birth, Sep 16
Jones, Andruw: Birth, Apr 23
Jones, Bobby: Birth Anniv, Mar 17
Jones, Bobby: Wins First Grand Slam: Anniv, Jul 12
Jones, Casey: Birth Anniv, Mar 14
Jones, Chipper: Birth, Apr 24
Jones, Chuck: Birth Anniv, Sep 21
Jones, Cobi: Birth, Jun 16
Jones, Davy: Birth, Dec 30
Jones, Dean: Birth, Jan 25
Jones, Eddie: Birth, Oct 20
Jones, Edward "Too Tall": Birth, Feb 23
Jones, George: Birth, Sep 12
Jones, Grace: Birth, May 19
Jones, Howard: Birth, Feb 23
Jones, James Earl: Birth, Jan 17
Jones, Jeffrey: Birth, Sep 28
Jones, Jennifer: Birth, Mar 2
Jones, Jenny: Birth, Jun 7
Jones, John Paul: Birth Anniv, Jul 6
Jones, K.C.: Birth, May 25
Jones, LeRoi (Amiri Baraka): Birth, Oct 7
Jones, Marion: Birth, Oct 12
Jones, Mary H.: Birth Anniv, May 1
Jones, Norah: Birth, Mar 30
Jones, Quincy: Birth, Mar 14
Jones, Ricki Lee: Birth, Nov 8
Jones, Sam J.: Birth, Aug 12
Jones, Shirley: Birth, Mar 31
Jones, Star: Birth, Mar 24
Jones, Terry: Birth, Feb 1
Jones, Tom: Birth, Jun 7
Jones, Tommy Lee: Birth, Sep 15
Jonestown Massacre: Anniv, Nov 18
Jong, Erica: Birth, Mar 26
Jonson, Ben: Birth Anniv, Jun 11
Joplin, Janis: Birth Anniv, Jan 19
Joplin, Scott: Birth Anniv, Nov 24
Jordan
- Accession Day, Jun 9
- Great Arab Revolt and Army Day, Jun 10
- Independence Day, May 25
- King Hussein: Birth Anniv, Nov 14
- King's Birthday, Jan 30

Jordan, Louis: Birth Anniv, Jul 8
Jordan, Michael: Birth, Feb 17
Jordan, Michael: Bulls Sign: Anniv, Sep 12
Jordan, Neil: Birth, Feb 25
Jordan, Vernon, Jr: Birth, Aug 15
Joseph, Chief, Surrender: Anniv, Oct 5
Joseph, Chief: Death Anniv, Sep 21
Jouett, Jack: Ride Anniv, Jun 3
Joule, James: Birth Anniv, Dec 24
Journalism
- All the News That's Fit to Print: Anniv, Feb 10
- Around the World in 72 Days: Anniv, Jan 25
- Beginning of the Penny Press: Anniv, Sep 3
- Brinkley, David: Birth Anniv, Jul 10
- Columnist's Day, Natl, Jun 23
- Dewey Defeats Truman Headline: Anniv, Nov 3
- Ebony Magazine: Anniv, Nov 1
- First American Daily Newspaper Published: Anniv, May 30
- First American Newspaper: Anniv, Sep 25
- First Magazine Published in America: Anniv, Feb 13
- First Newspaper Comic Strip: Anniv, Oct 18
- First Photos Used in a Newspaper Report: Anniv, Jul 1
- First Televised Presidential News Conf: Anniv, Jan 25
- Inspirational News Week, Natl, Apr 19
- Japan: Newspaper Week, Oct 15
- Life Magazine Debuts: Anniv, Nov 23
- NAB/National Broadcasters Convention (Las Vegas, NV), Apr 17
- New York Times First Published: Anniv, Sep 18
- New York Weekly Journal First Issue: Anniv, Nov 5
- New Yorker Published: Anniv, Feb 21
- Newspaper Assn of America Conv (San Diego, CA), Apr 5
- Newspaper Carrier Day, Sep 4
- Newspaper Carrier Day, Intl, Oct 10
- Newspaper in Education Week, Mar 2
- Newspaper Week, Natl, Oct 4
- Nixon's "Last" Press Conf: Anniv, Nov 7
- People Magazine: Anniv, Mar 4
- Pulitzer, Joseph: Birth Anniv, Apr 10
- Pyle, Ernest: Birth Anniv, Aug 3
- Thomas, Lowell: Birth Anniv, Apr 6
- Time Magazine First Published: Anniv, Mar 3
- UN: World Press Freedom Day, May 3
- USA Today First Published: Anniv, Sep 15
- Zenger, John P.: Arrest Anniv, Nov 17

Joust of the Quintana (Ascoli/Piceno, Italy), Aug 2
Joy of Cooking: Publication Anniv, Nov 30
Joy of Sex Published: Anniv, Oct 1

Joy, Robert: Birth, Aug 17
Joyce, James: Birth Anniv, Feb 2
Joyce, James: Bloomsday: Anniv, Jun 16
Joygerm Day, Natl, Jan 8
Joyner-Kersee, Jackie: Birth, Mar 3
Juarez, Benito: Birth Anniv, Mar 21
Jubilee Days Fest (Zion, IL), Sep 5
Judd, Ashley: Birth, Apr 19
Judd, Naomi: Birth, Jan 11
Judd, Wynonna: Birth, May 30
Judgment Day, Jan 17
Juggling Day, World, Jun 20
Julia, Raul: Birth Anniv, Mar 9
Julian, Percy: Birth Anniv, Apr 11
Jumbo the Elephant Arrives in America: Anniv, Apr 9
June Is Perennial Gardening Month, Jun 1
June Is Turkey Lovers' Month, Jun 1
Juneteenth, Jun 19
Junkanoo (Bahamas), Dec 26
Jupiter Effect: Anniv, Mar 10
Jupiter, Comet Crashes into: Anniv, Jul 16
Jurgensen, Sonny: Birth, Aug 23
Jury, First All-Woman: Anniv, Sep 22
Just for Laughs Fest (Montreal, QC, Canada), Jul 16
Just Pray No: Worldwide Weekend Prayer, Apr 18
Just, Ernest E.: Birth Anniv, Aug 14
Justice, David: Birth, Apr 14
Justice, US Dept of: Anniv, Jun 22

K

Kaczmarek, Jane: Birth, Dec 21
Kahanamoku, Duke: Birth Anniv, Aug 24
Kahlo, Frida: Birth Anniv, Jul 6
Kaine, Tim: Birth, Feb 26
Kaka: Birth, May 15
Kalb, Marvin: Birth, Jun 9
Kamali, Norma: Birth, Jun 27
Kamehameha Day (HI), Jun 11
Kanakaredes, Melina: Birth, Apr 23
Kanawa, Kiri Te: Birth, Mar 6
Kander, John: Birth, Mar 18
Kane, Bob: Batman Debuts: Anniv, May 1
Kane, Carol: Birth, Jun 18
Kansas
- Admission Day, Jan 29
- Apple Fest (Topeka), Oct 4
- Barbed Wire Swap/Sell (La Crosse), May 1
- Beef Empire Days (Garden City), May 27
- Brownback, Sam: Birth, Sep 12
- Columbus Day Fest/Hot Air Balloon Regatta (Columbus), Oct 9
- Dalton Defenders Day (Coffeyville), Oct 2
- Dodge City Days (Dodge City), Jul 24
- Eagle Day at the Lake (Kansas City), Jan 17
- Eagle Days (Junction City), Jan 17
- Fiesta Bullwhacker/Wild West Show (Olathe), Sep 26
- Guitar Flat-Picking Chmpshps/Walnut Valley Fest, Natl (Winfield), Sep 16
- Hoisington Celebration (Hoisington), Sep 4
- Inter-State Fair/Rodeo (Coffeyville), Aug 8
- Mennonite Relief Sale (Hutchinson), Apr 17
- Monster Myths by Moonlight (Milford), Oct 10
- Orphan Train Heritage Society Reunion (Concordia), Sep 18
- Oz Fest (Liberal), Oct 9
- Pancake Day, Intl (Liberal), Feb 24
- Pony Express Fest (Hanover), Aug 30
- Quantrill's Raid on Lawrence, KS: Anniv, Aug 21
- Roberts, Pat: Birth, Apr 20
- Salter Elected First Woman Mayor in US: Anniv, Apr 4
- Sebelius, Kathleen: Birth, May 15
- State Fair (Hutchinson), Sep 11
- Winfield Art-in-the-Park Fest (Winfield), Oct 3
- Woofstock (Wichita), Oct 3

Kansas City Hotel Disaster: Anniv, Jul 17
Kanu, Nwankwo: Birth, Aug 1
Kaplan, Gabe: Birth, Mar 31
Kapoor, Shashi: Birth, Mar 18
Karan, Donna: Birth, Oct 2
Karaoke Week, Natl, Apr 19
Kariya, Paul: Birth, Oct 16
Karloff, Boris: Birth Anniv, Nov 23
Karn, Richard: Birth, Feb 17
Karras, Alex: Birth, Jul 15
Kasdan, Lawrence: Birth, Jan 14
Kasem, Casey: Birth, Apr 27
Kasparov, Garry: Birth, Apr 13
Kasparov, Garry: First Computer Chess Victory: Anniv, Feb 10
Katmai Natl Park: Anniv, Dec 2
Katrina Strikes Gulf Coast: Anniv, Aug 29
Katt, William: Birth, Feb 16
Kauffmann, Stanley J.: Birth, Apr 24
Kaufmann, Christine: Birth, Jan 11
Kavner, Julie: Birth, Sep 7
Kaye, Danny: Birth Anniv, Jan 18
Kazakhstan
- Constitution Day, Aug 31
- Independence Day, Dec 16

Kazan, Elia: Birth Anniv, Sep 7
Kazan, Lainie: Birth, May 15
Kazurinsky, Tim: Birth, Mar 3
Keach, Stacy, Jr: Birth, Jun 2
Keane, Bil: Birth, Oct 5
Keaton, Buster: Birth Anniv, Oct 4
Keaton, Diane: Birth, Jan 5
Keaton, Michael: Birth, Sep 9
Keats, John: Birth Anniv, Oct 31
Keegan, Andrew: Birth, Jan 29
Keene, Donald: Birth, Jun 18
Keener, Catherine: Birth, Mar 26
Keep Kids Alive—Drive 25 Day, May 1
Keep Kids Creative Week, Natl, Sep 20
Keeshan, Bob: Birth Anniv, Jun 27
Keillor, Garrison: Birth, Aug 7
Keitel, Harvey: Birth, May 13
Keith, David: Birth, May 8
Keith, Toby: Birth, Jul 8
Keller, Helen, Fest (Tuscumbia, AL), Jun 25
Keller, Helen: Birth Anniv, Jun 27
Keller, Helen: Miracle: Anniv, Apr 5
Keller, Kasey: Birth, Nov 29
Kellerman, Sally: Birth, Jun 2
Kelley, Kitty: Birth, Apr 4
Kelly, Emmett: Birth Anniv, Dec 9
Kelly, Gene: Birth Anniv, Aug 23
Kelly, Gene: Singin' in the Rain Film Premiere: Anniv, Mar 27
Kelly, Grace: Birth Anniv, Nov 12
Kelly, Ned: Last Stand: Anniv, Jun 27
Kelly, Walt: Birth Anniv, Aug 25
Kelsey, Linda: Birth, Jul 28
Kemble, Fanny: Birth Anniv, Nov 27
Kemmler, William: First Electrocution for Death Penalty: Anniv, Aug 6
Kemp, Jack: Birth, Jul 13
Kemp, Shawn: Birth, Nov 26
Kempthorne, Dirk: Birth, Oct 29
Kenai Fjords Natl Park: Anniv, Dec 2
Keneally, Thomas: Birth, Oct 7
Kennan, George: Birth Anniv, Feb 16
Kennedy Intl Airport Dedication: Anniv, Jul 31
Kennedy, Anthony M.: Birth, Jul 23
Kennedy, Cortez: Birth, Aug 23
Kennedy, Edward Moore: Birth, Feb 22
Kennedy, Ethel: Birth, Apr 11
Kennedy, George: Birth, Feb 18
Kennedy, Jamie: Birth, May 25
Kennedy, John F., Jr: Birth Anniv, Nov 25
Kennedy, John Fitzgerald
- Assassination Anniv, Nov 22
- Birth Anniv, May 29
- Committee on Assassinations Report, Mar 29
- Day (MA), Nov 29
- First Televised Presidential Debate: Anniv, Sep 26
- First Televised Presidential News Conf: Anniv, Jan 25
- Profiles in Courage Published: Anniv, Jan 1
- Warren Commission Report Anniv, Sep 27

Kennedy, Robert
- Assassination Anniv, Jun 5
- Birth Anniv, Nov 20
- Committee on Assassinations Report, Mar 29

Kennedy, William: Birth, Jan 16
Kennerly, David Hume: Birth, Mar 9
Kensit, Patsy: Birth, Mar 4
Kent State Commemoration (Kent, OH), May 3
Kent State Students' Memorial Day, May 4
Kent, Jeff: Birth, Mar 7
Kentucky
- Admission Day, Jun 1
- American Quilter's Society Quilt Show (Paducah), Apr 22
- Battle of Blue Licks Celebration (Mount Olivet), Aug 15
- Beshear, Steve: Birth, Sept 21
- Boone Day, Jun 7
- Bunning, Jim: Birth, Oct 23
- Christmas Candlelight Tour (Bardstown), Nov 27
- Confederate Memorial Day, Jun 3
- Daniel Boone Pioneer Fest (Winchester), Sep 4
- Everly Brothers/Central City Rock 'n' Roll Cruise-In and Concert (Central City), Sep 5
- Fancy Farm Picnic (Fancy Farm), Aug 1
- Gospel Fest (Central City), Aug 26
- Great American Brass Band Fest (Danville), Jun 11
- Kentucky Apple Fest (Paintsville), Oct 2
- Kentucky Bourbon Fest (Bardstown), Sep 15
- Kentucky Derby (Louisville), May 2
- Kentucky Derby Fest (Louisville), Apr 17
- Kentucky State Chmpshp Fiddler's Contest (Falls of Rough), Jul 17
- Lincoln's Birthplace Cabin Wreath Laying (Hodgenville), Feb 12
- Maifest (Covington), May 15
- MainStrasse Village Original Goettafest (Covington), Jun 12
- Mammoth Cave Natl Park Established: Anniv, Jul 1
- Marion County Country Ham Days (Lebanon), Sep 26
- McConnell, Mitch: Birth, Feb 20
- Memory Days (Grayson), May 16

Oktoberfest (Covington), Sep 11
Scarecrow Fest (Winchester), Oct 3
State Fair (Louisville), Aug 20
Surrender of Fort Donelson: Anniv, Feb 16
Swappin' Meetin' (Cumberland), Oct 2
VentHaven Ventriloquist Convention (Fort Mitchell), Jul 16
Kentucky Derby, First: Anniv, May 17
Kenya
Jamhuri Day, Dec 12
Kenyatta Day, Oct 20
Madaraka Day, Jun 1
Keoghan, Phil: Birth, May 31
Kepler, Johannes: Birth Anniv, Dec 27
Kercheval, Ken: Birth, Jul 15
Kern, Jerome: Birth Anniv, Jan 27
Kerns, Joanna: Birth, Feb 12
Kerouac, Jack: Birth Anniv, Mar 12
Kerr, Deborah: Birth Anniv, Sep 30
Kerr, Steve: Birth, Sep 27
Kerrigan, Nancy: Birth, Oct 13
Kerry, John F.: Birth, Dec 11
Kerwin, Brian: Birth, Oct 25
Kerwin, Lance: Birth, Nov 6
Kewpie Doll: Rose C. O'Neill: Birth Anniv, Jun 25
Key, Francis Scott: Birth Anniv, Aug 1
Key, Francis Scott: Star-Spangled Banner Inspired: Anniv, Sep 13
Keynes, John Maynard: Birth Anniv, Jun 5
Keys, Alicia: Birth, Jan 25
Khachaturian, Aram: Birth Anniv, Jun 6
Khan, Chaka: Birth, Mar 23
Khomeini, Ayatollah: Death Anniv, Jun 3
Kick-Butt Day, Natl, Oct 12
Kid Inventors' Day, Jan 17
Kidd, Jason: Birth, Mar 23
Kidd, Michael: Birth Anniv, Aug 12
Kidder, Margot: Birth, Oct 17
KidFilm® Fest (Dallas, TX), Jan 12
Kidman, Nicole: Birth, Jun 20
Kidnapping, Lindbergh: Anniv, Mar 1
Kidney Day, World, Mar 12
Kidney Month, Natl, Mar 1
Kids' Goal Setting Week, Oct 5
KidsDay, Natl, Sep 19
KidSpree (Aurora, CO), Jul 18
Kiel, Richard: Birth, Sep 13
Kilborn, Craig: Birth, Aug 24
Killebrew, Harmon: Birth, Jun 29
Killy, Jean-Claude: Birth, Aug 30
Kilmer, Joyce: Birth Anniv, Dec 6
Kilmer, Val: Birth, Dec 31
Kilpatrick, James: Birth, Nov 1
Kim Il Sung: Death Anniv, Jul 8
Kim, Daniel Dae: Birth, Aug 4
Kimbrough, Charles: Birth, May 23
Kimmel, Jimmy: Birth, Nov 13
Kind, Richard: Birth, Nov 22
Kindergarten Day, Apr 21
Kindergarten: Get Ready for Kindergarten Month, Aug 1
Kindness Day, World, Nov 13
King Family Show TV Premiere: Anniv, Jan 23
King James Bible Published: Anniv, May 2
King Kong Film Premiere: Anniv, Mar 2
King Tut Tomb Discovery: Anniv, Nov 4
King, B.B.: Birth, Sep 16
King, Ben E.: Birth, Sep 28
King, Billie Jean, Wins Battle of Sexes: Anniv, Sep 20
King, Billie Jean: Birth, Nov 22
King, Carole: Birth, Feb 9
King, Coretta Scott: Birth Anniv, Apr 27
King, Don: Birth, Aug 20
King, Frank: Birth Anniv, Apr 9
King, Larry: Birth, Nov 19
King, Martin Luther, Jr
Assassination Anniv, Apr 4
Awarded Nobel Peace Prize: Anniv, Oct 14
Birth Anniv, Jan 15
Birthday Observed, Jan 19
Committee on Assassinations Report, Mar 29
March on Washington: Anniv, Aug 28
Martin Luther King, Jr, Federal Holiday, Jan 19
Stock Exchange Holiday, Jan 19
King, Perry: Birth, Apr 30
King, Rodney: Los Angeles Riots: Anniv, Apr 29
King, Stephen: Birth, Sep 21
King, W.L. MacKenzie: Birth Anniv, Dec 17
King, William R.: Birth Anniv, Apr 7
Kingsley, Ben: Birth, Dec 31
Kingston, Alex: Birth, Mar 11
Kingsville Intl Young Performers' Competitions (Kingsville, TX), Apr 2
Kinnear, Greg: Birth, Jun 17
Kinney, Kathy: Birth, Nov 3
Kinsey, Alfred: Birth Anniv, Jun 23
Kinski, Nastassja: Birth, Jan 24
Kipling, Rudyard: Birth Anniv, Dec 30
Kiribati: Independence Day, Jul 12
Kirshner, Don: Birth, Apr 17
Kiss-and-Make-Up Day, Aug 25
Kissinger, Henry: Birth, May 27
Kite, Tom: Birth, Dec 9
Kites, Kite-Flying
Kite Fest of Santiago Sacatepequez (Guatemala), Nov 1
Kite Month, Natl, Apr 1
Kitsch, Taylor: Birth, Apr 9
Kitt, Eartha: Birth, Jan 17
Kiwanis
Kiwanis Intl: Anniv, Jan 21
Klein, Calvin: Birth, Nov 19
Klein, Robert: Birth, Feb 8
Kliban, B(ernard): Birth Anniv, Jan 1
Kline, Kevin: Birth, Oct 24
Klobucher, Amy: Birth, May 25
Klondike Days (Eagle River, WI), Feb 21
Klondike Eldorado Gold Discovery: Anniv, Aug 31
Klondike Gold Discovery: Anniv, Aug 16
Klose, Miroslav: Birth, Jun 9
Klugman, Jack: Birth, Apr 27
Knight Rider TV Premiere: Anniv, Sep 26
Knight, Bobby: Birth, Oct 25
Knight, Gladys: Birth, May 28
Knight, O. Raymond: Birth Anniv, Apr 8
Knight, Shirley: Birth, Jul 5
Knight, T.R.: Birth, Mar 26
Knightley, Keira: Birth, Mar 26
Knights of Columbus Founder's Day, Mar 29
Knights of Pythias: Founding Anniv, Feb 19
Knock-Knock Day, Natl, Oct 31
Knowles, Beyonce: Birth, Sep 4
Knox County Scenic Drive (Galesburg, IL), Oct 3
Knuckles Down Month, Natl, Apr 1
Kobuk Valley Natl Park: Anniv, Dec 2
Koch, Edward: Birth, Dec 12
Koenig, Walter: Birth, Sep 14
Koestler, Arthur: Birth Anniv, Sep 5
Kohl, Herb: Birth, Feb 7
Koko the Gorilla: Birthday, Jul 4
Kokoschka, Oskar: Birth Anniv, Mar 1
Kolzig, Olaf: Birth, Apr 6
Konerko, Paul: Birth, May 5
Koop, C. Everett: Birth, Oct 14
Kopell, Bernie: Birth, Jun 21
Koppel, Ted: Birth, Feb 8
Korbut, Olga: Birth, May 16
Korea
Alphabet Day (Hangul), Oct 9
Chusok, Oct 3
Constitution Day, Jul 17
Independence Day, Aug 15
Korea, North and South, End War: Anniv, Dec 13
Korean Air Lines Flight 007 Disaster: Anniv, Sep 1
Korean War Armistice: Anniv, Jul 27
Korean War Began: Anniv, Jun 25
Memorial Day, Jun 6
National Day, Sep 9
National Foundation Day, Oct 3
Samiljol (Independence Movement Day), Mar 1
Seoul Recaptured by UN Forces, Mar 14
Tano Day, May 28
Kosar, Bernie: Birth, Nov 25
Kosciuszko, Tadeusz: Birth Anniv, Feb 4
Kotto, Yaphet: Birth, Nov 15
Koufax, Sandy: Birth, Dec 30
Kournikova, Anna: Birth, Jun 7
Kovacs, Ernie: Birth Anniv, Jan 23
Kozak, Harley Jane: Birth, Jan 28
Krabbe, Jeroen: Birth, Dec 5
Kraft Nabisco Chmpshp (Rancho Mirage, CA), Mar 30
Kraft Television Theatre TV Premiere: Anniv, May 7
Krakatoa Eruption: Anniv, Aug 26
Krakowski, Jane: Birth, Oct 11
Krall, Diana: Birth, Nov 16
Krampuslauf (Austria), Dec 5
Krantz, Judith: Birth, Jan 9
Krasinski, John: Birth, Oct 20
Krassner, Paul: Birth, Apr 9
Krause, Peter: Birth, Aug 12
Kravitz, Lenny: Birth, May 26
Kreis, Jason: Birth, Dec 29
Kreuk, Kristin: Birth, Dec 30
Kreutzmann, Bill, Jr: Birth, Jun 7
Krewe of Bacchus Parade (New Orleans, LA), Feb 22
Krewe of Carrollton Parade (New Orleans, LA), Feb 15
Krewe of Endymion Parade (New Orleans, LA), Feb 21
Krewe of Rex Mardi Gras Parade (New Orleans, LA), Feb 24
Krige, Alice: Birth, Jun 28
Krim, Mathilde: Birth, Jul 9
Krishna Janmashtami (India), Aug 14
Kristallnacht: Anniv, Nov 9
Kristofferson, Kris: Birth, Jun 22
Kroft, Steve: Birth, Aug 22
Krone, Julie: Birth, Jul 24
Krumholtz, David: Birth, May 15
Krupp, Alfried: Birth Anniv, Aug 13
Kubek, Tony: Birth, Oct 12
Kubrick, Stanley: Birth Anniv, Jul 26
Kudrow, Lisa: Birth, Jul 30
Kuhn, Margaret: Birth Anniv, Aug 3
Kukla, Fran and Ollie TV Premiere: Anniv, Nov 29
Kulongoski, Ted: Birth, Nov 5
Kung Fu TV Premiere: Anniv, Oct 1
Kunis, Mila: Birth, Aug 14
Kunstler, William: Birth Anniv, Jul 7
Kupets, Courtney: Birth, Jul 27
Kuralt, Charles: Birth Anniv, Sep 10

Kurban Bayram: See Eid-al-Adha, Nov 28
Kurosawa, Akira: Birth Anniv, Mar 23
Kurri, Jari: Birth, May 18
Kurtis, Bill: Birth, Sep 21
Kurtz, Swoosie: Birth, Sep 6
Kurtzman, Harvey: Birth Anniv, Oct 3
Kutcher, Ashton: Birth, Feb 7
Kutner, Luis: Birth Anniv, Jun 9
Kuwait
  Iraq Invades Kuwait: Anniv, Aug 2
  Kuwait Liberated: Anniv, Feb 27
  National Day, Feb 25
Kuznetsova, Svetlana: Birth, Jun 27
Kwan, Michelle: Birth, Jul 7
Kwanzaa, Dec 26
Kyl, Jon: Birth, Apr 25
Kyrgyzstan: Independence Day, Aug 31
Kyser, Kay: Birth Anniv, Jun 18

L
La Befana (Italy), Jan 6
La Guardia, Fiorello: Birth Anniv, Dec 11
LA Law TV Premiere: Anniv, Oct 3
La Placa, Alison: Birth, Dec 16
La Russa, Tony, Jr: Birth, Oct 4
La Salle, Eriq: Birth, Jul 23
LaBelle, Patti: Birth, May 24
Labonte, Bobby: Birth, May 8
Labor. See also Careers
  AFL Founded: Anniv, Dec 8
  AFL-CIO Founded: Anniv, Dec 5
  Day of the Holy Cross, May 3
  First Labor Day Observance: Anniv, Sep 5
  Five-Dollar-a-Day Minimum Wage: Anniv, Jan 5
  Haymarket Pardon: Anniv, Jun 26
  Haymarket Square Riot: Anniv, May 4
  Industrial Workers of the World (IWW) Founded: Anniv, Jun 27
  Jones, Mary H.: Birth Anniv, May 1
  Labor Day, May 1
  Labor Day, Sep 7
  Labor Day (Bahamas), Jun 5
  Labor Relations Act, Natl: Anniv, Jul 5
  Ludlow Mine Incident: Anniv, Apr 20
  Montgomery Ward Seized: Anniv, Apr 26
  Murray, Philip: Birth Anniv, May 25
  Schneiderman, Rose: Birth Anniv, Apr 6
  White Shirt Day, Feb 11
Lachey, Drew: Birth, Aug 8
Lachey, Nick: Birth, Nov 9
Lacoste, Rene: Birth Anniv, Jul 2
Lacroix, Christian: Birth, May 17
Lacrosse: NCAA Div I Women's Chmpshp (Towson, MD), May 22
Ladd, Cheryl: Birth, Jul 12
Ladd, David Alan: Birth, Feb 5
Ladd, Diane: Birth, Nov 29
Ladies' Day Initiated in Baseball: Anniv, Jun 16
Laennec, Rene: Birth Anniv, Feb 17
Laettner, Christian: Birth, Aug 17
Lafayette, Marquis de: Birth Anniv, Sep 6
Laffer, Arthur: Birth, Aug 14
Lafferty, James: Birth, Jul 25
LaFleur, Guy: Birth, Sep 20
Lag B'Omer, May 12
Lagerfeld, Karl: Birth, Sep 10
Lagerlof, Selma: Birth Anniv, Nov 20
Lahti, Christine: Birth, Apr 4
Laimbeer, Bill, Jr: Birth, May 19
Lake Clark Natl Park: Anniv, Dec 2
Lake, Ricki: Birth, Sep 21
Lalas, Alexi: Birth, Jun 1
Lamas, Lorenzo: Birth, Jan 20
Lamb, Charles: Birth Anniv, Feb 10
Lambert, Christopher: Birth, Mar 29
Lamour, Dorothy: Birth Anniv, Dec 10
L'Amour, Louis: Birth Anniv, Mar 22
Lampard, Frank: Birth, Jun 20
Lancaster, Burt: Birth Anniv, Nov 2
Land Mine Ban: Anniv, Mar 1
Landau, Martin: Birth, Jun 20
Landers, Ann: Birth Anniv, Jul 4
Landesberg, Steve: Birth, Nov 3
Landis, Kenesaw: Birth Anniv, Nov 20
Lando, Joe: Birth, Dec 9
Landon, Michael, Jr: Birth, Jun 20
Landon, Michael: Birth Anniv, Oct 31
Landrieu, Mary L.: Birth, Nov 23
Landscape Architecture Month, Natl, Apr 1
Landsgemeinde (Switzerland), Apr 26
Lane, Diane: Birth, Jan 22
Lane, Mark: Birth, Feb 24
Lane, Nathan: Birth, Feb 3
lang, k.d.: Birth, Nov 2
Lang, Stephen: Birth, Jul 11
Lange, Jessica: Birth, Apr 20
Langella, Frank: Birth, Jan 1
Langer, A.J.: Birth, May 22
Langer, Susanne: Birth Anniv, Dec 20
Langley, Samuel Pierpont: Birth Anniv, Aug 22
Langston, Mark: Birth, Aug 20
Lansbury, Angela: Birth, Oct 16
Lansky, Aaron: Birth, Jul 17
Lantz, Walter: Birth Anniv, Apr 27
Laos: Natl Holiday, Dec 2
Lappe, Frances Moore: Birth, Feb 10
Lardner, Ring Jr: Birth Anniv, Aug 19
Lardner, Ring: Birth Anniv, Mar 6
Largent, Steve: Birth, Sep 28
Larkin, Barry: Birth, Apr 28
Larroquette, John: Birth, Nov 25
Larry King Show TV Premiere: Anniv, Mar 13
Larson, Gary: Birth, Aug 14
Larter, Ali: Birth, Feb 28
Lasek, Bucky: Birth, Dec 3
Laser Patented: Anniv, Mar 22
Lasorda, Tommy: Birth, Sep 22
Lassen Volcanic Natl Park Established: Anniv, Aug 9
Lasser, Louise: Birth, Apr 11
Lassie TV Premiere: Anniv, Sep 12
Late Night with David Letterman TV Premiere: Anniv, Feb 1
Lathrop, Julia C.: Birth Anniv, Jun 29
Latin Fest (Hollywood, FL), Hollywood Beach, Sep 20
Latino Books Month, May 1
Latvia
  Baltic States' Independence Recognized: Anniv, Sep 6
  Independence Day, Nov 18
  John's Day (Midsummer Night Day), Jun 24
Lauder, Estee: Birth Anniv, Jul 1
Lauer, Andy: Birth, Jun 19
Lauer, Matt: Birth, Dec 30
Laugh and Get Rich Day, Feb 8
Laugh at Work Week, Apr 1
Laugh-Friendly Month, Natl, Feb 1
Laugh-In TV Premiere: Anniv, Jan 22
Lauper, Cyndi: Birth, Jun 20
Laurel and Hardy: Cuckoo Dancing Week, Jan 11
Laurel, Stan: Birth Anniv, Jun 16
Lauren, Ralph: Birth, Oct 14
Lauria, Dan: Birth, Apr 12
Laurie, Hugh, Jun 11
Laurie, Piper: Birth, Jan 22
Laurier, Sir Wilfred: Birth Anniv, Nov 20
Lautenberg, Frank: Birth, Jan 23
Lauter, Ed: Birth, Oct 30
Lavallette Heritage Arts & Crafts Show (Lavallette, NJ), Jul 26
Laver, Rod: Birth, Aug 9
Laverne and Shirley TV Premiere: Anniv, Jan 27
Lavin, Linda: Birth, Oct 15
Lavoisier, Antoine-Lavoisier: Execution Anniv, May 8
Law & Order TV Premiere: Anniv, Sep 13
Law Day, USA (Pres Proc), May 1
Law Enforcement Appreciation Month in Florida, May 1
Law, Jude: Birth, Dec 29
Law: Mansfield, Arabella: Birth Anniv, May 23
Lawless, Lucy: Birth, Mar 29
Lawn Mower Race, Sta-Bil Natl Chmpshp (Mansfield, OH), Sep 5
Lawrence (of Arabia), T.E.: Birth Anniv, Aug 16
Lawrence Welk Show TV Premiere: Anniv, Jul 2
Lawrence, Carol: Birth, Sep 5
Lawrence, David H.: Birth Anniv, Sep 11
Lawrence, Jacob: Birth Anniv, Sep 7
Lawrence, James: Birth Anniv, Oct 1
Lawrence, Joey: Birth, Apr 20
Lawrence, Martin: Birth, Apr 16
Lawrence, Sharon: Birth, Jun 29
Lawrence, Steve: Birth, Jul 8
Lawrence, Vicki: Birth, Mar 26
Lawyers: Be Kind to Lawyers Day, Natl, Apr 14
Lazar, Irving "Swifty": Birth Anniv, Mar 28
Lazarus Saturday, Apr 11
Lazarus, Procession of Icon of Saint (Cyprus), Apr 11
Le Mat, Paul: Birth, Sep 22
Leach, Robin: Birth, Aug 29
Leachman, Cloris: Birth, Apr 30
Leacock, Stephen: Birth Anniv, Dec 30
Leadership: Courageous Follower Day, Mar 4
League of Nations: Anniv, Jan 10
League of United Latin American Citizens (LULAC) Founded: Anniv, Feb 17
League of Women Voters Formed: Anniv, Feb 14
Leahy, Patrick J.: Birth, Mar 31
Leakey, Richard E.: Birth, Dec 19
Lean, Sir David: Birth Anniv, Mar 25
Leap Second Adjustment Time, Jun 30
Leap Second Adjustment Time, Dec 31
Lear, Edward: Birth Anniv, May 12
Lear, Evelyn: Birth, Jan 18
Lear, Norman: Birth, Jul 27
Learned, Michael: Birth, Apr 9
Learning Disabilities Assn Intl Conf (Salt Lake City, UT), Feb 25
Leary, Timothy: Birth Anniv, Oct 22
Leaud, Jean-Pierre: Birth, May 5
Leave It to Beaver TV Premiere: Anniv, Oct 4
Leave the Office Earlier Day, Natl, Jun 2
Leavitt, Mike: Birth, Feb 11
Lebanon
  Independence Day, Nov 22
  Last American Hostage Released: Anniv, Dec 4
  Palestinian Massacre: Anniv, Sep 16
  St. Maron's Day, Feb 9
LeBlanc, Matt: Birth, Jul 25

LeBon, Simon: Birth, Oct 27
Lebowitz, Fran: Birth, Oct 27
LeCarre, John: Birth, Oct 19
Lee, Ang: Birth, Oct 23
Lee, Brenda: Birth, Dec 11
Lee, Bruce: Birth Anniv, Nov 27
Lee, Christopher: Birth, May 27
Lee, Francis Lightfoot: Birth Anniv, Oct 14
Lee, Harper: Birth, Apr 28
Lee, Harper: To Kill a Mockingbird Published: Anniv, Jul 11
Lee, Jason: Birth, Apr 25
Lee, Michele: Birth, Jun 24
Lee, Peggy: Birth Anniv, May 26
Lee, Richard Henry: Birth Anniv, Jan 20
Lee, Robert E.
  Battle of the Wilderness: Anniv, May 5
  Birth Anniv, Jan 19
  Defeat at Five Forks: Anniv, Apr 1
  Fall of Richmond: Anniv, Apr 3
  Lee-Jackson Day, Jan 16
  Seven Days Campaign: Anniv, Jun 25
Lee, Spike: Birth, Mar 20
Leetch, Brian: Birth, Mar 3
Leeves, Jane: Birth, Apr 18
Legal Assistants Day, Mar 26
Legal Awareness Day, Employee, Feb 13
Legend, John: Birth, Dec 28
Legrand, Michel: Birth, Feb 24
LeGuin, Ursula K.: Birth, Oct 21
Leguizamo, John: Birth, Jul 22
Lehrer, James: Birth, May 19
Lehrer, Tom: Birth, Apr 9
Lei Day (Hawaii), May 1
Leibman, Ron: Birth, Oct 11
Leif Ericson Day Celebration (Philadelphia, PA), Oct 11
Leigh, Janet: Birth Anniv, Jul 6
Leigh, Janet: Psycho Film Premiere: Anniv, Jun 16
Leigh, Jennifer Jason: Birth, Feb 5
Leigh, Vivian: Gone with the Wind Film Premiere: Anniv, Dec 15
Leinart, Matt: Birth, May 11
Leland, David: Birth, Apr 20
Lemieux, Mario: Birth, Oct 5
Lemmon, Jack: Birth Anniv, Feb 8
Lemon, Meadowlark: Birth, Apr 25
LeMond, Greg: Birth, Jun 26
Lendl, Ivan: Birth, Mar 7
L'Enfant, Pierre C.: Birth Anniv, Aug 2
Lenin, Nikolai: Birth Anniv, Apr 22
Leningrad: Corridor of Death: Anniv, Jan 13
Lennon, John
  Bed-in for Peace: Anniv, Mar 25
  Birth Anniv, Oct 9
  Death Anniv, Dec 8
  Lennon-Ono Album Confiscation: Anniv, Jan 3
  Meets McCartney: Anniv, Jul 6
Lennon, Julian: Birth, Apr 8
Lennox, Annie: Birth, Dec 25
Leno, Jay: Birth, Apr 28
Lent, Feb 25
Lent, Orthodox, Mar 2
Lenz, Kay: Birth, Mar 4
Leo Begins, Jul 23
Leonard, Elmore: Birth, Oct 11
Leonard, Justin: Birth, Jun 15
Leonard, Robert Sean: Birth, Feb 28
Leonard, Sugar Ray: Birth, May 17
Leonardo da Vinci: Death Anniv, May 2
Leoni, Tea: Birth, Feb 25
Leopold, Aldo: Aldo Leopold Weekend (WI), Mar 6
Lerner, Michael: Birth, Jun 22
Leroux, Charles: Last Jump: Anniv, Sep 12
Leslie, Lisa: Birth, Jul 7
Lesotho
  Army Day, Jan 20
  Independence Day, Oct 4
  Moshoeshoe's Day, Mar 12
  Tree Planting Day, Natl, Mar 21
Lester, Richard: Birth, Jan 19
Let It Go Day, Jun 23
Lethem, Jonathan: Birth, Feb 19
Let's Make a Deal TV Premiere: Anniv, Dec 30
Letter Carriers "Stamp Out Humor" Food Drive, May 9
Letter from America Radio Premiere: Anniv, Mar 24
Letterman, David: Birth, Apr 12
Leutze, Emanuel: Birth Anniv, May 24
Levin, Carl: Birth, Jun 28
Levine, Charles A.: Death Anniv, Dec 6
Levine, David: Birth, Dec 20
Levine, Irving R.: Birth, Aug 26
Levine, James: Birth, Jun 23
Levinson, Barry: Birth, Apr 6
Levy, Eugene: Birth, Dec 17
Lewis & Clark Expedition
  Clark, William: Birth Anniv, Aug 1
  Commissioned: Anniv, Jan 18
  Lewis and Clark Heritage Days (St. Charles, MO), May 15
  Lewis, Meriwether: Birth Anniv, Aug 18
  Reaches the Pacific Ocean: Anniv, Nov 16
  Returns: Anniv, Sep 23
  Sacagawea: Death Anniv, Dec 20
  Sets Out: Anniv, May 14
Lewis, Anthony: Birth, Mar 27
Lewis, C.S.: Birth Anniv, Nov 29
Lewis, Carl: Birth, Jul 1
Lewis, Clea: Birth, Jul 19
Lewis, Emmanuel: Birth, Mar 9
Lewis, Francis: Birth Anniv, Mar 21
Lewis, Gary: Birth, Jul 31
Lewis, Huey: Birth, Jul 5
Lewis, Jerry Lee: Birth, Sep 29
Lewis, Jerry: Birth, Mar 16
Lewis, John L.: Birth Anniv, Feb 12
Lewis, Juliette: Birth, Jun 21
Lewis, Leona: Birth, Apr 3
Lewis, Meriwether: Birth Anniv, Aug 18
Lewis, Ramsey: Birth, May 27
Lewis, Sinclair: Birth Anniv, Feb 7
Lewis, Sinclair: Sinclair Lewis Days (Sauk Centre, MN), Jul 12
Lewis, Vicki: Birth, Mar 17
Li, Jet: Birth, Apr 26
Liar's Contest, Big Whopper (New Harmony, IN), Sep 19
Libby, Willard F.: Birth Anniv, Dec 17
Liberace
  Birth Anniv, May 16
  Commemoration (Las Vegas, NV), Feb 4
  Piano Competition (Las Vegas, NV), Sep 20
  TV Show Premiere: Anniv, Jul 1
Liberation Day (Poland), Jan 17
Liberia
  Flag Day, Aug 24
  Independence Day, Jul 26
  J.J. Roberts Day, Mar 15
Liberty Day, Mar 23
Liberty Fall Fest (Liberty, MO), Sep 25
Libra Begins, Sep 23
Libraries Remember, Sep 11
Library/Librarians
  American Library Assn Annual Conf (Chicago, IL), Jul 9
  Boston Public Library: Anniv, Apr 3
  Church Library Month, Oct 1
  Federation of Library Assns Annual Conf, Intl (Milan, Italy), Aug 23
  First Presidential Library: Anniv, Nov 19
  Folk Tales and Fables Week, World, Mar 1
  Freedom of Information Day, Mar 16
  Friends of Lake Forest Library Book Sale (Lake Forest, IL), Sep 18
  Library Assn, American: Founding, Oct 6
  Library Card Sign-up Month, Sep 1
  Library Legislative Day, May 12
  Library Lovers' Month, Feb 1
  Library of Congress: Anniv, Apr 24
  Library Week, Natl, Apr 12
  Medical Librarians Month, Natl, Oct 1
  New York Public Library: Anniv, May 23
  School Library Media Month, Apr 1
  Teen Read Week, Oct 18
  Teen Tech Week, Mar 8
Libya
  British Bases Evacuation Day, Mar 28
  Evacuation Day, Jun 11
  Independence Day, Dec 24
  Revolution Day, Sep 1
License Plates, First: Anniv, Apr 25
Lichtenstein, Roy: Birth Anniv, Oct 27
Licorice Day, Natl, Apr 12
Liddy, G. Gordon: Birth, Nov 30
Lieberman, Joseph: Birth, Feb 24
Liebling, A.J.: Birth Anniv, Oct 18
Liechtenstein: National Day, Aug 15
Life Magazine Debuts: Anniv, Nov 23
Life Month, Celebration of, Jan 1
LifeLight Outdoor Music Fest (Sioux Falls, SD), Sep 4
Lifewriting Month, Natl, Nov 1
Light, Judith: Birth, Feb 9
Lightfoot, Gordon: Birth, Nov 17
Lil Margaret's Bluegrass and Old-Time Music Fest (Leonardtown, MD), Aug 6
Lilac Fest (Mackinac Island, MI), Jun 5
Liliuokalani Deposed, Queen: Anniv, Jan 17
Lillard, Matthew: Birth, Jan 24
Lilly, Evangeline: Birth, Aug 3
Lilly, Kristine: Birth, Jul 22
Lilly, William: Birth Anniv, Apr 30
Limbaugh, Rush, Natl Radio Show Premiere: Anniv, Aug 1
Limbaugh, Rush: Birth, Jan 12
Limerick Day, May 12
Lincoln, Abraham
  Assassination Anniv, Apr 14
  Assassination Conspirators Hanging: Anniv, Jul 7
  Birth Anniv, Feb 12
  Emancipation Proclamation Takes Effect: Anniv, Jan 1
  Emancipation Proclamation: Anniv, Sep 22
  Gettysburg Address: Anniv, Nov 19
  House Divided Speech: Anniv, Jun 16
  Lincoln Memorial Dedication: Anniv, May 30
  Lincoln-Douglas Debates: Anniv, Aug 21
  Lincoln's Birthplace Cabin Wreath Laying (Hodgenville, KY), Feb 12
  Oregon Birthday Observance, Feb 2
  Peninsula Campaign Intensified: Anniv, May 9
  Signs Income Tax: Anniv, Jul 1
Lincoln, Blanche Lambert: Birth, Sep 30
Lincoln, Mary Todd: Birth Anniv, Dec 13
Lind, Jenny: Birth Anniv, Oct 6
Lind, Jenny: US Premiere, Sep 11
Lindbergh Flight: Anniv, May 20

Lindbergh Kidnapping: Anniv, Mar 1
Lindbergh Kidnapping: Hauptmann Execution: Anniv, Apr 3
Lindbergh, Anne M.: Birth Anniv, Jun 22
Lindbergh, Charles A.: Birth Anniv, Feb 4
Linden, Hal: Birth, Mar 20
Lindros, Eric: Birth, Feb 28
Lindsay, Robert: Birth, Dec 12
Line Dance Week, Sep 14
Lingle, Linda: Birth, Jun 4
Linn-Baker, Mark: Birth, Jun 17
Linney, Laura: Birth, Feb 5
Liotta, Ray: Birth, Dec 18
Lipinski, Tara: Birth, Jun 10
Lippmann, Walter: Birth Anniv, Sep 23
Lips Appreciation Day, Mar 16
Lipton, Peggy: Birth, Aug 30
Lisbon Earthquake: Anniv, Nov 1
Lisi, Virna: Birth, Nov 8
Listening Awareness Month, Intl, Mar 1
Lister, Joseph: Birth Anniv, Apr 5
Liston, Sonny: Birth Anniv, May 8
Liszt, Franz: Birth Anniv, Oct 22
Litchfield Open House Tour (Litchfield, CT), Jul 10
Literacy Day, Intl (UN), Sep 8
Literature
  American Poet Laureate Establishment: Anniv, Dec 20
  Amis, Kingsley: Birth Anniv, Apr 16
  Anne Bradstreet Day, Sep 16
  Asimov, Isaac: Birth Anniv, Jan 2
  Authors' Day, Natl, Nov 1
  Bad Poetry Day, Aug 18
  Be Kind to Editors and Writers Month, Sep 1
  Beckett, Samuel: Birth Anniv, Apr 13
  Biographers Day, May 16
  Bollingen Prize Award: Anniv, Feb 19
  Buck, Pearl S.: Birth Anniv, Jun 26
  Child, Lydia Maria: Birth Anniv, Feb 11
  Cooper, James Fenimore: Birth Anniv, Sep 15
  Dickens, Charles: Birth Anniv, Feb 7
  Edgar Allan Poe Evermore (Manheim, PA), Oct 30
  Eliot, T.S.: Birth Anniv, Sep 26
  Eliza Doolittle Day, May 20
  Emerson, Ralph Waldo: Birth Anniv, May 25
  First Magazine Published in America: Anniv, Feb 13
  Grapes of Wrath Published: Anniv, Apr 14
  Haiku Poetry Day, Natl, Dec 21
  Hay-on-Wye Fest of Literature (Hay-on-Wye, Wales), May 21
  Hobbit Day, Sep 22
  I Love to Write Day, Nov 15
  Merriam, Eve: Birth Anniv, Jul 19
  Mystery Series Week, Oct 4
  Orwell, George: Birth Anniv, Jun 25
  Poe, Edgar Allan: Birth Anniv, Jan 19
  Poetry Month, Natl, Apr 1
  Pulitzer Prizes First Awarded: Anniv, Jun 4
  Silent Spring Publication: Anniv, Apr 13
  Solzhenitsyn Goes Home: Anniv, May 25
  Stowe, Harriet Beecher: Birth Anniv, Jun 14
  Texas Book Fest (Austin, TX), Oct 31
  The Duchess Who Wasn't Day, Aug 27
  Tolkien Week, Sep 20
  Tolkien, J.R.R.: Birth Anniv, Jan 3
  Underdog Day, Dec 18
  Vercors, Jean: Birth Anniv, Feb 26
  Ways with Words (Dartington, England), Jul 10
  Wheatley, Phillis: Death Anniv, Dec 5
  White, E.B.: Birth Anniv, Jul 11
  Whitman, Walt: Birth Anniv, May 31
  Wilde, Oscar: Birth Anniv, Oct 16
  Words by the Water: A Cumbrian Literature Fest (Lake District, England), Feb 27
Lithgow, John: Birth, Oct 19
Lithuania
  Baltic States' Independence Recognized: Anniv, Sep 6
  Day of Statehood, Jul 6
  Independence Day, Feb 16
  Restitution of Independence Day, Mar 11
Little House on the Prairie TV Premiere: Anniv, Sep 11
Little League Baseball World Series (Williamsport, PA), Aug 21
Little Orphan Annie: Gray, Harold Lincoln: Birth Anniv, Jan 20
Little Richard: Birth, Dec 5
Little Rock Nine: Anniv, Sep 4
Little Women Publication Anniv, Sep 30
Little, Cleavon: Birth Anniv, Jun 1
Little, Malcolm: Assassination Anniv, Feb 21
Little, Rich: Birth, Nov 26
Liu, Lucy: Birth, Dec 2
Live Aid Concerts: Anniv, Jul 13
Lively, Blake: Birth, Aug 25
Liver Awareness Month, Natl, Oct 1
Livermore, Mary: Birth Anniv, Dec 19
Livestock Show, Rio Grande Valley (Mercedes, TX), Mar 13
Livestock Show/Rodeo, Southwestern Expo (Fort Worth, TX), Jan 16
Livingston, Philip: Birth Anniv, Jan 15
Livingston, Robert: Birth Anniv, Nov 27
Livingston, Stanley: Birth, Nov 24
Livingstone, David: Birth Anniv, Mar 19
Livingstone, Stanley Finds: Anniv, Nov 10
Lizard Race, World's Greatest (Lovington, NM), Jul 4
Ljungberg, Freddie: Birth, Apr 16
Lloyd Webber, Andrew: Birth, Mar 22
Lloyd, Christopher: Birth, Oct 22
Lloyd, Emily: Birth, Sep 29
Lloyd, Eric: Birth, May 19
Lloyd, Harold: Birth Anniv, Apr 20
Lloyd, Pop: Birth Anniv, Apr 25
Lloyd, Sabrina: Birth, Nov 20
Lobo, Rebecca: Birth, Oct 6
Lobster Days (Mystic, CT), May 23
Lobster Fest, Maine (Rockland, ME), Jul 29
Locke, John: Birth Anniv, Aug 29
Locke, Sondra: Birth, May 28
Lockhart, June: Birth, Jun 25
Lockhart, Keith: Birth, Nov 7
Locklear, Heather: Birth, Sep 25
Lockport Old Canal Days (Lockport, IL), Jun 20
Lockwood, Belva A. Bennett: Birth Anniv, Oct 24
Lockwood, Gary: Birth, Feb 21
Locust Plague of 1874: Anniv, Jul 20
Loewy, Raymond: Birth Anniv, Nov 5
Lofgren, Nils: Birth, Jun 21
Lofton, James: Birth, Jul 5
Lofton, Kenny: Birth, May 31
Log Cabin Day (Michigan), Jun 28
Log Home Show and Natl Fest of the West (Scottsdale, AZ), Mar 19
Loggia, Robert: Birth, Jan 3
Logging and Timber Industry; Logger Competition
  Logging Museum Fest Days (Rangeley, ME), Jul 24
  Lumberjack World Chmpshps (Hayward, WI), Jul 23
Loggins, Kenny: Birth, Jan 7
Lohan, Lindsay: Birth, Jul 2
Lollobrigida, Gina: Birth, Jul 4
Loloma, Charles: Birth Anniv, Jun 9
Lombardi, Vince: Birth Anniv, Jun 11
Lombroso, Cesare: Birth Anniv, Nov 18
London Book Fair (England), Apr 20
London Marathon (London, England), Apr 26
London Terrorist Bombings: Anniv, Jul 7
London to Brighton Veteran Car Run (England), Nov 1
London, Jack: Birth Anniv, Jan 12
London, Jeremy: Birth, Nov 7
Lone Ranger TV Premiere: Anniv, Sep 15
Long Beach Bayou Fest (Long Beach, CA), Jun 21
Long Count Day, Sep 22
Long, Crawford: First Use Anesthetic (Doctor's Day), Mar 30
Long, Howie: Birth, Jan 6
Long, Huey P.: Day, Aug 30
Long, Shelley: Birth, Aug 23
Longest Dam Race (Fort Peck, MT), Jun 20
Longest War in History Ends: Anniv, Feb 5
Longfellow, Henry Wadsworth: Birth Anniv, Feb 27
Longoria, Eva: Birth, Mar 15
Long-Term Care Awareness Month, Natl, Nov 1
Long-Term Care Planning Month, Oct 1
Longwood Gardens Easter Celebration (Kennett Square, PA), Apr 11
Longwood Gardens Orchid Extravaganza (Kennett Square, PA), Jan 24
Longyear, John M.: Birth Anniv, Apr 15
Look Up and Live TV Premiere: Anniv, Jan 3
Loomis Day, May 30
Loos, Anita: Birth Anniv, Apr 26
Loosen Up, Lighten Up Day, Nov 14
Lopez, Javy: Birth, Nov 5
Lopez, Jennifer: Birth, Jul 24
Lopez, Mario: Birth, Oct 10
Lopez, Nancy: Birth, Jan 6
Lopez, Trini: Birth, May 15
Lopiano, Donna: Birth, Sep 11
Lord Mayor's Show (London, England), Nov 14
Lord of the Rings, First Part Published: Anniv, Jul 19
Lord, Jack: Hawaii Five-O TV Premiere: Anniv, Sep 26
Loren, Sophia: Birth, Sep 20
Loring, Gloria: Birth, Dec 10
Los Angeles, CA, Founded: Anniv, Sep 4
Los Angeles, CA: Chicken Boy's Birthday, Sep 1
Lost Dutchman Days (Apache Junction, AZ), Feb 20
Lott, Ronnie: Birth, May 8
Lott, Trent: Birth, Oct 9
Lotus 1-2-3 Released: Anniv, Jan 26
Louganis, Greg: Birth, Jan 29
Loughlin, Lori: Birth, Jul 28
Louie Louie Day, Intl, Apr 11
Louis v Braddock/Schmeling Fight Anniv, Jun 22
Louis, Joe: Birth Anniv, May 13
Louis-Dreyfus, Julia: Birth, Jan 13

Louise, Tina: Birth, Feb 11
Louisiana
Admission Day, Apr 30
Allstate Sugar Bowl (New Orleans), Jan 2
Art & Folk Fest (Columbia), Oct 10
Caldwell Country Christmas Parade & Fireworks (Columbia), Dec 5
Christmas Fest of Lights (Natchitoches), Dec 5
Christmas New Orleans Style (New Orleans), Dec 1
Farragut Captures New Orleans: Anniv, Apr 25
French Quarter Fest (New Orleans), Apr 17
Gumbo Fest (Bridge City), Oct 9
Holiday in Dixie (Shreveport and Bossier City), Apr 17
Holiday Tour of Homes (Natchitoches), Dec 9
Hot Heads Chili Cook-off (Ruston), Jan 17
Huey P. Long Day, Aug 30
Jindal, Bobby: Birth, Jun 10
Krewe of Bacchus Parade (New Orleans), Feb 22
Krewe of Carrollton Parade (New Orleans), Feb 15
Krewe of Endymion Parade (New Orleans), Feb 21
Krewe of Rex Mardi Gras Parade (New Orleans), Feb 24
Landrieu, Mary L.: Birth, Nov 23
Louisiana Purchase Day, Apr 30
Louisiana State Fiddle Chmpshp (Natchitoches), Jul 17
Louisiana Yambilee Fest (Opelousas), Oct 22
Lousiana Sportsmen's Show and Fest (Gonzales), Mar 5
Marksville Easter Egg Knocking Contest (Marksville), Apr 12
Melrose Plantation Arts/Crafts Fest (Melrose), Jun 13
Mudbug Madness (Shreveport), May 21
Natchitoches Fest of Lights (Natchitoches), Nov 21
Natchitoches Historic Pilgrimage (Natchitoches), Oct 10
Natchitoches Jazz Fest (Natchitoches), Apr 17
Natchitoches-NW State Univ Folk Fest (Natchitoches), Jul 17
New Orleans Boat Show (New Orleans), Jan 7
New Orleans Jazz/Heritage Fest (New Orleans), Apr 24
Ouachita River Big Bass Fishing Tourn (West Monroe), May 16
Peach Fest, Louisiana (Ruston), Jun 26
Riverboat Fest (Columbia), May 16
Saint Patrick's Day Parade (Baton Rouge), Mar 14
Satchmo Summerfest (New Orleans), Jul 30
Scholarship Providers Assn Conf, Natl (New Orleans), Oct 27
Shrimp and Petroleum Fest, Louisiana (Morgan City), Sep 3
Speech-Language-Hearing Conv, American (New Orleans), Nov 19
State Fair of Louisiana (Shreveport), Oct 22
Twin Cities Krewe of Janus Mardi Gras Parade (Monroe), Feb 7
Vitter, David: Birth, May 3
Zulu Mardi Gras Parade (New Orleans), Feb 24
Lousma, Jack: Birth, Feb 29
Love a Mensch Week, Feb 14
Love Boat TV Premiere: Anniv, Sep 24
Love Canal Declared Disaster Area: Anniv, Aug 7
Love Is a Many Splendored Thing TV Premiere: Anniv, Sep 18
Love Litigating Lawyers Day, Aug 31
Love May Make World Go 'Round, but Laughter Keeps Us from Getting Dizzy Week, Feb 8
Love Note Day, Sep 25
Love of Life TV Premiere: Anniv, Sep 24
Love the Children Day, Texas, Mar 29
Love, Courtney: Birth, Jul 9
Love, Davis, III: Birth, Apr 13
Love, Mike: Birth, Mar 15
Lovecraft, H.P.: Birth Anniv, Aug 20
Lovejoy, Elijah P.: Birth Anniv, Nov 9
Lovell, James: Birth, Mar 25
Lovera, Juan: Birth Anniv, Dec 26
Lover's Day, Book Day and (Spain), Apr 23
Lover's Fair (Belgium), Dec 3
Lovett, Lyle: Birth, Nov 1
Loving v Virginia: Anniv, Jun 12
Lovitz, Jon: Birth, Jul 21
Low Country Shrimp Fest (McClellanville, SC), May 2
Low, Juliet: Birth Anniv, Oct 31
Lowe, Chad: Birth, Jan 15
Lowe, Rob: Birth, Mar 17
Lowell, Amy: Birth Anniv, Feb 9
Lowell, Carey: Birth, Feb 11
Lowell, James R.: Birth Anniv, Feb 22
Lowell, Percival: Birth Anniv, Mar 13
Loy, Myrna: Birth Anniv, Aug 2
Loyalty Day (Pres Proc), May 1
Lucas, George: Birth, May 14
Lucas, Josh: Birth, Mar 26
Lucci, Susan: Birth, Dec 23
Luce, Clare Boothe: Birth Anniv, Mar 10
Luce, Henry: Birth Anniv, Apr 3
Lucid, Shannon: Birth, Jan 14
Luck: Open an Umbrella Indoors Day, Natl, Mar 13
Luckinbill, Laurence: Birth, Nov 21
Ludendorff, Erich: Birth Anniv, Apr 9
Luft, Lorna: Birth, Nov 21
Lugar, Richard G.: Birth, Apr 4
Lughnasadh, Aug 1
Lugosi, Bela: Birth Anniv, Oct 20
Lugosi, Bela: Dracula Premiere: Anniv, Feb 12
LULAC (League of United Latin American Citizens) Founded: Anniv, Feb 17
Lully, Jean Baptiste: Birth Anniv, Nov 28
Lumberjack World Chmpshps (Hayward, WI), Jul 23
Lumet, Sidney: Birth, Jun 25
Lumiere, Auguste: Birth Anniv, Oct 19
Lumiere, Louis: Birth Anniv, Oct 5
Lumpy Rug Day, May 3
Lunden, Joan: Birth, Sep 19
Lundgren, Dolph: Birth, Nov 3
Luner, Jamie: Birth, May 12
Lung Assn, American: Christmas Seal Campaign, Oct 1
Lung Cancer Awareness Month, Nov 1
Lunsford, Bascom Lamar: Birth Anniv, Mar 21
Lupercalia, Feb 15
LuPone, Patti: Birth, Apr 21
Lurie, Alison: Birth, Sep 3
Lusitania Sinking: Anniv, May 7
Luther, Martin: Birth Anniv, Nov 10
Luxembourg
Beer Fest, Jul 19
Blessing of the Wine (Greiveldange), Dec 26
Bretzelsonndeg (Pretzel Sunday), Mar 22
Burgsonndeg, Mar 1
Candlemas, Feb 2
Emaishen, Apr 13
Ettelbruck Remembrance Day, Jul 6
Liberation Ceremony, Sep 9
National Holiday, Jun 23
Osweiler, Mar 27
Schuebermess Shepherd's Fair, Aug 23
Luyts, Jan: Birth Anniv, Sep 19
Lydon, John (Johnny Rotten): Birth, Jan 31
Lyman, Dorothy: Birth, Apr 18
Lynch, David: Birth, Jan 20
Lynch, John: Birth, Nov 25
Lynch, Kelly: Birth, Jan 31
Lynch, Thomas: Birth Anniv, Aug 5
Lynley, Carol: Birth, Feb 13
Lynn, Jonathan: Birth, Apr 3
Lynn, Loretta: Birth, Apr 14
Lyon, Mary: Birth Anniv, Feb 28
Lyon, Sue: Birth, Jul 10

M

M*A*S*H Final Episode: Anniv, Feb 28
M*A*S*H TV Premiere: Anniv, Sep 17
Ma, Yo-Yo: Birth, Oct 7
Maass, Clara: Birth Anniv, Jun 28
Maastricht European Fine Art Fair (Maastricht, Netherlands), Mar 13
Mabius, Eric: Birth, Apr 22
Mabon, Sep 22
MacArthur Returns: US Landings on Leyte, Philippines: Anniv, Oct 20
MacArthur, Douglas: Birth Anniv, Jan 26
MacArthur, James: Birth, Dec 8
Macau: Reverts to Chinese Control: Anniv, Dec 20
Macaulay, Thomas B.: Birth Anniv, Oct 25
Macchio, Ralph: Birth, Nov 4
MacCorkindale, Simon: Birth, Feb 12
MacDonald, Anne Thompson: Death Anniv, Oct 12
MacDonald, John A.: Birth Anniv, Jan 11
Macdonald, Norm: Birth, Oct 17
MacDowell, Andie: Birth, Apr 21
Macedonia
Independence Day, Sep 8
National Day, Aug 2
Saint Elias Day (Uprising): Anniv, Aug 2
MacFadden, Bernarr: Birth Anniv, Aug 16
MacGraw, Ali: Birth, Apr 1
Machias Wild Blueberry Fest (Machias, ME), Aug 21
Machiavelli, Niccolo: Birth Anniv, May 3
MacInnis, Al: Birth, Jul 11
Macintosh Debuts: Anniv, Jan 25
MacKenzie, Alexander: Birth Anniv, Jan 28
Mackie, Bob: Birth, Mar 24
Mackinac Bridge Walk (St. Ignace, MI), Sep 7
MacLachlan, Kyle: Birth, Feb 22
MacLaine, Shirley: Birth, Apr 24
MacLeish, Archibald: Birth Anniv, May 7
MacMurray, Fred: Birth Anniv, Aug 30
MacNeil, Robert: Birth, Jan 19
MacNeil-Lehrer Newshour TV Premiere: Anniv, Sep 5
MacNicol, Peter: Birth, Apr 10
Macpherson, Elle: Birth, Mar 29

MacRae, Sheila: Birth, Sep 24
Macy, William H.: Birth, Mar 13
Mad Magazine: Gaines, William M.: Birth Anniv, Mar 1
Mad Magazine: Kurtzman, Harvey: Birth Anniv, Oct 3
Madagascar
Commemoration Day, Mar 29
Independence Day, Jun 26
Madama Butterfly Premiere: Anniv, Feb 17
Madden, John: Birth, Apr 10
Maddux, Greg: Birth, Apr 14
Madigan, Amy: Birth, Sep 11
Madison, Dolly: Birth Anniv, May 20
Madison, James: Birth Anniv, Mar 16
Madonna: Birth, Aug 16
Madrid Train Bombings: Anniv, Mar 11
Madsen, Michael: Birth, Sep 25
Madsen, Virginia: Birth, Sep 11
Maffia, Roma: Birth, May 31
Magazine Month, Children's, Oct 1
Magazine, First Published in America: Anniv, Feb 13
Magellan, Ferdinand: Death Anniv, Apr 27
Magic Day, Oct 31
Magic Week, Intl, Oct 25
Magic: Robert-Houdin, Jean Eugene: Birth Anniv, Dec 6
Magna Carta Day, Jun 15
Magnum, PI TV Premiere: Anniv, Dec 11
Magnuson, Ann: Birth, Jan 4
Maguire, Tobey: Birth, Jun 27
Maher, Bill: Birth, Jan 20
Mahoney, John: Birth, Jun 20
Maifest (Covington, KY), May 15
Mail: Pony Express, Inauguration of: Anniv, Apr 3
Mail: V-Mail Delivery: Anniv, Jun 22
Mail-Order Catalog: Anniv, Aug 18
Mailorder Gardening Month, Natl, Jan 1
Maine
Acadia Natl Park Established: Anniv, Jan 1
Acton Fair (Acton), Aug 27
Admission Day, Mar 15
Apple Saturdays (New Gloucester), Sep 26
Baldacci, John: Birth, Jan 30
Bangor State Fair (Bangor), Jul 31
Blue Hill Fair (Blue Hill), Sep 3
Chester Greenwood Day Parade (Farmington), Dec 5
Coats & Toys for Kids Day, Dec 5
Collins, Susan M.: Birth, Dec 7
Common Ground Country Fair (Unity), Sep 25
Down East Spring Birding Fest (Eastport, Whiting, Lubec), May 22
Eastport "Old Home Week" Celebration (Eastport), Jul 1
Fryeburg Fair (Fryeburg), Oct 4
Logging Museum Fest Days (Rangeley), Jul 24
Machias Wild Blueberry Fest (Machias), Aug 21
Maine Highland Games (Brunswick), Aug 15
Maine Law: Anniv, Jun 2
Maine Lobster Fest (Rockland), Jul 29
Patriots' Day, Apr 20
Shaker Christmas Fair (New Gloucester), Dec 5
Shaker Museum Opening Day (New Gloucester), May 22
Sidewalk Art Fest (Portland), Aug 22
Skowhegan State Fair (Skowhegan), Aug 13
Snowe, Olympia J.: Birth, Feb 21
Thomas Point Beach Bluegrass Fest (Brunswick), Sep 3
West Quoddy Head Light Keepers Association Anniv Celebration (Lubec), Jul 11
Windjammer Days (Boothbay Harbor), Jun 23
Yarmouth Clam Fest (Yarmouth), Jul 17
Maines, Natalie: Birth, Oct 14
MainStrasse Village Original Goettafest (Covington, KY), Jun 12
Maize Day, Nov 27
Majerle, Dan: Birth, Sep 9
Major, John: Birth, Mar 29
Majors, Lee: Birth, Apr 23
Make a Difference to Children Month, Natl, Jul 1
Make Room for Daddy TV Premiere: Anniv, Sep 29
Make Up Your Mind Day, Dec 31
Make Up Your Own Holiday Day, Mar 26
Makeba, Miriam: Birth, Mar 4
Makepeace, Chris: Birth, Apr 22
Malaria Awareness Day (Pres Proc), Apr 25
Malaria Day, World, Apr 25
Malawi
Freedom Day, Jun 14
John Chilembwe Day, Jan 16
Martyr's Day, Mar 3
Republic Day, Jul 6
Malaysia
Freedom Day, Aug 31
Head of State's Official Birthday, Jun 6
Malcolm X: Assassination Anniv, Feb 21
Malcolm X: Birth Anniv, May 19
Malden, Karl: Birth, Mar 22
Maldives
Independence Day, Jul 26
Republic Day, Nov 11
Maleska, Eugene T.: Birth Anniv, Jan 6
Mali: Independence Day, Sep 22
Malick, Wendie: Birth, Dec 13
Malinowski, Bronislaw: Birth Anniv, Apr 7
Malkovich, John: Birth, Dec 9
Malle, Louis: Birth Anniv, Oct 30
Mallory, George L.: Birth Anniv, Jun 18
Malone, Dorothy: Birth, Jan 30
Malone, Karl: Birth, Jul 24
Malone, Moses: Birth, Mar 23
Maloney, Janel: Birth, Oct 3
Malta
Carnival, Feb 21
Feast of St. Paul's Shipwreck (Valletta), Feb 10
Independence Day, Sep 21
Mnarja, Jun 22
National Day, Jun 7
Republic Day, Dec 13
Siege Broken: Anniv, Sep 8
Maltese Falcon: Publication Anniv, Feb 14
Malthus, Thomas: Birth Anniv, Feb 17
Maltin, Leonard: Birth, Dec 18
Mama TV Premiere: Anniv, Jul 1
Mamet, David: Birth, Nov 30
Mammography Day, Natl, Oct 16
Mammoth Cave Natl Park Established: Anniv, Jul 1
Man Day, Feb 8
Mananitas, Las (Ponce, Puerto Rico), Dec 12
Manchester United Plane Crash: Anniv, Feb 6
Manchester, Melissa: Birth, Feb 15
Manchin, Joe, III: Birth, Aug 24
Mancini, Henry: Birth Anniv, Apr 16
Mandan, Robert: Birth, Feb 2
Mandarich, Tony: Birth, Sep 23
Mandel, Howie: Birth, Nov 29
Mandela, Nelson
Birthday, Jul 18
Inauguration: Anniv, May 10
Prison Release Anniv, Feb 11
Mandrell, Barbara: Birth, Dec 25
Mandrell, Louise: Birth, Jul 13
Manet, Edouard: Birth Anniv, Jan 23
Mangano, Silvana: Birth Anniv, Apr 21
Mangione, Chuck: Birth, Nov 29
Manheim, Camryn: Birth, Mar 8
Manilow, Barry: Birth, Jun 17
Mankiewicz, Joseph L.: Birth Anniv, Feb 11
Mankiller, Wilma: Birth, Nov 18
Mann, Horace: Birth Anniv, May 4
Mann, James: Birth Anniv, Oct 20
Mann, Marty: Birth Anniv, Oct 15
Manners, Miss (Judith Martin): Birth, Sep 13
Manning, Danny: Birth, May 17
Manning, Eli: Birth, Jan 3
Manning, Peyton: Birth, Mar 24
Mannix TV Premiere: Anniv, Sep 16
Manoff, Dinah: Birth, Jan 25
Man-Powered Flight, First: Anniv, Aug 23
Mansfield, Arabella: Birth Anniv, May 23
Manson, Patrick: Birth Anniv, Oct 3
Manstein, Erich von: Birth Anniv, Nov 24
Mantegna, Joe: Birth, Nov 13
Mantle, Mickey: Birth Anniv, Oct 20
Mantooth, Randolph: Birth, Sep 19
Manuel, Jay: Birth, Aug 14
Mao Tse-Tung: Birth Anniv, Dec 26
Mao Tse-Tung: Death Anniv, Sep 9
Maple Fair, Parke County (Rockville, IN), Feb 21
Maple Fest, Highland County (Highland County, VA), Mar 14
Maple Syrup Saturday (Appleton, WI), Mar 21
Maples, Marla: Birth, Oct 27
Mapplethorpe, Robert: Birth Anniv, Nov 4
Maradona, Diego: Birth, Oct 30
Marathon, Battle of: Anniv, Sep 9
Marathon, Historic Runs: Anniv, Sep 2
Marbles
Knuckles Down Month, Natl, Apr 1
Marble Meet, Northeast (Marlborough, MA), Oct 10
Marbles Chmpshp, British and World (England), Apr 10
Marbury, Stephon: Birth, Feb 20
Marceau, Sophie: Birth, Nov 17
March Forth—Do Something Day, Mar 4
March into Literacy Month, Natl, Mar 1
March, Fredric: Birth Anniv, Aug 8
Marciano, Rocky: Birth Anniv, Sep 1
Marconi, Guglielmo: Birth Anniv, Apr 25
Marcos, Ferdinand: Birth Anniv, Sep 11
Marcovicci, Andrea: Birth, Nov 18
Mardi Gras, Feb 24
Marfan Syndrome Awareness Month, Feb 1
Margolin, Stuart: Birth, Jan 31
Margulies, Julianna: Birth, Jun 8
Mariachi Conf, Tucson Intl (Tucson, AZ), Apr 20
Marie Antoinette: Execution Anniv, Oct 16
Marilyn Monroe's First Screen Test: Anniv, Jul 19
Marin, Cheech: Birth, Jul 13
Marinaro, Ed: Birth, Mar 31
Marine Corps Birthday: Anniv, Nov 10
Marino, Dan: Birth, Sep 15
Mario Day, Mar 10
Marion, Shawn: Birth, May 7

Maris Breaks Ruth Home Run Record: Anniv, Oct 1
Maris, Roger: Birth Anniv, Sep 10
Maritime Day, Natl, May 22
Maritime Day, Natl (Pres Proc), May 22
Markert, Russell: Birth Anniv, Aug 8
Marketing: Entrepreneurs "Do It Yourself" Marketing Month, Jun 1
Marley, Bob: Birth Anniv, Feb 6
Maroon Fest (Jamaica), Jan 6
Marquette, Jacques: Birth Anniv, Jun 1
Marriage Day, World, Feb 8
Marriage of Elizabeth and Philip: Anniv, Nov 20
Marriage: Loving v Virginia: Anniv, Jun 12
Marriage: Proposal Day!, Mar 20
Marriage: UK Allows Same-Sex Civil Partnerships: Anniv, Dec 21
Married Day, Decide to Be, Jun 27
Married to a Scorpio Support Day, Nov 18
Married with Children TV Premiere: Anniv, Apr 5
Marsalis, Branford: Birth, Aug 26
Marsalis, Wynton: Birth, Oct 18
Marsh, Jean: Birth, Jul 1
Marshall Islands: National Day, May 1
Marshall Plan: Anniv, Apr 3
Marshall, Garry: Birth, Nov 13
Marshall, George: Birth Anniv, Dec 31
Marshall, John: Appointed Chief Justice: Anniv, Jan 20
Marshall, John: Birth Anniv, Sep 24
Marshall, Penny: Birth, Oct 15
Marshall, Peter: Birth, Mar 30
Marshall, Thomas Riley: Birth Anniv, Mar 14
Marshall, Thurgood: Birth Anniv, Jul 2
Marshall, Thurgood: Resigns from Supreme Court: Anniv, Jun 27
Marshall, Thurgood: Sworn in to Supreme Court: Anniv, Oct 2
Marti, Jose Julian: Birth Anniv, Jan 28
Martin Z. Mollusk Day (Ocean City, NJ), May 7
Martin, Andrea: Birth, Jan 15
Martin, Ann M.: Birth, Aug 12
Martin, Billy: Birth Anniv, May 16
Martin, Chris: Birth, Mar 2
Martin, Curtis: Birth, May 1
Martin, Dean: Birth Anniv, Jun 7
Martin, Jesse L.: Birth, Jan 18
Martin, Judith: Birth, Sep 13
Martin, Kellie: Birth, Oct 16
Martin, Kenyon: Birth, Dec 30
Martin, Mary: Birth Anniv, Dec 1
Martin, Pamela Sue: Birth, Jan 5
Martin, Paul: Birth, Aug 28
Martin, Ricky: Birth, Dec 24
Martin, Steve: Birth, Aug 14
Martinez, Edgar: Birth, Jan 2
Martinez, Jose: Birth, May 14
Martinez, Mel: Birth, Oct 23
Martinez, Pedro: Birth, Oct 25
Martinez, Tino: Birth, Dec 7
Martinique: Mount Pelee Eruption: Anniv, May 8
Martinmas, Nov 11
Martinmas Goose (Switzerland), Nov 11
Martino, Al: Birth, Oct 7
Martyrs Day (Bangladesh), Feb 21
Martyrs' Day (Panama), Jan 9
Marvell, Andrew: Birth Anniv, Mar 31
Marx, Groucho: Birth Anniv, Oct 2
Marx, Harpo: Birth Anniv, Nov 23
Marx, Karl: Birth Anniv, May 5
Marx, Richard: Birth, Sep 16
Mary Tyler Moore Show TV Premiere: Anniv, Sep 19
Mary, Queen of Scots: Execution Anniv, Feb 8
Maryland
  Adopts Articles of Confederation: Anniv, Jan 30
  Autumn Arts Fest (Hagerstown), Sep 12
  Baltimore Book Fest (Baltimore), Sep 25
  Boonesborough Days (Boonsboro), Sep 12
  Cardin, Ben: Birth, Oct 5
  Catoctin ColorFest Arts/Crafts (Thurmont), Oct 10
  Celtic Fest, Southern Maryland (St. Leonard), Apr 25
  Country Fest and Auction (Deep Creek Lake), Aug 22
  Defenders Day, Sep 12
  Delmarva Chicken Fest (Centreville), Jun 19
  Fairmount Academy 1800s Fest (Fairmount), May 30
  Fell's Point Fun Fest (Baltimore), Oct 3
  Grand Militia Muster (St. Mary's City), Oct 17
  Grantsville Days (Grantsville), Jun 26
  Hard Crab Derby and Fair, Natl (Crisfield), Sep 4
  Hearth and Home in Early Maryland (St. Mary's City), Nov 27
  Heritage Days Fest (Cumberland), Jun 13
  John Wilkes Booth Escape Route Tour (Clinton), Apr 11
  Lil Margaret's Bluegrass and Old-Time Music Fest (Leonardtown), Aug 6
  Maryland Constitution Ratification: Anniv, Apr 28
  Maryland Day, Mar 25
  Maryland Home and Garden Show (Baltimore), Mar 6
  Maryland Renaissance Fest (Annapolis), Aug 29
  Mikulski, Barbara Ann: Birth, Jul 20
  Montgomery County Agricultural Fair (Gaithersburg), Aug 7
  O'Malley, Martin: Birth, Jan 18
  Preakness Stakes (Baltimore), May 16
  St. Mary's County Oyster Fest (Leonardtown), Oct 17
  State Fair (Timonium), Aug 28
  Sugarloaf Crafts Fest (Gaithersburg), Apr 3
  Sugarloaf Crafts Fest (Gaithersburg), Oct 9
  Sugarloaf Crafts Fest (Gaithersburg), Nov 20
  Sugarloaf Crafts Fest (Timonium), Oct 2
  Sugarloaf Crafts Fest (Timonium), Apr 24
  Tidewater Archaeology Dig (St. Mary's City), Jul 25
  Towsontown Spring Fest (Towson), May 2
  Victorian Christmas Celebration (Cumberland), Nov 27
  Ward World Chmpshp Waterfowl Carving Competition (Ocean City), Apr 24
  Waterfowl Fest (Easton), Nov 13
  Woodland Indian Discovery Day (St. Mary's City), Sep 12
Mason, Bobbie Ann: Birth, May 1
Mason, Dave: Birth, May 10
Mason, Jackie: Birth, Jun 9
Mason, Marsha: Birth, Apr 3
Massachusetts
  American Heroine Rewarded: Anniv, Jun 8
  Big E (West Springfield), Sep 18
  Boston Fire: Anniv, Nov 9
  Boston Marathon (Boston), Apr 20
  Boston Public Library: Anniv, Apr 3
  Bridge over the Neponset: Anniv, Apr 1
  Bunker Hill Day (Suffolk County), Jun 17
  Children's Day, Jun 14
  Christmas Stroll Weekend (Nantucket Island), Dec 4
  Craft Brewers Conf & BrewExpo America (Boston), Apr 21
  Daffodil Fest Weekend (Nantucket Island), Apr 24
  Evacuation Day (Boston), Mar 17
  Fall on Nantucket (Nantucket Island), Sep 1
  First Night (Boston), Dec 31
  Haitian Heritage Month, May 1
  Ig Nobel Prize Ceremony (Cambridge), Oct 1
  John F. Kennedy Day, Nov 29
  Kennedy, Edward Moore: Birth, Feb 22
  Kerry, John F.: Birth, Dec 11
  Northeast Marble Meet (Marlborough), Oct 10
  Original Massachusetts Home & Garden Show (West Springfield), Mar 26
  Patrick, Deval: Birth, Jul 31
  Patriots' Day, Apr 20
  Plymouth Plantation Earthquake: Anniv, Jun 1
  Railroad and Hobby Show (Springfield), Jan 24
  Ratification Day, Feb 6
  Romney, Mitt: Birth, Mar 12
  Sandcastle & Sculpture Day (Nantucket Island), Aug 15
  Student Government Day, Apr 3
  34th St Express (Boston), Dec 19
  US Women's Amateur Public Links Chmpshp (Devens), Jun 22
  WMAS Annual Halloween Ball (Springfield), Oct 31
  WMAS Valentine's Ball (Springfield), Feb 14
Massacre at Fort Pillow: Anniv, Apr 12
Massage: Baby Massage Day, Apr 11
Massey, Anna: Birth, Aug 11
Masterpiece Theatre TV Premiere: Anniv, Jan 10
Masters, Ben: Birth, May 6
Masters, Edgar Lee: Birth Anniv, Aug 23
Masterson, Bat: Birth Anniv, Nov 27
Masterson, Christopher: Birth, Jan 22
Masterson, Mary Stuart: Birth, Jun 28
Mastrantonio, Mary Elizabeth: Birth, Nov 17
Mastrioeni, Pablo: Birth, Aug 29
Mastroianni, Marcello: Birth Anniv, Sep 28
Masur, Richard: Birth, Nov 20
Mata Hari: Birth Anniv, Aug 7
Mata Hari: Execution Anniv, Oct 15
Matanzas Mule Day, Apr 27
Mathematics: Pi Day, Mar 14
Mathers, Jerry: Birth, Jun 2
Mathers, Marshall (Eminem): Birth, Oct 17
Matheson, Tim: Birth, Dec 31
Mathewson, Christy: Birth Anniv, Aug 12
Mathis, Johnny: Birth, Sep 30
Matisse, Henri: Birth Anniv, Dec 31
Matlin, Marlee: Birth, Aug 24
Matson, Boyd: Birth, Apr 26
Matsui, Hideki: Birth, Jun 12
Matsuzake, Daisuke: Birth, Sep 13
Matthau, Walter: Birth Anniv, Oct 1
Matthews, Dave: Birth, Jan 9

Matthews, DeLane: Birth, Aug 7
Mattingly, Don: Birth, Apr 20
Maude TV Premiere: Anniv, Sep 12
Maugham, W. Somerset: Birth Anniv, Jan 25
Maundy Thursday (Holy Thursday), Apr 9
Maura, Carmen: Birth, Sep 15
Mauresmo, Amelie: Birth, Jul 5
Mauritania: Independence Day, Nov 28
Mauritius: Independence Day, Mar 12
Maury, Matthew Fontaine: Birth Anniv, Jan 14
Maverick TV Premiere: Anniv, Sep 22
Mawlid al Nabi: Birthday of Prophet Muhammad, Mar 9
Max, Peter: Birth, Oct 19
Maxwell, James Clerk: Birth Anniv, Nov 13
Maxwell, Robert: Death Anniv, Nov 5
May Day, May 1
May Day Bank Holiday (United Kingdom), May 4
May Day Fairie Fest (Glen Rock, PA), May 1
May Ray Day, May 19
May, Elaine: Birth, Apr 21
Mayall, John: Birth, Nov 29
Mayer, John: Birth, Oct 16
Mayer, Maria Goeppert: Birth Anniv, Jun 28
Mayflower Day, Sep 16
Mayo, Charles: Birth Anniv, Jul 19
Mayo, William J.: Birth Anniv, Jun 29
Mayron, Melanie: Birth, Oct 20
Mays, Willie: Birth, May 6
Mayweather, Floyd, Jr: Birth, Feb 24
Mazowiecki, Tadeusz: Poland: Solidarity Founded: Anniv, Aug 31
Mazursky, Paul: Birth, Apr 25
McAliskey, Bernadette Devlin: Birth, Apr 23
McArdle, Andrea: Birth, Nov 4
McAuliffe, Christa: Birth Anniv, Sep 2
McAvoy, James: Birth, Jan 1
McBrayer, Jack: Birth, May 27
McBride, Brian: Birth, Jun 19
McBride, Martina: Birth, Jul 29
McBride, Patricia: Birth, Aug 23
McCain, John Sidney, III: Birth, Aug 29
McCallum, David: Birth, Sep 19
McCarthy Silenced by Senate: Anniv, Dec 2
McCarthy, Andrew: Birth, Nov 29
McCarthy, Cormac: Birth, Jul 20
McCarthy, Eugene: Birth Anniv, Mar 29
McCarthy, Jenny: Birth, Nov 1
McCarthy, Joseph: Birth Anniv, Nov 14
McCarthy, Kevin: Birth, Feb 15
McCartney, Paul: Beatles Break Up: Anniv, Apr 10
McCartney, Paul: Birth, Jun 18
McCartney, Paul: Meets John Lennon: Anniv, Jul 6
McCartney, Stella: Birth, Sep 13
McCaskill, Claire: Birth, July 24
McClanahan, Rue: Birth, Feb 21
McClure, Marc: Birth, Mar 31
McClure, Samuel S.: Birth Anniv, Feb 17
McClurg, Edie: Birth, Jul 23
McConaughey, Matthew: Birth, Nov 4
McConnell, Mitch: Birth, Feb 20
McCoo, Marilyn: Birth, Sep 30
McCormack, Eric: Birth, Apr 18
McCormick, Cyrus H.: Birth Anniv, Feb 15
McCourt, Frank: Birth, Aug 19
McCoy-Hatfield Feud Erupts: Anniv, Aug 7
McCrea, Joel: Birth Anniv, Nov 5
McDaniel, Hattie: Birth Anniv, Jun 10
McDermott, Dylan: Birth, Oct 26
McDonald's Opens, First: Anniv, Apr 15
McDonnell, Mary: Birth, Apr 28
McDormand, Frances: Birth, Jun 23
McDowell, Jack Burns: Birth, Jan 16
McDowell, Malcolm: Birth, Jun 13
McEnroe, John Patrick, Jr: Birth, Feb 16
McEntire, Reba: Birth, Mar 28
McEwan, Ian: Birth, May 21
McEwen, Mark: Birth, Sep 16
McFarland, George (Spanky): Birth Anniv, Oct 2
McFerrin, Bobby: Birth, Mar 11
McGillis, Kelly: Birth, Jul 9
McGinley, John: Birth, Aug 3
McGinley, Ted: Birth, May 30
McGoohan, Patrick: Birth, Mar 19
McGovern, Elizabeth: Birth, Jul 18
McGovern, George: Birth, Jul 19
McGovern, Maureen: Birth, Jul 27
McGowan, Rose: Birth, Sep 5
McGrady, Tracy: Birth, May 24
McGrath, Mark: Birth, Mar 15
McGraw, Dr. Phil: Birth, Sep 1
McGraw, John: Birth Anniv, Apr 7
McGraw, Tim: Birth, May 1
McGregor, Ewan: Birth, Mar 31
McGriff, Fred: Birth, Oct 31
McGuffey, William H.: Birth Anniv, Sep 23
McGuinn, Roger: Birth, Jul 13
McGwire Breaks Home Run Record: Anniv, Sep 8
McGwire, Mark: Birth, Oct 1
McHale, Kevin: Birth, Dec 19
McInerney, Jay: Birth, Jan 13
McKean, Michael: Birth, Oct 17
McKean, Thomas: Birth Anniv, Mar 19
McKellar, Danica: Birth, Jan 3
McKellen, Sir Ian: Birth, May 25
McKenzie, Benjamin: Birth, Sep 12
McKeon, Doug: Birth, Jun 10
McKeon, Nancy: Birth, Apr 4
McKinley, Ida Saxton: Birth Anniv, Jun 8
McKinley, William: Birth Anniv, Jan 29
McKinley, William: Death Anniv, Sep 14
McKnight, Brian: Birth, Jun 5
McKuen, Rod: Birth, Apr 29
McLachlan, Sarah: Birth, Jan 28
McLaughlin, John: Birth, Mar 29
McLean, Don: Birth, Oct 2
McLuhan, Marshall: Birth Anniv, Jul 21
McMahon, Ed: Birth, Mar 6
McMahon, Jim: Birth, Aug 21
McMahon, Julian: Birth, Jul 27
McMillan, Terry: Birth, Oct 18
McMurtry, Larry: Birth, Jun 3
McNair, Ronald E.: Birth Anniv, Oct 12
McNamara, Robert S.: Birth, Jun 9
McNichol, Jimmy: Birth, Jul 2
McNichol, Kristy: Birth, Sep 11
McPartland, Marian: Birth, Mar 20
McRae, Carmen: Birth Anniv, Apr 8
McRaney, Gerald: Birth, Aug 19
McShane, Ian: Birth, Sep 29
McTeer, Janet: Birth, May 8
McVie, Christine: Birth, Jul 12
Mead, Margaret: Birth Anniv, Dec 16
Meadows, Jayne: Birth, Sep 27
Meaney, Colm: Birth, May 30
Means, Russell: Birth, Nov 10
Meany, George: Birth Anniv, Aug 16
Meara, Anne: Birth, Sep 20
Mears, Rick: Birth, Dec 3
Meat Loaf: Birth, Sep 27
Meatout, Great American, Mar 20
Mecklenburg Day (NC), May 20
Medal of Honor, First World War II: Anniv, Feb 10
Medal of Honor, Irwin Earns First: Anniv, Feb 13
Medical Group Practice Week, Natl, Jan 19
Medical Librarians Month, Natl, Oct 1
Medical Orphans Month, Awareness of, May 1
Medical School for Women Opened at Boston: Anniv, Nov 1
Medical Science Liaison (MSL) Awareness and Appreciation Day, Natl, Nov 6
Medicare: Anniv, Jul 1
Medication Safety Week, Apr 1
Medieval Fair (Norman, OK), Apr 3
Medieval Faire, Hoggetowne (Gainesville, FL), Jan 24
Meditation Day, Garden, May 3
Meditation Month, Natl, May 1
Meditation, World Peace, Annual, Dec 31
Medvedev, Dmitry: Birth, Sep 14
Meester, Leighton: Birth, Apr 9
Meet the Press TV Premiere: Anniv, Nov 6
Mehta, Zubin: Birth, Apr 29
Meir, Golda: Birth Anniv, May 3
Mekka, Eddie: Birth, Jun 14
Melanoma Monday, May 4
Melanoma/Skin Cancer Detection and Prevention Month, May 1
Melbourne Cup (Melbourne, Australia), Nov 3
Mellencamp, John: Birth, Oct 7
Mellon, Andrew W.: Birth Anniv, Mar 24
Meloni, Christopher: Birth, Apr 2
Melvill, Michael: First Manned Private Spaceflight: Anniv, Jun 21
Melville (Moby-Dick) Marathon (Mystic, CT), Jul 31
Melville, Herman: Birth Anniv, Aug 1
Memento Mori, Jan 3
Memorial Day (Observed), May 25
Memorial Day (Pres Proc), May 25
Memorial Day (Traditional), May 30
Memorial Day Ceremonies (Andersonville, GA), May 24
Memorial Day Parade and Ceremonies (Gettysburg, PA), May 25
Memory Chmpshp, USA (New York, NY), Mar 21
Memory Day, Mar 21
Memory Days (Grayson, KY), May 16
Men Make Dinner Day, Natl, Nov 5
Mencken, Henry Louis: Birth Anniv, Sep 12
Mend a Broken Heart Month, Natl, Feb 1
Mendel, Gregor Johann: Birth Anniv, Jul 22
Mendes, Sergio: Birth, Feb 11
Menendez de Aviles, Pedro: Birth Anniv, Feb 15
Menendez, Robert: Birth, Jan 1
Menken, Alan: Birth, Jul 22
Mennonite Relief Sale (Hutchinson, KS), Apr 17
Menopause Day, World, Oct 18
Menotti, Gian Carlo: Birth Anniv, Jul 7
Men's Grooming Day, Natl, Aug 21
Men's Month, Intl, Jun 1
Mensch Week, Love a, Feb 14
Mental Health Month, Natl, May 1
Mental Illness Awareness Week, Oct 4
Mentoring Month, Natl, Jan 1
Menzies, Robert: Birth Anniv, Dec 20
Mercator, Gerhardus: Birth Anniv, Mar 5
Mercer, John Herndon (Johnny): Birth Anniv, Nov 18
Merchant, Natalie: Birth, Oct 26
Mercouri, Melina: Birth Anniv, Oct 18

Meredith (James) Enrolls at Ole Miss: Anniv, Sep 30
Meredith, Burgess: Birth Anniv, Nov 16
Meredith, Don: Birth, Apr 10
Meriwether, Lee: Birth, May 27
Merkerson, S. Epatha: Birth, Nov 28
Merman, Ethel: Birth Anniv, Jan 16
Merriam, Eve: Birth Anniv, Jul 19
Merrill, Dina: Birth, Dec 9
Merrimac Destroyed: Anniv, May 11
Merv Griffin Show TV Premiere: Anniv, Oct 1
Mesmer, Franz: Birth Anniv, May 23
Messi, Lionel: Birth, Jun 24
Messiah, Premiere of: Anniv, Apr 13
Messick, Dale: Birth Anniv, Apr 11
Messier, Mark: Birth, Jan 18
Messina Earthquake Anniv, Dec 28
Messina, Jim: Birth, Dec 5
Messing, Debra: Birth, Aug 15
Metcalf, Laurie: Birth, Jun 16
Metcalfe, Jesse: Birth, Dec 9
Meteor Showers, Perseid, Aug 9
Meteorological Day, World (UN), Mar 23
Metheny, Pat: Birth, Aug 12
Metric Conversion Act: Anniv, Dec 23
Metric System Developed: Anniv, Apr 7
Metric Week, Natl, Oct 4
Metropolitan Opera House: Opening Anniv, Oct 22
Metropolitan Opera Radio Broadcasts Premiere: Anniv, Dec 25
Mexican Fiesta Internacional (Milwaukee, WI), Aug 21
Mexican War Declared: Anniv, May 13
Mexico
- Battle of Puebla: Anniv, May 5
- Blessing of Animals at the Cathedral, Jan 17
- Calderon, Felipe: Birth, Aug 18
- Cinco de Mayo, May 5
- Constitution Day, Feb 5
- Cortes Conquers Mexico: Anniv, Nov 8
- Day of the Dead, Nov 1
- Day of the Holy Cross, May 3
- Dia de la Candelaria, Feb 2
- Dia de la Raza, Oct 12
- Feast of Our Lady of Solitude, Dec 18
- Feast of the Radishes (Oaxaca), Dec 23
- Flag Day, Feb 24
- Guadalajara Intl Book Fair (Guadalajara), Nov 28
- Guadalupe Day, Dec 12
- Independence Day, Sep 16
- Juarez, Benito: Birth Anniv, Mar 21
- Mainly Mozart Fest (Baja California), Jun 8
- Mexico City Earthquake: Anniv, Sep 19
- Mexico City Explosion: Anniv, Nov 19
- Posadas, Dec 16
- Postman's Day, Nov 12
- President's State of the Union Address, Sep 1
- Revolution Day, Nov 20
- San Isidro Day, May 15
- Treaty of Guadalupe Hidalgo (with US): Anniv, Feb 2
- Zapatista Rebellion: Anniv, Jan 1

Mfume, Kweisi: Birth, Oct 24
Miami Intl Boat/Sailboat Show (Miami Beach, FL), Feb 12
Mice: AFRMA Display at America's Family Pet Expo (Costa Mesa, CA), Apr 10
Mice: AFRMA Fancy Rat & Mouse Display (Costa Mesa, CA), Jul 28
Michael, George: Birth, Jun 25
Michaelmas, Sep 29
Michaels, Lorne: Birth, Nov 17
Michelangelo: Birth Anniv, Mar 6
Michele, Michael: Birth, Aug 30
Michelin, Andre: Birth Anniv, Jan 16
Michelson, Albert: First US Scientist Receives Nobel Prize: Anniv, Dec 10
Michener, James: Birth Anniv, Feb 3
Michigan
- Admission Day, Jan 26
- Alma Highland Fest and Games (Alma), May 23
- Alpenfest (Gaylord), Jul 14
- America's Thanksgiving Day Parade (Detroit), Nov 26
- Ann Arbor Film Fest (Ann Arbor), Mar 24
- Antiques by the Bay (St. Ignace), Jun 19
- Arcadia Daze (Arcadia), Jul 24
- Baby Food Fest, Natl (Fremont), Jul 21
- Battle Creek Cereal Fest (with World's Largest Breakfast Table) (Battle Creek), Jun 13
- Big Mac Shoreline Fall Scenic Bike Tour (Mackinaw City), Sep 12
- Big Mac Spring Scenic Bike Tour (Mackinaw City), Jun 13
- Big Ten Men's Gymnastics Chmpshps (Ann Arbor), Apr 3
- Big Ten Men's Tennis Chmpshp (Ann Arbor), Apr 23
- Big Ten Women's Swimming/Diving Chmpshps (Ann Arbor), Feb 19
- Blueberry Fest, Natl (South Haven), Aug 6
- Carry Nation Fest (Holly), Sep 10
- Cherry Pit Spitting Chmpshp, Intl (Eau Claire), Jul 4
- Corvette Show (Mackinaw City), Aug 28
- Curwood Fest (Owosso), Jun 4
- Detroit Founded: Anniv, Jul 24
- Dickens Fest (Holly), Dec 4
- Do-Dah Parade (Kalamazoo), Jun 6
- Essence of Motown Literary Jam (Detroit), Nov 14
- Fallasburg Fall Fest (Lowell), Sep 26
- Fourth of July Fireworks (Mackinaw City), Jul 4
- Grand Rapids Boat Show (Grand Rapids), Feb 18
- Granholm, Jennifer: Birth, Feb 5
- Great Fire of 1881: Anniv, Sep 5
- Holland Tulip Time Fest (Holland), May 2
- Isle Royale Natl Park Established: Anniv, Apr 3
- KCQ Country Music Fest (Saginaw), Jun 20
- Lakestride Half-Marathon (Ludington), Jun 20
- Levin, Carl: Birth, Jun 28
- Lilac Fest (Mackinac Island), Jun 5
- Log Cabin Day, Jun 28
- Mackinac Bridge Walk (St. Ignace), Sep 7
- MiAEYC Early Childhood Conf (Grand Rapids), Mar 26
- Michigan Home & Garden Show at Ford Field (Detroit), Mar 13
- Midwinter's Day Celebration (Ann Arbor), Feb 6
- Month of the Young Child, Apr 1
- New Year's Fest (Kalamazoo), Dec 31
- North American Intl Auto Show (Detroit), Jan 11
- On the Waterfront Swap Meet/Car Show (St. Ignace), Sep 18
- PGA Golf Chmpshp (Bloomfield Township), Aug 10
- Ribfest (Kalamazoo), Aug 6
- Richard Crane Memorial Truck Show (St. Ignace), Sep 18
- Silver Bells in the City (Lansing), Nov 20
- Snowman Burning (Sault Ste. Marie), Mar 20
- Spirit of the Woods Folk Fest (Brethren), Jun 20
- St. Ignace Auto Show (St. Ignace), Jun 25
- Stabenow, Debbie: Birth, Apr 29
- State Fair (Detroit), Aug 28
- Sugarloaf Art Fair (Novi), Apr 17
- Sugarloaf Art Fair (Novi), Oct 23
- Tip-Up Town USA (Houghton Lake), Jan 16
- Ultimate Fishing Show (Novi), Jan 8
- Ultimate Sport Show (Grand Rapids), Mar 19
- Victorian Christmas Sleigh Bell Parade (Manistee), Dec 3
- Wyandotte Street Art Fair (Wyandotte), Jul 8
- Zehnder's Snowfest (Frankenmuth), Jan 21

Mickelson, Phil: Birth, Jun 16
Mickey Mouse Club TV Premiere: Anniv, Oct 3
Mickey Mouse's Birthday, Nov 18
Micronesia, Federated States of: Constitution Day, May 10
Micronesia, Federated States of: Independence Day, Nov 3
Microsoft Releases Windows: Anniv, Nov 10
Mid-Autumn Fest (China), Oct 3
Middlemark, Marvin: Birth Anniv, Sep 16
Middleton, Arthur: Birth Anniv, Jun 26
Midler, Bette: Birth, Dec 1
Midnight Sun Baseball Game (Fairbanks, AK), Jun 21
Midnight Sun Fest (Nome, AK), Jun 20
Midori: Birth, Oct 25
Mid-South Fair (Memphis, TN), Sep 18
Midsummer (Wiccan), Jun 21
Midsummer Day/Eve Celebrations, Jun 21
Midwife's Day (Greece), Jan 8
Midwinter's Day Celebration (Ann Arbor, MI), Feb 6
Mighty Mouse Playhouse TV Premiere: Anniv, Dec 10
Migrants Day, Intl (UN), Dec 18
Migratory Bird Day, Intl, May 9
Mikita, Stan: Birth, May 20
Mikulski, Barbara Ann: Birth, Jul 20
Milano, Alyssa: Birth, Dec 19
Milbrett, Tiffeny: Birth, Oct 23
Miles, Sarah: Birth, Dec 31
Miles, Sylvia: Birth, Sep 9
Miles, Vera: Birth, Aug 23
Military Appreciation Month, Natl, May 1
Military Child, Month of the, Apr 1
Military Dictatorship Ended in Chile: Anniv, Dec 15
Military Family, Month of the, Nov 1
Military Spouse Appreciation Day, May 8
Military Spouse Appreciation Day (Pres Proc), May 8
Military Through the Ages (Williamsburg, VA), Mar 21
Milk Days Fest, Harvard (Harvard, IL), Jun 5
Millay, Edna St. Vincent: Birth Anniv, Feb 22
Millennium Summit, UN: Anniv, Sep 6
Miller, Arthur: Birth Anniv, Oct 17
Miller, Arthur: Death of a Salesman Premiere: Anniv, Feb 10

Miller, Barry: Birth, Feb 6
Miller, Christa: Birth, May 28
Miller, Dennis: Birth, Nov 3
Miller, Glenn: Birth Anniv, Mar 1
Miller, Glenn: Birthplace Society Fest (Clarinda, IA), Jun 11
Miller, Henry: Birth Anniv, Dec 26
Miller, Jonny Lee: Birth, Nov 15
Miller, Penelope Ann: Birth, Jan 13
Miller, Reggie: Birth, Aug 24
Miller, Roger: Birth Anniv, Jan 2
Miller, Shannon: Birth, Mar 10
Miller, Sienna: Birth, Dec 28
Miller, Steve: Birth, Oct 5
Miller, Wentworth: Birth, Jun 2
Miller's, Joe: Joke Day, Aug 16
Millett, Kate: Birth, Sep 14
Million Man March: Anniv, Oct 16
Million Minute Family Challenge™, Sep 1
Millionaire TV Premiere: Anniv, Jan 19
Mills, Donna: Birth, Dec 11
Mills, Florence: Birth Anniv, Jan 25
Mills, Hayley: Birth, Apr 18
Mills, John: Birth Anniv, Feb 22
Mills, Juliet: Birth, Nov 21
Milne, A.A.: Birth Anniv (Pooh Day), Jan 18
Milsap, Ronnie: Birth, Jan 16
Milton Berle Show: Texaco Star Theater, Sep 21
Milton, John: Birth Anniv, Dec 9
Milwaukee Irish Fest (Milwaukee, WI), Aug 13
Mind Day, Make Up Your, Dec 31
Mine Awareness and Assistance in Mine Action, Intl Day for (UN), Apr 4
Mineral Collecting Field Trips (Bancroft, ON, Canada), Jul 1
Miner's Day in West Virginia, Dec 6
Mineta, Norman: Birth, Nov 12
Ming, Yao: Birth, Sep 12
Miniature Golf Day, Natl, May 9
Mining: Boom Days (Leadville, CO), Jul 31
Minnelli, Liza: Birth, Mar 12
Minner, Ruth Ann: Birth, Jan 17
Minnesota
- Administrative Professionals Intl Conv (Minneapolis), Jul 26
- Admission Day, May 11
- Braham Pie Day (Braham), Aug 7
- Buffalo Days Celebration (Luverne), Jun 5
- Calithumpian Parade (Biwabik), Jul 4
- Coleman, Norm: Birth, Aug 17
- Defeat of Jesse James Days (Northfield), Sep 9
- Edmund Fitzgerald Beacon Lighting (Two Harbors), Nov 10
- Farm Toy Show & Auction (Sauk Centre), Feb 14
- Fest of Adventures (Aitkin), Sep 19
- Fest of Nations (St. Paul), Apr 30
- Fest of Owls, Intl (Houston), Mar 6
- Hot Dog Night (Luverne), Jul 9
- Inventors Congress (Redwood Falls), Jun 12
- Johnny Appleseed Days (Lake City), Oct 3
- King Turkey Days (Worthington), Sep 19
- Klobucher, Amy: Birth, May 25
- Little Falls Arts/Crafts (Little Falls), Sep 12
- Minnesota Renaissance Fest (Shakopee), Aug 15
- Nobel Conference (St. Peter), Oct 6
- Oktoberfest (New Ulm), Oct 2
- Pawlenty, Tim: Birth, Nov 1
- Rochesterfest (Rochester), Jun 20
- Saint Olaf Christmas Fest (Northfield), Dec 3
- Saint Paul Winter Carnival (St. Paul), Jan 22
- Scandinavian Hjemkomst Fest (Moorhead), Jun 26
- Sinclair Lewis Days (Sauk Centre), Jul 12
- South St. Paul Kaposia Days (South St. Paul), Jun 26
- State Fair (St. Paul), Aug 27
- Tall Timber Days Fest (Grand Rapids), Aug 1
- Tetonkaha Rendezvous (Lake Benton), Aug 7
- Tri-State Band Fest (Luverne), Sep 26
- Voyageurs Natl Park Established: Anniv, Apr 8
- Windsurfing Regatta/Unvarnished Music Fest (Worthington), Jun 12
- Winterfest (Luverne), Dec 4
- World Famous Fish House Parade (Aitkin), Nov 27

Minority Enterprise Development Week (Pres Proc), Aug 30
Minow, Newton: Birth, Jan 17
Minow, Newton: Vast Wasteland Speech: Anniv, May 9
Mint, US: Anniv, Apr 2
Miou-Miou: Birth, Feb 22
Mir Space Station, Feb 20
Mirabel Sisters Murdered: Anniv, Nov 25
Miracle on Ice: US Hockey Team Defeats USSR: Anniv, Feb 22
Miranda Decision: Anniv, Jun 13
Mirra, Dave: Birth, Apr 4
Mirren, Helen: Birth, Jul 26
Mirth Month, Intl, Mar 1
Mischief Night, Nov 4
Miss America Pageant, First: Anniv, Sep 8
Miss American Rose Day, Oct 20
Missile (Titan II) Explosion: Anniv, Sep 19
Missile, First Surface-to-Surface Missile: Anniv, Dec 24
Missing Children's Day, Natl, May 25
Mission Delores: Founding Anniv, Oct 9
Mission San Antonio de Padua: Founding Anniv, Jul 14
Mission San Carlos Borromeo de Carmelo: Founding Anniv, Jun 3
Mission San Diego de Alcala: Founding Anniv, Jul 16
Mission San Gabriel Archangel: Founding Anniv, Sep 8
Mission San Juan Capistrano: Founding Anniv, Nov 1
Mission San Luis Obispo de Tolosa: Founding Anniv, Sep 1
Mission San Luis Rey de Francia: Founding Anniv, Jun 13
Mission Santa Barbara: Founding Anniv, Dec 4
Mission Santa Clara de Asis: Founding Anniv, Jan 12
Mission: Impossible TV Premiere: Anniv, Sep 17
Mississinewa 1812 (Marion, IN), Oct 2
Mississippi
- Admission Day, Dec 10
- Barbour, Haley: Birth, Oct 22
- Cellular South Gum Tree Fest (Tupelo), May 9
- Civil Rights Workers Found Slain: Anniv, Aug 4
- Cochran, Thad: Birth, Dec 7
- Confederate Memorial Day, Apr 27
- Meredith (James) Enrolls at Ole Miss: Anniv, Sep 30
- Natchez Powwow (Natchez), Mar 28
- Natchez Spring Pilgrimage (Natchez), Mar 7
- Neshoba County Fair (Philadelphia), Jul 24
- State Fair (Jackson), Oct 7
- Vicksburg Surrenders: Anniv, Jul 3
- Wicker, Roger: Birth, Jul 5

Mississippi River Valley Scenic Drive (Cape Girardeau, MO), Apr 24
Missouri
- Admission Day, Aug 10
- Adoration Parade (Branson), Dec 6
- Apple Butter Makin' Days (Mount Vernon), Oct 9
- Art Fair and Winefest (Washington), May 15
- Benton Neighbor Day (Benton), Sep 4
- Black Walnut Fest (Stockton), Sep 23
- Blueberry Hill Open Dart Tourn (St. Louis), May 8
- Blunt, Matt: Birth, Nov 20
- Bond, Christopher S.: Birth, Mar 6
- Centralia Anchor Fest (Centralia), May 29
- Chili Cook-off and Fall Fest of Arts and Crafts (Washington), Sep 25
- Christmas Traditions (St. Charles), Nov 29
- Coal Miner Days (Novinger), May 24
- Concordia Fall Fest (Concordia), Sep 8
- Cow Milked While Flying: Anniv, Feb 18
- Dam Experience (Warsaw), Jul 4
- Deutsch Country Days (Marthasville), Oct 17
- Dogwood Fest (Camdenton), Apr 16
- Eagle Days in Springfield (Springfield), Jan 17
- Earth Day Community Fest (St. Louis), Apr 26
- Earthquakes: Anniv, Dec 6
- Eldon Turkey Fest (Eldon), Oct 10
- Emmett Kelly Clown Fest (Houston), May 1
- Fall Fest (Monett), Sep 19
- Farmington Country Days (Farmington), Jun 5
- Festival of the Little Hills (St. Charles), Aug 14
- Greater Springfield Garage Sale (Springfield), Jan 31
- Groundhog Run (Kansas City), Jan 25
- Japanese Fest (St. Louis), Sep 5
- Jours de Fete (Ste. Genevieve), Aug 8
- Lewis and Clark Heritage Days (St. Charles), May 15
- Liberty Fall Fest (Liberty), Sep 25
- Madison County Fair (Fredericktown), Oct 1
- Magic Dragon Street Meet Nationals and Extreme Car Shows (Lake Ozark), May 1
- Major League Baseball All-Star Game (St. Louis), Jul 7
- Mississippi River Valley Scenic Drive (Cape Girardeau), Apr 24
- Missouri Day, Oct 21
- Missouri Day Fest (Trenton), Oct 17
- Missouri State Chmpshp Racking Horse Show (Dexter), Jun 6
- NAIA Div I Men's Basketball Chmpshp (Kansas City), Mar 18
- NAIA Div II Men's Basketball Chmpshp (Point Lookout), Mar 11
- NAIA Men's and Women's Outdoor Track and Field Chmpshps (St. Louis), May 21

NAIA Natl Men's and Women's Swimming/Diving Chmpshps (St. Louis), Mar 4
Natl Soccer Coaches Assn of America Natl Conv (St. Louis), Jan 14
NCAA Div I Women's Chmpshp (St. Louis), Apr 5
Northeast Missouri Triathlon (Kirksville), Sep 13
Old Time Music Ozark Heritage Fest (West Plains), Jun 19
Orchid Show (St. Louis), Jan 31
Osage River Mountain Man Fest and Black Powder Shoot (Lake Ozark), Sep 19
Ozark Fall Farmfest (Springfield), Oct 2
Ozark Mountain Christmas/Branson Fest of Lights (Branson), Nov 1
Richmond's Mushroom Fest (Richmond), May 1
Route 66 Summerfest (Rolla), Jun 5
Saint Louis Race Riots: Anniv, Jul 2
Saint Piran's Day Celebration (Kansas City), Mar 7
Santa-Cali-Gon-Days Fest (Independence), Sep 4
Sheldon Old Settlers' Picnic (Sheldon), Aug 20
Show Me State Games (Columbia), Jul 17
Southeast Missouri District Fair (Cape Girardeau), Sep 12
State Fair (Sedalia), Aug 13
Strawberry Fest (Independence), Jun 6
Street Machine Fall Nationals (Springfield), Sep 18
Texas County Fair/Old Settlers Reunion (Houston), Aug 5
Tom Sawyer Days, Natl (Hannibal), Jul 1
US Women's Amateur (Golf) Chmpshp (St. Louis), Aug 3
Missouri Compromise: Anniv, Mar 3
Mister Rogers' Neighborhood TV Premiere: Anniv, May 22
Mitchell, Andrea: Birth, Oct 30
Mitchell, Chad: Birth, Dec 5
Mitchell, James: Birth, Feb 29
Mitchell, Joni: Birth, Nov 7
Mitchell, Margaret: Birth Anniv, Nov 8
Mitchell, Margaret: Gone with the Wind Published: Anniv, May 19
Mitchell, Maria: Birth Anniv, Aug 1
Mitchum, Robert: Birth Anniv, Aug 6
Mix, Tom: Birth Anniv, Jan 6
Mize, Larry: Birth, Sep 23
Mobius Awards (Los Angeles, CA), Feb 7
Mobius, August: Birth Anniv, Nov 17
Moby: Birth, Sep 11
Moby-Dick (Melville) Marathon (Mystic, CT), Jul 31
Moceanu, Dominique: Birth, Sep 30
Mochrie, Colin: Birth, Nov 30
Modano, Mike: Birth, Jun 7
Model T Introduced: Anniv, Oct 1
Modine, Matthew: Birth, Mar 22
Mohr, Jay: Birth, Aug 23
Mold Awareness Month, Sep 1
Moldova
Independence Day, Aug 27
National Language Day, Aug 31
Mole Day, Natl, Oct 23
Moliere Day: Baptism Anniv, Jan 15
Molina, Alfred: Birth, May 24
Molineaux, Tom: First US Heavyweight Defeated: Anniv, Dec 10
Molitor, Paul: Birth, Aug 22
Moll, Richard: Birth, Jan 13
Molson, John: Birth Anniv, Dec 28
Mom and Pop Business Owners Day, Natl, Mar 29
Moment of Frustration Scream Day, Intl, Oct 12
Moment of Silence (Nagasaki, Japan), Aug 9
Momsen, Taylor: Birth, Jul 26
Monaco
Grand Prix de Monaco (Monte Carlo), May 21
National Holiday, Nov 19
Monaghan, Dominic: Birth, Dec 8
Mondale, Walter Frederick (Fritz): Birth, Jan 5
Monday Holiday Law: Anniv, Jun 28
Monday Night Football TV Premiere: Anniv, Sep 21
Monday: Natl Thank God It's Monday! Day, Jan 5
Mondesi, Raul: Birth, Mar 12
Monet, Claude: Birth Anniv, Nov 14
Money Show, Natl (Portland, OR), Mar 13
Money, Eddie: Birth, Mar 2
Money, Paper, Issued: Anniv, Mar 10
Mongolia
Naadam National Holiday, Jul 11
Republic Day, Nov 26
Monica: Birth, Oct 24
Monitor Sinking: Anniv, Dec 30
Monk, Art: Birth, Dec 5
Monkees TV Premiere: Anniv, Sep 12
Monkey Trial: John T. Scopes Birth Anniv, Aug 3
Monroe Doctrine: Anniv, Dec 2
Monroe, Elizabeth K.: Birth Anniv, Jun 30
Monroe, Harriet: Birth Anniv, Dec 23
Monroe, James: Birth Anniv, Apr 28
Monroe, Marilyn: Birth Anniv, Jun 1
Monroe, Marilyn: Death Anniv, Aug 5
Monroe, Marilyn: First Screen Test: Anniv, Jul 19
Montag, Heidi: Birth, Sep 15
Montagnier, Luc: Birth, Aug 18
Montaigne, Michel de: Birth Anniv, Feb 28
Montalban, Ricardo: Birth, Nov 20
Montana
Admission Day, Nov 8
Arts in the Park (Kalispell), Jul 24
Bannack Days (Bannack), Jul 18
Battle of Little Bighorn: Anniv, Jun 25
Baucus, Max: Birth, Dec 11
Big Sky State Games (Billings), Jul 17
Buzzard Day Fest (Glendive), Jun 13
Christmas to Remember (Laurel), Dec 6
Ennis Rodeo & Parade (Ennis), Jul 3
Glacier Natl Park: Anniv, May 11
Helena Railroad Fair (Helena), Apr 26
Ice Fishing Derby (Fort Peck), Feb 21
Little Bighorn Days (Hardin), Jun 24
Longest Dam Race (Fort Peck), Jun 20
Miles City Bucking Horse Sale (Miles City), May 14
Montana Governor's Cup Walleye Tourn (Fort Peck), Jul 9
Montana Winter Fair (Lewistown), Jan 22
MontanaFair (Billings), Aug 7
Nordicfest (Libby), Sep 11
Northeast Montana Threshing Bee/Antique Show (Culbertson), Sep 26
Northern Intl Livestock Expo (Billings), Oct 10
Schweitzer, Brian: Birth, Sep 5
State Fair (Great Falls), Jul 24
Tester, Jon: Birth, Aug 21
Wild Horse Stampede (Wolf Point), Jul 9
Wildlife Film Fest, Intl (Missoula), May 9
Wolf Point's Annual Christmas Parade (Wolf Point), Dec 4
Montana, Joe: Birth, Jun 11
Montand, Yves: Birth Anniv, Oct 13
Monte Cassino Bombed: Anniv, Feb 15
Montenegro, Republic of: National Day, Jul 13
Monterey Jazz Fest (Monterey, CA), Sep 18
Montessori, Maria: Birth Anniv, Aug 31
Montgolfier, Jacques: Birth Anniv, Jan 7
Montgolfier, Joseph M.: Birth Anniv, Aug 26
Montgomery Boycott Arrests: Anniv, Feb 22
Montgomery Bus Boycott Begins: Anniv, Dec 5
Montgomery Bus Boycott Ends: Anniv, Dec 20
Montgomery, Belinda: Birth, Jul 23
Montgomery, Bernard Law: Birth Anniv, Nov 17
Montgomery, Poppy: Birth, Jun 19
Month of Freethought, Oct 1
Montoya, Carlos: Birth Anniv, Dec 3
Montserrat: Volcano Erupts: Anniv, Jun 25
Monty Python's Flying Circus TV Premiere: Anniv, Oct 5
Moody, Helen Wills: Birth Anniv, Oct 6
Moon Day (First Moon Landing), Jul 20
Moon Fest (China), Oct 3
Moon Phases
First Quarter, Jan 4
First Quarter, Feb 2
First Quarter, Mar 4
First Quarter, Apr 2
First Quarter, May 1
First Quarter, May 30
First Quarter, Jun 29
First Quarter, Jul 28
First Quarter, Aug 27
First Quarter, Sep 26
First Quarter, Oct 25
First Quarter, Nov 24
First Quarter, Dec 24
Full Moon, Jan 10
Full Moon, Feb 9
Full Moon, Mar 10
Full Moon, Apr 9
Full Moon, May 9
Full Moon, Jun 7
Full Moon, Jul 7
Full Moon, Aug 5
Full Moon, Sep 4
Full Moon, Oct 4
Full Moon, Nov 2
Full Moon, Dec 2
Full Moon, Dec 31
Last Quarter, Jan 17
Last Quarter, Feb 16
Last Quarter, Mar 18
Last Quarter, Apr 17
Last Quarter, May 17
Last Quarter, Jun 15
Last Quarter, Jul 15
Last Quarter, Aug 13
Last Quarter, Sep 11
Last Quarter, Oct 11
Last Quarter, Nov 9
Last Quarter, Dec 8
New Moon, Jan 26
New Moon, Feb 24
New Moon, Mar 26
New Moon, Apr 24
New Moon, May 24
New Moon, Jun 22
New Moon, Jul 21

New Moon, Aug 20
New Moon, Sep 18
New Moon, Oct 18
New Moon, Nov 16
New Moon, Dec 16
Moon, Warren: Birth, Nov 18
Moons, Native American Full
Moon, Beaver, Nov 2
Moon, Buck, Jul 7
Moon, Cold, Dec 2
Moon, Flower, May 9
Moon, Harvest, Sep 4
Moon, Hunter's, Oct 4
Moon, Pink, Apr 9
Moon, Snow, Feb 9
Moon, Strawberry, Jun 7
Moon, Sturgeon, Aug 5
Moon, Wolf, Jan 10
Moon, Worm, Mar 10
Moonlighting TV Premiere: Anniv, Mar 3
Moore, Archie: Birth Anniv, Dec 13
Moore, Clement: Birth Anniv, Jul 15
Moore, Demi: Birth, Nov 11
Moore, Dudley: Birth Anniv, Apr 19
Moore, Garry: Birth Anniv, Jan 31
Moore, Henry: Birth Anniv, Jul 30
Moore, Julia A. Davis: Birth Anniv, Dec 1
Moore, Julianne: Birth, Dec 3
Moore, Lenny: Birth, Nov 25
Moore, Mary Tyler: Birth, Dec 29
Moore, Melba: Birth, Oct 29
Moore, Michael: Birth, Apr 23
Moore, Roger: Birth, Oct 14
Moore, Shemar: Birth, Apr 20
Morales, Esai: Birth, Oct 1
Moran, Erin: Birth, Oct 18
Moranis, Rick: Birth, Apr 18
Moravian Easter Sunrise Service (Winston-Salem, NC), Apr 12
Morazan, Francisco: Holiday (Honduras), Oct 3
More Herbs, Less Salt Day, Aug 29
More, Sir Thomas: Birth Anniv, Feb 7
Moreau, Jeanne: Birth, Jan 23
Moreno, Rita: Birth, Dec 11
Morgan, Harry: Birth, Apr 10
Morgan, Jaye P.: Birth, Dec 3
Morgan, Joe: Birth, Sep 19
Morgan, John P.: Birth Anniv, Apr 17
Morgan, Michele: Birth, Feb 29
Morgan, Tracy: Birth, Nov 10
Morganfield, McKinley: Waters, Muddy: Birth Anniv, Apr 4
Moriarty, Cathy: Birth, Nov 29
Moriarty, Michael: Birth, Apr 5
Morione's Fest (Marinduque Island, Philippines), Apr 9
Morissette, Alanis: Birth, Jun 1
Morley, Robert: Birth Anniv, May 26
Mormon
Amnesty for Polygamists: Anniv, Jan 4
Church of Jesus Christ of Latter-day Saints: Anniv, Apr 6
Female Relief Society of Nauvoo: Anniv, Mar 17
Mormon Battalion Arrival in California: Anniv, Jan 29
Mormon Choir First Performs: Anniv, Aug 22
Nauvoo Legion Chartered: Anniv, Feb 3
Pioneer Day, Jul 24
Smith, Joseph, Jr, and Hyrum Smith: Death Anniv, Jun 27
Smith, Joseph, Jr: Birth Anniv, Dec 23
Strang, James Jesse: Birth Anniv, Mar 21
Young, Brigham: Birth Anniv, Jun 1
Morneau, Justin: Birth, May 15
Morocco
Anniv of the Green March, Nov 6
Fes Festival of World Sacred Music (Fes), Jun 5
Independence Day, Jan 11
Natl Day, May 23
Revolution of the King and the People, Aug 20
Youth Day, Jul 9
Morrill Land Grant Act Passed: Anniv, Jul 1
Morris, Esther Hobart McQuigg: Birth Anniv, Aug 8
Morris, Garrett: Birth, Feb 1
Morris, Jack: Birth, May 16
Morris, Kathryn: Birth, Jan 28
Morris, Lewis: Birth Anniv, Apr 8
Morris, Mark: Birth, Aug 29
Morris, Robert: Birth Anniv, Jan 31
Morris, Sarah Jane: Birth, Apr 12
Morris, William: Birth Anniv, Mar 24
Morrison, Jennifer: Birth, Aug 19
Morrison, Jim: Birth Anniv, Dec 8
Morrison, Toni: Birth, Feb 18
Morrison, Van: Birth, Aug 31
Morro Bay Harbor Fest (Morro Bay, CA), Oct 3
Morrow, Rob: Birth, Sep 21
Morse, David: Birth, Oct 11
Morse, Samuel F.: Birth Anniv, Apr 27
Morse, Samuel F.: Opens First US Telegraph Line: Anniv, May 24
Mortensen, Viggo: Birth, Oct 20
Morton, Jelly Roll: Birth Anniv, Sep 20
Morton, Joe: Birth, Oct 18
Morton, Levi P.: Birth Anniv, May 16
Moscow Soccer Tragedy: Anniv, Oct 20
Moses, Anna: Grandma Moses Day, Sep 7
Moses, Edwin: Birth, Aug 31
Moshoeshoe's Day (Lesotho), Mar 12
Mosquito Fest, Great Texas (Clute, TX), Jul 23
Moss, Randy: Birth, Feb 13
Moth-er Day, Mar 14
Mother Goose Day, May 1
Mother Goose Parade (El Cajon, CA), Nov 22
Mother Language Day, Intl, Feb 21
Mother Ocean Day, May 9
Mother Teresa: Birth Anniv, Aug 27
Mother, Father Deaf Day, Apr 26
Mothering Sunday (England), Mar 22
Mother-in-Law-Day, Oct 25
Mother's Day, May 10
Mother's Day (Pres Proc), May 10
Mother's Day at the Wall (Washington, DC), May 10
Motor Voter Bill Signed: Anniv, May 20
Motorcycles
AHRMA Vintage Motorcycle Races (Daytona Beach, FL), Mar 2
AspenCash Motorcycle Rally (Ruidoso, NM), May 14
Biketoberfest (Daytona Beach, FL), Oct 15
Dakar Rally (Argentina and Chile), Jan 3
Daytona 200 by Honda Classic (Daytona Beach, FL), Mar 7
Daytona Supercross by Honda (Daytona Beach, FL), Mar 6
Fall Cycle Scene Motorcycle Races (Daytona Beach, FL), Oct 15
Golden Aspen Motorcycle Rally (Ruidoso, NM), Sep 16
Motorcycle Mass/Blessing of the Bikes (Paterson, NJ), May 3
Motorcycle Safety Month, May 1
Sturgis Rally (Sturgis, SD), Aug 3
Tourist Trophy (Isle of Man), May 30
Women's Motorcycle Month, Jul 1
Motorsports Awareness Month, Aug 1
Mott, Lucretia (Coffin): Birth Anniv, Jan 3
Mott, Stewart Rawlings: Birth, Dec 4
Moulin, Jean: Death Anniv, Jul 8
Mount Everest Summit Reached: Anniv, May 29
Mount Everest, First Woman to Climb: Anniv, May 16
Mount Holyoke College Founded: Anniv, Nov 8
Mount Ogura Plane Crash: Anniv, Aug 12
Mount Pelee Eruption: Anniv, May 8
Mount Rainier Natl Park: Anniv, Mar 2
Mount Rushmore Completion: Anniv, Oct 31
Mount Rushmore Independence Day Celebration (Mount Rushmore, SD), Jul 3
Mount Saint Helens Eruption: Anniv, May 18
Mountain Dance and Folk Fest (Asheville, NC), Jul 30
Mountain Day, Intl (UN), Dec 11
Mountain Fair (Hiawassee, GA), Jul 15
Mountain Glory Fest (Marion, NC), Oct 10
Mountain Meadows Massacre: Anniv, Sep 11
Mountbatten, Louis: Assassination Anniv, Aug 27
Mourning, Alonzo: Birth, Feb 8
Move Hollywood & Broadway to Lebanon, PA, Day, Feb 5
Movie Theater Opens, First : Anniv, Apr 23
Moving Month, Natl, May 1
Moya, Carlos: Birth, Aug 27
Moyers, Bill: Birth, Jun 5
Mozambique
Armed Forces Day, Sep 24
Heroes' Day, Feb 3
Independence Day, Jun 25
Mozart Fest (Bartlesville, OK), Jun 12
Mozart Fest, Mainly (San Diego, CA), Jun 8
Mozart, Wolfgang Amadeus: Birth Anniv, Jan 27
Mr Peepers TV Premiere: Anniv, Jul 3
Mr Wizard TV Premiere: Anniv, Mar 3
MTV Premiere: Anniv, Aug 1
Mudbug Madness (Shreveport, LA), May 21
Mudd Day, Dec 20
Mudd, Roger: Birth, Feb 9
Muddy Frogwater Country Classic Fest (Milton-Freewater, OR), Aug 14
Muhammad: Isra al Mi'raj: Ascent of Prophet, Jul 19
Muhammad: Mawlid al Nabi: Birth of Muhammad, Mar 9
Muharram: Islamic New Year, Dec 18
Muir, John: Birth Anniv, Apr 21
Mukasey, Michael: Birth, Jul 27
Muldaur, Diana: Birth, Aug 19
Muldaur, Maria: Birth, Sep 12
Mule Day, Oct 26
Mule Day (Columbia, TN), Apr 2
Mulgrew, Kate: Birth, Apr 29
Mulhern, Matt: Birth, Jul 21
Mulholland, Terry: Birth, Mar 9
Mull, Martin: Birth, Aug 18
Mullally, Megan: Birth, Nov 12
Mullen, Larry: Birth, Oct 31
Mulligan Day, Oct 17
Mulligan, Gerry: Birth Anniv, Apr 6
Mullin, Chris: Birth, Jul 30
Mulroney, Brian: Birth, Mar 20
Mulroney, Dermot: Birth, Oct 31

Multicultural American Child Awareness Day, Jun 14
Multicultural Fest (Dartmouth, NS, Canada), Jun 19
Multiple Sclerosis Awareness Week, Mar 2
Multiple Sclerosis Education & Awareness Month, Natl, Mar 1
Mummies: Iceman Discovered: Anniv, Sep 19
Mummies: King Tut Tomb Discovery: Anniv, Nov 4
Mumy, Bill: Birth, Feb 1
Munich Founded: Anniv, Jun 14
Muniz, Frankie: Birth, Dec 5
Munoz-Rivera, Luis: Birth Anniv, Jul 17
Munsel, Patrice: Birth, May 14
Munsters TV Premiere: Anniv, Sep 24
Muppet Show Premiere: Anniv, Sep 13
Muppets: Henson, Jim: Birth Anniv, Sep 24
Mural-in-a-Day (Toppenish, WA), Jun 6
Murder, She Wrote TV Premiere: Anniv, Sep 30
Murdoch, Rupert: Birth, Mar 11
Murkowski, Lisa: Birth, May 22
Murphy Brown TV Premiere: Anniv, Nov 14
Murphy, Audie: Birth Anniv, Jun 20
Murphy, Ben: Birth, Mar 6
Murphy, Brittany: Birth, Nov 10
Murphy, Dale: Birth, Mar 12
Murphy, Eddie: Birth, Apr 3
Murphy, Michael: Birth, May 5
Murray, Anne: Birth, Jun 20
Murray, Bill: Birth, Sep 21
Murray, Chad Michael: Birth, Aug 24
Murray, Don: Birth, Jul 31
Murray, Eddie: Birth, Feb 24
Murray, Ken: Birth Anniv, Jul 14
Murray, Patty: Birth, Oct 11
Murray, Philip: Birth Anniv, May 25
Murrow, Edward R.: Birth Anniv, Apr 25
Musburger, Brent: Birth, May 26
Museum Day, Intl, May 18
Musgrave, Story: Birth, Aug 19
Mushroom Fest (Kennett Square, PA), Sep 12
Mushroom Fest, Richmond's (Richmond, MO), May 1
Mushroom Month, Natl, Sep 1
Musial, Stan: Birth, Nov 21
Music. See also Bluegrass, Country & Western, Fiddlers, Gospel, Jazz and Blues, Rock 'n' Roll
Aberdeen Intl Youth Fest (Aberdeen, Scotland), Jul 29
Accordion Awareness Month, Natl, Jun 1
Accordion Chmpshps, Kimberley Intl Old-Time (Kimberley, BC, Canada), Jul 6
All-Northwest Barbershop Ballad Contest (Forest Grove, OR), Feb 27
Arizona Musicfest (Carefree, AZ), Feb 4
Bach Fest (Leipzig, Germany), Jun 11
Barbershop Quartet Day, Apr 11
Blondie and Deborah Harry Month, Intl, Jul 1
Burlington Steamboat Days/Music Fest (Burlington, IA), Jun 16
Calgary Folk Music Fest (Calgary, AB, Canada), Jul 23
Canmore Folk Music Fest (Canmore, AB, Canada), Aug 1
Cape May Music Fest (Cape May, NJ), May 17
Carillon Fest, Intl (Springfield, IL), May 31
Carry a Tune Week, Natl, Oct 4
Celtic Fest, Southern Maryland (St. Leonard, MD), Apr 25
Cheltenham Music Fest (Cheltenham, England), Jul 3
Cisco Ottawa Bluesfest (Ottawa, ON, Canada), Jul 9
Eastern Music Fest (Greensboro, NC), Jun 27
Edinburgh Intl Fest (Edinburgh, Scotland), Aug 14
Edmonton Folk Music Fest (Edmonton, AB, Canada), Aug 6
Everly Brothers/Central City Rock 'n' Roll Cruise-In and Concert (Central City, KY), Sep 5
Exeter Fest (Exeter, England), Jun 19
Fes Festival of World Sacred Music (Fes, Morocco), Jun 5
Fest at Sandpoint (Sandpoint, ID), Aug 6
Gettysburg Brass Band Fest (Gettysburg, PA), Jun 18
Glastonbury Fest (Glastonbury, England), Jun 26
Glenn Miller Birthplace Society Fest (Clarinda, IA), Jun 11
Grammy Awards, Feb 8
Grand Teton Music Fest (Teton Village, WY), Jun 30
Great American Brass Band Fest (Danville, KY), Jun 11
Guitar Flat-Picking Chmpshps, Natl (Winfield, KS), Sep 16
Harrison Fest of Arts (Harrison Hot Springs, BC, Canada), Jul 11
Heritage Craft and Dulcimer Music Fest (Coshocton, OH), Jun 19
Heritage Green Concerts by the Springs (Sandy Springs, GA), May 3
Hodag Country Fest (Rhinelander, WI), Jul 9
Hot August Nights (Reno and Sparks, NV), Aug 1
Jamboree in the Hills (St. Clairsville, OH), Jul 16
Jazz Appreciation Month, Apr 1
Jazz Day, Intl, May 23
Joseph Brackett Day, May 6
Karaoke Week, Natl, Apr 19
KCQ Country Music Fest (Saginaw, MI), Jun 20
Kingsville Intl Young Performers' Competitions (Kingsville, TX), Apr 2
Levitt Pavilion Performing Arts/Music Fest (Westport, CT), Jun 28
Liberace Piano Competition (Las Vegas, NV), Sep 20
Live Aid Concerts: Anniv, Jul 13
Llangollen Intl Musical Eisteddfod (Llangollen, Wales), Jul 7
Louie Louie Day, Intl, Apr 11
Lucerne Fest at Easter (Lucerne, Switzerland), Mar 28
Lucerne Fest in Summer (Lucerne, Switzerland), Aug 12
Mainly Mozart Fest (San Diego, CA), Jun 8
Mardi Gras Fiesta Tropicale (Hollywood, FL), Feb 21
Midnight at the Oasis (Yuma, AZ), Mar 6
Military Music Fest (Belgium), Jun 14
Missouri Day Fest (Trenton, MO), Oct 17
Music in Our Schools Month, Mar 1
Musikfest (Bethlehem, PA), Aug 7
Natl Eisteddfod of Wales (Swansea, Wales), Aug 1
Newport Music Fest (Newport, RI), Jul 10
OK Mozart Fest (Bartlesville, OK), Jun 12
Old-Time Country Music Contest, Fest & Expo, Natl (Le Mars, IA), Aug 31
On the Waterfront (Rockford, IL), Sep 4
One-Hit Wonder Day, Natl, Sep 25
Oregon Bach Fest (Eugene, OR), Jun 26
Ottawa Folk Fest (Ottawa, ON, Canada), Aug 20
Piano Month, Natl, Sep 1
Piano Playing Contest, World Chmpshp Old-Time (Peoria, IL), May 22
Play-the-Recorder Month, Mar 1
Quirky Country Music Song Titles Day, Mar 27
Rounds Resounding Day, Aug 1
Saint Olaf Christmas Fest (Northfield, MN), Dec 3
Santa Fe Chamber Music Fest (Santa Fe, NM), Jul 19
Saxophone Day, Nov 6
Sea Music Fest (Mystic, CT), Jun 12
Silent Record Week, Jan 1
South by Southwest (Austin, TX), Mar 13
Southern Appalachian Dulcimer Fest (McCalla, AL), May 2
Spirit of the Woods Folk Fest (Brethren, MI), Jun 20
Spoleto Fest USA (Charleston, SC), May 22
Stars and Stripes Forever Day, May 14
Stresa Fest (Stresa, Italy), Aug 21
Summer Music Fest (Sitka, AK), Jun 5
Tennessee Fall Homecoming (Norris, TN), Oct 7
Traditional Sousa Concert (Kohler, WI), Jul 4
Tri-State Band Fest (Luverne, MN), Sep 26
Tucson Intl Mariachi Conf (Tucson, AZ), Apr 20
Universal Music Day, Oct 10
Vancouver Folk Music Fest (Vancouver, BC, Canada), Jul 17
Vinyl Record Day, Aug 12
W.C. Handy Fest (Florence, AL), Jul 17
Wagner Festspiele (Bayreuth, Germany), Jul 25
Windsurfing Regatta/Unvarnished Music Fest (Worthington, MN), Jun 12
Musical Anniversaries. See also Beatles; Presley, Elvis; Opera
Altamont Concert: Anniv, Dec 6
America the Beautiful Published: Anniv, Jul 4
American Top 40 Radio Premiere: Anniv, Jul 4
Anderson, Marian: Easter Concert: Anniv, Apr 9
Beethoven's Ninth Symphony Premiere: Anniv, May 7
Brahms Requiem Premiere: Anniv, Apr 10
Charlie Parker at the LA Philharmonic: Anniv, Mar 25
Day the Music Died (Holly, Richardson, Valens: Death Anniv), Feb 3
Ella Fitzgerald Wins Apollo Amateur Night: Anniv, Nov 21
God Bless America First Performed: Anniv, Nov 11
Happy Birthday to "Happy Birthday to You," Jun 27
Lennon-Ono Album Confiscation: Anniv, Jan 3
Mormon Choir First Performs: Anniv, Aug 22
Music Man Premiere: Anniv, Dec 19

New World Symphony Premiere: Anniv, Dec 16
Parker, Charlie: First Recorded: Anniv, Apr 30
Pop Music Chart Introduced: Anniv, Jan 4
Premiere of Handel's Messiah: Anniv, Apr 13
Rite of Spring Premiere and Riot: Anniv, May 29
Space Oddity Song Release: Anniv, Jun 11
Van Cliburn Conquers Moscow: Anniv, Apr 14
Vietnam Moratorium Concert: Anniv, Mar 28
Muslim Observances
Ashura: Tenth Day (1430), Jan 7
Ashura: Tenth Day (1431), Dec 27
Eid-al-Adha: Feast of the Sacrifice, Nov 28
Eid-al-Fitr: Celebrating the Fast, Sep 21
Isra al Mi'raj: Ascent of Prophet Muhammad, Jul 19
Mawlid al Nabi: Birthday of Prophet Muhammad, Mar 9
Muharram (New Year), Dec 18
Rabi' I: Month of the Migration, Feb 27
Ramadan: Islamic Month of Fasting, Aug 22
Yawm Arafat: The Standing at Arafat, Nov 27
Mussina, Mike: Birth, Dec 8
Mussolini Ousted: Anniv, Jul 25
Mussolini, Benito: Birth Anniv, Jul 29
Mustang: Ford Mustang Day, Intl, Apr 17
Mustard Day, Natl, Aug 1
Mutiny on the Bounty: Anniv, Apr 28
Mutombo, Dikembe: Birth, Jun 25
Mutt and Jeff Debut: Anniv, Mar 29
Muybridge, Eadweard: Birth Anniv, Apr 9
My Friend Flicka TV Premiere: Anniv, Feb 10
My Lai Massacre: Anniv, Mar 16
My Little Margie TV Premiere: Anniv, Jun 15
My Way Day, Feb 17
Myanmar
Independence Day, Jan 4
Resistance Day, Mar 27
Union Day, Feb 12
Myers, Mike: Birth, May 25
Myers, Russell: Birth, Oct 9
Myerson, Bess: Birth, Jul 16
Mysterio, Rey, Jr: Birth, Dec 12
Mystery Series Week, Oct 4

N

NAACP Founded: Anniv, Feb 12
Nabokov, Evgeni: Birth, Jul 25
Nabors, Jim: Birth, Jun 12
Nadal, Rafael: Birth, Jun 3
Nader, Ralph: Birth, Feb 27
Nafels Pilgrimage (Canton Glarus, Switzerland), Apr 2
NAFTA Signed: Anniv, Dec 8
Nagra, Parminder K.: Birth, Oct 5
Nagurski, Bronko: Birth Anniv, Nov 3
Naismith, James: Birth Anniv, Nov 6
Najimy, Kathy: Birth, Feb 6
Namath, Joe: Birth, May 31
Name That Tune TV Premiere: Anniv, Jul 6
Names
Celebrate Your Name Week, Mar 1
Fun Facts About Names Day, Mar 2
Get a Different Name Day, Feb 13
Learn What Your Name Means Day, Mar 4
Mario Day, Mar 10
Middle Name Pride Day, Mar 6
Name Your PC Day, Nov 20
Namesake Day, Mar 1
Nametag Day, Mar 5
Unique Names Day, Mar 3
Z Day, Jan 1
Nametag Day, Mar 5
Namibia
Heroes' Day, Aug 26
Independence Day, Mar 21
Nanak, Guru: Birth Anniv, Nov 2
Nanakusa (Japan), Jan 7
Nanticoke Indian Powwow (Millsboro, DE), Sep 12
Napolitano, Janet: Birth, Nov 29
Napping Day, Natl, Mar 9
Nash, Graham: Birth, Feb 2
Nash, Ogden: Birth Anniv, Aug 19
Nash, Steve: Birth, Feb 7
Nast, Thomas: Birth Anniv, Sep 27
Nastase, Ilie: Birth, Jul 19
Nat King Cole Show TV Premiere: Anniv, Nov 5
Natchez Spring Pilgrimage (Natchez, MS), Mar 7
Natchitoches Historic Pilgrimage (Natchitoches, LA), Oct 10
Natchitoches Jazz Fest (Natchitoches, LA), Apr 17
Natchitoches-NW State Univ Folk Fest (Natchitoches, LA), Jul 17
Nation, Carry, Fest (Holly, MI), Sep 10
Nation, Carry: Birth Anniv, Nov 25
National Bank, First Chartered by Congress: Anniv, Feb 25
National Broadcasters Convention (Las Vegas, NV), Apr 17
Nations, Fest of (St. Paul, MN), Apr 30
Native-American
American Indian Heritage Day (AL), Oct 12
American Indian Heritage Month, Natl, Nov 1
Americana Indian and Western Art Show/Sale (Yuma, AZ), Jan 30
Apache Wars Began: Anniv, Feb 4
Battle of Little Bighorn: Anniv, Jun 25
Bureau of Indian Affairs Established, Mar 11
Chief Joseph Surrender: Anniv, Oct 5
Cochise: Death Anniv, Jun 8
Coeur d'Alene Indian Pilgrimage (Cataldo, ID), Aug 15
Crow Reservation Opened for Settlement: Anniv, Oct 15
Hayes, Ira Hamilton: Birth Anniv, Jan 12
Iroquois Arts Fest (Howes Cave, NY), Sep 5
Joseph, Chief: Death Anniv, Sep 21
Kiamichi Owa-Chito Fest of the Forest (Broken Bow, OK), Jun 18
Last Formal Surrender of Confederate Troops: Anniv, Jun 23
Loloma, Charles: Birth Anniv, Jun 9
Maize Day, Nov 27
Minority Enterprise Development Week (Pres Proc), Aug 30
Nanticoke Indian Powwow (Millsboro, DE), Sep 12
Natchez Powwow (Natchez, MS), Mar 28
Native American Citizenship Day, Jun 15
Native Americans' Day (SD), Oct 12
Navajo Nation Navajo Code Talkers Day, Aug 14
Occoneechee State Park Native American Fest and Pow Wow (Clarksville, VA), May 9
Osceola: Death Anniv, Jan 30
Pendleton Round-Up (Pendleton, OR), Sep 12
Pocahontas: Death Anniv, Mar 21
Red Cloud: Death Anniv, Dec 10
Rights Recognized: Anniv, May 12
Sedona Arts Fest (Sedona, AZ), Oct 10
Seminole Tribe of Florida Legally Established: Anniv, Aug 21
Sitting Bull: Death Anniv, Dec 15
Totah Fest (Farmington, NM), Sep 5
Trail of Courage Living-History Fest (Rochester, IN), Sep 19
White Woman Made Indian Chief: Anniv, Sep 18
Woodland Indian Discovery Day (St. Mary's City, MD), Sep 12
Wounded Knee Massacre: Anniv, Dec 29
NATO Forces Attack Yugoslavia: Anniv, Mar 25
NATO Planes Down Serb Jets: Anniv, Feb 28
NATO: Anniv, Apr 4
Natural Bridges Natl Monument: Anniv, Apr 16
Nature Photography Day, Jun 15
Naughton, David: Birth, Feb 13
Naughton, James: Birth, Dec 6
Nauru: National Day, Jan 31
Nautilus: First Nuclear-Powered Submarine Voyage: Anniv, Jan 17
Nauvoo Legion Chartered: Anniv, Feb 3
Navajo Nation Navajo Code Talkers Day, Aug 14
Navratilova, Martina: Birth, Oct 18
Navy Birthday, Oct 13
Navy Day, Oct 27
Neal, Patricia: Birth, Jan 20
Nealon, Kevin: Birth, Nov 18
Near Death Experiences, Fest of (As Neves, Galicia, Spain), Jul 29
Near Miss Day, Mar 23
Neas, Ralph: Birth, May 14
Nebraska
Admission Day, Mar 1
Applejack Fest (Nebraska City), Sep 18
Arbor Day Fest (Nebraska City), Apr 24
BCHS Christmas Open House (Ainsworth), Dec 6
Christmas on the Prairie (Wahoo), Dec 5
Clarkson Czech Fest (Clarkson), Jun 26
Clearwater Chamber of Commerce Rodeo (Clearwater), Jun 26
Cobblestone Fest (Falls City), Aug 21
Crane Watch (Kearney), Mar 1
Czech Fest, Natl (Wilber), Jul 31
Fairfest (Hastings), Jul 22
Gage County Fair (Beatrice), Jul 14
Gateway Farm Expo (Kearney), Nov 18
Hagel, Chuck: Birth, Oct 4
Heineman, Dave: Birth, May 12
Homestead Days (Beatrice), Jun 16
Husker Harvest Days (Grand Island), Sep 15
Kool-Aid Days (Hastings), Aug 14
Light of the World Christmas Pageant (Minden), Nov 28
Nebraska State Fair (Lincoln), Aug 28
Nelson, Ben: Birth, May 17
Oregon Trail Days (Gering), Jul 9
Oregon Trail Rodeo (Hastings), Sep 4
Shakespeare on the Green (Omaha), Jun 18

Wayne Chicken Show (Wayne), Jul 10
Wings over the Platte Spring Migration Celebration (Grand Island), Feb 14
Neeson, Liam: Birth, Jun 7
Nehru, Jawaharlal: Birth Anniv, Nov 14
Neighbor Day (RI), May 24
Neill, Sam: Birth, Sep 14
Neither Snow nor Rain Day: Anniv, Sep 7
Nelligan, Kate: Birth, Mar 16
Nelson, Ben: Birth, May 17
Nelson, Bill: Birth, Sep 29
Nelson, Byron: Birth Anniv, Feb 4
Nelson, Cindy: Birth, Aug 19
Nelson, Craig T.: Birth, Apr 4
Nelson, David: Birth, Oct 24
Nelson, Horatio: Birth Anniv, Sep 29
Nelson, Judd: Birth, Nov 28
Nelson, Thomas: Birth Anniv, Dec 26
Nelson, Willie: Birth, Apr 30
Nelson: Ozzie and Harriet Radio Debut: Anniv, Oct 8
Nemec, Corin: Birth, Nov 5
Nepal
Birthday of His Majesty the King, Jul 7
Democracy Day, Natl, Feb 18
National Unity Day, Jan 11
Neptune Discovery: Anniv, Sep 23
Nero, Peter: Birth, May 22
Nerve Gas Attack on Japanese Subway: Anniv, Mar 20
Neshoba County Fair (Philadelphia, MS), Jul 24
Nesmith, Michael: Birth, Dec 30
Ness, Eliot: Birth Anniv, Apr 19
Nestbox Week, Natl, Feb 14
Netherlands
European Fine Art Fair (Maastricht), Mar 13
Liberation Day, May 5
Midwinter Horn Blowing, Nov 29
Natl Windmill Day, May 9
Netherlands–US: Diplomatic Anniv, Apr 19
Pan Amsterdam (Amsterdam), Nov 22
Prinsjesdag (Parliament opening), Sep 15
Queen's Birthday, Apr 30
Relief of Leiden Day, Oct 3
Scilly Isles Peace Anniv, Apr 17
Networking Week, Intl, Feb 2
Networking Week, Natl, Apr 6
Neuharth, Allen: Birth, Mar 22
Neurosurgery Outreach Month, Aug 1
Neutrality Appeal, American: Anniv, Aug 18
Neuwirth, Bebe: Birth, Dec 31
Nevada
Admission Day, Oct 31
Artown (Reno), Jul 1
Chmpshp Air Races, Natl (Reno), Sep 16
Consumer Electronics Show, Intl (Las Vegas), Jan 8
Cowboy Poetry Gathering, Natl (Elko), Jan 24
Ensign, John: Birth, Mar 25
Family Day, Nov 27
Geographers Annual Mtg, Assn of American (Las Vegas), Mar 22
Gibbons, James: Birth, Dec 16
Great Intl Chicken Wing Society Cook-off (Reno), Jul 10
Hot August Nights (Reno and Sparks), Aug 1
Liberace Commemoration (Las Vegas), Feb 4
Liberace Piano Competition (Las Vegas), Sep 20
NAB/National Broadcasters Convention (Las Vegas), Apr 17
Nevadapex Coin and Stamp Expo (Laughlin), Nov 6
Nugget Best in the West Rib Cook-Off (Sparks), Sep 2
Reid, Harry: Birth, Dec 2
Reno: Anniversary, May 9
State Fair (Reno), Aug 26
Vegaspex (Las Vegas), Jan 23
XTERRA Nevada Trail Run (Incline Village), Oct 3
Neville, Aaron: Birth, Jan 24
Nevis: Independence Day, Sep 19
New Amsterdam (New York) Incorporated as City: Anniv, Feb 2
New England, Dark Day in: Anniv, May 19
New Hampshire
Artists in the Park (Wolfeboro), Aug 19
Gregg, Judd: Birth, Feb 14
Hopkinton State Fair (Contoocook), Sep 3
League of NH Craftsmen Annual Craftsmen's Fair (Newbury), Aug 1
Lynch, John: Birth, Nov 25
New Hampshire Highland Games (Lincoln), Sep 18
Ratification Day, Jun 21
Sununu, John: Birth, Sep 10
New Jersey
Antiques at Memorial Day (Cape May), May 24
Arts & Crafts Fest (Loveladies), Jul 25
Baymen's Seafood and Music Fest (Tuckerton), Jun 20
Be Nice to New Jersey Week, Jul 5
Black Maria Studio: Anniv, Feb 1
Cape May Kids Playhouse (Cape May), Jul 6
Cape May Music Fest (Cape May), May 17
Cattus Island Nature Fest (Toms River), Oct 4
Chowderfest (Beach Haven), Oct 3
Christmas Candlelight House Tours (Cape May), Dec 5
Classic Boat Show (Tuckerton), Sep 5
Corzine, Jon: Birth, Jan 1
COSAC Annual Conference (Atlantic City), Oct 8
Cruisin' Downtown (Toms River), May 13
Crustacean Beauty Pageant/Ocean City Creep (Ocean City), Aug 5
Day of the Seal Celebration, Intl (Point Pleasant Beach), Mar 14
Dickens' Christmas Extravaganza (Cape May), Dec 6
Eggsibit (Phillipsburg), Mar 28
Father's Day Celebration (Point Pleasant Beach), Jun 21
Festival of the Sea (Point Pleasant Beach), Sep 19
Fishing Contest (Lakewood), May 2
Founders' Day (Toms River), Jun 6
Halloween Parade (Toms River), Oct 31
Heritage Day Fest (Lavallette), Sep 12
Independence Extravaganza Weekend (Lavallette), Jul 5
Ladies of Country Music Show (Waretown), Jun 27
Lautenberg, Frank: Birth, Jan 23
Lavallette Heritage Arts & Crafts Show (Lavallette), Jul 26
Long Beach Island Chowder Cook-Off (Beach Haven), Oct 3
Long Beach Island Surf Fishing Tourn (Long Beach Island), Oct 10
Martin Z. Mollusk Day (Ocean City), May 7
Menendez, Robert: Birth, Jan 1
Mother's Day Celebration (Point Pleasant Beach), May 10
Motorcycle Mass/Blessing of the Bikes (Paterson), May 3
New Jersey State Fair/Sussex Farm and Horse Show (Augusta), Jul 31
Ocean County Bluegrass Fest (Waretown), Feb 8
Ocean County Columbus Day Parade and Italian Fest (Seaside Heights), Oct 9
Ocean County Decoy/Gun Show (Tuckerton), Sep 26
Picatinny Peak Fall Hawkwatch (Dover), Sep 1
Pine Barrens Jamboree (Waretown), Oct 10
Positively Penguins (Point Pleasant Beach), Jan 10
Ratification Day: Anniv, Dec 18
Red Wine and Blues Fest (Tuckerton), Jul 4
Respect Your Mother (Point Pleasant Beach), Apr 18
Scandinavian Fest (Budd Lake), Sep 6
Seashore Open House Tour (Loveladies), Aug 5
Sherlock Holmes Weekend (Cape May), Mar 6
Spring Fest (Cape May), Apr 24
State Chili & Salsa Cook-Off (Toms River), May 16
State Ice Cream Fest (Toms River), Jul 18
Suffragists' Voting Attempt: Anniv, Nov 19
Sugarloaf Crafts Fest (Somerset), Mar 13
Sugarloaf Crafts Fest (Somerset), Oct 30
Toms River Canoe and Kayak Race (Toms River), May 17
Tour of Somerville (Somerville), May 25
US Girl's Junior (Golf) Chmpshp (Bedminster), Jul 20
US Junior Amateur (Golf) Chmpshp (Bedminster), Jul 20
Weird Contest Week (Ocean City), Aug 17
Wings 'n' Water Fest (Stone Harbor), Sep 19
New Mexico
Admission Day, Jan 6
Albuquerque Intl Balloon Fiesta (Albuquerque), Oct 3
AspenCash Motorcycle Rally (Ruidoso), May 14
Bingaman, Jeff: Birth, Oct 3
Carlsbad Caverns Natl Park Established: Anniv, May 14
Domenici, Pete V.: Birth, May 7
Electric Light Parade (Lovington), Dec 7
Extraterrestrial Culture Day, Feb 12
Farmington Invitational Balloon Fest (Farmington), May 22
Freedom Days (Farmington), Jul 2
Golden Aspen Motorcycle Rally (Ruidoso), Sep 16
Lovington Fall Arts/Crafts Fest (Lovington), Nov 7
New Mexico State Fair (Albuquerque), Sep 4
Outdoor Summer Theater (Farmington), Jun 19
Richardson, Bill: Birth, Nov 15
Santa Fe Chamber Music Fest (Santa Fe), Jul 19
Totah Fest (Farmington), Sep 5
World's Greatest Lizard Race (Lovington), Jul 4

New Orleans, Battle of: Anniv, Jan 8
New World Symphony Premiere: Anniv, Dec 16
New Year
Chinese New Year, Jan 26
Chinese New Year Fest & Parade (San Francisco, CA), Jan 24
Ethiopia: New Year's Day, Sep 11
First Night (Boston, MA), Dec 31
First Nights (Canada), Dec 31
First Nights (US), Dec 31
Hogmanay (Scotland), Dec 31
India: New Year's Day, Mar 22
Iranian New Year (Persian), Mar 21
Japanese Era New Year, Jan 1
Muharram (Islamic New Year), Dec 27
Naw-Ruz (Baha'i New Year's Day), Mar 21
New Year's Day, Jan 1
New Year's Day (Gregorian), Jan 1
New Year's Day Observance (Russia), Jan 1
New Year's Day Parade (London, England), Jan 1
New Year's Dishonor List, Jan 1
New Year's Eve, Dec 31
New Year's Fest (Kalamazoo, MI), Dec 31
New Year's Resolutions Week, Jan 4
Old New Year's Day, Mar 25
Rosh Hashanah (Jewish New Year), Sep 19
Russia: Old New Year's Eve, Jan 13
Sinhala and Tamil New Year (Sri Lanka), Apr 13
Songkran Fest (Thailand), Apr 13
Stock Exchange Holiday, Jan 1
United Kingdom New Year's Holiday, Jan 1
Vaisakhi (Sikh), Apr 13
New York
African Burial Ground Natl Monument Established: Anniv, Feb 27
Albany Riverfront Jazz Fest (Albany), Sep 5
Albany Tulip Fest (Albany), May 8
American Crossword Puzzle Tourn (Brooklyn), Feb 27
American Historical Assn Annual Mtg (New York), Jan 2
Belmont Stakes (Belmont Park), Jun 6
Belmont Stakes, First Running of: Anniv, Jun 19
BookExpo America (New York), May 28
Brooklyn Bridge Opened: Anniv, May 24
Clinton, Hillary Rodham: Birth, Oct 26
Cohocton Fall Foliage Fest (Cohocton), Oct 2
Colton Country Day (Colton), Jul 18
Columbia County Fair (Chatham), Sep 2
Corn Hill Arts Fest (Rochester), Jul 11
Decoy and Wildlife Art Show (Clayton), Jul 17
Farm Sanctuary Hoedown (Watkins Glen), Aug 1
Five Boro Bike Tour (New York), May 3
Great Wellsville Balloon Rally (Wellsville), Jul 17
Hang Around Victor Day (Victor), Sep 5
Highlights Foundation Writer's Workshop (Chautauqua), Jul 11
Iroquois Arts Fest (Howes Cave), Sep 5
Johnson City Field Days (Johnson City), Sep 4
Lilac Fest (Rochester), May 8
Macy's Thanksgiving Day Parade (New York), Nov 26
Mae West Birthday Gala (New York), Aug 14
Martin Van Buren Wreath-Laying (Kinderhook), Dec 5
Memory Chmpshp, USA (New York), Mar 21
New Amsterdam (New York) Incorporated as City: Anniv, Feb 2
New York City Marathon (New York), Nov 1
New York City Subway: Anniv, Oct 27
New York Comic Con (New York), Feb 6
New York Film Fest (New York), Sep 25
New York Public Library: Anniv, May 23
Paterson, David: Birth, May 20
Ratification Day, Jul 26
Renaissance Fest (Sterling), Jul 11
Rockefeller Center Christmas Tree Lighting (New York), Dec 1
Saint Patrick's Day Parade (Hornell), Mar 14
Saint Patrick's Day Parade (New York), Mar 17
Saranac Lake Winter Carnival (Saranac Lake), Feb 6
Scared Silly: Halloween in Prospect Park (Brooklyn), Oct 31
Schumer, Charles E.: Birth, Nov 23
Stamp & Coin Expo (New York), Apr 17
State Fair (Syracuse), Aug 27
Stationery Show, Natl (New York), May 17
Stone House Day (Hurley), Jul 11
Subway Accident: Anniv, Nov 2
Toy Tips Executive Toy Test (New York), Sep 1
US Open (Golf) Chmpshp (Farmingdale), Jun 18
Westminster Kennel Club Dog Show (New York), Feb 9
New York Stock Exchange Established: Anniv, May 17
New York Times First Published: Anniv, Sep 18
New York Weekly Journal First Issue: Anniv, Nov 5
New Yorker Published: Anniv, Feb 21
New Yorker: Addams, Charles: Birth Anniv, Jan 7
New Zealand
ANZAC Day, Apr 25
Labor Day, Oct 26
New Zealand First Sighted by Europeans, Dec 13
Otago/Southland Provincial Anniv, Mar 23
Waitangi Day, Feb 6
Newby, Marcia: Birth, Mar 8
Newcomb, Simon: Birth Anniv, Mar 12
Newhart TV Premiere: Anniv, Oct 25
Newhart, Bob: Birth, Sep 5
Newhouse, Samuel: Birth Anniv, May 24
Newlywed Game TV Premiere: Anniv, Jul 11
Newman, Barry: Birth, Nov 7
Newman, Edwin: Birth, Jan 25
Newman, Laraine: Birth, Mar 2
Newman, Paul: Birth, Jan 26
Newman, Randy: Birth, Nov 28
Newmar, Julie: Birth, Aug 16
Newmark, Craig: Birth, Dec 6
Newport Flower Show (Newport, RI), Jun 26
Newport Seafood and Wine Fest (Newport, OR), Feb 20
Newspaper Assn of America Conv (San Diego, CA), Apr 5
Newspaper Carrier Day, Intl, Oct 10
Newspaper in Education Week, Mar 2
Newspaper Week (Japan), Oct 15
Newspaper Week, Natl, Oct 4
Newspaper, First American: Anniv, Sep 25
Newton, Becki: Birth, Jul 4
Newton, Isaac: Birth Anniv, Jan 4
Newton, Juice: Birth, Feb 18
Newton, Thandie: Birth, Nov 6
Newton, Wayne: Birth, Apr 3
Newton-John, Olivia: Birth, Sep 26
Nez Perce: Chief Joseph Surrender: Anniv, Oct 5
Niagara Falls Runs Dry: Anniv, Mar 29
Niagara Falls, Charles Blondin's Conquest of: Anniv, Jun 30
Niagara Falls: First Barrel Jump: Anniv, Oct 24
Niagara Movement Founded: Anniv, Jul 11
Nicaragua
Battle of San Jacinto Day, Sep 14
Civil War Truce: Anniv, Apr 19
Independence Day, Sep 15
Natl Liberation Day, Jul 19
Nicholas II and Family Executed: Anniv, Jul 17
Nicholas, Denise: Birth, Jul 12
Nichols, Mike: Birth, Nov 6
Nichols, Stephen: Birth, Feb 19
Nicholson, Jack: Birth, Apr 22
Nick at Nite Debut: Anniv, Jul 1
Nickelodeon Debut: Anniv, Apr 2
Nickerson, Camille: Birth Anniv, Mar 30
Nicklaus, Jack: Birth, Jan 21
Nicks, Stevie: Birth, May 26
Nidetch, Jean: Birth, Oct 12
Nielsen, Arthur Charles: Birth Anniv, Sep 5
Nielsen, Leslie: Birth, Feb 11
Nietzsche, Friedrich Wilhelm: Birth Anniv, Oct 15
Nieuwendyk, Joe: Birth, Sep 10
Niger: Independence Day, Aug 3
Niger: Republic Day, Dec 18
Nigeria: Independence Day, Oct 1
Night Court TV Premiere: Anniv, Jan 4
Night of the Living Dead Released: Anniv, Oct 1
Night Out, Natl, Aug 4
Night Watch (France), Jul 13
Nightingale, Florence: Birth Anniv, May 12
Nightshift Workers Day, Natl, May 13
Nijinsky, Vaslav: Rite of Spring Premiere and Riot: Anniv, May 29
Nimoy, Leonard: Birth, Mar 26
Nininger, Alexander, Jr: First WWII Medal of Honor, Feb 10
Nixon Birthday Holiday (Yorba Linda, CA), Jan 9
Nixon, Cynthia: Birth, Apr 9
Nixon, John: Death Anniv, Dec 31
Nixon, Pat: Birth Anniv, Mar 16
Nixon, Richard M.
"Last" Press Conf: Anniv, Nov 7
Birth Anniv, Jan 9
Checkers Day, Sep 23
First American President to Visit Moscow: Anniv, May 22
First Televised Presidential Debate: Anniv, Sep 26
Meets Elvis Presley: Anniv, Dec 21
Moscow Communique: Anniv, May 29
Pardoned: Anniv, Sep 8
Presidential Resignation: Anniversary, Aug 9
Rejection of Senate Order: Anniv, Jan 4
Saturday Night Massacre: Anniv, Oct 20
Shanghai Communique: Anniv, Feb 27
Trip to China: Anniv, Feb 21

No Homework Day, May 6
No Housework Day, Apr 7
No Interruptions Day, Dec 31
No Pants Day, May 1
No Socks Day, May 8
Noah, Yannick: Birth, May 18
Nobel Conference (St. Peter, MN), Oct 6
Nobel Prize Ceremonies (Oslo, Norway/Stockholm, Sweden), Dec 10
Nobel Prize, First US Scientist Receives: Anniv, Dec 10
Nobel, Alfred: Birth Anniv, Oct 21
Nock, Bello: Birth, Sep 27
Nolte, Nick: Birth, Feb 8
Nomo, Hideo: Birth, Aug 31
Noone, Kathleen: Birth, Jan 8
Nordicfest (Libby, MT), Sep 11
Norgay, Tensing: Everest Summit Reached: Anniv, May 29
Noriega, Manuel: US Invasion of Panama: Anniv, Dec 20
Norman, Greg: Birth, Feb 10
Norman, Jessye: Birth, Sep 15
Norris, Chuck: Birth, Mar 10
Norris, Lee: Birth, Sep 25
Norskedalen's Midsummer Fest (Coon Valley, WI), Jun 20
Norskedalen's Old-Fashioned Christmas (Coon Valley, WI), Dec 5
North American Intl Auto Show (Detroit, MI), Jan 11
North Atlantic Treaty Ratified: Anniv, Apr 4
North Carolina
- Bele Chere (Asheville), Jul 24
- Big Band/Swing Dance Weekend (Asheville), Jan 23
- Burr, Richard: Birth, Nov 30
- Confederate Memorial Day, May 10
- Craftsmen's Christmas Classic Arts & Crafts Fest (Greensboro), Nov 27
- Dole, Elizabeth: Birth, Jul 29
- Easley, Mike: Birth, Mar 23
- Eastern Music Fest (Greensboro), Jun 27
- Everybody's Day Fest (Thomasville), Sep 26
- Folkmoot USA: The NC Intl Folk Fest (Waynesville), Jul 13
- Great Smoky Mountains Natl Park Established: Anniv, Jun 15
- Halifax Independence Day, Apr 12
- Holiday Market (Greensboro), Nov 6
- Home Furnishings Market, Intl (High Point), Apr 27
- Lucky May Show and Sale (Chapel Hill), May 2
- Mecklenburg Day, May 20
- Moravian Easter Sunrise Service (Winston-Salem), Apr 12
- Mountain Dance and Folk Fest (Asheville), Jul 30
- Mountain Glory Fest (Marion), Oct 10
- Ratification Day, Nov 21
- Singing on the Mountain (Linville), Jun 28
- Soldiers' Reunion Celebration (Newton), Aug 20
- State Fair (Raleigh), Oct 16
- Surrender at Durham Station: Anniv, Apr 18
- Whistlers Convention, Intl (Louisburg), Apr 22
- Woolly Worm Fest (Banner Elk), Oct 17

North Cascades Natl Park Established: Anniv, Oct 2
North Dakota
- Adams County Fair/Rodeo (Hettinger), Jul 29
- Admission Day, Nov 2
- Conrad, Kent: Birth, Mar 12
- Dorgan, Byron L.: Birth, May 14
- Fort Abraham Lincoln Fest (Mandan), Jun 20
- Fort Union Trading Post Rendezvous (Williston), Jun 18
- Fourth of July Celebration (Hettinger), Jul 3
- Hoeven, John: Birth, Mar 13
- North Star Classic (Valley City), Dec 3
- Sheyenne Valley Arts/Crafts Fest (Fort Ransom), Sep 26
- Sodbuster Days (Fort Ransom), Jul 11
- Sodbuster Days—Harvest (Fort Ransom), Sep 12
- State Fair (Minot), Jul 24
- Taylor Horsefest (Taylor), Jul 25
- Theodore Roosevelt Natl Park Established: Anniv, Apr 25
- White Cloud Days (Jamestown), Jul 9
- Winter Show (Valley City), Mar 3

North Pole Discovered: Anniv, Apr 6
North Pole, Solo Trip to: Anniv, Apr 22
North Sea Oil Rig Disaster: Anniv, Mar 27
North, Oliver Laurence: Birth, Oct 7
Northern Exposure TV Premiere: Anniv, Jul 12
Northern Hemisphere Hoodie-Hoo Day, Feb 20
Northern Ireland
- Belfast Fest at Queen's (Belfast), Oct 16
- Bloody Sunday: Anniv, Jan 30
- Christmas Holiday, Dec 25
- Good Friday Peace Agreement: Anniv, Apr 10
- Orangemen's Day, Jul 12
- Saint Patrick's Day, Mar 17

Northern Pacific Railroad Completed: Anniv, Sep 8
Northwest Folklife Fest (Seattle, WA), May 22
Northwest Ordinance: Anniv, Jul 13
Norton, Edward: Birth, Aug 18
Norton, Ken: Birth, Aug 9
Norton, Mary: Birth Anniv, Dec 10
Noruz (Iranian New Year), Mar 21
Norville, Deborah: Birth, Aug 8
Norwalk Seaport Oyster Fest (Norwalk, CT), Sep 11
Norway
- Birkebeinerrennet (Rena and Lillehammer), Mar 21
- Constitution Day or Independence Day, May 17
- Edvard Grieg Birth Anniv Celebration, Jun 15
- Midnight Sun at North Cape, May 14
- Nobel Prize Awards Ceremony (Oslo), Dec 10
- Olsok Eve, Jul 29
- Pageantry in Oslo (Oslo), Oct 1
- Tyvendedagen, Jan 13

Nosso Senhor Do Bonfim Fest (Brazil), Jan 20
Nostradamus: Birth Anniv, Dec 14
Noth, Chris: Birth, Nov 13
Nothing Day, Natl, Jan 16
Nottingham Goose Fair (Nottingham, England), Oct 7
Nouri, Michael: Birth, Dec 9
Nova Scotia Bluegrass/Oldtime Music Fest (Stewiacke, NS), Jul 24
Nova Scotia Intl Tattoo, Royal (Halifax, NS, Canada), Jul 1
Novak, Kim: Birth, Feb 13
Novello, Antonia: Birth, Aug 23
Novello, Don: Birth, Jan 1
NOW Founded: Anniv, Jun 30
Nowitzki, Dirk: Birth, Jun 19
Nuclear Chain Reaction, First Self-Sustaining: Anniv, Dec 2
Nuclear Medicine Week, Oct 5
Nuclear Power Plant Accident, Three Mile Island: Anniv, Mar 28
Nuclear Weapons: Russell-Einstein Manifesto: Anniv, Jul 9
Nuclear-Free World, First Step Toward a: Anniv, Dec 8
Nuclear-Powered Submarine Voyage, First: Anniv, Jan 17
Nude Recreation Week, Jul 6
Nugent, Ted: Birth, Dec 13
Numismatics: Money Show, Natl (Portland, OR), Mar 13
Nunavut Independence: Anniv, Apr 1
Nuremberg War Crimes Trials: Anniv, Nov 20
Nureyev, Rudolf: Birth Anniv, Mar 17
Nurses, Nursing. See also Health
- Delano, Jane: Birth Anniv, Mar 26
- Emergency Nurses Day, Oct 14
- Emergency Nurses Week, Oct 11
- NAPNAP Annual Conf (San Diego, CA), Mar 19
- Nurse Anesthetists Week, Natl, Jan 25
- Nurses Week, Natl, May 6
- Nursing Assistants Day and Week, Natl, Jun 11
- School Nurse Day, Natl, May 6
- WOC Nurse Week, Apr 19

Nursing Home Week, Natl, May 10
Nutrition Month, Natl, Mar 1
Nutrition Week, Natl Women's, Apr 5
Nutrition: Eat Better, Eat Together Month, Oct 1
Nutt Day, Emma M., Sep 1
Nuyen, France: Birth, Jul 31
Nylon Stockings: Anniv, May 15
NYPD Blue TV Premiere: Anniv, Sep 21
Nyquist, Ryan: Birth, Mar 6

O

O.K. Corral, Gunfight: Anniv, Oct 26
O.K. First Appearance in Print: Anniv, Mar 23
Oakley, Annie: Birth Anniv, Aug 13
Oakley, Charles: Birth, Dec 18
Oates, John: Birth, Apr 7
Oates, Joyce Carol: Birth, Jun 16
Oatmeal Fest (Bertram/Oatmeal, TX), Sep 4
Oatmeal Month, Jan 1
Obama, Barack: Birth, Aug 4
O'Brian, Hugh: Birth, Apr 19
O'Brien, Conan: Birth, Apr 18
O'Brien, Edna: Birth, Dec 15
O'Brien, Margaret: Birth, Jan 15
O'Brien, Soledad: Birth, Sep 19
O'Brien, Tim: Birth, Oct 1
O'Casey, Sean: Birth Anniv, Mar 30
Occoneechee State Park Native American Fest and Pow Wow (Clarksville, VA), May 9
Occupational Therapy Month, Natl, Apr 1
Ocean Fest Sea-Son, Natl Week of (Fort Lauderdale, FL), Mar 5
Ocean, Billy: Birth, Jan 21

Ocean, Natl Week of the, Apr 5
O'Connell, Daniel: Birth Anniv, Aug 6
O'Connor, Carroll: Birth Anniv, Aug 2
O'Connor, Donald: Birth Anniv, Aug 28
O'Connor, Donald: Singin' in the Rain Film Premiere: Anniv, Mar 27
O'Connor, Frances: Birth, Jun 12
O'Connor, Glynnis: Birth, Nov 19
O'Connor, Sandra Day: Birth, Mar 26
O'Connor, Sandra Day: First Woman Supreme Court Justice: Anniv, Sep 25
O'Connor, Sinead: Birth, Dec 8
October War (Yom Kippur War): Anniv, Oct 6
O'Dell, William "Spike": Birth, May 21
Oden, Greg: Birth, Jan 22
Odessa Retaken: Anniv, Apr 10
Odets, Clifford: Birth Anniv, Jul 18
Odetta: Birth, Dec 31
Odie: Birthday, Aug 8
Odometer Invented: Anniv, May 12
O'Donnell, Chris: Birth, Jun 26
O'Donnell, Rosie: Birth, Mar 21
Ogden, Jonathan: Birth, Jul 31
Oglethorpe Day, Feb 12
Oglethorpe, James: Birth Anniv, Dec 22
O'Grady, Gail: Birth, Jan 23
Oh, Sandra: Birth, Nov 30
O'Hara, Catherine: Birth, Mar 4
O'Hara, Maureen: Birth, Aug 17
O'Higgins, Bernardo: Birth Anniv, Aug 20
Ohio
- Admission Day, Mar 1
- Algonquin Mill Fall Fest (Carrollton), Oct 9
- All-American Soap Box Derby (Akron), Jul 25
- Antique Power Exhibition (Burton), Jul 24
- Anti-Saloon League Founded: Anniv (Oberlin), May 24
- Apple Butter Stirrin' (Coshocton), Oct 16
- Avon Heritage Duct Tape Fest (Avon), Jun 19
- Banana Split Fest (Wilmington), Jun 12
- Barnesville Pumpkin Fest (Barnesville), Sep 24
- Big Ten Women's Rowing Chmpshps (Columbus), May 2
- Brown, Sherrod: Birth, Nov 9
- Christkindl Markt (Canton), Nov 13
- Christmas Candlelightings (Coshocton), Dec 5
- Circleville Pumpkin Show (Circleville), Oct 21
- Cleveland Natl Air Show (Cleveland), Sep 5
- Clinton County Corn Fest (Wilmington), Sep 11
- Dandelion May Fest (Dover), May 1
- Fall Fest of Leaves (Ross County), Oct 16
- Geneva Area Grape Jamboree (Geneva), Sep 26
- Heritage Craft and Dulcimer Music Fest (Coshocton), Jun 19
- Holiday Happiness (Upper Arlington), Dec 5
- Hoof-Care Summit, Intl (Cincinnati), Feb 3
- Jackson County Apple Fest (Jackson), Sep 22
- Jamboree in the Hills (St. Clairsville), Jul 16
- Kent State Commemoration (Kent), May 3
- Lawn Mower Race, Sta-Bil Natl Chmpshp (Mansfield), Sep 5
- Marion Popcorn Fest (Marion), Sep 10
- Miss Ohio Pageant (Mansfield), Jun 12
- Ohio River Sternwheel Fest (Marietta), Sep 11
- Ohio State Fair (Columbus), Aug 5
- Origins Intl Game Expo (Columbus), Jun 25
- PGA Seniors' Chmpshp (Beechwood), May 21
- Red, White & Boom (Columbus), Jul 3
- Stokes Becomes First Black Mayor in US: Anniv, Nov 13
- Strickland, Ted: Birth, Aug 4
- Taste of Cincinnati (Cincinnati), May 23
- Tecumseh! Epic Outdoor Drama (Chillicothe), Jun 12
- Twins Day Fest (Twinsburg), Aug 7
- Utica Old-Fashioned Ice Cream Fest (Utica), May 23
- Voinovich, George V.: Birth, Jul 15

Oil Embargo Lifted, Arab: Anniv, Mar 13
Oil Well, First Commercial: Anniv, Aug 27
Oka, Masi: Birth, Dec 27
Okafor, Emeka: Birth, Sep 28
O'Keefe, Michael: Birth, Apr 24
O'Keeffe, Georgia: Birth Anniv, Nov 15
Oklahoma
- Admission Day, Nov 16
- Azalea Fest (Muskogee), Apr 1
- Cherokee Strip Celebration (Perry), Sep 19
- Cherokee Strip Day, Sep 16
- Cimarron Territory Celebration (Beaver), Apr 11
- Coburn, Tom: Birth, Mar 14
- Eighty-Niner Celebration (Guthrie), Apr 21
- Garden of Lights (Muskogee), Nov 26
- Henry, Brad: Birth, Jul 10
- Historical Day, Oct 10
- Inhofe, James M.: Birth, Nov 17
- Kiamichi Owa-Chito Fest of the Forest (Broken Bow), Jun 18
- Land Rush Begins, Apr 22
- Last Formal Surrender of Confederate Troops: Anniv, Jun 23
- Medieval Fair (Norman), Apr 3
- OK Mozart Fest (Bartlesville), Jun 12
- Oklahoma City Bombing: Anniv, Apr 19
- Oklahoma Day, Apr 22
- Oklahoma State Fair (Oklahoma City), Sep 17
- Rattlesnake Derby (Mangum), Apr 24
- Territorial Christmas Celebration (Guthrie), Nov 26
- US Amateur (Golf) Chmpshp (Tulsa), Aug 24
- US Amateur Public Links (Golf) Chmpshp (Norman), Jul 13
- Watermelon Fest (Rush Springs), Aug 8
- Will Rogers & Wiley Post Fly-In (Oologah), Aug 16
- Will Rogers Days (Claremore and Oologah), Nov 4
- World Cow Chip-Throwing Chmpshp (Beaver), Apr 11

Oklahoma City Bombing: Anniv, Apr 19
Oklahoma! Broadway Premiere: Anniv, Mar 31
Oktoberfest (Covington, KY), Sep 11
Oktoberfest (New Ulm, MN), Oct 2
Olajuwon, Hakeem: Birth, Jan 21
Old Inauguration Day, Mar 4
Old Ironsides Launched: Anniversary, Oct 21
Old Ironsides Saved by Poem: Anniv, Sep 16
Old New Year's Day, Mar 25
Old Threshers Reunion (Mount Pleasant, IA), Sep 3
Oldenburg, Claes: Birth, Jan 28
Older Americans Month (Pres Proc), May 1
Oldest Man in Space: Discovery, Oct 29
Oldman, Gary: Birth, Mar 21
Old-Time Country Music Contest, Fest & Expo, Natl (Le Mars, IA), Aug 31
Old-Time Fiddlers' Jamboree (Smithville, TN), Jul 3
Olerud, John: Birth, Aug 5
Olin, Ken: Birth, Jul 30
Oliphant, Pat: Birth, Jul 24
Olive Branch Petition: Anniv, Jul 8
Oliver, Jamie: Birth, May 27
Olivier, Laurence: Birth Anniv, May 22
Olmos, Edward James: Birth, Feb 24
Olmsted, Frederick L.: Birth Anniv, Apr 26
O'Loughlin, Gerald: Birth, Dec 23
Olowokandi, Michael: Birth, Apr 3
Olsen, Ashley: Birth, Jun 13
Olsen, Mary-Kate: Birth, Jun 13
Olsen, Merlin: Birth, Sep 15
Olympic Games
- First Modern Olympics Began: Anniv, Apr 6
- First Perfect Score: Anniv, Jul 18
- First Winter Olympics: Anniv, Jan 25
- Israeli Olympiad Massacre: Anniv, Sep 5
- Special Olympics Day, Jul 20
- Special Olympics World Winter Games (Boise, ID), Feb 6

Olympic Natl Park Established: Anniv, Jun 29
O'Malley, Martin: Birth, Jan 18
Oman: National Holiday, Nov 18
Omarr, Sydney: Birth Anniv, Aug 5
Omnibus TV Premiere: Anniv, Nov 9
On the Origin of Species Published: Anniv, Nov 22
Onassis, Aristotle: Birth Anniv, Jan 7
Onassis, Jacqueline Kennedy: Birth Anniv, Jul 28
One Arm Dove Hunt (Olney, TX), Sep 11
One Day at a Time TV Premiere: Anniv, Dec 16
One Life to Live TV Premiere: Anniv, Jul 15
One Voice, Jul 26
O'Neal, Jermaine: Birth, Oct 13
O'Neal, Ryan: Birth, Apr 20
O'Neal, Shaquille: Birth, Mar 6
O'Neal, Tatum: Birth, Nov 5
One-Hit Wonder Day, Natl, Sep 25
O'Neill, Ed: Birth, Apr 12
O'Neill, Eugene: Birth Anniv, Oct 16
O'Neill, Jennifer: Birth, Feb 20
O'Neill, Rose Cecil: Birth Anniv, Jun 25
One-on-One Month, Sep 1
Onions: Natl Sweet Vidalia Month, May 1
Onizuka, Ellison S.: Birth Anniv, Jun 24
Ono, Yoko: Bed-in for Peace: Anniv, Mar 25
Ono, Yoko: Birth, Feb 18
Ontkean, Michael: Birth, Jan 24
Open That Bottle Night, Feb 28
Open-Heart Surgery, First: Anniv, Jul 9
Opera
- Aida Premieres: Anniv, Dec 24
- Callas's Last Performance: Anniv, Jul 5
- Donizetti's Lucia Di Lammermoor Premiere: Anniv, Sep 26
- Madama Butterfly Premiere: Anniv, Feb 17

Marian Anderson Performs with Metropolitan Opera: Anniv, Jan 7
Metropolitan Opera House: Opening Anniv, Oct 22
Metropolitan Opera Radio Broadcasts Premiere: Anniv, Dec 25
Opera Debut in the Colonies: Anniv, Feb 8
Ponselle, Rosa: Birth Anniv, Jan 22
Verdi, Giuseppi: Birth Anniv, Oct 10
Wagner, Richard: Birth Anniv, May 22
Operation Iraqi Freedom: Anniv, Mar 19
Oprah Winfrey Show TV Premiere: Anniv, Sep 8
Optimism Month, Mar 1
O'Quinn, Terry: Birth, Jul 15
Orange Bowl (Miami, FL), Jan 1
Orangemen's Day (Northern Ireland), Jul 12
Orbach, Jerry: Birth Anniv, Oct 20
Orchid Show (St. Louis, MO), Jan 31
Ordonez, Reynaldo: Birth, Nov 11
Oregon
Admission Day, Feb 14
All-Northwest Barbershop Ballad Contest (Forest Grove), Feb 27
Brookings-Harbor Azalea Fest (Brookings), May 22
Columbia River Cross Channel Swim (Hood River), Sep 7
Concours d'Elegance (Forest Grove), Jul 19
Crater Lake Natl Park Established: Anniv, May 22
Crater Lake Rim Runs and Marathon (Klamath Falls), Aug 8
Footbag Chmpshps, World (Portland), Jul 27
Hangover Handicap Run (Klamath Falls), Jan 1
Holiday Ale Fest (Portland), Dec 3
Hood River County Fair (Hood River), Jul 22
Kulongoski, Ted: Birth, Nov 5
Lincoln, Abraham: Birthday Observance, Feb 2
Marion County Fair (Salem), Jul 9
Medford Jazz Jubilee (Medford), Oct 9
Miss Oregon Scholarship Pageant (Seaside), Jul 9
Money Show, Natl (Portland), Mar 13
Mother's Day Annual Rhododendron Show (Portland), May 9
Muddy Frogwater Country Classic Fest (Milton-Freewater), Aug 14
Newport Seafood and Wine Fest (Newport), Feb 20
Oregon Bach Fest (Eugene), Jun 26
Oregon Brewers Fest (Portland), Jul 23
Oregon State Fair (Salem), Aug 28
Pendleton Round-Up (Pendleton), Sep 12
Portland Historic Races (Portland), Jul 10
Portland Rose Fest (Portland), May 28
Portland's Birthday, Apr 6
Rhododendron Fest (Florence), May 15
Romance Reader's Luncheon (Portland), Apr 25
Sherwood Robin Hood Fest (Sherwood), Jul 17
Smith, Gordon: Birth, May 25
South Coast Writers Conf (Gold Beach), Feb 13
Sternwheeler Days (Cascade Locks), Jun 26
Turkey Rama (McMinnville), Jul 9
Verboort Sausage and Kraut Dinner (Forest Grove), Nov 7
Wyden, Ron: Birth, May 3
XTERRA Trail Running Chmpshp, Natl (Bend), Sep 26
Organic Act Day (US Virgin Islands), Jun 15
Organization of American States Founded: Anniv, Apr 30
Organization, Organizing
Clean-Off-Your-Desk Day, Natl, Jan 12
Garage Sale Day, Natl, Aug 8
Get Organized Month, Jan 1
Love Your Files Week, Natl, Sep 21
Organize Your Home Day, Jan 12
Organize Your Home Office Day, Mar 10
Organize Your Medical Information Month, Oct 1
Single-Tasking Day, Feb 21
Origins Intl Game Expo (Columbus, OH), Jun 25
Orlando, Tony: Birth, Apr 3
Ormond, Julia: Birth, Jan 4
Orphan Train Heritage Society Reunion (Concordia, KS), Sep 18
Orphans Day, World, Nov 9
Orr, Bobby: Birth, Mar 20
Orthodontic Health Month, Natl, Oct 1
Orthodox Christian Observances
Ascension Day, May 28
Cheesefare Sunday, Mar 1
Dormition of Theotokos, Aug 15
Dumb Week (Greece), Apr 5
Easter Sunday, Apr 19
Festival of All Saints, Jun 14
Green Monday, Mar 2
Lazarus Saturday, Apr 11
Lent, Mar 2
Meatfare Sunday, Feb 22
Palm Sunday, Apr 12
Pentecost, Jun 7
Roman Catholic/Eastern Orthodox Meeting: Anniv, Jan 5
Ortiz, Ana: Birth, Jan 25
Orwell, George: Birth Anniv, Jun 25
Osage River Mountain Man Fest and Black Powder Shoot (Lake Ozark, MO), Sep 19
Osborne, Jeffrey: Birth, Mar 9
Osbourne, Ozzy: Birth, Dec 3
Oscars Presentation, Feb 22
Osceola: Death Anniv, Jan 30
Osgood, Charles: Birth, Jan 8
O'Shea, Milo: Birth, Jun 2
Osment, Haley Joel: Birth, Apr 10
Osmond, Donny: Birth, Dec 9
Osmond, Marie: Birth, Oct 13
Ostara, Mar 20
Osteopathic Medicine Month, Natl, Sep 1
Osteoporosis Awareness and Prevention Month, Natl, May 1
Oswalt, Roy: Birth, Aug 29
O'Toole, Annette: Birth, Apr 1
O'Toole, Peter: Birth, Aug 2
Ott, Melvin (Mel): Birth Anniv, Mar 2
Otter, Butch: Birth, May 3
Ouimet, Francis DeSales: Birth Anniv, May 8
Our Miss Brooks TV Premiere: Anniv, Oct 3
Outback Bowl (Tampa, FL), Jan 1
Outcault, Richard Felton: Birth Anniv, Jan 14
Outdoors Month, Great (Pres Proc), Jun 1
Ovarian Cancer Awareness Month, Sep 1
Ovarian Cancer Awareness Month, Natl (Pres Proc), Sep 1
Overall, Park: Birth, Mar 15
Overseas Chinese Day (Taiwan), Oct 21
Owen, Clive: Birth, Oct 3
Owen, Michael: Birth, Dec 14
Owen, Robert: Birth Anniv, May 14
Owens, Buck: Birth Anniv, Aug 12
Owens, Gary: Birth, May 10
Owens, Jesse: Birth Anniv, Sep 12
Owens, Jesse: Greatest Day in Track and Field: Anniv, May 25
Oxenberg, Catherine: Birth, Sep 22
Oyster Fest, St. Mary's County (Leonardtown, MD), Oct 17
Oz Fest (Liberal, KS), Oct 9
Oz, Frank: Birth, May 24
Ozark Heritage Fest (West Plains, MO), Jun 19
Ozark Jubilee TV Premiere: Anniv, Jan 22
Ozawa, Seiji: Birth, Sep 1
Ozick, Cynthia: Birth, Apr 17
Ozzie and Harriet (Nelson) Radio Debut: Anniv, Oct 8
Ozzie and Harriet TV Premiere: Anniv, Oct 3

P

Paar, Jack: Birth Anniv, May 1
Paca, William: Birth Anniv, Oct 31
Pace, Lee: Birth, Mar 25
Pace, Orlando: Birth, Nov 4
Pacific Ocean Discovered: Anniv, Sep 25
Pacific: Eastern Pacific Hurricane Season, May 15
Pacing the Bounds (Liestal, Switzerland), May 18
Pacino, Al: Birth, Apr 25
Paderewski, Ignacy J.: Birth Anniv, Nov 6
Paganini, Nicolo: Birth Anniv, Oct 27
Page, Ellen: Birth, Feb 21
Page, Patti: Birth, Nov 8
Pagett, Nicola: Birth, Jun 15
Paglia, Camille: Birth, Apr 2
Paige, Janis: Birth, Sep 16
Paige, Satchel: Birth Anniv, Jul 7
Paine, Robert Treat: Birth Anniv, Mar 11
Paine, Thomas: Birth Anniv, Jan 29
Paine, Thomas: Day, Jan 29
Paine, Thomas: Freethinker's Day, Jan 29
Paisley, Brad: Birth, Oct 28
Pajamas: Wear Your Pajamas to Work Day, Natl, Apr 16
Pak, Se Ri: Birth, Sep 28
Pakistan
Defense of Pakistan Day, Sep 6
Founder's Death Anniv (Qaid-e-Azam), Sep 11
Independence Day, Aug 14
Jinnah, Mohammed Ali (Qaid-e-Azam): Birth Anniv, Dec 25
Republic Day, Mar 23
Palestinian Massacre: Anniv, Sep 16
Palestinian People, Intl Day of Solidarity with the (UN), Nov 29
Palffy, Ziggy: Birth, May 5
Palin, Michael: Birth, May 5
Palin, Sarah: Birth, Feb 11
Palm Sunday, Apr 5
Palm Sunday, Orthodox, Apr 12
Palme, Olof: Assassination Anniv, Feb 28
Palmeiro, Rafael: Birth, Sep 24
Palmer, Alice Freeman: Birth Anniv, Feb 21
Palmer, Arnold: Birth, Sep 10
Palmer, Betsy: Birth, Nov 1
Palmer, Carson: Birth, Dec 27
Palmer, Jim: Birth, Oct 15
Palmer, Lilli: Birth Anniv, May 24
Palminteri, Chazz: Birth, May 15

Palomares Hydrogen Bomb Accident: Anniv, Jan 17
Paltrow, Gwyneth: Birth, Sep 28
Pamuk, Orhan: Birth, Jun 7
Pan Am Circles Earth: Anniv, Jan 6
Pan American Flight 103 Explosion: Anniv, Dec 21
Pan American Week (Pres Proc), Apr 12
Panama
Assumes Control of Canal: Anniv, Dec 31
First Shout of Independence, Nov 10
Flag Day, Nov 4
Independence Day, Nov 3
Independence from Spain, Nov 28
Martyrs' Day, Jan 9
Panama City Foundation Day, Aug 15
US Invasion of Panama: Anniv, Dec 20
Panama Canal Opens: Anniv, Aug 15
Pan-American Day (Pres Proc), Apr 14
Pan-American Day in Florida, Apr 14
Pancake Day, Intl (Liberal, KS), Feb 24
Pancake Week, Natl, Feb 22
Pandemic of 1918 Hits US: Anniv, Mar 11
Panettiere, Hayden: Birth, Aug 21
Panic Day, Mar 9
Panini Month, Natl, Aug 1
Panizzi, Anthony: Birth Anniv, Sep 16
Pankin, Stuart: Birth, Apr 8
Pankow, John: Birth, Apr 18
Panoply (Huntsville, AL), Apr 24
Panther Day, Save the Florida, Mar 21
Pantoliano, Joe: Birth, Sep 12
Pants Day, No, May 1
Paper Money Issued: Anniv, Mar 10
Paperback Books Introduced: Anniv, Jul 30
Paperboard Packaging Week, Natl, Apr 20
Papp, Joseph: Birth Anniv, Jun 22
Papua New Guinea: Independence Day, Sep 16
Paquin, Anna: Birth, Jul 24
Parades
America's Thanksgiving Day Parade (Detroit, MI), Nov 26
Boom Box Parade (Willimantic, CT), Jul 4
Bristol Civic, Military/Firemen's Parade (Bristol, RI), Jul 4
Bud Billiken Parade (Chicago, IL), Aug 8
Calithumpian Parade (Biwabik, MN), Jul 4
Chester Greenwood Day Parade (Farmington, ME), Dec 5
Chinese New Year Parade (San Francisco, CA), Feb 7
Christmas on the River (Demopolis, AL), Nov 29
Do-Dah Parade (Kalamazoo, MI), Jun 6
Electric Light Parade (Lovington, NM), Dec 7
Gasparilla Extravaganza and Pirate Fest (Tampa, FL), Jan 24
George Washington Birthday (Alexandria, VA), Feb 16
Halloween Parade (Toms River, NJ), Oct 31
Holidays in the City Grand Illumination Parade (Norfolk, VA), Nov 21
Hollywood Beach Candy Cane Parade (Hollywood, FL), Dec 5
Jersey Battle of Flowers (St. Lawrence, Channel Islands), Aug 13
Joe Cain Procession (Mobile, AL), Feb 22
Lord Mayor's Show (London, England), Nov 14
Macy's Thanksgiving Day Parade (New York, NY), Nov 26
Memorial Day Parade (Aurora, IL), May 25
Memorial Day Parade and Ceremonies (Gettysburg, PA), May 25
Mother Goose Parade (El Cajon, CA), Nov 22
Mummers Parade (Philadelphia, PA), Jan 1
New Year's Day Parade (London, England), Jan 1
Pasadena Doo Dah Parade (Pasadena, CA), Jan 18
Pulaski Day Parade (Philadelphia, PA), Oct 4
Saint Patrick's Day Parade (Baton Rouge, LA), Mar 14
Saint Patrick's Day Parade (Hornell, NY), Mar 14
Saint Patrick's Day Parade (New York, NY), Mar 17
Tournament of Roses Parade (Pasadena, CA), Jan 1
Twin Cities Krewe of Janus Mardi Gras Parade (Monroe, LA), Feb 7
Victorian Christmas Sleigh Bell Parade (Manistee, MI), Dec 3
Wolf Point's Annual Christmas Parade (Wolf Point, MT), Dec 4
World Famous Fish House Parade (Aitkin, MN), Nov 27
Paraguay
Battle of Boqueron Day, Sep 29
Independence Day, May 15
Natl Heroes' Day, Mar 1
Peace with Bolivia Day, Jun 12
Paranormal Day, May 3
Paraprofessional Appreciation Day, Apr 1
Parcells, Bill: Birth, Aug 22
Pare, Michael: Birth, Oct 9
Parent Leadership Month, Natl, Feb 1
Parent, Bernie: Birth, Apr 3
Parents as Teachers Day, Natl, Nov 8
Parents' Day (Pres Proc), Jul 26
Parents: Prepare Tomorrow's Parents Month, May 10
Paretsky, Sara: Birth, Jun 8
Paris, Treaty of, Ends American Rev, Sep 3
Parish, Robert: Birth, Aug 30
Park Week, Natl (Pres Proc), Apr 19
Park, Grace: Birth, Mar 14
Parker Day, John, Apr 19
Parker, Bonnie: Bonnie and Clyde: Death Anniv, May 23
Parker, Charlie: At the LA Philharmonic: Anniv, Mar 25
Parker, Charlie: Birth Anniv, Aug 29
Parker, Charlie: First Recorded: Anniv, Apr 30
Parker, Colonel Tom: Birth Anniv, Jun 26
Parker, Dave: Birth, Jun 9
Parker, Fess: Birth, Aug 16
Parker, George: Death Anniv, Mar 17
Parker, Jameson: Birth, Nov 18
Parker, Mary-Louise: Birth, Aug 2
Parker, Robert Leroy (Butch Cassidy): Birth Anniv, Apr 13
Parker, Sarah Jessica: Birth, Mar 25
Parker, Tony: Birth, May 17
Parker, Trey: Birth, May 30
Parkinson Awareness Month, Natl, Apr 1
Parkinson, James: Death Anniv, Dec 21
Parkman, Francis: Birth Anniv, Sep 16
Parks Month, Natl Recreation and, Jul 1
Parks, Bert: Birth Anniv, Dec 30
Parks, Gordon: Birth Anniv, Nov 30
Parks, Michael: Birth, Apr 4
Parks, Rosa: Birth Anniv, Feb 4
Parks, Rosa: Day, Dec 1
Parnell, Charles S.: Birth Anniv, Jun 27
Parrineau, Harold: Birth, Aug 7
Parry, William: Birth Anniv, Dec 19
Parseghian, Ara: Birth, May 10
Parsons, Estelle: Birth, Nov 20
Parsons, Louella: Birth Anniv, Aug 6
Particularly Preposterous Packaging Day, Aug 7
Parton, Dolly: Birth, Jan 19
Pascal, Blaise: Birth Anniv, Jun 19
Pascua Florida Day (FL), Apr 2
Pasdar, Adrian: Birth, Apr 30
Passion Week, Mar 29
Passiontide, Mar 29
Passover, Apr 9
Passover Begins, Apr 8
Passport Presentation (Russia), Jan 2
Pasternak, Boris: Birth Anniv, Feb 10
Pasteur, Louis: Birth Anniv, Dec 27
Pasteur, Louis: First Successful Antirabies Inoculation: Anniv, Jul 6
Pastimes of Colonial Virginia (Williamsburg, VA), Aug 1
Pastoral Care Week, Oct 25
Pat Boone Show TV Premiere: Anniv, Oct 3
Patent Issued for First Adding Machine: Anniv, Oct 11
Patent Office Opens, US: Anniv, Jul 31
Paterno, Joe: Birth, Dec 21
Paterson, David: Birth, May 20
Patient Accessibility Week, Natl, Nov 1
Patient Recognition Week, Natl, Feb 1
Patinkin, Mandy: Birth, Nov 30
Patric, Jason: Birth, Jun 27
Patrick, Dan: Birth, May 15
Patrick, Danica: Birth, Mar 25
Patrick, Deval: Birth, Jul 31
Patriot Day, Sep 11
Patriots' Day (MA, ME), Apr 20
Patriots' Day in Florida, Apr 19
Patterson, Floyd: Birth Anniv, Jan 4
Patterson, James: Birth, Mar 22
Patton, Antwan (Big Boi): Birth, Feb 1
Patton, George S., Jr: Birth Anniv, Nov 11
Patton, Will: Birth, Jun 14
Paul, Adrian: Birth, May 29
Paul, Alexandra: Birth, Jul 29
Paul, Alice: Birth Anniv, Jan 11
Paul, Les: Birth, Jun 9
Pauley, Jane: Birth, Oct 31
Paulsen, Henry M., Jr: Birth, Mar 28
Paulus, Friedrich: Birth Anniv, Sep 23
Pause for Pledge (Natl Flag Day USA), Jun 14
Pavarotti, Luciano: Birth Anniv, Oct 12
Pavlova, Anna: Birth Anniv, Feb 12
Pawlenty, Tim: Birth, Nov 1
Pawnbrokers Day, Natl, Dec 6
Paxson, John: Birth, Sep 29
Paxton, Bill: Birth, May 17
Paymer, David: Birth, Aug 30
Payne, John H.: Birth Anniv, Jun 9
Payroll Week, Natl, Sep 7
Pays, Amanda: Birth, Jun 6
Payton, Gary: Birth, Jul 23
Peña, Elizabeth: Birth, Sep 23
Peabody, Elizabeth Palmer: Birth Anniv, May 16
Peabody, George: Birth Anniv, Feb 18
Peace
Annual World Peace Meditation, Dec 31
Day of Radiant Peace, Intl, Sep 22
Day of United Nations Peacekeepers, Intl, May 29

Disarmament Week (UN), Oct 24
Dream 2009 Day, Mar 11
Intl Day of (UN), Sep 21
Peace Fest (Hiroshima, Japan), Aug 6
Peace Officer Memorial Day (Pres Proc), May 15
Versailles Peace Conference (WWI): Anniv, Jan 18
World Hello Day, Nov 21
Peace Corps Day, Mar 3
Peace Corps Founded: Anniv, Mar 1
Peace Covenant, Universal: One Voice, Jul 26
Peace Rose Introduced to World: Anniv, Apr 29
Peach Fest, Louisiana (Ruston, LA), Jun 26
Peachtree Road Race (Atlanta, GA), Jul 4
Peake, Dr. James: Birth, Jun 18
Peale, Anna Claypoole: Birth Anniv, Mar 6
Peale, Charles W.: Birth Anniv, Apr 15
Peale, Norman Vincent: Birth Anniv, May 31
Peanut Butter Lovers' Month, Nov 1
Peanuts Debuts: Anniv, Oct 2
Pearl Harbor Day, Dec 7
Pearl Harbor Remembrance Day, Natl (Pres Proc), Dec 7
Pearl, Daniel: Birth Anniv, Oct 10
Pearl, Minnie: Birth Anniv, Oct 25
Pearse, Richard: Flight Anniv, Mar 31
Pearson, Lester B.: Birth Anniv, Apr 23
Peary, Robert E.: Birth Anniv, May 6
Peary, Robert E.: North Pole Discovered: Anniv, Apr 6
Pecan Day, Mar 25
Pecan Month, Natl, Apr 1
Pecan Month, Natl Georgia, Nov 1
Peck, Annie S.: Birth Anniv, Oct 19
Peck, Gregory: Birth Anniv, Apr 5
Peddler's Village Scarecrow Fest (Lahaska, PA), Sep 19
Pediatric Cancer Awareness Month, Sep 1
Pediatric Nurse Practitioner Week, Mar 15
Pediculosis Prevention Month, Natl, Sep 1
Peel, Robert: Birth Anniv, Feb 5
Peet, Amanda: Birth, Jan 11
Peete, Calvin: Birth, Jul 18
Pele Scores 1,000th Goal: Anniv, Nov 19
Pele: Birth, Oct 23
Pelosi, Nancy: Birth, Mar 26
Pencil Patented: Anniv, Mar 30
Penderecki, Krzysztof: Birth, Nov 23
Pendergrass, Teddy: Birth, Mar 26
Pendleton, Austin: Birth, Mar 27
Penn, Arthur Heller: Birth, Sep 27
Penn, Irving: Birth, Jun 16
Penn, John: Birth Anniv, May 6
Penn, Kal: Birth, Apr 23
Penn, Sean: Birth, Aug 17
Penn, William: Birth Anniv, Oct 14
Penn, William: Pennsylvania Deeded to: Anniv, Mar 4
Penniman, Little Richard: Birth, Dec 5
Pennington, Ty: Birth, Oct 19
Pennsylvania
Antique Show (Somerset), Aug 8
Antiques on the Diamond (Ligonier), Jun 13
Apple Blossom Fest (Gettysburg), May 2
Apple Fest (Lahaska), Nov 7
Apple Harvest Fest, Natl (Gettysburg), Oct 3
Art in the Garden (Washington), Sep 13
Battle of Bushy Run Reenactment (Harrison City), Aug 1
Battle of Germantown Reenactment (Philadelphia), Oct 3
Battle of Gettysburg: Anniv, Jul 1
Belsnickel Craft Show (Boyertown), Nov 27
Big Ten Men's Golf Chmpshps (University Park), May 1
Big Ten Men's Indoor Track/Field Chmpshps (University Park), Feb 28
Big Ten Wrestling Chmpshps (University Park), Mar 7
Blueberry Fest (Montrose), Aug 7
Casey, Robert: Birth, Apr 13
Celtic Classic Highland Games & Fest (Bethlehem), Sep 25
Celtic Fling (Manheim), Jun 26
Chadds Ford Days (Chadds Ford), Sep 12
Christkindlmarkt (Bethlehem), Nov 27
Christmas Craft Show (York), Dec 13
Covered Bridge Fest (Washington County), Sep 19
Dickens of a Christmas at Mount Hope Mansion (Manheim), Nov 27
Easter Craft Show (York), Mar 22
Edgar Allan Poe Evermore (Manheim), Oct 30
Eisenhower World War II Weekend (Gettysburg), Sep 19
Everything Autumn at Longwood Gardens (Kennett Square), Sep 7
Fabulous 1890s Weekend (Mansfield), Sep 25
Farm Show (Harrisburg), Jan 10
Farmers & Threshermens Jubilee (New Centerville), Sep 9
Festifall (Point Marion), Sep 26
Firestorm (Altoona), Jul 4
First American Abolition Society Founded: Anniv, Apr 14
First Commercial Oil Well: Anniv, Aug 27
First Natl Convention for Blacks: Anniv, Sep 15
First Night Football Game (Mansfield), Sep 28
First US Zoo: Anniv (Philadelphia), Jul 1
Flax Scutching Fest (Stahlstown), Sep 12
Fort Ligonier Days (Ligonier), Oct 9
Gettysburg Address Memorial Ceremony (Gettysburg), Nov 19
Gettysburg Brass Band Fest (Gettysburg), Jun 18
Gettysburg Holiday Fest (Gettysburg), Nov 28
Gettysburg Outdoor Antique Show (Gettysburg), May 16
Gettysburg Outdoor Antique Show (Gettysburg), Sep 19
Grand Illumination (Lahaska), Nov 20
Greater Pittsburgh Arts & Crafts Holiday Spectacular (Monroeville), Nov 20
Groundhog Day (Punxsutawney), Feb 2
Hanover Dutch Fest (Hanover), Jul 25
History Meets the Arts (Gettysburg), Apr 17
Holiday Lights on the Lake (Altoona), Nov 26
Home and Garden Fest (Chestnut Hill), May 3
Ice Fest (Ligonier), Jan 24
Johnstown Flood: Anniv, May 31
Leif Ericson Day Celebration (Philadelphia), Oct 11
Ligonier Highland Games (Ligonier), Sep 11
Little League Baseball World Series (Williamsport), Aug 21
Longwood Gardens Christmas Display (Kennett Square), Nov 26
Longwood Gardens Easter Celebration (Kennett Square), Apr 11
Longwood Gardens Fest of Fountains (Kennett Square), May 23
Longwood Gardens Orchid Extravaganza (Kennett Square), Jan 24
Longwood Gardens Spring Blooms (Kennett Square), Apr 1
May Day Fairie Fest (Glen Rock), May 1
Memorial Day Parade and Ceremonies (Gettysburg), May 25
Mount Pleasant Glass & Ethnic Fest (Mount Pleasant), Sep 25
Mummers Parade (Philadelphia), Jan 1
Mushroom Fest (Kennett Square), Sep 12
Musikfest (Bethlehem), Aug 7
New Oxford Outdoor Antique Show (New Oxford), Jun 20
Peddler's Village Fine Art & Crafts Show (Lahaska), Jun 6
Peddler's Village Gingerbread House Competition & Display (Lahaska), Nov 20
Peddler's Village Quilt Competition/Display (Lahaska), Jan 12
Peddler's Village Scarecrow Contest and Outdoor Display (Lahaska), Sep 13
Peddler's Village Scarecrow Fest (Lahaska), Sep 19
Penn State's Ag Progress Days (Rock Springs), Aug 18
Pennsylvania Arts & Crafts Christmas Fest (Washington), Oct 16
Pennsylvania Arts & Crafts Colonial Fest (Greensburg), Sep 4
Pennsylvania Deeded to William Penn: Anniv, Mar 4
Pennsylvania Renaissance Faire (Manheim), Aug 8
Pennsylvania RV & Camping Show (Hershey), Sep 14
Philadelphia Flower Show (Philadelphia), Mar 1
Pittsburgh Arts & Crafts Spring Fever Fest (Greensburg), Mar 27
Pittsburgh Renaissance Fest (West Newton), Aug 23
Polish Christmas Open House (Philadelphia), Dec 12
PSFCA East West All-Star Game (Altoona), Jun 20
Pulaski Day Parade (Philadelphia), Oct 4
Punxsutawney Groundhog Fest (Punxsutawney), Jun 28
Quilt Odyssey (Hershey), Jul 30
Rain Day (Waynesburg), Jul 29
Ratification Day, Dec 12
Remembrance Day (Gettysburg), Nov 21
Rendell, Ed: Birth, Jan 5
Rhubarb Fest (Intercourse), May 15
Seven Sweets & Sours Fest (Intercourse), Sep 18
Slow Pitch Softball Tourn (Williamsport), Jul 10
Snake Hunt (Cross Fork), Jun 27
South Mountain Fair (Arendtsville), Aug 18
Specter, Arlen: Birth, Feb 12
Springs Folk Fest (Springs), Oct 2
Strawberry Fest (Lahaska), May 2
US Women's Open (Golf) Chmpshp (Bethlehem), Jul 9
Walker Cup (Ardmore), Sep 12

Westmoreland Arts & Heritage Fest (Greensburg), Jul 2
York Intl Postcard Fair (York), Nov 20
Penny Press, Beginning of the: Anniv, Sep 3
Pentagon Completed: Anniv, Jan 15
Pentagon, Vietnam War Protesters Storm Pentagon: Anniv, Oct 21
Pentecost, May 31
People Magazine: Anniv, Mar 4
People Skills Month, Intl, Sep 1
Pepitone, Joe: Birth, Oct 9
Pepper, Barry: Birth, Apr 4
Pepper, Claude Denson: Birth Anniv, Sep 8
Peppercorn Ceremony (Bermuda), Apr 23
Pepys, Samuel: Birth Anniv, Feb 23
Perdue, Sonny: Birth, Dec 20
Perdue, Will: Birth, Aug 29
Perez, Rosie: Birth, Sep 6
Perez, Tony: Birth, May 14
Perigean Spring Tides, Jan 11
Perigean Spring Tides, Jun 22
Perigean Spring Tides, Jul 21
Perihelion, Earth at, Jan 4
Perkins, Anthony: Birth Anniv, Apr 4
Perkins, Anthony: Psycho Film Premiere: Anniv, Jun 16
Perkins, Elizabeth: Birth, Nov 18
Perkins, Frances: Appointed to Cabinet, Mar 4
Perkins, Frances: Birth Anniv, Apr 10
Perkins, Maxwell: Birth Anniv, Sep 20
Perkins, Millie: Birth, May 12
Perkins, Sam: Birth, Jun 14
Perlman, Itzhak: Birth, Aug 31
Perlman, Rhea: Birth, Mar 31
Perlman, Ron: Birth, Apr 13
Perot, H. Ross: Birth, Jun 27
Perreau, Gigi: Birth, Feb 6
Perrine, Valerie: Birth, Sep 3
Perry Como Show TV Premiere: Anniv, Dec 24
Perry Mason TV Premiere: Anniv, Sep 21
Perry, Gaylord Jackson: Birth, Sep 15
Perry, Jeff: Birth, Aug 16
Perry, Luke: Birth, Oct 11
Perry, Matthew: Birth, Aug 19
Perry, Matthew: Commodore Perry Day: Birth Anniv, Apr 10
Perry, Oliver H.: Birth Anniv, Aug 23
Perry, Rick: Birth, Mar 4
Perry, Steve: Birth, Jan 22
Perry, William "The Refrigerator": Birth, Dec 16
Perseid Meteor Showers, Aug 9
Pershing, John J.: Birth Anniv, Sep 13
Persian Gulf War
Desert Shield: Anniv, Aug 7
Ground War Begins: Anniv, Feb 23
Kuwait Liberated: Anniv, Feb 27
Person, Chuck Connors: Birth, Jun 27
Personal Chef Day, Natl, Feb 23
Personal Finance
Financial Wellness Month, Jan 1
Get Smart About Credit Day, Oct 15
Teach Children to Save Day, Natl, Apr 21
Wealth Mentality Month, Intl, Jan 1
Personal History Month, May 1
Personal Self-Defense Awareness Month, Natl, Jan 1
Personal Training Week, Natl, Apr 12
Peru
Countryman's Day, Jun 24
Day of Natl Honor, Oct 9
Independence Day, Jul 28
Saint Rose of Lima Day, Aug 30
Pesach (Passover), Apr 9
Pesach Begins, Apr 8
Pesci, Joe: Birth, Feb 9
Pescow, Donna: Birth, Mar 24
Peshtigo Forest Fire: Anniv, Oct 8
Pet Cancer Awareness Month, Natl, Nov 1
Peter and Paul Day, Saint, Jun 29
Peter I: Birth Anniv, May 30
Peters, Bernadette: Birth, Feb 28
Peters, Mary E.: Birth, Dec 4
Peters, Roberta: Birth, May 4
Petersen, Paul: Birth, Sep 23
Petersen, William: Birth, Feb 21
Peterson, Cassandra: Birth, Sep 17
Peterson, Oscar: Birth Anniv, Aug 15
Peterson, Roger Tory: Birth Anniv, Aug 28
Peterson, Seth: Birth, Aug 16
Petrified Forest Natl Park Established: Anniv, Dec 9
Petroleum Fest, Louisiana Shrimp and (Morgan City, LA), Sep 3
Pets (see also Animals; Cats; Dogs; Rats)
Holistic Pet Day, Natl, Aug 30
Pet Cancer Awareness Month, Natl, Nov 1
Pet Dental Health Month, Natl, Feb 1
Pet First Aid Awareness Month, Intl, Apr 1
Pet Owners Independence Day, Apr 18
Pet Week, Natl, May 3
Professional Pet Sitters Week, Mar 1
Wishbones for Pets, Oct 15
World Animal Remembrance Month, Sep 1
Pettit, Bob: Birth, Dec 12
Petty, Richard: Birth, Jul 2
Petty, Tom: Birth, Oct 20
Pfeiffer, Michelle: Birth, Apr 29
Phair, Liz: Birth, Apr 17
Phantom of the Opera Broadway Premiere: Anniv, Jan 26
Pharmacists Declare War on Alcoholism, Jun 1
Pharmacists' War on Diabetes, Apr 1
Phil Donahue Show TV Premiere: Anniv, Nov 6
Phil Silvers Show TV Premiere: Anniv, Sep 20
Philadelphia Flower Show, Mar 1
Philadelphia Police Bombing: Anniv, May 13
Philbin, Regis: Birth, Aug 25
Philip, King: Assassination Anniv, Aug 12
Philip, Prince: Birth, Jun 10
Philippines
Aquino, Benigno: Assassination Anniv, Aug 21
Araw ng Kagitingan (Day of Valor), Apr 9
Ati-Atihan Fest, Jan 17
Black Nazarene Fiesta, Jan 1
Bonifacio Day, Nov 30
Carabao Fest, May 14
Christmas Observance, Dec 16
Earthquake Jolts: Anniv, Jul 16
Feast of Our Lady of Peace/Good Voyage, May 1
Feast of the Black Nazarene, Jan 9
Fil-American Friendship Day, Jul 4
Holy Week, Apr 5
Independence Day, Jun 12
Morione's Fest (Marinduque Island), Apr 9
Mount Pinatubo Erupts in Philippines: Anniv, Jun 11
National Heroes' Day, Aug 30
Philippine Independence: Anniv, Mar 24
Rizal Day, Dec 30
Santacruzan, May 1
Simbang Gabi, Dec 16
US Military Leaves: Anniv, Nov 24
Phillips, Bobbie: Birth, Jan 29
Phillips, Chynna: Birth, Feb 12
Phillips, Julianne: Birth, May 13
Phillips, Lou Diamond: Birth, Feb 17
Phillips, Mackenzie: Birth, Nov 10
Phillips, Michelle: Birth, Jun 4
Phillips, Stone: Birth, Dec 2
Phillips, Wendy: Birth, Jan 2
Photo Month, Natl, May 1
Photography
First Photos Used in a Newspaper Report: Anniv, Jul 1
First Picture of Earth from Space: Anniv, Aug 7
First Presidential Photograph: Anniv, Feb 14
Nature Photography Day, Jun 15
Photographer Appreciation Month, Oct 1
Physical Fitness and Sports Month, Natl, May 1
Physical Therapy Month, Natl, Oct 1
Physical Wellness Month, Apr 1
Physician Assistants Day, Natl, Oct 6
Pi Day, Mar 14
Piano Competitions and Performances
Lucerne Fest, Piano (Lucerne, Switzerland), Nov 23
Piano Month, Natl, Sep 1
Van Cliburn Intl Competition (Fort Worth, TX), May 22
World Chmpshp Old-Time Piano Playing Contest (Peoria, IL), May 22
Piazza, Mike: Birth, Sep 4
Piazzetta, Giovanni Battista: Birth Anniv, Feb 13
Picasso, Pablo: Birth Anniv, Oct 25
Picatinny Peak Fall Hawkwatch (Dover, NJ), Sep 1
Piccard, Auguste: Birth Anniv, Jan 28
Piccard, Jacques: Birth, Jul 28
Piccard, Jean Felix: Birth Anniv, Jan 28
Piccard, Jeannette Ridlon: Birth Anniv, Jan 5
Pickens, James, Jr: Birth, Oct 26
Pickett, Bill: Birth Anniv, Dec 5
Pickett, George: Defeat at Five Forks: Anniv, Apr 1
Pickett's Charge: Battle of Gettysburg: Anniv, Jul 1
Pidgeon, Walter: Birth Anniv, Sep 23
Pied Piper of Hamelin: Anniv, Jul 22
Pied Piper: Rat-Catchers Day, Jul 22
Pierce, David Hyde: Birth, Apr 3
Pierce, Franklin: Birth Anniv, Nov 23
Pierce, Jane: Birth Anniv, Mar 12
Pierce, Paul: Birth, Oct 13
Pierpont, Julia: Day, May 23
Pietz, Amy: Birth, Mar 6
Pig Day, Natl, Mar 1
Pigott-Smith, Tim: Birth, May 13
Pileggi, Mitch: Birth, Apr 5
Pilgrim Landing: Anniv, Dec 21
Pinchot, Bronson: Birth, May 20
Pine Barrens Jamboree (Waretown, NJ), Oct 10
Piniella, Lou: Birth, Aug 28
Pink Moon, Apr 9
Pink: Birth, Sep 8
Pinkerton, Allan: Birth Anniv, Aug 25
Pinkett Smith, Jada: Birth, Sep 18
Pinochet, Augusto: Military Dictatorship Ended, Dec 15
Pinter, Harold: Birth, Oct 10
Pinzon, Martin: Arrival Anniv, Mar 1
Pippen, Scottie: Birth, Sep 25
Piquet, Nelson: Birth, Aug 17

Pirate Day, Talk Like a, Intl, Sep 19
Pisces Begins, Feb 20
Piscopo, Joe: Birth, Jun 17
Pisier, Marie-France: Birth, May 10
Pitcher, Molly: Birth Anniv, Oct 13
Pitt, Brad: Birth, Dec 18
Pitt, William: Birth Anniv, May 28
Pittsburgh Arts & Crafts Spring Fever Fest (Greensburg, PA), Mar 27
Piven, Jeremy: Birth, Jul 26
Pizarro, Francesco: Death Anniv, Jun 26
Pizza Party Day, Natl, May 15
Place, Mary Kay: Birth, Sep 23
Plana, Tony: Birth, Apr 19
Planck, Max: Birth Anniv, Apr 23
Plant the Seeds of Greatness Month, Feb 1
Plant, Robert: Birth, Aug 20
Platt, Oliver: Birth, Jan 12
Play Days, Sep 8
Play Presented in North American Colonies, First: Anniv, Aug 27
Playboy First Published: Anniv, Dec 1
Player, Gary: Birth, Nov 1
Playground Safety Week, Natl, Apr 19
Play-the-Recorder Month, Mar 1
Please Take My Children to Work Day, Jun 29
Pleasure Your Mate Month, Sep 1
Pledge Across America/Constitution Day, Sep 17
Pledge of Allegiance Recognized: Anniv, Dec 28
Pledge of Allegiance, Pause for (Natl Flag Day USA), Jun 14
Plimpton, George: Birth Anniv, Mar 18
Plimpton, Martha: Birth, Nov 16
Plimsoll Day (Samuel Plimsoll Birth Anniv), Feb 10
Plough Monday (England), Jan 12
Plum Digestive Health Month, California Dried, Jan 1
Plumb, Eve: Birth, Apr 29
Plummer, Amanda: Birth, Mar 23
Plummer, Christopher: Birth, Dec 13
Plushenko, Evgeny: Birth, Nov 3
Pluto Demoted: Anniv, Aug 24
Pluto Discovery: Anniv, Feb 18
Plutonium First Weighed: Anniv, Aug 20
Plymouth Plantation Earthquake: Anniv, Jun 1
Pocahontas: Death Anniv, Mar 21
Poe, Edgar Allan, Evermore (Manheim, PA), Oct 30
Poe, Edgar Allan: Birth Anniv, Jan 19
Poe, Edgar Allan: Raven Published: Anniv, Jan 29
Poehler, Amy: Birth, Sep 16
Poetry
  American Poet Laureate Establishment: Anniv, Dec 20
  Bad Poetry Day, Aug 18
  Baseball's Sad Lexicon Published: Anniv, Jul 10
  Clerihew Day, Jul 10
  Cowboy Poetry Gathering, Natl (Elko, NV), Jan 24
  Hammon, Jupiter: Birth Anniv, Oct 17
  Limerick Day, May 12
  Mighty Casey Has Struck Out: Anniv, Jun 3
  Poetry & the Creative Mind (New York, NY), Apr 1
  Poetry Contest (El Paso, TX), Jan 1
  Poetry Day in Florida, May 25
  Poetry Month, Natl, Apr 1
  Poet's Day, Aug 21
  Raven Published: Anniv, Jan 29
  Texas Cowboy Poetry Gathering (Alpine, TX), Feb 27
  Wheatley, Phillis: Poetry Collection Published: Anniv, Sep 1
Poinsett, Joel Roberts: Death Anniv, Dec 12
Poinsettia Day, Dec 12
Pointer, Bonnie: Birth, Jul 11
Poison Prevention Awareness Month, Mar 1
Poison Prevention Week, Natl, Mar 15
Poison Prevention Week, Natl (Pres Proc), Mar 15
Poitier, Sidney: Birth, Feb 20
Pol Pot Overthrown: Anniv, Jan 7
Poland
  Constitution Day, May 3
  Germany Invades: Anniv, Sep 1
  Independence Day, Nov 11
  Liberation Day, Jan 17
  Solidarity Founded: Anniv, Aug 31
  Solidarity Granted Legal Status: Anniv, Apr 17
Polanski, Roman: Birth, Aug 18
Polar Bear Swim (Nome, AK), Jun 20
Police
  Peace Officer Memorial Day (Pres Proc), May 15
  Peace Officer Memorial Day, Natl, May 15
  Police Officers Who Gave Their Lives in the Line of Duty Week, Apr 19
  Police Week (Pres Proc), May 10
  Police Week, Natl, May 10
Polio Vaccine: Anniv, Apr 12
Polish
  Polish Christmas Open House (Philadelphia, PA), Dec 12
  Polish-American Heritage Month, Oct 1
Polito, Jon: Birth, Dec 29
Polk, James: Birth Anniv, Nov 2
Polk, James: First Presidential Photograph: Anniv, Feb 14
Polk, Sarah Childress: Birth Anniv, Sep 4
Poll Tax Outlawed: Anniv, Apr 8
Pollak, Kevin: Birth, Oct 30
Pollan, Tracy: Birth, Jun 22
Pollard, Michael J.: Birth, May 30
Polo: Cartier Polo World Cup on Snow (St. Moritz, Switzerland), Jan 29
Polygamists, Amnesty for: Anniv, Jan 4
Pomegranate Month, Natl, Nov 1
Pompeii Destroyed (Vesuvius Day): Anniv, Aug 24
Pompeo, Ellen: Birth, Nov 10
Ponce de Leon Discovers Florida: Anniv, Apr 2
Ponselle, Rosa: Birth Anniv, Jan 22
Pony Express Fest (Hanover, KS), Aug 30
Pony Express, Inauguration of: Anniv, Apr 3
Pooh Day (A.A. Milne Birth Anniv), Jan 18
Poole, Cecil: First Black US State's Attorney: Anniv, Jul 6
Poor Richard's Almanack: Anniv, Dec 28
Pop Music Chart Introduced: Anniv, Jan 4
Pop, Iggy: Birth, Apr 21
Popcorn Fest (Valparaiso, IN), Sep 12
Popcorn Fest, Marion (Marion, OH), Sep 10
Popcorn Poppin' Month, Natl, Oct 1
Pope, Alexander: Birth Anniv, May 21
Pope, John: Birth Anniv, Mar 16
Popes, Roman Catholic
  Benedict XV: Birth Anniv, Nov 21
  Benedict XVI: Birth, Apr 16
  Benedict XVI: Election Anniv, Apr 19
  John Paul I: Birth Anniv, Oct 17
  John Paul II: Assassination Attempt: Anniv, May 13
  John Paul II: Birth Anniv, May 18
  John Paul II: Death Anniv, Apr 2
  John XXIII: Birth Anniv, Nov 25
  Paul VI: Birth Anniv, Sep 26
  Pius XI: Birth Anniv, May 31
  Pius XII: Birth Anniv, Mar 2
  Saint Pius X: Birth Anniv, Jun 2
Popeye Debuts: Anniv, Jan 17
Population Day, World (UN), Jul 11
Population: Day of Five Billion: Anniv, Jul 11
Population: Day of the Six Billion: Anniv, Oct 12
Porter, Cole: Birth Anniv, Jun 9
Porter, Katherine Anne: Birth Anniv, May 15
Porter, Sylvia: Birth Anniv, Jun 18
Porter, Terry: Birth, Apr 8
Porter, William S. (O. Henry): Birth Anniv, Sep 11
Portman, Natalie: Birth, Jun 9
Portugal
  Day of Portugal, Jun 10
  Independence Day, Dec 1
  Liberty Day, Apr 25
  Lisbon Earthquake: Anniv, Nov 1
  Pilgrimage to Fatima, May 12
  Republic Day, Oct 5
  Saint Anthony of Padua: Feast Day, Jun 13
Posey, Parker: Birth, Nov 8
Positive Attitude Month, Oct 1
Positively Penguins (Point Pleasant Beach, NJ), Jan 10
Post Day, World (UN), Oct 9
Post, Emily: Birth Anniv, Oct 30
Post, Markie: Birth, Nov 4
Post, Wiley: Birth Anniv, Nov 22
Postcard Shows: York Intl Postcard Fair (York, PA), Nov 20
Postell, Ashley: Birth, Jun 9
Postlethwaite, Pete: Birth, Feb 7
Postman's Day (Mexico), Nov 12
Postmaster General Established, US: Anniv, Sep 22
Potsdam Declaration: Anniv, Jul 26
Potter, Beatrix: Birth Anniv, Jul 28
Potts, Annie: Birth, Oct 28
Potty Training Awareness Month, Jun 1
Pound, Ezra: Birth Anniv, Oct 30
Pound, Ezra: Bollingen Prize Award, Feb 19
Poundstone, Paula: Birth, Dec 29
Poverty in America Awareness Month, Natl, Jan 1
Poverty, Intl Day for Eradication of (UN), Oct 17
Poverty, War on: Anniv, Jan 8
Povich, Maury: Birth, Jan 17
POW/MIA Recognition Day, Natl (Pres Proc), Sep 18
Powell, Colin: Birth, Apr 5
Powell, Cristen: Birth, Mar 22
Powell, Jane: Birth, Apr 1
Powell, John W.: Birth Anniv, Mar 24
Powell, Lewis F., Jr: Birth Anniv, Sep 19
Power Show, Fulton County Historical (Rochester, IN), Jun 19
Power, Tyrone: Birth Anniv, May 5
PowerPoint Week, Just Say No to, Feb 9
Powers, Francis Gary: Birth Anniv, Aug 17
Powers, Francis Gary: U-2 Incident: Anniv, May 1
Powers, Richard: Birth, Jun 18
Powers, Stefanie: Birth, Nov 2

Prairie Home Companion Premiere: Anniv, Feb 17
Prater's Mill Country Fair (Dalton, GA), Oct 10
Prayer
Just Pray No: Worldwide Weekend Prayer, Apr 18
National Day of Prayer (Pres Proc), May 7
Supreme Court Bans School Prayer: Anniv, Jun 25
World Day of Prayer, Mar 6
Preakness Stakes (Baltimore, MD), May 16
Preakness Stakes: Anniv, May 27
Prematurity Awareness Day, Nov 1
Prentiss, Paula: Birth, Mar 4
Preparedness Month, Natl, Sep 1
Prescott, William: Birth Anniv, Feb 20
Prescription Errors Education & Awareness Week, Oct 24
Prescriptions Month, Talk About, Oct 1
Presentation of the Lord (Candlemas Day), Feb 2
Preservation Month, Natl, May 1
Preservation of the Ozone Layer, Intl Day for (UN), Sep 16
President Occupies the White House: Anniv, Nov 1
President: Inauguration Day, Jan 20
Presidential Debate, First Televised: Anniv, Sep 26
Presidential Inaugural Ball: Anniv, May 7
Presidential Inauguration Anniv, George Washington, Apr 30
Presidential Inauguration, Cleveland's Second: Anniv, Mar 4
Presidential Joke Day, Aug 11
Presidential Photograph, First: Anniv, Feb 14
Presidential Resignation: Anniversary, Aug 9
Presidential Telecast, First: Anniv, Apr 30
Presidents' Day, Feb 16
Presidents' Day: Live from Delaware St (Indianapolis, IN), Feb 16
President's Environmental Youth Award Natl Competition, Oct 31
Presley, Elvis
Birth Anniv, Jan 8
Death Anniv, Aug 16
Elvis Presley's Birthday Celebration (Memphis, TN), Jan 8
Elvis Week (Memphis, TN), Aug 8
First Concert Appearance: Anniv, Jul 30
First Single Released: Anniv, Jul 19
Inducted into the Army: Anniv, Mar 24
Meets President Nixon: Anniv, Dec 21
Presley, Lisa Marie: Birth, Feb 1
Presley, Priscilla: Birth, May 24
Press Freedom Day, World (UN), May 3
Pressly, Jaime: Birth, Jul 30
Pressman, Lawrence: Birth, Jul 10
Preston, Kelly: Birth, Oct 13
Prevention of Eye Injuries Awareness Week, Natl, Jun 28
Previn, Andre: Birth, Apr 6
Price Is Right TV Premiere: Anniv, Nov 26
Price, Alan: Birth, Apr 19
Price, Leontyne: Birth, Feb 10
Price, Ray: Birth, Jan 12
Price, Vincent: Birth Anniv, May 27
Price, William Mark: Birth, Feb 15
Pride, Charley: Birth, Mar 18
Priesand, Sally: First Woman Rabbi in US: Anniv, Jun 3
Priestley, Jason: Birth, Aug 28
Priestly, Joseph: Birth Anniv, Mar 13
Prime Beef Month, Natl, Sep 1
Prime Meridian Set: Anniv, Nov 1
Primeau, Keith: Birth, Nov 24
Primetime Live TV Premiere: Anniv, Aug 3
Primus, Barry: Birth, Feb 16
Prince Harry: Birth, Sep 15
Prince Jonah Kuhio Kalanianole Day (HI), Mar 26
Prince William: Birth, Jun 21
Prince: Birth, Jun 7
Princess Diana: Death Anniv, Aug 31
Princeton, USS, Explosion: Anniv, Feb 28
Principal, Victoria: Birth, Jan 3
Principals' Day, School, May 1
Prine, Andrew: Birth, Feb 14
Printing Week, Intl, Jan 11
Prinze, Freddie, Jr: Birth, Mar 8
Prison, Union Officers Escape Libby: Anniv, Feb 9
Prisoner of War Recognition Day, Natl Former (Pres Proc), Apr 9
Prisoner TV Premiere: Anniv, Jun 1
Prix de l'Arc de Triomphe (Paris, France), Oct 4
Pro Sports Wives Day, Feb 11
Problem-Solving: It's About Time Week, Dec 25
Probst, Jeff: Birth, Oct 26
Procession of the Addolorata and Mysteries (Taranto, Italy), Apr 9
Procession of the Holy Blood (Belgium), May 21
Procrastination Week, Natl, Mar 2
Professional Speakers Day, Aug 7
Professional Wellness Month, Jun 1
Profiles in Courage Published: Anniv, Jan 1
Prohibition: 18th Amendment: Anniv, Jan 16
Prohibition Repealed: 21st Amendment Ratified, Dec 5
Prohibition: Maine Law: Anniv, Jun 2
Promotion Month, Shameless, Sep 1
Pronger, Chris: Birth, Oct 10
Proposal Day!, Mar 20
Proposition 13: Anniv, Jun 6
Prosky, Robert: Birth, Dec 13
Prostate Cancer Awareness Week, Sep 20
Protocol Officers Week, Natl, Mar 23
Proulx, E. Annie: Birth, Aug 22
Proust, Marcel: Birth Anniv, Jul 10
Prout, Mary Ann: Birth Anniv, Feb 14
Prowse, Juliet: Birth Anniv, Sep 25
Pryce, Jonathan: Birth, Jun 1
Pryor, Mark: Birth, Jan 10
Pryor, Richard: Birth Anniv, Dec 1
Psychic Week, Aug 3
Psycho Film Premiere: Anniv, Jun 16
PTA Founders' Day, Natl, Feb 17
Public Lands Day, Natl, Sep 26
Public Radio, Natl: Anniv, May 3
Public Relations: Getting the World to Beat a Path to Door Week, Oct 11
Public School, First in America: Anniv, Apr 23
Public Service Day (UN), Jun 23
Public Speaking: Freedom from Fear of Speaking Week, Jun 28
Public Television Debuts: Anniv, Nov 3
Publicity for Profit Week, Feb 1
Publishing: Small Press Month, Mar 1
Puccini, Giacomo: Birth Anniv, Dec 22
Puccini, Giacomo: Madama Butterfly Premiere: Anniv, Feb 17
Pueblo, USS, Seized by North Korea: Anniv, Jan 23
Puente, Tito: Birth Anniv, Apr 20
Puerto Rico
Acevedo Vila, Anibal: Birth, Feb 13
Barbosa, Jose Celso: Birth Anniv, Jul 27
Carnival de Ponce (Ponce), Feb 18
Constitution Day, Jul 25
Diego, Jose de: Birth Anniv, Apr 16
Discovery Day, Nov 19
Emancipation Day, Mar 22
Hostos, Eugenio Maria: Birth Anniv, Jan 11
Las Mananitas, Dec 12
Loiza Aldea Fiesta, Jul 25
Munoz-Rivera Day, Jul 17
Navidades, Dec 15
Virgin Islands–Puerto Rico Friendship Day, Oct 12
Pujols, Albert: Birth, Jan 16
Pulaski, Casimir: Birth Anniv, Mar 4
Pulaski, General: Memorial Day (Pres Proc), Oct 11
Pulitzer Prizes First Awarded: Anniv, Jun 4
Pulitzer, Joseph: Birth Anniv, Apr 10
Pulliam, Keshia Knight: Birth, Apr 9
Pullman, Bill: Birth, Dec 17
Pullman, George: Birth Anniv, Mar 3
Pumpkin Fest, Morton (Morton, IL), Sep 9
Pumpkin Regatta, Windsor (Windsor, NS, Canada), Oct 10
Pumpkin Show, Circleville (Circleville, OH), Oct 21
Pumpkins: Jack-o-Launch (Aurora, CO), Oct 10
Pumpkins: World Chmpshp Punkin Chunkin (Bridgeville, DE), Nov 6
Punctuation Day, Natl, Sep 24
Pun-Off, O. Henry Museum (Austin, TX), May 16
Punsters Day, Abet and Aid, Nov 8
Puppy Day, Natl, Mar 23
Purcell, Henry: Death Anniv, Nov 21
Purcell, Sarah: Birth, Oct 8
Purgatory Banquet (Gradoli, Italy), Feb 25
Purim, Mar 10
Purl, Linda: Birth, Sep 2
Purple Heart: Anniv, Aug 7
Push-Button Telephone Debuts: Anniv, Nov 18
Pushkin, Alexander: Birth Anniv, Jun 6
Putin, Vladimir: Birth, Oct 7
Puyallup Fair (Puyallup, WA), Sep 11
Puyallup Spring Fair (Puyallup, WA), Apr 16
Pyle, Ernest: Birth Anniv, Aug 3
Pynchon, Thomas: Birth, May 8

Q

Qatar: Independence Day, Sep 3
Qing Ming Fest or Tomb Sweeping Day, Apr 4
Quadrangle Fest (Texarkana, AR and TX), Oct 10
Quaid, Dennis: Birth, Apr 9
Quaid, Randy: Birth, Oct 1
Quality of Life Month, Intl, Jan 1
Quantrill's Raid on Lawrence, KS: Anniv, Aug 21
Quark, Physicists Discover Top: Anniv, Apr 23
Quasthoff, Thomas: Birth, Nov 9
Quayle, Dan: Birth, Feb 4
Quebec City Hunting, Fishing, Camping & Boat Show (Quebec City, QC, Canada), Mar 12
Quebec Founded: Anniv, Jul 3

Queen Elizabeth I: Accession: Anniv, Nov 17
Queen Elizabeth I: Birth Anniv, Sep 7
Queen Elizabeth II: Accession Anniv, Feb 6
Queen Elizabeth II: Agrees to Pay Taxes: Anniv, Nov 26
Queen for a Day TV Premiere: Anniv, Jan 3
Queen Latifah: Birth, Mar 18
Queen Mary, RMS: Maiden Voyage: Anniv, May 27
Queen Victoria: Death Anniv, Jan 22
Queen's Official Birthday, Jun 8
Queen's Official Birthday/Trooping Colours (England), Jun 13
Quentin, Carlos: Birth, Aug 28
Question Day, Intl Ask a, Mar 14
Quilt (quilts, quilting, quilt shows)
Peddler's Village Quilt Competition/Display (Lahaska, PA), Jan 12
Quilt Odyssey (Hershey, PA), Jul 30
Quilt Show (Woodstock, VT), Aug 1
Quilter's Society Show, American (Paducah, KY), Apr 22
Quilting Day, Natl, Mar 21
Suwannee River Quilt Show and Sale (White Springs, FL), Oct 16
Quincy TV Premiere: Anniv, Oct 3
Quinlan, Karen Ann: Birth Anniv, Mar 29
Quinlan, Kathleen: Birth, Nov 19
Quinn, Aidan: Birth, Mar 8
Quinn, Anthony: Birth Anniv, Apr 21
Quinn, Jane Bryant: Birth, Feb 5
Quinto, Zachary: Birth, Jun 2
Quirky Country Music Song Titles Day, Mar 27
Quiz Kids TV Premiere: Anniv, Jul 6

R

Ra, Sun: Birth Anniv, May 22
Rabbi: First Woman Rabbi in US: Anniv, Jun 3
Rabbit Week, Natl, Jul 15
Rabe, David: Birth, Mar 10
Rabi' I: Month of the Migration (Islamic), Feb 27
Rabinowitz, Solomon: Birth Anniv, Feb 18
Race Relations Day, Feb 14
Race Riots, Saint Louis: Anniv, Jul 2
Race Unity Day, Jun 14
Race Your Mouse Around the Icons Day, Aug 28
Racial Discrimination, Intl Day for Elimination of (UN), Mar 21
Racism/Racial Discrimination, Solidarity Against (UN), Mar 21
Radcliffe, Ann: Birth Anniv, Jul 9
Radcliffe, Daniel: Birth, Jul 23
Radio
Amateur Radio Day, Intl, Apr 18
American Top 40 Premiere: Anniv, Jul 4
ARRL Field Day, Jun 27
Breakfast Club Premiere: Anniv, Jun 23
Car Talk Natl Premiere: Anniv, Oct 31
Federal Communications Commission Created: Anniv, Feb 26
First Grand Ole Opry Broadcast: Anniv, Dec 10
First Play-by-Play Football Game Broadcast: Anniv, Nov 23
First Radio Broadcast from Space: Anniv, Dec 19
First Radio Broadcast of a Prizefight: Anniv, Sep 6
First Scheduled Radio Broadcast: Anniv, Nov 2
Howard Stern Show Premiere: Anniv, Nov 18
Imus in the Morning Radio Premiere: Anniv, Dec 2
Letter from America Premiere: Anniv, Mar 24
Loomis Day, May 30
Metropolitan Opera Radio Broadcasts Premiere: Anniv, Dec 25
Natl Traffic Directors Day, Nov 2
Ozzie and Harriet Debut: Anniv, Oct 8
Prairie Home Companion Premiere: Anniv, Feb 17
Public Radio, Natl: Anniv, May 3
Radio Broadcast by a President, First, Jun 14
Radio Broadcasting: Anniv, Jan 13
Radio Commercials: Anniv, Aug 28
Rest of the Story Premiere: Anniv, May 10
Rush Limbaugh Show Natl Premiere: Anniv, Aug 1
Shadow Premiere: Anniv, Jul 31
Transistor Unveiled: Anniv, Dec 23
War of the Worlds Broadcast: Anniv, Oct 30
Wolfman Jack: Birth Anniv, Jan 21
Your Hit Parade Radio Premiere: Anniv, Apr 12
Radio City Music Hall: Anniv, Dec 27
Radiological Soc of North America Scientific Assembly and Annual Mtg (Chicago, IL), Nov 29
Radishes, Feast of (Oaxaca, Mexico), Dec 23
Radium Discovered: Anniv, Dec 26
Radner, Gilda: Birth Anniv, Jun 28
Radnor, Josh: Birth, Jul 29
Radon Action Month, Natl, Jan 1
Radosavljevic, Predrag: Birth, Jun 24
Radziwill, Lee: Birth, Mar 3
Rae, Charlotte: Birth, Apr 22
Rafalski, Brian: Birth, Sep 28
Raffi: Birth, Jul 8
Raffin, Deborah: Birth, Mar 13
Raffles, Stamford: Birth Anniv, Jul 5
Rafter, Patrick: Birth, Dec 28
RAGBRAI—Register's Bicycle Ride Across Iowa (Des Moines, IA), Jul 19
Raggedy Ann & Andy Fest, Original (Arcola, IL), Jun 13
Ragsdale, William: Birth, Jan 19
Raid on Entebbe: Anniv, Jul 3
Raid on Richmond: Anniv, Mar 1
Railroad
Amtrak: Anniv, May 1
Antique Power Exhibition (Burton, OH), Jul 24
Circus Train Wreck: Anniv, Jun 22
Galesburg Railroad Days (Galesburg, IL), Jun 27
Golden Spike Driving: Anniv, May 10
Helena Railroad Fair (Helena, MT), Apr 26
Iron Horse Outraced by Horse: Anniv, Sep 18
New York City Subway: Anniv, Oct 27
Northern Pacific Railroad Completed: Anniv, Sep 8
Railroad and Hobby Show (Springfield, MA), Jan 24
Stevenson Depot Days (Stevenson, AL), Jun 8
34th St Express (Boston, MA), Dec 19
Train Day, Natl, May 9
Transcontinental US Railway Completion: Anniv, Aug 15
Rain Day (Waynesburg, PA), Jul 29
Rainbow Warrior Sinking: Anniv, Jul 10
Rainer, Luise: Birth, Jan 12
Raines, Tim: Birth, Sep 16
Rainey, Joseph: First Black in US House of Reps: Anniv, Dec 12
Rainey, Ma (Gertrude B.): Birth Anniv, Apr 3
Rainforest Week, World, Oct 12
Rainier, Prince: Birth Anniv, May 31
Raitt, Bonnie: Birth, Nov 8
Ram, Jagjivan: Birth Anniv, Apr 1
Ramadan: Islamic Month of Fasting, Aug 22
Ramamurthy, Sendhil: Birth, May 17
Rameau, Jean P.: Baptism Anniv, Sep 25
Ramirez, Hanley: Birth, Dec 23
Ramirez, Manny: Birth, May 30
Ramis, Harold: Birth, Nov 21
Ramo, Roberta Cooper: Birth, Aug 8
Rampling, Charlotte: Birth, Feb 5
Ramsay, Gordon: Birth, Nov 8
Ramses II Unearthed, Statue of: Anniv, Nov 30
Rand, Ayn: Birth Anniv, Feb 2
Rand, Sally: Birth Anniv, Apr 3
Randall, Tony: Birth Anniv, Feb 26
Randolph, Peyton: Death Anniv, Oct 22
Rankin, Ian: Birth, Apr 28
Rankin, Jeannette: Birth Anniv, Jun 11
Raphael, Sally Jessy: Birth, Feb 25
Raphael: Birth Anniv, Apr 6
Raptor Month, Oct 1
Rashad, Ahmad: Birth, Nov 19
Rashad, Phylicia: Birth, Jun 19
Rasputin, Grigori: Assassination Anniv, Dec 29
Rather, Dan: Birth, Oct 31
Ratification Day, Jan 14
Rats (see also Animals, Mice, Pets)
AFRMA Display at America's Family Pet Expo (Costa Mesa, CA), Apr 10
AFRMA Fancy Rat & Mouse Display (Costa Mesa, CA), Jul 28
Pied Piper of Hamelin: Anniv, Jul 22
Rat and Mouse Annual Show, Fancy (Riverside, CA), Jan 24
Rat-Catchers Day, Jul 22
Rattle, Simon: Birth, Jan 19
Rattlesnake Derby (Mangum, OK), Apr 24
Rattlesnake Roundup, World's Largest (Sweetwater, TX), Mar 13
Ratzenberger, John: Birth, Apr 6
Ratzinger, Joseph: Pope Benedict XVI: Election Anniv, Apr 19
Rauh, Joseph L., Jr: Birth Anniv, Jan 3
Raven Published: Anniv, Jan 29
Raver, Kim: Birth, Mar 15
Rawhide TV Premiere: Anniv, Jan 9
Rawlings, Marjorie Kinnan: Birth Anniv, Aug 8
Rawls, Lou: Birth Anniv, Dec 1
Ray, Rachael: Birth, Aug 25
Ray, Satyajit: Birth Anniv, May 2
Raye, Martha: Birth Anniv, Aug 27
Raymond, Alex: Birth Anniv, Oct 2
Razor, Electric, First Marketed: Anniv, Mar 18
Rea, Stephen: Birth, Oct 31
REACT Month, May 1
Read Across America Day, Mar 2
R.E.A.D. in America Day (Washington, DC), Sep 26

Read an E-Book Week, Mar 8
Read in the Bathtub Day, Feb 9
Read Me Week (TN), Feb 23
Read, Allen, Discovers O.K. Origin: Anniv, Mar 23
Read, George: Birth Anniv, Sep 18
Reader's Day, Natl Young, Nov 10
Reading Group Month, Natl, Oct 1
Reading Is Fun Week, May 10
Reading: Get Caught Reading Month, May 1
Reading: March into Literacy Month, Natl, Mar 1
Reagan, Nancy: Birth, Jul 6
Reagan, Ronald Prescott: Birth, May 20
Reagan, Ronald Wilson
  Assassination Attempt on: Anniv, Mar 30
  Birth Anniv, Feb 6
  Presidential Joke Day, Aug 11
  Tear Down This Wall Speech: Anniv, Jun 12
Real McCoys TV Premiere: Anniv, Oct 3
Real People TV Premiere: Anniv, Apr 18
Reason, Natl Day of, May 7
Reasoner, Harry: Birth Anniv, Apr 17
Rebuild Your Life Month, Jun 1
Rebuilding Day, Natl, Apr 25
Receptionists Day, Natl, May 13
Recess at Work Day, Jun 18
Recipe Greetings for the Holidays, Dec 1
Reckell, Peter: Birth, May 7
Reconciliation Day, Apr 2
Reconciliation, Intl Year of (UN), Jan 1
Record Store Day, Apr 18
Recreation and Parks Month, Natl, Jul 1
Recreation Week, Special, Jun 28
Red Army Departs Berlin: Anniv, Jun 11
Red Cloud: Death Anniv, Dec 10
Red Cross Day, World, May 8
Red Cross Month, Mar 1
Red Cross Month, American (Pres Proc), Mar 1
Red Skelton Show TV Premiere: Anniv, Sep 30
Reddy, Helen: Birth, Oct 25
Redford, Robert: Birth, Aug 18
Redgrave, Lynn: Birth, Mar 8
Redgrave, Vanessa: Birth, Jan 30
Redwood Natl Park Established: Anniv, Oct 2
Reece, Gabrielle: Birth, Jan 6
Reed, Donna: It's a Wonderful Life Film Premiere: Anniv, Dec 20
Reed, Jack: Birth, Nov 12
Reed, Jerry: Birth, Mar 20
Reed, Pamela: Birth, Apr 2
Reed, Rex: Birth, Oct 2
Reed, Walter: Birth Anniv, Sep 13
Reed, Willis: Birth, Jun 25
Reenactments (Historical, Military)
  Battle of Blue Licks Celebration (Mount Olivet, KY), Aug 15
  Battle of Bushy Run Reenactment (Harrison City, PA), Aug 1
  Battle of Germantown Reenactment (Philadelphia, PA), Oct 3
  Battle of Olustee (Olustee, FL), Feb 13
  Civil War Reenactment (Keokuk, IA), Apr 24
  Grand Militia Muster (St. Mary's City, MD), Oct 17
  Klondike Days (Eagle River, WI), Feb 21
  Little Bighorn Days (Hardin, MT), Jun 24
  Military Through the Ages (Williamsburg, VA), Mar 21
  Natural Bridge Battle (Tallahassee, FL), Mar 6
  Reenactment of Cowtown's Last Gunfight (Fort Worth, TX), Feb 8
  Trail of History (Ringwood, IL), Oct 17
  Upper Canada Village (Morrisburg, ON, Canada), May 16
Reese, Della: Birth, Jul 6
Reese, Pee Wee: Birth Anniv, Jul 23
Reeve, Christopher: Birth Anniv, Sep 25
Reeves, Jim: Birth Anniv, Aug 20
Reeves, Keanu: Birth, Sep 2
Reeves, Martha: Birth, Jul 18
Refired, not Retired, Day, Mar 1
Reformation Day, Oct 31
Reformation Sunday, Oct 25
Refugee Day, World (UN), Jun 20
Regifting Day, Natl, Dec 17
Registered Dietitian Day, Mar 11
Rehabilitation Awareness Celebration, Natl, Sep 20
Rehnquist, William Hubbs: Birth Anniv, Oct 1
Reid, Harry: Birth, Dec 2
Reid, Tara: Birth, Nov 8
Reid, Tim: Birth, Dec 19
Reina, Pepe: Birth, Aug 31
Reiner, Carl: Birth, Mar 20
Reiner, Rob: Birth, Mar 6
Reinhold, Judge: Birth, May 21
Reinking, Ann: Birth, Nov 10
Reiser, Paul: Birth, Mar 30
Reitman, Ivan: Birth, Oct 26
Rejection/Risk Awareness Week, Feb 7
Relationship Wellness Month, Feb 1
Relaxation Day, Natl, Aug 15
Religion Day, World, Jan 18
Religious Freedom Day, Jan 16
Religious Freedom Day (Pres Proc), Jan 16
Religious Travel Expo, World (Nashville, TN), Oct 28
Rell, M. Jodi: Birth, Jun 16
Remar, James: Birth, Dec 31
Rembrandt: Birth Anniv, Jul 15
Remember the Maine Day: Anniv, Feb 15
Remembrance Day (Canada), Nov 11
Remembrance Day (Gettysburg, PA), Nov 21
Remembrance Sunday (England), Nov 8
Remick, Lee: Birth Anniv, Dec 14
Remington Steele TV Premiere: Anniv, Oct 1
Remington, Frederic S.: Birth Anniv, Oct 4
Remini, Leah: Birth, Jun 15
Renaissance Fairs
  Alabama Renaissance Faire (Florence, AL), Oct 24
  Arizona Renaissance Fest (Apache Junction, AZ), Feb 7
  Georgia Renaissance Spring Fest (Atlanta, GA), Apr 18
  Hoggetowne Medieval Faire (Gainesville), Jan 24
  Maryland Renaissance Fest (Annapolis, MD), Aug 29
  Medieval Fair (Norman, OK), Apr 3
  Medieval Fest (Savannah, GA), Sep 26
  Minnesota Renaissance Fest (Shakopee, MN), Aug 15
  Pennsylvania Renaissance Faire (Manheim, PA), Aug 8
  Pittsburgh Renaissance Fest (West Newton, PA), Aug 23
  Sterling Renaissance Fest (Sterling, NY), Jul 11
Rendell, Ed: Birth, Jan 5
Rendezvous, Redbud Trail (Rochester, IN), Apr 25
Reno, Janet: Birth, Jul 21
Renoir, Pierre: Birth Anniv, Feb 25
Republican Party Formed: Anniv, Jul 6
Republican Symbol: Anniv, Nov 7
Research Council, Natl: First Meeting: Anniv, Sep 20
Resnik, Judith A.: Birth Anniv, Apr 5
Resolutions: Second Half of the New Year Day, Jul 1
Respect Day, Natl, Sep 18
Respect for Parents Day, Aug 1
Respect for the Aged Day (Japan), Sep 21
Respighi, Ottorino: Birth Anniv, Jul 9
Rest of the Story Radio Premiere: Anniv, May 10
Restless Leg Syndrome (RLS) Education and Awareness Week, Jul 18
Resurrect Romance Week, Natl, Aug 9
Retailers Week, Natl Independent, Jul 19
Retrocession Day (Taiwan), Oct 25
Rett Syndrome Awareness Month, Oct 1
Retton, Mary Lou: Birth, Jan 24
Return Day (Georgetown, DE), Nov 5
Return Shopping Carts to the Supermarket Month, Feb 1
Return the Borrowed Books Week, Mar 1
Reuben, Gloria: Birth, Jun 9
Reubens, Paul: Birth, Aug 27
Reunification of Germany: Anniv, Oct 3
Reunion Planning Month, Sep 1
Reunions: Class Reunion Month, Oct 1
Reunions: Family Reunion Month, Jul 1
Reuther, Walter: Birth Anniv, Sep 1
Revere, Anne: Birth Anniv, Jun 25
Revere, Paul: Birth, Jan 7
Revere, Paul: Birth Anniv, Jan 1
Revere, Paul: Ride Anniv, Apr 18
Revolution, American
  Battle of Blue Licks Celebration (Mount Olivet, KY), Aug 15
  Battle of Brandywine: Anniv, Sep 11
  Battle of Germantown Reenactment (Philadelphia, PA), Oct 3
  Battle of Lexington and Concord: Anniv, Apr 19
  Bennington Battle Day: Anniv, Aug 16
  Boston Tea Party: Anniv, Dec 16
  Camden, Battle of: Anniv, Aug 16
  Cessation of Hostilities: Anniv, Jan 20
  Evacuation Day (Boston, MA), Mar 17
  Great Britain–US: Articles of Peace: Anniv, Nov 30
  Hale, Nathan: Birth Anniv, Jun 6
  Henry, Patrick: Birth Anniv, May 29
  Independence Day (US), Jul 4
  John Parker Day, Apr 19
  Liberty Celebration (Yorktown, VA), Jul 4
  Liberty Day, Mar 23
  Middleton, Arthur: Birth Anniv, Jun 26
  Olive Branch Petition: Anniv, Jul 8
  Paris, Treaty of: Signing Anniv, Sep 3
  Paul Revere's Ride: Anniv, Apr 18
  Salvador, Francis: Death Anniv, Jul 31
  Sampson, Deborah: Birth Anniv, Dec 17
  Shays's Rebellion: Anniv, Aug 29
  Washington Crosses the Delaware: Anniv, Dec 25
  Washington Takes Command of Continental Army: Anniv, Jul 3
  Yorktown Day, Oct 19
  Yorktown Day (Yorktown, VA), Oct 19
  Yorktown Victory Celebration (Yorktown, VA), Oct 17
  Yorktown Victory Day (VA), Oct 12

Revolution, Russian: Anniv, Nov 7
Revson, Charles: Birth Anniv, Oct 11
Rex Allen Days (Willcox, AZ), Oct 2
Rey, Margaret: Birth Anniv, May 16
Reyna, Claudio: Birth, Jul 20
Reynolds, Burt: Birth, Feb 11
Reynolds, Debbie: Birth, Apr 1
Reynolds, Debbie: Singin' in the Rain Film Premiere: Anniv, Mar 27
Reynolds, Joshua: Birth Anniv, Jul 16
Reznor, Trent: Birth, May 17
Rhames, Ving: Birth, May 12
Rhoda TV Premiere: Anniv, Sep 9
Rhode Island
  Anne Hutchinson Memorial Day (Portsmouth), Jul 19
  Bristol Civic, Military/Firemen's Parade (Bristol), Jul 4
  Carcieri, Donald: Birth, Dec 16
  Children's Party at Green Animals (Newport), Jul 14
  Independence Day, May 4
  Neighbor Day, May 24
  New England Mid-Winter Surfing Chmpshp (Narragansett), Feb 21
  Newport Flower Show (Newport), Jun 26
  Newport Intl Boat Show (Newport), Sep 17
  Newport Music Fest (Newport), Jul 10
  Newport Spring Boat Show (Newport), May 15
  Newport Winter Fest (Newport), Feb 13
  Providence Boat Show (Providence), Jan 29
  Ratification Day, May 29
  Reed, Jack: Birth, Nov 12
  Victory Day, Aug 10
  Voters Reject Constitution: Anniv, Mar 24
  Whitehouse, Sheldon: Birth, Oct 20
Rhodes, Cecil: Birth Anniv, Jul 5
Rhodes, Cynthia: Birth, Nov 21
Rhododendron Fest (Florence, OR), May 15
Rhubarb Fest (Intercourse, PA), May 15
Rhys-Meyers, Jonathan: Birth, Jul 27
Ricardo, David: Birth Anniv, Apr 19
Ricci, Christina: Birth, Feb 12
Rice Month, Natl, Sep 1
Rice, Anne: Birth, Oct 4
Rice, Condoleezza: Birth, Nov 14
Rice, Glen: Birth, May 28
Rice, Jerry Lee: Birth, Oct 13
Rice, Jim: Birth, Mar 8
Rice, Tim: Birth, Nov 10
Rich, Adam: Birth, Oct 12
Richard, Rocket: Birth Anniv, Aug 4
Richards, Denise: Birth, Feb 17
Richards, Keith: Birth, Dec 18
Richards, Michael: Birth, Aug 24
Richards, Todd: Birth, Dec 28
Richardson, Bill: Birth, Nov 15
Richardson, J.P. (Big Bopper). See Day the Music Died: Anniv, Feb 3
Richardson, Joely: Birth, Jan 9
Richardson, Miranda: Birth, Mar 3
Richardson, Natasha: Birth, May 11
Richardson, Patricia: Birth, Feb 23
Richie, Lionel: Birth, Jun 20
Richie, Nicole: Birth, Sep 21
Richmond, Lee: First Perfect Game: Anniv, Jun 12
Richmond, Mitch: Birth, Jun 30
Richter Scale Day, Apr 26
Richter, Andy: Birth, Oct 28
Richter, Mike: Birth, Sep 22
Rickenbacker, Edward V.: Birth Anniv, Oct 8
Rickey, Branch: Birth Anniv, Dec 20
Rickles, Don: Birth, May 8
Rickover, Hyman George: Birth Anniv, Jan 27
Riddles, Libby: Birth, Apr 1
Ride, Sally K.: Birthday, May 26
Ridgeley, Andrew: Birth, Jan 26
Ridgway, Matthew Bunker: Birth Anniv, Mar 3
Riefenstahl, Leni: Birth Anniv, Aug 22
Riegert, Peter: Birth, Apr 11
Riel, Louis: Hanging Anniv, Nov 16
Rifkin, Ron: Birth, Oct 31
Rigby, Cathy: Birth, Dec 12
Rigg, Diana: Birth, Jul 20
Riggs, Bobby: Billie Jean King Wins: Anniv, Sep 20
Right-Brainers Rule Month, Oct 1
Riley, Bob: Birth, Oct 3
Riley, James Whitcomb: Death Anniv, Jul 22
Riley, Pat: Birth, Mar 20
Rimes, LeAnn: Birth, Aug 28
Ringgold, Faith: Birth, Oct 8
Ringwald, Molly: Birth, Feb 18
Rios, Marcelo: Birth, Dec 26
Riot Act: Anniv, Jul 20
Riot, Watts: Anniv, Aug 11
Ripa, Kelly: Birth, Oct 2
Ripken Streak Begins: Anniv, May 30
Ripken, Cal, Jr: Birth, Aug 24
Ripper, Jack the: Letter: Anniv, Sep 27
Ripper, Jack the: Whitechapel Murders Begin: Anniv, Aug 31
Rite of Spring Premiere and Riot: Anniv, May 29
Ritt, Martin: Birth Anniv, Mar 2
Ritter, Bill: Birth, Sep 6
Rivera, Chita: Birth, Jan 23
Rivera, Diego: Birth Anniv, Dec 8
Rivera, Geraldo: Birth, Jul 4
Rivera, Mariano: Birth, Nov 29
Riverbend Fest (Chattanooga, TN), Jun 5
Riverfest (LaCrosse, WI), Jul 1
Rivers Month, Natl, Jun 1
Rivers, Glenn: Birth, Oct 13
Rivers, Joan: Birth, Jun 8
Rivers, Johnny: Birth, Nov 7
Rizzuto, Phil: Birth Anniv, Sep 25
Roach, Hal: Birth Anniv, Jan 14
Road Traffic Victims, World Day of Remembrance for (UN), Nov 15
Roasting Month, Natl, Nov 1
Robards, Jason: Birth Anniv, Jul 26
Robbins, Jerome: Birth Anniv, Oct 11
Robbins, Tim: Birth, Oct 16
Robert the Hermit: Death Anniv, Apr 1
Robert-Houdin, Jean Eugene: Birth Anniv, Dec 6
Robert's Rules Day, May 2
Roberts, Cokie: Birth, Dec 27
Roberts, Doris: Birth, Nov 4
Roberts, Eric: Birth, Apr 18
Roberts, John: Birth, Jan 27
Roberts, Julia: Birth, Oct 28
Roberts, Nora: Birth, Oct 10
Roberts, Oral: Birth, Jan 24
Roberts, Pat: Birth, Apr 20
Roberts, Pernell: Birth, May 18
Roberts, Tony: Birth, Oct 22
Robertson, Cliff: Birth, Sep 9
Robertson, Oscar Palmer: Birth, Nov 24
Robertson, Pat: Birth, Mar 22
Robertson, Robbie: Birth, Jul 5
Robeson, Paul: Birth Anniv, Apr 9
Robin Hood Fest, Sherwood (Sherwood, OR), Jul 17
Robinson Crusoe Day, Feb 1
Robinson, Bill "Bojangles": Birth Anniv, May 25
Robinson, Brooks: Birth, May 18
Robinson, Cliff: Birth, Dec 16
Robinson, David: Birth, Aug 6
Robinson, Edwin Arlington: Birth Anniv, Dec 22
Robinson, Frank: Birth, Aug 31
Robinson, Frank: Named Baseball's First Black Manager: Anniv, Oct 3
Robinson, Glenn: Birth, Jan 10
Robinson, Jackie: Birth Anniv, Jan 31
Robinson, Jackie: Breaks Baseball Color Line: Anniv, Apr 15
Robinson, Roscoe, Jr: Birth Anniv, Oct 11
Robinson, Smokey: Birth, Feb 19
Robinson, Sugar Ray: Birth Anniv, May 3
Robot Enters World Lexicon: Anniv, Jan 25
Robot Homicide, First: Anniv, Jul 21
Rocco, Alex: Birth, Feb 29
Rochesterfest (Rochester, MN), Jun 20
Rochon, Lela: Birth, Apr 17
Rock Show, Mineral Capital (Bancroft, ON, Canada), Jul 26
Rock, Chris: Birth, Feb 7
Rockefeller, Abby Greene Aldrich: Birth Anniv, Oct 26
Rockefeller, David: Birth, Jun 12
Rockefeller, John D., IV: Birth, Jun 18
Rockefeller, Nelson: Birth Anniv, Jul 8
Rockhound Gemboree (Bancroft, ON, Canada), Jul 30
Rockne, Knute: Birth Anniv, Mar 4
Rockwell, Norman: Birth Anniv, Feb 3
Rockwell, Norman: First Post Cover: Anniv, May 20
Rocky and His Friends TV Premiere: Anniv, Nov 19
Rocky Mountain Natl Park Established: Anniv, Jan 26
Roddenberry, Gene: Birth Anniv, Aug 19
Roddick, Andy: Birth, Aug 30
Rodeo
  Adams County Fair/Rodeo (Hettinger, ND), Jul 29
  Beef Empire Days (Garden City, KS), May 27
  Black Hills Stock Show and Rodeo (Rapid City, SD), Jan 30
  Calgary Stampede (Calgary, AB, Canada), Jul 3
  Canadian Western Agribition (Regina, SK, Canada), Nov 23
  Cheyenne Frontier Days (Cheyenne, WY), Jul 17
  Clearwater Chamber of Commerce Rodeo (Clearwater, NE), Jun 26
  Dinosaur Roundup Rodeo (Vernal, UT), Jul 8
  Eighty-Niner Celebration (Guthrie, OK), Apr 21
  Ennis Rodeo & Parade (Ennis, MT), Jul 3
  Fiesta De Los Vaqueros (Tucson, AZ), Feb 21
  First Intercollegiate Rodeo (Apple Valley, CA), Apr 8
  Houston Livestock Show/Rodeo (Houston, TX), Mar 3
  Inter-State Fair/Rodeo (Coffeyville, KS), Aug 8
  Lost Dutchman Days (Apache Junction, AZ), Feb 20
  Oregon Trail Rodeo (Hastings, NE), Sep 4

Pendleton Round-Up (Pendleton, OR), Sep 12
Snake River Stampede (Nampa, ID), Jul 14
Southwestern Expo Livestock Show/Rodeo (Fort Worth, TX), Jan 16
Western Stock Show and Rodeo, Natl (Denver, CO), Jan 10
Wild Horse Stampede (Wolf Point, MT), Jul 9
Rodgers, Richard: Oklahoma! Broadway Premiere: Anniv, Mar 31
Rodin, Auguste: Birth Anniv, Nov 12
Rodman, Dennis: Birth, May 13
Rodney, Caesar: Birth Anniv, Oct 7
Rodriguez, Alex: Birth, Jul 27
Rodriguez, Ivan "Pudge": Birth, Nov 30
Rodriguez, Juan "Chi-Chi": Birth, Oct 23
Rodriguez, Robert: Birth, Jun 20
Roe v Wade Decision: Anniv, Jan 22
Roeper, Richard: Birth, Oct 17
Rogation Sunday, May 17
Rogers, Edith Nourse: Birth Anniv, Mar 19
Rogers, Fred: Birth Anniv, Mar 20
Rogers, Ginger: Birth Anniv, Jul 16
Rogers, Kenny: Birth, Aug 21
Rogers, Mimi: Birth, Jan 27
Rogers, Roy: Birth Anniv, Nov 5
Rogers, Wayne: Birth, Apr 7
Rogers, Will: Birth Anniv, Nov 4
Rogers, Will: Will Rogers Days (Claremore and Oologah, OK), Nov 4
Roget, Peter Mark: Birth Anniv, Jan 18
Roker, Al: Birth, Aug 20
Role Models Month, Natl Inspirational, Nov 1
Rolen, Scott: Birth, Apr 4
Roller Coaster, First, Opens: Anniv, Jun 13
Roller Skating Month, Natl, Oct 1
Rolling Stones: Altamont Concert: Anniv, Dec 6
Rollins, Jimmy: Birth, Nov 27
Roman Catholic/Eastern Orthodox Meeting: Anniv, Jan 5
Roman Catholic: New Catechism: Anniv, Nov 16
Romance (including dating, love, relationships)
Couple Appreciation Month, Apr 1
Dating and Life Coach Recognition Week, May 4
Decide to Be Married Day, Jun 27
Dump Your "Significant Jerk" Week, Feb 7
Flirting Week, Intl, Feb 9
Kiss-and-Make-Up Day, Aug 25
Love a Mensch Week, Feb 14
Love Note Day, Sep 25
Meet a Mate Week, Jun 15
Pleasure Your Mate Month, Sep 1
Proposal Day!, Mar 20
Rejection/Risk Awareness Week, Feb 7
Relationship Wellness Month, Feb 1
Resurrect Romance Week, Natl, Aug 9
Saint Valentine's Day, Feb 14
Share a Sunset with Your Lover Month, Natl, Jul 1
Singles Week, Natl, Sep 20
Weddings Month, Natl, Feb 1
Wife Appreciation Day, Sep 19
World Marriage Day, Feb 8
Romania
Ceausescu, Nicolae: Death Anniv, Dec 25
National Day, Dec 1
Surrender to USSR: Anniv, Aug 23
Romano, Ray: Birth, Dec 21
Rombauer, Irma: Joy of Cooking: Publication Anniv, Nov 30
Rome Executions: Anniv, Mar 25
Rome Liberated: Anniv, Jun 4
Rome, Sack of: Anniv, May 6
Rome: Birthday (Italy), Apr 21
Romijn, Rebecca: Birth, Nov 6
Rommel, Erwin: Birth Anniv, Nov 15
Romney, Mitt: Birth, Mar 12
Romo, Tony: Birth, Apr 21
Ronaldinho: Birth, Mar 21
Ronaldo, Cristiano: Birth, Feb 5
Ronaldo: Birth, Sep 22
Ronan, Saoirse: Birth, Apr 12
Ronstadt, Linda: Birth, Jul 15
Rontgen, Wilhelm K.: Birth Anniv, Mar 27
Rontgen, Wilhelm: X-Ray Discovery Day: Anniv, Nov 8
Rookies TV Premiere: Anniv, Sep 11
Room of One's Own Day, Jan 25
Rooney, Andy: Birth, Jan 14
Rooney, Mickey: Birth, Sep 23
Rooney, Wayne: Birth, Oct 24
Roosevelt, Alice: Birth Anniv, Jul 29
Roosevelt, Edith: Birth Anniv, Aug 6
Roosevelt, Eleanor, Day (Raymond, WA), Aug 8
Roosevelt, Eleanor: Birth Anniv, Oct 11
Roosevelt, Franklin Delano
Birth Anniv, Jan 30
Commemorative Ceremony (Warm Springs, GA), Apr 12
Death Anniv, Apr 12
Elected to Fourth Term: Anniv, Nov 7
Fala Day (Warm Springs, GA), Nov 7
First Fireside Chat: Anniv, Mar 12
First Presidential Telecast: Anniv, Apr 30
Unconditional Surrender Statement: Anniv, Jan 24
US Bank Holiday: Anniv, Mar 5
Roosevelt, Theodore: Birth Anniv, Oct 27
Roosevelt, Theodore: First Secret Service Agent to Die in the Line of Duty: Anniv, Sep 3
Root Canal Appreciation Day, May 13
Root Canal Awareness Week, Mar 29
Rorschach, Hermann: Birth Anniv, Nov 8
Rosacea Awareness Month, Apr 1
Rose Bowl Game (Pasadena, CA), Jan 1
Rose Fest, Portland (Portland, OR), May 28
Rose Month, Natl, Jun 1
Rose, Billy: Birth Anniv, Sep 6
Rose, Charlie: Birth, Jan 5
Rose, Jalen: Birth, Jan 30
Rose, Peace: Introduced to World: Anniv, Apr 29
Rose, Pete: Birth, Apr 14
Roseanne TV Premiere: Anniv, Oct 18
Roseanne: Birth, Nov 3
Rosenbaum, Michael: Birth, Jul 11
Rosenberg Execution: Anniv, Jun 19
Roses Parade, Tournament of (Pasadena, CA), Jan 1
Roses, Orangeburg Fest of (Orangeburg, SC), May 1
Rosh Hashanah, Sep 19
Rosh Hashanah Begins, Sep 18
Ross, Betsy: Birth Anniv, Jan 1
Ross, Diana: Birth, Mar 26
Ross, George: Birth Anniv, May 10
Ross, Katharine: Birth, Jan 29
Ross, Marion: Birth, Oct 25
Ross, Nellie Tayloe: Birth Anniv, Nov 29
Ross, Nellie Tayloe: Wyoming Inaugurates First US Woman Gov: Anniv, Jan 5
Rossellini, Isabella: Birth, Jun 18
Rossetti, Christina: Birth Anniv, Dec 5
Rossovich, Rick: Birth, Aug 28
Rossum, Emmy: Birth, Sep 12
Rostropovich, Mstislav: Birth Anniv, Mar 27
Rotary Tiller Race, World Chmpshp/Purplehull Pea Fest (Emerson, AR), Jun 26
Roth, David Lee: Birth, Oct 10
Roth, Philip: Birth, Mar 19
Roth, Tim: Birth, May 14
Roughhouse Fest (Japan), Oct 14
Rounds Resounding Day, Aug 1
Rounds, Mike: Birth, Oct 24
Roundtree, Richard: Birth, Sep 7
Rourke, Mickey: Birth, Sep 16
Rousseau, Henri: Birth Anniv, May 20
Rousseau, Jean J.: Birth Anniv, Jun 28
Route 66 Summerfest (Rolla, MO), Jun 5
Routh, Brandon: Birth, Oct 9
Rove, Karl: Birth, Dec 25
Rowan and Martin's Laugh-In, Jan 22
Rowlands, Gena: Birth, Jun 19
Rowling, J.K.: Birth, Jul 31
Roy Rogers Show TV Premiere: Anniv, Dec 30
Roy, Brandon: Birth, Jul 23
Roy, Patrick: Birth, Oct 5
Royko, Mike: Birth Anniv, Sep 19
Rozelle, Pete: Birth Anniv, Mar 1
Rozier, Jean Francois Pilatre de: First Fatal Aviation Accident: Anniv, Jun 15
RSV Awareness Month, Natl, Oct 1
Rubens, Peter P.: Birth Anniv, Jun 28
Rubik, Erno: Birth, Jul 13
Ruck, Alan: Birth, Jul 1
Rucker, Darius: Birth, May 13
Rudd, Paul: Birth, Apr 6
Rudner, Rita: Birth, Sep 17
Rudolph, Maya: Birth, Jul 27
Rudolph, Wilma: Birth Anniv, Jun 23
Ruffin, Davis Eli (David): Birth Anniv, Jan 18
Ruffin, Edmund: Birth Anniv, Jan 5
Rundgren, Todd: Birth, Jun 22
Running
Anvil Mountain Run (Nome, AK), Jul 4
Atlanta Marathon and Half Marathon, Weather Channel (Atlanta, GA), Nov 26
Bank of America Chicago Marathon (Chicago, IL), Oct 11
Berlin Marathon (Berlin, Germany), Sep 27
Bolder Boulder 10k (Boulder, CO), May 25
Boston Marathon (Boston, MA), Apr 20
Briggs & Al's Run & Walk (Milwaukee, WI), Sep 19
California Artichoke Fest (Castroville, CA), May 16
Carlsbad Marathon (Carlsbad, CA), Jan 25
Crater Lake Rim Runs and Marathon (Klamath Falls, OR), Aug 8
Dallas YMCA Turkey Trot (Dallas, TX), Nov 26
Easter Beach Run (Daytona Beach, FL), Apr 11
Egg Races (Switzerland), Apr 13
59 Min 37 Sec Anvil Mountain Challenge (Nome, AK), Sep 24
Groundhog Run (Kansas City, MO), Jan 25
Hangover Handicap Run (Klamath Falls, OR), Jan 1
Historic Marathon Runs: Anniv, Sep 2
Houston Marathon (Houston, TX), Jan 18

Ing Bay to Breakers Race (San Francisco, CA), May 17
Lakestride Half-Marathon (Ludington, MI), Jun 20
London Marathon (London, England), Apr 26
Longest Dam Race (Fort Peck, MT), Jun 20
New York City Marathon (New York, NY), Nov 1
Peachtree Road Race (Atlanta, GA), Jul 4
Romp in the Swamp Fun Walk (Appleton, WI), Oct 17
Runyan, Damon: Birth Anniv, Oct 4
RuPaul: Birth, Nov 17
Rural Life Sunday, May 17
Rush, Barbara: Birth, Jan 4
Rush, Benjamin: Birth Anniv, Jan 4
Rush, Geoffrey: Birth, Jul 6
Rush, William: Death Anniv, Jan 17
Rushdie, Salman, Death Sentence: Anniv, Feb 14
Rushdie, Salman: Birth, Jun 19
Rusk, (David) Dean: Birth Anniv, Feb 9
Russell, Bill: Birth, Feb 12
Russell, Charles M.: Birth Anniv, Mar 19
Russell, Jane: Birth, Jun 21
Russell, Keri: Birth, Mar 23
Russell, Kurt: Birth, Mar 17
Russell, Leon: Birth, Apr 2
Russell, Lillian: Birth Anniv, Dec 4
Russell, Mark: Birth, Aug 23
Russell, Theresa: Birth, Mar 20
Russell-Einstein Manifesto: Anniv, Jul 9
Russia
Army and Navy Day, Feb 23
Baltic States' Independence Recognized: Anniv, Sep 6
Battle of Stalingrad Begins: Anniv, Aug 22
Boris Yeltsin Inaugurated as President: Anniv, Jul 10
Christmas Bells Ring Again: Anniv, Dec 24
Christmas Day, Jan 7
COMECON and Warsaw Pact Disband: Anniv, Jun 28
Constitution Day, Dec 12
Corridor of Death: Anniv (Leningrad), Jan 13
Czar Nicholas II and Family Executed: Anniv, Jul 17
Day of National Reconciliation and Agreement, Nov 7
German Surrender at Stalingrad: Anniv, Feb 2
Great October Socialist Revolution: Anniv, Nov 7
Independence Day, Jun 12
Intl Labor Day, May 1
New Year's Day Observance, Jan 1
October Revolution, Nov 7
Old New Year's Eve, Jan 13
Passport Presentation, Jan 2
Saint Petersburg Founded: Anniv, May 27
Saint Petersburg Massacre: Anniv, Jan 9
Saint Petersburg Name Restored: Anniv, Sep 6
Soviet Communist Party Suspended: Anniv, Aug 29
Soviet Cosmonaut Returns to New Country: Anniv, Mar 26
Soviet Union Dissolved: Anniv, Dec 8
Soviet Union Invaded: Anniv, Jun 22
USSR Established: Anniv, Dec 30
Victory Day, May 9
Women's Day, Intl, Mar 8
Russo, Rene: Birth, Feb 17
Russo, Richard: Birth, Jul 15
Rustin, Bayard: Birth Anniv, Mar 17
Ruth, George Herman
Babe Ruth Day: Anniv, Apr 27
Baseball Hall of Fame's Charter Members: Anniv, Feb 2
Birth Anniv, Feb 6
Calls His Shot?: Anniv, Oct 1
Death Anniv, Aug 16
Debut in Majors: Anniv, Jul 11
First Major League Home Run: Anniv, May 6
First Pro Homer: Anniv, Sep 5
House That Ruth Built: Anniv, Apr 18
Last Game as Yankee: Anniv, Sep 30
Pitching Debut: Anniv, Apr 22
Sets Home Run Record: Anniv, Sep 30
Rutherford, Ernest: Birth Anniv, Aug 30
Rutherford, Kelly: Birth, Nov 6
Rutledge, Edward: Birth Anniv, Nov 23
Rutledge, John: Death Anniv, Jul 18
Ruttan, Susan: Birth, Sep 16
Rwanda
Genocide Remembrance Day, Apr 7
Independence Day, Jul 1
Republic Day, Sep 25
Tragedy in Rwanda: Anniv, Apr 6
Ryan, Amy: Birth, Nov 30
Ryan, Jeri: Birth, Feb 22
Ryan, Meg: Birth, Nov 19
Ryan, Nolan: Birth, Jan 31
Ryan's Hope TV Premiere: Anniv, Jul 7
Rydell, Bobby: Birth, Apr 26
Ryder, Albert Pinkham: Birth Anniv, Mar 19
Ryder, Winona: Birth, Oct 29

S

Saarinen, Eero: Birth Anniv, Aug 20
Saarinen, Eliel: Birth Anniv, Aug 20
Sabathia, C.C.: Birth, Jul 21
Sabatini, Gabriela: Birth, May 16
Sabato, Antonio, Jr: Birth, Feb 29
Saberhagen, Bret: Birth, Apr 11
Sabin, Albert Bruce: Birth Anniv, Aug 26
Sacagawea: Death Anniv, Dec 20
Sacco-Vanzetti Memorial Day, Aug 23
Sackhoff, Katee: Birth, Apr 8
Sacramento Jazz Jubilee (Sacramento, CA), May 22
Sadat, Anwar El: Assassination Anniv, Oct 6
Sadie Hawkins Day, Nov 7
Safe Boating Week, Natl, May 16
Safer, Morley: Birth, Nov 8
Safety Pin Patented: Anniv, Apr 10
Safety Razor Patented: Anniv, Dec 2
Safety. See also Crime
Automobile Speed Reduction: Anniv, Nov 25
Check Your Batteries Day, Mar 8
Child Safety Council Founded, Natl: Anniv, Nov 9
Chimney Safety Week, Natl, Sep 27
Church Safety and Security Month, Oct 1
Crime Prevention Month, Natl, Oct 1
Day of Natl Concern about Young People and Gun Violence, Oct 28
Dog Bite Prevention Week, Natl, May 17
Drowsy Driver Awareness Day, Apr 6
Drunk and Drugged Driving Prevention Month, Natl (Pres Proc), Dec 1
Farm Safety Week, Natl (Pres Proc), Sep 20
Fire Prevention Week, Oct 4
Fire Prevention Week (Pres Proc), Oct 4
Fire Safety Council, Natl: Anniv, Dec 7
Firepup's Birthday, Oct 1
Fireworks Safety Month, Jun 1
Halloween Safety Month, Oct 1
Heimlich Maneuver Introduced: Anniv, Jun 1
Home Office Safety and Security Week, Jan 5
Keep Kids Alive—Drive 25 Day, May 1
Missing Children's Day, Natl, May 25
Motorcycle Safety Month, May 1
Night Out, Natl, Aug 4
Personal Self-Defense Awareness Month, Natl, Jan 1
Playground Safety Week, Natl, Apr 19
Poison Prevention Week, Natl, Mar 15
Poison Prevention Week, Natl (Pres Proc), Mar 15
Preparedness Month, Natl, Sep 1
Prevention of Eye Injuries Awareness Week, Natl, Jun 28
REACT Month, May 1
Safe at Home Week, Natl, Aug 24
Safe Boating Week, Natl, May 16
Safe Boating Week, Natl (Pres Proc), May 16
Safe Toys and Gifts Month, Dec 1
Safety Month, Natl, Jun 1
Safetypup's Birthday, Feb 12
Sexual Assault Awareness and Prevention Month, Natl, Apr 1
SOS Adopted: Anniv, Nov 3
Sports & Home Eye Safety Month, Sep 1
Student Safety Month, Jun 1
Teens Don't Text and Drive Week, Natl, Nov 22
Window Safety Week, Natl, Apr 20
Workers Memorial Day, Apr 28
Youth Sports Safety Month, Natl, Apr 1
Safire, William: Birth, Dec 17
Sagal, Katey: Birth, Nov 18
Sagan, Carl: Birth Anniv, Nov 9
Sager, Carole Bayer: Birth, Mar 8
Saget, Bob: Birth, May 17
Sagittarius Begins, Nov 22
Sahl, Mort: Birth, May 11
Saint Aubin, Helen "Callaghan": Birth Anniv, Mar 13
Saint Bartholomew's Day Massacre: Anniv, Aug 24
Saint Basil's Cathedral: Christmas Bells Again: Anniv, Dec 24
Saint Christopher: Independence Day, Sep 19
Saint Elias Day: Macedonian Uprising: Anniv, Aug 2
Saint Elsewhere TV Premiere: Anniv, Oct 26
Saint Eustatius, West Indies: Statia and America Day, Nov 16
Saint Gotthard Auto Tunnel: Opening Anniv, Sep 5
Saint James, Susan: Birth, Aug 14
Saint Lawrence Seaway Act: Anniv, May 13
Saint Lawrence Seaway: Dedication Anniv, Jun 26
Saint Lucia: Independence Day, Feb 22
Saint Olaf Christmas Fest (Northfield, MN), Dec 3
Saint Patrick's Day Parade (Baton Rouge, LA), Mar 14
Saint Patrick's Day Parade (Hornell, NY), Mar 14
Saint Patrick's Day Parade (New York, NY), Mar 17
Saint Petersburg Massacre: Anniv, Jan 9

Saint Petersburg Name Restored: Anniv, Sep 6
Saint Piran's Day Celebration (Kansas City, MO), Mar 7
Saint Swithun's Celebration (Toronto, ON, Canada), Jul 15
Saint Vincent and the Grenadines: Independence Day, Oct 27
Saint, Eva Marie: Birth, Jul 4
Sainte-Marie, Buffy: Birth, Feb 20
Saint-Gaudens, Augustus: Birth Anniv, Mar 1
Saints, Saints' Days
Andrew's Day, Nov 30
Anthony of Padua: Feast Day (Portugal), Jun 13
Anthony's Day, Jan 17
Apollinaris: Feast Day, Jul 23
Augustine of Canterbury, Feast of, May 26
Augustine, Feast of, Aug 28
Barbara's Day, Dec 4
Basil's Day, Jan 1
Bernard of Montjoux: Feast Day, May 28
Cabrini, Mother Frances Xavier, Canonized: Anniv, Jul 7
Catherine of Siena: Feast Day, Apr 29
Catherine's Day, Nov 25
Cecilia: Feast Day, Nov 22
Clare of Assisi: Feast Day, Aug 11
Crispin's Day, Oct 25
David's Day (Wales), Mar 1
Edward, the Confessor: Feast Day, Oct 13
Erasmus (Elmo) Day, Jun 2
Fiesta de Santa Marta de Ribarteme (As Neves, Galicia, Spain), Jul 29
Frances of Rome: Feast Day, Mar 9
Frances Xavier Cabrini: Birth Anniv, Jul 15
Francis of Assisi: Feast Day, Oct 4
Gabriel: Feast Day, Mar 24
George: Feast Day (England), Apr 23
George's Day (Newfoundland, Canada), Apr 20
Gudula: Feast Day, Jan 8
Ignatius of Loyola, Feast of, Jul 31
Isidro Day (Mexico), May 15
James Day (Spain), Jul 25
Januarius: Feast Day, Sep 19
Jerome, Feast of, Sep 30
Joan of Arc: Feast Day, May 30
John Nepomucene Neumann: Birth Anniv, Mar 28
John of Capistrano: Death Anniv, Oct 23
John the Baptist Day, Jun 24
John, Apostle-Evangelist: Feast Day, Dec 27
Joseph's Day, Mar 19
Juan Diego: First Indian Saint: Anniv, Jul 31
Jude's Day, Oct 28
Lasarus' Day (Bulgaria), Apr 1
Lucia Day (Sweden), Dec 13
Luke: Feast Day, Oct 18
Martin's Day (Sweden), Nov 11
Nicholas Day, Dec 6
Oswald of Worcester: Feast Day, Feb 28
Patrick's Day, Mar 17
Paul's Feast (Cyprus), Jun 28
Peter and Paul Day, Jun 29
Peter's Day (Turkey), Jun 29
Piran's Day, Mar 5
Pius X: Birth Anniv, Jun 2
Sebastian's Day (Brazil), Jan 20
Stephen's Day, Dec 26
Swithin's Day, Jul 15
Sylvester's Day, Dec 31
Thomas of Canterbury: Feast Day, Dec 29
Valentine's Day, Feb 14
Vincent De Paul: Feast Day, Sep 27
Vincent De Paul: Old Feast Day, Jul 19
Vincent: Feast Day, Jan 22
Sajak, Pat: Birth, Oct 26
Sakharov, Andrey Dmitriyevich: Birth Anniv, May 21
Sakic, Joe: Birth, Jul 7
Salaam, Rashaan: Birth, Oct 8
Salad Month, Natl, May 1
Salazar, Alberto: Birth, Aug 7
Salazar, Ken: Birth, Mar 2
Saldana, Theresa: Birth, Aug 20
Salem Witch Hysteria Begins: Anniv, Mar 1
Salem Witch Trials Begin: Anniv, Jun 2
Sales, Soupy: Birth, Jan 8
Salesperson's Day, Natl, Oct 12
Salinger, J.D.: Birth, Jan 1
Salisbury, Harrison: Birth Anniv, Nov 14
Salk, Jonas: Birth Anniv, Oct 28
Salk, Lee: Birth Anniv, Dec 27
Salomon, Haym: Death Anniv, Jan 6
Salsa Month, Natl, May 1
Salt, Jennifer: Birth, Sep 4
Salt: No Salt Week, Oct 2
Salter, Susanna, Elected First Woman Mayor in US: Anniv, Apr 4
Salute to 35+ Moms Week, May 10
Salvador, Francis: Death Anniv, Jul 31
Salvation Army Founder's Day, Apr 10
Salvation Army in US: Anniv, Mar 10
Salvation Army: Booth, William: Birth Anniv, Apr 10
Sambora, Richie: Birth, Jul 11
Same-Sex Marriages, First US: Anniv, May 17
Samhain, Oct 31
Samms, Emma: Birth, Aug 28
Samoa
ANZAC Day, Apr 25
Arbor Day, Nov 6
Independence Day, Jun 1
Samoan Fire Dance, Dec 31
White Sunday, Oct 11
Samoa, American: Flag Day, Apr 17
Sampras, Pete: Birth, Aug 12
Sampson, Deborah: Birth Anniv, Dec 17
Sampson, Ralph: Birth, Jul 7
Samuelson, Joan Benoit: Birth, May 16
San Francisco 1906 Earthquake: Anniv, Apr 18
San Francisco 1989 Earthquake: Anniv, Oct 17
San Francisco Chinese New Year Parade, Feb 7
San Francisco Silent Film Fest (San Francisco, CA), Jul 10
San Giacomo, Laura: Birth, Nov 14
San Isidro Day (Mexico), May 15
San Jacinto Day (TX), Apr 21
San Marino: National Day, Sep 3
San Sebastian's Day (Brazil), Jan 20
Sanborn, David: Birth, Jul 30
Sand, George: Birth Anniv, Jul 1
Sand, Paul: Birth, Mar 5
Sanda, Dominique: Birth, Mar 11
Sandberg, Ryne: Birth, Sep 18
Sandburg, Carl: Birth Anniv, Jan 6
Sanders, Barry: Birth, Jul 16
Sanders, Bernie: Birth, Sep 8
Sanders, Colonel Harland David: Birth Anniv, Sep 9
Sanders, Deion: Birth, Aug 9
Sanders, Jay O.: Birth, Apr 16
Sanders, Reggie: Birth, Dec 1
Sanders, Richard: Birth, Aug 23
Sandino, Cesar: Assassination Anniv, Feb 21
Sandler, Adam: Birth, Sep 9
Sands, Tommy: Birth, Aug 27
Sandwich Day: John Montague Birth Anniv, Nov 3
Sandwich Generation Month, Jul 1
Sandy Springs Fest (Atlanta, GA), Sep 19
Sandy, Gary: Birth, Dec 25
Sandys, Edwin: Birth Anniv, Dec 9
Sanford and Son TV Premiere: Anniv, Jan 14
Sanford, Mark: Birth, May 28
Sanger, Margaret (Higgins): Birth Anniv, Sep 14
Santa Fe Chamber Music Fest, Jul 19
Santa Lucia Day (Sweden), Dec 13
Santa-Cali-Gon Days Fest (Independence, MO), Sep 4
Santana, Carlos: Birth, Jul 20
Santayana, George: Birth Anniv, Dec 16
Santiago, Benito: Birth, Mar 9
Santiago, Saundra: Birth, Apr 13
Sao Tome and Principe: Independence Day, Jul 12
Sarah, Duchess of York: Birth, Oct 15
Sarandon, Chris: Birth, Jul 24
Sarandon, Susan: Birth, Oct 4
Sarazen, Gene: Birth Anniv, Feb 27
Sarcastics Awareness Month, Natl, Oct 1
Sarcoidosis Awareness Day, Natl, Aug 29
Sargent, John Singer: Birth Anniv, Jan 12
Sarkozy, Nicolas: Birth, Jan 28
Saroyan, William: Birth Anniv, Aug 31
Sarrazin, Michael: Birth, May 22
Sarto, Andrea Del: Birth Anniv, Jul 14
Sartre, Jean-Paul: Birth Anniv, Jun 21
Sasaki, Kazuhiro: Birth, Feb 22
Sassoon, Vidal: Birth, Jan 17
Satchmo Summerfest (New Orleans, LA), Jul 30
Satisfied Staying Single Day, Feb 11
Saturday Night Live TV Premiere: Anniv, Oct 11
Saturday Night Massacre: Anniv, Oct 20
Saturn: Cassini-Huygens Reaches, Jul 1
Saturnalia, Dec 17
Saudi Arabia: Kingdom Unification, Sep 23
Sauntering Day, World, Jun 19
Savage, Adam: Birth, Jul 15
Savage, Ben: Birth, Sep 13
Savage, Fred: Birth, Jul 9
Savage, John: Birth, Aug 25
Savant, Doug: Birth, Jun 21
Savant, Marilyn vos: Birth, Aug 11
Save Your Vision Month, Mar 1
Save Your Vision Week (Pres Proc), Mar 1
Savings and Loan: Home Owners Loan Act: Anniv, Jun 13
Sawa, Devon: Birth, Sep 7
Sawyer, Diane K.: Birth, Dec 22
Sax, Adolphe: Birth Anniv (Saxophone Day), Nov 6
Saxon, John: Birth, Aug 5
Saxophone Day, Nov 6
Sayer, Leo: Birth, May 21
Sayers, Gale: Birth, May 30
Scacchi, Greta: Birth, Feb 18
Scaggs, Boz: Birth, Jun 8
Scalia, Antonin: Birth, Mar 11
Scaliger, Joseph J.: Birth Anniv, Aug 4
Scandinavian Hjemkomst Fest (Moorhead, MN), Jun 26
Scandinavian: Dalesburg Midsummer Fest (Vermillion, SD), Jun 19

Scarecrow and Mrs King TV Premiere: Anniv, Oct 3
Scarecrow Contest and Outdoor Display, Peddler's Village (Lahaska, PA), Sep 13
Scarecrow Fest (St. Charles, IL), Oct 9
Scarecrow Fest (Winchester, KY), Oct 3
Scarlatti, Domenico: Birth Anniv, Oct 26
Scarry, Richard M.: Birth Anniv, Jun 5
Scenic Drive Fest (Van Buren County, IA), Oct 10
Schafer, Ed: Birth, Aug 8
Schell, Maximilian: Birth, Dec 8
Schiaparelli, Elsa: Birth Anniv, Sep 10
Schieffer, Bob: Birth, Feb 25
Schiff, Richard: Birth, May 27
Schiffer, Claudia: Birth, Aug 25
Schilling, Curt: Birth, Nov 14
Schirra, Wally: Birth Anniv, Mar 12
Schlafly, Phyllis: Birth, Aug 15
Schlatter, Charlie: Birth, May 1
Schmeling, Max: Birth Anniv, Sep 28
Schmidt, Mike: Birth, Sep 27
Schneider, John: Birth, Apr 8
Schneider, Maria: Birth, Mar 27
Schneider, Rob: Birth, Oct 31
Schneiderman, Rose: Birth Anniv, Apr 6
Schnitzler, Arthur: Birth Anniv, May 15
Scholarship Month, Natl, Nov 1
Scholes, Paul: Birth, Nov 16
School
 Breakfast Week, Natl, Mar 2
 Library Media Month, Apr 1
 Lunch Week, Natl, Oct 12
 Nurse Day, Natl, May 6
 Pizza Party Day, Natl, May 15
 Principals' Day, May 1
 School Bus Safety Week, Natl, Oct 18
 Spirit Season, Intl, Apr 30
Schoolhouse Triangle Project Month, Sep 1
Schopenhauer, Arthur: Birth Anniv, Feb 22
Schorr, Daniel: Birth, Aug 31
Schrempf, Detlef: Birth, Jan 21
Schroder, Rick: Birth, Apr 13
Schroeder, Gerhard: Birth, Apr 7
Schroeder, Patricia: Birth, Jun 30
Schubert, Franz: Birth Anniv, Jan 31
Schuck, John: Birth, Feb 4
Schultz, Dwight: Birth, Nov 24
Schulz, Charles: Birth Anniv, Nov 26
Schuman Plan Anniv: European Union, May 9
Schuman, William Howard: Birth Anniv, Aug 4
Schumer, Charles E.: Birth, Nov 23
Schurz, Carl: Birth Anniv, Mar 2
Schutz, Heinrich: Birth Anniv, Oct 8
Schwartzman, Jason: Birth, Jun 26
Schwarzenegger, Arnold: Birth, Jul 30
Schwarzkopf, Norman H.: Birth, Aug 22
Schweitzer, Albert: Birth Anniv, Jan 14
Schweitzer, Brian: Birth, Sep 5
Schwenkfelder Thanksgiving, Sep 24
Schwikert, Tasha: Birth, Nov 21
Schwimmer, David: Birth, Nov 12
Schygulla, Hanna: Birth, Dec 25
Scialfa, Patty: Birth, Jul 29
Science
 American Assn for the Advancement of Science Annual Mtg (Chicago, IL), Feb 12
 Astronomy Day, May 2
 Astronomy Week, Apr 27
 Biological Clock Gene Discovered: Anniv, Apr 28
 Brain Awareness Week, Intl, Mar 16
 Bunsen Burner Day, Mar 31
 Camcorder Developed: Anniv, Jan 20
 Cellophane Tape Patented: Anniv, May 27
 Chemistry Week, Natl, Oct 18
 Cloning of an Adult Animal, First: Anniv, Feb 23
 Darwin Day, Feb 12
 Diesel Engine Patented: Anniv, Feb 23
 Earth's Rotation Proved: Anniv, Jan 8
 First Self-Sustaining Nuclear Chain Reaction: Anniv, Dec 2
 First US Scientist Receives Nobel Prize: Anniv, Dec 10
 Geographers Annual Mtg, Assn of American (Las Vegas, NV), Mar 22
 Human Genome Mapped: Anniv, Jun 26
 Ig Nobel Prize Ceremony (Cambridge, MA), Oct 1
 Laser Patented: Anniv, Mar 22
 Metric Conversion Act: Anniv, Dec 23
 Metric System Developed: Anniv, Apr 7
 Mole Day, Natl, Oct 23
 Nobel Conference (St. Peter, MN), Oct 6
 Nuclear Medicine Week, Oct 5
 Odometer Invented: Anniv, May 12
 Physicists Discover Top Quark: Anniv, Apr 23
 Plutonium First Weighed: Anniv, Aug 20
 Radiological Soc of North America Scientific Assembly and Annual Mtg (Chicago, IL), Nov 29
 Radium Discovered: Anniv, Dec 26
 Science Fest, Edinburgh Intl (Edinburgh, Scotland), Apr 6
 Sky Awareness Week, Apr 19
 Vitamin C Isolated: Anniv, Apr 4
 Woman Inducted into Natl Inventors Hall of Fame: Anniv, May 18
 X-Ray Discovery Day: Anniv, Nov 8
Science Fiction
 Asimov, Isaac: Birth Anniv, Jan 2
 Cyberspace Coined: Neuromancer Publication Anniv, Oct 1
 Robot Enters World Lexicon: Anniv, Jan 25
 Star Trek TV Premiere: Anniv, Sep 8
 Star Wars Released: Anniv, May 25
 2001: A Space Odyssey Premiere: Anniv, Apr 3
 X-Files TV Premiere: Anniv, Sep 10
Sciorra, Annabella: Birth, Mar 24
Scobee, Francis R.: Birth Anniv, May 19
Scoggins, Tracy: Birth, Nov 13
Scolari, Peter: Birth, Sep 12
Scooby-Doo, Where Are You? TV Premiere: Anniv, Sep 13
Scoop the Poop Week, Natl, Apr 24
Scopes, John T.: Birth Anniv, Aug 3
Scorpio Begins, Oct 23
Scorsese, Martin: Birth, Nov 17
Scotland
 Aberdeen Intl Youth Fest (Aberdeen), Jul 29
 Bannockburn Day, Jun 24
 Braemar Royal Highland Gathering (Braemar), Sep 5
 Burns' Nights, Jan 25
 Christmas Holiday, Dec 25
 Edinburgh Fest Fringe (Edinburgh), Aug 7
 Edinburgh Intl Fest (Edinburgh), Aug 14
 Edinburgh Intl Science Fest (Edinburgh), Apr 6
 Edinburgh Military Tattoo (Edinburgh), Aug 7
 Hogmanay, Dec 31
 Mary, Queen of Scots: Execution Anniv, Feb 8
 New Year's Bank Holiday, Jan 2
 Open Golf Chmpshp (British Open) (Turnberry), Jul 12
 Scottish Intl Badminton Chmpshp (Edinburgh), Nov 25
 Summer Bank Holiday, Aug 3
 Tartan Day, Apr 6
 Up Helly Aa, Jan 27
Scotland Yard First Appearance Anniv, Sep 29
Scott Thomas, Kristin: Birth, May 24
Scott, Campbell: Birth, Jul 19
Scott, Ridley: Birth, Nov 30
Scott, Robert: Birth Anniv, Jun 6
Scott, Sir Walter: Birth Anniv, Aug 15
Scott, Willard: Birth, Mar 7
Scott, Winfield: Birth Anniv, Jun 13
Scottish and Celtic
 Alma Highland Fest and Games (Alma, MI), May 23
 Celtic Classic Highland Games & Fest (Bethlehem, PA), Sep 25
 Celtic Fling (Manheim, PA), Jun 26
 Ligonier Highland Games (Ligonier, PA), Sep 11
 Longs Peak Scottish/Irish Highland Fest (Estes Park, CO), Sep 10
 Maine Highland Games (Brunswick, ME), Aug 15
 New Hampshire Highland Games (Lincoln, NH), Sep 18
Scotto, Renata: Birth, Feb 24
Scottsboro Trial: Anniv, Apr 6
Scottsdale Culinary Fest (Scottsdale, AZ), Apr 14
Scowcroft, Brent: Birth, Mar 19
Scrabble Inventor: Butts, Alfred M.: Birth Anniv, Apr 13
Scrapbooking Industry Day, Intl, Mar 4
Scripps Natl Spelling Bee Finals, May 27
Scruggs, Earl: Birth, Jan 6
SCUD Day (Savor the Comic, Unplug the Drama), Jul 8
Scully, Vin: Birth, Nov 29
Scurry, Briana: Birth, Sep 7
Sea Cadet Month, Sep 1
Seabiscuit Defeats War Admiral: Anniv, Nov 1
Seaborg, Glen: Plutonium First Weighed: Anniv, Aug 20
Seacrest, Ryan: Birth, Dec 24
Seafair (Seattle, WA), Jun 28
Seagal, Steven: Birth, Apr 10
Seal, Intl Day of the, Mar 22
Seal: Birth, Feb 19
Search for Tomorrow TV Premiere: Anniv, Sep 3
Seaver, Tom: Birth, Nov 17
Sebelius, Kathleen: Birth, May 15
Second Chances: Mulligan Day, Oct 17
Second Day of Christmas, Dec 26
Second Half of the New Year Day, Jul 1
Secondhand Wardrobe Day, Natl, Aug 25
Secor, Kyle: Birth, May 31
Secret Agent TV Premiere: Anniv, Apr 5
Secret Service Agent, First to Die in the Line of Duty: Anniv, Sep 3
Secret Storm TV Premiere: Anniv, Feb 1
Secretaries Day: See Administrative Professionals Day, Apr 22
Secretaries Week: See Administrative Professionals Week, Apr 19
Securities and Exchange Commission Created: Anniv, Jun 6
Sedaka, Neil: Birth, Mar 13
Sedgwick, Kyra: Birth, Aug 19

See It Now TV Premiere: Anniv, Nov 18
Seed Swap Day, Natl, Jan 31
Seeger, Pete: Birth, May 3
Seeing Eye Established: Anniv, Jan 29
Segal, Erich: Birth, Jun 16
Segal, George: Birth, Feb 13
Segar, E.C.: Birth Anniv, Dec 8
Segel, Jason: Birth, Jan 18
Seger, Bob: Birth, May 6
Sehorn, Jason: Birth, Apr 15
Seibert, Florence: Birth Anniv, Oct 6
Seidelman, Susan: Birth, Dec 11
Seikaly, Rony: Birth, May 10
Seinfeld TV Premiere: Anniv, May 31
Seinfeld, Jerry: Birth, Apr 29
Selanne, Teemu: Birth, Jul 3
Selby, David: Birth, Feb 5
Selena: Birth Anniv, Apr 16
Seles, Monica: Birth, Dec 2
Self-Awareness Month, Intl, Sep 1
Self-Esteem Month, Intl Boost, Feb 1
Self-Esteem Month, Teen, May 1
Self-Promotion Month, Oct 1
Selfridge, Thomas E.: Death Anniv, Sep 17
Self-University Week, Sep 1
Selig, Bud: Birth, Jul 30
Sellecca, Connie: Birth, May 25
Selleck, Tom: Birth, Jan 29
Sellers, Peter: Birth Anniv, Sep 8
Selma Civil Rights March: Anniv, Mar 21
Selznick, David: Gone with the Wind Film Premiere: Anniv, Dec 15
Seminole Tribe of Florida Legally Established: Anniv, Aug 21
Semmes, Raphael: Birth Anniv, Sep 27
Senate: Black Page Appointed: Anniv, Apr 8
Sendak, Maurice: Birth, Jun 10
Seneca Falls Convention Survivor Votes: Anniv, Nov 2
Senegal: Independence Day, Apr 4
Senior Citizens
  Assisted Living Week, Natl, Sep 13
  Family Caregivers Month, Natl, Nov 1
  First Social Security Check Issued: Anniv, Jan 31
  Gorgeous Grandma Day, Jul 23
  Medicare: Anniv, Jul 1
  Older Americans Month (Pres Proc), May 1
  Older Persons, Intl Day of (UN), Oct 1
  Refired, not Retired, Day, Mar 1
  Senior Health and Fitness Day, Natl, May 27
  Senior Independence Month, Natl, Feb 1
  September Is Healthy Aging Month, Sep 1
  Shut-In Visitation Day, Natl, Feb 11
  South Florida Senior Games (Hollywood, FL), Jan 21
  Spunky Old Broads Month, Feb 1
  Wellderly Week, Mar 16
Senses, Celebration of the, Jun 24
Seoul Recaptured by UN Forces, Mar 14
Sequim Irrigation Fest (Sequim, WA), May 2
Sequoia and Kings Canyon Natl Park Established: Anniv, Sep 25
Serbia: National Day, Feb 15
Sgt Pepper's Lonely Hearts Club Band Released: Anniv, Jun 1
Serkin, Peter: Birth, Jul 24
Service Dogs: Assistance Dog Week, Aug 9
Service, Robert William: Birth Anniv, Jan 16
Sesame Street TV Premiere: Anniv, Nov 10
Sessions, Jeff: Birth, Dec 24
Seton, Elizabeth Ann Bayley: Feast Day, Jan 4
Seton, Elizabeth Ann: Canonization Anniv, Sep 14
Setsubun (Japan), Feb 3
Settle, Matthew: Birth, Nov 17
Seurat, Georges: Birth Anniv, Dec 2
Seuss, Dr.: Geisel, Theodor: Birth Anniv, Mar 2
Sevareid, Eric: Birth Anniv, Nov 26
Severinsen, Doc: Birth, Jul 7
Seward's Day (AK), Mar 30
Sex and the City TV Premiere: Anniv, Jun 6
Sex: Joy of Sex Published: Anniv, Oct 1
Sexual Assault Awareness and Prevention Month, Natl, Apr 1
Sexuality Education Month, Natl Family, Oct 1
Sexually Transmitted Diseases (STDs) Awareness Month, Natl, Apr 1
Seychelles
  Constitution Day, Jun 18
  Independence Day, Jun 29
Seymour, Jane: Birth, Feb 15
Shabbat Across America/Canada, Mar 20
Shackelford, Ted: Birth, Jun 23
Shackleton, Ernest: Birth Anniv, Feb 15
Shadow Radio Premiere: Anniv, Jul 31
Shaffer, Paul: Birth, Nov 28
Shakespeare, William: Birth and Death Anniv, Apr 23
Shakespeare, Wm: Rev F. Gastrell's Ejectment: Anniv, Nov 27
Shakira: Birth, Feb 9
Shalhoub, Tony: Birth, Oct 9
Shalikashvili: Appointed Chair of Joint Chiefs: Anniv, Aug 11
Shamu's Birthday, Sep 26
Shandling, Garry: Birth, Nov 29
Shange, Ntozake: Birth, Oct 18
Shannon, Molly: Birth, Sep 16
Shanty Days (Algoma, WI), Aug 14
Sharapova, Maria: Birth, Apr 19
Shareware Day, Intl, Dec 12
Sharif, Omar: Birth, Apr 10
Sharm al-Sheikh Bombings: Anniv, Jul 23
Shatner, William: Birth, Mar 22
Shaughnessy, Charles: Birth, Feb 9
Shaver, Helen: Birth, Feb 24
Shavuot, May 29
Shavuot Begins, May 28
Shaw, George Bernard: Birth Anniv, Jul 26
Shaw, Patty Hearst: Birth, Feb 20
Shawn, Ted: Birth Anniv, Oct 21
Shawn, William: Birth Anniv, Aug 31
Shays's Rebellion: Anniv, Aug 29
Sheedy, Ally: Birth, Jun 13
Sheehy, Gail: Birth, Nov 27
Sheen, Charlie: Birth, Sep 3
Sheen, Martin: Birth, Aug 3
Sheep Market, Ho (Denmark), Aug 29
Sheffield, Gary: Birth, Nov 18
Sheik Film Release: Anniv, Nov 20
Shelby, Richard C.: Birth, May 6
Sheldon, Sidney: Birth Anniv, Feb 11
Shelley, Mary Wollstonecraft: Birth Anniv, Aug 30
Shelley, Percy Bysshe: Birth Anniv, Aug 4
Shemini Atzeret, Oct 10
Shenandoah Natl Park Established: Anniv, Dec 26
Shepard, Alan: Birth Anniv, Nov 18
Shepard, Sam: Birth, Nov 5
Shepherd, Cybill: Birth, Feb 18
Shepherd's Fair/Schuebermess (Luxembourg), Aug 23
Sheridan, Jamey: Birth, Jul 12
Sheridan, Nicollette: Birth, Nov 21
Sheridan, Richard B.: Birth Anniv, Oct 30
Sherlock Holmes Weekend (Cape May, NJ), Mar 6
Sherman Enters Atlanta: Anniv, Sep 2
Sherman, Bobby: Birth, Jul 22
Sherman, James S.: Birth Anniv, Oct 24
Sherman, Roger: Birth Anniv, Apr 19
Sherman, William Tecumseh
  Birth Anniv, Feb 8
  Surrender at Durham Station: Anniv, Apr 18
  Takes Savannah: Anniv, Dec 21
  War Is Hell: Anniv, Jun 19
Sherwood, Brad: Birth, Nov 24
Sherwood, Madeline: Birth, Nov 13
She's Funny That Way Day, Natl, Mar 31
Shevchenko, Andriy: Birth, Sep 29
Shields, Brooke: Birth, May 31
Shilts, Randy: Birth Anniv, Aug 8
Shire, Talia: Birth, Apr 25
Shirer, William L.: Birth Anniv, Feb 23
Shirley Temple Theatre TV Premiere: Anniv, Sep 18
Shoemaker-Levy: Comet Crashes into Jupiter: Anniv, Jul 16
Shopping Carts to the Supermarket Month, Return, Feb 1
Shopping Reminder Day, Nov 25
Shopping: Buy Nothing Day, Nov 27
Shore, Dinah: Birth Anniv, Mar 1
Shore, Pauly: Birth, Feb 1
Short, Martin: Birth, Mar 26
Shorter, Wayne: Birth, Aug 25
Shostakovich, Dmitri: Birth Anniv, Sep 25
Show and Tell Day at Work, Jan 8
Show, Grant: Birth, Feb 27
Shrimp and Petroleum Fest, Louisiana (Morgan City, LA), Sep 3
Shrimp Fest, Isle of Eight Flags (Fernandina Beach, FL), May 1
Shriver, Eunice Mary Kennedy: Birth, Jul 10
Shriver, Maria: Birth, Nov 6
Shriver, Pam: Birth, Jul 4
Shrove Monday, Feb 23
Shrove Tuesday, Feb 24
Shrove Tuesday: Pancake Week, Natl, Feb 22
Shrovetide, Feb 22
Shue, Andrew: Birth, Feb 19
Shue, Elisabeth: Birth, Oct 6
Shula, Don: Birth, Jan 4
Shuster, Joe: Superman Debuts: Anniv, Jun 1
Shut-In Visitation Day, Natl, Feb 11
Shyamalan, M. Night: Birth, Aug 6
Siberian Explosion: Anniversary, Jun 30
Siblings Day, Natl, Apr 10
Sickle Cell Awareness Month, Natl, Sep 1
Sidney, Philip: Birth Anniv, Nov 30
Siegel, Bugsy: Birth Anniv, Feb 28
Siegel, Jerry: Superman Debuts: Anniv, Jun 1
Siegmeister, Elie: Birth Anniv, Jan 15
Sierra Club Founded: Anniv, May 28
Sierra Leone: Independence Day, Apr 27
Sierra Leone: National Holiday, Apr 19
Sigler, Jamie-Lynn: Birth, May 15
Sikh: Vaisakhi (India), Apr 13
Sikorsky, Igor: Birth Anniv, May 25
Silent Record Week, Jan 1
Silent Spring Publication: Anniv, Apr 13
Sills, Beverly: Birth Anniv, May 25
Silver Bells in the City (Lansing, MI), Nov 20
Silver, Joel: Birth, Jul 14

Silver, Ron: Birth, Jul 2
Silverman, Fred: Birth, Sep 13
Silverman, Jonathan: Birth, Aug 5
Silverstein, Shel: Birth Anniv, Oct 18
Silverstone, Alicia: Birth, Oct 4
Simchat Torah, Oct 11
Simenon, Georges: Birth Anniv, Feb 12
Simmons, Gene: Birth, Aug 25
Simmons, J.K.: Birth, Jan 9
Simmons, Jean: Birth, Jan 31
Simmons, Joseph "Run": Birth, Nov 14
Simmons, Richard: Birth, Jul 12
Simms, Hilda: Birth Anniv, Apr 15
Simms, Phil: Birth, Nov 3
Simon, Carly: Birth, Jun 25
Simon, Neil: Birth, Jul 4
Simon, Paul: Birth, Oct 13
Simone, Nina: Birth Anniv, Feb 21
Simplon Tunnel Opening: Anniv, May 19
Simpson, Jessica: Birth, Jul 10
Simpson, O.J.: Birth, Jul 9
Simpsons TV Premiere: Anniv, Dec 17
Sinai Day (Egypt), Apr 25
Sinatra, Frank: Birth Anniv, Dec 12
Sinatra, Nancy: Birth, Jun 8
Sinbad: Birth, Nov 10
Sinclair, Upton: Birth Anniv, Sep 20
Sinden, Donald: Birth, Oct 9
Singapore
National Day, Aug 9
Vesak Day, May 10
Singh, Vijay: Birth, Feb 22
Singin' in the Rain Film Premiere: Anniv, Mar 27
Singing Telegram: Anniv, Jul 28
Single: Satisfied Staying Single Day, Feb 11
Singles Week, Natl, Sep 20
Singletary, Mike: Birth, Oct 9
Single-Tasking Day, Feb 21
Singleton, John: Birth, Jan 6
Singleton, Raynoma Gordy: Birth, Mar 8
Sinise, Gary: Birth, Mar 17
Sinkie Day, Nov 27
Sioux Empire Fair (Sioux Falls, SD), Aug 11
Sioux Empire Farm Show (Sioux Falls, SD), Jan 27
Sirica, John: Birth Anniv, Mar 19
Sirk, Douglas: Birth Anniv, Apr 26
Sisley, Alfred: Birth Anniv, Oct 30
Sisters' Day, Aug 2
Sisters: Siblings Day, Natl, Apr 10
Sisto, Jeremy: Birth, Oct 6
Sitting Bull: Death Anniv, Dec 15
Six Million Dollar Man TV Premiere: Anniv, Oct 20
$64,000 Question TV Premiere: Anniv, Jun 7
16th Street Baptist Church Bombing: Anniv, Sep 15
Sixty Minutes TV Premiere: Anniv, Sep 24
Skaggs, Ricky: Birth, Jul 18
Skagit Valley Tulip Fest (Burlington, WA), Apr 1
Skating (Ice, Inline, Figure, Roller, Speed)
Roller Skating Month, Natl, Oct 1
Skating Month, Natl, Jan 1
Skerritt, Tom: Birth, Aug 25
Skiing
American Birkebeiner (Cable to Hayward, WI), Feb 19
Birkebeinerrennet (Rena and Lillehammer, Norway), Mar 21
Coca-Cola Spring Splash (Winter Park, CO), Apr 12
NCAA Men's & Women's Skiing Chmpshps (Bethel/Rumford, ME), Mar 11
Toronto Ski, Snowboard and Travel Show (Toronto, ON, Canada), Oct 15
Skin Care Awareness Month, Natl, Sep 1
Skin: Rosacea Awareness Month, Apr 1
Skinner, B.F.: Birth Anniv, Mar 20
Skowhegan State Fair (Skowhegan, ME), Aug 13
Sky Awareness Week, Apr 19
Skye, Ione: Birth, Sep 4
Skylab Falls to Earth, Jul 11
Skyscraper, First: Anniv, May 1
Slamdance (Park City, UT), Jan 15
Slater, Christian: Birth, Aug 18
Slater, Helen: Birth, Dec 15
Slave Revolt, New York: Anniv, Apr 7
Slavery Abolished in District of Columbia: Anniv, Apr 16
Slavery, Abolition of (Jamaica), Aug 1
Slavery: First American Abolition Society Founded: Anniv, Apr 14
Slavery: Remembrance of the Slave Trade and Its Abolition, Intl Day for the (UN), Aug 23
Slayton, Donald "Deke" K.: Birth Anniv, Mar 1
Sled Dog
Iditarod Trail Sled Dog Race (Anchorage, AK), Mar 7
Sled Dogs Save Nome: Anniv, Feb 2
Yukon Quest Intl 1,000-Mile Sled Dog Race (Whitehorse, YT, Canada), Feb 14
Sleep Awareness Week, Natl, Mar 1
Sleidanus, Johannes: Death Anniv, Oct 31
Slezak, Erika: Birth, Aug 5
Slick, Grace: Birth, Oct 30
Sloan, Jerry: Birth, Mar 28
Sloane, Hans: Birth Anniv, Apr 16
Slovakia
Constitution Day, Sep 1
Czech-Slovak Divorce: Anniv, Jan 1
Liberation Day, May 8
National Uprising Day, Aug 29
St. Cyril and Methodius Day, Jul 5
Slovenia
Culture Day, Feb 8
Independence Day, Dec 26
Insurrection Day, Apr 27
National Day, Jun 25
Slovenian: St. Cyril's Parish Fest (Sheboygan, WI), Jul 19
Slovik, Eddie: Execution Anniv, Jan 31
Slovo, Joe: Birth Anniv, May 23
Slow Pitch Softball Tourn (Williamsport, PA), Jul 10
Slugs Return from Capistrano Day, May 28
Small Press Month, Mar 1
Smallpox Vaccine Discovered: Anniv, May 14
Smart, Jean: Birth, Sep 13
Smile Day, World, Oct 2
Smile Month, Natl, May 1
Smiley, Jane: Birth, Sep 26
Smirnoff, Yakov: Birth, Jan 24
Smith, Adam: Birth Anniv, Jun 5
Smith, Anna Nicole: Birth Anniv, Nov 28
Smith, Bessie: Birth Anniv, Apr 15
Smith, Bubba: Birth, Feb 28
Smith, Charles Martin: Birth, Oct 30
Smith, Emmitt: Birth, May 15
Smith, Gordon: Birth, May 25
Smith, Holland: Birth Anniv, Apr 20
Smith, Jaclyn: Birth, Oct 26
Smith, James: Death Anniv, Jul 11
Smith, Jedediah Strong: Birth Anniv, Jan 6
Smith, Joseph, Jr, and Hyrum Smith: Death Anniv, Jun 27
Smith, Joseph, Jr: Birth Anniv, Dec 23
Smith, Kate: Birth Anniv, May 1
Smith, Kate: God Bless America First Performed: Anniv, Nov 11
Smith, Kurtwood: Birth, Jul 3
Smith, Liz: Birth, Feb 2
Smith, Maggie: Birth, Dec 28
Smith, Margaret: Birth Anniv, Dec 14
Smith, Michael J.: Birth Anniv, Apr 30
Smith, Ozzie: Birth, Dec 26
Smith, Patti: Birth, Dec 30
Smith, Red: Birth Anniv, Sep 25
Smith, Robert: Alcoholics Anonymous: Founding Anniv, Jun 10
Smith, Shepard: Birth, Jan 14
Smith, Steve: Birth, Mar 31
Smith, Thorne: Birth Anniv, Mar 27
Smith, Will: Birth, Sep 25
Smith, Zadie: Birth, Oct 27
Smithson, James: Death Anniv, Jun 27
Smithsonian Institution Founded: Anniv, Aug 10
Smitrovich, Bill: Birth, May 16
Smits, Jimmy: Birth, Jul 9
Smits, Rik: Birth, Aug 23
Smokeout, Great American, Nov 19
Smoking, Take a New Year's Resolution to Stop Smoking, Dec 8
Smoltz, John: Birth, May 15
Smothers Brothers Fired: Anniv, Apr 4
Smothers, Dick: Birth, Nov 20
Smothers, Tom: Birth, Feb 2
Smulders, Cobie: Birth, Apr 3
Snake Hunt (Cross Fork, PA), Jun 27
Snake River Duck Race (Nome, AK), Sep 7
Snake River Stampede (Nampa, ID), Jul 14
Snead, Sam: Birth Anniv, May 27
Sneak Some Zucchini onto Your Neighbors' Porch Night, Aug 8
Snider, Dee: Birth, Mar 15
Snipes, Wesley: Birth, Jul 31
Snodgrass, W.D.: Birth, Jan 5
Snow Fest (Japan), Feb 8
Snow Moon, Feb 9
Snow Sculpting Competition (Rockford, IL), Jan 21
Snow White and the Seven Dwarfs Film Premiere: Anniv, Dec 21
Snow, Phoebe: Birth, Jul 17
Snowbirds Pancake Breakfast (El Centro, CA), Jan 10
Snowe, Olympia J.: Birth, Feb 21
Snowman Burning (Sault Ste. Marie, MI), Mar 20
Snowplow Mailbox Hockey Day, Jan 23
Snowshoe Chmpshps, US Natl, Mar 7
Soap Box Derby, All-American (Akron, OH), Jul 25
Soap TV Premiere: Anniv, Sep 13
Sobieski, Leelee: Birth, Jun 10
Soccer
Dallas Cup (Frisco, TX), Apr 5
Moscow Soccer Tragedy: Anniv, Oct 20
NAIA Men's Natl Chmpshp (Fresno, CA), Nov 30
NAIA Women's Natl Chmpshp, Nov 30
Natl Soccer Coaches Assn of America Natl Conv (St. Louis, MO), Jan 14
NCAA Div I Men's Soccer Chmpshp (Cary, NC), Dec 11
NCAA Div I Women's Soccer Chmpshp (College Station, TX), Dec 4
Pele Scores 1,000th Goal: Anniv, Nov 19

Soccer Tragedy (Belgium): Anniv, May 29
World Cup Inaugurated: Anniv, Jul 13
Social Justice, World Day for (UN), Feb 20
Social Security Act: Anniv, Aug 14
Social Security Check Issued, First: Anniv, Jan 31
Social Wellness Month, Jul 1
Social Work Month, Natl, Mar 1
Soderbergh, Steven: Birth, Jan 14
Softball. See also Baseball
NAIA Natl Chmpshp, May 15
NCAA Div I Chmpshp (Oklahoma City, OK), May 28
Slow Pitch Tourn (Williamsport, PA), Jul 10
365-Inning Softball Game: Anniv, Aug 14
Soil Stewardship Sunday: See Rural Life Sunday, May 17
Soldiers' Reunion Celebration (Newton, NC), Aug 20
Solemnity of Mary, Jan 1
Solidarity Granted Legal Status: Anniv, Apr 17
Solidarity with the Palestinian People, Intl Day of (UN), Nov 29
Solidarity with the Peoples of Non-Self-Governing Territories, Week of (UN), May 25
Solo Diners Eat Out Week, Feb 1
Solo, Hope: Birth, Jul 30
Solomon Islands: Independence Day, Jul 7
Solstice, Summer, Jun 21
Solstice, Winter, Dec 21
Solti, Georg: Birth Anniv, Oct 21
Solzhenitsyn Goes Home: Anniv, May 25
Somalia: National Day, Jul 1
Someday We'll Laugh About This Week, Jan 2
Somerhalder, Ian: Birth, Dec 8
Somers, Suzanne: Birth, Oct 16
Sommer, Elke: Birth, Nov 5
Sondheim, Stephen: Birth, Mar 22
Sopranos TV Premiere: Anniv, Jan 13
Sorbo, Kevin: Birth, Sep 24
Sorenstam, Annika: Birth, Oct 9
Soriano, Alfonso: Birth, Jan 7
Soros, George: Birth, Aug 12
Sorry Charlie Day, Apr 1
Sorvino, Paul: Birth, Apr 13
SOS Adopted: Anniv, Nov 3
Sosa, Sammy: Birth, Nov 12
Soto, Geovany: Birth, Jan 20
Soul Food Month, Natl, Jun 1
Soul, David: Birth, Aug 28
Sound Barrier Broken: Anniv, Oct 14
Sound of Music Film Premiere: Anniv, Mar 2
Soupy Sales TV Premiere: Anniv, Jul 4
Sour Herring Premiere (Sweden), Aug 20
Sourest Day, Oct 25
Sousa, John P.: Birth Anniv, Nov 6
Sousa: Stars and Stripes Forever Day, May 14
Souter, David H.: Birth, Sep 17
South Africa
African Natl Congress Ban Lifted: Anniv, Feb 2
Boer War: Anniv, Oct 12
Day of Goodwill, Dec 26
Family Day, Apr 13
Freedom Day, Apr 27
Heritage Day, Sep 24
Human Rights Day, Mar 21
Mandela Inauguration: Anniv, May 10
Multiracial Elections: Anniv, Apr 26
New Constitution: Anniv, Nov 18
Reconciliation Day, Dec 16
Repeals Last Apartheid Law: Anniv, Jun 17
Whites Vote to End Minority Rule: Anniv, Mar 17
Women's Day, Natl, Aug 9
Youth Day, Jun 16
South by Southwest (Austin, TX), Mar 13
South Carolina
Attack on Fort Sumter: Anniv, Apr 12
Attack on Fort Wagner: Anniv, Jul 19
Charleston Earthquake: Anniv, Aug 31
Charleston Intl Antiques Show (Charleston), Mar 20
Confederate Memorial Day, May 10
Craftsmen's Classic Arts & Crafts Fest (Columbia), Mar 6
Craftsmen's Classic Arts & Crafts Fest (Myrtle Beach), Aug 7
DeMint, Jim: Birth, Sep 2
Fest of Houses and Gardens (Charleston), Mar 19
Fort Sumter Returned to Union Control: Anniv, Feb 17
Fort Sumter Shelled by North: Anniv, Aug 17
Graham, Lindsey: Birth, Jul 9
Historic Pendleton Spring Jubilee (Pendleton), Apr 4
Low Country Shrimp Fest (McClellanville), May 2
Miss South Carolina Pageant (Spartanburg), Jun 30
Miss South Carolina Teen Competition (Spartanburg), Jun 30
Orangeburg Fest of Roses (Orangeburg), May 1
Palmetto Sportsmen's Classic (Columbia), Mar 27
Ratification Day, May 23
Sanford, Mark: Birth, May 28
Secession Anniv, Dec 20
South Carolina Fest of Flowers (Greenwood), Jun 5
Southern Cyclone: Anniv, Aug 24
Spoleto Fest USA (Charleston), May 22
State Fair (Columbia), Oct 14
Sumter Iris Fest (Sumter), May 22
US Mid-Amateur (Golf) Chmpshp (Charleston), Oct 3
South Coast Writers Conf (Gold Beach, OR), Feb 13
South Dakota
Admission Day, Nov 2
Badlands Natl Park Established: Anniv, Nov 10
Black Hills Passion Play (Spearfish), Jun 2
Black Hills Stock Show and Rodeo (Rapid City), Jan 30
Buffalo Roundup (Custer), Sep 28
Buffalo Roundup Arts Fest (Custer), Sep 26
Corn Palace Fest (Mitchell), Aug 26
Custer State Park Buffalo Auction (Custer), Nov 21
Czech Days (Tabor), Jun 18
Dalesburg Midsummer Fest (Vermillion), Jun 19
Fort Sisseton Historical Fest (Lake City), Jun 5
Gold Discovery Days (Custer), Jul 24
Johnson, Tim: Birth, Dec 28
Laura Ingalls Wilder Pageant (De Smet), Jul 10
LifeLight Outdoor Music Fest (Sioux Falls), Sep 4
Mount Rushmore Independence Day Celebration (Mount Rushmore), Jul 3
NAIA Women's Golf Natl Chmpshps (Rapid City), May 12
Native Americans' Day, Oct 12
Prairie Village Jamboree (Madison), Aug 28
Rounds, Mike: Birth, Oct 24
Schmeckfest (Freeman), Mar 27
Sidewalk Arts Fest (Sioux Falls), Sep 5
Sioux Empire Fair (Sioux Falls), Aug 11
Sioux Empire Farm Show (Sioux Falls), Jan 27
State Fair (Huron), Sep 3
Sturgis Rally (Sturgis), Aug 3
Thune, John R.: Birth, Jan 7
Wind Cave Natl Park Established: Anniv, Jan 3
South Korea
Armed Forces Day, Oct 1
Children's Day, May 5
South Pole Discovery: Anniv, Dec 14
Southeast Missouri District Fair (Cape Girardeau, MO), Sep 12
Southern Fest of Books (Nashville, TN), Oct 9
Southern Hemisphere Hoodie-Hoo Day, Aug 22
Soviet Georgia Votes Independence: Anniv, Mar 31
Soviet Union Invaded: Anniv, Jun 22
Sowerby, Leo: Birth Anniv, May 1
Soyinka, Wole: Birth, Jul 13
Space (excluding Space Milestones)
Aerospace Walk of Honor (Lancaster, CA), Sep 19
Apollo I: Spacecraft Fire: Anniv, Jan 27
Astronomers Find New Solar System: Anniv, Apr 15
Challenger Space Shuttle Explosion: Anniv, Jan 28
Closest Approach of a Comet to Earth: Anniv, Feb 20
Comet Crashes into Jupiter: Anniv, Jul 16
First Radio Broadcast from Space: Anniv, Dec 19
Jupiter Effect: Anniv, Mar 10
NASA Established: Anniv, Jul 29
Near Miss Day, Mar 23
Ozark UFO Conf (Eureka Springs, AR), Apr 10
Pluto Demoted: Anniv, Aug 24
Soviet Cosmonaut Returns to New Country: Anniv, Mar 26
Space Oddity Song Release: Anniv, Jun 11
Space Shuttle Columbia Disaster: Anniv, Feb 1
Titan 34-D Rocket Failure: Anniv, Apr 18
Uranus, Discovery of: Anniv, Mar 13
US Natl Commission on Space, Oct 13
Windstorms Discovered: Anniv, Nov 7
World Space Week (UN), Oct 4
Year of Astronomy, Intl (UN), Jan 1
Space Milestones
Year 1 (1957)
Sputnik 1, Oct 4
Sputnik 2, Nov 3
Year 2 (1958)
Explorer 1, Jan 31
Vanguard 1, Mar 17
Atlas—Christmas Greetings from Space, Dec 19
Year 3 (1959)
Luna 1, Jan 2
First Picture of Earth from Space, Aug 7
Luna 2, Sep 12
Luna 3, Oct 4
Year 4 (1960)
Echo 1, Aug 12
Sputnik 5, Aug 19

Year 5 (1961)
Project Mercury Test, Jan 31
Vostok 1, Apr 12
Freedom 7, May 5
Vostok 2, Aug 6
Year 6 (1962)
Friendship 7, Feb 20
Aurora 7, May 24
Telstar, Jul 10
Vostok 3, Aug 11
Year 7 (1963)
Faith 7, May 15
Vostok 5, Jun 14
Vostok 6, Jun 16
Year 8 (1964)
Mariner 4, Nov 28
Year 9 (1965)
Voskhod 2, Mar 18
Gemini 4, Jun 3
Gemini 5, Aug 21
Venera 3, Nov 16
Year 10 (1966)
Luna 9, Jan 31
Gemini 8, Mar 16
Gemini 12, Nov 11
Year 11 (1967)
Venera 4, Jun 12
Mariner 5, Jun 14
Year 12 (1968)
OGO 5, Mar 4
Soyuz 3, Oct 26
Apollo 8, Dec 21
Year 13 (1969)
Soyuz 4, Jan 14
Apollo 10, May 18
Apollo 11, Jul 16
Moon Day, Jul 20
Apollo 12, Nov 14
Year 14 (1970)
Osumi, Feb 11
Apollo 13, Apr 11
China 1, Apr 24
Space Rescue Agreement, Oct 28
Year 15 (1971)
Apollo 14, Jan 31
Salyut, Apr 19
Mars 2 and Mars 3, May 19
Mariner 9, May 30
Soyuz 11, Jun 6
Apollo 15, Jul 26
Intelsat 4 F-3, Dec 19
Year 16 (1972)
Pioneer 10, Mar 2
Venera 8, Mar 27
Apollo 16, Apr 16
Copernicus OAO 4, Apr 21
Apollo 17, Dec 7
Year 17 (1973)
Skylab, May 14
Skylab 2, May 25
Skylab 3, Jul 28
Intelsat-4 F-7, Aug 23
Soyuz 12, Sep 27
Skylab 4, Nov 16
Year 19 (1975)
Venera 9 and 10, Jun 8
Apollo-Soyuz Test Project, Jul 17
Viking 1 and 2, Aug 20
Year 20 (1976)
Soyuz 21, Jul 6
Year 21 (1977)
Enterprise, Aug 12
Voyager 2, Aug 20
Voyager 1, Sep 5
Salyut 6, Sep 29
Soyuz 26, Dec 10
Year 22 (1978)
Cosmos 954 Falls, Jan 24
Soyuz 28, Mar 2
Pioneer Venus 1, May 20
Pioneer Venus Multiprobe, Aug 8
Soyuz 31, Aug 26
Pegasus 1, Sep 17
Year 23 (1979)
Soyuz 32, Feb 25
Skylab Falls to Earth, Jul 11
Year 24 (1980)
Soyuz 35, Apr 9
Soyuz T-2, Jun 5
Rohini 1, Jul 18
Soyuz 37, Jul 23
Year 25 (1981)
Columbia STS-1, Apr 12
Ariane, Jun 19
Columbia STS-2, Nov 12
Year 26 (1982)
Kosmos 1383, Jul 1
Soyuz T-7, Aug 19
Columbia STS-5, Nov 11
Year 27 (1983)
NOAA 8, Mar 28
Challenger STS-6, Apr 4
First American Woman in Space (Challenger STS-7), Jun 18
Challenger STS-8, Aug 30
Year 28 (1984)
Challenger STS-10, Feb 3
Soyuz T-12, Jul 17
Discovery, Aug 30
Challenger STS 41-G, Oct 5
Vega 1, Dec 15
Year 29 (1985)
Discovery, Jan 24
Arabsat-1, Feb 8
Brasilsat 1, Feb 8
Discovery, Apr 12
Challenger STS 51-B, Apr 29
Year 30 (1986)
Mir Space Station, Feb 20
Delta 3914 Rocket Failure, May 3
Year 31 (1987)
Soyuz TM-3, Jul 22
Ariane-3, Sep 15
Year 32 (1988)
Phobos 2, Jul 12
Discovery, Sep 29
Buran, Nov 15
Year 33 (1989)
Atlantis, May 4
Voyager 2 Reaches Neptune, Aug 24
Year 34 (1990)
First Soviet Commercial Satellite, Feb 11
Hubble Space Telescope, Apr 25
Year 36 (1992)
Endeavour, May 13
Year 39 (1995)
Record Time in Space, Mar 22
Atlantis Docks with Mir, Jun 29
Galileo, Dec 7
Year 41 (1997)
Columbia Neurolab, Apr 17
Mars Pathfinder, Jul 4
Mars Global Surveyor, Sep 11
Cassini, Oct 15
Year 42 (1998)
Lunar Explorer, Jan 6
Discovery: Oldest Man in Space, Oct 29
International Space Station Launch, Dec 4
Year 43 (1999)
Stardust, Feb 7
Columbia: First Female Commander, Jul 23
Year 44 (2000)
Endeavour Mapping Mission, Feb 11
Near Orbits Asteroid, Feb 14
100th Space Shuttle Flight, Oct 11
International Space Station Inhabited, Nov 2
Year 45 (2001)
100th Spacewalk, Feb 14
Mir Abandoned, Mar 23
Mars Odyssey, Apr 7
First Tourist in Space, Apr 28
Genesis, Aug 8
Helios Solar Wing, Aug 13
Year 48 (2004)
Mars Exploration Rover Spirit, Jan 3
First Manned Private Spaceflight, Jun 21
Cassini-Huygens Reaches Saturn, Jul 1
Year 49 (2005)
Deep Impact Smashes into Tempel 1, Jul 4
Year 52 (2008)
Phoenix Lands on Mars, May 26
Spacek, Sissy: Birth, Dec 25
Spacey, Kevin: Birth, Jul 26
Spade, David: Birth, Jul 22
Spader, James: Birth, Feb 7
Spain
Book Day and Lover's Day, Apr 23
Canary Islands Plane Disaster: Anniv, Mar 27
Civil War Begins: Anniv, Jul 18
Constitution Day, Dec 6
Fiesta de Las Fallas (Valencia), Mar 12
Fiesta de Santa Marta de Ribarteme (As Neves, Galicia), Jul 29
La Tomatina (Bunol), Aug 26
Madrid Train Bombings: Anniv, Mar 11
National Holiday, Oct 12
Running of the Bulls, Jul 7
Saint James Day, Jul 25
Spain Captures Granada: Anniv, Jan 2
Spanish Flu: Pandemic of 1918 Hits US: Anniv, Mar 11
Spanish-American War
Maine Memorial Day (MA), Feb 15
Matanzas Mule Day, Apr 27
Remember the Maine Day: Anniv, Feb 15
Spanish-American War: Surrender of Guam to US: Anniv, Jun 20
Treaty of Paris Signed: Anniv, Dec 10
Spank Out Day USA, Apr 30
Spano, Vincent: Birth, Oct 18
Spassky, Boris: Birth, Jan 30
Spay Day USA, Feb 24
Speak Up and Succeed Day, Natl, Jan 27
Speaking: Freedom from Fear of Speaking Week, Jun 28
Speaking: Professional Speakers Day, Aug 7
Spears, Britney: Birth, Dec 2
Special Education Day, Dec 2
Special Kids Day (Elmhurst, IL), Dec 2
Special Olympics Day, Jul 20
Special Olympics World Winter Games (Boise, ID), Feb 6
Special Recreation Day, Jun 28
Specter, Arlen: Birth, Feb 12
Spector, Phil: Birth, Dec 26
Speech Month, Better Hearing and, May 1
Speech-Language-Hearing Conv, American (New Orleans, LA), Nov 19
Spelling Bee Finals, Scripps Natl, May 27
Spelling, Tori: Birth, May 16

Spellings, Margaret: Birth, Nov 30
Spelman College Established: Anniv, Apr 11
Spelvin, George: Day, Nov 15
Spencer, Diana: Death Anniv, Aug 31
Spencer, Jesse: Birth, Feb 12
Spengler, Oswald: Birth Anniv, May 29
Spider-Man Debuts: Anniv, Aug 1
Spielberg, Steven: Birth, Dec 18
Spielberg, Steven: Jaws Film Release: Anniv, Jun 20
Spina Bifida Awareness Month, Natl, Oct 1
Spinach Lovers Month, Oct 1
Spinal Muscular Atrophy Awareness Month, Aug 1
Spinks, Leon: Birth, Jul 11
Spinks, Michael: Birth, Jul 13
Spinning and Weaving Week, Oct 5
Spinoza, Baruch: Birth Anniv, Nov 24
Spirit of Freedom Celebration (Florence, AL), Jul 4
Spirit of NSA Day, Nov 14
Spirit of the Woods Folk Fest (Brethren, MI), Jun 20
Spiritual Literacy Month, Dec 1
Spiritual Wellness Month, Mar 1
Spitz, Mark: Birth, Feb 10
Spock, Benjamin: Birth Anniv, May 2
Spoleto Fest USA (Charleston, SC), May 22
Spoon River Valley Scenic Drive (Lewistown, IL), Oct 3
Spoon River Valley: Knox County Scenic Drive (Galesburg, IL), Oct 3
Spooner, William: Birth Anniv, Jul 22
Spooner's Day, Jul 22
Sporting Goods Assn Mgmt Conf, Natl (San Antonio, TX), May 3
Sports & Home Eye Safety Month, Sep 1
Sports America Kids Month, Jun 1
Sports Cliche Week, Jul 5
Sports Show, Milwaukee Journal Sentinel (Milwaukee, WI), Mar 11
Sports, Physical Fitness and, Month, Natl, May 1
Sportsmen's Show, Toronto (Toronto, ON, Canada), Mar 18
Spradlin, G.D.: Birth, Aug 31
Sprewell, Latrell: Birth, Sep 8
Spring Begins, Mar 20
Spring Fairy Fun Day, Mar 22
Spring Fest, Towsontown (Towson, MD), May 2
Spring Fever Week, Natl, Mar 16
Springer, Jerry: Birth, Feb 13
Springfield, Rick: Birth, Aug 23
Springs Folk Fest (Springs, PA), Oct 2
Springsteen, Bruce: Birth, Sep 23
Spruce Goose Flight: Anniv, Nov 2
Spunky Old Broads Month, Feb 1
Spurrier, Steve: Birth, Apr 20
Sputnik 1: Anniv, Oct 4
Squirrel Awareness Month, Oct 1
Sri Lanka
  Independence Day, Feb 4
  Natl Heroes Day, May 22
  Sinhala and Tamil New Year, Apr 13
St. John, Jill: Birth, Aug 19
St. Laurent, Louis Stephen: Birth Anniv, Feb 1
St. Petersburg Founded: Anniv, May 27
Stabenow, Debbie: Birth, Apr 29
Stackhouse, Jerry: Birth, Nov 5
Stade, Frederica von: Birth, Jun 1
Stagg, Amos Alonzo: Birth Anniv, Aug 16
Stahl, Lesley: Birth, Dec 16
Staley, Dawn: Birth, May 4
Stalin, Joseph: Birth Anniv, Dec 21
Stalingrad, German Surrender at: Anniv, Feb 2
Stallone, Sylvester: Birth, Jul 6
Stamos, John: Birth, Aug 19
Stamp, Terence: Birth, Jul 22
Stamps
  Coin & Stamp Expo (Anaheim, CA), May 1
  Coin & Stamp Expo (Anaheim, CA), Sep 4
  Coin & Stamp Expo (Anaheim, CA), Oct 2
  Coin & Stamp Expo (Los Angeles, CA), Mar 27
  Coin & Stamp Expo (Pasadena, CA), Feb 13
  Coin & Stamp Expo (Pasadena, CA), May 22
  Coin & Stamp Expo (Pasadena, CA), Jul 3
  Coin & Stamp Expo (Sherman Oaks, CA), Jun 12
  Coin & Stamp Expo: America (Anaheim, CA), Nov 13
  Coin & Stamp Expo: Arizona (Mesa, AZ), Jan 2
  Coin & Stamp Expo: California (Pasadena, CA), Nov 13
  Nevadapex Coin and Stamp Expo (Laughlin, NV), Nov 6
  Postage Stamps, First US: Anniv, Jul 1
  Stamp & Coin Expo (New York, NY), Apr 17
  Stamp Collecting Month, Natl, Oct 1
Standard Time Act, US: Anniv, Mar 19
Standing Bear: Native American Rights Recognized: Anniv, May 12
Stanhope, Philip D.: Birth Anniv, Sep 22
Stanley Finds Livingstone: Anniv, Nov 10
Stanley, Henry Morton: Birth Anniv, Jan 28
Stanton, Elizabeth Cady: Birth Anniv, Nov 12
Stanton, Harry Dean: Birth, Jul 14
Stanwyck, Barbara: Birth Anniv, Jul 16
Stapleton, Jean: Birth, Jan 19
Star Fest (Tanabata) (Japan), Jul 7
Star Trek TV Premiere: Anniv, Sep 8
Star Wars Released: Anniv, May 25
Stark, USS Attacked: Anniv, May 17
Starker, Janos: Birth, Jul 5
Starman Month, Intl, Oct 1
Starr, Bart: Birth, Jan 9
Starr, Ringo: Birth, Jul 7
Stars and Stripes Forever Day, May 14
Star-Spangled Banner Inspired: Anniv, Sep 13
State Dept Founded, US: Anniv, Jul 27
State Fairs
  Alabama Natl Fair (Montgomery, AL), Oct 9
  Alaska State Fair (Palmer, AK), Aug 27
  Arizona State Fair (Phoenix, AZ), Oct 9
  Arkansas State Fair (Little Rock, AR), Oct 9
  Bangor State Fair (Bangor, ME), Jul 31
  California State Fair (Sacramento, CA), Aug 21
  Colorado State Fair (Pueblo, CO), Aug 29
  Delaware State Fair (Harrington, DE), Jul 23
  Eastern Idaho State Fair (Blackfoot, ID), Sep 5
  Florida State Fair (Tampa, FL), Feb 5
  Georgia National Fair (Perry, GA), Oct 8
  Illinois State Fair (Springfield, IL), Aug 14
  Indiana State Fair (Indianapolis, IN), Aug 7
  Iowa State Fair (Des Moines, IA), Aug 13
  Kansas State Fair (Hutchinson, KS), Sep 11
  Kentucky State Fair (Louisville, KY), Aug 20
  Louisiana, State Fair of (Shreveport, LA), Oct 22
  Maryland State Fair (Timonium, MD), Aug 28
  Michigan State Fair (Detroit, MI), Aug 28
  Minnesota State Fair (St. Paul, MN), Aug 27
  Mississippi State Fair (Jackson, MS), Oct 7
  Missouri State Fair (Sedalia, MO), Aug 13
  Montana State Fair (Great Falls, MT), Jul 24
  Nebraska State Fair (Lincoln, NE), Aug 28
  Nevada State Fair (Reno, NV), Aug 26
  New Jersey State Fair/Sussex Farm and Horse Show (Augusta, NJ), Jul 31
  New Mexico State Fair (Albuquerque, NM), Sep 4
  New York State Fair (Syracuse, NY), Aug 27
  North Carolina State Fair (Raleigh, NC), Oct 16
  North Dakota State Fair (Minot, ND), Jul 24
  Ohio State Fair (Columbus, OH), Aug 5
  Oklahoma State Fair (Oklahoma City, OK), Sep 17
  Oregon State Fair (Salem, OR), Aug 28
  South Carolina State Fair (Columbia, SC), Oct 14
  South Dakota State Fair (Huron, SD), Sep 3
  State Fair of Texas (Dallas, TX), Sep 25
  Tennessee State Fair (Nashville, TN), Sep 4
  Utah State Fair (Salt Lake City, UT), Sep 10
  Vermont State Fair (Rutland, VT), Sep 4
  Virginia, State Fair of (Richmond, VA), Sep 24
  West Virginia State Fair (Lewisburg, WV), Aug 14
  Western Idaho Fair (Boise, ID), Aug 14
  Wisconsin State Fair (Milwaukee, WI), Aug 6
  Wyoming State Fair & Rodeo (Douglas, WY), Aug 8
Stationery Show, Natl (New York, NY), May 17
Statue of Liberty: Dedication Anniv, Oct 28
Staub, Rusty: Birth, Apr 1
Staubach, Roger: Birth, Feb 5
Staunton, Imelda: Birth, Jan 9
Stay Home Because You're Well Day, Nov 30
Stay Out of the Sun Day, Jul 3
Stay Up All Night Night, May 9
Steakhouse Month, Natl, Jun 1
Stealth Bomber Flight: Anniv, Jul 17
Steel Mills, Fed Government Seizure: Anniv, Apr 8
Steel, Danielle: Birth, Aug 14
Steele, Tommy: Birth, Dec 17
Steenburgen, Mary: Birth, Feb 8
Steeplechase at Callaway Gardens (Pine Mountain, GA), Nov 7
Steeples, Eddie: Birth, Nov 25
Stefani, Gwen: Birth, Oct 3
Steichen, Edward: Birth Anniv, Mar 27
Steig, William: Birth Anniv, Nov 14
Steiger, Rod: Birth Anniv, Apr 17
Stein, Ben: Birth, Nov 25
Stein, Gertrude: Birth Anniv, Feb 3

Steinberg, David: Birth, Aug 9
Steinbrenner, George: Birth, Jul 4
Steinem, Gloria: Birth, Mar 25
Stella, Frank: Birth, May 12
Stendhal: Birth Anniv, Jan 23
Stengel, Casey: Birth Anniv, Jul 30
Stephens, James: Birth, May 18
Stephenson, George: Birth Anniv, Jun 9
Stephenson, Jan: Birth, Dec 22
Stepmothers Day, May 1
Sterling Renaissance Fest (Sterling, NY), Jul 11
Stern, Daniel: Birth, Aug 28
Stern, Howard: Birth, Jan 12
Stern, Howard: Radio Show Premiere: Anniv, Nov 18
Sterne, Laurence: Birth Anniv, Nov 24
Sternhagen, Frances: Birth, Jan 13
Sternwheel Fest, Ohio River (Marietta, OH), Sep 11
Steve Allen Show TV Premiere: Anniv, Dec 25
Stevens, Cat: Birth, Jul 21
Stevens, Connie: Birth, Aug 8
Stevens, Fisher: Birth, Nov 27
Stevens, John Paul: Birth, Apr 20
Stevens, Stella: Birth, Oct 1
Stevens, Ted: Birth, Nov 18
Stevenson, Adlai: Birth Anniv, Feb 5
Stevenson, Adlai: Birth Anniv, Oct 23
Stevenson, Alexandra: Birth, Dec 15
Stevenson, Parker: Birth, Jun 4
Stevenson, Robert Louis: Birth Anniv, Nov 13
Stewart, Earnie: Birth, Mar 28
Stewart, French: Birth, Feb 20
Stewart, Jackie: Birth, Jun 11
Stewart, James: Birth Anniv, May 20
Stewart, James: It's a Wonderful Life Film Premiere: Anniv, Dec 20
Stewart, Jon: Birth, Nov 28
Stewart, Kordell: Birth, Oct 16
Stewart, Martha: Birth, Aug 3
Stewart, Patrick: Birth, Jul 13
Stewart, Potter: Birth Anniv, Jan 23
Stewart, Rod: Birth, Jan 10
Stiers, David Ogden: Birth, Oct 31
Stiles, Julia: Birth, Mar 28
Stiles, Ryan: Birth, Apr 22
Still, Valerie: Birth, May 14
Stiller, Ben: Birth, Nov 30
Stiller, Jerry: Birth, Jun 8
Stills, Stephen: Birth, Jan 3
Stilts: Walk on Stilts Day, Jul 27
Stine, R.L.: Birth, Oct 8
Sting (Gordon Sumner): Birth, Oct 2
Stipe, Michael: Birth, Jan 4
Stock Exchange Holiday, Jan 1
Stock Exchange Holiday, Jan 19
Stock Exchange Holiday, Feb 16
Stock Exchange Holiday, Apr 10
Stock Exchange Holiday, May 25
Stock Exchange Holiday, Jul 3
Stock Exchange Holiday, Sep 7
Stock Exchange Holiday, Nov 26
Stock Exchange Holiday, Dec 25
Stock Exchange, NY, Established: Anniv, May 17
Stock Market Crash of 1893: Anniv, May 5
Stock Market Crash of 1929: Anniv, Oct 29
Stock Market Panic: Anniv, Oct 24
Stockholm Syndrome Bank Robbery: Anniv, Aug 23
Stockings, Nylon: Anniv, May 15
Stockton, David: Birth, Nov 2
Stockton, John: Birth, Mar 26
Stockton, Richard: Birth Anniv, Oct 1
Stockwell, Dean: Birth, Mar 5
Stockwell, John: Birth, Mar 25
Stojakovic, Peja: Birth, Jun 9
Stojko, Elvis: Birth, Mar 22
Stokes, Carl: Becomes First Black Mayor in US: Anniv, Nov 13
Stoltz, Eric: Birth, Sep 30
Stone, Dee Wallace: Birth, Dec 14
Stone, Harlan Fiske: Birth Anniv, Oct 11
Stone, Lucy: Birth Anniv, Aug 13
Stone, Oliver: Birth, Sep 15
Stone, Sharon: Birth, Mar 10
Stone, Sly: Birth, Mar 15
Stone, Steve: Birth, Jul 14
Stone, Thomas: Death Anniv, Oct 5
Stonewall Riot: Anniv, Jun 28
Stookey, Noel Paul: Birth, Nov 30
Stop the Music TV Premiere: Anniv, May 5
Stoppard, Tom: Birth, Jul 3
Storey, David: Birth, Jul 13
Storm, Gale: Birth, Apr 5
Story, Joseph: Birth Anniv, Sep 18
Storytelling
  Family Stories Month, Nov 1
  Iowa Storytelling Fest (Clear Lake, IA), Jul 24
  Smoky Mountains Storytelling Fest (Pigeon Forge, TN), Jun 4
  Storytelling Fest, Natl (Jonesborough, TN), Oct 2
Stotz, Carl E.: Birth Anniv, Feb 20
Stoudamire, Damon: Birth, Sep 3
Stoudemire, Amare: Birth, Nov 16
Stowe, Harriet Beecher: Birth Anniv, Jun 14
Stowe, Madeleine: Birth, Aug 18
Stradivari, Antonio: Death Anniv, Dec 18
Strait, George: Birth, May 18
Straith, Claire: Birth Anniv, Aug 30
Strang, James Jesse: Birth Anniv, Mar 21
Strange, Curtis: Birth, Jan 30
Strange, Sarah: Birth, Sep 6
Strassman, Marcia: Birth, Apr 28
Strategic Planning Month, Intl, Oct 1
Strategic Thinking Month, Intl, Sep 1
Stratemeyer, Edward L.: Birth Anniv, Oct 4
Strathairn, David: Birth, Jan 26
Stratton, Dorothy C.: Birth Anniv, Mar 24
Strauss, Levi: Birth Anniv, Feb 26
Strauss, Peter: Birth, Feb 20
Strauss, Richard G.: Birth Anniv, Jun 11
Stravinsky, Igor F.: Birth Anniv, Jun 17
Stravinsky, Igor: Rite of Spring Premiere and Riot: Anniv, May 29
Straw Hat Month, Apr 1
Strawberry Fest (Lahaska, PA), May 2
Strawberry Fest (Plant City, FL), Feb 26
Strawberry Fest, Poteet (Poteet, TX), Apr 3
Strawberry Hill Races (Richmond, VA), Apr 11
Strawberry Month, February Is Fabulous Florida, Feb 1
Strawberry Moon, Jun 7
Strawberry, Darryl: Birth, Mar 12
Streep, Meryl: Birth, Jun 22
Street Machine Fall Nationals (Springfield, MO), Sep 18
Street, Huston: Birth, Aug 2
Street, Picabo: Birth, Apr 3
Streetcar Named Desire Broadway Opening: Anniv, Dec 3
Streeter, Ruth Cheney: Birth Anniv, Oct 2
Streisand, Barbra: Birth, Apr 24
Stresa Fest (Stresa, Italy), Aug 21
Stress Awareness Day, Natl, Apr 16
Stress Awareness Month, Apr 1
Stress Management: Zero-Tasking Day, Nov 1
Strickland, Rod: Birth, Jul 11
Strickland, Ted: Birth, Aug 4
Strindberg, August: Birth Anniv, Jan 22
Stringfield, Sherry: Birth, Jun 24
Stritch, Elaine: Birth, Feb 2
Stroke Awareness Month, Natl, May 1
Strokes Month, Strike Out, May 1
Strong, Rider: Birth, Dec 11
Stroud, Don: Birth, Sep 1
Strug, Kerri: Birth, Nov 19
Struthers, Sally: Birth, Jul 28
Stuart, Gilbert: Birth Anniv, Dec 3
Student Government Day (MA), Apr 3
Student Safety Month, Jun 1
Students' Memorial Day, Kent State, May 4
Stupid Guy Thing Day, Jun 22
Sturgeon Moon, Aug 5
Sturges, John: Birth Anniv, Jan 3
Sturgess, Jim: Birth, May 16
Sturgis Rally and Races, Aug 3
Stuttering Awareness Day, Intl, Oct 22
Stuttering Awareness Week, Natl, May 11
Styron, William: Birth Anniv, Jun 11
Subliminal Communications Month, Sep 1
Submarine: First Nuclear-Powered Voyage: Anniv, Jan 17
Substitute Teacher Appreciation Week, Sep 14
Subway Accident, New York: Anniv, Nov 2
Subway, New York City: Anniv, Oct 27
Success Month, Intl Expect, Mar 1
Succoth, Oct 3
Suchet, David: Birth, May 2
Sudan
  Independence Day, Jan 1
  Revolution Day, Jun 30
Suez Canal Formal Opening: Anniv, Nov 17
Suez Canal Opens: Anniv, Mar 7
Suez Canal: Evacuation Day (Egypt), Jun 18
Suffrage Parade Attacked, Woman: Anniv, Mar 3
Sugar Bowl, Allstate (New Orleans, LA), Jan 2
Suicide Prevention Week, Natl, Sep 7
Sukkot, Oct 3
Sukkot Begins, Oct 2
Sullivan, Anne: Birth Anniv, Apr 14
Sullivan, Anne: Helen Keller's Miracle: Anniv, Apr 5
Sullivan, Arthur: Birth Anniv, May 13
Sullivan, Ed: Birth Anniv, Sep 28
Sullivan, Erik Per: Birth, Jul 12
Sullivan, John L.: Birth Anniv, Oct 15
Sullivan, Louis: Birth Anniv, Sep 3
Sullivan, Susan: Birth, Nov 18
Sultana Explosion: Anniv, Apr 27
Sulzberger, Arthur O.: Birth, Sep 22
Sumac, Yma: Birth, Sep 10
Sumatran-Andaman Earthquake and Tsunamis: Anniv, Dec 26
Summer Arrival: Martin Z. Mollusk Day (Ocean City, NJ), May 7
Summer Begins, Jun 21
Summer Daylight-Saving Time (Europe), Mar 29
Summer Fairy Fun Day, Jun 28
Summer Market Fair, Eighteenth-Century (McLean, VA), Jul 18
Summer Music Fest (Sitka, AK), Jun 5
Summer Time (United Kingdom), Mar 29
Summer, Donna: Birth, Dec 31
Summer: May Ray Day, May 19
Summers, Andy: Birth, Dec 31
Summitt, Patricia (Pat): Birth, Jun 14

Sumner, Charles, Attacked in the Senate: Anniv, May 22
Sumner, Gordon (Sting): Birth, Oct 2
Sumter Iris Fest (Sumter, SC), May 22
Sun Bowl (El Paso, TX), Dec 31
Sun Yat-sen: Birth Anniv, Nov 12
Sun Yat-sen: Death Anniv, Mar 12
Sundance Film Fest (Park City, UT), Jan 15
Sunday, Billy: Birth Anniv, Nov 19
Sununu, John: Birth, Sep 10
Super Bowl (Tampa Bay, FL), Feb 1
Super Bowl, First: Anniv, Jan 15
Superman Celebration (Metropolis, IL), Jun 11
Superman Debuts: Anniv, Jun 1
Suplee, Ethan: Birth, May 25
Supply Chain Mgmt Professionals, Council of, Annual Conf (Chicago, IL), Sep 20
Support Your Local Chamber of Commerce Day, Natl, Oct 21
Supreme Court
Abortion Notification Ruling: Anniv, Jun 25
Bans School Prayer: Anniv, Jun 25
Brown v Board of Education: Anniv, May 17
Dred Scott Decision: Anniv, Mar 6
First Session of: Anniv, Feb 1
First Woman Justice: Anniv, Sep 25
Loving v Virginia: Anniv, Jun 12
Miranda Decision: Anniv, Jun 13
Rehnquist, William Hubbs: Birth Anniv, Oct 1
Roe v Wade Decision: Anniv, Jan 22
Rules for Bush: Anniv, Dec 12
Strikes Down Connecticut Law Banning Contraception: Anniv, Jun 7
Term Begins, Oct 5
Thurgood Marshall Resigns: Anniv, Jun 27
Upholds Ban on Abortion Counseling: Anniv, May 23
Upholds Right to Die: Anniv, Jun 25
Woman Presides over: Anniv, Apr 3
Surfing
Kahanamoku, Duke: Birth Anniv, Aug 24
New England Mid-Winter (Narragansett, RI), Feb 21
Triple Crown of Surfing (Oahu, HI), Nov 12
Suriname
Independence Day, Nov 25
Liberation Day, Jul 1
Surratt, Mary: Lincoln Assassination Conspirators Hanging: Anniv, Jul 7
Survivor TV Premiere: Anniv, May 31
Susskind, David: Birth Anniv, Dec 19
Sutcliffe, Rick: Birth, Jun 21
Sutherland, Donald: Birth, Jul 17
Sutherland, Joan: Birth, Nov 7
Sutherland, Kiefer: Birth, Dec 21
Sutter, John A.: Birth Anniv, Feb 15
Sutton Hoo Ship Burial Discovered: Anniv, May 11
Suvari, Mena: Birth, Feb 9
Suzman, Janet: Birth, Feb 9
Suzuki, Ichiro: Birth, Oct 22
Svenson, Bo: Birth, Feb 13
Swallows Depart from San Juan Capistrano (CA), Oct 23
Swallows Return to San Juan Capistrano (CA), Mar 19
Swank, Hilary: Birth, Jul 30
Swanson, Gloria: Birth Anniv, Mar 27
Swanson, Kristy: Birth, Dec 19
Swappin' Meetin' (Cumberland, KY), Oct 2
Swayze, John Cameron: Birth Anniv, Apr 4
Swayze, Patrick: Birth, Aug 18
Swaziland
Independence Day, Sep 6
King's Birthday, Apr 19
Natl Flag Day, Apr 25
Sweat, Keith: Birth, Jul 22
Sweden
All Saints' Day, Oct 31
Crayfish Premiere, Aug 12
Feast of Valborg, Apr 30
Flag Day, Jun 6
Gustavus Adolphus Day, Nov 6
Linnaeus Day (Stenbrohult), May 23
Midsummer, Jun 23
Nobel Prize Awards Ceremony (Stockholm), Dec 10
Saint Knut's Day, Jan 13
Saint Martin's Day, Nov 11
Santa Lucia Day, Dec 13
Sour Herring Premiere, Aug 20
Swedenborg, Emanuel: Birth Anniv, Jan 29
Swedish Days (Geneva, IL), Jun 23
Sweeney, D.B.: Birth, Nov 14
Sweet Potato Month, Feb 1
Sweetcorn Fest, Natl (Hoopeston, IL), Sep 3
Sweetest Day, Oct 17
Swift, Jonathan: Birth Anniv, Nov 30
Swift, Taylor: Birth, Dec 13
Swimming and Diving
Big Ten Men's Swimming/Diving Chmpshps (West Lafayette, IN), Feb 26
Big Ten Women's Swimming/Diving Chmpshps (Ann Arbor, MI), Feb 19
Columbia River Cross Channel Swim (Hood River, OR), Sep 7
First Woman Swims English Channel: Anniv, Aug 6
Kahanamoku, Duke: Birth Anniv, Aug 24
NAIA Natl Men's and Women's Swimming/Diving Chmpshps (St. Louis, MO), Mar 4
NCAA Men's Div I Swimming/Diving Chmpshps (College Station, TX), Mar 26
NCAA Women's Div I Swimming/Diving Chmpshps (College Station, TX), Mar 19
Polar Bear Swim (Nome, AK), Jun 20
Swimming School Opens, First US: Anniv, Jul 23
Waikiki Roughwater Swim (Honolulu, HI), Sep 1
Weissmuller, Johnny: Birth Anniv, Jun 2
Swinton, Tilda: Birth, Nov 5
Swit, Loretta: Birth, Nov 4
Switzerland
Berchtoldstag, Jan 2
Cartier Polo World Cup on Snow (St. Moritz), Jan 29
Chalandra Marz, Mar 1
Confederation Day, Aug 1
Dornach Battle Commemoration, Jul 19
Egg Races, Apr 13
Homstrom (Scuol), Feb 1
Landsgemeinde, Apr 26
Lucerne Fest at Easter (Lucerne), Mar 28
Lucerne Fest in Summer (Lucerne), Aug 12
Lucerne Fest, Piano (Lucerne), Nov 23
Martinmas Goose, Nov 11
Meitlisunntig, Jan 11
Morat Battle: Anniv, Jun 22
Nafels Pilgrimage (Canton Glarus), Apr 2
Onion Market (Zibelemarit), Nov 23
Pacing the Bounds (Liestal), May 18
Saint Gotthard Auto Tunnel Opened: Anniv, Sep 5
Sempach Battle Commemoration, Jul 6
Swoopes, Sheryl: Birth, Mar 25
Sword Swallowers Awareness Day, Intl, Feb 28
Sydney Opera House Opens: Anniv, Oct 20
Synge, John M.: Birth Anniv, Apr 16
Syrian Arab Republic
Independence Day, Apr 17
Revolution Day, Mar 8
Szold, Henrietta: Birth Anniv, Dec 21
Szymanowski, Karol: Birth Anniv, Oct 6

T
T, Mr: Birth, May 21
Ta'anit Esther (Fast of Esther), Mar 9
Tabaski: See Eid-al-Adha, Nov 28
Tabei, Junko: Birth, Sep 22
Tabei, Junko: First Woman to Climb Mount Everest, May 16
Tabernacles, Feast of: First Day, Oct 3
Tabori, Kristoffer: Birth, Aug 4
Tacoma Holiday Food and Gift Fest (Tacoma, WA), Oct 21
Taft, Helen Herron: Birth Anniv, Jan 2
Taft, William H.: Birth Anniv, Sep 15
Taft, William: Opens Baseball Season: Anniv, Apr 14
Tagore, Rabindranath: Birth Anniv, May 6
Tai Chi and Qigong Day, World, Apr 25
Tailors Day, Natl, Jun 3
Taiwan
Birthday of Cheng Huang, Jun 5
Birthday of Kuan Yin, Goddess of Mercy, Mar 15
Cheng Cheng Kung Landing Day, Apr 29
Chiang Kai-Shek Day, Oct 31
Confucius's Birthday and Teachers' Day, Sep 28
Constitution Day, Dec 25
Double Tenth Day, Oct 10
Expelled from UN: Anniv, Oct 25
Foundation Days, Jan 1
Overseas Chinese Day, Oct 21
Retrocession Day, Oct 25
Tomb-Sweeping Day, Natl, Apr 5
Youth Day, Mar 29
Tajikistan: Independence Day, Sep 9
Take Back Your Time Week, Natl, Jan 26
Take Our Daughters and Sons to Work Day, Apr 23
Take Your Webmaster to Lunch Day, Jul 6
Talent Scouts TV Premiere: Anniv, Dec 6
Tales of Wells Fargo TV Premiere: Anniv, Mar 18
Talese, Gay: Birth, Feb 7
Talk Like a Pirate Day, Intl, Sep 19
Tall Timber Days Fest (Grand Rapids, MN), Aug 1
Tallchief, Maria: Birth, Jan 24
Tamale Fiesta (El Centro, CA), Dec 5
Tamblyn, Amber: Birth, May 14
Tamblyn, Russ: Birth, Dec 30
Tambor, Jeffrey: Birth, Jul 8
Tammuz, Fast of, Jul 9
Tan, Amy: Birth, Feb 19
Tandy, Jessica: Birth Anniv, Jun 7
Tandy, Jessica: Streetcar Named Desire Broadway Opening: Anniv, Dec 3
Taney, Roger B.: Birth Anniv, Mar 17
Tangible Karma Day, Apr 4
Tanner, Henry Ossawa: Birth Anniv, Jun 21
Tano Day (Korea), May 28

Tanzania
Farmers' Day, Aug 8
Independence and Republic Day, Dec 9
Saba Saba Day, Jul 7
Union Day, Apr 26
Zanzibar Revolution Day, Jan 12
Tap Dance Day, Natl, May 25
Tarantino, Quentin: Birth, Mar 27
Tarbell, Ida M.: Birth Anniv, Nov 5
Tarkenton, Fran: Birth, Feb 3
Tarkington, Booth: Birth Anniv, Jul 29
Tartan Day, Apr 6
Tarzan TV Premiere: Anniv, Sep 8
Tasso, Torquato: Birth Anniv, Mar 11
Tati, Jacques: Birth Anniv, Oct 9
Tattoo, Royal Nova Scotia Intl (Halifax, NS, Canada), Jul 1
Taurus Begins, Apr 20
Tautou, Audrey: Birth, Aug 9
Tax, Income, Pay Day, Apr 15
Taxes: Clean Up Your IRS Act Month, Natl, Mar 1
Taylor, Annie: First Barrel Jump over Niagara Falls: Anniv, Oct 24
Taylor, Billy: Birth, Jul 24
Taylor, Delores: Birth, Sep 27
Taylor, Elizabeth: Birth, Feb 27
Taylor, Frederick W.: Birth Anniv, Mar 20
Taylor, George: Death Anniv, Feb 23
Taylor, Holland: Birth, Jan 14
Taylor, James: Birth, Mar 12
Taylor, Lawrence: Birth, Feb 4
Taylor, Lili: Birth, Feb 20
Taylor, Lucy Hobbs: Birth Anniv, Mar 14
Taylor, Margaret S.: Birth Anniv, Sep 21
Taylor, Meshach: Birth, Apr 11
Taylor, Paul: Birth, Jul 29
Taylor, Renee: Birth, Mar 19
Taylor, Rod: Birth, Jan 11
Taylor, Zachary: Birth Anniv, Nov 24
Taylor-Young, Leigh: Birth, Jan 25
Tchaikovsky, Peter Ilich: Birth Anniv, May 7
Tea Month, Natl Hot, Jan 1
Teach Children to Save Day, Natl, Apr 21
Teach Your Daughter to Volunteer Day, Apr 18
Teacher Appreciation Week, May 3
Teacher Day, Natl, May 5
Teacher's Day in Florida, May 15
Teachers' Day, Confucius's Birthday and (Taiwan), Sep 28
Teachers' Day, World (UN), Oct 5
Tear Down This Wall Speech: Anniv, Jun 12
Technology: iPod Unveiled: Anniv, Oct 23
Tecumseh: Death Anniv, Oct 5
Tecumseh: Epic Outdoor Drama (Chillicothe, OH), Jun 12
Ted Mack's Original Amateur Hour TV Premiere: Anniv, Jan 18
Teddy Bear to Work Day, Natl Bring Your, Oct 14
Teen Read Week, Oct 18
Teen Self-Esteem Month, May 1
Teen Tech Week, Mar 8
Teens Don't Text and Drive Week, Natl, Nov 22
Teflon Invented: Anniv, Apr 6
Telecommunication Day, World (UN), May 17
Telecommuter Appreciation Week, Mar 1
Telegram, Singing: Anniv, Jul 28
Telegraph Line, Morse Opens First US: Anniv, May 24
Telegraph, Atlantic Cable Laid: Anniv, Jul 27
Telephone
Area Codes Introduced: Anniv, Nov 10
AT&T Divestiture: Anniv, Jan 8
Bell, Alexander Graham: Birth Anniv, Mar 3
Cell Phone Courtesy Month, Jul 1
First Telephone Operator: Emma M. Nutt Day, Sep 1
Inane Answering Message Day, Jan 30
Invention: Anniv, Mar 10
On-Hold Month, Natl, Mar 1
Push-Button Debuts: Anniv, Nov 18
Television
Abbott and Costello Show TV Premiere: Anniv, Dec 5
Addams Family Premiere: Anniv, Sep 18
Adventures of Ellery Queen Premiere: Anniv, Oct 14
Alfred Hitchcock Presents Premiere: Anniv, Oct 2
Alice Premiere: Anniv, Aug 31
All in the Family Premiere: Anniv, Jan 12
All My Children Premiere: Anniv, Jan 5
Alvin Show Premiere: Anniv, Oct 4
American Bandstand Premiere: Anniv, Aug 5
American Idol Premiere: Anniv, Jun 11
America's Most Wanted Premiere: Anniv, Feb 7
Amos 'n' Andy Premiere: Anniv, Jun 28
Andy Griffith Show Premiere: Anniv, Oct 3
Andy Williams Show Premiere: Anniv, Jul 2
Another World Premiere: Anniv, May 4
Arsenio Hall Show Premiere: Anniv, Jan 3
Art Linkletter's House Party Premiere: Anniv, Sep 1
Arthur Murray Party Premiere: Anniv, Jul 20
As the World Turns Premiere: Anniv, Apr 2
Bachelor Father Premiere: Anniv, Sep 15
Barnaby Jones Premiere: Anniv, Jan 28
Barney & Friends Premiere: Anniv, Apr 6
Barney Miller Premiere: Anniv, Jan 23
Batman Premiere: Anniv, Jan 12
Baywatch Premiere: Anniv, Apr 23
Beat the Clock Premiere: Anniv, Mar 23
Beauty and the Beast Premiere: Anniv, Sep 25
Believe It or Not Premiere: Anniv, Mar 1
Beverly Hillbillies Premiere: Anniv, Sep 26
Bewitched Premiere: Anniv, Sep 17
Big Top Premiere: Anniv, Jul 1
Bob Hope Show Premiere: Anniv, Oct 12
Bob Newhart Show Premiere: Anniv, Oct 10
Bold and the Beautiful Premiere: Anniv, Mar 23
Brady Bunch Premiere: Anniv, Sep 26
Brothers Premiere: Anniv, Jul 13
Buck Rogers Premiere: Anniv, Apr 15
Buffy the Vampire Slayer Premiere: Anniv, Mar 10
Burns and Allen Show Premiere: Anniv, Oct 12
Cagney & Lacey Premiere: Anniv, Mar 25
Candid Camera Premiere: Anniv, Aug 10
Captain Kangaroo Premiere: Anniv, Oct 3
Captain Midnight Premiere: Anniv, Sep 4
Captain Video and His Video Rangers Premiere: Anniv, Jun 27
Carol Burnett Show Premiere: Anniv, Sep 11
Cathode-Ray Tube Patented: Anniv, Dec 20
Catholic Hour Premiere: Anniv, Jan 4
Cavalcade of Stars Premiere: Anniv, Jun 4
CBS Evening News Premiere: Anniv, May 3
Charlie's Angels Premiere: Anniv, Sep 22
Cheers Premiere: Anniv, Sep 30
China Beach Premiere: Anniv, Apr 26
CHiPs Premiere: Anniv, Sep 15
CNN Debut: Anniv, Jun 1
College Bowl Premiere: Anniv, Jan 4
Columbo Premiere: Anniv, Sep 15
Cops Premiere: Anniv, Mar 11
Cosby Show Premiere: Anniv, Sep 20
Court TV Debut: Anniv, Jul 1
CSI: Crime Scene Investigation Premiere: Anniv, Oct 6
Dallas Premiere: Anniv, Apr 2
Daniel Boone Premiere: Anniv, Sep 24
Dark Shadows Premiere: Anniv, Jun 27
Dating Game Premiere: Anniv, Dec 20
Davy Crockett Premiere: Anniv, Dec 15
Days of Our Lives Premiere: Anniv, Nov 8
Dick Cavett Show Premiere: Anniv, Mar 4
Dick Clark Retires from American Bandstand: Anniv, Mar 23
Dick Van Dyke Show Premiere: Anniv, Oct 3
Dinah Shore Show Premiere: Anniv, Nov 27
Ding Dong School Premiere: Anniv, Dec 22
Doctor Who Premiere: Anniv, Nov 23
Doctors Premiere: Anniv, Apr 1
Donny and Marie Premiere: Anniv, Jan 16
Dragnet Premiere: Anniv, Dec 16
Dukes of Hazzard Premiere: Anniv, Jan 26
Dynasty Premiere: Anniv, Jan 12
Ebert & Roeper and the Movies (Sneak Previews) Premiere: Anniv, Oct 12
Ed Sullivan Show Premiere: Anniv, Jun 20
Edge of Night Premiere: Anniv, Apr 2
Eight Is Enough Premiere: Anniv, Mar 15
Emergency Premiere: Anniv, Jan 22
ER Premiere: Anniv, Sep 19
Ernie Kovacs Premiere: Anniv, May 14
Evening at Pops Premiere: Anniv, Jul 12
Face the Nation Premiere: Anniv, Nov 7
Facts of Life Premiere: Anniv, Aug 24
Falcon Crest Premiere: Anniv, Dec 4
Fame Premiere: Anniv, Jan 7
Family Feud Premiere: Anniv, Jul 12
Family Ties Premiere: Anniv, Sep 22
Fantasy Island Premiere: Anniv, Jan 28
Farnsworth, Philo: Birth Anniv, Aug 19
Fat Albert and the Cosby Kids Premiere: Anniv, Sep 9
Fireside Theatre Premiere: Anniv, Apr 5
First Baseball Games Televised: Anniv, Aug 26
First Color TV Broadcast: Anniv, Jun 25
First Presidential Telecast: Anniv, Apr 30
First Scheduled Broadcast: Anniv, Jul 1
First Televised Presidential Debate: Anniv, Sep 26
First Televised Presidential News Conf: Anniv, Jan 25
Flintstones Premiere: Anniv, Sep 30
Flipper Premiere: Anniv, Sep 19
Flying Nun Premiere: Anniv, Sep 7
48 Hours Premiere: Anniv, Jan 19
Frasier Premiere: Anniv, Sep 16
Fred Waring Show Premiere: Anniv, Apr 17
French Chef Premiere: Anniv, Feb 11

Friends Premiere: Anniv, Sep 22
Frontline Premiere: Anniv, Jan 17
Fugitive Premiere: Anniv, Sep 17
Gene Autry Show Premiere: Anniv, Jul 23
General Electric Theater Premiere: Anniv, Feb 1
General Hospital Premiere: Anniv, Apr 1
Gentle Ben Premiere: Anniv, Sep 10
George Gobel Show Premiere: Anniv, Oct 2
Get Smart Premiere: Anniv, Sep 18
Gilligan's Island Premiere: Anniv, Sep 26
Goldbergs Premiere: Anniv, Jan 17
Golden Girls Premiere: Anniv, Sep 14
Golden Globe Awards, Jan 11
Gong Show Premiere: Anniv, Jun 14
Good Morning America Premiere: Anniv, Nov 6
Good Sex! with Dr. Ruth Westheimer Premiere: Anniv, Aug 27
Good Times Premiere: Anniv, Feb 1
Guiding Light Premiere: Anniv, Jun 26
Gumby Show Premiere: Anniv, Mar 16
Gunsmoke Premiere: Anniv, Sep 10
Hallmark Hall of Fame Premiere: Anniv, Jan 6
Happy Days Premiere: Anniv, Jan 15
Have Gun Will Travel Premiere: Anniv, Sep 14
Hawaii Five-O Premiere: Anniv, Sep 26
Hazel Premiere: Anniv, Sep 28
Hee Haw Premiere: Anniv, Jun 15
Hill Street Blues Premiere: Anniv, Jan 15
Hollywood Squares Premiere: Anniv, Oct 17
Home Improvement Premiere: Anniv, Sep 17
Hopalong Cassidy Premiere: Anniv, Jun 24
Howdy Doody Premiere: Anniv, Dec 27
I Love Lucy Premiere: Anniv, Oct 15
I Spy Premiere: Anniv, Sep 15
In Living Color Premiere: Anniv, Apr 15
Incredible Hulk Premiere: Anniv, Mar 10
Ironside Premiere: Anniv, Sep 14
It Takes a Thief Premiere: Anniv, Jan 9
I've Got a Secret Premiere: Anniv, Jun 19
Jack Benny Program Premiere: Anniv, Oct 28
Jeffersons Premiere: Anniv, Jan 18
Jeopardy Premiere: Anniv, Mar 30
Jetsons Premiere: Anniv, Sep 23
Jimmy Durante Show Premiere: Anniv, Oct 2
Joe Franklin Day, Mar 9
Johnny Carson's Final Show: Anniv, May 22
King Family Show Premiere: Anniv, Jan 23
Knight Rider Premiere: Anniv, Sep 26
Kraft Television Theatre Premiere: Anniv, May 7
Kukla, Fran and Ollie Premiere: Anniv, Nov 29
Kung Fu Premiere: Anniv, Oct 1
LA Law Premiere: Anniv, Oct 3
Larry King Show Premiere: Anniv, Mar 13
Lassie Premiere: Anniv, Sep 12
Late Night with David Letterman Premiere: Anniv, Feb 1
Laugh-In Premiere: Anniv, Jan 22
Laverne and Shirley Premiere: Anniv, Jan 27
Law & Order Premiere: Anniv, Sep 13
Lawrence Welk Show Premiere: Anniv, Jul 2
Leave It to Beaver Premiere: Anniv, Oct 4
Let's Make a Deal Premiere: Anniv, Dec 30
Liberace Show Premiere: Anniv, Jul 1
Little House on the Prairie Premiere: Anniv, Sep 11
Lone Ranger Premiere: Anniv, Sep 15
Look Up and Live Premiere: Anniv, Jan 3
Love Boat Premiere: Anniv, Sep 24
Love Is a Many Splendored Thing Premiere: Anniv, Sep 18
Love of Life Premiere: Anniv, Sep 24
M*A*S*H Final Episode: Anniv, Feb 28
M*A*S*H Premiere: Anniv, Sep 17
MacNeil-Lehrer Newshour Premiere: Anniv, Sep 5
Magnum, PI Premiere: Anniv, Dec 11
Make Room for Daddy Premiere: Anniv, Sep 29
Mama Premiere: Anniv, Jul 1
Mannix Premiere: Anniv, Sep 16
Married with Children Premiere: Anniv, Apr 5
Mary Tyler Moore Show Premiere: Anniv, Sep 19
Masterpiece Theatre Premiere: Anniv, Jan 10
Maude Premiere: Anniv, Sep 12
Maverick Premiere: Anniv, Sep 22
Meet the Press Premiere: Anniv, Nov 6
Merv Griffin Show Premiere: Anniv, Oct 1
Mickey Mouse Club Premiere: Anniv, Oct 3
Middlemark, Marvin: Birth Anniv, Sep 16
Mighty Mouse Playhouse Premiere: Anniv, Dec 10
Millionaire Premiere: Anniv, Jan 19
Minow, Newton: Birth, Jan 17
Mission: Impossible Premiere: Anniv, Sep 17
Mister Rogers' Neighborhood Premiere: Anniv, May 22
Monday Night Football Premiere: Anniv, Sep 21
Monkees Premiere: Anniv, Sep 12
Monty Python's Flying Circus Premiere: Anniv, Oct 5
Moonlighting Premiere: Anniv, Mar 3
Mr Peepers Premiere: Anniv, Jul 3
Mr Wizard Premiere: Anniv, Mar 3
MTV Premiere: Anniv, Aug 1
Munsters Premiere: Anniv, Sep 24
Muppet Show Premiere: Anniv, Sep 13
Murder, She Wrote Premiere: Anniv, Sep 30
Murphy Brown Premiere: Anniv, Nov 14
My Friend Flicka Premiere: Anniv, Feb 10
My Little Margie Premiere: Anniv, Jun 15
Name That Tune Premiere: Anniv, Jul 6
Nat King Cole Show Premiere: Anniv, Nov 5
Natl Traffic Directors Day, Nov 2
Newhart Premiere: Anniv, Oct 25
Newlywed Game Premiere: Anniv, Jul 11
Nick at Nite Debut: Anniv, Jul 1
Nickelodeon Debut: Anniv, Apr 2
Nielsen, Arthur Charles: Birth Anniv, Sep 5
Night Court Premiere: Anniv, Jan 4
Northern Exposure Premiere: Anniv, Jul 12
NYPD Blue Premiere: Anniv, Sep 21
Omnibus Premiere: Anniv, Nov 9
One Day at a Time Premiere: Anniv, Dec 16
One Life to Live Premiere: Anniv, Jul 15
Oprah Winfrey Show Premiere: Anniv, Sep 8
Our Miss Brooks Premiere: Anniv, Oct 3
Ozark Jubilee Premiere: Anniv, Jan 22
Ozzie and Harriet Premiere: Anniv, Oct 3
Pat Boone Show Premiere: Anniv, Oct 3
Perry Como Show Premiere: Anniv, Dec 24
Perry Mason Premiere: Anniv, Sep 21
Phil Donahue Show Premiere: Anniv, Nov 6
Phil Silvers Show Premiere: Anniv, Sep 20
Price Is Right Premiere: Anniv, Nov 26
Primetime Live Premiere: Anniv, Aug 3
Prisoner Premiere: Anniv, Jun 1
Public Television Debuts: Anniv, Nov 3
Queen for a Day Premiere: Anniv, Jan 3
Quincy Premiere: Anniv, Oct 3
Quiz Kids Premiere: Anniv, Jul 6
Rawhide Premiere: Anniv, Jan 9
Real McCoys Premiere: Anniv, Oct 3
Real People Premiere: Anniv, Apr 18
Red Skelton Show Premiere: Anniv, Sep 30
Remington Steele Premiere: Anniv, Oct 1
Rhoda Premiere: Anniv, Sep 9
Rocky and His Friends Premiere: Anniv, Nov 19
Rookies Premiere: Anniv, Sep 11
Roseanne Premiere: Anniv, Oct 18
Roy Rogers Show Premiere: Anniv, Dec 30
Ryan's Hope Premiere: Anniv, Jul 7
Saint Elsewhere Premiere: Anniv, Oct 26
Sanford and Son Premiere: Anniv, Jan 14
Saturday Night Live Premiere: Anniv, Oct 11
Scarecrow and Mrs King Premiere: Anniv, Oct 3
Scooby-Doo, Where Are You? Premiere: Anniv, Sep 13
Search for Tomorrow Premiere: Anniv, Sep 3
Secret Agent Premiere: Anniv, Apr 5
Secret Storm Premiere: Anniv, Feb 1
See It Now Premiere: Anniv, Nov 18
Seinfeld Premiere: Anniv, May 31
Sesame Street Premiere: Anniv, Nov 10
Sex and the City Premiere: Anniv, Jun 6
Shirley Temple Theatre Premiere: Anniv, Sep 18
Simpsons Premiere: Anniv, Dec 17
Six Million Dollar Man Premiere: Anniv, Oct 20
$64,000 Question Premiere: Anniv, Jun 7
Sixty Minutes Premiere: Anniv, Sep 24
Smothers Brothers Fired: Anniv, Apr 4
Sneak Previews Premiere: Anniv, Oct 12
Soap Premiere: Anniv, Sep 13
Sopranos Premiere: Anniv, Jan 13
Soupy Sales Show Premiere: Anniv, Jul 4
Star Trek Premiere: Anniv, Sep 8
Starman Month, Intl, Oct 1
Steve Allen Show Premiere: Anniv, Dec 25
Stop the Music Premiere: Anniv, May 5
Survivor Premiere: Anniv, May 31
Switches from Analog to Digital (US), Feb 17
Talent Scouts Premiere: Anniv, Dec 6
Tales of Wells Fargo Premiere: Anniv, Mar 18
Tarzan Premiere: Anniv, Sep 8
Ted Mack's Original Amateur Hour Premiere: Anniv, Jan 18
Television Academy Hall of Fame First Inductees, Mar 4
Texaco Star Theater Premiere: Anniv, Sep 21
That Girl Premiere: Anniv, Sep 8
3rd Rock from the Sun Premiere: Anniv, Jan 9

Thirtysomething Premiere: Anniv, Sep 29
This Is Your Life Premiere: Anniv, Oct 1
Three's Company Premiere: Anniv, Mar 15
Tiny Tim Weds Miss Vicki on The Tonight Show: Anniv, Dec 17
To Tell the Truth Premiere: Anniv, Dec 18
Today Premiere: Anniv, Jan 14
Tom Corbett, Space Cadet Premiere: Anniv, Oct 1
Tonight Show Premiere: Anniv, Sep 27
Tracey Ullman Show Premiere: Anniv, Apr 5
Truth or Consequences Premiere: Anniv, Sep 7
20/20 Premiere: Anniv, Jun 6
21 Jump Street Premiere: Anniv, Apr 12
Twenty Questions Premiere: Anniv, Nov 26
Twilight Zone Premiere: Anniv, Oct 2
Upstairs, Downstairs Premiere: Anniv, Oct 10
Vast Wasteland Speech: Anniv, May 9
Virginian Premiere: Anniv, Sep 19
Wagon Train Premiere: Anniv, Sep 18
Walt Disney Premiere: Anniv, Oct 27
Waltons Premiere: Anniv, Sep 14
Welcome Back, Kotter Premiere: Anniv, Sep 9
Welk, Lawrence: Birth Anniv, Mar 11
What's My Line? Premiere: Anniv, Feb 2
Wheel of Fortune Premiere: Anniv, Jan 6
Wonder Years Premiere: Anniv, Mar 15
World Television Day (UN), Nov 21
Wyatt Earp Premiere: Anniv, Sep 6
X-Files Premiere: Anniv, Sep 10
You Are There Premiere: Anniv, Feb 1
You Bet Your Life Premiere: Anniv, Oct 5
Young and the Restless Premiere: Anniv, Mar 26
Your Hit Parade Premiere: Anniv, Oct 7
Your Show of Shows Premiere: Anniv, Feb 25
Zane Grey Theater Premiere: Anniv, Oct 5
Zoo Parade Premiere: Anniv, May 28
Tell the Truth Day, Jul 7
Teller, Edward: Birth Anniv, Jan 15
Teller: Birth, Feb 14
Telluride Blues & Brews Fest (Telluride, CO), Sep 18
Telluride Wine Fest (Telluride, CO), Jun 25
Telstar: Space Milestone, Jul 10
Temple, Shirley: Birth, Apr 23
Ten Most Wanted List Debuts: Anniv, Mar 14
Ten-Four Day, Oct 4
Tennant, David: Birth, Apr 18
Tennant, Victoria: Birth, Sep 30
Tennessee
Admission Day, Jun 1
Alexander, Lamar: Birth, Jul 30
Battle of Chattanooga: Anniv, Nov 24
Battle of Nashville: Anniv, Dec 16
Battle of Shiloh: Anniv, Apr 6
Bredesen, Phil: Birth, Nov 21
Christmas in Old Appalachia (Clinton), Dec 6
Corker, Bob: Birth, Aug 24
Elvis Presley's Birthday Celebration (Memphis), Jan 8
Elvis Week (Memphis), Aug 8
Family Day, Aug 30
Family, Career and Community Leaders of America Natl Leadership Mtg (Nashville), Jul 12
Field Trial Chmpshp, Natl (Bird Dogs) (Grand Junction), Feb 9
First Grand Ole Opry Broadcast: Anniv, Dec 10
Great Smoky Mountains Natl Park Established: Anniv, Jun 15
July Fourth Celebration & Anvil Shoot (Clinton), Jul 4
Mid-South Fair (Memphis), Sep 18
Miss Tennessee Pageant (Jackson), Jun 17
Mule Day (Columbia), Apr 2
NAIA Div I Women's Basketball Chmpshp (Jackson), Mar 18
Oak Ridge Atomic Plant Begun: Anniv, Aug 1
Old-Time Fiddlers' Jamboree (Smithville), Jul 3
Polk County Ramp Tramp Fest (Benton), Apr 24
Religious Travel Expo, World (Nashville), Oct 28
Riverbend Fest (Chattanooga), Jun 5
Rock of Chickamauga: Anniv, Sep 20
Smoky Mountains Storytelling Fest (Pigeon Forge), Jun 4
Southern Fest of Books (Nashville), Oct 9
State Fair (Nashville), Sep 4
Storytelling Fest, Natl (Jonesborough), Oct 2
TACA Fall Craft Fair (Nashville), Sep 25
Tennessee Fall Homecoming (Norris), Oct 7
Tennessee Walking Horse Natl Celebration (Shelbyville), Aug 26
World's Biggest Fish Fry (Paris), Apr 20
Tenney, Jon: Birth, Dec 16
Tenniel, John: Birth Anniv, Feb 28
Tennille, Toni: Birth, May 8
Tennis
Big Ten Men's Chmpshp (Ann Arbor, MI), Apr 23
Big Ten Women's Chmpshp (Madison, WI), Apr 23
Lawn Tennis Chmpshps at Wimbledon (London, England), Jun 22
NAIA Men's & Women's Natl Chmpshps (Mobile, AL), May 11
NCAA Div I Men's and Women's Chmpshps (College Station, TX), May 14
Tennis Month, May 1
Tennyson, Alfred, Lord: Birth Anniv, Aug 6
Teresa, Mother: Birth Anniv, Aug 27
Tereshkova-Nikolaeva, Valentina: Birth, Mar 6
Terkel, Studs: Birth, May 16
Terrorism: Attack on America: Anniv, Sep 11
Terrorism: Bali Bombing: Anniv, Oct 12
Terrorism: London Bombings: Anniv, Jul 7
Terrorism: Madrid Train Bombings: Anniv, Mar 11
Terrorism: World Trade Center Bombing of 1993: Anniv, Feb 26
Terry, Ellen: Birth Anniv, Feb 27
Terry, John: Birth, Dec 7
Tesh, John: Birth, Jul 9
Testaverde, Vinny: Birth, Nov 13
Tester, Jon: Birth, Aug 21
Testicular Cancer Awareness Week, Apr 1
Test-Tube Baby: Birthday, Jul 25
Tet Offensive Begins: Anniv, Jan 30
Tet: See Chinese New Year, Jan 26
Tetonkaha Rendezvous (Lake Benton, MN), Aug 7
Teutul, Paul, Jr: Birth, Oct 2
Teutul, Paul, Sr: Birth, May 1
Texaco Star Theater TV Premiere: Anniv, Sep 21
Texas
Admission Day, Dec 29
Aggie Muster (College Station), Apr 21
AT&T Cotton Bowl Classic (Dallas), Jan 2
Bayfest (Corpus Christi), Sep 25
Big Bend Natl Park Established: Anniv, Jun 12
Bob Wills Day (Turkey), Apr 25
Branch Davidian Fire at Waco: Anniv, Apr 19
Celebration of the Horse (Houston), Jul 18
Charro Days Fiesta (Brownsville), Feb 26
Clear Lake Crawfish Fest (Seabrook), Apr 3
Clute's Christmas in the Park (Clute), Dec 8
Comal County Fair (New Braunfels), Sep 23
Come and Take It Fest (Gonzales), Oct 2
Confederate Heroes Day, Jan 19
Cornyn, John: Birth, Feb 2
Cowboy Poetry Gathering (Alpine), Feb 27
Dallas Cup (Frisco), Apr 5
Dallas YMCA Turkey Trot (Dallas), Nov 26
Dickens on the Strand (Galveston), Dec 5
East Texas Poultry Fest (Center), Oct 1
East Texas Yamboree (Gilmer), Oct 14
Electra Goat BBQ Cook-Off (Electra), May 8
Emancipation Day, Jun 19
Fall Citywide Garage Sale (Electra), Oct 3
Fiesta San Antonio (San Antonio), Apr 17
Fireant Fest (Marshall), Oct 10
Galveston Historic Homes Tour (Galveston Island), May 2
Galveston Hurricane: Anniv, Sep 8
Great Texas Mosquito Fest (Clute), Jul 23
Guadalupe Natl Park Established: Anniv, Sep 30
Hogeye Fest (Elgin), Oct 24
Hotter 'n Hell Hundred Bike Race (Wichita Falls), Aug 27
Houston Art Car Parade (Houston), May 9
Houston Livestock Show/Rodeo (Houston), Mar 3
Houston Marathon (Houston), Jan 18
Hummer/Bird Celebration (Rockport, Fulton), Sep 17
Hutchison, Kay Bailey: Birth, Jul 22
Independence Day, Mar 2
Juneteenth, Jun 19
KidFilm® Fest (Dallas), Jan 12
Kingsville Intl Young Performers' Competitions (Kingsville), Apr 2
O. Henry Museum Pun-Off (Austin), May 16
Oatmeal Fest (Bertram/Oatmeal), Sep 4
Oil Bowl Football Classic (Wichita Falls), Jun 20
One Arm Dove Hunt (Olney), Sep 11
Parade of Lights (Kingsville), Dec 5
Perry, Rick: Birth, Mar 4
Poetry Contest (El Paso), Jan 1
Posada de Kingsville (Kingsville), Nov 26
Poteet Strawberry Fest (Poteet), Apr 3
Prairie Dog Chili Cook-off/Quail-Egg Eat (Grand Prairie), Apr 4
Quadrangle Fest (Texarkana), Oct 10
Ranch Hand Breakfast (Kingsville), Nov 21

Re/Max Ballunar Liftoff Fest (Houston), Oct 30
Reenactment of Cowtown's Last Gunfight (Fort Worth), Feb 8
Rio Grande Valley Livestock Show (Mercedes), Mar 13
Rockport Seafair (Rockport), Oct 9
San Jacinto Day, Apr 21
South by Southwest (Austin), Mar 13
South Texas Wildlife and Birding Fest (Kingsville), Nov 19
Southwestern Expo Livestock Show/Rodeo (Fort Worth), Jan 16
Sporting Goods Assn Mgmt Conf, Natl (San Antonio), May 3
Spring Swing City Garage Sale (Electra), Apr 4
State Fair (Dallas), Sep 25
Summer Reading Club (El Paso), Jun 6
Sun Bowl (El Paso), Dec 31
Texas Book Fest (Austin), Oct 31
Texas City Disaster: Anniv, Apr 16
Texas Folklife Fest (San Antonio), Jun 12
Texas Hill Country Wine & Food Fest (Austin), Apr 16
Texas Love the Children Day, Mar 29
Texas Panhandle Tornado: Anniv, Apr 9
USA Film Fest (Dallas), Apr 29
Van Cliburn Intl Piano Competition (Fort Worth), May 22
Washington's Birthday Celebration (Laredo), Jan 22
Watermelon Thump (Luling), Jun 25
Western Days (Elgin), Jun 23
Westfest (West), Sep 4
Wonderland of Lights (Marshall), Nov 25
World Chmpshp BBQ Goat Cook-off/Crafts Fair (Brady), Sep 5
World's Largest Rattlesnake Roundup (Sweetwater), Mar 13
Texas County Fair/Old Settlers Reunion (Houston, MO), Aug 5
Thackeray, William: Birth Anniv, Jul 18
Thailand
Birthday of the Queen, Aug 12
Chakri Day, Apr 6
Chulalongkorn Day, Oct 23
Constitution Day, Dec 10
Coronation Day, May 5
Elephant Roundup at Surin, Nov 21
King's Birthday and National Day, Dec 5
Midyear Day (Half-Year Day), Jul 1
Songkran Fest, Apr 13
Thank God It's Monday! Day, Natl, Jan 5
Thank You Note Day, Natl, Dec 26
Thanksgiving Day, Nov 26
Thanksgiving Day (Canada), Oct 12
Thanksgiving Day (Pres Proc), Nov 26
Thanksgiving, Turkey-Free, Nov 26
Thanksgiving: Tie One on Day, Nov 25
Tharp, Twyla: Birth, Jul 1
That Girl TV Premiere: Anniv, Sep 8
That Sucks Day, Natl, Apr 15
Thatcher, Margaret: Birthday, Oct 13
Thatcher, Margaret: First Woman British Prime Minister: Anniv, May 4
Thayer, Ernest L.: Birth Anniv, Aug 14
Thayer, Sylvanus: Birth Anniv, Jun 9
Theater. See also Opera
Astor Place Riot: Anniv, May 10
Black Hills Passion Play (Spearfish, SD), Jun 2
Cats Premiere: Anniv, Oct 7
Coward, Noel: Birth Anniv, Dec 16
Death of a Salesman Premiere: Anniv, Feb 10
Donna Reed Performing Arts Fest (Denison, IA), Jun 15
Edmonton Intl Fringe Theatre Fest (Edmonton, AB, Canada), Aug 13
First Actor to Perform in Two Cities Same Day: Anniv, Feb 10
First Play Presented in North American Colonies: Anniv, Aug 27
First Tony Awards Presented: Anniv, Apr 6
George Spelvin Day, Nov 15
Hair Broadway Opening: Anniv, Mar 28
Harrison Fest of Arts (Harrison Hot Springs, BC, Canada), Jul 11
Laura Ingalls Wilder Pageant (De Smet, SD), Jul 10
Music Man Premiere: Anniv, Dec 19
Odets, Clifford: Birth Anniv, Jul 18
Oklahoma! Broadway Premiere: Anniv, Mar 31
Outdoor Summer Theater (Farmington, NM), Jun 19
Papp, Joseph: Birth Anniv, Jun 22
Phantom of the Opera Broadway Premiere: Anniv, Jan 26
Shakespeare on the Green (Omaha, NE), Jun 18
Streetcar Named Desire Broadway Opening: Anniv, Dec 3
Tecumseh! Epic Outdoor Drama (Chillicothe, OH), Jun 12
Theater in North America, First Performance: Anniv, Apr 30
Walter Plinge Day (England), Dec 2
West Side Story Premiere: Anniv, Sep 26
Williams, Tennessee: Birth Anniv, Mar 26
Winnipeg Fringe Theatre Fest (Winnipeg, MB, Canada), Jul 15
Ziegfeld Follies of 1907: Anniv, Jul 8
Theisman, Joe: Birth, Sep 9
Theodore Roosevelt Natl Park Established: Anniv, Apr 25
Theodosius I: Birth Anniv, Jan 11
Theron, Charlize: Birth, Aug 7
Theroux, Paul: Birth, Apr 10
Thewlis, David: Birth, Mar 20
3rd Rock from the Sun TV Premiere: Anniv, Jan 9
Thible, Marie: First Free Flight by a Woman: Anniv, Jun 4
Thicke, Alan: Birth, Mar 1
Thiessen, Tiffani-Amber: Birth, Jan 23
Thinking, Intl Strategic, Month, Sep 1
Thinking: Ask a Question Day, Intl, Mar 14
Thinking: Use Your Common Sense Day, Nov 4
Thinnes, Roy: Birth, Apr 6
Third Punic War: Ends: Anniv, Feb 5
Third Shift Workers Day, Natl, May 13
Third World Day: Anniv, Apr 18
Thirtysomething TV Premiere: Anniv, Sep 29
This Is Your Life TV Premiere: Anniv, Oct 1
Thomas Jefferson Day (Pres Proc), Apr 13
Thomas, B.J.: Birth, Aug 7
Thomas, Betty: Birth, Jul 27
Thomas, Clarence: Birth, Jun 23
Thomas, Danny: Birth Anniv, Jan 6
Thomas, Dylan: Birth Anniv, Oct 27
Thomas, Frank: Birth, May 27
Thomas, Helen: Birth, Aug 4
Thomas, Henry: Birth, Sep 8
Thomas, Isaiah: Birth Anniv, Jan 30
Thomas, Isiah: Birth, Apr 30
Thomas, Jonathan Taylor: Birth, Sep 8
Thomas, Kurt: Birth, Mar 29
Thomas, Lowell: Birth Anniv, Apr 6
Thomas, Marlo: Birth, Nov 21
Thomas, Martha Carey: Birth Anniv, Jan 2
Thomas, Michael Tilson: Birth, Dec 21
Thomas, Philip Michael: Birth, May 26
Thomas, Richard: Birth, Jun 13
Thomas, Robert B.: Birth Anniv, Apr 24
Thomas, Sean Patrick: Birth, Dec 17
Thome, Jim: Birth, Aug 27
Thompson, Emma: Birth, Apr 14
Thompson, Fred: Birth, Aug 19
Thompson, Hunter S.: Birth Anniv, Jul 18
Thompson, Jack: Birth, Aug 31
Thompson, John: Birth, Sep 2
Thompson, LaMarcus: First Roller Coaster Opens: Anniv, Jun 13
Thompson, Lea: Birth, May 31
Thompson, Sada: Birth, Sep 27
Thomson, Charles: Birth Anniv, Nov 29
Thoreau, Henry David: Birth Anniv, Jul 12
Thorne-Smith, Courtney: Birth, Nov 8
Thornton, Billy Bob: Birth, Aug 4
Thornton, Matthew: Death Anniv, Jun 24
Thorpe, James: Birth Anniv, May 28
Three Kings Day, Jan 6
300 Millionth American Born: Anniv, Oct 17
Three Stooges
De Rita, Joe: Birth Anniv, Jul 12
Fine, Larry: Birth Anniv, Oct 5
Howard, Curly: Birth Anniv, Oct 22
Howard, Moe: Birth Anniv, Jun 19
Howard, Shemp: Birth Anniv, Mar 17
Three's Company TV Premiere: Anniv, Mar 15
Threshing Bee, Norskedalen's (Coon Valley, WI), Sep 26
Thumb, Tom: Birth Anniv, Jan 4
Thune, John R.: Birth, Jan 7
Thurber, James: Birth Anniv, Dec 8
Thurman, Uma: Birth, Apr 29
Thurmond, Nate: Birth, Jul 25
Thurmond, Strom: Birth Anniv, Dec 5
Tiananmen Square Massacre: Anniv, Jun 4
Tibet: Dalai Lama Flees Tibet: Anniv, Mar 31
Tick Tock Day, Dec 29
Ticotin, Rachel: Birth, Nov 1
Tides, Perigean Spring, Jan 11
Tides, Perigean Spring, Jun 22
Tides, Perigean Spring, Jul 21
Tidewater Archaeology Dig (St. Mary's City, MD), Jul 25
Tie Month, Natl, Dec 1
Tierney, Gene: Birth Anniv, Nov 20
Tierney, Maura: Birth, Feb 3
Tiffany, Charles L.: Birth Anniv, Feb 15
Tiffany, Louis C.: Birth Anniv, Feb 18
Tiffin, Pamela: Birth, Oct 13
Tighe, Kevin: Birth, Aug 13
Tilbrook, Glenn: Birth, Aug 31
Tilden, Bill: Birth Anniv, Feb 10
Till, Emmett: Death Anniv, Aug 28
Tillis, Mel: Birth, Aug 8
Tilly, Jennifer: Birth, Sep 16
Tilly, Meg: Birth, Feb 14
Timberlake, Justin: Birth, Jan 31
Time; Calendars
Be Late for Something Day, Sep 5
Daylight Saving Time Begins (US), Mar 8
Daylight Saving Time Ends (US), Nov 1
Greenwich Mean Time Begins: Anniv, Sep 25
Leap Second Adjustment Time, Jun 30
Leap Second Adjustment Time, Dec 31
Prime Meridian Set: Anniv, Nov 1

Summer Daylight-Saving Time (Europe), Mar 29
Summer Time (United Kingdom), Mar 29
Time Zone Plan, US Uniform: Anniv, Nov 18
US Standard Time Act: Anniv, Mar 19
War Time: Anniv, Feb 9
Time Magazine First Published: Anniv, Mar 3
Time Management
It's About Time Week, Dec 25
Revise Your Work Schedule Month, May 1
Take Back Your Time Week, Natl, Jan 26
Time Management Month, Natl, Feb 1
Zero-Tasking Day, Nov 1
Tin Can Patent: Anniv, Jan 19
Tinker to Evers to Chance Lines in "Baseball's Sad Lexicon" First Published: Anniv, Jul 10
Tinker to Evers to Chance: First Double Play Anniv, Sep 15
Tinker, Grant: Birth, Jan 11
Tinker, Joe: Birth Anniv, Jul 27
Tinsley, Jamaal: Birth, Feb 28
Tiny Tim Weds Miss Vicki on The Tonight Show: Anniv, Dec 17
Tip-Up Town USA (Houghton Lake, MI), Jan 16
Tisdale, Ashley: Birth, Jul 2
Tisha B'Av (Fast of Ab), Jul 30
Titan II Missile Explosion: Anniv, Sep 19
Titanic (Film) Released: Anniv, Dec 19
Titanic Discovered: Anniv, Sep 1
Titanic, Sinking of the: Anniv, Apr 15
Tito (Josip Broz): Birth Anniv, May 25
Tittle, Y.A.: Birth, Oct 24
Tivoli Gardens Season (Copenhagen, Denmark), May 1
Tkachuk, Keith: Birth, Mar 28
To Kill a Mockingbird Published: Anniv, Jul 11
To Tell the Truth TV Premiere: Anniv, Dec 18
Toad Hollow Day of Encouragement, Jan 26
Toad Hollow Day of Thank You, Jun 20
Toad Hollow Week, Natl, Mar 14
Toad Suck Daze (Conway, AR), May 1
Tobago
Emancipation Day, Aug 1
Independence Day, Aug 31
Spiritual Baptist Liberation Shouter Day, Mar 30
Tobolowsky, Stephen: Birth, May 30
Tocqueville, Alexis de: Birth Anniv, Jul 29
Today TV Premiere: Anniv, Jan 14
Todd, Beverly: Birth, Jul 11
Toffler, Alvin: Birth, Oct 4
Togo
Independence Day, Apr 27
Liberation Day, Jan 13
Tojo Hideki: Execution Anniv, Dec 23
Tolerance, Intl Day for (UN), Nov 16
Tolkan, James: Birth, Jun 20
Tolkien Week, Sep 20
Tolkien, J.R.R.: Birth Anniv, Jan 3
Tolkien, J.R.R.: Hobbit Day, Sep 22
Tolkien, J.R.R.: Lord of the Rings, First Part Published: Anniv, Jul 19
Toll Collection Machine, First Automatic: Anniv, Nov 19
Tolstoy, Leo: Birth Anniv, Sep 9
Tom Corbett, Space Cadet TV Premiere: Anniv, Oct 1
Tom Sawyer Days, Natl (Hannibal, MO), Jul 1
Tomatina, La (Spain), Aug 26
Tomato Month, Fresh Florida, Apr 1
Tomb-Sweeping Day (China), Apr 4
Tomb-Sweeping Day, Natl (Taiwan), Apr 5
Tomczak, Mike: Birth, Oct 23
Tomei, Concetta: Birth, Dec 30
Tomei, Marisa: Birth, Dec 4
Tomjanovich, Rudy: Birth, Nov 24
Tomlin, Lily: Birth, Sep 1
Tomlinson, LaDanian: Birth, Jun 23
Tompkins, Daniel D.: Birth Anniv, Jun 21
Tonga: Emancipation Day, Jun 4
Tonight Show TV Premiere: Anniv, Sep 27
Tonight Show: Tiny Tim Weds Miss Vicki: Anniv, Dec 17
Tony Awards Presented, First: Anniv, Apr 6
Toomey, William: Birth, Jan 10
Tooth Fairy Day, Natl, Feb 28
Top Spinning Day, Intl, Oct 14
Tork, Peter: Birth, Feb 13
Torn, Rip: Birth, Feb 6
Torquemada, Tomas de: Death Anniv, Sep 16
Torre, Joe: Birth, Jul 18
Torres, Fernando: Birth, Mar 20
Toscanini, Arturo: Birth Anniv, Mar 25
Toss Away the "Could Haves" and "Should Haves" Day, Jul 18
Totenberg, Nina: Birth, Jan 14
Totti, Francesco: Birth, Sep 27
Toulouse-Lautrec, Henri de: Birth Anniv, Nov 24
Tour de France, Jul 4
Tourism Day, World, Sep 27
Tourism Week, Natl, May 9
Town Criers Day, Intl, Jul 13
Town Meeting Day (Vermont), Mar 3
Towne, Benjamin: First American Daily Newspaper Published: Anniv, May 30
Townsend, Robert: Birth, Feb 6
Townshend, Pete: Birth, May 19
Toynbee, Arnold J.: Birth Anniv, Apr 14
Toys
Barbie Debuts: Anniv, Mar 9
Coats & Toys for Kids Day (ME), Dec 5
Farm Toy Show & Auction (Sauk Centre, MN), Feb 14
Farm Toy Show, Natl (Dyersville, IA), Nov 6
G.I. Joe Introduced: Anniv, Feb 1
Safe Toys and Gifts Month, Dec 1
Summer Farm Toy Show (Dyersville, IA), Jun 5
Top Spinning Day, Intl, Oct 14
Toy Tips Executive Toy Test (New York, NY), Sep 1
Tracey Ullman Show TV Premiere: Anniv, Apr 5
Track and Field
Bannister Breaks Four-Minute Mile: Anniv, May 6
Big Ten Men's and Women's Outdoor Track/Field Chmpshps (Iowa City, IA), May 15
Big Ten Men's Indoor Track/Field Chmpshps (University Park, PA), Feb 28
Big Ten Women's Indoor Track/Field Chmpshps (Bloomington, IN), Feb 28
Jesse Owens's Remarkable Records: Anniv, May 25
NAIA Men's and Women's Cross-Country Natl Chmpshps, Nov 21
NAIA Men's and Women's Indoor Chmpshps, Mar 5
NAIA Men's and Women's Outdoor Chmpshps (St. Louis, MO), May 21
NCAA Div I Men's and Women's Track Chmpshps (Fayetteville, AR), Jun 10
NCAA Indoor Track/Field Chmpshps (College Station, TX), Mar 13
Simplot Games (Pocatello, ID), Feb 19
Tracy, Spencer: Birth Anniv, Apr 5
Trade Fair, Canton Autumn (China), Oct 15
Trade Show Image Week, Build a Better, Feb 15
Trade Week, World (Pres Proc), May 17
Trafalgar, Battle of: Anniv, Oct 21
Trail of Courage Living-History Fest (Rochester, IN), Sep 19
Trails Day, Natl, Jun 6
Train Day, Natl, May 9
Transatlantic Flight, First Nonstop: Anniv, Jun 14
Transatlantic Phoning: Anniv, Jan 7
Transcontinental Flight, First Scheduled: Anniv, Jan 25
Transfer Day (US Virgin Islands), Mar 31
Transistor Unveiled: Anniv, Dec 23
Transportation Week, Natl (Pres Proc), May 10
Travalena, Fred: Birth, Oct 6
Travanti, Daniel J.: Birth, Mar 7
Travel: American Adventures Month, Aug 1
Travelers with Disabilities Awareness Week, Nov 29
Travers, Mary: Birth, Nov 7
Travis, Nancy: Birth, Sep 21
Travis, Randy: Birth, May 4
Travis, William Barret: Birth Anniv, Aug 9
Travolta, John: Birth, Feb 18
Treasury Dept, US: Anniv, Sep 2
Treaty of Guadalupe Hidalgo: Anniv, Feb 2
Treaty of Paris Ends French and Indian War: Anniv, Feb 10
Trebek, Alex: Birth, Jul 22
Tree Planting Day, Natl (Lesotho), Mar 21
Tree-Sitting: Cohocton Fall Foliage Fest (Cohocton, NY), Oct 2
Trelawney, Edward J.: Birth Anniv, Nov 13
Trevino, Lee: Birth, Dec 1
Triangle Shirtwaist Fire: Anniv, Mar 25
Triathlon
Northeast Missouri Triathlon (Kirksville, MO), Sep 13
Winterlude (Ottawa, ON, Canada), Feb 6
Trick or Treat Night, Oct 31
Trillin, Calvin: Birth, Dec 5
Trinidad
Carnival (Port of Spain), Feb 23
Emancipation Day, Aug 1
Independence Day, Aug 31
Indian Arrival Day (Port of Spain), May 30
Spiritual Baptist Liberation Shouter Day, Mar 30
Trinity Sunday, Jun 7
Tripplehorn, Jeanne: Birth, Jun 10
Tritt, Travis: Birth, Feb 9
Trivia Contest, World's Largest (Stevens Point, WI), Apr 17
Trivia Day, Jan 4
Trollope, Anthony: Birth Anniv, Apr 24
Truancy Law: Anniv, Apr 12
Trudeau, Garry: Birth, Jul 21
Trudeau, Pierre Elliott: Birth Anniv, Oct 18
True Confessions Day, Mar 15
Truffaut, Francois: Birth Anniv, Feb 6
Truman Doctrine: Anniv, May 22
Truman, Bess (Elizabeth): Birth Anniv, Feb 13
Truman, Harry S: Birth Anniv, May 8

Truman, Harry S: Dewey Defeats Truman Headline: Anniv, Nov 3
Trumbull, Jonathan: Birth Anniv, Oct 12
Trump, Donald: Birth, Jun 14
Truth or Consequences TV Premiere: Anniv, Sep 7
Truth, Sojourner: Death Anniv, Nov 26
Truth: Tell the Truth Day, Jul 7
Tsunami: Highest in Recorded History: Anniv, Jul 9
Tsunami: Sumatran-Andaman Earthquake and Tsunamis: Anniv, Dec 26
Tu B'Shvat, Feb 9
Tubb, Ernest: Birth Anniv, Feb 9
Tubman, Harriet: Death Anniv, Mar 10
Tucci, Stanley: Birth, Jan 11
Tuchman, Barbara W.: Birth Anniv, Jan 30
Tucker, Chris: Birth, Aug 31
Tucker, Michael: Birth, Feb 6
Tucker, Tanya: Birth, Oct 10
Tug Fest, Great River (Port Byron, IL; LeClaire, IA), Aug 7
Tulip Fest, Albany (Albany, NY), May 8
Tulip Time Fest, Holland (Holland, MI), May 2
Tune, Tommy: Birth, Feb 28
Tunie, Tamara: Birth, Mar 14
Tunisia
  Independence Day, Mar 20
  Martyrs' Day, Apr 9
  Republic Day, Jul 25
  Tree Fest, Nov 8
  Women's Day, Aug 13
Tunney, Gene: Long Count Day, Sep 22
Tunney, James Joseph (Gene): Birth Anniv, May 25
Turgeon, Pierre: Birth, Aug 29
Turkey
  Constantinople Falls to the Turks: Anniv, May 29
  Natl Sovereignty/Children's Day, Apr 23
  Republic Day, Oct 29
  Saint Peter's Day, Jun 29
  Turkish Earthquake: Anniv, Aug 17
  Victory Day, Aug 30
  Youth and Sports Day, May 19
Turkey Days, King (Worthington, MN), Sep 19
Turkey Lovers' Month, June Is, Jun 1
Turkey Rama (McMinnville, OR), Jul 9
Turkey Vultures Return to the Living Sign (Canisteo, NY), Mar 11
Turkey-Free Thanksgiving, Nov 26
Turkmenistan
  Independence Day, Oct 27
  Neutrality Day, Dec 12
  Revival and Unity Day, May 18
Turkoglu, Hedo: Birth, Mar 19
Turlington, Christy: Birth, Jan 2
Turn Beauty Inside Out Day, May 20
Turner, Janine: Birth, Dec 6
Turner, John Napier: Birth, Jun 7
Turner, Kathleen: Birth, Jun 19
Turner, Ted: Birth, Nov 19
Turner, Tina: Birth, Nov 26
Turner's Frontier Address: Anniv, Jul 12
Turtle Day, World, May 23
Turtle Races (Danville, IL), Jun 13
Turturro, John: Birth, Feb 28
Turturro, Nick: Birth, Jan 29
Tushingham, Rita: Birth, Mar 14
Tuskegee Airmen Activated: Anniv, Mar 22
Tuskegee Institute Opening: Anniv, Jul 4
Tussaud, Marie: Birth Anniv, Dec 7
Tut, King: Tomb Discovery: Anniv, Nov 4
Tutu, Desmond: Birth, Oct 7
Tuvalu: National Holiday, Oct 1
Tuxedo Created: Anniv, Oct 10
Twain, Mark (Samuel Clemens): Birth Anniv, Nov 30
Twain, Mark: Natl Tom Sawyer Days (Hannibal, MO), Jul 1
Twain, Shania: Birth, Aug 28
20/20 TV Premiere: Anniv, Jun 6
21 Jump Street TV Premiere: Anniv, Apr 12
Tweed Day, Apr 3
Tweed, Shannon: Birth, Mar 10
Twelfth Day (Epiphany), Jan 6
Twelfth Night, Jan 5
Twellman, Taylor: Birth, Feb 29
Twenty Questions TV Premiere: Anniv, Nov 26
Twiggy: Birth, Sep 19
Twilight Zone TV Premiere: Anniv, Oct 2
Twins Day Fest (Twinsburg, OH), Aug 7
TWIT Award Month, Intl, Apr 1
Twitty, Conway: Birth Anniv, Sep 1
Two Different Colored Shoes Day, Natl, May 3
2001: A Space Odyssey Premiere: Anniv, Apr 3
Tybee 500 (Hollywood, FL; and Tybee Island, GA), May 10
Tyler, Aisha: Birth, Sep 18
Tyler, Anne: Birth, Oct 25
Tyler, John: Birth Anniv, Mar 29
Tyler, Julia G.: Birth Anniv, May 4
Tyler, Letitia Christian: Birth Anniv, Nov 12
Tyler, Liv: Birth, Jul 1
Tyler's Cabinet Resigns: Anniv, Sep 11
Tynan, Ronan: Birth, May 14
Tynwald Day (Isle of Man), Jul 6
Typewriter, First: Anniv, Jun 23
Tyson Bites Holyfield: Anniv, Jun 28
Tyson, Cicely: Birth, Dec 19
Tyson, Mike: Birth, Jun 30

U
U-2 Incident: Anniv, May 1
Ueberroth, Peter: Birth, Sep 2
Uecker, Bob: Birth, Jan 26
UFO Conf, Ozark (Eureka Springs, AR), Apr 10
Uganda
  Independence Day, Oct 9
  Liberation Day, Apr 11
Uggams, Leslie: Birth, May 25
Ukraine
  Chernobyl Reactor Disaster: Anniv, Apr 26
  Independence Day, Aug 24
  October Revolution, Nov 7
  Odessa Retaken: Anniv, Apr 10
  Ukrainian Day, Jan 22
Ukrainian Fest, Canada's Natl (Dauphin, MB, Canada), Jul 31
Ullman, Tracey: Birth, Dec 30
Ullmann, Liv: Birth, Dec 16
Ulrich, Skeet: Birth, Jan 20
Ultimate Sport Show (Grand Rapids, MI), Mar 19
Ultraviolet Awareness Month, May 1
Umbrella Month, Natl, Mar 1
Umbrella: Open an Umbrella Indoors Day, Natl, Mar 13
Underdog Day, Dec 18
Underwood, Blair: Birth, Aug 25
Underwood, Carrie: Birth, Mar 10
UNESCO: Anniv, Nov 4
UNICEF (UN): Anniv, Dec 11
UNICEF Day, Natl (Pres Proc), Oct 31
Union of Soviet Socialist Republics
  Moscow Communique: Anniv, May 29
  Saint Petersburg Name Restored: Anniv, Sep 6
  Soviet Union Dissolved: Anniv, Dec 8
  Troop Withdrawal/Afghanistan Deadline, Feb 15
Union, Gabrielle: Birth, Oct 29
Unique Talent Day, Celebrate Your, Nov 24
Unitas, Johnny: Birth Anniv, May 7
United Arab Emirates
  Dubai Desert Classic (Dubai), Jan 26
  Natl Day (Independence), Dec 2
United Kingdom. See also individual countries
  Accession of Queen Elizabeth II: Anniv, Feb 6
  Allows Same-Sex Civil Partnerships: Anniv, Dec 21
  Battle of Britain Day, Sep 15
  Battle of Britain Week, Sep 13
  Boxing Day, Dec 26
  Boxing Day Bank Holiday, Dec 26
  Brown, Gordon: Birth, Feb 20
  Cedes Claim to Hong Kong: Anniv, Jun 30
  Commonwealth Day, Mar 9
  Coronation Day, Jun 2
  Easter Monday Bank Holiday, Apr 13
  Good Friday Bank Holiday, Apr 10
  Holocaust Memorial Day, Jan 27
  May Day Bank Holiday, May 4
  New Year's Holiday, Jan 1
  Spring Bank Holiday, May 25
  Summer Bank Holiday, Aug 31
  Summer Time, Mar 29
United Nations
  Abolition of Slavery, Intl Day for the, Dec 2
  Africa Industrialization Day, Nov 20
  AIDS Day, World, Dec 1
  Biological Diversity, Intl Day for, May 22
  Charter Signed: Anniv, Jun 26
  Civil Aviation Day, Intl, Dec 7
  Cooperatives, Intl Day of, Jul 4
  Day for Mine Awareness and Assistance in Mine Action, Intl, Apr 4
  Day for Preventing the Exploitation of the Environment in War and Armed Conflict, Intl, Nov 6
  Day for South-South Cooperation, Dec 19
  Day for Women's Rights & Intl Peace, Mar 8
  Day of United Nations Peacekeepers, Intl, May 29
  Diabetes Day, World, Nov 14
  Disarmament Week, Oct 24
  Drug Abuse/Illicit Trafficking, Intl Day Against, Jun 26
  Elimination of Violence Against Women, Intl Day for the, Nov 25
  Eradication of Poverty, Intl Day for, Oct 17
  Families, Intl Day of, May 15
  First General Assembly: Anniv, Jan 10
  General Assembly Opening Day, Sep 15
  Human Rights Day, Dec 10
  Human Solidarity Day, Intl, Dec 20
  Innocent Children Victims of Aggression, Intl Day of, Jun 4
  Intl Day for Preservation of the Ozone Layer, Sep 16
  Intl Day for Tolerance, Nov 16
  Intl Day of Peace, Sep 21
  Land Mine Ban: Anniv, Mar 1
  Literacy Day, Intl, Sep 8

Migrants Day, Intl, Dec 18
Millennium Summit: Anniv, Sep 6
Mother Language Day, Intl, Feb 21
Mountain Day, Intl, Dec 11
Natural Disaster Reduction, Intl Day for, Oct 14
Older Persons, Intl Day of, Oct 1
Persons with Disabilities, Intl Day of, Dec 3
Public Service Day, Jun 23
Racial Discrimination, Intl Day for Elimination of, Mar 21
Racism/Racial Discrimination, Solidarity Against, Mar 21
Remembrance of the Slave Trade and Its Abolition, Intl Day for the, Aug 23
Revokes Resolution on Zionism: Anniv, Dec 16
Social Justice, World Day for, Feb 20
Solidarity with the Palestinian People, Intl Day of, Nov 29
Taiwan Expelled: Anniv, Oct 25
Telecommunication Day, World, May 17
Time of Remembrance and Reconciliation for Those Who Lost Their Lives During WWII, May 8
UNESCO: Anniv, Nov 4
UNICEF Day, Natl (Pres Proc), Oct 31
UNICEF: Anniv, Dec 11
United Nations Day, Oct 24
United Nations Day (Pres Proc), Oct 24
Universal Children's Day, Nov 20
Victims of Torture, Intl Day in Support of, Jun 26
Volunteer Day for Economic/Social Development, Intl, Dec 5
Water, World Day for, Mar 22
Week of Solidarity with the Peoples of Non-Self-Governing Territories, May 25
World Book and Copyright Day, Apr 23
World Day for Cultural Diversity for Dialogue and Development, May 21
World Day of Remembrance for Road Traffic Victims, Nov 15
World Day to Combat Desertification and Drought, Jun 17
World Development Information Day, Oct 24
World Environment Day, Jun 5
World Food Day, Oct 16
World Habitat Day, Oct 5
World Health Day, Apr 7
World Health Organization: Anniv, Apr 7
World Information Society Day, May 17
World Maritime Day, Sep 28
World Mental Health Day, Oct 10
World Meteorological Day, Mar 23
World No-Tobacco Day, May 31
World Population Day, Jul 11
World Post Day, Oct 9
World Press Freedom Day, May 3
World Refugee Day, Jun 20
World Space Week, Oct 4
World Teachers' Day, Oct 5
World Television Day, Nov 21
World's Indigenous People, Intl Day of the, Aug 9
Year of Astronomy, Intl, Jan 1
Year of Human Rights Learning, Intl, Jan 1
Year of Natural Fibers, Intl, Jan 1
Year of Reconciliation, Intl, Jan 1
Youth Day, Intl, Aug 12

United States (government and history)
Air Force Established: Anniv, Sep 18
Anne and Samantha Day, Jun 21
Armed Forces Unified: Anniv, Jul 26
Army Established: Anniv, Jun 14
Attack on America: Anniv, Sep 11
Attack on the USS Liberty: Anniv, Jun 8
Attempt to Free Iran Hostages: Anniv, Apr 24
Bank Bailout Bill: Anniv, Nov 27
Bank Holiday: Anniv, Mar 5
Bureau of Indian Affairs Established, Mar 11
Capitol Cornerstone Laid: Anniv, Sep 18
Civil Rights Act of 1964: Anniv, Jul 2
Civil Rights Act of 1968: Anniv, Apr 11
Civilian Auto Production Halted: Anniv, Feb 10
Clinton Impeachment Proceedings: Anniv, Dec 20
Coins Stamped "In God We Trust": Anniv, Apr 22
Congress Assembles, Jan 5
Congress Authorized Force Against Iraq: Anniv, Jan 12
Congress First Meets at Washington: Anniv, Nov 21
Congress: First Meeting Under Constitution: Anniv, Mar 4
Constitution of the US: Anniv, Sep 17
Customs: Anniv, Aug 1
Death Penalty Banned: Anniv, Jun 29
Declaration of Independence Approval and Signing: Anniv, Jul 4
Dept of Justice: Anniv, Jun 22
Dept of State Founded: Anniv, Jul 27
Distinguished Service Medal: Anniv, Mar 7
District of Columbia Establishing Legislation: Anniv, Jul 16
Dred Scott Decision: Anniv, Mar 6
Family-Leave Bill: Anniv, Feb 5
Federal Communications Commission Created: Anniv, Feb 26
Federal Credit Union Act: Anniv, Jun 26
Federal Government Seizure of Steel Mills: Anniv, Apr 8
Female House Page, First Formal: Anniv, May 14
55-mph Speed Limit: Anniv, Jan 2
First Brawl in US House of Representatives: Anniv, Jan 30
First Census: Anniv, Aug 1
First Elected Woman Senator: Anniv, Jan 12
First Foreign-Born Chair of Joint Chiefs: Anniv, Aug 11
First Mint in America: Anniv, Jun 10
First US Government Building: Anniv, Jul 31
First White House Easter Egg Roll: Anniv, Apr 2
First Woman Ambassador Appointed: Anniv, Oct 28
First Woman US Senator: Anniv, Oct 3
Fiscal Year, US Federal, Oct 1
Ford, Gerald: Assassination Attempts: Anniv, Sep 5
General Election Day, Nov 3
Great Seal of the US: Anniv, Sep 16
Great Seal of the US: Authorization Anniv, Jan 28
Great Seal of the US: Proposed: Anniv, Jul 4
Ground War Against Iraq Begins: Anniv, Feb 23
Gulf War Begins: Anniv, Jan 16
Home Owners Loan Act: Anniv, Jun 13
Hostages in Iran Released: Anniv, Jan 20
House Divided Speech: Anniv, Jun 16
Inauguration Day, Jan 20
Income Tax: Anniv, Mar 8
Independence Day, Jul 4
Invades Cambodia: Anniv, Apr 30
Invasion of Panama: Anniv, Dec 20
Irwin Earns First Medal of Honor: Anniv, Feb 13
Japan Bombed: Anniv, Apr 18
Japanese Internment: Anniv, Feb 19
Johnson Impeachment Proceedings: Anniv, Feb 24
Kuwait Liberated: Anniv, Feb 27
Labor Relations Act, Natl: Anniv, Jul 5
Lewis & Clark Expedition Returns: Anniv, Sep 23
Lewis and Clark Expedition Commissioned: Anniv, Jan 18
Lewis and Clark Expedition Sets Out: Anniv, May 14
Library of Congress: Anniv, Apr 24
Lincoln Signs Income Tax: Anniv, Jul 1
Lincoln-Douglas Debates: Anniv, Aug 21
Military Ban on Homosexuals Eased: Anniv, Jan 29
Moscow Communique: Anniv, May 29
Motor Voter Bill Signed: Anniv, May 20
NAFTA Signed: Anniv, Dec 8
Native American Rights Recognized: Anniv, May 12
Nixon First American President to Visit Moscow: Anniv, May 22
Nixon's Trip to China: Anniv, Feb 21
Nuclear-Free World, First Step Toward a: Anniv, Dec 8
Operation Iraqi Freedom: Anniv, Mar 19
Paper Money Issued: Anniv, Mar 10
Peace Corps Founded: Anniv, Mar 1
Philippine Independence: Anniv, Mar 24
Pony Express, Inauguration of: Anniv, Apr 3
Postmaster General Established: Anniv, Sep 22
President Occupies the White House, Nov 1
Presidential Succession Act: Anniv, Jul 18
Ratification Day, Jan 14
Sanctions Against South Africa Lifted: Anniv, Jul 10
Securities and Exchange Commission Created: Anniv, Jun 6
Senate Achieves a Quorum: Anniv, Apr 6
Senate Acquits Clinton: Anniv, Feb 12
Shanghai Communique: Anniv, Feb 27
Standard Time Act: Anniv, Mar 19
Sumner Attacked in the Senate: Anniv, May 22
Supreme Court Abortion Notification Ruling: Anniv, Jun 25
Supreme Court Bans School Prayer: Anniv, Jun 25
Supreme Court Right to Die Ruling: Anniv, Jun 25
Supreme Court Upholds Ban on Abortion Counseling: Anniv, May 23
300 Millionth American Born: Anniv, Oct 17
Treasury Department: Anniv, Sep 2
Treaty of Guadalupe Hidalgo (with Mexico): Anniv, Feb 2
Truman Doctrine: Anniv, May 22
Tyler's Cabinet Resigns: Anniv, Sep 11
Uniform Time Zone Plan: Anniv, Nov 18
US Capital Established at NYC: Anniv, Sep 13
US Enters WWI: Anniv, Apr 6

US Mint: Anniv, Apr 2
US Takes Out Its First Loan: Anniv, Sep 18
Vietnam Peace Agreement Signed: Anniv, Jan 27
Vietnam War Protesters Storm Pentagon: Anniv, Oct 21
Voting Rights Act Signed: Anniv, Aug 6
WAAC: Anniv, May 14
War Department Established: Anniv, Aug 7
War of 1812: Declaration Anniv, Jun 18
War on Poverty: Anniv, Jan 8
Washington Crosses the Delaware: Anniv, Dec 25
Water Pollution Control Act: Anniv, Oct 18
Woman Runs the US House of Representatives: Anniv, Jun 20
UNIVAC Computer: Anniv, Jun 14
Universal Children's Day (UN), Nov 20
Universal Hour of Peace, Dec 31
Unser, Al, Jr: Birth, Apr 19
Unser, Al: Birth, May 29
Unser, Bobby: Birth, Feb 20
Up Helly Aa (Scotland), Jan 27
Update Your References Week, May 3
Update Your Resume Month, Sep 1
Updike, John: Birth, Mar 18
Upjohn, Richard: Birth Anniv, Jan 22
Upshaw, Dawn: Birth, Jul 17
Upstairs, Downstairs TV Premiere: Anniv, Oct 10
Upsy Daisy Day, Jun 8
Uranus, Discovery of Planet: Anniv, Mar 13
Urban Eden Day, Natl, Sep 13
Urban, Keith: Birth, Oct 26
Urie, Michael: Birth, Aug 8
Uris, Leon: Birth Anniv, Aug 3
Urlacher, Brian: Birth, May 25
Uruguay
Artigas Day, Jun 19
Battle of Las Piedras Day, May 18
Constitution Day, Jul 18
Independence Day, Aug 25
Landing of the 33 Patriots Day, Apr 19
US Air Force Academy Established: Anniv, Apr 1
US Amateur (Golf) Chmpshp (Tulsa, OK), Aug 24
US Amateur Public Links (Golf) Chmpshp (Norman, OK), Jul 13
US and Vatican Reestablish Diplomatic Relations: Anniv, Jan 10
US House, Black Page Appointed: Anniv, Apr 9
US Junior Amateur (Golf) Chmpshp (Bedminster, NJ), Jul 20
US Mid-Amateur (Golf) Chmpshp (Charleston, SC), Oct 3
US Military Academy Founded: Anniv, Mar 16
US Natl Snow Sculpting Competition (Lake Geneva, WI), Feb 4
US Naval Academy Founded: Anniv, Oct 10
US Navy: Authorization Anniv, Oct 13
US Open (Golf) Chmpshp (Farmingdale, NY), Jun 18
US Senior Open (Golf) Chmpshp (Carmel, IN), Jul 30
US Senior Women's Amateur Chmpshp (Hot Springs, VA), Sep 12
US Virgin Islands
Danish West Indies Emancipation Day, Jul 3
Liberty Day, Nov 1
Natl Park Established: Anniv, Aug 2
Organic Act Day, Jun 15
Transfer Day, Mar 31
US Women's Amateur (Golf) Chmpshp (St. Louis, MO), Aug 3
US Women's Amateur Public Links (Golf) Chmpshp (Devens, MA), Jun 22
US Women's Mid-Amateur (Golf) Chmpshp (Ocala, FL), Oct 3
US Women's Open (Golf) Chmpshp (Bethlehem, PA), Jul 9
USA Film Fest (Dallas, TX), Apr 29
USA Today First Published: Anniv, Sep 15
USGA Senior Amateur (Golf) Chmpshp (Chicago, IL), Sep 12
Usher: Birth, Oct 14
USO Founded: Anniv, Feb 4
USS Constitution Launched: Anniversary, Oct 21
USS Constitution Saved by Poem: Anniv, Sep 16
USS Iowa, Explosion on: Anniv, Apr 19
USS Liberty, Attack on: Anniv, Jun 8
USS Princeton Explosion: Anniv, Feb 28
USS Pueblo Seized: Anniv, Jan 23
USS Stark Attacked: Anniv, May 17
USSR Established: Anniv, Dec 30
Ustinov, Peter: Birth Anniv, Apr 16
Utah
Admission Day, Jan 4
America's First Department Store: Anniv (Salt Lake City), Oct 16
Bennett, Robert F.: Birth, Sep 18
Bryce Canyon Natl Park Established: Anniv, Jan 1
Canyonlands Natl Park Established: Anniv, Sep 12
Capitol Reef Natl Park Established: Anniv, Dec 18
Dinosaur Roundup Rodeo (Vernal), Jul 8
Hatch, Orrin: Birth, Mar 22
Huntsman, John, Jr: Birth, Mar 26
Jell-O Week, Feb 8
Learning Disabilities Assn Intl Conf (Salt Lake City), Feb 25
Mountain Meadows Massacre: Anniv, Sep 11
Payson Golden Onion Days (Payson), Sep 4
Pioneer Day, Jul 24
Salt Lake's Family Christmas Gift Show (Sandy), Nov 13
Slamdance (Park City), Jan 15
State Fair (Salt Lake City), Sep 10
Sundance Film Fest (Park City), Jan 15
Utah Women Given Vote: Anniv, Feb 12
XTERRA Wheeler Canyon Xduro (Ogden), Aug 15
Zion Natl Park Established: Anniv, Nov 19
Utley, Chase: Birth, Dec 17
Utley, Garrick: Birth, Nov 19
Uzbekistan
Army Day, Jan 14
Constitution Day, Dec 8
Day of Memory and Honor, May 9
Independence Day, Sep 1

V

Vacation Day, Plan a Solo, Mar 1
Vacation: American Adventures Month, Aug 1
Vaccaro, Brenda: Birth, Nov 18
Vachon, Rogie: Birth, Sep 8
Vaisakhi (India), Apr 13
Valderrama, Carlos: Birth, Sep 2
Valens, Richie. See Day the Music Died: Anniv, Feb 3
Valentine, Bobby: Birth, May 13
Valentine, Karen: Birth, May 25
Valentine, Scott: Birth, Jun 3
Valentine's Ball, WMAS (Springfield, MA), Feb 14
Valentine's Day, Feb 14
Valentine's Day Massacre: Anniv, Feb 14
Valentine's Day, Chinese (Double Seven Fest), Aug 26
Valentino (Rudolph) Memorial Service, Aug 23
Valentino, Rudolph: Birth Anniv, May 6
Valentino, Rudolph: Sheik Film Release: Anniv, Nov 20
Valenzuela, Fernando: Birth, Nov 1
Vallee, Rudy: Birth Anniv, Jul 28
Valli, Frankie: Birth, May 3
Van Amstel, Louis: Birth, Jun 23
Van Ark, Joan: Birth, Jun 16
Van Brocklin, Norm: Birth Anniv, Mar 15
Van Buren, Abigail: Birth, Jul 4
Van Buren, Hannah Hoes: Birth Anniv, Mar 8
Van Buren, Martin: Annual Wreath Laying Ceremony (Kinderhook, NY), Dec 5
Van Buren, Martin: Birth Anniv, Dec 5
Van Cleef, Lee: Birth Anniv, Jan 9
Van Damme, Jean-Claude: Birth, Oct 18
Van Der Beek, James: Birth, Mar 8
Van Devere, Trish: Birth, Mar 9
Van Doren, Mamie: Birth, Feb 6
Van Dyke, Dick: Birth, Dec 13
Van Dyke, Jerry: Birth, Jul 27
Van Exel, Nick: Birth, Nov 27
Van Gogh, Vincent: Birth Anniv, Mar 30
Van Gundy, Jeff: Birth, Jan 19
Van Halen, Eddie: Birth, Jan 26
Van Heusen, Jimmy: Birth Anniv, Jan 26
Van Horn, Keith: Birth, Oct 23
Van Patten, Dick: Birth, Dec 9
Van Patten, Joyce: Birth, Mar 9
Van Peebles, Mario: Birth, Jan 15
Van Peebles, Melvin: Birth, Aug 21
Van Slyke, Andy: Birth, Dec 21
VanCamp, Emily: Birth, May 12
Vancouver, George: Birth Anniv, Jun 22
Vanderbilt, Amy: Birth Anniv, Jul 22
Vanderbilt, Gloria: Birth, Feb 20
Vanilla Ice: Birth, Oct 31
Vanuatu: Independence Day, Jul 30
Vardalos, Nia: Birth, Sep 24
Vargas, Elizabeth: Birth, Sep 6
Vatican and US Reestablish Diplomatic Relations: Anniv, Jan 10
Vatican City: Independence Anniv, Feb 11
Vatican Council II: Anniv, Oct 11
Vaughan Williams, Ralph: Birth Anniv, Oct 12
Vaughan, Sarah: Birth Anniv, Mar 27
Vaughn, Robert: Birth, Nov 22
Vaughn, Vince: Birth, Mar 28
VCR Introduced: Anniv, Jun 7
V-E Day, May 8
Veblen, Thorstein: Birth Anniv, Jul 30
Veeck, Bill: Birth Anniv, Feb 9
Veep Day, Aug 9
Vega, Suzanne: Birth, Jul 11
Vegetarian Events and Observances
Great American Meatout, Mar 20
Have-a-Heart Day, Natl, Feb 14
Independence-from-Meat Day, Jul 4
Turkey-Free Thanksgiving, Nov 26
Vegan Month, Nov 1
Vegetarian Day, World, Oct 1

Vegetarian Month, Oct 1
Vegetarian Resource Group's Essay Contest for Kids, May 1
VelJohnson, Reginald: Birth, Aug 16
Venezuela
Battle of Carabobo Day, Jun 24
Independence Day, Jul 5
VentHaven Ventriloquist Convention (Fort Mitchell, KY), Jul 16
Ventimiglia, Milo: Birth, Jul 8
Ventura, Jesse: Birth, Jul 15
Ventura, Robin: Birth, Jul 14
Verboort Sausage and Kraut Dinner (Forest Grove, OR), Nov 7
Vercors, Jean: Birth Anniv, Feb 26
Verdi, Giuseppi: Birth Anniv, Oct 10
Verdon, Gwen: Birth Anniv, Jan 13
Vereen, Ben: Birth, Oct 10
Verlander, Justin: Birth, Feb 20
Vermeil, Dick: Birth, Oct 30
Vermont
Admission Day, Mar 4
Bennington Battle Day: Anniv, Aug 16
Bennington Car Show (Bennington), Sep 18
Brookfield Ice Harvest (Brookfield), Jan 31
Champlain Valley Fair (Essex Junction), Aug 29
Children's Day (Woodstock), Jul 11
Cow Appreciation Day (Woodstock), Jul 25
Douglas, Jim: Birth, Jun 21
Family Halloween (Woodstock), Oct 25
Harvest Weekend (Woodstock), Oct 10
Leahy, Patrick J.: Birth, Mar 31
Northeast Kingdom Fall Foliage Fest (Walden), Sep 28
Old Vermont Fourth (Woodstock), Jul 4
Pumpkin and Apple Celebration (Woodstock), Oct 3
Quilt Show (Woodstock), Aug 1
Sanders, Bernie: Birth, Sep 8
Sheep Herding with Border Collies (Woodstock), Aug 9
State Fair (Rutland), Sep 4
Town Meeting Day, Mar 3
Traditional Plowing Match (Woodstock), May 3
Vermont Maple Fest (St. Albans), Apr 24
Wassail Celebration (Woodstock), Dec 11
Verne, Jules: Birth Anniv, Feb 8
Verrazano Day, Apr 17
Versailles Peace Conference: Anniv, Jan 18
Vesak, Day of: See Birthday of the Buddha, Apr 8
Vesey, Denmark: Death Anniv, Jul 2
Vespucci, Amerigo: Birth Anniv, Mar 9
Vesuvius Day, Aug 24
Veterans
ANZAC Day, Apr 25
Branson Veterans Homecoming (Branson, MO), Nov 5
Military Appreciation Month, Natl, May 1
Pearl Harbor Remembrance Day, Natl (Pres Proc), Dec 7
Remembrance Day (Gettysburg, PA), Nov 21
Soldiers' Reunion Celebration (Newton, NC), Aug 20
Veterans Bonus Army Eviction: Anniv, Jul 28
Veterans Day, Nov 11
Veterans Day (Pres Proc), Nov 11
Veterans of Foreign Wars Established: Anniv, Sep 29
VFW Ladies Auxiliary Organized: Anniv, Sep 17
Vietnam Veterans Memorial Statue Unveiling: Anniv, Nov 9
Vietnam Women's Memorial Dedicated: Anniv, Nov 11
Vice-Presidential Candidate, First Woman: Anniv, Jul 19
Vice-Presidential Resignation: Anniv, Dec 28
Victims of Torture, Intl Day in Support of (UN), Jun 26
Victims of Violence Wholly Day, Apr 4
Victor Emmanuel III: Birth Anniv, Nov 11
Victor, James: Birth, Jul 27
Victoria Day (Canada), May 18
Victory Day (RI), Aug 10
Victory in Europe Day, May 8
Vidal, Gore: Birth, Oct 3
Vidalia Onion Month, Natl Sweet, May 1
Video Games Day, Sep 12
Vieira, Meredith: Birth, Dec 30
Vietnam
Ho Chi Minh: Birth Anniv, May 19
Independence Day, Sep 2
Liberation Day, Apr 30
Natl Holiday, Feb 3
Vietnam War (US undeclared)
Battle of Hamburger Hill: Anniv, May 11
Cambodia Invaded by US: Anniv, Apr 30
Dien Bien Phu Falls: Anniv, May 7
Gulf of Tonkin Resolution: Anniv, Aug 7
My Lai Massacre: Anniv, Mar 16
Saigon Falls to Vietcong: Anniv, Apr 30
Tet Offensive Begins, Jan 30
Vietnam and US Resume Relations: Anniv, May 26
Vietnam Conflict Begins (with French): Anniv, Aug 22
Vietnam Moratorium Concert: Anniv, Mar 28
Vietnam Peace Agreement Signed: Anniv, Jan 27
Vietnam Veterans Memorial Statue Unveiling: Anniv, Nov 9
Vietnam War Protesters Storm Pentagon: Anniv, Oct 21
Women's Memorial Dedicated: Anniv, Nov 11
Vigoda, Abe: Birth, Feb 24
Viking Fest (Frederiksund, Denmark), Jun 19
Viking: Up Helly Aa (Scotland), Jan 27
Vila, Bob: Birth, Jun 20
Vilas, Guillermo: Birth, Aug 17
Villeneueve, Jacques: Birth, Apr 9
Vincent, Fay: Birth, May 29
Vincent, Jan-Michael: Birth, Jul 15
Vinegar Day, Jun 20
Vinegar Month, Natl, May 1
Vinson, Fred M.: Birth Anniv, Jan 22
Vinton, Bobby: Birth, Apr 16
Vinyl Record Day, Aug 12
Violence, YWCA Week Without, Oct 18
Virchow, Rudolf: Birth Anniv, Oct 13
Virgen de la Guadalupe: Las Mananitas (Ponce, Puerto Rico), Dec 12
Virgin Islands
Hurricane Supplication Day, Jul 27
Hurricane Thanksgiving Day, Oct 19
Virgin Islands–Puerto Rico Friendship Day, Oct 12
Virginia
Apple Day at Stonewall Jackson House (Lexington), Oct 17
Battle of Bull Run: Anniv, Jul 21
Battle of Cold Harbor: Anniv, Jun 3
Battle of Spotsylvania: Anniv, May 12
Battle of the Wilderness: Anniv, May 5
Blue Ridge Folklife Fest (Ferrum), Oct 24
Bonnie Blue Natl Horse Show (Lexington), May 14
Children's Day at Jamestown (Williamsburg), Sep 12
Chincoteague Easter Decoy Show (Chincoteague Island), Apr 10
Chincoteague Pony Penning (Chincoteague Island), Jul 29
Christmas Remembered at Stonewall Jackson House (Lexington), Dec 5
Civil War Peace Talks: Anniv, Feb 3
Colonial Christmas (Williamsburg), Dec 1
Craftsmen's Christmas Classic Arts & Crafts Fest (Richmond), Nov 6
Craftsmen's Classic Arts & Crafts Fest (Chantilly), Mar 27
Craftsmen's Classic Arts & Crafts Fest (Chantilly), Oct 16
Craftsmen's Classic Arts & Crafts Fest (Richmond), Mar 13
Craftsmen's Classic Arts & Crafts Fest (Roanoke), Oct 9
Defeat at Five Forks: Anniv, Apr 1
Eighteenth-Century Autumn Market Fair (McLean), Oct 17
Eighteenth-Century Christmas Wassail (McLean), Dec 13
Eighteenth-Century Spring Market Fair (McLean), May 16
Eighteenth-Century Summer Market Fair (McLean), Jul 18
Fall of Richmond: Anniv, Apr 3
First US Breach of Promise Suit: Anniv, Jun 14
Foods/Feasts of Colonial Virginia (Williamsburg), Nov 26
Foxfield Races (Charlottesville), Apr 25
From Africa to Virginia Month (Williamsburg), Feb 1
George Washington Birthday Parade (Alexandria), Feb 16
George Washington Birthnight Banquet/Ball (Alexandria), Feb 14
Highland County Maple Fest (Highland County), Mar 14
Historic Garden Week, Apr 18
Holidays in the City Grand Illumination Parade (Norfolk), Nov 21
Jamestown and Bermuda (Williamsburg), Mar 1
Jamestown Day (Williamsburg), May 16
Kaine, Tim: Birth, Feb 26
Keep Norfolk Beautiful Day (Norfolk), Mar 28
Lee-Jackson Day, Jan 16
Lexington's Fourth of July Balloon Rally (Lexington), Jul 4
Liberty Celebration (Yorktown), Jul 4
Migratory Bird Celebration, Intl (Chincoteague), May 9
Military Through the Ages (Williamsburg), Mar 21
Miss Virginia Pageant (Roanoke), Jun 25
Occoneechee State Park Native American Fest and Pow Wow (Clarksville), May 9
Old Fiddlers' Conv (Galax), Aug 3
Oyster Fest (Chincoteague Island), Oct 10
Pastimes of Colonial Virginia (Williamsburg), Aug 1
Peninsula Campaign Intensified: Anniv, May 9

Raid on Richmond: Anniv, Mar 1
Ratification Day, Jun 25
Seven Days Campaign: Anniv, Jun 25
Shenandoah Natl Park Established: Anniv, Dec 26
State Chmpshp Chili Cook-Off (Roanoke), May 2
State Fair (Richmond), Sep 24
Stonewall Jackson's Birthday Celebration (Lexington), Jan 21
Strawberry Hill Races (Richmond), Apr 11
Streetscene (Covington), Aug 8
Sugarloaf Crafts Fest (Chantilly), Jan 30
Sugarloaf Crafts Fest (Chantilly), May 1
Sugarloaf Crafts Fest (Chantilly), Dec 11
Sugarloaf Crafts Fest (Manassas), Sep 11
Suntrust Big Lick Blues Fest (Roanoke), Sep 19
Tools of the Trade (Williamsburg), Jun 1
Union Officers Escape Libby Prison: Anniv, Feb 9
US Senior Women's Amateur Chmpshp (Hot Springs), Sep 12
Virginia Christmas Show (Richmond), Nov 5
Virginia Gold Cup (Warrenton), May 2
Virginia Lake Fest (Clarksville), Jul 16
Virginia Peanut Fest (Emporia), Sep 25
Virginia Spring Show (Richmond), Mar 13
Warner, John: Birth, Feb 18
Washington's Birthday at Mount Vernon (Mount Vernon), Feb 14
Washington's Birthday Party (Fredericksburg), Feb 14
Webb, James: Birth, Feb 9
XTERRA Richmond Xduro and James River Scramble (Richmond), Jun 13
Yorktown Day (Yorktown), Oct 19
Yorktown Victory Celebration (Yorktown), Oct 17
Yorktown Victory Day, Oct 12
Virginia Company Expedition to America: Anniv, Dec 20
Virginia Plan Proposed: Anniv, May 29
Virginia Tech Shootings: Anniv, Apr 16
Virginian TV Premiere: Anniv, Sep 19
Virgo Begins, Aug 23
Virtual Assistants Day, Intl, May 15
Virtual Worlds Day, Aug 20
Vision and Learning Month, Children's, Aug 1
Vision Research Month, Jun 1
Vision, Healthy, Month, May 1
Vision: AMD/Low Vision Awareness Month, Feb 1
Visit Your Relatives Day, May 18
Visnjic, Goran: Birth, Sep 9
Vitale, Dick: Birth, Jun 9
Vitamin C Isolated: Anniv, Apr 4
Viticulturists' Day (Bulgaria), Feb 14
Vitter, David: Birth, May 3
Vitti, Monica: Birth, Nov 3
V-J Day (Announcement): Anniv, Aug 14
V-J Day (Ratification), Sep 2
V-Mail Delivery: Anniv, Jun 22
Voight, Jon: Birth, Dec 29
Voinovich, George V.: Birth, Jul 15
Volcanoes
Cameroon: Eruption: Anniv, Aug 22
Laki Volcano Eruption: Anniv, Jun 8
Montserrat: Volcano Erupts: Anniv, Jun 25
Mount Pelee Eruption: Anniv, May 8
Mount Pinatubo Erupts in Philippines: Anniv, Jun 11
Mount Saint Helens Eruption: Anniv, May 18
Vesuvius Day (Pompeii Destroyed: Anniv), Aug 24
Volksfest (New Glarus, WI), Aug 2
Volleyball: NAIA Women's Natl Chmpshp (Sioux City, IA), Nov 21
Voltaire: Birth Anniv, Nov 21
Volunteers, Volunteering
Community Spirit Days, Apr 1
Family Volunteer Day, Nov 21
Join Hands Day, May 2
Make a Difference Day, Oct 24
Rebuilding Day, Natl, Apr 25
Teach Your Daughter to Volunteer Day, Apr 18
Volunteer Day for Economic/Social Development, Intl (UN), Dec 5
Volunteer Week, Natl (Pres Proc), Apr 19
Von Braun: First Surface-to-Surface Missile: Anniv, Dec 24
von Furstenberg, Diane: Birth, Dec 31
Von Oy, Jenna: Birth, May 2
Von Richtofen: Red Baron Shot Down: Anniv, Apr 21
von Schiller, Friedrich: Birth Anniv, Nov 10
Von Steuben, Baron Friedrich: Birth Anniv, Sep 17
Von Sydow, Max: Birth, Apr 10
Vonnegut, Kurt, Jr: Birth Anniv, Nov 11
Voting
Blacks Ruled Eligible to Vote: Anniv, Apr 3
Last Week to Register to Vote in US General Elections, Sep 27
League of Women Voters Formed: Anniv, Feb 14
Motor Voter Bill Signed: Anniv, May 20
Seneca Falls Convention Survivor Votes: Anniv, Nov 2
Suffragists' Voting Attempt: Anniv, Nov 19
Susan B. Anthony Fined for Voting, Jun 6
Voting Age Changed (26th Amendment): Anniv, Jul 1
Voting Rights Act Signed: Anniv, Aug 6
Women Denied Vote: Anniv, Jan 12
Women's Rights Convention at Seneca Falls: Anniv, Jul 19
Women's Suffrage Amendment Introduced: Anniv, Jan 10
Voyageurs Natl Park Established: Anniv, Apr 8

W

Wachowski, Andy: Birth, Dec 29
Wachowski, Larry: Birth, Jun 21
Wade, Dwyane: Birth, Jan 17
Wade, Virginia: Birth, Jul 10
Wadlow, Robert Pershing: Birth Anniv, Feb 22
Waffle Week, Natl, Sep 6
Waggoner, Lyle: Birth, Apr 13
Wagner, Billy: Birth, Jun 25
Wagner, Honus: Birth Anniv, Feb 24
Wagner, Jack P.: Birth, Oct 3
Wagner, Kurt: Birth, Jun 22
Wagner, Lindsay: Birth, Jun 22
Wagner, Richard: Birth Anniv, May 22
Wagner, Robert: Birth, Feb 10
Wagon Train TV Premiere: Anniv, Sep 18
Wahl, Ken: Birth, Dec 11
Wahlberg, Donnie: Birth, Aug 17
Wahlberg, Mark: Birth, Jun 5
Waikiki Roughwater Swim (Honolulu, HI), Sep 1
Waitangi Day (New Zealand), Feb 6
Waite, Morrison R.: Birth Anniv, Nov 29
Waite, Terry: Birth, May 31
Waits, Tom: Birth, Dec 7
Waitstaff Day, Natl, May 21
Waitz, Grete: Birth, Oct 1
Walden, Robert: Birth, Sep 25
Waldseemuller, Martin: Cosmographiae Introductio: Publication Anniv, Apr 25
Wales
Christmas Holiday, Dec 25
Hay-on-Wye Fest of Literature (Hay-on-Wye), May 21
Llangollen Intl Musical Eisteddfod (Llangollen, Denbighshire), Jul 7
Natl Eisteddfod of Wales (Swansea), Aug 1
Saint David's Day, Mar 1
Walesa, Lech: Birth, Sep 29
Walesa, Lech: Solidarity Founded: Anniv, Aug 31
Walk on Stilts Day, Jul 27
Walk on Your Wild Side Day, Apr 12
Walken, Christopher: Birth, Mar 31
Walker Cup (Ardmore, PA), Sep 12
Walker, Alice: Birth, Feb 9
Walker, Ally: Birth, Aug 25
Walker, Antoine: Birth, Aug 12
Walker, Clint: Birth, May 30
Walker, Doak: Birth Anniv, Jan 1
Walker, Herschel: Birth, Mar 3
Walker, Jimmie: Birth, Jun 25
Walker, Larry: Birth, Dec 1
Walker, Mary E.: Birth Anniv, Nov 26
Walker, Mort: Birth, Sep 3
Walking
Mackinac Bridge Walk (St. Ignace, MI), Sep 7
Sauntering Day, World, Jun 19
Wallace, Chris: Birth, Oct 12
Wallace, George, Shot: Anniv, May 15
Wallace, Henry A.: Birth Anniv, Oct 7
Wallace, Mike: Birth, May 9
Wallace, Rasheed: Birth, Sep 17
Wallace, Rusty: Birth, Aug 14
Wallach, Eli: Birth, Dec 7
Wallenberg, Raoul: Birth Anniv, Aug 5
Wallet, Skeezix: Birthday, Feb 14
Walpurgis Night, Apr 30
Walsh, Dylan: Birth, Nov 17
Walsh, Kate: Birth, Oct 13
Walsh, M. Emmet: Birth, Mar 22
Walt Disney TV Premiere: Anniv, Oct 27
Walter Plinge Day (England), Dec 2
Walter, Jessica: Birth, Jan 31
Walters, Barbara: Birth, Sep 25
Walters, Julie: Birth, Feb 22
Walton, Bill: Birth, Nov 5
Walton, George: Death Anniv, Feb 2
Walton, Izaak: Birth Anniv, Aug 9
Walton, Sam: Birth Anniv, Mar 29
Waltons TV Premiere: Anniv, Sep 14
Waltrip, Darrell: Birth, Feb 5
Wambach, Abby: Birth, Jun 20
Wambaugh, Joseph: Birth, Jan 22
Wang, Garrett: Birth, Dec 15
Wapner, Joseph: Birth, Nov 15
War Crimes Trial (Japan): Anniv, Jan 19
War Criminals (German) Execution: Anniv, Oct 16
War Is Hell: Anniv, Jun 19
War of 1812: Declaration Anniv, Jun 18
War of the Worlds Broadcast: Anniv, Oct 30
War on Poverty: Anniv, Jan 8
War Time: Anniv, Feb 9
Ward, Burt: Birth, Jul 6
Ward, Montgomery, Seized: Anniv, Apr 26
Ward, Rachel: Birth, Sep 12

Ward, Sela: Birth, Jul 11
Ward, Simon: Birth, Oct 19
Warfield, Marsha: Birth, Mar 5
Warhol, Andy: Birth Anniv, Aug 6
Warner Weather Quotation: Anniv, Aug 24
Warner, Charles Dudley: Birth Anniv, Sep 12
Warner, David: Birth, Jul 29
Warner, John: Birth, Feb 18
Warner, Malcolm-Jamal: Birth, Aug 18
Warner, Mark: Birth, Dec 15
Warren Commission Report: Anniv, Sep 27
Warren, Earl: Birth Anniv, Mar 19
Warren, Lesley Ann: Birth, Aug 16
Warren, Michael: Birth, Mar 5
Warren, Robert Penn: Birth Anniv, Apr 24
Warrens Cranberry Fest (Warrens, WI), Sep 25
Warwick, Dionne: Birth, Dec 12
Washington
Admission Day, Nov 11
Bumbershoot: Seattle's Music & Arts Fest (Seattle), Sep 5
Cantwell, Maria: Birth, Oct 13
Corvette and High Performance Meet (Puyallup), Feb 7
Coupeville Arts & Crafts Fest (Coupeville), Aug 8
Eleanor Roosevelt Day (Raymond), Aug 8
Gregoire, Christine: Birth, Mar 24
Issaquah Salmon Days Fest (Issaquah), Oct 3
Maritime Gig Fest (Gig Harbor), Jun 6
Mount Rainier Natl Park: Anniv, Mar 2
Mural-in-a-Day (Toppenish), Jun 6
Murray, Patty: Birth, Oct 11
North Cascades Natl Park Established: Anniv, Oct 2
Northwest Folklife Fest (Seattle), May 22
Olympic Natl Park Established: Anniv, Jun 29
Puyallup Fair (Puyallup), Sep 11
Puyallup Spring Fair (Puyallup), Apr 16
Seafair (Seattle), Jun 28
Sequim Irrigation Fest (Sequim), May 2
Skagit Valley Tulip Fest (Burlington), Apr 1
Tacoma Holiday Food and Gift Fest (Tacoma), Oct 21
Toppenish Western Art Show (Toppenish), Aug 14
Washington State Apple Blossom Fest (Wenatchee), Apr 23
Washington, Booker T.: Birth Anniv, Apr 5
Washington, Denzel: Birth, Dec 28
Washington, District of Columbia
American Council on Education Annual Mtg, Feb 7
Cherry Blossom Fest, Mar 28
Davidson Fellows Award Reception, Sep 30
District-Establishing Legislation: Anniv, Jul 16
Geographic Bee Finals, Natl, May 19
Invasion Anniv, Aug 24
Mother's Day at the Wall, May 10
R.E.A.D. in America Day, Sep 26
Spelling Bee Finals, Scripps Natl, May 27
Vietnam Veterans Memorial Statue Unveiling: Anniv, Nov 9
Vietnam Women's Memorial Dedicated: Anniv, Nov 11
Washington Boat Show, Feb 19
Washington Home, Garden & Flower Show, Mar 19
Washington Monument Dedicated: Anniv, Feb 21
White House Easter Egg Roll, Apr 13
Washington, George
Address to Continental Army Officers: Anniv, Mar 15
Birth Anniv, Feb 22
Birthday at Mount Vernon (Mount Vernon, VA), Feb 14
Birthday Observance (Legal Holiday), Feb 16
Birthday Parade (Alexandria, VA), Feb 16
Birthday Party (Fredericksburg, VA), Feb 14
Crosses the Delaware: Anniv, Dec 25
Death Anniv, Dec 14
George Washington Birthnight Banquet/Ball (Alexandria, VA), Feb 14
Presidential Inauguration Anniv, Apr 30
Takes Command of Continental Army: Anniv, Jul 3
Washington's Birthday Celebration (Laredo, TX), Jan 22
White House Cornerstone Laid: Anniv, Oct 13
Washington, Harold: Birth Anniv, Apr 15
Washington, Harold: Elected Chicago's First Black Mayor: Anniv, Apr 11
Washington, Isaiah: Birth, Aug 3
Washington, Martha: Birth Anniv, Jun 21
Wasson, Craig: Birth, Mar 15
Watanabe, Ken: Birth, Oct 21
Water, World Day for (UN), Mar 22
Water-Drawing Fest (Japan), Mar 1
Waterfowl Fest (Easton, MD), Nov 13
Watergate Day, Jun 17
Waterloo, Battle of: Anniv, Jun 18
Watermelon Fest (Rush Springs, OK), Aug 8
Watermelon Fest, Hope (Hope, AR), Aug 6
Watermelon Thump (Luling, TX), Jun 25
Waters, Ethel: Birth Anniv, Oct 31
Waters, John: Birth, Apr 22
Waters, Muddy: Birth Anniv, Apr 4
Waterston, Sam: Birth, Nov 15
Watie, Stand: Birth Anniv, Dec 12
Watley, Jody: Birth, Jan 30
Watros, Cynthia: Birth, Sep 2
Watson, Doc: Birth, Mar 2
Watson, Emily: Birth, Jan 14
Watson, Emma: Birth, Apr 15
Watson, James: Birth, Apr 6
Watson, Tom: Birth, Sep 4
Watt, James: Birth Anniv, Jan 19
Wattleton, Alyce Faye: Birth, Jul 8
Watts Riot: Anniv, Aug 11
Watts, Andre: Birth, Jun 20
Watts, Charlie: Birth, Jun 2
Watts, Rolonda: Birth, Jul 12
Wave All Your Fingers at Your Neighbors Day, Feb 7
Wayans, Damon: Birth, Sep 4
Wayans, Keenen Ivory: Birth, Jun 8
Wayans, Marlon: Birth, Jul 23
Wayans, Shawn: Birth, Jan 19
Wayfinding Month, Intl, Jan 1
Wayne, John: Birth Anniv, May 26
Wayne, Mad Anthony: Birth Anniv, Jan 1
Wealth Mentality Month, Intl, Jan 1
Wear Red Day, Natl, Feb 6
Weather
Big Wind: Anniv, Apr 12
Great Blizzard of '88: Anniv, Mar 12
Meteorological Day, World (UN), Mar 23
Warner Quotation: Anniv, Aug 24
Weatherman's Day, Feb 5
Weathers, Carl: Birth, Jan 14
Weaver, Fritz: Birth, Jan 19
Weaver, Robert C.: First Black US Cabinet Member: Anniv, Jan 18
Weaver, Sigourney: Birth, Oct 8
Webb, James: Birth, Feb 9
Webb, Karrie: Birth, Dec 21
Webb, Spud: Birth, Jul 13
Webber, Chris: Birth, Mar 1
Weber, Carl Maria von: Birth Anniv, Nov 18
Weber, Steven: Birth, Mar 4
Webster, Daniel: Birth Anniv, Jan 18
Webster, Noah: Birth Anniv, Oct 16
Webster-Ashburton Treaty Signed: Anniv, Aug 9
Wedding of the Sea (Venice, Italy), May 24
Wedding: George H.W. and Barbara Bush: Anniv, Jan 6
Wedding: George W. and Laura Bush: Anniv, Nov 5
Wedding: Jimmy and Rosalynn Carter: Anniv, Jul 7
Wedding: William and Hillary Clinton: Anniv, Oct 11
Weddings Month, Natl, Feb 1
Wedgwood, Josiah: Birth Anniv, Jul 12
Weems, Mason L. (Parson): Birth Anniv, Oct 11
Wegman, William: Birth, Dec 2
Weights and Measures Day, May 20
Weil, Andrew: Birth, Jun 8
Weil, Simone: Birth Anniv, Feb 3
Weinberg, Max M.: Birth, Apr 13
Weir, Bob: Birth, Oct 16
Weir, Peter: Birth, Aug 21
Weird Contest Week (Ocean City, NJ), Aug 17
Weiskopf, Tom: Birth, Nov 9
Weiss, Michael: Birth, Aug 2
Weiss, Michael T.: Birth, Feb 2
Weissmuller, Johnny: Birth Anniv, Jun 2
Weisz, Rachel: Birth, Mar 7
Weitz, Bruce: Birth, May 27
Weizmann, Chaim: Birth Anniv, Nov 27
Welch, Jack: Birth, Nov 19
Welch, Raquel: Birth, Sep 5
Welcome Back, Kotter TV Premiere: Anniv, Sep 9
Welcomegiving Day, You're, Nov 27
Weld, Tuesday: Birth, Aug 27
Welfare: See Health and Welfare, Aug 14
Welk, Lawrence: Birth Anniv, Mar 11
Wellderly Week, Mar 16
Weller, Peter: Birth, Jun 24
Welles, Orson: Birth Anniv, May 6
Welles, Orson: Citizen Kane Film Premiere: Anniv, May 1
Welles, Orson: The Shadow Radio Premiere: Anniv, Jul 31
Welling, Tom: Birth, Apr 26
Wells, H.G.: Birth Anniv, Sep 21
Wells, Ida B.: Birth Anniv, Jul 16
Wells, Kitty: Birth, Aug 30
Wells, Mary: Birth Anniv, May 13
Welty, Eudora: Birth Anniv, Apr 13
Wen, Ming-Na: Birth, Nov 20
Wendt, George: Birth, Oct 17
Wenner, Jann: Birth, Jan 7
Werfel, Franz: Birth Anniv, Sep 10
Wesley, John: Birth Anniv, Jun 17
West Side Story Premiere: Anniv, Sep 26
West Virginia
Admission Day, Jun 20
Apple Butter Fest (Berkeley Springs), Oct 10
Bridge Day (Fayetteville), Oct 17
Byrd, Robert C.: Birth, Nov 20

Head-of-the-Mon-River Horseshoe Tourn (Fairmont), May 23
Manchin, Joe, III: Birth, Aug 24
Miner's Day, Dec 6
Preston County Buckwheat Fest (Kingwood), Sep 24
Rockefeller, John D., IV: Birth, Jun 18
State Fair (Lewisburg), Aug 14
West Virginia Italian Heritage Fest (Clarksburg), Sep 4
West, Adam: Birth, Sep 19
West, Dottie: Birth Anniv, Oct 11
West, Kanye: Birth, Jun 8
West, Mae, Birthday Gala (New York, NY), Aug 14
West, Mae: Birth Anniv, Aug 17
West, Rebecca: Birth Anniv, Dec 25
Western Stock Show and Rodeo, Natl (Denver, CO), Jan 10
Westheimer, Dr. Ruth: Birth, Jun 4
Westinghouse, George: Birth Anniv, Oct 6
Westminster Kennel Club Dog Show (New York, NY), Feb 9
Westwick, Ed: Birth, Jun 27
Wettig, Patricia: Birth, Dec 4
Whales: Shamu's Birthday, Sep 26
Whalin, Justin: Birth, Sep 6
Whalley, Joanne: Birth, Aug 25
Whang, Suzanne: Birth, Sep 28
Wharton, Edith: Birth Anniv, Jan 24
What Will Be Your Legacy Month, Aug 1
What You Think Upon Grows Day, May 31
What's My Line? TV Premiere: Anniv, Feb 2
Wheatley, Phillis: Death Anniv, Dec 5
Wheatley, Phillis: Poetry Collection Published: Anniv, Sep 1
Wheaton, Wil: Birth, Jul 29
Wheel of Fortune TV Premiere: Anniv, Jan 6
Wheelchair Beautification Month, Natl, Jul 1
Wheeler, William A.: Birth Anniv, Jun 30
Whelchel, Lisa: Birth, May 29
Whiner's Day, Natl, Dec 26
Whipple, William: Birth Anniv, Jan 14
Whistler, James: Birth Anniv, Jul 10
Whistlers Convention, Intl (Louisburg, NC), Apr 22
Whitaker, Forest: Birth, Jul 15
White Cane Safety Day (Pres Proc), Oct 15
White House Cornerstone Laid: Anniv, Oct 13
White House Easter Egg Roll (Washington, DC), Apr 13
White Shirt Day, Feb 11
White Sunday (Samoa, American Samoa), Oct 11
White, Betty: Birth, Jan 17
White, Byron R.: Birth Anniv, Jun 8
White, Charles: Birth Anniv, Apr 2
White, E.B.: Birth Anniv, Jul 11
White, Edward Douglass: Birth Anniv, Nov 3
White, Gilbert: Birth Anniv, Jul 18
White, Jaleel: Birth, Nov 27
White, Stanford: Birth Anniv, Nov 9
White, Vanna: Birth, Feb 18
Whitechapel Murders Begin: Anniv, Aug 31
Whitehouse, Sheldon: Birth, Oct 20
Whitelaw, Billie: Birth, Jun 6
Whitfield, Lynn: Birth, May 6
Whitman, Christine T.: Birth, Sep 26
Whitman, Slim (Otis): Birth, Jan 20
Whitman, Stuart: Birth, Feb 1
Whitman, Walt: Birth Anniv, May 31
Whitmire, Kathryn: Birth, Aug 15
Whitmonday, Jun 1
Whitney, Eli: Birth Anniv, Dec 8
Whitsunday, May 31
Whittier, John Greenleaf: Birth Anniv, Dec 17
Wiccan Observances
Beltane, Apr 30
Imbolc, Feb 2
Lughnasadh, Aug 1
Mabon, Sep 22
Midsummer, Jun 21
Ostara, Mar 20
Samhain, Oct 31
Yule, Dec 21
Wicker, Roger: Birth, Jul 5
Wicker, Tom: Birth, Jun 18
Wiesel, Elie: Birth, Sep 30
Wiesenthal, Simon: Birth Anniv, Dec 31
Wiest, Dianne: Birth, Mar 28
Wife Appreciation Day, Sep 19
Wig Out Day, Natl, May 22
Wiggin, Kate Douglas: Birth Anniv, Sep 28
Wilbur, Richard: Birth, Mar 1
Wilby, James: Birth, Feb 20
Wilcox, Dave: Birth, Sep 29
Wilde, Oscar: Birth Anniv, Oct 16
Wilder Pageant, Laura Ingalls (De Smet, SD), Jul 10
Wilder, Billy: Birth Anniv, Jun 22
Wilder, Gene: Birth, Jun 11
Wilder, L. Douglas: First Black Governor Elected: Anniv, Nov 7
Wilder, Thornton: Birth Anniv, Apr 17
Wildflower Week, Natl, May 4
Wildlife Week, Natl, Apr 18
Wilkins, Roy: Birth Anniv, Aug 30
Wilkinson, Tom: Birth, Dec 12
Will Rogers Day (OK), Nov 4
Will, George F.: Birth, May 4
Willard, Archibald M.: Birth Anniv, Aug 22
Willard, Emma Hart: Birth Anniv, Feb 23
Willard, Frances E.C.: Birth Anniv, Sep 28
William the Conqueror: Death Anniv, Sep 9
William, Prince: Birth, Jun 21
Williams, Andy: Birth, Dec 3
Williams, Archie: Birth Anniv, May 1
Williams, Bernie: Birth, Sep 13
Williams, Billy Dee: Birth, Apr 6
Williams, Cindy: Birth, Aug 22
Williams, Clarence, III: Birth, Aug 21
Williams, Curtis: Birth, Dec 11
Williams, Deniece: Birth, Jun 3
Williams, Esther: Birth, Aug 8
Williams, Hank, Jr: Birth, May 26
Williams, Hank, Sr: Birth Anniv, Sep 17
Williams, Jayson: Birth, Feb 22
Williams, Jimy: Birth, Oct 4
Williams, JoBeth: Birth, Dec 6
Williams, John: Birth, Feb 8
Williams, Mason: Birth, Aug 24
Williams, Matt: Birth, Nov 28
Williams, Michelle: Birth, Sep 9
Williams, Montel: Birth, Jul 3
Williams, Paul: Birth, Sep 19
Williams, Robin: Birth, Jul 21
Williams, Serena: Birth, Sep 26
Williams, Ted: Birth Anniv, Aug 30
Williams, Tennessee: Birth Anniv, Mar 26
Williams, Tennessee: Streetcar Named Desire Broadway Opening: Anniv, Dec 3
Williams, Treat: Birth, Dec 1
Williams, Vanessa: Birth, Mar 18
Williams, Venus: Birth, Jun 17
Williams, William: Birth Anniv, Apr 8
Williamson, Fred: Birth, Mar 5
Williamson, Nicol: Birth, Sep 14
Willis, Bruce: Birth, Mar 19
Willkie, Wendell L.: Birth Anniv, Feb 18
Wills, Bob: Birth Anniv, Mar 6
Wills, Bob: Day (Turkey, TX), Apr 25
Wills, Garry: Birth, May 22
Willson, Meredith: Birth Anniv, May 18
Wilson, Ann: Birth, Jun 19
Wilson, Blaine: Birth, Aug 3
Wilson, Brian: Birth, Jun 20
Wilson, Carnie: Birth, Apr 29
Wilson, Cassandra: Birth, Dec 4
Wilson, Chandra: Birth, Aug 27
Wilson, Edith: Birth Anniv, Oct 15
Wilson, Ellen L.: Birth Anniv, May 15
Wilson, Ellis: Birth Anniv, Apr 30
Wilson, Gretchen: Birth, Jun 26
Wilson, Harold: Birth Anniv, Mar 11
Wilson, Henry: Birth Anniv, Feb 16
Wilson, James: Birth Anniv, Sep 14
Wilson, Luke: Birth, Sep 21
Wilson, Mary: Birth, Mar 4
Wilson, Nancy: Birth, Feb 20
Wilson, Owen: Birth, Nov 18
Wilson, Rainn: Birth, Jan 20
Wilson, Tom: Birth, Aug 1
Wilson, William G.: Alcoholics Anonymous: Founding Anniv, Jun 10
Wilson, William Julius: Birth, Dec 20
Wilson, Woodrow: Birth Anniv, Dec 28
Wilson, Woodrow: Fourteen Points Proposed: Anniv, Jan 8
Wimbledon: Lawn Tennis Chmpshps at (London, England), Jun 22
Winchell, Walter: Birth Anniv, Apr 7
Wind Cave Natl Park Established: Anniv, Jan 3
Windjammer Days (Boothbay Harbor, ME), Jun 23
Windmill Day, Natl (Netherlands), May 9
Windom, William: Birth, Sep 28
Window Safety Week, Natl, Apr 20
Windsor, Duke of, Marriage: Anniv, Jun 3
Wine, Blessing of the (Greiveldange, Luxembourg), Dec 26
Wine: Open That Bottle Night, Feb 28
Wine: Telluride Wine Fest (Telluride, CO), Jun 25
Winehouse, Amy: Birth, Sep 14
Winfield, Dave: Birth, Oct 3
Winfrey, Oprah: Birth, Jan 29
Winger, Debra: Birth, May 17
Wings 'n' Water Fest (Stone Harbor, NJ), Sep 19
Wings over the Platte Spring Migration Celebration (Grand Island, NE), Feb 14
Winkler, Henry: Birth, Oct 30
Winningham, Mare: Birth, May 16
Winslet, Kate: Birth, Oct 5
Winstone, Ray: Birth, Feb 19
Winter Begins, Dec 21
Winter Fairy Fun Day, Dec 27
Winter Festivals and Celebrations
Brookfield Ice Harvest (Brookfield, VT), Jan 31
Illinois Snow Sculpting Competition (Rockford, IL), Jan 21
Nenana Tripod Raising Fest (Nenana, AK), Mar 7
Newport Winter Fest (Newport, RI), Feb 13
Saint Paul Winter Carnival (St. Paul, MN), Jan 22
Snowman Burning (Sault Ste. Marie, MI), Mar 20
Tip-Up Town USA (Houghton Lake, MI), Jan 16

US Natl Snow Sculpting Competition (Lake Geneva, WI), Feb 4
Winter Carnival Bon Soo (Sault Ste. Marie, ON, Canada), Feb 6
Winterfest (Flagstaff, AZ), Feb 1
Winterfest (Luverne, MN), Dec 4
Winterlude (Ottawa, ON, Canada), Feb 6
Wisconsin Dells Flake Out Fest (Wisconsin Dells, WI), Jan 17
Zehnder's Snowfest (Frankenmuth, MI), Jan 21
Winter Olympics, First: Anniv, Jan 25
Winter Solstice: Yalda (Iran), Dec 21
Winter, Alex: Birth, Jul 17
Winter, Edgar: Birth, Dec 28
Winter, Johnny: Birth, Feb 23
Winterlude (Ottawa, ON, Canada), Feb 6
Winters, Jonathan: Birth, Nov 11
Winthrop, John: Birth Anniv, Jan 12
Winwood, Steve: Birth, May 12
Wisconsin
Admission Day: Anniv, May 29
Aldo Leopold Weekend, Mar 6
Amcore Bank Faire on the Square Art & Craft Fair (Baraboo), May 16
American Birkebeiner (Cable to Hayward), Feb 19
Art Armada (Sheboygan), Jul 4
Art Fair on the Square (Madison), Jul 11
Automotion (Wisconsin Dells), May 16
Badger State Summer Games (Madison), Jun 19
Big Ten Women's Tennis Chmpshp (Madison), Apr 23
Briggs & Al's Run & Walk (Milwaukee), Sep 19
Cambridge Pottery Fest and US Pottery Games (Cambridge), Jun 13
Community Affair (Menomonee Falls), Oct 17
Country Christmas (Cambridge), Dec 5
Doyle, Jim: Birth, Nov 23
Ducktona 500 (Sheboygan Falls), Jul 5
EAA Airventure Oshkosh (Oshkosh), Jul 27
Feingold, Russell D.: Birth, Mar 2
Fishing Has No Boundaries (Hayward), May 15
Great Wisconsin Cheese Fest (Little Chute), Jun 5
Groundhog Day Celebration and Prognostication (Sun Prairie), Jan 31
Hodag Country Fest (Rhinelander), Jul 9
Holiday Folk Fair Intl (Milwaukee), Nov 20
Kettle Moraine Jazz Fest (West Bend), Sep 11
Klondike Days (Eagle River), Feb 21
Kohl, Herb: Birth, Feb 7
Lumberjack World Chmpshps (Hayward), Jul 23
Maple Syrup Saturday (Appleton), Mar 21
Mexican Fiesta Internacional (Milwaukee), Aug 21
Milwaukee Boat Show (Milwaukee), Jan 16
Milwaukee Irish Fest (Milwaukee), Aug 13
Milwaukee Journal Sentinel Sports Show (Milwaukee), Mar 11
Morel Mushroom Fest (Muscoda), May 16
Music by the Mile (West Allis), Jul 23
Norskedalen's Midsummer Fest (Coon Valley), Jun 20
Norskedalen's Old-Fashioned Christmas (Coon Valley), Dec 5
Norskedalen's Threshing Bee (Coon Valley), Sep 26
Northeastern Wisconsin Antique Power and Machinery Show Thresheree (Sturgeon Bay), Aug 14
Prairie Villa Rendezvous (Prairie du Chien), Jun 18
Riverfest (LaCrosse), Jul 1
Romp in the Swamp Fun Walk (Appleton), Oct 17
Saint Cyril's Parish Fest (Sheboygan), Jul 19
Shanty Days (Algoma), Aug 14
State Fair (Milwaukee), Aug 6
Sun Prairie's Sweet Corn Fest (Sun Prairie), Aug 20
Taste of Madison (Madison), Sep 5
Tongue Twister Contest, Intl (Burlington), Nov 7
Traditional Sousa Concert (Kohler), Jul 4
US Natl Snow Sculpting Competition (Lake Geneva), Feb 4
Volksfest (New Glarus), Aug 2
Warrens Cranberry Fest (Warrens), Sep 25
Wisconsin Cow-Chip Throw (Prairie du Sac), Aug 28
Wisconsin Dells Autumn Harvest Fest (Wisconsin Dells), Oct 17
Wisconsin Dells Flake Out Fest (Wisconsin Dells), Jan 17
World Dairy Expo (Madison), Sep 29
World's Largest Trivia Contest (Stevens Point), Apr 17
Wo-Zha-Wa Fall Fest (Wisconsin Dells), Sep 18
Yo-Yo and Skill Toy Conv (Burlington), Mar 13
Wise Health Care Consumer Month, Feb 1
Wise, Thomas J.: Birth Anniv, Oct 7
Wishbones for Pets, Oct 15
Witches: Salem Hysteria Begins: Anniv, Mar 1
Witches: Salem Trials Begin: Anniv, Jun 2
Witherspoon, John: Birth Anniv, Feb 5
Witherspoon, Reese: Birth, Mar 22
Witt, Alicia: Birth, Aug 21
Witt, Katarina: Birth, Dec 3
Witt, Paul Junger: Birth, Mar 20
Wizard of Oz Film Released: Anniv, Aug 25
WMAS Annual Halloween Ball (Springfield, MA), Oct 31
Wodehouse, P.G.: Birth Anniv, Oct 15
Wojtyla: Pope John Paul II: Birth Anniv, May 18
Wojtyla: Pope John Paul II: Death Anniv, Apr 2
Wolcott, Oliver: Birth Anniv, Nov 20
Wolf Moon, Jan 10
Wolf, Peter: Birth, Mar 7
Wolf, Scott: Birth, Jun 4
Wolfe, James: Birth Anniv, Jan 2
Wolfe, Tom: Birth, Mar 2
Wolff, Geoffrey: Birth, Nov 5
Wolff, Josh: Birth, Feb 25
Wolfman Jack: Birth Anniv, Jan 21
Wollstonecraft, Mary: Birth Anniv, Apr 27
Women
Abused Women and Children's Awareness Day, Jun 14
Alpha Kappa Alpha Sorority Founded: Anniv, Jan 15
American Heroine Rewarded: Anniv, Jun 8
Around the World in 72 Days: Anniv, Jan 25
Aspinwall Crosses US on Horseback: Anniv, Jul 8
Be Heard Day, Natl, Mar 7
Billie Jean King Wins Battle of Sexes: Anniv, Sep 20
Blackwell, Elizabeth, Awarded MD: Anniv, Jan 23
Bloomer, Amelia Jenks: Birth Anniv, May 27
Breast Cancer Awareness Month, Natl, Oct 1
Business Women's Day, American, Sep 22
Business Women's Week, Natl, Oct 19
Canada: Persons Day, Oct 18
Canada's First Woman Prime Minister: Anniv, Jun 25
Cervical Cancer Screening Month, Jan 1
Day for Women's Rights & Intl Peace (UN), Mar 8
Elimination of Violence Against Women, Intl Day for the (UN), Nov 25
English Channel, First Woman Swims: Anniv, Aug 6
Equal Rights Party Founding: Anniv, Sep 20
Female House Page, First Formal: Anniv, May 14
Female Relief Society of Nauvoo: Anniv, Mar 17
Feminine Mystique Published: Anniv, Feb 19
First All-Woman Jury: Anniv, Sep 22
First Doctor of Science Degree Earned by a Woman, Jun 20
First Elected Woman Senator: Anniv, Jan 12
First Episcopal Bishop: Anniv, Feb 11
First Female Congressional Page: Anniv, Jan 3
First Female FBI Agents: Anniv, Oct 25
First Free Flight by a Woman: Anniv, Jun 4
First to Climb Mount Everest, May 16
First US Woman Governor Inaugurated, Jan 5
First Woman in Space: Space Milestone, Jun 16
First Woman Rabbi in US: Anniv, Jun 3
First Woman to Walk in Space, Jul 17
First Woman US Ambassador Appointed: Anniv, Oct 28
First Woman US Senator: Anniv, Oct 3
First Woman Vice-Presidential Candidate: Anniv, Jul 19
First Women's Collegiate Basketball Game: Anniv, Mar 22
Fuller, Margaret: Birth Anniv, May 23
Girlfriend's Day, Aug 1
Girls and Women in Sports Day, Natl, Feb 4
Girls Write Now Day, Mar 8
Gorgeous Grandma Day, Jul 23
Gynecologic Cancer Awareness Month, Sep 1
Informed Woman Month, Apr 1
Introduce a Girl to Engineering Day, Feb 19
Jane Addams Day, Dec 10
Ladies' Day Initiated in Baseball: Anniv, Jun 16
League of Women Voters Formed: Anniv, Feb 14
Links, Inc: Anniv, Nov 9
Mansfield, Arabella: Birth Anniv, May 23
Margaret Brent Demands a Political Voice: Anniv, Jan 21
Mayer, Maria G.: Birth Anniv, Jun 28

Medical School Opened at Boston: Anniv, Nov 1
Meitlisunntig (Switzerland), Jan 11
Merriam, Eve: Birth Anniv, Jul 19
Nineteenth Amendment Ratified, Aug 18
NOW Founded: Anniv, Jun 30
Perkins, Frances (First Woman Appointed to US Cabinet), Mar 4
Personal Self-Defense Awareness Month, Natl, Jan 1
Pro Sports Wives Day, Feb 11
Russia: Women's Day, Intl, Mar 8
Salter Elected First Woman Mayor in US: Anniv, Apr 4
Seneca Falls Convention Survivor Votes: Anniv, Nov 2
She's Funny That Way Day, Natl, Mar 31
Single Working Women's Week, Aug 2
Space Milestone: First American Woman in Space, Jun 18
Spunky Old Broads Month, Feb 1
Suffrage Parade Attacked: Anniv, Mar 3
Suffragists' Voting Attempt: Anniv, Nov 19
Supreme Court Abortion Notification Ruling: Anniv, Jun 25
Susan B. Anthony Fined for Voting, Jun 6
Teach Your Daughter to Volunteer Day, Apr 18
Utah Women Given Vote: Anniv, Feb 12
Victorious Woman Month, Intl, May 1
WAAC: Anniv, May 14
Wear Red Day, Natl, Feb 6
White Woman Made Indian Chief: Anniv, Sep 18
Woman Inducted into Natl Inventors Hall of Fame: Anniv, May 18
Woman Presides over US Supreme Court: Anniv, Apr 3
Woman Road Warrior Day, Natl, Sep 21
Woman Runs the US House of Representatives: Anniv, Jun 20
Women Denied Vote: Anniv, Jan 12
Women in Blue Jeans Days, Jan 15
Women's Day, Natl (South Africa), Aug 9
Women's Ecommerce Day, Intl, Sep 21
Women's Equality Day, Aug 26
Women's Equality Day (Pres Proc), Aug 26
Women's Eye Health and Safety Month, Apr 1
Women's Friendship Day, Sep 20
Women's Hall of Fame, Natl: Anniv, Jul 21
Women's Health and Fitness Day, Natl, Sep 30
Women's Health Care Month, May 1
Women's Healthy Weight Day, Jan 22
Women's Heart Week, Feb 1
Women's History Month (Pres Proc), Mar 1
Women's History Month, Natl, Mar 1
Women's Motorcycle Month, Jul 1
Women's Nutrition Week, Natl, Apr 5
Women's Rights Convention at Seneca Falls: Anniv, Jul 19
Women's Self-Empowerment Week, Jan 5
Women's Small Business Month, Oct 1
Women's Suffrage Amendment Introduced: Anniv, Jan 10
Work at Home Moms Week, May 18
Working Women's Day, Intl, Mar 8
World Menopause Day, Oct 18
Women's Christian Temperance Union Organized: Anniv, Nov 19
Wonder Years TV Premiere: Anniv, Mar 15
Wonder, Stevie: Birth, May 13
Wonderful Weirdos Day, Sep 9
Wood, Elijah: Birth, Jan 28
Wood, Evan Rachel: Birth, Sep 7
Wood, Grant, Art Fest (Anamosa, IA), Jun 14
Wood, Grant: Birth Anniv, Feb 13
Wood, Kerry: Birth, Jun 16
Wood, Ron: Birth, Jun 1
Woodard, Alfre: Birth, Nov 8
Woodhull, Victoria C.: Birth Anniv, Sep 23
Woodie Wagon Day, Natl, Jul 18
Woodland Indian Discovery Day (St. Mary's City, MD), Sep 12
Woodruff, Judy: Birth, Nov 20
Woods, Eldrick "Tiger": Birth, Dec 30
Woods, Granville T.: Birth Anniv, Apr 23
Woods, James: Birth, Apr 18
Woodson, Carter Godwin: Birth Anniv, Dec 19
Woodstock Fair (Woodstock, CT), Sep 4
Woodstock: Anniv, Aug 15
Woodward, Bob: Birth, Mar 26
Woodward, Edward: Birth, Jun 1
Woodward, Joanne: Birth, Feb 27
Woodward, Robert B.: Birth Anniv, Apr 10
Woofstock (Wichita, KS), Oct 3
Woolery, Chuck: Birth, Mar 16
Woolf, Virginia: Birth Anniv, Jan 25
Woolly Worm Fest (Banner Elk, NC), Oct 17
Woolworth's First Opened: Anniv, Feb 22
Wopat, Tom: Birth, Sep 9
Word Origins
Boycott, Charles C.: Birth Anniv, Mar 12
Chauvin Day, Aug 15
Cyberspace Coined: Neuromancer Publication Anniv, Oct 1
De Silhouette, Etienne: Birth Anniv, Jul 8
O.K. First Appearance in Print: Anniv, Mar 23
Robot Enters World Lexicon: Anniv, Jan 25
Words by the Water: A Cumbrian Literature Fest (Lake District, England), Feb 27
Words Matter Week, Natl, Mar 1
Wordsworth, William: Birth Anniv, Apr 7
Work and Family Month, Natl, Oct 1
Work at Home Moms Week, May 18
Work from Home Week, Natl, Oct 4
Work Schedule Month, Revise Your, May 1
Work@Home Father's Day, Jun 19
Workers Memorial Day, Apr 28
Working Women's Day, Intl, Mar 8
Workplace Conflict Awareness Month, Apr 1
Workplace Eye Health and Safety Month, Mar 1
Workplace Politics Awareness Month, Oct 1
World AIDS Day (Pres Proc), Dec 1
World Chmpshp Punkin Chunkin (Bridgeville, DE), Nov 6
World Communion Sunday, Oct 4
World Cup Inaugurated: Anniv, Jul 13
World Day of Prayer, Mar 6
World Food Day, Oct 16
World Habitat Awareness Month, Apr 1
World Health Organization: Anniv, Apr 7
World Human Spirit Day, Feb 17
World Juggling Day, Jun 20
World Lupus Day, May 10
World Maritime Day (UN), Sep 28
World Tourism Day, Sep 27
World Trade Center Attack (9-11): Anniv, Sep 11
World Trade Center Bombing of 1993: Anniv, Feb 26
World Trade Center Recovery and Cleanup Ends: Anniv, May 30
World Trade Week (Pres Proc), May 17
World Turtle Day, May 23
World War I
Alvin C. York Day, Oct 8
ANZAC Day, Apr 25
Armistice: Anniv, Nov 11
Baseball Declared Nonessential: Anniv, Jul 20
Battle of Amiens, Second: Anniv, Aug 8
Battle of Cambrai–Saint Quentin: Anniv, Sep 27
Battle of Gallipoli, Apr 25
Battle of Lys River: Anniv, Apr 7
Battle of Meuse-Argonne Forest: Anniv, Sep 26
Battle of Saint-Mihiel: Anniv, Sep 12
Battle of Somme, Second: Anniv, Mar 21
Battle of the Marne: Anniv, Jul 15
Battle of Verdun, Feb 21
Battle of Vittorio Veneto: Anniv, Oct 24
Begins: Anniv, Jul 28
Big Bertha Paris Gun: Anniv, Mar 23
Campbell Becomes First American Air Ace: Anniv, Apr 14
Death/Duty Day, Nov 11
Fourteen Points Proposed: Anniv, Jan 8
German Revolution of 1918: Anniv, Oct 28
Ludendorff, Erich: Birth Anniv, Apr 9
Mata Hari: Birth Anniv, Aug 7
Mata Hari: Execution Anniv, Oct 15
Neutrality Appeal, American: Anniv, Aug 18
Red Baron Shot Down: Anniv, Apr 21
Treaty of Versailles: Anniv, Jun 28
US Enters WWI: Anniv, Apr 6
Versailles Peace Conference: Anniv, Jan 18
Veterans Bonus Army Eviction: Anniv, Jul 28
Wilhelm II Abdicates: Anniv, Nov 9
World War II
Allied Invasion of Sicily: Anniv, Jul 10
Allied Landing at Anzio: Anniv, Jan 22
Allied Landings in South of France: Anniv, Aug 15
Allies Break Out of Normandy Beachhead: Anniv, Jul 25
Allies Capture Monte Cassino: Anniv, May 18
Allies Retake Guadalcanal: Anniv, Feb 9
Allies Take New Guinea: Anniv, Jan 22
Allies Take Palermo: Anniv, Jul 22
Allies Take Sicily: Anniv, Aug 17
America Enters WWII, Dec 8
Arnold, Henry H.: Birth Anniv, Jun 25
Atomic Bomb Dropped on Hiroshima: Anniv, Aug 6
Atomic Bomb Dropped on Nagasaki: Anniv, Aug 9
Atomic Bomb Tested: Anniv, Jul 16
Attempt on Hitler's Life: Anniv, Jul 20
Auschwitz Liberated: Anniv, Jan 27
Austria Invaded by Nazi Germany: Anniv, Mar 12
Bataan Death March: Anniv, Apr 10
Battle of Bismarck Sea: Anniv, Mar 2
Battle of Kursk: Anniv, Jul 12
Battle of Leyte Gulf: Anniv, Oct 23
Battle of Midway: Anniv, Jun 4
Battle of Okinawa Begins: Anniv, Apr 1
Battle of Okinawa Ends: Anniv, Jun 21
Battle of Philippine Sea, Jun 19
Battle of Salerno: Anniv, Sep 9
Battle of San Pietro: Anniv, Dec 15

Battle of Stalingrad Begins: Anniv, Aug 22
Battle of Tarawa-Makin: Anniv, Nov 20
Battle of the Aleutian Islands: Anniv, May 30
Battle of the Bulge: Anniv, Dec 16
Battle of the Coral Sea: Anniv, May 8
Begins: Germany Invades Poland: Anniv, Sep 1
Berlin Surrenders: Anniv, May 2
Britain Declares War on Germany: Anniv, Sep 3
British Air Raid on Berlin: Anniv, Jan 16
British Capture Enigma Machine: Anniv, May 9
Civil Air Patrol Founded: Anniv, Dec 1
Civilian Auto Production Halted: Anniv, Feb 10
Clark, Mark: Birth Anniv, May 1
Corridor of Death: Anniv, Jan 13
Corsica Liberated: Anniv, Oct 4
Czechoslovakia: Rape of Lidice: Anniv, Jun 10
Davis, Benjamin O., Jr: Birth Anniv, Dec 18
D-Day: Anniv, Jun 6
De Gaulle, Charles: Birth Anniv, Nov 22
Diary of Anne Frank: Last Entry: Anniv, Aug 1
Dresden Firebombing: Anniv, Feb 13
Dunkirk Evacuated: Anniv, May 26
East Meets West: Anniv, Apr 25
Eisenhower Assumes Command: Anniv, Jan 16
FDR's Unconditional Surrender Statement: Anniv, Jan 24
First Medal of Honor: Anniv, Feb 10
First Surface-to-Surface Missile: Anniv, Dec 24
Four Chaplains Memorial Day, Feb 3
German Surrender at Stalingrad: Anniv, Feb 2
Germany's First Surrender: Anniv, May 7
Germany's Second Surrender: Anniv, May 8
Gersdorff Hitler Assassination Attempt: Anniv, Mar 21
Gilbert Islands Taken: Anniv, Nov 23
Gillars, Mildred E.: Death Anniv, Jun 25
Graham, Calvin "Baby Vet": Birth Anniv, Apr 3
Gypsy Condemnation Order: Anniv, Nov 15
Halsey, William "Bull": Birth Anniv, Oct 30
Hamburg Firestorm: Anniv, Jul 28
Hitler Youth Deployed: Anniv, Jan 26
Howard, Leslie: Birth Anniv, Apr 3
Indianapolis Sunk: Anniv, Jul 29
Italy Surrenders: Anniv, Sep 3
Iwo Jima Day: Anniv, Feb 23
Japan Bombed: Anniv, Apr 18
Japanese Attack US Mainland: Anniv, Feb 23
Japanese Internment: Anniv, Feb 19
Japan's Unconditional Surrender: Anniv, Aug 10
Krupp, Alfried: Birth Anniv, Aug 13
Lady Be Good Lost: Anniv, Apr 4
Leningrad Liberated: Anniv, Jan 27
Liberation of Buchenwald: Anniv, Apr 11
Liberation of Dachau: Anniv, Apr 29
MacArthur Returns: US Landings on Leyte, Philippines: Anniv, Oct 20
Manstein, Erich von: Birth Anniv, Nov 24
Marshall Islands Landings: Anniv, Jan 31
Marshall, George C.: Birth Anniv, Dec 31
Monte Cassino Bombed: Anniv, Feb 15
Montgomery, Bernard Law: Birth Anniv, Nov 17
Moulin, Jean: Death Anniv, Jul 8
Mussolini Executed: Anniv, Apr 28
Mussolini Ousted: Anniv, Jul 25
Napalm Used: Anniv, Jul 11
Navajo Nation Navajo Code Talkers Day, Aug 14
Nimitz, Chester: Birth Anniv, Feb 24
Oak Ridge Atomic Plant Begun: Anniv, Aug 1
Odessa Retaken: Anniv, Apr 10
Operation Flash: Anniv, Mar 13
Operation Overcast: Anniv, Jul 6
Paris Liberated: Anniv, Aug 25
Paulus, Friedrich: Birth Anniv, Sep 23
Peace Rose Introduced to World: Anniv, Apr 29
Pearl Harbor Day, Dec 7
Potsdam Declaration: Anniv, Jul 26
RAF Bombs Hitler Celebration: Anniv, Jan 30
RAF Bombs Ruhr Dams: Anniv, May 16
RAF Jams Nazi Radar: Anniv, Jul 24
Raising Flag on Iwo Jima: Hayes, Ira: Birth Anniv, Jan 12
Remagen Bridge Capture: Anniv, Mar 7
Ridgway, Matthew Bunker: Birth Anniv, Mar 3
Rogers, Edith Nourse: Birth Anniv, Mar 19
Romania Surrenders to USSR: Anniv, Aug 23
Rome Executions: Anniv, Mar 25
Rome Liberated: Anniv, Jun 4
Rommel, Erwin: Birth Anniv, Nov 15
Roosevelt, Franklin D.: Death Anniv, Apr 12
Russia: Victory Day, May 9
Smith, Holland: Birth Anniv, Apr 20
Soviet Union Invaded: Anniv, Jun 22
Tehran Conference: Anniv, Nov 28
Time of Remembrance and Reconciliation for Those Who Lost Their Lives During WWII (UN), May 8
Tokyo Blanket Bombing: Anniv, Mar 9
Truman Doctrine: Anniv, May 22
Tunis Campaign Victory: Anniv, May 13
Tuskegee Airmen Activated: Anniv, Mar 22
US Forces Land in Mindoro, Philippines: Anniv, Dec 15
US Landing on Iwo Jima: Anniv, Feb 19
US Landing on Luzon: Anniv, Jan 9
US Landing on Saipan, Jun 15
US Troops Enter Germany: Anniv, Sep 15
V-E Day, May 8
V-J Day (Announcement): Anniv, Aug 14
V-J Day (Ratification), Sep 2
V-Mail Delivery: Anniv, Jun 22
WAAC: Anniv, May 14
War Time: Anniv, Feb 9
Warsaw Ghetto Revolt: Anniv, Apr 19
Warsaw Uprising: Anniv, Aug 1
Yalta Agreement Signed: Anniv, Feb 11
Yamamoto, Isoroku: Birth Anniv, Apr 4
World Wide Web: Anniv, Aug 1
WorldFuture 2009 (Chicago, IL), Jul 17
World's Biggest Fish Fry (Paris, TN), Apr 20
World's End Day, Oct 22
World's Fair of Money (Los Angeles, CA), Aug 5
World's Indigenous People, Intl Day of the (UN), Aug 9
Worley, Jo Anne: Birth, Sep 6
Worm Moon, Mar 10
Woronov, Mary: Birth, Dec 8
Worthy, James: Birth, Feb 27
Wouk, Herman: Birth, May 27
Wounded Knee Massacre: Anniv, Dec 29
Wozniak, Stephen: Birth, Aug 11
Wrangell-Saint Elias Natl Park: Anniv, Dec 2
Wray, Fay: Birth Anniv, Sep 15
Wray, Fay: King Kong Film Premiere: Anniv, Mar 2
Wren, Christopher: Birth Anniv, Oct 20
Wren, Day of the (Ireland), Dec 26
Wrestling
Big Ten Chmpshps (University Park, PA), Mar 7
NAIA Chmpshps (Sioux City, IA), Mar 5
NCAA Div I Chmpshps (St. Louis, MO), Mar 19
Wright Brothers Day (Pres Proc), Dec 17
Wright Brothers First Powered Flight: Anniv, Dec 17
Wright Brothers: First Flight 100th Anniv Celebration (Kill Devil Hills, NC), Dec 17
Wright, Amy: Birth, Apr 15
Wright, Frank Lloyd: Birth Anniv, Jun 8
Wright, Frank Lloyd: Robie House Secrets & Shadows Tour (Chicago, IL), Oct 23
Wright, Frank Lloyd: Wright Plus (Oak Park, IL), May 16
Wright, Gary: Birth, Apr 26
Wright, Orville: Birth Anniv, Aug 19
Wright, Richard: Birth Anniv, Sep 4
Wright, Rick: Birth, Jul 28
Wright, Robin: Birth, Apr 8
Wright, Steven: Birth, Dec 6
Wright, Wilbur: Birth Anniv, Apr 16
Write a Business Plan Month, Natl, Dec 1
Writing. See also Journalism
Freelance Writers Appreciation Week, Feb 8
Ghostwriters Week, Natl, Mar 1
Highlights Foundation Writer's Workshop (Chautauqua, NY), Jul 11
I Love to Write Day, Nov 15
Lifewriting Month, Natl, Nov 1
Write a Letter of Appreciation Week, Natl, Mar 1
Write to Your Father Day, Jun 7
Writing: Card and Letter Writing Month, Natl, Apr 1
Writing: Grammar Day, Natl, Mar 4
Wuhl, Robert: Birth, Oct 9
Wyatt Earp TV Premiere: Anniv, Sep 6
Wyatt, Jane: Birth Anniv, Aug 12
Wyden, Ron: Birth, May 3
Wyle, Noah: Birth, Jun 4
Wyman, Bill: Birth, Oct 24
Wyoming
Admission Day, Jul 10
Barrasso, John: Birth, Jul 21
Bluegrass Fest (Alta), Aug 7
Cheyenne Frontier Days (Cheyenne), Jul 17
Enzi, Michael B.: Birth, Feb 1
First US Woman Governor Inaugurated, Jan 5
Fort Bridger Rendezvous (Fort Bridger), Sep 4
Freudenthal, Dave: Birth, Oct 12
Grand Teton Music Fest (Teton Village), Jun 30
Grand Teton Natl Park Established: Anniv, Feb 26
State Fair & Rodeo (Douglas), Aug 8
Targhee Fest (Alta), Jul 17
Wythe, George: Death Anniv, Jun 8

X
X-Files TV Premiere: Anniv, Sep 10
X-Ray Discovery Day: Anniv, Nov 8
XTERRA World Chmpshp (Maui, HI), Oct 25

Y
Yacht Race, Intl: Anniv, Aug 22
Yagudin, Alexei: Birth, Mar 18
Yalda (Iran), Dec 21
Yale Univ Founded: Anniv, Oct 16
Yale, Linus: Birth Anniv, Apr 4
Yalow, Rosalyn: Birthday, Jul 19
Yalta Agreement Signed: Anniv, Feb 11
Yamaguchi, Kristi: Birth, Jul 12
Yamamoto, Isoroku: Birth Anniv, Apr 4
Yambilee Fest, Louisiana (Opelousas, LA), Oct 22
Yamboree, East Texas (Gilmer, TX), Oct 14
Yankee Stadium Opens, Apr 18
Yankovic, Weird Al: Birth, Oct 23
Yanni: Birth, Nov 14
Yarborough, Cale: Birth, Mar 27
Yarrow, Peter: Birth, May 31
Yasbeck, Amy: Birth, Sep 12
Yastrzemski, Carl: Birth, Aug 22
Yawm Arafat (Islamic): The Standing at Arafat, Nov 27
Yeager, Chuck: Birth, Feb 13
Yeager, Chuck: Sound Barrier Broken: Anniv, Oct 14
Yearwood, Trisha: Birth, Sep 19
Yeats, William B.: Birth Anniv, Jun 13
Yell "Fudge" at the Cobras in North America Day, Jun 2
Yellow Daisy Fest (Stone Mountain, GA), Sep 10
Yellow Kid: First Newspaper Comic Strip: Anniv, Oct 18
Yellowstone Natl Park Established: Anniv, Mar 1
Yeltsin, Boris, Inaugurated as Russian President: Anniv, Jul 10
Yeltsin, Boris: Birth Anniv, Feb 1
Yemen: Natl Day, May 22
Yeoh, Michelle: Birth, Aug 6
Yevtushenko, Yevgeny: Birth, Jul 18
YMCA Organized: Anniv, Dec 29
Yoakam, Dwight: Birth, Oct 23
Yom Hashoah (Israel), Apr 21
Yom Kippur, Sep 28
Yom Kippur Begins, Sep 27
Yom Kippur War: Anniv, Oct 6
York, Alvin C.: Day, Oct 8
York, Michael: Birth, Mar 27
York, Susannah: Birth, Jan 9
Yorktown Day, Oct 19
Yorktown Day (Yorktown, VA), Oct 19
Yorktown Victory Day (VA), Oct 12
Yosemite Natl Park Established: Anniv, Oct 1
Yothers, Tina: Birth, May 5
You Are There TV Premiere: Anniv, Feb 1
You Bet Your Life TV Premiere: Anniv, Oct 5
Young Achievers/Leaders of Tomorrow Month, May 1
Young and the Restless TV Premiere: Anniv, Mar 26
Young, Andrew: Birth, Mar 12
Young, Brigham: Anniv of Last Marriage, Apr 6
Young, Brigham: Birth Anniv, Jun 1
Young, Burt: Birth, Apr 30
Young, Chic: Birth Anniv, Jan 9
Young, Cy: Birth Anniv, Mar 29
Young, Loretta: Birth Anniv, Jan 6
Young, Michael: Birth, Oct 19
Young, Neil: Birth, Nov 12
Young, Sean: Birth, Nov 20
Young, Steve: Birth, Oct 11
Young, Vince: Birth, May 18
Yount, Robin: Birth, Sep 16
Your Hit Parade Radio Premiere: Anniv, Apr 12
Your Hit Parade TV Premiere: Anniv, Oct 7
Your Show of Shows TV Premiere: Anniv, Feb 25
You're Welcomegiving Day, Nov 27
Youth Art Month, Mar 1
Youth Day (Cameroon), Feb 11
Youth Day (People's Republic of China), May 4
Youth Day, Intl (UN), Aug 12
Youth Leadership Month, Feb 1
Youth Service Day, Global, Apr 24
Youth Sports Safety Month, Natl, Apr 1
Yo-Yo and Skill Toy Conv (Burlington, WI), Mar 13
Yu, Jessica: Birth, Feb 14
Yugoslavia
  Civil War: Anniv, Jun 25
  NATO Forces Attack: Anniv, Mar 25
  Slovenia and Croatia Independence: Anniv, Jun 25
  Tito (Josip Broz): Birth Anniv, May 25
Yukon Gold Panning Chmpshps (Dawson City, YT, Canada), Jul 1
Yukon Quest Intl 1,000-Mile Sled Dog Race (Fairbanks, AK), Feb 14
Yukon Sourdough Rendezvous (Whitehorse, YT, Canada), Feb 20
Yule (Wiccan), Dec 21
YWCA Week Without Violence, Oct 18
Yzerman, Steve: Birth, May 9

Z
Z Day, Jan 1
Zadora, Pia: Birth, May 4
Zaharias, Mildred Babe Didrikson: Birth Anniv, Jun 26
Zahn, Paula: Birth, Feb 24
Zahn, Steve: Birth, Nov 13
Zaire: Congo (Dem Rep of the): Independence Day, Jun 30
Zambia
  African Freedom Day, May 25
  Heroes Day, Jul 6
  Independence Day, Oct 24
  Unity Day, Jul 7
  Youth Day, Aug 3
Zambrano, Carlos: Birth, Jun 1
Zane Grey TV Premiere: Anniv, Oct 5
Zane, Billy: Birth, Feb 24
Zanuck, Darryl F.: Birth Anniv, Sep 5
Zappa, Dweezil: Birth, Sep 5
Zappa, Frank: Birth Anniv, Dec 21
Zeffirelli, Franco: Birth, Feb 12
Zellweger, Renee: Birth, Apr 25
Zemeckis, Robert: Birth, May 14
Zenger, John P.: Arrest Anniv, Nov 17
Zerbe, Anthony: Birth, May 20
Zero-Tasking Day, Nov 1
Zeta-Jones, Catherine: Birth, Sep 25
Zetkin, Clara: Birth Anniv, Jul 5
Zhang, Ziyi: Birth, Feb 9
Zidane, Zinedine: Birth, Jun 23
Ziegfeld Follies of 1907: Anniv, Jul 8
Zimbabwe
  Heroes' Day, Aug 11
  Independence Day, Apr 18
Zimbalist, Efrem, Jr: Birth, Nov 30
Zimbalist, Stephanie: Birth, Oct 6
Zimmer, Don: Birth, Jan 17
Zion Natl Park Established: Anniv, Nov 19
Zionism, UN Revokes Resolution on: Anniv, Dec 16
Zip Codes Inaugurated: Anniv, Jul 1
Zipper Patented: Anniv, Apr 29
Zoeller, Fuzzy: Birth, Nov 11
Zola, Emile: Birth Anniv, Apr 2
Zolotow, Charlotte: Birth, Jun 26
Zoo Parade TV Premiere: Anniv, May 28
Zoo: First US Zoo: Anniv (Philadelphia, PA), Jul 1
Zoot Suit Riots: Anniv, Jun 3
Zucker, David: Birth, Oct 6
Zucker, Jerry: Birth, Mar 11
Zukerman, Pinchas: Birth, Jul 16
Zulu Mardi Gras Parade (New Orleans, LA), Feb 24
Zwingli, Ulrich: Birth Anniv, Jan 1

Yes! Please send me additional copies of *Chase's 2009 Calendar of Events*.

Ship to ______________________________

Address ______________________________

City, State, Zip ______________________________

Phone ( ) ______________________________

Please send me ______ copies of the 2009 edition of
CHASE'S CALENDAR OF EVENTS at $74.95 each (0-07-159954-1) $__________

Add applicable sales tax for all states **except** AK, DE, MT, NH, OR $__________

Shipping & Handling: Add $6.75 for the first copy,
$3.50 for each additional copy $__________

Total $__________

❑ Check or money order enclosed payable to: The McGraw-Hill Companies

Charge my ❑ Visa ❑ MasterCard ❑ American Express ❑ Discover Card

Acct. # ______________________________ Exp. Date ____/____

X ______________________________

Signature (if charging to bankcard)

Name (please print) ______________________________

STANDING ORDER AUTHORIZATION

To make sure that I receive each year's new edition, please accept this Standing Order Authorization to ship me ___ copies of Chase's Calendar of Events beginning with the 2009 edition. Bill me at the address shown at the top of this order form. I understand that I may cancel my Standing Order at any time.

X ______________________________

Signature Date

______________________________ ( )

Name (please print) Phone

GUARANTEE: Any book you order is unconditionally guaranteed and may be returned within 10 days of receipt for full refund.

Prices subject to change without notice. 9353

Mail to: **McGraw-Hill Customer Service**
P.O. Box 545
Blacklick, OH 43004-0545

Phone: (800) 722-4726 • Fax: (614) 755-5645 • Website: www.chases.com

HOW TO SUBMIT AN ENTRY

There is no charge for being listed in *Chase's*. Use the form below to submit new entries for forthcoming editions of *Chase's Calendar of Events*. Background information about your entry is also appreciated. Please be sure your dates are confirmed for **2010**, or clearly indicate if dates are tentative. Use a separate sheet for each entry submitted. Information selected by the editors may be used and publicized through their books, electronic formats, syndicated services and/or other related products and services. The editors reserve the right to select and edit information received. Please mail all information to: Calendar Editor, Chase's Calendar of Events, McGraw-Hill, 130 E. Randolph St., Ste 900, Chicago, IL 60601.

☞ **DEADLINE FOR 2010 EDITION: APRIL 15, 2009.** PLEASE TYPE OR PRINT VERY CLEARLY.

1. Exact name of entry:
2. Exact INCLUSIVE DATES for **2010**:
3. If applicable, estimated attendance (one figure—grand total all days):
4. Location (site [not address], city and state):
5. Brief description:
6. Formula—ONLY if used to set date(s) each year (Example: Annually, the third Monday in May):
7. For public use, complete contact info to be printed in book—name, address, phone, fax, e-mail, web.
8. For Chase's staff use, complete mailing address to send our update form to you next year—name, title or department, organization name, address—as well as a name, phone and e-mail of person we can contact with questions about your entry:
9. Person furnishing information: (print) ______________________________

   (print) (sign)
10. PLEASE CIRCLE THE EXACT INCLUSIVE DATES FOR YOUR 2010 EVENT ON THE CALENDAR BELOW.

2010

Key dates

M. L. King Birthday, Jan 18
Chinese New Year, Feb 14
Washington's Birthday, Feb 15
Lent begins, Feb 17
Spring, Mar 20
Passover, Mar 30
Easter, Apr 4
Mother's Day, May 9
Memorial Day, May 31
Father's Day, June 20
Summer, June 21
Ramadan, Aug 11
Labor Day, Sept 6
Rosh Hashanah, Sept 9–10
Yom Kippur, Sept 18
Autumn, Sept 22
Columbus Day, Oct 11
Thanksgiving, Nov 25
Chanukah, Dec 2–9
Winter, Dec 21

JAN	S	M	T	W	T	F	S
						1	2
	3	4	5	6	7	8	9
	10	11	12	13	14	15	16
	17	18	19	20	21	22	23
	24	25	26	27	28	29	30
	31						

FEB	S	M	T	W	T	F	S
		1	2	3	4	5	6
	7	8	9	10	11	12	13
	14	15	16	17	18	19	20
	21	22	23	24	25	26	27
	28						

MAR	S	M	T	W	T	F	S
		1	2	3	4	5	6
	7	8	9	10	11	12	13
	14	15	16	17	18	19	20
	21	22	23	24	25	26	27
	28	29	30	31			

APR	S	M	T	W	T	F	S
					1	2	3
	4	5	6	7	8	9	10
	11	12	13	14	15	16	17
	18	19	20	21	22	23	24
	25	26	27	28	29	30	

MAY	S	M	T	W	T	F	S
							1
	2	3	4	5	6	7	8
	9	10	11	12	13	14	15
	16	17	18	19	20	21	22
	23	24	25	26	27	28	29
	30	31					

JUNE	S	M	T	W	T	F	S
			1	2	3	4	5
	6	7	8	9	10	11	12
	13	14	15	16	17	18	19
	20	21	22	23	24	25	26
	27	28	29	30			

JULY	S	M	T	W	T	F	S
					1	2	3
	4	5	6	7	8	9	10
	11	12	13	14	15	16	17
	18	19	20	21	22	23	24
	25	26	27	28	29	30	31

AUG	S	M	T	W	T	F	S
	1	2	3	4	5	6	7
	8	9	10	11	12	13	14
	15	16	17	18	19	20	21
	22	23	24	25	26	27	28
	29	30	31				

SEPT	S	M	T	W	T	F	S
				1	2	3	4
	5	6	7	8	9	10	11
	12	13	14	15	16	17	18
	19	20	21	22	23	24	25
	26	27	28	29	30		

OCT	S	M	T	W	T	F	S
						1	2
	3	4	5	6	7	8	9
	10	11	12	13	14	15	16
	17	18	19	20	21	22	23
	24	25	26	27	28	29	30
	31						

NOV	S	M	T	W	T	F	S
		1	2	3	4	5	6
	7	8	9	10	11	12	13
	14	15	16	17	18	19	20
	21	22	23	24	25	26	27
	28	29	30				

DEC	S	M	T	W	T	F	S
				1	2	3	4
	5	6	7	8	9	10	11
	12	13	14	15	16	17	18
	19	20	21	22	23	24	25
	26	27	28	29	30	31	

2010

Note: This page may be photocopied in order to submit additional event entries to *Chase's 2010 Calendar of Events*

130 E. Randolph St., Ste 900, Chicago, IL 60601 • Phone (312) 233-7560 • Fax (312) 233-7569 • www.chases.com

	Team	Year	Pitcher	Team
sage	Chicago	1975—	Al Hrabosky	St. Louis
bell	Minnesota	1976—	Rawly Eastwick	Cincinnati
bell	Boston	1977—	Rollie Fingers	San Diego
sage	New York	1978—	Rollie Fingers	San Diego
shall	Minnesota	1979—	Bruce Sutter	Chicago
	Texas			
enberry	Kansas City	1980—	Rollie Fingers	San Diego
			Tom Hume	Cincinnati
gers	Milwaukee	1981—	Bruce Sutter	St. Louis
enberry	Kansas City	1982—	Bruce Sutter	St. Louis
enberry	Kansas City	1983—	Al Holland	Philadelphia
			Lee Smith	Chicago
enberry	Kansas City	1984—	Bruce Sutter	St. Louis
enberry	Kansas City	1985—	Jeff Reardon	Montreal
netti	New York	1986—	Todd Worrell	St. Louis
netti	New York	1987—	Steve Bedrosian	Philadelphia
don	Minnesota			
ckersley	Oakland	1988—	John Franco	Cincinnati
ell	Texas	1989—	Mark Davis	San Diego
igpen	Chicago	1990—	John Franco	New York
ckersley	Oakland	1991—	Lee Smith	St. Louis
rvey	California			
ckersley	Oakland	1992—	Doug Jones	Houston
			Lee Smith	St. Louis
gomery	Kansas City	1993—	Randy Myers	Chicago
n	Baltimore	1994—	John Franco	New York
a	Cleveland	1995—	Randy Myers	Chicago

MAJOR LEAGUE PLAYER OF THE YEAR

	Team
ll	New York N.L.
en	Cleveland A.L.
der Meer	Cincinnati N.L.
gio	New York A.L.
	Cleveland A.L.
ns	Boston A.L.
s	Boston A.L.
dler	New York A.L.
on	St. Louis N.L.
user	Detroit A.L.
l	St. Louis N.L.
s	Boston A.L.
eau	Cleveland A.L.
s	Boston A.L.
	New York A.L.
	St. Louis N.L.
erts	Philadelphia N.L.
	Cleveland A.L.
	New York N.L.
r	Brooklyn N.L.
ntle	New York A.L.

Year	Player	Team
1957—	Ted Williams	Boston A.L.
1958—	Bob Turley	New York A.L.
1959—	Early Wynn	Chicago A.L.
1960—	Bill Mazeroski	Pittsburgh N.L.
1961—	Roger Maris	New York A.L.
1962—	Maury Wills	Los Angeles N.L.
	Don Drysdale	Los Angeles N.L.
1963—	Sandy Koufax	Los Angeles N.L.
1964—	Ken Boyer	St. Louis N.L.
1965—	Sandy Koufax	Los Angeles N.L.
1966—	Frank Robinson	Baltimore A.L.
1967—	Carl Yastrzemski	Boston A.L.
1968—	Denny McLain	Detroit A.L.
1969—	Willie McCovey	San Francisco N.L.
1970—	Johnny Bench	Cincinnati N.L.
1971—	Joe Torre	St. Louis N.L.
1972—	Billy Williams	Chicago N.L.
1973—	Reggie Jackson	Oakland A.L.
1974—	Lou Brock	St. Louis N.L.
1975—	Joe Morgan	Cincinnati N.L.
1976—	Joe Morgan	Cincinnati N.L.
1977—	Rod Carew	Minnesota A.L.
1978—	Ron Guidry	New York A.L.
1979—	Willie Stargell	Pittsburgh N.L.
1980—	George Brett	Kansas City A.L.
1981—	Fernando Valenzuela	Los Angeles N.L.
1982—	Robin Yount	Milwaukee A.L.
1983—	Cal Ripken Jr.	Baltimore A.L.
1984—	Ryne Sandberg	Chicago N.L.
1985—	Don Mattingly	New York A.L.
1986—	Roger Clemens	Boston A.L.
1987—	George Bell	Toronto A.L.
1988—	Orel Hershiser	Los Angeles N.L.
1989—	Kevin Mitchell	San Francisco N.L.
1990—	Barry Bonds	Pittsburgh N.L.
1991—	Cal Ripken Jr.	Baltimore A.L.
1992—	Gary Sheffield	San Diego N.L.
1993—	Frank Thomas	Chicago A.L.
1994—	Jeff Bagwell	Houston N.L.
1995—	Albert Belle	Cleveland A.L.

MAJOR LEAGUE MANAGER OF THE YEAR

	Team
ny	New York A.L.
nie	Boston N.L.
hy	New York A.L.
er	Brooklyn N.L.
nie	Cincinnati N.L.
vorth	St. Louis N.L.
vorth	St. Louis N.L.
ny	New York A.L.
	St. Louis A.L.
e	Washington A.L.
	St. Louis N.L.
s	New York A.L.
	Pittsburgh N.L.
gel	New York A.L.
	Detroit A.L.
er	New York N.L.
y	St. Louis N.L.
el	New York A.L.
er	New York N.L.
n	Brooklyn N.L.
tts	Cincinnati N.L.
nson	St. Louis N.L.
el	New York A.L.
ton	Los Angeles N.L.

Year	Manager	Team
1960—	Danny Murtaugh	Pittsburgh N.L.
1961—	Ralph Houk	New York A.L.
1962—	Bill Rigney	Los Angeles A.L.
1963—	Walter Alston	Los Angeles N.L.
1964—	Johnny Keane	St. Louis N.L.
1965—	Sam Mele	Minnesota A.L.
1966—	Hank Bauer	Baltimore A.L.
1967—	Dick Williams	Boston A.L.
1968—	Mayo Smith	Detroit A.L.
1969—	Gil Hodges	New York N.L.
1970—	Danny Murtaugh	Pittsburgh N.L.
1971—	Charlie Fox	San Francisco N.L.
1972—	Chuck Tanner	Chicago A.L.
1973—	Gene Mauch	Montreal N.L.
1974—	Bill Virdon	New York A.L.
1975—	Darrell Johnson	Boston A.L.
1976—	Danny Ozark	Philadelphia N.L.
1977—	Earl Weaver	Baltimore A.L.
1978—	George Bamberger	Milwaukee A.L.
1979—	Earl Weaver	Baltimore A.L.
1980—	Bill Virdon	Houston N.L.
1981—	Billy Martin	Oakland A.L.
1982—	Whitey Herzog	St. Louis N.L.
1983—	Tony La Russa	Chicago A.L.
1984—	Jim Frey	Chicago N.L.
1985—	Bobby Cox	Toronto A.L.
1986—	John McNamara	Boston A.L.
	Hal Lanier	Houston N.L.
1987—	Sparky Anderson	Detroit A.L.
	Buck Rodgers	Montreal N.L.
1988—	Tony La Russa	Oakland A.L.
	Tom Lasorda	L.A. N.L. (tie)
	Jim Leyland	Pit. N.L. (tie)
1989—	Frank Robinson	Baltimore A.L.
	Don Zimmer	Chicago N.L.
1990—	Jeff Torborg	Chicago A.L.
	Jim Leyland	Pittsburgh N.L.
1991—	Tom Kelly	Minnesota A.L.
	Bobby Cox	Atlanta N.L.
1992—	Tony La Russa	Oakland A.L.
	Jim Leyland	Pittsburgh N
1993—	Johnny Oates	Baltimore
	Bobby Cox	Atlanta N
1994—	Buck Showalter	New Yo
	Felipe Alou	Montr
1995—	Mike Hargrove	Cleve
	Don Baylor	Colo

AWARD WINNERS

THE SPORTING NEWS

MOST VALUABLE PLAYER

AMERICAN LEAGUE

Year	Player	Team	Pos.	Points
1929—	Al Simmons	Philadelphia	OF	40
1930—	Joe Cronin	Washington	SS	52
1931—	Lou Gehrig	New York	1B	40
1932—	Jimmie Foxx	Philadelphia	1B	46
1933—	Jimmie Foxx	Philadelphia	1B	49
1934—	Lou Gehrig	New York	1B	51
1935—	Hank Greenberg	Detroit	1B	64
1936—	Lou Gehrig	New York	1B	55
1937—	Charley Gehringer	Detroit	2B	78
1938—	Jimmie Foxx	Boston	1B	304
1939—	Joe DiMaggio	New York	OF	280
1940—	Hank Greenberg	Detroit	OF	292
1941—	Joe DiMaggio	New York	OF	291
1942—	Joe Gordon	New York	2B	270
1943—	Spud Chandler	New York	P	246
1944—	Bobby Doerr	Boston	2B	
1945—	Eddie Mayo	Detroit	2B	

NATIONAL LEAGUE

Year	Player	Team	Pos.	Points
1929—	No selection			
1930—	Bill Terry	New York	1B	47
1931—	Chuck Klein	Philadelphia	OF	40
1932—	Chuck Klein	Philadelphia	OF	46
1933—	Carl Hubbell	New York	P	64
1934—	Dizzy Dean	St. Louis	P	57
1935—	Arky Vaughan	Pittsburgh	SS	42
1936—	Carl Hubbell	New York	P	61
1937—	Joe Medwick	St. Louis	OF	70
1938—	Ernie Lombardi	Cincinnati	C	229
1939—	Bucky Walters	Cincinnati	P	303
1940—	Frank McCormick	Cincinnati	1B	274
1941—	Dolf Camilli	Brooklyn	1B	300
1942—	Mort Cooper	St. Louis	P	263
1943—	Stan Musial	St. Louis	OF	267
1944—	Marty Marion	St. Louis	SS	
1945—	Tommy Holmes	Boston	OF	

PLAYER AND PITCHER OF THE YEAR

AMERICAN LEAGUE

Year	Player	Team	Pos.
1944—	Bobby Doerr	Boston	2B
	Hal Newhouser	Detroit	P
1945—	Eddie Mayo	Detroit	2B
	Hal Newhouser	Detroit	P
1946—	No selections		
1947—	No selections		
1948—	Lou Boudreau	Cleveland	SS
	Bob Lemon	Cleveland	P
1949—	Ted Williams	Boston	OF
	Ellis Kinder	Boston	P
1950—	Phil Rizzuto	New York	SS
	Bob Lemon	Cleveland	P
1951—	Ferris Fain	Philadelphia	1B
	Bob Feller	Cleveland	P
1952—	Luke Easter	Cleveland	1B
	Bobby Shantz	Philadelphia	P
1953—	Al Rosen	Cleveland	3B
	Bob Porterfield	Washington	P
1954—	Bobby Avila	Cleveland	2B
	Bob Lemon	Cleveland	P
1955—	Al Kaline	Detroit	OF
	Whitey Ford	New York	P
1956—	Mickey Mantle	New York	OF
	Billy Pierce	Chicago	P
1957—	Ted Williams	Boston	OF
	Billy Pierce	Chicago	P
1958—	Jackie Jensen	Boston	OF
	Bob Turley	New York	P
1959—	Nellie Fox	Chicago	2B
	Early Wynn	Chicago	P
1960—	Roger Maris	New York	OF
	Chuck Estrada	Baltimore	P
1961—	Roger Maris	New York	OF
	Whitey Ford	New York	P
1962—	Mickey Mantle	New York	OF
	Dick Donovan	Cleveland	P
1963—	Al Kaline	Detroit	OF
	Whitey Ford	New York	P
1964—	Brooks Robinson	Baltimore	3B
	Dean Chance	Los Angeles	P
1965—	Tony Oliva	Minnesota	OF
	Jim Grant	Minnesota	P
1966—	Frank Robinson	Baltimore	OF
	Jim Kaat	Minnesota	P
1967—	Carl Yastrzemski	Boston	OF
	Jim Lonborg	Boston	P
1968—	Ken Harrelson	Boston	OF
	Denny McLain	Detroit	P
1969—	Harmon Killebrew	Minnesota	1B-3B
	Denny McLain	Detroit	P
1970—	Harmon Killebrew	Minnesota	3B
	Sam McDowell	Cleveland	P

NATIONAL LEAGUE

Year	Player	Team	Pos.
1944—	Marty Marion	St. Louis	SS
	Bill Voiselle	New York	P
1945—	Tommy Holmes	Boston	OF
	Hank Borowy	Chicago	P
1946—	No selections		
1947—	No selections		
1948—	Stan Musial	St. Louis	OF-1B
	Johnny Sain	Boston	P
1949—	Enos Slaughter	St. Louis	OF
	Howard Pollet	St. Louis	P
1950—	Ralph Kiner	Pittsburgh	OF
	Jim Konstanty	Philadelphia	P
1951—	Stan Musial	St. Louis	OF
	Preacher Roe	Brooklyn	P
1952—	Hank Sauer	Chicago	OF
	Robin Roberts	Philadelphia	P
1953—	Roy Campanella	Brooklyn	C
	Warren Spahn	Milwaukee	P
1954—	Willie Mays	New York	OF
	Johnny Antonelli	New York	P
1955—	Duke Snider	Brooklyn	OF
	Robin Roberts	Philadelphia	P
1956—	Hank Aaron	Milwaukee	OF
	Don Newcombe	Brooklyn	P
1957—	Stan Musial	St. Louis	1B
	Warren Spahn	Milwaukee	P
1958—	Ernie Banks	Chicago	SS
	Warren Spahn	Milwaukee	P
1959—	Ernie Banks	Chicago	SS
	Sam Jones	San Francisco	P
1960—	Dick Groat	Pittsburgh	SS
	Vern Law	Pittsburgh	P
1961—	Frank Robinson	Cincinnati	OF
	Warren Spahn	Milwaukee	P
1962—	Maury Wills	Los Angeles	SS
	Don Drysdale	Los Angeles	P
1963—	Hank Aaron	Milwaukee	OF
	Sandy Koufax	Los Angeles	P
1964—	Ken Boyer	St. Louis	3B
	Sandy Koufax	Los Angeles	P
1965—	Willie Mays	San Francisco	OF
	Sandy Koufax	Los Angeles	P
1966—	Roberto Clemente	Pittsburgh	OF
	Sandy Koufax	Los Angeles	P
1967—	Orlando Cepeda	St. Louis	1B
	Mike McCormick	San Francisco	P
1968—	Pete Rose	Cincinnati	OF
	Bob Gibson	St. Louis	P
1969—	Willie McCovey	San Francisco	1B
	Tom Seaver	New York	P
1970—	Johnny Bench	Cincinnati	C
	Bob Gibson	St. Louis	P

Year	Player	Team	Pos.
1971—	Tony Oliva	Minnesota	OF
	Vida Blue	Oakland	P
1972—	Dick Allen	Chicago	1B
	Wilbur Wood	Chicago	P
1973—	Reggie Jackson	Oakland	OF
	Jim Palmer	Baltimore	P
1974—	Jeff Burroughs	Texas	OF
	Jim Hunter	Oakland	P
1975—	Fred Lynn	Boston	OF
	Jim Palmer	Baltimore	P
1976—	Thurman Munson	New York	C
	Jim Palmer	Baltimore	P
1977—	Rod Carew	Minnesota	1B
	Nolan Ryan	California	P
1978—	Jim Rice	Boston	OF
	Ron Guidry	New York	P
1979—	Don Baylor	California	OF
	Mike Flanagan	Baltimore	P
1980—	George Brett	Kansas City	3B
	Steve Stone	Baltimore	P
1981—	Tony Armas	Oakland	OF
	Jack Morris	Detroit	P
1982—	Robin Yount	Milwaukee	SS
	Dave Stieb	Toronto	P
1983—	Cal Ripken Jr.	Baltimore	SS
	LaMarr Hoyt	Chicago	P
1984—	Don Mattingly	New York	1B
	Willie Hernandez	Detroit	P
1985—	Don Mattingly	New York	1B
	Bret Saberhagen	Kansas City	P
1986—	Don Mattingly	New York	1B
	Roger Clemens	Boston	P
1987—	George Bell	Toronto	OF
	Jimmy Key	Toronto	P
1988—	Jose Canseco	Oakland	OF
	Frank Viola	Minnesota	P
1989—	Ruben Sierra	Texas	OF
	Bret Saberhagen	Kansas City	P
1990—	Cecil Fielder	Detroit	1B
	Bob Welch	Oakland	P
1991—	Cal Ripken Jr.	Baltimore	SS
	Roger Clemens	Boston	P

Year	Player	Team	Pos.
1971—	Joe Torre	St. Louis	3B
	Ferguson Jenkins	Chicago	P
1972—	Billy Williams	Chicago	OF
	Steve Carlton	Philadelphia	P
1973—	Bobby Bonds	San Francisco	OF
	Ron Bryant	San Francisco	P
1974—	Lou Brock	St. Louis	OF
	Mike Marshall	Los Angeles	P
1975—	Joe Morgan	Cincinnati	2B
	Tom Seaver	New York	P
1976—	George Foster	Cincinnati	OF
	Randy Jones	San Diego	P
1977—	George Foster	Cincinnati	OF
	Steve Carlton	Philadelphia	P
1978—	Dave Parker	Pittsburgh	OF
	Vida Blue	San Francisco	P
1979—	Keith Hernandez	St. Louis	1B
	Joe Niekro	Houston	P
1980—	Mike Schmidt	Philadelphia	3B
	Steve Carlton	Philadelphia	P
1981—	Andre Dawson	Montreal	OF
	Fernando Valenzuela	Los Angeles	P
1982—	Dale Murphy	Atlanta	OF
	Steve Carlton	Philadelphia	P
1983—	Dale Murphy	Atlanta	OF
	John Denny	Philadelphia	P
1984—	Ryne Sandberg	Chicago	2B
	Rick Sutcliffe	Chicago	P
1985—	Willie McGee	St. Louis	OF
	Dwight Gooden	New York	P
1986—	Mike Schmidt	Philadelphia	3B
	Mike Scott	Houston	P
1987—	Andre Dawson	Chicago	OF
	Rick Sutcliffe	Chicago	P
1988—	Andy Van Slyke	Pittsburgh	OF
	Orel Hershiser	Los Angeles	P
1989—	Kevin Mitchell	San Francisco	OF
	Mark Davis	San Diego	P
1990—	Barry Bonds	Pittsburgh	OF
	Doug Drabek	Pittsburgh	P
1991—	Barry Bonds	Pittsburgh	OF
	Tom Glavine	Atlanta	P

PITCHER OF THE YEAR

AMERICAN LEAGUE

Year	Pitcher	Team
1992—	Dennis Eckersley	Oakland
1993—	Jack McDowell	Chicago
1994—	Jimmy Key	New York
1995—	Randy Johnson	Seattle

NATIONAL LEAGUE

Year	Pitcher	Team
1992—	Greg Maddux	Chicago
1993—	Greg Maddux	Atlanta
1994—	Greg Maddux	Atlanta
1995—	Greg Maddux	Atlanta

ROOKIE OF THE YEAR

1946—Combined selection—Del Ennis, Philadelphia N.L., OF
1947—Combined selection—Jackie Robinson, Brooklyn N.L., 1B
1948—Combined selection—Richie Ashburn, Philadelphia N.L., OF

AMERICAN LEAGUE

Year	Player	Team	Pos.
1949—	Roy Sievers	St. Louis	OF
1950—	Whitey Ford	New York	P
1951—	Minnie Minoso	Chicago	OF
1952—	Clint Courtney	St. Louis	C
1953—	Harvey Kuenn	Detroit	SS
1954—	Bob Grim	New York	P
1955—	Herb Score	Cleveland	P
1956—	Luis Aparicio	Chicago	SS
1957—	Tony Kubek	New York	IF-OF
	(No pitcher named)		
1958—	Albie Pearson	Washington	OF
	Ryne Duren	New York	P
1959—	Bob Allison	Washington	OF
1960—	Ron Hansen	Baltimore	SS
1961—	Dick Howser	Kansas City	SS
	Don Schwall	Boston	P
1962—	Tom Tresh	New York	OF-SS
1963—	Pete Ward	Chicago	3B
	Gary Peters	Chicago	P
1964—	Tony Oliva	Minnesota	OF
	Wally Bunker	Baltimore	P
1965—	Curt Blefary	Baltimore	OF
	Marcelino Lopez	California	P
1966—	Tommie Agee	Chicago	OF
	Jim Nash	Kansas City	P
1967—	Rod Carew	Minnesota	2B
	Tom Phoebus	Baltimore	P
1968—	Del Unser	Washington	OF
	Stan Bahnsen	New York	P
1969—	Carlos May	Chicago	OF
	Mike Nagy	Boston	P
1970—	Roy Foster	Cleveland	OF
	Bert Blyleven	Minnesota	P
1971—	Chris Chambliss	Cleveland	1B
	Bill Parsons	Milwaukee	P
1972—	Carlton Fisk	Boston	C
	Dick Tidrow	Cleveland	P
1973—	Al Bumbry	Baltimore	OF
	Steve Busby	Kansas City	P
1974—	Mike Hargrove	Texas	1B
	Frank Tanana	California	P
1975—	Fred Lynn	Boston	OF
	Dennis Eckersley	Cleveland	P
1976—	Butch Wynegar	Minnesota	C
	Mark Fidrych	Detroit	P
1977—	Mitchell Page	Oakland	OF
	Dave Rozema	Detroit	P
1978—	Paul Molitor	Milwaukee	2B
	Rich Gale	Kansas City	P
1979—	Pat Putnam	Texas 1B	
	Mark Clear	California	P
1980—	Joe Charboneau	Cleveland	OF
	Britt Burns	Chicago	P
1981—	Rich Gedman	Boston	C
	Dave Righetti	New York	P
1982—	Cal Ripken Jr.	Baltimore	SS-3B
	Ed Vande Berg	Seattle	P
1983—	Ron Kittle	Chicago	OF
	Mike Boddicker	Baltimore	P
1984—	Alvin Davis	Seattle	1B
	Mark Langston	Seattle	P
1985	Ozzie Gullen	Chicago	SS
	Teddy Higuera	Milwaukee	P
1986—	Jose Canseco	Oakland	OF
	Mark Eichhorn	Toronto	P
1987—	Mark McGwire	Oakland	1B
	Mike Henneman	Detroit	P
1988—	Walt Weiss	Oakland	SS
	Bryan Harvey	California	P
1989—	Craig Worthington	Baltimore	3B
	Tom Gordon	Kansas City	P
1990—	Sandy Alomar Jr.	Cleveland	C
	Kevin Appier	Kansas City	P
1991—	Chuck Knoblauch	Minnesota	2B
	Juan Guzman	Toronto	P
1992—	Pat Listach	Milwaukee	SS
	Cal Eldred	Milwaukee	P
1993—	Tim Salmon	California	OF
	Aaron Sele	Boston	P
1994—	Bob Hamelin	Kansas City	DH
	Brian Anderson	California	P
1995—	Garret Anderson	California	OF
	Julian Tavarez	Cleveland	P

NATIONAL LEAGUE

Year	Player	Team	Pos.
1949—	Don Newcombe	Brooklyn	P
1950—	Combined A.L.-N.L. selection		
1951—	Willie Mays	New York	OF
1952—	Joe Black	Brooklyn	P
1953—	Jim Gilliam	Brooklyn	2B
1954—	Wally Moon	St. Louis	OF
1955—	Bill Virdon	St. Louis	OF
1956—	Frank Robinson	Cincinnati	OF
1957—	Ed Bouchee	Philadelphia	1B
	Jack Sanford	Philadelphia	P
1958—	Orlando Cepeda	San Francisco	1B
	Carlton Willey	Milwaukee	P
1959—	Willie McCovey	San Francisco	1B
1960—	Frank Howard	Los Angeles	OF
1961—	Billy Williams	Chicago	OF
	Ken Hunt	Cincinnati	P
1962—	Ken Hubbs	Chicago	2B
1963—	Pete Rose	Cincinnati	2B
	Ray Culp	Philadelphia	P
1964—	Dick Allen	Philadelphia	3B
	Billy McCool	Cincinnati	P

Year	Player
1965—	Joe Morgan
	Frank Linzy
1966—	Tommy Helms
	Don Sutton
1967—	Lee May
	Dick Hughes
1968—	Johnny Bench
	Jerry Koosman
1969—	Coco Laboy
	Tom Griffin
1970—	Bernie Carbo
	Carl Morton
1971—	Earl Williams
	Reggie Clevelanc
1972—	Dave Rader
	Jon Matlack
1973—	Gary Matthews
	Steve Rogers
1974—	Greg Gross
	John D'Acquisto
1975—	Gary Carter
	John Montefusco
1976—	Larry Herndon
	Butch Metzger
1977—	Andre Dawson
	Bob Owchinko
1978—	Bob Horner
	Don Robinson
1979—	Jeff Leonard
	Rick Sutcliffe
1980—	Lonnie Smith
	Bill Gullickson
1981—	Tim Raines
	Fernando Valenzu
1982—	Johnny Ray
	Steve Bedrosian
1983—	Darryl Strawberry
	Craig McMurtry
1984—	Juan Samuel
	Dwight Gooden
1985—	Vince Coleman
	Tom Browning
1986—	Robby Thompson
	Todd Worrell
1987—	Benito Santiago
	Mike Dunne
1988—	Mark Grace
	Tim Belcher
1989—	Jerome Walton
	Andy Benes
1990—	David Justice
	Mike Harkey
1991—	Jeff Bagwell
	Al Osuna
1992—	Eric Karros
	Tim Wakefield
1993—	Mike Piazza
	Kirk Rueter
1994—	Raul Mondesi
	Steve Trachsel
1995—	Chipper Jones
	Hideo Nomo

FIREMAN OF THE YEAR

AMERICAN LEAGUE

Year	Pitcher	Team
1960—	Mike Fornieles	Boston
1961—	Luis Arroyo	New York
1962—	Dick Radatz	Boston
1963—	Stu Miller	Baltimore
1964—	Dick Radatz	Boston
1965—	Eddie Fisher	Chicago
1966—	Jack Aker	Kansas City
1967—	Minnie Rojas	California
1968—	Wilbur Wood	Chicago
1969—	Ron Perranoski	Minnesota
970—	Ron Perranoski	Minnesota
971—	Ken Sanders	Milwaukee
972—	Sparky Lyle	New York
73—	John Hiller	Detroit
74—	Terry Forster	Chicago

NATIONA

Year	Pitcher
1960—	Lindy McDaniel
1961—	Stu Miller
1962—	Roy Face
1963—	Lindy McDaniel
1964—	Al McBean
1965—	Ted Abernathy
1966—	Phil Regan
1967—	Ted Abernathy
1968—	Phil Regan
1969—	Wayne Granger
1970—	Wayne Granger
1971—	Dave Giusti
1972—	Clay Carroll
1973—	Mike Marshall
1974—	Mike Marshall

Year	Pitche
1975—	Rich G
1976—	Bill Ca
1977—	Bill Ca
1978—	Rich G
1979—	Mike I
	Jim K
1980—	Dan Q
1981—	Rollie
1982—	Dan C
1983—	Dan C
1984—	Dan C
1985—	Dan C
1986—	Dave
1987—	Dave
	Jeff R
1988—	Denn
1989—	Jeff R
1990—	Bobb
1991—	Denn
	Brya
1992—	Denn
1993—	Jeff
1994—	Lee
1995—	Jose

Year	Playe
1936—	Carl H
1937—	John
1938—	Johnr
1939—	Joe D
1940—	Bob
1941—	Ted
1942—	Ted
1943—	Spud
1944—	Mart
1945—	Hal
1946—	Stan
1947—	Ted
1948—	Lou
1949—	Ted
1950—	Phil
1951—	Star
1952—	Rob
1953—	Al F
1954—	Wil
1955—	Duk
1956—	Mic

Year	Ma
1936—	Joe
1937—	Bil
1938—	Jo
1939—	Le
1940—	Bi
1941—	Bi
1942—	Bi
1943—	Jo
1944—	Lu
1945—	O
1946—	E
1947—	B
1948—	B
1949—	C
1950—	F
1951—	L
1952—	E
1953—	(
1954—	
1955—	
1956—	
1957—	
1958—	
1959—	

MAJOR LEAGUE EXECUTIVE OF THE YEAR

Year	Executive	Team
1936	Branch Rickey	St. Louis N.L.
1937	Ed Barrow	New York A.L.
1938	Warren Giles	Cincinnati N.L.
1939	Larry MacPhail	Brooklyn N.L.
1940	Walter Briggs Sr.	Detroit A.L.
1941	Ed Barrow	New York A.L.
1942	Branch Rickey	St. Louis N.L.
1943	Clark Griffith	Washington A.L.
1944	Billy DeWitt	St. Louis A.L.
1945	Phil Wrigley	Chicago N.L.
1946	Tom Yawkey	Boston A.L.
1947	Branch Rickey	Brooklyn N.L.
1948	Bill Veeck	Cleveland A.L.
1949	Bob Carpenter	Philadelphia N.L.
1950	George Weiss	New York A.L.
1951	George Weiss	New York A.L.
1952	George Weiss	New York A.L.
1953	Lou Perini	Milwaukee N.L.
1954	Horace Stoneham	New York N.L.
1955	Walter O'Malley	Brooklyn N.L.
1956	Gabe Paul	Cincinnati N.L.
1957	Frank Lane	St. Louis N.L.
1958	Joe Brown	Pittsburgh N.L.
1959	Buzzie Bavasi	L.A. N.L.
1960	George Weiss	New York A.L.
1961	Dan Topping	New York A.L.
1962	Fred Haney	Los Angeles A.L.
1963	Bing Devine	St. Louis N.L.
1964	Bing Devine	St. Louis N.L.
1965	Cal Griffith	Minnesota A.L.
1966	Lee MacPhail	Commissioner's Office
1967	Dick O'Connell	Boston A.L.
1968	Jim Campbell	Detroit A.L.
1969	John Murphy	New York N.L.
1970	Harry Dalton	Baltimore A.L.
1971	Cedric Tallis	Kansas City A.L.
1972	Roland Hemond	Chicago A.L.
1973	Bob Howsam	Cincinnati N.L.
1974	Gabe Paul	New York A.L.
1975	Dick O'Connell	Boston A.L.
1976	Joe Burke	Kansas City A.L.
1977	Bill Veeck	Chicago A.L.
1978	Spec Richardson	San Francisco N.L.
1979	Hank Peters	Baltimore A.L.
1980	Tal Smith	Houston N.L.
1981	John McHale	Montreal N.L.
1982	Harry Dalton	Milwaukee A.L.
1983	Hank Peters	Baltimore A.L.
1984	Dallas Green	Chicago N.L.
1985	John Schuerholz	Kansas City A.L.
1986	Frank Cashen	New York N.L.
1987	Al Rosen	San Francisco N.L.
1988	Fred Claire	Los Angeles N.L.
1989	Roland Hemond	Baltimore A.L.
1990	Bob Quinn	Cincinnati N.L.
1991	Andy MacPhail	Minnesota A.L.
1992	Dan Duquette	Montreal N.L.
1993	Lee Thomas	Philadelphia N.L.
1994	John Hart	Cleveland A.L.
1995	John Hart	Cleveland A.L.

GOLD GLOVE TEAMS

1957

MAJORS

P— Bobby Shantz, New York A.L.
C— Sherm Lollar, Chicago A.L.
1B— Gil Hodges, Brooklyn N.L.
2B— Nellie Fox, Chicago A.L.
3B— Frank Malzone, Boston A.L.
SS— Roy McMillan, Cincinnati N.L.
OF— Minnie Minoso, Chicago A.L.
OF— Willie Mays, New York N.L.
OF— Al Kaline, Detroit A.L.

1958

AMERICAN LEAGUE

P— Bobby Shantz, New York
C— Sherm Lollar, Chicago
1B— Vic Power, Cleveland
2B— Frank Bolling, Detroit
3B— Frank Malzone, Boston
SS— Luis Aparicio, Chicago
OF— Norm Siebern, New York
OF— Jimmy Piersall, Boston
OF— Al Kaline, Detroit

NATIONAL LEAGUE

P— Harvey Haddix, Cincinnati
C— Del Crandall, Milwaukee
1B— Gil Hodges, Los Angeles
2B— Bill Mazeroski, Pittsburgh
3B— Ken Boyer, St. Louis
SS— Roy McMillan, Cincinnati
OF— Frank Robinson, Cincinnati
OF— Willie Mays, San Francisco
OF— Hank Aaron, Milwaukee

1959

AMERICAN LEAGUE

P— Bobby Shantz, New York
C— Sherm Lollar, Chicago
1B— Vic Power, Cleveland
2B— Nellie Fox, Chicago
3B— Frank Malzone, Boston
SS— Luis Aparicio, Chicago
OF— Minnie Minoso, Cleveland
OF— Al Kaline, Detroit
OF— Jackie Jensen, Boston

NATIONAL LEAGUE

P— Harvey Haddix, Pittsburgh
C— Del Crandall, Milwaukee
1B— Gil Hodges, Los Angeles
2B— Charley Neal, Los Angeles
3B— Ken Boyer, St. Louis
SS— Roy McMillan, Cincinnati
OF— Jackie Brandt, San Francisco
OF— Willie Mays, San Francisco
OF— Hank Aaron, Milwaukee

1960

AMERICAN LEAGUE

P— Bobby Shantz, New York
C— Earl Battey, Washington
1B— Vic Power, Cleveland
2B— Nellie Fox, Chicago
3B— Brooks Robinson, Baltimore
SS— Luis Aparicio, Chicago
OF— Minnie Minoso, Chicago
OF— Jim Landis, Chicago
OF— Roger Maris, New York

NATIONAL LEAGUE

P— Harvey Haddix, Pittsburgh
C— Del Crandall, Milwaukee
1B— Bill White, St. Louis
2B— Bill Mazeroski, Pittsburgh
3B— Ken Boyer, St. Louis
SS— Ernie Banks, Chicago
OF— Wally Moon, Los Angeles
OF— Willie Mays, San Francisco
OF— Hank Aaron, Milwaukee

1961

AMERICAN LEAGUE

P— Frank Lary, Detroit
C— Earl Battey, Chicago
1B— Vic Power, Cleveland
2B— Bobby Richardson, New York
3B— Brooks Robinson, Baltimore
SS— Luis Aparicio, Chicago
OF— Al Kaline, Detroit
OF— Jimmy Piersall, Cleveland
OF— Jim Landis, Chicago

NATIONAL LEAGUE

P— Bobby Shantz, Pittsburgh
C— John Roseboro, Los Angeles
1B— Bill White, St. Louis
2B— Bill Mazeroski, Pittsburgh
3B— Ken Boyer, St. Louis
SS— Maury Wills, Los Angeles
OF— Willie Mays, San Francisco
OF— Roberto Clemente, Pittsburgh
OF— Vada Pinson, Cincinnati

1962

AMERICAN LEAGUE

P— Jim Kaat, Minnesota
C— Earl Battey, Minnesota
1B— Vic Power, Minnesota
2B— Bobby Richardson, New York
3B— Brooks Robinson, Baltimore
SS— Luis Aparicio, Chicago
OF— Jim Landis, Chicago
OF— Mickey Mantle, New York
OF— Al Kaline, Detroit

NATIONAL LEAGUE

P— Bobby Shantz, St. Louis
C— Del Crandall, Milwaukee
1B— Bill White, St. Louis
2B— Ken Hubbs, Chicago
3B— Jim Davenport, San Francisco
SS— Maury Wills, Los Angeles
OF— Willie Mays, San Francisco
OF— Roberto Clemente, Pittsburgh
OF— Bill Virdon, Pittsburgh

1963

AMERICAN LEAGUE

P— Jim Kaat, Minnesota
C— Elston Howard, New York
1B— Vic Power, Minnesota
2B— Bobby Richardson, New York
3B— Brooks Robinson, Baltimore
SS— Zoilo Versalles, Minnesota
OF— Al Kaline, Detroit
OF— Carl Yastrzemski, Boston
OF— Jim Landis, Chicago

NATIONAL LEAGUE

P— Bobby Shantz, St. Louis
C— Johnny Edwards, Cincinnati
1B— Bill White, St. Louis
2B— Bill Mazeroski, Pittsburgh
3B— Ken Boyer, St. Louis
SS— Bobby Wine, Philadelphia
OF— Willie Mays, San Francisco
OF— Roberto Clemente, Pittsburgh
OF— Curt Flood, St. Louis

1964

AMERICAN LEAGUE

P— Jim Kaat, Minnesota
C— Elston Howard, New York
1B— Vic Power, Los Angeles
2B— Bobby Richardson, New York
3B— Brooks Robinson, Baltimore
SS— Luis Aparicio, Baltimore
OF— Al Kaline, Detroit
OF— Jim Landis, Chicago
OF— Vic Davalillo, Cleveland

NATIONAL LEAGUE

P— Bobby Shantz, Philadelphia
C— Johnny Edwards, Cincinnati
1B— Bill White, St. Louis
2B— Bill Mazeroski, Pittsburgh
3B— Ron Santo, Chicago
SS— Ruben Amaro, Philadelphia
OF— Willie Mays, San Francisco
OF— Roberto Clemente, Pittsburgh
OF— Curt Flood, St. Louis

1965

AMERICAN LEAGUE

P— Jim Kaat, Minnesota
C— Bill Freehan, Detroit
1B— Joe Pepitone, New York
2B— Bobby Richardson, New York
3B— Brooks Robinson, Baltimore
SS— Zoilo Versalles, Minnesota
OF— Al Kaline, Detroit
OF— Tom Tresh, New York
OF— Carl Yastrzemski, Boston

NATIONAL LEAGUE

P— Bob Gibson, St. Louis
C— Joe Torre, Atlanta
1B— Bill White, St. Louis
2B— Bill Mazeroski, Pittsburgh
3B— Ron Santo, Chicago
SS— Leo Cardenas, Cincinnati
OF— Willie Mays, San Francisco
OF— Roberto Clemente, Pittsburgh
OF— Curt Flood, St. Louis

1966

AMERICAN LEAGUE

P— Jim Kaat, Minnesota
C— Bill Freehan, Detroit
1B— Joe Pepitone, New York
2B— Bobby Knoop, California
3B— Brooks Robinson, Baltimore
SS— Luis Aparicio, Baltimore
OF— Al Kaline, Detroit
OF— Tommie Agee, Chicago
OF— Tony Oliva, Minnesota

NATIONAL LEAGUE

P— Bob Gibson, St. Louis
C— John Roseboro, Los Angeles
1B— Bill White, Philadelphia
2B— Bill Mazeroski, Pittsburgh
3B— Ron Santo, Chicago
SS— Gene Alley, Pittsburgh
OF— Willie Mays, San Francisco
OF— Curt Flood, St. Louis
OF— Roberto Clemente, Pittsburgh

1967

AMERICAN LEAGUE

P— Jim Kaat, Minnesota
C— Bill Freehan, Detroit
1B— George Scott, Boston
2B— Bobby Knoop, California
3B— Brooks Robinson, Baltimore
SS— Jim Fregosi, California
OF— Carl Yastrzemski, Boston
OF— Paul Blair, Baltimore
OF— Al Kaline, Detroit

NATIONAL LEAGUE

P— Bob Gibson, St. Louis
C— Randy Hundley, Chicago
1B— Wes Parker, Los Angeles
2B— Bill Mazeroski, Pittsburgh
3B— Ron Santo, Chicago
SS— Gene Alley, Pittsburgh
OF— Roberto Clemente, Pittsburgh
OF— Curt Flood, St. Louis
OF— Willie Mays, San Francisco

1968

AMERICAN LEAGUE

P— Jim Kaat, Minnesota
C— Bill Freehan, Detroit
1B— George Scott, Boston
2B— Bobby Knoop, California
3B— Brooks Robinson, Baltimore
SS— Luis Aparicio, Chicago
OF— Mickey Stanley, Detroit
OF— Carl Yastrzemski, Boston
OF— Reggie Smith, Boston

NATIONAL LEAGUE

P— Bob Gibson, St. Louis
C— Johnny Bench, Cincinnati
1B— Wes Parker, Los Angeles
2B— Glenn Beckert, Chicago
3B— Ron Santo, Chicago
SS— Dal Maxvill, St. Louis
OF— Willie Mays, San Francisco
OF— Roberto Clemente, Pittsburgh
OF— Curt Flood, St. Louis

1969

AMERICAN LEAGUE

P— Jim Kaat, Minnesota
C— Bill Freehan, Detroit
1B— Joe Pepitone, New York
2B— Dave Johnson, Baltimore
3B— Brooks Robinson, Baltimore
SS— Mark Belanger, Baltimore
OF— Paul Blair, Baltimore
OF— Mickey Stanley, Detroit
OF— Carl Yastrzemski, Boston

NATIONAL LEAGUE

P— Bob Gibson, St. Louis
C— Johnny Bench, Cincinnati
1B— Wes Parker, Los Angeles
2B— Felix Millan, Atlanta
3B— Clete Boyer, Atlanta
SS— Don Kessinger, Chicago
OF— Roberto Clemente, Pittsburgh
OF— Curt Flood, St. Louis
OF— Pete Rose, Cincinnati

1970

AMERICAN LEAGUE

P— Jim Kaat, Minnesota
C— Ray Fosse, Cleveland
1B— Jim Spencer, California
2B— Dave Johnson, Baltimore
3B— Brooks Robinson, Baltimore
SS— Luis Aparicio, Chicago
OF— Mickey Stanley, Detroit
OF— Paul Blair, Baltimore
OF— Ken Berry, Chicago

NATIONAL LEAGUE

P— Bob Gibson, St. Louis
C— Johnny Bench, Cincinnati
1B— Wes Parker, Los Angeles
2B— Tommy Helms, Cincinnati
3B— Doug Rader, Houston
SS— Don Kessinger, Chicago
OF— Roberto Clemente, Pittsburgh
OF— Tommie Agee, New York
OF— Pete Rose, Cincinnati

1971

AMERICAN LEAGUE

P— Jim Kaat, Minnesota
C— Ray Fosse, Cleveland
1B— George Scott, Boston
2B— Dave Johnson, Baltimore
3B— Brooks Robinson, Baltimore
SS— Mark Belanger, Baltimore
OF— Paul Blair, Baltimore
OF— Amos Otis, Kansas City
OF— Carl Yastrzemski, Boston

NATIONAL LEAGUE

P— Bob Gibson, St. Louis
C— Johnny Bench, Cincinnati
1B— Wes Parker, Los Angeles
2B— Tommy Helms, Cincinnati
3B— Doug Rader, Houston
SS— Bud Harrelson, New York
OF— Roberto Clemente, Pittsburgh
OF— Bobby Bonds, San Francisco
OF— Willie Davis, Los Angeles

1972

AMERICAN LEAGUE

P— Jim Kaat, Minnesota
C— Carlton Fisk, Boston
1B— George Scott, Milwaukee
2B— Doug Griffin, Boston
3B— Brooks Robinson, Baltimore
SS— Ed Brinkman, Detroit
OF— Paul Blair, Baltimore
OF— Bobby Murcer, New York
OF— Ken Berry, California

NATIONAL LEAGUE

P— Bob Gibson, St. Louis
C— Johnny Bench, Cincinnati
1B— Wes Parker, Los Angeles
2B— Felix Millan, Atlanta
3B— Doug Rader, Houston
SS— Larry Bowa, Philadelphia
OF— Roberto Clemente, Pittsburgh
OF— Cesar Cedeno, Houston
OF— Willie Davis, Los Angeles

1973

AMERICAN LEAGUE

P— Jim Kaat, Chicago
C— Thurman Munson, New York
1B— George Scott, Milwaukee
2B— Bobby Grich, Baltimore
3B— Brooks Robinson, Baltimore
SS— Mark Belanger, Baltimore
OF— Paul Blair, Baltimore
OF— Amos Otis, Kansas City
OF— Mickey Stanley, Detroit

NATIONAL LEAGUE

P— Bob Gibson, St. Louis
C— Johnny Bench, Cincinnati
1B— Mike Jorgensen, Montreal
2B— Joe Morgan, Cincinnati
3B— Doug Rader, Houston
SS— Roger Metzger, Houston
OF— Bobby Bonds, San Francisco
OF— Cesar Cedeno, Houston
OF— Willie Davis, Los Angeles

1974

AMERICAN LEAGUE

P— Jim Kaat, Chicago
C— Thurman Munson, New York
1B— George Scott, Milwaukee
2B— Bobby Grich, Baltimore
3B— Brooks Robinson, Baltimore
SS— Mark Belanger, Baltimore
OF— Paul Blair, Baltimore
OF— Amos Otis, Kansas City
OF— Joe Rudi, Oakland

NATIONAL LEAGUE

P— Andy Messersmith, Los Angeles
C— Johnny Bench, Cincinnati
1B— Steve Garvey, Los Angeles
2B— Joe Morgan, Cincinnati
3B— Doug Rader, Houston
SS— Dave Concepcion, Cincinnati
OF— Cesar Cedeno, Houston
OF— Cesar Geronimo, Cincinnati
OF— Bobby Bonds, San Francisco

1975

AMERICAN LEAGUE

P— Jim Kaat, Chicago
C— Thurman Munson, New York
1B— George Scott, Milwaukee
2B— Bobby Grich, Baltimore
3B— Brooks Robinson, Baltimore
SS— Mark Belanger, Baltimore
OF— Paul Blair, Baltimore
OF— Joe Rudi, Oakland
OF— Fred Lynn, Boston

NATIONAL LEAGUE
P— Andy Messersmith, Los Angeles
C— Johnny Bench, Cincinnati
1B— Steve Garvey, Los Angeles
2B— Joe Morgan, Cincinnati
3B— Ken Reitz, St. Louis
SS— Dave Concepcion, Cincinnati
OF— Cesar Cedeno, Houston
OF— Cesar Geronimo, Cincinnati
OF— Garry Maddox, Philadelphia

1976

AMERICAN LEAGUE
P— Jim Palmer, Baltimore
C— Jim Sundberg, Texas
1B— George Scott, Milwaukee
2B— Bobby Grich, Baltimore
3B— Aurelio Rodriguez, Detroit
SS— Mark Belanger, Baltimore
OF— Joe Rudi, Oakland
OF— Dwight Evans, Boston
OF— Rick Manning, Cleveland

NATIONAL LEAGUE
P— Jim Kaat, Philadelphia
C— Johnny Bench, Cincinnati
1B— Steve Garvey, Los Angeles
2B— Joe Morgan, Cincinnati
3B— Mike Schmidt, Philadelphia
SS— Dave Concepcion, Cincinnati
OF— Cesar Cedeno, Houston
OF— Cesar Geronimo, Cincinnati
OF— Garry Maddox, Philadelphia

1977

AMERICAN LEAGUE
P— Jim Palmer, Baltimore
C— Jim Sundberg, Texas
1B— Jim Spencer, Chicago
2B— Frank White, Kansas City
3B— Graig Nettles, New York
SS— Mark Belanger, Baltimore
OF— Juan Beniquez, Texas
OF— Carl Yastrzemski, Boston
OF— Al Cowens, Kansas City

NATIONAL LEAGUE
P— Jim Kaat, Philadelphia
C— Johnny Bench, Cincinnati
1B— Steve Garvey, Los Angeles
2B— Joe Morgan, Cincinnati
3B— Mike Schmidt, Philadelphia
SS— Dave Concepcion, Cincinnati
OF— Cesar Geronimo, Cincinnati
OF— Garry Maddox, Philadelphia
OF— Dave Parker, Pittsburgh

1978

AMERICAN LEAGUE
P— Jim Palmer, Baltimore
C— Jim Sundberg, Texas
1B— Chris Chambliss, New York
2B— Frank White, Kansas City
3B— Graig Nettles, New York
SS— Mark Belanger, Baltimore
OF— Fred Lynn, Boston
OF— Dwight Evans, Boston
OF— Rick Miller, California

NATIONAL LEAGUE
P— Phil Niekro, Atlanta
C— Bob Boone, Philadelphia
1B— Keith Hernandez, St. Louis
2B— Dave Lopes, Los Angeles
3B— Mike Schmidt, Philadelphia
SS— Larry Bowa, Philadelphia
OF— Garry Maddox, Philadelphia
OF— Dave Parker, Pittsburgh
OF— Ellis Valentine, Montreal

1979

AMERICAN LEAGUE
P— Jim Palmer, Baltimore
C— Jim Sundberg, Texas
1B— Cecil Cooper, Milwaukee
2B— Frank White, Kansas City
3B— Buddy Bell, Texas
SS— Rick Burleson, Boston
OF— Dwight Evans, Boston
OF— Sixto Lezcano, Milwaukee
OF— Fred Lynn, Boston

NATIONAL LEAGUE
P— Phil Niekro, Atlanta
C— Bob Boone, Philadelphia
1B— Keith Hernandez, St. Louis
2B— Manny Trillo, Philadelphia
3B— Mike Schmidt, Philadelphia
SS— Dave Concepcion, Cincinnati
OF— Garry Maddox, Philadelphia
OF— Dave Parker, Pittsburgh
OF— Dave Winfield, San Diego

1980

AMERICAN LEAGUE
P— Mike Norris, Oakland
C— Jim Sundberg, Texas
1B— Cecil Cooper, Milwaukee
2B— Frank White, Kansas City
3B— Buddy Bell, Texas
SS— Alan Trammell, Detroit
OF— Fred Lynn, Boston
OF— Dwayne Murphy, Oakland
OF— Willie Wilson, Kansas City

NATIONAL LEAGUE
P— Phil Niekro, Atlanta
C— Gary Carter, Montreal
1B— Keith Hernandez, St. Louis
2B— Doug Flynn, New York
3B— Mike Schmidt, Philadelphia
SS— Ozzie Smith, San Diego
OF— Andre Dawson, Montreal
OF— Garry Maddox, Philadelphia
OF— Dave Winfield, San Diego

1981

AMERICAN LEAGUE
P— Mike Norris, Oakland
C— Jim Sundberg, Texas
1B— Mike Squires, Chicago
2B— Frank White, Kansas City
3B— Buddy Bell, Texas
SS— Alan Trammell, Detroit
OF— Dwayne Murphy, Oakland
OF— Dwight Evans, Boston
OF— Rickey Henderson, Oakland

NATIONAL LEAGUE
P— Steve Carlton, Philadelphia
C— Gary Carter, Montreal
1B— Keith Hernandez, St. Louis
2B— Manny Trillo, Philadelphia
3B— Mike Schmidt, Philadelphia
SS— Ozzie Smith, San Diego
OF— Andre Dawson, Montreal
OF— Garry Maddox, Philadelphia
OF— Dusty Baker, Los Angeles

1982

AMERICAN LEAGUE
P— Ron Guidry, New York
C— Bob Boone, California
1B— Eddie Murray, Baltimore
2B— Frank White, Kansas City
3B— Buddy Bell, Texas
SS— Robin Yount, Milwaukee
OF— Dwight Evans, Boston
OF— Dave Winfield, New York
OF— Dwayne Murphy, Oakland

NATIONAL LEAGUE
P— Phil Niekro, Atlanta
C— Gary Carter, Montreal
1B— Keith Hernandez, St. Louis
2B— Manny Trillo, Philadelphia
3B— Mike Schmidt, Philadelphia
SS— Ozzie Smith, St. Louis
OF— Andre Dawson, Montreal
OF— Dale Murphy, Atlanta
OF— Garry Maddox, Philadelphia

1983

AMERICAN LEAGUE
P— Ron Guidry, New York
C— Lance Parrish, Detroit
1B— Eddie Murray, Baltimore
2B— Lou Whitaker, Detroit
3B— Buddy Bell, Texas
SS— Alan Trammell, Detroit
OF— Dwight Evans, Boston
OF— Dave Winfield, New York
OF— Dwayne Murphy, Oakland

NATIONAL LEAGUE
P— Phil Niekro, Atlanta
C— Tony Pena, Pittsburgh
1B— Keith Hernandez, St.L.-N.Y.
2B— Ryne Sandberg, Chicago
3B— Mike Schmidt, Philadelphia
SS— Ozzie Smith, St. Louis
OF— Andre Dawson, Montreal
OF— Dale Murphy, Atlanta
OF— Willie McGee, St. Louis

1984

AMERICAN LEAGUE
P— Ron Guidry, New York
C— Lance Parrish, Detroit
1B— Eddie Murray, Baltimore
2B— Lou Whitaker, Detroit
3B— Buddy Bell, Texas
SS— Alan Trammell, Detroit
OF— Dwight Evans, Boston
OF— Dave Winfield, New York
OF— Dwayne Murphy, Oakland

NATIONAL LEAGUE
P— Joaquin Andujar, St. Louis
C— Tony Pena, Pittsburgh
1B— Keith Hernandez, New York
2B— Ryne Sandberg, Chicago
3B— Mike Schmidt, Philadelphia
SS— Ozzie Smith, St. Louis
OF— Dale Murphy, Atlanta
OF— Bob Dernier, Chicago
OF— Andre Dawson, Montreal

1985

AMERICAN LEAGUE
P— Ron Guidry, New York
C— Lance Parrish, Detroit
1B— Don Mattingly, New York
2B— Lou Whitaker, Detroit
3B— George Brett, Kansas City
SS— Alfredo Griffin, Oakland
OF— Gary Pettis, California
OF— Dave Winfield, New York
OF— Dwight Evans, Boston (tie)
Dwayne Murphy, Oakland (tie)

NATIONAL LEAGUE
P— Rick Reuschel, Pittsburgh
C— Tony Pena, Pittsburgh
1B— Keith Hernandez, New York
2B— Ryne Sandberg, Chicago
3B— Tim Wallach, Montreal
SS— Ozzie Smith, St. Louis
OF— Willie McGee, St. Louis
OF— Dale Murphy, Atlanta
OF— Andre Dawson, Montreal

1986

AMERICAN LEAGUE

P— Ron Guidry, New York
C— Bob Boone, California
1B— Don Mattingly, New York
2B— Frank White, Kansas City
3B— Gary Gaetti, Minnesota
SS— Tony Fernandez, Toronto
OF— Gary Pettis, California
OF— Jesse Barfield, Toronto
OF— Kirby Puckett, Minnesota

NATIONAL LEAGUE

P— Fernando Valenzuela, Los Angeles
C— Jody Davis, Chicago
1B— Keith Hernandez, New York
2B— Ryne Sandberg, Chicago
3B— Mike Schmidt, Philadelphia
SS— Ozzie Smith, St. Louis
OF— Tony Gwynn, San Diego
OF— Dale Murphy, Atlanta
OF— Willie McGee, St. Louis

1987

AMERICAN LEAGUE

P— Mark Langston, Seattle
C— Bob Boone, California
1B— Don Mattingly, New York
2B— Frank White, Kansas City
3B— Gary Gaetti, Minnesota
SS— Tony Fernandez, Toronto
OF— Jesse Barfield, Toronto
OF— Kirby Puckett, Minnesota
OF— Dave Winfield, New York

NATIONAL LEAGUE

P— Rick Reuschel, Pit.-S.F.
C— Mike LaValliere, Pittsburgh
1B— Keith Hernandez, New York
2B— Ryne Sandberg, Chicago
3B— Terry Pendleton, St. Louis
SS— Ozzie Smith, St. Louis
OF— Eric Davis, Cincinnati
OF— Tony Gwynn, San Diego
OF— Andre Dawson, Chicago

1988

AMERICAN LEAGUE

P— Mark Langston, Seattle
C— Bob Boone, California
1B— Don Mattingly, New York
2B— Harold Reynolds, Seattle
3B— Gary Gaetti, Minnesota
SS— Tony Fernandez, Toronto
OF— Kirby Puckett, Minnesota
OF— Devon White, California
OF— Gary Pettis, Detroit

NATIONAL LEAGUE

P— Orel Hershiser, Los Angeles
C— Benito Santiago, San Diego
1B— Keith Hernandez, New York
2B— Ryne Sandberg, Chicago
3B— Tim Wallach, Montreal
SS— Ozzie Smith, St. Louis
OF— Andy Van Slyke, Pittsburgh
OF— Eric Davis, Cincinnati
OF— Andre Dawson, Chicago

1989

AMERICAN LEAGUE

P— Bret Saberhagen, Kansas City
C— Bob Boone, Kansas City
1B— Don Mattingly, New York
2B— Harold Reynolds, Seattle
3B— Gary Gaetti, Minnesota
SS— Tony Fernandez, Toronto
OF— Kirby Puckett, Minnesota
OF— Devon White, California
OF— Gary Pettis, Detroit

NATIONAL LEAGUE

P— Ron Darling, New York
C— Benito Santiago, San Diego
1B— Andres Galarraga, Montreal
2B— Ryne Sandberg, Chicago
3B— Terry Pendleton, St. Louis
SS— Ozzie Smith, St. Louis
OF— Andy Van Slyke, Pittsburgh
OF— Tony Gwynn, San Diego
OF— Eric Davis, Cincinnati

1990

AMERICAN LEAGUE

P— Mike Boddicker, Boston
C— Sandy Alomar Jr., Cleveland
1B— Mark McGwire, Oakland
2B— Harold Reynolds, Seattle
3B— Kelly Gruber, Toronto
SS— Ozzie Guillen, Chicago
OF— Ken Griffey Jr., Seattle
OF— Ellis Burks, Boston
OF— Gary Pettis, Texas

NATIONAL LEAGUE

P— Greg Maddux, Chicago
C— Benito Santiago, San Diego
1B— Andres Galarraga, Montreal
2B— Ryne Sandberg, Chicago
3B— Tim Wallach, Montreal
SS— Ozzie Smith, St. Louis
OF— Barry Bonds, Pittsburgh
OF— Andy Van Slyke, Pittsburgh
OF— Tony Gwynn, San Diego

1991

AMERICAN LEAGUE

P— Mark Langston, California
C— Tony Pena, Boston
1B— Don Mattingly, New York
2B— Roberto Alomar, Toronto
3B— Robin Ventura, Chicago
SS— Cal Ripken, Baltimore
OF— Ken Griffey Jr., Seattle
OF— Kirby Puckett, Minnesota
OF— Devon White, Toronto

NATIONAL LEAGUE

P— Greg Maddux, Chicago
C— Tom Pagnozzi, St. Louis
1B— Will Clark, San Francisco
2B— Ryne Sandberg, Chicago
3B— Matt Williams, San Francisco
SS— Ozzie Smith, St. Louis
OF— Barry Bonds, Pittsburgh
OF— Andy Van Slyke, Pittsburgh
OF— Tony Gwynn, San Diego

1992

AMERICAN LEAGUE

P— Mark Langston, California
C— Ivan Rodriguez, Texas
1B— Don Mattingly, New York
2B— Roberto Alomar, Toronto
3B— Robin Ventura, Chicago
SS— Cal Ripken, Baltimore
OF— Ken Griffey Jr., Seattle
OF— Kirby Puckett, Minnesota
OF— Devon White, Toronto

NATIONAL LEAGUE

P— Greg Maddux, Chicago
C— Tom Pagnozzi, St. Louis
1B— Mark Grace, Chicago
2B— Jose Lind, Pittsburgh
3B— Terry Pendleton, Atlanta
SS— Ozzie Smith, St. Louis
OF— Barry Bonds, Pittsburgh
OF— Andy Van Slyke, Pittsburgh
OF— Larry Walker, Montreal

1993

AMERICAN LEAGUE

P— Mark Langston, California
C— Ivan Rodriguez, Texas
1B— Don Mattingly, New York
2B— Roberto Alomar, Toronto
3B— Robin Ventura, Chicago
SS— Omar Vizquel, Seattle
OF— Ken Griffey Jr., Seattle
OF— Kenny Lofton, Cleveland
OF— Devon White, Toronto

NATIONAL LEAGUE

P— Greg Maddux, Atlanta
C— Kirt Manwaring, San Francisco
1B— Mark Grace, Chicago
2B— Robby Thompson, San Fran.
3B— Matt Williams, San Francisco
SS— Jay Bell, Pittsburgh
OF— Barry Bonds, San Francisco
OF— Marquis Grissom, Montreal
OF— Larry Walker, Montreal

1994

AMERICAN LEAGUE

P— Mark Langston, California
C— Ivan Rodriguez, Texas
1B— Don Mattingly, New York
2B— Roberto Alomar, Toronto
3B— Wade Boggs, New York
SS— Omar Vizquel, Cleveland
OF— Ken Griffey Jr., Seattle
OF— Kenny Lofton, Cleveland
OF— Devon White, Toronto

NATIONAL LEAGUE

P— Greg Maddux, Atlanta
C— Tom Pagnozzi, St. Louis
1B— Jeff Bagwell, Houston
2B— Craig Biggio, Houston
3B— Matt Williams, San Francisco
SS— Barry Larkin, Cincinnati
OF— Barry Bonds, San Francisco
OF— Marquis Grissom, Montreal
OF— Darren Lewis, San Francisco

1995

AMERICAN LEAGUE

P— Mark Langston, California
C— Ivan Rodriguez, Texas
1B— J.T. Snow, California
2B— Roberto Alomar, Toronto
3B— Wade Boggs, New York
SS— Omar Vizquel, Cleveland
OF— Ken Griffey Jr., Seattle
OF— Kenny Lofton, Cleveland
OF— Devon White, Toronto

NATIONAL LEAGUE

P— Greg Maddux, Atlanta
C— Charles Johnson, Florida
1B— Mark Grace, Chicago
2B— Craig Biggio, Houston
3B— Ken Caminiti, San Diego
SS— Barry Larkin, Cincinnati
OF— Raul Mondesi, Los Angeles
OF— Marquis Grissom, Atlanta
OF— Steve Finley, San Diego

SILVER SLUGGER TEAMS

1980

AMERICAN LEAGUE

1B— Cecil Cooper, Milwaukee
2B— Willie Randolph, New York
3B— George Brett, Kansas City
SS— Robin Yount, Milwaukee
OF— Ben Oglivie, Milwaukee
OF— Al Oliver, Texas
OF— Willie Wilson, Kansas City
C— Lance Parrish, Detroit
DH— Reggie Jackson, New York

NATIONAL LEAGUE

1B— Keith Hernandez, St. Louis
2B— Manny Trillo, Philadelphia
3B— Mike Schmidt, Philadelphia
SS— Garry Templeton, St. Louis
OF— Dusty Baker, Los Angeles
OF— Andre Dawson, Montreal
OF— George Hendrick, St. Louis
C— Ted Simmons, St. Louis
P— Bob Forsch, St. Louis

1981

AMERICAN LEAGUE

1B— Cecil Cooper, Milwaukee
2B— Bobby Grich, California
3B— Carney Lansford, Boston
SS— Rick Burleson, California
OF— Rickey Henderson, Oakland
OF— Dwight Evans, Boston
OF— Dave Winfield, New York
C— Carlton Fisk, Chicago
DH— Al Oliver, Texas

NATIONAL LEAGUE

1B— Pete Rose, Philadelphia
2B— Manny Trillo, Philadelphia
3B— Mike Schmidt, Philadelphia
SS— Dave Concepcion, Cincinnati
OF— Andre Dawson, Montreal
OF— George Foster, Cincinnati
OF— Dusty Baker, Los Angeles
C— Gary Carter, Montreal
P— Fernando Valenzuela, Los Angeles

1982

AMERICAN LEAGUE

1B— Cecil Cooper, Milwaukee
2B— Damaso Garcia, Toronto
3B— Doug DeCinces, California
SS— Robin Yount, Milwaukee
OF— Dave Winfield, New York
OF— Willie Wilson, Kansas City
OF— Reggie Jackson, California
C— Lance Parrish, Detroit
DH— Hal McRae, Kansas City

NATIONAL LEAGUE

1B— Al Oliver, Montreal
2B— Joe Morgan, San Francisco
3B— Mike Schmidt, Philadelphia
SS— Dave Concepcion, Cincinnati
OF— Dale Murphy, Atlanta
OF— Pedro Guerrero, Los Angeles
OF— Leon Durham, Chicago
C— Gary Carter, Montreal
P— Don Robinson, Pittsburgh

1983

AMERICAN LEAGUE

1B— Eddie Murray, Baltimore
2B— Lou Whitaker, Detroit
3B— Wade Boggs, Boston
SS— Cal Ripken Jr., Baltimore
OF— Jim Rice, Boston
OF— Dave Winfield, New York
OF— Lloyd Moseby, Toronto
C— Lance Parrish, Detroit
DH— Don Baylor, New York

NATIONAL LEAGUE

1B— George Hendrick, St. Louis
2B— Johnny Ray, Pittsburgh
3B— Mike Schmidt, Philadelphia
SS— Dickie Thon, Houston
OF— Andre Dawson, Montreal
OF— Dale Murphy, Atlanta
OF— Jose Cruz, Houston
C— Terry Kennedy, San Diego
P— Fernando Valenzuela, Los Angeles

1984

AMERICAN LEAGUE

1B— Eddie Murray, Baltimore
2B— Lou Whitaker, Detroit
3B— Buddy Bell, Texas
SS— Cal Ripken Jr., Baltimore
OF— Tony Armas, Boston
OF— Jim Rice, Boston
OF— Dave Winfield, New York
C— Lance Parrish, Detroit
DH— Andre Thornton, Cleveland

NATIONAL LEAGUE

1B— Keith Hernandez, New York
2B— Ryne Sandberg, Chicago
3B— Mike Schmidt, Philadelphia
SS— Garry Templeton, San Diego
OF— Dale Murphy, Atlanta
OF— Jose Cruz, Houston
OF— Tony Gwynn, San Diego
C— Gary Carter, Montreal
P— Rick Rhoden, Pittsburgh

1985

AMERICAN LEAGUE

1B— Don Mattingly, New York
2B— Lou Whitaker, Detroit
3B— George Brett, Kansas City
SS— Cal Ripken Jr., Baltimore
OF— Rickey Henderson, New York
OF— Dave Winfield, New York
OF— George Bell, Toronto
C— Carlton Fisk, Chicago
DH— Don Baylor, New York

NATIONAL LEAGUE

1B— Jack Clark, St. Louis
2B— Ryne Sandberg, Chicago
3B— Tim Wallach, Montreal
SS— Hubie Brooks, Montreal
OF— Willie McGee, St. Louis
OF— Dale Murphy, Atlanta
OF— Dave Parker, Cincinnati
C— Gary Carter, New York
P— Rick Rhoden, Pittsburgh

1986

AMERICAN LEAGUE

1B— Don Mattingly, New York
2B— Frank White, Kansas City
3B— Wade Boggs, Boston
SS— Cal Ripken Jr., Baltimore
OF— George Bell, Toronto
OF— Kirby Puckett, Minnesota
OF— Jesse Barfield, Toronto
C— Lance Parrish, Detroit
DH— Don Baylor, Boston

NATIONAL LEAGUE

1B— Glenn Davis, Houston
2B— Steve Sax, Los Angeles
3B— Mike Schmidt, Philadelphia
SS— Hubie Brooks, Montreal
OF— Tony Gwynn, San Diego
OF— Tim Raines, Montreal
OF— Dave Parker, Cincinnati
C— Gary Carter, New York
P— Rick Rhoden, Pittsburgh

1987

AMERICAN LEAGUE

1B— Don Mattingly, New York
2B— Lou Whitaker, Detroit
3B— Wade Boggs, Boston
SS— Alan Trammell, Detroit
OF— George Bell, Toronto
OF— Dwight Evans, Boston
OF— Kirby Puckett, Minnesota
C— Matt Nokes, Detroit
DH— Paul Molitor, Milwaukee

NATIONAL LEAGUE

1B— Jack Clark, St. Louis
2B— Juan Samuel, Philadelphia
3B— Tim Wallach, Montreal
SS— Ozzie Smith, St. Louis
OF— Andre Dawson, Chicago
OF— Eric Davis, Cincinnati
OF— Tony Gwynn, San Diego
C— Benito Santiago, San Diego
P— Bob Forsch, St. Louis

1988

AMERICAN LEAGUE

1B— George Brett, Kansas City
2B— Julio Franco, Cleveland
3B— Wade Boggs, Boston
SS— Alan Trammell, Detroit
OF— Kirby Puckett, Minnesota
OF— Jose Canseco, Oakland
OF— Mike Greenwell, Boston
C— Carlton Fisk, Chicago
DH— Paul Molitor, Milwaukee

NATIONAL LEAGUE

1B— Andres Galarraga, Montreal
2B— Ryne Sandberg, Chicago
3B— Bobby Bonilla, Pittsburgh
SS— Barry Larkin, Cincinnati
OF— Darryl Strawberry, New York
OF— Andy Van Slyke, Pittsburgh
OF— Kirk Gibson, Los Angeles
C— Benito Santiago, San Diego
P— Tim Leary, Los Angeles

1989

AMERICAN LEAGUE

1B— Fred McGriff, Toronto
2B— Julio Franco, Texas
3B— Wade Boggs, Boston
SS— Cal Ripken Jr., Baltimore
OF— Kirby Puckett, Minnesota
OF— Ruben Sierra, Texas
OF— Robin Yount, Milwaukee
C— Mickey Tettleton, Baltimore
DH— Harold Baines, Chi.-Tex.

NATIONAL LEAGUE

1B— Will Clark, San Francisco
2B— Ryne Sandberg, Chicago
3B— Howard Johnson, New York
SS— Barry Larkin, Cincinnati
OF— Kevin Mitchell, San Francisco
OF— Tony Gwynn, San Diego
OF— Eric Davis, Cincinnati
C— Craig Biggio, Houston
P— Don Robinson, San Francisco

1990

AMERICAN LEAGUE

1B— Cecil Fielder, Detroit
2B— Julio Franco, Texas
3B— Kelly Gruber, Toronto
SS— Alan Trammell, Detroit
OF— Rickey Henderson, Oakland
OF— Jose Canseco, Oakland
OF— Ellis Burks, Boston
C— Lance Parrish, California
DH— Dave Parker, Milwaukee

NATIONAL LEAGUE
1B— Eddie Murray, Los Angeles
2B— Ryne Sandberg, Chicago
3B— Matt Williams, San Francisco
SS— Barry Larkin, Cincinnati
OF— Barry Bonds, Pittsburgh
OF— Bobby Bonilla, Pittsburgh
OF— Darryl Strawberry, New York
C— Benito Santiago, San Diego
P— Don Robinson, San Francisco

1991

AMERICAN LEAGUE
1B— Cecil Fielder, Detroit
2B— Julio Franco, Texas
3B— Wade Boggs, Boston
SS— Cal Ripken Jr., Baltimore
OF— Jose Canseco, Oakland
OF— Joe Carter, Toronto
OF— Ken Griffey Jr., Seattle
C— Mickey Tettleton, Detroit
DH— Frank Thomas, Chicago

NATIONAL LEAGUE
1B— Will Clark, San Francisco
2B— Ryne Sandberg, Chicago
3B— Howard Johnson, New York
SS— Barry Larkin, Cincinnati
OF— Barry Bonds, Pittsburgh
OF— Bobby Bonilla, Pittsburgh
OF— Ron Gant, Atlanta
C— Benito Santiago, San Diego
P— Tom Glavine, Atlanta

1992

AMERICAN LEAGUE
1B— Mark McGwire, Oakland
2B— Roberto Alomar, Toronto
3B— Edgar Martinez, Seattle
SS— Travis Fryman, Detroit
OF— Joe Carter, Toronto
OF— Juan Gonzalez, Texas
OF— Kirby Puckett, Minnesota
C— Mickey Tettleton, Detroit
DH— Dave Winfield, Toronto

NATIONAL LEAGUE
1B— Fred McGriff, San Diego
2B— Ryne Sandberg, Chicago
3B— Gary Sheffield, San Diego
SS— Barry Larkin, Cincinnati
OF— Barry Bonds, Pittsburgh
OF— Andy Van Slyke, Pittsburgh
OF— Larry Walker, Montreal
C— Darren Daulton, Philadelphia
P— Dwight Gooden, New York

1993

AMERICAN LEAGUE
1B— Frank Thomas, Chicago
2B— Carlos Baerga, Cleveland
3B— Wade Boggs, New York
SS— Cal Ripken Jr., Baltimore
OF— Albert Belle, Cleveland
OF— Juan Gonzalez, Texas
OF— Ken Griffey Jr., Seattle
C— Mike Stanley, New York
DH— Paul Molitor, Toronto

NATIONAL LEAGUE
1B— Fred McGriff, S.D.-Atl.
2B— Robby Thompson, San Fran.
3B— Matt Williams, San Francisco
SS— Jay Bell, Pittsburgh
OF— Barry Bonds, San Francisco
OF— Lenny Dykstra, Philadelphia
OF— David Justice, Atlanta
C— Mike Piazza, Los Angeles
P— Orel Hershiser, Los Angeles

1994

AMERICAN LEAGUE
1B— Frank Thomas, Chicago
2B— Carlos Baerga, Cleveland
3B— Wade Boggs, New York
SS— Cal Ripken Jr., Baltimore
OF— Albert Belle, Cleveland
OF— Ken Griffey Jr., Seattle
OF— Kirby Puckett, Minnesota
C— Ivan Rodriguez, Texas
DH— Julio Franco, Chicago

NATIONAL LEAGUE
1B— Jeff Bagwell, Houston
2B— Craig Biggio, Houston
3B— Matt Williams, San Francisco
SS— Wil Cordero, Montreal
OF— Moises Alou, Montreal
OF— Barry Bonds, San Francisco
OF— Tony Gwynn, San Diego
C— Mike Piazza, Los Angeles
P— Mark Portugal, San Francisco

1995

AMERICAN LEAGUE
1B— Mo Vaughn, Boston
2B— Chuck Knoblauch, Minnesota
3B— Gary Gaetti, Kansas City
SS— John Valentin, Boston
OF— Albert Belle, Cleveland
OF— Tim Salmon, California
OF— Manny Ramirez, Cleveland
C— Ivan Rodriguez, Texas
DH— Edgar Martinez, Seattle

NATIONAL LEAGUE
1B— Eric Karros, Los Angeles
2B— Craig Biggio, Houston
3B— Vinny Castilla, Colorado
SS— Barry Larkin, Cincinnati
OF— Dante Bichette, Colorado
OF— Tony Gwynn, San Diego
OF— Sammy Sosa, Chicago
C— Mike Piazza, Los Angeles
P— Tom Glavine, Atlanta

MAJOR LEAGUE ALL-STAR TEAMS

1925

1B— Jim Bottomley, St. Louis N.L.
2B— Rogers Hornsby, St. Louis N.L.
SS— Glenn Wright, Pittsburgh N.L.
3B— Pie Traynor, Pittsburgh N.L.
OF— Kiki Cuyler, Pittsburgh N.L.
OF— Max Carey, Pittsburgh N.L.
OF— Goose Goslin, Washington A.L.
C— Mickey Cochrane, Phil. A.L.
P— Walter Johnson, Washington A.L.
P— Ed Rommel, Philadelphia A.L.
P— Dazzy Vance, Brooklyn N.L.

1926

1B— George Burns, Cleveland A.L.
2B— Rogers Hornsby, St. Louis N.L.
SS— Joe Sewell, Cleveland A.L.
3B— Pie Traynor, Pittsburgh N.L.
OF— Goose Goslin, Washington A.L.
OF— John Mostil, Chicago A.L.
OF— Babe Ruth, New York A.L.
C— Bob O'Farrell, St. Louis N.L.
P— Herb Pennock, New York A.L.
P— George Uhle, Cleveland A.L.
P— Grover Alexander, St. Louis N.L.

1927

1B— Lou Gehrig, New York A.L.
2B— Rogers Hornsby, New York N.L.
SS— Travis Jackson, New York N.L.
3B— Pie Traynor, Pittsburgh N.L.
OF— Babe Ruth, New York A.L.
OF— Al Simmons, Philadelphia A.L.
OF— Paul Waner, Pittsburgh N.L.
C— Gabby Hartnett, Chicago N.L.
P— Charley Root, Chicago N.L.
P— Ted Lyons, Chicago A.L.

1928

1B— Lou Gehrig, New York A.L.
2B— Rogers Hornsby, Boston N.L.
SS— Travis Jackson, New York N.L.
3B— Fred Lindstrom, New York N.L.
OF— Babe Ruth, New York A.L.
OF— Heinie Manush, St. Louis A.L.
OF— Paul Waner, Pittsburgh N.L.
C— Mickey Cochrane, Phil. A.L.
P— Lefty Grove, Philadelphia A.L.
P— Waite Hoyt, New York A.L.

1929

1B— Jimmie Foxx, Philadelphia A.L.
2B— Rogers Hornsby, Chicago N.L.
SS— Travis Jackson, New York N.L.
3B— Pie Traynor, Pittsburgh, N.L.
OF— Al Simmons, Philadelphia A.L.
OF— Hack Wilson, Chicago N.L.
OF— Babe Ruth, New York A.L.
C— Mickey Cochrane, Phil. A.L.
P— Lefty Grove, Philadelphia A.L.
P— Burleigh Grimes, Pittsburgh N.L.

1930

1B— Bill Terry, New York N.L.
2B— Frank Frisch, St. Louis N.L.
SS— Joe Cronin, Washington A.L.
3B— Fred Lindstrom, New York N.L.
OF— Al Simmons, Philadelphia A.L.
OF— Hack Wilson, Chicago N.L.
OF— Babe Ruth, New York A.L.
C— Mickey Cochrane, Phil. A.L.
P— Lefty Grove, Philadelphia A.L.
P— Wes Ferrell, Cleveland A.L.

1931

1B— Lou Gehrig, New York A.L.
2B— Frank Frisch, St. Louis N.L.
SS— Joe Cronin, Washington A.L.
3B— Pie Traynor, Pittsburgh N.L.
OF— Al Simmons, Philadelphia A.L.
OF— Earl Averill, Cleveland A.L.
OF— Babe Ruth, New York A.L.
C— Mickey Cochrane, Phil. A.L.
P— Lefty Grove, Philadelphia A.L.
P— George Earnshaw, Phil. A.L.

1932

1B— Jimmie Foxx, Philadelphia A.L.
2B— Tony Lazzeri, New York A.L.
SS— Joe Cronin, Washington A.L.
3B— Pie Traynor, Pittsburgh N.L.
OF— Lefty O'Doul, Brooklyn N.L.
OF— Earl Averill, Cleveland A.L.
OF— Chuck Klein, Philadelphia N.L.
C— Bill Dickey, New York A.L.
P— Lefty Grove, Philadelphia A.L.
P— Lon Warneke, Chicago N.L.

1933

1B— Jimmie Foxx, Philadelphia A.L.
2B— Charley Gehringer, Detroit A.L.
SS— Joe Cronin, Washington A.L.
3B— Pie Traynor, Pittsburgh N.L.
OF— Al Simmons, Chicago A.L.
OF— Wally Berger, Boston N.L.
OF— Chuck Klein, Philadelphia N.L.
C— Bill Dickey, New York A.L.
P— Alvin Crowder, Washington A.L.
P— Carl Hubbell, New York N.L.

1934
1B— Lou Gehrig, New York A.L.
2B— Charley Gehringer, Detroit A.L.
SS— Joe Cronin, Washington A.L.
3B— Mike Higgins, Philadelphia A.L.
OF— Al Simmons, Chicago A.L.
OF— Earl Averill, Cleveland A.L.
OF— Mel Ott, New York N.L.
C— Mickey Cochrane, Detroit A.L.
P— Lefty Gomez, New York A.L.
P— Schoolboy Rowe, Detroit A.L.
P— Dizzy Dean, St. Louis N.L.

1935
1B— Hank Greenberg, Detroit A.L.
2B— Charley Gehringer, Detroit A.L.
SS— Arky Vaughan, Pittsburgh N.L.
3B— Pepper Martin, St. Louis N.L.
OF— Joe Medwick, St. Louis N.L.
OF— Doc Cramer, Philadelphia A.L.
OF— Mel Ott, New York N.L.
C— Mickey Cochrane, Detroit A.L.
P— Carl Hubbell, New York N.L.
P— Dizzy Dean, St. Louis N.L.

1936
1B— Lou Gehrig, New York A.L.
2B— Charley Gehringer, Detroit A.L.
SS— Luke Appling, Chicago A.L.
3B— Mike Higgins, Philadelphia A.L.
OF— Joe Medwick, St. Louis N.L.
OF— Earl Averill, Cleveland A.L.
OF— Mel Ott, New York N.L.
C— Bill Dickey, New York A.L.
P— Carl Hubbell, New York N.L.
P— Dizzy Dean, St. Louis N.L.

1937
1B— Lou Gehrig, New York A.L.
2B— Charley Gehringer, Detroit A.L.
SS— Dick Bartell, New York N.L.
3B— Red Rolfe, New York A.L.
OF— Joe Medwick, St. Louis N.L.
OF— Joe DiMaggio, New York A.L.
OF— Paul Waner, Pittsburgh N.L.
C— Gabby Hartnett, Chicago N.L.
P— Carl Hubbell, New York N.L.
P— Red Ruffing, New York A.L.

1938
1B— Jimmie Foxx, Boston A.L.
2B— Charley Gehringer, Detroit A.L.
SS— Joe Cronin, Boston A.L.
3B— Red Rolfe, New York A.L.
OF— Joe Medwick, St. Louis N.L.
OF— Joe DiMaggio, New York A.L.
OF— Mel Ott, New York N.L.
C— Bill Dickey, New York A.L.
P— Red Ruffing, New York A.L.
P— Lefty Gomez, New York A.L.
P— Johnny Vander Meer, Cin. N.L.

1939
1B— Jimmie Foxx, Boston A.L.
2B— Joe Gordon, New York A.L.
SS— Joe Cronin, Boston A.L.
3B— Red Rolfe, New York A.L.
OF— Joe Medwick, St. Louis N.L.
OF— Joe DiMaggio, New York A.L.
OF— Ted Williams, Boston A.L.
C— Bill Dickey, New York A.L.
P— Red Ruffing, New York A.L.
P— Bob Feller, Cleveland A.L.
P— Bucky Walters, Cincinnati N.L.

1940
1B— Frank McCormick, Cincinnati N.L.
2B— Joe Gordon, New York A.L.
SS— Luke Appling, Chicago A.L.
3B— Stan Hack, Chicago N.L.
OF— Hank Greenberg, Detroit A.L.
OF— Joe DiMaggio, New York A.L.
OF— Ted Williams, Boston A.L.
C— Harry Danning, New York N.L.
P— Bob Feller, Cleveland A.L.
P— Bucky Walters, Cincinnati N.L.
P— Paul Derringer, Cincinnati N.L.

1941
1B— Dolf Camilli, Brooklyn N.L.
2B— Joe Gordon, New York A.L.
SS— Cecil Travis, Washington A.L.
3B— Stan Hack, Chicago N.L.
OF— Ted Williams, Boston A.L.
OF— Joe DiMaggio, New York A.L.
OF— Pete Reiser, Brooklyn N.L.
C— Bill Dickey, New York A.L.
P— Bob Feller, Cleveland A.L.
P— Whitlow Wyatt, Brooklyn N.L.
P— Thornton Lee, Chicago A.L.

1942
1B— Johnny Mize, New York N.L.
2B— Joe Gordon, New York A.L.
SS— Johnny Pesky, Boston A.L.
3B— Stan Hack, Chicago N.L.
OF— Ted Williams, Boston A.L.
OF— Joe DiMaggio, New York A.L.
OF— Enos Slaughter, St. Louis N.L.
C— Mickey Owen, Brooklyn N.L.
P— Mort Cooper, St. Louis N.L.
P— Tiny Bonham, New York A.L.
P— Tex Hughson, Boston A.L.

1943
1B— Rudy York, Detroit A.L.
2B— Billy Herman, Brooklyn N.L.
SS— Luke Appling, Chicago A.L.
3B— Billy Johnson, New York A.L.
OF— Dick Wakefield, Detroit A.L.
OF— Stan Musial, St. Louis N.L.
OF— Bill Nicholson, Chicago N.L.
C— Walker Cooper, St. Louis N.L.
P— Spud Chandler, New York A.L.
P— Mort Cooper, St. Louis N.L.
P— Rip Sewell, Pittsburgh N.L.

1944
1B— Ray Sanders, St. Louis N.L.
2B— Bobby Doerr, Boston A.L.
SS— Marty Marion, St. Louis N.L.
3B— Bob Elliott, Pittsburgh N.L.
OF— Stan Musial, St. Louis N.L.
OF— Dick Wakefield, Detroit A.L.
OF— Dixie Walker, Brooklyn, N.L.
C— Walker Cooper, St. Louis N.L.
P— Hal Newhouser, Detroit A.L.
P— Mort Cooper, St. Louis N.L.
P— Dizzy Trout, Detroit A.L.

1945
1B— Phil Cavarretta, Chicago N.L.
2B— George Stirnweiss, N.Y. A.L.
SS— Marty Marion, St. Louis N.L.
3B— Whitey Kurowski, St. Louis N.L.
OF— Tommy Holmes, Boston N.L.
OF— Andy Pafko, Chicago N.L.
OF— Goody Rosen, Brooklyn N.L.
C— Paul Richards, Detroit A.L.
P— Hal Newhouser, Detroit A.L.
P— Boo Ferriss, Boston A.L.
P— Hank Borowy, Chicago N.L.

1946
1B— Stan Musial, St. Louis N.L.
2B— Bobby Doerr, Boston A.L.
SS— Johnny Pesky, Boston A.L.
3B— George Kell, Detroit A.L.
OF— Ted Williams, Boston A.L.
OF— Dom DiMaggio, Boston A.L.
OF— Enos Slaughter, St. Louis N.L.
C— Aaron Robinson, New York A.L.
P— Hal Newhouser, Detroit A.L.
P— Bob Feller, Cleveland A.L.
P— Boo Ferriss, Boston A.L.

1947
1B— Johnny Mize, New York N.L.
2B— Joe Gordon, Cleveland A.L.
SS— Lou Boudreau, Cleveland A.L.
3B— George Kell, Detroit A.L.
OF— Ted Williams, Boston A.L.
OF— Joe DiMaggio, New York A.L.
OF— Ralph Kiner, Pittsburgh N.L.
C— Walker Cooper, New York N.L.
P— Ewell Blackwell, Cincinnati N.L.
P— Bob Feller, Cleveland A.L.
P— Ralph Branca, Brooklyn N.L.

1948
1B— Johnny Mize, New York N.L.
2B— Joe Gordon, Cleveland A.L.
SS— Lou Boudreau, Cleveland A.L.
3B— Bob Elliott, Boston N.L.
OF— Ted Williams, Boston A.L.
OF— Joe DiMaggio, New York A.L.
OF— Stan Musial, St. Louis N.L.
C— Birdie Tebbetts, Boston A.L.
P— Johnny Sain, Boston N.L.
P— Bob Lemon, Cleveland A.L.
P— Harry Brecheen, St. Louis N.L.

1949
1B— Tommy Henrich, New York A.L.
2B— Jackie Robinson, Brooklyn N.L.
SS— Phil Rizzuto, New York A.L.
3B— George Kell, Detroit A.L.
OF— Ted Williams, Boston A.L.
OF— Stan Musial, St. Louis N.L.
OF— Ralph Kiner, Pittsburgh N.L.
C— Roy Campanella, Brooklyn N.L.
P— Mel Parnell, Boston A.L.
P— Ellis Kinder, Boston A.L.
P— Joe Page, New York A.L.

1950
1B— Walt Dropo, Boston A.L.
2B— Jackie Robinson, Brooklyn N.L.
SS— Phil Rizzuto, New York A.L.
3B— George Kell, Detroit A.L.
OF— Stan Musial, St. Louis N.L.
OF— Ralph Kiner, Pittsburgh N.L.
OF— Larry Doby, Cleveland A.L.
C— Yogi Berra, New York A.L.
P— Vic Raschi, New York A.L.
P— Bob Lemon, Cleveland A.L.
P— Jim Konstanty, Phil. N.L.

1951
1B— Ferris Fain, Philadelphia A.L.
2B— Jackie Robinson, Brooklyn N.L.
SS— Phil Rizzuto, New York A.L.
3B— George Kell, Detroit A.L.
OF— Stan Musial, St. Louis N.L.
OF— Ted Williams, Boston A.L.
OF— Ralph Kiner, Pittsburgh N.L.
C— Roy Campanella, Brooklyn N.L.
P— Sal Maglie, New York N.L.
P— Preacher Roe, Brooklyn N.L.
P— Allie Reynolds, New York A.L.

1952

1B— Ferris Fain, Philadelphia A.L.
2B— Jackie Robinson, Brooklyn N.L.
SS— Phil Rizzuto, New York A.L.
3B— George Kell, Boston A.L.
OF— Stan Musial, St. Louis N.L.
OF— Hank Sauer, Chicago N.L.
OF— Mickey Mantle, New York A.L.
C— Yogi Berra, New York A.L.
P— Robin Roberts, Philadelphia N.L.
P— Bobby Shantz, Philadelphia A.L.
P— Allie Reynolds, New York A.L.

1953

1B— Mickey Vernon, Washington A.L.
2B— Red Schoendienst, St. Louis N.L.
SS— Pee Wee Reese, Brooklyn N.L.
3B— Al Rosen, Cleveland A.L.
OF— Stan Musial, St. Louis N.L.
OF— Duke Snider, Brooklyn N.L.
OF— Carl Furillo, Brooklyn N.L.
C— Roy Campanella, Brooklyn N.L.
P— Robin Roberts, Philadelphia N.L.
P— Warren Spahn, Milwaukee N.L.
P— Bob Porterfield, Washington A.L.

1954

1B— Ted Kluszewski, Cincinnati N.L.
2B— Bobby Avila, Cleveland A.L.
SS— Alvin Dark, New York N.L.
3B— Al Rosen, Cleveland A.L.
OF— Willie Mays, New York N.L.
OF— Stan Musial, St. Louis N.L.
OF— Duke Snider, Brooklyn N.L.
C— Yogi Berra, New York A.L.
P— Bob Lemon, Cleveland A.L.
P— Johnny Antonelli, New York N.L.
P— Robin Roberts, Philadelphia N.L.

1955

1B— Ted Kluszewski, Cincinnati N.L.
2B— Nellie Fox, Chicago A.L.
SS— Ernie Banks, Chicago N.L.
3B— Ed Mathews, Milwaukee N.L.
OF— Duke Snider, Brooklyn N.L.
OF— Ted Williams, Boston A.L.
OF— Al Kaline, Detroit A.L.
C— Roy Campanella, Brooklyn N.L.
P— Robin Roberts, Philadelphia N.L.
P— Don Newcombe, Brooklyn N.L.
P— Whitey Ford, New York A.L.

1956

1B— Ted Kluszewski, Cincinnati N.L.
2B— Nellie Fox, Chicago A.L.
SS— Harvey Kuenn, Detroit A.L.
3B— Ken Boyer, St. Louis N.L.
OF— Mickey Mantle, New York A.L.
OF— Hank Aaron, Milwaukee N.L.
OF— Ted Williams, Boston A.L.
C— Yogi Berra, New York A.L.
P— Don Newcombe, Brooklyn N.L.
P— Whitey Ford, New York A.L.
P— Billy Pierce, Chicago A.L.

1957

1B— Stan Musial, St. Louis N.L.
2B— Red Schoendienst, N.Y.-Mil. N.L.
SS— Gil McDougald, New York A.L.
3B— Ed Mathews, Milwaukee N.L.
OF— Mickey Mantle, New York A.L.
OF— Ted Williams, Boston A.L.
OF— Willie Mays, New York N.L.
C— Yogi Berra, New York A.L.
P— Warren Spahn, Milwaukee N.L.
P— Billy Pierce, Chicago N.L.
P— Jim Bunning, Detroit A.L.

1958

1B— Stan Musial, St. Louis N.L.
2B— Nellie Fox, Chicago A.L.
SS— Ernie Banks, Chicago N.L.
3B— Frank Thomas, Pittsburgh N.L.
OF— Ted Williams, Boston A.L.
OF— Willie Mays, San Francisco N.L.
OF— Hank Aaron, Milwaukee N.L.
C— Del Crandall, Milwaukee N.L.
P— Bob Turley, New York A.L.
P— Warren Spahn, Milwaukee N.L.
P— Bob Friend, Pittsburgh N.L.

1959

1B— Orlando Cepeda, S.F. N.L.
2B— Nellie Fox, Chicago A.L.
SS— Ernie Banks, Chicago N.L.
3B— Ed Mathews, Milwaukee N.L.
OF— Minnie Minoso, Cleveland A.L.
OF— Willie Mays, San Francisco N.L.
OF— Hank Aaron, Milwaukee N.L.
C— Sherm Lollar, Chicago A.L.
P— Early Wynn, Chicago A.L.
P— Sam Jones, San Francisco N.L.
P— Johnny Antonelli, S.F. N.L.

1960

1B— Bill Skowron, New York A.L.
2B— Bill Mazeroski, Pittsburgh N.L.
SS— Ernie Banks, Chicago N.L.
3B— Ed Mathews, Milwaukee N.L.
OF— Minnie Minoso, Chicago A.L.
OF— Willie Mays, San Francisco N.L.
OF— Roger Maris, New York A.L.
C— Del Crandall, Milwaukee N.L.
P— Vernon Law, Pittsburgh N.L.
P— Warren Spahn, Milwaukee N.L.
P— Ernie Broglio, St. Louis N.L.

1961

AMERICAN LEAGUE

1B— Norm Cash, Detroit
2B— Bobby Richardson, New York
SS— Tony Kubek, New York
3B— Brooks Robinson, Baltimore
OF— Mickey Mantle, New York
OF— Roger Maris, New York
OF— Rocky Colavito, Detroit
C— Elston Howard, New York
P— Whitey Ford, New York
P— Frank Lary, Detroit

NATIONAL LEAGUE

1B— Orlando Cepeda, San Francisco
2B— Frank Bolling, Milwaukee
SS— Maury Wills, Los Angeles
3B— Ken Boyer, St. Louis
OF— Willie Mays, San Francisco
OF— Frank Robinson, Cincinnati
OF— Roberto Clemente, Pittsburgh
C— Smoky Burgess, Pittsburgh
P— Joey Jay, Cincinnati
P— Warren Spahn, Milwaukee

1962

AMERICAN LEAGUE

1B— Norm Siebern, Kansas City
2B— Bobby Richardson, New York
SS— Tom Tresh, New York
3B— Brooks Robinson, Baltimore
OF— Leon Wagner, Los Angeles
OF— Mickey Mantle, New York
OF— Al Kaline, Detroit
C— Earl Battey, Minnesota
P— Ralph Terry, New York
P— Dick Donovan, Cleveland

NATIONAL LEAGUE

1B— Orlando Cepeda, San Francisco
2B— Bill Mazeroski, Pittsburgh
SS— Maury Wills, Los Angeles
3B— Ken Boyer, St. Louis
OF— Tommy Davis, Los Angeles
OF— Willie Mays, San Francisco
OF— Frank Robinson, Cincinnati
C— Del Crandall, Milwaukee
P— Don Drysdale, Los Angeles
P— Bob Purkey, Cincinnati

1963

AMERICAN LEAGUE

1B— Joe Pepitone, New York
2B— Bobby Richardson, New York
SS— Luis Aparicio, Baltimore
3B— Frank Malzone, Boston
OF— Carl Yastrzemski, Boston
OF— Albie Pearson, Los Angeles
OF— Al Kaline, Detroit
C— Elston Howard, New York
P— Whitey Ford, New York
P— Gary Peters, Chicago

NATIONAL LEAGUE

1B— Bill White, St. Louis
2B— Jim Gilliam, Los Angeles
SS— Dick Groat, St. Louis
3B— Ken Boyer, St. Louis
OF— Tommy Davis, Los Angeles
OF— Willie Mays, San Francisco
OF— Hank Aaron, Milwaukee
C— John Edwards, Cincinnati
P— Sandy Koufax, Los Angeles
P— Juan Marichal, San Francisco

1964

AMERICAN LEAGUE

1B— Dick Stuart, Boston
2B— Bobby Richardson, New York
SS— Jim Fregosi, Los Angeles
3B— Brooks Robinson, Baltimore
OF— Harmon Killebrew, Minnesota
OF— Mickey Mantle, New York
OF— Tony Oliva, Minnesota
C— Elston Howard, New York
P— Dean Chance, Los Angeles
P— Gary Peters, Chicago

NATIONAL LEAGUE

1B— Bill White, St. Louis
2B— Ron Hunt, New York
SS— Dick Groat, St. Louis
3B— Ken Boyer, St. Louis
OF— Billy Williams, Chicago
OF— Willie Mays, San Francisco
OF— Roberto Clemente, Pittsburgh
C— Joe Torre, Milwaukee
P— Sandy Koufax, Los Angeles
P— Jim Bunning, Philadelphia

1965

AMERICAN LEAGUE

1B— Fred Whitfield, Cleveland
2B— Bobby Richardson, New York
SS— Zoilo Versalles, Minnesota
3B— Brooks Robinson, Baltimore
OF— Carl Yastrzemski, Boston
OF— Jimmie Hall, Minnesota
OF— Tony Oliva, Minnesota
C— Earl Battey, Minnesota
P— Jim Grant, Minnesota
P— Mel Stottlemyre, New York

NATIONAL LEAGUE
1B— Willie McCovey, San Francisco
2B— Pete Rose, Cincinnati
SS— Maury Wills, Los Angeles
3B— Deron Johnson, Cincinnati
OF— Willie Stargell, Pittsburgh
OF— Willie Mays, San Francisco
OF— Hank Aaron, Milwaukee
C— Joe Torre, Milwaukee
P— Sandy Koufax, Los Angeles
P— Juan Marichal, San Francisco

1966

AMERICAN LEAGUE
1B— Boog Powell, Baltimore
2B— Bobby Richardson, New York
SS— Luis Aparicio, Baltimore
3B— Brooks Robinson, Baltimore
OF— Frank Robinson, Baltimore
OF— Al Kaline, Detroit
OF— Tony Oliva, Minnesota
C— Paul Casanova, Washington
P— Jim Kaat, Minnesota
P— Earl Wilson, Detroit

NATIONAL LEAGUE
1B— Felipe Alou, Atlanta
2B— Pete Rose, Cincinnati
SS— Gene Alley, Pittsburgh
3B— Ron Santo, Chicago
OF— Willie Stargell, Pittsburgh
OF— Willie Mays, San Francisco
OF— Roberto Clemente, Pittsburgh
C— Joe Torre, Atlanta
P— Sandy Koufax, Los Angeles
P— Juan Marichal, San Francisco

1967

AMERICAN LEAGUE
1B— Harmon Killebrew, Minnesota
2B— Rod Carew, Minnesota
SS— Jim Fregosi, California
3B— Brooks Robinson, Baltimore
OF— Carl Yastrzemski, Boston
OF— Al Kaline, Detroit
OF— Frank Robinson, Baltimore
C— Bill Freehan, Detroit
P— Jim Lonborg, Boston
P— Earl Wilson, Detroit

NATIONAL LEAGUE
1B— Orlando Cepeda, St. Louis
2B— Bill Mazeroski, Pittsburgh
SS— Gene Alley, Pittsburgh
3B— Ron Santo, Chicago
OF— Hank Aaron, Atlanta
OF— Jim Wynn, Houston
OF— Roberto Clemente, Pittsburgh
C— Tim McCarver, St. Louis
P— Mike McCormick, San Francisco
P— Ferguson Jenkins, Chicago

1968

AMERICAN LEAGUE
1B— Boog Powell, Baltimore
2B— Rod Carew, Minnesota
SS— Luis Aparicio, Chicago
3B— Brooks Robinson, Baltimore
OF— Ken Harrelson, Boston
OF— Willie Horton, Detroit
OF— Frank Howard, Washington
C— Bill Freehan, Detroit
P— Dave McNally, Baltimore
P— Denny McLain, Detroit

NATIONAL LEAGUE
1B— Willie McCovey, San Francisco
2B— Tommy Helms, Cincinnati
SS— Don Kessinger, Chicago
3B— Ron Santo, Chicago
OF— Billy Williams, Chicago
OF— Curt Flood, St. Louis
OF— Pete Rose, Cincinnati
C— Johnny Bench, Cincinnati
P— Bob Gibson, St. Louis
P— Juan Marichal, San Francisco

1969

AMERICAN LEAGUE
1B— Boog Powell, Baltimore
2B— Rod Carew, Minnesota
SS— Rico Petrocelli, Boston
3B— Harmon Killebrew, Minnesota
OF— Frank Howard, Washington
OF— Paul Blair, Baltimore
OF— Reggie Jackson, Oakland
C— Bill Freehan, Detroit
RHP— Denny McLain, Detroit
LHP— Mike Cuellar, Baltimore

NATIONAL LEAGUE
1B— Willie McCovey, San Francisco
2B— Glenn Beckert, Chicago
SS— Don Kessinger, Chicago
3B— Ron Santo, Chicago
OF— Cleon Jones, New York
OF— Matty Alou, Pittsburgh
OF— Hank Aaron, Atlanta
C— Johnny Bench, Cincinnati
RHP— Tom Seaver, New York
LHP— Steve Carlton, St. Louis

1970

AMERICAN LEAGUE
1B— Boog Powell, Baltimore
2B— Dave Johnson, Baltimore
SS— Luis Aparicio, Chicago
3B— Harmon Killebrew, Minnesota
OF— Frank Howard, Washington
OF— Reggie Smith, Boston
OF— Tony Oliva, Minnesota
C— Ray Fosse, Cleveland
RHP— Jim Perry, Minnesota
LHP— Sam McDowell, Cleveland

NATIONAL LEAGUE
1B— Willie McCovey, San Francisco
2B— Glenn Beckert, Chicago
SS— Don Kessinger, Chicago
3B— Tony Perez, Cincinnati
OF— Billy Williams, Chicago
OF— Bobby Tolan, Cincinnati
OF— Hank Aaron, Atlanta
C— Johnny Bench, Cincinnati
RHP— Bob Gibson, St. Louis
LHP— Jim Merritt, Cincinnati

1971

AMERICAN LEAGUE
1B— Norm Cash, Detroit
2B— Cookie Rojas, Kansas City
SS— Leo Cardenas, Minnesota
3B— Brooks Robinson, Baltimore
OF— Merv Rettenmund, Baltimore
OF— Bobby Murcer, New York
OF— Tony Oliva, Minnesota
C— Bill Freehan, Detroit
RHP— Jim Palmer, Baltimore
LHP— Vida Blue, Oakland

NATIONAL LEAGUE
1B— Lee May, Cincinnati
2B— Glenn Beckett, Chicago
SS— Bud Harrelson, New York
3B— Joe Torre, St. Louis
OF— Willie Stargell, Pittsburgh
OF— Willie Davis, Los Angeles
OF— Hank Aaron, Atlanta
C— Manny Sanguillen, Pittsburgh
RHP— Ferguson Jenkins, Chicago
LHP— Steve Carlton, St. Louis

1972

AMERICAN LEAGUE
1B— Dick Allen, Chicago
2B— Rod Carew, Minnesota
SS— Luis Aparicio, Boston
3B— Brooks Robinson, Baltimore
OF— Joe Rudi, Oakland
OF— Bobby Murcer, New York
OF— Richie Scheinblum, Kansas City
C— Carlton Fisk, Boston
RHP— Gaylord Perry, Cleveland
LHP— Wilbur Wood, Chicago

NATIONAL LEAGUE
1B— Willie Stargell, Pittsburgh
2B— Joe Morgan, Cincinnati
SS— Chris Speier, San Francisco
3B— Ron Santo, Chicago
OF— Billy Williams, Chicago
OF— Cesar Cedeno, Houston
OF— Roberto Clemente, Pittsburgh
C— Johnny Bench, Cincinnati
RHP— Ferguson Jenkins, Chicago
LHP— Steve Carlton, Philadelphia

1973

AMERICAN LEAGUE
1B— John Mayberry, Kansas City
2B— Rod Carew, Minnesota
SS— Bert Campaneris, Oakland
3B— Sal Bando, Oakland
OF— Reggie Jackson, Oakland
OF— Amos Otis, Kansas City
OF— Bobby Murcer, New York
C— Thurman Munson, New York
RHP— Jim Palmer, Baltimore
LHP— Ken Holtzman, Oakland

NATIONAL LEAGUE
1B— Tony Perez, Cincinnati
2B— Dave Johnson, Atlanta
SS— Bill Russell, Los Angeles
3B— Darrell Evans, Atlanta
OF— Bobby Bonds, San Francisco
OF— Cesar Cedeno, Houston
OF— Pete Rose, Cincinnati
C— Johnny Bench, Cincinnati
RHP— Tom Seaver, New York
LHP— Ron Bryant, San Francisco

1974

AMERICAN LEAGUE
1B— Dick Allen, Chicago
2B— Rod Carew, Minnesota
SS— Bert Campaneris, Oakland
3B— Sal Bando, Oakland
OF— Joe Rudi, Oakland
OF— Paul Blair, Baltimore
OF— Jeff Burroughs, Texas
C— Thurman Munson, New York
DH— Tommy Davis, Baltimore
RHP— Jim Hunter, Oakland
LHP— Mike Cuellar, Baltimore

NATIONAL LEAGUE
1B— Steve Garvey, Los Angeles
2B— Joe Morgan, Cincinnati
SS— Dave Concepcion, Cincinnati
3B— Mike Schmidt, Philadelphia
OF— Lou Brock, St. Louis
OF— Jim Wynn, Los Angeles
OF— Richie Zisk, Pittsburgh
C— Johnny Bench, Cincinnati
RHP— Andy Messersmith, Los Angeles
LHP— Don Gullett, Cincinnati

1975

AMERICAN LEAGUE
1B— John Mayberry, Kansas City
2B— Rod Carew, Minnesota
SS— Toby Harrah, Texas
3B— Graig Nettles, New York
OF— Jim Rice, Boston
OF— Fred Lynn, Boston
OF— Reggie Jackson, Oakland
C— Thurman Munson, New York
DH— Willie Horton, Detroit
RHP— Jim Palmer, Baltimore
LHP— Jim Kaat, Chicago

NATIONAL LEAGUE
1B— Steve Garvey, Los Angeles
2B— Joe Morgan, Cincinnati
SS— Larry Bowa, Philadelphia
3B— Bill Madlock, Chicago
OF— Greg Luzinski, Philadelphia
OF— Al Oliver, Pittsburgh
OF— Dave Parker, Pittsburgh
C— Johnny Bench, Cincinnati
RHP— Tom Seaver, New York
LHP— Randy Jones, San Diego

1976

AMERICAN LEAGUE
1B— Chris Chambliss, New York
2B— Bobby Grich, Baltimore
3B— George Brett, Kansas City
SS— Mark Belanger, Baltimore
OF— Joe Rudi, Oakland
OF— Mickey Rivers, New York
OF— Reggie Jackson, Baltimore
C— Thurman Munson, New York
DH— Hal McRae, Kansas City
RHP— Jim Palmer, Baltimore
LHP— Frank Tanana, California

NATIONAL LEAGUE
1B— Willie Montanez, S.F.-Atl.
2B— Joe Morgan, Cincinnati
3B— Mike Schmidt, Philadelphia
SS— Dave Concepcion, Cincinnati
OF— George Foster, Cincinnati
OF— Cesar Cedeno, Houston
OF— Ken Griffey, Cincinnati
C— Bob Boone, Philadelphia
RHP— Don Sutton, Los Angeles
LHP— Randy Jones, San Diego

1977

AMERICAN LEAGUE
1B— Rod Carew, Minnesota
2B— Willie Randolph, New York
3B— Graig Nettles, New York
SS— Rick Burleson, Boston
OF— Jim Rice, Boston
OF— Larry Hisle, Minnesota
OF— Bobby Bonds, California
C— Carlton Fisk, Boston
DH— Hal McRae, Kansas City
RHP— Nolan Ryan, California
LHP— Frank Tanana, California

NATIONAL LEAGUE
1B— Steve Garvey, Los Angeles
2B— Joe Morgan, Cincinnati
3B— Mike Schmidt, Philadelphia
SS— Garry Templeton, St. Louis
OF— George Foster, Cincinnati
OF— Dave Parker, Pittsburgh
OF— Greg Luzinski, Philadelphia
C— Ted Simmons, St. Louis
RHP— Rick Reuschel, Chicago
LHP— Steve Carlton, Philadelphia

1978

AMERICAN LEAGUE
1B— Rod Carew, Minnesota
2B— Frank White, Kansas City
3B— Graig Nettles, New York
SS— Robin Yount, Milwaukee
OF— Jim Rice, Boston
OF— Larry Hisle, Milwaukee
OF— Fred Lynn, Boston
C— Jim Sundberg, Texas
DH— Rusty Staub, Detroit
RHP— Jim Palmer, Baltimore
LHP— Ron Guidry, New York

NATIONAL LEAGUE
1B— Steve Garvey, Los Angeles
2B— Dave Lopes, Los Angeles
3B— Pete Rose, Cincinnati
SS— Larry Bowa, Philadelphia
OF— George Foster, Cincinnati
OF— Dave Parker, Pittsburgh
OF— Jack Clark, San Francisco
C— Ted Simmons, St. Louis
RHP— Gaylord Perry, San Diego
LHP— Vida Blue, San Francisco

1979

AMERICAN LEAGUE
1B— Cecil Cooper, Milwaukee
2B— Bobby Grich, California
3B— George Brett, Kansas City
SS— Roy Smalley, Minnesota
OF— Jim Rice, Boston
OF— Fred Lynn, Boston
OF— Ken Singleton, Baltimore
C— Darrell Porter, Kansas City
DH— Don Baylor, California
RHP— Jim Kern, Texas
LHP— Mike Flanagan, Baltimore

NATIONAL LEAGUE
1B— Keith Hernandez, St. Louis
2B— Dave Lopes, Los Angeles
3B— Mike Schmidt, Philadelphia
SS— Garry Templeton, St. Louis
OF— Dave Kingman, Chicago
OF— Omar Moreno, Pittsburgh
OF— Dave Winfield, San Diego
C— Ted Simmons, St. Louis
RHP— Joe Niekro, Houston
LHP— Steve Carlton, Philadelphia

1980

AMERICAN LEAGUE
1B— Cecil Cooper, Milwaukee
2B— Willie Randolph, New York
3B— George Brett, Kansas City
SS— Robin Yount, Milwaukee
OF— Ben Oglivie, Milwaukee
OF— Al Bumbry, Baltimore
OF— Reggie Jackson, New York
DH— Reggie Jackson, New York
C— Rick Cerone, New York
RHP— Steve Stone, Baltimore
LHP— Tommy John, New York

NATIONAL LEAGUE
1B— Keith Hernandez, St. Louis
2B— Manny Trillo, Philadelphia
3B— Mike Schmidt, Philadelphia
SS— Garry Templeton, St. Louis
OF— Dusty Baker, Los Angeles
OF— Cesar Cedeno, Houston
OF— George Hendrick, St. Louis
C— Gary Carter, Montreal
RHP— Jim Bibby, Pittsburgh
LHP— Steve Carlton, Philadelphia

1981

AMERICAN LEAGUE
1B— Cecil Cooper, Milwaukee
2B— Bobby Grich, California
3B— Buddy Bell, Texas
SS— Rick Burleson, California
OF— Rickey Henderson, Oakland
OF— Dwayne Murphy, Oakland
OF— Tony Armas, Oakland
C— Jim Sundberg, Texas
DH— Richie Zisk, Seattle
RHP— Jack Morris, Detroit
LHP— Ron Guidry, New York

NATIONAL LEAGUE
1B— Pete Rose, Philadelphia
2B— Manny Trillo, Philadelphia
3B— Mike Schmidt, Philadelphia
SS— Dave Concepcion, Cincinnati
OF— George Foster, Cincinnati
OF— Andre Dawson, Montreal
OF— Pedro Guerrero, Los Angeles
C— Gary Carter, Montreal
RHP— Tom Seaver, Cincinnati
LHP— Fernando Valenzuela, Los Angeles

1982

AMERICAN LEAGUE
1B— Cecil Cooper, Milwaukee
2B— Damaso Garcia, Toronto
3B— Doug DeCinces, California
SS— Robin Yount, Milwaukee
OF— Dave Winfield, New York
OF— Gorman Thomas, Milwaukee
OF— Dwight Evans, Boston
C— Lance Parrish, Detroit
DH— Hal McRae, Kansas City
RHP— Dave Stieb, Toronto
LHP— Geoff Zahn, California

NATIONAL LEAGUE
1B— Al Oliver, Montreal
2B— Manny Trillo, Philadelphia
3B— Mike Schmidt, Philadelphia
SS— Ozzie Smith, St. Louis
OF— Lonnie Smith, St. Louis
OF— Dale Murphy, Atlanta
OF— Pedro Guerrero, Los Angeles
C— Gary Carter, Montreal
RHP— Steve Rogers, Montreal
LHP— Steve Carlton, Philadelphia

1983

AMERICAN LEAGUE
1B— Eddie Murray, Baltimore
2B— Lou Whitaker, Detroit
3B— Wade Boggs, Boston
SS— Cal Ripken, Baltimore
OF— Jim Rice, Boston
OF— Dave Winfield, New York
OF— Lloyd Moseby, Toronto
C— Carlton Fisk, Chicago
DH— Greg Luzinski, Chicago
RHP— LaMarr Hoyt, Chicago
LHP— Ron Guidry, New York

NATIONAL LEAGUE

1B— George Hendrick, St. Louis
2B— Glenn Hubbard, Atlanta
3B— Mike Schmidt, Philadelphia
SS— Dickie Thon, Houston
OF— Dale Murphy, Atlanta
OF— Andre Dawson, Montreal
OF— Tim Raines, Montreal
C— Tony Pena, Pittsburgh
RHP— John Denny, Philadelphia
LHP— Larry McWilliams, Pittsburgh

1984

AMERICAN LEAGUE

1B— Don Mattingly, New York
2B— Lou Whitaker, Detroit
3B— Buddy Bell, Texas
SS— Cal Ripken, Baltimore
OF— Tony Armas, Boston
OF— Dwight Evans, Boston
OF— Dave Winfield, New York
C— Lance Parrish, Detroit
DH— Dave Kingman, Oakland
RHP— Mike Boddicker, Baltimore
LHP— Willie Hernandez, Detroit

NATIONAL LEAGUE

1B— Keith Hernandez, New York
2B— Ryne Sandberg, Chicago
3B— Mike Schmidt, Philadelphia
SS— Ozzie Smith, St. Louis
OF— Dale Murphy, Atlanta
OF— Jose Cruz, Houston
OF— Tony Gwynn, San Diego
C— Gary Carter, Montreal
RHP— Rick Sutcliffe, Chicago
LHP— Mark Thurmond, San Diego

1985

AMERICAN LEAGUE

1B— Don Mattingly, New York
2B— Damaso Garcia, Toronto
3B— Wade Boggs, Boston
SS— Cal Ripken, Baltimore
OF— Rickey Henderson, New York
OF— Harold Baines, Chicago
OF— Phil Bradley, Seattle
C— Carlton Fisk, Chicago
DH— Don Baylor, New York
RHP— Bret Saberhagen, Kansas City
LHP— Ron Guidry, New York

NATIONAL LEAGUE

1B— Keith Hernandez, New York
2B— Tom Herr, St. Louis
3B— Tim Wallach, Montreal
SS— Ozzie Smith, St. Louis
OF— Dave Parker, Cincinnati
OF— Willie McGee, St. Louis
OF— Dale Murphy, Atlanta
C— Gary Carter, New York
RHP— Dwight Gooden, New York
LHP— John Tudor, St. Louis

1986

AMERICAN LEAGUE

1B— Don Mattingly, New York
2B— Tony Bernazard, Cleveland
3B— Wade Boggs, Boston
SS— Tony Fernandez, Toronto
OF— Jim Rice, Boston
OF— George Bell, Toronto
OF— Kirby Puckett, Minnesota
C— Rich Gedman, Boston
DH— Don Baylor, Boston
RHP— Roger Clemens, Boston
LHP— Teddy Higuera, Milwaukee

NATIONAL LEAGUE

1B— Keith Hernandez, New York
2B— Steve Sax, Los Angeles
3B— Mike Schmidt, Philadelphia
SS— Ozzie Smith, St. Louis
OF— Tim Raines, Montreal
OF— Tony Gwynn, San Diego
OF— Dave Parker, Cincinnati
C— Gary Carter, New York
RHP— Mike Scott, Houston
LHP— Fernando Valenzuela, Los Angeles

1987

AMERICAN LEAGUE

1B— Don Mattingly, New York
2B— Willie Randolph, New York
3B— Wade Boggs, Boston
SS— Alan Trammell, Detroit
OF— George Bell, Toronto
OF— Kirby Puckett, Minnesota
OF— Dwight Evans, Boston
C— Matt Nokes, Detroit
DH— Paul Molitor, Milwaukee
RHP— Roger Clemens, Boston
LHP— Jimmy Key, Toronto

NATIONAL LEAGUE

1B— Jack Clark, St. Louis
2B— Juan Samuel, Philadelphia
3B— Tim Wallach, Montreal
SS— Ozzie Smith, St. Louis
OF— Andre Dawson, Chicago
OF— Tony Gwynn, San Diego
OF— Eric Davis, Cincinnati
C— Benito Santiago, San Diego
RHP— Rick Sutcliffe, Chicago
LHP— Zane Smith, Atlanta

1988

AMERICAN LEAGUE

1B— George Brett, Kansas City
2B— Johnny Ray, California
3B— Wade Boggs, Boston
SS— Alan Trammell, Detroit
OF— Kirby Puckett, Minnesota
OF— Mike Greenwell, Boston
OF— Jose Canseco, Oakland
C— Ernie Whitt, Toronto
DH— Harold Baines, Chicago
RHP— Dave Stewart, Oakland
LHP— Frank Viola, Minnesota

NATIONAL LEAGUE

1B— Will Clark, San Francisco
2B— Ryne Sandberg, Chicago
3B— Bobby Bonilla, Pittsburgh
SS— Barry Larkin, Cincinnati
OF— Darryl Strawberry, New York
OF— Andy Van Slyke, Pittsburgh
OF— Kevin McReynolds, New York
C— Mike LaValliere, Pittsburgh
RHP— Orel Hershiser, Los Angeles
LHP— Danny Jackson, Cincinnati

1989

AMERICAN LEAGUE

1B— Fred McGriff, Toronto
2B— Julio Franco, Texas
3B— Carney Lansford, Oakland
SS— Cal Ripken, Baltimore
OF— Ruben Sierra, Texas
OF— Kirby Puckett, Minnesota
OF— Robin Yount, Milwaukee
C— Mickey Tettleton, Baltimore
DH— Harold Baines, Chi.-Tex.
RHP— Bret Saberhagen, Kansas City
LHP— Chuck Finley, California

NATIONAL LEAGUE

1B— Will Clark, San Francisco
2B— Ryne Sandberg, Chicago
3B— Howard Johnson, New York
SS— Shawon Dunston, Chicago
OF— Tony Gwynn, San Diego
OF— Kevin Mitchell, San Francisco
OF— Eric Davis, Cincinnati
C— Benito Santiago, San Diego
RHP— Mike Scott, Houston
LHP— Mark Davis, San Diego

1990

AMERICAN LEAGUE

1B— Cecil Fielder, Detroit
2B— Julio Franco, Texas
3B— Kelly Gruber, Toronto
SS— Alan Trammell, Detroit
OF— Rickey Henderson, Oakland
OF— Jose Canseco, Oakland
OF— Ellis Burks, Boston
C— Carlton Fisk, Chicago
DH— Dave Parker, Milwaukee
RHP— Bob Welch, Oakland
LHP— Chuck Finley, California

NATIONAL LEAGUE

1B— Eddie Murray, Los Angeles
2B— Ryne Sandberg, Chicago
3B— Matt Williams, San Francisco
SS— Barry Larkin, Cincinnati
OF— Barry Bonds, Pittsburgh
OF— Bobby Bonilla, Pittsburgh
OF— Darryl Strawberry, New York
C— Mike Scioscia, Los Angeles
RHP— Doug Drabek, Pittsburgh
LHP— Frank Viola, New York

1991

AMERICAN LEAGUE

1B— Cecil Fielder, Detroit
2B— Julio Franco, Texas
3B— Wade Boggs, Boston
SS— Cal Ripken, Baltimore
OF— Jose Canseco, Oakland
OF— Joe Carter, Toronto
OF— Ken Griffey Jr., Seattle
C— Mickey Tettleton, Detroit
RHP— Roger Clemens, Boston
LHP— Jim Abbott, California

NATIONAL LEAGUE

1B— Will Clark, San Francisco
2B— Ryne Sandberg, Chicago
3B— Terry Pendleton, Atlanta
SS— Barry Larkin, Cincinnati
OF— Barry Bonds, Pittsburgh
OF— Bobby Bonilla, Pittsburgh
OF— Ron Gant, Atlanta
C— Benito Santiago, San Diego
RHP— Jose Rijo, Cincinnati
LHP— Tom Glavine, Atlanta

1992

AMERICAN LEAGUE

1B— Mark McGwire, Oakland
2B— Roberto Alomar, Toronto
3B— Edgar Martinez, Seattle
SS— Travis Fryman, Detroit
OF— Joe Carter, Toronto
OF— Mike Devereaux, Baltimore
OF— Kirby Puckett, Minnesota
C— Mickey Tettleton, Detroit
RHP— Jack McDowell, Chicago
LHP— Dave Fleming, Seattle

NATIONAL LEAGUE

1B— Fred McGriff, San Diego
2B— Ryne Sandberg, Chicago
3B— Gary Sheffield, San Diego
SS— Barry Larkin, Cincinnati
OF— Barry Bonds, Pittsburgh
OF— Andy Van Slyke, Pittsburgh
OF— Larry Walker, Montreal
C— Darren Daulton, Philadelphia
RHP— Greg Maddux, Chicago
LHP— Tom Glavine, Atlanta

1993

AMERICAN LEAGUE

1B— Frank Thomas, Chicago
2B— Carlos Baerga, Cleveland
3B— Travis Fryman, Detroit
SS— Cal Ripken Jr., Baltimore
OF— Albert Belle, Cleveland
OF— Juan Gonzalez, Texas
OF— Ken Griffey Jr., Seattle
C— Mike Stanley, New York
DH— Paul Molitor, Toronto
RHP— Jack McDowell, Chicago
LHP— Jimmy Key, New York

NATIONAL LEAGUE

1B— Fred McGriff, S.D.-Atl.
2B— Robby Thompson, San Francisco
3B— Matt Williams, San Francisco
SS— Jay Bell, Pittsburgh
OF— Barry Bonds, San Francisco
OF— Lenny Dykstra, Philadelphia
OF— David Justice, Atlanta
C— Mike Piazza, Los Angeles
RHP— Greg Maddux, Atlanta
LHP— Steve Avery, Atlanta

1994

AMERICAN LEAGUE

1B— Frank Thomas, Chicago
2B— Chuck Knoblauch, Minnesota
3B— Wade Boggs, New York
SS— Cal Ripken Jr., Baltimore
OF— Albert Belle, Cleveland
OF— Ken Griffey Jr., Seattle
OF— Kirby Puckett, Minnesota
C— Ivan Rodriguez, Texas
DH— Paul Molitor, Toronto
RHP— David Cone, Kansas City
LHP— Jimmy Key, New York

NATIONAL LEAGUE

1B— Jeff Bagwell, Houston
2B— Craig Biggio, Houston
3B— Matt Williams, San Francisco
SS— Barry Larkin, Cincinnati
OF— Moises Alou, Montreal
OF— Barry Bonds, San Francisco
OF— Tony Gwynn, San Diego
C— Mike Piazza, Los Angeles
RHP— Greg Maddux, Atlanta
LHP— Danny Jackson, Philadelphia

1995

AMERICAN LEAGUE

1B— Mo Vaughn, Boston
2B— Carlos Baerga, Cleveland
3B— Jim Thome, Cleveland
SS— Cal Ripken Jr., Baltimore
OF— Albert Belle, Cleveland
OF— Tim Salmon, California
OF— Jim Edmonds, California
C— Ivan Rodriguez, Texas
DH— Edgar Martinez, Seattle
RHP— Mike Mussina, Baltimore
LHP— Randy Johnson, Seattle

NATIONAL LEAGUE

1B— Eric Karros, Los Angeles
2B— Craig Biggio, Houston
3B— Vinny Castilla, Colorado
SS— Barry Larkin, Cincinnati
OF— Reggie Sanders, Cincinnati
OF— Dante Bichette, Colorado
OF— Sammy Sosa, Chicago
C— Mike Piazza, Los Angeles
RHP— Greg Maddux, Atlanta
LHP— Pete Schourek, Cincinnati

MINOR LEAGUE PLAYER OF THE YEAR

Year Player, Team, League

1936—John Vander Meer, Durham, Piedmont
1937—Charlie Keller, Newark, International
1938—Fred Hutchinson, Seattle, Pacific Coast
1939—Lou Novikoff, Tulsa, Texas; Los Angeles, Pacific Coast
1940—Phil Rizzuto, Kansas City, American Association
1941—John Lindell, Newark, International
1942—Dick Barrett, Seattle, Pacific Coast
1943—Chet Covington, Scranton, Eastern
1944—Rip Collins, Albany, Eastern
1945—Gil Coan, Chattanooga, Southern
1946—Sibby Sisti, Indianapolis, American Association
1947—Hank Sauer, Syracuse, International
1948—Gene Woodling, San Francisco, Pacific Coast
1949—Orie Arntzen, Albany, Eastern
1950—Frank Saucier, San Antonio, Texas
1951—Gene Conley, Hartford, Eastern
1952—Bill Skowron, Kansas City, American Association
1953—Gene Conley, Toledo, American Association
1954—Herb Score, Indianapolis, American Association
1955—John Murff, Dallas, Texas
1956—Steve Bilko, Los Angeles, Pacific Coast
1957—Norm Siebern, Denver, American Association
1958—Jim O'Toole, Nashville, Southern
1959—Frank Howard, Victoria-Spokane
1960—Willie Davis, Spokane, Pacific Coast
1961—Howie Koplitz, Birmingham, Southern
1962—Bob Bailey, Columbus, International
1963—Don Buford, Indianapolis, International
1964—Mel Stottlemyre, Richmond, International
1965—Joe Foy, Toronto, International
1966—Mike Epstein, Rochester, International

Year Player, Team, League

1967—Johnny Bench, Buffalo, International
1968—Merv Rettenmund, Rochester, International
1969—Danny Walton, Oklahoma City, American Association
1970—Don Baylor, Rochester, International
1971—Bobby Grich, Rochester, International
1972—Tom Paciorek, Albuquerque, Pacific Coast
1973—Steve Ontiveros, Phoenix, Pacific Coast
1974—Jim Rice, Pawtucket, International
1975—Hector Cruz, Tulsa, American Association
1976—Pat Putnam, Asheville, Western Carolina
1977—Ken Landreaux, S.L.C., Pacific Coast; El Paso, Texas
1978—Champ Summers, Indianapolis, American Association
1979—Mark Bomback, Vancouver, Pacific Coast
1980—Tim Raines, Denver, American Association
1981—Mike Marshall, Albuquerque, Pacific Coast
1982—Ron Kittle, Edmonton, Pacific Coast
1983—Kevin McReynolds, Las Vegas, Pacific Coast
1984—Alan Knicely, Wichita, American Association
1985—Jose Canseco, Hunt., Southern-Tac., Pacific Coast
1986—Tim Pyznarski, Las Vegas, Pacific Coast
1987—Randy Milligan, Tidewater, International
1988—Sandy Alomar Jr., Las Vegas, Pacific Coast
Gary Sheffield, Denver, American Association (tie)
1989—Sandy Alomar Jr., Las Vegas, Pacific Coast
1990—Jose Offerman, Albuquerque, Pacific Coast
1991—Pedro Martinez, Albuquerque, Pacific Coast
1992—Tim Salmon, Edmonton, Pacific Coast
1993—Cliff Floyd, Harrisburg, Eastern
1994—Derek Jeter, Tampa, Florida State; Albany, Eastern; Columbus, International
1995—Karim Garcia, Albuquerque, Pacific Coast

MINOR LEAGUE MANAGER OF THE YEAR

Year Manager, Team, League

1936—Al Sothoron, Milwaukee, American Association
1937—Jake Flowers, Salisbury, Eastern Shore
1938—Paul Richards, Atlanta, Southern
1939—Bill Meyer, Kansas City, American Association

Year Manager, Team, League

1940—Larry Gilbert, Nashville, Southern
1941—Burt Shotton, Columbus, American Association
1942—Eddie Dyer, Columbus, American Association
1943—Nick Cullop, Columbus, American Association

Year	Manager, Team, League
1944	Al Thomas, Baltimore, International
1945	Lefty O'Doul, San Francisco, Pacific Coast
1946	Clay Hopper, Montreal, International
1947	Nick Cullop, Milwaukee, American Association
1948	Casey Stengel, Oakland, Pacific Coast
1949	Fred Haney, Hollywood, Pacific Coast
1950	Rollie Hemsley, Columbus, American Association
1951	Charlie Grimm, Milwaukee, American Association
1952	Luke Appling, Memphis, Southern
1953	Bobby Bragan, Hollywood, Pacific Coast
1954	Kerby Farrell, Indianapolis, American Association
1955	Bill Rigney, Minneapolis, American Association
1956	Kerby Farrell, Indianapolis, American Association
1957	Ben Geraghty, Wichita, American Association
1958	Cal Ermer, Birmingham, Southern
1959	Pete Reiser, Victoria, Texas
1960	Mel McGaha, Toronto, International
1961	Kerby Farrell, Buffalo, International
1962	Ben Geraghty, Jacksonville, International
1963	Rollie Hemsley, Indianapolis, International
1964	Harry Walker, Jacksonville, International
1965	Grady Hatton, Oklahoma City, Pacific Coast
1966	Bob Lemon, Seattle, Pacific Coast
1967	Bob Skinner, San Diego, Pacific Coast
1968	Jack Tighe, Toledo, International
1969	Clyde McCullough, Tidewater, International
1970	Tom Lasorda, Spokane, Pacific Coast
1971	Del Rice, Salt Lake City, Pacific Coast
1972	Hank Bauer, Tidewater, International
1973	Joe Morgan, Charleston, International
1974	Joe Altobelli, Rochester, International
1975	Joe Frazier, Tidewater, International
1976	Vern Rapp, Denver, American Association
1977	Tommy Thompson, Arkan., Texas
1978	Les Moss, Evansville, American Association
1979	Vern Benson, Syracuse, International
1980	Hal Lanier, Springfield, American Association
1981	Del Crandall, Albuquerque, Pacific Coast
1982	George Scherger, Indianapolis, American Association
1983	Bill Dancy, Reading, Eastern
1984	Bob Rodgers, Indianapolis, American Association
1985	Jim Fregosi, Louisville, American Association
1986	Joe Sparks, Indianapolis, American Association
1987	Terry Collins, Albuquerque, Pacific Coast
1988	Joe Sparks, Indianapolis, American Association
1989	Bob Bailor, Syracuse, International
1990	Sal Rende, Omaha, American Association
1991	Chris Chambliss, Greenville, Southern
1992	Grady Little, Greenville, Southern
1993	Jim Tracy, Harrisburg, Eastern
1994	Mike Jirschele, Wilmington, Carolina
1995	Pete Mackanin, Ottawa, International

MINOR LEAGUE EXECUTIVE OF THE YEAR (HIGHER CLASSIFICATIONS, 1936-1992)

(Restricted to Class AAA starting in 1963)

Year	Executive, Team, League
1936	Earl Mann, Atlanta, Southern
1937	Robert LaMotte, Savannah, Sally
1938	Louis McKenna, St. Paul, American Association
1939	Bruce Dudley, Louisville, American Association
1940	Roy Hamey, Kansas City, American Association
1941	Emil Sick, Seattle, Pacific Coast
1942	Bill Veeck, Milwaukee, American Association
1943	Clarence Rowland, Los Angeles, Pacific Coast
1944	William Mulligan, Seattle, Pacific Coast
1945	Bruce Dudley, Louisville, American Association
1946	Earl Mann, Atlanta, Southern
1947	William Purnhage, Waterloo, I.I.I.
1948	Edward Glennon, Birmingham, Southern
1949	Ted Sullivan, Indianapolis, American Association
1950	Clearnce (Brick) Laws, Oakland, Pacific Coast
1951	Robert Howsam, Denver, West
1952	Jack Cooke, Toronto, International
1953	Richard Burnett, Dallas, Texas
1954	Edward Stumpf, Indianapolis, American Association
1955	Dewey Soriano, Seattle, Pacific Coast
1956	Robert Howsam, Denver American Association
1957	John Stiglmeier, Buffalo, International
1958	Edward Glennon, Birmingham, Southern
1959	Edward Leishman, Salt Lake City, Pacific Coast
1960	Ray Winder, Little Rock, Southern
1961	Elten Schiller, Omaha, American Association
1962	George Sisler Jr., Rochester, International
1963	Lewis Matlin, Hawaii, Pacific Coast
1964	Edward Leishman, San Diego, Pacific Coast
1965	Harold Cooper, Columbus, International
1966	John Quinn Jr., Hawaii, Pacific Coast
1967	Hillman Lyons, Richmond, International
1968	Gabe Paul Jr., Tulsa, Pacific Coast
1969	Bill Gardner, Louisville, International
1970	Dick King, Wichita, American Association
1971	Carl Steinfeldt Jr., Rochester, International
1972	Don Labbruzzo, Evansville, American Association
1973	Merle Miller, Tucson, Pacific Coast
1974	John Carbray, Sacramento, Pacific Coast
1975	Stan Naccarato, Tacoma, Pacific Coast
1976	Art Teece, Salt Lake City, Pacific Coast
1977	George Sisler Jr., Columbus, International
1978	Willie Sanchez, Albuquerque, Pacific Coast
1979	George Sisler Jr., Columbus, International
1980	Jim Burris, Denver, American Association
1981	Pat McKernan, Albuquerque, Pacific Coast
1982	A. Ray Smith, Louisville, American Association
1983	A. Ray Smith, Louisville, American Association
1984	Mike Tamburro, Pawtucket, International
1985	Patty Cox Hampton, Oklahoma City, American Association
1986	Bob Goughan, Rochester, International
1987	Stu Kehoe, Vancouver, Pacific Coast
1988	Bob Rich, Buffalo, American Association
1989	Larry Schmittou, Nashville, American Association
1990	Greg Corns, Phoenix, Pacific Coast
1991	Tom Maloney, Denver, American Association
1992	Lou Schwechheimer, Pawtucket, International

MINOR LEAGUE EXECUTIVE OF THE YEAR (LOWER CLASSIFICATIONS, 1950-1990)

(Separate awards for Class AA and Class A started in 1963; for Short Class A in 1988)

Year	Executive, Team, League
1950	H. Cooper, Hutchinson, Western Association
1951	O. W. (Bill) Hayes, Triple, B.S.
1952	Hillman Lyons, Danville, MOV
1953	Carl Roth, Peoria, I.I.I.
1954	James Meagham, Cedar Rapids, I.I.I.
1955	John Petrakis, Dubuque, MOV
1956	Marvin Milkes, Fresno, California
1957	Richard Wagner, Lincoln, West.
1958	Gerald Waring, Macon, Sally
1959	Clay Dennis, Des Moines, I.I.I.
1960	Hubert Kittle, Yakima, Northwest
1961	David Steele, Fresno, California
1962	John Quinn Jr., San Jose, California
1963	Hugh Finnerty, Tulsa, Texas Ben Jewell, M. Valley, Pioneer
1964	Glynn West, Birmingham, Southern James Bayens, Rock Hill, W. Carolina
1965	Dick Butler, Dallas-Ft. Worth, Texas Ken. Blackman, Quad Cities, Midwest
1966	Tom Fleming, Evansville, Southern Cappy Harada, Lodi, California
1967	Robert Quinn, Reading, Eastern Pat Williams, Spar'burg, W.C.
1968	Phil Howser, Charlotte, Southern Merle Miller, Burlington, Midwest
1969	Charlie Blaney, Albuquerque, Texas Bill Gorman, Visalia, California
1970	Carl Sawatski, Arkansas, Texas Bob Williams, Bakersfield, California
1971	Miles Wolff, Savannah, Dixie Association Ed Holtz, Appleton, Midwest

Year	Executive, Team, League
1972	John Begzos, S. Antonio, Texas
	Bob Piccinini, Modesto, California
1973	Dick Kravitz, Jacksonville, Southern
	Fritz Colschen, Clinton, Midwest
1974	Jim Paul, El Paso, Texas
	Bing Russell, Portland, Northwest
1975	Jim Paul, El Paso, Texas
	Cordy Jensen, Eugene, Northwest
1976	Woodrow Reid, Chattanooga, Southern
	Don Buchheister, Cedar Rapids, Midwest
1977	Jim Paul, El Paso, Texas
	Harry Pells, Quad Cities, Midwest
1978	Larry Schmittou, Nashville, Southern
	Dave Hersh, Appleton, Midwest
1979	Bill Rigney Jr., Midland, Texas
	Tom Romenesko, Greensboro, W.C.
1980	Frances Crockett, Charlotte, Southern
	Tom Romenesko, Greensboro, W.C.
1981	Allie Prescott, Memphis, Southern
	Dan Overstreet, Hagerstown, Caro.
1982	Art Clarkson, Birmingham, Southern
	Bob Carruesco, Stockton, California
1983	Edward Kenney, New Britain, Eastern
	Terry Reynolds, Vero Beach, Florida State
1984	Bruce Baldwin, Greenville, Southern
	Dave Tarrolly, Beloit, Midwest
1985	Ben Bernard, Albany-Colonie, Eastern
	Pete Vonachen, Peoria, Midwest
1986	Bill Davidson, Midland, Texas
	Rob Dlugozima, Durham, Carolina
1987	Joe Preseren, Tulsa, Texas
	Skip Weisman, Greensboro, South Atlantic
1988	Bill Valentine, Arkansas, Texas
	Dennis Bastien, Charleston (W.Va.), South Atlantic
	Bob Beban, Eugene, Northwest
1989	Chuck Domino, Reading, Eastern
	John Baxter, South Bend, Midwest
	Bill Pereira, Boise, Northwest
1990	Joe Preseren, Tulsa, Texas
	Dan Chapman, Stockton, California
	Dave Baggott, Salt Lake City, Pioneer

MINOR LEAGUE EXECUTIVE OF THE YEAR

Year	Executive, Team, League
1993	Todd Vander Woude, Harrisburg, Eastern (AA)
1994	Scott Lane, West Michigan, Midwest (A)
1995	Jack and Mary Cain, Portland, Northwest (A)

BASEBALL WRITERS' ASSOCIATION OF AMERICA

MOST VALUABLE PLAYER

AMERICAN LEAGUE

Year	Player	Team	Pos.	Points
1931	Lefty Grove	Philadelphia	P	78
1932	Jimmie Foxx	Philadelphia	1B	75
1933	Jimmie Foxx	Philadelphia	1B	74
1934	Mickey Cochrane	Detroit	C	67
1935	Hank Greenberg	Detroit	1B	*80
1936	Lou Gehrig	New York	1B	73
1937	Charley Gehringer	Detroit	2B	78
1938	Jimmie Foxx	Boston	1B	305
1939	Joe DiMaggio	New York	OF	280
1940	Hank Greenberg	Detroit	OF	292
1941	Joe DiMaggio	New York	OF	291
1942	Joe Gordon	New York	2B	270
1943	Spud Chandler	New York	P	246
1944	Hal Newhouser	Detroit	P	236
1945	Hal Newhouser	Detroit	P	236
1946	Ted Williams	Boston	OF	224
1947	Joe DiMaggio	New York	OF	202
1948	Lou Boudreau	Cleveland	SS	324
1949	Ted Williams	Boston	OF	272
1950	Phil Rizzuto	New York	SS	284
1951	Yogi Berra	New York	C	184
1952	Bobby Shantz	Philadelphia	P	280
1953	Al Rosen	Cleveland	3B	*336
1954	Yogi Berra	New York	C	230
1955	Yogi Berra	New York	C	218
1956	Mickey Mantle	New York	OF	*336
1957	Mickey Mantle	New York	OF	233
1958	Jackie Jensen	Boston	OF	233
1959	Nellie Fox	Chicago	2B	295
1960	Roger Maris	New York	OF	225
1961	Roger Maris	New York	OF	202
1962	Mickey Mantle	New York	OF	234
1963	Elston Howard	New York	C	248
1964	Brooks Robinson	Baltimore	3B	269
1965	Zoilo Versalles	Minnesota	SS	275
1966	Frank Robinson	Baltimore	OF	*280
1967	Carl Yastrzemski	Boston	OF	275
1968	Denny McLain	Detroit	P	*280
1969	Harmon Killebrew	Minnesota	1B-3B	294
1970	Boog Powell	Baltimore	1B	234
1971	Vida Blue	Oakland	P	268
1972	Dick Allen	Chicago	1B	321
1973	Reggie Jackson	Oakland	OF	*336
1974	Jeff Burroughs	Texas	OF	248
1975	Fred Lynn	Boston	OF	326

NATIONAL LEAGUE

Year	Player	Team	Pos.	Points
1931	Frank Frisch	St. Louis	2B	65
1932	Chuck Klein	Philadelphia	OF	78
1933	Carl Hubbell	New York	P	77
1934	Dizzy Dean	St. Louis	P	78
1935	Gabby Hartnett	Chicago	C	75
1936	Carl Hubbell	New York	P	60
1937	Joe Medwick	St. Louis	OF	70
1938	Ernie Lombardi	Cincinnati	C	229
1939	Bucky Walters	Cincinnati	P	303
1940	Frank McCormick	Cincinnati	1B	274
1941	Dolf Camilli	Brooklyn	1B	300
1942	Mort Cooper	St. Louis	P	263
1943	Stan Musial	St. Louis	OF	267
1944	Marty Marion	St. Louis	SS	190
1945	Phil Cavarretta	Chicago	1B	279
1946	Stan Musial	St. Louis	1B	319
1947	Bob Elliott	Boston	3B	205
1948	Stan Musial	St. Louis	OF	303
1949	Jackie Robinson	Brooklyn	2B	264
1950	Jim Konstanty	Philadelphia	P	286
1951	Roy Campanella	Brooklyn	C	243
1952	Hank Sauer	Chicago	OF	226
1953	Roy Campanella	Brooklyn	C	297
1954	Willie Mays	New York	OF	283
1955	Roy Campanella	Brooklyn	C	226
1956	Don Newcombe	Brooklyn	P	223
1957	Hank Aaron	Milwaukee	OF	239
1958	Ernie Banks	Chicago	SS	283
1959	Ernie Banks	Chicago	SS	2321/2
1960	Dick Groat	Pittsburgh	SS	276
1961	Frank Robinson	Cincinnati	OF	219
1962	Maury Wills	Los Angeles	SS	209
1963	Sandy Koufax	Los Angeles	P	237
1964	Ken Boyer	St. Louis	3B	243
1965	Willie Mays	San Francisco	OF	224
1966	Roberto Clemente	Pittsburgh	OF	218
1967	Orlando Cepeda	St. Louis	1B	*280
1968	Bob Gibson	St. Louis	P	242
1969	Willie McCovey	San Francisco	1B	265
1970	Johnny Bench	Cincinnati	C	326
1971	Joe Torre	St. Louis	3B	318
1972	Johnny Bench	Cincinnati	C	263
1973	Pete Rose	Cincinnati	OF	274
1974	Steve Garvey	Los Angeles	1B	270
1975	Joe Morgan	Cincinnati	2B	3211/2

Year	Player	Team	Pos.	Points
1976—	Thurman Munson	New York	C	304
1977—	Rod Carew	Minnesota	1B	273
1978—	Jim Rice	Boston	OF	352
1979—	Don Baylor	California	OF	347
	Keith Hernandez	St. Louis	1B	216
1980—	George Brett	Kansas City	3B	335
1981—	Rollie Fingers	Milwaukee	P	319
1982—	Robin Yount	Milwaukee	SS	385
1983—	Cal Ripken Jr.	Baltimore	SS	322
1984—	Willie Hernandez	Detroit	P	306
1985—	Don Mattingly	New York	1B	367
1986—	Roger Clemens	Boston	P	339
1987—	George Bell	Toronto	OF	332
1988—	Jose Canseco	Oakland	OF	*392
1989—	Robin Yount	Milwaukee	OF	256
1990—	Rickey Henderson	Oakland	OF	317
1991—	Cal Ripken Jr.	Baltimore	SS	318
1992—	Dennis Eckersley	Oakland	P	306
1993—	Frank Thomas	Chicago	1B	*392
1994—	Frank Thomas	Chicago	1B	372
1995—	Mo Vaughn	Boston	1B	308

Year	Player	Team	Pos.	Points
1976—	Joe Morgan	Cincinnati	2B	311
1977—	George Foster	Cincinnati	OF	291
1978—	Dave Parker	Pittsburgh	OF	320
1979—	Willie Stargell	Pittsburgh	1B	216
1980—	Mike Schmidt	Philadelphia	3B	*336
1981—	Mike Schmidt	Philadelphia	3B	321
1982—	Dale Murphy	Atlanta	OF	283
1983—	Dale Murphy	Atlanta	OF	318
1984—	Ryne Sandberg	Chicago	2B	326
1985—	Willie McGee	St. Louis	OF	280
1986—	Mike Schmidt	Philadelphia	3B	287
1987—	Andre Dawson	Chicago	OF	269
1988—	Kirk Gibson	Los Angeles	OF	272
1989—	Kevin Mitchell	San Francisco	OF	314
1990—	Barry Bonds	Pittsburgh	OF	331
1991—	Terry Pendleton	Atlanta	3B	274
1992—	Barry Bonds	Pittsburgh	OF	304
1993—	Barry Bonds	San Francisco	OF	372
1994—	Jeff Bagwell	Houston	1B	*392
1995—	Barry Larkin	Cincinnati	SS	281

*Unanimous selection.

CY YOUNG MEMORIAL AWARD

Year	Pitcher	Team	Votes
1956—	Don Newcombe	Brooklyn	10
1957—	Warren Spahn	Milwaukee	15
1958—	Bob Turley	New York A.L.	5
1959—	Early Wynn	Chicago A.L.	13
1960—	Vernon Law	Pittsburgh	8
1961—	Whitey Ford	New York A.L.	9
1962—	Don Drysdale	Los Angeles N.L.	14
1963—	Sandy Koufax	Los Angeles N.L.	*20
1964—	Dean Chance	Los Angeles A.L.	17
1965—	Sandy Koufax	Los Angeles N.L.	*20
1966—	Sandy Koufax	Los Angeles N.L.	*20
1967—	A.L.—Jim Lonborg	Boston	18
	N.L.—Mike McCormick	San Francisco	18
1968—	A.L.—Denny McLain	Detroit	*20
	N.L.—Bob Gibson	St. Louis	*20
1969—	A.L.—Denny McLain	Detroit	10
	Mike Cuellar	Baltimore	10
	N.L.—Tom Seaver	New York	23
1970—	A.L.—Jim Perry	Minnesota	55
	N.L.—Bob Gibson	St. Louis	118
1971—	A.L.—Vida Blue	Oakland	98
	N.L.—Fergie Jenkins	Chicago	97
1972—	A.L.—Gaylord Perry	Cleveland	64
	N.L.—Steve Carlton	Philadelphia	*120
1973—	A.L.—Jim Palmer	Baltimore	88
	N.L.—Tom Seaver	New York	71
1974—	A.L.—Jim Hunter	Oakland	90
	N.L.—Mike Marshall	Los Angeles	96
1975—	A.L.—Jim Palmer	Baltimore	98
	N.L.—Tom Seaver	New York	98
1976—	A.L.—Jim Palmer	Baltimore	108
	N.L.—Randy Jones	San Diego	96
1977—	A.L.—Sparky Lyle	New York	56½
	N.L.—Steve Carlton	Philadelphia	*104
1978—	A.L.—Ron Guidry	New York	*140
	N.L.—Gaylord Perry	San Diego	116
1979—	A.L.—Mike Flanagan	Baltimore	136
	N.L.—Bruce Sutter	Chicago	72
1980—	A.L.—Steve Stone	Baltimore	100
	N.L.—Steve Carlton	Philadelphia	118
1981—	A.L.—Rollie Fingers	Milwaukee	126
	N.L.—Fernando Valenzuela	Los Angeles	70
1982—	A.L.—Pete Vuckovich	Milwaukee	87
	N.L.—Steve Carlton	Philadelphia	112
1983—	A.L.—LaMarr Hoyt	Chicago	116
	N.L.—John Denny	Philadelphia	103
1984—	A.L.—Willie Hernandez	Detroit	88
	N.L.—Rick Sutcliffe	Chicago	*120
1985—	A.L.—Bret Saberhagen	Kansas City	127
	N.L.—Dwight Gooden	New York	*120
1986—	A.L.—Roger Clemens	Boston	*140
	N.L.—Mike Scott	Houston	98
1987—	A.L.—Roger Clemens	Boston	124
	N.L.—Steve Bedrosian	Philadelphia	57
1988—	A.L.—Frank Viola	Minnesota	138
	N.L.—Orel Hershiser	Los Angeles	*120
1989—	A.L.—Bret Saberhagen	Kansas City	138
	N.L.—Mark Davis	San Diego	107
1990—	A.L.—Bob Welch	Oakland	107
	N.L.—Doug Drabek	Pittsburgh	118
1991—	A.L.—Roger Clemens	Boston	119
	N.L.—Tom Glavine	Atlanta	110
1992—	A.L.—Dennis Eckersley	Oakland	107
	N.L.—Greg Maddux	Chicago	112
1993—	A.L.—Jack McDowell	Chicago	124
	N.L.—Greg Maddux	Atlanta	119
1994—	A.L.—David Cone	Kansas City	108
	N.L.—Greg Maddux	Atlanta	*140
1995—	A.L.—Randy Johnson	Seattle	136
	N.L.—Greg Maddux	Atlanta	*140

*Unanimous selection.

ROOKIE OF THE YEAR

1947—Combined selection—Jackie Robinson, Brooklyn N.L., 1B
1948—Combined selection—Alvin Dark, Boston N.L., SS

AMERICAN LEAGUE

Year	Player	Team	Pos.	Votes
1949—	Roy Sievers	St. Louis	OF	10
1950—	Walt Dropo	Boston	1B	15
1951—	Gil McDougald	New York	3B	13
1952—	Harry Byrd	Philadelphia	P	9
1953—	Harvey Kuenn	Detroit	SS	23
1954—	Bob Grim	New York	P	15
1955—	Herb Score	Cleveland	P	18
1956—	Luis Aparicio	Chicago	SS	22
1957—	Tony Kubek	New York	IF-OF	23
1958—	Albie Pearson	Washington	OF	14
1959—	Bob Allison	Washington	OF	18

NATIONAL LEAGUE

Year	Player	Team	Pos.	Votes
1949—	Don Newcombe	Brooklyn	P	21
1950—	Sam Jethroe	Boston	OF	11
1951—	Willie Mays	New York	OF	18
1952—	Joe Black	Brooklyn	P	19
1953—	Jim Gilliam	Brooklyn	2B	11
1954—	Wally Moon	St. Louis	OF	17
1955—	Bill Virdon	St. Louis	OF	15
1956—	Frank Robinson	Cincinnati	OF	*24
1957—	Jack Sanford	Philadelphia	P	16
1958—	Orlando Cepeda	San Francisco	1B	*†21
1959—	Willie McCovey	San Francisco	1B	*24

Year	Player	Team	Pos.	Votes
1960—	Ron Hansen	Baltimore	SS	22
1961—	Don Schwall	Boston	P	7
1962—	Tom Tresh	New York	OF-SS	13
1963—	Gary Peters	Chicago	P	10
1964—	Tony Oliva	Minnesota	OF	19
1965—	Curt Blefary	Baltimore	OF	12
1966—	Tommie Agee	Chicago	OF	16
1967—	Rod Carew	Minnesota	2B	19
1968—	Stan Bahnsen	New York	P	17
1969—	Lou Piniella	Kansas City	OF	9
1970—	Thurman Munson	New York	C	23
1971—	Chris Chambliss	Cleveland	1B	11
1972—	Carlton Fisk	Boston	C	*24
1973—	Al Bumbry	Baltimore	OF	13½
1974—	Mike Hargrove	Texas	1B	16½
1975—	Fred Lynn	Boston	OF	23
1976—	Mark Fidrych	Detroit	P	22
1977—	Eddie Murray	Baltimore	DH-1B	12½
1978—	Lou Whitaker	Detroit	2B	21
1979—	John Castino	Minnesota	3B	7
	Alfredo Griffin	Toronto	SS	7
1980—	Joe Charboneau	Cleveland	OF	103
1981—	Dave Righetti	New York	P	127
1982—	Cal Ripken	Baltimore	SS-3B	132
1983—	Ron Kittle	Chicago	OF	104
1984—	Alvin Davis	Seattle	1B	134
1985—	Ozzie Guillen	Chicago	SS	101
1986—	Jose Canseco	Oakland	OF	110
1987—	Mark McGwire	Oakland	1B	*140
1988—	Walt Weiss	Oakland	SS	103
1989—	Gregg Olson	Baltimore	P	136
1990—	Sandy Alomar Jr.	Cleveland	C	*140
1991—	Chuck Knoblauch	Minnesota	2B	136
1992—	Pat Listach	Milwaukee	SS	122
1993—	Tim Salmon	California	OF	*140
1994—	Bob Hamelin	Kansas City	DH	134
1995—	Marty Cordova	Minnesota	3B	105

*Unanimous selection. †Three writers did not vote.

Year	Player	Team	Pos.	Votes
1960—	Frank Howard	Los Angeles	OF	12
1961—	Billy Williams	Chicago	OF	10
1962—	Ken Hubbs	Chicago	2B	19
1963—	Pete Rose	Cincinnati	2B	17
1964—	Dick Allen	Philadelphia	3B	18
1965—	Jim Lefebvre	Los Angeles	2B	13
1966—	Tommy Helms	Cincinnati	3B	12
1967—	Tom Seaver	New York	P	11
1968—	Johnny Bench	Cincinnati	C	10½
1969—	Ted Sizemore	Los Angeles	2B	14
1970—	Carl Morton	Montreal	P	11
1971—	Earl Williams	Atlanta	C	18
1972—	Jon Matlack	New York	P	19
1973—	Gary Matthews	San Francisco	OF	11
1974—	Bake McBride	St. Louis	OF	16
1975—	John Montefusco	San Francisco	P	12
1976—	Butch Metzger	San Diego	P	11
	Pat Zachry	Cincinnati	P	11
1977—	Andre Dawson	Montreal	OF	10
1978—	Bob Horner	Atlanta	3B	12½
1979—	Rick Sutcliffe	Los Angeles	P	20
1980—	Steve Howe	Los Angeles	P	80
1981—	Fernando Valenzuela	Los Angeles	P	107
1982—	Steve Sax	Los Angeles	2B	63
1983—	Darryl Strawberry	New York	OF	109
1984—	Dwight Gooden	New York	P	118
1985—	Vince Coleman	St. Louis	OF	*120
1986—	Todd Worrell	St. Louis	P	118
1987—	Benito Santiago	San Diego	C	*120
1988—	Chris Sabo	Cincinnati	3B	79
1989—	Jerome Walton	Chicago	OF	116
1990—	Dave Justice	Atlanta	OF	118
1991—	Jeff Bagwell	Houston	1B	118
1992—	Eric Karros	Los Angeles	1B	116
1993—	Mike Piazza	Los Angeles	C	*140
1994—	Raul Mondesi	Los Angeles	OF	*140
1995—	Hideo Nomo	Los Angeles	P	118

MANAGER OF THE YEAR

AMERICAN LEAGUE

Year	Manager	Team	Points
1983—	Tony La Russa	Chicago	17
1984—	Sparky Anderson	Detroit	96
1985—	Bobby Cox	Toronto	104
1986—	John McNamara	Boston	95
1987—	Sparky Anderson	Detroit	90
1988—	Tony La Russa	Oakland	103
1989—	Frank Robinson	Baltimore	125
1990—	Jeff Torborg	Chicago	128
1991—	Tom Kelly	Minnesota	138
1992—	Tony La Russa	Oakland	132
1993—	Gene Lamont	Chicago	72
1994—	Buck Showalter	New York	132
1995—	Lou Piniella	Seattle	86

NATIONAL LEAGUE

Year	Manager	Team	Points
1983—	Tommy Lasorda	Los Angeles	10
1984—	Jim Frey	Chicago	101
1985—	Whitey Herzog	St. Louis	86
1986—	Hal Lanier	Houston	108
1987—	Buck Rodgers	Montreal	92
1988—	Tommy Lasorda	Los Angeles	101
1989—	Don Zimmer	Chicago	118
1990—	Jim Leyland	Pittsburgh	99
1991—	Bobby Cox	Atlanta	96
1992—	Jim Leyland	Pittsburgh	109
1993—	Dusty Baker	San Francisco	105
1994—	Felipe Alou	Montreal	138
1995—	Don Baylor	Colorado	122

EARLY MOST VALUABLE PLAYER AWARDS

CHALMERS AWARD

AMERICAN LEAGUE

Year	Player	Team	Pos.	Points
1911—	Ty Cobb	Detroit	OF	64
1912—	Tris Speaker	Boston	OF	59
1913—	Walter Johnson	Washington	P	54
1914—	Eddie Collins	Philadelphia	2B	63

NATIONAL LEAGUE

Year	Player	Team	Pos.	Points
1911—	Frank Schulte	Chicago	OF	29
1912—	Larry Doyle	New York	2B	48
1913—	Jake Daubert	Brooklyn	1B	50
1914—	Johnny Evers	Boston	2B	50

LEAGUE AWARDS

AMERICAN LEAGUE

Year	Player	Team	Pos.	Points
1922—	George Sisler	St. Louis	1B	59
1923—	Babe Ruth	New York	OF	64
1924—	Walter Johnson	Washington	P	55
1925—	Roger Peckinpaugh	Washington	SS	45
1926—	George Burns	Cleveland	1B	63
1927—	Lou Gehrig	New York	1B	56
1928—	Mickey Cochrane	Philadelphia	C	53
1929—	No selection			

NATIONAL LEAGUE

Year	Player	Team	Pos.	Points
1922—	No selection			
1923—	No selection			
1924—	Dazzy Vance	Brooklyn	P	74
1925—	Rogers Hornsby	St. Louis	2B	73
1926—	Bob O'Farrell	St. Louis	C	79
1927—	Paul Waner	Pittsburgh	OF	72
1928—	Jim Bottomley	St. Louis	1B	76
1929—	Rogers Hornsby	Chicago	2B	60

HALL OF FAME

ROSTER OF MEMBERS

Name	Des.*	Elec. year	Votes rec.†	Votes cast‡	% of vote	Teams as player
Aaron, Hank	P	1982	406	415	97.8	Milwaukee NL, Atlanta NL, Milwaukee AL
Alexander, Grover C.	P	1938	212	262	80.9	Philadelphia NL, Chicago NL, St. Louis NL
Alston, Walter	M	1983	CV	—	—	St. Louis NL
Anson, Cap	P	1939	C1	—	—	Chicago NL
Aparicio, Luis	P	1984	341	403	84.6	Chicago AL, Baltimore AL, Boston AL
Appling, Luke	P	1964	189	225	84	Chicago AL
Ashburn, Richie	P	1995	CV	—	—	Philadelphia NL, Chicago NL, New York NL
Averill, Earl	P	1975	CV	—	—	Cleveland AL, Detroit AL, Boston AL
Baker, Home Run	P	1955	CV	—	—	Philadelphia AL, New York AL
Bancroft, Dave	P	1971	CV	—	—	Philadelphia NL, New York NL, Boston NL, Brooklyn NL
Banks, Ernie	P	1977	321	383	83.8	Chicago NL
Barlick, Al	U	1989	CV	—	—	
Barrow, Ed	E	1953	CV	—	—	
Beckley, Jake	P	1971	CV	—	—	Pittsburgh NL, Pittsburgh PL, New York NL, Cincinnati NL, St. Louis NL
Bell, Cool Papa	P	1974	SCNL	—	—	Negro Leagues
Bench, Johnny	P	1989	431	447	96.4	Cincinnati NL
Bender, Chief	P	1953	CV	—	—	Philadelphia AL, Philadelphia NL, Chicago AL
Berra, Yogi	P	1972	339	396	85.6	New York AL, New York NL
Bottomley, Jim	P	1974	CV	—	—	St. Louis NL, Cincinnati NL, St. Louis AL
Boudreau, Lou	P	1970	232	300	77.3	Cleveland AL, Boston AL
Bresnahan, Roger	P	1945	C2	—	—	Washington NL, Chicago NL, Baltimore AL, New York NL, St. Louis NL
Brock, Lou	P	1985	315	395	79.7	Chicago NL, St. Louis NL
Brouthers, Dan	P	1945	C2	—	—	Troy NL, Buffalo NL, Detroit NL, Boston NL, Boston PL, Boston AA,Brooklyn NL, Baltimore NL,Louisville NL, Philadelphia NL, New York NL
Brown, Three Finger	P	1949	C2	—	—	St. Louis NL, Chicago NL, Cincinnati NL
Bulkeley, Morgan	E	1937	CC	—	—	
Burkett, Jesse	P	1946	C2	—	—	New York NL, Cleveland NL, St. Louis NL, St. Louis AL, Boston AL
Campanella, Roy	P	1969	270	340	79.4	Brooklyn NL
Carew, Rod	P	1991	401	447	89.7	Minnesota AL, California AL
Carey, Max	P	1961	CV	—	—	Pittsburgh NL, Brooklyn NL
Carlton, Steve	P	1994	436	455	95.8	St. Louis NL, Philadelphia NL, San Francisco NL, Chicago AL, Cleveland AL, Minnesota AL
Cartwright, Alexander	O	1938	CC	—	—	
Chadwick, Henry	O	1938	CC	—	—	
Chance, Frank	P	1946	C2	—	—	Chicago NL, New York AL
Chandler, Happy	E	1982	CV	—	—	
Charleston, Oscar	P	1976	SCNL	—	—	Negro Leagues
Chesbro, Jack	P	1946	C2	—	—	Pittsburgh NL, New York AL, Boston AL
Clarke, Fred	P	1945	C2	—	—	Louisville NL, Pittsburgh NL
Clarkson, John	P	1963	CV	—	—	Worcester NL, Chicago NL, Boston NL, Cleveland NL
Clemente, Roberto	P	1973	393	424	92.7	Pittsburgh NL
Cobb, Ty	P	1936	222	226	98.2	Detroit AL, Philadelphia AL
Cochrane, Mickey	P	1947	128	161	79.5	Philadelphia AL, Detroit AL
Collins, Eddie	P	1939	213	274	77.7	Philadelphia AL, Chicago AL
Collins, Jimmy	P	1945	C2	—	—	Boston NL, Louisville NL, Boston AL, Philadelphia AL
Combs, Earle	P	1970	CV	—	—	New York AL
Comiskey, Charley	F/P	1939	C1	—	—	St. Louis AA, Chicago PL, Cincinnati NL
Conlan, Jocko	U	1974	CV	—	—	Chicago AL
Connolly, Tommy	U	1953	CV	—	—	
Connor, Roger	P	1976	CV	—	—	Troy NL, New York NL, New York PL, Philadelphia NL, St. Louis NL
Coveleski, Stan	P	1969	CV	—	—	Philadelphia AL, Cleveland AL, Washington AL, New York AL
Crawford, Sam	P	1957	CV	—	—	Cincinnati NL, Detroit AL
Cronin, Joe	P	1956	152	193	78.8	Pittsburgh NL, Washington AL, Boston AL
Cummings, Candy	P	1939	C1	—	—	Hartford NL, Cincinnati NL
Cuyler, Kiki	P	1968	CV	—	—	Pittsburgh NL, Chicago NL, Cincinnati NL, Brooklyn NL
Dandridge, Ray	P	1987	CV	—	—	Negro Leagues
Day, Leon	P	1995	CV	—	—	Negro Leagues
Dean, Dizzy	P	1953	209	264	79.2	St. Louis NL, Chicago NL, St. Louis AL
Delahanty, Ed	P	1945	C2	—	—	Philadelphia NL, Cleveland PL, Washington AL
Dickey, Bill	P	1954	202	252	80.2	New York AL
Dihigo, Martin	P	1977	SCNL	—	—	Negro Leagues

Name	Des.*	Elec. year	Votes rec.†	Votes cast‡	% of vote	Teams as player
DiMaggio, Joe	P	1955	223	251	88.8	New York AL
Doerr, Bobby	P	1986	CV	—	—	Boston AL
Drysdale, Don	P	1984	316	403	78.4	Brooklyn NL, Los Angeles NL
Duffy, Hugh	P	1945	C2	—	—	Chicago NL, Chicago PL, Boston AA, Boston NL, Milwaukee AL, Philadelphia NL
Durocher, Leo	M	1994	CV	—	—	New York AL, Cincinnati NL, St. Louis NL, Brooklyn NL
Evans, Billy	U	1973	CV	—	—	
Evers, Johnny	P	1946	C2	—	—	Chicago NL, Boston NL, Philadelphia NL, Chicago AL
Ewing, Buck	P	1939	C1	—	—	Troy NL, New York NL, New York PL, Cleveland NL, Cincinnati NL
Faber, Red	P	1964	CV	—	—	Chicago AL
Feller, Bob	P	1962	150	160	93.8	Cleveland AL
Ferrell, Rick	P	1984	CV	—	—	St. Louis AL, Boston AL, Washington AL
Fingers, Rollie	P	1992	349	430	81.2	Oakland AL, San Diego NL, Milwaukee AL
Flick, Elmer	P	1963	CV	—	—	Philadelphia NL, Philadelphia AL, Cleveland AL
Ford, Whitey	P	1974	284	365	77.8	New York AL
Foster, Rube	P	1981	CV	—	—	Negro Leagues
Foxx, Jimmie	P	1951	179	226	79.2	Philadelphia AL, Boston AL, Chicago NL, Philadelphia NL
Frick, Ford	E	1970	CV	—	—	
Frisch, Frank	P	1947	136	161	84.5	New York NL, St. Louis NL
Galvin, Pud	P	1965	CV	—	—	Buffalo NL, Pittsburgh AA, Pittsburgh NL, Pittsburgh PL, St. Louis NL
Gehrig, Lou	P	1939	SE	—	—	New York AL
Gehringer, Charley	P	1949	159	187	85.0	Detroit AL
Gibson, Bob	P	1981	337	401	84.0	St. Louis NL
Gibson, Josh	P	1972	SCNL	—	—	Negro Leagues
Giles, Warren	E	1979	CV	—	—	
Gomez, Lefty	P	1972	CV	—	—	New York AL, Washington AL
Goslin, Goose	P	1968	CV	—	—	Washington AL, St. Louis AL, Detroit AL
Greenberg, Hank	P	1956	164	193	85.0	Detroit AL, Pittsburgh NL
Griffith, Clark	M	1946	C2	—	—	St. Louis AA, Boston AA, Chicago NL, Chicago AL, New York AL, Cincinnati NL, Washington AL
Grimes, Burleigh	P	1964	CV	—	—	Pittsburgh NL, Brooklyn NL, New York NL, Boston NL, St. Louis NL, Chicago NL, New York AL
Grove, Lefty	P	1947	123	161	76.4	Philadelphia AL, Boston AL
Hafey, Chick	P	1971	CV	—	—	St. Louis NL, Cincinnati NL
Haines, Jesse	P	1970	CV	—	—	Cincinnati NL, St. Louis NL
Hamilton, Billy	P	1961	CV	—	—	Kansas City AA, Philadelphia NL, Boston NL
Harridge, Will	E	1972	CV	—	—	
Harris, Bucky	M	1975	CV	—	—	Washington AL, Detroit AL
Hartnett, Gabby	P	1955	195	251	77.7	Chicago NL, New York NL
Heilmann, Harry	P	1952	203	234	86.8	Detroit AL, Cincinnati NL
Herman, Billy	P	1975	CV	—	—	Chicago NL, Brooklyn NL, Boston NL, Pittsburgh NL
Hooper, Harry	P	1971	CV	—	—	Boston AL, Chicago AL
Hornsby, Rogers	P	1942	182	233	78.1	St. Louis NL, New York NL, Boston NL, Chicago NL, St. Louis AL
Hoyt, Waite	P	1969	CV	—	—	New York NL, Boston AL, New York AL, Detroit AL, Philadelphia AL, Brooklyn NL, Pittsburgh NL
Hubbard, Cal	U	1976	CV	—	—	
Hubbell, Carl	P	1947	140	161	87.0	New York NL
Huggins, Miller	M	1964	CV	—	—	Cincinnati NL, St. Louis NL
Hulbert, William	F	1995	CV	—	—	
Hunter, Catfish	P	1987	315	413	76.3	Kansas City AL, Oakland AL, New York AL
Irvin, Monte	P	1973	SCNL	—	—	New York NL, Chicago NL, Negro Leagues
Jackson, Reggie	P	1993	396	423	93.6	Kansas City AL, Oakland AL, Baltimore AL, New York AL, California AL
Jackson, Travis	P	1982	CV	—	—	New York NL
Jenkins, Ferguson	P	1991	334	447	74.7	Philadelphia NL, Chicago NL, Texas AL, Boston AL
Jennings, Hugh	P	1945	C2	—	—	Louisville AA, Louisville NL, Baltimore NL, Brooklyn NL, Philadelphia NL, Detroit AL
Johnson, Ban	E	1937	CC	—	—	
Johnson, Judy	P	1975	SCNL	—	—	Negro Leagues
Johnson, Walter	P	1936	189	226	83.6	Washington AL
Joss, Addie	P	1978	CV	—	—	Cleveland AL
Kaline, Al	P	1980	340	385	88.3	Detroit AL
Keefe, Tim	P	1964	CV	—	—	Troy NL, New York AA, New York NL, New York PL, Philadelphia NL
Keeler, Willie	P	1939	207	274	75.5	New York NL, Brooklyn, NL, Baltimore NL, New York AL
Kell, George	P	1983	CV	—	—	Philadelphia AL, Detroit AL, Boston AL, Chicago AL, Baltimore AL

Name	Des.*	Elec. year	Votes rec.†	Votes cast‡	% of vote	Teams as player
Kelley, Joe	P	1971	CV	—	—	Boston NL, Pittsburgh NL, Baltimore NL, Brooklyn NL, Baltimore AL, Cincinnati NL
Kelly, George	P	1973	CV	—	—	New York NL, Pittsburgh NL, Cincinnati NL, Chicago NL, Brooklyn NL
Kelly, Mike	P	1945	C2	—	—	Cincinnati NL, Chicago NL, Boston NL, Boston PL, Cincinnati AA, Boston AA, New York NL
Killebrew, Harmon	P	1984	335	403	83.1	Washington AL, Minnesota AL, Kansas City AL
Kiner, Ralph	P	1975	273	362	75.4	Pittsburgh NL, Chicago NL, Cleveland AL
Klein, Chuck	P	1980	CV	—	—	Philadelphia NL, Chicago NL, Pittsburgh NL
Klem, Bill	U	1953	CV	—	—	
Koufax, Sandy	P	1972	344	396	86.9	Brooklyn NL, Los Angeles NL
Lajoie, Nap	P	1937	168	201	83.6	Philadelphia NL, Philadelphia AL, Cleveland AL
Landis, Kenesaw M.	E	1944	C2	—	—	
Lazzeri, Tony	P	1991	CV	—	—	New York AL, Chicago NL, Brooklyn NL, New York NL
Lemon, Bob	P	1976	305	388	78.6	Cleveland AL
Leonard, Buck	P	1972	SCNL	—	—	Negro Leagues
Lindstrom, Fred	P	1976	CV	—	—	New York NL, Pittsburgh NL, Chicago NL, Brooklyn NL
Lloyd, John Henry	P	1977	SCNL	—	—	Negro Leagues
Lombardi, Ernie	P	1986	CV	—	—	Brooklyn NL, Cincinnati NL, Boston NL, New York NL
Lopez, Al	M	1977	CV	—	—	Brooklyn NL, Boston NL, Pittsburgh NL, Cleveland AL
Lyons, Ted	P	1955	217	251	86.5	Chicago AL
Mack, Connie	M	1937	CC	—	—	Washington NL, Buffalo PL, Pittsburgh NL
MacPhail, Larry	E	1978	CV	—	—	
Mantle, Mickey	P	1974	322	365	88.2	New York AL
Manush, Heinie	P	1964	CV	—	—	Detroit AL, St. Louis AL, Washington AL, Boston AL, Brooklyn NL, Pittsburgh NL
Maranville, Rabbit	P	1954	209	252	82.9	Boston NL, Pittsburgh NL, Chicago NL, Brooklyn NL, St. Louis NL
Marichal, Juan	P	1983	313	374	83.7	San Francisco NL, Boston AL, Los Angeles NL
Marquard, Rube	P	1971	CV	—	—	New York NL, Brooklyn NL, Cincinnati NL, Boston NL
Mathews, Eddie	P	1978	301	379	79.4	Boston NL, Milwaukee NL, Atlanta NL, Houston NL, Detroit AL
Mathewson, Christy	P	1936	205	226	90.7	New York NL, Cincinnati NL
Mays, Willie	P	1979	409	432	94.7	New York (Giants)NL, San Francisco NL, New York (Mets)NL
McCarthy, Joe	M	1957	CV	—	—	
McCarthy, Tommy	P	1946	C2	—	—	Boston UA, Boston NL, Philadelphia NL, St. Louis AA, Brooklyn NL
McCovey, Willie	P	1986	346	425	81.4	San Francisco NL, San Diego NL, Oakland AL
McGinnity, Joe	P	1946	C2	—	—	Baltimore NL, Brooklyn NL, Baltimore AL, New York NL
McGowan, Bill	U	1992	CV	—	—	
McGraw, John	M	1937	CC	—	—	Baltimore AA, Baltimore NL, St. Louis NL, Baltimore AL, New York NL
McKechnie, Bill	M	1962	CV	—	—	Pittsburgh NL, Boston NL, New York AL, New York NL, Cincinnati
Medwick, Joe	P	1968	240	283	84.8	St. Louis NL, Brooklyn NL, New York NL, Boston NL
Mize, Johnny	P	1981	CV	—	—	St. Louis NL, New York NL, New York AL
Morgan, Joe	P	1990	363	444	81.8	Houston NL, Cincinnati NL, San Francisco NL, Philadelphia NL, Oakland AL
Musial, Stan	P	1969	317	340	93.2	St. Louis NL
Newhouser, Hal	P	1992	CV	—	—	Detroit AL, Cleveland AL
Nichols, Kid	P	1949	C2	—	—	Boston NL, St. Louis NL, Philadelphia NL
O'Rourke, Jim	P	1945	C2	—	—	Boston NL, Providence NL, Buffalo NL, New York NL, Washington NL, New York PL
Ott, Mel	P	1951	197	226	87.2	New York NL
Paige, Satchel	P	1971	SCNL	—	—	Cleveland AL, St. Louis AL, Kansas City AL, Negro Leagues
Palmer, Jim	P	1990	411	444	92.6	Baltimore AL
Pennock, Herb	P	1948	94	121	77.7	Philadelphia AL, Boston AL, New York AL
Perry, Gaylord	P	1991	342	447	76.5	San Francisco NL, Cleveland AL, Texas AL, San Diego NL, New York AL, Atlanta NL, Seattle AL, Kansas City AL
Plank, Eddie	P	1946	C2	—	—	Philadelphia AL, St. Louis AL
Radbourn, Hoss	P	1939	C1	—	—	Buffalo NL, Providence NL, Boston NL, Boston PL, Cincinnati NL
Reese, Pee Wee	P	1984	CV	—	—	Brooklyn NL, Los Angeles NL
Rice, Sam	P	1963	CV	—	—	Washington AL, Cleveland AL
Rickey, Branch	E	1967	CV	—	—	St. Louis AL, New York AL
Rixey, Eppa	P	1963	CV	—	—	Philadelphia NL, Cincinnati NL
Rizzuto, Phil	P	1994	CV	—	—	New York AL
Roberts, Robin	P	1976	337	388	86.9	Philadelphia NL, Baltimore AL, Houston NL, Chicago NL

Name	Des.*	Elec. year	Votes rec.†	Votes cast‡	% of vote	Teams as player
Robinson, Brooks	P	1983	344	374	92.0	Baltimore AL
Robinson, Frank	P	1982	370	415	89.2	Cincinnati NL, Baltimore AL, Los Angeles NL, California AL, Cleveland AL
Robinson, Jackie	P	1962	124	160	77.5	Brooklyn NL
Robinson, Wilbert	M	1945	C2	—	—	Philadelphia AA, Baltimore AA, Baltimore NL, St. Louis NL, Baltimore AL
Roush, Edd	P	1962	CV	—	—	Chicago AL, New York NL, Cincinnati NL
Ruffing, Red	P	1967	266	306	86.9	Boston AL, New York AL, Chicago AL
Rusie, Amos	P	1977	CV	—	—	Indianapolis NL, New York NL, Cincinnati NL
Ruth, Babe	P	1936	215	226	95.1	Boston AL, New York AL, Boston NL
Schalk, Ray	P	1955	CV	—	—	Chicago AL, New York NL
Schmidt, Mike	P	1995	444	460	96.5	Philadelphia NL
Schoendienst, Red	P	1989	CV	—	—	St. Louis NL, New York (Giants) NL, Milwaukee NL
Seaver, Tom	P	1992	425	430	98.8	New York NL, Cincinnati NL, Chicago AL, Boston AL
Sewell, Joe	P	1977	CV	—	—	Cleveland AL, New York AL
Simmons, Al	P	1953	199	264	75.4	Philadelphia AL, Chicago AL, Detroit AL, Washington AL, Boston NL, Cincinnati NL, Boston AL
Sisler, George	P	1939	235	274	85.8	St. Louis AL, Washington AL, Boston NL
Slaughter, Enos	P	1985	CV	—	—	St. Louis NL, New York AL, Kansas City AL, Milwaukee NL
Snider, Duke	P	1980	333	385	86.5	Brooklyn NL, Los Angeles NL, New York NL, San Francisco NL
Spahn, Warren	P	1973	316	380	83.2	Boston NL, Milwaukee NL, New York NL, San Francisco NL
Spalding, Al	P	1939	C1	—	—	Chicago NL
Speaker, Tris	P	1937	165	201	82.1	Boston AL, Cleveland AL, Washington AL, Philadelphia AL
Stargell, Willie	P	1988	352	427	82.4	Pittsburgh NL
Stengel, Casey	M	1966	CV	—	—	Brooklyn NL, Pittsburgh NL, Philadelphia NL, New York NL, Boston NL
Terry, Bill	P	1954	195	252	77.4	New York NL
Thompson, Sam	P	1974	CV	—	—	Detroit NL, Philadelphia NL, Detroit AL
Tinker, Joe	P	1946	C2	—	—	Chicago NL, Cincinnati NL
Traynor, Pie	P	1948	93	121	76.9	Pittsburgh NL
Vance, Dazzy	P	1955	205	251	81.7	Pittsburgh NL, New York AL, Brooklyn NL, St. Louis NL, Cincinnati NL
Vaughan, Arky	P	1985	CV	—	—	Pittsburgh NL, Brooklyn NL
Veeck, Bill	E	1991	CV	—	—	
Waddell, Rube	P	1946	C2	—	—	Louisville NL, Pittsburgh NL, Chicago NL, Philadelphia AL, St. Louis AL
Wagner, Honus	P	1936	215	226	95.1	Louisville NL, Pittsburgh NL
Wallace, Bobby	P	1953	CV	—	—	Cleveland NL, St. Louis NL, St. Louis AL
Walsh, Ed	P	1946	C2	—	—	Chicago AL, Boston NL
Waner, Lloyd	P	1967	CV	—	—	Pittsburgh NL, Boston NL, Cincinnati NL, Philadelphia NL, Brooklyn NL
Waner, Paul	P	1952	195	234	83.3	Pittsburgh NL, Brooklyn NL, Boston NL, New York AL
Ward, John Montgomery	P	1964	CV	—	—	Providence NL, New York NL, Brooklyn PL, Brooklyn NL
Weiss, George	E	1971	CV	—	—	
Welch, Mickey	P	1973	CV	—	—	Troy NL, New York NL
Wheat, Zack	P	1959	CV	—	—	Brooklyn NL, Philadelphia AL
Wilhelm, Hoyt	P	1985	331	395	83.8	New York NL, St. Louis NL, Cleveland AL, Baltimore AL, Chicago AL California AL, Atlanta NL, Chicago NL, Los Angeles NL
Williams, Billy	P	1987	354	413	85.7	Chicago NL, Oakland AL
Williams, Ted	P	1966	282	302	93.4	Boston AL
Willis, Vic	P	1995	CV	—	—	Boston NL, Pittsburgh NL, St. Louis NL
Wilson, Hack	P	1979	CV	—	—	New York NL, Chicago NL, Brooklyn NL, Philadelphia NL
Wright, George	M	1937	CC	—	—	Boston NL, Providence NL
Wright, Harry	M	1953	CV	—	—	Boston NL
Wynn, Early	P	1972	301	396	76.0	Washington AL, Cleveland AL, Chicago AL
Yastrzemski, Carl	P	1989	423	447	94.6	Boston AL
Yawkey, Tom	E	1980	CV	—	—	
Young, Cy	P	1937	153	201	76.1	Cleveland NL, St. Louis NL, Boston AL, Cleveland AL, Boston NL
Youngs, Ross	P	1972	CV	—	—	New York NL

*Designation for which he was honored. Abbreviations: E—executive; F—founder; M—manager; O—organizer; P—player; U—umpire.
†Where an abbreviation is listed rather than a vote total, the enshrinee was selected by one of the following groups: Centennial Commission (CC), committee of old-time players and writers (C1), committee on old-timers (C2), Committee on Veterans (CV), special election by Baseball Writers' Association of America (SE) or Special Committee on Negro Leagues (SCNL).
‡Votes cast by eligible members of the Baseball Writers' Association of America.
League abbreviations: AA—American Association; AL—American League; NL—National League; PL—Players League; UA—Union Association.

TEAM BY TEAM

AMERICAN LEAGUE

BALTIMORE ORIOLES

YEARLY FINISHES

Year	Position	W	L	Pct.	*GB	Manager	Attendance
1901†	8th	48	89	.350	35 1/2	Hugh Duffy	139,034
1902‡	2nd	78	58	.574	5	Jimmy McAleer	272,283
1903‡	6th	65	74	.468	26 1/2	Jimmy McAleer	380,405
1904‡	6th	65	87	.428	29	Jimmy McAleer	318,108
1905‡	8th	54	99	.354	40 1/2	Jimmy McAleer	339,112
1906‡	5th	76	73	.510	16	Jimmy McAleer	389,157
1907‡	6th	69	83	.454	24	Jimmy McAleer	419,025
1908‡	4th	83	69	.546	6 1/2	Jimmy McAleer	618,947
1909‡	7th	61	89	.407	36	Jimmy McAleer	366,274
1910‡	8th	47	107	.305	57	John O'Connor	249,889
1911‡	8th	45	107	.296	56 1/2	Bobby Wallace	207,984
1912‡	7th	53	101	.344	53	Bobby Wallace, George Stovall	214,070
1913‡	8th	57	96	.373	39	George Stovall, Branch Rickey	250,330
1914‡	5th	71	82	.464	28 1/2	Branch Rickey	244,714
1915‡	6th	63	91	.409	39 1/2	Branch Rickey	150,358
1916‡	5th	79	75	.513	12	Fielder Jones	335,740
1917‡	7th	57	97	.370	43	Fielder Jones	210,486
1918‡	5th	58	64	.475	15	Fielder Jones, Jimmy Austin, Jimmy Burke	122,076
1919‡	5th	67	72	.482	20 1/2	Jimmy Burke	349,350
1920‡	4th	76	77	.497	21 1/2	Jimmy Burke	419,311
1921‡	3rd	81	73	.526	17 1/2	Lee Fohl	355,978
1922‡	2nd	93	61	.604	1	Lee Fohl	712,918
1923‡	5th	74	78	.487	24	Lee Fohl, Jimmy Austin	430,296
1924‡	4th	74	78	.487	17	George Sisler	533,349
1925‡	3rd	82	71	.536	15	George Sisler	462,898
1926‡	7th	62	92	.403	29	George Sisler	283,986
1927‡	7th	59	94	.336	50 1/2	Dan Howley	247,879
1928‡	3rd	82	72	.532	19	Dan Howley	339,497
1929‡	4th	79	73	.520	26	Dan Howley	280,697
1930‡	6th	64	90	.416	38	Bill Killefer	152,088
1931‡	5th	63	91	.409	45	Bill Killefer	179,126
1932‡	6th	63	91	.409	44	Bill Killefer	112,558
1933‡	8th	55	96	.364	43 1/2	Bill Killefer, Allen Sothoron, Rogers Hornsby	88,113
1934‡	6th	67	85	.441	33	Rogers Hornsby	115,305
1935‡	7th	65	87	.428	28 1/2	Rogers Hornsby	80,922
1936‡	7th	57	95	.375	44 1/2	Rogers Hornsby	93,267
1937‡	8th	46	108	.299	56	Rogers Hornsby, Jim Bottomley	123,121
1938‡	7th	55	97	.362	44	Gabby Street	130,417
1939‡	8th	43	111	.279	64 1/2	Fred Haney	109,159
1940‡	6th	67	87	.435	23	Fred Haney	239,591
1941‡	6th (tied)	70	84	.455	31	Fred Haney, Luke Sewell	176,240
1942‡	3rd	82	69	.543	19 1/2	Luke Sewell	255,617
1943‡	6th	72	80	.474	25	Luke Sewell	214,392
1944‡	1st	89	65	.578	+1	Luke Sewell	508,644
1945‡	3rd	81	70	.536	6	Luke Sewell	482,986
1946‡	7th	66	88	.429	38	Luke Sewell, Zack Taylor	526,435
1947‡	8th	59	95	.383	38	Muddy Ruel	320,474
1948‡	6th	59	94	.386	37	Zack Taylor	335,546
1949‡	7th	53	101	.344	44	Zack Taylor	270,936
1950‡	7th	58	96	.377	40	Zack Taylor	247,131
1951‡	8th	52	102	.338	46	Zack Taylor	293,790
1952‡	7th	64	90	.416	31	Rogers Hornsby, Marty Marion	518,796
1953‡	8th	54	100	.351	46 1/2	Marty Marion	297,238
1954	7th	54	100	.351	57	Jimmie Dykes	1,060,910
1955	7th	57	97	.370	39	Paul Richards	852,039
1956	6th	69	85	.448	28	Paul Richards	901,201
1957	5th	76	76	.500	21	Paul Richards	1,029,581
1958	6th	74	79	.484	17 1/2	Paul Richards	829,991
1959	6th	74	80	.481	20	Paul Richards	891,926
1960	2nd	89	65	.578	8	Paul Richards	1,187,849
1961	3rd	95	67	.586	14	Paul Richards, Luman Harris	951,089
1962	7th	77	85	.475	19	Billy Hitchcock	790,254
1963	4th	86	76	.531	18 1/2	Billy Hitchcock	774,343
1964	3rd	97	65	.599	2	Hank Bauer	1,116,215
1965	3rd	94	68	.580	8	Hank Bauer	781,649
1966	1st	97	63	.606	+9	Hank Bauer	1,203,366

Year	Position	W	L	Pct.	*GB	Manager	Attendance
1967	6th (tied)	76	85	.472	15 1/2	Hank Bauer	955,053
1968	2nd	91	71	.562	12	Hank Bauer, Earl Weaver	943,977

EAST DIVISION

Year	Position	W	L	Pct.	*GB	Manager	Attendance
1969	1st§	109	53	.673	+19	Earl Weaver	1,058,168
1970	1st§	108	54	.667	+15	Earl Weaver	1,057,069
1971	1st§	101	57	.639	+12	Earl Weaver	1,023,037
1972	3rd	80	74	.519	5	Earl Weaver	899,950
1973	1st∞	97	65	.599	+8	Earl Weaver	958,667
1974	1st∞	91	71	.562	+2	Earl Weaver	962,572
1975	2nd	90	69	.566	4 1/2	Earl Weaver	1,002,157
1976	2nd	88	74	.543	10 1/2	Earl Weaver	1,058,609
1977	2nd (tied)	97	64	.602	2 1/2	Earl Weaver	1,195,769
1978	4th	90	71	.559	9	Earl Weaver	1,051,724
1979	1st§	102	57	.642	+8	Earl Weaver	1,681,009
1980	2nd	100	62	.617	3	Earl Weaver	1,797,438
1981	2nd/4th	59	46	.562	▲	Earl Weaver	1,024,652
1982	2nd	94	68	.580	1	Earl Weaver	1,613,031
1983	1st§	98	64	.605	+6	Joe Altobelli	2,042,071
1984	5th	85	77	.525	19	Joe Altobelli	2,045,784
1985	4th	83	78	.516	16	Joe Altobelli, Earl Weaver	2,132,387
1986	7th	73	89	.451	22 1/2	Earl Weaver	1,973,176
1987	6th	67	95	.414	31	Cal Ripken Sr.	1,835,692
1988	7th	54	107	.335	34 1/2	Cal Ripken Sr., Frank Robinson	1,660,738
1989	2nd	87	75	.537	2	Frank Robinson	2,535,208
1990	5th	76	85	.472	11 1/2	Frank Robinson	2,415,189
1991	6th	67	95	.414	24	Frank Robinson, Johnny Oates	2,552,753
1992	3rd	89	73	.549	7	Johnny Oates	3,567,819
1993	3rd (tied)	85	77	.525	10	Johnny Oates	3,644,965
1994	2nd	63	49	.563	6 1/2	Johnny Oates	2,535,359
1995	3rd	71	73	.493	15	Phil Regan	3,098,475

*Games behind winner. †Milwaukee Brewers. ‡St. Louis Browns. §Won championship series. ∞Lost championship series. ▲First half 31-23; second half 28-23.

MANAGERIAL RECORDS

Joe Altobelli 212-167, Jimmy Austin 29-38, Hank Bauer 407-318, Jim Bottomley 21-56, Jimmy Burke 172-180, Hugh Duffy 48-89, Jimmie Dykes 54-100, Lee Fohl 226-183, Fred Haney 125-227, Lum Harris 17-10, Billy Hitchcock 163-161, Rogers Hornsby 255-381, Dan Howley 220-239, Fielder Jones 158-196, Bill Killefer 224-329, Marty Marion 96-161, Jimmy McAleer 551-632, Johnny Oates 291-270, Jack O'Connor 47-107, Phil Regan 71-73, Paul Richards 517-539, Branch Rickey 139-179, Cal Ripken Sr. 67-101, Frank Robinson 230-285, Luke Sewell 432-410, George Sisler 218-241, Al Sothoron 2-6, George Stovall 91-158, Gabby Street 55-97, Zack Taylor 235-410, Bobby Wallace 57-134, Earl Weaver 1,481-1,060.

BOSTON RED SOX

YEARLY FINISHES

Year	Position	W	L	Pct.	*GB	Manager	Attendance
1901	2nd	79	57	.581	4	Jimmy Collins	289,448
1902	3rd	77	60	.562	6 1/2	Jimmy Collins	348,567
1903	1st	91	47	.659	+14 1/2	Jimmy Collins	379,338
1904	1st	95	59	.617	+1 1/2	Jimmy Collins	623,295
1905	4th	78	74	.513	16	Jimmy Collins	468,828
1906	8th	49	105	.318	45 1/2	Jimmy Collins, Chick Stahl	410,209
1907	7th	59	90	.396	32 1/2	George Huff, Bob Unglaub, Deacon McGuire	436,777
1908	5th	75	79	.487	15 1/2	Deacon McGuire, Fred Lake	473,048
1909	3rd	88	63	.583	9 1/2	Fred Lake	668,965
1910	4th	81	72	.529	22 1/2	Patsy Donovan	584,619
1911	5th	78	75	.510	24	Patsy Donovan	503,961
1912	1st	105	47	.691	+14	Jake Stahl	597,096
1913	4th	79	71	.527	15 1/2	Jake Stahl, Bill Carrigan	437,194
1914	2nd	91	62	.595	8 1/2	Bill Carrigan	481,359
1915	1st	101	50	.669	+2 1/2	Bill Carrigan	539,885
1916	1st	91	63	.591	+2	Bill Carrigan	496,397
1917	2nd	90	62	.592	9	Jack Barry	387,856
1918	1st	75	51	.595	+2 1/2	Ed Barrow	249,513
1919	6th	66	71	.482	20 1/2	Ed Barrow	417,291
1920	5th	72	81	.471	25 1/2	Ed Barrow	402,445
1921	5th	75	79	.487	23 1/2	Hugh Duffy	279,273
1922	8th	61	93	.396	33	Hugh Duffy	259,184
1923	8th	61	91	.401	37	Frank Chance	229,668
1924	7th	67	87	.435	25	Lee Fohl	448,556
1925	8th	47	105	.309	49 1/2	Lee Fohl	267,782
1926	8th	46	107	.301	44 1/2	Lee Fohl	285,155

Year	Position	W	L	Pct.	*GB	Manager	Attendance
1927	8th	51	103	.331	59	Bill Carrigan	305,275
1928	8th	57	96	.373	43 1/2	Bill Carrigan	396,920
1929	8th	58	96	.377	48	Bill Carrigan	394,620
1930	8th	52	102	.338	50	Heinie Wagner	444,045
1931	6th	62	90	.408	45	Shano Collins	350,975
1932	8th	43	111	.279	64	Shano Collins, Marty McManus	182,150
1933	7th	63	86	.423	34 1/2	Marty McManus	268,715
1934	4th	76	76	.500	24	Bucky Harris	610,640
1935	4th	78	75	.510	16	Joseph Cronin	558,568
1936	6th	74	80	.481	28 1/2	Joe Cronin	626,895
1937	5th	80	72	.526	21	Joe Cronin	559,659
1938	2nd	88	61	.591	9 1/2	Joe Cronin	646,459
1939	2nd	89	62	.589	17	Joe Cronin	573,070
1940	4th (tied)	82	72	.532	8	Joe Cronin	716,234
1941	2nd	84	70	.545	17	Joe Cronin	718,497
1942	2nd	93	59	.612	9	Joe Cronin	730,340
1943	7th	68	84	.447	29	Joe Cronin	358,275
1944	4th	77	77	.500	12	Joe Cronin	506,975
1945	7th	71	83	.461	17 1/2	Joe Cronin	603,794
1946	1st	104	50	.675	+12	Joe Cronin	1,416,944
1947	3rd	83	71	.539	14	Joe Cronin	1,427,315
1948	2nd†	96	59	.619	1	Joe McCarthy	1,558,798
1949	2nd	96	58	.623	1	Joe McCarthy	1,596,650
1950	3rd	94	60	.610	4	Joe McCarthy, Steve O'Neill	1,344,080
1951	3rd	87	67	.565	11	Steve O'Neill	1,312,282
1952	6th	76	78	.494	19	Lou Boudreau	1,115,750
1953	4th	84	69	.549	16	Lou Boudreau	1,026,133
1954	4th	69	85	.448	42	Lou Boudreau	931,127
1955	4th	84	70	.545	12	Pinky Higgins	1,203,200
1956	4th	84	70	.545	13	Pinky Higgins	1,137,158
1957	3rd	82	72	.532	16	Pinky Higgins	1,181,087
1958	3rd	79	75	.513	13	Pinky Higgins	1,077,047
1959	5th	75	79	.487	19	Pinky Higgins, Billy Jurges	984,102
1960	7th	65	89	.422	32	Billy Jurges, Pinky Higgins	1,129,866
1961	6th	76	86	.469	33	Pinky Higgins	850,589
1962	8th	76	84	.475	19	Pinky Higgins	733,080
1963	7th	76	85	.472	28	Johnny Pesky	942,642
1964	8th	72	90	.444	27	Johnny Pesky, Billy Herman	883,276
1965	9th	62	100	.383	40	Billy Herman	652,201
1966	9th	72	90	.444	26	Billy Herman, Pete Runnels	811,172
1967	1st	92	70	.568	+1	Dick Williams	1,727,832
1968	4th	86	76	.531	17	Dick Williams	1,940,788

EAST DIVISION

Year	Position	W	L	Pct.	*GB	Manager	Attendance
1969	3rd	87	75	.537	22	Dick Williams, Eddie Popowski	1,833,246
1970	3rd	87	75	.537	21	Eddie Kasko	1,595,278
1971	3rd	85	77	.525	18	Eddie Kasko	1,678,732
1972	2nd	85	70	.548	1/2	Eddie Kasko	1,441,718
1973	2nd	89	73	.549	8	Eddie Kasko	1,481,002
1974	3rd	84	78	.519	7	Darrell Johnson	1,556,411
1975	1st‡	95	65	.594	+4 1/2	Darrell Johnson	1,748,587
1976	3rd	83	79	.512	15 1/2	Darrell Johnson, Don Zimmer	1,895,846
1977	2nd (tied)	97	64	.602	2 1/2	Don Zimmer	2,074,549
1978	2nd§	99	64	.607	1	Don Zimmer	2,320,643
1979	3rd	91	69	.569	11 1/2	Don Zimmer	2,353,114
1980	4th	83	77	.519	19	Don Zimmer, Johnny Pesky	1,956,092
1981	5th/2nd (tied)	59	49	.546	∞	Ralph Houk	1,060,379
1982	3rd	89	73	.549	6	Ralph Houk	1,950,124
1983	6th	78	84	.481	20	Ralph Houk	1,782,285
1984	4th	86	76	.531	18	Ralph Houk	1,661,618
1985	5th	81	81	.500	18 1/2	John McNamara	1,786,633
1986	1st‡	95	66	.590	+5 1/2	John McNamara	2,147,641
1987	5th	78	84	.481	20	John McNamara	2,231,551
1988	1st▲	89	73	.549	+1	John McNamara, Joe Morgan	2,464,851
1989	3rd	83	79	.512	6	Joe Morgan	2,510,012
1990	1st▲	88	74	.543	+2	Joe Morgan	2,528,986
1991	2nd (tied)	84	78	.519	7	Joe Morgan	2,562,435
1992	7th	73	89	.451	23	Butch Hobson	2,468,574
1993	5th	80	82	.494	15	Butch Hobson	2,422,021
1994	4th	54	61	.470	17	Butch Hobson	1,775,818
1995	1st◆	86	58	.597	+7	Kevin Kennedy	2,164,410

*Games behind winner. †Lost pennant playoff. ‡Won championship series. §Lost division playoff. ∞First half 30-26; second half 29-23. ▲Lost championship series. ◆Lost division series.

MANAGERIAL RECORDS

Ed Barrow 213-203, Jack Barry 90-62, Lou Boudreau 229-232, Bill Carrigan 489-500, Frank Chance 61-91, Jimmy Collins 455-376, Shano Collins 73-134, Joe Cronin 1,071-916, Patsy Donovan 159-147, Hugh Duffy 136-172, Lee Fohl 160-299, Bucky Harris 76-76, Billy Herman 128-182, Pinky Higgins 560-556, Butch Hobson 207-232, Ralph Houk 312-282, George Huff 2-6, Darrell Johnson 220-188, Billy Jurges 59-63, Eddie Kasko 346-295, Kevin Kennedy 86-58, Fred Lake 110-80, Joe McCarthy 223-145, Deacon McGuire 98-123, Marty McManus 95-153, John McNamara 297-273, Joe Morgan 301-262, Steve O'Neill 150-99, Johnny Pesky 147-179, Eddie Popowski 5-4, Pete Runnels 8-8, Chick Stahl 14-26, Jake Stahl 144-88, Bob Unglaub 9-20, Heinie Wagner 52-102, Dick Williams 260-217, Don Zimmer 411-304.

CALIFORNIA ANGELS

YEARLY FINISHES

Year	Position	W	L	Pct.	*GB	Manager	Attendance
1961†	8th	70	91	.435	38 1/2	Bill Rigney	603,510
1962†	3rd	86	76	.531	10	Bill Rigney	1,144,063
1963†	9th	70	91	.435	34	Bill Rigney	821,015
1964†	5th	82	80	.506	17	Bill Rigney	760,439
1965†	7th	75	87	.463	27	Bill Rigney	566,727
1966	6th	80	82	.494	18	Bill Rigney	1,400,321
1967	5th	84	77	.522	7 1/2	Bill Rigney	1,317,713
1968	8th	67	95	.414	36	Bill Rigney	1,025,956

WEST DIVISION

Year	Position	W	L	Pct.	*GB	Manager	Attendance
1969	3rd	71	91	.438	26	Bill Rigney, Lefty Phillips	758,388
1970	3rd	86	76	.531	12	Lefty Phillips	1,077,741
1971	4th	76	86	.469	25 1/2	Lefty Phillips	926,373
1972	5th	75	80	.484	18	Del Rice	744,190
1973	4th	79	83	.488	15	Bobby Winkles	1,058,206
1974	6th	68	94	.420	22	Bobby Winkles, Dick Williams	917,269
1975	6th	72	89	.447	25 1/2	Dick Williams	1,058,163
1976	4th (tied)	76	86	.469	14	Dick Williams, Norm Sherry	1,006,774
1977	5th	74	88	.457	28	Norm Sherry, Dave Garcia	1,432,633
1978	2nd (tied)	87	75	.537	5	Dave Garcia, Jim Fregosi	1,755,386
1979	1st‡	88	74	.543	+3	Jim Fregosi	2,523,575
1980	6th	65	95	.406	31	Jim Fregosi	2,297,327
1981	4th/7th	51	59	.464	§	Jim Fregosi, Gene Mauch	1,441,545
1982	1st‡	93	69	.574	+3	Gene Mauch	2,807,360
1983	5th (tied)	70	92	.432	29	John McNamara	2,555,016
1984	2nd (tied)	81	81	.500	3	John McNamara	2,402,997
1985	2nd	90	72	.556	1	Gene Mauch	2,567,427
1986	1st‡	92	70	.568	+5	Gene Mauch	2,655,872
1987	6th (tied)	75	87	.463	10	Gene Mauch	2,696,299
1988	4th	75	87	.463	29	Cookie Rojas	2,340,925
1989	3rd	91	71	.562	8	Doug Rader	2,647,291
1990	4th	80	82	.494	23	Doug Rader	2,555,688
1991	7th	81	81	.500	14	Doug Rader, Buck Rodgers	2,416,236
1992	5th (tied)	72	90	.444	24	Buck Rodgers	2,065,444
1993	5th (tied)	71	91	.438	23	Buck Rodgers	2,057,460
1994	4th	47	68	.409	5 1/2	Buck Rodgers, Marcel Lachemann	1,512,622
1995	2nd	78	67	.538	1	Marcel Lachemann	1,748,680

*Games behind winner. †Los Angeles Angels through September 1, 1965. ‡Lost championship series. §First half 31-29; second half 20-30.

MANAGERIAL RECORDS

Jim Fregosi 237-249, Dave Garcia 60-66, Marcel Lachemann 109-111, Gene Mauch 379-332, John McNamara 151-173, Lefty Phillips 222-225, Doug Rader 232-216, Del Rice 75-80, Bill Rigney 625-707, Buck Rodgers 179-223, Cookie Rojas 75-87, Norm Sherry 76-71, Dick Williams 147-194, Bobby Winkles 109-127.

CHICAGO WHITE SOX

YEARLY FINISHES

Year	Position	W	L	Pct.	*GB	Manager	Attendance
1901	1st	83	53	.610	+4	Clark Griffith	354,350
1902	4th	74	60	.552	8	Clark Griffith	337,898
1903	7th	60	77	.438	30 1/2	Nixey Callahan	286,183
1904	3rd	89	65	.578	6	Nixey Callahan, Fielder Jones	557,123
1905	2nd	92	60	.605	2	Fielder Jones	687,419
1906	1st	93	58	.616	+3	Fielder Jones	585,202
1907	3rd	87	64	.576	5 1/2	Fielder Jones	666,307
1908	3rd	88	64	.579	1 1/2	Fielder Jones	636,096

Year	Position	W	L	Pct.	*GB	Manager	Attendance
1909	4th	78	74	.513	20	Billy Sullivan	478,400
1910	6th	68	85	.444	35 1/2	Hugh Duffy	552,084
1911	4th	77	74	.510	24	Hugh Duffy	583,208
1912	4th	78	76	.506	28	Nixey Callahan	602,241
1913	5th	78	74	.513	17 1/2	Nixey Callahan	644,501
1914	6th (tied)	70	84	.455	30	Nixey Callahan	469,290
1915	3rd	93	61	.604	9 1/2	Pants Rowland	539,461
1916	2nd	89	65	.578	2	Pants Rowland	679,923
1917	1st	100	54	.649	+9	Pants Rowland	684,521
1918	6th	57	67	.460	17	Pants Rowland	195,081
1919	1st	88	52	.629	+3 1/2	Kid Gleason	627,186
1920	2nd	96	58	.623	2	Kid Gleason	833,492
1921	7th	62	92	.403	36 1/2	Kid Gleason	543,650
1922	5th	77	77	.500	17	Kid Gleason	602,860
1923	7th	69	85	.448	30	Kid Gleason	573,778
1924	8th	66	87	.431	25 1/2	Johnny Evers	606,658
1925	5th	79	75	.513	18 1/2	Eddie Collins	832,231
1926	5th	81	72	.529	9 1/2	Eddie Collins	710,339
1927	5th	70	83	.458	29 1/2	Ray Schalk	614,423
1928	5th	72	82	.468	29	Ray Schalk, Lena Blackburne	494,152
1929	7th	59	93	.388	46	Lena Blackburne	426,795
1930	7th	62	92	.403	40	Donie Bush	406,123
1931	8th	56	97	.366	51	Donie Bush	403,550
1932	7th	49	102	.325	56 1/2	Lew Fonseca	233,198
1933	6th	67	83	.447	31	Lew Fonseca	397,789
1934	8th	53	99	.349	47	Lew Fonseca, Jimmie Dykes	236,559
1935	5th	74	78	.487	19 1/2	Jimmie Dykes	470,281
1936	3rd	81	70	.536	20	Jimmie Dykes	440,810
1937	3rd	86	68	.558	16	Jimmie Dykes	589,245
1938	6th	65	83	.439	32	Jimmie Dykes	338,278
1939	4th	85	69	.552	22 1/2	Jimmie Dykes	594,104
1940	4th (tied)	82	72	.532	8	Jimmie Dykes	660,336
1941	3rd	77	77	.500	24	Jimmie Dykes	677,077
1942	6th	66	82	.446	34	Jimmie Dykes	425,734
1943	4th	82	72	.532	16	Jimmie Dykes	508,962
1944	7th	71	83	.461	18	Jimmie Dykes	563,539
1945	6th	71	78	.477	15	Jimmie Dykes	657,981
1946	5th	74	80	.481	30	Jimmie Dykes, Ted Lyons	983,403
1947	6th	70	84	.455	27	Ted Lyons	876,948
1948	8th	51	101	.336	44 1/2	Ted Lyons	777,844
1949	6th	63	91	.409	34	Jack Onslow	937,151
1950	6th	60	94	.390	38	Jack Onslow, Red Corriden	781,330
1951	4th	81	73	.526	17	Paul Richards	1,328,234
1952	3rd	81	73	.526	14	Paul Richards	1,231,675
1953	3rd	89	65	.578	11 1/2	Paul Richards	1,191,353
1954	3rd	94	60	.610	17	Paul Richards, Marty Marion	1,231,629
1955	3rd	91	63	.591	5	Marty Marion	1,175,684
1956	3rd	85	69	.552	12	Marty Marion	1,000,090
1957	2nd	90	64	.584	8	Al Lopez	1,135,668
1958	2nd	82	72	.532	10	Al Lopez	797,451
1959	1st	94	60	.610	+5	Al Lopez	1,423,144
1960	3rd	87	67	.565	10	Al Lopez	1,644,460
1961	4th	86	76	.531	23	Al Lopez	1,146,019
1962	5th	85	77	.525	11	Al Lopez	1,131,562
1963	2nd	94	68	.580	10 1/2	Al Lopez	1,158,848
1964	2nd	98	64	.605	1	Al Lopez	1,250,053
1965	2nd	95	67	.586	7	Al Lopez	1,130,519
1966	4th	83	79	.512	15	Eddie Stanky	990,016
1967	4th	89	73	.549	3	Eddie Stanky	985,634
1968	8th (tied)	67	95	.414	36	Eddie Stanky, Al Lopez	803,775

WEST DIVISION

Year	Position	W	L	Pct.	*GB	Manager	Attendance
1969	5th	68	94	.420	29	Al Lopez, Don Gutteridge	589,546
1970	6th	56	106	.346	42	Don Gutteridge, Chuck Tanner	495,355
1971	3rd	79	83	.488	22 1/2	Chuck Tanner	833,891
1972	2nd	87	67	.565	5 1/2	Chuck Tanner	1,177,318
1973	5th	77	85	.475	17	Chuck Tanner	1,302,527
1974	4th	80	80	.500	9	Chuck Tanner	1,149,596
1975	5th	75	86	.466	22 1/2	Chuck Tanner	750,802
1976	6th	64	97	.398	25 1/2	Paul Richards	914,945
1977	3rd	90	72	.556	12	Bob Lemon	1,657,135
1978	5th	71	90	.441	20 1/2	Bob Lemon, Larry Doby	1,491,100
1979	5th	73	87	.456	14	Don Kessinger, Tony La Russa	1,280,702
1980	5th	70	90	.438	26	Tony La Russa	1,200,365
1981	3rd/6th	54	52	.509	†	Tony La Russa	946,651
1982	3rd	87	75	.537	6	Tony La Russa	1,567,787

Year	Position	W	L	Pct.	*GB	Manager	Attendance
1983	1st‡	99	63	.611	+20	Tony La Russa	2,132,821
1984	5th (tied)	74	88	.457	10	Tony La Russa	2,136,988
1985	3rd	85	77	.525	6	Tony La Russa	1,669,888
1986	5th	72	90	.444	20	Tony La Russa, Jim Fregosi	1,424,313
1987	5th	77	85	.475	8	Jim Fregosi	1,208,060
1988	5th	71	90	.441	32 1/2	Jim Fregosi	1,115,749
1989	7th	69	92	.429	29 1/2	Jeff Torborg	1,045,651
1990	2nd	94	68	.580	9	Jeff Torborg	2,002,357
1991	2nd	87	75	.537	8	Jeff Torborg	2,934,154
1992	3rd	86	76	.531	10	Gene Lamont	2,681,156
1993	1st‡	94	68	.580	+8	Gene Lamont	2,581,091

CENTRAL DIVISION

Year	Position	W	L	Pct.	*GB	Manager	Attendance
1994	1st	67	46	.593	+1	Gene Lamont	1,697,398
1995	3rd	68	76	.472	32	Gene Lamont, Terry Bevington	1,609,773

*Games behind winner. †First half 31-22; second half 23-30. ‡Lost championship series.

MANAGERIAL RECORDS

Terry Bevington 57-56, Lena Blackburne 99-133, Donie Bush 118-189, Nixey Callahan 309-329, Eddie Collins 160-147, Red Corriden 52-72, Larry Doby 37-50, Hugh Duffy 145-159, Jimmie Dykes 899-940, Johnny Evers 66-87, Lew Fonseca 120-196, Jim Fregosi 193-226, Kid Gleason 392-364, Clark Griffith 157-113, Don Gutteridge 109-172, Fielder Jones 426-293, Don Kessinger 46-60, Tony La Russa 522-510, Gene Lamont 258-210, Bob Lemon 124-112, Al Lopez 840-650, Ted Lyons 185-245, Marty Marion 179-138, Jack Onslow 71-133, Paul Richards 406-362, Pants Rowland 339-247, Ray Schalk 102-125, Eddie Stanky 206-197, Billy Sullivan 78-74, Chuck Tanner 401-414, Jeff Torborg 250-235.

CLEVELAND INDIANS

YEARLY FINISHES

Year	Position	W	L	Pct.	*GB	Manager	Attendance
1901	7th	54	82	.397	29	James McAleer	131,380
1902	5th	69	67	.507	14	Bill Armour	275,395
1903	3rd	77	63	.550	15	Bill Armour	311,280
1904	4th	86	65	.570	7 1/2	Bill Armour	264,749
1905	5th	76	78	.494	19	Nap Lajoie	316,306
1906	3rd	89	64	.582	5	Nap Lajoie	325,733
1907	4th	85	67	.559	8	Nap Lajoie	382,046
1908	2nd	90	64	.584	1/2	Nap Lajoie	422,242
1909	6th	71	82	.464	27 1/2	Nap Lajoie, Deacon McGuire	354,627
1910	5th	71	81	.467	32	Deacon McGuire	293,456
1911	3rd	80	73	.523	22	Deacon McGuire, George Stovall	406,296
1912	5th	75	78	.490	30 1/2	Harry Davis, J.L. Birmingham	336,844
1913	3rd	86	66	.566	9 1/2	J.L. Birmingham	541,000
1914	8th	51	102	.333	48 1/2	J.L. Birmingham	185,997
1915	7th	57	95	.375	44 1/2	J.L. Birmingham, Lee Fohl	159,285
1916	6th	77	77	.500	14	Lee Fohl	492,106
1917	3rd	88	66	.571	12	Lee Fohl	477,298
1918	2nd	73	54	.575	2 1/2	Lee Fohl	295,515
1919	2nd	84	55	.604	3 1/2	Lee Fohl, Tris Speaker	538,135
1920	1st	98	56	.636	+2	Tris Speaker	912,832
1921	2nd	94	60	.610	4 1/2	Tris Speaker	748,705
1922	4th	78	76	.507	16	Tris Speaker	528,145
1923	3rd	82	71	.536	16 1/2	Tris Speaker	558,856
1924	6th	67	86	.438	24 1/2	Tris Speaker	481,905
1925	6th	70	84	.455	27 1/2	Tris Speaker	419,005
1926	2nd	88	66	.571	3	Tris Speaker	627,426
1927	6th	66	87	.431	43 1/2	Jack McAllister	373,138
1928	7th	62	92	.403	39	Roger Peckinpaugh	375,907
1929	3rd	81	71	.533	24	Roger Peckinpaugh	536,210
1930	4th	81	73	.536	21	Roger Peckinpaugh	528,657
1931	4th	78	76	.506	30	Roger Peckinpaugh	483,027
1932	4th	87	65	.572	19	Roger Peckinpaugh	468,953
1933	4th	75	76	.497	23 1/2	Roger Peckinpaugh, Walter Johnson	387,936
1934	3rd	85	69	.552	16	Walter Johnson	391,338
1935	3rd	82	71	.536	12	Walter Johnson, Steve O'Neill	397,615
1936	5th	80	74	.519	22 1/2	Steve O'Neill	500,391
1937	4th	83	71	.539	19	Steve O'Neill	564,849
1938	3rd	86	66	.566	13	Ossie Vitt	652,006
1939	3rd	87	67	.565	20 1/2	Ossie Vitt	563,926
1940	2nd	89	65	.578	1	Ossie Vitt	902,576

Year	Position	W	L	Pct.	*GB	Manager	Attendance
1941	4th (tied)	75	79	.487	26	Roger Peckinpaugh	745,948
1942	4th	75	79	.487	28	Lou Boudreau	459,447
1943	3rd	82	71	.536	15 1/2	Lou Boudreau	438,894
1944	5th (tied)	72	82	.468	17	Lou Boudreau	475,272
1945	5th	73	72	.503	11	Lou Boudreau	558,182
1946	6th	68	86	.442	36	Lou Boudreau	1,057,289
1947	4th	80	74	.519	17	Lou Boudreau	1,521,978
1948	1st†	97	58	.626	+1	Lou Boudreau	2,620,627
1949	3rd	89	65	.578	8	Lou Boudreau	2,233,771
1950	4th	92	62	.597	6	Lou Boudreau	1,727,464
1951	2nd	93	61	.604	5	Al Lopez	1,704,984
1952	2nd	93	61	.604	2	Al Lopez	1,444,607
1953	2nd	92	62	.597	8 1/2	Al Lopez	1,069,176
1954	1st	111	43	.721	+8	Al Lopez	1,335,472
1955	2nd	93	61	.604	3	Al Lopez	1,221,780
1956	2nd	88	66	.571	9	Al Lopez	865,467
1957	6th	76	77	.497	21 1/2	Kerby Farrell	722,256
1958	4th	77	76	.503	14 1/2	Bobby Bragan, Joe Gordon	663,805
1959	2nd	89	65	.578	5	Joe Gordon	1,497,976
1960	4th	76	78	.494	21	Joe Gordon, Jimmie Dykes	950,985
1961	5th	78	83	.484	30 1/2	Jimmie Dykes	725,547
1962	6th	80	82	.494	16	Mel McGaha	716,076
1963	5th (tied)	79	83	.488	25 1/2	Birdie Tebbetts	562,507
1964	6th (tied)	79	83	.488	20	Birdie Tebbetts	653,293
1965	5th	87	75	.537	15	Birdie Tebbetts	934,786
1966	5th	81	81	.500	17	Birdie Tebbetts, George Strickland	903,359
1967	8th	75	87	.463	17	Joe Adcock	662,980
1968	3rd	86	75	.534	16 1/2	Alvin Dark	857,994

EAST DIVISION

Year	Position	W	L	Pct.	*GB	Manager	Attendance
1969	6th	62	99	.385	46 1/2	Alvin Dark	619,970
1970	5th	76	86	.469	32	Alvin Dark	729,752
1971	6th	60	102	.370	43	Alvin Dark, John Lipon	591,361
1972	5th	72	84	.462	14	Ken Aspromonte	626,354
1973	6th	71	91	.438	26	Ken Aspromonte	615,107
1974	4th	77	85	.475	14	Ken Aspromonte	1,114,262
1975	4th	79	80	.497	15 1/2	Frank Robinson	977,039
1976	4th	81	78	.509	16	Frank Robinson	948,776
1977	5th	71	90	.441	28 1/2	Frank Robinson, Jeff Torborg	900,365
1978	6th	69	90	.434	29	Jeff Torborg	800,584
1979	6th	81	80	.503	22	Jeff Torborg, Dave Garcia	1,011,644
1980	6th	79	81	.494	23	Dave Garcia	1,033,827
1981	6th/5th	52	51	.504	‡	Dave Garcia	661,395
1982	6th (tied)	78	84	.481	17	Dave Garcia	1,044,021
1983	7th	70	92	.432	28	Mike Ferraro, Pat Corrales	768,941
1984	6th	75	87	.463	29	Pat Corrales	734,079
1985	7th	60	102	.370	39 1/2	Pat Corrales	655,181
1986	5th	84	78	.519	11 1/2	Pat Corrales	1,471,805
1987	7th	61	101	.377	37	Pat Corrales, Doc Edwards	1,077,898
1988	6th	78	84	.481	11	Doc Edwards	1,411,610
1989	6th	73	89	.451	16	Doc Edwards, John Hart	1,285,542
1990	4th	77	85	.475	11	John McNamara	1,225,240
1991	7th	57	105	.352	34	John McNamara, Mike Hargrove	1,051,863
1992	4th (tied)	76	86	.469	20	Mike Hargrove	1,224,274
1993	6th	76	86	.469	19	Mike Hargrove	2,177,908

CENTRAL DIVISION

Year	Position	W	L	Pct.	*GB	Manager	Attendance
1994	2nd	66	47	.584	1	Mike Hargrove	1,995,174
1995	1st§∞	100	44	.694	+30	Mike Hargrove	2,842,745

*Games behind winner. †Won pennant playoff. ‡First half 26-24; second half 26-27. §Won division series. ∞Won championship series.

MANAGERIAL RECORDS

Joe Adcock 75-87, Bill Armour 232-195, Ken Aspromonte 220-260, Joe Birmingham 170-191, Lou Boudreau 728-649, Bobby Bragan 31-36, Pat Corrales 280-355, Alvin Dark 266-321, Harry Davis 54-71, Jimmie Dykes 103-115, Doc Edwards 173-207, Kerby Farrell 76-77, Mike Ferraro 40-60, Lee Fohl 327-310, Dave Garcia 247-244, Joe Gordon 184-151, Mike Hargrove 350-316, John Hart 8-11, Walter Johnson 179-168, Nap Lajoie 377-309, Johnny Lipon 18-41, Al Lopez 570-354, Jimmy McAleer 54-82, Jack McCallister 66-87, Mel McGaha 80-82, Deacon McGuire 91-117, John McNamara 102-137, Steve O'Neill 199-168, Roger Peckinpaugh 490-481, Frank Robinson 186-189, Tris Speaker 617-520, George Stovall 74-62, George Strickland 15-24, Birdie Tebbetts 269-298, Jeff Torborg 157-201, Oscar Vitt 262-198.

DETROIT TIGERS

YEARLY FINISHES

Year	Position	W	L	Pct.	*GB	Manager	Attendance
1901	3rd	74	61	.548	8 1/2	George Stallings	259,430
1902	7th	52	83	.385	30 1/2	Frank Dwyer	189,469
1903	5th	65	71	.478	25	Ed Barrow	224,523
1904	7th	62	90	.408	32	Ed Barrow, Bobby Lowe	177,796
1905	3rd	79	74	.516	15 1/2	Bill Armour	193,384
1906	6th	71	78	.477	21	Bill Armour	174,043
1907	1st	92	58	.613	+1 1/2	Hughey Jennings	297,079
1908	1st	90	63	.588	+ 1/2	Hughey Jennings	436,199
1909	1st	98	54	.645	+3 1/2	Hughey Jennings	490,490
1910	3rd	86	68	.558	18	Hughey Jennings	391,288
1911	2nd	89	65	.578	13 1/2	Hughey Jennings	484,988
1912	6th	69	84	.451	36 1/2	Hughey Jennings	402,870
1913	6th	66	87	.431	30	Hughey Jennings	398,502
1914	4th	80	73	.523	19 1/2	Hughey Jennings	416,225
1915	2nd	100	54	.649	2 1/2	Hughey Jennings	476,105
1916	3rd	87	67	.565	4	Hughey Jennings	616,772
1917	4th	78	75	.510	21 1/2	Hughey Jennings	457,289
1918	7th	55	71	.437	20	Hughey Jennings	203,719
1919	4th	80	60	.571	8	Hughey Jennings	643,805
1920	7th	61	93	.396	37	Hughey Jennings	579,650
1921	6th	71	82	.464	27	Ty Cobb	661,527
1922	3rd	79	75	.513	15	Ty Cobb	861,206
1923	2nd	83	71	.539	16	Ty Cobb	911,377
1924	3rd	86	68	.558	6	Ty Cobb	1,015,136
1925	4th	81	73	.526	16 1/2	Ty Cobb	820,766
1926	6th	79	75	.513	12	Ty Cobb	711,914
1927	4th	82	71	.536	27 1/2	George Moriarty	773,716
1928	6th	68	86	.442	33	George Moriarty	474,323
1929	6th	70	84	.455	36	Bucky Harris	869,318
1930	5th	75	79	.487	27	Bucky Harris	649,450
1931	7th	61	93	.396	47	Bucky Harris	434,056
1932	5th	76	75	.503	29 1/2	Bucky Harris	397,157
1933	5th	75	79	.487	25	Del Baker	320,972
1934	1st	101	53	.656	+7	Mickey Cochrane	919,161
1935	1st	93	58	.616	+3	Mickey Cochrane	1,034,929
1936	2nd	83	71	.539	19 1/2	Mickey Cochrane	875,948
1937	2nd	89	65	.578	13	Mickey Cochrane	1,072,276
1938	4th	84	70	.545	16	Mickey Cochrane, Del Baker	799,557
1939	5th	81	73	.526	26 1/2	Del Baker	836,279
1940	1st	90	64	.584	+1	Del Baker	1,112,693
1941	4th (tied)	75	79	.487	26	Del Baker	684,915
1942	5th	73	81	.474	30	Del Baker	580,087
1943	5th	78	76	.506	20	Steve O'Neill	606,287
1944	2nd	88	66	.571	1	Steve O'Neill	923,176
1945	1st	88	65	.575	+1 1/2	Steve O'Neill	1,280,341
1946	2nd	92	62	.597	12	Steve O'Neill	1,722,590
1947	2nd	85	69	.552	12	Steve O'Neill	1,398,093
1948	5th	78	76	.506	18 1/2	Steve O'Neill	1,743,035
1949	4th	87	67	.565	10	Red Rolfe	1,821,204
1950	2nd	95	59	.617	3	Red Rolfe	1,951,474
1951	5th	73	81	.474	25	Red Rolfe	1,132,641
1952	8th	50	104	.325	45	Red Rolfe, Fred Hutchinson	1,026,846
1953	6th	60	94	.390	40 1/2	Fred Hutchinson	884,658
1954	5th	68	86	.442	43	Fred Hutchinson	1,079,847
1955	5th	79	75	.513	17	Bucky Harris	1,181,838
1956	5th	82	72	.532	15	Bucky Harris	1,051,182
1957	4th	78	76	.506	20	Jack Tighe	1,272,346
1958	5th	77	77	.500	15	Jack Tighe, Bill Norman	1,098,924
1959	4th	76	78	.494	18	Bill Norman, Jimmie Dykes	1,221,221
1960	6th	71	83	.461	26	Jimmie Dykes, Billy Hitchcock, Joe Gordon	1,167,669
1961	2nd	101	61	.623	8	Bob Scheffing	1,600,710
1962	4th	85	76	.528	10 1/2	Bob Scheffing	1,207,881
1963	5th (tied)	79	83	.488	25 1/2	Bob Scheffing, Charlie Dressen	821,952
1964	4th	85	77	.525	14	Charlie Dressen	816,139
1965	4th	89	73	.549	13	Charlie Dressen, Bob Swift	1,029,645
1966	3rd	88	74	.543	10	Charlie Dressen, Bob Swift, Frank Skaff	1,124,293
1967	2nd	91	71	.562	1	Mayo Smith	1,447,143
1968	1st	103	59	.636	+12	Mayo Smith	2,031,847

EAST DIVISION

Year	Position	W	L	Pct.	*GB	Manager	Attendance
1969	2nd	90	72	.556	19	Mayo Smith	1,577,481
1970	4th	79	83	.488	29	Mayo Smith	1,501,293
1971	2nd	91	71	.562	12	Billy Martin	1,591,073

Year	Position	W	L	Pct.	*GB	Manager	Attendance
1972	1st†	86	70	.551	+1/2	Billy Martin	1,892,386
1973	3rd	85	77	.525	12	Billy Martin, Joe Schultz	1,724,146
1974	6th	72	90	.444	19	Ralph Houk	1,243,080
1975	6th	57	102	.358	37 1/2	Ralph Houk	1,058,836
1976	5th	74	87	.460	24	Ralph Houk	1,467,020
1977	4th	74	88	.457	26	Ralph Houk	1,359,856
1978	5th	86	76	.531	13 1/2	Ralph Houk	1,714,893
1979	5th	85	76	.528	18	Les Moss, Dick Tracewski, Sparky Anderson	1,630,929
1980	5th	84	78	.519	19	Sparky Anderson	1,785,293
1981	4th/2nd (tied)	60	49	.550	‡	Sparky Anderson	1,149,144
1982	4th	83	79	.512	12	Sparky Anderson	1,636,058
1983	2nd	92	70	.568	6	Sparky Anderson	1,829,636
1984	1st§	104	58	.642	+15	Sparky Anderson	2,704,794
1985	3rd	84	77	.522	15	Sparky Anderson	2,286,609
1986	3rd	87	75	.537	8 1/2	Sparky Anderson	1,899,437
1987	1st†	98	64	.605	+2	Sparky Anderson	2,061,830
1988	2nd	88	74	.543	1	Sparky Anderson	2,081,162
1989	7th	59	103	.364	30	Sparky Anderson	1,543,656
1990	3rd	79	83	.488	9	Sparky Anderson	1,495,785
1991	2nd	84	78	.519	7	Sparky Anderson	1,641,661
1992	6th	75	87	.463	21	Sparky Anderson	1,423,963
1993	3rd (tied)	85	77	.525	10	Sparky Anderson	1,971,421
1994	5th	53	62	.461	18	Sparky Anderson	1,184,783
1995	4th	60	84	.417	26	Sparky Anderson	1,180,979

*Games behind winner. †Lost championship series. ‡First half 31-26; second half 29-23. §Won championship series.

MANAGERIAL RECORDS

Sparky Anderson 1,431-1,248, Bill Armour 150-152, Del Baker 392-336, Ed Barrow 97-117, Ty Cobb 479-444, Mickey Cochrane 379-278, Chuck Dressen 221-189, Frank Dwyer 52-83, Jimmie Dykes 118-115, Joe Gordon 26-31, Bucky Harris 516-557, Ralph Houk 366-443, Fred Hutchinson 155-235, Hugh Jennings 1,131-972, Bobby Lowe 30-44, Billy Martin 248-204, George Moriarty 150-157, Les Moss 27-26, Bill Norman 58-64, Steve O'Neill 509-414, Red Rolfe 278-256, Bob Scheffing 210-173, Joe Schultz 14-14, Frank Skaff 40-39, Mayo Smith 363-285, George Stallings 74-61, Bob Swift 56-43, Jack Tighe 99-104.

KANSAS CITY ROYALS

YEARLY FINISHES

WEST DIVISION

Year	Position	W	L	Pct.	*GB	Manager	Attendance
1969	4th	69	93	.429	28	Joe Gordon	902,414
1970	4th (tied)	65	97	.401	33	Charlie Metro, Bob Lemon	693,047
1971	2nd	85	76	.528	16	Bob Lemon	910,784
1972	4th	76	78	.494	16 1/2	Bob Lemon	707,656
1973	2nd	88	74	.543	6	Jack McKeon	1,345,341
1974	5th	77	85	.475	13	Jack McKeon	1,173,292
1975	2nd	91	71	.562	7	Jack McKeon, Whitey Herzog	1,151,836
1976	1st†	90	72	.556	+2 1/2	Whitey Herzog	1,680,265
1977	1st†	102	60	.630	+8	Whitey Herzog	1,852,603
1978	1st†	92	70	.568	+5	Whitey Herzog	2,255,493
1979	2nd	85	77	.525	3	Whitey Herzog	2,261,845
1980	1st‡	97	65	.599	+14	Jim Frey	2,288,714
1981	5th/1st∞	50	53	.485	§	Jim Frey, Dick Howser	1,279,403
1982	2nd	90	72	.556	3	Dick Howser	2,284,464
1983	2nd	79	83	.488	20	Dick Howser	1,963,875
1984	1st†	84	78	.519	+3	Dick Howser	1,810,018
1985	1st‡	91	71	.562	+1	Dick Howser	2,162,717
1986	3rd (tied)	76	86	.469	16	Dick Howser, Mike Ferraro	2,320,794
1987	2nd	83	79	.512	2	Billy Gardner, John Wathan	2,392,471
1988	3rd	84	77	.522	19 1/2	John Wathan	2,350,181
1989	2nd	92	70	.568	7	John Wathan	2,477,700
1990	6th	75	86	.466	27 1/2	John Wathan	2,244,956
1991	6th	82	80	.506	13	John Wathan, Hal McRae	2,161,537
1992	5th (tied)	72	90	.444	24	Hal McRae	1,867,689
1993	3rd	84	78	.519	10	Hal McRae	1,934,578

CENTRAL DIVISION

Year	Position	W	L	Pct.	*GB	Manager	Attendance
1994	3rd	64	51	.557	4	Hal McRae	1,400,494
1995	2nd	70	74	.486	30	Bob Boone	1,233,530

*Games behind winner. †Lost championship series. ‡Won championship series. §First half 20-30; second half 30-23. ∞Lost division series.

MANAGERIAL RECORDS

Bob Boone 70-74, Mike Ferraro 36-38, Jim Frey 127-105, Billy Gardner 62-64, Joe Gordon 69-93, Whitey Herzog 410-304, Dick Howser 404-365, Bob Lemon 207-218, Jack McKeon 215-205, Hal McRae 286-277, Charlie Metro 19-33, John Wathan 288-270.

MILWAUKEE BREWERS

YEARLY FINISHES

WEST DIVISION

Year	Position	W	L	Pct.	*GB	Manager	Attendance
1969†	6th	64	98	.395	33	Joe Schultz	677,944
1970	4th	65	97	.401	33	Dave Bristol	933,690
1971	6th	69	92	.429	32	Dave Bristol	731,531

EAST DIVISION

Year	Position	W	L	Pct.	*GB	Manager	Attendance
1972	6th	65	91	.417	21	Dave Bristol, Del Crandall	600,440
1973	5th	74	88	.457	23	Del Crandall	1,092,158
1974	5th	76	86	.469	15	Del Crandall	955,741
1975	5th	68	94	.420	28	Del Crandall	1,213,357
1976	6th	66	95	.410	32	Alex Grammas	1,012,164
1977	6th	67	95	.414	33	Alex Grammas	1,114,938
1978	3rd	93	69	.574	6 1/2	George Bamberger	1,601,406
1979	2nd	95	66	.590	8	George Bamberger	1,918,343
1980	3rd	86	76	.531	17	George Bamberger, Buck Rodgers	1,857,408
1981	3rd/1st§	62	47	.569	‡	Buck Rodgers	878,432
1982	1st∞	95	67	.586	+1	Buck Rodgers, Harvey Kuenn	1,978,896
1983	5th	87	75	.537	11	Harvey Kuenn	2,397,131
1984	7th	67	94	.416	36 1/2	Rene Lachemann	1,608,509
1985	6th	71	90	.441	28	George Bamberger	1,360,265
1986	6th	77	84	.478	18	George Bamberger, Tom Trebelhorn	1,265,041
1987	3rd	91	71	.562	7	Tom Trebelhorn	1,909,244
1988	3rd (tied)	87	75	.537	2	Tom Trebelhorn	1,923,238
1989	4th	81	81	.500	8	Tom Trebelhorn	1,970,735
1990	6th	74	88	.457	14	Tom Trebelhorn	1,752,900
1991	4th	83	79	.512	8	Tom Trebelhorn	1,478,729
1992	2nd	92	70	.568	4	Phil Garner	1,857,314
1993	7th	69	93	.426	26	Phil Garner	1,688,080

CENTRAL DIVISION

Year	Position	W	L	Pct.	*GB	Manager	Attendance
1994	5th	53	62	.461	15	Phil Garner	1,268,399
1995	4th	65	79	.451	35	Phil Garner	1,087,560

*Games behind winner. †Seattle Pilots. ‡First half 31-25; second half 31-22. §Lost division series. ∞Won championship series.

MANAGERIAL RECORDS

George Bamberger 377-351, Dave Bristol 144-209, Del Crandall 271-338, Phil Garner 279-304, Alex Grammas 133-190, Harvey Kuenn 160-118, Rene Lachemann 67-94, Buck Rodgers 124-102, Joe Schultz 64-98, Tom Trebelhorn 422-397.

MINNESOTA TWINS

YEARLY FINISHES

Year	Position	W	L	Pct.	*GB	Manager	Attendance
1901†	6th	61	72	.459	20 1/2	Jimmy Manning	161,661
1902†	6th	61	75	.449	22	Tom Loftus	188,158
1903†	8th	43	94	.314	47 1/2	Tom Loftus	128,878
1904†	8th	38	113	.251	55 1/2	Patsy Donovan	131,744
1905†	7th	64	87	.421	29 1/2	Jake Stahl	252,027
1906†	7th	55	95	.367	37 1/2	Jake Stahl	129,903
1907†	8th	49	102	.325	43 1/2	Joe Cantillon	221,929
1908†	7th	67	85	.441	22 1/2	Joe Cantillon	264,252
1909†	8th	42	110	.276	56	Joe Cantillon	205,199
1910†	7th	66	85	.437	36 1/2	Jimmy McAleer	254,591
1911†	7th	64	90	.416	38 1/2	Jimmy McAleer	244,884
1912†	2nd	91	61	.599	14	Clark Griffith	350,663
1913†	2nd	90	64	.584	6 1/2	Clark Griffith	325,831
1914†	3rd	81	73	.526	19	Clark Griffith	243,888
1915†	4th	85	68	.556	17	Clark Griffith	167,332
1916†	7th	76	77	.497	14 1/2	Clark Griffith	177,265
1917†	5th	74	79	.484	25 1/2	Clark Griffith	89,682
1918†	3rd	72	56	.563	4	Clark Griffith	182,122
1919†	7th	56	84	.400	32	Clark Griffith	234,096
1920†	6th	68	84	.447	29	Clark Griffith	359,260
1921†	4th	80	73	.523	18	George McBride	456,069
1922†	6th	69	85	.448	25	Clyde Milan	458,552
1923†	4th	75	78	.490	23 1/2	Donie Bush	357,406

Year	Position	W	L	Pct.	*GB	Manager	Attendance
1924†	1st	92	62	.597	+2	Bucky Harris	534,310
1925†	1st	96	55	.636	+8 1/2	Bucky Harris	817,199
1926†	4th	81	69	.540	8	Bucky Harris	551,580
1927†	3rd	85	69	.552	25	Bucky Harris	528,976
1928†	4th	75	79	.487	26	Bucky Harris	378,501
1929†	5th	71	81	.467	34	Walter Johnson	355,506
1930†	2nd	94	60	.610	8	Walter Johnson	614,474
1931†	3rd	92	62	.597	16	Walter Johnson	492,657
1932†	3rd	93	61	.604	14	Walter Johnson	371,396
1933†	1st	99	53	.651	+7	Joe Cronin	437,533
1934†	7th	66	86	.434	34	Joe Cronin	330,074
1935†	6th	67	86	.438	27	Bucky Harris	255,011
1936†	4th	82	71	.536	20	Bucky Harris	379,525
1937†	6th	73	80	.477	28 1/2	Bucky Harris	397,799
1938†	5th	75	76	.497	23 1/2	Bucky Harris	522,694
1939†	6th	65	87	.428	41 1/2	Bucky Harris	339,257
1940†	7th	64	90	.416	26	Bucky Harris	381,241
1941†	6th (tied)	70	84	.455	31	Bucky Harris	415,663
1942†	7th	62	89	.411	39 1/2	Bucky Harris	403,493
1943†	2nd	84	69	.549	13 1/2	Ossie Bluege	574,694
1944†	8th	64	90	.416	25	Ossie Bluege	525,235
1945†	2nd	87	67	.565	1 1/2	Ossie Bluege	652,660
1946†	4th	76	78	.494	28	Ossie Bluege	1,027,216
1947†	7th	64	90	.416	33	Ossie Bluege	850,758
1948†	7th	56	97	.366	40	Joe Kuhel	795,254
1949†	8th	50	104	.325	47	Joe Kuhel	770,745
1950†	5th	67	87	.435	31	Bucky Harris	699,697
1951†	7th	62	92	.403	36	Bucky Harris	695,167
1952†	5th	78	76	.506	17	Bucky Harris	699,457
1953†	5th	76	76	.500	23 1/2	Bucky Harris	595,594
1954†	6th	66	88	.429	45	Bucky Harris	503,542
1955†	8th	53	101	.344	43	Chuck Dressen	425,238
1956†	7th	59	95	.383	38	Chuck Dressen	431,647
1957†	8th	55	99	.357	43	Chuck Dressen, Cookie Lavagetto	457,079
1958†	8th	61	93	.396	31	Cookie Lavagetto	475,288
1959†	8th	63	91	.409	31	Cookie Lavagetto	615,372
1960†	5th	73	81	.474	24	Cookie Lavagetto	743,404
1961	7th	70	90	.438	38	Cookie Lavagetto, Sam Mele	1,256,723
1962	2nd	91	71	.562	5	Sam Mele	1,433,116
1963	3rd	91	70	.565	13	Sam Mele	1,406,652
1964	6th (tied)	79	83	.488	20	Sam Mele	1,207,514
1965	1st	102	60	.630	+7	Sam Mele	1,463,258
1966	2nd	89	73	.549	9	Sam Mele	1,259,374
1967	2nd (tied)	91	71	.562	1	Sam Mele, Cal Ermer	1,483,547
1968	7th	79	83	.488	24	Cal Ermer	1,143,257

WEST DIVISION

Year	Position	W	L	Pct.	*GB	Manager	Attendance
1969	1st‡	97	65	.599	+9	Billy Martin	1,349,328
1970	1st‡	98	64	.605	+9	Bill Rigney	1,261,887
1971	5th	74	86	.463	26 1/2	Bill Rigney	940,858
1972	3rd	77	77	.500	15 1/2	Bill Rigney, Frank Quilici	797,901
1973	3rd	81	81	.500	13	Frank Quilici	907,499
1974	3rd	82	80	.506	8	Frank Quilici	662,401
1975	4th	76	83	.478	20 1/2	Frank Quilici	737,156
1976	3rd	85	77	.525	5	Gene Mauch	715,394
1977	4th	84	77	.522	17 1/2	Gene Mauch	1,162,727
1978	4th	73	89	.451	19	Gene Mauch	787,878
1979	4th	82	80	.506	6	Gene Mauch	1,070,521
1980	3rd	77	84	.478	19 1/2	Gene Mauch, Johnny Goryl	769,206
1981	7th/4th	41	68	.376	§	Johnny Goryl, Billy Gardner	469,090
1982	7th	60	102	.370	33	Billy Gardner	921,186
1983	5th (tied)	70	92	.432	29	Billy Gardner	858,939
1984	2nd (tied)	81	81	.500	3	Billy Gardner	1,598,422
1985	4th (tied)	77	85	.475	14	Billy Gardner, Ray Miller	1,651,814
1986	6th	71	91	.438	21	Ray Miller, Tom Kelly	1,255,453
1987	1st∞	85	77	.525	+2	Tom Kelly	2,081,976
1988	2nd	91	71	.562	13	Tom Kelly	3,030,672
1989	5th	80	82	.494	19	Tom Kelly	2,277,438
1990	7th	74	88	.457	29	Tom Kelly	1,751,584
1991	1st∞	95	67	.586	+8	Tom Kelly	2,293,842
1992	2nd	90	72	.556	6	Tom Kelly	2,482,428
1993	5th (tied)	71	91	.438	23	Tom Kelly	2,048,673

CENTRAL DIVISION

Year	Position	W	L	Pct.	*GB	Manager	Attendance
1994	4th	53	60	.469	14	Tom Kelly	1,398,565
1995	5th	56	88	.389	44	Tom Kelly	1,057,667

*Games behind winner. †Washington Senators (original club). ‡Lost championship series. §First half 17-39; second half 24-29. ∞Won championship series.

MANAGERIAL RECORDS

Ossie Bluege 375-394, Donie Bush 75-78, Joe Cantillon 158-297, Joe Cronin 165-139, Patsy Donovan 38-113, Chuck Dressen 116-212, Cal Ermer 145-129, Billy Gardner 268-353, Johnny Goryl 34-38, Clark Griffith 693-646, Bucky Harris 1,336-1,416, Walter Johnson 350-264, Tom Kelly 707-707, Joe Kuhel 106-201, Cookie Lavagetto 271-384, Tom Loftus 104-169, Jimmy Manning 61-72, Billy Martin 97-65, Gene Mauch 378-394, Jimmy McAleer 130-175, George McBride 80-73, Sam Mele 524-436, Clyde Milan 69-85, Ray Miller 109-130, Frank Quilici 280-287, Bill Rigney 208-184, Jake Stahl 119-182.

NEW YORK YANKEES

YEARLY FINISHES

Year	Position	W	L	Pct.	*GB	Manager	Attendance
1901†	5th	68	65	.511	13 1/2	John McGraw	141,952
1902	8th	50	88	.362	34	John McGraw, Wilbert Robinson	174,606
1903	4th	72	62	.537	17	Clark Griffith	211,808
1904	2nd	92	59	.609	1 1/2	Clark Griffith	438,919
1905	6th	71	78	.477	21 1/2	Clark Griffith	309,100
1906	2nd	90	61	.596	3	Clark Griffith	434,709
1907	5th	70	78	.473	21	Clark Griffith	350,020
1908	8th	51	103	.331	39 1/2	Clark Griffith, Kid Elberfeld	305,500
1909	5th	74	77	.490	23 1/2	George Stallings	501,000
1910	2nd	88	63	.583	14 1/2	George Stallings, Hal Chase	355,857
1911	6th	76	76	.500	25 1/2	Hal Chase	302,444
1912	8th	50	102	.329	55	Harry Wolverton	242,194
1913	7th	57	94	.377	38	Frank Chance	357,551
1914	6th (tied)	70	84	.455	30	Frank Chance, Roger Peckinpaugh	359,477
1915	5th	69	83	.454	32 1/2	Bill Donovan	256,035
1916	4th	80	74	.519	11	Bill Donovan	469,211
1917	6th	71	82	.464	28 1/2	Bill Donovan	330,294
1918	4th	60	63	.488	13 1/2	Miller Huggins	282,047
1919	3rd	80	59	.576	7 1/2	Miller Huggins	619,164
1920	3rd	95	59	.617	3	Miller Huggins	1,289,422
1921	1st	98	55	.641	+4 1/2	Miller Huggins	1,230,696
1922	1st	94	60	.610	+1	Miller Huggins	1,026,134
1923	1st	98	54	.645	+16	Miller Huggins	1,007,066
1924	2nd	89	63	.586	2	Miller Huggins	1,053,533
1925	7th	69	85	.448	30	Miller Huggins	697,267
1926	1st	91	63	.591	+3	Miller Huggins	1,027,095
1927	1st	110	44	.714	+19	Miller Huggins	1,164,015
1928	1st	101	53	.656	+2 1/2	Miller Huggins	1,072,132
1929	2nd	88	66	.571	18	Miller Huggins, Art Fletcher	960,148
1930	3rd	86	68	.558	16	Bob Shawkey	1,169,230
1931	2nd	94	59	.614	13 1/2	Joe McCarthy	912,437
1932	1st	107	47	.695	+13	Joe McCarthy	962,320
1933	2nd	91	59	.607	7	Joe McCarthy	728,014
1934	2nd	94	60	.610	7	Joe McCarthy	854,682
1935	2nd	89	60	.597	3	Joe McCarthy	657,508
1936	1st	102	51	.667	+19 1/2	Joe McCarthy	976,913
1937	1st	102	52	.662	+13	Joe McCarthy	998,148
1938	1st	99	53	.651	+9 1/2	Joe McCarthy	970,916
1939	1st	106	45	.702	+17	Joe McCarthy	859,785
1940	3rd	88	66	.571	2	Joe McCarthy	988,975
1941	1st	101	53	.656	+17	Joe McCarthy	964,722
1942	1st	103	51	.669	+9	Joe McCarthy	988,251
1943	1st	98	56	.636	+13 1/2	Joe McCarthy	645,006
1944	3rd	83	71	.539	6	Joe McCarthy	822,864
1945	4th	81	71	.533	6 1/2	Joe McCarthy	881,846
1946	3rd	87	67	.565	17	Joe McCarthy, Bill Dickey, Johnny Neun	2,265,512
1947	1st	97	57	.630	+12	Bucky Harris	2,178,937
1948	3rd	94	60	.610	2 1/2	Bucky Harris	2,373,901
1949	1st	97	57	.630	+1	Casey Stengel	2,281,676
1950	1st	98	56	.636	+3	Casey Stengel	2,081,380
1951	1st	98	56	.636	+5	Casey Stengel	1,950,107
1952	1st	95	59	.617	+2	Casey Stengel	1,629,665
1953	1st	99	52	.656	+8 1/2	Casey Stengel	1,537,811
1954	2nd	103	51	.669	8	Casey Stengel	1,475,171
1955	1st	96	58	.623	+3	Casey Stengel	1,490,138

Year	Position	W	L	Pct.	*GB	Manager	Attendance
1956	1st	97	57	.630	+9	Casey Stengel	1,491,784
1957	1st	98	56	.636	+8	Casey Stengel	1,497,134
1958	1st	92	62	.597	+10	Casey Stengel	1,428,438
1959	3rd	79	75	.513	15	Casey Stengel	1,552,030
1960	1st	97	57	.630	+8	Casey Stengel	1,627,349
1961	1st	109	53	.673	+8	Ralph Houk	1,747,725
1962	1st	96	66	.593	+5	Ralph Houk	1,493,574
1963	1st	104	57	.646	+10 1/2	Ralph Houk	1,308,920
1964	1st	99	63	.611	+1	Yogi Berra	1,305,638
1965	6th	77	85	.475	25	Johnny Keane	1,213,552
1966	10th	70	89	.440	26 1/2	Johnny Keane, Ralph Houk	1,124,648
1967	9th	72	90	.444	20	Ralph Houk	1,259,514
1968	5th	83	79	.512	20	Ralph Houk	1,185,666

EAST DIVISION

Year	Position	W	L	Pct.	*GB	Manager	Attendance
1969	5th	80	81	.497	28 1/2	Ralph Houk	1,067,996
1970	2nd	93	69	.574	15	Ralph Houk	1,136,879
1971	4th	82	80	.506	21	Ralph Houk	1,070,771
1972	4th	79	76	.510	6 1/2	Ralph Houk	966,328
1973	4th	80	82	.494	17	Ralph Houk	1,262,103
1974	2nd	89	73	.549	2	Bill Virdon	1,273,075
1975	3rd	83	77	.519	12	Bill Virdon, Billy Martin	1,288,048
1976	1st‡	97	62	.610	+10 1/2	Billy Martin	2,012,434
1977	1st‡	100	62	.617	+2 1/2	Billy Martin	2,103,092
1978	1st§‡	100	63	.613	+1	Billy Martin, Bob Lemon	2,335,871
1979	4th	89	71	.556	13 1/2	Bob Lemon, Billy Martin	2,537,765
1980	1st∞	103	59	.636	+3	Dick Howser	2,627,417
1981	1st/6th◆‡	59	48	.551	▲	Gene Michael, Bob Lemon	1,614,533
1982	5th	79	83	.488	16	Bob Lemon, Gene Michael, Clyde King	2,041,219
1983	3rd	91	71	.562	7	Billy Martin	2,257,976
1984	3rd	87	75	.537	17	Yogi Berra	1,821,815
1985	2nd	97	64	.602	2	Yogi Berra, Billy Martin	2,214,587
1986	2nd	90	72	.556	5 1/2	Lou Piniella	2,268,030
1987	4th	89	73	.549	9	Lou Piniella	2,427,672
1988	5th	85	76	.528	3 1/2	Billy Martin, Lou Piniella	2,633,701
1989	5th	74	87	.460	14 1/2	Dallas Green, Bucky Dent	2,170,485
1990	7th	67	95	.414	21	Bucky Dent, Stump Merrill	2,006,436
1991	5th	71	91	.438	20	Stump Merrill	1,863,733
1992	4th (tied)	76	86	.469	20	Buck Showalter	1,748,733
1993	2nd	88	74	.543	7	Buck Showalter	2,416,965
1994	1st	70	43	.619	+6 1/2	Buck Showalter	1,675,556
1995	2nd■	79	65	.549	7	Buck Showalter	1,705,263

*Games behind winner. †Baltimore Orioles. ‡Won championship series. §Won pennant playoff. ∞Lost championship series. ▲First half 34-22; second half 25-26. ◆Won division series. ■Lost division series.

MANAGERIAL RECORDS

Yogi Berra 192-148, Frank Chance 117-168, Hal Chase 86-80, Bucky Dent 36-53, Bill Dickey 57-48, Bill Donovan 220-239, Kid Elberfeld 27-71, Art Fletcher 6-5, Dallas Green 56-65, Clark Griffith 419-370, Bucky Harris 191-117, Ralph Houk 944-806, Dick Howser 103-59, Miller Huggins 1,067-719, Johnny Keane 81-101, Clyde King 29-33, Bob Lemon 99-73, Billy Martin 501-385, Joe McCarthy 1,460-867, John McGraw 94-96, Stump Merrill 120-155, Gene Michael 92-76, Johnny Neun 8-6, Roger Peckinpaugh 10-10, Lou Piniella 224-193, Wilbert Robinson 24-57, Bob Shawkey 86-68, Buck Showalter 311-268, George Stallings 152-136, Casey Stengel 1,149-696, Bill Virdon 142-124, Harry Wolverton 50-102.

OAKLAND ATHLETICS

YEARLY FINISHES

Year	Position	W	L	Pct.	*GB	Manager	Attendance
1901†	4th	74	62	.544	9	Connie Mack	206,329
1902†	1st	83	53	.610	+5	Connie Mack	442,473
1903†	2nd	75	60	.556	14 1/2	Connie Mack	420,078
1904†	5th	81	70	.536	12 1/2	Connie Mack	512,294
1905†	1st	92	56	.622	+2	Connie Mack	554,576
1906†	4th	78	67	.538	12	Connie Mack	489,129
1907†	2nd	88	57	.607	1 1/2	Connie Mack	625,581
1908†	6th	68	85	.444	22	Connie Mack	455,062
1909†	2nd	95	58	.621	3 1/2	Connie Mack	674,915
1910†	1st	102	48	.680	+14 1/2	Connie Mack	588,905
1911†	1st	101	50	.669	+13 1/2	Connie Mack	605,749
1912†	3rd	90	62	.592	15	Connie Mack	517,653
1913†	1st	96	57	.627	+6 1/2	Connie Mack	571,896
1914†	1st	99	53	.651	+8 1/2	Connie Mack	346,641
1915†	8th	43	109	.283	58 1/2	Connie Mack	146,223
1916†	8th	36	117	.235	54 1/2	Connie Mack	184,471
1917†	8th	55	98	.359	44 1/2	Connie Mack	221,432

Year	Position	W	L	Pct.	*GB	Manager	Attendance
1918†	8th	52	76	.406	24	Connie Mack	177,926
1919†	8th	36	104	.257	52	Connie Mack	225,209
1920†	8th	48	106	.312	50	Connie Mack	287,888
1921†	8th	53	100	.346	45	Connie Mack	344,430
1922†	7th	65	89	.422	29	Connie Mack	425,356
1923†	6th	69	83	.454	29	Connie Mack	534,122
1924†	5th	71	81	.467	20	Connie Mack	531,992
1925†	2nd	88	64	.579	8 1/2	Connie Mack	869,703
1926†	3rd	83	67	.553	6	Connie Mack	714,308
1927†	2nd	91	63	.591	19	Connie Mack	605,529
1928†	2nd	98	55	.641	2 1/2	Connie Mack	689,756
1929†	1st	104	46	.693	+18	Connie Mack	839,176
1930†	1st	102	52	.662	+8	Connie Mack	721,663
1931†	1st	107	45	.704	+13 1/2	Connie Mack	627,464
1932†	2nd	94	60	.610	13	Connie Mack	405,500
1933†	3rd	79	72	.523	19 1/2	Connie Mack	297,138
1934†	5th	68	82	.453	31	Connie Mack	305,847
1935†	8th	58	91	.389	34	Connie Mack	233,173
1936†	8th	53	100	.346	49	Connie Mack	285,173
1937†	7th	54	97	.358	46 1/2	Connie Mack	430,733
1938†	8th	53	99	.349	46	Connie Mack	385,357
1939†	7th	55	97	.362	51 1/2	Connie Mack	395,022
1940†	8th	54	100	.351	36	Connie Mack	432,145
1941†	8th	64	90	.416	37	Connie Mack	528,894
1942†	8th	55	99	.357	48	Connie Mack	423,487
1943†	8th	49	105	.318	49	Connie Mack	376,735
1944†	5th (tied)	72	82	.468	17	Connie Mack	505,322
1945†	8th	52	98	.347	34 1/2	Connie Mack	462,631
1946†	8th	49	105	.318	55	Connie Mack	621,793
1947†	5th	78	76	.506	19	Connie Mack	911,566
1948†	4th	84	70	.545	12 1/2	Connie Mack	945,076
1949†	5th	81	73	.526	16	Connie Mack	816,514
1950†	8th	52	102	.338	46	Connie Mack	309,805
1951†	6th	70	84	.455	28	Jimmie Dykes	465,469
1952†	4th	79	75	.513	16	Jimmie Dykes	627,100
1953†	7th	59	95	.383	41 1/2	Jimmie Dykes	362,113
1954†	8th	51	103	.331	60	Ed Joost	304,666
1955‡	6th	63	91	.409	33	Lou Boudreau	1,393,054
1956‡	8th	52	102	.338	45	Lou Boudreau	1,015,154
1957‡	7th	59	94	.386	38 1/2	Lou Boudreau, Harry Craft	901,067
1958‡	7th	73	81	.474	19	Harry Craft	925,090
1959‡	7th	66	88	.429	28	Harry Craft	963,683
1960‡	8th	58	96	.377	39	Bob Elliot	774,944
1961‡	9th (tied)	61	100	.379	47 1/2	Joe Gordon, Hank Bauer	683,817
1962‡	9th	72	90	.444	24	Hank Bauer	635,675
1963‡	8th	73	89	.451	31 1/2	Ed Lopat	762,364
1964‡	10th	57	105	.352	42	Ed Lopat, Mel McGaha	642,478
1965‡	10th	59	103	.364	43	Mel McGaha, Haywood Sullivan	528,344
1966‡	7th	74	86	.463	23	Alvin Dark	773,929
1967‡	10th	62	99	.385	29 1/2	Alvin Dark, Luke Appling	726,639
1968	6th	82	80	.506	21	Bob Kennedy	837,466

WEST DIVISION

Year	Position	W	L	Pct.	*GB	Manager	Attendance
1969	2nd	88	74	.543	9	Hank Bauer, John McNamara	778,232
1970	2nd	89	73	.549	9	John McNamara	778,355
1971	1st§	101	60	.627	+16	Dick Williams	914,993
1972	1st∞	93	62	.600	+5 1/2	Dick Williams	921,323
1973	1st∞	94	68	.580	+6	Dick Williams	1,000,763
1974	1st∞	90	72	.556	+5	Alvin Dark	845,693
1975	1st§	98	64	.605	+7	Alvin Dark	1,075,518
1976	2nd	87	74	.540	2 1/2	Chuck Tanner	780,593
1977	7th	63	98	.391	38 1/2	Jack McKeon, Bobby Winkles	495,599
1978	6th	69	93	.426	23	Bobby Winkles, Jack McKeon	526,999
1979	7th	54	108	.333	34	Jim Marshall	306,763
1980	2nd	83	79	.512	14	Billy Martin	842,259
1981	1st/2nd◆§	64	45	.587	▲	Billy Martin	1,304,054
1982	5th	68	94	.420	25	Billy Martin	1,735,489
1983	4th	74	88	.457	25	Steve Boros	1,294,941
1984	4th	77	85	.475	7	Steve Boros, Jackie Moore	1,353,281
1985	4th (tied)	77	85	.475	14	Jackie Moore	1,334,599
1986	3rd (tied)	76	86	.469	16	Jackie Moore, Tony La Russa	1,314,646
1987	3rd	81	81	.500	4	Tony La Russa	1,678,921
1988	1st∞	104	58	.642	+13	Tony La Russa	2,287,335
1989	1st∞	99	63	.611	+7	Tony La Russa	2,667,225

Year	Position	W	L	Pct.	*GB	Manager	Attendance
1990	1st∞	103	59	.636	+9	Tony La Russa	2,900,217
1991	4th	84	78	.519	11	Tony La Russa	2,713,493
1992	1st§	96	66	.593	+6	Tony La Russa	2,494,160
1993	7th	68	94	.420	26	Tony La Russa	2,035,025
1994	2nd	51	63	.447	1	Tony La Russa	1,242,692
1995	4th	67	77	.465	11 1/2	Tony La Russa	1,174,310

*Games behind winner. †Philadelphia Athletics. ‡Kansas City Athletics. §Lost championship series. ∞Won championship series. ▲First half 37-23; second half 27-22. ◆Won division series.

MANAGERIAL RECORDS

Luke Appling 10-30, Hank Bauer 187-226, Steve Boros 94-112, Lou Boudreau 151-260, Harry Craft 162-196, Alvin Dark 314-291, Jimmie Dykes 198-254, Bob Elliott 58-96, Joe Gordon 26-33, Eddie Joost 51-103, Bob Kennedy 82-80, Tony La Russa 695-614, Eddie Lopat 90-124, Connie Mack 3,582-3,814, Jim Marshall 54-108, Billy Martin 215-218, Mel McGaha 45-91, Jack McKeon 71-105, John McNamara 97-78, Jackie Moore 163-190, Haywood Sullivan 54-82, Chuck Tanner 87-74, Dick Williams 288-190, Bobby Winkles 61-86.

SEATTLE MARINERS

YEARLY FINISHES

WEST DIVISION

Year	Position	W	L	Pct.	*GB	Manager	Attendance
1977	6th	64	98	.395	38	Darrell Johnson	1,338,511
1978	7th	56	104	.350	35	Darrell Johnson	877,440
1979	6th	67	95	.414	21	Darrell Johnson	844,447
1980	7th	59	103	.364	38	Darrell Johnson, Maury Wills	836,204
1981	6th/5th	44	65	.404	†	Maury Wills, Rene Lachemann	636,276
1982	4th	76	86	.469	17	Rene Lachemann	1,070,404
1983	7th	60	102	.370	39	Rene Lachemann, Del Crandall	813,537
1984	5th (tied)	74	88	.457	10	Del Crandall, Chuck Cottier	870,372
1985	6th	74	88	.457	17	Chuck Cottier	1,128,696
1986	7th	67	95	.414	25	Chuck Cottier, Marty Martinez, Dick Williams	1,029,045
1987	4th	78	84	.481	7	Dick Williams	1,134,255
1988	7th	68	93	.422	35 1/2	Dick Williams, Jim Snyder	1,022,398
1989	6th	73	89	.451	26	Jim Lefebvre	1,298,443
1990	5th	77	85	.475	26	Jim Lefebvre	1,509,727
1991	5th	83	79	.512	12	Jim Lefebvre	2,147,905
1992	7th	64	98	.395	32	Bill Plummer	1,651,398
1993	4th	82	80	.506	12	Lou Piniella	2,051,853
1994	3rd	49	63	.438	2	Lou Piniella	1,104,206
1995	1st‡§	79	66	.545	+1	Lou Piniella	1,643,203

*Games behind winner. †First half 21-36; second half 23-29. ‡Won division series. §Lost championship series.

MANAGERIAL RECORDS

Chuck Cottier 98-120, Del Crandall 93-141, Darrell Johnson 226-362, Rene Lachemann 140-180, Jim Lefebvre 233-253, Lou Piniella 210-209, Bill Plummer 64-98, Jimmy Snyder 45-60, Dick Williams 159-192, Maury Wills 26-56.

TEXAS RANGERS

YEARLY FINISHES

Year	Position	W	L	Pct.	*GB	Manager	Attendance
1961†	9th (tied)	61	100	.379	47 1/2	Mickey Vernon	597,287
1962†	10th	60	101	.373	35 1/2	Mickey Vernon	729,775
1963†	10th	56	106	.346	48 1/2	Mickey Vernon, Gil Hodges	535,604
1964†	9th	62	100	.383	37	Gil Hodges	600,106
1965†	8th	70	92	.432	32	Gil Hodges	560,083
1966†	8th	71	88	.447	25 1/2	Gil Hodges	576,260
1967†	6th (tied)	76	85	.472	15 1/2	Gil Hodges	770,863
1968†	10th	65	96	.404	37 1/2	Jim Lemon	546,661

EAST DIVISION

Year	Position	W	L	Pct.	*GB	Manager	Attendance
1969†	4th	86	76	.531	23	Ted Williams	918,106
1970†	6th	70	92	.432	38	Ted Williams	824,789
1971†	5th	63	96	.396	38 1/2	Ted Williams	655,156

WEST DIVISION

Year	Position	W	L	Pct.	*GB	Manager	Attendance
1972	6th	54	100	.351	38 1/2	Ted Williams	662,974
1973	6th	57	105	.352	37	Whitey Herzog, Del Wilber, Billy Martin	686,085
1974	2nd	84	76	.525	5	Billy Martin	1,193,902
1975	3rd	79	83	.488	19	Billy Martin, Frank Lucchesi	1,127,924

Year	Position	W	L	Pct.	*GB	Manager	Attendance
1976	4th (tied)	76	86	.469	14	Frank Lucchesi	1,164,982
1977	2nd	94	68	.580	8	Frank Lucchesi, Eddie Stanky, Connie Ryan, Billy Hunter	1,250,722
1978	2nd (tied)	87	75	.537	5	Billy Hunter, Pat Corrales	1,447,963
1979	3rd	83	79	.512	5	Pat Corrales	1,519,671
1980	4th	76	85	.472	20 1/2	Pat Corrales	1,198,175
1981	2nd/3rd	57	48	.543	‡	Don Zimmer	850,076
1982	6th	64	98	.395	29	Don Zimmer, Darrell Johnson	1,154,432
1983	3rd	77	85	.475	22	Doug Rader	1,363,469
1984	7th	69	92	.429	14 1/2	Doug Rader	1,102,471
1985	7th	62	99	.385	28 1/2	Doug Rader, Bobby Valentine	1,112,497
1986	2nd	87	75	.537	5	Bobby Valentine	1,692,002
1987	6th (tied)	75	87	.463	10	Bobby Valentine	1,763,053
1988	6th	70	91	.435	33 1/2	Bobby Valentine	1,581,901
1989	4th	83	79	.512	16	Bobby Valentine	2,043,993
1990	3rd	83	79	.512	20	Bobby Valentine	2,057,911
1991	3rd	85	77	.525	10	Bobby Valentine	2,297,720
1992	4th	77	85	.475	19	Bobby Valentine, Toby Harrah	2,198,231
1993	2nd	86	76	.531	8	Kevin Kennedy	2,244,616
1994	1st	52	62	.456	+1	Kevin Kennedy	2,503,198
1995	3rd	74	70	.514	4 1/2	Johnny Oates	1,985,910

*Games behind winner. †Washington Senators (second club). ‡First half 33-22; second half 24-26.

MANAGERIAL RECORDS

Pat Corrales 160-164, Toby Harrah 32-44, Whitey Herzog 47-91, Gil Hodges 321-444, Billy Hunter 146-108, Darrell Johnson 26-40, Kevin Kennedy 138-138, Jim Lemon 65-96, Frank Lucchesi 142-149, Billy Martin 137-141, Johnny Oates 74-70, Doug Rader 155-200, Connie Ryan 2-4, Eddie Stanky 1-0, Bobby Valentine 581-605, Mickey Vernon 135-227, Del Wilber 1-0, Ted Williams 273-364, Don Zimmer 95-106.

TORONTO BLUE JAYS

YEARLY FINISHES

EAST DIVISION

Year	Position	W	L	Pct.	*GB	Manager	Attendance
1977	7th	54	107	.335	45 1/2	Roy Hartsfield	1,701,052
1978	7th	59	102	.366	40	Roy Hartsfield	1,562,585
1979	7th	53	109	.327	50 1/2	Roy Hartsfield	1,431,651
1980	7th	67	95	.414	36	Bobby Mattick	1,400,327
1981	7th/7th	37	69	.349	†	Bobby Mattick	755,083
1982	6th (tied)	78	84	.481	17	Bobby Cox	1,275,978
1983	4th	89	73	.549	9	Bobby Cox	1,930,415
1984	2nd	89	73	.549	15	Bobby Cox	2,110,009
1985	1st‡	99	62	.615	+2	Bobby Cox	2,468,925
1986	4th	86	76	.531	9 1/2	Jimy Williams	2,455,477
1987	2nd	96	66	.593	2	Jimy Williams	2,778,429
1988	3rd (tied)	87	75	.537	2	Jimy Williams	2,595,175
1989	1st‡	89	73	.549	+2	Jimy Williams, Cito Gaston	3,375,883
1990	2nd	86	76	.531	2	Cito Gaston	3,885,284
1991	1st‡	91	71	.562	+7	Cito Gaston	4,001,527
1992	1st§	96	66	.593	+4	Cito Gaston	4,028,318
1993	1st§	95	67	.586	+7	Cito Gaston	4,057,947
1994	3rd	55	60	.478	16	Cito Gaston	2,907,933
1995	5th	56	88	.389	30	Cito Gaston	2,826,483

*Games behind winner. †First half 16-42; second half 21-27. ‡Lost championship series. §Won championship series.

MANAGERIAL RECORDS

Bobby Cox 355-292, Cito Gaston 556-477, Roy Hartsfield 166-318, Bobby Mattick 104-164, Jimy Williams 281-241.

NATIONAL LEAGUE

ATLANTA BRAVES

YEARLY FINISHES

Year	Position	W	L	Pct.	*GB	Manager	Attendance
1901†	5th	69	69	.500	20 1/2	Frank Selee	146,502
1902†	3rd	73	64	.533	29	Al Buckenberger	116,960
1903†	6th	58	80	.420	32	Al Buckenberger	143,155
1904†	7th	55	98	.359	51	Al Buckenberger	140,694
1905†	7th	51	103	.331	54 1/2	Fred Tenney	150,003
1906†	8th	49	102	.325	66 1/2	Fred Tenney	143,280
1907†	7th	58	90	.392	47	Fred Tenney	203,221

Year	Position	W	L	Pct.	*GB	Manager	Attendance
1908†	6th	63	91	.409	36	Joe Kelley	253,750
1909†	8th	45	108	.294	65 1/2	Frank Bowerman, Harry Smith	195,188
1910†	8th	53	100	.346	50 1/2	Fred Lake	149,027
1911†	8th	44	107	.291	54	Fred Tenney	116,000
1912†	8th	52	101	.340	52	Johnny Kling	121,000
1913†	5th	69	82	.457	31 1/2	George Stallings	208,000
1914†	1st	94	59	.614	+10 1/2	George Stallings	382,913
1915†	2nd	83	69	.546	7	George Stallings	376,283
1916†	3rd	89	63	.586	4	George Stallings	313,495
1917†	6th	72	81	.471	25 1/2	George Stallings	174,253
1918†	7th	53	71	.427	28 1/2	George Stallings	84,938
1919†	6th	57	82	.410	38 1/2	George Stallings	167,401
1920†	7th	62	90	.408	30	George Stallings	162,483
1921†	4th	79	74	.516	15	Fred Mitchell	318,627
1922†	8th	53	100	.346	39 1/2	Fred Mitchell	167,965
1923†	7th	54	100	.351	41 1/2	Fred Mitchell	227,802
1924†	8th	53	100	.346	40	Dave Bancroft	117,478
1925†	5th	70	83	.458	25	Dave Bancroft	313,528
1926†	7th	66	86	.434	22	Dave Bancroft	303,598
1927†	7th	60	94	.390	34	Dave Bancroft	288,685
1928†	7th	50	103	.327	44 1/2	Jack Slattery, Rogers Hornsby	227,001
1929†	8th	56	98	.364	43	Emil Fuchs	372,351
1930†	6th	70	84	.455	22	Bill McKechnie	464,835
1931†	7th	64	90	.416	37	Bill McKechnie	515,005
1932†	5th	77	77	.500	13	Bill McKechnie	507,606
1933†	4th	83	71	.539	9	Bill McKechnie	517,803
1934†	4th	78	73	.517	16	Bill McKechnie	303,205
1935†	8th	38	115	.248	61 1/2	Bill McKechnie	232,754
1936†	6th	71	83	.461	21	Bill McKechnie	340,585
1937†	5th	79	73	.520	16	Bill McKechnie	385,339
1938†	5th	77	75	.507	12	Casey Stengel	341,149
1939†	7th	63	88	.417	32 1/2	Casey Stengel	285,994
1940†	7th	65	87	.428	34 1/2	Casey Stengel	241,616
1941†	7th	62	92	.403	38	Casey Stengel	263,680
1942†	7th	59	89	.399	44	Casey Stengel	285,332
1943†	6th	68	85	.444	36 1/2	Casey Stengel	271,289
1944†	6th	65	89	.422	40	Bob Coleman	208,691
1945†	6th	67	85	.441	30	Bob Coleman, Del Bissonette	374,178
1946†	4th	81	72	.529	15 1/2	Billy Southworth	969,673
1947†	3rd	86	68	.558	8	Billy Southworth	1,277,361
1948†	1st	91	62	.595	+6 1/2	Billy Southworth	1,455,439
1949†	4th	75	79	.487	22	Billy Southworth	1,081,795
1950†	4th	83	71	.539	8	Billy Southworth	944,391
1951†	4th	76	78	.494	20 1/2	Billy Southworth, Tommy Holmes	487,475
1952†	7th	64	89	.418	32	Tommy Holmes, Charlie Grimm	281,278
1953‡	2nd	92	62	.597	13	Charlie Grimm	1,826,397
1954‡	3rd	89	65	.578	8	Charlie Grimm	2,131,388
1955‡	2nd	85	69	.552	13 1/2	Charlie Grimm	2,005,836
1956‡	2nd	92	62	.597	1	Charlie Grimm, Fred Haney	2,046,331
1957‡	1st	95	59	.617	+8	Fred Haney	2,215,404
1958‡	1st	92	62	.597	+8	Fred Haney	1,971,101
1959‡	2nd§	86	70	.551	2	Fred Haney	1,749,112
1960‡	2nd	88	66	.571	7	Chuck Dressen	1,497,799
1961‡	4th	83	71	.539	10	Chuck Dressen, Birdie Tebbetts	1,101,441
1962‡	5th	86	76	.531	15 1/2	Birdie Tebbetts	766,921
1963‡	6th	84	78	.519	15	Bobby Bragan	773,018
1964‡	5th	88	74	.543	5	Bobby Bragan	910,911
1965‡	5th	86	76	.531	11	Bobby Bragan	555,584
1966	5th	85	77	.525	10	Bobby Bragan, Billy Hitchcock	1,539,801
1967	7th	77	85	.475	24 1/2	Billy Hitchcock, Ken Silvestri	1,389,222
1968	5th	81	81	.500	16	Lum Harris	1,126,540

WEST DIVISION

Year	Position	W	L	Pct.	*GB	Manager	Attendance
1969	1st∞	93	69	.574	+3	Lum Harris	1,458,320
1970	5th	76	86	.469	26	Lum Harris	1,078,848
1971	3rd	82	80	.506	8	Lum Harris	1,006,320
1972	4th	70	84	.455	25	Lum Harris, Eddie Mathews	752,973
1973	5th	76	85	.472	22 1/2	Eddie Mathews	800,655
1974	3rd	88	74	.543	14	Eddie Mathews, Clyde King	981,085
1975	5th	67	94	.416	40 1/2	Clyde King, Connie Ryan	534,672
1976	6th	70	92	.432	32	Dave Bristol	818,179
1977	6th	61	101	.377	37	Dave Bristol, Ted Turner	872,464
1978	6th	69	93	.426	26	Bobby Cox	904,494
1979	6th	66	94	.413	23 1/2	Bobby Cox	769,465
1980	4th	81	80	.503	11	Bobby Cox	1,048,411

Year	Position	W	L	Pct.	*GB	Manager	Attendance
1981	4th/5th	50	56	.472	▲	Bobby Cox	535,418
1982	1st∞	89	73	.549	+1	Joe Torre	1,801,985
1983	2nd	88	74	.543	3	Joe Torre	2,119,935
1984	2nd (tied)	80	82	.494	12	Joe Torre	1,724,892
1985	5th	66	96	.407	29	Eddie Haas, Bobby Wine	1,350,137
1986	6th	72	89	.447	23 1/2	Chuck Tanner	1,387,181
1987	5th	69	92	.429	20 1/2	Chuck Tanner	1,217,402
1988	6th	54	106	.338	39 1/2	Chuck Tanner, Russ Nixon	848,089
1989	6th	63	97	.394	28	Russ Nixon	984,930
1990	6th	65	97	.401	26	Russ Nixon, Bobby Cox	980,129
1991	1st◆	94	68	.580	+1	Bobby Cox	2,140,217
1992	1st◆	98	64	.605	+8	Bobby Cox	3,077,400
1993	1st∞	104	58	.642	+1	Bobby Cox	3,884,725

EAST DIVISION

Year	Position	W	L	Pct.	*GB	Manager	Attendance
1994	2nd	68	46	.596	6	Bobby Cox	2,539,240
1995	1st■◆	90	54	.625	+21	Bobby Cox	2,561,831

*Games behind winner. †Boston Braves. ‡Milwaukee Braves. §Lost pennant playoff. ∞Lost championship series. ▲First half 25-29; second half 25-27. ◆Won championship series. ■Won division series.

MANAGERIAL RECORDS

Dave Bancroft 249-363, Del Bissonette 25-34, Frank Bowerman 23-55, Bobby Bragan 310-287, Dave Bristol 131-192, Al Buckenberger 186-242, Bob Coleman 107-140, Bobby Cox 760-670, Chuck Dressen 159-124, Emil Fuchs 56-98, Charlie Grimm 341-285, Eddie Haas 50-71, Fred Haney 341-231, Lum Harris 379-373, Billy Hitchcock 110-100, Tommy Holmes 61-69, Rogers Hornsby 39-83, Joe Kelley 63-91, Clyde King 96-101, Johnny Kling 52-101, Fred Lake 53-100, Eddie Mathews 149-161, Bill McKechnie 560-666, Fred Mitchell 186-274, Russ Nixon 130-216, Connie Ryan 9-18, Frank Selee 69-69, Ken Silvestri 0-3, Jack Slattery 11-20, Harry Smith 22-53, Billy Southworth 424-358, George Stallings 579-597, Casey Stengel 394-516, Chuck Tanner 153-208, Birdie Tebbetts 98-89, Fred Tenney 202-402, Joe Torre 257-229, Ted Turner 0-1, Bobby Wine 16-25.

CHICAGO CUBS

YEARLY FINISHES

Year	Position	W	L	Pct.	*GB	Manager	Attendance
1901	6th	53	86	.381	37	Tom Loftus	205,071
1902	5th	68	69	.496	34	Frank Selee	263,700
1903	3rd	82	56	.594	8	Frank Selee	386,205
1904	2nd	93	60	.608	13	Frank Selee	439,100
1905	3rd	92	61	.601	13	Frank Selee, Frank Chance	509,900
1906	1st	116	36	.763	+20	Frank Chance	654,300
1907	1st	107	45	.704	+17	Frank Chance	422,550
1908	1st	99	55	.643	+1	Frank Chance	665,325
1909	2nd	104	49	.680	6 1/2	Frank Chance	633,480
1910	1st	104	50	.675	+13	Frank Chance	526,152
1911	2nd	92	62	.597	7 1/2	Frank Chance	576,000
1912	3rd	91	59	.607	11 1/2	Frank Chance	514,000
1913	3rd	88	65	.575	13 1/2	Johnny Evers	419,000
1914	4th	78	76	.506	16 1/2	Hank O'Day	202,516
1915	4th	73	80	.477	17 1/2	Roger Bresnahan	217,058
1916	5th	67	86	.438	26 1/2	Joe Tinker	453,685
1917	5th	74	80	.481	24	Fred Mitchell	360,218
1918	1st	84	45	.651	+10 1/2	Fred Mitchell	337,256
1919	3rd	75	65	.536	21	Fred Mitchell	424,430
1950	5th (tied)	75	79	.487	18	Fred Mitchell	480,783
1921	7th	64	89	.418	30	Johnny Evers, Bill Killefer	410,107
1922	5th	80	74	.519	13	Bill Killefer	542,283
1923	4th	83	71	.539	12 1/2	Bill Killefer	703,705
1924	5th	81	72	.529	12	Bill Killefer	716,922
1925	8th	68	86	.442	27 1/2	Bill Killefer, Rabbit Maranville, George Gibson	622,610
1926	4th	82	72	.532	7	Joe McCarthy	885,063
1927	4th	85	68	.556	8 1/2	Joe McCarthy	1,159,168
1928	3rd	91	63	.591	4	Joe McCarthy	1,143,740
1929	1st	98	54	.645	+10 1/2	Joe McCarthy	1,485,166
1930	2nd	90	64	.584	2	Joe McCarthy, Rogers Hornsby	1,463,624
1931	3rd	84	70	.545	17	Rogers Hornsby	1,086,422
1932	1st	90	64	.584	+4	Rogers Hornsby, Charlie Grimm	974,688
1933	3rd	86	68	.558	6	Charlie Grimm	594,112
1934	3rd	86	65	.570	8	Charlie Grimm	707,525
1935	1st	100	54	.649	+4	Charlie Grimm	692,604
1936	2nd (tied)	87	67	.565	5	Charlie Grimm	699,370
1937	2nd	93	61	.604	3	Charlie Grimm	895,020
1938	1st	89	63	.586	+2	Charlie Grimm, Gabby Hartnett	951,640

Year	Position	W	L	Pct.	*GB	Manager	Attendance
1939	4th	84	70	.545	13	Gabby Hartnett	726,663
1940	5th	75	79	.487	25 1/2	Gabby Hartnett	534,878
1941	6th	70	84	.455	30	Jimmy Wilson	545,159
1942	6th	68	86	.442	38	Jimmy Wilson	590,872
1943	5th	74	79	.484	30 1/2	Jimmy Wilson	508,247
1944	4th	75	79	.487	30	Jimmy Wilson, Charlie Grimm	640,110
1945	1st	98	56	.636	+3	Charlie Grimm	1,036,386
1946	3rd	82	71	.536	14 1/2	Charlie Grimm	1,342,970
1947	6th	69	85	.448	25	Charlie Grimm	1,364,039
1948	8th	64	90	.416	27 1/2	Charlie Grimm	1,237,792
1949	8th	61	93	.396	36	Charlie Grimm, Frankie Frisch	1,143,139
1950	7th	64	89	.418	26 1/2	Frankie Frisch	1,165,944
1951	8th	62	92	.403	34 1/2	Frankie Frisch, Phil Cavarretta	894,415
1952	5th	77	77	.500	19 1/2	Phil Cavarretta	1,024,826
1953	7th	65	89	.422	40	Phil Cavarretta	763,658
1954	7th	64	90	.416	33	Stan Hack	748,183
1955	6th	72	81	.471	26	Stan Hack	875,800
1956	8th	60	94	.390	33	Stan Hack	720,118
1957	7th (tied)	62	92	.403	33	Bob Scheffing	670,629
1958	5th (tied)	72	82	.468	20	Bob Scheffing	979,904
1959	5th (tied)	74	80	.481	13	Bob Scheffing	858,255
1960	7th	60	94	.390	35	Charlie Grimm, Lou Boudreau	809,770
1961	7th	64	90	.416	29	Vedie Himsl, Harry Craft, Elvin Tappe, Lou Klein	673,057
1962	9th	59	103	.364	42 1/2	Charlie Metro, Elvin Tappe, Lou Klein	609,802
1963	7th	82	80	.506	17	Bob Kennedy	979,551
1964	8th	76	86	.469	17	Bob Kennedy	751,647
1965	8th	72	90	.444	25	Bob Kennedy, Lou Klein	641,361
1966	10th	59	103	.364	36	Leo Durocher	635,891
1967	3rd	87	74	.540	14	Leo Durocher	977,226
1968	3rd	84	78	.519	13	Leo Durocher	1,043,409

EAST DIVISION

Year	Position	W	L	Pct.	*GB	Manager	Attendance
1969	2nd	92	70	.568	8	Leo Durocher	1,674,993
1970	2nd	84	78	.519	5	Leo Durocher	1,642,705
1971	3rd (tied)	83	79	.512	14	Leo Durocher	1,653,007
1972	2nd	85	70	.548	11	Leo Durocher, Whitey Lockman	1,299,163
1973	5th	77	84	.478	5	Whitey Lockman	1,351,705
1974	6th	66	96	.407	22	Whitey Lockman, Jim Marshall	1,015,378
1975	5th (tied)	75	87	.463	17 1/2	Jim Marshall	1,034,819
1976	4th	75	87	.463	26	Jim Marshall	1,026,217
1977	4th	81	81	.500	20	Herman Franks	1,439,834
1978	3rd	79	83	.488	11	Herman Franks	1,525,311
1979	5th	80	82	.494	18	Herman Franks, Joe Amalfitano	1,648,587
1980	6th	64	98	.395	27	Preston Gomez, Joe Amalfitano	1,206,776
1981	6th/5th	38	65	.369	†	Joe Amalfitano	565,637
1982	5th	73	89	.451	19	Lee Elia	1,249,278
1983	5th	71	91	.438	19	Lee Elia, Charlie Fox	1,479,717
1984	1st‡	96	65	.596	+6 1/2	Jim Frey	2,104,219
1985	4th	77	84	.478	23 1/2	Jim Frey	2,161,534
1986	5th	70	90	.438	37	Jim Frey, John Vukovich, Gene Michael	1,859,102
1987	6th	76	85	.472	18 1/2	Gene Michael, Frank Lucchesi	2,035,130
1988	4th	77	85	.475	24	Don Zimmer	2,089,034
1989	1st‡	93	69	.574	+6	Don Zimmer	2,491,942
1990	4th	77	85	.475	18	Don Zimmer	2,243,791
1991	4th	77	83	.481	20	Don Zimmer, Joe Altobelli, Jim Essian	2,314,250
1992	4th	78	84	.481	18	Jim Lefebvre	2,126,720
1993	4th	84	78	.519	13	Jim Lefebvre	2,653,763

CENTRAL DIVISION

Year	Position	W	L	Pct.	*GB	Manager	Attendance
1994	5th	49	64	.434	16 1/2	Tom Trebelhorn	1,845,208
1995	3rd	73	71	.507	12	Jim Riggleman	1,918,265

*Games behind winner. †First half 15-37; second half 23-28. ‡Lost championship series.

MANAGERIAL RECORDS

Joe Amalfitano 66-116, Lou Boudreau 54-83, Roger Bresnahan 73-80, Phil Cavarretta 169-213, Frank Chance 753-379, Harry Craft 7-9, Leo Durocher 535-526, Lee Elia 127-158, Jim Essian 59-63, Johnny Evers 130-121, Charlie Fox 17-22, Herman Franks 238-241, Jim Frey 196-182, Frank Frisch 141-196, George Gibson 12-14, Preston Gomez 38-52, Charlie Grimm 946-784, Stan Hack 196-265, Gabby Hartnett 203-176, Vedie Himsl 10-21, Rogers Hornsby 141-114, Roy Johnson 0-1, Bob Kennedy 182-198, Bill Killefer 299-292, Lou Klein 65-83, Jim Lefebvre 162-162, Whitey Lockman 157-162, Tom Loftus 53-86, Frank Lucchesi 8-17, Rabbit Maranville 23-30, Jim Marshall 175-218, Joe McCarthy 442-321, Charlie Metro 43-69, Gene Michael 114-124, Fred Mitchell 308-269, Hank O'Day 78-76, Jim Riggleman 73-71, Bob Scheffing 208-254, Frank Selee 295-223, Elvin Tappe 46-69, Joe Tinker 67-86, Tom Trebelhorn 49-64, John Vukovich 1-1, Jimmy Wilson 213-258, Don Zimmer 265-259.

CINCINNATI REDS

YEARLY FINISHES

Year	Position	W	L	Pct.	*GB	Manager	Attendance
1901	8th	52	87	.374	38	Bid McPhee	205,728
1902	4th	70	70	.500	33 1/2	Bid McPhee, Frank Bancroft, Joe Kelley	217,300
1903	4th	74	65	.532	16 1/2	Joe Kelley	351,680
1904	3rd	88	65	.575	18	Joe Kelley	391,915
1905	5th	79	74	.516	26	Joe Kelley	313,927
1906	6th	64	87	.424	51 1/2	Ned Hanlon	330,056
1907	6th	66	87	.431	41 1/2	Ned Hanlon	317,500
1908	5th	73	81	.474	26	John Ganzel	399,200
1909	4th	77	76	.503	33 1/2	Clark Griffith	424,643
1910	5th	75	79	.487	29	Clark Griffith	380,622
1911	6th	70	83	.458	29	Clark Griffith	300,000
1912	4th	75	78	.490	29	Hank O'Day	344,000
1913	7th	64	89	.418	37 1/2	Joe Tinker	258,000
1914	8th	60	94	.390	34 1/2	Buck Herzog	100,791
1915	7th	71	83	.461	*20	Buck Herzog	218,878
1916	7th (tied)	60	93	.392	33 1/2	Buck Herzog, Christy Mathewson	255,846
1917	4th	78	76	.506	20	Christy Mathewson	269,056
1918	3rd	68	60	.531	15 1/2	Christy Mathewson, Heinie Groh	163,009
1919	1st	96	44	.686	+9	Pat Moran	532,501
1920	3rd	82	71	.536	10 1/2	Pat Moran	568,107
1921	6th	70	83	.458	24	Pat Moran	311,227
1922	2nd	86	68	.558	7	Pat Moran	493,754
1923	2nd	91	63	.591	4 1/2	Pat Moran	575,063
1924	4th	83	70	.542	10	Jack Hendricks	437,707
1925	3rd	80	73	.523	15	Jack Hendricks	464,920
1926	2nd	87	67	.565	2	Jack Hendricks	672,987
1927	5th	75	78	.490	18 1/2	Jack Hendricks	442,164
1928	5th	78	74	.513	16	Jack Hendricks	490,490
1929	7th	66	88	.429	33	Jack Hendricks	295,040
1930	7th	59	95	.383	33	Dan Howley	386,727
1931	8th	58	96	.377	43	Dan Howley	263,316
1932	8th	60	94	.390	30	Dan Howley	356,950
1933	8th	58	94	.382	33	Donie Bush	218,281
1934	8th	52	99	.344	42	Bob O'Farrell, Chuck Dressen	206,773
1935	6th	68	85	.444	31 1/2	Chuck Dressen	448,247
1936	5th	74	80	.481	18	Chuck Dressen	466,245
1937	8th	56	98	.364	40	Chuck Dressen, Bobby Wallace	411,221
1938	4th	82	68	.547	6	Bill McKechnie	706,756
1939	1st	97	57	.630	+4 1/2	Bill McKechnie	981,443
1940	1st	100	53	.654	+12	Bill McKechnie	850,180
1941	3rd	88	66	.571	12	Bill McKechnie	643,513
1942	4th	76	76	.500	29	Bill McKechnie	427,031
1943	2nd	87	67	.565	18	Bill McKechnie	379,122
1944	3rd	89	65	.578	16	Bill McKechnie	409,567
1945	7th	61	93	.396	37	Bill McKechnie	290,070
1946	6th	67	87	.435	30	Bill McKechnie	715,751
1947	5th	73	81	.474	21	Johnny Neun	899,975
1948	7th	64	89	.418	27	Johnny Neun, Bucky Walters	823,386
1949	7th	62	92	.403	35	Bucky Walters	707,782
1950	6th	66	87	.431	24 1/2	Luke Sewell	538,794
1951	6th	68	86	.442	28 1/2	Luke Sewell	588,268
1952	6th	69	85	.448	27 1/2	Luke Sewell, Rogers Hornsby	604,197
1953	6th	68	86	.442	37	Rogers Hornsby, Buster Mills	548,086
1954	5th	74	80	.481	23	Birdie Tebbetts	704,167
1955	5th	75	79	.487	23 1/2	Birdie Tebbetts	693,662
1956	3rd	91	63	.591	2	Birdie Tebbetts	1,125,928
1957	4th	80	74	.519	15	Birdie Tebbetts	1,070,850
1958	4th	76	78	.494	16	Birdie Tebbetts, Jimmie Dykes	788,582
1959	5th (tied)	74	80	.481	13	Mayo Smith, Fred Hutchinson	801,289
1960	6th	67	87	.435	28	Fred Hutchinson	663,486
1961	1st	93	61	.604	+4	Fred Hutchinson	1,117,603
1962	3rd	98	64	.605	3 1/2	Fred Hutchinson	982,085
1963	5th	86	76	.531	13	Fred Hutchinson	858,805
1964	2nd (tied)	92	70	.549	1	Fred Hutchinson, Dick Sisler	862,466
1965	4th	89	73	.549	8	Dick Sisler	1,047,824
1966	7th	76	84	.475	18	Don Heffner, Dave Bristol	742,958
1967	4th	87	75	.537	14 1/2	Dave Bristol	958,300
1968	4th	83	79	.512	14	Dave Bristol	733,354

WEST DIVISION

Year	Position	W	L	Pct.	*GB	Manager	Attendance
1969	3rd	89	73	.549	4	Dave Bristol	987,991
1970	1st†	102	60	.630	+14 1/2	Sparky Anderson	1,803,568
1971	4th (tied)	79	83	.488	11	Sparky Anderson	1,501,122
1972	1st†	95	59	.617	+10 1/2	Sparky Anderson	1,611,459
1973	1st‡	99	63	.611	+3 1/2	Sparky Anderson	2,017,601
1974	2nd	98	64	.605	4	Sparky Anderson	2,164,307
1975	1st†	108	54	.667	+20	Sparky Anderson	2,315,603
1976	1st†	102	60	.630	+10	Sparky Anderson	2,629,708
1977	2nd	88	74	.543	10	Sparky Anderson	2,519,670
1978	2nd	92	69	.571	2 1/2	Sparky Anderson	2,532,497
1979	1st‡	90	71	.559	+1 1/2	John McNamara	2,356,933
1980	3rd	89	73	.549	3 1/2	John McNamara	2,022,450
1981	2nd/2nd	66	42	.611	§	John McNamara	1,093,730
1982	6th	61	101	.377	28	John McNamara, Russ Nixon	1,326,528
1983	6th	74	88	.457	17	Russ Nixon	1,190,419
1984	5th	70	92	.432	22	Vern Rapp, Pete Rose	1,275,887
1985	2nd	89	72	.553	5 1/2	Pete Rose	1,834,619
1986	2nd	86	76	.531	10	Pete Rose	1,692,432
1987	2nd	84	78	.519	6	Pete Rose	2,185,205
1988	2nd	87	74	.540	7	Pete Rose	2,072,528
1989	5th	75	87	.463	17	Pete Rose, Tommy Helms	1,979,320
1990	1st†	91	71	.562	+5	Lou Piniella	2,400,892
1991	5th	74	88	.457	20	Lou Piniella	2,372,377
1992	2nd	90	72	.556	8	Lou Piniella	2,315,946
1993	5th	73	89	.451	31	Tony Perez, Dave Johnson	2,453,232

CENTRAL DIVISION

Year	Position	W	L	Pct.	*GB	Manager	Attendance
1994	1st	66	48	.579	+ 1/2	Dave Johnson	1,897,681
1995	1st∞‡	85	59	.590	+9	Dave Johnson	1,837,649

*Games behind winner. †Won championship series. ‡Lost championship series. §First half 35-21; second half 31-21. ∞Won division series.

MANAGERIAL RECORDS

Sparky Anderson 863-586, Frank Bancroft 9-7, Dave Bristol 298-265, Donie Bush 58-94, Chuck Dressen 214-282, Jimmie Dykes 24-17, John Ganzel 73-81, Clark Griffith 222-238, Heinie Groh 7-3, Ned Hanlon 130-174, Don Heffner 37-46, Tommy Helms 14-21, Jack Hendricks 469-450, Buck Herzog 165-226, Rogers Hornsby 91-106, Dan Howley 177-285, Fred Hutchinson 443-372, Dave Johnson 204-172, Joe Kelley 275-230, Christy Mathewson 164-176, Bill McKechnie 747-632, John McNamara 279-244, Bid McPhee 79-124, Buster Mills 4-4, Pat Moran 425-329, Johnny Neun 117-137, Russ Nixon 101-131, Hank O'Day 75-78, Bob O'Farrell 30-60, Tony Perez 20-24, Lou Piniella 255-231, Vern Rapp 51-70, Pete Rose 426-388, Luke Sewell 176-234, Dick Sisler 121-94, Mayo Smith 35-45, Birdie Tebbetts 372-357, Joe Tinker 64-89, Bobby Wallace 5-20, Bucky Walters 81-123.

COLORADO ROCKIES

YEARLY FINISHES

WEST DIVISION

Year	Position	W	L	Pct.	*GB	Manager	Attendance
1993	6th	67	95	.414	37	Don Baylor	4,483,350
1994	3rd	53	64	.453	6 1/2	Don Baylor	3,281,511
1995	2nd†	77	67	.535	1	Don Baylor	3,390,037

*Games behind winner. †Lost division series.

MANAGERIAL RECORDS

Don Baylor 197-226.

FLORIDA MARLINS

YEARLY FINISHES

EAST DIVISION

Year	Position	W	L	Pct.	*GB	Manager	Attendance
1993	6th	64	98	.395	33	Rene Lachemann	3,064,847
1994	5th	51	64	.443	23 1/2	Rene Lachemann	1,937,467
1995	4th	67	76	.469	22 1/2	Rene Lachemann	1,700,466

*Games behind winner.

MANAGERIAL RECORDS

Rene Lachemann 182-238.

HOUSTON ASTROS

YEARLY FINISHES

Year	Position	W	L	Pct.	*GB	Manager	Attendance
1962†	8th	64	96	.400	36 1/2	Harry Craft	924,456
1963†	9th	66	96	.407	33	Harry Craft	719,502
1964†	9th	66	96	.407	27	Harry Craft, Luman Harris	725,773
1965	9th	65	97	.401	32	Luman Harris	2,151,470
1966	8th	72	90	.444	23	Grady Hatton	1,872,108
1967	9th	69	93	.426	32 1/2	Grady Hatton	1,348,303
1968	10th	72	90	.444	25	Grady Hatton, Harry Walker	1,312,887

WEST DIVISION

Year	Position	W	L	Pct.	*GB	Manager	Attendance
1969	5th	81	81	.500	12	Harry Walker	1,442,995
1970	4th	79	83	.488	23	Harry Walker	1,253,444
1971	4th (tied)	79	83	.488	11	Harry Walker	1,261,589
1972	2nd	84	69	.549	10 1/2	Harry Walker, Leo Durocher, Salty Parker	1,469,247
1973	4th	82	80	.506	17	Leo Durocher, Preston Gomez	1,394,004
1974	4th	81	81	.500	21	Preston Gomez	1,090,728
1975	6th	64	97	.398	43 1/2	Preston Gomez, Bill Virdon	858,002
1976	3rd	80	82	.494	22	Bill Virdon	886,146
1977	3rd	81	81	.500	17	Bill Virdon	1,109,560
1978	5th	74	88	.457	21	Bill Virdon	1,126,145
1979	2nd	89	73	.549	1 1/2	Bill Virdon	1,900,312
1980	1st‡§	93	70	.571	+1	Bill Virdon	2,278,217
1981	3rd/1st▲	61	49	.555	∞	Bill Virdon	1,321,282
1982	5th	77	85	.475	12	Bill Virdon, Bob Lillis	1,558,555
1983	3rd	85	77	.525	6	Bob Lillis	1,351,962
1984	2nd (tied)	80	82	.494	12	Bob Lillis	1,229,862
1985	3rd (tied)	83	79	.512	12	Bob Lillis	1,184,314
1986	1st§	96	66	.593	+10	Hal Lanier	1,734,276
1987	3rd	76	86	.469	14	Hal Lanier	1,909,902
1988	5th	82	80	.506	12 1/2	Hal Lanier	1,933,505
1989	3rd	86	76	.531	6	Art Howe	1,834,908
1990	4th (tied)	75	87	.463	16	Art Howe	1,310,927
1991	6th	65	97	.401	29	Art Howe	1,196,152
1992	4th	81	81	.500	17	Art Howe	1,211,412
1993	3rd	85	77	.525	19	Art Howe	2,084,546

CENTRAL DIVISION

Year	Position	W	L	Pct.	*GB	Manager	Attendance
1994	2nd	66	49	.574	1/2	Art Howe	1,561,136
1995	2nd	76	68	.528	9	Terry Collins	1,363,801

*Games behind winner. †Houston Colt .45s. ‡Won division playoff. §Lost championship series. ∞First half 28-29; second half 33-20. ▲Lost division series.

MANAGERIAL RECORDS

Terry Collins 142-117, Harry Craft 191-280, Leo Durocher 98-95, Preston Gomez 128-161, Lum Harris 70-105, Grady Hatton 164-221, Art Howe 392-418, Hal Lanier 254-232, Bob Lillis 276-261, Bill Virdon 544-522, Harry Walker 355-353.

LOS ANGELES DODGERS

YEARLY FINISHES

Year	Position	W	L	Pct.	*GB	Manager	Attendance
1901†	3rd	79	57	.581	9 1/2	Ned Hanlon	189,200
1902†	2nd	75	63	.543	27 1/2	Ned Hanlon	199,868
1903†	5th	70	66	.515	19	Ned Hanlon	224,670
1904†	6th	56	97	.366	50	Ned Hanlon	214,600
1905†	8th	48	104	.316	56 1/2	Ned Hanlon	227,924
1906†	5th	66	86	.434	50	Patsy Donovan	227,400
1907†	5th	65	83	.439	40	Patsy Donovan	312,500
1908†	7th	53	101	.344	46	Patsy Donovan	275,600
1909†	6th	55	98	.359	55 1/2	Harry Lumley	321,300
1910†	6th	64	90	.416	40	Bill Dahlen	279,321
1911†	7th	64	86	.427	33 1/2	Bill Dahlen	269,000
1912†	7th	58	95	.379	46	Bill Dahlen	243,000
1913†	6th	65	84	.436	34 1/2	Bill Dahlen	347,000
1914†	5th	75	79	.487	19 1/2	Wilbert Robinson	122,671
1915†	3rd	80	72	.526	10	Wilbert Robinson	297,766
1916†	1st	94	60	.610	+2 1/2	Wilbert Robinson	447,747
1917†	7th	70	81	.464	26 1/2	Wilbert Robinson	221,619
1918†	5th	57	69	.452	25 1/2	Wilbert Robinson	83,831

Year	Position	W	L	Pct.	*GB	Manager	Attendance
1919†	5th	69	71	.493	27	Wilbert Robinson	360,721
1920†	1st	93	61	.604	+7	Wilbert Robinson	808,722
1921†	5th	77	75	.507	16 1/2	Wilbert Robinson	613,245
1922†	6th	76	78	.494	17	Wilbert Robinson	498,856
1923†	6th	76	78	.494	19 1/2	Wilbert Robinson	564,666
1924†	2nd	92	62	.597	1 1/2	Wilbert Robinson	818,883
1925†	6th (tied)	68	85	.444	27	Wilbert Robinson	659,435
1926†	6th	71	82	.464	17 1/2	Wilbert Robinson	650,819
1927†	6th	65	88	.425	28 1/2	Wilbert Robinson	637,230
1928†	6th	77	76	.503	17 1/2	Wilbert Robinson	664,863
1929†	6th	70	83	.458	28 1/2	Wilbert Robinson	731,886
1930†	4th	86	68	.558	6	Wilbert Robinson	1,097,339
1931†	4th	79	73	.520	21	Wilbert Robinson	753,133
1932†	3rd	81	73	.526	9	Max Carey	681,827
1933†	6th	65	88	.425	26 1/2	Max Carey	526,815
1934†	6th	71	81	.467	23 1/2	Casey Stengel	434,188
1935†	5th	70	83	.458	29 1/2	Casey Stengel	470,517
1936†	7th	67	87	.435	25	Casey Stengel	489,618
1937†	6th	62	91	.405	33 1/2	Burleigh Grimes	482,481
1938†	7th	69	80	.463	18 1/2	Burleigh Grimes	663,087
1939†	3rd	84	69	.549	12 1/2	Leo Durocher	955,668
1940†	2nd	88	65	.575	12	Leo Durocher	975,978
1941†	1st	100	54	.649	+2 1/2	Leo Durocher	1,214,910
1942†	2nd	104	50	.675	2	Leo Durocher	1,037,765
1943†	3rd	81	72	.529	23 1/2	Leo Durocher	661,739
1944†	7th	63	91	.409	42	Leo Durocher	605,905
1945†	3rd	87	67	.565	11	Leo Durocher	1,059,220
1946†	2nd‡	96	60	.615	2	Leo Durocher	1,796,824
1947†	1st	94	60	.610	+5	Clyde Sukeforth, Burt Shotton	1,807,526
1948†	3rd	84	70	.545	7 1/2	Leo Durocher, Burt Shotton	1,398,967
1949†	1st	97	57	.630	+1	Burt Shotton	1,633,747
1950†	2nd	89	65	.578	2	Burt Shotton	1,185,896
1951†	2nd‡	97	60	.618	1	Chuck Dressen	1,282,628
1952†	1st	96	57	.627	+4 1/2	Chuck Dressen	1,088,704
1953†	1st	105	49	.682	+13	Chuck Dressen	1,163,419
1954†	2nd	92	62	.597	5	Walter Alston	1,020,531
1955†	1st	98	55	.641	+13 1/2	Walter Alston	1,033,589
1956†	1st	93	61	.604	+1	Walter Alston	1,213,562
1957†	3rd	84	70	.545	11	Walter Alston	1,028,258
1958	7th	71	83	.461	21	Walter Alston	1,845,556
1959	1st§	88	68	.564	+2	Walter Alston	2,071,045
1960	4th	82	72	.532	13	Walter Alston	2,253,887
1961	2nd	89	65	.578	4	Walter Alston	1,804,250
1962	2nd‡	102	63	.618	1	Walter Alston	2,755,184
1963	1st	99	63	.611	+6	Walter Alston	2,538,602
1964	6th (tied)	80	82	.494	13	Walter Alston	2,228,751
1965	1st	97	65	.599	+2	Walter Alston	2,553,577
1966	1st	95	67	.586	+1 1/2	Walter Alston	2,617,029
1967	8th	73	89	.451	28 1/2	Walter Alston	1,664,362
1968	7th	76	86	.469	21	Walter Alston	1,581,093

WEST DIVISION

Year	Position	W	L	Pct.	*GB	Manager	Attendance
1969	4th	85	77	.525	8	Walter Alston	1,784,527
1970	2nd	87	74	.540	14 1/2	Walter Alston	1,697,142
1971	2nd	89	73	.549	1	Walter Alston	2,064,594
1972	3rd	85	70	.548	10 1/2	Walter Alston	1,860,858
1973	2nd	95	66	.590	3 1/2	Walter Alston	2,136,192
1974	1st∞	102	60	.630	+4	Walter Alston	2,632,474
1975	2nd	88	74	.543	20	Walter Alston	2,539,349
1976	2nd	92	70	.568	10	Walter Alston, Tommy Lasorda	2,386,301
1977	1st∞	98	64	.605	+10	Tommy Lasorda	2,955,087
1978	1st∞	95	67	.586	+2 1/2	Tommy Lasorda	3,347,845
1979	3rd	79	83	.488	11 1/2	Tommy Lasorda	2,860,954
1980	2nd▲	92	71	.564	1	Tommy Lasorda	3,249,287
1981	1st/4th§∞	63	47	.573	◆	Tommy Lasorda	2,381,292
1982	2nd	88	74	.543	1	Tommy Lasorda	3,608,881
1983	1st▼	91	71	.652	+3	Tommy Lasorda	3,510,313
1984	4th	79	83	.488	13	Tommy Lasorda	3,134,824
1985	1st▼	95	67	.586	+5 1/2	Tommy Lasorda	3,264,593
1986	5th	73	89	.451	23	Tommy Lasorda	3,023,208
1987	4th	73	89	.451	17	Tommy Lasorda	2,797,409
1988	1st∞	94	67	.584	+7	Tommy Lasorda	2,980,262
1989	4th	77	83	.481	14	Tommy Lasorda	2,944,653
1990	2nd	86	76	.531	5	Tommy Lasorda	3,002,396

Year	Position	W	L	Pct.	*GB	Manager	Attendance
1991	2nd	93	69	.574	1	Tommy Lasorda	3,348,170
1992	6th	63	99	.389	35	Tommy Lasorda	2,473,266
1993	4th	81	81	.500	23	Tommy Lasorda	3,170,392
1994	1st	58	56	.509	+3 1/2	Tommy Lasorda	2,279,355
1995	1st	78	66	.542	+1	Tommy Lasorda	2,766,251

*Games behind winner. †Brooklyn Dodgers. ‡Lost pennant playoff. §Won pennant playoff. ∞Won championship series. ▲Lost division playoff. ◆First half 36-21; second half 27-26. ■Won division series. ▼Lost championship series.

MANAGERIAL RECORDS

Walter Alston 2,040-1,613, Max Carey 146-161, Bill Dahlen 251-355, Patsy Donovan 184-270, Chuck Dressen 298-166, Leo Durocher 738-565, Burleigh Grimes 131-171, Ned Hanlon 328-387, Tommy Lasorda 1,558-1,404, Harry Lumley 55-98, Wilbert Robinson 1,375-1,341, Burt Shotton 326-215, Casey Stengel 208-251, Clyde Sukeforth 2-0.

MONTREAL EXPOS

YEARLY FINISHES

EAST DIVISION

Year	Position	W	L	Pct.	*GB	Manager	Attendance
1969	6th	52	110	.321	48	Gene Mauch	1,212,608
1970	6th	73	89	.451	16	Gene Mauch	1,424,683
1971	5th	71	90	.441	25 1/2	Gene Mauch	1,290,963
1972	5th	70	86	.449	26 1/2	Gene Mauch	1,142,145
1973	4th	79	83	.488	3 1/2	Gene Mauch	1,246,863
1974	4th	79	82	.491	8 1/2	Gene Mauch	1,019,134
1975	5th (tied)	75	87	.463	17 1/2	Gene Mauch	908,292
1976	6th	55	107	.340	46	Karl Kuehl, Charlie Fox	646,704
1977	5th	75	87	.463	26	Dick Williams	1,433,757
1978	4th	76	86	.469	14	Dick Williams	1,427,007
1979	2nd	95	65	.594	2	Dick Williams	2,102,173
1980	2nd	90	72	.556	1	Dick Williams	2,208,175
1981	3rd/1st‡§	60	48	.556	†	Dick Williams, Jim Fanning	1,534,564
1982	3rd	86	76	.531	6	Jim Fanning	2,318,292
1983	3rd	82	80	.506	8	Bill Virdon	2,320,651
1984	5th	78	83	.484	18	Bill Virdon, Jim Fanning	1,606,531
1985	3rd	84	77	.522	16 1/2	Buck Rodgers	1,502,494
1986	4th	78	83	.484	29 1/2	Buck Rodgers	1,128,981
1987	3rd	91	71	.562	4	Buck Rodgers	1,850,324
1988	3rd	81	81	.500	20	Buck Rodgers	1,478,659
1989	4th	81	81	.500	12	Buck Rodgers	1,783,533
1990	3rd	85	77	.525	10	Buck Rodgers	1,373,087
1991	6th	71	90	.441	26 1/2	Buck Rodgers, Tom Runnells	934,742
1992	2nd	87	75	.537	9	Tom Runnells, Felipe Alou	1,669,077
1993	2nd	94	68	.580	3	Felipe Alou	1,641,437
1994	1st	74	40	.649	+6	Felipe Alou	1,276,250
1995	5th	66	78	.458	24	Felipe Alou	1,309,618

*Games behind winner. †First half 30-25; second half 30-23. ‡Won division series. §Lost championship series.

MANAGERIAL RECORDS

Felipe Alou 304-241, Jim Fanning 116-103, Charlie Fox 12-22, Karl Kuehl 43-85, Gene Mauch 499-627, Buck Rodgers 520-499, Tom Runnells 68-81, Bill Virdon 146-147, Dick Williams 380-347.

NEW YORK METS

YEARLY FINISHES

Year	Position	W	L	Pct.	*GB	Manager	Attendance
1962	10th	40	120	.250	60 1/2	Casey Stengel	922,530
1963	10th	51	111	.315	48	Casey Stengel	1,080,108
1964	10th	53	109	.327	40	Casey Stengel	1,732,597
1965	10th	50	112	.309	47	Casey Stengel, Wes Westrum	1,768,389
1966	9th	66	95	.410	28 1/2	Wes Westrum	1,932,693
1967	10th	61	101	.377	40 1/2	Wes Westrum, Salty Parker	1,565,492
1968	9th	73	89	.451	24	Gil Hodges	1,781,657

EAST DIVISION

Year	Position	W	L	Pct.	*GB	Manager	Attendance
1969	1st†	100	62	.617	+8	Gil Hodges	2,175,373
1970	3rd	83	79	.512	6	Gil Hodges	2,697,479
1971	3rd (tied)	83	79	.512	14	Gil Hodges	2,266,680
1972	3rd	83	73	.532	13 1/2	Yogi Berra	2,134,185
1973	1st†	82	79	.509	+1 1/2	Yogi Berra	1,912,390
1974	5th	71	91	.438	17	Yogi Berra	1,722,209

Year	Position	W	L	Pct.	*GB	Manager	Attendance
1975	3rd (tied)	82	80	.506	10 1/2	Yogi Berra, Roy McMillan	1,730,566
1976	3rd	86	76	.531	15	Joe Frazier	1,468,754
1977	6th	64	98	.395	37	Joe Frazier, Joe Torre	1,066,825
1978	6th	66	96	.407	24	Joe Torre	1,007,328
1979	6th	63	99	.389	35	Joe Torre	788,905
1980	5th	67	95	.414	24	Joe Torre	1,192,073
1981	5th/4th	41	62	.398	‡	Joe Torre	704,244
1982	6th	65	97	.401	27	George Bamberger	1,323,036
1983	6th	68	94	.420	22	George Bamberger, Frank Howard	1,112,774
1984	2nd	90	72	.556	6 1/2	Dave Johnson	1,842,695
1985	2nd	98	64	.605	3	Dave Johnson	2,761,601
1986	1st†	108	54	.667	+21 1/2	Dave Johnson	2,767,601
1987	2nd	92	70	.568	3	Dave Johnson	3,034,129
1988	1st§	100	60	.625	+15	Dave Johnson	3,055,445
1989	2nd	87	75	.537	6	Dave Johnson	2,918,710
1990	2nd	91	71	.562	4	Dave Johnson, Bud Harrelson	2,732,745
1991	5th	77	84	.478	20 1/2	Bud Harrelson, Mike Cubbage	2,284,484
1992	5th	72	90	.444	24	Jeff Torborg	1,779,534
1993	7th	59	103	.364	38	Jeff Torborg, Dallas Green	1,873,183
1994	3rd	55	58	.487	18 1/2	Dallas Green	1,151,471
1995	2nd (tied)	69	75	.479	21	Dallas Green	1,273,183

*Games behind winner. †Won championship series. ‡First half 17-34; second half 24-28. §Lost championship series.

MANAGERIAL RECORDS

George Bamberger 81-127, Yogi Berra 292-296, Mike Cubbage 3-4, Joe Frazier 101-106, Dallas Green 170-211, Bud Harrelson 145-129, Gil Hodges 339-309, Frank Howard 52-64, Davey Johnson 595-417, Roy McMillan 26-27, Salty Parker 4-7, Casey Stengel 175-404, Jeff Torborg 85-115, Joe Torre 286-420, Wes Westrum 142-237.

PHILADELPHIA PHILLIES

YEARLY FINISHES

Year	Position	W	L	Pct.	*GB	Manager	Attendance
1901	2nd	83	57	.593	7 1/2	Bill Shettsline	234,937
1902	7th	56	81	.409	46	Bill Shettsline	112,066
1903	7th	49	86	.363	39 1/2	Chief Zimmer	151,729
1904	8th	52	100	.342	53 1/2	Hugh Duffy	140,771
1905	4th	83	69	.546	21 1/2	Hugh Duffy	317,932
1906	4th	71	82	.464	45 1/2	Hugh Duffy	294,680
1907	3rd	83	64	.565	21 1/2	Bill Murray	341,216
1908	4th	83	71	.539	16	Bill Murray	420,660
1909	5th	74	79	.484	36 1/2	Bill Murray	303,177
1910	4th	78	75	.510	25 1/2	Red Dooin	296,597
1911	4th	79	73	.520	19 1/2	Red Dooin	416,000
1912	5th	73	79	.480	30 1/2	Red Dooin	250,000
1913	2nd	88	63	.583	12 1/2	Red Dooin	470,000
1914	6th	74	80	.481	20 1/2	Red Dooin	138,474
1915	1st	90	62	.592	+7	Pat Moran	449,898
1916	2nd	91	62	.595	2 1/2	Pat Moran	515,365
1917	2nd	87	65	.572	10	Pat Moran	354,428
1918	6th	55	68	.447	26	Pat Moran	122,266
1919	8th	47	90	.343	47 1/2	Jack Coombs, Gavvy Cravath	240,424
1920	8th	62	91	.405	30 1/2	Gavvy Cravath	330,998
1921	8th	51	103	.331	43 1/2	Bill Donovan, Kaiser Wilhelm	273,961
1922	7th	57	96	.373	35 1/2	Kaiser Wilhelm	232,471
1923	8th	50	104	.325	45 1/2	Art Fletcher	228,168
1924	7th	55	96	.364	37	Art Fletcher	299,818
1925	6th (tied)	68	85	.444	27	Art Fletcher	304,905
1926	8th	58	93	.384	29 1/2	Art Fletcher	240,600
1927	8th	51	103	.331	43	Stuffy McInnis	305,420
1928	8th	43	109	.283	51	Burt Shotton	182,168
1929	5th	71	82	.464	27 1/2	Burt Shotton	281,200
1930	8th	52	102	.338	40	Burt Shotton	299,007
1931	6th	66	88	.429	35	Burt Shotton	284,849
1932	4th	78	76	.506	12	Burt Shotton	268,914
1933	7th	60	92	.395	31	Burt Shotton	156,421
1934	7th	56	93	.376	37	Jimmy Wilson	169,885
1935	7th	64	89	.418	35 1/2	Jimmy Wilson	205,470
1936	8th	54	100	.351	38	Jimmy Wilson	249,219
1937	7th	61	92	.399	34 1/2	Jimmy Wilson	212,790
1938	8th	45	105	.300	43	Jimmy Wilson, Hans Lobert	166,111
1939	8th	45	106	.298	50 1/2	Doc Prothro	277,973
1940	8th	50	103	.327	50	Doc Prothro	207,177
1941	8th	43	111	.279	57	Doc Prothro	231,401
1942	8th	42	109	.278	62 1/2	Hans Lobert	230,183

Year	Position	W	L	Pct.	*GB	Manager	Attendance
1943	7th	64	90	.416	41	Bucky Harris, Fred Fitzsimmons	466,975
1944	8th	61	92	.399	43 1/2	Fred Fitzsimmons	369,586
1945	8th	46	108	.299	52	Fred Fitzsimmons, Ben Chapman	285,057
1946	5th	69	85	.448	28	Ben Chapman	1,045,247
1947	7th (tied)	62	92	.403	32	Ben Chapman	907,332
1948	6th	66	88	.429	25 1/2	Ben Chapman, Dusty Cooke, Eddie Sawyer	767,429
1949	3rd	81	73	.526	16	Eddie Sawyer	819,698
1950	1st	91	63	.591	+2	Eddie Sawyer	1,217,035
1951	5th	73	81	.474	23 1/2	Eddie Sawyer	937,658
1952	4th	87	67	.565	9 1/2	Eddie Sawyer, Steve O'Neill	775,417
1953	3rd (tied)	83	71	.539	22	Steve O'Neill	853,644
1954	4th	75	79	.487	22	Steve O'Neill, Terry Moore	738,991
1955	4th	77	77	.500	21 1/2	Mayo Smith	922,886
1956	5th	71	83	.461	22	Mayo Smith	934,798
1957	5th	77	77	.500	19	Mayo Smith	1,146,230
1958	8th	69	85	.448	23	Mayo Smith, Eddie Sawyer	931,110
1959	8th	64	90	.416	23	Eddie Sawyer	802,815
1960	8th	59	95	.383	36	Eddie Sawyer, Andy Cohen, Gene Mauch	862,205
1961	8th	47	107	.305	46	Gene Mauch	590,039
1962	7th	81	80	.503	20	Gene Mauch	762,034
1963	4th	87	75	.537	12	Gene Mauch	907,141
1964	2nd (tied)	92	70	.568	1	Gene Mauch	1,425,891
1965	6th	85	76	.528	11 1/2	Gene Mauch	1,166,376
1966	4th	87	75	.537	8	Gene Mauch	1,108,201
1967	5th	82	80	.506	19 1/2	Gene Mauch	828,888
1968	7th (tied)	76	86	.469	21	Gene Mauch, George Myatt, Bob Skinner	664,546

EAST DIVISION

Year	Position	W	L	Pct.	*GB	Manager	Attendance
1969	5th	63	99	.389	37	Bob Skinner, George Myatt	519,414
1970	5th	73	88	.453	15 1/2	Frank Lucchesi	708,247
1971	6th	67	95	.414	30	Frank Lucchesi	1,511,223
1972	6th	59	97	.378	37 1/2	Frank Lucchesi, Paul Owens	1,343,329
1973	6th	71	91	.438	11 1/2	Danny Ozark	1,475,934
1974	3rd	80	82	.494	8	Danny Ozark	1,808,648
1975	2nd	86	76	.531	6 1/2	Danny Ozark	1,909,233
1976	1st†	101	61	.623	+9	Danny Ozark	2,480,150
1977	1st†	101	61	.623	+5	Danny Ozark	2,700,070
1978	1st†	90	72	.556	+1 1/2	Danny Ozark	2,583,389
1979	4th	84	78	.519	14	Danny Ozark, Dallas Green	2,775,011
1980	1st‡	91	71	.562	+1	Dallas Green	2,651,650
1981	1st/3rd∞	59	48	.551	§	Dallas Green	1,638,752
1982	2nd	89	73	.549	3	Pat Corrales	2,376,394
1983	1st‡	90	72	.556	+6	Pat Corrales, Paul Owens	2,128,339
1984	4th	81	81	.500	15 1/2	Paul Owens	2,062,693
1985	5th	75	87	.463	26	John Felske	1,830,350
1986	2nd	86	75	.534	21 1/2	John Felske	1,933,335
1987	4th (tied)	80	82	.494	15	John Felske, Lee Elia	2,100,110
1988	6th	65	96	.404	35 1/2	Lee Elia, John Vukovich	1,990,041
1989	6th	67	95	.414	26	Nick Leyva	1,861,985
1990	4th (tied)	77	85	.475	18	Nick Leyva	1,992,484
1991	3rd	78	84	.481	20	Nick Leyva, Jim Fregosi	2,050,012
1992	6th	70	92	.432	26	Jim Fregosi	1,927,448
1993	1st‡	97	65	.599	+3	Jim Fregosi	3,137,674
1994	4th	54	61	.470	20 1/2	Jim Fregosi	2,290,971
1995	2nd (tied)	69	75	.479	21	Jim Fregosi	2,043,598

*Games behind winner. †Lost championship series. ‡Won championship series. §First half 34-21; second half 25-27. ∞Lost division series.

MANAGERIAL RECORDS

Ben Chapman 197-277, Andy Cohen 1-0, Dusty Cooke 6-6, Jack Coombs 18-44, Pat Corrales 132-115, Gavvy Cravath 91-137, Bill Donovan 31-71, Red Dooin 392-370, Hugh Duffy 206-251, Lee Elia 111-142, John Felske 190-194, Fred Fitzsimmons 102-179, Art Fletcher 231-378, Jim Fregosi 364-368, Dallas Green 169-130, Bucky Harris 40-53, Nick Leyva 148-189, Hans Lobert 42-111, Frank Lucchesi 166-233, Gene Mauch 645-684, Stuffy McInnis 51-103, Terry Moore 35-42, Pat Moran 323-257, Bill Murray 240-214, George Myatt 21-35, Steve O'Neill 182-140, Paul Owens 161-158, Danny Ozark 594-510, Doc Prothro 138-320, Eddie Sawyer 390-424, Bill Shettsline 139-138, Burt Shotton 370-549, Bob Skinner 92-123, Mayo Smith 264-281, John Vukovich 5-4, Kaiser Wilhelm 77-128, Jimmy Wilson 280-477, Chief Zimmer 49-86.

PITTSBURGH PIRATES

YEARLY FINISHES

Year	Position	W	L	Pct.	*GB	Manager	Attendance
1901	1st	90	49	.647	+7 1/2	Fred Clarke	251,955
1902	1st	103	36	.741	+27 1/2	Fred Clarke	243,826

Year	Position	W	L	Pct.	*GB	Manager	Attendance
1903	1st	91	49	.650	+6 1/2	Fred Clarke	326,855
1904	4th	87	66	.569	19	Fred Clarke	340,615
1905	2nd	96	57	.627	9	Fred Clarke	369,124
1906	3rd	93	60	.608	23 1/2	Fred Clarke	394,877
1907	2nd	91	63	.591	17	Fred Clarke	319,506
1908	2nd	98	56	.636	1	Fred Clarke	382,444
1909	1st	110	42	.724	+6 1/2	Fred Clarke	534,950
1910	3rd	86	67	.562	17 1/2	Fred Clarke	436,586
1911	3rd	85	69	.552	14 1/2	Fred Clarke	432,000
1912	2nd	93	58	.616	10	Fred Clarke	384,000
1913	4th	78	71	.523	21 1/2	Fred Clarke	296,000
1914	7th	69	85	.448	25 1/2	Fred Clarke	139,620
1915	5th	73	81	.474	18	Fred Clarke	225,743
1916	6th	65	89	.422	29	Jimmy Callahan	289,132
1917	8th	51	103	.331	47	Jimmy Callahan, Honus Wagner, Hugo Bezdek	192,807
1918	4th	65	60	.520	17	Hugo Bezdek	213,610
1919	4th	71	68	.511	24 1/2	Hugo Bezdek	276,810
1920	4th	79	75	.513	14	George Gibson	429,037
1921	2nd	90	63	.588	4	George Gibson	701,567
1922	3rd (tied)	85	69	.552	8	George Gibson, Bill McKechnie	523,675
1923	3rd	87	67	.565	8 1/2	Bill McKechnie	611,082
1924	3rd	90	63	.588	3	Bill McKechnie	736,883
1925	1st	95	58	.621	+8 1/2	Bill McKechnie	804,354
1926	3rd	84	69	.549	4 1/2	Bill McKechnie	798,542
1927	1st	94	60	.610	+1 1/2	Donie Bush	869,720
1928	4th	85	67	.559	9	Donie Bush	495,070
1929	2nd	88	65	.575	10 1/2	Donie Bush, Jewel Ens	491,377
1930	5th	80	74	.519	12	Jewel Ens	357,795
1931	5th	75	79	.487	26	Jewel Ens	260,392
1932	2nd	86	68	.558	4	George Gibson	287,262
1933	2nd	87	67	.565	5	George Gibson	288,747
1934	5th	74	76	.493	19 1/2	George Gibson, Pie Traynor	322,622
1935	4th	86	67	.562	13 1/2	Pie Traynor	352,885
1936	4th	84	70	.545	8	Pie Traynor	372,524
1937	3rd	86	68	.558	10	Pie Traynor	459,679
1938	2nd	86	64	.573	2	Pie Traynor	641,033
1939	6th	68	85	.444	28 1/2	Pie Traynor	376,734
1940	4th	78	76	.506	22 1/2	Frankie Frisch	507,934
1941	4th	81	73	.526	19	Frankie Frisch	482,241
1942	5th	66	81	.449	36 1/2	Frankie Frisch	448,897
1943	4th	80	74	.519	25	Frankie Frisch	604,278
1944	2nd	90	63	.588	14 1/2	Frankie Frisch	498,740
1945	4th	82	72	.532	16	Frankie Frisch	604,694
1946	7th	63	91	.409	34	Frankie Frisch, Spud Davis	749,962
1947	7th (tied)	62	92	.403	32	Billy Herman, Bill Burwell	1,283,531
1948	4th	83	71	.539	8 1/2	Billy Meyer	1,517,021
1949	6th	71	83	.461	26	Billy Meyer	1,499,435
1950	8th	57	96	.373	33 1/2	Billy Meyer	1,166,267
1951	7th	64	90	.416	32 1/2	Billy Meyer	980,590
1952	8th	42	112	.273	54 1/2	Billy Meyer	686,673
1953	8th	50	104	.325	55	Fred Haney	572,757
1954	8th	53	101	.344	44	Fred Haney	475,494
1955	8th	60	94	.390	38 1/2	Fred Haney	469,397
1956	7th	66	88	.429	27	Bobby Bragan	949,878
1957	7th (tied)	62	92	.403	33	Bobby Bragan, Danny Murtaugh	850,732
1958	2nd	84	70	.545	8	Danny Murtaugh	1,311,988
1959	4th	78	76	.506	9	Danny Murtaugh	1,359,917
1960	1st	95	59	.617	+7	Danny Murtaugh	1,705,828
1961	6th	75	79	.487	18	Danny Murtaugh	1,199,128
1962	4th	93	68	.578	8	Danny Murtaugh	1,090,648
1963	8th	74	88	.457	25	Danny Murtaugh	783,648
1964	6th (tied)	80	82	.494	13	Danny Murtaugh	759,496
1965	3rd	90	72	.556	7	Harry Walker	909,279
1966	3rd	92	70	.568	3	Harry Walker	1,196,618
1967	6th	81	81	.500	20 1/2	Harry Walker, Danny Murtaugh	907,012
1968	6th	80	82	.494	17	Larry Shepard	693,485

EAST DIVISION

Year	Position	W	L	Pct.	*GB	Manager	Attendance
1969	3rd	88	74	.543	12	Larry Shepard, Alex Grammas	769,369
1970	1st†	89	73	.549	+5	Danny Murtaugh	1,341,947
1971	1st‡	97	65	.599	+7	Danny Murtaugh	1,501,132
1972	1st†	96	59	.619	+11	Bill Virdon	1,427,460
1973	3rd	80	82	.494	2 1/2	Bill Virdon, Danny Murtaugh	1,319,913
1974	1st†	88	74	.543	+1 1/2	Danny Murtaugh	1,110,552

Year	Position	W	L	Pct.	*GB	Manager	Attendance
1975	1st†	92	69	.571	+6 1/2	Danny Murtaugh	1,270,018
1976	2nd	92	70	.568	9	Danny Murtaugh	1,025,945
1977	2nd	96	66	.593	5	Chuck Tanner	1,237,349
1978	2nd	88	73	.547	1 1/2	Chuck Tanner	964,106
1979	1st‡	98	64	.605	+2	Chuck Tanner	1,435,454
1980	3rd	83	79	.512	8	Chuck Tanner	1,646,757
1981	4th/6th	46	56	.451	§	Chuck Tanner	541,789
1982	4th	84	78	.519	8	Chuck Tanner	1,024,106
1983	2nd	84	78	.519	6	Chuck Tanner	1,225,916
1984	6th	75	87	.463	21 1/2	Chuck Tanner	773,500
1985	6th	57	104	.354	43 1/2	Chuck Tanner	735,900
1986	6th	64	98	.395	44	Jim Leyland	1,000,917
1987	4th (tied)	80	82	.494	15	Jim Leyland	1,161,193
1988	2nd	85	75	.531	15	Jim Leyland	1,866,713
1989	5th	74	88	.457	19	Jim Leyland	1,374,141
1990	1st†	95	67	.586	+4	Jim Leyland	2,049,908
1991	1st†	98	64	.605	+14	Jim Leyland	2,065,302
1992	1st†	96	66	.593	+9	Jim Leyland	1,829,395
1993	5th	75	87	.463	22	Jim Leyland	1,650,593

CENTRAL DIVISION

Year	Position	W	L	Pct.	*GB	Manager	Attendance
1994	3rd (tied)	53	61	.465	13	Jim Leyland	1,222,520
1995	5th	58	86	.403	27	Jim Leyland	905,517

*Games behind winner. †Lost championship series. ‡Won championship series. §First half 25-23; second half 21-33.

MANAGERIAL RECORDS

Hugo Bezdek 166-187, Bobby Bragan 102-155, Bill Burwell 1-0, Donie Bush 246-178, Jimmy Callahan 85-129, Fred Clarke 1,343-909, Spud Davis 1-2, Jewel Ens 176-167, Frank Frisch 539-528, George Gibson 401-330, Alex Grammas 4-1, Fred Haney 163-299, Billy Herman 61-92, Jim Leyland 778-774, Bill McKechnie 409-293, Billy Meyer 317-452, Danny Murtaugh 1,115-950, Larry Shepard 164-155, Chuck Tanner 711-685, Pie Traynor 457-406, Bill Virdon 163-128, Honus Wagner 1-4, Harry Walker 224-184.

ST. LOUIS CARDINALS

YEARLY FINISHES

Year	Position	W	L	Pct.	*GB	Manager	Attendance
1901	4th	76	64	.543	14 1/2	Patsy Donovan	379,988
1902	6th	56	78	.418	44 1/2	Patsy Donovan	226,417
1903	8th	43	94	.314	46 1/2	Patsy Donovan	226,538
1904	5th	75	79	.487	31 1/2	Kid Nichols	386,750
1905	6th	58	96	.377	47 1/2	Kid Nichols, Jimmy Burke, Matt Robison	292,800
1906	7th	52	98	.347	63	John McCloskey	283,770
1907	8th	52	101	.340	55 1/2	John McCloskey	185,377
1908	8th	49	105	.318	50	John McCloskey	205,129
1909	7th	54	98	.355	56	Roger Bresnahan	299,982
1910	7th	63	90	.412	40 1/2	Roger Bresnahan	355,668
1911	5th	75	74	.503	22	Roger Bresnahan	447,768
1912	6th	63	90	.412	41	Roger Bresnahan	241,759
1913	8th	51	99	.340	49	Miller Huggins	203,531
1914	3rd	81	72	.529	13	Miller Huggins	256,099
1915	6th	72	81	.471	18 1/2	Miller Huggins	252,666
1916	7th (tied)	60	93	.392	33 1/2	Miller Huggins	224,308
1917	3rd	82	70	.539	15	Miller Huggins	288,491
1918	8th	51	78	.395	33	Jack Hendricks	110,599
1919	7th	54	83	.394	40 1/2	Branch Rickey	167,059
1920	5th (tied)	75	79	.487	18	Branch Rickey	326,836
1921	3rd	87	66	.569	7	Branch Rickey	384,773
1922	3rd (tied)	85	69	.552	8	Branch Rickey	536,998
1923	5th	79	74	.516	16	Branch Rickey	338,551
1924	6th	65	89	.422	28 1/2	Branch Rickey	272,885
1925	4th	77	76	.503	18	Branch Rickey, Rogers Hornsby	404,959
1926	1st	89	65	.578	+2	Rogers Hornsby	668,428
1927	2nd	92	61	.601	1 1/2	Bob O'Farrell	749,340
1928	1st	95	59	.617	+2	Bill McKechnie	761,574
1929	4th	78	74	.513	20	Bill McKechnie, Billy Southworth	399,887
1930	1st	92	62	.597	+2	Gabby Street	508,501
1931	1st	101	53	.656	+13	Gabby Street	608,535
1932	6th (tied)	72	82	.468	18	Gabby Street	279,219
1933	5th	82	71	.536	9 1/2	Gabby Street, Frankie Frisch	256,171
1934	1st	95	58	.621	+2	Frankie Frisch	325,056
1935	2nd	96	58	.623	4	Frankie Frisch	506,084
1936	2nd (tied)	87	67	.565	5	Frankie Frisch	448,078
1937	4th	81	73	.526	15	Frankie Frisch	430,811

Year	Position	W	L	Pct.	*GB	Manager	Attendance
1938	6th	71	80	.470	17 1/2	Frankie Frisch, Mike Gonzalez	291,418
1939	2nd	92	61	.601	4 1/2	Ray Blades	400,245
1940	3rd	84	69	.549	16	Ray Blades, Mike Gonzalez, Billy Southworth	324,078
1941	2nd	97	56	.634	2 1/2	Billy Southworth	633,645
1942	1st	106	48	.688	+2	Billy Southworth	553,552
1943	1st	105	49	.682	+18	Billy Southworth	517,135
1944	1st	105	49	.682	+14 1/2	Billy Southworth	461,968
1945	2nd	95	59	.617	3	Billy Southworth	594,630
1946	1st†	98	58	.628	+2	Eddie Dyer	1,061,807
1947	2nd	89	65	.578	5	Eddie Dyer	1,247,913
1948	2nd	85	69	.552	6 1/2	Eddie Dyer	1,111,440
1949	2nd	96	58	.623	1	Eddie Dyer	1,430,676
1950	5th	78	75	.510	12 1/2	Eddie Dyer	1,093,411
1951	3rd	81	73	.526	15 1/2	Marty Marion	1,013,429
1952	3rd	88	66	.571	8 1/2	Eddie Stanky	913,113
1953	3rd (tied)	83	71	.539	22	Eddie Stanky	880,242
1954	6th	72	82	.468	25	Eddie Stanky	1,039,698
1955	7th	68	86	.442	30 1/2	Eddie Stanky, Harry Walker	849,130
1956	4th	76	78	.494	17	Fred Hutchinson	1,029,773
1957	2nd	87	67	.565	8	Fred Hutchinson	1,183,575
1958	5th (tied)	72	82	.468	20	Fred Hutchinson, Stan Hack	1,063,730
1959	7th	71	83	.461	16	Solly Hemus	929,953
1960	3rd	86	68	.558	9	Solly Hemus	1,096,632
1961	5th	80	74	.519	13	Solly Hemus, Johnny Keane	855,305
1962	6th	84	78	.519	17 1/2	Johnny Keane	953,895
1963	2nd	93	69	.574	6	Johnny Keane	1,170,546
1964	1st	93	69	.574	+1	Johnny Keane	1,143,294
1965	7th	80	81	.497	16 1/2	Red Schoendienst	1,241,201
1966	6th	83	79	.512	12	Red Schoendienst	1,712,980
1967	1st	101	60	.627	+10 1/2	Red Schoendienst	2,090,145
1968	1st	97	65	.599	+9	Red Schoendienst	2,011,167

EAST DIVISION

Year	Position	W	L	Pct.	*GB	Manager	Attendance
1969	4th	87	75	.537	13	Red Schoendienst	1,682,783
1970	4th	76	86	.469	13	Red Schoendienst	1,629,736
1971	2nd	90	72	.556	7	Red Schoendienst	1,604,671
1972	4th	75	81	.481	21 1/2	Red Schoendienst	1,196,894
1973	2nd	81	81	.500	1 1/2	Red Schoendienst	1,574,046
1974	2nd	86	75	.534	1 1/2	Red Schoendienst	1,838,413
1975	3rd (tied)	82	80	.506	10 1/2	Red Schoendienst	1,695,270
1976	5th	72	90	.444	29	Red Schoendienst	1,207,079
1977	3rd	83	79	.512	18	Vern Rapp	1,659,287
1978	5th	69	93	.426	21	Vern Rapp, Jack Krol, Ken Boyer	1,278,215
1979	3rd	86	76	.531	12	Ken Boyer	1,627,256
1980	4th	74	88	.457	17	Ken Boyer, Jack Krol, Whitey Herzog, Red Schoendienst	1,385,147
1981	2nd/2nd	59	43	.578	‡	Whitey Herzog	1,010,247
1982	1st§	92	70	.568	+3	Whitey Herzog	2,111,906
1983	4th	79	83	.488	11	Whitey Herzog	2,317,914
1984	3rd	84	78	.519	12 1/2	Whitey Herzog	2,037,448
1985	1st§	101	61	.623	+3	Whitey Herzog	2,637,563
1986	3rd	79	82	.491	28 1/2	Whitey Herzog	2,471,974
1987	1st§	95	67	.586	+3	Whitey Herzog	3,072,122
1988	5th	76	86	.469	25	Whitey Herzog	2,892,799
1989	3rd	86	76	.531	7	Whitey Herzog	3,080,980
1990	6th	70	92	.432	25	Whitey Herzog, Red Schoendienst, Joe Torre	2,573,225
1991	2nd	84	78	.519	14	Joe Torre	2,448,699
1992	3rd	83	79	.512	13	Joe Torre	2,418,483
1993	3rd	87	75	.537	10	Joe Torre	2,844,328

CENTRAL DIVISION

Year	Position	W	L	Pct.	*GB	Manager	Attendance
1994	3rd (tied)	53	61	.465	13	Joe Torre	1,866,544
1995	4th	62	81	.434	22 1/2	Joe Torre, Mike Jorgensen	1,756,727

*Games behind winner. †Won pennant playoff. ‡First half 30-20; second half 29-23. §Won championship series.

MANAGERIAL RECORDS

Ray Blades 106-85, Ken Boyer 166-190, Roger Bresnahan 255-352, Jimmy Burke 17-32, Patsy Donovan 175-236, Eddie Dyer 446-325, Frank Frisch 458-354, Mike Gonzalez 9-13, Stan Hack 3-7, Solly Hemus 190-192, Jack Hendricks 51-78, Whitey Herzog 835-739, Rogers Hornsby 153-116, Miller Huggins 346-415, Fred Hutchinson 232-220, Mike Jorgensen 42-54, Johnny Keane 317-249, Marty Marion 81-73, John McCloskey 153-304, Bill McKechnie 129-88, Kid Nichols 94-108, Bob O'Farrell 92-61, Vern Rapp 89-90, Branch Rickey 458-485, Stanley Robison 22-35, Red Schoendienst 1,028-944, Billy Southworth 620-346, Eddie Stanky 260-238, Gabby Street 312-242, Joe Torre 351-354, Harry Walker 51-67.

SAN DIEGO PADRES

YEARLY FINISHES

WEST DIVISION

Year	Position	W	L	Pct.	*GB	Manager	Attendance
1969	6th	52	110	.321	41	Preston Gomez	512,970
1970	6th	63	99	.389	39	Preston Gomez	643,679
1971	6th	61	100	.379	28 1/2	Preston Gomez	557,513
1972	6th	58	95	.379	36 1/2	Preston Gomez, Don Zimmer	644,273
1973	6th	60	102	.370	39	Don Zimmer	611,826
1974	6th	60	102	.370	42	John McNamara	1,075,399
1975	4th	71	91	.438	37	John McNamara	1,281,747
1976	5th	73	89	.451	29	John McNamara	1,458,478
1977	5th	69	93	.426	29	John McNamara, Bob Skinner, Alvin Dark	1,376,269
1978	4th	84	78	.519	11	Roger Craig	1,670,107
1979	5th	68	93	.422	22	Roger Craig	1,456,967
1980	6th	73	89	.451	19 1/2	Jerry Coleman	1,139,026
1981	6th/6th	41	69	.373	†	Frank Howard	519,161
1982	4th	81	81	.500	8	Dick Williams	1,607,516
1983	4th	81	81	.500	10	Dick Williams	1,539,815
1984	1st‡	92	70	.568	+12	Dick Williams	1,983,904
1985	3rd (tied)	83	79	.512	12	Dick Williams	2,210,352
1986	4th	74	88	.457	22	Steve Boros	1,805,716
1987	6th	65	97	.401	25	Larry Bowa	1,454,061
1988	3rd	83	78	.516	11	Larry Bowa, Jack McKeon	1,506,896
1989	2nd	89	73	.549	3	Jack McKeon	2,009,031
1990	4th (tied)	75	87	.463	16	Jack McKeon, Greg Riddoch	1,856,396
1991	3rd	84	78	.519	10	Greg Riddoch	1,804,289
1992	3rd	82	80	.506	16	Greg Riddoch, Jim Riggleman	1,722,102
1993	7th	61	101	.377	43	Jim Riggleman	1,375,432
1994	4th	47	70	.402	12 1/2	Jim Riggleman	953,857
1995	3rd	70	74	.486	8	Bruce Bochy	1,041,805

*Games behind winner. †First half 23-33; second half 18-36. ‡Won championship series.

MANAGERIAL RECORDS

Bruce Bochy 70-74, Steve Boros 74-88, Larry Bowa 81-127, Jerry Coleman 73-89, Roger Craig 152-171, Alvin Dark 49-65, Preston Gomez 180-316, Frank Howard 41-69, Jack McKeon 193-164, John McNamara 224-310, Greg Riddoch 200-194, Jim Riggleman 112-179, Dick Williams 337-311, Don Zimmer 114-190.

SAN FRANCISCO GIANTS

YEARLY FINISHES

Year	Position	W	L	Pct.	*GB	Manager	Attendance
1901†	7th	52	85	.380	37	George Davis	297,650
1902†	8th	48	88	.353	53 1/2	Horace Fogel, Heinie Smith, John McGraw	302,875
1903†	2nd	84	55	.604	6 1/2	John McGraw	579,530
1904†	1st	106	47	.693	+13	John McGraw	609,826
1905†	1st	105	48	.686	+9	John McGraw	552,700
1906†	2nd	96	56	.632	20	John McGraw	402,850
1907†	4th	82	71	.536	25 1/2	John McGraw	538,350
1908†	2nd (tied)	98	56	.636	1	John McGraw	910,000
1909†	3rd	92	61	.601	18 1/2	John McGraw	783,700
1910†	2nd	91	63	.591	13	John McGraw	511,785
1911†	1st	99	54	.647	+7 1/2	John McGraw	675,000
1912†	1st	103	48	.682	+10	John McGraw	638,000
1913†	1st	101	51	.664	+12 1/2	John McGraw	630,000
1914†	2nd	84	70	.545	10 1/2	John McGraw	364,313
1915†	8th	69	83	.454	21	John McGraw	391,850
1916†	4th	86	66	.566	7	John McGraw	552,056
1917†	1st	98	56	.636	+10	John McGraw	500,264
1918†	2nd	71	53	.573	10 1/2	John McGraw	256,618
1919†	2nd	87	53	.621	9	John McGraw	708,857
1920†	2nd	86	68	.558	7	John McGraw	929,609
1921†	1st	94	59	.614	+4	John McGraw	773,477
1922†	1st	93	61	.604	+7	John McGraw	945,809
1923†	1st	95	58	.621	+4 1/2	John McGraw	820,780
1924†	1st	93	60	.608	+1 1/2	John McGraw	844,068
1925†	2nd	86	66	.566	8 1/2	John McGraw	778,993
1926†	5th	74	77	.490	13 1/2	John McGraw	700,362
1927†	3rd	92	62	.597	2	John McGraw	858,190
1928†	2nd	93	61	.604	2	John McGraw	916,191
1929†	3rd	84	67	.556	13 1/2	John McGraw	868,806
1930†	3rd	87	67	.565	5	John McGraw	868,714

Year	Position	W	L	Pct.	*GB	Manager	Attendance
1931†	2nd	87	65	.572	13	John McGraw	812,163
1932†	6th (tied)	72	82	.468	18	John McGraw, Bill Terry	484,868
1933†	1st	91	61	.599	+5	Bill Terry	604,471
1934†	2nd	93	60	.608	2	Bill Terry	730,851
1935†	3rd	91	62	.595	8 1/2	Bill Terry	748,748
1936†	1st	92	62	.597	+5	Bill Terry	837,952
1937†	1st	95	57	.625	+3	Bill Terry	926,887
1938†	3rd	83	67	.553	5	Bill Terry	799,633
1939†	5th	77	74	.510	18 1/2	Bill Terry	702,457
1940†	6th	72	80	.474	27 1/2	Bill Terry	747,852
1941†	5th	74	79	.484	25 1/2	Bill Terry	763,098
1942†	3rd	85	67	.559	20	Mel Ott	779,621
1943†	8th	55	98	.359	49 1/2	Mel Ott	466,095
1944†	5th	67	87	.435	38	Mel Ott	674,083
1945†	5th	78	74	.513	19	Mel Ott	1,016,468
1946†	8th	61	93	.396	36	Mel Ott	1,219,873
1947†	4th	81	73	.526	13	Mel Ott	1,600,793
1948†	5th	78	76	.506	13 1/2	Mel Ott, Leo Durocher	1,459,269
1949†	5th	73	81	.474	24	Leo Durocher	1,218,446
1950†	3rd	86	68	.558	5	Leo Durocher	1,008,876
1951†	1st‡	98	59	.624	+1	Leo Durocher	1,059,539
1952†	2nd	92	62	.597	4 1/2	Leo Durocher	984,940
1953†	5th	70	84	.455	35	Leo Durocher	811,518
1954†	1st	97	57	.630	+5	Leo Durocher	1,155,067
1955†	3rd	80	74	.519	18 1/2	Leo Durocher	824,112
1956†	6th	67	87	.435	26	Bill Rigney	629,179
1957†	6th	69	85	.448	26	Bill Rigney	653,923
1958	3rd	80	74	.519	12	Bill Rigney	1,272,625
1959	3rd	83	71	.539	4	Bill Rigney	1,422,130
1960	5th	79	75	.513	16	Bill Rigney, Tom Sheehan	1,795,356
1961	3rd	85	69	.552	8	Alvin Dark	1,390,679
1962	1st‡	103	62	.624	+1	Alvin Dark	1,592,594
1963	3rd	88	74	.543	11	Alvin Dark	1,571,306
1964	4th	90	72	.556	3	Alvin Dark	1,504,364
1965	2nd	95	67	.586	2	Herman Franks	1,546,075
1966	2nd	93	68	.578	1 1/2	Herman Franks	1,657,192
1967	2nd	91	71	.562	10 1/2	Herman Franks	1,242,480
1968	2nd	88	74	.543	9	Herman Franks	837,220

WEST DIVISION

Year	Position	W	L	Pct.	*GB	Manager	Attendance
1969	2nd	90	72	.556	3	Clyde King	873,603
1970	3rd	86	76	.531	16	Clyde King, Charlie Fox	740,720
1971	1st§	90	72	.556	+1	Charlie Fox	1,106,043
1972	5th	69	86	.445	26 1/2	Charlie Fox	647,744
1973	3rd	88	74	.543	11	Charlie Fox	834,193
1974	5th	72	90	.444	30	Charlie Fox, Wes Westrum	519,987
1975	3rd	80	81	.497	27 1/2	Wes Westrum	522,919
1976	4th	74	88	.457	28	Bill Rigney	626,868
1977	4th	75	87	.463	23	Joe Altobelli	700,056
1978	3rd	89	73	.549	6	Joe Altobelli	1,740,477
1979	4th	71	91	.438	19 1/2	Joe Altobelli, Dave Bristol	1,456,402
1980	5th	75	86	.466	17	Dave Bristol	1,096,115
1981	5th/3rd	56	55	.505	∞	Frank Robinson	632,274
1982	3rd	87	75	.537	2	Frank Robinson	1,200,948
1983	5th	79	83	.488	12	Frank Robinson	1,251,530
1984	6th	66	96	.407	26	Frank Robinson, Danny Ozark	1,001,545
1985	6th	62	100	.383	33	Jim Davenport, Roger Craig	818,697
1986	3rd	83	79	.512	13	Roger Craig	1,528,748
1987	1st§	90	72	.556	+6	Roger Craig	1,917,168
1988	4th	83	79	.512	11 1/2	Roger Craig	1,785,297
1989	1st▲	92	70	.568	+3	Roger Craig	2,059,701
1990	3rd	85	77	.525	6	Roger Craig	1,975,528
1991	4th	75	87	.463	19	Roger Craig	1,737,478
1992	5th	72	90	.444	26	Roger Craig	1,561,987
1993	2nd	103	59	.636	1	Dusty Baker	2,606,354
1994	2nd	55	60	.478	3 1/2	Dusty Baker	1,704,608
1995	4th	67	77	.465	11	Dusty Baker	1,241,500

*Games behind winner. †New York Giants. ‡Won pennant playoff. §Lost championship series. ∞First half 27-32; second half 29-23. ▲Won championship series.

MANAGERIAL RECORDS

Joe Altobelli 225-239, Dusty Baker 225-196, Dave Bristol 85-98, Roger Craig 586-566, Alvin Dark 366-277, Jim Davenport 56-88, George Davis 52-85, Leo Durocher 637-523, Horace Fogel 18-23, Charlie Fox 348-327, Herman Franks 367-280, Clyde King 109-95, John McGraw 2,604-1,801, Mel Ott 464-530, Danny Ozark 24-32, Bill Rigney 406-430, Frank Robinson 264-277, Tom Sheehan 46-50, Heinie Smith 5-27, Bill Terry 823-661, Wes Westrum 118-129.

MINOR LEAGUES

Farm systems

American Association

International League

Mexican League

Pacific Coast League

Eastern League

Southern League

Texas League

California League

Carolina League

Florida League

Midwest League

New York-Pennsylvania League

Northwest League

South Atlantic League

Appalachian League

Arizona League

Dominican Summer League

Gulf Coast League

Pioneer League

Minor league index

FARM SYSTEMS

AMERICAN LEAGUE

BALTIMORE (6): AAA—Rochester. AA—Bowie. A—High Desert, Frederick. Rookie—Bluefield, Gulf Coast Orioles.
BOSTON (6): AAA—Pawtucket. AA—Trenton. A—Sarasota, Michigan, Lowell. Rookie—Gulf Coast Red Sox.
CALIFORNIA (6): AAA—Vancouver. AA—Midland. A—Cedar Rapids, Lake Elsinore, Boise. Rookie—Mesa Angels.
CHICAGO (7): AAA—Nashville. AA—Birmingham. A—South Bend, Hickory, Prince William. Rookie—Bristol, Gulf Coast White Sox.
CLEVELAND (6): AAA—Buffalo. AA—Canton-Akron. A—Kinston, Columbus, Watertown. Rookie—Burlington.
DETROIT (6): AAA—Toledo. AA—Jacksonville. A—Lakeland, Fayetteville, Jamestown. Rookie—Gulf Coast Tigers.
KANSAS CITY (6): AAA—Omaha. AA—Wichita. A—Lansing, Wilmington, Spokane. Rookie—Gulf Coast Royals.
MILWAUKEE (5): AAA—New Orleans. AA—El Paso. A—Stockton, Beloit. Rookie—Helena.
MINNESOTA (6): AAA—Salt Lake. AA—Hardware City. A—Fort Myers, Fort Wayne. Rookie—Elizabethton, Gulf Coast Twins.
NEW YORK (6): AAA—Columbus. AA—Norwich. A—Tampa, Greensboro, Oneonta. Rookie—Gulf Coast Yankees.
OAKLAND (6): AAA—Edmonton. AA—Huntsville. A—Modesto, West Michigan, Southern Oregon. Rookie—Scottsdale A's.
SEATTLE (6): AAA—Tacoma. AA—Port City. A—Lancaster, Wisconsin, Everett. Rookie—Peoria Mariners.
TEXAS (6): AAA—Oklahoma City. AA—Tulsa. A—Charlotte, Charleston (SC), Hudson Valley. Rookie—Gulf Coast Rangers.
TORONTO (6): AAA—Syracuse. AA—Knoxville. A—Dunedin, Hagerstown, St. Catharines. Rookie—Medicine Hat.

NATIONAL LEAGUE

ATLANTA (7): AAA—Richmond. AA—Greenville. A—Durham, Macon, Eugene. Rookie—Danville, Gulf Coast Braves.
CHICAGO (6): AAA—Iowa. AA—Orlando. A—Daytona, Rockford, Williamsport. Rookie—Gulf Coast Cubs.
CINCINNATI (6): AAA—Indianapolis. AA—Chattanooga. A—Winston-Salem, Charleston (WV). Rookie—Billings, Princeton.
COLORADO (6): AAA—Colorado Springs. AA—New Haven. A—Salem, Asheville, Portland. Rookie—Mesa Rockies.
FLORIDA (6): AAA—Charlotte. AA—Portland. A—Brevard County, Kane County, Utica. Rookie—Gulf Coast Marlins.
HOUSTON (6): AAA—Tucson. AA—Jackson. A—Kissimmee, Quad City, Auburn. Rookie—Gulf Coast Astros.
LOS ANGELES (7): AAA—Albuquerque. AA—San Antonio. A—San Bernardino, Savannah, Vero Beach, Yakima. Rookie—Great Falls.
MONTREAL (6): AAA—Ottawa. AA—Harrisburg. A—West Palm Beach, Delmarva, Vermont. Rookie—Gulf Coast Expos.
NEW YORK (7): AAA—Norfolk. AA—Binghamton. A—St. Lucie, Capital City, Pittsfield. Rookie—Kingsport, Gulf Coast Mets.
PHILADELPHIA (6): AAA—Scranton/Wilkes-Barre. AA—Reading. A—Clearwater, Piedmont, Batavia. Rookie—Martinsville.
PITTSBURGH (6): AAA—Calgary. AA—Carolina. A—Lynchburg, Augusta, Erie. Rookie—Gulf Coast Pirates.
ST. LOUIS (6): AAA—Louisville. AA—Arkansas. A—St. Petersburg, Peoria (IL), New Jersey. Rookie—Johnson City.
SAN DIEGO (6): AAA—Las Vegas. AA—Memphis. A—Rancho Cucamonga, Clinton. Rookie—Idaho Falls, Peoria (AZ) Padres.
SAN FRANCISCO (5): AAA—Phoenix. AA—Shreveport. A—San Jose, Burlington, Bellingham.

AMERICAN ASSOCIATION

LEAGUE OFFICE

President
Branch Rickey

Address
6801 Miami Ave., Suite 3
Cincinnati, OH 45243

Phone
513-271-4800

TEAMS

BUFFALO BISONS

General manager
Mike Buczowski
Manager
Brian Graham
Ballpark (capacity, surface)
Pilot Field (21,050, grass)
Affiliation
Indians
Address
P.O. Box 450
Buffalo, NY 14203
Phone
716-846-2003

INDIANAPOLIS INDIANS

General manager
Max Schumacher
Manager
Dave Miley
Ballpark (capacity, surface)
Bush Stadium (12,000, grass)
Affiliation
Reds
Address
1501 W. 16th St.
Indianapolis, IN 46202
Phone
317-269-3545

IOWA CUBS

General manager
Sam Bernabe
Manager
Ron Clark
Ballpark (capacity, surface)
Sec Taylor Stadium (10,500, grass)
Affiliation
Cubs
Address
350 SW 1 St.
Des Moines, IA 50309
Phone
515-243-6111

LOUISVILLE REDBIRDS

General manager
Dale Owens
Manager
Joe Pettini
Ballpark (capacity, surface)
Cardinal Stadium (33,000, artificial)
Affiliation
Cardinals
Address
P.O. Box 36407
Louisville, KY 40233
Phone
502-367-9121

NASHVILLE SOUNDS

General manager
Larry Schmittou
Manager
Rick Renick
Ballpark (capacity, surface)
Greer Stadium (17,000, grass)
Affiliation
White Sox
Address
P.O. Box 23290
Nashville, TN 37202
Phone
615-242-4371

NEW ORLEANS ZEPHYRS

General manager
Jay Miller
Manager
Tim Ireland
Ballpark (capacity, surface)
Privateer Park (4,700, grass)
Affiliation
Brewers
Address
P.O. Box 24672
New Orleans, LA 70184
Phone
504-282-6777

OKLAHOMA CITY 89ERS

General Manager
Dorsena Picknell
Manager
Greg Biagini
Ballpark (capacity, surface)
All Sports Stadium (15,000, grass)
Affiliation
Rangers
Address
P.O. Box 75089
Oklahoma City, OK 73147
Phone
405-946-8989

OMAHA ROYALS

Vice president/general manager
Bill Gorman
Manager
Mike Jirschele
Ballpark (capacity, surface)
Rosenblatt Stadium (23,000, grass)
Affiliation
Royals
Address
P.O. Box 3665
Omaha, NE 68103
Phone
402-734-2550

1995 FINAL STANDINGS

COMPOSITE

Team	Ind.	Buf.	Oma.	Lou.	Iowa	Nash.	N.O.	O.C.	W	L	T	Pct.	GB
Indianapolis (Reds)	....	10	9	16	11	14	16	12	88	56	0	.611	....
Buffalo (Indians)	14	....	9	16	10	11	9	13	82	62	0	.569	6
Omaha (Royals)	9	9	....	7	14	9	10	18	76	68	0	.528	12
Louisville (Cardinals)	8	8	11	....	11	15	9	12	74	70	0	.514	14
Iowa (Cubs)	7	8	10	7	....	8	15	14	69	74	0	.483	18½
Nashville (White Sox)	10	13	9	9	10	....	8	9	68	76	0	.472	20
New Orleans (Brewers)	2	9	14	9	8	10	....	11	63	79	0	.444	24
Oklahoma City (Rangers)	6	5	6	6	10	9	12	....	54	89	0	.378	33½

Major league affiliations in parentheses.
Iowa club represented Des Moines, Iowa.

PLAYOFFS: Louisville defeated Indianapolis, three games to none; Buffalo defeated Omaha, three games to one; Louisville defeated Buffalo, three games to two, to win league championship.

REGULAR-SEASON ATTENDANCE: Buffalo, 900,782; Indianapolis, 366,254; Iowa, 466,320; Louisville, 556,211; Nashville, 355,133; New Orleans, 142,675; Oklahoma City, 259,198; Omaha, 417,761. Total—3,464,334. Playoffs (12 games)—72,847. Class AAA All-Star Game at Scranton/Wilkes-Barre—10,965.

MANAGERS: Buffalo, Brian Graham; Indianapolis, Marc Bombard; Iowa, Ron Clark; Louisville, Joe Pettini; Nashville, Rick Renick; New Orleans, Chris Bando; Oklahoma City, Greg Biagini; Omaha, Mike Jirschele.

ALL-STAR TEAM: 1B—Jeff Grotewald, Omaha; 2B—Eric Owens, Indianapolis; 3B—Tracy Woodson, Louisville; SS—Mark Loretta, New Orleans; OF—Steve Gibralter, Indianapolis; Brian Giles, Buffalo; Brooks Kieschnick, Iowa; C—John Marzano, Oklahoma City; DH—Drew Denson, Indianapolis; RHP—Joe Roa, Buffalo; LHP—Eric Bell, Buffalo; Relief Pitcher—Cory Bailey, Louisville; Most Valuable Player—Eric Owens, Indianapolis; Rookie of the Year—Eric Owens, Indianapolis; Manager of the Year—Marc Bombard, Indianapolis.

1995 BATTING

TEAM

Team	Avg.	G	TPA	AB	R	H	TB	2B	3B	HR	RBI	SH	SF	HP	BB	IBB	SO	SB	CS	GDP	LOB	SHO	Slg.	OBP
Buffalo	.276	144	5461	4847	708	1338	2068	261	41	129	658	35	55	63	461	31	660	63	28	119	1035	5	.427	.343
Indianapolis	.275	144	5500	4890	791	1344	2267	286	29	193	746	25	39	54	492	30	1001	93	50	109	961	3	.464	.345
Omaha	.273	144	5401	4772	698	1305	2065	266	31	144	643	57	45	52	473	37	859	69	49	101	1004	6	.433	.343
Iowa	.268	143	5282	4790	552	1285	1851	226	32	92	507	54	38	38	362	30	781	55	44	109	995	13	.386	.322
Nashville	.263	144	5452	4906	621	1288	1916	239	25	113	577	39	34	53	420	32	872	109	59	123	986	7	.391	.325
Louisville	.259	144	5299	4697	617	1217	1882	245	27	122	570	33	46	49	474	31	933	113	54	118	971	10	.401	.330
New Orleans	.253	142	5202	4611	572	1166	1687	206	30	85	520	45	45	58	442	24	862	107	66	98	969	14	.366	.323
Oklahoma City	.253	143	5215	4696	572	1186	1757	241	42	82	529	28	41	49	401	31	856	68	37	125	929	10	.374	.315

INDIVIDUAL

TOP QUALIFIERS FOR BATTING CHAMPIONSHIP

Minimum 389 plate appearances. *Lefthanded batter. †Switch-hitter.

Player, Team	Avg.	G	TPA	AB	R	H	TB	2B	3B	HR	RBI	SH	SF	HP	BB	IBB	SO	SB	CS	GDP	Slg.	OBP
Carter, Mike, Iowa	.325	107	447	421	57	137	183	16	3	8	40	3	3	6	14	3	46	12	12	5	.435	.354
Snopek, Chris, Nashville	.323	113	456	393	56	127	194	23	4	12	55	6	3	4	50	1	72	2	5	5	.494	.402
Owens, Eric, Indianapolis	.314	108	485	427	86	134	210	24	8	12	63	3	2	1	52	2	61	33	12	7	.492	.388
Ramsey, Fernando, Nashville	.310	98	428	406	61	126	166	19	3	5	45	4	2	3	13	2	47	26	8	9	.409	.335
Giles, Brian, Buffalo*	.310	123	486	413	67	128	207	18	8	15	67	5	6	8	54	4	40	7	3	9	.501	.395
Marzano, John, Oklahoma City	.309	120	474	427	55	132	206	41	3	9	56	0	6	8	33	2	54	3	4	17	.482	.365
Saenz, Olmedo, Nashville	.304	111	478	415	60	126	193	26	1	13	74	3	3	12	45	1	60	0	2	11	.465	.385
Brady, Doug, Nashville†	.298	125	488	450	71	134	176	15	6	5	27	4	3	0	31	3	76	32	6	4	.391	.341
Kieschnick, Brooks, Iowa*	.295	138	570	505	61	149	250	30	1	23	73	0	3	4	58	7	91	2	3	11	.495	.370
Giannelli, Ray, Louisville*	.295	119	441	390	56	115	184	19	1	16	70	0	4	3	44	5	85	3	7	6	.472	.367
Grotewold, Jeff, Omaha*	.294	105	441	350	70	103	173	19	0	17	60	3	1	5	82	5	88	0	2	14	.494	.434
Ripken, Billy, Buffalo	.292	130	492	448	51	131	179	34	1	4	56	6	8	2	28	0	38	6	4	14	.400	.331
Martinez, Manny, Iowa	.290	122	429	397	63	115	172	17	8	8	49	7	2	3	20	0	64	11	8	3	.433	.327
Loretta, Mark, New Orleans	.286	127	534	479	48	137	190	22	5	7	79	5	7	9	34	1	47	8	9	12	.397	.340
Burnitz, Jeromy, Buffalo*	.284	128	500	443	72	126	223	26	7	19	85	1	3	3	50	8	83	13	5	6	.503	.359

DEPARTMENTAL LEADERS: G—Robertson, 139; AB—Valrie, 544; R—Owens, 86; H—Kieschnick, 149; TB—Kieschnick, 250; 2B—Marzano, 41; 3B—Bradshaw, Giles, M. Martinez, Owens, 8; HR—Kieschnick, 23; RBI—Burnitz, 85; SH—Halter, 19; SF—Dorsett, Ripken, 8; HP—Denson, 19; BB—Grotewold, 82; IBB—Burnitz, 8; SO—Valrie, 107; SB—Owens, 33; CS—Singleton, Valrie, 15; GIDP—Kosco, 18; Slg.—Burnitz, .503; OBP—Grotewold, .434.

ALL PLAYERS

*Lefthanded batter. †Switch-hitter.

Player, Team	Avg.	G	TPA	AB	R	H	TB	2B	3B	HR	RBI	SH	SF	HP	BB	IBB	SO	SB	CS	GDP	Slg.	OBP
Abbott, Paul, Iowa	.000	46	4	2	0	0	0	0	0	0	0	1	0	1	0	0	1	0	0	0	.000	.333
Amaro, Ruben, Buffalo†	.305	54	242	213	42	65	104	15	3	6	22	3	1	7	18	1	29	6	1	5	.488	.377
Anderson, Mike, Iowa	.000	27	14	11	0	0	0	0	0	0	0	2	0	0	1	0	5	0	0	0	.000	.083
Anthony, Eric, Indianapolis*	.292	7	30	24	7	7	19	0	0	4	8	0	0	0	6	3	4	2	0	2	.792	.433
Arias, Amador, Indianapolis†	.400	5	17	15	2	6	6	0	0	0	1	0	0	0	2	0	1	1	0	0	.400	.471
Aversa, Joe, Louisville†	.220	85	172	141	23	31	37	6	0	0	9	3	2	0	26	2	29	7	3	1	.262	.337
Barber, Brian, Louisville	.400	20	6	5	1	2	3	1	0	0	2	0	0	0	1	0	3	0	0	0	.600	.500
Barker, Tim, New Orleans	.258	80	306	264	44	68	90	9	5	1	24	8	1	4	29	0	39	10	8	2	.341	.339
Basse, Mike, New Orleans*	.247	121	455	381	49	94	112	14	2	0	35	7	6	3	58	3	62	15	9	5	.294	.346
Batchelor, Richard, Louisville	.000	50	3	1	0	0	0	0	0	0	0	1	0	0	1	0	0	0	0	1	.000	.500
Battle, Allen, Louisville	.280	47	198	164	28	46	69	12	1	3	18	5	0	1	28	0	32	7	1	3	.421	.389
Beatty, Blaine, Indianapolis*	.200	20	6	5	2	1	1	0	0	0	0	1	0	0	0	0	1	0	0	0	.200	.200
Belk, Tim, Indianapolis	.301	57	212	193	30	58	81	11	0	4	18	1	0	2	16	0	30	2	5	9	.420	.360
Bell, David, Buf.-Lou.	.273	88	366	330	43	90	135	14	2	9	43	2	3	7	24	1	47	4	3	6	.409	.332
Beltran, Rigo, Louisville*	.333	25	21	18	3	6	8	2	0	0	2	0	1	0	2	0	4	0	0	0	.444	.381
Benavides, Freddie, Iowa	.241	106	347	315	30	76	110	14	4	4	26	1	1	5	25	0	47	2	3	12	.349	.306
Benes, Alan, Louisville	.300	11	11	10	2	3	9	0	0	2	4	1	0	0	0	0	4	0	0	0	.900	.300
Bess, Johnny, Indianapolis†	.000	2	5	5	0	0	0	0	0	0	0	0	0	0	0	0	2	0	0	0	.000	.000
Bolick, Frank, Buffalo†	.246	20	69	65	11	16	31	6	0	3	10	0	0	1	3	0	13	0	1	3	.477	.290
Borrelli, Dean, Oklahoma City	.200	54	207	185	17	37	54	9	1	2	17	0	2	2	18	0	50	0	1	7	.292	.275
Bradshaw, Terry, Louisville*	.283	111	453	389	65	110	174	24	8	8	42	7	1	3	53	0	60	20	7	4	.447	.372
Brady, Doug, Nashville†	.298	125	488	450	71	134	176	15	6	5	27	4	3	0	31	3	76	32	6	4	.391	.341
Bream, Scott, Iowa†	.159	29	96	82	10	13	20	1	0	2	9	3	0	0	11	0	20	1	0	1	.244	.258
Briley, Greg, Indianapolis*	.233	46	169	146	17	34	51	8	0	3	17	1	0	0	22	3	34	9	2	1	.349	.333
Brooks, Jerry, Indianapolis	.283	90	355	325	41	92	157	19	2	14	52	0	3	5	22	0	38	3	1	16	.483	.335
Brown, Chris, Indianapolis	.000	3	8	7	0	0	0	0	0	0	0	0	0	0	1	0	0	0	0	0	.000	.125
Brown, Kevin, Oklahoma City	.400	3	12	10	1	4	5	1	0	0	0	0	0	0	2	0	4	0	0	0	.500	.500
Brown, Marty, Oklahoma City	.168	30	112	101	12	17	31	5	0	3	12	0	1	2	8	1	25	0	0	3	.307	.241
Bruett, J.T., Omaha*	.279	44	155	129	20	36	50	6	1	2	14	5	3	1	17	1	19	6	4	3	.388	.360
Buckels, Gary, Louisville	.000	13	1	1	0	0	0	0	0	0	0	0	0	0	0	0	1	0	0	0	.000	.000
Buckley, Travis, Indianapolis	.000	23	17	14	1	0	0	0	0	0	0	3	0	0	0	0	6	0	0	0	.000	.000
Buechele, Steve, Oklahoma City	.308	3	14	13	1	4	7	0	0	1	3	0	0	0	1	0	1	0	0	0	.538	.357
Burnitz, Jeromy, Buffalo*	.284	128	500	443	72	126	223	26	7	19	85	1	3	3	50	8	83	13	5	6	.503	.359
Burton, Darren, Omaha†	.000	2	5	5	0	0	0	0	0	0	0	0	0	0	0	0	1	0	0	0	.000	.000
Busby, Mike, Louisville	.200	6	6	5	1	1	1	0	0	0	0	0	0	1	0	0	3	0	0	0	.200	.333
Byington, John, N.O.-O.C.	.259	122	473	437	49	113	142	16	2	3	32	4	6	5	21	2	41	7	2	16	.325	.296
Caceres, Edgar, Omaha†	.206	37	117	107	13	22	27	3	1	0	12	1	1	0	8	3	10	3	1	2	.252	.259
Cadaret, Greg, Louisville*	.000	12	1	1	1	0	0	0	0	0	0	0	0	0	0	0	0	0	0	0	.000	.000
Cameron, Stanton, Okla. City	.167	5	16	12	2	2	3	1	0	0	0	0	0	0	4	0	3	0	0	0	.250	.375
Campbell, Mike, Iowa	.000	21	8	8	0	0	0	0	0	0	0	0	0	0	0	0	6	0	0	0	.000	.000
Candaele, Casey, Buffalo†	.247	97	399	364	50	90	126	10	7	4	38	4	7	2	22	1	42	9	2	6	.346	.289
Cappuccio, Carmine, Nashville*	.273	66	248	216	30	59	88	14	0	5	24	1	1	1	29	4	26	0	2	6	.407	.360

Player, Team	Avg.	G	TPA	AB	R	H	TB	2B	3B	HR	RBI	SH	SF	HP	BB	IBB	SO	SB	CS	GDP	Slg.	OBP
Caraballo, Ramon, Louisville†	.318	69	276	245	38	78	114	10	1	8	25	4	4	4	19	1	42	14	4	5	.465	.371
Carpenter, Cris, Louisville	.000	49	1	1	0	0	0	0	0	0	0	0	0	0	0	0	1	0	0	0	.000	.000
Carter, Mike, Iowa	.325	107	447	421	57	137	183	16	3	8	40	3	3	6	14	3	46	12	12	5	.435	.354
Chamberlain, Wes, Omaha	.219	16	69	64	2	14	20	3	0	1	6	0	1	2	2	0	15	0	0	4	.313	.261
Chance, Tony, Oklahoma City	.214	63	213	196	19	42	60	12	0	2	20	1	1	0	15	0	55	1	1	5	.306	.269
Cholowsky, Dan, Louisville	.218	76	285	238	27	52	84	9	1	7	25	0	6	5	36	0	64	10	4	5	.353	.326
Clinton, Jim, Oklahoma City	.000	8	14	13	0	0	0	0	0	0	0	0	0	0	1	0	6	0	0	1	.000	.071
Coleman, Vince, Omaha†	.395	9	40	38	7	15	20	2	0	1	5	0	0	0	2	2	6	3	0	0	.526	.425
Colon, Cris, Iowa†	.260	106	391	366	35	95	127	18	1	4	36	3	1	4	17	4	51	1	0	5	.347	.299
Cookson, Brent, Omaha	.401	40	160	137	28	55	80	13	0	4	20	0	2	4	17	0	24	0	0	3	.584	.475
Costo, Tim, Buffalo	.247	105	369	324	41	80	128	11	2	11	60	3	7	8	27	0	65	2	0	7	.395	.314
Cotto, Henry, Nashville	.131	17	62	61	4	8	12	1	0	1	4	0	0	0	1	0	20	0	1	3	.197	.145
Coughlin, Kevin, Nashville*	.182	10	26	22	0	4	5	1	0	0	0	0	0	0	4	0	3	0	1	1	.227	.308
Courtright, John, Indianapolis*	.250	13	4	4	1	1	1	0	0	0	0	0	0	0	0	0	2	0	0	0	.250	.250
Cox, Darron, Iowa	.234	33	110	94	7	22	31	6	0	1	14	2	4	2	8	0	21	0	0	0	.330	.296
Creek, Doug, Louisville*	.000	26	1	1	0	0	0	0	0	0	0	0	0	0	0	0	0	0	0	0	.000	.000
Cron, Chris, Nashville	.217	21	78	69	3	15	23	2	0	2	10	1	0	0	8	2	20	0	0	2	.333	.299
Dabney, Fred, Iowa	.000	33	2	2	0	0	0	0	0	0	0	0	0	0	0	0	0	0	0	0	.000	.000
Deak, Brian, Louisville	.228	54	193	162	19	37	60	5	0	6	31	1	1	3	26	0	47	2	0	3	.370	.344
Deak, Darrel, Louisville†	.241	106	400	336	42	81	127	21	2	7	34	0	6	5	53	6	90	2	2	5	.378	.348
Denson, Drew, Indianapolis	.277	107	412	357	59	99	174	21	0	19	69	0	3	18	34	5	68	1	0	10	.487	.367
DeLaRosa, Francisco, Louisville†	.222	28	12	9	0	2	5	1	1	0	5	3	0	0	0	0	5	0	0	0	.556	.222
DiFelice, Mike, Louisville	.270	21	68	63	8	17	21	4	0	0	3	0	0	0	5	0	11	1	0	4	.333	.324
Diggs, Tony, Louisville†	.250	23	41	36	4	9	12	3	0	0	0	0	0	0	5	1	4	2	1	1	.333	.341
Dismuke, Jamie, Indianapolis*	.250	13	39	36	6	9	10	1	0	0	2	0	0	0	3	1	3	0	0	1	.278	.308
Dodson, Bo, New Orleans*	.281	62	244	203	29	57	91	5	1	9	34	0	5	0	36	6	27	0	0	4	.448	.381
Dorsett, Brian, Indianapolis	.262	91	350	313	40	82	157	25	1	16	58	0	8	4	25	0	47	1	1	11	.502	.317
Dostal, Bruce, Oklahoma City*	.212	88	331	293	35	62	100	14	6	4	31	4	1	3	30	0	49	11	3	7	.341	.291
Elster, Kevin, Omaha	.238	11	48	42	5	10	14	4	0	0	6	0	1	0	5	0	8	0	0	0	.333	.313
Fanning, Steve, Iowa	.000	4	6	5	0	0	0	0	0	0	0	0	0	0	1	0	4	0	0	0	.000	.167
Fariss, Monty, Iowa	.182	10	42	33	5	6	9	0	0	1	2	0	0	0	9	2	7	0	0	0	.273	.357
Figueroa, Bien, Oklahoma City	.100	9	22	20	1	2	2	0	0	0	2	1	1	0	0	0	2	1	0	0	.100	.095
Finn, John, New Orleans	.325	35	136	117	20	38	53	4	1	3	19	4	0	2	13	2	7	9	2	1	.453	.402
Flores, Miguel, Buffalo	.283	31	120	113	13	32	42	8	1	0	12	1	0	1	5	0	13	5	0	4	.372	.319
Fordyce, Brook, Buffalo	.250	58	195	176	18	44	57	13	0	0	9	3	0	2	14	0	20	1	0	2	.324	.313
Fox, Eric, Oklahoma City†	.278	92	388	349	52	97	147	22	5	6	50	4	3	2	30	7	68	5	5	7	.421	.336
Franco, Matt, Iowa*	.281	121	499	455	51	128	184	28	5	6	58	1	6	0	37	5	44	1	1	11	.404	.331
Fraraccio, Dan, Nashville	.250	10	30	28	2	7	7	0	0	0	3	1	0	0	1	0	6	2	0	1	.250	.276
Frascatore, John, Louisville	.000	28	2	2	0	0	0	0	0	0	0	0	0	0	0	0	0	0	0	0	.000	.000
Garber, Jeff, Omaha	.143	6	14	14	1	2	2	0	0	0	0	0	0	0	0	0	5	0	0	1	.143	.143
Gardner, Jeff, Iowa*	.323	65	262	235	35	76	96	11	0	3	24	2	1	1	23	0	27	1	2	5	.409	.385
Giannelli, Ray, Louisville*	.295	119	441	390	56	115	184	19	1	16	70	0	4	3	44	5	85	3	7	6	.472	.367
Gibralter, Steve, Indianapolis	.316	79	295	263	49	83	162	19	3	18	63	1	2	4	25	3	70	0	2	6	.616	.381
Giles, Brian, Buffalo*	.310	123	486	413	67	128	207	18	8	15	67	5	6	8	54	4	40	7	3	9	.501	.395
Gilkey, Bernard, Louisville	.333	2	7	6	3	2	6	1	0	1	1	0	0	0	1	0	0	0	0	0	1.000	.429
Glanville, Doug, Iowa	.270	112	449	419	48	113	145	16	2	4	37	7	4	3	16	0	64	13	9	4	.346	.299
Goldberg, Lonnie, Oklahoma City	.233	10	32	30	2	7	13	3	0	1	5	0	0	0	2	0	4	1	0	1	.433	.281
Gonzalez, Javier, New Orleans	.248	43	127	113	20	28	54	11	0	5	15	2	1	4	7	0	24	0	0	0	.478	.312
Gordon, Keith, Indianapolis	.264	89	281	265	36	70	104	14	1	6	38	1	0	0	15	0	94	3	4	3	.392	.304
Gousha, Sean, Iowa	.000	2	5	5	0	0	0	0	0	0	0	0	0	0	0	0	3	0	0	0	.000	.000
Gozzo, Mauro, Iowa	.000	6	1	1	0	0	0	0	0	0	0	0	0	0	0	0	1	0	0	0	.000	.000
Grant, Mark, Iowa	.000	11	10	10	0	0	0	0	0	0	0	0	0	0	0	0	7	0	0	0	.000	.000
Green, Gary, Omaha	.169	26	75	71	5	12	14	2	0	0	3	1	0	0	3	0	14	0	0	1	.197	.203
Greene, Willie, Indianapolis*	.243	91	370	325	57	79	152	12	2	19	45	0	4	3	38	2	67	3	3	6	.468	.324
Grotewold, Jeff, Omaha*	.294	105	441	350	70	103	173	19	0	17	60	3	1	5	82	5	88	0	2	14	.494	.434
Grott, Matt, Indianapolis*	.300	25	13	10	0	3	4	1	0	0	2	0	0	0	3	0	3	0	0	0	.400	.462
Gulan, Mike, Louisville	.236	58	210	195	21	46	79	10	4	5	27	0	2	3	10	1	53	2	2	6	.405	.281
Halter, Shane, Omaha	.230	124	452	392	42	90	139	19	3	8	39	19	1	0	40	0	97	2	3	6	.355	.300
Hamelin, Bob, Omaha*	.294	36	152	119	25	35	77	12	0	10	32	0	2	0	31	5	34	2	3	1	.647	.434
Haney, Todd, Iowa	.313	90	366	326	38	102	138	20	2	4	30	4	2	6	28	0	21	2	2	17	.423	.376
Hare, Shawn, Oklahoma City*	.265	68	267	238	27	63	94	13	3	4	30	1	1	4	23	2	47	3	1	9	.395	.338
Harris, Donald, Oklahoma City	.200	12	44	40	4	8	11	1	1	0	7	0	1	0	3	0	7	0	2	2	.275	.250
Harris, Mike, New Orleans*	.232	21	60	56	3	13	16	3	0	0	5	0	0	0	4	1	9	1	1	1	.286	.283
Hatcher, Billy, Omaha	.276	26	117	105	14	29	39	5	1	1	12	0	1	2	9	2	6	4	2	5	.371	.342
Hecht, Steve, Oklahoma City*	.261	67	261	238	26	62	83	6	3	3	14	3	1	3	16	3	45	9	5	1	.349	.314
Hemond, Scott, Louisville	.000	1	3	3	1	0	0	0	0	0	0	0	0	0	0	0	0	0	0	0	.000	.000
Hiatt, Phil, Omaha	.158	20	79	76	7	12	23	5	0	2	8	0	1	0	2	0	25	0	0	0	.303	.177
Hinzo, Tommy, Oklahoma City†	.252	82	277	254	33	64	76	10	1	0	20	3	3	4	13	1	38	8	3	3	.299	.296
Holbert, Aaron, Louisville	.257	112	434	401	57	103	154	16	4	9	40	3	5	5	20	1	60	14	6	10	.384	.297
Horn, Sam, Oklahoma City*	.308	46	182	156	26	48	93	9	0	12	42	0	1	0	25	3	49	0	2	4	.596	.401
Hosey, Dwayne, Omaha†	.295	75	304	271	59	80	145	21	4	12	50	1	2	1	29	2	45	15	6	1	.535	.363
Howard, Tim, Nashville*	.233	37	118	103	8	24	35	3	1	2	13	0	1	1	13	0	12	4	3	3	.340	.322
Howitt, Dann, Nas.-Buf.*	.262	86	284	252	35	66	109	14	4	7	33	0	2	0	30	6	62	0	3	7	.433	.338
Hubbard, Mike, Iowa	.260	75	289	254	28	66	93	6	3	5	23	6	3	0	26	1	60	6	1	5	.366	.325
Hughes, Keith, Omaha*	.289	103	378	342	51	99	158	22	2	11	46	1	4	1	30	3	41	4	2	4	.462	.345
Hulett, Tim, Lou.-O.C.	.219	42	160	151	15	33	45	7	1	1	10	0	0	0	9	1	33	0	1	1	.298	.263
Humphreys, Mike, Buffalo	.246	34	141	126	17	31	38	4	0	1	5	1	1	5	8	0	22	5	1	0	.302	.314
Hunter, Brian, Indianapolis	.361	9	42	36	7	13	30	5	0	4	11	0	0	0	6	1	11	0	1	0	.833	.452
Jaha, John, New Orleans	.400	3	12	10	2	4	8	1	0	1	3	0	0	0	2	1	1	0	0	1	.800	.500
James, Chris, Omaha	.167	3	13	12	3	2	6	1	0	1	3	0	0	0	1	0	2	0	0	0	.500	.231
Jarvis, Kevin, Indianapolis*	.571	10	8	7	1	4	4	0	0	0	3	0	0	0	1	0	1	0	0	0	.571	.625
Johns, Keith, Louisville	.000	5	10	10	0	0	0	0	0	0	0	0	0	0	0	0	2	0	0	0	.000	.000
Jose, Felix, Iowa†	.135	10	39	37	2	5	8	3	0	0	1	0	0	1	1	0	6	0	0	1	.216	.179

Player, Team	Avg.	G	TPA	AB	R	H	TB	2B	3B	HR	RBI	SH	SF	HP	BB	IBB	SO	SB	CS	GDP	Slg.	OBP
Kennedy, Darryl, Oklahoma City	.182	3	11	11	1	2	5	0	0	1	3	0	0	0	0	0	2	0	0	0	.455	.182
Kessinger, Keith, Iowa†	.229	68	245	210	21	48	65	11	0	2	20	7	2	1	25	2	23	1	1	6	.310	.311
Kieschnick, Brooks, Iowa*	.295	138	570	505	61	149	250	30	1	23	73	0	3	4	58	7	91	2	3	11	.495	.370
Kmak, Joe, Iowa	.173	34	109	98	6	17	26	3	0	2	7	3	2	0	6	0	24	0	0	4	.265	.217
Knapp, Mike, Indianapolis	.256	14	43	39	8	10	15	2	0	1	6	0	0	1	3	0	7	1	0	0	.385	.326
Kosco, Bryn, Iowa*	.251	119	399	363	50	91	166	24	3	15	52	2	3	1	30	5	85	2	2	18	.457	.307
Koslofski, Kevin, New Orleans*	.212	105	364	321	41	68	115	18	4	7	35	3	3	2	34	2	100	4	2	1	.358	.289
Kremblas, Frank, Indianapolis	.160	27	89	75	7	12	14	2	0	0	3	2	0	0	12	1	25	4	2	2	.187	.276
Lee, Manuel, Louisville†	.273	6	22	22	2	6	6	0	0	0	0	0	0	0	0	0	2	1	0	1	.273	.273
Levis, Jesse, Buffalo*	.311	66	231	196	26	61	89	16	0	4	20	1	0	2	32	0	11	0	3	7	.454	.413
Lindeman, Jim, Oklahoma City	.252	83	335	294	52	74	132	16	3	12	36	0	3	5	33	4	54	0	1	11	.449	.334
Lockhart, Keith, Omaha*	.378	44	166	148	24	56	80	7	1	5	19	1	0	1	16	3	10	1	3	0	.541	.442
Lofton, Rodney, New Orleans	.217	102	260	240	30	52	62	7	0	1	18	2	2	1	15	1	48	9	3	11	.258	.264
Long, Kevin, Omaha*	.250	22	70	64	7	16	19	3	0	0	0	1	0	0	5	0	8	1	2	3	.297	.304
Lopez, Luis, Buffalo	.262	123	499	455	62	119	193	21	1	17	66	0	7	8	29	3	47	1	1	15	.424	.313
Lopez, Pedro, New Orleans	.000	3	8	8	0	0	0	0	0	0	0	0	0	0	0	0	3	0	0	0	.000	.000
Loretta, Mark, New Orleans	.286	127	534	479	48	137	190	22	5	7	79	5	7	9	34	1	47	8	9	12	.397	.340
Lovullo, Torey, Buffalo†	.255	132	552	474	84	121	199	20	5	16	61	1	5	2	70	7	62	3	1	12	.420	.350
Luce, Roger, Oklahoma City	.000	1	3	3	0	0	0	0	0	0	0	0	0	0	0	0	2	0	0	0	.000	.000
Lyden, Mitch, Omaha	.253	71	259	237	26	60	106	8	1	12	44	3	6	2	11	2	66	0	0	5	.447	.285
Lyons, Barry, Nashville	.257	71	294	265	37	68	110	16	1	8	38	1	4	4	20	4	56	0	0	7	.415	.314
Mabry, John, Louisville*	.083	4	12	12	0	1	1	0	0	0	0	0	0	0	0	0	0	0	0	0	.083	.083
Machado, Robert, Nashville	.143	16	56	49	7	7	13	3	0	1	5	0	0	0	7	0	12	0	1	1	.265	.250
Magdaleno, Ricky, Indianapolis	.125	4	9	8	1	1	4	0	0	1	1	1	0	0	0	0	3	0	0	0	.500	.125
Marini, Marc, Buffalo*	.271	32	93	85	12	23	37	5	0	3	15	0	1	0	7	0	14	0	0	3	.435	.323
Martindale, Ryan, Buffalo	.161	11	31	31	4	5	6	1	0	0	0	0	0	0	0	0	9	1	0	1	.194	.161
Martinez, Carmelo, Buffalo	.278	11	43	36	8	10	17	1	0	2	9	0	0	0	7	0	10	0	0	1	.472	.395
Martinez, Domingo, Louisville	.261	64	245	222	26	58	100	15	0	9	31	0	4	4	15	2	49	0	0	7	.450	.314
Martinez, Frankie, Louisville	.000	38	1	1	0	0	0	0	0	0	0	0	0	0	0	0	1	0	0	0	.000	.000
Martinez, Manny, Iowa	.290	122	429	397	63	115	172	17	8	8	49	7	2	3	20	0	64	11	8	3	.433	.327
Marzano, John, Oklahoma City	.309	120	474	427	55	132	206	41	3	9	56	0	6	8	33	2	54	3	4	17	.482	.365
Massarelli, John, Buffalo	.000	3	2	1	0	0	0	0	0	0	0	0	0	0	1	0	0	0	0	0	.000	.500
Matheny, Mike, New Orleans	.353	6	20	17	3	6	17	2	0	3	4	0	0	3	0	0	5	0	0	0	1.000	.450
Mathile, Mike, Indianapolis	.000	14	1	1	0	0	0	0	0	0	0	0	0	0	0	0	1	0	0	0	.000	.000
McCarty, Dave, Indianapolis	.336	37	158	140	31	47	83	10	1	8	32	1	1	1	15	0	30	0	0	5	.593	.401
McClendon, Lloyd, Buffalo	.278	37	130	108	19	30	51	6	0	5	19	0	0	2	20	3	20	0	0	5	.472	.400
McCoy, Trey, Oklahoma City	.310	9	36	29	4	9	10	1	0	0	2	0	0	0	7	1	7	0	0	1	.345	.444
McNeely, Jeff, Louisville	.236	109	295	271	31	64	72	6	1	0	19	0	1	0	23	0	53	5	8	8	.266	.295
Mercedes, Henry, Omaha	.215	86	307	275	37	59	104	12	0	11	37	6	1	3	22	0	90	2	0	7	.378	.279
Miller, Keith, Omaha	.250	7	25	20	3	5	7	2	0	0	2	0	1	0	4	0	2	1	0	0	.350	.360
Milstien, Dave, Nashville	.235	11	37	34	1	8	9	1	0	0	2	0	0	0	3	0	4	0	0	1	.265	.297
Minchey, Nate, Louisville	.067	26	17	15	0	1	1	0	0	0	0	1	0	0	1	0	8	0	0	0	.067	.125
Mitchell, Keith, Indianapolis	.244	70	260	213	40	52	100	11	2	11	36	1	4	1	40	3	40	4	4	7	.469	.363
Morris, Hal, Indianapolis*	.400	2	6	5	2	2	2	0	0	0	1	0	0	0	1	0	0	0	0	0	.400	.500
Morton, Kevin, Iowa	.000	28	3	3	0	0	0	0	0	0	0	0	0	0	0	0	0	0	0	0	.000	.000
Mota, Jose, Omaha†	.322	27	100	87	6	28	32	4	0	0	10	4	2	1	6	0	9	1	2	3	.368	.365
Mottola, Chad, Indianapolis	.259	69	261	239	40	62	99	11	1	8	37	1	1	0	20	0	50	8	1	6	.414	.315
Mouton, Lyle, Nashville	.296	71	295	267	40	79	120	17	0	8	41	0	4	1	23	2	58	10	4	9	.449	.349
Nabholz, Chris, Iowa*	.000	6	3	3	0	0	0	0	0	0	0	0	0	0	0	0	0	0	0	0	.000	.000
Nilsson, Dave, New Orleans*	.444	3	11	9	1	4	7	0	0	1	4	0	0	0	2	0	0	0	0	0	.778	.545
Nitkowski, C.J., Indianapolis*	.000	6	3	2	0	0	0	0	0	0	0	1	0	0	0	0	2	0	0	0	.000	.000
Noriega, Rey, Nashville†	.164	20	60	55	6	9	16	4	0	1	3	1	1	0	3	0	20	0	0	0	.291	.203
Norman, Les, Omaha	.284	83	340	313	46	89	141	19	3	9	33	3	2	4	18	2	48	5	3	3	.450	.329
O'Halloran, Greg, Iowa*	.158	7	20	19	1	3	4	1	0	0	1	0	1	0	0	0	7	0	0	0	.211	.150
Oliver, Joe, New Orleans	.077	4	13	13	0	1	2	1	0	0	0	0	0	0	0	0	3	0	0	0	.154	.077
Ortiz, Javier, Nashville	.167	7	25	24	3	4	7	0	0	1	1	0	0	0	1	0	5	0	0	1	.292	.200
Ortiz, Junior, Nashville	.186	64	191	172	13	32	44	9	0	1	16	2	1	4	12	0	27	0	0	8	.256	.254
Ortiz, Luis, Oklahoma City	.306	47	182	170	19	52	78	10	5	2	20	1	3	0	8	2	20	1	1	7	.459	.331
Osborne, Donovan, Louisville*	.000	1	2	2	0	0	0	0	0	0	0	0	0	0	0	0	1	0	0	0	.000	.000
Owens, Eric, Indianapolis	.314	108	485	427	86	134	210	24	8	12	63	3	2	1	52	2	61	33	12	7	.492	.388
Pagnozzi, Tom, Louisville	.500	5	17	16	4	8	13	2	0	1	3	0	0	0	1	0	0	0	0	1	.813	.529
Parra, Franklin, Oklahoma City†	.167	6	21	18	0	3	4	1	0	0	1	0	1	0	2	0	4	1	0	1	.222	.238
Pena, Geronimo, Louisville†	.381	6	24	21	5	8	15	1	0	2	6	0	0	0	3	2	1	0	0	0	.714	.458
Perez, Danny, New Orleans	.294	12	39	34	5	10	11	1	0	0	0	0	0	0	5	1	9	0	0	0	.324	.385
Perry, Herbert, Buffalo	.317	49	203	180	27	57	79	14	1	2	17	3	2	3	15	2	18	1	0	4	.439	.375
Petkovsek, Mark, Louisville	.091	8	11	11	0	1	2	1	0	0	0	0	0	0	0	0	1	0	0	0	.182	.091
Pledger, Kinnis, Iowa*	.083	9	26	24	1	2	2	0	0	0	0	0	0	0	2	0	12	0	0	1	.083	.154
Prager, Howard, Louisville*	.255	54	121	102	9	26	49	5	0	6	15	0	0	0	19	0	25	1	1	2	.480	.372
Pratt, Todd, Iowa	.328	23	62	58	3	19	20	1	0	0	5	0	0	0	4	1	17	0	0	0	.345	.371
Pugh, Tim, Indianapolis	.286	6	8	7	1	2	2	0	0	0	0	1	0	0	0	0	2	0	0	0	.286	.286
Raczka, Mike, Louisville*	.000	55	1	0	0	0	0	0	0	0	0	1	0	0	0	0	0	0	0	0	.000	.000
Ramsey, Fernando, Nashville	.310	98	428	406	61	126	166	19	3	5	45	4	2	3	13	2	47	26	8	9	.409	.335
Randa, Joe, Omaha	.275	64	259	233	33	64	102	10	2	8	33	1	1	2	22	0	33	2	2	9	.438	.341
Reed, Rick, Indianapolis	.182	22	13	11	2	2	3	1	0	0	1	2	0	0	0	0	0	0	0	0	.273	.182
Reese, Pokey, Indianapolis	.239	89	387	343	51	82	135	21	1	10	46	1	3	4	36	0	81	8	5	3	.394	.316
Remlinger, Mike, Indianapolis*	.500	41	2	2	0	1	2	1	0	0	0	0	0	0	0	0	0	0	0	0	1.000	.500
Reynolds, Harold, Omaha†	.202	38	124	109	12	22	33	6	1	1	11	0	2	0	13	1	10	2	3	2	.303	.282
Riles, Ernest, Buffalo*	.278	6	23	18	5	5	8	0	0	1	7	0	1	1	3	0	1	0	0	2	.444	.391
Ripken, Billy, Buffalo	.292	130	492	448	51	131	179	34	1	4	56	6	8	2	28	0	38	6	4	14	.400	.331
Ritchie, Gregg, Oklahoma City*	.179	9	34	28	5	5	8	0	0	1	4	0	0	0	6	1	4	1	0	0	.286	.324
Rivera, Luis, Oklahoma City	.138	19	60	58	3	8	15	4	0	1	3	0	0	1	1	0	6	0	0	1	.259	.167
Robertson, Mike, Nashville*	.248	139	565	499	55	124	206	17	4	19	52	3	2	11	50	7	72	2	4	8	.413	.329
Rohrmeier, Dan, Indianapolis	.176	10	34	34	5	6	11	3	1	0	3	0	0	0	0	0	4	0	0	1	.324	.176

Player, Team	Avg.	G	TPA	AB	R	H	TB	2B	3B	HR	RBI	SH	SF	HP	BB	IBB	SO	SB	CS	GDP	Slg.	OBP
Rolls, David, Oklahoma City	.000	2	7	5	0	0	0	0	0	0	1	0	0	1	1	0	4	0	0	0	.000	.286
Ronan, Marc, Louisville*	.213	78	241	225	15	48	56	8	0	0	8	2	0	0	14	2	42	4	3	10	.249	.259
Roper, John, Indianapolis	.000	8	2	1	0	0	0	0	0	0	0	1	0	0	0	0	1	0	0	0	.000	.000
Ruffin, Johnny, Indianapolis	.000	36	1	1	0	0	0	0	0	0	0	0	0	0	0	0	0	0	0	0	.000	.000
Sabo, Chris, Louisville	.393	9	30	28	5	11	14	0	0	1	4	0	0	1	1	0	4	0	0	0	.500	.433
Saenz, Olmedo, Nashville	.304	111	478	415	60	126	193	26	1	13	74	3	3	12	45	1	60	0	2	11	.465	.385
Sagmoen, Marc, Oklahoma City*	.223	56	211	188	20	42	68	11	3	3	25	1	4	2	16	0	31	5	2	2	.362	.286
Salkeld, Roger, Indianapolis	.375	21	8	8	2	3	5	2	0	0	1	0	0	0	0	0	4	0	0	0	.625	.375
Sauveur, Rich, Indianapolis*	.000	52	1	1	0	0	0	0	0	0	0	0	0	0	0	0	1	0	0	0	.000	.000
Schu, Rick, Oklahoma City	.271	110	445	398	49	108	169	19	3	12	57	0	2	5	40	1	63	5	3	8	.425	.344
Scudder, Scott, Indianapolis	.500	7	2	2	0	1	2	1	0	0	0	0	0	0	0	0	0	0	0	0	1.000	.500
Sellers, Rick, Indianapolis	.263	5	20	19	3	5	15	1	0	3	7	0	0	0	1	0	3	0	0	0	.789	.300
Service, Scott, Indianapolis	.000	36	3	3	0	0	0	0	0	0	0	0	0	0	0	0	1	0	0	0	.000	.000
Shave, Jon, Oklahoma City	.205	32	92	83	10	17	18	1	0	0	5	1	0	1	7	0	28	1	0	1	.217	.275
Simmons, Scott, Louisville	.500	2	2	2	0	1	1	0	0	0	0	0	0	0	0	0	0	0	0	0	.500	.500
Singleton, Duane, New Orleans*	.268	106	401	355	48	95	125	10	4	4	29	3	1	3	39	2	63	31	15	7	.352	.344
Sisco, Steve, Omaha	.208	7	27	24	4	5	6	1	0	0	0	1	0	0	2	0	8	0	0	0	.250	.269
Smith, Ed, Buffalo	.323	13	35	31	4	10	21	0	1	3	9	0	1	0	3	0	5	0	1	0	.677	.371
Smith, Greg, N.O.-Ind.†	.212	63	208	184	19	39	44	3	1	0	9	2	1	2	19	1	25	11	7	6	.239	.291
Smith, Ottis, Iowa	.400	5	5	5	0	2	2	0	0	0	0	0	0	0	0	0	3	0	0	0	.400	.400
Snopek, Chris, Nashville	.323	113	456	393	56	127	194	23	4	12	55	6	3	4	50	1	72	2	5	5	.494	.402
Staton, Dave, New Orleans	.252	108	381	325	42	82	152	11	1	19	46	1	1	8	46	0	96	0	3	6	.468	.358
Steenstra, Kennie, Iowa	.000	29	16	16	0	0	0	0	0	0	0	0	0	0	0	0	9	0	0	0	.000	.000
Stefanski, Mike, New Orleans	.246	78	253	228	30	56	76	10	2	2	24	5	5	1	14	0	28	2	0	8	.333	.286
Stewart, Andy, Omaha	.301	44	176	156	24	47	67	11	0	3	21	0	0	8	12	1	18	0	1	4	.429	.381
Stillwell, Kurt, Indianapolis†	.264	100	390	341	50	90	131	14	3	7	30	0	3	1	45	1	51	4	3	6	.384	.349
Strickland, Chad, Omaha	.273	8	24	22	3	6	8	2	0	0	5	0	1	0	1	0	4	0	0	1	.364	.292
Sturtze, Tanyon, Iowa	.000	23	4	4	0	0	0	0	0	0	0	0	0	0	0	0	1	0	0	0	.000	.000
Stynes, Chris, Omaha	.275	83	349	306	51	84	133	12	5	9	42	4	5	5	27	0	24	4	5	7	.435	.338
Sutko, Glenn, New Orleans	.208	42	109	101	7	21	38	8	0	3	14	1	0	0	7	0	35	0	0	1	.376	.259
Swartzbaugh, Dave, Iowa	.000	30	1	1	0	0	0	0	0	0	0	0	0	0	0	0	1	0	0	0	.000	.000
Sweeney, Mark, Louisville*	.368	22	94	76	15	28	42	8	0	2	22	0	2	2	14	1	8	2	0	0	.553	.468
Talanoa, Scott, New Orleans	.143	31	107	98	9	14	21	4	0	1	3	0	1	2	6	0	26	0	0	5	.214	.206
Taylor, Rob, Iowa	.000	54	2	2	0	0	0	0	0	0	0	0	0	0	0	0	2	0	0	0	.000	.000
Thomas, Skeets, Louisville*	.249	84	292	273	29	68	112	15	1	9	34	0	0	1	18	0	76	0	0	14	.410	.298
Trafton, Todd, Indianapolis	.000	5	5	5	0	0	0	0	0	0	0	0	0	0	0	0	2	0	0	0	.000	.000
Tremie, Chris, Nashville	.200	67	209	190	13	38	48	4	0	2	16	4	0	2	13	0	37	0	0	6	.253	.259
Tucker, Michael, Omaha*	.305	71	307	275	37	84	122	18	4	4	28	2	2	4	24	5	39	11	4	3	.444	.367
Unroe, Tim, New Orleans	.261	102	402	371	43	97	140	21	2	6	45	1	5	7	18	1	94	4	3	9	.377	.304
Valrie, Kerry, Nashville	.250	138	593	544	75	136	193	30	3	7	55	2	4	3	40	0	107	22	15	15	.355	.303
Vargas, Hector, Oklahoma City	.275	98	343	305	38	84	98	10	2	0	27	4	2	2	30	1	54	6	1	9	.321	.342
Vasquez, Marcos, Indianapolis	.500	2	2	2	0	1	1	0	0	0	0	0	0	0	0	0	0	0	0	0	.500	.500
Viola, Frank, Indianapolis*	.333	6	4	3	0	1	1	0	0	0	0	1	0	0	0	0	0	0	0	0	.333	.333
Vitiello, Joe, Omaha	.279	59	249	229	33	64	118	14	2	12	42	0	2	6	12	0	50	0	1	9	.515	.329
Wachter, Derek, New Orleans	.257	112	432	384	44	98	147	23	1	8	45	0	3	5	40	2	69	2	2	11	.385	.331
Walker, Mike, Iowa	.000	16	1	1	0	0	0	0	0	0	0	0	0	0	0	0	1	0	0	0	.000	.000
Ward, Turner, New Orleans†	.242	11	37	33	3	8	14	1	1	1	3	0	0	0	4	0	10	0	0	1	.424	.324
Warren, Brian, Indianapolis	1.000	41	1	1	1	1	1	0	0	0	0	0	0	0	0	0	0	0	0	0	1.000	1.000
Watson, Allen, Louisville*	.000	4	3	2	0	0	0	0	0	0	0	0	0	0	1	0	0	0	0	0	.000	.333
Weger, Wes, New Orleans	.286	64	247	234	28	67	89	16	0	2	24	1	1	1	10	0	31	0	2	5	.380	.317
Wilson, Brandon, Nas.-Ind.	.278	31	104	97	11	27	35	5	0	1	10	1	0	0	6	0	12	3	1	3	.361	.320
Wilson, Nigel, Indianapolis*	.313	82	326	304	53	95	179	27	3	17	51	0	1	8	13	4	95	5	3	2	.589	.356
Wolak, Jerry, Nashville	.229	108	419	385	43	88	153	21	1	14	63	5	2	7	20	1	83	5	3	12	.397	.278
Woodson, Tracy, Louisville	.262	118	469	431	62	113	202	35	0	18	76	0	6	5	27	5	43	12	4	18	.469	.309
Worthington, Craig, Indianapolis	.318	81	313	277	48	88	134	19	0	9	41	1	4	0	31	1	51	1	1	5	.484	.381
Wrona, Rick, Buf.-Lou.	.226	47	135	124	10	28	40	7	1	1	12	2	2	2	5	0	25	0	1	8	.323	.263
Yelding, Eric, Buffalo	.346	29	88	81	13	28	38	7	0	1	9	0	1	0	6	0	12	3	1	0	.469	.386
Young, Dmitri, Louisville†	.286	2	8	7	3	2	2	0	0	0	0	0	0	0	1	0	1	0	0	0	.286	.375
Zeile, Todd, Louisville	.125	2	8	8	0	1	1	0	0	0	0	0	0	0	0	0	2	0	0	0	.125	.125
Zupcic, Bob, Nashville	.244	13	55	41	9	10	18	2	0	2	5	0	1	0	13	1	6	1	0	2	.439	.418

GRAND SLAMS: Burnitz, Gibralter, 3 each; Giannelli, Hamelin, McCarty, Mottola, Snopek, 2 each; Brooks, Bruett, Carter, Deak, Dodson, Dorsett, Dostal, Fox, Gordon, Grotewold, Horn, Hunter, Kosco, Koslofski, Mitchell, Pena, Ramsey, Weger, Worthington, 1 each.

AWARDED FIRST BASE ON CATCHER'S INTERFERENCE: Stynes 2 (Martindale, J. Ortiz); Koslofski (Tremie).

PLAYERS WITH TWO OR MORE TEAMS

Player, Team	Avg.	G	TPA	AB	R	H	TB	2B	3B	HR	RBI	SH	SF	HP	BB	IBB	SO	SB	CS	GDP	Slg.	OBP
Bell, David, Buffalo	.272	70	284	254	34	69	106	11	1	8	34	1	3	4	22	0	37	0	3	4	.417	.336
Bell, David, Louisville	.276	18	82	76	9	21	29	3	1	1	9	1	0	3	2	1	10	4	0	2	.382	.321
Byington, John, New Orleans	.255	13	52	47	5	12	16	1	0	1	3	0	2	1	2	0	4	1	0	1	.340	.288
Byington, John, Oklahoma City	.259	109	421	390	44	101	126	15	2	2	29	4	4	4	19	2	37	6	2	16	.323	.297
Duncan, Chip, Oklahoma City	.000	3	0	0	0	0	0	0	0	0	0	0	0	0	0	0	0	0	0	0	.000	.000
Duncan, Chip, New Orleans	.000	15	3	2	0	0	0	0	0	0	0	0	0	0	1	0	2	0	0	0	.000	.333
Howitt, Dann, Nashville*	.226	45	151	133	16	30	47	6	1	3	15	0	2	0	16	4	32	0	3	5	.353	.305
Howitt, Dann, Buffalo*	.303	41	133	119	19	36	62	8	3	4	18	0	0	0	14	2	30	0	0	2	.521	.376
Hulett, Tim, Louisville	.300	3	12	10	1	3	4	1	0	0	3	0	0	0	2	1	0	0	1	0	.400	.417
Hulett, Tim, Oklahoma City	.213	39	148	141	14	30	41	6	1	1	7	0	0	0	7	0	33	0	0	1	.291	.250
Smith, Greg, New Orleans†	.212	59	192	170	18	36	41	3	1	0	9	2	1	2	17	1	22	11	7	6	.241	.289
Smith, Greg, Indianapolis†	.214	4	16	14	1	3	3	0	0	0	0	0	0	0	2	0	3	0	0	0	.214	.313
Wilson, Brandon, Nashville	.294	27	90	85	8	25	33	5	0	1	10	1	0	0	4	0	11	3	1	3	.388	.326
Wilson, Brandon, Indianapolis	.167	4	14	12	3	2	2	0	0	0	0	0	0	0	2	0	1	0	0	0	.167	.286
Wrona, Rick, Buffalo	.226	31	101	93	9	21	27	6	0	0	10	2	1	2	3	0	19	0	1	7	.290	.263
Wrona, Rick, Louisville	.226	16	34	31	1	7	13	1	1	1	2	0	1	0	2	0	6	0	0	1	.419	.265

1995 PITCHING

TEAM

Team	W	L	Pct.	ERA	G	CG	ShO	Sv.	IP	H	TBF	R	ER	HR	SH	SF	HB	BB	IBB	SO	WP	Bk.
Louisville	74	70	.514	3.79	144	10	8	42	1241.0	1208	5307	623	522	106	47	40	45	406	41	840	60	5
Buffalo	82	62	.569	3.91	144	13	8	45	1251.0	1278	5350	604	543	91	27	48	61	396	15	820	44	4
Indianapolis	88	56	.611	3.91	144	12	8	41	1262.0	1178	5348	642	548	111	33	46	40	434	33	883	67	5
New Orleans	63	79	.444	3.98	142	11	8	32	1213.2	1274	5221	606	537	113	29	32	50	445	29	806	67	10
Iowa	69	74	.483	4.03	143	13	8	32	1240.1	1224	5329	614	555	140	46	38	56	496	38	889	59	3
Nashville	68	76	.472	4.04	144	8	11	39	1276.2	1338	5502	673	573	145	44	50	40	405	40	931	49	9
Omaha	76	68	.528	4.26	144	12	10	36	1238.1	1301	5328	660	586	132	43	44	53	423	25	820	51	8
Oklahoma City	54	89	.378	4.56	143	11	7	26	1220.2	1328	5427	709	618	122	47	45	71	520	25	835	71	12

INDIVIDUAL

TOP QUALIFIERS FOR EARNED-RUN AVERAGE TITLE

Minimum 115 innings. *Lefthanded pitcher.

Pitcher, Team	W	L	Pct.	ERA	G	GS	CG	ShO	GF	Sv.	IP	H	TBF	R	ER	HR	SH	SF	HB	BB	IBB	SO	WP	Bk.
Bolton, Rodney, Nashville	14	3	.824	2.88	20	20	3	1	0	0	131.1	127	534	44	42	13	2	2	7	23	1	76	2	0
Reed, Rick, Indianapolis	11	4	.733	3.33	22	21	3	1	0	0	135.0	127	551	60	50	16	4	2	2	26	2	92	0	0
Anderson, Mike, Iowa	7	9	.438	3.46	27	27	3	1	0	0	171.2	156	715	71	66	23	3	3	12	69	3	123	7	1
Roa, Joe, Buffalo	17	3	.850	3.50	25	24	3	0	1	0	164.2	168	678	71	64	9	2	5	7	28	1	93	1	2
Taylor, Scott, N.O.-O.C.	8	8	.500	3.55	24	21	1	1	0	0	129.1	132	557	62	51	12	4	2	7	41	0	74	5	0
Abbott, Paul, Iowa	7	7	.500	3.67	46	11	0	0	7	0	115.1	104	498	50	47	12	4	1	0	64	4	127	12	0
Minchey, Nate, Louisville	8	7	.533	3.73	26	24	1	0	0	0	147.1	153	633	77	61	9	4	5	7	42	0	67	9	1
Steenstra, Kennie, Iowa	9	12	.429	3.89	29	26	6	2	1	0	171.1	174	722	85	74	15	6	6	8	48	3	96	6	0
Bell, Eric, Buffalo*	13	9	.591	3.90	28	24	3	1	1	0	161.1	177	687	76	70	18	1	4	7	47	0	86	3	0
DeLaRosa, Francisco, Louisville	2	5	.286	4.06	28	19	1	0	1	0	115.1	104	483	56	52	15	2	3	2	38	4	66	2	1
Salkeld, Roger, Indianapolis	12	2	.857	4.22	20	20	1	0	0	0	119.1	96	497	60	56	13	3	4	2	57	1	86	3	0
Farrell, John, Buffalo	11	9	.550	4.54	29	28	2	0	1	0	184.1	198	792	97	93	17	2	9	16	61	1	92	11	1
Farrell, Mike, New Orleans*	8	10	.444	4.57	25	24	0	0	0	0	141.2	173	619	84	72	19	2	5	4	38	3	74	2	1
Buckley, Travis, Indianapolis	10	9	.526	4.70	23	18	3	2	0	0	132.0	141	561	80	69	8	3	4	3	33	3	85	4	0
Beltran, Rigo, Louisville*	8	9	.471	5.21	24	24	0	0	0	0	129.2	156	575	81	75	12	2	8	5	34	0	92	4	2

DEPARTMENTAL LEADERS: W—Roa, 17; L—Perez, Steenstra, 12; Pct.—Salkeld, .857; G—Munoz, 57; GS—J. Farrell, 28; CG—Steenstra, 6; ShO—Buckley, Milacki, Nichting, Steenstra, 2; GF—Sauveur, 43; Sv.—Bailey, 25; IP—J. Farrell, 184.1; H—J. Farrell, 198; TBF—J. Farrell, 792; R—J. Farrell, 97; ER—J. Farrell, 93; HR—Baldwin, 27; SH—Raczka, 8; SF—J. Farrell, 9; HB—J. Farrell, 16; BB—M. Anderson, 69; IBB—Carpenter, 10; SO—Abbott, 127; WP—Jean, 14; Bk.—Baldwin, Jean, 3.

ALL PITCHERS

*Lefthanded pitcher.

Pitcher, Team	W	L	Pct.	ERA	G	GS	CG	ShO	GF	Sv.	IP	H	TBF	R	ER	HR	SH	SF	HB	BB	IBB	SO	WP	Bk.
Abbott, Paul, Iowa	7	7	.500	3.67	46	11	0	0	7	0	115.1	104	498	50	47	12	4	1	0	64	4	127	12	0
Adams, Terry, Iowa	0	0	.000	0.00	7	0	0	0	6	5	6.1	3	25	0	0	0	0	0	0	2	0	10	1	0
Alberro, Jose, Oklahoma City	4	2	.667	3.36	20	10	0	0	7	0	77.2	73	331	34	29	4	2	3	4	27	2	55	6	0
Anderson, Mike, Iowa	7	9	.438	3.46	27	27	3	1	0	0	171.2	156	715	71	66	23	3	3	12	69	3	123	7	1
Anderson, Scott, Omaha	5	3	.625	4.17	15	11	1	0	0	0	73.1	63	294	37	34	9	0	1	2	16	0	47	0	0
Archer, Kurt, New Orleans	2	6	.250	3.25	38	0	0	0	11	2	61.0	57	256	23	22	5	6	3	5	17	2	41	5	0
Austin, Jim, Buffalo	1	1	.500	12.00	2	1	0	0	0	0	3.0	7	19	6	4	1	0	0	0	2	0	1	1	0
Bailey, Cory, Louisville	5	3	.625	4.55	55	0	0	0	40	25	59.1	51	258	30	30	6	6	2	0	30	4	49	7	0
Baldwin, James, Nashville	5	9	.357	5.85	18	18	0	0	0	0	95.1	120	448	76	62	27	1	3	2	44	1	89	10	3
Barber, Brian, Louisville	6	5	.545	4.70	20	19	0	0	0	0	107.1	105	465	67	56	14	2	6	4	40	1	94	1	0
Barfield, John, Oklahoma City*	0	0	.000	0.00	4	0	0	0	1	1	7.1	4	26	2	0	0	0	0	0	1	0	2	0	0
Batchelor, Richard, Louisville	5	4	.556	3.28	50	6	0	0	7	0	85.0	85	352	39	31	5	4	3	7	16	2	61	0	0
Beatty, Blaine, Indianapolis*	7	1	.875	3.61	20	8	0	0	1	0	67.1	80	293	33	27	7	4	1	2	16	0	37	3	2
Belcher, Tim, Indianapolis	0	0	.000	1.80	2	2	0	0	0	0	10.0	6	36	2	2	2	0	0	1	1	0	8	0	0
Bell, Eric, Buffalo*	13	9	.591	3.90	28	24	3	1	1	0	161.1	177	687	76	70	18	1	4	7	47	0	86	3	0
Beltran, Rigo, Louisville*	8	9	.471	5.21	24	24	0	0	0	0	129.2	156	575	81	75	12	2	8	5	34	0	92	4	2
Benes, Alan, Louisville	4	2	.667	2.41	11	11	2	1	0	0	56.0	37	215	16	15	5	0	0	1	14	1	54	2	0
Bere, Jason, Nashville	1	0	1.000	3.38	1	1	0	0	0	0	5.1	6	24	2	2	0	0	0	0	2	0	7	0	0
Bertotti, Mike, Nashville*	2	3	.400	8.72	7	6	0	0	1	0	32.0	41	154	34	31	8	0	1	3	17	0	35	0	0
Bevil, Brian, Omaha	1	3	.250	9.41	6	6	0	0	0	0	22.0	40	119	31	23	7	1	0	3	14	1	10	2	0
Bluma, Jaime, Omaha	0	0	.000	3.04	18	0	0	0	10	4	23.2	21	101	13	8	1	3	3	0	14	4	12	3	0
Bolton, Rodney, Nashville	14	3	.824	2.88	20	20	3	1	0	0	131.1	127	534	44	42	13	2	2	7	23	1	76	2	0
Bolton, Tom, Nashville*	5	7	.417	4.43	19	17	1	1	1	0	101.2	106	433	52	50	10	0	1	3	31	0	82	3	2
Boze, Marshall, New Orleans	3	9	.250	4.27	23	19	1	0	1	1	111.2	134	495	65	53	10	2	2	2	45	1	47	6	1
Brandenburg, Mark, Okla. City	0	5	.000	2.02	35	0	0	0	15	2	58.0	52	235	16	13	2	3	1	2	15	5	51	0	2
Brewer, Billy, Omaha*	0	0	.000	0.00	6	0	0	0	1	0	7.0	1	25	0	0	0	0	0	0	7	0	5	2	1
Bronkey, Jeff, New Orleans	0	1	.000	2.25	2	1	0	0	0	0	8.0	8	29	2	2	0	1	0	0	1	0	2	1	0
Brown, Kevin, Omaha*	0	0	.000	7.62	7	1	0	0	0	0	13.0	20	71	13	11	0	3	2	0	12	1	5	1	0
Browning, Tom, Omaha*	2	1	.667	3.43	5	5	0	0	0	0	21.0	13	78	8	8	1	1	0	0	5	0	5	1	0
Brumley, Duff, Oklahoma City	1	1	.500	5.40	3	0	0	0	1	1	5.0	6	24	4	3	0	1	0	0	2	0	3	0	0
Buckels, Gary, Louisville	1	2	.333	5.51	13	0	0	0	6	5	16.1	18	80	11	10	3	2	1	0	13	2	8	3	0
Buckley, Travis, Indianapolis	10	9	.526	4.70	23	18	3	2	0	0	132.0	141	561	80	69	8	3	4	3	33	3	85	4	0
Bunch, Mel, Omaha	1	7	.125	4.57	12	11	1	0	0	0	65.0	63	272	37	33	10	3	4	0	20	2	50	8	1
Burrows, Terry, Oklahoma City*	0	1	.000	10.13	5	0	0	0	0	0	2.2	5	16	4	3	0	0	0	0	2	0	4	1	0
Busby, Mike, Louisville	2	2	.500	3.29	6	6	1	0	0	0	38.1	28	154	18	14	2	2	2	3	11	0	26	2	0
Bushing, Chris, Oklahoma City	0	0	.000	13.50	3	0	0	0	2	0	1.1	5	10	2	2	2	0	1	0	0	0	2	0	0
Caceres, Edgar, Omaha	0	0	.000	9.00	1	0	0	0	1	0	2.0	4	11	2	2	0	0	0	0	1	0	1	1	0
Cadaret, Greg, Louisville*	1	0	1.000	3.09	12	0	0	0	2	0	11.2	14	50	4	4	0	1	0	0	1	0	7	0	0
Campbell, Mike, Iowa	9	3	.750	2.45	21	15	0	0	2	0	102.2	93	419	31	28	10	4	4	3	29	5	88	2	0
Carpenter, Cris, Louisville	2	5	.286	2.43	49	0	0	0	20	5	66.2	59	273	18	18	6	6	2	1	20	10	41	3	0
Casian, Larry, Iowa*	0	0	.000	2.13	13	0	0	0	4	1	12.2	9	48	3	3	0	1	1	1	2	1	9	0	0

Pitcher, Team	W	L	Pct.	ERA	G	GS	CG	ShO	GF	Sv.	IP	H	TBF	R	ER	HR	SH	SF	HB	BB	IBB	SO	WP	Bk.
Chapin, Darrin, Buffalo	0	1	.000	8.31	6	0	0	0	3	0	8.2	12	42	10	8	2	2	1	0	2	1	4	1	0
Cimorelli, Frank, Louisville	1	1	.500	9.00	6	0	0	0	2	0	5.0	12	26	7	5	2	0	0	0	0	0	3	0	0
Clark, Mark, Buffalo	4	0	1.000	3.57	5	5	0	0	0	0	35.1	39	151	14	14	0	1	2	2	10	0	17	0	0
Combs, Pat, New Orleans*	1	1	.500	5.40	12	2	0	0	5	0	15.0	19	78	11	9	1	0	1	1	13	0	10	5	0
Converse, Jim, Omaha	1	0	1.000	0.00	4	0	0	0	0	0	5.0	1	19	0	0	0	0	0	0	1	0	9	1	0
Costello, Fred, Nashville	0	2	.000	5.11	7	0	0	0	5	0	12.1	17	61	9	7	1	1	0	0	7	0	6	2	0
Courtright, John, Indianapolis*	2	1	.667	4.28	13	2	0	0	1	0	33.2	29	147	18	16	2	2	1	2	15	1	13	4	1
Crawford, Carlos, Buffalo	0	1	.000	5.64	13	3	0	0	3	1	30.1	36	137	22	19	2	2	0	0	12	0	15	0	0
Creek, Doug, Louisville*	3	2	.600	3.23	26	0	0	0	5	0	30.2	20	132	12	11	1	0	0	1	21	0	29	4	0
Curtis, Chris, Oklahoma City	3	5	.375	5.00	51	0	0	0	22	5	77.1	81	358	53	43	5	6	3	5	39	3	40	2	0
Dabney, Fred, Iowa*	4	6	.400	5.95	33	1	0	0	4	0	56.0	68	262	42	37	8	5	3	3	29	3	33	5	0
Darwin, Danny, Oklahoma City	0	0	.000	0.00	1	1	0	0	0	0	3.0	1	10	0	0	0	0	0	0	0	0	4	0	0
Davis, Clint, Louisville	0	0	.000	12.27	4	0	0	0	0	0	3.2	6	19	5	5	1	0	0	0	2	1	4	0	1
Davis, John, Nashville	1	1	.500	0.00	4	0	0	0	3	1	3.1	3	16	2	0	0	0	0	0	3	1	0	0	0
Davis, Storm, Indianapolis	0	0	.000	3.38	4	0	0	0	1	0	5.1	4	22	2	2	0	0	1	0	3	0	4	1	0
DeJesus, Jose, Omaha	3	6	.333	6.13	36	6	0	0	19	10	61.2	56	288	45	42	10	2	5	2	52	3	49	7	0
DeLaRosa, Francisco, Louisville	2	5	.286	4.06	28	19	1	0	1	0	115.1	104	483	56	52	15	2	3	2	38	4	66	2	1
DeLeon, Luis, Iowa	0	1	.000	13.50	2	0	0	0	1	0	2.0	6	12	3	3	0	0	0	0	0	0	3	0	1
Dettmer, John, Oklahoma City	0	0	.000	2.08	5	0	0	0	3	0	8.2	10	37	3	2	1	1	0	0	4	0	10	1	1
Dibble, Rob, New Orleans	0	1	.000	0.00	4	0	0	0	1	0	4.0	1	16	2	0	0	0	0	1	2	0	6	0	0
Dixon, Steve, Iowa*	6	3	.667	2.85	53	0	0	0	19	0	41.0	34	176	16	13	4	0	2	5	19	4	38	2	0
Donnelly, Brendan, Indianapolis	1	1	.500	23.63	3	0	0	0	0	0	2.2	7	18	8	7	2	0	1	1	2	0	1	2	0
Dorlarque, Aaron, Omaha	2	2	.500	4.24	24	1	0	0	13	4	40.1	38	166	19	19	7	1	3	3	15	1	24	1	0
Drahman, Brian, O.C.-Ind.	2	2	.500	2.83	24	0	0	0	15	4	35.0	39	157	11	11	3	1	1	2	15	3	22	0	0
Duncan, Chip, O.C.-N.O.	1	4	.200	5.90	17	5	0	0	6	0	39.2	50	183	28	26	7	2	3	2	19	2	26	5	1
Eddy, Chris, Omaha*	1	1	.500	7.27	14	0	0	0	6	0	17.1	20	84	15	14	1	1	2	2	12	2	12	0	0
Edens, Tom, Iowa	2	0	1.000	3.46	20	3	0	0	5	1	41.2	36	175	17	16	3	1	0	3	17	1	28	2	0
Ellis, Robert, Nashville	1	1	.500	2.18	4	4	0	0	0	0	20.2	16	85	7	5	2	0	1	1	10	0	9	1	0
Embree, Alan, Buffalo*	3	4	.429	0.89	30	0	0	0	19	5	40.2	31	170	10	4	0	1	2	1	19	2	56	0	0
Farrell, John, Buffalo	11	9	.550	4.54	29	28	2	0	1	0	184.1	198	792	97	93	17	2	9	16	61	1	92	11	1
Farrell, Mike, New Orleans*	8	10	.444	4.57	25	24	0	0	0	0	141.2	173	619	84	72	19	2	5	4	38	3	74	2	1
Ferry, Mike, Indianapolis	1	2	.333	5.19	3	3	0	0	0	0	17.1	21	76	15	10	3	0	2	0	3	0	3	0	0
Fleming, Dave, Omaha*	1	0	1.000	3.38	3	3	0	0	0	0	16.0	17	72	6	6	1	1	0	2	7	0	8	0	0
Franco, Matt, Iowa	0	0	.000	0.00	1	0	0	0	1	0	1.0	1	5	0	0	0	0	0	0	1	0	1	1	0
Frascatore, John, Louisville	2	8	.200	3.95	28	10	1	0	15	5	82.0	89	370	54	36	5	5	2	3	34	3	55	5	0
Fritz, John, New Orleans	6	3	.667	3.97	41	6	0	0	6	1	81.2	70	348	38	36	11	1	0	4	42	4	56	5	0
Frohwirth, Todd, Buffalo	0	1	.000	3.34	26	0	0	0	11	3	32.1	31	137	13	12	4	1	1	1	12	1	33	0	0
Fyhrie, Mike, Omaha	3	4	.429	4.45	14	11	0	0	2	0	60.2	71	259	34	30	7	0	2	4	14	0	39	0	0
Gajkowski, Steve, Nashville	0	1	.000	2.55	15	0	0	0	5	0	24.2	26	103	15	7	2	0	1	1	8	1	12	1	0
Ganote, Joe, New Orleans	7	4	.636	3.42	14	13	2	1	1	0	81.2	88	348	35	31	6	5	2	6	21	2	56	6	0
Garces, Rich, Iowa	0	2	.000	2.86	23	0	0	0	15	7	28.1	25	116	10	9	3	0	0	1	8	1	36	0	1
Garrelts, Scott, Omaha	1	2	.333	5.30	9	1	0	0	3	1	18.2	17	84	12	11	2	0	0	2	13	1	15	2	0
Geeve, Dave, Oklahoma City	2	5	.286	5.66	10	10	2	0	0	0	55.2	72	249	36	35	7	3	5	4	13	1	30	0	2
Givens, Brian, New Orleans*	7	4	.636	2.55	16	11	2	1	1	0	77.2	67	320	28	22	2	2	3	0	33	1	75	2	2
Goetz, Barry, Oklahoma City	4	6	.400	5.72	40	6	0	0	15	1	89.2	97	399	60	57	8	3	6	4	49	3	46	1	2
Gozzo, Mauro, Iowa	0	3	.000	4.15	6	6	0	0	0	0	30.1	37	131	22	14	4	2	0	0	11	1	11	3	0
Grant, Mark, Iowa	5	2	.714	3.13	11	11	2	0	0	0	69.0	58	276	28	24	6	0	2	2	10	0	39	1	0
Graves, Daniel, Buffalo	0	0	.000	3.00	3	0	0	0	3	0	3.0	5	16	4	1	0	0	0	0	1	0	2	1	0
Green, Gary, Omaha	0	0	.000	10.80	2	0	0	0	2	0	1.2	5	10	2	2	0	0	1	0	0	0	1	0	0
Grimsley, Jason, Buffalo	5	3	.625	2.91	10	10	2	0	0	0	68.0	61	285	26	22	4	2	3	3	19	0	40	4	0
Grott, Matt, Indianapolis*	7	3	.700	4.24	25	18	2	1	2	2	114.2	99	468	61	54	10	2	5	3	24	2	74	11	0
Hammaker, Atlee, Nashville*	1	2	.333	1.27	15	0	0	0	5	1	28.1	27	115	4	4	1	1	0	0	7	2	20	0	0
Harris, Pep, Buffalo	2	1	.667	2.48	14	0	0	0	3	0	32.2	32	141	11	9	2	0	0	0	15	0	18	0	0
Harris, Reggie, Omaha	0	1	.000	18.00	2	0	0	0	0	0	2.0	5	12	4	4	1	0	0	0	1	0	2	1	0
Harrison, Brian, Omaha	4	2	.667	6.13	16	8	1	0	1	0	54.1	76	248	39	37	7	3	3	1	10	0	12	1	0
Helling, Rick, Oklahoma City	4	8	.333	5.33	20	20	3	0	0	0	109.2	132	493	73	65	13	2	6	10	41	1	80	3	1
Heredia, Wilson, Oklahoma City	1	4	.200	6.82	8	7	0	0	0	0	31.2	40	158	26	24	3	1	1	5	25	1	21	1	0
Huisman, Rick, Omaha	0	0	.000	1.80	5	0	0	0	3	1	5.0	3	19	1	1	1	0	0	0	1	0	13	0	0
Hurst, James, O.C.-Ind.*	1	5	.167	7.20	31	7	0	0	13	5	50.0	73	249	42	40	7	2	0	3	26	0	43	4	0
Ignasiak, Mike, New Orleans	1	1	.500	2.50	4	2	0	0	1	0	18.0	9	71	5	5	2	0	0	0	8	0	19	1	0
Jackson, Danny, Louisville*	1	0	1.000	1.29	1	1	1	0	0	0	7.0	8	30	1	1	0	0	0	1	2	0	2	0	0
Jackson, Mike, Indianapolis	0	0	.000	0.00	2	1	0	0	1	0	2.0	0	6	0	0	0	0	0	0	0	0	1	0	0
Jarvis, Kevin, Indianapolis	4	2	.667	4.45	10	10	2	1	0	0	60.2	62	262	33	30	2	0	2	0	18	1	37	5	0
Jean, Domingo, O.C.-Ind.	4	8	.333	6.00	26	13	1	0	9	1	90.0	103	425	70	60	12	5	2	1	61	1	73	14	3
Johnson, Dane, Nashville	4	4	.500	2.41	46	0	0	0	28	15	56.0	48	240	24	15	2	5	1	1	28	6	51	3	1
Jones, Calvin, Nashville	0	0	.000	6.75	5	0	0	0	0	0	6.2	13	38	8	5	3	0	0	0	3	1	5	0	0
Jones, Stacy, New Orleans	3	2	.600	3.02	34	0	0	0	25	6	47.2	51	197	16	16	3	1	1	2	12	2	39	3	0
Karchner, Matt, Nashville	3	3	.500	1.45	28	0	0	0	21	9	37.1	39	156	7	6	3	5	0	0	10	5	29	2	0
Karl, Scott, New Orleans*	3	4	.429	3.30	8	6	1	1	1	0	46.1	47	191	18	17	3	0	1	2	12	2	29	1	0
Keyser, Brian, Nashville	2	4	.333	2.36	10	10	2	1	0	0	72.1	49	273	23	19	4	3	3	1	9	0	40	1	0
Kiefer, Mark, New Orleans	8	2	.800	2.82	12	12	1	0	0	0	70.1	60	290	22	22	5	1	0	5	19	0	52	6	0
Kilgo, Rusty, Indianapolis*	0	0	.000	4.50	2	0	0	0	0	0	2.0	4	10	2	1	0	0	0	0	1	0	1	0	0
Klink, Joe, Buffalo*	2	1	.667	3.00	45	0	0	0	21	8	39.0	31	161	13	13	0	3	5	1	15	0	32	3	0
Kutzler, Jerry, Omaha	8	5	.615	4.02	37	7	0	0	12	4	103.0	128	449	48	46	8	3	2	5	27	2	45	0	0
Lacy, Kerry, Oklahoma City	0	0	.000	0.00	1	0	0	0	1	1	2.1	0	7	0	0	0	0	0	0	0	0	1	0	0
Lancaster, Les, Buffalo	4	5	.444	4.31	45	3	1	0	10	0	87.2	90	372	45	42	6	2	1	2	19	5	68	4	0
Levine, Alan, Nashville	0	2	.000	5.14	3	3	0	0	0	0	14.0	20	69	10	8	1	0	0	0	7	0	14	3	0
Lewis, James, Buffalo	6	4	.600	3.64	18	16	1	0	2	1	94.0	101	405	42	38	7	1	3	9	25	0	50	4	0
Linton, Doug, Omaha	7	7	.500	4.40	18	18	2	1	0	0	108.1	129	472	60	53	9	5	3	7	24	2	85	3	1
Lopez, Albie, Buffalo	5	10	.333	4.44	18	18	1	1	0	0	101.1	101	448	57	50	10	0	5	2	51	0	82	8	0
Lorraine, Andrew, Nashville*	4	1	.800	6.00	7	7	0	0	0	0	39.0	51	184	29	26	4	1	3	1	12	0	26	2	0
Lynch, David, Buffalo*	1	2	.333	4.30	14	0	0	0	3	0	14.2	16	66	8	7	0	1	1	0	7	1	14	0	0
Magnante, Mike, Omaha*	5	1	.833	2.84	15	8	0	0	3	0	57.0	55	235	23	18	3	1	3	1	13	0	38	5	0

Pitcher, Team	W	L	Pct.	ERA	G	GS	CG	ShO	GF	Sv.	IP	H	TBF	R	ER	HR	SH	SF	HB	BB	IBB	SO	WP	Bk.
Mallicoat, Rob, Omaha*	0	1	.000	3.00	3	0	0	0	1	0	3.0	1	12	1	1	0	1	0	0	3	0	1	0	0
Marquez, Isidrio, Nashville	7	4	.636	4.75	46	0	0	0	17	4	72.0	80	315	41	38	8	6	3	2	27	5	57	0	0
Martinez, Frankie, Louisville	2	1	.667	3.61	38	0	0	0	8	0	52.1	60	230	25	21	4	1	0	2	21	5	23	10	0
Mathews, T.J., Louisville	9	4	.692	2.70	32	7	0	0	10	1	66.2	60	298	35	20	2	0	3	3	27	2	50	1	0
Mathile, Mike, Indianapolis	0	2	.000	2.51	14	3	0	0	4	0	28.2	22	113	10	8	1	1	4	0	8	0	16	0	0
McAndrew, Jamie, New Orleans	7	5	.583	3.97	17	17	3	1	0	0	104.1	102	443	48	46	8	1	3	2	44	1	62	1	1
McClellan, Paul, New Orleans	0	3	.000	6.06	3	3	1	0	0	0	16.1	19	71	11	11	0	0	0	0	8	0	8	0	1
Meier, Kevin, Iowa	1	2	.333	8.44	3	2	0	0	0	0	10.2	18	51	10	10	6	0	0	0	3	0	7	1	0
Melendez, Jose, Omaha	3	4	.429	4.89	21	1	0	0	8	0	35.0	44	163	21	19	8	1	0	4	14	2	30	0	0
Milacki, Bob, Omaha	8	3	.727	3.33	15	15	2	2	0	0	105.1	90	421	42	39	8	1	0	2	31	0	63	3	0
Minchey, Nate, Louisville	8	7	.533	3.73	26	24	1	0	0	0	147.1	153	633	77	61	9	4	5	7	42	0	67	9	1
Mongiello, Mike, Nashville	3	3	.500	5.14	31	8	1	0	7	1	91.0	104	408	59	52	10	1	6	4	37	3	72	3	0
Moore, Marcus, Indianapolis	1	0	1.000	4.97	7	1	0	0	2	1	12.2	13	62	8	7	0	1	0	0	14	2	6	0	0
Morton, Kevin, Iowa*	1	7	.125	4.79	28	12	1	0	5	0	92.0	97	405	52	49	13	4	4	2	42	3	49	3	0
Munoz, J.J., Omaha*	2	3	.400	3.38	57	0	0	0	21	6	56.0	48	235	23	21	3	4	2	6	19	2	51	5	1
Myers, Rod, Omaha	4	5	.444	4.10	38	0	0	0	17	2	48.1	52	212	26	22	5	2	3	0	19	1	38	1	1
Nabholz, Chris, Iowa*	0	2	.000	6.41	6	5	0	0	0	0	19.2	27	98	17	14	3	0	0	3	12	0	16	3	0
Nichting, Chris, Oklahoma City	5	5	.500	2.13	23	7	3	2	8	1	67.2	58	275	19	16	4	4	2	2	19	0	72	2	0
Nitkowski, C.J., Indianapolis*	0	2	.000	5.20	6	6	0	0	0	0	27.2	28	120	16	16	3	0	2	1	10	0	21	0	1
Noriega, Rey, Nashville	0	0	.000	0.00	1	0	0	0	1	0	1.0	0	3	0	0	0	0	0	0	0	0	1	0	0
Novoa, Rafael, Nashville*	0	1	.000	10.80	3	3	0	0	0	0	10.0	17	58	13	12	0	0	1	2	9	0	3	0	0
Ogea, Chad, Buffalo	0	1	.000	4.58	4	4	0	0	0	0	17.2	16	79	12	9	1	0	0	2	8	0	11	0	0
Olsen, Steve, Nashville	1	7	.125	4.79	14	14	0	0	0	0	77.0	85	329	44	41	10	3	5	0	16	0	45	4	0
Olson, Gregg, Buf.-Oma.	0	0	.000	0.00	1	0	0	0	1	0	1.0	0	4	0	0	0	0	0	0	1	0	1	1	0
Osborne, Donovan, Louisville*	0	1	.000	3.86	1	1	0	0	0	0	7.0	8	30	3	3	0	1	0	0	0	0	3	0	0
Pall, Donn, Nashville	4	3	.571	3.98	44	0	0	0	13	3	86.0	89	365	40	38	10	5	3	4	20	7	79	3	0
Parker, Clay, New Orleans	0	0	.000	6.75	2	0	0	0	0	0	1.1	3	9	2	1	0	0	0	0	2	0	2	0	0
Patterson, Danny, Okla. City	1	0	1.000	1.65	14	0	0	0	3	2	27.1	23	111	8	5	0	3	2	1	9	2	9	4	0
Pennington, Brad, Indianapolis*	0	0	.000	10.29	11	2	0	0	1	0	14.0	17	79	19	16	3	0	1	0	21	1	11	2	0
Perez, David, Oklahoma City	5	12	.294	5.57	20	20	1	0	0	0	103.1	120	461	71	64	16	0	0	13	34	1	74	5	0
Perry, Pat, Omaha*	0	0	.000	5.79	5	0	0	0	4	3	4.2	5	21	3	3	0	0	0	0	2	1	4	0	0
Perschke, Greg, Buffalo	1	1	.500	5.74	3	3	0	0	0	0	15.2	13	65	10	10	2	0	1	0	6	0	11	0	0
Petkovsek, Mark, Louisville	4	1	.800	2.32	8	8	2	1	0	0	54.1	38	209	16	14	3	1	1	1	8	0	30	1	0
Pierce, Ed, Omaha*	0	0	.000	7.36	3	0	0	0	1	0	3.2	9	21	4	3	0	0	0	0	1	0	1	0	0
Pittsley, Jim, Omaha	4	1	.800	3.21	8	8	0	0	0	0	47.2	38	189	20	17	5	0	0	2	16	0	39	0	2
Poole, Jim, Buffalo*	0	0	.000	27.00	1	1	0	0	0	0	2.2	7	17	8	8	1	0	0	1	2	0	0	0	0
Popplewell, Tom, New Orleans	0	2	.000	6.75	10	0	0	0	1	0	13.1	13	64	11	10	0	0	2	1	11	1	16	2	0
Prager, Howard, Louisville*	0	0	.000	0.00	2	0	0	0	2	0	2.0	1	7	0	0	0	0	0	0	0	0	1	0	0
Pugh, Tim, Indianapolis	2	4	.333	4.68	6	6	1	1	0	0	42.1	42	184	24	22	4	1	4	5	14	1	20	1	0
Raczka, Mike, Louisville*	5	3	.625	3.86	55	0	0	0	16	1	49.0	49	216	23	21	7	8	2	3	20	6	43	3	0
Rambo, Dan, New Orleans	0	4	.000	5.20	7	6	0	0	1	0	36.1	39	155	23	21	6	2	0	2	9	1	22	1	0
Rasmussen, Dennis, Omaha*	6	3	.667	2.89	10	10	3	1	0	0	65.1	63	269	22	21	7	1	1	2	17	0	51	1	0
Reed, Rick, Indianapolis	11	4	.733	3.33	22	21	3	1	0	0	135.0	127	551	60	50	16	4	2	2	26	2	92	0	0
Remlinger, Mike, Indianapolis*	5	3	.625	4.05	41	1	0	0	7	0	46.2	40	210	24	21	4	2	1	2	32	4	58	8	0
Righetti, Dave, Nashville*	4	5	.444	3.23	16	15	1	1	0	0	83.2	81	344	40	30	9	3	4	1	20	0	44	2	2
Rightnowar, Ron, New Orleans	1	1	.500	2.67	25	0	0	0	20	10	30.1	37	135	16	9	3	2	1	2	9	1	22	3	0
Roa, Joe, Buffalo	17	3	.850	3.50	25	24	3	0	1	0	164.2	168	678	71	64	9	2	5	7	28	1	93	1	2
Roberson, Sid, New Orleans*	0	2	.000	7.62	4	3	0	0	0	0	13.0	20	69	11	11	1	0	2	1	10	0	8	0	0
Roper, John, Indianapolis	2	5	.286	4.97	8	8	0	0	0	0	41.2	47	186	26	23	9	0	0	1	16	1	23	4	0
Ruffcorn, Scott, Nashville	0	0	.000	108.00	2	2	0	0	0	0	0.1	3	9	4	4	0	0	0	2	3	0	0	1	0
Ruffin, Johnny, Indianapolis	3	1	.750	2.90	36	1	0	0	4	0	49.2	27	213	19	16	3	2	1	0	37	2	58	7	0
Salkeld, Roger, Indianapolis	12	2	.857	4.22	20	20	1	0	0	0	119.1	96	497	60	56	13	3	4	2	57	1	86	3	0
Santana, Julio, Oklahoma City	0	2	.000	39.00	2	2	0	0	0	0	3.0	9	25	14	13	3	0	0	0	7	0	6	1	1
Sauveur, Rich, Indianapolis*	5	2	.714	2.05	52	0	0	0	43	15	57.0	43	228	17	13	3	1	1	2	18	3	47	3	0
Scanlan, Bob, New Orleans	0	1	.000	5.40	3	3	0	0	0	0	11.2	17	51	7	7	0	0	0	1	3	0	5	1	0
Schuermann, Lance, Okla. City*	4	7	.364	4.67	33	13	0	0	6	0	88.2	101	398	51	46	12	1	4	2	40	0	44	8	0
Scudder, Scott, Indianapolis	1	4	.200	5.17	7	7	0	0	0	0	38.1	43	161	24	22	4	0	1	1	9	1	13	3	0
Seminara, Frank, New Orleans	2	3	.400	7.96	11	7	0	0	2	0	37.1	54	171	35	33	3	0	3	2	14	1	19	1	1
Service, Scott, Indianapolis	4	1	.800	2.18	36	0	0	0	32	18	41.1	33	175	13	10	4	2	1	3	15	2	48	1	0
Shifflett, Steve, Iowa	5	1	.833	5.33	26	0	0	0	8	0	27.0	30	116	18	16	2	3	4	1	6	1	10	0	0
Shinall, Zak, New Orleans	0	0	.000	7.62	9	0	0	0	1	0	13.0	15	58	11	11	4	0	0	1	7	1	5	2	0
Shuey, Paul, Buffalo	1	2	.333	2.63	25	0	0	0	19	11	27.1	21	108	9	8	2	3	0	0	7	0	27	2	0
Simas, Bill, Nashville	1	1	.500	3.86	7	0	0	0	3	0	11.2	12	50	5	5	0	1	0	0	3	1	12	0	0
Simmons, Scott, Louisville*	0	2	.000	8.00	2	2	0	0	0	0	9.0	11	40	9	8	3	0	0	1	1	0	2	0	0
Sirotka, Mike, Nashville*	1	5	.167	2.83	8	8	0	0	0	0	54.0	51	217	21	17	4	2	3	1	13	1	34	1	0
Slusarski, Joe, Buf.-N.O.	2	2	.500	2.39	37	2	0	0	23	11	64.0	55	255	22	17	6	1	2	1	15	2	39	0	0
Smith, Ottis, Iowa*	1	3	.250	10.45	5	5	0	0	0	0	20.2	34	108	25	24	3	0	1	1	13	0	12	0	0
Steenstra, Kennie, Iowa	9	12	.429	3.89	29	26	6	2	1	0	171.1	174	722	85	74	15	6	6	8	48	3	96	6	0
Strange, Don, Omaha	0	0	.000	7.47	9	0	0	0	3	1	15.2	24	75	13	13	2	0	1	0	6	0	11	0	0
Sturtze, Tanyon, Iowa	4	7	.364	6.80	23	17	1	1	0	0	86.0	108	398	66	65	18	5	2	5	42	1	48	5	0
Sullivan, Scott, Indianapolis	4	3	.571	3.53	44	0	0	0	21	1	58.2	51	253	31	23	2	3	4	2	24	4	54	3	0
Swartzbaugh, Dave, Iowa	3	0	1.000	1.53	30	0	0	0	9	0	47.0	33	187	10	8	1	2	0	1	18	1	38	1	0
Swingle, Paul, New Orleans	1	4	.200	4.57	35	0	0	0	9	0	43.1	42	185	25	22	7	1	0	1	15	2	41	5	0
Talanoa, Scott, New Orleans	0	0	.000	0.00	2	0	0	0	2	0	1.1	1	5	0	0	0	0	0	0	0	0	0	0	0
Taylor, Rob, Iowa	4	2	.667	2.81	54	0	0	0	40	18	57.2	42	241	20	18	3	5	3	2	28	2	48	4	0
Taylor, Scott, N.O.-O.C.	8	8	.500	3.55	24	21	1	1	0	0	129.1	132	557	62	51	12	4	2	7	41	0	74	5	0
Telford, Anthony, Buffalo	4	1	.800	3.46	16	2	0	0	4	0	39.0	35	161	15	15	1	1	4	2	10	3	24	1	0
Thomas, Mike, New Orleans*	0	1	.000	4.05	35	0	0	0	14	1	33.1	37	151	18	15	3	0	0	2	18	0	28	3	2
Torres, Dilson, Omaha	3	1	.750	2.63	5	5	1	1	0	0	27.1	28	113	11	8	2	2	1	1	7	0	12	1	1
Toth, Robert, Omaha	1	2	.333	3.61	8	8	1	0	0	0	47.1	53	205	25	19	7	3	2	2	8	0	31	0	0
Turner, Matt, Buffalo	0	1	.000	5.23	13	0	0	0	10	3	10.1	16	54	7	6	0	1	0	1	5	0	10	0	1
Urbani, Tom, Louisville*	1	1	.500	2.93	2	2	0	0	0	0	15.1	16	65	6	5	0	0	0	0	5	0	11	0	0
Vasquez, Marcos, Indianapolis	0	0	.000	0.00	2	0	0	0	1	1	4.0	1	13	0	0	0	0	0	0	0	0	1	0	0

Pitcher, Team	W	L	Pct.	ERA	G	GS	CG	ShO	GF	Sv.	IP	H	TBF	R	ER	HR	SH	SF	HB	BB	IBB	SO	WP	Bk.
Vierra, Joey, Nashville*	2	2	.500	4.17	56	1	0	0	22	4	58.1	47	237	28	27	6	1	5	1	19	4	57	4	0
Viola, Frank, Indianapolis*	3	3	.500	4.09	6	6	0	0	0	0	33.0	33	138	17	15	3	0	2	2	6	0	25	0	0
Vosberg, Ed, Oklahoma City*	1	0	1.000	0.00	1	0	0	0	0	0	1.2	1	7	0	0	0	0	0	0	1	0	2	0	0
Walker, Mike, Iowa	1	1	.500	4.10	16	1	0	0	3	0	26.1	22	122	13	12	3	1	1	3	19	4	13	0	0
Warren, Brian, Indianapolis	2	1	.667	1.61	41	0	0	0	9	2	56.0	56	234	18	10	2	1	1	5	9	2	35	2	1
Watson, Allen, Louisville*	2	2	.500	2.63	4	4	1	1	0	0	24.0	20	97	10	7	1	0	0	0	6	0	19	3	0
Wilson, Steve, Nashville*	2	2	.500	4.56	20	7	0	0	4	1	51.1	60	234	32	26	7	3	4	3	17	1	26	1	1
Wishnevski, Rob, Okla. City	6	3	.667	3.47	41	8	0	0	12	3	109.0	101	466	51	42	9	5	5	7	53	2	78	13	0
Young, Anthony, Iowa	0	1	.000	11.25	3	1	0	0	0	0	4.0	9	23	5	5	0	0	1	0	4	0	6	0	0

COMBINATION SHUTOUTS: **Buffalo (6)**—Bell-Embree, Bell-Turner, Lewis-Embree-Olson, Grimsley-Frohwirth-Klink-Shuey, Grimsley-Klink-Shuey, Lewis-Klink-Frohwirth. **Indianapolis (2)**—Grott-Warren-Sauveur, Reed-Sullivan. **Iowa (4)**—Abbott-Morton-Taylor-Swartzbaugh, Campbell-Swartzbaugh-Dixon-Taylor, Edens-Swartzbaugh-Taylor, Sturtze-Garces. **Louisville (5)**—Beltran-Cimorelli, Beltran-Mathews-Raczka-Bailey, Benes-Batchelor-Raczka-Mathews, Benes-Batchelor-Carpenter-Raczka, Benes-Raczka-Buckels. **Nashville (7)**—Baldwin-Hammaker-Marquez, Bolton-Karchner, Bolton-Marquez, Bolton-Wilson, Ellis-Righetti-Karchner, Mongiello-Pall, Olsen-Karchner-Johnson-Gajkowski-Vierra-Pall. **New Orleans (4)**—Farrell-Archer-Thomas-Jones, Ganote-Swingle-Jones, Kiefer-Boze-Fritz, Kiefer-Jones. **Oklahoma City (4)**—Alberro-Schuermann-Goetz-Curtis, Perez-Nichting-Hurst, Schuermann-Goetz-Hurst-Curtis, Taylor-Wishnevski. **Omaha (5)**—Bevil-Anderson-Garrelts, Brown-Kutzler-Perry-Dorlarque, Fleming-Converse-Huisman, Linton-Perry, Magnante-Harrison-Munoz-DeJesus.

NO-HIT GAMES: None.

PITCHERS WITH TWO OR MORE TEAMS

Pitcher, Team	W	L	Pct.	ERA	G	GS	CG	ShO	GF	Sv.	IP	H	TBF	R	ER	HR	SH	SF	HB	BB	IBB	SO	WP	Bk.
Drahman, Brian, Okla. City	2	2	.500	3.09	22	0	0	0	15	4	32.0	36	145	11	11	3	1	1	2	14	3	19	0	0
Drahman, Brian, Indianapolis	0	0	.000	0.00	2	0	0	0	0	0	3.0	3	12	0	0	0	0	0	0	1	0	3	0	0
Duncan, Chip, Oklahoma City	0	0	.000	3.38	3	0	0	0	1	0	5.1	6	22	2	2	0	1	1	0	1	0	3	0	0
Duncan, Chip, New Orleans	1	4	.200	6.29	14	5	0	0	5	0	34.1	44	161	26	24	7	1	2	2	18	2	23	5	1
Hurst, James, Okla. City*	1	5	.167	7.33	28	7	0	0	11	4	46.2	71	236	40	38	6	2	0	3	25	0	42	4	0
Hurst, James, Indianapolis*	0	0	.000	5.40	3	0	0	0	2	1	3.1	2	13	2	2	1	0	0	0	1	0	1	0	0
Jean, Domingo, Okla. City	3	8	.273	6.14	24	13	1	0	9	1	88.0	102	418	70	60	12	4	2	1	61	1	72	14	3
Jean, Domingo, Indianapolis	1	0	1.000	0.00	2	0	0	0	0	0	2.0	1	7	0	0	0	1	0	0	0	0	1	0	0
Olson, Gregg, Buffalo	1	0	1.000	2.49	18	0	0	0	17	13	21.2	16	92	6	6	0	1	0	3	9	0	25	0	0
Olson, Gregg, Omaha	0	0	.000	0.00	1	0	0	0	1	0	1.0	0	4	0	0	0	0	0	0	1	0	1	1	0
Slusarski, Joe, Buffalo	1	1	.500	6.32	4	2	0	0	0	0	15.2	18	67	12	11	2	0	1	1	4	0	9	0	0
Slusarski, Joe, New Orleans	1	1	.500	1.12	33	0	0	0	23	11	48.1	37	188	10	6	4	1	1	0	11	2	30	0	0
Taylor, Scott, New Orleans	1	0	1.000	2.38	2	2	0	0	0	0	11.1	10	47	3	3	0	0	0	1	3	0	9	0	0
Taylor, Scott, Oklahoma City	7	8	.467	3.66	22	19	1	1	0	0	118.0	122	510	59	48	12	4	2	6	38	0	65	5	0

1995 FIELDING

TEAM

Team	Pct.	G	PO	A	E	TC	DP	PB
New Orleans	.980	142	3641	1572	107	5320	163	17
Buffalo	.979	144	3753	1592	115	5460	137	10
Iowa	.978	143	3721	1503	120	5344	137	11
Omaha	.975	144	3715	1479	134	5328	158	21
Louisville	.972	144	3723	1455	147	5325	107	15
Oklahoma City	.972	143	3662	1506	151	5319	156	19
Nashville	.971	144	3830	1600	163	5593	144	16
Indianapolis	.971	144	3786	1441	157	5384	114	20

TRIPLE PLAY: Iowa.

INDIVIDUAL

FIRST BASEMEN

NOTE: All caps denotes fielding-percentage leader based on 72 games for catchers, 96 for all other non-pitchers and 144 innings for pitchers. *Throws lefthanded.

Player, Team	Pct.	G	PO	A	E	TC	DP
Anthony, Eric, Indianapolis*	.909	2	9	1	1	11	1
Aversa, Joe, Louisville	1.000	1	1	0	0	1	0
Barker, Tim, New Orleans	1.000	10	62	4	0	66	7
Belk, Tim, Indianapolis	.989	50	428	20	5	453	24
Bolick, Frank, Buffalo	1.000	1	9	0	0	9	1
Borrelli, Dean, Oklahoma City	.972	3	33	2	1	36	4
Brooks, Jerry, Indianapolis	1.000	7	64	5	0	69	5
Brown, Marty, Oklahoma City	1.000	2	22	2	0	24	2
Byington, John, Oklahoma City	.994	22	151	9	1	161	13
Caceres, Edgar, Omaha	1.000	2	23	0	0	23	1
Cholowsky, Dan, Louisville	.961	6	48	1	2	51	3
Clinton, Jim, Oklahoma City	1.000	3	20	3	0	23	1
Colon, Cris, Iowa	.984	52	357	24	6	387	31
Costo, Tim, Buffalo	.991	66	584	47	6	637	56
Coughlin, Kevin, Nashville*	1.000	2	14	0	0	14	1
Cron, Chris, Nashville	1.000	2	9	0	0	9	2
Deak, Darrel, Louisville	.983	45	333	16	6	355	28
Denson, Drew, Indianapolis	.983	15	108	9	2	119	19
Dismuke, Jamie, Indianapolis	.981	11	91	10	2	103	9
Dodson, Bo, New Orleans*	.995	47	400	32	2	434	40
Fariss, Monty, Iowa	1.000	7	62	3	0	65	5
Franco, Matt, Iowa	.996	36	222	18	1	241	26
Giannelli, Ray, Louisville	.988	17	71	9	1	81	10
Grotewold, Jeff, Omaha	.981	85	745	49	15	809	84
Hamelin, Bob, Omaha*	.967	19	157	19	6	182	21
Horn, Sam, Oklahoma City*	1.000	2	11	0	0	11	0
Hunter, Brian, Indianapolis*	1.000	4	35	1	0	36	0
Jaha, John, New Orleans	1.000	1	9	2	0	11	3
Kieschnick, Brooks, Iowa	1.000	7	13	3	0	16	2
Kosco, Bryn, Iowa	.993	70	548	43	4	595	57
Lindeman, Jim, Oklahoma City	.989	74	640	48	8	696	67
Lopez, Luis, Buffalo	.989	27	252	17	3	272	23
Lovullo, Torey, Buffalo	.974	11	70	6	2	78	6
Lyden, Mitch, Omaha	1.000	6	18	3	0	21	2
Lyons, Barry, Nashville	.993	17	128	7	1	136	10
Martinez, Carmelo, Buffalo	.500	1	0	1	1	2	0
Martinez, Domingo, Louisville	.988	35	299	30	4	333	24
McCarty, Dave, Indianapolis*	.994	37	335	14	2	351	27
McCoy, Trey, Oklahoma City	1.000	7	64	3	0	67	11
Morris, Hal, Indianapolis*	1.000	2	13	2	0	15	0
Norman, Les, Omaha	1.000	1	0	1	0	1	0
Ortiz, Luis, Oklahoma City	1.000	1	6	0	0	6	2
Perry, Herbert, Buffalo	.994	48	419	44	3	466	42
Prager, Howard, Louisville*	.980	33	188	13	4	205	13
Pratt, Todd, Iowa	.963	6	23	3	1	27	0
ROBERTSON, Mike, Nashville*	.992	137	1172	75	10	1257	111
Sabo, Chris, Louisville	1.000	7	32	4	0	36	2
Schu, Rick, Oklahoma City	1.000	18	130	11	0	141	17
Singleton, Duane, New Orleans	1.000	1	3	0	0	3	0
Smith, Ed, Buffalo	1.000	1	1	0	0	1	0
Staton, Dave, New Orleans	.993	54	419	33	3	455	45
Stefanski, Mike, New Orleans	1.000	1	8	0	0	8	3
Stewart, Andy, Omaha	1.000	11	72	13	0	85	5
Sweeney, Mark, Louisville*	.990	22	176	19	2	197	14
Talanoa, Scott, New Orleans	1.000	5	30	3	0	33	3
Unroe, Tim, New Orleans	1.000	47	321	23	0	344	46
Vargas, Hector, Oklahoma City	1.000	22	154	10	0	164	18

Player, Team	Pct.	G	PO	A	E	TC	DP
Vitiello, Joe, Omaha	.984	28	221	21	4	246	26
Wachter, Derek, New Orleans	1.000	1	1	0	0	1	0
Woodson, Tracy, Louisville	.965	12	102	9	4	115	4
Worthington, Craig, Indianapolis	.996	30	217	26	1	244	15
Zeile, Todd, Louisville	.923	2	11	1	1	13	0

TRIPLE PLAY: Kosco.

SECOND BASEMEN

Player, Team	Pct.	G	PO	A	E	TC	DP
Arias, Amador, Indianapolis	.938	5	10	20	2	32	7
Aversa, Joe, Louisville	.951	32	28	49	4	81	5
Barker, Tim, New Orleans	1.000	23	48	55	0	103	19
Bell, David, Buf.-Lou.	.991	21	43	62	1	106	11
Benavides, Freddie, Iowa	1.000	1	2	5	0	7	2
BRADY, Doug, Nashville	.975	116	238	304	14	556	88
Bream, Scott, Iowa	.980	25	43	57	2	102	17
Brown, Marty, Oklahoma City	.955	6	8	13	1	22	1
Byington, John, Oklahoma City	.941	15	26	38	4	68	8
Caceres, Edgar, Omaha	.977	8	18	25	1	44	7
Candaele, Casey, Buffalo	.985	52	103	165	4	272	27
Caraballo, Ramon, Louisville	.981	58	126	178	6	310	39
Cholowsky, Dan, Louisville	.950	6	7	12	1	20	0
Clinton, Jim, Oklahoma City	1.000	1	1	1	0	2	0
Colon, Cris, Iowa	.990	23	39	61	1	101	16
Deak, Darrel, Louisville	.959	45	71	92	7	170	16
Finn, John, New Orleans	.961	14	17	32	2	51	5
Flores, Miguel, Buffalo	.980	29	53	92	3	148	22
Gardner, Jeff, Iowa	.988	49	103	153	3	259	39
Giannelli, Ray, Louisville	1.000	2	1	2	0	3	1
Halter, Shane, Omaha	.921	21	42	51	8	101	15
Haney, Todd, Iowa	.975	33	64	95	4	163	16
Hecht, Steve, Oklahoma City	.965	32	65	99	6	170	28
Hinzo, Tommy, Oklahoma City	.955	56	112	122	11	245	41
Howard, Tim, Nashville	.984	12	32	28	1	61	8
Hulett, Tim, Lou.-O.C.	1.000	7	11	12	0	23	2
Johns, Keith, Louisville	1.000	3	7	4	0	11	1
Kessinger, Keith, Iowa	1.000	23	44	70	0	114	16
Kremblas, Frank, Indianapolis	.966	7	13	15	1	29	3
Lofton, Rodney, New Orleans	.983	57	98	134	4	236	35
Loretta, Mark, New Orleans	1.000	1	1	1	0	2	1
Lovullo, Torey, Buffalo	.984	69	132	175	5	312	47
Milstien, Dave, Nashville	1.000	2	5	5	0	10	2
Mota, Jose, Omaha	1.000	9	13	23	0	36	6
Owens, Eric, Indianapolis	.967	105	219	274	17	510	63
Pena, Geronimo, Louisville	.926	5	9	16	2	27	3
Reynolds, Harold, Omaha	.966	33	63	80	5	148	22
Ripken, Bill, Buffalo	1.000	4	13	12	0	25	2
Schu, Rick, Oklahoma City	1.000	3	6	7	0	13	1
Shave, Jon, Oklahoma City	.964	28	43	64	4	111	16
Sisco, Steve, Omaha	.956	7	16	27	2	45	8
Smith, Greg, N.O.-Ind.	.968	23	41	49	3	93	11
Stillwell, Kurt, Indianapolis	.980	28	39	61	2	102	7
Stynes, Chris, Omaha	.966	69	136	176	11	323	51
Vargas, Hector, Oklahoma City	.958	17	33	35	3	71	8
Weger, Wes, New Orleans	.974	53	115	145	7	267	48
Wilson, Brandon, Nash.-Ind.	.951	21	33	64	5	102	8

SECOND BASEMEN WITH TWO OR MORE TEAMS

Player, Team	Pct.	G	PO	A	E	TC	DP
Bell, David, Buffalo	1.000	3	4	8	0	12	4
Bell, David, Louisville	.989	18	39	54	1	94	7
Hulett, Tim, Louisville	1.000	3	6	5	0	11	0
Hulett, Tim, Oklahoma City	1.000	4	5	7	0	12	2
Smith, Greg, New Orleans	.973	19	31	40	2	73	8
Smith, Greg, Indianapolis	.950	4	10	9	1	20	3
Wilson, Brandon, Nashville	.950	20	32	63	5	100	8
Wilson, Brandon, Indianapolis	1.000	1	1	1	0	2	0

THIRD BASEMEN

Player, Team	Pct.	G	PO	A	E	TC	DP
Anderson, Charlie, Louisville	1.000	1	1	0	0	1	0
Aversa, Joe, Louisville	.957	16	3	19	1	23	2
Barker, Tim, New Orleans	.902	18	6	31	4	41	3
Bell, David, Buffalo	.954	66	37	151	9	197	9
Benavides, Freddie, Iowa	.903	17	7	21	3	31	3
Bolick, Frank, Buffalo	.943	17	8	25	2	35	1
Bream, Scott, Iowa	1.000	1	0	2	0	2	0
Brooks, Jerry, Indianapolis	1.000	2	1	7	0	8	1
Brown, Chris, Indianapolis	1.000	2	1	2	0	3	0
Brown, Marty, Oklahoma City	.938	20	12	48	4	64	6
Buechele, Steve, Oklahoma City	.818	3	3	6	2	11	0
Byington, John, N.O.-O.C.	.945	77	66	163	15	244	25
Caceres, Edgar, Omaha	1.000	15	8	32	0	40	0
Candaele, Casey, Buffalo	1.000	1	0	4	0	4	0
Cholowsky, Dan, Louisville	1.000	1	1	0	0	1	0
Colon, Cris, Iowa	.945	21	8	44	3	55	5
Costo, Tim, Buffalo	.750	3	1	2	1	4	0
Cron, Chris, Nashville	.833	10	8	17	5	30	1
Deak, Darrel, Louisville	.929	9	5	8	1	14	0
Dodson, Bo, New Orleans*	1.000	1	0	1	0	1	0
Finn, John, New Orleans	.667	1	1	1	1	3	0
Franco, Matt, Iowa	.925	95	61	161	18	240	11
Garber, Jeff, Omaha	1.000	3	0	2	0	2	0
Gardner, Jeff, Iowa	.857	7	4	8	2	14	2
Giannelli, Ray, Louisville	.900	5	3	6	1	10	1
Green, Gary, Omaha	.846	5	3	8	2	13	0
Greene, Willie, Indianapolis	.952	62	41	118	8	167	6
Grotewold, Jeff, Omaha	1.000	3	5	3	0	8	1
Gulan, Mike, Louisville	.948	54	38	90	7	135	2
Haney, Todd, Iowa	.938	16	12	33	3	48	4
Howard, Tim, Nashville	.930	19	10	43	4	57	5
Hubbard, Mike, Iowa	1.000	1	1	1	0	2	0
Hulett, Tim, Oklahoma City	1.000	4	4	9	0	13	2
Kosco, Bryn, Iowa	.833	8	5	5	2	12	0
Kremblas, Frank, Indianapolis	.900	12	3	24	3	30	4
Lockhart, Keith, Omaha	.928	37	31	72	8	111	10
Lofton, Rodney, New Orleans	.963	31	20	57	3	80	8
Lopez, Luis, Buffalo	.958	11	3	20	1	24	2
Loretta, Mark, New Orleans	1.000	4	3	9	0	12	0
Lovullo, Torey, Buffalo	.930	58	30	116	11	157	13
McClendon, Lloyd, Buffalo	1.000	2	0	1	0	1	0
Mercedes, Henry, Omaha	.895	7	1	16	2	19	2
Milstien, Dave, Nashville	1.000	4	4	7	0	11	1
Ortiz, Luis, Oklahoma City	.931	38	29	93	9	131	7
Randa, Joe, Omaha	.958	64	42	96	6	144	8
Reynolds, Harold, Omaha	1.000	2	1	7	0	8	0
SAENZ, Olmedo, Nashville	.939	111	82	289	24	395	24
Schu, Rick, Oklahoma City	.889	21	9	31	5	45	4
Singleton, Duane, New Orleans	1.000	1	0	1	0	1	0
Smith, Ed, Buffalo	1.000	2	3	1	0	4	0
Smith, Greg, New Orleans	.913	30	19	54	7	80	8
Snopek, Chris, Nashville	.714	3	0	5	2	7	0
Staton, Dave, New Orleans	1.000	2	0	1	0	1	0
Stefanski, Mike, New Orleans	1.000	3	1	2	0	3	0
Stewart, Andy, Omaha	.000	1	0	0	2	2	0
Stillwell, Kurt, Indianapolis	.904	24	17	49	7	73	6
Stynes, Chris, Omaha	.947	13	8	28	2	38	5
Sutko, Glenn, New Orleans	.750	2	1	5	2	8	1
Unroe, Tim, New Orleans	.940	67	51	137	12	200	16
Vargas, Hector, Oklahoma City	1.000	2	0	3	0	3	0
Weger, Wes, New Orleans	.941	5	6	10	1	17	1
Wolak, Jerry, Nashville	.667	1	0	2	1	3	0
Woodson, Tracy, Louisville	.960	75	58	160	9	227	16
Worthington, Craig, Indianapolis	.947	52	28	114	8	150	11

THIRD BASEMEN WITH TWO OR MORE TEAMS

Player, Team	Pct.	G	PO	A	E	TC	DP
Byington, John, New Orleans	.885	11	3	20	3	26	1
Byington, John, Oklahoma City	.945	66	63	143	12	218	24

SHORTSTOPS

Player, Team	Pct.	G	PO	A	E	TC	DP
Aversa, Joe, Louisville	.985	35	43	87	2	132	14
Barker, Tim, New Orleans	1.000	2	4	9	0	13	2
Bell, David, Buffalo	.900	5	5	13	2	20	4
Benavides, Freddie, Iowa	.968	85	113	220	11	344	49
Brady, Doug, Nashville	.800	1	1	3	1	5	0
Bream, Scott, Iowa	.857	2	3	3	1	7	0
Brown, Marty, Oklahoma City	.778	1	1	6	2	9	1
Caceres, Edgar, Omaha	.913	6	9	12	2	23	6
Candaele, Casey, Buffalo	.881	19	20	32	7	59	8
Caraballo, Ramon, Louisville	.969	8	8	23	1	32	5
Clinton, Jim, Oklahoma City	1.000	3	3	0	0	3	0
Elster, Kevin, Omaha	1.000	11	22	30	0	52	12
Fanning, Steve, Iowa	1.000	1	0	2	0	2	0
Figueroa, Bien, Oklahoma City	.974	9	11	26	1	38	4
Fraraccio, Dan, Nashville	.933	8	17	39	4	60	8
Goldberg, Lonnie, Okla. City	.975	8	7	32	1	40	4
Green, Gary, Omaha	1.000	19	20	52	0	72	8
Greene, Willie, Indianapolis	.933	14	14	42	4	60	5
Halter, Shane, Omaha	.9779	103	183	304	11	498	75
Haney, Todd, Iowa	.975	22	26	53	2	81	13
Hinzo, Tommy, Oklahoma City	.957	26	27	63	4	94	14
Holbert, Aaron, Louisville	.936	109	153	302	31	486	53
Hulett, Tim, Oklahoma City	.921	27	45	72	10	127	19

Player, Team	Pct.	G	PO	A	E	TC	DP
Johns, Keith, Louisville	1.000	1	0	5	0	5	0
Kessinger, Keith, Iowa	.931	41	47	115	12	174	28
Lee, Manuel, Louisville	1.000	6	4	3	0	7	2
Lofton, Rodney, New Orleans	1.000	5	6	13	0	19	4
Loretta, Mark, New Orleans	.958	123	200	366	25	591	79
Lovullo, Torey, Buffalo	1.000	2	3	6	0	9	2
Magdaleno, Ricky, Indianapolis	.833	3	1	4	1	6	0
Milstien, Dave, Nashville	.947	5	4	14	1	19	1
Mota, Jose, Omaha	.918	13	17	28	4	49	5
Noriega, Rey, Nashville	.871	17	23	31	8	62	5
Parra, Franklin, Oklahoma City	.800	4	3	9	3	15	1
Reese, Pokey, Indianapolis	.935	88	131	258	27	416	37
RIPKEN, Bill, Buffalo	.9782	126	150	389	12	551	80
Rivera, Luis, Oklahoma City	.962	19	24	51	3	78	11
Schu, Rick, Oklahoma City	.961	63	85	162	10	257	34
Smith, Greg, New Orleans	.974	15	21	53	2	76	13
Snopek, Chris, Nashville	.942	110	133	353	30	516	71
Stillwell, Kurt, Indianapolis	.960	44	56	113	7	176	27
Weger, Wes, New Orleans	.909	2	3	7	1	11	2
Wilson, Brandon, Nash.-Ind.	.902	10	9	28	4	41	6

TRIPLE PLAY: Benavides.

SHORTSTOPS WITH TWO OR MORE TEAMS

Player, Team	Pct.	G	PO	A	E	TC	DP
Wilson, Brandon, Nashville	.933	7	6	22	2	30	6
Wilson, Brandon, Indianapolis	.818	3	3	6	2	11	0

OUTFIELDERS

Player, Team	Pct.	G	PO	A	E	TC	DP
Amaro, Ruben, Buffalo	.990	49	102	2	1	105	0
Anthony, Eric, Indianapolis*	1.000	2	2	0	0	2	0
Barker, Tim, New Orleans	1.000	34	41	2	0	43	0
Basse, Mike, New Orleans*	.988	91	150	8	2	160	0
Battle, Allen, Louisville	.982	47	106	1	2	109	0
Belk, Tim, Indianapolis	1.000	7	12	1	0	13	0
Bess, Johnny, Indianapolis	1.000	1	1	0	0	1	0
Bradshaw, Terry, Louisville	.969	107	248	1	8	257	0
Briley, Greg, Indianapolis	.972	44	69	1	2	72	0
Brooks, Jerry, Indianapolis	.932	32	39	2	3	44	0
Brown, Marty, Oklahoma City	1.000	1	1	0	0	1	0
Bruett, J.T., Omaha*	.977	39	84	0	2	86	0
Burnitz, Jeromy, Buffalo	.981	127	241	12	5	258	0
Burton, Darren, Omaha	1.000	2	6	0	0	6	0
Caceres, Edgar, Omaha	1.000	2	1	0	0	1	0
Cameron, Stanton, Okla. City	1.000	5	8	2	0	10	1
Candaele, Casey, Buffalo	.962	30	49	1	2	52	0
Cappuccio, Carmine, Nashville	.978	51	86	3	2	91	2
Carter, Mike, Iowa	.980	97	189	7	4	200	1
Chamberlain, Wes, Omaha	1.000	14	24	2	0	26	1
Chance, Tony, Oklahoma City	.990	58	90	6	1	97	1
Cholowsky, Dan, Louisville	.973	61	104	4	3	111	0
Coleman, Vince, Omaha	.950	9	19	0	1	20	0
Cookson, Brent, Omaha	1.000	26	56	3	0	59	1
Costo, Tim, Buffalo	.909	12	10	0	1	11	0
Cotto, Henry, Nashville	.833	5	5	0	1	6	0
Coughlin, Kevin, Nashville*	1.000	6	12	0	0	12	0
Diggs, Tony, Louisville	1.000	18	21	1	0	22	0
Dodson, Bo, New Orleans*	1.000	7	10	1	0	11	0
Dostal, Bruce, Oklahoma City*	.986	81	204	7	3	214	1
Finn, John, New Orleans	.972	23	33	2	1	36	0
Fox, Eric, Oklahoma City*	.982	87	157	4	3	164	0
Giannelli, Ray, Louisville	.983	95	164	9	3	176	2
Gibralter, Steve, Indianapolis	.977	78	207	2	5	214	0
Giles, Brian, Buffalo*	.981	118	248	4	5	257	0
Gilkey, Bernard, Louisville	1.000	2	2	0	0	2	0
Glanville, Doug, Iowa	.982	101	209	9	4	222	3
Gordon, Keith, Indianapolis	.988	80	155	3	2	160	2
Greene, Willie, Indianapolis	1.000	3	5	0	0	5	0
Haney, Todd, Iowa	.957	13	21	1	1	23	1
Hare, Shawn, Oklahoma City*	.966	63	110	4	4	118	2
Harris, Donald, Oklahoma City	1.000	10	23	1	0	24	0
Harris, Mike, New Orleans*	1.000	4	5	1	0	6	0
Hatcher, Billy, Omaha	.981	26	52	0	1	53	0
Hecht, Steve, Oklahoma City	.985	30	64	3	1	68	0
Hiatt, Phil, Omaha	.974	19	37	1	1	39	0
Hosey, Dwayne, Omaha	.971	62	125	10	4	139	2
Howitt, Dann, Nash.-Buf.	.973	45	67	4	2	73	0
Hughes, Keith, Omaha*	.965	74	130	9	5	144	2
Humphreys, Mike, Buffalo	1.000	33	80	4	0	84	1
Hunter, Brian, Indianapolis*	.889	7	7	1	1	9	0
Jose, Felix, Iowa	1.000	8	12	0	0	12	0
Kieschnick, Brooks, Iowa	.989	117	166	12	2	180	1
KOSLOFSKI, Kevin, New Orleans	.996	101	231	19	1	251	2
Kremblas, Frank, Indianapolis	1.000	2	6	0	0	6	0
Lindeman, Jim, Oklahoma City	1.000	1	1	0	0	1	0
Long, Kevin, Omaha*	1.000	18	32	0	0	32	0
Lopez, Luis, Buffalo	1.000	7	5	1	0	6	0
Mabry, John, Louisville	.889	4	8	0	1	9	0
Marini, Marc, Buffalo*	1.000	18	17	1	0	18	0
Martinez, Carmelo, Buffalo	1.000	2	2	0	0	2	0
Martinez, Manny, Iowa	.983	108	281	16	5	302	2
McClendon, Lloyd, Buffalo	.941	24	32	0	2	34	0
McNeely, Jeff, Louisville	.993	98	144	1	1	146	0
Miller, Keith, Omaha	1.000	1	2	0	0	2	0
Mitchell, Keith, Indianapolis	.979	65	136	4	3	143	1
Mota, Jose, Omaha	1.000	3	4	1	0	5	0
Mottola, Chad, Indianapolis	.976	69	151	11	4	166	2
Mouton, Lyle, Nashville	.978	62	123	8	3	134	1
Nilsson, Dave, New Orleans	1.000	1	2	0	0	2	0
Norman, Les, Omaha	.979	81	180	8	4	192	1
Pledger, Kinnis, Iowa	1.000	5	7	0	0	7	0
Ramsey, Fernando, Nashville	.973	87	211	4	6	221	1
Ritchie, Gregg, Oklahoma City*	1.000	6	11	0	0	11	0
Robertson, Mike, Nashville*	.889	5	8	0	1	9	0
Rohrmeier, Dan, Indianapolis	1.000	8	10	0	0	10	0
Sagmoen, Marc, Oklahoma City*	.980	54	97	3	2	102	0
Schu, Rick, Oklahoma City	.917	7	11	0	1	12	0
Singleton, Duane, New Orleans	.978	85	165	12	4	181	2
Smith, Ed, Buffalo	.750	9	9	0	3	12	0
Staton, Dave, New Orleans	1.000	2	1	0	0	1	0
Thomas, Skeets, Louisville	.969	57	87	7	3	97	1
Tucker, Michael, Omaha	.986	70	133	11	2	146	1
Unroe, Tim, New Orleans	1.000	1	1	0	0	1	0
Valrie, Kerry, Nashville	.972	124	265	11	8	284	6
Vargas, Hector, Oklahoma City	.971	47	62	6	2	70	2
Vitiello, Joe, Omaha	1.000	2	4	0	0	4	0
Wachter, Derek, New Orleans	.983	107	157	17	3	177	3
Ward, Turner, New Orleans	.900	9	9	0	1	10	0
Wilson, Nigel, Indianapolis*	.958	69	111	4	5	120	1
Wolak, Jerry, Nashville	.970	83	155	8	5	168	0
Yelding, Eric, Buffalo	.979	19	45	2	1	48	0
Young, Dmitri, Louisville	.750	2	3	0	1	4	0
Zupcic, Bob, Nashville	.923	9	9	3	1	13	0

TRIPLE PLAY: M. Martinez.

OUTFIELDERS WITH TWO OR MORE TEAMS

Player, Team	Pct.	G	PO	A	E	TC	DP
Howitt, Dann, Nashville	1.000	14	14	2	0	16	0
Howitt, Dann, Buffalo	.965	31	53	2	2	57	0

CATCHERS

Player, Team	Pct.	G	PO	A	E	TC	DP	PB
Borrelli, Dean, Oklahoma City	.997	49	282	24	1	307	4	14
Brooks, Jerry, Indianapolis	.986	52	323	22	5	350	1	12
Brown, Kevin, Oklahoma City	.750	2	6	0	2	8	0	0
Cox, Darron, Iowa	.986	28	187	18	3	208	4	1
Deak, Brian, Louisville	.993	51	247	18	2	267	0	4
DiFelice, Mike, Louisville	.984	21	111	10	2	123	2	2
Dorsett, Brian, Indianapolis	.982	87	506	34	10	550	4	5
Fordyce, Brook, Buffalo	.991	51	306	18	3	327	2	2
Gonzalez, Javier, New Orleans	.996	43	239	27	1	267	5	4
Gousha, Sean, Iowa	1.000	2	7	0	0	7	0	0
Hemond, Scott, Louisville	1.000	1	6	0	0	6	0	1
Hubbard, Mike, Iowa	.982	71	446	33	9	488	3	8
Kennedy, Darryl, Okla. City	.931	3	24	3	2	29	0	0
Kmak, Joe, Iowa	.992	33	209	26	2	237	3	1
Knapp, Mike, Indianapolis	1.000	13	60	3	0	63	0	1
Levis, Jesse, Buffalo	.994	60	338	20	2	360	5	3
Lopez, Luis, Buffalo	1.000	4	12	1	0	13	1	0
Lopez, Pedro, New Orleans	1.000	2	14	1	0	15	0	0
Luce, Roger, Oklahoma City	1.000	1	6	0	0	6	0	0
Lyden, Mitch, Omaha	.993	44	269	28	2	299	5	5
Lyons, Barry, Nashville	1.000	31	172	15	0	187	3	1
Machado, Robert, Nashville	.972	15	87	17	3	107	1	2
Martindale, Ryan, Buffalo	.978	11	41	4	1	46	0	1
Marzano, John, Okla. City	.992	93	551	64	5	620	12	4
Matheny, Mike, New Orleans	1.000	6	30	4	0	34	0	0
Mercedes, Henry, Omaha	.987	78	418	55	6	479	9	12
O'Halloran, Greg, Iowa	.935	5	28	1	2	31	0	1
Oliver, Joe, New Orleans	1.000	3	14	7	0	21	1	0
Ortiz, Junior, Nashville	.985	56	301	31	5	337	4	8
Pagnozzi, Tom, Louisville	1.000	5	19	0	0	19	0	0
Pratt, Todd, Iowa	.985	8	59	5	1	65	0	0
Rolls, David, Oklahoma City	1.000	2	15	1	0	16	0	1
RONAN, Marc, Louisville	.993	76	417	35	3	455	1	8
Sellers, Rick, Indianapolis	1.000	5	19	4	0	23	0	2

Player, Team	Pct.	G	PO	A	E	TC	DP	PB
Stefanski, Mike, New Orleans	.995	70	355	35	2	392	5	7
Stewart, Andy, Omaha	.981	25	140	16	3	159	2	3
Strickland, Chad, Omaha	1.000	8	32	3	0	35	0	1
Sutko, Glenn, New Orleans	.991	39	192	20	2	214	2	6
Tremie, Chris, Nashville	.998	67	394	30	1	425	5	5
Wrona, Rick, Buf.-Lou.	.992	44	224	20	2	246	4	4

CATCHERS WITH TWO OR MORE TEAMS

Player, Team	Pct.	G	PO	A	E	TC	DP	PB
Wrona, Rick, Buffalo	.995	31	167	16	1	184	3	4
Wrona, Rick, Louisville	.984	13	57	4	1	62	1	0

PITCHERS

Player, Team	Pct.	G	PO	A	E	TC	DP
Abbott, Paul, Iowa	.941	46	6	10	1	17	4
Adams, Terry, Iowa	1.000	7	1	2	0	3	0
Alberro, Jose, Okla. City	1.000	20	6	15	0	21	0
Anderson, Mike, Iowa	.971	27	17	17	1	35	0
Anderson, Scott, Omaha	.944	15	8	9	1	18	1
Archer, Kurt, New Orleans	1.000	38	1	7	0	8	0
Austin, Jim, Buffalo	.750	2	0	3	1	4	0
Bailey, Cory, Louisville	1.000	55	6	10	0	16	0
Baldwin, James, Nashville	.947	18	3	15	1	19	0
Barber, Brian, Louisville	.850	20	4	13	3	20	1
Barfield, John, Okla. City*	1.000	4	1	1	0	2	0
Batchelor, Richard, Louisville	.882	50	9	6	2	17	0
Beatty, Blaine, Indianapolis*	1.000	20	2	9	0	11	1
BELL, Eric, Buffalo*	1.000	28	11	27	0	38	3
Beltran, Rigo, Louisville*	.913	24	9	12	2	23	0
Benes, Alan, Louisville	1.000	11	6	5	0	11	1
Bere, Jason, Nashville	.500	1	0	1	1	2	0
Bertotti, Mike, Nashville*	1.000	7	1	1	0	2	0
Bevil, Brian, Omaha	1.000	6	0	1	0	1	0
Bluma, Jaime, Omaha	1.000	18	5	3	0	8	2
Bolton, Rodney, Nashville	1.000	20	12	20	0	32	6
Bolton, Tom, Nashville*	.944	19	3	14	1	18	0
Boze, Marshall, New Orleans	1.000	23	9	11	0	20	3
Brandenburg, Mark, Okla. City	.800	35	2	6	2	10	1
Brewer, Billy, Omaha*	1.000	6	1	1	0	2	0
Bronkey, Jeff, New Orleans	1.000	2	0	1	0	1	0
Brown, Kevin, Omaha*	.800	7	1	3	1	5	0
Browning, Tom, Omaha*	1.000	5	3	1	0	4	0
Brumley, Duff, Okla. City	.500	3	0	1	1	2	0
Buckels, Gary, Louisville	.875	13	5	2	1	8	0
Buckley, Travis, Indianapolis	.938	23	10	20	2	32	1
Bunch, Mel, Omaha	1.000	12	6	7	0	13	1
Busby, Mike, Louisville	.833	6	4	1	1	6	0
Bushing, Chris, Okla. City	.000	3	0	0	1	1	0
Caceres, Edgar, Omaha	1.000	1	2	0	0	2	0
Cadaret, Greg, Louisville*	.750	12	0	3	1	4	0
Campbell, Mike, Iowa	1.000	21	5	15	0	20	0
Carpenter, Cris, Louisville	1.000	49	5	9	0	14	0
Casian, Larry, Iowa*	1.000	13	0	7	0	7	0
Chapin, Darrin, Buffalo	1.000	6	1	1	0	2	0
Cimorelli, Frank, Louisville	1.000	6	0	2	0	2	1
Clark, Mark, Buffalo	1.000	5	4	6	0	10	1
Combs, Pat, New Orleans*	1.000	12	0	1	0	1	0
Costello, Fred, Nashville	.667	7	1	1	1	3	0
Courtright, John, Indianapolis*	1.000	13	2	3	0	5	0
Crawford, Carlos, Buffalo	.833	13	0	5	1	6	1
Creek, Doug, Louisville*	1.000	26	4	3	0	7	0
Curtis, Chris, Okla. City	.750	51	2	10	4	16	0
Dabney, Fred, Iowa*	1.000	33	5	10	0	15	0
Davis, Storm, Indianapolis	1.000	4	1	1	0	2	1
DeJesus, Jose, Omaha	1.000	36	0	8	0	8	0
DeLaRosa, Francisco, Louisville	.947	28	8	10	1	19	0
Dettmer, John, Okla. City	1.000	5	0	1	0	1	0
Dibble, Rob, New Orleans	1.000	4	1	0	0	1	0
Dixon, Steve, Iowa*	.875	53	2	5	1	8	0
Dorlarque, Aaron, Omaha	.900	24	1	8	1	10	0
Drahman, Brian, O.C.-Ind.	1.000	24	2	3	0	5	0
Duncan, Chip, O.C.-N.O.	1.000	17	0	2	0	2	0
Eddy, Chris, Omaha*	1.000	14	0	1	0	1	0
Edens, Tom, Iowa	1.000	20	2	3	0	5	0
Ellis, Robert, Nashville	1.000	4	1	3	0	4	0
Embree, Alan, Buffalo*	1.000	30	2	3	0	5	0
Farrell, John, Buffalo	.911	29	14	27	4	45	1
Farrell, Mike, New Orleans*	1.000	25	9	17	0	26	4
Ferry, Mike, Indianapolis	1.000	3	0	2	0	2	0
Fleming, Dave, Omaha*	1.000	3	0	2	0	2	0
Frascatore, John, Louisville	.895	28	10	7	2	19	0
Fritz, John, New Orleans	.923	41	6	6	1	13	0
Frohwirth, Todd, Buffalo	1.000	26	1	5	0	6	0
Fyhrie, Mike, Omaha	1.000	14	7	6	0	13	1

Player, Team	Pct.	G	PO	A	E	TC	DP
Gajkowski, Steve, Nashville	1.000	15	4	2	0	6	0
Ganote, Joe, New Orleans	1.000	14	4	15	0	19	0
Garces, Rich, Iowa	1.000	23	3	2	0	5	0
Garrelts, Scott, Omaha	1.000	9	2	1	0	3	1
Geeve, Dave, Okla. City	1.000	10	3	7	0	10	0
Givens, Brian, New Orleans*	.867	16	3	10	2	15	0
Goetz, Barry, Oklahoma City	.895	40	5	12	2	19	4
Gozzo, Mauro, Iowa	.875	6	4	3	1	8	0
Grant, Mark, Iowa	1.000	11	7	7	0	14	1
Graves, Daniel, Buffalo	1.000	3	0	1	0	1	0
Grimsley, Jason, Buffalo	1.000	10	6	10	0	16	2
Grott, Matt, Indianapolis*	.833	25	4	6	2	12	0
Hammaker, Atlee, Nashville*	1.000	15	3	5	0	8	0
Harris, Pep, Buffalo	.875	14	3	4	1	8	1
Harrison, Brian, Omaha	1.000	16	2	6	0	8	0
Helling, Rick, Okla. City	1.000	20	4	14	0	18	0
Heredia, Wilson, Okla. City	1.000	8	3	0	0	3	0
Hurst, James, O.C.-Ind.*	1.000	31	2	2	0	4	0
Ignasiak, Mike, New Orleans	1.000	4	0	2	0	2	0
Jarvis, Kevin, Indianapolis	1.000	10	7	3	0	10	0
Jean, Domingo, O.C.-Ind.	.900	26	7	11	2	20	0
Johnson, Dane, Nashville	.800	46	0	4	1	5	0
Jones, Calvin, Nashville	1.000	5	1	0	0	1	0
Jones, Stacy, New Orleans	1.000	34	4	3	0	7	0
Karchner, Matt, Nashville	.833	28	4	6	2	12	3
Karl, Scott, New Orleans*	.923	8	2	10	1	13	2
Keyser, Brian, Nashville	1.000	10	8	14	0	22	0
Kiefer, Mark, New Orleans	1.000	12	8	9	0	17	2
Kilgo, Rusty, Indianapolis*	1.000	2	0	1	0	1	0
Klink, Joe, Buffalo*	.889	45	2	6	1	9	1
KUTZLER, Jerry, Omaha	1.000	37	19	19	0	38	2
Lacy, Kerry, Oklahoma City	1.000	1	0	1	0	1	0
Lancaster, Les, Buffalo	.944	45	7	10	1	18	0
Levine, Alan, Nashville	1.000	3	1	0	0	1	0
Lewis, James, Buffalo	1.000	18	9	12	0	21	0
Linton, Doug, Omaha	.824	18	2	12	3	17	1
Lopez, Albie, Buffalo	.929	18	5	8	1	14	2
Lorraine, Andrew, Nashville*	1.000	7	0	2	0	2	0
Lynch, David, Buffalo*	1.000	14	5	1	0	6	0
Magnante, Mike, Omaha*	.941	15	4	12	1	17	1
Mallicoat, Rob, Omaha*	1.000	3	0	1	0	1	0
Marquez, Isidrio, Nashville	1.000	46	2	11	0	13	1
Martinez, Frankie, Louisville	1.000	38	4	11	0	15	0
Mathews, T.J., Louisville	1.000	32	5	5	0	10	0
Mathile, Mike, Indianapolis	1.000	14	5	2	0	7	2
McAndrew, Jamie, New Orleans	.923	17	11	13	2	26	2
McClellan, Paul, New Orleans	1.000	3	1	3	0	4	0
Meier, Kevin, Iowa	1.000	3	0	3	0	3	1
Melendez, Jose, Omaha	1.000	21	1	4	0	5	0
Milacki, Bob, Omaha	.944	15	7	10	1	18	1
Minchey, Nate, Louisville	.920	26	7	16	2	25	1
Mongiello, Mike, Nashville	1.000	31	9	8	0	17	0
Moore, Marcus, Indianapolis	1.000	7	0	1	0	1	0
Morton, Kevin, Iowa*	.950	28	8	11	1	20	1
Munoz, J.J., Omaha*	.875	57	8	6	2	16	0
Myers, Rod, Omaha	1.000	38	4	7	0	11	0
Nabholz, Chris, Iowa*	1.000	6	0	2	0	2	0
Nichting, Chris, Okla. City	1.000	23	6	6	0	12	1
Nitkowski, C.J., Indianapolis*	1.000	6	1	5	0	6	0
Novoa, Rafael, Nashville*	1.000	3	1	1	0	2	0
Ogea, Chad, Buffalo	1.000	4	1	5	0	6	0
Olsen, Steve, Nashville	1.000	14	4	6	0	10	0
Olson, Gregg, Buf.-Oma.	1.000	19	1	6	0	7	0
Osborne, Donovan, Louisville*	1.000	1	2	1	0	3	0
Pall, Donn, Nashville	1.000	44	5	14	0	19	0
Parker, Clay, New Orleans	1.000	2	1	0	0	1	0
Patterson, Danny, Okla. City	.818	14	5	4	2	11	1
Perez, David, Oklahoma City	.875	20	6	22	4	32	3
Perry, Pat, Omaha*	1.000	5	0	1	0	1	0
Perschke, Greg, Buffalo	1.000	3	1	3	0	4	0
Petkovsek, Mark, Louisville	.905	8	6	13	2	21	0
Pittsley, Jim, Omaha	1.000	8	1	4	0	5	0
Popplewell, Tom, New Orleans	1.000	10	0	2	0	2	0
Prager, Howard, Louisville*	1.000	2	1	0	0	1	0
Pugh, Tim, Indianapolis	.750	6	2	1	1	4	0
Raczka, Mike, Louisville*	.889	55	7	9	2	18	2
Rambo, Dan, New Orleans	1.000	7	5	3	0	8	0
Rasmussen, Dennis, Omaha*	1.000	10	1	14	0	15	1
Reed, Rick, Indianapolis	.964	22	7	20	1	28	1
Remlinger, Mike, Indianapolis*	.889	41	4	4	1	9	0
Righetti, Dave, Nashville*	.750	16	1	11	4	16	0
Rightnowar, Ron, New Orleans	1.000	25	4	7	0	11	1
Roa, Joe, Buffalo	.950	25	13	25	2	40	3

Player, Team	Pct.	G	PO	A	E	TC	DP
Roberson, Sid, New Orleans*	1.000	4	1	1	0	2	0
Roper, John, Indianapolis	1.000	8	3	7	0	10	0
Ruffin, Johnny, Indianapolis	.875	36	4	3	1	8	0
Salkeld, Roger, Indianapolis	.929	20	3	10	1	14	1
Sauveur, Rich, Indianapolis*	1.000	52	6	13	0	19	2
Scanlan, Bob, New Orleans	1.000	3	1	0	0	1	0
Schuermann, Lance, Okla. City*	1.000	33	3	8	0	11	0
Scudder, Scott, Indianapolis	.889	7	1	7	1	9	0
Seminara, Frank, New Orleans	.571	11	2	2	3	7	0
Service, Scott, Indianapolis	1.000	36	5	3	0	8	0
Shifflett, Steve, Iowa	.929	26	7	6	1	14	1
Shinall, Zak, New Orleans	1.000	9	1	2	0	3	0
Shuey, Paul, Buffalo	.667	25	0	2	1	3	0
Simas, Bill, Nashville	1.000	7	0	2	0	2	0
Simmons, Scott, Louisville*	1.000	2	1	3	0	4	0
Sirotka, Mike, Nashville*	.818	8	1	8	2	11	2
Slusarski, Joe, Buf.-N.O.	1.000	37	4	6	0	10	0
Smith, Ottis, Iowa*	1.000	5	0	4	0	4	0
Steenstra, Kennie, Iowa	.978	29	14	31	1	46	2
Strange, Don, Omaha	1.000	9	1	3	0	4	0
Sturtze, Tanyon, Iowa	1.000	23	3	16	0	19	0
Sullivan, Scott, Indianapolis	.846	44	4	7	2	13	1
Swartzbaugh, Dave, Iowa	1.000	30	3	6	0	9	1
Swingle, Paul, New Orleans	1.000	35	4	1	0	5	0
Taylor, Rob, Iowa	.909	54	2	8	1	11	0
Taylor, Scott, N.O.-O.C.	1.000	24	12	17	0	29	1
Telford, Anthony, Buffalo	.933	16	9	5	1	15	0
Thomas, Mike, New Orleans*	1.000	35	1	2	0	3	1
Torres, Dilson, Omaha	.833	5	4	1	1	6	0
Toth, Robert, Omaha	.857	8	3	3	1	7	0
Turner, Matt, Buffalo	1.000	13	0	1	0	1	0
Urbani, Tom, Louisville*	1.000	2	1	1	0	2	0
Vasquez, Marcos, Indianapolis	1.000	2	2	0	0	2	0
Vierra, Joey, Nashville*	1.000	56	2	6	0	8	1
Viola, Frank, Indianapolis*	.857	6	4	2	1	7	1
Vosberg, Ed, Oklahoma City*	1.000	1	0	1	0	1	0
Walker, Mike, Iowa	1.000	16	4	4	0	8	1
Warren, Brian, Indianapolis	.933	41	2	12	1	15	1
Watson, Allen, Louisville*	1.000	4	3	5	0	8	1
Wilson, Steve, Nashville*	.900	20	3	6	1	10	0
Wishnevski, Rob, Okla. City	.963	41	16	10	1	27	2

PITCHERS WITH TWO OR MORE TEAMS

Player, Team	Pct.	G	PO	A	E	TC	DP
Drahman, Brian, Okla. City	1.000	22	2	3	0	5	0
Drahman, Brian, Indianapolis	.000	2	0	0	0	0	0
Duncan, Chip, Oklahoma City	.000	3	0	0	0	0	0
Duncan, Chip, New Orleans	1.000	14	0	2	0	2	0
Hurst, James, Okla. City*	1.000	28	2	2	0	4	0
Hurst, James, Indianapolis*	.000	3	0	0	0	0	0
Jean, Domingo, Okla. City	.889	24	7	9	2	18	0
Jean, Domingo, Indianapolis	1.000	2	0	2	0	2	0
Olson, Gregg, Buffalo	1.000	18	1	6	0	7	0
Olson, Gregg, Omaha	.000	1	0	0	0	0	0
Slusarski, Joe, Buffalo	1.000	4	1	1	0	2	0
Slusarski, Joe, New Orleans	1.000	33	3	5	0	8	0
Taylor, Scott, New Orleans	1.000	2	2	0	0	2	0
Taylor, Scott, Oklahoma City	1.000	22	10	17	0	27	1

The following players did not have any fielding statistics at the positions indicated or appeared only as a designated hitter, pinch-hitter or pinch-runner: Aversa, of; Belcher, p; Bolick, ss; Burrows, p; Converse, p; Darwin, p; C. Davis, p; J. Davis, p; DeLeon, p; Diggs, ss; Donnelly, p; Fordyce, of; Franco, c, p; Fraraccio, 3b; Goldberg, 3b; Green, p; M. Harris, 1b; R. Harris, p; Howard, ss, of; Howitt, 1b; Huisman, p; D. Jackson, p; M. Jackson, p; James, dh; Johns, 3b; Lofton, c; Magdaleno, 3b; Massarelli, dh, ph, pr; Noriega, p; O'Halloran, of; J. Ortiz, dh, ph; Parra, of; Pennington, p; Dan. Perez, dh, ph, pr; Pierce, p; Poole, p; Riles, dh, ph; Ruffcorn, p; Santana, p; Stefanski, of; Stewart, of; Talanoa, p; Trafton, ph; B. Wilson, of; A. Young, p.

LEAGUE CHAMPIONS

Year	Team	Pct.
1902	Indianapolis	.683
1903	St. Paul	.657
1904	St. Paul	.646
1905	Columbus	.658
1906	Columbus	.615
1907	Columbus	.584
1908	Indianapolis	.601
1909	Louisville	.554
1910	Minneapolis	.637
1911	Minneapolis	.600
1912	Minneapolis	.636
1913	Milwaukee	.599
1914	Milwaukee	.590
1915	Minneapolis	.597
1916	Louisville	.605
1917	Indianapolis	.588
1918	Kansas City	.589
1919	St. Paul	.610
1920	St. Paul	.701
1921	Louisville	.583
1922	St. Paul	.641
1923	Kansas City	.675
1924	St. Paul	.578
1925	Louisville	.635
1926	Louisville	.629
1927	Toledo	.601
1928	Indianapolis	.593
1929	Kansas City	.665
1930	Louisville	.608
1931	St. Paul	.623
1932	Minneapolis	.595
1933	Columbus*	.604
	Minneapolis	.562
1934	Minneapolis	.570
	Columbus*	.556
1935	Minneapolis	.591
1936	Milwaukee†	.584
1937	Columbus†	.584
1938	St. Paul	.596
	Kansas City (2nd)‡	.556
1939	Kansas City	.695
	Louisville (4th)‡	.490
1940	Kansas City	.625
	Louisville (4th)‡	.500
1941	Columbus†	.621
1942	Kansas City	.549
	Columbus (3rd)‡	.532
1943	Milwaukee	.596
	Columbus (3rd)‡	.532
1944	Milwaukee	.667
	Louisville (3rd)‡	.574
1945	Milwaukee	.604
	Louisville (3rd)‡	.545
1946	Louisville†	.601
1947	Kansas City	.608
	Milwaukee (3rd)†	.513
1948	Indianapolis	.649
	St. Paul (3rd)‡	.558
1949	St. Paul	.608
	Indianapolis (2nd)‡	.604
1950	Minneapolis	.584
	Columbus (3rd)‡	.549
1951	Milwaukee†	.623
1952	Milwaukee	.656
	Kansas City (2nd)‡	.578
1953	Toledo	.584
	Kansas City (2nd)‡	.571
1954	Indianapolis	.625
	Louisville (2nd)‡	.556
1955	Minneapolis†	.597
1956	Indianapolis†	.597
1957	Wichita	.604
	Denver (2nd)†	.584
1958	Charleston	.589
	Minneapolis (3rd)‡	.536
1959	Louisville§	.599
	Omaha§	.516
	Minneapolis (2nd)‡	.586
1960	Denver	.571
	Louisville (2nd)‡	.556
1961	Indianapolis	.573
	Louisville (2nd)‡	.553
1962	Indianapolis	.605
	Louisville (4th)‡	.486
1963-1968	Did not operate.	
1969	Omaha	.607
1970	Omaha*	.529
	Denver	.504
1971	Indianapolis	.604
	Denver*	.521
1972	Wichita	.621
	Evansville*	.593
1973	Iowa	.610
	Tulsa*	.504
1974	Indianapolis	.578
	Tulsa*	.567
1975	Evansville*	.566
	Denver	.569
1976	Denver*	.632
	Omaha	.574
1977	Omaha	.563
	Denver*	.522
1978	Indianapolis	.578
	Omaha*	.489
1979	Evansville*	.574
	Oklahoma City	.533
1980	Denver	.676
	Springfield*	.551
1981	Omaha	.581
	Denver*	.559
1982	Indianapolis*	.551
	Omaha	.518
1983	Louisville	.578
	Denver‡	.545
1984	Denver	.513
	Louisville‡	.510
1985	Oklahoma City	.556
	Louisville*	.521
1986	Indianapolis*	.563
	Denver	.535
1987	Denver	.564
	Indianapolis‡	.536
1988	Indianapolis	.627
	Omaha	.570
1989	Indianapolis*	.596
	Omaha	.507
1990	Omaha*	.589
	Nashville	.585
1991	Buffalo	.566
	Denver*	.549
1992	Buffalo	.604
	Oklahoma City*	.514
1993	Iowa*	.590
	Nashville	.566
1994	Indianapolis‡	.601
	Nashville	.576
1995	Indianapolis	.611
	Louisville‡	.514

*Won playoff (East vs. West). †Won championship and four-team playoff. ‡Won four-team playoff. §Respective Eastern and Western division winners.

INTERNATIONAL LEAGUE

LEAGUE OFFICE

President
Randy Mobley

Address
55 S. High St., Suite 202
Dublin, OH 43017

Phone
614-791-9300

TEAMS

CHARLOTTE KNIGHTS

General manager
Bill Lavelle
Manager
Sal Rende
Ballpark (capacity, surface)
Knights Stadium (10,000, grass)
Affiliation
Marlins
Address
P.O. Box 1207
Fort Mill, SC 29716
Phone
803-548-8050

COLUMBUS CLIPPERS

General manager
Ken Schnacke
Manager
Stump Merrill
Ballpark (capacity, surface)
Cooper Stadium (15,000, artificial)
Affiliation
Yankees
Address
1155 W. Mound St.
Columbus, OH 43223
Phone
614-462-5250

NORFOLK TIDES

General manager
Dave Rosenfield
Manager
Bobby Valentine
Ballpark (capacity, surface)
Harbor Park (12,059, grass)
Affiliation
Mets
Address
150 Park Ave.
Norfolk, VA 23510
Phone
804-622-2222

OTTAWA LYNX

General manager
P.J. Loyello
Manager
Pete Mackanin
Ballpark (capacity, surface)
Ottawa Stadium (10,332, grass)
Affiliation
Expos
Address
300 Coventry Rd.
Ottawa, Ontario K1K 4P5
Phone
613-747-5969

PAWTUCKET RED SOX

General manager
Lou Schwechheimer
Manager
Buddy Bailey
Ballpark (capacity, surface)
McCoy Stadium (7,002, grass)
Affiliation
Red Sox
Address
P.O. Box 2365
Pawtucket, RI 02861
Phone
401-724-7300

RICHMOND BRAVES

General manager
Bruce Baldwin
Manager
Bill Dancy
Ballpark (capacity, surface)
The Diamond (12,156, grass)
Affiliation
Braves
Address
P.O. Box 6667
Richmond, VA 23230
Phone
804-359-4444

ROCHESTER RED WINGS

General manager
Joe Altobelli
Manager
Marv Foley
Ballpark (capacity, surface)
Silver Stadium (10,503, grass)
Affiliation
Orioles
Address
500 Norton St.
Rochester, NY 14621
Phone
716-467-3000

SCRANTON/WILKES-BARRE BARONS

General manager
Bill Terlecky
Manager
Butch Hobson
Ballpark (capacity, surface)
Lackawanna County Stadium (10,832, artificial)
Affiliation
Phillies
Address
P.O. Box 3449
Scranton, PA 18505
Phone
717-969-2255

SYRACUSE CHIEFS

General manager
Anthony "Tex" Simone
Manager
Richie Hebner
Ballpark (capacity, surface)
MacArthur Stadium (10,000, grass)
Affiliation
Blue Jays
Address
MacArthur Stadium
Syracuse, NY 13208
Phone
315-474-7833

TOLEDO MUD HENS

General manager
Gene Cook
Manager
Tom Runnells
Ballpark (capacity, surface)
Ned Skeldon Stadium (10,025, grass)
Affiliation
Tigers
Address
P.O. Box 6212
Toledo, OH 43614
Phone
419-893-9483

1995 FINAL STANDINGS

EAST DIVISION

Team	W	L	T	Pct.	GB
Rochester (Orioles)	73	69	0	.514	....
Ottawa (Expos)	72	70	0	.507	1
Pawtucket (Red Sox)	70	71	0	.496	2½
Scranton/Wilkes-Barre (Phillies)	70	72	0	.493	3
Syracuse (Blue Jays)	59	82	0	.418	13½

WEST DIVISION

Team	W	L	T	Pct.	GB
Norfolk (Mets)	86	56	0	.606	....
Richmond (Braves)	75	66	0	.532	10½
Columbus (Yankees)	71	68	0	.511	13½
Toledo (Tigers)	71	71	0	.500	15
Charlotte (Marlins)	59	81	0	.421	26

COMPOSITE

Team	Nor.	Rich.	Roc.	Col.	Ott.	Tol.	Paw.	SWB	Char.	Syr.	W	L	T	Pct.	GB
Norfolk (Mets)	....	11	7	8	9	12	10	6	13	10	86	56	0	.606	....
Richmond (Braves)	7	....	6	11	7	10	7	10	10	7	75	66	0	.532	10½
Rochester (Orioles)	7	8	....	9	7	5	10	9	9	9	73	69	0	.514	13
Columbus (Yankees)	10	7	5	....	8	10	7	6	10	8	71	68	0	.511	13½
Ottawa (Expos)	5	7	11	6	....	5	7	10	8	13	72	70	0	.507	14
Toledo (Tigers)	6	8	9	8	9	....	8	9	7	7	71	71	0	.500	15
Pawtucket (Red Sox)	4	7	8	6	11	6	....	10	7	11	70	71	0	.496	15½
Scranton/Wilkes-Barre (Phillies)	8	4	9	8	8	5	8	....	9	11	70	72	0	.493	16
Charlotte (Marlins)	5	8	5	6	6	11	7	5	....	6	59	81	0	.421	26
Syracuse (Blue Jays)	4	6	9	6	5	7	7	7	8	....	59	82	0	.418	26½

Major league affiliations in parentheses.

PLAYOFFS: Norfolk defeated Richmond, three games to two; Ottawa defeated Rochester, three games to two; Ottawa defeated Norfolk, three games to one, to win league championship.

REGULAR-SEASON ATTENDANCE: Charlotte, 336,001; Columbus, 541,451; Norfolk, 586,317; Ottawa, 511,865; Pawtucket, 486,029; Richmond, 524,210; Rochester, 402,127; Scranton/Wilkes-Barre, 489,040; Syracuse, 303,208; Toledo, 306,906. Total—4,487,154. Playoffs (14 games)—63,732. Class AAA All-Star Game at Scranton/Wilkes-Barre—10,965.

MANAGERS: Charlotte, Sal Rende; Columbus, Bill Evers; Norfolk, Toby Harrah; Ottawa, Pete Mackanin; Pawtucket, Buddy Bailey; Richmond, Grady Little; Rochester, Marv Foley; Scranton/Wilkes-Barre, Mike Quade; Syracuse, Bob Didier (April 6 through June 21), Hector Torres (June 22) and Richie Hebner (June 23 through end of season); Toledo, Tom Runnells. Managerial record of team with more than one manager: Syracuse, Didier, 25-43, Torres 1-0, Hebner 33-39.

ALL-STAR TEAM: 1B—Don Sparks, Columbus; 2B—Kevin Jordan, Scranton/Wilkes-Barre; 3B—Butch Huskey, Norfolk; SS—Derek Jeter, Columbus; OF—Alex Ochoa, Rochester-Norfolk; Robert Perez, Syracuse; Mark Smith, Rochester; C—Jorge Posada, Columbus; DH—Carlos Delgado, Syracuse; Starting Pitcher—Jason Isringhausen, Norfolk; Relief Pitcher—Rod Nichols, Richmond; Most Valuable Player—Butch Huskey, Norfolk; Most Valuable Pitcher—Jason Isringhausen, Norfolk; Rookie of the Year—Jason Isringhausen, Norfolk; Manager of the Year—Toby Harrah, Norfolk.

1995 BATTING

TEAM

Team	Avg.	G	TPA	AB	R	H	TB	2B	3B	HR	RBI	SH	SF	HP	BB	IBB	SO	SB	CS	GDP	LOB	ShO	Slg.	OBP
Scr./Wil.-Bar.	.272	142	5374	4734	645	1286	1849	248	48	73	602	58	50	72	459	19	777	95	55	129	1015	4	.391	.342
Columbus	.271	140	5308	4730	687	1281	1940	222	61	105	629	38	46	36	456	20	911	104	57	109	951	12	.410	.337
Pawtucket	.264	142	5302	4732	676	1249	1995	240	19	156	630	32	36	45	456	21	951	94	63	111	930	6	.422	.332
Rochester	.262	142	5303	4735	669	1242	1936	256	36	122	616	27	46	48	446	21	820	125	65	108	947	7	.409	.329
Charlotte	.260	140	5281	4695	620	1220	1775	218	17	101	582	42	45	35	464	15	729	119	70	97	951	12	.378	.328
Norfolk	.260	142	5269	4697	650	1219	1798	229	40	90	602	52	42	42	434	20	823	132	94	110	888	5	.383	.325
Richmond	.259	141	5272	4710	559	1222	1716	194	33	78	510	39	42	40	441	30	794	70	69	115	975	12	.364	.325
Syracuse	.258	141	5276	4764	615	1227	1936	243	41	128	561	18	39	39	416	21	885	76	58	104	940	11	.406	.320
Ottawa	.257	142	5242	4644	618	1195	1751	225	35	87	566	65	30	44	454	31	824	161	53	104	946	8	.377	.327
Toledo	.257	142	5337	4755	600	1222	1840	224	35	108	546	39	45	56	442	11	962	93	70	107	985	11	.387	.325

INDIVIDUAL

TOP QUALIFIERS FOR BATTING CHAMPIONSHIP

Minimum 383 plate appearances. *Lefthanded batter. †Switch-hitter.

Player, Team	Avg.	G	TPA	AB	R	H	TB	2B	3B	HR	RBI	SH	SF	HP	BB	IBB	SO	SB	CS	GDP	Slg.	OBP
Perez, Robert, Syracuse	.343	122	522	502	70	172	249	38	6	9	67	1	4	2	13	4	60	7	5	17	.496	.359
Giovanola, Ed, Richmond*	.321	99	385	321	45	103	137	18	2	4	36	4	4	1	55	3	37	8	7	10	.427	.417
Delgado, Carlos, Syracuse*	.318	91	387	333	59	106	203	23	4	22	74	0	4	5	45	7	78	0	4	8	.610	.403
Jeter, Derek, Columbus	.317	123	558	486	96	154	205	27	9	2	45	2	5	4	61	1	56	20	12	9	.422	.394
Schall, Gene, Scr./W.-B.	.313	92	383	320	52	100	169	25	4	12	63	0	4	10	49	2	54	3	3	14	.528	.415
Sparks, Don, Columbus	.312	137	585	545	67	170	237	26	10	7	90	1	9	1	29	3	75	2	0	17	.435	.342
Jordan, Kevin, Scr./W.-B.	.310	106	453	410	61	127	179	29	4	5	60	1	6	8	28	0	36	3	0	14	.437	.361
Garcia, Omar, Norfolk	.309	115	459	430	55	133	177	21	7	3	64	1	7	0	21	3	58	3	4	13	.412	.336
Castleberry, Kevin, Ottawa*	.294	118	489	428	65	126	173	18	4	7	56	5	4	0	52	3	59	9	7	5	.404	.368
Crespo, Felipe, Syracuse†	.294	88	392	347	56	102	171	20	5	13	41	1	1	2	41	4	56	12	7	5	.493	.371
Munoz, Jose, Richmond†	.290	135	588	520	65	151	188	18	5	3	45	5	6	4	53	4	65	7	10	18	.362	.357
Zuber, Jon, Scr./W.-B.*	.287	119	471	418	53	120	158	19	5	3	50	1	2	0	49	2	68	1	2	12	.378	.360
Huskey, Butch, Norfolk	.284	109	442	394	66	112	216	18	1	28	87	0	3	6	39	4	88	8	6	9	.548	.355
Ochoa, Alex, Roch.-Nor.	.283	125	505	459	58	130	192	24	4	10	61	1	3	2	40	1	62	24	10	12	.418	.341
Kowitz, Brian, Richmond*	.280	100	400	353	53	99	129	14	5	2	34	3	0	3	41	1	43	11	8	4	.365	.360
Yan, Julian, Ottawa	.280	114	392	372	49	104	198	22	3	22	79	2	1	2	15	2	90	5	1	10	.532	.310

DEPARTMENTAL LEADERS: G—Sparks, 137; AB—Sparks, 545; R—Jeter, 96; H—R. Perez, 172; TB—R. Perez, 249; 2B—R. Perez, 38; 3B—Sparks, 10; HR—Huskey, 28; RBI—Sparks, 90; SH—Buccheri, A. Rodriguez, 11; SF—Sparks, 9; HP—G. Murray, 11; BB—Tyler, 71; IBB—C. Delgado, 7; SO—Clark, 129; SB—Buccheri, 44; CS—Alicea, Ordonez, Otero, 13; GIDP—Munoz, 18; Slg.—C. Delgado, .610; OBP—Giovanola, .417.

ALL PLAYERS

*Lefthanded batter. †Switch-hitter.

Player, Team	Avg.	G	TPA	AB	R	H	TB	2B	3B	HR	RBI	SH	SF	HP	BB	IBB	SO	SB	CS	GDP	Slg.	OBP
Abbott, Kurt, Charlotte	.278	5	19	18	3	5	8	0	0	1	3	0	0	0	1	0	3	1	0	0	.444	.316
Abner, Shawn, Norfolk	.258	11	32	31	3	8	8	0	0	0	1	0	0	0	1	0	7	0	0	0	.258	.281
Acevedo, Juan, Norfolk	.000	2	1	0	0	0	0	0	0	0	0	0	0	0	1	0	0	0	0	0	.000	1.000
Adamson, Joel, Charlotte*	.071	19	14	14	0	1	1	0	0	0	0	0	0	0	0	0	5	0	0	0	.071	.071
Alfonzo, Edgar, Rochester	.185	18	60	54	5	10	16	3	0	1	6	3	1	0	2	0	10	0	0	3	.296	.211
Alicea, Ed, Norfolk†	.245	122	491	436	63	107	141	17	4	3	39	6	2	2	45	2	78	21	13	11	.323	.318
Alvarez, Clemente, Ottawa	.231	50	159	143	15	33	52	7	0	4	20	3	0	2	10	1	34	0	0	2	.364	.290
Alvarez, Jose, Richmond	.000	5	2	2	0	0	0	0	0	0	0	0	0	0	0	0	1	0	0	0	.000	.000
Azuaje, Jesus, Norfolk	.429	5	16	14	1	6	7	1	0	0	0	0	0	0	2	0	2	1	1	0	.500	.500
Baez, Kevin, Toledo	.231	116	411	376	30	87	116	13	2	4	37	10	2	1	22	1	57	1	6	13	.309	.274
Barbara, Don, Pawtucket*	.217	40	141	129	19	28	42	8	0	2	10	0	0	0	12	0	18	2	0	3	.326	.284
Bark, Brian, Rich.-Paw.*	.000	43	2	2	0	0	0	0	0	0	0	0	0	0	0	0	0	0	0	0	.000	.000
Barnwell, Rich, Columbus	.231	46	146	130	22	30	41	4	2	1	17	2	0	1	13	0	32	7	3	4	.315	.306
Barron, Tony, Ottawa	.245	50	164	147	20	36	76	10	0	10	22	0	1	2	14	1	22	0	2	3	.517	.317
Barry, Jeff, Norfolk†	.220	12	47	41	3	9	11	2	0	0	6	0	2	1	3	0	6	0	0	2	.268	.277
Bartee, Kimera, Rochester†	.154	15	55	52	5	8	12	2	1	0	3	2	1	0	0	0	16	0	0	0	.231	.151
Batista, Miguel, Charlotte	.083	34	13	12	0	1	1	0	0	0	0	0	0	0	1	0	6	0	0	0	.083	.154
Batiste, Kim, Scr./W.B.-Roc.	.264	98	397	382	41	101	143	17	2	7	47	1	1	3	10	0	41	5	8	13	.374	.288
Battle, Howard, Syracuse	.251	118	488	443	43	111	160	17	4	8	48	1	2	3	39	2	73	10	11	7	.361	.314
Bautista, Danny, Toledo	.241	18	63	58	6	14	17	3	0	0	4	1	0	3	1	0	10	1	2	1	.293	.290
Baxter, Robert, Ottawa*	.125	39	11	8	2	1	1	0	0	0	0	1	0	0	2	0	2	0	0	0	.125	.300
Bell, Juan, Pawtucket†	.263	68	284	262	42	69	107	18	1	6	23	1	0	0	21	0	46	4	5	7	.408	.318
Benitez, Yamil, Ottawa	.259	127	524	474	66	123	213	24	6	18	69	2	2	2	44	3	128	14	6	10	.449	.324
Bennett, Gary, Scr./W.-B.	.150	7	23	20	1	3	3	0	0	0	1	1	0	0	2	1	2	0	0	0	.150	.227
Benzinger, Todd, Columbus†	.280	12	52	50	4	14	20	3	0	1	4	0	0	0	2	1	10	0	0	2	.400	.308
Bieser, Steve, Scr./W.-B.†	.269	95	285	245	37	66	93	12	6	1	33	6	2	10	22	1	56	14	5	5	.380	.351
Birkbeck, Mike, Norfolk	.222	9	10	9	2	2	3	1	0	0	0	0	0	0	1	0	3	0	0	0	.333	.300
Blosser, Greg, Pawtucket*	.200	17	56	50	5	10	13	0	0	1	4	0	1	0	5	0	13	0	0	0	.260	.268
Boka, Ben, Norfolk	.143	19	22	21	0	3	3	0	0	0	1	1	0	0	0	0	8	0	0	0	.143	.143
Boston, Daryl, Charlotte*	.188	18	70	64	7	12	20	5	0	1	2	0	0	0	6	0	12	0	0	1	.313	.257
Boucher, Denis, Ottawa	.375	14	11	8	1	3	5	2	0	0	2	1	0	0	2	0	0	0	0	0	.625	.500
Bournigal, Rafael, Ottawa	.204	19	58	54	2	11	15	4	0	0	6	1	0	1	2	0	4	0	0	2	.278	.246
Bowers, Brent, Syracuse*	.252	111	318	305	38	77	118	16	5	5	26	1	1	1	10	0	57	5	1	3	.387	.278
Brewer, Rod, Charlotte*	.322	69	279	236	31	76	120	15	1	9	55	0	5	5	33	3	45	0	0	3	.508	.409
Briley, Greg, Toledo*	.238	31	90	84	8	20	29	4	1	1	7	0	0	0	6	0	25	0	2	3	.345	.289
Brito, Tilson, Syracuse	.242	90	363	327	49	79	122	16	3	7	32	2	1	4	29	0	69	17	8	6	.373	.310
Brock, Chris, Richmond	.000	23	9	8	0	0	0	0	0	0	0	0	0	0	1	0	3	0	0	1	.000	.111
Brock, Tarrik, Toledo*	.194	9	33	31	4	6	7	1	0	0	0	0	0	0	2	0	17	2	2	0	.226	.242
Brooks, Eric, Syracuse	.192	47	133	120	12	23	28	3	1	0	5	1	0	0	12	0	27	0	2	2	.233	.265
Brophy, E.J., Scr./W.-B.	.200	34	76	65	7	13	18	2	0	1	6	3	0	0	8	1	15	0	0	3	.277	.288
Brown, Jarvis, Nor.-Roch.	.294	62	251	218	41	64	90	16	5	0	21	4	0	1	28	0	49	7	4	5	.413	.377
Brown, Randy, Pawtucket	.250	74	232	212	27	53	67	6	1	2	12	4	2	4	10	0	53	5	1	4	.316	.294
Buccheri, Jim, Ottawa	.268	133	537	470	64	126	150	16	4	0	30	11	2	3	49	5	58	44	11	7	.319	.340
Buford, Damon, Rochester	.309	46	208	188	40	58	88	12	3	4	18	1	1	1	17	0	26	17	4	2	.468	.367
Butler, Rich, Syracuse*	.161	69	210	199	20	32	46	4	2	2	14	1	1	0	9	0	45	2	3	5	.231	.196
Butler, Robert, Scr./W.-B.*	.300	92	365	327	46	98	131	16	4	3	35	4	4	6	24	2	39	5	8	14	.401	.355
Byrd, Paul, Norfolk	.250	22	4	4	0	1	1	0	0	0	0	0	0	0	0	0	0	0	0	0	.250	.250
Cabrera, Francisco, Richmond	.231	36	111	104	7	24	32	5	0	1	14	0	2	0	5	2	22	0	1	3	.308	.261
Cairo, Sergio, Ottawa	.333	2	6	6	1	2	3	1	0	0	0	0	0	0	0	0	1	0	0	0	.500	.333
Canate, Willie, Syracuse	.238	114	382	345	48	82	112	17	2	3	30	3	2	9	23	0	62	8	5	9	.325	.301
Canseco, Jose, Pawtucket	.167	2	8	6	1	1	1	0	0	0	1	0	1	0	1	0	5	0	0	0	.167	.250
Capra, Nick, Charlotte	.256	119	465	406	60	104	150	17	1	9	51	2	2	1	54	0	45	22	12	5	.369	.343
Carey, Paul, Rochester*	.236	89	335	284	39	67	107	13	0	9	50	1	5	5	40	5	68	1	2	2	.377	.335
Carpenter, Bubba, Columbus*	.246	116	420	374	57	92	143	12	3	11	49	2	3	1	40	2	70	13	6	2	.382	.318
Carr, Chuck, Charlotte†	.217	7	25	23	5	5	10	0	1	1	2	0	0	0	2	1	1	2	0	0	.435	.280
Carter, Jeff, Charlotte†	.269	124	505	428	78	115	141	20	3	0	22	9	1	5	62	0	86	22	10	5	.329	.367
Carter, Steve, Charlotte*	.250	24	80	72	9	18	27	0	0	3	15	0	1	0	7	0	6	0	0	1	.375	.313
Castaldo, Vince, Charlotte*	.200	7	14	10	2	2	2	0	0	0	1	0	1	0	3	0	3	0	0	0	.200	.357
Castillo, Alberto, Norfolk	.267	69	249	217	23	58	85	13	1	4	31	3	2	1	26	0	32	2	3	6	.392	.346
Castleberry, Kevin, Ottawa*	.294	118	489	428	65	126	173	18	4	7	56	5	4	0	52	3	59	9	7	5	.404	.368
Chamberlain, Wes, Pawtucket	.350	48	190	183	28	64	119	17	1	12	40	0	1	3	3	0	45	5	3	3	.650	.368
Clark, Tony, Toledo†	.242	110	463	405	50	98	161	17	2	14	63	0	3	3	52	1	129	0	2	8	.398	.330
Clary, Marty, Charlotte	.500	9	4	2	0	1	1	0	0	0	0	2	0	0	0	0	0	0	0	0	.500	.500
Coffman, Kevin, Richmond	.000	2	1	0	0	0	0	0	0	0	0	0	0	0	1	0	0	0	0	0	.000	1.000
Combs, Pat, Scr./W.-B.*	.000	22	1	1	0	0	0	0	0	0	0	0	0	0	0	0	1	0	0	0	.000	.000
Cornelius, Reid, Ott.-Nor.	.063	14	19	16	0	1	1	0	0	0	0	3	0	0	0	0	10	0	0	0	.063	.063
Crawford, Joe, Norfolk*	.000	8	1	1	0	0	0	0	0	0	0	0	0	0	0	0	1	0	0	0	.000	.000
Crespo, Felipe, Syracuse†	.294	88	392	347	56	102	171	20	5	13	41	1	1	2	41	4	56	12	7	5	.493	.371
Crowley, Jim, Rochester	.173	34	110	98	7	17	23	3	0	1	6	1	0	4	7	0	21	0	1	2	.235	.257
Cruz, Ivan, Toledo*	.194	11	43	36	5	7	9	2	0	0	3	0	1	0	6	0	9	0	0	1	.250	.302
Cuyler, Milt, Toledo†	.305	54	232	203	33	62	98	10	4	6	28	0	4	5	20	0	40	6	7	1	.483	.375
Dascenzo, Doug, Charlotte†	.260	75	295	265	51	69	90	9	0	4	26	1	4	0	25	0	30	14	9	7	.340	.320
Daubach, Brian, Norfolk*	.000	2	9	7	0	0	0	0	0	0	0	0	0	0	2	1	0	0	0	0	.000	.222
Davis, Jay, Norfolk*	.192	10	26	26	1	5	8	1	1	0	3	0	0	0	0	0	2	0	1	1	.308	.192
Davis, Russ, Columbus	.250	20	95	76	12	19	31	4	1	2	15	0	1	1	17	3	23	0	0	0	.408	.389
DeBerry, Joe, Columbus*	.292	10	25	24	3	7	13	2	2	0	4	0	0	0	1	0	6	0	0	1	.542	.320
Dejardin, Bobby, Rochester†	.314	9	40	35	6	11	13	2	0	0	3	0	2	0	3	0	3	1	0	0	.371	.350
Delgado, Alex, Pawtucket	.252	44	114	107	14	27	45	3	0	5	12	0	0	1	6	0	12	0	0	4	.421	.298
Delgado, Carlos, Syracuse*	.318	91	387	333	59	106	203	23	4	22	74	0	4	5	45	7	78	0	4	8	.610	.403
Delima, Rafael, Ottawa*	.259	10	33	27	4	7	7	0	0	0	3	1	0	0	5	0	3	2	0	2	.259	.375

Player, Team	Avg.	G	TPA	AB	R	H	TB	2B	3B	HR	RBI	SH	SF	HP	BB	IBB	SO	SB	CS	GDP	Slg.	OBP
Dellicarri, Joe, Toledo	.250	4	15	12	4	3	6	0	0	1	1	0	0	2	1	0	2	1	0	0	.500	.400
Deshaies, Jim, Scr./W.-B.*	.067	19	19	15	0	1	1	0	0	0	3	4	0	0	0	0	8	0	0	0	.067	.067
Devarez, Cesar, Rochester	.250	67	249	240	32	60	77	12	1	1	21	1	1	0	7	0	25	2	2	8	.321	.270
Diaz, Cesar, Norfolk	.182	3	11	11	2	2	2	0	0	0	0	0	0	0	0	0	2	0	0	0	.182	.182
Diaz, Edgar, Syracuse	.302	15	52	43	5	13	15	0	1	0	2	1	0	1	7	0	6	0	0	0	.349	.412
Diaz, Rafael, Ottawa	.000	32	4	2	0	0	0	0	0	0	0	0	0	0	2	0	1	0	0	0	.000	.500
Donnels, Chris, Pawtucket*	.400	4	16	15	1	6	9	0	0	1	4	0	0	0	1	0	3	0	0	0	.600	.438
Eenhoorn, Robert, Columbus	.252	92	349	318	36	80	112	11	3	5	32	6	2	3	20	0	54	2	4	5	.352	.300
Eischen, Joey, Ottawa*	.000	11	1	1	0	0	0	0	0	0	0	0	0	0	0	0	0	0	0	0	.000	.000
Elster, Kevin, Scr./W.-B.	.294	5	19	17	2	5	8	3	0	0	2	0	0	0	2	0	3	0	0	1	.471	.368
Engle, Tom, Norfolk	.000	1	1	1	0	0	0	0	0	0	0	0	0	0	0	0	0	0	0	0	.000	.000
Epps, Scott, Columbus	.143	4	8	7	0	1	1	0	0	0	0	1	0	0	0	0	1	0	0	0	.143	.143
Everett, Carl, Norfolk†	.300	67	286	260	52	78	120	16	4	6	35	1	1	4	20	1	47	12	6	2	.462	.358
Eversgerd, Bryan, Ottawa	.000	38	2	1	0	0	0	0	0	0	0	0	0	0	1	0	1	0	0	0	.000	.500
Felix, Junior, Ottawa†	.225	51	179	160	22	36	58	7	3	3	24	1	0	3	15	1	48	1	2	6	.363	.303
Figga, Mike, Columbus	.280	8	29	25	2	7	11	1	0	1	3	1	0	0	3	0	5	0	0	0	.440	.357
Fleming, Carlton, Columbus†	.221	32	95	86	9	19	25	6	0	0	5	1	0	0	8	0	6	0	2	3	.291	.287
Fletcher, Paul, Scr./W.-B.	.000	52	2	2	0	0	0	0	0	0	0	0	0	0	0	0	1	0	0	0	.000	.000
Florence, Don, Norfolk	.000	41	2	0	2	0	0	0	0	0	0	0	0	0	2	0	0	0	0	0	.000	1.000
Foley, Tom, Ottawa*	.306	23	72	62	13	19	24	5	0	0	7	2	0	0	8	0	7	1	0	4	.387	.386
Ford, Curt, Charlotte*	.305	57	179	167	18	51	70	10	0	3	17	0	0	3	9	1	29	2	4	4	.419	.352
Fox, Andy, Columbus*	.348	82	354	302	61	105	160	16	6	9	37	2	3	4	43	1	41	22	4	5	.530	.432
Fraser, Willie, Ottawa	.048	19	25	21	0	1	1	0	0	0	0	3	0	0	1	0	12	0	0	0	.048	.091
Frazier, Lou, Ottawa†	.218	31	126	110	11	24	30	3	0	1	10	1	1	1	13	0	20	10	1	2	.273	.304
Friedman, Jason, Paw.-Roch.*	.339	39	123	112	15	38	63	7	0	6	18	1	1	1	8	1	11	0	0	3	.563	.385
Fulton, Ed, Pawtucket*	.294	9	21	17	0	5	7	2	0	0	2	0	0	0	3	1	6	0	0	0	.412	.400
Gaddy, Bob, Scr./W.-B.	.000	17	12	9	0	0	0	0	0	0	0	2	0	0	1	0	2	0	0	0	.000	.100
Garcia, Omar, Norfolk	.309	115	459	430	55	133	177	21	7	3	64	1	7	0	21	3	58	3	4	13	.412	.336
Geisler, Phil, Scr./W.-B.*	.186	20	46	43	2	8	16	5	0	1	7	1	0	0	2	0	13	0	0	2	.372	.222
Gilbert, Shawn, Scr./W.-B.	.263	136	614	536	84	141	177	26	2	2	42	4	4	6	64	0	102	16	11	8	.330	.346
Giovanola, Ed, Richmond*	.321	99	385	321	45	103	137	18	2	4	36	4	4	1	55	3	37	8	7	10	.427	.417
Givens, Jim, Toledo†	.237	79	247	219	23	52	59	5	1	0	14	0	1	1	26	0	40	7	5	4	.269	.320
Gonzalez, Pete, Toledo	.211	6	23	19	0	4	5	1	0	0	2	0	0	1	3	0	6	0	0	0	.263	.348
Goodwin, Curtis, Rochester*	.264	36	156	140	24	37	46	3	3	0	7	3	0	1	12	0	15	17	3	4	.329	.327
Grable, Rob, Scr./W.-B.	.229	26	92	83	7	19	32	4	0	3	11	1	0	1	7	0	34	3	0	1	.386	.297
Grace, Mike, Scr./W.-B.	.000	2	4	3	0	0	0	0	0	0	1	1	0	0	0	0	2	0	0	0	.000	.000
Graffanino, Tony, Richmond	.190	50	198	179	20	34	52	6	0	4	17	1	2	1	15	0	49	2	2	4	.291	.254
Graham, Greg, Norfolk†	.197	47	141	122	14	24	29	5	0	0	9	2	1	1	15	1	23	1	2	5	.238	.288
Greene, Charlie, Norfolk	.193	27	92	88	6	17	20	3	0	0	4	1	0	0	3	0	28	0	1	1	.227	.220
Greene, Tommy, Scr./W.-B.	.125	4	10	8	0	1	1	0	0	0	0	1	0	0	1	0	3	0	0	0	.125	.222
Greenwell, Mike, Pawtucket*	.500	1	5	4	0	2	4	2	0	0	0	0	0	0	1	0	0	1	0	0	1.000	.600
Gregg, Tommy, Charlotte*	.387	34	147	124	30	48	87	10	1	9	32	0	1	1	21	2	13	7	0	3	.702	.476
Gresham, Kris, Rochester	.250	21	70	64	5	16	20	2	1	0	4	0	0	2	4	0	15	0	0	2	.313	.314
Grijak, Kevin, Richmond*	.298	106	342	309	35	92	154	16	5	12	56	0	4	4	25	4	47	1	3	10	.498	.354
Grudzielanek, Mark, Ottawa	.298	49	201	181	26	54	68	9	1	1	22	2	4	4	10	0	17	12	1	6	.376	.342
Hall, Joe, Toledo	.320	91	360	319	52	102	158	19	2	11	47	1	2	2	36	1	50	4	1	7	.495	.390
Hardge, Mike, Pawtucket	.253	29	99	91	9	23	29	3	0	1	5	0	0	0	8	0	16	1	3	2	.319	.313
Hardtke, Jason, Norfolk†	.286	4	9	7	1	2	3	1	0	0	0	0	0	0	2	0	0	1	1	0	.429	.444
Harris, Greg, Ottawa†	.000	11	1	1	0	0	0	0	0	0	0	0	0	0	0	0	0	0	0	0	.000	.000
Harrison, Tom, Richmond	.250	9	6	4	0	1	1	0	0	0	1	1	0	0	1	0	0	0	0	0	.250	.400
Hatteberg, Scott, Pawtucket*	.271	85	299	251	36	68	106	15	1	7	27	1	3	4	40	2	39	2	0	8	.422	.376
Hayden, Dave, Scr./W.-B.	.293	20	47	41	6	12	19	1	0	2	3	0	0	0	6	0	13	0	2	1	.463	.383
Heble, Kurt, Syracuse	.000	4	1	1	0	0	0	0	0	0	0	0	0	0	0	0	1	0	0	0	.000	.000
Hecht, Steve, Toledo*	.236	25	84	72	14	17	24	5	1	0	6	1	2	2	7	0	6	5	0	0	.333	.313
Heffernan, Bert, Ottawa*	.216	36	115	102	13	22	30	5	0	1	12	3	1	2	7	0	13	1	0	3	.294	.277
Hernandez, Jeremy, Charlotte	.000	15	2	1	0	0	0	0	0	0	1	0	0	0	1	0	0	0	0	0	.000	.500
Hernandez, Kiki, Charlotte	.240	60	170	150	13	36	65	8	0	7	28	0	3	1	16	1	26	0	0	5	.433	.312
Hill, Eric, Scr./W.-B.	.000	21	1	0	0	0	0	0	0	0	0	0	0	0	1	0	0	0	0	0	.000	1.000
Hill, Lew, Columbus†	.271	54	150	144	15	39	56	5	0	4	20	0	0	1	5	1	36	6	5	2	.389	.300
Holifield, Rick, Scr./W.-B.*	.206	76	257	223	32	46	67	6	3	3	24	1	3	6	24	0	52	21	5	1	.300	.297
Houston, Tyler, Richmond*	.255	103	374	349	41	89	141	10	3	12	42	1	2	4	18	3	62	3	5	6	.404	.298
Howard, Tim, Pawtucket*	.311	38	99	90	13	28	35	5	1	0	11	1	0	1	7	0	11	7	3	3	.389	.367
Huskey, Butch, Norfolk	.284	109	442	394	66	112	216	18	1	28	87	0	3	6	39	4	88	8	6	9	.548	.355
Huson, Jeff, Rochester*	.251	60	252	223	28	56	74	9	0	3	21	2	1	0	26	2	29	16	5	7	.332	.328
Ilsley, Blaise, Scr./W.-B.*	.357	30	22	14	1	5	7	2	0	0	2	3	0	0	5	0	2	0	0	0	.500	.526
Isringhausen, Jason, Norfolk	.133	12	16	15	2	2	2	0	0	0	0	1	0	0	0	0	2	0	0	1	.133	.133
Jacobs, Frank, Nor.-Ott.*	.246	19	69	57	11	14	24	3	2	1	10	0	0	1	11	0	7	0	1	2	.421	.377
Jacome, Jason, Norfolk*	.000	8	7	7	0	0	0	0	0	0	0	0	0	0	0	0	1	0	0	0	.000	.000
Jeter, Derek, Columbus	.317	123	558	486	96	154	205	27	9	2	45	2	5	4	61	1	56	20	12	9	.422	.394
Johnson, Matt, Syracuse	.500	5	7	6	1	3	5	2	0	0	0	0	0	1	0	0	1	0	0	0	.833	.571
Jones, Chris, Norfolk	.333	33	129	114	20	38	61	12	1	3	19	0	3	1	11	1	20	5	2	2	.535	.388
Jordan, Kevin, Scr./W.-B.	.310	106	453	410	61	127	179	29	4	5	60	1	6	8	28	0	36	3	0	14	.437	.361
Jorgensen, Terry, Charlotte	.264	99	401	356	38	94	129	14	0	7	52	1	4	1	39	1	40	3	3	9	.362	.335
Juden, Jeff, Scr./W.-B.	.000	14	15	14	0	0	0	0	0	0	1	1	0	0	0	0	5	0	0	0	.000	.000
Karp, Ryan, Scr./W.-B.*	.071	13	18	14	1	1	1	0	0	0	2	3	1	0	0	0	2	0	0	0	.071	.067
Kelly, Mike, Richmond	.289	15	52	45	5	13	20	1	0	2	8	0	0	2	5	0	17	0	1	0	.444	.385
Kelly, Pat, Rich.-Syr.	.144	41	104	90	8	13	21	2	0	2	10	2	2	4	6	0	20	0	1	2	.233	.225
Kerley, Collin, Ottawa	.000	5	1	0	0	0	0	0	0	0	1	0	1	0	0	0	0	0	0	0	.000	.000
Knapp, Mike, Rochester	.183	40	140	126	10	23	29	1	1	1	12	0	1	1	12	0	26	1	1	3	.230	.257
Knorr, Randy, Syracuse	.269	18	73	67	6	18	28	5	1	1	6	0	1	0	5	0	14	0	0	1	.418	.315
Koelling, Brian, Scr./W.-B.	.264	16	55	53	5	14	15	1	0	0	3	0	1	0	1	0	14	3	1	1	.283	.273
Kowitz, Brian, Richmond*	.280	100	400	353	53	99	129	14	5	2	34	3	0	3	41	1	43	11	8	4	.365	.360
Layana, Tim, Ottawa	.000	26	2	2	0	0	0	0	0	0	0	0	0	0	0	0	1	0	0	0	.000	.000

Player, Team	Avg.	G	TPA	AB	R	H	TB	2B	3B	HR	RBI	SH	SF	HP	BB	IBB	SO	SB	CS	GDP	Slg.	OBP
Leach, Jalal, Columbus*	.243	88	302	272	37	66	106	12	5	6	31	1	4	2	22	1	60	11	4	5	.390	.300
Ledesma, Aaron, Norfolk	.299	56	213	201	26	60	74	12	1	0	28	1	0	1	10	1	22	6	3	5	.368	.335
Lee, Derek, Norfolk*	.254	112	415	351	56	89	160	17	0	18	60	2	5	7	48	4	62	11	6	11	.456	.350
Leiper, Dave, Ottawa*	.000	2	1	1	0	0	0	0	0	0	0	0	0	0	0	0	1	0	0	0	.000	.000
Leiper, Tim, Toledo*	.212	18	71	66	3	14	15	1	0	0	6	0	1	0	4	0	8	0	0	3	.227	.254
Lemon, Don, Charlotte	.000	6	1	1	0	0	0	0	0	0	0	0	0	0	0	0	1	0	0	0	.000	.000
Lennon, Pat, Pawtucket	.273	40	146	128	20	35	54	6	2	3	20	0	1	1	16	0	42	6	4	6	.422	.356
Levangie, Dana, Pawtucket	.235	6	20	17	1	4	4	0	0	0	0	1	0	0	2	0	3	0	0	0	.235	.316
Lewis, Richie, Charlotte	.091	18	14	11	1	1	1	0	0	0	0	2	0	0	1	0	0	0	0	0	.091	.167
Lewis, T.R., Rochester	.295	22	87	78	12	23	42	7	0	4	19	0	1	1	7	0	14	1	1	2	.538	.356
Lieberthal, Mike, Scr./W.-B.	.281	85	340	278	44	78	120	20	2	6	42	2	7	9	44	2	26	1	4	14	.432	.388
Lis, Joe, Syracuse	.262	130	538	485	68	127	219	33	4	17	56	0	5	2	46	1	54	6	2	8	.452	.325
Livesey, Jeff, Columbus	.264	42	99	91	8	24	27	3	0	0	7	0	1	0	7	0	18	0	0	5	.297	.313
Lomon, Kevin, Richmond	.200	33	5	5	0	1	1	0	0	0	0	0	0	0	0	0	0	0	0	0	.200	.200
Long, Steve, Charlotte	.111	33	10	9	0	1	1	0	0	0	0	1	0	0	0	0	3	0	0	0	.111	.111
Ludwick, Eric, Norfolk	.250	4	4	4	1	1	1	0	0	0	0	0	0	0	0	0	2	0	0	0	.250	.250
Lukachyk, Rob, Toledo*	.254	104	387	346	43	88	147	24	7	7	26	3	3	2	33	0	75	8	5	5	.425	.320
Luke, Matt, Columbus*	.299	23	81	77	11	23	38	4	1	3	12	1	0	1	2	0	12	1	1	3	.494	.325
Lutz, Brent, Syracuse	.163	35	90	86	5	14	17	0	0	1	5	0	0	0	4	0	23	1	2	3	.198	.200
Maas, Kevin, Columbus*	.280	44	188	161	28	45	83	7	2	9	33	0	2	2	23	0	40	0	0	1	.516	.372
Magrane, Joe, Ottawa	.200	12	12	10	1	2	5	0	0	1	1	1	0	0	1	0	2	0	0	0	.500	.273
Mahay, Ron, Pawtucket*	.318	11	48	44	5	14	18	4	0	0	3	0	0	0	4	1	9	1	0	2	.409	.375
Malave, Jose, Pawtucket	.270	91	350	318	55	86	169	12	1	23	57	0	0	2	30	1	67	0	1	4	.531	.337
Malzone, John, Pawtucket*	.111	6	18	18	0	2	2	0	0	0	2	0	0	0	0	0	4	0	0	1	.111	.111
Manahan, Anthony, Scr./W.-B.	.288	90	333	299	36	86	108	11	1	3	32	2	0	4	28	4	39	6	1	7	.361	.356
Manuel, Barry, Ottawa	.077	35	18	13	3	1	1	0	0	0	0	2	0	0	3	0	4	0	0	0	.077	.250
Marsh, Tom, Scr./W.-B.	.307	78	315	296	46	91	153	22	5	10	47	0	2	4	13	1	39	9	3	10	.517	.343
Martin, Chris, Ottawa	.257	126	473	412	55	106	136	19	1	3	40	8	3	4	46	1	59	30	5	12	.330	.335
Martinez, Pablo, Richmond†	.229	14	50	48	5	11	15	0	2	0	4	0	0	0	2	0	7	1	1	3	.313	.260
Martinez, Ray, Ottawa	.250	39	119	108	17	27	33	6	0	0	9	3	1	0	6	0	17	3	0	3	.306	.287
Mashore, Justin, Toledo	.220	72	251	223	32	49	71	4	3	4	21	9	2	3	14	1	62	12	9	1	.318	.273
Massarelli, John, Charlotte	.244	65	284	254	37	62	79	7	2	2	8	1	1	2	26	0	55	14	10	2	.311	.318
Masse, Billy, Columbus	.224	49	195	165	19	37	59	6	2	4	24	0	2	4	24	1	31	3	3	7	.358	.333
May, Darrell, Richmond*	.000	10	8	5	1	0	0	0	0	0	0	1	0	0	2	0	4	0	0	0	.000	.286
McClain, Scott, Rochester	.251	61	226	199	32	50	85	9	1	8	22	1	2	1	23	0	34	0	1	5	.427	.329
McCoy, Trey, Norfolk	.209	25	74	67	6	14	28	5	0	3	7	0	0	2	5	0	11	0	0	2	.418	.284
McDowell, Oddibe, Columbus*	.217	14	54	46	5	10	15	0	1	1	2	2	0	0	6	0	9	0	1	1	.326	.308
McGee, Willie, Pawtucket†	.476	5	21	21	9	10	10	0	0	0	2	0	0	0	0	0	4	2	0	0	.476	.476
McGinnis, Russ, Rochester	.182	20	77	55	8	10	21	2	0	3	11	0	3	2	17	0	19	0	0	4	.382	.377
McGriff, Terry, Toledo	.271	58	208	188	14	51	71	8	0	4	23	0	0	0	20	0	29	0	0	9	.378	.341
McNair, Fred, Scr./W.-B.	.240	9	29	25	1	6	7	1	0	0	2	0	1	0	3	0	6	0	0	1	.280	.310
Melvin, Bob, Columbus	.288	19	69	66	7	19	27	5	0	1	4	0	0	0	3	1	12	0	0	3	.409	.319
Mendenhall, Kirk, Toledo	.200	11	36	30	2	6	10	1	0	1	4	1	0	0	5	0	1	2	0	1	.333	.314
Miller, Kurt, Charlotte	.167	22	28	24	1	4	4	0	0	0	0	3	0	0	1	0	8	0	0	0	.167	.200
Millette, Joe, Charlotte	.187	74	212	193	22	36	54	6	0	4	20	1	4	4	10	0	36	1	1	4	.280	.237
Milne, Darren, Toledo	.150	7	21	20	0	3	4	1	0	0	4	0	0	0	1	0	4	0	0	1	.200	.190
Minutelli, Gino, Richmond*	.000	5	2	2	0	0	0	0	0	0	0	0	0	0	0	0	1	0	0	0	.000	.000
Mitchell, John, Ottawa	.000	6	1	1	0	0	0	0	0	0	0	0	0	0	0	0	0	0	0	0	.000	.000
Montalvo, Rob, Syracuse	.038	11	28	26	0	1	1	0	0	0	1	0	0	0	2	0	8	0	0	1	.038	.107
Montoya, Al, Syracuse*	.000	7	1	1	0	0	0	0	0	0	0	0	0	0	0	0	0	0	0	0	.000	.000
Montoyo, Charlie, Scr./W.-B.	.243	92	347	288	32	70	94	13	1	3	34	5	3	1	50	1	45	2	3	4	.326	.354
Moore, Bobby, Richmond	.258	108	365	329	45	85	116	18	2	3	27	3	2	4	27	1	27	9	7	6	.353	.320
Morgan, Kevin, Norfolk	.323	19	67	62	10	20	21	1	0	0	8	0	0	1	4	0	8	1	3	1	.339	.373
Morman, Russ, Charlotte	.314	44	187	169	28	53	80	7	1	6	36	0	3	1	14	3	22	2	2	4	.473	.364
Munoz, Jose, Richmond†	.290	135	588	520	65	151	188	18	5	3	45	5	6	4	53	4	65	7	10	18	.362	.357
Murray, Glenn, Pawtucket	.244	104	387	336	66	82	172	15	0	25	66	1	5	11	34	1	109	5	6	4	.512	.329
Murray, Matt, Richmond*	.200	19	19	15	2	3	3	0	0	0	3	1	0	0	3	0	2	0	0	0	.200	.333
Mutis, Jeff, Charlotte*	.000	27	3	3	0	0	0	0	0	0	0	0	0	0	0	0	1	0	0	0	.000	.000
Natal, Rob, Charlotte	.314	53	204	191	23	60	83	14	0	3	24	0	0	2	11	1	23	0	0	4	.435	.358
Nevin, Phil, Toledo	.304	7	24	23	3	7	12	2	0	1	3	0	0	0	1	0	5	0	0	2	.522	.333
Nichols, Rod, Richmond	.500	41	2	2	0	1	2	1	0	0	0	0	0	0	0	0	0	0	0	0	1.000	.500
Noboa, Junior, Rochester	.100	6	21	20	1	2	2	0	0	0	2	0	1	0	0	0	0	0	0	1	.100	.095
Obando, Sherman, Rochester	.296	85	360	324	42	96	161	26	6	9	53	0	4	3	29	3	57	1	1	11	.497	.356
Ochoa, Alex, Roch.-Nor.	.283	125	505	459	58	130	192	24	4	10	61	1	3	2	40	1	62	24	10	12	.418	.341
O'Connor, Kevin, Richmond*	.222	94	231	203	33	45	65	2	3	4	14	0	0	1	27	2	42	14	4	3	.320	.316
Olivares, Omar, Scr./W.-B.	.444	8	12	9	2	4	7	1	1	0	2	2	1	0	0	0	2	0	0	0	.778	.400
Olmeda, Jose, Richmond†	.253	80	263	241	22	61	81	11	3	1	24	3	2	1	16	2	41	2	1	5	.336	.300
Ordonez, Rey, Norfolk	.214	125	486	439	49	94	129	21	4	2	50	10	7	3	27	2	50	11	13	12	.294	.261
Orton, John, Rich.-Nor.	.264	73	243	220	26	58	81	11	0	4	26	1	1	4	17	0	67	3	5	5	.368	.326
Osuna, Al, Norfolk	.000	14	3	3	0	0	0	0	0	0	0	0	0	0	0	0	2	0	0	0	.000	.000
Otero, Ricky, Norfolk†	.268	72	325	295	37	79	102	8	6	1	23	2	0	1	27	0	33	16	13	2	.346	.331
Owens, Billy, Rochester†	.143	9	29	28	2	4	4	0	0	0	1	0	0	0	1	0	6	0	0	0	.143	.172
Pappas, Erik, Charlotte	.221	122	461	389	48	86	150	28	3	10	52	1	4	6	61	0	78	10	7	11	.386	.333
Payton, Jay, Norfolk	.240	50	215	196	33	47	78	11	4	4	30	4	2	2	11	0	22	11	3	5	.398	.284
Pecorilli, Aldo, Richmond	.260	49	150	127	16	33	54	3	0	6	17	2	0	2	19	2	20	0	0	5	.425	.365
Pemberton, Rudy, Toledo	.344	67	247	224	31	77	119	15	3	7	23	0	3	5	15	2	36	8	4	5	.531	.393
Penn, Shannon, Toledo†	.248	63	249	218	41	54	63	4	1	1	15	2	2	10	17	0	40	15	9	4	.289	.328
Perez, Eddie, Richmond	.265	92	341	324	31	86	120	19	0	5	40	1	2	2	12	0	58	1	2	12	.370	.294
Perez, Robert, Syracuse	.343	122	522	502	70	172	249	38	6	9	67	1	4	2	13	4	60	7	5	17	.496	.359
Perezchica, Tony, Columbus	.257	101	394	358	43	92	133	12	4	7	44	7	5	5	18	2	74	3	3	8	.372	.298
Person, Robert, Norfolk	.167	5	9	6	1	1	1	0	0	0	0	3	0	0	0	0	0	0	0	0	.167	.167
Posada, Jorge, Columbus†	.255	108	432	368	60	94	160	32	5	8	51	6	3	1	54	2	101	4	4	14	.435	.350
Potts, Mike, Richmond*	.000	38	4	4	0	0	0	0	0	0	0	0	0	0	0	0	3	0	0	0	.000	.000

Player, Team	Avg.	G	TPA	AB	R	H	TB	2B	3B	HR	RBI	SH	SF	HP	BB	IBB	SO	SB	CS	GDP	Slg.	OBP
Pough, Pork Chop, Pawtucket	.232	30	108	99	12	23	48	8	1	5	23	0	1	1	7	1	27	0	0	2	.485	.287
Pride, Curtis, Ottawa*	.279	42	168	154	25	43	69	8	3	4	24	0	0	2	12	4	35	8	4	2	.448	.339
Pulsipher, Bill, Norfolk*	.091	13	13	11	1	1	1	0	0	0	1	0	1	0	1	0	2	0	0	0	.091	.154
Ramos, John, Syracuse	.252	116	463	413	59	104	190	24	1	20	75	1	5	6	38	1	83	2	2	11	.460	.320
Reed, Darren, Richmond	.265	57	151	136	11	36	58	7	0	5	22	0	3	1	11	0	28	0	0	4	.426	.318
Rhodes, Karl, Pawtucket*	.285	69	285	246	40	70	119	13	3	10	43	1	3	1	34	3	46	8	6	7	.484	.370
Rice, Lance, Toledo†	.268	15	46	41	2	11	15	1	0	1	6	1	0	0	4	0	6	0	3	0	.366	.333
Rivera, Ruben, Columbus	.270	48	204	174	37	47	104	8	2	15	35	0	1	3	26	0	62	8	4	5	.598	.373
Roa, Hector, Richmond†	.258	40	126	120	15	31	42	5	0	2	7	1	1	1	3	1	23	0	1	4	.350	.280
Roberts, Chris, Norfolk	.158	27	22	19	1	3	4	1	0	0	0	2	0	0	1	0	5	0	0	0	.211	.200
Robertson, Rod, Rochester†	.278	101	370	338	54	94	164	21	2	15	58	4	2	4	22	1	63	8	7	8	.485	.328
Rodriguez, Carlos, Pawtucket†	.293	40	157	133	19	39	46	7	0	0	13	1	2	1	20	0	8	1	0	4	.346	.385
Rodriguez, Henry, Ottawa*	.200	4	16	15	0	3	4	1	0	0	2	0	0	0	1	0	4	0	0	0	.267	.250
Rodriguez, Steve, Pawtucket	.241	82	358	324	39	78	103	16	3	1	24	2	3	4	25	1	34	12	10	7	.318	.301
Rodriguez, Tony, Pawtucket	.268	96	353	317	37	85	104	15	2	0	21	11	4	6	15	0	39	11	5	8	.328	.310
Rodriguez, Victor, Pawtucket	.276	31	122	116	10	32	37	5	0	0	8	3	1	0	2	0	13	1	1	3	.319	.286
Rogers, Bryan, Norfolk	.000	56	4	3	0	0	0	0	0	0	0	1	0	0	0	0	2	0	0	0	.000	.000
Rowland, Rich, Pawtucket	.258	34	133	124	20	32	63	7	0	8	24	0	1	1	7	1	24	0	1	2	.508	.301
Rudolph, Mason, Charlotte	.250	2	4	4	1	1	1	0	0	0	0	0	0	0	0	0	1	0	0	0	.250	.250
Rueter, Kirk, Ottawa*	.294	20	18	17	1	5	5	0	0	0	2	0	0	0	1	0	4	0	0	0	.294	.333
Rundels, Matt, Ottawa	.250	14	46	36	7	9	12	1	1	0	4	2	0	1	7	0	8	1	1	1	.333	.386
Sanders, Tracy, Norfolk*	.227	64	148	110	21	25	43	6	0	4	14	0	0	4	34	0	34	3	1	2	.391	.426
Santangelo, F.P., Ottawa†	.255	95	315	267	37	68	95	15	3	2	25	6	4	6	32	3	22	7	4	2	.356	.343
Saunders, Chris, Norfolk	.232	16	65	56	9	13	27	3	1	3	7	0	0	0	9	0	15	1	1	1	.482	.338
Sawkiw, Warren, Syracuse†	.190	11	47	42	3	8	9	1	0	0	0	0	0	0	5	0	8	2	0	1	.214	.277
Schall, Gene, Scr./W.-B.	.313	92	383	320	52	100	169	25	4	12	63	0	4	10	49	2	54	3	3	14	.528	.415
Scheid, Rich, Charlotte*	.000	19	4	2	0	0	0	0	0	0	0	2	0	0	0	0	1	0	0	0	.000	.000
Schmidt, Curt, Ottawa	.000	43	1	1	0	0	0	0	0	0	0	0	0	0	0	0	0	0	0	0	.000	.000
Schmidt, Jason, Richmond	.150	19	20	20	1	3	3	0	0	0	0	0	0	0	0	0	9	0	0	1	.150	.150
Schunk, Jerry, Charlotte	.224	101	372	343	36	77	108	13	0	6	33	4	4	2	19	2	31	8	0	16	.315	.266
Scott, Gary, Richmond	.151	27	98	86	7	13	14	1	0	0	2	0	1	1	10	0	13	0	1	0	.163	.245
Seefried, Tate, Columbus*	.164	29	113	110	7	18	27	6	0	1	12	0	2	0	1	0	34	0	0	2	.245	.168
Seelbach, Chris, Richmond	.000	14	11	9	0	0	0	0	0	0	0	2	0	0	0	0	4	0	0	0	.000	.000
Sefcik, Kevin, Scr./W.-B.	.346	7	30	26	5	9	17	6	1	0	6	0	1	0	3	0	1	0	0	1	.654	.400
Sharperson, Mike, Richmond	.319	87	343	298	42	95	122	16	1	3	47	1	7	2	35	3	34	7	2	6	.409	.386
Shumpert, Terry, Pawtucket	.271	37	150	133	17	36	49	7	0	2	11	2	0	1	14	0	27	10	4	3	.368	.345
Siddall, Joe, Ottawa*	.214	83	278	248	26	53	74	14	2	1	23	2	0	4	23	0	42	3	3	6	.298	.291
Small, Aaron, Syr.-Char.	.000	34	2	2	0	0	0	0	0	0	0	0	0	0	0	0	2	0	0	0	.000	.000
Smith, Greg, Rochester†	.229	52	235	210	32	48	68	6	1	4	21	2	0	2	21	1	24	14	3	2	.324	.305
Smith, Mark, Rochester	.277	96	404	364	55	101	168	25	3	12	66	1	7	7	24	1	69	7	3	8	.462	.328
Smith, Pete, Charlotte	.125	10	9	8	0	1	1	0	0	0	0	0	0	0	1	0	4	0	0	1	.125	.222
Snyder, Cory, Pawtucket	.227	20	71	66	9	15	28	4	0	3	8	0	0	0	5	0	25	0	0	1	.424	.282
Sparks, Don, Columbus	.312	137	585	545	67	170	237	26	10	7	90	1	9	1	29	3	75	2	0	17	.435	.342
Spencer, Stan, Charlotte	.000	9	6	5	0	0	0	0	0	0	0	1	0	0	0	0	3	0	0	0	.000	.000
Spiers, Bill, Norfolk*	.220	12	51	41	4	9	11	2	0	0	4	1	1	0	8	0	6	0	1	4	.268	.340
Spradlin, Jerry, Charlotte†	.333	41	3	3	1	1	4	0	0	1	2	0	0	0	0	0	1	0	0	0	1.333	.333
Springer, Dennis, Scr./W.-B.	.048	30	26	21	1	1	1	0	0	0	0	5	0	0	0	0	12	0	0	0	.048	.048
Springer, Steve, Toledo	.265	25	108	102	14	27	42	7	1	2	10	0	2	0	4	1	18	1	1	3	.412	.287
Stairs, Matt, Pawtucket*	.284	75	305	271	40	77	133	17	0	13	56	1	3	1	29	3	41	3	3	10	.491	.352
Steverson, Todd, Toledo	.107	9	33	28	6	3	6	0	0	1	1	0	0	0	5	0	13	0	2	1	.214	.242
Stidham, Phil, Norfolk	.000	34	5	5	0	0	0	0	0	0	0	0	0	0	0	0	1	0	0	0	.000	.000
Strawberry, Darryl, Columbus*	.301	22	101	83	20	25	51	3	1	7	29	0	2	1	15	1	17	1	1	1	.614	.406
Swann, Pedro, Richmond*	.211	15	40	38	2	8	9	1	0	0	3	0	0	1	1	0	2	0	2	0	.237	.250
Tackett, Jeff, Toledo	.269	96	349	301	32	81	114	15	0	6	30	5	1	7	35	0	46	2	1	6	.379	.358
Tavarez, Jesus, Charlotte†	.300	39	151	140	15	42	55	6	2	1	8	0	2	0	9	0	19	7	7	1	.393	.338
Taylor, Sam, Scr./W.-B.*	.143	3	8	7	3	1	1	0	0	0	1	0	0	0	1	0	2	0	0	0	.143	.250
Telgheder, Dave, Norfolk	.000	29	13	12	0	0	0	0	0	0	0	1	0	0	0	0	8	0	0	0	.000	.000
Thobe, J.J, Ottawa	.333	55	3	3	0	1	1	0	0	0	0	0	0	0	0	0	1	0	0	0	.333	.333
Thobe, Tom, Richmond*	.250	48	5	4	0	1	2	1	0	0	0	1	0	0	0	0	2	0	0	0	.500	.250
Thomas, Royal, Richmond	.333	39	7	6	1	2	2	0	0	0	1	1	0	0	0	0	1	0	0	0	.333	.333
Thompson, Ryan, Norfolk	.340	15	61	53	7	18	27	3	0	2	11	0	4	0	4	0	15	4	1	0	.509	.361
Thoutsis, Paul, Columbus*	.215	52	137	130	10	28	34	4	1	0	15	1	1	1	4	0	16	1	0	4	.262	.243
Tokheim, David, Scr./W.-B.*	.271	127	483	450	64	122	189	18	8	11	66	3	7	5	18	2	55	6	7	11	.420	.302
Torres, Ricky, Ottawa	.250	32	9	8	2	2	3	1	0	0	1	1	0	0	0	0	4	0	0	0	.375	.250
Toth, David, Richmond	.231	7	14	13	1	3	3	0	0	0	1	0	0	0	1	0	2	0	1	1	.231	.286
Tovar, Raul, Ottawa	.304	20	64	56	8	17	19	2	0	0	7	0	0	0	8	0	5	0	0	3	.339	.391
Townley, Jason, Syracuse	.261	96	313	264	25	69	104	11	0	8	30	3	8	0	38	0	71	0	3	6	.394	.345
Tranberg, Mark, Scr./W.-B.	.200	11	5	5	0	1	1	0	0	0	0	0	0	0	0	0	3	0	0	0	.200	.200
Tucker, Scooter, Richmond	.167	22	76	66	5	11	16	3	1	0	6	0	1	1	8	0	16	0	0	2	.242	.263
Twardoski, Mike, Richmond*	.138	19	69	58	7	8	9	1	0	0	5	1	0	0	10	2	8	1	1	0	.155	.265
Tyler, Brad, Rochester*	.258	114	441	361	60	93	167	17	3	17	52	0	5	4	71	4	63	10	5	3	.463	.381
Urbina, Ugueth, Ottawa	.000	13	16	16	1	0	0	0	0	0	0	0	0	0	0	0	9	0	0	0	.000	.000
Valdes, Marc, Charlotte	.125	27	29	24	1	3	5	2	0	0	3	5	0	0	0	0	7	0	0	0	.208	.125
Vatcher, Jim, Scr./W.-B.	.375	9	25	24	4	9	10	1	0	0	2	0	0	0	1	0	4	1	0	1	.417	.400
Velasquez, Guillermo, Ottawa*	.250	45	120	112	11	28	36	5	0	1	9	0	0	0	8	1	14	1	2	3	.321	.300
Villanueva, Hector, Richmond	.211	10	21	19	1	4	8	1	0	1	3	0	1	0	1	0	3	0	0	0	.421	.238
Wade, Scott, Pawtucket	.148	7	27	27	2	4	5	1	0	0	0	0	0	0	0	0	11	0	0	0	.185	.148
Wade, Terrell, Richmond*	.207	24	32	29	2	6	8	2	0	0	4	2	0	0	1	0	9	0	0	0	.276	.233
Waggoner, Aubrey, Pawtucket*	.188	16	59	48	3	9	10	1	0	0	8	1	0	0	10	1	22	2	2	0	.208	.328
Walker, Pete, Norfolk	.000	34	3	2	0	0	0	0	0	0	0	1	0	0	0	0	1	0	0	0	.000	.000
Warner, Mike, Richmond*	.206	28	110	97	10	20	32	4	1	2	8	2	0	1	10	0	21	0	3	0	.330	.287
Wawruck, Jim, Rochester*	.302	39	167	149	21	45	66	12	3	1	23	1	2	2	13	0	23	5	4	3	.443	.361
Weathers, David, Charlotte	.000	1	1	1	0	0	0	0	0	0	0	0	0	0	0	0	0	0	0	0	.000	.000

Player, Team	Avg.	G	TPA	AB	R	H	TB	2B	3B	HR	RBI	SH	SF	HP	BB	IBB	SO	SB	CS	GDP	Slg.	OBP
Wedge, Eric, Pawtucket	.234	108	444	376	52	88	167	17	1	20	68	0	3	2	63	4	96	1	3	9	.444	.345
Weinke, Chris, Syracuse*	.226	113	388	341	42	77	123	12	2	10	41	0	2	1	44	2	74	4	3	10	.361	.314
West, David, Scr./W.-B.*	.000	1	2	1	0	0	0	0	0	0	0	1	0	0	0	0	0	0	0	0	.000	.000
White, Derrick, Toledo	.265	87	346	309	50	82	145	15	3	14	49	0	4	4	29	3	65	6	6	12	.469	.332
White, Gabe, Ottawa*	.000	12	3	3	0	0	0	0	0	0	0	0	0	0	0	0	2	0	0	0	.000	.000
Whiten, Mark, Pawtucket†	.284	28	121	102	19	29	46	3	1	4	13	0	0	0	19	0	30	4	2	3	.451	.397
Wiegandt, Scott, Scr./W.-B.*	.000	47	3	2	0	0	0	0	0	0	1	0	1	0	0	0	2	0	0	0	.000	.000
Williams, Jimmy, Nor.-Roch.* ...	.143	32	19	14	2	2	3	1	0	0	2	2	0	1	2	0	7	0	0	0	.214	.294
Williams, Juan, Richmond*	.264	45	147	129	18	34	54	5	0	5	11	0	1	0	17	0	38	1	3	5	.419	.347
Wilson, Craig, Toledo	.263	121	518	468	56	123	181	31	0	9	65	3	7	3	37	0	61	8	2	11	.387	.317
Wilson, Paul, Norfolk	.000	10	14	10	2	0	0	0	0	0	0	1	0	0	3	0	8	0	0	0	.000	.231
Wilson, Tom, Columbus	.258	22	73	62	11	16	21	3	1	0	9	2	0	0	9	0	10	0	0	0	.339	.352
Wilstead, Randy, Ottawa*	.292	9	34	24	6	7	11	2	1	0	3	0	2	2	6	0	3	0	0	1	.458	.441
Wood, Ted, Ottawa*	.267	98	369	326	35	87	129	16	1	8	49	1	3	2	37	6	63	9	2	8	.396	.342
Woodall, Brad, Richmond†	.222	14	12	9	2	2	3	1	0	0	0	1	0	0	2	0	3	0	0	0	.333	.364
Woods, Tyrone, Rochester	.261	70	265	238	30	62	105	17	1	8	31	0	2	1	24	1	68	2	3	6	.441	.328
Yan, Julian, Ottawa	.280	114	392	372	49	104	198	22	3	22	79	2	1	2	15	2	90	5	1	10	.532	.310
Zaun, Greg, Rochester†	.293	42	158	140	26	41	74	13	1	6	18	0	1	3	14	2	21	0	3	0	.529	.367
Zimmerman, Mike, Charlotte	.400	31	5	5	0	2	2	0	0	0	0	0	0	0	0	0	0	0	0	0	.400	.400
Zinter, Alan, Toledo†	.222	101	379	334	42	74	136	15	4	13	48	2	5	2	36	1	102	4	1	5	.407	.297
Zosky, Eddie, Charlotte	.247	92	326	312	27	77	105	15	2	3	42	5	1	1	7	0	48	2	3	8	.337	.265
Zuber, Jon, Scr./W.-B.*	.287	119	471	418	53	120	158	19	5	3	50	1	2	0	49	2	68	1	2	12	.378	.360
Zupcic, Bob, Charlotte	.295	72	283	254	34	75	120	12	0	11	47	1	4	0	24	0	35	2	2	3	.472	.351

GRAND SLAMS: Wedge, 2; Battle, Benitez, Bowers, Brewer, Ri. Butler, Capra, S. Carter, C. Delgado, Felix, Geisler, Hall, Houston, Leach, Lee, Lennon, Lewis, Lis, Malave, Morman, Perezchica, Ramos, Tyler, 1 each.

AWARDED FIRST BASE ON CATCHER'S INTERFERENCE: Buccheri 2 (Hernandez 2); Lee 2 (Alvarez, Gonzalez); Alvarez (Brooks); Fulton (Alvarez); Leach (Lutz); R. Martinez (Hernandez); Perezchica (Orton); Siddall (Tackett); M. Smith (Tackett); Zuber (Knorr).

PLAYERS WITH TWO OR MORE TEAMS

Player, Team	Avg.	G	TPA	AB	R	H	TB	2B	3B	HR	RBI	SH	SF	HP	BB	IBB	SO	SB	CS	GDP	Slg.	OBP
Bark, Brian, Richmond*	.000	13	2	2	0	0	0	0	0	0	0	0	0	0	0	0	0	0	0	0	.000	.000
Bark, Brian, Pawtucket*	.000	30	0	0	0	0	0	0	0	0	0	0	0	0	0	0	0	0	0	0	.000	.000
Batiste, Kim, Scr./W.-B.	.230	32	126	122	10	28	46	4	1	4	18	0	0	2	2	0	14	1	0	3	.377	.254
Batiste, Kim, Rochester	.281	66	271	260	31	73	97	13	1	3	29	1	1	1	8	0	27	4	8	10	.373	.304
Brown, Jarvis, Norfolk	.284	45	169	148	29	42	60	12	3	0	17	2	0	1	18	0	29	6	3	3	.405	.365
Brown, Jarvis, Rochester	.314	17	82	70	12	22	30	4	2	0	4	2	0	0	10	0	20	1	1	2	.429	.400
Cornelius, Reid, Ottawa	.000	4	1	1	0	0	0	0	0	0	0	0	0	0	0	0	1	0	0	0	.000	.000
Cornelius, Reid, Norfolk	.067	10	18	15	0	1	1	0	0	0	0	3	0	0	0	0	9	0	0	0	.067	.067
Friedman, Jason, Pawtucket* ...	.294	14	55	51	6	15	24	3	0	2	9	1	1	0	2	1	3	0	0	1	.471	.315
Friedman, Jason, Rochester*	.377	25	68	61	9	23	39	4	0	4	9	0	0	1	6	0	8	0	0	2	.639	.441
Jacobs, Frank, Norfolk*	.240	8	25	25	2	6	10	1	0	1	6	0	0	0	0	0	4	0	0	1	.400	.240
Jacobs, Frank, Ottawa*	.250	11	44	32	9	8	14	2	2	0	4	0	0	1	11	0	3	0	1	1	.438	.455
Kelly, Pat, Richmond	.182	11	24	22	2	4	5	1	0	0	2	0	0	2	0	0	5	0	1	1	.227	.250
Kelly, Pat, Syracuse	.132	30	80	68	6	9	16	1	0	2	8	2	2	2	6	0	15	0	0	1	.235	.218
Ochoa, Alex, Rochester	.274	91	367	336	41	92	138	18	2	8	46	1	2	2	26	1	50	17	7	8	.411	.328
Ochoa, Alex, Norfolk	.309	34	138	123	17	38	54	6	2	2	15	0	1	0	14	0	12	7	3	4	.439	.377
Orton, John, Richmond	.180	17	56	50	6	9	15	3	0	1	6	1	1	1	3	0	22	2	2	1	.300	.236
Orton, John, Norfolk	.288	56	187	170	20	49	66	8	0	3	20	0	0	3	14	0	45	1	3	4	.388	.353
Small, Aaron, Syracuse	.000	1	0	0	0	0	0	0	0	0	0	0	0	0	0	0	0	0	0	0	.000	.000
Small, Aaron, Charlotte	.000	33	2	2	0	0	0	0	0	0	0	0	0	0	0	0	2	0	0	0	.000	.000
Williams, Jimmy, Norfolk*	.143	27	19	14	2	2	3	1	0	0	2	2	0	1	2	0	7	0	0	0	.214	.294
Williams, Jimmy, Rochester* ...	.000	5	0	0	0	0	0	0	0	0	0	0	0	0	0	0	0	0	0	0	.000	.000

1995 PITCHING

TEAM

Team	W	L	Pct.	ERA	G	CG	ShO	Sv.	IP	H	TBF	R	ER	HR	SH	SF	HB	BB	IBB	SO	WP	Bk.
Norfolk	86	56	.606	3.01	142	15	18	35	1258.2	1153	5219	493	421	79	52	34	39	419	7	921	47	10
Richmond.........	75	66	.532	3.46	141	4	14	41	1247.2	1196	5283	545	480	67	52	36	25	466	36	898	48	6
Toledo	71	71	.500	3.47	142	10	10	39	1253.1	1241	5304	571	483	108	38	40	41	411	31	735	52	2
Rochester.........	73	69	.514	3.80	142	9	5	36	1236.1	1263	5265	616	522	119	45	52	30	398	10	899	60	11
Ottawa..............	72	70	.507	3.92	142	9	11	28	1224.1	1190	5174	611	533	87	51	48	50	410	13	761	53	6
Scr./W.-B.	70	72	.493	4.03	142	12	8	39	1236.1	1211	5271	646	554	96	49	40	61	435	38	882	74	6
Columbus..........	71	68	.511	4.07	140	5	8	33	1223.2	1220	5280	643	553	84	33	36	62	478	18	822	84	11
Pawtucket.........	70	71	.496	4.54	142	6	1	33	1230.1	1310	5368	711	621	138	30	48	57	438	15	849	76	8
Syracuse	59	82	.418	4.57	141	1	4	29	1229.2	1259	5437	768	624	137	32	40	35	530	30	946	67	7
Charlotte..........	59	81	.421	4.72	140	6	9	29	1225.1	1320	5363	735	642	133	28	47	57	483	11	763	90	8

INDIVIDUAL

TOP QUALIFIERS FOR EARNED-RUN AVERAGE TITLE

Minimum 114 innings. *Lefthanded pitcher.

Pitcher, Team	W	L	Pct.	ERA	G	GS	CG	ShO	GF	Sv.	IP	H	TBF	R	ER	HR	SH	SF	HB	BB	IBB	SO	WP	Bk.
Schmidt, Jason, Richmond....	8	6	.571	2.25	19	19	0	0	0	0	116.0	97	484	40	29	2	15	1	3	48	3	95	4	1
Murray, Matt, Richmond	10	3	.769	2.78	19	19	0	0	0	0	123.0	108	501	41	38	6	1	4	3	34	1	78	9	1
Weston, Mickey, Toledo	11	7	.611	2.90	28	27	2	1	0	0	180.0	170	734	68	58	14	2	5	7	41	1	69	4	0
Rueter, Kirk, Ottawa*	9	7	.563	3.06	20	20	3	1	0	0	120.2	120	498	50	41	7	8	3	1	25	0	67	2	1
Adamson, Joel, Charlotte*	8	4	.667	3.29	19	18	2	0	0	0	115.0	113	471	51	42	12	0	3	6	20	0	80	4	2
Haynes, Jimmy, Rochester	12	8	.600	3.29	26	25	3	1	0	0	167.0	162	691	77	61	16	4	7	0	49	0	140	6	1

Pitcher, Team	W	L	Pct.	ERA	G	GS	CG	ShO	GF	Sv.	IP	H	TBF	R	ER	HR	SH	SF	HB	BB	IBB	SO	WP	Bk.
Deshaies, Jim, Scr./W.-B.*	7	8	.467	3.45	19	19	2	1	0	0	117.1	105	476	51	45	82		3	5	26	0	79	2	1
Williams, Jimmy, Nor.-Roc.*	12	6	.667	3.48	32	16	0	0	6	2	119.0	110	522	55	46	3	1	5	2	65	0	100	12	4
Ilsley, Blaise, Scr./W.-B.*	8	10	.444	3.88	29	29	2	1	0	0	185.1	210	786	96	80	17	8	4	5	34	2	102	6	0
Flener, Huck, Syracuse*	6	11	.353	3.94	30	23	1	0	3	0	134.2	131	572	70	59	20	1	6	6	41	2	83	2	2
Ojala, Kirt, Columbus*	8	7	.533	3.95	32	20	0	0	5	1	145.2	138	619	74	64	15	6	2	3	54	3	107	7	1
Carrara, Giovanni, Syracuse	7	7	.500	3.96	21	21	0	0	0	0	131.2	116	565	72	58	11	3	2	4	56	2	81	3	0
DeSilva, John, Rochester	11	9	.550	4.18	26	25	2	0	1	0	150.2	156	644	78	70	19	3	3	6	51	0	82	2	1
Carlyle, Ken, Toledo	8	8	.500	4.33	32	20	0	0	0	0	124.2	139	541	65	60	10	2	5	4	44	2	63	7	0
Bottenfield, Kent, Toledo	5	11	.313	4.54	27	19	2	1	3	1	136.2	148	601	80	69	15	6	4	4	55	4	68	6	1

DEPARTMENTAL LEADERS: W—Haynes, J. Williams, 12; L—Roberts, Valdes, 13; Pct.—Isringhausen, .900; G—Ricci, 68; GS—Ilsley, 29; CG—Pulsipher, Springer, Wilson, 4; ShO—Isringhausen, 3; GF—Ricci, 48; Sv.—Nichols, Ricci, 25; IP—Ilsley, 185.1; H—Ilsley, 210; TBF—Ilsley, 786; R—Springer, 101; ER—Roberts, Valdes, 92; HR—Roberts, 24; SH—J. Schmidt, 15; SF—Springer, 10; HB—Rumer, 16; BB—Rumer, 76; IBB—Wiegandt, 8; SO—Haynes, 140; WP—Long, 14; Bk.—J. Williams, 4.

ALL PITCHERS

*Lefthanded pitcher.

Pitcher, Team	W	L	Pct.	ERA	G	GS	CG	ShO	GF	Sv.	IP	H	TBF	R	ER	HR	SH	SF	HB	BB	IBB	SO	WP	Bk.
Acevedo, Juan, Norfolk	0	0	.000	0.00	2	2	0	0	0	0	3.0	0	9	0	0	0	0	0	1	1	0	2	0	0
Adamson, Joel, Charlotte*	8	4	.667	3.29	19	18	2	0	0	0	115.0	113	471	51	42	12	0	3	6	20	0	80	4	2
Ahearne, Pat, Toledo	7	9	.438	4.70	25	23	1	1	0	0	139.2	165	599	83	73	11	2	5	5	37	3	54	2	0
Alvarez, Jose, Richmond	1	3	.250	3.62	5	5	0	0	0	0	27.1	26	113	15	11	2	0	0	1	7	0	16	2	0
Alvarez, Tavo, Ottawa	2	1	.667	2.49	3	3	0	0	0	0	21.2	17	83	6	6	1	0	0	1	5	0	11	1	0
Ausanio, Joe, Columbus	1	0	1.000	7.50	11	0	0	0	9	3	12.0	12	53	10	10	1	1	2	1	5	0	20	1	0
Bakkum, Scott, Pawtucket	1	0	1.000	1.71	15	0	0	0	4	2	26.1	21	114	13	5	3	0	1	2	7	0	15	4	0
Baptist, Travis, Syracuse*	3	4	.429	4.33	15	13	0	0	0	0	79.0	83	356	56	38	12	2	3	2	32	2	52	4	1
Bark, Brian, Rich.-Paw.*	5	3	.625	2.99	43	5	0	0	15	7	72.1	63	291	24	24	3	2	2	1	31	0	43	4	0
Barnes, Brian, Pawtucket*	7	5	.583	4.23	21	18	2	0	0	0	106.1	107	454	62	50	12	0	2	4	30	0	90	5	1
Barnwell, Rich, Columbus	0	0	.000	0.00	1	0	0	0	1	0	1.0	0	3	0	0	0	0	0	0	0	0	1	0	0
Batista, Miguel, Charlotte	6	12	.333	4.80	34	18	0	0	4	0	116.1	118	516	79	62	11	1	1	1	60	2	58	12	1
Bauer, Matt, Toledo*	2	1	.667	3.46	13	0	0	0	4	0	13.0	17	59	7	5	0	0	2	0	4	1	10	0	1
Baxter, Robert, Ottawa*	5	5	.500	3.92	39	13	0	0	10	0	101.0	125	426	51	44	6	4	5	0	25	1	39	3	0
Benitez, Armando, Rochester	2	2	.500	1.25	17	0	0	0	17	8	21.2	10	81	4	3	2	0	0	0	7	0	37	1	0
Bennett, Joel, Pawtucket	2	4	.333	5.84	20	13	0	0	2	0	77.0	91	357	57	50	6	0	4	3	45	3	50	6	0
Bergman, Sean, Toledo	0	1	.000	6.00	1	1	0	0	0	0	3.0	4	13	2	2	1	0	0	1	0	0	4	0	0
Birkbeck, Mike, Norfolk	5	3	.625	2.36	9	9	0	0	0	0	53.1	52	215	20	14	2	3	0	1	13	0	39	1	0
Blair, Dirk, Richmond	1	1	.500	6.48	8	0	0	0	5	0	8.1	12	41	8	6	1	1	0	1	4	0	2	0	0
Blomdahl, Ben, Toledo	5	4	.556	3.54	41	0	0	0	23	3	56.0	55	232	24	22	6	1	1	2	13	4	39	3	0
Boehringer, Brian, Columbus	8	6	.571	2.77	17	17	3	0	0	0	104.0	101	439	39	32	6	3	3	4	31	1	58	9	0
Borland, Toby, Scr./W.-B.	0	0	.000	0.00	8	0	0	0	3	1	11.1	5	45	0	0	0	0	0	0	6	1	15	2	0
Borowski, Joe, Rochester	1	3	.250	4.04	28	0	0	0	22	6	35.2	32	149	16	16	3	5	1	0	18	2	32	1	0
Bottenfield, Kent, Toledo	5	11	.313	4.54	27	19	2	1	3	1	136.2	148	601	80	69	15	6	4	4	55	4	68	6	1
Boucher, Denis, Ottawa*	2	3	.400	5.69	14	11	0	0	1	0	55.1	65	254	39	35	1	3	3	0	31	0	22	4	0
Bowen, Ryan, Charlotte	0	1	.000	9.64	1	1	0	0	0	0	4.2	5	22	5	5	1	0	0	0	4	0	3	0	0
Brock, Chris, Richmond	2	8	.200	5.40	22	9	0	0	5	0	60.0	68	270	37	36	2	3	3	1	27	2	43	1	2
Brow, Scott, Syracuse	1	5	.167	9.00	11	5	0	0	1	0	31.0	52	164	39	31	7	2	3	1	18	1	14	1	0
Brown, Chad, Syracuse*	1	1	.500	3.27	11	0	0	0	5	0	22.0	21	106	11	8	1	2	2	0	20	3	14	4	0
Brown, Jeff, Richmond*	1	2	.333	3.22	12	0	0	0	6	1	22.1	23	94	10	8	1	1	0	1	5	3	12	1	0
Brown, Keith, Charlotte	0	1	.000	2.45	4	0	0	0	2	0	7.1	6	31	3	2	1	0	0	1	2	0	3	1	0
Brown, Tim, Syracuse	3	8	.273	6.27	19	12	0	0	3	0	74.2	95	351	69	52	10	3	4	2	28	1	54	2	1
Buckels, Gary, Toledo	2	2	.500	2.15	31	0	0	0	7	0	46.0	37	193	14	11	2	1	1	0	20	2	38	10	0
Byrd, Paul, Norfolk	3	5	.375	2.79	22	10	1	0	10	6	87.0	71	341	29	27	6	0	1	5	21	0	61	1	0
Cain, Tim, Pawtucket	4	0	1.000	2.28	14	0	0	0	5	4	27.2	24	111	7	7	0	1	1	1	8	1	19	1	0
Capra, Nick, Charlotte	0	0	.000	0.00	1	0	0	0	1	0	0.1	1	3	0	0	0	0	0	0	1	0	0	0	0
Carlyle, Ken, Toledo	8	8	.500	4.33	32	20	0	0	0	0	124.2	139	541	65	60	10	2	5	4	44	2	63	7	0
Carper, Mark, Columbus	8	9	.471	4.82	33	14	0	0	3	1	106.1	114	478	61	57	10	2	2	7	55	0	61	10	0
Carrara, Giovanni, Syracuse	7	7	.500	3.96	21	21	0	0	0	0	131.2	116	565	72	58	11	3	2	4	56	2	81	3	0
Carter, Andy, Scr./W.-B.*	1	2	.333	4.35	14	1	0	0	5	0	20.2	17	91	10	10	2	0	1	3	13	2	18	1	1
Chavez, Carlos, Rochester	0	0	.000	10.80	1	0	0	0	0	0	1.2	3	11	2	2	0	0	1	0	3	0	1	2	0
Chitren, Steve, Rochester	0	0	.000	2.45	2	0	0	0	1	0	3.2	6	18	3	1	0	0	1	0	3	0	0	0	0
Christopher, Mike, Toledo	2	4	.333	2.23	36	0	0	0	35	21	36.1	38	160	14	9	1	3	3	1	8	4	32	1	0
Ciccarella, Joe, Pawtucket*	0	1	.000	3.86	11	5	0	0	2	0	25.2	22	112	15	11	2	3	0	4	10	1	13	4	0
Clark, Terry, Rochester	1	2	.333	2.70	9	0	0	0	7	5	10.0	5	37	3	3	2	0	1	0	2	1	10	0	1
Clary, Marty, Charlotte	2	2	.500	4.74	9	2	0	0	5	0	19.0	26	86	16	10	1	1	4	2	1	0	8	1	0
Clemens, Roger, Pawtucket	0	0	.000	0.00	1	1	0	0	0	0	5.0	1	19	0	0	0	0	0	0	3	0	5	0	0
Coffman, Kevin, Richmond	1	0	1.000	3.00	2	1	0	0	0	0	6.0	4	25	2	2	0	0	0	0	4	0	7	0	0
Combs, Pat, Scr./W.-B.*	4	4	.500	5.43	22	6	0	0	7	0	56.1	71	251	37	34	6	2	2	1	25	3	36	1	0
Cook, Andy, Columbus	2	3	.400	3.36	37	2	0	0	12	2	56.1	53	235	24	21	2	3	1	3	19	1	28	3	2
Coppinger, Rocky, Rochester	3	0	1.000	1.04	5	5	0	0	0	0	34.2	23	140	5	4	2	0	2	1	17	0	19	0	0
Cornelius, Reid, Ott.-Nor.	8	1	.889	1.67	14	13	1	0	0	0	81.0	73	341	22	15	3	3	2	8	24	0	50	3	0
Cornett, Brad, Syracuse	0	1	.000	4.91	3	3	0	0	0	0	11.0	13	49	6	6	1	0	1	0	4	0	3	0	0
Cox, Danny, Syracuse	0	0	.000	0.00	4	0	0	0	1	0	7.0	2	28	0	0	0	0	0	0	5	0	9	0	0
Crabtree, Tim, Syracuse	0	2	.000	5.40	26	0	0	0	16	5	31.2	38	148	25	19	1	1	1	1	12	2	22	5	1
Crawford, Joe, Norfolk*	1	1	.500	1.93	8	0	0	0	1	0	18.2	9	70	5	4	0	1	0	0	4	0	13	0	0
Croghan, Andy, Columbus	1	1	.500	3.60	20	0	0	0	13	4	25.0	21	113	10	10	1	0	0	1	22	0	22	1	2
Crowley, Jim, Rochester	0	0	.000	13.50	1	0	0	0	1	0	2.0	4	11	3	3	0	0	0	0	1	0	3	0	0
Culberson, Calvain, Pawtucket	0	0	.000	6.39	6	0	0	0	1	0	12.2	18	65	12	9	0	0	3	0	11	0	4	1	0
Dascenzo, Doug, Charlotte*	0	0	.000	0.00	1	0	0	0	1	0	1.0	1	4	0	0	0	0	0	0	0	0	0	0	0
Davis, Mark, Charlotte*	0	0	.000	5.00	9	0	0	0	0	0	9.0	13	44	8	5	0	0	1	1	1	0	5	2	0
Dedrick, Jim, Rochester	4	0	1.000	1.77	24	2	0	0	4	1	45.2	45	190	9	9	0	2	4	1	14	1	31	4	0
Deshaies, Jim, Scr./W.-B.*	7	8	.467	3.45	19	19	2	1	0	0	117.1	105	476	51	45	8	2	3	5	26	0	79	2	1
DeSilva, John, Rochester	11	9	.550	4.18	26	25	2	0	1	0	150.2	156	644	78	70	19	3	3	6	51	0	82	2	1
Dettmer, John, Rochester	4	7	.364	4.68	21	11	1	1	3	1	82.2	98	359	52	43	9	2	3	2	16	0	46	2	1
Diaz, Rafael, Ottawa	0	3	.000	6.56	32	2	0	0	7	0	48.0	51	218	38	35	6	2	4	4	25	2	31	4	1

Pitcher, Team	W	L	Pct.	ERA	G	GS	CG	ShO	GF	Sv.	IP	H	TBF	R	ER	HR	SH	SF	HB	BB	IBB	SO	WP	Bk.
Drahman, Brian, Charlotte	2	1	.667	6.30	21	0	0	0	15	4	20.0	28	99	14	14	1	2	1	0	11	1	17	3	0
Dunbar, Matt, Columbus*	2	3	.400	4.06	36	0	0	0	9	0	44.1	50	201	22	20	1	0	1	3	19	2	33	5	1
DuBois, Brian, Scr./W.-B.*	1	5	.167	4.56	49	0	0	0	19	1	51.1	58	230	31	26	4	3	2	1	25	5	48	5	0
Eiland, Dave, Columbus	8	7	.533	3.14	19	18	1	1	0	0	109.0	109	444	44	38	0	2	1	3	22	2	62	1	0
Eischen, Joey, Ottawa*	2	1	.667	1.72	11	0	0	0	3	0	15.2	9	61	4	3	0	1	0	0	8	1	13	0	0
Engle, Tom, Norfolk	0	1	.000	12.00	1	1	0	0	0	0	3.0	5	17	4	4	0	0	0	0	3	0	5	0	0
Eversgerd, Bryan, Ottawa*	6	2	.750	2.38	38	0	0	0	9	2	53.0	49	232	21	14	1	2	3	1	26	1	45	2	0
Fajardo, Hector, Ottawa	0	0	.000	4.11	11	0	0	0	5	0	15.1	18	69	7	7	2	1	0	0	6	0	9	1	0
Falteisek, Steve, Ottawa	2	0	1.000	1.17	3	3	1	1	0	0	23.0	17	86	4	3	0	0	0	1	5	0	18	0	1
Finnvold, Gar, Pawtucket	0	0	.000	0.00	1	1	0	0	0	0	3.2	1	15	1	0	0	0	0	0	1	0	3	0	0
Flener, Huck, Syracuse*	6	11	.353	3.94	30	23	1	0	3	0	134.2	131	572	70	59	20	1	6	6	41	2	83	2	2
Fletcher, Paul, Scr./W.-B.	4	1	.800	3.10	52	0	0	0	7	2	61.0	45	257	33	21	7	7	3	1	28	4	48	8	0
Florence, Don, Norfolk*	0	1	.000	0.96	41	0	0	0	16	4	47.0	37	191	6	5	0	5	1	1	17	3	29	2	0
Forney, Rick, Rochester	0	0	.000	3.94	3	3	0	0	0	0	16.0	19	72	9	7	2	2	1	0	6	0	12	2	0
Fraser, Willie, Ottawa	7	6	.538	3.19	19	19	1	1	0	0	107.1	94	434	44	38	11	3	3	3	18	0	84	2	0
Frazier, Ron, Columbus	1	2	.333	4.50	24	5	0	0	9	0	54.0	54	240	33	27	4	4	2	4	23	2	31	7	1
Frey, Steve, Scr./W.-B.*	0	0	.000	1.80	4	0	0	0	2	0	5.0	3	21	1	1	0	1	0	1	2	1	3	1	0
Fuller, Mark, Norfolk	0	0	.000	2.08	4	0	0	0	4	1	4.1	7	18	2	1	0	0	0	0	0	0	2	0	0
Gaddy, Bob, Scr./W.-B.*	5	7	.417	6.28	17	17	0	0	0	0	86.0	100	407	72	60	7	8	5	9	56	1	42	10	0
Gakeler, Dan, Pawtucket	0	2	.000	6.10	4	4	0	0	0	0	20.2	24	97	14	14	2	1	2	2	9	1	13	3	0
Ganote, Joe, Syracuse	0	2	.000	10.13	3	3	0	0	0	0	10.2	16	51	15	12	3	0	1	0	4	0	3	0	0
Garcia, Miguel, Ottawa*	0	0	.000	1.35	5	0	0	0	1	0	6.2	6	27	1	1	1	0	0	0	3	0	4	0	0
Gardiner, Mike, Toledo	0	1	.000	4.41	11	1	0	0	4	0	16.1	19	77	8	8	2	1	1	0	13	0	10	1	0
Gibson, Paul, Syracuse*	0	1	.000	4.81	26	0	0	0	8	3	24.1	24	106	16	13	0	1	0	2	6	2	28	1	0
Gohr, Greg, Toledo	0	2	.000	2.87	6	4	0	0	1	0	15.2	16	68	9	5	1	0	0	0	8	0	15	1	0
Gonzales, Frank, Toledo*	3	2	.600	3.31	49	0	0	0	6	0	51.2	43	217	23	19	4	2	0	3	17	1	54	2	0
Grace, Mike, Scr./W.-B.	2	0	1.000	1.59	2	2	1	0	0	0	17.0	17	68	3	3	0	0	0	0	2	0	13	2	0
Gray, Dennis, Syracuse*	2	2	.500	4.44	15	0	0	0	3	0	24.1	27	106	16	12	3	0	0	2	10	0	15	3	0
Greene, Tommy, Scr./W.-B.	3	0	1.000	2.22	4	4	0	0	0	0	28.1	18	105	8	7	1	1	1	0	6	0	19	5	0
Groom, Buddy, Toledo*	2	3	.400	1.91	6	5	1	0	0	0	33.0	31	132	14	7	4	1	0	0	4	0	24	0	0
Guzman, Juan, Syracuse	0	0	.000	0.00	1	1	0	0	0	0	5.0	1	18	0	0	0	0	0	0	3	0	5	1	0
Hammond, Chris, Charlotte*	0	0	.000	0.00	1	1	0	0	0	0	4.0	3	19	1	0	0	0	0	0	2	0	3	1	0
Hancock, Chris, Charlotte*	0	1	.000	13.50	3	0	0	0	1	0	3.1	6	20	6	5	0	0	1	0	4	0	2	0	0
Hansen, Brent, Pawtucket	7	5	.583	4.29	14	14	2	0	0	0	92.1	90	385	48	44	12	0	3	5	23	0	50	1	0
Harris, Greg, Ottawa	3	0	1.000	1.06	11	0	0	0	8	1	17.0	7	60	3	2	1	1	1	0	3	0	17	0	0
Harrison, Tom, Richmond	2	1	.667	3.21	9	6	0	0	1	1	42.0	34	182	17	15	2	4	3	2	20	1	16	0	1
Hartley, Mike, Paw.- Roc.	1	2	.333	3.43	34	1	0	0	16	1	57.2	51	235	22	22	7	1	2	3	14	1	51	2	2
Haynes, Jimmy, Rochester	12	8	.600	3.29	26	25	3	1	0	0	167.0	162	691	77	61	16	4	7	0	49	0	140	6	1
Heble, Kurt, Syracuse	0	0	.000	5.79	4	0	0	0	1	0	4.2	6	23	4	3	0	0	0	0	2	0	5	1	0
Heffernan, Bert, Ottawa	0	0	.000	0.00	1	0	0	0	1	0	0.1	1	3	0	0	0	0	0	0	1	0	0	1	0
Henry, Dwayne, Toledo	1	1	.500	3.35	41	0	0	0	28	11	48.1	43	212	21	18	3	1	3	3	24	0	52	5	0
Hernandez, Jeremy, Charlotte	0	2	.000	5.58	15	3	0	0	6	0	30.2	37	142	20	19	6	1	1	0	15	0	24	5	0
Hernandez, Willie, Columbus*	2	1	.667	7.67	22	0	0	0	10	0	27.0	43	134	24	23	3	0	3	2	12	0	16	2	1
Hill, Chris, Pawtucket*	2	3	.400	6.10	10	6	0	0	2	0	31.0	31	147	24	21	3	1	3	2	25	1	20	4	0
Hill, Eric, Scr./W.-B.	4	3	.571	4.30	21	0	0	0	7	2	23.0	24	99	13	11	4	1	0	0	9	0	16	2	0
Hoeme, Steve, Pawtucket	0	2	.000	4.62	15	2	0	0	5	1	39.0	40	165	21	20	2	0	1	1	15	0	21	1	0
Holman, Brad, Rochester	0	1	.000	0.00	1	1	0	0	0	0	1.2	5	12	4	0	0	0	1	0	2	0	0	1	0
Howard, Chris, Pawtucket*	3	1	.750	3.92	17	0	0	0	2	0	20.2	25	91	11	9	6	0	2	0	4	1	19	0	0
Hurst, James, Rochester*	1	1	.500	3.79	10	0	0	0	2	0	19.0	17	74	8	8	2	0	1	0	4	1	17	4	0
Hutton, Mark, Columbus	2	6	.250	8.43	11	11	0	0	0	0	52.1	64	243	51	49	7	0	3	4	24	1	23	2	0
Ilsley, Blaise, Scr./W.-B.*	8	10	.444	3.88	29	29	2	1	0	0	185.1	210	786	96	80	17	8	4	5	34	2	102	6	0
Innis, Jeff, Scr./W.-B.	0	2	.000	4.30	15	0	0	0	10	6	14.2	13	64	8	7	0	0	1	0	8	1	14	1	0
Isringhausen, Jason, Norfolk	9	1	.900	1.55	12	12	3	3	0	0	87.0	64	343	17	15	2	2	0	2	24	0	75	4	1
Jacome, Jason, Norfolk*	2	4	.333	3.92	8	8	0	0	0	0	43.2	40	181	21	19	5	4	1	1	13	0	31	1	0
Johnston, Joel, Pawtucket	1	2	.333	6.75	30	0	0	0	13	6	41.1	54	194	31	31	4	1	2	2	19	1	39	3	1
Jones, Calvin, Pawtucket	5	2	.714	4.03	33	0	0	0	27	8	38.0	37	165	23	17	5	3	2	0	15	1	36	6	0
Jordan, Ricardo, Syracuse*	0	0	.000	6.57	13	0	0	0	5	0	12.1	15	59	9	9	1	0	0	1	7	1	17	2	0
Juden, Jeff, Scr./W.-B.	6	4	.600	4.10	14	13	0	0	0	0	83.1	73	354	43	38	4	4	3	9	33	1	65	4	1
Juhl, Mike, Scr./W.-B.*	0	0	.000	0.00	1	0	0	0	1	0	0.1	0	1	0	0	0	0	0	0	0	0	1	0	0
Kamieniecki, Scott, Columbus	1	0	1.000	0.00	1	1	0	0	0	0	6.2	2	23	0	0	0	0	0	0	1	0	10	0	0
Karp, Ryan, Scr./W.-B.*	7	1	.875	4.20	13	13	0	0	0	0	81.1	81	357	43	38	6	2	2	4	31	0	73	2	0
Kerley, Collin, Ottawa	2	0	1.000	2.16	5	0	0	0	1	0	8.1	11	39	3	2	0	1	0	0	3	0	3	0	0
Kiely, John, Toledo	0	0	.000	1.46	14	0	0	0	5	0	12.1	13	56	4	2	1	0	0	0	6	2	8	0	0
King, Richard, Richmond	1	1	.500	2.57	14	0	0	0	5	0	14.0	13	63	8	4	1	0	0	0	6	0	3	0	0
Klingenbeck, Scott, Rochester	3	1	.750	2.72	8	7	0	0	0	0	43.0	46	177	14	13	2	3	2	1	10	0	29	2	0
Kramer, Tommy, Toledo	3	1	.750	4.61	6	5	0	0	0	0	27.1	23	116	15	14	6	0	2	0	16	0	15	0	0
Krivda, Rick, Rochester*	6	5	.545	3.19	16	16	1	0	0	0	101.2	96	429	44	36	11	6	4	2	32	0	74	3	3
Lane, Aaron, Rochester*	0	0	.000	6.30	9	0	0	0	2	0	10.0	11	47	11	7	2	0	0	2	5	0	9	2	0
Langbehn, Gregg, Pawtucket*	0	0	.000	0.00	7	0	0	0	0	0	2.0	0	12	0	0	0	0	1	0	6	0	1	1	0
Layana, Tim, Ottawa	1	1	.500	8.50	26	0	0	0	9	4	36.0	56	178	35	34	7	1	2	2	20	1	27	4	0
Lee, Mark, Rochester*	4	2	.667	1.57	25	0	0	0	8	3	28.2	18	108	6	5	0	1	0	0	5	0	35	1	0
Leiper, Dave, Ottawa*	0	0	.000	0.00	2	0	0	0	0	0	3.0	1	11	0	0	0	0	0	0	1	0	2	0	0
Lemon, Don, Charlotte	0	0	.000	5.40	6	0	0	0	0	0	11.2	11	50	7	7	2	0	0	0	3	0	8	0	0
Lemp, Chris, Rochester	0	1	.000	11.25	3	0	0	0	1	0	4.0	7	21	5	5	1	0	1	0	3	0	4	1	0
Lewis, Richie, Charlotte	5	2	.714	3.20	17	8	1	0	4	0	59.0	50	243	22	21	5	2	4	0	20	0	45	4	2
Lewis, Scott, Pawtucket	0	0	.000	3.86	3	0	0	0	1	0	4.2	7	19	2	2	2	0	0	0	0	0	1	1	0
Lima, Jose, Toledo	5	3	.625	3.01	11	11	1	0	0	0	74.2	69	301	26	25	9	3	4	1	14	2	40	2	0
Lomon, Kevin, Richmond	1	2	.333	3.00	32	3	0	0	8	1	60.0	62	261	23	20	2	4	4	0	32	4	52	4	0
Long, Steve, Charlotte	5	4	.556	5.96	33	6	0	0	10	4	74.0	71	344	57	49	7	1	2	8	46	1	46	14	0
Looney, Brian, Pawtucket*	4	7	.364	3.49	18	18	1	0	0	0	100.2	106	438	44	39	9	2	0	3	33	0	78	7	2
Ludwick, Eric, Norfolk	1	1	.500	5.85	4	3	0	0	0	0	20.0	22	88	15	13	3	0	0	1	7	0	9	1	0
MacDonald, Bob, Columbus*	2	1	.667	2.33	13	0	0	0	2	0	19.1	22	84	7	5	1	1	1	0	5	0	13	0	0
Magee, Bo, Rochester*	0	0	.000	13.50	2	0	0	0	1	0	2.0	4	11	3	3	0	0	0	0	1	0	1	0	0

Pitcher, Team	W	L	Pct.	ERA	G	GS	CG	ShO	GF	Sv.	IP	H	TBF	R	ER	HR	SH	SF	HB	BB	IBB	SO	WP	Bk.
Magrane, Joe, Ottawa*	3	6	.333	4.84	12	12	0	0	0	0	67.0	69	295	43	36	5	5	1	3	31	0	37	7	0
Mantei, Matt, Charlotte	0	1	.000	2.57	6	0	0	0	1	0	7.0	1	27	3	2	1	0	1	1	5	0	10	0	0
Manuel, Barry, Ottawa	5	12	.294	4.59	35	22	1	0	8	1	127.1	125	554	71	65	4	4	9	14	50	1	85	6	2
Marshall, Randy, Toledo*	7	3	.700	2.30	20	17	2	1	0	0	109.1	99	445	38	28	7	4	3	2	29	3	67	2	0
Martel, Ed, Toledo	0	1	.000	1.59	4	0	0	0	1	0	5.2	4	28	1	1	0	1	0	1	5	0	3	0	0
Martin, Tom, Richmond*	0	0	.000	9.00	7	0	0	0	2	0	9.0	10	45	9	9	4	0	0	0	10	2	3	0	0
Mathews, Terry, Charlotte	0	0	.000	4.91	2	0	0	0	0	0	3.2	5	15	2	2	0	0	0	0	0	0	5	0	0
Maxcy, Brian, Toledo	1	3	.250	5.26	20	0	0	0	9	2	25.2	32	120	20	15	3	4	0	1	11	1	11	3	0
May, Darrell, Richmond*	4	2	.667	3.71	9	9	0	0	0	0	51.0	53	216	21	21	1	1	3	0	16	1	42	2	0
McCready, Jim, Norfolk	0	1	.000	2.01	28	0	0	0	8	0	40.1	41	175	14	9	0	5	1	0	20	1	21	1	0
McDonald, Ben, Rochester	0	0	.000	2.45	1	1	0	0	0	0	3.2	1	17	2	1	0	0	0	0	4	0	1	1	0
McGehee, Kevin, Rochester	11	9	.550	5.83	27	20	0	0	0	0	126.2	150	554	89	82	18	3	7	5	33	0	84	5	1
Melendez, Jose, Scr./W.-B.	0	0	.000	6.00	2	0	0	0	0	0	3.0	6	19	4	2	0	1	1	1	2	0	1	0	0
Mendoza, Ramiro, Columbus	1	0	1.000	2.57	2	2	0	0	0	0	14.0	10	51	4	4	0	0	1	0	2	0	13	1	0
Menhart, Paul, Syracuse	2	4	.333	6.31	10	10	0	0	0	0	51.1	62	234	42	36	5	2	3	0	25	0	30	3	1
Miller, Kurt, Charlotte	8	11	.421	4.62	22	22	0	0	0	0	126.2	143	563	76	65	13	5	3	7	55	0	83	6	0
Mills, Alan, Rochester	0	1	.000	0.00	1	1	0	0	0	0	2.2	2	17	6	0	0	0	1	0	5	0	2	1	0
Minutelli, Gino, Richmond*	0	0	.000	4.41	5	3	0	0	0	0	16.1	20	70	8	8	0	1	1	0	3	0	8	0	0
Mitchell, John, Ottawa	0	1	.000	4.32	6	0	0	0	1	0	8.1	8	35	4	4	1	1	0	0	3	1	5	0	0
Montoya, Al, Syracuse*	0	0	.000	0.00	7	0	0	0	0	0	4.1	3	18	1	0	0	0	0	0	3	1	2	0	0
Munoz, Bobby, Scr./W.-B.	1	0	1.000	0.56	2	2	1	1	0	0	16.0	8	57	2	1	0	0	0	2	3	1	10	1	0
Murphy, Rob, Charlotte*	0	0	.000	0.00	3	0	0	0	3	2	3.0	2	11	0	0	0	0	0	0	0	0	1	1	0
Murray, Matt, Richmond	10	3	.769	2.78	19	19	0	0	0	0	123.0	108	501	41	38	6	1	4	3	34	1	78	9	1
Musset, Jose, Columbus	0	0	.000	6.23	5	0	0	0	1	0	4.1	4	19	4	3	2	0	0	0	2	0	4	1	0
Mutis, Jeff, Charlotte*	0	1	.000	3.72	27	0	0	0	5	2	36.1	31	153	18	15	2	2	4	1	14	2	21	1	0
Myers, Jimmy, Rochester	0	4	.000	3.06	55	0	0	0	28	6	64.2	72	289	28	22	2	3	2	1	29	1	31	1	0
Myers, Mike, Char.- Tol.*	0	5	.000	5.40	43	0	0	0	14	0	45.0	47	197	29	27	7	2	0	1	18	1	32	5	0
Newlin, Jim, Charlotte	0	0	.000	4.26	5	0	0	0	2	0	6.1	6	24	3	3	3	0	0	0	1	0	5	1	0
Nichols, Rod, Richmond	1	2	.333	2.53	41	3	0	0	37	25	57.0	54	232	16	16	5	0	1	2	6	1	57	1	0
Ojala, Kirt, Columbus*	8	7	.533	3.95	32	20	0	0	5	1	145.2	138	619	74	64	15	6	2	3	54	3	107	7	1
Olivares, Omar, Scr./W.-B.	0	3	.000	4.87	7	7	0	0	0	0	44.1	49	197	25	24	2	2	0	4	20	2	28	3	0
Oquist, Mike, Rochester	0	0	.000	5.25	7	0	0	0	3	2	12.0	17	56	8	7	0	0	0	0	5	1	11	0	0
Osuna, Al, Norfolk*	3	1	.750	3.00	14	4	0	0	2	0	42.0	39	175	14	14	5	0	3	1	12	0	31	1	0
Pacheco, Alex, Ottawa	1	0	1.000	6.23	4	0	0	0	0	0	8.2	8	35	6	6	2	0	0	0	5	0	4	0	0
Patterson, Jeff, Columbus	5	3	.625	3.61	33	0	0	0	8	0	62.1	56	268	30	25	0	0	3	3	30	2	36	9	0
Pavlas, Dave, Columbus	3	3	.500	2.61	48	0	0	0	32	18	58.2	43	233	19	17	2	4	1	1	20	2	51	4	0
Paxton, Darrin, Norfolk*	0	0	.000	9.00	1	0	0	0	0	0	2.0	3	10	2	2	0	0	0	0	2	0	0	0	0
Pena, Alejandro, Charlotte	0	0	.000	0.96	9	0	0	0	8	5	9.1	2	31	1	1	0	0	0	0	1	0	7	0	0
Pena, Jim, Ottawa*	0	0	.000	3.68	7	0	0	0	2	0	7.1	4	34	3	3	1	1	0	2	8	1	7	3	0
Perigny, Don, Charlotte	1	1	.500	5.14	6	0	0	0	3	0	7.0	8	30	6	4	1	0	1	1	1	0	10	2	0
Person, Robert, Norfolk	2	1	.667	4.50	5	4	0	0	0	0	32.0	30	138	17	16	2	1	1	0	13	0	33	4	0
Pettitte, Andy, Columbus*	0	0	.000	0.00	2	2	0	0	0	0	11.2	7	38	0	0	0	0	0	0	0	0	8	1	0
Pierce, Jeff, Pawtucket	4	2	.667	4.14	23	3	0	0	8	0	41.1	34	172	21	19	5	2	2	2	16	1	43	2	1
Plummer, Dale, Pawtucket	9	9	.500	5.19	34	10	1	0	9	0	100.2	140	457	73	58	13	5	5	6	18	2	47	0	1
Polley, Dale, Richmond*	3	2	.600	1.56	47	0	0	0	22	7	63.1	51	261	15	11	2	2	3	2	20	5	60	2	0
Potts, Mike, Richmond*	5	5	.500	3.79	38	1	0	0	17	1	73.2	79	320	35	31	4	3	1	0	37	4	52	6	0
Pulsipher, Bill, Norfolk*	6	4	.600	3.14	13	13	4	2	0	0	91.2	84	377	36	32	3	5	3	1	33	0	63	2	3
Quirico, Rafael, Columbus*	0	0	.000	4.70	20	0	0	0	8	0	23.0	15	96	14	12	1	0	1	3	14	0	21	5	2
Rapp, Pat, Charlotte	0	1	.000	6.00	1	1	0	0	0	0	6.0	6	23	4	4	0	0	0	0	1	0	5	2	0
Reed, Darren, Richmond	0	0	.000	0.00	1	0	0	0	1	0	1.0	1	5	0	0	0	0	0	0	1	0	1	0	0
Rhodes, Arthur, Rochester*	2	1	.667	2.70	4	4	1	0	0	0	30.0	27	125	12	9	2	3	0	1	8	0	33	1	0
Ricci, Chuck, Scr./W.-B.	4	3	.571	2.49	68	0	0	0	48	25	65.0	48	269	22	18	6	4	1	4	24	5	66	1	0
Rivera, Mariano, Columbus	2	2	.500	2.10	7	7	1	1	0	0	30.0	25	114	10	7	2	0	1	0	3	0	30	0	0
Roberts, Chris, Norfolk*	7	13	.350	5.52	25	25	2	0	0	0	150.0	197	676	99	92	24	6	4	8	58	0	88	5	0
Robertson, Rod, Rochester	0	0	.000	15.43	1	0	0	0	0	0	2.1	6	13	4	4	2	0	0	0	0	0	2	0	0
Robinson, Ken, Syracuse	5	3	.625	3.22	38	0	0	0	12	2	50.1	37	201	18	18	6	2	2	2	12	2	61	2	0
Rodriguez, Frank, Pawtucket	1	1	.500	4.00	13	2	0	0	8	2	27.0	19	109	12	12	2	0	0	3	8	0	18	1	0
Rogers, Bryan, Norfolk	8	3	.727	2.21	56	0	0	0	34	10	77.1	58	303	22	19	4	4	3	0	22	1	50	8	0
Rogers, Jimmy, Syracuse	3	4	.429	3.05	38	0	0	0	9	1	73.2	65	308	26	25	4	3	3	3	31	2	82	6	0
Rojas, Euclides, Charlotte	0	1	.000	3.00	2	0	0	0	1	0	3.0	2	13	1	1	0	0	0	0	2	0	2	0	0
Rueter, Kirk, Ottawa*	9	7	.563	3.06	20	20	3	1	0	0	120.2	120	498	50	41	7	8	3	1	25	0	67	2	1
Rumer, Tim, Columbus*	10	8	.556	5.22	28	25	0	0	1	0	141.1	156	654	98	82	13	7	5	16	76	1	110	5	1
Ryan, Ken, Pawtucket	0	1	.000	6.30	9	0	0	0	5	0	10.0	12	42	7	7	1	0	1	0	4	0	6	1	0
Ryan, Kevin, Rochester	0	3	.000	9.35	6	2	0	0	0	0	17.1	27	83	20	18	3	0	1	1	4	0	7	1	0
Sackinsky, Brian, Rochester	3	3	.500	4.60	14	11	0	0	0	0	62.2	70	260	33	32	6	1	4	1	10	0	42	4	0
Santos, Henry, Toledo*	0	1	.000	6.75	1	0	0	0	0	0	2.2	3	13	2	2	1	0	0	0	2	0	4	0	0
Satre, Jason, Pawtucket	1	5	.167	6.16	9	5	0	0	1	0	30.2	38	143	23	21	3	2	2	2	16	0	14	2	0
Scheid, Rich, Charlotte*	1	4	.200	5.93	19	8	0	0	1	0	54.2	74	246	40	36	10	1	4	2	15	0	37	1	0
Schmidt, Curt, Ottawa	5	0	1.000	2.22	43	0	0	0	38	15	52.2	40	206	14	13	1	0	1	4	18	0	38	2	0
Schmidt, Jason, Richmond	8	6	.571	2.25	19	19	0	0	0	0	116.0	97	484	40	29	2	15	1	3	48	3	95	4	1
Seelbach, Chris, Richmond	4	6	.400	4.66	14	14	1	0	0	0	73.1	64	314	39	38	7	0	3	2	39	0	65	3	0
Segura, Jose, Columbus	0	2	.000	8.71	11	0	0	0	8	4	10.1	18	59	12	10	0	0	0	0	8	0	8	2	0
Sele, Aaron, Pawtucket	0	0	.000	9.00	2	2	0	0	0	0	5.0	9	25	5	5	3	0	0	1	2	0	1	0	0
Seminara, Frank, Rochester	1	0	1.000	3.28	29	0	0	0	5	0	35.2	31	149	13	13	2	3	2	1	14	0	20	3	1
Senior, Shawn, Pawtucket*	0	1	.000	6.00	1	1	0	0	0	0	6.0	9	29	4	4	0	1	0	0	2	0	1	0	0
Shea, John, Rochester*	0	1	.000	2.95	38	0	0	0	19	4	39.2	38	172	16	13	8	1	1	1	17	2	37	2	0
Shepherd, Keith, Charlotte	1	1	.500	21.21	4	0	0	0	1	0	4.2	11	29	11	11	1	0	1	1	3	0	2	0	0
Small, Aaron, Syr.- Char.	2	1	.667	2.98	34	0	0	0	17	10	42.1	39	179	16	14	3	0	1	2	11	1	33	3	0
Smith, Daryl, Columbus	0	3	.000	4.03	13	7	0	0	2	0	51.1	54	225	31	23	5	0	3	4	20	1	23	5	0
Smith, Pete, Charlotte	2	1	.667	3.86	10	8	0	0	1	0	49.0	51	206	21	21	5	1	2	1	17	0	20	2	2
Smith, Zane, Pawtucket*	0	0	.000	0.00	1	1	0	0	0	0	7.0	5	23	0	0	0	0	0	0	0	0	5	0	0
Sodowsky, Clint, Toledo	5	1	.833	2.85	9	9	1	0	0	0	60.0	47	247	21	19	5	2	0	3	30	1	32	1	0
Spencer, Stan, Charlotte	1	4	.200	7.84	9	9	0	0	0	0	41.1	61	198	37	36	9	0	0	3	24	1	19	0	0

Pitcher, Team	W	L	Pct.	ERA	G	GS	CG	ShO	GF	Sv.	IP	H	TBF	R	ER	HR	SH	SF	HB	BB	IBB	SO	WP	Bk.
Spoljaric, Paul, Syracuse*	2	10	.167	4.93	43	9	0	0	27	10	87.2	69	382	51	48	133	1	2	54	3	108	8	0	
Spradlin, Jerry, Charlotte	3	3	.500	3.03	41	0	0	0	14	1	59.1	59	244	26	20	6	2	3	3	15	1	38	5	0
Springer, Dennis, Scr./W.-B.	10	11	.476	4.68	30	23	4	0	3	0	171.0	163	715	101	89	19	0	10	7	47	1	115	8	0
Steed, Rick, Syracuse	4	3	.571	3.72	31	0	0	0	15	1	55.2	51	239	29	23	2	2	2	0	23	1	34	1	1
Stidham, Phil, Norfolk	6	2	.750	3.21	34	6	0	0	12	1	70.0	56	305	33	25	4	2	6	5	36	1	56	5	0
Stoddard, Bob, Norfolk	0	1	.000	6.75	3	0	0	0	1	0	2.2	5	14	2	2	0	0	0	0	1	0	1	1	1
Suppan, Jeff, Pawtucket	2	3	.400	5.32	7	7	0	0	0	0	45.2	50	191	29	27	9	0	1	1	9	0	32	2	0
Sutherland, John, Columbus	0	0	.000	9.00	3	0	0	0	2	0	3.0	5	14	3	3	0	0	0	0	0	0	2	0	0
Telgheder, Dave, Norfolk	5	4	.556	2.24	29	11	0	0	8	3	92.1	77	356	34	23	7	5	2	1	8	0	75	0	2
Thobe, J.J, Ottawa	5	8	.385	3.27	55	0	0	0	25	5	88.0	79	354	37	32	8	6	2	1	16	3	36	1	0
Thobe, Tom, Richmond*	7	0	1.000	1.84	48	2	1	1	15	5	88.0	65	350	27	18	2	3	1	1	26	5	57	5	0
Thomas, Royal, Richmond	7	7	.500	3.48	39	8	1	1	12	0	88.0	103	389	43	34	6	3	2	2	24	2	39	1	0
Tilmon, Pat, Syracuse	0	0	.000	1.50	4	0	0	0	0	0	6.0	8	28	3	1	0	0	0	0	4	0	2	0	0
Timlin, Mike, Syracuse	1	1	.500	1.04	8	0	0	0	2	0	17.1	13	70	6	2	2	0	0	0	4	0	13	0	0
Torres, Ricky, Ottawa	3	8	.273	5.01	32	11	1	0	4	0	91.2	90	391	58	51	9	3	4	6	26	1	58	5	0
Tranberg, Mark, Scr./W.-B.	1	4	.200	7.23	11	2	0	0	3	0	23.2	32	107	19	19	3	2	1	2	6	0	15	4	0
Tunnell, Lee, Toledo	0	1	.000	3.14	7	0	0	0	1	0	14.1	9	53	5	5	0	2	0	1	2	0	7	0	0
Urbina, Ugueth, Ottawa	6	2	.750	3.04	13	11	2	1	0	0	68.0	46	273	26	23	1	3	2	1	26	0	55	1	0
Valdes, Marc, Charlotte	9	13	.409	4.86	27	27	3	2	0	0	170.1	189	728	98	92	19	3	5	12	59	1	104	2	1
VanEgmond, Tim, Pawtucket	5	3	.625	3.92	12	12	0	0	0	0	66.2	66	279	32	29	10	1	2	4	21	1	47	5	0
Veres, Randy, Charlotte	1	0	1.000	2.70	6	0	0	0	6	1	6.2	3	29	2	2	1	1	0	0	5	0	5	1	0
Wade, Terrell, Richmond*	10	9	.526	4.56	24	23	1	0	0	0	142.0	137	600	76	72	10	3	5	1	63	1	124	5	1
Wainhouse, David, Syr.- Char.	3	2	.600	4.50	30	0	0	0	22	5	28.0	35	132	19	14	2	1	3	1	15	3	20	6	0
Wakefield, Tim, Pawtucket	2	1	.667	2.52	4	4	0	0	0	0	25.0	23	105	10	7	1	0	1	4	9	0	14	0	0
Walker, Pete, Norfolk	5	2	.714	3.91	34	1	0	0	25	8	48.1	51	207	24	21	4	3	1	1	16	1	39	2	1
Wallace, Kent, Columbus	4	1	.800	3.02	9	9	0	0	0	0	50.2	44	200	19	17	8	0	0	0	11	0	31	3	0
Ward, Duane, Syracuse	1	1	.500	15.00	6	0	0	0	1	0	6.0	14	33	10	10	0	1	0	0	2	1	4	0	0
Ware, Jeff, Syracuse	7	0	1.000	3.00	16	16	0	0	0	0	75.0	62	319	29	25	8	0	1	2	46	0	76	3	0
Weathers, David, Charlotte	0	1	.000	9.00	1	1	0	0	0	0	5.0	10	27	5	5	0	0	0	0	5	0	0	1	0
Weber, Ben, Syracuse	4	5	.444	5.40	25	15	0	0	3	1	91.2	111	403	62	55	10	2	1	3	27	1	38	5	0
Wegmann, Tom, Rochester	3	2	.600	3.44	9	5	1	0	2	0	34.0	30	140	15	13	3	3	1	3	9	0	23	0	0
Wengert, Bill, Pawtucket	0	1	.000	5.40	7	0	0	0	1	0	11.2	17	53	7	7	1	0	0	0	4	0	10	0	0
Wertz, Bill, Pawtucket	4	5	.444	5.80	29	6	0	0	12	2	63.2	74	298	47	41	11	4	4	1	31	1	55	7	0
West, David, Scr./W.-B.*	1	0	1.000	0.00	1	1	1	1	0	0	7.0	2	22	0	0	0	0	0	0	0	0	6	0	0
Weston, Mickey, Toledo	11	7	.611	2.90	28	27	2	1	0	0	180.0	170	734	68	58	14	2	5	7	41	1	69	4	0
White, Gabe, Ottawa*	2	3	.400	3.90	12	12	0	0	0	0	62.1	58	264	31	27	10	1	4	4	17	0	37	2	1
Whitehurst, Wally, Paw.- Syr.	4	4	.500	5.17	12	10	0	0	0	0	55.2	68	242	37	32	7	2	0	0	12	0	34	4	0
Wickander, Kevin, Toledo*	2	1	.667	2.13	16	0	0	0	3	1	12.2	11	52	3	3	1	0	1	1	5	0	8	0	0
Wiegandt, Scott, Scr./W.-B.*	1	3	.250	2.98	47	0	0	0	15	2	54.1	55	234	19	18	0	1	0	2	27	8	41	5	2
Wiggs, Johnny, Pawtucket*	1	0	1.000	5.79	14	0	0	0	3	0	9.1	11	40	6	6	0	0	0	0	3	0	6	0	0
Williams, Jimmy, Nor.-Roc.*	12	6	.667	3.48	32	16	0	0	6	2	119.0	110	522	55	46	3	1	5	2	65	0	100	12	4
Williams, Mike, Scr./W.-B.	0	1	.000	4.66	3	3	1	0	0	0	9.2	8	39	5	5	0	0	0	0	2	0	8	0	1
Williams, Woody, Syracuse	0	0	.000	3.52	5	1	0	0	1	1	7.2	5	34	3	3	0	0	0	0	5	0	13	0	0
Wilson, Paul, Norfolk	5	3	.625	2.85	10	10	4	2	0	0	66.1	59	270	25	21	3	2	1	3	20	0	67	2	0
Woodall, Brad, Richmond*	4	4	.500	5.10	13	11	0	0	1	0	65.1	70	279	39	37	5	6	0	3	17	1	44	1	0
York, Mike, Syracuse	1	4	.200	7.00	20	5	0	0	3	0	45.0	55	227	50	35	11	0	2	1	27	0	37	5	0
Zimmerman, Mike, Charlotte	2	2	.500	5.30	31	7	0	0	9	0	69.2	84	319	46	41	6	3	3	4	41	0	30	10	0

COMBINATION SHUTOUTS: **Charlotte (7)**—Adamson-Hancock, Adamson-Lewis-Myers-Small, Lewis-Scheid-Spradlin, Long-Mutis, Miller-Myers, Miller-Small, Valdes-Myers. **Columbus (6)**—Boehringer-Pavlas, Eiland-Ausanio, Kamieniecki-Dunbar-Cook-Ausanio, Ojala-Carper, Ojala-Frazier, Pettitte-Ojala-Pavlas. **Norfolk (11)**—Cornelius-Byrd, Cornelius-Walker, Cornelius-Rogers-Florence-Byrd, Isringhausen-Florence-Walker, Jacome-Rogers-Florence-Byrd, Roberts-Stidham-Walker, Stidham-Crawford-McCready-Rogers-Walker, Stidham-Rogers-Walker, Telgheder-Stidham-Walker, Telgheder-Walker, Williams-Walker-Rogers. **Ottawa (7)**—Alvarez-Eversgerd, Fraser-Eversgerd-Thobe, Fraser-Pena-Layana, Fraser-Schmidt, Manuel-Eversgerd-Schmidt, Urbina-Layana-Eversgerd, Fraser-Urbina-Thobe-Schmidt. **Pawtucket (1)**—Hansen-Culberson-Wengert-Wiggs-Johnston. **Richmond (12)**—Murray-Nichols 2, Bark-Polley, May-Lomon-Polley, Murray-Brock-Nichols, Nichols-Thomas-Polley-Minutelli-Martin, Schmidt-Thobe-Lomon, Schmidt-Thobe-Nichols, Seelbach-Potts, Thobe-King-Brown, Wade-Lomon-Nichols, Woodall-Nichols. **Rochester (3)**—Coppinger-Oquist, Haynes-Benitez, Klingenbeck-Shea. **Scr./Wilkes-Barre (4)**—Ilsley-Ricci-Innis, Juden-DuBois-Fletcher, Juden-Wiegandt-DuBois, Springer-Wiegandt-Hill. **Syracuse (4)**—Brown-Montoya-Wainhouse, Flener-Steed, Ware-Crabtree, Whitehurst-Steed. **Toledo (6)**—Ahearne-Bauer-Christopher, Groom-Christopher, Marshall-Blomdahl-Maxcy-Christopher, Marshall-Buckels-Christopher, Sodowsky-Blomdahl-Gonzales-Buckels-Henry, Weston-Martel-Christopher.

NO-HIT GAMES: Rivera, Columbus, defeated Rochester, 3-0 (second game, five innings), June 26.

PITCHERS WITH TWO OR MORE TEAMS

Pitcher, Team	W	L	Pct.	ERA	G	GS	CG	ShO	GF	Sv.	IP	H	TBF	R	ER	HR	SH	SF	HB	BB	IBB	SO	WP	Bk.
Bark, Brian, Richmond*	2	2	.500	3.54	13	5	0	0	0	0	40.2	42	168	16	16	2	1	1	0	17	0	22	1	0
Bark, Brian, Pawtucket*	3	1	.750	2.27	30	0	0	0	15	7	31.2	21	123	8	8	1	1	1	1	14	0	21	3	0
Cornelius, Reid, Ottawa	1	1	.500	6.75	4	3	0	0	0	0	10.2	16	54	12	8	1	0	1	2	5	0	7	2	0
Cornelius, Reid, Norfolk	7	0	1.000	0.90	10	10	1	0	0	0	70.1	57	287	10	7	2	3	1	6	19	0	43	1	0
Hartley, Mike, Pawtucket	1	1	.500	4.05	26	1	0	0	10	1	46.2	47	196	21	21	7	1	2	3	12	0	39	2	2
Hartley, Mike, Rochester	0	1	.000	0.82	8	0	0	0	6	0	11.0	4	39	1	1	0	0	0	0	2	1	12	0	0
Myers, Mike, Charlotte*	0	5	.000	5.65	37	0	0	0	12	0	36.2	41	162	25	23	6	2	0	0	15	1	24	3	0
Myers, Mike, Toledo*	0	0	.000	4.32	6	0	0	0	2	0	8.1	6	35	4	4	1	0	0	1	3	0	8	2	0
Small, Aaron, Syracuse	0	0	.000	5.40	1	0	0	0	0	0	1.2	3	9	1	1	1	0	0	0	1	0	2	0	0
Small, Aaron, Charlotte	2	1	.667	2.88	33	0	0	0	17	10	40.2	36	170	15	13	2	0	1	2	10	1	31	3	0
Wainhouse, Dave, Syracuse	3	2	.600	3.70	26	0	0	0	21	5	24.1	29	111	13	10	1	1	2	1	11	3	18	4	0
Wainhouse, Dave, Charlotte	0	0	.000	9.82	4	0	0	0	1	0	3.2	6	21	6	4	1	0	1	0	4	0	2	2	0
Whitehurst, Wally, Pawtucket	1	3	.250	6.51	6	6	0	0	0	0	27.2	36	123	21	20	3	1	0	0	5	0	13	3	0
Whitehurst, Wally, Syracuse	3	1	.750	3.86	6	4	0	0	0	0	28.0	32	119	16	12	4	1	0	0	7	0	21	1	0
Williams, Jimmy, Norfolk*	11	4	.733	3.05	27	13	0	0	6	2	106.1	89	453	42	36	3	1	5	1	56	0	88	5	2
Williams, Jimmy, Rochester*	1	2	.333	7.11	5	3	0	0	0	0	12.2	21	69	13	10	0	0	0	1	9	0	12	7	2

1995 FIELDING

TEAM

Team	Pct.	G	PO	A	E	TC	DP	PB
Ottawa	.976	142	3673	1644	131	5448	136	14
Richmond	.975	141	3743	1558	134	5435	122	10
Scr./W-B	.975	142	3709	1467	133	5309	134	19
Columbus	.975	140	3671	1606	137	5414	149	15
Norfolk	.974	142	3776	1639	147	5562	147	8
Charlotte	.973	140	3676	1630	145	5451	154	11
Toledo	.972	142	3760	1735	157	5652	168	8
Rochester	.971	142	3709	1477	154	5340	127	11
Pawtucket	.971	142	3691	1425	152	5268	104	21
Syracuse	.964	141	3689	1490	195	5374	116	13

TRIPLE PLAYS: Ottawa, Toledo.

INDIVIDUAL

FIRST BASEMEN

NOTE: All caps denotes fielding-percentage leader based on 71 games for catchers, 95 for all other non-pitchers and 142 innings for pitchers. *Throws lefthanded.

Player, Team	Pct.	G	PO	A	E	TC	DP
Barbara, Don, Pawtucket*	.985	29	235	20	4	259	15
Barry, Jeff, Norfolk	.984	12	117	9	2	128	10
Benzinger, Todd, Columbus	.986	12	131	8	2	141	12
Brewer, Rod, Charlotte*	.990	65	541	50	6	597	57
Cabrera, Francisco, Richmond	1.000	10	79	3	0	82	5
Capra, Nick, Charlotte	1.000	1	7	0	0	7	0
Carey, Paul, Rochester	.991	76	633	47	6	686	61
Carpenter, Bubba, Columbus*	1.000	3	20	1	0	21	3
Chamberlain, Wes, Pawtucket	1.000	1	1	0	0	1	0
Clark, Tony, Toledo	.981	62	615	51	13	679	73
Crowley, Jim, Rochester	1.000	2	21	0	0	21	1
Cruz, Ivan, Toledo*	.969	9	89	6	3	98	9
Daubach, Brian, Norfolk	1.000	2	21	3	0	24	3
Davis, Russ, Columbus	1.000	2	8	1	0	9	1
DeBerry, Joe, Columbus*	.974	5	36	2	1	39	1
Delgado, Alex, Pawtucket	1.000	5	16	2	0	18	1
Delgado, Carlos, Syracuse	.995	79	696	47	4	747	63
Friedman, Jason, Paw.-Roc.*	1.000	21	161	13	0	174	15
Garcia, Omar, Norfolk	.988	107	963	67	12	1042	89
Gregg, Tommy, Charlotte*	.993	13	123	12	1	136	14
Grijak, Kevin, Richmond	.992	51	355	25	3	383	26
Houston, Tyler, Richmond	.987	61	421	33	6	460	44
Huskey, Butch, Norfolk	.988	18	155	6	2	163	21
Jacobs, Frank, Nor.-Ott.*	1.000	3	21	0	0	21	2
Jorgensen, Terry, Charlotte	1.000	4	13	1	0	14	1
Ledesma, Aaron, Norfolk	1.000	3	33	0	0	33	4
Lis, Joe, Syracuse	1.000	2	16	0	0	16	1
Lukachyk, Rob, Toledo	.929	2	13	0	1	14	1
Lutz, Brent, Syracuse	1.000	1	2	0	0	2	1
Maas, Kevin, Columbus*	1.000	11	89	8	0	97	13
McCoy, Trey, Norfolk	.952	3	16	4	1	21	1
McGinnis, Russ, Rochester	1.000	4	29	1	0	30	2
McNair, Fred, Scr./W.-B.	1.000	3	25	2	0	27	3
Melvin, Bob, Columbus	1.000	1	11	1	0	12	1
Montoyo, Charlie, Scr./W.-B.	1.000	2	3	0	0	3	0
Morman, Russ, Charlotte	.998	40	407	23	1	431	42
Natal, Rob, Charlotte	1.000	1	8	2	0	10	1
Obando, Sherman, Rochester	.962	16	137	14	6	157	15
O'Connor, Kevin, Richmond	1.000	1	2	0	0	2	0
Owens, Billy, Rochester	.985	9	60	4	1	65	3
Pappas, Erik, Charlotte	.995	23	187	17	1	205	22
Pecorilli, Aldo, Richmond	1.000	27	170	11	0	181	16
Perez, Eddie, Richmond	1.000	2	1	0	0	1	0
Pough, Pork Chop, Pawtucket	.994	20	144	20	1	165	11
Ramos, John, Syracuse	.983	14	108	8	2	118	9
Robertson, Rod, Rochester	.944	4	17	0	1	18	1
Rodriguez, Tony, Pawtucket	1.000	1	2	0	0	2	0
Rodriguez, Victor, Pawtucket	.985	10	62	4	1	67	10
Rowland, Rich, Pawtucket	1.000	3	28	1	0	29	1
Sanders, Tracy, Norfolk	1.000	3	14	1	0	15	3
Schall, Gene, Scr./W.-B.	.992	43	355	20	3	378	34
Seefried, Tate, Columbus	.993	28	271	25	2	298	27
Sharperson, Mike, Richmond	1.000	6	43	7	0	50	5
Snyder, Cory, Pawtucket	1.000	3	23	4	0	27	4
Sparks, Don, Columbus	.994	80	762	55	5	822	76
Thoutsis, Paul, Columbus	1.000	5	28	3	0	31	4
Townley, Jason, Syracuse	.935	6	22	7	2	31	3
Twardoski, Mike, Richmond*	1.000	19	165	15	0	180	8
Velasquez, Guillermo, Ottawa	.996	29	216	16	1	233	14
Villanueva, Hector, Richmond	1.000	4	26	1	0	27	2
Wedge, Eric, Pawtucket	.995	74	554	40	3	597	49
Weinke, Chris, Syracuse	.991	50	379	46	4	429	28
White, Derrick, Toledo	.985	26	241	16	4	261	22
Wilstead, Randy, Ottawa*	1.000	3	35	2	0	37	3
Wood, Ted, Ottawa*	.986	33	260	20	4	284	21
Woods, Tyrone, Rochester	.988	30	227	18	3	248	22
YAN, Julian, Ottawa	.997	105	876	57	3	936	88
Zinter, Alan, Toledo	.992	48	476	32	4	512	48
Zuber, Jon, Scr./W.-B.*	.996	104	825	63	4	892	86
Zupcic, Bob, Charlotte	1.000	4	21	1	0	22	1

TRIPLE PLAYS: Clark, Yan.

FIRST BASEMEN WITH TWO OR MORE TEAMS

Player, Team	Pct.	G	PO	A	E	TC	DP
Friedman, Jason, Pawtucket*	1.000	10	79	3	0	82	7
Friedman, Jason, Rochester*	1.000	11	82	10	0	92	8
Jacobs, Frank, Norfolk*	1.000	2	12	0	0	12	0
Jacobs, Frank, Ottawa*	1.000	1	9	0	0	9	2

SECOND BASEMEN

Player, Team	Pct.	G	PO	A	E	TC	DP
Alfonzo, Edgar, Rochester	1.000	1	1	3	0	4	0
Alicea, Ed, Norfolk	.965	114	224	325	20	569	75
Azuaje, Jesus, Norfolk	1.000	3	10	6	0	16	2
Bell, Juan, Pawtucket	.981	23	49	55	2	106	11
Bournigal, Rafael, Ottawa	1.000	1	0	2	0	2	0
Briley, Greg, Toledo	.957	8	13	31	2	46	6
Brito, Tilson, Syracuse	1.000	4	3	5	0	8	0
Brown, Randy, Pawtucket	1.000	2	3	6	0	9	0
Buccheri, Jim, Ottawa	.973	12	14	22	1	37	7
Capra, Nick, Charlotte	1.000	3	2	1	0	3	0
Carter, Jeff, Charlotte	.951	68	148	199	18	365	40
CASTLEBERRY, Kevin, Ottawa	.977	96	205	257	11	473	58
Crespo, Felipe, Syracuse	.938	86	160	220	25	405	38
Crowley, Jim, Rochester	.982	24	49	61	2	112	19
Dejardin, Bobby, Rochester	.974	8	15	23	1	39	5
Dellicarri, Joe, Toledo	.970	4	14	18	1	33	6
Diaz, Edgar, Syracuse	.667	2	0	2	1	3	0
Eenhoorn, Robert, Columbus	.979	82	162	219	8	389	63
Fleming, Carlton, Columbus	.934	20	37	62	7	106	12
Foley, Tom, Ottawa	.984	10	27	34	1	62	11
Fox, Andy, Columbus	1.000	4	2	5	0	7	2
Givens, Jim, Toledo	.972	39	56	116	5	177	29
Graffanino, Tony, Richmond	.983	50	102	127	4	233	30
Graham, Greg, Norfolk	.963	7	7	19	1	27	5
Hall, Joe, Toledo	1.000	1	0	1	0	1	0
Hardge, Mike, Pawtucket	.959	16	32	39	3	74	7
Hardtke, Jason, Norfolk	1.000	2	5	2	0	7	0
Hecht, Steve, Toledo	.989	15	43	51	1	95	16
Huson, Jeff, Rochester	1.000	8	25	28	0	53	9
Jordan, Kevin, Scr./W.-B.	.976	102	217	279	12	508	70
Kelly, Pat, Rich.-Syr.	.957	12	18	26	2	46	4
Koelling, Brian, Scr./W.-B.	.935	16	39	33	5	77	9
Leiper, Tim, Toledo	.933	6	17	11	2	30	2
Lis, Joe, Syracuse	.994	42	64	111	1	176	22
Manahan, Anthony, Scr./W.-B.	.976	24	64	58	3	125	10
Martin, Chris, Ottawa	1.000	7	19	18	0	37	4
Martinez, Pablo, Richmond	.875	2	5	2	1	8	1
Millette, Joe, Charlotte	.951	47	75	139	11	225	32
Montalvo, Rob, Syracuse	.917	7	14	19	3	36	5
Montoyo, Charlie, Scr./W.-B.	1.000	2	3	1	0	4	0
Morgan, Kevin, Norfolk	1.000	10	25	26	0	51	8
Munoz, Jose, Richmond	.988	51	111	146	3	260	36
Noboa, Junior, Rochester	.909	6	9	11	2	22	0
O'Connor, Kevin, Richmond	1.000	1	4	3	0	7	1
Olmeda, Jose, Richmond	.968	23	40	50	3	93	10
Penn, Shannon, Toledo	.962	58	106	173	11	290	37
Perezchica, Tony, Columbus	.981	48	75	128	4	207	28
Roa, Hector, Richmond	.969	13	23	40	2	65	5
Robertson, Rod, Rochester	.907	12	22	27	5	54	11
Rodriguez, Steve, Pawtucket	.975	80	167	191	9	367	37
Rodriguez, Tony, Pawtucket	.986	33	65	80	2	147	13

Player, Team	Pct.	G	PO	A	E	TC	DP
Rundels, Matt, Ottawa	.967	10	13	45	2	60	5
Santangelo, F.P., Ottawa	1.000	20	32	54	0	86	9
Schunk, Jerry, Charlotte	.978	32	50	82	3	135	27
Scott, Gary, Richmond	1.000	4	10	5	0	15	1
Sefcik, Kevin, Scr./W.-B.	1.000	7	13	16	0	29	4
Sharperson, Mike, Richmond	1.000	3	3	6	0	9	3
Shumpert, Terry, Pawtucket	1.000	3	2	1	0	3	0
Spiers, Bill, Norfolk	.936	8	19	25	3	47	7
Springer, Steve, Toledo	.976	22	46	75	3	124	19
Tyler, Brad, Rochester	.970	94	171	252	13	436	46
Wilson, Craig, Toledo	.966	7	8	20	1	29	4
Zosky, Eddie, Charlotte	.970	13	20	44	2	66	14

TRIPLE PLAY: Hecht.

SECOND BASEMEN WITH TWO OR MORE TEAMS

Player, Team	Pct.	G	PO	A	E	TC	DP
Kelly, Pat, Richmond	.833	1	3	2	1	6	1
Kelly, Pat, Syracuse	.975	11	15	24	1	40	3

THIRD BASEMEN

Player, Team	Pct.	G	PO	A	E	TC	DP
Alfonzo, Edgar, Rochester	.750	3	0	3	1	4	0
Alicea, Ed, Norfolk	.929	3	4	9	1	14	0
Azuaje, Jesus, Norfolk	1.000	2	1	6	0	7	0
Batiste, Kim, S/WB-Roc.	.940	91	75	160	15	250	16
Battle, Howard, Syracuse	.913	90	40	192	22	254	11
Bell, Juan, Pawtucket	.833	2	3	2	1	6	0
Bieser, Steve, Scr./W.-B.	.714	2	2	3	2	7	0
Bournigal, Rafael, Ottawa	1.000	1	0	1	0	1	0
Capra, Nick, Charlotte	.892	23	22	36	7	65	5
Castaldo, Vince, Charlotte	1.000	2	1	1	0	2	0
Castleberry, Kevin, Ottawa	.873	23	16	46	9	71	5
Crowley, Jim, Rochester	1.000	8	3	10	0	13	3
Davis, Russ, Columbus	.848	19	9	30	7	46	1
Dejardin, Bobby, Rochester	1.000	2	1	1	0	2	0
Delgado, Alex, Pawtucket	1.000	4	1	5	0	6	1
Donnels, Chris, Pawtucket	.833	3	2	3	1	6	0
Eenhoorn, Robert, Columbus	1.000	5	3	6	0	9	0
Epps, Scott, Columbus	1.000	1	1	0	0	1	0
Foley, Tom, Ottawa	1.000	5	5	9	0	14	0
Fox, Andy, Columbus	.968	69	59	184	8	251	22
Gilbert, Shawn, Scr./W.-B.	.929	3	2	11	1	14	2
Giovanola, Ed, Richmond	1.000	2	0	2	0	2	0
Givens, Jim, Toledo	.839	12	8	18	5	31	3
Grable, Rob, Scr./W.-B.	.846	4	4	7	2	13	2
Graham, Greg, Norfolk	.926	23	9	41	4	54	7
Hall, Joe, Toledo	.885	12	3	20	3	26	1
Hardge, Mike, Pawtucket	.906	13	8	21	3	32	0
Hayden, Dave, Scr./W.-B.	.917	13	7	15	2	24	2
Houston, Tyler, Richmond	.939	13	9	22	2	33	5
Huskey, Butch, Norfolk	.943	56	28	122	9	159	9
Johnson, Matt, Syracuse	1.000	1	0	1	0	1	0
JORGENSEN, Terry, Charlotte	.962	97	73	208	11	292	21
Kelly, Pat, Rich.-Syr.	1.000	6	1	9	0	10	1
Ledesma, Aaron, Norfolk	.929	48	39	91	10	140	8
Leiper, Tim, Toledo	1.000	2	3	6	0	9	0
Lieberthal, Mike, Scr./W.-B.	.500	1	0	1	1	2	0
Lis, Joe, Syracuse	.914	35	35	82	11	128	4
Lutz, Brent, Syracuse	.714	3	1	4	2	7	0
Malzone, John, Pawtucket	.833	5	2	8	2	12	1
Manahan, Anthony, Scr./W.-B.	.901	37	28	63	10	101	6
Martin, Chris, Ottawa	.921	46	36	115	13	164	12
Martinez, Ray, Ottawa	.944	31	16	68	5	89	3
McClain, Scott, Rochester	.940	61	41	130	11	182	9
McGriff, Terry, Toledo	.786	3	4	7	3	14	3
Millette, Joe, Charlotte	.857	1	1	5	1	7	1
Montalvo, Rob, Syracuse	1.000	2	1	2	0	3	1
Montoyo, Charlie, Scr./W.-B.	.952	71	46	114	8	168	9
Munoz, Jose, Richmond	.930	36	24	56	6	86	5
Natal, Rob, Charlotte	.909	4	4	6	1	11	0
Pecorilli, Aldo, Richmond	1.000	6	0	1	0	1	0
Perezchica, Tony, Columbus	.923	19	15	33	4	52	3
Pough, Pork Chop, Pawtucket	.778	1	1	6	2	9	1
Roa, Hector, Richmond	1.000	15	4	23	0	27	0
Robertson, Rod, Rochester	.935	10	5	24	2	31	3
Rodriguez, Tony, Pawtucket	.938	59	44	122	11	177	10
Rodriguez, Victor, Pawtucket	1.000	24	14	45	0	59	2
Rowland, Rich, Pawtucket	1.000	1	0	1	0	1	0
Rundels, Matt, Ottawa	1.000	2	2	4	0	6	0
Santangelo, F.P., Ottawa	.946	53	27	113	8	148	4
Saunders, Chris, Norfolk	.923	16	8	28	3	39	1
Sawkiw, Warren, Syracuse	.813	7	4	9	3	16	0
Schunk, Jerry, Charlotte	.914	15	9	23	3	35	0
Scott, Gary, Richmond	.909	23	14	46	6	66	4
Sharperson, Mike, Richmond	.969	69	32	125	5	162	9
Shumpert, Terry, Pawtucket	.896	30	27	68	11	106	12
Siddall, Joe, Ottawa	.750	1	2	1	1	4	0
Snyder, Cory, Pawtucket	.907	14	15	24	4	43	4
Sparks, Don, Columbus	.975	39	25	92	3	120	15
Spiers, Bill, Norfolk	.889	4	4	4	1	9	0
Springer, Steve, Toledo	.944	6	3	14	1	18	3
Tackett, Jeff, Toledo	1.000	1	2	2	0	4	0
Weinke, Chris, Syracuse	.875	18	9	19	4	32	1
Wilson, Craig, Toledo	.921	113	72	256	28	356	18
Zosky, Eddie, Charlotte	.975	13	16	23	1	40	8

TRIPLE PLAY: Wilson.

THIRD BASEMEN WITH TWO OR MORE TEAMS

Player, Team	Pct.	G	PO	A	E	TC	DP
Batiste, Kim, Scr./W.-B.	.952	28	24	56	4	84	7
Batiste, Kim, Rochester	.934	63	51	104	11	166	9
Kelly, Pat, Richmond	1.000	4	1	9	0	10	1
Kelly, Pat, Syracuse	.000	2	0	0	0	0	0

SHORTSTOPS

Player, Team	Pct.	G	PO	A	E	TC	DP
Abbott, Kurt, Charlotte	.909	5	5	15	2	22	3
Alfonzo, Edgar, Rochester	.971	9	13	21	1	35	5
BAEZ, Kevin, Toledo	.975	116	205	414	16	635	92
Batiste, Kim, Rochester	1.000	3	3	3	0	6	0
Battle, Howard, Syracuse	.923	34	42	89	11	142	11
Bell, Juan, Pawtucket	.929	43	56	87	11	154	11
Bournigal, Rafael, Ottawa	.984	15	15	48	1	64	10
Brito, Tilson, Syracuse	.952	88	120	235	18	373	48
Brown, Randy, Pawtucket	.949	67	102	161	14	277	33
Capra, Nick, Charlotte	1.000	1	1	0	0	1	0
Diaz, Edgar, Syracuse	.950	12	28	29	3	60	7
Eenhoorn, Robert, Columbus	1.000	5	3	6	0	9	2
Elster, Kevin, Scr./W.-B.	.947	5	6	12	1	19	4
Foley, Tom, Ottawa	1.000	6	13	19	0	32	4
Fox, Andy, Columbus	.970	10	10	22	1	33	3
Gilbert, Shawn, Scr./W.-B.	.953	107	156	347	25	528	71
Giovanola, Ed, Richmond	.965	90	125	284	15	424	52
Givens, Jim, Toledo	.952	28	37	83	6	126	17
Graham, Greg, Norfolk	.918	12	14	31	4	49	5
Grudzielanek, Mark, Ottawa	.939	49	58	156	14	228	29
Hayden, Dave, Scr./W.-B.	1.000	1	0	3	0	3	0
Huson, Jeff, Rochester	.974	54	85	175	7	267	43
Jeter, Derek, Columbus	.953	123	189	394	29	612	74
Johnson, Matt, Syracuse	1.000	5	2	7	0	9	1
Kelly, Pat, Syracuse	.950	15	19	38	3	60	9
Ledesma, Aaron, Norfolk	1.000	1	1	3	0	4	0
Lis, Joe, Syracuse	1.000	2	0	3	0	3	0
Manahan, Anthony, Scr./W.-B.	.925	17	31	43	6	80	12
Martin, Chris, Ottawa	.952	70	101	195	15	311	45
Martinez, Pablo, Richmond	.982	12	16	38	1	55	5
Martinez, Ray, Ottawa	.875	5	2	5	1	8	1
Mendenhall, Kirk, Toledo	.955	9	14	28	2	44	10
Millette, Joe, Charlotte	.934	19	25	46	5	76	10
Montalvo, Rob, Syracuse	1.000	1	2	5	0	7	1
Montoyo, Charlie, Scr./W.-B.	.947	16	23	31	3	57	3
Morgan, Kevin, Norfolk	.976	7	12	29	1	42	2
Munoz, Jose, Richmond	.916	36	44	119	15	178	9
Olmeda, Jose, Richmond	.824	3	6	8	3	17	4
Ordonez, Rey, Norfolk	.967	124	188	436	21	645	88
Perezchica, Tony, Columbus	.956	11	24	41	3	68	7
Roa, Hector, Richmond	.957	9	10	34	2	46	5
Robertson, Rod, Rochester	.926	33	40	86	10	136	16
Rodriguez, Carlos, Pawtucket	.962	38	51	99	6	156	13
Rodriguez, Tony, Pawtucket	.963	12	10	16	1	27	1
Santangelo, F.P., Ottawa	.958	5	7	16	1	24	5
Schunk, Jerry, Charlotte	.966	60	104	177	10	291	44
Smith, Greg, Rochester	.963	52	83	149	9	241	26
Zosky, Eddie, Charlotte	.966	66	125	212	12	349	52

TRIPLE PLAY: Martin.

OUTFIELDERS

Player, Team	Pct.	G	PO	A	E	TC	DP
Abner, Shawn, Norfolk	1.000	3	2	0	0	2	0
Barnwell, Rich, Columbus	.986	44	66	2	1	69	1
Barron, Tony, Ottawa	1.000	31	59	2	0	61	0
Bartee, Kimera, Rochester	1.000	15	37	2	0	39	0
Bautista, Danny, Toledo	.943	18	32	1	2	35	0
Benitez, Yamil, Ottawa	.964	116	177	10	7	194	2
Bieser, Steve, Scr./W.-B.	.988	39	82	1	1	84	0
Blosser, Greg, Pawtucket*	.886	16	30	1	4	35	0

Player, Team	Pct.	G	PO	A	E	TC	DP
Boston, Daryl, Charlotte*	1.000	8	12	1	0	13	0
Bowers, Brent, Syracuse	.945	94	150	5	9	164	0
Briley, Greg, Toledo	.973	16	36	0	1	37	0
Brock, Tarrik, Toledo*	.929	9	12	1	1	14	0
Brown, Jarvis, Nor.-Roc.	.955	60	126	2	6	134	1
Brown, Randy, Pawtucket	1.000	4	3	0	0	3	0
Buccheri, Jim, Ottawa	.984	116	235	7	4	246	0
Buford, Damon, Rochester	.983	46	115	2	2	119	0
Butler, Rich, Syracuse	.965	64	101	9	4	114	2
Butler, Robert, Scr./W.-B.*	.974	85	147	4	4	155	1
Cairo, Sergio, Ottawa	1.000	2	3	0	0	3	0
Canate, Willie, Syracuse	.963	112	223	14	9	246	4
Capra, Nick, Charlotte	.972	85	133	7	4	144	0
Carpenter, Bubba, Columbus*	.982	104	211	4	4	219	2
Carr, Chuck, Charlotte	1.000	7	9	0	0	9	0
Carter, Jeff, Charlotte	1.000	43	73	5	0	78	2
Carter, Steve, Charlotte	.900	12	15	3	2	20	0
Chamberlain, Wes, Pawtucket	.945	33	66	3	4	73	0
Cuyler, Milt, Toledo	.960	51	95	1	4	100	0
Dascenzo, Doug, Charlotte*	1.000	70	157	3	0	160	0
Davis, Jay, Norfolk*	1.000	8	11	0	0	11	0
Delgado, Carlos, Syracuse	1.000	14	28	2	0	30	0
Delima, Rafael, Ottawa*	1.000	8	6	2	0	8	0
Everett, Carl, Norfolk	1.000	64	133	7	0	140	0
Felix, Junior, Ottawa	1.000	33	60	0	0	60	0
Ford, Curt, Charlotte	.987	45	69	5	1	75	1
Fox, Andy, Columbus	1.000	8	13	0	0	13	0
Frazier, Lou, Ottawa	.974	30	73	3	2	78	0
Friedman, Jason, Rochester*	1.000	4	5	0	0	5	0
Geisler, Phil, Scr./W.-B.*	1.000	12	19	1	0	20	0
Gilbert, Shawn, Scr./W.-B.	.967	23	55	3	2	60	0
Goodwin, Curtis, Rochester*	.965	36	81	1	3	85	0
Grable, Rob, Scr./W.-B.	1.000	14	25	0	0	25	0
Gregg, Tommy, Charlotte*	1.000	13	17	1	0	18	0
Grijak, Kevin, Richmond	1.000	4	4	0	0	4	0
Hall, Joe, Toledo	.993	73	145	5	1	151	1
Hecht, Steve, Toledo	1.000	7	13	0	0	13	0
Heffernan, Bert, Ottawa	.800	1	4	0	1	5	0
Hill, Lew, Columbus	.984	37	62	0	1	63	0
Holifield, Rick, Scr./W.-B.*	.964	72	131	4	5	140	0
Houston, Tyler, Richmond	.963	15	25	1	1	27	0
Howard, Tim, Pawtucket	.965	31	55	0	2	57	0
Huskey, Butch, Norfolk	.972	41	65	4	2	71	0
Jones, Chris, Norfolk	.985	30	62	4	1	67	2
Kelly, Mike, Richmond	1.000	12	24	0	0	24	0
Kelly, Pat, Rich.-Syr.	1.000	8	12	1	0	13	0
Kowitz, Brian, Richmond*	.969	97	217	2	7	226	0
Leach, Jalal, Columbus*	.943	64	97	2	6	105	0
Lee, Derek, Norfolk	.959	65	86	8	4	98	1
Leiper, Tim, Toledo	1.000	4	11	0	0	11	0
Lennon, Pat, Pawtucket	.951	35	54	4	3	61	1
Lewis, T.R., Rochester	.905	10	19	0	2	21	0
Lis, Joe, Syracuse	.980	31	48	2	1	51	1
Lukachyk, Rob, Toledo	.988	96	157	2	2	161	1
Luke, Matt, Columbus*	.949	23	36	1	2	39	0
Lutz, Brent, Syracuse	.923	13	12	0	1	13	0
Maas, Kevin, Columbus*	1.000	22	26	0	0	26	0
Mahay, Ron, Pawtucket*	1.000	11	30	2	0	32	0
Malave, Jose, Pawtucket	.966	65	113	2	4	119	0
Marsh, Tom, Scr./W.-B.	.994	75	156	4	1	161	2
Mashore, Justin, Toledo	.986	68	140	6	2	148	1
Massarelli, John, Charlotte	.983	64	110	8	2	120	0
Masse, Billy, Columbus	.961	44	72	1	3	76	0
McCoy, Trey, Norfolk	1.000	2	4	0	0	4	0
McDowell, Oddibe, Columbus*	1.000	14	26	0	0	26	0
McGee, Willie, Pawtucket	.875	3	7	0	1	8	0
Milne, Darren, Toledo	1.000	6	3	1	0	4	0
MOORE, Bobby, Richmond	1.000	100	179	9	0	188	3
Morman, Russ, Charlotte	.900	3	9	0	1	10	0
Munoz, Jose, Richmond	.957	25	20	2	1	23	1
Murray, Glenn, Pawtucket	.975	95	227	5	6	238	0
Nevin, Phil, Toledo	1.000	4	2	0	0	2	0
Obando, Sherman, Rochester	.960	29	47	1	2	50	0
Ochoa, Alex, Roch.-Nor.	.974	124	249	10	7	266	1
O'Connor, Kevin, Richmond	.976	79	118	4	3	125	0
Olmeda, Jose, Richmond	.946	48	84	4	5	93	1
Otero, Ricky, Norfolk	.970	72	147	12	5	164	5
Pappas, Erik, Charlotte	.956	21	38	5	2	45	0
Payton, Jay, Norfolk	.982	49	106	3	2	111	0
Pecorilli, Aldo, Richmond	1.000	11	18	0	0	18	0
Pemberton, Rudy, Toledo	.953	43	59	2	3	64	2
Perez, Robert, Syracuse	.964	119	208	7	8	223	0
Perezchica, Tony, Columbus	.957	20	21	1	1	23	0
Pride, Curtis, Ottawa	.974	37	69	5	2	76	1
Ramos, John, Syracuse	.917	7	11	0	1	12	0
Reed, Darren, Richmond	1.000	30	52	1	0	53	0
Rhodes, Karl, Pawtucket*	.967	65	172	6	6	184	3
Rivera, Ruben, Columbus	.975	48	113	6	3	122	2
Robertson, Rod, Rochester	.909	39	57	3	6	66	0
Rundels, Matt, Ottawa	1.000	1	1	0	0	1	0
Sanders, Tracy, Norfolk	.980	27	47	1	1	49	0
Santangelo, F.P., Ottawa	.952	12	18	2	1	21	1
Sawkiw, Warren, Syracuse	.933	7	13	1	1	15	0
Schall, Gene, Scr./W.-B.	.988	45	76	5	1	82	0
Smith, Mark, Rochester	.961	95	167	4	7	178	1
Snyder, Cory, Pawtucket	1.000	2	2	0	0	2	0
Sparks, Don, Columbus	1.000	2	1	0	0	1	0
Stairs, Matt, Pawtucket	1.000	51	79	13	0	92	2
Steverson, Todd, Toledo	.818	7	8	1	2	11	0
Strawberry, Darryl, Columbus*	1.000	9	9	0	0	9	0
Swann, Pedro, Richmond	1.000	9	9	1	0	10	0
Tavarez, Jesus, Charlotte	.979	38	92	2	2	96	0
Taylor, Sam, Scr./W.-B.*	1.000	1	2	0	0	2	0
Thompson, Ryan, Norfolk	1.000	13	15	2	0	17	0
Thoutsis, Paul, Columbus	.953	31	41	0	2	43	0
Tokheim, David, Scr./W.-B.*	.982	92	158	8	3	169	2
Tovar, Raul, Ottawa	.963	14	26	0	1	27	0
Tyler, Brad, Rochester	.964	15	26	1	1	28	0
Vatcher, Jim, Scr./W.-B.	1.000	4	8	0	0	8	0
Wade, Scott, Pawtucket	1.000	7	15	1	0	16	0
Waggoner, Aubrey, Pawtucket	.939	13	31	0	2	33	0
Warner, Mike, Richmond*	.950	27	57	0	3	60	0
Wawruck, Jim, Rochester*	1.000	30	75	6	0	81	1
Weinke, Chris, Syracuse	.915	28	43	0	4	47	0
White, Derrick, Toledo	.947	48	86	4	5	95	0
Whiten, Mark, Pawtucket	.940	20	43	4	3	50	0
Williams, Juan, Richmond	.961	40	69	5	3	77	1
Wood, Ted, Ottawa*	.987	50	73	4	1	78	0
Woods, Tyrone, Rochester	.938	14	14	1	1	16	0
Yan, Julian, Ottawa	.600	3	3	0	2	5	0
Zinter, Alan, Toledo	.955	15	21	0	1	22	0
Zupcic, Bob, Charlotte	.977	54	81	4	2	87	0

OUTFIELDERS WITH TWO OR MORE TEAMS

Player, Team	Pct.	G	PO	A	E	TC	DP
Brown, Jarvis, Norfolk	.960	43	71	1	3	75	0
Brown, Jarvis, Rochester	.949	17	55	1	3	59	1
Kelly, Pat, Richmond	1.000	7	11	1	0	12	0
Kelly, Pat, Syracuse	1.000	1	1	0	0	1	0
Ochoa, Alex, Rochester	.975	91	183	9	5	197	1
Ochoa, Alex, Norfolk	.971	33	66	1	2	69	0

CATCHERS

Player, Team	Pct.	G	PO	A	E	TC	DP	PB
Alvarez, Clemente, Ottawa	.988	48	292	26	4	322	3	3
Bennett, Gary, Scr./W.-B.	1.000	7	38	4	0	42	0	1
Bieser, Steve, Scr./W.-B.	.973	39	230	25	7	262	3	7
Boka, Ben, Norfolk	.970	14	28	4	1	33	1	4
Brooks, Eric, Syracuse	.988	46	235	15	3	253	0	5
Brophy, E.J., Scr./W.-B.	.980	30	132	16	3	151	2	3
Cabrera, Francisco, Richmond	1.000	3	7	2	0	9	1	2
Castillo, Alberto, Norfolk	.987	67	469	44	7	520	4	1
Delgado, Alex, Pawtucket	.974	33	157	32	5	194	1	7
Devarez, Cesar, Rochester	.995	52	331	40	2	373	4	5
Diaz, Cesar, Norfolk	.938	3	13	2	1	16	1	0
Epps, Scott, Columbus	.941	4	15	1	1	17	0	0
Figga, Mike, Columbus	1.000	5	29	4	0	33	0	1
Fulton, Ed, Pawtucket	.971	7	31	2	1	34	1	2
Gonzalez, Pete, Toledo	.957	6	40	5	2	47	0	0
Greene, Charlie, Norfolk	1.000	27	157	25	0	182	1	0
Gresham, Kris, Rochester	.965	21	127	12	5	144	3	0
Hatteberg, Scott, Pawtucket	.984	77	446	45	8	499	5	7
Heffernan, Bert, Ottawa	.987	28	140	15	2	157	3	3
Hernandez, Kiki, Charlotte	.964	30	119	16	5	140	0	1
Houston, Tyler, Richmond	.986	21	124	13	2	139	2	1
Knapp, Mike, Rochester	.996	36	203	23	1	227	1	3
Knorr, Randy, Syracuse	.979	17	129	14	3	146	3	0
Levangie, Dana, Pawtucket	1.000	6	32	4	0	36	0	0
Lieberthal, Mike, Scr./W.-B.	.9927	83	503	45	4	552	2	8
Livesey, Jeff, Columbus	.984	26	113	7	2	122	0	0
Lutz, Brent, Syracuse	.975	19	71	8	2	81	0	2
Massarelli, John, Charlotte	1.000	2	11	0	0	11	0	1
McGinnis, Russ, Rochester	1.000	2	12	1	0	13	0	1
McGriff, Terry, Toledo	1.000	40	167	18	0	185	1	2
Melvin, Bob, Columbus	.971	12	66	2	2	70	0	0
Natal, Rob, Charlotte	.997	43	259	41	1	301	3	4

Player, Team	Pct.	G	PO	A	E	TC	DP	PB
Orton, John, Rich.-Nor.	.995	63	373	48	2	423	6	3
Pappas, Erik, Charlotte	.982	75	398	37	8	443	4	5
Pecorilli, Aldo, Richmond	1.000	2	1	2	0	3	0	0
Perez, Eddie, Richmond	.989	83	539	69	7	615	7	2
POSADA, Jorge, Columbus	.9928	93	500	58	4	562	7	14
Ramos, John, Syracuse	.959	10	68	2	3	73	0	0
Reed, Darren, Richmond	.978	7	41	3	1	45	0	1
Rice, Lance, Toledo	1.000	15	70	9	0	79	1	0
Robertson, Rod, Rochester	1.000	2	7	2	0	9	0	1
Rowland, Rich, Pawtucket	.984	27	177	8	3	188	0	3
Rudolph, Mason, Charlotte	1.000	2	6	0	0	6	0	0
Santangelo, F.P., Ottawa	1.000	1	5	0	0	5	0	0
Siddall, Joe, Ottawa	.990	78	346	56	4	406	6	8
Tackett, Jeff, Toledo	.987	93	485	58	7	550	5	6
Tijerina, Tony, Norfolk	1.000	1	1	0	0	1	0	0
Toth, David, Richmond	.947	5	15	3	1	19	0	0
Townley, Jason, Syracuse	.990	74	473	32	5	510	5	6
Tucker, Scooter, Richmond	.984	20	107	16	2	125	1	4
Villanueva, Hector, Richmond	1.000	2	5	1	0	6	0	0
Wedge, Eric, Pawtucket	1.000	9	42	6	0	48	0	2
Wilson, Tom, Columbus	.962	22	109	16	5	130	2	0
Zaun, Greg, Rochester	.989	34	243	18	3	264	1	1
Zinter, Alan, Toledo	1.000	3	5	1	0	6	0	0

CATCHERS WITH TWO OR MORE TEAMS

Player, Team	Pct.	G	PO	A	E	TC	DP	PB
Orton, John, Richmond	1.000	17	83	10	0	93	1	0
Orton, John, Norfolk	.994	46	290	38	2	330	5	3

PITCHERS

Player, Team	Pct.	G	PO	A	E	TC	DP
Adamson, Joel, Charlotte*	1.000	19	9	14	0	23	2
Ahearne, Pat, Toledo	1.000	25	10	16	0	26	0
Alvarez, Jose, Richmond	.800	5	0	4	1	5	0
Alvarez, Tavo, Ottawa	1.000	3	3	2	0	5	0
Ausanio, Joe, Columbus	1.000	11	0	3	0	3	0
Bakkum, Scott, Pawtucket	.667	15	2	0	1	3	0
Baptist, Travis, Syracuse*	1.000	15	4	10	0	14	1
Bark, Brian, Rich.-Paw.*	1.000	43	3	12	0	15	0
Barnes, Brian, Pawtucket*	.917	21	6	16	2	24	1
Batista, Miguel, Charlotte	.903	34	13	15	3	31	1
Bauer, Matt, Toledo*	.800	13	0	4	1	5	0
Baxter, Robert, Ottawa*	.957	39	8	14	1	23	2
Benitez, Armando, Rochester	1.000	17	1	2	0	3	0
Bennett, Joel, Pawtucket	1.000	20	6	12	0	18	1
Birkbeck, Mike, Norfolk	1.000	9	7	13	0	20	2
Blair, Dirk, Richmond	.667	8	1	1	1	3	0
Blomdahl, Ben, Toledo	1.000	41	3	7	0	10	0
Boehringer, Brian, Columbus	.842	17	4	12	3	19	1
Borland, Toby, Scr./W.-B.	.800	8	1	3	1	5	0
Borowski, Joe, Rochester	.750	28	1	2	1	4	0
Bottenfield, Kent, Toledo	.966	27	6	22	1	29	1
Boucher, Denis, Ottawa*	.909	14	4	6	1	11	3
Brock, Chris, Richmond	.929	22	5	8	1	14	0
Brow, Scott, Syracuse	.818	11	5	4	2	11	0
Brown, Chad, Syracuse*	1.000	11	1	8	0	9	1
Brown, Jeff, Richmond*	1.000	12	2	6	0	8	0
Brown, Keith, Charlotte	1.000	4	0	1	0	1	0
Brown, Tim, Syracuse	1.000	19	11	6	0	17	0
Buckels, Gary, Toledo	1.000	31	2	5	0	7	0
Byrd, Paul, Norfolk	.750	22	5	7	4	16	0
Cain, Tim, Pawtucket	1.000	14	3	3	0	6	0
Carlyle, Ken, Toledo	.967	32	8	21	1	30	4
Carper, Mark, Columbus	.909	33	7	13	2	22	2
Carrara, Giovanni, Syracuse	.900	21	17	19	4	40	2
Carter, Andy, Scr./W.-B.*	1.000	14	0	2	0	2	0
Chitren, Steve, Rochester	1.000	2	0	1	0	1	0
Christopher, Mike, Toledo	1.000	36	5	8	0	13	1
Ciccarella, Joe, Pawtucket*	1.000	11	3	4	0	7	1
Clark, Terry, Rochester	1.000	9	2	0	0	2	0
Clary, Marty, Charlotte	.714	9	1	4	2	7	0
Coffman, Kevin, Richmond	1.000	2	0	1	0	1	0
Combs, Pat, Scr./W.-B.*	.833	22	1	4	1	6	2
Cook, Andy, Columbus	.941	37	5	11	1	17	1
Coppinger, Rocky, Rochester	1.000	5	2	3	0	5	0
Cornelius, Reid, Ott.-Nor.	1.000	14	6	20	0	26	0
Cornett, Brad, Syracuse	1.000	3	2	2	0	4	0
Cox, Danny, Syracuse	1.000	4	0	2	0	2	0
Crabtree, Tim, Syracuse	.900	26	3	6	1	10	0
Crawford, Joe, Norfolk*	1.000	8	1	5	0	6	0
Croghan, Andy, Columbus	1.000	20	1	1	0	2	0
Culberson, Calvain, Pawtucket	1.000	6	0	2	0	2	0
Davis, Mark, Charlotte*	.750	9	1	2	1	4	0
Dedrick, Jim, Rochester	1.000	24	5	11	0	16	1
Deshaies, Jim, Scr./W.-B.*	.970	19	6	26	1	33	1
DeSilva, John, Rochester	.914	26	10	22	3	35	1
Dettmer, John, Rochester	.929	21	5	8	1	14	1
Diaz, Rafael, Ottawa	.867	32	6	7	2	15	0
Drahman, Brian, Charlotte	1.000	21	1	2	0	3	1
DuBois, Brian, Scr./W.-B.*	1.000	49	0	11	0	11	1
Dunbar, Matt, Columbus*	.857	36	1	5	1	7	0
Eiland, Dave, Columbus	1.000	19	10	22	0	32	3
Eischen, Joey, Ottawa*	1.000	11	3	1	0	4	0
Eversgerd, Bryan, Ottawa*	1.000	38	2	12	0	14	1
Fajardo, Hector, Ottawa	1.000	11	1	5	0	6	0
Falteisek, Steve, Ottawa	1.000	3	2	5	0	7	0
Flener, Huck, Syracuse*	.921	30	9	26	3	38	4
Fletcher, Paul, Scr./W.-B.	.714	52	2	3	2	7	0
Florence, Don, Norfolk*	.846	41	3	8	2	13	1
Forney, Rick, Rochester	.667	3	0	2	1	3	0
Fraser, Willie, Ottawa	.938	19	6	9	1	16	0
Frazier, Ron, Columbus	.769	24	2	8	3	13	0
Gaddy, Bob, Scr./W.-B.*	1.000	17	6	21	0	27	2
Gakeler, Dan, Pawtucket	1.000	4	2	2	0	4	0
Ganote, Joe, Syracuse	1.000	3	0	1	0	1	0
Garcia, Miguel, Ottawa*	1.000	5	1	4	0	5	1
Gardiner, Mike, Toledo	1.000	11	1	0	0	1	0
Gibson, Paul, Syracuse*	1.000	26	2	3	0	5	0
Gohr, Greg, Toledo	1.000	6	2	1	0	3	1
Gonzales, Frank, Toledo*	1.000	49	2	6	0	8	0
Grace, Mike, Scr./W.-B.	1.000	2	2	0	0	2	0
Gray, Dennis, Syracuse*	.875	15	2	5	1	8	0
Greene, Tommy, Scr./W.-B.	.833	4	0	5	1	6	0
Groom, Buddy, Toledo*	1.000	6	2	5	0	7	0
Guzman, Juan, Syracuse	1.000	1	0	1	0	1	0
Hammond, Chris, Charlotte*	1.000	1	0	1	0	1	0
Hancock, Chris, Charlotte*	1.000	3	1	1	0	2	0
Hansen, Brent, Pawtucket	1.000	14	9	7	0	16	1
Harris, Greg, Ottawa	1.000	11	2	5	0	7	1
Harrison, Tom, Richmond	.700	9	4	3	3	10	0
Hartley, Mike, Paw.-Roc.	1.000	34	1	5	0	6	0
Haynes, Jimmy, Rochester	.889	26	14	18	4	36	2
Heble, Kurt, Syracuse	1.000	4	1	1	0	2	0
Henry, Dwayne, Toledo	.857	41	3	3	1	7	1
Hernandez, Jeremy, Charlotte	1.000	15	3	2	0	5	0
Hernandez, Willie, Columbus*	1.000	22	2	4	0	6	1
Hill, Chris, Pawtucket*	1.000	10	1	1	0	2	0
Hill, Eric, Scr./W.-B.	1.000	21	3	2	0	5	0
Hoeme, Steve, Pawtucket	1.000	15	1	6	0	7	0
Holman, Brad, Rochester	.000	1	0	0	1	1	0
Howard, Chris, Pawtucket*	.800	17	3	1	1	5	0
Hurst, James, Rochester*	1.000	10	0	2	0	2	0
Hutton, Mark, Columbus	1.000	11	3	6	0	9	0
ILSLEY, Blaise, Scr./W.-B.*	1.000	29	13	36	0	49	6
Innis, Jeff, Scr./W.-B.	1.000	15	2	2	0	4	0
Isringhausen, Jason, Norfolk	.947	12	5	13	1	19	2
Jacome, Jason, Norfolk*	1.000	8	0	7	0	7	1
Johnston, Joel, Pawtucket	1.000	30	0	3	0	3	0
Jones, Calvin, Pawtucket	1.000	33	1	5	0	6	0
Jordan, Ricardo, Syracuse*	1.000	13	1	3	0	4	0
Juden, Jeff, Scr./W.-B.	.769	14	3	7	3	13	1
Karp, Ryan, Scr./W.-B.*	.875	13	2	5	1	8	1
Kerley, Collin, Ottawa	1.000	5	0	3	0	3	0
Kiely, John, Toledo	1.000	14	0	4	0	4	1
King, Richard, Richmond	1.000	14	3	1	0	4	0
Klingenbeck, Scott, Rochester	1.000	8	7	7	0	14	0
Kramer, Tommy, Toledo	1.000	6	2	0	0	2	0
Krivda, Rick, Rochester*	.917	16	2	9	1	12	0
Lane, Aaron, Rochester*	1.000	9	0	2	0	2	0
Layana, Tim, Ottawa	1.000	26	0	2	0	2	1
Lee, Mark, Rochester*	1.000	25	1	1	0	2	0
Leiper, Dave, Ottawa*	1.000	2	0	1	0	1	0
Lemon, Don, Charlotte	1.000	6	0	1	0	1	0
Lewis, Richie, Charlotte	.889	17	1	7	1	9	0
Lima, Jose, Toledo	.929	11	4	9	1	14	1
Lomon, Kevin, Richmond	1.000	32	5	10	0	15	1
Long, Steve, Charlotte	.875	33	5	9	2	16	0
Looney, Brian, Pawtucket*	1.000	18	5	9	0	14	0
Ludwick, Eric, Norfolk	1.000	4	0	2	0	2	0
MacDonald, Bob, Columbus*	1.000	13	1	4	0	5	0
Magrane, Joe, Ottawa*	.929	12	2	11	1	14	0
Mantei, Matt, Charlotte	1.000	6	1	0	0	1	0
Manuel, Barry, Ottawa	1.000	35	5	9	0	14	1
Marshall, Randy, Toledo*	.920	20	4	19	2	25	1
Martel, Ed, Toledo	1.000	4	0	2	0	2	0
Martin, Tom, Richmond*	.667	7	0	2	1	3	0

Player, Team	Pct.	G	PO	A	E	TC	DP
Mathews, Terry, Charlotte	1.000	2	1	0	0	1	0
Maxcy, Brian, Toledo	.833	20	3	2	1	6	0
May, Darrell, Richmond*	.875	9	3	4	1	8	0
McCready, Jim, Norfolk	.917	28	1	10	1	12	1
McDonald, Ben, Rochester	1.000	1	1	1	0	2	0
McGehee, Kevin, Rochester	.885	27	16	7	3	26	1
Mendoza, Ramiro, Columbus	1.000	2	1	0	0	1	0
Menhart, Paul, Syracuse	1.000	10	3	7	0	10	0
Miller, Kurt, Charlotte	1.000	22	5	11	0	16	0
Minutelli, Gino, Richmond*	1.000	5	0	3	0	3	0
Mitchell, John, Ottawa	1.000	6	0	2	0	2	0
Montoya, Al, Syracuse*	1.000	7	3	3	0	6	1
Munoz, Bobby, Scr./W.-B.	1.000	2	1	2	0	3	0
Murphy, Rob, Charlotte*	1.000	3	0	1	0	1	0
Murray, Matt, Richmond	1.000	19	13	7	0	20	1
Mutis, Jeff, Charlotte*	.909	27	2	8	1	11	1
Myers, Jimmy, Rochester	.947	55	6	12	1	19	1
Myers, Mike, Char.-Tol.*	1.000	43	2	5	0	7	0
Newlin, Jim, Charlotte	1.000	5	0	2	0	2	1
Nichols, Rod, Richmond	.857	41	2	4	1	7	0
Ojala, Kirt, Columbus*	.971	32	10	23	1	34	2
Olivares, Omar, Scr./W.-B.	1.000	7	8	6	0	14	1
Oquist, Mike, Rochester	1.000	7	0	2	0	2	0
Osuna, Al, Norfolk*	1.000	14	4	5	0	9	0
Patterson, Jeff, Columbus	1.000	33	5	9	0	14	0
Pavlas, Dave, Columbus	.929	48	3	10	1	14	0
Pena, Jim, Ottawa*	1.000	7	0	2	0	2	0
Perigny, Don, Charlotte	1.000	6	0	1	0	1	0
Person, Robert, Norfolk	1.000	5	1	1	0	2	0
Pettitte, Andy, Columbus*	1.000	2	0	3	0	3	0
Pierce, Jeff, Pawtucket	1.000	23	0	5	0	5	0
Plummer, Dale, Pawtucket	.968	34	12	18	1	31	2
Polley, Dale, Richmond*	.789	47	2	13	4	19	0
Potts, Mike, Richmond*	1.000	38	8	13	0	21	2
Pulsipher, Bill, Norfolk*	.895	13	2	15	2	19	0
Quirico, Rafael, Columbus*	.800	20	1	3	1	5	0
Rapp, Pat, Charlotte	1.000	1	1	1	0	2	0
Rhodes, Arthur, Rochester*	1.000	4	0	6	0	6	1
Ricci, Chuck, Scr./W.-B.	1.000	68	6	12	0	18	1
Rivera, Mariano, Columbus	1.000	7	5	4	0	9	0
Roberts, Chris, Norfolk*	.968	25	7	23	1	31	2
Robinson, Ken, Syracuse	.750	38	0	3	1	4	0
Rodriguez, Frank, Pawtucket	.778	13	1	6	2	9	0
Rogers, Bryan, Norfolk	1.000	56	9	13	0	22	2
Rogers, Jimmy, Syracuse	1.000	38	1	9	0	10	0
Rojas, Euclides, Charlotte	1.000	2	0	1	0	1	0
Rueter, Kirk, Ottawa*	1.000	20	4	31	0	35	2
Rumer, Tim, Columbus*	.944	28	1	16	1	18	0
Ryan, Ken, Pawtucket	1.000	9	2	0	0	2	0
Ryan, Kevin, Rochester	1.000	6	3	3	0	6	0
Sackinsky, Brian, Rochester	1.000	14	3	4	0	7	0
Satre, Jason, Pawtucket	1.000	9	2	4	0	6	0
Scheid, Rich, Charlotte*	.875	19	2	12	2	16	0
Schmidt, Curt, Ottawa	1.000	43	6	8	0	14	1
Schmidt, Jason, Richmond	.950	19	4	15	1	20	0
Seelbach, Chris, Richmond	.917	14	5	6	1	12	2
Segura, Jose, Columbus	.667	11	1	1	1	3	0
Sele, Aaron, Pawtucket	1.000	2	1	1	0	2	0
Seminara, Frank, Rochester	.800	29	1	7	2	10	0
Senior, Shawn, Pawtucket*	1.000	1	2	3	0	5	0
Shea, John, Rochester*	1.000	38	1	4	0	5	0
Shepherd, Keith, Charlotte	1.000	4	1	0	0	1	0
Small, Aaron, Syr.-Char.	1.000	34	0	5	0	5	1
Smith, Daryl, Columbus	1.000	13	5	10	0	15	1
Smith, Pete, Charlotte	.933	10	4	10	1	15	2
Smith, Zane, Pawtucket*	1.000	1	0	2	0	2	1
Sodowsky, Clint, Toledo	1.000	9	5	8	0	13	0
Spencer, Stan, Charlotte	1.000	9	5	3	0	8	0
Spoljaric, Paul, Syracuse*	.882	43	6	9	2	17	1
Spradlin, Jerry, Charlotte	.769	41	4	6	3	13	0
Springer, Dennis, Scr./W.-B.	1.000	30	12	13	0	25	1
Steed, Rick, Syracuse	.875	31	2	5	1	8	0
Stidham, Phil, Norfolk	.762	34	7	9	5	21	1
Suppan, Jeff, Pawtucket	1.000	7	5	4	0	9	0
Sutherland, John, Columbus	1.000	3	1	0	0	1	0
Telgheder, Dave, Norfolk	1.000	29	6	16	0	22	1
Thobe, J.J., Ottawa	1.000	55	8	26	0	34	2
Thobe, Tom, Richmond*	1.000	48	5	11	0	16	0
Thomas, Royal, Richmond	.875	39	12	16	4	32	0
Tilmon, Pat, Syracuse	1.000	4	1	2	0	3	0
Timlin, Mike, Syracuse	1.000	8	0	4	0	4	0
Torres, Ricky, Ottawa	.813	32	4	9	3	16	1
Tranberg, Mark, Scr./W.-B.	1.000	11	3	2	0	5	0
Tunnell, Lee, Toledo	1.000	7	2	1	0	3	0
Urbina, Ugueth, Ottawa	1.000	13	6	8	0	14	0
Valdes, Marc, Charlotte	.972	27	8	27	1	36	1
VanEgmond, Tim, Pawtucket	.941	12	6	10	1	17	0
Wade, Terrell, Richmond*	1.000	24	5	20	0	25	0
Wainhouse, Dave, Syr.-Char.	.800	30	2	6	2	10	0
Wakefield, Tim, Pawtucket	1.000	4	0	4	0	4	0
Walker, Pete, Norfolk	.923	34	6	6	1	13	1
Wallace, Kent, Columbus	.929	9	6	7	1	14	0
Ward, Duane, Syracuse	1.000	6	0	1	0	1	0
Ware, Jeff, Syracuse	.917	16	2	9	1	12	0
Weathers, David, Charlotte	1.000	1	2	1	0	3	0
Weber, Ben, Syracuse	.958	25	12	11	1	24	1
Wegmann, Tom, Rochester	.909	9	1	9	1	11	0
Wengert, Bill, Pawtucket	1.000	7	1	2	0	3	1
Wertz, Bill, Pawtucket	1.000	29	5	8	0	13	1
West, David, Scr./W.-B.*	1.000	1	1	1	0	2	0
Weston, Mickey, Toledo	.978	28	19	25	1	45	0
White, Gabe, Ottawa*	1.000	12	2	4	0	6	0
Whitehurst, Wally, Paw.-Syr.	1.000	12	1	7	0	8	1
Wickander, Kevin, Toledo*	1.000	16	2	2	0	4	1
Wiegandt, Scott, Scr./W.-B.*	1.000	47	2	6	0	8	1
Wiggs, Johnny, Pawtucket*	1.000	14	0	1	0	1	0
Williams, Jimmy, Nor.-Roch.*	.733	32	2	9	4	15	0
Williams, Woody, Syracuse	1.000	5	0	1	0	1	0
Wilson, Paul, Norfolk	1.000	10	4	11	0	15	0
Woodall, Brad, Richmond*	.944	13	5	12	1	18	2
York, Mike, Syracuse	.667	20	2	4	3	9	0
Zimmerman, Mike, Charlotte	.960	31	7	17	1	25	1

PITCHERS WITH TWO OR MORE TEAMS

Player, Team	Pct.	G	PO	A	E	TC	DP
Bark, Brian, Richmond*	1.000	13	2	6	0	8	0
Bark, Brian, Pawtucket*	1.000	30	1	6	0	7	0
Cornelius, Reid, Ottawa	1.000	4	2	3	0	5	0
Cornelius, Reid, Norfolk	1.000	10	4	17	0	21	0
Hartley, Mike, Pawtucket	1.000	26	1	5	0	6	0
Hartley, Mike, Rochester	.000	8	0	0	0	0	0
Myers, Mike, Charlotte*	1.000	37	2	4	0	6	0
Myers, Mike, Toledo*	1.000	6	0	1	0	1	0
Small, Aaron, Syracuse	.000	1	0	0	0	0	0
Small, Aaron, Charlotte	1.000	33	0	5	0	5	1
Wainhouse, Dave, Syracuse	.889	26	2	6	1	9	0
Wainhouse, Dave, Charlotte	.000	4	0	0	1	1	0
Whitehurst, Wally, Pawtucket	1.000	6	0	3	0	3	0
Whitehurst, Wally, Syracuse	1.000	6	1	4	0	5	1
Williams, Jimmy, Norfolk*	.733	27	2	9	4	15	0
Williams, Jimmy, Rochester*	.000	5	0	0	0	0	0

The following players did not have any fielding statistics at the positions indicated or appeared only as a designated hitter, pinch-hitter or pinch-runner: Acevedo, p; Barnwell, p; Bergman, p; Bowen, p; Brooks, of; Canseco, dh; Capra, p; Chavez, p; Clemens, p; Crowley, p; Dascenzo, p; E. Diaz, 3b; Engle, p; Finnvold, p; Frey, p; Fuller, p; Gonzales, of; Greenwell, dh; Heffernan, p; Juhl, p; Kamieniecki, p; Knapp, 3b; Langbehn, p; Lemp, p; S. Lewis, p; Livesey, 1b; Magee, p; Melendez, p; Mills, p; Montalvo, of; Musset, p; Pacheco, p; Paxton, p; A. Pena, p; Reed, p; Robertson, p; H. Rodriguez, dh; Santos, p; Schall, 3b; Shumpert, of; S. Springer, ss; Stoddard, p; Twardoski, of; Veres, p; M. Williams, p; Zupcic, 3b.

LEAGUE CHAMPIONS

Year	Team	Pct.	Year	Team	Pct.	Year	Team	Pct.
1884—	Trenton	.520	1892—	Providence	.615	1900—	Providence	.616
1885—	Syracuse	.584		Binghamton*	.667	1901—	Rochester	.642
1886—	Utica	.646	1893—	Erie	.606	1902—	Toronto	.669
1887—	Toronto	.644	1894—	Providence	.696	1903—	Jersey City	.742
1888—	Syracuse	.723	1895—	Springfield	.687	1904—	Buffalo	.657
1889—	Detroit	.649	1896—	Providence	.602	1905—	Providence	.638
1890—	Detroit	.617	1897—	Syracuse	.632	1906—	Buffalo	.607
1891—	Buffalo (reg. season)	.727	1898—	Montreal	.586	1907—	Toronto	.619
	Buffalo (supplemental)	.680	1899—	Rochester	.624	1908—	Baltimore	.593

Year	Team	Pct.
1909—	Rochester	.596
1910—	Rochester	.601
1911—	Rochester	.645
1912—	Toronto	.595
1913—	Newark	.625
1914—	Providence	.617
1915—	Buffalo	.632
1916—	Buffalo	.586
1917—	Toronto	.604
1918—	Toronto	.693
1919—	Baltimore	.671
1920—	Baltimore	.719
1921—	Baltimore	.717
1922—	Baltimore	.689
1923—	Baltimore	.677
1924—	Baltimore	.709
1925—	Baltimore	.633
1926—	Toronto	.657
1927—	Buffalo	.667
1928—	Rochester	.549
1929—	Rochester	.613
1930—	Rochester	.629
1931—	Rochester	.601
1932—	Newark	.649
1933—	Newark	.622
	Buffalo (4th)†	.494
1934—	Newark	.608
	Toronto (3rd)†	.559
1935—	Montreal	.597
	Syracuse (2nd)†	.565
1936—	Buffalo‡	.610
1937—	Newark‡	.717
1938—	Newark‡	.684
1939—	Jersey City	.582
	Rochester (2nd)†	.556
1940—	Rochester	.611
	Newark (2nd)†	.594
1941—	Newark	.649
	Montreal (2nd)†	.584
1942—	Newark	.601
	Syracuse (3rd)†	.513
1943—	Toronto	.625
	Syracuse (3rd)†	.536
1944—	Baltimore‡	.553
1945—	Montreal	.621
	Newark (2nd)†	.582
1946—	Montreal‡	.649
1947—	Jersey City	.610
	Syracuse (3rd)†	.575
1948—	Montreal‡	.614
1949—	Buffalo	.584
	Montreal (3rd)†	.545
1950—	Rochester	.609
	Baltimore (3rd)†	.556
1951—	Montreal‡	.617
1952—	Montreal	.629
	Rochester (3rd)†	.619
1953—	Rochester	.630
	Montreal (2nd)†	.586
1954—	Toronto	.630
	Syracuse (4th)§	.510
1955—	Montreal	.617
	Rochester (4th)†	.497
1956—	Toronto	.566
	Rochester (2nd)†	.553
1957—	Toronto	.575
	Buffalo (2nd)†	.571
1958—	Montreal‡	.588
1959—	Buffalo	.582
	Havana (3rd)†	.523
1960—	Toronto‡	.649
1961—	Columbus	.597
	Buffalo (3rd)†	.559
1962—	Jacksonville	.610
	Atlanta (3rd)†	.539
1963—	Syracuse∞	.533
	Indianapolis‡	.562
1964—	Jacksonville	.589
	Rochester (4th)†	.532
1965—	Columbus	.582
	Toronto (3rd)†	.556
1966—	Rochester	.565
	Toronto (2nd-tied)†	.558
1967—	Richmond	.574
	Toledo (3rd)†	.525
1968—	Toledo	.565
	Jacksonville (4th)†	.514
1969—	Tidewater	.563
	Syracuse (3rd)†	.536
1970—	Syracuse‡	.600
1971—	Rochester‡	.614
1972—	Louisville	.563
	Tidewater (3rd)†	.545
1973—	Charleston	.586
	Pawtucket▲†	.534
1974—	Memphis	.613
	Rochester ∞‡	.611
1975—	Tidewater‡	.610
1976—	Rochester	.638
	Syracuse (2nd)†	.590
1977—	Pawtucket	.571
	Charleston (2nd)‡	.557
1978—	Charleston	.607
	Richmond (4th)†	.511
1979—	Columbus‡	.612
1980—	Columbus‡	.593
1981—	Columbus‡	.633
1982—	Richmond	.590
	Tidewater (3rd)†	.540
1983—	Columbus	.593
	Tidewater (4th)†	.511
1984—	Columbus	.590
	Pawtucket (4th)†	.536
1985—	Syracuse	.564
	Tidewater (4th)†	.540
1986—	Richmond‡	.571
1987—	Tidewater	.579
	Columbus†	.550
1988—	Rochester◆	.546
	Tidewater	.546
1989—	Syracuse	.572
	Richmond◆	.555
1990—	Rochester◆	.614
	Columbus	.596
1991—	Columbus◆	.590
	Pawtucket	.552
1992—	Columbus◆	.660
	Scr. W.B.	.592
1993—	Charlotte◆	.610
	Rochester	.525
1994—	Richmond◆	.567
	Pawtucket	.549
1995—	Norfolk	.606
	Ottawa◆	.507

*Won split-season playoff. †Won four-team playoff. ‡Won championship and four-team playoff. §Defeated Havana in game to decide fourth place, then won four-team playoff. ∞League was divided into Northern, Southern divisions. ▲League divided into American, National divisions. ◆League divided into Eastern, Western divisions; won playoffs. (NOTE—Known as Eastern League in 1884, New York State League in 1885, International League in 1886-87, International Association in 1888, International League in 1889-90, Eastern Association in 1891 and Eastern League from 1892 until 1912.)

MEXICAN LEAGUE

1995 FINAL STANDINGS

FIRST HALF

NORTHERN ZONE

Team	W	L	T	Pct.	GB
Reynosa	39	19	1	.672	....
Saltillo	34	25	0	.576	5½
Monterrey	31	27	1	.597	8
Aguascalientes	30	28	0	.517	9
Nuevo Laredo	27	32	0	.458	12½
Monclova	26	33	0	.441	13½
Torreon	22	36	1	.379	17
Jalisco	19	39	1	.328	20

SOUTHERN ZONE

Team	W	L	T	Pct.	GB
Mexico City Red Devils	39	18	1	.684	....
Mexico City Tigers	33	26	0	.559	7
Campeche	32	27	0	.542	8
Tabasco	30	27	2	.526	9
Puebla	29	29	1	.500	10½
Yucatan	28	30	1	.483	11½
Aguila	26	33	0	.441	14
Minatitlan	21	37	1	.362	18½

SECOND HALF

NORTHERN ZONE

Team	W	L	T	Pct.	GB
Reynosa	34	21	2	.618	....
Torreon	34	21	1	.618	....
Nuevo Laredo	35	22	0	.614	....
Monterrey	34	22	1	.607	½
Saltillo	29	28	0	.509	6
Aguascalientes	27	27	2	.500	6½
Monclova	20	36	1	.357	14½
Jalisco	11	43	1	.204	22½

SOUTHERN ZONE

Team	W	L	T	Pct.	GB
Mexico City Red Devils	41	15	0	.732	....
Tabasco	31	23	2	.574	9
Yucatan	31	25	0	.554	10
Campeche	28	27	1	.5090	12½
Mexico City Tigers	29	28	0	.5087	12½
Puebla	23	34	0	.404	18½
Minatitlan	20	36	1	.357	21
Aguila	19	38	0	.333	22½

COMPOSITE

NORTHERN ZONE

Team	W	L	T	Pct.	GB
Reynosa	73	40	3	.646	....
Monterrey	65	49	2	.570	8½
Saltillo	63	53	0	.543	11½
Nuevo Laredo	62	54	0	.534	12½
Aguascalientes	57	55	2	.509	15½
Torreon	56	57	2	.496	17
Monclova	46	69	1	.400	28
Jalisco	30	82	2	.268	42½

SOUTHERN ZONE

Team	W	L	T	Pct.	GB
Mexico City Red Devils	80	33	1	.708	....
Tabasco	61	50	4	.550	18
Mexico City Tigers	62	54	0	.534	19½
Campeche	60	54	1	.526	20½
Yucatan	59	55	1	.518	21½
Puebla	52	63	1	.452	29
Aguila	45	71	0	.388	36½
Minatitlan	41	73	2	.360	39½

PLAYOFFS—Reynosa defeated Nuevo Laredo, four games to three; Monterrey defeated Saltillo, four games to one, in Northern Zone first round. Mexico City Red Devils defeated Campeche, four games to two; Mexico City Tigers defeated Tabasco, four games to one, in Southern Zone first round. Monterrey defeated Reynosa, four games to two, in Northern Zone finals; Mexico City Red Devils defeated Mexico City Tigers, four games to two, in Southern Zone finals. Monterrey defeated Mexico City Red Devils, four games to none, in final series to capture league championship.

(Compiled by Ana Luisa Perea Talarico, League Statistician, Mexico, D.F.)

1995 BATTING

TEAM

Team	Avg.	G	TPA	AB	R	H	TB	2B	3B	HR	RBI	SH	SF	HP	BB	IBB	SO	SB	CS	GDP	LOB	ShO	Slg.	OBP
M.C. Red Devils	.317	114	4195	3683	660	1166	1680	173	22	99	609	40	38	27	407	42	397	84	45	81	804	4	.456	.385
Reynosa	.304	116	4424	3815	680	1160	1626	201	35	65	616	45	51	42	471	31	524	14	21	138	851	3	.426	.382
Monterrey	.301	116	4280	3720	566	1118	1597	193	38	70	524	52	29	24	455	28	516	100	61	124	849	6	.429	.378
Torreon	.295	115	4214	3669	588	1081	1571	160	36	86	520	78	31	37	399	25	516	47	33	109	803	7	.428	.367
Aguascalientes	.295	114	4177	3629	571	1072	1534	162	33	78	522	61	43	48	396	37	481	45	34	102	804	5	.423	.368
M.C. Tigers	.293	116	4261	3681	646	1080	1682	162	37	122	587	56	32	26	466	26	567	85	50	78	790	7	.457	.374
Puebla	.285	116	4074	3602	531	1025	1435	176	24	62	486	52	32	38	350	25	515	34	25	115	754	10	.398	.351
Saltillo	.278	116	4363	3725	578	1036	1544	178	39	84	524	63	31	30	514	33	604	56	34	98	887	3	.414	.367
Tabasco	.275	115	4088	3581	444	983	1333	157	26	47	403	72	25	30	380	40	484	45	39	117	827	12	.372	.347
Campeche	.273	115	4030	3459	454	944	1287	142	15	57	401	78	24	30	439	27	521	101	69	119	779	12	.372	.358
Monclova	.273	116	4161	3633	475	993	1350	137	35	50	443	66	40	28	394	22	446	49	45	100	804	13	.372	.346
Jalisco	.273	114	4065	3531	445	964	1288	166	13	44	392	48	39	37	410	24	530	45	51	133	792	7	.365	.351
Yucatan	.272	115	4204	3494	519	951	1326	139	22	64	474	84	29	38	559	32	462	45	26	120	875	6	.380	.376
Nuevo Laredo	.270	116	4280	3728	500	1005	1404	151	16	72	455	61	24	54	413	26	514	41	41	120	852	8	.377	.349
Aguila	.250	116	4089	3572	356	893	1134	120	17	29	303	83	29	32	373	32	472	55	26	88	802	19	.317	.324
Minatitlan	.249	116	4099	3627	343	904	1179	128	9	43	315	69	24	31	348	23	420	22	24	111	794	23	.325	.318

INDIVIDUAL

TOP QUALIFIERS FOR BATTING CHAMPIONSHIP

Minimum 313 plate appearances.

Player, Team	Avg.	G	TPA	AB	R	H	TB	2B	3B	HR	RBI	SH	SF	HP	BB	IBB	SO	SB	CS	GDP	Slg.	OBP
Gainey, Ty, MCRD	.411	86	352	285	69	117	221	19	2	27	115	0	2	1	64	13	44	4	0	6	.775	.517
Canizalez, Juan C., Mont	.358	104	414	386	58	138	183	14	5	7	54	2	3	3	20	0	33	8	10	11	.474	.391
Mendez, Jesus, Agu.-Tab	.356	113	460	399	54	142	181	21	3	4	54	5	1	0	55	13	17	2	2	12	.454	.433

Player, Team	Avg.	G	TPA	AB	R	H	TB	2B	3B	HR	RBI	SH	SF	HP	BB	IBB	SO	SB	CS	GDP	Slg.	OBP
Casillas, Adam, Rey.	.356	102	448	382	82	136	170	22	3	2	53	1	8	5	52	5	13	0	5	20	.445	.432
Garcia, Cornelio, Mont.	.348	104	451	391	83	136	188	24	11	2	47	4	3	1	52	2	51	34	17	6	.481	.423
Romero, Oscar, Tab.	.344	115	482	410	72	141	195	24	0	10	47	11	1	2	58	5	42	10	6	19	.476	.427
Tolentino, Jose, Mont.	.342	83	346	304	49	104	176	24	0	16	79	1	2	2	37	6	37	1	2	15	.579	.414
Gonzalez, Denio, Sal.	.341	109	459	384	74	131	228	23	1	24	95	0	4	1	70	2	55	4	3	9	.594	.440
Rivera, German, Pue.	.340	110	430	344	59	117	170	19	2	10	53	4	3	2	77	10	43	3	0	10	.494	.460
Arredondo, Luis A., MCRD	.340	112	485	421	90	143	192	19	3	8	58	4	5	1	54	3	49	15	7	7	.456	.412

DEPARTMENTAL LEADERS: G—Several players tied with 116; AB—Iturbe, 440; R—J. Robles, 93; H—Tellez, 144; 2B—A. Jimenez, 40; 3B—Co. Garcia, F. Villegas, 11; HR—Gainey, 27; RBI—Gainey, 115; SH—Luna, 21; SF—J. Castillo, 10; HP—G. Sanchez, 19; BB—R. Torres, 96; IBB—G. Wright, 14; SO—B. Castillo, 84; SB—Brinkley, 55; CS—Brinkley, 23; GIDP—Three players tied with 20; Slg.—Gainey, .775.

ALL PLAYERS

Player, Team	Avg.	G	TPA	AB	R	H	TB	2B	3B	HR	RBI	SH	SF	HP	BB	IBB	SO	SB	CS	GDP	Slg.	OBP
Abrego, Jesus, Jal.	.258	99	415	353	55	91	120	19	2	2	27	4	3	3	52	2	47	7	13	15	.340	.355
Aganza, Ruben, Monc.	.296	116	476	412	66	122	201	24	2	17	66	2	5	2	55	4	31	0	1	12	.488	.378
Agramon, Antonio, Jal.	.244	41	145	131	16	32	54	7	0	5	21	3	1	1	9	1	36	1	0	5	.412	.296
Aguilar, Enrique, Ags.	.325	113	455	428	59	139	207	21	1	15	74	3	3	4	17	2	22	2	5	13	.484	.354
Aguilera, Armando, Sal.	.000	13	9	9	0	0	0	0	0	0	0	0	0	0	0	0	3	0	0	0	.000	.000
Almeida, Shammar, Sal.	.272	97	350	287	43	78	128	6	1	14	42	3	4	7	49	6	79	0	2	5	.446	.386
Almendra, Gregorio, Tab.	.167	26	40	36	5	6	9	0	0	1	2	1	1	0	2	1	10	0	0	2	.250	.205
Alverez, Hector, Pue.	.295	116	474	413	77	122	160	27	1	3	58	9	6	2	44	1	56	5	2	13	.387	.361
Alvarez, Ivan, Jal.	.250	2	4	4	0	1	1	0	0	0	0	0	0	0	0	0	2	0	0	0	.250	.250
Alvarez, Luis, Jal.	.372	24	84	78	11	29	39	8	1	0	7	0	0	0	6	0	8	1	1	1	.500	.417
Ansley, Willie, Agu.	.282	30	121	103	14	29	38	5	2	0	6	1	1	0	16	2	31	5	1	6	.369	.375
Arano, Wilfrido, N.L.	.333	13	16	12	5	4	7	1	1	0	2	0	0	1	3	0	2	2	0	0	.583	.500
Arauz, Ignacio, Monc.	.226	46	119	106	10	24	31	4	0	1	13	2	2	0	9	1	30	0	1	4	.292	.282
Arce, Francisco J., Min.	.304	90	331	303	18	92	115	17	0	2	28	4	3	1	20	2	21	0	0	14	.380	.346
Arevalo, Guadalupe, Ags.	.321	66	181	162	27	52	64	8	2	0	13	2	0	0	17	2	14	2	1	3	.395	.385
Arias, Everardo, Pue.	.205	49	154	127	17	26	34	4	2	0	12	4	2	0	21	0	31	1	0	1	.268	.313
Arredondo, Hernando, Pue.	.291	77	171	158	16	46	52	4	1	0	12	2	1	1	9	1	25	1	2	4	.329	.331
Arredondo, Jesus A., Ags.	.322	113	486	388	79	125	157	16	8	0	49	10	3	13	72	0	37	7	4	10	.405	.441
Arredondo, Luis A., MCRD	.340	112	485	421	90	143	192	19	3	8	58	4	5	1	54	3	49	15	7	7	.456	.412
Arvizu, Javier, Cam.	.307	100	348	287	35	88	116	18	2	2	27	3	2	2	54	2	45	4	6	9	.404	.417
Arzate, Martin, Jal.	.230	80	209	178	17	41	48	5	1	0	20	5	6	1	19	0	19	1	3	12	.270	.299
Avila, Roberto, Min.	.125	7	11	8	1	1	1	0	0	0	0	1	0	0	2	0	3	0	0	0	.125	.300
Avila, Ruben, Tor.	.270	114	456	403	58	109	175	19	1	15	63	6	6	3	38	2	70	3	2	9	.434	.333
Ayala, Armenta M., Monc.	.200	4	6	5	1	1	1	0	0	0	0	1	0	0	0	0	1	0	0	0	.200	.200
Balderas, S. Abelardo, Min.	.183	61	121	104	12	19	20	1	0	0	10	2	3	0	12	0	20	0	0	3	.192	.261
Barrera, Jesus A., Min.	.294	5	17	17	0	5	5	0	0	0	0	0	0	0	0	0	3	0	0	0	.294	.294
Barrera, Nelson, MCRD	.292	93	327	298	38	87	155	17	0	17	71	4	2	4	19	5	43	0	0	12	.520	.341
Bellazetin, Jose Juan, MCT	.192	9	38	26	8	5	5	0	0	0	2	0	1	0	11	0	3	0	1	0	.192	.421
Beltran, Gerardo, Min.	.253	85	293	265	22	67	95	11	1	5	22	6	0	4	18	2	28	1	4	6	.358	.310
Brinkley, Darrell, Cam.	.338	106	446	397	79	134	203	26	2	13	50	3	4	5	37	4	38	55	23	10	.511	.397
Brumley, Duff, Mont.-Ags.	.000	1	0	0	0	0	0	0	0	0	0	0	0	0	0	0	0	0	0	0	.000	.000
Burguillos, Carlos M., Min.	.252	98	377	337	41	85	115	14	2	4	35	7	2	1	30	1	20	10	4	10	.341	.314
Cabreja, Alexis, Pue.	.297	59	226	212	42	63	84	10	4	1	19	0	1	4	9	1	17	9	5	3	.396	.336
Cairo, Sergio, Yuc.	.313	58	221	195	26	61	81	2	0	6	35	5	3	0	18	1	21	3	1	6	.415	.366
Camacho, Adulfo, Yuc.	.245	113	478	372	69	91	118	14	2	3	34	20	2	8	76	0	47	4	7	9	.317	.382
Campos, Oscar, Agu.	.250	11	12	12	2	3	3	0	0	0	0	0	0	0	0	0	5	0	0	0	.250	.250
Canizalez, Juan C., Mont.	.358	104	414	386	58	138	183	14	5	7	54	2	3	3	20	0	33	8	10	11	.474	.391
Cano, Jose, Ags.	.000	1	1	1	0	0	0	0	0	0	0	0	0	0	0	0	0	0	0	0	.000	.000
Cantu, Gerardo, Pue.	.214	72	146	126	13	27	41	2	0	4	19	0	2	1	17	2	23	0	1	6	.325	.308
Caraballo, Gari, Mont.	.304	26	93	79	11	24	38	5	0	3	15	1	0	1	12	0	19	0	1	3	.481	.402
Carrasco, Ernesto, N.L.	.259	113	430	378	43	98	113	13	1	0	27	5	2	4	41	5	47	9	9	11	.299	.336
Carrillo, Matias, MCT	.331	97	398	338	81	112	194	14	4	20	78	2	3	3	52	7	43	20	7	8	.574	.422
Carter, Steve, Monc.	.273	14	50	44	5	12	16	1	0	1	7	0	0	0	6	0	1	0	0	1	.364	.360
Casillas, Adam, Rey.	.356	102	448	382	82	136	170	22	3	2	53	1	8	5	52	5	13	0	5	20	.445	.432
Castaldo, Vince, Cam.	.250	40	155	132	21	33	56	6	1	5	22	0	0	1	22	1	23	3	2	4	.424	.361
Castaneda, Nick, Yuc.	.395	14	56	43	7	17	26	4	1	1	9	0	2	0	11	2	7	0	0	1	.605	.500
Castaneda, Rafael, N.L.	.278	116	468	406	52	113	150	16	3	5	43	8	3	2	49	3	42	5	6	20	.369	.357
Castillo, Braulio, Rey.	.312	95	416	356	77	111	200	30	7	15	81	0	4	4	52	1	84	3	1	16	.562	.401
Castillo, Juan, Ags.	.335	106	456	376	73	126	179	16	8	7	58	10	10	2	58	5	58	6	3	14	.476	.417
Castro, Arnoldo, Min.	.253	109	438	380	39	96	119	9	1	4	32	19	0	3	36	0	24	2	2	11	.313	.322
Castro, Eddie, Min.-Sal.	.246	59	243	191	16	47	63	7	0	3	24	0	2	3	47	5	38	0	0	4	.330	.399
Castro, Leonel, Jal.	.000	3	4	4	0	0	0	0	0	0	0	0	0	0	0	0	2	0	0	1	.000	.000
Cazarin, Manuel, Agu.	.244	113	422	386	28	94	130	22	1	4	38	7	4	4	21	4	16	2	1	13	.337	.287
Canedo, Alberto, Cam.	.179	36	48	39	7	7	12	2	0	1	4	2	0	1	6	0	12	0	1	1	.308	.304
Cecena, Manuel, Min.	.273	3	11	11	2	3	3	0	0	0	1	0	0	0	0	0	1	0	0	0	.273	.273
Cervera, Francisco, Jal.	.263	95	342	274	47	72	103	13	3	4	31	3	5	10	50	5	59	4	5	6	.376	.389
Chan, Armando, Monc.	.274	81	228	201	31	55	70	8	2	1	19	3	1	0	23	1	35	0	1	5	.348	.347
Clement, Wes, Ags.	.167	9	33	30	2	5	6	1	0	0	3	0	0	0	3	0	11	0	0	1	.200	.242
Cobos, Rogelio, MCRD	.200	7	6	5	1	1	1	0	0	0	0	0	0	0	1	0	2	0	1	0	.200	.333
Contreras, Cuitlahuac, Tor.-Monc.	.202	39	113	94	10	19	31	1	1	3	12	1	1	2	15	4	28	2	1	1	.330	.321
Cornejo, Edgar, Sal.	.183	41	111	93	12	17	21	2	1	0	8	0	0	0	18	0	15	0	1	1	.226	.315
Corrales, Virgilio, N.L.	.111	15	20	18	2	2	4	2	0	0	3	0	0	0	2	0	4	0	0	1	.222	.200
Cruz, Luis Alfonso, Rey.	.301	108	450	418	64	126	190	26	1	12	80	2	8	6	16	2	37	1	0	19	.455	.330
Cruz, Marco Antonio, N.L.	.240	115	392	333	32	80	106	12	1	4	36	11	1	11	36	0	64	0	1	7	.318	.333
Cueto, Raul, Tab.	.100	5	11	10	2	1	1	0	0	0	0	0	0	1	0	0	2	0	0	1	.100	.182
Cuevas, Angelo, Tab.-Min.	.270	104	418	371	44	100	137	14	1	7	33	5	2	0	40	5	31	2	7	10	.369	.339
Dattola, Kevin, Tor.	.265	29	130	117	15	31	41	2	1	2	13	1	0	1	11	1	15	3	1	4	.350	.333
Delgado, Tomas, Tab.	.284	28	79	67	13	19	28	1	1	2	6	1	0	0	11	0	8	0	1	2	.418	.385
DeLima, Rafael, Tab.	.300	72	303	257	40	77	93	12	2	0	15	4	2	1	39	9	35	10	5	4	.362	.391

Player, Team	Avg.	G	TPA	AB	R	H	TB	2B	3B	HR	RBI	SH	SF	HP	BB	IBB	SO	SB	CS	GDP	Slg.	OBP
Diaz, Luis Fernando, MCT	.311	95	333	267	49	83	124	12	4	7	47	6	0	1	59	4	47	7	5	5	.464	.437
Diaz, Remigio, Mont.	.233	95	290	258	24	60	79	4	6	1	20	6	1	0	25	0	28	5	2	14	.306	.299
Dominguez, David, MCT-Min.	.297	88	332	263	36	78	118	11	1	9	37	4	3	0	62	0	46	1	3	6	.449	.427
Dominguez, Fausto, Tab.	.000	3	5	5	0	0	0	0	0	0	0	0	0	0	0	0	4	0	0	1	.000	.000
Duarte C., Rene, Min.	.264	74	213	197	23	52	65	7	0	2	16	4	1	3	8	0	23	2	1	6	.330	.301
Duran, Felipe, MCRD	.279	54	148	136	29	38	47	6	0	1	11	0	2	4	6	0	10	2	2	1	.346	.324
Elvira, Ramon H., Tab.	.000	2	2	2	0	0	0	0	0	0	0	0	0	0	0	0	1	0	0	0	.000	.000
Enriquez, Graciano, Ags.	.288	65	245	219	36	63	85	9	2	3	19	3	1	2	20	1	52	5	3	2	.388	.351
Enriquez, Martin, Ags.	.000	1	1	1	0	0	0	0	0	0	0	0	0	0	0	0	1	0	0	0	.000	.000
Escalante, Marcelo, Sal.	.245	83	240	220	19	54	77	10	2	3	29	5	3	2	10	1	63	1	0	7	.350	.281
Espinoza, Javier, Cam.	.247	83	257	198	24	49	61	7	1	1	19	8	3	2	46	5	24	2	3	4	.308	.390
Espinoza, Jose M., Monc.	.229	45	114	105	9	24	27	3	0	0	9	0	1	1	7	0	20	0	0	3	.257	.281
Esquer, Ramon, Rey.	.289	86	357	287	52	83	111	11	7	1	40	6	4	3	57	2	50	3	2	1	.387	.407
Estrada, Hector, Pue.	.313	116	450	418	51	131	187	23	0	11	78	1	7	2	22	3	47	1	4	17	.447	.345
Estrada, Ricardo, Min.-Agu.	.206	46	122	107	10	22	30	5	0	1	8	3	1	0	11	1	27	0	0	3	.280	.277
Estrada, Ruben, N.L.	.232	84	195	168	20	39	43	4	0	0	16	3	0	2	22	3	20	2	2	4	.256	.328
Fariss, Monty, Mont.	.259	43	144	112	20	29	45	7	0	3	14	0	0	1	31	1	26	1	0	3	.402	.424
Felix, Arturo, Yuc.	.246	107	391	333	42	82	102	14	3	0	32	6	2	3	47	1	50	7	1	13	.306	.343
Fentanes, Oscar, Tab.	.311	100	374	341	33	106	146	11	4	7	51	6	3	5	19	1	42	1	3	9	.428	.353
Fernandez, Carlos, Jal.	.260	13	54	50	5	13	21	2	0	2	7	0	0	1	3	0	16	0	0	0	.420	.315
Fernandez, Daniel, MCRD	.316	106	466	386	89	122	168	14	7	6	45	6	1	4	69	4	24	23	9	3	.435	.424
Fernandez, Fabian, Rey.	.200	6	11	10	2	2	3	1	0	0	0	0	0	0	1	0	1	0	0	1	.300	.273
Flores, Miguel, Mont.	.292	36	152	120	20	35	48	8	1	1	18	6	1	2	23	2	17	8	2	3	.400	.411
Franco, Manuel, Mont.	.280	72	245	225	29	63	94	14	4	3	41	1	5	3	11	0	49	7	6	9	.418	.316
Franklin, Jay, Mont.-Ags.	.000	1	0	0	1	0	0	0	0	0	0	0	0	0	0	0	0	0	0	0	.000	.000
Gainey, Ty, MCRD	.411	86	352	285	69	117	221	19	2	27	115	0	2	1	64	13	44	4	0	6	.775	.517
Gamboa, Jose A., Agu.	.234	81	235	205	20	48	64	6	2	2	15	4	1	5	20	1	24	2	2	5	.312	.316
Garcia, Carlos, Agu.	.207	97	297	246	31	51	62	8	0	1	14	11	1	2	37	1	48	3	3	3	.252	.315
Garcia, Cornelio, Mont.	.348	104	451	391	83	136	188	24	11	2	47	4	3	1	52	2	51	34	17	6	.481	.423
Garcia, Hector, Tor.	.294	109	464	405	60	119	144	11	7	0	42	13	3	4	39	0	43	11	6	18	.356	.359
Garcia, Heriberto, Agu.	.284	115	478	433	55	123	143	7	5	1	25	13	1	3	28	1	29	14	4	10	.330	.331
Garcia, Jose Luis, Mont.	.286	4	17	14	1	4	4	0	0	0	5	0	0	1	2	0	5	0	0	0	.286	.412
Garcia, Rosario, Rey.	.100	12	13	10	3	1	1	0	0	0	1	1	0	0	2	0	6	0	0	0	.100	.250
Garza, Gerardo, Tor.	.326	111	399	350	57	114	156	15	0	9	44	11	1	5	32	4	30	6	6	7	.446	.389
Garzon, Eliseo, Tab.	.223	100	350	292	31	65	97	11	0	7	37	9	3	3	43	3	49	0	2	3	.332	.326
Gastelum, Carlos, Min.	.239	59	178	163	11	39	42	3	0	0	1	5	0	2	8	0	25	1	0	2	.258	.283
Gastelum G., Sergio O., MCT	.000	3	4	3	0	0	0	0	0	0	0	1	0	0	0	0	2	0	0	0	.000	.000
Gavia, Jesus, Agu.-Min.	.237	52	141	131	10	31	42	2	0	3	12	0	1	2	7	0	21	0	0	5	.321	.284
Gil, Geronimo, MCRD	.286	4	7	7	1	2	2	0	0	0	0	0	0	0	0	0	1	0	0	0	.286	.286
Gonzalez, Denio, Sal.	.341	109	459	384	74	131	228	23	1	24	95	0	4	1	70	2	55	4	3	9	.594	.440
Gonzalez, Jesus, Jal.	.254	104	390	347	43	88	122	13	0	7	36	3	3	3	34	2	33	1	5	11	.352	.323
Gonzalez, Jose, Mont.	.313	103	427	368	74	115	188	23	4	14	67	1	4	2	52	3	61	19	7	15	.511	.397
Gonzalez, Pedro, Sal.	.217	33	93	69	19	15	32	2	3	3	9	2	0	3	19	1	20	4	0	2	.464	.407
Guerrero, Francisco, Tor.	.267	85	335	270	44	72	90	12	3	0	33	8	4	4	49	0	31	4	1	8	.333	.382
Guerrero, Jaime, Ags.	.235	72	232	217	23	51	74	9	1	4	22	4	0	1	10	0	50	2	2	5	.341	.272
Guerrero, Javier, Ags.	.251	75	240	203	30	51	85	9	2	7	27	4	0	1	32	4	51	3	1	5	.419	.356
Guizar, Hector, Cam.	.247	101	309	279	28	69	83	10	2	0	24	6	3	1	20	0	32	3	4	17	.297	.297
Gutierrez, Andres, Pue.	.196	54	108	97	16	19	25	4	1	0	6	3	0	0	8	0	16	1	0	1	.258	.257
Gutierrez, Arturo, Agu.	.000	1	0	0	0	0	0	0	0	0	0	0	0	0	0	0	0	0	0	0	.000	.000
Gutierrez, Felipe, Monc.	.205	20	49	44	6	9	17	2	0	2	7	0	2	1	2	0	8	0	0	1	.386	.245
Gutierrez, Jose Luis, Agu.	.247	90	263	227	18	56	65	6	0	1	21	4	3	7	22	1	34	0	1	7	.286	.328
Guzman, Marco A., Yuc.	.269	100	360	316	28	85	109	15	0	3	43	8	0	1	35	3	27	1	0	18	.345	.344
Harris, Donald, Agu.-Monc.	.271	53	216	188	26	51	90	7	4	8	31	2	2	4	20	0	45	5	3	4	.479	.350
Heath, Robert Lee, MCT	.321	99	329	305	40	98	126	12	5	2	30	1	3	4	16	0	52	10	7	4	.413	.360
Hecht, Steve, Monc.	.333	5	19	18	2	6	6	0	0	0	2	0	0	0	1	0	4	1	1	0	.333	.368
Hernandez, Miguel, Agu.	.257	59	178	152	10	39	42	3	0	0	9	11	1	1	13	0	14	1	0	2	.276	.317
Hernandez A., Martin, Cam.	.287	51	107	101	9	29	43	2	0	4	15	1	0	0	5	0	25	2	1	0	.426	.321
Hernandez B., Juan C., Pue.	.167	42	80	66	15	11	15	4	0	0	3	2	0	3	9	0	12	2	1	3	.227	.295
Hernandez W., Ger'do, Min.	.216	80	244	218	21	47	63	14	1	0	12	3	0	6	17	0	50	2	1	4	.289	.290
Herrera, Isidro, Cam.	.246	108	448	349	51	86	97	11	0	0	23	16	1	4	78	2	31	18	9	10	.278	.389
Horn, Sam, MCRD	.316	11	46	38	9	12	22	1	0	3	12	0	1	0	7	1	11	0	0	1	.579	.413
Housie, Wayne, Yuc.	.239	46	206	184	27	44	64	5	6	1	21	2	3	0	17	1	26	6	3	4	.348	.299
Howell, Patrick, MCT	.321	87	363	336	63	108	137	9	7	2	22	4	0	3	20	0	51	23	10	2	.408	.365
Hurst, Jonathan, Jal.-Mont.	.000	1	0	0	1	0	0	0	0	0	0	0	0	0	0	0	0	0	0	0	.000	.000
Hurtado, Hector, Mont.	.245	70	192	163	13	40	48	5	0	1	18	4	1	2	22	3	28	0	2	8	.294	.340
Infante, Alexis, Tab.	.299	95	394	354	52	106	122	10	3	0	26	8	4	4	24	1	25	3	3	15	.345	.347
Iturbe, Pedro, Pue.	.323	113	474	440	77	142	185	21	8	2	61	10	1	5	18	1	54	4	4	10	.420	.356
Jelks, Greg, Cam.	.211	54	206	175	20	37	66	6	1	7	29	1	1	3	26	1	32	5	5	9	.377	.322
Jeter, Shawn, Sal.	.337	24	96	89	17	30	43	4	3	1	7	1	0	0	6	0	15	4	3	1	.483	.379
Jimenez, Alfonso, Sal.	.337	112	475	398	79	134	200	40	4	6	59	7	5	1	64	2	47	6	2	6	.503	.425
Jimenez, Eduardo, Yuc.	.316	115	463	373	67	118	222	26	3	24	90	3	4	4	79	12	53	4	0	15	.595	.437
Jimenez, Ulises, Jal.	.233	30	93	86	7	20	22	2	0	0	7	4	0	0	3	0	12	1	2	2	.256	.258
Laurencio, Rodfer, Cam.	.182	10	22	22	2	4	4	0	0	0	0	0	0	0	0	0	5	0	0	2	.182	.182
Leal, Jose Guadalupe, Cam.	.269	100	344	308	37	83	111	12	2	4	51	6	3	0	27	2	62	1	7	5	.360	.325
Leyva, German, Monc.	.285	104	473	358	49	102	128	13	2	3	39	11	2	52	50	4	31	3	2	7	.358	.442
Lopez, Alfredo, Jal.	.293	26	104	92	11	27	34	4	0	1	11	1	2	2	7	0	12	2	1	2	.370	.350
Lopez, Fabian, MCRD	.214	9	15	14	2	3	3	0	0	0	1	0	0	0	1	0	1	1	0	0	.214	.267
Lopez, Gonzalo, Monc.	.323	101	393	362	35	117	160	18	5	5	66	4	8	2	17	4	22	1	4	15	.442	.350
Lopez, Miguel, Yuc.	.308	10	18	13	2	4	4	0	0	0	0	4	0	1	0	0	1	0	0	1	.308	.357
Lopez, Salvador, Rey.	.284	43	122	109	16	31	36	5	0	0	15	5	1	2	5	0	18	0	0	7	.330	.325
Lopez A., Victor M., Jal.	.286	79	271	255	24	73	91	13	1	1	31	5	2	2	7	0	37	5	3	6	.357	.308
Loredo, Jorge Luis, Cam.	.257	89	310	269	27	69	95	10	2	4	31	7	1	4	29	0	51	0	3	15	.353	.337
Luna, Jose Luis, Sal.	.224	93	296	254	21	57	71	12	1	0	26	21	0	2	19	0	27	0	3	8	.280	.284

Player, Team	Avg.	G	TPA	AB	R	H	TB	2B	3B	HR	RBI	SH	SF	HP	BB	IBB	SO	SB	CS	GDP	Slg.	OBP
Machiria, Pablo, Ags.	.333	112	454	406	61	135	194	21	1	12	72	6	8	5	29	5	35	3	2	13	.478	.377
Machorro, Roberto, Monc.	.171	22	43	41	1	7	11	2	1	0	5	0	0	0	2	0	2	1	0	1	.268	.209
Maclin, Lonnie, Agu.	.236	37	174	140	27	33	43	4	3	0	10	1	2	2	29	4	17	13	2	4	.307	.370
Magallanes, Ever, Mont.	.255	54	171	149	20	38	47	3	0	2	15	6	3	0	13	3	10	2	1	3	.315	.309
Magallanes, William, Tab.	.260	64	259	215	30	56	82	9	1	5	28	4	0	1	39	5	37	5	1	7	.381	.376
Magana, Gabriel, Yuc.	.222	24	43	36	7	8	9	1	0	0	2	0	0	3	4	0	4	0	0	1	.250	.349
Malpica, Enrique, Agu.	.239	79	201	176	16	42	43	1	0	0	14	6	3	0	16	1	34	1	1	3	.244	.297
Marrujo, Hector, Tab.	.233	95	327	292	29	68	84	8	4	0	18	8	1	3	23	1	44	2	1	13	.288	.295
Martinez, Carmelo, Mont.	.296	43	177	142	23	42	84	12	0	10	30	0	0	1	34	3	23	1	0	6	.592	.435
Martinez, Enrique, Mont.	.250	15	14	12	1	3	3	0	0	0	0	0	0	1	1	0	0	0	0	1	.250	.357
Martinez, Grimaldo, Monc.	.272	103	439	393	55	107	135	10	6	2	45	6	5	2	33	1	30	7	6	12	.344	.328
Martinez, Luis Carlos, Sal.	.227	46	72	66	10	15	19	4	0	0	4	6	0	0	0	0	5	0	0	3	.288	.227
Martinez, Raul, Sal.	.357	9	15	14	0	5	5	0	0	0	1	0	0	0	1	0	3	0	0	0	.357	.400
McCoy, Trey, N.L.	.321	9	35	28	7	9	15	0	0	2	3	0	0	0	7	0	4	0	1	1	.536	.457
Medina, Jose Ramon, Cam.	.224	56	111	98	15	22	25	1	1	0	6	3	1	2	7	1	23	0	0	3	.255	.287
Mendez, Jesus, Agu.-Tab.	.356	113	460	399	54	142	181	21	3	4	54	5	1	0	55	13	17	2	2	12	.454	.433
Mendez, Ramon, Ags.	.264	42	126	110	16	29	39	5	1	1	12	3	3	0	10	0	16	1	0	3	.355	.317
Mendez, Roberto C., MCRD	.304	99	360	309	50	94	132	8	3	8	47	8	5	4	34	4	29	9	7	7	.427	.375
Mendiola, Juan C., Agu.	.098	32	60	51	3	5	7	2	0	0	3	1	0	0	8	1	10	0	0	0	.137	.220
Mercedes, Luis, Yuc.	.316	52	224	196	35	62	74	5	2	1	10	2	0	2	24	1	26	7	5	7	.378	.396
Merchand, Mark, Rey.	.152	9	39	33	4	5	10	2	0	1	4	1	0	0	5	2	7	0	0	3	.303	.263
Mere, Pedro, MCT	.286	95	356	304	53	87	128	14	0	9	48	3	4	0	45	2	40	3	3	8	.421	.374
Meza, Alfredo, Mont.	.172	35	60	58	5	10	13	0	0	1	2	0	0	0	2	0	9	0	0	3	.224	.200
Michel, Domingo, Cam.	.323	44	164	127	30	41	76	8	0	9	32	2	2	0	33	0	25	2	1	2	.598	.457
Mitchell, Keith, Tab.	.333	24	100	81	15	27	53	6	1	6	26	0	1	0	18	0	10	0	6	1	.654	.450
Monroy, Francisco, Mont.	.333	4	3	3	0	1	1	0	0	0	1	0	0	0	0	0	1	0	0	0	.333	.333
Monroy, Victor Hugo, Rey.	.380	41	114	108	16	41	55	8	0	2	24	0	0	1	5	0	8	0	0	4	.509	.412
Montalvo, Ivan, MCT	.285	70	166	144	18	41	61	8	3	2	22	4	4	0	14	1	32	1	1	1	.424	.340
Mora, Andres, N.L.	.263	50	159	137	12	36	59	5	0	6	18	0	1	1	20	2	16	0	0	4	.431	.358
Morales, Alejandro, Tor.	.000	4	8	6	0	0	0	0	0	0	1	1	1	0	0	0	2	0	0	1	.000	.000
Morales, Florentino, N.L.	.254	99	397	342	49	87	113	19	2	1	21	5	2	6	42	2	54	2	1	10	.330	.344
Moreno, David, Sal.	.133	14	15	15	0	2	3	1	0	0	0	0	0	0	0	0	1	0	0	0	.200	.133
Morones, Martin, Monc.	.259	97	387	317	53	82	109	8	5	3	34	6	2	1	61	0	39	19	8	9	.344	.378
Motley, Darryl, Tor.-Agu.	.276	32	139	116	16	32	46	8	0	2	22	1	1	2	19	1	15	1	1	1	.397	.384
Munoz, Noe, Rey.	.314	36	141	121	23	38	49	8	0	1	22	0	1	0	19	1	17	0	0	7	.405	.404
Navarrete, Alejandro, Tab.	.000	1	1	1	0	0	0	0	0	0	0	0	0	0	0	0	1	0	0	0	.000	.000
Naveda, Edgar, Jal.	.290	103	402	352	45	102	135	25	1	2	37	1	3	1	45	6	30	8	6	19	.384	.369
Noris, Rogelio, N.L.	.205	65	140	122	15	25	34	4	1	1	13	3	1	0	14	1	32	2	0	5	.279	.285
Nunez Avina, Jose J., Jal.	.191	32	53	47	7	9	10	1	0	0	7	1	0	1	4	0	12	1	0	3	.213	.269
Nunez Garcia, Jose J., Jal.	.125	20	40	40	1	5	5	0	0	0	1	0	0	0	0	0	12	0	1	0	.125	.125
Ochoa, Marin Edgar, MCT	.228	52	104	92	10	21	36	6	0	3	12	3	1	1	7	0	20	0	0	6	.391	.287
Ojeda, Miguel, MCRD	.280	50	163	150	14	42	64	5	1	5	24	0	2	2	9	0	29	2	1	3	.427	.325
Olvera, Sergio, Monc.	.246	68	219	203	25	50	72	8	1	4	12	4	0	1	11	0	39	2	2	3	.355	.288
Orantes, Ramon, Mont.	.265	79	221	196	26	52	69	9	4	0	17	4	1	0	20	0	31	4	7	10	.352	.332
Ortega, Roberto, Tab.	.218	77	222	193	15	42	62	11	0	3	16	4	2	1	22	4	29	0	1	7	.321	.298
Ortiz, Alejandro, MCT	.282	97	384	330	53	93	151	13	0	15	64	1	3	3	47	2	44	4	5	13	.458	.373
Osuna, Hector, Yuc.	.185	31	68	54	7	10	10	0	0	0	11	2	0	2	10	1	11	0	0	1	.185	.333
Pacho, Juan Jose, Yuc.	.273	104	365	322	31	88	105	13	2	0	23	9	1	2	31	0	27	2	2	12	.326	.340
Paez, Raul, MCRD	.341	93	257	232	32	79	113	19	3	3	28	2	0	2	21	2	24	1	1	3	.487	.400
Palacios, Alfonso, P., Tab.	.167	5	6	6	1	1	1	0	0	0	0	0	0	0	0	0	1	0	0	0	.167	.167
Pardo, Victor, Manuel, Pue.	.260	104	334	288	36	75	109	12	2	6	27	5	1	2	38	2	42	2	1	10	.378	.350
Paredes, Johnny, Agu.	.179	7	31	28	4	5	5	0	0	0	1	0	0	0	3	0	3	0	1	1	.179	.258
Payro, Edison, Cam.	.233	28	33	30	2	7	8	1	0	0	7	0	0	1	2	0	6	0	0	1	.267	.303
Peralta, Amado, Yuc.-Jal.	.280	90	335	268	34	75	98	20	0	1	26	1	2	4	60	0	44	1	5	7	.366	.416
Perez, Alejandro, N.L.	.200	10	12	10	3	2	2	0	0	0	1	2	0	0	0	0	3	0	0	0	.200	.200
Perez, Alfredo, Pue.	.000	2	2	2	0	0	0	0	0	0	0	0	0	0	0	0	0	0	0	0	.000	.000
Perez, Francisco, Rey.	.281	51	106	96	13	27	40	3	2	2	21	0	3	1	6	1	34	0	1	1	.417	.321
Perez, Juan Luis, Tor.	.286	33	63	56	6	16	24	2	3	0	8	3	0	0	4	0	15	0	1	0	.429	.333
Pena, Carlos, Yuc.	.250	14	34	28	3	7	8	1	0	0	5	3	0	0	3	0	10	0	0	0	.286	.323
Pena, Luis Alberto, Pue.	.310	108	364	326	36	101	152	18	0	11	61	2	3	2	31	3	59	1	1	11	.466	.370
Pena, M. Joel, Agu	.000	9	10	9	1	0	0	0	0	0	0	0	0	0	1	0	2	0	0	1	.000	.100
Pierce, Dominique, Jal.	.160	7	29	25	0	4	5	1	0	0	0	0	0	0	4	1	6	0	0	2	.200	.276
Pledger, Kinnis E., Tor.	.234	14	54	47	7	11	16	0	1	1	5	0	0	1	6	0	14	0	0	0	.340	.333
Ponce, Hector, Cam.	.000	5	8	8	0	0	0	0	0	0	0	0	0	0	0	0	1	0	0	0	.000	.000
Precichi, Jorge, Sal.	.212	80	328	283	46	60	81	10	4	1	18	7	2	2	34	0	42	6	3	13	.286	.299
Pulido, Jesus, N.L.	.118	15	19	17	0	2	2	0	0	0	0	0	0	1	1	0	7	0	0	1	.118	.211
Quintana, Carlos, Min.-Yuc.	.325	78	329	268	47	87	112	9	2	4	37	6	1	3	51	2	23	2	1	19	.418	.437
Quintero, Guillermo, Mont.	.377	70	84	69	24	26	30	2	1	0	6	6	1	1	7	0	13	7	1	1	.435	.436
Quiroz, Jose Julian, Ags.	.239	60	179	155	21	37	57	9	1	3	28	0	2	1	21	5	28	1	0	5	.368	.330
Quinones, Luis, Yuc.	.235	44	190	153	31	36	50	5	0	3	19	5	4	0	28	2	17	4	1	2	.327	.346
Ramirez, Efren, Ags.	.252	87	284	246	27	62	86	6	3	4	23	8	1	11	18	0	42	0	6	6	.350	.330
Ramirez, Enrique, N.L.	.241	112	422	394	43	95	104	7	1	0	27	15	0	1	12	0	19	5	6	16	.264	.265
Ramirez G., Jesus A., MCRD	.175	47	42	40	13	7	8	1	0	0	4	1	0	0	1	0	3	2	2	0	.200	.195
Ramon, Reyes, Agu.	.077	5	13	13	0	1	1	0	0	0	0	0	0	0	0	0	6	0	0	0	.077	.077
Rendina, Mike, Monc.	.128	12	44	39	2	5	6	1	0	0	3	0	2	0	3	0	7	0	1	1	.154	.182
Renteria, Edison, Agu.-Cam.	.300	45	165	150	21	45	56	6	1	1	14	2	0	1	12	4	16	3	2	5	.373	.356
Reyes, Gilberto, Cam.	.277	111	406	361	37	100	131	10	0	7	36	8	1	3	33	4	56	2	2	15	.363	.342
Reyna, Luis, Monc.-Tab.	.272	50	194	173	23	47	64	5	0	4	31	1	4	1	15	2	17	6	3	5	.370	.326
Ritchie, Greg, Tab.	.345	17	66	55	7	19	28	3	3	0	8	1	0	2	8	0	8	2	2	4	.509	.446
Rivera, Alberto, Jal.	.263	55	162	133	18	35	39	2	1	0	9	3	3	4	19	1	20	4	0	8	.293	.365
Rivera, Eleazar, Monc.	.227	12	26	22	3	5	5	0	0	0	0	2	0	1	1	0	5	0	0	1	.227	.292
Rivera, German, Pue.	.340	110	430	344	59	117	170	19	2	10	53	4	3	2	77	10	43	3	0	10	.494	.460
Roa, Hector, MCT	.250	33	136	128	18	32	50	9	0	3	22	1	1	1	5	0	23	0	0	5	.391	.281

Player, Team	Avg.	G	TPA	AB	R	H	TB	2B	3B	HR	RBI	SH	SF	HP	BB	IBB	SO	SB	CS	GDP	Slg.	OBP
Robles, Javier, MCT	.311	113	474	409	93	127	218	24	8	17	53	13	5	3	44	1	61	7	6	6	.533	.377
Robles, Ricardo, Sal.	.222	12	12	9	2	2	2	0	0	0	1	0	0	0	3	2	5	0	0	0	.222	.417
Robles, Trinidad, MCT-Min.	.105	14	22	19	3	2	3	1	0	0	2	2	0	0	1	0	7	0	0	0	.158	.150
Rodriguez, Boi, N.L.	.307	82	340	293	54	90	178	18	2	22	77	0	5	1	41	4	47	5	3	3	.608	.388
Rodriguez, Fernando, Tor.	.320	105	397	347	49	111	168	17	2	12	49	4	2	8	36	4	43	3	5	12	.484	.394
Rodriguez, Genaro, N.L.	.267	75	210	187	12	50	64	4	2	2	25	5	1	2	15	1	28	1	3	7	.342	.327
Rodriguez, Hector, Rey.	.291	107	412	351	65	102	144	11	5	7	52	5	5	5	46	0	78	0	3	8	.410	.376
Rodriguez, Jose Luis, Agu.	.241	86	264	237	13	57	69	12	0	0	12	3	0	2	22	6	38	3	3	9	.291	.310
Rodriguez, Juan F., Rey.-Agu.	.178	52	209	174	18	31	33	2	0	0	12	7	1	1	26	0	7	0	1	3	.190	.287
Rodriguez, Ruben, Monc.	.258	19	66	62	8	16	20	4	0	0	4	1	0	2	1	0	4	1	0	0	.323	.292
Rodriguez, Serafin, Pue.	.286	5	15	14	2	4	4	0	0	0	0	1	0	0	0	0	1	0	0	0	.286	.286
Rodriguez S., Noel, Agu.	.316	10	21	19	3	6	6	0	0	0	1	2	0	0	0	0	4	1	1	1	.316	.316
Rojas, Francisco, Tab.	.169	32	71	65	6	11	13	2	0	0	5	1	0	1	4	0	11	0	0	1	.200	.229
Rojas, Homar, MCRD	.332	90	355	319	51	106	134	13	0	5	53	3	6	1	26	2	25	3	2	14	.420	.378
Romero, Marco A., MCT	.297	107	437	381	61	113	198	18	2	21	96	1	6	4	45	3	39	5	2	8	.520	.372
Romero, Oscar, Tab.	.344	115	482	410	72	141	195	24	0	10	47	11	1	2	58	5	42	10	6	19	.476	.427
Rubio, Marco A., Cam.-Min.	.224	80	264	232	10	52	62	7	0	1	14	8	4	1	19	2	19	1	1	11	.267	.281
Rubio, Sergio, Yuc.	.239	36	76	71	13	17	20	3	0	0	6	0	0	1	4	0	12	1	1	5	.282	.289
Ruiz, Demetrio, Jal.-Tab.	.214	36	96	84	4	18	21	1	1	0	7	4	2	0	6	0	4	0	0	2	.250	.261
Ruiz, Juan De Dios, Tor.	.306	105	409	360	70	110	176	16	10	10	67	5	6	1	37	4	38	9	2	13	.489	.366
Sabino, Miguel, Jal.	.167	7	23	18	1	3	3	0	0	0	3	0	0	0	5	2	4	0	1	2	.167	.348
Saenz, Ricardo, N.L.	.321	116	479	433	72	139	220	25	1	18	83	3	3	3	37	2	74	3	5	10	.508	.376
Saiz, Herminio, Tor.	.000	1	2	2	0	0	0	0	0	0	0	0	0	0	0	0	1	0	0	0	.000	.000
Salas, Heriberto, Tor.	.263	40	93	80	14	21	32	7	2	0	13	1	1	2	9	0	15	1	0	4	.400	.348
Salgado, Eduardo, MCT	.231	10	14	13	2	3	5	0	1	0	2	0	0	0	1	0	3	0	0	0	.385	.286
Samaniego, Manuel, Monc.	.327	68	198	171	19	56	74	9	3	1	30	3	1	4	19	0	15	1	2	5	.433	.405
Sanchez, Armando, Mont.	.293	92	334	290	35	85	100	13	1	0	29	5	1	0	38	2	22	2	0	5	.345	.374
Sanchez, Gerardo, N.L.	.323	116	490	400	72	129	184	20	1	11	59	1	5	19	65	3	38	5	3	20	.460	.436
Sanchez, Roque, Cam.	.266	56	115	109	9	29	33	4	0	0	9	5	1	0	0	0	9	1	0	5	.303	.264
Sandoval, Jose Luis, MCRD	.311	106	399	354	52	110	158	22	1	8	59	3	6	4	32	4	40	3	4	10	.446	.369
Santos, Julio, Jal.	.285	52	151	130	15	37	46	6	0	1	11	4	1	3	13	0	31	2	1	6	.354	.361
Santos, Luis Angel, Ags.	.250	3	4	4	3	1	1	0	0	0	1	0	0	0	0	0	1	0	0	0	.250	.250
Sasser, Mike, Min.	.286	15	59	56	4	16	23	1	0	2	11	0	0	0	3	0	6	0	0	0	.411	.322
Sievers, Carlos, Yuc.	.158	14	23	19	1	3	6	0	0	1	2	0	0	0	4	0	5	0	1	0	.316	.304
Snider, Van, Tor.	.325	81	336	302	61	98	192	22	0	24	67	0	2	1	31	5	57	0	0	8	.636	.387
Solis, Roberto, Pue.	.000	4	1	1	0	0	0	0	0	0	0	0	0	0	0	0	1	0	0	0	.000	.000
Sommers, Jesus, Pue.-Agu.	.224	96	351	317	12	71	87	11	1	1	20	2	1	2	29	1	36	1	0	11	.274	.292
Soriano, Ricardo, Tor.	.143	27	30	28	6	4	4	0	0	0	2	0	0	0	2	0	4	1	0	0	.143	.200
Soto, Emison, Pue.	.286	90	349	304	54	87	151	21	2	13	52	4	2	11	28	1	47	2	3	14	.497	.365
Sparks, Greg, MCT	.245	20	69	53	11	13	25	3	0	3	14	1	1	1	13	2	20	1	0	1	.472	.397
Stark, Matt, Rey.	.332	95	402	322	66	107	169	26	0	12	83	0	7	6	67	7	35	0	0	14	.525	.448
Tatis, Bernardo, MCRD	.303	84	358	304	69	92	121	13	2	4	45	2	2	0	50	4	27	17	3	4	.398	.399
Tatum, Willie, Yuc.	.000	3	10	9	0	0	0	0	0	0	1	0	0	0	1	0	3	0	0	0	.000	.100
Tejeda, Arturo, N.L.	.116	22	49	43	6	5	6	1	0	0	1	0	0	0	6	0	11	0	1	0	.140	.224
Tellez, Alonso, Rey.	.331	116	478	435	67	144	205	25	6	8	63	0	2	0	41	6	51	2	1	13	.471	.387
Tillman, Rusty, Agu.-Tab.	.248	63	256	202	30	50	90	7	0	11	34	1	5	2	46	4	69	6	2	2	.446	.384
Tiquet, Lazaro, Tab.	.281	101	387	352	35	99	146	29	3	4	52	6	4	4	21	2	51	4	6	14	.415	.325
Tolentino, Jose, Mont.	.342	83	346	304	49	104	176	24	0	16	79	1	2	2	37	6	37	1	2	15	.579	.414
Torres, Eduardo, Sal.	.222	104	398	338	46	75	129	13	4	11	52	4	3	0	53	3	74	6	5	10	.382	.325
Torres, Raymundo, Yuc.	.233	107	418	309	45	72	130	11	1	15	62	4	3	6	96	6	74	2	2	4	.421	.420
Tovar, Jose De Jesus, Sal.-Monc.	.228	56	185	167	15	38	40	2	0	0	15	5	1	2	10	0	26	1	2	4	.240	.278
Trafton, Todd, Tor.	.336	45	192	152	35	51	78	7	1	6	34	0	1	4	35	2	16	1	0	5	.513	.469
Trapaga, Miguel, MCT	.202	52	123	109	17	22	32	4	0	2	9	2	0	1	11	0	24	0	1	2	.294	.281
Trejo, David, Agu.	.000	1	4	4	1	0	0	0	0	0	0	0	0	0	0	0	0	0	0	0	.000	.000
Trevino, Alejandro, Mont.	.317	93	311	262	32	83	108	17	1	2	28	5	3	3	38	2	26	1	3	7	.412	.405
Valdez, Francisco J., Rey.	.267	81	261	217	36	58	75	12	1	1	30	4	3	4	33	4	27	0	1	11	.346	.370
Valdez, Jesus, Yuc.	.302	81	221	192	28	58	76	12	0	2	36	6	4	1	18	0	14	2	0	6	.396	.358
Valencia, Carlos, Ags.	.269	55	202	160	19	43	58	9	0	2	27	2	5	2	33	6	14	2	0	3	.363	.390
Valenzuela, Armando, Rey.	.256	97	424	367	62	94	110	10	3	0	31	16	3	2	36	0	38	4	4	7	.300	.324
Valenzuela, Eduardo, Sal.	.273	67	139	128	15	35	47	7	1	1	16	1	1	2	7	1	6	0	0	4	.367	.319
Valenzuela, Horacio, Min.-Jal.	.196	78	270	235	17	46	65	10	0	3	24	1	4	1	29	5	31	0	1	11	.277	.283
Valenzuela, Jose Luis, Ags.	.311	40	119	106	15	33	43	4	3	0	7	2	0	0	11	1	12	1	0	6	.406	.376
Valenzuela S., Joel, Tor.	.125	6	10	8	0	1	1	0	0	0	0	1	0	0	1	0	1	0	0	0	.125	.222
Valle, Jorge Luis, Tor.	.292	101	377	325	46	95	123	13	3	3	36	14	2	2	34	1	43	2	7	9	.378	.361
Valle, Jose Luis, Min.	.221	104	369	339	35	75	99	10	1	4	35	9	1	4	16	2	27	1	0	8	.292	.264
Valverde, Raul, Jal.	.302	75	251	242	23	73	103	13	1	5	33	2	1	0	6	0	33	1	3	9	.426	.317
Vargas, Trinidad, Pue.	.200	65	188	170	14	34	40	4	1	0	14	5	3	1	9	0	31	2	1	6	.235	.240
Vazquez, Felipe, MCRD	.333	26	28	27	3	9	11	2	0	0	1	0	0	0	1	0	5	0	0	2	.407	.357
Vega V., Edgar, MCT	.208	78	220	192	16	40	47	3	2	0	9	6	0	0	22	0	29	2	1	2	.245	.290
Velazquez, Armando, Agu.	.222	21	52	45	2	10	10	0	0	0	5	4	1	0	2	0	10	0	1	3	.222	.250
Velazquez, Guillermo, Mont.	.252	34	134	119	16	30	51	9	0	4	18	0	0	0	15	1	27	0	0	1	.429	.336
Verdugo, Guadalupe, Tor.	.222	28	58	45	7	10	12	2	0	0	5	3	0	0	10	0	10	1	0	1	.267	.364
Verdugo, Sostenes, Yuc.	.429	5	9	7	2	3	3	0	0	0	0	0	0	0	2	0	1	0	0	0	.429	.556
Verdugo, Vicente, MCRD	.285	106	381	358	48	102	128	14	0	4	35	7	4	0	12	0	30	2	6	8	.358	.305
Villaescusa, Fernando, Jal.	.352	60	203	179	26	63	72	7	1	0	14	4	2	2	16	2	4	4	1	5	.402	.407
Villanueva, Hector, MCT	.374	53	225	182	41	68	115	11	0	12	47	1	0	1	41	4	19	1	0	6	.632	.491
Villanueva, Luis, Ags.	.000	1	1	1	0	0	0	0	0	0	0	0	0	0	0	0	0	0	0	0	.000	.000
Villarreal, Alejandro, N.L.	.000	8	7	7	1	0	0	0	0	0	0	0	0	0	0	0	2	0	0	0	.000	.000
Villegas, Fernando, Sal.	.323	98	415	372	65	120	169	12	11	5	40	3	0	7	33	0	41	9	5	10	.454	.388
Villegas, Jose Angel, Ags.	.000	3	3	2	0	0	0	0	0	0	0	0	0	0	1	0	2	0	0	0	.000	.333
Vizcarra, Marco A., Rey.	.294	68	214	177	32	52	56	1	0	1	16	4	2	3	28	0	19	1	3	6	.316	.395
Vizcarra, Roberto, Ags.	.290	112	475	414	80	120	199	19	0	20	87	4	7	6	44	6	35	10	7	13	.481	.361
Wearing, Mel, Jal.-Sal.	.287	85	342	268	52	77	129	9	2	13	59	0	4	1	69	2	79	4	2	10	.481	.430

Player, Team	Avg.	G	TPA	AB	R	H	TB	2B	3B	HR	RBI	SH	SF	HP	BB	IBB	SO	SB	CS	GDP	Slg.	OBP
Wong Medrano, J., Monc.	.228	48	137	114	11	26	34	3	1	1	10	7	2	0	14	1	17	0	3	4	.298	.308
Wright, George, Sal.	.335	116	491	409	70	137	200	23	2	12	76	0	7	0	75	14	38	12	5	12	.489	.432
Wright, Tom, Jal.	.143	2	8	7	0	1	2	1	0	0	0	0	0	0	1	0	2	0	0	0	.286	.250
Yuriar, Jesus, Monc.	.278	101	365	313	40	87	104	9	4	0	35	8	2	3	39	0	43	2	6	12	.332	.361
Zambrano, Roberto, Pue.	.286	5	16	14	3	4	7	0	0	1	5	0	0	1	1	0	3	0	0	0	.500	.375
Zamudio, Rafael, Mont.-Agu.	.308	37	110	107	9	33	48	10	1	1	5	0	0	0	3	0	22	1	0	1	.449	.327
Zazueta, Juan Carlos, Tab.	.269	54	141	130	15	35	42	3	2	0	13	2	0	1	8	0	24	5	1	3	.323	.317
Zazueta, Maurico, Tor.	.298	81	325	299	45	89	116	9	3	4	28	8	2	1	15	1	52	2	2	10	.388	.331
Zulueta, Felix, Tab.	.140	14	47	43	4	6	6	0	0	0	0	1	0	0	3	0	9	0	0	3	.140	.196

GRAND SLAMS: Ro. Mendez, R. Vizcarra, 2 each; Ru. Avila, Cairo, Camacho, Carter, B. Castillo, L. Cruz, Fentanes, Gainey, Jav. Guerrero, Horn, Machiria, W. Magallanes, C. Martinez, G. Martinez, Montalvo, Munoz, Saenz, Snider, Stark, Tellez, F. Valdez, M. Vizcarra, Wearing, Zambrano, 1 each.

AWARDED FIRST BASE ON CATCHER'S INTERFERENCE: Morones 3 (V. Lopez 2, Vega); Camacho (Cazarin); A. Castro (Cazarin); Jo. Espinoza (M. Cruz); Ru. Estrada (Machorro); D. Gonzalez (V. Lopez); Nunez Avina (M. Cruz); G. Sanchez (V. Lopez).

1995 PITCHING

TEAM

Team	W	L	Pct.	ERA	G	CG	ShO	Sv.	IP	H	TBF	R	ER	HR	SH	SF	HB	BB	IBB	SO	WP	Bk.
Tabasco	61	50	.550	3.31	115	28	12	23	944.1	947	3566	413	347	44	74	24	38	284	14	490	23	5
Campeche	60	54	.526	3.35	115	23	10	27	934.0	924	3513	442	348	58	73	32	31	409	48	374	30	3
Minatitlan	41	73	.360	3.60	116	12	5	21	973.0	1003	3649	451	389	59	67	25	27	430	51	431	20	3
M.C. Red Devils	80	33	.708	3.71	114	19	5	29	932.2	950	3501	442	384	64	56	35	20	421	9	621	53	3
Monterrey	65	49	.570	3.84	116	9	5	31	960.0	965	3628	473	410	56	64	27	31	408	22	546	52	2
Nuevo Laredo	62	54	.534	4.15	116	16	0	35	982.1	1018	3732	508	453	82	61	28	29	401	48	557	46	5
Saltillo	63	53	.543	4.18	116	13	3	24	969.0	1003	3644	523	450	63	56	31	45	478	14	538	43	5
Aguila	45	71	.388	4.19	116	13	3	24	964.2	1007	3630	500	449	69	58	30	46	417	24	459	22	5
Reynosa	73	40	.646	4.26	116	16	5	32	980.2	1066	3795	532	464	69	65	23	33	430	24	560	36	3
Puebla	52	63	.452	4.32	116	35	5	14	925.1	1030	3562	538	444	79	77	33	32	405	30	405	31	3
Yucatan	59	55	.518	4.41	115	18	6	23	938.0	1048	3627	530	460	62	80	23	27	426	26	480	65	2
Monclova	46	69	.400	4.41	116	16	1	30	949.2	1071	3692	547	465	70	49	41	30	430	35	539	56	2
Aguascalientes	57	55	.509	4.62	114	18	3	23	937.2	1056	3611	546	481	75	61	37	46	446	28	500	35	4
M.C. Tigers	62	54	.534	4.85	116	22	8	19	948.1	970	3609	575	511	72	49	36	44	513	30	539	56	1
Torreon	56	57	.496	4.98	115	23	3	26	943.2	1083	3654	599	522	83	52	48	36	432	38	473	50	2
Jalisco	30	82	.268	6.08	114	23	1	15	913.2	1234	3736	737	617	67	66	48	37	444	32	457	69	5

INDIVIDUAL

TOP QUALIFIERS FOR EARNED-RUN AVERAGE TITLE

Minimum 93 innings.

Pitcher, Team	W	L	Pct.	ERA	G	GS	CG	ShO	GF	Sv.	IP	H	TBF	R	ER	HR	SH	SF	HB	BB	IBB	SO	WP	Bk.
Ruiz, Cecilio, Tab.	13	5	.722	1.71	24	23	7	5	1	0	162.2	132	584	41	31	6	20	4	4	33	1	92	1	0
Solarte, Jose A., Min.	8	4	.667	1.72	45	6	3	1	39	4	115.0	93	397	23	22	2	9	3	1	42	9	64	1	0
Munoz, Ricardo, Tab.	12	6	.667	2.46	22	22	7	3	0	0	142.2	128	514	49	39	5	14	2	7	36	1	69	1	1
Ramirez, Roberto, MCRD	13	3	.813	2.56	20	20	8	3	0	0	137.1	125	502	50	39	9	5	3	5	35	0	70	3	2
Zappelli, Mark, Sal.	6	8	.429	2.63	33	9	2	0	24	6	106.0	109	396	40	31	2	9	0	6	47	0	45	3	0
Sierra, Abel, Cam.	11	9	.550	2.64	24	21	10	5	3	0	153.1	132	578	60	45	7	9	3	0	48	4	80	4	1
Vazquez, Adrian, Cam.	11	6	.647	2.64	21	21	3	0	0	0	136.1	118	487	48	40	8	10	1	5	72	3	39	4	1
Munoz, Miguel, Agu.-Rey.	11	3	.786	2.67	20	20	2	1	0	0	138.0	140	522	47	41	3	8	1	4	22	1	62	1	2
Cuervo, Bernardo, Cam.	12	4	.750	2.74	28	18	6	4	10	0	125.0	122	460	50	38	7	15	3	2	45	7	40	4	0
Martinez, Filiberto, Sal.	8	5	.615	2.76	19	19	3	2	0	0	107.2	98	399	39	33	2	5	2	7	57	0	57	3	1

DEPARTMENTAL LEADERS: W—A. Moreno, 16; L—Gomez Rios, F. Soto, 14; Pct.—Cordova, 1.000; G—J. Villegas, 52; GS—Soto, 25; CG—E. Lopez, Sierra, 10; ShO—Ruiz, Sierra, 5; GF—J. Villegas, 50; Sv.—Murillo, 30; IP—E. Lopez, 163.1; H—F. Soto, 182; TBF—; R—V. Gonzalez, 93; ER—Renteria, 74; HR—Rios, 17; SH—Ruiz, 20; SF—J. Moreno, 9; HB—J. Moreno, Palafox, 11; BB—Barraza, 73; IBB—Grajales, 13; SO—A. Moreno, A. Quiroz, 108; WP—Pina, Segura, 10; Bk.—L. Castro, 3.

ALL PITCHERS

Pitcher, Team	W	L	Pct.	ERA	G	GS	CG	ShO	GF	Sv.	IP	H	TBF	R	ER	HR	SH	SF	HB	BB	IBB	SO	WP	Bk.
Acosta, Aaron, Tor.	9	3	.750	4.08	21	21	4	1	0	0	128.0	138	477	66	58	9	6	4	3	56	1	76	8	0
Acosta, Francisco, Yuc.	0	0	.000	4.50	2	0	0	0	2	0	4.0	8	20	3	2	0	0	0	0	2	1	2	0	0
Acosta, Gerardo, MCRD	1	0	1.000	0.00	2	0	0	0	2	0	2.1	1	7	0	0	0	0	0	0	2	0	1	1	0
Agosto, Juan, Mont.-Ags.	1	4	.200	6.15	17	6	0	0	11	4	45.1	62	187	37	31	6	3	2	5	15	0	18	4	0
Aguilar, Jose M., Min.-Tab.	4	10	.286	6.91	24	16	1	0	8	0	71.2	94	302	61	55	5	3	0	1	37	2	36	3	0
Aguirre, Gaudencio, Tab.	0	0	.000	11.81	3	0	0	0	3	0	5.1	11	26	7	7	1	0	0	1	1	0	4	2	0
Alicea, Miguel, Tor.	0	2	.000	3.46	28	0	0	0	28	15	26.0	31	107	18	10	4	3	2	0	8	1	11	0	0
Alvarez, Ivan, Jal.	0	4	.000	7.27	6	3	1	0	3	1	17.1	20	68	16	14	1	2	2	1	8	1	8	1	1
Alvarez, Juan Jesus, MCT	12	8	.600	3.70	23	23	4	0	0	0	153.1	158	578	71	63	10	9	2	8	59	3	65	6	0
Antunez, Martin, Jal.	3	8	.273	4.43	26	11	4	0	15	1	91.1	109	357	51	45	6	11	4	2	21	2	38	7	0
Arano, Ramon, Agu.	2	2	.500	6.86	5	5	1	1	0	0	21.0	28	89	17	16	2	1	1	1	6	0	7	0	0
Arce, Francisco J., Min.	0	0	.000	0.00	1	0	0	0	1	1	1.0	0	3	0	0	0	0	0	0	0	0	0	0	0
Arrington, Tom, Jal.	5	9	.357	5.26	16	16	6	0	0	0	92.1	129	371	65	54	6	6	8	3	32	4	47	3	0
Arzate, Martin, Jal.	0	0	.000	4.26	3	0	0	0	3	0	6.1	9	25	5	3	0	0	1	0	2	0	2	2	0
Austin, Jim, MCT	0	0	.000	5.40	3	0	0	0	3	0	1.2	2	7	2	1	0	0	0	0	2	0	0	2	0
Ayrault, Bob, Monc.	0	2	.000	8.60	7	7	1	0	0	0	30.1	43	123	29	29	8	1	4	2	17	2	15	1	0
Baez, Sixto, Agu.	3	5	.375	5.29	28	13	0	0	15	2	78.1	89	294	50	46	4	6	3	4	46	3	22	2	1
Baller, Jay, MCRD	0	1	.000	2.37	16	0	0	0	16	6	19.0	10	62	8	5	1	1	2	1	17	0	13	3	0
Barfield, John David, N.L.	5	2	.714	2.70	34	1	1	0	33	24	63.1	50	219	19	19	2	4	1	0	13	4	36	4	0
Barraza, Ernesto, MCT	10	4	.714	3.15	24	17	4	3	7	0	125.2	111	454	58	44	1	6	3	1	73	3	78	7	0
Barron, Avelino, Sal.	1	4	.200	4.33	35	5	0	0	30	2	79.0	83	297	52	38	7	7	1	4	39	4	40	4	0

Pitcher, Team	W	L	Pct.	ERA	G	GS	CG	ShO	GF	Sv.	IP	H	TBF	R	ER	HR	SH	SF	HB	BB	IBB	SO	WP	Bk.
Bencomo, Omar, Sal.-Jal.	6	7	.462	4.33	35	1	0	0	34	2	70.2	73	268	37	34	3	5	3	1	27	2	56	5	0
Benitez, Francisco, Ags.-Jal.	0	2	.000	9.26	11	2	0	0	9	0	23.1	39	100	29	24	2	2	2	1	26	1	8	2	0
Browning, Mike, Cam.	1	3	.250	6.14	9	0	0	0	9	3	7.1	10	29	5	5	0	0	1	0	5	0	4	2	0
Brumley, Duff, Mont.-Ags.	1	3	.250	3.86	7	5	0	0	2	0	28.0	25	104	15	12	1	2	1	0	20	1	22	3	0
Burcham, Tim, Jal.	1	2	.333	3.18	6	6	2	1	0	0	28.1	25	105	10	10	1	2	0	0	9	1	17	4	0
Burlingame, Dennis, Monc.	0	1	.000	4.26	2	2	0	0	0	0	12.2	12	46	7	6	1	2	1	0	8	2	5	0	0
Cabrales, Gabriel, Tab.	3	2	.600	4.70	32	2	0	0	30	2	69.0	84	277	41	36	2	6	3	1	15	1	43	1	0
Calderon, Manaces, Min.	0	0	.000	1.59	3	0	0	0	3	0	5.2	2	19	2	1	0	0	0	0	4	0	3	1	0
Camacho, Adrian, Min.	2	2	.500	5.40	22	2	0	0	20	0	38.1	43	144	25	23	4	3	1	4	22	1	14	2	1
Camacho, Adulfo, Yuc.	0	0	.000	10.80	1	0	0	0	1	0	3.1	4	13	4	4	0	0	0	0	4	0	0	0	0
Campos, Francisco, Cam.	0	0	.000	1.93	5	1	0	0	4	0	9.1	9	35	2	2	0	0	1	0	3	0	2	1	0
Cano, Ezequiel, Jal.	3	12	.200	5.36	17	16	3	0	1	0	102.1	119	408	66	61	10	3	4	3	39	3	58	6	1
Cano, Jose, Ags.	9	7	.563	5.02	21	21	3	0	0	0	118.1	137	465	73	66	8	4	2	7	53	0	73	4	0
Cardenas, Benito, N.L.	0	0	.000	2.70	5	0	0	0	5	0	6.2	7	24	4	2	0	0	0	0	4	0	3	0	0
Carranza, Javier, Rey.	10	6	.625	4.86	21	20	2	0	1	0	113.0	128	451	67	61	8	6	2	4	45	2	72	7	0
Carrasco, Alejandro, MCRD	2	2	.500	4.91	30	2	0	0	28	1	47.2	54	175	29	26	4	1	3	0	18	1	13	5	0
Castaneda, Aurelio, Jal.	2	0	1.000	7.36	4	0	0	0	4	0	3.2	3	13	3	3	1	0	0	0	2	0	3	0	0
Castillo, Felipe, MCRD	3	1	.750	1.75	17	0	0	0	17	5	25.2	19	83	6	5	1	3	2	0	18	2	15	1	0
Castillo, Luis Trinidad, Monc.	1	1	.500	10.13	4	4	0	0	0	0	13.1	20	61	16	15	5	0	1	1	6	0	8	1	0
Castro, Gerardo, MCT	1	0	1.000	10.38	5	1	0	0	4	0	8.2	13	40	10	10	1	0	0	1	6	0	3	1	0
Castro, Leonel, Jal.	3	10	.231	6.04	19	19	2	0	0	0	107.1	141	444	91	72	7	9	3	4	45	3	49	6	3
Cazares, Juan, Jal.-Mont.	3	3	.500	4.81	35	1	0	0	34	2	33.2	43	137	19	18	2	0	0	1	20	2	18	4	0
Cazares, Rosario, Tab.	0	4	.000	3.47	34	1	0	0	33	3	46.2	37	170	21	18	4	4	3	2	16	2	22	0	1
Cazares, Tomas, MCRD-Rey.	1	0	1.000	5.96	15	1	0	0	14	0	22.2	31	92	16	15	2	2	1	1	10	0	10	0	0
Cecena, Jose Isabel, Sal.	4	4	.500	4.40	38	0	0	0	38	14	45.0	34	156	25	22	2	8	1	5	40	3	47	9	0
Cervantes, Lauro, Ags.-Agu.	3	5	.375	7.25	14	14	1	0	0	0	58.1	88	247	53	47	4	3	3	5	24	3	25	0	0
Chapin, Darrin, Rey.	1	1	.500	1.48	11	3	0	0	8	3	30.1	24	112	10	5	1	1	0	0	13	1	17	4	0
Cimorelli, Frank, Cam.	1	3	.250	3.26	19	0	0	0	19	4	30.1	38	118	15	11	0	4	2	0	13	2	13	2	0
Conde, Ricardo, Yuc.	0	0	.000	13.50	2	0	0	0	2	0	0.2	2	3	1	1	0	0	0	1	1	0	1	0	0
Contreras, Cuitlahuac, Tor.-Monc.	0	0	.000	0.00	1	0	0	0	1	0	3.1	6	15	1	0	0	0	0	0	2	0	0	0	0
Cordova, Francisco, MCRD	13	0	1.000	3.10	27	20	1	0	7	4	125.0	131	490	52	43	8	4	2	3	42	0	88	2	1
Cota, Guadalupe, N.L.	0	0	.000	6.75	1	0	0	0	1	0	1.1	2	5	1	1	0	0	0	0	1	0	0	0	0
Cota C., Armando, Tab.	0	2	.000	9.82	15	1	0	0	14	1	11.0	18	45	14	12	3	2	0	1	9	0	5	0	1
Couoh, Enrique, MCT	6	5	.545	3.70	39	10	4	2	29	8	97.1	82	348	45	40	8	3	8	4	65	4	67	8	0
Cruz, Andres, Yuc.	4	11	.267	4.73	23	21	4	0	2	0	125.2	146	485	74	66	8	14	6	5	48	5	61	8	0
Cruz, Javier, Rey.	8	5	.615	4.32	35	8	1	0	27	2	89.2	99	351	49	43	10	6	1	3	37	3	51	2	1
Cruz, Juan Alonso, Jal.	2	1	.667	5.77	26	1	0	0	25	0	53.0	76	228	38	34	3	1	0	4	29	1	31	2	0
Cruz, Juan Diego, Yuc.	0	2	.000	3.06	17	0	0	0	17	0	32.1	27	118	11	11	3	0	0	1	12	0	20	1	0
Cruz Soto, Antonio, Pue.	1	4	.200	3.73	14	5	1	0	9	0	41.0	35	151	23	17	6	4	2	2	39	4	23	0	0
Cuervo, Bernardo, Cam.	12	4	.750	2.74	28	18	6	4	10	0	125.0	122	460	50	38	7	15	3	2	45	7	40	4	0
Dehesa, Noel, Tab.	0	0	.000	6.10	6	0	0	0	6	0	10.1	14	46	9	7	2	0	0	1	2	0	2	0	0
Delfin, Adolfo, MCT	1	6	.143	5.19	37	0	0	0	37	3	69.1	81	278	45	40	6	3	5	8	30	3	30	3	0
Del Toro, Miguel, MCRD-Rey.	5	4	.556	2.25	37	0	0	0	37	16	68.0	54	253	23	17	2	5	2	4	43	1	49	4	0
Del Valle, Enrique, MCT-Agu.	1	0	1.000	14.59	11	1	0	0	10	0	12.1	29	61	21	20	0	1	2	1	13	0	7	1	0
Diaz, Alejandro, Agu.	2	4	.333	4.01	24	1	0	0	23	2	51.2	52	188	25	23	5	3	2	3	20	1	22	0	0
Diaz, Cesar, N.L.	4	3	.571	3.42	29	9	1	0	20	0	71.0	64	259	29	27	8	7	4	4	27	2	25	3	0
Diaz, Marcos, Mont.	4	2	.667	3.89	21	9	0	0	12	0	69.1	74	267	37	30	2	4	3	3	32	1	32	4	0
Diaz, Octavio, Ags.	0	0	.000	18.00	4	0	0	0	4	0	5.0	9	22	10	10	1	0	1	1	7	0	5	2	0
Dojaquez, Omar, Monc.	0	0	.000	13.50	1	0	0	0	1	0	0.2	2	5	1	1	0	0	0	0	0	0	1	1	0
Dominguez, Herminio, Cam.	4	2	.667	2.89	39	1	0	0	38	12	37.1	32	135	17	12	2	1	0	1	18	1	25	0	0
Draper, Mike, MCT	4	4	.500	3.62	22	0	0	0	22	5	32.1	26	117	13	13	2	4	0	1	16	3	11	1	0
Elvira, Narciso, Mont.	10	5	.667	5.13	18	18	1	1	0	0	93.0	98	363	59	53	12	1	0	3	40	0	70	3	0
Enriquez, Graciano, Ags.	0	1	.000	5.68	3	1	0	0	2	0	6.1	10	28	5	4	1	0	0	0	2	0	0	1	0
Enriquez, Martin, Ags.	8	8	.500	3.92	24	20	6	1	4	1	144.2	155	555	73	63	11	6	6	9	50	2	96	1	0
Espinoza, Mario, Yuc.	0	0	.000	....	1	0	0	0	1	0	0.0	2	2	2	2	0	0	0	0	0	0	0	0	0
Espinoza, Rogelio, Jal.	0	1	.000	9.00	7	0	0	0	7	1	6.0	14	29	6	6	0	1	0	1	5	1	3	0	0
Esquer, Mercedes, Yuc.-Mont.	7	3	.700	2.64	13	13	1	1	0	0	71.2	72	272	30	21	4	6	3	1	21	1	33	2	1
Farmer, Gorman, Pue.	0	1	.000	1.93	3	0	0	0	3	0	4.2	4	17	1	1	0	0	0	0	4	0	2	0	0
Felix, Arturo, Yuc.	0	0	.000	21.00	1	0	0	0	1	0	3.0	8	17	7	7	1	0	0	0	2	0	1	0	0
Figueroa, Fernando, Tor.	11	5	.688	4.72	17	17	2	0	0	0	114.1	124	443	69	60	8	0	3	1	46	2	54	7	0
Flores, Ignacio, Tor.	0	2	.000	6.44	21	1	0	0	20	0	29.1	42	124	27	21	7	1	1	1	19	1	12	0	0
Flynt, Will, MCRD	7	1	.875	2.24	10	9	3	0	1	0	56.1	51	210	18	14	0	2	2	0	27	0	49	5	0
Fonseca L., Pabel R., Min.	0	0	.000	0.00	1	0	0	0	1	0	0.2	1	3	0	0	0	0	0	0	1	0	0	0	0
Franklin, Jay, Mont.-Ags.	9	6	.600	3.52	22	21	3	2	1	0	122.2	127	459	65	48	4	8	3	7	57	2	60	6	0
Galvez, Rosario, N.L.	0	0	.000	15.00	6	0	0	0	6	0	6.0	13	29	10	10	0	0	1	0	5	0	4	2	1
Garcia, David, Monc.	0	0	.000	4.00	16	1	0	0	15	0	18.0	18	66	9	8	0	0	1	1	18	0	20	1	0
Garcia, Mike, Tab.	2	1	.667	1.94	26	2	1	0	24	14	46.1	36	165	10	10	0	6	3	0	6	1	30	1	0
Garcia Cruz, Jose Luis, MCT	4	6	.400	5.86	36	7	0	0	29	2	58.1	77	247	42	38	4	4	0	3	27	4	31	1	0
Garcia R., Miguel, Min.	4	3	.571	3.39	38	2	1	1	36	0	74.1	72	269	30	28	6	4	3	1	32	5	26	1	0
Garibay, Roberto, Pue.	4	3	.571	3.58	40	0	0	0	40	11	50.1	59	194	27	20	1	3	4	1	29	5	17	3	0
Garibay, Salvaror, Ags.	0	0	.000	3.00	23	1	0	0	22	0	54.0	60	197	20	18	1	4	5	2	24	1	31	2	0
Garibay Bravo, Daniel, MCT	2	0	1.000	6.40	21	5	0	0	16	0	45.0	49	176	32	32	3	1	0	4	29	3	26	2	0
Garza, Roberto, Rey.-N.L.	2	3	.400	6.71	19	7	0	0	12	0	51.0	54	194	40	38	9	3	4	0	31	7	20	3	1
Gomez, Jesus, A., Monc.	1	1	.500	4.70	10	3	0	0	7	0	23.0	28	93	16	12	2	2	0	1	19	2	15	2	0
Gomez Rios, Martin, Min.	4	14	.222	3.89	23	23	1	0	0	0	125.0	131	455	59	54	5	10	4	1	63	1	40	4	1
Gonzalez, Arturo, Mont.	7	8	.467	4.55	18	18	0	0	0	0	97.0	108	383	56	49	5	8	2	5	37	0	39	3	1
Gonzalez, Gilberto, Tor.	0	0	.000	40.50	3	0	0	0	3	0	0.2	4	6	3	3	1	0	0	0	3	0	0	2	0
Gonzalez, Victor Manuel, Jal.	1	6	.143	7.21	32	11	0	0	21	2	87.1	133	369	93	70	4	7	5	4	49	4	34	3	0
Grajales, Norberto, Tor.	4	1	.800	3.41	41	0	0	0	41	1	68.2	71	244	28	26	3	6	5	2	35	13	31	1	1
Green, Otis, Mont.	3	3	.500	1.95	21	0	0	0	21	4	32.1	19	106	7	7	2	2	1	0	15	0	39	1	0
Guerra, Esmili, Pue.	1	2	.333	3.86	8	3	0	0	5	0	18.2	26	71	13	8	0	3	0	1	8	0	7	1	0
Guerrero, Omar, Rey.	0	2	.000	11.12	7	2	0	0	5	0	11.1	23	51	14	14	1	1	0	1	9	2	6	1	0
Gutierrez, Arturo, Agu.	0	1	.000	4.19	8	2	0	0	6	0	19.1	19	69	9	9	0	0	2	1	13	0	6	0	0

Pitcher, Team	W	L	Pct.	ERA	G	GS	CG	ShO	GF	Sv.	IP	H	TBF	R	ER	HR	SH	SF	HB	BB	IBB	SO	WP	Bk.
Henry, John, Pue.	7	4	.636	4.10	15	10	5	1	5	0	68.0	67	254	31	31	5	4	2	4	24	1	37	3	1
Heredia, Hector, Mont.	9	9	.500	3.30	22	22	5	2	0	0	142.0	148	544	57	52	7	8	3	1	40	2	66	4	0
Hernandez, Dimas, C., Monc.	0	0	.000	4.81	13	0	0	0	13	0	24.1	21	88	17	13	4	0	3	0	19	1	12	2	0
Hernandez, Encarn'cn, Jal.-Monc.	2	1	.667	5.73	36	2	0	0	34	1	59.2	95	257	49	38	7	6	4	2	17	2	21	3	0
Hernandez, Jose Manuel, N.L.	7	4	.636	3.19	47	4	0	0	43	6	98.2	94	360	41	35	6	9	4	1	38	7	52	4	0
Hernandez, Julio, Agu.	5	11	.313	4.33	21	19	3	1	2	0	99.2	98	369	56	48	9	8	0	1	53	2	53	2	1
Hernandez, Manuel, A., MCRD	11	4	.733	3.18	23	23	5	2	0	0	141.2	142	531	54	50	9	10	1	2	54	0	98	4	0
Hernandez, Martin, Yuc.	11	3	.786	3.62	24	21	7	3	3	0	121.2	135	479	57	49	10	6	2	1	48	1	65	8	0
Hernandez, Ramon, Mont.	0	0	.000	10.53	13	0	0	0	13	0	19.2	28	88	25	23	1	1	1	0	18	0	11	6	0
Hernandez V., Manuel, Jal.	0	0	.000	7.71	1	0	0	0	1	0	2.1	4	9	2	2	1	0	1	0	1	0	0	0	0
Herrera, Calixto, Monc.	9	9	.500	3.69	50	3	1	1	47	0	92.2	82	332	42	38	3	11	3	9	59	11	69	8	0
Herrera, Enrique, Agu.	2	4	.333	2.64	34	3	0	0	31	1	71.2	83	275	25	21	6	2	3	3	23	1	35	4	0
Huerta, Luis Enrique, Pue.	9	7	.563	3.28	22	22	8	2	0	0	145.1	134	544	65	53	10	9	4	3	48	1	55	1	0
Hurst, Jonathan, Jal.-Mont.	4	1	.800	2.16	28	1	0	0	27	9	50.0	40	177	12	12	1	7	1	2	13	1	49	4	0
Inzunza, Jorge, Tab.	1	0	1.000	3.50	11	0	0	0	11	0	18.0	21	72	9	7	0	0	0	3	11	0	9	4	0
Iniguez, Dario, Jal.	2	7	.222	10.47	11	10	0	0	1	0	38.2	76	186	51	45	4	3	0	2	22	1	34	3	0
Jimenez, Cesar D., Monc.	3	6	.333	3.87	14	12	1	0	2	0	74.1	84	287	34	32	1	3	2	3	28	3	26	1	0
Jimenez, German, Yuc.-Ags.	6	4	.600	3.25	18	18	4	0	0	0	102.1	121	405	46	37	9	11	2	2	32	1	43	5	0
Jimenez, Issac, Yuc.	6	8	.429	3.20	19	19	3	0	0	0	112.2	117	422	46	40	3	8	0	9	56	1	54	5	0
Jones, Al, Tor.	4	9	.308	4.34	17	13	4	1	4	0	85.0	78	308	49	41	8	5	4	0	44	2	65	1	0
Juarez, Fernando, Tor.	1	0	1.000	4.26	10	0	0	0	10	0	6.1	7	26	3	3	0	0	1	1	3	0	1	0	0
Kelley, Drum Richard, Monc.	3	8	.273	3.10	12	12	2	0	0	0	72.2	68	267	33	25	2	5	1	2	39	3	48	8	0
Kiely, John, MCT	0	0	.000	0.00	1	0	0	0	1	0	0.1	0	0	0	0	0	1	0	0	0	0	0	0	0
Klvac, David John, Tor.	0	0	.000	10.80	3	0	0	0	3	1	5.0	5	19	6	6	0	0	0	0	6	0	4	0	0
Lara, Hugo, Cam.	8	5	.615	4.14	24	21	3	0	3	1	126.0	126	478	66	58	9	8	4	10	53	9	54	3	0
Lara, Jorge, Rey.	7	2	.778	2.33	39	1	0	0	37	4	73.1	53	261	28	19	2	4	3	0	38	3	45	1	0
Leal, Gerardo, Monc.	2	5	.286	7.13	25	6	0	0	19	0	70.2	109	299	62	56	8	3	4	1	30	0	28	8	0
Ledon, Juan Carlos, Jal.	0	2	.000	7.62	9	4	0	0	5	0	26.0	36	111	26	22	3	3	1	2	15	3	14	0	0
Leon, Danilo, Yuc.	1	3	.250	9.00	5	0	0	0	5	1	8.0	12	30	9	8	1	4	0	0	5	3	4	1	0
Lewis, Craig, Monc.	0	2	.000	6.28	3	3	0	0	0	0	14.1	19	58	12	10	0	0	1	0	11	1	10	2	0
Lewis, Scott, Mont.	2	1	.667	1.50	30	0	0	0	30	15	42.0	24	143	7	7	2	3	0	0	10	3	27	1	0
Leyva, Carlos Armando, MCT	1	0	1.000	7.30	26	0	0	0	26	0	24.2	33	100	24	20	0	3	2	1	27	3	9	7	0
Leyva, Filiberto, Agu.	1	2	.333	7.33	21	0	0	0	21	2	23.1	34	95	24	19	5	2	1	4	15	3	8	1	0
Lind, Orlando, Rey.	5	3	.625	2.60	12	12	3	1	0	0	72.2	72	263	24	21	5	11	0	2	32	0	42	1	0
Lizarraga, Andres, N.L.	0	0	.000	5.79	6	0	0	0	6	0	4.2	6	18	4	3	1	0	2	1	1	0	3	0	0
Lizarraga, Hugo, Cam.	3	4	.429	2.78	24	8	0	0	16	3	68.0	70	260	24	21	5	3	1	1	32	3	36	0	0
Llanes, Emeterio, Yuc.	0	1	.000	6.89	11	1	0	0	10	0	15.2	19	62	12	12	1	0	0	3	7	0	5	1	0
Loaiza, Sabino, Cam.	0	5	.000	6.31	9	6	0	0	3	0	25.2	22	94	20	18	1	1	1	2	21	2	6	1	0
Lopez, Emigdio, Tab.	14	6	.700	3.09	25	23	10	3	2	0	163.1	169	630	62	56	11	4	4	7	38	2	82	3	0
Lopez, Gilberto, Agu.	0	0	.000	7.43	8	0	0	0	8	0	13.1	16	53	11	11	0	0	0	0	9	0	6	0	0
Lopez, Jesus Nain, Rey.	0	0	.000	18.00	1	0	0	0	1	0	1.0	4	5	3	2	1	0	0	0	3	0	0	0	0
Lopez, Jonas, Ags.	3	3	.500	4.06	20	7	0	0	13	0	44.1	55	179	23	20	5	2	2	4	9	1	19	1	0
Lopez, De La T., J.J., Min.	4	7	.364	2.57	36	0	0	0	36	16	56.0	46	201	19	16	3	1	1	2	23	6	37	3	0
Lozano, Miguel Angel, Min.	0	0	.000	12.27	3	0	0	0	3	0	3.2	8	16	5	5	0	0	1	0	4	0	1	0	0
Lucio, Martin, Pue.	0	0	.000	0.00	1	0	0	0	1	0	1.0	1	3	0	0	0	0	1	0	0	0	1	0	0
Luevano, Juan, Agu.	6	8	.429	3.30	41	4	0	0	37	12	84.2	71	303	33	31	3	8	3	3	24	1	50	2	0
Lynch, Dave, MCT	2	2	.500	2.75	8	4	2	0	4	0	36.0	32	131	11	11	1	2	1	2	15	1	31	1	0
Macias, Abraham, Agu.	0	1	.000	9.58	6	1	0	0	5	1	10.1	15	43	12	11	2	0	1	0	11	2	4	0	0
Mack, Tony Len, Tor.	0	2	.000	7.20	4	1	0	0	3	0	10.0	19	45	8	8	1	0	0	0	6	0	2	0	0
Maclin, Lonnie, Agu.	0	0	.000	0.00	1	0	0	0	1	0	1.0	1	4	0	0	0	0	0	0	0	0	1	0	0
Mansur, Jeff, Pue.	0	0	.000	4.50	13	1	0	0	12	1	12.0	16	45	8	6	1	4	0	0	10	1	4	1	0
Manzano, Adrian, MCT	0	0	.000	0.00	2	1	0	0	1	0	3.2	3	13	0	0	0	1	0	0	2	0	1	0	0
Marquez, Miguel, Mont.-Agu.	0	0	.000	18.00	1	0	0	0	1	0	1.0	5	8	2	2	0	0	0	0	0	0	1	0	0
Martin, Daniel, Yuc.	0	0	.000	9.00	5	0	0	0	5	0	3.0	7	14	3	3	0	1	0	0	4	0	2	1	0
Martin, Thomas, MCT	0	1	.000	27.00	1	1	0	0	0	0	1.1	5	9	5	4	0	0	0	0	1	0	0	0	0
Martinez, Filiberto, Sal.	8	5	.615	2.76	19	19	3	2	0	0	107.2	98	399	39	33	2	5	2	7	57	0	57	3	1
Martnez, Mauricio, Sal.	0	1	.000	4.87	11	1	0	0	10	0	20.1	20	77	13	11	1	0	0	0	16	1	12	0	0
Martinez, Ramon, Pue.	0	0	.000	12.27	7	0	0	0	7	0	3.2	12	23	5	5	0	0	0	0	0	0	2	0	0
Martinez, Sean, Pue.	0	0	.000	15.75	2	0	0	0	2	0	4.0	12	23	7	7	1	0	0	0	2	0	2	0	0
Medina, Jose Ramon, Cam.	0	0	.000	0.00	1	0	0	0	1	0	1.1	1	5	0	0	0	0	0	0	1	0	0	0	0
Mejia, Cesar, Cam.	4	6	.400	4.85	24	5	1	0	19	2	55.2	56	204	38	30	6	5	5	5	31	6	27	1	0
Mendez, Luis Fernando, Rey.	6	6	.500	4.57	21	21	3	0	0	0	106.1	129	413	62	54	7	7	2	5	41	1	68	4	0
Meza, Leobardo, Agu.	2	1	.667	0.69	7	5	0	0	2	0	26.0	15	85	3	2	1	2	2	0	5	0	13	0	0
Minutelli, Gino, MCT	2	3	.400	8.26	12	5	1	0	7	1	28.1	43	123	29	26	2	3	2	2	15	0	15	2	0
Miranda, Julio Cesar, Tor.	6	6	.500	6.44	41	1	0	0	40	8	58.2	67	229	43	42	7	7	3	2	20	9	25	7	0
Molina, Joaquin, Tor.	0	1	.000	5.34	17	0	0	0	17	1	30.1	29	111	19	18	3	2	3	2	17	0	17	3	0
Montano, Francisco, Monc.	8	9	.471	4.15	22	22	3	0	0	0	128.0	134	490	68	59	7	5	3	1	38	2	78	5	0
Mora, Eleazar, Agu.	6	10	.375	4.53	23	21	3	0	2	0	117.1	133	454	67	59	12	6	5	10	43	2	58	2	1
Moreno, Angel, N.L.	16	3	.842	3.20	22	22	8	0	0	0	160.1	136	586	61	57	9	5	2	4	44	2	108	0	0
Moreno, Claudio, MCRD	3	1	.750	5.19	27	1	0	0	26	1	59.0	66	224	39	34	5	5	2	3	35	2	36	5	0
Moreno, Jesus, Sal.	10	4	.714	4.95	22	22	1	0	0	0	131.0	147	499	82	72	12	2	9	11	50	0	60	1	0
Moreno, Leobardo, MCRD	6	1	.857	5.02	21	8	1	0	13	0	52.0	61	205	32	29	6	2	3	1	23	0	41	1	0
Moreno Alvarez, Ricardo, N.L.	0	0	.000	8.18	10	1	0	0	9	0	11.0	14	42	11	10	2	0	0	0	18	1	7	4	0
Moreno V., Ricardo, Jal.	0	2	.000	1.85	9	2	2	0	7	1	24.1	26	93	9	5	0	2	1	0	10	0	11	0	0
Murillo, Felipe, Monc.	1	1	.500	2.16	43	0	0	0	43	30	58.1	57	219	18	14	1	2	4	1	13	1	40	0	0
Munoz, Miguel, Agu.-Rey.	11	3	.786	2.67	20	20	2	1	0	0	138.0	140	522	47	41	3	8	1	4	22	1	62	1	2
Munoz, Pablo, Pue.	0	0	.000	6.35	10	0	0	0	10	0	5.2	8	22	4	4	1	1	0	0	3	1	1	2	0
Munoz, Ricardo, Tab.	12	6	.667	2.46	22	22	7	3	0	0	142.2	128	514	49	39	5	14	2	7	36	1	69	1	1
Navarro, Adolfo, Ags.	1	5	.167	7.22	9	7	1	0	2	0	33.2	39	128	29	27	2	3	4	3	24	0	12	0	0
Navarro, Luis A., Sal.	3	4	.429	5.61	19	8	0	0	11	0	51.1	53	200	36	32	6	1	2	5	29	0	24	2	0
Neri, Braulio, Yuc.-Tor.	1	1	.500	12.56	21	0	0	0	21	0	14.1	26	64	25	20	1	1	3	0	20	3	5	5	0
Neri, Eduardo, Agu.	4	5	.444	3.59	51	3	0	0	48	4	102.2	86	359	46	41	5	6	0	3	71	3	61	5	2
Nunez Avina, J.J., Jal.	0	1	.000	7.62	17	0	0	0	17	0	28.1	41	117	24	24	3	0	3	0	15	0	11	5	0

Pitcher, Team	W	L	Pct.	ERA	G	GS	CG	ShO	GF	Sv.	IP	H	TBF	R	ER	HR	SH	SF	HB	BB	IBB	SO	WP	Bk.
Ochoa, Porfirio, N.L.	0	1	.000	8.22	7	1	0	0	6	0	7.2	15	35	8	7	1	1	1	1	2	1	1	0	0
Olague, Jesus, Mont.	0	0	.000	4.58	7	2	0	0	5	0	19.2	20	69	10	10	0	1	4	2	14	0	9	2	1
Orozco, Jaime, Pue.	8	10	.444	4.24	23	22	5	0	1	0	140.0	154	541	80	66	9	12	6	6	48	5	67	5	1
Ortega, Pablo, N.L.	0	1	.000	5.93	5	2	1	0	3	0	13.2	11	52	9	9	2	0	0	2	5	0	7	1	0
Osuna, Ricardo, Tab.	2	4	.333	4.26	8	8	0	0	0	0	38.0	45	147	25	18	0	2	2	3	20	0	16	0	0
Osuna, Roberto, N.L.	6	13	.316	4.45	25	22	1	0	3	0	127.1	148	499	75	63	14	8	4	3	55	3	74	1	1
Palafox, Juan Manuel, Tor.	10	7	.588	4.73	21	21	9	1	0	0	139.0	155	537	82	73	13	7	3	11	44	1	63	5	1
Pelcastregui, Leonardo, Tor.	0	0	.000	13.50	5	0	0	0	5	0	2.0	2	7	3	3	0	1	0	0	3	0	1	1	0
Perez, Joaquin, Min.	0	0	.000	3.86	1	0	0	0	1	0	2.1	2	9	1	1	0	0	0	0	0	0	0	1	0
Perez, Leonardo, Mont.	8	4	.667	2.48	34	6	1	0	28	4	83.1	69	299	31	23	6	8	4	5	47	7	56	3	0
Perez, Vladimir, Rey.	1	1	.500	2.82	14	0	0	0	14	6	22.1	17	76	7	7	1	2	0	1	13	4	6	2	0
Perry, Jeff, N.L.	4	11	.267	4.86	25	19	1	0	6	0	109.1	113	418	62	59	9	11	1	3	63	8	61	5	1
Pena, Alejandro, Mont.	0	0	.000	0.00	2	0	0	0	2	1	2.2	1	9	0	0	0	0	0	0	0	0	2	0	0
Pimentel, Roberto, Tor.-Monc.	5	6	.455	5.51	39	5	0	0	34	0	47.1	59	187	32	29	4	8	2	3	32	1	20	2	1
Pina, Rafael, MCRD	6	3	.667	3.38	42	0	0	0	42	3	69.1	66	266	29	26	2	6	2	1	39	3	63	10	0
Pinero, Hugo Jose, Min.	0	0	.000	5.40	3	0	0	0	3	0	6.2	4	23	5	4	0	1	0	1	3	2	3	0	0
Pruneda, Armando, Monc.	2	3	.400	5.63	10	3	0	0	7	0	24.0	27	92	16	15	4	0	1	0	18	0	4	3	1
Puig, Benny, Ags.-Tor.	4	5	.444	3.23	16	15	4	0	1	0	97.2	94	363	41	35	7	7	3	5	46	0	38	6	0
Pulido, Raymundo, MCT	0	0	.000	11.81	2	2	0	0	0	0	5.1	5	19	7	7	2	0	0	0	7	0	4	3	0
Purata, Julio, Rey.	13	5	.722	3.60	22	22	5	3	0	0	132.2	126	493	61	53	11	7	1	2	50	1	74	0	0
Quijada, Mario, Tor.	0	0	.000	0.00	2	0	0	0	2	0	3.2	2	13	0	0	0	0	0	0	2	0	2	0	0
Quintanilla, Enrique, N.L.	2	2	.500	7.04	33	5	0	0	28	1	61.1	89	255	51	48	8	4	2	5	27	4	30	8	1
Quintero, Victor H., Tor.	1	0	1.000	6.75	5	0	0	0	5	0	8.0	10	36	11	6	2	0	1	0	3	0	5	0	0
Quiroz, Aaron, N.L.	11	7	.611	3.11	23	22	3	0	1	0	139.0	136	527	54	48	11	6	0	3	56	3	108	9	0
Quiroz, Jose J., Ags.	4	2	.667	3.67	23	0	0	0	23	1	34.1	28	119	14	14	2	4	2	0	20	3	27	1	0
Quinones, Enrique, Yuc.	1	4	.200	4.66	25	2	0	0	23	1	58.0	71	227	35	30	7	6	2	0	25	3	34	1	0
Ramirez, Martin, Ags.	1	0	1.000	10.80	5	0	0	0	5	0	8.1	13	36	10	10	0	1	1	1	2	0	4	1	0
Ramirez, Miguel, A., Jal.	0	1	.000	8.72	8	1	0	0	7	0	21.2	28	82	22	21	2	2	1	2	19	1	9	6	0
Ramirez, Roberto, MCRD	13	3	.813	2.56	20	20	8	3	0	0	137.1	125	502	50	39	9	5	3	5	35	0	70	3	2
Ramos, Jorge Luis, Pue.	1	4	.200	3.97	23	1	0	0	22	1	47.2	53	187	27	21	5	2	0	5	19	0	19	1	0
Raygoza, Martin, Monc.	7	10	.412	3.47	21	21	6	0	0	0	140.0	154	555	71	54	9	2	6	3	40	4	77	4	0
Renteria, Hilario, Tor.	5	10	.333	6.00	22	22	0	0	0	0	111.0	146	459	87	74	13	4	7	5	31	6	58	4	0
Retes, Lorenzo, Tab.-Min.	2	5	.286	5.24	24	17	0	0	7	0	87.2	119	359	61	51	6	11	4	0	40	2	38	1	0
Reyes, Dennis, MCRD	5	5	.500	6.60	17	15	1	0	2	0	58.2	76	228	49	43	4	7	5	0	41	0	44	2	0
Rincon, Ricardo, MCRD	6	6	.500	5.16	27	11	0	0	16	3	75.0	86	285	45	43	7	7	5	1	41	0	41	3	0
Rios, Jesus, MCT	10	6	.625	4.25	25	23	7	3	2	0	146.0	121	541	78	69	17	4	5	6	50	1	103	2	0
Rivera, Eleazar, Monc.	1	0	1.000	0.00	1	1	0	0	0	0	8.0	6	28	2	0	0	0	0	0	4	0	6	1	0
Rivera, Hector, Rey.-Agu.	6	8	.429	5.38	23	15	3	1	8	0	87.0	97	348	58	52	7	3	3	5	39	1	35	4	0
Rivera, Lino, Monc.	1	3	.250	8.42	5	5	0	0	0	0	25.2	41	111	29	24	4	1	1	1	13	0	17	3	0
Rivera, Paul, Ags.	2	1	.667	5.82	14	7	1	0	7	0	38.2	45	151	27	25	3	0	3	2	34	0	27	6	2
Rodriguez, Fernando, Pue.	0	0	.000	6.00	5	0	0	0	5	0	3.0	2	10	2	2	0	0	1	0	3	0	2	0	0
Rodriguez, Mario A., Rey.	0	1	.000	11.77	12	0	0	0	12	0	26.0	47	123	35	34	3	0	0	1	11	1	9	1	0
Rodriguez, Mario, Min.	3	9	.250	4.53	26	17	1	0	9	0	109.1	131	419	63	55	11	12	2	4	46	5	31	1	0
Rodriguez, Raul, Sal.	14	4	.778	3.30	23	22	3	1	1	0	144.2	126	527	59	53	6	6	4	3	55	0	106	2	1
Rodriguez, Rene, N.L.	3	3	.500	3.96	32	1	0	0	31	4	36.1	46	147	26	16	0	3	1	2	19	6	10	1	0
Rodriguez, Rosario, Mont.	0	0	.000	10.38	11	0	0	0	11	0	4.1	6	19	5	5	0	0	0	0	5	1	5	2	0
Rodriguez, Salvador, Yuc.	0	3	.000	6.08	10	3	0	0	7	1	26.2	28	102	19	18	3	1	0	0	20	0	14	2	1
Rojo, Oscar, Cam.-Rey.	3	1	.750	5.73	34	2	0	0	32	1	59.2	69	236	43	38	6	5	5	2	33	4	26	4	0
Romero, Juan, Tab.	3	5	.375	3.49	29	5	0	0	24	1	69.2	71	258	34	27	3	5	1	3	29	1	23	3	1
Romo, Guillermo, Tor.	1	3	.250	5.96	15	9	0	0	6	0	45.1	59	174	33	30	2	5	3	2	38	1	15	4	0
Ruiz, Cecilio, Tab.	13	5	.722	1.71	24	23	7	5	1	0	162.2	132	584	41	31	6	20	4	4	33	1	92	1	0
Sadecki, Steve, Jal.	0	5	.000	7.59	5	5	1	0	0	0	21.1	33	90	24	18	3	1	2	2	18	0	7	4	0
Saenz, Alfredo, Pue.	8	10	.444	3.60	26	20	9	1	6	1	132.1	143	507	73	53	13	12	3	6	52	4	71	6	1
Saldana, Edgardo, Agu.-Tab.	6	8	.429	3.22	23	20	4	1	3	0	117.1	121	451	47	42	6	8	3	4	42	1	70	4	1
Saldana, Gerardo, Pue.	0	1	.000	9.64	2	1	0	0	1	0	4.2	9	20	5	5	1	0	0	0	7	1	3	0	0
Salgado, Eduardo, MCT	0	0	.000	3.86	11	0	0	0	11	0	14.0	16	55	6	6	2	0	1	1	7	0	6	1	0
Sanchez, Hector, Agu.-Mont.	2	3	.400	5.44	24	0	0	0	24	1	44.2	60	180	30	27	8	2	2	4	11	3	16	2	0
Sanchez, Jose Luis, Jal.	1	4	.200	6.32	14	6	2	0	8	0	47.0	59	190	50	33	2	0	6	3	47	2	18	7	0
Sandoval, Carlos, Min.	0	1	.000	3.28	32	1	0	0	31	0	35.2	32	130	14	13	3	5	0	2	16	5	17	1	0
Sandoval, Guillermo, Mont.	2	4	.333	5.03	33	4	0	0	29	1	59.0	62	214	36	33	2	7	4	1	31	1	36	0	0
Segura, Jose, Yuc.	10	2	.833	4.47	38	0	0	0	38	14	54.1	47	199	29	27	3	7	0	0	27	3	38	10	0
Serna, Ramon, Ags.	4	3	.571	4.64	30	3	0	0	27	2	64.0	68	243	39	33	7	4	1	3	35	2	36	3	1
Sierra, Abel, Cam.	11	9	.550	2.64	24	21	10	5	3	0	153.1	132	578	60	45	7	9	3	0	48	4	80	4	1
Silverio, Victor, Agu.-Ags.	0	0	.000	6.75	2	0	0	0	2	0	1.1	2	6	1	1	0	0	0	0	5	0	1	0	0
Smith, Daryl, Sal.	3	2	.600	4.11	7	4	1	0	3	0	30.2	30	116	17	14	1	1	0	0	22	0	20	0	0
Solarte, Jose A., Min.	8	4	.667	1.72	45	6	3	1	39	4	115.0	93	397	23	22	2	9	3	1	42	9	64	1	0
Solis, Ricardo, Yuc.	9	9	.500	4.92	23	20	1	1	3	0	115.1	143	452	66	63	7	13	0	2	43	1	51	5	0
Sombra, Francisco, Sal.	2	3	.400	3.18	37	4	1	0	33	0	51.0	52	190	21	18	2	5	4	0	15	2	25	4	0
Soto, Fernando, Min.	7	14	.333	3.63	25	25	4	2	0	0	161.1	182	638	77	65	10	6	2	0	51	9	67	2	0
Soto, Ramon E., Agu.	0	0	.000	1.80	3	0	0	0	3	0	5.0	3	18	1	1	0	0	0	0	3	0	4	1	0
Strauss, Julio Cesar, Tab.	2	2	.500	2.13	12	0	0	0	12	2	12.2	9	41	3	3	0	2	0	0	10	4	9	0	0
Tapia, Jose, Cam.	0	0	.000	9.00	1	0	0	0	1	0	1.0	3	6	1	1	0	0	0	0	0	0	0	0	0
Tatum, Willie, Yuc.	0	1	.000	....	1	0	0	0	1	0	0.0	2	3	2	2	0	0	0	0	1	1	0	0	0
Tejeda, Juan, Cam.	3	4	.429	3.24	27	9	1	1	18	2	66.2	75	262	34	24	4	8	3	0	17	3	18	1	0
Tinoco, Ruben, Cam.	0	2	.000	4.34	25	1	0	0	24	0	56.0	70	223	35	27	6	6	4	3	21	5	16	4	1
Toledo, Mario, Cam.	2	2	.500	4.15	26	4	0	0	22	0	43.1	45	169	31	20	5	4	3	1	28	2	16	2	0
Tunnell, Lee, MCT	4	5	.444	5.91	14	4	0	0	10	0	35.0	34	132	27	23	4	1	1	1	14	1	25	2	0
Uribe, Juan Carlos, Yuc.	6	3	.667	1.93	43	1	1	1	42	6	70.0	52	244	19	15	1	5	3	3	30	5	43	5	0
Valdez, Armando, Sal.-Pue.-Tor.	0	1	.000	24.16	10	0	0	0	10	0	6.1	26	44	18	17	3	1	0	1	8	1	5	0	1
Valdez, Jose Luis, N.L.	2	1	.667	3.80	15	1	0	0	14	0	21.1	28	90	11	9	1	1	2	0	5	1	11	2	0
Valdez, Rafael, Rey.-Yuc.	8	1	.889	5.51	22	21	2	1	1	0	96.1	124	393	65	59	6	7	5	4	49	1	67	5	0
Valencia, Jorge, Sal.	6	5	.545	5.54	29	17	2	0	12	0	102.1	131	395	72	63	12	6	5	1	62	2	38	5	2
Valenzuela, Aurelio, Yuc.	1	0	1.000	6.23	7	1	0	0	6	0	13.0	15	54	16	9	1	0	2	0	7	0	3	0	0

Pitcher, Team	W	L	Pct.	ERA	G	GS	CG	ShO	GF	Sv.	IP	H	TBF	R	ER	HR	SH	SF	HB	BB	IBB	SO	WP	Bk.
Valenzuela, Jorge, Pue.	0	0	.000	22.50	6	0	0	0	6	0	4.0	10	22	10	10	3	0	0	0	5	0	3	1	0
Valenzuela, Saul, Pue.	10	8	.556	3.94	22	22	7	1	0	0	146.1	156	551	75	64	10	16	6	3	54	3	52	5	0
Vargas, Ignacio, Pue.	3	8	.273	6.08	18	8	0	0	10	0	53.1	67	207	44	36	6	5	2	0	31	1	17	1	0
Vargas, Joel, Tab.	0	0	.000	5.40	4	0	0	0	4	0	5.0	6	20	3	3	0	0	0	1	2	0	4	2	0
Vazquez, Adrian, Cam.	11	6	.647	2.64	21	21	3	0	0	0	136.1	118	487	48	40	8	10	1	5	72	3	39	4	1
Vazquez, Aguedo, Ags.	6	0	1.000	3.97	22	12	1	1	10	1	77.0	74	288	35	34	7	1	2	3	31	2	33	1	0
Vega, Obed, MCT	5	5	.500	5.75	18	14	0	0	4	0	76.2	78	289	58	49	10	5	3	1	58	2	41	6	1
Velazquez, Ernesto A., Tor.-Sal.	0	4	.000	8.65	19	7	0	0	12	0	42.2	63	179	43	41	8	2	3	2	33	0	10	4	0
Velazquez, Ildefonso, Yuc.	0	0	.000	10.13	3	0	0	0	3	0	2.2	4	13	4	3	1	1	0	0	3	0	1	1	0
Velazquez, Israel, Min.	4	12	.250	3.28	23	22	2	1	1	0	120.2	114	450	58	44	9	7	4	10	63	3	77	1	1
Veliz A., Francisco, Sal.-Monc.	0	0	.000	2.96	19	0	0	0	19	0	24.1	22	83	8	8	2	2	1	2	14	0	15	4	0
Verdugo, Orlando, Yuc.	0	0	.000	54.00	2	0	0	0	2	0	0.2	3	5	4	4	0	0	0	0	4	0	0	2	0
Villalobos, Noe, Mont.	0	0	.000	11.25	2	1	0	0	1	0	4.0	6	18	5	5	1	0	0	0	3	0	1	2	0
Villanueva, Luis, Ags.	2	2	.500	6.00	28	0	0	0	28	3	18.0	23	69	15	12	1	2	1	0	8	1	13	0	1
Villarreal, Antonio, Mont.-Yuc.	5	2	.714	2.95	34	2	0	0	32	1	76.1	78	288	33	25	4	7	3	2	35	5	43	7	0
Villegas, Jose Angel, Ags.	9	7	.563	3.70	52	2	0	0	50	7	82.2	86	310	38	34	7	9	2	2	46	7	35	5	0
Villegas, Ramon, Pue.	0	1	.000	5.97	17	1	0	0	16	0	37.2	50	153	28	25	5	1	2	1	14	2	16	1	0
Vizcarra A., Rodrigo, Ags.	0	0	.000	3.60	3	0	0	0	3	0	5.0	8	22	4	2	0	0	0	0	3	0	0	0	0
Wagner, Hector, Ags.	1	5	.167	6.03	15	3	0	0	12	5	31.1	46	130	21	21	2	4	0	0	21	5	18	1	0
Walker, Mike, MCRD	2	3	.400	4.01	19	5	0	0	14	4	42.2	41	152	21	19	5	1	2	2	20	1	23	4	0
Wayne, Gary, MCRD-Monc.	4	5	.444	3.41	22	6	2	0	16	2	58.0	60	220	26	22	6	5	2	1	14	1	51	7	0
Zappelli, Mark, Sal.	6	8	.429	2.63	33	9	2	0	24	6	106.0	109	396	40	31	2	9	0	6	47	0	45	3	0
Zavala, Marcos, MCT	0	0	.000	4.50	4	0	0	0	4	0	2.0	2	7	1	1	0	0	1	0	2	0	2	0	0

COMBINATION SHUTOUTS: A total of 70 combination shutouts were pitched in the Mexican League in 1995. Aguila led the league with 11.

NO-HIT GAMES: Ramirez, Mexico City Red Devils, defeated Tabasco, 2-0, June 6; Hernandez, Aguila, defeated Mexico City Red Devils, 1-0, June 20; Henry, Puebla, defeated Aguila, 3-0, July 1; Cuervo, Campeche, defeated Minatitlan, 4-0, July 2.

1995 FIELDING

TEAM

Team	Pct.	G	PO	A	E	TC	DP	PB
Aguascalientes	.981	114	2813	1272	80	4165	126	9
M.C. Red Devils	.979	114	2798	1292	86	4176	120	13
Minatitlan	.979	116	2919	1293	90	4302	131	11
Nuevo Laredo	.978	116	2947	1291	96	4334	122	11
Mexico City Tigers	.977	116	2845	1240	96	4181	91	8
Yucatan	.977	115	2814	1305	99	4218	107	12
Torreon	.977	115	2831	1308	96	4235	134	12
Aguila	.976	116	2894	1363	106	4363	137	10
Reynosa	.975	116	2942	1306	107	4355	128	4
Monterrey	.975	116	2880	1269	105	4254	114	8
Saltillo	.972	116	2907	1358	123	4388	149	7
Puebla	.971	116	2776	1312	122	4210	116	9
Tabasco	.969	115	2833	1289	131	4253	118	4
Campeche	.967	115	2802	1245	137	4184	120	8
Monclova	.966	116	2849	1236	145	4230	128	9
Jalisco	.965	114	2741	1254	147	4142	126	10

TRIPLE PLAYS: Aguila, Mexico City Tigers, Monclova, Nuevo Laredo, Torreon, Puebla.

INDIVIDUAL

FIRST BASEMEN

Player, Team	Pct.	G	PO	A	E	TC	DP
Estrada, Ruben, N.L.	1.000	66	381	29	0	410	45
Valdez, Jesus, Yuc.	1.000	41	273	21	0	294	26
Peralta, Amado, Yuc.-Jal.	1.000	29	256	11	0	267	23
Arce, Francisco J., Min.	1.000	23	179	11	0	190	23
Velazquez, Guillermo, Mont.	1.000	16	138	4	0	142	11
Sasser, Mike, Min.	1.000	15	150	7	0	157	15
Fariss, Monty, Mont.	1.000	13	100	3	0	103	12
Castaneda, Rafael, N.L.	1.000	12	76	6	0	82	4
Tillman, Rusty, Agu.-Tab.	1.000	11	91	4	0	95	10
Gonzalez, Denio, Sal.	1.000	11	85	7	0	92	10
Rendina, Mike, Monc.	1.000	11	81	9	0	90	8
Alvarez, Luis, Jal.	1.000	11	83	6	0	89	10
Carrillo, Matias, MCT	1.000	10	62	0	0	62	3
Guerrero, Javier, Ags.	.998	58	475	28	1	504	48
Romero, Marco Antonio, MCT	.996	105	929	61	4	994	78
Gavia, Jesus, Agu.-Min.	.996	29	209	13	1	223	22
Machiria, Pablo, Ags.	.996	26	215	21	1	237	31
Tolentino, Jose, Mont.	.995	76	691	41	4	736	67
Quintana, Carlos, Min.-Yuc.	.995	71	615	43	3	661	57
Valenzuela, Horacio, Min.-Jal.	.995	52	402	22	2	426	48
Pena, Luis Alberto, Pue.	.994	85	742	39	5	786	63
Paez, Raul, MCRD	.994	84	507	34	3	544	58
Zulueta, Felix, Tab.	.992	13	115	8	1	124	8
Avila, Ruben, Tor.	.991	112	1022	71	10	1103	117
Casillas, Adam, Rey.	.991	90	785	76	8	869	80
Torres, Eduardo, Sal.	.991	15	108	4	1	113	10
Mendez, Jesus, Agu.-Tab.	.990	105	927	76	10	1013	102
Almeida, Shammar, Sal.	.990	93	757	57	8	822	101
Ortega, Roberto, Tab.	.990	49	376	35	4	415	54
Rodriguez, Genaro, N.L.	.989	56	329	21	4	354	43
Tejeda, Arturo, N.L.	.989	15	80	6	1	87	11
Aganza, Ruben, Monc.	.988	92	825	59	11	895	79
Naveda, Edgar, Jal.	.988	57	455	42	6	503	51
Quiroz, Jose Julian, Ags.	.988	16	80	4	1	85	9
Orantes, Ramon, Mont.	.988	11	80	4	1	85	8
Guerrero, Jaime, Ags.	.988	11	76	8	1	85	8
Stark, Matt, Rey.	.987	17	147	7	2	156	17
Barrera, Nelson, MCRD	.986	67	475	27	7	509	51
Castro, Eddie, Min.-Sal.	.986	32	262	19	4	285	38
Arvizu, Javier, Cam.	.985	92	798	47	13	858	83
Sommers, Jesus, Pue.-Agu.	.985	21	186	11	3	200	15
Michel, Domingo, Cam.	.985	18	129	5	2	136	11
Arevalo, Guadalupe, Ags.	.982	10	52	3	1	56	11
Chan, Armando, Monc.	.981	13	99	4	2	105	21
Zamudio, Rafael, Mont.-Agu.	.978	13	87	4	2	93	12
Estrada, Ricardo, Min.-Agu.	.976	38	316	15	8	339	32
Rivera, German, Pue.	.963	20	123	8	5	136	16
Reyna, Luis, Monc.-Tab.	.958	10	65	4	3	72	4
Hernandez A., Martin, Cam.	.948	17	53	2	3	58	5

FIRST BASEMEN WITH FEWER THAN 10 GAMES

Player, Team	Pct.	G	PO	A	E	TC	DP
Diaz, Luis Fernando, MCT	1.000	9	41	1	0	42	2
Infante, Alexis, Tab.	1.000	9	40	5	0	45	6
Rodriguez, Boi, N.L.	1.000	9	44	1	0	45	2
Merchand, Mark, Rey.	1.000	9	96	5	0	101	11
Cornejo, Edgar, Sal.	1.000	6	28	2	0	30	2
Mora, Andres, N.L.	1.000	6	46	2	0	48	8
Rubio, Marco A., Cam.-Min.	1.000	5	13	1	0	14	3
Ritchie, Greg, Tab.	1.000	4	31	3	0	34	3
Soto, Emison, Pue.	1.000	4	18	0	0	18	2
Leal, Jose Guadalupe, Cam.	1.000	4	26	1	0	27	5
Cobos, Rogelio, MCRD	1.000	3	11	2	0	13	0
Ojeda, Miguel, MCRD	1.000	3	17	2	0	19	1
Trevino, Alejandro, Mont.	1.000	3	10	0	0	10	0
Perez, Juan Luis, Tor.	1.000	3	20	0	0	20	2
Valverde, Raul, Jal.	1.000	3	17	2	0	19	4
Villanueva, Hector, MCT	1.000	2	12	0	0	12	0
Sparks, Greg, MCT	1.000	2	19	0	0	19	1
Pardo, Victor Manuel, Pue.	1.000	2	5	0	0	5	1
Canedo, Alberto, Cam.	1.000	2	8	0	0	8	1
Tatum, Willie, Yuc.	1.000	2	21	2	0	23	1
McCoy, Trey, N.L.	1.000	2	13	2	0	15	0
Motley, Darryl, Tor.-Agu.	1.000	2	8	1	0	9	0
Snider, Van, Tor.	1.000	2	8	2	0	10	1

Player, Team	Pct.	G	PO	A	E	TC	DP
Cervera, Francisco, Jal.	1.000	2	23	1	0	24	4
Nunez Avina, Jose Juan, Jal.	1.000	2	1	0	0	1	0
Mendez, Roberto C., MCRD	1.000	1	1	0	0	1	0
Mere, Pedro, MCT	1.000	1	0	1	0	1	0
Ortiz, Alejandro, MCT	1.000	1	1	0	0	1	0
Rojas, Francisco, Tab.	1.000	1	2	0	0	2	1
Valenzuela, Eduardo, Sal.	1.000	1	1	0	0	1	0
Martinez, Raul, Sal.	1.000	1	1	0	0	1	1
Robles, Ricardo, Sal.	1.000	1	3	0	0	3	2
Flores, Miguel, Mont.	1.000	1	10	0	0	10	0
Perez, Francisco, Rey.	1.000	1	1	0	0	1	0
Lopez, Gonzalo, Monc.	1.000	1	1	0	0	1	0
Enriquez, Graciano, Ags.	1.000	1	3	0	0	3	0
Lopez A., Victor M., Jal.	1.000	1	10	1	0	11	0
Alvarez, Ivan, Jal.	1.000	1	13	1	0	14	0
Clement, Wes, Ags.	.985	8	59	8	1	68	4
Guzman, Marco A., Yuc.	.977	6	40	3	1	44	5
Cantu, Gerardo, Pue.	.970	8	32	0	1	33	2
Garcia, Cornelio, Mont.	.969	5	29	2	1	32	6
Cruz, Luis Alfonso, Rey.	.958	6	39	7	2	48	8
Sabino, Miguel, Jal.	.955	5	39	3	2	44	7
Cuevas, Angelo, Tab.-Min.	.950	6	34	4	2	40	5
Payro, Edison, Cam.	.947	6	17	1	1	19	3
Cairo, Sergio, Yuc.	.900	2	15	3	2	20	2
Rivera, Alberto, Jal.	.750	1	3	0	1	4	0
Martinez, Grimaldo, Monc.	.667	1	1	1	1	3	1

TRIPLE PLAYS: Aganza, Avila, Ri. Estrada, Ru. Estrada, Romero, Sommers.

SECOND BASEMEN

Player, Team	Pct.	G	PO	A	E	TC	DP
Balderas, S., Abelardo, Min.	1.000	12	16	24	0	40	4
Verdugo, Guadalupe, Tor.	1.000	11	26	23	0	49	6
Sanchez, Armando, Mont.	.994	64	151	164	2	317	45
Morales, Florentino, N.L.	.990	39	97	95	2	194	34
Camacho, Adulfo, Yuc.	.989	112	269	340	7	616	73
Esquer, Ramon, Rey.	.989	85	227	234	5	466	68
Zazueta, Mauricio, Tor.	.988	78	189	235	5	429	60
Ruiz, Juan De Dios, Tor.	.986	17	34	38	1	73	10
Rivera, Alberto, Jal.	.986	14	34	35	1	70	11
Renteria, Edison, Agu.-Cam.	.985	29	50	78	2	130	18
Zazueta, Juan Carlos, Tab.	.984	47	90	90	3	183	18
Martinez, Grimaldo, Monc.	.983	101	230	303	9	542	78
Vizcarra, Roberto, Ags.	.981	104	282	285	11	578	83
Rodriguez, Juan F., Rey.-Agu.	.981	49	119	144	5	268	38
Martinez, Luis Carlos, Sal.	.981	13	22	29	1	52	10
Castro, Arnoldo, Min.	.980	109	318	322	13	653	88
Verdugo, Vicente, MCRD	.979	105	213	306	11	530	76
Carrasco, Ernesto, N.L.	.979	93	225	235	10	470	67
Tovar, Jose De Jesus, Sal.-Monc.	.979	36	95	95	4	194	31
Mendiola, Juan Carlos, Agu.	.979	28	41	52	2	95	11
Garcia, Carlos, Agu.	.978	49	105	117	5	227	37
Mere, Pedro, MCT	.977	89	205	271	11	487	57
Pardo, Victor Manuel, Pue.	.975	102	222	281	13	516	69
Flores, Miguel, Mont.	.975	34	103	91	5	199	23
Duran, Felipe, MCRD	.975	14	23	16	1	40	5
Gonzalez, Jesus, Jal.	.974	84	224	225	12	461	74
Trapaga, Miguel, MCT	.970	31	39	59	3	101	7
Wong Medrano, Julian, Monc.	.969	10	14	17	1	32	7
Infante, Alexis, Tab.	.967	86	236	231	16	483	66
Hernandez B., Juan C., Pue.	.967	19	27	32	2	61	8
Loredo, Jorge Luis, Cam.	.966	68	137	180	11	328	47
Vizcarra, Marco, A., Rey.	.965	35	74	90	6	170	20
Precichi, Jorge, Sal.	.963	78	216	256	18	490	78
Magallanes, Ever, Mont.	.962	11	25	25	2	52	5
Salas, Heriberto, Tor.	.955	13	21	21	2	44	5
Sanchez, Roque, Cam.	.952	23	26	31	3	62	7
Santos, Julio, Jal.	.947	15	30	42	4	76	16
Arevalo, Guadalupe, Ags.	.941	10	7	25	2	34	5
Quintero, Guillermo, Mont.	.935	43	33	39	5	77	10
Rubio, Marco A., Cam.-Min.	.909	10	13	17	3	33	4

SECOND BASEMEN WITH FEWER THAN 10 GAMES

Player, Team	Pct.	G	PO	A	E	TC	DP
Lopez, Miguel, Yuc.	1.000	9	16	13	0	29	6
Paredes, Johnny, Agu.	1.000	7	19	18	0	37	5
Fernandez, Fabian, Rey.	1.000	6	6	4	0	10	4
Estrada, Ruben, N.L.	1.000	5	4	1	0	5	1
Gutierrez, Felipe, Monc.	1.000	5	12	10	0	22	4
Nunez Garcia, Jose J., Jal.	1.000	5	6	10	0	16	0
Ramirez, G., Jesus A., MCRD	1.000	4	1	8	0	9	1
Lopez, Fabian, MCRD	1.000	4	6	10	0	16	1
Arredondo, Jesus, A., Ags.	1.000	4	12	15	0	27	4
Robles, Trinidad, MCT-Min.	1.000	3	3	2	0	5	0

Player, Team	Pct.	G	PO	A	E	TC	DP
Vargas, Trinidad, Pue.	1.000	3	8	11	0	19	4
Perez, Alejandro, N.L.	1.000	3	4	1	0	5	0
Felix, Arturo, Yuc.	1.000	2	2	0	0	2	0
Malpica, Enrique, Agu.	1.000	2	3	5	0	8	1
Monroy, Francisco, Mont.	1.000	2	2	0	0	2	0
Ayala Armenta, Mario, Monc.	1.000	2	4	1	0	5	1
Roa, Hector, MCT	1.000	1	4	3	0	7	0
Gastelum, G., Sergio, O., MCT	1.000	1	0	3	0	3	0
Marrujo, Hector, Tab.	1.000	1	2	2	0	4	0
Perez, Alfredo, Pue.	1.000	1	1	1	0	2	0
Soto, Emison, Pue.	1.000	1	0	4	0	4	1
Brinkley, Darrell, Cam.	1.000	1	2	2	0	4	0
Diaz, Remigio, Mont.	1.000	1	1	1	0	2	1
Rodriguez, Genaro, N.L.	1.000	1	4	0	0	4	0
Rodriguez, Hector, Rey.	1.000	1	1	0	0	1	0
Contreras, Cuitlahuac, Tor.-Monc.	1.000	1	0	1	0	1	0
Olvera, Sergio, Monc.	1.000	1	1	1	0	2	1
Leyva, German, Monc.	1.000	1	3	4	0	7	0
Laurencio, Rodfer, Cam.	.975	9	16	23	1	40	1
Arredondo, Hernando, Pue.	.960	8	7	17	1	25	1
Cervera, Francisco, Jal.	.955	3	14	7	1	22	2
Canizalez, Juan Carlos, Mont.	.923	6	7	5	1	13	1
Montalvo, Ivan, MCT	.909	7	7	13	2	22	1
Valenzuela S., Joel, Tor.	.889	6	3	5	1	9	0
Barrera, Jesus Antonio, Min.	.875	1	2	5	1	8	0
Valenzuela, Armando, Rey.	.833	1	1	4	1	6	0

TRIPLE PLAYS: Carrasco, Garcia, Mere.

THIRD BASEMEN

Player, Team	Pct.	G	PO	A	E	TC	DP
Garcia, Carlos, Agu.	.990	46	27	69	1	97	10
Arevalo, Guadalupe, Ags.	.982	25	14	42	1	57	4
Sanchez, Roque, Cam.	.981	28	12	39	1	52	3
Balderas, S. Abelardo, Min.	.977	30	18	24	1	43	1
Castaneda, Rafael, N.L.	.973	107	112	245	10	367	33
Cornejo, Edgar, Sal.	.973	34	22	50	2	74	10
Roa, Hector, MCT	.972	28	18	51	2	71	1
Aguilar, Enrique, Ags.	.968	61	47	103	5	155	9
Cruz, Luis Alfonso, Rey.	.967	11	6	23	1	30	2
Rivera, Alberto, Jal.	.964	19	15	39	2	56	3
Duran, Felipe, MCRD	.962	26	23	52	3	78	4
Valle, Jorge Luis, Tor.	.960	27	24	73	4	101	10
Ortiz, Alejandro, MCT	.958	87	55	174	10	239	14
Orantes, Ramon, Mont.	.957	35	14	53	3	70	5
Peralta, Amado, Yuc.-Jal.	.955	54	46	101	7	154	15
Cazarin, Manuel, Agu.	.955	19	13	29	2	44	5
Tatis, Bernardo, MCRD	.949	83	71	190	14	275	15
Aganza, Ruben, Monc.	.947	22	28	44	4	76	11
Ruiz, Juan De Dios, Tor.	.945	86	73	183	15	271	20
Sanchez, Armando, Mont.	.945	28	14	38	3	55	3
Rivera, German, Pue.	.943	96	67	199	16	282	23
Arce, Francisco J., Min.	.943	55	37	112	9	158	15
Carrasco, Ernesto, N.L.	.943	12	9	24	2	35	3
Jimenez, Ulises, Jal.	.938	26	31	45	5	81	3
Leyva, German, Monc.	.934	93	84	170	18	272	23
Rubio, Marco A., Cam.-Min.	.933	63	48	120	12	180	13
Quinones, Luis, Yuc.	.933	42	32	107	10	149	13
Malpica, Enrique, Agu.	.929	57	37	119	12	168	13
Rodriguez, Hector, Rey.	.928	106	103	192	23	318	17
Guerrero, Jaime, Ags.	.927	34	29	60	7	96	10
Franco, Manuel, Mont.	.925	56	42	94	11	147	14
Gonzalez, Denio, Sal.	.922	90	78	160	20	258	22
Felix, Arturo, Yuc.	.922	69	59	131	16	206	10
Jelks, Greg, Cam.	.921	16	13	45	5	63	8
Barrera, Nelson, MCRD	.912	11	4	27	3	34	2
Loredo, Jorge Luis, Cam.	.909	13	6	24	3	33	2
Romero, Oscar, Tab.	.907	113	96	227	33	356	18
Santos, Julio, Jal.	.905	10	4	15	2	21	2
Arredondo, Hernando, Pue.	.900	33	13	50	7	70	3
Renteria, Edison, Agu.-Cam.	.900	17	18	27	5	50	0
Castaldo, Vince, Cam.	.894	39	26	67	11	104	8
Naveda, Edgar, Jal.	.825	10	9	24	7	40	3

THIRD BASEMEN WITH FEWER THAN 10 GAMES

Player, Team	Pct.	G	PO	A	E	TC	DP
Magallanes, Ever, Mont.	1.000	8	5	9	0	14	0
Vizcarra, Marco A., Rey.	1.000	8	0	3	0	3	0
Michel, Domingo, Cam.	1.000	7	4	10	0	14	2
Verdugo, Sostenes, Yuc.	1.000	5	2	6	0	8	1
Verdugo, Vincente, MCRD	1.000	4	0	2	0	2	0
Camacho, Adulfo, Yuc.	1.000	4	1	7	0	8	0
Estrada, Ricardo, Min.-Agu.	1.000	4	5	2	0	7	0
Barrera, Jesus Antonio, Min.	1.000	4	2	7	0	9	1

Player, Team	Pct.	G	PO	A	E	TC	DP
Villarreal, Alejandro, N.L.	1.000	4	0	1	0	1	0
Salas, Heriberto, Tor.	1.000	4	1	10	0	11	0
Trapaga, Miguel, MCT	1.000	3	0	2	0	2	0
Rojas, Francisco, Tab.	1.000	3	1	6	0	7	0
Romero, Marco A., MCT	1.000	2	1	5	0	6	0
Montalvo, Ivan, MCT	1.000	2	0	1	0	1	0
Arias, Everardo, Pue.	1.000	2	1	5	0	6	1
Vargas, Trinidad, Pue.	1.000	2	2	7	0	9	0
Fariss, Monty, Mont.	1.000	2	4	1	0	5	0
Hernandez B., Juan C., Pue.	1.000	1	1	2	0	3	1
Laurencio, Rodfer, Cam.	1.000	1	0	2	0	2	0
Jimenez, Alfonso, Sal.	1.000	1	3	1	0	4	0
Martinez, Luis Carlos, Sal.	1.000	1	0	1	0	1	0
Diaz, Remigio, Mont.	1.000	1	2	2	0	4	1
Contreras, Cuitlahuac, Tor.-Monc.	1.000	1	1	0	0	1	0
Rodriguez S., Noel, Agu.	.933	7	4	10	1	15	1
Valle, Jose Luis, Min.	.900	3	2	7	1	10	3
Castillo, Juan, Ags.	.875	2	3	4	1	8	1
Cervera, Francisco, Jal.	.818	3	3	6	2	11	0
Canizalez, Juan Carlos, Mont.	.800	4	2	6	2	10	1
Caraballo, Gari, Mont.	.778	9	3	18	6	27	1
Wong Medrano, Julian, Monc.	.700	5	2	5	3	10	1

TRIPLE PLAYS: Castaneda, Malpica, Ortiz.

SHORTSTOPS

Player, Team	Pct.	G	PO	A	E	TC	DP
Quintero, Guillermo, Mont.	1.000	17	13	41	0	54	3
Trapaga, Miguel, MCT	1.000	11	11	20	0	31	5
Sandoval, Jose Luis, MCRD	.979	106	172	344	11	527	76
Arredondo, Jesus, A., Ags.	.976	108	211	387	15	613	84
Valle, Jose Luis, Min.	.975	101	181	328	13	522	67
Magana, Gabriel, Yuc.	.975	20	26	52	2	80	10
Diaz, Remigio, Mont.	.973	92	114	283	11	408	46
Loredo, Jorge Luis, Cam.	.973	13	13	23	1	37	2
Pacho, Juan Jose, Yuc.	.972	104	163	317	14	494	58
Garcia, Heriberto, Agu.	.971	115	240	420	20	680	86
Guerrero, Jaime, Ags.	.970	10	11	21	1	33	6
Guerrero, Francisco, Tor.	.966	83	153	520	14	687	49
Ramirez, Enrique, N.L.	.965	111	169	354	19	542	66
Jimenez, Alfonso, Sal.	.965	109	189	383	21	593	83
Robles, Javier, MCT	.963	112	189	330	20	539	61
Valenzuela, Armando, Rey.	.962	96	153	300	18	471	61
Vargas, Trinidad, Pue.	.960	60	79	158	10	247	22
Guizar, Hector, Cam.	.959	99	195	302	21	518	72
Cervera, Francisco, Jal.	.959	83	135	261	17	413	65
Nunez Garcia, Jose J., Jal.	.959	10	15	32	2	49	7
Rojas, Francisco, Tab.	.958	26	22	46	3	71	7
Magallanes, Ever, Mont.	.956	28	47	84	6	137	17
Hernandez B., Juan C., Pue.	.955	18	23	40	3	66	4
Marrujo, Hector, Tab.	.954	93	161	272	21	454	68
Martinez, Luis Carlos, Sal.	.954	25	19	43	3	65	11
Arias, Everardo, Pue.	.950	47	92	156	13	261	41
Carrasco, Ernesto, N.L.	.947	11	14	22	2	38	6
Wong Medrano, Julian, Monc.	.946	17	26	44	4	74	8
Valle, Jorge Luis, Tor.	.945	27	40	80	7	127	21
Balderas, S. Abelardo, Min.	.943	18	20	30	3	53	7
Vizcarra, Marco A., Rey.	.942	21	30	83	7	120	23
Duran, Felipe, MCRD	.941	15	21	27	3	51	6
Contreras, Cuitlahuac, Tor.-Monc.	.927	21	22	54	6	82	6
Nunez Avina, Jose Juan, Jal.	.927	11	12	26	3	41	6
Olvera, Sergio, Monc.	.919	68	86	175	23	284	37
Lopez, Gonzalo, Monc.	.909	13	12	28	4	44	5
Rivera, Alberto, Jal.	.906	18	17	41	6	64	11
Salas, Heriberto, Tor.	.880	10	9	13	3	25	4
Jelks, Greg, Cam.	.842	13	28	36	12	76	10

SHORTSTOPS WITH FEWER THAN 10 GAMES

Player, Team	Pct.	G	PO	A	E	TC	DP
Avila, Roberto, Min.	1.000	7	3	15	0	18	4
Rubio, Marco A., Cam.-Min.	1.000	6	10	24	0	34	5
Pardo, Victor Manuel, Pue.	1.000	3	0	7	0	7	0
Solis, Roberto, Pue.	1.000	3	2	2	0	4	0
Felix, Arturo, Yuc.	1.000	2	0	4	0	4	0
Escalante, Marcelo, Sal.	1.000	2	6	0	0	6	0
Perez, Alejandro, N.L.	1.000	2	0	2	0	2	0
Verdugo, Vicente, MCRD	1.000	1	1	2	0	3	0
Garzon, Eliseo, Tab.	1.000	1	2	4	0	6	0
Cantu, Gerardo, Pue.	1.000	1	0	1	0	1	0
Camacho, Adulfo, Yuc.	1.000	1	1	0	0	1	0
Gonzalez, Denio, Sal.	1.000	1	0	4	0	4	0
Cornejo, Edgar, Sal.	1.000	1	0	2	0	2	0
Flores, Miguel, Mont.	1.000	1	2	3	0	5	0
Castaneda, Rafael, N.L.	1.000	1	2	4	0	6	1

Player, Team	Pct.	G	PO	A	E	TC	DP
Esquer, Ramon, Rey.	1.000	1	3	3	0	6	1
Rodriguez, Juan F., Rey.-Agu.	1.000	1	3	2	0	5	1
Rodriguez, Hector, Rey.	1.000	1	1	0	0	1	0
Martinez, Grimaldo, Monc.	1.000	1	1	1	0	2	1
Leyva, German, Monc.	1.000	1	3	2	0	5	0
Ayala Armenta, Mario, Monc.	1.000	1	1	6	0	7	1
Arevalo, Guadalupe, Ags.	1.000	1	1	1	0	2	0
Castillo, Juan, Ags.	1.000	1	2	0	0	2	0
Santos, Luis Angel, Ags.	1.000	1	1	2	0	3	1
Castro, Leonel, Jal.	1.000	1	1	1	0	2	0
Santos, Julio, Jal.	.963	6	8	18	1	27	5
Verdugo, Guadalupe, Tor.	.950	7	9	10	1	20	3
Zazueta, Juan Carlos, Tab.	.917	5	5	6	1	12	2
Infante, Alexis, Tab.	.913	6	7	14	2	23	3
Gutierrez, Felipe, Monc.	.900	3	5	4	1	10	1
Estrada, Ruben, N.L.	.857	2	3	3	1	7	0
Arredondo, Hernando, Pue.	.846	4	3	8	2	13	2
Tovar, Jose de Jesus, Sal.-Monc.	.833	9	11	29	8	48	10
Garcia, Carlos, Agu.	.750	4	0	3	1	4	0
Quinones, Luis, Yuc.	.714	1	2	3	2	7	0
Perez, Alfredo, Pue.	.667	1	1	1	1	3	0
Franco, Manuel, Mont.	.500	1	1	0	1	2	0

TRIPLE PLAYS: Arias, Olvera, Jor. Valle.

OUTFIELDERS

Player, Team	Pct.	G	PO	A	E	TC	DP
Cruz, Luis Alfonso, Rey.	1.000	95	198	8	0	206	0
Cabreja, Alexis, Pue.	1.000	59	105	8	0	113	2
Valencia, Carlos, Ags.	1.000	49	89	7	0	96	0
Medina, Jose Ramon, Cam.	1.000	47	65	8	0	73	0
Tillman, Rusty, Agu.-Tab.	1.000	46	97	4	0	101	2
Espinoza, Jose M., Monc.	1.000	40	52	8	0	60	2
Maclin, Lonnie, Agu.	1.000	37	67	0	0	67	0
Valenzuela, Jose Luis, Ags.	1.000	33	56	2	0	58	1
Motley, Darryl, Tor.-Agu.	1.000	30	42	3	0	45	1
Soriano, Ricardo, Tor.	1.000	22	18	0	0	18	0
Ojeda, Miguel, MCRD	1.000	21	13	1	0	14	0
Valdez, Jesus, Yuc.	1.000	20	25	1	0	26	0
Santos, Julio, Jal.	1.000	15	31	2	0	33	0
Fariss, Monty, Mont.	1.000	14	22	2	0	24	0
Casillas, Adam, Rey.	1.000	13	18	1	0	19	1
Malpica, Enrique, Agu.	1.000	12	9	2	0	11	0
Moreno, David, Sal.	1.000	12	8	0	0	8	0
Quiroz, Jose Julian, Ags.	1.000	12	19	2	0	21	0
Ortega, Roberto, Tab.	1.000	11	11	0	0	11	0
Payro, Edison, Cam.	1.000	10	5	1	0	6	0
Michel, Domingo, Cam.	1.000	10	17	1	0	18	0
Contreras, Cuitlahuac, Tor.-Monc.	1.000	10	16	1	0	17	0
Tellez, Alonso, Rey.	.995	116	176	10	1	187	1
Arredondo, Luis A., MCRD	.995	111	184	15	1	200	3
Fernandez, Daniel, MCRD	.995	106	186	7	1	194	1
Diaz, Luis Fernando, MCT	.991	70	106	4	1	111	0
Villegas, Fernando, Sal.	.990	92	179	10	2	191	2
Cuevas, Angelo, Tab.-Min.	.990	66	100	3	1	104	0
Torres, Raymundo, Yuc.	.989	45	80	8	1	89	0
Lopez, Gonzalo, Monc.	.988	91	145	13	2	160	4
Noris, Rogelio, N.L.	.988	55	81	3	1	85	0
Valle, Jorge Luis, Tor.	.988	39	71	9	1	81	1
Mendez, Roberto C., MCRD	.987	98	146	5	2	153	0
Dattola, Kevin, Tor.	.987	28	73	4	1	78	1
Herrera, Isidro, Cam.	.984	96	179	2	3	184	1
Enriquez, Graciano, Ags.	.984	62	111	9	2	122	1
Canizalez, Juan Carlos, Mont.	.983	95	164	5	3	172	2
Iturbe, Pedro, Pue.	.982	113	207	13	4	224	0
Fentanes, Oscar, Tab.	.982	60	104	4	2	110	1
Harris, Donald, Agu.-Monc.	.982	51	106	4	2	112	1
Sanchez, Gerardo, N.L.	.981	113	201	6	4	211	0
Arzate, Martin, Jal.	.981	78	146	7	3	156	1
Rubio, Sergio, Yuc.	.981	30	47	5	1	53	0
Gutierrez, Andres, Pue.	.979	36	39	8	1	48	1
Burguillos, Carlos M., Min.	.976	98	193	10	5	208	2
Gutierrez, Jose Luis, Agu.	.976	62	75	5	2	82	0
Mercedes, Luis, Yuc.	.976	52	113	7	3	123	1
Valverde, Raul, Jal.	.976	37	79	1	2	82	0
Brinkley, Darrell, Cam.	.974	98	219	9	6	234	3
Heath, Robert Lee, MCT	.974	93	146	6	4	156	0
Magallanes, William, Tab.	.974	60	110	3	3	116	1
Zamudio, Rafael, Mont.-Agu.	.974	25	38	0	1	39	0
Garcia, Cornelio, Mont.	.973	99	140	5	4	149	1
Rodriguez, Fernando, Tor.	.972	73	99	6	3	108	0
Snider, Van, Tor.	.972	61	97	7	3	107	0
Yuriar, Jesus, Monc.	.971	99	227	9	7	243	3

Player, Team	Pct.	G	PO	A	E	TC	DP
Espinoza, Javier, Cam.	.971	69	130	5	4	139	2
Velazquez, Armando, Agu.	.971	21	34	0	1	35	0
Delgado, Tomas, Tab.	.971	20	29	4	1	34	1
Saenz, Ricardo, N.L.	.970	115	245	17	8	270	1
Castillo, Juan, Ags.	.970	104	216	9	7	232	2
Torres, Eduardo, Sal.	.970	86	122	9	4	135	0
Howell, Patrick, MCT	.970	84	148	11	5	164	0
Agramon, Antonio, Jal.	.970	39	62	3	2	67	0
Alvarez, Hector, Pue.	.969	116	240	14	8	262	3
Cairo, Sergio, Yuc.	.968	45	60	0	2	62	0
Jeter, Shawn, Sal.	.968	17	30	0	1	31	0
Reyna, Luis, Monc.-Tab.	.968	17	29	1	1	31	0
Hernandez, W. Gerardo, Min.	.967	75	165	11	6	182	0
Gamboa, Jose A., Agu.	.967	74	114	4	4	122	0
De Lima, Rafael, Tab.	.967	71	144	3	5	152	1
Garcia, Hector, Tor.	.966	105	185	12	7	204	1
Machiria, Pablo, Ags.	.966	84	134	6	5	145	0
Carrillo, Matias, MCT	.965	86	162	5	6	173	0
Felix, Arturo, Yuc.	.964	36	51	3	2	56	0
Leal, Jose Guadalupe, Cam.	.963	54	99	6	4	109	3
Beltran, Gerardo, Min.	.961	70	119	3	5	127	2
Dominguez, David, MCT-Min.	.961	63	95	4	4	103	0
Housie, Wayne, Yuc.	.960	46	92	3	4	90	0
Gonzalez, Jose, Mont.	.959	103	209	3	9	221	0
Soto, Emison, Pue.	.958	34	39	7	2	48	0
Escalante, Marcelo, Sal.	.957	57	84	4	4	92	1
Ansley, Willie, Agu.	.957	28	41	3	2	46	0
Lopez, Alfredo, Jal.	.957	25	44	0	2	46	0
Pledger, Kinnis E., Tor.	.957	13	21	1	1	23	0
Wright, George, Sal.	.956	110	201	17	10	228	1
Jimenez, Eduardo, Yuc.	.956	91	142	11	7	160	1
Naveda, Edgar, Jal.	.955	38	63	1	3	67	0
Morones, Martin, Monc.	.952	84	154	5	8	167	2
Montalvo, Ivan, MCT	.952	20	20	0	1	21	0
Castillo, Braulio, Rey.	.949	91	159	7	9	175	3
Rodriguez, Boi, N.L.	.946	80	134	6	8	148	0
Orantes, Ramon, Mont.	.946	26	51	2	3	56	1
Tiquet, Lazaro, Tab.	.943	54	78	5	5	88	0
Wearing, Mel, Jal.-Sal.	.943	45	78	5	5	88	1
Abrego, Jesus, Jal.	.941	54	87	9	6	102	0
Guerrero, Jaime, Ags.	.941	12	16	0	1	17	0
Ramirez G., Jesus A., MCRD	.938	33	13	2	1	16	0
Rodriguez, Jose Luis, Agu.	.935	62	99	2	7	108	0
Almendra, Gregorio, Tab.	.929	16	13	0	1	14	0
Ritchie, Greg, Tab.	.929	14	13	0	1	14	0
Trevino, Alejandro, Mont.	.923	21	35	1	3	39	1
Fernandez, Carlos, Jal.	.909	13	20	0	2	22	0
Lopez, Salvador, Rey.	.905	35	35	3	4	42	1
Mitchell, Keith, Tab.	.875	24	28	0	4	32	0
Martinez, Enrique, Mont.	.875	10	6	1	1	8	0

OUTFIELDERS WITH FEWER THAN 10 GAMES

Player, Team	Pct.	G	PO	A	E	TC	DP
Garcia, Rosario, Rey.	1.000	9	5	1	0	6	0
Salgado, Eduardo, MCT	1.000	8	8	0	0	8	0
Robles, Trinidad, MCT-Min.	1.000	7	9	2	0	11	0
Pena, M., Joel, Agu.	1.000	7	8	2	0	10	0
Nunez Avina, Jose Juan, Jal.	1.000	7	9	0	0	9	0
Tejeda, Arturo, N.L.	1.000	6	4	0	0	4	0
Ponce, Hector, Cam.	1.000	5	4	0	0	4	0
Reyes, Ramon, Agu.	1.000	5	4	0	0	4	0
Estrada, Ruben, N.L.	1.000	5	8	0	0	8	0
Arano, Wilfrido, N.L.	1.000	5	2	0	0	2	0
Perez, Francisco, Rey.	1.000	5	7	0	0	7	0
Tatis, Bernardo, MCRD	1.000	4	2	0	0	2	0
Palacios, Alfonso, P., Tab.	1.000	4	1	0	0	1	0
Zambrano, Roberto, Pue.	1.000	4	2	0	0	2	0
Sievers, Carlos, Yuc.	1.000	4	4	0	0	4	0
Morales, Alejandro, Tor.	1.000	4	8	0	0	8	0
Lopez A., Victor M., Jal.	1.000	4	7	0	0	7	0
Gil, Geronimo, MCRD	1.000	3	2	1	0	3	1
Sparks, Greg, MCT	1.000	3	0	1	0	1	0
Aguilera, Armando, Sal.	1.000	3	1	0	0	1	0
Tapia, Jose, Cam.	1.000	2	1	0	0	1	0
Salas, Heriberto, Tor.	1.000	2	2	0	0	2	0
Verdugo, Guadalupe, Tor.	1.000	2	0	1	0	1	0
Wright, Tom, Jal.	1.000	2	3	1	0	4	0
Pena, Luis Alberto, Pue.	1.000	1	3	0	0	3	0
Arvizu, Javier, Cam.	1.000	1	1	0	0	1	0
Jimenez, German, Yuc.-Ags.	1.000	1	2	0	0	2	0
Mendiola, Juan Carlos, Agu.	1.000	1	1	0	0	1	0
Estrada, Ricardo, Min.-Agu.	1.000	1	1	0	0	1	0
Trejo, David, Agu.	1.000	1	2	0	0	2	0

Player, Team	Pct.	G	PO	A	E	TC	DP
Balderas S., Abelardo, Min.	1.000	1	1	0	0	1	0
Stark, Matt, Rey.	1.000	1	2	0	0	2	0
Perez, Juan Luis, Tor.	1.000	1	1	0	0	1	0
Miranda, Julio Cesar, Tor.	1.000	1	3	1	0	4	0
Arevalo, Guadalupe, Ags.	1.000	1	0	1	0	1	0
Nunez Garcia, Jose J., Jal.	1.000	1	1	0	0	1	0
Quintana, Carlos, Min.-Yuc.	.947	8	17	1	1	19	0
Wong Medrano, Julian, Monc.	.929	8	13	0	1	14	0
Paez, Raul, MCRD	.889	7	7	1	1	9	0
Chan, Armando, Monc.	.889	7	8	0	1	9	0
Cecena, Manuel, Min.	.875	3	7	0	1	8	0
Rodriguez, Serafin, Pue.	.857	5	6	0	1	7	0
Alvarez, Luis, Jal.	.850	7	15	2	3	20	0
Hecht, Steve, Monc.	.750	2	3	0	1	4	0
Cervera, Francisco, Jal.	.333	1	0	1	2	3	1
Gainey, Ty, MCRD	.000	1	0	0	1	1	0

CATCHERS

Player, Team	Pct.	G	PO	A	E	TC	DP	PB
Meza, Alfredo, Mont.	1.000	32	89	12	0	101	1	1
Vazquez, Felipe, MCRD	1.000	26	62	6	0	68	0	3
Pena, Carlos, Yuc.	1.000	14	49	4	0	53	1	2
Campos, Oscar, Agu.	1.000	10	15	1	0	16	0	2
Mendez, Ramon, Ags.	.994	41	158	15	1	174	3	5
Ruiz, Demetrio, Jal.-Tab.	.993	34	122	24	1	147	2	1
Ojeda, Miguel, MCRD	.992	24	106	11	1	118	2	2
Hernandez, Miguel, Agu.	.991	49	187	35	2	224	6	1
Valdez, Francisco J., Rey.	.989	73	328	39	4	371	4	3
Gastelum, Carlos, Min.	.989	59	248	28	3	279	2	2
Duarte C., Rene, Min.	.988	63	209	35	3	247	4	8
Reyes, Gilberto, Cam.	.987	110	390	59	6	455	8	8
Abrego, Jesus, Jal.	.987	40	188	33	3	224	3	4
Vega V., Edgar, MCT	.986	77	330	37	5	372	2	3
Cazarin, Manuel, Agu.	.986	77	295	58	5	358	7	6
Villanueva, Hector, MCT	.986	27	136	9	2	147	1	4
Garzon, Eliseo, Tab.	.985	99	459	61	8	528	6	3
Ramirez, Efren, Ags.	.985	87	385	68	7	460	7	4
Cruz, Marco Antonio, N.L.	.984	115	572	54	10	636	6	8
Luna, Jose Luis, Sal.	.984	93	424	53	8	485	7	7
Samaniego, Manuel, Monc.	.984	53	218	27	4	249	3	2
Arauz, Ignacio, Monc.	.984	39	154	26	3	183	4	4
Rojas, Homar, MCRD	.983	89	489	39	9	537	2	8
Canedo, Alberto, Cam.	.983	31	53	6	1	60	1	0
Garza, Gerardo, Tor.	.982	108	470	73	10	553	9	9
Estrada, Hector, Pue.	.981	85	336	33	7	376	5	5
Trevino, Alejandro, Mont.	.981	66	262	44	6	312	6	2
Hurtado, Hector, Mont.	.981	55	228	24	5	257	4	4
Gavia, Jesus, Agu.-Min.	.980	14	38	10	1	49	1	1
Rivera, Eleazar, Monc.	.980	11	47	3	1	51	0	1
Ochoa, Marin Edgar, MCT	.979	46	128	15	3	146	2	1
Osuna, Hector, Yuc.	.977	30	111	15	3	129	2	1
Rodriguez, Ruben, Monc.	.973	19	98	12	3	113	2	1
Munoz, Noe, Rey.	.972	35	185	25	6	216	2	0
Monroy, Victor Hugo, Rey.	.971	24	86	15	3	104	0	1
Machorro, Roberto, Monc.	.969	16	56	7	2	65	0	1
Guzman, Marco A., Yuc.	.967	96	359	49	14	422	4	9
Perez, Juan Luis, Tor.	.962	21	44	7	2	53	1	2
Valenzuela, Eduardo, Sal.	.960	48	128	15	6	149	0	0
Lopez A., Victor M., Jal.	.957	63	240	33	12	285	5	5
Cantu, Gerardo, Pue.	.957	24	60	6	3	69	3	0
Pulido, Jesus, N.L.	.941	11	14	2	1	17	0	1
Soto, Emison, Pue.	.928	17	65	12	6	83	1	4
Corrales, Virgilio, N.L.	.895	12	15	2	2	19	0	2

CATCHERS WITH FEWER THAN 10 GAMES

Player, Team	Pct.	G	PO	A	E	TC	DP	PB
Aguilera, Armando, Sal.	1.000	8	5	0	0	5	0	0
Dominguez, Fausto, Tab.	1.000	3	6	0	0	6	0	1
Elvira, Ramon H., Tab.	1.000	2	2	0	0	2	0	0
Martinez, Raul, Sal.	1.000	1	1	0	0	1	0	0
Avila, Ruben, Sal.	1.000	1	2	0	0	2	0	0
Cueto, Raul, Tab.	.933	4	14	0	1	15	0	0

PITCHERS

Player, Team	Pct.	G	PO	A	E	TC	DP
Villegas, Jose Angel, Ags.	1.000	52	4	9	0	13	1
Herrera, Calixto, Monc.	1.000	50	2	20	0	22	1
Murillo, Felipe, Monc.	1.000	43	0	6	0	6	0
Pina, Rafael, MCRD	1.000	42	4	11	0	15	0
Miranda, Julio Cesar, Tor.	1.000	41	4	4	0	8	0
Grajales, Norberto, Tor.	1.000	41	5	21	0	26	3
Pimentel, Roberto, Tor.-Monc.	1.000	39	4	8	0	12	1

Player, Team	Pct.	G	PO	A	E	TC	DP
Segura, Jose, Yuc.	1.000	38	5	7	0	12	0
Garcia, R. Miguel, Min.	1.000	38	7	16	0	23	2
Cecena, Jose Isabel, Sal.	1.000	38	1	7	0	8	0
Del Toro, Miguel, MCRD-Rey.	1.000	37	6	9	0	15	0
Sombra, Francisco, Sal.	1.000	37	3	9	0	12	0
Garcia Cruz, Jose Luis, MCT	1.000	36	1	10	0	11	1
Lopez, De La T., Jose J., Min.	1.000	36	4	4	0	8	0
Hernandez, Encarn'cn, Jal.-Monc.	1.000	36	2	11	0	13	1
Bencomo, Omar, Sal.-Jal.	1.000	35	2	11	0	13	1
Barron, Avelino, Sal.	1.000	35	3	12	0	15	2
Cruz, Javier, Rey.	1.000	35	2	11	0	13	1
Cazares, Juan, Jal.-Mont.	1.000	35	1	7	0	8	0
Villarreal, Antonio, Mont.-Yuc.	1.000	34	2	19	0	21	1
Perez, Leonardo, Mont.	1.000	34	1	7	0	8	0
Zappelli, Mark, Sal.	1.000	33	12	17	0	29	0
Quintanilla, Enrique, N.L.	1.000	33	3	9	0	12	1
Cabrales, Gabriel, Tab.	1.000	32	1	18	0	19	1
Sandoval, Carlos, Min.	1.000	32	2	9	0	11	0
Carrasco, Alejandro, MCRD	1.000	30	2	5	0	7	1
Lewis, Scott, Mont.	1.000	30	0	6	0	6	0
Valencia, Jorge, Sal	1.000	29	8	22	0	30	0
Alicea, Miguel, Tor.	1.000	28	2	4	0	6	1
Villanueva, Luis, Ags.	1.000	28	1	3	0	4	1
Rincon, Ricardo, MCRD	1.000	27	2	12	0	14	2
Leyva, Carlos Armando, MCT	1.000	26	1	4	0	5	0
Garcia, Mike, Tab.	1.000	26	4	9	0	13	0
Toledo, Mario, Cam.	1.000	26	1	6	0	7	0
Rodriguez, Mario A., Min.	1.000	26	4	16	0	20	2
Antunez, Martin, Jal.	1.000	26	6	11	0	17	0
Lopez, Emigdio, Tab.	1.000	25	18	32	0	50	1
Tinoco, Ruben, Cam.	1.000	25	0	16	0	16	2
Sierra, Abel, Cam.	1.000	24	3	9	0	12	1
Hernandez, Martin, Yuc.	1.000	24	3	12	0	15	2
Sanchez, Hector, Agu.-Mont.	1.000	24	5	7	0	12	1
Diaz, Alejandro, Agu.	1.000	24	7	12	0	19	3
Aguilar, Jose Miguel, Min.-Tab.	1.000	24	4	18	0	22	1
Enriquez, Martin, Ags.	1.000	24	5	18	0	23	0
Ramos, Jorge Luis, Pue.	1.000	23	2	7	0	9	0
Solis, Ricardo, Yuc.	1.000	23	6	24	0	30	2
Rivera, Hector, Rey.-Agu.	1.000	23	7	18	0	25	1
Garibay, Salvador, Ags.	1.000	23	4	7	0	11	1
Quiroz, Jose Julian, Ags.	1.000	23	4	4	0	8	2
Draper, Mike, MCT	1.000	22	4	3	0	7	0
Valenzuela, Saul, Pue.	1.000	22	9	35	0	44	1
Camacho, Adrian, Min.	1.000	22	1	7	0	8	0
Heredia, Hector, Mont.	1.000	22	8	24	0	32	1
Moreno, Angel, N.L.	1.000	22	11	33	0	44	3
Renteria, Hilario, Tor.	1.000	22	7	17	0	24	1
Vazquez, Aguedo, Ags.	1.000	22	9	10	0	19	1
Moreno, Leobardo, MCRD	1.000	21	1	8	0	9	0
Garibay, Bravo Daniel, MCT	1.000	21	0	5	0	5	1
Neri, Braulio, Yuc.-Tor.	1.000	21	2	3	0	5	0
Leyva, Filiberto, Agu.	1.000	21	0	1	0	1	0
Diaz, Marcos, Mont.	1.000	21	1	12	0	13	1
Green, Otis, Mont.	1.000	21	2	7	0	9	0
Mendez, Luis Fernando, Rey.	1.000	21	10	13	0	23	2
Palafox, Juan Manuel, Tor.	1.000	21	10	17	0	27	1
Flores, Ignacio, Tor.	1.000	21	1	2	0	3	0
Ramirez, Roberto, MCRD	1.000	20	6	35	0	41	7
Munoz, Miguel, Agu.-Rey.	1.000	20	6	31	0	37	3
Lopez, Jonas, Ags.	1.000	20	3	3	0	6	1
Cimorelli, Frank, Cam.	1.000	19	3	4	0	7	1
Garza, Roberto, Rey.-N.L.	1.000	19	3	6	0	9	0
Velazquez, Ernesto A., Tor.-Sal.	1.000	19	5	2	0	7	0
Vargas, Ignacio, Pue.	1.000	18	3	15	0	18	5
Jimenez, German, Yuc.-Ags.	1.000	18	3	15	0	18	0
Gonzalez, Arturo, Mont.	1.000	18	0	19	0	19	3
Elvira, Narciso, Mont.	1.000	18	3	12	0	15	2
Castillo, Felipe, MCRD	1.000	17	2	2	0	4	1
Villegas, Ramon, Pue.	1.000	17	2	2	0	4	0
Cruz, Juan Diego, Yuc.	1.000	17	1	3	0	4	0
Molina, Joaquin, Tor.	1.000	17	4	8	0	12	0
Figueroa, Fernando, Tor.	1.000	17	12	28	0	40	3
Nunez Avina, Jose Juan, Jal.	1.000	17	1	7	0	8	0
Garcia, David, Monc.	1.000	16	0	2	0	2	0
Arrington, Tom, Jal.	1.000	16	4	16	0	20	0
Cazares, Tomas, MCRD-Rey.	1.000	15	2	6	0	8	0
Cota, Armando, Tab.	1.000	15	0	5	0	5	1
Henry, John, Pue.	1.000	15	10	10	0	20	0
Valdez, Jose Luis, N.L.	1.000	15	0	3	0	3	0
Wagner, Hector, Ags.	1.000	15	1	8	0	9	0
Perez, Vladimir, Rey.	1.000	14	1	3	0	4	0
Mansur, Jeff, Pue.	1.000	13	1	5	0	6	0

Player, Team	Pct.	G	PO	A	E	TC	DP
Hernandez, Ramon, Mont.	1.000	13	1	2	0	3	0
Hernandez, Dimas C., Monc.	1.000	13	2	4	0	6	0
Strauss, Julio Cesar, Tab.	1.000	12	0	4	0	4	1
Salgado, Eduardo, MCT	1.000	11	1	1	0	2	0
Del Valle, Enrique, MCT-Agu.	1.000	11	1	2	0	3	1
Inzunza, Jorge, Tab.	1.000	11	1	1	0	2	0
Llanes, Emeterio, Yuc.	1.000	11	1	0	0	1	0
Rodriguez, Rosario, Mont.	1.000	11	0	1	0	1	0
Chapin, Darrin, Rey.	1.000	11	2	3	0	5	0
Moreno, Ricardo, MCT-N.L.	1.000	10	0	1	0	1	0
Juarez, Fernando, Tor.	1.000	10	0	4	0	4	0
Gomez, Jesus A., Monc.	1.000	10	0	3	0	3	0
Ruiz, Cecilio, Tab.	.978	24	6	39	1	46	2
Purata, Julio, Rey.	.974	22	4	33	1	38	2
Huerta, Luis Enrique, Pue.	.972	22	9	26	1	36	1
Jimenez, Issac, Yuc.	.971	19	6	28	1	35	1
Vazquez, Adrian, Cam.	.969	21	10	21	1	32	1
Carranza, Javier, Rey.	.967	21	9	20	1	30	0
Hernandez, Jose M., N.L.	.966	47	9	19	1	29	1
Moreno, Jesus, Sal.	.964	22	6	21	1	28	2
Acosta, Aaron, Tor.	.964	21	11	16	1	28	1
Soto, Fernando, Min.	.962	25	5	20	1	26	1
Cruz, Andres, Yuc.	.962	23	6	19	1	26	0
Herrera, Enrique, Agu.	.960	34	5	19	1	25	0
Kelley, Drum Richard, Monc.	.960	12	3	21	1	25	2
Orozco, Jaime, Pue.	.952	23	10	30	2	42	3
Osuna, Roberto, N.L.	.950	25	4	15	1	20	0
Vega, Obed, MCT	.950	18	6	13	1	20	2
Lara, Jorge, Rey.	.947	39	7	11	1	19	1
Romero, Juan, Tab.	.947	29	8	10	1	19	1
Hernandez, Manuel A., MCRD.	.947	23	9	27	2	38	3
Jones, Al, Tor.	.947	17	4	14	1	19	4
Esquer, Mercedes, Yuc.-Mont.	.947	13	3	15	1	19	1
Lind, Orlando, Rey.	.947	12	6	12	1	19	1
Cuervo, Bernardo, Cam.	.946	28	7	28	2	37	1
Luevano, Juan, Agu.	.944	41	3	14	1	18	0
Couoh, Enrique, MCT	.944	39	7	10	1	18	0
Velazquez, Israel, Min.	.944	23	4	13	1	18	1
Cano, Ezequiel, Jal.	.944	17	2	15	1	18	0
Alvarez, Juan Jesus, MCT	.943	23	4	29	2	35	1
Barfield, John David, N.L.	.941	34	4	12	1	17	1
Cervantes, Lauro, Ags.-Agu.	.941	14	5	11	1	17	0
Saenz, Alfredo, Pue.	.939	26	6	25	2	33	0
Munoz, Ricardo, Tab.	.939	22	10	36	3	49	3
Raygoza, Martin, Monc.	.939	21	4	27	2	33	1
Barraza, Ernesto, MCT	.935	24	12	31	3	46	0
Cordova, Francisco, MCRD	.933	27	5	23	2	30	0
Valdez, Rafael, Rey.-Yuc.	.933	22	4	10	1	15	0
Cano, Jose, Ags.	.933	21	8	20	2	30	4
Rojo, Oscar, Cam.-Rey.	.929	34	3	10	1	14	1
Solarte, Jose A., Min.	.926	45	7	18	2	27	1
Puig, Benny, Ags.-Tor.	.926	16	3	22	2	27	3
Neri, Eduardo, Agu.	.923	51	5	31	3	39	5
Garibay, Roberto, Pue.	.923	40	5	7	1	13	0
Serna, Ramon, Ags.	.923	30	3	9	1	13	0
Rios, Jesus, MCT	.923	25	4	20	2	26	0
Saldana, Edgardo, Agu.-Tab.	.923	23	5	19	2	26	0
Gomez Rios, Martin, Min.	.923	23	9	15	2	26	1
Baez, Sixto, Agu.	.917	28	5	17	2	24	3
Quinones, Enrique, Yuc.	.917	25	1	10	1	12	2
Lara, Hugo, Cam.	.917	24	6	27	3	36	1
Reyes, Dennis, MCRD	.917	17	3	8	1	12	0
Romo, Guillermo, Tor.	.917	15	2	9	1	12	0
Cruz Soto, Antonio, Pue.	.917	14	1	10	1	12	1
Iniguez, Dario, Jal.	.917	11	4	7	1	12	0
Quiroz, Aaron, N.L.	.913	23	3	18	2	23	2
Lizarraga, Hugo, Cam.	.909	24	2	8	1	11	0
Wayne, Gary, MCRD-Monc.	.909	22	2	8	1	11	0
Martinez, Filiberto, Sal.	.909	19	3	18	2	23	1
Rodriguez, Raul, Sal.	.903	23	5	23	3	31	4
Dominguez, Herminio, Cam.	.900	39	0	9	1	10	1
Cazares, Rosario, Tab.	.900	34	4	5	1	10	1
Diaz, Cesar, N.L.	.900	29	3	6	1	10	0
Hurst, Jonathan, Jal.-Mont.	.900	28	5	4	1	10	1
Retes, Lorenzo, Tab.-Min.	.900	24	6	12	2	20	1
Walker, Mike, MCRD	.900	19	2	7	1	10	2
Franklin, Jay, Mont.-Ags.	.897	22	7	19	3	29	1
Mejia, Cesar, Cam.	.895	24	5	12	2	19	1
Perry, Jeff, N.L.	.889	25	6	10	2	18	0
Hernandez, Julio, Agu.	.886	21	9	22	4	35	3
Sandoval, Guillermo, Mont.	.882	33	2	13	2	17	0
Uribe, Juan Carlos, Yuc.	.875	43	2	5	1	8	0
Tejeda, Juan, Cam.	.875	27	2	12	2	16	1

Player, Team	Pct.	G	PO	A	E	TC	DP
Navarro, Luis A., Sal.	.875	19	4	3	1	8	0
Rodriguez, Mario A., Rey.	.875	12	4	3	1	8	0
Flynt, Will, MCRD	.875	10	2	5	1	8	0
Castro, Leonel, Jal.	.871	19	9	18	4	31	1
Mora, Eleazar, Agu.	.864	23	8	11	3	22	3
Veliz, A., Francisco, Sal.-Monc.	.857	19	1	5	1	7	2
Sanchez, Jose Luis, Jal.	.857	14	2	4	1	7	0
Jimenez, Cesar D., Monc.	.846	14	4	7	2	13	0
Delfin, Adolfo, MCT	.833	37	1	9	2	12	2
Cruz, Juan Alonso, Jal.	.833	26	0	5	1	6	0
Benitez, Francisco, Ags.-Jal.	.833	11	0	5	1	6	0
Rodriguez, Rene, N.L.	.818	32	2	7	2	11	0
Leal, Gerardo, Monc.	.818	25	3	6	2	11	0
Montano, Francisco, Monc.	.818	22	6	12	4	22	0
Moreno, Claudio, MCRD	.786	27	4	7	3	14	1
Tunnell, Lee, MCT	.778	14	0	7	2	9	0
Rivera, Paul, Ags.	.778	14	0	7	2	9	0
Agosto, Juan, Mont.-Ags.	.750	17	1	5	2	8	0
Martinez, Mauricio, Sal.	.750	11	0	3	1	4	0
Rodriguez, Salvador, Yuc.	.750	10	0	3	1	4	1
Pruneda, Armando, Monc.	.750	10	0	3	1	4	0
Gonzalez, Victor M., Jal.	.739	32	6	11	6	23	3
Minutelli, Gino, MCT	.667	12	1	3	2	6	0
Baller, Jay, MCRD	.600	16	0	3	2	5	0
Munoz, Pablo, Pue.	.000	10	0	0	1	1	0

PITCHERS WITH FEWER THAN 10 GAMES

Player, Team	Pct.	G	PO	A	E	TC	DP
Browning, Mike, Cam.	1.000	9	0	3	0	3	1
Loaiza, Sabino, Cam.	1.000	9	5	3	0	8	0
Navarro, Adolfo, Ags.	1.000	9	2	8	0	10	0
Moreno, Ricardo, Jal.	1.000	9	0	2	0	2	0
Lynch, Dave, MCT	1.000	8	1	9	0	10	1
Osuna, Ricardo, Tab.	1.000	8	2	9	0	11	2
Guerra, Esmili, Pue.	1.000	8	0	2	0	2	0
Gutierrez, Arturo, Agu.	1.000	8	0	6	0	6	1
Lopez, Gilberto, Agu.	1.000	8	2	3	0	5	0
Ramirez, Miguel A., Jal.	1.000	8	2	3	0	5	1
Martinez, Ramon, Pue.	1.000	7	0	1	0	1	0
Valenzuela, Aurelio, Yuc.	1.000	7	0	1	0	1	0
Meza, Leobardo, Agu.	1.000	7	2	4	0	6	1
Smith, Daryl, Sal.	1.000	7	0	5	0	5	0
Olague, Jesus, Mont.	1.000	7	0	3	0	3	0
Brumley, Duff, Mont.-Ags.	1.000	7	0	5	0	5	1
Ochoa, Porfirio, N.L.	1.000	7	0	2	0	2	0
Ayrault, Bob, Monc.	1.000	7	0	6	0	6	0
Espinoza, Rogelio, Jal.	1.000	7	0	1	0	1	0
Dehesa, Noel, Tab.	1.000	6	1	0	0	1	0
Valenzuela, Jorge, Pue.	1.000	6	1	0	0	1	0
Macias, Abraham, Agu.	1.000	6	2	2	0	4	0
Galvez, Rosario, N.L.	1.000	6	0	2	0	2	0
Burcham, Tim, Jal.	1.000	6	3	8	0	11	0
Campos, Francisco, Cam.	1.000	5	0	1	0	1	0
Leon, Danilo, Yuc.	1.000	5	0	2	0	2	0
Martin, Daniel, Yuc.	1.000	5	0	1	0	1	0
Ortega, Pablo, N.L.	1.000	5	1	2	0	3	0
Quintero, Victor Hugo, Tor.	1.000	5	0	1	0	1	0
Rivera, Lino, Monc.	1.000	5	0	5	0	5	0
Ramirez, Martin, Ags.	1.000	5	0	1	0	1	0
Vargas, Joel, Tab.	1.000	4	1	0	0	1	0
Mack, Tony Len, Tor.	1.000	4	0	3	0	3	0
Castillo, Luis Trinidad, Monc.	1.000	4	1	1	0	2	0
Soto, Ramon E., Agu.	1.000	3	0	1	0	1	0
Calderon, Manaces, Min.	1.000	3	0	1	0	1	0
Klvac, David John, Tor.	1.000	3	0	1	0	1	0
Lewis, Craig, Monc.	1.000	3	1	4	0	5	0
Pulido, Raymundo, MCT	1.000	2	0	1	0	1	0
Martinez, Sean, Pue.	1.000	2	1	0	0	1	0
Conde, Ricardo, Yuc.	1.000	2	1	1	0	2	0
Pena, Alejandro, Mont.	1.000	2	1	0	0	1	0
Burlingame, Dennis, Monc.	1.000	2	1	2	0	3	0
Camacho, Adulfo, Yuc.	1.000	1	1	1	0	2	0
Contreras, Cuitlahuac, Tor.-Monc.	1.000	1	0	1	0	1	0
Ledon, Juan Carlos, Jal.	.909	9	4	6	1	11	0
Sadecki, Steve, Jal.	.800	5	2	2	1	5	0
Alvarez, Ivan, Jal.	.750	6	2	1	1	4	0
Arano, Ramon, Agu.	.750	5	0	3	1	4	0
Pelcastregui, Leonardo, Tor.	.750	5	0	3	1	4	0
Cardenas, Benito, N.L.	.667	5	0	2	1	3	0
Pinero, Hugo Jose, Min.	.500	3	0	1	1	2	0

LEAGUE CHAMPIONS

Year	Team	Pct.
1955—	Mexico City Tigers*	.539
1956—	Mexico City Reds	.692
1957—	Yucatan	.567
	Mex. C. Reds (2nd)†	.550
1958—	Nuevo Laredo	.625
1959—	Poza Rica	.575
	Mex. C. Reds (3rd)†	.507
1960—	Mexico City Tigers	.538
1961—	Veracruz	.575
1962—	Monterrey	.592
1963—	Puebla	.606
1964—	Mexico City Reds	.586
1965—	Mexico City Tigers	.590
1966—	Mexico City Tigers‡	.614
	Mexico City Reds	.571
1967—	Jalisco	.607
1968—	Mexico City Reds	.586
1969—	Reynosa	.591
1970—	Aguila§	.580
	Mexico City Reds	.607
1971—	Jalisco§	.558
	Saltillo	.593
1972—	Saltillo	.636
	Cordoba§	.541
1973—	Saltillo	.656
	Mexico City Reds∞	.590
1974—	Jalisco	.627
	Mexico City Reds∞	.551
1975—	Tampico∞	.541
	Cordoba	.649
1976—	Mexico City Reds∞	.543
	Union Laguna	.547
1977—	Mexico City Reds	.623
	Nuevo Laredo∞	.507
1978—	Aguascalientes∞	.589
	Union Laguna	.523
1979—	Saltillo	.704
	Puebla∞	.628
1980—	No champion▲	
1981—	Mexico City Reds	.615
	Reynosa	.492
1982—	Ciudad Juarez∞	.570
	Mexico City Tigers	.508
1983—	Campeche◆	.614
	Ciudad Juarez	.535
1984—	Yucatan◆	.560
	Ciudad Juarez	.509
1985—	Mexico City Reds◆	.606
	Nuevo Laredo	.5275
1986—	Puebla◆	.682
	Monclova	.598
1987—	Mexico City Reds◆	.605
	Monterrey	.536
1988—	Mexico City Reds◆	.646
	Nuevo Laredo	.602
1989—	Nuevo Laredo◆	.621
	Yucatan	.539
1990—	Nuevo Laredo	.618
	Leon◆	.565
1991—	Monterrey◆	.683
	Mexico City Reds	.627
1992—	Mexico City Tigers◆	.594
	Nuevo Laredo	.538
1993—	Nuevo Laredo	.589
	Tabasco◆	.528
1994—	Mexico City Red Devils◆	.646
	Monterrey Sultans	.608
1995—	Mexico City Red Devils	.708
	Monterrey Sultans◆	.570

*Defeated Nuevo Laredo, two games to none, in playoff for pennant. †Won four-team playoff. ‡Won split-season playoff. §League divided into Northern, Southern divisions; won two-team playoff. ∞League divided into Northern, Southern zones; sub-divided into Eastern, Western divisions, won eight-team playoff. ▲A players strike on July 1 forced the cancellation of the regular season and playoff schedule. ◆League divided into Northern, Southern zones; four clubs from each zone qualified for postseason play. Won final series for league championship.

PACIFIC COAST LEAGUE

LEAGUE OFFICE

President/secretary-treasurer
Bill Cutler

Address
2345 S. Alma School Rd., Suite 110
Mesa, AZ 85210

Phone
602-838-2171

TEAMS

ALBUQUERQUE DUKES

General manager
Pat McKernan
Manager
Phil Regan
Ballpark (capacity, surface)
Albuquerque Sports Stadium (10,510, grass)
Affiliation
Dodgers
Address
1601 Stadium Blvd. SE
Albuquerque, NM 87106
Phone
505-243-1791

CALGARY CANNONS

General manager
Tom Valcke
Manager
Trent Jewitt
Ballpark (capacity, surface)
Name to be announced (7,500, grass)
Affiliation
Pirates
Address
P.O. Box 3690, Station B
Calgary, Alberta T2M 4M4
Phone
403-284-1111

COLORADO SPRINGS SKY SOX

General manager
Robert Goughan
Manager
Brad Mills
Ballpark (capacity, surface)
Sky Sox Stadium (8,500, grass)
Affiliation
Rockies
Address
4385 Tutt Blvd.
Colorado Springs, CO 80922
Phone
719-597-1449

EDMONTON TRAPPERS

President/general manager
Mel Kowalchuk
Manager
Gary Jones
Ballpark (capacity, surface)
John Ducey Park (10,000; artificial infield, grass outfield)
Affiliation
Athletics
Address
10233 96th Ave.
Edmonton, Alberta T5K 0A5
Phone
403-429-2934

LAS VEGAS STARS

General manager
Don Logan
Manager
Tim Flannery
Ballpark (capacity, surface)
Cashman Field (9,370, grass)
Affiliation
Padres
Address
850 Las Vegas Blvd. N
Las Vegas, NV 89101
Phone
702-386-7200

PHOENIX FIREBIRDS

Vice president/general manager
Craig Pletenik
Manager
Jim Davenport
Ballpark (capacity, surface)
Scottsdale Stadium (11,200, grass)
Affiliation
Giants
Address
P.O. Box 8528
Scottsdale, AZ 85252
Phone
602-275-0500

SALT LAKE BUZZ

Vice president/general manager
Tammy Felker-White
Manager
Phil Roof
Ballpark (capacity, surface)
Franklin-Quest Field (15,000, grass)
Affiliation
Twins
Address
P.O. Box 4108
Salt Lake City, UT 84110
Phone
801-485-3800

TACOMA RAINIERS

President/general manager
Dave Bean
Manager
Dave Myers
Ballpark (capacity, surface)
Cheney Stadium (10,106, grass)
Affiliation
Mariners
Address
P.O. Box 11087
Tacoma, WA 98411
Phone
206-752-7707

TUCSON TOROS

General manager
Mike Feder
Manager
Tim Tolman
Ballpark (capacity, surface)
Hi Corbett Field (8,000, grass)
Affiliation
Astros
Address
P.O. Box 27045
Tucson, AZ 85716
Phone
602-325-2621

VANCOUVER CANADIANS

Vice president/general manager
Brent Imlach
Manager
Don Long
Ballpark (capacity, surface)
Nat Bailey Stadium (6,500, grass)
Affiliation
Angels
Address
4601 Ontario St.
Vancouver, B.C. V5V 3H4
Phone
604-872-5232

1995 FINAL STANDINGS

FIRST HALF

NORTHERN DIVISION

Team	W	L	T	Pct.	GB
Vancouver (Angels)	45	27	0	.625	....
Salt Lake (Twins)	38	34	0	.528	7
Tacoma (Mariners)	37	35	0	.514	8
Edmonton (Athletics)	35	37	0	.486	10
Calgary (Pirates)	30	41	0	.423	14½

SOUTHERN DIVISION

Team	W	L	T	Pct.	GB
Colorado Springs (Rockies)	39	33	0	.542	....
Albuquerque (Dodgers)	38	34	0	.528	1
Tucson (Astros)	37	34	0	.521	1½
Phoenix (Giants)	34	38	0	.472	5
Las Vegas (Padres)	26	46	0	.361	13

SECOND HALF

NORTHERN DIVISION

Team	W	L	T	Pct.	GB
Salt Lake (Twins)	41	31	0	.569	....
Vancouver (Angels)	36	33	0	.522	3½
Edmonton (Athletics)	33	39	0	.458	8
Tacoma (Mariners)	31	41	0	.431	10
Calgary (Pirates)	28	42	0	.400	12

SOUTHERN DIVISION

Team	W	L	T	Pct.	GB
Tucson (Astros)	50	22	0	.694	....
Colorado Springs (Rockies)	38	33	0	.535	11½
Albuquerque (Dodgers)	37	35	0	.514	13
Las Vegas (Padres)	35	37	0	.486	15
Phoenix (Giants)	28	44	0	.389	22

COMPOSITE

Team	Tuc.	Van.	SLC	C.S.	Alb.	Tac.	Edm.	Phx.	L.V.	Cal.	W	L	T	Pct.	GB
Tucson (Astros)	....	8	9	8	4	12	10	14	10	12	87	56	0	.608	....
Vancouver (Angels)	8	....	8	6	8	12	8	12	9	10	81	60	0	.574	5
Salt Lake (Twins)	7	8	....	9	11	7	9	9	10	9	79	65	0	.549	8½
Colorado Springs (Rockies)	8	9	7	....	7	9	9	9	8	11	77	66	0	.538	10
Albuquerque (Dodgers)	12	8	5	9	....	7	7	9	8	10	75	69	0	.521	12½
Tacoma (Mariners)	4	4	9	7	9	....	11	7	11	6	68	76	0	.472	19½
Edmonton (Athletics)	6	8	7	7	9	5	....	9	8	9	68	76	0	.472	19½
Phoenix (Giants)	2	4	7	7	7	9	7	....	11	8	62	82	0	.431	25½
Las Vegas (Padres)	6	7	6	8	8	5	8	5	....	8	61	83	0	.424	26½
Calgary (Pirates)	3	4	7	5	6	10	7	8	8	....	58	83	0	.411	28

Major league affiliations in parentheses.

PLAYOFFS: Colorado Springs defeated Tucson, three games to one; Salt Lake defeated Vancouver, three games to one; Colorado Springs defeated Salt Lake, three games to two, to win league championship.

REGULAR-SEASON ATTENDANCE: Albuquerque, 340,050; Calgary, 279,054; Colorado Springs, 195,375; Edmonton, 426,012; Las Vegas, 330,869; Phoenix, 282,370; Salt Lake, 637,332; Tacoma, 316,103; Tucson, 301,963; Vancouver, 305,739. Total, 3,414,867. Playoffs (12 games)—43,642. Class AAA All-Star Game at Scranton/Wilkes-Barre—10,965.

MANAGERS: Albuquerque, Rick Dempsey; Calgary, Bobby Meacham; Colorado Springs, Brad Mills; Edmonton, Gary Jones; Las Vegas, Tim Flannery; Phoenix, Jim Davenport; Salt Lake, Phil Roof; Tacoma, Steve Smith; Tucson, Rick Sweet; Vancouver, Don Long.

ALL-STAR TEAM: 1B—Mike Busch, Albuquerque; 2B—Dave Hajek, Tucson; 3B—Ron Coomer, Albuquerque; SS—Fausto Cruz, Edmonton; OF—Trent Hubbard, Colorado Springs; Riccardo Ingram, Salt Lake; Karim Garcia, Albuquerque; C—George Williams, Edmonton; DH—Harvey Pulliam, Colorado Springs; RHP—Donne Wall, Tucson; LHP—Glenn Dishman, Las Vegas; Relief Pitcher—Scott Watkins, Salt Lake; Most Valuable Player—Donne Wall, Tucson; Manager of the Year—Don Long, Vancouver.

1995 BATTING

TEAM

Team	Avg.	G	TPA	AB	R	H	TB	2B	3B	HR	RBI	SH	SF	HP	BB	IBB	SO	SB	CS	GDP	LOB	ShO	Slg.	OBP
Salt Lake	.304	144	5589	4987	831	1516	2259	332	45	107	769	38	52	57	455	30	712	132	65	132	1025	6	.453	.365
Calgary	.302	141	5335	4812	743	1451	2145	306	35	106	697	37	50	38	398	39	704	98	58	110	987	10	.446	.356
Colo. Springs	.291	143	5395	4819	821	1403	2273	293	53	157	770	46	50	34	444	49	829	105	50	96	952	3	.472	.352
Tucson	.289	143	5514	4816	786	1393	2071	285	63	89	726	54	54	34	555	48	848	134	68	114	1034	4	.430	.363
Albuquerque	.285	144	5459	4901	754	1396	2110	277	52	111	691	46	27	32	452	38	821	92	71	134	968	10	.431	.347
Vancouver	.281	141	5359	4726	723	1328	1879	237	43	76	648	42	46	39	504	40	755	114	52	110	1007	14	.398	.352
Tacoma	.279	144	5429	4874	682	1358	2028	230	49	114	646	43	42	34	436	25	845	106	46	119	987	8	.416	.339
Edmonton	.278	144	5511	4816	759	1340	1979	295	43	86	685	49	61	44	541	35	811	80	45	126	1024	6	.411	.352
Las Vegas	.271	144	5363	4789	663	1300	1867	254	32	83	602	42	51	42	437	35	840	77	43	126	986	8	.390	.334
Phoenix	.265	144	5575	4871	658	1289	1878	258	44	81	604	63	62	54	525	38	791	66	58	115	1059	5	.386	.339

INDIVIDUAL

TOP QUALIFIERS FOR BATTING CHAMPIONSHIP

Minimum 389 plate appearances. *Lefthanded batter. †Switch-hitter.

Player, Team	Avg.	G	TPA	AB	R	H	TB	2B	3B	HR	RBI	SH	SF	HP	BB	IBB	SO	SB	CS	GDP	Slg.	OBP
Ingram, Riccardo, Salt Lake	.348	122	526	477	80	166	249	43	2	12	85	0	5	3	41	3	60	4	5	22	.522	.399
Hubbard, Trent, Colorado Springs	.340	123	553	480	102	163	242	29	7	12	66	2	5	5	61	5	59	37	14	2	.504	.416
Beamon, Trey, Calgary*	.334	118	498	452	74	151	205	29	5	5	62	2	3	2	39	4	55	18	8	7	.454	.387
Pulliam, Harvey, Colorado Springs	.327	115	465	407	90	133	250	30	6	25	91	0	6	3	49	10	59	6	2	11	.614	.398
Hajek, Dave, Tucson	.327	131	554	502	99	164	221	37	4	4	79	5	6	2	39	7	27	12	7	11	.440	.373
Simons, Mitch, Salt Lake	.325	130	543	480	87	156	207	34	4	3	46	4	2	10	47	2	45	32	16	9	.431	.395
Garcia, Karim, Albuquerque*	.319	124	519	474	88	151	257	26	10	20	91	2	3	2	38	5	102	12	6	12	.542	.369
Dunn, Steve, Salt Lake*	.316	109	439	402	57	127	196	31	1	12	83	0	6	1	30	4	63	3	2	6	.488	.360
Ramos, Ken, Tucson*	.315	112	391	327	57	103	152	24	8	3	47	4	5	3	51	3	27	14	5	3	.465	.407
Litton, Greg, Tacoma	.309	117	444	388	58	120	174	25	1	9	56	4	6	3	43	1	69	2	2	11	.448	.377
Palmeiro, Orlando, Vancouver*	.307	107	458	398	66	122	151	21	4	0	47	11	5	3	41	8	34	16	7	11	.379	.371
Cedeno, Roger, Albuquerque†	.305	99	429	367	67	112	155	19	9	2	44	4	3	2	53	2	56	23	18	5	.422	.393
Raabe, Brian, Salt Lake	.305	112	497	440	88	134	187	32	6	3	60	2	7	3	45	2	14	15	0	12	.425	.368
Benard, Marvin, Phoenix*	.304	111	441	378	70	115	159	14	6	6	32	5	3	5	50	3	66	10	13	2	.421	.390
Abreu, Bob, Tucson*	.304	114	491	415	72	126	214	24	17	10	75	0	8	1	67	9	120	16	14	6	.516	.395

DEPARTMENTAL LEADERS: G—Bowie, 141; AB—Bowie, 531; R—Hubbard, 102; H—R. Ingram, 166; TB—Garcia, 257; 2B—R. Ingram, 43; 3B—Abreu, 17; HR—Pulliam, 25; RBI—Garcia, Pulliam, 91; SH—Palmeiro, 11; SF—Wood, 12; HP—Quinlan, 15; BB—Leonard, 81; IBB—Pulliam, 10; SO—Quinlan, 124; SB—Hubbard, 37; CS—Cedeno, 18; GIDP—R. Ingram, 22; Slg.—Pulliam, .614; OBP—Hubbard, .416.

ALL PLAYERS

*Lefthanded batter. †Switch-hitter.

Player, Team	Avg.	G	TPA	AB	R	H	TB	2B	3B	HR	RBI	SH	SF	HP	BB	IBB	SO	SB	CS	GDP	Slg.	OBP
Abreu, Bob, Tucson*	.304	114	491	415	72	126	214	24	17	10	75	0	8	1	67	9	120	16	14	6	.516	.395
Acevedo, Juan, Colorado Springs	.000	3	5	4	0	0	0	0	0	0	0	1	0	0	0	0	2	0	0	0	.000	.000
Allensworth, Jermaine, Calgary	.316	51	209	190	46	60	90	13	4	3	11	1	0	5	13	0	30	13	4	3	.474	.375
Anderson, Garret, Vancouver*	.311	14	66	61	9	19	26	7	0	0	12	0	0	0	5	0	14	0	0	3	.426	.364
Aude, Rich, Calgary	.333	50	216	195	34	65	110	14	2	9	42	0	5	4	12	1	30	3	2	11	.564	.375
August, Don, Calgary	.000	2	2	2	0	0	0	0	0	0	0	0	0	0	0	0	1	0	0	0	.000	.000
Aurilia, Rich, Phoenix	.279	71	296	258	42	72	99	12	0	5	34	0	3	0	35	2	29	2	2	4	.384	.361
Backlund, Brett, Calgary	.143	12	7	7	1	1	2	1	0	0	0	0	0	0	0	0	2	0	0	0	.286	.143
Bailey, Roger, Colorado Springs	.250	3	5	4	1	1	2	1	0	0	0	0	0	0	1	0	1	0	0	0	.500	.400
Ball, Jeff, Tucson	.293	110	403	362	58	106	147	25	2	4	56	4	5	7	25	3	66	11	5	13	.406	.346
Barron, Tony, Tacoma	.200	9	28	25	4	5	5	0	0	0	2	0	0	1	2	0	3	0	0	0	.200	.286
Barton, Shawn, Phoenix	.000	15	2	2	0	0	0	0	0	0	0	0	0	0	0	0	1	0	0	0	.000	.000
Beamon, Trey, Calgary*	.334	118	498	452	74	151	205	29	5	5	62	2	3	2	39	4	55	18	8	7	.454	.387
Bean, Billy, Las Vegas*	.290	119	509	445	67	129	212	34	2	15	77	0	9	9	46	9	55	2	2	9	.476	.361
Beard, Garrett, Edmonton	.230	22	69	61	5	14	16	2	0	0	10	1	2	2	3	0	7	0	0	2	.262	.279
Beauchamp, Kash, Edmonton	.200	1	5	5	0	1	1	0	0	0	1	0	0	0	0	0	0	0	0	0	.200	.200
Becker, Rich, Salt Lake†	.309	36	152	123	26	38	63	7	0	6	28	0	2	1	26	0	24	6	1	1	.512	.428
Bellinger, Clay, Phoenix	.274	97	311	277	34	76	100	16	1	2	32	2	3	2	27	1	52	3	2	5	.361	.340
Benard, Marvin, Phoenix*	.304	111	441	378	70	115	159	14	6	6	32	5	3	5	50	3	66	10	13	2	.421	.390
Bennett, Chris, Calgary	.000	4	2	1	0	0	0	0	0	0	0	0	0	0	1	0	1	0	0	0	.000	.500
Bennett, Erik, Van.-Tuc.	.250	42	4	4	0	1	1	0	0	0	0	0	0	0	0	0	0	0	0	0	.250	.250
Blanco, Henry, Albuquerque	.227	29	110	97	11	22	34	4	1	2	13	1	2	0	10	1	23	0	0	3	.351	.294
Bochtler, Doug, Las Vegas	.000	18	2	2	0	0	0	0	0	0	0	0	0	0	0	0	2	0	0	0	.000	.000
Bolick, Frank, Colorado Springs†	.235	23	76	68	8	16	27	3	1	2	7	0	0	0	8	0	14	0	0	0	.397	.316
Bourgeois, Steve, Phoenix	.200	6	6	5	1	1	2	1	0	0	1	1	0	0	0	0	1	0	0	1	.400	.200
Bournigal, Rafael, Albuquerque	.129	15	33	31	2	4	5	1	0	0	1	0	0	1	1	0	2	0	0	0	.161	.182
Bowie, Jim, Edmonton*	.267	141	597	531	69	142	181	26	2	3	70	4	6	2	54	7	51	4	1	21	.341	.334
Bragg, Darren, Tacoma*	.307	53	236	212	24	65	96	13	3	4	31	0	1	0	23	1	39	10	3	3	.453	.373
Bream, Scott, Las Vegas†	.241	87	343	303	33	73	82	7	1	0	15	2	0	3	35	1	59	7	5	7	.271	.326
Brewer, Rod, Phoenix*	.244	15	55	45	8	11	18	4	0	1	8	0	2	5	3	0	10	1	1	1	.400	.345
Brink, Brad, Pho.-Edm.	.111	20	9	9	0	1	1	0	0	0	0	0	0	0	0	0	2	0	0	0	.111	.111
Brito, Bernardo, Salt Lake	.306	51	207	186	31	57	114	10	1	15	49	0	0	4	17	5	58	1	0	7	.613	.377
Brito, Jorge, Colorado Springs	.229	32	102	96	9	22	34	4	1	2	15	1	2	1	2	0	20	0	0	3	.354	.248
Brocail, Doug, Tucson*	1.000	3	2	1	0	1	1	0	0	0	0	1	0	0	0	0	0	0	0	0	1.000	1.000
Brosnan, Jason, Albuquerque*	.250	23	4	4	0	1	1	0	0	0	2	0	0	0	0	0	3	0	0	0	.250	.250
Brumley, Mike, Tucson†	.261	94	378	330	56	86	138	20	10	4	33	1	3	3	41	5	67	17	6	8	.418	.345
Bruno, Julio, Las Vegas	.245	38	148	139	13	34	42	6	1	0	6	0	1	0	8	0	24	1	3	6	.302	.284
Bruske, Jim, Albuquerque	.421	45	22	19	4	8	9	1	0	0	4	2	0	0	1	0	3	0	0	0	.474	.450
Bryant, Scott, Edmonton	.288	119	466	406	58	117	186	33	3	10	69	0	5	6	49	3	87	1	3	7	.458	.369
Bullock, Eric, Las Vegas*	.263	84	206	190	32	50	68	4	1	4	25	2	1	1	12	1	22	6	0	4	.358	.309
Burcham, Tim, Phoenix	.000	5	1	1	1	0	0	0	0	0	0	0	0	0	0	0	0	0	0	0	.000	.000
Burgos, Enrique, Phoenix*	.000	41	5	4	0	0	0	0	0	0	0	0	0	0	1	0	3	0	0	0	.000	.200
Burke, John, Colorado Springs†	.222	19	21	18	2	4	4	0	0	0	3	3	0	0	0	0	3	0	0	0	.222	.222
Burks, Ellis, Colorado Springs	.310	8	33	29	9	9	19	2	1	2	6	0	0	0	4	0	8	0	0	1	.655	.394
Busch, Mike, Albuquerque	.269	121	492	443	68	119	207	32	1	18	62	0	0	7	42	3	103	2	2	12	.467	.341
Bustillos, Albert, Colorado Springs	.167	34	28	24	1	4	4	0	0	0	2	1	0	0	3	0	6	0	0	0	.167	.259
Cadaret, Greg, Las Vegas*	.167	28	7	6	1	1	2	1	0	0	0	0	0	0	1	0	1	0	0	1	.333	.286
Cameron, Stanton, Calgary	.208	7	28	24	8	5	9	4	0	0	4	0	0	0	4	0	4	0	0	0	.375	.321
Candaele, Casey, Albuquerque†	.259	12	33	27	2	7	7	0	0	0	2	1	1	0	4	0	4	0	1	1	.259	.344
Cangelosi, John, Tucson†	.368	30	128	106	18	39	45	4	1	0	9	3	0	0	19	2	11	11	3	1	.425	.464
Carlson, Dan, Phoenix	.160	23	25	25	4	4	5	1	0	0	4	0	0	0	0	0	7	0	0	1	.200	.160
Carvajal, Jovino, Vancouver†	.325	41	168	163	25	53	65	3	3	1	10	1	0	1	3	0	18	10	7	6	.399	.341
Case, Mike, Colorado Springs	.286	7	14	14	2	4	5	1	0	0	0	0	0	0	0	0	4	1	1	0	.357	.286
Castellano, Pete, Colorado Springs	.266	99	368	334	40	89	143	23	2	9	47	3	5	2	24	1	56	2	0	10	.428	.315
Castillo, Juan, Tucson	.000	11	7	5	1	0	0	0	0	0	0	1	0	0	1	0	2	0	0	0	.000	.167
Castro, Juan, Albuquerque	.267	104	368	341	51	91	126	18	4	3	43	7	0	0	20	3	42	4	4	11	.370	.307
Cedeno, Roger, Albuquerque†	.305	99	429	367	67	112	155	19	9	2	44	4	3	2	53	2	56	23	18	5	.422	.393
Chavez, Raul, Tucson	.262	32	115	103	14	27	32	5	0	0	10	1	1	2	8	0	13	0	1	7	.311	.325
Chimelis, Joel, Phoenix	.259	118	442	398	48	103	158	32	1	7	66	3	8	5	28	4	53	1	2	7	.397	.310
Christopherson, Eric, Phoenix	.220	94	330	282	21	62	76	9	1	1	25	5	5	3	35	1	54	1	1	12	.270	.308
Cianfrocco, Archi, Las Vegas	.311	89	352	322	51	100	154	20	2	10	58	0	7	3	16	0	61	5	0	11	.478	.342
Clayton, Royal, Phoenix	.250	5	5	4	0	1	1	0	0	0	0	1	0	0	0	0	0	0	0	0	.250	.250
Cockrell, Alan, Colorado Springs	.313	106	388	355	58	111	171	22	1	12	58	1	0	2	30	3	65	0	3	8	.482	.370
Cohick, Emmitt, Vancouver*	.333	10	30	24	3	8	10	2	0	0	5	0	1	0	5	0	8	0	1	1	.417	.433
Colbert, Craig, Las Vegas	.249	74	264	241	30	60	73	8	1	1	24	1	1	0	21	0	44	1	0	14	.303	.308
Cole, Stu, Colorado Springs	.274	76	231	208	28	57	82	15	2	2	24	2	2	2	17	1	19	1	2	8	.394	.332
Cole, Victor, Las Vegas†	.000	4	6	5	0	0	0	0	0	0	1	0	0	0	1	0	1	0	0	0	.000	.167
Conroy, Brian, Colorado Springs†	.250	5	9	8	1	2	2	0	0	0	1	1	0	0	0	0	2	0	0	0	.250	.250
Cookson, Brent, Phoenix	.300	68	239	210	38	63	123	9	3	15	46	1	2	1	25	2	36	3	3	4	.586	.374
Coomer, Ron, Albuquerque	.322	85	347	323	54	104	179	23	2	16	76	0	4	2	18	1	28	5	2	16	.554	.357
Corbin, Archie, Calgary	.200	47	5	5	0	1	1	0	0	0	1	0	0	0	0	0	0	0	0	0	.200	.200
Corbin, Ted, Salt Lake†	.200	4	10	10	0	2	2	0	0	0	1	0	0	0	0	0	1	0	0	1	.200	.200
Correa, Ramser, Albuquerque	1.000	2	1	1	0	1	1	0	0	0	0	0	0	0	0	0	0	0	0	0	1.000	1.000
Correia, Rod, Vancouver	.303	73	298	264	42	80	99	6	5	1	39	4	4	0	26	3	33	8	4	7	.375	.361
Counsell, Craig, Colorado Springs*	.281	118	444	399	60	112	161	22	6	5	53	3	6	2	34	7	47	10	2	12	.404	.336
Cromwell, Nate, Las Vegas*	.333	9	3	3	1	1	2	1	0	0	2	0	0	0	0	0	0	0	1	0	.667	.333
Cruz, Fausto, Edmonton	.281	114	498	448	72	126	186	23	2	11	67	4	7	5	34	2	67	7	5	15	.415	.334
Cummings, Midre, Calgary*	.277	45	172	159	19	44	58	9	1	1	16	0	5	2	6	4	27	1	1	1	.365	.302
Czajkowski, Jim, Colorado Springs†	.000	60	2	1	0	0	0	0	0	0	0	1	0	0	0	0	0	0	0	0	.000	.000
Daal, Omar, Albuquerque*	.000	17	10	9	0	0	0	0	0	0	0	0	0	0	1	0	3	0	0	0	.000	.100

Player, Team	Avg.	G	TPA	AB	R	H	TB	2B	3B	HR	RBI	SH	SF	HP	BB	IBB	SO	SB	CS	GDP	Slg.	OBP
Dalesandro, Mark, Vancouver	.333	34	131	123	16	41	59	13	1	1	18	0	1	1	6	0	12	2	0	2	.480	.366
Daspit, Jim, Tuc.-Edm.	.200	38	6	5	0	1	1	0	0	0	0	1	0	0	0	0	2	0	0	0	.200	.200
Daugherty, Jack, Phoenix†	.152	10	36	33	4	5	6	1	0	0	3	0	1	0	2	1	4	0	0	1	.182	.194
Deer, Rob, Van.-L.V.	.290	89	353	303	54	88	173	23	4	18	65	0	3	0	47	6	89	2	2	4	.571	.382
DeLaRosa, Juan, Salt Lake	.224	31	54	49	7	11	13	2	0	0	5	3	1	0	1	1	6	0	0	2	.265	.235
DeLosSantos, Mariano, Calgary	.125	14	11	8	1	1	1	0	0	0	0	2	0	0	1	0	2	0	0	0	.125	.222
Demetral, Chris, Albuquerque*	.278	87	214	187	34	52	70	7	1	3	19	3	0	0	24	2	28	1	6	7	.374	.360
Diaz, Alex, Tacoma†	.250	10	42	40	3	10	11	1	0	0	4	0	0	0	2	0	5	1	2	0	.275	.286
Diaz, Eddy, Tacoma	.333	11	40	36	5	12	14	2	0	0	5	0	0	0	4	0	2	0	0	0	.389	.400
Dishman, Glenn, Las Vegas	.045	14	26	22	0	1	1	0	0	0	0	4	0	0	0	0	5	0	0	0	.045	.045
Dougherty, Jim, Tucson	.000	8	1	1	0	0	0	0	0	0	0	0	0	0	0	0	1	0	0	0	.000	.000
Duncan, Andres, Salt Lake†	.278	12	44	36	2	10	14	2	1	0	6	2	1	1	4	0	5	2	0	0	.389	.357
Dunn, Steve, Salt Lake*	.316	109	439	402	57	127	196	31	1	12	83	0	6	1	30	4	63	3	2	6	.488	.360
Durant, Mike, Salt Lake	.251	85	322	295	40	74	101	15	3	2	23	3	2	2	20	0	31	11	7	13	.342	.301
Durham, Leon, Vancouver*	.273	18	60	55	7	15	22	1	0	2	10	0	0	0	5	0	11	0	0	1	.400	.333
Ehmann, Kurt, Phoenix	.269	67	251	216	21	58	67	5	2	0	7	4	4	3	24	1	41	8	3	1	.310	.344
Eischen, Joey, Albuquerque*	.000	13	1	1	0	0	0	0	0	0	0	0	0	0	0	0	0	0	0	0	.000	.000
Encarnacion, Angelo, Calgary	.250	21	81	80	8	20	26	3	0	1	6	0	0	0	1	1	12	1	0	2	.325	.259
Ericks, John, Calgary	.143	5	8	7	0	1	1	0	0	0	0	1	0	0	0	0	2	0	0	0	.143	.143
Ettles, Mark, Las Vegas	.500	11	2	2	0	1	1	0	0	0	1	0	0	0	0	0	1	0	0	0	.500	.500
Fabregas, Jorge, Vancouver*	.247	21	83	73	9	18	33	3	0	4	10	0	1	0	9	3	12	0	0	1	.452	.325
Faneyte, Rikkert, Phoenix	.274	38	153	135	22	37	50	8	1	1	17	2	1	0	15	1	22	2	5	1	.370	.344
Faries, Paul, Edmonton	.300	117	472	424	67	127	146	15	2	0	46	7	5	2	34	1	47	14	8	14	.344	.351
Fermin, Felix, Tacoma	.333	1	3	3	0	1	1	0	0	0	0	0	0	0	0	0	0	0	0	0	.333	.333
Fesh, Sean, Tuc.-L.V.*	.000	40	1	1	0	0	0	0	0	0	0	0	0	0	0	0	0	0	0	0	.000	.000
Flora, Kevin, Vancouver	.298	38	142	124	22	37	53	7	0	3	14	1	1	0	16	0	33	7	4	2	.427	.376
Flynt, Bill, Calgary*	.000	12	2	1	1	0	0	0	0	0	0	0	0	0	1	0	1	0	0	0	.000	.500
Forbes, P.J., Vancouver	.274	109	411	369	47	101	132	22	3	1	52	7	10	2	21	0	46	4	6	4	.358	.308
Franklin, Micah, Calgary†	.293	110	411	358	64	105	196	28	0	21	71	0	5	1	47	8	95	3	3	7	.547	.372
Fredrickson, Scott, Col. Springs	.250	58	8	8	1	2	2	0	0	0	0	0	0	0	0	0	2	0	0	0	.250	.250
Gainer, Jay, Colorado Springs*	.291	112	410	358	57	104	194	19	1	23	86	0	6	0	42	9	64	2	3	7	.542	.360
Gallaher, Kevin, Tucson	.000	3	3	2	0	0	0	0	0	0	0	1	0	0	0	0	1	0	0	0	.000	.000
Gallego, Mike, Edmonton	.278	6	20	18	1	5	6	1	0	0	1	0	0	2	0	0	4	0	0	0	.333	.350
Gamez, Bob, Phoenix*	.167	36	13	12	1	2	4	0	1	0	2	0	0	0	1	0	2	0	0	0	.333	.231
Garcia, Karim, Albuquerque*	.319	124	519	474	88	151	257	26	10	20	91	2	3	2	38	5	102	12	6	12	.542	.369
Gardner, Chris, Tucson	1.000	16	2	2	1	2	3	1	0	0	1	0	0	0	0	0	0	0	0	0	1.500	1.000
Garrison, Webster, Col. Springs	.293	126	518	460	83	135	215	32	6	12	77	3	6	3	46	2	74	12	4	9	.467	.357
Giambi, Jason, Edmonton*	.342	55	229	190	34	65	102	26	1	3	41	0	3	2	34	4	26	0	0	4	.537	.441
Goff, Jerry, Tucson*	.222	68	238	207	23	46	77	11	1	6	34	0	2	0	29	3	56	0	0	3	.372	.315
Gonzales, Rene, Vancouver	.273	50	192	165	27	45	69	12	0	4	18	0	1	2	24	1	25	0	0	7	.418	.370
Grebeck, Brian, Vancouver	.245	81	292	241	41	59	89	11	2	5	30	5	3	5	38	1	38	4	0	6	.369	.355
Greene, Todd, Vancouver	.250	43	185	168	28	42	89	3	1	14	35	0	2	4	11	2	36	1	0	3	.530	.308
Greer, Ken, Phoenix	.000	38	4	3	0	0	0	0	0	0	0	1	0	0	0	0	2	0	0	0	.000	.000
Griffey, Ken, Tacoma*	.000	1	3	3	0	0	0	0	0	0	0	0	0	0	0	0	1	0	0	0	.000	.000
Guerrero, Juan, Tucson	.294	72	211	194	21	57	75	10	1	2	21	2	1	0	14	3	42	1	1	3	.387	.340
Guerrero, Wilton, Albuquerque	.327	14	52	49	10	16	19	1	1	0	2	2	0	0	1	1	7	2	3	1	.388	.340
Gutierrez, Ricky, Tucson	.301	64	270	236	46	71	94	12	4	1	26	1	2	3	28	4	28	9	7	6	.398	.379
Hajek, Dave, Tucson	.327	131	554	502	99	164	221	37	4	4	79	5	6	2	39	7	27	12	7	11	.440	.373
Hale, Chip, Salt Lake*	.286	16	56	49	5	14	18	4	0	0	2	0	0	0	7	1	5	0	1	2	.367	.375
Hall, Billy, Las Vegas†	.225	86	274	249	42	56	64	3	1	1	22	1	3	1	20	1	47	22	5	3	.257	.282
Hancock, Lee, Calgary*	.176	34	21	17	1	3	3	0	0	0	2	3	1	0	0	0	7	0	0	0	.176	.167
Hanel, Marcus, Calgary	.125	2	8	8	1	1	1	0	0	0	0	0	0	0	0	0	1	0	0	0	.125	.125
Hansell, Greg, Alb.-S.L.	.500	15	3	2	1	1	1	0	0	0	0	1	0	0	0	0	1	0	0	0	.500	.500
Hansen, Terrel, Tacoma	.220	20	54	50	5	11	21	1	0	3	10	0	1	1	2	0	12	0	0	5	.420	.259
Harriger, Denny, Las Vegas	.263	29	42	38	3	10	12	2	0	0	2	2	0	0	2	0	15	0	0	1	.316	.300
Hartgraves, Dean, Tucson	.000	14	2	2	0	0	0	0	0	0	0	0	0	0	0	0	0	0	0	0	.000	.000
Hatcher, Chris, Tucson	.286	94	339	290	59	83	148	19	2	14	50	1	2	4	42	2	107	7	3	9	.510	.382
Hathaway, Hilly, Las Vegas*	.214	15	16	14	2	3	3	0	0	0	2	2	0	0	0	0	2	1	0	3	.214	.214
Hawblitzel, Ryan, Col. Springs	.300	21	13	10	4	3	4	1	0	0	1	2	0	0	1	0	2	0	0	0	.400	.364
Hazlett, Steve, Salt Lake	.300	127	477	427	71	128	177	25	6	4	49	2	3	4	41	1	65	8	10	9	.415	.364
Helfand, Eric, Edmonton*	.214	19	71	56	5	12	23	4	2	1	12	5	1	0	9	1	10	0	1	3	.411	.318
Hernandez, Fernando, Las Vegas	.000	8	5	4	0	0	0	0	0	0	0	0	0	0	1	0	3	0	0	0	.000	.200
Hill, Milt, Calgary	.286	24	8	7	0	2	2	0	0	0	1	1	0	0	0	0	4	0	0	0	.286	.286
Hocking, Denny, Salt Lake†	.282	117	437	397	51	112	164	24	2	8	75	8	5	2	25	1	41	12	8	10	.413	.324
Holbert, Ray, Las Vegas	.115	9	31	26	3	3	4	1	0	0	3	0	0	0	5	0	10	1	1	1	.154	.258
Hollandsworth, Todd, Albuquerque*	.237	10	45	38	9	9	17	2	0	2	4	0	0	1	6	2	8	1	0	1	.447	.356
Holman, Shawn, Albuquerque	1.000	49	1	1	0	1	1	0	0	0	1	0	0	0	0	0	0	0	0	0	1.000	1.000
Holt, Chris, Tucson	.111	20	24	18	1	2	3	1	0	0	1	6	0	0	0	0	4	0	0	1	.167	.111
Hook, Chris, Phoenix†	.000	4	1	1	0	0	0	0	0	0	0	0	0	0	0	0	1	0	0	0	.000	.000
Hope, John, Calgary	.083	13	16	12	0	1	1	0	0	0	0	4	0	0	0	0	4	0	0	0	.083	.083
Horn, Jeff, Salt Lake	.500	3	10	10	0	5	6	1	0	0	2	0	0	0	0	0	1	0	0	0	.600	.500
Horn, Sam, Calgary*	.333	36	114	99	21	33	69	8	2	8	22	0	1	0	14	0	21	0	0	6	.697	.412
Hosey, Steve, Vancouver	.271	16	66	59	10	16	25	3	0	2	6	0	0	0	7	0	16	2	0	1	.424	.348
Howard, Chris, Tacoma	.243	83	294	268	33	65	91	14	0	4	31	4	2	2	18	2	70	0	1	9	.340	.293
Hubbard, Trent, Col. Springs	.340	123	553	480	102	163	242	29	7	12	66	2	5	5	61	5	59	37	14	2	.504	.416
Huckaby, Ken, Albuquerque	.324	89	298	278	30	90	113	16	2	1	40	3	1	4	12	1	26	3	1	16	.406	.359
Huisman, Rick, Tucson	.000	42	1	1	0	0	0	0	0	0	0	0	0	0	0	0	1	0	0	0	.000	.000
Humphreys, Mike, Tacoma	.200	18	39	35	3	7	9	2	0	0	1	0	1	0	3	0	11	0	0	0	.257	.256
Hunter, Brian, Tucson	.329	38	172	155	28	51	61	5	1	1	16	0	0	0	17	0	13	11	3	1	.394	.395
Hunter, Jim, Colorado Springs	.000	10	3	2	1	0	0	0	0	0	0	0	0	0	1	0	1	0	0	0	.000	.333
Hyers, Tim, Las Vegas*	.290	82	287	259	46	75	92	12	1	1	23	2	1	1	24	3	33	0	3	7	.355	.351
Ingram, Garey, Albuquerque	.246	63	259	232	28	57	79	11	4	1	30	0	3	3	21	1	40	10	4	4	.341	.313
Ingram, Riccardo, Salt Lake	.348	122	526	477	80	166	249	43	2	12	85	0	5	3	41	3	60	4	5	22	.522	.399

Player, Team	Avg.	G	TPA	AB	R	H	TB	2B	3B	HR	RBI	SH	SF	HP	BB	IBB	SO	SB	CS	GDP	Slg.	OBP
Jackson, John, Van.-S.L.*	.287	90	365	307	59	88	132	21	4	5	32	6	3	5	44	2	35	16	5	7	.430	.382
Jean, Domingo, Tucson	.000	3	3	3	0	0	0	0	0	0	0	0	0	0	0	0	3	0	0	0	.000	.000
Johnson, Erik, Calgary	.297	123	503	455	64	135	191	35	6	3	58	3	6	0	39	6	40	5	4	12	.420	.348
Johnson, Mark, Calgary*	.304	9	30	23	7	7	17	4	0	2	8	0	0	1	6	1	4	1	0	0	.739	.467
Johnston, Joel, Col. Springs	.000	18	2	2	0	0	0	0	0	0	0	0	0	0	0	0	1	0	0	0	.000	.000
Jones, Bobby, Col. Springs	.200	11	7	5	1	1	1	0	0	0	0	2	0	0	0	0	0	0	0	0	.200	.200
Jones, Dax, Phoenix	.267	112	444	404	47	108	141	21	3	2	45	2	5	2	31	3	52	11	10	8	.349	.319
Jones, Tim, Edmonton*	.500	2	6	6	1	3	4	1	0	0	1	0	0	0	0	0	0	0	0	0	.667	.500
Jordan, Ricky, Vancouver	.222	19	67	63	5	14	22	2	0	2	9	0	0	1	3	0	7	0	0	2	.349	.269
Keagle, Greg, Las Vegas	.000	14	8	6	0	0	0	0	0	0	0	2	0	0	0	0	2	0	0	0	.000	.000
Kellner, Frank, Tucson†	.180	28	106	89	11	16	21	3	1	0	7	1	1	0	15	0	12	1	0	2	.236	.295
Ketchen, Doug, Tucson	.063	19	17	16	1	1	1	0	0	0	0	0	0	0	1	0	2	0	0	0	.063	.118
Kile, Darryl, Tucson	.200	4	7	5	1	1	1	0	0	0	0	1	0	0	1	0	1	0	0	1	.200	.333
Kirkpatrick, Jay, Albuquerque*	.250	13	42	40	4	10	16	1	1	1	6	0	0	0	2	1	6	0	0	0	.400	.286
Knabenshue, Chris, Calgary*	.000	4	14	10	2	0	0	0	0	0	1	0	0	0	4	0	3	0	0	0	.000	.286
Knudsen, Kurt, Phoenix	.000	11	3	2	0	0	0	0	0	0	0	1	0	0	0	0	1	0	0	0	.000	.000
Kotarski, Mike, Col. Springs*	.000	22	5	4	0	0	0	0	0	0	0	1	0	0	0	0	2	0	0	0	.000	.000
Kreuter, Chad, Tacoma†	.292	15	56	48	6	14	22	5	0	1	11	0	0	0	8	0	11	0	0	3	.458	.393
Landrum, Ced, Col. Springs*	.259	82	185	166	31	43	58	5	2	2	19	5	2	1	11	1	29	12	5	2	.349	.306
Latham, Chris, Albuquerque†	.167	5	20	18	2	3	5	0	1	0	3	0	1	0	1	0	4	1	0	0	.278	.200
Lennon, Pat, Salt Lake	.400	34	129	115	26	46	79	15	0	6	29	0	1	1	12	2	29	2	1	1	.687	.457
Leonard, Mark, Phoenix*	.296	112	484	392	73	116	189	25	3	14	79	1	10	0	81	8	63	3	2	19	.482	.408
Lieber, Jon, Calgary*	.118	14	21	17	2	2	2	0	0	0	0	1	0	0	3	0	6	0	0	0	.118	.250
Lind, Jose, Vancouver	.222	10	37	36	2	8	10	2	0	0	5	0	0	0	1	0	4	1	0	0	.278	.243
Litton, Greg, Tacoma	.309	117	444	388	58	120	174	25	1	9	56	4	6	3	43	1	69	2	2	11	.448	.377
Loiselle, Rich, L.V.-Tuc.	.125	10	8	8	1	1	1	0	0	0	0	0	0	0	0	0	5	0	0	0	.125	.125
Lott, Billy, Albuquerque	.315	41	160	146	23	46	72	7	2	5	26	1	0	0	13	2	48	1	2	5	.493	.371
Lydy, Scott, Edmonton	.290	104	447	400	78	116	207	29	7	16	65	3	5	6	33	3	66	15	4	11	.518	.349
Mack, Quinn, Tacoma*	.265	70	230	204	30	54	68	11	0	1	17	1	0	1	24	5	21	9	2	6	.333	.345
Makarewicz, Scott, Tucson	.266	62	208	192	21	51	75	9	0	5	31	2	2	2	10	3	23	1	0	9	.391	.306
Maksudian, Mike, Edmonton*	.265	100	372	324	54	86	127	24	4	3	34	2	0	0	46	2	55	5	1	8	.392	.357
Marrero, Oreste, Albuquerque*	.348	7	24	23	5	8	16	2	0	2	6	0	0	0	1	0	5	0	0	0	.696	.375
Martin, Jim, Albuquerque*	.253	25	83	75	8	19	27	3	1	1	7	0	0	0	8	0	20	3	3	3	.360	.325
Martinez, Carlos, Vancouver	.247	25	106	97	17	24	30	3	0	1	6	0	0	2	7	2	17	1	2	4	.309	.311
Martinez, Chito, Col. Springs*	.155	42	122	110	18	17	37	8	0	4	6	0	0	0	12	0	32	0	2	0	.336	.238
Martinez, Jesus, Albuquerque*	.000	2	1	1	0	0	0	0	0	0	0	0	0	0	0	0	0	0	0	0	.000	.000
Martinez, Jose, Las Vegas	.045	27	26	22	0	1	2	1	0	0	0	3	0	0	1	0	10	0	0	1	.091	.087
Martinez, Pedro, Tucson*	.333	20	3	3	0	1	1	0	0	0	0	0	0	0	0	0	1	0	0	0	.333	.333
Marx, Tim, Calgary	.297	61	208	185	27	55	71	11	1	1	12	1	3	0	19	2	16	2	3	6	.384	.357
Mashore, Damon, Edmonton†	.300	117	390	337	50	101	133	19	5	1	37	3	3	5	42	0	77	17	5	9	.395	.382
Masteller, Dan, Salt Lake*	.303	48	174	152	25	46	82	10	7	4	18	1	3	3	15	3	17	4	1	3	.539	.370
Matos, Francisco, Calgary	.323	100	352	341	36	110	142	11	6	3	40	3	1	2	5	0	25	9	2	11	.416	.335
Maurer, Ron, Albuquerque	.259	84	209	185	29	48	81	14	2	5	25	1	1	3	19	2	34	1	2	1	.438	.337
Mauser, Tim, Las Vegas	.000	35	1	1	0	0	0	0	0	0	0	0	0	0	0	0	0	0	0	0	.000	.000
Maynard, Scott, Tacoma	.000	1	1	1	0	0	0	0	0	0	0	0	0	0	0	0	0	0	0	1	.000	.000
Maysey, Matt, Calgary	.118	44	17	17	0	2	2	0	0	0	1	0	0	0	0	0	5	0	0	0	.118	.118
McCarthy, Tom, Albuquerque	.364	13	11	11	0	4	6	2	0	0	4	0	0	0	0	0	3	0	0	0	.545	.364
McCarty, Dave, Phoenix	.351	37	175	151	31	53	88	19	2	4	19	0	1	6	17	1	27	1	1	6	.583	.434
McCracken, Quinton, Col. Springs†	.361	61	270	244	55	88	123	14	6	3	28	2	0	1	23	3	30	17	6	4	.504	.418
McDavid, Ray, Las Vegas*	.271	52	201	166	28	45	70	8	1	5	27	0	1	4	30	0	35	7	1	2	.422	.393
McFarlin, Terric, Las Vegas†	.143	59	9	7	2	1	1	0	0	0	0	2	0	0	0	0	3	0	0	0	.143	.143
McMurtry, Craig, Tucson	.167	17	13	12	2	2	2	0	0	0	1	0	0	0	1	0	3	0	1	0	.167	.231
Mejia, Roberto, Col. Springs	.294	38	153	143	18	42	62	10	2	2	14	2	0	1	7	2	29	0	2	6	.434	.331
Menendez, Tony, Phoenix	.000	50	3	3	0	0	0	0	0	0	0	0	0	0	0	0	2	0	0	0	.000	.000
Mercedes, Luis, Calgary	.262	25	98	84	18	22	26	1	0	1	8	0	0	3	11	0	10	1	2	2	.310	.367
Milchin, Mike, Albuquerque*	.364	18	12	11	0	4	6	2	0	0	1	1	0	0	0	0	1	0	0	0	.545	.364
Miller, Barry, Phoenix*	.224	71	180	156	18	35	51	8	1	2	21	0	1	0	23	0	35	0	2	4	.327	.322
Miller, Damian, Salt Lake	.285	83	320	295	39	84	118	23	1	3	41	5	2	3	15	1	39	2	4	11	.400	.324
Miller, Roger, Phoenix	.212	43	150	137	14	29	38	4	1	1	10	4	0	0	9	0	15	0	0	3	.277	.260
Mimbs, Mark, Albuquerque*	.048	23	23	21	1	1	2	1	0	0	0	2	0	0	0	0	3	0	0	0	.095	.048
Mintz, Steve, Phoenix*	.000	31	3	2	0	0	0	0	0	0	0	1	0	0	0	0	1	0	0	0	.000	.000
Mirabelli, Doug, Phoenix	.167	23	81	66	3	11	13	0	1	0	7	0	2	1	12	1	10	1	0	5	.197	.296
Mlicki, Doug, Tucson	.444	6	11	9	2	4	4	0	0	0	2	1	0	0	1	0	0	0	0	0	.444	.500
Molina, Ben, Vancouver	.000	1	2	2	0	0	0	0	0	0	0	0	0	0	0	0	1	0	0	0	.000	.000
Molina, Izzy, Edmonton	.167	2	6	6	0	1	1	0	0	0	0	0	0	0	0	0	2	0	0	0	.167	.167
Montalvo, Rafael, Albuquerque	.111	49	10	9	1	1	1	0	0	0	0	1	0	0	0	0	5	0	0	0	.111	.111
Montgomery, Ray, Tucson	.302	88	326	291	48	88	140	19	0	11	68	1	8	2	24	1	58	5	3	3	.481	.351
Monzon, Jose, Vancouver	.217	13	26	23	5	5	9	1	0	1	5	0	0	0	3	0	2	0	0	1	.391	.308
Moore, Kerwin, Edmonton†	.279	72	317	265	53	74	102	14	4	2	26	3	1	1	47	1	67	10	3	3	.385	.389
Mora, Melvin, Tucson	.600	2	7	5	3	3	5	0	1	0	1	0	0	0	2	1	0	1	0	0	1.000	.714
Mouton, James, Tucson	.455	3	11	11	1	5	8	0	0	1	1	0	0	0	0	0	2	0	1	0	.727	.455
Mueller, Bill, Phoenix†	.297	41	198	172	23	51	82	13	6	2	19	6	1	0	19	0	31	0	0	7	.477	.365
Mulligan, Sean, Las Vegas	.274	101	378	339	34	93	136	20	1	7	43	1	3	8	27	2	61	0	0	7	.401	.340
Munoz, Noe, Albuquerque	.224	23	60	58	1	13	14	1	0	0	3	0	0	0	2	0	8	0	0	3	.241	.250
Munoz, Orlando, Vancouver†	.100	4	10	10	0	1	1	0	0	0	0	0	0	0	0	0	3	0	1	1	.100	.100
Murray, Calvin, Phoenix	.180	13	56	50	8	9	22	1	0	4	10	1	1	0	4	0	6	2	2	2	.440	.236
Nevin, Phil, Tucson	.291	62	252	223	31	65	102	16	0	7	41	1	0	1	27	1	39	2	3	9	.457	.371
Newfield, Marc, Tac.-L.V.	.295	73	298	268	40	79	121	16	1	8	42	1	1	6	22	1	41	3	0	7	.451	.360
Nied, David, Colorado Springs	.000	7	6	6	0	0	0	0	0	0	0	0	0	0	0	0	4	0	0	0	.000	.000
Nokes, Matt, Colorado Springs*	.216	12	43	37	7	8	22	2	0	4	10	0	3	1	2	0	4	0	0	1	.595	.256
Noland, J.D., Tacoma*	.275	76	271	251	27	69	100	10	3	5	28	4	3	0	13	1	37	14	6	7	.398	.307
Northrup, Kevin, Edmonton	.182	17	50	44	4	8	10	2	0	0	1	1	0	0	5	1	8	0	0	0	.227	.265
O'Donoghue, John, Albuquerque*	.091	25	13	11	0	1	1	0	0	0	1	1	0	0	1	0	5	0	0	0	.091	.167

Player, Team	Avg.	G	TPA	AB	R	H	TB	2B	3B	HR	RBI	SH	SF	HP	BB	IBB	SO	SB	CS	GDP	Slg.	OBP
Olivares, Omar, Col. Springs	.000	3	4	4	0	0	0	0	0	0	0	0	0	0	0	0	0	0	0	0	.000	.000
Ortiz, Ray, Phoenix*	.242	66	204	190	22	46	72	10	2	4	29	0	1	0	13	3	36	1	0	2	.379	.289
Osik, Keith, Calgary	.336	90	331	301	40	101	158	25	1	10	59	0	4	5	21	2	42	2	2	5	.525	.384
Owens, Jayhawk, Col. Springs	.294	70	251	221	47	65	124	13	5	12	48	1	2	7	20	2	61	2	1	2	.561	.368
Painter, Lance, Col. Springs*	.000	11	3	2	0	0	0	0	0	0	0	1	0	0	0	0	1	0	0	0	.000	.000
Palmeiro, Orlando, Vancouver*	.307	107	458	398	66	122	151	21	4	0	47	11	5	3	41	8	34	16	7	11	.379	.371
Park, Chan Ho, Albuquerque	.074	23	29	27	2	2	3	1	0	0	2	0	1	0	1	0	12	0	0	0	.111	.103
Parker, Rick, Albuquerque	.280	58	209	175	33	49	63	7	2	1	14	1	1	3	27	4	17	1	6	4	.360	.383
Parra, Jose, Albuquerque	.000	12	9	6	1	0	0	0	0	0	0	3	0	0	0	0	3	0	0	0	.000	.000
Patrick, Bronswell, Tucson	.400	43	10	5	1	2	2	0	0	0	2	2	0	1	2	0	1	0	0	0	.400	.625
Peever, Lloyd, Col. Springs	.222	8	11	9	2	2	3	1	0	0	0	1	0	0	1	0	3	0	0	0	.333	.300
Peguero, Jose, Vancouver	.254	17	59	59	6	15	21	6	0	0	3	0	0	0	0	0	8	1	0	2	.356	.254
Peguero, Julio, Tacoma†	.200	11	26	25	2	5	7	0	1	0	1	0	0	0	1	0	7	0	0	0	.280	.231
Perez, Eduardo, Vancouver	.325	69	278	246	39	80	124	12	7	6	37	1	4	2	25	0	34	6	2	5	.504	.386
Perez, Neifi, Colorado Springs†	.278	11	37	36	4	10	14	4	0	0	2	1	0	0	0	0	5	1	1	0	.389	.278
Petagine, Roberto, Las Vegas*	.214	19	70	56	8	12	19	2	1	1	5	1	0	0	13	1	17	1	0	0	.339	.362
Pevey, Marty, Tacoma*	.105	7	20	19	2	2	2	0	0	0	0	0	0	0	1	0	5	0	0	0	.105	.150
Phillips, Randy, Phoenix	.167	25	20	18	1	3	3	0	0	0	0	1	0	0	1	0	7	0	0	0	.167	.211
Phoenix, Steve, Edmonton	.000	41	2	1	0	0	0	0	0	0	0	0	0	0	1	0	1	0	0	0	.000	.500
Pirkl, Greg, Tacoma	.293	47	190	174	29	51	108	8	2	15	44	0	1	1	14	1	28	1	1	3	.621	.347
Plantier, Phil, Tucson*	.250	10	29	24	6	6	11	2	0	1	4	0	0	0	5	0	4	0	0	1	.458	.379
Polcovich, Kevin, Calgary	.282	62	237	213	31	60	79	8	1	3	27	2	3	8	11	0	32	5	6	7	.371	.336
Pose, Scott, Alb.-S.L.*	.301	77	257	219	46	66	78	10	1	0	20	3	3	1	31	2	28	15	4	2	.356	.386
Powell, Ross, Tucson*	.000	13	6	6	0	0	0	0	0	0	0	0	0	0	0	0	3	0	0	0	.000	.000
Pozo, Arquimedez, Tacoma	.300	122	484	450	57	135	196	19	6	10	62	1	4	3	26	1	31	3	3	15	.436	.340
Prince, Tom, Albuquerque	.318	61	222	192	30	61	97	15	0	7	36	1	0	2	27	2	41	0	0	6	.505	.407
Pritchett, Chris, Vancouver*	.276	123	498	434	66	120	179	27	4	8	53	2	1	5	56	6	79	2	3	7	.412	.365
Pulliam, Harvey, Col. Springs	.327	115	465	407	90	133	250	30	6	25	91	0	6	3	49	10	59	6	2	11	.614	.398
Pyc, Dave, Albuquerque*	.000	1	2	2	0	0	0	0	0	0	0	0	0	0	0	0	0	0	0	0	.000	.000
Pye, Eddie, Albuquerque	.295	84	337	302	49	89	120	20	1	3	32	2	2	1	30	2	36	11	2	7	.397	.358
Quinlan, Tom, Salt Lake	.279	130	527	466	78	130	215	22	6	17	88	1	6	15	39	2	124	6	3	12	.461	.350
Raabe, Brian, Salt Lake	.305	112	497	440	88	134	187	32	6	3	60	2	7	3	45	2	14	15	0	12	.425	.368
Ralph, Curtis, Calgary	.000	28	2	1	0	0	0	0	0	0	1	0	0	1	0	0	0	0	0	0	.000	.500
Ramirez, J.D., Vancouver	.000	1	4	4	0	0	0	0	0	0	0	0	0	0	0	0	1	0	0	0	.000	.000
Ramos, Ken, Tucson*	.315	112	391	327	57	103	152	24	8	3	47	4	5	3	51	3	27	14	5	3	.465	.407
Rath, Gary, Albuquerque*	.000	8	4	3	0	0	0	0	0	0	1	1	0	0	0	0	1	0	0	0	.000	.000
Ratliff, Daryl, Calgary	.343	95	310	286	41	98	111	11	1	0	37	4	0	2	18	2	30	9	6	7	.388	.386
Raven, Luis, Vancouver	.244	37	152	135	18	33	61	11	1	5	26	1	1	0	15	0	35	3	1	6	.452	.318
Rekar, Bryan, Col. Springs	.250	7	6	4	0	1	1	0	0	0	2	2	0	0	0	0	2	0	0	0	.250	.250
Relaford, Desi, Tacoma†	.239	30	128	113	20	27	40	5	1	2	7	0	2	0	13	2	24	6	0	2	.354	.313
Reynoso, Armando, Col. Springs	.000	5	3	3	0	0	0	0	0	0	0	0	0	0	0	0	0	0	0	0	.000	.000
Richardson, Jeff, Calgary	.333	7	24	18	4	6	6	0	0	0	3	3	1	0	2	0	1	0	0	1	.333	.381
Riley, Marquis, Vancouver	.262	120	533	477	70	125	143	6	6	0	43	2	4	1	49	3	69	29	10	11	.300	.330
Roberson, Kevin, Tacoma†	.236	42	180	157	17	37	63	6	1	6	17	0	2	2	19	1	51	1	1	4	.401	.322
Roberts, Bip, Las Vegas†	.333	3	13	12	1	4	4	0	0	0	2	0	1	0	0	0	3	1	0	0	.333	.308
Robinson, Scott, Phoenix	.346	32	30	26	3	9	15	1	1	1	3	3	0	0	1	0	7	1	0	1	.577	.370
Rodriguez, Alex, Tacoma	.360	54	237	214	37	77	140	12	3	15	45	1	2	2	18	1	44	2	4	2	.654	.411
Rodriguez, Boi, Calgary*	.256	11	42	39	10	10	18	2	0	2	10	0	0	0	3	1	5	1	0	0	.462	.310
Rodriguez, Felix, Albuquerque	.429	14	7	7	1	3	6	0	0	1	2	0	0	0	0	0	4	0	0	0	.857	.429
Rogers, Kevin, Phoenix†	.000	3	1	1	0	0	0	0	0	0	0	0	0	0	0	0	1	0	0	0	.000	.000
Rohde, Dave, Tucson†	.276	73	210	170	27	47	59	8	2	0	20	6	2	0	32	1	17	2	2	5	.347	.387
Romanoli, Paul, Col. Springs*	.000	31	1	0	0	0	0	0	0	0	0	0	0	0	1	0	0	0	0	0	.000	1.000
Roper, John, Phoenix	1.000	1	1	1	0	1	1	0	0	0	0	0	0	0	0	0	0	0	0	0	1.000	1.000
Rosselli, Joe, Phoenix	.000	14	15	12	0	0	0	0	0	0	0	3	0	0	0	0	0	0	0	0	.000	.000
Rossy, Rico, Las Vegas	.301	98	381	316	44	95	113	11	2	1	45	2	6	2	55	2	36	3	7	13	.358	.401
Russo, Paul, Las Vegas	.297	44	160	148	17	44	66	10	0	4	19	1	2	0	9	2	31	0	1	4	.446	.333
Sager, A.J., Colorado Springs	.286	23	23	21	2	6	6	0	0	0	1	0	0	0	2	0	7	0	0	1	.286	.348
St. Claire, Randy, Calgary	.000	54	2	2	0	0	0	0	0	0	0	0	0	0	0	0	2	0	0	0	.000	.000
Sanders, Scott, Las Vegas	.000	1	1	1	0	0	0	0	0	0	0	0	0	0	0	0	1	0	0	0	.000	.000
Saunders, Doug, Edm.-Tac.	.272	55	162	151	21	41	69	7	3	5	28	1	2	1	7	0	32	0	0	3	.457	.304
Schofield, Dick, Vancouver	.189	16	60	53	5	10	14	4	0	0	9	1	2	1	3	0	3	0	0	1	.264	.237
Scott, Darryl, Colorado Springs	.000	59	5	5	0	0	0	0	0	0	0	0	0	0	0	0	5	0	0	0	.000	.000
Scott, Gary, Phoenix	.265	68	253	219	33	58	93	16	2	5	26	0	1	7	26	5	39	2	2	3	.425	.360
Sealy, Scot, Tacoma	.300	4	10	10	1	3	3	0	0	0	0	0	0	0	0	0	0	0	0	0	.300	.300
See, Larry, Las Vegas	.307	38	122	114	11	35	51	8	1	2	20	0	2	1	5	0	12	0	0	5	.447	.336
Sepeda, Jamie, Tucson	.167	8	6	6	1	1	1	0	0	0	1	0	0	0	0	0	3	0	0	0	.167	.167
Sheets, Andy, Tacoma	.293	132	483	437	57	128	181	29	9	2	47	10	4	0	32	2	83	8	3	9	.414	.338
Sheldon, Scott, Edmonton	.258	45	150	128	21	33	54	7	1	4	12	4	1	2	15	0	15	4	2	0	.422	.342
Shelton, Ben, Salt Lake	.242	9	39	33	7	8	14	1	1	1	6	0	0	0	6	0	16	0	0	0	.424	.359
Sherman, Darrell, Tacoma*	.257	119	421	350	59	90	111	9	3	2	31	10	4	3	54	0	49	19	6	6	.317	.358
Shifflett, Steve, Col. Springs	.250	23	4	4	0	1	1	0	0	0	1	0	0	0	0	0	1	0	0	0	.250	.250
Shouse, Brian, Calgary*	.333	8	8	6	0	2	2	0	0	0	1	2	0	0	0	0	0	0	0	0	.333	.333
Simmons, Nelson, Calgary†	.281	107	333	299	44	84	128	17	0	9	58	0	4	0	30	3	45	1	1	5	.428	.342
Simms, Mike, Tucson	.295	85	361	319	56	94	175	26	8	13	66	0	4	3	35	0	65	10	2	6	.549	.366
Simons, Mitch, Salt Lake	.325	130	543	480	87	156	207	34	4	3	46	4	2	10	47	2	45	32	16	9	.431	.395
Small, Mark, Tucson	.600	51	5	5	2	3	3	0	0	0	2	0	0	0	0	0	1	0	0	0	.600	.600
Smiley, Reuben, Las Vegas*	.219	34	106	96	10	21	36	4	1	3	17	0	2	0	8	1	19	6	3	2	.375	.274
Smith, Ira, Las Vegas	.325	59	229	209	39	68	106	19	5	3	22	4	1	2	13	0	25	5	4	3	.507	.369
Snider, Van, Salt Lake*	.357	32	123	115	25	41	69	7	0	7	28	1	0	0	7	0	17	1	0	5	.600	.393
Snyder, Cory, Las Vegas	.265	8	35	34	4	9	10	1	0	0	5	0	0	0	1	0	10	0	0	2	.294	.286
Sojo, Luis, Tacoma	.176	4	17	17	1	3	6	0	0	1	1	0	0	0	0	0	2	0	0	0	.353	.176
Spearman, Vernon, Albuquerque*	.172	22	40	29	7	5	7	0	1	0	2	0	0	0	11	0	4	2	2	2	.241	.400
Springer, Steve, L.V.	.218	35	90	87	7	19	25	3	0	1	10	0	1	0	2	1	17	1	1	5	.287	.233

Player, Team	Avg.	G	TPA	AB	R	H	TB	2B	3B	HR	RBI	SH	SF	HP	BB	IBB	SO	SB	CS	GDP	Slg.	OBP
Stahoviak, Scott, Salt Lake*	.303	9	39	33	6	10	11	1	0	0	5	0	0	0	6	0	3	2	0	0	.333	.410
Stankiewicz, Andy, Tucson	.276	25	104	87	16	24	31	4	0	1	15	2	1	0	14	0	8	3	1	3	.356	.373
Strittmatter, Mark, Col. Springs	.294	5	17	17	1	5	7	2	0	0	3	0	0	0	0	0	3	0	0	0	.412	.294
Sveum, Dale, Calgary†	.284	118	462	408	71	116	188	34	1	12	70	1	5	0	48	2	78	2	2	9	.461	.356
Sweeney, Mark, Vancouver*	.345	69	275	226	48	78	117	14	2	7	59	1	1	2	43	4	33	3	1	6	.518	.452
Tatum, Jim, Colorado Springs	.323	27	102	93	17	30	55	7	0	6	18	0	2	1	6	0	21	0	1	2	.591	.363
Taylor, Kerry, Las Vegas	.273	8	11	11	1	3	4	1	0	0	1	0	0	0	0	0	6	0	0	0	.364	.273
Taylor, Scott, Calgary*	.111	27	27	27	1	3	3	0	0	0	0	0	0	0	0	0	9	0	0	0	.111	.111
Tejero, Fausto, Vancouver	.260	37	107	96	10	25	28	3	0	0	8	1	0	0	10	1	22	2	0	0	.292	.330
Thompson, Mark, Col. Springs	.300	11	12	10	3	3	6	0	0	1	1	2	0	0	0	0	4	0	0	0	.600	.300
Thurman, Gary, Tacoma	.300	93	392	363	65	109	158	10	12	5	46	3	1	5	20	0	62	22	8	2	.435	.344
Thurston, Jerrey, Las Vegas	.200	5	21	20	2	4	5	1	0	0	0	0	0	1	0	0	5	0	0	0	.250	.238
Tomberlin, Andy, Edmonton*	.250	14	59	52	9	13	22	3	0	2	7	1	0	1	5	0	15	0	0	1	.423	.328
Traxler, Brian, Albuquerque*	.283	110	378	353	46	100	159	24	1	11	50	1	0	0	24	3	27	1	3	11	.450	.329
Treadwell, Jody, Albuquerque	.400	30	20	15	2	6	6	0	0	0	5	3	1	0	1	0	3	0	0	0	.400	.412
Trlicek, Rick, Phoenix	.000	38	4	2	1	0	0	0	0	0	0	0	0	0	2	0	2	0	0	0	.000	.500
Turang, Brian, Tacoma	.240	59	215	196	22	47	56	4	1	1	18	3	3	0	13	0	35	7	4	7	.286	.283
Turner, Chris, Vancouver	.266	80	324	282	44	75	108	20	2	3	48	1	2	5	34	2	54	3	0	5	.383	.353
Valdez, Carlos, Phoenix	.000	18	2	2	0	0	0	0	0	0	0	0	0	0	0	0	1	0	0	0	.000	.000
Valdez, Sergio, Phoenix	.100	18	28	20	2	2	3	1	0	0	1	5	0	0	3	0	4	0	0	0	.150	.217
Van Burkleo, Ty, Col. Springs*	.286	76	264	231	43	66	126	14	2	14	57	1	2	1	29	2	57	2	1	1	.545	.365
Vanderweele, Doug, Phoenix	.000	11	2	2	0	0	0	0	0	0	0	0	0	0	0	0	2	0	0	0	.000	.000
Vatcher, Jim, Las Vegas	.292	101	399	356	56	104	162	31	3	7	43	2	5	3	33	6	46	3	4	6	.455	.353
Vaughn, Derek, Vancouver	.667	1	3	3	0	2	2	0	0	0	0	0	0	0	0	0	0	1	0	0	.667	.667
Velandia, Jorge, Las Vegas	.262	66	230	206	25	54	72	12	3	0	25	7	2	2	13	1	37	0	0	5	.350	.309
Wagner, Billy, Tucson*	.400	13	14	10	1	4	4	0	0	0	0	2	0	0	2	0	5	0	0	0	.400	.500
Wakamatsu, Don, Tacoma	.156	9	35	32	3	5	6	1	0	0	6	0	0	1	2	0	8	0	0	4	.188	.229
Wall, Donne, Tucson	.083	28	39	36	0	3	3	0	0	0	1	3	0	0	0	0	6	0	0	3	.083	.083
Wallach, Tim, Albuquerque	.333	1	3	3	1	1	1	0	0	0	1	0	0	0	0	0	2	0	0	0	.333	.333
Walters, Dan, Col. Springs	.284	52	165	155	15	44	66	9	2	3	23	1	1	1	7	1	20	0	0	6	.426	.317
Waring, Jim, Tucson*	.286	5	7	7	1	2	5	0	0	1	1	0	0	0	0	0	1	0	0	0	.714	.286
Weber, Wes, Tac.-L.V.	.167	29	7	6	1	1	1	0	0	0	0	0	0	0	1	0	3	0	0	0	.167	.286
Wehner, John, Calgary	.329	40	173	158	30	52	80	12	2	4	24	1	0	2	12	1	16	8	4	3	.506	.384
Westbrook, Destry, Tucson	.000	5	1	1	0	0	0	0	0	0	0	0	0	0	0	0	1	0	0	0	.000	.000
Whitaker, Steve, Phoenix*	.333	16	13	12	2	4	6	0	1	0	0	1	0	0	0	0	2	0	0	1	.500	.333
White, Chris, Tucson	.000	5	1	1	0	0	0	0	0	0	0	0	0	0	0	0	1	0	0	0	.000	.000
White, Rick, Calgary	.133	14	16	15	0	2	2	0	0	0	0	1	0	0	0	0	3	0	0	0	.133	.133
Whitehurst, Wally, Phoenix	.000	4	2	1	0	0	0	0	0	0	0	0	0	0	1	0	1	0	0	0	.000	.500
Widger, Chris, Tacoma	.276	50	184	174	29	48	88	11	1	9	21	1	0	0	9	0	29	0	0	4	.506	.311
Wilkerson, Curtis, Tacoma†	.222	5	19	18	1	4	4	0	0	0	3	0	0	0	1	0	3	0	0	0	.222	.263
Wilkins, Rick, Tucson*	.333	4	15	12	0	4	4	0	0	0	4	0	1	0	2	0	0	0	0	0	.333	.400
Willard, Jerry, Tacoma*	.268	85	279	228	33	61	104	16	0	9	47	0	3	3	45	6	43	0	0	7	.456	.391
Williams, George, Edmonton†	.310	81	347	290	53	90	149	20	0	13	55	3	2	2	50	6	52	0	4	9	.514	.413
Williams, Keith, Phoenix	.301	24	95	83	7	25	37	4	1	2	14	4	2	1	5	0	11	0	0	4	.446	.341
Williams, Reggie, Albuquerque†	.312	66	269	234	44	73	116	15	5	6	29	1	3	1	30	0	46	6	4	3	.496	.388
Williams, Todd, Albuquerque	.000	25	4	4	0	0	0	0	0	0	0	0	0	0	0	0	4	0	0	0	.000	.000
Willis, Travis, Calgary	1.000	22	1	1	0	1	1	0	0	0	1	0	0	0	0	0	0	0	0	0	1.000	1.000
Wilson, Gary, Calgary	.500	6	3	2	0	1	1	0	0	0	0	1	0	0	0	0	1	0	0	0	.500	.500
Wimmer, Chris, Phoenix	.263	132	503	449	55	118	155	23	4	2	44	5	5	13	31	1	49	13	7	10	.345	.325
Winston, Darrin, Calgary	.000	53	2	2	0	0	0	0	0	0	0	0	0	0	0	0	0	0	0	0	.000	.000
Wojciechowski, Steve, Edm.*	.000	14	1	1	0	0	0	0	0	0	0	0	0	0	0	0	0	0	0	0	.000	.000
Wolfe, Joel, Edmonton	.205	11	43	39	4	8	11	3	0	0	4	1	1	0	2	0	7	0	2	1	.282	.238
Womack, Tony, Calgary*	.280	30	119	107	12	30	35	3	1	0	6	0	0	0	12	1	11	7	5	1	.327	.353
Wood, Jason, Edmonton	.235	127	471	421	49	99	135	20	5	2	50	6	12	3	29	3	72	1	4	13	.321	.282
Worrell, Tim, Las Vegas	.000	10	4	4	0	0	0	0	0	0	0	0	0	0	0	0	3	0	0	0	.000	.000
Young, Ernie, Edmonton	.277	95	407	347	70	96	170	21	4	15	72	1	7	3	49	1	73	2	2	5	.490	.365
Young, Kevin, Calgary	.356	45	181	163	24	58	107	23	1	8	34	0	3	0	15	0	21	6	3	4	.656	.403

GRAND SLAMS: Deer, Gainer, Hajek, Pulliam, 2 each; Abreu, Bean, Burks, Cockrell, Coomer, Dalesandro, Demetral, Dunn, Garcia, Goff, Greene, Hocking, Makarewicz, McDavid, Murray, Pozo, A. Rodriguez, Russo, Saunders, Simms, Snider, Wehner, K. Williams, E. Young, 1 each.

AWARDED FIRST BASE ON CATCHER'S INTERFERENCE: Cianfrocco 2 (Chavez, Huckaby); Gainer 2 (Mulligan 2); Forbes (Geo. Williams); Parker (Geo. Williams); Ramos (Geo. Williams); Sweeney (Geo. Williams).

PLAYERS WITH TWO OR MORE TEAMS

Player, Team	Avg.	G	TPA	AB	R	H	TB	2B	3B	HR	RBI	SH	SF	HP	BB	IBB	SO	SB	CS	GDP	Slg.	OBP
Bennett, Erik, Vancouver	.000	28	0	0	0	0	0	0	0	0	0	0	0	0	0	0	0	0	0	0	.000	.000
Bennett, Erik, Tucson	.250	14	4	4	0	1	1	0	0	0	0	0	0	0	0	0	0	0	0	0	.250	.250
Brink, Brad, Phoenix	.111	11	9	9	0	1	1	0	0	0	0	0	0	0	0	0	2	0	0	0	.111	.111
Brink, Brad, Edmonton	.000	9	0	0	0	0	0	0	0	0	0	0	0	0	0	0	0	0	0	0	.000	.000
Daspit, Jim, Tucson	.200	36	6	5	0	1	1	0	0	0	0	1	0	0	0	0	2	0	0	0	.200	.200
Daspit, Jim, Edmonton	.000	2	0	0	0	0	0	0	0	0	0	0	0	0	0	0	0	0	0	0	.000	.000
Deer, Rob, Vancouver	.288	25	98	80	16	23	42	5	1	4	20	0	2	0	16	2	32	0	0	1	.525	.398
Deer, Rob, Las Vegas	.291	64	255	223	38	65	131	18	3	14	45	0	1	0	31	4	57	2	2	3	.587	.376
Fesh, Sean, Tucson*	.000	10	0	0	0	0	0	0	0	0	0	0	0	0	0	0	0	0	0	0	.000	.000
Fesh, Sean, Las Vegas*	.000	30	1	1	0	0	0	0	0	0	0	0	0	0	0	0	0	0	0	0	.000	.000
Hansell, Greg, Albuquerque	.500	8	3	2	1	1	1	0	0	0	0	1	0	0	0	0	1	0	0	0	.500	.500
Hansell, Greg, Salt Lake	.000	7	0	0	0	0	0	0	0	0	0	0	0	0	0	0	0	0	0	0	.000	.000
Jackson, John, Vancouver*	.301	35	140	113	20	34	46	7	1	1	11	3	0	2	22	2	15	8	3	3	.407	.423
Jackson, John, Salt Lake*	.278	55	225	194	39	54	86	14	3	4	21	3	3	3	22	0	20	8	2	4	.443	.356
Loiselle, Rich, Las Vegas	.125	8	8	8	1	1	1	0	0	0	0	0	0	0	0	0	5	0	0	0	.125	.125
Loiselle, Rich, Tucson	.000	2	0	0	0	0	0	0	0	0	0	0	0	0	0	0	0	0	0	0	.000	.000
Newfield, Marc, Tacoma	.278	53	222	198	30	55	81	11	0	5	30	0	0	5	19	1	30	1	0	6	.409	.356
Newfield, Marc, Las Vegas	.343	20	76	70	10	24	40	5	1	3	12	1	1	1	3	0	11	2	0	1	.571	.373

Player, Team	Avg.	G	TPA	AB	R	H	TB	2B	3B	HR	RBI	SH	SF	HP	BB	IBB	SO	SB	CS	GDP	Slg.	OBP
Pose, Scott, Albuquerque*	.188	7	18	16	5	3	4	1	0	0	1	0	0	0	2	0	0	2	0	0	.250	.278
Pose, Scott, Salt Lake*............	.310	70	239	203	41	63	74	9	1	0	19	3	3	1	29	2	28	13	4	2	.365	.394
Saunders, Doug, Edmonton.....	.188	5	16	16	2	3	7	2	1	0	4	0	0	0	0	0	2	0	0	0	.438	.188
Saunders, Doug, Tacoma.........	.281	50	146	135	19	38	62	5	2	5	24	1	2	1	7	0	30	0	0	3	.459	.317
Weber, Wes, Tacoma	.000	20	0	0	0	0	0	0	0	0	0	0	0	0	0	0	0	0	0	0	.000	.000
Weber, Wes, Las Vegas............	.167	9	7	6	1	1	1	0	0	0	0	0	0	0	1	0	3	0	0	0	.167	.286

1995 PITCHING

TEAM

Team	W	L	Pct.	ERA	G	CG	ShO	Sv.	IP	H	TBF	R	ER	HR	SH	SF	HB	BB	IBB	SO	WP	Bk.
Vancouver.........	81	60	.574	4.08	141	14	11	26	1215.2	1242	5223	620	551	99	44	44	46	421	25	782	63	3
Albuquerque	75	69	.521	4.12	144	6	7	42	1248.2	1340	5441	688	571	98	40	42	31	490	47	919	60	8
Tucson...............	87	56	.608	4.50	143	1	8	41	1244.2	1425	5468	698	623	63	51	51	52	427	17	859	66	8
Tacoma	68	76	.472	4.55	144	10	8	40	1249.0	1354	5469	734	631	105	33	57	43	471	45	771	47	18
Las Vegas	61	83	.424	4.75	144	15	8	29	1230.1	1337	5544	780	649	108	61	53	46	543	37	794	69	5
Phoenix.............	62	82	.431	4.86	144	8	5	28	1275.2	1436	5609	765	689	105	60	54	25	496	50	852	83	9
Colo. Springs....	77	66	.538	4.91	143	4	11	32	1212.0	1359	5408	760	661	96	53	53	45	509	35	803	62	11
Salt Lake...........	79	65	.549	5.03	144	10	5	40	1249.2	1446	5512	773	698	116	39	44	34	448	39	754	60	11
Edmonton	68	76	.472	5.13	144	6	5	32	1239.1	1384	5499	790	706	109	39	55	43	541	55	703	90	12
Calgary..............	58	83	.411	5.32	141	7	6	26	1195.0	1451	5356	812	707	111	40	42	43	401	27	719	50	7

INDIVIDUAL

TOP QUALIFIERS FOR EARNED-RUN AVERAGE TITLE

Minimum 115 innings. *Lefthanded pitcher.

Pitcher, Team	W	L	Pct.	ERA	G	GS	CG	ShO	GF	Sv.	IP	H	TBF	R	ER	HR	SH	SF	HB	BB	IBB	SO	WP	Bk.
Wall, Donne, Tucson	17	6	.739	3.30	28	28	0	0	0	0	177.1	190	732	72	65	5	6	4	5	32	1	119	5	1
Williams, Shad, Vancouver	9	7	.563	3.37	25	25	3	1	0	0	149.2	142	627	65	56	16	3	3	4	48	2	114	7	1
Johns, Doug, Edmonton*	9	5	.643	3.41	23	21	0	0	1	0	132.0	148	567	55	50	8	3	1	3	43	3	70	6	3
Sager, A.J., Colorado Springs ...	8	5	.615	3.50	23	22	1	1	0	0	133.2	153	564	61	52	14	4	3	2	23	1	80	0	0
Hawkins, LaTroy, Salt Lake	9	7	.563	3.55	22	22	4	1	0	0	144.1	150	601	63	57	7	5	2	1	40	1	74	6	1
Treadwell, Jody, Albuquerque ...	7	5	.583	3.96	30	15	1	1	4	1	125.0	121	510	61	55	15	2	5	2	32	4	79	9	1
McFarlin, Terric, Las Vegas.......	7	6	.538	3.96	58	2	0	0	20	7	122.2	120	535	67	54	11	6	3	2	59	4	85	18	0
Harriger, Denny, Las Vegas.......	9	9	.500	4.07	29	28	7	2	0	0	177.0	187	776	94	80	12	6	5	4	60	2	97	4	1
Holt, Chris, Tucson....................	5	8	.385	4.10	20	19	0	0	0	0	118.2	155	524	65	54	5	7	3	7	32	1	69	6	0
Taylor, Scott, Calgary*	5	8	.385	4.11	27	25	1	0	0	0	140.0	144	578	73	64	10	3	4	3	35	2	83	3	0
Harikkala, Tim, Tacoma	5	12	.294	4.24	25	24	4	1	0	0	146.1	151	638	78	69	13	3	4	2	55	3	73	7	0
Carlson, Dan, Phoenix...............	9	5	.643	4.27	23	22	2	0	1	0	132.2	138	582	67	63	11	7	7	3	66	0	93	6	1
Bustillos, Albert, Col. Springs.......	8	4	.667	4.61	34	19	0	0	5	3	132.2	151	572	82	68	15	4	2	4	33	0	77	8	0
Robinson, Scott, Phoenix	5	7	.417	4.66	31	15	0	0	9	0	123.2	134	519	68	64	14	2	3	4	37	1	61	4	0
Weber, Wes, Las Vegas............	6	11	.353	4.67	29	21	2	0	3	0	150.1	170	663	92	78	16	5	6	4	50	10	86	6	3

DEPARTMENTAL LEADERS: W—Wall, 17; L—Barcelo, R. Phillips, 13; Pct.—E. Bennett, .900; G—Czajkowski, 60; GS—Barcelo, Harriger, Wall, Wasdin, 28; CG—Harriger, 7; ShO—Harriger, 2; GF—Czajkowski, 44; Sv.—Watkins, 20; IP—Wall, 177.1; H—Barcelo, 214; TBF—Harriger, 776; R—Barcelo, 131; ER—Barcelo, 112; HR—Wasdin, 26; SH—Jo. Martinez, 9; SF—Mauser, 13; HB—Misuraca, 8; BB—Shaw, 88; IBB—Weber, 10; SO—Wall, 119; WP—McFarlin, 18; Bk.—Converse, Kubinski, 4.

ALL PITCHERS

*Lefthanded pitcher.

Pitcher, Team	W	L	Pct.	ERA	G	GS	CG	ShO	GF	Sv.	IP	H	TBF	R	ER	HR	SH	SF	HB	BB	IBB	SO	WP	Bk.
Acevedo, Juan, Col. Springs	1	1	.500	6.14	3	3	0	0	0	0	14.2	18	68	11	10	0	1	1	2	7	0	7	2	1
Adams, Willie, Edmonton..........	2	5	.286	4.37	11	10	1	0	1	0	68.0	73	288	35	33	2	2	2	6	15	5	40	3	0
Akerfelds, Darrel, Vancouver.....	3	3	.500	4.50	9	9	0	0	0	0	48.0	60	216	24	24	5	3	3	4	19	1	27	3	1
Alicea, Miguel, Albuquerque......	1	1	.500	4.05	7	0	0	0	5	3	6.2	6	31	5	3	0	2	0	0	4	1	0	3	0
Apana, Matt, Tacoma	8	8	.500	4.95	21	20	0	0	0	0	103.2	121	481	72	57	9	3	6	5	61	0	58	6	0
Arvesen, Scott, Las Vegas	0	0	.000	15.00	2	0	0	0	2	0	3.0	4	16	5	5	1	0	0	1	2	0	0	2	0
August, Don, Calgary	0	2	.000	4.50	2	2	0	0	0	0	8.0	10	39	7	4	0	2	1	0	4	0	4	0	0
Ayrault, Bob, Calgary	0	0	.000	4.91	6	0	0	0	3	0	7.1	7	35	4	4	0	0	1	1	4	1	3	0	0
Backlund, Brett, Calgary............	2	3	.400	5.22	12	8	0	0	3	0	50.0	59	213	29	29	6	1	2	0	9	0	29	0	0
Bailey, Roger, Col. Springs........	0	0	.000	2.70	3	3	0	0	0	0	16.2	15	71	9	5	0	0	0	0	8	0	7	0	0
Baker, Scott, Edmonton*	4	7	.364	5.28	22	20	1	0	0	0	107.1	123	474	69	63	9	2	2	3	46	4	56	4	0
Bankhead, Scott, Edmonton......	1	3	.250	7.85	12	0	0	0	5	1	18.1	28	90	18	16	2	3	1	1	7	2	15	0	0
Barcelo, Marc, Salt Lake	8	13	.381	7.05	28	28	2	0	0	0	143.0	214	684	131	112	19	5	5	6	59	2	63	4	2
Barton, Shawn, Phoenix*..........	2	0	1.000	1.80	15	0	0	0	2	0	25.0	20	95	5	5	2	1	0	0	5	0	25	0	0
Bennett, Chris, Calgary	0	0	.000	5.14	4	0	0	0	1	0	7.0	11	35	7	4	0	0	2	0	1	0	7	0	0
Bennett, Erik, Van.-Tuc.............	9	1	.900	4.42	42	1	0	0	16	3	73.1	71	316	41	36	6	0	5	5	32	4	63	4	1
Berumen, Andres, Las Vegas	0	0	.000	5.40	3	0	0	0	0	0	3.1	4	16	2	2	0	0	0	1	2	0	3	0	0
Bielecki, Mike, Vancouver	1	0	1.000	0.00	3	1	0	0	0	0	5.0	2	21	3	0	0	0	0	0	2	0	4	0	0
Bittiger, Jeff, Edmonton	2	0	1.000	5.28	6	1	0	0	0	0	15.1	17	70	10	9	1	1	2	0	7	0	10	3	0
Bochtler, Doug, Las Vegas	2	3	.400	4.25	18	2	0	0	7	1	36.0	31	161	18	17	5	1	2	1	26	6	32	2	0
Boskie, Shawn, Vancouver........	1	0	1.000	3.00	1	1	0	0	0	0	6.0	4	25	2	2	1	0	0	0	4	0	1	0	0
Bourgeois, Steve, Phoenix	1	1	.500	3.38	6	5	0	0	0	0	34.2	38	153	18	13	2	0	0	2	13	0	23	4	1
Bowie, Jim, Edmonton*	0	0	.000	7.50	7	0	0	0	7	0	6.0	8	28	5	5	2	0	1	1	3	0	4	0	0
Bream, Scott, Las Vegas...........	0	1	.000	0.00	1	0	0	0	1	0	0.1	1	5	1	0	0	1	0	0	2	0	0	0	0
Brink, Brad, Pho.-Edm.	2	6	.250	6.29	20	12	0	0	4	0	68.2	79	327	55	48	5	1	5	4	46	3	48	2	0
Briscoe, John, Edmonton..........	0	0	.000	3.00	3	3	0	0	0	0	6.0	5	26	2	2	0	0	0	0	5	0	3	0	0
Brocail, Doug, Tucson	1	0	1.000	3.86	3	3	0	0	0	0	16.1	18	74	9	7	1	0	1	2	4	0	16	0	0

Pitcher, Team	W	L	Pct.	ERA	G	GS	CG	ShO	GF	Sv.	IP	H	TBF	R	ER	HR	SH	SF	HB	BB	IBB	SO	WP	Bk.
Brock, Russ, Edmonton	1	8	.111	6.87	18	8	0	0	2	1	55.0	75	266	44	42	6	0	3	3	31	4	44	2	1
Brosnan, Jason, Albuquerque*	2	0	1.000	4.35	23	1	0	0	11	2	31.0	30	128	16	15	3	0	2	0	9	1	18	0	1
Bruske, Jim, Albuquerque	7	5	.583	4.11	43	6	0	0	13	4	114.0	128	492	54	52	6	4	4	3	41	2	99	3	0
Bryant, Scott, Edmonton	0	0	.000	0.00	2	0	0	0	1	0	3.1	3	14	0	0	0	0	0	0	0	0	3	1	0
Bryant, Shawn, Salt Lake*	4	1	.800	4.88	31	0	0	0	8	0	48.0	62	221	31	26	1	3	0	2	16	2	27	1	2
Bullard, Jason, Col. Springs	0	0	.000	7.27	4	0	0	0	1	0	8.2	18	48	13	7	1	0	0	1	5	1	5	0	1
Burcham, Tim, Phoenix	1	0	1.000	5.06	5	0	0	0	1	0	10.2	18	50	7	6	1	0	1	0	2	0	6	3	0
Burgos, Enrique, Phoenix*	2	6	.250	6.14	41	2	0	0	13	2	58.2	63	273	44	40	7	5	3	0	40	5	77	4	1
Burke, John, Col. Springs	7	1	.875	4.55	19	17	0	0	1	1	87.0	79	376	46	44	7	2	3	1	48	0	65	5	1
Bustillos, Albert, Col. Springs	8	4	.667	4.61	34	19	0	0	5	3	132.2	151	572	82	68	15	4	2	4	33	0	77	8	0
Butler, Mike, Vancouver*	0	0	.000	4.50	3	0	0	0	0	0	6.0	4	25	3	3	0	2	0	1	2	0	3	0	0
Cadaret, Greg, Las Vegas*	3	5	.375	5.88	28	4	0	0	6	0	52.0	56	234	40	34	6	2	3	0	22	0	52	10	0
Campbell, Kevin, Tacoma	3	2	.600	3.67	31	0	0	0	8	1	49.0	50	211	28	20	6	0	2	5	14	3	34	3	1
Carlson, Dan, Phoenix	9	5	.643	4.27	23	22	2	0	1	0	132.2	138	582	67	63	11	7	7	3	66	0	93	6	1
Carmona, Rafael, Tacoma	4	3	.571	5.06	8	8	1	1	0	0	48.0	52	212	29	27	6	1	2	3	19	1	37	1	3
Castillo, Juan, Tucson	0	4	.000	10.93	11	10	0	0	1	0	40.1	66	206	51	49	4	1	3	5	27	0	21	5	0
Castro, Nelson, Albuquerque	0	0	.000	0.00	2	0	0	0	2	1	2.1	0	7	0	0	0	0	0	1	0	0	2	1	0
Chavez, Tony, Vancouver	2	0	1.000	1.50	8	0	0	0	5	1	12.0	7	46	4	2	0	1	0	0	4	0	8	0	0
Clayton, Royal, Phoenix	0	2	.000	5.87	5	5	0	0	0	0	23.0	35	108	18	15	1	2	0	0	6	2	13	0	0
Colbert, Craig, Las Vegas	0	0	.000	0.00	1	0	0	0	1	0	1.0	1	5	0	0	0	0	0	0	1	0	1	0	0
Cole, Victor, Las Vegas	0	2	.000	6.41	4	4	0	0	0	0	19.2	19	86	17	14	4	1	1	0	10	0	12	1	1
Conroy, Brian, Col. Springs	0	2	.000	6.11	5	5	0	0	0	0	28.0	36	128	19	19	0	0	0	0	11	1	9	0	0
Converse, Jim, Tacoma	4	7	.364	5.99	17	12	0	0	3	0	73.2	96	337	57	49	5	4	5	1	36	1	43	4	4
Corbin, Archie, Calgary	1	5	.167	8.56	47	1	0	0	13	1	61.0	76	309	63	58	6	0	5	3	55	0	54	7	0
Correa, Ramser, Albuquerque	0	0	.000	0.00	2	0	0	0	0	0	4.0	5	16	0	0	0	0	0	0	1	1	3	0	0
Corsi, Jim, Edmonton	0	0	.000	0.00	3	0	0	0	3	3	3.0	0	10	0	0	0	0	0	0	1	0	3	0	0
Courtright, John, Salt Lake*	3	7	.300	6.80	18	17	1	0	0	0	84.2	108	384	70	64	6	5	7	0	36	7	42	4	2
Cromwell, Nate, Las Vegas*	0	2	.000	13.50	9	3	0	0	3	0	15.1	35	94	27	23	5	1	0	1	14	1	11	0	0
Crowther, Brent, Col. Springs	0	1	.000	7.50	1	1	0	0	0	0	6.0	11	30	6	5	1	0	1	0	2	0	1	0	0
Cummings, John, Tacoma*	0	1	.000	7.71	1	1	0	0	0	0	2.1	6	16	4	2	1	0	0	0	3	0	3	0	0
Czajkowski, Jim, Col. Springs	3	10	.231	5.06	60	0	0	0	44	17	83.2	90	382	54	47	8	6	8	2	52	7	56	4	0
Daal, Omar, Albuquerque*	2	3	.400	3.88	17	9	0	0	3	1	53.1	56	232	28	23	3	0	0	1	26	2	46	1	0
Darwin, Jeff, Tacoma	7	2	.778	2.70	46	0	0	0	31	12	63.1	51	256	21	19	2	3	3	1	21	5	51	0	0
Daspit, Jim, Tuc.-Edm.	5	2	.714	4.10	38	0	0	0	11	1	68.0	69	294	36	31	5	2	5	2	24	1	54	7	0
Davis, Tim, Tacoma*	0	1	.000	5.40	2	2	0	0	0	0	13.1	15	57	8	8	2	0	0	0	4	0	13	0	0
Davison, Scott, Tacoma	1	1	.500	5.32	8	3	0	0	2	0	22.0	21	91	14	13	1	1	1	0	4	0	12	1	1
Deer, Rob, Las Vegas	0	0	.000	0.00	1	0	0	0	1	0	1.0	1	6	0	0	0	0	0	0	1	0	0	1	0
DeLosSantos, Mariano, Calgary	3	6	.333	6.15	14	14	0	0	0	0	71.2	85	321	57	49	4	4	4	3	22	0	36	2	1
Demetral, Chris, Albuquerque	0	0	.000	0.00	1	0	0	0	0	0	0.0	0	0	0	0	0	0	0	0	0	0	0	0	0
Dishman, Glenn, Las Vegas*	6	3	.667	2.55	14	14	3	1	0	0	106.0	91	430	37	30	12	4	1	0	20	2	64	3	1
Dougherty, Jim, Tucson	1	0	1.000	3.27	8	0	0	0	3	1	11.0	11	46	4	4	1	0	0	0	5	0	12	0	1
Edenfield, Ken, Vancouver	7	2	.778	3.45	33	0	0	0	4	0	60.0	56	259	24	23	2	3	3	5	25	2	44	5	0
Edwards, Wayne, Albuquerque*	1	2	.333	5.06	14	0	0	0	3	1	16.0	17	82	16	9	1	2	1	0	17	3	12	2	0
Eischen, Joey, Albuquerque*	3	0	1.000	0.00	13	0	0	0	6	2	16.1	8	59	0	0	0	0	0	1	3	0	14	1	0
Elliott, Donnie, Las Vegas	1	0	1.000	4.50	7	0	0	0	3	1	8.0	8	35	4	4	1	1	1	0	4	1	2	0	0
Ericks, John, Calgary	2	1	.667	2.48	5	5	0	0	0	0	29.0	20	116	8	8	2	1	0	0	13	0	25	3	0
Ettles, Mark, Las Vegas	0	0	.000	7.82	10	0	0	0	3	0	12.2	21	62	11	11	4	0	1	0	3	0	10	1	0
Evans, Dave, Tucson	0	0	.000	0.00	2	0	0	0	0	0	3.0	2	12	0	0	0	0	0	0	1	0	4	0	0
Fesh, Sean, Tuc.-L.V.*	3	1	.750	2.81	40	0	0	0	12	1	51.1	64	237	23	16	2	4	0	3	19	5	25	1	1
Flynt, Bill, Calgary*	1	0	1.000	5.40	12	1	0	0	3	0	21.2	27	103	15	13	4	1	1	0	12	0	12	1	0
Fortugno, Tim, Vancouver*	1	1	.500	1.54	10	0	0	0	7	1	11.2	8	45	2	2	1	0	0	0	4	1	7	0	0
Fredrickson, Scott, Col. Springs	11	3	.786	3.45	58	1	0	0	20	4	75.2	70	348	40	29	2	8	3	5	47	5	70	15	2
Gallaher, Kevin, Tucson	1	1	.500	6.43	3	3	0	0	0	0	14.0	19	70	11	10	1	0	2	2	9	0	11	2	0
Gamez, Bob, Phoenix*	3	5	.375	5.59	36	9	0	0	5	2	66.0	76	292	46	41	6	4	1	0	27	4	41	7	0
Gandarillas, Gus, Salt Lake	2	3	.400	6.44	22	0	0	0	13	2	29.1	34	135	23	21	5	3	1	1	19	4	17	5	0
Garcia, Jose, Albuquerque	1	3	.250	6.32	11	0	0	0	4	0	15.2	19	73	11	11	3	2	4	0	7	1	10	0	0
Gardella, Mike, Phoenix*	0	0	.000	13.50	3	0	0	0	1	0	4.0	9	21	6	6	0	0	0	0	1	0	3	0	0
Gardner, Chris, Tucson	1	4	.200	8.54	16	2	0	0	6	0	26.1	43	127	26	25	0	2	1	0	19	1	6	1	1
Gavaghan, Sean, Salt Lake	1	4	.200	5.51	35	0	0	0	15	5	47.1	53	221	32	29	3	6	1	3	31	3	28	3	0
Gibson, Paul, Calgary*	0	2	.000	3.72	19	0	0	0	9	1	19.1	21	86	11	8	1	0	2	1	9	1	17	3	0
Glinatsis, George, Tacoma	1	2	.333	7.34	8	8	0	0	0	0	30.2	39	138	25	25	4	0	2	1	13	0	13	0	0
Gomez, Pat, Phoenix*	0	0	.000	27.00	2	0	0	0	0	0	1.1	5	12	5	4	0	0	0	0	3	2	1	1	0
Gould, Clint, Tacoma	0	0	.000	0.00	1	0	0	0	1	0	0.1	0	1	0	0	0	0	0	0	0	0	0	0	0
Grahe, Joe, Col. Springs	1	1	.500	3.27	2	2	1	0	0	0	11.0	7	41	4	4	1	1	1	0	3	0	4	0	0
Graybill, Dave, Tacoma	0	0	.000	6.75	6	0	0	0	4	0	9.1	12	43	8	7	1	0	2	0	6	0	1	0	0
Green, Otis, Tacoma*	4	1	.800	5.76	18	0	0	0	3	0	25.0	26	113	19	16	3	0	1	1	12	2	17	3	0
Greer, Ken, Phoenix	5	2	.714	3.98	38	0	0	0	13	1	63.1	65	270	29	28	1	3	2	2	19	1	41	5	0
Grundt, Ken, Col. Springs*	0	0	.000	4.76	9	0	0	0	1	0	5.2	9	30	5	3	0	0	0	0	4	0	5	0	0
Guetterman, Lee, Tacoma*	1	2	.333	2.95	33	1	0	0	9	4	36.2	33	147	12	12	2	0	1	0	9	2	21	1	0
Hancock, Lee, Calgary*	6	10	.375	5.07	34	17	1	0	5	0	113.2	146	510	78	64	9	5	0	4	27	2	49	4	1
Hansell, Greg, Alb.-S.L.	4	2	.667	6.14	15	6	0	0	3	1	48.1	64	218	35	33	5	2	1	2	10	2	32	3	1
Harikkala, Tim, Tacoma	5	12	.294	4.24	25	24	4	1	0	0	146.1	151	638	78	69	13	3	4	2	55	3	73	7	0
Harriger, Denny, Las Vegas	9	9	.500	4.07	29	28	7	2	0	0	177.0	187	776	94	80	12	6	5	4	60	2	97	4	1
Hartgraves, Dean, Tucson*	3	2	.600	2.11	14	0	0	0	9	5	21.1	21	91	6	5	0	0	1	1	5	2	15	0	0
Hathaway, Hilly, Las Vegas*	4	6	.400	6.22	14	14	1	0	0	0	63.2	76	285	49	44	4	4	3	1	27	0	37	6	0
Hawblitzel, Ryan, Col. Springs	5	3	.625	4.55	21	14	0	0	1	0	83.0	88	352	47	42	7	3	5	3	17	1	40	2	0
Hawkins, LaTroy, Salt Lake	9	7	.563	3.55	22	22	4	1	0	0	144.1	150	601	63	57	7	5	2	1	40	1	74	6	1
Haynes, Heath, Edmonton	2	0	1.000	6.27	12	0	0	0	1	0	18.2	21	87	14	13	1	0	3	0	11	3	13	2	0
Henry, Jon, Salt Lake	1	0	1.000	6.75	3	2	0	0	0	0	12.0	15	53	9	9	3	1	0	0	2	0	3	0	0
Heredia, Julian, Vancouver	5	3	.625	3.63	51	0	0	0	37	10	74.1	69	319	34	30	8	5	1	5	23	3	65	9	0
Hermanson, Dustin, Las Vegas	0	1	.000	3.50	31	0	0	0	22	11	36.0	35	174	23	14	5	0	0	2	29	0	42	1	1
Hernandez, Fernando, Las Vegas	1	6	.143	7.65	8	8	0	0	0	0	37.2	43	186	32	32	3	0	2	3	31	3	40	4	0
Hill, Milt, Calgary	1	3	.250	4.90	24	5	0	0	5	0	60.2	69	260	38	33	8	3	3	1	14	2	31	2	1

Pitcher, Team	W	L	Pct.	ERA	G	GS	CG	ShO	GF	Sv.	IP	H	TBF	R	ER	HR	SH	SF	HB	BB	IBB	SO	WP	Bk.
Holdridge, David, Vancouver	0	2	.000	4.61	11	0	0	0	6	1	13.2	18	68	10	7	0	2	0	1	7	1	13	3	0
Hollins, Stacy, Edmonton	0	7	.000	10.31	7	7	0	0	0	0	29.2	47	156	43	34	4	0	1	1	21	3	25	6	0
Holman, Brad, Tacoma	1	0	1.000	8.10	5	0	0	0	1	0	6.2	9	31	6	6	0	0	0	0	3	0	1	0	0
Holman, Shawn, Albuquerque	5	6	.455	5.13	49	1	0	0	22	5	79.0	107	386	58	45	3	5	5	5	39	7	60	7	0
Holt, Chris, Tucson	5	8	.385	4.10	20	19	0	0	0	0	118.2	155	524	65	54	5	7	3	7	32	1	69	6	0
Holzemer, Mark, Vancouver*	3	2	.600	2.47	28	4	0	0	11	2	54.2	45	228	18	15	2	5	0	3	24	4	35	2	0
Hook, Chris, Phoenix	0	0	.000	1.50	4	0	0	0	0	0	6.0	2	22	1	1	0	0	0	0	3	0	5	0	1
Hope, John, Calgary	7	1	.875	2.79	13	13	3	1	0	0	80.2	76	322	29	25	3	3	1	3	11	0	41	1	0
Horsman, Vince, Salt Lake*	1	0	1.000	10.38	16	0	0	0	7	0	13.0	23	64	15	15	3	0	0	0	4	2	10	1	0
Hostetler, Tom, Edmonton	0	0	.000	12.60	4	0	0	0	1	0	5.0	9	31	7	7	2	0	0	0	8	1	7	1	0
Huisman, Rick, Tucson	6	1	.857	4.45	42	0	0	0	28	6	54.2	58	246	33	27	1	0	3	1	28	3	47	3	1
Hunter, Jim, Col. Springs	2	2	.500	6.96	10	4	0	0	0	0	32.1	43	154	27	25	1	2	2	2	17	2	13	2	0
Janicki, Pete, Vancouver	1	4	.200	7.03	9	9	0	0	0	0	48.2	64	227	38	38	8	1	4	1	23	0	34	0	0
Jean, Domingo, Tucson	2	1	.667	6.59	3	3	0	0	0	0	13.2	15	62	10	10	1	0	0	0	7	0	14	3	0
Jimenez, Miguel, Edmonton	0	0	.000	12.27	6	3	0	0	2	0	7.1	12	43	10	10	0	0	1	0	10	0	4	0	0
Johns, Doug, Edmonton*	9	5	.643	3.41	23	21	0	0	1	0	132.0	148	567	55	50	8	3	1	3	43	3	70	6	3
Johnson, Judd, Salt Lake*	1	1	.500	3.43	17	0	0	0	7	1	21.0	27	103	11	8	1	1	4	0	12	5	11	2	1
Johnston, Joel, Col. Springs	2	2	.500	5.96	18	0	0	0	6	0	22.2	26	106	16	15	1	3	2	2	12	0	14	0	0
Jones, Bobby, Col. Springs*	1	2	.333	7.30	11	8	0	0	0	0	40.2	50	204	38	33	5	4	1	2	33	1	48	4	1
Jones, Stacy, Phoenix	0	1	.000	8.53	4	0	0	0	0	0	6.1	8	35	9	6	0	0	2	0	6	1	4	0	0
Keagle, Greg, Las Vegas	7	6	.538	4.28	14	13	0	0	1	0	75.2	76	351	47	36	3	6	5	6	42	2	49	2	0
Keling, Korey, Vancouver	0	2	.000	4.08	3	3	0	0	0	0	17.2	18	75	9	8	1	0	0	0	6	0	16	0	0
Ketchen, Doug, Tucson	3	6	.333	6.28	19	12	0	0	2	1	71.2	101	332	55	50	8	3	2	2	26	0	30	3	1
Kile, Darryl, Tucson	2	1	.667	8.51	4	4	0	0	0	0	24.1	29	113	23	23	0	1	0	4	12	0	15	5	0
King, Kevin, Tacoma*	0	0	.000	7.56	16	0	0	0	6	0	16.2	33	85	14	14	2	1	0	0	7	1	10	2	1
Knudsen, Kurt, Phoenix	0	1	.000	5.03	11	1	0	0	4	1	19.2	18	86	13	11	2	0	2	0	11	0	20	0	0
Kotarski, Mike, Col. Springs*	2	2	.500	10.80	22	0	0	0	11	0	30.0	48	162	37	36	5	1	2	2	20	1	21	4	0
Krueger, Bill, Tacoma*	5	3	.625	4.26	10	8	0	0	0	0	50.2	52	213	30	24	4	1	1	2	9	0	39	2	0
Kubinski, Tim, Edmonton*	1	2	.333	4.78	6	5	0	0	0	0	32.0	34	136	18	17	4	0	0	4	10	0	12	0	4
Leftwich, Phil, Vancouver	2	0	1.000	3.19	6	5	1	0	0	0	36.2	28	142	13	13	4	2	1	0	9	0	25	3	0
Leiper, Dave, Edmonton*	1	0	1.000	13.50	2	0	0	0	1	0	1.1	4	10	2	2	0	0	0	1	2	1	1	0	0
Lewis, Scott, Tacoma	1	1	.500	9.64	3	2	0	0	0	0	9.1	13	47	10	10	1	1	1	3	4	0	11	0	1
Lieber, Jon, Calgary	1	5	.167	7.01	14	14	0	0	0	0	77.0	122	365	69	60	6	1	0	0	19	0	34	0	0
Lilliquist, Derek, Albuquerque*	0	0	.000	2.70	13	0	0	0	12	5	13.1	18	55	4	4	1	0	0	0	3	2	9	0	0
Logsdon, Kevin, Col. Springs*	0	0	.000	24.00	2	0	0	0	1	0	3.0	8	21	8	8	1	0	0	0	5	0	2	0	1
Loiselle, Rich, L.V.-Tuc.	2	2	.500	5.97	10	8	1	1	0	0	37.2	44	175	31	25	5	1	0	2	13	0	20	0	1
Long, Joey, Las Vegas*	1	3	.250	4.60	25	0	0	0	9	0	31.1	38	143	22	16	1	0	4	0	16	2	13	0	0
Lorraine, Andrew, Vancouver*	6	6	.500	3.96	18	18	4	1	0	0	97.2	105	420	49	43	7	4	3	3	30	0	51	4	0
Mack, Tony, Vancouver	0	1	.000	4.50	4	3	0	0	0	0	20.0	19	83	10	10	4	1	1	0	6	0	15	1	0
Manzanillo, Ravelo, Calgary*	0	2	.000	12.75	8	1	0	0	0	0	12.0	23	65	18	17	4	0	1	1	10	0	2	1	3
Martinez, Jesus, Albuquerque*	1	1	.500	4.50	2	0	0	0	1	0	4.0	4	20	2	2	0	1	1	1	4	2	5	0	0
Martinez, Jose, Las Vegas	6	10	.375	4.75	27	25	2	1	0	0	151.2	156	646	86	80	9	9	5	7	44	2	64	5	0
Martinez, Pedro, Tucson*	1	1	.500	6.62	20	3	0	0	6	2	34.0	44	158	28	25	2	2	4	2	13	1	21	0	0
Maurer, Ron, Albuquerque	0	0	.000	0.00	1	0	0	0	1	0	1.0	0	3	0	0	0	0	0	0	0	0	1	0	0
Mauser, Tim, Las Vegas	3	4	.429	4.80	35	0	0	0	15	0	50.2	63	233	39	27	6	4	13	1	20	2	32	1	0
Maysey, Matt, Calgary	8	7	.533	5.50	44	12	0	0	4	1	103.0	122	468	67	63	9	2	3	7	44	3	71	7	0
McCarthy, Tom, Albuquerque	3	3	.500	6.00	13	8	0	0	1	0	48.0	61	223	41	32	4	1	2	1	22	2	28	2	0
McCurry, Jeff, Calgary	0	0	.000	1.80	3	0	0	0	0	0	5.0	3	22	1	1	0	0	0	2	2	0	2	0	0
McFarlin, Terric, Las Vegas	7	6	.538	3.96	58	2	0	0	20	7	122.2	120	535	67	54	11	6	3	2	59	4	85	18	0
McMurtry, Craig, Tucson	6	1	.857	1.29	13	13	1	0	0	0	69.2	54	275	11	10	2	3	1	4	19	1	41	5	0
Mecir, Jim, Tacoma	1	4	.200	3.10	40	0	0	0	22	8	69.2	63	298	29	24	3	3	1	1	28	7	46	5	0
Menendez, Tony, Phoenix	5	6	.455	3.92	50	0	0	0	31	13	64.1	67	288	34	28	6	5	4	2	32	9	61	3	0
Merriman, Brett, Las Vegas	2	2	.500	8.25	11	0	0	0	4	0	12.0	14	59	12	11	1	0	0	0	12	1	7	2	0
Milacki, Bob, Tacoma	6	4	.600	5.27	12	12	1	0	0	0	71.2	94	322	50	42	5	2	3	0	23	1	31	0	0
Milchin, Mike, Albuquerque*	8	4	.667	4.32	18	17	2	1	0	0	83.1	94	359	43	40	2	1	2	0	30	1	50	5	0
Mimbs, Mark, Albuquerque*	6	5	.545	2.97	23	16	1	0	2	0	106.0	105	433	40	35	7	3	3	1	22	0	96	7	1
Mintz, Steve, Phoenix	5	2	.714	2.39	31	0	0	0	19	7	49.0	42	205	16	13	4	3	0	2	21	4	36	4	0
Misuraca, Mike, Salt Lake	9	6	.600	5.34	31	19	1	0	2	0	143.1	174	628	93	85	15	0	6	8	36	1	67	7	0
Mlicki, Doug, Tucson	1	2	.333	5.56	6	6	0	0	0	0	34.0	44	155	27	21	3	2	1	2	6	0	22	1	0
Mohler, Mike, Edmonton*	2	1	.667	2.60	29	0	0	0	17	5	45.0	40	191	16	13	0	3	0	0	20	2	28	4	0
Montalvo, Rafael, Albuquerque	3	5	.375	2.65	49	0	0	0	19	4	98.1	105	430	44	29	5	2	3	4	34	7	65	1	0
Monteleone, Rich, Vancouver	1	0	1.000	3.24	7	1	0	0	1	1	16.2	19	73	7	6	1	0	1	0	3	0	7	0	0
Morman, Alvin, Tucson*	5	1	.833	3.91	45	0	0	0	10	3	48.1	50	211	26	21	6	5	8	0	20	1	36	2	0
Morrison, Keith, Vancouver	14	9	.609	4.93	28	26	4	1	1	0	160.2	178	685	97	88	16	2	11	6	40	0	84	4	0
Mulholland, Terry, Phoenix*	0	0	.000	2.25	1	1	0	0	0	0	4.0	4	18	3	1	0	0	0	0	1	0	4	0	0
Munoz, Oscar, Salt Lake	8	6	.571	4.95	19	19	1	1	0	0	112.2	121	486	67	62	9	0	7	3	35	1	74	7	0
Murphy, Dan, Edmonton	0	1	.000	5.40	1	0	0	0	0	0	1.2	1	8	1	1	1	0	0	0	3	0	2	0	0
Naulty, Dan, Salt Lake	2	6	.250	5.18	42	8	0	0	19	4	90.1	92	393	55	52	10	2	1	2	47	2	76	6	0
Nied, David, Colorado Springs	1	1	.500	4.99	7	7	0	0	0	0	30.2	31	141	18	17	0	4	0	2	25	2	21	2	0
O'Donoghue, John, Albuquerque*	5	6	.455	3.82	25	18	1	1	3	0	92.0	97	394	58	39	10	1	1	0	25	0	59	3	0
Olivares, Omar, Col. Springs	0	1	.000	5.40	3	2	0	0	0	0	11.2	14	52	7	7	1	1	1	1	2	0	6	0	0
Osik, Keith, Calgary	0	0	.000	4.50	2	0	0	0	1	0	2.0	1	8	1	1	1	0	0	0	1	0	3	0	0
Osuna, Antonio, Albuquerque	0	1	.000	4.42	19	0	0	0	17	11	18.1	15	76	9	9	2	0	1	0	9	0	19	2	0
Painter, Lance, Col. Springs*	0	3	.000	5.96	11	4	0	0	3	0	25.2	32	117	20	17	3	0	0	1	11	1	12	0	1
Park, Chan Ho, Albuquerque	6	7	.462	4.91	23	22	0	0	0	0	110.0	93	487	64	60	10	3	2	6	76	2	101	8	2
Parra, Jose, Albuquerque	3	2	.600	5.13	12	10	1	1	1	1	52.2	62	232	33	30	7	4	2	1	17	3	33	2	0
Patrick, Bronswell, Tucson	5	1	.833	4.19	43	4	0	0	10	1	81.2	91	352	42	38	3	2	3	1	21	1	62	4	0
Patterson, Ken, Vancouver*	0	0	.000	0.82	8	0	0	0	3	1	11.0	12	46	1	1	0	0	0	0	4	1	4	1	0
Peek, Tim, Edmonton	0	0	.000	4.57	12	0	0	0	3	0	21.2	20	87	11	11	3	0	1	0	7	0	6	2	0
Peever, Lloyd, Col. Springs	3	2	.600	5.36	8	8	0	0	0	0	42.0	45	185	26	25	5	0	3	1	16	0	25	3	0
Phillips, Randy, Phoenix	4	13	.235	5.11	25	24	2	1	0	0	132.0	155	574	83	75	11	4	6	4	40	2	66	8	2
Phillips, Tony, Tacoma	3	2	.600	4.12	47	1	0	0	19	1	87.1	98	370	44	40	6	3	7	6	14	7	44	0	2
Phoenix, Steve, Edmonton	4	3	.571	4.50	40	0	0	0	25	5	64.0	66	280	36	32	6	5	3	1	28	4	28	5	0

Pitcher, Team	W	L	Pct.	ERA	G	GS	CG	ShO	GF	Sv.	IP	H	TBF	R	ER	HR	SH	SF	HB	BB	IBB	SO	WP	Bk.
Piatt, Doug, Phoenix	0	1	.000	5.87	6	0	0	0	2	0	7.2	7	34	5	5	0	1	1	0	5	1	3	0	0
Plantenberg, Erik, Las Vegas*	0	0	.000	81.00	2	0	0	0	0	0	0.1	3	5	3	3	0	0	0	1	0	0	1	0	0
Pose, Scott, Salt Lake	0	0	.000	0.00	1	0	0	0	1	0	1.0	0	4	0	0	0	0	0	0	1	0	0	0	0
Powell, Ross, Tucson*	3	3	.500	3.08	13	4	0	0	5	1	38.0	37	169	16	13	3	5	0	1	15	0	34	1	0
Pulido, Carlos, Salt Lake*	8	1	.889	4.67	43	3	0	0	9	3	71.1	87	321	42	37	10	1	0	2	20	4	38	0	1
Pyc, Dave, Albuquerque*	0	1	.000	3.86	1	1	0	0	0	0	7.0	7	31	5	3	1	0	1	0	2	1	3	0	0
Ralph, Curtis, Calgary	1	4	.200	8.44	28	0	0	0	11	1	32.0	43	159	35	30	2	2	0	2	23	4	27	3	0
Ratekin, Mark, Vancouver	3	2	.600	5.33	19	3	0	0	3	0	50.2	62	223	35	30	7	6	3	1	18	2	14	3	0
Rath, Gary, Albuquerque*	3	5	.375	5.08	8	8	0	0	0	0	39.0	46	178	31	22	4	1	1	2	20	0	23	2	0
Rekar, Bryan, Colorado Springs	4	2	.667	1.49	7	7	2	1	0	0	48.1	29	182	10	8	0	1	0	2	13	0	39	3	0
Renko, Steve, Vancouver	2	5	.286	4.21	10	9	0	0	0	0	51.1	53	226	29	24	2	0	3	0	18	0	22	5	0
Revenig, Todd, Edmonton	4	5	.444	4.31	45	0	0	0	30	10	54.1	53	230	32	26	5	3	3	2	15	1	28	2	0
Reynoso, Armando, Col. Springs	2	1	.667	1.57	5	5	0	0	0	0	23.0	14	86	4	4	1	0	1	0	6	1	17	0	1
Risley, Bill, Tacoma	0	0	.000	0.00	1	0	0	0	0	0	1.0	0	4	0	0	0	0	0	0	1	0	2	0	0
Robertson, Rich, Salt Lake*	5	0	1.000	2.44	7	7	1	0	0	0	44.1	31	172	13	12	2	2	0	0	12	1	40	1	0
Robinson, Scott, Phoenix	5	7	.417	4.66	31	15	0	0	9	0	123.2	134	519	68	64	14	2	3	4	37	1	61	4	0
Rodriguez, Felix, Albuquerque	3	2	.600	4.24	14	11	0	0	0	0	51.0	52	224	29	24	5	4	1	0	26	0	46	0	1
Rogers, Kevin, Phoenix*	0	0	.000	4.15	3	1	0	0	0	0	4.1	9	22	2	2	0	0	0	0	2	0	1	2	0
Rohde, Dave, Tucson	0	0	.000	0.00	1	0	0	0	1	0	1.0	0	4	0	0	0	0	0	0	1	0	0	0	0
Romanoli, Paul, Col. Springs*	3	1	.750	4.50	31	0	0	0	9	3	20.0	27	99	13	10	2	1	1	1	10	2	23	1	0
Roper, John, Phoenix	0	1	.000	9.00	1	1	0	0	0	0	3.0	5	14	3	3	0	0	1	0	0	0	2	0	0
Rose, Scott, Edmonton	0	2	.000	6.30	5	1	0	0	2	0	10.0	13	45	7	7	0	1	0	0	7	0	0	0	0
Rosselli, Joe, Phoenix*	4	3	.571	4.99	13	13	1	0	0	0	79.1	94	332	47	44	8	2	4	0	12	0	34	2	0
Ryan, Matt, Calgary	0	0	.000	1.93	5	0	0	0	4	1	4.2	5	20	1	1	0	0	0	1	1	1	2	0	0
Rychel, Kevin, Calgary	0	1	.000	10.38	10	0	0	0	3	0	8.2	14	45	11	10	3	0	0	0	6	0	4	1	0
Sager, A.J., Col. Springs	8	5	.615	3.50	23	22	1	1	0	0	133.2	153	564	61	52	14	4	3	2	23	1	80	0	0
St. Claire, Randy, Calgary	3	5	.375	5.00	54	0	0	0	40	19	54.0	72	258	31	30	5	8	3	3	21	5	43	1	0
Salkeld, Roger, Tacoma	1	0	1.000	1.80	4	3	0	0	1	1	15.0	8	59	4	3	0	0	0	0	7	0	11	0	0
Sanchez, Alex, Edmonton	0	0	.000	5.19	8	0	0	0	0	0	17.1	18	75	12	10	0	0	2	0	10	0	8	2	0
Sanders, Scott, Las Vegas	0	0	.000	0.00	1	1	0	0	0	0	3.0	3	14	0	0	0	0	0	0	1	0	2	0	0
Sanford, Mo, Salt Lake	0	1	.000	6.35	4	0	0	0	0	0	5.2	6	27	4	4	1	0	0	0	4	0	8	0	0
Schmitt, Todd, Las Vegas	0	2	.000	7.82	12	0	0	0	8	2	12.2	16	61	11	11	0	0	1	2	9	0	6	2	0
Schullstrom, Erik, Salt Lake	2	0	1.000	4.66	10	0	0	0	7	2	9.2	12	43	5	5	1	0	0	0	4	0	8	0	0
Scott, Darryl, Col. Springs	4	10	.286	4.70	59	1	0	0	27	4	95.2	113	429	63	50	7	4	7	3	41	7	77	7	0
Sepeda, Jamie, Tucson	3	2	.600	4.91	8	8	0	0	0	0	40.1	52	178	22	22	1	4	0	2	12	0	19	1	2
Serafini, Dan, Salt Lake*	0	0	.000	6.75	1	0	0	0	1	1	4.0	4	17	3	3	2	0	0	0	1	0	4	0	0
Shaw, Curtis, Edmonton*	6	5	.545	4.67	42	3	0	0	11	2	98.1	91	454	60	51	4	5	6	6	88	8	52	17	1
Shifflett, Steve, Col. Springs	4	3	.571	6.87	23	0	0	0	9	0	38.0	61	184	33	29	6	1	4	0	13	2	21	0	2
Shouse, Brian, Calgary*	4	4	.500	6.18	8	8	1	0	0	0	39.1	62	185	35	27	2	1	1	1	7	0	17	3	0
Simas, Bill, Vancouver	6	3	.667	3.55	30	0	0	0	24	6	38.0	44	175	19	15	1	1	1	4	14	2	44	1	0
Small, Mark, Tucson	3	3	.500	4.09	51	0	0	0	40	19	66.0	74	285	32	30	5	1	2	1	19	2	51	8	0
Smith, Tim, Edmonton	3	2	.600	6.03	9	7	0	0	0	0	37.1	44	174	27	25	2	2	2	1	22	2	22	4	0
Springer, Russ, Vancouver	2	0	1.000	3.44	6	6	0	0	0	0	34.0	24	146	16	13	3	0	0	3	23	0	23	3	0
Stanhope, Chuck, Edmonton	1	1	.500	4.50	6	0	0	0	4	0	6.0	8	25	3	3	0	2	1	0	1	0	2	0	0
Stevens, Matt, Salt Lake	0	0	.000	3.52	7	0	0	0	3	1	7.2	9	34	4	3	1	0	1	1	2	0	5	0	0
Sveum, Dale, Calgary	0	0	.000	0.00	2	0	0	0	1	0	2.0	1	7	0	0	0	0	0	0	0	0	2	0	0
Swan, Russ, Edmonton*	3	3	.500	4.34	17	0	0	0	12	4	18.2	23	85	9	9	2	1	1	0	11	4	10	4	0
Tabaka, Jeff, Las Vegas*	0	1	.000	1.99	19	0	0	0	12	6	22.2	16	95	6	5	0	2	1	1	14	3	27	2	0
Taylor, Kerry, Las Vegas	2	2	.500	4.38	8	8	0	0	0	0	37.0	44	174	21	18	3	4	0	2	21	1	21	0	0
Taylor, Scott, Calgary*	5	8	.385	4.11	27	25	1	0	0	0	140.0	144	578	73	64	10	3	4	3	35	2	83	3	0
Telford, Anthony, Edmonton	3	2	.600	7.18	8	6	0	0	0	0	36.1	47	173	32	29	5	2	2	2	16	0	17	2	0
Thompson, John, Tacoma	0	1	.000	0.00	1	0	0	0	0	0	2.2	3	12	2	0	0	1	0	0	0	0	0	0	0
Thompson, Mark, Col. Springs	5	3	.625	6.10	11	10	0	0	0	0	62.0	73	276	43	42	2	2	2	6	25	0	38	0	0
Torres, Salomon, Pho.-Tac.	1	1	.500	3.00	6	4	0	0	1	0	30.0	22	122	10	10	2	2	1	2	13	1	24	2	1
Treadwell, Jody, Albuquerque	7	5	.583	3.96	30	15	1	1	4	1	125.0	121	510	61	55	15	2	5	2	32	4	79	9	1
Trlicek, Rick, Phoenix	5	4	.556	5.29	38	0	0	0	19	0	63.0	72	279	44	37	7	4	3	0	21	6	43	6	1
Trombley, Mike, Salt Lake	5	3	.625	3.62	12	12	0	0	0	0	69.2	71	301	32	28	3	0	5	2	26	1	59	4	1
Valdez, Carlos, Phoenix	1	0	1.000	2.76	18	0	0	0	12	2	29.1	29	131	10	9	2	2	0	0	13	2	30	3	0
Valdez, Sergio, Phoenix	6	7	.462	4.45	18	18	2	0	0	0	109.1	117	456	58	54	6	3	3	2	25	4	64	14	0
Valera, Julio, Vancouver	2	5	.286	5.70	13	13	2	0	0	0	71.0	85	314	54	45	2	0	0	2	21	0	43	1	0
Vanderweele, Doug, Phoenix	2	4	.333	6.10	11	4	1	0	1	0	38.1	57	178	29	26	9	2	3	1	11	3	20	1	1
VanRyn, Ben, Vancouver*	2	0	1.000	3.07	11	5	0	0	2	0	29.1	29	123	10	10	1	2	2	0	9	1	20	2	0
Villone, Ron, Tacoma*	1	0	1.000	0.61	22	0	0	0	16	13	29.2	9	117	6	2	1	1	2	0	19	0	43	1	0
Wagner, Billy, Tucson*	5	3	.625	3.18	13	13	0	0	0	0	76.1	70	325	28	27	3	4	2	1	32	0	80	4	0
Wagner, Matt, Tacoma	1	5	.167	6.27	6	6	1	0	0	0	33.0	43	157	29	23	3	0	1	1	17	1	33	2	0
Waldron, Joe, Tucson*	1	0	1.000	4.32	4	0	0	0	1	0	8.1	6	31	4	4	0	0	0	0	2	0	11	0	0
Wall, Donne, Tucson	17	6	.739	3.30	28	28	0	0	0	0	177.1	190	732	72	65	5	6	4	5	32	1	119	5	1
Waring, Jim, Tucson	2	2	.500	8.46	5	5	0	0	0	0	22.1	30	108	24	21	1	0	2	5	8	0	5	0	0
Wasdin, John, Edmonton	12	8	.600	5.52	29	28	2	1	0	0	174.1	193	744	117	107	26	3	11	4	38	3	111	10	1
Watkins, Scott, Salt Lake*	4	2	.667	2.80	45	0	0	0	33	20	54.2	45	217	18	17	4	1	3	1	13	1	57	1	0
Watson, Ron, Vancouver	0	1	.000	4.76	5	0	0	0	2	0	5.2	3	26	3	3	0	1	0	0	6	1	3	0	0
Weber, Wes, Tac.-L.V.	6	11	.353	4.67	29	21	2	0	3	0	150.1	170	663	92	78	16	5	6	4	50	10	86	6	3
Wengert, Don, Edmonton	1	1	.500	7.38	16	6	0	0	4	1	39.0	55	178	32	32	5	0	1	1	16	2	20	3	0
Westbrook, Destry, Tucson	0	0	.000	7.30	5	0	0	0	2	0	12.1	20	60	10	10	2	0	0	0	7	0	8	2	0
Whitaker, Steve, Phoenix*	0	5	.000	7.00	16	10	0	0	3	0	54.0	72	261	47	42	2	6	4	0	36	2	30	3	1
White, Chris, Tucson	1	1	.500	8.71	5	1	0	0	2	0	10.1	16	44	10	10	1	1	0	0	2	0	6	0	0
White, Rick, Calgary	6	4	.600	4.20	14	11	1	0	1	0	79.1	97	338	40	37	13	0	4	3	10	0	56	2	0
Whitehurst, Wally, Phoenix	0	1	.000	7.16	4	4	0	0	0	0	16.1	20	76	13	13	0	2	0	1	8	1	7	2	0
Williams, Jeff, Tacoma	0	3	.000	8.22	8	3	0	0	4	0	23.0	31	109	21	21	1	0	3	2	12	0	8	0	0
Williams, Shad, Vancouver	9	7	.563	3.37	25	25	3	1	0	0	149.2	142	627	65	56	16	3	3	4	48	2	114	7	1
Williams, Todd, Albuquerque	4	1	.800	3.38	25	0	0	0	5	0	45.1	59	203	21	17	4	1	1	1	15	4	23	1	2
Willis, Carl, Vancouver	2	2	.500	4.11	20	0	0	0	9	1	35.0	40	154	17	16	2	0	2	0	11	2	17	2	0
Willis, Travis, Calgary	2	2	.500	7.15	22	0	0	0	7	0	39.0	57	188	35	31	4	2	0	4	15	4	13	2	0

Pitcher, Team	W	L	Pct.	ERA	G	GS	CG	ShO	GF	Sv.	IP	H	TBF	R	ER	HR	SH	SF	HB	BB	IBB	SO	WP	Bk.
Wilson, Gary, Calgary	1	2	.333	5.51	6	4	0	0	0	0	16.1	19	75	16	10	1	1	2	0	9	0	12	2	1
Winston, Darrin, Calgary*	4	6	.400	4.80	53	0	0	0	20	2	50.2	59	226	33	27	8	0	2	0	17	2	40	2	0
Wissler, Bill, Salt Lake	3	3	.500	4.62	37	2	0	0	9	1	60.1	69	262	32	31	7	3	0	1	24	1	26	5	0
Wojciechowski, Steve, Edm.*	6	3	.667	3.69	14	12	2	1	1	0	78.0	75	320	37	32	5	1	4	1	21	0	39	4	2
Wolcott, Bob, Tacoma	6	3	.667	4.08	13	13	2	1	0	0	79.1	94	347	49	36	10	1	4	5	16	0	43	2	1
Worrell, Tim, Las Vegas	0	2	.000	6.00	10	3	0	0	0	0	24.0	27	121	21	16	1	2	0	3	17	0	18	0	0

COMBINATION SHUTOUTS: **Albuquerque (3)**—McCarthy-Montalvo-Brosnan, Mimbs-Rodriguez-Montalvo, O'Donoghue-Bruske-Daal. **Calgary (5)**—DeLosSantos-Flynt-McCurry-St. Claire, Ericks-Backlund, Ericks-Corbin-Winston-St. Claire, Hope-Ralph-Winston, Taylor-Maysey-Ryan. **Colorado Springs (10)**—Peever-Bustillos 2, Fredrickson-Czajkowski, Nied-Sager-Scott, Rekar-Romanoli, Rekar-Scott, Reynoso-Hawblitzel-Czajkowski, Sager-Czajkowski, Sager-Scott, Sager-Shifflett. **Edmonton (3)**—Baker-Mohler, Johns-Mohler, Wojciechowski-Brock-Mohler. **Las Vegas (3)**—Harriger-McFarlin-Hermanson, Martinez-McFarlin-Tabaka, Taylor-Merriman-McFarlin-Hermanson. **Phoenix (4)**—Brink-Knudsen, Carlson-Rogers-Trlicek-Greer, Whitaker-Menendez, Whitehurst-Phillips-Burcham-Barton-Trlicek. **Salt Lake (3)**—Hawkins-Gavaghan, Munoz-Bryant-Schullstrom-Watkins, Trombley-Watkins. **Tacoma (5)**—Apana-Darwin, Apana-Mecir, Carmona-Darwin, Milacki-Phillips, Salkeld-Mecir. **Tucson (8)**—Jean-Small-Daspit, McMurtry-Ketchen-Huisman, McMurtry-Powell-Ketchen, Sepeda-Patrick-Hartgraves, Wall-Huisman, Wagner-Daspit-Bennett, Wagner-Morman-Huisman, Wagner-Small. **Vancouver (8)**—Akerfelds-Chavez, Holzemer-Patterson-Simas, Janicki-Edenfield-Holzemer, Morrison-Butler-Holdridge, Springer-Ratekin-Simas, VanRyn-Bennett-Simas, Williams-Heredia, Williams-Monteleone-Fortugno-Heredia.

NO-HIT GAMES: Milchin, Albuquerque, defeated Vancouver, 2-0 (second game), June 13.

PITCHERS WITH TWO OR MORE TEAMS

Pitcher, Team	W	L	Pct.	ERA	G	GS	CG	ShO	GF	Sv.	IP	H	TBF	R	ER	HR	SH	SF	HB	BB	IBB	SO	WP	Bk.
Bennett, Erik, Vancouver	6	0	1.000	4.26	28	0	0	0	12	2	50.2	44	206	24	24	5	0	2	3	18	2	39	4	1
Bennett, Erik, Tucson	3	1	.750	4.76	14	1	0	0	4	1	22.2	27	110	17	12	1	0	3	2	14	2	24	0	0
Brink, Brad, Phoenix	2	5	.286	7.05	11	9	0	0	0	0	44.2	55	215	35	35	3	1	4	2	30	0	33	1	0
Brink, Brad, Edmonton	0	1	.000	4.88	9	3	0	0	4	0	24.0	24	112	20	13	2	0	1	2	16	3	15	1	0
Daspit, Jim, Tucson	5	1	.833	3.57	36	0	0	0	11	1	63.0	63	272	30	25	3	2	5	2	22	1	49	5	0
Daspit, Jim, Edmonton	0	1	.000	10.80	2	0	0	0	0	0	5.0	6	22	6	6	2	0	0	0	2	0	5	2	0
Fesh, Sean, Tucson*	1	0	1.000	1.35	10	0	0	0	1	0	13.1	11	52	2	2	0	0	0	0	3	0	7	0	0
Fesh, Sean, Las Vegas*	2	1	.667	3.32	30	0	0	0	11	1	38.0	53	185	21	14	2	4	0	3	16	5	18	1	1
Hansell, Greg, Albuquerque	1	1	.500	8.44	8	1	0	0	3	1	16.0	25	77	15	15	2	1	0	1	6	1	15	0	0
Hansell, Greg, Salt Lake	3	1	.750	5.01	7	5	0	0	0	0	32.1	39	141	20	18	3	1	1	1	4	1	17	3	1
Loiselle, Rich, Las Vegas	2	2	.500	7.24	8	7	1	1	0	0	27.1	36	131	27	22	5	1	0	2	9	0	16	0	0
Loiselle, Rich, Tucson	0	0	.000	2.61	2	1	0	0	0	0	10.1	8	44	4	3	0	0	0	0	4	0	4	0	1
Torres, Salomon, Phoenix	0	0	.000	0.00	1	0	0	0	0	0	2.0	2	8	0	0	0	1	0	0	0	0	5	0	0
Torres, Salomon, Tacoma	1	1	.500	3.21	5	4	0	0	1	0	28.0	20	114	10	10	2	1	1	2	13	1	19	2	1
Weber, Weston, Tacoma	3	7	.300	4.60	20	13	1	0	3	0	101.2	111	443	55	52	12	3	4	2	41	10	54	5	3
Weber, Weston, Las Vegas	3	4	.429	4.81	9	8	1	0	0	0	48.2	59	220	37	26	4	2	2	2	9	0	32	1	0

1995 FIELDING

TEAM

Team	Pct.	G	PO	A	E	TC	DP	PB
Salt Lake	.981	144	3749	1647	103	5499	131	11
Vancouver	.978	141	3647	1459	117	5223	131	14
Phoenix	.976	144	3827	1627	134	5588	165	11
Albuquerque	.974	144	3746	1663	144	5553	152	15
Col. Springs	.974	143	3636	1532	139	5307	152	9
Edmonton	.973	144	3718	1678	148	5544	151	13
Tucson	.973	143	3734	1592	148	5474	146	19
Tacoma	.971	144	3747	1576	159	5482	130	16
Calgary	.968	141	3585	1667	174	5426	150	15
Las Vegas	.967	144	3691	1591	181	5463	133	20

TRIPLE PLAYS: Phoenix, Tacoma.

INDIVIDUAL

FIRST BASEMEN

NOTE: All caps denotes fielding-percentage leader based on 72 games for catchers, 96 for all other non-pitchers and 144 innings for pitchers. *Throws lefthanded.

Player, Team	Pct.	G	PO	A	E	TC	DP
Aude, Rich, Calgary	.988	49	447	31	6	484	58
Ball, Jeff, Tucson	.990	35	272	16	3	291	25
Barron, Tony, Tacoma	1.000	1	1	0	0	1	0
Bean, Billy, Las Vegas*	1.000	9	77	3	0	80	8
Bellinger, Clay, Phoenix	1.000	3	10	1	0	11	2
Blanco, Henry, Albuquerque	1.000	11	97	6	0	103	3
Bolick, Frank, C.S.	1.000	1	8	1	0	9	1
BOWIE, Jim, Edmonton*	.996	138	1215	126	6	1347	127
Brewer, Rod, Phoenix*	1.000	13	134	14	0	148	12
Brumley, Mike, Tucson	1.000	2	3	0	0	3	0
Bryant, Scott, Edmonton	.980	10	45	4	1	50	5
Bullock, Eric, Las Vegas*	.667	1	2	0	1	3	0
Busch, Mike, Albuquerque	.994	40	303	21	2	326	30
Castellano, Pedro, C.S.	.995	26	186	9	1	196	24
Chimelis, Joel, Phoenix	.998	51	395	25	1	421	41
Cianfrocco, Archi, Las Vegas	.985	42	371	35	6	412	33
Colbert, Craig, Las Vegas	.857	2	6	0	1	7	0
Coomer, Ron, Albuquerque	.979	35	314	17	7	338	33
Dalesandro, Mark, Vancouver	1.000	1	9	0	0	9	0
Deer, Rob, Van.-L.V.	.976	17	113	11	3	127	10
Dunn, Steve, Salt Lake*	.991	102	916	59	9	984	75
Durant, Mike, Salt Lake	.917	1	11	0	1	12	0
Durham, Leon, Vancouver*	1.000	2	5	0	0	5	0
Gainer, Jay, C.S.*	.986	63	508	48	8	564	57
Giambi, Jason, Edmonton	1.000	3	7	0	0	7	1
Goff, Jerry, Tucson	.938	3	15	0	1	16	0
Gonzales, Rene, Vancouver	1.000	1	8	2	0	10	2
Hale, Chip, Salt Lake	1.000	3	25	2	0	27	5
Hansen, Terrel, Tacoma	1.000	9	71	6	0	77	5
Hatcher, Chris, Tucson	.977	73	590	40	15	645	62
Horn, Sam, Calgary*	.976	16	157	5	4	166	15
Huckaby, Ken, Albuquerque	1.000	1	3	0	0	3	0
Hyers, Tim, Las Vegas*	.998	54	450	24	1	475	40
Ingram, Riccardo, Salt Lake	1.000	1	1	0	0	1	0
Johnson, Mark, Calgary*	.972	8	65	5	2	72	4
Jordan, Ricky, Vancouver	1.000	1	4	0	0	4	0
Kirkpatrick, Jay, Albuquerque	1.000	6	51	4	0	55	1
Leonard, Mark, Phoenix	.989	13	89	1	1	91	11
Litton, Greg, Tacoma	.990	79	575	48	6	629	53
Maksudian, Mike, Edmonton	1.000	4	16	1	0	17	0
Marrero, Oreste, Albuquerque*	1.000	1	6	0	0	6	2
Martinez, Chito, C.S.*	.941	3	16	0	1	17	3
Masteller, Dan, Salt Lake*	.990	10	84	12	1	97	4
Maurer, Ron, Albuquerque	1.000	1	1	0	0	1	0
McCarty, Dave, Phoenix*	.994	35	327	31	2	360	39
Miller, Barry, Phoenix*	.994	38	290	17	2	309	31
Munoz, Orlando, Vancouver	1.000	1	1	0	0	1	0
Newfield, Marc, Las Vegas	1.000	1	10	1	0	11	1
Ortiz, Ray, Phoenix*	.990	13	91	5	1	97	15
Osik, Keith, Calgary	1.000	11	83	9	0	92	3
Perez, Eduardo, Vancouver	.986	8	67	4	1	72	3
Petagine, Roberto, Las Vegas*	.975	14	110	7	3	120	13
Pirkl, Greg, Tacoma	.983	33	276	19	5	300	31
Pritchett, Chris, Vancouver	.989	117	995	92	12	1099	99
Quinlan, Tom, Salt Lake	1.000	21	149	7	0	156	18
Raven, Luis, Vancouver	.971	3	32	1	1	34	6
Rodriguez, Boi, Calgary	.975	7	73	4	2	79	5
Saunders, Doug, Tacoma	1.000	4	35	3	0	38	2

Player, Team	Pct.	G	PO	A	E	TC	DP
See, Larry, Las Vegas	.995	24	195	15	1	211	18
Sheldon, Scott, Edmonton	1.000	3	21	2	0	23	2
Shelton, Ben, Salt Lake*	.970	7	59	5	2	66	10
Simmons, Nelson, Calgary	.956	9	62	3	3	68	7
Simms, Mike, Tucson	.985	48	376	24	6	406	43
Snider, Van, Salt Lake	.986	7	66	3	1	70	6
Springer, Steve, Las Vegas	1.000	3	32	3	0	35	2
Stahoviak, Scott, Salt Lake	1.000	5	32	1	0	33	2
Sveum, Dale, Calgary	.986	36	313	39	5	357	32
Sweeney, Mark, Vancouver*	.958	3	22	1	1	24	2
Traxler, Brian, Albuquerque*	.992	66	569	23	5	597	61
Turang, Brian, Tacoma	1.000	1	6	0	0	6	0
Turner, Chris, Vancouver	1.000	6	45	3	0	48	7
Van Burkleo, Ty, C.S.*	.982	65	521	29	10	560	53
Willard, Jerry, Tacoma	.976	46	324	35	9	368	26
Young, Kevin, Calgary	.978	12	124	11	3	138	11

TRIPLE PLAYS: Litton, McCarty.

FIRST BASEMEN WITH TWO OR MORE TEAMS

Player, Team	Pct.	G	PO	A	E	TC	DP
Deer, Rob, Vancouver	.977	5	40	2	1	43	4
Deer, Rob, Las Vegas	.976	12	73	9	2	84	6

SECOND BASEMEN

Player, Team	Pct.	G	PO	A	E	TC	DP
Abreu, Bob, Tucson	1.000	1	3	0	0	3	1
Bellinger, Clay, Phoenix	.956	16	15	28	2	45	3
Bream, Scott, Las Vegas	.975	65	134	177	8	319	42
Brumley, Mike, Tucson	.929	4	3	10	1	14	1
Candaele, Casey, Albuquerque	.958	6	23	23	2	48	8
Castro, Juan, Albuquerque	1.000	10	4	17	0	21	2
Chimelis, Joel, Phoenix	.958	20	34	34	3	71	15
Cole, Stu, C.S.	.987	14	34	41	1	76	15
Corbin, Ted, Salt Lake	.875	2	3	4	1	8	1
Correia, Rod, Vancouver	.944	8	15	19	2	36	5
Demetral, Chris, Albuquerque	.978	40	59	115	4	178	23
Diaz, Eddy, Tacoma	.966	7	10	18	1	29	4
Duncan, Andres, Salt Lake	1.000	1	4	0	0	4	1
Ehmann, Kurt, Phoenix	1.000	2	5	5	0	10	3
Faries, Paul, Edmonton	.984	105	230	261	8	499	75
FORBES, P.J., Vancouver	.986	103	180	257	6	443	63
Gallego, Mike, Edmonton	1.000	2	3	2	0	5	0
Garrison, Webster, C.S.	.971	100	193	307	15	515	66
Gonzales, Rene, Vancouver	.903	7	10	18	3	31	5
Grebeck, Brian, Vancouver	.973	16	37	34	2	73	11
Guerrero, Juan, Tucson	.947	5	10	8	1	19	0
Hajek, Dave, Tucson	.982	124	269	398	12	679	100
Hale, Chip, Salt Lake	1.000	5	3	13	0	16	2
Hall, Billy, Las Vegas	.928	69	108	149	20	277	32
Hocking, Denny, Salt Lake	1.000	1	2	3	0	5	0
Holbert, Ray, Las Vegas	.972	9	9	26	1	36	5
Ingram, Garey, Albuquerque	.975	48	90	144	6	240	38
Johnson, Erik, Calgary	.974	81	159	218	10	387	66
Jones, Tim, Edmonton	1.000	1	0	1	0	1	0
Kellner, Frank, Tucson	1.000	1	1	2	0	3	0
Lind, Jose, Vancouver	1.000	10	23	21	0	44	8
Matos, Francisco, Calgary	.967	48	84	123	7	214	29
Maurer, Ron, Albuquerque	.977	25	38	46	2	86	12
Mejia, Roberto, C.S.	.973	35	80	97	5	182	28
Mueller, Bill, Phoenix	1.000	1	3	3	0	6	1
Munoz, Orlando, Vancouver	1.000	3	3	5	0	8	1
Parker, Rick, Albuquerque	1.000	3	4	2	0	6	0
Pozo, Arquimedez, Tacoma	.971	81	162	245	12	419	49
Pye, Eddie, Albuquerque	.971	41	83	116	6	205	26
Raabe, Brian, Salt Lake	.989	56	98	169	3	270	37
Ramirez, J.D., Vancouver	1.000	1	1	5	0	6	0
Relaford, Desi, Tacoma	.958	29	50	88	6	144	18
Richardson, Jeff, Calgary	.963	5	11	15	1	27	7
Roberts, Bip, Las Vegas	1.000	1	0	2	0	2	0
Rohde, Dave, Tucson	.982	16	28	26	1	55	5
Rossy, Rico, Las Vegas	.973	14	30	43	2	75	12
Saunders, Doug, Edm.-Tac.	.986	11	33	37	1	71	11
Sheets, Andy, Tacoma	1.000	8	9	31	0	40	5
Sheldon, Scott, Edmonton	1.000	1	0	2	0	2	0
Simons, Mitch, Salt Lake	.984	90	195	244	7	446	63
Sojo, Luis, Tacoma	1.000	2	3	6	0	9	0
Stankiewicz, Andy, Tucson	.947	4	7	11	1	19	3
Turang, Brian, Tacoma	.947	12	25	29	3	57	5
Wehner, John, Calgary	.931	5	15	12	2	29	4
Wilkerson, Curtis, Tacoma	1.000	5	8	19	0	27	4
Wimmer, Chris, Phoenix	.983	127	224	371	10	605	96
Womack, Tony, Calgary	.967	15	15	44	2	61	4
Wood, Jason, Edmonton	.968	39	84	98	6	188	17

TRIPLE PLAYS: Pozo, Wimmer.

SECOND BASEMEN WITH TWO OR MORE TEAMS

Player, Team	Pct.	G	PO	A	E	TC	DP
Saunders, Doug, Edmonton	1.000	4	16	17	0	33	5
Saunders, Doug, Tacoma	.974	7	17	20	1	38	6

THIRD BASEMEN

Player, Team	Pct.	G	PO	A	E	TC	DP
Ball, Jeff, Tucson	.957	46	19	93	5	117	11
Bellinger, Clay, Phoenix	.981	27	15	37	1	53	5
Blanco, Henry, Albuquerque	.967	19	17	41	2	60	6
Bolick, Frank, C.S.	.927	17	12	26	3	41	1
Brumley, Mike, Tucson	.938	17	5	25	2	32	0
Bruno, Julio, Las Vegas	.925	38	25	99	10	134	10
Bryant, Scott, Edmonton	.700	2	4	3	3	10	1
Busch, Mike, Albuquerque	.941	75	31	143	11	185	14
Candaele, Casey, Albuquerque	1.000	1	0	1	0	1	0
Case, Mike, C.S.	.625	3	1	4	3	8	0
Castellano, Pedro, C.S.	.973	73	36	110	4	150	15
Chimelis, Joel, Phoenix	.938	24	15	45	4	64	4
Cianfrocco, Archi, Las Vegas	.880	31	17	64	11	92	3
Cole, Stu, C.S.	.912	18	8	23	3	34	3
Coomer, Ron, Albuquerque	.980	44	21	76	2	99	5
Correia, Rod, Vancouver	.875	6	4	10	2	16	1
Dalesandro, Mark, Vancouver	.846	7	4	7	2	13	0
Diaz, Eddy, Tacoma	1.000	4	2	5	0	7	1
Ehmann, Kurt, Phoenix	.913	13	7	14	2	23	2
Faries, Paul, Edmonton	.857	3	3	3	1	7	0
Gallego, Mike, Edmonton	1.000	1	0	2	0	2	1
Garrison, Webster, C.S.	.914	22	12	41	5	58	4
Giambi, Jason, Edmonton	.935	48	31	98	9	138	10
Gonzales, Rene, Vancouver	.966	11	10	18	1	29	2
Grebeck, Brian, Vancouver	.957	11	6	16	1	23	3
Guerrero, Juan, Tucson	.900	28	16	38	6	60	5
Hale, Chip, Salt Lake	1.000	9	5	11	0	16	2
Johnson, Erik, Calgary	1.000	11	7	25	0	32	0
Jones, Tim, Edmonton	1.000	1	1	4	0	5	0
Litton, Greg, Tacoma	.948	39	33	59	5	97	7
Maksudian, Mike, Edmonton	1.000	11	7	23	0	30	3
Martinez, Carlos, Vancouver	.970	24	17	48	2	67	3
Maurer, Ron, Albuquerque	.967	17	5	24	1	30	1
Mueller, Bill, Phoenix	.938	40	23	82	7	112	8
Munoz, Orlando, Vancouver	1.000	1	2	1	0	3	1
Nevin, Phil, Tucson	.923	57	39	128	14	181	17
Osik, Keith, Calgary	1.000	1	2	2	0	4	0
Parker, Rick, Albuquerque	1.000	3	1	4	0	5	0
Peguero, Jose, Vancouver	.929	17	6	33	3	42	2
Perez, Eduardo, Vancouver	.958	42	27	86	5	118	11
Pozo, Arquimedez, Tacoma	.946	33	29	59	5	93	2
Pye, Eddie, Albuquerque	1.000	3	1	2	0	3	0
QUINLAN, Tom, Salt Lake	.940	110	66	231	19	316	18
Raabe, Brian, Salt Lake	.975	31	16	63	2	81	1
Raven, Luis, Vancouver	.873	21	9	46	8	63	6
Rodriguez, Boi, Calgary	.625	2	0	5	3	8	1
Rohde, Dave, Tucson	.893	15	6	19	3	28	1
Rossy, Rico, Las Vegas	.894	27	20	56	9	85	3
Russo, Paul, Las Vegas	.960	43	30	91	5	126	10
Saunders, Doug, Tacoma	.947	34	18	54	4	76	9
Scott, Gary, Phoenix	.921	60	33	107	12	152	8
Sheets, Andy, Tacoma	.913	33	11	83	9	103	2
Sheldon, Scott, Edmonton	.959	32	20	74	4	98	8
Snyder, Cory, Las Vegas	.600	2	1	2	2	5	0
Springer, Steve, Las Vegas	.957	9	6	16	1	23	1
Stahoviak, Scott, Salt Lake	1.000	7	4	15	0	19	2
Stankiewicz, Andy, Tucson	1.000	2	2	8	0	10	1
Sveum, Dale, Calgary	.963	70	40	196	9	245	20
Tatum, Jim, C.S.	.945	23	13	39	3	55	6
Turang, Brian, Tacoma	.917	14	9	24	3	36	3
Turner, Chris, Vancouver	.909	14	7	23	3	33	2
Wallach, Tim, Albuquerque	1.000	1	0	1	0	1	0
Wehner, John, Calgary	.909	31	14	86	10	110	7
Wood, Jason, Edmonton	.939	59	48	136	12	196	15
Young, Kevin, Calgary	.913	31	20	74	9	103	4

SHORTSTOPS

Player, Team	Pct.	G	PO	A	E	TC	DP
Aurilia, Rich, Phoenix	.975	71	104	246	9	359	56
Bellinger, Clay, Phoenix	.960	29	42	79	5	126	19
Bournigal, Rafael, Albuquerque	.951	12	7	32	2	41	4
Bream, Scott, Las Vegas	.967	24	26	63	3	92	11
Brumley, Mike, Tucson	.961	24	22	52	3	77	9
Castro, Juan, Albuquerque	.971	92	148	327	14	489	67
Chimelis, Joel, Phoenix	.911	8	16	25	4	45	2
Cole, Stu, C.S.	.964	23	24	57	3	84	14

Player, Team	Pct.	G	PO	A	E	TC	DP
Corbin, Ted, Salt Lake	1.000	2	3	5	0	8	3
Correia, Rod, Vancouver	.961	60	106	193	12	311	35
Counsell, Craig, C.S.	.950	115	182	386	30	598	86
Cruz, Fausto, Edmonton	.958	113	196	355	24	575	72
Duncan, Andres, Salt Lake	.966	11	25	32	2	59	6
Ehmann, Kurt, Phoenix	.949	51	79	165	13	257	45
Faries, Paul, Edmonton	1.000	3	2	15	0	17	2
Forbes, P.J., Vancouver	1.000	6	10	14	0	24	1
Gallego, Mike, Edmonton	1.000	1	0	4	0	4	0
Gonzales, Rene, Vancouver	.947	26	25	82	6	113	18
Grebeck, Brian, Vancouver	.959	38	53	109	7	169	19
Guerrero, Juan, Tucson	1.000	2	0	1	0	1	1
Guerrero, Wilton, Albuquerque	.852	14	13	39	9	61	6
Gutierrez, Ricky, Tucson	.977	61	91	167	6	264	34
HOCKING, Denny, Salt Lake	.966	114	171	390	20	581	72
Johnson, Erik, Calgary	.920	26	32	71	9	112	9
Kellner, Frank, Tucson	.974	25	39	72	3	114	22
Litton, Greg, Tacoma	1.000	2	0	4	0	4	0
Matos, Francisco, Calgary	.944	45	56	145	12	213	32
Maurer, Ron, Albuquerque	1.000	13	12	33	0	45	3
Perez, Neifi, C.S.	.936	11	16	28	3	47	5
Polcovich, Kevin, Calgary	.959	61	90	215	13	318	49
Pye, Eddie, Albuquerque	.947	29	48	78	7	133	17
Raabe, Brian, Salt Lake	.958	9	6	17	1	24	4
Relaford, Desi, Tacoma	1.000	2	2	5	0	7	0
Roberts, Bip, Las Vegas	.938	3	2	13	1	16	1
Rodriguez, Alex, Tacoma	.961	51	90	157	10	257	28
Rohde, Dave, Tucson	.948	32	30	62	5	97	11
Rossy, Rico, Las Vegas	.951	58	88	205	15	308	34
Schofield, Dick, Vancouver	.932	16	24	44	5	73	9
Sheets, Andy, Tacoma	.957	93	137	268	18	423	59
Sheldon, Scott, Edmonton	.933	3	3	11	1	15	2
Simons, Mitch, Salt Lake	.949	15	24	50	4	78	5
Sojo, Luis, Tacoma	1.000	1	1	3	0	4	1
Springer, Steve, Las Vegas	.920	4	4	19	2	25	3
Stankiewicz, Andy, Tucson	.978	20	27	62	2	91	9
Sveum, Dale, Calgary	.778	1	3	4	2	9	3
Velandia, Jorge, Las Vegas	.903	66	97	190	31	318	39
Womack, Tony, Calgary	.960	15	22	50	3	75	5
Wood, Jason, Edmonton	.945	30	41	97	8	146	20

OUTFIELDERS

Player, Team	Pct.	G	PO	A	E	TC	DP
Abreu, Bob, Tucson	.969	111	204	18	7	229	5
Allensworth, Jermaine, Calgary	.989	46	90	2	1	93	0
Anderson, Garret, Vancouver*	.957	11	22	0	1	23	0
Ball, Jeff, Tucson	1.000	15	19	0	0	19	0
Barron, Tony, Tacoma	1.000	5	11	0	0	11	0
Beamon, Trey, Calgary	.960	110	201	14	9	224	0
Bean, Billy, Las Vegas*	.983	110	219	6	4	229	2
Beauchamp, Kash, Edmonton	1.000	1	3	0	0	3	0
Becker, Rich, Salt Lake*	.991	36	108	5	1	114	0
Bellinger, Clay, Phoenix	1.000	23	32	0	0	32	0
Benard, Marvin, Phoenix*	.959	97	183	5	8	196	2
Blanco, Henry, Albuquerque	1.000	1	1	0	0	1	0
Bragg, Darren, Tacoma	.968	47	115	7	4	126	2
Brito, Bernardo, Salt Lake	1.000	4	15	0	0	15	0
Brumley, Mike, Tucson	.948	42	68	5	4	77	2
Bryant, Scott, Edmonton	.942	53	93	5	6	104	0
Bullock, Eric, Las Vegas*	.959	35	46	1	2	49	0
Burks, Ellis, C.S.	1.000	7	16	0	0	16	0
Busch, Mike, Albuquerque	.800	6	4	0	1	5	0
Cameron, Stanton, Calgary	1.000	7	10	0	0	10	0
Cangelosi, John, Tucson*	.986	29	67	2	1	70	0
Carvajal, Jovino, Vancouver	.980	38	92	5	2	99	0
Cedeno, Roger, Albuquerque	.985	94	189	3	3	195	0
Cianfrocco, Archi, Las Vegas	1.000	14	23	1	0	24	0
Cockrell, Alan, C.S.	.981	87	153	5	3	161	1
Cohick, Emmitt, Vancouver*	.905	7	19	0	2	21	0
Colbert, Craig, Las Vegas	1.000	2	3	1	0	4	0
Cookson, Brent, Phoenix	.967	56	86	2	3	91	1
Cummings, Midre, Calgary	.943	41	96	4	6	106	1
Dalesandro, Mark, Vancouver	1.000	18	33	1	0	34	0
Daugherty, Jack, Phoenix*	.909	7	10	0	1	11	0
Deer, Rob, Van.-L.V.	.963	49	77	0	3	80	0
Delarosa, Juan, Salt Lake	1.000	23	42	1	0	43	0
Demetral, Chris, Albuquerque	.952	16	18	2	1	21	1
Diaz, Alex, Tacoma	1.000	9	15	1	0	16	0
Durant, Mike, Salt Lake	1.000	3	5	0	0	5	0
Faneyte, Rikkert, Phoenix	.944	36	83	2	5	90	1
Flora, Kevin, Vancouver	.986	35	65	4	1	70	1
Franklin, Micah, Calgary	.965	100	162	3	6	171	0
Garcia, Karim, Albuquerque*	.932	122	185	7	14	206	0
Grebeck, Brian, Vancouver	1.000	12	11	0	0	11	0
Guerrero, Juan, Tucson	1.000	4	10	0	0	10	0
Hajek, Dave, Tucson	1.000	1	2	0	0	2	0
Hansen, Terrel, Tacoma	1.000	5	3	0	0	3	0
Hatcher, Chris, Tucson	1.000	6	9	0	0	9	0
Hazlett, Steve, Salt Lake	.986	124	273	13	4	290	0
Hollandsworth, Todd, Albuq.*	1.000	10	19	3	0	22	0
Hosey, Steve, Vancouver	.962	15	22	3	1	26	0
Hubbard, Trent, C.S.	.980	120	285	11	6	302	0
Humphreys, Mike, Tacoma	.955	15	21	0	1	22	0
Hunter, Brian, Tucson	1.000	37	91	1	0	92	0
Hyers, Tim, Las Vegas*	.953	23	40	1	2	43	0
Ingram, Garey, Albuquerque	1.000	19	25	0	0	25	0
Ingram, Riccardo, Salt Lake	.990	112	197	10	2	209	0
Jackson, John, Van.-S.L.*	.981	83	155	4	3	162	0
Jones, Dax, Phoenix	.980	105	284	9	6	299	0
Knabenshue, Chris, Calgary	1.000	2	1	0	0	1	0
Landrum, Ced, C.S.	.961	46	70	3	3	76	0
Latham, Chris, Albuquerque	1.000	5	7	0	0	7	0
Lennon, Pat, Salt Lake	1.000	6	10	0	0	10	0
Leonard, Mark, Phoenix	.976	89	154	9	4	167	3
Litton, Greg, Tacoma	1.000	3	2	1	0	3	0
Lott, Billy, Albuquerque	.988	40	76	4	1	81	3
Lydy, Scott, Edmonton	.968	92	202	12	7	221	1
Mack, Quinn, Tacoma*	.960	56	94	3	4	101	3
Maksudian, Mike, Edmonton	1.000	19	23	1	0	24	0
Marrero, Oreste, Albuquerque*	1.000	5	8	0	0	8	0
Martin, Jim, Albuquerque	.971	24	34	0	1	35	0
Martinez, Chito, C.S.*	.981	27	50	1	1	52	0
Mashore, Damon, Edmonton	.981	114	197	12	4	213	1
Masteller, Dan, Salt Lake*	1.000	31	53	2	0	55	0
Maurer, Ron, Albuquerque	1.000	8	12	0	0	12	0
McCarty, Dave, Phoenix*	1.000	3	3	1	0	4	0
McCracken, Quinton, C.S.	.991	57	104	5	1	110	1
McDavid, Ray, Las Vegas	1.000	49	134	0	0	134	0
Mercedes, Luis, Calgary	.940	25	43	4	3	50	2
Miller, Damian, Salt Lake	1.000	1	1	0	0	1	0
Montgomery, Ray, Tucson	.965	87	182	10	7	199	3
Moore, Kerwin, Edmonton	.974	63	147	5	4	156	2
Mora, Melvin, Tucson	1.000	2	2	0	0	2	0
Mouton, James, Tucson	.500	3	1	0	1	2	0
Murray, Calvin, Phoenix	1.000	13	19	2	0	21	0
Newfield, Marc, Tac.-L.V.	.971	49	99	2	3	104	0
Noland, J.D., Tacoma	.947	42	68	4	4	76	1
Northrup, Kevin, Edmonton	.933	10	12	2	1	15	0
Ortiz, Ray, Phoenix*	1.000	26	29	2	0	31	0
Osik, Keith, Calgary	1.000	3	1	0	0	1	0
PALMEIRO, Orlando, Vancouver	.995	103	192	4	1	197	2
Parker, Rick, Albuquerque	.975	44	78	1	2	81	0
Peguero, Julio, Tacoma	1.000	7	9	1	0	10	0
Plantier, Phil, Tucson	1.000	9	9	0	0	9	0
Pose, Scott, Alb.-S.L.	.980	66	92	8	2	102	0
Pritchett, Chris, Vancouver	1.000	1	4	0	0	4	0
Pulliam, Harvey, C.S.	.985	112	186	8	3	197	6
Ramos, Ken, Tucson*	.988	100	165	5	2	172	1
Ratliff, Daryl, Calgary	.978	79	177	4	4	185	0
Riley, Marquis, Vancouver	.994	119	326	2	2	330	0
Roberson, Kevin, Tacoma	.981	29	51	2	1	54	0
Shelton, Ben, Salt Lake*	1.000	2	3	0	0	3	0
Sherman, Darrell, Tacoma*	.974	112	252	12	7	271	1
Simmons, Nelson, Calgary	.965	35	51	4	2	57	2
Simms, Mike, Tucson	.964	34	48	6	2	56	1
Simons, Mitch, Salt Lake	1.000	12	12	0	0	12	0
Smiley, Reuben, Las Vegas*	.933	26	41	1	3	45	0
Smith, Ira, Las Vegas	.957	54	87	3	4	94	1
Snider, Van, Salt Lake	1.000	22	33	2	0	35	0
Snyder, Cory, Las Vegas	1.000	6	8	1	0	9	0
Spearman, Vernon, Albuquerque*	1.000	8	11	0	0	11	0
Springer, Steve, Las Vegas	.800	3	4	0	1	5	0
Sweeney, Mark, Vancouver*	.988	38	80	1	1	82	0
Thurman, Gary, Tacoma	.965	86	180	13	7	200	2
Tomberlin, Andy, Edmonton*	.929	12	25	1	2	28	0
Turang, Brian, Tacoma	.982	30	56	0	1	57	0
Turner, Chris, Vancouver	1.000	3	11	0	0	11	0
Vatcher, Jim, Las Vegas	.994	95	164	8	1	173	3
Vaughn, Derek, Vancouver	1.000	1	3	0	0	3	0
Wehner, John, Calgary	1.000	5	7	0	0	7	0
Widger, Chris, Tacoma	1.000	6	13	1	0	14	0
Williams, Keith, Phoenix	1.000	19	38	1	0	39	0
Williams, Reggie, Albuquerque	1.000	61	141	10	0	151	4
Wolfe, Joel, Edmonton	.923	11	12	0	1	13	0
Young, Ernie, Edmonton	.971	90	194	7	6	207	0

OUTFIELDERS WITH TWO OR MORE TEAMS

Player, Team	Pct.	G	PO	A	E	TC	DP
Deer, Rob, Vancouver	.917	9	11	0	1	12	0
Deer, Rob, Las Vegas	.971	40	66	0	2	68	0
Jackson, John, Vancouver*	1.000	31	56	3	0	59	0
Jackson, John, Salt Lake*	.971	52	99	1	3	103	0
Newfield, Marc, Tacoma	.966	30	55	1	2	58	0
Newfield, Marc, Las Vegas	.978	19	44	1	1	46	0
Pose, Scott, Albuquerque	1.000	4	2	0	0	2	0
Pose, Scott, Salt Lake	.980	62	90	8	2	100	0

CATCHERS

Player, Team	Pct.	G	PO	A	E	TC	DP	PB
Beard, Garrett, Edmonton	.977	17	75	10	2	87	1	0
Bellinger, Clay, Phoenix	1.000	1	2	0	0	2	0	0
Brito, Jorge, C.S.	.983	31	163	13	3	179	2	2
Chavez, Raul, Tucson	.980	32	203	39	5	247	3	4
Christopherson, Eric, Phoenix	.993	91	543	44	4	591	6	5
Cianfrocco, Archi, Las Vegas	1.000	1	1	0	0	1	0	0
Colbert, Craig, Las Vegas	.985	69	343	42	6	391	4	8
Dalesandro, Mark, Vancouver	1.000	4	10	0	0	10	0	0
Durant, Mike, Salt Lake	.990	70	354	30	4	388	3	2
Ehmann, Kurt, Phoenix	.750	1	3	0	1	4	0	2
Encarnacion, Angelo, Calgary	.984	21	113	14	2	129	1	3
Fabregas, Jorge, Vancouver	.969	21	112	12	4	128	2	0
Goff, Jerry, Tucson	.989	62	336	39	4	379	5	12
Greene, Todd, Vancouver	.995	30	175	17	1	193	1	5
Hanel, Marcus, Calgary	.923	2	12	0	1	13	0	1
Helfand, Eric, Edmonton	.968	16	79	11	3	93	2	1
Horn, Jeff, Salt Lake	1.000	3	18	1	0	19	0	2
Howard, Chris, Tacoma	.987	77	405	47	6	458	3	8
Huckaby, Ken, Albuquerque	.973	80	515	61	16	592	5	9
Kreuter, Chad, Tacoma	.988	14	70	10	1	81	3	1
Litton, Greg, Tacoma	1.000	2	2	0	0	2	0	0
Makarewicz, Scott, Tucson	.981	61	338	28	7	373	8	2
Maksudian, Mike, Edmonton	.989	54	241	33	3	277	2	8
Marx, Tim, Calgary	.977	54	268	27	7	302	5	5
Maurer, Ron, Albuquerque	1.000	5	18	3	0	21	0	0
Maynard, Scott, Tacoma	1.000	1	6	0	0	6	0	0
MILLER, Damian, Salt Lake	.998	76	394	52	1	447	5	7
Miller, Roger, Phoenix	.972	41	221	23	7	251	5	2
Mirabelli, Doug, Phoenix	.985	23	115	17	2	134	4	2
Molina, Ben, Vancouver	1.000	1	4	0	0	4	0	0
Molina, Izzy, Edmonton	1.000	2	9	1	0	10	0	0
Monzon, Jose, Vancouver	1.000	13	41	5	0	46	0	2
Mulligan, Sean, Las Vegas	.987	82	439	33	6	478	5	11
Munoz, Noe, Albuquerque	.991	19	89	16	1	106	1	3
Nokes, Matt, C.S.	.979	8	43	3	1	47	1	0
Osik, Keith, Calgary	.990	74	372	24	4	400	3	6
Owens, Jayhawk, C.S.	.989	68	390	46	5	441	8	4
Pevey, Marty, Tacoma	1.000	7	36	1	0	37	0	1
Prince, Tom, Albuquerque	.989	55	310	34	4	348	7	3
Sealy, Scot, Tacoma	.933	4	14	0	1	15	0	1
Strittmatter, Mark, C.S.	.973	5	32	4	1	37	0	0
Tatum, Jim, C.S.	.667	1	2	0	1	3	0	0
Tejero, Fausto, Vancouver	.995	37	186	29	1	216	3	2
Thurston, Jerrey, Las Vegas	.976	5	36	4	1	41	0	1
Turner, Chris, Vancouver	.990	51	282	23	3	308	2	5
Wakamatsu, Don, Tacoma	.952	9	53	6	3	62	1	0
Walters, Dan, C.S.	.984	48	222	17	4	243	2	3
Widger, Chris, Tacoma	.980	37	176	21	4	201	3	4
Wilkins, Rick, Tucson	1.000	4	27	4	0	31	0	1
Willard, Jerry, Tacoma	1.000	12	38	0	0	38	0	1
Williams, George, Edmonton	.981	64	310	44	7	361	6	4

PITCHERS

Player, Team	Pct.	G	PO	A	E	TC	DP
Acevedo, Juan, C.S.	1.000	3	2	0	0	2	0
Adams, Willie, Edmonton	1.000	11	5	8	0	13	0
Akerfelds, Darrel, Vancouver	1.000	9	3	7	0	10	0
Alicea, Miguel, Albuquerque	1.000	7	1	2	0	3	0
Apana, Matt, Tacoma	.895	21	7	10	2	19	1
Arvesen, Scott, Las Vegas	1.000	2	0	2	0	2	0
August, Don, Calgary	1.000	2	1	0	0	1	0
Ayrault, Bob, Calgary	.500	6	0	1	1	2	0
Backlund, Brett, Calgary	1.000	12	4	4	0	8	0
Bailey, Roger, C.S.	1.000	3	0	1	0	1	0
Baker, Scott, Edmonton*	.955	22	4	17	1	22	0
Bankhead, Scott, Edmonton	1.000	12	1	2	0	3	0
Barcelo, Marc, Salt Lake	.938	28	8	22	2	32	0
Barton, Shawn, Phoenix*	.667	15	2	2	2	6	0
Bennett, Erik, Van.-Tuc.	1.000	42	3	7	0	10	0
Bittiger, Jeff, Edmonton	.833	6	3	2	1	6	0
Bochtler, Doug, Las Vegas	1.000	18	1	3	0	4	0
Bourgeois, Steve, Phoenix	1.000	6	4	2	0	6	0
Bowie, Jim, Edmonton*	1.000	7	0	3	0	3	2
Brink, Brad, Pho.-Edm.	1.000	20	6	12	0	18	0
Briscoe, John, Edmonton	1.000	3	1	0	0	1	0
Brocail, Doug, Tucson	.750	3	0	3	1	4	0
Brock, Russ, Edmonton	.875	18	2	5	1	8	1
Brosnan, Jason, Albuquerque*	1.000	23	1	0	0	1	0
Bruske, Jim, Albuquerque	.958	43	2	21	1	24	1
Bryant, Shawn, Salt Lake*	.875	31	1	6	1	8	0
Bullard, Jason, C.S.	1.000	4	0	1	0	1	0
Burcham, Tim, Phoenix	1.000	5	1	1	0	2	0
Burgos, Enrique, Phoenix*	.800	41	0	4	1	5	0
Burke, John, C.S.	.933	19	4	10	1	15	2
Bustillos, Albert, C.S.	.962	34	6	19	1	26	1
Butler, Mike, Vancouver*	1.000	3	0	3	0	3	0
Cadaret, Greg, Las Vegas*	.923	28	1	11	1	13	2
Campbell, Kevin, Tacoma	.909	31	3	7	1	11	1
Carlson, Dan, Phoenix	.960	23	11	13	1	25	1
Carmona, Rafael, Tacoma	.929	8	5	8	1	14	0
Castillo, Juan, Tucson	.750	11	4	2	2	8	0
Chavez, Tony, Vancouver	1.000	8	1	2	0	3	0
Clayton, Royal, Phoenix	1.000	5	5	12	0	17	1
Cole, Victor, Las Vegas	.750	4	2	1	1	4	0
Conroy, Brian, C.S.	1.000	5	3	2	0	5	0
Converse, Jim, Tacoma	1.000	17	3	7	0	10	2
Corbin, Archie, Calgary	.882	47	9	6	2	17	2
Courtright, John, Salt Lake*	.960	18	5	19	1	25	0
Cromwell, Nate, Las Vegas*	1.000	9	1	6	0	7	0
Crowther, Brent, C.S.	1.000	1	0	2	0	2	0
Czajkowski, Jim, C.S.	.941	60	6	10	1	17	1
Daal, Omar, Albuquerque*	.900	17	1	8	1	10	2
Darwin, Jeff, Tacoma	1.000	46	3	6	0	9	1
Daspit, Jim, Tuc.-Edm.	.909	38	3	7	1	11	0
Davis, Tim, Tacoma*	1.000	2	1	0	0	1	0
Davison, Scott, Tacoma	1.000	8	2	2	0	4	0
DeLosSantos, Mariano, Calgary	.882	14	6	9	2	17	0
Dishman, Glenn, Las Vegas*	1.000	14	6	21	0	27	0
Dougherty, Jim, Tucson	1.000	8	0	1	0	1	0
Edenfield, Ken, Vancouver	.857	33	2	10	2	14	3
Edwards, Wayne, Albuquerque*	.909	14	5	5	1	11	1
Eischen, Joey, Albuquerque*	1.000	13	1	0	0	1	0
Elliott, Donnie, Las Vegas	1.000	7	0	1	0	1	0
Ericks, John, Calgary	1.000	5	2	3	0	5	0
Ettles, Mark, Las Vegas	1.000	10	1	0	0	1	1
Evans, Dave, Tucson	1.000	2	0	1	0	1	0
Fesh, Sean, Tuc.-L.V.*	1.000	40	1	9	0	10	0
Flynt, Bill, Calgary*	1.000	12	0	3	0	3	0
Fortugno, Tim, Vancouver*	1.000	10	0	2	0	2	0
Fredrickson, Scott, C.S.	1.000	58	4	16	0	20	0
Gallaher, Kevin, Tucson	1.000	3	1	0	0	1	0
Gamez, Bob, Phoenix*	1.000	36	1	10	0	11	1
Gandarillas, Gus, Salt Lake	1.000	22	3	8	0	11	1
Garcia, Jose, Albuquerque	1.000	11	1	5	0	6	0
Gardner, Chris, Tucson	.857	16	0	6	1	7	1
Gavaghan, Sean, Salt Lake	.923	35	2	10	1	13	1
Gibson, Paul, Calgary*	.500	19	0	1	1	2	0
Glinatsis, George, Tacoma	1.000	8	2	7	0	9	1
Gomez, Pat, Phoenix*	.667	2	0	2	1	3	1
Grahe, Joe, C.S.	1.000	2	0	3	0	3	0
Graybill, Dave, Tacoma	1.000	6	1	0	0	1	0
Green, Otis, Tacoma*	1.000	18	2	5	0	7	0
Greer, Ken, Phoenix	1.000	38	3	8	0	11	0
Grundt, Ken, C.S.*	1.000	9	1	1	0	2	0
Guetterman, Lee, Tacoma*	1.000	33	7	9	0	16	0
Hancock, Lee, Calgary*	.964	34	5	22	1	28	2
Hansell, Greg, Alb.-S.L.	1.000	15	4	8	0	12	0
Harikkala, Tim, Tacoma	.926	25	11	14	2	27	3
Harriger, Denny, Las Vegas	.977	29	16	27	1	44	4
Hartgraves, Dean, Tucson*	1.000	14	0	1	0	1	0
Hathaway, Hilly, Las Vegas*	.944	14	4	13	1	18	1
Hawblitzel, Ryan, C.S.	.933	21	4	10	1	15	0
Hawkins, LaTroy, Salt Lake	.912	22	10	21	3	34	1
Haynes, Heath, Edmonton	1.000	12	1	4	0	5	1
Henry, Jon, Salt Lake	1.000	3	3	2	0	5	0
Heredia, Julian, Vancouver	.900	51	3	6	1	10	0
Hermanson, Dustin, Las Vegas	1.000	31	0	2	0	2	0
Hernandez, Fernando, Las Vegas	1.000	8	2	0	0	2	0
Hill, Milt, Calgary	1.000	24	2	8	0	10	0
Holdridge, David, Vancouver	.800	11	1	3	1	5	0
Hollins, Stacy, Edmonton	1.000	7	2	5	0	7	0
Holman, Brad, Tacoma	.500	5	1	0	1	2	0
Holman, Shawn, Albuquerque	1.000	49	3	12	0	15	0

Player, Team	Pct.	G	PO	A	E	TC	DP
Holt, Chris, Tucson	.943	20	9	24	2	35	1
Holzemer, Mark, Vancouver*	.944	28	7	10	1	18	0
Hook, Chris, Phoenix	1.000	4	0	1	0	1	0
Hope, John, Calgary	1.000	13	14	17	0	31	2
Horsman, Vince, Salt Lake*	1.000	16	1	0	0	1	0
Hostetler, Tom, Edmonton	1.000	4	2	1	0	3	0
Huisman, Rick, Tucson	.818	42	5	4	2	11	1
Hunter, Jim, C.S.	1.000	10	0	8	0	8	0
Janicki, Pete, Vancouver	1.000	9	2	4	0	6	0
Johns, Doug, Edmonton*	.907	23	13	26	4	43	1
Johnson, Judd, Salt Lake*	1.000	17	1	6	0	7	0
Johnston, Joel, C.S.	1.000	18	0	2	0	2	0
Jones, Bobby, C.S.*	.889	11	2	6	1	9	0
Jones, Stacy, Phoenix	1.000	4	0	1	0	1	0
Keagle, Greg, Las Vegas	.933	14	5	9	1	15	0
Keling, Korey, Vancouver	1.000	3	0	3	0	3	0
Ketchen, Doug, Tucson	.824	19	6	8	3	17	1
Kile, Darryl, Tucson	1.000	4	2	5	0	7	0
King, Kevin, Tacoma*	.750	16	0	3	1	4	0
Knudsen, Kurt, Phoenix	1.000	11	0	3	0	3	0
Kotarski, Mike, C.S.*	1.000	22	1	2	0	3	0
Krueger, Bill, Tacoma*	.917	10	1	10	1	12	0
Kubinski, Tim, Edmonton*	.889	6	2	6	1	9	0
Leftwich, Phil, Vancouver	1.000	6	4	7	0	11	0
Leiper, Dave, Edmonton*	1.000	2	1	0	0	1	0
Lewis, Scott, Tacoma	1.000	3	1	1	0	2	0
Lieber, Jon, Calgary	.867	14	7	6	2	15	0
Lilliquist, Derek, Albuquerque*	1.000	13	1	4	0	5	1
Logsdon, Kevin, C.S.*	1.000	2	1	0	0	1	0
Loiselle, Rich, L.V.-Tuc.	.800	10	2	2	1	5	0
Long, Joey, Las Vegas*	.833	25	1	4	1	6	0
Lorraine, Andrew, Vancouver*	1.000	18	7	15	0	22	2
Mack, Tony, Vancouver	1.000	4	1	5	0	6	0
Manzanillo, Ravelo, Calgary*	1.000	8	1	2	0	3	0
Martinez, Jose, Las Vegas	.970	27	11	21	1	33	1
Martinez, Pedro, Tucson*	.889	20	0	8	1	9	1
Mauser, Tim, Las Vegas	.778	35	1	6	2	9	0
Maysey, Matt, Calgary	.947	44	5	13	1	19	0
McCarthy, Tom, Albuquerque	.900	13	3	6	1	10	0
McCurry, Jeff, Calgary	1.000	3	0	2	0	2	0
McFarlin, Terric, Las Vegas	.949	58	11	26	2	39	1
McMurtry, Craig, Tucson	.938	13	5	10	1	16	1
Mecir, Jim, Tacoma	.933	40	6	8	1	15	0
Menendez, Tony, Phoenix	1.000	50	4	9	0	13	2
Merriman, Brett, Las Vegas	1.000	11	0	2	0	2	0
Milacki, Bob, Tacoma	.905	12	9	10	2	21	1
Milchin, Mike, Albuquerque*	1.000	18	2	13	0	15	0
Mimbs, Mark, Albuquerque*	1.000	23	4	15	0	19	1
Mintz, Steve, Phoenix	.800	31	1	3	1	5	0
Misuraca, Mike, Salt Lake	.973	31	8	28	1	37	3
Mlicki, Doug, Tucson	1.000	6	6	1	0	7	0
Mohler, Mike, Edmonton*	1.000	29	2	11	0	13	0
Montalvo, Rafael, Albuquerque	.833	49	7	18	5	30	1
Monteleone, Rich, Vancouver	1.000	7	1	4	0	5	0
Morman, Alvin, Tucson*	.917	45	3	8	1	12	0
Morrison, Keith, Vancouver	.974	28	14	23	1	38	0
Mulholland, Terry, Phoenix*	.000	1	0	0	1	1	0
Munoz, Oscar, Salt Lake	.909	19	8	12	2	22	2
Naulty, Dan, Salt Lake	1.000	42	3	5	0	8	1
Nied, David, C.S.	1.000	7	4	6	0	10	1
O'Donoghue, John, Albuquerque*	1.000	25	6	12	0	18	1
Olivares, Omar, C.S.	1.000	3	0	2	0	2	0
Osuna, Antonio, Albuquerque	1.000	19	0	2	0	2	0
Painter, Lance, C.S.*	.875	11	1	6	1	8	0
Park, Chan Ho, Albuquerque	.958	23	7	16	1	24	1
Parra, Jose, Albuquerque	.667	12	3	3	3	9	0
Patrick, Bronswell, Tucson	1.000	43	7	4	0	11	0
Patterson, Ken, Vancouver*	1.000	8	1	0	0	1	0
Peek, Tim, Edmonton	1.000	12	2	3	0	5	0
Peever, Lloyd, C.S.	1.000	8	1	4	0	5	0
Phillips, Randy, Phoenix	.882	25	4	11	2	17	2
Phillips, Tony, Tacoma	.957	47	9	13	1	23	1
Phoenix, Steve, Edmonton	1.000	40	8	7	0	15	1
Piatt, Doug, Phoenix	1.000	6	1	2	0	3	0
Powell, Ross, Tucson*	.800	13	0	4	1	5	0
Pulido, Carlos, Salt Lake*	1.000	43	1	11	0	12	1
Pyc, Dave, Albuquerque*	1.000	1	0	1	0	1	0
Ralph, Curtis, Calgary	1.000	28	2	5	0	7	0
Ratekin, Mark, Vancouver	1.000	19	2	8	0	10	0
Rath, Gary, Albuquerque*	1.000	8	0	4	0	4	0
Rekar, Bryan, C.S.	1.000	7	4	8	0	12	2
Renko, Steve, Vancouver	1.000	10	5	3	0	8	0
Revenig, Todd, Edmonton	.933	45	6	8	1	15	0
Reynoso, Armando, C.S.	.833	5	2	3	1	6	0
Robertson, Rich, Salt Lake*	1.000	7	2	6	0	8	1
Robinson, Scott, Phoenix	.974	31	12	26	1	39	3
Rodriguez, Felix, Albuquerque	1.000	14	3	8	0	11	1
Rogers, Kevin, Phoenix*	1.000	3	0	1	0	1	0
Rohde, Dave, Tucson	1.000	1	0	1	0	1	0
Romanoli, Paul, C.S.*	.750	31	1	2	1	4	0
Roper, John, Phoenix	1.000	1	0	1	0	1	0
Rose, Scott, Edmonton	1.000	5	1	1	0	2	0
Rosselli, Joe, Phoenix*	1.000	13	1	7	0	8	1
Ryan, Matt, Calgary	1.000	5	0	1	0	1	0
Rychel, Kevin, Calgary	1.000	10	1	2	0	3	0
Sager, A.J., C.S.	.968	23	10	20	1	31	1
St. Claire, Randy, Calgary	.947	54	2	16	1	19	1
Salkeld, Roger, Tacoma	1.000	4	2	0	0	2	0
Sanchez, Alex, Edmonton	1.000	8	1	6	0	7	0
Schullstrom, Erik, Salt Lake	1.000	10	1	0	0	1	0
Scott, Darryl, C.S.	1.000	59	6	15	0	21	1
Sepeda, Jamie, Tucson	1.000	8	5	8	0	13	0
Shaw, Curtis, Edmonton*	.862	42	6	19	4	29	4
Shifflett, Steve, C.S.	1.000	23	4	6	0	10	0
Shouse, Brian, Calgary*	.833	8	2	3	1	6	0
Simas, Bill, Vancouver	.875	30	3	4	1	8	0
Small, Mark, Tucson	1.000	51	6	5	0	11	1
Smith, Tim, Edmonton	1.000	9	9	5	0	14	0
Springer, Russ, Vancouver	.857	6	3	3	1	7	0
Stanhope, Chuck, Edmonton	1.000	6	0	1	0	1	0
Stevens, Matt, Salt Lake	1.000	7	1	2	0	3	1
Sveum, Dale, Calgary	1.000	2	0	1	0	1	0
Swan, Russ, Edmonton*	.889	17	1	7	1	9	0
Tabaka, Jeff, Las Vegas*	1.000	19	1	1	0	2	0
Taylor, Kerry, Las Vegas	1.000	8	1	5	0	6	0
Taylor, Scott, Calgary*	1.000	27	8	27	0	35	6
Telford, Anthony, Edmonton	.857	8	5	7	2	14	0
Thompson, John, Tacoma	.000	1	0	0	1	1	0
Thompson, Mark, C.S.	1.000	11	3	5	0	8	1
Torres, Salomon, Pho.-Tac.	.900	6	3	6	1	10	1
Treadwell, Jody, Albuquerque	.826	30	1	18	4	23	2
Trlicek, Rick, Phoenix	.875	38	2	12	2	16	1
Trombley, Mike, Salt Lake	1.000	12	7	6	0	13	0
Valdez, Carlos, Phoenix	.800	18	0	4	1	5	0
Valdez, Sergio, Phoenix	1.000	18	9	14	0	23	2
Valera, Julio, Vancouver	.800	13	3	5	2	10	0
Vanderweele, Doug, Phoenix	.889	11	5	3	1	9	0
VanRyn, Ben, Vancouver*	1.000	11	3	3	0	6	0
Villone, Ron, Tacoma*	.800	22	0	4	1	5	0
Wagner, Billy, Tucson*	.933	13	2	12	1	15	0
Wagner, Matt, Tacoma	1.000	6	0	2	0	2	1
Waldron, Joe, Tucson*	1.000	4	0	1	0	1	0
WALL, Donne, Tucson	1.000	28	13	40	0	53	2
Waring, Jim, Tucson	1.000	5	1	2	0	3	0
Wasdin, John, Edmonton	.909	29	15	15	3	33	0
Watkins, Scott, Salt Lake*	.818	45	2	7	2	11	0
Watson, Ron, Vancouver	1.000	5	1	0	0	1	0
Weber, Weston, Tac.-L.V.	.971	29	17	17	1	35	1
Wengert, Don, Edmonton	1.000	16	2	5	0	7	1
Westbrook, Destry, Tucson	1.000	5	1	0	0	1	1
Whitaker, Steve, Phoenix*	1.000	16	1	14	0	15	1
White, Chris, Tucson	1.000	5	0	2	0	2	0
White, Rick, Calgary	1.000	14	5	4	0	9	0
Williams, Jeff, Tacoma	1.000	8	2	3	0	5	0
Williams, Shad, Vancouver	1.000	25	11	18	0	29	2
Williams, Todd, Albuquerque	.909	25	3	7	1	11	1
Willis, Carl, Vancouver	1.000	20	2	4	0	6	0
Willis, Travis, Calgary	1.000	22	8	7	0	15	0
Wilson, Gary, Calgary	1.000	6	1	6	0	7	0
Winston, Darrin, Calgary*	1.000	53	2	6	0	8	0
Wissler, Bill, Salt Lake	1.000	37	3	11	0	14	2
Wojciechowski, Steve, Edmonton*	1.000	14	6	17	0	23	0
Wolcott, Bob, Tacoma	1.000	13	3	8	0	11	0
Worrell, Tim, Las Vegas	1.000	10	0	4	0	4	0

PITCHERS WITH TWO OR MORE TEAMS

Player, Team	Pct.	G	PO	A	E	TC	DP
Bennett, Erik, Vancouver	1.000	28	3	4	0	7	0
Bennett, Erik, Tucson	1.000	14	0	3	0	3	0
Brink, Brad, Phoenix	1.000	11	4	8	0	12	0
Brink, Brad, Edmonton	1.000	9	2	4	0	6	0
Daspit, Jim, Tucson	.909	36	3	7	1	11	0
Daspit, Jim, Edmonton	.000	2	0	0	0	0	0
Fesh, Sean, Tucson*	1.000	10	1	1	0	2	0
Fesh, Sean, Las Vegas*	1.000	30	0	8	0	8	0
Hansell, Greg, Albuquerque	1.000	8	0	4	0	4	0

Player, Team	Pct.	G	PO	A	E	TC	DP
Hansell, Greg, Salt Lake	1.000	7	4	4	0	8	0
Loiselle, Rich, Las Vegas	1.000	8	2	1	0	3	0
Loiselle, Rich, Tucson	.500	2	0	1	1	2	0
Torres, Salomon, Phoenix	1.000	1	0	1	0	1	0
Torres, Salomon, Tacoma	.889	5	3	5	1	9	1
Weber, Weston, Tacoma	1.000	20	14	15	0	29	1
Weber, Weston, Las Vegas	.833	9	3	2	1	6	0

The following players did not have any fielding statistics at the positions indicated or appeared only as a designated hitter, pinch-hitter or pinch-runner: Ball, 2b; Beard, 1b; C. Bennett, p; Berumen, p; Bielecki, p; Boskie, p; Bream, of, p; Sc. Bryant, p; N. Castro, p; Colbert, 3b, p; Correa, p; Corsi, p; J. Cummings, p; Deer, p; Demetral, p; Fermin, ss; Gardella, p; Goff, 3b; Gould, p; Griffey, dh; W. Guerrero, of; Hall, of; Jean, p; Jimenez, p; Je. Martinez, p; Maurer, p; Murphy, p; Osik, p; Parker, ss; Plantenberg, p; Pose, p; Risley, p; Rohde, of; Sanders, p; Sanford, p; Saunders, ss; Schmitt, p; Serafini, p; I. Smith, 3b; Whitehurst, p; G. Williams, of.

LEAGUE CHAMPIONS

Year	Team	Pct.
1903—	Los Angeles	.630
1904—	Tacoma	.589
	Tacoma§	.571
	Los Angeles§	.571
1905—	Tacoma	.583
	Los Angeles*	.604
1906—	Portland	.657
1907—	Los Angeles	.608
1908—	Los Angeles	.585
1909—	San Francisco	.623
1910—	Portland	.567
1911—	Portland	.589
1912—	Oakland	.591
1913—	Portland	.559
1914—	Portland	.574
1915—	San Francisco	.570
1916—	Los Angeles	.601
1917—	San Francisco	.561
1918—	Vernon	.569
	Los Angeles (2nd)◆	.548
1919—	Vernon	.613
1920—	Vernon	.556
1921—	Los Angeles	.574
1922—	San Francisco	.638
1923—	San Francisco	.617
1924—	Seattle	.545
1925—	San Francisco	.643
1926—	Los Angeles	.599
1927—	Oakland	.615
1928—	San Francisco*	.630
	Sacramento∞	.626
	San Francisco∞	.626
1929—	Mission	.643
	Hollywood*	.592
1930—	Los Angeles	.576
	Hollywood*	.650
1931—	Hollywood	.626
	San Francisco*	.608
1932—	Portland	.587
1933—	Los Angeles	.610
1934—	Los Angeles▼	.786
	Los Angeles▼	.689
1935—	Los Angeles	.648
	San Francisco*	.608
1936—	Portland‡	.549
1937—	Sacramento	.573
	San Diego (3rd)†	.545
1938—	Los Angeles	.590
	Sacramento (3rd)†	.537
1939—	Seattle	.589
	Sacramento (4th)†	.500
1940—	Seattle‡	.629
1941—	Seattle‡	.598
1942—	Sacramento	.590
	Seattle (3rd)†	.539
1943—	Los Angeles	.710
	S. Francisco (2nd)†	.574
1944—	Los Angeles	.586
	S. Francisco (3rd)†	.509
1945—	Portland	.622
	S. Francisco (4th)†	.525
1946—	San Francisco‡	.628
1947—	Los Angeles▲	.567
1948—	Oakland‡	.606
1949—	Hollywood‡	.583
1950—	Oakland	.590
1951—	Seattle‡	.593
1952—	Hollywood	.606
1953—	Hollywood	.589
1954—	San Diego■	.604
1955—	Seattle	.552
1956—	Los Angeles	.637
1957—	San Francisco	.601
1958—	Phoenix	.578
1959—	Salt Lake City	.552
1960—	Spokane	.601
1961—	Tacoma	.630
1962—	San Diego	.604
1963—	Spokane	.620
	Oklahoma City•	.632
1964—	Arkansas	.609
	San Diego•	.576
1965—	Oklahoma City a	.628
	Portland	.547
1966—	Seattle•	.561
	Tulsa	.578
1967—	San Diego•	.574
	Spokane	.541
1968—	Tulsa•	.642
	Spokane	.586
1969—	Tacoma•	.589
	Eugene	.603
1970—	Spokane•	.644
	Hawaii	.671
1971—	Salt Lake City	.534
	Tacoma	.545
1972—	Albuquerque	.622
	Eugene	.534
1973—	Tucson	.583
	Spokane•	.563
1974—	Spokane•	.549
	Albuquerque	.535
1975—	Salt Lake City	.556
	Hawaii•	.611
1976—	Salt Lake City	.625
	Hawaii•	.531
1977—	Phoenix•	.579
	Hawaii	.541
1978—	Tacoma††	.584
	Albuquerque††	.557
1979—	Albuquerque	.581
	Salt Lake City‡‡	.541
1980—	Albuquerque	.578
	Hawaii	.539
1981—	Albuquerque*	.712
	Tacoma	.561
1982—	Albuquerque*	.594
	Spokane	.545
1983—	Albuquerque	.594
	Portland*	.528
1984—	Hawaii	.621
	Edmonton*	.486
1985—	Vancouver*	.522
	Phoenix	.563
1986—	Vancouver	.616
	Las Vegas*	.563
1987—	Calgary	.596
	Albuquerque*	.542
1988—	Vancouver	.599
	Las Vegas*	.529
1989—	Albuquerque	.563
	Vancouver*	.514
1990—	Albuquerque*	.641
	Edmonton	.553
1991—	Albuquerque	.580
	Tucson*	.564
1992—	Colorado Springs*	.596
	Portland	.576
1993—	Portland	.608
	Tucson*	.580
1994—	Albuquerque*	.597
	Vancouver	.542
1995—	Salt Lake	.549
	Colorado Springs*	.538

*Won split-season playoff. †Won four-team playoff. ‡Won pennant and four-team playoff. §Tied for second-half title with Tacoma winning playoff. ∞Tied for second-half title, with Sacramento winning playoff. ▲Ended regular season in tie with San Francisco and won one-game playoff for pennant, then won four-club playoff. ◆Won playoff from first-place Vernon and awarded championship. ■Defeated Hollywood in one-game playoff for pennant. ▼Won both halves, no playoff. •League was divided into Northern, Southern divisions in 1963, 1969-70-71, and Eastern, Western divisions in 1964 through 1968 and 1972 through 1977, won two-team playoff. ††League divided into Eastern and Western divisions, Tacoma and Albuquerque declared co-champions following cancellation of four-team playoff due to continuing rain and wet grounds. ‡‡Won second-half title and defeated Hawaii in four-team playoff.

EASTERN LEAGUE

LEAGUE OFFICE

President
John Levenda

Address
P.O. Box 60687
Harrisburg, PA 17106

Phone
717-233-4909

TEAMS

BINGHAMTON METS

General manager
R.C. Reuteman

Manager
John Tamargo

Ballpark (capacity, surface)
Binghamton Municipal Stadium (6,064, grass)

Affiliation
Mets

Address
P.O. Box 598
Binghamton, NY 13902

Phone
607-723-6387

BOWIE BAYSOX

General manager
Jon Danos

Manager
Jon Danos

Ballpark (capacity, surface)
Prince George's Stadium (10,000, grass)

Affiliation
Orioles

Address
P.O. Box 1661
Bowie, MD 20717

Phone
301-805-6000

CANTON/AKRON INDIANS

General manager
Jeff Auman

Manager
Jeff Datz

Ballpark (capacity, surface)
Thurman Munson Memorial Stadium (5,708, grass)

Affiliation
Indians

Address
2501 Allen Ave. SE
Canton, OH 44707

Phone
216-456-5100

HARDWARE CITY ROCK CATS

General manager
Gerry Berthiaume

Manager
Al Newman

Ballpark (capacity, surface)
Beehive Field (4,700, grass)

Affiliation
Twins

Address
P.O. Box 1718
New Britain, CT 06050

Phone
203-224-8383

HARRISBURG SENATORS

General manager
Todd Vander Woude

Manager
Pat Kelly

Ballpark (capacity, surface)
RiverSide Stadium (6,300, grass)

Affiliation
Expos

Address
P.O. Box 15757
Harrisburg, PA 17105

Phone
717-231-4444

NEW HAVEN RAVENS

General manager
Charles Dowd

Manager
Bill Hayes

Ballpark (capacity, surface)
Yale Field (6,200, grass)

Affiliation
Rockies

Address
63 Grove St.
New Haven, CT 06511

Phone
1-800-728-3671

NORWICH NAVIGATORS

General manager
George Brzezinski

Manager
Jim Essian

Ballpark (capacity, surface)
Name to be announced (7,000, grass)

Affiliation
Yankees

Address
P.O. Box 6003
Yantic, CT 06389

Phone
203-887-7962

PORTLAND SEA DOGS

General manager
Charles Eshbach

Manager
Carlos Tosca

Ballpark (capacity, surface)
Hadlock Field (6,000, grass)

Affiliation
Marlins

Address
P.O. Box 636
Portland, ME 04104

Phone
207-874-9300

READING PHILLIES

General manager
Chuck Domino

Manager
Bill Robinson

Ballpark (capacity, surface)
Municipal Memorial Stadium (8,000, grass)

Affiliation
Phillies

Address
P.O. Box 15050
Reading, PA 19610

Phone
610-375-8469

TRENTON THUNDER

General manager
Wayne Hodes

Manager
Ken Macha

Ballpark (capacity, surface)
Mercer County Waterfront Park (6,300, grass)

Affiliation
Red Sox

Address
One Thunder Road
Trenton, NJ 08611

Phone
609-394-8326

1995 FINAL STANDINGS

NORTHERN DIVISION

Team	W	L	T	Pct.	GB
Portland (Marlins)	86	56	0	.606	....
New Haven (Rockies)	79	63	0	.556	7
Norwich (Yankees)	70	71	0	.496	15½
Binghamton (Mets)	67	75	0	.472	19
New Britain (Twins)	65	77	0	.458	21

SOUTHERN DIVISION

Team	W	L	T	Pct.	GB
Trenton (Red Sox)	73	69	0	.514	....
Reading (Phillies)	73	69	0	.514	....
Bowie (Orioles)	68	74	0	.479	5
Canton/Akron (Indians)	67	75	0	.472	6
Harrisburg (Expos)	61	80	0	.433	11½

COMPOSITE

Team	Por.	N.H.	Tre.	Rea.	Nor.	Bow.	C.A.	Bin.	N.B.	Har.	W	L	T	Pct.	GB
Portland (Marlins)	....	10	5	9	13	10	10	10	10	9	86	56	0	.606	....
New Haven (Rockies)	8	....	6	8	7	9	10	11	10	10	79	63	0	.556	7
Trenton (Red Sox)	9	8	....	7	4	5	8	10	9	13	73	69	0	.514	13
Reading (Phillies)	5	6	11	....	7	9	7	8	10	10	73	69	0	.514	13
Norwich (Yankees)	5	11	10	7	....	6	10	6	10	5	70	71	0	.496	15½
Bowie (Orioles)	4	5	13	9	8	....	9	7	5	8	68	74	0	.479	18
Canton/Akron (Indians)	4	4	10	11	4	9	....	9	7	9	67	75	0	.472	19
Binghamton (Mets)	8	7	4	6	12	7	5	....	10	8	67	75	0	.472	19
New Britain (Twins)	8	8	5	4	8	9	7	8	....	8	65	77	0	.458	21
Harrisburg (Expos)	5	4	5	8	8	10	9	6	6	....	61	80	0	.433	24½

Major league affiliations in parentheses.

PLAYOFFS: Reading defeated Trenton, three games to none; New Haven defeated Portland, three games to one; Reading defeated New Haven, three game to two, to win league championship.

REGULAR-SEASON ATTENDANCE: Binghamton, 200,077; Bowie, 463,976; Canton/Akron, 195,049; Harrisburg, 240,488; New Britain, 124,560; New Haven, 283,766; Norwich, 281,473; Portland, 429,763; Reading, 383,984; Trenton, 453,915. Total—3,057,051. Playoffs (12 games)—45,913. Class AA All-Star Game at Shreveport—6,247.

MANAGERS: Binghamton, John Tamargo; Bowie, Bob Miscik; Canton/Akron, Ted Kubiak; Harrisburg, Pat Kelly; New Britain, Sal Butera; New Haven, Paul Zuvella; Norwich, Jimmy Johnson; Portland, Carlos Tosca; Reading, Bill Dancy; Trenton, Ken Macha.

ALL-STAR TEAM: 1B—David Kennedy, New Haven; 2B—Todd Walker, New Britain; 3B—Rob Grable, Reading; SS—Nomar Garciaparra, Trenton; OF—Angel Echevarria, New Haven; Billy McMillon, Portland; Jay Payton, Binghamton; C—Mike Figga, Norwich; DH—Clyde "Pork Chop" Pough, Trenton; P—Paul Wilson, Binghamton; Eric Ludwick, Binghamton; Jay Powell, Portland; Dan Serafini, New Britain; Most Valuable Player—Jay Payton, Binghamton; Pitcher of the Year—Paul Wilson, Binghamton; Rookie of the Year—Jay Payton, Binghamton; Manager of the Year—Bill Dancy, Reading.

1995 BATTING

TEAM

Team	Avg.	G	TPA	AB	R	H	TB	2B	3B	HR	RBI	SH	SF	HP	BB	IBB	SO	SB	CS	GDP	LOB	ShO	Slg.	OBP
Portland	.269	142	5541	4783	745	1286	1878	223	45	93	674	63	53	63	577	45	846	140	64	104	1067	4	.393	.352
New Haven	.261	142	5382	4771	699	1243	1784	226	27	87	641	47	38	52	471	20	951	145	57	100	990	7	.374	.331
Norwich	.258	141	5384	4666	635	1206	1802	237	46	89	600	38	50	71	559	33	1066	116	59	91	1053	12	.386	.343
Binghamton	.256	142	5466	4803	638	1231	1770	247	35	74	568	56	55	64	488	30	864	103	58	87	1046	9	.369	.330
Trenton	.256	142	5525	4829	649	1234	1848	239	33	103	584	51	52	64	529	36	935	135	84	99	1044	13	.383	.334
Bowie	.255	142	5370	4678	663	1193	1730	229	16	92	605	29	49	70	542	22	838	126	51	120	1011	11	.370	.338
Canton/Akron	.252	142	5239	4599	557	1158	1680	228	21	84	525	58	41	60	480	26	939	97	65	82	1018	9	.365	.328
Reading	.252	142	5367	4712	672	1186	1834	236	29	118	621	50	42	69	494	30	853	100	66	99	957	10	.389	.329
New Britain	.249	142	5335	4717	627	1175	1776	218	28	109	575	24	43	44	507	22	965	139	58	123	953	11	.377	.325
Harrisburg	.243	141	5215	4591	587	1116	1672	217	24	97	544	66	33	51	469	37	940	89	66	91	938	7	.364	.318

INDIVIDUAL

TOP QUALIFIERS FOR BATTING CHAMPIONSHIP

Minimum 383 plate appearances. *Lefthanded batter. †Switch-hitter.

Player, Team	Avg.	G	TPA	AB	R	H	TB	2B	3B	HR	RBI	SH	SF	HP	BB	IBB	SO	SB	CS	GDP	Slg.	OBP
Payton, Jay, Binghamton	.345	85	390	357	59	123	191	20	3	14	54	0	2	2	29	2	32	16	7	11	.535	.395
McGuire, Ryan, Trenton*	.333	109	477	414	59	138	190	29	1	7	59	4	1	0	58	5	51	11	8	10	.459	.414
McMillon, Billy, Portland*	.313	141	628	518	92	162	239	29	3	14	93	1	5	7	96	5	90	15	9	10	.461	.423
Jacobs, Frank, Bing.-Har.*	.312	101	402	337	56	105	166	22	0	13	60	0	2	5	58	7	56	1	3	5	.493	.418
Kennedy, David, New Haven	.306	128	541	484	75	148	240	22	2	22	96	0	4	5	48	1	131	4	1	12	.496	.372
Katzaroff, Rob, Portland	.304	116	505	441	87	134	188	16	4	10	49	4	4	7	49	3	33	18	10	4	.426	.379
Grable, Rob, Reading	.300	103	427	353	71	106	180	24	1	16	67	1	5	1	67	3	85	15	11	8	.510	.408
Echevarria, Angel, New Haven	.300	124	524	453	78	136	231	30	1	21	100	0	7	8	56	3	93	8	3	8	.510	.382
Horne, Tyrone, Har.-Nor.*	.291	133	554	460	82	134	225	33	5	16	69	3	6	1	84	3	101	18	10	7	.489	.397
Walker, Todd, New Britain*	.290	137	587	513	83	149	245	27	3	21	85	1	8	2	63	1	101	23	9	13	.478	.365
Renteria, Edgar, Portland	.289	135	558	508	70	147	197	15	7	7	68	8	8	2	32	2	85	30	11	10	.388	.329
Selby, Bill, Trenton*	.286	117	510	451	64	129	201	29	2	13	68	2	8	3	46	3	52	4	6	14	.446	.350
Hardtke, Jason, Binghamton†	.286	121	536	455	65	130	192	42	4	4	52	2	9	4	66	1	58	6	8	7	.422	.375
Ogden, Jamie, New Britain*	.284	117	438	384	54	109	172	22	1	13	61	0	5	1	48	5	90	6	5	10	.448	.361
Rogers, Lamarr, New Haven	.283	109	447	371	68	105	120	15	0	0	31	8	3	1	64	1	50	21	7	15	.323	.387

DEPARTMENTAL LEADERS: G—McMillon, 141; AB—Doster, 551; R—Milliard, 104; H—McMillon, 162; TB—Doster, 254; 2B—Hardtke, 42; 3B—Robertson, 10; HR—McNair, 23; RBI—Echevarria, 100; SH—Milliard, 13; SF—Barry, Hardtke, 9; HP—Delvecchio, 23; BB—McMillon, 96; IBB—Clark, 12; SO—Delvecchio, 133; SB—T. Jones, 51; CS—D. Jackson, 22; GIDP—Lucca, 18; Slg.—Pough, .543; OBP—McMillon, .423.

ALL PLAYERS

*Lefthanded batter. †Switch-hitter.

Player, Team	Avg.	G	TPA	AB	R	H	TB	2B	3B	HR	RBI	SH	SF	HP	BB	IBB	SO	SB	CS	GDP	Slg.	OBP
Abad, Andy, Trenton*	.240	89	335	287	29	69	101	14	3	4	32	6	3	3	36	2	58	5	7	6	.352	.328
Agbayani, Benny, Binghamton	.275	88	341	295	38	81	99	11	2	1	26	1	1	5	39	0	51	12	3	6	.336	.368
Alcantara, Israel, Harrisburg	.211	71	262	237	25	50	96	12	2	10	29	1	1	2	21	1	81	1	1	5	.405	.280
Alfonseca, Antonio, Portland	.059	19	18	17	1	1	4	0	0	1	2	1	0	0	0	0	8	0	0	1	.235	.059
Alfonzo, Edgar, Bowie	.304	28	123	112	14	34	43	6	0	1	19	0	1	0	10	1	16	1	2	2	.384	.358
Allen, Matt, Harrisburg	.143	5	16	14	2	2	2	0	0	0	1	0	0	0	2	0	2	0	0	0	.143	.250
Alomar, Sandy, Canton/Akron	.400	6	16	15	3	6	7	1	0	0	1	0	0	0	1	0	1	0	0	1	.467	.438
Alston, Garvin, New Haven	.000	47	5	5	0	0	0	0	0	0	0	0	0	0	0	0	1	0	0	1	.000	.000
Alvarez, Tavo, Harrisburg	1.000	3	4	3	1	3	3	0	0	0	1	1	0	0	0	0	0	0	0	0	1.000	1.000
Aminoff, Matt, New Haven	.000	6	1	1	0	0	0	0	0	0	0	0	0	0	0	0	0	0	0	0	.000	.000
Arnold, Ken, Bowie	.000	10	28	22	3	0	0	0	0	0	0	0	0	0	6	0	8	0	0	1	.000	.214
Arteaga, Ivan, New Haven*	.111	14	9	9	0	1	2	1	0	0	0	0	0	0	0	0	1	0	0	0	.222	.111
Aucoin, Derek, Harrisburg	.000	29	1	1	0	0	0	0	0	0	0	0	0	0	0	0	0	0	0	0	.000	.000
Avila, Rolando, Bowie	.233	16	51	43	8	10	12	2	0	0	4	1	1	0	6	0	8	2	2	0	.279	.320
Azuaje, Jesus, Binghamton	.198	24	102	86	10	17	22	5	0	0	8	3	0	2	11	0	25	1	1	1	.256	.303
Barron, Tony, Harrisburg	.291	29	116	103	20	30	65	5	0	10	23	0	0	2	10	0	21	0	0	8	.631	.365
Barry, Jeff, Binghamton†	.269	80	339	290	49	78	140	17	6	11	53	0	9	9	31	6	61	4	1	4	.483	.348
Bartee, Kimera, Bowie†	.284	53	247	218	45	62	82	9	1	3	19	3	2	1	23	1	45	22	7	1	.376	.352
Bates, Fletcher, Binghamton†	.000	2	9	8	1	0	0	0	0	0	0	0	0	0	1	0	6	0	0	0	.000	.111
Batiste, Kim, Bowie	.358	24	102	95	16	34	51	5	0	4	27	0	1	0	6	0	14	2	0	5	.537	.392
Bautista, Juan, Bowie	.105	13	44	38	3	4	6	2	0	0	0	1	0	2	3	0	5	1	0	3	.158	.209
Beech, Matt, Reading*	.091	14	13	11	0	1	1	0	0	0	0	1	0	0	1	0	4	0	0	0	.091	.167
Benbow, Lou, Binghamton	1.000	3	2	1	0	1	1	0	0	0	0	0	0	0	1	0	0	0	0	0	1.000	1.000
Bennett, Gary, Reading	.236	86	301	271	27	64	87	11	0	4	40	3	2	3	22	1	36	0	0	12	.321	.299
Berrios, Harry, Bowie	.245	56	236	208	32	51	79	13	0	5	21	1	0	1	26	1	44	12	2	6	.380	.332
Biasucci, Joe, Canton/Akron	.244	41	159	135	19	33	47	8	0	2	16	1	1	2	20	0	35	0	0	2	.348	.348
Bigler, Jeff, Reading*	.091	13	53	44	4	4	5	1	0	0	2	1	1	1	6	2	10	0	0	1	.114	.212
Blasingame, Kent, Reading*	.205	86	236	195	38	40	51	4	2	1	17	5	2	5	29	0	43	9	7	3	.262	.320
Blazier, Ron, Reading	.000	57	8	8	0	0	0	0	0	0	0	0	0	0	0	0	2	0	0	0	.000	.000
Blosser, Greg, Trenton*	.246	49	196	179	25	44	90	13	0	11	34	1	3	0	13	0	42	3	2	4	.503	.292
Bournigal, Rafael, Harrisburg	.221	29	114	95	12	21	26	3	1	0	7	6	1	1	11	0	8	1	0	2	.274	.306
Brede, Brent, New Britain*	.274	134	532	449	71	123	164	28	2	3	39	6	5	3	69	2	82	14	6	13	.365	.371
Brito, Luis, Reading†	.333	2	3	3	1	1	1	0	0	0	1	0	0	0	0	0	0	1	0	0	.333	.333
Brophy, E.J., Reading	.500	2	4	4	0	2	3	1	0	0	0	0	0	0	0	0	1	0	0	0	.750	.500
Brown, Jarvis, Bowie	.279	58	259	219	50	61	93	12	1	6	23	2	1	4	33	0	49	12	3	5	.425	.381
Brown, Matt, Trenton	.182	4	12	11	1	2	2	0	0	0	0	0	0	0	1	0	2	0	0	0	.182	.250
Brownson, Mark, New Haven	.000	1	2	2	0	0	0	0	0	0	0	0	0	0	0	0	1	0	0	0	.000	.000
Bryant, Pat, Canton/Akron	.259	127	485	421	60	109	188	22	3	17	59	5	3	4	52	0	116	16	8	5	.447	.344
Buckley, Troy, Harrisburg	.291	48	169	158	16	46	62	10	0	2	15	1	1	0	9	2	19	0	1	2	.392	.327
Bullinger, Kirk, Harrisburg	.000	56	1	1	0	0	0	0	0	0	0	0	0	0	0	0	0	0	0	0	.000	.000
Bullock, Craig, Binghamton	.000	11	1	1	0	0	0	0	0	0	0	0	0	0	0	0	0	0	0	0	.000	.000
Burke, Alan, Reading	.200	11	25	20	5	4	9	2	0	1	3	1	0	3	1	1	6	0	0	0	.450	.333
Burnett, Roger, Norwich	.222	104	398	356	32	79	102	14	0	3	29	7	3	4	28	2	64	3	3	9	.287	.284
Byrd, Anthony, New Britain	.247	123	483	442	54	109	154	20	8	3	51	5	5	3	28	2	85	21	10	13	.348	.293
Byrne, Clayton, Bowie	.218	14	63	55	5	12	19	2	1	1	6	2	2	0	4	0	8	2	1	3	.345	.262
Cabreja, Alexis, Norwich	.091	6	14	11	1	1	1	0	0	0	1	0	0	0	3	0	0	1	0	0	.091	.286
Cabrera, Jolbert, Harrisburg	.286	9	38	35	4	10	12	2	0	0	1	2	0	0	1	0	3	3	1	1	.343	.306
Cairo, Sergio, Harrisburg	.000	4	15	13	0	0	0	0	0	0	0	0	0	1	1	0	2	0	0	1	.000	.133
Cameron, Stanton, Cant./Akron	.256	35	100	82	11	21	32	8	0	1	12	2	2	4	10	0	18	1	0	1	.390	.357
Campbell, Darrin, Cant./Akron	.000	2	7	7	1	0	0	0	0	0	0	0	0	0	0	0	1	0	0	0	.000	.000
Carey, Todd, Trenton*	.272	76	263	228	30	62	99	11	1	8	36	1	2	4	28	0	44	3	4	2	.434	.359
Case, Mike, New Haven	.245	102	364	310	55	76	126	16	2	10	46	3	4	4	43	4	72	6	2	6	.406	.341
Castaldo, Gregg, Bowie	.234	104	322	265	37	62	86	12	3	2	26	7	2	9	39	0	61	5	3	5	.325	.349
Castaneda, Hector, Bowie*	.154	34	76	65	3	10	12	2	0	0	6	0	1	0	10	0	10	0	0	1	.185	.263
Castillo, Ben, Canton/Akron	.224	32	129	116	15	26	43	7	2	2	15	0	1	1	11	0	23	1	2	2	.371	.295
Charbonnet, Mark, Harrisburg*	.251	120	443	407	34	102	148	14	4	8	57	4	6	4	19	6	104	3	6	12	.364	.287
Chavez, Eric, Bowie	.196	14	57	51	5	10	18	2	0	2	4	0	0	1	4	0	17	0	0	1	.353	.268
Chergey, Dan, Portland	.000	55	2	2	0	0	0	0	0	0	0	0	0	0	0	0	2	0	0	0	.000	.000
Chick, Bruce, Harrisburg	.268	12	41	41	4	11	15	2	1	0	6	0	0	0	0	0	9	0	0	1	.366	.268
Clapinski, Chris, Portland†	.236	87	248	208	32	49	76	9	3	4	30	5	5	2	28	2	44	5	2	4	.365	.325
Clark, Tim, Portland*	.271	134	568	499	62	135	197	34	2	8	88	0	7	3	59	12	86	0	5	13	.395	.347
Cosman, Jeff, Binghamton	.417	10	12	12	0	5	5	0	0	0	1	0	0	0	0	0	2	0	1	0	.417	.417
Cradle, Cobi, Binghamton*	.000	2	2	2	0	0	0	0	0	0	0	0	0	0	0	0	0	0	0	0	.000	.000
Crawford, Joe, Binghamton*	.667	42	4	3	1	2	3	1	0	0	2	1	0	0	0	0	0	0	0	0	1.000	.667
Crosby, Mike, Canton/Akron*	.165	75	245	224	18	37	59	5	1	5	20	7	1	3	10	0	60	1	1	4	.263	.210
Crowley, Jim, Bowie	.214	29	123	98	11	21	32	5	0	2	13	0	0	2	23	0	23	1	1	0	.327	.374
Cunnane, Will, Portland	.143	21	10	7	0	1	2	1	0	0	1	3	0	0	0	0	5	0	0	0	.286	.143
Daly, Bob, Binghamton	.000	1	5	4	1	0	0	0	0	0	0	0	0	0	1	1	1	0	0	0	.000	.200
Daubach, Brian, Binghamton*	.245	135	535	469	61	115	174	25	2	10	72	1	7	7	51	5	104	6	2	5	.371	.324
Dauphin, Phil, Harrisburg*	.244	111	454	398	53	97	136	20	2	5	38	3	7	2	43	8	61	17	7	1	.342	.316
Davenport, Adell, Canton/Akron	.276	9	33	29	2	8	9	1	0	0	5	0	0	1	3	0	5	0	0	0	.310	.364
Davis, Jay, Binghamton*	.255	116	484	443	64	113	151	17	6	3	50	1	6	8	26	1	68	11	5	7	.341	.304
Davis, Tommy, Bowie	.313	9	34	32	5	10	22	3	0	3	10	0	0	1	1	0	9	0	0	1	.688	.353
DeBerry, Joe, Norwich*	.000	2	4	4	0	0	0	0	0	0	0	0	0	0	0	0	2	0	0	0	.000	.000
DeHart, Rick, Harrisburg*	.167	35	12	12	0	2	2	0	0	0	2	0	0	0	0	0	6	0	0	0	.167	.167
Delgado, Alex, Trenton	.333	23	86	72	13	24	34	1	0	3	14	1	1	3	9	0	8	0	0	2	.472	.424
Delvecchio, Nick, Norwich*	.260	125	531	430	66	112	200	23	4	19	74	0	6	23	72	8	133	2	1	6	.465	.390
Diaz, Cesar, Binghamton	.170	13	53	47	5	8	10	2	0	0	5	0	0	0	6	0	20	0	1	3	.213	.264
Dixon, Colin, New Haven	.191	14	51	47	3	9	11	2	0	0	7	0	0	2	2	0	7	0	1	2	.234	.255
Doolan, Blake, Reading	.000	60	3	3	0	0	0	0	0	0	0	0	0	0	0	0	1	0	0	0	.000	.000

Player, Team	Avg.	G	TPA	AB	R	H	TB	2B	3B	HR	RBI	SH	SF	HP	BB	IBB	SO	SB	CS	GDP	Slg.	OBP
Doster, David, Reading	.265	139	621	551	84	146	254	39	3	21	79	8	4	7	51	2	61	11	7	11	.461	.333
Duncan, Andres, New Britain†	.226	83	252	230	28	52	61	5	2	0	10	2	3	3	14	1	51	10	5	2	.265	.276
Eason, Tommy, Reading	.255	96	364	333	43	85	151	18	3	14	50	7	5	1	18	1	61	2	2	3	.453	.291
Echevarria, Angel, New Haven	.300	124	524	453	78	136	231	30	1	21	100	0	7	8	56	3	93	8	3	8	.510	.382
Edmondson, Brian, Binghamton	.231	23	13	13	1	3	4	1	0	0	5	0	0	0	0	0	4	0	0	0	.308	.231
Engle, Tom, Binghamton	.000	13	3	2	0	0	0	0	0	0	0	0	0	0	1	0	2	0	0	0	.000	.333
Epperson, Chad, Binghamton†	.059	7	18	17	0	1	3	0	1	0	0	0	0	0	1	1	8	1	0	0	.176	.111
Epps, Scott, Norwich	.247	33	85	73	6	18	24	6	0	0	7	2	1	0	9	0	21	0	0	1	.329	.325
Estalella, Bobby, Reading	.235	10	39	34	5	8	15	1	0	2	9	0	0	1	4	1	7	0	0	1	.441	.333
Everson, Darin, Harrisburg*	.214	5	15	14	0	3	4	1	0	0	1	1	0	0	0	0	2	0	0	0	.286	.214
Falteisek, Steve, Harrisburg	.320	26	28	25	4	8	10	2	0	0	2	3	0	0	0	0	3	0	0	1	.400	.320
Farmer, Mike, New Haven†	.313	42	16	16	4	5	10	0	1	1	7	0	0	0	0	0	4	0	1	0	.625	.313
Fiegel, Todd, Binghamton*	.000	4	1	1	0	0	0	0	0	0	0	0	0	0	0	0	1	0	0	0	.000	.000
Figga, Mike, Norwich	.271	109	451	399	59	108	177	22	4	13	61	2	6	1	43	3	90	1	0	10	.444	.339
Fisher, David, Reading	.230	79	227	204	18	47	70	18	1	1	20	2	4	3	14	0	29	4	4	0	.343	.284
Fitzpatrick, Robert, Harrisburg	.167	15	51	42	3	7	11	1	0	1	3	1	0	2	6	0	11	0	0	1	.262	.300
Fleming, Carlton, Norwich†	.304	40	140	125	15	38	43	3	1	0	16	2	1	0	12	0	10	5	3	4	.344	.362
Foster, Mark, Reading*	.000	25	1	1	0	0	0	0	0	0	0	0	0	0	0	0	0	0	0	0	.000	.000
Fox, Andy, Norwich*	.206	44	196	175	23	36	64	3	5	5	17	1	1	0	19	0	36	8	1	3	.366	.282
Friedman, Jason, Bowie*	.232	63	248	228	22	53	73	11	0	3	27	1	1	2	16	2	23	1	1	7	.320	.287
Fuller, Aaron, Trenton†	.196	58	225	204	27	40	55	7	4	0	10	3	1	2	15	0	45	16	4	2	.270	.257
Fuller, Mark, Binghamton*	.400	47	5	5	2	2	3	1	0	0	0	0	0	0	0	0	3	0	0	0	.600	.400
Fully, Ed, Bing.-Bowie	.213	52	164	155	19	33	48	6	0	3	9	2	0	1	6	0	28	2	5	0	.310	.247
Garcia, Omar, Binghamton	.526	5	23	19	4	10	13	1	1	0	1	0	0	0	4	1	0	0	0	1	.684	.609
Garciaparra, Nomar, Trenton	.267	125	581	513	77	137	197	20	8	8	47	4	6	8	50	3	42	35	12	10	.384	.338
Garrow, David, New Britain	.143	6	16	14	0	2	2	0	0	0	1	0	0	0	2	0	2	0	0	1	.143	.250
Geisler, Phil, Reading*	.232	76	299	272	27	63	85	10	3	2	35	0	2	4	21	3	65	4	2	5	.313	.294
Gentile, Scott, Harrisburg	.000	37	1	1	0	0	0	0	0	0	0	0	0	0	0	0	1	0	0	0	.000	.000
Gerald, Ed, New Britain†	.111	6	20	18	1	2	3	1	0	0	3	0	0	0	2	0	9	0	0	1	.167	.200
Gilmore, Joel, Reading	.000	18	4	4	0	0	0	0	0	0	0	0	0	0	0	0	1	0	0	0	.000	.000
Gomes, Wayne, Reading	.154	22	15	13	3	2	3	1	0	0	0	1	0	0	1	0	6	0	0	1	.231	.214
Gonzalez, Mauricio, New Haven†	.268	73	173	164	20	44	55	5	3	0	12	1	0	1	7	0	29	0	1	1	.335	.302
Grable, Rob, Reading	.300	103	427	353	71	106	180	24	1	16	67	1	5	1	67	3	85	15	11	8	.510	.408
Grace, Mike, Reading	.111	24	20	18	1	2	2	0	0	0	2	2	0	0	0	0	8	0	0	0	.111	.111
Graham, Tim, Trenton*	.160	8	27	25	2	4	5	1	0	0	0	1	0	0	1	0	5	0	1	0	.200	.192
Greene, Charlie, Binghamton	.237	100	373	346	26	82	101	13	0	2	34	3	4	5	15	4	47	2	1	10	.292	.276
Gresham, Kris, Bowie	.077	5	16	13	1	1	1	0	0	0	0	0	0	0	3	0	5	1	0	0	.077	.250
Grifol, Pedro, New Britain	.177	77	252	226	23	40	58	9	0	3	21	1	1	1	23	1	33	1	0	8	.257	.255
Grissom, Antonio, Harrisburg	.257	82	279	237	32	61	83	10	0	4	23	4	1	4	33	0	48	13	8	6	.350	.356
Grundt, Ken, New Haven*	.000	28	1	0	0	0	0	0	0	0	0	1	0	0	0	0	0	0	0	0	.000	.000
Guerra, Mark, Binghamton	.250	6	4	4	1	1	1	0	0	0	0	0	0	0	0	0	2	0	0	0	.250	.250
Hagy, Gary, Canton/Akron	.294	6	18	17	2	5	7	2	0	0	3	0	0	0	1	0	2	0	0	0	.412	.333
Hammonds, Jeffrey, Bowie	.387	9	42	31	7	12	20	3	1	1	11	0	1	0	10	0	7	3	0	0	.645	.524
Hanselman, Carl, Reading*	.000	24	7	5	1	0	0	0	0	0	0	1	0	0	1	0	1	0	0	0	.000	.167
Hardge, Mike, Trenton	.244	40	141	127	18	31	37	4	1	0	12	1	2	0	11	0	26	3	4	7	.291	.300
Hardtke, Jason, Binghamton†	.286	121	536	455	65	130	192	42	4	4	52	2	9	4	66	1	58	6	8	7	.422	.375
Hartung, Andy, New Haven	.097	12	33	31	4	3	5	2	0	0	0	0	0	0	2	0	7	1	0	0	.161	.152
Harvey, Ray, Canton/Akron*	.259	122	499	444	52	115	146	20	1	3	32	7	2	3	43	1	75	1	4	6	.329	.327
Hawkins, Kraig, Norwich†	.222	12	54	45	5	10	10	0	0	0	3	2	0	0	7	0	11	7	2	0	.222	.327
Hayden, Dave, Reading	.234	68	221	192	22	45	60	6	0	3	11	0	2	1	26	3	39	0	3	6	.313	.326
Hecker, Doug, Trenton	.204	61	248	221	20	45	76	16	0	5	32	4	3	2	18	2	43	2	0	8	.344	.266
Held, Dan, Reading	.500	2	6	4	2	2	6	1	0	1	3	0	0	0	2	0	1	1	0	0	1.500	.667
Henderson, Rod, Harrisburg	.000	12	10	8	0	0	0	0	0	0	0	1	0	0	1	0	4	0	0	0	.000	.111
Heredia, Wilson, Portland	.222	4	10	9	1	2	2	0	0	0	0	1	0	0	0	0	2	0	0	1	.222	.222
Higgins, Mike, New Haven	.245	17	56	49	4	12	12	0	0	0	6	3	1	0	3	0	10	0	0	1	.245	.283
Hiljus, Erik, Binghamton	.091	10	14	11	1	1	1	0	0	0	1	2	0	0	1	0	2	0	0	0	.091	.167
Hill, Eric, Reading	.000	38	3	2	0	0	0	0	0	0	0	0	0	0	1	0	2	0	0	0	.000	.333
Hinds, Robert, Norwich	.252	132	516	445	71	112	125	8	1	1	37	6	3	12	50	0	102	27	10	4	.281	.341
Hinton, Steve, Harrisburg*	.222	10	25	18	4	4	4	0	0	0	0	0	0	0	7	0	5	0	0	0	.222	.440
Hodge, Roy, Bowie	.172	29	120	99	11	17	20	1	1	0	9	0	2	1	18	0	15	2	0	5	.202	.300
Holifield, Rick, Reading*	.247	30	118	93	18	23	31	3	1	1	5	2	0	1	22	3	18	5	2	0	.333	.397
Holman, Brad, New Haven	.000	7	1	1	0	0	0	0	0	0	0	0	0	0	0	0	0	0	0	0	.000	.000
Holman, Craig, Reading†	.000	33	5	3	0	0	0	0	0	0	0	2	0	0	0	0	1	0	0	1	.000	.000
Hood, Dennis, Canton/Akron	.217	8	26	23	6	5	6	1	0	0	2	0	0	0	2	0	7	1	0	0	.261	.280
Horne, Tyrone, Har.-Nor.*	.291	133	554	460	82	134	225	33	5	16	69	3	6	1	84	3	101	18	10	7	.489	.397
Howard, Matt, Bowie	.303	70	289	251	42	76	91	8	2	1	15	3	1	5	29	1	27	22	4	6	.363	.385
Hughes, Troy, Norwich	.327	15	61	55	7	18	25	2	1	1	8	0	1	1	4	0	11	0	2	3	.455	.377
Hugo, Sean, Bowie*	.222	43	139	117	15	26	29	3	0	0	10	0	1	1	20	3	29	1	1	0	.248	.338
Hunter, Greg, New Britain*	.077	6	14	13	1	1	1	0	0	0	0	0	0	0	1	0	1	1	0	0	.077	.143
Hunter, Rich, Reading	.000	3	6	6	0	0	0	0	0	0	0	0	0	0	0	0	0	0	0	0	.000	.000
Hutchins, Jason, New Haven	.000	12	1	1	0	0	0	0	0	0	0	0	0	0	0	0	1	0	0	0	.000	.000
Hymel, Lou, Harrisburg	.189	95	335	302	35	57	104	10	2	11	36	1	2	8	22	0	97	3	2	3	.344	.260
Isringhausen, Jason, Bingham.	.357	6	15	14	1	5	7	2	0	0	0	1	0	0	0	0	2	0	0	0	.500	.357
Jackson, Damian, Cant./Akron	.248	131	565	484	67	120	153	20	2	3	34	7	0	9	65	0	103	40	22	6	.316	.348
Jackson, John, New Britain*	.298	16	69	57	8	17	30	2	1	3	8	0	0	1	11	0	7	3	4	0	.526	.420
Jacobs, Frank, Bing.-Har.*	.312	101	402	337	56	105	166	22	0	13	60	0	2	5	58	7	56	1	3	5	.493	.418
Johnson, Charles, Portland	.000	2	8	7	0	0	0	0	0	0	0	0	0	0	1	0	3	0	0	0	.000	.125
Johnson, J.J., Trenton	.500	2	6	6	1	3	3	0	0	0	1	0	0	0	0	0	0	0	0	0	.500	.500
Johnson, Jason, New Haven	.000	19	9	7	0	0	0	0	0	0	0	0	0	1	1	0	1	0	0	0	.000	.222
Jones, Bobby, New Haven	.286	27	10	7	1	2	2	0	0	0	0	1	0	0	2	0	3	0	0	0	.286	.444
Jones, Terry, New Haven†	.269	124	521	472	78	127	144	12	1	1	26	3	3	3	39	0	104	51	19	6	.305	.327
Juday, Rob, Trenton†	.100	3	12	10	0	1	1	0	0	0	0	0	0	0	2	1	4	0	0	0	.100	.250
Juelsgaard, Jarod, Portland	.200	48	10	10	0	2	2	0	0	0	0	0	0	0	0	0	4	0	0	0	.200	.200

Player, Team	Avg.	G	TPA	AB	R	H	TB	2B	3B	HR	RBI	SH	SF	HP	BB	IBB	SO	SB	CS	GDP	Slg.	OBP
Karp, Ryan, Reading*	.333	7	4	3	1	1	1	0	0	0	0	0	0	0	1	0	0	0	0	1	.333	.500
Katzaroff, Rob, Portland	.304	116	505	441	87	134	188	16	4	10	49	4	4	7	49	3	33	18	10	4	.426	.379
Keister, Tripp, Binghamton*	.219	66	182	146	23	32	44	7	1	1	10	2	0	5	29	1	26	3	4	0	.301	.367
Kendrena, Ken, Harrisburg	.000	31	4	2	1	0	0	0	0	0	0	1	0	0	1	0	1	0	0	0	.000	.333
Kennedy, David, New Haven	.306	128	541	484	75	148	240	22	2	22	96	0	4	5	48	1	131	4	1	12	.496	.372
Kerley, Collin, Harrisburg	.000	2	2	0	1	0	0	0	0	0	0	2	0	0	0	0	0	0	0	0	.000	.000
Knackert, Brent, Binghamton	.167	48	8	6	0	1	1	0	0	0	0	1	0	0	1	1	1	0	0	0	.167	.286
Kontorinis, Andrew, New Britain*	.289	36	133	114	12	33	43	4	0	2	17	0	0	5	14	0	18	1	1	3	.377	.391
Kotarski, Mike, New Haven*	.000	31	1	1	0	0	0	0	0	0	0	0	0	0	0	0	1	0	0	0	.000	.000
Kounas, Tony, Harrisburg	.235	66	218	196	15	46	54	5	0	1	22	0	1	2	19	1	27	1	1	7	.276	.307
Kremers, Jimmy, Portland*	.223	85	294	264	32	59	101	11	5	7	37	1	2	0	27	3	70	1	0	3	.383	.294
Lamb, David, Bowie†	.250	1	4	4	0	1	1	0	0	0	1	0	0	0	0	0	1	0	0	0	.250	.250
Lane, Dan, Harrisburg	.123	39	88	81	5	10	11	1	0	0	1	1	0	3	3	0	21	0	1	3	.136	.184
Lantigua, Eduardo, Cant./Akron	.196	13	49	46	5	9	14	2	0	1	4	1	0	1	1	0	14	0	0	2	.304	.229
Larkin, Andy, Portland	.000	9	6	6	0	0	0	0	0	0	0	0	0	0	0	0	5	0	0	0	.000	.000
Lawton, Matt, New Britain*	.269	114	485	412	75	111	179	19	5	13	54	2	3	12	56	1	70	26	9	8	.434	.371
Leahy, Pat, Portland	.000	13	6	3	1	0	0	0	0	0	1	0	0	1	2	0	1	1	0	0	.000	.500
LeGree, Keith, New Britain*	.200	43	131	110	10	22	24	2	0	0	6	0	0	0	21	0	33	3	1	3	.218	.328
Lemon, Don, Portland	.000	30	6	6	0	0	0	0	0	0	0	0	0	0	0	0	2	0	0	0	.000	.000
Lennon, Pat, Trenton	.398	27	113	98	19	39	49	7	0	1	8	0	0	1	14	0	22	7	2	3	.500	.478
Levangie, Dana, Trenton	.178	42	142	129	10	23	28	3	1	0	7	0	1	1	11	0	30	1	3	3	.217	.246
Lewis, T.R., Bowie	.294	86	357	309	57	91	127	19	1	5	44	1	6	1	40	2	43	12	3	8	.411	.371
List, Lou, New Haven	.278	82	234	212	26	59	95	10	4	6	44	0	1	1	20	0	43	2	2	4	.448	.342
Loewer, Carlton, Reading*	.200	8	13	10	3	2	2	0	0	0	0	1	0	0	2	0	5	0	0	0	.200	.333
Long, R.D., Norwich†	.212	9	40	33	4	7	10	3	0	0	5	0	0	0	7	0	11	2	1	1	.303	.350
Lopez, Rene, New Britain	.246	82	298	264	22	65	82	8	0	3	26	5	2	0	27	0	48	0	0	5	.311	.314
Lucca, Lou, Portland	.276	112	454	388	57	107	164	28	1	9	64	0	2	5	59	5	77	4	4	18	.423	.377
Ludwick, Eric, Binghamton	.071	23	18	14	2	1	2	1	0	0	1	3	0	0	1	0	3	0	0	0	.143	.133
Luke, Matt, Norwich*	.260	93	394	365	48	95	146	17	5	8	53	3	4	2	20	2	68	5	4	6	.400	.299
Magee, Wendell, Reading	.294	39	161	136	17	40	60	9	1	3	21	0	4	0	21	1	17	3	4	3	.441	.379
Mahalik, John, Binghamton	.225	67	213	187	19	42	65	6	1	5	19	5	1	1	19	1	34	1	1	6	.348	.298
Mahay, Ron, Trenton*	.235	93	363	310	37	73	106	12	3	5	28	2	4	3	44	3	90	5	6	5	.342	.332
Mantei, Matt, Portland	.000	8	1	1	0	0	0	0	0	0	0	0	0	0	0	0	1	0	0	0	.000	.000
Manto, Jeff, Bowie	.250	1	4	4	1	1	1	0	0	0	0	0	0	0	0	0	2	0	0	0	.250	.250
Marabella, Tony, Harrisburg*	.225	30	100	89	10	20	24	1	0	1	11	3	1	0	7	0	11	0	1	3	.270	.278
Marini, Marc, Canton/Akron*	.306	83	348	310	41	95	134	28	1	3	56	0	8	0	30	7	51	3	3	9	.432	.359
Martin, Jeff, Trenton	.217	78	284	254	25	55	79	10	1	4	30	6	3	5	16	0	83	3	3	10	.311	.273
Martindale, Ryan, Cant./Akron	.375	2	9	8	2	3	3	0	0	0	1	0	0	0	1	0	0	0	1	1	.375	.444
Martinez, Ray, Harrisburg	.237	48	173	152	18	36	45	6	0	1	13	0	0	1	20	2	24	3	2	6	.296	.329
Massarelli, John, Cant./Akron	.281	55	198	178	17	50	70	10	2	2	22	1	3	0	16	0	28	17	6	1	.393	.335
Maxwell, Pat, Canton/Akron*	.247	84	293	267	19	66	85	7	0	4	25	6	1	4	15	1	26	1	0	5	.318	.296
McCall, Rod, Canton/Akron*	.274	26	108	95	16	26	58	5	0	9	18	0	0	1	12	3	21	1	1	3	.611	.361
McClain, Scott, Bowie	.278	70	291	259	41	72	127	14	1	13	61	0	4	3	25	1	44	2	1	13	.490	.344
McConnell, Chad, Reading	.276	94	359	319	46	88	135	12	1	11	52	1	2	10	27	1	59	8	3	8	.423	.349
McCracken, Quinton, New Hav.†	.357	55	247	221	33	79	101	11	4	1	26	1	1	3	21	3	32	26	8	2	.457	.419
McDill, Allen, Binghamton*	.000	12	7	4	1	0	0	0	0	0	0	2	0	0	1	0	1	0	0	0	.000	.200
McGraw, Tom, Portland*	.125	51	9	8	0	1	1	0	0	0	0	1	0	0	0	0	1	0	0	0	.125	.125
McGuire, Ryan, Trenton*	.333	109	477	414	59	138	190	29	1	7	59	4	1	0	58	5	51	11	8	10	.459	.414
McKeel, Walt, Trenton	.238	29	94	84	11	20	31	3	1	2	11	0	2	0	8	0	15	2	1	1	.369	.298
McMillon, Billy, Portland*	.313	141	628	518	92	162	239	29	3	14	93	1	5	7	96	5	90	15	9	10	.461	.423
McNabb, Buck, Cant./Akron*	.167	19	57	48	3	8	8	0	0	0	1	2	0	1	6	0	14	0	1	0	.167	.273
McNair, Fred, Reading	.271	108	437	395	64	107	202	24	1	23	68	1	0	3	38	1	86	3	2	12	.511	.339
Mendoza, Reynol, Portland	.077	27	19	13	0	1	1	0	0	0	0	2	0	0	4	0	4	0	0	0	.077	.294
Mercedes, Feliciano, Bowie†	.150	28	89	80	10	12	13	1	0	0	7	1	1	1	6	0	14	2	3	2	.163	.216
Merloni, Lou, Trenton	.277	93	381	318	42	88	109	16	1	1	30	11	2	11	39	3	50	7	7	1	.343	.373
Michael, Jeff, Bowie	.167	4	16	12	2	2	2	0	0	0	0	0	0	0	4	0	4	0	0	0	.167	.375
Mikkelsen, Linc, Harrisburg†	.000	22	7	7	2	0	0	0	0	0	0	0	0	0	0	0	1	0	0	0	.000	.000
Millan, Adan, Reading	.350	10	26	20	3	7	13	3	0	1	7	0	1	1	4	0	3	0	0	1	.650	.462
Millares, Jose, Bowie	.248	120	459	411	50	102	150	30	3	4	50	2	6	19	20	0	62	7	6	14	.365	.309
Miller, Ryan, Binghamton	.053	9	22	19	3	1	1	0	0	0	0	1	0	0	2	0	4	1	0	0	.053	.143
Milliard, Ralph, Portland	.267	128	581	464	104	124	185	22	3	11	40	13	4	14	85	3	83	22	10	5	.399	.393
Mitchell, Larry, Reading	.000	25	13	12	0	0	0	0	0	0	1	0	1	0	0	0	4	0	0	0	.000	.000
Mix, Greg, Portland	.053	24	22	19	1	1	1	0	0	0	0	2	0	0	1	0	8	0	0	1	.053	.100
Moler, Jason, Reading	.265	22	96	83	17	22	31	3	0	2	14	0	1	0	12	2	13	2	2	1	.373	.354
Moore, Joel, New Haven*	.182	27	27	22	1	4	5	1	0	0	2	3	0	0	2	0	6	0	0	0	.227	.250
Moore, Tim, New Britain†	.241	90	343	311	39	75	123	19	1	9	45	0	2	6	24	4	86	4	2	7	.395	.306
Morgan, Kevin, Binghamton	.277	114	488	430	63	119	154	21	1	4	51	7	2	5	44	4	52	9	9	2	.358	.349
Mota, Gary, Reading	.227	33	119	110	13	25	36	4	2	1	9	1	0	0	8	2	23	0	2	2	.327	.280
Munoz, Bobby, Reading	.000	4	1	1	0	0	0	0	0	0	0	0	0	0	0	0	1	0	0	0	.000	.000
Murphy, Mike, Canton/Akron	.043	10	27	23	3	1	1	0	0	0	0	0	0	0	4	0	3	0	1	0	.043	.185
Murphy, Pat, Trenton*	.228	35	123	114	17	26	30	4	0	0	11	1	1	1	6	1	21	10	6	1	.263	.270
Myrow, John, New Haven	.246	96	394	353	52	87	116	18	1	3	50	3	3	8	25	2	67	16	5	13	.329	.308
Nava, Lipso, Trenton	.216	20	57	51	7	11	17	3	0	1	7	1	1	3	1	0	5	1	0	1	.333	.268
Neal, Mike, Canton/Akron	.267	134	511	419	64	112	155	24	2	5	46	4	8	9	71	3	79	5	6	7	.370	.379
Neier, Chris, New Haven	.143	38	15	14	0	2	2	0	0	0	1	0	0	0	1	0	2	0	0	1	.143	.200
Nixon, Trot, Trenton*	.160	25	105	94	9	15	26	3	1	2	8	2	2	0	7	0	20	2	1	0	.277	.214
Norman, Kenny, New Britain†	.290	12	36	31	4	9	10	1	0	0	1	0	0	0	5	0	9	0	1	1	.323	.389
Northrup, Kevin, Harrisburg	.309	40	163	152	23	47	64	14	0	1	27	0	1	0	10	1	16	0	1	3	.421	.350
Ogden, Jamie, New Britain*	.284	117	438	384	54	109	172	22	1	13	61	0	5	1	48	5	90	6	5	10	.448	.361
Owens, Billy, Bowie†	.269	122	505	453	57	122	200	27	0	17	91	0	8	1	43	6	87	2	1	13	.442	.329
Pacheco, Alex, Harrisburg	.000	45	4	4	0	0	0	0	0	0	0	0	0	0	0	0	3	0	0	0	.000	.000
Paniagua, Jose, Harrisburg	.250	25	15	12	1	3	5	2	0	0	1	2	0	0	1	0	7	0	0	0	.417	.308
Paxton, Darrin, Har.-Bing.*	.000	28	4	3	0	0	0	0	0	0	0	0	0	0	1	0	0	0	0	1	.000	.250

Player, Team	Avg.	G	TPA	AB	R	H	TB	2B	3B	HR	RBI	SH	SF	HP	BB	IBB	SO	SB	CS	GDP	Slg.	OBP
Payton, Jay, Binghamton	.345	85	390	357	59	123	191	20	3	14	54	0	2	2	29	2	32	16	7	11	.535	.395
Perez, Neifi, New Haven†	.253	116	458	427	59	108	157	28	3	5	43	4	1	2	24	2	52	5	2	6	.368	.295
Person, Robert, Binghamton	.000	26	4	4	0	0	0	0	0	0	0	0	0	0	0	0	2	0	0	0	.000	.000
Pettit, Doug, Portland*	.000	21	2	2	0	0	0	0	0	0	0	0	0	0	0	0	0	0	0	0	.000	.000
Phillips, Steve, Norwich*	.258	11	38	31	2	8	15	1	0	2	7	1	0	0	6	2	8	0	0	0	.484	.378
Pote, Lou, Harrisburg	.000	9	3	3	0	0	0	0	0	0	0	0	0	0	0	0	1	0	0	0	.000	.000
Pough, Pork Chop, Trenton	.278	97	424	363	68	101	197	23	5	21	69	0	4	7	50	8	101	11	5	1	.543	.373
Powell, Jay, Portland	.000	50	1	1	0	0	0	0	0	0	0	0	0	0	0	0	0	0	0	0	.000	.000
Ramirez, Alex, Canton/Akron	.248	33	140	133	15	33	47	3	4	1	11	1	1	0	5	1	24	3	5	5	.353	.273
Ramirez, Hector, Binghamton	.158	20	23	19	0	3	3	0	0	0	1	3	1	0	0	0	8	0	0	0	.158	.150
Ramirez, Omar, Canton/Akron	.324	10	38	34	6	11	11	0	0	0	3	1	0	0	3	0	3	0	0	0	.324	.378
Redmond, Mike, Portland	.255	105	365	333	37	85	107	11	1	3	39	4	3	3	22	2	27	2	2	9	.321	.305
Rekar, Bryan, New Haven	.091	12	16	11	0	1	1	0	0	0	2	5	0	0	0	0	5	0	0	0	.091	.091
Renteria, Dave, Norwich	.105	15	42	38	4	4	4	0	0	0	0	1	0	0	3	0	13	1	0	0	.105	.171
Renteria, Edgar, Portland	.289	135	558	508	70	147	197	15	7	7	68	8	8	2	32	2	85	30	11	10	.388	.329
Riggs, Kevin, Norwich*	.330	57	238	179	38	59	89	16	1	4	36	0	4	4	51	3	28	5	5	4	.497	.479
Rivera, Ruben, Norwich	.293	71	306	256	49	75	134	16	8	9	39	0	2	11	37	2	77	16	8	4	.523	.402
Robertson, Jason, Norwich*	.276	117	507	456	60	126	193	29	10	6	54	4	5	1	41	3	106	19	12	5	.423	.334
Rodriguez, Nerio, Bowie	.000	3	6	4	0	0	0	0	0	0	0	0	0	0	2	0	2	0	0	0	.000	.333
Rogers, Lamarr, New Haven	.283	109	447	371	68	105	120	15	0	0	31	8	3	1	64	1	50	21	7	15	.323	.387
Rojas, Euclides, Portland	.000	14	2	2	0	0	0	0	0	0	0	0	0	0	0	0	2	0	0	0	.000	.000
Rolen, Scott, Reading	.289	20	86	76	16	22	34	3	0	3	15	1	1	1	7	0	14	1	0	2	.447	.353
Romano, Scott, Norwich	.246	100	414	353	43	87	125	15	1	7	51	4	2	7	48	1	57	7	2	13	.354	.346
Roper, Chad, New Britain	.226	120	478	443	41	100	161	22	3	11	61	1	4	3	27	3	86	2	3	9	.363	.273
Rudolph, Mason, Portland	.197	41	80	76	9	15	33	4	1	4	16	0	1	2	1	0	29	0	1	2	.434	.225
Rundels, Matt, Harrisburg	.247	120	526	462	72	114	185	30	4	11	55	8	1	8	47	1	112	19	11	5	.400	.326
Saffer, Jon, Harrisburg*	.237	20	82	76	9	18	22	4	0	0	4	0	0	0	6	0	14	2	1	2	.289	.293
Salamon, John, New Haven	.000	6	3	2	0	0	0	0	0	0	0	1	0	0	0	0	2	0	0	0	.000	.000
Salcedo, Edwin, Norwich	.000	3	2	2	0	0	0	0	0	0	0	0	0	0	0	0	2	0	0	0	.000	.000
Sanders, Tracy, Binghamton*	.281	10	37	32	6	9	18	3	0	2	8	0	0	0	5	0	11	1	0	0	.563	.378
Saunders, Chris, Binghamton	.259	122	503	441	58	114	170	22	5	8	66	5	7	5	45	1	98	3	6	7	.385	.329
Scalzitti, Will, New Haven	.187	39	137	123	9	23	32	6	0	1	14	1	2	1	10	0	17	0	0	0	.260	.250
Schmidt, Tom, New Haven	.217	115	458	423	55	92	141	25	3	6	49	1	5	5	24	2	99	2	1	13	.333	.265
Schneider, Phil, New Haven*	.000	2	1	1	0	0	0	0	0	0	0	0	0	0	0	0	1	0	0	0	.000	.000
Schorr, Brad, Binghamton	.000	4	6	5	0	0	0	0	0	0	0	0	0	0	1	0	3	0	0	0	.000	.167
Seefried, Tate, Norwich*	.226	77	314	274	34	62	97	18	1	5	33	1	4	4	31	4	86	0	1	6	.354	.310
Sefcik, Kevin, Reading	.272	128	564	508	68	138	176	18	4	4	46	3	3	12	38	0	48	14	11	5	.346	.335
Selby, Bill, Trenton*	.286	117	510	451	64	129	201	29	2	13	68	2	8	3	46	3	52	4	6	14	.446	.350
Sexton, Chris, New Haven	.000	1	3	3	0	0	0	0	0	0	0	0	0	0	0	0	0	0	0	0	.000	.000
Shaw, Cedric, Harrisburg*	.000	5	2	1	0	0	0	0	0	0	0	0	0	0	1	0	1	0	0	0	.000	.500
Sheff, Chris, Portland	.276	131	557	471	85	130	205	25	7	12	91	1	8	5	72	6	84	23	6	10	.435	.372
Shelton, Ben, N.B.-Tre.	.218	91	370	294	60	64	122	7	0	17	43	0	3	6	67	4	89	5	1	10	.415	.370
Smith, Brandon, Binghamton	.000	2	2	2	0	0	0	0	0	0	0	0	0	0	0	0	1	0	0	0	.000	.000
Smith, Bubba, New Britain	.243	42	155	148	20	36	65	11	0	6	21	0	1	0	6	1	41	0	0	5	.439	.271
Smith, Ed, Canton/Akron	.241	103	412	365	41	88	143	18	2	11	52	7	3	1	36	4	93	0	2	6	.392	.309
Smith, Eric, Reading	.000	4	1	1	0	0	0	0	0	0	0	0	0	0	0	0	0	0	0	0	.000	.000
Smith, John, Binghamton	.083	9	15	12	2	1	2	1	0	0	1	0	0	1	2	0	6	0	0	0	.167	.267
Snyder, Randy, New Haven	.235	5	18	17	2	4	5	1	0	0	2	0	1	0	0	0	3	0	2	0	.294	.222
Soliz, Steve, Canton/Akron	.173	32	96	81	9	14	23	3	0	2	7	1	1	0	13	0	16	0	0	3	.284	.284
Solomon, Steve, Reading*	.228	119	420	356	50	81	121	19	6	3	42	3	2	11	48	3	82	17	4	11	.340	.336
Spencer, Stan, Portland	.000	8	7	4	0	0	0	0	0	0	0	1	0	0	2	0	0	0	0	1	.000	.333
Stidham, Phil, Binghamton	.000	7	1	1	0	0	0	0	0	0	0	0	0	0	0	0	0	0	0	0	.000	.000
Strittmatter, Mark, New Haven	.243	90	344	288	44	70	105	12	1	7	42	1	2	6	47	1	51	1	0	5	.365	.359
Stull, Everett, Harrisburg	.214	24	17	14	2	3	4	1	0	0	1	3	0	0	0	0	6	0	0	0	.286	.214
Tam, Jeff, Binghamton	.000	14	1	1	0	0	0	0	0	0	0	0	0	0	0	0	1	0	0	0	.000	.000
Taylor, Jamie, Canton/Akron*	.000	4	13	11	0	0	0	0	0	0	0	1	0	1	0	0	4	0	0	0	.000	.083
Tellers, Dave, New Haven	.000	33	5	4	0	0	0	0	0	0	0	1	0	0	0	0	3	0	0	0	.000	.000
Thompson, Ryan, Binghamton	.500	2	9	8	2	4	7	0	0	1	4	0	0	0	1	0	2	0	0	0	.875	.556
Thomson, John, New Haven	.000	26	19	12	0	0	0	0	0	0	0	5	0	0	2	0	2	0	0	0	.000	.143
Tijerina, Tony, Binghamton†	.178	32	124	118	3	21	26	5	0	0	9	0	2	3	1	0	22	0	0	2	.220	.202
Tinsley, Lee, Trenton†	.389	4	19	18	3	7	8	1	0	0	3	0	0	0	1	0	5	1	0	0	.444	.421
Tirpack, Ken, New Britain*	.250	7	21	16	4	4	12	2	0	2	3	0	0	0	5	1	3	1	0	1	.750	.429
Torres, Tony, Portland	.296	58	101	81	15	24	31	3	2	0	4	8	0	1	11	0	23	9	0	1	.383	.387
Tovar, Edgar, Harrisburg	.202	81	277	247	28	50	70	7	2	3	21	9	1	4	16	2	24	1	3	5	.283	.261
Townsend, Chad, Cant./Akron*	.262	116	447	404	39	106	157	22	1	9	50	1	3	8	31	4	90	3	2	6	.389	.325
Tranberg, Mark, Reading	.214	18	17	14	1	3	4	1	0	0	1	2	0	0	1	0	2	0	0	1	.286	.267
Trisler, John, Reading	.182	30	11	11	2	2	2	0	0	0	0	0	0	0	0	0	6	0	0	0	.182	.182
Turner, Brian, Norwich*	.296	86	343	311	39	92	131	21	3	4	43	2	4	1	25	2	72	3	2	5	.421	.346
Valette, Ramon, New Britain	.214	111	371	346	40	74	101	11	2	4	32	1	2	1	21	0	52	19	2	14	.292	.259
Van Slyke, Andy, Bowie*	.500	2	9	6	2	3	3	0	0	0	2	0	0	0	3	1	0	0	0	0	.500	.667
Ventress, Leroy, Harrisburg†	.220	11	46	41	4	9	9	0	0	0	0	0	0	0	5	0	19	3	0	0	.220	.304
Viano, Jake, New Haven	.000	57	3	3	0	0	0	0	0	0	0	0	0	0	0	0	1	0	0	0	.000	.000
Vidro, Jose, Harrisburg†	.260	64	274	246	33	64	96	16	2	4	38	4	3	1	20	2	37	3	7	5	.390	.315
Virgilio, George, Har.-Bowie†	.202	68	201	163	20	33	42	3	0	2	18	1	2	2	33	2	22	1	1	8	.258	.340
Waco, David, Reading	.300	5	10	10	1	3	3	0	0	0	1	0	0	0	0	0	2	0	0	0	.300	.300
Wakamatsu, Don, Cant./Akron	.266	51	171	143	16	38	60	10	0	4	23	3	2	6	17	2	21	0	0	7	.420	.363
Walker, Todd, New Britain*	.290	137	587	513	83	149	245	27	3	21	85	1	8	2	63	1	101	23	9	13	.478	.365
Wallace, Derek, Binghamton	.000	15	1	1	0	0	0	0	0	0	0	0	0	0	0	0	0	0	0	0	.000	.000
Waller, Casey, Portland†	.222	14	42	36	4	8	12	2	1	0	5	0	0	0	6	0	4	1	0	2	.333	.333
Ward, Bryan, Portland*	.200	20	16	15	3	3	3	0	0	0	1	0	0	0	1	0	4	0	0	0	.200	.250
Waszgis, B.J., Bowie	.253	130	521	438	53	111	163	22	0	10	50	1	3	9	70	1	91	2	4	5	.372	.365
Wawruck, Jim, Bowie*	.278	56	239	212	29	59	86	7	1	6	30	1	3	3	20	2	31	7	3	7	.406	.345
Weber, Neil, Harrisburg*	.091	28	24	22	2	2	4	2	0	0	2	1	0	0	1	0	11	0	0	1	.182	.130

Player, Team	Avg.	G	TPA	AB	R	H	TB	2B	3B	HR	RBI	SH	SF	HP	BB	IBB	SO	SB	CS	GDP	Slg.	OBP
Wells, Forry, New Haven*	.214	4	16	14	3	3	3	0	0	0	1	0	0	1	1	1	2	0	0	1	.214	.313
Whisenant, Matt, Portland†	.000	23	19	16	1	0	0	0	0	0	1	2	0	0	1	0	8	0	0	0	.000	.059
White, Billy, New Haven	.232	58	208	181	25	42	62	9	1	3	34	0	0	0	27	0	44	2	2	3	.343	.332
White, Don, Binghamton	.236	94	365	314	48	74	104	17	2	3	20	6	3	2	40	0	56	25	6	10	.331	.323
Wilson, Paul, Binghamton	.200	16	20	15	0	3	5	2	0	0	1	5	0	0	0	0	5	0	0	1	.333	.200
Wilson, Pookie, Portland*	.273	107	386	348	51	95	127	13	5	3	44	5	4	11	18	2	51	9	4	9	.365	.325
Wilson, Thomas, Norwich	.143	28	101	84	6	12	16	4	0	0	4	0	0	0	17	0	22	0	0	3	.190	.287
Wipf, Mark, Binghamton†	.091	4	13	11	1	1	1	0	0	0	1	0	1	0	1	0	8	1	0	0	.091	.154
Yelding, Eric, Canton/Akron	.351	10	40	37	5	13	14	1	0	0	7	0	1	1	1	0	6	3	0	0	.378	.375
Zambrano, Eddie, Trenton	.147	19	76	68	5	10	14	1	0	1	7	0	1	1	6	1	25	0	0	1	.206	.224
Zambrano, Jose, Trenton	.242	22	76	62	7	15	27	6	0	2	7	0	0	3	11	0	15	2	1	3	.435	.382
Zolecki, Mike, New Haven	.111	9	10	9	0	1	1	0	0	0	0	1	0	0	0	0	3	0	0	0	.111	.111
Zuniga, David, Binghamton	.000	3	1	1	1	0	0	0	0	0	0	0	0	0	0	0	1	0	0	0	.000	.000

GRAND SLAMS: Estallela, Strittmatter, Townsend, 2 each; Alcantara, Barry, Blosser, Bryant, Carey, Clark, Echevarria, Garciaparra, Grissom, Holifield, Jacobs, Kennedy, List, Luke, Magee, Mahay, McClain, Ogden, Owens, E. Renteria, Rivera, Roper, Selby, Shelton, B. Smith, Solomon, 1 each.

AWARDED FIRST BASE ON CATCHER'S INTERFERENCE: Charbonnet 3 (Crosby, Grifol, Wakamatsu); Myrow 2 (Gresham, Kounas); Barron (Crosby); Chavez (Allen); Dauphin (Waszgis); Hood (Grifol); T. Jones (Epps); McMillon (Diaz); Millares (Kounas); Milliard (Strittmatter).

PLAYERS WITH TWO OR MORE TEAMS

Player, Team	Avg.	G	TPA	AB	R	H	TB	2B	3B	HR	RBI	SH	SF	HP	BB	IBB	SO	SB	CS	GDP	Slg.	OBP
Fully, Ed, Binghamton	.194	18	37	36	4	7	11	1	0	1	3	1	0	0	0	0	5	0	2	0	.306	.194
Fully, Ed, Bowie	.218	34	127	119	15	26	37	5	0	2	6	1	0	1	6	0	23	2	3	0	.311	.262
Horne, Tyrone, Harrisburg*	.296	87	359	294	59	87	154	17	4	14	47	3	3	1	58	2	65	14	8	3	.524	.410
Horne, Tyrone, Norwich*	.283	46	195	166	23	47	71	16	1	2	22	0	3	0	26	1	36	4	2	4	.428	.374
Jacobs, Frank, Binghamton*	.294	23	78	68	12	20	35	3	0	4	9	0	0	0	10	0	15	0	0	3	.515	.385
Jacobs, Frank, Harrisburg*	.316	78	324	269	44	85	131	19	0	9	51	0	2	5	48	7	41	1	3	2	.487	.426
Paxton, Darrin, Harrisburg*	.000	7	0	0	0	0	0	0	0	0	0	0	0	0	0	0	0	0	0	0	.000	.000
Paxton, Darrin, Binghamton*	.000	21	4	3	0	0	0	0	0	0	0	0	0	0	1	0	0	0	0	1	.000	.250
Shelton, Ben, New Britain	.239	56	221	176	37	42	86	5	0	13	30	0	2	3	40	0	58	4	0	6	.489	.385
Shelton, Ben, Trenton	.186	35	149	118	23	22	36	2	0	4	13	0	1	3	27	4	31	1	1	4	.305	.349
Virgilio, George, Harrisburg†	.143	27	77	56	9	8	11	0	0	1	5	0	1	0	20	2	11	1	1	2	.196	.364
Virgilio, George, Bowie†	.234	41	124	107	11	25	31	3	0	1	13	1	1	2	13	0	11	0	0	6	.290	.325

1995 PITCHING

TEAM

Team	W	L	Pct.	ERA	G	CG	ShO	Sv.	IP	H	TBF	R	ER	HR	SH	SF	HB	BB	IBB	SO	WP	Bk.
New Haven	79	63	.556	3.61	142	3	14	37	1239.2	1185	5332	592	497	68	51	42	53	521	29	951	53	18
Trenton	73	69	.514	3.78	142	15	8	35	1279.2	1197	5461	624	538	97	42	46	90	452	22	905	57	24
Portland	86	56	.606	3.79	142	6	9	40	1255.0	1184	5373	592	528	93	61	35	59	497	41	979	59	11
Binghamton	67	75	.472	3.91	142	15	10	28	1259.1	1162	5334	625	547	103	42	48	52	487	33	897	57	21
Reading	73	69	.514	3.99	142	7	8	31	1247.0	1211	5369	634	553	112	45	29	41	513	33	991	56	24
New Britain	65	77	.458	4.01	142	7	12	26	1246.2	1236	5430	653	555	81	58	54	51	500	18	935	64	10
Bowie	68	74	.479	4.13	142	7	10	32	1231.0	1225	5408	681	565	125	43	56	55	530	32	892	75	17
Canton/Akron	67	75	.472	4.24	142	9	9	33	1215.1	1187	5280	672	573	102	54	48	46	519	32	786	48	11
Harrisburg	61	80	.433	4.31	141	7	6	26	1219.2	1176	5354	682	584	94	50	45	80	543	28	981	58	10
Norwich	70	71	.496	4.32	141	6	7	39	1231.2	1265	5483	717	591	71	36	53	81	554	33	880	81	12

INDIVIDUAL

TOP QUALIFIERS FOR EARNED-RUN AVERAGE TITLE

Minimum 114 innings. *Lefthanded pitcher.

Pitcher, Team	W	L	Pct.	ERA	G	GS	CG	ShO	GF	Sv.	IP	H	TBF	R	ER	HR	SH	SF	HB	BB	IBB	SO	WP	Bk.
Wilson, Paul, Binghamton	6	3	.667	2.17	16	16	4	1	0	0	120.1	89	464	34	29	5	3	4	5	24	2	127	4	3
Falteisek, Steve, Harrisburg	9	6	.600	2.95	25	25	5	0	0	0	168.0	152	707	74	55	3	7	5	11	64	4	112	6	1
Ludwick, Eric, Binghamton	12	5	.706	2.95	23	22	3	2	0	0	143.1	108	590	52	47	9	4	6	2	68	1	131	6	0
Orellano, Rafael, Trenton*	11	7	.611	3.09	27	27	2	0	0	0	186.2	146	772	68	64	18	4	1	11	72	0	160	9	4
Moore, Joel, New Haven	14	6	.700	3.20	27	26	1	1	0	0	157.1	156	682	69	56	8	6	6	8	67	2	102	5	1
Whitten, Casey, Canton/Akron*	9	8	.529	3.31	20	20	2	1	0	0	114.1	100	469	49	42	10	1	2	3	38	0	91	5	2
Serafini, Dan, New Britain*	12	9	.571	3.38	27	27	1	1	0	0	162.2	155	692	74	61	7	3	4	12	72	0	123	3	4
Roberts, Brett, New Britain	11	9	.550	3.41	28	28	5	1	0	0	174.0	162	729	72	66	9	4	5	5	50	0	135	6	0
Mendoza, Reynol, Portland	9	10	.474	3.43	27	27	1	1	0	0	168.0	163	715	73	64	6	10	4	9	69	3	120	15	0
Whisenant, Matt, Portland*	10	6	.625	3.50	23	22	2	0	0	0	128.2	106	544	57	50	8	7	4	9	65	3	107	8	0
Grace, Mike, Reading	13	6	.684	3.54	24	24	2	0	0	0	147.1	137	606	65	58	13	5	0	6	35	0	118	3	2
Stephenson, Garrett, Bowie	7	10	.412	3.64	29	29	1	0	0	0	175.1	154	743	87	71	23	5	7	18	47	0	139	4	2
Cunnane, Will, Portland	9	2	.818	3.67	21	21	1	1	0	0	117.2	120	497	48	48	10	3	0	5	34	1	83	2	0
Steph, Rod, Canton/Akron	8	10	.444	3.81	32	20	1	0	5	0	137.0	150	595	74	58	6	7	2	9	33	1	82	5	0
Brooks, Wes, Trenton	5	11	.313	4.12	29	23	5	0	0	0	161.2	149	670	87	74	17	4	7	11	43	0	85	5	6

DEPARTMENTAL LEADERS: W—Moore, 14; L—Buddie, Paniagua, Ramirez, Stull, 12; Pct.—Cunnane, .818; G—Doolan, 60; GS—Stephenson, 29; CG—Brooks, Falteisek, Roberts, 5; ShO—Tranberg, 3; GF—Viano, 49; Sv.—Powell, 24; IP—Orellano, 186.2; H—Miller, 172; TBF—Orellano, 772; R—Buddie, 102; ER—Weber, 85; HR—Stephenson, 23; SH—Norris, Weber, 11; SF—Senior, 11; HB—Stephenson, 18; BB—Weber, 90; IBB—Knackert, 8; SO—Orellano, 160; WP—Re. Mendoza, 15; Bk.—Brooks, Gomes, 6.

ALL PITCHERS

*Lefthanded pitcher.

Pitcher, Team	W	L	Pct.	ERA	G	GS	CG	ShO	GF	Sv.	IP	H	TBF	R	ER	HR	SH	SF	HB	BB	IBB	SO	WP	Bk.
Alfonseca, Antonio, Portland	9	3	.750	3.64	19	17	1	0	0	0	96.1	81	405	43	39	6	3	3	4	42	1	75	5	4
Alston, Garvin, New Haven	4	4	.500	2.84	47	0	0	0	20	6	66.2	47	271	24	21	1	4	2	3	26	3	73	4	0
Alvarez, Tavo, Harrisburg	2	1	.667	2.25	3	3	0	0	0	0	16.0	17	70	8	4	0	0	0	0	5	0	14	0	0
Aminoff, Matt, New Haven	0	2	.000	1.54	6	0	0	0	2	0	11.2	9	51	7	2	0	2	0	0	6	1	10	0	0
Amos, Chad, Trenton	0	0	.000	12.60	6	0	0	0	1	0	5.0	10	25	8	7	2	0	0	0	3	0	1	2	0
Andersen, Larry, Reading	0	0	.000	6.23	5	0	0	0	1	0	4.1	6	21	3	3	0	0	0	1	1	0	7	0	0
Antolick, Jeff, Norwich	1	1	.500	6.75	2	2	0	0	0	0	9.1	17	46	9	7	2	0	2	1	2	0	5	1	0
Arffa, Steve, Binghamton	0	0	.000	4.50	1	1	0	0	0	0	6.0	7	25	3	3	0	0	0	0	1	0	1	0	1
Arteaga, Ivan, New Haven	2	4	.333	5.56	14	11	0	0	0	0	34.0	36	162	26	21	3	1	2	5	21	0	18	1	3
Aucoin, Derek, Harrisburg	2	4	.333	4.96	29	0	0	0	10	1	52.2	52	242	34	29	3	0	5	8	28	2	48	2	0
Bakkum, Scott, Trenton	6	4	.600	1.34	28	0	0	0	10	0	47.0	31	181	12	7	4	1	1	2	9	2	24	1	0
Beech, Matt, Reading*	2	4	.333	2.96	14	13	0	0	0	0	79.0	67	345	33	26	7	6	2	6	33	1	70	4	1
Bennett, Shayne, Trenton	0	1	.000	5.06	10	0	0	0	6	3	10.2	16	48	6	6	0	3	1	0	3	0	6	1	0
Blais, Mike, Trenton	2	0	1.000	2.52	13	0	0	0	7	0	25.0	19	96	8	7	1	1	2	1	7	0	20	0	0
Blazier, Ron, Reading	4	5	.444	3.29	56	3	0	0	17	1	106.2	93	431	44	39	11	5	2	0	31	7	102	2	1
Bogott, Kurt, Trenton*	0	1	.000	2.70	2	0	0	0	2	0	3.1	3	13	1	1	1	0	0	0	1	0	2	0	0
Borowski, Joe, Bowie	2	2	.500	3.92	16	0	0	0	14	7	20.2	16	83	9	9	2	0	0	0	7	1	32	1	0
Botkin, Alan, Harrisburg*	0	0	.000	8.31	3	0	0	0	2	1	4.1	5	19	4	4	2	0	0	0	2	0	4	2	0
Brooks, Wes, Trenton	5	11	.313	4.12	29	23	5	0	0	0	161.2	149	670	87	74	17	4	7	11	43	0	85	5	6
Brown, Dan, Reading	1	0	1.000	7.71	2	0	0	0	1	0	2.1	4	12	4	2	1	0	0	0	0	0	2	0	0
Brown, Dickie, Canton/Akron	8	5	.615	4.67	37	9	0	0	11	3	98.1	88	449	56	51	9	7	3	4	67	7	51	9	0
Brownson, Mark, New Haven	0	0	.000	1.50	1	1	0	0	0	0	6.0	4	24	2	1	1	0	0	0	1	0	4	0	0
Buddie, Mike, Norwich	10	12	.455	4.81	29	27	2	0	1	1	149.2	155	689	102	80	4	6	8	15	81	2	106	13	1
Bullinger, Kirk, Harrisburg	5	3	.625	2.42	56	0	0	0	39	7	67.0	61	282	22	18	4	4	1	0	25	5	42	2	2
Bullock, Craig, Binghamton	0	3	.000	6.89	11	0	0	0	4	0	15.2	20	74	12	12	1	0	2	0	7	0	12	0	0
Cabrera, Jose, Canton/Akron	5	3	.625	3.28	24	11	1	1	4	0	85.0	83	350	32	31	7	1	6	1	21	1	61	0	2
Cain, Tim, Trenton	4	3	.571	3.73	29	1	0	0	8	4	50.2	46	215	25	21	1	4	0	6	17	3	45	3	0
Carper, Mark, Norwich	0	0	.000	10.80	1	1	0	0	0	0	5.0	9	26	6	6	2	0	1	2	1	0	3	2	0
Carter, Glenn, Trenton	1	1	.500	3.07	14	0	0	0	12	8	14.2	15	63	8	5	0	0	0	1	4	0	10	1	1
Carter, John, Canton/Akron	1	2	.333	3.95	5	5	0	0	0	0	27.1	27	118	13	12	0	0	0	3	13	2	14	1	0
Carter, Tom, Norwich*	3	7	.300	5.57	28	15	0	0	2	0	97.0	128	467	69	60	4	3	4	3	47	3	65	10	0
Caruso, Joe, Trenton	1	1	.500	11.37	11	0	0	0	5	0	12.2	21	64	16	16	1	0	0	2	8	0	8	2	0
Case, Mike, New Haven	0	0	.000	0.00	2	0	0	0	2	0	3.0	0	10	0	0	0	0	0	1	0	0	2	0	0
Cederblad, Brett, Trenton	3	2	.600	3.63	8	5	2	1	1	0	44.2	43	182	19	18	4	2	2	0	11	1	36	2	0
Chapin, Darrin, Canton/Akron	0	1	.000	4.50	4	0	0	0	2	0	8.0	12	38	7	4	0	1	0	0	2	0	6	0	1
Chavez, Carlos, Bowie	0	0	.000	0.00	1	0	0	0	0	0	2.0	0	6	0	0	0	0	0	0	1	0	2	0	0
Chergey, Dan, Portland	6	7	.462	3.47	55	0	0	0	27	5	80.1	62	331	35	31	7	7	2	3	26	6	75	2	0
Ciccarella, Joe, Trenton*	2	1	.667	2.73	22	2	0	0	6	0	33.0	31	138	13	10	3	1	3	0	12	0	33	0	0
Coleman, Billy, Norwich	6	4	.600	4.05	46	0	0	0	12	2	73.1	56	335	52	33	5	3	4	4	57	5	64	12	1
Conner, Scott, Bowie	5	1	.833	4.17	44	0	0	0	9	0	82.0	57	378	43	38	7	4	7	10	74	2	82	13	2
Coppinger, Rocky, Bowie	6	2	.750	2.69	13	13	2	2	0	0	83.2	58	352	33	25	7	0	4	3	43	0	62	4	1
Cosman, Jeff, Binghamton	2	4	.333	7.08	10	10	0	0	0	0	48.1	57	219	40	38	4	1	1	2	18	0	23	2	0
Crawford, Carlos, Cant./Akron	2	2	.500	2.61	8	8	2	0	0	0	51.2	47	212	19	15	1	1	0	1	15	0	36	2	0
Crawford, Joe, Binghamton*	7	2	.778	2.23	42	1	0	0	15	0	60.2	48	239	17	15	4	3	7	5	17	4	43	3	1
Cunnane, Will, Portland	9	2	.818	3.67	21	21	1	1	0	0	117.2	120	497	48	48	10	3	0	5	34	1	83	2	0
Dedrick, Jim, Bowie	4	2	.667	2.98	10	10	0	0	0	0	60.1	59	267	24	20	7	2	2	5	25	2	48	5	1
DeHart, Rick, Harrisburg	6	7	.462	4.84	35	12	0	0	4	0	93.0	94	417	62	50	13	4	6	5	39	3	64	4	4
DeJean, Mike, Norwich	5	5	.500	2.99	59	0	0	0	40	20	78.1	58	323	29	26	5	2	3	5	34	2	57	4	1
DeJesus, Javier, New Britain*	0	0	.000	1.59	4	0	0	0	2	0	5.2	8	26	2	1	0	0	1	0	1	0	3	1	0
DeLaMaza, Roland, Cant./Akron	2	1	.667	4.10	7	7	0	0	0	0	37.1	35	162	19	17	5	0	0	2	18	0	27	1	0
DeLaRosa, Maximo, Cant./Akron	0	0	.000	54.00	1	0	0	0	0	0	0.1	1	3	2	2	1	0	0	0	1	0	0	0	0
Devereux, Charles, Bowie	0	1	.000	5.21	12	0	0	0	3	0	19.0	24	100	13	11	2	0	2	0	17	3	27	1	0
Diaz, Ralph, Harrisburg	2	2	.500	5.59	11	1	0	0	2	0	19.1	17	83	13	12	3	2	0	1	9	2	16	1	0
Dodd, Robert, Reading*	0	0	.000	0.00	1	0	0	0	0	0	1.1	0	5	0	0	0	0	0	0	2	0	0	0	0
Doolan, Blake, Reading	11	5	.688	2.22	60	0	0	0	45	16	73.0	63	300	22	18	3	3	5	0	27	4	50	4	1
Driskill, Travis, Canton/Akron	3	4	.429	4.66	33	0	0	0	22	4	46.1	46	200	24	24	3	1	1	1	19	1	39	0	1
Edmondson, Brian, Binghamton	7	11	.389	4.76	23	22	2	1	0	0	134.1	150	601	82	71	17	5	5	6	59	2	69	7	0
Emerson, Scott, Bowie-Tre.*	0	2	.000	4.98	8	4	0	0	0	0	21.2	28	111	21	12	3	0	1	0	16	0	18	4	0
Engle, Tom, Binghamton	2	1	.667	5.40	13	2	0	0	5	0	28.1	28	118	19	17	5	2	0	3	7	0	15	2	0
Eshelman, Vaughn, Trenton*	0	1	.000	0.00	2	2	0	0	0	0	7.0	3	25	1	0	0	0	0	1	0	0	7	0	0
Faino, Jeff, Tre.-Bowie*	1	3	.250	2.66	36	0	0	0	15	0	50.2	43	207	21	15	3	3	3	2	16	1	22	2	0
Falteisek, Steve, Harrisburg	9	6	.600	2.95	25	25	5	0	0	0	168.0	152	707	74	55	3	7	5	11	64	4	112	6	1
Farmer, Mike, New Haven*	10	5	.667	4.89	40	12	0	0	7	0	110.1	117	475	63	60	8	6	2	5	35	4	77	5	3
Fernandez, Jared, Trenton	5	4	.556	3.90	11	10	1	0	0	0	67.0	64	290	32	29	4	3	1	5	28	1	40	2	0
Fernandez, Sid, Bowie*	1	0	1.000	0.75	2	2	1	1	0	0	12.0	4	41	2	1	0	0	0	0	3	0	10	1	0
Fiegel, Todd, Binghamton*	0	1	.000	15.00	4	0	0	0	1	0	3.0	4	21	5	5	1	0	1	4	3	0	3	1	1
Fisher, David, Reading	0	0	.000	0.00	2	0	0	0	2	0	2.1	1	8	0	0	0	0	0	1	0	0	1	0	0
Forney, Rick, Bowie	7	7	.500	5.75	23	19	1	1	2	0	97.0	110	437	69	62	14	2	6	3	42	0	73	7	1
Foster, Mark, Reading*	1	1	.500	5.66	25	0	0	0	4	1	20.2	25	106	15	13	1	2	1	1	17	3	15	2	4
Fronio, Jason, Canton/Akron	1	3	.250	7.22	8	5	1	0	1	0	28.2	32	137	25	23	2	0	3	4	16	0	23	5	0
Fuller, Mark, Binghamton	4	3	.571	2.95	47	1	0	0	12	1	79.1	83	330	33	26	7	2	3	5	22	5	34	0	4
Fultz, Aaron, New Britain*	0	2	.000	6.60	3	3	0	0	0	0	15.0	11	64	12	11	1	0	2	0	9	0	12	0	0
Gandarillas, Gus, New Britain	2	4	.333	6.12	25	0	0	0	18	7	32.1	38	152	26	22	1	2	0	3	16	0	25	3	0
Gavaghan, Sean, New Britain	2	1	.667	2.20	21	0	0	0	21	5	28.2	18	119	10	7	0	2	2	2	10	2	30	0	1
Gentile, Scott, Harrisburg	2	2	.500	3.44	37	0	0	0	26	11	49.2	36	202	19	19	3	2	1	4	15	2	48	1	0
Gilmore, Joel, Reading	2	0	1.000	6.25	18	3	0	0	4	0	36.0	45	168	27	25	6	1	2	3	18	2	27	3	1
Gomes, Wayne, Reading	7	4	.636	3.96	22	22	1	1	0	0	104.2	89	462	54	46	8	3	1	1	70	0	102	6	6
Grace, Mike, Reading	13	6	.684	3.54	24	24	2	0	0	0	147.1	137	606	65	58	13	5	0	6	35	0	118	3	2
Graves, Dan, Canton/Akron	1	0	1.000	0.00	17	0	0	0	17	10	23.1	10	82	1	0	0	4	0	1	2	0	11	0	0
Grundt, Ken, New Haven*	2	2	.500	2.13	28	0	0	0	8	3	38.0	26	146	14	9	1	2	0	1	10	2	27	2	0

Pitcher, Team	W	L	Pct.	ERA	G	GS	CG	ShO	GF	Sv.	IP	H	TBF	R	ER	HR	SH	SF	HB	BB	IBB	SO	WP	Bk.
Guerra, Mark, Binghamton	2	1	.667	5.79	6	5	1	0	0	0	32.2	35	139	24	21	6	1	0	0	9	1	24	0	0
Hancock, Chris, Portland*	0	0	.000	0.00	1	0	0	0	0	0	0.0	2	2	1	1	0	0	0	0	0	0	0	0	0
Hanselman, Carl, Reading	4	3	.571	6.37	24	1	0	0	4	2	41.0	45	186	29	29	7	1	1	4	17	1	35	2	0
Hansen, Brent, Trenton	4	5	.444	3.26	11	11	3	1	0	0	77.1	70	327	32	28	5	3	2	12	17	1	52	1	2
Harris, Doug, Bowie	3	5	.375	4.01	11	11	2	0	0	0	60.2	66	259	30	27	6	1	1	0	15	1	32	2	2
Harris, Pep, Canton/Akron	6	3	.667	2.39	32	7	0	0	20	10	83.0	78	346	34	22	4	8	4	4	23	3	40	2	2
Heflin, Bronson, Reading	0	0	.000	0.00	1	0	0	0	1	0	1.0	0	4	0	0	0	0	0	0	1	0	2	0	0
Henderson, Chris, New Haven	0	0	.000	0.00	3	0	0	0	3	0	4.0	1	15	0	0	0	1	0	0	2	0	2	1	0
Henderson, Rod, Harrisburg	3	6	.333	4.31	12	12	0	0	0	0	56.1	51	240	28	27	4	0	1	5	18	0	53	1	0
Heredia, Wilson, Portland	4	0	1.000	2.00	4	4	0	0	0	0	27.0	22	115	7	6	2	1	1	1	14	0	19	0	0
Hiljus, Erik, Binghamton	2	4	.333	5.86	10	10	0	0	0	0	55.1	60	252	38	36	8	2	1	1	32	1	40	4	2
Hill, Chris, Trenton*	0	0	.000	9.00	7	0	0	0	2	0	6.0	7	30	6	6	0	0	0	0	6	0	10	1	0
Hill, Eric, Reading	4	3	.571	2.90	38	0	0	0	16	4	59.0	55	251	23	19	1	3	3	0	27	6	52	2	1
Hines, Rich, Norwich*	3	5	.375	3.63	54	0	0	0	28	7	62.0	58	283	38	25	2	1	4	5	34	7	50	7	2
Hoeme, Steve, Trenton	2	0	1.000	3.33	20	0	0	0	14	6	24.1	23	108	9	9	1	2	2	3	8	0	17	3	0
Holman, Brad, New Haven	0	0	.000	3.38	7	1	0	0	4	0	16.0	8	58	6	6	0	0	1	0	5	0	9	1	1
Holman, Craig, Reading	1	1	.500	3.49	32	1	0	0	13	1	56.2	55	235	27	22	10	2	2	2	16	2	40	2	1
Hrusovsky, John, Cant./Akron	1	7	.125	7.11	35	4	0	0	11	1	69.2	77	323	64	55	12	4	6	2	35	3	59	1	0
Hubbard, Mark, Norwich*	4	4	.500	4.21	13	12	0	0	1	1	72.2	81	310	38	34	2	2	2	6	25	1	39	1	1
Hudson, Joe, Trenton	0	1	.000	1.71	22	0	0	0	17	8	31.2	20	133	8	6	0	1	0	1	17	3	24	2	1
Hunter, Rich, Reading	3	0	1.000	2.05	3	3	0	0	0	0	22.0	14	86	6	5	1	0	1	0	6	0	17	2	0
Hurst, James, Bowie*	0	0	.000	0.00	1	0	0	0	0	0	1.1	2	8	3	0	0	1	0	0	1	0	1	0	0
Hutchins, Jason, New Haven	0	0	.000	3.86	12	1	0	0	4	1	14.0	13	70	6	6	0	0	0	2	14	0	14	3	0
Ingram, Todd, Trenton	1	1	.500	5.84	18	0	0	0	7	0	24.2	27	125	19	16	2	2	2	1	21	4	16	1	1
Isringhausen, Jason, Bingham.	2	1	.667	2.85	6	6	1	0	0	0	41.0	26	164	15	13	1	0	0	3	12	0	59	6	0
Janzen, Marty, Norwich	1	2	.333	4.95	3	3	0	0	0	0	20.0	17	85	11	11	2	0	0	2	7	0	16	2	0
Jarvis, Matt, Bowie*	9	8	.529	5.11	26	21	0	0	1	0	118.0	154	531	71	67	11	4	4	4	42	1	60	5	3
Johnson, Dom, Trenton	1	2	.333	9.42	5	2	0	0	1	0	14.1	19	74	16	15	2	0	0	1	12	0	11	2	1
Johnson, Jason, New Haven	6	3	.667	5.32	19	12	0	0	1	0	67.2	77	297	43	40	2	1	4	3	29	1	37	6	0
Jones, Bobby, New Haven*	5	2	.714	2.58	27	8	0	0	9	3	73.1	61	315	27	21	4	3	3	8	36	2	70	7	0
Juelsgaard, Jarod, Portland	3	1	.750	3.89	48	0	0	0	13	2	71.2	65	313	35	31	3	1	2	2	44	2	44	5	0
Juhl, Mike, Reading*	1	8	.111	4.27	49	0	0	0	16	6	46.1	43	208	32	22	4	4	1	1	28	1	39	2	1
Karp, Ryan, Reading*	1	2	.333	3.06	7	7	0	0	0	0	47.0	44	190	18	16	4	3	0	0	15	0	37	1	2
Kendrena, Ken, Harrisburg	3	2	.600	2.51	30	0	0	0	8	1	64.2	58	277	27	18	5	2	1	4	25	2	46	3	0
Kerley, Collin, Harrisburg	0	0	.000	0.00	2	0	0	0	0	0	6.2	5	26	0	0	0	0	0	0	1	0	3	1	0
Kindell, Scott, Binghamton*	0	0	.000	0.00	1	0	0	0	0	0	1.0	2	5	0	0	0	0	0	0	0	0	0	0	0
Kirkreit, Daron, Cant./Akron	2	9	.182	5.69	14	14	1	0	0	0	80.2	74	360	54	51	13	5	5	6	46	1	67	2	0
Kline, Steve, Cant./Akron*	2	3	.400	2.42	14	14	0	0	0	0	89.1	86	377	34	24	6	4	1	1	30	3	45	1	1
Knackert, Brent, Binghamton	7	7	.500	2.30	48	0	0	0	28	11	82.1	53	324	23	21	4	5	2	3	26	8	69	3	0
Knowles, Greg, Bowie	5	2	.714	4.14	37	1	0	0	13	2	74.0	83	327	44	34	6	5	2	1	26	7	37	3	0
Koller, Rod, Canton/Akron	0	0	.000	7.23	9	1	0	0	2	1	18.2	26	89	17	15	2	0	1	2	4	0	3	0	0
Konieczki, Dom, New Britain*	0	1	.000	1.95	39	0	0	0	15	1	32.1	28	146	10	7	1	2	1	1	19	2	35	3	0
Kotarski, Mike, New Haven*	2	3	.400	3.24	31	0	0	0	10	2	50.0	43	234	25	18	4	4	2	1	36	4	54	3	5
Kozeniewski, Blaise, Norwich	1	0	1.000	4.91	29	0	0	0	13	0	55.0	53	250	35	30	2	1	2	6	27	0	33	3	0
Lane, Aaron, Bowie*	5	3	.625	4.17	40	0	0	0	18	2	45.1	45	200	23	21	2	5	0	1	21	3	31	3	1
Langbehn, Gregg, Trenton*	0	1	.000	5.40	14	0	0	0	2	1	13.1	9	57	9	8	0	0	0	1	9	0	11	0	0
Larkin, Andy, Portland	1	2	.333	3.38	9	9	0	0	0	0	40.0	29	160	16	15	5	4	0	6	11	2	23	1	0
Leahy, Pat, Portland	3	1	.750	4.50	13	6	0	0	1	0	42.0	32	175	24	21	5	5	1	1	20	3	37	2	0
Legault, Kevin, New Britain	6	1	.857	3.21	47	1	0	0	17	3	87.0	79	367	31	31	3	6	5	4	28	4	52	5	0
Lehman, Toby, Bowie	1	3	.250	7.94	4	4	0	0	0	0	17.0	20	77	15	15	4	0	0	0	11	0	14	0	0
Lemon, Don, Portland	1	6	.143	3.61	30	3	0	0	11	1	62.1	60	263	30	25	3	4	4	0	19	3	47	0	2
Lemp, Chris, Bowie	2	4	.333	5.40	18	0	0	0	16	4	20.0	28	94	13	12	0	1	2	2	7	3	14	3	0
Loewer, Carlton, Reading	4	1	.800	2.16	8	8	0	0	0	0	50.0	42	212	17	12	3	1	0	1	31	0	35	4	0
Long, Joe, Norwich	4	2	.667	4.85	43	1	0	0	15	2	81.2	103	391	54	44	4	2	6	6	48	3	34	3	0
Ludwick, Eric, Binghamton	12	5	.706	2.95	23	22	3	2	0	0	143.1	108	590	52	47	9	4	6	2	68	1	131	6	0
Maduro, Calvin, Bowie	0	6	.000	5.09	7	7	0	0	0	0	35.1	39	165	28	20	3	1	2	0	27	0	26	3	0
Magee, Bo, C-A/Bowie*	1	3	.250	6.63	26	1	0	0	11	1	38.0	43	185	34	28	2	0	2	0	34	2	32	5	0
Maldonado, Jay, New Britain	0	0	.000	11.81	5	0	0	0	1	0	5.1	7	28	8	7	0	1	0	0	3	0	4	0	3
Malloy, Chuck, Trenton	0	0	.000	4.76	1	1	0	0	0	0	5.2	9	28	5	3	0	0	2	2	1	0	1	1	0
Mansur, Jeff, New Britain*	0	0	.000	1.42	5	0	0	0	2	1	6.1	5	26	1	1	1	0	0	0	2	0	3	0	0
Mantei, Matt, Portland	1	0	1.000	2.38	8	0	0	0	4	1	11.1	10	48	3	3	0	1	0	1	5	0	15	0	0
Matthews, Mike, Cant./Akron*	5	8	.385	5.93	15	15	1	0	0	0	74.1	82	345	62	49	6	2	8	2	43	1	37	8	1
McCready, Jim, Binghamton	1	1	.500	3.23	32	0	0	0	16	4	39.0	42	178	21	14	4	3	2	2	14	1	17	5	0
McDill, Allen, Binghamton*	3	5	.375	4.56	12	12	1	0	0	0	73.0	69	324	42	37	5	1	4	3	38	2	44	3	1
McGraw, Tom, Portland*	5	0	1.000	1.81	51	0	0	0	11	2	74.2	69	322	21	15	2	7	3	4	31	3	60	4	0
Mendoza, Ramiro, Norwich	5	6	.455	3.21	19	19	2	1	0	0	89.2	87	380	39	32	4	1	1	2	33	0	68	2	1
Mendoza, Reynol, Portland	9	10	.474	3.43	27	27	1	1	0	0	168.0	163	715	73	64	6	10	4	9	69	3	120	15	0
Mikkelsen, Linc, Harrisburg	1	2	.333	5.37	21	5	0	0	5	0	53.2	57	243	33	32	1	5	2	4	24	0	39	1	1
Miller, Travis, New Britain*	7	9	.438	4.37	28	27	1	1	1	0	162.2	172	723	93	79	17	6	3	4	65	2	151	5	0
Mitchell, Larry, Reading	6	11	.353	5.54	25	24	1	1	1	0	128.1	136	584	85	79	13	2	2	4	72	4	107	7	1
Mix, Greg, Portland	6	4	.600	4.68	24	13	0	0	1	0	92.1	98	401	51	48	9	2	4	4	25	5	56	3	0
Moore, Joel, New Haven	14	6	.700	3.20	27	26	1	1	0	0	157.1	156	682	69	56	8	6	6	8	67	2	102	5	1
Moten, Scott, New Britain	8	5	.615	3.94	40	1	0	0	18	3	75.1	65	323	40	33	8	6	3	0	36	2	43	5	0
Munoz, Bobby, Reading	0	4	.000	10.80	4	4	0	0	0	0	15.0	28	74	19	18	4	0	0	0	3	0	8	1	0
Musselwhite, James, Norwich	5	9	.357	4.58	24	24	1	0	0	0	131.2	136	566	75	67	11	5	6	6	34	3	96	8	1
Musset, Jose, Norwich	4	1	.800	3.33	34	0	0	0	12	4	48.2	43	217	21	18	2	3	3	7	24	2	42	4	0
Neier, Chris, New Haven	10	4	.714	4.16	38	18	1	0	5	0	123.1	164	550	62	57	10	4	3	1	47	5	74	2	1
Newlin, Jim, Bowie	3	5	.375	3.68	40	1	0	0	26	11	63.2	69	283	35	26	6	3	5	2	22	3	51	9	1
Nied, David, New Haven	0	0	.000	8.10	1	1	0	0	0	0	3.1	4	14	3	3	2	0	0	0	0	0	0	0	0
Nieto, Tony, Bowie	0	0	.000	15.00	1	1	0	0	0	0	3.0	6	18	5	5	2	0	0	0	3	0	3	0	0
Norris, Joe, New Britain	5	6	.455	3.59	46	0	0	0	20	5	82.2	79	364	42	33	4	11	3	2	36	5	81	4	0
Novoa, Rafael, Binghamton*	0	1	.000	2.25	4	0	0	0	2	0	8.0	6	34	2	2	0	1	0	0	5	0	6	0	0
Ohme, Kevin, New Britain*	3	4	.429	3.46	35	11	0	0	7	0	101.1	89	427	51	39	5	7	7	3	45	1	52	7	0

Pitcher, Team	W	L	Pct.	ERA	G	GS	CG	ShO	GF	Sv.	IP	H	TBF	R	ER	HR	SH	SF	HB	BB	IBB	SO	WP	Bk.
Orellano, Rafael, Trenton*	11	7	.611	3.09	27	27	2	0	0	0	186.2	146	772	68	64	18	4	1	11	72	0	160	9	4
Pacheco, Alex, Harrisburg	9	7	.563	4.27	45	0	0	0	29	4	86.1	76	371	45	41	8	1	1	8	31	4	88	4	0
Paniagua, Jose, Harrisburg	7	12	.368	5.34	25	25	2	1	0	0	126.1	140	575	84	75	9	5	5	12	62	0	89	8	0
Pantoja, Johnny, Norwich	1	2	.333	6.48	11	2	0	0	2	0	25.0	29	119	23	18	1	1	1	2	14	0	19	0	0
Paxton, Darrin, Har.-Bing.*	1	2	.333	3.48	28	3	0	0	10	0	44.0	46	184	22	17	3	0	2	0	13	1	27	1	1
Percibal, Billy, Bowie	1	0	1.000	0.00	2	2	0	0	0	0	14.0	7	52	0	0	0	0	0	0	7	0	7	0	1
Perez, Melido, Norwich	1	0	1.000	0.00	2	2	0	0	0	0	9.0	7	35	0	0	0	0	0	0	3	0	9	0	1
Perschke, Greg, Cant./Akron	1	0	1.000	3.38	3	0	0	0	1	0	5.1	4	21	2	2	1	0	0	0	2	0	4	1	0
Person, Robert, Binghamton	5	4	.556	3.11	26	7	1	0	13	7	66.2	46	263	27	23	4	4	1	0	25	0	65	1	0
Peterson, Dean, Trenton	4	8	.333	5.38	20	14	1	0	2	0	88.2	96	389	57	53	7	3	3	4	27	3	47	3	4
Pettit, Doug, Portland	3	1	.750	3.69	21	0	0	0	9	2	31.2	30	129	13	13	1	2	0	2	6	3	24	0	0
Pierce, Ed, Bowie*	0	2	.000	6.43	7	4	0	0	1	1	21.0	32	102	16	15	2	1	2	0	9	0	16	2	0
Pollard, Damon, Harrisburg	0	0	.000	8.64	6	0	0	0	1	0	8.1	11	42	11	8	2	1	2	0	4	0	10	5	0
Popplewell, Tom, Cant./Akron	2	0	1.000	9.74	15	0	0	0	3	0	20.1	33	103	22	22	6	1	2	0	16	1	14	0	0
Pote, Lou, Harrisburg	0	1	.000	5.40	9	4	0	0	2	0	28.1	32	123	17	17	3	0	2	1	7	0	24	1	0
Powell, Jay, Portland	5	4	.556	1.87	50	0	0	0	44	24	53.0	42	213	12	11	2	3	1	2	15	1	53	2	1
Puig, Benny, Harrisburg*	0	0	.000	0.00	1	0	0	0	0	0	1.2	3	9	2	0	0	0	0	0	1	0	0	0	0
Ramirez, Hector, Binghamton	4	12	.250	4.60	20	20	2	0	0	0	123.1	127	534	69	63	12	2	2	3	48	2	63	3	5
Rekar, Bryan, New Haven	6	3	.667	2.13	12	12	1	1	0	0	80.1	65	325	28	19	4	3	0	3	16	1	80	0	0
Ricken, Ray, Norwich	4	2	.667	2.72	8	8	1	1	0	0	53.0	44	217	21	16	2	2	0	1	24	2	43	3	0
Riley, Ed, Trenton*	0	0	.000	2.76	16	0	0	0	7	1	16.1	14	74	6	5	1	0	2	4	9	1	10	0	0
Ritchie, Todd, New Britain	4	9	.308	5.73	24	21	0	0	0	0	113.0	135	515	78	72	12	4	5	6	54	0	60	8	0
Roberts, Brett, New Britain	11	9	.550	3.41	28	28	5	1	0	0	174.0	162	729	72	66	9	4	5	5	50	0	135	6	0
Rojas, Euclides, Portland	1	1	.500	7.77	14	1	0	0	5	1	22.0	27	104	20	19	3	0	0	1	13	1	22	2	1
Ruffin, Bruce, New Haven*	0	0	.000	0.00	2	2	0	0	0	0	2.0	1	7	0	0	0	0	0	0	0	0	2	0	0
Ryan, Ken, Trenton	0	2	.000	5.82	11	0	0	0	7	2	17.0	23	79	13	11	1	1	0	0	5	0	16	0	0
Ryan, Kevin, Bowie	4	3	.571	3.43	39	1	0	0	14	5	63.0	67	267	31	24	5	2	2	1	15	2	31	1	0
Saccavino, Craig, New Britain	1	6	.143	5.66	27	1	0	0	12	1	41.1	48	213	36	26	6	3	3	2	32	0	34	8	0
Salamon, John, New Haven	1	0	1.000	6.10	6	0	0	0	0	0	10.1	9	54	7	7	0	1	2	0	16	1	9	1	0
Schneider, Phil, New Haven*	0	1	.000	7.71	2	2	0	0	0	0	7.0	8	37	8	6	1	1	0	0	9	0	3	0	0
Schorr, Brad, Binghamton	0	2	.000	9.18	4	4	0	0	0	0	16.2	21	87	21	17	1	0	1	0	20	1	6	2	0
Sele, Aaron, Trenton	0	1	.000	3.38	2	2	0	0	0	0	8.0	8	33	3	3	0	0	1	2	2	0	9	0	0
Senior, Shawn, Trenton*	11	7	.611	4.52	27	27	0	0	0	0	151.1	154	673	91	76	15	5	11	9	68	2	90	10	4
Serafini, Dan, New Britain*	12	9	.571	3.38	27	27	1	1	0	0	162.2	155	692	74	61	7	3	4	12	72	0	123	3	4
Shaw, Cedric, Harrisburg*	0	1	.000	4.66	5	2	0	0	0	0	19.1	25	83	10	10	2	1	0	0	6	0	13	2	0
Shenk, Larry, Bowie	0	0	.000	6.52	6	0	0	0	1	0	9.2	6	45	8	7	1	1	0	1	8	0	8	2	0
Smith, Eric, Reading	0	1	.000	20.25	4	0	0	0	0	0	4.0	11	28	9	9	1	0	0	1	4	1	5	2	0
Spencer, Stan, Portland	1	4	.200	7.38	8	8	0	0	0	0	39.0	57	193	39	32	9	0	4	2	19	0	32	0	0
Standish, Scott, Norwich	4	3	.571	5.67	17	9	0	0	0	0	60.1	73	280	43	38	3	2	3	5	30	3	47	4	2
Steph, Rod, Canton/Akron	8	10	.444	3.81	32	20	1	0	5	0	137.0	150	595	74	58	6	7	2	9	33	1	82	5	0
Stephenson, Garrett, Bowie	7	10	.412	3.64	29	29	1	0	0	0	175.1	154	743	87	71	23	5	7	18	47	0	139	4	2
Stidham, Phil, Binghamton	0	0	.000	4.66	7	0	0	0	4	0	9.2	9	47	6	5	0	1	0	0	9	0	7	0	0
Stull, Everett, Harrisburg	3	12	.200	5.54	24	24	0	0	0	0	126.2	114	569	88	78	12	5	5	9	79	2	132	7	1
Sullivan, Grant, Norwich*	0	0	.000	54.00	1	0	0	0	0	0	0.2	4	6	4	4	1	0	0	0	0	0	0	0	0
Sullivan, Mike, Trenton	3	1	.750	1.37	15	0	0	0	9	2	19.2	17	79	5	3	1	1	0	2	3	0	16	0	0
Suppan, Jeff, Trenton	6	2	.750	2.36	15	15	1	1	0	0	99.0	86	409	35	26	5	1	3	8	26	1	88	4	0
Sutherland, John, Norwich	1	0	1.000	2.77	13	0	0	0	6	2	13.0	12	51	5	4	3	0	1	1	3	0	12	0	0
Tam, Jeff, Binghamton	0	2	.000	4.50	14	0	0	0	7	3	18.0	20	83	11	9	1	2	1	4	4	2	9	3	0
Taylor, Tommy, Canton/Akron	1	1	.500	3.72	5	0	0	0	3	0	9.2	9	41	4	4	2	1	1	0	6	0	3	0	0
Telford, Anthony, Canton/Akron	2	0	1.000	0.82	2	2	0	0	0	0	11.0	6	42	2	1	0	0	0	0	4	1	4	0	0
Tellers, Dave, New Haven	2	5	.286	2.87	33	3	0	0	4	1	69.0	60	278	29	22	3	2	3	4	14	1	63	3	0
Thomson, John, New Haven	7	8	.467	4.18	26	24	0	0	0	0	131.1	132	572	69	61	8	2	7	2	56	0	82	3	2
Tirado, Aris, Harrisburg	1	0	1.000	0.77	8	0	0	0	4	1	11.2	8	48	1	1	1	0	1	0	5	0	10	0	0
Tranberg, Mark, Reading	6	6	.500	3.73	18	18	3	3	0	0	111.0	110	458	50	46	7	3	3	3	30	0	62	5	0
Trinidad, Hector, New Britain	4	11	.267	4.61	23	22	0	0	1	0	121.0	137	516	67	62	6	1	10	7	22	0	92	6	2
Trisler, John, Reading	2	4	.333	5.16	30	10	0	0	10	0	82.0	96	366	51	47	6	1	3	6	26	1	50	2	2
Trlicek, Rick, Canton/Akron	5	3	.625	3.05	24	0	0	0	16	3	38.1	33	158	16	13	4	4	2	0	16	3	27	1	1
Turner, Brian, Norwich*	0	0	.000	9.00	2	0	0	0	2	0	2.0	2	12	2	2	1	0	0	1	2	0	0	0	0
Viano, Jake, New Haven	3	6	.333	3.38	57	0	0	0	49	19	72.0	51	304	31	27	5	7	3	2	38	1	85	2	0
Virgilio, George, Bowie	0	0	.000	0.00	1	0	0	0	0	0	1.0	0	4	0	0	0	0	0	0	0	0	0	0	0
Voisard, Mark, New Haven	2	0	1.000	3.23	27	0	0	0	10	2	30.2	31	132	12	11	1	0	1	2	14	0	22	4	0
Wainhouse, David, Portland	2	1	.667	7.20	17	0	0	0	5	0	25.0	39	122	22	20	3	0	1	1	8	1	16	1	0
Wallace, Derek, Binghamton	0	1	.000	5.28	15	0	0	0	11	2	15.1	11	62	9	9	1	0	3	1	9	1	8	1	2
Wallace, Kent, Norwich	7	6	.538	3.52	18	16	0	0	1	0	94.2	93	395	41	37	9	2	2	1	24	0	72	2	1
Ward, Bryan, Portland*	7	3	.700	4.50	20	11	1	1	5	2	72.0	70	321	42	36	9	1	1	2	31	3	71	7	3
Weber, Neil, Harrisburg*	6	11	.353	5.01	28	28	0	0	0	0	152.2	157	696	98	85	16	11	7	8	90	1	119	7	1
Wegmann, Tom, Bowie	2	3	.400	4.18	14	11	0	0	0	0	64.2	56	272	35	30	8	2	2	2	22	2	49	0	2
Welch, Mike, Binghamton	0	0	.000	0.00	1	0	0	0	1	0	1.0	0	3	0	0	0	0	0	0	0	0	2	0	0
West, David, Reading*	0	0	.000	1.50	1	1	0	0	0	0	6.0	2	23	1	1	1	0	0	0	3	0	8	0	0
Whisenant, Matt, Portland*	10	6	.625	3.50	23	22	2	0	0	0	128.2	106	544	57	50	8	7	4	9	65	3	107	8	0
Whitten, Casey, Canton/Akron*	9	8	.529	3.31	20	20	2	1	0	0	114.1	100	469	49	42	10	1	2	3	38	0	91	5	2
Williams, Greg, Canton/Akron*	0	0	.000	4.23	24	0	0	0	7	0	27.2	15	115	14	13	2	2	1	0	21	3	17	0	0
Wilson, Paul, Binghamton	6	3	.667	2.17	16	16	4	1	0	0	120.1	89	464	34	29	5	3	4	5	24	2	127	4	3
Wright, Jamey, New Haven	0	1	.000	9.00	1	1	0	0	0	0	3.0	6	20	6	3	0	0	0	1	3	0	0	0	0
Zolecki, Mike, New Haven	3	4	.429	3.25	9	7	0	0	1	0	55.1	56	229	25	20	2	1	1	1	20	1	32	0	2

COMBINATION SHUTOUTS: **Binghamton (6)**—Crawford-McCready-Paxton, Isringhausen-Knackert, Ludwick-Engle, Ludwick-Knackert, Ramirez-Person, Wilson-Knackert. **Bowie (6)**—Forney-Borowski, Forney-Newlin-Lane, Jarvis-Conner-Newlin, Percibal-Conner, Stephenson-Newlin, Wegmann-Conner-Lane-Lemp. **Canton/Akron (7)**—Brown-Harris-Graves, Crawford-Graves, Harris-Steph-Graves, Kline-Driskill, Kline-Steph-Trlicek, Whitten-Harris, Whitten-Brown-Magee-Hrusovsky. **Harrisburg (5)**—DeHart-Bullinger, Falteisek-Mikkelsen, Stull-DeHart-Pacheco, Stull-Pacheco, Weber-Aucoin. **New Britain (9)**—Serafini-Gandarillas 3, Legault-Moten, Miller-Gandarillas, Ohme-Gavaghan, Roberts-Gavaghan, Roberts-Norris, Serafini-Mansur-Norris. **New Haven (12)**—Arteaga-Grundt, Farmer-Kotarski-Henderson, Johnson-Kotarski, Johnson-Kotarski-Tellers-Viano, Jones-Voisard, Moore-Jones-Viano, Moore-Tellers-Voisard, Rekar-Alston-Hutchins, Rekar-Kotarski, Ruffin-Farmer, Thomson-Alston-Viano, Thomson-Aminoff-Hutchins. **Norwich (5)**—Buddie-DeJean, Hubbard-DeJean, Perez-Buddie, Standish-Coleman-Kozeniewski, Wallace-Musset-Long. **Portland (6)**—Alfonseca-Juelsgaard, Cunnane-Ward, Larkin-Pettit, Mendoza-McGraw, Mendoza-McGraw-Mantei, Mendoza-Powell-Chergey. **Reading (3)**—Gilmore-Hill, Mitchell-Hill, Mitchell-Holman. **Trenton (5)**—Brooks-Langbehn-Caruso, Orellano-Ciccarella, Senior-Cain, Senior-Caruso-Langbehn, Suppan-Hudson.

NO-HIT GAMES: None.

PITCHERS WITH TWO OR MORE TEAMS

Pitcher, Team	W	L	Pct.	ERA	G	GS	CG	ShO	GF	Sv.	IP	H	TBF	R	ER	HR	SH	SF	HB	BB	IBB	SO	WP	Bk.
Emerson, Scott, Bowie*	0	2	.000	5.06	4	4	0	0	0	0	16.0	19	82	18	9	3	0	1	0	14	0	13	3	0
Emerson, Scott, Trenton*	0	0	.000	4.76	4	0	0	0	0	0	5.2	9	29	3	3	0	0	0	0	2	0	5	1	0
Faino, Jeff, Trenton*	1	1	.500	2.35	5	0	0	0	1	0	7.2	9	32	3	2	1	0	0	0	1	0	5	0	0
Faino, Jeff, Bowie*	0	2	.000	2.72	31	0	0	0	14	0	43.0	34	175	18	13	2	3	3	2	15	1	17	2	0
Magee, Bo, Canton/Akron*	0	2	.000	6.98	21	0	0	0	8	1	29.2	33	145	26	23	0	0	0	0	28	1	25	4	0
Magee, Bo, Bowie*	1	1	.500	5.40	5	1	0	0	3	0	8.1	10	40	8	5	2	0	2	0	6	1	7	1	0
Paxton, Darrin, Harrisburg*	0	1	.000	1.29	7	0	0	0	2	0	7.0	5	30	2	1	0	0	0	0	3	1	7	0	0
Paxton, Darrin, Binghamton*	1	1	.500	3.89	21	3	0	0	8	0	37.0	41	154	20	16	3	0	2	0	10	0	20	1	1

1995 FIELDING

TEAM

Team	Pct.	G	PO	A	E	TC	DP	PB
Binghamton	.978	142	3778	1545	117	5440	129	24
Reading	.977	142	3741	1481	122	5344	137	19
Portland	.976	142	3765	1633	134	5532	116	15
Trenton	.972	142	3839	1575	156	5570	108	23
New Haven	.970	142	3719	1494	159	5372	130	13
Canton/Akron	.968	142	3646	1512	173	5331	136	13
New Britain	.967	142	3740	1549	180	5469	120	17
Harrisburg	.967	141	3659	1438	175	5272	118	28
Norwich	.965	141	3695	1525	188	5408	119	20
Bowie	.965	142	3693	1485	188	5366	118	26

TRIPLE PLAYS: Bowie, New Britain.

INDIVIDUAL

FIRST BASEMEN

NOTE: All caps denotes fielding-percentage leader based on 71 games for catchers, 95 for all other non-pitchers and 142 innings for pitchers. *Throws lefthanded.

Player, Team	Pct.	G	PO	A	E	TC	DP
Arnold, Ken, Bowie	1.000	2	1	0	0	1	0
Barry, Jeff, Binghamton	1.000	4	13	1	0	14	1
Bigler, Jeff, Reading*	.992	13	125	6	1	132	8
Brede, Brent, New Britain*	1.000	10	69	7	0	76	5
Cameron, Stanton, Cant./Akron	1.000	1	2	0	0	2	0
Carey, Todd, Trenton	1.000	8	49	4	0	53	3
Case, Mike, New Haven	.984	39	222	18	4	244	22
Charbonnet, Mark, Harrisburg*	.983	6	50	8	1	59	5
Chavez, Eric, Bowie	.981	12	99	7	2	108	8
Clapinski, Chris, Portland	.900	1	9	0	1	10	1
Clark, Tim, Portland*	.991	129	1158	98	11	1267	93
Daly, Bob, Binghamton	1.000	1	8	2	0	10	1
DAUBACH, Brian, Binghamton	.992	131	1137	98	10	1245	111
Davenport, Adell, Canton/Akron	1.000	6	45	2	0	47	3
Davis, Tommy, Bowie	1.000	3	28	2	0	30	4
Delvecchio, Nick, Norwich	.985	58	498	43	8	549	38
Eason, Tommy, Reading	.987	26	209	18	3	230	17
Epps, Scott, Norwich	1.000	1	7	0	0	7	0
Everson, Darin, Harrisburg	1.000	3	19	0	0	19	1
Fisher, David, Reading	1.000	1	6	0	0	6	0
Friedman, Jason, Bowie*	.987	44	359	35	5	399	31
Fully, Ed, Binghamton	1.000	1	1	0	0	1	1
Garcia, Omar, Binghamton	.978	4	43	2	1	46	3
Geisler, Phil, Reading*	.987	18	137	11	2	150	10
Hardge, Mike, Trenton	1.000	1	0	1	0	1	0
Hartung, Andy, New Haven	.966	3	26	2	1	29	1
Harvey, Ray, Canton/Akron*	.987	10	71	7	1	79	8
Hecker, Doug, Trenton	.994	30	283	26	2	311	16
Held, Dan, Reading	1.000	1	6	0	0	6	2
Hinton, Steve, Harrisburg*	.978	8	45	0	1	46	1
Hymel, Lou, Harrisburg	.985	25	186	17	3	206	19
Jacobs, Frank, Bing.-Har.*	.976	83	670	63	18	751	57
Kennedy, David, New Haven	.984	117	938	70	16	1024	105
Kontorinis, Andrew, New Britain	.991	14	107	8	1	116	5
Kounas, Tony, Harrisburg	.977	18	121	7	3	131	7
Kremers, Jimmy, Portland	.987	18	142	6	2	150	8
Lane, Dan, Harrisburg	1.000	1	2	0	0	2	0
Marabella, Tony, Harrisburg	1.000	7	42	4	0	46	5
Martinez, Ray, Harrisburg	.986	8	58	10	1	69	5
McCall, Rod, Canton/Akron	.992	12	111	7	1	119	15
McGuire, Ryan, Trenton*	.989	70	642	48	8	698	51
McKeel, Walt, Trenton	1.000	3	4	0	0	4	0
McNair, Fred, Reading	.987	88	765	46	11	822	73
Millan, Adan, Reading	1.000	1	8	0	0	8	1
Millares, Jose, Bowie	.966	3	24	4	1	29	3
Moler, Jason, Reading	1.000	1	9	1	0	10	0
Ogden, Jamie, New Britain*	.987	66	582	41	8	631	49
Owens, Billy, Bowie	.988	82	665	60	9	734	62
Pough, Pork Chop, Trenton	.980	32	262	31	6	299	17
Riggs, Kevin, Norwich	.966	3	27	1	1	29	1
Saunders, Chris, Binghamton	1.000	1	7	2	0	9	1
Seefried, Tate, Norwich	.989	58	497	39	6	542	52
Shelton, Ben, N.B.-Tre.*	.987	55	505	36	7	548	43
Smith, Bubba, New Britain	1.000	7	48	3	0	51	6
Smith, Ed, Canton/Akron	.987	12	70	4	1	75	6
Tirpack, Ken, New Britain	.953	5	38	3	2	43	3
Townsend, Chad, Canton/Akron*	.985	111	904	73	15	992	92
Turner, Brian, Norwich*	.990	26	197	11	2	210	20
Virgilio, George, Harrisburg	1.000	2	11	0	0	11	2
Waco, David, Reading	1.000	1	1	0	0	1	0
Waszgis, B.J., Bowie	1.000	1	1	0	0	1	0

TRIPLE PLAYS: Ogden, Owens.

FIRST BASEMEN WITH TWO OR MORE TEAMS

Player, Team	Pct.	G	PO	A	E	TC	DP
Jacobs, Frank, Binghamton*	.962	9	69	6	3	78	4
Jacobs, Frank, Harrisburg*	.978	74	601	57	15	673	53
Shelton, Ben, New Britain*	.988	49	446	36	6	488	40
Shelton, Ben, Trenton*	.983	6	59	0	1	60	3

SECOND BASEMEN

Player, Team	Pct.	G	PO	A	E	TC	DP
Alfonzo, Edgar, Bowie	1.000	19	36	38	0	74	10
Azuaje, Jesus, Binghamton	.989	20	31	63	1	95	16
Biasucci, Joe, Canton/Akron	1.000	4	11	11	0	22	1
Carey, Todd, Trenton	.973	21	46	63	3	112	15
Castaldo, Gregg, Bowie	.971	48	86	116	6	208	28
Clapinski, Chris, Portland	1.000	15	32	28	0	60	9
Crowley, Jim, Bowie	.976	8	19	21	1	41	6
Doster, David, Reading	.983	137	261	420	12	693	91
Duncan, Andres, New Britain	1.000	6	8	7	0	15	1
Fisher, David, Reading	1.000	9	5	18	0	23	2
Fleming, Carlton, Norwich	.950	32	57	75	7	139	14
Gonzalez, Mauricio, New Haven	.986	17	31	40	1	72	7
Hardge, Mike, Trenton	.951	13	17	41	3	61	7
Hardtke, Jason, Binghamton	.970	115	197	346	17	560	68
Hinds, Robert, Norwich	.960	111	248	322	24	594	73
Hunter, Greg, New Britain	1.000	2	1	1	0	2	0
Juday, Rob, Trenton	1.000	3	2	3	0	5	0
Lane, Dan, Harrisburg	1.000	10	21	16	0	37	1
Long, R.D., Norwich	1.000	2	1	4	0	5	0
Mahalik, John, Binghamton	.976	10	16	25	1	42	5
Marabella, Tony, Harrisburg	1.000	1	0	1	0	1	0
Martinez, Ray, Harrisburg	1.000	17	29	39	0	68	7
Maxwell, Pat, Canton/Akron	.960	20	40	57	4	101	10
Mercedes, Feliciano, Bowie	.982	26	44	67	2	113	11
Merloni, Lou, Trenton	.952	72	149	168	16	333	25
Millares, Jose, Bowie	.938	30	54	51	7	112	15
Miller, Ryan, Binghamton	1.000	2	1	4	0	5	0
Milliard, Ralph, Portland	.975	128	299	357	17	673	71
Murphy, Pat, Trenton	.951	7	17	22	2	41	7
Neal, Mike, Canton/Akron	.959	121	238	340	25	603	78
Renteria, Dave, Norwich	1.000	3	5	1	0	6	1
ROGERS, Lamarr, New Haven	.984	104	203	290	8	501	61
Rundels, Matt, Harrisburg	.954	93	196	241	21	458	64
Selby, Bill, Trenton	.966	35	70	70	5	145	14
Smith, Ed, Canton/Akron	1.000	1	0	1	0	1	1
Torres, Tony, Portland	.970	10	14	18	1	33	4
Valette, Ramon, New Britain	.963	26	38	91	5	134	26
Vidro, Jose, Harrisburg	.964	27	61	73	5	139	12
Virgilio, George, Bowie	.947	26	46	62	6	114	12

Player, Team	Pct.	G	PO	A	E	TC	DP
Walker, Todd, New Britain	.961	117	210	328	22	560	65
White, Billy, New Haven	.963	31	57	101	6	164	27
Zuniga, David, Binghamton	1.000	1	0	1	0	1	1

TRIPLE PLAY: Walker.

THIRD BASEMEN

Player, Team	Pct.	G	PO	A	E	TC	DP
Alcantara, Israel, Harrisburg	.892	68	48	118	20	186	9
Alfonzo, Edgar, Bowie	1.000	1	0	1	0	1	0
Azuaje, Jesus, Binghamton	.833	3	3	2	1	6	0
Batiste, Kim, Bowie	.881	23	14	38	7	59	1
Biasucci, Joe, Canton/Akron	.941	7	4	12	1	17	3
Burnett, Roger, Norwich	.915	21	7	47	5	59	3
Carey, Todd, Trenton	.925	27	16	46	5	67	3
Case, Mike, New Haven	1.000	12	8	8	0	16	1
Castaldo, Gregg, Bowie	1.000	2	2	0	0	2	0
Chavez, Eric, Bowie	.875	2	1	6	1	8	1
Clapinski, Chris, Portland	.978	30	24	64	2	90	4
Crowley, Jim, Bowie	.964	20	15	38	2	55	6
Dixon, Colin, New Haven	.815	12	9	13	5	27	0
Epps, Scott, Norwich	.500	3	0	1	1	2	0
Garrow, David, New Britain	1.000	3	2	5	0	7	1
Gonzalez, Mauricio, New Haven	1.000	5	1	3	0	4	0
Grable, Rob, Reading	.956	34	25	40	3	68	6
Hardge, Mike, Trenton	.920	9	7	16	2	25	2
Hardtke, Jason, Binghamton	.875	5	4	10	2	16	0
Hartung, Andy, New Haven	.923	5	6	6	1	13	1
Hayden, Dave, Reading	.924	58	33	89	10	132	7
Hinds, Robert, Norwich	.769	13	6	14	6	26	1
Hunter, Greg, New Britain	.667	1	0	2	1	3	0
Kontorinis, Andrew, New Britain	.750	3	1	2	1	4	0
Lane, Dan, Harrisburg	1.000	2	0	1	0	1	0
Lantigua, Eduardo, Cant./Akron	.811	13	8	22	7	37	1
Long, R.D., Norwich	.750	1	1	2	1	4	1
Lopez, Rene, New Britain	1.000	2	3	5	0	8	0
LUCCA, Lou, Portland	.952	111	56	261	16	333	23
Mahalik, John, Binghamton	.938	25	12	48	4	64	6
Marabella, Tony, Harrisburg	.904	17	16	31	5	52	1
Martinez, Ray, Harrisburg	.932	16	10	31	3	44	8
Maxwell, Pat, Canton/Akron	.944	42	20	82	6	108	6
McClain, Scott, Bowie	.933	70	57	165	16	238	15
Merloni, Lou, Trenton	.945	20	16	53	4	73	5
Millares, Jose, Bowie	.874	25	20	56	11	87	3
Moler, Jason, Reading	.967	21	15	43	2	60	4
Murphy, Pat, Trenton	.900	10	9	18	3	30	1
Nava, Lipso, Trenton	1.000	4	4	10	0	14	0
Neal, Mike, Canton/Akron	.947	6	6	12	1	19	1
Pough, Pork Chop, Trenton	.969	8	9	22	1	32	0
Redmond, Mike, Portland	1.000	1	1	0	0	1	0
Renteria, Dave, Norwich	1.000	6	5	10	0	15	0
Rolen, Scott, Reading	.934	20	10	47	4	61	3
Romano, Scott, Norwich	.913	99	70	236	29	335	19
Roper, Chad, New Britain	.938	117	69	248	21	338	21
Rundels, Matt, Harrisburg	.750	1	1	2	1	4	0
Saunders, Chris, Binghamton	.951	118	47	223	14	284	17
Schmidt, Tom, New Haven	.897	113	79	181	30	290	21
Sefcik, Kevin, Reading	1.000	21	9	33	0	42	5
Selby, Bill, Trenton	.885	74	49	136	24	209	11
Smith, Ed, Canton/Akron	.938	81	38	160	13	211	15
Taylor, Jamie, Canton/Akron	1.000	3	2	6	0	8	1
Torres, Tony, Portland	1.000	12	2	18	0	20	3
Tovar, Edgar, Harrisburg	.958	12	6	17	1	24	2
Vidro, Jose, Harrisburg	.963	19	8	44	2	54	4
Virgilio, George, Har.-Bowie	.930	17	10	30	3	43	2
Walker, Todd, New Britain	.865	21	5	27	5	37	1
Waller, Casey, Portland	1.000	1	0	6	0	6	1
White, Billy, New Haven	1.000	8	6	12	0	18	3
Wilson, Thomas, Norwich	.800	7	6	14	5	25	0

THIRD BASEMEN WITH TWO OR MORE TEAMS

Player, Team	Pct.	G	PO	A	E	TC	DP
Virgilio, George, Harrisburg	.921	16	9	26	3	38	2
Virgilio, George, Bowie	1.000	1	1	4	0	5	0

SHORTSTOPS

Player, Team	Pct.	G	PO	A	E	TC	DP
Alfonzo, Edgar, Bowie	.889	12	13	27	5	45	6
Arnold, Ken, Bowie	.964	7	6	21	1	28	5
Batiste, Kim, Bowie	.833	1	1	4	1	6	0
Bautista, Juan, Bowie	.907	12	21	28	5	54	8
Bournigal, Rafael, Harrisburg	.968	29	27	64	3	94	14
Brito, Luis, Reading	1.000	2	2	4	0	6	1
Burnett, Roger, Norwich	.931	75	116	194	23	333	39
Cabrera, Jolbert, Harrisburg	.935	9	11	18	2	31	5
Carey, Todd, Trenton	.985	14	20	45	1	66	7
Castaldo, Gregg, Bowie	.948	46	64	120	10	194	16
Clapinski, Chris, Portland	.971	10	9	25	1	35	2
Duncan, Andres, New Britain	.941	68	119	184	19	322	43
Fisher, David, Reading	.935	40	50	80	9	139	17
Fox, Andy, Norwich	.958	44	77	127	9	213	23
Garciaparra, Nomar, Trenton	.963	125	205	396	23	624	61
Garrow, David, New Britain	1.000	2	3	5	0	8	0
Gonzalez, Mauricio, New Haven	.933	22	22	61	6	89	13
Hagy, Gary, Canton/Akron	.963	5	8	18	1	27	3
Hardge, Mike, Trenton	.786	3	3	8	3	14	0
Hinds, Robert, Norwich	.926	13	22	28	4	54	9
Howard, Matt, Bowie	.972	67	86	196	8	290	38
Hunter, Greg, New Britain	.800	3	2	2	1	5	0
Jackson, Damian, Canton/Akron	.939	122	220	337	36	593	80
Lamb, David, Bowie	.800	1	1	3	1	5	2
Lane, Dan, Harrisburg	.935	20	11	32	3	46	4
Long, R.D., Norwich	.800	6	6	14	5	25	3
Mahalik, John, Binghamton	.944	27	30	72	6	108	11
Martinez, Ray, Harrisburg	1.000	3	3	11	0	14	1
Maxwell, Pat, Canton/Akron	.907	15	29	49	8	86	7
Merloni, Lou, Trenton	1.000	1	1	1	0	2	0
Michael, Jeff, Bowie	.750	4	8	7	5	20	2
Miller, Ryan, Binghamton	1.000	3	9	8	0	17	6
Morgan, Kevin, Binghamton	.962	114	192	340	21	553	73
Nava, Lipso, Trenton	1.000	3	6	5	0	11	1
Neal, Mike, Canton/Akron	.793	6	11	12	6	29	2
PEREZ, Neifi, New Haven	.967	114	175	358	18	551	80
Renteria, Dave, Norwich	.800	5	7	9	4	20	3
Renteria, Edgar, Portland	.944	134	179	379	33	591	55
Roper, Chad, New Britain	1.000	2	3	10	0	13	1
Rundels, Matt, Harrisburg	.875	9	11	24	5	40	4
Sefcik, Kevin, Reading	.963	112	157	316	18	491	63
Sexton, Chris, New Haven	1.000	1	0	3	0	3	0
Torres, Tony, Portland	.935	9	8	21	2	31	6
Tovar, Edgar, Harrisburg	.949	63	92	171	14	277	35
Valette, Ramon, New Britain	.927	84	90	215	24	329	34
Vidro, Jose, Harrisburg	.973	20	28	45	2	75	9
Virgilio, George, Harrisburg	.750	3	2	7	3	12	1
White, Billy, New Haven	.917	10	10	23	3	36	6

TRIPLE PLAYS: Bautista, Valette.

OUTFIELDERS

Player, Team	Pct.	G	PO	A	E	TC	DP
Abad, Andy, Trenton*	.987	86	143	9	2	154	1
Agbayani, Benny, Binghamton	.972	60	100	3	3	106	0
Avila, Rolando, Bowie	.935	13	28	1	2	31	0
Barron, Tony, Harrisburg	.975	22	37	2	1	40	0
Barry, Jeff, Binghamton	1.000	74	116	5	0	121	0
Bartee, Kimera, Bowie	.964	53	155	4	6	165	1
Bates, Fletcher, Binghamton	1.000	2	7	0	0	7	0
Berrios, Harry, Bowie	.979	54	94	1	2	97	0
Blasingame, Kent, Reading*	.904	46	64	2	7	73	0
Blosser, Greg, Trenton*	1.000	35	59	5	0	64	1
Brede, Brent, New Britain*	.962	120	238	12	10	260	3
Brown, Jarvis, Bowie	.972	58	135	4	4	143	1
Bryant, Pat, Canton/Akron	.975	120	302	8	8	318	1
Burke, Alan, Reading	.875	6	7	0	1	8	0
Byrd, Anthony, New Britain	.977	119	247	7	6	260	1
Byrne, Clayton, Bowie	1.000	14	27	2	0	29	1
Cabreja, Alexis, Norwich	.800	5	4	0	1	5	0
Cairo, Sergio, Harrisburg	1.000	3	4	0	0	4	0
Cameron, Stanton, Cant./Akron	.955	23	38	4	2	44	2
Case, Mike, New Haven	.979	52	86	8	2	96	1
Castillo, Ben, Canton/Akron	.941	31	59	5	4	68	0
Charbonnet, Mark, Harrisburg*	.995	91	182	3	1	186	1
Chick, Bruce, Harrisburg	.875	10	13	1	2	16	0
Clapinski, Chris, Portland	1.000	5	6	0	0	6	0
Dauphin, Phil, Harrisburg*	.977	104	207	4	5	216	0
Davis, Jay, Binghamton*	.965	112	210	9	8	227	1
Delvecchio, Nick, Norwich	.957	42	62	4	3	69	0
Duncan, Andres, New Britain	1.000	1	1	0	0	1	0
Echevarria, Angel, New Haven	.978	105	202	20	5	227	0
Epps, Scott, Norwich	1.000	2	1	0	0	1	0
Fleming, Carlton, Norwich	1.000	3	3	0	0	3	0
Friedman, Jason, Bowie*	1.000	2	2	0	0	2	0
Fuller, Aaron, Trenton	.972	56	135	6	4	145	2
Fully, Ed, Bing.-Bowie	.944	42	96	5	6	107	4
Geisler, Phil, Reading*	.984	58	121	6	2	129	2
Gerald, Ed, New Britain	.750	2	2	1	1	4	0

Player, Team	Pct.	G	PO	A	E	TC	DP
Grable, Rob, Reading	.980	72	94	2	2	98	0
Graham, Tim, Trenton	1.000	8	14	0	0	14	0
Grissom, Antonio, Harrisburg	.956	59	106	3	5	114	0
Hammonds, Jeffrey, Bowie	.923	7	12	0	1	13	0
Hardge, Mike, Trenton	.955	14	18	3	1	22	0
Harvey, Ray, Canton/Akron*	.977	51	85	0	2	87	0
Hawkins, Kraig, Norwich	1.000	12	28	0	0	28	0
Hayden, Dave, Reading	1.000	2	3	0	0	3	0
Hecker, Doug, Trenton	.929	18	24	2	2	28	0
Held, Dan, Reading	1.000	1	2	0	0	2	0
Hodge, Roy, Bowie	.968	27	54	6	2	62	0
Holifield, Rick, Reading*	.989	30	84	3	1	88	1
Hood, Dennis, Canton/Akron	1.000	8	10	1	0	11	1
Horne, Tyrone, Har.-Nor.	.955	90	164	7	8	179	0
Hughes, Troy, Norwich	.875	12	21	0	3	24	0
Hugo, Sean, Bowie*	1.000	34	64	2	0	66	0
Jackson, John, New Britain*	.880	13	21	1	3	25	1
Johnson, J.J., Trenton	1.000	2	1	0	0	1	0
Jones, Terry, New Haven	.966	121	264	18	10	292	0
Katzaroff, Rob, Portland	.985	99	193	1	3	197	0
Keister, Tripp, Binghamton*	.952	18	16	4	1	21	0
LAWTON, Matt, New Britain	.991	110	221	12	2	235	2
LeGree, Keith, New Britain	.957	28	44	0	2	46	0
Lennon, Pat, Trenton	.919	22	32	2	3	37	0
Lewis, T.R., Bowie	.942	76	128	1	8	137	0
List, Lou, New Haven	.920	18	22	1	2	25	0
Luke, Matt, Norwich*	.979	93	178	12	4	194	1
Magee, Wendell, Reading	.932	39	65	4	5	74	0
Mahay, Ron, Trenton*	.970	91	187	9	6	202	2
Marabella, Tony, Harrisburg	1.000	1	2	0	0	2	0
Marini, Marc, Canton/Akron*	.994	83	150	3	1	154	0
Massarelli, John, Canton/Akron	.983	52	114	2	2	118	1
McConnell, Chad, Reading	.975	85	149	7	4	160	2
McCracken, Quinton, New Haven	.971	53	92	10	3	105	0
McGuire, Ryan, Trenton*	.973	37	66	7	2	75	1
McMillon, Billy, Portland*	.982	131	207	14	4	225	3
McNabb, Buck, Canton/Akron	1.000	18	31	0	0	31	0
Millares, Jose, Bowie	1.000	20	23	2	0	25	0
Moore, Tim, New Britain*	.882	15	15	0	2	17	0
Mota, Gary, Reading	.946	24	33	2	2	37	1
Murphy, Mike, Canton/Akron	1.000	9	18	1	0	19	1
Murphy, Pat, Trenton	.944	14	17	0	1	18	0
Myrow, John, New Haven	.977	94	161	11	4	176	0
Nava, Lipso, Trenton	1.000	11	18	0	0	18	0
Nixon, Trot, Trenton*	1.000	25	66	2	0	68	0
Norman, Kenny, New Britain	1.000	5	6	1	0	7	0
Northrup, Kevin, Harrisburg	.959	32	46	1	2	49	0
Ogden, Jamie, New Britain*	.988	40	78	3	1	82	0
Payton, Jay, Binghamton	.988	83	230	7	3	240	1
Phillips, Steve, Norwich*	1.000	11	21	0	0	21	0
Ramirez, Alex, Canton/Akron	.975	32	72	5	2	79	2
Ramirez, Omar, Canton/Akron	1.000	3	2	0	0	2	0
Rivera, Ruben, Norwich	.984	71	176	7	3	186	1
Robertson, Jason, Norwich*	.979	116	227	4	5	236	0
Rundels, Matt, Harrisburg	.978	20	44	1	1	46	0
Saffer, Jon, Harrisburg	.972	17	35	0	1	36	0
Sanders, Tracy, Binghamton	.909	7	10	0	1	11	0
Sheff, Chris, Portland	.985	113	191	4	3	198	0
Smith, Ed, Canton/Akron	.923	14	23	1	2	26	0
Smith, John, Binghamton	1.000	3	3	0	0	3	0
Solomon, Steve, Reading*	.990	97	197	8	2	207	0
Thompson, Ryan, Binghamton	1.000	2	2	0	0	2	0
Tinsley, Lee, Trenton	1.000	3	4	0	0	4	0
Tovar, Edgar, Harrisburg	1.000	1	1	0	0	1	0
Turner, Brian, Norwich*	.990	50	98	2	1	101	1
Van Slyke, Andy, Bowie	1.000	2	4	0	0	4	0
Ventress, Leroy, Harrisburg	1.000	9	18	2	0	20	2
Wawruck, Jim, Bowie*	.986	51	68	3	1	72	0
Wells, Forry, New Haven	1.000	4	5	0	0	5	0
White, Don, Binghamton	.984	78	180	7	3	190	0
Wilson, Pookie, Portland*	.988	88	159	3	2	164	1
Wipf, Mark, Binghamton	.750	4	6	0	2	8	0
Yelding, Eric, Canton/Akron	1.000	9	20	1	0	21	0
Zambrano, Eddie, Trenton	1.000	16	38	2	0	40	1
Zambrano, Jose, Trenton	.975	21	38	1	1	40	0

OUTFIELDERS WITH TWO OR MORE TEAMS

Player, Team	Pct.	G	PO	A	E	TC	DP
Fully, Ed, Binghamton	1.000	9	16	3	0	19	3
Fully, Ed, Bowie	.932	33	80	2	6	88	1
Horne, Tyrone, Harrisburg	.971	70	130	5	4	139	0
Horne, Tyrone, Norwich	.900	20	34	2	4	40	0

CATCHERS

Player, Team	Pct.	G	PO	A	E	TC	DP	PB
Allen, Matt, Harrisburg	.943	5	31	2	2	35	0	0
Alomar, Sandy, Canton/Akron	.958	5	23	0	1	24	0	0
Bennett, Gary, Reading	.994	82	551	65	4	620	13	6
Brophy, E.J., Reading	1.000	2	3	0	0	3	0	0
Brown, Matt, Trenton	1.000	4	19	1	0	20	0	0
Buckley, Troy, Harrisburg	.997	43	313	36	1	350	6	5
Campbell, Darrin, Cant./Akron	.923	2	11	1	1	13	0	0
Castaneda, Hector, Bowie	.984	32	113	12	2	127	2	3
Crosby, Mike, Canton/Akron	.984	73	389	53	7	449	7	5
Delgado, Alex, Trenton	.978	19	114	19	3	136	1	1
Diaz, Cesar, Binghamton	.987	13	72	2	1	75	0	5
Eason, Tommy, Reading	.990	58	368	32	4	404	7	10
Epperson, Chad, Binghamton	1.000	5	12	2	0	14	0	0
Epps, Scott, Norwich	.971	27	120	15	4	139	0	2
Estalella, Bobby, Reading	.986	10	60	9	1	70	1	3
Everson, Darin, Harrisburg	1.000	2	12	1	0	13	0	0
Figga, Mike, Norwich	.985	105	640	92	11	743	4	15
Fitzpatrick, Robert, Harrisburg	.991	14	98	9	1	108	3	3
GREENE, Charlie, Binghamton	.995	100	670	54	4	728	3	9
Gresham, Kris, Bowie	.971	5	33	1	1	35	0	0
Grifol, Pedro, New Britain	.980	74	442	42	10	494	2	12
Higgins, Mike, New Haven	.980	17	92	7	2	101	0	4
Hymel, Lou, Harrisburg	.986	49	324	30	5	359	0	16
Johnson, Charles, Portland	.958	2	21	2	1	24	0	0
Kounas, Tony, Harrisburg	.975	38	234	34	7	275	4	4
Kremers, Jimmy, Portland	.980	45	263	32	6	301	3	5
Levangie, Dana, Trenton	.996	42	248	26	1	275	3	5
Lopez, Rene, New Britain	.983	79	498	69	10	577	4	5
Martin, Jeff, Trenton	.989	75	484	43	6	533	4	13
Martindale, Ryan, Cant./Akron	1.000	2	13	0	0	13	0	0
McKeel, Walt, Trenton	.979	17	84	11	2	97	1	4
Millan, Adan, Reading	1.000	5	30	0	0	30	0	0
Redmond, Mike, Portland	.992	104	656	95	6	757	6	9
Rodriguez, Nerio, Bowie	1.000	3	13	1	0	14	0	0
Rudolph, Mason, Portland	1.000	16	44	2	0	46	0	1
Salcedo, Edwin, Norwich	1.000	3	8	0	0	8	0	0
Scalzitti, Will, New Haven	.996	39	220	28	1	249	0	4
Smith, Brandon, Binghamton	1.000	2	3	1	0	4	1	0
Snyder, Randy, New Haven	.941	5	30	2	2	34	0	1
Soliz, Steve, Canton/Akron	.979	32	161	24	4	189	1	3
Strittmatter, Mark, New Haven	.990	90	664	48	7	719	3	4
Tijerina, Tony, Binghamton	.991	32	199	14	2	215	1	10
Wakamatsu, Don, Cant./Akron	.992	47	219	22	2	243	2	5
Waszgis, B.J., Bowie	.982	125	782	89	16	887	6	23
Wilson, Thomas, Norwich	.993	19	129	12	1	142	0	3

TRIPLE PLAY: Waszgis.

PITCHERS

Player, Team	Pct.	G	PO	A	E	TC	DP
Alfonseca, Antonio, Portland	.889	19	9	15	3	27	0
Alston, Garvin, New Haven	.933	47	8	6	1	15	0
Alvarez, Tavo, Harrisburg	1.000	3	2	2	0	4	0
Aminoff, Matt, New Haven	.500	6	1	0	1	2	0
Amos, Chad, Trenton	1.000	6	1	0	0	1	0
Andersen, Larry, Reading	.500	5	0	1	1	2	0
Antolick, Jeff, Norwich	.833	2	2	3	1	6	0
Arffa, Steve, Binghamton*	.000	1	0	0	1	1	0
Arteaga, Ivan, New Haven	.917	14	3	8	1	12	1
Aucoin, Derek, Harrisburg	1.000	29	4	4	0	8	0
Bakkum, Scott, Trenton	.917	28	5	6	1	12	0
Beech, Matt, Reading*	1.000	14	2	9	0	11	0
Bennett, Shayne, Trenton	1.000	10	0	2	0	2	0
Blais, Mike, Trenton	1.000	13	0	1	0	1	0
Blazier, Ron, Reading	1.000	56	9	14	0	23	3
Borowski, Joe, Bowie	.750	16	0	3	1	4	1
Botkin, Alan, Harrisburg*	1.000	3	0	1	0	1	0
Brooks, Wes, Trenton	.929	29	11	28	3	42	1
Brown, Dan, Reading	.000	2	0	0	1	1	0
Brown, Dickie, Canton/Akron	.882	37	3	12	2	17	0
Buddie, Mike, Norwich	.941	29	10	22	2	34	1
Bullinger, Kirk, Harrisburg	.949	56	14	23	2	39	3
Bullock, Craig, Binghamton	1.000	11	3	5	0	8	0
Cabrera, Jose, Canton/Akron	1.000	24	5	4	0	9	1
Cain, Tim, Trenton	1.000	29	4	11	0	15	0
Carper, Mark, Norwich	1.000	1	1	1	0	2	0
Carter, Glenn, Trenton	.500	14	1	0	1	2	0
Carter, John, Canton/Akron	.857	5	2	4	1	7	0
Carter, Tom, Norwich*	.929	28	2	11	1	14	1
Caruso, Joe, Trenton	1.000	11	1	3	0	4	1
Case, Mike, New Haven	1.000	2	0	1	0	1	0
Cederblad, Brett, Trenton	1.000	8	6	7	0	13	0

Player, Team	Pct.	G	PO	A	E	TC	DP
Chapin, Darrin, Canton/Akron	1.000	4	0	2	0	2	0
Chergey, Dan, Portland	.867	55	4	9	2	15	2
Ciccarella, Joe, Trenton*	1.000	22	4	2	0	6	0
Coleman, Billy, Norwich	1.000	46	10	5	0	15	2
Conner, Scott, Bowie	.778	44	2	12	4	18	0
Coppinger, Rocky, Bowie	.938	13	11	4	1	16	1
Cosman, Jeff, Binghamton	1.000	10	5	9	0	14	0
Crawford, Carlos, Canton/Akron	1.000	8	5	8	0	13	1
Crawford, Joe, Binghamton*	1.000	42	2	12	0	14	1
CUNNANE, Will, Portland	1.000	21	14	20	0	34	2
Dedrick, Jim, Bowie	.966	10	10	18	1	29	3
DeHart, Rick, Harrisburg*	.789	35	6	9	4	19	2
DeJean, Mike, Norwich	.957	59	2	20	1	23	3
DeLaMaza, Roland, Cant./Akron	1.000	7	0	3	0	3	0
Diaz, Ralph, Harrisburg	.600	11	2	1	2	5	0
Doolan, Blake, Reading	.857	60	5	13	3	21	0
Driskill, Travis, Canton/Akron	1.000	33	1	2	0	3	0
Edmondson, Brian, Binghamton	.931	23	9	18	2	29	1
Emerson, Scott, Bowie-Tre.*	.571	8	2	2	3	7	1
Engle, Tom, Binghamton	1.000	13	2	2	0	4	0
Eshelman, Vaughn, Trenton*	1.000	2	0	3	0	3	0
Faino, Jeff, Tre.-Bowie*	.818	36	3	6	2	11	0
Falteisek, Steve, Harrisburg	.937	25	16	43	4	63	4
Farmer, Mike, New Haven*	.952	40	4	16	1	21	1
Fernandez, Jared, Trenton	1.000	11	2	12	0	14	0
Fernandez, Sid, Bowie*	1.000	2	0	2	0	2	1
Forney, Rick, Bowie	1.000	23	4	10	0	14	0
Foster, Mark, Reading*	1.000	25	1	3	0	4	0
Fronio, Jason, Canton/Akron	.833	8	2	3	1	6	0
Fuller, Mark, Binghamton	1.000	47	8	10	0	18	1
Fultz, Aaron, New Britain*	1.000	3	0	4	0	4	0
Gandarillas, Gus, New Britain	.800	25	2	2	1	5	0
Gavaghan, Sean, New Britain	1.000	21	2	6	0	8	1
Gentile, Scott, Harrisburg	1.000	37	2	7	0	9	0
Gilmore, Joel, Reading	1.000	18	4	7	0	11	0
Gomes, Wayne, Reading	.941	22	6	10	1	17	1
Grace, Mike, Reading	1.000	24	9	23	0	32	1
Graves, Dan, Canton/Akron	1.000	17	1	12	0	13	0
Grundt, Ken, New Haven*	.917	28	4	7	1	12	2
Guerra, Mark, Binghamton	1.000	6	4	4	0	8	0
Hanselman, Carl, Reading	.857	24	2	4	1	7	0
Hansen, Brent, Trenton	.938	11	6	9	1	16	0
Harris, Doug, Bowie	1.000	11	5	7	0	12	0
Harris, Pep, Canton/Akron	1.000	32	2	14	0	16	0
Henderson, Chris, New Haven	1.000	3	0	1	0	1	0
Henderson, Rod, Harrisburg	.857	12	3	3	1	7	0
Heredia, Wilson, Portland	.800	4	0	4	1	5	0
Hiljus, Erik, Binghamton	.923	10	6	6	1	13	0
Hill, Chris, Trenton*	1.000	7	0	1	0	1	0
Hill, Eric, Reading	.889	38	3	5	1	9	1
Hines, Rich, Norwich*	.941	54	3	13	1	17	0
Hoeme, Steve, Trenton	1.000	20	1	3	0	4	0
Holman, Brad, New Haven	1.000	7	1	0	0	1	0
Holman, Craig, Reading	1.000	32	5	12	0	17	0
Hrusovsky, John, Canton/Akron	.929	35	2	11	1	14	0
Hubbard, Mark, Norwich*	1.000	13	3	22	0	25	1
Hudson, Joe, Trenton	1.000	22	4	12	0	16	0
Hunter, Rich, Reading	1.000	3	1	2	0	3	1
Hurst, James, Bowie*	.000	1	0	0	1	1	0
Hutchins, Jason, New Haven	.750	12	1	2	1	4	0
Ingram, Todd, Trenton	1.000	18	1	1	0	2	0
Isringhausen, Jason, Binghamton	.857	6	1	5	1	7	0
Janzen, Marty, Norwich	1.000	3	1	3	0	4	0
Jarvis, Matt, Bowie*	.970	26	10	22	1	33	1
Johnson, Dom, Trenton	.800	5	0	4	1	5	0
Johnson, Jason, New Haven	.846	19	5	6	2	13	0
Jones, Bobby, New Haven*	.882	27	5	10	2	17	0
Juelsgaard, Jarod, Portland	.880	48	4	18	3	25	2
Juhl, Mike, Reading*	.917	49	2	9	1	12	1
Karp, Ryan, Reading*	1.000	7	4	10	0	14	0
Kendrena, Ken, Harrisburg	1.000	30	6	14	0	20	0
Kerley, Collin, Harrisburg	1.000	2	0	1	0	1	0
Kindell, Scott, Binghamton*	1.000	1	0	1	0	1	0
Kirkreit, Daron, Canton/Akron	.933	14	6	8	1	15	1
Kline, Steve, Canton/Akron*	.960	14	7	17	1	25	1
Knackert, Brent, Binghamton	.957	48	7	15	1	23	0
Knowles, Greg, Bowie	1.000	37	8	16	0	24	1
Koller, Rod, Canton/Akron	1.000	9	6	5	0	11	0
Konieczki, Dom, New Britain*	1.000	39	4	7	0	11	0
Kotarski, Mike, New Haven*	.917	31	1	10	1	12	0
Kozeniewski, Blaise, Norwich	1.000	29	2	9	0	11	1
Lane, Aaron, Bowie*	1.000	40	4	7	0	11	1
Langbehn, Gregg, Trenton*	1.000	14	0	4	0	4	0
Larkin, Andy, Portland	1.000	9	3	10	0	13	0
Leahy, Pat, Portland	.818	13	0	9	2	11	0
Legault, Kevin, New Britain	1.000	47	6	20	0	26	1
Lehman, Toby, Bowie	.833	4	2	3	1	6	0
Lemon, Don, Portland	.923	30	5	7	1	13	0
Lemp, Chris, Bowie	1.000	18	2	4	0	6	0
Loewer, Carlton, Reading	1.000	8	3	4	0	7	0
Long, Joe, Norwich	.929	43	6	7	1	14	0
Ludwick, Eric, Binghamton	.966	23	11	17	1	29	1
Maduro, Calvin, Bowie	1.000	7	2	6	0	8	0
Magee, Bo, C-A/Bowie*	1.000	26	5	6	0	11	0
Maldonado, Jay, New Britain	1.000	5	1	1	0	2	0
Mansur, Jeff, New Britain*	1.000	5	1	1	0	2	0
Mantei, Matt, Portland	1.000	8	1	2	0	3	0
Matthews, Mike, Cant./Akron*	1.000	15	2	15	0	17	1
McCready, Jim, Binghamton	1.000	32	3	6	0	9	0
McDill, Allen, Binghamton*	1.000	12	7	9	0	16	0
McGraw, Tom, Portland*	1.000	51	10	13	0	23	3
Mendoza, Ramiro, Norwich	1.000	19	8	10	0	18	0
Mendoza, Reynol, Portland	.896	27	16	27	5	48	2
Mikkelsen, Linc, Harrisburg	.950	21	5	14	1	20	1
Miller, Travis, New Britain*	.815	28	10	12	5	27	0
Mitchell, Larry, Reading	.963	25	10	16	1	27	1
Mix, Greg, Portland	1.000	24	6	15	0	21	1
Moore, Joel, New Haven	.971	27	8	25	1	34	3
Moten, Scott, New Britain	.867	40	4	9	2	15	0
Munoz, Bobby, Reading	.667	4	1	1	1	3	0
Musselwhite, James, Norwich	1.000	24	12	19	0	31	0
Musset, Jose, Norwich	1.000	34	3	3	0	6	1
Neier, Chris, New Haven	1.000	38	13	10	0	23	1
Newlin, Jim, Bowie	.944	40	9	8	1	18	0
Nied, David, New Haven	1.000	1	1	0	0	1	0
Nieto, Tony, Bowie	1.000	1	1	0	0	1	0
Norris, Joe, New Britain	1.000	46	6	13	0	19	0
Novoa, Rafael, Binghamton*	1.000	4	2	0	0	2	0
Ohme, Kevin, New Britain*	.921	35	8	27	3	38	2
Orellano, Rafael, Trenton*	1.000	27	6	23	0	29	1
Pacheco, Alex, Harrisburg	.944	45	5	12	1	18	1
Paniagua, Jose, Harrisburg	.962	25	11	14	1	26	2
Pantoja, Johnny, Norwich	1.000	11	4	5	0	9	0
Paxton, Darrin, Har.-Bing.*	1.000	28	2	12	0	14	2
Percibal, Billy, Bowie	1.000	2	0	1	0	1	0
Perez, Melido, Norwich	1.000	2	0	2	0	2	0
Perschke, Greg, Canton/Akron	.500	3	0	1	1	2	0
Person, Robert, Binghamton	1.000	26	8	6	0	14	1
Peterson, Dean, Trenton	.952	20	7	13	1	21	0
Pettit, Doug, Portland	1.000	21	2	5	0	7	1
Pierce, Ed, Bowie*	.833	7	0	5	1	6	0
Pollard, Damon, Harrisburg	.500	6	0	1	1	2	0
Popplewell, Tom, Canton/Akron	1.000	15	0	2	0	2	0
Pote, Lou, Harrisburg	1.000	9	0	1	0	1	0
Powell, Jay, Portland	1.000	50	3	9	0	12	0
Puig, Benny, Harrisburg*	1.000	1	1	1	0	2	0
Ramirez, Hector, Binghamton	1.000	20	7	19	0	26	1
Rekar, Bryan, New Haven	.947	12	6	12	1	19	1
Ricken, Ray, Norwich	1.000	8	4	10	0	14	0
Riley, Ed, Trenton*	1.000	16	1	4	0	5	0
Ritchie, Todd, New Britain	.963	24	9	17	1	27	0
Roberts, Brett, New Britain	1.000	28	16	16	0	32	0
Rojas, Euclides, Portland	1.000	14	2	4	0	6	0
Ryan, Ken, Trenton	1.000	11	1	0	0	1	0
Ryan, Kevin, Bowie	1.000	39	9	9	0	18	1
Saccavino, Craig, New Britain	.889	27	3	5	1	9	0
Salamon, John, New Haven	.667	6	0	2	1	3	0
Schneider, Phil, New Haven*	1.000	2	0	2	0	2	0
Schorr, Brad, Binghamton	1.000	4	1	2	0	3	0
Sele, Aaron, Trenton	1.000	2	0	2	0	2	0
Senior, Shawn, Trenton*	1.000	27	8	24	0	32	2
Serafini, Dan, New Britain*	.864	27	4	15	3	22	0
Shaw, Cedric, Harrisburg*	.833	5	1	4	1	6	0
Shenk, Larry, Bowie	.667	6	1	1	1	3	0
Spencer, Stan, Portland	.500	8	0	1	1	2	0
Standish, Scott, Norwich	.909	17	7	3	1	11	0
Steph, Rod, Canton/Akron	.960	32	10	14	1	25	1
Stephenson, Garrett, Bowie	.800	29	14	22	9	45	1
Stidham, Phil, Binghamton	1.000	7	0	2	0	2	0
Stull, Everett, Harrisburg	.941	24	8	8	1	17	1
Sullivan, Mike, Trenton	1.000	15	4	5	0	9	0
Suppan, Jeff, Trenton	1.000	15	11	14	0	25	2
Sutherland, John, Norwich	1.000	13	1	2	0	3	0
Tam, Jeff, Binghamton	1.000	14	3	5	0	8	0
Taylor, Tommy, Canton/Akron	1.000	5	0	1	0	1	0
Telford, Anthony, Canton/Akron	1.000	2	1	2	0	3	0

Player, Team	Pct.	G	PO	A	E	TC	DP
Tellers, Dave, New Haven	.909	33	4	6	1	11	0
Thomson, John, New Haven	.885	26	12	11	3	26	0
Tirado, Aris, Harrisburg	1.000	8	3	1	0	4	0
Tranberg, Mark, Reading	1.000	18	6	15	0	21	2
Trinidad, Hector, New Britain	.958	23	7	16	1	24	1
Trisler, John, Reading	.933	30	3	11	1	15	0
Trlicek, Rick, Canton/Akron	1.000	24	1	6	0	7	0
Viano, Jake, New Haven	.846	57	5	6	2	13	0
Virgilio, George, Bowie	1.000	1	0	1	0	1	0
Voisard, Mark, New Haven	1.000	27	1	5	0	6	0
Wainhouse, David, Portland	.857	17	3	3	1	7	0
Wallace, Derek, Binghamton	1.000	15	6	1	0	7	0
Wallace, Kent, Norwich	1.000	18	4	13	0	17	0
Ward, Bryan, Portland*	.800	20	2	2	1	5	0
Weber, Neil, Harrisburg*	.968	28	7	23	1	31	1
Wegmann, Tom, Bowie	1.000	14	5	6	0	11	0
West, David, Reading*	1.000	1	1	0	0	1	0
Whisenant, Matt, Portland*	.919	23	8	26	3	37	4
Whitten, Casey, Canton/Akron*	1.000	20	8	11	0	19	0
Williams, Greg, Canton/Akron*	1.000	24	1	8	0	9	0
Wilson, Paul, Binghamton	.964	16	10	17	1	28	1
Wright, Jamey, New Haven	.667	1	0	2	1	3	0
Zolecki, Mike, New Haven	.900	9	5	4	1	10	0

PITCHERS WITH TWO OR MORE TEAMS

Player, Team	Pct.	G	PO	A	E	TC	DP
Emerson, Scott, Bowie*	.667	4	2	2	2	6	1
Emerson, Scott, Trenton*	.000	4	0	0	1	1	0
Faino, Jeff, Trenton*	.000	5	0	0	1	1	0
Faino, Jeff, Bowie*	.900	31	3	6	1	10	0
Magee, Bo, Canton/Akron*	1.000	21	3	4	0	7	0
Magee, Bo, Bowie*	1.000	5	2	2	0	4	0
Paxton, Darrin, Harrisburg*	1.000	7	1	2	0	3	1
Paxton, Darrin, Binghamton*	1.000	21	1	10	0	11	1

The following players did not have any fielding statistics at the positions indicated or appeared only as a designated hitter, pinch-hitter or pinch-runner: Benbow, ph; Biasucci, of; Bogott, p; Brownson, p; Cameron, 3b; C. Chavez, p; Clark, of; Cradle, dh; Daubach, 3b; DeBerry, dh, ph; DeJesus, p; Delarosa, p; Delgado, 3b; Devereux, p; Dodd, p; Doster, of; Fiegel, p; Fisher, 3b, p; Hagy, 3b; Hancock, p; Hayden, ss; Heflin, p; Malloy, p; Manto, dh; Romano, of; Ruffin, p; Eric Smith, p; G. Sullivan, p; Turner, p; Valdez, of; Virgilio, of; Welch, p.

LEAGUE CHAMPIONS

Year	Team	Pct.
1923—	Williamsport	.661
1924—	Williamsport	.654
1925—	York§	.583
	Williamsport§	.583
1926—	Scranton	.627
1927—	Harrisburg	.630
1928—	Harrisburg	.603
1929—	Binghamton	.597
1930—	Wilkes-Barre	.572
1931—	Harrisburg	.597
1932—	Wilkes-Barre	.561
1933—	Binghamton	.690
1934—	Binghamton	.694
	Williamsport*	.603
1935—	Scranton	.657
	Binghamton*	.580
1936—	Scranton*	.609
	Elmira	.629
1937—	Elmira†	.622
1938—	Binghamton	.622
	Elmira (3rd)‡	.522
1939—	Scranton†	.571
1940—	Scranton	.568
	Binghamton (2nd)‡	.554
1941—	Wilkes-Barre	.630
	Elmira (3rd)‡	.514
1942—	Albany	.600
	Scranton (2nd)‡	.593
1943—	Scranton	.630
	Elmira (2nd)‡	.568
1944—	Hartford	.723
	Binghamton (4th)‡	.474
1945—	Utica	.615
	Albany (3rd)‡	.564
1946—	Scranton†	.691
1947—	Utica†	.652
1948—	Scranton†	.636
1949—	Albany	.664
	Binghamton (4th)‡	.500
1950—	Wilkes-Barre‡	.652
1951—	Wilkes-Barre‡	.612
	Scranton (2nd)†	.562
1952—	Albany	.603
	Binghamton (2nd)‡	.562
1953—	Reading	.682
	Binghamton (2nd)‡	.636
1954—	Wilkes-Barre	.576
	Albany (3rd)‡	.540
1955—	Reading	.613
	Allentown (2nd)‡	.565
1956—	Schenectady†	.609
1957—	Binghamton	.607
	Reading (3rd)‡	.529
1958—	Lancaster∞	.568
	Binghamton (6th)‡	.493
1959—	Springfield†	.607
1960—	Williamsport▲	.551
	Springfield (3rd)▲	.496
1961—	Springfield	.612
1962—	Williamsport	.593
	Elmira (2nd)‡	.514
1963—	Charleston	.593
1964—	Elmira	.586
1965—	Pittsfield	.607
1966—	Elmira	.633
1967—	Binghamton◆	.586
	Elmira	.532
1968—	Pittsfield	.604
	Reading (2nd)‡	.579
1969—	York	.640
1970—	Waterbury■	.560
	Reading■	.553
1971—	Three Rivers	.569
	Elmira▼	.561
1972—	West Haven▼	.600
	Three Rivers	.559
1973—	Reading▼	.551
	Pittsfield	.551
1974—	Thetford Miners (2nd)•	.536
	Pittsfield (2nd)	.496
1975—	Reading	.613
	Bristol*	.587
1976—	Three Rivers	.601
	West Haven††	.576
1977—	West Haven‡‡	.623
	Three Rivers	.551
1978—	Reading	.642
	Bristol*	.580
1979—	West Haven§§	.597
1980—	Holyoke*	.561
	Waterbury	.540
1981—	Glens Falls	.615
	Bristol*	.577
1982—	West Haven*	.614
	Lynn	.590
1983—	Lynn	.554
	New Britain‡	.518
1984—	Waterbury	.543
	Vermont‡	.536
1985—	Albany	.540
	Vermont‡	.514
1986—	Reading	.566
	Vermont‡	.554
1987—	Pittsfield	.630
	Harrisburg‡	.550
1988—	Glens Falls	.584
	Albany‡	.522
1989—	Albany‡	.657
	Harrisburg	.522
1990—	Albany	.568
	London‡	.547
1991—	Harrisburg	.621
	Albany‡	.543
1992—	Canton/Akron	.580
	Binghamton‡	.572
1993—	Harrisburg‡	.681
	Canton/Akron	.543
1994—	Harrisburg	.633
	Binghamton‡	.582
1995—	New Haven	.556
	Reading‡	.514

*Won split-season playoff. †Won championship and four-team playoff. ‡Won four-team playoff. §Tied for pennant, York winning playoff. ∞League was divided into Northern, Southern divisions and played a split season; Lancaster was overall season leader. ▲Playoff finals canceled after one game because of rain with Williamsport and Springfield declared playoff co-champions. ◆League was divided into Eastern, Western divisions; Binghamton won playoff. ■Tied for pennant, Waterbury winning playoff. ▼League was divided into American, National divisions; won playoff. •League was divided into American and National divisions; won four-team playoff. ††League was divided into Northern, Southern divisions, won playoff. ‡‡League was divided into New England and Canadian-American divisions; won playoff. §§Won both halves of split season (no playoffs). (NOTE—Known as New York-Pennsylvania League prior to 1938.)

SOUTHERN LEAGUE

LEAGUE OFFICE

President/secretary-treasurer
Arnold Fielkow

Address
1 Depot St., Suite 300
Marietta, GA 30060

Phone
770-428-4749

TEAMS

BIRMINGHAM BARONS

President/general manager
Bill Hardekopf
Manager
To be announced
Ballpark (capacity, surface)
Hoover Metropolitan Stadium (10,500, grass)
Affiliation
White Sox
Address
P.O. Box 360007
Birmingham, AL 35236
Phone
205-988-3200

CAROLINA MUDCATS

General manager
Joe Kremer
Manager
Marc Hill
Ballpark (capacity, surface)
Five County Stadium (6,000, grass)
Affiliation
Pirates
Address
P.O. Drawer 1218
Zebulon, NC 27597
Phone
919-269-2287

CHATTANOOGA LOOKOUTS

President/general manager
J. Frank Burke
Manager
Mark Berry
Ballpark (capacity, surface)
Historic Engel Stadium (7,500, grass)
Affiliation
Reds
Address
P.O. Box 11002
Chattanooga, TN 37401
Phone
615-267-2208

GREENVILLE BRAVES

General manager
Steve DeSalvo
Manager
Jeff Cox
Ballpark (capacity, surface)
Greenville Municipal Stadium (7,027, grass)
Affiliation
Braves
Address
P.O. Box 16683
Greenville, SC 29606
Phone
803-299-3456

HUNTSVILLE STARS

President/general manager
Don Mincher
Manager
Dick Scott
Ballpark (capacity, surface)
Joe W. Davis Stadium (10,400, grass)
Affiliation
Athletics
Address
P.O. Box 2769
Huntsville, AL 35804
Phone
205-882-2562

JACKSONVILLE SUNS

Vice president/general manager
Peter Bragan Jr.
Manager
To be announced
Ballpark (capacity, surface)
Wolfson Park (to be announced, grass)
Affiliation
Tigers
Address
P.O. Box 4756
Jacksonville, FL 32201
Phone
904-358-2846

KNOXVILLE SMOKIES

General manager
Dan Rajkowski
Manager
Omar Malave
Ballpark (capacity, surface)
Bill Meyer Stadium (6,412, grass)
Affiliation
Blue Jays
Address
633 Jessamine St.
Knoxville, TN 37917
Phone
615-637-9494

MEMPHIS CHICKS

President/general manager
David Hersh
Manager
Ed Romero
Ballpark (capacity, surface)
Tim McCarver Stadium (10,000, artificial infield, grass outfield)
Affiliation
Padres
Address
800 Home Run Lane
Memphis, TN 38104
Phone
901-272-1687

ORLANDO CUBS

General manager
Roger Wexelberg
Manager
Bruce Kimm
Ballpark (capacity, surface)
Tinker Field (6,000, grass)
Affiliation
Cubs
Address
287 S. Tampa Ave.
Orlando, FL 32805
Phone
407-245-2827

PORT CITY ROOSTERS

General manager
David Kotarba
Manager
Orlando Gomez
Ballpark (capacity, surface)
Brooks Field at UNC-Wilmington (3,500, grass)
Affiliation
Mariners
Address
P.O. Box 7217
Wilmington, NC 28406
Phone
910-350-7000

1995 FINAL STANDINGS

FIRST HALF

EAST DIVISION

Team	W	L	T	Pct.	GB
Carolina (Pirates)	45	27	0	.625	....
Orlando (Cubs)	41	30	0	.577	3½
Greenville (Braves)	35	37	0	.486	10
Port City (Mariners)	32	39	0	.451	12½
Jacksonville (Tigers)	32	40	0	.444	13

WEST DIVISION

Team	W	L	T	Pct.	GB
Memphis (Padres)	40	32	0	.556	....
Chattanooga (Reds)	36	36	0	.500	4
Huntsville (Athletics)	35	37	0	.486	5
Birmingham (White Sox)	33	39	0	.458	7
Knoxville (Blue Jays)	30	42	0	.417	10

SECOND HALF

EAST DIVISION

Team	W	L	T	Pct.	GB
Carolina (Pirates)	44	28	0	.611	....
Jacksonville (Tigers)	43	29	0	.597	1
Orlando (Cubs)	35	37	0	.486	9
Port City (Mariners)	30	41	0	.423	13½
Greenville (Braves)	24	46	0	.343	19

WEST DIVISION

Team	W	L	T	Pct.	GB
Chattanooga (Reds)	47	24	0	.662	....
Birmingham (White Sox)	47	25	0	.653	½
Huntsville (Athletics)	35	37	0	.486	12½
Memphis (Padres)	28	42	0	.400	18½
Knoxville (Blue Jays)	24	48	0	.333	23½

COMPOSITE

Team	Caro.	Chat.	Bir.	Orl.	Jax.	Hun.	Mem.	P.C.	Grn.	Knx.	W	L	T	Pct.	GB
Carolina (Pirates)	....	5	5	12	15	6	4	18	10	14	89	55	0	.618	....
Chattanooga (Reds)	3	....	17	4	5	13	13	4	12	12	83	60	0	.580	5½
Birmingham (White Sox)	3	15	....	5	5	14	16	5	8	9	80	64	0	.556	9
Orlando (Cubs)	12	4	3	....	16	3	5	15	9	9	76	67	0	.531	12½
Jacksonville (Tigers)	9	3	3	16	....	5	7	13	9	10	75	69	0	.521	14
Huntsville (Athletics)	2	11	10	5	3	....	15	5	9	10	70	74	0	.486	19
Memphis (Padres)	4	11	8	3	1	17	....	5	10	9	68	74	0	.479	20
Port City (Mariners)	14	3	3	8	11	3	3	....	9	8	62	80	0	.437	26
Greenville (Braves)	6	4	8	7	7	7	4	7	....	9	59	83	0	.415	29
Knoxville (Blue Jays)	2	4	7	7	6	6	7	8	7	....	54	90	0	.375	35

Carolina's home games played in Zebulon, N.C.

Port City's home games played in Wilmington, N.C.

Major league affiliations in parentheses.

PLAYOFFS: Carolina defeated Orlando, three games to two; Chattanooga defeated Memphis, three games to two; Carolina defeated Chattanooga, three games to two, to win league championship.

REGULAR-SEASON ATTENDANCE: Birmingham, 303,066; Carolina, 317,802; Chattanooga, 290,002; Greenville, 223,225; Huntsville, 243,179; Jacksonville, 237,433; Knoxville, 123,428; Memphis, 221,302; Orlando, 191,080; Port City, 110,233. Total, 2,260,750. Playoffs (15 games)—26,846. Class AA All-Star Game at Shreveport—6,247.

MANAGERS: Birmingham, Terry Francona; Carolina, Trent Jewett; Chattanooga, Dave Miley; Greenville, Bruce Benedict; Huntsville, Dick Scott; Jacksonville, Bill Plummer; Knoxville, Garth Iorg; Memphis, Jerry Royster; Orlando, Bruce Kimm; Port City, Dave Myers.

ALL-STAR TEAM: 1B—Jim Bonnici, Port City; 2B—Brian Koelling, Chattanooga; 3B—Scott Spiezio, Huntsville; SS—Desi Relaford, Port City; Utility IF—Ruben Santana, Chattanooga; OF—Jermaine Dye, Greenville; Robin Jennings, Orlando; Charles Poe, Birmingham; Pedro Valdes, Orlando; C—Jason Kendall, Carolina; DH—Ivan Cruz, Jacksonville; RHP—(tie) Luis Andujar, Birmingham, and Elmer Dessens, Carolina; LHP—Matt Ruebel, Carolina; Most Valuable Player—Jason Kendall, Carolina; Most Outstanding Pitcher—Luis Andujar, Birmingham; Manager of the Year—Bruce Kimm, Orlando.

1995 BATTING

TEAM

Team	Avg.	G	TPA	AB	R	H	TB	2B	3B	HR	RBI	SH	SF	HP	BB	IBB	SO	SB	CS	GDP	LOB	ShO	Slg.	OBP
Chattanooga	.280	143	5506	4885	730	1366	2078	259	36	127	680	45	40	53	480	38	808	91	58	136	1037	7	.425	.348
Carolina	.270	144	5650	5023	689	1358	1935	257	31	86	629	67	48	67	445	42	826	129	72	116	1040	8	.385	.335
Greenville	.268	142	5337	4772	680	1278	1995	263	29	132	630	47	48	39	431	26	1006	90	87	98	918	6	.418	.330
Birmingham	.264	144	5449	4726	688	1249	1769	225	23	83	608	62	50	55	554	36	868	155	72	104	1038	12	.374	.345
Orlando	.261	143	5315	4736	617	1235	1770	233	28	82	560	50	39	34	454	30	786	83	73	127	940	4	.374	.327
Memphis	.258	142	5251	4753	624	1225	1856	205	39	116	573	32	34	36	389	26	1057	165	68	90	920	11	.390	.317
Port City	.253	142	5451	4814	604	1216	1772	229	24	93	540	35	37	58	500	35	948	107	74	117	1021	13	.368	.328
Huntsville	.251	144	5472	4779	643	1200	1819	202	30	119	592	34	45	59	552	22	1027	113	68	94	1076	9	.381	.333
Knoxville	.244	144	5203	4619	577	1125	1610	221	39	62	502	43	32	67	442	21	989	181	98	100	906	9	.349	.317
Jacksonville	.231	144	5385	4720	620	1091	1751	214	25	132	573	56	33	69	506	45	1055	103	61	97	913	9	.371	.313

INDIVIDUAL

TOP QUALIFIERS FOR BATTING CHAMPIONSHIP

Minimum 389 plate appearances. *Lefthanded batter. †Switch-hitter.

Player, Team	Avg.	G	TPA	AB	R	H	TB	2B	3B	HR	RBI	SH	SF	HP	BB	IBB	SO	SB	CS	GDP	Slg.	OBP
Coughlin, Kevin, Birmingham*	.385	96	376	327	56	126	168	29	2	3	49	8	2	5	34	7	43	5	2	3	.514	.448
Kendall, Jason, Carolina	.326	117	508	429	87	140	192	26	1	8	71	1	8	14	56	5	22	10	7	10	.448	.414
Rohrmeier, Dan, Chattanooga	.326	118	482	426	77	139	221	31	0	17	76	1	7	7	41	5	63	0	1	9	.519	.389
Swann, Pedro, Greenville*	.324	102	390	339	57	110	171	24	2	11	64	0	3	3	45	2	63	14	11	8	.504	.405
Valdes, Pedro, Orlando*	.300	114	474	426	57	128	183	28	3	7	68	0	6	5	37	3	77	3	6	7	.430	.359
Larregui, Ed, Orlando	.300	122	460	423	55	127	180	18	1	11	60	0	4	1	32	2	39	3	10	15	.426	.348
Koelling, Brian, Chattanooga	.296	107	486	432	71	128	172	21	7	3	44	8	3	3	40	1	63	30	12	9	.398	.358
Jennings, Robin, Orlando*	.296	132	543	490	71	145	237	27	7	17	79	0	5	4	44	5	61	7	14	11	.484	.355
Santana, Ruben, Chattanooga	.293	142	625	556	89	163	239	23	10	11	79	6	5	8	50	5	77	2	5	17	.430	.357

Player, Team	Avg.	G	TPA	AB	R	H	TB	2B	3B	HR	RBI	SH	SF	HP	BB	IBB	SO	SB	CS	GDP	Slg.	OBP
Ladell, Cleveland, Chattanooga	.292	135	565	517	76	151	208	28	7	5	43	4	2	2	39	1	88	28	15	12	.402	.343
Watkins, Pat, Chattanooga	.291	105	398	358	57	104	170	26	2	12	57	0	4	3	33	4	53	5	5	7	.475	.352
Wilson, Craig, Birmingham	.289	132	531	471	56	136	169	19	1	4	46	10	2	5	43	0	44	2	2	21	.359	.353
Canale, George, Carolina*	.287	130	545	487	71	140	245	30	6	21	102	0	8	4	46	6	83	1	3	15	.503	.349
Stewart, Shannon, Knoxville	.287	138	601	498	89	143	194	24	6	5	55	3	5	6	89	3	61	42	16	13	.390	.398
Relaford, Desmond, Port City†	.287	90	397	352	51	101	137	11	2	7	27	2	0	2	41	2	58	25	9	4	.389	.365

DEPARTMENTAL LEADERS: G—E. Burton, Coolbaugh, Santana, 142; AB—Santana, 556; R—E. Burton, 95; H—Santana, 163; TB—Bonnici, 246; 2B—Bonnici, 36; 3B—Delacruz, 12; HR—Cruz, 31; RBI—Canale, 102; SH—E. Burton, Sanchez, 15; SF—Spiezio, 14; HP—Delacruz, 15; BB—Stewart, 89; IBB—Bonnici, Cruz, 15; SO—Barker, 143; SB—E. Burton, 60; CS—E. Burton, 22; GIDP—C. Wilson, 21; Slg.—Cruz, .564; OBP—Kendall, .414.

ALL PLAYERS

*Lefthanded batter. †Switch-hitter.

Player, Team	Avg.	G	TPA	AB	R	H	TB	2B	3B	HR	RBI	SH	SF	HP	BB	IBB	SO	SB	CS	GDP	Slg.	OBP
Abbott, Jeff, Birmingham	.320	55	223	197	25	63	85	11	1	3	28	3	2	2	19	2	20	1	3	3	.431	.382
Adams, Tommy, Port City	.220	30	127	118	10	26	42	7	0	3	16	0	1	2	6	0	27	5	3	1	.356	.268
Adriana, Sharnol, Knoxville	.284	75	301	261	33	74	102	17	1	3	33	2	2	4	32	1	64	12	13	6	.391	.368
Allensworth, Jermaine, Carolina	.269	56	251	219	37	59	80	14	2	1	14	2	0	5	25	0	34	13	8	4	.365	.357
Alvarez, Gabe, Memphis	.556	2	10	9	0	5	6	1	0	0	4	0	0	0	1	0	1	0	0	0	.667	.600
Arias, Amador, Chattanooga†	.222	71	115	108	17	24	29	3	1	0	4	1	0	0	6	0	15	3	2	4	.269	.263
Arnold, Jamie, Greenville	.091	10	12	11	0	1	3	0	1	0	1	1	0	0	0	0	2	0	0	1	.273	.091
Austin, Jake, Carolina*	.236	102	376	352	29	83	118	19	2	4	40	2	3	2	17	4	51	5	3	13	.335	.273
Ayrault, Joe, Greenville	.245	89	328	302	27	74	115	20	0	7	42	7	3	3	13	5	70	2	4	8	.381	.280
Backlund, Brett, Carolina	.333	22	12	12	2	4	6	2	0	0	2	0	0	0	0	0	2	0	0	0	.500	.333
Baker, Jared, Memphis*	.500	4	2	2	0	1	1	0	0	0	1	0	0	0	0	0	1	0	0	0	.500	.500
Barker, Glen, Jacksonville	.239	133	562	507	74	121	185	26	4	10	49	12	1	9	33	0	143	39	16	1	.365	.296
Barnes, Jon, Memphis	.000	2	3	3	0	0	0	0	0	0	0	0	0	0	0	0	1	0	0	1	.000	.000
Batista, Tony, Huntsville	.255	120	459	419	55	107	180	23	1	16	61	6	3	2	29	0	98	7	8	8	.430	.305
Beard, Garrett, Huntsville	.190	43	144	126	18	24	29	2	0	1	8	0	2	1	15	1	21	2	3	4	.230	.278
Beasley, Tony, Carolina	.281	105	380	335	59	94	124	16	4	2	34	4	6	4	31	2	44	20	4	6	.370	.343
Beatty, Blaine, Chattanooga*	.125	8	8	8	0	1	1	0	0	0	0	0	0	0	0	0	2	0	0	0	.125	.125
Beckett, Robbie, Memphis	.000	36	8	8	0	0	0	0	0	0	0	0	0	0	0	0	6	0	0	0	.000	.000
Bennett, Chris, Carolina	.333	18	3	3	0	1	1	0	0	0	0	0	0	0	0	0	1	0	0	1	.333	.333
Blair, Dirk, Greenville	.000	40	2	2	0	0	0	0	0	0	0	0	0	0	0	0	1	0	0	0	.000	.000
Bonnici, James, Port City	.283	138	596	508	75	144	246	36	3	20	91	0	3	9	76	15	97	2	2	14	.484	.384
Boone, Aaron, Chattanooga	.227	23	74	66	6	15	18	3	0	0	3	1	2	0	5	0	12	2	0	5	.273	.274
Boston, D.J., Knoxville*	.244	132	533	479	51	117	179	27	1	11	71	2	3	2	47	1	100	12	8	12	.374	.313
Bradford, Troy, Orlando	.000	4	2	2	0	0	0	0	0	0	0	0	0	0	0	0	0	0	0	0	.000	.000
Briggs, Stoney, Memphis	.247	118	440	385	60	95	147	14	7	8	46	1	3	10	40	5	133	17	8	13	.382	.331
Briley, Greg, Jacksonville*	.087	8	26	23	2	2	5	0	0	1	4	0	1	0	2	0	6	0	1	0	.217	.154
Brock, Tarrik, Jacksonville*	.115	9	31	26	4	3	3	0	0	0	2	1	0	1	3	0	14	2	0	0	.115	.233
Brooks, Eric, Knoxville	.283	21	68	53	6	15	30	3	0	4	12	0	0	3	12	1	9	0	1	0	.566	.441
Brown, Adam, Chattanooga*	.266	77	259	233	24	62	95	14	2	5	32	0	1	1	24	4	36	0	1	9	.408	.336
Brown, Brant, Orlando*	.271	121	502	446	67	121	174	27	4	6	53	11	3	3	39	2	77	8	5	6	.390	.332
Brown, Chad, Knoxville*	.000	40	1	1	0	0	0	0	0	0	0	0	0	0	0	0	1	0	0	0	.000	.000
Brown, Michael, Carolina*	.238	60	253	223	29	53	92	13	1	8	33	0	0	2	28	7	62	0	3	1	.413	.328
Brumfield, Jacob, Carolina	.417	3	13	12	2	5	11	0	0	2	2	0	0	0	1	0	2	0	2	0	.917	.462
Brumley, Duff, Chattanooga	.000	25	2	2	0	0	0	0	0	0	0	0	0	0	0	0	0	0	0	1	.000	.000
Bruno, Julio, Memphis	.270	59	211	196	16	53	71	6	3	2	25	3	2	2	8	0	35	3	2	9	.362	.303
Buckley, Travis, Chattanooga	.000	3	3	2	0	0	0	0	0	0	0	0	0	0	1	0	1	0	0	0	.000	.333
Buckley, Troy, Chattanooga	.241	10	29	29	1	7	7	0	0	0	0	0	0	0	0	0	6	0	0	0	.241	.241
Bullinger, Jim, Orlando	.000	1	2	0	0	0	0	0	0	0	0	2	0	0	0	0	0	0	0	0	.000	.000
Burgos, John, Chattanooga*	.286	44	8	7	0	2	2	0	0	0	0	0	0	0	1	0	1	0	0	0	.286	.375
Burlingame, Ben, Orlando	.167	37	14	12	0	2	2	0	0	0	3	2	0	0	0	0	3	0	0	0	.167	.167
Burton, Darren, Orlando†	.306	62	249	222	40	68	100	16	2	4	21	0	0	0	27	2	42	7	4	5	.450	.382
Burton, Essex, Birmingham	.255	142	656	554	95	141	163	15	2	1	43	15	2	5	80	4	79	60	22	9	.294	.353
Bush, Homer, Memphis	.280	108	454	432	53	121	158	12	5	5	37	4	0	2	15	0	83	34	12	6	.366	.307
Butler, Rich, Knoxville*	.267	58	245	217	27	58	88	12	3	4	33	1	0	2	25	1	41	11	3	5	.406	.348
Cameron, Mike, Birmingham	.249	107	419	350	64	87	150	20	5	11	60	5	4	6	54	0	104	21	12	9	.429	.355
Canale, George, Carolina*	.287	130	545	487	71	140	245	30	6	21	102	0	8	4	46	6	83	1	3	15	.503	.349
Cappuccio, Carmine, Birming.*	.278	65	277	248	34	69	100	13	3	4	38	3	2	2	22	4	21	2	2	10	.403	.339
Cardenas, John, Port City	.226	57	206	195	17	44	53	9	0	0	17	1	1	0	9	1	45	1	3	9	.272	.259
Casanova, Raul, Memphis	.271	89	342	306	42	83	137	18	0	12	44	0	4	4	25	2	51	4	1	7	.448	.330
Catalanotto, Frank, Jacksonville*	.226	134	559	491	66	111	164	19	5	8	48	6	4	9	49	4	56	13	8	9	.334	.306
Cole, Victor, Memphis†	.000	8	2	2	0	0	0	0	0	0	0	0	0	0	0	0	0	0	0	0	.000	.000
Coleman, Ken, Orlando†	.277	127	479	394	82	109	146	19	3	4	37	4	2	3	76	0	55	25	7	16	.371	.396
Colon, Felix, Jacksonville	.259	31	96	81	5	21	34	7	0	2	8	0	0	2	13	0	13	0	0	2	.420	.375
Conger, Jeff, Carolina*	.289	39	150	128	15	37	48	6	1	1	17	2	1	1	18	2	31	8	2	0	.375	.378
Coolbaugh, Mike, Knoxville	.240	142	555	500	71	120	183	32	2	9	56	4	3	11	37	3	110	7	11	13	.366	.305
Cooper, Gary, Jacksonville	.276	99	405	337	66	93	171	22	1	18	66	0	3	6	59	4	83	8	4	11	.507	.390
Cora, Manny, Port City†	.226	80	270	261	17	59	73	8	3	0	15	0	1	0	8	0	38	1	6	8	.280	.248
Cotton, John, Memphis*	.253	121	459	407	60	103	174	19	8	12	47	6	4	4	38	0	101	15	6	2	.428	.320
Coughlin, Kevin, Birmingham*	.385	96	376	327	56	126	168	29	2	3	49	8	2	5	34	7	43	5	2	3	.514	.448
Cox, Darron, Orlando	.284	33	115	102	8	29	46	5	0	4	15	2	2	1	8	0	16	3	3	3	.451	.336
Cradle, Rickey, Knoxville	.179	41	139	117	17	21	40	5	1	4	13	1	1	3	17	0	29	3	3	3	.342	.297
Cranford, Jay, Carolina	.229	93	353	288	30	66	95	12	1	5	42	2	7	4	52	1	67	3	4	6	.330	.348
Cruz, Ivan, Jacksonville*	.282	108	460	397	65	112	224	17	1	31	93	0	3	0	60	15	94	0	0	7	.564	.374
Dabney, Fred, Orlando	.000	13	2	2	0	0	0	0	0	0	0	0	0	0	0	0	0	0	0	0	.000	.000
Danapilis, Eric, Jacksonville	.258	129	488	415	47	107	163	24	1	10	63	0	3	9	61	6	100	3	3	13	.393	.363
D'Andrea, Mike, Greenville	.500	40	11	8	2	4	4	0	0	0	0	1	0	0	2	0	0	0	0	0	.500	.600
Davis, Josh, Memphis	.500	1	3	2	0	1	1	0	0	0	0	0	0	0	1	0	1	0	0	0	.500	.667
DeLaCruz, Lorenzo, Knoxville	.274	140	560	508	63	139	207	20	12	8	61	1	0	15	36	3	129	11	11	14	.407	.340
DeLaNuez, Rex, Jacksonville	.263	111	399	331	47	87	138	22	1	9	41	8	3	8	49	3	74	10	6	5	.417	.368

Player, Team	Avg.	G	TPA	AB	R	H	TB	2B	3B	HR	RBI	SH	SF	HP	BB	IBB	SO	SB	CS	GDP	Slg.	OBP
DeLeon, Luis, Orlando	.000	5	2	1	1	0	0	0	0	0	0	1	0	0	0	0	1	0	0	0	.000	.000
DeLeon, Roberto, Memphis	.267	73	252	236	24	63	94	10	0	7	34	1	1	2	12	0	32	2	2	1	.398	.307
Delgado, Wilson, Port City†	.195	13	47	41	3	8	12	4	0	0	1	0	0	0	6	0	8	0	0	1	.293	.298
Dessens, Elmer, Carolina	.313	27	19	16	0	5	6	1	0	0	2	3	0	0	0	0	5	0	0	0	.375	.313
Diaz, Eddy, Port City	.261	110	474	421	66	110	180	22	0	16	47	1	4	8	40	3	39	9	7	9	.428	.334
DiSarcina, Glenn, Birmingham*	.269	9	28	26	4	7	8	1	0	0	2	0	0	0	2	0	3	0	0	0	.308	.321
Dismuke, Jamie, Chattanooga*	.285	99	402	347	56	99	170	11	0	20	69	0	1	10	44	10	45	0	0	11	.490	.381
Dotel, Mariano, Memphis†	.280	8	27	25	7	7	9	2	0	0	5	0	0	0	2	0	10	0	1	0	.360	.333
Dowler, Dee, Orlando	.226	9	33	31	6	7	9	2	0	0	1	0	0	0	2	0	5	1	0	0	.290	.273
Dreyer, Darren, Orlando	.000	14	1	1	0	0	0	0	0	0	0	0	0	0	0	0	1	0	0	0	.000	.000
Drinkwater, Sean, Memphis	.240	102	319	287	29	69	101	12	1	6	26	2	3	1	26	1	49	3	4	6	.352	.303
Duross, Gabe, Orlando*	.262	68	257	244	23	64	85	10	1	3	40	0	2	1	10	3	20	3	2	12	.348	.292
Dye, Jermaine, Greenville	.285	104	437	403	50	115	194	26	4	15	71	2	4	1	27	2	74	4	8	9	.481	.329
Edge, Tim, Carolina	.214	45	137	126	15	27	44	5	0	4	19	0	1	0	10	0	33	0	0	4	.349	.270
Erdman, Brad, Orlando	.111	14	39	36	4	4	4	0	0	0	0	0	0	2	1	0	6	0	0	4	.111	.179
Espinosa, Ramon, Carolina	.286	134	520	489	69	140	181	28	2	3	48	8	1	5	17	3	64	14	6	15	.370	.316
Etheridge, Roger, Greenville*	.214	32	14	14	1	3	5	0	1	0	0	0	0	0	0	0	2	0	0	1	.357	.214
Evans, Sean, Carolina	.000	29	1	1	0	0	0	0	0	0	0	0	0	0	0	0	0	0	0	0	.000	.000
Farmer, Howard, Chattanooga	.000	1	1	1	0	0	0	0	0	0	0	0	0	0	0	0	0	0	0	0	.000	.000
Farrell, Jon, Carolina	.220	94	339	314	34	69	112	13	0	10	47	3	3	4	15	0	82	3	4	9	.357	.262
Felix, Lauro, Huntsville	.111	10	29	27	3	3	6	0	0	1	1	0	0	0	2	0	8	0	0	1	.222	.172
Fermin, Carlos, Jacksonville	.173	59	132	127	10	22	29	4	0	1	9	0	0	0	5	0	16	0	2	2	.228	.205
Fernandez, Daniel, Jacksonville	.165	94	268	230	18	38	55	5	0	4	16	3	2	4	29	1	60	1	3	3	.239	.268
Ferry, Mike, Chattanooga	.190	24	28	21	2	4	4	0	0	0	1	5	0	0	2	0	6	0	0	0	.190	.261
Fox, Chad, Chattanooga	.200	20	11	10	0	2	2	0	0	0	1	1	0	0	0	0	3	0	0	0	.200	.200
Francisco, David, Huntsville	.279	129	534	477	75	133	167	17	1	5	48	5	3	11	38	0	92	30	8	10	.350	.344
Freitas, Mike, Memphis	.000	54	1	1	0	0	0	0	0	0	0	0	0	0	0	0	1	0	0	0	.000	.000
Fryman, Troy, Birmingham*	.222	112	416	356	48	79	122	13	3	8	41	2	3	6	49	6	97	9	1	4	.343	.324
Garcia, Luis, Jacksonville	.277	17	49	47	6	13	13	0	0	0	5	0	0	1	1	0	8	2	1	0	.277	.306
Gennaro, Brad, Memphis*	.267	104	428	397	46	106	142	19	1	5	60	3	5	2	21	2	62	11	8	9	.358	.304
Gipson, Charles, Port City	.223	112	437	391	36	87	102	11	2	0	29	7	1	8	30	0	66	10	12	13	.261	.291
Gomez, Fabio, Port City	.237	29	109	93	7	22	29	4	0	1	11	1	2	0	12	0	20	1	3	1	.312	.318
Gomez, Rudy, Orlando	.192	93	239	214	18	41	57	11	1	1	16	5	3	2	15	1	45	0	0	8	.266	.248
Gonzalez, Paul, Birmingham*	.269	8	28	26	4	7	14	1	0	2	4	0	0	0	2	0	7	0	1	0	.538	.321
Griffey, Craig, Port City	.177	96	365	299	43	53	66	11	1	0	24	3	3	9	46	0	77	13	3	5	.221	.303
Grijak, Kevin, Greenville*	.432	21	85	74	14	32	43	5	0	2	11	0	2	2	7	0	9	0	1	0	.581	.482
Gubanich, Creighton, Huntsville	.219	94	336	274	37	60	108	7	1	13	43	2	5	7	48	0	82	1	0	2	.394	.344
Haas, David, Orlando	.000	3	1	1	0	0	0	0	0	0	0	0	0	0	0	0	0	0	0	0	.000	.000
Hanel, Marcus, Carolina	.183	21	67	60	1	11	12	1	0	0	3	1	1	1	4	0	18	0	1	2	.200	.242
Hansen, Terrel, Jacksonville	.223	55	199	179	22	40	75	8	0	9	22	0	2	8	10	1	40	0	1	2	.419	.291
Hanson, Craig, Memphis	.000	25	2	2	0	0	0	0	0	0	0	0	0	0	0	0	1	0	0	0	.000	.000
Harley, Quentin, Memphis†	.245	50	174	159	21	39	59	5	3	3	14	0	1	1	13	1	34	7	1	2	.371	.305
Harmes, Kris, Knoxville*	.228	86	299	259	28	59	89	14	2	4	29	1	3	0	36	5	47	0	1	8	.344	.319
Harrah, Doug, Orlando	.000	44	2	2	0	0	0	0	0	0	0	0	0	0	0	0	1	0	0	0	.000	.000
Harrison, Brian, Memphis*	.000	38	1	1	0	0	0	0	0	0	0	0	0	0	0	0	0	0	0	0	.000	.000
Harrison, Tom, Greenville	.222	14	9	9	2	2	3	1	0	0	0	0	0	0	0	0	3	0	1	0	.333	.222
Hart, Chris, Huntsville	.262	36	120	103	11	27	40	3	2	2	20	3	2	2	10	1	30	1	3	1	.388	.333
Henry, Santiago, Knoxville	.220	138	481	454	47	100	139	25	4	2	30	7	5	5	10	0	91	16	6	7	.306	.243
Hernandez, Fernando, Memphis	.000	12	5	4	0	0	0	0	0	0	0	1	0	0	0	0	4	0	0	0	.000	.000
Herrera, Jose, Huntsville*	.282	92	389	358	37	101	138	11	4	6	45	0	2	2	27	2	58	9	8	8	.385	.334
Hickey, Mike, Port City†	.262	120	521	447	59	117	161	24	1	6	59	4	4	5	60	2	83	6	3	9	.360	.353
Hill, Milt, Carolina	.091	10	12	11	0	1	1	0	0	0	0	1	0	0	0	0	2	0	0	0	.091	.091
Hollinger, Adrian, Greenville*	.143	7	7	7	0	1	2	1	0	0	1	0	0	0	0	0	5	0	0	0	.286	.143
Hollins, Damon, Greenville	.247	129	520	466	64	115	199	26	2	18	77	0	6	4	44	6	120	6	6	7	.427	.313
Hostetler, Marcus, Greenville	.000	33	2	2	0	0	0	0	0	0	0	0	0	0	0	0	2	0	0	0	.000	.000
Hostetler, Mike, Greenville	.105	28	22	19	1	2	2	0	0	0	3	2	0	0	1	0	1	0	1	0	.105	.150
Hughes, Troy, Greenville	.255	73	221	200	24	51	78	7	1	6	25	0	2	2	17	0	52	3	6	1	.390	.317
Hurst, Jimmy, Birmingham	.189	91	339	301	47	57	104	11	0	12	34	0	2	1	33	0	95	12	5	5	.346	.270
Hutcheson, David, Orlando	.000	28	28	21	2	0	0	0	0	0	0	3	0	0	4	0	13	0	0	0	.000	.160
Hyzdu, Adam, Chattanooga	.263	102	364	312	55	82	137	14	1	13	48	2	1	4	45	2	56	3	2	4	.439	.362
Ingram, Todd, Knoxville	.000	21	1	1	0	0	0	0	0	0	0	0	0	0	0	0	1	0	0	0	.000	.000
Jenkins, Dee, Chattanooga*	.059	8	20	17	1	1	2	1	0	0	1	0	0	0	3	0	7	0	1	0	.118	.200
Jennings, Robin, Orlando*	.296	132	543	490	71	145	237	27	7	17	79	0	5	4	44	5	61	7	14	11	.484	.355
Johnson, Chris, Orlando	.000	46	2	2	0	0	0	0	0	0	0	0	0	0	0	0	2	0	0	0	.000	.000
Johnson, Earl, Memphis†	.200	2	11	10	0	2	2	0	0	0	0	0	0	0	1	0	0	0	1	0	.200	.273
Johnson, Jack, Orlando	.221	25	77	68	3	15	15	0	0	0	4	0	1	1	7	0	11	1	3	1	.221	.299
Johnson, Matt, Knoxville	.181	57	170	144	8	26	30	4	0	0	11	2	2	5	17	0	32	1	1	5	.208	.286
Kaufman, Brad, Memphis	.083	28	27	24	4	2	3	1	0	0	1	2	0	0	1	0	12	0	0	0	.125	.120
Keagle, Greg, Memphis	.143	15	9	7	2	1	1	0	0	0	0	1	0	0	1	0	0	0	0	0	.143	.250
Kelly, Pat, Knoxville	.242	47	180	161	22	39	53	6	1	2	14	5	0	1	13	1	30	1	1	1	.329	.303
Kendall, Jason, Carolina	.326	117	508	429	87	140	192	26	1	8	71	1	8	14	56	5	22	10	7	10	.448	.414
Kessinger, Keith, Orlando†	.258	18	71	62	8	16	21	5	0	0	5	2	0	1	6	0	3	0	0	1	.339	.333
Kilgo, Rusty, Chattanooga*	.000	54	2	2	0	0	0	0	0	0	0	0	0	0	0	0	1	0	0	0	.000	.000
Killeen, Tim, Memphis*	.235	77	258	230	27	54	95	14	0	9	40	0	1	0	27	6	71	2	0	5	.413	.314
Kimsey, Keith, Jacksonville	.161	34	128	118	8	19	28	4	1	1	10	0	1	2	7	0	39	1	1	6	.237	.219
Kingston, Mark, Orlando†	.266	66	226	199	17	53	81	13	0	5	24	2	2	1	22	5	41	0	1	4	.407	.339
Klesko, Ryan, Greenville*	.231	4	15	13	1	3	6	0	0	1	4	0	0	0	2	0	1	0	0	1	.462	.333
Koehler, Jim, Port City*	.000	2	2	2	0	0	0	0	0	0	0	0	0	0	0	0	1	0	0	0	.000	.000
Koelling, Brian, Chattanooga	.296	107	486	432	71	128	172	21	7	3	44	8	3	3	40	1	63	30	12	9	.398	.358
Koller, Jerry, Greenville	.200	25	27	25	0	5	5	0	0	0	1	2	0	0	0	0	6	0	0	1	.200	.200
Kopriva, Dan, Chattanooga	.281	51	138	121	14	34	45	8	0	1	11	2	0	2	11	0	14	1	1	5	.372	.351
Kramer, Tommy, Chattanooga†	.294	21	19	17	0	5	6	1	0	0	2	1	0	0	1	0	1	0	0	2	.353	.333
Kremblas, Frank, Chattanooga	.149	19	77	67	8	10	15	2	0	1	6	0	2	1	7	0	10	1	1	2	.224	.234

Player, Team	Avg.	G	TPA	AB	R	H	TB	2B	3B	HR	RBI	SH	SF	HP	BB	IBB	SO	SB	CS	GDP	Slg.	OBP
Krevokuch, Jim, Carolina	.282	70	197	174	20	49	65	13	0	1	11	4	2	5	12	1	20	1	1	6	.374	.342
Kroon, Marc, Memphis†	.000	22	15	13	1	0	0	0	0	0	1	1	0	0	1	0	4	0	0	0	.000	.071
Ladd, Jeff, Knoxville	.292	9	31	24	1	7	10	1	1	0	2	1	0	1	5	0	8	0	0	0	.417	.433
Ladell, Cleveland, Chattanooga	.292	135	565	517	76	151	208	28	7	5	43	4	2	2	39	1	88	28	15	12	.402	.343
LaRocca, Greg, Memphis	.143	2	7	7	0	1	1	0	0	0	0	0	0	0	0	0	1	0	1	1	.143	.143
Larregui, Ed, Orlando	.300	122	460	423	55	127	180	18	1	11	60	0	4	1	32	2	39	3	10	15	.426	.348
Lawrence, Sean, Carolina*	.000	12	1	1	0	0	0	0	0	0	0	0	0	0	0	0	1	0	0	0	.000	.000
Leary, Rob, Carolina*	.305	67	289	243	38	74	112	14	3	6	42	0	3	3	40	2	38	3	3	7	.461	.405
Lee, Derrek, Memphis	.111	2	9	9	0	1	1	0	0	0	1	0	0	0	0	0	2	0	0	0	.111	.111
Leiper, Tim, Jacksonville*	.259	110	435	375	60	97	142	19	1	8	46	3	6	3	48	6	30	3	3	11	.379	.343
Lesher, Brian, Huntsville	.261	127	538	471	78	123	207	23	2	19	71	0	1	2	64	2	110	7	8	7	.439	.351
Lidle, Kevin, Jacksonville	.163	36	82	80	12	13	23	7	0	1	5	1	0	0	1	0	31	1	0	1	.288	.173
Loiselle, Rich, Memphis	.125	13	9	8	1	1	2	1	0	0	1	0	0	0	1	0	3	0	0	0	.250	.222
Long, Joey, Memphis	.000	25	2	2	0	0	0	0	0	0	0	0	0	0	0	0	1	0	0	1	.000	.000
Luebbers, Larry, Chattanooga	.333	30	25	21	2	7	9	2	0	0	4	2	0	0	2	0	1	0	0	0	.429	.391
Lutz, Brent, Knoxville	.132	52	167	144	14	19	31	6	0	2	12	2	0	6	15	0	59	4	1	1	.215	.242
Mack, Quinn, Memphis*	.238	20	74	63	6	15	22	1	0	2	6	1	0	2	8	1	8	2	1	1	.349	.342
Madsen, Dan, Orlando†	.192	15	32	26	6	5	7	0	1	0	6	0	0	0	6	0	2	0	1	0	.269	.344
Magdaleno, Ricky, Chattanooga	.175	11	44	40	2	7	12	2	0	1	2	0	0	0	4	0	13	0	0	3	.300	.250
Malloy, Marty, Greenville*	.278	124	515	461	73	128	184	20	3	10	59	7	8	0	39	1	58	11	12	6	.399	.329
Manahan, Austin, Orlando†	.212	94	280	260	34	55	76	12	0	3	19	2	0	2	16	0	57	13	6	9	.292	.263
Manning, Henry, Birmingham	.300	11	34	30	3	9	16	1	0	2	11	0	3	0	1	0	1	0	0	0	.533	.294
Martinez, Angel, Knoxville*	.229	41	152	144	14	33	49	8	1	2	22	0	2	0	6	0	34	0	1	2	.340	.257
Martinez, Pablo, Greenville†	.255	120	510	462	70	118	163	22	4	5	29	8	1	2	37	0	89	12	12	7	.353	.313
Mashore, Justin, Jacksonville	.243	40	160	148	26	36	60	8	2	4	15	3	0	3	6	0	41	5	1	2	.405	.287
Mattson, Rob, Memphis*	.235	33	35	34	3	8	9	1	0	0	4	1	0	0	0	0	9	2	0	0	.265	.235
May, Darrell, Greenville*	.167	15	6	6	0	1	1	0	0	0	0	0	0	0	0	0	3	0	0	0	.167	.167
Meier, Kevin, Orlando	.167	11	7	6	0	1	2	1	0	0	0	0	0	0	1	0	2	0	0	0	.333	.286
Merchant, Mark, Chattanooga†	.208	25	60	53	4	11	14	0	0	1	6	0	0	0	7	1	15	0	0	4	.264	.300
Molina, Izzy, Huntsville	.259	83	337	301	38	78	120	16	1	8	26	0	2	8	26	0	62	3	4	6	.399	.332
Moore, Marcus, Chattanooga†	.000	36	3	3	0	0	0	0	0	0	0	0	0	0	0	0	3	0	0	0	.000	.000
Morales, Francisco, Orlando	.167	2	7	6	0	1	1	0	0	0	0	0	0	0	1	0	2	0	0	0	.167	.286
Morel, Ramon, Carolina	.000	10	12	12	1	0	0	0	0	0	0	0	0	0	0	0	2	0	0	0	.000	.000
Morland, Mike, Knoxville	.179	11	29	28	6	5	6	1	0	0	1	0	0	0	1	0	4	0	0	1	.214	.207
Mota, Domingo, Chattanooga	.000	5	6	6	0	0	0	0	0	0	0	0	0	0	0	0	1	0	0	1	.000	.000
Mottola, Chad, Chattanooga	.293	51	196	181	32	53	98	13	1	10	39	0	1	1	13	0	32	1	2	2	.541	.342
Moultrie, Pat, Knoxville*	.255	13	60	51	3	13	13	0	0	0	7	4	1	0	4	1	6	2	1	0	.255	.304
Munoz, Omer, Carolina	.265	67	249	234	29	62	80	10	1	2	25	5	2	3	5	0	23	2	0	7	.342	.287
Murray, Heath, Memphis*	.500	14	8	6	0	3	3	0	0	0	0	2	0	0	0	0	0	0	0	0	.500	.500
Murray, Matt, Greenville*	.250	5	4	4	0	1	1	0	0	0	0	0	0	0	0	0	1	0	0	0	.250	.250
Neill, Mike, Huntsville*	.299	33	120	107	11	32	46	6	1	2	16	0	1	0	12	1	29	1	0	1	.430	.367
Nitkowski, C.J., Chattanooga*	.000	8	8	7	1	0	0	0	0	0	0	1	0	0	0	0	4	0	0	0	.000	.000
Nix, Jim, Chattanooga	.000	40	5	5	0	0	0	0	0	0	0	0	0	0	0	0	1	0	0	0	.000	.000
Noriega, Rey, Birmingham†	.190	42	114	100	9	19	24	5	0	0	5	2	0	1	11	0	27	1	2	3	.240	.277
Norton, Greg, Birmingham†	.249	133	551	469	65	117	162	23	2	6	60	3	10	5	64	7	90	19	12	10	.345	.339
Nunez, Ramon, Greenville	.261	81	262	241	34	63	109	15	2	9	34	0	3	3	15	0	63	1	1	8	.452	.309
Olmeda, Jose, Greenville†	.250	31	115	108	16	27	46	5	1	4	10	0	0	0	7	0	18	1	0	4	.426	.296
Ortiz, Hector, Orlando	.234	96	325	299	13	70	82	12	0	0	18	1	4	1	20	0	39	0	5	10	.274	.281
Paige, Carey, Greenville	.167	7	6	6	0	1	2	1	0	0	0	0	0	0	0	0	2	0	0	0	.333	.167
Parris, Steve, Carolina	.083	14	15	12	1	1	1	0	0	0	0	3	0	0	0	0	3	0	0	0	.083	.083
Pearson, Eddie, Birmingham*	.224	50	211	201	20	45	64	13	0	2	25	0	2	1	7	0	36	1	0	9	.318	.251
Pecorilli, Aldo, Greenville	.385	70	298	265	51	102	144	17	2	7	42	1	4	6	22	2	39	2	8	4	.543	.438
Peguero, Julio, Port City†	.316	71	278	256	42	81	107	15	1	3	18	4	1	1	16	1	34	12	8	3	.418	.358
Perona, Joe, Jacksonville	.147	13	37	34	2	5	8	3	0	0	3	0	1	0	2	0	5	0	0	2	.235	.189
Peters, Chris, Carolina*	.000	2	3	2	0	0	0	0	0	0	0	1	0	0	0	0	1	0	0	0	.000	.000
Petersen, Chris, Orlando	.212	125	439	382	48	81	109	10	3	4	36	5	3	4	45	3	97	7	3	14	.285	.300
Petersen, Matt, Orlando	.154	24	14	13	1	2	2	0	0	0	0	1	0	0	0	0	3	0	0	0	.154	.154
Peterson, Charles, Carolina	.329	20	82	70	13	23	28	3	1	0	7	0	1	2	9	1	15	2	1	1	.400	.415
Pevey, Marty, Jacksonville*	.259	20	66	58	2	15	20	2	0	1	7	2	2	0	4	0	17	0	2	4	.345	.297
Pickett, Ricky, Chattanooga*	1.000	40	1	1	0	1	1	0	0	0	1	0	0	0	0	0	0	0	0	0	1.000	1.000
Pisciotta, Marc, Carolina	.000	56	2	2	0	0	0	0	0	0	0	0	0	0	0	0	1	0	0	0	.000	.000
Poe, Charles, Birmingham	.283	120	500	427	75	121	192	28	2	13	60	7	5	10	51	4	79	19	4	7	.450	.369
Polcovich, Kevin, Carolina	.317	64	244	221	27	70	87	8	0	3	18	3	1	5	14	1	29	10	5	3	.394	.369
Pratte, Evan, Jacksonville†	.250	18	61	52	2	13	15	2	0	0	1	0	0	2	7	3	9	0	3	2	.288	.361
Rackley, Keifer, Port City*	.256	114	484	430	55	110	149	17	2	6	40	6	5	4	39	2	96	8	4	11	.347	.320
Ralph, Curtis, Carolina	.000	18	1	1	0	0	0	0	0	0	0	0	0	0	0	0	1	0	0	0	.000	.000
Ramirez, Roberto, Port City	.278	129	540	490	67	136	223	24	6	17	82	3	6	6	35	4	98	11	10	14	.455	.330
Ratliff, Daryl, Carolina	.286	16	73	63	10	18	25	4	0	1	5	2	0	0	8	1	10	2	1	1	.397	.366
Ratliff, Jon, Orlando	.043	26	25	23	1	1	1	0	0	0	0	2	0	0	0	0	8	0	0	0	.043	.043
Relaford, Desmond, Port City†	.287	90	397	352	51	101	137	11	2	7	27	2	0	2	41	2	58	25	9	4	.389	.365
Rendina, Mike, Jacksonville*	.224	31	106	98	12	22	36	5	0	3	16	0	0	0	7	2	20	0	0	3	.367	.276
Rice, Lance, Jacksonville†	.123	65	167	154	8	19	31	1	1	3	11	2	0	0	11	0	23	0	0	5	.201	.182
Ripplemeyer, Brad, Greenville	.182	53	183	165	8	30	44	8	0	2	16	5	2	0	11	0	54	1	0	5	.267	.230
Rivera, Roberto, Orlando*	.400	50	6	5	1	2	6	1	0	1	4	1	0	0	0	0	0	0	0	0	1.200	.400
Roberts, Lonell, Knoxville†	.236	116	492	454	66	107	128	12	3	1	29	4	4	3	27	1	97	57	18	7	.282	.281
Robinson, Don, Greenville*	.214	13	34	28	2	6	9	1	1	0	3	1	1	0	4	0	4	1	0	0	.321	.303
Rodarte, Raul, Carolina	.370	16	66	54	8	20	27	5	1	0	11	2	0	0	10	3	14	2	2	2	.500	.469
Rohrmeier, Dan, Chattanooga	.326	118	482	426	77	139	221	31	0	17	76	1	7	7	41	5	63	0	1	9	.519	.389
Rose, Pete, Birmingham*	.385	5	16	13	1	5	6	1	0	0	2	0	0	0	3	0	3	0	0	0	.462	.500
Ruebel, Matt, Carolina*	.130	27	25	23	1	3	3	0	0	0	1	1	0	0	1	0	10	0	0	0	.130	.167
Rumfield, Toby, Chattanooga	.264	92	310	273	32	72	110	12	1	8	53	3	5	3	26	2	47	0	3	14	.403	.329
Russo, Paul, Memphis	.311	45	145	122	19	38	67	9	1	6	18	0	0	1	22	1	33	1	0	3	.549	.421
Ryan, Matt, Carolina	.000	44	1	1	0	0	0	0	0	0	0	0	0	0	0	0	1	0	0	0	.000	.000

Player, Team	Avg.	G	TPA	AB	R	H	TB	2B	3B	HR	RBI	SH	SF	HP	BB	IBB	SO	SB	CS	GDP	Slg.	OBP
Rychel, Kevin, Carolina	.000	40	4	3	0	0	0	0	0	0	0	1	0	0	0	0	1	0	0	0	.000	.000
Samuels, Scott, Orlando*	.286	5	24	21	3	6	10	1	0	1	4	0	0	0	3	0	4	2	0	0	.476	.375
Sanchez, Yuri, Jacksonville*	.213	121	396	342	52	73	113	8	7	6	26	15	0	1	38	0	116	15	6	3	.330	.294
Sanders, Deion, Chattanooga*	.571	2	7	7	1	4	7	0	0	1	2	0	0	0	0	0	1	1	0	0	1.000	.571
Sanford, Chance, Carolina*	.278	16	42	36	6	10	24	3	1	3	10	0	0	1	5	1	7	3	1	0	.667	.381
Santana, Ruben, Chattanooga	.293	142	625	556	89	163	239	23	10	11	79	6	5	8	50	5	77	2	5	17	.430	.357
Saunders, Doug, Port City	.263	28	128	114	13	30	53	9	1	4	16	0	2	2	10	1	28	2	0	4	.465	.328
Sawkiw, Warren, Knoxville†	.248	44	138	121	11	30	39	4	1	1	11	3	1	0	13	0	36	2	2	2	.322	.319
Schmitt, Todd, Memphis	.000	26	1	1	0	0	0	0	0	0	0	0	0	0	0	0	1	0	0	0	.000	.000
Schutz, Carl, Greenville*	1.000	51	1	1	0	1	1	0	0	0	0	0	0	0	0	0	0	0	0	0	1.000	1.000
Schwenke, Matt, Memphis	.242	23	69	62	7	15	18	3	0	0	4	1	1	1	3	0	16	0	0	0	.290	.284
Seelbach, Chris, Greenville	.200	9	12	10	0	2	2	0	0	0	0	1	0	0	1	0	2	0	0	0	.200	.273
Sellers, Rick, Chattanooga	.238	89	337	281	40	67	110	13	3	8	41	2	4	5	45	3	66	2	1	8	.391	.349
Sheldon, Scott, Huntsville	.217	66	263	235	25	51	77	10	2	4	15	3	1	1	23	0	60	5	0	7	.328	.288
Shouse, Brian, Carolina*	.250	22	20	16	2	4	5	1	0	0	1	4	0	0	0	0	3	0	1	0	.313	.250
Simmons, John, Greenville*	.250	48	5	4	0	1	1	0	0	0	0	0	0	0	1	0	0	0	0	0	.250	.400
Slaught, Don, Carolina	.250	3	12	12	1	3	4	1	0	0	1	0	0	0	0	0	3	0	0	0	.333	.250
Smith, Ira, Memphis	.303	64	267	238	40	72	106	13	3	5	36	0	3	2	23	0	32	11	4	6	.445	.365
Smith, Ottis, Orlando	.364	17	15	11	4	4	7	1	1	0	0	3	0	0	1	0	1	0	0	0	.636	.417
Smith, Robert, Greenville	.261	127	496	444	75	116	191	27	3	14	58	4	1	7	40	2	109	12	6	12	.430	.331
Snyder, Jared, Orlando	.500	1	4	4	2	2	2	0	0	0	0	0	0	0	0	0	0	0	0	0	.500	.500
Sobolewski, Mark, Huntsville	.205	83	340	307	35	63	100	14	1	7	34	2	1	8	22	1	62	2	1	11	.326	.275
Sparks, Greg, Greenville*	.214	65	168	145	15	31	52	6	0	5	21	2	2	2	17	1	41	0	0	3	.359	.301
Spiezio, Scott, Huntsville†	.282	141	616	528	78	149	237	33	8	13	86	2	14	4	67	2	78	10	3	10	.449	.359
Stewart, Shannon, Knoxville	.287	138	601	498	89	143	194	24	6	5	55	3	5	6	89	3	61	42	16	13	.390	.398
Sutherland, Alex, Port City	.205	13	49	44	1	9	12	3	0	0	3	0	0	0	5	0	7	1	0	3	.273	.286
Swann, Pedro, Greenville*	.324	102	390	339	57	110	171	24	2	11	64	0	3	3	45	2	63	14	11	8	.504	.405
Swartzbaugh, Dave, Orlando	.000	16	2	2	0	0	0	0	0	0	0	0	0	0	0	0	1	0	0	0	.000	.000
Telemaco, Amaury, Orlando	.250	22	17	16	2	4	4	0	0	0	0	1	0	0	0	0	3	0	0	0	.250	.250
Thomas, Keith, Memphis†	.253	109	378	356	66	90	141	13	4	10	33	1	0	1	20	0	85	43	11	6	.396	.294
Thompson, Jason, Memphis*	.272	137	542	475	62	129	211	20	1	20	64	0	5	0	62	4	131	7	3	7	.444	.352
Tolar, Kevin, Carolina	1.000	12	1	1	0	1	1	0	0	0	1	0	0	0	0	0	0	0	0	0	1.000	1.000
Torres, Paul, Orlando	.298	63	262	228	38	68	114	14	1	10	45	0	2	1	29	4	40	0	3	1	.500	.377
Tranbarger, Mark, Chattanooga*	.000	48	2	2	0	0	0	0	0	0	0	0	0	0	0	0	1	0	0	0	.000	.000
Tredaway, Chad, Memphis†	.267	10	33	30	5	8	9	1	0	0	4	0	0	0	3	1	5	1	0	0	.300	.333
Triessl, Mike, Memphis	.167	4	6	6	0	1	1	0	0	0	0	0	0	0	0	0	0	0	0	0	.167	.167
Tsamis, George, Car.-P.C.	.000	19	1	0	0	0	0	0	0	0	0	0	0	0	1	0	0	0	0	0	.000	1.000
Turnier, Aaron, Greenville*	.000	8	1	1	0	0	0	0	0	0	0	0	0	0	0	0	1	0	0	0	.000	.000
Tuttle, Dave, Chattanooga	.000	8	4	2	0	0	0	0	0	0	1	2	0	0	0	0	1	0	0	0	.000	.000
Valdes, Pedro, Orlando*	.300	114	474	426	57	128	183	28	3	7	68	0	6	5	37	3	77	3	6	7	.430	.359
VanRyn, Ben, Chattanooga*	.500	5	2	2	1	1	2	1	0	0	2	0	0	0	0	0	1	0	0	0	1.000	.500
Varitek, Jason, Port City†	.224	104	421	352	42	79	127	14	2	10	44	3	3	2	61	4	126	0	1	8	.361	.340
Vasquez, Chris, Chattanooga*	.400	7	17	15	3	6	10	1	0	1	1	0	0	0	2	0	3	0	0	0	.667	.471
Vasquez, Marcos, Chattanooga	.158	27	20	19	2	3	3	0	0	0	1	1	0	0	0	0	6	0	0	0	.158	.158
Velandia, Jorge, Memphis	.204	63	203	186	23	38	64	10	2	4	17	1	1	1	14	2	37	0	2	4	.344	.262
Viera, Jose, Orlando	.121	12	36	33	2	4	7	0	0	1	2	0	0	1	2	0	8	0	0	0	.212	.194
Vinas, Julio, Birmingham	.269	102	421	372	47	100	138	16	2	6	61	0	7	5	37	1	80	3	3	6	.371	.337
Vollmer, Scott, Birmingham	.236	81	309	258	35	61	84	5	0	6	39	4	4	1	42	1	39	0	1	5	.326	.341
Waggoner, Jim, Huntsville*	.200	51	149	110	18	22	29	5	1	0	15	3	0	2	34	0	29	1	2	1	.264	.397
Walker, Dane, Huntsville*	.232	110	436	370	46	86	109	13	2	2	35	2	3	2	57	6	84	9	7	9	.295	.336
Warner, Mike, Greenville*	.237	53	225	173	31	41	53	12	0	0	7	2	2	1	47	0	36	12	4	1	.306	.399
Watkins, Pat, Chattanooga	.291	105	398	358	57	104	170	26	2	12	57	0	4	3	33	4	53	5	5	7	.475	.352
White, Jason, Huntsville	.234	48	196	167	20	39	69	4	1	8	27	0	3	2	24	2	49	2	1	3	.413	.332
Wilkins, Marc, Carolina	.000	37	7	5	0	0	0	0	0	0	1	1	0	0	1	0	4	0	0	1	.000	.167
Williams, Juan, Greenville*	.313	62	214	192	40	60	123	14	2	15	39	0	3	0	19	3	44	4	3	5	.641	.369
Wilson, Brandon, Chattanooga	.328	75	343	308	56	101	159	29	1	9	50	2	2	3	28	0	52	12	6	7	.516	.387
Wilson, Craig, Birmingham	.289	132	531	471	56	136	169	19	1	4	46	10	2	5	43	0	44	2	2	21	.359	.353
Wolfe, Joel, Huntsville	.256	108	466	399	58	102	157	15	2	12	41	6	2	5	54	4	75	23	12	5	.393	.350
Wollenburg, Doug, Greenville	.191	66	180	162	22	31	39	5	0	1	12	1	1	3	13	2	31	4	3	6	.241	.263
Womack, Tony, Carolina*	.256	82	364	332	52	85	105	9	4	1	19	11	0	2	19	2	36	27	10	2	.316	.300
Wooten, Shawn, Jacksonville	.129	20	73	70	4	9	16	1	0	2	7	0	1	1	1	0	17	0	0	3	.229	.151

GRAND SLAMS: Cameron, 3; Danapilis, Killeen, Rohrmeier, Thompson, 2 each; Austin, Barker, Butler, Canale, Coolbaugh, Cooper, Cruz, Diaz, Dismuke, Gennaro, Gubanich, Hart, Hickey, Hollins, Kendall, Larregui, C. Petersen, Ramirez, Rendina, Rivera, Santana, Sellers, Spiezio, Swann, Watkins, Williams, 1 each.

AWARDED FIRST BASE ON CATCHER'S INTERFERENCE: Griffey 5 (Erdman, Kendall, Lutz, Molina, Ortiz); Casanova 3 (Brooks, Harmes, Pecorilli); Hurst 2 (Beard, Harmes); Kopriva 2 (A. Martinez 2); Torres 2 (Cardenas, Varitek); Walker 2 (A. Brown, Cox); Briggs (Vollmer); Bush (Pecorilli); F. Gomez (Perona); Hickey (Kendall); Ladell (Lidle); Rendina (Kendall); Schwenke (Vollmer); I. Smith (Pecorilli); Spiezio (Cox).

PLAYERS WITH TWO OR MORE TEAMS

Player, Team	Avg.	G	TPA	AB	R	H	TB	2B	3B	HR	RBI	SH	SF	HP	BB	IBB	SO	SB	CS	GDP	Slg.	OBP
Tsamis, George, Carolina	.000	12	1	0	0	0	0	0	0	0	0	0	0	0	1	0	0	0	0	0	.000	1.000
Tsamis, George, Port City	.000	7	0	0	0	0	0	0	0	0	0	0	0	0	0	0	0	0	0	0	.000	.000

PITCHING

TEAM

Team	W	L	Pct.	ERA	G	CG	ShO	Sv.	IP	H	TBF	R	ER	HR	SH	SF	HB	BB	IBB	SO	WP	Bk.
Orlando	76	67	.531	3.41	143	6	14	43	1257.2	1174	5274	563	477	113	44	41	66	413	54	892	64	11
Carolina	89	55	.618	3.48	144	7	14	44	1322.1	1267	5603	611	511	86	57	34	63	418	40	979	71	5
Port City	62	80	.437	3.62	142	5	6	27	1264.0	1179	5382	617	508	89	52	33	78	475	18	989	79	13
Birmingham	80	64	.556	3.73	144	8	9	35	1248.1	1208	5282	599	517	94	36	44	39	413	18	962	67	10
Jacksonville	75	69	.521	3.73	144	13	8	36	1286.2	1303	5476	621	533	112	43	32	41	476	28	854	60	10
Chattanooga	83	60	.580	3.78	143	4	9	44	1258.1	1239	5439	633	528	85	60	49	39	488	29	1033	60	8
Huntsville	70	74	.486	4.03	144	1	7	39	1249.0	1230	5299	637	559	102	57	30	42	433	36	865	82	8
Memphis	68	74	.479	4.32	142	15	5	32	1236.0	1191	5513	704	593	103	31	43	88	652	51	1058	101	13
Greenville	59	83	.415	4.65	142	7	4	34	1234.2	1303	5401	726	638	134	52	46	44	477	35	819	66	8
Knoxville	54	90	.375	4.76	144	6	12	32	1222.1	1249	5350	761	646	114	39	54	37	508	12	919	84	7

INDIVIDUAL

TOP QUALIFIERS FOR EARNED-RUN AVERAGE TITLE

Minimum 115 innings. *Lefthanded pitcher.

Pitcher, Team	W	L	Pct.	ERA	G	GS	CG	ShO	GF	Sv.	IP	H	TBF	R	ER	HR	SH	SF	HB	BB	IBB	SO	WP	Bk.
Dessens, Elmer, Carolina	15	8	.652	2.49	27	27	1	0	0	0	152.0	170	638	62	42	10	11	4	3	21	3	68	7	2
Sodowsky, Clint, Jacksonville	5	5	.500	2.55	19	19	5	3	0	0	123.2	102	497	46	35	4	2	2	5	50	1	77	3	0
Miller, Trever, Jacksonville*	8	2	.800	2.72	31	16	3	2	4	0	122.1	122	512	46	37	5	4	2	5	34	0	77	1	0
Ruebel, Matt, Carolina*	13	5	.722	2.76	27	27	4	3	0	0	169.1	150	699	68	52	7	4	7	7	45	1	136	7	1
Wagner, Matt, Port City	5	8	.385	2.82	23	23	0	0	0	0	137.0	121	566	57	43	9	3	4	4	33	1	111	5	1
Andujar, Luis, Birmingham	14	8	.636	2.85	27	27	2	1	0	0	167.1	147	689	64	53	10	1	5	7	44	0	146	3	1
Telemaco, Amaury, Orlando	8	8	.500	3.29	22	22	3	1	0	0	147.2	112	587	60	54	13	8	3	4	42	3	151	7	1
Kramer, Tommy, Chattanooga	12	1	.923	3.33	21	18	2	0	1	0	127.0	117	513	54	47	8	5	5	2	28	4	126	4	0
Ratliff, Jon, Orlando	10	5	.667	3.47	26	25	1	1	1	0	140.0	143	599	67	54	9	2	8	10	42	1	94	13	0
Kroon, Marc, Memphis	7	5	.583	3.51	22	19	0	0	2	2	115.1	90	497	49	45	12	2	2	6	61	1	123	16	1
Fernandez, Osvaldo, Port City*	12	7	.632	3.57	27	26	0	0	0	0	156.1	139	654	78	62	6	4	1	5	60	1	160	12	1
Chouinard, Bobby, Huntsville	14	8	.636	3.62	29	29	1	1	0	0	166.2	155	694	81	67	10	9	1	4	50	5	106	4	0
Vasquez, Marcos, Chattanooga	7	6	.538	3.68	26	18	0	0	1	1	120.0	125	531	63	49	12	6	5	4	46	1	80	5	1
Moore, Tim, Birmingham	7	5	.583	3.68	29	19	0	0	3	0	120.0	118	521	58	49	10	7	6	4	40	1	78	6	2
Thompson, Justin, Jacksonville*	6	7	.462	3.73	18	18	3	0	0	0	123.0	110	502	55	51	7	4	2	3	38	2	98	3	0

DEPARTMENTAL LEADERS: W—Dessens, 15; L—Mattson, 13; Pct.—Kramer, .923; G—Kelly, 66; GS—Chouinard, 29; CG—Mattson, 11; ShO—Mattson, Ruebel, Sodowsky, 3; GF—Kelly, 58; Sv.—Kelly, Kilgo, 29; IP—Mattson, 201.2; H—Mattson, 199; TBF—Mattson, 862; R—Kaufman, 112; ER—Mi. Hostetler, Kaufman, 95; HR—Mi. Hostetler, 24; SH—Dessens, Franklin, 11; SF—Mattson, 15; HB—Mattson, 20; BB—Kaufman, 90; IBB—Veras, 11; SO—Fernandez, 160; WP—Beckett, 19; Bk.—Drumright, 5.

ALL PITCHERS

*Lefthanded pitcher.

Pitcher, Team	W	L	Pct.	ERA	G	GS	CG	ShO	GF	Sv.	IP	H	TBF	R	ER	HR	SH	SF	HB	BB	IBB	SO	WP	Bk.
Abbott, Todd, Huntsville	0	0	.000	4.05	4	0	0	0	1	0	6.2	6	28	3	3	1	1	0	0	3	0	4	1	0
Adam, Dave, Port City	6	10	.375	4.34	31	13	0	0	9	0	112.0	107	492	58	54	10	4	0	11	48	1	85	5	1
Adams, Terry, Orlando	2	3	.400	1.43	37	0	0	0	30	19	37.2	23	149	9	6	2	0	1	2	16	1	26	4	1
Adams, Willie, Huntsville	6	5	.545	3.01	13	13	0	0	0	0	80.2	75	330	33	27	8	2	1	2	17	0	72	1	0
Aldred, Scott, Jacksonville*	1	0	1.000	0.00	2	2	0	0	0	0	12.0	9	42	0	0	0	0	0	0	1	0	11	0	0
Almanzar, Carlos, Knoxville	3	12	.200	3.99	35	19	0	0	7	2	126.1	144	546	77	56	10	3	6	3	32	1	93	4	1
Andujar, Luis, Birmingham	14	8	.636	2.85	27	27	2	1	0	0	167.1	147	689	64	53	10	1	5	7	44	0	146	3	1
Apana, Matt, Port City	1	3	.250	4.32	6	6	0	0	0	0	33.1	34	154	24	16	4	1	0	2	24	1	28	2	0
Arnold, Jamie, Greenville	1	5	.167	6.35	10	10	0	0	0	0	56.2	76	266	42	40	8	0	2	7	25	1	19	6	0
Backlund, Brett, Carolina	5	6	.455	3.58	22	14	0	0	1	0	93.0	81	388	46	37	10	4	3	5	35	2	80	2	0
Baker, Jared, Memphis	1	0	1.000	14.73	4	0	0	0	1	1	7.1	10	39	12	12	1	0	1	0	8	0	6	1	0
Banks, Jim, Huntsville	3	2	.600	4.73	44	1	0	0	19	2	66.2	72	305	39	35	5	3	4	3	40	3	52	7	0
Barnes, Jon, Memphis	0	1	.000	3.24	2	1	0	0	0	0	8.1	9	34	3	3	0	0	0	0	2	0	2	1	0
Bauer, Matt, Jacksonville*	1	1	.500	4.12	27	0	0	0	7	0	43.2	43	195	22	20	8	2	2	2	22	1	30	1	0
Beard, Garrett, Huntsville	0	0	.000	0.00	1	0	0	0	1	0	3.0	3	13	0	0	0	0	0	0	1	0	1	0	0
Beatty, Blaine, Chattanooga*	3	2	.600	3.46	8	8	1	0	0	0	52.0	60	225	22	20	2	3	3	1	17	2	34	2	1
Beckett, Robbie, Memphis*	3	4	.429	4.80	36	8	2	1	11	0	86.1	65	400	57	46	3	2	3	10	73	4	98	19	0
Beltran, Alonso, Knoxville	3	6	.333	5.69	28	6	0	0	7	1	87.0	111	399	60	55	8	3	4	5	32	0	54	6	2
Bene, Bill, Chattanooga	0	0	.000	13.50	4	0	0	0	1	0	4.0	7	27	6	6	2	0	0	0	9	0	4	1	0
Bennett, Bob, Huntsville	10	7	.588	4.22	23	21	0	0	0	0	117.1	119	482	62	55	13	4	3	3	28	0	70	3	1
Bennett, Chris, Carolina	0	1	.000	6.67	18	0	0	0	5	1	27.0	42	128	22	20	2	2	0	0	9	2	13	3	0
Berlin, Mike, Jacksonville	0	0	.000	2.45	3	0	0	0	1	0	3.2	3	14	1	1	0	1	0	0	0	0	1	1	0
Bertotti, Mike, Birmingham*	2	7	.222	5.00	12	12	1	0	0	0	63.0	60	279	38	35	4	0	4	2	36	0	53	8	0
Blair, Dirk, Greenville	2	2	.500	4.21	40	0	0	0	19	2	62.0	69	261	29	29	7	3	0	3	11	2	38	1	0
Bradford, Troy, Orlando	1	1	.500	4.91	4	4	0	0	0	0	22.0	22	92	13	12	3	1	0	1	9	0	6	4	0
Brandow, Derek, Knoxville	5	6	.455	4.29	25	21	1	0	1	1	107.0	95	466	60	51	13	1	8	6	50	1	106	9	0
Brown, Chad, Knoxville*	1	3	.250	4.57	40	0	0	0	14	1	41.1	38	181	23	21	2	1	1	1	22	1	35	5	0
Brumley, Duff, Chattanooga	5	1	.833	1.68	25	0	0	0	9	1	48.1	31	193	11	9	0	3	2	2	16	2	60	3	2
Buckley, Travis, Chattanooga	1	2	.333	7.53	3	3	0	0	0	0	14.1	21	69	12	12	4	0	1	1	5	0	10	1	0
Bullinger, Jim, Orlando	0	0	.000	0.00	1	1	0	0	0	0	4.0	3	16	0	0	0	0	0	0	1	0	2	0	0
Burgess, Kurt, Greenville*	1	1	.500	7.20	8	0	0	0	3	0	10.0	16	48	8	8	0	1	1	0	2	0	3	1	0
Burgos, John, Chattanooga*	3	5	.375	2.78	44	3	0	0	9	0	100.1	95	424	42	31	7	5	3	4	19	4	82	2	1
Burlingame, Ben, Orlando	9	2	.818	3.53	37	10	0	0	10	1	97.0	93	415	39	38	7	3	6	4	38	8	73	4	0
Carmona, Rafael, Port City	0	1	.000	1.80	15	0	0	0	15	4	15.0	11	59	5	3	0	1	1	1	3	0	17	2	0
Carpenter, Chris, Knoxville	3	7	.300	5.18	12	12	0	0	0	0	64.1	71	287	47	37	3	1	4	1	31	1	53	9	0
Cedeno, Blas, Jacksonville	3	2	.600	3.46	48	5	0	0	13	0	80.2	71	329	34	31	7	1	1	1	36	1	53	2	1
Chouinard, Bobby, Huntsville	14	8	.636	3.62	29	29	1	1	0	0	166.2	155	694	81	67	10	9	1	4	50	5	106	4	0

Pitcher, Team	W	L	Pct.	ERA	G	GS	CG	ShO	GF	Sv.	IP	H	TBF	R	ER	HR	SH	SF	HB	BB	IBB	SO	WP	Bk.
Christman, Scott, Birmingham*	2	5	.286	6.39	12	12	0	0	0	0	62.0	76	284	49	44	6	2	4	3	24	1	37	6	0
Clark, Dera, Memphis	2	2	.500	2.39	23	0	0	0	13	5	26.1	18	111	7	7	1	0	0	0	14	3	29	5	0
Cole, Victor, Memphis	1	0	1.000	1.35	8	2	0	0	3	0	20.0	15	81	5	3	0	0	0	0	8	1	17	0	0
Connolly, Matt, Orlando	3	4	.429	4.08	21	4	0	0	11	2	39.2	34	165	18	18	5	0	0	2	11	3	43	1	0
Connors, Chad, Chattanooga	0	1	.000	2.79	10	0	0	0	8	0	9.2	9	46	3	3	1	0	1	0	9	1	15	1	0
Cooke, Steve, Carolina*	0	0	.000	7.20	1	1	0	0	0	0	5.0	5	27	4	4	0	0	0	0	5	0	4	1	0
Cullop, Glen, Chattanooga	0	0	.000	7.90	8	0	0	0	3	0	13.2	15	63	13	12	1	1	2	0	7	1	8	0	0
Dabney, Fred, Orlando*	2	1	.667	2.08	13	0	0	0	4	1	17.1	13	78	9	4	0	2	0	2	10	4	9	1	1
D'Andrea, Mike, Greenville	3	6	.333	4.88	40	7	0	0	11	2	99.2	110	447	65	54	5	4	9	3	53	8	61	7	1
Davison, Scott, Port City	2	0	1.000	0.89	34	0	0	0	28	10	40.2	22	156	4	4	1	6	2	1	16	1	50	2	0
DeLeon, Luis, Orlando	0	1	.000	2.00	4	0	0	0	2	0	9.0	7	35	2	2	1	2	0	0	2	1	3	0	0
DeLeon, Roberto, Memphis	0	0	.000	7.71	2	0	0	0	2	0	2.1	3	11	2	2	1	0	0	0	2	0	3	0	0
DeLosSantos, Mariano, Carolina	1	0	1.000	3.62	21	0	0	0	3	0	27.1	28	122	16	11	5	1	0	2	14	3	20	1	0
Dessens, Elmer, Carolina	15	8	.652	2.49	27	27	1	0	0	0	152.0	170	638	62	42	10	11	4	3	21	3	68	7	2
Dibble, Rob, Birmingham	0	1	.000	7.36	8	0	0	0	1	1	7.1	4	32	6	6	0	1	0	1	5	0	15	2	0
Doman, Roger, Knoxville	0	3	.000	5.87	14	0	0	0	6	0	30.2	42	140	25	20	2	1	1	1	11	0	16	3	0
Dressendorfer, Kirk, Huntsville	0	1	.000	3.15	9	4	0	0	1	0	20.0	13	79	7	7	1	0	0	2	5	0	18	1	0
Dreyer, Darren, Orlando	1	3	.250	4.18	14	0	0	0	5	0	23.2	24	98	11	11	1	3	1	3	3	1	10	0	0
Drinkwater, Sean, Memphis	0	1	.000	18.00	1	0	0	0	1	0	1.0	2	6	2	2	1	0	0	0	1	0	0	0	0
Drumright, Mike, Jacksonville	0	1	.000	3.69	5	5	0	0	0	0	31.2	30	137	13	13	4	0	0	2	15	1	34	1	5
Etheridge, Roger, Greenville*	2	10	.167	5.67	32	16	1	0	6	0	101.2	120	462	73	64	10	4	5	3	52	1	47	8	1
Evans, Sean, Carolina	5	2	.714	5.33	29	2	0	0	10	0	49.0	47	218	35	29	1	0	1	3	25	1	44	5	0
Farmer, Howard, Chattanooga	0	1	.000	6.75	1	1	0	0	0	0	4.0	5	21	6	3	1	0	0	0	1	0	2	0	0
Fermin, Ramon, Huntsville	6	7	.462	3.86	32	13	0	0	16	7	100.1	105	435	53	43	5	6	1	6	45	5	58	6	1
Fernandez, Osvaldo, Port City*	12	7	.632	3.57	27	26	0	0	0	0	156.1	139	654	78	62	6	4	1	5	60	1	160	12	1
Ferry, Mike, Chattanooga	9	5	.643	3.77	24	24	1	0	0	0	155.0	191	660	75	65	8	10	6	5	23	1	74	3	0
Figueroa, Fernando, Carolina*	0	0	.000	3.38	6	0	0	0	1	0	8.0	12	37	5	3	2	0	0	0	2	0	4	1	0
Fitzer, Doug, Port City*	0	0	.000	5.40	4	0	0	0	1	0	5.0	3	20	4	3	1	0	0	0	1	0	4	0	0
Flynt, Bill, Carolina*	0	0	.000	0.00	4	0	0	0	1	0	3.2	3	16	0	0	0	1	0	0	2	0	6	0	0
Fordham, Tom, Birmingham*	6	3	.667	3.38	14	14	2	1	0	0	82.2	79	348	35	31	9	2	2	0	28	2	61	3	0
Fox, Chad, Chattanooga	4	5	.444	5.06	20	17	0	0	1	0	80.0	76	363	49	45	2	2	2	3	52	1	56	14	0
Franklin, Ryan, Port City	6	10	.375	4.32	31	20	1	1	2	0	146.0	153	627	84	70	13	11	3	12	43	4	102	6	2
Freeman, Chris, Knoxville	2	3	.400	5.42	39	5	0	0	16	8	81.1	78	354	53	49	12	5	5	1	38	0	80	1	0
Freitas, Mike, Memphis	0	6	.000	3.66	54	0	0	0	16	2	59.0	55	246	26	24	3	2	3	2	26	8	36	3	1
Gaillard, Eddie, Jacksonville	0	1	.000	5.63	8	0	0	0	2	0	8.0	11	42	5	5	0	2	1	0	5	1	4	0	0
Gajkowski, Steve, Birmingham	4	4	.500	4.18	35	0	0	0	14	2	51.2	64	230	27	24	4	2	0	2	16	1	29	1	0
Glinatsis, George, Port City	6	7	.462	5.30	18	18	1	0	0	0	93.1	104	427	63	55	6	2	4	13	44	1	68	7	1
Goldsmith, Gary, Jacksonville	4	7	.364	4.61	15	15	0	0	0	0	82.0	78	347	52	42	14	1	4	2	31	1	42	5	0
Gray, Dennis, Knoxville*	0	3	.000	6.34	24	0	0	0	10	0	32.2	29	143	25	23	2	2	0	1	20	0	22	5	0
Greene, Rick, Jacksonville	6	2	.750	3.49	32	0	0	0	6	0	38.2	45	177	19	15	3	1	0	3	15	2	29	0	0
Grigsby, Benji, Huntsville	3	5	.375	4.01	30	6	0	0	8	3	76.1	66	306	40	34	7	0	3	1	20	1	55	6	0
Grimm, John, Jacksonville	2	1	.667	8.62	13	0	0	0	5	0	15.2	23	82	17	15	5	0	0	1	10	0	9	0	0
Guilfoyle, Michael, Jacksonville*	5	1	.833	2.88	56	0	0	0	14	3	59.1	55	256	23	19	2	2	2	0	31	3	50	1	0
Gutierrez, Jim, Jacksonville	8	4	.667	2.76	45	1	0	0	14	4	58.2	60	243	22	18	2	3	2	0	25	4	36	3	0
Haas, David, Orlando	0	3	.000	4.97	3	3	0	0	0	0	12.2	18	69	10	7	1	0	0	3	10	0	4	1	0
Hanson, Craig, Memphis	0	3	.000	6.43	25	3	0	0	8	1	49.0	64	247	36	35	8	0	3	2	39	4	33	5	0
Harrah, Doug, Orlando	5	2	.714	1.94	44	0	0	0	21	5	69.2	58	296	21	15	6	4	1	5	34	6	49	4	0
Harrison, Brian, Memphis*	2	1	.667	3.25	38	0	0	0	7	0	36.0	32	170	21	13	0	1	0	4	33	2	29	4	0
Harrison, Tom, Greenville	6	4	.600	4.38	14	14	1	0	0	0	88.1	87	370	50	43	9	7	1	2	27	3	57	5	0
Hart, Jason, Orlando	0	1	.000	2.12	14	0	0	0	10	3	17.0	14	69	5	4	0	1	3	1	4	0	20	1	0
Haught, Gary, Huntsville	1	1	.500	4.30	9	3	0	0	3	0	23.0	23	97	14	11	4	1	0	1	8	1	20	0	0
Heble, Kurt, Knoxville	3	7	.300	6.02	47	0	0	0	25	6	52.1	52	231	36	35	7	0	1	1	24	0	44	6	1
Hernandez, Fernando, Memphis	4	6	.400	5.16	12	12	0	0	0	0	66.1	72	303	46	38	4	0	0	3	42	1	74	8	1
Hickey, Mike, Port City	0	1	.000	18.00	1	0	0	0	1	0	1.0	2	6	2	2	0	0	0	1	0	0	0	0	0
Hill, Milt, Carolina	2	2	.500	4.02	10	10	0	0	0	0	56.0	53	226	27	25	6	4	1	2	6	0	46	0	0
Hollinger, Adrian, Greenville	1	4	.200	4.63	7	6	1	0	0	0	44.2	43	196	26	23	2	0	4	1	20	1	28	2	1
Hollins, Stacy, Huntsville	3	8	.273	5.33	15	15	0	0	0	0	82.2	80	364	52	49	10	4	2	4	42	6	62	8	2
Hostetler, Marcus, Greenville	5	2	.714	4.12	33	0	0	0	19	2	43.2	47	199	30	20	6	4	3	2	21	2	24	3	0
Hostetler, Mike, Greenville	10	10	.500	5.26	28	28	0	0	0	0	162.2	182	711	102	95	24	8	4	6	46	4	93	6	1
Huber, Jeff, Memphis*	0	0	.000	11.57	5	0	0	0	0	0	4.2	7	22	6	6	2	0	0	1	0	0	6	0	0
Hurtado, Edwin, Knoxville	2	4	.333	4.45	11	11	0	0	0	0	54.2	54	240	34	27	7	1	4	0	25	0	38	4	0
Hutcheson, David, Orlando	8	10	.444	4.01	28	27	1	1	1	0	168.1	178	708	84	75	23	5	3	8	45	3	103	6	0
Ingram, Todd, Knoxville	1	1	.500	3.71	20	0	0	0	9	3	34.0	26	143	17	14	3	1	2	0	16	0	19	1	0
Jackson, Mike, Chattanooga	0	0	.000	0.00	3	2	0	0	0	0	3.0	2	11	0	0	0	0	0	0	0	0	2	0	0
Janzen, Marty, Knoxville	5	1	.833	2.63	7	7	2	1	0	0	48.0	35	188	14	14	2	0	2	1	14	0	44	1	1
Jersild, Aaron, Knoxville*	2	2	.500	5.98	14	5	0	0	4	0	40.2	47	184	28	27	6	1	0	1	21	1	29	2	1
Jimenez, Miguel, Huntsville	3	2	.600	3.60	6	6	0	0	0	0	30.0	25	124	12	12	3	1	0	0	11	0	28	1	0
Johnson, Barry, Birmingham	7	4	.636	1.85	47	0	0	0	10	0	78.0	64	308	21	16	1	2	1	2	15	1	53	2	1
Johnson, Chris, Orlando	5	4	.556	3.45	46	0	0	0	21	5	70.1	68	296	34	27	6	4	3	1	24	7	49	3	0
Johnston, Sean, Birmingham*	5	2	.714	4.21	34	13	0	0	8	0	98.1	120	432	53	46	6	2	2	2	36	0	44	2	1
Kaufman, Brad, Memphis	11	10	.524	5.76	27	27	0	0	0	0	148.1	142	676	112	95	17	6	5	14	90	4	119	10	0
Keagle, Greg, Memphis	4	9	.308	5.11	15	15	1	0	0	0	81.0	82	365	52	46	11	1	3	6	41	2	82	8	3
Kelley, Rich, Jacksonville*	1	0	1.000	4.50	7	0	0	0	1	0	6.0	9	24	3	3	1	1	1	0	0	0	2	0	1
Kelly, John, Jacksonville	7	7	.500	2.09	66	0	0	0	58	29	77.1	76	322	24	18	4	6	2	0	21	5	47	3	1
Kilgo, Rusty, Chattanooga*	8	2	.800	2.32	54	0	0	0	47	29	66.0	67	273	21	17	0	2	0	0	13	5	61	4	0
King, Kevin, Port City*	1	2	.333	3.77	20	0	0	0	6	0	31.0	35	136	15	13	2	1	1	3	11	1	19	4	1
Koller, Jerry, Greenville	9	12	.429	4.94	25	25	3	0	0	0	147.2	163	629	86	81	16	5	7	2	37	4	84	5	1
Konuszewski, Dennis, Carolina	7	7	.500	3.65	48	0	0	0	18	2	61.2	63	278	33	25	3	3	1	1	26	5	48	5	1
Kotes, Chris, Knoxville	3	9	.250	4.91	36	11	1	0	9	1	106.1	109	470	66	58	7	4	3	4	45	2	74	9	1
Kramer, Tommy, Chattanooga	12	1	.923	3.33	21	18	2	0	1	0	127.0	117	513	54	47	8	5	5	2	28	4	126	4	0
Kroon, Marc, Memphis	7	5	.583	3.51	22	19	0	0	2	2	115.1	90	497	49	45	12	2	2	6	61	1	123	16	1
Lawrence, Sean, Carolina*	0	2	.000	5.48	12	3	0	0	3	0	21.1	27	96	13	13	2	0	0	1	8	1	19	0	0
Lemke, Steve, Huntsville	4	9	.308	4.38	25	19	0	0	1	0	125.1	144	544	72	61	5	7	3	8	29	4	65	9	0

Pitcher, Team	W	L	Pct.	ERA	G	GS	CG	ShO	GF	Sv.	IP	H	TBF	R	ER	HR	SH	SF	HB	BB	IBB	SO	WP	Bk.
Levine, Alan, Birmingham	4	3	.571	2.34	43	1	0	0	31	7	73.0	61	305	22	19	2	2	2	2	25	5	68	7	1
Loiselle, Rich, Memphis	6	3	.667	3.55	13	13	1	0	0	0	78.2	82	357	46	31	5	1	1	6	33	2	48	3	1
Long, Joey, Memphis*	0	2	.000	3.32	25	0	0	0	3	0	21.2	28	104	15	8	0	1	1	1	10	2	18	0	0
Lowe, Derek, Port City	1	6	.143	6.08	10	10	1	0	0	0	53.1	70	244	41	36	8	3	2	3	22	1	30	2	0
Luebbers, Larry, Chattanooga	10	6	.625	4.65	28	21	0	0	4	0	118.0	112	514	71	61	7	6	6	7	59	1	87	1	0
Manning, Derek, Huntsville*	1	2	.333	4.50	5	5	0	0	0	0	28.0	26	114	14	14	4	1	0	0	7	0	22	0	0
Mattson, Rob, Memphis	12	13	.480	4.11	30	28	11	3	1	0	201.2	199	862	109	92	20	7	15	20	73	2	139	4	4
Maurer, Mike, Huntsville	0	2	.000	6.53	17	0	0	0	14	6	20.2	34	100	18	15	0	2	1	0	5	2	19	2	0
May, Darrell, Greenville*	2	8	.200	3.55	15	15	0	0	0	0	91.1	81	377	44	36	18	2	5	3	20	0	79	4	0
McCarthy, Greg, Birmingham*	3	3	.500	5.04	38	0	0	0	13	3	44.2	37	195	28	25	4	4	2	2	29	3	48	3	1
Meier, Kevin, Orlando	4	1	.800	2.64	11	11	0	0	0	0	64.2	55	257	24	19	6	0	2	5	13	4	52	4	0
Meinershagen, Adam, Knoxville	1	1	.500	10.80	3	3	0	0	0	0	11.2	17	55	14	14	2	1	0	1	2	0	4	0	0
Michalak, Chris, Huntsville*	1	1	.500	11.12	7	0	0	0	4	1	5.2	10	32	7	7	1	1	0	1	5	0	4	2	0
Miller, Trever, Jacksonville*	8	2	.800	2.72	31	16	3	2	4	0	122.1	122	512	46	37	5	4	2	5	34	0	77	1	0
Moehler, Brian, Jacksonville	8	10	.444	4.82	28	27	0	0	1	0	162.1	176	696	94	87	14	3	5	6	52	1	89	15	0
Mongiello, Mike, Birmingham	3	1	.750	1.99	7	5	0	0	1	0	31.2	23	120	8	7	2	1	0	1	6	0	23	0	0
Moore, Marcus, Chattanooga	6	1	.857	4.98	36	0	0	0	8	2	43.1	31	192	24	24	6	2	2	2	34	1	57	3	1
Moore, Tim, Birmingham	7	5	.583	3.68	29	19	0	0	3	0	120.0	118	521	58	49	10	7	6	4	40	1	78	6	2
Morel, Ramon, Carolina	3	3	.500	3.52	10	10	0	0	0	0	69.0	71	281	31	27	4	1	2	2	10	0	34	2	0
Morgan, Mike, Orlando	0	2	.000	7.59	2	2	0	0	0	0	10.2	13	48	9	9	1	1	0	1	7	0	5	0	0
Murray, Heath, Memphis*	5	4	.556	3.38	14	14	0	0	0	0	77.1	83	363	36	29	1	3	3	4	42	1	71	7	1
Murray, Matt, Greenville	4	0	1.000	1.53	5	5	0	0	0	0	29.1	20	111	5	5	0	1	0	1	8	0	25	2	0
Nezelek, Andy, Carolina	1	0	1.000	5.14	6	0	0	0	1	1	14.0	16	64	9	8	3	0	0	0	3	0	14	0	0
Nickell, Jackie, Port City	5	8	.385	3.73	27	9	0	0	7	0	89.1	74	367	40	37	11	2	4	8	30	0	81	4	4
Nitkowski, C.J., Chattanooga*	4	2	.667	2.50	8	8	0	0	0	0	50.1	39	204	20	14	1	3	0	1	20	0	52	1	1
Nix, Jim, Chattanooga	3	5	.375	3.20	40	5	0	0	14	2	84.1	84	360	43	30	8	6	4	2	30	1	71	7	1
Norman, Scott, Jacksonville	1	3	.250	2.48	4	4	2	0	0	0	29.0	31	122	12	8	4	1	0	1	6	0	9	1	0
Olsen, Steve, Birmingham	8	3	.727	3.48	14	14	2	1	0	0	85.1	84	357	44	33	4	3	7	1	21	2	56	1	0
Pace, Scott, Knoxville*	6	8	.429	4.57	18	18	1	1	0	0	102.1	117	462	66	52	8	6	6	4	48	3	71	7	0
Paige, Carey, Greenville	1	4	.200	5.01	7	7	0	0	0	0	41.1	45	182	30	23	5	1	0	2	11	0	26	2	0
Parris, Steve, Carolina	9	1	.900	2.51	14	14	2	2	0	0	89.2	61	344	25	25	2	3	1	4	16	1	86	3	0
Peters, Chris, Carolina*	2	0	1.000	1.29	2	2	0	0	0	0	14.0	9	56	2	2	0	0	1	0	2	0	7	2	0
Petersen, Matt, Orlando	3	9	.250	5.87	24	15	1	1	2	0	89.0	107	414	66	58	15	5	4	7	39	5	59	2	2
Pett, Jose, Knoxville	8	9	.471	4.26	26	25	1	1	0	0	141.2	132	602	87	67	16	4	4	4	48	0	89	8	0
Pickett, Ricky, Chattanooga*	4	5	.444	3.28	40	0	0	0	19	9	46.2	22	203	20	17	3	2	0	0	44	3	69	1	0
Pierce, Rob, Huntsville	1	1	.500	9.87	15	0	0	0	5	0	17.1	26	92	21	19	2	0	1	1	14	1	16	8	1
Pierson, Jason, Birmingham*	0	2	.000	8.10	4	4	0	0	0	0	23.1	29	102	22	21	6	0	1	2	6	0	15	0	1
Pisciotta, Marc, Carolina	6	4	.600	4.15	56	0	0	0	27	9	69.1	60	313	37	32	2	7	3	6	45	8	57	4	0
Plantenberg, Erik, Memphis*	2	0	1.000	1.66	20	0	0	0	9	2	21.2	19	80	4	4	2	1	0	1	2	1	16	1	0
Plaster, Allen, Huntsville	1	0	1.000	3.18	43	0	0	0	14	2	68.0	63	290	26	24	4	4	2	0	26	0	47	7	0
Ralph, Curtis, Carolina	1	1	.500	2.42	18	1	0	0	2	1	26.0	23	105	8	7	3	0	0	0	10	0	17	1	0
Ratliff, Jon, Orlando	10	5	.667	3.47	26	25	1	1	1	0	140.0	143	599	67	54	9	2	8	10	42	1	94	13	0
Resendez, Oscar, Port City	0	2	.000	4.24	11	0	0	0	3	0	17.0	16	76	8	8	0	0	0	1	8	0	15	2	0
Rivera, Lino, Carolina	0	0	.000	6.00	4	0	0	0	1	0	6.0	10	31	6	4	0	0	0	0	3	0	4	0	0
Rivera, Roberto, Orlando*	6	2	.750	2.38	49	0	0	0	14	6	68.0	50	257	18	18	4	0	4	0	11	3	34	3	1
Roper, John, Chattanooga	0	0	.000	1.00	3	3	0	0	0	0	9.0	5	33	1	1	0	0	0	0	1	0	6	0	0
Rose, Scott, Huntsville	4	6	.400	2.59	38	5	0	0	23	13	80.0	70	316	24	23	2	5	3	2	23	5	35	6	0
Rosengren, John, Jacksonville*	2	7	.222	4.52	14	13	0	0	0	0	67.2	73	308	39	34	7	2	2	5	40	0	59	12	2
Ruebel, Matt, Carolina*	13	5	.722	2.76	27	27	4	3	0	0	169.1	150	699	68	52	7	4	7	7	45	1	136	7	1
Ruffcorn, Scott, Birmingham	0	2	.000	5.63	3	3	0	0	0	0	16.0	17	71	11	10	0	0	0	0	10	0	13	2	0
Russell, LaGrande, Port City	4	3	.571	3.24	39	0	0	0	13	1	72.1	68	329	32	26	7	4	3	1	43	3	54	9	0
Ryan, Matt, Carolina	2	1	.667	1.57	44	0	0	0	38	26	46.0	33	188	10	8	0	4	0	2	19	2	23	3	0
Rychel, Kevin, Carolina	3	2	.600	3.33	40	0	0	0	14	1	51.1	35	210	21	19	1	1	1	6	24	4	60	8	0
Sawkiw, Warren, Knoxville	0	0	.000	0.00	1	0	0	0	1	0	1.0	0	4	0	0	0	0	0	0	1	0	1	0	0
Schmitt, Todd, Memphis	0	0	.000	1.30	26	0	0	0	24	18	27.2	18	108	4	4	2	0	1	1	11	2	27	0	0
Schutz, Carl, Greenville*	3	7	.300	4.94	51	0	0	0	46	26	58.1	53	258	36	32	4	2	2	1	36	3	56	3	0
Seelbach, Chris, Greenville	6	0	1.000	1.64	9	9	1	1	0	0	60.1	38	249	15	11	2	5	3	4	30	0	65	3	1
Shafer, Bill, Greenville	2	2	.500	5.01	42	0	0	0	16	1	59.1	69	283	37	33	7	3	0	4	38	3	44	2	2
Shoemaker, Steve, Huntsville	4	4	.500	3.43	43	0	0	0	24	5	76.0	62	318	33	29	8	3	4	1	31	2	63	7	0
Shouse, Brian, Carolina*	7	6	.538	4.47	21	20	0	0	0	0	114.2	126	480	64	57	14	5	3	4	19	2	76	1	1
Silva, Jose, Knoxville	0	0	.000	9.00	3	0	0	0	0	0	2.0	3	15	2	2	0	1	1	0	6	0	2	0	0
Simmons, John, Greenville*	1	5	.167	4.62	48	0	0	0	15	1	60.1	67	266	35	31	9	1	0	0	22	2	54	3	0
Sirotka, Mike, Birmingham*	7	6	.538	3.20	16	16	1	0	0	0	101.1	95	412	42	36	11	3	3	2	22	0	79	4	1
Smith, Mike, Chattanooga	0	2	.000	17.47	3	2	0	0	0	0	5.2	11	37	13	11	0	0	0	1	5	0	5	1	0
Smith, Ottis, Orlando*	4	5	.444	3.07	17	17	0	0	0	0	108.1	109	461	50	37	9	2	1	4	38	4	51	5	4
Snyder, John, Birmingham	1	0	1.000	6.64	5	4	0	0	0	0	20.1	24	87	16	15	6	0	1	2	6	0	13	1	0
Sodowsky, Clint, Jacksonville	5	5	.500	2.55	19	19	5	3	0	0	123.2	102	497	46	35	4	2	2	5	50	1	77	3	0
Steed, Rick, Knoxville	2	4	.333	3.69	27	0	0	0	23	9	31.2	23	136	15	13	1	3	2	2	16	2	29	4	0
Swartzbaugh, Dave, Orlando	4	0	1.000	2.48	16	0	0	0	3	0	29.0	18	111	10	8	1	1	1	2	7	0	37	1	1
Taylor, Aaron, Huntsville	1	1	.500	2.13	5	4	0	0	0	0	25.1	26	106	7	6	3	1	1	1	6	0	24	1	1
Telemaco, Amaury, Orlando	8	8	.500	3.29	22	22	3	1	0	0	147.2	112	587	60	54	13	8	3	4	42	3	151	7	1
Thomas, Carlos, Hun.-Mem.	3	3	.500	7.62	18	0	0	0	7	0	26.0	28	127	24	22	3	3	1	1	19	1	24	2	1
Thomas, Larry, Birmingham*	4	1	.800	1.34	35	0	0	0	9	2	40.1	24	156	9	6	0	2	2	2	15	1	47	3	0
Thompson, Justin, Jacksonville*	6	7	.462	3.73	18	18	3	0	0	0	123.0	110	502	55	51	7	4	2	3	38	2	98	3	0
Tolar, Kevin, Carolina*	1	0	1.000	3.65	12	0	0	0	3	0	12.1	16	59	5	5	0	0	2	0	7	0	9	2	0
Tranbarger, Mark, Chattanooga*	3	1	.750	1.95	48	0	0	0	12	0	55.1	50	236	15	12	4	2	4	2	20	1	46	2	0
Tsamis, George, Car.-P.C.*	0	0	.000	3.38	19	0	0	0	6	0	21.1	23	97	9	8	1	1	0	1	16	3	10	2	0
Turnier, Aaron, Greenville*	0	1	.000	5.19	8	0	0	0	0	0	17.1	17	86	13	10	2	1	0	0	18	1	16	3	0
Tuttle, Dave, Chattanooga	1	6	.143	7.01	8	7	0	0	1	0	34.2	40	165	29	27	6	2	1	1	21	0	20	4	0
Urso, Sal, Port City*	2	0	1.000	2.17	51	0	0	0	8	1	45.2	41	185	13	11	0	0	0	0	21	0	44	7	1
VanRyn, Ben, Chattanooga*	0	1	.000	9.24	5	3	0	0	0	0	12.2	22	69	18	13	2	0	2	1	6	0	6	0	0
Vasquez, Chris, Chattanooga	0	0	.000	18.00	1	0	0	0	1	0	1.0	2	7	2	2	0	0	0	0	3	0	0	0	0
Vasquez, Marcos, Chattanooga	7	6	.538	3.68	26	18	0	0	1	1	120.0	125	531	63	49	12	6	5	4	46	1	80	5	1

Pitcher, Team	W	L	Pct.	ERA	G	GS	CG	ShO	GF	Sv.	IP	H	TBF	R	ER	HR	SH	SF	HB	BB	IBB	SO	WP	Bk.
Veras, Dario, Memphis	7	3	.700	3.81	58	0	0	0	22	1	82.2	81	360	38	35	8	3	1	7	27	11	70	5	1
Waggoner, Jim, Huntsville	0	0	.000	0.00	1	0	0	0	1	0	2.0	1	7	0	0	0	0	0	0	0	0	1	0	0
Wagner, Matt, Port City	5	8	.385	2.82	23	23	0	0	0	0	137.0	121	566	57	43	9	3	4	4	33	1	111	5	1
Walker, Dane, Huntsville	0	0	.000	0.00	1	0	0	0	1	0	0.2	0	4	0	0	0	0	0	0	2	0	0	0	0
Watkins, Jason, Birmingham	0	0	.000	3.95	10	0	0	0	3	0	13.2	18	64	7	6	1	0	0	1	3	0	10	1	1
Weber, Ben, Knoxville	4	1	.800	3.91	12	1	0	0	6	0	25.1	26	104	12	11	3	0	0	0	6	0	16	0	0
Wendell, Turk, Orlando	1	0	1.000	3.86	5	0	0	0	2	1	7.0	6	30	3	3	0	0	0	1	4	0	7	0	0
Whiteside, Sean, Jacksonville*	2	0	1.000	3.78	27	1	0	0	4	0	33.1	34	148	17	14	4	2	3	0	20	4	17	4	0
Wilkins, Marc, Carolina	5	3	.625	3.99	37	12	0	0	1	0	99.1	91	436	47	44	8	5	3	11	44	2	80	9	0
Willis, Travis, Carolina	1	1	.500	2.91	16	0	0	0	6	3	21.2	23	101	10	7	0	1	1	3	10	2	12	2	0
Wilson, Gary, Carolina	0	0	.000	0.00	1	1	0	0	0	0	4.2	0	16	0	0	0	0	0	0	3	0	5	0	0
Withem, Shannon, Jacksonville	5	8	.385	5.75	19	18	0	0	1	0	108.0	142	481	77	69	17	5	1	5	24	1	80	4	0
Witte, Trey, Port City	3	2	.600	1.73	48	0	0	0	34	11	62.1	48	250	17	12	0	6	3	5	14	0	39	0	1
Wolcott, Bob, Port City	7	3	.700	2.20	12	12	2	1	0	0	86.0	60	320	26	21	6	0	3	3	13	0	53	2	0
Wolfe, Joel, Huntsville	0	0	.000	0.00	1	0	0	0	1	0	1.0	0	3	0	0	0	0	0	0	1	0	0	0	0
Woodfin, Chris, Birmingham	3	3	.500	4.50	48	0	0	0	41	20	64.0	59	269	34	32	6	2	2	1	24	1	72	10	0
Worley, Robert, Port City	1	7	.125	4.58	22	5	0	0	6	0	57.0	60	263	42	29	5	3	2	4	30	1	26	8	0
Worrell, Steve, Birmingham*	0	1	.000	8.31	4	0	0	0	2	0	4.1	5	21	5	4	2	0	0	0	2	0	2	2	0
Young, Anthony, Orlando	0	0	.000	0.00	2	2	0	0	0	0	5.0	6	24	1	0	0	0	0	0	3	0	5	0	0
Zongor, Steve, Huntsville*	2	0	1.000	7.62	9	0	0	0	3	0	13.0	13	60	11	11	4	0	0	1	9	0	11	1	1

COMBINATION SHUTOUTS: **Birmingham (6)**—Andujar-McCarthy-Woodfin, Andujar-Thomas, Andujar-Thomas-Woodfin, Fordham-Gajkowski, Johnston-Johnson-Woodfin, Sirotka-Gajkowski-Woodfin. **Carolina (9)**—Dessens-Backlund-Konuszewski, Dessens-Konuszewski-Pisciotta, Parris-Figueroa-Rychel-Pisciotta, Parris-Rychel-Ryan, Ruebel-Konuszewski-Pisciotta, Ruebel-Ryan, Ruebel-Wilkins-Pisciotta-Ryan, Ruebel-Wilkins-Ryan, Wilson-Shouse-Ryan. **Chattanooga (9)**—Ferry-Brumley-Fox, Fox-Pickett, Kramer-Burgos, Luebbers-Brumley, Luebbers-Kilgo, Luebbers-Tranbarger-Burgos, Roper-Jackson-Kramer-Pickett, Vasquez-Pickett, Vasquez-Pickett-Kilgo. **Greenville (3)**—Murray-Schutz, Murray-Shafer-Schutz, Seelbach-Schutz. **Huntsville (6)**—Bennett-Banks, Chouinard-Plaster, Dressendorfer-Banks-Plaster-Rose, Fermin-Rose, Hollins-Shoemaker-Banks, Lemke-Pierce-Plaster-Banks. **Jacksonville (3)**—Gutierrez-Whiteside-Kelly, Sodowsky-Moehler, Thompson-Greene. **Knoxville (9)**—Almanzar-Freeman-Steed, Almanzar-Ingram-Steed, Beltran-Almanzar, Beltran-Brown, Brandow-Doman-Ingram, Carpenter-Beltran, Carpenter-Freeman, Kotes-Freeman, Pace-Ingram. **Memphis (1)**—Kaufman-Schmitt. **Orlando (10)**—Hutcheson-Johnson-Adams 2, Burlingame-Dabney-Hart, Burlingame-Rivera-Harrah, Burlingame-Rivera-Johnson, Bullinger-Ratliff, Ratliff-Rivera-Harrah-Adams, Ratliff-Rivera-Hart, Ratliff-Rivera-Wendell, Telemaco-Johnson-Adams. **Port City (4)**—Fernandez-Adam-Urso, Nickell-Franklin-Witte, Nickell-Witte, Wagner-King-Witte.

NO-HIT GAMES: Andujar, Birmingham, defeated Memphis, 1-0, August 8; Beckett, Memphis, lost to Chattanooga, 1-0 (second game), September 2.

PITCHERS WITH TWO OR MORE TEAMS

Pitcher, Team	W	L	Pct.	ERA	G	GS	CG	ShO	GF	Sv.	IP	H	TBF	R	ER	HR	SH	SF	HB	BB	IBB	SO	WP	Bk.
Thomas, Carlos, Huntsville	2	2	.500	4.97	7	0	0	0	3	0	12.2	13	56	8	7	2	2	0	1	5	1	12	1	1
Thomas, Carlos, Memphis	1	1	.500	10.13	11	0	0	0	4	0	13.1	15	71	16	15	1	1	1	0	14	0	12	1	0
Tsamis, George, Carolina*	0	0	.000	4.09	12	0	0	0	2	0	11.0	12	46	5	5	1	0	0	1	5	1	7	2	0
Tsamis, George, Port City*	0	0	.000	2.61	7	0	0	0	4	0	10.1	11	51	4	3	0	1	0	0	11	2	3	0	0

1995 FIELDING

TEAM

Team	Pct.	G	PO	A	E	TC	DP	PB
Jacksonville	.976	144	3860	1779	139	5778	167	10
Orlando	.973	143	3773	1531	146	5450	121	10
Huntsville	.971	144	3747	1663	161	5571	151	22
Carolina	.971	144	3967	1639	168	5774	139	19
Port City	.971	142	3792	1610	163	5565	161	31
Memphis	.971	142	3708	1411	155	5274	122	27
Birmingham	.970	144	3745	1507	165	5417	132	16
Chattanooga	.969	143	3775	1358	163	5296	122	19
Greenville	.969	142	3704	1466	165	5335	111	7
Knoxville	.966	144	3667	1479	183	5329	129	19

TRIPLE PLAYS: Carolina, Chattanooga.

INDIVIDUAL

FIRST BASEMEN

NOTE: All caps denotes fielding-percentage leader based on 72 games for catchers, 96 for all other non-pitchers and 144 innings for pitchers. *Throws lefthanded.

Player, Team	Pct.	G	PO	A	E	TC	DP
Beard, Garrett, Huntsville	1.000	2	5	0	0	5	0
BONNICI, James, Port City	.995	137	1274	87	7	1368	136
Boston, D.J., Knoxville*	.986	132	1129	91	17	1237	117
Brown, Brant, Orlando*	.990	107	917	92	10	1019	75
Brown, Michael, Carolina*	.991	56	503	36	5	544	33
Canale, George, Carolina	.994	38	294	22	2	318	34
Cardenas, John, Port City	1.000	5	25	0	0	25	2
Colon, Felix, Jacksonville	1.000	15	137	13	0	150	13
Coolbaugh, Mike, Knoxville	1.000	7	65	5	0	70	0
Cooper, Gary, Jacksonville	1.000	5	38	3	0	41	3
Cotton, John, Memphis	1.000	1	2	0	0	2	1
Coughlin, Kevin, Birmingham*	.989	26	160	13	2	175	15
Cruz, Ivan, Jacksonville*	.992	81	795	60	7	862	86
DeLeon, Roberto, Memphis	1.000	1	1	0	0	1	1
Dismuke, Jamie, Chattanooga	.989	95	647	69	8	724	64
Drinkwater, Sean, Memphis	.982	10	50	4	1	55	2
Duross, Gabe, Orlando*	.992	38	328	24	3	355	31
Farrell, Jon, Carolina	1.000	1	2	0	0	2	0
Fryman, Troy, Birmingham	.985	86	655	53	11	719	67
Gonzalez, Paul, Birmingham	1.000	2	21	0	0	21	1
Grijak, Kevin, Greenville	.986	20	202	7	3	212	16
Gubanich, Creighton, Huntsville	.990	21	179	22	2	203	20
Hanel, Marcus, Carolina	1.000	1	2	0	0	2	1
Harmes, Kris, Knoxville	1.000	3	28	0	0	28	2
Hickey, Mike, Port City	1.000	7	44	4	0	48	7
Killeen, Tim, Memphis	1.000	1	1	0	0	1	0
Kingston, Mark, Orlando	1.000	4	10	0	0	10	1
Koehler, Jim, Port City*	1.000	1	1	0	0	1	0
Kopriva, Dan, Chattanooga	1.000	3	4	0	0	4	0
Leary, Rob, Carolina*	.985	59	557	36	9	602	51
Lee, Derrek, Memphis	1.000	2	16	3	0	19	1
Leiper, Tim, Jacksonville	.986	26	250	23	4	277	23
Lesher, Brian, Huntsville*	.941	3	14	2	1	17	2
Lutz, Brent, Knoxville	1.000	1	6	1	0	7	0
Merchant, Mark, Chattanooga	1.000	1	1	0	0	1	0
Molina, Izzy, Huntsville	.889	1	7	1	1	9	0
Munoz, Omer, Carolina	1.000	1	1	0	0	1	0
Nunez, Ramon, Greenville	.985	45	305	25	5	335	29
Olmeda, Jose, Greenville	1.000	1	5	1	0	6	0
Pearson, Eddie, Birmingham	.987	33	286	25	4	315	25
Pecorilli, Aldo, Greenville	.996	34	245	24	1	270	15
Perona, Joe, Jacksonville	1.000	1	1	0	0	1	0
Pevey, Marty, Jacksonville	1.000	4	27	2	0	29	2
Rendina, Mike, Jacksonville*	1.000	23	219	10	0	229	20
Rohrmeier, Dan, Chattanooga	.969	7	29	2	1	32	4
Rumfield, Toby, Chattanooga	.983	55	353	53	7	413	38
Russo, Paul, Memphis	1.000	1	12	2	0	14	0
Santana, Ruben, Chattanooga	1.000	1	8	4	0	12	0
Sawkiw, Warren, Knoxville	.947	3	16	2	1	19	1
Sheldon, Scott, Huntsville	.991	10	103	5	1	109	9
Sparks, Greg, Greenville*	.983	55	340	12	6	358	29
Spiezio, Scott, Huntsville	1.000	2	17	0	0	17	3
Swann, Pedro, Greenville	.954	7	59	3	3	65	6
Thompson, Jason, Memphis*	.994	135	1044	88	7	1139	102

Player, Team	Pct.	G	PO	A	E	TC	DP
Torres, Paul, Orlando	1.000	2	15	0	0	15	0
Vinas, Julio, Birmingham	1.000	8	69	3	0	72	7
White, Jason, Huntsville*	.986	48	445	32	7	484	45
Wolfe, Joel, Huntsville	.992	62	592	48	5	645	60
Wollenburg, Doug, Greenville	.977	5	41	2	1	44	3

TRIPLE PLAYS: M. Brown, Rohrmeier.

SECOND BASEMEN

Player, Team	Pct.	G	PO	A	E	TC	DP
Alvarez, Gabe, Memphis	.833	2	0	5	1	6	1
Arias, Amador, Chattanooga	.966	40	40	45	3	88	10
Batista, Tony, Huntsville	.970	18	35	61	3	99	14
Beasley, Tony, Carolina	.968	80	146	217	12	375	44
Burton, Essex, Birmingham	.957	140	311	337	29	677	94
Bush, Homer, Memphis	.969	106	235	268	16	519	69
CATALANOTTO, Frank, Jacks'ville	.974	133	252	411	18	681	98
Coleman, Ken, Orlando	.974	79	121	180	8	309	33
Coolbaugh, Mike, Knoxville	1.000	6	8	12	0	20	2
Cora, Manny, Port City	.968	67	155	213	12	380	50
Cotton, John, Memphis	.800	2	3	1	1	5	1
DeLeon, Roberto, Memphis	1.000	3	2	3	0	5	1
Diaz, Eddy, Port City	.978	36	65	112	4	181	26
Drinkwater, Sean, Memphis	.974	6	13	24	1	38	4
Fermin, Carlos, Jacksonville	1.000	7	4	12	0	16	2
Gipson, Charles, Port City	.900	2	2	7	1	10	2
Gomez, Rudy, Orlando	.972	77	106	136	7	249	31
Harley, Quentin, Memphis	.970	26	41	55	3	99	9
Henry, Santiago, Knoxville	.972	106	209	269	14	492	69
Hickey, Mike, Port City	.945	34	74	99	10	183	23
Jenkins, Dee, Chattanooga	.917	7	11	11	2	24	3
Johnson, Matt, Knoxville	.988	28	27	58	1	86	13
Kelly, Pat, Knoxville	1.000	1	1	4	0	5	0
Kessinger, Keith, Orlando	.970	13	31	33	2	66	9
Koelling, Brian, Chattanooga	.980	56	132	117	5	254	23
Kremblas, Frank, Chattanooga	.956	19	44	42	4	90	12
Krevokuch, Jim, Carolina	.987	24	31	47	1	79	8
Leiper, Tim, Jacksonville	1.000	10	13	32	0	45	7
Malloy, Marty, Greenville	.973	124	246	321	16	583	69
Manahan, Austin, Orlando	.898	21	42	46	10	98	9
Munoz, Omer, Carolina	.987	48	103	130	3	236	28
Noriega, Rey, Birmingham	1.000	8	14	10	0	24	1
Nunez, Ramon, Greenville	.978	10	26	19	1	46	5
Olmeda, Jose, Greenville	1.000	3	10	13	0	23	2
Pratte, Evan, Jacksonville	1.000	4	14	15	0	29	7
Relaford, Desmond, Port City	.941	5	5	11	1	17	2
Rodarte, Raul, Carolina	.800	3	3	5	2	10	2
Sanchez, Yuri, Jacksonville	1.000	2	4	3	0	7	0
Santana, Ruben, Chattanooga	.945	50	76	114	11	201	21
Sawkiw, Warren, Knoxville	.974	11	15	23	1	39	5
Sheldon, Scott, Huntsville	.974	27	57	90	4	151	19
Sobolewski, Mark, Huntsville	.964	83	160	238	15	413	58
Spiezio, Scott, Huntsville	1.000	1	1	4	0	5	1
Tredaway, Chad, Memphis	.929	7	10	16	2	28	4
Waggoner, Jim, Huntsville	.979	21	39	55	2	96	12
Wollenburg, Doug, Greenville	.956	16	31	34	3	68	8
Womack, Tony, Carolina	.956	11	16	27	2	45	5

THIRD BASEMEN

Player, Team	Pct.	G	PO	A	E	TC	DP
Adriana, Sharnol, Knoxville	1.000	3	1	3	0	4	0
Beard, Garrett, Huntsville	1.000	1	0	1	0	1	0
Beasley, Tony, Carolina	1.000	2	0	2	0	2	0
Boone, Aaron, Chattanooga	.875	22	14	28	6	48	4
Bruno, Julio, Memphis	.934	52	32	109	10	151	15
Canale, George, Carolina	.942	26	18	31	3	52	2
Coleman, Ken, Orlando	.942	77	23	91	7	121	8
Coolbaugh, Mike, Knoxville	.935	126	83	279	25	387	30
Cooper, Gary, Jacksonville	.957	75	38	162	9	209	11
Cotton, John, Memphis	1.000	1	0	1	0	1	0
Cranford, Jay, Carolina	.914	86	69	177	23	269	14
DeLeon, Roberto, Memphis	.875	7	1	6	1	8	0
Diaz, Eddy, Port City	.932	29	25	44	5	74	6
Drinkwater, Sean, Memphis	.963	62	43	113	6	162	17
Fermin, Carlos, Jacksonville	.889	18	6	26	4	36	2
Gomez, Fabio, Port City	.914	17	13	40	5	58	6
Gonzalez, Paul, Birmingham	1.000	5	3	11	0	14	0
Gubanich, Creighton, Huntsville	.765	5	3	10	4	17	1
Harley, Quentin, Memphis	.737	7	4	10	5	19	2
Harmes, Kris, Knoxville	.667	3	2	2	2	6	0
Hickey, Mike, Port City	.927	73	35	142	14	191	10
Johnson, Matt, Knoxville	1.000	5	1	7	0	8	0
Kelly, Pat, Knoxville	1.000	9	5	25	0	30	1
Kessinger, Keith, Orlando	1.000	1	0	1	0	1	0
Kingston, Mark, Orlando	.946	58	38	85	7	130	6
Kopriva, Dan, Chattanooga	.848	33	19	48	12	79	2
Krevokuch, Jim, Carolina	.918	38	22	68	8	98	5
Leiper, Tim, Jacksonville	.944	33	21	80	6	107	12
Lidle, Kevin, Jacksonville	.786	6	2	9	3	14	2
Manahan, Austin, Orlando	.808	19	8	13	5	26	0
Noriega, Rey, Birmingham	.941	6	5	11	1	17	0
NORTON, Greg, Birmingham	.938	131	102	277	25	404	23
Nunez, Ramon, Greenville	.667	1	0	2	1	3	0
Olmeda, Jose, Greenville	1.000	1	0	5	0	5	0
Pecorilli, Aldo, Greenville	.867	3	2	11	2	15	0
Perona, Joe, Jacksonville	.900	7	2	7	1	10	1
Pratte, Evan, Jacksonville	.933	9	5	23	2	30	1
Rodarte, Raul, Carolina	.871	9	6	21	4	31	2
Rohrmeier, Dan, Chattanooga	.889	12	14	10	3	27	2
Rose, Pete, Birmingham	1.000	4	4	8	0	12	0
Russo, Paul, Memphis	.961	35	20	53	3	76	3
Santana, Ruben, Chattanooga	.929	98	64	160	17	241	14
Saunders, Doug, Port City	.963	28	14	63	3	80	7
Sawkiw, Warren, Knoxville	.833	5	1	14	3	18	1
Sheldon, Scott, Huntsville	1.000	2	3	5	0	8	2
Smith, Robert, Greenville	.937	126	120	265	26	411	25
Spiezio, Scott, Huntsville	.932	134	104	291	29	424	34
Torres, Paul, Orlando	.913	38	19	65	8	92	4
Tredaway, Chad, Memphis	1.000	2	0	1	0	1	0
Viera, Jose, Orlando	.913	9	7	14	2	23	1
Waggoner, Jim, Huntsville	1.000	6	5	6	0	11	1
Wollenburg, Doug, Greenville	.852	21	11	35	8	54	1
Wooten, Shawn, Jacksonville	.921	20	8	50	5	63	3

TRIPLE PLAY: Canale.

SHORTSTOPS

Player, Team	Pct.	G	PO	A	E	TC	DP
Adriana, Sharnol, Knoxville	.928	71	88	209	23	320	36
Alvarez, Gabe, Memphis	1.000	1	0	1	0	1	0
Arias, Amador, Chattanooga	.871	9	8	19	4	31	3
Batista, Tony, Huntsville	.945	102	133	310	26	469	59
Beasley, Tony, Carolina	.960	23	36	60	4	100	11
Coleman, Ken, Orlando	.917	4	7	4	1	12	2
Cora, Manny, Port City	.944	6	5	12	1	18	3
Cotton, John, Memphis	.941	24	30	34	4	68	7
Cranford, Jay, Carolina	.800	1	3	1	1	5	0
DeLeon, Roberto, Memphis	.941	54	73	134	13	220	19
Delgado, Wilson, Port City	.917	13	10	45	5	60	7
Diaz, Eddy, Port City	.940	46	75	129	13	217	30
DiSarcina, Glenn, Birmingham	1.000	3	5	4	0	9	2
Dotel, Mariano, Memphis	1.000	8	9	19	0	28	4
Drinkwater, Sean, Memphis	.935	14	18	25	3	46	4
Felix, Lauro, Huntsville	.964	9	7	20	1	28	6
Fermin, Carlos, Jacksonville	.939	32	53	85	9	147	25
Garcia, Luis, Jacksonville	.929	15	19	46	5	70	8
Gomez, Rudy, Orlando	.958	26	28	64	4	96	17
Harley, Quentin, Memphis	1.000	1	0	2	0	2	0
Henry, Santiago, Knoxville	.918	32	51	94	13	158	14
Johnson, Matt, Knoxville	.833	8	3	12	3	18	1
Kelly, Pat, Knoxville	.939	37	45	94	9	148	24
Kessinger, Keith, Orlando	.913	5	8	13	2	23	2
Koelling, Brian, Chattanooga	.932	51	87	117	15	219	28
Krevokuch, Jim, Carolina	1.000	1	1	0	0	1	0
LaRocca, Greg, Memphis	.889	2	6	2	1	9	1
Magdaleno, Ricky, Chattanooga	.839	11	20	32	10	62	6
MARTINEZ, Pablo, Greenville	.966	118	167	340	18	525	55
Noriega, Rey, Birmingham	.909	14	15	25	4	44	7
Olmeda, Jose, Greenville	.959	22	36	58	4	98	12
Petersen, Chris, Orlando	.964	125	212	357	21	590	66
Polcovich, Kevin, Carolina	.943	63	88	208	18	314	36
Pratte, Evan, Jacksonville	.857	4	3	3	1	7	0
Relaford, Desi, Port City	.929	84	129	265	30	424	62
Sanchez, Yuri, Jacksonville	.957	116	170	366	24	560	70
Sheldon, Scott, Huntsville	.948	25	40	88	7	135	23
Velandia, Jorge, Memphis	.952	60	88	152	12	252	29
Waggoner, Jim, Huntsville	.986	17	22	50	1	73	9
Wilson, Brandon, Chattanooga	.951	75	97	195	15	307	37
Wilson, Craig, Birmingham	.945	132	193	389	34	616	80
Wollenburg, Doug, Greenville	.909	6	8	12	2	22	6
Womack, Tony, Carolina	.953	68	110	214	16	340	49

TRIPLE PLAYS: Koelling, Womack.

OUTFIELDERS

Player, Team	Pct.	G	PO	A	E	TC	DP
Abbott, Jeff, Birmingham*	.966	42	55	1	2	58	0
Adams, Tommy, Port City	1.000	19	27	3	0	30	1
Allensworth, Jermaine, Carolina	.985	54	131	3	2	136	1
Austin, Jake, Carolina	.974	93	136	12	4	152	2
Barker, Glen, Jacksonville	.973	120	284	9	8	301	3
Beasley, Tony, Carolina	1.000	1	1	0	0	1	0
Briggs, Stoney, Memphis	.959	89	136	6	6	148	1
Briley, Greg, Jacksonville	1.000	7	11	0	0	11	0
Brock, Tarrik, Jacksonville*	.929	9	12	1	1	14	0
Brown, Brant, Orlando*	1.000	8	14	0	0	14	0
Brumfield, Jacob, Carolina	1.000	3	9	0	0	9	0
Burton, Darren, Orlando	.981	49	101	4	2	107	1
Butler, Rich, Knoxville	.974	48	106	5	3	114	1
Cameron, Mike, Birmingham	.985	107	250	7	4	261	1
Canale, George, Carolina	.962	30	45	5	2	52	0
Cappuccio, Carmine, Birmingham	.985	65	119	9	2	130	0
Conger, Jeff, Carolina*	.969	39	90	3	3	96	3
Coolbaugh, Mike, Knoxville	1.000	2	3	0	0	3	0
Cotton, John, Memphis	.969	90	178	10	6	194	1
Coughlin, Kevin, Birmingham*	.971	73	128	7	4	139	3
Cradle, Rickey, Knoxville	.980	31	45	3	1	49	0
Danapilis, Eric, Jacksonville	.981	78	100	4	2	106	1
DeLaCruz, Lorenzo, Knoxville	.964	119	224	14	9	247	1
DeLaNuez, Rex, Jacksonville	.992	82	117	9	1	127	1
Dowler, Dee, Orlando	1.000	9	16	3	0	19	0
Drinkwater, Sean, Memphis	1.000	2	2	0	0	2	0
Duross, Gabe, Orlando*	1.000	1	1	0	0	1	0
Dye, Jermaine, Greenville	.981	103	234	22	5	261	2
Espinosa, Ramon, Carolina	.956	125	232	9	11	252	2
Farrell, Jon, Carolina	.957	79	147	10	7	164	2
Francisco, David, Huntsville	.979	128	267	15	6	288	4
Fryman, Troy, Birmingham	1.000	11	15	0	0	15	0
Gennaro, Brad, Memphis*	.984	102	172	10	3	185	1
Gipson, Charles, Port City	.980	110	233	12	5	250	4
Griffey, Craig, Port City	.982	92	152	8	3	163	1
Hansen, Terrel, Jacksonville	.986	44	69	3	1	73	1
Harley, Quentin, Memphis	1.000	5	7	0	0	7	0
Hart, Chris, Huntsville	.980	28	48	2	1	51	1
Herrera, Jose, Huntsville*	.958	90	176	6	8	190	0
Hollins, Damon, Greenville*	.978	129	330	18	8	356	3
Hughes, Troy, Greenville	.968	53	83	7	3	93	1
Hurst, Jimmy, Birmingham	.931	66	131	3	10	144	0
HYZDU, Adam, Chattanooga	.995	99	182	4	1	187	0
Jennings, Robin, Orlando*	.963	126	242	15	10	267	2
Johnson, Earl, Memphis	.800	2	4	0	1	5	0
Johnson, Matt, Knoxville	.750	2	3	0	1	4	0
Kimsey, Keith, Jacksonville	.984	30	57	5	1	63	1
Klesko, Ryan, Greenville*	1.000	2	2	0	0	2	0
Krevokuch, Jim, Carolina	1.000	1	2	0	0	2	0
Ladell, Cleveland, Chattanooga	.985	135	312	6	5	323	2
Larregui, Ed, Orlando	.976	92	156	6	4	166	2
Leary, Rob, Carolina*	1.000	2	5	0	0	5	0
Leiper, Tim, Jacksonville	.988	57	75	7	1	83	1
Lesher, Brian, Huntsville*	.974	114	184	5	5	194	2
Lidle, Kevin, Jacksonville	.500	1	1	0	1	2	0
Lutz, Brent, Knoxville	.923	8	11	1	1	13	0
Mack, Quinn, Memphis*	1.000	16	33	0	0	33	0
Madsen, Dan, Orlando*	1.000	9	16	1	0	17	0
Manahan, Austin, Orlando	.963	32	52	0	2	54	0
Mashore, Justin, Jacksonville	1.000	40	88	2	0	90	1
Merchant, Mark, Chattanooga	1.000	4	1	0	0	1	0
Mottola, Chad, Chattanooga	.974	50	106	6	3	115	2
Moultrie, Pat, Knoxville*	1.000	13	22	0	0	22	0
Neill, Mike, Huntsville*	1.000	13	24	0	0	24	0
Noriega, Rey, Birmingham	1.000	12	13	0	0	13	0
Pecorilli, Aldo, Greenville	.923	6	12	0	1	13	0
Peguero, Julio, Port City	.961	36	72	2	3	77	1
Peterson, Charles, Carolina	.977	20	40	2	1	43	0
Pevey, Marty, Jacksonville	1.000	6	8	0	0	8	0
Poe, Charles, Birmingham	.968	78	143	7	5	155	1
Rackley, Keifer, Port City	.960	78	116	4	5	125	0
Ramirez, Roberto, Port City	.961	102	165	8	7	180	3
Ratliff, Daryl, Carolina	.967	15	29	0	1	30	0
Roberts, Lonell, Knoxville	.947	81	159	3	9	171	0
Robinson, Don, Greenville	1.000	6	5	1	0	6	1
Rohrmeier, Dan, Chattanooga	1.000	56	103	7	0	110	2
Rumfield, Toby, Chattanooga	1.000	12	12	0	0	12	0
Samuels, Scott, Orlando	1.000	5	11	0	0	11	0
Sanders, Deion, Chattanooga*	1.000	1	3	1	0	4	1
Santana, Ruben, Chattanooga	1.000	1	2	0	0	2	0
Sawkiw, Warren, Knoxville	1.000	5	6	0	0	6	0
Smith, Ira, Memphis	.972	59	98	5	3	106	1
Stewart, Shannon, Knoxville	.980	132	283	6	6	295	1
Swann, Pedro, Greenville	.966	48	83	3	3	89	0
Thomas, Keith, Memphis	.982	88	160	7	3	170	1
Torres, Paul, Orlando	1.000	37	59	3	0	62	1
Valdes, Pedro, Orlando*	.979	106	172	11	4	187	6
Vasquez, Chris, Chattanooga	1.000	3	5	0	0	5	0
Walker, Dane, Huntsville	.944	50	65	2	4	71	0
Warner, Mike, Greenville*	.953	48	100	1	5	106	0
Watkins, Pat, Chattanooga	.960	104	185	8	8	201	1
Williams, Juan, Greenville	.991	51	104	2	1	107	0
Wolfe, Joel, Huntsville	1.000	24	44	2	0	46	0
Wollenburg, Doug, Greenville	1.000	1	1	0	0	1	0

TRIPLE PLAY: Farrell.

CATCHERS

Player, Team	Pct.	G	PO	A	E	TC	DP	PB
Ayrault, Joe, Greenville	.986	88	516	64	8	588	4	3
Beard, Garrett, Huntsville	.978	29	162	17	4	183	1	3
Brooks, Eric, Knoxville	.986	19	122	16	2	140	1	3
Brown, Adam, Chattanooga	.992	65	440	35	4	479	7	7
Buckley, Troy, Chattanooga	1.000	8	61	3	0	64	0	1
Cardenas, John, Port City	.989	48	328	34	4	366	5	10
Casanova, Raul, Memphis	.980	75	531	55	12	598	6	12
Cox, Darron, Orlando	.973	31	157	24	5	186	1	2
Davis, Josh, Memphis	1.000	1	6	0	0	6	0	0
Edge, Tim, Carolina	.983	34	198	31	4	233	3	2
Erdman, Brad, Orlando	.986	14	70	3	1	74	0	0
Fernandez, Daniel, Jacksonville	.991	93	464	61	5	530	7	5
Gubanich, Creighton, Huntsville	.997	43	253	47	1	301	4	5
Hanel, Marcus, Carolina	1.000	18	103	13	0	116	4	6
Harmes, Kris, Knoxville	.974	43	275	24	8	307	3	2
Johnson, Jack, Orlando	.977	21	111	14	3	128	2	2
Kendall, Jason, Carolina	.989	98	692	54	8	754	7	11
Killeen, Tim, Memphis	.985	59	408	55	7	470	5	11
Kingston, Mark, Orlando	1.000	4	3	1	0	4	0	1
Ladd, Jeff, Knoxville	.977	7	38	4	1	43	0	0
Lidle, Kevin, Jacksonville	.990	20	90	10	1	101	1	0
Lutz, Brent, Knoxville	.971	39	217	19	7	243	1	9
Manning, Henry, Birmingham	.985	11	57	10	1	68	2	1
Martinez, Angel, Knoxville	.980	38	219	30	5	254	0	4
Molina, Izzy, Huntsville	.980	78	455	74	11	540	11	14
Morales, Francisco, Orlando	1.000	2	6	1	0	7	0	2
Morland, Mike, Knoxville	.985	9	60	5	1	66	0	1
Ortiz, Hector, Orlando	.991	94	567	72	6	645	5	3
Pecorilli, Aldo, Greenville	.913	6	39	3	4	46	0	0
Perona, Joe, Jacksonville	.909	6	17	3	2	22	0	0
Pevey, Marty, Jacksonville	.952	5	19	1	1	21	0	0
Rice, Lance, Jacksonville	.994	63	284	43	2	329	9	5
Ripplemeyer, Brad, Greenville	.972	53	287	28	9	324	3	4
Rumfield, Toby, Chattanooga	1.000	2	2	0	0	2	0	0
Schwenke, Matt, Memphis	.972	20	130	8	4	142	1	4
Sellers, Rick, Chattanooga	.987	88	567	55	8	630	7	11
Slaught, Don, Carolina	1.000	3	24	1	0	25	0	0
Snyder, Jared, Orlando	1.000	1	6	1	0	7	0	0
Sutherland, Alex, Port City	.990	13	91	10	1	102	0	0
Triessl, Mike, Memphis	.889	3	8	0	1	9	0	0
Varitek, Jason, Port City	.988	89	589	59	8	656	7	21
Vinas, Julio, Birmingham	.976	57	356	50	10	416	4	5
VOLLMER, Scott, Birmingham	.992	79	554	70	5	629	8	10

PITCHERS

Player, Team	Pct.	G	PO	A	E	TC	DP
Abbott, Todd, Huntsville	1.000	4	0	1	0	1	0
Adam, Dave, Port City	.923	31	7	17	2	26	0
Adams, Terry, Orlando	.667	37	1	3	2	6	1
Adams, Willie, Huntsville	.857	13	4	8	2	14	0
Aldred, Scott, Jacksonville*	1.000	2	1	1	0	2	0
Almanzar, Carlos, Knoxville	.968	35	17	13	1	31	1
Andujar, Luis, Birmingham	.960	27	13	11	1	25	3
Apana, Matt, Port City	1.000	6	1	5	0	6	0
Arnold, Jamie, Greenville	1.000	10	2	5	0	7	0
Backlund, Brett, Carolina	1.000	22	4	14	0	18	0
Banks, Jim, Huntsville	.800	44	4	4	2	10	0
Barnes, Jon, Memphis	1.000	2	0	1	0	1	0
Bauer, Matt, Jacksonville*	1.000	27	4	5	0	9	0
Beatty, Blaine, Chattanooga*	.900	8	3	6	1	10	1
Beckett, Robbie, Memphis*	.500	36	1	2	3	6	0
Beltran, Alonso, Knoxville	.933	28	4	10	1	15	0
Bene, Bill, Chattanooga	1.000	4	1	0	0	1	0
Bennett, Bob, Huntsville	1.000	23	21	16	0	37	1
Bennett, Chris, Carolina	1.000	18	2	3	0	5	0
Berlin, Mike, Jacksonville	1.000	3	0	1	0	1	0

Player, Team	Pct.	G	PO	A	E	TC	DP
Bertotti, Mike, Birmingham*	.824	12	2	12	3	17	0
Blair, Dirk, Greenville	.875	40	2	5	1	8	1
Bradford, Troy, Orlando	1.000	4	0	1	0	1	0
Brandow, Derek, Knoxville	1.000	25	9	7	0	16	2
Brown, Chad, Knoxville*	.938	40	6	9	1	16	1
Brumley, Duff, Chattanooga	.909	25	6	4	1	11	2
Buckley, Travis, Chattanooga	1.000	3	1	0	0	1	0
Burgess, Kurt, Greenville*	.667	8	0	2	1	3	0
Burgos, John, Chattanooga*	.947	44	9	9	1	19	0
Burlingame, Ben, Orlando	1.000	37	5	12	0	17	1
Carmona, Rafael, Port City	1.000	15	0	2	0	2	0
Carpenter, Chris, Knoxville	.875	13	5	9	2	16	1
Cedeno, Blas, Jacksonville	.952	48	5	15	1	21	1
Chouinard, Bobby, Huntsville	.938	29	7	23	2	32	4
Christman, Scott, Birmingham*	.941	12	4	12	1	17	0
Clark, Dera, Memphis	1.000	23	2	3	0	5	0
Cole, Victor, Memphis	1.000	8	1	3	0	4	1
Connolly, Matt, Orlando	1.000	21	3	2	0	5	0
Connors, Chad, Chattanooga	1.000	10	1	0	0	1	0
Cooke, Steve, Carolina*	1.000	1	0	1	0	1	0
Cullop, Glen, Chattanooga	.667	8	1	1	1	3	0
Dabney, Fred, Orlando*	.833	13	2	3	1	6	0
D'Andrea, Mike, Greenville	.864	40	8	11	3	22	2
Davison, Scott, Port City	.889	34	4	4	1	9	0
DeLeon, Luis, Orlando	1.000	4	2	3	0	5	0
DeLosSantos, Mariano, Carolina	.889	21	3	5	1	9	0
Dessens, Elmer, Carolina	1.000	27	11	26	0	37	2
Doman, Roger, Knoxville	1.000	14	2	3	0	5	0
Dressendorfer, Kirk, Huntsville	1.000	9	2	3	0	5	0
Dreyer, Darren, Orlando	1.000	14	6	5	0	11	0
Drinkwater, Sean, Memphis	1.000	1	0	1	0	1	0
Drumright, Mike, Jacksonville	.875	5	2	5	1	8	0
Etheridge, Roger, Greenville*	.962	32	2	23	1	26	0
Evans, Sean, Carolina	.846	29	4	7	2	13	0
Farmer, Howard, Chattanooga	1.000	1	0	1	0	1	0
Fermin, Ramon, Huntsville	.952	32	6	14	1	21	3
Fernandez, Osvaldo, Port City*	1.000	27	8	28	0	36	4
Ferry, Mike, Chattanooga	1.000	24	19	10	0	29	1
Figueroa, Fernando, Carolina*	1.000	6	1	2	0	3	0
Fordham, Tom, Birmingham*	.750	14	2	10	4	16	0
Fox, Chad, Chattanooga	.765	20	9	4	4	17	2
Franklin, Ryan, Port City	.946	31	5	30	2	37	3
Freeman, Chris, Knoxville	1.000	39	4	7	0	11	1
Freitas, Mike, Memphis	1.000	54	2	9	0	11	3
Gaillard, Eddie, Jacksonville	1.000	8	0	1	0	1	1
Gajkowski, Steve, Birmingham	1.000	35	4	12	0	16	1
Glinatsis, George, Port City	1.000	18	4	12	0	16	3
Goldsmith, Gary, Jacksonville	.833	15	5	10	3	18	1
Gray, Dennis, Knoxville*	.875	24	1	6	1	8	1
Greene, Rick, Jacksonville	1.000	32	2	4	0	6	0
Grigsby, Benji, Huntsville	.875	30	8	6	2	16	0
Grimm, John, Jacksonville	.750	13	2	1	1	4	0
Guilfoyle, Michael, Jacksonville*	1.000	56	1	3	0	4	0
Gutierrez, Jim, Jacksonville	1.000	45	5	9	0	14	1
Haas, David, Orlando	1.000	3	0	1	0	1	0
Hanson, Craig, Memphis	1.000	25	2	1	0	3	0
Harrah, Doug, Orlando	1.000	44	4	6	0	10	1
Harrison, Brian, Memphis*	1.000	38	0	3	0	3	0
Harrison, Tom, Greenville	.944	14	9	8	1	18	0
Hart, Jason, Orlando	1.000	14	1	3	0	4	0
Haught, Gary, Huntsville	1.000	9	3	4	0	7	0
Heble, Kurt, Knoxville	.875	47	2	5	1	8	0
Hernandez, Fernando, Memphis	.750	12	1	2	1	4	1
Hill, Milt, Carolina	1.000	10	0	8	0	8	0
Hollinger, Adrian, Greenville	1.000	7	6	4	0	10	0
Hollins, Stacy, Huntsville	1.000	15	4	9	0	13	0
Hostetler, Marcus, Greenville	.833	32	1	4	1	6	0
Hostetler, Mike, Greenville	.846	28	5	17	4	26	0
Huber, Jeff, Memphis*	1.000	5	0	1	0	1	0
Hurtado, Edwin, Knoxville	.875	11	7	7	2	16	0
Hutcheson, David, Orlando	.974	28	20	18	1	39	0
Ingram, Todd, Knoxville	1.000	20	3	3	0	6	0
Janzen, Marty, Knoxville	1.000	7	1	10	0	11	1
Jersild, Aaron, Knoxville*	1.000	14	0	7	0	7	1
Jimenez, Miguel, Huntsville	1.000	6	2	0	0	2	0
Johnson, Barry, Birmingham	1.000	47	6	15	0	21	0
Johnson, Chris, Orlando	1.000	46	4	9	0	13	1
Johnston, Sean, Birmingham*	1.000	34	11	20	0	31	1
Kaufman, Brad, Memphis	.886	27	12	19	4	35	1
Keagle, Greg, Memphis	1.000	15	8	10	0	18	0
Kelley, Rich, Jacksonville*	1.000	7	1	1	0	2	0
Kelly, John, Jacksonville	.933	66	3	11	1	15	1
Kilgo, Rusty, Chattanooga*	1.000	54	8	16	0	24	1

Player, Team	Pct.	G	PO	A	E	TC	DP
King, Kevin, Port City*	.909	20	2	8	1	11	0
Koller, Jerry, Greenville	1.000	25	8	17	0	25	0
Konuszewski, Dennis, Carolina	.923	48	5	7	1	13	1
Kotes, Chris, Knoxville	.889	36	10	14	3	27	2
Kramer, Tommy, Chattanooga	1.000	21	9	15	0	24	0
Kroon, Marc, Memphis	.800	22	4	4	2	10	1
Lawrence, Sean, Carolina*	1.000	12	1	2	0	3	0
Lemke, Steve, Huntsville	.968	25	10	20	1	31	2
Levine, Alan, Birmingham	1.000	43	3	17	0	20	1
Loiselle, Rich, Memphis	.957	13	15	7	1	23	1
Long, Joey, Memphis*	1.000	25	1	6	0	7	0
Lowe, Derek, Port City	1.000	10	2	8	0	10	0
LUEBBERS, Larry, Chattanooga	1.000	28	13	30	0	43	6
Manning, Derek, Huntsville*	1.000	5	0	5	0	5	0
Mattson, Rob, Memphis	.953	30	10	31	2	43	3
Maurer, Mike, Huntsville	1.000	17	1	0	0	1	0
May, Darrell, Greenville*	1.000	15	4	11	0	15	0
McCarthy, Greg, Birmingham*	1.000	38	2	8	0	10	1
Meier, Kevin, Orlando	.882	11	3	12	2	17	0
Meinershagen, Adam, Knoxville	1.000	3	0	2	0	2	0
Michalak, Chris, Huntsville*	1.000	7	1	3	0	4	0
Miller, Trever, Jacksonville*	.971	31	8	25	1	34	2
Moehler, Brian, Jacksonville	.977	28	19	24	1	44	1
Mongiello, Mike, Birmingham	1.000	7	1	3	0	4	0
Moore, Marcus, Chattanooga	.800	36	1	3	1	5	0
Moore, Tim, Birmingham	1.000	29	11	11	0	22	0
Morel, Ramon, Carolina	1.000	10	4	10	0	14	0
Morgan, Mike, Orlando	.833	2	1	4	1	6	1
Murray, Heath, Memphis*	.867	14	6	7	2	15	0
Murray, Matt, Greenville	1.000	5	1	2	0	3	0
Nezelek, Andy, Carolina	1.000	6	2	1	0	3	0
Nickell, Jackie, Port City	.882	27	4	11	2	17	1
Nitkowski, C.J., Chattanooga*	1.000	8	8	9	0	17	0
Nix, Jim, Chattanooga	.957	40	7	15	1	23	0
Norman, Scott, Jacksonville	1.000	4	1	4	0	5	0
Olsen, Steve, Birmingham	1.000	14	6	7	0	13	1
Pace, Scott, Knoxville*	.889	18	4	12	2	18	0
Paige, Carey, Greenville	.857	7	1	5	1	7	0
Parris, Steve, Carolina	.938	14	5	10	1	16	0
Peters, Chris, Carolina*	1.000	2	1	1	0	2	0
Petersen, Matt, Orlando	1.000	24	4	13	0	17	0
Pett, Jose, Knoxville	.950	26	5	14	1	20	0
Pickett, Ricky, Chattanooga*	.875	40	1	6	1	8	0
Pierce, Rob, Huntsville	1.000	15	1	1	0	2	0
Pierson, Jason, Birmingham*	1.000	4	1	2	0	3	0
Pisciotta, Marc, Carolina	.882	56	5	10	2	17	0
Plantenberg, Erik, Memphis*	1.000	20	2	2	0	4	0
Plaster, Allen, Huntsville	.846	43	2	9	2	13	1
Ralph, Curtis, Carolina	1.000	18	1	2	0	3	0
Ratliff, Jon, Orlando	.938	26	8	7	1	16	0
Resendez, Oscar, Port City	1.000	11	1	2	0	3	0
Rivera, Lino, Carolina	1.000	4	0	1	0	1	0
Rivera, Roberto, Orlando*	1.000	49	5	15	0	20	1
Roper, John, Chattanooga	1.000	3	3	0	0	3	0
Rose, Scott, Huntsville	1.000	38	11	13	0	24	0
Rosengren, John, Jacksonville*	1.000	14	2	12	0	14	0
Ruebel, Matt, Carolina*	.949	27	10	27	2	39	2
Ruffcorn, Scott, Birmingham	1.000	3	3	2	0	5	0
Russell, LaGrande, Port City	.909	39	2	8	1	11	1
Ryan, Matt, Carolina	.955	44	1	20	1	22	0
Rychel, Kevin, Carolina	1.000	40	3	6	0	9	2
Schmitt, Todd, Memphis	1.000	26	4	3	0	7	0
Schutz, Carl, Greenville*	1.000	51	2	5	0	7	0
Seelbach, Chris, Greenville	1.000	9	1	4	0	5	0
Shafer, Bill, Greenville	.333	42	0	1	2	3	0
Shoemaker, Steve, Huntsville	1.000	43	8	7	0	15	0
Shouse, Brian, Carolina*	.950	21	5	14	1	20	1
Simmons, John, Greenville*	.571	48	1	3	3	7	0
Sirotka, Mike, Birmingham*	.947	16	3	15	1	19	2
Smith, Mike, Chattanooga	1.000	3	1	0	0	1	0
Smith, Ottis, Orlando*	.963	17	8	18	1	27	1
Snyder, John, Birmingham	1.000	5	1	2	0	3	0
Sodowsky, Clint, Jacksonville	.850	19	7	10	3	20	1
Steed, Rick, Knoxville	.833	27	7	3	2	12	0
Swartzbaugh, Dave, Orlando	.800	16	1	3	1	5	0
Taylor, Aaron, Huntsville	1.000	5	1	5	0	6	1
Telemaco, Amaury, Orlando	.933	22	14	14	2	30	1
Thomas, Carlos, Hun.-Mem.	.750	18	2	4	2	8	0
Thomas, Larry, Birmingham*	1.000	35	3	6	0	9	0
Thompson, Justin, Jacksonville*	.920	18	4	19	2	25	0
Tolar, Kevin, Carolina*	1.000	12	0	1	0	1	0
Tranbarger, Mark, Chattanooga*	1.000	48	6	7	0	13	1
Tsamis, George, Car.-P.C.*	1.000	19	1	2	0	3	0

Player, Team	Pct.	G	PO	A	E	TC	DP
Turnier, Aaron, Greenville*	1.000	8	1	0	0	1	0
Tuttle, Dave, Chattanooga	1.000	8	5	8	0	13	0
Urso, Sal, Port City*	1.000	51	3	18	0	21	2
VanRyn, Ben, Chattanooga*	1.000	5	2	3	0	5	0
Vasquez, Marcos, Chattanooga	1.000	26	12	20	0	32	2
Veras, Dario, Memphis	.875	58	8	6	2	16	0
Wagner, Matt, Port City	.862	23	9	16	4	29	2
Watkins, Jason, Birmingham	1.000	10	0	2	0	2	0
Weber, Ben, Knoxville	1.000	12	3	4	0	7	1
Wendell, Turk, Orlando	1.000	5	0	1	0	1	0
Whiteside, Sean, Jacksonville*	1.000	27	1	7	0	8	0
Wilkins, Marc, Carolina	1.000	37	1	12	0	13	1
Willis, Travis, Carolina	.833	16	3	2	1	6	0
Wilson, Gary, Carolina	1.000	1	0	2	0	2	0
Withem, Shannon, Jacksonville	1.000	19	10	12	0	22	2
Witte, Trey, Port City	.950	48	4	15	1	20	0
Wolcott, Bob, Port City	.941	12	9	7	1	17	1
Woodfin, Chris, Birmingham	.882	48	5	10	2	17	0
Worley, Robert, Port City	.857	22	2	4	1	7	0
Young, Anthony, Orlando	1.000	2	1	1	0	2	0
Zongor, Steve, Huntsville*	1.000	9	2	2	0	4	0

TRIPLE PLAY: Nitkowski.

PITCHERS WITH TWO OR MORE TEAMS

Player, Team	Pct.	G	PO	A	E	TC	DP
Thomas, Carlos, Huntsville	1.000	7	0	1	0	1	0
Thomas, Carlos, Memphis	.714	11	2	3	2	7	0
Tsamis, George, Carolina*	.000	12	0	0	0	0	0
Tsamis, George, Port City*	1.000	7	1	2	0	3	0

The following players did not have any fielding statistics at the positions indicated or appeared only as a designated hitter, pinch-hitter or pinch-runner: Baker, p; Beard, p; Briggs, 3b; A. Brown, 1b; Bullinger, p; Cooper, ss; R. DeLeon, p; Dibble, p; Felix, of; Fitzer, p; Flynt, p; Garcia, 3b; R. Gomez, 3b; Gubanich, of; Hickey, p; Jackson, p; Kaufman, of; Mashore, 2b; Mota, 2b, of; Munoz, 3b; Sanford, dh, ph, pr; Sawkiw, p; Silva, p; K. Thomas, 3b; C. Vazquez, p; Waggoner, p; Walker, p; Wolfe, p; Worrell, p.

LEAGUE CHAMPIONS

Year	Team	Pct.
1904—	Macon	.598
1905—	Macon	.625
1906—	Savannah	.637
1907—	Charleston	.620
1908—	Jackonsville	.694
1909—	Chattanooga*	.738
	Augusta	.702
1910—	Columbus	.588
1911—	Columbus*	.681
	Columbia	.710
1912—	Jacksonville*	.679
	Columbus	.632
1913—	Savannah	.754
	Savannah	.593
1914—	Savannah*	.667
	Albany	.650
1915—	Macon	.588
	Columbus*	.686
1916—	Augusta*	.617
	Columbia	.631
1917—	Charleston	.741
	Columbia*	.667
1918—	Did not operate.	
1919—	Columbia	.585
1920—	Columbia	.633
1921—	Columbia	.642
1922—	Charleston	.625
1923—	Charlotte*	.653
	Macon	.580
1924—	Augusta	.612
1925—	Spartanburg	.620
1926—	Greenville	.662
1927—	Greenville	.622
1928—	Asheville	.664
1929—	Asheville	.605
	Knoxville*	.634
1930—	Greenville*	.620
	Macon	.643
1931-35—	Did not operate.	
1936—	Jacksonville	.652
	Columbus*	.650
1937—	Columbus	.572
	Savannah (3rd)†	.565
1938—	Savannah	.574
	Macon (2nd)†	.570
1939—	Columbus	.601
	Augusta (2nd)†	.597
1940—	Savannah	.627
	Columbus (2nd)†	.583
1941—	Macon	.643
	Columbia (2nd)†	.636
1942—	Charleston	.620
	Macon (2nd)†	.585
1943-45—	Did not operate.	
1946—	Columbus	.568
	Augusta (4th)†	.547
1947—	Columbus	.575
	Savannah (2nd)†	.563
1948—	Charleston	.572
	Greenville (3rd)†	.549
1949—	Macon‡	.623
1950—	Macon‡	.588
1951—	Montgomery	.607
1952—	Columbia	.649
	Montgomery (3rd)†	.558
1953—	Jacksonville	.679
	Savannah (2nd)†	.571
1954—	Jacksonville	.593
	Savannah (2nd)†	.571
1955—	Columbia	.636
	Augusta (3rd)†	.543
1956—	Jacksonville‡	.621
1957—	Augusta	.636
	Charlotte (2nd)†	.562
1958—	Augusta	.550
	Macon (3rd)†	.500
1959—	Knoxville	.557
	Gastonia (4th)†	.504
1960—	Columbia	.597
	Savannah (3rd)†	.561
1961—	Asheville	.635
1962—	Savannah	.662
	Macon (3rd)†	.576
1963—	Augusta*	.661
	Lynchburg	.662
1964—	Lynchburg	.579
1965—	Columbus	.572
1966—	Mobile	.629
1967—	Birmingham	.604
1968—	Asheville	.614
1969—	Charlotte	.579
1970—	Columbus	.569
1971—	Did not operate as league—clubs were members of Dixie Association.	
1972—	Asheville	.583
	Montgomery§	.561
1973—	Montgomery§	.580
	Jacksonville	.559
1974—	Jacksonville	.565
	Knoxville§	.533
1975—	Orlando	.587
	Montgomery§	.545
1976—	Montgomery∞	.591
	Orlando	.540
1977—	Montgomery∞	.628
	Jacksonville	.522
1978—	Knoxville∞	.611
	Savannah	.500
1979—	Columbus	.587
	Nashville∞	.576
1980—	Memphis	.576
	Charlotte∞	.500
1981—	Nashville	.566
	Orlando∞	.556
1982—	Jacksonville	.576
	Nashville∞	.535
1983—	Birmingham∞	.628
	Jacksonville	.531
1984—	Charlotte∞	.510
	Knoxville	.483
1985—	Charlotte	.545
	Huntsville∞	.542
1986—	Huntsville	.553
	Columbus∞	.500
1987—	Charlotte	.586
	Birmingham∞	.476
1988—	Greenville	.604
	Chattanooga∞	.566
1989—	Birmingham∞	.615
	Greenville	.504
1990—	Orlando	.590
	Memphis∞	.507
1991—	Greenville	.611
	Orlando∞	.535
1992—	Greenville∞	.699
	Chattanooga	.629
1993—	Birmingham∞	.549
	Knoxville	.500
1994—	Huntsville∞	.587
	Carolina	.529
1995—	Carolina∞	.618
	Chattanooga	.580

*Won split season playoff. †Won four-club playoff. ‡Won championship and four-club playoff. §League was divided into Eastern and Western divisions; won playoff. ∞League was divided into Eastern and Western divisions and played split season; won playoff.

TEXAS LEAGUE

LEAGUE OFFICE

President/treasurer
Tom Kayser

Address
2442 Facet Oak
San Antonio, TX 78232

Phone
210-545-5297

TEAMS

ARKANSAS TRAVELERS

General manager
Bill Valentine
Manager
Rick Mahler
Ballpark (capacity, surface)
Ray Winder Field (6,783, grass)
Affiliation
Cardinals
Address
P.O. Box 5599
Little Rock, AR 72215
Phone
501-664-1555

EL PASO DIABLOS

General manager
Rick Parr
Manager
Dave Machemer
Ballpark (capacity, surface)
Cohen Stadium (9,765, grass)
Affiliation
Brewers
Address
P.O. Drawer 4797
El Paso, TX 79914
Phone
915-755-2000

JACKSON GENERALS

General manager
Bill Blackwell
Manager
Dave Engle
Ballpark (capacity, surface)
Smith-Wills Stadium (5,200, grass)
Affiliation
Astros
Address
P.O. Box 4209
Jackson, MS 39296
Phone
601-981-4664

MIDLAND ANGELS

General manager
Monty Hoppel
Manager
Mario Mendoza
Ballpark (capacity, surface)
Christensen Stadium (5,000, grass)
Affiliation
Angels
Address
P.O. Box 51187
Midland, TX 79710
Phone
915-683-4251

SAN ANTONIO MISSIONS

General manager
Burl Yarbrough
Manager
John Shelby
Ballpark (capacity, surface)
Nelson Wolf Stadium (6,300, grass)
Affiliation
Dodgers
Address
5757 Highway 90 West
San Antonio, TX 78227
Phone
210-675-7275

SHREVEPORT CAPTAINS

General manager
Gilbert Little
Manager
Frank Cacciatore
Ballpark (capacity, surface)
Fair Grounds Field (6,200, grass)
Affiliation
Giants
Address
P.O. Box 3448
Shreveport, LA 71133
Phone
318-636-5555

TULSA DRILLERS

Executive v.p./general manager
Chuck Lamson
Manager
Bobby Jones
Ballpark (capacity, surface)
Drillers Stadium (10,813, grass)
Affiliation
Rangers
Address
P.O. Box 4448
Tulsa, OK 74159
Phone
918-744-5998

WICHITA WRANGLERS

General manager
Steve Shaad
Manager
Ron Johnson
Ballpark (capacity, surface)
Lawrence-Dumont Stadium (6,067, artificial infield, grass outfield)
Affiliation
Royals
Address
P.O. Box 1420
Wichita, KS 67201
Phone
316-267-3372

1995 FINAL STANDINGS

FIRST HALF

EAST DIVISION

Team	W	L	T	Pct.	GB
Shreveport (Giants)	43	24	0	.642	....
Arkansas (Cardinals)	37	30	0	.552	6
Jackson (Astros)	32	35	0	.478	11
Tulsa (Rangers)	21	46	0	.313	22

WEST DIVISION

Team	W	L	T	Pct.	GB
Midland (Angels)	36	32	0	.529	....
San Antonio (Dodgers)	35	33	0	.515	1
El Paso (Brewers)	35	33	0	.515	1
Wichita (Royals)	31	37	0	.456	5

SECOND HALF

EAST DIVISION

Team	W	L	T	Pct.	GB
Shreveport (Giants)	45	23	0	.662	....
Arkansas (Cardinals)	33	35	0	.485	12
Tulsa (Rangers)	31	37	0	.456	14
Jackson (Astros)	30	38	0	.441	15

WEST DIVISION

Team	W	L	T	Pct.	GB
Wichita (Royals)	41	27	0	.603	....
El Paso (Brewers)	33	35	0	.485	8
Midland (Angels)	30	38	0	.441	11
San Antonio (Dodgers)	29	39	0	.426	12

COMPOSITE

Team	Shr.	Wch.	Ark.	E.P.	Mid.	S.A.	Jac.	Tul.	W	L	T	Pct.	GB
Shreveport (Giants)	....	7	18	7	7	7	22	20	88	47	0	.652	....
Wichita (Royals)	3	....	5	19	15	16	6	8	72	64	0	.529	16½
Arkansas (Cardinals)	14	5	....	6	3	7	16	19	70	65	0	.519	18
El Paso (Brewers)	3	13	4	....	17	19	4	8	68	68	0	.500	20½
Midland (Angels)	3	17	7	15	....	13	5	6	66	70	0	.485	22½
San Antonio (Dodgers)	3	16	3	13	19	....	4	6	64	72	0	.471	24½
Jackson (Astros)	9	4	16	6	5	6	....	16	62	73	0	.459	26
Tulsa (Rangers)	12	2	12	2	4	4	16	....	52	83	0	.385	36

Arkansas club represented Little Rock, Ark.

Major league affiliations in parentheses.

PLAYOFFS: Midland defeated Wichita, three games to two; Shreveport defeated Midland, four games to one, to win league championship.

REGULAR-SEASON ATTENDANCE: Arkansas, 248,340; El Paso, 329,233; Jackson, 171,508; Midland, 202,830; San Antonio, 387,090; Shreveport, 173,996; Tulsa, 321,662; Wichita, 203,134. Total—2,037,793. Playoffs (10 games)—28,569. Class AA All-Star Game at Shreveport—6,247. Texas League All-Star Game at El Paso—2,906.

MANAGERS: Arkansas, Mike Ramsey; El Paso, Tim Ireland; Jackson, Tim Tolman; Midland, Mario Mendoza; San Antonio, John Shelby; Shreveport, Ron Wotus; Tulsa, Bobby Jones; Wichita, Ron Johnson.

ALL-STAR TEAM: 1B—Todd Landry, El Paso; 2B—Jeff Berblinger, Arkansas; 3B—George Arias, Midland; SS—Wil Guerrero, San Antonio; OF—Brian Banks, El Paso; Jacob Cruz, Shreveport; Johnny Damon, Wichita; C—Todd Greene, Midland; DH—Oreste Marrero, San Antonio; Utility—Jay Canizaro, Shreveport; LHP—David Pyc, San Antonio; Gary Rath, San Antonio; Billy Wagner, Jackson; RHP—Steve Bourgeois, Shreveport; Edwin Corps, Shreveport; Steve Montgomery, Arkansas; Player of the Year—Johnny Damon, Wichita; Pitcher of the Year—Steve Bourgeois, Shreveport; Manager of the Year—Ron Johnson, Wichita.

1995 BATTING

TEAM

Team	Avg.	G	TPA	AB	R	H	TB	2B	3B	HR	RBI	SH	SF	HP	BB	IBB	SO	SB	CS	GDP	LOB	ShO	Slg.	OBP
El Paso	.286	136	5316	4656	733	1331	1993	274	68	84	665	32	48	53	527	22	888	84	54	130	990	1	.428	.362
Midland	.284	136	5292	4681	726	1328	2071	235	50	136	660	48	54	40	468	23	856	110	85	93	960	3	.442	.350
Wichita	.282	136	5278	4701	685	1328	1937	244	34	99	616	61	28	59	429	32	668	143	95	109	970	7	.412	.348
Shreveport	.280	135	5349	4644	733	1302	1894	267	35	85	663	57	48	54	546	40	742	108	66	114	1013	4	.408	.359
Arkansas	.268	135	5006	4387	617	1176	1739	199	32	100	570	52	26	47	492	31	787	86	63	116	938	3	.396	.346
San Antonio	.265	136	5115	4556	585	1209	1763	228	34	86	531	25	41	45	446	22	834	119	108	98	914	9	.387	.334
Jackson	.262	135	5058	4488	541	1174	1683	203	24	86	490	47	50	45	427	23	689	78	74	114	958	12	.375	.329
Tulsa	.257	135	5080	4513	540	1160	1648	202	35	72	501	53	42	46	424	18	683	54	50	121	949	12	.365	.324

INDIVIDUAL

TOP QUALIFIERS FOR BATTING CHAMPIONSHIP

Minimum 367 plate appearances. *Lefthanded batter. †Switch-hitter.

Player, Team	Avg.	G	TPA	AB	R	H	TB	2B	3B	HR	RBI	SH	SF	HP	BB	IBB	SO	SB	CS	GDP	Slg.	OBP
Guerrero, Wilton, San Antonio	.348	95	414	382	53	133	158	13	6	0	26	4	1	1	26	3	63	21	22	10	.414	.390
Damon, Johnny, Wichita*	.343	111	503	423	83	145	226	15	9	16	54	10	1	2	67	13	35	26	15	3	.534	.434
Berblinger, Jeff, Arkansas	.319	87	392	332	66	106	144	15	4	5	29	1	2	9	48	1	40	16	16	2	.434	.417
Carvajal, Jovino, Midland†	.313	79	374	348	58	109	138	13	5	2	23	5	2	1	18	2	42	39	21	3	.397	.347
Lopez, Roberto, El Paso†	.312	114	509	417	80	130	171	22	8	1	44	6	5	4	77	2	63	9	4	4	.410	.419
Mueller, Bill, Shreveport†	.309	88	393	330	56	102	125	16	2	1	39	1	5	4	53	2	36	6	5	9	.379	.406
Williamson, Antone, El Paso*	.309	104	446	392	62	121	184	30	6	7	90	0	4	3	47	3	57	3	1	10	.469	.383
Banks, Brian, El Paso†	.308	128	536	441	81	136	231	39	10	12	78	3	8	3	81	6	113	9	9	10	.524	.413
Myers, Rod, Wichita*	.307	131	548	499	71	153	208	22	6	7	62	8	3	4	34	3	77	29	16	7	.417	.354
Monell, Johnny, Tulsa†	.306	121	513	434	55	133	189	18	1	12	64	0	6	6	67	6	53	0	1	10	.435	.402
Wolff, Mike, Midland	.303	127	524	445	76	135	211	28	3	14	70	4	7	3	65	3	83	10	9	10	.474	.390
Romero, Mandy, Wichita†	.302	121	515	440	73	133	230	32	1	21	82	0	1	5	69	10	60	1	3	15	.523	.402
Bridges, Kary, Jackson*	.301	118	477	418	56	126	165	22	4	3	43	6	4	0	49	3	17	10	12	12	.395	.372
Mora, Melvin, Jackson	.298	123	522	467	63	139	180	32	0	3	45	7	7	9	32	1	57	22	11	11	.385	.350
Cruz, Jacob, Shreveport*	.297	127	529	458	88	136	210	33	1	13	77	4	2	8	57	6	72	9	8	15	.459	.383

DEPARTMENTAL LEADERS: G—Arias, 134; AB—Arias, 520; R—Arias, 91; H—Myers, 153; TB—Arias, 274; 2B—Banks, 39; 3B—Glenn, 11; HR—Arias, 30; RBI—Arias, 104; SH—R. Martinez, 18; SF—R. Martinez, 9; HP—Fasano, 16; BB—Banks, 81; IBB—Damon, 13; SO—Glenn, 126; SB—F. Martinez, 44; CS—W. Guerrero, 22; GIDP—Landry, 20; Slg.—Damon, .534; OBP—Damon, .434.

ALL PLAYERS

*Lefthanded batter. †Switch-hitter.

Player, Team	Avg.	G	TPA	AB	R	H	TB	2B	3B	HR	RBI	SH	SF	HP	BB	IBB	SO	SB	CS	GDP	Slg.	OBP
Alguacil, Jose, Shreveport*	.250	1	4	4	1	1	1	0	0	0	1	0	0	0	0	0	1	1	0	0	.250	.250
Allen, Ron, Jackson	.333	4	4	3	0	1	1	0	0	0	0	1	0	0	0	0	0	0	0	0	.333	.333
Anderson, Charlie, Arkansas	.283	77	262	240	31	68	99	15	2	4	29	0	1	0	21	1	55	1	2	10	.413	.340
Anderson, Paul, Arkansas	.250	38	5	4	0	1	3	0	1	0	1	1	0	0	0	0	0	0	0	1	.750	.250
Arias, George, Midland	.279	134	594	520	91	145	274	19	10	30	104	1	5	5	63	1	119	3	1	11	.527	.359
Arrandale, Matt, Arkansas	.000	47	2	2	0	0	0	0	0	0	0	0	0	0	0	0	1	0	0	0	.000	.000
Aurilia, Rich, Shreveport	.327	64	261	226	29	74	105	17	1	4	42	5	2	1	27	3	26	10	3	8	.465	.398
Badorek, Mike, Arkansas	.000	18	17	17	0	0	0	0	0	0	0	0	0	0	0	0	6	0	0	1	.000	.000
Bagwell, Jeff, Jackson	.167	4	16	12	0	2	2	0	0	0	0	0	0	1	3	1	2	0	0	0	.167	.375
Banks, Brian, El Paso†	.308	128	536	441	81	136	231	39	10	12	78	3	8	3	81	6	113	9	9	10	.524	.413
Berblinger, Jeff, Arkansas	.319	87	392	332	66	106	144	15	4	5	29	1	2	9	48	1	40	16	16	2	.434	.417
Bethea, Scott, Arkansas*	.176	11	39	34	6	6	7	1	0	0	4	2	1	0	2	0	5	1	0	0	.206	.216
Blanco, Henry, San Antonio	.255	88	335	302	37	77	139	18	4	12	48	0	0	4	29	2	52	1	1	4	.460	.328
Bourgeois, Steve, Shreveport	.323	24	35	31	6	10	17	2	1	1	8	2	0	0	2	0	2	0	0	1	.548	.364

Player, Team	Avg.	G	TPA	AB	R	H	TB	2B	3B	HR	RBI	SH	SF	HP	BB	IBB	SO	SB	CS	GDP	Slg.	OBP
Boykin, Tyrone, Midland	.271	62	235	210	34	57	95	11	3	7	25	1	3	0	21	1	36	2	1	3	.452	.333
Brannon, Cliff, Shreveport	.000	3	1	1	0	0	0	0	0	0	0	0	0	0	0	0	0	0	0	1	.000	.000
Brewington, Jamie, Shreveport	.143	16	18	14	1	2	2	0	0	0	2	1	0	0	3	0	3	0	0	0	.143	.294
Bridges, Kary, Jackson*	.301	118	477	418	56	126	165	22	4	3	43	6	4	0	49	3	17	10	12	12	.395	.372
Brosnan, Jason, San Antonio*	.000	19	1	1	0	0	0	0	0	0	0	0	0	0	0	0	1	0	0	0	.000	.000
Brunson, William, San Antonio*	.000	14	5	5	0	0	0	0	0	0	0	0	0	0	0	0	2	0	0	0	.000	.000
Burton, Darren, Wichita†	.239	41	185	163	13	39	53	9	1	1	20	9	0	1	12	0	27	6	6	2	.325	.295
Busby, Mike, Arkansas	.167	20	24	18	1	3	3	0	0	0	1	5	1	0	0	0	7	0	0	0	.167	.158
Butterfield, Chris, San Antonio†	.000	2	8	6	0	0	0	0	0	0	0	0	0	0	2	0	3	0	0	0	.000	.250
Cairo, Miguel, San Antonio	.278	107	474	435	53	121	146	20	1	1	41	4	4	5	26	0	32	33	16	6	.336	.323
Canizaro, Jay, Shreveport	.293	126	513	440	83	129	204	25	7	12	60	4	5	6	58	4	98	16	9	9	.464	.379
Carpenter, Brian, Arkansas	.000	17	6	6	0	0	0	0	0	0	0	0	0	0	0	0	2	0	0	0	.000	.000
Carpenter, Jerry, Midland	.000	2	2	2	1	0	0	0	0	0	0	0	0	0	0	0	1	0	0	0	.000	.000
Caruso, Gene, El Paso*	.000	46	1	1	0	0	0	0	0	0	0	0	0	0	0	0	0	0	0	0	.000	.000
Carvajal, Jovino, Midland†	.313	79	374	348	58	109	138	13	5	2	23	5	2	1	18	2	42	39	21	3	.397	.347
Castillo, Juan, Jackson	.091	12	13	11	2	1	1	0	0	0	0	1	0	0	1	0	3	0	0	0	.091	.167
Castillo, Mariano, Shreveport	.000	22	3	3	0	0	0	0	0	0	0	0	0	0	0	0	2	0	0	0	.000	.000
Castro, Nelson, San Antonio	.000	48	1	1	0	0	0	0	0	0	0	0	0	0	0	0	0	0	0	0	.000	.000
Centeno, Henri, Jackson†	.256	92	204	172	24	44	55	3	1	2	12	3	2	3	24	2	31	6	4	7	.320	.353
Charles, Frank, Tulsa	.253	126	510	479	51	121	190	24	3	13	72	1	4	4	22	0	92	1	0	19	.397	.289
Chavez, Raul, Jackson	.287	58	205	188	16	54	74	8	0	4	25	4	2	3	8	1	17	0	4	7	.394	.323
Cholowsky, Dan, Arkansas	.311	54	221	190	41	59	92	12	0	7	35	0	2	5	24	2	41	7	6	2	.484	.398
Christopher, Chris, Arkansas	.274	23	63	62	7	17	21	1	0	1	3	0	0	0	1	0	6	4	1	2	.339	.286
Clinton, Jim, Tulsa	.193	28	69	57	6	11	16	2	0	1	7	3	1	1	7	0	16	2	0	3	.281	.288
Cohick, Emmitt, Midland*	.229	56	193	153	25	35	58	13	2	2	23	2	3	2	33	1	45	3	2	0	.379	.366
Colon, Dennis, Jackson*	.224	106	415	379	33	85	110	10	0	5	31	2	6	4	24	2	38	3	6	8	.290	.274
Corps, Edwin, Shreveport	.360	27	32	25	3	9	10	1	0	0	4	2	0	0	5	0	5	0	0	0	.400	.467
Creek, Ryan, Jackson	.150	26	24	20	2	3	3	0	0	0	0	1	0	0	3	0	9	0	1	1	.150	.261
Cruz, Jacob, Shreveport*	.297	127	529	458	88	136	210	33	1	13	77	4	2	8	57	6	72	9	8	15	.459	.383
Damon, Johnny, Wichita*	.343	111	503	423	83	145	226	15	9	16	54	10	1	2	67	13	35	26	15	3	.534	.434
Dandridge, Brad, San Antonio	.417	3	12	12	1	5	5	0	0	0	1	0	0	0	0	0	1	0	1	0	.417	.417
Daniels, Moe, Midland	.202	25	100	84	9	17	25	5	0	1	4	0	0	2	14	0	22	2	4	0	.298	.330
Davis, Ray, Arkansas	.111	21	21	18	2	2	2	0	0	0	0	1	0	0	2	0	9	0	1	0	.111	.200
Diaz, Alfredo, Midland†	.240	8	27	25	3	6	9	3	0	0	4	2	0	0	0	0	12	0	0	1	.360	.240
Diaz, Lino, Wichita	.350	62	247	226	40	79	118	15	3	6	43	0	1	6	14	0	21	0	3	5	.522	.401
DiFelice, Mike, Arkansas	.267	62	205	176	14	47	62	10	1	1	24	2	1	3	23	0	29	0	2	13	.352	.360
Diggs, Tony, Arkansas†	.268	78	275	235	33	63	94	9	8	2	21	2	1	2	35	5	41	7	6	3	.400	.366
Dodson, Bo, El Paso*	.359	63	267	223	46	80	129	20	4	7	43	0	0	7	37	2	42	1	1	6	.578	.464
Donnels, Chris, Jackson*	.167	4	16	12	1	2	3	1	0	0	1	0	0	0	4	0	4	0	0	0	.250	.375
Dumas, Mike, El Paso	.217	12	27	23	5	5	7	0	1	0	4	0	1	0	3	0	0	2	1	0	.304	.296
Edwards, Mike, Tulsa	.216	38	130	111	11	24	38	3	1	3	13	1	1	2	15	0	13	0	0	5	.342	.318
Ehmann, Kurt, Shreveport	.231	38	163	130	24	30	38	5	0	1	17	4	2	5	22	1	15	1	2	5	.292	.358
Ellis, Paul, Arkansas*	.227	78	287	229	17	52	64	6	0	2	25	4	1	4	49	4	18	0	1	9	.279	.371
Estes, Shawn, Shreveport	.667	4	3	3	0	2	2	0	0	0	1	0	0	0	0	0	0	1	0	0	.667	.667
Estrada, Osmani, Tulsa	.266	120	463	410	44	109	147	23	3	3	43	5	4	9	35	2	49	0	2	9	.359	.334
Evans, Dave, Jackson	.000	49	2	2	0	0	0	0	0	0	0	0	0	0	0	0	0	0	0	0	.000	.000
Fasano, Sal, Wichita	.290	87	362	317	60	92	175	19	2	20	66	0	2	16	27	1	61	3	6	8	.552	.373
Felder, Ken, El Paso	.272	114	425	367	51	100	168	24	4	12	55	0	4	6	48	3	94	2	6	10	.458	.362
Felix, Lauro, El Paso	.277	83	276	220	51	61	85	13	1	3	25	5	2	4	45	0	44	6	1	4	.386	.406
Florez, Tim, Shreveport	.268	100	331	295	37	79	121	11	2	9	46	3	3	4	26	1	49	4	3	7	.410	.332
Forkner, Tim, Jackson*	.269	35	140	119	19	32	52	11	0	3	23	0	0	2	19	0	14	1	3	3	.437	.379
Frias, Hanley, Tulsa†	.281	93	416	360	44	101	127	18	4	0	27	8	2	1	45	0	53	14	12	6	.353	.360
Frontera, Chad, Shreveport	.077	20	17	13	0	1	1	0	0	0	0	2	0	0	2	0	5	0	0	0	.077	.200
Gallaher, Kevin, Jackson	.200	6	12	10	0	2	3	1	0	0	1	1	0	0	1	0	1	0	0	0	.300	.273
Gamez, Francisco, El Paso	.000	28	1	1	0	0	0	0	0	0	0	0	0	0	0	0	0	0	0	0	.000	.000
Garcia, Jose, San Antonio	.000	38	1	1	0	0	0	0	0	0	0	0	0	0	0	0	1	0	0	0	.000	.000
Gilmore, Tony, Jackson	.212	53	159	146	10	31	37	3	0	1	15	1	2	0	10	0	27	0	0	3	.253	.259
Glenn, Leon, Midland*	.254	120	475	433	68	110	202	19	11	17	65	3	3	2	34	1	126	16	11	9	.467	.309
Gonzales, Rene, Midland	.176	5	21	17	1	3	3	0	0	0	2	0	0	0	4	0	1	0	1	0	.176	.333
Gonzalez, Raul, Wichita	.291	22	87	79	14	23	36	3	2	2	11	0	0	0	8	0	13	4	0	1	.456	.356
Greene, Todd, Midland	.327	82	346	318	59	104	203	19	1	26	57	1	5	5	17	4	55	3	5	6	.638	.365
Griffin, Ty, Arkansas†	.274	94	302	263	38	72	117	16	1	9	44	0	3	0	36	2	59	17	2	5	.445	.358
Groppuso, Mike, Jackson	.215	24	97	79	5	17	25	3	1	1	5	0	1	1	16	3	17	2	1	1	.316	.351
Grzanich, Mike, Jackson	.000	50	4	3	0	0	0	0	0	0	0	0	0	0	1	0	1	0	0	0	.000	.250
Guerrero, Mike, El Paso†	.310	23	79	71	14	22	26	1	0	1	7	0	1	0	7	0	5	0	0	1	.366	.367
Guerrero, Pedro, Midland	.302	66	282	252	40	76	110	13	0	7	40	0	0	2	28	2	34	0	2	16	.437	.376
Guerrero, Wilton, San Antonio	.348	95	414	382	53	133	158	13	6	0	26	4	1	1	26	3	63	21	22	10	.414	.390
Gulan, Mike, Arkansas	.314	64	260	242	47	76	134	16	3	12	48	0	1	6	11	1	52	4	2	4	.554	.358
Harkrider, Timothy, Midland†	.291	124	529	460	66	134	170	22	4	2	39	14	4	2	48	3	36	3	5	7	.370	.358
Harris, Mike, El Paso*	.333	8	27	24	4	8	13	2	0	1	5	0	1	0	2	0	3	0	0	0	.542	.370
Hatcher, Chris, Jackson	.308	11	45	39	5	12	16	1	0	1	3	0	1	1	4	0	6	0	2	1	.410	.378
Hidalgo, Richard, Jackson	.266	133	530	489	59	130	212	28	6	14	59	0	7	2	32	1	76	8	9	11	.434	.309
Hingle, Larry, Jackson*	.000	9	1	0	0	0	0	0	0	0	0	1	0	0	0	0	0	0	0	0	.000	.000
Holt, Chris, Jackson	.333	5	6	3	0	1	1	0	0	0	0	2	0	0	1	0	0	0	0	0	.333	.500
Hosey, Steve, Midland	.239	30	103	88	16	21	31	4	0	2	16	0	1	2	12	1	31	5	4	2	.352	.340
Hubbs, Dan, San Antonio	.000	31	2	1	0	0	0	0	0	0	0	1	0	0	0	0	0	0	0	0	.000	.000
Hughes, Bobby, El Paso	.266	51	189	173	11	46	79	12	0	7	27	0	2	2	12	1	30	0	2	4	.457	.317
Hunter, Brian, Jackson	.500	2	7	6	1	3	3	0	0	0	0	0	0	0	1	0	0	0	0	1	.500	.571
Hyde, Rich, Shreveport	.000	33	6	6	0	0	0	0	0	0	0	0	0	0	0	0	3	0	0	0	.000	.000
Jaime, Angel, San Antonio	.364	9	24	22	5	8	11	0	0	1	2	0	0	0	2	0	3	2	1	1	.500	.417
Jenkins, Bernie, Shreveport	.167	5	14	12	1	2	5	0	0	1	1	0	0	0	2	0	5	0	0	1	.417	.286
Jenkins, Geoff, El Paso*	.278	22	88	79	12	22	33	4	2	1	13	0	1	0	8	0	23	3	1	1	.418	.341
Jennings, Lance, Wichita	.182	13	47	44	2	8	8	0	0	0	3	1	1	0	1	0	8	0	0	1	.182	.196

Player, Team	Avg.	G	TPA	AB	R	H	TB	2B	3B	HR	RBI	SH	SF	HP	BB	IBB	SO	SB	CS	GDP	Slg.	OBP
Jensen, Marcus, Shreveport†	.283	95	378	321	55	91	141	22	8	4	45	5	8	3	41	1	68	0	0	4	.439	.362
Johns, Keith, Arkansas	.280	111	466	396	69	111	134	13	2	2	28	11	2	2	55	0	53	14	7	11	.338	.369
Johnson, Russ, Jackson	.248	132	540	475	65	118	165	16	2	9	53	2	5	8	50	1	60	10	5	11	.347	.327
Jones, Keith, Arkansas*	.226	50	97	84	11	19	21	2	0	0	4	4	0	0	9	0	12	3	3	3	.250	.301
Kappesser, Bob, El Paso	.191	61	132	115	17	22	34	5	2	1	17	2	3	0	12	0	19	2	2	4	.296	.262
Kellner, Frank, Jackson†	.316	75	315	269	31	85	102	15	1	0	29	4	5	2	35	2	52	1	7	2	.379	.392
Kennedy, Darryl, Tulsa	.251	61	222	195	26	49	69	9	1	3	26	3	4	3	17	0	22	0	0	5	.354	.315
Ketchen, Doug, Jackson	.125	17	8	8	0	1	1	0	0	0	0	0	0	0	0	0	0	0	0	0	.125	.125
Landrum, Tito, San Antonio	.238	87	296	260	42	62	101	13	1	8	25	0	2	7	26	0	64	5	6	9	.388	.322
Landry, Todd, El Paso	.292	132	557	511	76	149	238	33	4	16	79	2	4	7	33	1	99	9	7	20	.466	.341
Latham, Chris, San Antonio†	.299	58	251	214	38	64	115	14	5	9	37	1	1	2	33	0	59	11	11	2	.537	.396
Lewis, Anthony, Arkansas*	.251	115	454	407	55	102	201	21	3	24	85	0	1	2	44	5	117	0	2	7	.494	.326
Lidle, Cory, El Paso	.000	45	1	1	0	0	0	0	0	0	0	0	0	0	0	0	0	0	0	0	.000	.000
Lister, Martin, Jackson*	.000	15	13	10	0	0	0	0	0	0	0	0	0	0	3	0	5	0	0	0	.000	.231
LoDuca, Paul, San Antonio	.246	61	227	199	27	49	60	8	0	1	8	0	0	2	26	0	25	5	5	12	.302	.339
Long, Kevin, Wichita*	.292	67	293	250	38	73	92	14	1	1	26	0	0	2	41	2	29	9	6	3	.368	.396
Long, Ryan, Wichita	.231	102	358	342	36	79	120	26	0	5	34	1	0	5	10	1	48	4	4	9	.351	.263
Long, Tony, Arkansas*	.000	32	3	3	0	0	0	0	0	0	0	0	0	0	0	0	1	0	0	0	.000	.000
Lopez, Pedro, El Paso	.312	84	243	218	32	68	99	15	2	4	28	3	0	4	18	1	45	0	3	8	.454	.375
Lopez, Roberto, El Paso†	.312	114	509	417	80	130	171	22	8	1	44	6	5	4	77	2	63	9	4	4	.410	.419
Lowe, Sean, Arkansas	.208	24	25	24	2	5	9	1	0	1	2	0	0	0	1	0	8	0	0	0	.375	.240
Luce, Roger, Jackson	.212	18	55	52	4	11	18	2	1	1	4	0	0	0	3	0	12	0	0	3	.346	.255
Luzinski, Ryan, San Antonio	.229	44	163	144	18	33	41	5	0	1	9	2	1	3	13	1	32	1	1	6	.285	.304
Maness, Dwight, San Antonio	.223	57	211	179	29	40	63	2	3	5	24	5	2	5	20	0	44	4	6	3	.352	.316
Marrero, Oreste, San Antonio*	.258	125	515	445	60	115	209	25	3	21	86	0	3	3	64	5	98	5	2	4	.470	.353
Marshall, Jason, Wichita	.226	60	156	146	14	33	36	1	1	0	9	5	0	1	4	0	23	0	0	8	.247	.252
Martin, Jim, San Antonio*	.235	95	372	327	43	77	115	20	3	4	36	0	4	5	36	2	83	18	10	4	.352	.317
Martinez, Felix, Wichita†	.263	127	468	426	53	112	142	15	3	3	30	4	1	6	31	0	71	44	20	5	.333	.321
Martinez, Francisco, Arkansas	.000	11	1	1	0	0	0	0	0	0	0	0	0	0	0	0	1	0	0	0	.000	.000
Martinez, Gabby, El Paso†	.278	44	141	133	13	37	44	3	2	0	11	3	1	2	2	0	22	5	1	2	.331	.297
Martinez, Jesus, San Antonio*	.083	24	14	12	1	1	2	1	0	0	0	1	0	0	0	0	7	0	0	0	.167	.083
Martinez, Ramon, Wichita	.275	103	466	393	58	108	141	20	2	3	51	18	9	4	42	1	50	11	8	11	.359	.344
Mayes, Craig, Shreveport*	.222	3	9	9	0	2	3	1	0	0	3	0	0	0	0	0	2	0	0	0	.333	.222
McEwing, Joe, Arkansas	.248	42	137	121	16	30	40	4	0	2	12	6	0	1	9	2	13	3	2	4	.331	.305
McFarlin, Jason, Shreveport*	.337	93	293	252	39	85	120	13	2	6	37	4	2	10	25	7	26	8	7	8	.476	.415
McLain, Mike, Shreveport*	.000	11	2	2	0	0	0	0	0	0	0	0	0	0	0	0	1	0	0	0	.000	.000
McNabb, Buck, Jackson*	.260	15	55	50	4	13	14	1	0	0	3	0	0	0	5	0	11	1	0	1	.280	.327
Medrano, Anthony, Wichita	.000	1	5	5	0	0	0	0	0	0	0	0	0	0	0	0	3	0	0	0	.000	.000
Melendez, Dan, San Antonio*	.261	128	522	464	46	121	172	28	1	7	59	0	6	1	51	5	66	0	3	11	.371	.331
Mercado, Hector, Jackson*	.000	8	8	7	1	0	0	0	0	0	0	0	0	0	1	0	5	0	0	1	.000	.125
Mercedes, Guillermo, Tulsa†	.119	15	47	42	4	5	6	1	0	0	1	1	0	0	4	0	6	0	0	2	.143	.196
Mesewicz, Mark, Arkansas*	.000	5	2	2	0	0	0	0	0	0	0	0	0	0	0	0	1	0	0	0	.000	.000
Metcalfe, Mike, San Antonio†	.244	10	50	41	10	10	11	1	0	0	2	1	1	0	7	0	2	1	2	0	.268	.347
Millan, Bernie, El Paso†	.242	13	35	33	2	8	12	1	0	1	3	0	1	1	0	0	3	0	0	6	.364	.257
Miller, Roger, Shreveport	.274	19	73	62	11	17	29	6	0	2	10	2	1	2	6	0	1	0	0	1	.468	.352
Mirabelli, Doug, Shreveport	.302	40	148	126	14	38	51	13	0	0	16	2	0	0	20	1	14	1	0	3	.405	.397
Mitchell, Tony, Jackson†	.266	96	371	331	45	88	166	17	2	19	61	0	3	1	35	1	83	1	2	10	.502	.335
Mlicki, Doug, Jackson	.000	16	13	9	0	0	0	0	0	0	0	3	0	0	1	0	2	0	0	0	.000	.100
Monell, Johnny, Tulsa†	.306	121	513	434	55	133	189	18	1	12	64	0	6	6	67	6	53	0	1	10	.435	.402
Montgomery, Ray, Jackson	.299	35	146	127	24	38	78	8	1	10	24	0	1	5	13	2	13	6	3	3	.614	.384
Montgomery, Steve, Arkansas	.000	55	1	1	0	0	0	0	0	0	0	0	0	0	0	0	0	0	0	0	.000	.000
Montoya, Norm, El Paso*	1.000	52	1	1	1	1	1	0	0	0	0	0	0	0	0	0	0	0	0	0	1.000	1.000
Monzon, Jose, Midland	.289	57	209	180	29	52	68	11	1	1	19	3	2	2	22	0	36	0	0	6	.378	.369
Mora, Melvin, Jackson	.298	123	522	467	63	139	180	32	0	3	45	7	7	9	32	1	57	22	11	11	.385	.350
Morrow, Chris, Shreveport*	.246	83	272	240	31	59	97	17	0	7	35	0	0	1	31	4	44	1	1	8	.404	.335
Mueller, Bill, Shreveport†	.309	88	393	330	56	102	125	16	2	1	39	1	5	4	53	2	36	6	5	9	.379	.406
Munoz, Orlando, Midland†	.314	87	355	309	39	97	127	19	4	1	44	5	6	2	33	2	33	9	5	4	.411	.377
Murphy, Steve, Wichita*	.333	18	46	39	9	13	15	2	0	0	4	2	1	0	4	1	5	0	1	2	.385	.386
Murray, Calvin, Shreveport	.236	110	509	441	77	104	133	17	3	2	29	5	1	3	59	2	70	26	10	5	.302	.329
Myers, Rod, Wichita*	.307	131	548	499	71	153	208	22	6	7	62	8	3	4	34	3	77	29	16	7	.417	.354
Narcisse, Tyrone, Jackson	.115	27	29	26	2	3	4	1	0	0	2	1	0	0	2	0	12	0	0	0	.154	.179
Nevers, Tom, Jac.-E.P.	.245	118	458	416	55	102	149	12	4	9	47	0	2	5	35	2	79	7	3	16	.358	.310
Nicholas, Darrell, El Paso	.205	15	40	39	4	8	10	0	1	0	2	1	0	0	0	0	11	4	0	0	.256	.205
Nilsson, Dave, El Paso*	.467	5	15	15	1	7	11	1	0	1	4	0	0	0	0	0	1	1	0	0	.733	.467
Norton, Chris, Arkansas	.240	10	37	25	6	6	8	2	0	0	6	0	1	0	11	2	5	0	0	0	.320	.459
Nunez, Rogelio, Tulsa†	.224	82	290	263	27	59	69	4	0	2	17	8	1	8	10	0	43	0	7	10	.262	.273
Odor, Rouglas, El Paso	.294	6	19	17	2	5	5	0	0	0	2	0	0	0	2	0	2	0	0	1	.294	.368
Oehrlein, Dave, Arkansas*	.182	23	13	11	2	2	3	1	0	0	0	1	0	0	1	0	4	0	0	1	.273	.250
Ortiz, Bo, Midland	.275	96	388	360	48	99	139	10	3	8	56	4	5	2	17	2	40	12	11	6	.386	.307
Osborne, Donovan, Arkansas*	.000	2	3	3	0	0	0	0	0	0	0	0	0	0	0	0	2	0	0	0	.000	.000
Otanez, Willis, San Antonio	.240	27	108	100	8	24	33	4	1	1	7	0	2	0	6	0	25	0	1	3	.330	.278
Parra, Franklin, Tulsa†	.245	71	283	261	27	64	83	9	2	2	26	5	5	0	12	0	51	7	9	5	.318	.273
Perez, Danny, El Paso	.276	22	82	76	16	21	24	1	1	0	7	0	1	1	4	0	14	1	0	0	.316	.317
Peterson, Mark, Shreveport*	.167	37	14	12	0	2	2	0	0	0	0	1	0	0	1	0	0	1	0	1	.167	.231
Pimentel, Wander, Arkansas	.000	2	2	2	0	0	0	0	0	0	0	0	0	0	0	0	0	0	0	0	.000	.000
Pote, Lou, Shreveport	.500	28	2	2	1	1	1	0	0	0	0	0	0	0	0	0	0	0	0	0	.500	.500
Prado, Jose, San Antonio	.125	28	10	8	1	1	1	0	0	0	0	2	0	0	0	0	2	0	0	0	.125	.125
Probst, Alan, Jackson	.236	28	99	89	11	21	29	5	0	1	8	0	2	1	7	0	25	0	0	3	.326	.293
Puchales, Javier, San Antonio*	.228	31	62	57	4	13	14	1	0	0	1	1	1	0	3	1	6	0	2	5	.246	.262
Pyc, Dave, San Antonio*	.333	26	13	12	0	4	4	0	0	0	1	1	0	0	0	0	1	0	0	0	.333	.333
Radziewicz, Doug, Arkansas*	.233	34	135	116	15	27	35	5	0	1	13	0	0	0	18	1	14	0	0	2	.302	.336
Ramirez, J.D., Midland	.271	80	285	251	34	68	116	16	1	10	36	2	5	5	22	0	49	1	1	5	.462	.336
Rath, Gary, San Antonio*	.154	18	13	13	0	2	2	0	0	0	1	0	0	0	0	0	4	0	0	1	.154	.154

Player, Team	Avg.	G	TPA	AB	R	H	TB	2B	3B	HR	RBI	SH	SF	HP	BB	IBB	SO	SB	CS	GDP	Slg.	OBP
Raven, Luis, Midland	.267	21	92	86	9	23	42	2	1	5	15	0	1	1	4	0	30	1	1	2	.488	.304
Redington, Tom, Midland	.250	9	38	32	5	8	10	2	0	0	3	0	0	0	6	0	5	0	0	1	.313	.368
Reid, Derek, Shreveport	.143	8	14	14	2	2	4	0	1	0	1	0	0	0	0	0	4	0	0	0	.286	.143
Richardson, Scott, El Paso	.254	82	279	256	29	65	89	9	6	1	29	2	0	5	16	0	42	8	6	13	.348	.310
Richey, Jeff, Shreveport	.000	8	2	1	0	0	0	0	0	0	0	1	0	0	0	0	1	0	0	0	.000	.000
Rios, Eddie, San Antonio	.285	98	392	365	43	104	149	22	4	5	53	1	5	1	20	2	47	2	4	8	.408	.320
Rodriques, Cecil, El Paso	.266	72	264	244	36	65	94	9	7	2	24	0	4	1	15	0	51	5	2	2	.385	.307
Romero, Mandy, Wichita†	.302	121	515	440	73	133	230	32	1	21	82	0	1	5	69	10	60	1	3	15	.523	.402
Romero, Willie, San Antonio	.266	105	427	376	46	100	143	20	1	7	44	0	6	5	40	1	69	10	12	7	.380	.340
Rupp, Brian, Arkansas	.325	23	84	77	10	25	28	3	0	0	6	1	0	0	6	0	12	0	1	3	.364	.373
Sagmoen, Marc, Tulsa*	.231	63	272	242	36	56	92	8	5	6	22	1	2	4	23	0	23	5	4	2	.380	.306
Samples, Todd, El Paso	.000	2	5	4	1	0	0	0	0	0	0	0	0	0	1	0	1	0	0	0	.000	.200
Sepeda, Jaime, Jackson	.000	1	1	0	0	0	0	0	0	0	0	0	0	0	1	0	0	0	0	0	.000	1.000
Shabazz, Basil, El Paso	.216	47	122	102	19	22	30	2	3	0	7	4	2	0	14	1	23	9	5	2	.294	.305
Silvia, Brian, Arkansas	.241	12	34	29	4	7	8	1	0	0	3	0	0	1	4	0	9	0	0	1	.276	.353
Simmons, Scott, Arkansas	.056	22	25	18	0	1	1	0	0	0	1	4	1	1	1	0	3	0	0	0	.056	.143
Simonton, Benji, Shreveport	.306	38	123	108	18	33	60	9	3	4	30	1	1	2	11	0	32	3	1	1	.556	.377
Sims, Wesley, Tulsa†	.233	12	49	43	4	10	13	1	1	0	5	0	0	0	6	0	3	0	1	1	.302	.327
Sisco, Steve, Wichita	.301	54	227	209	29	63	86	12	1	3	23	1	1	1	15	0	31	3	1	5	.411	.350
Smiley, Rueben, Wichita*	.240	41	114	104	16	25	36	3	1	2	13	0	2	0	8	0	20	1	3	3	.346	.289
Smith, Mike, Tulsa	.257	132	571	499	65	128	204	22	3	16	64	5	5	2	60	1	72	11	6	13	.409	.336
Soderstrom, Steve, Shreveport	.043	22	25	23	1	1	1	0	0	0	1	1	0	1	0	0	8	0	0	0	.043	.083
Steed, Dave, San Antonio	.252	40	137	123	13	31	52	10	1	3	16	0	2	1	11	0	32	0	1	2	.423	.314
Stefanski, Mike, El Paso	.407	6	27	27	5	11	17	3	0	1	6	0	0	0	0	0	3	1	0	0	.630	.407
Stewart, Andy, Wichita	.259	60	233	216	28	56	83	18	0	3	32	0	2	4	11	0	31	1	2	9	.384	.305
Strickland, Chad, Wichita	.224	51	191	183	16	41	51	7	0	1	21	2	1	0	5	0	22	0	0	9	.279	.243
Sutko, Glenn, El Paso	.277	44	141	119	18	33	56	9	1	4	20	0	2	0	20	1	34	1	0	5	.471	.376
Sutton, Larry, Wichita*	.269	53	227	197	31	53	81	11	1	5	32	0	2	2	26	0	33	1	1	3	.411	.357
Takayoshi, Todd, Midland*	.278	7	20	18	2	5	7	0	1	0	0	1	0	0	1	0	4	1	0	0	.389	.316
Talanoa, Scott, El Paso	.222	2	10	9	0	2	4	2	0	0	1	0	0	0	1	0	0	0	0	1	.444	.300
Taulbee, Andy, Shreveport	.077	14	15	13	2	1	4	0	0	1	3	1	0	1	0	0	3	0	0	0	.308	.143
Tejero, Fausto, Midland	.226	16	56	53	7	12	18	3	0	1	11	0	1	1	1	0	13	0	1	1	.340	.250
Texidor, Jose, Tulsa	.269	129	532	494	55	133	183	33	1	5	64	2	2	3	31	3	61	1	1	19	.370	.315
Thomas, Brian, Tulsa*	.269	131	522	458	61	123	177	24	9	4	35	5	5	2	50	6	87	8	4	8	.386	.340
Thompson, Fletcher, El Paso*	.192	11	27	26	3	5	5	0	0	0	3	0	0	0	1	0	9	0	0	1	.192	.222
Torres, Paul, Arkansas	.225	66	258	231	24	52	93	11	0	10	33	1	0	5	21	0	56	2	1	9	.403	.304
Troutman, Keith, San Antonio	.000	38	1	1	0	0	0	0	0	0	0	0	0	0	0	0	0	0	0	0	.000	.000
Turco, Frank, Tulsa	.208	53	173	149	23	31	39	3	1	1	12	5	0	1	18	0	34	4	3	2	.262	.298
Urso, Joe, Midland	.324	12	44	37	6	12	15	3	0	0	4	0	1	1	5	0	3	0	0	0	.405	.409
Valdez, Carlos, Shreveport	.000	22	6	6	0	0	0	0	0	0	0	0	0	0	0	0	1	0	0	0	.000	.000
Vanderweele, Doug, Shreveport	.214	13	17	14	0	3	3	0	0	0	0	2	0	0	1	0	2	0	0	0	.214	.267
Velez, Jose, Arkansas†	.296	107	307	287	37	85	121	13	1	7	41	2	2	2	13	1	36	5	4	8	.422	.329
Verduzco, Steven, Jackson	.241	18	29	29	4	7	13	3	0	1	1	0	0	0	0	0	8	0	1	1	.448	.241
Voigt, Jack, Tulsa	.188	4	18	16	1	3	6	0	0	1	3	0	0	0	2	0	5	1	0	2	.375	.278
Wagner, Billy, Jackson*	.286	12	17	14	1	4	6	0	1	0	1	2	0	0	1	0	3	0	0	0	.429	.333
Wagner, Bret, Arkansas*	.143	6	9	7	0	1	1	0	0	0	2	1	0	0	1	0	1	0	0	0	.143	.250
Waldron, Joe, Jackson*	.167	28	7	6	0	1	1	0	0	0	0	0	0	0	1	0	3	0	0	0	.167	.286
Walker, Jamie, Jackson*	.000	50	5	5	0	0	0	0	0	0	0	0	0	0	0	0	4	0	0	0	.000	.000
Waring, Jim, Jackson*	.200	18	7	5	1	1	2	1	0	0	0	2	0	0	0	0	1	0	0	0	.400	.200
Warner, Ron, Arkansas	.245	47	120	98	9	24	27	3	0	0	8	3	2	1	16	1	15	0	0	3	.276	.350
Weaver, Eric, San Antonio	.000	27	10	9	0	0	0	0	0	0	0	1	0	0	0	0	4	0	0	0	.000	.000
Weger, Wes, El Paso	.256	45	172	160	22	41	54	9	2	0	19	1	1	0	10	1	14	1	1	9	.338	.298
Wesson, Barry, Jackson	.667	4	3	3	2	2	4	0	1	0	1	0	0	0	0	0	0	0	0	0	1.333	.667
Whitaker, Steve, Shreveport*	.000	4	3	3	0	0	0	0	0	0	0	0	0	0	0	0	0	0	0	0	.000	.000
White, Chad, Jackson†	.273	32	88	77	11	21	25	4	0	0	3	3	0	0	8	1	9	2	1	3	.325	.341
White, Chris, Jackson	.375	39	8	8	2	3	3	0	0	0	2	0	0	0	0	0	1	0	0	0	.375	.375
White, Jimmy, Jackson*	.000	2	2	1	1	0	0	0	0	0	0	0	0	0	1	0	0	0	0	0	.000	.500
Wilkins, Rick, Jackson*	.000	4	14	11	0	0	0	0	0	0	0	0	0	0	3	0	2	0	0	0	.000	.214
Williams, Keith, Shreveport	.305	75	305	275	39	84	133	20	1	9	55	0	7	0	23	3	39	5	3	5	.484	.351
Williams, Ted, Wichita†	.000	1	0	0	1	0	0	0	0	0	0	0	0	0	0	0	0	0	0	0	.000	.000
Williamson, Antone, El Paso*	.309	104	446	392	62	121	184	30	6	7	90	0	4	3	47	3	57	3	1	10	.469	.383
Wilson, Desi, Shreveport*	.286	122	530	482	77	138	186	27	3	5	72	0	7	1	40	2	68	11	9	18	.386	.338
Witasick, Jay, Arkansas	.000	7	9	9	0	0	0	0	0	0	0	0	0	0	0	0	7	0	0	1	.000	.000
Witkowski, Matt, Shreveport	.289	17	50	38	7	11	12	1	0	0	5	2	1	1	8	1	7	0	0	0	.316	.417
Wolff, Mike, Midland	.303	127	524	445	76	135	211	28	3	14	70	4	7	3	65	3	83	10	9	10	.474	.390
Woods, Kenny, Shreveport	.254	89	236	209	30	53	73	11	0	3	23	2	1	1	23	2	29	4	5	4	.349	.329
Yard, Bruce, San Antonio*	.359	16	44	39	7	14	17	3	0	0	4	0	0	0	5	0	6	0	1	0	.436	.432
Young, Dmitri, Arkansas†	.292	97	403	367	54	107	167	18	6	10	62	0	3	3	30	3	46	2	4	11	.455	.347

GRAND SLAMS: Blanco, 3; Fasano, Glenn, Landry, 2 each; Charles, Chavez, Cohick, Cruz, Forkner, P. Guerrero, Johnson, Lewis, Marrero, McFarlin, Melendez, Simonton, Williamson, 1 each.

AWARDED FIRST BASE ON CATCHER'S INTERFERENCE: Thomas 2 (Ellis, Silvia); Harkrider (P. Lopez); Landrum (Monzon); J. Martinez (Jensen); Mitchell (Monzon); Radziewicz (Monzon); Velez (P. Lopez).

PLAYERS WITH TWO OR MORE TEAMS

Player, Team	Avg.	G	TPA	AB	R	H	TB	2B	3B	HR	RBI	SH	SF	HP	BB	IBB	SO	SB	CS	GDP	Slg.	OBP
Nevers, Tom, Jackson	.242	83	326	298	36	72	109	7	3	8	35	0	2	2	24	2	58	5	2	10	.366	.301
Nevers, Tom, El Paso	.254	35	132	118	19	30	40	5	1	1	12	0	0	3	11	0	21	2	1	6	.339	.333

1995 PITCHING

TEAM

Team	W	L	Pct.	ERA	G	CG	ShO	Sv.	IP	H	TBF	R	ER	HR	SH	SF	HB	BB	IBB	SO	WP	Bk.
Shreveport	88	47	.652	3.28	135	6	14	44	1221.0	1181	5164	530	445	82	40	39	55	432	21	748	61	8
San Antonio	64	72	.471	3.77	136	6	5	38	1202.0	1214	5184	586	503	66	54	43	45	482	6	783	76	18
Jackson	62	73	.459	3.90	135	8	7	35	1185.2	1123	5083	607	514	85	57	44	59	495	36	815	81	9
Arkansas	70	65	.519	3.95	135	7	7	41	1154.0	1178	4953	602	506	71	60	37	40	374	21	751	53	5
Wichita	72	64	.529	4.30	136	3	5	45	1211.2	1243	5230	668	579	115	32	39	40	478	21	821	90	6
Tulsa	52	83	.385	4.54	135	9	6	24	1177.1	1318	5188	692	594	128	44	35	34	485	49	651	68	9
El Paso	68	68	.500	4.58	136	7	4	38	1199.1	1372	5438	764	610	90	48	54	59	558	38	867	86	4
Midland	66	70	.485	4.68	136	13	3	29	1196.1	1379	5254	711	622	111	40	46	57	455	19	711	93	12

INDIVIDUAL

TOP QUALIFIERS FOR EARNED-RUN AVERAGE TITLE

Minimum 109 innings. *Lefthanded pitcher.

Pitcher, Team	W	L	Pct.	ERA	G	GS	CG	ShO	GF	Sv.	IP	H	TBF	R	ER	HR	SH	SF	HB	BB	IBB	SO	WP	Bk.
Rath, Gary, San Antonio*	13	3	.813	2.77	18	18	3	1	0	0	117.0	96	483	42	36	6	3	2	4	48	0	81	4	2
Bourgeois, Steve, Shreveport	12	3	.800	2.85	22	22	2	2	0	0	145.1	140	604	50	46	8	4	5	4	53	1	91	11	1
Narcisse, Tyrone, Jackson	5	14	.263	3.24	27	27	2	0	0	0	163.2	140	686	76	59	8	10	8	10	60	5	93	8	0
Busby, Mike, Arkansas	7	6	.538	3.29	20	20	1	0	0	0	134.0	125	565	63	49	8	3	3	6	35	1	95	5	0
Lidle, Cory, El Paso	5	4	.556	3.36	45	9	0	0	12	2	109.2	126	480	52	41	6	6	1	6	36	3	78	6	0
Pyc, Dave, San Antonio*	12	6	.667	3.38	26	26	1	0	0	0	157.0	170	676	72	59	6	6	4	3	49	1	78	3	1
Soderstrom, Steve, Shreveport	9	5	.643	3.41	22	22	0	0	0	0	116.0	106	508	53	44	6	5	2	10	51	0	91	12	2
Browne, Byron, El Paso	10	4	.714	3.43	25	20	2	1	3	0	126.0	106	541	55	48	7	3	9	6	78	2	110	7	0
Simmons, Scott, Arkansas*	11	9	.550	3.43	22	22	1	1	0	0	139.0	145	569	66	53	9	5	6	1	28	1	73	5	0
Keling, Korey, Midland	8	5	.615	3.46	29	12	1	1	7	1	122.1	113	518	53	47	7	0	1	1	52	3	101	9	2
Prado, Jose, San Antonio	7	11	.389	3.48	28	22	0	0	3	1	144.2	126	621	70	56	9	7	9	7	64	0	93	13	2
Martinez, Jesus, San Antonio*	6	9	.400	3.54	24	24	1	0	0	0	139.2	129	603	64	55	6	7	4	7	71	0	83	16	4
Creek, Ryan, Jackson	9	7	.563	3.63	26	24	1	1	1	0	143.2	137	622	74	58	11	6	8	6	64	0	120	12	2
Corps, Edwin, Shreveport	13	6	.684	3.86	27	27	2	0	0	0	165.2	195	712	80	71	16	2	6	8	41	2	53	4	2
Wiley, Chad, Tulsa	6	9	.400	3.89	26	23	0	0	2	0	159.2	165	672	78	69	19	5	3	6	52	3	69	6	4

DEPARTMENTAL LEADERS: W—Corps, Rath, 13; L—Narcisse, 14; Pct.—Rath, .813; G—Montgomery, 55; GS—Hancock, 28; CG—Hancock, 5; ShO—Badorek, Bourgeois, 2; GF—Montgomery, 53; Sv.—Montgomery, 36; IP—Hancock, 175.2; H—Hancock, 222; TBF—Hancock, 764; R—Hancock, 107; ER—Hancock, 89; HR—Wiley, 19; SH—Narcisse, 10; SF—Browne, Prado, Rodriguez, 9; HB—Several pitchers tied with 10; BB—Rodriguez, 80; IBB—Maloney, 9; SO—Rodriguez, 129; WP—Schmidt, 18; Bk.—J. Martinez, Wiley, 4.

ALL PITCHERS

*Lefthanded pitcher.

Pitcher, Team	W	L	Pct.	ERA	G	GS	CG	ShO	GF	Sv.	IP	H	TBF	R	ER	HR	SH	SF	HB	BB	IBB	SO	WP	Bk.
Akerfelds, Darrel, Midland	3	1	.750	3.44	29	1	0	0	5	0	55.0	46	235	21	21	3	1	2	6	26	3	16	2	0
Alkire, Jeff, Arkansas*	0	0	.000	3.00	2	0	0	0	0	0	3.0	4	13	1	1	0	1	0	0	0	0	2	1	0
Allen, Ron, Jackson	2	0	1.000	5.91	4	0	0	0	0	0	10.2	13	49	7	7	0	2	2	0	5	1	3	0	0
Anderson, Paul, Arkansas	1	0	1.000	3.26	38	1	0	0	15	0	58.0	60	243	27	21	1	4	2	1	11	1	31	5	1
Archer, Kurt, El Paso	0	0	.000	3.00	4	0	0	0	2	1	6.0	4	24	2	2	0	0	0	0	1	0	5	0	0
Arrandale, Matt, Arkansas	3	5	.375	3.28	47	3	0	0	23	2	68.2	72	296	28	25	1	2	2	1	22	4	28	1	0
Atkinson, Neil, Wichita*	3	0	1.000	4.80	40	0	0	0	8	1	50.2	52	223	29	27	7	1	2	1	21	2	32	3	1
Badorek, Mike, Arkansas	7	5	.583	4.35	18	17	4	2	1	1	101.1	119	446	61	49	4	4	5	3	30	0	50	2	0
Bevil, Brian, Wichita	5	7	.417	5.84	15	15	0	0	0	0	74.0	85	334	51	48	7	0	3	3	35	0	57	7	0
Bluma, Jaime, Wichita	4	3	.571	3.09	42	0	0	0	40	22	55.1	38	214	19	19	9	3	1	1	9	2	31	1	0
Blyleven, Todd, Midland	3	1	.750	5.02	8	0	0	0	2	0	14.1	13	57	8	8	1	2	2	0	3	1	8	0	1
Bonanno, Rob, Midland	1	1	.500	9.45	3	3	0	0	0	0	13.1	24	68	16	14	5	0	1	0	6	0	6	0	0
Bourgeois, Steve, Shreveport	12	3	.800	2.85	22	22	2	2	0	0	145.1	140	604	50	46	8	4	5	4	53	1	91	11	1
Bovee, Mike, Wichita	8	6	.571	4.18	20	20	1	0	0	0	114.0	118	486	60	53	12	2	4	2	43	0	72	4	0
Brannon, Cliff, Shreveport	0	0	.000	5.40	3	1	0	0	0	0	10.0	13	47	7	6	0	1	0	0	4	0	7	2	2
Brewer, Nevin, Wichita	3	2	.600	3.96	19	4	1	1	4	0	50.0	54	218	31	22	6	0	1	1	21	1	21	9	1
Brewington, Jamie, Shreveport	8	3	.727	3.06	16	16	1	1	0	0	88.1	72	376	39	30	8	2	7	0	55	0	74	4	0
Bridges, Kary, Jackson	0	0	.000	9.00	1	0	0	0	1	0	1.0	1	4	1	1	1	0	0	0	0	0	1	0	0
Brosnan, Jason, San Antonio*	1	0	1.000	3.57	19	0	0	0	7	2	22.2	24	94	9	9	1	1	0	0	4	0	21	1	0
Brown, Willard, Midland	9	10	.474	5.18	27	27	2	0	0	0	147.2	188	651	92	85	17	9	3	9	47	1	80	9	0
Browne, Byron, El Paso	10	4	.714	3.43	25	20	2	1	3	0	126.0	106	541	55	48	7	3	9	6	78	2	110	7	0
Browning, Tom, Wichita*	1	0	1.000	7.50	1	1	0	0	0	0	6.0	10	28	5	5	0	0	2	0	1	0	5	0	0
Brunson, William, San Anton.*	4	5	.444	4.95	14	14	0	0	0	0	80.0	105	356	46	44	4	3	1	4	22	0	44	5	1
Busby, Mike, Arkansas	7	6	.538	3.29	20	20	1	0	0	0	134.0	125	565	63	49	8	3	3	6	35	1	95	5	0
Butler, Mike, Midland*	1	1	.500	4.50	19	0	0	0	7	0	24.0	24	104	12	12	4	0	2	2	9	1	14	0	0
Camacho, Dan, San Antonio	1	1	.500	1.59	11	0	0	0	10	2	11.1	9	47	2	2	0	0	0	0	8	0	8	2	0
Carpenter, Brian, Arkansas	2	1	.667	4.96	17	4	0	0	1	0	52.2	57	232	32	29	6	6	2	3	21	1	35	1	1
Caruso, Gene, El Paso*	2	1	.667	6.08	46	1	0	0	19	2	71.0	87	331	55	48	6	3	2	3	36	3	53	4	0
Castillo, Felipe, Tulsa	2	2	.500	3.82	14	0	0	0	5	0	33.0	42	147	19	14	2	2	0	1	11	1	16	3	0
Castillo, Juan, Jackson	4	4	.500	4.01	12	12	0	0	0	0	67.1	68	301	39	30	5	2	1	7	27	0	38	4	0
Castillo, Mariano, Shreveport	3	1	.750	3.13	22	0	0	0	4	0	37.1	38	161	17	13	4	4	0	0	13	3	31	0	0
Castro, Nelson, San Antonio	5	7	.417	5.20	48	1	0	0	14	3	81.1	98	360	51	47	5	4	3	1	30	1	51	5	0
Cather, Mike, Tulsa	0	2	.000	3.32	18	0	0	0	12	0	21.2	20	90	11	8	0	4	1	1	7	5	15	0	0
Chavez, Tony, Midland	0	1	.000	8.00	7	0	0	0	6	2	9.0	13	42	9	8	1	0	0	1	1	0	4	1	0
Cimorelli, Frank, El Paso	0	0	.000	4.50	2	0	0	0	0	0	2.0	1	11	1	1	0	0	1	2	2	0	0	0	0
Cole, Jim, El Paso	1	4	.200	8.75	6	6	0	0	0	0	23.2	42	121	28	23	3	0	3	0	11	0	14	1	1
Connolly, Chris, Wichita*	1	0	1.000	5.68	13	0	0	0	2	0	12.2	18	64	11	8	0	1	1	2	11	0	2	2	0
Corona, John, Arkansas*	1	1	.500	7.20	5	0	0	0	2	0	5.0	7	28	5	4	0	1	0	1	6	1	3	0	0
Corps, Edwin, Shreveport	13	6	.684	3.86	27	27	2	0	0	0	165.2	195	712	80	71	16	2	6	8	41	2	53	4	2

Pitcher, Team	W	L	Pct.	ERA	G	GS	CG	ShO	GF	Sv.	IP	H	TBF	R	ER	HR	SH	SF	HB	BB	IBB	SO	WP	Bk.
Correa, Ramser, San Antonio	1	4	.200	4.53	42	0	0	0	32	17	49.2	54	221	29	25	5	0	2	0	21	0	34	4	0
Creek, Doug, Arkansas*	4	2	.667	2.88	26	0	0	0	11	1	34.1	24	143	12	11	4	3	0	3	16	2	50	1	0
Creek, Ryan, Jackson	9	7	.563	3.63	26	24	1	1	1	0	143.2	137	622	74	58	11	6	8	6	64	0	120	12	2
Cummings, John, San Antonio*	0	2	.000	3.95	6	5	0	0	0	0	27.1	28	113	13	12	0	2	1	1	7	0	13	3	2
Davidson, Jackie, Tulsa	0	2	.000	21.86	2	2	0	0	0	0	7.0	21	42	18	17	1	0	0	0	1	0	5	0	0
Davis, Jeff, Tulsa	1	0	1.000	0.00	1	1	0	0	0	0	7.0	2	24	0	0	0	0	0	0	1	0	4	1	0
Davis, Ray, Arkansas	7	6	.538	4.50	21	18	0	0	1	0	110.0	112	467	67	55	14	5	5	4	30	0	70	6	1
Dorlarque, Aaron, Wichita	1	1	.500	1.15	20	1	0	0	4	0	47.0	37	179	8	6	2	2	0	3	10	4	32	2	0
Dreyer, Steve, Tulsa	2	4	.333	2.89	10	10	1	0	0	0	62.1	56	252	22	20	6	2	1	2	19	1	48	4	0
Duda, Steve, El Paso	1	3	.250	4.87	24	4	0	0	7	1	44.1	58	212	33	24	0	2	2	5	16	1	29	0	0
Duey, Kyle, Jackson	0	2	.000	5.40	7	0	0	0	6	2	6.2	11	32	4	4	1	1	0	0	2	0	4	0	0
Duncan, Chip, Tulsa	2	1	.667	3.00	17	1	0	0	11	1	36.0	34	153	12	12	2	1	0	1	17	6	31	4	0
Eddy, Chris, Wichita*	1	0	1.000	4.00	9	0	0	0	5	1	9.0	8	38	4	4	1	0	0	1	3	0	10	0	0
Edsell, Geoff, Midland	2	3	.400	5.91	5	5	1	0	0	0	32.0	39	140	26	21	5	1	2	0	16	0	19	5	0
Escamilla, Jaime, Tulsa*	0	0	.000	1.80	4	0	0	0	0	0	5.0	6	23	4	1	1	0	0	0	2	0	5	1	0
Estes, Shawn, Shreveport*	2	0	1.000	2.01	4	4	0	0	0	0	22.1	14	90	5	5	1	0	1	3	10	0	18	3	0
Evans, Bart, Wichita	0	4	.000	10.48	7	7	0	0	0	0	22.1	22	123	28	26	3	1	0	1	45	0	13	7	1
Evans, Dave, Jackson	2	9	.182	3.33	49	0	0	0	37	18	67.2	50	278	29	25	2	5	3	4	28	6	54	0	1
Frontera, Chad, Shreveport	3	5	.375	4.17	20	13	0	0	2	1	82.0	88	368	45	38	9	2	3	6	39	0	52	2	0
Fyhrie, Mike, Wichita	3	2	.600	3.04	17	9	0	0	3	1	74.0	76	312	31	25	4	1	1	1	23	0	41	3	1
Gallaher, Kevin, Jackson	2	2	.500	3.40	6	6	1	0	0	0	42.1	31	179	18	16	1	3	1	0	23	1	28	4	0
Gamez, Francisco, El Paso	2	1	.667	5.29	27	8	0	0	6	2	68.0	79	316	46	40	8	5	2	4	39	5	33	6	0
Ganote, Joe, El Paso	5	1	.833	1.61	12	7	0	0	1	1	50.1	40	207	18	9	3	2	1	3	16	0	39	4	0
Garcia, Jose, San Antonio	2	6	.250	4.03	38	0	0	0	15	2	58.0	50	242	32	26	4	4	4	6	24	0	36	6	2
Geeve, Dave, Tulsa	3	8	.273	5.17	15	14	3	1	0	0	94.0	108	400	61	54	16	1	2	2	20	0	38	1	0
Gerstein, Ron, El Paso*	8	12	.400	4.55	28	22	1	0	2	1	126.2	155	584	90	64	14	4	6	2	58	3	69	4	1
Granger, Jeff, Wichita*	4	7	.364	5.93	18	18	0	0	0	0	95.2	122	439	76	63	9	3	4	1	40	0	81	10	0
Grundy, Phil, Wichita	1	1	.500	8.31	6	2	0	0	1	0	17.1	16	75	17	16	6	1	1	1	7	0	11	3	0
Grzanich, Mike, Jackson	5	3	.625	2.74	50	0	0	0	23	8	65.2	55	276	22	20	0	5	3	6	38	5	44	4	0
Guerrero, Mike, El Paso	0	0	.000	3.38	2	0	0	0	2	0	2.2	3	11	1	1	0	0	0	0	0	0	0	0	0
Hancock, Ryan, Midland	12	9	.571	4.56	28	28	5	1	0	0	175.2	222	764	107	89	17	5	4	8	45	1	79	7	3
Harris, Bryan, Midland*	6	5	.545	4.94	39	4	0	0	10	0	78.1	105	359	50	43	9	4	3	4	32	1	60	9	2
Harrison, Brian, Wichita	1	1	.500	4.73	15	0	0	0	5	2	26.2	35	120	18	14	1	1	1	1	7	1	11	0	0
Heredia, Wilson, Tulsa	4	2	.667	3.18	8	7	1	1	1	1	45.1	42	194	19	16	4	3	1	2	21	3	34	1	3
Herges, Matt, San Antonio	0	3	.000	4.88	19	0	0	0	13	8	27.2	34	130	16	15	2	3	0	0	16	1	18	3	0
Hingle, Larry, Jackson*	0	2	.000	11.12	9	0	0	0	1	0	11.1	11	58	15	14	1	2	1	0	15	1	5	7	1
Holdridge, David, Midland	1	0	1.000	1.78	14	0	0	0	11	1	25.1	20	100	8	5	1	1	0	1	8	0	23	2	0
Holt, Chris, Jackson	2	2	.500	1.67	5	5	1	1	0	0	32.1	27	126	8	6	2	1	0	0	5	1	24	1	0
Hubbs, Dan, San Antonio	2	1	.667	3.54	31	0	0	0	6	0	61.0	58	248	25	24	3	3	1	1	16	0	52	0	1
Humphrey, Rich, Jackson	1	1	.500	1.69	9	0	0	0	1	0	16.0	11	66	5	3	0	2	1	0	9	2	9	1	0
Hyde, Rich, Shreveport	5	1	.833	3.89	33	0	0	0	16	7	44.0	48	188	21	19	2	1	1	4	10	3	24	1	0
Jones, Stacy, El Paso	1	1	.500	2.03	8	0	0	0	5	3	13.1	12	58	7	3	0	1	0	0	4	0	14	1	0
Kappesser, Bob, El Paso	0	0	.000	9.28	8	0	0	0	7	0	10.2	18	56	11	11	3	0	1	1	5	0	2	0	1
Keling, Korey, Midland	8	5	.615	3.46	29	12	1	1	7	1	122.1	113	518	53	47	7	0	1	1	52	3	101	9	2
Kellner, Frank, Jackson	0	0	.000	4.50	1	0	0	0	0	0	2.0	3	10	1	1	0	0	0	0	1	0	1	0	0
Ketchen, Doug, Jackson	3	3	.500	3.59	15	5	0	0	5	1	52.2	55	216	23	21	5	0	0	1	15	0	45	8	0
Keusch, Joseph, Tulsa	0	0	.000	0.00	2	0	0	0	2	0	2.2	1	10	0	0	0	0	0	0	0	0	0	0	0
Kimel, Jack, Tulsa*	2	2	.500	7.32	17	2	0	0	5	0	35.2	52	181	33	29	7	1	3	0	23	2	10	0	0
Kloek, Kevin, El Paso	7	11	.389	4.93	28	27	3	1	0	0	157.0	196	699	103	86	6	2	5	10	48	0	121	12	0
Knox, Kerry, Tulsa*	2	2	.500	3.41	5	4	0	0	1	0	29.0	28	124	12	11	2	1	0	1	9	1	14	2	0
Kosenski, John, El Paso	3	1	.750	5.72	16	0	0	0	6	0	28.1	41	141	19	18	1	1	1	2	17	2	25	4	0
Lacy, Kerry, Tulsa	2	7	.222	4.28	28	7	0	0	16	9	82.0	94	363	47	39	5	3	3	3	39	7	49	7	0
Langbehn, Gregg, El Paso*	2	1	.667	5.24	16	0	0	0	3	0	22.1	19	97	16	13	6	0	2	1	12	1	20	2	0
Lidle, Cory, El Paso	5	4	.556	3.36	45	9	0	0	12	2	109.2	126	480	52	41	6	6	1	6	36	3	78	6	0
Linares, Yfrain, El Paso	1	1	.500	9.45	8	0	0	0	1	0	13.1	21	70	15	14	1	0	2	1	12	1	9	2	0
Lister, Martin, Jackson*	4	3	.571	4.00	15	13	1	1	1	0	69.2	80	299	35	31	2	3	2	1	24	0	27	6	0
Long, Tony, Arkansas*	4	4	.500	3.74	32	0	0	0	8	0	55.1	58	241	28	23	5	3	3	2	14	0	35	0	1
Lowe, Sean, Arkansas	9	8	.529	4.88	24	24	0	0	0	0	129.0	143	578	84	70	2	5	4	5	64	0	77	9	0
Mack, Tony, Midland	0	0	.000	0.00	3	0	0	0	0	0	5.2	3	21	0	0	0	1	0	0	1	0	5	0	0
Maloney, Sean, El Paso	7	5	.583	4.18	43	0	0	0	27	15	64.2	69	292	41	30	4	4	4	3	28	9	54	5	0
Marshall, Jason, Wichita	0	0	.000	9.00	1	0	0	0	1	0	1.0	4	6	1	1	1	0	0	0	0	0	0	0	0
Martin, Jerry, Tulsa	3	7	.300	5.18	22	17	0	0	1	0	88.2	100	405	55	51	12	4	3	2	51	1	46	7	0
Martinez, Francisco, Arkansas	1	1	.500	1.29	11	0	0	0	4	1	21.0	10	80	3	3	0	3	1	1	7	1	13	2	0
Martinez, Jesus, San Antonio*	6	9	.400	3.54	24	24	1	0	0	0	139.2	129	603	64	55	6	7	4	7	71	0	83	16	4
Martinez, Ramiro, Tulsa*	0	5	.000	5.17	13	5	0	0	0	0	47.0	53	220	29	27	5	0	3	1	34	2	37	3	0
Matranga, Jeff, Arkansas	0	0	.000	0.00	7	0	0	0	4	0	8.0	1	27	0	0	0	0	0	0	3	0	4	0	0
McDill, Allen, Wichita*	1	0	1.000	2.11	12	1	0	0	5	1	21.1	16	85	7	5	2	0	0	1	5	0	20	1	0
McLain, Mike, Shreveport	2	1	.667	3.12	11	0	0	0	4	1	17.1	13	66	7	6	1	1	0	1	3	0	11	0	0
Mercado, Hector, Jackson*	1	4	.200	7.80	8	7	0	0	0	0	30.0	36	157	33	26	5	2	1	2	32	1	20	4	0
Mesewicz, Mark, Arkansas*	0	1	.000	6.75	5	0	0	0	1	0	9.1	13	41	7	7	0	2	0	0	1	1	7	0	0
Mlicki, Doug, Jackson	8	3	.727	2.79	16	16	2	0	0	0	96.2	73	390	41	30	6	1	2	4	33	0	72	5	0
Montgomery, Steve, Arkansas	5	2	.714	3.25	55	0	0	0	53	36	61.0	52	259	22	22	6	7	1	4	22	6	56	5	1
Montoya, Norm, El Paso*	2	5	.286	3.42	51	0	0	0	9	2	76.1	88	330	36	29	3	5	2	2	18	5	43	4	0
Moody, Ritchie, Tulsa*	0	1	.000	6.97	11	0	0	0	5	0	20.2	24	94	18	16	2	1	1	1	18	1	9	2	0
Morones, Geno, Wichita	3	6	.333	4.10	17	16	0	0	0	0	79.0	85	353	49	36	5	4	6	3	39	0	32	3	0
Morvay, Joe, Tulsa	5	8	.385	5.21	37	0	0	0	28	8	65.2	82	305	45	38	4	6	1	4	28	6	30	4	0
Narcisse, Tyrone, Jackson	5	14	.263	3.24	27	27	2	0	0	0	163.2	140	686	76	59	8	10	8	10	60	5	93	8	0
Nieves, Ernesto, Midland	0	1	.000	4.05	6	1	0	0	1	0	13.1	15	62	7	6	1	2	1	1	10	1	3	1	0
Oehrlein, Dave, Arkansas*	4	7	.364	4.87	23	10	1	0	4	0	77.2	80	338	48	42	6	5	2	4	28	1	52	5	0
Oropesa, Eddie, San Antonio*	1	1	.500	3.12	16	0	0	0	7	1	17.1	22	87	8	6	2	1	2	3	12	1	16	0	1
Osborne, Donovan, Arkansas*	0	1	.000	2.45	2	2	0	0	0	0	11.0	12	46	4	3	0	0	0	1	2	0	6	0	0
Paskievitch, Tom, Wichita	1	1	.500	5.06	5	0	0	0	1	0	5.1	6	21	3	3	1	0	1	0	2	0	3	1	0
Patterson, Danny, Tulsa	2	2	.500	6.19	26	0	0	0	22	5	36.1	45	163	27	25	2	0	1	2	13	2	24	5	0

Pitcher, Team	W	L	Pct.	ERA	G	GS	CG	ShO	GF	Sv.	IP	H	TBF	R	ER	HR	SH	SF	HB	BB	IBB	SO	WP	Bk.
Perez, David, Tulsa	3	2	.600	5.24	8	7	0	0	0	0	46.1	49	204	30	27	5	5	0	1	18	2	25	1	0
Peterson, Mark, Shreveport*	4	3	.571	1.27	37	0	0	0	14	2	64.0	51	248	15	9	2	2	5	4	6	2	38	0	0
Pickett, Ricky, Shreveport*	2	0	1.000	1.71	14	0	0	0	9	3	21.0	9	82	5	4	1	0	1	0	9	0	23	2	0
Popplewell, Tom, El Paso	0	0	.000	15.00	4	0	0	0	0	0	3.0	7	21	5	5	0	0	0	1	6	0	1	2	0
Pote, Lou, Shreveport	2	2	.500	5.33	28	0	0	0	11	3	50.2	53	226	41	30	8	4	1	0	26	1	30	4	0
Powell, John, Tulsa	1	4	.200	3.89	7	7	0	0	0	0	39.1	45	174	21	17	9	0	1	2	16	0	27	1	1
Prado, Jose, San Antonio	7	11	.389	3.48	28	22	0	0	3	1	144.2	126	621	70	56	9	7	9	7	64	0	93	13	2
Pricher, John, Midland	0	0	.000	4.50	8	0	0	0	6	1	10.0	16	48	7	5	1	0	1	0	6	0	7	0	0
Purdy, Shawn, Shreveport	6	3	.667	3.75	52	1	0	0	40	21	62.1	61	260	31	26	7	1	3	1	18	2	33	3	0
Pyc, Dave, San Antonio*	12	6	.667	3.38	26	26	1	0	0	0	157.0	170	676	72	59	6	6	4	3	49	1	78	3	1
Ralston, Kris, Wichita	9	4	.692	3.56	18	16	0	0	0	0	93.2	85	389	40	37	10	3	2	7	28	0	84	6	0
Ratekin, Mark, Midland	0	0	.000	5.94	11	0	0	0	4	0	16.2	19	72	12	11	1	0	2	2	3	0	11	2	0
Rath, Gary, San Antonio*	13	3	.813	2.77	18	18	3	1	0	0	117.0	96	483	42	36	6	3	2	4	48	0	81	4	2
Rawitzer, Kevin, Wichita*	6	4	.600	5.25	28	3	0	0	7	1	48.0	48	209	30	28	4	0	2	1	19	0	42	1	0
Ray, Ken, Wichita	4	5	.444	5.97	14	14	0	0	0	0	75.1	83	342	55	50	7	1	0	1	46	0	53	8	1
Renko, Steve, Midland	3	5	.375	4.81	22	9	0	0	4	1	76.2	100	352	51	41	3	2	5	0	28	2	44	5	0
Richey, Jeff, Shreveport	1	2	.333	2.45	8	0	0	0	4	1	22.0	20	94	7	6	0	2	0	1	8	3	11	3	0
Rodriguez, Frankie, El Paso	9	8	.529	4.98	28	27	1	0	1	0	142.2	157	650	90	79	9	9	9	5	80	2	129	16	1
Santana, Julio, Tulsa	6	4	.600	3.15	15	15	3	0	0	0	103.0	91	438	40	36	8	2	4	0	52	2	71	8	1
Schmidt, Jeff, Midland	4	12	.250	5.83	20	20	0	0	0	0	100.1	127	466	75	65	12	2	4	5	48	1	46	18	1
Schooler, Mike, Midland	3	3	.500	1.79	54	0	0	0	47	20	65.1	49	257	16	13	5	5	4	0	19	3	55	5	0
Sebach, Kyle, Midland	1	2	.333	10.31	5	5	0	0	0	0	18.1	31	93	24	21	1	2	2	3	12	0	7	3	0
Sepeda, Jaime, Jackson	0	1	.000	9.00	1	1	0	0	0	0	4.0	7	21	4	4	0	0	1	0	2	0	1	0	0
Sheehan, Chris, Wichita	0	2	.000	5.51	31	0	0	0	10	2	50.2	51	221	35	31	5	4	2	2	16	6	31	5	0
Simmons, Scott, Arkansas*	11	9	.550	3.43	22	22	1	1	0	0	139.0	145	569	66	53	9	5	6	1	28	1	73	5	0
Smith, Scotty, Tulsa	5	8	.385	6.02	29	13	1	0	12	0	101.2	144	469	83	68	15	3	6	2	31	4	38	5	0
Snyder, John, Midland	8	9	.471	5.74	21	21	4	0	0	0	133.1	158	591	93	85	12	3	6	10	48	1	81	7	3
Soderstrom, Steve, Shreveport	9	5	.643	3.41	22	22	0	0	0	0	116.0	106	508	53	44	6	5	2	10	51	0	91	12	2
Strange, Don, Wichita	0	1	.000	1.50	24	0	0	0	17	8	36.0	28	136	7	6	2	0	1	0	7	0	36	5	0
Taulbee, Andy, Shreveport	4	5	.444	3.95	14	14	1	1	0	0	86.2	107	388	47	38	5	6	3	3	27	2	38	3	1
Thibert, John, Midland	0	0	.000	4.18	12	0	0	0	5	2	23.2	19	104	12	11	1	0	1	2	17	0	15	3	0
Toth, Robert, Wichita	8	4	.667	2.17	21	9	1	0	2	0	103.2	95	427	30	25	6	3	3	4	27	1	77	6	1
Troutman, Keith, San Antonio	1	2	.333	3.15	38	0	0	0	22	2	65.2	64	268	24	23	3	1	3	1	18	1	50	3	0
Valdez, Carlos, Shreveport	3	2	.600	1.27	22	3	0	0	8	5	64.0	40	240	11	9	0	1	0	3	14	2	51	1	0
Vanderweele, Doug, Shreveport	5	2	.714	2.52	13	9	0	0	0	0	64.1	61	253	18	18	3	1	0	2	13	0	22	3	0
VanRyn, Ben, Midland*	1	1	.500	2.78	19	0	0	0	8	1	32.1	33	133	10	10	4	0	0	2	12	0	24	2	0
Wagner, Billy, Jackson*	2	2	.500	2.57	12	12	0	0	0	0	70.0	49	288	25	20	7	1	1	4	36	1	77	4	1
Wagner, Bret, Arkansas*	1	2	.333	3.19	6	6	0	0	0	0	36.2	34	161	14	13	1	1	1	0	18	0	31	3	0
Wagner, Joe, El Paso	0	4	.000	9.95	5	5	0	0	0	0	19.0	32	109	31	21	7	0	0	2	22	0	8	4	0
Waldron, Joe, Jackson*	1	2	.333	3.71	28	0	0	0	12	2	51.0	57	215	22	21	5	4	2	4	11	1	39	2	1
Walker, Jamie, Jackson*	4	2	.667	4.50	50	0	0	0	19	2	58.0	59	250	29	29	6	3	2	2	24	5	38	4	1
Wallace, Derek, Wichita	4	3	.571	4.40	26	0	0	0	18	6	43.0	51	188	23	21	5	1	1	2	13	4	24	3	0
Wanke, Chuck, Shreveport*	2	3	.400	4.35	43	0	0	0	17	0	41.1	35	183	23	20	1	0	1	5	22	0	40	2	0
Waring, Jim, Jackson	1	4	.200	8.01	17	5	0	0	5	2	51.2	77	243	49	46	7	3	2	3	15	2	27	2	0
Watson, Allen, Arkansas*	1	0	1.000	0.00	1	1	0	0	0	0	5.0	4	19	1	0	0	0	0	0	0	0	7	0	0
Watson, Ron, Midland	0	0	.000	4.91	3	0	0	0	0	0	3.2	2	17	2	2	0	0	0	0	6	0	3	3	0
Weaver, Eric, San Antonio	8	11	.421	4.07	27	26	1	0	1	0	141.2	147	635	83	64	10	9	7	7	72	1	105	8	2
Webb, Doug, El Paso	2	1	.667	4.42	18	0	0	0	16	8	18.1	11	77	9	9	3	1	1	0	13	1	11	2	0
Wheeler, Earl, Tulsa	1	1	.500	5.40	5	0	0	0	3	0	8.1	14	41	8	5	1	0	1	0	2	0	6	2	0
Whitaker, Steve, Shreveport*	2	0	1.000	3.86	4	3	0	0	0	0	16.1	17	70	8	7	0	1	0	0	10	0	10	1	0
White, Chad, Jackson	0	0	.000	18.00	1	0	0	0	0	0	1.0	1	6	2	2	0	0	0	0	2	0	0	1	0
White, Chris, Jackson	6	3	.667	5.09	38	2	0	0	15	0	70.2	71	311	45	40	10	1	3	5	24	4	45	4	2
Wiley, Chad, Tulsa	6	9	.400	3.89	26	23	0	0	2	0	159.2	165	672	78	69	19	5	3	6	52	3	69	6	4
Witasick, Jay, Arkansas	2	4	.333	6.88	7	7	0	0	0	0	34.0	46	161	29	26	4	0	0	0	16	1	26	2	0

COMBINATION SHUTOUTS: **Arkansas (4)**—Lowe-Arrandale-Montgomery, Lowe-Long, Simmons-Montgomery, Witasick-Long-Anderson. **El Paso (2)**—Gamez-Browne, Lidle-Montoya-Duda. **Jackson (4)**—Gallaher-Walker, Lister-Grzanich-Evans, Wagner-Grzanich, Waring-Waldron-Evans. **Midland (1)**—Brown-Schooler. **San Antonio (4)**—Castro-Hubbs-Brosnan-Correa, Martinez-Castro-Correa, Martinez-Correa, Rath-Correa. **Shreveport (10)**—Corps-Hyde 2, Corps-Purdy 2, Bourgeois-Frontera, Brewington-Richey-Purdy, Corps-Valdez, Estes-Hyde-Purdy, Soderstrom-Castillo-Purdy, Soderstrom-Whitaker-Purdy. **Tulsa (4)**—Dreyer-Smith, Heredia-Morvay, Santana-Lacy, Smith-Cather. **Wichita (4)**—Morones-Atkinson-Wallace, Ralston-Fyhrie, Ralston-Strange, Ralston-Wallace.

NO-HIT GAMES: None.

1995 FIELDING

TEAM

Team	Pct.	G	PO	A	E	TC	DP	PB
Shreveport	.975	135	3663	1578	136	5377	150	17
Jackson	.973	135	3557	1538	144	5239	144	25
San Antonio	.972	136	3606	1568	148	5322	137	17
Arkansas	.971	135	3462	1621	154	5237	125	7
Midland	.971	136	3589	1624	158	5371	169	20
Tulsa	.969	135	3532	1549	162	5243	143	12
Wichita	.968	136	3635	1511	169	5315	125	11
El Paso	.960	136	3598	1552	213	5363	136	23

TRIPLE PLAYS: None.

INDIVIDUAL

FIRST BASEMEN

NOTE: All caps denotes fielding-percentage leader based on 68 games for catchers, 91 for all other non-pitchers and 136 innings for pitchers. *Throws lefthanded.

Player, Team	Pct.	G	PO	A	E	TC	DP
Anderson, Charlie, Arkansas	.986	13	65	6	1	72	5
Bagwell, Jeff, Jackson	1.000	3	24	6	0	30	3
Banks, Brian, El Paso	.975	5	37	2	1	40	1
Boykin, Tyrone, Midland	.980	19	131	17	3	151	14
Charles, Frank, Tulsa	.984	123	1108	73	19	1200	117
Cholowsky, Dan, Arkansas	.979	32	263	22	6	291	22
Clinton, Jim, Tulsa	.972	7	64	5	2	71	7
Colon, Dennis, Jackson	.985	101	892	79	15	986	89
Dodson, Bo, El Paso*	1.000	11	100	7	0	107	12
Fasano, Sal, Wichita	.982	35	303	30	6	339	36

Player, Team	Pct.	G	PO	A	E	TC	DP
Florez, Tim, Shreveport	.875	1	7	0	1	8	1
Glenn, Leon, Midland	.988	110	1009	60	13	1082	112
Greene, Todd, Midland	1.000	2	3	0	0	3	0
Groppuso, Mike, Jackson	1.000	8	56	4	0	60	4
Guerrero, Mike, El Paso	1.000	1	1	0	0	1	0
Guerrero, Pedro, Midland	.895	2	16	1	2	19	1
Hatcher, Chris, Jackson	1.000	3	28	4	0	32	1
Kellner, Frank, Jackson	1.000	23	200	17	0	217	20
Kennedy, Darryl, Tulsa	1.000	1	2	0	0	2	0
Landry, Todd, El Paso*	.989	121	1014	123	13	1150	101
Lewis, Anthony, Arkansas*	.917	3	20	2	2	24	1
LoDuca, Paul, San Antonio	1.000	2	7	0	0	7	1
Long, Kevin, Wichita*	.970	4	31	1	1	33	1
Lopez, Pedro, El Paso	.875	5	6	1	1	8	1
Luce, Roger, Jackson	1.000	1	9	1	0	10	0
Marrero, Oreste, San Antonio*	.994	19	154	13	1	168	17
Marshall, Jason, Wichita	.989	11	82	4	1	87	5
MELENDEZ, Dan, San Antonio*	.997	120	1068	98	3	1169	103
Millan, Bernie, El Paso	1.000	3	2	0	0	2	0
Mirabelli, Doug, Shreveport	1.000	3	27	0	0	27	2
Montgomery, Ray, Jackson	.980	5	43	5	1	49	2
Montoya, Norm, El Paso*	1.000	1	1	0	0	1	0
Morrow, Chris, Shreveport*	1.000	2	19	2	0	21	0
Munoz, Orlando, Midland	1.000	3	23	3	0	26	4
Myers, Rod, Wichita*	.857	2	6	0	1	7	0
Nevers, Tom, El Paso	1.000	3	10	0	0	10	3
Norton, Chris, Arkansas	.980	5	47	2	1	50	6
Radziewicz, Doug, Arkansas*	.994	33	330	27	2	359	37
Raven, Luis, Midland	1.000	6	45	5	0	50	10
Redington, Tom, Midland	1.000	7	62	6	0	68	8
Richardson, Scott, El Paso	.750	1	3	0	1	4	0
Romero, Mandy, Wichita	.933	2	13	1	1	15	3
Rupp, Brian, Arkansas	.963	12	70	7	3	80	4
Simonton, Benji, Shreveport	1.000	9	81	5	0	86	11
Stewart, Andy, Wichita	.994	41	328	28	2	358	33
Sutko, Glenn, El Paso	1.000	2	3	1	0	4	0
Sutton, Larry, Wichita*	.986	52	452	25	7	484	39
Torres, Paul, Arkansas	.987	54	560	34	8	602	37
Turco, Frank, Tulsa	.932	8	35	6	3	44	5
Voigt, Jack, Tulsa	1.000	1	8	1	0	9	0
Warner, Ron, Arkansas	1.000	1	1	0	0	1	0
Williamson, Antone, El Paso	1.000	6	32	1	0	33	8
Wilson, Desi, Shreveport*	.992	118	1113	72	9	1194	112
Witkowski, Matt, Shreveport	.960	8	45	3	2	50	8
Woods, Kenny, Shreveport	1.000	3	21	0	0	21	5

SECOND BASEMEN

Player, Team	Pct.	G	PO	A	E	TC	DP
Berblinger, Jeff, Arkansas	.968	87	183	270	15	468	61
Bridges, Kary, Jackson	.975	68	118	198	8	324	42
Cairo, Miguel, San Antonio	.963	80	159	227	15	401	50
Canizaro, Jay, Shreveport	.965	105	228	295	19	542	84
Centeno, Henri, Jackson	.966	58	82	116	7	205	41
Diaz, Alfredo, Midland	1.000	3	5	4	0	9	2
Diaz, Lino, Wichita	.833	2	1	4	1	6	1
Dumas, Mike, El Paso	.960	5	12	12	1	25	1
Estrada, Osmani, Tulsa	1.000	5	12	16	0	28	6
Felix, Lauro, El Paso	.957	20	40	49	4	93	18
Florez, Tim, Shreveport	.977	42	65	102	4	171	23
Gonzales, Rene, Midland	.964	5	11	16	1	28	6
Griffin, Ty, Arkansas	.978	40	84	136	5	225	24
Guerrero, Mike, El Paso	1.000	1	2	2	0	4	0
Kappesser, Bob, El Paso	1.000	8	2	6	0	8	2
Kellner, Frank, Jackson	1.000	20	30	59	0	89	18
Lopez, Roberto, El Paso	.972	110	229	295	15	539	69
Marshall, Jason, Wichita	1.000	16	19	28	0	47	3
MARTINEZ, Ramon, Wichita	.984	100	182	299	8	489	67
McEwing, Joe, Arkansas	1.000	4	7	11	0	18	1
Medrano, Anthony, Wichita	.909	1	3	7	1	11	0
Millan, Bernie, El Paso	1.000	5	3	10	0	13	2
Mueller, Bill, Shreveport	1.000	2	5	1	0	6	0
Munoz, Orlando, Midland	.994	69	131	185	2	318	50
Nevers, Tom, Jac.-E.P.	.938	14	28	33	4	64	8
Odor, Rouglas, El Paso	.833	1	1	4	1	6	1
Ortiz, Bo, Midland	1.000	1	0	3	0	3	0
Ramirez, J.D., Midland	.974	62	143	200	9	352	42
Richardson, Scott, El Paso	.000	2	0	0	1	1	0
Rios, Eddie, San Antonio	.974	62	107	156	7	270	34
Sims, Wesley, Tulsa	1.000	1	3	2	0	5	1
Sisco, Steve, Wichita	.993	29	59	80	1	140	15
Smith, Mike, Tulsa	.982	131	310	412	13	735	94
Thompson, Fletcher, El Paso	1.000	6	13	26	0	39	3
Urso, Joe, Midland	.956	9	17	26	2	45	11
Warner, Ron, Arkansas	1.000	7	17	7	0	24	4
Witkowski, Matt, Shreveport	.966	4	12	16	1	29	5
Woods, Kenny, Shreveport	.857	1	3	3	1	7	1
Yard, Bruce, San Antonio	1.000	1	2	3	0	5	1

SECOND BASEMEN WITH TWO OR MORE TEAMS

Player, Team	Pct.	G	PO	A	E	TC	DP
Nevers, Tom, Jackson	.938	13	27	33	4	64	8
Nevers, Tom, El Paso	1.000	1	1	0	0	1	0

THIRD BASEMEN

Player, Team	Pct.	G	PO	A	E	TC	DP
Anderson, Charlie, Arkansas	.921	48	21	108	11	140	6
ARIAS, George, Midland	.936	129	127	300	29	456	40
Banks, Brian, El Paso	1.000	2	1	1	0	2	0
Blanco, Henry, San Antonio	.963	88	79	210	11	300	21
Centeno, Henri, Jackson	1.000	2	0	1	0	1	0
Diaz, Alfredo, Midland	1.000	1	1	4	0	5	0
Diaz, Lino, Wichita	.965	61	40	124	6	170	13
Donnels, Chris, Jackson	.929	4	6	7	1	14	0
Dumas, Mike, El Paso	.833	3	3	7	2	12	0
Edwards, Mike, Tulsa	.911	25	28	44	7	79	6
Estrada, Osmani, Tulsa	.926	92	73	164	19	256	17
Felix, Lauro, El Paso	.951	16	5	34	2	41	4
Florez, Tim, Shreveport	.920	48	22	81	9	112	12
Forkner, Tim, Jackson	.900	34	27	63	10	100	8
Glenn, Leon, Midland	.889	3	3	5	1	9	0
Griffin, Ty, Arkansas	.818	17	7	29	8	44	0
Groppuso, Mike, Jackson	.965	15	14	41	2	57	3
Guerrero, Mike, El Paso	.333	2	0	1	2	3	0
Gulan, Mike, Arkansas	.929	63	33	150	14	197	12
Kappesser, Bob, El Paso	.882	11	4	11	2	17	0
Kellner, Frank, Jackson	.919	21	12	22	3	37	2
LoDuca, Paul, San Antonio	.833	2	0	5	1	6	0
Long, Ryan, Wichita	.912	69	43	134	17	194	6
Marshall, Jason, Wichita	.929	9	2	11	1	14	1
Millan, Bernie, El Paso	.833	2	2	3	1	6	0
Mora, Melvin, Jackson	.667	1	0	2	1	3	0
Mueller, Bill, Shreveport	.977	85	47	168	5	220	13
Munoz, Orlando, Midland	.778	3	1	6	2	9	1
Nevers, Tom, Jac.-E.P.	.881	100	77	204	38	319	16
Otanez, Willis, San Antonio	.957	27	18	48	3	69	4
Parra, Franklin, Tulsa	.944	22	18	33	3	54	4
Raven, Luis, Midland	.929	4	4	9	1	14	1
Rios, Eddie, San Antonio	1.000	26	15	65	0	80	8
Rupp, Brian, Arkansas	.905	6	4	15	2	21	1
Sisco, Steve, Wichita	1.000	6	1	15	0	16	1
Stefanski, Mike, El Paso	.842	6	2	14	3	19	2
Stewart, Andy, Wichita	1.000	2	0	2	0	2	0
Thompson, Fletcher, El Paso	.714	3	2	3	2	7	1
Verduzco, Steven, Jackson	1.000	3	2	0	0	2	0
Warner, Ron, Arkansas	1.000	9	6	11	0	17	1
Weger, Wes, El Paso	1.000	1	0	3	0	3	0
Williamson, Antone, El Paso	.862	76	47	134	29	210	6
Witkowski, Matt, Shreveport	.833	2	1	4	1	6	0
Woods, Kenny, Shreveport	.895	21	14	37	6	57	2

THIRD BASEMEN WITH TWO OR MORE TEAMS

Player, Team	Pct.	G	PO	A	E	TC	DP
Nevers, Tom, Jackson	.907	68	57	158	22	237	13
Nevers, Tom, El Paso	.805	32	20	46	16	82	3

SHORTSTOPS

Player, Team	Pct.	G	PO	A	E	TC	DP
Alguacil, Jose, Shreveport	.750	1	2	1	1	4	1
Arias, George, Midland	1.000	1	1	0	0	1	0
Aurilia, Rich, Shreveport	.962	63	122	237	14	373	52
Bethea, Scott, Arkansas	.943	10	13	37	3	53	8
Cairo, Miguel, San Antonio	.946	30	51	89	8	148	22
Canizaro, Jay, Shreveport	.941	19	26	38	4	68	10
Centeno, Henri, Jackson	1.000	1	0	1	0	1	0
Clinton, Jim, Tulsa	1.000	2	1	4	0	5	1
Diaz, Alfredo, Midland	1.000	4	5	6	0	11	2
Dumas, Mike, El Paso	.818	2	5	4	2	11	1
Ehmann, Kurt, Shreveport	.973	38	53	126	5	184	23
Estrada, Osmani, Tulsa	.966	18	30	56	3	89	13
Felix, Lauro, El Paso	.939	47	71	99	11	181	24
Florez, Tim, Shreveport	.941	6	6	10	1	17	3
Frias, Hanley, Tulsa	.948	93	137	301	24	462	65
Guerrero, Mike, El Paso	.938	18	35	40	5	80	7
Guerrero, Wilton, San Antonio	.953	88	121	263	19	403	46
Harkrider, Timothy, Midland	.948	124	177	402	32	611	95
Jaime, Angel, San Antonio	.944	4	4	13	1	18	1

Player, Team	Pct.	G	PO	A	E	TC	DP
Johns, Keith, Arkansas	.952	111	159	354	26	539	66
JOHNSON, Russ, Jackson	.978	128	182	383	13	578	78
Kellner, Frank, Jackson	.933	7	12	16	2	30	4
Lopez, Roberto, El Paso	.909	6	4	6	1	11	0
Marshall, Jason, Wichita	.969	21	26	37	2	65	8
Martinez, Felix, Wichita	.922	125	222	371	50	643	76
Martinez, Gabby, El Paso	.949	43	65	103	9	177	27
Martinez, Ramon, Wichita	.941	2	4	12	1	17	1
Mercedes, Guillermo, Tulsa	.938	15	23	52	5	80	10
Metcalfe, Mike, San Antonio	.957	10	14	31	2	47	7
Munoz, Orlando, Midland	.949	13	16	40	3	59	6
Nevers, Tom, Jac.-E.P.	.947	7	7	11	1	19	3
Odor, Rouglas, El Paso	.962	5	11	14	1	26	6
Parra, Franklin, Tulsa	1.000	1	0	2	0	2	1
Pimentel, Wander, Arkansas	1.000	2	1	2	0	3	0
Sims, Wesley, Tulsa	.939	10	15	31	3	49	10
Warner, Ron, Arkansas	.939	22	31	62	6	99	14
Weger, Wes, El Paso	.931	37	62	100	12	174	16
Woods, Kenny, Shreveport	.906	21	32	55	9	96	12
Yard, Bruce, San Antonio	.950	9	19	19	2	40	6

SHORTSTOPS WITH TWO OR MORE TEAMS

Player, Team	Pct.	G	PO	A	E	TC	DP
Nevers, Tom, Jackson	1.000	5	5	8	0	13	1
Nevers, Tom, El Paso	.833	2	2	3	1	6	2

OUTFIELDERS

Player, Team	Pct.	G	PO	A	E	TC	DP
Anderson, Charlie, Arkansas	1.000	4	4	0	0	4	0
Banks, Brian, El Paso	.960	117	207	8	9	224	1
Boykin, Tyrone, Midland	.970	34	61	3	2	66	0
Bridges, Kary, Jackson	.955	28	39	3	2	44	0
Burton, Darren, Wichita	.963	41	73	4	3	80	1
Carvajal, Jovino, Midland	.983	79	161	10	3	174	2
Cholowsky, Dan, Arkansas	1.000	24	42	1	0	43	0
Christopher, Chris, Arkansas	.931	18	26	1	2	29	0
Clinton, Jim, Tulsa	1.000	14	13	1	0	14	1
Cohick, Emmitt, Midland*	.945	36	49	3	3	55	1
CRUZ, Jacob, Shreveport*	.996	114	235	16	1	252	2
Damon, Johnny, Wichita*	.984	108	296	11	5	312	2
Daniels, Moe, Midland	.962	24	46	4	2	52	2
Diggs, Tony, Arkansas	.972	71	164	8	5	177	0
Dodson, Bo, El Paso*	1.000	1	1	0	0	1	0
Felder, Ken, El Paso	.966	108	156	14	6	176	0
Glenn, Leon, Midland	1.000	5	9	1	0	10	0
Gonzalez, Raul, Wichita	.957	21	38	6	2	46	0
Hatcher, Chris, Jackson	.875	6	13	1	2	16	1
Hidalgo, Richard, Jackson	.981	129	238	14	5	257	3
Hosey, Steve, Midland	1.000	22	35	1	0	36	0
Hunter, Brian, Jackson	1.000	2	5	0	0	5	0
Jaime, Angel, San Antonio	1.000	4	3	0	0	3	0
Jenkins, Bernie, Shreveport	.833	4	5	0	1	6	0
Jenkins, Geoff, El Paso*	.857	21	41	1	7	49	0
Jones, Keith, Arkansas*	1.000	17	32	1	0	33	0
Landrum, Tito, San Antonio	.955	82	144	5	7	156	2
Landry, Todd, El Paso*	.875	17	13	1	2	16	0
Latham, Chris, San Antonio	.972	58	135	2	4	141	0
Lewis, Anthony, Arkansas*	1.000	77	105	4	0	109	0
Long, Kevin, Wichita*	.986	60	129	8	2	139	0
Long, Ryan, Wichita	1.000	22	40	1	0	41	0
Maness, Dwight, San Antonio	.952	55	156	1	8	165	0
Marrero, Oreste, San Antonio*	.984	34	60	0	1	61	0
Marshall, Jason, Wichita	1.000	3	3	0	0	3	0
Martin, Jim, San Antonio	.916	81	125	6	12	143	1
McEwing, Joe, Arkansas	1.000	30	54	1	0	55	1
McFarlin, Jason, Shreveport*	.956	64	84	3	4	91	1
McNabb, Buck, Jackson	1.000	13	23	0	0	23	0
Mitchell, Tony, Jackson	.933	73	118	7	9	134	2
Montgomery, Ray, Jackson	1.000	25	59	5	0	64	0
Mora, Melvin, Jackson	.981	119	244	14	5	263	6
Morrow, Chris, Shreveport*	1.000	56	90	4	0	94	1
Murphy, Steve, Wichita	.960	14	24	0	1	25	0
Murray, Calvin, Shreveport	.993	109	286	9	2	297	1
Myers, Rod, Wichita*	.967	129	256	8	9	273	2
Nicholas, Darrell, El Paso	.903	14	28	0	3	31	0
Nilsson, Dave, El Paso	1.000	5	4	0	0	4	0
Ortiz, Bo, Midland	.974	92	165	20	5	190	5
Parra, Franklin, Tulsa	.902	45	81	2	9	92	0
Puchales, Javier, San Antonio*	.963	18	22	4	1	27	0
Radziewicz, Doug, Arkansas*	1.000	3	4	1	0	5	0
Raven, Luis, Midland	.909	8	8	2	1	11	2
Reid, Derek, Shreveport	1.000	5	3	0	0	3	0
Richardson, Scott, El Paso	.958	75	109	5	5	119	3
Rodriques, Cecil, El Paso	.976	65	118	2	3	123	0
Romero, Willie, San Antonio	.966	103	215	14	8	237	6
Rupp, Brian, Arkansas	.929	7	13	0	1	14	0
Sagmoen, Marc, Tulsa*	.993	62	135	7	1	143	3
Samples, Todd, El Paso	1.000	1	3	0	0	3	0
Shabazz, Basil, El Paso	.938	40	53	8	4	65	1
Simonton, Benji, Shreveport	.938	18	29	1	2	32	1
Sisco, Steve, Wichita	1.000	2	2	0	0	2	0
Smiley, Rueben, Wichita*	.938	24	28	2	2	32	1
Stewart, Andy, Wichita	1.000	2	1	1	0	2	0
Strickland, Chad, Wichita	1.000	1	1	0	0	1	0
Texidor, Jose, Tulsa	.993	128	264	9	2	275	2
Thomas, Brian, Tulsa	.992	131	340	16	3	359	2
Torres, Paul, Arkansas	1.000	8	14	0	0	14	0
Turco, Frank, Tulsa	.987	36	66	8	1	75	2
Velez, Jose, Arkansas*	.972	95	130	8	4	142	2
Verduzco, Steven, Jackson	.818	6	9	0	2	11	0
Wesson, Barry, Jackson	1.000	2	3	0	0	3	0
White, Chad, Jackson	.981	30	51	1	1	53	0
Williams, Keith, Shreveport	.966	63	109	4	4	117	0
Wolff, Mike, Midland	.973	127	309	18	9	336	3
Woods, Kenny, Shreveport	.974	38	34	3	1	38	2
Young, Dmitri, Arkansas	.931	91	116	5	9	130	1

CATCHERS

Player, Team	Pct.	G	PO	A	E	TC	DP	PB
Banks, Brian, El Paso	.947	3	17	1	1	19	0	2
Blanco, Henry, San Antonio	1.000	1	2	0	0	2	0	0
Carpenter, Jerry, Midland	1.000	1	1	0	0	1	0	0
Chavez, Raul, Jackson	.987	55	316	52	5	373	8	7
Dandridge, Brad, San Antonio	1.000	2	9	0	0	9	0	1
DiFelice, Mike, Arkansas	.984	61	327	48	6	381	5	3
Ehmann, Kurt, Shreveport	.000	1	0	0	1	1	0	0
ELLIS, Paul, Arkansas	.998	76	408	39	1	448	5	4
Fasano, Sal, Wichita	.976	44	286	34	8	328	5	3
Gilmore, Tony, Jackson	.991	50	285	29	3	317	2	12
Glenn, Leon, Midland	1.000	1	6	1	0	7	0	0
Greene, Todd, Midland	.992	65	311	44	3	358	3	9
Hughes, Bobby, El Paso	.976	51	298	29	8	335	2	6
Jennings, Lance, Wichita	1.000	13	61	10	0	71	0	1
Jensen, Marcus, Shreveport	.991	89	471	70	5	546	5	11
Kappesser, Bob, El Paso	.975	35	157	37	5	199	0	7
Kennedy, Darryl, Tulsa	.979	59	280	43	7	330	6	5
LoDuca, Paul, San Antonio	.975	56	346	38	10	394	5	5
Lopez, Pedro, El Paso	.985	48	231	37	4	272	7	8
Luce, Roger, Jackson	.949	16	71	4	4	79	1	2
Luzinski, Ryan, San Antonio	.986	43	246	33	4	283	6	5
Mayes, Craig, Shreveport	1.000	3	11	4	0	15	0	0
Miller, Roger, Shreveport	.984	19	116	11	2	129	3	4
Mirabelli, Doug, Shreveport	.984	35	166	21	3	190	1	2
Monzon, Jose, Midland	.976	57	312	61	9	382	9	6
Nunez, Rogelio, Tulsa	.967	82	420	73	17	510	6	7
Probst, Alan, Jackson	.994	25	137	19	1	157	3	4
Romero, Mandy, Wichita	.982	26	146	17	3	166	1	1
Silvia, Brian, Arkansas	.936	11	39	5	3	47	0	0
Steed, Dave, San Antonio	.981	40	227	27	5	259	2	3
Stewart, Andy, Wichita	.964	17	74	6	3	83	1	1
Strickland, Chad, Wichita	.977	50	285	50	8	343	2	5
Sutko, Glenn, El Paso	.975	34	198	34	6	238	2	3
Takayoshi, Todd, Midland	1.000	6	28	2	0	30	0	0
Tejero, Fausto, Midland	.990	16	90	13	1	104	0	5
Wilkins, Rick, Jackson	1.000	4	23	1	0	24	0	0
Yard, Bruce, San Antonio	1.000	2	3	0	0	3	0	0

PITCHERS

Player, Team	Pct.	G	PO	A	E	TC	DP
Akerfelds, Darrel, Midland	.933	29	5	9	1	15	0
Alkire, Jeff, Arkansas*	1.000	2	0	2	0	2	0
Allen, Ron, Jackson	1.000	4	1	4	0	5	1
Anderson, Paul, Arkansas	.917	38	5	17	2	24	3
Archer, Kurt, El Paso	1.000	4	0	3	0	3	0
Arrandale, Matt, Arkansas	.909	47	3	17	2	22	0
Atkinson, Neil, Wichita*	1.000	40	1	3	0	4	0
Badorek, Mike, Arkansas	1.000	18	4	13	0	17	2
Bevil, Brian, Wichita	1.000	15	6	6	0	12	1
Bluma, Jaime, Wichita	1.000	42	4	11	0	15	1
Blyleven, Todd, Midland	1.000	8	0	2	0	2	0
Bonanno, Rob, Midland	1.000	3	1	0	0	1	0
Bourgeois, Steve, Shreveport	.967	22	9	20	1	30	1
Bovee, Mike, Wichita	1.000	20	8	9	0	17	1
Brewer, Nevin, Wichita	.875	19	5	2	1	8	0
Brewington, Jamie, Shreveport	.941	16	7	9	1	17	2

Player, Team	Pct.	G	PO	A	E	TC	DP
Brosnan, Jason, San Antonio*	1.000	19	3	4	0	7	0
Brown, Willard, Midland	.882	27	5	10	2	17	0
Browne, Byron, El Paso	.966	25	10	18	1	29	6
Brunson, William, San Antonio*	.955	14	4	17	1	22	1
Busby, Mike, Arkansas	.966	20	8	20	1	29	0
Butler, Mike, Midland*	1.000	19	1	0	0	1	0
Camacho, Dan, San Antonio	1.000	11	1	0	0	1	1
Carpenter, Brian, Arkansas	1.000	17	0	6	0	6	0
Caruso, Gene, El Paso*	1.000	46	6	9	0	15	1
Castillo, Felipe, Tulsa	.900	14	3	6	1	10	0
Castillo, Juan, Jackson	1.000	12	9	9	0	18	0
Castillo, Mariano, Shreveport	1.000	22	1	5	0	6	0
Castro, Nelson, San Antonio	.917	48	8	14	2	24	1
Cather, Mike, Tulsa	1.000	18	3	6	0	9	0
Chavez, Tony, Midland	1.000	7	1	1	0	2	0
Cimorelli, Frank, El Paso	1.000	2	0	2	0	2	0
Cole, Jim, El Paso	1.000	6	2	3	0	5	0
Connolly, Chris, Wichita*	1.000	13	0	4	0	4	0
Corona, John, Arkansas*	1.000	5	0	2	0	2	1
Corps, Edwin, Shreveport	.947	27	13	23	2	38	2
Correa, Ramser, San Antonio	1.000	42	5	4	0	9	0
Creek, Doug, Arkansas*	.833	26	1	4	1	6	0
Creek, Ryan, Jackson	.926	26	7	18	2	27	0
Cummings, John, San Antonio*	1.000	6	2	5	0	7	0
Davis, Jeff, Tulsa	1.000	1	1	1	0	2	0
Davis, Ray, Arkansas	1.000	21	6	16	0	22	1
Dorlarque, Aaron, Wichita	1.000	20	1	5	0	6	0
Dreyer, Steve, Tulsa	.929	10	3	10	1	14	0
Duda, Steve, El Paso	.909	24	4	6	1	11	0
Duey, Kyle, Jackson	1.000	7	1	2	0	3	0
Duncan, Chip, Tulsa	.900	17	2	7	1	10	0
Edsell, Geoff, Midland	1.000	5	3	7	0	10	1
Escamilla, Jaime, Tulsa*	1.000	4	0	2	0	2	0
Estes, Shawn, Shreveport*	.833	4	0	5	1	6	1
Evans, Bart, Wichita	.833	7	3	2	1	6	0
Evans, Dave, Jackson	.875	49	1	13	2	16	0
Frontera, Chad, Shreveport	1.000	20	7	18	0	25	3
Fyhrie, Mike, Wichita	1.000	17	9	14	0	23	2
Gallaher, Kevin, Jackson	1.000	6	6	6	0	12	0
Gamez, Francisco, El Paso	1.000	27	13	13	0	26	0
Ganote, Joe, El Paso	.889	12	8	8	2	18	0
Garcia, Jose, San Antonio	.950	38	9	10	1	20	1
Geeve, Dave, Tulsa	1.000	15	9	13	0	22	0
Gerstein, Ron, El Paso*	.961	28	13	36	2	51	3
Granger, Jeff, Wichita*	.870	18	4	16	3	23	0
Grundy, Phil, Wichita	1.000	6	1	1	0	2	0
Grzanich, Mike, Jackson	.929	50	7	6	1	14	0
Hancock, Ryan, Midland	.943	28	13	20	2	35	2
Harris, Bryan, Midland*	1.000	39	1	14	0	15	1
Harrison, Brian, Wichita	1.000	15	0	4	0	4	0
Heredia, Wilson, Tulsa	1.000	8	1	6	0	7	1
Herges, Matt, San Antonio	.889	19	2	6	1	9	1
Hingle, Larry, Jackson*	1.000	9	2	3	0	5	0
Holdridge, David, Midland	.750	14	2	1	1	4	0
Holt, Chris, Jackson	1.000	5	5	6	0	11	0
Hubbs, Dan, San Antonio	1.000	31	6	10	0	16	2
Humphrey, Rich, Jackson	1.000	9	1	2	0	3	0
Hyde, Rich, Shreveport	1.000	33	3	4	0	7	0
Jones, Stacy, El Paso	1.000	8	1	0	0	1	0
Kappesser, Bob, El Paso	1.000	8	0	1	0	1	0
Keling, Korey, Midland	.938	29	9	21	2	32	4
Ketchen, Doug, Jackson	1.000	15	6	7	0	13	0
Keusch, Joseph, Tulsa	.500	2	0	1	1	2	0
Kimel, Jack, Tulsa*	.909	17	2	8	1	11	1
Kloek, Kevin, El Paso	.950	28	17	21	2	40	4
Knox, Kerry, Tulsa*	1.000	5	2	8	0	10	0
Kosenski, John, El Paso	1.000	16	4	4	0	8	0
Lacy, Kerry, Tulsa	.929	28	7	19	2	28	4
Langbehn, Gregg, El Paso*	1.000	16	1	6	0	7	0
Lidle, Cory, El Paso	1.000	45	5	20	0	25	1
Linares, Yfrain, El Paso	1.000	8	0	1	0	1	0
Lister, Martin, Jackson*	.857	15	2	10	2	14	1
Long, Tony, Arkansas*	.917	32	2	9	1	12	0
Lowe, Sean, Arkansas	.914	24	13	19	3	35	0
Mack, Tony, Midland	1.000	3	0	1	0	1	0
Maloney, Sean, El Paso	1.000	43	6	18	0	24	1
Marshall, Jason, Wichita	1.000	1	0	2	0	2	1
Martin, Jerry, Tulsa	.818	22	4	5	2	11	0
Martinez, Francisco, Arkansas	1.000	11	3	3	0	6	0
Martinez, Jesus, San Antonio*	.903	24	5	23	3	31	0
Martinez, Ramiro, Tulsa*	1.000	13	0	3	0	3	0
Matranga, Jeff, Arkansas	1.000	7	0	1	0	1	0
McDill, Allen, Wichita*	.500	12	0	1	1	2	0
McLain, Mike, Shreveport	1.000	11	0	2	0	2	0
Mercado, Hector, Jackson*	1.000	8	1	5	0	6	0
Mesewicz, Mark, Arkansas*	1.000	5	0	2	0	2	0
Mlicki, Doug, Jackson	.895	16	8	9	2	19	1
Montgomery, Steve, Arkansas	1.000	55	2	7	0	9	0
Montoya, Norm, El Paso*	.900	51	11	7	2	20	1
Moody, Ritchie, Tulsa*	1.000	11	3	3	0	6	2
Morones, Geno, Wichita	.833	17	4	16	4	24	3
Morvay, Joe, Tulsa	.813	37	0	13	3	16	0
Narcisse, Tyrone, Jackson	.878	27	18	18	5	41	2
Nieves, Ernesto, Midland	1.000	6	0	3	0	3	0
Oehrlein, Dave, Arkansas*	1.000	23	4	12	0	16	0
Oropesa, Eddie, San Antonio*	1.000	16	1	0	0	1	0
Osborne, Donovan, Arkansas*	1.000	2	1	3	0	4	0
Patterson, Danny, Tulsa	.900	26	5	4	1	10	1
Perez, David, Tulsa	.786	8	0	11	3	14	1
Peterson, Mark, Shreveport*	.952	37	4	16	1	21	0
Pickett, Ricky, Shreveport*	.000	14	0	0	1	1	0
Pote, Lou, Shreveport	.800	28	2	10	3	15	1
Powell, John, Tulsa	1.000	7	0	5	0	5	0
Prado, Jose, San Antonio	.940	28	23	24	3	50	2
Pricher, John, Midland	1.000	8	1	1	0	2	0
Purdy, Shawn, Shreveport	1.000	52	1	8	0	9	0
Pyc, Dave, San Antonio*	1.000	26	6	42	0	48	4
Ralston, Kris, Wichita	.900	18	3	6	1	10	0
Ratekin, Mark, Midland	1.000	11	0	5	0	5	1
Rath, Gary, San Antonio*	1.000	18	1	15	0	16	0
Rawitzer, Kevin, Wichita*	.800	28	4	4	2	10	1
Ray, Ken, Wichita	.941	14	4	12	1	17	0
Renko, Steve, Midland	.857	22	4	8	2	14	2
Richey, Jeff, Shreveport	1.000	8	0	4	0	4	1
Rodriguez, Frankie, El Paso	.976	28	10	30	1	41	1
Santana, Julio, Tulsa	.957	15	7	15	1	23	2
Schmidt, Jeff, Midland	.636	20	2	5	4	11	0
Schooler, Mike, Midland	1.000	54	4	8	0	12	1
Sebach, Kyle, Midland	.833	5	2	3	1	6	2
Sepeda, Jaime, Jackson	1.000	1	0	1	0	1	0
Sheehan, Chris, Wichita	1.000	31	6	5	0	11	0
SIMMONS, Scott, Arkansas*	1.000	22	9	41	0	50	1
Smith, Scotty, Tulsa	1.000	29	5	14	0	19	0
Snyder, John, Midland	.833	21	8	17	5	30	1
Soderstrom, Steve, Shreveport	.895	22	8	9	2	19	1
Strange, Don, Wichita	1.000	24	3	2	0	5	0
Taulbee, Andy, Shreveport	.850	14	8	9	3	20	2
Thibert, John, Midland	1.000	12	1	2	0	3	0
Toth, Robert, Wichita	1.000	21	8	9	0	17	0
Troutman, Keith, San Antonio	1.000	38	4	7	0	11	1
Valdez, Carlos, Shreveport	.944	22	4	13	1	18	1
Vanderweele, Doug, Shreveport	1.000	13	6	11	0	17	5
VanRyn, Ben, Midland*	1.000	19	4	5	0	9	1
Wagner, Billy, Jackson*	.889	12	2	6	1	9	0
Wagner, Bret, Arkansas*	1.000	6	1	7	0	8	0
Wagner, Joe, El Paso	1.000	5	0	2	0	2	0
Waldron, Joe, Jackson*	1.000	28	3	4	0	7	1
Walker, Jamie, Jackson*	1.000	50	5	15	0	20	0
Wallace, Derek, Wichita	.778	26	1	6	2	9	0
Wanke, Chuck, Shreveport*	.778	43	0	7	2	9	1
Waring, Jim, Jackson	1.000	17	7	10	0	17	1
Watson, Allen, Arkansas*	1.000	1	0	1	0	1	0
Weaver, Eric, San Antonio	.889	27	15	17	4	36	0
Webb, Doug, El Paso	1.000	18	0	3	0	3	0
Whitaker, Steve, Shreveport*	1.000	4	0	3	0	3	0
White, Chris, Jackson	.938	38	5	10	1	16	0
Wiley, Chad, Tulsa	.902	26	9	28	4	41	2
Witasick, Jay, Arkansas	1.000	7	0	5	0	5	0

The following players did not have any fielding statistics at the positions indicated or appeared only as a designated hitter, pinch-hitter or pinch-runner: Brannon, p; Bridges, p; Browning, p; Butterfield, dh; Caruso, of; Charles, c; R. Chavez, 3b; Davidson, p; Eddy, p; Gamez, of; M. Guerrero, p; M. Harris, dh, ph; Kappesser, of; Kellner, p; Langbehn, of; Monell, dh, ph; Mora, 2b; Munoz, of; Paskievitch, p; Dan. Perez, dh, ph, pr; Popplewell, p; Ramirez, of; Redington, 2b; Richardson, 3b; Sparks, pr; Sutko, of; Talanoa, dh; Urso, 1b; Voigt, of; R. Watson, p; Wheeler, p; Chad White, p; J. White, ph; T. Williams, pr; Yard, 3b.

LEAGUE CHAMPIONS

Year	Team	Pct.
1888—	Dallas	.671
1889—	Houston	.551
1890—	Galveston	.705
1892—	Houston	.741
	Houston	.613
1895—	Dallas	.754
	Fort Worth*	.750
1896—	Fort Worth	.757
	Houston*	.679
	Galveston	.548
1897—	San Antonio†	.657
	Galveston†	.717
1898—	League disbanded.	
1899—	Galveston	.632
	Galveston	.762
1900-01—	Did not operate.	
1902—	Corsicana	.866
	Corsicana	.682
1903—	Paris-Waco	.615
	Dallas*	.648
1904—	Corsicana*	.615
	Fort Worth	.800
1905—	Fort Worth	.545
1906—	Fort Worth	.677
	Cleburne∞	.609
1907—	Austin	.629
1908—	San Antonio	.664
1909—	Houston	.601
1910—	Dallas†	.586
	Houston†	.586
1911—	Austin	.575
1912—	Houston	.626
1913—	Houston	.620
1914—	Houston†	.671
	Waco†	.671
1915—	Waco	.592
1916—	Waco	.587
1917—	Dallas	.600
1918—	Dallas	.584
1919—	Shreveport*	.677
	Fort Worth	.651
1920—	Fort Worth	.703
	Fort Worth	.750
1921—	Fort Worth	.691
	Fort Worth	.662
1922—	Fort Worth	.694
	Fort Worth	.711
1923—	Fort Worth	.632
1924—	Fort Worth	.689
	Fort Worth	.763
1925—	Fort Worth	.711
	Fort Worth▲	.653
1926—	Dallas	.574
1927—	Wichita Falls	.654
1928—	Houston*	.679
	Wichita Falls	.731
1929—	Dallas*	.588
	Wichita Falls	.620
1930—	Wichita Falls	.697
	Fort Worth*	.632
1931—	Houston◆	.625
	Houston	.734
1932—	Beaumont*	.640
	Dallas	.727
1933—	Houston	.623
	San Antonio (4th)§	.523
1934—	Galveston‡	.579
1935—	Oklahoma City‡	.590
1936—	Dallas	.604
	Tulsa (3rd)§	.519
1937—	Oklahoma City	.635
	Fort Worth (3rd)§	.535
1938—	Beaumont	.635
1939—	Houston	.606
	Fort Worth (4th)§	.540
1940—	Houston‡	.652
1941—	Houston	.673
	Dallas (4th)§	.519
1942—	Beaumont	.605
	Shreveport (2nd)§	.576
1943-44-45—	Did not operate.	
1946—	Fort Worth	.656
	Dallas (2nd)§	.591
1947—	Houston‡	.623
1948—	Fort Worth‡	.601
1949—	Fort Worth	.649
	Tulsa (2nd)§	.584
1950—	Beaumont	.595
	San Antonio (4th)§	.513
1951—	Houston‡	.619
1952—	Dallas	.571
	Shreveport (3rd)§	.522
1953—	Dallas‡	.571
1954—	Shreveport	.559
	Houston (2nd)§	.553
1955—	Dallas	.581
	Shreveport (3rd)§	.540
1956—	Houston‡	.623
1957—	Dallas	.662
	Houston (2nd)§	.630
1958—	Fort Worth	.582
	Cor. Christi (3rd)§	.507
1959—	Victoria	.589
	Austin (2nd)§	.548
1960—	Rio Grande Valley	.590
	Tulsa (3rd)	.528
1961—	Amarillo	.643
	San Antonio (3rd)§	.532
1962—	El Paso	.571
	Tulsa (2nd)§	.550
1963—	San Antonio	.564
	Tulsa (3rd)§	.529
1964—	San Antonio‡	.607
1965—	Tulsa	.574
	Albuquerque■	.550
1966—	Arkansas	.579
1967—	Albuquerque	.557
1968—	Arkansas	.586
	El Paso■	.562
1969—	Amarillo	.593
	Memphis■	.504
1970—	Albuquerque◆	.615
	Memphis	.507
1971—	Did not operate as league—clubs were members of Dixie Association.	
1972—	Alexandria	.600
	El Paso■	.557
1973—	San Antonio	.590
	Memphis■	.558
1974—	Victoria■	.581
	El Paso	.555
1975—	Lafayette▼	.558
	Midland▼	.604
1976—	Amarillo■	.600
	Shreveport	.515
1977—	El Paso	.600
	Arkansas•	.485
1978—	El Paso•	.593
	Jackson	.567
1979—	Arkansas•	.571
	Midland	.563
1980—	Arkansas•	.596
	San Antonio	.544
1981—	San Antonio	.571
	Jackson•	.507
1982—	El Paso	.559
	Tulsa•	.515
1983—	Jackson	.507
	Beaumont•	.500
1984—	Beaumont	.654
	Jackson•	.610
1985—	El Paso	.632
	Jackson•	.537
1986—	El Paso•	.630
	Jackson	.533
1987—	Wichita•	.515
	Jackson	.515
1988—	El Paso	.552
	Tulsa•	.522
1989—	Arkansas•	.585
	Wichita	.537
1990—	San Antonio	.582
	Shreveport•	.489
1991—	Shreveport•	.632
	El Paso	.596
1992—	Shreveport	.566
	Wichita•	.515
1993—	El Paso	.563
	Jackson•	.541
1994—	El Paso•	.647
	Jackson	.548
1995—	Shreveport•	.652
	Midland	.485

*Won split-season playoff. †Won playoff for title. ‡Finished first and won four-club playoff. §Won four-club playoff. ∞Title to Cleburne by default. ▲Tied with Dallas in second half and won playoff for championship. ◆Tied with Beaumont at end of first half and won title in best-of-five series played as part of second-half schedule. ■League divided into Eastern, Western divisions; won two-team playoff. ▼League divided into Eastern, Western divisions; declared co-champions when playoffs were not completed. •League divided into Eastern and Western divisions and played split-season; won playoffs. NOTE—Championship awarded to winner of four-team playoff, 1933-51; first-place team and playoff winner co-champions, 1952-64.

CALIFORNIA LEAGUE

LEAGUE OFFICE

President/treasurer
Joe Gagliardi
Address
2380 S. Bascom Ave., Suite 200
Campbell, CA 95008
Phone
408-369-8038

Teams (affiliation)
Bakersfield Blaze (independent)
High Desert Mavericks (Orioles)
Lake Elsinore Storm (Angels)
Modesto A's (A's)
Rancho Cucamonga Quakes (Padres)
Lancaster Jethawks (Mariners)
San Bernardino Stampede (Dodgers)
San Jose Giants (Giants)
Stockton Ports (Brewers)
Visalia Oaks (independent)

1995 FINAL STANDINGS

FIRST HALF

NORTHERN DIVISION

Team	W	L	T	Pct.	GB
Modesto (Athletics)	40	30	0	.571	....
San Jose (Giants)	36	34	0	.514	4
Stockton (Brewers)	35	34	0	.507	4½
Visalia (Co-op)	35	35	0	.500	5
Bakersfield (Co-op)	31	39	0	.443	9

SOUTHERN DIVISION

Team	W	L	T	Pct.	GB
San Bernardino (Dodgers)	44	25	0	.638	....
Lake Elsinore (Angels)	37	32	0	.536	7
Riverside (Mariners)	35	34	0	.507	9
Rancho Cucamonga (Padres)	32	36	0	.471	11½
High Desert (Orioles)	22	48	0	.314	22½

SECOND HALF

NORTHERN DIVISION

Team	W	L	T	Pct.	GB
San Jose (Giants)	41	29	0	.586	....
Stockton (Brewers)	39	31	0	.557	2
Modesto (Athletics)	38	32	0	.543	3
Bakersfield (Co-op)	27	43	0	.386	14
Visalia (Co-op)	23	47	0	.329	18

SOUTHERN DIVISION

Team	W	L	T	Pct.	GB
Lake Elsinore (Angels)	44	25	0	.638	....
San Bernardino (Dodgers)	40	29	0	.580	4
Riverside (Mariners)	37	33	0	.529	7½
Rancho Cucamonga (Padres)	36	34	0	.514	8½
High Desert (Orioles)	24	46	0	.343	20½

COMPOSITE

Team	S.B.	L.E.	Mod.	S.J.	Stk.	Riv.	R.C.	Vis.	Bak.	H.D.	W	L	T	Pct.	GB
San Bernardino (Dodgers)	...	11	7	10	4	8	14	9	5	17	85	54	0	.612	....
Lake Elsinore (Angels)	8	....	7	6	9	12	10	8	9	13	82	57	0	.590	3
Modesto (Athletics)	5	5	....	8	11	7	8	14	14	6	78	62	0	.557	7½
San Jose (Giants)	2	6	12	....	9	8	9	11	10	10	77	63	0	.550	8½
Stockton (Brewers)	8	3	9	11	....	6	4	10	12	11	74	66	0	.529	11½
Riverside (Mariners)	12	8	5	4	6	....	8	6	11	12	72	67	0	.518	13
Rancho Cucamonga (Padres)	6	10	4	3	8	11	....	6	7	13	68	71	0	.489	17
Visalia (Co-op)	3	4	6	9	10	6	6	....	7	7	58	82	0	.414	27½
Bakersfield (Co-op)	7	3	6	10	8	1	5	13	....	5	58	82	0	.414	27½
High Desert (Orioles)	3	7	6	2	1	8	7	5	7	....	46	94	0	.329	39½

Major league affiliations in parentheses.

High Desert played home games in Adelanto, Calif.

PLAYOFFS: San Jose defeated Stockton, two games to none; Lake Elsinore defeated Riverside, two games to one; San Jose defeated Modesto, three games to none; San Bernardino defeated Lake Elsinore, three games to none; San Bernardino defeated San Jose, three games to none, to win league championship.

REGULAR-SEASON ATTENDANCE: Bakersfield, 105,890; High Desert, 146,355; Lake Elsinore, 383,297; Modesto, 100,108; Rancho Cucamonga, 446,146; Riverside, 56,601; San Bernardino, 119,434; San Jose, 140,976; Stockton, 107,140; Visalia, 71,513. Total, 1,677,460. Playoffs (14 games)—31,796. All-Star Game at Lake Elsinore—5,870.

MANAGERS: Bakersfield, Greg Mahlberg; High Desert, Tim Blackwell; Lake Elsinore, Mitch Seoane; Modesto, Glenn Ezell; Rancho Cucamonga, Marty Barrett; Riverside, Dave Brundage; San Bernardino, Ron Roenicke; San Jose, Carlos Lezcano; Stockton, Bob Mariano; Visalia, Lyle Yates.

ALL-STAR TEAM: 1B—Steve Cox, Modesto; 2B—Adam Riggs, San Bernardino; 3B—Rick Ladjevich, Riverside; SS—Greg LaRocca, Rancho Cucamonga; OF—Alex Ramirez, Bakersfield; Armando Rios, San Jose; Greg Shockey, Lake Elsinore; C—Raul Ibanez, Riverside; DH—Rod McCall, Bakersfield; P—Matt Beaumont, Lake Elsinore; Carlos Castillo, Lake Elsinore; Keith Foulke, San Jose; Doug Webb, Stockton; Most Valuable Player—Adam Riggs, San Bernardino; Pitcher of the Year—Matt Beaumont, Lake Elsinore; Rookie of the Year—Adam Riggs, San Bernardino; Manager of the Year—Ron Roenicke, San Bernardino.

1995 BATTING

TEAM

Team	Avg.	G	TPA	AB	R	H	TB	2B	3B	HR	RBI	SH	SF	HP	BB	IBB	SO	SB	CS	GDP	LOB	ShO	Slg.	OBP
San Bernardino	.284	139	5466	4803	823	1362	2132	250	29	154	738	51	43	65	502	11	988	246	100	82	941	4	.444	.356
Stockton	.281	140	5406	4778	730	1341	1911	244	43	80	626	74	49	47	458	11	872	220	97	100	971	2	.400	.346
Lake Elsinore	.275	139	5492	4773	800	1312	2013	275	51	108	731	41	39	62	575	18	973	114	62	108	1045	4	.422	.358
Riverside	.274	139	5465	4813	799	1319	1875	213	44	85	698	30	54	86	482	12	914	153	72	81	992	5	.390	.347
R. Cucamonga	.272	139	5415	4733	742	1288	1850	220	30	94	676	36	50	73	522	14	980	169	62	104	1019	4	.391	.350
Modesto	.267	140	5534	4678	773	1251	1970	245	30	138	703	80	44	72	659	15	1064	137	79	104	1083	9	.421	.363
Bakersfield	.267	140	5327	4690	626	1250	1749	229	21	76	551	60	33	68	475	14	952	149	97	120	1003	11	.373	.340
San Jose	.260	140	5552	4835	695	1256	1801	227	54	70	602	66	43	68	528	19	1011	217	77	90	1069	10	.372	.338
High Desert	.259	140	5371	4710	669	1218	1871	215	39	120	601	44	41	91	484	5	1033	181	103	87	950	15	.397	.337
Visalia	.255	140	5358	4756	591	1211	1695	210	38	66	529	51	40	50	459	6	1025	116	83	105	1000	11	.356	.324

INDIVIDUAL

TOP QUALIFIERS FOR BATTING CHAMPIONSHIP

Minimum 378 plate appearances. *Lefthanded batter. †Switch-hitter.

Player, Team	Avg.	G	TPA	AB	R	H	TB	2B	3B	HR	RBI	SH	SF	HP	BB	IBB	SO	SB	CS	GDP	Slg.	OBP
Riggs, Adam, San Bernardino	.362	134	622	542	111	196	317	39	5	24	106	7	4	10	59	1	93	31	10	9	.585	.431
Hamlin, Jonas, Stockton	.332	99	416	388	65	129	219	32	5	16	69	1	6	4	17	2	86	5	4	7	.564	.361
Ibanez, Raul, Riverside*	.332	95	414	361	59	120	221	23	9	20	108	1	9	2	41	1	49	4	3	7	.612	.395
McCall, Rod, Bakersfield*	.330	96	399	345	61	114	195	19	1	20	70	2	4	8	40	7	90	2	5	6	.565	.408
Shockey, Greg, Lake Elsinore*	.327	114	492	441	85	144	242	32	3	20	88	0	2	6	42	2	88	2	2	6	.549	.391
Ramirez, Alex, Bakersfield	.323	98	428	406	56	131	190	25	2	10	52	0	1	3	18	1	76	13	9	9	.468	.355
LaRocca, Greg, R.C.	.322	125	524	466	77	150	220	36	5	8	74	0	2	12	44	0	77	15	4	13	.472	.393
Nicholas, Darrell, Stockton	.320	87	386	350	54	112	149	16	3	5	39	11	1	1	23	1	75	26	8	6	.426	.363
Barger, Mike, Riverside	.317	82	390	344	77	109	127	10	1	2	41	5	1	2	38	1	45	33	14	3	.369	.387
Ladjevich, Rick, Riverside	.309	122	525	470	74	145	192	26	0	7	71	3	4	22	26	2	65	3	2	8	.409	.370
Seitzer, Brad, Stockton	.308	127	507	428	66	132	184	28	3	6	56	2	2	3	72	2	68	7	4	10	.430	.410
Berry, Michael, Visalia	.307	98	434	368	69	113	176	28	4	9	61	1	3	5	57	1	70	12	6	9	.478	.404
Morillo, Cesar, Bakersfield†	.305	108	412	371	41	113	143	25	1	1	37	5	1	4	31	2	71	4	12	6	.385	.364
Sbrocco, Jon, San Jose*	.301	120	508	425	66	128	158	14	5	2	46	17	1	10	55	3	43	12	10	5	.372	.393
Lee, Derrek, R.C.	.301	128	565	502	82	151	249	25	2	23	95	0	7	7	49	2	130	14	7	8	.496	.366
Ortega, Hector, Stockton	.301	137	601	539	81	162	221	27	4	8	76	6	7	10	39	0	109	26	13	8	.410	.355

DEPARTMENTAL LEADERS: G—H. Ortega, 137; AB—Riggs, 542; R—Riggs, 111; H—Riggs, 196; TB—Riggs, 317; 2B—Riggs, 39; 3B—D'Aquila, 11; HR—Cox, 30; RBI—Cox, 110; SH—Martins, 18; SF—Cox, 10; HP—Ladjevich, 22; BB—McDonald, 110; IBB—Redington, 8; SO—Hust, 169; SB—McDonald, 70; CS—Carr, 21; GIDP—Wingate, 25; Slg.—Ibanez, .612; OBP—Riggs, .431.

ALL PLAYERS

*Lefthanded batter. †Switch-hitter.

Player, Team	Avg.	G	TPA	AB	R	H	TB	2B	3B	HR	RBI	SH	SF	HP	BB	IBB	SO	SB	CS	GDP	Slg.	OBP
Adams, Tommy, Riverside	.287	69	290	251	46	72	121	17	4	8	40	1	3	7	28	0	40	12	4	5	.482	.370
Alguacil, Jose, San Jose*	.236	58	253	225	30	53	69	10	3	0	17	8	2	4	14	0	44	11	6	2	.307	.290
Alimena, Charles, San Jose*	.205	54	184	171	17	35	45	3	2	1	18	0	1	1	11	0	44	1	0	8	.263	.255
Allanson, Andy, Lake Elsinore	.317	22	100	82	22	26	47	9	0	4	22	0	1	1	16	0	8	2	2	4	.573	.430
Alvarez, Gabe, R.C.	.344	59	248	212	41	73	112	17	2	6	36	0	2	5	29	0	30	1	0	3	.528	.431
Asencio, Alex, San Bernardino*	.257	29	114	105	15	27	42	1	4	2	18	1	0	2	6	0	31	2	0	0	.400	.310
Avila, Rolando, High Desert	.239	52	218	180	26	43	61	10	1	2	10	5	0	4	29	0	26	19	8	0	.339	.357
Banks, Tony, Modesto*	.198	28	99	81	10	16	22	3	0	1	10	4	1	0	13	0	17	3	0	0	.272	.305
Barger, Mike, Riverside	.317	82	390	344	77	109	127	10	1	2	41	5	1	2	38	1	45	33	14	3	.369	.387
Bautista, Juan, High Desert	.262	99	408	374	54	98	152	13	4	11	51	6	3	7	18	0	74	22	9	8	.406	.306
Bellhorn, Mark, Modesto†	.258	56	262	229	35	59	89	12	0	6	31	2	0	4	27	0	52	5	2	9	.389	.346
Bengoechea, Brandy, Modesto	.261	134	537	467	60	122	164	19	4	5	44	11	3	9	47	1	96	7	10	10	.351	.338
Berry, Michael, Visalia	.307	98	434	368	69	113	176	28	4	9	61	1	3	5	57	1	70	12	6	9	.478	.404
Bethea, Scott, Visalia	.241	105	433	370	51	89	112	17	3	0	27	9	3	4	47	1	35	14	9	4	.303	.330
Bishop, Steve, High Desert	.116	12	48	43	5	5	8	1	1	0	3	0	0	1	4	0	12	1	0	1	.186	.208
Bogle, Bryan, High Desert	.172	19	72	64	7	11	15	2	1	0	4	0	0	0	8	0	18	3	1	1	.234	.264
Bonds, Bobby, Visalia	.223	109	423	373	56	83	140	12	6	11	30	3	1	4	42	1	114	26	12	5	.375	.307
Bordick, Mike, Modesto	.000	1	3	2	0	0	0	0	0	0	0	0	0	1	0	0	0	0	1	0	.000	.333
Brakebill, Mark, Lake Elsinore	.143	2	8	7	0	1	1	0	0	0	0	0	0	0	1	0	2	0	0	0	.143	.250
Breuer, Jim, Bakersfield	.048	10	26	21	0	1	1	0	0	0	3	0	2	1	2	0	13	0	0	0	.048	.154
Brock, Tarrick, Visalia*	.225	45	161	138	21	31	43	5	2	1	15	2	0	4	17	0	52	11	1	2	.312	.327
Burke, Jamie, Lake Elsinore	.274	106	421	365	47	100	133	15	6	2	56	11	4	9	32	1	53	6	4	12	.364	.344
Byrne, Clayton, High Desert	.236	54	209	199	24	47	64	10	2	1	19	0	0	3	7	0	36	7	5	1	.322	.273
Cabrera, Jairo, High Desert	.205	14	46	39	2	8	8	0	0	0	3	2	1	1	3	0	7	1	0	2	.205	.273
Campillo, Rob, Stockton	.302	35	119	106	10	32	35	3	0	0	17	3	2	1	7	0	13	0	0	4	.330	.345
Carpenter, Jerry, Lake Elsinore	.000	1	3	2	0	0	0	0	0	0	0	0	0	0	1	0	0	0	0	1	.000	.333
Carr, Jeremy, Bakersfield	.257	128	595	499	92	128	157	22	2	1	38	6	0	11	79	0	73	52	21	9	.315	.370
Carrasquel, Domingo, Stockton†	.269	67	189	160	19	43	53	10	0	0	20	10	1	0	18	0	21	2	5	3	.331	.341
Cavanagh, Mike, San Jose	.125	6	20	16	2	2	4	0	1	0	3	2	0	0	2	0	8	0	0	0	.250	.222
Chavez, Eric, High Desert	.232	74	288	254	38	59	116	15	0	14	37	0	2	4	27	0	74	4	2	4	.457	.314
Clark, Howie, High Desert*	.258	100	371	329	50	85	124	20	2	5	40	3	3	4	32	0	51	12	6	4	.377	.329
Claudio, Patricio, Bakersfield	.281	32	145	128	19	36	54	9	3	1	9	2	0	2	13	0	26	5	7	3	.422	.357
Clyburn, Danny, High Desert	.281	45	184	160	20	45	86	3	1	12	37	0	3	4	17	1	41	2	1	3	.538	.359
Conway, Jeff, R.C.*	.254	28	73	67	9	17	18	1	0	0	5	2	0	0	4	0	10	1	1	3	.269	.296
Cook, Jason, Riverside	.190	6	26	21	9	4	5	1	0	0	3	0	0	0	5	0	4	0	0	0	.238	.346
Corps, Erick, R.C.†	.191	73	213	183	21	35	44	6	0	1	13	4	2	2	22	0	54	1	1	5	.240	.282
Cox, Steve, Modesto*	.298	132	591	483	95	144	269	29	3	30	110	0	10	14	84	6	88	5	4	12	.557	.409
Cromer, D.T., Modesto*	.259	108	430	378	59	98	168	18	5	14	52	6	6	4	36	1	66	5	7	10	.444	.325
Cruz, Jose, Riverside†	.257	35	170	144	34	37	67	7	1	7	29	0	2	0	24	1	50	3	1	1	.465	.359
Cuellar, Jose, Riverside	.111	19	57	45	7	5	5	0	0	0	2	0	0	0	12	0	9	0	0	0	.111	.298
Cuevas, Eduardo, R.C.	.243	43	150	140	14	34	46	5	2	1	24	0	3	0	7	1	16	5	1	6	.329	.273
Cunningham, Earl, Lake Elsinore	.239	78	308	284	50	68	130	13	2	15	55	0	2	6	15	0	97	8	3	7	.458	.290
Curtis, Kevin, High Desert	.293	112	470	399	70	117	208	26	1	21	70	0	5	12	54	1	83	8	6	7	.521	.389
Dandridge, Brad, San Bernardino	.320	82	342	322	56	103	154	14	2	11	61	1	2	3	14	0	34	16	5	11	.478	.352
Daniels, Moe, Lake Elsinore	.305	39	170	151	26	46	58	8	2	0	11	0	0	1	18	0	35	6	4	2	.384	.382
D'Aquila, Tom, High Desert	.264	110	438	386	48	102	167	10	11	11	63	0	3	4	45	1	111	8	7	11	.433	.345
Davis, Doug, Lake Elsinore	.333	1	4	3	0	1	1	0	0	0	0	0	0	0	1	0	1	0	0	0	.333	.500
Dean, Chris, Riverside†	.251	116	482	407	56	102	152	16	8	6	45	3	7	16	49	1	98	13	10	6	.373	.349
Delgado, Wilson, San Jose†	.000	1	2	2	1	0	0	0	0	0	0	0	0	0	0	0	0	0	0	0	.000	.000
Derotal, Francisco, R.C.	.196	29	62	56	9	11	19	2	0	2	5	1	0	2	3	0	20	1	0	0	.339	.262
Diaz, Alfredo, Lake Elsinore†	.235	49	169	149	25	35	54	12	2	1	25	3	6	0	11	0	54	1	1	6	.362	.277
Dobrolsky, Bill, Stockton	.270	88	290	252	28	68	94	14	3	2	30	2	5	6	25	0	37	3	4	4	.373	.344

Player, Team	Avg.	G	TPA	AB	R	H	TB	2B	3B	HR	RBI	SH	SF	HP	BB	IBB	SO	SB	CS	GDP	Slg.	OBP
Doty, Derrin, Lake Elsinore	.247	94	368	324	46	80	116	12	0	8	35	2	2	3	37	0	54	16	6	4	.358	.328
Dressendorfer, Kirk, Modesto	.000	27	1	1	0	0	0	0	0	0	0	0	0	0	0	0	1	0	0	0	.000	.000
Dumas, Mike, Stockton	.235	74	278	243	41	57	73	7	3	1	17	6	1	1	27	0	26	21	12	8	.300	.313
Dunn, Todd, Stockton	.293	67	272	249	44	73	118	20	2	7	40	1	1	2	19	2	67	14	3	5	.474	.347
Durkin, Chris, San Bernardino*	.268	57	197	164	24	44	80	10	1	8	31	1	3	1	28	0	48	9	6	3	.488	.372
Eaddy, Keith, High Desert	.244	99	395	336	58	82	143	17	4	12	42	3	3	10	43	0	107	20	9	8	.426	.344
Ealy, Tracey, San Jose†	.156	12	35	32	7	5	5	0	0	0	2	0	0	1	2	0	12	0	0	2	.156	.229
Erstad, Darin, Lake Elsinore*	.363	25	120	113	24	41	69	7	3	5	24	0	1	0	6	0	22	3	0	2	.611	.392
Faircloth, Kevin, San Bernardino	.185	56	176	146	23	27	30	3	0	0	6	4	2	10	14	0	40	7	3	2	.205	.297
Fernandez, Antonio, Visalia	.227	90	327	309	25	70	88	10	1	2	32	1	2	1	14	0	48	1	0	18	.285	.261
Fitzpatrick, Will, Stockton*	.207	13	37	29	5	6	10	1	0	1	4	0	0	0	8	0	16	0	0	0	.345	.378
Fuller, Aaron, Visalia†	.253	49	211	186	27	47	63	7	3	1	19	3	2	1	19	0	32	11	10	0	.339	.322
Fully, Ed, High Desert	.369	38	159	149	28	55	84	11	0	6	34	1	0	2	7	0	22	9	6	3	.564	.405
Galarza, Joel, San Jose	.292	58	235	209	28	61	97	13	1	7	44	4	5	2	11	0	35	6	2	4	.464	.326
Garcia, Manuel, Visalia	.100	12	44	40	3	4	8	2	1	0	4	0	1	2	1	0	18	3	0	0	.200	.159
Gargiulo, Mike, High Desert*	.206	14	36	34	2	7	8	1	0	0	4	1	0	0	1	0	9	0	1	1	.235	.229
Gibbs, Kevin, San Bernardino†	.231	5	13	13	1	3	4	1	0	0	0	0	0	0	0	0	2	1	0	0	.308	.231
Graham, John, Visalia*	.248	98	353	306	45	76	89	8	1	1	30	4	3	4	36	0	77	12	6	2	.291	.332
Grass, Darren, R.C.	.241	23	63	58	6	14	23	6	0	1	9	3	0	0	2	0	15	0	0	1	.397	.267
Gresham, Kris, High Desert	.257	47	160	140	25	36	59	8	0	5	15	2	2	4	12	1	31	1	3	6	.421	.329
Grieve, Ben, Modesto*	.262	28	124	107	17	28	39	5	0	2	14	0	2	0	15	1	22	2	0	3	.364	.347
Guevara, Giomar, Riverside†	.243	83	335	292	53	71	95	12	3	2	34	6	6	1	30	1	71	7	4	4	.325	.310
Guiel, Aaron, Lake Elsinore*	.269	113	493	409	73	110	170	25	7	7	58	4	4	7	69	0	96	7	6	7	.416	.380
Guillen, Jose, Modesto†	.257	41	129	113	16	29	36	2	1	1	11	5	0	0	11	0	24	9	3	3	.319	.323
Gulseth, Mark, San Jose*	.234	22	74	64	8	15	21	4	1	0	6	0	0	0	10	2	16	1	0	0	.328	.338
Hamlin, Jonas, Stockton	.332	99	416	388	65	129	219	32	5	16	69	1	6	4	17	2	86	5	4	7	.564	.361
Harmer, Frank, High Desert†	.250	6	17	12	3	3	7	1	0	1	1	0	0	0	5	0	5	0	0	0	.583	.471
Haught, Gary, Modesto†	.000	34	1	1	0	0	0	0	0	0	0	0	0	0	0	0	1	0	0	0	.000	.000
Hayashi, Hiroyasu, Visalia*	.268	40	169	138	19	37	43	6	0	0	15	4	0	1	26	1	27	2	3	4	.312	.388
Hecker, Doug, Visalia	.071	8	17	14	2	1	1	0	0	0	0	0	0	0	3	0	5	0	1	0	.071	.235
Hemphill, Bret, Lake Elsinore†	.199	45	170	146	12	29	39	7	0	1	17	0	3	3	18	0	36	2	1	4	.267	.294
Hence, Sam, Bakersfield	.125	4	9	8	1	1	1	0	0	0	0	1	0	0	0	0	1	0	0	0	.125	.125
Hilo, Johnny, San Bernardino†	.247	38	111	93	14	23	30	2	1	1	9	3	0	0	15	0	23	3	2	1	.323	.352
Hodge, Roy, High Desert	.300	42	180	140	31	42	61	8	1	3	15	0	1	3	36	0	24	8	7	3	.436	.450
Hollandsworth, Todd, San Bern.*	.500	1	2	2	0	1	1	0	0	0	0	0	0	0	0	0	1	0	1	0	.500	.500
Hostetler, Brian, Stockton*	.000	3	7	7	0	0	0	0	0	0	0	0	0	0	0	0	3	0	0	0	.000	.000
Hughes, Bobby, Stockton	.235	52	200	179	22	42	79	9	2	8	31	0	3	1	17	1	41	2	2	10	.441	.300
Hugo, Sean, High Desert*	.240	28	90	75	8	18	26	3	1	1	13	0	2	1	12	0	21	1	1	2	.347	.344
Hunter, Scott, San Bernardino	.285	113	428	379	68	108	166	19	3	11	59	4	1	6	36	1	83	27	8	0	.438	.355
Hust, Gary, Modesto	.238	128	539	467	85	111	216	20	2	27	87	4	3	4	61	3	169	10	4	4	.463	.329
Ibanez, Raul, Riverside*	.332	95	414	361	59	120	221	23	9	20	108	1	9	2	41	1	49	4	3	7	.612	.395
Ibarra, Jesse, San Jose†	.333	3	10	9	1	3	5	2	0	0	4	0	0	0	1	0	1	0	0	2	.556	.400
Jenkins, Geoff, Stockton*	.255	13	59	47	13	12	23	2	0	3	12	0	2	0	10	0	12	2	0	0	.489	.373
Jennings, Lance, Visalia	.301	85	356	316	31	95	130	15	1	6	41	0	2	2	36	2	56	0	2	8	.411	.374
Jimenez, Miguel, Modesto	.000	4	1	1	0	0	0	0	0	0	0	0	0	0	0	0	1	0	0	0	.000	.000
Johnson, Earl, R. Cucamonga†	.293	81	372	341	51	100	117	11	3	0	25	5	0	1	25	0	51	34	12	5	.343	.343
Johnson, Keith, San Bernardino	.242	111	451	417	64	101	180	26	1	17	68	11	2	4	17	0	83	20	12	4	.432	.277
Johnson, Todd, Bakersfield	.360	9	28	25	2	9	13	2	1	0	2	0	0	0	3	0	4	0	1	1	.520	.429
Jorgensen, Randy, Riverside*	.299	133	564	495	78	148	220	32	2	12	97	0	8	15	46	1	74	4	2	13	.444	.371
Keel, David, Modesto*	.200	9	29	25	4	5	8	0	0	1	3	1	0	0	3	0	7	0	0	0	.320	.286
Keene, Andre, San Jose*	.254	103	414	323	62	82	144	15	1	15	62	0	6	9	76	2	101	7	6	7	.446	.403
Keifer, Greg, San Jose	.212	28	75	66	9	14	22	2	0	2	12	0	0	0	9	0	31	2	0	0	.333	.307
King, Brett, San Jose	.274	107	451	394	61	108	154	29	4	3	41	5	6	5	41	1	86	28	8	8	.391	.345
Kirkpatrick, Jay, San Bernardino*	.270	71	309	267	38	72	136	19	0	15	50	0	2	0	40	3	75	3	0	3	.509	.362
Knapp, Mike, High Desert	.267	5	18	15	1	4	5	1	0	0	1	0	1	0	2	0	6	0	1	0	.333	.333
Konerko, Paul, San Bernardino	.277	118	519	448	77	124	204	21	1	19	77	2	6	4	59	2	88	3	1	12	.455	.362
Koscielniak, Dwain, R.C.	.222	7	13	9	1	2	5	0	0	1	2	0	1	0	3	0	2	0	0	0	.556	.385
Kruger, Andy, Visalia*	.253	100	391	356	46	90	125	9	7	4	32	3	1	2	28	0	65	10	15	4	.351	.310
Ladjevich, Rick, Riverside	.309	122	525	470	74	145	192	26	0	7	71	3	4	22	26	2	65	3	2	8	.409	.370
LaRocca, Greg, R.C.	.322	125	524	466	77	150	220	36	5	8	74	0	2	12	44	0	77	15	4	13	.472	.393
Lee, Derrek, R.C.	.301	128	565	502	82	151	249	25	2	23	95	0	7	7	49	2	130	14	7	8	.496	.366
Lemons, Rich, Bakersfield*	.282	36	139	124	18	35	52	5	0	4	16	1	0	1	13	1	42	4	2	2	.419	.355
Luuloa, Keith, Lake Elsinore	.263	102	418	380	50	100	151	22	7	5	53	7	1	6	24	0	47	1	5	9	.397	.316
Marnell, Anthony, R.C.	.043	16	24	23	3	1	1	0	0	0	1	0	0	0	1	0	13	0	0	0	.043	.083
Marquez, Jesus, Riverside*	.237	84	340	312	42	74	93	9	2	2	26	2	4	4	18	0	62	4	5	5	.298	.284
Martin, Lincoln, High Desert†	.240	54	184	150	27	36	50	7	2	1	12	4	2	0	28	0	37	7	4	2	.333	.356
Martinez, Gabby, Stockton†	.258	64	237	213	25	55	77	13	3	1	20	9	3	2	10	0	25	13	6	6	.362	.294
Martinez, Greg, Stockton†	.276	114	492	410	80	113	125	8	2	0	43	10	1	2	69	1	64	55	9	7	.305	.382
Martins, Eric, Modesto	.290	106	496	407	71	118	148	17	5	1	54	18	4	4	62	0	74	7	8	8	.364	.386
Marval, Raul, San Jose	.278	10	39	36	1	10	10	0	0	0	3	2	0	0	1	0	5	1	1	0	.278	.297
Mayes, Craig, San Jose*	.252	90	348	318	34	80	105	17	4	0	39	1	2	0	27	1	50	3	1	7	.330	.308
McCall, Rod, Bakersfield*	.330	96	399	345	61	114	195	19	1	20	70	2	4	8	40	7	90	2	5	6	.565	.408
McDonald, Jason, Modesto†	.262	133	619	493	109	129	186	25	7	6	50	8	2	6	110	0	84	70	20	6	.377	.401
McGonigle, Bill, Stockton	.262	78	248	210	33	55	65	8	1	0	21	8	3	4	23	0	35	3	4	3	.310	.342
McKinnis, Leroy, R.C.	.245	15	62	49	9	12	16	1	0	1	6	0	2	1	10	1	10	1	0	3	.327	.371
McNabb, Buck, Bakersfield*	.300	63	281	237	34	71	81	8	1	0	27	4	2	0	38	1	38	11	1	5	.342	.394
Meade, Paul, Bakersfield†	.000	24	1	1	0	0	0	0	0	0	0	0	0	0	0	0	1	0	0	0	.000	.000
Meilan, Tony, Bakersfield	.211	12	42	38	3	8	9	1	0	0	2	1	0	1	2	0	4	1	1	0	.237	.268
Mejia, Miguel, High Desert	.269	37	137	119	14	32	40	6	1	0	12	2	1	1	14	0	17	16	7	3	.336	.348
Mercedes, Feliciano, High Desert†	.234	31	113	107	10	25	31	4	1	0	10	1	0	0	5	0	24	5	0	1	.290	.268
Miller, Roy, Riverside	.183	65	194	175	21	32	39	4	0	1	18	1	1	5	12	0	49	3	4	4	.223	.254
Milstien, Dave, Stockton	.276	58	244	214	36	59	87	14	1	4	37	0	1	4	25	1	16	6	3	5	.407	.361
Moeder, Tony, Lake Elsinore	.238	68	283	252	39	60	98	18	1	6	26	0	1	3	27	2	61	2	3	7	.389	.318

Player, Team	Avg.	G	TPA	AB	R	H	TB	2B	3B	HR	RBI	SH	SF	HP	BB	IBB	SO	SB	CS	GDP	Slg.	OBP
Molina, Ben, Lake Elsinore	.385	27	112	96	21	37	54	7	2	2	12	3	1	4	8	1	7	0	0	2	.563	.450
Moore, Kerwin, Modesto†	.245	15	69	53	8	13	21	3	1	1	6	2	1	2	11	0	20	4	4	0	.396	.388
Moore, Mark, Modesto	.261	77	312	261	40	68	114	16	0	10	48	0	3	6	42	0	76	3	2	9	.437	.372
Moore, Vince, R.C.*	.227	84	337	299	50	68	126	11	1	15	57	0	1	2	35	0	102	10	5	5	.421	.312
Morales, William, Modesto	.277	109	460	419	49	116	160	32	0	4	60	2	4	7	28	1	75	1	4	13	.382	.330
Morillo, Cesar, Bakersfield†	.305	108	412	371	41	113	143	25	1	1	37	5	1	4	31	2	71	4	12	6	.385	.364
Morreale, John, Stockton	.239	30	98	88	13	21	25	2	1	0	8	1	1	0	8	0	16	0	3	4	.284	.299
Moschetti, Mike, Modesto	.351	23	87	77	5	27	33	6	0	0	9	3	1	0	6	0	16	0	2	2	.429	.393
Mowry, Dave, R.C.*	.239	50	164	142	19	34	53	10	0	3	23	0	1	0	21	1	38	0	0	3	.373	.335
Nadeau, Mike, High Desert	.246	22	71	57	5	14	14	0	0	0	4	3	0	5	6	0	12	3	2	1	.246	.368
Neill, Mike, Modesto*	.276	71	299	257	39	71	108	17	1	6	36	5	1	2	34	2	65	4	4	6	.420	.364
Nelson, Charles, San Bern.*	.250	1	4	4	0	1	1	0	0	0	0	0	0	0	0	0	0	0	0	0	.250	.250
Nevers, Tom, Stockton	.286	4	16	14	2	4	4	0	0	0	3	0	0	2	0	0	6	1	0	0	.286	.375
Newstrom, Doug, San Bern.*	.291	97	367	316	53	92	134	22	1	6	58	6	3	2	40	0	58	19	9	7	.424	.371
Nicholas, Darrell, Stockton	.320	87	386	350	54	112	149	16	3	5	39	11	1	1	23	1	75	26	8	6	.426	.363
Ohmura, Iwao, Visalia	.261	45	170	153	15	40	54	9	1	1	18	4	4	0	9	0	32	1	1	5	.353	.295
Ortega, Hector, Stockton	.301	137	601	539	81	162	221	27	4	8	76	6	7	10	39	0	109	26	13	8	.410	.355
Ortega, Randy, Modesto	.174	10	31	23	2	4	5	1	0	0	1	1	0	1	6	0	7	0	0	0	.217	.367
Owen, Spike, Lake Elsinore†	.200	3	12	10	1	2	3	1	0	0	0	0	0	0	2	0	2	0	0	0	.300	.333
Pagan, Angel, High Desert†	.157	35	125	115	12	18	26	3	1	1	10	2	1	3	4	0	29	3	2	4	.226	.203
Pagee, Shawn, Visalia†	.114	22	48	44	1	5	5	0	0	0	4	2	0	0	2	0	17	0	1	1	.114	.152
Parker, Alan, Visalia	.230	121	439	395	40	91	113	18	2	0	36	9	6	1	27	0	81	6	7	4	.286	.277
Patel, Manny, Riverside*	.285	83	314	274	45	78	98	8	6	0	32	1	1	5	33	0	30	9	4	5	.358	.371
Paulino, Arturo, Modesto	.111	5	14	9	2	1	1	0	0	0	0	1	0	0	4	0	4	1	0	1	.111	.385
Phillips, Gary, San Jose	.264	106	406	363	51	96	132	17	8	1	32	6	2	9	26	0	68	3	1	6	.364	.328
Pinoni, Scott, Visalia	.320	73	298	259	44	83	144	19	0	14	45	0	1	5	33	0	50	1	1	8	.556	.406
Powell, Chris, Lake Elsinore*	.200	13	56	40	7	8	15	2	1	1	2	0	0	3	13	0	10	0	2	1	.375	.429
Powell, Dante, San Jose	.248	135	559	505	74	125	194	23	8	10	70	1	4	3	46	2	131	43	12	8	.384	.312
Powell, Gordon, Stockton	.254	111	418	389	58	99	164	19	5	12	48	3	5	0	21	1	85	22	6	3	.422	.289
Priest, Chris, Visalia	.232	55	214	185	18	43	54	8	0	1	15	2	3	5	19	0	34	3	3	6	.292	.316
Prieto, Chris, R.C.*	.273	114	448	366	80	100	130	12	6	2	35	8	5	5	64	2	55	39	14	10	.355	.384
Prieto, Rick, Bakersfield†	.222	74	286	248	34	55	77	12	2	2	22	6	0	3	29	0	46	15	2	1	.310	.311
Ramirez, Alex, Bakersfield	.323	98	428	406	56	131	190	25	2	10	52	0	1	3	18	1	76	13	9	9	.468	.355
Rasmussen, Nate, Bakersfield*	.197	23	84	71	12	14	18	4	0	0	6	0	1	0	12	0	23	0	0	3	.254	.310
Raven, Luis, Lake Elsinore	.417	6	30	24	5	10	20	2	1	2	6	0	0	1	5	0	7	1	0	0	.833	.533
Redington, Tom, Lake Elsinore	.328	76	325	271	50	89	135	26	1	6	54	0	2	1	51	8	43	2	1	4	.498	.434
Reese, Matthew, Modesto*	.200	15	54	50	4	10	17	4	0	1	6	0	0	0	4	0	23	0	2	0	.340	.259
Richardson, Brian, San Bernardino	.284	127	513	462	68	131	187	18	1	12	58	6	3	7	35	2	122	17	16	11	.405	.341
Richardson, Scott, Stockton	.225	24	90	80	12	18	30	4	1	2	14	1	0	3	6	0	16	8	3	3	.375	.303
Riggs, Adam, San Bernardino	.362	134	622	542	111	196	317	39	5	24	106	7	4	10	59	1	93	31	10	9	.585	.431
Rios, Armando, San Jose*	.293	128	574	488	76	143	207	34	3	8	75	4	7	1	74	3	75	51	10	8	.424	.382
Rivera, Santiago, R. Cucamonga†	.215	61	147	130	11	28	35	5	1	0	10	2	1	1	13	0	36	2	0	3	.269	.290
Roberge, J.P., San Bernardino	.287	116	497	450	92	129	204	22	1	17	59	2	3	8	34	0	62	31	8	9	.453	.345
Roberts, Bip, R.C.†	.000	1	4	3	1	0	0	0	0	0	0	0	0	0	1	0	1	1	0	0	.000	.250
Roberts, John, R.C.	.278	98	389	327	59	91	131	16	3	6	51	2	2	14	44	2	86	27	8	9	.401	.385
Rodriguez, Miguel, Stockton	.300	12	12	10	2	3	6	1	1	0	1	0	0	1	1	0	4	0	0	0	.600	.417
Rodriguez, Nerio, High Desert	.236	58	166	144	20	34	53	7	0	4	12	2	1	1	18	0	50	5	3	0	.368	.323
Rodriques, Cecil, Stockton	.266	45	190	173	21	46	70	6	3	4	20	1	3	0	13	0	31	4	8	4	.405	.312
Rossiter, Michael, Modesto	.000	18	1	1	0	0	0	0	0	0	0	0	0	0	0	0	0	0	0	0	.000	.000
Sbrocco, Jon, San Jose*	.301	120	508	425	66	128	158	14	5	2	46	17	1	10	55	3	43	12	10	5	.372	.393
Schaaf, Bob, San Bernardino	.252	52	165	151	18	38	60	7	0	5	21	0	0	2	12	0	32	4	4	4	.397	.315
Schneider, Dan, San Jose	.167	13	38	36	3	6	7	1	0	0	2	1	0	0	1	0	7	0	0	1	.194	.189
Schwenke, Matt, R.C.	.179	22	60	56	7	10	12	2	0	0	7	1	1	0	2	0	20	0	0	0	.214	.203
Sealy, Scot, Riverside	.243	58	225	206	23	50	61	5	0	2	30	1	1	1	16	0	36	2	2	4	.296	.299
See, Larry, R.C.	.345	49	191	171	34	59	111	10	0	14	50	0	2	4	14	1	31	0	2	4	.649	.403
Seitzer, Brad, Stockton	.308	127	507	428	66	132	184	28	3	6	56	2	2	3	72	2	68	7	4	10	.430	.410
Serra, Jose, High Desert	.261	76	262	234	30	61	69	6	1	0	22	3	1	6	18	0	30	11	5	2	.295	.328
Shepherd, Brian, San Jose	.156	13	46	32	2	5	5	0	0	0	1	2	0	1	11	0	6	0	2	0	.156	.386
Shockey, Greg, Lake Elsinore*	.327	114	492	441	85	144	242	32	3	20	88	0	2	6	42	2	88	2	2	6	.549	.391
Short, Rick, High Desert	.418	29	110	98	14	41	56	3	0	4	12	0	0	2	10	0	5	1	2	2	.571	.482
Simmons, Mark, Lake Elsinore†	.202	81	274	238	35	48	60	7	1	1	25	2	0	2	32	0	61	10	8	4	.252	.301
Simonton, Benji, San Jose	.289	61	279	225	38	65	110	9	6	8	37	0	4	10	40	2	78	7	0	5	.489	.412
Singleton, Chris, San Jose*	.277	94	441	405	55	112	141	13	5	2	31	5	1	5	17	1	49	33	13	5	.348	.313
Smith, Demond, Lake Elsinore†	.351	34	162	148	32	52	85	8	2	7	26	0	1	2	11	0	36	14	3	1	.574	.401
Smith, Frank, San Bernardino	.205	58	158	122	19	25	43	7	1	3	15	0	2	4	30	1	54	9	3	0	.352	.373
Smith, Joel, Vis.-L.E.	.266	97	387	350	44	93	151	16	3	12	62	2	6	3	26	0	80	0	1	13	.431	.317
Smith, Scott, Riverside	.235	56	200	179	28	42	54	6	0	2	20	0	0	0	21	1	60	2	1	7	.302	.315
Soliz, Steve, Bakersfield	.245	44	176	159	9	39	47	5	0	1	11	0	0	2	15	0	34	2	1	6	.296	.318
Spearman, Vernon, San Bern.*	.288	93	433	365	78	105	143	15	7	3	36	8	4	0	56	1	50	43	12	5	.392	.379
Stare, Lonny, Bakersfield	.272	104	422	372	54	101	153	21	2	9	59	8	2	7	33	1	65	14	10	9	.411	.341
Stuckenschneider, Eric, S.B.	.250	8	30	20	2	5	6	1	0	0	2	0	1	2	7	0	6	1	0	0	.300	.467
Sturdivant, Marcus, Riverside*	.274	99	393	347	60	95	121	13	5	1	34	2	4	1	39	1	41	31	13	3	.349	.345
Tachikawa, Takashi, Visalia	.176	47	128	119	10	21	28	2	1	1	14	0	1	0	8	0	28	1	1	7	.235	.227
Takayoshi, Todd, Lake Elsinore*	.242	60	201	157	19	38	55	6	1	3	30	2	0	0	42	1	30	1	1	5	.350	.402
Tejcek, John, Riverside	.260	105	458	416	72	108	166	22	3	10	54	4	2	4	32	1	116	23	3	5	.399	.317
Tejero, Fausto, Lake Elsinore	.238	8	27	21	5	5	6	1	0	0	3	0	1	0	5	0	6	1	0	1	.286	.370
Tena, Dario, R.C.†	.172	11	34	29	1	5	6	1	0	0	0	1	0	1	3	0	4	2	1	1	.207	.273
Thielen, D.J., San Jose	.213	91	328	282	38	60	99	13	1	8	34	3	2	3	38	1	81	4	5	5	.351	.311
Thurston, Jerrey, R.C.	.220	76	235	200	24	44	56	9	0	1	13	4	3	7	21	0	64	1	0	2	.280	.312
Tohyama, Shoji, Visalia*	.297	51	168	155	15	46	65	9	2	2	24	1	1	3	8	0	38	1	1	3	.419	.341
Tredaway, Chad, R. Cucamonga†	.277	109	449	408	53	113	152	17	2	6	57	1	8	3	29	3	43	4	2	10	.373	.324
Triessl, Mike, Riv.-R.C.	.292	71	238	212	28	62	81	10	0	3	34	1	2	5	17	1	47	1	0	6	.382	.356
Tyrus, Jason, Bakersfield	.173	25	91	81	12	14	26	0	0	4	10	0	1	2	7	0	28	4	2	1	.321	.253

Player, Team	Avg.	G	TPA	AB	R	H	TB	2B	3B	HR	RBI	SH	SF	HP	BB	IBB	SO	SB	CS	GDP	Slg.	OBP
Urbina, William, Modesto	.000	30	3	3	0	0	0	0	0	0	0	0	0	0	0	0	2	0	0	0	.000	.000
Urso, Joe, Lake Elsinore	.316	65	284	244	48	77	106	16	2	3	34	1	2	3	34	1	41	7	5	6	.434	.403
Vaughn, Derek, Lake Elsinore	.265	94	380	328	66	87	134	15	7	6	50	6	2	1	43	2	61	22	5	9	.409	.350
Wallace, Brian, San Jose	.222	25	93	81	15	18	25	1	0	2	8	2	0	1	9	1	18	3	0	2	.309	.308
Wallach, Tim, San Bernardino	.467	4	15	15	2	7	10	3	0	0	4	0	0	0	0	0	3	0	0	0	.667	.467
Walsh, Matthew, Modesto	.000	44	1	1	0	0	0	0	0	0	0	0	0	0	0	0	1	0	0	0	.000	.000
Whitaker, Ryan, Modesto	.000	32	2	1	0	0	0	0	0	0	0	0	0	0	1	0	1	0	0	0	.000	.500
White, Jason, Modesto	.307	76	339	267	63	82	166	16	1	22	71	7	3	8	54	0	71	1	2	9	.622	.434
Williams, Matt, San Jose	.182	4	12	11	2	2	5	0	0	1	2	0	0	1	0	0	3	0	0	0	.455	.250
Williamson, Joel, High Desert	.167	24	72	66	5	11	13	2	0	0	1	3	0	0	3	0	18	1	0	1	.197	.203
Wilson, Todd, San Jose	.239	37	128	117	14	28	37	7	1	0	13	3	0	2	6	0	19	1	0	5	.316	.288
Wingate, Ervan, Bakersfield	.234	121	501	445	51	104	153	23	1	8	59	4	4	6	42	0	86	5	8	25	.344	.306
Wittig, Paul, Bakersfield	.278	93	368	331	44	92	132	17	1	7	53	5	5	6	20	0	66	6	3	8	.399	.326
Wolff, Mike, High Desert*	.271	94	324	292	32	79	117	17	3	5	44	1	6	9	16	1	53	3	5	5	.401	.322
Woodridge, Dickie, R.C.*	.282	116	438	358	67	101	125	9	3	3	58	2	5	2	71	1	40	9	4	5	.349	.399
Wyngarden, Brett, Visalia	.263	76	289	270	21	71	94	14	0	3	24	1	3	3	12	0	81	1	2	6	.348	.299
Yard, Bruce, Bakersfield*	.230	59	228	191	19	44	57	8	1	1	17	7	2	1	27	0	22	2	5	10	.298	.326
Zahner, Kevin, Bakersfield	.233	82	282	257	25	60	77	7	2	2	31	6	5	2	12	0	37	4	1	10	.300	.268
Zellers, Kevin, Bakersfield	.241	96	384	332	39	80	113	16	1	5	27	2	3	8	39	1	106	5	6	6	.340	.332
Zongor, Steven, Modesto	.000	37	1	1	0	0	0	0	0	0	0	0	0	0	0	0	1	0	0	0	.000	.000

GRAND SLAMS: Adams, Alvarez, Riggs, 2 each; Asencio, Barger, Berry, Chavez, Dandridge, Dobrolsky, Guevara, Hunter, Hust, Ibanez, K. Johnson, Kirkpatrick, Ladjevich, Lee, Martins, McDonald, M. Moore, D. Powell, Redington, Shockey, Stare, Thielen, Treadway, White, 1 each.

AWARDED FIRST BASE ON CATCHER'S INTERFERENCE: Singleton 8 (Hughes 2, Triessl 2, Dandridge, Hemphill, M. Moore, Thurston); Galarza 4 (Dandridge, M. Rodriguez, Tejero, Wittig); Hunter 2 (Zahner 2); Chavez (Cuellar); Cunningham (Zahner); Kruger (Dobrolsky); Martins (Ibanez); Parker (Newstrom); Shockey (Harmer); Triessl (Newstrom); Wittig (Hemphill).

PLAYERS WITH TWO OR MORE TEAMS

Player, Team	Avg.	G	TPA	AB	R	H	TB	2B	3B	HR	RBI	SH	SF	HP	BB	IBB	SO	SB	CS	GDP	Slg.	OBP
Smith, Joel, Visalia	.286	67	285	262	32	75	120	12	3	9	43	2	3	3	15	0	65	0	1	9	.458	.329
Smith, Joel, Lake Elsinore	.205	30	102	88	12	18	31	4	0	3	19	0	3	0	11	0	15	0	0	4	.352	.284
Triessl, Mike, Riverside	.365	22	88	74	15	27	38	2	0	3	14	0	1	1	12	1	15	0	0	1	.514	.455
Triessl, Mike, R.C.	.254	49	150	138	13	35	43	8	0	0	20	1	1	4	5	0	32	1	0	5	.312	.297

1995 PITCHING

TEAM

Team	W	L	Pct.	ERA	G	CG	ShO	Sv.	IP	H	TBF	R	ER	HR	SH	SF	HB	BB	IBB	SO	WP	Bk.
San Jose	77	63	.550	3.05	140	5	17	35	1270.0	1147	5236	516	430	75	71	33	48	388	11	1013	56	14
Lake Elsinore	82	57	.590	3.73	139	5	9	36	1227.1	1246	5292	646	509	92	33	46	62	429	8	1022	58	10
Modesto	78	62	.557	4.13	140	0	5	41	1234.1	1260	5387	676	566	102	62	43	62	464	9	1077	98	15
San Bernardino	85	54	.612	4.25	139	3	8	41	1248.0	1311	5518	719	589	101	60	40	60	493	14	980	80	9
Stockton	74	66	.529	4.30	140	5	7	40	1239.2	1311	5523	694	592	93	68	38	85	555	19	880	68	24
R. Cucamonga	68	71	.489	4.45	139	10	8	30	1216.1	1212	5397	718	601	95	41	48	87	605	21	1074	100	17
Bakersfield	58	82	.414	4.53	140	3	4	33	1222.0	1299	5431	757	615	116	54	37	59	553	6	851	120	13
Riverside	72	67	.518	4.54	139	2	6	34	1226.1	1290	5483	767	618	83	55	52	67	577	21	981	90	17
Visalia	58	82	.414	4.66	140	11	9	24	1243.1	1322	5401	759	644	102	42	38	81	447	3	974	92	22
High Desert	46	94	.329	5.78	140	3	2	30	1227.2	1410	5718	996	789	132	47	61	71	633	13	960	115	31

INDIVIDUAL

TOP QUALIFIERS FOR EARNED-RUN AVERAGE TITLE

Minimum 112 innings. *Lefthanded pitcher.

Pitcher, Team	W	L	Pct.	ERA	G	GS	CG	ShO	GF	Sv.	IP	H	TBF	R	ER	HR	SH	SF	HB	BB	IBB	SO	WP	Bk.
Price, Tom, San Bernardino*	10	5	.667	2.20	42	13	2	0	9	3	151.2	145	605	49	37	5	5	1	3	14	4	82	5	0
Bonanno, Rob, Lake Elsinore	8	4	.667	3.05	17	17	4	2	0	0	112.0	112	455	49	38	10	2	4	3	16	0	72	0	0
Janicki, Pete, Lake Elsinore	9	4	.692	3.06	20	20	0	0	0	0	123.1	130	532	66	42	7	3	6	5	28	0	106	6	1
Moore, Trey, Riverside*	14	6	.700	3.09	24	24	0	0	0	0	148.1	122	605	65	51	6	2	5	2	58	1	134	6	1
Smith, Ryan, Riverside	10	7	.588	3.11	23	23	2	1	0	0	141.2	142	609	68	49	7	7	5	10	50	1	108	5	3
Percibal, Billy, High Desert	7	6	.538	3.23	21	20	2	0	0	0	128.0	123	547	63	46	10	2	2	3	55	0	105	7	4
Dixon, Bubba, R.C.*	10	7	.588	3.24	47	12	2	0	15	5	141.2	118	572	61	51	14	5	1	8	46	0	133	6	2
Beaumont, Matt, Lake Elsinore*	16	9	.640	3.29	27	26	0	0	0	0	175.1	162	724	80	64	15	1	6	7	57	1	149	1	1
Edwards, Wayne, Bakersfield*	9	8	.529	3.36	21	21	1	0	0	0	128.2	125	557	63	48	7	2	2	10	56	0	83	10	0
Foulke, Keith, San Jose	13	6	.684	3.50	28	26	2	1	0	0	177.1	166	723	85	69	16	10	3	7	32	0	168	6	2
DeClue, Jon, Vis.-L.E.*	11	6	.647	3.52	30	18	0	0	3	0	143.1	145	590	64	56	16	4	3	5	32	0	112	4	1
Howry, Bobby, San Jose	12	10	.545	3.54	27	25	1	0	1	0	165.1	171	695	79	65	6	12	4	8	54	0	107	7	3
Iglesias, Mike, Bak.-S.B.	8	12	.400	3.57	28	26	2	1	0	0	158.2	150	660	79	63	12	5	3	13	40	0	120	10	0
Edsell, Geoff, Lake Elsinore	8	12	.400	3.67	23	22	1	1	0	0	139.2	127	600	81	57	11	7	3	7	67	0	134	6	1
Endo, Masataka, Visalia	9	9	.500	3.76	28	27	6	1	0	0	186.2	162	763	87	78	13	7	2	7	62	1	178	17	8

DEPARTMENTAL LEADERS: W—Beaumont, 16; L—Griffin, 15; Pct.—Brunson, 1.000; G—Holtz, 56; GS—Clayton, LaChappa, 28; CG—Endo, 6; ShO—Bonanno, Murray, 2; GF—C. Castillo, R. Linares, 52; Sv.—C. Castillo, 32; IP—Endo, 186.2; H—Griffin, 182; TBF—Endo, 763; R—Griffin, 129; ER—Griffin, 108; HR—LaChappa, Macey, 17; SH—Howry, 12; SF—Griffin, 10; HB—Griffin, 17; BB—LaChappa, 88; IBB—Arroyo, 6; SO—Endo, 178; WP—Griffin, 21; Bk.—Endo, 8.

ALL PITCHERS

*Lefthanded pitcher.

Pitcher, Team	W	L	Pct.	ERA	G	GS	CG	ShO	GF	Sv.	IP	H	TBF	R	ER	HR	SH	SF	HB	BB	IBB	SO	WP	Bk.
Aguirre, Jose, Lake Elsinore*	0	1	.000	3.83	29	0	0	0	11	0	47.0	48	207	26	20	2	1	2	1	20	0	35	2	1
Anderson, Brian, Lake Elsinore*	1	1	.500	1.93	3	3	0	0	0	0	14.0	10	51	3	3	0	0	1	0	1	0	13	1	0
Andrakin, Rob, San Jose	2	1	.667	2.36	29	0	0	0	20	7	45.2	38	193	14	12	1	7	3	3	19	2	49	2	1
Aquino, Julio, San Bernardino	2	2	.500	7.84	25	3	0	0	6	0	59.2	96	293	59	52	5	2	2	1	23	0	42	5	1
Aquino, Luis, San Jose	0	0	.000	0.00	4	4	0	0	0	0	10.1	9	38	1	0	0	0	0	1	1	0	13	1	0
Arroyo, Luis, R.C.*	7	10	.412	5.25	26	24	0	0	0	0	128.2	158	599	97	75	9	8	6	12	62	6	102	7	3
Baker, Jared, R.C.	7	2	.778	4.44	31	15	1	1	3	1	101.1	98	442	57	50	9	3	4	8	49	1	98	3	1
Baldwin, Scott, Modesto*	0	1	.000	6.08	5	3	0	0	0	0	13.1	16	75	11	9	1	1	3	0	19	0	10	5	0
Barnes, Jon, R.C.	0	0	.000	1.69	5	1	0	0	3	0	10.2	6	39	3	2	0	0	0	0	2	0	10	0	0
Baron, Jim, R.C.*	0	0	.000	16.88	3	0	0	0	1	0	2.2	7	22	8	5	1	1	0	0	6	0	3	2	0
Barrett, Mark, R.C.*	1	0	1.000	3.58	32	0	0	0	11	1	32.2	39	149	18	13	2	2	1	2	11	1	29	0	0
Baxter, Herbert, Modesto*	4	7	.364	6.60	29	14	0	0	3	0	91.1	104	434	75	67	10	4	4	3	64	0	73	20	6
Beaumont, Matt, Lake Elsinore*	16	9	.640	3.29	27	26	0	0	0	0	175.1	162	724	80	64	15	1	6	7	57	1	149	1	1
Berumen, Andres, R.C.	0	0	.000	2.45	4	0	0	0	1	1	7.1	6	28	2	2	1	0	0	0	1	0	11	0	0
Bielecki, Mike, Lake Elsinore	0	0	.000	4.91	3	2	0	0	0	0	3.2	2	15	2	2	0	1	0	0	2	0	2	1	0
Bland, Nathan, Bakersfield*	4	9	.308	5.22	27	23	0	0	1	0	122.1	155	562	89	71	13	5	3	1	55	0	46	12	2
Blyleven, Todd, Lake Elsinore	0	1	.000	4.32	6	0	0	0	0	0	8.1	12	44	9	4	2	0	2	2	5	0	8	1	0
Bonanno, Rob, Lake Elsinore	8	4	.667	3.05	17	17	4	2	0	0	112.0	112	455	49	38	10	2	4	3	16	0	72	0	0
Boskie, Shawn, Lake Elsinore	0	0	.000	4.09	3	3	0	0	0	0	11.0	15	53	7	5	1	0	0	0	4	0	8	0	0
Brewer, Brian, High Desert*	1	9	.100	5.47	17	15	1	0	0	0	80.2	96	376	66	49	2	4	0	5	42	1	65	5	2
Briscoe, John, Modesto	0	0	.000	1.59	4	4	0	0	0	0	5.2	5	22	1	1	0	0	0	0	2	0	5	0	0
Brohawn, Troy, San Jose*	7	3	.700	1.65	11	10	0	0	1	0	65.1	45	246	14	12	4	1	1	1	20	0	57	5	1
Brown, Cory, High Desert	2	7	.222	5.36	30	10	0	0	8	3	94.0	104	417	66	56	15	5	5	6	32	0	80	3	1
Brown, Keith, Stockton*	1	0	1.000	1.62	12	0	0	0	3	0	16.2	11	65	4	3	1	0	0	1	6	2	8	1	0
Brunson, William, San Bern.*	10	0	1.000	2.05	13	13	0	0	0	0	83.1	68	334	24	19	4	3	5	5	21	0	70	3	0
Cafaro, Rocco, High Desert	4	5	.444	4.46	44	1	0	0	39	8	66.2	69	290	42	33	10	2	4	2	25	0	52	6	1
Camacho, Dan, San Bernardino	6	2	.750	3.95	43	1	0	0	27	9	68.1	66	295	32	30	7	5	1	1	30	3	79	5	1
Castillo, Carlos, Lake Elsinore	2	1	.667	2.41	52	0	0	0	52	32	52.1	55	223	18	14	2	1	0	5	15	0	40	2	1
Castillo, Mariano, San Jose	4	4	.500	1.59	21	0	0	0	8	3	56.2	49	226	14	10	1	2	0	2	13	0	51	1	0
Castro, Tony, Lake Elsinore	0	0	.000	5.56	8	0	0	0	2	0	11.1	15	57	9	7	1	1	1	0	8	0	9	2	0
Chavez, Tony, Lake Elsinore	4	2	.667	4.23	33	0	0	0	14	0	44.2	51	206	28	21	2	2	3	4	19	2	49	5	0
Clark, Howie, High Desert	0	0	.000	0.00	1	0	0	0	0	0	0.0	0	2	2	2	0	0	0	0	2	0	0	0	0
Clayton, Craig, Riverside	9	8	.529	5.00	28	28	0	0	0	0	160.1	171	738	102	89	16	11	6	7	83	3	156	7	1
Clement, Matt, R.C.	3	4	.429	4.24	12	12	0	0	0	0	57.1	61	267	37	27	1	2	4	5	49	0	33	12	0
Cole, Jim, Stockton	7	4	.636	3.48	14	13	1	0	0	0	85.1	88	359	43	33	7	1	2	5	20	0	52	1	1
Colon, Julio, San Bernardino	6	3	.667	4.33	49	0	0	0	30	12	79.0	68	343	47	38	7	1	1	2	37	2	75	12	0
Cope, Robin, Riverside	2	4	.333	7.39	11	5	0	0	0	0	31.2	50	162	31	26	2	0	1	0	18	1	13	3	2
Crills, Brad, High Desert	1	2	.333	5.51	5	3	0	0	1	0	16.1	19	78	15	10	0	0	1	1	8	0	10	3	2
Cromwell, Nate, R.C.*	0	1	.000	3.52	4	4	0	0	0	0	15.1	15	64	7	6	1	1	0	1	6	0	14	0	1
Crow, Dean, Riverside	3	4	.429	2.63	51	0	0	0	47	22	61.2	54	249	21	18	1	3	2	3	13	0	46	2	0
Dafun, George, Lake Elsinore	0	2	.000	5.54	3	3	0	0	0	0	13.0	8	53	8	8	0	0	0	1	11	0	13	2	1
Daigle, Tim, High Desert*	0	1	.000	4.95	19	0	0	0	9	4	43.2	46	203	33	24	7	1	1	0	20	0	36	4	0
Davis, Eddie, San Bernardino	0	0	.000	3.77	5	1	0	0	2	1	14.1	17	68	10	6	1	1	0	3	6	0	6	0	1
DeClue, Jon, Vis.-L.E.*	11	6	.647	3.52	30	18	0	0	3	0	143.1	145	590	64	56	16	4	3	5	32	0	112	4	1
Dennis, Shane, R.C.*	8	2	.800	2.51	11	11	2	1	0	0	79.0	63	316	27	22	8	3	2	0	22	1	77	1	0
Dixon, Bubba, R.C.*	10	7	.588	3.24	47	12	2	0	15	5	141.2	118	572	61	51	14	5	1	8	46	0	133	6	2
Dobrolsky, Bill, Stockton	0	0	.000	5.40	3	0	0	0	3	0	3.1	5	16	2	2	1	0	0	0	0	0	2	0	0
Dressendorfer, Kirk, Modesto	0	6	.000	4.62	27	16	0	0	2	0	37.0	39	171	24	19	5	2	2	2	18	0	50	6	0
Drewien, Dan, R.C.	1	2	.333	6.35	17	0	0	0	1	1	28.1	30	127	20	20	3	1	1	2	11	1	26	2	0
Drysdale, Brooks, Lake Elsinore	1	0	1.000	2.00	8	0	0	0	2	0	9.0	8	41	3	2	1	1	1	0	4	1	8	2	0
Duda, Steve, Stockton	3	6	.333	4.33	12	12	2	1	0	0	79.0	87	343	48	38	7	5	2	6	20	0	59	0	3
Dyess, Todd, High Desert	6	9	.400	5.10	23	22	0	0	0	0	125.1	145	573	94	71	9	5	5	9	58	0	118	17	5
Dykhoff, Radhames, High Desert*	1	5	.167	5.02	34	2	0	0	10	3	80.2	95	389	68	45	8	7	7	0	44	2	88	0	2
Eaddy, Brad, Bakersfield*	4	5	.444	2.95	42	1	0	0	19	5	79.1	66	328	29	26	4	4	0	0	36	1	68	3	0
Edsell, Geoff, Lake Elsinore	8	12	.400	3.67	23	22	1	1	0	0	139.2	127	600	81	57	11	7	3	7	67	0	134	6	1
Edwards, Wayne, Bakersfield*	9	8	.529	3.36	21	21	1	0	0	0	128.2	125	557	63	48	7	2	2	10	56	0	83	10	0
Endo, Masataka, Visalia	9	9	.500	3.76	28	27	6	1	0	0	186.2	162	763	87	78	13	7	2	7	62	1	178	17	8
Enoki, Yasuhiro, Visalia	4	7	.364	5.45	13	13	2	1	0	0	74.1	104	335	52	45	8	1	3	2	11	0	51	2	0
Erdos, Todd, R.C.	0	0	.000	13.50	1	0	0	0	0	0	2.2	5	13	4	4	0	0	1	0	0	0	4	0	0
Estes, Shawn, San Jose*	5	2	.714	2.17	9	8	0	0	0	0	49.2	32	191	13	12	1	0	3	1	17	0	61	7	0
Ettles, Mark, R.C.	0	0	.000	6.35	3	0	0	0	1	0	5.2	7	26	5	4	1	0	0	1	1	0	7	1	0
Felix, Ruben, Stockton*	0	2	.000	12.79	6	0	0	0	2	0	6.1	9	34	9	9	2	1	0	2	5	2	3	0	2
Fetchel, Tony, Visalia	0	1	.000	6.66	18	1	0	0	5	0	24.1	22	132	20	18	0	0	0	11	32	0	11	7	0
Fitzer, Douglas, Riverside*	0	0	.000	4.61	25	0	0	0	7	0	27.1	26	123	15	14	3	0	2	0	15	1	13	3	0
Foulke, Keith, San Jose	13	6	.684	3.50	28	26	2	1	0	0	177.1	166	723	85	69	16	10	3	7	32	0	168	6	2
Gambs, Chris, High Desert	0	0	.000	12.00	3	0	0	0	2	0	3.0	4	16	4	4	0	0	0	0	4	0	1	0	0
Gamez, Francisco, Stockton	2	1	.667	2.78	4	3	0	0	0	0	22.2	20	96	8	7	0	0	0	1	11	0	7	1	0
Garrett, Hal, R.C.	0	4	.000	2.79	23	1	0	0	5	0	42.0	40	196	21	13	2	2	5	2	25	0	43	7	1
Gates, Sean, R.C.	0	0	.000	0.00	1	0	0	0	0	0	2.2	1	10	0	0	0	0	0	1	0	0	2	0	0
Gomez, Dennys, San Jose	2	0	1.000	2.08	13	0	0	0	5	0	30.1	27	136	13	7	0	3	0	2	15	0	23	1	0
Gomez, Marcial, Lake Elsinore	1	0	1.000	5.84	7	0	0	0	0	0	12.1	11	56	10	8	0	0	1	1	10	0	10	2	1
Gomez, Pat, San Jose*	0	0	.000	1.42	3	2	0	0	0	0	6.1	5	29	2	1	0	1	0	0	5	0	5	1	1
Griffin, Ryan, High Desert	6	15	.286	6.80	31	25	0	0	4	3	143.0	182	686	129	108	14	4	10	17	80	0	96	21	2
Hackett, Jason, High Desert*	3	1	.750	5.18	18	2	0	0	9	1	40.0	43	195	30	23	6	2	1	2	31	2	29	6	0
Hanson, Craig, R.C.	3	4	.429	6.14	9	9	0	0	0	0	36.2	43	175	29	25	6	1	2	6	19	1	31	3	1
Hartmann, Pete, Stockton*	2	0	1.000	4.50	12	0	0	0	5	1	14.0	9	61	7	7	1	1	0	0	11	0	9	1	1
Hartvigson, Chad, San Jose*	4	4	.500	3.54	32	7	0	0	8	4	84.0	85	357	38	33	4	6	3	0	24	1	63	3	1
Hathaway, Hilly, R.C.*	0	1	.000	3.46	3	3	0	0	0	0	13.0	11	52	6	5	0	0	0	2	4	1	10	0	0
Haught, Gary, Modesto	9	5	.643	2.60	34	4	0	0	6	4	86.2	76	355	29	25	10	10	0	6	24	1	81	0	0
Hecker, Doug, Visalia	0	0	.000	0.00	2	0	0	0	2	0	2.0	1	9	1	0	0	0	1	1	1	0	2	1	0

Pitcher, Team	W	L	Pct.	ERA	G	GS	CG	ShO	GF	Sv.	IP	H	TBF	R	ER	HR	SH	SF	HB	BB	IBB	SO	WP	Bk.
Henrikson, Dan, San Jose*	0	1	.000	7.71	7	0	0	0	0	0	7.0	8	32	6	6	0	0	0	0	4	0	6	0	0
Herges, Matt, San Bernardino	5	2	.714	3.66	22	2	0	0	4	1	51.2	58	231	29	21	3	2	1	2	15	0	35	0	0
Hermanson, Mike, R.C.	4	6	.400	5.67	42	0	0	0	13	0	74.2	69	352	52	47	4	1	5	11	49	2	74	8	2
Hill, Chris, High Desert*	0	2	.000	9.00	5	1	0	0	2	0	13.0	20	66	13	13	5	0	3	1	7	0	10	1	0
Hinchliffe, Brett, Riverside	3	8	.273	6.61	15	15	0	0	0	0	77.2	110	373	69	57	10	5	3	8	35	3	68	4	0
Hinson, Dean, Vis.-L.E.	1	1	.500	4.17	28	0	0	0	18	3	41.0	38	186	27	19	2	3	1	5	22	0	39	10	2
Holdridge, David, Lake Elsinore	3	0	1.000	0.98	12	0	0	0	8	0	18.1	13	74	3	2	0	1	1	2	5	1	24	3	0
Holtz, Mike, Lake Elsinore*	4	4	.500	2.29	56	0	0	0	19	3	82.2	70	341	26	21	7	5	4	5	23	3	101	2	0
Howry, Bobby, San Jose	12	10	.545	3.54	27	25	1	0	1	0	165.1	171	695	79	65	6	12	4	8	54	0	107	7	3
Huber, Aaron, Modesto	0	0	.000	0.00	4	0	0	0	1	0	5.1	7	27	3	0	0	0	0	0	3	0	5	0	0
Hyde, Rich, San Jose	0	2	.000	2.00	16	0	0	0	15	7	18.0	19	77	6	4	1	2	0	0	5	1	13	3	0
Idemoto, Kenichiro, Visalia*	5	6	.455	4.10	31	8	2	0	5	2	101.0	104	428	54	46	11	4	2	4	27	0	83	1	0
Iglesias, Mike, Bak.-S.B.	8	12	.400	3.57	28	26	2	1	0	0	158.2	150	660	79	63	12	5	3	13	40	0	120	10	0
Ippolito, Rob, Riverside	1	3	.250	4.20	35	0	0	0	11	1	60.0	59	272	41	28	4	4	1	6	31	2	43	8	0
Isom, Jeff, R.C.*	1	0	1.000	9.00	4	0	0	0	3	0	4.0	6	21	4	4	1	0	1	1	0	0	2	0	0
Jacobsen, Joe, San Bernardino	0	0	.000	0.00	4	0	0	0	3	2	3.2	4	17	2	0	0	0	0	0	2	0	5	1	0
James, Mike, Lake Elsinore	0	0	.000	9.53	5	1	0	0	1	0	5.2	9	29	6	6	1	0	0	0	3	0	8	0	0
Janicki, Pete, Lake Elsinore	9	4	.692	3.06	20	20	0	0	0	0	123.1	130	532	66	42	7	3	6	5	28	0	106	6	1
Jaye, Jamie, Bakersfield*	1	2	.333	4.39	5	5	0	0	0	0	26.2	30	118	16	13	1	1	0	1	10	0	22	3	3
Jenkins, Jon, Visalia	1	1	.500	5.55	33	1	0	0	22	0	47.0	43	223	34	29	3	2	5	5	38	0	38	5	1
Jimenez, Miguel, Modesto	1	2	.333	6.00	4	4	0	0	0	0	18.0	14	83	13	12	5	0	1	2	14	0	11	4	0
Karns, Tim, High Desert	1	0	1.000	0.59	7	0	0	0	2	0	15.1	10	67	6	1	0	0	0	0	9	0	9	2	0
Keagle, Greg, R.C.	0	0	.000	4.50	2	2	0	0	0	0	14.0	14	59	9	7	1	0	1	2	2	0	11	1	0
Kenady, Jake, Bakersfield*	4	10	.286	6.72	23	16	0	0	1	0	87.0	107	419	76	65	7	1	3	3	68	0	69	10	1
Kramer, Jeff, Stockton	12	7	.632	4.47	32	24	0	0	2	1	149.0	174	662	87	74	9	8	4	12	58	0	108	9	6
Kubinski, Tim, Modesto*	6	10	.375	4.95	25	17	0	0	4	2	109.0	126	485	73	60	12	6	5	8	24	0	83	10	1
Kyslinger, Dan, Stockton	4	1	.800	3.59	37	0	0	0	11	1	52.2	58	253	24	21	2	4	2	2	37	1	44	6	2
LaChappa, Matt, R.C.*	11	7	.611	5.56	28	28	1	0	0	0	153.2	163	691	103	95	17	1	3	10	88	2	106	15	2
LaGarde, Joe, S.B-Bak	4	10	.286	6.72	23	16	0	0	1	0	87.0	107	419	76	65	7	1	3	3	68	0	69	10	1
LaRocca, Todd, High Desert	0	7	.000	7.41	15	7	0	0	2	1	51.0	68	248	53	42	7	0	2	1	29	0	31	7	2
Linares, Rich, Bakersfield	4	4	.500	2.27	55	0	0	0	52	20	67.1	64	272	18	17	2	4	1	3	17	2	57	3	0
Linares, Yfrain, Stockton	2	0	1.000	1.17	7	3	0	0	1	0	23.0	20	98	7	3	1	1	0	0	16	1	17	3	0
Locklear, Dean, Visalia*	3	3	.500	3.93	9	9	0	0	0	0	52.2	50	225	29	23	4	1	1	5	21	0	27	6	0
Macey, Fausto, San Jose	8	9	.471	3.89	28	25	1	0	0	0	171.0	167	709	84	74	17	7	5	6	50	1	94	6	4
Magnelli, Anthony, Visalia	2	5	.286	4.24	29	0	0	0	25	11	40.1	40	161	20	19	2	4	1	0	6	0	30	5	1
Manning, Derek, Modesto*	10	1	.909	2.43	25	12	0	0	4	3	111.0	112	467	43	30	7	6	4	1	25	0	102	3	1
Martin, Jeff, San Jose	5	6	.455	3.30	36	0	0	0	28	5	71.0	60	305	34	26	5	5	2	3	25	3	63	1	0
Maurer, Mike, Modesto	2	2	.500	1.79	39	0	0	0	37	18	40.1	27	157	9	8	3	2	2	2	9	0	44	2	0
McGonigle, Bill, Stockton	0	0	.000	6.75	4	0	0	0	3	0	4.0	5	20	3	3	1	0	0	1	3	0	3	1	0
McLain, Mike, San Jose	0	1	.000	2.29	9	0	0	0	3	2	19.2	16	77	5	5	0	0	1	0	6	0	21	1	0
Meade, Paul, Bakersfield	2	2	.500	7.55	24	0	0	0	9	0	53.2	70	253	47	45	15	3	3	5	25	1	32	4	2
Meadows, Jimmy, Visalia	7	6	.538	4.37	27	21	1	1	2	0	125.2	136	543	71	61	14	3	5	11	51	1	94	12	2
Michalak, Chris, Modesto*	3	2	.600	2.62	44	0	0	0	16	2	65.1	56	266	26	19	3	4	3	4	27	1	49	2	1
Mitchell, Kendrick, Bakersfield*	1	2	.333	5.34	36	0	0	0	12	0	57.1	61	271	46	34	7	1	1	2	38	0	36	18	2
Montane, Ivan, Riverside	5	5	.500	5.63	24	16	0	0	6	0	92.2	101	442	67	58	3	3	6	10	71	0	79	19	0
Moore, Trey, Riverside*	14	6	.700	3.09	24	24	0	0	0	0	148.1	122	605	65	51	6	2	5	2	58	1	134	6	1
Murphy, Matt, Stockton*	2	1	.667	5.91	5	4	0	0	0	0	21.1	25	100	14	14	2	2	1	1	13	0	9	0	0
Murray, Heath, R.C.*	9	4	.692	3.12	14	14	4	2	0	0	92.1	80	381	37	32	5	3	2	4	38	1	81	6	3
Muto, Junichiro, Visalia	1	2	.333	3.52	17	0	0	0	10	5	38.1	33	149	16	15	1	1	1	2	5	0	35	1	0
Myers, Tom, Visalia*	3	8	.273	6.43	30	13	0	0	5	0	85.1	108	406	81	61	6	3	6	10	45	0	34	7	1
Nelson, Chris, Modesto	2	0	1.000	0.90	2	2	0	0	0	0	10.0	4	37	1	1	0	0	0	0	4	0	8	1	0
Newton, Geronimo, Riverside*	4	4	.500	3.15	46	0	0	0	11	2	71.1	74	307	35	25	1	3	3	4	24	3	42	2	4
Nomo, Hideo, Bakersfield	0	1	.000	3.38	1	1	0	0	0	0	5.1	6	24	2	2	0	0	0	1	1	0	6	1	0
Oropesa, Eddie, San Bernardino*	0	0	.000	0.00	1	0	0	0	1	1	1.0	0	3	0	0	0	0	0	0	0	0	0	0	0
Ortiz, Russell, San Jose	0	1	.000	1.50	5	0	0	0	5	0	6.0	4	24	1	1	0	0	1	0	2	0	7	0	0
Osuna, Antonio, San Bernardino	0	0	.000	1.29	5	0	0	0	2	0	7.0	3	31	1	1	1	1	0	2	5	0	11	3	1
Paluk, Jeff, San Bernardino	6	3	.667	5.71	41	0	0	0	19	1	52.0	65	255	34	33	2	4	3	7	30	2	52	1	0
Parra, Julio, San Bernardino	4	5	.444	5.19	14	13	0	0	0	0	69.1	76	310	45	40	7	2	2	3	29	0	65	2	3
Patterson, Ken, Lake Elsinore*	0	0	.000	0.00	6	0	0	0	2	1	9.2	7	35	0	0	0	0	0	0	1	0	9	1	0
Paul, Andy, Stockton	7	5	.583	4.06	38	13	0	0	11	1	106.1	116	473	59	48	7	5	1	8	42	4	87	6	3
Pearsall, J.J., San Bernardino*	0	1	.000	8.44	6	0	0	0	2	0	10.2	15	54	10	10	3	3	0	0	7	0	5	1	0
Pena, Alex, High Desert	3	4	.429	6.66	34	6	0	0	20	3	77.0	97	363	68	57	4	7	1	4	28	2	44	6	3
Percibal, Billy, High Desert	7	6	.538	3.23	21	20	2	0	0	0	128.0	123	547	63	46	10	2	2	3	55	0	105	7	4
Perisho, Matt, Lake Elsinore*	8	9	.471	6.32	24	22	0	0	0	0	115.1	137	541	91	81	10	0	8	6	60	0	68	7	0
Peters, Don, San Jose	3	3	.500	4.24	20	13	0	0	5	2	68.0	68	284	33	32	6	1	3	4	24	0	38	1	1
Pincavitch, Kevin, San Bern.	2	0	1.000	2.70	3	0	0	0	0	0	10.0	8	46	5	3	1	1	0	0	6	1	10	0	0
Pivaral, Hugo, San Bernardino	6	4	.600	4.63	24	24	0	0	0	0	103.0	106	460	61	53	14	6	2	7	43	0	89	13	0
Prater, Pete, San Jose	2	0	1.000	3.18	5	4	0	0	0	0	22.2	18	90	8	8	0	1	1	1	7	0	14	0	0
Price, Tom, San Bernardino*	10	5	.667	2.20	42	13	2	0	9	3	151.2	145	605	49	37	5	5	1	3	14	4	82	5	0
Pricher, John, Lake Elsinore	1	0	1.000	3.38	5	0	0	0	1	0	8.0	9	37	4	3	0	0	0	0	4	0	3	2	0
Ramos, Cesar, Bakersfield	6	3	.667	3.56	24	4	0	0	6	2	60.2	63	257	28	24	2	6	2	1	17	0	35	7	1
Ricabal, Dan, San Bernardino	4	1	.800	3.88	43	0	0	0	13	2	72.0	63	315	35	31	7	0	2	5	33	1	62	2	1
Rigby, Brad, Modesto	11	4	.733	3.84	31	23	0	0	4	2	154.2	135	653	79	66	5	2	7	12	48	0	145	8	2
Roach, Peter, San Bernardino*	1	2	.333	3.00	30	0	0	0	14	8	33.0	28	143	16	11	2	2	2	2	14	1	38	5	0
Rodriguez, Nerio, High Desert	0	0	.000	1.80	7	0	0	0	3	0	10.0	8	44	2	2	0	0	0	0	7	0	10	0	0
Rogers, Jason, High Desert*	1	3	.250	7.83	5	5	0	0	0	0	23.0	32	121	26	20	0	1	2	0	18	0	10	5	0
Rogers, Kevin, San Jose*	0	2	.000	1.80	4	4	0	0	0	0	10.0	10	38	2	2	0	0	0	0	1	0	5	0	0
Rolocut, Brian, San Bernardino	1	0	1.000	5.68	11	3	0	0	2	0	12.2	15	70	10	8	0	2	3	1	16	0	10	0	0
Rosenkranz, Terry, Stockton*	1	2	.333	6.20	35	1	0	0	14	0	49.1	44	234	34	34	4	5	4	1	49	2	43	4	0
Rossiter, Michael, Modesto	7	2	.778	4.19	18	7	0	0	3	0	68.2	68	290	33	32	5	2	2	2	19	0	70	1	1
Rowland, Thad, Visalia*	0	1	.000	4.91	7	0	0	0	3	0	11.0	18	53	8	6	1	0	0	1	4	0	5	1	0
Ryan, Reid, Visalia	0	6	.000	9.38	12	5	0	0	4	0	31.2	51	170	43	33	3	1	4	7	26	0	14	2	3
Sadler, Al, Stockton	4	9	.308	4.42	37	14	1	1	10	2	114.0	113	501	62	56	9	3	2	8	59	0	82	6	2

Pitcher, Team	W	L	Pct.	ERA	G	GS	CG	ShO	GF	Sv.	IP	H	TBF	R	ER	HR	SH	SF	HB	BB	IBB	SO	WP	Bk.
Salazar, Luis, Stockton	6	2	.750	2.32	52	0	0	0	26	10	89.1	66	350	28	23	6	5	3	7	18	5	71	0	1
Saneaux, Francisco, High Desert	0	8	.000	10.59	23	11	0	0	4	1	52.2	56	296	77	62	8	0	6	11	72	1	64	10	4
Santana, Marino, Riverside	3	5	.375	6.19	9	9	0	0	0	0	48.0	44	214	47	33	10	3	4	2	25	0	57	2	3
Sauritch, Chris, High Desert	1	0	1.000	6.14	7	0	0	0	4	0	14.2	20	68	10	10	3	0	0	0	8	1	10	1	0
Sawyer, Zach, Modesto	7	1	.875	5.40	55	0	0	0	16	3	70.0	88	328	45	42	8	5	0	5	28	0	72	15	0
Scafa, Bob, Bakersfield*	5	8	.385	4.23	42	5	0	0	13	4	78.2	92	349	56	37	13	2	3	4	26	1	61	4	0
Scheffler, Craig, Bakersfield*	3	8	.273	5.62	32	19	0	0	3	0	105.2	118	490	85	66	15	7	5	4	65	0	51	15	0
Schenbeck, T.J., Stockton	1	5	.167	7.05	31	1	0	0	11	2	44.2	66	222	41	35	3	5	3	4	16	1	32	4	0
Schlutt, Jason, R.C.*	0	1	.000	4.91	11	0	0	0	5	2	14.2	16	67	9	8	0	1	1	1	4	0	11	3	0
Schramm, Carl, San Jose	6	4	.600	2.54	37	0	0	0	19	3	71.0	57	297	23	20	4	8	2	2	24	3	68	5	0
Seanez, Rudy, San Bernardino	2	0	1.000	0.00	4	0	0	0	2	1	6.0	2	23	0	0	0	0	0	0	3	0	5	0	0
Sebach, Kyle, Lake Elsinore	7	2	.778	4.60	14	13	0	0	0	0	76.1	91	340	40	39	10	1	1	4	29	0	60	6	0
Seki, Kiyokazu, Visalia	5	6	.455	4.94	35	3	0	0	16	3	85.2	79	360	53	47	11	1	0	1	29	0	84	1	0
Shenk, Larry, High Desert	0	0	.000	16.88	2	0	0	0	1	1	2.2	6	16	5	5	2	0	0	0	3	0	2	0	0
Slade, Shawn, Lake Elsinore	1	0	1.000	5.14	15	0	0	0	6	0	14.0	15	65	11	8	1	2	0	1	5	0	15	0	2
Smith, Hut, High Desert	3	4	.429	9.13	11	9	0	0	1	0	46.1	58	216	54	47	10	2	5	8	15	0	38	4	1
Smith, Ryan, Riverside	10	7	.588	3.11	23	23	2	1	0	0	141.2	142	609	68	49	7	7	5	10	50	1	108	5	3
Spiller, Derron, Visalia*	5	8	.385	6.03	32	11	0	0	8	0	88.0	114	390	64	59	6	6	3	5	16	1	52	5	2
Stone, Ricky, San Bernardino	3	5	.375	6.52	12	12	0	0	0	0	58.0	79	273	50	42	7	6	3	2	25	0	31	5	0
Sullivan, Dan, Riverside	4	4	.500	4.13	53	0	0	0	26	8	85.0	98	383	49	39	3	2	4	3	38	3	59	4	0
Suzuki, Mac, Riverside	0	1	.000	4.70	6	0	0	0	1	0	7.2	10	39	4	4	0	0	1	0	6	0	6	2	0
Takayoshi, Todd, Lake Elsinore	0	0	.000	40.50	1	0	0	0	1	0	0.2	1	6	3	3	0	0	0	1	2	0	0	0	0
Tapia, Elias, Bakersfield	0	1	.000	3.90	17	0	0	0	10	1	32.1	35	152	22	14	3	1	1	2	14	0	14	4	1
Taulbee, Andy, San Jose	3	2	.600	3.02	10	9	1	1	0	0	62.2	50	251	27	21	7	4	0	4	22	0	33	2	0
Theron, Greg, Riverside	4	2	.667	5.03	40	0	0	0	20	1	68.0	72	299	44	38	8	4	2	7	23	0	45	8	0
Thomas, Robbie, Bakersfield*	1	6	.143	7.48	26	6	0	0	4	0	49.1	55	247	51	41	8	4	4	5	36	0	39	6	0
Trimarco, Mike, High Desert	6	6	.500	5.27	40	1	0	0	16	2	100.2	109	441	70	59	12	5	6	1	36	4	52	7	2
Urbina, William, Modesto	2	0	1.000	5.27	30	0	0	0	11	1	41.0	51	185	28	24	4	0	1	4	16	0	18	4	0
Vanhof, John, Riverside*	1	1	.500	10.59	4	4	0	0	0	0	17.0	26	88	25	20	3	1	2	0	12	0	12	2	1
VanLandingham, William, San Jose	1	0	1.000	0.00	1	1	0	0	0	0	6.2	4	26	0	0	0	0	0	0	2	0	5	0	0
Villano, Mike, San Jose	0	1	.000	1.65	21	0	0	0	16	1	32.2	27	137	7	6	2	0	1	3	11	0	42	3	0
Wada, Takashi, Visalia	1	0	1.000	4.62	17	1	0	0	5	0	37.0	44	173	23	19	3	0	2	2	18	0	43	4	1
Wagner, Joe, Stockton	7	6	.538	4.35	20	18	0	0	1	0	107.2	124	494	62	52	8	8	3	4	53	0	76	7	0
Walsh, Matthew, Modesto	2	7	.222	4.65	44	9	0	0	21	5	100.2	98	445	64	52	11	5	3	6	45	4	108	5	2
Watson, Ron, Lake Elsinore	1	0	1.000	4.76	10	0	0	0	6	0	11.1	6	50	6	6	0	1	0	2	6	0	8	1	1
Webb, Doug, Stockton	0	0	.000	1.70	32	0	0	0	31	22	37.0	17	140	7	7	3	1	0	1	8	0	34	0	0
Whitaker, Ryan, Modesto	5	10	.333	4.41	32	25	0	0	3	0	151.0	177	669	90	74	10	8	3	4	54	2	88	10	1
Whitaker, Steve, San Jose*	0	0	.000	4.50	2	0	0	0	1	1	6.0	7	26	3	3	0	0	0	0	2	0	2	0	0
White, Darell, R.C.	0	5	.000	6.22	42	0	0	0	17	0	59.1	69	285	49	41	3	3	2	3	43	3	49	8	0
Whitman, Ryan, R.C.	1	2	.333	4.96	14	0	0	0	5	0	16.1	23	79	13	9	0	1	0	0	7	0	13	0	1
Williams, Matt, Bakersfield*	2	0	1.000	2.36	7	7	0	0	0	0	34.1	34	150	9	9	1	3	2	3	14	0	30	1	1
Williard, Brian, Lake Elsinore	2	4	.333	4.26	29	3	0	0	5	0	61.1	64	252	32	29	3	2	0	2	13	0	44	1	0
Wilson, Trevor, San Jose*	0	1	.000	1.35	2	2	0	0	0	0	6.2	5	29	4	1	0	1	0	0	3	0	5	0	0
Wilstead, Judd, Stockton	8	9	.471	5.09	31	21	0	0	1	0	139.2	165	653	94	79	15	10	5	14	71	1	72	12	3
Winchester, Marty, Riverside*	3	1	.750	4.57	35	4	0	0	8	0	67.0	67	305	40	34	2	5	3	2	45	3	56	5	0
Wolff, Bryan, R.C.	2	7	.222	3.32	54	0	0	0	43	18	57.0	39	262	23	21	4	4	3	3	54	0	77	15	0
Worley, Robert, Riverside	6	4	.600	5.31	11	11	0	0	0	0	61.0	64	275	44	36	4	2	2	3	30	0	44	8	2
Worrell, Tim, R.C.	0	2	.000	5.16	9	3	0	0	2	1	22.2	25	103	17	13	2	0	1	2	6	1	17	0	0
Wunsch, Kelly, Stockton*	5	6	.455	5.33	14	13	1	1	0	0	74.1	89	349	51	44	4	8	1	7	39	0	62	6	0
York, Charles, Bakersfield*	4	2	.667	5.82	31	5	0	0	7	1	68.0	75	298	47	44	6	5	4	3	24	1	69	7	0
Yoshida, Atsushi, Visalia	5	7	.417	3.60	13	13	0	0	0	0	75.0	88	310	37	30	4	2	0	0	12	0	68	3	0
Zerbe, Chad, San Bernardino*	11	7	.611	4.57	28	27	1	0	0	0	163.1	168	718	103	83	15	10	5	3	64	0	94	4	0
Zongor, Steven, Modesto*	7	2	.778	4.07	37	0	0	0	9	1	55.1	57	238	29	25	3	5	3	1	21	1	55	2	0

COMBINATION SHUTOUTS: **Bakersfield (3)**—Edwards-Linares, Iglesias-Linares, Thomas-Scafa. **High Desert (2)**—Percibal-Saneaux, Percibal-Trimarco. **Lake Elsinore (6)**—Beaumont-Aguirre-Watson, Bonanno-Holdridge, Janicki-Holtz, Perisho-Holtz-Castillo, Sebach-Aguirre, Sebach-Holtz-Castillo. **Modesto (5)**—Baxter-Walsh, Briscoe-Haught-Michalak-Zongor, Manning-Rigby, Rossiter-Sawyer-Maurer, Rossiter-Urbina-Sawyer. **Rancho Cucamonga (4)**—Clement-Dixon-Wolff, Dennis-Wolff, Dixon-White, LaChappa-Hermanson-Schlutt. **Riverside (5)**—Clayton-Newton-Crow, Clayton-Sullivan-Crow, Moore-Newton-Theron-Winchester, Smith-Sullivan-Crow, Winchester-Ippolito-Fitzer. **San Bernardino (8)**—Brunson-Price-Camacho-Colon-Paluk-Roach, Brunson-Roach-Camacho, Brunson-Camacho-Ricabal, Herges-Camacho, Lagarde-Camacho, Pivaral-Herges-Colon, Price-Camacho, Stone-Ricabal-Roach. **San Jose (15)**—Aquino-Howry, Brohawn-Andrakin, Brohawn-Villano, Estes-Martin, Estes-Peters, Foulke-Castillo, Foulke-Peters, Howry-Andrakin-Hartvigson, Howry-Schramm, Howry-Schramm-Hyde, Macey-Andrakin-Peters, Peters-Castillo, Prater-Hartvigson-Andrakin, VanLandingham-McLain, Wilson-Martin-Schramm-Ortiz. **Stockton (4)**—Kramer-Salazar, Linares-Paul-Webb, Paul-Sadler, Rosenkranz-Paul-Sadler-Schenbeck. **Visalia (6)**—Endo-Magnelli, Meadows-DeClue-Jenkins, Meadows-Seki, Myers-Muto, Spiller-Wada, Yoshida-DeClue.

NO-HIT GAMES: None.

PITCHERS WITH TWO OR MORE TEAMS

Pitcher, Team	W	L	Pct.	ERA	G	GS	CG	ShO	GF	Sv.	IP	H	TBF	R	ER	HR	SH	SF	HB	BB	IBB	SO	WP	Bk.
DeClue, Jon, Visalia*	6	5	.545	3.50	21	14	0	0	3	0	103.0	95	421	48	40	11	3	2	3	27	0	90	3	1
DeClue, Jon, Lake Elsinore*	5	1	.833	3.57	9	4	0	0	0	0	40.1	50	169	16	16	5	1	1	2	5	0	22	1	0
Hinson, Dean, Visalia	1	1	.500	3.93	23	0	0	0	14	3	34.1	30	150	18	15	1	3	0	4	16	0	35	9	2
Hinson, Dean, Lake Elsinore	0	0	.000	5.40	5	0	0	0	4	0	6.2	8	36	9	4	1	0	1	1	6	0	4	1	0
Iglesias, Mike, Bakersfield	7	10	.412	3.26	24	23	2	1	0	0	143.2	124	586	65	52	11	5	3	11	38	0	108	7	0
Iglesias, Mike, San Bernardino	1	2	.333	6.60	4	3	0	0	0	0	15.0	26	74	14	11	1	0	0	2	2	0	12	3	0
LaGarde, Joe, San Bernardino	5	10	.333	4.60	24	24	0	0	0	0	123.1	135	557	83	63	9	4	7	9	68	0	102	10	1
LaGarde, Joe, Bakersfield	1	1	.500	2.91	4	4	0	0	0	0	21.2	19	98	8	7	1	0	0	0	13	0	25	5	0

1995 FIELDING

TEAM

Team	Pct.	G	PO	A	E	TC	DP	PB
San Jose	.968	140	3810	1446	174	5430	120	16
San Bernardino	.968	139	3744	1562	177	5483	94	29
Stockton	.965	140	3719	1564	192	5475	120	22
Visalia	.964	140	3730	1530	199	5459	143	29
Lake Elsinore	.964	139	3682	1493	196	5371	124	22
Rancho Cucamonga	.963	139	3649	1463	199	5311	128	29
Riverside	.960	139	3679	1534	217	5430	124	46
Bakersfield	.959	140	3666	1639	224	5529	142	23
Modesto	.959	140	3703	1511	222	5436	112	16
High Desert	.950	140	3683	1508	275	5466	112	36

TRIPLE PLAY: Rancho Cucamonga.

INDIVIDUAL

FIRST BASEMEN

NOTE: All caps denotes fielding-percentage leader based on 70 games for catchers, 93 for all other non-pitchers and 140 innings for pitchers. *Throws lefthanded.

Player, Team	Pct.	G	PO	A	E	TC	DP
Alguacil, Jose, San Jose	1.000	1	1	0	0	1	0
Alimena, Charles, San Jose*	.987	35	280	15	4	299	22
Bengoechea, Brandy, Modesto	.927	4	37	1	3	41	3
Brakebill, Mark, Lake Elsinore	1.000	1	9	1	0	10	0
Breuer, Jim, Bakersfield	1.000	2	16	1	0	17	0
Burke, Jamie, Lake Elsinore	.987	21	152	5	2	159	15
Chavez, Eric, High Desert	.974	4	35	3	1	39	0
Cox, Steve, Modesto*	.984	114	991	77	17	1085	85
Cromer, D.T., Modesto*	1.000	4	34	8	0	42	2
Curtis, Kevin, High Desert	.983	70	576	53	11	640	52
Diaz, Alfredo, Lake Elsinore	1.000	1	4	0	0	4	0
Fernandez, Antonio, Visalia	.982	13	99	8	2	109	15
Galarza, Joel, San Jose	1.000	5	40	2	0	42	2
Gulseth, Mark, San Jose	1.000	16	112	11	0	123	6
Hamlin, Jonas, Stockton	.984	98	851	65	15	931	81
Hecker, Doug, Visalia	.974	6	35	3	1	39	2
Hughes, Bobby, Stockton	1.000	1	1	0	0	1	0
Ibanez, Raul, Riverside	.959	9	66	5	3	74	7
JORGENSEN, Randy, Riverside*	.989	131	1081	116	13	1210	101
Keene, Andre, San Jose*	.974	50	431	22	12	465	35
Kirkpatrick, Jay, San Bernardino	.994	52	462	39	3	504	33
Ladjevich, Rick, Riverside	1.000	6	40	4	0	44	8
Lee, Derrek, R.C.	.983	121	970	86	18	1074	96
McCall, Rod, Bakersfield	.979	52	490	26	11	527	52
Moeder, Tony, Lake Elsinore	.974	61	508	44	15	567	50
Morales, William, Modesto	.964	3	25	2	1	28	3
Mowry, Dave, R.C.*	1.000	8	38	2	0	40	3
Newstrom, Doug, San Bern.	.988	51	467	47	6	520	29
Ortega, Hector, Stockton	1.000	2	7	1	0	8	0
Ortega, Randy, Modesto	1.000	1	1	0	0	1	1
Pagee, Shawn, Visalia	.900	1	9	0	1	10	1
Pinoni, Scott, Visalia	.993	68	631	35	5	671	50
Powell, Gordon, Stockton	1.000	4	28	4	0	32	2
Rasmussen, Nate, Bakersfield*	.994	19	167	3	1	171	17
Redington, Tom, Lake Elsinore	.990	56	456	30	5	491	45
Richardson, Brian, San Bern.	1.000	6	41	4	0	45	2
Roberge, J.P., San Bernardino	.995	35	339	30	2	371	21
Sealy, Scot, Riverside	1.000	1	10	1	0	11	1
See, Larry, R.C.	.966	11	75	10	3	88	6
Seitzer, Brad, Stockton	.992	47	348	38	3	389	27
Shockey, Greg, Lake Elsinore*	1.000	1	5	0	0	5	0
Simonton, Benji, San Jose	.991	35	309	19	3	331	27
Smith, Frank, San Bernardino	1.000	1	2	0	0	2	0
Smith, Joel, Vis.-L.E.	.978	15	124	8	3	135	13
Smith, Scott, Riverside	1.000	2	5	1	0	6	0
Takayoshi, Todd, Lake Elsinore	.974	6	38	0	1	39	2
Tohyama, Shoji, Visalia*	.988	46	308	31	4	343	33
Triessl, Mike, R.C.	1.000	4	31	0	0	31	1
Wallace, Brian, San Jose	1.000	1	6	0	0	6	1
White, Jason, Modesto*	1.000	16	132	7	0	139	11
Wilson, Todd, San Jose	1.000	6	47	3	0	50	7
Wingate, Ervan, Bakersfield	.991	56	508	35	5	548	50
Wittig, Paul, Bakersfield	.964	2	25	2	1	28	2
Wolff, Mike, High Desert*	.988	79	576	71	8	655	49
Wyngarden, Brett, Visalia	.939	7	58	4	4	66	8
Zahner, Kevin, Bakersfield	.962	15	87	13	4	104	9

FIRST BASEMEN WITH TWO OR MORE TEAMS

Player, Team	Pct.	G	PO	A	E	TC	DP
Smith, Joel, Visalia	1.000	12	105	8	0	113	9
Smith, Joel, Lake Elsinore	.864	3	19	0	3	22	4

SECOND BASEMEN

Player, Team	Pct.	G	PO	A	E	TC	DP
Alguacil, Jose, San Jose	.990	25	44	58	1	103	17
Bengoechea, Brandy, Modesto	1.000	4	8	9	0	17	1
Berry, Michael, Visalia	.980	46	68	77	3	148	18
Bethea, Scott, Visalia	.969	74	163	184	11	358	53
Carr, Jeremy, Bakersfield	.970	121	325	346	21	692	102
Carrasquel, Domingo, Stockton	.957	31	48	84	6	138	18
Clark, Howie, High Desert	.938	9	16	14	2	32	1
Corps, Erick, R.C.	1.000	15	11	23	0	34	5
Cuevas, Eduardo, R.C.	.931	14	29	25	4	58	9
Dean, Chris, Riverside	.939	115	207	304	33	544	68
Diaz, Alfredo, Lake Elsinore	1.000	2	4	3	0	7	1
Dumas, Mike, Stockton	.967	34	79	69	5	153	14
Faircloth, Kevin, San Bernardino	.944	12	11	23	2	36	3
Fernandez, Antonio, Visalia	.957	13	15	30	2	47	4
Fuller, Aaron, Visalia	.833	1	3	2	1	6	0
Garcia, Manuel, Visalia	.980	11	19	30	1	50	8
Guiel, Aaron, Lake Elsinore	.958	108	214	294	22	530	72
Guillen, Jose, Modesto	.962	12	18	33	2	53	4
LaRocca, Greg, R.C.	.929	24	42	63	8	113	12
Martin, Lincoln, High Desert	.937	36	53	81	9	143	19
Martins, Eric, Modesto	.956	98	188	242	20	450	51
Marval, Raul, San Jose	1.000	4	4	10	0	14	1
McDonald, Jason, Modesto	.943	14	22	28	3	53	4
Mercedes, Feliciano, High Desert	.976	24	28	52	2	82	8
Morillo, Cesar, Bakersfield	.944	10	20	31	3	54	12
Morreale, John, Stockton	.982	11	24	32	1	57	7
Moschetti, Mike, Modesto	.940	20	38	56	6	100	11
Nadeau, Mike, High Desert	.947	20	30	42	4	76	5
Nevers, Tom, Stockton	.833	2	3	2	1	6	1
Owen, Spike, Lake Elsinore	1.000	1	0	1	0	1	0
Pagan, Angel, High Desert	.913	11	15	27	4	46	5
Patel, Manny, Riverside	.984	27	46	81	2	129	18
Phillips, Gary, San Jose	1.000	1	2	2	0	4	1
Powell, Gordon, Stockton	.959	73	130	217	15	362	43
Priest, Chris, Visalia	1.000	1	0	8	0	8	0
Richardson, Scott, Stockton	1.000	1	1	2	0	3	1
Riggs, Adam, San Bernardino	.928	121	223	303	41	567	47
Rivera, Santiago, R.C.	1.000	1	1	0	0	1	0
Roberge, J.P., San Bernardino	1.000	5	4	6	0	10	3
Sbrocco, Jon, San Jose	.962	114	226	311	21	558	60
Schaaf, Bob, San Bernardino	1.000	9	19	27	0	46	6
Serra, Jose, High Desert	.904	40	75	123	21	219	19
Short, Rick, High Desert	.939	25	48	59	7	114	12
Simmons, Mark, Lake Elsinore	.967	16	28	30	2	60	5
Tredaway, Chad, R.C.	1.000	4	8	10	0	18	1
Urso, Joe, Lake Elsinore	.969	22	40	54	3	97	15
Wallace, Brian, San Jose	.889	3	6	10	2	18	1
Wingate, Ervan, Bakersfield	.982	9	19	36	1	56	5
WOODRIDGE, Dickie, R.C.	.988	97	178	235	5	418	64

THIRD BASEMEN

Player, Team	Pct.	G	PO	A	E	TC	DP
Alguacil, Jose, San Jose	.950	14	19	19	2	40	2
Alvarez, Gabe, R.C.	.960	9	5	19	1	25	0
Bengoechea, Brandy, Modesto	.895	129	82	226	36	344	13
Berry, Michael, Visalia	.885	48	25	98	16	139	10
Bogle, Bryan, High Desert	.927	16	12	26	3	41	2
Brakebill, Mark, Lake Elsinore	1.000	1	0	1	0	1	0
Burke, Jamie, Lake Elsinore	.927	89	68	186	20	274	20
Chavez, Eric, High Desert	.882	37	18	49	9	76	3
Clark, Howie, High Desert	.917	82	60	151	19	230	12
Corps, Erick, R.C.	.704	9	3	16	8	27	1
Diaz, Alfredo, Lake Elsinore	.922	30	26	69	8	103	7
Fernandez, Antonio, Visalia	.922	60	42	111	13	166	14
Fuller, Aaron, Visalia	.800	2	1	3	1	5	0
Guillen, Jose, Modesto	.950	7	6	13	1	20	1

Player, Team	Pct.	G	PO	A	E	TC	DP
Johnson, Keith, San Bernardino	.857	5	4	8	2	14	1
Koscielniak, Dwain, R.C.	.833	4	1	4	1	6	1
LADJEVICH, Rick, Riverside	.936	94	72	176	17	265	21
LaRocca, Greg, R.C.	.933	11	5	23	2	30	2
Martins, Eric, Modesto	.967	11	5	24	1	30	2
Miller, Roy, Riverside	.900	21	11	25	4	40	4
Milstien, Dave, Stockton	1.000	1	0	1	0	1	0
Morales, William, Modesto	1.000	1	0	3	0	3	0
Morillo, Cesar, Bakersfield	.938	18	11	50	4	65	2
Morreale, John, Stockton	.933	8	3	11	1	15	1
Nadeau, Mike, High Desert	1.000	2	0	1	0	1	0
Nevers, Tom, Stockton	1.000	1	1	1	0	2	0
Ortega, Hector, Stockton	.911	72	75	120	19	214	10
Ortega, Randy, Modesto	1.000	2	1	2	0	3	0
Owen, Spike, Lake Elsinore	1.000	1	0	2	0	2	0
Pagan, Angel, High Desert	.818	10	5	22	6	33	1
Parker, Alan, Visalia	1.000	2	1	3	0	4	0
Patel, Manny, Riverside	.904	34	21	73	10	104	6
Phillips, Gary, San Jose	.906	103	66	194	27	287	18
Priest, Chris, Visalia	.889	35	30	58	11	99	7
Raven, Luis, Lake Elsinore	1.000	5	5	15	0	20	3
Redington, Tom, Lake Elsinore	.500	1	1	0	1	2	0
Richardson, Brian, San Bernardino	.926	122	82	254	27	363	18
Rivera, Santiago, R.C.	.909	24	9	21	3	33	4
Roberge, J.P., San Bernardino	1.000	1	0	1	0	1	0
Schaaf, Bob, San Bernardino	.923	18	6	30	3	39	2
Seitzer, Brad, Stockton	.925	67	47	150	16	213	15
Serra, Jose, High Desert	1.000	2	1	0	0	1	0
Short, Rick, High Desert	1.000	5	3	8	0	11	0
Simmons, Mark, Lake Elsinore	.935	23	13	30	3	46	4
Smith, Scott, Riverside	1.000	4	4	8	0	12	0
Tredaway, Chad, R.C.	.923	97	73	202	23	298	24
Urso, Joe, Lake Elsinore	.500	1	1	0	1	2	0
Wallace, Brian, San Jose	.929	5	3	10	1	14	1
Wallach, Tim, San Bernardino	.909	4	2	8	1	11	1
Williams, Matt, San Jose	1.000	4	0	4	0	4	0
Wilson, Todd, San Jose	.960	25	17	55	3	75	5
Wingate, Ervan, Bakersfield	.905	33	27	59	9	95	4
Zellers, Kevin, Bakersfield	.912	94	68	223	28	319	21

SHORTSTOPS

Player, Team	Pct.	G	PO	A	E	TC	DP
Alguacil, Jose, San Jose	.969	19	28	35	2	65	7
Alvarez, Gabe, R.C.	.884	43	47	113	21	181	13
Bautista, Juan, High Desert	.911	96	154	253	40	447	46
Bellhorn, Mark, Modesto	.927	55	94	172	21	287	29
Bengoechea, Brandy, Modesto	1.000	1	2	4	0	6	1
Bethea, Scott, Visalia	.938	27	34	72	7	113	11
Bordick, Mike, Modesto	1.000	1	2	1	0	3	0
Carrasquel, Domingo, Stockton	.943	30	31	68	6	105	14
Cook, Jason, Riverside	.897	5	12	14	3	29	4
Corps, Erick, R.C.	.846	6	5	6	2	13	1
Delgado, Wilson, San Jose	1.000	1	1	2	0	3	1
Diaz, Alfredo, Lake Elsinore	.957	12	17	27	2	46	3
Dumas, Mike, Stockton	1.000	1	1	3	0	4	0
Faircloth, Kevin, San Bernardino	.961	42	47	102	6	155	11
Guevara, Giomar, Riverside	.929	83	123	231	27	381	47
Guillen, Jose, Modesto	1.000	5	3	5	0	8	2
JOHNSON, Keith, San Bernardino	.963	105	170	319	19	508	42
King, Brett, San Jose	.950	107	165	269	23	457	52
LaRocca, Greg, R.C.	.931	87	131	220	26	377	49
Luuloa, Keith, Lake Elsinore	.921	101	155	290	38	483	54
Martinez, Gabby, Stockton	.924	64	96	158	21	275	33
Marval, Raul, San Jose	.871	7	17	10	4	31	2
McDonald, Jason, Modesto	.885	78	119	213	43	375	44
Meilan, Tony, Bakersfield	.891	12	10	31	5	46	5
Mercedes, Feliciano, High Desert	.839	8	12	14	5	31	2
Miller, Roy, Riverside	.929	38	60	96	12	168	21
Milstien, Dave, Stockton	.954	56	104	168	13	285	28
Morillo, Cesar, Bakersfield	.917	73	109	222	30	361	42
Nevers, Tom, Stockton	.800	1	2	2	1	5	0
Pagan, Angel, High Desert	.944	14	19	32	3	54	8
Parker, Alan, Visalia	.949	118	202	352	30	584	81
Patel, Manny, Riverside	.923	21	33	51	7	91	9
Paulino, Arturo, Modesto	1.000	4	3	10	0	13	1
Phillips, Gary, San Jose	1.000	1	0	1	0	1	0
Prieto, Rick, Bakersfield	1.000	2	3	7	0	10	1
Rivera, Santiago, R.C.	.891	15	24	25	6	55	6
Schaaf, Bob, San Bernardino	.933	4	6	8	1	15	3
Serra, Jose, High Desert	.887	35	38	64	13	115	17
Simmons, Mark, Lake Elsinore	.923	8	6	18	2	26	3
Stare, Lonny, Bakersfield	.500	1	0	1	1	2	0
Urso, Joe, Lake Elsinore	.938	24	30	61	6	97	11
Wallace, Brian, San Jose	.908	16	34	45	8	87	10
Wingate, Ervan, Bakersfield	.929	2	5	8	1	14	0
Yard, Bruce, Bakersfield	.957	53	77	192	12	281	49

TRIPLE PLAY: Alvarez (unassisted).

OUTFIELDERS

Player, Team	Pct.	G	PO	A	E	TC	DP
Adams, Tommy, Riverside	.979	48	91	2	2	95	0
Alguacil, Jose, San Jose	.857	4	6	0	1	7	0
Alimena, Charles, San Jose*	1.000	3	1	0	0	1	0
Asencio, Alex, San Bernardino*	.942	29	48	1	3	52	0
Avila, Rolando, High Desert	.955	49	105	2	5	112	1
Banks, Tony, Modesto*	.977	25	41	1	1	43	0
Barger, Mike, Riverside	.982	78	160	6	3	169	0
Bishop, Steve, High Desert	.917	9	9	2	1	12	0
Bogle, Bryan, High Desert	1.000	1	1	0	0	1	0
Bonds, Bobby, Visalia	.947	103	225	9	13	247	2
Breuer, Jim, Bakersfield	1.000	7	7	0	0	7	0
Brock, Tarrick, Visalia*	.949	39	90	4	5	99	1
Byrne, Clayton, High Desert	.945	51	113	7	7	127	3
Carr, Jeremy, Bakersfield	1.000	1	1	0	0	1	0
Chavez, Eric, High Desert	1.000	8	9	2	0	11	1
Claudio, Patricio, Bakersfield	.960	32	67	5	3	75	0
Clyburn, Danny, High Desert	.932	42	63	6	5	74	0
Conway, Jeff, R.C.*	1.000	25	33	2	0	35	2
Corps, Erick, R.C.	.982	34	50	4	1	55	0
Cromer, D.T., Modesto*	.944	95	126	8	8	142	0
Cruz, Jose, Riverside	.961	33	70	4	3	77	1
Cunningham, Earl, Lake Elsinore	1.000	8	5	0	0	5	0
Curtis, Kevin, High Desert	1.000	2	2	0	0	2	0
Dandridge, Brad, San Bernardino	.976	23	39	1	1	41	0
Daniels, Moe, Lake Elsinore	.990	38	91	4	1	96	0
D'Aquila, Tom, High Desert	.917	73	120	2	11	133	0
Derotal, Francisco, R.C.	.960	27	23	1	1	25	0
Doty, Derrin, Lake Elsinore	.971	91	128	4	4	136	0
Dumas, Mike, Stockton	.985	34	62	2	1	65	0
Dunn, Todd, Stockton	.968	63	116	6	4	126	1
Durkin, Chris, San Bernardino*	.946	53	83	4	5	92	0
Eaddy, Keith, High Desert	.957	84	151	4	7	162	0
Ealy, Tracey, San Jose	1.000	3	5	0	0	5	0
Erstad, Darin, Lake Elsinore*	.985	25	65	2	1	68	0
Fuller, Aaron, Visalia	.967	47	114	5	4	123	3
Fully, Ed, High Desert	.963	34	76	3	3	82	0
Gibbs, Kevin, San Bernardino	1.000	5	5	0	0	5	0
Graham, John, Visalia*	.972	65	97	7	3	107	0
Grieve, Ben, Modesto	.951	27	37	2	2	41	0
Guillen, Jose, Modesto	1.000	2	1	0	0	1	0
Hayashi, Hiroyasu, Visalia*	.967	26	55	3	2	60	0
Hence, Sam, Bakersfield	1.000	2	1	1	0	2	0
Hilo, Johnny, San Bernardino*	.930	34	39	1	3	43	0
Hodge, Roy, High Desert	.922	36	55	4	5	64	0
Hugo, Sean, High Desert*	.941	24	45	3	3	51	0
Hunter, Scott, San Bernardino	.953	111	177	7	9	193	0
Hust, Gary, Modesto	.974	128	214	11	6	231	3
Jenkins, Geoff, Stockton*	.895	13	14	3	2	19	0
Johnson, Earl, R.C.	.972	81	225	16	7	248	2
Keel, David, Modesto	1.000	9	12	0	0	12	0
Keifer, Greg, San Jose	1.000	22	20	0	0	20	0
Kruger, Andy, Visalia*	.940	71	123	2	8	133	1
Lemons, Rich, Bakersfield	.942	35	46	3	3	52	0
Marquez, Jesus, Riverside*	.971	68	123	9	4	136	0
Martin, Lincoln, High Desert	1.000	4	1	0	0	1	0
Martinez, Greg, Stockton	.985	109	253	7	4	264	0
McDonald, Jason, Modesto	.965	43	106	5	4	115	1
McGonigle, Bill, Stockton	.976	60	114	10	3	127	3
McNabb, Buck, Bakersfield	.991	63	101	8	1	110	1
Mejia, Miguel, High Desert	.952	34	58	2	3	63	0
Miller, Roy, Riverside	1.000	1	1	0	0	1	0
Moore, Kerwin, Modesto	.966	15	27	1	1	29	0
Moore, Vince, R.C.*	.960	84	154	15	7	176	3
Neill, Mike, Modesto*	.968	59	113	7	4	124	0
Nelson, Charles, San Bernardino*	1.000	1	2	0	0	2	0
Newstrom, Doug, San Bernardino	1.000	10	4	2	0	6	0
Nicholas, Darrell, Stockton	.936	53	97	6	7	110	0
Ohmura, Iwao, Visalia	.969	42	58	5	2	65	2
Ortega, Hector, Stockton	.988	46	79	6	1	86	1
Powell, Chris, Lake Elsinore*	.957	13	21	1	1	23	0
Powell, Dante, San Jose	.967	130	308	18	11	337	3
Priest, Chris, Visalia	1.000	15	14	2	0	16	1
Prieto, Chris, R.C.*	.957	89	146	10	7	163	2
Prieto, Rick, Bakersfield	.970	68	156	4	5	165	2

Player, Team	Pct.	G	PO	A	E	TC	DP
Ramirez, Alex, Bakersfield	.941	84	150	9	10	169	2
Reese, Matthew, Modesto*	1.000	6	11	0	0	11	0
Richardson, Scott, Stockton	.900	20	26	1	3	30	0
Rios, Armando, San Jose*	.963	118	220	16	9	245	5
Rivera, Santiago, R.C.	1.000	9	9	0	0	9	0
Roberge, J.P., San Bernardino	.986	46	67	2	1	70	1
Roberts, John, R.C.	.978	95	165	13	4	182	2
Rodriques, Cecil, Stockton	.952	45	94	5	5	104	2
Schaaf, Bob, San Bernardino	1.000	5	4	1	0	5	0
Shockey, Greg, Lake Elsinore*	.976	107	187	16	5	208	1
Simmons, Mark, Lake Elsinore	.959	34	46	1	2	49	0
Singleton, Chris, San Jose*	.955	91	142	6	7	155	0
Smith, Demond, Lake Elsinore	.929	34	62	3	5	70	0
Smith, Frank, San Bernardino	.971	51	63	5	2	70	1
Smith, Scott, Riverside	.938	32	59	1	4	64	0
SPEARMAN, Vernon, San Bern.*	.987	93	224	9	3	236	2
Stare, Lonny, Bakersfield	.964	99	170	16	7	193	0
Stuckenschneider, Eric, San Bern.	1.000	2	3	0	0	3	0
Sturdivant, Marcus, Riverside*	.958	78	130	7	6	143	0
Tachikawa, Takashi, Visalia	.973	36	65	6	2	73	3
Tejcek, John, Riverside	.955	92	183	9	9	201	1
Tena, Dario, R.C.	.889	11	8	0	1	9	0
Thielen, D.J., San Jose	.974	79	144	7	4	155	4
Tyrus, Jason, Bakersfield	.942	24	47	2	3	52	0
Vaughn, Derek, Lake Elsinore	.969	92	181	9	6	196	1
White, Jason, Modesto*	.927	26	36	2	3	41	0
Wingate, Ervan, Bakersfield	1.000	18	26	0	0	26	0
Woodridge, Dickie, R.C.	1.000	4	3	0	0	3	0

CATCHERS

Player, Team	Pct.	G	PO	A	E	TC	DP	PB
Allanson, Andy, Lake Elsinore	.993	22	122	11	1	134	1	3
Cabrera, Jairo, High Desert	.969	14	78	16	3	97	0	1
Campillo, Rob, Stockton	.978	35	192	30	5	227	1	7
Carpenter, Jerry, Lake Elsinore	1.000	1	9	3	0	12	0	0
Cavanagh, Mike, San Jose	1.000	6	45	3	0	48	0	1
Chavez, Eric, High Desert	.941	12	42	6	3	51	0	2
Cuellar, Jose, Riverside	.972	19	92	11	3	106	1	6
Dandridge, Brad, San Bern.	.984	43	267	34	5	306	3	10
Dobrolsky, Bill, Stockton	.984	79	431	73	8	512	3	9
Galarza, Joel, San Jose	.983	37	267	28	5	300	3	3
Gargiulo, Mike, High Desert	1.000	14	76	8	0	84	2	3
Grass, Darren, R.C.	.994	21	138	23	1	162	1	2
Gresham, Kris, High Desert	.975	47	270	46	8	324	1	11
Harmer, Frank, High Desert	.962	5	22	3	1	26	0	1
Hemphill, Bret, Lake Elsinore	.976	45	354	47	10	411	1	6
Hughes, Bobby, Stockton	.987	45	251	50	4	305	4	5
Ibanez, Raul, Riverside	.980	63	399	49	9	457	3	25
Jennings, Lance, Visalia	.988	76	501	71	7	579	10	9
Johnson, Todd, Bakersfield	1.000	7	36	4	0	40	0	1
Knapp, Mike, High Desert	.949	5	32	5	2	39	1	1
Konerko, Paul, San Bernardino	.985	95	676	68	11	755	0	18
Ladjevich, Rick, Riverside	1.000	4	15	0	0	15	0	0
Marnell, Anthony, R.C.	.968	16	82	8	3	93	0	1
MAYES, Craig, San Jose	.992	84	576	61	5	642	9	9
McKinnis, Leroy, R.C.	1.000	10	88	15	0	103	3	4
Molina, Ben, Lake Elsinore	.995	27	195	16	1	212	0	4
Moore, Mark, Modesto	.970	37	269	18	9	296	2	7
Morales, William, Modesto	.991	101	772	100	8	880	9	8
Newstrom, Doug, San Bern.	.962	14	49	2	2	53	0	1
Ortega, Randy, Modesto	1.000	7	57	2	0	59	0	1
Pagee, Shawn, Visalia	.964	17	92	15	4	111	2	2
Rodriguez, Miguel, Stockton	.957	11	21	1	1	23	0	1
Rodriguez, Nerio, High Desert	.978	50	324	33	8	365	3	10
Schneider, Dan, San Jose	.989	12	80	6	1	87	0	0
Schwenke, Matt, R.C.	.981	22	135	16	3	154	0	4
Sealy, Scot, Riverside	.981	54	408	50	9	467	1	8
See, Larry, R.C.	1.000	1	1	0	0	1	0	0
Shepherd, Brian, San Jose	.978	13	76	14	2	92	0	3
Smith, Joel, Vis.-L.E.	.991	45	297	45	3	345	5	6
Soliz, Steve, Bakersfield	.989	44	237	43	3	283	2	4
Takayoshi, Todd, Lake Elsinore	.987	35	198	23	3	224	2	5
Tejero, Fausto, Lake Elsinore	.982	8	48	8	1	57	2	1
Thurston, Jerrey, R.C.	.980	75	489	57	11	557	5	9
Triessl, Mike, Riv.-R.C.	.971	40	208	25	7	240	6	16
Williamson, Joel, High Desert	.962	24	136	16	6	158	1	7
Wittig, Paul, Bakersfield	.974	61	368	48	11	427	4	14
Wyngarden, Brett, Visalia	.977	36	189	19	5	213	3	15
Zahner, Kevin, Bakersfield	.969	47	231	21	8	260	2	4

CATCHERS WITH TWO OR MORE TEAMS

Player, Team	Pct.	G	PO	A	E	TC	DP	PB
Smith, Joel, Visalia	.991	28	192	30	2	224	4	3
Smith, Joel, Lake Elsinore	.992	17	105	15	1	121	1	3
Triessl, Mike, Riverside	.962	11	68	7	3	78	2	7
Triessl, Mike, R.C.	.975	29	140	18	4	162	4	9

PITCHERS

Player, Team	Pct.	G	PO	A	E	TC	DP
Aguirre, Jose, Lake Elsinore*	.800	29	0	4	1	5	0
Anderson, Brian, Lake Elsinore*	1.000	3	1	4	0	5	0
Andrakin, Rob, San Jose	.900	29	6	3	1	10	0
Aquino, Julio, San Bernardino	.875	25	8	6	2	16	0
Arroyo, Luis, R.C.*	.943	26	11	22	2	35	0
Baker, Jared, R.C.	1.000	31	8	9	0	17	0
Baldwin, Scott, Modesto*	.833	5	1	4	1	6	1
Barnes, Jon, R.C.	1.000	5	0	1	0	1	0
Baron, Jim, R.C.*	.500	3	0	1	1	2	0
Barrett, Mark, R.C.*	1.000	32	0	3	0	3	0
Baxter, Herbert, Modesto*	.893	29	4	21	3	28	1
Beaumont, Matt, Lake Elsinore*	.962	27	9	41	2	52	2
Berumen, Andres, R.C.	1.000	4	1	0	0	1	0
Bielecki, Mike, Lake Elsinore	1.000	3	0	1	0	1	0
Bland, Nathan, Bakersfield*	.900	27	3	24	3	30	0
Blyleven, Todd, Lake Elsinore	1.000	6	0	3	0	3	0
Bonanno, Rob, Lake Elsinore	.926	17	8	17	2	27	1
Brewer, Brian, High Desert*	.920	17	3	20	2	25	0
Briscoe, John, Modesto	1.000	4	1	0	0	1	0
Brohawn, Troy, San Jose*	1.000	11	4	10	0	14	0
Brown, Cory, High Desert	.950	30	9	10	1	20	0
Brown, Keith, Stockton*	1.000	12	1	5	0	6	0
Brunson, William, San Bernardino*	.962	13	4	21	1	26	0
Cafaro, Rocco, High Desert	.909	44	3	7	1	11	0
Camacho, Dan, San Bernardino	1.000	43	5	10	0	15	1
Castillo, Carlos, Lake Elsinore	1.000	52	5	6	0	11	2
Castillo, Mariano, San Jose	.833	21	1	4	1	6	0
Castro, Tony, Lake Elsinore	1.000	8	0	2	0	2	0
Chavez, Tony, Lake Elsinore	1.000	33	1	5	0	6	0
Clayton, Craig, Riverside	.960	28	12	12	1	25	0
Clement, Matt, R.C.	.923	12	3	9	1	13	1
Cole, Jim, Stockton	.882	14	1	14	2	17	2
Colon, Julio, San Bernardino	1.000	49	9	13	0	22	1
Cope, Robin, Riverside	.625	11	2	3	3	8	0
Crills, Brad, High Desert	1.000	5	1	3	0	4	0
Cromwell, Nate, R.C.*	1.000	4	1	5	0	6	0
Crow, Dean, Riverside	1.000	51	2	8	0	10	1
Dafun, George, Lake Elsinore	1.000	3	0	1	0	1	0
Daigle, Tim, High Desert*	.944	19	9	8	1	18	0
Davis, Eddie, San Bernardino	1.000	5	1	2	0	3	0
DeClue, Jon, Vis.-L.E.*	.931	30	5	22	2	29	0
Dennis, Shane, R.C.*	.938	11	4	11	1	16	0
Dixon, Bubba, R.C.*	.897	47	8	27	4	39	1
Dressendorfer, Kirk, Modesto	.875	27	1	6	1	8	1
Drewien, Dan, R.C.	1.000	17	0	4	0	4	0
Drysdale, Brooks, Lake Elsinore	1.000	8	1	1	0	2	0
Duda, Steve, Stockton	.941	12	3	13	1	17	1
Dyess, Todd, High Desert	.909	23	17	23	4	44	1
Dykhoff, Radhames, High Desert*	.941	34	6	10	1	17	0
Eaddy, Brad, Bakersfield*	.810	42	4	13	4	21	0
Edsell, Geoff, Lake Elsinore	.875	23	4	24	4	32	0
Edwards, Wayne, Bakersfield*	.882	21	2	13	2	17	0
Endo, Masataka, Visalia	.943	28	13	37	3	53	4
Enoki, Yasuhiro, Visalia	1.000	13	5	6	0	11	0
Estes, Shawn, San Jose*	.818	9	2	7	2	11	0
Ettles, Mark, R.C.	1.000	3	1	2	0	3	1
Felix, Ruben, Stockton*	1.000	6	1	1	0	2	0
Fetchel, Tony, Visalia	.900	18	1	8	1	10	0
Fitzer, Douglas, Riverside*	.714	25	3	2	2	7	1
Foulke, Keith, San Jose	.972	28	10	25	1	36	2
Gamez, Francisco, Stockton	1.000	4	3	4	0	7	0
Garrett, Hal, R.C.	.778	23	3	4	2	9	0
Gates, Sean, R.C.	1.000	1	0	1	0	1	0
Gomez, Dennys, San Jose	1.000	13	1	4	0	5	0
Gomez, Marcial, Lake Elsinore	1.000	7	2	1	0	3	0
Gomez, Pat, San Jose*	1.000	3	0	1	0	1	0
Griffin, Ryan, High Desert	.878	31	13	23	5	41	0
Hackett, Jason, High Desert*	1.000	18	2	5	0	7	0
Hanson, Craig, R.C.	.750	9	2	1	1	4	0
Hartmann, Pete, Stockton*	1.000	12	2	2	0	4	0
Hartvigson, Chad, San Jose*	.917	32	0	11	1	12	0

Player, Team	Pct.	G	PO	A	E	TC	DP
Hathaway, Hilly, R.C.*	1.000	3	1	3	0	4	0
Haught, Gary, Modesto	.893	34	3	22	3	28	1
Hecker, Doug, Visalia	1.000	2	0	1	0	1	0
Herges, Matt, San Bernardino	.857	22	3	9	2	14	0
Hermanson, Mike, R.C.	1.000	42	3	6	0	9	0
Hill, Chris, High Desert*	1.000	5	0	1	0	1	0
Hinchliffe, Brett, Riverside	.875	15	2	12	2	16	0
Hinson, Dean, Vis.-L.E.	.909	28	4	6	1	11	1
Holdridge, David, Lake Elsinore	1.000	12	4	1	0	5	1
Holtz, Mike, Lake Elsinore*	.733	56	5	6	4	15	1
Howry, Bobby, San Jose	.969	27	14	17	1	32	3
Hyde, Rich, San Jose	1.000	16	1	1	0	2	0
Idemoto, Kenichiro, Visalia*	.846	31	3	19	4	26	2
Iglesias, Mike, Bak.-S.B.	.960	28	5	19	1	25	0
Ippolito, Rob, Riverside	1.000	35	4	7	0	11	0
Isom, Jeff, R.C.*	1.000	4	0	1	0	1	0
Jacobsen, Joe, San Bernardino	1.000	4	1	0	0	1	0
James, Mike, Lake Elsinore	.000	5	0	0	1	1	0
Janicki, Pete, Lake Elsinore	.833	20	6	14	4	24	1
Jaye, Jamie, Bakersfield*	1.000	5	0	4	0	4	0
Jenkins, Jon, Visalia	.833	33	1	9	2	12	0
Jimenez, Miguel, Modesto	1.000	4	2	2	0	4	0
Karns, Tim, High Desert	1.000	7	1	0	0	1	0
Keagle, Greg, R.C.	1.000	2	1	0	0	1	0
Kenady, Jake, Bakersfield*	.813	23	3	10	3	16	1
Kramer, Jeff, Stockton	.927	32	19	19	3	41	1
Kubinski, Tim, Modesto*	1.000	25	6	22	0	28	2
Kyslinger, Dan, Stockton	.857	37	3	3	1	7	0
LaChappa, Matt, R.C.*	.964	28	12	15	1	28	0
LaGarde, Joe, S.B.-Bak.	.943	28	19	31	3	53	3
LaRocca, Todd, High Desert	.889	15	13	11	3	27	1
Linares, Rich, Bakersfield	.944	55	6	11	1	18	0
Linares, Yfrain, Stockton	.714	7	3	2	2	7	1
Locklear, Dean, Visalia*	1.000	9	2	10	0	12	0
Macey, Fausto, San Jose	.922	28	9	38	4	51	3
Magnelli, Anthony, Visalia	.923	29	3	9	1	13	0
Manning, Derek, Modesto*	.923	25	7	17	2	26	2
Martin, Jeff, San Jose	.857	36	2	4	1	7	0
Maurer, Mike, Modesto	1.000	39	0	3	0	3	0
McLain, Mike, San Jose	.833	9	2	3	1	6	0
Meade, Paul, Bakersfield	1.000	24	4	6	0	10	0
Meadows, Jimmy, Visalia	.902	27	16	30	5	51	3
Michalak, Chris, Modesto*	.946	44	5	30	2	37	0
Mitchell, Kendrick, Bakersfield*	.727	36	5	3	3	11	0
Montane, Ivan, Riverside	.771	24	8	19	8	35	2
Moore, Trey, Riverside*	.970	24	5	27	1	33	2
Murphy, Matt, Stockton*	1.000	5	0	2	0	2	0
Murray, Heath, R.C.*	.950	14	3	16	1	20	1
Muto, Junichiro, Visalia	1.000	17	2	4	0	6	1
Myers, Tom, Visalia*	.813	30	4	22	6	32	1
Nelson, Chris, Modesto	1.000	2	0	1	0	1	0
Newton, Geronimo, Riverside*	1.000	46	5	25	0	30	2
Ortiz, Russell, San Jose	.000	5	0	0	1	1	0
Osuna, Antonio, San Bernardino	1.000	5	0	3	0	3	0
Paluk, Jeff, San Bernardino	.909	41	2	8	1	11	0
Parra, Julio, San Bernardino	.909	14	3	7	1	11	0
Patterson, Ken, Lake Elsinore*	1.000	6	1	0	0	1	0
Paul, Andy, Stockton	.955	38	6	15	1	22	0
Pearsall, J.J., San Bernardino*	1.000	6	0	1	0	1	0
Pena, Alex, High Desert	1.000	34	12	17	0	29	1
Percibal, Billy, High Desert	1.000	21	13	19	0	32	3
Perisho, Matt, Lake Elsinore*	.944	24	3	14	1	18	0
Peters, Don, San Jose	.917	20	0	11	1	12	1
Pincavitch, Kevin, San Bernardino	.500	3	1	0	1	2	0
Pivaral, Hugo, San Bernardino	.813	24	6	7	3	16	1
Prater, Pete, San Jose	1.000	5	0	5	0	5	0
Price, Tom, San Bernardino*	.978	42	14	30	1	45	2
Ramos, Cesar, Bakersfield	.864	24	8	11	3	22	0
Ricabal, Dan, San Bernardino	.933	43	8	6	1	15	1
Rigby, Brad, Modesto	.938	31	12	18	2	32	3
Roach, Peter, San Bernardino*	.909	30	2	8	1	11	2
Rodriguez, Nerio, High Desert	1.000	7	1	1	0	2	0
Rogers, Jason, High Desert*	.875	5	2	5	1	8	0
Rogers, Kevin, San Jose*	1.000	4	0	2	0	2	0
Rolocut, Brian, San Bernardino	1.000	11	1	2	0	3	1
Rosenkranz, Terry, Stockton*	.857	35	4	2	1	7	0
Rossiter, Michael, Modesto	1.000	18	3	7	0	10	0
Rowland, Thad, Visalia*	1.000	7	1	1	0	2	0
Ryan, Reid, Visalia	.875	12	1	6	1	8	0
Sadler, Al, Stockton	1.000	37	11	13	0	24	0
Salazar, Luis, Stockton	.933	52	6	22	2	30	1
Saneaux, Francisco, High Desert	.625	23	2	3	3	8	0
Santana, Marino, Riverside	.889	9	5	3	1	9	0
Sauritch, Chris, High Desert	1.000	7	2	1	0	3	0
Sawyer, Zach, Modesto	.733	55	7	4	4	15	0
Scafa, Bob, Bakersfield*	.885	42	1	22	3	26	0
Scheffler, Craig, Bakersfield*	.852	32	3	20	4	27	1
Schenbeck, T.J., Stockton	.929	31	6	7	1	14	0
Schlutt, Jason, R.C.*	1.000	11	1	2	0	3	0
Schramm, Carl, San Jose	1.000	37	6	17	0	23	0
Seanez, Rudy, San Bernardino	1.000	4	0	1	0	1	0
Sebach, Kyle, Lake Elsinore	1.000	14	5	11	0	16	0
Seki, Kiyokazu, Visalia	.941	35	5	11	1	17	1
Shenk, Larry, High Desert	1.000	2	1	0	0	1	0
Slade, Shawn, Lake Elsinore	1.000	15	1	2	0	3	0
Smith, Hut, High Desert	.833	11	4	11	3	18	1
Smith, Ryan, Riverside	.977	23	21	21	1	43	3
Spiller, Derron, Visalia*	.900	32	0	9	1	10	0
Stone, Ricky, San Bernardino	.882	12	9	6	2	17	0
Sullivan, Dan, Riverside	.913	53	8	13	2	23	1
Suzuki, Mac, Riverside	.500	6	1	0	1	2	0
Tapia, Elias, Bakersfield	.867	17	3	10	2	15	0
Taulbee, Andy, San Jose	.923	10	1	11	1	13	0
Theron, Greg, Riverside	.941	40	4	12	1	17	1
Thomas, Robbie, Bakersfield*	.667	26	2	4	3	9	0
Trimarco, Mike, High Desert	.917	40	7	15	2	24	1
Urbina, William, Modesto	1.000	30	1	10	0	11	1
Vanhof, John, Riverside*	.857	4	0	6	1	7	0
Villano, Mike, San Jose	1.000	21	3	3	0	6	0
Wada, Takashi, Visalia	1.000	17	1	9	0	10	2
Wagner, Joe, Stockton	.826	20	4	15	4	23	0
Walsh, Matthew, Modesto	1.000	44	3	10	0	13	2
Watson, Ron, Lake Elsinore	1.000	10	1	0	0	1	0
Webb, Doug, Stockton	.889	32	5	3	1	9	0
Whitaker, Ryan, Modesto	.936	32	12	32	3	47	0
Whitaker, Steve, San Jose*	1.000	2	0	2	0	2	0
White, Darell, R.C.	.941	42	7	9	1	17	0
Whitman, Ryan, R.C.	.750	14	1	2	1	4	1
Williams, Matt, Bakersfield*	1.000	7	3	4	0	7	0
Williard, Brian, Lake Elsinore	.941	29	7	9	1	17	2
Wilson, Trevor, San Jose*	1.000	2	0	1	0	1	0
Wilstead, Judd, Stockton	.960	31	8	16	1	25	1
Winchester, Marty, Riverside*	.950	35	2	17	1	20	1
Wolff, Bryan, R.C.	.833	54	1	4	1	6	0
Worley, Robert, Riverside	.647	11	5	6	6	17	0
Worrell, Tim, R.C.	.857	9	2	4	1	7	0
Wunsch, Kelly, Stockton*	.929	14	3	10	1	14	0
York, Charles, Bakersfield*	.938	31	2	13	1	16	0
Yoshida, Atsushi, Visalia	.952	13	2	18	1	21	1
ZERBE, Chad, San Bernardino*	1.000	28	14	47	0	61	1
Zongor, Steven, Modesto*	.917	37	2	9	1	12	1

PITCHERS WITH TWO OR MORE TEAMS

Player, Team	Pct.	G	PO	A	E	TC	DP
DeClue, Jon, Visalia*	.923	21	3	21	2	26	0
DeClue, Jon, Lake Elsinore*	1.000	9	2	1	0	3	0
Hinson, Dean, Visalia	.900	23	4	5	1	10	0
Hinson, Dean, Lake Elsinore	1.000	5	0	1	0	1	1
Iglesias, Mike, Bakersfield	.958	24	4	19	1	24	0
Iglesias, Mike, San Bernardino	1.000	4	1	0	0	1	0
LaGarde, Joe, San Bernardino	.939	24	17	29	3	49	3
LaGarde, Joe, Bakersfield	1.000	4	2	2	0	4	0

The following players did not have any fielding statistics at the positions indicated or appeared only as a designated hitter, pinch-hitter or pinch-runner: L. Aquino, p; Boskie, p; Carrasquel, 3b; Clark, 1b, ss, of, c, p; Cook, 3b; Cuevas, of; D. Davis, dh; Dobrolsky, p; Erdos, p; Fitzpatrick, dh, ph; Gambs, p; Henrikson, p; Hollandsworth, of; Hostetler, dh, ph; Huber, p; Ibarra, dh, ph; Keene, of; McGonigle, p; Mowry, of; Nomo, p; Oropesa, p; Paulino, 3b; Pricher, p; Rivera, 1b; L. Roberts, dh; Short, ss; Sturdivant, 1b; Takayoshi, p; Thielen, 3b; VanLandingham, p; Zahner, of.

LEAGUE CHAMPIONS

Year	Team	Pct.
1914—	Fresno	.571
1915—	Modesto	.857
1916-40—	Did not operate.	
1941—	Fresno	.643
	Santa Barbara (2nd)*	.597
1942—	Santa Barbara†	.642
1943-44-45—	Did not operate.	
1946—	Stockton‡	.600
1947—	Stockton‡	.679
1948—	Fresno	.607
	Santa Barbara (3rd)*	.529
1949—	Bakersfield	.612
	San Jose (4th)*	.543
1950—	Ventura	.607
	Modesto (2nd)*	.586
1951—	Santa Barbara‡	.599
1952—	Fresno‡	.629
1953—	San Jose‡	.664
1954—	Modesto‡	.623
1955—	Stockton	.733
	Fresno§	.718
1956—	Fresno§	.650
1957—	Visalia∞	.622
	Salinas (4th)*	.504
1958—	Fresno*	.639
	Bakersfield	.672
1959—	Bakersfield	.592
	Modesto§	.643
1960—	Reno	.614
	Reno	.657
1961—	Reno	.743
	Reno	.643
1962—	San Jose§	.686
	Reno	.587
1963—	Modesto	.589
	Stockton§	.687
1964—	Fresno	.638
	Fresno	.600
1965—	San Jose	.586
	Stockton§	.614
1966—	Modesto	.577
	Modesto	.671
1967—	San Jose§	.676
	Modesto	.586
1968—	San Jose	.629
	Fresno§	.623
1969—	Stockton§	.600
	Visalia	.614
1970—	Bakersfield	.667
	Bakersfield	.671
1971—	Visalia§	.583
	Fresno	.500
1972—	Modesto§	.547
	Bakersfield	.629
1973—	Lodi§	.657
	Bakersfield	.571
1974—	Fresno§	.607
	San Jose	.579
1975—	Reno	.614
	Reno	.614
1976—	Salinas	.650
	Reno§	.547
1977—	Salinas	.564
	Lodi§	.579
1978—	Visalia§	.698
	Lodi	.607
1979—	San Jose§	.636
	Reno	.525
1980—	Stockton§	.638
	Visalia	.507
1981—	Visalia	.621
	Lodi§	.521
1982—	Modesto§	.671
	Visalia	.586
1983—	Visalia	.621
	Redwood§	.529
1984—	Modesto§	.597
	Bakersfield	.486
1985—	Fresno§	.575
	Stockton	.566
1986—	Palm Springs	.613
	Stockton§	.585
1987—	Fresno§	.559
	Reno	.535
1988—	Stockton	.657
	Riverside§	.599
1989—	Stockton	.627
	Bakersfield§	.577
1990—	Visalia	.638
	Stockton§	.582
1991—	San Jose	.676
	High Desert§	.537
1992—	Stockton§	.610
	Visalia	.551
1993—	High Desert§	.620
	Modesto	.529
1994—	Modesto	.706
	Rancho Cucamonga§	.566
1995—	San Bernardino§	.612
	San Jose	.550

*Won four-club playoff. †League disbanded June 28. ‡Won championship and four-club playoff. §Won split-season playoff. ∞Won both halves of split season.

CAROLINA LEAGUE

LEAGUE OFFICE

President/treasurer
John Hopkins
Address
P.O. Box 9503
Greensboro, NC 27429
Phone
910-691-9030

Teams (affiliation)
Durham Bulls (Braves)
Frederick Keys (Orioles)
Kinston Indians (Indians)
Lynchburg Hillcats (Pirates)
Prince William Cannons (White Sox)
Salem Avalanche (Rockies)
Wilmington Blue Rocks (Royals)
Winston-Salem Warthogs (Reds)

1995 FINAL STANDINGS

FIRST HALF

NORTHERN DIVISION

Team	W	L	T	Pct.	GB
Prince William (White Sox)	37	33	0	.529	....
Wilmington (Royals)	35	34	0	.507	1½
Lynchburg (Pirates)	33	36	0	.478	3½
Frederick (Orioles)	27	41	0	.397	9

SOUTHERN DIVISION

Team	W	L	T	Pct.	GB
Kinston (Indians)	45	24	0	.652	....
Winston-Salem (Reds)	36	34	0	.514	9½
Salem (Rockies)	34	36	0	.486	11½
Durham (Braves)	30	39	0	.435	15

SECOND HALF

NORTHERN DIVISION

Team	W	L	T	Pct.	GB
Wilmington (Royals)	48	21	0	.696	....
Lynchburg (Pirates)	34	35	0	.493	14
Frederick (Orioles)	31	38	0	.449	17
Prince William (White Sox)	27	43	0	.386	21½

SOUTHERN DIVISION

Team	W	L	T	Pct.	GB
Kinston (Indians)	36	32	0	.529	....
Winston-Salem (Reds)	33	34	0	.493	2½
Salem (Rockies)	34	36	0	.486	3
Durham (Braves)	33	37	0	.471	4

COMPOSITE

Team	Wil.	Kin.	W.S.	Sal.	Lyn.	P.W.	Dur.	Fre.	W	L	T	Pct.	GB
Wilmington (Royals)	....	9	10	11	11	15	13	14	83	55	0	.601	....
Kinston (Indians)	11	....	9	15	10	10	13	13	81	56	0	.591	1½
Winston-Salem (Reds)	10	9	....	8	10	12	13	7	69	68	0	.504	13½
Salem (Rockies)	9	5	12	....	13	7	9	13	68	72	0	.486	16
Lynchburg (Pirates)	8	10	10	7	....	12	12	8	67	71	0	.486	16
Prince William (White Sox)	5	10	8	13	8	....	8	12	64	76	0	.457	20
Durham (Braves)	7	7	7	11	7	12	....	12	63	76	0	.453	20½
Frederick (Orioles)	5	6	12	7	12	8	8	....	58	79	0	.423	24½

Major league affiliations in parentheses.

PLAYOFFS: Wilmington defeated Prince William, two games to none; Kinston defeated Wilmington, three games to none, to win league championship.

REGULAR-SEASON ATTENDANCE: Durham, 390,486; Frederick, 300,968; Kinston, 140,116; Lynchburg, 111,654; Prince William, 215,250; Salem, 140,111; Wilmington, 358,766; Winston-Salem, 158,842. Total, 1,816,193. Playoffs (5 games)—15,694. All-Star Game at Lynchburg—5,690.

MANAGERS: Durham, Matt West; Frederick, Mike O'Berry; Kinston, Gordy MacKenzie; Lynchburg, Marc Hill; Prince William, Dave Huppert; Salem, Bill Hayes; Wilmington, John Mizerock; Winston-Salem, Mark Berry.

ALL-STAR TEAM: 1B—Richie Sexson, Kinston; 2B—Ricky Gutierrez, Kinston; 3B—Aaron Boone, Winston-Salem; SS—Enrique Wilson, Kinston; Utility IF—Anthony Medrano, Wilmington; Edgard Velasquez, Salem; OF—James Betzsold, Kinston; Charles Peterson, Lynchburg; Utility OF—Bruce Aven, Kinston; C—Mike Sweeney, Wilmington; DH—Reed Secrist, Lynchburg; Starting Pitcher—Bartolo Colon, Kinston; Relief Pitcher—Dan Graves, Kinston; Most Valuable Player—Richie Sexson, Kinston; Pitcher of the Year—Bartolo Colon, Kinston; Manager of the Year—John Mizerock, Wilmington.

1995 BATTING

TEAM

Team	Avg.	G	TPA	AB	R	H	TB	2B	3B	HR	RBI	SH	SF	HP	BB	IBB	SO	SB	CS	GDP	LOB	ShO	Slg.	OBP
Lynchburg	.264	138	5128	4483	655	1185	1774	214	27	107	577	45	40	59	501	31	880	156	107	102	915	8	.396	.343
Wilmington	.255	138	5144	4591	550	1173	1668	204	33	75	485	70	33	57	393	24	771	135	87	89	938	4	.363	.320
Kinston	.254	137	5114	4509	605	1145	1786	222	31	119	555	35	48	63	459	30	900	139	85	63	912	8	.396	.328
Salem	.252	140	5347	4699	619	1186	1802	231	29	109	562	42	33	55	516	35	991	69	51	101	1015	13	.383	.331
Durham	.249	139	4981	4447	566	1109	1661	197	14	109	519	32	25	77	399	32	1007	150	100	101	838	16	.374	.320
Prince William	.247	140	5169	4576	572	1130	1666	210	28	90	520	24	35	57	477	26	878	96	48	135	963	9	.364	.323
Winston-Salem	.246	137	5094	4508	601	1110	1752	204	21	132	562	40	35	53	458	43	961	105	72	83	895	8	.389	.321
Frederick	.234	137	4999	4430	497	1038	1488	197	26	67	424	47	31	64	426	29	979	110	78	96	892	12	.336	.309

INDIVIDUAL

TOP QUALIFIERS FOR BATTING CHAMPIONSHIP

Minimum 378 plate appearances. *Lefthanded batter. †Switch-hitter.

Player, Team	Avg.	G	TPA	AB	R	H	TB	2B	3B	HR	RBI	SH	SF	HP	BB	IBB	SO	SB	CS	GDP	Slg.	OBP
Sweeney, Mike, Wilmington	.310	99	407	332	61	103	182	23	1	18	53	1	5	9	60	7	39	6	1	4	.548	.424
Sexson, Richie, Kinston	.306	131	554	494	80	151	251	34	0	22	85	0	7	10	43	5	115	4	6	8	.508	.368
Velazquez, Edgard, Salem	.300	131	553	497	74	149	225	25	6	13	69	3	7	4	40	4	102	7	10	17	.453	.352

Player, Team	Avg.	G	TPA	AB	R	H	TB	2B	3B	HR	RBI	SH	SF	HP	BB	IBB	SO	SB	CS	GDP	Slg.	OBP
Zapata, Ramon, Lynchburg	.298	119	469	416	59	124	179	27	2	8	45	9	0	2	42	0	58	6	8	13	.430	.365
Rodarte, Raul, Lynchburg	.286	104	388	346	57	99	157	18	2	12	48	2	1	4	35	2	49	19	13	8	.454	.358
Medrano, Anthony, Wilmington	.285	123	518	460	69	131	172	20	6	3	43	15	4	5	34	2	42	11	6	10	.374	.338
Williams, Harold, Prince William*	.282	129	534	472	56	133	207	30	1	14	72	1	2	11	48	11	98	4	2	16	.439	.360
Secrist, Reed, Lynchburg*	.282	112	442	380	60	107	188	18	3	19	75	1	4	3	54	7	88	3	4	6	.495	.372
Culp, Brian, Salem	.279	128	539	459	69	128	187	33	1	8	63	0	5	4	71	4	80	8	3	8	.407	.377
Collier, Lou, Lynchburg	.276	114	463	399	68	110	147	19	3	4	38	3	3	7	51	4	60	31	11	13	.368	.365
Peterson, Charles, Lynchburg	.274	107	447	391	61	107	145	9	4	7	51	6	5	2	43	1	73	31	17	11	.371	.345
Mendez, Carlos, Wilmington	.273	107	420	396	46	108	152	19	2	7	61	1	5	0	18	1	36	0	4	17	.384	.301
Betts, Todd, Kinston*	.272	109	430	331	52	90	138	15	3	9	44	1	4	6	88	2	56	2	3	5	.417	.429
Lopez, Mendy, Wilmington	.271	130	470	428	42	116	157	29	3	2	36	7	2	5	28	0	73	18	10	12	.367	.322
Sexton, Chris, W-S/Salem	.271	127	587	476	84	129	172	16	6	5	37	12	1	1	97	2	55	14	11	11	.361	.395

DEPARTMENTAL LEADERS: G—Menechino, 137; AB—Velazquez, 497; R—Sexton, 84; H—Sexson, 151; TB—Sexson, 251; 2B—Sexson, 34; 3B—Delaney, Gutierrez, E. Wilson, 7; HR—J. Thomas, 26; RBI—Sexson, 85; SH—Medrano, 15; SF—E. Wilson, 10; HP—Knott, 15; BB—Sexton, 97; IBB—Simon, 14; SO—J. Thomas, 156; SB—Gutierrez, 43; CS—Pagano, Valdez, 21; GIDP—Polidor, 18; Slg.—Sweeney, .548; OBP—Betts, .429.

ALL PLAYERS

*Lefthanded batter. †Switch-hitter.

Player, Team	Avg.	G	TPA	AB	R	H	TB	2B	3B	HR	RBI	SH	SF	HP	BB	IBB	SO	SB	CS	GDP	Slg.	OBP
Abbott, Jeff, Prince William	.348	70	298	264	41	92	120	16	0	4	47	1	5	2	26	0	25	7	1	8	.455	.404
Akers, Chad, Winston-Salem	.260	103	399	361	41	94	116	14	1	2	29	7	3	1	27	1	49	25	8	7	.321	.311
Anderson, Milt, Kinston†	.000	4	5	5	1	0	0	0	0	0	0	0	0	0	0	0	0	0	0	0	.000	.000
Arnold, Jamie, Durham	.000	15	2	2	1	0	0	0	0	0	0	0	0	0	0	0	0	0	0	0	.000	.000
Austin, Jake, Lynchburg*	.270	18	79	74	7	20	29	6	0	1	11	0	2	0	3	0	8	0	3	1	.392	.291
Aven, Bruce, Kinston	.261	130	534	479	70	125	227	23	5	23	69	0	1	13	41	3	109	15	9	7	.474	.335
Avila, Rolando, Frederick	.263	52	197	175	26	46	59	8	1	1	13	5	0	3	14	0	27	15	5	2	.337	.328
Bako, Paul, Winston-Salem*	.285	82	299	249	29	71	107	11	2	7	27	6	1	1	42	6	66	3	1	6	.430	.389
Benbow, Lou, Durham	.220	82	262	245	20	54	73	7	0	4	17	3	0	3	11	0	53	2	3	8	.298	.263
Bernhardt, Steven, Salem	.217	59	200	180	18	39	58	3	2	4	16	5	2	5	8	0	38	2	3	5	.322	.267
Berrios, Harry, Frederick	.208	71	278	240	33	50	89	5	2	10	28	0	2	4	32	3	66	10	6	3	.371	.309
Bess, Johnny, Winston-Salem†	.187	88	286	246	35	46	72	10	2	4	21	2	0	8	30	4	83	12	4	4	.293	.296
Betts, Todd, Kinston*	.272	109	430	331	52	90	138	15	3	9	44	1	4	6	88	2	56	2	3	5	.417	.429
Betzsold, James, Kinston	.268	126	524	455	77	122	223	22	2	25	71	0	4	10	55	3	137	3	5	4	.490	.357
Bonifay, Ken, Lynchburg*	.245	116	453	375	57	92	148	22	2	10	54	0	4	11	63	4	88	3	5	6	.395	.366
Boone, Aaron, Winston-Salem	.261	108	453	395	61	103	166	19	1	14	50	4	2	9	43	7	77	11	7	4	.420	.345
Bridgers, Brandon, Frederick	.161	10	44	31	3	5	8	3	0	0	5	1	1	0	11	0	5	1	1	0	.258	.372
Broach, Donald, Winston-Salem	.261	117	522	460	74	120	175	23	4	8	34	5	2	5	50	2	73	16	14	9	.380	.338
Brooks, Eddie, Lynchburg	.118	27	79	68	6	8	9	1	0	0	2	1	1	1	8	0	21	0	1	1	.132	.218
Brooks, Ramy, Wilmington	.218	94	359	326	41	71	111	16	0	8	30	1	1	6	25	1	82	2	1	7	.340	.285
Brown, Adrian, Lynchburg†	.242	54	233	215	30	52	64	5	2	1	14	4	1	1	12	0	20	11	6	3	.298	.284
Brown, Ray, Winston-Salem*	.265	122	512	445	63	118	201	26	0	19	77	0	4	11	52	12	85	3	2	8	.452	.354
Brown, Todd, Frederick†	.237	32	69	59	6	14	18	4	0	0	2	4	0	1	5	0	21	6	2	1	.305	.308
Buchanan, Shawn, Prince William	.000	4	1	1	2	0	0	0	0	0	0	0	0	0	0	0	0	0	0	0	.000	.000
Byington, Jimmie, Wilmington	.223	92	295	273	24	61	69	6	1	0	23	3	2	4	13	0	33	12	6	3	.253	.267
Byrne, Clayton, Frederick	.228	35	142	136	16	31	47	7	0	3	13	0	0	0	5	0	29	3	4	4	.346	.255
Cabrera, Jairo, Frederick	.183	25	70	60	7	11	12	1	0	0	1	2	0	1	7	0	13	0	1	1	.200	.279
Canetto, John, Lynchburg†	.250	13	32	28	5	7	9	2	0	0	2	0	1	0	3	0	13	0	0	0	.321	.313
Carpenter, Matt, Salem	.000	1	1	0	0	0	0	0	0	0	0	0	0	1	0	0	0	0	0	0	.000	1.000
Carr, Jeremy, Wilmington	.231	5	14	13	1	3	4	1	0	0	0	0	0	0	1	0	3	0	1	0	.308	.286
Carranza, Pete, Salem	.216	18	60	51	9	11	25	2	0	4	8	0	0	0	9	0	8	2	0	0	.490	.333
Castaneda, Hector, Frederick*	.213	17	56	47	6	10	13	1	1	0	4	2	1	0	6	0	9	0	0	2	.277	.296
Cawhorn, Gerad, Kinston	.210	85	300	262	23	55	70	12	0	1	22	5	2	2	29	2	60	4	1	7	.267	.292
Claudio, Patricio, Kinston	.265	89	330	298	37	79	109	7	4	5	27	5	1	0	26	2	73	27	11	2	.366	.323
Clyburn, Danny, W-S/Fre.	.250	74	297	272	31	68	119	14	2	11	45	0	2	6	17	1	77	3	5	5	.438	.306
Collier, Lou, Lynchburg	.276	114	463	399	68	110	147	19	3	4	38	3	3	7	51	4	60	31	11	13	.368	.365
Conger, Jeff, Lynchburg*	.264	90	369	318	44	84	116	13	5	3	23	7	3	6	35	1	74	26	16	1	.365	.345
Cornelius, Brian, Lynchburg*	.154	12	44	39	2	6	9	3	0	0	4	1	0	0	4	0	11	0	1	1	.231	.233
Correa, Miguel, Durham†	.236	118	425	398	43	94	172	19	1	19	70	2	3	3	19	2	95	9	13	6	.432	.274
Cradle, Cobi, Winston-Salem*	.183	23	94	71	14	13	15	2	0	0	2	1	1	0	21	0	8	9	2	0	.211	.366
Culp, Brian, Salem	.279	128	539	459	69	128	187	33	1	8	63	0	5	4	71	4	80	8	3	8	.407	.377
Daniel, Mike, Lynchburg	.284	50	202	169	31	48	91	11	1	10	35	2	1	1	29	4	36	0	2	7	.538	.390
Davis, Tommy, Frederick	.268	130	545	496	62	133	210	26	3	15	57	1	3	4	41	7	105	7	1	14	.423	.327
Delaney, Donovan, Wilmington	.250	114	395	360	22	90	126	13	7	3	39	4	2	4	25	0	82	6	9	8	.350	.304
Dellucci, David, Frederick*	.281	28	111	96	16	27	33	3	0	1	10	0	0	3	12	1	10	1	2	3	.344	.378
Diaz, Einar, Kinston	.263	104	398	373	46	98	137	21	0	6	43	1	4	8	12	2	29	3	6	6	.367	.297
Diaz, Lino, Wilmington	.301	51	190	173	20	52	68	6	2	2	23	2	0	4	11	0	9	0	5	2	.393	.356
Dixon, Colin, Salem	.291	57	240	220	25	64	94	13	1	5	30	0	2	5	13	1	30	0	0	10	.427	.342
Durso, Joe, Prince William	.213	58	198	178	16	38	57	3	2	4	22	1	1	2	16	1	31	0	0	2	.320	.284
Evans, Michael, Wilmington*	.218	96	351	317	26	69	110	15	1	8	36	4	1	2	27	3	79	0	2	2	.347	.282
Fasano, Sal, Wilmington	.227	23	94	88	12	20	30	2	1	2	7	0	0	1	5	0	16	0	0	4	.341	.277
Foster, Jim, Frederick	.261	128	493	429	44	112	163	27	3	6	56	0	5	8	51	5	63	2	3	10	.380	.347
Fraraccio, Dan, Prince William	.230	24	83	74	11	17	28	5	0	2	6	1	0	0	8	0	12	0	0	1	.378	.305
French, Anton, Durham†	.269	7	30	26	3	7	8	1	0	0	2	0	0	1	3	0	2	4	1	0	.308	.367
Frye, Dan, Winston-Salem	.182	7	16	11	3	2	6	1	0	1	2	0	0	0	5	0	4	0	0	0	.545	.438
Gann, Steve, Winston-Salem	.244	15	48	41	5	10	12	2	0	0	5	2	1	2	2	0	5	0	1	0	.293	.304
Garcia, Adrian, Durham	.250	5	16	12	2	3	4	1	0	0	2	0	0	0	4	0	4	1	0	0	.333	.438
Garcia, Guillermo, Winston-Salem	.237	78	278	245	26	58	81	10	2	3	29	2	2	1	28	0	32	2	2	7	.331	.315
Garcia, Jesse, Frederick	.225	124	432	365	52	82	108	11	3	3	27	7	2	9	49	0	75	5	10	5	.296	.329
Garcia, Vincente, Salem	.243	119	518	457	62	111	169	26	1	10	41	5	2	1	53	3	73	5	0	10	.370	.322
Gargiulo, Mike, Frederick*	.273	6	12	11	1	3	3	0	0	0	0	0	0	1	0	0	4	0	0	0	.273	.333
Giudice, John, Salem	.258	99	387	356	49	92	142	21	4	7	48	0	3	4	24	2	81	7	4	7	.399	.310
Goligoski, Jason, Prince William*	.217	95	360	300	42	65	76	7	2	0	24	2	3	3	52	0	47	16	5	4	.253	.335

Player, Team	Avg.	G	TPA	AB	R	H	TB	2B	3B	HR	RBI	SH	SF	HP	BB	IBB	SO	SB	CS	GDP	Slg.	OBP
Gonzalez, Paul, Prince William*	.207	92	328	290	25	60	91	10	0	7	34	1	3	3	31	3	85	1	1	7	.314	.287
Gonzalez, Raul, Wilmington	.292	86	334	308	36	90	148	19	3	11	49	3	7	2	14	3	34	6	4	3	.481	.320
Grunewald, Keith, Salem†	.265	118	473	412	48	109	151	22	1	6	45	2	3	10	46	8	84	8	4	8	.367	.350
Gutierrez, Ricky, Kinston	.262	117	521	439	63	115	162	21	7	4	46	7	4	4	67	3	62	43	16	3	.369	.362
Hagy, Gary, Kinston	.134	52	162	142	12	19	31	3	0	3	9	5	2	1	12	1	34	3	2	1	.218	.204
Hanel, Marcus, Lynchburg	.185	40	142	135	14	25	40	4	1	3	8	2	0	1	4	0	33	0	1	1	.296	.214
Harriss, Robin, Kinston	.245	15	54	49	8	12	23	3	1	2	6	1	1	0	3	0	8	0	0	1	.469	.283
Hawkins, Wes, Frederick	.211	78	219	199	13	42	56	10	2	0	16	4	1	4	11	0	49	4	1	9	.281	.265
Hendricks, Ryan, Frederick*	.133	5	17	15	1	2	6	1	0	1	3	0	0	0	2	0	6	0	0	1	.400	.235
Hicks, Jamie, Durham	.219	41	111	105	9	23	29	6	0	0	14	0	1	0	5	2	18	0	2	5	.276	.252
Higgins, Mike, Salem	.241	53	182	158	9	38	47	9	0	0	18	2	4	1	17	1	30	1	3	0	.297	.311
Hodge, Roy, Frederick	.256	48	191	172	19	44	61	12	1	1	17	0	2	1	16	0	31	4	3	8	.355	.319
Holdren, Nate, Salem	.245	119	464	420	48	103	168	16	2	15	69	2	2	6	34	0	126	6	3	7	.400	.310
House, Mitch, Lynchburg	.180	16	61	50	7	9	15	3	0	1	6	0	1	1	9	1	13	0	1	2	.300	.311
Hugo, Sean, Frederick*	.281	29	112	89	13	25	41	4	0	4	13	0	2	0	21	1	24	0	0	4	.461	.411
Hunter, Lanier, Frederick†	.143	7	15	14	1	2	3	1	0	0	0	0	0	0	1	0	7	0	0	0	.214	.200
Izquierdo, Sergio, Prince William	.188	10	36	32	6	6	8	2	0	0	2	0	0	2	2	0	3	0	0	2	.250	.278
Jacobs, Ryan, Durham	.000	29	1	1	0	0	0	0	0	0	0	0	0	0	0	0	0	0	0	0	.000	.000
Jenkins, Demetrish, Winst.-Salem*	.289	50	168	149	25	43	64	7	1	4	14	0	1	0	18	0	25	0	6	1	.430	.363
Jimenez, Manny, Durham	.245	121	400	375	40	92	118	16	2	2	23	3	0	5	17	1	71	8	6	11	.315	.287
Jimenez, Oscar, Wilmington	.251	121	446	374	42	94	123	18	4	1	31	6	3	10	53	2	92	11	8	3	.329	.357
Johnson, Todd, Kinston	.232	21	58	56	4	13	17	2	1	0	9	2	0	0	0	0	13	0	0	1	.304	.232
Jones, Pookie, Salem	.208	16	58	53	9	11	17	3	0	1	3	1	0	1	3	0	16	1	1	4	.321	.263
King, Andre, Dur.-P.W.	.245	120	519	453	63	111	169	23	4	9	36	6	4	10	45	1	135	16	13	7	.373	.324
Kirgan, Chris, Frederick*	.201	124	410	378	25	76	131	18	2	11	47	1	3	3	25	3	107	3	2	7	.347	.254
Knoblauh, Jay, Lynchburg	.277	87	292	264	40	73	117	16	2	8	47	1	5	6	16	0	62	3	2	3	.443	.326
Knott, John, Durham	.267	112	426	344	55	92	145	14	3	11	46	2	2	15	63	2	100	11	13	5	.422	.401
Knowles, Brian, Wilmington	.000	9	27	25	1	0	0	0	0	0	1	2	0	0	0	0	5	0	0	2	.000	.000
Kopriva, Dan, Winston-Salem	.345	17	64	58	4	20	26	4	1	0	5	0	1	1	4	0	6	1	0	2	.448	.391
Lamb, David, Frederick†	.222	124	497	436	39	97	121	14	2	2	34	8	5	10	38	5	81	6	7	10	.278	.297
Larkin, Stephen, Winston-Salem*	.220	13	54	50	2	11	12	1	0	0	4	0	1	0	3	1	12	2	2	0	.240	.259
Leary, Rob, Lynchburg*	.260	63	259	208	42	54	87	9	0	8	31	0	2	5	44	4	43	9	4	3	.418	.398
LeCronier, Jason, Frederick*	.282	40	143	131	17	37	65	8	1	6	19	0	0	0	12	2	40	1	0	3	.496	.343
Lemons, Rich, Kinston*	.250	5	14	12	1	3	4	1	0	0	0	0	0	0	2	0	4	1	0	1	.333	.357
Lezeau, James, Salem*	.000	4	6	5	0	0	0	0	0	0	0	0	0	0	1	0	3	0	0	1	.000	.167
Lofton, James, Winston-Salem†	.220	38	134	123	15	27	34	5	1	0	14	2	0	1	8	1	22	1	4	0	.276	.273
Lopez, Mendy, Wilmington	.271	130	470	428	42	116	157	29	3	2	36	7	2	5	28	0	73	18	10	12	.367	.322
Machado, Robert, Prince William	.254	83	322	272	37	69	101	14	0	6	31	2	1	7	40	5	47	0	0	6	.371	.363
Mader, Chris, Kinston	.074	11	30	27	1	2	2	0	0	0	2	1	0	1	1	0	5	0	0	0	.074	.138
Magdaleno, Ricky, Winston-Salem	.223	91	332	309	30	69	105	13	1	7	40	3	3	2	15	0	69	3	1	4	.340	.261
Magee, Danny, Durham	.256	76	290	266	38	68	93	11	1	4	29	1	0	12	11	0	46	7	5	5	.350	.315
Manto, Jeff, Frederick	.375	2	8	8	1	3	6	0	0	1	3	0	0	0	0	0	1	0	0	0	.750	.375
McBride, Gator, Durham	.236	102	422	360	60	85	141	15	1	13	59	1	2	5	54	1	109	11	4	5	.392	.342
McKinnon, Sandy, Prince William	.253	125	540	494	64	125	160	19	5	2	23	3	1	3	39	0	93	35	17	6	.324	.311
Medrano, Anthony, Wilmington	.285	123	518	460	69	131	172	20	6	3	43	15	4	5	34	2	42	11	6	10	.374	.338
Meggers, Mike, Winston-Salem	.246	76	309	272	45	67	147	18	1	20	54	0	4	1	32	5	69	7	3	5	.540	.324
Meluskey, Mitch, Kinston†	.241	8	31	29	5	7	12	5	0	0	2	0	0	0	2	0	9	0	0	1	.414	.290
Mendez, Carlos, Wilmington	.273	107	420	396	46	108	152	19	2	7	61	1	5	0	18	1	36	0	4	17	.384	.301
Mendez, Sergio, Lynchburg	.246	65	252	236	30	58	95	13	0	8	35	2	2	3	9	1	49	9	4	9	.403	.280
Menechino, Frank, Prince William	.261	137	594	476	65	124	179	31	3	6	58	3	8	11	96	2	75	6	2	17	.376	.391
Michael, Jeff, Frederick	.246	66	236	203	19	50	62	12	0	0	17	5	3	1	24	1	46	3	4	4	.305	.325
Monds, Wonderful, Durham	.279	81	317	297	44	83	118	17	0	6	33	1	1	1	17	1	63	28	7	7	.397	.320
Montilla, Julio, Wilmington†	.222	8	32	27	0	6	6	0	0	0	1	1	0	0	4	0	6	0	0	0	.222	.323
Murphy, Mike, Kinston	.232	67	197	177	26	41	50	6	0	1	15	1	1	3	15	1	30	13	4	2	.282	.301
Newell, Brett, Durham	.215	33	87	79	10	17	18	1	0	0	3	2	1	1	4	0	20	0	1	2	.228	.259
Newhouse, Andre, Prince William	.213	78	278	258	28	55	73	10	1	2	21	1	2	1	16	0	59	7	2	6	.283	.260
Nunez, Ramon, Durham	.370	17	64	54	13	20	39	4	0	5	15	1	1	0	8	0	9	0	0	4	.722	.444
Nunez, Sergio, Wilmington	.237	124	528	460	63	109	135	10	2	4	25	13	1	3	51	4	66	33	19	8	.293	.317
Oglesby, Luke, Wilmington*	.200	53	69	60	18	12	12	0	0	0	1	4	0	1	4	0	21	19	6	0	.200	.262
Ordonez, Magglio, Prince William	.238	131	535	487	61	116	180	24	2	12	65	0	4	3	41	0	71	11	5	16	.370	.299
Oyas, Danny, Winston-Salem	.214	50	190	173	19	37	67	6	0	8	31	3	2	2	10	0	45	1	1	6	.387	.262
Pagan, Angel, Frederick	.194	31	78	72	8	14	22	3	1	1	6	1	0	0	5	0	19	0	1	2	.306	.247
Pagano, Scott, Durham†	.266	110	405	354	47	94	111	12	1	1	26	7	1	5	38	5	75	41	21	8	.314	.344
Paul, Kortney, Wilmington	.111	8	11	9	1	1	1	0	0	0	0	1	0	0	1	0	2	0	0	1	.111	.200
Peterson, Charles, Lynchburg	.274	107	447	391	61	107	145	9	4	7	51	6	5	2	43	1	73	31	17	11	.371	.345
Polidor, Wil, Prince William†	.249	95	362	346	34	86	108	14	4	0	24	5	2	0	9	0	33	2	6	18	.312	.266
Pozo, Yohel, Salem	.170	43	142	135	7	23	27	4	0	0	3	4	0	1	2	0	21	0	1	4	.200	.188
Prieto, Rick, Kinston†	.193	26	102	88	12	17	24	2	1	1	10	1	0	0	13	0	20	3	1	2	.273	.297
Quillin, Ty, Frederick*	.122	16	45	41	4	5	5	0	0	0	3	0	0	0	4	0	15	0	1	0	.122	.200
Reynolds, Chance, Lynchburg†	.200	5	20	15	0	3	3	0	0	0	2	0	0	2	3	0	2	0	1	1	.200	.400
Richardson, Eric, Prince William	.167	9	19	18	2	3	3	0	0	0	1	0	0	0	1	0	3	0	1	2	.167	.211
Riemer, Matt, Frederick	.182	27	81	77	6	14	19	2	0	1	10	0	0	0	4	0	22	0	1	1	.247	.222
Robertson, Robbie, Winst.-Salem*	.216	91	304	278	34	60	95	11	0	8	32	1	2	1	22	3	77	2	4	7	.342	.274
Robertson, Tommy, Lynchburg*	.273	61	185	161	16	44	54	7	0	1	23	1	2	1	20	2	41	3	7	2	.335	.353
Rodarte, Raul, Lynchburg	.286	104	388	346	57	99	157	18	2	12	48	2	1	4	35	2	49	19	13	8	.454	.358
Rodriguez, Roman, Lynchburg	.254	44	143	130	11	33	37	4	0	0	9	3	1	2	7	0	25	1	0	9	.285	.300
Sanford, Chance, Lynchburg*	.333	16	74	66	8	22	35	4	0	3	14	0	1	0	7	0	13	1	0	1	.530	.392
Sauritch, Chris, Frederick†	.067	9	23	15	2	1	1	0	0	0	1	0	0	3	5	0	6	2	1	0	.067	.391
Scalzitti, Will, Salem	.200	11	41	35	4	7	8	1	0	0	0	1	0	1	4	1	5	0	1	1	.229	.300
Secrist, Reed, Lynchburg*	.282	112	442	380	60	107	188	18	3	19	75	1	4	3	54	7	88	3	4	6	.495	.372
Sexson, Richie, Kinston	.306	131	554	494	80	151	251	34	0	22	85	0	7	10	43	5	115	4	6	8	.508	.368
Sexton, Chris, W-S/Salem	.271	127	587	476	84	129	172	16	6	5	37	12	1	1	97	2	55	14	11	11	.361	.395
Short, Rick, Frederick	.077	5	14	13	1	1	1	0	0	0	2	0	0	0	1	0	2	1	0	0	.077	.143

Player, Team	Avg.	G	TPA	AB	R	H	TB	2B	3B	HR	RBI	SH	SF	HP	BB	IBB	SO	SB	CS	GDP	Slg.	OBP
Simon, Randall, Durham*	.264	122	466	420	56	111	185	18	1	18	79	0	5	5	36	14	63	6	5	15	.440	.326
Smith, Jason, Salem	.093	30	99	86	4	8	14	1	1	1	5	1	0	1	11	0	38	0	0	1	.163	.204
Smith, Sean, Durham*	.280	32	103	93	10	26	43	8	0	3	13	1	0	0	9	1	22	1	0	3	.462	.343
Snyder, Randy, Salem	.289	23	95	76	19	22	36	5	0	3	14	0	0	1	18	0	13	2	1	3	.474	.432
Spinello, Joe, Prince William	.133	10	32	30	1	4	5	1	0	0	2	1	0	1	0	0	9	0	0	2	.167	.161
Sweeney, Mike, Wilmington	.310	99	407	332	61	103	182	23	1	18	53	1	5	9	60	7	39	6	1	4	.548	.424
Teeters, Brian, Wilmington*	.228	64	184	162	25	37	62	7	0	6	26	2	0	1	19	1	51	11	5	3	.383	.313
Thomas, Greg, Kinston*	.219	102	365	329	32	72	126	21	0	11	43	1	7	3	25	4	98	0	2	2	.383	.275
Thomas, Juan, Prince William	.235	132	515	464	64	109	215	20	4	26	69	1	2	8	40	4	156	4	5	16	.463	.305
Thomas, Rod, Winston-Salem	.222	20	63	54	7	12	20	2	0	2	7	0	0	1	8	0	22	2	3	0	.370	.333
Toth, Dave, Durham	.245	85	289	257	20	63	87	6	0	6	26	0	1	6	25	1	42	3	3	6	.339	.325
Valdez, Trovin, Frederick†	.245	112	405	375	51	92	112	12	4	0	13	6	1	5	18	0	77	34	21	2	.299	.288
Van Slyke, Andy, Frederick*	.000	1	5	2	1	0	0	0	0	0	0	0	0	1	2	1	1	1	0	0	.000	.600
Velazquez, Edgard, Salem	.300	131	553	497	74	149	225	25	6	13	69	3	7	4	40	4	102	7	10	17	.453	.352
Walker, Joe, Prince William†	.333	1	4	3	1	1	3	0	1	0	2	0	0	0	1	0	1	0	0	0	1.000	.500
Warner, Ken, Durham	.226	51	154	137	12	31	50	11	1	2	13	3	2	0	12	1	32	1	2	1	.365	.285
Watkins, Pat, Winston-Salem	.206	27	120	107	14	22	39	3	1	4	13	1	2	0	10	0	24	1	0	5	.364	.269
Watson, Marty, Prince William	.259	23	91	85	12	22	44	3	2	5	14	0	1	0	5	0	21	2	1	4	.518	.297
Weaver, Colby, Durham	.278	8	22	18	2	5	7	2	0	0	2	0	0	0	4	0	6	0	0	0	.389	.409
Webb, Kevin, Durham	.182	43	144	121	17	22	41	4	0	5	11	0	1	4	18	0	39	2	0	5	.339	.306
Wells, Forry, Salem*	.254	119	469	402	60	102	187	23	4	18	67	3	1	7	56	6	105	6	3	2	.465	.354
Wells, Mark, Salem*	.195	66	252	236	24	46	84	8	0	10	31	1	1	1	13	3	83	0	3	2	.356	.239
White, Jimmy, Winston-Salem*	.261	31	119	111	15	29	57	5	1	7	18	1	1	2	4	0	33	1	1	1	.514	.297
Wieser, Mike, Durham	.210	28	65	62	5	13	18	2	0	1	3	0	0	1	2	0	12	0	1	0	.290	.246
Williams, Harold, Prince William*	.282	129	534	472	56	133	207	30	1	14	72	1	2	11	48	11	98	4	2	16	.439	.360
Wilson, Brian, Winston-Salem	.224	20	65	58	10	13	20	1	0	2	8	0	0	0	7	0	16	1	2	2	.345	.308
Wilson, Enrique, Kinston†	.267	117	505	464	55	124	180	24	7	6	52	4	10	2	25	2	38	18	19	10	.388	.301
Zapata, Ramon, Lynchburg	.298	119	469	416	59	124	179	27	2	8	45	9	0	2	42	0	58	6	8	13	.430	.365

GRAND SLAMS: Correa, Secrist, 3 each; Betts, Betzsold, Cawhorn, Collier, Davis, G. Garcia, P. Gonzalez, Gutierrez, Holdren, Magdaleno, McBride, Meggers, Menechino, Ordonez, R. Robertson, Simon, Sweeney, G. Thomas, F. Wells, M. Wells, White, 1 each.

AWARDED FIRST BASE ON CATCHER'S INTERFERENCE: Velazquez 2 (R. Brooks, S. Smith); Byrne (Johnson); King (Higgins).

PLAYERS WITH TWO OR MORE TEAMS

Player, Team	Avg.	G	TPA	AB	R	H	TB	2B	3B	HR	RBI	SH	SF	HP	BB	IBB	SO	SB	CS	GDP	Slg.	OBP
Clyburn, Danny, Winston-Salem	.260	59	246	227	27	59	106	10	2	11	41	0	2	4	13	1	59	2	4	5	.467	.309
Clyburn, Danny, Frederick	.200	15	51	45	4	9	13	4	0	0	4	0	0	2	4	0	18	1	1	0	.289	.294
King, Andre, Durham	.252	111	480	421	59	106	161	22	3	9	33	5	4	10	39	1	126	15	13	5	.382	.327
King, Andre, Prince William	.156	9	39	32	4	5	8	1	1	0	3	1	0	0	6	0	9	1	0	2	.250	.289
Sexton, Chris, Winston-Salem	.400	4	19	15	3	6	9	0	0	1	5	0	0	0	4	0	0	0	0	0	.600	.526
Sexton, Chris, Salem	.267	123	568	461	81	123	163	16	6	4	32	12	1	1	93	2	55	14	11	11	.354	.390

1995 PITCHING

TEAM

Team	W	L	Pct.	ERA	G	CG	ShO	Sv.	IP	H	TBF	R	ER	HR	SH	SF	HB	BB	IBB	SO	WP	Bk.
Wilmington	83	55	.601	2.84	138	2	17	46	1232.2	1017	5054	459	389	63	35	29	57	405	33	1005	86	13
Kinston	81	56	.591	3.24	137	8	10	37	1214.0	1056	5006	500	437	98	44	35	74	408	23	943	69	7
Winston-Salem	69	68	.504	3.33	137	12	11	30	1198.0	1065	4983	538	443	102	34	24	60	427	19	850	57	14
Prince William	64	76	.457	3.91	140	12	11	32	1206.0	1176	5147	594	524	114	40	44	58	432	28	962	81	6
Frederick	58	79	.423	3.92	137	10	11	32	1190.2	1123	5130	617	518	101	45	38	68	487	25	1018	103	16
Salem	68	72	.486	4.10	140	8	6	34	1237.0	1238	5355	667	563	115	42	34	57	536	54	871	114	22
Lynchburg	67	71	.486	4.16	138	5	9	27	1182.2	1213	5091	640	547	106	44	36	51	393	34	893	83	16
Durham	63	76	.453	4.25	139	6	3	39	1186.2	1188	5210	650	560	109	51	40	60	541	34	825	74	9

INDIVIDUAL

TOP QUALIFIERS FOR EARNED-RUN AVERAGE TITLE

Minimum 112 innings. *Lefthanded pitcher.

Pitcher, Team	W	L	Pct.	ERA	G	GS	CG	ShO	GF	Sv.	IP	H	TBF	R	ER	HR	SH	SF	HB	BB	IBB	SO	WP	Bk.
Rusch, Glendon, Wilmington*	14	6	.700	1.74	26	26	1	1	0	0	165.2	110	629	41	32	5	4	3	4	34	3	147	3	1
Colon, Bartolo, Kinston	13	3	.813	1.96	21	21	0	0	0	0	128.2	91	493	31	28	8	1	2	0	39	0	152	4	3
Byrdak, Tim, Wilmington*	11	5	.688	2.16	27	26	0	0	0	0	166.1	118	657	46	40	7	3	3	10	45	2	127	1	0
Peters, Chris, Lynchburg*	11	5	.688	2.43	24	24	3	3	0	0	144.2	126	586	57	39	5	7	4	5	35	2	132	12	1
Wright, Jamey, Salem	10	8	.556	2.47	26	26	2	1	0	0	171.0	160	732	74	47	7	3	6	13	72	3	95	16	2
Maduro, Calvin, Frederick	8	5	.615	2.94	20	20	2	2	0	0	122.1	109	499	43	40	16	3	2	6	34	0	120	2	0
Lyons, Curt, Winston-Salem	9	9	.500	2.98	26	26	0	0	0	0	160.1	139	672	66	53	10	6	2	15	67	3	122	9	3
Robbins, Jason, Winston-Salem	9	6	.600	3.06	23	23	3	1	0	0	141.0	113	571	62	48	16	0	5	7	42	1	106	5	1
Rosado, Jose, Wilmington*	10	7	.588	3.13	25	25	0	0	0	0	138.0	128	562	53	48	9	2	7	3	30	6	117	1	5
Pratt, Rich, Prince William*	5	11	.313	3.14	25	25	2	1	0	0	152.0	139	619	66	53	12	2	5	4	42	0	120	10	2
Pfaff, Jason, Lynchburg	5	6	.455	3.23	35	10	0	0	4	0	114.1	115	488	56	41	6	5	2	8	31	3	95	8	0
Reed, Chris, Winston-Salem	10	7	.588	3.32	24	24	3	1	0	0	149.0	116	613	63	55	11	3	1	4	68	1	104	3	1
Vaught, Jay, Kinston	8	12	.400	3.37	27	26	4	1	0	0	171.0	184	717	80	64	19	8	5	15	28	3	82	6	1
Jacobs, Ryan, Durham*	11	6	.647	3.51	29	25	1	0	3	0	148.2	145	640	72	58	12	6	5	3	57	3	99	10	0
Mathews, Del, Durham*	7	8	.467	3.54	33	16	1	0	8	1	112.0	117	478	53	44	6	4	1	10	38	2	77	6	0

DEPARTMENTAL LEADERS: W—Rusch, 14; L—Woods, 15; Pct.—Colon, .813; G—Byrd, 60; GS—Pool, 28; CG—Vaught, 4; ShO—Peters, 3; GF—Byrd, 53; Sv.—Byrd, 27; IP—Vaught, Wright, 171.0; H—Pool, 191; TBF—Wright, 732; R—Pool, 90; ER—Pool, 88; HR—Vaught, 19; SH—Bowie, 13; SF—Marenghi, 8; HB—Lyons, Vaught, 15; BB—Green, Million, 79; IBB—Bock, Rizzo, 8; SO—Colon, 152; WP—Heathcott, 18; Bk.—Dillinger, 7.

ALL PITCHERS

*Lefthanded pitcher.

Pitcher, Team	W	L	Pct.	ERA	G	GS	CG	ShO	GF	Sv.	IP	H	TBF	R	ER	HR	SH	SF	HB	BB	IBB	SO	WP	Bk.
Abramavicius, Jason, Lynchburg*	1	0	1.000	7.30	9	0	0	0	2	0	12.1	22	64	13	10	0	0	0	0	5	1	11	1	0
Aminoff, Matt, Salem	4	6	.400	3.21	39	0	0	0	32	16	53.1	53	237	28	19	3	7	3	4	22	4	31	6	0
Anderson, Eric, Wilmington	3	1	.750	2.93	16	0	0	0	10	2	27.2	28	109	9	9	1	0	0	0	4	0	19	4	1
Anderson, Jimmy, Lynchburg*	1	5	.167	4.13	10	9	0	0	1	0	52.1	56	231	29	24	1	4	1	5	21	1	32	7	3
Arnold, Jamie, Durham	4	8	.333	3.94	15	14	1	0	0	0	80.0	86	347	42	35	5	4	1	9	21	0	44	4	0
Atkinson, Neil, Wilmington*	1	1	.500	2.86	8	0	0	0	5	3	22.0	21	93	7	7	1	2	0	1	6	3	20	3	0
Barnes, Keith, Salem*	4	5	.444	5.35	15	15	1	0	0	0	79.0	90	335	52	47	11	1	3	3	24	0	43	4	0
Binkley, Brett, Durham*	2	2	.500	5.97	24	0	0	0	6	0	28.2	34	138	20	19	2	2	1	1	21	1	20	4	1
Bliss, Bill, Salem	3	2	.600	4.23	34	0	0	0	17	4	44.2	38	193	24	21	4	2	1	1	25	6	23	9	2
Bock, Jeff, Durham	5	1	.833	3.36	32	4	0	0	11	2	67.0	58	282	31	25	9	4	3	1	31	8	45	3	0
Bowie, Micah, Durham*	4	11	.267	3.59	23	23	1	0	0	0	130.1	119	561	65	52	8	13	3	8	61	3	91	4	3
Brabant, Dan, Kinston	7	4	.636	4.23	47	0	0	0	12	1	93.2	81	405	47	44	9	3	4	6	49	3	89	9	0
Brewer, Brian, Frederick*	2	4	.333	2.53	14	8	0	0	3	1	67.2	49	263	22	19	2	3	2	3	19	1	48	5	2
Brewer, Nevin, Wilmington	1	1	.500	0.93	17	0	0	0	13	8	29.0	19	120	4	3	0	3	0	1	15	2	20	3	0
Brownson, Mark, Salem	2	1	.667	4.02	9	1	0	0	5	1	15.2	16	71	8	7	0	0	0	1	10	4	9	4	0
Burgess, Kurt, Durham*	2	4	.333	7.83	34	0	0	0	11	0	43.2	48	219	44	38	3	3	2	8	34	2	25	4	1
Byrd, Matt, Durham	5	4	.556	2.97	60	0	0	0	53	27	69.2	52	296	24	23	8	0	3	3	32	4	79	9	0
Byrdak, Tim, Wilmington*	11	5	.688	2.16	27	26	0	0	0	0	166.1	118	657	46	40	7	3	3	10	45	2	127	1	0
Call, Mike, Prince William	4	7	.364	5.42	28	9	3	1	8	1	104.2	114	462	66	63	14	3	3	7	37	1	62	5	0
Callistro, Rob, Prince William	1	1	.500	4.00	8	0	0	0	1	0	18.0	19	79	8	8	3	1	0	0	7	0	18	1	1
Caruso, Joe, Lynchburg	4	0	1.000	2.95	29	0	0	0	14	4	39.2	36	168	13	13	0	4	4	3	16	4	27	2	1
Chaves, Rafael, Lynchburg	1	3	.250	2.66	42	0	0	0	41	22	47.1	35	191	17	14	3	4	0	1	13	3	45	5	1
Chavez, Carlos, Frederick	5	5	.500	2.55	43	1	0	0	16	6	81.1	62	342	38	23	4	1	0	2	40	2	107	16	1
Christman, Scott, Prince William*	4	4	.500	3.59	13	13	1	0	0	0	85.1	83	346	38	34	7	1	6	2	19	2	56	3	0
Christmas, Maurice, Durham	2	7	.222	4.83	31	18	0	0	2	0	113.2	135	493	68	61	15	2	3	4	19	2	68	2	0
Clemons, Chris, Prince William	7	12	.368	4.73	27	27	1	0	0	0	137.0	136	606	78	72	18	4	4	11	64	2	92	2	0
Colon, Bartolo, Kinston	13	3	.813	1.96	21	21	0	0	0	0	128.2	91	493	31	28	8	1	2	0	39	0	152	4	3
Conley, Curt, Salem*	4	1	.800	3.61	39	0	0	0	20	3	47.1	42	211	22	19	4	2	3	2	27	3	35	4	2
Connolly, Chris, Wilmington*	5	2	.714	3.48	27	0	0	0	13	1	44.0	38	196	23	17	2	1	1	5	23	2	29	10	1
Connors, Chad, Winston-Salem	2	2	.500	6.86	16	0	0	0	8	2	19.2	28	95	16	15	3	0	0	3	11	1	13	2	0
Coppinger, Rocky, Frederick	7	1	.875	1.57	11	11	2	1	0	0	68.2	46	272	16	12	3	3	1	0	24	0	91	1	0
Crills, Brad, Frederick	2	5	.286	3.06	9	9	3	1	0	0	61.2	63	259	26	21	2	3	2	3	12	1	33	2	2
Crowther, Brent, Salem	3	6	.333	2.76	12	12	3	1	0	0	78.1	70	322	31	24	4	5	0	2	25	5	60	7	2
Cruz, Nelson, Prince William	2	1	.667	0.47	9	0	0	0	7	1	19.1	12	75	1	1	1	0	0	2	6	0	18	0	0
Cullop, Glen, Winston-Salem	0	1	.000	0.90	6	0	0	0	5	0	10.0	7	39	1	1	0	0	1	0	5	0	4	1	0
Daigle, Tim, Frederick*	0	2	.000	8.53	6	0	0	0	0	0	6.1	9	38	12	6	1	0	2	1	5	0	9	2	0
Daniels, Lee, Durham	1	4	.200	4.24	21	0	0	0	7	4	23.1	26	113	13	11	1	3	0	1	14	1	24	4	2
Dawley, Joey, Frederick	1	2	.333	6.34	24	0	0	0	8	1	32.2	41	163	28	23	4	1	1	3	22	1	29	5	1
DeLaMaza, Roland, Kinston	6	0	1.000	2.37	26	12	0	0	5	1	110.1	99	445	31	29	13	7	0	3	28	3	100	3	0
DeLaRosa, Maximo, Kinston	5	2	.714	2.19	43	0	0	0	21	8	61.2	46	266	23	15	0	5	2	4	37	3	61	7	1
DeLeon, Elcilio, Lynchburg	2	0	1.000	4.24	13	0	0	0	3	0	17.0	12	74	9	8	2	1	1	3	11	0	9	0	0
Dickens, John, Wilmington*	3	1	.750	1.77	48	0	0	0	27	9	76.1	57	296	17	15	1	2	3	3	17	3	59	5	0
Dietrich, Jason, Salem	1	0	1.000	8.59	6	0	0	0	1	0	7.1	9	39	7	7	2	0	0	1	8	0	9	0	0
Dillinger, John, Lynchburg	6	6	.500	4.02	27	22	0	0	1	0	123.0	111	540	62	55	10	5	5	7	67	4	97	9	7
Donnelly, Brendan, Winston-Salem	1	2	.333	1.02	23	0	0	0	14	2	35.1	20	138	6	4	1	2	0	2	14	2	32	0	1
Doorneweerd, Dave, Lynchburg	0	1	.000	6.75	5	0	0	0	2	0	8.0	8	38	6	6	0	0	0	1	5	0	9	1	0
Downs, John, Wilmington	1	0	1.000	5.40	8	0	0	0	5	0	11.2	19	55	7	7	2	0	1	0	2	1	7	2	0
Doyle, Tom, Winston-Salem*	3	1	.750	3.45	21	3	0	0	3	1	31.1	32	140	18	12	2	1	0	3	12	0	22	5	0
Driskill, Travis, Kinston	0	2	.000	2.74	15	0	0	0	9	0	23.0	17	90	7	7	2	0	3	1	5	1	24	1	0
Dyess, Todd, Frederick	0	2	.000	6.59	3	3	0	0	0	0	13.2	17	61	10	10	1	0	1	1	5	0	8	3	0
Etler, Todd, Winston-Salem	6	12	.333	3.69	24	23	3	0	0	0	153.2	148	628	71	63	13	4	5	2	49	2	78	3	2
Evans, Bart, Wilmington	4	1	.800	2.89	16	6	0	0	4	2	46.2	30	215	21	15	0	0	1	5	44	0	47	7	0
Faino, Jeff, Frederick*	0	0	.000	4.76	4	0	0	0	2	0	5.2	7	26	5	3	0	1	0	0	2	0	8	1	0
Farson, Bryan, Lynchburg*	7	3	.700	5.82	27	6	0	0	7	0	51.0	51	228	41	33	13	1	2	2	19	4	35	3	0
Flury, Pat, Wilmington	1	0	1.000	2.45	15	0	0	0	6	1	22.0	18	89	6	6	2	0	1	1	9	1	14	1	1
Fordham, Tom, Prince William*	9	0	1.000	2.04	13	13	1	1	0	0	84.0	66	340	20	19	7	2	1	2	35	2	78	1	0
Gamboa, Javier, Wilmington	3	4	.429	4.04	8	8	0	0	0	0	49.0	42	202	23	22	6	3	0	1	13	0	33	2	0
Garrett, Neil, Salem	1	0	1.000	12.27	5	0	0	0	0	0	3.2	5	24	8	5	0	1	0	1	5	0	3	3	0
Giron, Emiliano, Winston-Salem	2	0	1.000	2.30	17	0	0	0	11	0	27.1	23	121	15	7	1	0	0	3	10	0	29	2	2
Goldman, Barry, Salem	0	3	.000	5.79	8	0	0	0	6	0	9.1	8	41	7	6	0	0	0	0	7	1	6	2	0
Graves, Dan, Kinston	3	1	.750	0.82	38	0	0	0	37	21	44.0	30	177	11	4	0	1	0	0	12	2	46	0	0
Green, Jason, Durham	2	4	.333	5.58	39	1	0	0	14	3	50.0	31	248	31	31	1	2	4	1	79	1	59	13	1
Grundy, Phillip, Wilmington	6	6	.500	3.31	20	16	0	0	3	1	106.0	106	445	46	39	7	4	1	5	32	2	90	7	0
Hagan, Danny, Winston-Salem*	1	0	1.000	1.80	1	1	0	0	0	0	5.0	5	21	1	1	0	0	0	0	4	0	2	0	0
Hale, Shane, Frederick*	0	2	.000	10.93	6	2	0	0	0	0	14.0	21	69	18	17	1	1	3	1	6	2	6	1	0
Hanson, Kris, Kinston	5	6	.455	5.04	20	18	1	0	0	0	96.1	102	404	56	54	11	1	3	5	24	1	53	3	0
Harrison, Tom, Durham	3	1	.750	0.96	7	6	0	0	0	0	37.2	22	145	5	4	1	0	0	1	13	1	25	0	0
Hartzog, Cullen, Lynchburg	6	4	.600	3.34	43	1	0	0	17	0	59.1	49	254	23	22	5	1	1	2	30	2	45	8	0
Harvell, Pete, Winston-Salem*	0	1	.000	12.60	4	0	0	0	1	0	5.0	9	28	7	7	1	0	1	0	4	0	1	1	0
Heathcott, Mike, Prince William	4	9	.308	4.67	27	14	1	0	4	3	88.2	96	387	56	46	8	2	7	2	36	3	68	18	0
Heiserman, Rick, Kinston	9	3	.750	3.74	19	19	1	0	0	0	113.0	97	470	55	47	13	3	4	9	42	1	86	6	1
Hernandez, Francisco, Frederick	0	1	.000	6.00	3	0	0	0	3	1	3.0	3	15	2	2	1	0	1	0	3	0	3	0	0
Hodges, Kevin, Wilmington	2	3	.400	4.53	12	10	0	0	1	0	53.2	53	232	31	27	1	1	1	3	25	1	27	4	0
Hostetler, Marcus, Durham	1	1	.500	6.61	12	0	0	0	3	0	16.1	23	80	13	12	3	1	2	1	7	0	6	0	0
Huber, Jeff, Frederick*	2	0	1.000	5.21	21	0	0	0	4	0	19.0	29	92	16	11	5	1	2	0	5	1	11	2	0
Jacobs, Ryan, Durham*	11	6	.647	3.51	29	25	1	0	3	0	148.2	145	640	72	58	12	6	5	3	57	3	99	10	0
Jesperson, Bob, Winston-Salem	2	1	.667	4.26	5	0	0	0	4	0	6.1	5	26	3	3	0	0	0	0	4	1	1	0	0
Johnson, Jason, Lynchburg	1	4	.200	4.91	10	10	0	0	0	0	55.0	58	236	37	30	9	0	3	2	20	0	41	2	0
Johnson, Jason, Salem	1	2	.333	2.05	5	4	0	0	0	0	22.0	23	94	6	5	0	1	0	1	5	0	9	1	0
Kirkreit, Daron, Kinston	0	1	.000	5.93	3	3	0	0	0	0	13.2	14	63	9	9	1	1	1	2	6	0	14	1	0

Pitcher, Team	W	L	Pct.	ERA	G	GS	CG	ShO	GF	Sv.	IP	H	TBF	R	ER	HR	SH	SF	HB	BB	IBB	SO	WP	Bk.
Kitchen, Ron, Frederick	2	2	.500	7.23	30	0	0	0	11	0	37.1	55	179	35	30	6	3	2	1	10	3	10	1	1
Kummerfeldt, Jason, Winst.-Sal.	4	6	.400	3.48	37	3	0	0	14	3	77.2	78	326	37	30	7	1	1	7	19	5	51	1	0
Kusiewicz, Michael, Salem*	0	0	.000	1.50	1	1	0	0	0	0	6.0	7	26	1	1	0	0	0	2	0	0	7	0	1
Larock, Scott, Salem	5	4	.556	3.90	52	1	0	0	18	4	101.2	96	423	52	44	10	4	2	0	27	7	92	5	3
Lavenia, Mark, Durham*	0	1	.000	5.56	6	0	0	0	1	0	11.1	14	51	8	7	1	0	1	0	5	0	9	3	0
Lawrence, Sean, Lynchburg*	5	8	.385	4.22	20	19	0	0	0	0	111.0	115	465	56	52	16	3	3	1	25	0	82	3	0
LaPlante, Michel, Lynchburg	1	1	.500	8.22	5	2	0	0	0	0	15.1	21	73	14	14	4	0	1	1	3	0	13	2	0
LaRocca, Todd, Frederick	3	1	.750	1.76	5	5	0	0	0	0	30.2	22	132	7	6	0	2	0	2	16	0	24	4	0
Lehman, Toby, Frederick	0	5	.000	4.25	19	10	1	0	2	0	55.0	44	237	30	26	9	3	1	3	27	1	48	6	0
Lemp, Chris, Frederick	2	3	.400	2.38	41	0	0	0	36	19	45.1	44	194	16	12	4	3	2	0	17	2	50	8	0
Leroy, John, Durham	6	9	.400	5.44	24	22	1	0	0	0	125.2	128	545	82	76	17	2	5	5	57	1	77	5	1
Lindemann, Wayne, Prince William*	2	0	1.000	5.86	19	0	0	0	14	1	43.0	54	196	30	28	7	1	5	2	20	2	32	3	0
Locklear, Jeff, Salem*	0	0	.000	12.79	6	0	0	0	2	0	6.1	10	33	9	9	2	0	2	0	4	0	3	0	0
Lombardi, John, Frederick	0	4	.000	7.16	6	3	0	0	0	0	16.1	22	75	13	13	2	0	1	2	6	0	13	2	0
Lyons, Curt, Winston-Salem	9	9	.500	2.98	26	26	0	0	0	0	160.1	139	672	66	53	10	6	2	15	67	3	122	9	3
Maberry, Louis, Winston-Salem	1	0	1.000	4.34	20	0	0	0	12	0	37.1	40	154	20	18	5	1	0	2	7	0	19	7	0
Maduro, Calvin, Frederick	8	5	.615	2.94	20	20	2	2	0	0	122.1	109	499	43	40	16	3	2	6	34	0	120	2	0
Magee, Bo, Frederick*	2	1	.667	4.05	5	5	0	0	0	0	26.2	28	111	15	12	4	2	0	2	5	0	28	2	0
Magre, Pete, Winston-Salem	1	1	.500	3.09	17	0	0	0	4	2	32.0	39	150	14	11	3	2	0	3	15	1	27	3	3
Maine, Dalton, Frederick	1	1	.500	3.68	19	0	0	0	10	0	22.0	20	98	10	9	2	0	1	2	11	0	21	5	0
Mansur, Jeff, Frederick*	0	0	.000	4.70	12	0	0	0	6	0	15.1	20	70	8	8	1	1	1	2	5	1	12	0	0
Marenghi, Matt, Frederick	4	13	.235	5.08	30	16	0	0	8	2	113.1	108	475	73	64	14	1	8	9	41	2	85	6	1
Martinez, Johnny, Kinston	3	0	1.000	1.64	6	0	0	0	5	2	11.0	9	44	2	2	0	0	0	1	4	0	13	1	0
Mathews, Del, Durham*	7	8	.467	3.54	33	16	1	0	8	1	112.0	117	478	53	44	6	4	1	10	38	2	77	6	0
Mattson, Craig, Lynchburg	2	0	1.000	3.09	11	0	0	0	5	0	11.2	11	46	5	4	1	0	0	1	0	0	5	0	0
Mayse, Robert, Frederick	1	0	1.000	3.72	6	0	0	0	1	0	9.2	9	42	5	4	0	0	0	1	8	0	7	0	0
McKenzie, Scott, Winston-Salem	3	4	.429	2.75	49	0	0	0	41	20	72.0	42	294	27	22	7	5	0	5	30	2	55	7	0
Mesa, Rafael, Kinston	4	3	.571	2.94	35	1	0	0	24	0	52.0	34	206	19	17	5	4	3	4	20	2	29	4	0
Mesewicz, Mark, Lynchburg*	0	1	.000	23.14	6	0	0	0	1	0	4.2	13	29	12	12	2	0	0	0	2	0	3	1	0
Million, Doug, Salem*	5	7	.417	4.62	24	23	0	0	0	0	111.0	111	513	71	57	6	6	1	9	79	4	85	9	4
Montoya, Wilmer, Kinston	1	0	1.000	5.40	1	0	0	0	0	0	3.1	4	15	2	2	0	1	0	0	1	0	2	0	0
Morel, Ramon, Lynchburg	3	7	.300	3.47	12	12	1	1	0	0	72.2	80	304	35	28	2	2	3	3	13	2	44	2	0
Murphy, Chris, Winston-Salem*	2	1	.667	2.70	4	3	0	0	1	0	20.0	13	75	7	6	2	1	1	0	5	0	22	1	0
Najera, Noe, Kinston*	0	1	.000	2.25	8	3	0	0	2	0	20.0	10	78	6	5	0	1	0	2	9	1	14	0	0
Nelson, Earl, Durham*	0	1	.000	4.95	15	0	0	0	9	2	20.0	27	105	17	11	4	1	1	3	17	2	17	2	0
Nieto, Tony, Frederick	1	4	.200	3.92	21	0	0	0	6	0	39.0	38	162	19	17	4	2	1	5	9	2	14	1	1
Oropeza, Igor, Kinston	2	3	.400	4.50	20	2	0	0	2	1	38.0	24	164	19	19	4	3	2	3	29	2	31	3	0
Paige, Carey, Durham	5	3	.625	3.38	10	10	1	0	0	0	64.0	53	252	24	24	8	2	3	1	15	1	37	1	0
Perkins, Paul, Lynchburg	0	3	.000	3.94	25	0	0	0	14	1	29.2	34	135	15	13	1	0	0	2	10	3	28	1	0
Peters, Chris, Lynchburg*	11	5	.688	2.43	24	24	3	3	0	0	144.2	126	586	57	39	5	7	4	5	35	2	132	12	1
Pfaff, Jason, Lynchburg	5	6	.455	3.23	35	10	0	0	4	0	114.1	115	488	56	41	6	5	2	8	31	3	95	8	0
Pickford, Kevin, Lynchburg*	0	3	.000	4.94	4	4	0	0	0	0	27.1	31	110	15	15	5	0	1	0	0	0	15	2	1
Pierson, Jason, Prince William*	5	4	.556	4.42	21	12	0	0	5	0	91.2	91	382	48	45	9	1	4	2	22	0	69	1	0
Place, Mike, Durham	2	1	.667	10.57	7	0	0	0	1	0	7.2	11	36	11	9	0	0	0	0	6	0	2	0	0
Pontbriant, Matt, Lynchburg*	7	7	.500	5.05	27	17	1	1	4	0	108.2	137	476	67	61	16	5	2	1	28	3	60	2	1
Pool, Matt, Salem	9	9	.500	4.80	28	28	2	0	0	0	165.0	191	705	90	88	18	5	2	6	50	5	95	16	1
Pratt, Rich, Prince William*	5	11	.313	3.14	25	25	2	1	0	0	152.0	139	619	66	53	12	2	5	4	42	0	120	10	2
Priest, Eddie, Winston-Salem*	5	5	.500	3.63	12	12	1	1	0	0	67.0	60	275	32	27	7	2	2	0	22	0	60	2	0
Raines, Ken, Durham*	1	0	1.000	4.94	19	0	0	0	3	0	23.2	38	118	19	13	3	2	1	0	12	2	15	0	0
Ramos, Cesar, Kinston	1	2	.333	3.65	8	0	0	0	2	0	12.1	16	56	6	5	0	2	0	2	3	1	4	0	0
Rawitzer, Kevin, Wilmington*	2	0	1.000	2.33	15	1	0	0	7	3	27.0	21	111	8	7	0	1	0	3	8	1	22	1	0
Ray, Ken, Wilmington	6	4	.600	2.69	13	13	1	0	0	0	77.0	74	320	32	23	3	3	3	1	22	2	63	17	2
Reed, Chris, Winston-Salem	10	7	.588	3.32	24	24	3	1	0	0	149.0	116	613	63	55	11	3	1	4	68	1	104	3	1
Rhodes, Joe, Frederick	0	1	.000	4.50	2	1	0	0	1	0	6.0	8	28	3	3	0	1	0	0	2	0	2	1	0
Riemer, Matt, Frederick	0	0	.000	0.00	1	0	0	0	1	0	1.0	1	5	0	0	0	0	0	1	0	0	0	0	0
Rizzo, Todd, Prince William*	3	5	.375	2.78	36	0	0	0	10	1	68.0	68	307	30	21	2	2	1	3	39	8	59	13	0
Robbins, Jason, Winston-Salem	9	6	.600	3.06	23	23	3	1	0	0	141.0	113	571	62	48	16	0	5	7	42	1	106	5	1
Roberts, Ray, Wilmington*	1	2	.333	3.32	13	0	0	0	6	4	19.0	18	79	7	7	2	0	1	0	2	0	16	0	0
Rogers, Jason, Frederick*	1	3	.250	4.32	15	14	1	0	0	0	66.2	64	309	38	32	1	2	2	3	45	3	39	6	2
Rosado, Jose, Wilmington*	10	7	.588	3.13	25	25	0	0	0	0	138.0	128	562	53	48	9	2	7	3	30	6	117	1	5
Runion, Tony, Kinston	7	11	.389	4.09	28	24	0	0	2	0	143.0	131	599	70	65	9	2	6	13	57	0	84	10	0
Rusch, Glendon, Wilmington*	14	6	.700	1.74	26	26	1	1	0	0	165.2	110	629	41	32	5	4	3	4	34	3	147	3	1
Ruyak, Todd, Winston-Salem*	5	6	.455	3.99	34	9	0	0	7	0	85.2	99	369	44	38	8	6	3	1	20	0	48	2	1
Saipe, Mike, Salem	4	5	.444	3.48	21	9	0	0	7	3	85.1	68	347	35	33	7	1	1	2	32	4	90	9	1
Salamon, John, Salem	1	0	1.000	6.14	8	0	0	0	4	1	14.2	13	60	10	10	5	0	0	0	5	0	9	0	0
Sauritch, Chris, Frederick	0	0	.000	9.00	1	0	0	0	1	0	1.0	1	4	1	1	1	0	0	0	0	0	1	0	0
Sexton, Jeff, Kinston	5	1	.833	2.53	8	8	2	1	0	0	57.0	52	226	17	16	3	0	0	2	7	0	41	6	1
Sheehan, Chris, Wilmington	2	1	.667	1.86	13	0	0	0	5	3	19.1	7	67	5	4	0	2	0	2	2	0	27	1	0
Sinnes, David, Wilmington	0	2	.000	3.04	18	0	0	0	11	3	23.2	15	115	12	8	0	1	1	5	24	1	34	6	0
Smith, Hut, Frederick	3	2	.600	6.47	20	2	0	0	7	2	32.0	39	162	23	23	4	2	1	4	31	1	28	7	1
Smith, Toby, Wilmington	5	7	.417	3.08	30	7	0	0	13	4	79.0	67	320	32	27	9	2	1	3	20	2	65	6	2
Sobkoviak, Jeff, Salem	5	3	.625	4.80	40	5	0	0	10	2	86.1	96	371	52	46	13	3	4	5	37	5	44	7	0
Sosa, Jose, Lynchburg	0	0	.000	6.88	10	0	0	0	6	0	17.0	27	82	14	13	1	1	0	0	6	1	12	4	1
Stewart, Chris, Salem	0	2	.000	8.53	10	0	0	0	4	0	12.2	18	64	15	12	3	0	1	0	11	2	10	3	2
Stewart, Rachaad, Frederick*	8	8	.500	3.64	26	26	1	1	0	0	150.2	126	635	71	61	8	5	1	10	66	1	140	12	4
Tagle, Hank, Prince William*	3	2	.600	3.09	33	0	0	0	16	2	70.0	58	275	28	24	4	4	2	5	15	1	66	3	0
Tolar, Kevin, Lynchburg*	2	0	1.000	2.79	18	0	0	0	4	0	19.1	13	77	7	6	1	0	1	1	6	0	19	3	0
Towns, Ryan, Wilmington	1	0	1.000	5.63	12	0	0	0	2	1	16.0	12	75	11	10	0	0	0	0	18	0	8	1	0
Tuttle, Dave, Winston-Salem	3	3	.500	3.18	10	10	2	1	0	0	62.1	49	248	28	22	5	0	2	3	19	0	54	3	0
Vaught, Jay, Kinston	8	12	.400	3.37	27	26	4	1	0	0	171.0	184	717	80	64	19	8	5	15	28	3	82	6	1
Vazquez, Archie, Prince William	3	4	.429	3.59	47	0	0	0	45	20	57.2	53	261	26	23	5	9	1	1	30	4	70	8	0
Voisard, Mark, Salem	0	0	.000	7.36	6	0	0	0	2	0	7.1	8	33	6	6	4	0	1	1	4	0	5	0	0
Waldron, Joe, Salem*	1	2	.333	2.51	9	0	0	0	3	0	14.1	23	64	5	4	0	0	0	0	1	0	17	0	0

Pitcher, Team	W	L	Pct.	ERA	G	GS	CG	ShO	GF	Sv.	IP	H	TBF	R	ER	HR	SH	SF	HB	BB	IBB	SO	WP	Bk.
Walker, James, Frederick	2	2	.500	3.48	9	0	0	0	1	0	20.2	15	90	12	8	0	1	0	1	9	1	19	2	0
Walls, Doug, Salem	5	5	.500	3.84	15	15	0	0	0	0	79.2	61	344	39	34	10	1	3	3	49	1	79	5	2
Wells, David, Durham	0	0	.000	4.73	7	0	0	0	1	0	13.1	21	63	8	7	2	0	1	0	2	0	6	0	0
White, Gary, Frederick*	1	0	1.000	3.00	1	1	0	0	0	0	6.0	3	23	2	2	1	0	0	0	2	0	4	0	0
Williams, Greg, Kinston*	2	1	.667	2.45	30	0	0	0	8	3	22.0	15	88	9	6	1	1	0	2	8	0	18	5	0
Winkle, Ken, Wilmington	1	1	.500	10.54	11	0	0	0	5	1	13.2	16	67	18	16	5	1	1	1	10	1	14	1	0
Woods, Brian, Prince William	9	15	.375	5.17	27	27	3	0	0	0	139.1	155	632	89	80	14	5	4	14	53	1	102	12	3
Worrell, Steve, Prince William*	3	1	.750	1.52	29	0	0	0	18	3	47.1	32	180	10	8	3	3	1	1	7	2	52	1	0
Wright, Jamey, Salem	10	8	.556	2.47	26	26	2	1	0	0	171.0	160	732	74	47	7	3	6	13	72	3	95	16	2
Young, Danny, Lynchburg*	2	4	.333	7.40	24	2	0	0	7	0	41.1	52	196	37	34	3	1	2	2	27	1	34	5	0
Zolecki, Mike, Salem	0	1	.000	7.20	9	0	0	0	1	0	15.0	22	73	15	12	2	0	1	0	7	0	12	4	0

COMBINATION SHUTOUTS: **Durham (3)**—Harrison-Nelson, Jacobs-Bock, Jacobs-Byrd. **Frederick (6)**—Brewer-Marenghi, Coppinger-Smith-Lemp, Dyess-Mayse-Maine-Smith, Maduro-Chavez-Lemp, Magee-Marenghi, Rogers-Kitchen-Lemp-Maine. **Kinston (8)**—Colon-DeLaMaza, Colon-Oropeza-Williams-Brabant, DeLaMaza-Martinez, Mesa-Delarosa-Graves, Najera-Martinez, Runion-Delarosa, Runion-Williams-Delarosa, Vaught-Mesa. **Lynchburg (4)**—Anderson-Farson, Dillinger-Pfaff, Farson-Caruso-Perkins, Lawrence-Chaves. **Prince William (8)**—Fordham-Vazquez 2, Christman-Cruz, Christman-Worrell, Fordham-Heathcott-Call, Heathcott-Tagle-Vazquez, Pratt-Vazquez, Woods-Vazquez. **Salem (4)**—Barnes-Larock-Sobkoviak-Goldman, Pool-Aminoff, Saipe-Aminoff-Bliss, Walls-Aminoff. **Wilmington (16)**—Rusch-Brewer 2, Byrdak-Anderson, Byrdak-Brewer, Byrdak-Dickens, Gamboa-Evans, Grundy-Anderson, Grundy-Dickens, Hodges-Smith, Ray-Dickens, Ray-Sheehan-Rawitzer-Sinnes, Rosado-Atkinson, Rosado-Flury, Rosado-Sinnes-Connolly, Rusch-Smith-Connolly, Smith-Sinnes-Roberts-Flury. **Winston-Salem (7)**—Doyle-Kummerfeldt-Donnelly-McKenzie, Etler-McKenzie, Lyons-McKenzie, Lyons-Ruyak-Giron, Priest-Kummerfeldt, Robbins-Doyle-McKenzie, Robbins-Kummerfeldt-Ruyak-Harvell.

NO-HIT GAMES: Woods-Vazquez, Prince William, defeated Salem, 8-0, April 8; Rosado-Flury, Wilmington, defeated Winston-Salem, 3-0, April 15; Harrison-Nelson, Durham, defeated Prince William, 4-0, April 30; Pratt, Prince William, defeated Frederick, 3-0 (second game), May 19.

1995 FIELDING

TEAM

Team	Pct.	G	PO	A	E	TC	DP	PB
Kinston	.978	137	3642	1555	119	5316	136	17
Wilmington	.974	138	3698	1533	139	5370	107	14
Prince William	.970	140	3618	1525	157	5300	99	12
Salem	.970	140	3711	1667	166	5544	134	23
Winston-Salem	.969	137	3594	1543	165	5302	127	29
Durham	.968	139	3560	1353	160	5073	134	23
Lynchburg	.967	138	3548	1569	175	5292	130	16
Frederick	.966	137	3572	1461	179	5212	105	23

TRIPLE PLAYS: Lynchburg, Wilmington.

INDIVIDUAL

FIRST BASEMEN

NOTE: All caps denotes fielding-percentage leader based on 70 games for catchers, 93 for all other non-pitchers and 140 innings for pitchers. *Throws lefthanded.

Player, Team	Pct.	G	PO	A	E	TC	DP
Bernhardt, Steven, Salem	1.000	2	9	0	0	9	1
Bess, Johnny, Winston-Salem	.977	19	115	11	3	129	16
Bonifay, Ken, Lynchburg	.995	57	541	25	3	569	53
Brown, Ray, Winston-Salem	.981	100	919	52	19	990	81
Byington, Jimmie, Wilmington	1.000	8	63	6	0	69	9
Cawhorn, Gerad, Kinston	1.000	4	22	3	0	25	4
Culp, Brian, Salem	1.000	2	11	1	0	12	2
Daniel, Mike, Lynchburg	.967	8	80	7	3	90	9
Dixon, Colin, Salem	.993	38	377	24	3	404	37
Evans, Michael, Wilmington	.971	43	315	22	10	347	21
Fasano, Sal, Wilmington	1.000	2	17	2	0	19	1
Garcia, Guillermo, Winst.-Salem	.990	10	95	8	1	104	7
Hagy, Gary, Kinston	1.000	1	2	0	0	2	0
Hanel, Marcus, Lynchburg	1.000	1	1	0	0	1	0
Hendricks, Ryan, Frederick	1.000	2	12	1	0	13	1
Holdren, Nate, Salem	.982	90	764	63	15	842	74
House, Mitch, Lynchburg	.992	12	114	7	1	122	16
Hugo, Sean, Frederick*	.893	4	22	3	3	28	2
Kirgan, Chris, Frederick*	.989	115	872	50	10	932	68
Knoblauh, Jay, Lynchburg	.966	4	26	2	1	29	1
Knott, John, Durham	.987	20	153	4	2	159	13
Larkin, Stephen, Winston-Salem*	.917	3	21	1	2	24	3
Leary, Rob, Lynchburg*	.983	23	168	6	3	177	12
MENDEZ, Carlos, Wilmington	.993	95	831	57	6	894	67
Michael, Jeff, Frederick	1.000	28	174	11	0	185	16
Nunez, Ramon, Durham	.983	7	53	4	1	58	3
Riemer, Matt, Frederick	1.000	12	74	8	0	82	4
Robertson, Robbie, Winst.-Sal.*	.980	12	96	4	2	102	9
Rodarte, Raul, Lynchburg	.957	2	21	1	1	23	1
Secrist, Reed, Lynchburg	.995	38	370	9	2	381	27
Sexson, Richie, Kinston	.990	125	1135	79	12	1226	109
Simon, Randall, Durham*	.989	113	864	51	10	925	89
Smith, Jason, Salem	1.000	1	7	1	0	8	0
Thomas, Greg, Kinston*	.990	12	94	5	1	100	9
Thomas, Juan, Prince William	.994	68	619	36	4	659	49
Webb, Kevin, Durham	.980	7	47	2	1	50	7
Wells, Forry, Salem	.981	19	147	11	3	161	11
Wieser, Mike, Durham	1.000	2	9	1	0	10	2
Williams, Harold, Prince William*	.985	72	617	40	10	667	40

TRIPLE PLAYS: Mendez, Secrist.

SECOND BASEMEN

Player, Team	Pct.	G	PO	A	E	TC	DP
Akers, Chad, Winston-Salem	.978	75	169	225	9	403	52
Benbow, Lou, Durham	.938	7	5	10	1	16	0
Bernhardt, Steven, Salem	.977	25	59	66	3	128	20
Brooks, Eddie, Lynchburg	.972	18	35	34	2	71	7
Byington, Jimmie, Wilmington	.862	9	16	9	4	29	1
Carr, Jeremy, Wilmington	1.000	1	1	3	0	4	1
Cawhorn, Gerad, Kinston	1.000	13	29	20	0	49	4
Gann, Steve, Winston-Salem	1.000	1	2	3	0	5	1
Garcia, Jesse, Frederick	.952	123	283	278	28	589	69
Garcia, Vincente, Salem	.984	114	252	295	9	556	70
Grunewald, Keith, Salem	1.000	2	3	8	0	11	1
GUTIERREZ, Ricky, Kinston	.986	116	250	318	8	576	90
Hagy, Gary, Kinston	.936	14	17	27	3	47	4
Jenkins, Demetrish, Winst.-Salem	.981	31	72	82	3	157	25
Jimenez, Manny, Durham	.976	95	204	200	10	414	65
Lofton, James, Winston-Salem	.932	36	74	76	11	161	17
Medrano, Anthony, Wilmington	1.000	12	20	29	0	49	5
Menechino, Frank, Prince William	.975	137	293	295	15	603	76
Michael, Jeff, Frederick	.891	12	19	22	5	46	6
Montilla, Julio, Wilmington	1.000	5	5	6	0	11	1
Newell, Brett, Durham	1.000	3	4	3	0	7	0
Nunez, Sergio, Wilmington	.954	124	231	313	26	570	70
Pagan, Angel, Frederick	.975	13	19	20	1	40	1
Polidor, Wil, Prince William	.929	5	3	10	1	14	1
Prieto, Rick, Kinston	1.000	1	3	2	0	5	1
Rodarte, Raul, Lynchburg	1.000	5	7	6	0	13	2
Rodriguez, Roman, Lynchburg	.979	13	22	25	1	48	6
Sanford, Chance, Lynchburg	.961	16	34	39	3	76	9
Sauritch, Chris, Frederick	1.000	1	2	3	0	5	1
Sexton, Chris, Salem	1.000	3	6	9	0	15	2
Warner, Ken, Durham	.957	47	71	84	7	162	25
Wieser, Mike, Durham	.500	1	1	1	2	4	0
Zapata, Ramon, Lynchburg	.976	98	209	246	11	466	68

TRIPLE PLAY: Medrano.

THIRD BASEMEN

Player, Team	Pct.	G	PO	A	E	TC	DP
Benbow, Lou, Durham	.894	18	12	30	5	47	6
Bernhardt, Steven, Salem	.909	21	15	55	7	77	1
Betts, Todd, Kinston	.929	92	50	184	18	252	19
Bonifay, Ken, Lynchburg	.931	24	25	56	6	87	6
BOONE, Aaron, Winston-Salem	.940	108	59	272	21	352	21
Brooks, Eddie, Lynchburg	1.000	5	0	9	0	9	0

Player, Team	Pct.	G	PO	A	E	TC	DP
Byington, Jimmie, Wilmington	.947	12	8	28	2	38	1
Carranza, Pete, Salem	.842	13	5	27	6	38	2
Cawhorn, Gerad, Kinston	.961	50	32	117	6	155	11
Davis, Tommy, Frederick	.897	120	83	240	37	360	13
Diaz, Einar, Kinston	.800	2	0	4	1	5	0
Diaz, Lino, Wilmington	.969	32	23	70	3	96	4
Fraraccio, Dan, Prince William	.945	24	13	56	4	73	3
Frye, Dan, Winston-Salem	.929	5	2	11	1	14	1
Gann, Steve, Winston-Salem	.926	7	3	22	2	27	1
Garcia, Guillermo, Winst.-Salem	.933	6	0	14	1	15	2
Goligoski, Jason, Prince William	.907	38	18	99	12	129	10
Gonzalez, Paul, Prince William	.931	84	58	210	20	288	12
Grunewald, Keith, Salem	.944	87	65	224	17	306	23
Hagy, Gary, Kinston	.933	6	5	9	1	15	1
Holdren, Nate, Salem	.500	1	1	0	1	2	0
Jimenez, Manny, Durham	.966	21	16	41	2	59	3
Knott, John, Durham	.912	55	40	94	13	147	7
Kopriva, Dan, Winston-Salem	.956	16	9	34	2	45	1
Lopez, Mendy, Wilmington	.939	108	55	271	21	347	11
Manto, Jeff, Frederick	1.000	1	0	2	0	2	0
Michael, Jeff, Frederick	.956	15	11	32	2	45	7
Montilla, Julio, Wilmington	1.000	1	1	2	0	3	1
Newell, Brett, Durham	.917	26	20	35	5	60	3
Newhouse, Andre, Prince William	1.000	1	0	3	0	3	0
Pagan, Angel, Frederick	1.000	9	0	11	0	11	0
Polidor, Wil, Prince William	1.000	1	0	3	0	3	0
Riemer, Matt, Frederick	1.000	1	0	4	0	4	1
Rodarte, Raul, Lynchburg	.920	95	56	267	28	351	27
Rodriguez, Roman, Lynchburg	1.000	11	6	35	0	41	3
Secrist, Reed, Lynchburg	.915	18	7	36	4	47	2
Short, Rick, Frederick	.800	1	0	4	1	5	0
Webb, Kevin, Durham	.849	32	23	39	11	73	3
Wells, Forry, Salem	.853	26	19	45	11	75	2
Wieser, Mike, Durham	.889	16	13	19	4	36	2

SHORTSTOPS

Player, Team	Pct.	G	PO	A	E	TC	DP
Akers, Chad, Winston-Salem	.948	24	37	55	5	97	13
Benbow, Lou, Durham	.948	57	71	165	13	249	35
Brooks, Eddie, Lynchburg	.923	8	7	17	2	26	1
Byington, Jimmie, Wilmington	.932	13	12	29	3	44	4
Collier, Lou, Lynchburg	.937	112	156	361	35	552	68
Fraraccio, Dan, Prince William	1.000	2	1	2	0	3	0
Frye, Dan, Winston-Salem	.000	1	0	0	1	1	0
Gann, Steve, Winston-Salem	.933	3	5	9	1	15	3
Garcia, Guillermo, Winst.-Sal	1.000	1	6	7	0	13	0
Goligoski, Jason, Prince William	.953	56	77	167	12	256	24
Grunewald, Keith, Salem	.957	26	37	73	5	115	17
Hagy, Gary, Kinston	.983	24	41	76	2	119	19
Jimenez, Manny, Durham	.917	9	13	20	3	36	5
Lamb, David, Frederick	.954	120	151	348	24	523	53
Lopez, Mendy, Wilmington	.959	22	29	64	4	97	13
Magdaleno, Ricky, Winst.-Sal.	.929	91	145	274	32	451	57
Magee, Danny, Durham	.934	73	94	176	19	289	39
Medrano, Anthony, Wilmington	.963	113	160	308	18	486	54
Michael, Jeff, Frederick	.963	15	18	34	2	54	7
Montilla, Julio, Wilmington	1.000	3	2	4	0	6	1
Newell, Brett, Durham	.933	4	6	8	1	15	3
Pagan, Angel, Frederick	.952	5	4	16	1	21	4
Polidor, Wil, Prince William	.950	89	106	271	20	397	31
Rodriguez, Roman, Lynchburg	.909	18	18	52	7	77	4
Sauritch, Chris, Frederick	1.000	1	0	6	0	6	0
SEXTON, Chris, W-S/Salem	.966	120	201	423	22	646	73
Wieser, Mike, Durham	.857	9	5	13	3	21	3
Wilson, Brian, Winston-Salem	.926	20	20	55	6	81	9
Wilson, Enrique, Kinston	.964	114	181	375	21	577	68
Zapata, Ramon, Lynchburg	.936	13	11	33	3	47	3

TRIPLE PLAYS: Collier, Lopez.

SHORTSTOPS WITH TWO OR MORE TEAMS

Player, Team	Pct.	G	PO	A	E	TC	DP
Sexton, Chris, Winston-Salem	1.000	4	6	17	0	23	2
Sexton, Chris, Salem	.965	116	195	406	22	623	71

OUTFIELDERS

Player, Team	Pct.	G	PO	A	E	TC	DP
Abbott, Jeff, Prince William*	.958	62	88	3	4	95	0
Austin, Jake, Lynchburg	.971	18	30	3	1	34	0
Aven, Bruce, Kinston	.983	110	158	11	3	172	1
Avila, Rolando, Frederick	.991	51	106	7	1	114	0
Bernhardt, Steven, Salem	1.000	3	2	1	0	3	0
Berrios, Harry, Frederick	.973	46	71	1	2	74	0
Bess, Johnny, Winston-Salem	1.000	21	28	3	0	31	0
Betzsold, James, Kinston	.959	123	196	13	9	218	3
Bonifay, Ken, Lynchburg	.964	17	26	1	1	28	0
Bridgers, Brandon, Frederick	1.000	10	23	0	0	23	0
Broach, Donald, Winston-Salem	.985	116	258	11	4	273	2
Brown, Adrian, Lynchburg	.983	54	110	6	2	118	0
Brown, Todd, Frederick	.970	27	31	1	1	33	1
Byington, Jimmie, Wilmington	.989	48	86	0	1	87	0
Byrne, Clayton, Frederick	.948	34	85	7	5	97	2
Carr, Jeremy, Wilmington	1.000	1	1	0	0	1	0
Claudio, Patricio, Kinston	.988	89	233	5	3	241	2
Clyburn, Danny, W-S/Fre.	.945	59	79	6	5	90	1
Conger, Jeff, Lynchburg*	.953	85	156	5	8	169	1
Cornelius, Brian, Lynchburg	.941	12	15	1	1	17	0
Correa, Miguel, Durham	.972	92	198	12	6	216	1
Cradle, Cobi, Winston-Salem*	1.000	21	38	2	0	40	0
Culp, Brian, Salem	.970	106	153	9	5	167	1
Daniel, Mike, Lynchburg	1.000	2	1	1	0	2	0
Delaney, Donovan, Wilmington	.950	110	138	14	8	160	2
Dellucci, David, Frederick*	.966	23	26	2	1	29	0
Evans, Michael, Wilmington	1.000	15	23	1	0	24	0
French, Anton, Durham	1.000	7	19	0	0	19	0
Giudice, John, Salem	.981	98	193	13	4	210	4
Gonzalez, Raul, Wilmington	.966	76	137	5	5	147	1
Hawkins, Wes, Frederick	.980	41	49	0	1	50	0
Hodge, Roy, Frederick	.981	47	99	4	2	105	0
Hugo, Sean, Frederick*	1.000	19	22	0	0	22	0
Hunter, Lanier, Frederick	1.000	3	7	0	0	7	0
Jimenez, Oscar, Wilmington	.969	119	239	12	8	259	1
KING, Andre, Dur.-P.W.	1.000	106	279	9	0	288	3
Knoblauh, Jay, Lynchburg	.985	54	61	3	1	65	0
Knott, John, Durham	1.000	32	37	4	0	41	0
Knowles, Brian, Wilmington	1.000	7	12	3	0	15	0
Larkin, Stephen, Winston-Salem*	1.000	10	19	0	0	19	0
Leary, Rob, Lynchburg*	.889	34	31	1	4	36	0
LeCronier, Jason, Frederick	.957	27	43	1	2	46	0
Lemons, Rich, Kinston	.750	2	3	0	1	4	0
Lezeau, James, Salem	1.000	3	5	0	0	5	0
McBride, Gator, Durham	.930	78	123	10	10	143	1
McKinnon, Sandy, Prince William	.978	123	263	6	6	275	4
Meggers, Mike, Winston-Salem	.976	67	116	6	3	125	1
Monds, Wonderful, Durham	.984	51	112	9	2	123	2
Murphy, Mike, Kinston	.977	57	78	7	2	87	0
Newhouse, Andre, Prince William	.964	72	103	5	4	112	1
Oglesby, Luke, Wilmington	.957	39	45	0	2	47	0
Ordonez, Magglio, Prince William	.978	130	256	5	6	267	1
Oyas, Danny, Winston-Salem	.973	42	70	3	2	75	1
Pagano, Scott, Durham	.976	84	154	12	4	170	3
Peterson, Charles, Lynchburg	.962	104	192	11	8	211	1
Prieto, Rick, Kinston	.982	25	52	3	1	56	1
Quillin, Ty, Frederick	.900	8	9	0	1	10	0
Richardson, Eric, Prince William	1.000	6	6	1	0	7	0
Riemer, Matt, Frederick	1.000	7	9	2	0	11	0
Robertson, Robbie, Winst.-Sal.*	.977	54	80	6	2	88	0
Robertson, Tommy, Lynchburg	.952	42	38	2	2	42	1
Secrist, Reed, Lynchburg	.976	25	39	1	1	41	1
Sexton, Chris, Salem	1.000	3	3	0	0	3	0
Teeters, Brian, Wilmington*	1.000	51	99	1	0	100	0
Thomas, Greg, Kinston*	.943	20	31	2	2	35	0
Thomas, Rod, Winston-Salem	.964	18	24	3	1	28	0
Valdez, Trovin, Frederick	.934	106	167	16	13	196	4
Van Slyke, Andy, Frederick	1.000	1	3	0	0	3	0
Velazquez, Edgard, Salem	.976	131	273	16	7	296	1
Watkins, Pat, Winston-Salem	.982	26	51	5	1	57	0
Watson, Marty, Prince William	.933	22	41	1	3	45	0
Wells, Forry, Salem	.969	39	62	1	2	65	1
Wells, Mark, Salem	.963	56	73	6	3	82	1

OUTFIELDERS WITH TWO OR MORE TEAMS

Player, Team	Pct.	G	PO	A	E	TC	DP
Clyburn, Danny, Winst.-Salem	.947	49	66	6	4	76	1
Clyburn, Danny, Frederick	.929	10	13	0	1	14	0
King, Andre, Durham	1.000	97	261	9	0	270	3
King, Andre, Prince William	1.000	9	18	0	0	18	0

CATCHERS

Player, Team	Pct.	G	PO	A	E	TC	DP	PB
Bako, Paul, Winston-Salem	.989	78	478	49	6	533	3	15
Bess, Johnny, Winston-Salem	.993	20	122	14	1	137	1	3
Brooks, Ramy, Wilmington	.992	53	326	36	3	365	4	4
Cabrera, Jairo, Frederick	.976	25	136	29	4	169	1	6
Canetto, John, Lynchburg	1.000	11	50	8	0	58	0	2

Player, Team	Pct.	G	PO	A	E	TC	DP	PB
Castaneda, Hector, Frederick	.984	10	55	6	1	62	0	1
Daniel, Mike, Lynchburg	.992	19	115	7	1	123	1	1
DIAZ, Einar, Kinston	.9924	103	676	107	6	789	7	13
Dixon, Colin, Salem	1.000	2	4	0	0	4	0	0
Durso, Joe, Prince William	.974	50	310	25	9	344	2	4
Fasano, Sal, Wilmington	1.000	17	115	10	0	125	2	1
Foster, Jim, Frederick	.988	112	804	89	11	904	4	15
Garcia, Adrian, Durham	.966	5	24	4	1	29	0	1
Garcia, Guillermo, Winst.-Sal.	.983	54	301	38	6	345	2	11
Gargiulo, Mike, Frederick	1.000	3	20	4	0	24	0	1
Hanel, Marcus, Lynchburg	.993	40	241	38	2	281	4	4
Harriss, Robin, Kinston	1.000	15	94	11	0	105	0	1
Hicks, Jamie, Durham	.991	39	199	14	2	215	0	8
Higgins, Mike, Salem	.978	51	359	48	9	416	5	6
Izquierdo, Sergio, Prince William	.972	10	61	8	2	71	0	3
Johnson, Todd, Kinston	.971	21	117	16	4	137	2	1
Machado, Robert, Prince William	.9921	76	548	78	5	631	2	5
Mader, Chris, Kinston	.923	1	11	1	1	13	0	1
Meluskey, Mitch, Kinston	.985	7	58	6	1	65	1	1
Mendez, Carlos, Wilmington	1.000	1	3	1	0	4	0	1
Mendez, Sergio, Lynchburg	.985	60	409	55	7	471	3	8
Paul, Kortney, Wilmington	.962	7	23	2	1	26	0	0
Pozo, Yohel, Salem	.976	42	205	37	6	248	2	7
Reynolds, Chance, Lynchburg	1.000	5	32	4	0	36	0	0
Rodarte, Raul, Lynchburg	1.000	2	5	0	0	5	0	0
Scalzitti, Will, Salem	1.000	11	55	11	0	66	0	5
Secrist, Reed, Lynchburg	.979	14	44	2	1	47	0	1
Smith, Jason, Salem	.966	24	125	19	5	149	3	2
Smith, Sean, Durham	.989	27	152	25	2	179	2	1
Snyder, Randy, Salem	1.000	23	149	23	0	172	0	3
Spinello, Joe, Prince William	1.000	9	61	4	0	65	0	0
Sweeney, Mike, Wilmington	.989	72	575	45	7	627	5	8
Toth, Dave, Durham	.989	82	472	57	6	535	10	11
Walker, Joe, Prince William	.889	1	8	0	1	9	0	0
Weaver, Colby, Durham	.964	5	24	3	1	28	0	2
Webb, Kevin, Durham	.500	1	1	0	1	2	0	0

PITCHERS

Player, Team	Pct.	G	PO	A	E	TC	DP
Abramavicius, Jason, Lynchburg*	1.000	9	0	1	0	1	0
Aminoff, Matt, Salem	.882	39	4	11	2	17	4
Anderson, Eric, Wilmington	1.000	16	2	7	0	9	2
Anderson, Jimmy, Lynchburg*	1.000	10	4	6	0	10	0
Arnold, Jamie, Durham	.957	15	8	14	1	23	1
Atkinson, Neil, Wilmington*	1.000	8	0	5	0	5	0
Barnes, Keith, Salem*	.870	15	1	19	3	23	0
Binkley, Brett, Durham*	1.000	24	1	12	0	13	1
Bliss, Bill, Salem	1.000	34	1	6	0	7	0
Bock, Jeff, Durham	.900	32	2	7	1	10	1
Bowie, Micah, Durham*	.850	23	5	12	3	20	1
Brabant, Dan, Kinston	.952	47	7	13	1	21	2
Brewer, Brian, Frederick*	.917	14	3	8	1	12	0
Brewer, Nevin, Wilmington	1.000	17	4	5	0	9	1
Brownson, Mark, Salem	1.000	9	3	3	0	6	0
Burgess, Kurt, Durham*	.929	34	3	10	1	14	1
Byrd, Matt, Durham	1.000	60	2	7	0	9	0
Byrdak, Tim, Wilmington*	.977	27	15	27	1	43	2
Call, Mike, Prince William	1.000	28	1	13	0	14	0
Callistro, Rob, Prince William	1.000	8	1	1	0	2	0
Caruso, Joe, Lynchburg	1.000	29	1	4	0	5	0
Chaves, Rafael, Lynchburg	1.000	42	0	8	0	8	0
Chavez, Carlos, Frederick	.875	43	3	11	2	16	2
Christman, Scott, Prince Will.*	.893	13	6	19	3	28	0
Christmas, Maurice, Durham	1.000	31	6	16	0	22	2
Clemons, Chris, Prince William	.971	27	11	23	1	35	0
Colon, Bartolo, Kinston	.952	21	7	13	1	21	1
Conley, Curt, Salem*	1.000	39	2	6	0	8	0
Connolly, Chris, Wilmington*	1.000	27	3	7	0	10	0
Connors, Chad, Winst.-Salem	1.000	16	1	2	0	3	0
Coppinger, Rocky, Frederick	1.000	11	0	5	0	5	1
Crills, Brad, Frederick	1.000	9	4	13	0	17	0
Crowther, Brent, Salem	.895	12	6	11	2	19	0
Cruz, Nelson, Prince William	1.000	9	1	2	0	3	0
Cullop, Glen, Winston-Salem	1.000	6	0	1	0	1	1
Daniels, Lee, Durham	1.000	21	1	4	0	5	0
Dawley, Joey, Frederick	1.000	24	3	6	0	9	0
DeLaMaza, Roland, Kinston	1.000	26	5	18	0	23	1
DeLaRosa, Maximo, Kinston	.833	43	5	10	3	18	1
DeLeon, Elcilio, Lynchburg	1.000	13	1	0	0	1	0
Dickens, John, Wilmington*	.941	48	3	13	1	17	1
Dillinger, John, Lynchburg	.786	27	2	9	3	14	0
Donnelly, Brendan, Winst.-Sal.	.857	23	2	4	1	7	0
Doorneweerd, Dave, Lynchburg	1.000	5	0	1	0	1	0
Downs, John, Wilmington	1.000	8	1	2	0	3	0
Doyle, Tom, Winston-Salem*	1.000	21	1	4	0	5	0
Dyess, Todd, Frederick	1.000	3	1	2	0	3	0
Etler, Todd, Winston-Salem	1.000	24	19	19	0	38	4
Evans, Bart, Wilmington	.889	16	6	2	1	9	0
Faino, Jeff, Frederick*	1.000	4	0	1	0	1	0
Farson, Bryan, Lynchburg*	.750	27	0	3	1	4	0
Flury, Pat, Wilmington	1.000	15	0	4	0	4	0
Fordham, Tom, Prince William*	.857	13	3	15	3	21	0
Gamboa, Javier, Wilmington	1.000	8	5	4	0	9	0
Garrett, Neil, Salem	.000	5	0	0	2	2	0
Goldman, Barry, Salem	1.000	8	1	2	0	3	0
Graves, Dan, Kinston	1.000	38	5	9	0	14	0
Green, Jason, Durham	.900	39	3	6	1	10	0
Grundy, Phillip, Wilmington	.909	20	12	8	2	22	0
Hagan, Danny, Winston-Salem*	1.000	1	0	3	0	3	1
Hale, Shane, Frederick*	.800	6	0	4	1	5	1
Hanson, Kris, Kinston	.962	20	7	18	1	26	0
Harrison, Tom, Durham	1.000	7	3	8	0	11	1
Hartzog, Cullen, Lynchburg	.727	43	2	6	3	11	0
Harvell, Pete, Winston-Salem*	1.000	4	1	0	0	1	0
Heathcott, Mike, Prince William	1.000	27	3	15	0	18	0
Heiserman, Rick, Kinston	1.000	19	4	10	0	14	0
Hernandez, Francisco, Frederick	1.000	3	0	2	0	2	0
Hodges, Kevin, Wilmington	.857	12	0	6	1	7	1
Hostetler, Marcus, Durham	.500	12	0	1	1	2	0
Huber, Jeff, Frederick*	1.000	21	1	2	0	3	0
Jacobs, Ryan, Durham*	.976	29	8	32	1	41	2
Jesperson, Bob, Winston-Salem	1.000	5	1	1	0	2	0
Johnson, Jason M., Lynchburg	.765	10	3	10	4	17	1
Johnson, Jason S., Salem	1.000	5	0	1	0	1	0
Kirkreit, Daron, Kinston	1.000	3	1	3	0	4	0
Kitchen, Ron, Frederick	.895	30	4	13	2	19	0
Kummerfeldt, Jason, Winst.-Sal.	1.000	37	5	12	0	17	1
Kusiewicz, Michael, Salem*	1.000	1	0	2	0	2	0
LaPlante, Michel, Lynchburg	1.000	5	0	1	0	1	0
LaRocca, Todd, Frederick	1.000	5	4	8	0	12	0
Larock, Scott, Salem	.842	52	5	11	3	19	0
Lavenia, Mark, Durham*	1.000	6	0	1	0	1	0
Lawrence, Sean, Lynchburg*	.895	20	4	13	2	19	0
Lehman, Toby, Frederick	1.000	19	2	7	0	9	1
Lemp, Chris, Frederick	1.000	41	2	5	0	7	1
Leroy, John, Durham	1.000	24	5	14	0	19	1
Lindemann, Wayne, Prince Will.*	.909	19	1	9	1	11	1
Lombardi, John, Frederick	1.000	6	0	2	0	2	0
Lyons, Curt, Winston-Salem	.923	26	13	23	3	39	0
Maberry, Louis, Winston-Salem	.900	20	3	6	1	10	0
Maduro, Calvin, Frederick	.972	20	2	33	1	36	1
Magee, Bo, Frederick*	1.000	5	2	4	0	6	0
Magre, Pete, Winston-Salem	.833	17	1	4	1	6	0
Maine, Dalton, Frederick	1.000	19	1	1	0	2	0
Mansur, Jeff, Frederick*	1.000	12	1	4	0	5	0
Marenghi, Matt, Frederick	.850	30	5	12	3	20	0
Martinez, Johnny, Kinston	1.000	6	0	1	0	1	1
Mathews, Del, Durham*	.962	33	6	19	1	26	1
Mattson, Craig, Lynchburg	.500	11	1	0	1	2	0
Mayse, Robert, Frederick	1.000	6	1	0	0	1	0
McKenzie, Scott, Winst.-Salem	.929	49	2	11	1	14	1
Mesa, Rafael, Kinston	.900	35	2	7	1	10	1
Million, Doug, Salem*	.957	24	4	18	1	23	0
Montoya, Wilmer, Kinston	1.000	1	2	1	0	3	0
Morel, Ramon, Lynchburg	1.000	12	5	9	0	14	2
Murphy, Chris, Winston-Salem*	1.000	4	0	3	0	3	0
Najera, Noe, Kinston*	1.000	8	2	2	0	4	0
Nelson, Earl, Durham*	.800	15	0	4	1	5	0
Nieto, Tony, Frederick	.875	21	2	12	2	16	1
Oropeza, Igor, Kinston	.857	20	3	3	1	7	0
Paige, Carey, Durham	1.000	10	5	11	0	16	0
Perkins, Paul, Lynchburg	1.000	25	1	1	0	2	0
Peters, Chris, Lynchburg*	.968	24	1	29	1	31	3
Pfaff, Jason, Lynchburg	.968	35	6	24	1	31	2
Pickford, Kevin, Lynchburg*	1.000	4	1	2	0	3	0
Pierson, Jason, Prince William*	1.000	21	4	18	0	22	0
Place, Mike, Durham	.800	7	1	3	1	5	1
Pontbriant, Matt, Lynchburg*	.900	27	3	15	2	20	2
Pool, Matt, Salem	.955	28	20	22	2	44	1
Pratt, Rich, Prince William*	.939	25	1	30	2	33	1
Priest, Eddie, Winston-Salem*	.938	12	1	14	1	16	0
Raines, Ken, Durham*	1.000	19	1	11	0	12	1
Ramos, Cesar, Kinston	.800	8	2	2	1	5	0
Rawitzer, Kevin, Wilmington*	1.000	15	3	5	0	8	1

Player, Team	Pct.	G	PO	A	E	TC	DP
Ray, Ken, Wilmington	.952	13	3	17	1	21	1
Reed, Chris, Winston-Salem	.977	24	17	25	1	43	1
Rhodes, Joe, Frederick	.500	2	0	1	1	2	0
Rizzo, Todd, Prince William*	.800	36	0	8	2	10	0
Robbins, Jason, Winston-Salem	.931	23	12	15	2	29	0
Roberts, Ray, Wilmington*	1.000	13	0	3	0	3	0
Rogers, Jason, Frederick*	.889	15	5	11	2	18	1
Rosado, Jose, Wilmington*	1.000	25	8	14	0	22	1
Runion, Tony, Kinston	.875	28	5	9	2	16	0
RUSCH, Glendon, Wilmington*	1.000	26	10	29	0	39	5
Ruyak, Todd, Winston-Salem*	.938	34	6	9	1	16	0
Saipe, Mike, Salem	.875	21	4	10	2	16	2
Salamon, John, Salem	.750	8	0	3	1	4	0
Sexton, Jeff, Kinston	1.000	8	4	9	0	13	1
Sheehan, Chris, Wilmington	1.000	13	0	3	0	3	0
Sinnes, David, Wilmington	1.000	18	2	2	0	4	0
Smith, Hut, Frederick	.429	20	0	3	4	7	0
Smith, Toby, Wilmington	1.000	30	6	12	0	18	0
Sobkoviak, Jeff, Salem	1.000	40	3	6	0	9	0
Sosa, Jose, Lynchburg	1.000	10	1	1	0	2	0
Stewart, Chris, Salem	1.000	10	1	0	0	1	0
Stewart, Rachaad, Frederick*	1.000	26	2	23	0	25	0
Tagle, Hank, Prince William*	.952	33	6	14	1	21	0
Tolar, Kevin, Lynchburg*	1.000	18	2	0	0	2	0
Towns, Ryan, Wilmington	1.000	12	3	2	0	5	0
Tuttle, Dave, Winston-Salem	.923	10	3	9	1	13	0
Vaught, Jay, Kinston	.943	27	11	22	2	35	0
Vazquez, Archie, Prince William	.800	47	1	7	2	10	0
Voisard, Mark, Salem	.667	6	1	1	1	3	0
Waldron, Joe, Salem*	1.000	9	2	1	0	3	1
Walker, James, Frederick	1.000	9	2	6	0	8	0
Walls, Doug, Salem	.833	15	4	6	2	12	0
Wells, David, Durham	1.000	7	0	2	0	2	0
Williams, Greg, Kinston*	1.000	30	2	4	0	6	0
Winkle, Ken, Wilmington	1.000	11	1	3	0	4	0
Woods, Brian, Prince William	.867	27	10	16	4	30	0
Worrell, Steve, Prince William*	1.000	29	1	7	0	8	0
Wright, Jamey, Salem	.959	26	16	31	2	49	2
Young, Danny, Lynchburg*	.833	24	1	4	1	6	0
Zolecki, Mike, Salem	1.000	9	0	5	0	5	0

The following players did not have any fielding statistics at the positions indicated or appeared only as a designated hitter, pinch-hitter or pinch-runner: M. Anderson, of; Bess, ss; Buchanan, dh, pr; Carpenter, ph; Carranza, of; Daigle, p; Davis, of; Dietrich, p; Dixon, 3b; Driskill, p; M. Evans, c; Foster, 3b; Giron, p; P. Gonzalez, of; Grunewald, 1b; Gutierrez, ss; Jones, dh, ph; Knott, 2b; Lamb, 2b; Locklear, p; Mader, 3b; Mesewicz, p; Riemer, p; Sauritch, 3b, p; S. Smith, 3b; Sweeney, 3b; Toth, of; G. White, p; J. White, dh, ph; E. Wilson, 2b.

LEAGUE CHAMPIONS

Year	Team	Pct.
1945—	Danville	.681
1946—	Greensboro	.599
	Raleigh (2nd)†	.563
1947—	Burlington	.613
	Raleigh (3rd)†	.574
1948—	Raleigh	.592
	Martinsville (2nd)†	.570
1949—	Danville	.601
	Burlington (4th)†	.500
1950—	Winston-Salem*	.693
1951—	Durham	.600
	Wins-Salem (2nd)†	.583
1952—	Raleigh	.581
	Reidsville (4th)†	.536
1953—	Raleigh	.593
	Danville (2nd)†	.572
1954—	Fayetteville*	.628
1955—	HP-Thomasville	.580
	Danville (2nd)†	.533
1956—	HP-Thomasville	.591
	Fayetteville (4th)§	.523
1957—	Durham	.632
	HP-Thomasville	.622
1958—	Danville	.576
	Burlington (4th)†	.511
1959—	Raleigh	.600
	Wilson (2nd)†	.550
1960—	Greensboro‡	.636
	Burlington	.586
1961—	Wilson	.594
1962—	Durham	.636
	Wilson	.600
	Kinston (2nd)†	.593
1963—	Kinston§	.538
	Greensboro§	.590
	Wilson (2nd)†	.535
1964—	Kinston§	.572
	Winston-Salem§†	.590
1965—	Peninsula§	.597
	Durham§	.580
	Tidewater†	.528
1966—	Kinston§	.547
	Winston-Salem§	.586
	Rocky Mount†	.533
1967—	Durham∞(West.)	.536
	Raleigh (East.)	.542
1968—	Salem (West.)	.607
	Ral-Dur (East.)	.597
	HP-Thom.▲(W.)	.493
1969—	Rocky M (East.)	.569
	Salem (West.)	.542
	Ral-Dur◆(East.)	.560
1970—	Winston-Salem‡	.586
	Burlington	.597
1971—	Peninsula‡	.647
	Kinston	.623
1972—	Salem‡	.657
	Burlington	.632
1973—	Lynchburg	.588
	Winston-Salem‡	.557
1974—	Salem	.671
	Salem	.582
1975—	Rocky Mount	.667
	Rocky Mount	.614
1976—	Winston-Salem	.618
	Winston-Salem	.551
1977—	Lynchburg	.591
	Peninsula‡	.556
1978—	Peninsula	.696
	Lynchburg‡	.614
1979—	Winston-Salem■	.607
1980—	Peninsula‡	.714
	Durham	.600
1981—	Peninsula	.522
	Hagerstown‡	.507
1982—	Alexandria‡	.597
	Durham	.588
1983—	Lynchburg‡	.691
	Winston-Salem	.529
1984—	Lynchburg‡	.645
	Durham	.486
1985—	Lynchburg	.679
	Winston-Salem‡	.417
1986—	Hagerstown	.655
	Winston-Salem‡	.594
1987—	Salem‡	.576
	Kinston	.536
1988—	Kinston§	.629
	Lynchburg	.486
1989—	Durham	.609
	Prince William‡	.522
1990—	Kinston	.652
	Frederick‡	.544
1991—	Kinston‡	.645
	Lynchburg	.482
1992—	Lynchburg	.570
	Peninsula‡	.536
1993—	Wilmington	.532
	Winston-Salem‡	.514
1994—	Wilmington‡	.681
	Winston-Salem	.555
1995—	Wilmington	.601
	Kinston‡	.591

*Won championship and four-club playoff. †Won four-club playoff. ‡Won split-season playoff. §League was divided into Eastern, Western divisions. ∞Won eight-club, two-division playoff. ▲Won eight-club, two-division playoff against Raleigh-Durham. ◆Won eight-club, two-division playoff against Burlington. ■Won both halves of split season (no playoffs).

FLORIDA STATE LEAGUE

LEAGUE OFFICE

President
Chuck Murphy

Address
P.O. Box 349
Daytona Beach, FL 32115

Phone
904-252-7479

Teams (affiliation)
Brevard County Manatees (Marlins)
Charlotte Rangers (Rangers)
Clearwater Phillies (Phillies)
Daytona Cubs (Cubs)
Dunedin Blue Jays (Blue Jays)
Fort Myers Miracle (Twins)
Kissimmee Cobras (Astros)
Lakeland Tigers (Tigers)
St. Lucie Mets (Mets)
St. Petersburg Cardinals (Cardinals)
Sarasota Red Sox (Red Sox)
Tampa Yankees (Yankees)
Vero Beach Dodgers (Dodgers)
West Palm Beach Expos (Expos)

1995 FINAL STANDINGS

FIRST HALF

EAST DIVISION

Team	W	L	T	Pct.	GB
Daytona (Cubs)	41	28	0	.594	....
Vero Beach (Dodgers)	39	31	0	.557	2½
St. Lucie (Mets)	33	35	0	.485	7½
Brevard County (Marlins)	30	38	0	.441	10½
Kissimmee (Astros)	28	41	0	.406	13
West Palm Beach (Expos)	25	44	0	.362	16

WEST DIVISION

Team	W	L	T	Pct.	GB
Tampa (Yankees)	41	29	0	.586	....
Clearwater (Phillies)	38	32	0	.543	3
Lakeland (Tigers)	36	33	0	.522	4½
Dunedin (Blue Jays)	35	33	0	.515	5
Charlotte (Rangers)	35	33	0	.515	5
Fort Myers (Twins)	34	34	0	.500	6
Sarasota (Red Sox)	34	34	0	.500	6
St. Petersburg (Cardinals)	32	36	0	.471	8

SECOND HALF

EAST DIVISION

Team	W	L	T	Pct.	GB
Daytona (Cubs)	46	20	0	.697	....
Vero Beach (Dodgers)	35	28	0	.556	9½
Brevard County (Marlins)	31	36	0	.463	15½
West Palm Beach (Expos)	29	37	1	.439	17
St. Lucie (Mets)	28	38	1	.424	18
Kissimmee (Astros)	27	40	0	.403	19½

WEST DIVISION

Team	W	L	T	Pct.	GB
Fort Myers (Twins)	41	21	1	.661	....
Clearwater (Phillies)	41	27	0	.603	3
St. Petersburg (Cardinals)	32	31	0	.508	9½
Sarasota (Red Sox)	31	34	1	.477	11½
Tampa (Yankees)	31	35	0	.470	12
Charlotte (Rangers)	30	34	1	.469	12
Lakeland (Tigers)	28	36	1	.438	14
Dunedin (Blue Jays)	28	41	0	.406	16½

COMPOSITE

Team	Day.	Ft.M.	Clw.	V.B.	Tam.	Char.	Sar.	St.P.	Lak.	Dun.	StL	B.C.	Kis.	WPB	W	L	T	Pct.	GB
Daytona (Cubs)	....	5	4	6	8	6	2	6	4	6	8	10	10	12	87	48	0	.644	....
Fort Myers (Twins)	1	....	8	3	6	8	11	6	9	6	2	6	4	5	75	55	1	.577	9½
Clearwater (Phillies)	4	4	....	6	5	10	8	5	7	10	3	7	6	4	79	59	0	.572	9½
Vero Beach (Dodgers)	6	5	2	....	5	5	5	3	2	5	9	8	9	10	74	59	0	.556	12
Tampa (Yankees)	0	6	5	2	....	7	10	10	7	7	5	4	5	4	72	64	0	.529	15½
Charlotte (Rangers)	2	6	2	2	5	....	4	6	9	8	5	5	4	7	65	67	1	.492	20½
Sarasota (Red Sox)	4	5	4	3	2	8	....	4	9	6	5	5	5	5	65	68	1	.489	21
St. Petersburg (Cardinals)	2	6	11	2	6	4	7	....	4	5	4	5	4	4	64	67	0	.489	21
Lakeland (Tigers)	4	1	5	6	5	6	6	8	....	7	5	1	5	5	64	69	1	.481	22
Dunedin (Blue Jays)	2	6	6	3	9	2	6	7	4	....	7	3	4	4	63	74	0	.460	25
St. Lucie (Mets)	8	4	5	7	3	3	3	2	3	1	....	7	7	8	61	73	1	.455	25½
Brevard County (Marlins)	6	1	1	8	3	3	1	3	6	5	9	....	9	6	61	74	0	.452	26
Kissimmee (Astros)	5	4	2	5	3	4	3	4	3	4	4	7	....	7	55	81	0	.404	32½
West Palm Beach (Expos)	4	2	4	6	4	1	2	3	2	4	7	6	9	....	54	81	1	.400	33

Brevard County played home games in Melbourne, Fla.

Charlotte played home games in Port Charlotte, Fla.

Major league affiliations in parentheses.

PLAYOFFS: Fort Myers defeated Tampa, two games to one; Daytona defeated Fort Myers, three games to two, to win league championship.

REGULAR-SEASON ATTENDANCE: Brevard County, 140,109; Charlotte, 60,000; Clearwater, 71,761; Daytona, 90,071; Dunedin, 65,764; Fort Myers, 78,431; Kissimmee, 41,091; Lakeland, 21,635; St. Lucie, 80,734; St. Petersburg, 100,055; Sarasota, 65,223; Tampa, 48,598; Vero Beach, 42,702; West Palm Beach, 71,446. Total, 977,620. Playoffs (8 games), 4,392. All-Star Game, 3,587.

MANAGERS: Brevard County, Fredi Gonzalez; Charlotte, Butch Wynegar; Clearwater, Don McCormack; Daytona, Dave Trembley; Dunedin, Jim Nettles; Fort Myers, Al Newman; Kissimmee, Dave Engle; Lakeland, Dave Anderson; St. Lucie, Rafael Landestoy; St. Petersburg, Chris Maloney; Sarasota, Tommy Barrett; Tampa, Jake Gibbs; Vero Beach, Jon Debus; West Palm Beach, Gomer Hodge (April 6 through June 3) and Rick Sofield (June 4 through end of season). Managerial records of team with more than one manager: West Palm Beach, Hodge 19-36, Sofield 35-45.

ALL-STAR TEAM: 1B—Dan Held, Clearwater; 2B—Bobby Morris, Daytona; 3B—Gary Caraballo, Fort Myers; SS—Jason Maxwell, Daytona; Utility IF—Michael Metcalfe, Vero Beach; LF—Shane Spencer, Tampa; CF—Wendell Magee, Clearwater; RF—Scott Samuels, Daytona; Utility OF—Chris Latham, Vero Beach; C—Bobby Estalella, Clearwater, and Kevin Brown, Charlotte; DH—Bubba Trammell, Lakeland; RHP—Matt Drews, Tampa; Shane Bowers, Fort Myers; LHP—Benj Sampson, Fort Myers; Troy Carrasco, Fort Myers; Relievers—Joe Jacobsen, Vero Beach; Jason Hart, Daytona; Most Valuable Player—Shane Spencer, Tampa; Manager of the Year—Dave Trembley, Daytona.

1995 BATTING

TEAM

Team	Avg.	G	TPA	AB	R	H	TB	2B	3B	HR	RBI	SH	SF	HP	BB	IBB	SO	SB	CS	GDP	LOB	ShO	Slg.	OBP
Vero Beach	.261	133	4883	4280	583	1119	1540	182	22	65	507	41	42	68	451	23	755	184	87	99	918	11	.360	.338
Clearwater	.261	138	5209	4565	653	1192	1747	219	33	90	576	35	38	86	484	11	822	119	67	129	986	9	.383	.341
Lakeland	.261	135	4944	4460	553	1162	1623	190	38	65	493	29	33	33	388	13	935	133	68	83	920	10	.364	.322
Sarasota	.260	134	4923	4400	571	1146	1591	198	26	65	499	30	30	52	407	7	927	126	105	80	886	10	.362	.328
Daytona	.256	135	4995	4355	638	1114	1524	187	32	53	549	35	49	78	471	21	759	161	78	98	890	8	.350	.336
Charlotte	.253	133	4969	4375	543	1106	1548	210	32	56	483	34	33	78	449	12	839	96	96	94	956	11	.354	.331
Dunedin	.250	138	5238	4616	621	1156	1682	218	37	78	556	30	38	50	504	20	930	79	44	86	994	8	.364	.328
Brevard County	.248	135	5138	4492	556	1113	1530	197	23	58	490	39	52	52	502	11	891	83	53	118	998	8	.341	.327
Fort Myers	.248	131	4825	4220	552	1045	1447	196	22	54	471	62	32	70	440	20	784	84	73	99	883	9	.343	.327
Tampa	.247	136	5137	4438	580	1098	1570	191	31	73	512	44	35	56	557	15	911	98	56	84	1015	7	.354	.336
West Palm Bch.	.242	136	4861	4324	510	1045	1396	182	29	37	443	41	37	40	419	13	851	123	72	81	880	13	.323	.312
Kissimmee	.241	136	5051	4452	508	1073	1464	205	21	48	432	27	46	75	450	14	855	141	66	109	945	13	.329	.318
St. Lucie	.240	135	4875	4313	484	1034	1394	154	40	42	414	61	31	53	413	18	908	133	89	83	889	8	.323	.312
St. Petersburg	.234	131	4726	4175	468	975	1326	173	20	46	408	35	35	37	440	14	813	69	39	107	883	16	.318	.310

INDIVIDUAL

TOP QUALIFIERS FOR BATTING CHAMPIONSHIP

Minimum 378 plate appearances. *Lefthanded batter. †Switch-hitter.

Player, Team	Avg.	G	TPA	AB	R	H	TB	2B	3B	HR	RBI	SH	SF	HP	BB	IBB	SO	SB	CS	GDP	Slg.	OBP
Magee, Wendell, Clearwater	.353	96	432	388	67	137	189	24	5	6	46	1	5	4	33	3	40	7	10	15	.487	.405
Samuels, Scott, Daytona*	.327	112	473	388	92	127	186	29	12	2	42	3	4	8	69	7	63	38	14	8	.479	.435
Nelson, Bry, Kissimmee†	.327	105	423	395	47	129	182	34	5	3	52	1	6	1	20	0	37	14	10	8	.461	.355
Saffer, Jon, West Palm Beach*	.318	92	384	324	60	103	137	10	6	4	35	4	1	2	53	1	49	18	9	7	.423	.416
Morris, Bobby, Daytona*	.308	95	397	344	44	106	134	18	2	2	55	2	5	8	38	6	46	22	8	5	.390	.385
Roberts, David, Lakeland*	.303	92	401	357	67	108	137	10	5	3	30	2	2	1	39	2	43	30	8	7	.384	.371
Metcalfe, Mike, Vero Beach†	.301	120	509	435	86	131	159	13	3	3	35	6	5	3	60	2	37	60	27	8	.366	.386
Spencer, Shane, Tampa	.300	134	573	500	87	150	235	31	3	16	88	2	3	7	61	2	60	14	8	7	.470	.382
Berg, David, Brevard County	.298	114	474	382	71	114	143	18	1	3	39	7	9	8	68	1	61	9	4	5	.374	.407
Fick, Chris, St. Petersburg*	.293	113	399	348	56	102	172	25	3	13	52	0	3	10	38	2	79	1	2	9	.494	.376
Facione, Chris, Lakeland	.293	110	444	400	44	117	161	17	6	5	56	2	4	2	35	3	76	20	10	13	.403	.349
Tebbs, Nathan, Sarasota†	.291	118	487	440	58	128	157	15	4	2	52	4	1	3	39	0	80	25	15	7	.357	.352
Freeman, Sean, Lakeland*	.290	119	472	414	42	120	163	21	2	6	65	0	7	2	49	3	98	3	4	3	.394	.362
Millar, Kevin, Brevard County	.288	129	551	459	53	132	207	32	2	13	68	0	10	12	70	2	66	4	4	8	.451	.388
Cabrera, Jolbert, W. Palm Beach	.286	103	413	357	62	102	132	23	2	1	25	6	4	8	38	0	61	19	12	3	.370	.364

DEPARTMENTAL LEADERS: G—Held, Spencer, 134; AB—A. Ramirez, 541; R—Samuels, 92; H—Spencer, 150; TB—Spencer, 235; 2B—Held, 35; 3B—Samuels, 12; HR—Held, 21; RBI—Spencer, 88; SH—B. Jones, 16; SF—Millar, 10; HP—Cooney, 23; BB—Patzke, 85; IBB—Patzke, 8; SO—S. Smith, 136; SB—Metcalfe, 60; CS—Metcalfe, 27; GIDP—Kingman, 21; Slg.—Fick, .494; OBP—Samuels, .435.

ALL PLAYERS

*Lefthanded batter. †Switch-hitter.

Player, Team	Avg.	G	TPA	AB	R	H	TB	2B	3B	HR	RBI	SH	SF	HP	BB	IBB	SO	SB	CS	GDP	Slg.	OBP
Abad, Andy, Sarasota*	.288	18	65	59	5	17	20	3	0	0	10	0	0	0	6	0	13	4	3	0	.339	.354
Adolfo, Carlos, West Palm Beach	.185	28	86	81	6	15	19	1	0	1	7	0	0	0	5	0	22	1	0	1	.235	.233
Agbayani, Benny, St. Lucie	.310	44	191	155	24	48	69	9	3	2	29	1	4	5	26	1	27	8	3	4	.445	.416
Alcantara, Israel, W. Palm Beach	.276	39	148	134	16	37	57	7	2	3	22	2	1	2	9	0	35	3	0	0	.425	.329
Almanzar, Richard, Lakeland	.307	42	167	140	29	43	55	9	0	1	14	5	0	4	18	0	20	11	9	5	.393	.401
Alvarado, Basilio, W. Palm Beach	.222	6	19	18	0	4	4	0	0	0	0	0	0	0	1	0	5	0	0	1	.222	.263
Amador, Manuel, Clearwater†	.279	96	359	330	45	92	137	19	4	6	47	1	0	6	22	0	38	5	2	6	.415	.335
Anderson, Cliff, Vero Beach*	.271	113	391	365	48	99	141	20	2	6	44	6	2	8	10	1	58	1	4	4	.386	.304
Angeli, Doug, Clearwater	.191	16	54	47	4	9	12	3	0	0	3	2	1	1	3	0	13	0	1	0	.255	.250
Arano, Eloy, Lakeland†	.283	102	366	353	35	100	111	9	1	0	33	3	1	0	9	1	55	5	6	7	.314	.300
Asencio, Alex, Vero Beach*	.266	58	196	184	24	49	69	8	3	2	21	1	4	1	6	0	22	4	3	3	.375	.287
Aybar, Ramon, Lakeland*	.125	3	9	8	1	1	1	0	0	0	0	0	0	0	1	0	5	0	0	0	.125	.222
Azuaje, Jesus, St. Lucie	.239	91	362	306	35	73	86	5	1	2	20	11	0	7	36	1	55	14	9	5	.281	.332
Babin, Brady, Brevard County	.248	32	118	105	15	26	39	3	2	2	19	1	2	1	9	0	20	0	1	4	.371	.308
Baker, Jason, Fort Myers*	.239	91	324	276	35	66	75	9	0	0	26	8	3	7	30	1	38	8	8	5	.272	.326
Basey, Marsalis, Kissimmee	.230	91	344	317	37	73	79	6	0	0	16	2	3	4	18	1	35	12	5	6	.249	.278
Baugh, Gavin, Brevard County†	.188	81	286	250	24	47	65	11	2	1	21	2	3	4	26	0	70	10	3	3	.260	.272
Bell, Mike, Charlotte	.260	129	523	470	49	122	159	20	1	5	52	3	2	0	48	0	72	9	8	11	.338	.327
Bellum, Donnie, St. Petersburg	.195	64	136	118	16	23	26	3	0	0	9	4	2	0	12	0	23	0	2	5	.220	.265
Benbow, Lou, St. Lucie	.364	12	36	33	4	12	14	2	0	0	2	1	0	1	1	0	7	0	1	0	.424	.400
Benz, Jake, West Palm Beach*	.000	45	1	1	1	0	0	0	0	0	0	0	0	0	0	0	0	0	0	0	.000	.000
Berg, David, Brevard County	.298	114	474	382	71	114	143	18	1	3	39	7	9	8	68	1	61	9	4	5	.374	.407
Berry, Michael, W. Palm Beach	.165	24	92	79	16	13	21	3	1	1	2	0	0	0	13	0	16	0	1	1	.266	.283
Beyna, Terry, Kissimmee	.167	15	45	42	4	7	8	1	0	0	2	0	0	1	2	0	12	0	0	4	.190	.222
Bierek, Kurt, Tampa*	.248	126	517	447	60	111	143	16	2	4	53	2	2	4	61	3	73	3	4	11	.320	.342
Biltimier, Mike, Vero Beach*	.225	127	482	422	62	95	151	14	0	14	50	3	4	5	48	1	109	0	1	8	.358	.309
Blair, Brian, Charlotte*	.223	69	302	264	34	59	70	5	3	0	9	2	1	1	34	3	42	14	6	4	.265	.313
Blum, Geoffrey, W. Palm Beach†	.263	125	502	457	54	120	147	20	2	1	62	1	7	3	34	1	61	6	5	12	.322	.313
Bokemeier, Matt, Charlotte†	.236	105	417	385	42	91	133	16	1	8	34	4	0	2	26	1	76	7	7	11	.345	.288
Borel, Jamie, Lakeland	.122	16	48	41	8	5	6	1	0	0	1	0	0	1	6	0	6	2	1	2	.146	.250
Borrero, Rikchy, Sarasota	.204	34	108	98	9	20	25	5	0	0	4	1	2	2	5	0	22	0	1	1	.255	.252
Boyd, Quincy, Vero Beach	.152	31	75	66	4	10	12	2	0	0	1	0	0	0	9	1	20	0	0	2	.182	.253
Braddy, Junior, Sarasota	.264	114	455	413	41	109	137	12	5	2	36	2	4	5	31	0	99	13	12	10	.332	.320

Player, Team	Avg.	G	TPA	AB	R	H	TB	2B	3B	HR	RBI	SH	SF	HP	BB	IBB	SO	SB	CS	GDP	Slg.	OBP
Brito, Domingo, Clearwater	.000	1	1	1	0	0	0	0	0	0	0	0	0	0	0	0	1	0	0	0	.000	.000
Brito, Luis, Clearwater†	.274	109	409	383	42	105	134	14	3	3	41	5	3	1	17	0	35	12	5	14	.350	.304
Brock, Tarrick, Lakeland*	.209	28	104	91	12	19	22	3	0	0	5	1	0	0	12	0	32	5	3	2	.242	.301
Brown, Armann, Fort Myers	.190	23	68	63	6	12	20	2	3	0	9	0	1	1	3	0	15	1	0	1	.317	.235
Brown, Kevin, Charlotte	.265	107	419	355	48	94	154	25	1	11	57	1	4	9	50	0	96	2	3	9	.434	.366
Brown, Ron, Brevard County	.260	121	448	404	48	105	140	22	2	3	51	1	9	3	31	0	79	6	12	14	.347	.311
Brown, Shawn, Lakeland	.167	10	29	24	2	4	5	1	0	0	0	0	0	1	4	0	5	0	0	0	.208	.310
Brown, Willie, Brevard County*	.222	63	215	189	26	42	68	6	1	6	23	0	0	1	25	3	74	4	3	1	.360	.316
Browne, Jerry, Brevard County†	.286	3	9	7	0	2	2	0	0	0	2	0	1	0	1	0	1	0	0	0	.286	.333
Brunson, Matt, Lakeland†	.129	45	162	132	10	17	21	2	1	0	7	4	0	0	26	0	41	9	2	4	.159	.272
Burke, Alan, Clearwater	.222	3	9	9	2	2	5	0	0	1	2	0	0	0	0	0	2	0	0	1	.556	.222
Cabrera, Alex, Daytona	.294	54	229	214	26	63	83	14	0	2	35	0	2	4	9	0	36	2	4	8	.388	.332
Cabrera, Jolbert, W. Palm Beach	.286	103	413	357	62	102	132	23	2	1	25	6	4	8	38	0	61	19	12	3	.370	.364
Cabrera, Orlando, W. Palm Beach	.200	3	5	5	0	1	1	0	0	0	0	0	0	0	0	0	1	0	0	0	.200	.200
Campos, Jesus, W. Palm Beach	.221	107	361	326	32	72	82	6	2	0	21	6	2	2	25	0	40	18	7	5	.252	.279
Candelaria, Ben, Dunedin*	.259	125	532	471	66	122	168	21	5	5	49	3	5	0	53	1	98	11	4	11	.357	.331
Caraballo, Gary, Fort Myers	.307	85	351	309	51	95	144	24	2	7	55	0	3	5	34	3	44	5	6	10	.466	.382
Carey, Todd, Sarasota*	.306	25	94	85	15	26	44	6	0	4	19	0	0	0	9	0	17	2	1	3	.518	.372
Castro, Ramon, Kissimmee	.208	36	128	120	6	25	30	5	0	0	8	0	1	1	6	0	21	0	0	1	.250	.250
Champion, Jim, Fort Myers*	.227	99	354	308	38	70	101	14	4	3	33	5	3	12	26	0	88	3	1	3	.328	.309
Chick, Bruce, West Palm Beach	.100	3	11	10	0	1	1	0	0	0	1	0	0	0	1	0	3	0	0	1	.100	.182
Christmon, Drew, Lakeland*	.220	79	294	273	34	60	107	8	6	9	39	1	2	4	14	1	96	7	2	4	.392	.266
Clark, Kevin, Sarasota	.225	84	317	293	23	66	89	11	0	4	31	1	0	2	21	0	63	2	5	9	.304	.282
Collier, Dan, Sarasota	.256	67	270	242	30	62	112	12	1	12	44	0	3	5	20	0	83	5	9	3	.463	.322
Cooney, Kyle, Vero Beach	.278	105	400	356	44	99	132	11	2	6	54	1	2	23	17	1	50	4	3	15	.371	.349
Cooper, Tim, Tampa	.176	63	201	170	16	30	44	3	1	3	13	0	2	5	24	0	48	1	1	3	.259	.294
Cossins, Tim, Charlotte	.059	7	21	17	1	1	1	0	0	0	0	0	0	0	4	1	5	0	1	0	.059	.238
Costello, Brian, Clearwater	.249	112	445	406	52	101	151	19	2	9	56	0	0	2	37	0	88	14	9	9	.372	.315
Cradle, Cobi, St. Lucie*	.233	78	302	257	34	60	70	5	1	1	12	4	3	1	37	0	45	19	3	1	.272	.329
Cradle, Rickey, Dunedin	.275	50	211	178	33	49	86	10	3	7	27	1	2	2	28	0	49	6	2	2	.483	.376
Crespo, Mike, Charlotte†	.162	28	80	74	6	12	14	2	0	0	3	0	0	0	6	0	23	0	0	3	.189	.225
Cromer, Brandon, Dunedin*	.237	106	385	329	40	78	113	11	3	6	43	5	3	5	43	3	84	0	5	6	.343	.332
Dalton, Dee, St. Petersburg	.205	118	438	385	36	79	103	16	1	2	30	2	3	3	45	0	81	10	4	7	.268	.291
Davenport, Jeff, Sarasota	.000	10	28	22	1	0	0	0	0	0	3	0	2	0	1	0	8	0	0	0	.000	.040
Davila, Vic, Dunedin*	.257	109	370	331	48	85	127	14	5	6	45	3	4	8	24	2	66	1	3	4	.384	.319
Dawson, Andre, Brevard County	.100	3	10	10	0	1	1	0	0	0	0	0	0	0	0	0	2	0	0	1	.100	.100
Deares, Greg, St. Petersburg*	.235	20	54	51	3	12	13	1	0	0	6	0	0	0	2	0	8	0	0	0	.255	.264
DeBerry, Joe, Tampa*	.224	58	216	196	16	44	62	9	3	1	18	0	1	0	19	3	45	1	0	3	.316	.292
DeJesus, Malvin, Lakeland	.301	73	273	239	39	72	98	7	5	3	23	2	1	4	27	0	51	7	6	1	.410	.380
DeLaCruz, Carlos, Lakeland	.000	2	3	3	0	0	0	0	0	0	0	0	0	0	0	0	2	0	0	0	.000	.000
Delafield, Wil, Tampa	.269	7	29	26	4	7	11	1	0	1	6	0	0	1	2	0	11	1	0	0	.423	.345
Diaz, Cesar, St. Lucie	.233	102	386	361	33	84	123	17	2	6	40	3	1	2	19	1	91	0	5	13	.341	.274
Diaz, Edwin, Charlotte	.284	115	495	450	48	128	188	26	5	8	56	3	2	7	33	0	94	8	13	10	.418	.341
Diaz, Linardo, Clearwater	.212	11	37	33	1	7	8	1	0	0	1	0	1	0	3	0	7	0	0	1	.242	.270
Donato, Daniel, Tampa*	.250	3	9	8	1	2	5	0	0	1	1	0	0	1	0	0	2	0	0	0	.625	.333
Dowler, Dee, Daytona	.251	112	479	415	70	104	129	12	2	3	59	7	4	8	45	0	51	26	15	11	.311	.333
Driskell, Jeff, Lakeland	.262	23	67	61	8	16	26	4	0	2	8	0	1	0	5	0	17	0	0	1	.426	.313
Duross, Gabe, Daytona*	.241	60	240	224	20	54	72	9	0	3	34	0	3	2	11	2	12	4	4	6	.321	.279
Ellis, Kevin, Daytona	.270	120	471	430	57	116	163	17	6	6	66	0	4	10	26	1	73	6	3	11	.379	.323
Epperson, Chad, St. Lucie†	.190	42	141	121	7	23	35	7	1	1	14	1	2	0	17	2	32	1	0	7	.289	.286
Erdman, Brad, Daytona	.154	8	31	26	6	4	5	1	0	0	3	1	0	0	4	0	6	0	0	0	.192	.267
Estalella, Bobby, Clearwater	.260	117	469	404	61	105	176	24	1	15	58	3	4	2	56	2	76	0	3	12	.436	.350
Evans, Stan, Clearwater*	.248	89	322	286	34	71	82	5	3	0	32	4	3	0	29	0	33	10	5	6	.287	.314
Evans, Tom, Dunedin	.279	130	513	444	63	124	186	29	3	9	66	3	7	8	51	0	80	7	2	10	.419	.359
Everson, Darin, W. Palm Beach*	.219	38	124	105	7	23	28	2	0	1	13	0	1	6	12	2	22	0	0	3	.267	.331
Facione, Chris, Lakeland	.293	110	444	400	44	117	161	17	6	5	56	2	4	2	35	3	76	20	10	13	.403	.349
Ferrier, Ross, St. Lucie	.201	68	258	234	27	47	78	6	2	7	23	1	2	3	18	1	69	2	5	6	.333	.265
Fick, Chris, St. Petersburg*	.293	113	399	348	56	102	172	25	3	13	52	0	3	10	38	2	79	1	2	9	.494	.376
Fithian, Grant, Tampa	.250	3	4	4	0	1	1	0	0	0	1	0	0	0	0	0	2	0	0	0	.250	.250
Fitzpatrick, Robert, W. Palm Beach	.209	17	53	43	3	9	13	1	0	1	5	0	1	0	9	0	12	3	3	0	.302	.340
Flores, Jose, Clearwater	.222	49	212	185	25	41	54	4	3	1	19	7	1	4	15	0	27	12	5	4	.292	.293
Forkerway, Trey, Daytona	.202	75	214	188	22	38	45	4	0	1	11	4	1	1	20	0	29	10	1	5	.239	.281
Forkner, Tim, Kissimmee*	.284	89	367	296	42	84	115	20	4	1	34	2	4	5	60	2	40	4	2	11	.389	.408
Foster, Jeff, West Palm Beach*	.207	65	194	179	22	37	62	7	3	4	26	3	1	1	10	1	42	10	3	4	.346	.251
Freeman, Sean, Lakeland*	.290	119	472	414	42	120	163	21	2	6	65	0	7	2	49	3	98	3	4	3	.394	.362
Frias, Hanley, Charlotte†	.333	33	140	120	23	40	52	6	3	0	14	3	1	1	15	0	11	8	6	0	.433	.409
Froschauer, Trevor, Kissimmee	.197	102	390	325	32	64	110	8	1	12	40	0	3	13	49	0	121	2	0	10	.338	.323
Gallone, Santy, Clearwater	.244	90	357	283	45	69	104	15	1	6	40	2	7	18	47	1	39	5	3	11	.367	.377
Garcia, Luis, Lakeland	.280	102	378	361	39	101	125	10	4	2	35	4	4	1	8	0	42	9	10	6	.346	.294
Garcia, Osmel, St. Petersburg	.175	105	356	315	37	55	59	4	0	0	13	7	0	6	28	0	66	24	11	8	.187	.255
Gibbs, Kevin, Vero Beach†	.250	7	20	20	1	5	6	1	0	0	2	0	0	0	0	0	0	1	0	0	.300	.250
Gonzalez, Alex, Brevard County	.203	17	61	59	6	12	16	2	1	0	8	0	0	1	1	0	14	1	1	2	.271	.230
Gousha, Sean, Daytona	.250	5	9	8	1	2	4	2	0	0	0	0	0	0	1	0	0	0	0	1	.500	.333
Grissom, Antonio, W. Palm Beach	.200	8	24	20	3	4	5	1	0	0	1	0	0	0	4	0	6	2	1	0	.250	.333
Gross, Rafael, Vero Beach	.252	35	124	115	18	29	35	4	1	0	8	1	2	3	3	0	15	5	4	1	.304	.285
Gyselman, Jeff, Clearwater	.172	26	70	64	8	11	11	0	0	0	3	0	0	0	6	0	14	0	0	4	.172	.243
Halemanu, Joshua, Kissimmee*	.133	6	16	15	1	2	2	0	0	0	0	0	0	0	1	0	7	0	0	0	.133	.188
Hammell, Al, St. Lucie	.157	34	88	70	7	11	15	1	0	1	3	1	0	1	16	0	19	2	1	2	.214	.322
Hansen, Elston, Tampa	.193	61	222	187	28	36	56	12	1	2	19	5	3	4	23	0	45	0	1	4	.299	.290
Hare, Rich, Lakeland	.150	9	21	20	3	3	3	0	0	0	2	0	0	0	1	0	4	0	0	0	.150	.190
Hastings, Lionel, Brevard County	.273	120	523	469	60	128	169	20	0	7	45	5	2	3	44	0	64	3	3	14	.360	.338
Hawkins, Kraig, Tampa†	.243	111	512	432	56	105	123	9	3	1	19	11	1	2	66	0	95	28	14	6	.285	.345
Haws, Scott, Clearwater*	.000	2	2	1	0	0	0	0	0	0	0	0	0	0	1	0	0	0	0	0	.000	.500

Player, Team	Avg.	G	TPA	AB	R	H	TB	2B	3B	HR	RBI	SH	SF	HP	BB	IBB	SO	SB	CS	GDP	Slg.	OBP
Held, Daniel, Clearwater	.272	134	569	489	82	133	233	35	1	21	82	1	4	19	56	1	127	2	1	13	.476	.366
Henry, Antoine, Sarasota	.226	16	70	62	14	14	22	0	1	2	8	0	0	0	8	0	7	5	2	1	.355	.314
Hernaiz, Juan, Vero Beach	.212	50	170	156	17	33	42	1	1	2	9	4	0	1	9	1	39	5	1	4	.269	.259
Hilt, Scott, Fort Myers*	.167	19	46	42	3	7	10	0	0	1	3	0	0	1	3	0	12	0	0	4	.238	.239
Hollis, Ronald, Vero Beach*	.000	43	1	1	0	0	0	0	0	0	0	0	0	0	0	0	1	0	0	0	.000	.000
Horn, Jeff, Fort Myers	.266	66	245	199	25	53	60	5	1	0	20	1	3	4	38	1	30	2	3	4	.302	.389
Hunter, Torii, Fort Myers	.246	113	447	391	64	96	136	15	2	7	36	5	1	12	38	1	77	7	4	8	.348	.330
Jackson, Gavin, Sarasota	.266	100	402	342	61	91	112	19	1	0	36	8	4	6	40	3	43	11	12	8	.327	.349
Johnson, Andre, Daytona	.071	5	14	14	2	1	1	0	0	0	2	0	0	0	0	0	4	0	0	0	.071	.071
Johnson, Jack, Daytona	.375	4	9	8	1	3	6	0	0	1	2	0	0	0	1	0	4	0	0	0	.750	.444
Johnson, J.J., Sarasota	.276	107	427	391	49	108	162	16	4	10	43	2	2	6	26	0	74	7	8	9	.414	.329
Jones, Ben, Fort Myers	.239	109	399	335	60	80	94	10	2	0	31	16	1	6	41	2	53	19	6	10	.281	.332
Jones, Ryan, Dunedin	.249	127	531	478	65	119	201	28	0	18	78	0	5	7	41	3	92	1	1	7	.421	.315
Keister, Tripp, St. Lucie*	.330	28	111	94	15	31	40	5	2	0	14	0	1	2	14	0	11	5	4	1	.426	.423
Kelly, Pat, Tampa	.235	3	17	17	0	4	5	1	0	0	2	0	0	0	0	0	1	0	0	0	.294	.235
Kendall, Jeremey, Clearwater	.215	36	158	135	18	29	43	1	2	3	10	1	2	6	14	0	40	15	5	2	.319	.312
Kimsey, Keith, Lakeland	.217	54	197	175	30	38	68	8	2	6	16	0	0	0	22	0	58	1	1	4	.389	.305
Kingman, Brendan, Brevard County	.253	95	384	348	37	88	139	19	4	8	47	0	4	1	31	3	45	1	0	21	.399	.313
Kingston, Mark, Daytona†	.235	49	188	170	23	40	54	8	0	2	23	0	3	1	14	2	33	1	1	5	.318	.293
Knauss, Tom, Fort Myers	.237	99	353	316	37	75	99	19	1	1	26	1	2	6	28	1	72	2	8	4	.313	.310
Knowles, Eric, Tampa	.271	115	444	391	45	106	141	24	4	1	33	3	2	3	45	0	58	7	3	8	.361	.349
Koeyers, Ramsey, W. Palm Beach	.189	77	261	244	19	46	54	6	1	0	18	5	3	0	9	0	64	2	1	10	.221	.215
Landaker, Dave, Kissimmee	.206	96	348	287	30	59	70	7	2	0	18	4	5	10	42	0	47	8	10	6	.244	.323
Landry, Lonny, Lakeland	.161	19	59	56	2	9	10	1	0	0	4	1	0	0	2	0	16	0	0	0	.179	.190
Latham, Chris, Vero Beach†	.286	71	322	259	53	74	113	13	4	6	39	2	3	2	56	4	54	42	11	2	.436	.413
Lee, Manuel, St. Petersburg†	.353	6	19	17	2	6	7	1	0	0	3	0	0	0	2	0	3	0	0	0	.412	.421
Lewis, Tyrone, Vero Beach	.000	1	1	1	0	0	0	0	0	0	0	0	0	0	0	0	1	0	0	0	.000	.000
Little, Mark, Charlotte	.256	115	507	438	75	112	186	31	8	9	50	2	2	14	51	1	108	20	14	4	.425	.350
Loeb, Marc, Dunedin	.223	64	222	193	17	43	58	12	0	1	23	3	0	2	24	0	46	1	1	3	.301	.315
Lombardi, John, Sarasota	.263	7	20	19	2	5	7	2	0	0	1	0	0	1	0	0	4	0	0	0	.368	.300
Long, Justin, Brevard County	.118	9	18	17	3	2	2	0	0	0	1	0	0	0	1	0	11	0	0	0	.118	.167
Long, R.D., Tampa†	.250	110	475	384	70	96	143	15	10	4	36	9	2	2	72	1	100	28	13	4	.372	.370
Lopez, Jose, St. Lucie	1.000	1	4	2	0	2	2	0	0	0	1	0	0	0	2	0	0	0	0	0	1.000	1.000
Lowery, Terrell, Charlotte	.257	11	42	35	4	9	15	2	2	0	4	0	0	1	6	0	6	1	0	2	.429	.381
Luzinski, Ryan, Vero Beach	.336	38	144	134	15	45	72	12	0	5	23	0	1	0	9	3	21	1	0	4	.537	.375
Macon, Leland, Charlotte	.259	119	477	405	52	105	132	15	3	2	38	2	7	22	41	1	85	14	12	10	.326	.354
Madonna, Chris, St. Lucie*	.000	3	5	5	0	0	0	0	0	0	0	0	0	0	0	0	1	0	0	0	.000	.000
Madsen, Dan, Daytona†	.194	13	41	36	7	7	11	1	0	1	3	1	0	1	3	0	11	4	2	0	.306	.275
Madsen, Dave, St. Petersburg	.281	121	469	388	48	109	147	20	3	4	64	0	9	2	70	1	62	1	0	14	.379	.386
Magee, Wendell, Clearwater	.353	96	432	388	67	137	189	24	5	6	46	1	5	4	33	3	40	7	10	15	.487	.405
Majeski, Brian, Vero Beach	.224	69	178	147	22	33	44	3	1	2	11	3	0	2	26	2	34	9	8	0	.299	.349
Malone, Scott, Charlotte*	.236	100	369	314	33	74	96	14	1	2	40	5	3	2	45	1	41	5	2	8	.306	.332
Maness, Dwight, V.B.-St.L.	.225	57	219	187	20	42	58	7	0	3	28	3	5	6	18	0	35	14	7	2	.310	.306
Mangham, Rodney, Kissimmee†	.209	42	160	134	19	28	37	7	1	0	12	3	1	0	22	0	31	5	3	1	.276	.318
Marabella, Tony, W. Palm Beach*	.259	60	217	201	22	52	60	6	1	0	21	0	3	0	13	0	23	1	1	4	.299	.300
Marine, Del, Lakeland	.241	77	278	257	27	62	88	14	0	4	25	0	3	5	13	0	63	5	1	3	.342	.288
Marrero, Elieser, St. Petersburg	.211	107	415	383	43	81	129	16	1	10	55	0	7	1	23	2	55	9	4	10	.337	.254
Marsh, Roy, Kissimmee	.216	114	437	393	51	85	121	18	3	4	23	2	0	4	38	0	95	22	11	6	.308	.292
Martin, Mike, Lakeland	.176	6	21	17	1	3	3	0	0	0	1	1	0	0	3	0	1	0	0	1	.176	.300
Martinez, Dalvis, Lakeland	.189	38	126	111	12	21	26	5	0	0	5	2	0	1	12	0	26	0	1	6	.234	.274
Martinez, Ramon, Brevard County†	.263	99	410	372	47	98	115	7	2	2	24	4	1	4	29	2	84	21	4	0	.309	.323
Matvey, Mike, St. Petersburg	.273	87	350	304	32	83	106	15	4	0	20	2	1	3	40	1	67	1	5	2	.349	.362
Maxwell, Jason, Daytona	.263	117	466	388	66	102	151	13	3	10	58	1	8	6	63	1	68	12	7	6	.389	.368
McCalmont, Jim, Fort Myers	.228	92	323	285	30	65	94	13	2	4	21	3	4	8	23	1	54	2	7	8	.330	.300
McEwing, Joe, St. Petersburg	.228	75	317	281	33	64	80	13	0	1	23	6	4	1	25	3	49	2	3	5	.285	.289
McKeel, Walt, Sarasota	.333	62	231	198	26	66	104	14	0	8	35	0	5	3	25	0	28	6	3	4	.525	.407
McKinnon, Tom, St. Petersburg*	.267	53	178	172	15	46	68	16	0	2	10	0	1	0	5	2	39	1	1	4	.395	.287
McMullen, Jon, Clearwater*	.237	30	138	118	17	28	38	7	0	1	14	0	0	0	20	2	19	0	0	6	.322	.348
Melhuse, Adam, Dunedin†	.215	123	495	428	43	92	124	20	0	4	41	1	4	1	61	1	87	6	1	7	.290	.312
Meluskey, Mitch, Kissimmee†	.215	78	295	261	23	56	85	18	1	3	31	2	4	1	27	2	33	3	0	12	.326	.287
Mercedes, Guillermo, Charlotte†	.218	33	121	110	10	24	26	2	0	0	5	2	1	1	7	0	12	1	2	1	.236	.269
Metcalfe, Mike, Vero Beach†	.301	120	509	435	86	131	159	13	3	3	35	6	5	3	60	2	37	60	27	8	.366	.386
Micucci, Mike, Daytona*	.195	23	47	41	4	8	10	2	0	0	3	2	0	0	4	0	9	0	0	0	.244	.267
Mientkiewicz, Doug, Fort Myers*	.245	38	131	110	9	27	38	6	1	1	15	2	0	1	18	1	19	2	2	1	.345	.357
Millar, Kevin, Brevard County	.288	129	551	459	53	132	207	32	2	13	68	0	10	12	70	2	66	4	4	8	.451	.388
Miller, Ryan, St. Lucie	.244	89	309	279	32	68	90	10	3	2	23	8	2	7	13	0	42	5	3	7	.323	.292
Mitchell, Mike, Tampa*	.266	102	406	368	40	98	140	16	1	8	61	1	6	2	29	1	52	1	0	10	.380	.319
Molina, Jose, Daytona	.236	82	273	233	27	55	69	9	1	1	19	2	2	7	29	0	53	1	0	7	.296	.336
Moore, Mike, Vero Beach	.273	7	28	22	3	6	7	1	0	0	1	0	0	0	6	0	8	0	1	1	.318	.429
Morales, Francisco, Day.-St.P.	.229	64	221	188	27	43	78	11	0	8	33	0	2	4	27	0	57	2	1	5	.415	.335
Morris, Bobby, Daytona*	.308	95	397	344	44	106	134	18	2	2	55	2	5	8	38	6	46	22	8	5	.390	.385
Mota, Santo, St. Petersburg†	.156	64	190	173	27	27	38	8	0	1	11	2	0	0	15	0	40	6	0	2	.220	.223
Motes, Jeff, St. Lucie	.200	12	38	35	7	7	7	0	0	0	4	1	0	1	1	0	7	0	0	1	.200	.243
Motte, James, Fort Myers	.235	119	432	392	47	92	125	17	2	4	37	5	2	2	31	1	78	8	10	13	.319	.293
Motuzas, Jeff, Tampa	.159	28	76	69	6	11	14	0	0	1	8	1	0	2	4	0	24	1	0	0	.203	.227
Moultrie, Pat, Dunedin*	.246	92	385	349	40	86	105	8	4	1	29	3	3	3	27	1	65	15	4	5	.301	.304
Murphy, Jeffrey, St. Petersburg†	.180	50	143	122	9	22	33	3	1	2	14	0	0	2	19	0	36	0	0	5	.270	.301
Murphy, Pat, Sarasota*	.201	54	200	189	18	38	48	4	0	2	15	2	0	1	8	0	26	12	5	2	.254	.237
Nava, Lipso, Sarasota	.258	21	73	62	11	16	26	4	0	2	10	0	0	4	7	0	7	1	0	3	.419	.370
Nava, Marlon, Fort Myers	.242	112	413	376	47	91	112	18	0	1	37	11	2	2	22	1	45	5	9	6	.298	.286
Nelson, Bry, Kissimmee†	.327	105	423	395	47	129	182	34	5	3	52	1	6	1	20	0	37	14	10	8	.461	.355
Nelson, Charles, Vero Beach*	.271	80	327	277	37	75	92	13	2	0	30	3	1	0	46	2	50	33	13	7	.332	.373
Niethammer, Marc, W. Palm Beach*	.187	96	353	315	34	59	106	11	3	10	31	1	2	4	31	3	105	4	6	2	.337	.267

Player, Team	Avg.	G	TPA	AB	R	H	TB	2B	3B	HR	RBI	SH	SF	HP	BB	IBB	SO	SB	CS	GDP	Slg.	OBP
Nihart, Tim, Fort Myers	.200	4	11	10	1	2	4	2	0	0	2	0	0	0	1	0	3	0	0	0	.400	.273
Nixon, Trot, Sarasota*	.303	73	312	264	43	80	114	11	4	5	39	0	2	1	45	3	46	7	5	5	.432	.404
Northeimer, Jamie, Clearwater	.316	6	24	19	1	6	7	1	0	0	5	0	0	2	3	0	4	0	0	0	.368	.458
Northrup, Kevin, St. Lucie	.297	17	70	64	7	19	22	1	1	0	12	0	2	0	4	0	6	2	1	2	.344	.329
Nuneviller, Tom, Clearwater	.233	12	49	43	2	10	12	2	0	0	6	0	2	0	4	0	6	0	0	1	.279	.286
O'Brien, Joe, Clearwater	.140	13	54	50	6	7	11	1	0	1	7	0	0	1	3	0	13	1	0	4	.220	.204
Orie, Kevin, Daytona	.244	119	474	409	54	100	152	17	4	9	51	0	6	15	42	2	71	5	4	11	.372	.333
Ortiz, Nick, Sarasota	.247	91	337	304	38	75	112	20	1	5	38	1	1	4	27	0	68	6	4	3	.368	.315
Otanez, Willis, Vero Beach	.260	92	389	354	39	92	146	24	0	10	53	0	5	2	28	3	59	1	1	15	.412	.314
Ottavinia, Paul, W. Palm Beach*	.235	112	438	395	35	93	120	20	2	1	37	5	2	2	34	2	44	13	6	10	.304	.298
Pachot, John, West Palm Beach	.251	67	245	227	17	57	67	10	0	0	23	3	1	2	12	0	38	1	2	4	.295	.293
Parra, Julio, Vero Beach	.000	22	1	0	0	0	0	0	0	0	0	1	0	0	0	0	0	0	0	0	.000	.000
Patton, Greg, Sarasota	.217	8	25	23	1	5	5	0	0	0	0	0	0	0	2	0	8	0	0	0	.217	.280
Patzke, Jeff, Dunedin†	.264	129	560	470	68	124	201	32	6	11	75	1	2	2	85	8	81	5	3	10	.428	.377
Perez, Jhonny, Kissimmee	.271	65	244	214	24	58	82	12	0	4	31	0	0	7	22	1	37	23	7	5	.383	.358
Perez, Joe, Charlotte*	.257	24	86	74	8	19	26	4	0	1	9	0	1	2	9	0	12	1	1	0	.351	.349
Perez, Richard, Daytona	.220	85	289	255	31	56	64	8	0	0	26	4	1	1	28	0	41	4	2	5	.251	.298
Peterson, Nate, Kissimmee*	.280	76	283	257	34	72	101	17	0	4	22	0	1	4	21	2	42	3	1	5	.393	.343
Petrulis, Paul, St. Lucie	.227	104	347	291	33	66	79	10	0	1	16	8	1	2	45	0	51	3	11	8	.271	.333
Pichardo, Sandy, St. Lucie†	.274	125	522	478	55	131	153	10	6	0	27	12	1	3	28	3	64	29	17	6	.320	.318
Pico, Brandon, Daytona*	.245	16	58	49	4	12	14	2	0	0	4	2	0	0	7	0	8	1	1	0	.286	.339
Porter, Bo, Daytona	.217	113	377	336	54	73	98	12	2	3	19	4	3	2	32	0	104	22	10	5	.292	.287
Post, David, Vero Beach	.237	52	143	114	16	27	31	2	1	0	11	3	1	2	23	0	11	3	0	5	.272	.371
Prater, Andrew, Brevard County	.150	73	204	173	18	26	37	5	0	2	16	5	4	4	18	0	49	0	0	3	.214	.241
Querecuto, Juan, Dunedin	.179	53	151	140	16	25	34	4	1	1	10	0	0	3	8	1	31	0	0	5	.243	.238
Radmanovich, Ryan, Fort Myers*	.317	12	44	41	3	13	15	2	0	0	5	0	0	1	2	0	8	0	0	0	.366	.364
Raifstanger, John, Sarasota	.270	102	367	326	52	88	115	19	1	2	24	2	2	3	34	1	63	6	1	5	.353	.342
Raleigh, Matt, West Palm Beach	.207	66	243	179	29	37	54	11	0	2	18	1	3	6	54	1	64	4	2	4	.302	.401
Ramirez, Angel, Dunedin	.275	131	569	541	78	149	202	19	5	8	52	0	2	5	21	0	99	17	12	12	.373	.308
Ramirez, Hiram, Sarasota	.186	40	146	140	13	26	34	2	0	2	12	2	1	0	3	0	29	3	2	2	.243	.201
Ramos, Eddie, Kissimmee	.114	30	112	105	5	12	17	3	1	0	8	0	3	0	4	1	27	0	0	5	.162	.143
Reeves, Glen, Brevard County	.270	117	504	415	68	112	141	22	2	1	33	2	3	6	78	0	78	6	7	12	.340	.390
Renteria, David, Tampa	.217	33	78	69	6	15	23	3	1	1	4	2	2	1	4	0	16	1	1	1	.333	.263
Rijo, Rafael, Charlotte	.304	16	52	46	3	14	16	2	0	0	5	1	0	0	5	1	11	2	0	0	.348	.373
Roberge, John, Vero Beach	.000	3	9	9	1	0	0	0	0	0	0	0	0	0	0	0	2	0	0	0	.000	.000
Roberts, David, Lakeland*	.303	92	401	357	67	108	137	10	5	3	30	2	2	1	39	2	43	30	8	7	.384	.371
Robinson, Dan, Brevard County*	.237	105	395	354	38	84	128	17	3	7	52	2	3	1	35	0	81	10	6	14	.362	.305
Roche, Marlon, Kissimmee	.227	26	102	97	10	22	29	7	0	0	7	1	1	0	3	0	24	3	2	2	.299	.248
Rodriguez, Adam, Lakeland	.250	30	96	88	8	22	29	4	0	1	10	0	0	0	8	0	17	1	0	1	.330	.313
Rojas, Roberto, Lakeland*	.250	4	13	12	1	3	3	0	0	0	2	0	0	0	1	1	4	1	0	0	.250	.308
Rolen, Scott, Clearwater	.290	66	283	238	45	69	116	13	2	10	39	0	3	5	37	1	46	4	0	4	.487	.392
Rupp, Brian, St. Petersburg	.277	90	357	325	30	90	106	12	2	0	23	4	0	1	27	1	43	0	0	14	.326	.334
Rupp, Chad, Fort Myers	.266	107	420	376	44	100	161	23	1	12	52	0	3	2	38	1	77	14	3	10	.428	.334
Sabo, Chris, St. Petersburg	.231	14	51	39	10	9	15	0	0	2	7	0	0	1	10	0	6	1	0	2	.385	.400
Saffer, Jon, West Palm Beach*	.318	92	384	324	60	103	137	10	6	4	35	4	1	2	53	1	49	18	9	7	.423	.416
Samuels, Scott, Daytona*	.327	112	473	388	92	127	186	29	12	2	42	3	4	8	69	7	63	38	14	8	.479	.435
Sanchez, Omar, Dunedin	.250	39	147	120	25	30	35	5	0	0	8	2	1	3	21	0	22	6	4	0	.292	.372
Sanchez, Victor, Kissimmee	.268	78	308	272	34	73	105	11	0	7	38	1	4	8	23	1	69	6	3	6	.386	.339
Santucci, Steven, St. Petersburg	.236	106	324	292	25	69	92	5	3	4	25	2	3	0	27	0	60	9	3	8	.315	.298
Sauve, Erik, Charlotte	.143	31	79	70	9	10	13	3	0	0	4	0	0	0	9	0	13	0	2	1	.186	.241
Saylor, Jamie, Kissimmee*	.228	89	319	289	38	66	78	4	1	2	19	0	2	6	22	1	58	13	6	5	.270	.295
Schaaf, Rob, Vero Beach	.217	21	61	60	7	13	17	1	0	1	5	0	0	0	1	0	13	0	0	2	.283	.230
Schmitz, Mike, Tampa	.231	4	13	13	2	3	4	1	0	0	0	0	0	0	0	0	1	0	0	1	.308	.231
Scolaro, Donnie, Kissimmee	.302	23	74	63	9	19	22	3	0	0	3	2	2	0	7	0	12	1	0	1	.349	.361
Sell, Donald, Vero Beach*	.270	80	248	222	21	60	71	6	1	1	23	2	2	4	18	0	33	1	3	5	.320	.333
Sheffield, Tony, Sarasota*	.238	103	350	315	45	75	101	17	3	1	25	4	1	2	28	0	109	9	11	4	.321	.303
Shirley, Al, St. Lucie	.186	59	212	183	27	34	61	6	3	5	18	0	1	5	23	1	94	8	4	2	.333	.292
Shores, Scott, Clearwater	.254	133	530	460	74	117	171	23	5	7	52	3	2	10	55	1	127	30	16	11	.372	.345
Shugars, Shawn, Charlotte*	.348	10	27	23	4	8	11	1	1	0	3	0	0	1	3	0	4	0	0	2	.478	.444
Sims, Michael, Brevard County	.185	89	283	260	24	48	57	6	0	1	20	5	1	2	15	0	52	4	2	14	.219	.234
Sims, Wes, Charlotte†	.273	5	13	11	2	3	4	1	0	0	1	0	0	0	2	0	5	0	0	0	.364	.385
Smith, Bubba, Fort Myers	.330	60	195	176	27	58	112	15	0	13	51	0	3	0	16	4	38	1	2	8	.636	.379
Smith, Dave, Sarasota	.299	23	80	67	12	20	27	5	1	0	6	1	0	3	9	0	10	1	5	1	.403	.405
Smith, Sloan, Tampa†	.260	124	494	412	61	107	171	23	1	13	64	1	3	4	74	3	136	6	8	8	.415	.375
Snyder, Jared, Daytona	.167	18	42	36	2	6	6	0	0	0	6	2	1	1	2	0	4	0	1	2	.167	.225
Solano, Fausto, Dunedin	.208	41	167	144	19	30	42	5	2	1	10	5	0	1	17	0	30	3	2	4	.292	.296
Sosa, Juan, Vero Beach	.222	8	27	27	2	6	12	1	1	1	6	0	0	0	0	0	4	0	2	0	.444	.222
Southard, Scott, Brevard County	.210	68	245	219	18	46	61	7	1	2	21	5	0	1	20	0	40	4	3	2	.279	.279
Sowards, Ryan, Vero Beach*	.286	75	252	196	36	56	78	13	0	3	34	2	4	3	47	2	32	1	0	6	.398	.424
Spencer, Shane, Tampa	.300	134	573	500	87	150	235	31	3	16	88	2	3	7	61	2	60	14	8	7	.470	.382
Steed, David, Vero Beach	.251	59	218	195	11	49	65	16	0	0	24	1	1	3	18	0	53	0	0	5	.333	.323
Stewart, Tom, Kissimmee†	.251	52	191	167	9	42	51	4	1	1	15	3	1	3	17	0	48	0	2	3	.305	.330
Stovall, Darond, W. Palm Beach†	.232	121	510	461	52	107	145	22	2	4	51	2	3	0	44	2	117	18	12	4	.315	.297
Strawberry, Darryl, Tampa*	.222	2	10	9	1	2	6	1	0	1	2	0	0	0	1	0	2	0	0	1	.667	.300
Stricklin, Scott, Fort Myers*	.187	65	212	166	20	31	32	1	0	0	8	5	0	0	41	2	25	4	4	3	.193	.348
Subero, Carlos, Charlotte†	.136	17	45	44	3	6	7	1	0	0	4	1	0	0	0	0	10	0	0	1	.159	.136
Suplee, Ray, Tampa	.233	98	364	317	33	74	106	9	1	7	37	3	4	7	33	1	94	4	2	2	.334	.316
Taylor, Mike, St. Petersburg*	.239	70	192	159	13	38	49	3	1	2	15	4	1	0	28	2	24	0	2	2	.308	.351
Tebbs, Nathan, Sarasota†	.291	118	487	440	58	128	157	15	4	2	52	4	1	3	39	0	80	25	15	7	.357	.352
Terrell, Matt, St. Lucie	.197	86	216	193	24	38	48	6	2	0	9	3	1	1	18	0	53	11	2	3	.249	.268
Thompson, Billy, Lakeland	.242	73	243	223	26	54	84	13	1	5	28	1	3	1	15	0	45	4	0	2	.377	.289
Torborg, Dale, St.L-Tampa	.100	7	10	10	0	1	1	0	0	0	1	0	0	0	0	0	5	0	0	0	.100	.100
Torres, Jaime, Tampa	.239	107	408	364	45	87	128	17	0	8	45	3	3	10	28	1	29	1	1	14	.352	.309

Player, Team	Avg.	G	TPA	AB	R	H	TB	2B	3B	HR	RBI	SH	SF	HP	BB	IBB	SO	SB	CS	GDP	Slg.	OBP
Trammell, Bubba, Lakeland	.284	122	510	454	61	129	215	32	3	16	72	0	4	4	48	2	80	13	3	9	.474	.355
Troilo, Jason, Tampa	.000	1	3	2	0	0	0	0	0	0	0	0	0	1	0	0	2	0	0	0	.000	.333
Twitty, Sean, Tampa	.250	1	4	4	0	1	1	0	0	0	0	0	0	0	0	0	1	0	0	1	.250	.250
Ugueto, Jesus, St. Petersburg	.130	37	83	77	3	10	11	1	0	0	3	1	1	1	3	0	18	0	1	4	.143	.171
Unrat, Chris, Charlotte*	.250	66	201	172	22	43	56	8	1	1	17	4	2	0	23	1	38	1	2	6	.326	.335
Varriano, Mark, Sarasota	.000	8	17	16	0	0	0	0	0	0	0	0	0	0	1	0	9	0	0	0	.000	.059
Venezia, Danny, Fort Myers	.245	16	57	49	5	12	15	1	1	0	4	0	1	0	7	0	8	1	0	1	.306	.333
Verduzco, Steve, Kissimmee	.250	98	399	348	47	87	125	17	0	7	50	3	5	6	37	3	50	18	4	10	.359	.328
Vessel, Andrew, Charlotte	.265	129	553	498	67	132	189	26	2	9	78	1	7	15	32	2	75	3	17	11	.380	.324
Vidro, Jose, West Palm Beach†	.325	44	177	163	20	53	81	15	2	3	24	2	2	2	8	0	21	0	1	5	.497	.360
Waco, David, Clearwater	.223	59	226	193	22	43	53	8	1	0	13	5	0	5	23	0	27	2	2	5	.275	.321
Warner, Randy, St. Lucie	.260	122	480	446	43	116	181	23	6	10	70	0	4	3	27	0	86	6	7	9	.406	.304
Whatley, Gabe, Daytona*	.262	15	51	42	8	11	17	3	0	1	5	0	0	0	7	0	5	2	0	0	.405	.367
White, Jimmy, Kissimmee*	.182	16	66	55	6	10	15	3	1	0	3	1	0	1	9	0	9	4	0	2	.273	.308
Whitehurst, Todd, St. Lucie†	.222	58	216	189	13	42	51	7	1	0	18	1	1	4	21	2	37	2	3	1	.270	.312
Williams, Ed, Lakeland†	.267	4	15	15	1	4	7	1	1	0	1	0	0	0	0	0	4	0	0	0	.467	.267
Wilson, Tom, Tampa	.167	17	61	48	3	8	8	0	0	0	2	1	1	0	11	0	13	1	0	0	.167	.317
Wipf, Mark, St. Lucie†	.246	123	490	435	52	107	151	20	6	4	53	4	5	5	39	6	95	15	7	4	.347	.312
Wooten, Shawn, Lakeland	.230	38	148	135	11	31	49	10	1	2	11	0	1	2	10	0	28	0	1	2	.363	.291
Wyrick, Chris, St. Petersburg	.237	55	156	139	20	33	44	6	1	1	15	1	0	5	10	0	25	3	1	3	.317	.312
Zambrano, Jose, Sarasota	.367	10	43	30	4	11	18	1	0	2	8	0	0	1	12	0	11	1	1	0	.600	.558
Zuniga, David, St. Lucie	.172	10	30	29	1	5	5	0	0	0	0	0	0	0	1	0	6	0	1	1	.172	.200

GRAND SLAMS: Alcantara, Bierek, Collier, L. Garcia, Malone, Morales, Morris, M. Nava, Rolen, C. Rupp, B. Smith, Spencer, Torres, Vessel, 1 each.

AWARDED FIRST BASE ON CATCHER'S INTERFERENCE: R.D. Long 6 (Melhuse 2, Marine, Meluskey, Rodriguez, Thompson); Davenport 3 (K. Brown 2, Marine); Orie 3 (Stricklin 2, C. Diaz); Azuaje 2 (Luzinski 2); Whatley 2 (V. Sanchez 2); Wipf 2 (K. Brown, M. Sims); Baugh (Luzinski); Bierek (Melhuse); Cooney (Melhuse); Deares (Castro); Ellis (Melhuse); Facione (Marrero); Jackson (Castro); Magee (Marine); Marrero (C. Diaz); Jh. Perez (Melhuse); C. Rupp (Luzinski); Sabo (Torres); Samuels (Torres); Wyrick (Thompson).

PLAYERS WITH TWO OR MORE TEAMS

Player, Team	Avg.	G	TPA	AB	R	H	TB	2B	3B	HR	RBI	SH	SF	HP	BB	IBB	SO	SB	CS	GDP	Slg.	OBP
Maness, Dwight, Vero Beach	.231	43	167	143	16	33	45	3	0	3	23	2	5	6	11	0	29	13	5	2	.315	.303
Maness, Dwight, St. Lucie	.205	14	52	44	4	9	13	4	0	0	5	1	0	0	7	0	6	1	2	0	.295	.314
Morales, Francisco, Daytona	.257	36	122	101	17	26	50	6	0	6	23	0	2	3	16	0	28	1	1	2	.495	.369
Morales, Francisco, St. Petersburg	.195	28	99	87	10	17	28	5	0	2	10	0	0	1	11	0	29	1	0	3	.322	.293
Torborg, Dale, St. Lucie	.111	5	9	9	0	1	1	0	0	0	1	0	0	0	0	0	4	0	0	0	.111	.111
Torborg, Dale, Tampa	.000	2	1	1	0	0	0	0	0	0	0	0	0	0	0	0	1	0	0	0	.000	.000

1995 PITCHING

TEAM

Team	W	L	Pct.	ERA	G	CG	ShO	Sv.	IP	H	TBF	R	ER	HR	SH	SF	HB	BB	IBB	SO	WP	Bk.
Tampa	72	64	.529	2.81	136	7	13	44	1187.2	1054	4992	513	371	42	35	32	58	439	17	939	67	19
Daytona	87	48	.644	2.82	135	3	13	49	1173.0	1020	4853	484	368	60	33	20	49	382	12	980	77	11
Fort Myers	75	55	.577	2.85	131	10	12	31	1136.0	978	4719	450	360	60	36	44	62	409	13	823	66	9
St. Petersburg	64	67	.489	3.03	131	7	12	34	1121.1	947	4667	475	378	56	32	34	40	416	16	925	63	13
St. Lucie	61	73	.455	3.25	135	18	16	27	1161.2	1085	4875	504	419	50	44	33	50	412	24	793	71	22
Vero Beach	74	59	.556	3.40	133	3	7	40	1137.0	990	4889	521	429	64	43	38	35	563	14	939	115	23
Brevard County	61	74	.452	3.44	135	5	14	29	1191.1	1123	5109	582	456	65	44	40	79	462	20	828	57	12
West Palm Beach	54	81	.400	3.49	136	8	7	29	1146.1	1110	4960	550	445	43	41	53	70	478	18	745	92	17
Charlotte	65	67	.492	3.50	133	7	8	35	1154.1	1120	4916	538	449	77	38	33	50	394	9	758	55	23
Clearwater	79	59	.572	3.55	138	8	10	36	1201.2	1202	5151	583	474	59	49	43	40	416	20	891	67	29
Sarasota	65	68	.489	3.81	134	6	10	34	1153.0	1142	5027	606	488	57	35	33	66	466	28	819	82	25
Lakeland	64	69	.481	3.87	135	5	7	44	1156.2	1181	5015	617	498	56	36	46	72	450	8	887	75	19
Dunedin	63	74	.460	4.02	138	4	5	30	1200.0	1205	5286	668	536	93	37	33	79	541	8	840	77	22
Kissimmee	55	81	.404	4.19	136	5	7	30	1183.2	1221	5315	729	551	48	40	49	78	547	5	813	96	26

INDIVIDUAL

TOP QUALIFIERS FOR EARNED-RUN AVERAGE TITLE

Minimum 112 innings. *Lefthanded pitcher.

Pitcher, Team	W	L	Pct.	ERA	G	GS	CG	ShO	GF	Sv.	IP	H	TBF	R	ER	HR	SH	SF	HB	BB	IBB	SO	WP	Bk.
Pincavitch, Kevin, Vero Beach	10	7	.588	1.66	32	13	2	1	5	2	124.2	83	504	37	23	7	5	1	5	48	0	103	12	1
Bowers, Shane, Fort Myers	13	5	.722	2.16	23	23	1	0	0	0	145.2	119	580	43	35	6	2	4	12	32	1	103	6	1
Drews, Matthew, Tampa	15	7	.682	2.27	28	28	3	0	0	0	182.0	142	748	73	46	5	5	5	17	58	0	140	8	2
Nunez, Clemente, Brevard County	12	6	.667	2.48	19	19	4	2	0	0	123.1	99	490	48	34	3	2	2	5	22	1	79	3	5
Larson, Toby, St. Lucie	6	7	.462	2.52	19	18	3	1	0	0	121.2	122	508	44	34	5	4	0	7	30	2	82	7	1
Walker, Wade, Daytona	8	6	.571	2.53	25	24	2	1	0	0	135.0	113	541	50	38	5	3	2	2	36	0	117	8	1
King, Curtis, St. Petersburg	7	8	.467	2.58	28	21	3	0	1	0	136.0	117	567	49	39	3	4	2	11	49	2	65	6	0
Janzen, Marty, Tampa	10	3	.769	2.61	18	18	1	0	0	0	113.2	102	461	38	33	4	1	2	4	30	0	104	3	4
Guerra, Mark, St. Lucie	9	9	.500	2.64	23	23	4	3	0	0	160.0	148	644	55	47	5	4	4	4	33	1	110	2	3
Winslett, Dax, V.B.-Day.	12	6	.667	2.78	26	25	0	0	0	0	152.0	148	627	59	47	11	4	2	2	39	0	111	13	2
Davis, Jeff, Charlotte	12	7	.632	2.89	26	26	0	0	0	0	165.1	159	691	74	53	10	6	2	11	37	0	105	6	2
Box, Shawn, Daytona	8	6	.571	3.05	25	23	0	0	0	0	124.0	114	511	50	42	5	3	0	3	35	1	90	5	1
Yan, Esteban, W. Palm Beach	6	8	.429	3.07	24	21	1	0	1	1	137.2	139	580	63	47	3	7	5	10	33	0	89	8	3
Carrasco, Troy, Fort Myers*	12	4	.750	3.13	25	25	2	0	0	0	138.0	131	596	62	48	6	4	7	8	63	0	96	11	2
Dodd, Robert, Clearwater*	8	7	.533	3.16	26	26	0	0	0	0	151.0	144	636	64	53	4	3	6	1	58	0	110	3	7

DEPARTMENTAL LEADERS: W—Drews, 15; L—Granger, 12; Pct.—Debrino, .786; G—Metheney, 59; GS—Drews, 28; CG—Cosman, 6; ShO—Guerra, 3; GF—Rios, 52; Sv.—Jacobsen, 32; IP—Drews, 182.0; H—Granger, 176; TBF—Drews, 748; R—Brower, Granger, 93; ER—Granger, 79; HR—Brower, 16; SH—Lewis, Sampson, 8; SF—DaSilva, Norman, Walter, 9; HB—O'Malley, 18; BB—Forster, 80; IBB—McLaughlin, 7; SO—Detmers, 150; WP—Ashworth, 24; Bk.—Dodd, McCommon, 7.

ALL PITCHERS

*Lefthanded pitcher.

Pitcher, Team	W	L	Pct.	ERA	G	GS	CG	ShO	GF	Sv.	IP	H	TBF	R	ER	HR	SH	SF	HB	BB	IBB	SO	WP	Bk.
Adkins, Tim, Dunedin*	7	4	.636	3.75	45	0	0	0	37	17	48.0	36	215	29	20	2	3	2	1	33	0	49	7	0
Agostinelli, Peter, Clearwater*	4	4	.500	4.34	57	0	0	0	23	6	45.2	54	207	26	22	1	2	2	0	22	5	32	3	1
Albaladejo, Randy, Kissimmee	0	0	.000	11.42	7	0	0	0	4	0	8.2	13	51	13	11	0	1	1	3	10	0	5	2	0
Aldred, Scott, Lakeland*	4	2	.667	3.19	13	7	0	0	3	2	67.2	57	275	25	24	3	2	1	3	19	0	64	2	0
Andersen, Mark, Brevard County	0	1	.000	3.96	20	0	0	0	9	0	36.1	42	169	25	16	2	1	1	2	17	0	21	3	0
Antoszek, Chris, Sarasota	1	2	.333	4.15	3	3	0	0	0	0	17.1	21	77	10	8	0	0	1	0	4	0	9	2	2
Aquino, Julio, Vero Beach	0	0	.000	0.00	3	0	0	0	2	1	3.0	1	14	0	0	0	0	0	0	3	0	0	0	0
Arffa, Steve, St. Lucie*	5	5	.500	4.30	32	10	1	1	2	2	88.0	99	373	46	42	8	0	4	3	22	3	46	8	1
Ashworth, Kym, Vero Beach*	7	4	.636	3.53	24	24	1	1	0	0	120.0	111	515	56	47	8	6	5	1	64	0	97	24	2
Aybar, Manuel, St. Petersburg	2	5	.286	3.35	9	9	0	0	0	0	48.1	42	202	27	18	4	0	1	1	16	0	43	7	1
Baine, David, Charlotte*	1	3	.250	4.10	21	3	0	0	9	1	48.1	47	212	23	22	4	0	2	0	24	0	29	3	1
Barkley, Brian, Sarasota*	8	10	.444	3.25	24	24	2	2	0	0	146.2	147	611	66	53	5	2	3	5	37	3	70	4	1
Beech, Matt, Clearwater*	9	4	.692	4.19	15	15	0	0	0	0	86.0	87	363	45	40	5	3	2	3	30	0	85	6	0
Belinda, Stan, Sarasota	0	0	.000	4.50	1	1	0	0	0	0	2.0	2	7	1	1	1	0	0	0	0	0	2	0	0
Bennett, Shayne, Sarasota	2	5	.286	2.56	52	0	0	0	43	24	59.2	50	255	23	17	3	4	2	4	21	4	69	5	1
Benz, Jake, West Palm Beach*	0	2	.000	1.17	44	0	0	0	38	22	54.0	44	220	13	7	0	3	2	3	18	3	48	4	1
Berlin, Mike, Lakeland	2	1	.667	3.06	16	0	0	0	4	1	32.1	25	139	13	11	0	0	2	2	21	0	23	4	0
Berry, Jason, Tampa	2	0	1.000	0.92	7	0	0	0	1	0	19.2	14	78	3	2	0	0	1	1	10	0	14	1	0
Biehl, Rod, Fort Myers*	2	0	1.000	4.05	12	0	0	0	4	0	20.0	15	81	9	9	1	0	1	1	8	1	20	5	0
Blake, Todd, St. Petersburg*	2	2	.500	2.59	42	0	0	0	20	0	55.2	58	244	25	16	3	3	3	0	17	2	35	2	0
Bogott, Kurt, Sarasota*	6	4	.600	3.05	41	9	0	0	15	0	88.2	89	388	44	30	3	4	1	4	41	0	62	8	3
Borkowski, David, Lakeland	1	0	1.000	0.00	1	1	0	0	0	0	5.0	2	17	0	0	0	0	0	0	1	0	3	0	0
Bowen, Mitchel, Brevard County	0	2	.000	2.56	41	3	0	0	17	3	88.0	87	381	36	25	3	5	1	3	32	2	51	6	0
Bowen, Ryan, Brevard County	0	2	.000	2.45	3	3	0	0	0	0	11.0	6	43	3	3	1	0	0	0	6	0	10	0	0
Bowers, Shane, Fort Myers	13	5	.722	2.16	23	23	1	0	0	0	145.2	119	580	43	35	6	2	4	12	32	1	103	6	1
Box, Shawn, Daytona	8	6	.571	3.05	25	23	0	0	0	0	124.0	114	511	50	42	5	3	0	3	35	1	90	5	1
Breitenstein, Keith, Kissimmee*	0	1	.000	3.00	4	0	0	0	1	0	6.0	7	29	2	2	0	1	1	0	3	1	4	0	0
Briscoe, Janos, Charlotte	0	0	.000	0.00	1	0	0	0	1	0	2.0	3	10	0	0	0	0	0	0	0	0	2	0	0
Brower, Jim, Charlotte	7	10	.412	3.89	27	27	2	1	0	0	173.2	170	740	93	75	16	3	3	8	62	1	110	11	0
Brown, Alvin, Lakeland	2	3	.400	4.24	9	9	0	0	0	0	46.2	35	202	23	22	1	1	1	4	33	0	35	9	1
Brown, Brett, Kissimmee*	0	0	.000	0.00	1	0	0	0	1	0	0.2	1	3	0	0	0	0	0	0	0	0	0	0	0
Buckles, Bucky, Charlotte	2	9	.182	3.13	48	0	0	0	43	16	69.0	70	293	29	24	5	5	2	0	21	3	43	4	2
Bullock, Craig, St. Lucie	4	5	.444	2.52	40	0	0	0	28	5	50.0	47	203	15	14	2	6	2	1	13	3	27	1	2
Cain, Chance, St. Petersburg	1	0	1.000	3.27	7	0	0	0	2	0	11.0	18	51	6	4	0	0	1	0	2	0	4	0	1
Caridad, Ron, Fort Myers	2	3	.400	2.40	17	0	0	0	9	3	41.1	27	171	15	11	1	1	2	3	18	0	38	4	0
Carl, Todd, Brevard County	3	4	.429	3.96	15	7	0	0	3	1	52.1	44	224	26	23	3	1	2	2	27	0	19	3	0
Carpenter, Brian, St. Petersburg	5	3	.625	2.14	16	7	0	0	2	0	59.0	40	226	17	14	4	1	1	0	11	0	51	4	0
Carpenter, Chris, Dunedin	3	5	.375	2.17	15	15	0	0	0	0	99.1	83	420	29	24	3	2	0	4	50	0	56	9	3
Carrasco, Troy, Fort Myers*	12	4	.750	3.13	25	25	2	0	0	0	138.0	131	596	62	48	6	4	7	8	63	0	96	11	2
Cederblad, Brett, Sarasota	7	6	.538	4.09	24	12	0	0	2	0	92.1	98	384	50	42	4	0	4	6	21	0	71	7	2
Challinor, John, Vero Beach	2	6	.250	3.86	37	1	0	0	15	1	74.2	62	318	36	32	6	1	4	0	35	1	59	5	1
Cindrich, Jeff, Tampa	1	4	.200	4.35	24	0	0	0	9	0	39.1	50	177	28	19	4	0	3	0	17	1	32	5	0
Clelland, Rick, West Palm Beach	2	4	.333	2.69	35	5	0	0	10	0	70.1	59	316	30	21	3	3	5	8	46	1	66	10	0
Clemens, Roger, Sarasota	0	0	.000	0.00	1	1	0	0	0	0	4.0	0	14	0	0	0	0	0	0	2	0	7	0	0
Connolly, Matt, Daytona	7	1	.875	0.98	18	2	0	0	7	2	55.1	37	216	14	6	0	3	0	2	9	2	77	6	0
Corn, Chris, Tampa	0	1	.000	3.18	4	0	0	0	1	0	5.2	3	25	2	2	0	0	0	2	3	0	9	2	0
Cosman, Jeff, St. Lucie	4	9	.308	3.12	15	15	6	2	0	0	101.0	96	412	43	35	2	3	1	3	27	3	72	5	1
Costa, Tony, Clearwater	9	10	.474	3.85	25	25	2	1	0	0	145.0	155	631	75	62	5	6	5	10	39	0	71	11	4
Croushore, Rick, St. Petersburg	6	4	.600	3.51	12	11	0	0	0	0	59.0	44	251	25	23	2	3	1	4	32	0	57	5	0
Culberson, Don, Daytona	1	1	.500	4.56	12	0	0	0	6	0	23.2	27	113	15	12	2	0	2	4	15	0	15	2	1
Cumberland, Chris, Tampa*	1	2	.333	1.82	5	5	0	0	0	0	24.2	28	104	10	5	1	1	0	1	5	0	10	1	0
Dace, Derek, Kissimmee*	0	1	.000	16.88	1	1	0	0	0	0	2.2	4	17	5	5	0	0	1	0	5	0	1	0	0
DaSilva, Fernando, W. Palm Beach	7	10	.412	3.70	27	20	2	0	1	0	124.0	136	530	61	51	3	2	9	11	31	1	54	5	1
Dault, Donnie, Kissimmee	4	7	.364	3.08	41	5	0	0	16	6	108.0	95	445	52	37	2	4	0	5	36	0	95	8	5
Davis, Jeff, Charlotte	12	7	.632	2.89	26	26	0	0	0	0	165.1	159	691	74	53	10	6	2	11	37	0	105	6	2
Davis, Mark, Brevard County*	0	0	.000	0.00	3	0	0	0	1	0	5.0	2	16	0	0	0	0	0	0	0	0	4	0	0
DeBrino, Rob, Fort Myers	11	3	.786	3.14	41	0	0	0	18	4	48.2	38	206	24	17	2	0	2	5	25	3	30	2	0
DeLaHoya, Javier, Brevard County	1	0	1.000	1.74	5	0	0	0	1	0	10.1	6	40	2	2	1	0	0	2	2	0	8	0	0
Delgado, Ernie, Brevard County	1	6	.143	7.07	18	10	0	0	4	0	62.1	74	308	51	49	4	1	4	7	59	0	36	7	2
Detmers, Kris, St. Petersburg*	10	9	.526	3.25	25	25	1	0	0	0	146.2	120	606	64	53	12	3	7	2	57	0	150	3	2
DeVries, Andrew, Daytona*	1	0	1.000	3.57	21	1	0	0	9	0	45.1	45	203	21	18	2	2	2	5	22	0	21	6	0
Dodd, Robert, Clearwater*	8	7	.533	3.16	26	26	0	0	0	0	151.0	144	636	64	53	4	3	6	1	58	0	110	3	7
Dotel, Octavio, St. Lucie	1	0	1.000	5.63	3	0	0	0	2	0	8.0	10	38	5	5	1	1	2	0	4	0	9	2	0
Drews, Matthew, Tampa	15	7	.682	2.27	28	28	3	0	0	0	182.0	142	748	73	46	5	5	5	17	58	0	140	8	2
Dreyer, Darren, Daytona	3	5	.375	1.94	29	0	0	0	19	7	55.2	42	214	18	12	3	1	2	1	9	0	45	0	0
Drumheller, Al, Tampa*	3	3	.500	1.34	32	0	0	0	10	2	40.1	24	158	11	6	1	2	2	1	14	2	45	1	0
Drumright, Mike, Lakeland	1	1	.500	4.29	5	5	0	0	0	0	21.0	19	87	11	10	2	1	0	0	9	0	19	1	2
Duran, Roberto, Vero Beach*	7	4	.636	3.38	23	22	0	0	0	0	101.1	82	446	42	38	8	3	1	1	70	0	114	12	2
Ehler, Daniel, Brevard County	5	6	.455	3.57	16	15	0	0	0	0	88.1	88	380	46	35	2	4	3	8	26	1	66	0	1
Emerson, Scott, Sarasota*	2	5	.286	4.77	16	11	1	0	1	0	60.1	66	273	38	32	2	2	2	6	29	2	47	6	0
Engle, Tom, St. Lucie	3	3	.500	1.80	9	9	1	0	0	0	50.0	34	203	16	10	1	0	3	5	15	1	41	0	0
Evans, Stan, Clearwater	0	0	.000	0.00	1	0	0	0	0	0	2.0	2	11	2	0	0	0	0	0	2	0	1	0	0
Ferran, Alex, Sarasota*	0	0	.000	0.00	1	0	0	0	0	0	0.0	1	5	4	4	0	0	0	1	2	0	0	2	0
Fiore, Tony, Clearwater	6	2	.750	3.71	24	10	0	0	3	0	70.1	70	323	41	29	4	3	5	2	44	2	45	9	3
Forster, Scott, West Palm Beach*	6	11	.353	4.05	26	26	1	0	0	0	146.2	129	643	78	66	6	5	4	7	80	1	92	16	0
Foster, Mark, Clearwater*	0	1	.000	5.40	24	0	0	0	6	1	23.1	30	108	17	14	1	1	0	4	10	0	13	1	1
Franek, Tom, Clearwater	0	0	.000	3.55	9	0	0	0	5	0	12.2	12	54	6	5	2	0	0	0	3	1	9	0	1
Fultz, Aaron, Fort Myers*	3	6	.333	3.25	21	21	2	2	0	0	122.0	115	516	52	44	10	4	3	8	41	1	127	7	1
Gaillard, Eddy, Lakeland	2	4	.333	1.31	43	0	0	0	38	25	55.0	48	227	13	8	1	1	3	0	18	2	51	2	1
Gallaher, Kevin, Kissimmee	1	1	.500	5.71	7	7	0	0	0	0	17.1	8	86	11	11	0	0	0	3	24	0	21	2	0

Pitcher, Team	W	L	Pct.	ERA	G	GS	CG	ShO	GF	Sv.	IP	H	TBF	R	ER	HR	SH	SF	HB	BB	IBB	SO	WP	Bk.
Gallone, Santy, Clearwater	0	0	.000	0.00	1	0	0	0	1	0	1.0	1	4	0	0	0	0	0	0	0	0	2	0	0
Gandolph, Dave, Kissimmee*	0	2	.000	5.28	12	4	0	0	3	0	15.1	15	77	11	9	0	0	3	0	20	0	8	3	0
Garcia, Frank, St. Petersburg	0	1	.000	10.26	16	0	0	0	8	1	16.2	27	98	22	19	1	0	1	1	18	0	8	3	0
Gardner, Scott, Lakeland	0	0	.000	2.77	5	0	0	0	2	0	13.0	10	54	6	4	1	0	0	0	7	0	14	0	0
Gaspar, Cade, Lakeland	7	6	.538	3.90	23	23	0	0	0	0	99.1	95	422	48	43	5	1	3	9	44	0	97	13	3
Gonzalez, Generoso, Lakeland	0	0	.000	0.00	1	0	0	0	0	0	2.2	1	8	0	0	0	0	0	0	1	0	1	1	0
Gonzalez, Geremis, Daytona	5	1	.833	1.22	19	2	0	0	7	4	44.1	34	178	15	6	0	1	2	1	13	1	30	4	2
Gordon, Mike, Tampa-Dun.	5	8	.385	3.69	28	27	1	0	0	0	161.0	155	700	86	66	12	5	1	7	73	0	132	11	2
Gorecki, Rick, Vero Beach	1	2	.333	0.67	6	5	0	0	0	0	27.0	19	110	6	2	0	1	1	4	9	0	24	1	0
Granger, Greg, Lakeland	9	12	.429	5.01	27	25	1	1	0	0	142.0	176	639	93	79	7	6	7	15	46	0	91	8	2
Grasser, Craig, St. Petersburg	4	2	.667	1.36	26	0	0	0	7	0	33.0	26	133	5	5	2	0	0	2	12	1	27	2	0
Greene, Tommy, Clearwater	0	3	.000	3.15	3	3	0	0	0	0	20.0	12	77	7	7	2	0	0	2	7	0	20	1	0
Grennan, Steve, St. Lucie*	0	0	.000	2.16	9	0	0	0	3	0	8.1	8	38	3	2	0	0	0	1	4	0	10	0	0
Groot, Franz, Vero Beach	0	0	.000	5.83	14	1	0	0	10	1	29.1	28	127	21	19	4	2	5	3	18	0	15	2	1
Guerra, Mark, St. Lucie	9	9	.500	2.64	23	23	4	3	0	0	160.0	148	644	55	47	5	4	4	4	33	1	110	2	3
Gunderson, Mike, Kissimmee	0	0	.000	0.00	1	0	0	0	0	0	2.1	1	8	0	0	0	0	0	0	0	0	0	0	0
Halperin, Mike, Dunedin*	3	5	.375	3.62	14	12	0	0	0	0	69.2	70	298	36	28	4	1	0	3	29	1	63	2	0
Hammond, Chris, Brevard County*	0	0	.000	0.00	1	1	0	0	0	0	4.0	3	16	1	0	0	1	0	0	0	0	4	0	0
Harris, D.J., Dunedin	3	3	.500	3.22	42	0	0	0	16	2	67.0	54	294	29	24	6	3	3	6	41	1	56	2	0
Harris, Greg, Fort Myers	1	1	.500	0.95	3	3	1	0	0	0	19.0	12	69	3	2	1	1	0	0	4	0	11	1	1
Hart, Jason, Daytona	0	3	.000	2.21	37	0	0	0	34	24	40.2	29	172	15	10	2	2	0	1	18	2	50	0	0
Hartgrove, Lyle, Sarasota	3	1	.750	3.98	47	1	0	0	15	2	74.2	73	316	36	33	3	2	3	4	21	2	52	1	2
Hartmann, Pete, Charlotte*	2	4	.333	7.32	15	2	0	0	9	2	35.2	46	180	34	29	7	4	2	0	26	0	30	3	4
Hartmann, Rich, St. Petersburg	0	0	.000	1.65	13	0	0	0	1	0	16.1	13	65	5	3	2	0	0	0	3	0	12	3	0
Hartnett, Bill, Kissimmee	1	1	.500	4.01	32	2	0	0	7	2	74.0	87	346	52	33	3	1	2	4	32	1	61	6	1
Hecker, Doug, Sarasota	1	2	.333	3.43	10	1	0	0	2	1	21.0	24	96	9	8	0	1	1	1	7	0	16	4	1
Heflin, Bronson, Clearwater	2	3	.400	2.95	57	0	0	0	44	21	61.0	52	256	25	20	3	6	1	0	21	5	84	4	0
Heiserman, Rick, St. Petersburg	2	3	.400	5.46	6	5	0	0	1	0	28.0	28	118	18	17	2	0	2	1	11	0	18	4	0
Henderson, Ryan, Vero Beach	11	5	.688	3.88	39	6	0	0	10	2	104.1	98	453	53	45	1	6	1	5	58	3	86	9	2
Henriquez, Oscar, Kissimmee	3	4	.429	5.04	20	0	0	0	7	1	44.2	40	207	29	25	2	2	2	6	30	0	36	3	0
Heredia, Felix, Brevard County*	6	4	.600	3.57	34	8	0	0	3	1	95.2	101	420	52	38	6	0	7	4	36	1	76	6	1
Hernandez, Jeremy, Brevard County	0	0	.000	2.35	4	2	0	0	0	0	7.2	5	29	2	2	0	0	0	0	2	0	5	2	0
Herrmann, Gary, Clearwater*	7	2	.778	3.60	42	3	0	0	10	3	70.0	64	295	31	28	3	3	3	0	28	1	56	1	0
Hiljus, Erik, St. Lucie	8	4	.667	2.99	17	17	0	0	0	0	111.1	85	453	46	37	4	6	5	3	50	2	98	10	6
Hill, Shawn, Daytona	5	3	.625	3.68	37	0	0	0	22	3	58.2	48	241	31	24	6	1	0	2	17	3	71	0	1
Hingle, Larry, Kissimmee*	0	0	.000	18.78	10	0	0	0	6	0	7.2	15	48	18	16	1	0	0	0	11	0	2	1	0
Hmielewski, Chris, W. Palm Beach*	1	3	.250	3.59	36	2	0	0	15	0	57.2	57	259	31	23	4	3	2	2	28	4	41	6	0
Hollinger, Adrian, Brevard County	0	2	.000	5.40	11	4	0	0	4	2	25.0	26	118	17	15	1	0	1	1	18	0	18	1	1
Hollis, Ronald, Vero Beach	2	5	.286	2.47	43	0	0	0	13	0	73.0	55	306	22	20	1	3	2	2	38	6	56	1	0
Housely, Adam, Lakeland	0	1	.000	6.00	19	1	0	0	3	1	30.0	39	141	23	20	0	1	0	3	11	0	23	1	2
Howard, Chris, Sarasota*	0	2	.000	5.23	6	5	0	0	0	0	10.1	10	45	6	6	1	1	2	0	4	0	7	1	3
Hubbard, Mark, Tampa*	4	3	.571	1.84	13	11	1	0	0	0	68.1	52	269	22	14	2	1	2	4	21	0	40	2	0
Huffman, Jeff, Sarasota	4	4	.500	4.58	15	11	0	0	1	0	76.2	72	335	43	39	3	3	1	4	36	1	55	8	1
Humphrey, Rich, Kissimmee	3	1	.750	1.96	46	0	0	0	39	14	55.0	45	233	16	12	1	5	2	3	20	0	33	2	1
Hunter, Rich, Clearwater	6	0	1.000	2.93	9	9	0	0	0	0	58.1	62	242	23	19	3	3	2	5	7	0	46	3	3
Hurst, William, Brevard County	1	4	.200	3.02	39	4	0	0	29	12	50.2	33	228	20	17	1	3	1	8	41	4	35	4	0
Jacobsen, Joe, Vero Beach	1	3	.250	3.67	47	0	0	0	44	32	49.0	42	215	22	20	2	5	2	2	23	2	54	10	1
Janzen, Marty, Tampa	10	3	.769	2.61	18	18	1	0	0	0	113.2	102	461	38	33	4	1	2	4	30	0	104	3	4
Jersild, Aaron, Dunedin*	2	6	.250	4.81	22	3	0	0	10	1	48.2	54	219	30	26	1	2	2	6	17	0	39	2	5
Jerzembeck, Michael, Tampa	0	1	.000	9.00	2	0	0	0	0	0	3.0	5	17	4	3	1	0	0	0	2	0	1	1	0
Johnson, Jonathan, Charlotte	1	5	.167	2.70	8	7	1	0	1	0	43.1	34	178	14	13	2	2	0	1	16	0	25	3	3
Jordan, Jason, Lakeland	1	3	.250	5.95	4	4	0	0	0	0	19.2	32	94	20	13	1	0	4	1	7	0	8	1	0
Kamieniecki, Scott, Tampa	1	0	1.000	1.80	1	1	0	0	0	0	5.0	6	22	2	1	0	0	0	0	1	0	2	1	0
Kell, Rob, Charlotte*	1	0	1.000	3.05	11	0	0	0	5	1	20.2	16	93	9	7	1	0	0	2	15	0	21	2	0
Kendrena, Ken, W. Palm Beach	3	3	.500	3.04	16	0	0	0	5	2	23.2	23	102	9	8	2	1	1	0	11	2	19	3	0
Kenny, Sean, St. Lucie	4	9	.308	2.70	46	0	0	0	15	2	56.2	51	229	22	17	1	4	1	3	15	1	26	2	2
Kerley, Collin, West Palm Beach	1	3	.250	3.95	19	0	0	0	8	0	27.1	28	119	16	12	0	0	0	1	11	1	17	2	0
Keusch, Joseph, Charlotte	9	4	.692	1.82	40	0	0	0	27	8	64.1	56	257	19	13	3	2	3	2	14	2	36	3	1
Khoury, Tony, Daytona	2	0	1.000	4.05	7	0	0	0	5	0	6.2	10	30	3	3	1	0	1	0	2	0	4	0	0
King, Curtis, St. Petersburg	7	8	.467	2.58	28	21	3	0	1	0	136.0	117	567	49	39	3	4	2	11	49	2	65	6	0
Knieper, Aaron, W. Palm Beach	2	4	.333	3.95	32	6	0	0	10	0	70.2	67	317	38	31	0	3	4	4	46	2	48	12	4
Kostich, Bill, Lakeland*	1	0	1.000	0.00	4	0	0	0	2	0	6.0	2	21	0	0	0	1	0	1	2	0	2	0	0
Kozeniewski, Blaise, Tampa	3	1	.750	0.95	11	0	0	0	0	0	19.0	11	69	3	2	1	0	0	0	3	0	17	1	1
Kramer, Dan, Sarasota*	2	0	1.000	6.14	21	0	0	0	4	0	14.2	18	69	12	10	1	0	2	0	7	0	13	1	2
Lankford, Frank, Tampa	4	6	.400	2.59	55	0	0	0	36	15	73.0	64	305	29	21	0	7	0	2	22	6	58	1	0
Largusa, Levon, Dunedin*	4	4	.500	4.10	16	7	1	1	1	0	59.1	68	268	32	27	2	1	1	0	28	0	37	1	0
Larson, Toby, St. Lucie	6	7	.462	2.52	19	18	3	1	0	0	121.2	122	508	44	34	5	4	0	7	30	2	82	7	1
Leahy, Pat, Brevard County	4	4	.500	3.88	11	11	0	0	0	0	46.1	41	200	29	20	6	1	2	5	22	1	43	2	0
Lehoisky, Russ, Fort Myers	0	5	.000	3.29	26	0	0	0	10	0	52.0	45	240	25	19	0	7	2	4	38	3	29	5	0
Leshnock, Donnie, Tampa	10	6	.625	3.08	28	10	0	0	2	2	87.2	78	378	41	30	2	1	5	4	45	0	67	7	2
Lewis, Michael, Brevard County*	4	5	.444	2.32	43	0	0	0	8	1	62.0	48	251	22	16	5	8	0	2	22	3	44	1	0
Lima, Jose, Lakeland	3	1	.750	2.57	4	4	0	0	0	0	21.0	23	86	11	6	2	0	0	0	0	0	20	1	0
Linebarger, Keith, Fort Myers	7	4	.636	2.10	29	10	1	1	12	4	103.0	74	418	30	24	6	3	2	9	35	1	73	4	0
Liquet, Wilton, Vero Beach	0	0	.000	4.05	4	1	0	0	1	0	6.2	5	29	3	3	0	1	0	0	5	0	3	1	0
Loewer, Carlton, Clearwater	7	5	.583	3.30	20	20	1	0	0	0	114.2	124	502	59	42	6	3	5	5	36	0	83	7	3
Loiz, Niuman, Kissimmee	0	8	.000	5.56	13	13	0	0	0	0	56.2	71	271	48	35	2	2	3	2	30	0	33	10	0
Lopez, Johann, Kissimmee	5	5	.500	2.61	18	12	0	0	3	1	69.0	55	283	30	20	3	1	2	3	25	0	67	5	3
Lopez, Orlando, Daytona*	7	2	.778	2.68	44	0	0	0	15	8	80.2	75	342	30	24	6	5	1	3	32	1	76	6	2
Lovingier, Kevin, St. Petersburg*	1	0	1.000	1.66	22	0	0	0	6	0	21.2	9	82	4	4	0	1	1	2	10	1	14	1	0
Lukasiewicz, Mark, Dunedin*	3	6	.333	5.60	31	13	0	0	11	1	88.1	80	383	62	55	13	1	2	7	42	0	71	7	0
Maldonado, Jay, Fort Myers	0	1	.000	6.23	5	0	0	0	1	0	4.1	6	23	4	3	0	0	0	0	4	1	4	1	1
Mallory, Trevor, Dunedin	0	5	.000	5.01	37	3	0	0	10	0	70.0	80	326	53	39	4	1	3	3	41	0	46	7	0
Malloy, Charles, Sarasota	6	4	.600	3.54	16	12	2	1	2	0	86.1	72	354	38	34	5	2	2	0	39	2	51	6	1

Pitcher, Team	W	L	Pct.	ERA	G	GS	CG	ShO	GF	Sv.	IP	H	TBF	R	ER	HR	SH	SF	HB	BB	IBB	SO	WP	Bk.
Manning, David, Charlotte	9	5	.643	3.50	26	20	0	0	2	0	128.2	127	545	56	50	7	3	3	3	46	0	66	0	5
Markham, Andy, W. Palm Beach	7	11	.389	3.94	24	23	1	0	0	0	121.0	129	532	62	53	8	4	6	9	44	1	58	4	1
Marquardt, Scott, St. Petersburg	3	4	.429	3.78	9	9	0	0	0	0	52.1	55	222	24	22	4	1	1	3	15	0	39	4	4
Marquez, Ihosvany, Sarasota	1	1	.500	3.00	12	0	0	0	4	1	15.0	10	70	6	5	1	1	0	2	13	1	18	0	0
Marrero, Kenny, Lakeland	1	4	.200	3.72	37	0	0	0	18	5	55.2	54	239	28	23	5	1	2	0	28	1	46	6	1
Martinez, Cesar, Sarasota*	6	6	.500	3.75	34	10	0	0	2	0	110.1	108	477	62	46	6	3	2	4	40	2	61	9	1
Martinez, Ramiro, Charlotte*	2	2	.500	4.08	14	6	0	0	6	2	46.1	45	192	21	21	3	3	3	0	15	0	30	3	0
Matranga, Jeff, St. Petersburg	3	4	.429	2.74	53	0	0	0	17	3	65.2	49	272	27	20	2	3	3	9	20	3	71	2	0
Matulevich, Jeff, St. Petersburg	1	5	.167	2.76	51	0	0	0	48	30	58.2	50	253	20	18	3	2	1	0	30	3	61	4	0
McCommon, Jason, W. Palm Bch.	7	11	.389	3.75	26	26	3	1	0	0	156.0	153	650	75	65	13	7	6	10	38	0	94	6	7
McDill, Allen, St. Lucie*	4	2	.667	1.64	7	7	1	1	0	0	49.1	36	190	11	9	2	1	0	1	13	0	28	3	0
McLain, Mike, Lakeland	1	1	.500	3.58	21	0	0	0	11	1	27.2	33	118	13	11	3	1	0	1	7	0	27	3	0
McLaughlin, Denis, Sarasota	3	2	.600	3.26	54	0	0	0	30	6	66.1	57	305	31	24	3	4	1	7	46	7	79	5	3
Medina, Rafael, Tampa	2	2	.500	2.37	6	6	0	0	0	0	30.1	29	131	12	8	0	0	0	1	12	0	25	0	2
Meinershagen, Adam, Dunedin	5	9	.357	3.75	21	13	1	0	2	0	98.1	115	430	59	41	13	3	8	6	23	1	53	3	0
Mercado, Hector, Kissimmee*	6	8	.429	3.46	19	17	2	0	0	0	104.0	96	433	50	40	2	2	3	3	37	0	75	4	1
Merrill, Ethan, Sarasota*	11	7	.611	3.78	27	25	1	1	2	0	150.0	155	672	86	63	11	3	5	11	67	2	78	7	0
Metheney, Nelson, Clearwater	5	5	.500	3.00	59	0	0	0	11	1	72.0	65	310	32	24	2	7	4	0	25	3	38	3	2
Meyer, David, Tampa*	3	4	.429	6.52	12	11	0	0	0	0	58.0	84	281	49	42	3	2	3	4	29	0	29	6	4
Militello, Sam, Brevard County	0	1	.000	7.84	4	4	0	0	0	0	10.1	7	58	10	9	1	0	0	1	20	0	18	6	0
Miller, Shawn, Fort Myers	4	4	.500	1.90	30	2	0	0	16	4	71.0	68	288	16	15	4	2	2	2	13	1	35	2	0
Mix, Greg, Brevard County	3	1	.750	3.94	5	4	1	0	0	0	29.2	27	119	13	13	1	0	0	3	10	0	17	1	1
Moody, Eric, Charlotte	5	5	.500	2.75	13	13	2	2	0	0	88.1	84	353	30	27	2	3	1	5	13	0	57	0	0
Moody, Ritchie, Charlotte*	0	1	.000	6.23	1	1	0	0	0	0	4.1	3	22	3	3	0	1	0	0	8	0	0	0	0
Moraga, David, W. Palm Beach*	1	1	.500	3.94	3	3	0	0	0	0	16.0	20	75	7	7	0	0	0	0	10	0	10	0	0
Morris, Matt, St. Petersburg	3	2	.600	2.38	6	6	1	1	0	0	34.0	22	134	16	9	1	2	0	0	11	0	31	0	2
Morse, Paul, Fort Myers	3	1	.750	3.82	35	0	0	0	29	15	61.1	57	247	30	26	3	1	4	3	12	0	56	4	1
Mysel, David, Lakeland	1	1	.500	5.83	20	0	0	0	8	2	29.1	36	141	22	19	3	3	0	3	14	0	32	2	0
Newell, Brandon, St. Lucie	2	2	.500	2.96	39	0	0	0	16	3	48.2	42	211	18	16	1	5	2	3	29	2	39	4	0
Norman, Scott, Lakeland	7	7	.500	4.07	22	21	3	0	0	0	128.1	141	571	86	58	4	2	9	6	38	1	63	4	2
Nunez, Clemente, Brevard County	12	6	.667	2.48	19	19	4	2	0	0	123.1	99	490	48	34	3	2	2	5	22	1	79	3	5
Nye, Ryan, Clearwater	12	7	.632	3.40	27	27	5	1	0	0	167.0	164	681	71	63	8	5	5	6	33	1	116	4	3
O'Brien, Brian, Fort Myers*	0	3	.000	2.88	24	0	0	0	17	0	34.1	31	147	20	11	2	2	1	0	15	1	20	4	0
O'Malley, Paul, Kissimmee	8	10	.444	3.61	27	27	0	0	0	0	147.0	148	661	86	59	7	3	3	18	62	0	80	13	2
Oropesa, Eddie, Vero Beach*	3	1	.750	3.81	19	1	0	0	7	1	28.1	25	120	12	12	0	1	2	3	10	0	23	4	2
Pack, Steve, St. Lucie	0	0	.000	4.82	5	0	0	0	2	0	9.1	15	48	6	5	0	1	0	1	1	0	6	0	0
Paluk, Jeff, Vero Beach	1	0	1.000	6.75	2	0	0	0	0	0	4.0	5	19	3	3	0	0	0	0	2	0	4	0	0
Parra, Julio, Vero Beach	7	3	.700	2.85	22	1	0	0	12	0	41.0	39	176	21	13	2	1	2	1	20	1	36	4	1
Pena, Juan, Sarasota	1	1	.500	4.91	2	2	0	0	0	0	7.1	8	35	4	4	0	0	0	2	3	0	5	1	1
Perkins, Ron, Clearwater	1	1	.500	2.84	6	0	0	0	3	0	6.1	6	30	3	2	1	0	0	1	5	0	3	1	0
Perpetuo, Nelson, Charlotte*	0	0	.000	7.71	5	0	0	0	1	0	7.0	5	33	7	6	0	1	0	1	5	0	7	0	0
Petcka, Joe, St. Lucie	1	1	.500	5.98	30	1	0	0	12	0	46.2	39	213	35	31	1	2	0	3	35	0	28	7	0
Petersen, Matt, Daytona	2	1	.667	4.15	3	3	0	0	0	0	17.1	13	66	8	8	2	0	1	0	3	0	13	0	0
Peterson, Dean, Sarasota	1	3	.250	6.75	4	4	0	0	0	0	17.1	25	90	17	13	2	1	1	3	10	0	15	1	0
Pettit, Doug, Brevard County	2	5	.286	2.83	27	0	0	0	14	4	35.0	37	158	18	11	3	2	3	0	13	4	22	1	0
Phelps, Tommy, W. Palm Beach*	0	2	.000	16.20	2	2	0	0	0	0	5.0	10	33	10	9	0	0	0	0	11	0	5	2	0
Pincavitch, Kevin, Vero Beach	10	7	.588	1.66	32	13	2	1	5	2	124.2	83	504	37	23	7	5	1	5	48	0	103	12	1
Pisciotta, Scott, W. Palm Beach	5	4	.556	2.52	53	0	0	0	29	2	60.2	55	271	26	17	1	1	4	0	36	2	38	11	0
Pollard, Damon, W. Palm Beach	4	3	.571	3.35	28	0	0	0	6	1	51.0	38	208	21	19	0	1	4	2	26	0	43	3	0
Powell, John, Charlotte	4	1	.800	3.00	19	2	0	0	9	2	48.0	44	201	18	16	2	2	2	3	13	1	47	1	1
Querecuto, Juan, Dunedin	0	0	.000	0.00	1	0	0	0	1	0	2.0	1	9	0	0	0	0	0	0	1	0	2	0	0
Raggio, Brady, St. Petersburg	2	3	.400	3.80	20	3	0	0	4	0	47.1	43	195	24	20	2	3	1	1	13	2	35	2	1
Rama, Shelby, Clearwater	0	0	.000	4.32	4	0	0	0	1	0	8.1	12	36	4	4	0	0	0	0	1	0	2	1	0
Ramos, Edgar, Kissimmee	4	0	1.000	0.41	4	4	0	0	0	0	22.0	11	80	4	1	1	0	0	0	1	0	16	0	0
Rathbun, Jason, Tampa	1	0	1.000	4.05	10	5	0	0	3	0	26.2	27	118	17	12	2	1	0	2	10	0	14	2	0
Redman, Mark, Fort Myers*	2	1	.667	2.76	8	5	0	0	0	0	32.2	28	134	13	10	4	1	2	1	13	0	26	2	0
Reed, Jason, Vero Beach*	0	0	.000	3.42	21	0	0	0	9	0	23.2	18	102	9	9	3	0	0	1	11	1	17	0	0
Resz, Greg, Tampa	0	1	.000	3.38	12	0	0	0	3	1	13.1	10	61	9	5	0	0	0	1	9	2	16	3	0
Reyes, Dennis, Vero Beach*	1	0	1.000	1.80	3	2	0	0	0	0	10.0	8	43	2	2	0	1	0	0	6	0	9	0	1
Reyes, Jose, Charlotte	1	3	.250	4.40	30	2	0	0	11	3	61.1	67	274	38	30	7	0	3	4	22	0	41	5	0
Ricken, Ray, Tampa	3	4	.429	2.15	11	11	1	0	0	0	75.1	47	291	25	18	3	2	1	1	27	0	58	1	2
Rios, Dan, Tampa	0	4	.000	2.00	57	0	0	0	52	24	67.1	67	296	24	15	1	5	2	8	20	4	72	2	0
Rodriguez, Chris, Daytona	1	0	1.000	5.91	5	0	0	0	1	0	10.2	14	46	7	7	2	0	0	2	2	0	6	0	0
Rodriguez, Salvador, Tampa	0	1	.000	11.05	6	0	0	0	1	0	7.1	13	40	10	9	1	0	0	1	4	0	7	1	0
Rojano, Rafael, Tampa	0	2	.000	6.23	3	0	0	0	0	0	4.1	4	19	3	3	0	1	0	0	2	1	1	0	0
Roman, Dan, Charlotte*	2	2	.500	7.71	7	5	0	0	1	0	25.2	30	126	22	22	2	1	2	6	19	1	21	2	2
Romano, Michael, Dunedin	11	7	.611	4.13	28	26	1	1	1	0	150.1	141	654	79	69	15	4	3	11	75	0	102	5	3
Root, Derek, Kissimmee*	0	0	.000	4.50	5	0	0	0	1	0	6.0	10	29	3	3	0	0	0	0	2	0	3	0	0
Roque, Rafael, St. Lucie*	6	9	.400	3.56	24	24	2	1	0	0	136.2	114	582	65	54	7	2	4	4	72	1	81	11	4
Rosengren, John, Lakeland*	3	3	.500	3.99	13	8	0	0	1	0	56.1	46	253	33	25	6	2	2	7	36	0	35	2	0
Rushworth, Jim, W. Palm Beach	1	0	1.000	3.65	10	0	0	0	4	1	12.1	11	54	5	5	0	1	1	1	6	0	9	0	0
Ryan, Jason, Daytona	11	5	.688	3.48	26	26	0	0	0	0	134.2	128	579	61	52	10	3	2	9	54	0	98	13	1
Sacharko, Mark, Kissimmee	0	1	.000	6.59	6	1	0	0	2	0	13.2	16	68	10	10	0	0	2	2	11	0	6	2	0
Salazar, Mike, Lakeland*	7	3	.700	3.19	42	3	0	0	18	5	87.1	86	371	37	31	4	4	1	6	21	1	52	2	1
Sampson, Benj, Fort Myers*	11	9	.550	3.49	28	27	3	2	1	0	160.0	148	664	71	62	11	8	8	4	52	0	95	5	0
Sanchez, Victor, Kissimmee	0	0	.000	3.00	3	0	0	0	3	0	3.0	2	14	1	1	0	0	0	0	3	0	1	0	0
Santana, Julio, Charlotte	0	3	.000	3.73	5	5	1	0	0	0	31.1	32	136	16	13	1	1	1	0	16	0	27	7	2
Santiago, Sandi, Tampa	3	2	.600	3.90	34	3	0	0	12	0	57.2	54	251	28	25	1	1	3	0	29	1	55	6	0
Santos, Henry, Lakeland*	5	6	.455	4.24	35	10	0	0	7	0	97.2	111	434	59	46	3	5	4	6	40	0	80	10	0
Sauerbeck, Scott, St. Lucie*	0	1	.000	2.03	20	1	0	0	4	0	26.2	26	116	10	6	0	0	2	0	14	1	25	2	2
Saunders, Tony, Brevard County*	6	5	.545	3.04	13	13	0	0	0	0	71.0	60	275	29	24	6	1	4	7	15	0	54	3	0
Schlomann, Brett, Tampa	2	0	1.000	1.64	2	2	0	0	0	0	11.0	10	44	6	2	2	0	0	0	0	0	5	0	0
Schneider, Tom, W. Palm Beach*	0	1	.000	10.80	4	0	0	0	1	0	3.1	8	21	5	4	0	0	0	1	2	0	3	0	0

Pitcher, Team	W	L	Pct.	ERA	G	GS	CG	ShO	GF	Sv.	IP	H	TBF	R	ER	HR	SH	SF	HB	BB	IBB	SO	WP	Bk.
Seip, Rod, Charlotte	1	2	.333	2.00	6	4	0	0	1	0	27.0	26	116	9	6	1	0	2	1	6	1	23	1	0
Sele, Aaron, Sarasota	0	0	.000	0.00	2	2	0	0	0	0	7.0	6	27	0	0	0	0	0	0	1	0	8	0	0
Serna, Joe, Lakeland	0	1	.000	2.00	5	0	0	0	3	1	9.0	10	44	4	2	1	2	0	1	5	2	3	1	2
Shoemaker, Stephen, Tampa	0	1	.000	1.08	3	2	0	0	0	0	16.2	9	73	5	2	1	2	1	0	13	0	12	2	0
Shrum, Dennis, Kissimmee	7	6	.538	3.24	38	0	0	0	15	5	91.2	96	408	44	33	7	5	1	5	28	0	69	5	5
Sikes, Ken, Vero Beach	3	4	.429	5.06	14	12	0	0	1	0	64.0	64	291	44	36	4	0	2	2	36	0	50	4	1
Siler, Jeff, Lakeland*	2	2	.500	2.28	27	0	0	0	10	1	27.2	21	100	9	7	2	2	0	0	7	1	26	0	1
Sinacori, Chris, Dunedin	0	1	.000	6.75	12	0	0	0	11	2	12.0	13	53	9	9	1	0	0	3	4	1	11	1	0
Sinclair, Steve, Dunedin*	5	3	.625	2.59	46	0	0	0	18	2	73.0	69	297	26	21	4	1	1	3	17	1	52	2	3
Smith, Dan, Charlotte	5	1	.833	2.95	9	9	1	1	0	0	58.0	53	242	23	19	4	1	2	3	16	0	34	1	0
Smith, Eric, Clearwater	0	0	.000	0.00	8	0	0	0	7	4	8.0	3	27	0	0	0	0	0	0	1	0	7	0	0
Smith, Keilan, Dunedin	11	6	.647	4.11	26	24	1	0	1	0	149.0	164	663	83	68	11	6	2	15	53	1	85	16	3
Southard, Scott, Brevard County	0	0	.000	0.00	1	0	0	0	1	0	1.0	0	3	0	0	0	0	0	0	0	0	1	0	0
Spring, Josh, Dunedin	1	0	1.000	1.05	18	0	0	0	6	2	25.2	16	110	6	3	1	1	0	1	17	1	23	3	0
Standish, Scott, Tampa	0	0	.000	2.57	4	2	0	0	0	0	14.0	10	55	5	4	1	0	1	0	4	0	10	1	0
Stanifer, Robert, Brevard County	3	6	.333	4.14	18	13	0	0	0	0	82.2	97	360	47	38	4	4	5	7	15	0	45	2	0
Steinert, Robert, Dunedin	3	4	.429	4.70	17	11	0	0	1	0	74.2	82	329	48	39	4	4	4	3	29	0	41	6	4
Steinke, Brock, Kissimmee	0	3	.000	6.61	8	5	0	0	0	0	32.2	48	160	28	24	0	0	4	1	16	0	15	5	1
Stentz, Brent, Lakeland	0	0	.000	0.00	2	0	0	0	1	0	2.0	0	6	0	0	0	0	0	0	0	0	4	0	0
Stephenson, Brian, Daytona	10	9	.526	3.96	26	26	0	0	0	0	150.0	145	640	79	66	7	6	3	7	58	2	109	14	2
Stevenson, Jason, Daytona	2	0	1.000	2.95	8	0	0	0	3	1	18.1	11	71	6	6	0	1	0	1	6	0	15	1	0
Stewart, Chris, St. Petersburg	0	1	.000	5.35	30	0	0	0	7	0	33.2	29	150	22	20	2	2	2	1	25	1	36	2	1
Swan, Tyrone, Clearwater	2	3	.400	3.40	37	0	0	0	10	0	47.2	50	208	25	18	5	2	2	1	19	1	46	6	0
Tatar, Jason, Fort Myers	4	5	.444	2.61	21	15	0	0	4	1	82.2	64	339	33	24	3	0	4	2	36	0	60	3	2
Telgheder, Jim, Sarasota	0	3	.000	6.48	22	0	0	0	5	0	25.0	30	122	20	18	3	2	0	2	15	2	24	4	1
Tewksbury, Bob, Charlotte	1	0	1.000	0.00	1	1	0	0	0	0	6.0	3	22	0	0	0	0	0	0	0	0	4	0	0
Thompson, Justin, Lakeland*	2	1	.667	4.88	6	6	0	0	0	0	24.0	30	107	13	13	1	0	2	2	8	0	20	0	0
Thornton, Paul, Brevard County	4	5	.444	3.27	42	1	0	0	27	4	71.2	66	311	34	26	5	5	1	8	27	2	56	3	0
Tidwell, Jason, Brevard County	0	0	.000	0.00	4	1	0	0	0	0	7.0	5	31	3	0	0	0	0	0	3	0	3	0	0
Toney, Mike, Dunedin	1	2	.333	8.03	12	0	0	0	8	3	12.1	19	67	14	11	0	1	1	1	13	1	6	2	0
Tucker, Julien, Kissimmee	2	11	.154	5.00	19	15	0	0	0	0	68.1	86	327	61	38	3	1	6	5	27	0	28	5	3
Turrentine, Rich, St. Lucie	0	3	.000	6.05	4	4	0	0	0	0	19.1	17	92	14	13	3	1	0	2	17	0	14	3	0
Tuttle, Dave, Lakeland	1	4	.200	2.90	6	4	1	0	1	0	31.0	31	132	11	10	1	0	3	2	12	0	28	1	0
Twiggs, Greg, Daytona*	8	3	.727	1.41	18	13	1	0	1	0	89.1	64	355	30	14	3	1	1	5	28	0	80	4	0
Urbina, Dan, Vero Beach	5	7	.417	4.32	18	16	0	0	0	0	91.2	90	412	56	44	4	0	5	3	52	0	68	13	4
Urbina, Ugueth, W. Palm Beach	1	0	1.000	0.00	2	2	0	0	0	0	9.0	4	30	0	0	0	0	0	1	1	0	11	0	0
Valley, Jason, Clearwater	0	0	.000	12.46	4	0	0	0	0	0	4.1	9	23	6	6	0	1	0	0	4	0	4	1	0
Vandemark, John, Clearwater*	1	2	.333	5.67	24	0	0	0	6	0	27.0	24	127	21	17	4	1	1	0	21	1	18	2	1
Viola, Frank, Dunedin*	0	1	.000	3.97	3	3	0	0	0	0	11.1	12	53	9	5	2	0	1	1	3	0	8	0	0
Wagner, Bret, St. Petersburg*	5	4	.556	2.12	17	17	1	0	0	0	93.1	77	373	36	22	3	3	2	2	28	0	59	4	0
Walker, Wade, Daytona	8	6	.571	2.53	25	24	2	1	0	0	135.0	113	541	50	38	5	3	2	2	36	0	117	8	1
Walter, Michael, Kissimmee	4	3	.571	5.55	41	0	0	0	21	0	71.1	78	338	58	44	4	5	9	10	42	1	42	9	2
Ward, Bryan, Brevard County*	5	1	.833	2.88	11	11	0	0	0	0	72.0	68	296	27	23	5	4	0	2	17	0	65	1	1
Ward, Duane, Dunedin	0	1	.000	6.23	3	2	0	0	0	0	4.1	4	19	3	3	1	1	0	2	1	0	4	0	1
Waring, Jim, Kissimmee	2	1	.667	1.78	5	5	1	0	0	0	30.1	23	120	10	6	1	1	1	3	11	0	16	4	1
Watts, Brandon, Vero Beach*	5	3	.625	4.04	13	8	0	0	1	0	49.0	46	215	29	22	5	0	2	1	22	0	42	4	1
Weathers, Dave, Brevard County	0	0	.000	0.00	1	1	0	0	0	0	4.0	4	15	0	0	0	0	0	0	1	0	3	0	0
Welch, Mike, St. Lucie	4	4	.500	5.40	44	6	0	0	33	15	70.0	96	322	50	42	7	4	3	6	18	4	51	4	0
Wendell, Turk, Daytona	0	0	.000	1.17	4	2	0	0	0	0	7.2	5	30	2	1	0	1	0	0	1	0	8	1	0
Westbrook, Destry, Kissimmee	0	1	.000	10.07	10	0	0	0	2	1	19.2	34	106	24	22	2	1	0	0	13	1	22	2	0
Whiteman, Greg, Lakeland*	1	2	.333	6.05	4	4	0	0	0	0	19.1	18	87	16	13	0	0	2	0	15	0	20	1	1
Whitten, Michael, Brevard County*	1	4	.200	3.96	22	0	0	0	9	1	38.2	47	170	21	17	2	1	3	2	9	1	25	2	0
Williams, Matt, Kissimmee*	4	6	.400	4.63	19	18	2	0	0	0	101.0	115	446	60	52	7	5	3	2	44	1	71	5	1
Winslett, Dax, V.B.-Day.	12	6	.667	2.78	26	25	0	0	0	0	152.0	148	627	59	47	11	4	2	2	39	0	111	13	2
Witasick, Jay, St. Petersburg	7	7	.500	2.74	18	18	1	1	0	0	105.0	80	425	39	32	4	1	4	0	36	1	109	5	1
Wright, Howard, Kissimmee	1	0	1.000	3.60	2	0	0	0	0	0	5.0	1	21	3	2	0	0	0	0	4	0	3	0	0
Yan, Esteban, West Palm Beach	6	8	.429	3.07	24	21	1	0	1	1	137.2	139	580	63	47	3	7	5	10	33	0	89	8	3
Yocum, David, Vero Beach*	2	1	.667	2.96	8	7	0	0	0	0	27.1	22	116	12	9	2	3	2	0	12	0	20	3	1
Young, Anthony, Daytona	0	0	.000	5.63	6	1	0	0	3	0	8.0	5	36	5	5	0	0	0	0	4	0	3	0	0

COMBINATION SHUTOUTS: **Brevard County (12)**—Ward-Hurst 2, Carl-Lewis-Bowen-Hurst, Ehler-Heredia-Davis-Lewis-Hurst, Ehler-Lewis, Hollinger-Lewis-Carl-Andersen, Leahy-Heredia-Hurst, Nunez-Lewis, Nunez-Whitten, Saunders-Pettit, Saunders-Pettit-Hurst, Stanifer-Ehler-Pettit. **Charlotte (4)**—Davis-Buckels, Moody-Keusch-Buckles, Roman-Manning-Buckles, Seip-Buckels. **Clearwater (8)**—Beech-Swan-Foster, Costa-Herrmann-Franek, Dodd-Metheney-Agostinelli, Fiore-Metheney-Swan, Hunter-Agostinelli-Heflin, Loewer-Herrmann-Metheney-Agostinelli, Nye-Heflin-Perkins, Nye-Metheney-Heflin. **Daytona (12)**—Box-Connolly-Hart, Box-Stevenson, Gonzalez-Dreyer, Gonzalez-Lopez-Hart, Ryan-Rodriguez-Hart, Stephenson-Young-Hart, Twiggs-Hill, Walker-Gonzalez, Walker-Lopez, Walker-Lopez-Hart, Winslett-DeVries-Dreyer, Winslett-Lopez. **Dunedin (3)**—Carpenter-Sinclair, Largusa-Adkins, Smith-Harris-Sinacori. **Fort Myers (7)**—Bowers-Linebarger, Linebarger-DeBrino, Sampson-DeBrino-Morse, Sampson-Maldonado-Biehl, Tatar-Caridad-Linebarger, Tatar-DeBrino, Tatar-O'Brien-DeBrino. **Kissimmee (7)**—Gallaher-Lopez 2, Lopez-Dault, Mercado-Hartnett, Mercado-Shrum-Humphrey, Ramos-Shrum-Dault, Tucker-Wright-Shrum. **Lakeland (6)**—Borkowski-Stentz-Gaillard, Drumright-Gaillard, Gaspar-Salazar, Gaspar-Salazar-Housely-Marrero, Lima-Aldred, Thompson-Santos. **St. Lucie (7)**—Engle-Bullock-Welch, Engle-Kenny-Welch, Larsen-Kenny-Welch, McDill-Newell-Arffa, McDill-Petcka-Kenny, Roque-Bullock, Roque-Newell-Kenny. **St. Petersburg (10)**—Aybar-Lovingier-Matranga-Matulevich, Carpenter-Grasser, Croushore-Lovingier-Matranga, Croushore-King-Blake-Garcia, Croushore-Matranga-Matulevich, Detmers-Garcia, Detmers-Lovingier-Matulevich, Detmers-Stewart-Grasser-Matranga, King-Matranga-Matulevich, Wagner-Lovingier-Matulevich. **Sarasota (6)**—Barkley-Bogott-McLaughlin-Bennett, Cederblad-Bennett, Cederblad-Kramer-Telgheder-Martinez, Howard-Merrill, Malloy-Bogott-Bennett, Peterson-Bennett. **Tampa (13)**—Drews-Lankford 2, Janzen-Rios 2, Drews-Rios, Drews-Santiago-Cindrich, Hubbard-Rodriguez-Lankford, Hubbard-Kozeniewski-Santiago, Janzen-Rodriguez-Rios, Leshnock-Corn-Rios, Medina-Lankford-Resz-Santiago, Rathbun-Rios, Santiago-Berry-Lankford-Rios. **Vero Beach (5)**—Duran-Hollis-Jacobsen, Duran-Parra-Henderson-Jacobsen, Pincavitch-Jacobsen, Urbina-Hollis-Jacobsen, Watts-Aquino. **West Palm Beach (6)**—Yan-Benz 2, DaSilva-Benz-Pisciotta, Markham-Pollard-Pisciotta, McCommon-Benz, Urbina-Yan.

NO-HIT GAMES: Moody, Charlotte, defeated Sarasota, 11-0, April 20; Nunez, Brevard County, defeated West Palm Beach, 2-0, May 28; Roque, St. Lucie, defeated Dunedin, 6-1, June 28; Duran-Hollis-Jacobsen, Vero Beach, defeated West Palm Beach, 3-0 (second game), June 28.

PITCHERS WITH TWO OR MORE TEAMS

Pitcher, Team	W	L	Pct.	ERA	G	GS	CG	ShO	GF	Sv.	IP	H	TBF	R	ER	HR	SH	SF	HB	BB	IBB	SO	WP	Bk.
Gordon, Mike, Tampa	4	6	.400	3.04	21	21	1	0	0	0	124.1	111	521	54	42	6	3	1	4	49	0	96	9	2
Gordon, Mike, Dunedin	1	2	.333	5.89	7	6	0	0	0	0	36.2	44	179	32	24	6	2	0	3	24	0	36	2	0
Winslett, Dax, Vero Beach	6	4	.600	3.18	14	13	0	0	0	0	85.0	87	358	35	30	7	4	1	1	21	0	59	6	2
Winslett, Dax, Daytona	6	2	.750	2.28	12	12	0	0	0	0	67.0	61	269	24	17	4	0	1	1	18	0	52	7	0

1995 FIELDING

TEAM

Team	Pct.	G	PO	A	E	TC	DP	PB
Fort Myers	.974	131	3408	1382	129	4919	135	9
St. Petersburg	.971	131	3364	1219	138	4721	89	14
St. Lucie	.971	135	3485	1504	151	5140	137	18
Daytona	.969	135	3519	1384	158	5061	120	11
Charlotte	.969	133	3463	1404	158	5025	109	19
Tampa	.967	136	3563	1497	170	5230	106	24
Clearwater	.967	138	3605	1425	169	5199	102	21
Vero Beach	.967	133	3411	1415	165	4991	102	25
Brevard County	.967	135	3574	1628	179	5381	148	22
Lakeland	.966	135	3470	1522	177	5169	117	18
W. Palm Beach	.963	136	3439	1446	186	5071	110	20
Dunedin	.963	138	3600	1482	194	5276	122	24
Sarasota	.961	134	3459	1475	198	5132	124	38
Kissimmee	.955	136	3551	1520	240	5311	119	32

TRIPLE PLAY: Daytona.

INDIVIDUAL

FIRST BASEMEN

NOTE: All caps denotes fielding-percentage leader based on 69 games for catchers, 92 for all other non-pitchers and 138 innings for pitchers. *Throws lefthanded.

Player, Team	Pct.	G	PO	A	E	TC	DP
Abad, Andy, Sarasota*	.978	12	84	6	2	92	10
Baugh, Gavin, Brevard County	1.000	1	2	0	0	2	0
Beyna, Terry, Kissimmee	1.000	4	40	2	0	42	2
Biltimier, Mike, Vero Beach*	.991	127	1025	103	10	1138	89
Blair, Brian, Charlotte*	.982	8	56	0	1	57	6
Bokemeier, Matt, Charlotte	.983	13	107	7	2	116	10
Boyd, Quincy, Vero Beach	.941	5	31	1	2	34	3
Braddy, Junior, Sarasota	1.000	1	6	0	0	6	0
Brown, Kevin, Charlotte	1.000	1	12	0	0	12	1
Cabrera, Alex, Daytona	.989	39	335	16	4	355	31
Caraballo, Gary, Fort Myers	1.000	1	5	0	0	5	2
Carey, Todd, Sarasota	1.000	12	93	11	0	104	10
Champion, Jim, Fort Myers*	.990	57	442	43	5	490	46
Clark, Kevin, Sarasota	.975	46	411	18	11	440	36
Cooper, Tim, Tampa	.989	32	255	16	3	274	13
Davila, Vic, Dunedin	1.000	1	1	0	0	1	0
DeBerry, Joe, Tampa*	.984	49	414	26	7	447	36
Duross, Gabe, Daytona*	.988	60	526	28	7	561	48
Ellis, Kevin, Daytona	1.000	5	7	2	0	9	1
Epperson, Chad, St. Lucie	.972	15	123	17	4	144	16
Everson, Darin, W. Palm Beach	.994	21	158	15	1	174	12
FREEMAN, Sean, Lakeland*	.993	118	980	89	7	1076	91
Froschauer, Trevor, Kissimmee	.980	64	549	47	12	608	52
Halemanu, Joshua, Kissimmee*	1.000	1	10	0	0	10	0
Held, Daniel, Clearwater	.990	132	1115	72	12	1199	87
Johnson, Jack, Daytona	1.000	2	6	2	0	8	0
Jones, Ryan, Dunedin	.977	119	1041	67	26	1134	90
Kingman, Brendan, Brev. County	1.000	3	16	2	0	18	0
Kingston, Mark, Daytona	.986	37	320	33	5	358	33
Koeyers, Ramsey, W. Palm Beach	1.000	1	6	1	0	7	1
Landaker, Dave, Kissimmee	.981	10	94	9	2	105	9
Loeb, Marc, Dunedin	1.000	1	1	0	0	1	1
Long, R.D., Tampa	1.000	1	17	0	0	17	0
Madsen, Dave, St. Petersburg	.996	55	415	33	2	450	34
Malone, Scott, Charlotte	.990	99	830	68	9	907	73
Marabella, Tony, W. Palm Beach	.988	19	157	7	2	166	13
Marine, Del, Lakeland	.979	15	84	8	2	94	4
McKeel, Walt, Sarasota	1.000	2	15	0	0	15	0
Melhuse, Adam, Dunedin	1.000	3	18	5	0	23	1
Mientkiewicz, Doug, Fort Myers	.994	24	160	12	1	173	22
Millar, Kevin, Brevard County	.991	125	1213	95	12	1320	134
Mitchell, Mike, Tampa	.993	57	518	47	4	569	43
Murphy, Jeffrey, St. Petersburg	1.000	1	9	1	0	10	0
Niethammer, Marc, W. Palm Bch.	.976	73	575	38	15	628	56
Ottavinia, Paul, W. Palm Beach*	.981	11	95	6	2	103	5
Patton, Greg, Sarasota	1.000	2	8	0	0	8	0
Querecuto, Juan, Dunedin	.983	21	161	12	3	176	18
Raifstanger, John, Sarasota	.991	49	435	20	4	459	41
Raleigh, Matt, W. Palm Beach	.989	20	172	12	2	186	14
Ramirez, Hiram, Sarasota	.989	18	174	7	2	183	16
Ramos, Eddie, Kissimmee	.996	29	264	10	1	275	22
Roberge, John, Vero Beach	1.000	1	10	2	0	12	1
Robinson, Dan, Brevard County	.989	13	86	4	1	91	5
Rodriguez, Adam, Lakeland	.981	13	91	10	2	103	7
Rupp, Brian, St. Petersburg	.990	59	463	27	5	495	31
Rupp, Chad, Fort Myers	.994	55	468	24	3	495	41
Sabo, Chris, St. Petersburg	1.000	10	58	6	0	64	5
Sanchez, Victor, Kissimmee	.968	37	284	21	10	315	24
Sauve, Erik, Charlotte	1.000	13	65	3	0	68	5
Schaaf, Rob, Vero Beach	1.000	2	20	0	0	20	0
Schmitz, Mike, Tampa	1.000	3	21	5	0	26	1
Sell, Donald, Vero Beach	1.000	3	25	1	0	26	1
Smith, Bubba, Fort Myers	1.000	8	34	1	0	35	5
Sowards, Ryan, Vero Beach	.909	4	9	1	1	11	0
Taylor, Mike, St. Petersburg*	.982	20	101	7	2	110	7
Torborg, Dale, St.L.-Tampa	1.000	6	29	1	0	30	2
Unrat, Chris, Charlotte	.978	12	83	8	2	93	6
Waco, David, Clearwater	1.000	8	63	2	0	65	8
Warner, Randy, St. Lucie	.988	104	894	70	12	976	97
Whatley, Gabe, Daytona	1.000	1	1	1	0	2	0
Whitehurst, Todd, St. Lucie	.988	20	152	7	2	161	11

TRIPLE PLAY: Cabrera.

FIRST BASEMEN WITH TWO OR MORE TEAMS

Player, Team	Pct.	G	PO	A	E	TC	DP
Torborg, Dale, St. Lucie	1.000	5	29	1	0	30	2
Torborg, Dale, Tampa	.000	1	0	0	0	0	0

SECOND BASEMEN

Player, Team	Pct.	G	PO	A	E	TC	DP
Almanzar, Richard, Lakeland	.984	36	92	92	3	187	16
Amador, Manuel, Clearwater	.955	47	90	124	10	224	26
Anderson, Cliff, Vero Beach	.965	97	149	234	14	397	45
Arano, Eloy, Lakeland	.949	17	27	47	4	78	9
Aybar, Ramon, Lakeland	1.000	3	3	4	0	7	0
Azuaje, Jesus, St. Lucie	.955	50	123	133	12	268	40
Basey, Marsalis, Kissimmee	.971	73	159	213	11	383	49
Baugh, Gavin, Brevard County	.813	3	7	6	3	16	1
Berg, David, Brevard County	1.000	7	22	25	0	47	8
Berry, Michael, W. Palm Beach	.975	10	20	19	1	40	3
Blum, Geoffrey, W. Palm Beach	.982	60	102	167	5	274	33
Bokemeier, Matt, Charlotte	1.000	10	15	32	0	47	2
Brito, Luis, Clearwater	1.000	3	9	8	0	17	2
Brunson, Matt, Lakeland	.953	30	63	78	7	148	14
Cabrera, Jolbert, W. Palm Beach	.967	14	22	37	2	61	2
Dalton, Dee, St. Petersburg	.934	22	30	27	4	61	4
Davila, Vic, Dunedin	.967	24	33	56	3	92	14
DeJesus, Malvin, Lakeland	.952	45	98	118	11	227	35
Diaz, Edwin, Charlotte	.968	110	213	277	16	506	67
Flores, Jose, Clearwater	.955	9	21	21	2	44	6
Forkerway, Trey, Daytona	.976	40	62	99	4	165	29
Foster, Jeff, West Palm Beach	.958	19	38	30	3	71	5
Gallone, Santy, Clearwater	.946	42	78	96	10	184	22
Garcia, Luis, Lakeland	.932	9	21	20	3	44	5
Hansen, Elston, Tampa	.947	42	65	97	9	171	19
Hastings, Lionel, Brevard County	.9767	118	251	378	15	644	93
Kelly, Pat, Tampa	1.000	3	8	14	0	22	3
Landaker, Dave, Kissimmee	.600	1	2	1	2	5	0
Lee, Manuel, St. Petersburg	1.000	1	0	2	0	2	0
Long, R.D., Tampa	.965	94	195	272	17	484	45
Marabella, Tony, W. Palm Beach	.857	2	5	1	1	7	1
Martin, Mike, Lakeland	.929	6	11	15	2	28	3
McCalmont, Jim, Fort Myers	.982	71	132	147	5	284	46
McEwing, Joe, St. Petersburg	.954	72	133	176	15	324	35
Miller, Ryan, St. Lucie	.950	6	5	14	1	20	1
Morris, Bobby, Daytona	.910	64	109	133	24	266	33
Mota, Santo, St. Petersburg	.948	43	69	77	8	154	15
Murphy, Pat, Sarasota	.992	22	65	57	1	123	16
Nava, Marlon, Fort Myers	.953	61	85	116	10	211	24
Nelson, Bry, Kissimmee	.972	6	14	21	1	36	8
Ortiz, Nick, Sarasota	1.000	1	0	1	0	1	0
PATZKE, Jeff, Dunedin	.9774	117	255	307	13	575	59
Perez, Richard, Daytona	.953	47	64	98	8	170	18
Pichardo, Sandy, St. Lucie	.969	79	177	223	13	413	52
Post, David, Vero Beach	.975	39	74	82	4	160	20
Raifstanger, John, Sarasota	.957	33	67	67	6	140	20
Raleigh, Matt, W. Palm Beach	.750	3	1	5	2	8	0
Renteria, David, Tampa	1.000	8	6	16	0	22	3
Sauve, Erik, Charlotte	1.000	12	21	23	0	44	5

Player, Team	Pct.	G	PO	A	E	TC	DP
Saylor, Jamie, Kissimmee	.971	57	89	149	7	245	31
Schaaf, Rob, Vero Beach	.972	11	10	25	1	36	5
Scolaro, Donnie, Kissimmee	.968	8	9	21	1	31	2
Sims, Wes, Charlotte	.875	2	4	3	1	8	0
Smith, Dave, Sarasota	.929	19	35	57	7	99	15
Sosa, Juan, Vero Beach	1.000	5	8	13	0	21	2
Southard, Scott, Brevard County	.934	15	24	33	4	61	9
Sowards, Ryan, Vero Beach	.500	1	0	1	1	2	0
Subero, Carlos, Charlotte	1.000	9	13	21	0	34	6
Tebbs, Nathan, Sarasota	.977	71	153	185	8	346	43
Ugueto, Jesus, St. Petersburg	1.000	4	8	5	0	13	1
Venezia, Danny, Fort Myers	.941	15	30	50	5	85	10
Vidro, Jose, West Palm Beach	.979	35	91	93	4	188	35
Waco, David, Clearwater	.982	47	86	128	4	218	20
Zuniga, David, St. Lucie	1.000	6	12	11	0	23	4

Player, Team	Pct.	G	PO	A	E	TC	DP
Sims, Wes, Charlotte	1.000	1	0	3	0	3	0
Smith, Bubba, Fort Myers	.950	6	6	13	1	20	2
Southard, Scott, Brevard County	.884	15	10	28	5	43	5
Sowards, Ryan, Vero Beach	.895	12	5	12	2	19	2
Stewart, Tom, Kissimmee	.857	7	5	7	2	14	1
Tebbs, Nathan, Sarasota	.889	16	6	26	4	36	5
Ugueto, Jesus, St. Petersburg	.857	10	3	3	1	7	0
Verduzco, Steve, Kissimmee	.750	2	2	1	1	4	0
Vidro, Jose, West Palm Beach	1.000	3	2	5	0	7	0
Waco, David, Clearwater	.667	4	4	4	4	12	0
Whatley, Gabe, Daytona	1.000	1	2	2	0	4	0
Whitehurst, Todd, St. Lucie	.915	39	26	82	10	118	7
Wooten, Shawn, Lakeland	.942	38	23	90	7	120	5
Wyrick, Chris, St. Petersburg	.917	13	11	22	3	36	2

THIRD BASEMEN

Player, Team	Pct.	G	PO	A	E	TC	DP
Alcantara, Israel, W. Palm Beach	.906	29	30	57	9	96	3
Almanzar, Richard, Lakeland	.818	4	3	6	2	11	1
Amador, Manuel, Clearwater	.875	6	2	5	1	8	0
Anderson, Cliff, Vero Beach	1.000	1	0	3	0	3	0
Arano, Eloy, Lakeland	.968	55	36	116	5	157	8
Azuaje, Jesus, St. Lucie	.970	26	12	52	2	66	6
Baugh, Gavin, Brevard County	.921	72	51	181	20	252	31
Bell, Mike, Charlotte	.914	126	91	280	35	406	19
Benbow, Lou, St. Lucie	1.000	2	1	1	0	2	0
Berg, David, Brevard County	.943	52	39	144	11	194	13
Berry, Michael, W. Palm Beach	.846	11	7	15	4	26	4
Beyna, Terry, Kissimmee	.833	3	1	4	1	6	1
Bierek, Kurt, Tampa	.916	122	85	219	28	332	17
Blum, Geoffrey, W. Palm Beach	.921	13	14	21	3	38	5
Bokemeier, Matt, Charlotte	.850	6	3	14	3	20	1
Brito, Luis, Clearwater	1.000	11	11	19	0	30	1
Brown, Shawn, Lakeland	.826	9	4	15	4	23	1
Browne, Jerry, Brevard County	.667	1	1	1	1	3	0
Cabrera, Jolbert, W. Palm Beach	.931	10	10	17	2	29	1
Caraballo, Gary, Fort Myers	.934	83	74	197	19	290	22
Carey, Todd, Sarasota	.800	6	3	13	4	20	5
Cooper, Tim, Tampa	.818	16	8	28	8	44	0
DALTON, Dee, St. Petersburg	.931	100	66	191	19	276	15
Davila, Vic, Dunedin	.897	12	9	17	3	29	0
Donato, Daniel, Tampa	1.000	1	2	1	0	3	1
Evans, Tom, Dunedin	.922	129	92	309	34	435	16
Flores, Jose, Clearwater	.927	30	18	71	7	96	2
Forkner, Tim, Kissimmee	.916	89	66	196	24	286	15
Foster, Jeff, W. Palm Beach	.917	15	12	43	5	60	0
Gallone, Santy, Clearwater	.946	15	7	28	2	37	2
Gross, Rafael, Vero Beach	.947	35	21	69	5	95	6
Hansen, Elston, Tampa	.000	1	0	0	1	1	0
Jackson, Gavin, Sarasota	1.000	1	1	2	0	3	0
Landaker, Dave, Kissimmee	.915	36	28	80	10	118	3
Lopez, Jose, St. Lucie	1.000	1	0	2	0	2	0
Madsen, Dave, St. Petersburg	.941	11	7	9	1	17	0
Marabella, Tony, W. Palm Beach	.938	31	36	54	6	96	6
Martinez, Dalvis, Lakeland	.872	38	16	79	14	109	6
McCalmont, Jim, Fort Myers	.889	13	6	26	4	36	2
Mota, Santo, St. Petersburg	1.000	1	0	1	0	1	0
Motes, Jeff, St. Lucie	.926	9	5	20	2	27	0
Murphy, Pat, Sarasota	.965	21	19	36	2	57	3
Nava, Lipso, Sarasota	.927	14	5	33	3	41	2
Nava, Marlon, Fort Myers	.932	35	30	66	7	103	7
Nelson, Bry, Kissimmee	1.000	6	3	7	0	10	0
O'Brien, Joe, Clearwater	.973	12	6	30	1	37	1
Orie, Kevin, Daytona	.916	106	80	204	26	310	20
Ortiz, Nick, Sarasota	.887	76	50	186	30	266	25
Otanez, Willis, Vero Beach	.925	89	59	186	20	265	18
Patton, Greg, Sarasota	1.000	1	1	2	0	3	0
Perez, Jhonny, Kissimmee	1.000	1	2	0	0	2	0
Perez, Richard, Daytona	.922	37	26	68	8	102	6
Petrulis, Paul, St. Lucie	.984	69	41	140	3	184	13
Querecuto, Juan, Dunedin	.750	2	1	2	1	4	0
Radmanovich, Ryan, Ft. Myers	.806	11	7	22	7	36	0
Raifstanger, John, Sarasota	.880	8	4	18	3	25	3
Raleigh, Matt, W. Palm Beach	.900	29	20	52	8	80	4
Renteria, David, Tampa	1.000	1	1	1	0	2	0
Rolen, Scott, Clearwater	.899	65	43	135	20	198	13
Rupp, Brian, St. Petersburg	.879	13	12	17	4	33	2
Sabo, Chris, St. Petersburg	.750	2	0	3	1	4	0
Sauve, Erik, Charlotte	.800	2	2	2	1	5	0
Scolaro, Donnie, Kissimmee	1.000	3	0	5	0	5	0

SHORTSTOPS

Player, Team	Pct.	G	PO	A	E	TC	DP
Amador, Manuel, Clearwater	.966	23	37	47	3	87	11
Anderson, Cliff, Vero Beach	.961	17	21	53	3	77	9
Angeli, Doug, Clearwater	.957	16	17	49	3	69	12
Arano, Eloy, Lakeland	.945	27	38	66	6	110	14
Azuaje, Jesus, St. Lucie	.959	16	24	46	3	73	11
Babin, Brady, Brevard County	.914	32	55	73	12	140	17
Benbow, Lou, St. Lucie	.886	10	14	25	5	44	3
Berg, David, Brevard County	.948	56	96	179	15	290	34
Berry, Michael, W. Palm Beach	1.000	1	0	1	0	1	0
Blum, Geoffrey, W. Palm Beach	.941	38	50	110	10	170	17
Bokemeier, Matt, Charlotte	.954	62	99	173	13	285	35
Brito, Luis, Clearwater	.939	96	117	266	25	408	46
Brunson, Matt, Lakeland	.900	15	22	50	8	80	14
Cabrera, Jolbert, W. Palm Beach	.934	80	116	240	25	381	38
Cabrera, Orlando, W. Palm Beach	.833	2	2	3	1	6	0
Carey, Todd, Sarasota	.938	3	5	10	1	16	0
Cromer, Brandon, Dunedin	.964	94	146	259	15	420	57
DeJesus, Malvin, Lakeland	.957	4	3	19	1	23	0
Flores, Jose, Clearwater	.943	10	15	35	3	53	4
Forkerway, Trey, Daytona	.935	30	26	61	6	93	10
Foster, Jeff, W. Palm Beach	.937	19	45	44	6	95	14
Frias, Hanley, Charlotte	.932	33	45	106	11	162	25
Garcia, Luis, Lakeland	.932	92	146	282	31	459	45
Gonzalez, Alex, Brevard County	.906	17	26	51	8	85	12
Jackson, Gavin, Sarasota	.956	94	121	331	21	473	47
Knowles, Eric, Tampa	.939	115	191	382	37	610	53
Landaker, Dave, Kissimmee	.857	4	4	8	2	14	0
Lee, Manuel, St. Petersburg	.833	5	2	8	2	12	0
Long, R.D., Tampa	.943	7	12	21	2	35	4
Matvey, Mike, St. Petersburg	.968	87	116	218	11	345	28
MAXWELL, Jason, Daytona	.969	116	181	325	16	522	65
Mercedes, Guillermo, Charlotte	.977	33	42	83	3	128	12
Metcalfe, Mike, Vero Beach	.919	120	153	301	40	494	50
Miller, Ryan, St. Lucie	.954	82	124	225	17	366	49
Mota, Santo, St. Petersburg	.805	10	16	17	8	41	5
Motes, Jeff, St. Lucie	1.000	3	3	2	0	5	0
Motte, James, Fort Myers	.955	116	155	336	23	514	70
Murphy, Pat, Sarasota	.889	1	1	7	1	9	1
Nava, Lipso, Sarasota	1.000	6	6	13	0	19	3
Nava, Marlon, Fort Myers	.953	22	29	53	4	86	10
Nelson, Bry, Kissimmee	.905	59	89	159	26	274	35
Ortiz, Nick, Sarasota	.938	13	17	28	3	48	6
Patton, Greg, Sarasota	.923	4	3	9	1	13	1
Patzke, Jeff, Dunedin	.932	13	19	22	3	44	5
Perez, Jhonny, Kissimmee	.901	33	47	116	18	181	20
Perez, Richard, Daytona	.500	1	0	1	1	2	1
Petrulis, Paul, St. Lucie	.959	33	46	95	6	147	20
Renteria, David, Tampa	.920	20	27	53	7	87	12
Saylor, Jamie, Kissimmee	.917	22	35	75	10	120	17
Scolaro, Donnie, Kissimmee	.804	9	14	23	9	46	4
Sims, Wes, Charlotte	.857	1	2	4	1	7	2
Smith, Dave, Sarasota	.818	2	2	7	2	11	0
Solano, Fausto, Dunedin	.932	38	75	116	14	205	32
Sosa, Juan, Vero Beach	.909	2	2	8	1	11	2
Southard, Scott, Brevard County	.927	39	57	120	14	191	21
Stewart, Tom, Kissimmee	.877	19	26	38	9	73	8
Subero, Carlos, Charlotte	.964	6	8	19	1	28	2
Tebbs, Nathan, Sarasota	.897	23	26	52	9	87	8
Ugueto, Jesus, St. Petersburg	.982	20	23	32	1	56	8
Vidro, Jose, West Palm Beach	1.000	6	8	12	0	20	1
Wyrick, Chris, St. Petersburg	.920	30	30	62	8	100	12
Zuniga, David, St. Lucie	1.000	4	2	7	0	9	1

TRIPLE PLAY: Forkerway.

OUTFIELDERS

Player, Team	Pct.	G	PO	A	E	TC	DP
Abad, Andy, Sarasota*	1.000	8	6	0	0	6	0
Adolfo, Carlos, W. Palm Beach	.939	22	29	2	2	33	0
Agbayani, Benny, St. Lucie	.950	19	37	1	2	40	0
Alcantara, Israel, W. Palm Beach	1.000	3	4	1	0	5	0
Arano, Eloy, Lakeland	1.000	2	1	0	0	1	0
Asencio, Alex, Vero Beach*	.982	58	101	10	2	113	2
Baker, Jason, Fort Myers*	.979	84	136	1	3	140	0
Basey, Marsalis, Kissimmee	.943	18	31	2	2	35	0
Bellum, Donnie, St. Petersburg	1.000	59	77	1	0	78	0
Berry, Michael, W. Palm Beach	1.000	1	1	1	0	2	0
Beyna, Terry, Kissimmee	1.000	3	3	1	0	4	0
Blair, Brian, Charlotte*	.981	49	96	5	2	103	0
Borel, Jamie, Lakeland	1.000	12	26	1	0	27	0
Braddy, Junior, Sarasota	.951	99	167	7	9	183	0
Brock, Tarrick, Lakeland*	.966	28	56	1	2	59	0
Brown, Armann, Fort Myers	.970	19	32	0	1	33	0
Brown, Ron, Brevard County	.989	112	163	12	2	177	2
Brown, Willie, Brevard County	1.000	49	87	3	0	90	0
Browne, Jerry, Brevard County	1.000	1	2	0	0	2	0
Burke, Alan, Clearwater	1.000	1	5	0	0	5	0
Campos, Jesus, W. Palm Beach	.960	96	196	19	9	224	4
Candelaria, Ben, Dunedin	.971	121	189	10	6	205	0
Champion, Jim, Fort Myers*	1.000	31	42	3	0	45	1
Chick, Bruce, W. Palm Beach	1.000	2	3	0	0	3	0
Christmon, Drew, Lakeland	.946	54	77	10	5	92	0
Collier, Dan, Sarasota	.825	24	32	1	7	40	0
Cooney, Kyle, Vero Beach	1.000	1	1	0	0	1	0
Cooper, Tim, Tampa	1.000	2	1	0	0	1	0
Costello, Brian, Clearwater	.965	99	212	7	8	227	0
Cradle, Cobi, St. Lucie*	.976	57	120	3	3	126	0
Cradle, Rickey, Dunedin	1.000	48	94	4	0	98	1
Davila, Vic, Dunedin	.929	12	13	0	1	14	0
Deares, Greg, St. Petersburg	1.000	17	24	2	0	26	0
DeLaCruz, Carlos, Lakeland	1.000	2	3	0	0	3	0
Delafield, Wil, Tampa	1.000	3	3	0	0	3	0
Diaz, Linardo, Clearwater	1.000	11	17	2	0	19	0
Dowler, Dee, Daytona	.996	109	243	9	1	253	4
Ellis, Kevin, Daytona	.927	69	98	4	8	110	0
Evans, Stan, Clearwater	.973	72	135	9	4	148	1
Facione, Chris, Lakeland	.990	105	195	6	2	203	0
Ferrier, Ross, St. Lucie	.971	44	64	3	2	69	1
Fick, Chris, St. Petersburg	.956	105	145	7	7	159	1
Gallone, Santy, Clearwater	1.000	4	9	0	0	9	0
Garcia, Osmel, St. Petersburg	.982	102	211	11	4	226	1
Gibbs, Kevin, Vero Beach	1.000	7	12	0	0	12	0
Grissom, Antonio, W. Palm Bch.	1.000	4	6	0	0	6	0
Halemanu, Joshua, Kissimmee*	1.000	2	3	0	0	3	0
Hare, Rich, Lakeland	.889	7	16	0	2	18	0
Hawkins, Kraig, Tampa	.991	111	224	9	2	235	0
Henry, Antoine, Sarasota	1.000	12	28	1	0	29	1
Hernaiz, Juan, Vero Beach	.964	46	78	2	3	83	0
Hunter, Torii, Fort Myers	.973	103	242	15	7	264	7
Johnson, J.J., Sarasota	.954	97	159	8	8	175	1
JONES, Ben, Fort Myers	1.000	103	221	10	0	231	3
Keister, Tripp, St. Lucie*	1.000	16	27	3	0	30	0
Kendall, Jeremey, Clearwater	.945	36	83	3	5	91	0
Kimsey, Keith, Lakeland	.986	49	68	2	1	71	1
Knauss, Tom, Fort Myers	.976	88	152	9	4	165	2
Landaker, Dave, Kissimmee	.976	44	75	5	2	82	0
Landry, Lonny, Lakeland	.972	19	35	0	1	36	0
Latham, Chris, Vero Beach	.949	59	125	5	7	137	0
Little, Mark, Charlotte	.966	96	274	8	10	292	1
Long, Justin, Brevard County	1.000	6	7	0	0	7	0
Lowery, Terrell, Charlotte	1.000	11	18	0	0	18	0
Macon, Leland, Charlotte	.958	107	217	11	10	238	3
Madsen, Dan, Daytona*	1.000	13	15	1	0	16	0
Magee, Wendell, Clearwater	.973	93	166	12	5	183	0
Majeski, Brian, Vero Beach	.971	58	99	3	3	105	0
Maness, Dwight, V.B.-St.L.	.992	52	121	7	1	129	1
Mangham, Rodney, Kissimmee*	.959	42	90	4	4	98	0
Marsh, Roy, Kissimmee	.971	112	257	10	8	275	1
Martinez, Ramon, Brevard County	.958	93	178	5	8	191	0
McEwing, Joe, St. Petersburg	1.000	2	6	0	0	6	0
McKinnon, Tom, St. Petersburg	.948	52	87	4	5	96	1
Mota, Santo, St. Petersburg	1.000	3	7	1	0	8	0
Moultrie, Pat, Dunedin*	.966	77	132	9	5	146	0
Murphy, Pat, Sarasota	1.000	2	6	0	0	6	0
Nelson, Bry, Kissimmee	1.000	20	38	1	0	39	0
Nelson, Charles, Vero Beach*	.971	76	96	3	3	102	0
Nixon, Trot, Sarasota*	.986	69	140	4	2	146	1
Northrup, Kevin, St. Lucie	1.000	14	24	1	0	25	0
Nuneviller, Tom, Clearwater	.900	8	8	1	1	10	0
Ottavinia, Paul, W. Palm Beach*	.972	100	170	5	5	180	0
Perez, Joe, Charlotte*	1.000	15	30	2	0	32	0
Peterson, Nate, Kissimmee	.949	46	71	4	4	79	0
Pichardo, Sandy, St. Lucie	.970	22	31	1	1	33	0
Pico, Brandon, Daytona*	.895	11	17	0	2	19	0
Porter, Bo, Daytona	.980	110	183	10	4	197	3
Post, David, Vero Beach	1.000	4	3	0	0	3	0
Raifstanger, John, Sarasota	1.000	10	5	0	0	5	0
Ramirez, Angel, Dunedin	.968	130	320	17	11	348	0
Reeves, Glen, Brevard County	.969	111	172	13	6	191	2
Rijo, Rafael, Charlotte	1.000	10	13	0	0	13	0
Roberge, John, Vero Beach	1.000	1	2	0	0	2	0
Roberts, David, Lakeland*	.985	31	61	3	1	65	0
Robinson, Dan, Brevard County	.964	51	75	6	3	84	0
Roche, Marlon, Kissimmee	.976	26	38	2	1	41	0
Rojas, Roberto, Lakeland*	1.000	4	6	0	0	6	0
Rupp, Brian, St. Petersburg	.967	19	28	1	1	30	0
Saffer, Jon, West Palm Beach	.976	77	118	3	3	124	1
Samuels, Scott, Daytona	.989	106	170	6	2	178	2
Sanchez, Omar, Dunedin	.970	34	59	6	2	67	2
Santucci, Steven, St. Petersburg	.984	96	184	6	3	193	3
Schaaf, Rob, Vero Beach	1.000	6	9	0	0	9	0
Scolaro, Donnie, Kissimmee	1.000	2	0	1	0	1	0
Sell, Donald, Vero Beach	.990	67	98	1	1	100	0
Sheffield, Tony, Sarasota*	.971	95	198	5	6	209	3
Shirley, Al, St. Lucie	1.000	56	123	1	0	124	0
Shores, Scott, Clearwater	.965	103	236	11	9	256	2
Shugars, Shawn, Charlotte*	.909	6	10	0	1	11	0
Smith, Sloan, Tampa	.982	124	206	11	4	221	2
Sowards, Ryan, Vero Beach	.957	17	22	0	1	23	0
Spencer, Shane, Tampa	.966	109	166	6	6	178	0
Stewart, Tom, Kissimmee	.959	29	44	3	2	49	0
Stovall, Darond, W. Palm Beach*	.990	114	283	13	3	299	3
Suplee, Ray, Tampa	.919	66	96	6	9	111	1
Tebbs, Nathan, Sarasota	1.000	2	1	0	0	1	0
Terrell, Matt, St. Lucie	.977	70	124	3	3	130	0
Trammell, Bubba, Lakeland	.973	113	176	7	5	188	0
Verduzco, Steve, Kissimmee	.963	94	147	9	6	162	1
Vessel, Andrew, Charlotte	.974	110	218	9	6	233	1
Warner, Randy, St. Lucie	.500	4	2	0	2	4	0
Whatley, Gabe, Daytona	1.000	10	5	2	0	7	0
White, Jimmy, Kissimmee	1.000	5	5	2	0	7	0
Wipf, Mark, St. Lucie	.969	114	237	11	8	256	4
Zambrano, Jose, Sarasota	.917	6	10	1	1	12	0

OUTFIELDERS WITH TWO OR MORE TEAMS

Player, Team	Pct.	G	PO	A	E	TC	DP
Maness, Dwight, Vero Beach	.991	43	106	6	1	113	0
Maness, Dwight, St. Lucie	1.000	9	15	1	0	16	1

CATCHERS

Player, Team	Pct.	G	PO	A	E	TC	DP	PB
Alvarado, Basilio, W. Palm Bch	.968	6	25	5	1	31	0	0
Borrero, Rikchy, Sarasota	.980	30	189	9	4	202	0	14
Boyd, Quincy, Vero Beach	.982	13	54	2	1	57	0	1
Brown, Kevin, Charlotte	.985	96	523	60	9	592	3	11
Castro, Ramon, Kissimmee	.967	34	184	18	7	209	0	3
Clark, Kevin, Sarasota	.979	30	167	18	4	189	0	10
Cooney, Kyle, Vero Beach	.982	59	394	52	8	454	3	18
Cossins, Tim, Charlotte	1.000	3	12	2	0	14	0	1
Crespo, Mike, Charlotte	1.000	19	87	12	0	99	0	3
Davenport, Jeff, Sarasota	.975	9	36	3	1	40	0	1
Diaz, Cesar, St. Lucie	.982	96	569	85	12	666	7	8
Driskell, Jeff, Lakeland	1.000	13	50	7	0	57	1	0
Epperson, Chad, St. Lucie	.981	17	81	24	2	107	0	4
Erdman, Brad, Daytona	1.000	5	35	3	0	38	0	0
Estalella, Bobby, Clearwater	.987	114	771	82	11	864	1	17
Everson, Darin, W. Palm Beach	.957	5	19	3	1	23	1	0
Fithian, Grant, Tampa	1.000	3	6	3	0	9	0	1
Fitzpatrick, Robert, W. Palm Bch.	.986	12	62	8	1	71	0	0
Froschauer, Trevor, Kissimmee	.964	33	162	28	7	197	3	21
Gousha, Sean, Daytona	1.000	5	24	2	0	26	0	1
Gyselman, Jeff, Clearwater	.993	26	112	22	1	135	0	4
Hammell, Al, St. Lucie	.989	34	145	27	2	174	3	6
Hilt, Scott, Fort Myers	.983	13	56	3	1	60	0	1
Horn, Jeff, Fort Myers	.989	65	424	40	5	469	5	3
Johnson, Jack, Daytona	1.000	2	17	1	0	18	0	0
Kingston, Mark, Daytona	1.000	1	1	1	0	2	0	0
Koeyers, Ramsey, W. Palm Beach	.980	63	362	38	8	408	2	9
Loeb, Marc, Dunedin	.988	40	225	22	3	250	0	7
Lombardi, John, Sarasota	1.000	7	26	8	0	34	0	0
Luzinski, Ryan, Vero Beach	.955	23	148	23	8	179	2	1
Madonna, Chris, St. Lucie	.667	2	2	0	1	3	0	0

Player, Team	Pct.	G	PO	A	E	TC	DP	PB
Marine, Del, Lakeland	.970	58	312	47	11	370	3	5
Marrero, Elieser, St. Petersburg	.984	81	574	52	10	636	6	5
McKeel, Walt, Sarasota	.977	56	326	51	9	386	2	10
Melhuse, Adam, Dunedin	.980	94	574	55	13	642	8	14
Meluskey, Mitch, Kissimmee	.980	75	443	40	10	493	3	5
Micucci, Mike, Daytona	1.000	22	92	4	0	96	0	1
Molina, Jose, Daytona	.987	82	501	91	8	600	4	7
Morales, Francisco, Day.-St.P.	.988	51	364	38	5	407	3	7
Motuzas, Jeff, Tampa	1.000	28	122	13	0	135	1	2
Murphy, Jeffrey, St. Petersburg	.996	40	241	31	1	273	5	4
Nihart, Tim, Fort Myers	1.000	4	21	3	0	24	0	0
Northeimer, Jamie, Clearwater	1.000	6	47	6	0	53	0	0
Pachot, John, W. Palm Beach	.984	60	310	60	6	376	1	11
Prater, Andrew, Brevard County	.975	73	344	46	10	400	3	7
Querecuto, Juan, Dunedin	1.000	14	70	11	0	81	0	3
Ramirez, Hiram, Sarasota	.989	14	81	10	1	92	1	2
Rodriguez, Adam, Lakeland	.983	15	104	9	2	115	1	1
Sanchez, Victor, Kissimmee	.943	9	43	7	3	53	1	3
SIMS, Michael, Brevard County	.9911	89	505	53	5	563	3	15
Snyder, Jared, Daytona	.968	18	86	5	3	94	1	0
Steed, David, Vero Beach	.987	52	345	39	5	389	0	5
Stricklin, Scott, Fort Myers	.990	65	352	54	4	410	7	5
Thompson, Billy, Lakeland	.973	66	447	52	14	513	3	12
Torres, Jaime, Tampa	.9905	105	741	95	8	844	4	19
Troilo, Jason, Tampa	1.000	1	5	0	0	5	0	1
Unrat, Chris, Charlotte	.965	33	179	16	7	202	0	4
Varriano, Mark, Sarasota	.952	7	20	0	1	21	0	1
Williams, Ed, Lakeland	1.000	1	4	1	0	5	0	0
Wilson, Tom, Tampa	1.000	13	85	7	0	92	0	1

CATCHERS WITH TWO OR MORE TEAMS

Player, Team	Pct.	G	PO	A	E	TC	DP	PB
Morales, Francisco, Daytona	.988	29	222	22	3	247	1	2
Morales, Francisco, St. P'burg	.988	22	142	16	2	160	2	5

PITCHERS

Player, Team	Pct.	G	PO	A	E	TC	DP
Adkins, Tim, Dunedin*	.900	45	2	7	1	10	1
Agostinelli, Peter, Clearwater*	.875	57	9	5	2	16	0
Albaladejo, Randy, Kissimmee	1.000	7	1	0	0	1	0
Aldred, Scott, Lakeland*	.955	13	3	18	1	22	0
Andersen, Mark, Brevard County	.833	20	3	2	1	6	1
Antoszek, Chris, Sarasota	.750	3	0	3	1	4	0
Arffa, Steve, St. Lucie*	.938	32	5	10	1	16	1
Ashworth, Kym, Vero Beach*	.950	24	8	30	2	40	1
Aybar, Manuel, St. Petersburg	1.000	9	6	5	0	11	0
Baine, David, Charlotte*	.857	21	1	5	1	7	0
Barkley, Brian, Sarasota*	.941	24	6	26	2	34	1
Beech, Matt, Clearwater*	.769	15	5	5	3	13	1
Belinda, Stan, Sarasota	1.000	1	0	1	0	1	0
Bennett, Shayne, Sarasota	.750	52	1	5	2	8	0
Benz, Jake, W. Palm Beach*	.941	44	2	14	1	17	1
Berlin, Mike, Lakeland	1.000	16	2	6	0	8	1
Berry, Jason, Tampa	.750	7	0	3	1	4	1
Biehl, Rod, Fort Myers*	1.000	12	1	2	0	3	0
Blake, Todd, St. Petersburg*	1.000	42	1	3	0	4	0
Bogott, Kurt, Sarasota*	.895	41	5	12	2	19	1
Borkowski, David, Lakeland	1.000	1	0	3	0	3	1
Bowen, Mitchel, Brevard County	.960	41	9	15	1	25	1
Bowen, Ryan, Brevard County	.500	3	1	0	1	2	0
Bowers, Shane, Fort Myers	1.000	23	6	23	0	29	2
Box, Shawn, Daytona	.933	25	10	18	2	30	0
Breitenstein, Keith, Kissimmee*	1.000	4	0	1	0	1	0
Brower, Jim, Charlotte	.946	27	11	24	2	37	3
Brown, Alvin, Lakeland	1.000	9	5	10	0	15	1
Buckles, Bucky, Charlotte	1.000	48	7	14	0	21	0
Bullock, Craig, St. Lucie	.944	40	1	16	1	18	3
Cain, Chance, St. Petersburg	1.000	7	1	2	0	3	0
Caridad, Ron, Fort Myers	1.000	17	4	8	0	12	0
Carl, Todd, Brevard County	.800	15	2	6	2	10	0
Carpenter, Brian, St. Petersburg	1.000	16	3	4	0	7	0
Carpenter, Chris, Dunedin	.771	15	10	17	8	35	3
Carrasco, Troy, Fort Myers*	.917	25	4	18	2	24	1
Cederblad, Brett, Sarasota	1.000	24	4	13	0	17	0
Challinor, John, Vero Beach	1.000	37	2	7	0	9	0
Cindrich, Jeff, Tampa	1.000	24	1	3	0	4	0
Clelland, Rick, W. Palm Beach	.833	35	2	3	1	6	0
Connolly, Matt, Daytona	.750	18	1	2	1	4	0
Corn, Chris, Tampa	1.000	4	0	1	0	1	0
Cosman, Jeff, St. Lucie	.889	15	11	13	3	27	2
Costa, Tony, Clearwater	.900	25	10	17	3	30	3
Croushore, Rick, St. Petersburg	.875	12	2	5	1	8	0
Culberson, Don, Daytona	.500	12	0	2	2	4	0
Cumberland, Chris, Tampa*	.875	5	1	6	1	8	0
DaSilva, Fernando, W. Palm Beach	.947	27	7	11	1	19	1
Dault, Donnie, Kissimmee	.967	41	9	20	1	30	0
Davis, Jeff, Charlotte	.971	26	13	21	1	35	2
DeBrino, Rob, Fort Myers	1.000	41	2	3	0	5	1
DeLaHoya, Javier, Brevard County	1.000	5	1	1	0	2	0
Delgado, Ernie, Brevard County	1.000	18	4	8	0	12	0
Detmers, Kris, St. Petersburg*	.960	25	1	23	1	25	0
DeVries, Andrew, Daytona*	1.000	21	4	7	0	11	0
Dodd, Robert, Clearwater*	.950	26	3	16	1	20	1
Dotel, Octavio, St. Lucie	1.000	3	0	1	0	1	0
Drews, Matthew, Tampa	.944	28	18	16	2	36	5
Dreyer, Darren, Daytona	1.000	29	5	8	0	13	0
Drumheller, Al, Tampa*	1.000	32	3	5	0	8	1
Drumright, Mike, Lakeland	1.000	5	2	3	0	5	1
Duran, Roberto, Vero Beach*	.875	23	2	5	1	8	0
Ehler, Daniel, Brevard County	.895	16	4	13	2	19	1
Emerson, Scott, Sarasota*	.615	16	1	7	5	13	0
Engle, Tom, St. Lucie	1.000	9	5	4	0	9	0
Fiore, Tony, Clearwater	.960	24	9	15	1	25	3
Forster, Scott, W. Palm Beach*	.829	26	6	28	7	41	1
Foster, Mark, Clearwater*	1.000	24	1	3	0	4	0
Franek, Tom, Clearwater	1.000	9	1	1	0	2	0
Fultz, Aaron, Fort Myers*	1.000	21	7	18	0	25	0
Gaillard, Eddy, Lakeland	1.000	43	3	4	0	7	1
Gallaher, Kevin, Kissimmee	.667	7	1	1	1	3	1
Gallone, Santy, Clearwater	1.000	1	0	1	0	1	0
Gandolph, Dave, Kissimmee*	.500	12	0	1	1	2	0
Garcia, Frank, St. Petersburg	1.000	16	0	1	0	1	0
Gardner, Scott, Lakeland	.750	5	0	3	1	4	1
Gaspar, Cade, Lakeland	1.000	23	10	13	0	23	0
Gonzalez, Geremis, Daytona	.800	19	3	5	2	10	0
Gordon, Mike, Tampa-Dun.	.880	28	14	30	6	50	0
Gorecki, Rick, Vero Beach	1.000	6	2	3	0	5	0
Granger, Greg, Lakeland	1.000	27	7	14	0	21	0
Grasser, Craig, St. Petersburg	1.000	26	1	2	0	3	0
Greene, Tommy, Clearwater	1.000	3	1	1	0	2	0
Grennan, Steve, St. Lucie*	1.000	9	0	2	0	2	0
Groot, Franz, Vero Beach	1.000	14	3	2	0	5	0
Guerra, Mark, St. Lucie	.953	23	14	27	2	43	5
Gunderson, Mike, Kissimmee	1.000	1	0	1	0	1	0
Halperin, Mike, Dunedin*	.946	14	6	29	2	37	0
Hammond, Chris, Brev. County*	1.000	1	0	2	0	2	0
Harris, D.J., Dunedin	.905	42	7	12	2	21	0
Harris, Greg, Fort Myers	1.000	3	1	2	0	3	0
Hart, Jason, Daytona	1.000	37	2	6	0	8	1
Hartgrove, Lyle, Sarasota	1.000	47	5	9	0	14	1
Hartmann, Pete, Charlotte*	.667	15	0	6	3	9	0
Hartnett, Bill, Kissimmee	.923	32	4	8	1	13	0
Hecker, Doug, Sarasota	1.000	10	0	3	0	3	0
Heflin, Bronson, Clearwater	.923	57	3	9	1	13	0
Heiserman, Rick, St. Petersburg	1.000	6	2	3	0	5	0
Henderson, Ryan, Vero Beach	.962	39	8	17	1	26	4
Henriquez, Oscar, Kissimmee	1.000	20	4	6	0	10	1
Heredia, Felix, Brevard County*	.950	34	3	16	1	20	2
Hernandez, Jeremy, Brev. County	1.000	4	1	0	0	1	0
Herrmann, Gary, Clearwater*	.929	42	4	9	1	14	2
Hiljus, Erik, St. Lucie	.889	17	5	11	2	18	0
Hill, Shawn, Daytona	.875	37	3	4	1	8	0
Hingle, Larry, Kissimmee*	1.000	10	1	2	0	3	1
Hmielewski, Chris, W. Palm Bch.*	.933	36	1	13	1	15	0
Hollinger, Adrian, Brevard County	1.000	11	2	4	0	6	1
Hollis, Ronald, Vero Beach	1.000	43	13	14	0	27	3
Housely, Adam, Lakeland	1.000	19	4	6	0	10	0
Howard, Chris, Sarasota*	1.000	6	0	4	0	4	0
Hubbard, Mark, Tampa*	.958	13	5	18	1	24	1
Huffman, Jeff, Sarasota	.952	15	9	11	1	21	1
Humphrey, Rich, Kissimmee	1.000	46	5	18	0	23	0
Hunter, Rich, Clearwater	1.000	9	2	7	0	9	1
Hurst, William, Brevard County	.857	39	3	9	2	14	1
Jacobsen, Joe, Vero Beach	.929	47	3	10	1	14	1
Janzen, Marty, Tampa	.857	18	6	6	2	14	0
Jersild, Aaron, Dunedin*	.636	22	0	7	4	11	1
Johnson, Jonathan, Charlotte	1.000	8	5	9	0	14	1
Jordan, Jason, Lakeland	1.000	4	1	2	0	3	0
Kamieniecki, Scott, Tampa	1.000	1	2	1	0	3	0
Kell, Rob, Charlotte*	1.000	11	2	2	0	4	0
Kendrena, Ken, W. Palm Beach	.900	16	4	5	1	10	0
Kenny, Sean, St. Lucie	.923	46	0	12	1	13	0
Kerley, Collin, W. Palm Beach	.875	19	2	5	1	8	1
Keusch, Joseph, Charlotte	1.000	40	7	9	0	16	1
King, Curtis, St. Petersburg	.936	28	17	27	3	47	5
Knieper, Aaron, W. Palm Beach	.889	32	2	14	2	18	1

Player, Team	Pct.	G	PO	A	E	TC	DP
Kostich, Bill, Lakeland*	1.000	4	0	2	0	2	0
Kozeniewski, Blaise, Tampa	1.000	11	0	1	0	1	0
Lankford, Frank, Tampa	1.000	55	7	11	0	18	1
Largusa, Levon, Dunedin*	1.000	16	2	5	0	7	0
Larson, Toby, St. Lucie	.929	19	13	13	2	28	0
Leahy, Pat, Brevard County	.933	11	8	6	1	15	1
Lehoisky, Russ, Fort Myers	.818	26	4	5	2	11	0
Leshnock, Donnie, Tampa	.813	28	3	10	3	16	1
Lewis, Michael, Brevard County*	1.000	43	5	11	0	16	0
Lima, Jose, Lakeland	1.000	4	2	1	0	3	0
Linebarger, Keith, Fort Myers	.947	29	10	8	1	19	0
Liquet, Wilton, Vero Beach	1.000	4	1	2	0	3	0
Loewer, Carlton, Clearwater	.778	20	2	5	2	9	0
Loiz, Niuman, Kissimmee	.889	13	4	4	1	9	1
Lopez, Johann, Kissimmee	1.000	18	6	5	0	11	1
Lopez, Orlando, Daytona*	.909	44	6	14	2	22	2
Lovingier, Kevin, St. Petersburg*	1.000	22	2	5	0	7	1
Lukasiewicz, Mark, Dunedin*	.800	31	4	8	3	15	0
Mallory, Trevor, Dunedin	1.000	37	2	6	0	8	1
Malloy, Charles, Sarasota	1.000	16	4	6	0	10	1
Manning, David, Charlotte	1.000	26	7	18	0	25	3
Markham, Andy, W. Palm Beach	.913	24	6	15	2	23	0
Marquardt, Scott, St. Petersburg	1.000	9	4	6	0	10	0
Marrero, Kenny, Lakeland	.857	37	1	5	1	7	0
Martinez, Cesar, Sarasota*	1.000	34	2	12	0	14	0
Martinez, Ramiro, Charlotte*	1.000	14	3	6	0	9	0
Matranga, Jeff, St. Petersburg	.889	53	6	10	2	18	0
Matulevich, Jeff, St. Petersburg	1.000	51	2	5	0	7	0
McCommon, Jason, W. Palm Bch.	.974	26	8	30	1	39	2
McDill, Allen, St. Lucie*	.800	7	1	3	1	5	0
McLain, Mike, Lakeland	.667	21	1	3	2	6	0
McLaughlin, Denis, Sarasota	.800	54	3	9	3	15	0
Medina, Rafael, Tampa	.800	6	1	3	1	5	0
Meinershagen, Adam, Dunedin	.765	21	5	8	4	17	0
Mercado, Hector, Kissimmee*	.842	19	1	15	3	19	0
Merrill, Ethan, Sarasota*	.862	27	4	21	4	29	1
Metheney, Nelson, Clearwater	.813	59	2	11	3	16	0
Meyer, David, Tampa*	1.000	12	6	12	0	18	1
Militello, Sam, Brevard County	1.000	4	0	1	0	1	0
Miller, Shawn, Fort Myers	.818	30	5	4	2	11	1
Mix, Greg, Brevard County	.800	5	2	6	2	10	1
Moody, Eric, Charlotte	1.000	13	9	15	0	24	5
Moody, Ritchie, Charlotte*	1.000	1	0	3	0	3	0
Moraga, David, W. Palm Beach*	1.000	3	0	2	0	2	0
Morris, Matt, St. Petersburg	1.000	6	3	3	0	6	0
Morse, Paul, Fort Myers	1.000	35	10	8	0	18	1
Mysel, David, Lakeland	1.000	20	2	3	0	5	0
Newell, Brandon, St. Lucie	1.000	39	3	15	0	18	2
Norman, Scott, Lakeland	.810	22	8	9	4	21	1
Nunez, Clemente, Brevard County	.773	19	6	11	5	22	0
Nye, Ryan, Clearwater	1.000	27	10	15	0	25	1
O'Brien, Brian, Fort Myers*	.833	24	4	6	2	12	0
O'Malley, Paul, Kissimmee	.864	27	16	22	6	44	0
Oropesa, Eddie, Vero Beach*	1.000	19	6	5	0	11	0
Pack, Steve, St. Lucie	1.000	5	1	2	0	3	0
Paluk, Jeff, Vero Beach	1.000	2	0	2	0	2	0
Parra, Julio, Vero Beach	.750	22	3	3	2	8	3
Perkins, Ron, Clearwater	1.000	6	0	1	0	1	0
Perpetuo, Nelson, Charlotte*	.000	5	0	0	1	1	0
Petcka, Joe, St. Lucie	.909	30	3	7	1	11	0
Petersen, Matt, Daytona	1.000	3	0	2	0	2	0
Peterson, Dean, Sarasota	1.000	4	2	2	0	4	0
Pettit, Doug, Brevard County	1.000	27	4	4	0	8	1
Phelps, Tommy, W. Palm Beach*	1.000	2	0	1	0	1	0
Pincavitch, Kevin, Vero Beach	.844	32	8	19	5	32	1
Pisciotta, Scott, W. Palm Beach	.727	53	4	4	3	11	0
Pollard, Damon, W. Palm Beach	.923	28	4	8	1	13	2
Powell, John, Charlotte	1.000	19	2	1	0	3	0
Raggio, Brady, St. Petersburg	1.000	20	4	7	0	11	0
Rama, Shelby, Clearwater	1.000	4	1	1	0	2	0
Ramos, Edgar, Kissimmee	1.000	4	0	2	0	2	0
Rathbun, Jason, Tampa	.857	10	3	3	1	7	0
Redman, Mark, Fort Myers*	.875	8	2	5	1	8	0
Reed, Jason, Vero Beach*	1.000	21	0	4	0	4	0
Resz, Greg, Tampa	1.000	12	0	1	0	1	0
Reyes, Dennis, Vero Beach*	1.000	3	2	2	0	4	0
Reyes, Jose, Charlotte	.846	30	2	9	2	13	0
Ricken, Ray, Tampa	.933	11	2	12	1	15	0
Rios, Dan, Tampa	.933	57	5	9	1	15	2

Player, Team	Pct.	G	PO	A	E	TC	DP
Rodriguez, Chris, Daytona	1.000	5	0	2	0	2	1
Rodriguez, Salvador, Tampa	1.000	6	1	0	0	1	0
Rojano, Rafael, Tampa	1.000	3	1	1	0	2	0
Roman, Dan, Charlotte*	.833	7	1	4	1	6	0
Romano, Michael, Dunedin	.872	28	11	23	5	39	1
Root, Derek, Kissimmee*	.500	5	0	1	1	2	0
Roque, Rafael, St. Lucie*	.840	24	4	17	4	25	0
Rosengren, John, Lakeland*	.923	13	2	10	1	13	0
Rushworth, Jim, W. Palm Beach	1.000	10	0	3	0	3	0
Ryan, Jason, Daytona	.879	26	7	22	4	33	0
Sacharko, Mark, Kissimmee	1.000	6	2	1	0	3	0
Salazar, Mike, Lakeland*	.900	42	6	12	2	20	0
Sampson, Benj, Fort Myers*	1.000	28	6	17	0	23	1
Sanchez, Victor, Kissimmee	1.000	3	0	1	0	1	0
Santana, Julio, Charlotte	1.000	5	2	0	0	2	0
Santiago, Sandi, Tampa	1.000	34	6	2	0	8	0
Santos, Henry, Lakeland*	1.000	35	2	8	0	10	0
Sauerbeck, Scott, St. Lucie*	1.000	20	0	3	0	3	0
Saunders, Tony, Brevard County*	1.000	13	8	10	0	18	1
Schneider, Tom, W. Palm Beach*	1.000	4	0	1	0	1	0
Seip, Rod, Charlotte	.800	6	2	2	1	5	0
Serna, Joe, Lakeland	1.000	5	1	4	0	5	0
Shoemaker, Stephen, Tampa	1.000	3	0	2	0	2	0
Shrum, Dennis, Kissimmee	.867	38	5	21	4	30	0
Sikes, Ken, Vero Beach	.950	14	10	9	1	20	0
Siler, Jeff, Lakeland*	1.000	27	2	16	0	18	0
Sinacori, Chris, Dunedin	1.000	12	1	0	0	1	0
Sinclair, Steve, Dunedin*	.952	46	6	14	1	21	2
Smith, Dan, Charlotte	.833	9	0	5	1	6	0
Smith, Eric, Clearwater	1.000	8	0	1	0	1	0
Smith, Keilan, Dunedin	.926	26	7	18	2	27	1
Spring, Josh, Dunedin	.857	18	2	4	1	7	1
Stanifer, Robert, Brevard County	.920	18	7	16	2	25	2
Steinert, Robert, Dunedin	.786	17	2	9	3	14	2
Steinke, Brock, Kissimmee	1.000	8	2	1	0	3	0
Stephenson, Brian, Daytona	.882	26	4	11	2	17	1
Stevenson, Jason, Daytona	1.000	8	1	2	0	3	0
Stewart, Chris, St. Petersburg	1.000	30	1	3	0	4	0
Swan, Tyrone, Clearwater	1.000	37	0	2	0	2	0
Tatar, Jason, Fort Myers	1.000	21	1	11	0	12	3
Telgheder, Jim, Sarasota	1.000	22	0	3	0	3	1
Tewksbury, Bob, Charlotte	.500	1	1	0	1	2	0
Thompson, Justin, Lakeland*	1.000	6	2	6	0	8	0
Thornton, Paul, Brevard County	.957	42	7	15	1	23	0
Tidwell, Jason, Brevard County	1.000	4	2	0	0	2	0
Toney, Mike, Dunedin	1.000	12	2	1	0	3	0
Tucker, Julien, Kissimmee	.824	19	6	8	3	17	1
Turrentine, Rich, St. Lucie	1.000	4	2	4	0	6	0
Tuttle, Dave, Lakeland	1.000	6	6	6	0	12	2
Twiggs, Greg, Daytona*	.929	18	3	10	1	14	0
Urbina, Dan, Vero Beach	.852	18	6	17	4	27	0
Valley, Jason, Clearwater	1.000	4	1	0	0	1	0
Vandemark, John, Clearwater*	.857	24	1	5	1	7	0
Wagner, Bret, St. Petersburg*	.958	17	5	18	1	24	1
WALKER, Wade, Daytona	1.000	25	8	22	0	30	1
Walter, Michael, Kissimmee	.955	41	8	13	1	22	0
Ward, Bryan, Brevard County*	.769	11	0	10	3	13	0
Ward, Duane, Dunedin	1.000	3	1	1	0	2	0
Waring, Jim, Kissimmee	.889	5	3	5	1	9	0
Watts, Brandon, Vero Beach*	.857	13	1	5	1	7	1
Weathers, Dave, Brevard County	1.000	1	0	1	0	1	0
Welch, Mike, St. Lucie	.769	44	3	7	3	13	1
Wendell, Turk, Daytona	1.000	4	2	3	0	5	0
Westbrook, Destry, Kissimmee	.667	10	0	2	1	3	0
Whiteman, Greg, Lakeland*	1.000	4	0	5	0	5	0
Whitten, Michael, Bre. County*	1.000	22	3	3	0	6	0
Williams, Matt, Kissimmee*	1.000	19	3	11	0	14	0
Winslett, Dax, V.B.-Day.	.975	26	20	19	1	40	1
Witasick, Jay, St. Petersburg	.889	18	5	11	2	18	1
Yan, Esteban, W. Palm Beach	.854	24	9	26	6	41	0
Yocum, David, Vero Beach*	1.000	8	2	8	0	10	0
Young, Anthony, Daytona	1.000	6	2	1	0	3	0

PITCHERS WITH TWO OR MORE TEAMS

Player, Team	Pct.	G	PO	A	E	TC	DP
Gordon, Mike, Tampa	.897	21	12	23	4	39	0
Gordon, Mike, Dunedin	.818	7	2	7	2	11	0
Winslett, Dax, Vero Beach	1.000	14	16	10	0	26	1
Winslett, Dax, Daytona	.929	12	4	9	1	14	0

The following players did not have any fielding statistics at the positions indicated or appeared only as a designated hitter, pinch-hitter or pinch-runner: Aquino, p; Basey, 3b; Briscoe, p; D. Brito, 2b; B. Brown, p; Clemens, p; Dace, p; M. Davis, p; Dawson, dh; E. Diaz, ss; Donato, of; Epperson, 3b; S. Evans, p; Ferran, p; Forkerway, of; Gen. Gonzalez, p; R. Hartmann, p; Haws, ph; Jerzembeck, p; A. Johnson, of; Khoury, p; Kingman, c; Kramer, p; T. Lewis, ph; Maldonado, p; Malone, of; Marquez, p; McMullen, dh; Melhuse, of; Moore, dh; M. Nava, of; Pena, p; Querecuto, of, p; Raleigh, ss, c; A. Rodriguez, 3b; Sabo, of; Schlomann, p; Sele, p; Southard, p; Standish, p; Stentz, p; Strawberry, dh; Taylor, of; Twitty, dh; Unrat, ss; U. Urbina, p; Viola, p; Waco, of; Wright, p; Wyrick, 2b.

LEAGUE CHAMPIONS

Year	Team	Pct.
1919—	Sanford*	.605
	Orlando*	.703
1920—	Tampa	.654
	Tampa	.722
1921—	Orlando	.635
1922—	St. Petersburg	.503
	St. Petersburg	.618
1923—	Orlando	.667
	Orlando	.678
1924—	Lakeland	.695
	Lakeland	.683
1925—	St. Petersburg	.667
	Tampa†	.696
1926—	Sanford	.647
	Sanford	.623
1927—	Orlando†	.600
	Miami	.661
1928-35—	Did not operate.	
1936—	Gainesville	.542
	St. Augustine (4th)†	.492
1937—	Gainesville§	.616
1938—	Leesburg	.626
	Gainesville (2nd)‡	.615
1939—	Sanford§	.787
1940—	Daytona Beach	.619
	Orlando (4th)‡	.507
1941—	St. Augustine	.659
	Leesburg (4th)‡	.488
1942-45—	Did not operate.	
1946—	Orlando§	.681
1947—	St. Augustine	.625
	Gainesville (2nd)‡	.584
1948—	Orlando	.643
	Daytona Beach (2nd)‡	.616
1949—	Gainesville	.635
	St. Augustine (3rd)‡	.556
1950—	Orlando	.629
	DeLand (3rd)‡	.590
1951—	DeLand§	.643
1952—	DeLand∞	.704
	Palatka (3rd)‡	.569
1953—	Daytona Beach†	.657
	DeLand	.703
1954—	Jacksonville Beach	.629
	Lakeland†	.594
1955—	Orlando	.671
	Orlando	.643
1956—	Cocoa	.614
	Cocoa	.671
1957—	Palatka	.629
	Tampa†	.681
1958—	St. Petersburg	.732
	St. Petersburg	.681
1959—	Tampa	.591
	St. Petersburg†	.612
1960—	Lakeland	.731
	Palatka†	.614
1961—	Tampa†	.710
	Sarasota	.696
1962—	Sarasota	.689
	Fort Lauderdale†	.623
1963—	Sarasota	.645
	Sarasota	.667
1964—	Fort Lauderdale†	.629
	St. Petersburg	.594
1965—	Fort Lauderdale	.627
	Fort Lauderdale	.634
1966—	Leesburg†	.781
	St. Petersburg	.700
1967—	St. Petersburg▲	.691
	Orlando	.638
1968—	Miami	.613
	Orlando◆	.579
1969—	Miami■	.606
	Orlando	.606
1970—	Miami▼	.662
	St. Petersburg	.600
1971—	Miami▼	.667
	Daytona Beach	.586
1972—	Miami•	.562
	Daytona Beach	.606
1973—	St. Petersburg††	.575
	West Palm Beach	.580
1974—	West Palm Beach††	.598
	Fort Lauderdale	.626
1975—	St. Petersburg††	.652
	Miami	.581
1976—	Tampa	.559
	Lakeland††	.536
1977—	Lakeland††	.616
	West Palm Beach	.583
1978—	Lakeland	.565
	Miami§	.539
1979—	Fort Lauderdale	.643
	Winter Haven‡‡	.577
1980—	Daytona Beach	.628
	Fort Lauderdale††	.606
1981—	Fort Myers	.554
	Daytona Beach§§	.504
1982—	Fort Lauderdale§§	.621
	Tampa	.546
1983—	Daytona Beach	.634
	Vero Beach§§	.515
1984—	Tampa	.532
	Fort Lauderdale§§	.521
1985—	Fort Myers∞∞	.590
	Fort Lauderdale	.550
1986—	St. Petersburg∞∞	.647
	West Palm Beach	.593
1987—	Fort Lauderdale∞∞	.616
	Osceola	.576
1988—	Osceola	.606
	St. Lucie▲▲	.532
1989—	Port Charlotte▲▲	.540
	St. Petersburg	.540
1990—	West Palm Beach	.697
	Vero Beach▲▲	.585
1991—	Clearwater	.623
	West Palm Beach▲▲	.550
1992—	Sarasota	.639
	Lakeland◆◆	.530
1993—	St. Lucie	.600
	Clearwater§§	.556
1994—	Tampa§§	.606
	Brevard County	.561
1995—	Daytona§§	.644
	Fort Myers	.577

*Split-season playoff abandoned after each team won three games. †Won split-season playoff. ‡Won four-club playoff. §Won championship and four-club playoff. ∞Won both halves of split season. ▲League divided into Eastern and Western divisions with split season. St. Petersburg and Orlando won both halves of split season; St. Petersburg won playoff. ◆League divided into Eastern and Western divisions. Miami won regular-season pennant on basis of highest won-lost percentage. Orlando won four-club playoff involving first two teams in each division. ■League divided into Southern and Central divisions. Miami won playoff between division leaders. (NOTE—Pennant awarded to playoff winner in 1936.) ▼League divided into Eastern and Western divisions. Miami won regular-season pennant on basis of highest won-loss percentage, and also won four-club playoff involving first two teams in each division. •League divided into Eastern and Western divisions. Won four-club playoff involving first two teams in each division. ††League divided into Northern and Southern divisions. Won four-club playoff involving first two teams in each division. ‡‡League divided into Northern and Southern divisions. Same two clubs won both halves; won playoffs. §§Won split-season playoff. ∞∞League divided into Western, Central and Southern divisions. Won four-club playoff. ▲▲League divided into Eastern, Western and Central divisions; played split-season. Won six-club playoff. ◆◆League divided into Eastern, Western and Central divisions; played split-season. Won eight-club playoff.

MIDWEST LEAGUE

LEAGUE OFFICE

President
George H. Spelius
Address
P.O. Box 936
Beloit, WI 53512
Phone
608-364-1188

Teams (affiliation)
Beloit Snappers (Brewers)
Burlington Bees (Giants)
Cedar Rapids Kernels (Angels)
Clinton Lumber Kings (Padres)
Fort Wayne Wizards (Twins)
Kane County Cougars (Marlins)
Lansing Lugnuts (Royals)
Michigan Battle Cats (Red Sox)
Peoria Chiefs (Cardinals)
Quad City River Bandits (Astros)
Rockford Cubbies (Cubs)
South Bend Silver Hawks (White Sox)
West Michigan Whitecaps (A's)
Wisconsin Timber Rattlers (Mariners)

1995 FINAL STANDINGS

FIRST HALF

EASTERN DIVISION

Team	W	L	T	Pct.	GB
Michigan (Red Sox)	36	32	0	.529	....
West Michigan (Athletics)	35	33	0	.515	1
Fort Wayne (Twins)	35	35	0	.500	2
South Bend (White Sox)	31	36	0	.463	4½

CENTRAL DIVISION

Team	W	L	T	Pct.	GB
Beloit (Brewers)	45	25	0	.643	....
Kane County (Marlins)	39	31	0	.557	6
Rockford (Cubs)	34	36	0	.486	11
Wisconsin (Mariners)	30	38	0	.441	14

WESTERN DIVISION

Team	W	L	T	Pct.	GB
Quad City (Astros)	40	27	0	.597	....
Springfield (Royals)	38	31	0	.551	3
Cedar Rapids (Angels)	38	31	0	.551	3
Peoria (Cardinals)	32	35	0	.478	8
Burlington (Giants)	29	38	0	.433	11
Clinton (Padres)	17	51	0	.250	23½

SECOND HALF

EASTERN DIVISION

Team	W	L	T	Pct.	GB
Fort Wayne (Twins)	40	30	0	.571	....
Michigan (Red Sox)	39	31	0	.557	1
South Bend (White Sox)	35	33	0	.515	4
West Michigan (Athletics)	32	36	0	.471	7

CENTRAL DIVISION

Team	W	L	T	Pct.	GB
Beloit (Brewers)	43	26	0	.623	....
Rockford (Cubs)	41	29	0	.586	2½
Wisconsin (Mariners)	33	37	0	.471	10½
Kane County (Marlins)	30	38	0	.441	12½

WESTERN DIVISION

Team	W	L	T	Pct.	GB
Cedar Rapids (Angels)	38	31	0	.551	....
Quad City (Astros)	36	34	0	.514	2½
Clinton (Padres)	34	35	0	.493	4
Peoria (Cardinals)	30	37	0	.448	7
Springfield (Royals)	27	43	0	.386	11½
Burlington (Giants)	25	43	0	.368	12½

COMPOSITE

Team	Bel.	Q.C.	C.R.	Mch.	Rck.	F.W.	K.C.	W.M.	S.B.	Spr.	Peo.	Wis.	Bur.	Cln.	W	L	T	Pct.	GB
Beloit (Brewers)	...	4	5	7	11	6	11	6	6	5	3	14	5	5	88	51	0	.633	....
Quad City (Astros)	4	....	7	3	5	4	4	6	2	11	11	3	9	7	76	61	0	.555	11
Cedar Rapids (Angels)	3	9	....	3	4	5	6	3	3	6	10	3	11	10	76	62	0	.551	11½
Michigan (Red Sox)	1	3	5	....	3	10	6	7	14	5	5	7	3	6	75	63	0	.543	12½
Rockford (Cubs)	9	3	4	5	....	6	6	4	5	6	7	8	6	6	75	65	0	.536	13½
Fort Wayne (Twins)	2	4	3	10	2	....	5	14	10	7	4	4	3	7	75	65	0	.536	13½
Kane County (Marlins)	9	4	2	2	14	3	....	4	3	6	4	9	5	4	69	69	0	.500	18½
West Michigan (Athletics)	1	2	4	13	4	6	4	....	11	5	5	2	4	6	67	69	0	.493	19½
South Bend (White Sox)	2	6	5	6	3	10	3	8	....	2	4	5	7	5	66	69	0	.489	20
Springfield (Royals)	3	5	10	3	2	1	2	2	6	....	6	6	8	11	65	74	0	.468	23
Peoria (Cubs)	5	5	6	3	1	4	4	3	2	6	....	4	9	10	62	72	0	.463	23½
Wisconsin (Mariners)	6	4	5	1	12	4	11	6	3	2	3	....	2	4	63	75	0	.457	24½
Burlington (Giants)	3	3	4	5	2	5	3	4	1	8	5	6	....	5	54	81	0	.400	32
Clinton (Padres)	3	9	2	2	2	1	4	2	3	5	5	4	9	....	51	86	0	.372	36

Kane County's home games played in Geneva, Ill.

Michigan's home games played in Battle Creek, Mich.

Quad City's home games played in Davenport, Ia.

West Michigan's home games played in Comstock Park, Mich.

Major league affiliations in parentheses.

PLAYOFFS: Beloit defeated Rockford, two games to none; Michigan defeated Fort Wayne, two games to none; Quad City defeated Cedar Rapids, two games to one; West Michigan defeated Kane County, two games to one; Beloit defeated Quad City, two games to one; Michigan defeated West Michigan, two games to one; Beloit defeated Michigan, three games to none, to win league championship.

REGULAR-SEASON ATTENDANCE: Beloit, 60,816; Burlington, 69,412; Cedar Rapids, 135,840; Clinton, 50,126; Fort Wayne, 253,568; Kane County, 477,550; Michigan, 171,794; Peoria, 195,056; Quad City, 257,501; Rockford, 110,052; South Bend, 225,999; Springfield, 39,467; West Michigan, 507,989; Wisconsin, 209,159. Total, 2,764,329. Playoffs (19 games), 38,047. All-Star Game at West Michigan—8,483.

MANAGERS: Beloit, Dub Kilgo; Burlington, Mike Hart; Cedar Rapids, Tom Lawless; Clinton, Ed Romero; Fort Wayne, Dan Rohn; Kane County, Lynn Jones; Michigan, Demarlo Hale; Peoria, Roy Silver; Quad City, Jim Pankovits; Rockford, Steve Roadcap; South Bend, Fred Kendall; Springfield, Brian Poldberg; West Michigan, Jim Colborn; Wisconsin, Mike Goff.

ALL-STAR TEAM: 1B—Jesus Ibarra, Burlington; 2B—Luis Castillo, Kane County; 3B—Sean McNally, Springfield; SS—Donnie Sadler, Michigan; OF—Demond Smith, Cedar Rapids-West Michigan; Todd Dunwoody, Kane County; Ryan Jackson, Kane County; C—Jose Valentin, Fort Wayne; DH—Derek Hacopian, Beloit; LHP—Tony Mounce, Quad City; RHP—Jeff D'Amico, Beloit; LH Reliever—Jeff Keith, Burlington; RH Reliever—Travis Welch, Peoria; Most Valuable Player—Jesus Ibarra, Burlington; Prospect of the Year—Jose Valentin, Fort Wayne; Manager of the Year—Demarlo Hale, Michigan.

1995 BATTING

TEAM

Team	Avg.	G	TPA	AB	R	H	TB	2B	3B	HR	RBI	SH	SF	HP	BB	IBB	SO	SB	CS	GDP	LOB	ShO	Slg.	OBP
Quad City	.269	137	5036	4447	660	1195	1721	226	33	78	585	40	46	59	438	8	767	206	95	94	907	11	.387	.339
Kane County	.264	138	5240	4550	706	1201	1758	235	38	82	616	43	47	60	535	21	935	171	70	78	997	3	.386	.346
Cedar Rapids	.263	138	5180	4497	697	1184	1777	234	28	101	597	47	43	65	525	16	880	195	82	83	954	6	.395	.346
Beloit	.263	139	5227	4491	723	1181	1761	234	35	92	620	44	37	90	560	24	860	194	99	84	975	6	.392	.354
Rockford	.263	140	5368	4678	764	1229	1813	275	30	83	662	26	40	98	524	19	894	184	71	91	1015	7	.388	.347
Fort Wayne	.261	140	5397	4786	661	1251	1859	253	38	93	601	30	37	66	476	22	926	135	72	84	1034	8	.388	.334
South Bend	.257	135	5172	4507	630	1158	1628	198	40	64	563	41	55	57	511	18	857	143	72	80	983	4	.361	.336
Michigan	.252	138	5299	4601	684	1158	1780	233	34	107	607	38	39	86	534	16	1058	175	60	75	1004	3	.387	.338
Peoria	.249	134	4762	4271	534	1065	1473	175	37	53	454	50	29	52	356	16	738	131	72	94	839	7	.345	.313
Wisconsin	.245	138	5100	4444	593	1089	1546	230	31	55	529	60	48	89	452	24	926	166	59	81	962	8	.348	.324
Springfield	.245	139	5073	4503	638	1101	1670	217	41	90	563	39	38	68	425	15	980	187	59	92	900	6	.371	.317
Burlington	.240	135	4808	4255	569	1022	1563	166	18	113	497	37	24	61	429	8	960	103	46	98	879	7	.367	.317
Clinton	.234	137	4936	4316	521	1011	1343	188	18	36	451	39	31	38	510	13	910	160	72	75	951	18	.311	.318
West Michigan	.232	136	5104	4304	650	1000	1411	192	24	57	533	72	40	82	606	23	996	226	96	84	919	5	.328	.335

INDIVIDUAL

TOP QUALIFIERS FOR BATTING CHAMPIONSHIP

Minimum 378 plate appearances. *Lefthanded batter. †Switch-hitter.

Player, Team	Avg.	G	TPA	AB	R	H	TB	2B	3B	HR	RBI	SH	SF	HP	BB	IBB	SO	SB	CS	GDP	Slg.	OBP
Smith, Demond, C.R.-W.M.†	.338	87	397	349	70	118	187	26	8	9	44	6	1	7	34	3	69	40	14	3	.536	.407
Ibarra, Jesus, Burlington†	.330	129	519	437	72	144	278	30	1	34	96	0	1	4	77	6	94	1	2	8	.636	.434
Mitchell, Donovan, Quad City*	.329	111	422	383	72	126	163	23	1	4	42	5	3	2	29	0	38	21	15	10	.426	.376
Castillo, Luis, Kane County	.326	89	400	340	71	111	123	4	4	0	23	4	1	0	55	1	50	41	18	1	.362	.419
Hacopian, Derek, Beloit	.324	123	508	442	75	143	244	30	1	23	92	0	2	8	56	5	35	4	5	20	.552	.407
Valentin, Jose, Fort Wayne†	.321	112	433	383	59	123	216	26	5	19	65	1	0	2	47	7	75	0	5	7	.564	.398
Rodriguez, Noel, Quad City	.311	109	422	386	48	120	180	26	5	8	71	0	4	4	28	1	49	4	5	11	.466	.360
Koskie, Corey, Fort Wayne*	.310	123	515	462	64	143	238	37	5	16	78	1	5	9	38	3	79	2	4	10	.515	.370
Freire, Alejandro, Quad City	.305	125	482	417	71	127	197	23	1	15	65	2	7	6	50	1	83	9	5	9	.472	.381
Pico, Brandon, Rockford*	.300	96	428	383	59	115	162	27	4	4	47	4	3	2	34	0	53	7	7	7	.423	.358
Delgado, Wilson, Wis.-Bur.†	.299	112	477	435	65	130	174	23	3	5	44	4	1	2	35	1	72	12	9	12	.400	.353
Trammell, Gary, Quad City*	.298	103	378	336	44	100	124	12	3	2	33	5	3	1	33	0	62	14	8	4	.369	.359
Belliard, Ron, Beloit	.297	130	507	461	76	137	214	28	5	13	76	2	1	7	36	2	67	16	12	10	.464	.356
Roskos, John, Kane County	.297	114	472	418	74	124	202	36	3	12	88	0	6	6	42	1	86	2	0	6	.483	.364
Jackson, Ryan, Kane County*	.293	132	547	471	78	138	219	39	6	10	82	0	5	4	67	7	74	13	8	9	.465	.382
Betances, Junior, Beloit	.293	122	504	427	66	125	165	21	8	1	52	7	7	2	61	1	67	21	9	9	.386	.378

DEPARTMENTAL LEADERS: G—Robledo, Williams, 135; AB—Robledo, 537; R—Sadler, 103; H—Robledo, 153; TB—Ibarra, 278; 2B—Jackson, 39; 3B—R. Mendez, 11; HR—Ibarra, 34; RBI—Robledo, 108; SH—F. Soriano, 18; SF—Robledo, 16; HP—Dennis, 16; BB—Carone, 84; IBB—Several batters tied with 7; SO—Denbow, 143; SB—Hernandez, 58; CS—Hernandez, 21; GIDP—Hacopian, 20; Slg.—Ibarra, .636; OBP—Ibarra, .434.

ALL PLAYERS

*Lefthanded batter. †Switch-hitter.

Player, Team	Avg.	G	TPA	AB	R	H	TB	2B	3B	HR	RBI	SH	SF	HP	BB	IBB	SO	SB	CS	GDP	Slg.	OBP
Alexander, Chad, Quad City	.286	2	7	7	2	2	2	0	0	0	1	0	0	0	0	0	0	0	0	0	.286	.286
Alguacil, Jose, Burlington†	.221	38	148	136	15	30	32	2	0	0	5	3	0	2	7	0	27	13	1	2	.235	.269
Allen, Dustin, Clinton	.266	36	152	139	25	37	66	12	1	5	31	0	0	1	12	1	29	1	0	3	.475	.329
Allison, Chris, Michigan	.315	87	361	298	46	94	110	8	4	0	22	4	0	7	52	1	39	36	4	5	.369	.429
Altman, Heath, Burlington†	.125	20	29	24	4	3	6	0	0	1	2	0	0	1	4	0	15	1	0	0	.250	.276
Alvarez, Luis, Cedar Rapids*	.195	42	137	123	14	24	39	7	1	2	13	0	1	1	12	3	15	2	2	3	.317	.270
Alvarez, Rafael, Fort Wayne*	.283	99	416	374	62	106	148	17	5	5	36	2	4	2	34	1	53	15	11	5	.396	.343
Amerson, Gordon, Clinton*	.157	48	169	134	15	21	26	2	0	1	8	0	0	0	35	2	41	5	5	2	.194	.331
Amezcua, Adan, Quad City	.246	46	150	142	13	35	59	8	2	4	12	1	1	1	5	0	28	2	3	4	.415	.275
Andreopouls, Alex, Beloit*	.301	60	208	163	32	49	61	9	0	1	20	3	1	3	35	1	16	5	3	2	.374	.431
Augustine, Andy, Wisconsin	.171	56	160	129	17	22	25	0	0	1	6	4	0	8	19	0	43	3	1	5	.194	.314
Avalos, Gilbert, Rockford	.237	104	402	350	57	83	106	15	1	2	34	7	2	4	39	0	74	18	4	8	.303	.319
Ballara, Juan, Peoria	.255	86	262	243	33	62	110	12	6	8	27	0	0	2	17	1	53	5	3	5	.453	.309
Barnes, Kelvin, Rockford	.167	5	14	12	1	2	2	0	0	0	0	0	0	1	1	0	3	0	0	0	.167	.286
Barton, Scott, Rockford*	.231	14	30	26	2	6	9	3	0	0	2	1	0	0	3	0	6	0	1	0	.346	.310
Bautista, Juan, Peoria	.222	84	201	189	31	42	54	4	1	2	22	3	3	2	4	0	43	18	8	1	.286	.242
Bazzani, Matt, Michigan	.116	29	86	69	8	8	13	5	0	0	6	4	0	2	11	0	28	1	0	0	.188	.256
Belliard, Ron, Beloit	.297	130	507	461	76	137	214	28	5	13	76	2	1	7	36	2	67	16	12	10	.464	.356
Betances, Junior, Beloit	.293	122	504	427	66	125	165	21	8	1	52	7	7	2	61	1	67	21	9	9	.386	.378
Betten, Randy, Cedar Rapids	.233	36	74	60	8	14	16	2	0	0	4	0	1	0	13	0	8	6	2	0	.267	.365
Biermann, Steve, Peoria†	.238	59	143	122	10	29	32	3	0	0	10	2	0	4	15	1	16	4	3	5	.262	.340
Bogle, Bryan, Rockford	.206	36	106	97	13	20	29	3	0	2	11	0	1	0	8	0	20	4	1	2	.299	.264
Booty, Josh, Kane County	.101	31	121	109	6	11	16	2	0	1	6	0	1	0	11	0	45	1	0	1	.147	.182
Borrero, Rikchy, Michigan	.229	23	80	70	8	16	28	4	1	2	6	0	0	4	6	0	17	0	1	2	.400	.325
Boulware, Benjamin, S. Bend	.258	129	521	476	68	123	158	19	5	2	60	2	3	8	32	2	78	24	13	10	.332	.314
Bowers, R.J., Quad City	.242	110	426	372	52	90	147	19	1	12	58	0	6	13	35	1	119	10	9	7	.395	.324
Bowles, John, Michigan*	.241	106	415	352	48	85	115	18	0	4	46	5	3	9	46	1	70	5	8	13	.327	.341
Brandon, Jelani, Springfield	.243	74	272	230	32	56	79	12	1	3	37	2	3	2	35	0	37	6	2	4	.343	.344
Bray, Notorris, Burlington	.200	15	56	45	8	9	11	0	1	0	6	1	0	2	8	0	12	3	0	1	.244	.345
Brown, Armann, Fort Wayne	.233	78	293	253	35	59	75	9	2	1	25	2	0	8	30	0	57	26	7	8	.296	.333
Brown, Emil, West Michigan	.251	124	528	459	63	115	147	17	3	3	67	0	6	11	52	0	77	35	19	17	.320	.337

Player, Team	Avg.	G	TPA	AB	R	H	TB	2B	3B	HR	RBI	SH	SF	HP	BB	IBB	SO	SB	CS	GDP	Slg.	OBP
Buchanan, Shawn, S. Bend	.269	103	410	350	45	94	124	16	4	2	35	1	3	10	46	0	72	10	8	10	.354	.367
Buhner, Shawn, Wisconsin	.240	87	318	292	24	70	96	14	3	2	36	0	4	6	16	2	65	0	2	9	.329	.289
Burchel, Brad, Beloit	.147	13	39	34	4	5	6	1	0	0	3	0	0	2	3	0	11	0	3	0	.176	.256
Burgos, Carlos, Springfield	.181	27	83	72	8	13	15	2	0	0	8	0	1	3	7	0	11	0	0	2	.208	.277
Burt, Chris, Beloit	.000	37	1	1	0	0	0	0	0	0	0	0	0	0	0	0	0	0	0	0	.000	.000
Bustos, Saul, Rockford	.253	95	323	289	46	73	119	12	2	10	47	2	8	2	22	0	66	5	2	8	.412	.302
Cady, Todd, Kane County†	.251	115	448	387	47	97	155	23	1	11	66	0	4	9	47	3	104	1	0	4	.401	.342
Campillo, Rob, Beloit	.211	47	144	123	17	26	30	4	0	0	13	7	2	5	7	1	20	0	0	2	.244	.277
Carmona, Cesarin, Clinton†	.178	42	146	129	13	23	27	2	1	0	5	1	0	1	15	0	35	10	7	2	.209	.269
Carone, Richard, South Bend	.254	111	447	347	56	88	133	16	1	9	51	5	2	9	84	0	91	0	3	7	.383	.410
Carpenter, Jerry, Cedar Rapids	.100	11	34	30	2	3	3	0	0	0	2	0	0	0	4	0	9	0	0	0	.100	.206
Carroll, Doug, Wisconsin*	.225	90	311	276	29	62	95	18	0	5	40	0	3	14	18	3	60	3	0	7	.344	.302
Castillo, Alberto, Burlington*	.165	34	110	103	7	17	33	4	0	4	13	0	0	0	7	0	43	2	0	2	.320	.218
Castillo, Luis, Kane County	.326	89	400	340	71	111	123	4	4	0	23	4	1	0	55	1	50	41	18	1	.362	.419
Castro, Dennis, Kane County*	.246	46	156	138	12	34	58	9	0	5	21	2	1	0	15	1	33	1	0	0	.420	.318
Castro, Jose, West Michigan†	.240	113	509	409	76	98	128	20	2	2	40	13	0	11	76	2	94	51	20	2	.313	.373
Cedeno, Edwardo, Springfield	.224	81	234	210	30	47	79	7	2	7	27	3	2	5	14	0	67	7	3	1	.376	.286
Cephas, Ruben, Beloit*	.170	76	105	94	17	16	16	0	0	0	1	3	0	1	7	0	25	13	3	0	.170	.235
Chevalier, Virgil, Michigan	.667	2	7	6	2	4	5	1	0	0	0	0	0	0	1	0	0	1	0	0	.833	.714
Choi, Kyung, Cedar Rapids*	.228	36	136	123	14	28	39	4	2	1	14	1	2	1	9	0	12	4	1	4	.317	.281
Clifford, James, Wisconsin*	.244	101	371	307	46	75	137	26	3	10	44	1	5	13	40	2	87	8	4	3	.446	.351
Cline, Pat, Rockford	.272	112	464	390	65	106	172	27	0	13	77	0	5	11	58	3	93	6	1	6	.441	.377
Coe, Ryan, Quad City	.261	38	111	92	16	24	46	7	0	5	18	0	1	3	13	0	20	1	2	4	.500	.367
Cole, Abdul, Kane County	.123	56	150	122	10	15	21	3	0	1	7	3	2	6	17	0	48	3	1	4	.172	.259
Coleman, Michael, Michigan	.268	112	477	422	70	113	166	16	2	11	61	6	3	6	40	1	93	29	5	7	.393	.338
Contreras, Efrain, Peoria*	.258	98	305	271	35	70	113	9	2	10	48	1	3	3	27	3	45	1	3	12	.417	.329
Cook, Hayward, Kane County	.280	78	277	261	50	73	104	5	1	8	23	2	1	1	12	0	61	23	4	4	.398	.313
Cook, Jason, Wisconsin	.269	117	491	405	61	109	152	24	2	5	64	3	6	12	64	7	44	12	5	8	.375	.380
Cordero, Pablo, Burlington	.242	59	210	190	21	46	65	9	2	2	21	3	1	2	14	0	38	2	1	4	.342	.300
Corujo, Rey, Burlington	.133	14	47	45	2	6	7	1	0	0	0	0	0	0	2	0	8	1	1	2	.156	.170
Cruz, Deivi, Burlington	.138	16	63	58	2	8	12	1	0	1	9	1	0	0	4	0	7	1	1	1	.207	.194
Cuevas, Eduardo, Clinton	.259	69	276	263	39	68	87	11	1	2	31	1	3	0	9	1	31	17	3	5	.331	.280
D'Amico, Jeff, West Michigan	.226	125	511	434	56	98	145	24	1	7	55	4	7	10	56	2	94	8	5	12	.334	.323
Dantzler, Eric, Burlington	.167	30	100	84	6	14	18	1	0	1	7	1	3	0	12	0	24	2	0	5	.214	.263
Darcuiel, Faruq, Wisconsin*	.259	83	315	282	29	73	92	10	3	1	20	4	2	5	22	0	50	27	6	1	.326	.322
Darden, Tony, Kane County	.287	86	337	286	42	82	116	15	5	3	31	1	2	8	40	1	40	5	5	6	.406	.387
DaSilva, Manny, West Michigan	.316	7	25	19	5	6	13	2	1	1	3	1	0	1	4	0	4	0	0	1	.684	.458
Davalillo, David, Cedar Rapids	.270	44	153	141	17	38	47	7	1	0	16	4	1	0	7	0	32	1	0	3	.333	.302
Davis, Josh, Clinton	.200	8	16	15	2	3	3	0	0	0	2	0	0	0	1	0	5	1	0	0	.200	.250
Dean, Mark, Peoria†	.205	75	216	190	19	39	45	2	2	0	12	5	0	7	14	0	42	4	3	3	.237	.284
DeBoer, Rob, West Michigan	.242	104	406	339	57	82	129	25	2	6	50	1	4	4	58	1	110	11	6	6	.381	.356
Delaney, Sean, Springfield	.298	62	214	188	24	56	83	8	2	5	22	1	1	5	19	1	27	5	1	5	.441	.376
DeLeon, Raymond, Clinton*	.267	9	34	30	3	8	9	1	0	0	4	0	1	1	2	0	3	0	1	1	.300	.324
DeLeon, Santo, Wisconsin†	.105	9	24	19	0	2	2	0	0	0	0	2	0	0	3	0	5	1	0	0	.105	.227
Delgado, Wilson, Wis.-Bur.†	.299	112	477	435	65	130	174	23	3	5	44	4	1	2	35	1	72	12	9	12	.400	.353
Denbow, Don, Burlington	.178	105	374	326	42	58	103	7	1	12	33	1	0	5	42	0	143	14	2	2	.316	.282
Dennis, Brian, Rockford	.206	51	135	102	10	21	30	3	0	2	16	1	3	16	13	0	28	1	1	3	.294	.373
DePastino, Joe, Michigan	.277	98	368	325	47	90	148	20	4	10	53	0	5	8	30	1	70	3	3	5	.455	.348
Derosso, Tony, Michigan	.233	106	434	382	57	89	150	20	1	13	50	1	2	11	38	2	93	9	1	5	.393	.319
Donati, John, Cedar Rapids	.286	116	453	381	63	109	185	24	2	16	75	1	4	10	57	1	92	5	3	4	.486	.389
Dumas, Mike, Beloit	.254	20	83	71	11	18	23	1	2	0	4	1	0	0	11	0	11	9	6	0	.324	.354
Dunwoody, Todd, K. C.*	.283	132	565	494	89	140	218	20	8	14	89	2	9	8	52	7	105	39	11	7	.441	.355
Ebbert, Chad, Clinton	.000	2	5	5	0	0	0	0	0	0	0	0	0	0	0	0	1	0	0	0	.000	.000
Encarnacion, Anito, Ced. Rapids	.209	42	89	86	4	18	21	3	0	0	6	1	0	0	2	0	12	0	0	4	.244	.227
Espinal, Juan, Clinton	.208	116	400	336	28	70	102	11	0	7	46	6	7	4	47	2	79	3	3	8	.304	.307
Espiritu, Michael, Cedar Rapids	.167	9	31	24	1	4	4	0	0	0	2	0	0	0	7	1	3	1	1	2	.167	.355
Evans, Jason, South Bend†	.280	101	432	336	70	94	137	17	4	6	36	8	3	6	79	1	74	11	4	3	.408	.422
Faggett, Ethan, Michigan*	.243	115	445	399	56	97	146	11	7	8	47	3	2	4	37	3	112	23	7	9	.366	.312
Failla, Paul, Cedar Rapids†	.253	129	537	459	77	116	153	23	4	2	48	7	3	2	66	0	102	30	19	9	.333	.347
Fitzpatrick, Will, Beloit*	.200	55	158	115	18	23	36	5	1	2	14	0	1	4	38	1	35	5	3	0	.313	.411
Fortin, Troy, Fort Wayne	.258	112	458	407	49	105	149	21	1	7	48	0	3	8	38	1	69	4	5	7	.366	.331
Francisco, Vicente, W. Mich.†	.245	85	321	277	41	68	83	8	2	1	25	12	1	1	30	0	48	4	8	4	.300	.320
Fraser, Joe, Fort Wayne	.200	5	16	15	0	3	3	0	0	0	2	0	1	0	0	0	5	1	0	0	.200	.188
Freeman, Richard, Rockford	.273	131	535	466	89	127	203	33	5	11	67	0	1	7	61	3	57	8	3	11	.436	.364
Freire, Alejandro, Quad City	.305	125	482	417	71	127	197	23	1	15	65	2	7	6	50	1	83	9	5	9	.472	.381
French, Anton, Peoria†	.273	116	467	417	71	114	173	19	5	10	37	7	0	6	37	2	98	57	16	6	.415	.341
Fric, Sean, Rockford	.235	7	21	17	3	4	5	1	0	0	2	0	0	0	4	0	2	0	0	1	.294	.381
Garcia, Amaury, Kane County	.241	26	77	58	19	14	23	4	1	1	5	0	0	1	18	0	12	5	2	1	.397	.429
Garcia, Carlos, Fort Wayne	.189	34	105	95	13	18	23	5	0	0	10	3	0	0	7	0	13	11	0	0	.242	.245
Garcia, Franklin, Beloit	.230	26	68	61	7	14	16	2	0	0	6	1	1	0	5	0	14	5	2	2	.262	.284
Gazarek, Marty, Rockford	.261	107	439	399	57	104	139	24	1	3	53	2	3	8	27	1	58	7	5	8	.348	.318
Gerteisen, Aaron, Peoria*	.216	73	247	218	24	47	61	6	1	2	17	3	1	0	25	0	29	7	5	4	.280	.295
Gibralter, David, Michigan	.252	121	492	456	48	115	199	34	1	16	82	3	4	8	20	2	79	3	4	7	.436	.293
Glenn, Darrin, Burlington	.214	62	211	182	35	39	72	4	1	9	27	0	1	5	23	0	59	4	3	8	.396	.318
Gonzalez, Jimmy, Quad City	.244	35	88	78	4	19	27	3	1	1	14	0	1	1	8	0	13	1	2	2	.346	.318
Goodell, Steve, Kane County	.286	2	9	7	0	2	2	0	0	0	1	0	0	0	2	0	2	0	0	0	.286	.444
Gordon, Adrian, Fort Wayne	.240	75	253	217	34	52	70	10	1	2	18	1	3	6	26	1	63	16	7	3	.323	.333
Grandizio, Steve, Peoria	.280	117	438	379	65	106	135	18	4	1	33	2	5	10	42	1	63	21	8	10	.356	.362
Grieve, Ben, W. Michigan*	.261	102	445	371	53	97	127	16	1	4	62	0	6	8	60	6	75	11	3	10	.342	.371
Gugino, Mark, Kane County	.244	58	208	164	29	40	66	13	2	3	20	3	2	4	35	0	29	5	3	4	.402	.385
Gulseth, Mark, Burlington*	.277	41	159	137	15	38	57	7	0	4	19	0	2	2	18	0	30	3	3	4	.416	.365
Gunderson, Shane, Ft. Wayne	.253	26	103	87	17	22	35	7	0	2	12	4	0	2	10	1	17	2	1	0	.402	.343
Hacopian, Derek, Beloit	.324	123	508	442	75	143	244	30	1	23	92	0	2	8	56	5	35	4	5	20	.552	.407

Player, Team	Avg.	G	TPA	AB	R	H	TB	2B	3B	HR	RBI	SH	SF	HP	BB	IBB	SO	SB	CS	GDP	Slg.	OBP
Hall, Ryan, Peoria*	.271	108	378	317	38	86	131	24	0	7	44	3	5	4	49	2	70	1	2	7	.413	.371
Hamburg, Leon, W. Mich.	.183	85	317	268	40	49	75	16	2	2	32	2	1	4	42	0	78	12	3	5	.280	.302
Hamilton, Joe, Michigan*	.217	119	491	405	65	88	155	15	2	16	59	2	6	5	73	3	124	8	7	1	.383	.339
Hansen, Jed, Springfield	.258	122	506	414	86	107	175	27	7	9	50	6	1	7	78	0	73	44	10	8	.423	.384
Harris, Eric, West Michigan	.168	70	237	202	29	34	68	9	2	7	29	0	2	7	26	0	73	5	0	5	.337	.283
Harris, Mike, Beloit*	.341	12	45	41	8	14	17	1	1	0	5	0	0	0	4	0	5	7	1	0	.415	.400
Harvey, Aaron, Kane County*	.292	100	376	336	58	98	150	25	3	7	54	4	4	5	25	0	70	11	7	4	.446	.346
Hause, Brendan, W. Michigan*	.000	32	1	1	0	0	0	0	0	0	0	0	0	0	0	0	0	0	0	0	.000	.000
Heath, Jason, Wisconsin	.268	70	272	235	29	63	99	20	2	4	32	7	4	7	19	2	60	3	3	4	.421	.336
Hemphill, Bret, Cedar Rapids†	.252	72	264	234	36	59	96	11	1	8	28	1	4	4	21	0	54	0	2	7	.410	.319
Henderson, Juan, Ced. Rapids	.229	123	453	402	61	92	112	12	1	2	28	10	2	3	36	0	79	47	12	6	.279	.296
Hernandez, Carlos, Quad City	.260	126	530	470	74	122	165	19	6	4	40	9	1	11	39	1	68	58	21	4	.351	.330
Herrick, Jason, Cedar Rapids*	.285	104	404	358	54	102	164	21	4	11	57	3	3	2	38	2	84	19	3	7	.458	.354
Hightower, Vee, Rockford†	.265	64	284	238	51	63	97	11	1	7	36	0	1	6	39	1	52	23	6	6	.408	.380
Hilt, Scott, Fort Wayne*	.185	30	105	92	13	17	27	5	1	1	15	0	0	2	11	0	28	0	0	3	.293	.286
Hinds, Collin, Wisconsin	.071	5	16	14	0	1	1	0	0	0	1	0	0	0	2	0	8	1	0	0	.071	.188
Iatarola, Aaron, Cedar Rapids*	.260	115	445	388	62	101	171	20	1	16	69	1	7	5	44	1	92	7	4	2	.441	.338
Ibarra, Jesus, Burlington†	.330	129	519	437	72	144	278	30	1	34	96	0	1	4	77	6	94	1	2	8	.636	.434
Jackson, Ryan, Kane County*	.293	132	547	471	78	138	219	39	6	10	82	0	5	4	67	7	74	13	8	9	.465	.382
Jaha, John, Beloit	.000	1	4	4	1	0	0	0	0	0	0	0	0	0	0	0	1	0	0	0	.000	.000
Johnson, Jack, Rockford	.214	24	79	70	5	15	23	2	0	2	14	0	1	0	8	2	17	0	0	1	.329	.291
Johnson, James, Clinton	.118	8	19	17	0	2	2	0	0	0	0	1	0	0	1	0	3	0	1	1	.118	.167
Jones, Ken, Clinton	.184	31	84	76	8	14	16	2	0	0	7	1	0	1	6	0	20	1	0	1	.211	.253
Jumonville, Joe, Peoria	.228	113	393	378	37	86	124	18	4	4	45	1	4	1	9	0	47	2	1	12	.328	.245
Keefe, Jamie, Clinton	.240	67	203	175	28	42	50	3	1	1	10	3	0	2	23	0	42	12	3	2	.286	.335
Keifer, Greg, Burlington	.143	6	16	14	3	2	3	1	0	0	2	0	0	0	2	0	4	1	0	0	.214	.250
Kimbler, Doug, Rockford	.286	102	401	353	69	101	174	33	2	12	67	3	2	4	39	0	61	7	3	8	.493	.362
King, Bill, West Michigan	.000	30	2	2	0	0	0	0	0	0	0	0	0	0	0	0	1	0	0	0	.000	.000
Klassen, Danny, Beloit	.275	59	241	218	27	60	85	15	2	2	25	0	3	4	16	0	43	12	4	4	.390	.332
Kominek, Toby, Beloit	.278	55	218	187	38	52	91	14	2	7	30	0	2	10	18	1	56	12	2	1	.487	.369
Koskie, Corey, Fort Wayne*	.310	123	515	462	64	143	238	37	5	16	78	1	5	9	38	3	79	2	4	10	.515	.370
Krause, Scott, Beloit	.247	134	553	481	83	119	196	30	4	13	76	3	7	12	50	5	126	24	10	7	.407	.329
Kuilan, Hector, Kane County	.000	2	7	7	0	0	0	0	0	0	0	0	0	0	0	0	1	0	0	0	.000	.000
Kurek, Chris, Michigan	.193	52	166	145	14	28	40	8	2	0	18	1	2	5	13	0	47	0	0	2	.276	.279
Lane, Ryan, Fort Wayne	.266	115	514	432	69	115	172	37	1	6	56	6	4	7	65	0	92	17	9	9	.398	.368
Lanza, Mike, Wisconsin	.204	101	365	333	28	68	89	13	1	2	29	6	2	2	22	0	67	10	5	7	.267	.256
LaValliere, Mike, South Bend	.600	2	6	5	1	3	4	1	0	0	1	0	0	0	1	0	0	0	0	0	.800	.667
Levias, Andres, South Bend†	.234	25	87	77	13	18	19	1	0	0	12	1	3	0	6	1	14	7	3	2	.247	.279
Lewis, Marc, Michigan	.152	36	103	92	14	14	21	2	1	1	5	2	0	0	9	0	16	10	3	1	.228	.228
Linares, Yfrain, Beloit	.000	20	1	1	0	0	0	0	0	0	0	0	0	0	0	0	0	0	0	0	.000	.000
Livsey, Shane, Rockford†	.283	57	250	226	39	64	82	10	1	2	27	0	0	2	22	3	30	21	7	0	.363	.352
Llanos, Victor, Peoria	.277	21	50	47	7	13	15	2	0	0	3	0	0	0	3	0	7	0	1	0	.319	.320
Logan, Chris, Clinton	.000	53	1	1	0	0	0	0	0	0	0	0	0	0	0	0	1	0	0	0	.000	.000
Lowry, Curt, Clinton	.214	57	211	182	33	39	44	1	2	0	16	0	1	1	26	1	51	7	6	2	.242	.314
Lugo, Jesus, Peoria	.265	65	234	219	26	58	79	11	2	2	29	0	0	2	12	3	31	1	1	8	.361	.309
Madsen, Dan, Rockford†	.261	29	110	88	18	23	33	6	2	0	11	0	2	6	14	0	15	14	4	6	.375	.391
Martin, Mike, Clinton*	.189	51	158	127	10	24	27	3	0	0	14	2	4	1	24	0	24	2	0	2	.213	.314
Martinez, Erik, Clinton	.102	29	64	59	4	6	6	0	0	0	2	1	0	1	3	0	10	2	0	0	.102	.159
Marval, Raul, Burlington	.267	88	316	296	42	79	94	8	2	1	19	3	1	6	10	0	32	4	6	9	.318	.304
Mathews, Byron, S. Bend†	.199	97	378	332	40	66	88	11	4	1	34	7	4	3	32	2	70	16	11	6	.265	.272
Mathis, Joe, Wisconsin*	.266	117	427	376	59	100	141	17	3	6	43	5	2	0	43	1	91	26	6	7	.375	.340
Matthews, Gary, Clinton†	.238	128	501	421	57	100	132	18	4	2	40	3	3	6	68	1	109	28	8	8	.314	.349
McCalmont, Jim, Ft. Wayne	.333	7	36	33	5	11	23	3	0	3	7	0	0	0	3	0	3	2	0	1	.697	.389
McDonald, Keith, Peoria	.268	65	213	179	22	48	57	6	0	1	20	4	0	6	22	0	38	0	1	2	.318	.367
McNally, Sean, Springfield	.271	132	528	479	60	130	210	28	8	12	79	0	6	8	35	6	119	6	3	10	.438	.328
Mealing, Al, Beloit*	.220	19	44	41	4	9	11	2	0	0	2	0	0	0	3	0	17	2	1	0	.268	.273
Medina, Alger, Rockford	.194	26	71	62	8	12	16	1	0	1	8	0	0	2	7	0	15	6	1	2	.258	.296
Melo, Juan, Clinton†	.282	134	524	479	65	135	184	32	1	5	46	5	2	5	33	0	88	12	10	11	.384	.333
Mendez, Emilio, Beloit	.059	7	19	17	1	1	1	0	0	0	0	1	0	0	1	0	9	0	0	0	.059	.111
Mendez, Rudolfo, Springfield	.276	129	500	449	70	124	204	28	11	10	72	2	7	8	34	2	121	40	10	13	.454	.333
Mendoza, Francisco, Springfield	.253	96	339	308	38	78	131	18	1	11	49	0	5	2	24	1	65	4	1	7	.425	.307
Milstien, Dave, Beloit	.327	53	226	196	47	64	84	12	1	2	21	1	0	6	23	1	15	8	4	6	.429	.413
Miranda, Alex, W. Michigan*	.232	124	479	393	53	91	140	21	2	8	60	2	4	5	75	6	78	6	8	3	.356	.358
Mitchell, Donovan, Quad City*	.329	111	422	383	72	126	163	23	1	4	42	5	3	2	29	0	38	21	15	10	.426	.376
Moeder, Tony, Cedar Rapids	.268	48	194	168	32	45	103	11	1	15	47	0	3	4	19	0	36	2	2	2	.613	.351
Molina, Ben, Cedar Rapids	.293	39	151	133	15	39	60	9	0	4	17	1	1	1	15	0	11	1	1	4	.451	.367
Molina, Luis, Wisconsin	.255	109	401	337	45	86	115	18	1	3	42	7	7	8	42	3	72	7	9	5	.341	.345
Monahan, Shane, Wisconsin	.283	59	256	233	34	66	90	9	6	1	32	7	3	2	11	0	40	9	2	4	.386	.317
Montiel, David, Beloit†	.160	74	126	100	20	16	17	1	0	0	11	4	3	8	11	0	19	19	10	0	.170	.287
Moore, Brandon, S. Bend	.257	132	573	510	75	131	146	9	3	0	37	7	5	3	48	1	49	34	8	15	.286	.322
Moriarty, Mike, Fort Wayne	.227	62	237	203	26	46	70	6	3	4	26	2	3	2	27	1	44	8	0	1	.345	.319
Morris, Gregory, Ced. Rapids	.287	103	425	355	65	102	162	18	0	14	57	0	3	6	61	4	59	8	2	6	.456	.398
Moschetti, Mike, W. Michigan	.318	8	26	22	6	7	9	2	0	0	3	1	0	0	3	0	8	1	0	0	.409	.400
Mucker, Kelcey, Ft. Wayne*	.230	109	439	405	48	93	132	16	1	7	47	1	2	4	27	1	59	12	4	8	.326	.283
Mullins, Greg, Beloit*	.000	15	1	1	0	0	0	0	0	0	0	0	0	0	0	0	0	0	0	0	.000	.000
Nelson, Bryant, Quad City†	.038	6	26	26	1	1	2	1	0	0	2	0	0	0	0	0	3	0	0	2	.077	.038
Newhan, David, W. Michigan*	.219	25	112	96	9	21	35	5	0	3	8	1	1	1	13	1	26	3	2	2	.365	.315
Newman, Damon, W. Mich.	.000	21	1	1	0	0	0	0	0	0	0	0	0	0	0	0	1	0	0	0	.000	.000
Nilsson, Dave, Beloit*	.545	3	13	11	2	6	12	3	0	1	7	0	0	0	2	0	0	0	0	0	1.091	.615
Nunez, Isaias, Peoria*	.217	120	410	378	37	82	119	19	6	2	43	1	5	1	25	1	66	1	6	4	.315	.264
Oglesby, Luke, Springfield*	.197	50	149	122	27	24	30	0	0	2	6	3	0	5	19	0	26	24	5	0	.246	.329
Olinde, Chad, Rockford*	.238	54	196	164	21	39	53	11	0	1	26	3	1	5	23	0	42	3	2	0	.323	.347
Olmstead, Nate, Ced. Rapids†	.232	59	182	155	20	36	47	8	0	1	15	2	1	2	20	1	37	1	0	7	.303	.326

Player, Team	Avg.	G	TPA	AB	R	H	TB	2B	3B	HR	RBI	SH	SF	HP	BB	IBB	SO	SB	CS	GDP	Slg.	OBP
Ortega, Randy, W. Mich.	.216	48	177	162	8	35	39	4	0	0	13	1	0	1	13	0	27	0	2	8	.241	.278
Paez, Israel, Fort Wayne	.260	113	428	388	47	101	123	12	2	2	45	3	1	1	35	1	55	12	11	8	.317	.322
Patterson, Jake, Ft. Wayne*	.264	116	484	435	56	115	190	23	5	14	68	0	5	9	35	4	118	0	2	5	.437	.329
Patton, Greg, Michigan	.248	69	263	226	34	56	96	13	0	9	27	2	2	2	31	2	58	4	3	2	.425	.341
Pearce, Jeff, Wisconsin*	.000	28	1	1	0	0	0	0	0	0	0	0	0	0	0	0	0	0	0	0	.000	.000
Pearson, Kevin, Fort Wayne	.141	29	88	78	10	11	17	1	1	1	7	1	0	3	6	0	30	1	0	2	.218	.230
Perez, Mike, Rockford	.245	39	124	106	12	26	31	3	1	0	11	2	1	2	13	0	24	3	3	5	.292	.336
Pico, Brandon, Rockford*	.300	96	428	383	59	115	162	27	4	4	47	4	3	2	34	0	53	7	7	7	.423	.358
Pierzynski, A.J., Ft. Wayne*	.310	22	87	84	10	26	39	5	1	2	14	0	1	0	2	0	10	0	0	1	.464	.322
Polanco, Placido, Peoria	.266	103	394	361	43	96	117	7	4	2	41	11	2	2	18	0	30	7	6	8	.324	.303
Poor, Jeff, Burlington	.242	101	361	322	33	78	115	23	1	4	38	2	3	7	27	1	68	1	0	9	.357	.312
Powell, Chris, Cedar Rapids*	.159	25	76	63	11	10	15	3	1	0	4	0	1	1	11	1	17	6	0	2	.238	.289
Pratt, Wes, Quad City	.227	14	51	44	5	10	19	1	1	2	10	0	0	0	7	0	11	2	0	2	.432	.333
Price, Christopher, Springfield	.264	52	186	159	22	42	60	7	1	3	14	1	1	2	23	0	32	6	2	5	.377	.362
Prieto, Alejandro, Springfield†	.251	124	491	431	61	108	129	9	3	2	44	12	2	6	40	1	69	11	7	10	.299	.322
Probst, Alan, Quad City	.258	52	167	151	23	39	74	12	1	7	27	1	1	1	13	0	28	2	0	3	.490	.319
Rajotte, Jason, W. Michigan*	.000	44	2	1	1	0	0	0	0	0	0	0	0	0	1	0	0	0	0	0	.000	.500
Ramirez, Joel, Wisconsin	.083	7	24	24	1	2	3	1	0	0	1	0	0	0	0	0	4	1	0	0	.125	.083
Ramos, Jeff, Springfield*	.219	39	111	96	14	21	41	8	0	4	20	0	5	1	9	0	25	0	0	3	.427	.279
Reid, Derek, Burlington	.285	95	393	354	74	101	163	15	4	13	55	3	1	4	31	0	55	22	4	7	.460	.349
Rennhack, Mike, Quad City†	.271	100	351	299	46	81	100	14	1	1	47	4	8	1	39	1	37	15	4	3	.334	.349
Reyes, Michael, Kane County	.189	14	45	37	8	7	10	3	0	0	4	0	0	1	7	0	11	0	2	0	.270	.333
Richardson, Eric, South Bend	.231	63	223	199	32	46	59	11	1	0	19	2	1	1	19	0	39	23	6	3	.296	.300
Rincones, Wuarnner, S. Bend	.214	20	66	56	4	12	13	1	0	0	7	0	3	1	6	0	13	0	1	0	.232	.288
Robbins, Lance, Cedar Rapids	.235	38	93	81	18	19	23	4	0	0	6	0	1	2	9	0	16	1	3	0	.284	.323
Robinson, Darek, Peoria†	.240	113	411	363	36	87	108	15	0	2	23	7	1	2	37	2	60	2	5	7	.298	.313
Robledo, Nilson, S. Bend	.285	135	587	537	71	153	243	24	3	20	108	1	16	3	30	4	100	0	2	8	.453	.317
Rocha, Juan, Springfield	.233	94	314	292	33	68	121	21	1	10	41	1	1	4	16	0	65	5	2	4	.414	.281
Rodriguez, Maximo, K.C.	.191	72	260	236	18	45	69	7	1	5	30	1	2	2	18	0	65	0	1	7	.292	.252
Rodriguez, Noel, Quad City	.311	109	422	386	48	120	180	26	5	8	71	0	4	4	28	1	49	4	5	11	.466	.360
Rodriguez, Victor, K.C.	.235	127	535	472	65	111	122	9	1	0	43	16	4	2	40	0	47	18	6	17	.258	.295
Rondon, Alex, W. Michigan	.216	25	82	74	11	16	25	3	0	2	5	0	0	1	7	0	13	1	0	2	.338	.293
Root, Mitch, Clinton	.275	89	350	309	37	85	116	20	1	3	42	0	2	2	37	1	52	3	1	8	.375	.354
Rosario, Melvin, S. Bend†	.273	118	488	450	58	123	210	30	6	15	57	1	3	4	30	7	109	1	8	0	.467	.322
Rose, Pete, South Bend*	.277	116	491	423	56	117	165	24	6	4	65	2	7	5	54	0	45	2	0	6	.390	.360
Roskos, John, Kane County	.297	114	472	418	74	124	202	36	3	12	88	0	6	6	42	1	86	2	0	6	.483	.364
Ross, Tony, Quad City	.257	107	378	339	46	87	115	11	4	3	41	2	3	3	31	0	57	21	5	4	.339	.322
Ryder, Derek, Cedar Rapids	.095	17	29	21	1	2	2	0	0	0	2	3	0	0	5	0	7	0	1	1	.095	.269
Sadler, Donnie, Michigan	.283	118	529	438	103	124	192	25	8	9	55	3	3	6	79	0	85	41	13	5	.438	.397
Salzano, Jerry, Rockford	.286	6	22	21	0	6	9	1	1	0	2	0	0	0	1	0	1	0	1	1	.429	.318
Sanchez, Marcos, Clinton†	.111	6	19	18	0	2	3	1	0	0	0	0	0	0	1	0	6	0	0	2	.167	.158
Sanchez, Victor, Quad City	.235	13	40	34	3	8	8	0	0	0	1	0	0	0	6	0	10	1	0	2	.235	.350
Sanders, Pat, W. Michigan*	.208	11	29	24	4	5	5	0	0	0	3	0	1	0	4	0	6	0	0	0	.208	.310
Santana, Jose, Quad City†	.227	88	267	229	36	52	69	10	2	1	21	4	2	8	24	0	40	6	4	7	.301	.319
Schneider, Dan, Burlington	.213	51	157	141	13	30	40	4	0	2	12	3	0	3	10	0	27	1	1	6	.284	.279
Schwenke, Matt, Clinton	.190	36	107	100	3	19	29	5	1	1	8	2	1	1	2	0	34	0	0	3	.290	.212
Smith, Dave, Michigan	.219	61	217	187	18	41	55	11	0	1	23	1	4	5	20	0	46	1	1	3	.294	.306
Smith, Demond, C.R.-W.M.†	.338	87	397	349	70	118	187	26	8	9	44	6	1	7	34	3	69	40	14	3	.536	.407
Smith, John, Beloit	.211	76	288	261	38	55	109	16	4	10	44	1	2	4	20	1	88	8	2	4	.418	.275
Smith, Matt, Springfield*	.226	117	439	412	49	93	131	18	1	6	46	1	1	1	24	4	96	8	5	11	.318	.269
Smith, Scott, Wisconsin	.327	34	122	107	13	35	58	12	1	3	17	1	1	2	11	0	21	0	1	7	.542	.397
Snook, Robert, Beloit	.000	3	8	6	0	0	0	0	0	0	0	0	0	0	2	0	3	0	0	0	.000	.250
Snyder, Jarod, Rockford	.185	24	76	65	7	12	17	2	0	1	6	1	0	4	6	0	15	0	0	1	.262	.293
Soriano, Fred, W. Michigan†	.262	107	384	305	68	80	102	7	3	3	32	18	2	8	51	1	72	40	6	0	.334	.380
Soriano, Jose, W. Michigan	.213	123	474	413	64	88	122	12	2	6	43	15	5	8	33	3	103	35	12	7	.295	.281
Sparks, Rodney, Springfield	.219	43	105	96	11	21	28	4	0	1	7	1	0	0	8	0	14	0	0	0	.292	.279
Spinello, Joe, South Bend	.214	7	16	14	2	3	3	0	0	0	1	0	0	0	2	0	3	0	0	1	.214	.313
Stasio, Chris, Michigan	.305	87	348	315	44	96	141	22	1	7	47	1	3	4	25	0	78	1	0	7	.448	.360
Sutherland, Alex, Wisconsin	.224	90	327	303	36	68	92	17	2	1	35	2	1	2	19	2	56	2	0	5	.304	.274
Swift, Scott, Burlington†	.191	68	256	209	29	40	45	3	1	0	17	5	3	0	37	0	33	9	5	4	.215	.309
Tena, Dario, Clinton†	.183	99	328	295	30	54	60	6	0	0	19	5	2	1	25	0	41	33	10	3	.203	.248
Topham, Ryan, S. Bend*	.250	14	53	48	4	12	15	3	0	0	2	1	0	0	4	0	12	0	0	0	.313	.308
Totman, Jason, Clinton	.288	61	262	229	32	66	91	19	3	0	32	1	2	4	26	0	27	6	1	2	.397	.368
Towner, Kyle, Wisconsin†	.226	104	376	301	64	68	83	12	0	1	24	5	3	4	63	1	59	34	11	1	.276	.364
Trammell, Gary, Quad City*	.298	103	378	336	44	100	124	12	3	2	33	5	3	1	33	0	62	14	8	4	.369	.359
Treanor, Matt, Springfield	.185	75	240	211	17	39	58	6	2	3	19	2	2	4	21	0	59	1	1	1	.275	.269
Truby, Chris, Quad City	.233	118	451	400	68	93	151	23	4	9	64	3	3	3	41	0	66	27	8	11	.378	.306
Tyler, Josh, Beloit	.237	77	234	186	24	44	55	5	0	2	27	7	3	2	36	0	40	3	6	4	.296	.361
Tyrus, Jason, Clinton	.226	65	173	159	15	36	49	5	1	2	17	3	0	1	10	0	53	4	5	0	.308	.276
Ullan, Dave, Clinton	.208	43	122	96	8	20	24	1	0	1	11	2	1	3	20	1	16	0	2	1	.250	.358
Valentin, Jose, Fort Wayne†	.321	112	433	383	59	123	216	26	5	19	65	1	0	2	47	7	75	0	5	7	.564	.398
Villalobos, Carlos, Wisconsin	.260	110	436	389	64	101	152	16	4	9	53	4	5	3	35	1	76	16	4	3	.391	.322
Vizcaino, Romulo, Ft. Wayne†	.248	103	387	343	44	85	109	13	4	1	22	3	5	1	35	1	56	6	6	6	.318	.315
Walker, Joe, South Bend†	.000	6	10	6	0	0	0	0	0	0	0	0	0	0	4	0	4	0	0	0	.000	.400
Walker, Steve, Rockford†	.289	103	462	415	78	120	167	24	7	3	44	0	0	10	37	3	104	40	16	1	.402	.361
Wallace, Brian, Burlington	.213	97	390	338	48	72	111	12	0	9	38	7	5	6	34	0	65	7	5	7	.328	.292
Walls, Eric, Springfield*	.227	101	322	299	53	68	90	14	1	2	21	4	0	2	17	0	65	20	7	8	.301	.274
Wambach, James, S. Bend*	.214	9	30	28	1	6	6	0	0	0	2	0	0	0	2	0	6	0	0	1	.214	.267
Ward, Turner, Beloit†	.000	2	8	5	0	0	0	0	0	0	0	0	0	0	3	0	1	0	0	0	.000	.375
Wathan, Dusty, Wisconsin†	.091	5	12	11	1	1	4	0	0	1	3	0	0	1	0	0	3	0	0	0	.364	.167
Watson, Kevin, Burlington	.186	80	271	247	29	46	74	5	1	7	25	2	1	3	18	0	88	1	2	4	.300	.249
Welch, Coby, Springfield	.171	19	40	35	3	6	6	0	0	0	1	0	0	3	2	0	9	0	0	0	.171	.275
Whatley, Gabe, Rockford*	.257	95	396	339	54	87	135	23	2	7	54	0	6	6	45	3	58	11	3	6	.398	.348

Player, Team	Avg.	G	TPA	AB	R	H	TB	2B	3B	HR	RBI	SH	SF	HP	BB	IBB	SO	SB	CS	GDP	Slg.	OBP
White, Chad, Quad City†	.244	75	289	242	36	59	73	14	0	0	18	4	2	1	37	3	35	12	4	5	.302	.344
White, Walter, Kane County	.285	63	250	207	30	59	84	18	2	1	23	5	3	3	32	0	52	3	2	3	.406	.384
Whittaker, Jay, South Bend	.220	67	259	227	29	50	85	14	3	5	31	1	2	3	26	0	58	14	5	5	.374	.306
Williams, Drew, Beloit*	.267	135	517	427	66	114	181	21	2	14	66	1	2	6	81	4	76	8	8	9	.424	.390
Wilson, Chris, Beloit	.190	28	68	63	12	12	15	1	1	0	6	0	0	2	3	0	14	5	1	0	.238	.250
Wilson, Todd, Burlington	.257	30	115	105	8	27	38	5	0	2	11	0	0	4	6	0	12	1	0	1	.362	.322
Winget, Jeremy, Clinton*	.269	120	445	375	49	101	139	23	0	5	44	1	1	1	67	3	75	4	4	7	.371	.381
Wojtkowski, Steve, Michigan*	.000	6	17	14	2	0	0	0	0	0	0	0	0	0	3	0	3	0	0	1	.000	.176
Woodard, Steve, Beloit*	.000	22	1	1	0	0	0	0	0	0	1	0	0	0	0	0	0	0	0	0	.000	.000
Wulfert, Mark, Clinton	.245	48	167	147	17	36	51	10	1	1	16	1	1	1	17	0	34	9	2	1	.347	.325
Young, Kevin, Cedar Rapids	.291	119	459	395	58	115	147	22	2	2	46	7	4	15	37	0	42	17	12	7	.372	.370
Zaletel, Brian, Burlington	.227	27	105	97	9	22	32	4	0	2	5	0	1	3	4	0	19	0	0	5	.330	.276
Zerpa, Mauro, South Bend	.221	41	95	86	5	19	20	1	0	0	5	2	0	1	6	0	20	1	0	3	.233	.280
Zwisler, Josh, Beloit	.234	98	287	252	29	59	76	12	1	1	18	2	0	4	28	1	46	8	4	4	.302	.320

GRAND SLAMS: Carone, Donati, E. Harris, Moeder, 2 each; Bautista, Delgado, Faggett, Freeman, Freire, Hacopian, Hamilton, Herrick, Jackson, Livsey, Melo, Nilsson, Pratt, Robledo, Rocha, N. Rodriguez, Sadler, J. Soriano, Towner, Truby, Watson, Whittaker, 1 each.

AWARDED FIRST BASE ON CATCHER'S INTERFERENCE: Clifford 5 (Amezcua, Andreopoulos, Coe, Fortin, Welch); Andreopoulos 3 (Cline, Hilt, Valentin); C. White 3 (Valentin 3); Coe 2 (Ballara, Cline); Harvey 2 (Ballara, Cline); McDonald 2 (Espiritu, Roskos); Olmstead 2 (Rosario, Zwisler); Pico 2 (Schneider, Sutherland); Swift 2 (Cline, Rosario); Cady (Poor); J. Cook (DePastino); Fortin (B. Molina); Gibralter (Cline); Kominek (M. Rodriguez); Lowry (Valentin); Lugo (Rosario); Mathis (Valentin); Richardson (Ortega); Robinson (Rosario); M. Rodriguez (Barton); V. Rodriguez (Encarnacion); Schwenke (Campillo); Swift (Cline); Truby (Sutherland); Young (Cline); Zwisler (Cline).

PLAYERS WITH TWO OR MORE TEAMS

Player, Team	Avg.	G	TPA	AB	R	H	TB	2B	3B	HR	RBI	SH	SF	HP	BB	IBB	SO	SB	CS	GDP	Slg.	OBP
Delgado, Wilson, Wisconsin†	.243	19	75	70	13	17	20	3	0	0	7	2	0	0	3	0	15	3	0	5	.286	.274
Delgado, Wilson, Burlington†	.310	93	402	365	52	113	154	20	3	5	37	2	1	2	32	1	57	9	9	7	.422	.368
Smith, Demond, Cedar Rapids†	.341	79	361	317	64	108	168	25	7	7	41	5	1	6	32	2	61	37	12	3	.530	.410
Smith, Demond, West Michigan†	.313	8	36	32	6	10	19	1	1	2	3	1	0	1	2	1	8	3	2	0	.594	.371

1995 PITCHING

TEAM

Team	W	L	Pct.	ERA	G	CG	ShO	Sv.	IP	H	TBF	R	ER	HR	SH	SF	HB	BB	IBB	SO	WP	Bk.
Quad City	76	61	.555	3.19	137	7	11	35	1166.1	1011	4930	533	414	73	38	31	59	427	11	922	63	10
Wisconsin	63	75	.457	3.75	138	14	8	35	1180.0	1055	5062	599	492	74	36	36	60	501	28	917	82	13
South Bend	66	69	.489	3.76	135	13	8	27	1183.2	1169	5119	620	495	74	55	40	71	459	6	843	87	30
Peoria	62	72	.463	3.80	134	6	9	36	1131.0	1039	4864	605	478	72	41	33	39	466	6	937	55	15
Beloit	88	51	.633	3.93	139	8	9	49	1195.2	1114	5142	618	522	83	40	35	59	503	12	1064	89	28
West Michigan	67	69	.493	3.95	136	1	9	36	1174.2	1146	5209	664	515	62	36	30	81	550	11	893	83	26
Fort Wayne	75	65	.536	4.03	140	4	8	41	1236.1	1187	5365	660	554	83	50	42	74	515	13	1029	120	20
Michigan	75	63	.543	4.05	138	9	5	31	1208.2	1130	5227	665	544	81	50	55	71	502	13	975	82	13
Cedar Rapids	76	62	.551	4.06	138	16	6	40	1184.2	1184	5160	655	534	79	48	31	4	425	23	907	81	21
Rockford	75	65	.536	4.12	140	4	5	29	1201.0	1136	5226	663	550	76	36	52	73	508	8	829	123	16
Kane County	69	69	.500	4.20	138	5	8	26	1181.2	1168	5230	668	551	79	49	41	99	495	28	879	87	10
Springfield	65	74	.468	4.32	139	4	5	22	1175.1	1248	5161	680	564	103	41	45	54	429	3	729	95	7
Clinton	51	86	.372	4.32	137	19	4	25	1129.0	1146	5035	690	542	70	44	38	71	504	43	865	93	17
Burlington	54	81	.400	4.45	135	6	4	35	1103.0	1112	4972	710	545	95	42	45	56	597	38	898	114	13

INDIVIDUAL

TOP QUALIFIERS FOR EARNED-RUN AVERAGE TITLE

Minimum 112 innings. *Lefthanded pitcher.

Pitcher, Team	W	L	Pct.	ERA	G	GS	CG	ShO	GF	Sv.	IP	H	TBF	R	ER	HR	SH	SF	HB	BB	IBB	SO	WP	Bk.
Corrigan, Cory, Peoria	4	7	.364	2.32	47	10	0	0	5	0	112.2	90	450	36	29	3	5	5	2	23	0	84	4	1
D'Amico, Jeff, Beloit	13	3	.813	2.39	21	20	3	1	0	0	132.0	102	523	40	35	7	3	2	4	31	2	119	6	1
Mounce, Tony, Quad City*	16	8	.667	2.43	25	25	3	1	0	0	159.0	118	649	55	43	6	6	6	3	57	2	143	6	2
Smith, Charles, South Bend	10	10	.500	2.69	26	25	4	2	1	0	167.0	128	688	70	50	8	7	2	13	61	0	145	21	11
Walters, Brett, Clinton	8	7	.533	2.71	32	19	4	0	4	1	146.0	133	598	58	44	9	6	1	10	27	3	122	4	2
Dickson, Jason, Cedar Rapids	14	6	.700	2.86	25	25	9	1	0	0	173.0	151	708	71	55	12	4	3	8	45	0	134	7	2
Dale, Carl, Peoria	9	9	.500	2.94	24	24	2	1	0	0	143.2	124	613	66	47	8	3	2	1	62	0	104	4	1
Kester, Tim, Quad City	12	5	.706	2.97	28	23	2	0	3	0	160.2	158	665	80	53	8	5	6	10	20	1	111	4	0
Bieniasz, Derek, Wisconsin	11	10	.524	3.13	27	27	4	2	0	0	175.1	145	717	76	61	7	8	6	10	54	3	99	4	3
Cloude, Ken, Wisconsin	9	8	.529	3.24	25	25	4	0	0	0	161.0	137	677	64	58	8	1	7	8	63	4	140	10	1
Parisi, Michael, Kane County	11	8	.579	3.29	26	26	2	1	0	0	164.1	152	687	73	60	7	2	6	9	42	1	113	11	0
Bigham, Dave, South Bend*	8	7	.533	3.29	25	23	1	1	1	0	153.0	176	651	62	56	9	10	5	11	35	0	101	10	2
King, Bill, West Michigan	9	7	.563	3.34	30	18	0	0	3	2	148.1	152	633	75	55	6	5	1	5	41	0	95	6	5
Isom, Jeff, Clinton*	8	8	.500	3.40	35	15	2	1	8	2	116.1	123	501	56	44	7	7	5	6	42	5	94	5	1
Tollberg, Brian, Beloit	13	4	.765	3.41	22	22	1	1	0	0	132.0	119	529	59	50	10	2	5	6	27	0	110	5	4

DEPARTMENTAL LEADERS: W—Mounce, 16; L—Lock, 15; Pct.—D'Amico, .813; G—Reed, 63; GS—Several pitchers tied with 27; CG—Dickson, 9; ShO—C. Beck, Bieniasz, Raggio, C. Smith, 2; GF—Rain, 51; Sv.—Welch, 31; IP—Al. Garcia, 177.0; H—R. Smith, 179; TBF—Al. Garcia, 755; R—R. Smith, 100; ER—R. Smith, 89; HR—Mercado, 18; SH—Bigham, 10; SF—Barksdale, Faulkner, 9; HB—Al. Garcia, 15; BB—Miranda, 88; IBB—B. Smith, 7; SO—C. Smith, 145; WP—Mix, 29; Bk.—C. Smith, 11.

ALL PITCHERS

*Lefthanded pitcher.

Pitcher, Team	W	L	Pct.	ERA	G	GS	CG	ShO	GF	Sv.	IP	H	TBF	R	ER	HR	SH	SF	HB	BB	IBB	SO	WP	Bk.
Abreu, Jose, Burlington	1	0	1.000	3.46	8	0	0	0	1	0	13.0	9	61	8	5	0	1	1	1	12	0	14	0	2
Abreu, Juan, Burlington*	0	0	.000	0.00	2	0	0	0	1	0	2.0	1	11	3	0	0	0	1	0	4	1	0	0	0
Aguirre, Jose, Cedar Rapids*	0	0	.000	3.86	6	2	0	0	0	0	14.0	12	61	6	6	1	0	1	0	10	0	12	2	0
Alejo, Nigel, Kane County	4	1	.800	2.39	48	0	0	0	38	7	52.2	48	233	17	14	5	2	0	2	25	2	47	5	0
Ali, Sam, Burlington	0	0	.000	2.25	3	0	0	0	2	0	4.0	4	16	1	1	0	0	0	0	0	0	2	0	0
Altman, Heath, Burlington	0	0	.000	2.45	3	0	0	0	1	0	3.2	3	20	2	1	0	0	0	0	6	0	5	1	0
Alvarado, Luis, Fort Wayne	1	1	.500	2.92	16	1	0	0	6	2	37.0	41	165	18	12	2	0	1	1	14	1	24	1	0
Alvarez, Ivan, Burlington*	1	2	.333	4.85	4	2	0	0	0	0	13.0	17	59	12	7	2	1	0	0	5	0	12	3	0
Ambrose, John, South Bend	1	1	.500	5.40	3	3	1	0	0	0	16.2	18	77	13	10	2	1	0	0	10	0	15	2	0
Andersen, Mark, Kane County	1	2	.333	3.46	15	0	0	0	5	1	26.0	29	116	13	10	3	1	1	1	13	1	15	2	0
Anderson, Eric, Springfield	9	5	.643	3.40	21	14	1	1	2	1	92.2	89	391	39	35	4	0	2	4	34	1	52	8	0
Bair, Dennis, Rockford	4	2	.667	1.51	9	7	0	0	1	0	53.2	41	209	10	9	2	1	1	1	6	0	40	4	1
Barker, Richard, Rockford	2	0	1.000	3.71	32	0	0	0	15	1	43.2	45	196	20	18	2	1	0	2	20	1	23	5	0
Barksdale, Joe, Michigan	9	8	.529	4.53	24	24	1	0	0	0	141.0	139	643	91	71	7	6	9	14	78	1	93	11	3
Baron, Jim, Clinton*	0	8	.000	6.22	11	9	1	0	1	0	50.2	65	232	42	35	4	3	2	1	16	2	31	4	0
Barrios, Manuel, Quad City	1	5	.167	2.25	50	0	0	0	48	23	52.0	44	219	16	13	1	2	1	4	17	1	55	1	0
Beck, Chris, Wisconsin	12	8	.600	3.88	28	19	2	2	6	2	130.0	113	553	62	56	13	3	3	4	61	2	119	10	1
Beck, Greg, Beloit	5	2	.714	4.72	35	5	0	0	12	2	74.1	73	331	46	39	2	1	6	2	35	2	91	7	2
Bedinger, Doug, Fort Wayne	6	6	.500	4.61	46	0	0	0	35	9	66.1	74	301	37	34	8	7	5	4	28	3	62	5	0
Bell, Jason, Fort Wayne	3	1	.750	1.31	9	6	0	0	2	0	34.1	26	139	11	5	0	3	0	1	6	0	40	6	2
Bernal, Manuel, Springfield	1	5	.167	7.38	8	8	0	0	0	0	42.2	55	193	37	35	9	1	0	3	9	0	17	1	0
Betances, Junior, Beloit	0	0	.000	0.00	1	0	0	0	1	0	0.1	1	2	0	0	0	0	0	0	0	0	0	0	1
Betti, Rich, Michigan*	0	0	.000	0.00	1	0	0	0	0	0	2.0	0	7	0	0	0	0	0	0	1	0	1	0	0
Beverlin, Jason, West Michigan	3	9	.250	4.04	22	14	0	0	1	0	89.0	76	392	51	40	4	3	3	8	40	0	84	5	5
Bieniasz, Derek, Wisconsin	11	10	.524	3.13	27	27	4	2	0	0	175.1	145	717	76	61	7	8	6	10	54	3	99	4	3
Bigham, Dave, South Bend*	8	7	.533	3.29	25	23	1	1	1	0	153.0	176	651	62	56	9	10	5	11	35	0	101	10	2
Blais, Mike, Michigan	2	1	.667	1.96	32	0	0	0	26	10	46.0	34	184	12	10	0	3	4	1	11	3	35	4	0
Blanco, Alberto, Quad City*	3	3	.500	3.13	11	11	1	1	0	0	54.2	47	231	22	19	2	0	3	1	19	0	58	3	0
Bogle, Sean, Rockford	1	0	1.000	1.21	13	0	0	0	3	0	22.1	17	84	3	3	0	2	1	0	9	0	15	1	0
Bonilla, Welnis, Michigan	1	1	.500	6.17	12	0	0	0	8	1	11.2	12	58	12	8	1	1	0	1	10	0	7	0	1
Brewer, Billy, Springfield*	0	0	.000	0.00	1	0	0	0	1	1	2.0	2	9	1	0	0	0	0	0	1	0	2	0	0
Brixey, Dustin, Springfield	4	5	.444	3.79	36	8	0	0	6	2	102.0	101	438	51	43	3	3	6	7	40	0	44	6	0
Bronkey, Jeff, Beloit	0	1	.000	3.68	3	3	0	0	0	0	7.1	5	32	5	3	1	0	0	1	3	0	8	1	0
Broome, Curtis, South Bend	5	8	.385	4.48	29	4	1	0	10	1	90.1	101	399	53	45	9	3	2	3	39	0	62	5	1
Bryant, Chris, Rockford*	2	2	.500	6.43	21	0	0	0	9	0	35.0	32	152	26	25	5	0	1	3	17	1	29	3	0
Burt, Chris, Beloit	1	3	.250	3.80	36	0	0	0	32	27	42.2	34	176	19	18	2	4	2	1	17	1	42	2	0
Bush, Craig, Michigan	7	3	.700	3.82	34	2	0	0	18	6	75.1	68	320	37	32	8	2	0	3	30	0	78	4	0
Bushart, John, Cedar Rapids*	2	2	.500	7.36	19	3	0	0	7	0	36.2	47	179	34	30	6	0	0	4	17	0	24	3	0
Bussa, Todd, Kane County	0	1	.000	0.86	36	0	0	0	33	14	42.0	20	162	4	4	1	1	1	6	15	5	38	3	0
Byrne, Earl, Rockford*	4	3	.571	4.65	13	11	0	0	0	0	60.0	54	269	36	31	2	3	6	3	38	0	51	8	1
Cardona, Isbell, Burlington	0	4	.000	7.00	6	4	0	0	0	0	18.0	19	94	21	14	4	1	2	1	20	1	12	2	1
Carl, Todd, Kane County	0	5	.000	8.54	12	7	0	0	2	0	39.0	69	192	37	37	8	0	1	5	11	0	22	7	0
Carroll, David, Peoria*	2	2	.500	4.38	24	6	0	0	5	0	51.1	53	230	33	25	3	2	0	3	24	0	41	6	1
Carter, Lance, Springfield	9	5	.643	3.99	27	24	1	1	0	0	137.2	151	584	77	61	14	2	4	8	22	0	118	11	1
Casey, Ryan, Rockford	0	2	.000	6.05	16	0	0	0	8	1	19.1	19	89	15	13	1	1	1	1	11	0	12	3	1
Castro, Dennis, Kane County	0	0	.000	0.00	1	0	0	0	1	0	1.0	2	7	1	0	0	0	0	0	1	0	1	0	0
Chapman, Walker, Fort Wayne	2	6	.250	6.24	14	11	0	0	2	1	53.1	59	249	41	37	4	2	3	2	36	0	31	3	1
Charlton, Aaron, Burlington	0	1	.000	4.13	16	0	0	0	6	0	24.0	18	105	13	11	2	0	1	4	13	0	16	4	0
Cintron, Jose, Cedar Rapids	5	3	.625	3.84	13	9	1	1	0	0	68.0	65	280	36	29	4	2	2	2	9	0	38	2	1
Cloude, Ken, Wisconsin	9	8	.529	3.24	25	25	4	0	0	0	161.0	137	677	64	58	8	1	7	8	63	4	140	10	1
Cobb, Trevor, Fort Wayne*	4	4	.500	3.88	11	10	0	0	0	0	53.1	51	226	26	23	3	1	0	3	18	0	46	6	0
Cochrane, Chris, West Michigan	6	4	.600	3.07	41	4	0	0	29	9	85.0	79	357	37	29	7	4	1	5	28	3	48	3	1
Cook, Jake, Michigan	5	3	.625	4.83	21	11	1	0	3	0	76.1	68	333	48	41	3	5	1	2	39	0	50	12	2
Corrigan, Cory, Peoria	4	7	.364	2.32	47	10	0	0	5	0	112.2	90	450	36	29	3	5	5	2	23	0	84	4	1
Crossley, Chad, Cedar Rapids	0	0	.000	7.71	12	0	0	0	7	1	16.1	18	85	16	14	2	2	2	8	15	0	9	5	1
Crump, Jody, Peoria*	1	1	.500	6.19	25	0	0	0	7	0	36.1	40	167	25	25	3	1	1	0	26	0	16	3	1
Curran, Tighe, Peoria*	3	0	1.000	2.90	24	0	0	0	7	0	40.1	35	174	18	13	0	2	0	2	21	0	21	2	1
Dafun, George, Cedar Rapids	0	1	.000	3.27	5	1	0	0	2	0	11.0	15	56	5	4	1	0	1	0	10	1	13	1	0
Dale, Carl, Peoria	9	9	.500	2.94	24	24	2	1	0	0	143.2	124	613	66	47	8	3	2	1	62	0	104	4	1
Dalton, Brian, Beloit	4	3	.571	2.74	34	4	0	0	13	4	82.0	70	345	31	25	0	4	2	2	44	0	75	5	4
D'Amico, Jeff, Beloit	13	3	.813	2.39	21	20	3	1	0	0	132.0	102	523	40	35	7	3	2	4	31	2	119	6	1
Daniels, John, Wisconsin	4	5	.444	2.66	39	0	0	0	19	7	74.1	63	315	28	22	5	0	2	6	22	2	60	2	0
Davalillo, David, Cedar Rapids	0	0	.000	0.00	1	0	0	0	1	0	2.0	0	7	0	0	0	0	0	0	1	0	3	0	1
Davis, Keith, Clinton	2	5	.286	5.22	36	8	0	0	15	2	70.2	64	313	41	41	2	0	5	3	45	0	54	7	1
Deakman, Josh, Cedar Rapids	4	2	.667	3.59	13	13	0	0	0	0	72.2	67	301	33	29	5	3	2	7	24	0	53	5	0
Dean, Mark, Peoria	0	0	.000	0.00	2	0	0	0	2	0	2.0	0	7	0	0	0	0	0	1	0	0	1	0	0
Delvalle, Henry, West Michigan*	1	1	.500	3.38	3	0	0	0	0	0	5.1	4	24	4	2	0	0	0	0	4	0	8	1	0
Dennis, Brian, Rockford	0	0	.000	3.60	3	0	0	0	2	1	5.0	6	21	2	2	0	0	0	0	1	0	4	0	0
Dennis, Shane, Clinton*	3	9	.250	3.87	14	14	3	0	0	0	86.0	68	364	51	37	5	4	0	2	35	3	80	5	0
DeWitt, Scott, Kane County*	0	0	.000	0.00	1	1	0	0	0	0	3.0	0	10	0	0	0	0	0	1	1	0	2	0	0
Dickson, Jason, Cedar Rapids	14	6	.700	2.86	25	25	9	1	0	0	173.0	151	708	71	55	12	4	3	8	45	0	134	7	2
Diorio, Mike, Quad City	6	4	.600	3.24	33	11	0	0	4	1	91.2	82	391	39	33	6	4	0	4	36	1	81	13	2
Dixon, Jim, South Bend	1	2	.333	4.86	10	1	0	0	6	0	16.2	25	81	16	9	2	1	1	3	4	1	11	3	1
Domenico, Brian, Michigan	0	2	.000	2.89	6	1	0	0	1	0	9.1	11	48	12	3	3	3	0	0	11	1	5	0	0
Doughty, Brian, Wisconsin	5	7	.417	3.95	32	3	0	0	12	4	84.1	83	360	50	37	4	4	3	6	26	3	54	5	0
Dowhower, Deron, Fort Wayne	3	0	1.000	3.27	35	0	0	0	13	3	77.0	53	331	32	28	4	4	4	4	49	0	97	13	0
Droll, Jeff, South Bend	0	1	.000	3.21	8	0	0	0	4	1	14.0	25	72	11	5	0	0	1	0	4	1	9	0	0
Duncan, Sean, South Bend*	0	0	.000	0.79	12	0	0	0	7	0	11.1	8	44	2	1	0	0	0	0	3	0	8	0	0
Dutch, John, Michigan	2	4	.333	7.94	32	0	0	0	16	1	51.0	80	257	50	45	5	3	6	3	20	1	23	3	1
Elarton, Scott, Quad City	13	7	.650	4.45	26	26	0	0	0	0	149.2	149	668	86	74	12	8	4	8	71	2	112	12	0

Pitcher, Team	W	L	Pct.	ERA	G	GS	CG	ShO	GF	Sv.	IP	H	TBF	R	ER	HR	SH	SF	HB	BB	IBB	SO	WP	Bk.
Epstein, Ian, West Michigan*	5	0	1.000	5.89	18	0	0	0	7	0	18.1	24	89	14	12	2	1	1	2	10	0	16	3	0
Erdos, Todd, Clinton	0	0	.000	5.40	5	1	0	0	1	0	5.0	4	27	4	3	0	0	0	0	8	1	1	2	0
Estes, Shawn, Wis.-Bur.*	0	0	.000	2.84	6	6	0	0	0	0	25.1	18	110	9	8	2	0	1	2	17	0	33	4	1
Farmer, Jon, Kane County*	1	4	.200	6.98	29	11	0	0	4	0	78.2	97	369	65	61	9	1	5	8	32	1	60	7	2
Farrell, Jim, Michigan	3	2	.600	3.65	13	13	1	0	0	0	69.0	62	291	34	28	10	1	1	5	23	0	70	3	1
Faulkner, Neal, Rockford	2	3	.400	3.90	40	0	0	0	17	1	67.0	61	290	36	29	3	3	9	3	29	1	47	10	1
Felix, Ruben, Beloit*	4	3	.571	5.40	45	0	0	0	9	0	48.1	49	233	33	29	6	5	1	2	36	2	60	4	1
Fennell, Barry, Rockford*	2	1	.667	2.35	4	4	0	0	0	0	23.0	19	94	8	6	2	0	2	1	8	0	13	1	1
Fidge, Darren, Fort Wayne	6	5	.545	3.68	39	17	1	0	20	13	134.1	126	572	62	55	11	4	2	9	37	1	106	15	1
Filbeck, Ryan, Kane County	5	0	1.000	3.67	25	0	0	0	6	1	41.2	40	182	19	17	0	2	3	3	17	3	28	7	0
Fitzpatrick, Kenneth, Springfield	2	2	.500	3.92	12	7	0	0	1	0	43.2	36	187	26	19	3	1	1	1	17	0	29	4	1
Fitzpatrick, Will, Beloit	0	0	.000	2.45	3	0	0	0	3	0	3.2	3	17	1	1	1	0	0	1	2	0	2	0	0
Fletcher, Paul, South Bend*	4	4	.500	2.98	36	0	0	0	24	5	57.1	55	250	21	19	2	5	1	3	24	1	49	5	1
Flury, Pat, Springfield	2	6	.250	4.31	34	0	0	0	19	1	54.1	65	246	32	26	5	4	1	1	24	0	35	2	0
Foderaro, Kevin, Peoria	3	8	.273	6.20	15	14	0	0	0	0	69.2	80	316	58	48	4	3	5	1	24	1	36	3	0
Freehill, Michael, Cedar Rapids	4	5	.444	2.62	54	0	0	0	49	28	55.0	54	234	25	16	4	3	0	7	12	5	47	10	1
Gamboa, Javier, Springfield	6	6	.500	3.15	19	19	1	0	0	0	105.2	83	429	45	37	10	3	2	0	32	0	66	4	0
Garcia, Alfredo, Rockford	14	9	.609	3.76	27	27	1	1	0	0	177.0	176	755	94	74	13	4	4	15	43	0	120	10	0
Garcia, Ariel, South Bend	4	2	.667	3.14	10	10	0	0	0	0	57.1	54	246	23	20	3	3	2	8	19	0	46	4	2
Garrett, Hal, Clinton	3	8	.273	5.59	11	11	1	0	0	0	58.0	58	268	43	36	4	5	2	4	34	3	41	5	0
Gates, Sean, Clinton	0	2	.000	4.99	29	0	0	0	12	1	39.2	39	178	23	22	3	2	2	5	19	3	27	1	0
Gautreau, Mike, Peoria	4	3	.571	4.55	45	0	0	0	9	0	63.1	62	278	42	32	3	3	1	2	29	1	55	2	2
Gomez, Augustine, S. Bend	7	6	.538	4.13	25	25	1	0	0	0	144.0	120	615	85	66	7	4	7	8	68	0	99	9	6
Gomez, Dennys, Burlington	1	1	.500	3.74	14	0	0	0	9	0	21.2	25	97	11	9	2	1	0	0	11	1	26	6	0
Gonzalez, Gabe, Kane County*	4	4	.500	2.28	32	0	0	0	10	1	43.1	32	181	18	11	0	2	1	2	14	2	41	1	0
Gonzalez, Geremis, Rockford	4	4	.500	5.10	12	12	1	0	0	0	65.1	63	297	43	37	4	1	4	8	28	0	36	8	1
Gonzalez, Juan, Beloit	11	5	.688	4.16	42	6	0	0	17	6	88.2	86	386	50	41	4	3	4	6	37	1	53	16	0
Gooda, David, Beloit*	0	0	.000	3.77	3	3	0	0	0	0	14.1	13	61	8	6	1	1	0	1	7	0	9	0	0
Gould, Clint, Wisconsin	0	0	.000	5.77	25	0	0	0	15	0	34.1	34	164	24	22	4	1	0	2	28	1	20	1	0
Gourdin, Tom, Fort Wayne	6	6	.500	4.42	41	0	0	0	19	6	89.2	90	384	49	44	10	3	3	9	32	0	74	11	2
Green, Chris, Wisconsin	1	5	.167	3.67	35	0	0	0	18	2	56.1	55	244	31	23	3	3	3	5	21	6	43	3	3
Grenert, Geoff, Cedar Rapids	3	4	.429	4.13	27	4	0	0	7	1	72.0	76	319	43	33	4	1	4	9	23	1	55	3	1
Grote, Jason, Burlington	0	1	.000	9.35	6	0	0	0	2	1	8.2	10	41	10	9	2	0	0	2	5	0	5	1	0
Gunderson, Mike, Quad City	3	2	.600	2.74	44	0	0	0	10	1	65.2	46	270	25	20	1	0	0	5	27	0	48	4	2
Gunther, Kevin, W. Michigan	1	3	.250	3.71	17	0	0	0	7	2	26.2	28	117	16	11	1	0	2	2	3	1	17	2	1
Halama, John, Quad City*	1	2	.333	2.02	55	0	0	0	26	2	62.1	48	241	16	14	7	2	1	3	22	1	56	1	0
Hale, Chad, Michigan*	6	3	.667	2.48	42	0	0	0	14	2	69.0	68	280	27	19	4	2	5	2	13	1	49	3	0
Hall, Billy, Quad City	4	2	.667	2.15	36	0	0	0	20	7	50.1	29	199	18	12	3	0	0	2	18	2	36	3	1
Hall, Yates, Peoria	2	5	.286	4.53	9	8	0	0	0	0	45.2	45	197	25	23	4	0	1	0	24	0	47	5	0
Hammerschmidt, Andy, Clinton*	5	5	.500	3.87	14	14	1	0	0	0	86.0	89	355	40	37	7	3	3	6	18	2	51	0	2
Hause, Brendan, W. Michigan*	8	7	.533	3.87	31	18	0	0	4	0	137.1	136	595	75	59	10	5	5	4	57	0	106	6	0
Hebbert, Allan, Kane County	0	1	.000	12.38	5	2	0	0	2	0	8.0	9	46	12	11	1	0	1	2	15	0	3	2	0
Herbert, Russell, South Bend	2	4	.333	3.52	9	9	0	0	0	0	53.2	46	224	25	21	3	1	0	3	27	0	48	1	2
Hernandez, Santos, Burlington	5	8	.385	2.66	44	0	0	0	28	9	64.1	54	274	27	19	3	4	4	2	20	2	85	1	0
Hill, Jason, Cedar Rapids*	2	1	.667	4.55	48	0	0	0	17	2	59.1	59	276	38	30	4	8	1	5	41	6	49	2	1
Huntsman, Scott, Beloit	4	3	.571	2.72	43	0	0	0	14	1	49.2	42	229	17	15	3	2	1	5	34	2	49	5	0
Hutzler, Jeff, Burlington	3	5	.375	3.48	9	9	0	0	0	0	51.2	51	223	34	20	4	3	2	2	17	1	44	4	1
Ignasiak, Mike, Beloit	0	0	.000	0.00	1	1	0	0	0	0	3.0	0	11	0	0	0	0	0	0	2	0	4	0	0
Isom, Jeff, Clinton*	8	8	.500	3.40	35	15	2	1	8	2	116.1	123	501	56	44	7	7	5	6	42	5	94	5	1
Jenkins, A.J., Clinton	1	12	.077	6.60	33	13	2	0	5	0	91.1	109	437	80	67	10	3	6	5	55	5	54	10	0
Johnson, Ron, Peoria*	5	7	.417	3.17	22	19	0	0	0	0	102.1	105	449	56	36	9	4	4	4	36	0	61	1	0
Jones, Scott, Michigan	2	0	1.000	5.68	5	0	0	0	3	0	6.1	3	31	5	4	2	0	0	0	8	0	13	2	0
Keith, Jeffrey, Burlington*	1	3	.250	2.98	47	0	0	0	38	23	66.1	35	275	26	22	1	4	3	6	42	4	74	4	0
Kester, Tim, Quad City	12	5	.706	2.97	28	23	2	0	3	0	160.2	158	665	80	53	8	5	6	10	20	1	111	4	0
Khoury, Tony, Rockford	2	2	.500	4.60	28	1	0	0	13	0	45.0	49	213	37	23	4	2	2	5	26	1	38	6	0
King, Bill, West Michigan	9	7	.563	3.34	30	18	0	0	3	2	148.1	152	633	75	55	6	5	1	5	41	0	95	6	5
Knox, Jeffery, Cedar Rapids	7	6	.538	4.92	25	17	0	0	1	0	108.0	125	479	69	59	4	4	3	13	24	0	56	6	6
Krause, Kevin, Rockford	6	7	.462	3.81	30	13	0	0	5	0	99.1	96	431	53	42	7	2	1	5	41	0	58	10	1
Krueger, Robert, Wisconsin*	0	0	.000	4.50	19	0	0	0	5	0	22.0	21	99	12	11	0	0	0	2	11	0	20	4	0
Kurek, Chris, Michigan	0	0	.000	9.00	1	0	0	0	1	0	1.0	1	4	1	1	1	0	0	0	0	0	0	0	0
Lake, Kevin, Burlington*	10	7	.588	4.45	28	21	0	0	2	0	119.1	136	544	75	59	10	2	3	6	61	3	85	9	0
Leach, Jumaane, Clinton*	1	3	.250	3.71	19	0	0	0	7	0	26.2	30	123	17	11	1	1	0	2	7	2	12	2	0
Leibee, Skye, West Michigan*	0	1	.000	11.74	9	0	0	0	1	0	7.2	9	48	13	10	0	0	1	3	13	0	5	2	0
Leiber, Zane, South Bend	0	0	.000	6.91	14	0	0	0	8	1	28.2	35	134	26	22	3	1	1	2	9	0	21	2	3
Linares, Yfrain, Beloit	3	3	.500	4.29	19	12	0	0	3	0	71.1	75	324	42	34	2	1	3	5	43	0	63	5	3
Lindemann, Wayne, S. Bend	0	4	.000	7.36	7	6	0	0	1	0	22.0	32	117	21	18	5	1	1	2	16	0	15	0	0
Lintern, Cory, Burlington	1	0	1.000	6.00	8	0	0	0	4	0	15.0	19	67	10	10	4	1	0	1	5	1	8	1	0
Lock, Dan, Quad City*	8	15	.348	4.15	27	27	1	0	0	0	143.0	152	642	94	66	13	8	4	10	58	0	90	5	0
Logan, Chris, Clinton	4	6	.400	2.18	53	0	0	0	42	17	62.0	62	284	29	15	0	1	0	2	27	4	61	7	0
Lowe, Jason, West Michigan	0	0	.000	11.00	7	0	0	0	4	0	9.0	17	50	14	11	4	0	0	0	6	0	7	2	0
Lundquist, David, South Bend	8	4	.667	3.58	18	18	5	1	0	0	118.0	107	492	54	47	4	7	3	5	38	0	60	3	0
MacDonald, Mike, Springfield	6	5	.545	3.30	55	0	0	0	48	12	62.2	49	261	24	23	8	4	2	3	27	0	49	3	1
Mamott, Joe, Michigan	3	6	.333	5.96	14	13	1	0	0	0	77.0	76	352	56	51	4	1	7	8	50	0	66	5	3
Marquez, Ihosvany, Michigan	1	0	1.000	7.71	3	0	0	0	0	0	4.2	3	21	4	4	0	0	0	0	4	0	7	0	0
Martinez, Javier, Rockford	6	6	.500	3.96	18	18	1	0	0	0	104.2	100	455	56	46	6	5	4	12	39	0	53	15	2
Martinez, Uriel, Clinton	0	0	.000	5.19	11	0	0	0	2	0	17.1	27	84	15	10	2	0	1	0	3	0	8	5	2
May, Scott, Rockford	3	0	1.000	1.71	8	3	0	0	0	0	26.1	20	108	7	5	0	1	0	1	9	0	24	0	0
Mays, Marcus, Kane County*	1	2	.333	6.17	8	0	0	0	5	0	11.2	15	56	8	8	1	2	0	0	7	1	6	1	0
McCormack, Andy, South Bend*	1	2	.333	4.63	6	4	0	0	2	0	23.1	26	105	14	12	3	2	1	1	11	0	10	1	0
McMillan, Leonard, Burlington	1	0	1.000	5.27	8	0	0	0	1	0	13.2	15	65	8	8	2	0	0	1	10	1	4	3	0
McMullen, Mike, Burlington	4	10	.286	5.49	29	11	2	0	6	0	83.2	98	410	76	51	5	2	4	9	54	3	53	9	2
Meadows, Brian, Kane County	9	9	.500	4.22	26	26	1	1	0	0	147.0	163	646	90	69	11	8	4	12	41	0	103	3	2
Mercado, Gabby, Beloit	11	6	.647	5.36	24	23	0	0	1	0	129.1	138	565	89	77	18	3	3	5	50	1	89	6	3

Pitcher, Team	W	L	Pct.	ERA	G	GS	CG	ShO	GF	Sv.	IP	H	TBF	R	ER	HR	SH	SF	HB	BB	IBB	SO	WP	Bk.
Meyhoff, Jason, Fort Wayne*	2	1	.667	6.59	17	10	0	0	3	0	54.2	70	258	52	40	5	1	5	2	30	0	35	5	3
Micknich, Steve, Kane County	1	0	1.000	2.31	9	0	0	0	3	0	11.2	13	58	3	3	0	0	1	4	6	0	10	4	1
Miles, Chad, Kane County*	1	1	.500	7.24	19	0	0	0	4	0	27.1	35	145	33	22	3	4	4	4	23	1	14	2	1
Miranda, Walter, Kane County	8	7	.533	4.08	25	25	1	0	0	0	128.0	102	562	68	58	9	7	4	9	88	2	106	11	2
Mitchell, Alvin, Michigan	6	8	.429	5.31	30	17	0	0	4	1	115.1	120	513	75	68	9	7	8	7	64	1	74	10	1
Mix, Derek, Clinton	1	0	1.000	5.14	35	0	0	0	18	1	49.0	34	247	42	28	1	2	3	12	54	2	40	29	0
Montelongo, Joseph, Rockford	10	7	.588	4.26	20	20	1	0	0	0	118.1	109	512	62	56	8	4	5	6	49	0	82	8	1
Morgan, Eric, Wisconsin	0	0	.000	1.35	7	0	0	0	4	1	13.1	5	54	6	2	1	1	1	2	7	0	7	1	0
Morrison, Chris, West Michigan	4	1	.800	4.98	13	0	0	0	4	0	21.2	28	97	13	12	1	1	1	0	4	0	13	2	1
Mosman, Marc, Burlington	0	0	.000	0.00	8	0	0	0	5	0	9.0	5	34	0	0	0	0	0	0	4	0	6	1	0
Mott, Tom, Fort Wayne	13	4	.765	4.03	25	25	1	0	0	0	129.2	123	557	67	58	6	6	3	10	48	0	64	14	0
Mounce, Tony, Quad City*	16	8	.667	2.43	25	25	3	1	0	0	159.0	118	649	55	43	6	6	6	3	57	2	143	6	2
Mull, Blaine, Springfield	4	10	.286	4.88	25	25	0	0	0	0	125.1	142	564	79	68	12	9	7	6	50	1	71	14	0
Mullins, Greg, Beloit*	3	1	.750	3.96	15	4	0	0	6	2	36.1	26	151	16	16	2	0	1	5	14	0	48	2	3
Myers, Jason, Burlington*	2	9	.182	5.02	16	16	1	0	0	0	95.0	109	413	64	53	14	3	5	2	26	0	85	4	0
Nartker, Mike, Fort Wayne	5	5	.500	3.10	17	16	1	1	0	0	95.2	87	387	36	33	5	2	5	1	20	1	79	3	2
Nate, Scott, Beloit*	1	0	1.000	2.77	20	0	0	0	8	2	26.0	26	118	12	8	2	0	0	1	13	0	29	2	0
Nelson, Rodney, Springfield	6	10	.375	5.46	25	21	1	0	2	0	115.1	131	541	82	70	7	3	8	7	73	0	58	14	0
Newman, Damon, W. Michigan	3	4	.429	3.74	21	9	0	0	5	1	67.1	57	306	32	28	4	1	1	6	50	1	52	7	2
Newman, Eric, Clinton	1	7	.125	7.65	11	10	1	0	0	0	42.1	52	212	41	36	5	1	2	2	38	2	31	3	3
Ormonde, Troy, Rockford	0	3	.000	8.14	7	5	0	0	0	0	24.1	29	131	29	22	2	1	2	4	28	0	13	8	0
Padilla, Roy, Michigan*	0	1	.000	6.48	4	1	0	0	2	0	8.1	10	46	9	6	0	0	1	3	7	0	7	2	0
Parisi, Michael, Kane County	11	8	.579	3.29	26	26	2	1	0	0	164.1	152	687	73	60	7	2	6	9	42	1	113	11	0
Pavano, Carl, Michigan	6	6	.500	3.44	22	22	1	0	0	0	141.1	118	591	63	54	7	6	7	6	52	0	138	9	0
Pavicich, Paul, Fort Wayne*	4	3	.571	3.01	39	0	0	0	15	5	86.2	75	360	39	29	9	3	2	1	28	3	100	3	0
Pearce, Jeff, Wisconsin*	0	1	.000	7.03	27	0	0	0	9	0	24.1	21	122	21	19	1	1	1	6	25	0	19	1	1
Perez, Jayson, Clinton	0	1	.000	6.53	13	1	0	0	2	0	20.2	31	110	28	15	2	0	2	2	15	2	17	1	0
Perez, Juan, West Michigan*	11	8	.579	3.64	30	19	1	0	3	1	141.0	129	610	73	57	4	1	2	8	55	0	117	5	1
Perkins, Dan, Fort Wayne	7	12	.368	5.49	29	22	0	0	2	0	121.1	133	562	86	74	3	3	4	13	69	1	89	22	2
Peters, Brannon, Fort Wayne*	1	1	.500	4.38	11	1	0	0	5	0	24.2	29	115	17	12	1	2	0	1	16	1	24	3	0
Peterson, Jayson, Rockford	4	7	.364	6.47	13	13	0	0	0	0	65.1	67	312	56	47	5	1	2	0	47	0	45	9	1
Petroff, Daniel, Cedar Rapids	9	10	.474	4.62	27	27	2	0	0	0	146.0	153	635	86	75	9	5	4	14	47	0	98	9	2
Phillips, Marc, Springfield*	6	2	.750	3.05	38	2	0	0	14	3	85.2	88	387	47	29	5	3	5	3	38	0	41	10	0
Pineda, Leonel, Kane County	2	2	.500	3.51	5	5	1	0	0	0	33.1	44	142	14	13	0	2	2	0	6	1	10	3	0
Place, Mike, South Bend	4	5	.444	3.95	28	2	0	0	13	3	54.2	56	235	30	24	3	4	4	4	19	2	34	7	0
Pontes, Dan, Peoria	2	5	.286	1.60	34	6	0	0	9	1	67.2	47	267	19	12	1	4	1	4	15	1	88	1	0
Portillo, Alex, South Bend*	0	1	.000	4.91	2	0	0	0	1	0	3.2	5	15	2	2	0	0	0	0	0	0	4	0	0
Prater, Pete, Burlington	7	5	.583	3.69	21	20	2	0	1	0	114.2	112	499	58	47	13	4	6	2	56	3	80	13	2
Press, Greg, Kane County	10	8	.556	3.60	29	21	0	0	1	0	132.1	127	571	72	53	8	5	3	5	37	1	82	10	0
Putrich, Josh, Rockford	0	2	.000	7.45	6	1	0	0	3	0	9.2	10	41	8	8	1	0	1	0	5	1	6	1	0
Quirk, John, South Bend*	3	2	.600	3.96	22	1	0	0	9	0	52.1	52	245	32	23	4	1	6	1	36	0	30	4	0
Radinsky, Scott, South Bend*	0	0	.000	0.00	6	0	0	0	5	2	9.2	5	33	0	0	0	0	0	0	0	0	11	0	0
Radlosky, Robert, Fort Wayne	11	8	.579	4.03	30	18	1	0	5	0	120.2	111	522	64	54	11	7	5	11	55	2	102	5	2
Raggio, Brady, Peoria	3	0	1.000	1.85	8	8	3	2	0	0	48.2	42	181	13	10	1	1	1	0	2	0	34	0	0
Rain, Steve, Rockford	5	2	.714	1.21	53	0	0	0	51	23	59.1	38	234	12	8	0	3	2	2	23	3	66	8	0
Rajotte, Jason, W. Michigan*	2	2	.500	3.12	44	0	0	0	37	13	52.0	51	242	27	18	1	3	1	3	38	3	52	3	0
Ramos, Edgar, Quad City	0	1	.000	15.43	2	2	0	0	0	0	4.2	5	27	9	8	0	0	0	1	7	0	5	1	0
Rantz, Ron, Beloit*	0	1	.000	16.20	10	0	0	0	1	0	8.1	12	54	15	15	0	0	0	2	15	0	12	6	1
Ratliff, Chris, Burlington	2	6	.250	6.34	15	14	1	1	0	0	61.0	74	281	49	43	7	1	2	1	32	5	33	5	0
Rector, Bobby, Burlington	9	11	.450	4.11	27	24	0	0	0	0	135.2	135	589	78	62	7	4	5	6	59	3	102	9	2
Reed, Brian, Peoria	11	3	.786	1.79	63	0	0	0	30	4	90.1	55	357	29	18	5	5	3	6	25	2	119	3	1
Renfroe, Chad, Michigan	1	3	.250	3.13	12	3	0	0	6	2	31.2	28	138	16	11	1	0	1	2	15	2	25	4	0
Ritter, Jason, Springfield	1	0	1.000	12.34	7	0	0	0	2	0	11.2	19	65	20	16	1	0	1	2	6	0	12	3	0
Rivette, Scott, West Michigan	1	0	1.000	2.93	8	0	0	0	4	2	15.1	12	65	5	5	0	0	2	0	7	0	15	1	0
Robbins, Michael, Springfield*	2	3	.400	4.50	8	8	0	0	0	0	40.0	47	172	22	20	4	0	1	1	10	0	26	2	2
Roberts, Ray, Springfield*	2	5	.286	4.52	38	0	0	0	12	1	65.2	86	292	38	33	6	4	3	3	17	0	43	5	0
Roettgen, Mark, Peoria	0	4	.000	10.29	4	4	0	0	0	0	14.0	24	76	20	16	1	1	0	0	15	0	14	3	3
Rose, Brian, Michigan	8	5	.615	3.44	21	20	2	0	0	0	136.0	127	561	63	52	5	3	1	9	31	0	105	4	0
Rosenbohm, Jim, Burlington	0	0	.000	19.80	3	0	0	0	1	0	5.0	9	36	11	11	1	0	1	1	11	0	3	5	0
Rosenkranz, Terry, Beloit*	0	0	.000	0.00	4	0	0	0	2	0	8.0	2	30	2	0	0	0	0	0	2	0	4	0	0
Ruch, Rob, Fort Wayne	0	1	.000	2.73	9	3	0	0	1	1	26.1	17	108	8	8	1	0	0	2	16	0	27	1	0
Runyan, Sean, Quad City*	4	6	.400	3.66	22	11	0	0	2	0	76.1	67	327	37	31	10	1	2	3	29	0	65	4	0
Rushing, William, Ft. Wayne*	1	1	.500	1.78	13	0	0	0	5	1	25.1	15	100	11	5	0	0	0	0	10	0	25	4	2
Sak, James, Clinton	6	1	.857	1.98	7	7	3	0	0	0	50.0	42	200	12	11	2	1	2	0	14	0	37	0	3
Salmon, Fabian, South Bend	4	1	.800	3.80	15	0	0	0	8	3	23.2	18	103	15	10	1	0	0	1	11	0	15	2	0
Santana, Marino, Wisconsin	8	3	.727	1.77	15	15	2	1	0	0	96.2	57	368	26	19	5	2	2	1	25	0	110	6	0
Scheffer, Aaron, Wisconsin	0	1	.000	6.59	9	0	0	0	6	0	13.2	17	65	14	10	2	1	0	0	5	1	8	2	0
Schenbeck, T.J., Beloit	4	2	.667	3.62	18	1	0	0	9	5	37.1	35	171	18	15	3	3	3	2	23	1	37	5	0
Schiefelbein, Mike, Burlington	0	0	.000	0.00	1	0	0	0	0	0	0.0	0	1	0	0	0	0	0	0	1	0	0	0	0
Scott, Ron, Peoria*	0	2	.000	8.47	21	1	0	0	8	0	34.0	37	168	36	32	4	1	4	5	30	0	21	9	2
Shaver, Tony, Quad City	2	0	1.000	1.61	35	0	0	0	9	1	56.0	35	222	15	10	2	2	0	2	19	1	40	2	1
Sick, David, Cedar Rapids	6	5	.545	3.67	50	0	0	0	12	3	73.2	72	331	41	30	5	5	2	10	27	3	64	5	1
Sikorski, Brian, Quad City	1	0	1.000	0.00	2	0	0	0	1	0	3.0	1	11	1	0	0	0	0	0	0	0	4	0	0
Silva, Luis, West Michigan	1	0	1.000	6.75	10	1	0	0	1	0	21.1	31	102	16	16	2	1	1	2	7	0	24	2	3
Skuse, Nicholas, Cedar Rapids	13	7	.650	4.04	26	25	3	1	1	0	147.0	155	650	84	66	10	3	3	9	61	1	116	12	3
Slade, Shawn, Cedar Rapids	3	1	.750	4.25	30	0	0	0	14	3	42.1	42	186	24	20	1	3	2	2	19	2	35	4	1
Slininger, Dennis, Peoria	0	3	.000	10.97	3	3	0	0	0	0	10.2	16	54	13	13	5	0	0	0	7	0	12	0	0
Smith, Andy, West Michigan	4	10	.286	3.89	30	22	0	0	4	2	122.2	117	554	71	53	3	2	3	10	72	1	68	6	1
Smith, Brook, Burlington*	3	2	.600	5.01	39	4	0	0	12	1	88.0	85	414	67	49	7	7	3	3	72	7	70	19	2
Smith, Charles, South Bend	10	10	.500	2.69	26	25	4	2	1	0	167.0	128	688	70	50	8	7	2	13	61	0	145	21	11
Smith, John, West Michigan*	1	0	1.000	4.05	25	0	0	0	11	1	33.1	32	149	21	15	4	2	0	3	18	0	33	2	1
Smith, Mason, Burlington	0	4	.000	6.94	8	4	0	0	2	0	23.1	26	109	18	18	1	0	1	0	12	1	19	2	1
Smith, Roy, Wisconsin	7	14	.333	5.38	27	27	1	0	0	0	149.0	179	669	100	89	9	5	2	3	54	2	109	10	2

Pitcher, Team	W	L	Pct.	ERA	G	GS	CG	ShO	GF	Sv.	IP	H	TBF	R	ER	HR	SH	SF	HB	BB	IBB	SO	WP	Bk.
Smith, Shad, Burlington	0	1	.000	6.23	2	2	0	0	0	0	8.2	10	42	8	6	1	1	0	0	6	1	4	1	0
Sosa, Helpis, West Michigan	3	5	.375	4.70	21	6	0	0	5	2	53.2	59	255	47	28	5	3	4	4	26	0	37	5	1
Stark, Zachary, Kane County*	1	1	.500	15.51	5	4	0	0	0	0	15.2	27	94	30	27	2	1	0	2	17	0	5	1	0
Steed, Sam, Springfield*	2	0	1.000	2.45	8	0	0	0	6	0	14.2	14	64	4	4	0	1	0	0	6	0	14	2	0
Stein, Blake, Peoria	10	6	.625	3.80	27	27	1	0	0	0	139.2	122	596	69	59	12	1	4	5	61	0	133	2	1
Steinke, Brock, Quad City	2	1	.667	4.34	21	1	0	0	7	0	37.1	30	168	20	18	2	0	4	3	27	0	18	4	2
Stevenson, Jason, Rockford	4	3	.571	5.59	33	5	0	0	9	2	77.1	85	333	50	48	9	1	4	1	31	0	54	5	5
Surratt, Jamie, South Bend	3	3	.500	3.12	26	0	0	0	22	11	40.1	32	163	15	14	5	3	2	2	12	1	34	3	1
Telgheder, Jim, Michigan	5	1	.833	1.80	22	1	0	0	18	4	35.0	29	142	8	7	0	2	2	1	8	2	39	3	0
Theodile, Robert, South Bend	1	2	.333	7.62	7	4	0	0	0	0	26.0	45	130	30	22	1	1	1	1	13	0	16	5	0
Thomas, Carlos, Clinton	2	0	1.000	2.45	13	0	0	0	1	1	18.1	19	86	9	5	1	2	0	1	10	1	14	0	0
Thompson, John, Wisconsin	2	8	.200	4.13	38	7	0	0	29	19	69.2	65	314	41	32	8	2	2	2	43	2	69	13	1
Thurmond, Travis, Ced. Rapids	2	5	.286	5.31	14	2	0	0	4	2	39.0	36	172	25	23	4	2	0	1	20	4	55	3	0
Tidwell, Jason, Kane County	1	4	.200	8.62	6	4	0	0	0	0	15.2	19	80	17	15	2	1	0	4	14	0	13	3	0
Tillmon, Darrell, Michigan*	6	3	.667	2.24	13	10	2	0	2	0	76.1	56	293	25	19	8	2	0	0	12	0	53	1	0
Tollberg, Brian, Beloit	13	4	.765	3.41	22	22	1	1	0	0	132.0	119	529	59	50	10	2	5	6	27	0	110	5	4
Torres, Luis, Clinton	0	0	.000	13.50	3	0	0	0	0	0	2.0	5	16	3	3	0	0	0	1	5	0	1	0	2
Towns, Ryan, Springfield	0	1	.000	5.58	18	1	0	0	7	0	30.2	33	141	24	19	6	1	0	2	17	0	31	4	1
Tyrrell, Jim, Michigan*	2	3	.400	3.60	16	0	0	0	7	4	25.0	17	114	17	10	3	3	2	4	15	1	37	2	1
Upchurch, Wayne, Springfield	2	3	.400	4.25	18	2	0	0	11	1	29.2	40	137	19	14	3	2	2	2	4	1	13	0	1
Vandeweg, Ryan, Clinton	6	4	.600	4.15	15	15	1	0	0	0	91.0	92	400	56	42	5	3	2	7	32	3	89	3	1
Vanhof, Dave, Wisconsin*	4	5	.444	4.16	15	13	1	0	1	0	62.2	52	291	42	29	4	4	3	3	50	2	27	8	0
Vardijan, Daniel, Kane County	0	0	.000	6.00	1	1	0	0	0	0	3.0	5	17	3	2	0	0	0	1	2	0	2	1	0
Villano, Mike, Burlington	3	1	.750	2.84	16	0	0	0	7	1	25.1	20	120	12	8	1	2	1	4	21	0	29	5	0
Walls, Eric, Springfield*	0	0	.000	0.00	1	0	0	0	1	0	1.0	1	4	0	0	0	0	0	0	0	0	0	0	0
Walters, Brett, Clinton	8	7	.533	2.71	32	19	4	0	4	1	146.0	133	598	58	44	9	6	1	10	27	3	122	4	2
Warren, Deshawn, Ced. Rapids*	2	3	.400	3.26	7	7	1	1	0	0	30.1	20	122	12	11	2	1	0	2	13	0	26	1	0
Washburn, Jarrod, Ced. Rapids*	0	1	.000	3.44	3	3	0	0	0	0	18.1	17	79	7	7	1	2	1	3	7	0	20	1	0
Weinberg, Todd, W. Michigan*	4	5	.444	4.76	36	9	0	0	5	1	87.0	86	392	52	46	3	2	1	13	56	2	54	19	2
Welch, Travis, Peoria	3	4	.429	4.50	46	0	0	0	46	31	46.0	40	203	26	23	6	5	0	3	18	1	45	5	1
West, Adam, Peoria*	0	3	.000	12.08	4	4	0	0	0	0	12.2	22	81	21	17	0	0	1	0	24	0	5	2	0
Wiesner, Chad, Wisconsin	0	0	.000	3.00	1	0	0	0	0	0	3.0	3	12	1	1	0	0	0	0	1	0	2	0	0
Williams, Juan, Fort Wayne*	0	0	.000	4.50	3	0	0	0	3	0	6.0	7	29	4	3	0	2	0	0	3	0	4	0	3
Winkle, Ken, Springfield	1	1	.500	9.49	9	0	0	0	3	0	12.1	16	56	13	13	3	0	0	1	2	0	8	2	0
Woodard, Steve, Beloit	7	4	.636	4.54	21	21	1	0	0	0	115.0	113	490	68	58	12	6	2	5	31	0	94	6	5
Wunsch, Kelly, Beloit*	4	7	.364	4.20	14	14	3	1	0	0	85.2	90	364	47	40	7	2	0	3	37	0	66	6	0
Ybarra, Jamie, Kane County	5	5	.500	3.00	50	2	0	0	16	2	96.0	62	398	37	32	7	5	2	13	40	4	104	2	2
Zancanaro, Dave, W. Michigan*	0	2	.000	2.20	16	16	0	0	0	0	32.2	19	132	8	8	1	2	0	3	15	0	42	1	2
Zanolla, Dan, Kane County	4	4	.500	3.58	28	3	0	0	3	0	60.1	58	276	34	24	2	3	2	6	28	3	54	1	0

COMBINATION SHUTOUTS: **Beloit (6)**—Beck-Linares, D'Amico-Dalton-Burt, D'Amico-Mullins, Gonzalez-Dalton-Burt, Linares-Dalton, Tollberg-Huntsman. **Burlington (3)**—Lake-Keith, Prater-Hernandez, Rector-Hernandez. **Cedar Rapids (2)**—Skuse-Sick-Freehill, Warren-Sick. **Clinton (3)**—Dennis-Isom, Hammerschmidt-Isom, Isom-Davis. **Fort Wayne (7)**—Bell-Pavicich-Rushing-Fidge, Cobb-Rushing, Fidge-Bedinger, Nartker-Fidge, Perkins-Pavicich, Ruch-Pavicich-Fidge, Ruch-Perkins-Rushing. **Kane County (6)**—Meadows-Gonzalez-Alejo, Miranda-Alejo, Press-Andersen, Zanolla-Ybarra, Meadows-Zanolia-Bussa, Press-Miles-Bussa. **Michigan (5)**—Mitchell-Bush-Telgheder, Mitchell-Hale, Rose-Blais, Rose-Bush, Rose-Tillmon. **Peoria (6)**—Corrigan-Pontes-Welch, Dale-Corrigan, Foderaro-Corrigan-Carroll, Stein-Pontes-Reed, Stein-Reed, Stein-Welch. **Quad City (9)**—Blanco-Hall, Elarton-Halama-Barrios, Lock-Diorio, Mounce-Barrios, Mounce-Halama-Barrios, Mounce-Hall, Mounce-Kester, Runyan-Gunderson, Steinke-Halama-Barrios. **Rockford (4)**—Bair-Bogle, Garcia-Casey, Krause-Faulkner-Barker, Martinez-Rain. **South Bend (4)**—Bigham-Salmon, Garcia-Leiber, Gomez-Surratt, Herbert-Radinsky. **Springfield (3)**—Anderson-Roberts-MacDonald, Carter-Anderson-Brixey-MacDonald, Gamboa-Brixey. **West Michigan (9)**—Hause-Rajotte, King-Cochrane, King-Epstein-Hause-Rajotte, Newman-Weinberg-Beverlin-Sosa, Perez-Epstein-Smith, Perez-Gunther-Rajotte, Weinberg-Morrison-Rajotte, Zancanaro-Hause, Zancanaro-Perez-Gunther. **Wisconsin (3)**—Bieniasz-Daniels-Morgan-Green, Smith-Doughty, Smith-Krueger.

NO-HIT GAMES: None.

PITCHERS WITH TWO OR MORE TEAMS

Pitcher, Team	W	L	Pct.	ERA	G	GS	CG	ShO	GF	Sv.	IP	H	TBF	R	ER	HR	SH	SF	HB	BB	IBB	SO	WP	Bk.
Estes, Shawn, Wisconsin*	0	0	.000	0.90	2	2	0	0	0	0	10.0	5	38	1	1	0	0	1	0	5	0	11	2	1
Estes, Shawn, Burlington*	0	0	.000	4.11	4	4	0	0	0	0	15.1	13	72	8	7	2	0	0	2	12	0	22	2	0

1995 FIELDING

TEAM

Team	Pct.	G	PO	A	E	TC	DP	PB
Beloit	.968	139	3587	1508	168	5263	112	22
Michigan	.968	138	3626	1428	169	5223	106	32
Cedar Rapids	.966	138	3554	1517	176	5247	114	19
Wisconsin	.965	138	3540	1555	184	5279	114	27
South Bend	.964	135	3551	1488	186	5225	107	23
Peoria	.964	134	3393	1403	178	4974	103	25
Rockford	.964	140	3603	1552	193	5348	104	27
Kane County	.962	138	3545	1412	196	5153	118	21
Quad City	.962	137	3499	1546	200	5245	106	18
Fort Wayne	.962	140	3709	1542	210	5461	115	31
Burlington	.961	135	3309	1451	194	4954	111	34
Springfield	.960	139	3526	1579	215	5320	105	30
West Michigan	.956	136	3524	1511	231	5266	119	19
Clinton	.950	137	3387	1405	252	5044	102	25

TRIPLE PLAYS: South Bend, West Michigan.

INDIVIDUAL

FIRST BASEMEN

NOTE: All caps denotes fielding-percentage leader based on 70 games for catchers, 93 for all other non-pitchers and 144 innings for pitchers. *Throws lefthanded.

Player, Team	Pct.	G	PO	A	E	TC	DP
Allen, Dustin, Clinton	.967	23	137	10	5	152	17
Altman, Heath, Burlington	1.000	1	1	0	0	1	0
Ballara, Juan, Peoria	1.000	2	11	1	0	12	1
Bazzani, Matt, Michigan	.750	1	3	0	1	4	1
Bowles, John, Michigan	1.000	3	9	1	0	10	1
Buhner, Shawn, Wisconsin	.985	62	543	38	9	590	42
Burchel, Brad, Beloit	1.000	1	5	0	0	5	1
Burgos, Carlos, Springfield	1.000	8	81	2	0	83	6
Cady, Todd, Kane County	.982	88	724	46	14	784	62
Castillo, Alberto, Burlington*	.985	33	238	21	4	263	18
Castro, Dennis, Kane County	.857	1	12	0	2	14	2

Player, Team	Pct.	G	PO	A	E	TC	DP
Chevalier, Virgil, Michigan	1.000	1	4	2	0	6	1
Clifford, James, Wisconsin*	.985	81	729	49	12	790	59
Coe, Ryan, Quad City	1.000	2	9	0	0	9	0
Dantzler, Eric, Burlington	.973	12	69	3	2	74	8
DeLeon, Raymond, Clinton*	1.000	3	21	2	0	23	2
Dennis, Brian, Rockford	.900	9	16	2	2	20	0
DePastino, Joe, Michigan	1.000	9	75	3	0	78	10
Donati, John, Cedar Rapids	.976	72	658	30	17	705	43
Fitzpatrick, Will, Beloit	1.000	13	59	4	0	63	4
Fortin, Troy, Fort Wayne	.991	80	737	44	7	788	53
Francisco, Vicente, W. Michigan	.966	3	26	2	1	29	0
FREEMAN, Richard, Rockford	.9953	131	1181	82	6	1269	81
Freire, Alejandro, Quad City	.993	101	931	70	7	1008	73
Gibralter, David, Michigan	.988	92	788	54	10	852	61
Glenn, Darrin, Burlington	.967	5	29	0	1	30	1
Grandizio, Steve, Peoria	1.000	1	4	0	0	4	0
Gulseth, Mark, Burlington	.991	40	315	25	3	343	25
Gunderson, Shane, Ft. Wayne	1.000	4	34	3	0	37	4
Hacopian, Derek, Beloit	.988	27	160	11	2	173	13
Hall, Ryan, Peoria	.993	18	129	11	1	141	6
Harris, Eric, West Michigan	.989	24	164	10	2	176	11
Heath, Jason, Wisconsin	1.000	1	1	0	0	1	0
Ibarra, Jesus, Burlington	.976	56	457	35	12	504	45
Jackson, Ryan, Kane County*	.988	52	475	31	6	512	42
Johnson, Jack, Rockford	1.000	4	28	3	0	31	3
Kimbler, Doug, Rockford	1.000	1	2	0	0	2	0
Krause, Scott, Beloit	1.000	1	1	0	0	1	1
Llanos, Victor, Peoria	.965	9	53	2	2	57	6
Martin, Mike, Clinton	1.000	1	2	1	0	3	1
McNally, Sean, Springfield	1.000	1	11	1	0	12	0
Mendoza, Francisco, Springfield	.977	20	154	13	4	171	16
Milstien, Dave, Beloit	1.000	1	1	0	0	1	0
Miranda, Alex, W. Michigan*	.986	118	972	79	15	1066	89
Moeder, Tony, Cedar Rapids	1.000	40	396	19	0	415	30
Nunez, Isaias, Peoria*	.981	119	966	80	20	1066	78
Olmstead, Nate, Cedar Rapids	.979	33	256	24	6	286	24
Patterson, Jake, Fort Wayne*	.980	56	478	23	10	511	38
Patton, Greg, Michigan	1.000	2	8	0	0	8	0
Pearson, Kevin, Fort Wayne	.958	8	42	4	2	48	4
Robbins, Lance, Ced. Rapids	1.000	1	2	0	0	2	0
Robledo, Nilson, South Bend	.983	135	1224	82	22	1328	91
Rodriguez, Noel, Quad City	.990	46	382	14	4	400	24
Root, Mitch, Clinton	.981	56	498	25	10	533	40
Rose, Pete, South Bend	1.000	1	3	0	0	3	1
Salzano, Jerry, Rockford	1.000	3	22	0	0	22	2
Sanchez, Victor, Quad City	1.000	2	15	0	0	15	1
Sanders, Pat, W. Michigan*	1.000	6	19	3	0	22	0
Schwenke, Matt, Clinton	1.000	6	35	1	0	36	1
Smith, Matt, Springfield*	.988	116	1081	78	14	1173	72
Stasio, Chris, Michigan	.997	40	334	21	1	356	21
Tyler, Josh, Beloit	1.000	6	14	1	0	15	0
Whatley, Gabe, Rockford	.985	7	61	3	1	65	6
Williams, Drew, Beloit	.9946	124	1050	57	6	1113	79
Winget, Jeremy, Clinton*	.981	61	483	43	10	536	36
Zwisler, Josh, Beloit	1.000	2	6	0	0	6	0

TRIPLE PLAYS: Miranda, Robledo.

SECOND BASEMEN

Player, Team	Pct.	G	PO	A	E	TC	DP
Allison, Chris, Michigan	.969	83	160	211	12	383	53
Avalos, Gilbert, Rockford	.980	32	52	92	3	147	16
Belliard, Ron, Beloit	.955	119	219	314	25	558	69
Betances, Junior, Beloit	1.000	7	9	11	0	20	3
Betten, Randy, Cedar Rapids	.963	20	18	34	2	54	6
Biermann, Steve, Peoria	.941	9	3	13	1	17	1
Boulware, Benjamin, S. Bend	.962	129	244	332	23	599	72
Bowles, John, Michigan	.921	28	30	52	7	89	8
Carmona, Cesarin, Clinton	.928	36	50	78	10	138	16
Castillo, Luis, Kane County	.962	89	193	241	17	451	55
Castro, Jose, West Michigan	.954	99	230	247	23	500	53
Cedeno, Edwardo, Springfield	.944	7	2	15	1	18	0
Cook, Jason, Wisconsin	.989	59	104	174	3	281	31
Cruz, Deivi, Burlington	.962	14	16	35	2	53	6
Cuevas, Eduardo, Clinton	.900	6	7	11	2	20	3
Darden, Tony, Kane County	.979	10	21	25	1	47	7
Davalillo, David, Cedar Rapids	1.000	8	8	19	0	27	6
Dean, Mark, Peoria	.959	25	50	44	4	98	8
Dumas, Mike, Beloit	1.000	1	2	1	0	3	1
Francisco, Vicente, W. Michigan	.964	41	81	79	6	166	23
Fraser, Joe, Fort Wayne	.947	4	8	10	1	19	2
Garcia, Amaury, Kane County	.818	4	4	5	2	11	1
Garcia, Carlos, Fort Wayne	.974	9	19	18	1	38	4
Garcia, Franklin, Beloit	.943	20	27	39	4	70	10
Hamburg, Leon, W. Michigan	.938	8	16	14	2	32	3
Hansen, Jed, Springfield	.963	120	220	345	22	587	63
HENDERSON, Juan, Ced. Rapids	.974	114	251	304	15	570	72
Hernandez, Carlos, Quad City	.964	98	157	276	16	449	50
Keefe, Jamie, Clinton	.962	40	65	87	6	158	20
Kimbler, Doug, Rockford	1.000	5	4	4	0	8	1
Krause, Scott, Beloit	1.000	1	1	0	0	1	0
Lane, Ryan, Fort Wayne	.969	42	65	92	5	162	13
Lanza, Mike, Wisconsin	.963	39	76	105	7	188	18
Livsey, Shane, Rockford	.941	52	83	109	12	204	20
Martinez, Erik, Clinton	.913	8	6	15	2	23	4
Marval, Raul, Burlington	.962	79	149	182	13	344	51
McCalmont, Jim, Fort Wayne	.973	6	16	20	1	37	9
Milstien, Dave, Beloit	.923	2	7	5	1	13	2
Mitchell, Donovan, Quad City	.968	50	67	115	6	188	19
Molina, Luis, Wisconsin	.971	43	66	100	5	171	19
Moschetti, Mike, W. Michigan	.909	6	10	20	3	33	0
Olinde, Chad, Rockford	.943	39	42	91	8	141	11
Paez, Israel, Fort Wayne	.955	91	178	247	20	445	44
Patton, Greg, Michigan	1.000	7	11	15	0	26	3
Perez, Mike, Rockford	.967	37	37	82	4	123	15
Polanco, Placido, Peoria	1.000	1	2	3	0	5	1
Ramirez, Joel, Wisconsin	.912	5	9	22	3	34	4
Robbins, Lance, Cedar Rapids	.964	12	22	32	2	56	3
Robinson, Darek, Peoria	.960	111	208	276	20	504	59
Smith, Dave, Michigan	.951	36	47	70	6	123	14
Sparks, Rodney, Springfield	.923	23	30	42	6	78	7
Swift, Scott, Burlington	.948	53	84	99	10	193	16
Totman, Jason, Clinton	.949	57	106	137	13	256	30
Tyler, Josh, Beloit	1.000	1	1	0	0	1	0
White, Walter, Kane County	.943	44	89	110	12	211	24
Wojtkowski, Steve, Michigan	1.000	2	1	2	0	3	1
Zerpa, Mauro, South Bend	.923	8	10	14	2	26	1

TRIPLE PLAYS: Boulware, Castro.

THIRD BASEMEN

Player, Team	Pct.	G	PO	A	E	TC	DP
Avalos, Gilbert, Rockford	.885	72	51	157	27	235	4
Barnes, Kelvin, Rockford	.900	4	3	6	1	10	0
Belliard, Ron, Beloit	.971	15	2	32	1	35	2
BETANCES, Junior, Beloit	.932	102	59	216	20	295	18
Betten, Randy, Cedar Rapids	1.000	2	2	4	0	6	0
Biermann, Steve, Peoria	1.000	3	0	1	0	1	1
Booty, Josh, Kane County	.913	31	23	71	9	103	4
Bowles, John, Michigan	.931	19	17	50	5	72	6
Burchel, Brad, Beloit	1.000	1	1	0	0	1	0
Castro, Dennis, Kane County	.925	42	31	93	10	134	8
Cedeno, Edwardo, Springfield	.882	6	2	13	2	17	0
Cook, Jason, Wisconsin	.956	35	23	85	5	113	6
Cruz, Deivi, Burlington	1.000	2	4	6	0	10	1
Cuevas, Eduardo, Clinton	.907	30	11	57	7	75	0
D'Amico, Jeff, West Michigan	.916	108	93	247	31	371	25
Darden, Tony, Kane County	.888	47	30	97	16	143	10
Davalillo, David, Cedar Rapids	.938	30	12	63	5	80	1
Dean, Mark, Peoria	.899	34	19	52	8	79	6
Derosso, Tony, Michigan	.928	80	63	155	17	235	6
Donati, John, Cedar Rapids	1.000	2	0	2	0	2	0
Dumas, Mike, Beloit	1.000	3	0	14	0	14	0
Espinal, Juan, Clinton	.889	107	73	182	32	287	8
Francisco, Vicente, W. Michigan	.884	36	21	63	11	95	4
Garcia, Amaury, Kane County	.750	20	7	26	11	44	1
Garcia, Carlos, Fort Wayne	.862	14	9	16	4	29	1
Gibralter, David, Michigan	.900	16	17	28	5	50	5
Glenn, Darrin, Burlington	.758	11	2	23	8	33	1
Gugino, Mark, Kane County	.500	1	1	0	1	2	0
Jumonville, Joe, Peoria	.924	112	72	219	24	315	22
Keefe, Jamie, Clinton	1.000	4	4	4	0	8	1
Kimbler, Doug, Rockford	.952	49	46	92	7	145	11
Klassen, Danny, Beloit	1.000	2	3	5	0	8	1
Kominek, Toby, Beloit	1.000	3	1	1	0	2	0
Koskie, Corey, Fort Wayne	.900	109	80	244	36	360	23
Martinez, Erik, Clinton	.500	2	0	1	1	2	1
McCalmont, Jim, Fort Wayne	.889	2	2	6	1	9	1
McNally, Sean, Springfield	.927	128	91	278	29	398	12
Mendoza, Francisco, Springfield	.829	12	14	20	7	41	3
Mitchell, Donovan, Quad City	.909	4	3	7	1	11	0
Molina, Luis, Wisconsin	1.000	5	2	7	0	9	1
Morris, Gregory, Cedar Rapids	.909	102	65	226	29	320	15
Nelson, Bryant, Quad City	1.000	1	0	2	0	2	0
Olinde, Chad, Rockford	.870	17	15	32	7	54	2
Ortega, Randy, West Michigan	.857	2	2	4	1	7	0
Paez, Israel, Fort Wayne	.875	19	15	41	8	64	3
Patton, Greg, Michigan	.956	24	19	46	3	68	1

Player, Team	Pct.	G	PO	A	E	TC	DP
Rincones, Wuarnner, S. Bend	.912	20	25	37	6	68	8
Robbins, Lance, Cedar Rapids	.875	15	6	22	4	32	1
Root, Mitch, Clinton	1.000	2	0	5	0	5	0
Rose, Pete, South Bend	.921	113	124	249	32	405	23
Salzano, Jerry, Rockford	.429	3	1	2	4	7	0
Smith, Dave, Michigan	.875	2	1	6	1	8	0
Sparks, Rodney, Springfield	.833	4	0	5	1	6	1
Trammell, Gary, Quad City	.833	21	9	46	11	66	8
Truby, Chris, Quad City	.903	118	73	279	38	390	26
Tyler, Josh, Beloit	.957	40	28	60	4	92	4
Valentin, Jose, Fort Wayne	1.000	9	6	14	0	20	2
Villalobos, Carlos, Wisconsin	.878	104	76	234	43	353	16
Wallace, Brian, Burlington	.911	97	62	225	28	315	19
Whatley, Gabe, Rockford	.826	10	4	15	4	23	0
White, Walter, Kane County	.800	8	2	14	4	20	0
Wilson, Todd, Burlington	.920	29	12	57	6	75	1
Wojtkowski, Steve, Michigan	1.000	2	1	5	0	6	0
Zerpa, Mauro, South Bend	.882	15	9	21	4	34	2

TRIPLE PLAY: Francisco.

SHORTSTOPS

Player, Team	Pct.	G	PO	A	E	TC	DP
Alguacil, Jose, Burlington	.910	36	66	95	16	177	17
Allison, Chris, Michigan	1.000	1	2	2	0	4	1
Betances, Junior, Beloit	.920	23	24	57	7	88	10
Betten, Randy, Cedar Rapids	.750	2	1	2	1	4	1
Biermann, Steve, Peoria	.932	40	36	87	9	132	15
Burchel, Brad, Beloit	.844	9	5	22	5	32	4
BUSTOS, Saul, Rockford	.969	94	117	289	13	419	36
Castro, Jose, West Michigan	.896	14	17	26	5	48	4
Cedeno, Edwardo, Springfield	.910	26	26	55	8	89	5
Cruz, Deivi, Burlington	1.000	1	0	1	0	1	0
D'Amico, Jeff, West Michigan	.933	21	27	57	6	90	5
Darden, Tony, Kane County	1.000	1	0	1	0	1	0
Davalillo, David, Cedar Rapids	.923	4	4	8	1	13	2
Dean, Mark, Peoria	.917	11	7	26	3	36	4
Delgado, Wilson, Wis.-Bur.	.953	112	156	350	25	531	63
Dumas, Mike, Beloit	.930	9	12	28	3	43	4
Failla, Paul, Cedar Rapids	.935	129	162	343	35	540	65
Francisco, Vicente, W. Michigan	.769	11	9	21	9	39	4
Garcia, Franklin, Beloit	.333	2	1	0	2	3	0
Goodell, Steve, Kane County	.923	2	6	6	1	13	2
Henderson, Juan, Cedar Rapids	.952	7	5	15	1	21	0
Hernandez, Carlos, Quad City	.954	30	31	73	5	109	9
Keefe, Jamie, Clinton	.903	9	9	19	3	31	2
Kimbler, Doug, Rockford	.943	54	113	154	16	283	36
Klassen, Danny, Beloit	.917	56	70	128	18	216	23
Lane, Ryan, Fort Wayne	.943	75	111	222	20	353	38
Lanza, Mike, Wisconsin	.931	58	82	160	18	260	28
Martinez, Erik, Clinton	.913	7	8	13	2	23	1
Marval, Raul, Burlington	.949	12	14	23	2	39	5
Melo, Juan, Clinton	.922	132	183	372	47	602	70
Mendez, Emilio, Beloit	.895	7	6	11	2	19	2
Milstien, Dave, Beloit	.940	49	69	149	14	232	21
Mitchell, Donovan, Quad City	.925	42	46	103	12	161	8
Molina, Luis, Wisconsin	.957	63	106	180	13	299	32
Moore, Brandon, South Bend	.956	132	193	398	27	618	64
Moriarty, Mike, Fort Wayne	.956	62	96	165	12	273	22
Nelson, Bryant, Quad City	.750	1	1	2	1	4	1
Paez, Israel, Fort Wayne	1.000	8	8	13	0	21	2
Patton, Greg, Michigan	.958	19	24	45	3	72	8
Polanco, Placido, Peoria	.950	101	112	283	21	416	40
Prieto, Alejandro, Springfield	.936	123	199	358	38	595	70
Ramirez, Joel, Wisconsin	1.000	2	3	2	0	5	0
Robbins, Lance, Cedar Rapids	.500	2	0	2	2	4	1
Rodriguez, Victor, Kane County	.959	127	151	312	20	483	56
Sadler, Donnie, Michigan	.944	112	168	307	28	503	59
Santana, Jose, Quad City	.920	80	101	223	28	352	43
Smith, Dave, Michigan	.913	12	10	32	4	46	3
Soriano, Fred, West Michigan	.938	106	140	298	29	467	52
Sparks, Rodney, Springfield	.968	6	6	24	1	31	3
White, Walter, Kane County	.912	13	21	31	5	57	8
Zerpa, Mauro, South Bend	.960	12	6	18	1	25	1

TRIPLE PLAYS: D'Amico, Zerpa.

SHORTSTOPS WITH TWO OR MORE TEAMS

Player, Team	Pct.	G	PO	A	E	TC	DP
Delgado, Wilson, Wisconsin	.940	19	29	65	6	100	14
Delgado, Wilson, Burlington	.956	93	127	285	19	431	49

OUTFIELDERS

Player, Team	Pct.	G	PO	A	E	TC	DP
Alexander, Chad, Quad City	1.000	2	3	0	0	3	0
Allen, Dustin, Clinton	.902	18	34	3	4	41	1
Altman, Heath, Burlington	1.000	13	15	1	0	16	0
Alvarez, Luis, Cedar Rapids*	.667	3	2	0	1	3	0
Alvarez, Rafael, Fort Wayne*	.961	96	189	7	8	204	0
Amerson, Gordon, Clinton*	.864	47	49	2	8	59	0
Bautista, Juan, Peoria	.936	63	86	2	6	94	0
Bogle, Bryan, Rockford	.904	33	45	2	5	52	1
Bowers, R.J., Quad City	.957	107	148	7	7	162	0
Bowles, John, Michigan	.937	38	56	3	4	63	0
Brandon, Jelani, Springfield	.967	57	80	7	3	90	0
Bray, Notorris, Burlington	.974	15	37	1	1	39	0
Brown, Armann, Fort Wayne	.973	76	138	5	4	147	0
Brown, Emil, West Michigan	.957	109	165	12	8	185	4
Buchanan, Shawn, South Bend	.983	94	171	6	3	180	1
Carroll, Doug, Wisconsin	.918	47	59	8	6	73	0
Castro, Jose, West Michigan	1.000	2	3	1	0	4	0
Cedeno, Edwardo, Springfield	.980	29	45	5	1	51	0
Cephas, Ruben, Beloit	.929	63	50	2	4	56	0
Choi, Kyung, Cedar Rapids*	.960	33	42	6	2	50	1
Cole, Abdul, Kane County	.955	50	82	2	4	88	2
Coleman, Michael, Michigan	.981	111	251	5	5	261	0
Contreras, Efrain, Peoria	.951	77	112	5	6	123	2
Cook, Hayward, Kane County	.984	65	123	4	2	129	1
Cook, Jason, Wisconsin	.966	20	25	3	1	29	0
Cordero, Pablo, Burlington	.912	57	79	4	8	91	0
Corujo, Rey, Burlington	.846	13	11	0	2	13	0
Dantzler, Eric, Burlington	1.000	9	9	0	0	9	0
Darcuiel, Faruq, Wisconsin*	.925	76	119	5	10	134	1
Darden, Tony, Kane County	.975	26	37	2	1	40	1
DeLeon, Santo, Wisconsin	.909	9	10	0	1	11	0
Denbow, Don, Burlington	.973	105	176	7	5	188	0
Donati, John, Cedar Rapids	1.000	1	3	0	0	3	0
Dumas, Mike, Beloit	1.000	7	9	1	0	10	0
Dunwoody, Todd, Kane County*	.983	129	284	6	5	295	1
Evans, Jason, South Bend	.964	87	152	11	6	169	3
Faggett, Ethan, Michigan*	.966	107	168	5	6	179	0
Freire, Alejandro, Quad City	1.000	3	1	0	0	1	0
French, Anton, Peoria	.939	113	164	6	11	181	1
Fric, Sean, Rockford	.800	5	4	0	1	5	0
Garcia, Carlos, Fort Wayne	1.000	7	13	0	0	13	0
Gazarek, Marty, Rockford	.949	70	120	11	7	138	3
Gerteisen, Aaron, Peoria	.975	66	117	1	3	121	0
Glenn, Darrin, Burlington	1.000	14	22	2	0	24	0
Gordon, Adrian, Fort Wayne	.956	41	40	3	2	45	1
Grandizio, Steve, Peoria	.981	93	153	3	3	159	1
Grieve, Ben, West Michigan	.942	92	125	6	8	139	0
Gugino, Mark, Kane County	.951	36	58	0	3	61	0
Gunderson, Shane, Ft. Wayne	1.000	21	20	2	0	22	1
Hacopian, Derek, Beloit	.969	74	90	3	3	96	1
Hamburg, Leon, W. Michigan	.943	61	90	9	6	105	0
Hamilton, Joe, Michigan	.973	115	204	11	6	221	2
Harris, Eric, West Michigan	1.000	6	3	0	0	3	0
Harvey, Aaron, Kane County	.976	57	82	0	2	84	0
Herrick, Jason, Cedar Rapids*	.952	100	148	9	8	165	2
Hightower, Vee, Rockford	.968	17	29	1	1	31	0
Hinds, Collin, Wisconsin	1.000	4	5	0	0	5	0
Iatarola, Aaron, Cedar Rapids*	.955	72	83	2	4	89	0
Jackson, Ryan, Kane County*	.990	59	96	1	1	98	1
Johnson, James, Clinton	.917	7	10	1	1	12	0
Keifer, Greg, Burlington	.875	5	7	0	1	8	0
Kominek, Toby, Beloit	.976	51	80	2	2	84	0
KRAUSE, Scott, Beloit	.985	131	177	14	3	194	3
Levias, Andres, South Bend	.971	23	32	2	1	35	0
Lewis, Marc, Michigan	.981	31	48	3	1	52	0
Linares, Yfrain, Beloit	1.000	1	1	0	0	1	0
Lowry, Curt, Clinton	.957	56	103	7	5	115	2
Lugo, Jesus, Peoria	.984	36	58	2	1	61	1
Madsen, Dan, Rockford*	.984	29	61	0	1	62	0
Martinez, Erik, Clinton	.800	7	4	0	1	5	0
Mathews, Byron, South Bend	.959	89	201	7	9	217	2
Mathis, Joe, Wisconsin	.983	112	165	10	3	178	1
Matthews, Gary, Clinton	.966	127	245	9	9	263	3
Mealing, Al, Beloit	.857	14	11	1	2	14	0
Medina, Alger, Rockford	.941	20	16	0	1	17	0
Mendez, Rudolfo, Springfield	.932	124	185	20	15	220	3
Moeder, Tony, Cedar Rapids	1.000	7	13	0	0	13	0
Monahan, Shane, Wisconsin	.971	59	100	0	3	103	0

Player, Team	Pct.	G	PO	A	E	TC	DP
Montiel, David, Beloit	.981	55	49	2	1	52	0
Mucker, Kelcey, Fort Wayne	.957	105	147	10	7	164	2
Nelson, Bryant, Quad City	.909	5	9	1	1	11	1
Newhan, David, W. Michigan	.976	23	37	3	1	41	0
Oglesby, Luke, Springfield	1.000	42	81	1	0	82	0
Olmstead, Nate, Cedar Rapids	1.000	6	4	1	0	5	0
Pearson, Kevin, Fort Wayne	1.000	14	11	0	0	11	0
Pico, Brandon, Rockford*	.977	94	159	12	4	175	1
Powell, Chris, Cedar Rapids*	.977	23	41	1	1	43	0
Pratt, Wes, Quad City	1.000	14	25	0	0	25	0
Price, Christopher, Springfield	.957	48	88	1	4	93	0
Reid, Derek, Burlington	.975	95	187	7	5	199	1
Rennhack, Mike, Quad City*	.973	93	143	2	4	149	0
Reyes, Michael, Kane County	.875	13	20	1	3	24	0
Richardson, Eric, South Bend	.976	49	78	2	2	82	0
Robbins, Lance, Cedar Rapids	.833	5	4	1	1	6	1
Rocha, Juan, Springfield	.945	75	113	7	7	127	1
Ross, Tony, Quad City	.968	96	148	5	5	158	1
Salzano, Jerry, Rockford	1.000	1	1	0	0	1	0
Smith, Demond, C.R.-W.M.	.968	86	177	3	6	186	0
Smith, John, Beloit	1.000	73	126	5	0	131	0
Smith, Scott, Wisconsin	1.000	28	36	5	0	41	1
Soriano, Jose, West Michigan	.964	121	257	13	10	280	3
Stasio, Chris, Michigan	.925	33	37	0	3	40	0
Swift, Scott, Burlington	1.000	12	15	4	0	19	1
Tena, Dario, Clinton	.970	90	154	8	5	167	3
Topham, Ryan, South Bend*	.941	13	16	0	1	17	0
Towner, Kyle, Wisconsin	.983	98	165	10	3	178	2
Trammell, Gary, Quad City	.932	37	49	6	4	59	2
Tyler, Josh, Beloit	1.000	4	3	0	0	3	0
Tyrus, Jason, Clinton	.968	53	86	6	3	95	0
Vizcaino, Romulo, Fort Wayne	.968	98	137	13	5	155	0
Walker, Steve, Rockford	.974	99	254	12	7	273	2
Walls, Eric, Springfield*	.965	83	162	3	6	171	0
Ward, Turner, Beloit	1.000	2	1	0	0	1	0
Watson, Kevin, Burlington	.961	73	94	5	4	103	0
Whatley, Gabe, Rockford	.983	74	106	7	2	115	0
White, Chad, Quad City	.975	73	149	6	4	159	0
Whittaker, Jay, South Bend	.964	61	129	3	5	137	1
Williams, Drew, Beloit	.857	5	6	0	1	7	0
Wilson, Chris, Beloit	1.000	20	27	2	0	29	1
Wulfert, Mark, Clinton	.922	46	56	3	5	64	0
Young, Kevin, Cedar Rapids	.984	116	175	12	3	190	3
Zaletel, Brian, Burlington	1.000	21	19	0	0	19	0
Zwisler, Josh, Beloit	1.000	19	16	1	0	17	0

OUTFIELDERS WITH TWO OR MORE TEAMS

Player, Team	Pct.	G	PO	A	E	TC	DP
Smith, Demond, Cedar Rapids	.971	79	165	2	5	172	0
Smith, Demond, W. Michigan	.929	7	12	1	1	14	0

CATCHERS

Player, Team	Pct.	G	PO	A	E	TC	DP	PB
Amezcua, Adan, Quad City	.979	46	285	34	7	326	4	11
Andreopouls, Alex, Beloit	.978	55	361	45	9	415	1	3
Augustine, Andy, Wisconsin	.997	55	274	34	1	309	3	12
Ballara, Juan, Peoria	.986	52	310	35	5	350	3	10
Barton, Scott, Rockford	.960	5	20	4	1	25	1	1
Bazzani, Matt, Michigan	.986	23	126	11	2	139	2	10
Borrero, Rikchy, Michigan	.962	16	95	5	4	104	1	0
Burgos, Carlos, Springfield	.985	12	62	3	1	66	0	1
Cady, Todd, Kane County	1.000	7	33	6	0	39	1	2
Campillo, Rob, Beloit	.992	45	303	49	3	355	0	4
CARONE, Richard, S. Bend	.988	83	563	76	8	647	6	11
Carpenter, Jerry, Ced. Rapids	1.000	11	52	8	0	60	0	1
Chevalier, Virgil, Michigan	1.000	1	5	1	0	6	0	0
Cline, Pat, Rockford	.973	91	549	64	17	630	2	18
Coe, Ryan, Quad City	.988	30	150	17	2	169	0	1
DaSilva, Manny, W. Michigan	.951	5	36	3	2	41	0	2
Davis, Josh, Clinton	.952	8	37	3	2	42	1	1
DeBoer, Rob, W. Michigan	.982	83	494	54	10	558	2	13
Delaney, Sean, Springfield	.974	45	187	36	6	229	8	8
Dennis, Brian, Rockford	.986	17	65	6	1	72	2	14
DePastino, Joe, Michigan	.991	68	451	71	5	527	1	4
Ebbert, Chad, Clinton	1.000	2	10	1	0	11	0	1
Encarnacion, Anito, C. Rapids	.928	14	54	10	5	69	0	4
Espiritu, Michael, Ced. Rapids	.944	9	59	8	4	71	1	1
Fortin, Troy, Fort Wayne	.800	4	7	1	2	10	1	0
Glenn, Darrin, Burlington	1.000	4	6	0	0	6	0	0
Gonzalez, Jimmy, Quad City	.987	30	136	13	2	151	0	3
Hall, Ryan, Peoria	.992	39	228	27	2	257	2	11
Hamburg, Leon, W. Michigan	1.000	2	3	0	0	3	0	0
Heath, Jason, Wisconsin	.977	13	76	10	2	88	0	5
Hemphill, Bret, Ced. Rapids	.992	68	429	69	4	502	6	7
Hilt, Scott, Fort Wayne	.975	30	181	15	5	201	1	10
Ibarra, Jesus, Burlington	.943	22	121	12	8	141	0	11
Johnson, Jack, Rockford	.976	19	107	16	3	126	1	1
Jones, Ken, Clinton	.971	31	181	19	6	206	2	4
Kuilan, Hector, Kane Co.	.944	2	12	5	1	18	0	0
Kurek, Chris, Michigan	.975	49	303	43	9	355	2	9
LaValliere, Mike, S. Bend	1.000	2	3	0	0	3	0	0
Martin, Mike, Clinton	.978	50	281	35	7	323	3	7
McDonald, Keith, Peoria	.991	62	411	54	4	469	5	4
Molina, Ben, Cedar Rapids	.978	39	283	32	7	322	5	5
Ortega, Randy, W. Michigan	.984	42	278	22	5	305	3	5
Pierzynski, A.J., Ft. Wayne	.939	20	119	34	10	163	0	4
Poor, Jeff, Burlington	.985	74	469	54	8	531	3	18
Probst, Alan, Quad City	.992	52	318	42	3	363	1	1
Ramos, Jeff, Springfield	1.000	12	50	4	0	54	0	2
Rodriguez, Maximo, K. C.	.976	65	414	39	11	464	4	12
Rondon, Alex, W. Michigan	.958	21	124	14	6	144	2	5
Rosario, Melvin, S. Bend	.962	49	271	58	13	342	5	10
Roskos, John, Kane County	.986	71	431	47	7	485	5	7
Ryder, Derek, Cedar Rapids	.983	16	50	8	1	59	1	1
Sanchez, Marcos, Clinton	.973	6	32	4	1	37	0	4
Sanchez, Victor, Quad City	.980	6	43	5	1	49	0	2
Schneider, Dan, Burlington	.984	51	328	45	6	379	4	5
Schwenke, Matt, Clinton	.962	31	153	23	7	183	4	5
Snook, Robert, Beloit	1.000	3	19	2	0	21	0	0
Snyder, Jarod, Rockford	.962	24	112	13	5	130	0	3
Spinello, Joe, South Bend	.929	4	13	0	1	14	0	0
Sutherland, Alex, Wisconsin	.986	85	554	66	9	629	5	10
Treanor, Matt, Springfield	.976	74	390	66	11	467	4	10
Tyler, Josh, Beloit	1.000	2	8	0	0	8	0	1
Ullan, Dave, Clinton	.956	37	199	20	10	229	0	2
Valentin, Jose, Fort Wayne	.973	101	730	108	23	861	11	17
Walker, Joe, South Bend	1.000	6	20	1	0	21	0	2
Wathan, Dusty, Wisconsin	1.000	5	21	5	0	26	0	0
Welch, Coby, Springfield	.969	18	85	9	3	97	1	3
Williams, Drew, Beloit	1.000	2	6	0	0	6	0	0
Zwisler, Josh, Beloit	.974	67	325	45	10	380	1	14

PITCHERS

Player, Team	Pct.	G	PO	A	E	TC	DP
Aguirre, Jose, Cedar Rapids*	1.000	6	0	1	0	1	0
Alejo, Nigel, Kane County	.857	48	2	4	1	7	0
Ali, Sam, Burlington	1.000	3	0	2	0	2	0
Altman, Heath, Burlington	1.000	3	0	1	0	1	1
Alvarado, Luis, Fort Wayne	.800	16	1	3	1	5	1
Alvarez, Ivan, Burlington*	1.000	4	0	3	0	3	0
Ambrose, John, South Bend	.800	3	2	2	1	5	0
Andersen, Mark, Kane County	1.000	15	2	5	0	7	1
Anderson, Eric, Springfield	.923	21	4	8	1	13	0
Bair, Dennis, Rockford	1.000	9	1	8	0	9	0
Barker, Richard, Rockford	1.000	32	5	7	0	12	0
Barksdale, Joe, Michigan	.923	24	10	14	2	26	0
Baron, Jim, Clinton*	.875	11	0	7	1	8	0
Barrios, Manuel, Quad City	.778	50	1	6	2	9	0
Beck, Chris, Wisconsin	.923	28	10	14	2	26	2
Beck, Greg, Beloit	.833	35	9	6	3	18	0
Bedinger, Doug, Fort Wayne	.882	46	4	11	2	17	0
Bell, Jason, Fort Wayne	1.000	9	3	12	0	15	2
Bernal, Manuel, Springfield	.917	8	2	9	1	12	1
Betances, Junior, Beloit	1.000	1	0	1	0	1	0
Betti, Rich, Michigan*	1.000	1	1	0	0	1	0
Beverlin, Jason, W. Michigan	1.000	22	4	14	0	18	0
Bieniasz, Derek, Wisconsin	.933	27	13	29	3	45	1
Bigham, Dave, South Bend*	.923	25	5	31	3	39	0
Blais, Mike, Michigan	1.000	32	3	10	0	13	1
Blanco, Alberto, Quad City*	.833	11	2	8	2	12	0
Bogle, Sean, Rockford	1.000	13	4	5	0	9	0
Bonilla, Welnis, Michigan	1.000	12	0	3	0	3	0
Brixey, Dustin, Springfield	.923	36	6	18	2	26	0
Bronkey, Jeff, Beloit	1.000	3	0	1	0	1	0
Broome, Curtis, South Bend	1.000	29	9	16	0	25	1
Bryant, Chris, Rockford*	.900	21	0	9	1	10	0
Burt, Chris, Beloit	1.000	36	3	5	0	8	1
Bush, Craig, Michigan	.875	34	0	7	1	8	0
Bushart, John, Cedar Rapids*	1.000	19	2	4	0	6	0
Bussa, Todd, Kane County	1.000	36	2	5	0	7	0
Byrne, Earl, Rockford*	.905	13	1	18	2	21	1
Cardona, Isbell, Burlington	.000	6	0	0	1	1	0
Carl, Todd, Kane County	1.000	12	0	2	0	2	0
Carroll, David, Peoria*	.923	24	6	6	1	13	1
Carter, Lance, Springfield	.967	27	13	16	1	30	0

Player, Team	Pct.	G	PO	A	E	TC	DP
Casey, Ryan, Rockford	1.000	16	1	2	0	3	0
Chapman, Walker, Fort Wayne	1.000	14	2	5	0	7	1
Charlton, Aaron, Burlington	.750	16	1	2	1	4	0
Cintron, Jose, Cedar Rapids	1.000	13	4	12	0	16	1
Cloude, Ken, Wisconsin	.886	25	8	23	4	35	1
Cobb, Trevor, Fort Wayne*	.833	11	2	3	1	6	0
Cochrane, Chris, W. Michigan	1.000	41	9	24	0	33	3
Cook, Jake, Michigan	.897	21	9	17	3	29	1
Corrigan, Cory, Peoria	.967	47	10	19	1	30	2
Crossley, Chad, Cedar Rapids	1.000	12	0	1	0	1	0
Crump, Jody, Peoria*	1.000	25	3	6	0	9	0
Curran, Tighe, Peoria*	.952	24	7	13	1	21	1
Dafun, George, Cedar Rapids	1.000	5	1	1	0	2	0
Dale, Carl, Peoria	.943	24	9	24	2	35	2
Dalton, Brian, Beloit	1.000	34	5	7	0	12	1
D'Amico, Jeff, Beloit	.958	21	10	13	1	24	0
Daniels, John, Wisconsin	.895	39	6	11	2	19	1
Davis, Keith, Clinton	.857	36	6	6	2	14	0
Deakman, Josh, Ced. Rapids	.923	13	2	10	1	13	1
Dennis, Brian, Rockford	1.000	3	0	1	0	1	0
Dennis, Shane, Clinton*	.852	14	3	20	4	27	0
DeWitt, Scott, Kane County*	1.000	1	1	0	0	1	0
Dickson, Jason, Ced. Rapids	.980	25	14	35	1	50	2
Diorio, Mike, Quad City	.857	33	6	12	3	21	1
Dixon, Jim, South Bend	1.000	10	2	3	0	5	0
Domenico, Brian, Michigan	.750	6	2	1	1	4	0
Doughty, Brian, Wisconsin	.944	32	3	14	1	18	1
Dowhower, Deron, F.t Wayne	.917	35	4	7	1	12	0
Droll, Jeff, South Bend	1.000	8	0	2	0	2	0
Duncan, Sean, South Bend*	.667	12	0	2	1	3	0
Dutch, John, Michigan	1.000	32	3	5	0	8	0
Elarton, Scott, Quad City	.958	26	7	16	1	24	2
Epstein, Ian, West Michigan*	1.000	18	1	0	0	1	0
Erdos, Todd, Clinton	1.000	5	0	1	0	1	0
Estes, Shawn, Wis.-Bur.*	.875	6	2	5	1	8	1
Farmer, Jon, Kane County*	.917	29	4	7	1	12	1
Farrell, Jim, Michigan	1.000	13	3	4	0	7	0
Faulkner, Neal, Rockford	.900	40	4	5	1	10	0
Felix, Ruben, Beloit*	.833	45	0	5	1	6	0
Fennell, Barry, Rockford*	1.000	4	0	4	0	4	1
Fidge, Darren, Fort Wayne	.943	39	8	25	2	35	1
Filbeck, Ryan, Kane County	.857	25	3	9	2	14	0
Fitzpatrick, Kenneth, Springfield	1.000	12	3	7	0	10	0
Fitzpatrick, Will, Beloit	1.000	3	0	1	0	1	0
Fletcher, Paul, South Bend*	1.000	36	1	9	0	10	2
Flury, Pat, Springfield	1.000	34	3	13	0	16	1
Foderaro, Kevin, Peoria	.933	15	6	8	1	15	0
Freehill, Michael, Cedar Rapids	1.000	54	4	12	0	16	1
Gamboa, Javier, Springfield	.833	19	6	14	4	24	0
GARCIA, Alfredo, Rockford	1.000	27	12	29	0	41	3
Garcia, Ariel, South Bend	1.000	10	2	7	0	9	0
Garrett, Hal, Clinton	.933	11	4	10	1	15	0
Gates, Sean, Clinton	.714	29	3	2	2	7	0
Gautreau, Mike, Peoria	.813	45	4	9	3	16	0
Gomez, Augustine, S. Bend	.826	25	8	11	4	23	0
Gomez, Dennys, Burlington	1.000	14	1	3	0	4	0
Gonzalez, Gabe, Kane County*	.929	32	6	7	1	14	0
Gonzalez, Geremis, Rockford	.739	12	7	10	6	23	1
Gonzalez, Juan, Beloit	.909	42	8	12	2	22	0
Gooda, David, Beloit*	1.000	3	0	6	0	6	0
Gould, Clint, Wisconsin	1.000	25	3	6	0	9	0
Gourdin, Tom, Fort Wayne	.963	41	7	19	1	27	0
Green, Chris, Wisconsin	1.000	35	9	16	0	25	2
Grenert, Geoff, Cedar Rapids	.944	27	5	12	1	18	1
Grote, Jason, Burlington	1.000	6	0	2	0	2	0
Gunderson, Mike, Quad City	.938	44	3	12	1	16	0
Gunther, Kevin, W. Michigan	1.000	17	1	2	0	3	0
Halama, John, Quad City*	.920	55	3	20	2	25	1
Hale, Chad, Michigan*	1.000	42	2	13	0	15	0
Hall, Billy, Quad City	1.000	36	2	14	0	16	2
Hall, Yates, Peoria	1.000	9	1	4	0	5	0
Hammerschmidt, Andy, Clinton*	.935	14	2	27	2	31	3
Hause, Brendan, W. Michigan*	.911	31	10	31	4	45	1
Hebbert, Allan, Kane County	.667	5	1	3	2	6	0
Herbert, Russell, South Bend	.900	9	1	8	1	10	0
Hernandez, Santos, Burlington	1.000	44	1	10	0	11	1
Hill, Jason, Cedar Rapids*	1.000	48	4	12	0	16	1
Huntsman, Scott, Beloit	1.000	43	2	3	0	5	0
Hutzler, Jeff, Burlington	.900	9	2	7	1	10	0
Isom, Jeff, Clinton*	1.000	35	2	19	0	21	0
Jenkins, A.J., Clinton	.800	33	3	9	3	15	0
Johnson, Ron, Peoria*	.964	22	5	22	1	28	0
Keith, Jeffrey, Burlington*	.957	47	9	13	1	23	0

Player, Team	Pct.	G	PO	A	E	TC	DP
Kester, Tim, Quad City	.895	28	11	23	4	38	0
Khoury, Tony, Rockford	1.000	28	3	5	0	8	0
King, Bill, West Michigan	.892	30	14	19	4	37	0
Knox, Jeffery, Cedar Rapids	.885	25	10	13	3	26	1
Krause, Kevin, Rockford	.917	30	8	14	2	24	1
Krueger, Robert, Wisconsin*	1.000	19	2	2	0	4	0
Lake, Kevin, Burlington*	.923	28	8	28	3	39	1
Leach, Jumaane, Clinton*	1.000	19	0	7	0	7	0
Leibee, Skye, West Michigan*	1.000	9	2	1	0	3	0
Leiber, Zane, South Bend	.800	14	3	1	1	5	0
Linares, Yfrain, Beloit	.833	19	4	6	2	12	0
Lindemann, Wayne, S. Bend*	1.000	7	0	4	0	4	1
Lintern, Cory, Burlington	1.000	8	2	1	0	3	0
Lock, Dan, Quad City*	.849	27	9	36	8	53	4
Logan, Chris, Clinton	.889	53	4	12	2	18	0
Lowe, Jason, West Michigan	.667	7	0	2	1	3	0
Lundquist, David, South Bend	1.000	18	5	10	0	15	1
MacDonald, Mike, Springfield	.929	55	4	9	1	14	1
Mamott, Joe, Michigan	.889	14	4	12	2	18	0
Martinez, Javier, Rockford	.917	18	3	19	2	24	1
Martinez, Uriel, Clinton	1.000	11	2	4	0	6	0
May, Scott, Rockford	1.000	8	0	3	0	3	0
Mays, Marcus, Kane County*	1.000	8	0	2	0	2	0
McCormack, Andy, S. Bend*	1.000	6	1	3	0	4	0
McMillan, Leonard, Burlington	1.000	8	3	3	0	6	1
McMullen, Mike, Burlington	.895	29	6	11	2	19	1
Meadows, Brian, Kane County	.944	26	12	22	2	36	2
Mercado, Gabby, Beloit	.926	24	6	19	2	27	0
Meyhoff, Jason, Fort Wayne*	1.000	17	2	6	0	8	2
Micknich, Steve, Kane County	1.000	9	0	1	0	1	0
Miles, Chad, Kane County*	1.000	19	1	5	0	6	0
Miranda, Walter, Kane County	.932	25	15	26	3	44	2
Mitchell, Alvin, Michigan	.960	30	9	15	1	25	4
Mix, Derek, Clinton	.846	35	1	10	2	13	0
Montelongo, Joseph, Rockford	.889	20	11	21	4	36	1
Morgan, Eric, Wisconsin	.857	7	1	5	1	7	0
Morrison, Chris, W. Michigan	1.000	13	2	1	0	3	0
Mosman, Marc, Burlington	1.000	8	1	4	0	5	1
Mott, Tom, Fort Wayne	.914	25	14	18	3	35	3
Mounce, Tony, Quad City*	.907	25	9	30	4	43	1
Mull, Blaine, Springfield	.947	25	12	24	2	38	0
Mullins, Greg, Beloit*	.933	15	4	10	1	15	1
Myers, Jason, Burlington*	.938	16	3	12	1	16	0
Nartker, Mike, Fort Wayne	1.000	17	4	11	0	15	0
Nate, Scott, Beloit*	1.000	20	2	5	0	7	1
Nelson, Rodney, Springfield	.778	25	8	13	6	27	0
Newman, Damon, W. Michigan	.923	21	5	7	1	13	1
Newman, Eric, Clinton	1.000	11	2	11	0	13	2
Ormonde, Troy, Rockford	1.000	7	4	7	0	11	0
Padilla, Roy, Michigan*	.750	4	0	3	1	4	0
Parisi, Michael, Kane County	.886	26	10	21	4	35	1
Pavano, Carl, Michigan	.943	22	16	17	2	35	0
Pavicich, Paul, Fort Wayne*	1.000	39	1	11	0	12	0
Pearce, Jeff, Wisconsin*	1.000	27	0	5	0	5	0
Perez, Jayson, Clinton	.636	13	2	5	4	11	0
Perez, Juan, West Michigan*	.943	30	4	29	2	35	2
Perkins, Dan, Fort Wayne	.875	29	7	14	3	24	0
Peters, Brannon, Ft. Wayne*	1.000	11	1	2	0	3	0
Peterson, Jayson, Rockford	.778	13	3	4	2	9	0
Petroff, Daniel, Cedar Rapids	.953	28	13	28	2	43	1
Phillips, Marc, Springfield*	.826	38	6	13	4	23	2
Pineda, Leonel, Kane County	1.000	5	4	10	0	14	0
Place, Mike, South Bend	1.000	28	2	5	0	7	0
Pontes, Dan, Peoria	.833	34	5	10	3	18	2
Portillo, Alex, South Bend*	1.000	2	0	1	0	1	0
Prater, Pete, Burlington	.957	21	7	15	1	23	1
Press, Greg, Kane County	.905	29	8	30	4	42	1
Putrich, Josh, Rockford	1.000	6	2	0	0	2	0
Quirk, John, South Bend*	.800	22	0	8	2	10	0
Radinsky, Scott, S. Bend*	1.000	6	0	1	0	1	0
Radlosky, Robert, Ft. Wayne	.913	30	9	12	2	23	1
Raggio, Brady, Peoria	1.000	8	6	11	0	17	2
Rain, Steve, Rockford	.909	53	1	9	1	11	1
Rajotte, Jason, W. Michigan*	.944	44	4	13	1	18	2
Ramos, Edgar, Quad City	1.000	2	0	1	0	1	0
Ratliff, Chris, Burlington	.944	15	4	13	1	18	0
Rector, Bobby, Burlington	.929	27	7	19	2	28	1
Reed, Brian, Peoria	.833	64	4	11	3	18	1
Renfroe, Chad, Michigan	.909	12	5	5	1	11	0
Ritter, Jason, Springfield	1.000	7	1	0	0	1	0
Rivette, Scott, West Michigan	1.000	8	0	3	0	3	0
Robbins, Michael, Springfield*	.889	8	1	7	1	9	1
Roberts, Ray, Springfield*	1.000	38	2	9	0	11	0

Player, Team	Pct.	G	PO	A	E	TC	DP
Roettgen, Mark, Peoria	1.000	4	0	2	0	2	0
Rose, Brian, Michigan	.925	21	13	24	3	40	0
Rosenkranz, Terry, Beloit*	1.000	4	0	1	0	1	0
Ruch, Rob, Fort Wayne	1.000	9	3	1	0	4	0
Runyan, Sean, Quad City*	.895	22	7	10	2	19	0
Rushing, William, Ft. Wayne*	1.000	13	0	4	0	4	1
Sak, James, Clinton	1.000	7	3	6	0	9	0
Salmon, Fabian, South Bend	1.000	15	4	2	0	6	0
Santana, Marino, Wisconsin	.913	15	5	16	2	23	0
Scheffer, Aaron, Wisconsin	1.000	9	0	4	0	4	0
Schenbeck, T.J., Beloit	1.000	18	4	10	0	14	0
Scott, Ron, Peoria*	.800	21	3	1	1	5	0
Shaver, Tony, Quad City	.923	35	5	7	1	13	2
Sick, David, Cedar Rapids	.938	50	3	12	1	16	0
Sikorski, Brian, Quad City	1.000	2	0	1	0	1	0
Silva, Luis, West Michigan	.857	10	1	5	1	7	0
Skuse, Nicholas, Ced. Rapids	.972	27	12	23	1	36	1
Slade, Shawn, Cedar Rapids	1.000	30	1	7	0	8	0
Slininger, Dennis, Peoria	1.000	3	0	2	0	2	0
Smith, Andy, West Michigan	.771	30	8	19	8	35	1
Smith, Brook, Burlington*	.952	39	9	31	2	42	0
Smith, Charles, South Bend	.896	26	10	33	5	48	1
Smith, John, West Michigan*	.800	25	1	7	2	10	1
Smith, Mason, Burlington	1.000	8	0	6	0	6	0
Smith, Roy, Wisconsin	.960	27	10	14	1	25	0
Smith, Shad, Burlington	.600	2	2	1	2	5	0
Sosa, Helpis, West Michigan	.714	21	1	4	2	7	0
Stark, Zachary, Kane County*	.750	5	0	6	2	8	0
Steed, Sam, Springfield*	1.000	8	3	5	0	8	0
Stein, Blake, Peoria	.778	27	9	12	6	27	0
Steinke, Brock, Quad City	.800	21	2	2	1	5	0
Stevenson, Jason, Rockford	.941	33	7	9	1	17	2
Surratt, Jamie, South Bend	.917	26	5	6	1	12	0
Telgheder, Jim, Michigan	.857	22	2	4	1	7	0
Theodile, Robert, South Bend	.909	7	4	6	1	11	0
Thomas, Carlos, Clinton	1.000	13	5	1	0	6	0
Thompson, John, Wisconsin	.900	38	4	5	1	10	0
Thurmond, Travis, Ced. Rapids	1.000	14	2	6	0	8	0
Tidwell, Jason, Kane County	1.000	6	0	5	0	5	0
Tillmon, Darrell, Michigan*	.800	13	7	5	3	15	0
Tollberg, Brian, Beloit	.971	22	10	23	1	34	2
Towns, Ryan, Springfield	.750	18	1	2	1	4	0
Tyrrell, Jim, Michigan*	1.000	16	1	4	0	5	1
Upchurch, Wayne, Springfield	.875	18	6	1	1	8	1
Vanhof, Dave, Wisconsin*	.810	15	5	12	4	21	0
Vandeweg, Ryan, Clinton	.909	15	6	14	2	22	1
Villano, Mike, Burlington	.875	16	3	4	1	8	1
Walters, Brett, Clinton	.919	32	7	27	3	37	2
Warren, Deshawn, Ced. Rapids*	1.000	7	0	7	0	7	0
Washburn, Jarrod, Ced. Rapids*	1.000	3	2	3	0	5	0
Weinberg, Todd, W. Michigan*	.875	36	3	18	3	24	1
Welch, Travis, Peoria	1.000	46	4	8	0	12	0
West, Adam, Peoria*	.667	4	0	2	1	3	0
Wiesner, Chad, Wisconsin	1.000	1	1	0	0	1	0
Williams, Juan, Fort Wayne*	1.000	3	1	0	0	1	0
Woodard, Steve, Beloit	1.000	21	7	17	0	24	1
Wunsch, Kelly, Beloit*	.864	14	2	17	3	22	2
Ybarra, Jamie, Kane County	.917	50	9	13	2	24	1
Zancanaro, Dave, W. Michigan*	.800	16	0	4	1	5	0
Zanolla, Dan, Kane County	.909	28	3	7	1	11	0

PITCHERS WITH TWO OR MORE TEAMS

Player, Team	Pct.	G	PO	A	E	TC	DP
Estes, Shawn, Wisconsin*	1.000	2	2	2	0	4	1
Estes, Shawn, Burlington*	.750	4	0	3	1	4	0

The following players did not have any fielding statistics at the positions indicated or appeared only as a designated hitter, pinch-hitter or pinch-runner: Jose Abreu, p; Juan Abreu, p; Avalos, of; Betances, of; Boulware, of; Brewer, p; Buchanan, 3b; Bustos, 3b; D. Castro, p; Contreras, ss; Jason Cook, ss; Davalillo, p; Dean, of, c, p; Delvalle, p; Fraser, 3b; M. Harris, dh, ph, pr; Ignasiak, p; Jaha, dh; S. Jones, p; Keefe, of; Kurek, p; Lanza, 3b; Llanos, 3b; Marquez, p; Milstien, of; Nilsson, dh; Rantz, p; Root, 2b; Rosenbohm, p; Schiefelbein, p; Torres, p; Truby, of; Vardijan, p; Walls, p; Wambach, dh, ph; D. Williams, 3b; Winkle, p.

LEAGUE CHAMPIONS

Year	Team	Pct.
1947—	Belleville	.667
	Belleville	.672
1948—	West Frankfort*	.708
1949—	Centralia	.627
	Paducah (4th)†	.454
1950—	Centralia‡	.675
1951—	Paris§	.700
	Danville (4th)†	.432
1952—	Danville∞	.685
	Decatur (3rd)†	.584
1953—	Decatur*	.576
1954—	Decatur	.587
	Danville (2nd)‡	.528
1955—	Dubuque*	.587
1956—	Paris▲	.656
	Dubuque	.603
1957—	Decatur▲	.683
	Clinton	.623
1958—	Michigan City	.623
	Waterloo◆	.613
1959—	Waterloo	.613
	Waterloo	.613
1960—	Waterloo	.629
	Waterloo	.677
1961—	Waterloo	.613
	Quincy◆	.594
1962—	Dubuque◆	.667
	Waterloo	.625
1963—	Clinton	.710
	Clinton	.629
1964—	Clinton	.667
	Fox Cities◆	.667
1965—	Burlington	.667
	Burlington	.677
1966—	Fox Cities◆	.689
	Cedar Rapids	.762
1967—	Wisconsin Rapids	.685
	Appleton◆	.587
1968—	Decatur	.656
	Quad Cities◆	.648
1969—	Appleton	.648
	Appleton	.690
1970—	Quincy◆	.691
	Quad Cities	.581
1971—	Appleton	.642
	Quad Cities■	.548
1972—	Appleton	.598
	Danville■	.584
1973—	Wisconsin Rapids■	.562
	Danville	.537
1974—	Appleton	.593
	Danville■	.517
1975—	Waterloo■	.727
	Quad Cities	.624
1976—	Waterloo■	.600
	Cedar Rapids	.595
1977—	Waterloo	.580
	Burlington■	.511
1978—	Appleton■	.708
	Burlington	.500
1979—	Waterloo	.600
	Quad Cities■	.579
1980—	Waterloo■	.610
	Quad Cities	.532
1981—	Wausau■	.636
	Quad Cities	.570
1982—	Madison	.626
	Appleton▼	.579
1983—	Appleton•	.635
	Springfield	.576
1984—	Appleton•	.640
	Springfield	.504
1985—	Kenosha▼	.568
	Peoria	.536
1986—	Springfield	.621
	Waterloo▼	.557
1987—	Springfield	.671
	Kenosha▼	.586
1988—	Cedar Rapids■	.621
	Kenosha	.579
1989—	South Bend■	.644
	Springfield	.541
1990—	Cedar Rapids	.657
	Quad City■	.579
1991—	Clinton■	.583
	Madison	.558
1992—	Quad City	.664
	Cedar Rapids■	.594
1993—	Clinton	.597
	South Bend■	.566
1994—	Rockford	.640
	Cedar Rapids■	.554
1995—	Beloit††	.633
	Michigan	.543

*Won championship and four-club playoff. †Won four-club playoff. ‡Playoff finals canceled because of bad weather. §Won both halves of split season. ∞Won first half of split season and tied Paris for second-half title. ▲Won first-half title and four-team playoff. ◆Won split season playoff. ■League divided into Northern and Southern divisions and played split season. Playoff winner. ▼League divided into Northern, Central and Southern divisions. Playoff winner. •League divided into Northern, Central and Southern divisions; regular season and playoff winner. ††League divided into Eastern, Central and Western divisions; regular season and playoff winner. (NOTE—Known as Illinois State League in 1947-48 and Mississippi-Ohio Valley League from 1949 through 1955.)

NEW YORK-PENN LEAGUE

LEAGUE OFFICE

President
Bob Julian
Address
1629 Oneida St.
Utica, NY 13501
Phone
315-733-8036

Teams (affiliation)
Auburn Doubledays (Astros)
Batavia Clippers (Phillies)
Elmira Pioneers (Marlins)
Erie SeaWolves (Pirates)
Hudson Valley Renegades (Rangers)
Jamestown Jammers (Tigers)
New Jersey Cardinals (Cardinals)
Oneonta Yankees (Yankees)
Pittsfield Mets (Mets)
St. Catharines Blue Jays (Blue Jays)
Utica Blue Sox (Red Sox)
Vermont Expos (Expos)
Watertown Indians (Indians)
Williamsport Cubs (Cubs)

1995 FINAL STANDINGS

McNAMARA DIVISION

Team	W	L	T	Pct.	GB
Vermont (Expos)	49	27	0	.645	....
Hudson Valley (Rangers)	47	27	0	.635	1
New Jersey (Cardinals)	35	41	0	.461	14
Pittsfield (Mets)	34	42	0	.447	15

PINCKNEY DIVISION

Team	W	L	T	Pct.	GB
Batavia (Phillies)	41	34	0	.547	....
St. Catharines (Blue Jays)	38	37	0	.507	3
Erie (Pirates)	34	41	0	.453	7
Jamestown (Tigers)	32	44	0	.421	9½

STEDLER DIVISION

Team	W	L	T	Pct.	GB
Watertown (Indians)	46	27	0	.630	....
Auburn (Astros)	40	34	0	.541	6½
Williamsport (Cubs)	37	39	0	.487	10½
Oneonta (Yankees)	34	41	0	.453	13
Utica (Red Sox)	33	40	0	.452	13
Elmira (Marlins)	25	51	0	.329	22½

COMPOSITE

Team	Ver.	H.V.	Wat.	Bat.	Aub.	St.C.	Wpt.	N.J.	One.	Erie	Uti.	Pit.	Jam.	Elm.	W	L	T	Pct.	GB
Vermont (Expos)	....	7	4	3	2	3	2	7	2	2	2	9	4	2	49	27	0	.645	....
Hudson Valley (Rangers)	5	....	2	4	2	1	2	8	4	4	2	9	2	2	47	27	0	.635	1
Watertown (Indians)	0	1	....	2	5	3	4	4	7	4	6	1	3	6	46	27	0	.630	1½
Batavia (Phillies)	1	0	2	....	1	6	2	3	2	7	2	3	9	3	41	34	0	.547	7½
Auburn (Astros)	2	2	5	3	....	3	4	2	2	3	4	2	2	6	40	34	0	.541	8
St. Catharines (Blue Jays)	1	3	1	5	1	....	4	2	3	6	3	1	4	4	38	37	0	.507	10½
Williamsport (Cubs)	2	2	4	2	4	0	....	2	2	2	6	2	2	7	37	39	0	.487	12
New Jersey (Cardinals)	5	4	0	1	2	2	2	....	2	3	2	6	2	4	35	41	0	.461	14
Oneonta (Yankees)	2	0	1	2	6	1	6	2	....	1	4	1	3	5	34	41	0	.453	14½
Erie (Pirates)	2	0	0	5	1	6	2	1	3	....	1	3	7	3	34	41	0	.453	14½
Utica (Red Sox)	2	1	2	2	4	1	2	2	7	2	....	2	1	5	33	40	0	.452	14½
Pittsfield (Mets)	3	3	3	1	2	3	2	6	3	1	2	....	3	2	34	42	0	.447	15
Jamestown (Tigers)	0	2	1	3	2	8	2	2	1	5	3	1	....	2	32	44	0	.421	17
Elmira (Marlins)	2	2	2	1	2	0	5	0	3	1	3	2	2	....	25	51	0	.329	24

Major league affiliations in parentheses.

Hudson Valley home games played in Fishkill, N.Y.

New Jersey home games played in Augusta, N.J.

Vermont home games played in Winooski, Vt.

PLAYOFFS: Vermont defeated Hudson Valley, two games to none; Watertown defeated Batavia, two games to one; Watertown defeated Vermont, two games to one, to win league championship.

REGULAR-SEASON ATTENDANCE: Auburn, 58,972; Batavia, 38,313; Elmira, 43,759; Erie, 181,815; Hudson Valley, 161,673; Jamestown, 48,938; New Jersey, 176,788; Oneonta, 53,990; Pittsfield, 73,273; St. Catharines, 50,528; Utica, 64,487; Vermont, 120,917; Watertown, 45,202; Williamsport, 63,192. Total—1,181,847. Playoffs (8 games)—14,684.

MANAGERS: Auburn, Manny Acta; Batavia, Al LeBoeuf; Elmira, Paul Kirsch; Erie, Scott Little; Hudson Valley, Bump Wills; Jamestown, Bruce Fields; New Jersey, Luis Melendez; Oneonta, Rob Thomson; Pittsfield, Ron Gideon; St. Catharines, J.J. Cannon; Utica, Bob Geren; Vermont, Jim Gabella; Watertown, Joel Skinner; Williamsport, Oneri Fleita.

ALL-STAR TEAM: 1B—Steve Carver, Batavia; 2B—Marlon Anderson, Batavia; 3B—Clifford Brumbaugh, Hudson Valley; SS—Oscar Robles, Auburn; Utility IF—Jose Fernandez, Vermont; OF—Ed Bady, Vermont; Fletcher Bates, Pittsfield; Jose Guillen, Erie; Luke Wilcox, Oneonta; C—Ramon Castro, Auburn; Scott Vieira, Williamsport; DH—Virgil Chevalier, Utica; RHP—Chris Weidert, Vermont; Scott Mudd, Hudson Valley; LHP—Bryan Link, Hudson Valley; Michael Venafro, Hudson Valley; Most Valuable Player—Clifford Brumbaugh, Hudson Valley; Manager of the Year—Joel Skinner, Watertown.

1995 BATTING

TEAM

Team	Avg.	G	TPA	AB	R	H	TB	2B	3B	HR	RBI	SH	SF	HP	BB	IBB	SO	SB	CS	GDP	LOB	ShO	Slg.	OBP
Auburn	.267	74	2765	2444	383	653	897	112	18	32	331	10	24	29	258	5	410	71	27	69	533	1	.367	.341
Hudson Valley	.267	74	2859	2512	376	670	897	105	25	24	306	13	31	50	252	13	465	107	51	72	533	1	.357	.342
Erie	.264	75	2829	2503	368	661	941	92	25	46	307	23	20	50	232	3	502	81	50	62	498	5	.376	.336
Batavia	.262	75	2918	2592	389	680	941	106	31	31	336	22	17	50	236	5	474	88	35	49	536	1	.363	.334
St. Catharines	.257	75	2918	2557	344	658	911	119	25	28	289	40	20	53	248	9	570	96	45	25	565	8	.356	.333
Vermont	.257	76	2842	2505	354	643	865	94	28	24	287	17	27	36	257	9	457	152	72	36	515	2	.345	.331
Watertown	.257	73	2834	2456	360	630	896	127	26	29	306	21	24	34	299	11	529	49	23	61	564	3	.365	.342
Utica	.256	73	2708	2425	358	622	865	98	23	33	304	21	30	41	191	2	479	125	55	49	431	1	.357	.318
Williamsport	.255	76	2919	2561	379	654	907	122	34	21	324	12	24	47	275	7	523	85	44	51	543	6	.354	.336
Jamestown	.254	76	2963	2544	368	646	926	117	29	35	312	19	21	40	338	9	526	104	48	50	577	9	.364	.348

Team	Avg.	G	TPA	AB	R	H	TB	2B	3B	HR	RBI	SH	SF	HP	BB	IBB	SO	SB	CS	GDP	LOB	ShO	Slg.	OBP
New Jersey....	.250	76	2979	2603	370	651	849	105	27	13	314	29	14	53	280	6	477	93	43	54	550	3	.326	.334
Pittsfield........	.249	76	2858	2498	325	623	830	101	32	14	270	26	23	36	274	7	487	103	50	36	545	6	.332	.330
Elmira............	.243	76	2860	2534	316	616	884	106	30	34	261	14	17	42	253	11	552	111	52	61	532	6	.349	.320
Oneonta.........	.243	75	2812	2489	312	604	843	125	30	18	261	9	27	28	259	4	553	87	33	42	548	6	.339	.318

INDIVIDUAL

TOP QUALIFIERS FOR BATTING CHAMPIONSHIP

Minimum 205 plate appearances. *Lefthanded batter. †Switch-hitter.

Player, Team	Avg.	G	TPA	AB	R	H	TB	2B	3B	HR	RBI	SH	SF	HP	BB	IBB	SO	SB	CS	GDP	Slg.	OBP
Brumbaugh, Clifford, Hud. Valley....	.358	74	325	282	44	101	134	19	4	2	45	0	2	2	39	4	51	15	3	11	.475	.437
Bady, Edward, Vermont†.............	.329	72	326	295	51	97	124	15	3	2	25	2	0	5	24	3	52	34	19	3	.420	.389
Casey, Sean, Watertown*............	.329	55	229	207	26	68	92	18	0	2	37	0	3	1	18	4	21	3	0	6	.444	.380
Wilcox, Chris, Oneonta*..............	.327	59	246	223	25	73	106	16	7	1	28	0	2	1	20	3	28	9	3	4	.475	.382
Bates, Fletcher, Pittsfield†...........	.326	75	325	276	52	90	140	14	9	6	37	1	3	4	41	0	72	17	9	1	.507	.417
Jorgensen, Tim, Watertown*.......	.325	73	331	295	44	96	157	19	9	8	52	1	1	2	32	4	63	4	1	4	.532	.394
Vieira, Scott, Williamsport..........	.318	61	252	214	35	68	98	8	2	6	46	0	4	9	25	1	37	3	1	3	.458	.405
Rice, Charles, Erie†......................	.316	70	298	269	44	85	128	15	2	8	33	0	1	8	19	0	59	7	5	5	.476	.377
Dawkins, Walter, Batavia.............	.315	58	239	203	46	64	86	11	4	1	31	2	3	4	27	0	36	15	6	6	.424	.401
Winn, Randy, Elmira......................	.315	51	233	213	38	67	82	7	4	0	22	0	2	3	15	0	31	19	7	1	.385	.365
Guillen, Jose, Erie........................	.314	66	281	258	41	81	136	17	1	12	46	0	1	12	10	0	44	1	5	5	.527	.367
Bovender, Andy, Auburn..............	.313	71	278	243	42	76	114	15	4	5	41	0	1	4	30	2	70	1	2	7	.469	.396
Hall, Andy, New Jersey†..............	.310	64	279	252	30	78	101	10	5	1	34	4	0	4	19	2	44	19	6	2	.401	.367
Miyake, Chris, Erie.......................	.308	61	246	227	34	70	92	6	5	2	25	1	1	5	12	0	31	14	6	3	.405	.355
Chevalier, Virgil, Utica..................	.308	64	267	250	34	77	114	12	2	7	46	0	3	3	11	0	35	15	6	6	.456	.341

DEPARTMENTAL LEADERS: G—Daly, 76; AB—Anderson, 312; R—Sanchez, 62; H—Brumbaugh, 101; TB—Jorgensen, 157; 2B—Daly, 22; 3B—Joseph, 10; HR—Guillen, 12; RBI—Daly, 60; SH—Several players tied with 7; SF—Daly, Olsen, 7; HP—Goodell, 14; BB—M. Miller, 60; IBB—Weaver, 5; SO—Landers, 86; SB—Am. Garcia, 41; CS—Bady, 19; GIDP—Booty, 12; Slg.—Jorgensen, .532; OBP—Brumbaugh, .437.

ALL PLAYERS

*Lefthanded batter. †Switch-hitter.

Player, Team	Avg.	G	TPA	AB	R	H	TB	2B	3B	HR	RBI	SH	SF	HP	BB	IBB	SO	SB	CS	GDP	Slg.	OBP
Adams, Jason, Auburn..................	.215	51	212	181	28	39	45	6	0	0	18	1	0	3	27	1	19	3	1	5	.249	.327
Adamson, Jason, Erie..................	.286	2	7	7	0	2	2	0	0	0	2	0	0	0	0	0	1	0	0	0	.286	.286
Afenir, Tom, Watertown................	.200	6	17	15	2	3	5	2	0	0	3	1	0	1	0	0	3	0	0	1	.333	.250
Alexander, Chad, Auburn..............	.291	71	316	278	45	81	121	15	5	5	43	1	5	7	25	1	37	7	1	11	.435	.359
Anderson, Marlon, Batavia*..........	.295	74	337	312	52	92	122	13	4	3	40	2	4	4	15	2	20	22	8	2	.391	.331
Antrim, Patrick, Oneonta†............	.192	26	82	78	6	15	16	1	0	0	5	1	1	1	1	0	23	3	1	1	.205	.210
Arvelo, Tom, Pittsfield...................	.305	67	303	279	41	85	107	8	7	0	17	2	1	5	16	0	63	24	6	0	.384	.352
Austin, Lakevie, Utica...................	.242	34	101	91	10	22	28	3	0	1	6	1	0	1	8	0	38	5	2	1	.308	.310
Babin, Brady, Elmira......................	.350	6	24	20	4	7	10	1	1	0	2	1	0	0	3	0	1	0	0	0	.500	.435
Bady, Edward, Vermont†..............	.329	72	326	295	51	97	124	15	3	2	25	2	0	5	24	3	52	34	19	3	.420	.389
Barrett, Michael, Vermont.............	.100	3	12	10	0	1	1	0	0	0	1	0	1	0	1	0	1	0	0	0	.100	.167
Barton, Scott, Williamsport*.........	.222	16	51	45	3	10	19	5	2	0	13	1	1	0	4	0	13	0	1	2	.422	.280
Bates, Fletcher, Pittsfield†............	.326	75	325	276	52	90	140	14	9	6	37	1	3	4	41	0	72	17	9	1	.507	.417
Bazzani, Matt, Utica......................	.243	29	87	74	15	18	37	4	3	3	17	3	0	6	4	0	17	1	0	0	.500	.333
Bentley, Kevin, Williamsport.........	.217	50	130	115	14	25	41	4	3	2	13	1	0	0	14	0	48	1	3	1	.357	.302
Betts, Darrell, New Jersey†...........	.152	54	193	151	22	23	27	4	0	0	11	7	0	3	32	0	38	3	6	2	.179	.312
Blakeney, Mo, Vermont.................	.265	39	144	132	17	35	51	8	1	2	17	0	0	4	8	0	23	12	2	3	.386	.326
Booty, Josh, Elmira......................	.220	74	313	287	33	63	101	18	1	6	37	0	2	5	19	0	85	4	4	12	.352	.278
Borges, Mariano, Erie..................	.111	17	50	45	4	5	5	0	0	0	2	0	0	2	3	0	11	1	1	2	.111	.200
Boryczewski, Marty, Erie..............	.094	10	33	32	0	3	3	0	0	0	0	0	0	0	1	0	6	0	0	2	.094	.121
Bourne, Charles, St. Catharines....	.199	55	203	176	24	35	49	11	0	1	17	4	2	3	18	0	50	12	3	2	.278	.281
Bovender, Andy, Auburn..............	.313	71	278	243	42	76	114	15	4	5	41	0	1	4	30	2	70	1	2	7	.469	.396
Brannon, Tony, Utica....................	.216	42	139	125	11	27	37	5	1	1	18	1	2	2	9	0	20	5	2	5	.296	.275
Brinkley, Josh, Vermont................	.221	38	144	122	14	27	29	2	0	0	11	0	2	6	14	0	26	6	1	4	.238	.326
Briones, Christopher, Hud. Valley....	.221	48	174	163	18	36	65	12	1	5	26	1	3	3	4	0	53	0	0	2	.399	.249
Brito, Domingo, Batavia...............	.125	11	41	32	1	4	4	0	0	0	2	0	0	0	9	0	9	0	0	2	.125	.317
Brumbaugh, Clifford, Hud. Valley....	.358	74	325	282	44	101	134	19	4	2	45	0	2	2	39	4	51	15	3	11	.475	.437
Brunner, Michael, Auburn............	.193	26	88	83	7	16	28	6	0	2	11	0	0	0	5	0	25	2	1	3	.337	.239
Budzinski, Mark, Watertown*.......	.253	70	318	253	50	64	101	12	8	3	25	3	2	8	52	1	49	15	5	3	.399	.394
Caballero, Manuel, Jamestown*......	.197	52	177	142	23	28	49	4	1	5	20	0	2	1	32	0	42	3	2	10	.345	.345
Cabrera, Orlando, Vermont...........	.282	65	271	248	37	70	101	12	5	3	33	2	4	1	16	0	28	15	8	3	.407	.323
Cameron, Ken, New Jersey*..........	.239	39	154	138	18	33	44	9	1	0	10	2	0	2	12	0	20	5	0	2	.319	.309
Camfield, Eric, Oneonta*..............	.270	73	323	296	45	80	100	11	3	1	42	2	2	1	22	0	41	17	7	1	.338	.321
Camilli, Jason, Vermont...............	.243	63	280	243	37	59	76	10	2	1	21	3	2	2	30	1	52	17	10	4	.313	.329
Canetto, John, Erie†.....................	.160	11	32	25	5	4	4	0	0	0	1	0	0	0	7	0	7	0	0	1	.160	.344
Cardona, Ruben, New Jersey*........	.251	49	221	195	36	49	62	5	4	0	24	3	1	1	21	0	24	7	2	3	.318	.326
Carpenter, Matt, Watertown..........	.323	12	35	31	4	10	13	3	0	0	4	0	0	0	4	0	7	0	0	3	.419	.400
Carver, Steve, Batavia*................	.304	56	236	217	35	66	104	13	2	7	41	1	1	0	17	1	29	2	1	3	.479	.353
Casey, Sean, Watertown*............	.329	55	229	207	26	68	92	18	0	2	37	0	3	1	18	4	21	3	0	6	.444	.380
Castro, Ramon, Auburn................	.299	63	254	224	40	67	111	17	0	9	49	0	6	0	24	0	27	0	1	6	.496	.358
Chamblee, James, Utica...............	.255	62	231	200	36	51	68	9	1	2	16	1	1	6	23	0	45	9	7	5	.340	.348
Chevalier, Virgil, Utica.................	.308	64	267	250	34	77	114	12	2	7	46	0	3	3	11	0	35	15	6	6	.456	.341
Choate, Jonathan, Watertown*.......	.219	59	223	196	28	43	63	10	2	2	24	0	2	1	24	0	36	2	3	5	.321	.305
Coats, Nathan, Watertown............	.276	12	33	29	2	8	12	2	1	0	3	0	0	0	4	0	11	0	0	0	.414	.364
Conley, Brian, Williamsport...........	.251	69	292	259	42	65	88	18	1	1	23	2	3	4	24	0	49	7	3	4	.340	.321
Cornelius, Jonathon, Batavia.........	.262	68	295	263	29	69	97	11	4	3	41	3	2	5	22	0	59	4	2	4	.369	.329
Cox, Charles, Batavia..................	.218	38	135	124	13	27	35	4	2	0	11	0	0	0	11	0	41	2	0	5	.282	.281
Crane, Todd, Batavia....................	.246	27	84	69	15	17	20	3	0	0	8	1	0	1	13	0	25	2	0	2	.290	.373

Player, Team	Avg.	G	TPA	AB	R	H	TB	2B	3B	HR	RBI	SH	SF	HP	BB	IBB	SO	SB	CS	GDP	Slg.	OBP
Culp, Matt, Watertown*	.129	33	102	85	7	11	17	3	0	1	8	0	0	3	14	0	26	1	0	1	.200	.275
Culp, Randy, Vermont	.000	1	3	3	0	0	0	0	0	0	0	0	0	0	0	0	0	0	0	0	.000	.000
Daly, Rob, Pittsfield	.294	76	333	303	43	89	126	22	3	3	60	0	7	1	22	1	28	4	1	5	.416	.336
Davis, Albert, Erie	.230	44	178	152	31	35	53	12	0	2	12	2	3	2	19	0	26	8	2	3	.349	.318
Dawkins, Walter, Batavia	.315	58	239	203	46	64	86	11	4	1	31	2	3	4	27	0	36	15	6	6	.424	.401
DeLaRosa, Elvis, Jamestown	.238	14	44	42	3	10	12	2	0	0	5	0	1	0	1	0	15	1	1	1	.286	.250
Deluca, Nic, New Jersey	.250	3	8	8	1	2	2	0	0	0	0	0	0	0	0	0	2	0	0	0	.250	.250
Deman, Lou, New Jersey	.220	52	205	186	22	41	55	8	0	2	24	1	1	5	12	0	60	2	3	3	.296	.284
Denning, Wes, Vermont*	.196	56	202	168	30	33	37	0	2	0	17	4	3	4	23	0	45	16	5	1	.220	.303
Dennis, Les, Oneonta	.264	48	167	148	24	39	52	6	2	1	13	0	2	3	14	0	40	5	2	4	.351	.335
Deshenes, Marc, Watertown	.208	42	174	144	18	30	39	4	1	1	14	5	4	3	18	0	45	6	2	3	.271	.302
Diaz, Linardo, Batavia	.240	22	88	75	13	18	27	4	1	1	7	4	0	6	3	0	17	4	1	1	.360	.321
Dieguez, Mike, Pittsfield	.215	59	225	181	31	39	48	7	1	0	17	1	0	12	31	0	29	0	5	5	.265	.366
Doezie, Troy, New Jersey	.190	23	95	84	15	16	28	5	2	1	12	0	0	1	10	0	18	0	1	5	.333	.284
Echols, Mandell, Hudson Valley	.284	58	235	215	31	61	78	8	3	1	21	0	1	5	14	0	48	15	13	5	.363	.340
Edwards, Aaron, Erie	.264	15	60	53	10	14	14	0	0	0	3	1	0	0	6	1	10	7	2	2	.264	.339
Ellison, Tony, Williamsport	.222	5	21	18	5	4	7	0	0	1	2	0	0	1	2	0	5	0	0	0	.389	.333
Emmons, Scott, Oneonta	.198	67	277	242	25	48	75	15	3	2	32	2	5	3	25	0	62	1	1	5	.310	.276
Engleka, Douglas, Jamestown	.283	44	194	166	32	47	65	8	2	2	20	1	3	4	20	0	28	11	5	5	.392	.368
Erwin, Mat, Elmira	.262	68	290	260	22	68	96	12	2	4	39	0	2	6	22	2	36	2	1	10	.369	.331
Evans, Kyle, Hudson Valley*	.238	57	225	189	31	45	70	11	1	4	25	0	2	7	27	1	39	4	1	3	.370	.351
Fana, Alberto, Batavia	.262	20	64	61	5	16	17	1	0	0	4	1	0	0	2	0	11	0	0	1	.279	.286
Fernandez, Jose, Vermont	.274	66	287	270	38	74	106	6	7	4	41	1	2	1	13	2	51	29	4	2	.393	.308
Flanigan, Steven, Erie	.271	25	87	85	8	23	32	4	1	1	10	0	0	1	1	0	23	1	0	1	.376	.287
Freel, Ryan, St. Catharines	.280	65	284	243	30	68	97	10	5	3	29	7	5	7	22	0	49	12	7	3	.399	.350
Freitas, Joe, New Jersey	.191	14	55	47	8	9	15	6	0	0	9	0	2	1	5	0	18	2	0	1	.319	.273
Fuller, Brian, Jamestown	.270	40	159	137	28	37	66	9	1	6	24	0	0	3	19	1	26	4	2	0	.482	.371
Funaro, Joe, Elmira	.265	56	209	189	24	50	72	10	3	2	16	1	2	0	17	1	21	5	2	3	.381	.322
Gallagher, Shawn, Hudson Valley	.150	5	22	20	1	3	5	2	0	0	4	0	0	1	1	0	4	0	0	2	.250	.227
Garcia, Amaury, Elmira	.273	62	272	231	40	63	76	7	3	0	17	3	0	4	34	2	50	41	12	1	.329	.375
Garcia, Apostol, Jamestown	.235	60	221	200	25	47	61	8	3	0	21	7	1	3	10	0	36	10	6	3	.305	.280
Garcia, Jaime, Vermont	.242	50	183	149	22	36	53	7	2	2	16	2	1	4	27	2	30	1	1	1	.356	.370
Garman, Sean, New Jersey*	.195	50	159	133	20	26	31	5	0	0	8	3	1	1	21	0	25	1	0	4	.233	.308
Garrett, Jason, Elmira	.221	41	146	131	15	29	38	4	1	1	11	1	0	3	11	0	31	2	1	5	.290	.297
Gipner, Marcus, Oneonta†	.099	25	96	81	0	8	9	1	0	0	0	0	0	0	15	0	20	1	1	4	.111	.240
Gonzalez, Rich, Watertown	.266	55	207	184	24	49	58	4	1	1	17	4	2	0	17	0	19	1	0	7	.315	.325
Goodell, Steve, Elmira	.253	69	306	253	42	64	107	14	4	7	30	1	2	14	36	0	50	4	5	8	.423	.374
Goodwin, Joseph, Hudson Valley	.282	57	211	181	29	51	60	6	0	1	27	2	2	6	20	0	20	2	1	7	.331	.368
Goodwin, Keith, Utica	.260	39	164	146	26	38	50	4	1	2	16	3	1	0	14	0	22	10	1	5	.342	.323
Gorecki, Ryan, Hudson Valley*	.296	59	213	189	24	56	60	4	0	0	20	2	2	3	17	1	10	8	6	9	.317	.360
Gray, Ricky, Jamestown*	.152	32	97	79	15	12	23	3	1	2	8	0	0	1	17	1	30	4	0	2	.291	.309
Guillen, Jose, Erie	.314	66	281	258	41	81	136	17	1	12	46	0	1	12	10	0	44	1	5	5	.527	.367
Halemanu, Joshua, Auburn*	.197	52	193	157	25	31	58	6	0	7	25	0	4	3	29	0	60	2	2	0	.369	.326
Hall, Andy, New Jersey†	.310	64	279	252	30	78	101	10	5	1	34	4	0	4	19	2	44	19	6	2	.401	.367
Hare, Rich, Jamestown	.193	27	60	57	6	11	15	4	0	0	3	0	0	1	2	0	13	4	1	0	.263	.233
Hayes, Chris, St. Catharines	.306	70	304	271	39	83	112	17	3	2	36	1	1	7	24	0	50	8	7	2	.413	.376
Hayes, Heath, Watertown	.212	15	60	52	4	11	14	3	0	0	6	0	1	0	7	0	14	1	1	1	.269	.300
Hermansen, Chad, Erie	.273	44	189	165	30	45	77	8	3	6	25	0	2	4	18	0	39	4	2	6	.467	.354
Hernandez, Rob, Elmira†	.040	8	31	25	0	1	1	0	0	0	0	1	0	0	5	0	7	1	0	0	.040	.200
Holley, Jack, St. Catharines	.240	65	280	246	33	59	72	2	1	3	26	7	0	5	22	0	47	3	3	4	.293	.315
Horton, Eric, St. Catharines	.000	21	1	1	0	0	0	0	0	0	0	0	0	0	0	0	1	0	0	0	.000	.000
Imersek, Jason, Oneonta	.077	6	14	13	1	1	1	0	0	0	1	0	0	0	1	0	2	0	0	0	.077	.143
Insunza, Miguel, New Jersey	.242	55	240	207	30	50	56	6	0	0	21	3	1	5	24	0	8	11	8	8	.271	.333
Jaroncyk, Ryan, Pittsfield	.231	4	17	13	5	3	3	0	0	0	0	0	0	1	3	0	5	5	0	0	.231	.412
Jasco, Elinton, Williamsport	.320	6	26	25	2	8	10	2	0	0	4	1	0	0	0	0	5	2	0	0	.400	.320
Jefferson, Dave, Elmira	.077	5	14	13	1	1	1	0	0	0	0	0	0	0	1	0	3	2	0	3	.077	.143
Johnson, Damon, St. Catharines	.216	63	248	232	26	50	72	9	5	1	25	3	1	4	8	1	73	9	2	4	.310	.253
Johnson, Jason, Hudson Valley	.240	46	169	150	27	36	64	7	3	5	16	0	2	5	12	0	38	10	6	2	.427	.314
Jones, Jaime, Elmira*	.284	31	125	116	21	33	55	6	2	4	11	0	0	0	9	0	30	5	4	2	.474	.336
Jorgensen, Tim, Watertown*	.325	73	331	295	44	96	157	19	9	8	52	1	1	2	32	4	63	4	1	4	.532	.394
Joseph, Terry, Williamsport	.292	70	298	260	49	76	107	8	10	1	34	1	0	7	30	1	33	18	6	5	.412	.380
Kapler, Gabriel, Jamestown	.288	63	265	236	38	68	107	19	4	4	34	0	4	2	23	0	37	1	2	4	.453	.351
Kimm, Tyson, Batavia†	.270	14	44	37	8	10	12	2	0	0	6	0	0	1	6	0	6	0	0	0	.324	.386
Koonce, Graham, Jamestown*	.280	73	327	289	37	81	108	16	1	3	34	0	1	2	35	0	63	8	3	1	.374	.361
Lackey, Steve, Pittsfield	.240	21	80	75	7	18	23	5	0	0	6	1	1	1	2	0	16	1	0	1	.307	.266
Landers, Mark, St. Catharines*	.232	74	324	271	43	63	104	11	0	10	52	0	4	4	45	4	86	1	2	0	.384	.346
Lariviere, Jason, New Jersey	.280	33	116	100	13	28	33	3	1	0	9	2	0	0	14	0	10	8	2	2	.330	.368
Lauterhahn, Mike, Williamsport	.143	5	19	14	5	2	3	1	0	0	0	0	0	0	5	0	5	1	1	0	.214	.368
Leaman, Jeff, Batavia	.264	62	244	220	30	58	82	10	1	4	22	2	0	2	20	0	55	2	4	3	.373	.331
Lebron, Ruben, Utica†	.287	52	169	150	30	43	58	6	3	1	15	4	2	2	11	0	28	16	7	0	.387	.339
LeClair, Paul, Pittsfield	.180	31	111	100	10	18	21	3	0	0	6	1	1	1	7	0	35	0	1	0	.210	.239
Lemonis, Chris, Jamestown*	.236	57	216	191	19	45	56	7	2	0	21	3	1	2	18	0	32	5	1	4	.293	.307
Lewis, Marc, Utica	.301	69	294	272	47	82	122	15	5	5	39	2	3	0	17	0	32	24	9	6	.449	.339
Lobaton, Jose, Oneonta	.221	41	161	145	23	32	52	11	3	1	11	1	0	2	13	0	30	4	1	2	.359	.294
Long, Garrett, Erie	.278	29	126	108	17	30	40	4	0	2	16	0	2	1	15	0	25	2	2	6	.370	.365
Long, Justin, Elmira	.210	56	206	186	25	39	62	6	1	5	17	1	1	1	17	0	54	13	3	3	.333	.278
Long, Terrence, Pittsfield*	.257	51	208	187	24	48	77	9	4	4	31	1	1	1	18	2	36	11	4	2	.412	.324
Lowell, Mike, Oneonta	.260	72	313	281	36	73	94	18	0	1	27	0	6	3	23	0	34	3	1	5	.335	.316
Lugo, Julio, Auburn	.291	59	260	230	36	67	82	6	3	1	16	2	0	2	26	0	31	17	7	7	.357	.368
Macias, Jose, Vermont†	.239	53	199	176	24	42	50	4	2	0	9	2	0	2	19	0	19	11	7	3	.284	.320
Mackert, Jamie, Erie	.218	35	125	101	18	22	40	4	4	2	17	1	0	1	22	0	46	0	4	2	.396	.363
Maleski, Tom, Williamsport	.232	40	136	112	13	26	36	8	1	0	14	1	2	2	19	0	25	1	1	2	.321	.348
Martinez, Dave, Hudson Valley*	.250	44	142	124	19	31	37	6	0	0	17	0	2	3	13	1	25	1	1	1	.298	.331

Player, Team	Avg.	G	TPA	AB	R	H	TB	2B	3B	HR	RBI	SH	SF	HP	BB	IBB	SO	SB	CS	GDP	Slg.	OBP
Martinez, Roger, Pittsfield	.101	23	76	69	1	7	10	3	0	0	3	0	1	1	5	0	20	1	0	1	.145	.171
May, Freddie, Erie*	.267	27	98	90	10	24	32	3	1	1	12	1	1	1	5	0	23	5	5	2	.356	.309
Maynor, Tonka, Erie*	.129	11	37	31	2	4	8	1	0	1	3	0	0	2	4	0	2	0	0	0	.258	.270
McAulay, John, Hudson Valley	.212	24	66	52	7	11	11	0	0	0	4	1	3	2	8	0	9	1	1	1	.212	.323
McCartney, Sommer, Elmira	.179	33	120	112	11	20	27	4	0	1	5	0	0	2	6	0	29	1	3	1	.241	.233
McClendon, Travis, New Jersey	.286	50	178	161	25	46	60	9	1	1	18	1	1	5	10	1	25	6	3	5	.373	.345
McCormick, Cody, Oneonta	.276	74	305	268	33	74	112	16	2	6	32	1	2	4	30	1	60	4	2	2	.418	.355
McDonald, Ashanti, Williamsport*	.249	59	213	193	26	48	57	4	1	1	20	2	1	4	13	0	46	4	5	5	.295	.308
McHugh, Ryan, New Jersey	.194	26	109	98	7	19	26	4	0	1	14	1	1	1	8	0	39	2	0	3	.265	.259
McLendon, Craig, Hudson Valley	.000	4	6	6	0	0	0	0	0	0	0	0	0	0	0	0	3	0	0	0	.000	.000
McNally, Shawn, New Jersey	.256	24	104	90	11	23	31	5	0	1	10	1	0	5	8	0	18	5	1	1	.344	.350
Miller, Kumandac, Elmira	.201	47	169	154	9	31	41	4	3	0	15	2	3	2	8	0	40	2	4	4	.266	.246
Miller, Michael, Jamestown	.228	64	267	197	39	45	65	9	1	3	27	0	0	10	60	0	66	10	7	6	.330	.431
Milord, Clausel, Jamestown	.207	34	110	87	13	18	26	3	1	1	12	0	2	1	20	0	21	6	4	1	.299	.355
Minici, Jason, Watertown	.208	66	263	231	28	48	71	5	0	6	27	2	1	4	25	1	65	4	3	3	.307	.295
Mitchell, Rivers, Jamestown	.282	60	257	234	28	66	86	8	6	0	17	7	0	3	13	0	35	15	7	2	.368	.328
Miyake, Chris, Erie	.308	61	246	227	34	70	92	6	5	2	25	1	1	5	12	0	31	14	6	3	.405	.355
Morales, Eric, Pittsfield	.241	66	267	237	18	57	68	6	1	1	28	6	3	1	20	2	36	2	2	4	.287	.299
Morenz, Shea, Oneonta*	.276	33	135	116	11	32	46	5	3	1	20	0	1	3	15	0	27	1	4	4	.397	.370
Morgan, Scott, Watertown	.262	66	282	244	42	64	88	18	0	2	33	0	4	8	26	0	63	6	5	11	.361	.348
Mota, Gleydel, Pittsfield*	.162	14	42	37	4	6	6	0	0	0	2	1	0	0	4	0	11	2	2	0	.162	.244
Motes, Jeff, Pittsfield	.231	52	198	169	14	39	52	7	3	0	15	4	3	1	21	0	33	1	1	5	.308	.314
Mueller, Bret, New Jersey	.262	70	292	267	39	70	97	5	8	2	39	0	1	4	20	0	61	7	3	6	.363	.322
Nelson, Tray, Oneonta	.146	16	54	48	5	7	10	3	0	0	8	0	2	0	4	0	21	0	0	0	.208	.204
Nieves, Jose, Williamsport	.214	69	306	276	46	59	86	13	1	4	44	0	3	6	21	1	39	11	10	4	.312	.281
Norman, Ty, Utica	.252	49	175	159	23	40	54	5	0	3	15	2	4	2	8	0	28	8	4	5	.340	.289
Nova, Jose Feliz, Williamsport	.221	52	197	172	25	38	47	7	1	0	13	1	2	1	21	0	48	2	1	6	.273	.306
Olsen, Donald, Vermont	.256	70	300	270	33	69	108	16	1	7	44	0	7	3	20	0	52	3	4	5	.400	.307
Owens, Walter, Watertown	.273	23	52	44	9	12	13	1	0	0	3	2	0	0	6	0	10	2	1	1	.295	.360
Palmer, Jim, Oneonta	.070	15	51	43	4	3	3	0	0	0	4	0	0	1	7	0	16	0	0	0	.070	.216
Parker, Michael, Pittsfield	.500	3	2	2	0	1	1	0	0	0	0	0	0	0	0	0	1	0	0	0	.500	.500
Parsons, Jeff, Pittsfield	.227	49	212	172	31	39	43	4	0	0	10	3	0	0	37	0	33	25	7	1	.250	.364
Pelis, Andy, Pittsfield	.053	8	23	19	3	1	1	0	0	0	0	0	0	0	4	0	7	0	0	2	.053	.217
Perez, Mike, Williamsport	.294	7	24	17	2	5	7	0	1	0	3	0	1	3	3	0	3	0	0	0	.412	.458
Pettiford, Torrey, Batavia	.311	41	164	151	21	47	56	5	2	0	17	3	0	5	5	0	18	12	2	4	.371	.354
Pierce, Kirk, Batavia	.218	30	118	101	18	22	29	5	1	0	7	1	0	6	10	0	23	0	0	4	.287	.325
Pileski, Mark, Pittsfield	.161	8	33	31	2	5	6	1	0	0	4	1	0	0	1	0	2	1	0	2	.194	.188
Podsednik, Scott, Hudson Valley*	.266	65	291	252	42	67	70	3	0	0	20	1	2	1	35	3	31	20	6	9	.278	.355
Pollock, Elton, Erie	.299	43	189	174	29	52	67	7	1	2	21	1	1	1	12	1	30	12	5	4	.385	.346
Pratt, Wes, Auburn	.266	66	281	256	42	68	85	11	0	2	44	0	1	4	20	0	43	6	3	9	.332	.327
Prodanov, Peter, Utica	.244	55	192	172	26	42	61	10	0	3	22	1	3	0	16	1	31	12	2	2	.355	.304
Putko, James, Williamsport*	.270	47	159	141	18	38	59	12	0	3	23	0	0	2	16	1	34	0	1	3	.418	.352
Rascon, Rene, Elmira*	.219	34	137	114	12	25	31	4	1	0	11	2	1	0	20	3	34	3	3	3	.272	.333
Rathmell, Lance, Utica	.285	66	261	228	34	65	80	10	1	1	30	0	4	1	28	0	25	4	5	7	.351	.360
Raynor, Mark, Batavia	.262	66	309	267	49	70	101	10	6	3	37	1	1	2	38	1	42	13	4	1	.378	.357
Reed, Billy, Hudson Valley	.216	45	158	134	16	29	38	4	1	1	11	6	0	1	17	0	24	3	2	5	.284	.309
Reilly, John, St. Catharines	.260	32	96	77	8	20	29	2	2	1	10	2	1	10	6	0	20	0	0	0	.377	.383
Reynolds, Paul, Erie†	.242	37	142	120	17	29	31	2	0	0	18	1	4	3	14	0	18	0	2	5	.258	.326
Rice, Charles, Erie†	.316	70	298	269	44	85	128	15	2	8	33	0	1	8	19	0	59	7	5	5	.476	.377
Richard, Chris, New Jersey*	.282	75	339	284	36	80	109	14	3	3	43	0	2	6	47	3	31	6	6	3	.384	.392
Rivera, Wilfredo, Utica	.210	44	150	138	14	29	40	2	3	1	15	0	2	5	5	0	35	3	1	3	.290	.260
Robinson, David, Batavia*	.219	56	226	201	27	44	65	9	3	2	26	0	2	2	20	0	45	9	3	2	.323	.293
Robinson, Hassan, Auburn	.265	65	259	245	32	65	75	8	1	0	18	2	1	2	9	0	25	12	2	9	.306	.296
Robles, Oscar, Auburn*	.287	58	257	216	49	62	73	9	1	0	19	1	1	0	39	1	15	8	2	5	.338	.395
Rodriguez, Luis, St. Catharines	.276	66	271	257	22	71	94	16	2	1	20	2	1	1	10	1	49	2	4	7	.366	.305
Rojas, Ron, Jamestown*	.213	17	59	47	8	10	14	1	0	1	8	1	1	2	8	1	9	4	0	0	.298	.345
Rosado, Juan, Vermont*	.245	48	177	155	20	38	49	4	2	1	24	0	3	1	18	1	16	4	5	2	.316	.322
Rosario, Felix, St. Catharines	.226	64	244	217	24	49	58	6	0	1	21	5	3	1	18	1	44	9	3	1	.267	.285
Russell, Jason, Batavia	.191	40	161	141	9	27	38	3	1	2	18	1	3	5	11	0	25	0	2	4	.270	.269
Sagers, Kory, Utica†	.182	25	72	66	11	12	15	1	1	0	7	1	0	0	5	0	18	1	1	1	.227	.239
Salzano, Jerry, Williamsport	.298	62	245	218	28	65	82	13	2	0	23	0	1	4	22	0	28	4	3	6	.376	.371
Samuel, Cody, Oneonta	.274	37	139	124	15	34	55	7	1	4	17	0	3	2	10	0	42	2	0	3	.444	.331
Sanchez, Omar, St. Catharines	.301	74	341	292	62	88	125	16	6	3	23	2	0	8	39	1	50	26	10	0	.428	.398
Sapp, Damien, Utica	.198	37	133	111	19	22	32	5	1	1	14	2	1	5	14	0	34	0	2	2	.288	.313
Schreiber, Stan, Erie	.286	3	8	7	1	2	6	0	2	0	2	0	0	0	1	0	2	0	0	0	.857	.375
Schreimann, Eric, Batavia	.269	15	61	52	9	14	27	1	0	4	13	0	1	7	1	1	7	0	1	1	.519	.361
Scolaro, Donald, Auburn	.239	49	176	159	14	38	44	6	0	0	25	2	2	2	11	0	27	1	3	6	.277	.293
Segura, Juan, Erie	.257	26	110	105	10	27	41	2	3	2	9	2	0	0	3	1	24	1	1	1	.390	.278
Seidel, Ryan, Williamsport	.296	64	225	203	27	60	78	8	5	0	20	1	3	1	17	2	37	13	2	3	.384	.348
Shanahan, Jason, Elmira†	.239	64	265	230	19	55	84	9	4	4	28	1	2	2	30	3	50	7	3	5	.365	.330
Shumpert, Derek, Oneonta†	.209	62	229	196	25	41	54	7	3	0	11	2	0	2	29	0	58	13	3	6	.276	.317
Smith, Akili, Erie	.125	14	46	40	6	5	8	0	0	1	1	1	0	1	4	0	13	1	0	1	.200	.222
Smith, Rod, Oneonta†	.235	49	220	187	34	44	58	8	3	0	10	0	1	2	30	0	49	24	7	1	.310	.345
Snusz, Chris, Batavia	.227	21	72	66	9	15	19	1	0	1	5	0	0	0	6	0	6	1	1	4	.288	.292
Solano, Fausto, St. Catharines	.285	57	245	207	28	59	84	17	1	2	24	4	1	3	30	1	28	14	4	2	.406	.382
Soriano, Carlos, Pittsfield	.176	5	18	17	1	3	5	2	0	0	1	0	0	0	1	0	2	1	0	1	.294	.222
Speed, Dorian, Williamsport	.216	60	237	204	30	44	64	8	3	2	23	1	3	1	28	0	56	18	5	3	.314	.309
Springfield, Bo, Erie*	.263	25	92	76	11	20	28	1	2	1	6	2	1	0	13	0	20	8	4	2	.368	.367
Stadler, Mike, Watertown	.238	6	22	21	2	5	6	1	0	0	2	0	1	0	0	0	6	0	0	0	.286	.227
Steinkemper, Jacob, Vermont	.164	21	72	61	4	10	13	3	0	0	5	0	0	1	10	0	15	1	3	0	.213	.292
Stratton, Kelly, Hudson Valley*	.207	30	67	58	10	12	17	2	0	1	8	0	0	2	7	1	6	1	1	2	.293	.313
Taylor, Jerry, Watertown	.286	5	22	21	3	6	7	1	0	0	3	0	0	0	1	0	3	0	0	1	.333	.318
Thornhill, Chad, Watertown*	.250	55	204	164	34	41	51	8	1	0	16	1	1	1	37	1	31	0	0	5	.311	.389

Player, Team	Avg.	G	TPA	AB	R	H	TB	2B	3B	HR	RBI	SH	SF	HP	BB	IBB	SO	SB	CS	GDP	Slg.	OBP
Tippin, Greg, Utica*	.228	68	260	232	20	53	68	7	1	2	27	0	4	8	16	1	68	12	6	1	.293	.296
Tribolet, Scott, Auburn	.250	50	191	172	23	43	61	7	4	1	22	1	3	2	13	0	31	12	2	1	.355	.305
Turner, Rocky, Pittsfield	.259	33	128	116	9	30	34	4	0	0	10	1	1	3	7	0	17	8	7	0	.293	.315
Ugueto, Hector, New Jersey	.287	54	232	202	37	58	72	7	2	1	28	1	3	9	17	0	36	9	2	4	.356	.364
Valera, Willy, Watertown	.254	65	260	240	33	61	89	13	3	3	29	2	2	2	14	0	57	4	2	6	.371	.298
Varriano, Mark, Utica	.091	4	13	11	2	1	1	0	0	0	1	0	0	0	2	0	3	0	0	0	.091	.231
Vasquez, Danny, Hudson Valley	.267	69	263	240	38	64	93	9	4	4	31	0	4	3	15	1	58	16	5	4	.388	.313
Venezia, Richard, Erie	.204	38	127	108	11	22	27	2	0	1	10	4	2	0	13	0	24	5	1	1	.250	.285
Vieira, Scott, Williamsport	.318	61	252	214	35	68	98	8	2	6	46	0	4	9	25	1	37	3	1	3	.458	.405
Viruet, Willie, Pittsfield	.188	11	40	32	4	6	6	0	0	0	5	2	0	2	4	0	7	0	0	0	.188	.316
Vopata, Nathan, Hudson Valley*	.281	68	265	231	37	65	93	12	8	0	30	0	5	6	23	1	36	10	5	7	.403	.355
Waggoner, James, Jamestown*	.245	63	231	204	21	50	72	5	4	3	24	0	3	2	22	1	40	2	3	2	.353	.320
Walker, Rodney, Hudson Valley	.077	13	27	26	2	2	2	0	0	0	1	0	1	0	0	0	10	1	0	2	.077	.074
Weaver, Scott, Jamestown*	.301	65	279	236	33	71	101	11	2	5	34	0	2	3	38	5	33	16	4	9	.428	.401
Whipple, Boomer, Erie	.253	67	268	225	29	57	67	4	0	2	33	6	1	6	30	0	18	4	3	8	.298	.355
Wilcox, Chris, Oneonta*	.327	59	246	223	25	73	106	16	7	1	28	0	2	1	20	3	28	9	3	4	.475	.382
Williams, Brian, St. Catharines	.194	24	77	67	5	13	15	2	0	0	6	3	1	0	6	0	23	0	0	0	.224	.257
Winn, Randy, Elmira	.315	51	233	213	38	67	82	7	4	0	22	0	2	3	15	0	31	19	7	1	.385	.365
Wolger, Michael, Vermont*	.256	60	242	203	27	52	67	7	1	2	23	1	2	2	34	0	47	3	3	5	.330	.365
Yoder, Paul, Pittsfield*	.213	55	217	183	25	39	53	6	4	0	18	1	1	2	30	2	34	0	5	6	.290	.329
Zuleta, Julio, Williamsport	.173	30	88	75	9	13	18	3	1	0	6	0	0	2	11	1	12	0	1	4	.240	.295

GRAND SLAMS: Caballero, Engleka, Fuller, Nieves, Prodanov, Raynor, Speed, Tippin, Waggoner, 1 each.
AWARDED FIRST BASE ON CATCHER'S INTERFERENCE: LeClair (McAulay); Lemonis (Reynolds); Rice (Rodriguez); D. Robinson (Stadler); Vasquez (Morales).

1995 PITCHING

TEAM

Team	W	L	Pct.	ERA	G	CG	ShO	Sv.	IP	H	TBF	R	ER	HR	SH	SF	HB	BB	IBB	SO	WP	Bk.
Vermont	49	27	.645	2.86	76	1	9	30	667.2	558	2793	282	212	19	18	18	54	251	5	479	63	16
Watertown	46	27	.630	3.10	73	1	7	23	645.1	580	2695	268	222	27	11	21	30	228	18	508	41	17
Williamsport	37	39	.487	3.38	76	0	2	20	665.1	678	2905	362	250	25	23	19	44	193	3	494	34	18
Oneonta	34	41	.453	3.51	75	0	2	20	646.2	611	2869	368	252	12	19	23	39	287	4	595	68	11
Erie	34	41	.453	3.51	75	5	5	16	653.0	648	2861	350	255	31	27	17	35	256	12	434	48	9
Hudson Valley	47	27	.635	3.57	74	4	3	24	660.0	637	2817	325	262	25	27	16	38	236	12	536	98	24
St. Catharines	38	37	.507	3.71	75	1	3	19	669.2	652	2887	341	276	38	23	22	41	292	0	461	59	14
Pittsfield	34	42	.447	3.85	76	3	4	22	659.0	671	2876	369	282	25	18	22	31	265	4	451	56	14
New Jersey	35	41	.461	3.85	76	0	5	17	682.0	649	3002	372	292	28	19	35	52	303	9	607	61	25
Batavia	41	34	.547	3.93	75	4	8	14	666.0	716	2882	369	291	28	21	20	42	194	6	507	71	18
Utica	33	40	.452	4.00	73	7	2	19	636.1	643	2840	379	283	20	11	31	41	300	10	500	68	7
Auburn	40	34	.541	4.50	74	6	5	24	621.2	620	2764	366	311	28	15	24	42	300	7	431	52	7
Elmira	25	51	.329	4.55	76	0	2	16	658.0	675	2937	424	333	30	19	22	46	293	7	507	71	30
Jamestown	32	44	.421	4.59	76	1	1	15	666.2	673	2936	427	340	46	25	29	54	254	4	494	61	24

INDIVIDUAL

TOP QUALIFIERS FOR EARNED-RUN AVERAGE TITLE

Minimum 61 innings. *Lefthanded pitcher.

Pitcher, Team	W	L	Pct.	ERA	G	GS	CG	ShO	GF	Sv.	IP	H	TBF	R	ER	HR	SH	SF	HB	BB	IBB	SO	WP	Bk.
Weidert, Chris, Vermont	11	1	.917	1.79	15	15	1	1	0	0	95.1	67	378	31	19	4	0	2	4	21	0	52	8	0
Dixon, Timothy, Vermont*	7	2	.778	1.83	18	9	0	0	2	1	69.0	58	287	20	14	0	3	0	8	16	0	58	5	7
McNeese, John, Williamsport*	5	3	.625	1.86	13	12	0	0	0	0	72.2	73	297	24	15	2	1	1	2	10	1	47	2	2
Young, Joe, St. Catharines	6	5	.545	2.04	15	15	0	0	0	0	83.2	72	349	29	19	4	3	4	5	35	0	73	5	3
Mudd, Scott, Hudson Valley	7	1	.875	2.24	15	15	3	1	0	0	100.2	91	402	37	25	2	2	3	2	18	0	62	10	1
Bullock, Derek, Erie	4	4	.500	2.35	11	11	1	1	0	0	65.0	65	270	21	17	0	1	0	2	15	0	27	1	0
Yeager, Gary, Batavia	9	4	.692	2.56	19	8	1	0	4	0	81.0	74	327	33	23	2	0	0	3	16	0	57	7	4
Trumpour, Andy, Pittsfield	7	6	.538	2.57	15	15	2	1	0	0	105.0	95	427	44	30	2	3	3	5	32	0	75	7	0
Stephens, Shannon, Elmira	8	5	.615	2.58	17	12	0	0	2	0	90.2	72	364	38	26	4	3	0	4	17	1	74	6	2
Hamilton, Bo, Batavia	7	2	.778	2.58	14	13	1	0	0	0	83.2	73	348	30	24	2	3	0	5	23	0	62	10	1
Munro, Peter, Utica	5	4	.556	2.60	14	14	0	0	0	0	90.0	79	389	38	26	3	3	3	7	33	1	74	4	0
Jacobs, Mike, Utica	8	3	.727	2.71	13	13	2	1	0	0	86.1	83	371	35	26	1	2	0	1	37	2	51	8	0
Young, Ryan, Erie	5	2	.714	2.79	16	10	1	0	2	1	67.2	62	288	34	21	5	5	1	3	17	0	38	0	1
St. Pierre, Bob, Oneonta	5	3	.625	2.83	15	15	0	0	0	0	89.0	83	368	39	28	4	1	4	2	24	0	91	4	2
Horton, Eric, St. Catharines	6	2	.750	2.84	21	7	0	0	9	3	69.2	50	276	28	22	4	1	3	3	26	0	51	4	2

DEPARTMENTAL LEADERS: W—Weidert, 11; L—Bettencourt, 8; Pct.—Weidert, .917; G—Donnelly, 36; GS—Several pitchers tied with 15; CG—Mudd, 3; ShO—Several pitchers tied with 1; GF—Tessmer, 33; Sv.—R. Marquez, 21; IP—Trumpour, 105.0; H—Cordero, 96; TBF—Trumpour, 427; R—Cordero, 62; ER—Cordero, 51; HR—Martinez, 10; SH—Farrow, 6; SF—Miedreich, 7; HB—Mamott, 11; BB—Fuller, 51; IBB—Kahlon, 5; SO—St. Pierre, 91; WP—Bauer, Goedde, 13; Bk.—Dixon, Pailthorpe, 7.

ALL PITCHERS

*Lefthanded pitcher.

Pitcher, Team	W	L	Pct.	ERA	G	GS	CG	ShO	GF	Sv.	IP	H	TBF	R	ER	HR	SH	SF	HB	BB	IBB	SO	WP	Bk.
Adge, Jason, Watertown	5	1	.833	1.58	19	0	0	0	8	1	45.2	40	179	10	8	0	1	1	1	9	1	26	5	0
Albaladejo, Randy, Auburn	0	0	.000	5.23	9	0	0	0	6	2	10.1	12	48	6	6	0	0	2	2	5	0	7	2	0
Antonini, Adrian, Batavia	0	1	.000	9.53	3	3	0	0	0	0	5.2	12	30	6	6	0	0	0	1	1	0	8	0	0
Arellano, Carlos, Watertown	0	0	.000	3.60	2	2	0	0	0	0	5.0	3	21	2	2	1	0	0	0	4	0	4	1	0
Atkins, Dannon, Watertown	5	2	.714	3.26	13	10	0	0	1	1	60.2	52	255	28	22	2	1	2	2	26	0	46	5	2
Atwater, Joe, Pittsfield*	1	0	1.000	2.25	1	1	0	0	0	0	8.0	8	33	2	2	0	0	0	0	3	0	6	0	0
Bair, Dennis, Williamsport	2	3	.400	1.60	7	7	0	0	0	0	39.1	33	161	13	7	0	0	1	1	2	0	31	1	3
Bajda, Mike, Jamestown	2	2	.500	7.99	13	3	0	0	0	0	23.2	35	123	26	21	2	2	1	3	17	0	14	3	3

Pitcher, Team	W	L	Pct.	ERA	G	GS	CG	ShO	GF	Sv.	IP	H	TBF	R	ER	HR	SH	SF	HB	BB	IBB	SO	WP	Bk.
Baker, Jason, Vermont	6	5	.545	4.13	14	14	0	0	0	0	72.0	59	317	40	33	2	1	0	5	47	1	57	11	0
Ballew, Preston, Pittsfield*	1	0	1.000	0.00	1	1	0	0	0	0	5.0	2	20	0	0	0	0	0	0	3	0	4	1	0
Barker, Jeff, Jamestown	2	2	.500	3.94	14	0	0	0	2	0	16.0	15	70	10	7	2	2	0	2	8	0	14	0	0
Barnes, Monte, Oneonta*	0	0	.000	3.86	3	0	0	0	2	0	4.2	5	23	2	2	0	0	0	0	4	0	3	0	0
Barnett, Marty, Batavia	1	6	.143	6.20	10	10	0	0	0	0	49.1	67	228	45	34	3	2	4	5	10	1	32	9	3
Bauer, Charles, Hudson Valley	4	3	.571	3.17	15	15	0	0	0	0	82.1	81	357	42	29	0	1	1	8	32	0	62	13	6
Bazzani, Matt, Utica	0	0	.000	0.00	1	0	0	0	1	0	0.1	2	3	0	0	0	0	0	0	0	0	1	0	0
Beach, Scott, Erie	1	0	1.000	7.50	14	0	0	0	4	0	18.0	24	97	21	15	3	0	0	2	17	1	8	1	0
Beagle, Chad, Elmira*	1	3	.250	5.73	5	5	0	0	0	0	22.0	25	101	16	14	0	0	0	0	13	0	21	4	1
Becker, Tom, Oneonta	6	6	.500	5.33	15	15	0	0	0	0	77.2	83	353	55	46	0	4	4	2	40	0	65	12	2
Bell, Mike, Vermont*	0	0	.000	0.54	7	0	0	0	4	1	16.2	7	59	5	1	0	1	0	1	5	2	12	0	0
Benes, Adam, New Jersey	5	3	.625	3.36	19	10	0	0	3	0	75.0	71	311	30	28	3	0	4	3	23	0	47	5	2
Bennett, Jason, Watertown	3	3	.500	3.76	16	12	0	0	2	0	79.0	86	333	36	33	5	2	0	9	20	3	53	2	1
Bennett, Matt, New Jersey	3	0	1.000	3.42	23	0	0	0	7	0	47.1	49	203	30	18	0	2	2	2	13	1	34	3	5
Berry, Jason, Oneonta	2	0	1.000	0.00	8	0	0	0	0	0	12.2	9	50	1	0	0	1	0	0	4	0	19	1	0
Bettencourt, Justin, Jamestown*	2	8	.200	4.84	14	14	0	0	0	0	74.1	73	332	53	40	7	0	5	4	41	0	63	9	3
Betti, Rich, Utica*	2	1	.667	1.02	12	0	0	0	5	2	17.2	9	65	2	2	1	0	0	0	2	0	25	1	0
Bigler, Cory, Erie	0	6	.000	4.66	10	4	0	0	3	0	29.0	34	135	21	15	2	2	1	2	13	1	13	1	1
Boardman, Eric, Oneonta	3	4	.429	3.82	11	6	0	0	0	0	33.0	30	149	24	14	1	1	1	2	21	0	23	3	0
Bogle, Sean, Williamsport	1	0	1.000	2.05	12	0	0	0	5	1	22.0	22	99	12	5	0	2	1	1	8	0	15	2	1
Bowman, Paul, Pittsfield	0	1	.000	9.64	2	0	0	0	2	0	4.2	7	25	6	5	0	0	0	0	5	0	3	2	0
Brandt, Dale, Oneonta*	1	2	.333	3.73	23	0	0	0	14	0	31.1	36	143	21	13	0	1	1	1	15	1	24	2	0
Brown, Shawn, Jamestown	1	2	.333	6.05	18	0	0	0	11	0	19.1	27	97	16	13	1	0	1	3	6	0	10	2	1
Bullock, Derek, Erie	4	4	.500	2.35	11	11	1	1	0	0	65.0	65	270	21	17	0	1	0	2	15	0	27	1	0
Burgus, Travis, Elmira	7	5	.583	3.48	15	15	0	0	0	0	88.0	84	369	45	34	7	3	3	4	29	0	68	4	1
Cannon, Kevan, Utica*	3	4	.429	3.39	9	9	1	0	0	0	61.0	59	260	33	23	2	0	3	5	23	1	51	2	2
Centeno, Jose, Vermont*	0	0	.000	0.90	6	0	0	0	4	1	10.0	8	39	2	1	1	0	0	0	0	0	6	1	0
Chew, Greg, Erie	2	3	.400	3.23	24	0	0	0	13	3	30.2	37	141	18	11	1	0	1	2	15	4	23	4	1
Choi, Chang Yang, Batavia	1	3	.250	4.96	7	7	0	0	0	0	32.2	35	146	20	18	1	1	1	2	14	0	32	7	4
Civit, Xavier, Vermont	3	3	.500	2.85	19	0	0	0	6	1	53.2	44	222	21	17	0	1	2	3	21	0	44	5	0
Codd, Tim, Hudson Valley	3	0	1.000	3.08	25	0	0	0	5	0	38.0	36	170	15	13	2	1	0	2	21	0	38	12	0
Collie, Tim, Erie	3	6	.333	2.00	29	0	0	0	22	11	36.0	32	149	18	8	1	2	0	0	9	2	27	0	1
Conley, Brian, Williamsport	0	0	.000	18.00	1	0	0	0	1	0	1.0	4	10	5	2	0	0	0	0	2	0	0	1	0
Cordero, Francisco, Jamestown	4	7	.364	5.22	15	14	0	0	0	0	88.0	96	392	62	51	3	3	3	8	37	0	54	11	0
Corey, Bryan, Jamestown	2	2	.500	3.86	29	0	0	0	28	10	28.0	21	116	14	12	2	0	1	1	12	1	41	4	0
Corominus, Mike, Auburn*	2	1	.667	6.94	13	0	0	0	5	0	23.1	22	111	20	18	2	0	1	1	24	0	14	3	1
Coronado, Osvaldo, Pittsfield	4	5	.444	3.87	15	15	0	0	0	0	90.2	91	381	52	39	2	2	3	4	26	0	57	6	2
Crowell, Jim, Watertown*	5	2	.714	2.86	12	9	0	0	0	0	56.2	50	241	22	18	1	0	2	1	27	1	48	2	1
Crowther, John, St. Catharines	3	6	.333	5.40	15	14	0	0	0	0	68.1	87	305	43	41	7	1	2	3	34	0	44	9	4
Cummins, Brian, Jamestown*	2	1	.667	3.38	18	0	0	0	2	1	34.2	37	152	22	13	1	2	4	1	8	0	24	3	0
Davey, Tom, St. Catharines	4	3	.571	3.32	7	7	0	0	0	0	38.0	27	160	19	14	2	0	2	3	21	0	29	3	1
DeLaCruz, Narcisco, St. Cath.*	1	1	.500	7.20	21	0	0	0	10	0	35.0	39	170	31	28	5	2	3	4	22	0	19	5	0
Dempster, Ryan, Hudson Valley	1	0	1.000	3.18	1	1	0	0	0	0	5.2	7	24	2	2	0	1	0	0	1	0	6	0	0
Diaz, Jairo, Williamsport	1	7	.125	2.98	30	0	0	0	6	0	45.1	39	188	21	15	2	5	0	3	10	1	55	4	1
Dixon, Timothy, Vermont*	7	2	.778	1.83	18	9	0	0	2	1	69.0	58	287	20	14	0	3	0	8	16	0	58	5	7
Donnelly, Robert, New Jersey	1	3	.250	3.54	36	0	0	0	13	0	48.1	37	210	21	19	1	4	1	3	30	4	63	5	0
Draeger, Mark, Hudson Valley	3	4	.429	5.40	21	2	0	0	4	0	40.0	40	193	33	24	0	1	2	4	26	2	33	10	0
Duffy, Ryan, Erie	1	2	.333	4.76	19	8	0	0	4	0	51.0	59	223	33	27	1	0	0	1	14	0	31	2	0
Durkovic, Peter, Jamestown*	0	0	.000	5.92	14	1	0	0	4	1	24.1	28	115	17	16	4	0	4	1	10	0	10	2	1
Eby, Michael, Jamestown*	2	1	.667	1.52	23	0	0	0	9	2	29.2	20	118	7	5	1	3	0	1	5	0	33	1	4
Einertson, Darrel, Oneonta	0	4	.000	1.88	25	0	0	0	8	0	38.1	32	167	20	8	1	1	0	3	15	1	35	0	1
Enard, Tony, Elmira	0	5	.000	7.63	15	5	0	0	8	0	30.2	33	149	36	26	1	0	5	4	22	0	27	10	4
Farr, Mark, Elmira	0	5	.000	6.08	9	9	0	0	0	0	40.0	45	200	34	27	3	1	1	4	31	1	24	5	2
Farrow, Jason, Erie	3	1	.750	2.23	20	4	0	0	2	0	48.1	44	213	18	12	0	6	2	6	20	2	50	4	2
Ferguson, Tim, Vermont*	0	0	.000	7.71	3	0	0	0	1	0	4.2	2	20	4	4	0	0	0	2	2	0	2	0	0
Fernandes, Jamie, Utica	0	1	.000	4.66	3	1	0	0	1	1	9.2	9	41	5	5	0	0	1	0	3	0	7	1	0
Fernandez, Jared, Utica	3	2	.600	1.89	5	5	1	0	0	0	38.0	30	148	11	8	2	0	1	1	9	1	23	1	0
Ferullo, Matt, Pittsfield	1	0	1.000	0.00	2	0	0	0	1	0	5.0	3	19	0	0	0	0	0	0	1	0	6	0	0
Fitterer, Scott, St. Catharines	0	0	.000	1.14	22	0	0	0	17	9	23.2	18	101	7	3	1	1	0	1	13	0	22	2	0
Foran, John, Jamestown	1	2	.333	5.82	14	0	0	0	4	1	17.0	17	79	15	11	1	0	1	1	6	0	18	3	3
Ford, Ben, Oneonta	5	0	1.000	0.87	29	0	0	0	10	0	52.0	39	224	23	5	1	0	2	5	16	0	50	8	0
Ford, Brian, Batavia*	3	1	.750	1.18	29	0	0	0	26	10	38.0	24	143	8	5	1	2	2	0	5	0	44	2	0
Frascatore, Steve, New Jersey	4	6	.400	4.68	16	15	0	0	1	0	82.2	86	370	56	43	2	1	3	6	30	0	43	6	2
Fuller, Stephen, Auburn	6	5	.545	4.86	14	14	0	0	0	0	66.2	67	317	51	36	2	1	5	3	51	0	29	9	1
Gaiko, Robert, Batavia	1	1	.500	8.18	20	0	0	0	10	0	33.0	50	165	34	30	3	1	1	4	11	3	25	7	0
Gambs, Chris, Batavia	3	2	.600	5.50	7	7	0	0	0	0	34.1	31	148	21	21	0	1	1	0	22	0	21	4	0
Garcia, Rick, Elmira	1	7	.125	5.97	15	15	0	0	0	0	75.1	80	341	56	50	3	1	2	5	46	0	53	5	2
Glynn, Ryan, Hudson Valley	3	3	.500	4.70	9	8	0	0	0	0	44.0	56	192	27	23	0	0	1	3	16	1	21	10	3
Goedde, Roger, Erie	1	3	.250	7.97	5	5	0	0	0	0	20.1	31	110	23	18	1	2	4	0	17	0	8	13	0
Green, Jason, Auburn	8	2	.800	3.81	14	14	2	1	0	0	82.2	82	365	48	35	1	4	0	10	29	0	48	5	0
Greene, Brian, Williamsport	3	2	.600	3.33	18	5	0	0	3	0	46.0	52	203	28	17	1	2	1	2	16	0	25	4	1
Grife, Richard, Watertown	1	2	.333	2.53	5	0	0	0	2	0	10.2	10	44	5	3	0	1	0	0	5	0	8	1	0
Groves, Brian, Jamestown*	0	1	.000	4.44	16	0	0	0	6	0	24.1	21	111	17	12	0	0	0	2	17	0	15	5	0
Gulin, Lindsey, Pittsfield*	1	0	1.000	3.86	1	1	0	0	0	0	7.0	4	29	4	3	1	1	0	0	3	0	3	1	1
Hall, Yates, New Jersey	3	0	1.000	1.37	5	5	0	0	0	0	26.1	19	109	7	4	0	0	1	1	11	0	22	4	1
Hamilton, Bo, Batavia	7	2	.778	2.58	14	13	1	0	0	0	83.2	73	348	30	24	2	3	0	5	23	0	62	10	1
Hammack, Brandon, Williamspt	1	5	.167	4.18	27	0	0	0	17	6	32.1	32	151	20	15	3	2	1	2	14	1	40	2	2
Hartshorn, Tyson, St. Cath.	3	4	.429	4.26	13	13	1	1	0	0	69.2	83	307	45	33	6	3	1	3	25	0	25	6	1
Harvey, Terry, Watertown	6	2	.750	1.82	8	8	0	0	0	0	54.1	36	205	13	11	1	0	3	1	6	1	33	0	0
Helvey, Rob, New Jersey*	2	1	.667	0.73	11	0	0	0	8	2	12.1	7	45	1	1	0	1	1	0	5	0	15	0	0
Hernandez, Elvin, Erie	6	1	.857	2.89	14	14	2	1	0	0	90.1	82	377	40	29	8	5	3	4	22	0	54	2	1
Herr, David, Vermont	6	3	.667	3.76	18	7	0	0	4	1	55.0	53	229	26	23	0	1	2	4	18	1	35	5	0
Horn, Keith, Watertown	3	2	.600	2.86	8	8	0	0	0	0	44.0	39	180	18	14	4	0	1	0	12	0	36	0	2

Pitcher, Team	W	L	Pct.	ERA	G	GS	CG	ShO	GF	Sv.	IP	H	TBF	R	ER	HR	SH	SF	HB	BB	IBB	SO	WP	Bk.
Horton, Aaron, Oneonta*	0	2	.000	3.22	6	3	0	0	1	0	22.1	19	96	13	8	0	2	0	3	4	0	12	0	1
Horton, Eric, St. Catharines	6	2	.750	2.84	21	7	0	0	9	3	69.2	50	276	28	22	4	1	3	3	26	0	51	4	2
Howard, Tom, Elmira*	0	0	.000	7.43	10	0	0	0	5	0	13.1	9	69	13	11	0	0	1	0	21	0	7	6	0
Howatt, Jeff, Pittsfield	1	2	.333	4.15	17	0	0	0	5	1	39.0	37	167	22	18	2	1	3	0	15	0	26	3	3
Hoy, Wayne, St. Catharines	5	3	.625	2.21	24	1	0	0	9	3	57.0	39	228	20	14	0	1	0	3	23	0	34	5	1
Hritz, Derrick, Watertown*	0	1	.000	2.10	18	0	0	0	10	1	30.0	28	130	9	7	0	2	1	1	16	2	23	4	1
Imersek, Jason, Oneonta	0	0	.000	0.00	1	0	0	0	1	0	0.1	0	1	0	0	0	0	0	0	0	0	0	0	0
Jacobs, Mike, Utica	8	3	.727	2.71	13	13	2	1	0	0	86.1	83	371	35	26	1	2	0	1	37	2	51	8	0
Johnson, Scott, Elmira	0	0	.000	4.32	4	0	0	0	1	0	8.1	10	37	4	4	0	0	0	1	1	0	4	0	0
Jones, Scott, Utica	0	1	.000	1.35	20	0	0	0	20	13	20.0	11	78	3	3	0	1	2	0	9	1	26	3	0
Kahlon, Bobby, Hudson Valley	5	5	.500	2.32	30	0	0	0	16	3	54.1	35	220	16	14	3	5	0	1	21	5	76	10	1
Kast, Nick, New Jersey*	5	1	.833	1.38	29	0	0	0	7	0	45.2	29	188	11	7	0	1	2	7	21	1	64	3	4
Kawabata, Kyle, Batavia	2	0	1.000	3.58	18	0	0	0	4	0	32.2	34	140	16	13	3	2	1	3	5	1	30	2	1
Kelley, Jason, Williamsport	1	1	.500	1.62	3	3	0	0	0	0	16.2	14	70	3	3	0	0	0	1	7	0	6	1	0
Kendrick, Scott, Williamsport	2	1	.667	3.33	5	5	0	0	0	0	27.0	26	117	14	10	2	1	2	3	8	0	15	3	0
Kindell, Scott, Pittsfield*	4	1	.800	2.36	20	0	0	0	9	0	26.2	25	109	11	7	1	2	2	1	6	0	14	2	0
Koenig, Matthew, Pittsfield	4	5	.444	4.27	15	12	0	0	1	0	78.0	81	334	47	37	6	1	1	3	23	0	43	6	0
Lail, Jerry, Oneonta	5	6	.455	3.97	13	13	0	0	0	0	68.0	66	309	38	30	3	1	4	5	31	0	59	1	0
Link, Bryan, Hudson Valley*	5	3	.625	3.49	15	15	1	0	0	0	90.1	79	370	39	35	5	5	2	3	25	0	88	7	1
Lisio, Joseph, Pittsfield	2	2	.500	1.62	28	0	0	0	23	12	33.1	27	141	8	6	0	2	5	1	14	1	24	2	0
Loiz, Niuman, Auburn	1	1	.500	2.63	3	3	1	1	0	0	13.2	7	56	5	4	0	0	0	0	8	0	11	2	1
Long, Justin, Elmira	0	0	.000	0.00	1	0	0	0	1	0	1.0	0	3	0	0	0	0	0	0	0	0	2	0	0
Lowe, Ben, St. Catharines*	4	5	.444	4.35	15	15	0	0	0	0	78.2	89	358	43	38	3	3	3	9	40	0	61	10	1
Mamott, Joe, Utica	0	4	.000	6.68	9	6	0	0	1	0	32.1	40	173	35	24	1	0	3	11	28	0	36	10	0
Marquez, Ihosvany, Utica	0	0	.000	2.70	12	0	0	0	3	0	20.0	13	84	8	6	0	0	1	4	13	0	23	4	0
Marquez, Robert, Vermont	1	1	.500	0.84	29	0	0	0	29	21	32.0	15	122	5	3	0	1	0	1	11	0	32	1	0
Martineau, Brian, Hud. Valley	5	2	.714	1.30	30	0	0	0	26	18	41.2	30	166	10	6	1	5	0	3	10	1	39	4	5
Martinez, Osvaldo, Jamestown	4	4	.500	3.77	15	15	1	0	0	0	90.2	85	384	46	38	10	3	1	6	30	1	56	2	4
Mathis, Sammie, Watertown	4	1	.800	4.36	18	0	0	0	4	0	33.0	39	153	22	16	1	0	3	4	15	1	21	1	2
Mattes, Troy, Vermont	3	4	.429	3.72	10	10	0	0	0	0	46.0	51	209	34	19	3	5	4	5	25	0	23	7	0
McClurg, Clinton, Batavia	2	2	.500	4.30	10	5	1	0	1	0	37.2	41	171	26	18	2	3	2	4	21	0	14	4	0
McEntire, Ethan, Pittsfield*	4	2	.667	5.06	13	13	0	0	0	0	69.1	81	325	43	39	2	1	2	5	46	0	41	7	0
McHugh, Michael, Hud. Valley*	0	0	.000	8.40	10	0	0	0	3	0	15.0	26	85	17	14	0	0	0	2	14	0	9	4	0
McNeese, John, Williamsport*	5	3	.625	1.86	13	12	0	0	0	0	72.2	73	297	24	15	2	1	1	2	10	1	47	2	2
McNichol, Brian, Williamsport*	3	1	.750	3.08	9	9	0	0	0	0	49.2	57	215	28	17	1	1	1	2	8	0	35	1	1
Mejia, Carlos, Utica*	1	1	.500	4.73	10	0	0	0	5	1	13.1	15	62	8	7	0	1	1	0	5	0	14	4	2
Mendes, Jaime, Batavia	1	1	.500	3.92	30	0	0	0	14	3	41.1	50	177	23	18	3	2	2	2	6	0	35	4	0
Mensink, Brian, Batavia	4	1	.800	2.98	11	8	0	0	1	0	48.1	56	207	23	16	0	2	1	5	10	0	37	3	2
Merrick, Brett, Watertown*	2	1	.667	1.93	22	0	0	0	11	4	37.1	15	142	10	8	2	0	1	0	18	3	44	3	0
Micknich, Steve, Elmira	0	0	.000	0.00	4	0	0	0	4	2	5.1	1	20	0	0	0	0	0	1	2	0	6	0	0
Miedreich, Kevin, New Jersey	2	6	.250	4.70	15	15	0	0	0	0	74.2	84	340	47	39	2	2	7	8	33	0	39	5	1
Miles, Chad, Elmira*	1	1	.500	6.65	14	0	0	0	4	0	21.2	29	105	18	16	2	1	1	1	10	0	10	5	1
Miller, David, Elmira	1	1	.500	4.32	9	0	0	0	4	1	16.2	17	73	8	8	1	1	0	2	7	2	11	1	2
Mitchell, Courtney, Batavia*	0	5	.000	4.89	28	0	0	0	9	1	42.1	46	194	28	23	2	1	2	3	23	1	40	4	1
Mitchell, Scott, Vermont	3	1	.750	2.23	18	1	0	0	5	1	40.1	35	171	18	10	1	2	2	4	15	0	30	2	4
Moore, Robert, Hudson Valley	2	3	.400	5.43	13	13	0	0	0	0	63.0	77	280	45	38	5	2	5	4	13	0	45	10	3
Moore, Sam, Elmira	1	2	.333	1.84	15	0	0	0	9	3	29.1	23	112	8	6	1	1	0	1	4	0	22	3	1
Morris, Chad, Vermont	1	0	1.000	2.40	9	0	0	0	6	0	15.0	11	65	4	4	1	0	1	1	9	0	19	5	3
Morris, Matt, New Jersey	2	0	1.000	1.64	2	2	0	0	0	0	11.0	12	45	3	2	1	0	0	0	3	0	13	0	3
Mosley, Tim, Williamsport	2	0	1.000	4.28	23	0	0	0	6	1	33.2	40	161	23	16	0	2	2	4	16	0	26	2	0
Mudd, Scott, Hudson Valley	7	1	.875	2.24	15	15	3	1	0	0	100.2	91	402	37	25	2	2	3	2	18	0	62	10	1
Munro, Peter, Utica	5	4	.556	2.60	14	14	0	0	0	0	90.0	79	389	38	26	3	3	3	7	33	1	74	4	0
Murray, Dan, Pittsfield	0	6	.000	1.97	22	0	0	0	19	6	32.0	24	145	17	7	1	2	0	1	16	3	34	3	0
Neese, Josh, Jamestown	3	1	.750	3.72	20	2	0	0	5	0	36.1	29	153	15	15	2	4	3	4	14	2	38	4	4
Negrette, Richard, Watertown	3	3	.500	5.52	18	5	0	0	6	3	45.2	42	203	30	28	5	2	2	7	23	2	35	6	1
Noffke, Andrew, Utica	0	2	.000	7.71	23	0	0	0	9	0	25.2	34	137	30	22	1	0	2	3	24	0	24	5	0
Noone, Bill, Batavia	1	0	1.000	14.29	6	0	0	0	2	0	5.2	14	35	11	9	1	0	1	0	3	0	2	1	0
Nunez, Maximo, St. Catharines	1	0	1.000	9.39	7	0	0	0	4	0	7.2	11	42	10	8	1	2	0	1	7	0	6	1	0
Nuttle, Jamison, Erie	0	1	.000	3.07	13	0	0	0	9	1	14.2	8	59	8	5	1	0	1	0	7	0	13	0	0
Oakley, Matt, Jamestown	0	0	.000	18.00	1	0	0	0	0	0	1.0	3	7	2	2	0	0	0	0	1	0	0	0	0
Olivier, Rich, Oneonta	3	3	.500	3.88	12	12	0	0	0	0	60.1	63	264	36	26	2	3	2	4	21	0	50	8	0
Ormonde, Troy, Williamsport	2	4	.333	4.29	14	14	0	0	0	0	71.1	61	324	50	34	2	4	3	5	39	0	41	3	2
Pailthorpe, Bob, Elmira	2	7	.222	4.88	13	12	0	0	1	1	51.2	69	241	41	28	2	1	3	1	17	0	38	2	7
Patterson, Casey, Pittsfield	0	4	.000	9.53	12	4	0	0	3	0	34.0	47	181	43	36	4	1	1	6	28	0	18	4	2
Peguero, Jose, St. Catharines	2	1	.667	4.50	17	0	0	0	7	0	34.0	31	148	19	17	1	4	2	1	19	0	19	0	0
Pena, Jesus, Erie*	0	3	.000	12.66	3	3	0	0	0	0	10.2	18	56	16	15	1	1	0	2	7	0	5	0	1
Perez, Gil, Erie	2	2	.500	2.79	18	1	0	0	1	0	38.2	39	172	19	12	1	2	2	4	15	0	27	8	0
Perez, Hilario, Utica	2	2	.500	4.81	20	3	0	0	7	1	43.0	50	203	38	23	4	0	5	1	22	2	22	1	0
Peterman, Ernie, St. Catharines	1	1	.500	5.94	4	3	0	0	0	0	16.2	18	71	11	11	1	1	1	4	2	0	8	0	1
Peterson, Jayson, Williamsport	2	0	1.000	3.71	3	3	0	0	0	0	17.0	15	73	7	7	1	0	0	1	5	0	14	1	0
Phillips, Jon, Auburn*	2	0	1.000	0.00	2	0	0	0	1	0	5.1	6	23	0	0	0	0	0	1	1	0	5	0	0
Pinango, Simon, Utica*	2	4	.333	6.91	20	0	0	0	6	0	28.2	30	135	27	22	2	0	3	1	16	1	27	4	0
Powell, Brian, Jamestown	2	1	.667	3.08	5	5	0	0	0	0	26.1	19	108	12	9	1	0	1	5	8	0	15	3	0
Powell, Jeremy, Vermont	5	5	.500	4.34	15	15	0	0	0	0	87.0	88	373	48	42	5	2	2	6	34	1	47	6	2
Pyrtle, Joe, Pittsfield	0	1	.000	3.48	17	0	0	0	7	2	31.0	32	140	18	12	1	1	1	0	12	0	17	2	3
Rakers, Jason, Watertown	4	3	.571	3.00	14	14	1	1	0	0	75.0	72	315	27	25	3	0	2	0	24	1	73	6	2
Randolph, Steve, Oneonta*	0	3	.000	7.48	6	6	0	0	0	0	21.2	19	109	22	18	0	0	2	1	23	0	31	5	0
Reames, Britt, New Jersey	2	1	.667	1.52	5	5	0	0	0	0	29.2	19	121	7	5	1	1	0	3	12	0	42	5	0
Reichstein, Derek, Elmira	1	4	.200	5.23	22	2	0	0	8	1	51.2	52	234	37	30	2	2	4	5	27	1	37	5	4
Reid, Rayon, Erie	3	3	.500	2.45	8	7	0	0	0	0	47.2	37	189	16	13	2	0	0	3	11	0	47	4	1
Reilly, John, St. Catharines	0	1	.000	0.00	1	0	0	0	1	0	0.2	1	6	2	0	0	0	0	0	2	0	0	0	0
Reinfelder, David, Jamestown*	2	5	.286	4.60	16	14	0	0	0	0	78.1	85	334	48	40	6	5	3	6	17	0	55	5	0
Reyes, Jose, Erie	2	3	.400	3.39	19	7	1	0	1	0	58.1	53	253	25	22	2	1	0	1	29	1	44	3	0

Pitcher, Team	W	L	Pct.	ERA	G	GS	CG	ShO	GF	Sv.	IP	H	TBF	R	ER	HR	SH	SF	HB	BB	IBB	SO	WP	Bk.
Ricketts, Chad, Williamsport	4	5	.444	4.19	12	12	0	0	0	0	68.2	89	312	46	32	4	0	3	8	16	0	37	1	3
Robbins, Jake, Oneonta	0	0	.000	0.00	1	0	0	0	1	0	1.0	0	3	0	0	0	0	0	0	0	0	1	0	0
Romboli, Curtis, Utica*	2	3	.400	4.56	14	6	2	0	3	0	51.1	60	225	32	26	1	1	1	1	16	0	34	4	1
Root, Derek, Auburn*	2	0	1.000	3.29	17	3	0	0	5	1	38.1	28	165	14	14	0	2	1	2	24	0	37	4	1
Rosenbohm, Jim, Auburn	2	4	.333	3.66	22	1	0	0	6	1	51.2	48	236	23	21	0	1	0	10	32	3	50	5	0
Ross, Jeremy, Elmira	1	0	1.000	3.00	20	0	0	0	3	2	42.0	38	184	17	14	0	1	2	2	20	1	40	6	3
Sagedal, Brent, Hudson Valley	0	2	.000	7.08	14	5	0	0	4	1	34.1	42	158	29	27	7	2	1	1	18	1	25	7	1
St. Pierre, Bob, Oneonta	5	3	.625	2.83	15	15	0	0	0	0	89.0	83	368	39	28	4	1	4	2	24	0	91	4	2
Santiago, Antonio, Utica*	0	3	.000	5.30	4	4	0	0	0	0	18.2	24	91	17	11	0	1	1	0	13	0	11	7	0
Santoro, Gary, Elmira	1	4	.200	3.75	24	0	0	0	20	6	36.0	45	164	21	15	1	2	0	6	10	1	34	6	0
Santos, Rafael, Erie	0	0	.000	0.00	2	0	0	0	0	0	1.0	0	5	0	0	0	0	0	0	2	0	1	0	0
Sauve, Jeff, Utica	1	1	.500	4.70	11	0	0	0	5	1	15.1	19	72	12	8	1	1	1	1	8	1	16	2	1
Schulte, Troy, Auburn	1	2	.333	4.88	23	0	0	0	17	6	31.1	30	130	20	17	5	2	0	1	9	0	22	1	0
Schultz, Scott, Watertown	1	3	.250	4.70	9	5	0	0	3	2	30.2	39	141	24	16	2	0	1	2	11	0	20	2	3
Scolaro, Donald, Auburn	0	0	.000	54.00	1	0	0	0	1	0	0.1	2	3	2	2	2	0	0	0	0	0	0	0	0
Severino, Jose, New Jersey	3	3	.500	5.29	17	10	0	0	1	0	66.1	65	303	48	39	8	1	4	2	37	2	68	9	3
Short, Barry, Pittsfield	0	0	.000	4.50	2	0	0	0	1	1	2.0	4	10	1	1	0	0	0	0	0	0	3	1	0
Shumaker, Anthony, Batavia*	2	2	.500	1.62	9	4	1	1	0	0	39.0	38	157	10	7	0	0	0	0	4	0	31	2	0
Sikorski, Brian, Auburn	1	2	.333	2.10	23	0	0	0	19	12	34.1	22	137	8	8	1	0	1	0	14	2	35	1	0
Smart, J.D., Vermont	0	1	.000	2.28	5	5	0	0	0	0	27.2	29	118	9	7	1	1	3	3	7	0	21	0	0
Smith, Eric, Auburn	2	6	.250	3.93	14	14	0	0	0	0	71.0	70	314	37	31	4	0	4	5	30	0	56	5	3
Smith, Justin, Batavia	4	3	.571	4.26	15	10	0	0	0	0	61.1	71	266	35	29	5	1	2	5	20	0	37	5	2
Smith, Randy, St. Catharines	0	2	.000	3.27	18	0	0	0	9	2	33.0	34	141	14	12	0	0	0	1	9	0	26	1	0
Smyth, Gregg, Auburn*	6	6	.500	4.56	14	14	1	1	0	0	75.0	87	332	48	38	2	2	6	2	25	0	48	6	0
Spaulding, Scott, New Jersey	1	0	1.000	2.59	35	0	0	0	11	2	48.2	36	200	17	14	4	1	0	6	14	0	40	2	1
Speier, Justin, Williamsport	2	1	.667	1.49	30	0	0	0	22	12	36.1	27	142	6	6	1	2	2	1	4	0	39	0	0
Stachler, Eric, Auburn	1	2	.333	8.42	18	0	0	0	5	2	36.1	47	179	35	34	2	2	2	1	27	2	32	4	0
Steinke, Brock, Auburn	1	0	1.000	2.08	6	0	0	0	3	0	8.2	11	38	2	2	1	0	0	0	3	0	6	0	0
Stephens, Bill, Vermont	3	1	.750	1.65	13	0	0	0	8	3	27.1	17	111	5	5	0	0	0	5	7	0	30	5	0
Stephens, Shannon, Elmira	8	5	.615	2.58	17	12	0	0	2	0	90.2	72	364	38	26	4	3	0	4	17	1	74	6	2
Stern, Marty, Vermont	0	0	.000	3.38	8	0	0	0	4	0	13.1	12	57	5	5	1	0	0	1	6	0	10	1	0
Swenson, Mike, New Jersey*	2	4	.333	4.82	19	6	0	0	3	0	52.1	53	246	35	28	1	0	3	7	32	0	54	5	0
Tatis, Ramon, Pittsfield*	4	5	.444	3.63	13	13	1	1	0	0	79.1	88	341	40	32	2	1	1	3	27	0	69	8	3
Tessmer, Jay, Oneonta	2	0	1.000	0.95	34	0	0	0	33	20	38.0	27	156	8	4	0	0	0	3	12	2	52	3	2
Thomas, Rob, Erie*	1	1	.500	4.60	15	0	0	0	7	0	15.2	9	71	10	8	2	0	2	1	17	1	9	4	0
Tickell, Brian, Auburn	5	3	.625	5.57	13	11	2	0	0	0	72.2	79	310	47	45	6	1	2	4	18	0	31	5	0
Treend, Pat, Elmira	0	2	.000	6.29	17	1	0	0	6	0	34.1	43	171	32	24	3	2	0	5	16	0	29	3	0
Trumpour, Andy, Pittsfield	7	6	.538	2.57	15	15	2	1	0	0	105.0	95	427	44	30	2	3	3	5	32	0	75	7	0
Venafro, Michael, Hud. Valley*	9	1	.900	2.13	32	0	0	0	12	2	50.2	37	200	13	12	0	2	1	5	21	2	32	1	3
Viegas, Randy, Erie*	0	0	.000	6.30	8	1	0	0	2	0	10.0	14	53	9	7	0	0	0	2	9	0	9	1	0
Villafana, Jose, New Jersey	0	6	.000	4.91	27	0	0	0	21	13	29.1	35	141	17	16	0	4	2	0	21	1	28	4	2
Volkert, Oreste, St. Catharines	2	3	.400	2.67	22	0	0	0	8	2	54.0	53	225	20	16	3	1	1	0	14	0	44	8	0
Ward, Jon, New Jersey	0	7	.000	8.07	9	8	0	0	1	0	32.1	47	170	42	29	5	1	5	4	18	0	35	5	1
Weber, David, Williamsport	2	3	.400	7.94	22	2	0	0	9	0	34.0	51	165	38	30	3	1	0	2	15	0	28	2	2
Weber, Eric, Jamestown	2	2	.500	5.23	15	3	0	0	4	0	32.2	35	142	25	19	2	0	0	2	11	0	22	3	0
Weber, Lenny, Watertown	1	0	1.000	2.00	5	0	0	0	3	0	9.0	5	37	2	2	0	1	0	0	6	1	11	1	0
Weidert, Chris, Vermont	11	1	.917	1.79	15	15	1	1	0	0	95.1	67	378	31	19	4	0	2	4	21	0	52	8	0
Welch, Robb, Utica	4	4	.500	5.68	12	12	1	0	0	0	65.0	76	303	45	41	1	1	3	5	39	0	35	7	1
Whitworth, Clint, Oneonta	0	2	.000	5.93	12	1	0	0	2	0	27.1	31	136	23	18	0	0	2	5	15	0	15	9	0
Wilkinson, Arrow, Oneonta	0	2	.000	4.13	14	0	0	0	2	0	28.1	28	135	19	13	0	3	1	1	23	0	24	4	1
Wilson, Mike, Oneonta	2	4	.333	4.20	14	4	0	0	1	0	40.2	41	183	24	19	0	1	0	2	19	0	41	8	2
Wilson, Mike, Jamestown	1	3	.250	6.55	5	5	0	0	0	0	22.0	27	103	20	16	1	1	1	4	6	0	12	1	1
Winchester, Scott, Watertown	3	1	.750	2.83	23	0	0	0	22	11	28.2	24	116	10	9	0	1	2	2	6	2	27	2	2
Wolff, Thomas, Pittsfield	0	2	.000	8.00	4	1	0	0	2	0	9.0	15	49	11	8	1	0	0	2	5	0	8	1	0
Wolger, Michael, Vermont*	0	0	.000	16.88	2	0	0	0	2	0	2.2	2	16	5	5	0	0	0	1	7	0	1	1	0
Wood, Kerry,, Williamsport	0	0	.000	10.38	2	2	0	0	0	0	4.1	5	23	8	5	0	0	0	0	5	0	5	1	0
Wyatt, Cortez, Williamsport	4	3	.571	2.63	22	2	0	0	7	0	48.0	38	194	16	14	3	0	1	6	8	0	35	3	0
Yeager, Gary, Batavia	9	4	.692	2.56	19	8	1	0	4	0	81.0	74	327	33	23	2	0	0	3	16	0	57	7	4
Young, Joe, St. Catharines	6	5	.545	2.04	15	15	0	0	0	0	83.2	72	349	29	19	4	3	4	5	35	0	73	5	3
Young, Ryan, Erie	5	2	.714	2.79	16	10	1	0	2	1	67.2	62	288	34	21	5	5	1	3	17	0	38	0	1

COMBINATION SHUTOUTS: **Auburn (2)**—Rosenbohm-Root, Smith-Rosenbohm-Stachler-Albaladejo. **Batavia (7)**—Gambs-Ford, Gambs-McClurg-Mendes-Ford, Gambs-Mensink-Ford, Hamilton-Ford, Mensink-Mendes-Ford, Smith-Mendes, Yeager-Mitchell. **Elmira (2)**—Stephens-Miller-Santoro, Stephens-Reichstein. **Erie (3)**—Bullock-Perez-Viegas, Bullock-Reyes-Chew, Reid-Perez-Reyes-Nuttle. **Hudson Valley (2)**—Link-Venafro-Martineau, Mudd-Kahlon-Martineau. **Jamestown (1)**—Neese-Eby-Corey. **New Jersey (5)**—Frascatore-Spaulding-Donnelly, Hall-Donnelly-Spaulding, Miedreich-Kast-Donnelly-Helvey, Morris-Donnelly-Spaulding-Villafana, Reames-Bennett-Benes. **Oneonta (2)**—Becker-Einertson-Tessmer 2. **Pittsfield (2)**—Ballew-Pyrtle-Lisio, Coronado-Kindell-Lisio. **St. Catharines (2)**—Crowther-Hoy-Fitterer, Davey-Hoy. **Utica (1)**—Jacobs-Sauve. **Vermont (8)**—Baker-Civit-Marquez, Baker-Dixon-Marquez, Baker-Mitchell-Marquez, Baker-Stephens-Morris, Dixon-Civit, Dixon-Herr-Marquez, Herr-Stephens, Mattes-Civit-Marquez. **Watertown (6)**—Atkins-Merrick-Winchester, Atkins-Schultz, Atkins-Weber, Crowell-Atkins, Harvey-Hritz, Horn-Merrick. **Williamsport (2)**—Kelley-Mosley-Weber, Wood-Hammack-Mosley-Diaz-Speier.

NO-HIT GAMES: Hernandez, Erie, defeated Oneonta, 7-0, August 24.

1995 FIELDING

TEAM

Team	Pct.	G	PO	A	E	TC	DP	PB
Watertown	.972	73	1936	894	83	2913	72	16
Vermont	.962	76	2003	858	113	2974	79	26
Hudson Valley	.960	74	1980	864	120	2964	64	18
St. Catharines	.959	75	2009	917	126	3052	72	13
Batavia	.959	75	1998	877	124	2999	90	10
Auburn	.958	74	1865	832	119	2816	71	15
New Jersey	.957	76	2046	739	124	2909	55	16
Jamestown	.957	76	2000	896	131	3027	63	13
Elmira	.956	76	1974	894	133	3001	64	16
Pittsfield	.955	76	1977	880	135	2992	67	15
Utica	.952	73	1909	827	138	2874	62	29
Erie	.950	75	1959	897	150	3006	72	14
Williamsport	.947	76	1996	828	158	2982	57	29
Oneonta	.944	75	1940	827	165	2932	50	24

TRIPLE PLAYS: Auburn, Elmira, Erie, Hudson Valley, Oneonta, St. Catharines.

INDIVIDUAL

FIRST BASEMEN

NOTE: All caps denotes fielding-percentage leader based on 38 games for catchers, 51 for all other non-pitchers and 76 innings for pitchers. *Throws lefthanded.

Player, Team	Pct.	G	PO	A	E	TC	DP
Adams, Jason, Auburn	1.000	1	2	0	0	2	0
Brumbaugh, Clifford, Hud. Valley	1.000	2	6	0	0	6	1
Carver, Steve, Batavia	.983	50	451	17	8	476	46
Casey, Sean, Watertown	.985	52	510	24	8	542	37
Chevalier, Virgil, Utica	.994	19	166	10	1	177	14
Culp, Matt, Watertown	.987	9	72	5	1	78	9
Daly, Rob, Pittsfield	.989	76	724	60	9	793	58
Emmons, Scott, Oneonta	.966	13	136	7	5	148	9
EVANS, Kyle, Hudson Valley*	.996	53	467	24	2	493	35
Fana, Alberto, Batavia	.981	13	96	9	2	107	12
Gallagher, Shawn, Hud. Valley	.978	5	44	1	1	46	2
Garman, Sean, New Jersey	.917	5	11	0	1	12	0
Garrett, Jason, Elmira	1.000	19	177	8	0	185	10
Gipner, Marcus, Oneonta	.972	23	195	14	6	215	12
Halemanu, Joshua, Auburn*	.978	52	463	32	11	506	42
Hayes, Chris, St. Catharines	1.000	2	14	0	0	14	0
Hayes, Heath, Watertown	.993	13	131	9	1	141	13
Johnson, Jason, Hud. Valley	.500	1	1	0	1	2	0
Koonce, Graham, Jamestown*	.985	72	694	70	12	776	49
Landers, Mark, St. Catharines*	.988	74	704	41	9	754	61
Leaman, Jeff, Batavia	.964	19	145	17	6	168	16
Lewis, Marc, Utica	1.000	1	20	2	0	22	0
Long, Garrett, Erie	.977	17	161	12	4	177	14
Mackert, Jamie, Erie	.985	22	184	9	3	196	13
Maleski, Tom, Williamsport	1.000	3	16	2	0	18	0
Martinez, Dave, Hudson Valley*	1.000	24	173	11	0	184	18
Maynor, Tonka, Erie	.988	8	77	3	1	81	8
McCartney, Sommer, Elmira	1.000	1	7	1	0	8	1
Morales, Eric, Pittsfield	1.000	1	4	0	0	4	0
Olsen, Donald, Vermont	1.000	48	462	26	0	488	48
Palmer, Jim, Oneonta	.955	7	64	0	3	67	1
Prodanov, Peter, Utica	.833	4	9	1	2	12	2
Putko, James, Williamsport	.969	36	262	19	9	290	18
Rathmell, Lance, Utica	.917	2	10	1	1	12	2
Rice, Charles, Erie	.960	31	275	13	12	300	21
Richard, Chris, New Jersey*	.984	75	620	43	11	674	51
Salzano, Jerry, Williamsport	.986	53	403	27	6	436	33
Samuel, Cody, Oneonta	.974	37	319	12	9	340	20
Sapp, Damien, Utica	1.000	1	1	0	0	1	0
Scolaro, Donald, Auburn	1.000	24	207	14	0	221	22
Seidel, Ryan, Williamsport	1.000	2	14	2	0	16	0
Shanahan, Jason, Elmira	.995	57	563	51	3	617	49
Smith, Akili, Erie	.958	2	21	2	1	24	6
Thornhill, Chad, Watertown	.939	6	28	3	2	33	4
Tippin, Greg, Utica*	.984	56	453	32	8	493	35
Vieira, Scott, Williamsport	1.000	1	3	0	0	3	0
Waggoner, James, Jamestown	.979	5	43	4	1	48	4
Walker, Rodney, Hudson Valley	.778	2	7	0	2	9	0
Wolger, Michael, Vermont*	.990	28	267	17	3	287	21

TRIPLE PLAYS: Landers, Rice, Scolaro.

SECOND BASEMEN

Player, Team	Pct.	G	PO	A	E	TC	DP
Adams, Jason, Auburn	.949	47	73	151	12	236	35
ANDERSON, Marlon, Batavia	.9648	73	153	231	14	398	67
Antrim, Patrick, Oneonta	.500	1	1	0	1	2	0
Arvelo, Tom, Pittsfield	.944	67	133	173	18	324	38
Brinkley, Josh, Vermont	1.000	2	6	6	0	12	0
Brito, Domingo, Batavia	1.000	3	0	2	0	2	0
Cabrera, Orlando, Vermont	.964	53	115	152	10	277	38
Cardona, Ruben, New Jersey	.967	48	98	135	8	241	33
Conley, Brian, Williamsport	.930	50	100	125	17	242	22
DeLuca, Nic, New Jersey	1.000	1	0	1	0	1	0
Dennis, Les, Oneonta	.922	31	48	70	10	128	13
Deshenes, Marc, Watertown	.970	35	59	100	5	164	21
Engleka, Douglas, Jamestown	.957	21	33	56	4	93	9
Freel, Ryan, St. Catharines	.940	65	118	181	19	318	32
Funaro, Joe, Elmira	.963	17	30	49	3	82	13
Garcia, Amaury, Elmira	.944	60	128	178	18	324	33
Garcia, Apostol, Jamestown	.000	1	0	0	1	1	0
Gorecki, Ryan, Hudson Valley	.9647	53	92	154	9	255	35
Hall, Andy, New Jersey	1.000	4	6	10	0	16	1
Holley, Jack, St. Catharines	1.000	8	15	15	0	30	2
Insunza, Miguel, New Jersey	.939	25	45	63	7	115	8
Jasco, Elinton, Williamsport	1.000	6	11	17	0	28	1
Lebron, Ruben, Utica	.968	48	84	128	7	219	21
Lemonis, Chris, Jamestown	.960	51	99	140	10	249	29
Lugo, Julio, Auburn	.937	20	42	62	7	111	12
Macias, Jose, Vermont	.949	21	49	62	6	117	15
McDonald, Ashanti, Williamsport	.885	8	6	17	3	26	3
Miyake, Chris, Erie	.9647	38	89	130	8	227	25
Nieves, Jose, Williamsport	.960	9	21	27	2	50	8
Parsons, Jeff, Pittsfield	1.000	1	1	2	0	3	0
Perez, Mike, Williamsport	1.000	7	15	21	0	36	7
Pettiford, Torrey, Batavia	.947	3	7	11	1	19	1
Pollock, Elton, Erie	1.000	3	5	3	0	8	1
Rathmell, Lance, Utica	.911	20	31	41	7	79	11
Rojas, Ron, Jamestown	.942	10	26	23	3	52	6
Sagers, Kory, Utica	.962	15	31	45	3	79	8
Sanchez, Omar, St. Catharines	.911	7	18	23	4	45	7
Schreiber, Stan, Erie	.867	2	8	5	2	15	4
Scolaro, Donald, Auburn	.953	8	18	23	2	43	4
Segura, Juan, Erie	.944	12	25	43	4	72	7
Smith, Rod, Oneonta	.939	49	74	125	13	212	23
Soriano, Carlos, Pittsfield	1.000	2	2	7	0	9	0
Thornhill, Chad, Watertown	.978	48	107	112	5	224	32
Turner, Rocky, Pittsfield	.857	1	2	4	1	7	1
Venezia, Richard, Erie	.958	22	35	56	4	95	13
Viruet, Willie, Pittsfield	.957	9	21	24	2	47	6
Vopata, Nathan, Hudson Valley	.946	27	54	51	6	111	10
Walker, Rodney, Hudson Valley	1.000	1	2	0	0	2	0
Whipple, Boomer, Erie	1.000	2	3	1	0	4	0

TRIPLE PLAYS: Adams, Dennis, Am. Garcia, Holley.

THIRD BASEMEN

Player, Team	Pct.	G	PO	A	E	TC	DP
Adams, Jason, Auburn	.000	1	0	0	1	1	0
Booty, Josh, Elmira	.898	73	56	173	26	255	20
Bovender, Andy, Auburn	.900	58	42	102	16	160	12
Brannon, Tony, Utica	.879	41	31	85	16	132	6
Brinkley, Josh, Vermont	.933	7	6	8	1	15	0
Brumbaugh, Clifford, Hud. Valley	.914	73	54	149	19	222	11
Cox, Charles, Batavia	.400	1	1	1	3	5	0
DeLuca, Nic, New Jersey	1.000	2	1	3	0	4	0
DIEGUEZ, Mike, Pittsfield	.954	52	42	104	7	153	9
Engleka, Douglas, Jamestown	.917	6	1	10	1	12	3
Fernandez, Jose, Vermont	.907	63	48	157	21	226	13
Funaro, Joe, Elmira	1.000	1	1	2	0	3	0
Garman, Sean, New Jersey	.919	44	45	68	10	123	7
Hall, Andy, New Jersey	.773	38	19	39	17	75	2
Hayes, Chris, St. Catharines	.954	28	26	77	5	108	8
Holley, Jack, St. Catharines	.914	46	40	108	14	162	8
Insunza, Miguel, New Jersey	.800	3	2	2	1	5	0
Jorgensen, Tim, Watertown	.936	73	42	205	17	264	24
Leaman, Jeff, Batavia	.926	38	17	83	8	108	9
Lemonis, Chris, Jamestown	.900	4	4	5	1	10	0
Lowell, Mike, Oneonta	.911	72	59	188	24	271	8
Macias, Jose, Vermont	.950	9	5	14	1	20	1
Mackert, Jamie, Erie	.882	12	2	28	4	34	3
Maleski, Tom, Williamsport	.857	3	2	4	1	7	0
McDonald, Ashanti, Williamsport	.934	25	12	59	5	76	3
Miller, Michael, Jamestown	.908	64	36	141	18	195	8
Motes, Jeff, Pittsfield	.908	24	13	46	6	65	3
Nova, Jose Feliz, Williamsport	.853	52	24	86	19	129	4
Palmer, Jim, Oneonta	1.000	3	3	6	0	9	0
Prodanov, Peter, Utica	.923	22	12	48	5	65	4
Rathmell, Lance, Utica	.966	22	11	46	2	59	3
Rodriguez, Luis, St. Catharines	1.000	2	1	3	0	4	0
Rojas, Ron, Jamestown	.917	6	4	7	1	12	0
Russell, Jason, Batavia	.884	40	29	78	14	121	8
Scolaro, Donald, Auburn	.923	16	8	28	3	39	2
Segura, Juan, Erie	.750	2	0	3	1	4	0
Shanahan, Jason, Elmira	1.000	2	2	5	0	7	1
Soriano, Carlos, Pittsfield	.700	3	1	6	3	10	1
Venezia, Richard, Erie	1.000	3	2	3	0	5	1
Vieira, Scott, Williamsport	.833	2	1	4	1	6	1
Viruet, Willie, Pittsfield	1.000	1	2	2	0	4	0
Vopata, Nathan, Hudson Valley	1.000	5	0	4	0	4	0
Waggoner, James, Jamestown	1.000	3	0	5	0	5	0
Walker, Rodney, Hudson Valley	1.000	1	0	1	0	1	0
Whipple, Boomer, Erie	.947	64	67	146	12	225	14

TRIPLE PLAYS: Booty, Whipple.

SHORTSTOPS

Player, Team	Pct.	G	PO	A	E	TC	DP
Antrim, Patrick, Oneonta	.804	23	25	65	22	112	7
Arvelo, Tom, Pittsfield	1.000	1	1	3	0	4	0
Babin, Brady, Elmira	.963	5	5	21	1	27	2

Player, Team	Pct.	G	PO	A	E	TC	DP
Barrett, Michael, Vermont	1.000	1	1	3	0	4	0
Betts, Darrell, New Jersey	.900	51	73	117	21	211	23
Brinkley, Josh, Vermont	.900	1	2	7	1	10	2
Brito, Domingo, Batavia	.964	9	6	21	1	28	2
Cabrera, Orlando, Vermont	.891	12	20	37	7	64	4
Camilli, Jason, Vermont	.939	62	87	191	18	296	45
Chamblee, James, Utica	.892	62	87	162	30	279	33
Conley, Brian, Williamsport	.750	3	7	2	3	12	0
Dennis, Les, Oneonta	.958	17	19	50	3	72	10
Deshenes, Marc, Watertown	.897	12	10	25	4	39	4
Engleka, Douglas, Jamestown	.930	22	37	43	6	86	9
Funaro, Joe, Elmira	.917	3	5	6	1	12	1
Garcia, Apostol, Jamestown	.904	60	66	189	27	282	28
Goodell, Steve, Elmira	.899	66	85	209	33	327	34
Hayes, Chris, St. Catharines	.928	14	36	41	6	83	9
Hermansen, Chad, Erie	.839	39	52	104	30	186	15
Holley, Jack, St. Catharines	.926	5	11	14	2	27	4
Insunza, Miguel, New Jersey	.886	28	30	63	12	105	12
Jaroncyk, Ryan, Pittsfield	.900	4	4	14	2	20	0
Kimm, Tyson, Batavia	.800	1	1	3	1	5	0
Lackey, Steve, Pittsfield	.956	21	29	79	5	113	16
Leaman, Jeff, Batavia	1.000	2	1	4	0	5	1
Lobaton, Jose, Oneonta	.892	41	46	111	19	176	19
Lugo, Julio, Auburn	.947	19	36	54	5	95	10
McDonald, Ashanti, Williamsport	.941	23	43	84	8	135	15
Miyake, Chris, Erie	.941	18	26	69	6	101	12
Motes, Jeff, Pittsfield	.941	9	9	23	2	34	3
Nieves, Jose, Williamsport	.881	54	64	166	31	261	21
Parsons, Jeff, Pittsfield	.870	40	63	125	28	216	23
Pileski, Mark, Pittsfield	.900	3	5	13	2	20	1
Prodanov, Peter, Utica	.957	11	11	33	2	46	1
Rathmell, Lance, Utica	1.000	1	4	3	0	7	0
Raynor, Mark, Batavia	.950	66	109	231	18	358	56
Reed, Billy, Hudson Valley	.884	42	53	115	22	190	13
Robles, Oscar, Auburn	.949	55	105	190	16	311	39
Rojas, Ron, Jamestown	1.000	1	0	3	0	3	0
Sagers, Kory, Utica	.800	7	3	13	4	20	3
Segura, Juan, Erie	.975	12	24	53	2	79	12
Shanahan, Jason, Elmira	.889	2	1	7	1	9	0
SOLANO, Fausto, St. Catharines	.955	57	115	183	14	312	41
Thornhill, Chad, Watertown	1.000	1	0	4	0	4	0
Valera, Willy, Watertown	.953	65	96	211	15	322	32
Venezia, Richard, Erie	.977	8	15	27	1	43	5
Vopata, Nathan, Hudson Valley	.923	37	59	96	13	168	20
Walker, Rodney, Hudson Valley	.917	7	7	15	2	24	2

TRIPLE PLAYS: Lobaton, Lugo, Reed.

OUTFIELDERS

Player, Team	Pct.	G	PO	A	E	TC	DP
Adamson, Jason, Erie	1.000	2	2	0	0	2	0
Alexander, Chad, Auburn	.965	68	129	8	5	142	1
Austin, Lakevie, Utica	.886	29	37	2	5	44	0
Bady, Edward, Vermont	.962	71	166	11	7	184	4
Bates, Fletcher, Pittsfield	.912	70	119	6	12	137	1
Bazzani, Matt, Utica	1.000	1	1	0	0	1	0
Bentley, Kevin, Williamsport	.962	43	47	4	2	53	1
Blakeney, Mo, Vermont	.958	38	42	4	2	48	0
Borges, Mariano, Erie	.875	16	20	1	3	24	1
Bourne, Charles, St. Catharines	.896	53	91	12	12	115	1
Budzinski, Mark, Watertown*	.959	70	113	5	5	123	2
Cameron, Ken, New Jersey*	.986	28	69	3	1	73	0
Camfield, Eric, Oneonta*	.945	67	94	9	6	109	1
Chevalier, Virgil, Utica	1.000	1	4	0	0	4	0
Choate, Jonathan, Watertown	.946	40	50	3	3	56	0
Cornelius, Jonathon, Batavia	.927	63	105	10	9	124	3
Cox, Charles, Batavia	1.000	2	3	0	0	3	0
Crane, Todd, Batavia	.972	21	34	1	1	36	0
Culp, Matt, Watertown	1.000	4	1	0	0	1	0
Davis, Albert, Erie	.973	44	67	5	2	74	1
Dawkins, Walter, Batavia	.984	51	120	3	2	125	0
Denning, Wes, Vermont	.936	55	80	8	6	94	0
Diaz, Linardo, Batavia	.959	21	44	3	2	49	2
Echols, Mandell, Hudson Valley	.959	56	114	4	5	123	1
Edwards, Aaron, Erie	.917	13	21	1	2	24	0
Ellison, Tony, Williamsport	.857	3	5	1	1	7	0
Freitas, Joe, New Jersey	.970	14	32	0	1	33	0
Funaro, Joe, Elmira	.953	33	37	4	2	43	0
Goodwin, Keith, Utica	.900	36	60	3	7	70	0
Gray, Ricky, Jamestown*	.977	27	42	1	1	44	1
Guillen, Jose, Erie	.900	64	107	10	13	130	5
Hare, Rich, Jamestown	1.000	15	12	1	0	13	0
Hayes, Chris, St. Catharines	1.000	3	2	1	0	3	0
Jefferson, Dave, Elmira	.833	5	4	1	1	6	0
Johnson, Damon, St. Catharines	.957	60	84	5	4	93	0
Johnson, Jason, Hudson Valley	.944	36	48	3	3	54	0
Jones, Jaime, Elmira*	.907	30	38	1	4	43	0
Joseph, Terry, Williamsport	.955	66	103	3	5	111	1
Kapler, Gabriel, Jamestown	.926	61	103	9	9	121	3
Lariviere, Jason, New Jersey	.960	33	43	5	2	50	0
Lauterhahn, Mike, Williamsport	1.000	4	5	1	0	6	0
Leaman, Jeff, Batavia	.900	5	8	1	1	10	0
LeClair, Paul, Pittsfield	.981	29	50	2	1	53	2
Lewis, Marc, Utica	.969	66	115	9	4	128	3
Long, Garrett, Erie	.950	9	17	2	1	20	0
Long, Justin, Elmira	.979	52	87	7	2	96	1
LONG, Terrence, Pittsfield*	.9913	51	111	3	1	115	0
Lugo, Julio, Auburn	1.000	3	7	0	0	7	0
Macias, Jose, Vermont	.951	23	39	0	2	41	0
May, Freddie, Erie*	1.000	25	42	2	0	44	0
McHugh, Ryan, New Jersey	.980	24	45	3	1	49	0
McNally, Shawn, New Jersey	.976	24	39	2	1	42	1
Miller, Kumandac, Elmira	.928	42	63	1	5	69	0
Milord, Clausel, Jamestown	1.000	28	56	0	0	56	0
Minici, Jason, Watertown	.9908	63	106	2	1	109	1
Mitchell, Rivers, Jamestown	.935	52	92	9	7	108	2
Morenz, Shea, Oneonta	.964	31	26	1	1	28	0
Morgan, Scott, Watertown	.946	40	50	3	3	56	0
Mota, Gleydel, Pittsfield*	.941	11	16	0	1	17	0
Mueller, Bret, New Jersey	.945	66	134	3	8	145	0
Nelson, Tray, Oneonta	.824	13	14	0	3	17	0
Norman, Ty, Utica	.982	47	102	8	2	112	2
Owens, Walter, Watertown	1.000	18	18	1	0	19	0
Pettiford, Torrey, Batavia	.000	1	0	0	1	1	0
Podsednik, Scott, Hud.Valley*	.978	65	125	6	3	134	2
Pollock, Elton, Erie	.976	41	79	2	2	83	1
Pratt, Wes, Auburn	.955	54	122	5	6	133	3
Prodanov, Peter, Utica	1.000	14	16	3	0	19	1
Rascon, Rene, Elmira*	.933	26	28	0	2	30	0
Rivera, Wilfredo, Utica	.937	43	69	5	5	79	1
Robinson, David, Batavia*	.967	54	86	1	3	90	1
Robinson, Hassan, Auburn	.936	59	66	7	5	78	0
Rosado, Juan, Vermont*	1.000	48	77	7	0	84	1
Rosario, Felix, St. Catharines	.961	55	93	5	4	102	2
Salzano, Jerry, Williamsport	.933	17	27	1	2	30	0
Sanchez, Omar, St. Catharines	.969	60	117	9	4	130	0
Schreimann, Eric, Batavia	.917	14	22	0	2	24	0
Seidel, Ryan, Williamsport	.963	59	100	3	4	107	2
Shumpert, Derek, Oneonta	.964	60	101	6	4	111	2
Smith, Akili, Erie	.692	7	6	3	4	13	0
Speed, Dorian, Williamsport	.968	58	146	5	5	156	4
Springfield, Bo, Erie	.903	17	27	1	3	31	0
Stratton, Kelly, Hudson Valley*	.900	18	16	2	2	20	0
Tippin, Greg, Utica*	.750	6	5	1	2	8	0
Tribolet, Scott, Auburn	.916	40	74	2	7	83	0
Rocky, Pittsfield	.934	27	56	1	4	61	0
Ugueto, Hector, New Jersey	.990	53	96	5	1	102	0
Vasquez, Danny, Hudson Valley	.966	67	102	12	4	118	0
Vieira, Scott, Williamsport	.500	5	1	0	1	2	0
Waggoner, James, Jamestown	1.000	3	1	0	0	1	0
Weaver, Scott, Jamestown*	.943	62	81	2	5	88	0
Wilcox, Chris, Oneonta	.947	59	84	6	5	95	0
Winn, Randy, Elmira	.954	51	103	1	5	109	0
Yoder, Paul, Pittsfield	.938	46	68	7	5	80	1

TRIPLE PLAY: Johnson.

CATCHERS

Player, Team	Pct.	G	PO	A	E	TC	DP	PB
Afenir, Tom, Watertown	.955	6	39	3	2	44	0	1
Barton, Scott, Williamsport	.987	14	71	4	1	76	1	9
Bazzani, Matt, Utica	.979	23	121	17	3	141	2	4
Boryczewski, Marty, Erie	.945	10	64	5	4	73	1	3
Brinkley, Josh, Vermont	.981	16	87	14	2	103	2	15
Briones, Christopher, H. V.	1.000	5	7	2	0	9	0	1
Brunner, Michael, Auburn	.969	24	137	19	5	161	0	5
Caballero, Manuel, Jamestown	.984	37	229	24	4	257	2	4
Canetto, John, Erie	.967	10	55	3	2	60	1	3
Carpenter, Matt, Watertown	1.000	4	18	3	0	21	0	1
Castro, Ramon, Auburn	.994	54	297	46	2	345	4	10
Chevalier, Virgil, Utica	.992	21	112	12	1	125	0	5
Coats, Nathan, Watertown	1.000	12	45	8	0	53	2	4
Cox, Charles, Batavia	.980	34	225	21	5	251	2	3
DeLaRosa, Elvis, Jamestown	.956	14	96	12	5	113	0	3
Deman, Lou, New Jersey	1.000	22	173	27	0	200	0	5
Doezie, Troy, New Jersey	.947	14	94	13	6	113	0	3
Emmons, Scott, Oneonta	.975	37	315	32	9	356	1	10
Erwin, Mat, Elmira	.978	57	367	69	10	446	3	9

Player, Team	Pct.	G	PO	A	E	TC	DP	PB
Flanigan, Steven, Erie	.986	22	128	16	2	146	3	3
Fuller, Brian, Jamestown	.986	31	183	28	3	214	3	6
Garcia, Jaime, Vermont	.983	50	316	41	6	363	2	8
GONZALEZ, Rich, Watertown	1.000	55	371	41	0	412	4	6
Goodwin, Joseph, H.V.	.973	57	368	62	12	442	5	10
Hernandez, Rob, Elmira	.975	6	36	3	1	40	0	2
Imersek, Jason, Oneonta	1.000	1	1	0	0	1	0	0
Maleski, Tom, Williamsport	.957	28	154	22	8	184	1	10
Martinez, Roger, Pittsfield	.968	17	77	13	3	93	2	3
McAulay, John, Hud. Valley	.974	24	129	21	4	154	3	7
McCartney, Sommer, Elmira	.982	15	103	8	2	113	0	5
McClendon, Travis, N. Jersey	.993	46	341	61	3	405	4	8
McCormick, Cody, Oneonta	.987	38	283	26	4	313	2	14
McLendon, Craig, Hud. Valley	.958	4	22	1	1	24	0	0
Morales, Eric, Pittsfield	.973	57	340	63	11	414	2	11
Parker, Michael, Pittsfield	1.000	3	5	1	0	6	0	0
Pelis, Andy, Pittsfield	.976	8	34	6	1	41	0	1
Pierce, Kirk, Batavia	.974	27	167	24	5	196	4	0
Reilly, John, St. Catharines	.958	4	16	7	1	24	1	0
Reynolds, Paul, Erie	.972	36	204	37	7	248	0	5
Rodriguez, Luis, St. Catharines	.975	62	383	80	12	475	7	11
Sapp, Damien, Utica	.982	35	234	37	5	276	2	17
Schreimann, Eric, Batavia	1.000	1	7	2	0	9	0	1
Snusz, Chris, Batavia	.964	18	121	14	5	140	2	6
Stadler, Mike, Watertown	.955	5	38	4	2	44	2	4
Steinkemper, Jacob, Vermont	.954	15	75	8	4	87	0	3
Varriano, Mark, Utica	.939	4	29	2	2	33	0	3
Vieira, Scott, Williamsport	.976	27	157	9	4	170	1	5
Williams, Brian, St. Catharines	.989	16	80	12	1	93	0	2
Zuleta, Julio, Williamsport	.966	25	131	12	5	148	1	5

TRIPLE PLAY: Goodwin.

PITCHERS

Player, Team	Pct.	G	PO	A	E	TC	DP
Adge, Jason, Watertown	1.000	19	0	5	0	5	1
Antonini, Adrian, Batavia	.500	3	0	1	1	2	0
Arellano, Carlos, Watertown	1.000	2	2	1	0	3	0
Atkins, Dannon, Watertown	.905	13	7	12	2	21	1
Atwater, Joe, Pittsfield*	1.000	1	0	1	0	1	0
Bair, Dennis, Williamsport	1.000	7	1	8	0	9	1
Bajda, Mike, Jamestown	1.000	13	3	4	0	7	0
Baker, Jason, Vermont	.824	14	5	9	3	17	0
Ballew, Preston, Pittsfield*	1.000	1	1	3	0	4	0
Barker, Jeff, Jamestown	.667	14	0	2	1	3	0
Barnett, Marty, Batavia	.941	10	2	14	1	17	0
BAUER, Charles, Hudson Valley	1.000	15	3	18	0	21	1
Beach, Scott, Erie	1.000	14	2	4	0	6	1
Beagle, Chad, Elmira*	1.000	5	2	4	0	6	0
Becker, Tom, Oneonta	.963	15	7	19	1	27	3
Bell, Mike, Vermont*	1.000	7	2	3	0	5	1
Benes, Adam, New Jersey	1.000	19	5	7	0	12	1
Bennett, Jason, Watertown	.972	16	2	33	1	36	4
Bennett, Matt, New Jersey	.929	23	4	9	1	14	0
Berry, Jason, Oneonta	1.000	8	0	1	0	1	0
Bettencourt, Justin, Jamestown*	.950	14	6	13	1	20	1
Betti, Rich, Utica*	1.000	12	2	0	0	2	0
Bigler, Cory, Erie	.857	10	3	3	1	7	0
Boardman, Eric, Oneonta	1.000	11	4	10	0	14	1
Bogle, Sean, Williamsport	.625	12	1	4	3	8	0
Bowman, Paul, Pittsfield	1.000	2	1	0	0	1	0
Brandt, Dale, Oneonta*	.857	23	0	6	1	7	0
Brown, Shawn, Jamestown	1.000	18	2	4	0	6	0
Bullock, Derek, Erie	1.000	11	3	11	0	14	0
Burgus, Travis, Elmira	.950	15	2	17	1	20	0
Cannon, Kevan, Utica*	1.000	9	4	15	0	19	2
Centeno, Jose, Vermont*	1.000	6	0	1	0	1	0
Choi, Chang Yang, Batavia	1.000	7	0	1	0	1	0
Civit, Xavier, Vermont	.800	19	5	7	3	15	0
Codd, Tim, Hudson Valley	1.000	25	0	5	0	5	0
Collie, Tim, Erie	1.000	29	1	5	0	6	1
Cordero, Francisco, Jamestown	.850	15	12	22	6	40	0
Corey, Bryan, Jamestown	1.000	29	4	4	0	8	0
Corominus, Mike, Auburn*	1.000	13	3	3	0	6	0
Coronado, Osvaldo, Pittsfield	.880	15	9	13	3	25	2
Crowell, Jim, Watertown*	.933	12	1	13	1	15	0
Crowther, John, St. Catharines	.875	15	4	10	2	16	0
Cummins, Brian, Jamestown*	1.000	18	2	11	0	13	1
Davey, Tom, St. Catharines	.875	7	1	6	1	8	0
DeLaCruz, Narcisco, St. Cath.*	1.000	21	3	7	0	10	1
Dempster, Ryan, Hudson Valley	1.000	1	0	1	0	1	0
Diaz, Jairo, Williamsport	.867	30	2	11	2	15	0
Dixon, Timothy, Vermont*	.867	18	3	10	2	15	0
Donnelly, Robert, New Jersey	1.000	36	1	5	0	6	0
Draeger, Mark, Hudson Valley	.917	21	1	10	1	12	0
Duffy, Ryan, Erie	.929	19	3	10	1	14	0
Durkovic, Peter, Jamestown*	1.000	14	2	4	0	6	0
Eby, Michael, Jamestown*	1.000	23	8	4	0	12	0
Einertson, Darrel, Oneonta	.667	25	1	3	2	6	1
Enard, Tony, Elmira	.857	15	1	5	1	7	0
Farr, Mark, Elmira	1.000	9	5	6	0	11	0
Farrow, Jason, Erie	1.000	20	2	10	0	12	1
Fernandes, Jamie, Utica	1.000	3	0	2	0	2	0
Fernandez, Jared, Utica	1.000	5	0	4	0	4	0
Ferullo, Matt, Pittsfield	1.000	2	0	1	0	1	0
Fitterer, Scott, St. Catharines	.750	22	0	3	1	4	0
Foran, John, Jamestown	1.000	14	2	2	0	4	0
Ford, Ben, Oneonta	.545	29	1	5	5	11	0
Ford, Brian, Batavia*	1.000	29	2	5	0	7	0
Frascatore, Steve, New Jersey	.688	16	1	10	5	16	0
Fuller, Stephen, Auburn	.875	14	3	11	2	16	0
Gaiko, Robert, Batavia	.800	20	1	7	2	10	0
Gambs, Chris, Batavia	1.000	7	2	3	0	5	0
Garcia, Rick, Elmira	.846	15	7	15	4	26	0
Glynn, Ryan, Hudson Valley	.857	9	3	9	2	14	2
Goedde, Roger, Erie	.750	5	2	1	1	4	0
Green, Jason, Auburn	.800	14	4	16	5	25	0
Greene, Brian, Williamsport	.889	18	5	3	1	9	0
Grife, Richard, Watertown	1.000	5	0	2	0	2	0
Groves, Brian, Jamestown*	1.000	16	2	4	0	6	0
Gulin, Lindsey, Pittsfield*	1.000	1	0	2	0	2	0
Hall, Yates, New Jersey	.500	5	1	0	1	2	0
Hamilton, Bo, Batavia	.952	14	7	13	1	21	0
Hammack, Brandon, Williamspt	1.000	27	3	5	0	8	0
Hartshorn, Tyson, St. Catharines	.800	13	4	8	3	15	1
Harvey, Terry, Watertown	.895	8	7	10	2	19	0
Hernandez, Elvin, Erie	.864	14	7	12	3	22	0
Herr, David, Vermont	.778	18	1	6	2	9	1
Horn, Keith, Watertown	1.000	8	2	1	0	3	0
Horton, Aaron, Oneonta*	1.000	6	2	4	0	6	0
Horton, Eric, St. Catharines	.955	21	6	15	1	22	1
Howard, Tom, Elmira*	.800	10	1	3	1	5	0
Howatt, Jeff, Pittsfield	.800	17	3	1	1	5	0
Hoy, Wayne, St. Catharines	.944	24	4	13	1	18	1
Hritz, Derrick, Watertown*	1.000	18	2	6	0	8	0
Jacobs, Mike, Utica	.944	13	7	10	1	18	0
Johnson, Scott, Elmira	1.000	4	0	1	0	1	0
Jones, Scott, Utica	1.000	20	1	1	0	2	0
Kahlon, Bobby, Hudson Valley	1.000	30	0	15	0	15	0
Kast, Nick, New Jersey*	1.000	29	0	6	0	6	0
Kawabata, Kyle, Batavia	1.000	18	2	6	0	8	1
Kelley, Jason, Williamsport	1.000	3	0	1	0	1	0
Kendrick, Scott, Williamsport	.667	5	2	0	1	3	0
Kindell, Scott, Pittsfield*	.909	20	2	8	1	11	0
Koenig, Matthew, Pittsfield	.955	15	7	14	1	22	1
Lail, Jerry, Oneonta	.667	13	3	5	4	12	0
Link, Bryan, Hudson Valley*	.929	15	7	19	2	28	1
Lisio, Joseph, Pittsfield	1.000	28	3	2	0	5	1
Loiz, Niuman, Auburn	1.000	3	0	1	0	1	0
Lowe, Ben, St. Catharines*	.909	15	2	8	1	11	0
Mamott, Joe, Utica	.600	9	1	5	4	10	0
Marquez, Ihosvany, Utica	1.000	12	1	2	0	3	0
Marquez, Robert, Vermont	.857	29	3	3	1	7	0
Martineau, Brian, Hud. Valley	.917	30	1	10	1	12	0
Martinez, Osvaldo, Jamestown	.882	15	5	10	2	17	0
Mathis, Sammie, Watertown	1.000	18	2	6	0	8	0
Mattes, Troy, Vermont	1.000	10	0	8	0	8	0
McClurg, Clinton, Batavia	1.000	10	5	3	0	8	1
McEntire, Ethan, Pittsfield*	1.000	13	2	12	0	14	1
McHugh, Michael, Hud. Valley*	1.000	10	0	2	0	2	0
McNeese, John, Williamsport*	.952	13	0	20	1	21	0
McNichol, Brian, Williamsport*	1.000	9	3	7	0	10	0
Mejia, Carlos, Utica*	1.000	10	0	1	0	1	0
Mendes, Jaime, Batavia	1.000	30	1	3	0	4	0
Mensink, Brian, Batavia	.857	11	3	9	2	14	1
Merrick, Brett, Watertown*	.800	22	1	3	1	5	1
Miedreich, Kevin, New Jersey	1.000	15	6	9	0	15	0
Miles, Chad, Elmira*	1.000	14	1	1	0	2	0
Miller, David, Elmira	1.000	9	0	1	0	1	0
Mitchell, Courtney, Batavia*	.769	28	3	7	3	13	1
Mitchell, Scott, Vermont	.889	18	4	4	1	9	0
Moore, Robert, Hudson Valley	1.000	13	4	10	0	14	1
Moore, Sam, Elmira	.750	15	2	1	1	4	0
Morris, Chad, Vermont	1.000	9	0	1	0	1	0
Mosley, Tim, Williamsport	1.000	23	0	2	0	2	0
Mudd, Scott, Hudson Valley	.867	15	5	8	2	15	0
Munro, Peter, Utica	.957	14	9	13	1	23	0

Player, Team	Pct.	G	PO	A	E	TC	DP
Murray, Dan, Pittsfield	1.000	22	0	5	0	5	0
Neese, Josh, Jamestown	1.000	20	4	4	0	8	0
Negrette, Richard, Watertown	.889	18	1	7	1	9	0
Noffke, Andrew, Utica	.667	23	2	0	1	3	0
Noone, Bill, Batavia	1.000	6	1	0	0	1	0
Nunez, Maximo, St. Catharines	1.000	7	2	0	0	2	0
Nuttle, Jamison, Erie	1.000	13	1	1	0	2	0
Olivier, Rich, Oneonta	.909	12	2	8	1	11	0
Ormonde, Troy, Williamsport	.960	14	13	11	1	25	1
Pailthorpe, Bob, Elmira	1.000	13	9	8	0	17	3
Patterson, Casey, Pittsfield	1.000	12	1	4	0	5	0
Peguero, Jose, St. Catharines	.667	17	2	4	3	9	0
Pena, Jesus, Erie*	1.000	3	2	4	0	6	0
Perez, Gil, Erie	.938	18	3	12	1	16	1
Perez, Hilario, Utica	.909	20	3	7	1	11	0
Peterman, Ernie, St. Catharines	1.000	4	5	4	0	9	2
Peterson, Jayson, Williamsport	.667	3	2	0	1	3	0
Phillips, Jon, Auburn*	1.000	2	1	1	0	2	0
Pinango, Simon, Utica*	1.000	20	2	3	0	5	0
Powell, Brian, Jamestown	1.000	5	1	3	0	4	0
Powell, Jeremy, Vermont	.867	15	14	12	4	30	4
Pyrtle, Joe, Pittsfield	1.000	17	0	1	0	1	0
Rakers, Jason, Watertown	1.000	14	2	11	0	13	0
Randolph, Steve, Oneonta*	1.000	6	1	1	0	2	0
Reames, Britt, New Jersey	1.000	5	0	4	0	4	0
Reichstein, Derek, Elmira	1.000	22	4	5	0	9	0
Reid, Rayon, Erie	1.000	8	4	4	0	8	1
Reinfelder, David, Jamestown*	.905	16	4	15	2	21	1
Reyes, Jose, Erie	1.000	19	8	6	0	14	0
Ricketts, Chad, Williamsport	.727	12	3	5	3	11	0
Romboli, Curtis, Utica*	.778	14	3	4	2	9	2
Root, Derek, Auburn*	.929	17	7	6	1	14	0
Rosenbohm, Jim, Auburn	1.000	22	2	10	0	12	1
Ross, Jeremy, Elmira	1.000	20	0	1	0	1	0
Sagedal, Brent, Hudson Valley	1.000	14	1	6	0	7	0
Santiago, Antonio, Utica*	.800	4	0	4	1	5	0
Santoro, Gary, Elmira	.800	24	3	5	2	10	0
Santos, Rafael, Erie	1.000	2	0	1	0	1	0
Schulte, Troy, Auburn	.875	23	3	4	1	8	1
Schultz, Scott, Watertown	.889	9	0	8	1	9	0
Severino, Jose, New Jersey	.818	17	3	6	2	11	0
Shumaker, Anthony, Batavia*	1.000	9	3	5	0	8	1
Sikorski, Brian, Auburn	1.000	23	2	3	0	5	0
Smart, J.D., Vermont	1.000	5	2	3	0	5	0
Smith, Eric, Auburn	.870	14	5	15	3	23	2
Smith, Justin, Batavia	.875	15	2	5	1	8	0
Smith, Randy, St. Catharines	1.000	18	6	4	0	10	0
Smyth, Gregg, Auburn*	.769	14	3	7	3	13	0
Spaulding, Scott, New Jersey	1.000	35	6	5	0	11	0
Speier, Justin, Williamsport	1.000	30	2	6	0	8	0
St. Pierre, Bob, Oneonta	.913	15	7	14	2	23	0
Stachler, Eric, Auburn	1.000	18	1	3	0	4	0
Steinke, Brock, Auburn	1.000	6	0	2	0	2	0
Stephens, Bill, Vermont	1.000	13	3	5	0	8	0
Stephens, Shannon, Elmira	.926	17	10	15	2	27	0
Stern, Marty, Vermont	1.000	8	2	0	0	2	0
Swenson, Mike, New Jersey*	.889	19	2	6	1	9	2
Tatis, Ramon, Pittsfield*	.938	13	5	10	1	16	1
Tessmer, Jay, Oneonta	.909	34	3	7	1	11	0
Thomas, Rob, Erie*	.833	15	1	4	1	6	0
Tickell, Brian, Auburn	.909	13	3	7	1	11	0
Treend, Pat, Elmira	.667	17	1	1	1	3	0
Trumpour, Andy, Pittsfield	.917	15	8	14	2	24	0
Venafro, Michael, Hud. Valley*	.957	32	5	17	1	23	3
Villafana, Jose, New Jersey	.857	27	1	5	1	7	0
Volkert, Oreste, St. Catharines	.875	22	3	11	2	16	1
Ward, Jon, New Jersey	.500	9	0	1	1	2	0
Weber, David, Williamsport	.846	22	2	9	2	13	1
Weber, Eric, Jamestown	1.000	15	2	4	0	6	0
Weber, Lenny, Watertown	1.000	5	0	2	0	2	0
WEIDERT, Chris, Vermont	1.000	15	9	12	0	21	1
Welch, Robb, Utica	.800	12	5	7	3	15	0
Whitworth, Clint, Oneonta	1.000	12	0	1	0	1	0
Wilkinson, Arrow, Oneonta	.900	14	1	8	1	10	0
Wilson, Mike L., Oneonta	1.000	14	1	7	0	8	0
Wilson, Mike R., Jamestown	1.000	5	3	4	0	7	0
Winchester, Scott, Watertown	1.000	23	3	3	0	6	0
Wolff, Thomas, Pittsfield	.714	4	3	2	2	7	0
Wolger, Michael, Vermont*	1.000	2	0	1	0	1	1
Wyatt, Cortez, Williamsport	1.000	22	6	9	0	15	0
Yeager, Gary, Batavia	.929	19	6	7	1	14	2
Young, Joe, St. Catharines	1.000	15	3	7	0	10	0
Young, Ryan, Erie	.900	16	7	11	2	20	1

The following players did not have any fielding statistics at the positions indicated or appeared only as a designated hitter, pinch-hitter or pinch-runner: Albaladejo, p; Barnes, p; Bazzani, p; Chew, p; Conley, p; R. Culp, dh; Ferguson, p; Gorecki, 3b; Helvey, p; Imersek, p; Lebron, ss; J. Long, p; Micknich, p; M. Morris, p; Oakley, p; Pierce, 1b; Prodanov, 2b; Reilly, of, p; Robbins, p; Salzano, 3b; Sauve, p; Scolaro, p; Short, p; Taylor, dh; Viegas, p; Wood, p.

LEAGUE CHAMPIONS

Year	Team	Pct.
1939—	Olean*	.631
1940—	Olean*	.625
1941—	Jamestown	.618
	Bradford (2nd)†	.549
1942—	Jamestown*	.672
1943—	Lockport	.591
	Wellsville (3rd)†	.532
1944—	Lockport	.608
	Jamestown (2nd)†	.565
1945—	Batavia*	.677
1946—	Jamestown‡	.672
	Batavia‡	.672
1947—	Jamestown*	.690
1948—	Lockport*	.603
1949—	Bradford*	.635
1950—	Hornell	.653
	Olean (2nd)†	.568
1951—	Olean	.622
	Hornell (3rd)†	.568
1952—	Hamilton	.659
	Jamestown (2nd)†	.643
1953—	Jamestown*	.704
1954—	Corning*	.621
1955—	Hamilton*	.656
1956—	Wellsville*	.617
1957—	Wellsville	.632
	Erie (2nd)†	.598
1958—	Wellsville	.556
	Geneva (2nd)†	.548
1959—	Wellsville†	.635
1960—	Erie	.643
	Wellsville (2nd)†	.535
1961—	Geneva	.616
	Olean (4th)†	.512
1962—	Jamestown	.580
	Auburn (3rd)†	.521
1963—	Auburn	.585
	Batavia (3rd)†	.485
1964—	Auburn§	.622
1965—	Binghamton	.677
	Binghamton	.607
1966—	Auburn∞	.620
	Binghamton	.646
1967—	Auburn	.667
1968—	Auburn	.645
	Oneonta (2nd)*	.558
1969—	Oneonta	.662
1970—	Auburn	.623
1971—	Oneonta	.662
1972—	Niagara Falls	.686
1973—	Auburn	.667
1974—	Oneonta	.768
1975—	Newark	.688
	Newark	.714
1976—	Elmira	.727
	Elmira	.703
1977—	Oneonta▲	.671
	Batavia	.600
1978—	Oneonta	.729
	Geneva◆	.718
1979—	Geneva	.725
	Oneonta◆	.618
1980—	Oneonta▲	.662
	Geneva	.649
1981—	Oneonta▲	.658
	Jamestown	.649
1982—	Oneonta	.566
	Niagara Falls▲	.553
1983—	Utica▲	.649
	Newark	.649
1984—	Newark	.622
	Little Falls▲	.587
1985—	Oneonta*	.705
	Auburn	.603
1986—	Oneonta	.766
	St. Catharines◆	.632
1987—	Geneva▲	.632
	Watertown	.579
1988—	Oneonta▲	.632
	Jamestown	.618
1989—	Pittsfield	.697
	Jamestown▲	.579
1990—	Oneonta■	.667
	Geneva	.662
1991—	Pittsfield	.662
	Jamestown■	.654
1992—	Hamilton	.737
	Geneva▼	.547
1993—	Niagara Falls▼	.603
	Pittsfield	.533
1994—	Auburn	.592
	New Jersey▼	.573
1995—	Vermont	.645
	Watertown▼	.630

*Won championship and four-club playoff. †Won four-club playoff. ‡Jamestown and Batavia declared co-champions; Batavia defeated Jamestown in final of four-club playoff. §Won championship and two-club playoff. ∞Won split-season playoff. ▲League divided into Eastern and Western divisions; won playoff. ◆League divided into Wrigley and Yawkey divisions; won playoff. ■League divided into Eastern, Western and Stedler divisions; won playoff. ▼League divided into McNamara, Pinckney and Stedler divisions; won playoff. (NOTE—Known as Pennsylvania-Ontario-New York League from 1939 through 1956.)

NORTHWEST LEAGUE

LEAGUE OFFICE

President/treasurer
Bob Richmond

Address
P.O. Box 4941
Scottsdale, AZ 85261

Phone
602-483-8224

Teams (affiliation)
Bellingham Giants (Giants)
Boise Hawks (Angels)
Eugene Emeralds (Braves)
Everett AquaSox (Mariners)
Portland Rockies (Rockies)
Southern Oregon Timberjacks (A's)
Spokane Indians (Royals)
Yakima Bears (Dodgers)

1995 FINAL STANDINGS

NORTH DIVISION

Team	W	L	T	Pct.	GB
Bellingham (Giants)	43	33	0	.566	....
Everett (Mariners)	37	39	0	.487	6
Spokane (Royals)	36	40	0	.474	7
Yakima (Dodgers)	28	48	0	.368	15

SOUTH DIVISION

Team	W	L	T	Pct.	GB
Boise (Angels)	48	27	0	.640	....
Portland (Rockies)	41	34	0	.547	7
Eugene (Braves)	37	39	0	.487	11½
Southern Oregon (Athletics)	33	43	0	.434	15½

COMPOSITE

Team	Boi.	Bell.	Port.	Ever.	Eug.	Spo.	S.O.	Yak.	W	L	T	Pct.	GB
Boise (Angels)	....	7	8	7	5	7	6	8	48	27	0	.640	....
Bellingham (Giants)	3	....	4	6	6	7	9	8	43	33	0	.566	5½
Portland (Rockies)	3	6	....	6	7	4	10	5	41	34	0	.547	7
Everett (Mariners)	3	6	4	....	4	5	5	10	37	39	0	.487	11½
Eugene (Braves)	7	4	5	6	....	5	5	5	37	39	0	.487	11½
Spokane (Royals)	3	5	6	7	5	....	4	6	36	40	0	.474	12½
Southern Oregon (Athletics)	6	1	2	5	7	6	....	6	33	43	0	.434	15½
Yakima (Dodgers)	2	4	5	2	5	6	4	....	28	48	0	.368	20½

Southern Oregon played home games in Medford, Ore.

Major league affiliations in parentheses.

PLAYOFFS: Boise defeated Bellingham, two games to one, to win league championship.

REGULAR-SEASON ATTENDANCE: Bellingham, 54,104; Boise, 165,255; Eugene, 134,878; Everett, 89,950; Portland, 249,696; Southern Oregon, 84,682; Spokane, 162,344; Yakima, 81,570. Total—1,022,479. Playoffs (3 games)—7,181.

MANAGERS: Bellingham, Glenn Tufts; Boise, Tom Kotchman; Eugene, Paul Runge; Everett, Orlando Gomez; Portland, P.J. Carey; Southern Oregon, Tony DeFrancesco; Spokane, Al Pedrique; Yakima, Joe Vavra.

ALL-STAR TEAM: 1B—Danny Buxbaum, Boise; 2B—Jonathan Watson, Bellingham; 3B—Ryan Kane, Boise; SS—Miguel Tejada, Southern Oregon; OF—Kevin Gibbs, Yakima; Kevin Ham, Boise; Joe Trippy, Eugene; C—Patrick Hallmark, Spokane; DH—James Vida, Spokane; RHP—Travis Thurmond, Boise; LHP—Marc D'Alessandro, Portland; RH Reliever—Grant Vermillion, Boise; LH Reliever—Adam Butler, Eugene; Most Valuable Player—Danny Buxbaum, Boise; Manager of the Year—Glenn Tufts, Bellingham.

1995 BATTING

TEAM

Team	Avg.	G	TPA	AB	R	H	TB	2B	3B	HR	RBI	SH	SF	HP	BB	IBB	SO	SB	CS	GDP	LOB	ShO	Slg.	OBP
Boise	.265	75	2963	2523	411	669	965	117	16	49	358	24	19	44	350	16	506	68	30	59	621	1	.382	.362
Eugene	.249	76	2864	2534	364	630	926	104	24	48	307	19	20	58	233	7	578	137	62	34	492	3	.365	.324
Yakima	.244	76	2897	2560	288	624	853	116	25	21	240	20	26	26	260	13	565	122	36	53	575	5	.333	.317
Spokane	.242	76	2933	2575	333	623	845	110	11	30	281	19	18	50	271	9	546	54	36	65	556	3	.328	.324
Everett	.241	76	2996	2591	369	625	959	116	16	62	316	21	16	50	318	12	650	113	45	48	586	5	.370	.334
Bellingham	.239	76	2923	2563	334	613	878	111	11	44	290	20	24	40	276	25	654	79	42	44	544	5	.343	.320
Southern Oregon	.237	76	2970	2488	372	589	846	109	20	36	311	26	31	40	385	8	509	107	44	53	576	6	.340	.344
Portland	.223	75	2806	2407	316	536	729	92	19	21	255	19	19	48	307	10	542	126	54	46	517	4	.303	.320

INDIVIDUAL

TOP QUALIFIERS FOR BATTING CHAMPIONSHIP

Minimum 205 plate appearances. *Lefthanded batter. †Switch-hitter.

Player, Team	Avg.	G	TPA	AB	R	H	TB	2B	3B	HR	RBI	SH	SF	HP	BB	IBB	SO	SB	CS	GDP	Slg.	OBP
Buxbaum, Danny, Boise	.329	68	289	231	46	76	115	15	0	8	51	0	5	4	49	5	31	1	0	3	.498	.446
Vida, James, Spokane*	.323	74	311	291	38	94	121	13	1	4	39	0	0	1	19	5	32	0	0	5	.416	.367
Bilderback, Ty, Boise*	.322	61	210	177	35	57	81	11	2	3	25	0	1	3	29	0	29	10	5	4	.458	.424
Ham, Kevin, Boise	.315	69	287	238	39	75	109	7	3	7	43	0	1	8	40	2	57	2	2	9	.458	.429
Gibbs, Kevin, Yakima†	.313	52	228	182	36	57	74	6	4	1	18	2	3	5	36	1	46	38	5	3	.407	.434
Trippy, Joe, Eugene*	.309	75	300	259	48	80	102	16	0	2	38	2	2	13	24	0	31	29	13	1	.394	.393
Hallmark, Patrick, Spokane	.304	56	246	227	36	69	92	11	0	4	25	2	2	2	13	0	37	5	3	5	.405	.344
Watson, Jonathan, Bellingham	.299	65	262	231	42	69	84	9	0	2	27	4	3	4	20	2	41	16	9	3	.364	.360
Cruz, Deivi, Bellingham	.296	62	245	223	32	66	92	17	0	3	28	1	2	0	19	3	21	6	3	5	.413	.348
Hodges, Randy, Eugene*	.291	61	229	206	29	60	83	7	5	2	28	3	1	7	12	1	35	10	6	3	.403	.350
Tinoco, Luis, Everett	.286	62	242	203	34	58	99	10	2	9	31	0	1	3	35	1	41	9	3	6	.488	.397

Player, Team	Avg.	G	TPA	AB	R	H	TB	2B	3B	HR	RBI	SH	SF	HP	BB	IBB	SO	SB	CS	GDP	Slg.	OBP
Sheffer, Chad, Everett†	.280	56	232	193	31	54	65	9	1	0	18	6	4	2	27	0	38	28	8	3	.337	.367
Kane, Ryan, Boise	.276	74	318	283	39	78	138	14	2	14	59	0	5	5	25	4	57	0	0	10	.488	.340
Filchner, Duane, S. Oregon*	.275	62	231	189	34	52	74	4	0	6	34	1	3	3	35	2	28	12	8	4	.392	.391
Wathan, Dusty, Everett†	.271	53	206	181	32	49	78	9	1	6	25	1	0	7	17	0	26	2	1	4	.431	.356
Miranda, Tony, Spokane	.271	71	306	266	53	72	95	17	0	2	22	3	2	7	28	1	36	15	10	8	.357	.353

DEPARTMENTAL LEADERS: G—Trippy, 75; AB—Vida, 291; R—Miranda, 53; H—Vida, 94; TB—Kane, 138; 2B—Morales, 18; 3B—Hodges, Tejada, 5; HR—Kane, 14; RBI—Kane, 59; SH—Vallone, 8; SF—Amado, Buxbaum, Kane, 5; HP—Trippy, Whitley, 13; BB—Drizos, 54; IBB—Amado, Calderon, 6; SO—Vickers, 102; SB—Gibbs, 38; CS—Lombard, Trippy, 13; GIDP—Roland, 13; Slg.—Buxbaum, .498; OBP—Buxbaum, .446.

ALL PLAYERS

*Lefthanded batter. †Switch-hitter.

Player, Team	Avg.	G	TPA	AB	R	H	TB	2B	3B	HR	RBI	SH	SF	HP	BB	IBB	SO	SB	CS	GDP	Slg.	OBP
Alzualde, Daniel, Boise	.284	24	74	67	3	19	25	3	0	1	8	1	0	1	5	0	19	0	0	2	.373	.342
Amado, Jose, Everett	.265	57	250	215	33	57	98	15	1	8	33	0	5	6	24	6	19	15	5	4	.456	.348
Ardoin, Danny, S. Oregon	.234	58	224	175	28	41	58	9	1	2	23	5	4	9	31	0	50	2	1	2	.331	.370
Arias, Rogelio, Portland	.279	13	45	43	4	12	13	1	0	0	3	0	1	0	1	0	3	3	1	2	.302	.289
Backowski, Lance, Yakima	.193	34	125	114	8	22	25	1	1	0	8	2	1	0	8	1	16	4	1	7	.219	.244
Barthol, Blake, Portland	.236	56	221	191	20	45	62	10	2	1	25	1	3	4	22	0	32	5	2	5	.325	.323
Baughman, Justin, Boise	.233	58	243	215	26	50	63	4	3	1	20	4	1	2	18	0	38	19	4	2	.293	.297
Benner, Brian, Bellingham	.125	2	9	8	0	1	2	1	0	0	1	0	0	0	1	0	4	0	0	0	.250	.222
Betten, Randy, Boise	.375	2	9	8	2	3	3	0	0	0	2	0	0	0	1	0	2	0	0	0	.375	.444
Bilderback, Ty, Boise*	.322	61	210	177	35	57	81	11	2	3	25	0	1	3	29	0	29	10	5	4	.458	.424
Bray, Notorris, Bellingham	.500	2	7	4	3	2	2	0	0	0	0	0	0	0	3	0	1	0	1	0	.500	.714
Brown, Roosevelt, Eugene*	.309	57	183	165	28	51	92	12	4	7	32	0	2	3	13	2	30	6	3	1	.558	.366
Bryan, Leonardo, Boise	.200	42	96	80	8	16	21	3	1	0	6	0	0	0	16	0	18	3	2	3	.263	.333
Brzozoski, Marc, Portland	.233	66	272	240	22	56	72	6	2	2	25	1	2	4	25	3	71	6	4	4	.300	.314
Burrows, Mike, Everett*	.206	67	272	223	28	46	78	5	3	7	33	2	2	3	42	1	72	13	8	1	.350	.337
Buxbaum, Danny, Boise	.329	68	289	231	46	76	115	15	0	8	51	0	5	4	49	5	31	1	0	3	.498	.446
Calderon, Ricardo, Bellingham*	.227	67	245	216	23	49	76	9	0	6	35	1	2	4	22	6	73	1	2	5	.352	.307
Carpentier, Mike, Yakima	.255	53	208	188	20	48	76	8	4	4	28	3	3	1	13	0	23	4	5	2	.404	.302
Castillo, Alberto, Bellingham*	.213	74	302	263	19	56	82	11	0	5	23	0	3	1	35	4	99	0	1	2	.312	.305
Choi, Kyung, Boise*	.299	21	77	67	14	20	22	2	0	0	5	0	1	0	9	1	5	3	1	0	.328	.377
Christenson, Ryan, S. Oregon	.190	49	183	158	14	30	39	4	1	1	16	1	2	0	22	0	33	5	5	3	.247	.286
Corujo, Rey, Bellingham	.221	60	237	208	23	46	81	15	1	6	34	1	4	1	23	0	27	6	4	8	.389	.297
Cruz, Deivi, Bellingham	.296	62	245	223	32	66	92	17	0	3	28	1	2	0	19	3	21	6	3	5	.413	.348
Cruz, Jose, Everett†	.455	3	14	11	6	5	5	0	0	0	2	0	0	0	3	0	3	1	0	0	.455	.571
Cuevas, Trent, Yakima	.203	38	139	123	13	25	35	7	0	1	8	1	1	0	14	0	22	3	4	3	.285	.283
Dalton, Jed, Boise	.262	48	135	126	10	33	43	8	1	0	10	1	0	0	8	1	20	1	1	2	.341	.306
Dantzler, Eric, Bellingham	.118	6	17	17	2	2	6	1	0	1	1	0	0	0	0	0	5	0	0	1	.353	.118
DaSilva, Manny, S. Oregon	.246	55	231	195	31	48	79	14	4	3	33	1	3	6	26	1	25	3	1	9	.405	.348
Daugherty, Keith, Eugene	.125	2	8	8	0	1	1	0	0	0	0	0	0	0	0	0	3	0	0	0	.125	.125
Davalillo, David, Boise	.223	36	120	112	17	25	39	9	1	1	12	1	0	1	6	0	21	1	0	4	.348	.269
Davanon, Jeff, S. Oregon†	.251	57	207	167	29	42	55	6	2	1	17	5	1	0	34	0	49	6	5	1	.329	.376
DeLeon, Reymundo, Eugene	.189	50	142	127	14	24	33	2	2	1	11	0	1	1	13	0	48	2	3	3	.260	.268
Drizos, Justin, Portland*	.205	71	283	224	37	46	72	15	1	3	24	1	1	3	54	1	55	7	1	3	.321	.365
Durrington, Trent, Boise	.171	50	163	140	23	24	39	4	1	3	19	2	2	2	17	0	35	2	0	4	.279	.267
Elam, Brett, Portland	.143	33	105	84	11	12	12	0	0	0	8	2	1	1	17	0	17	3	2	3	.143	.291
Ellison, Skeeter, Eugene†	.133	19	21	15	5	2	2	0	0	0	1	0	1	0	5	0	7	4	2	0	.133	.333
Escandon, Emiliano, Spokane†	.318	13	51	44	7	14	20	1	1	1	12	0	0	1	6	0	11	1	0	0	.455	.412
Felix, Pedro, Bellingham	.274	43	124	113	14	31	35	2	1	0	16	2	2	0	7	0	33	1	1	2	.310	.311
Feuerstein, David, Portland	.268	70	300	269	40	72	103	10	3	5	44	3	3	2	23	2	41	20	8	9	.383	.327
Filchner, Duane, S. Oregon*	.275	62	231	189	34	52	74	4	0	6	34	1	3	3	35	2	28	12	8	4	.392	.391
Finnieston, Adam, Spokane	.237	10	42	38	4	9	9	0	0	0	4	1	1	1	1	0	9	0	1	0	.237	.268
Foote, Derek, Eugene*	.000	1	1	0	0	0	0	0	0	0	0	0	0	0	1	0	0	0	0	0	.000	1.000
Frazier, Tyrone, Spokane	.170	51	168	147	15	25	28	3	0	0	9	5	0	5	11	0	46	8	4	3	.190	.252
Gibbs, Kevin, Yakima†	.313	52	228	182	36	57	74	6	4	1	18	2	3	5	36	1	46	38	5	3	.407	.434
Granzow, Judd, Yakima*	.224	50	175	156	12	35	56	5	2	4	13	0	1	3	15	4	53	3	1	3	.359	.303
Graves, Bryan, Boise	.208	32	70	53	9	11	16	2	0	1	5	0	0	0	17	0	12	0	0	0	.302	.400
Griffin, Chad, Everett*	.183	36	99	82	11	15	20	2	0	1	5	1	0	0	16	1	36	1	0	0	.244	.316
Groseclose, Harold, Portland	.333	5	17	12	2	4	5	1	0	0	2	0	1	2	2	0	2	0	1	0	.417	.471
Gross, Rafael, Yakima	.254	40	158	142	17	36	51	4	1	3	15	1	1	1	13	1	17	12	2	3	.359	.318
Hacker, Steve, Eugene	.211	16	61	57	4	12	21	3	0	2	9	0	1	2	1	0	13	0	0	1	.368	.246
Hallead, John, Portland*	.168	45	164	143	17	24	36	5	2	1	16	2	2	2	15	0	49	9	5	1	.252	.253
Hallmark, Patrick, Spokane	.304	56	246	227	36	69	92	11	0	4	25	2	2	2	13	0	37	5	3	5	.405	.344
Ham, Kevin, Boise	.315	69	287	238	39	75	109	7	3	7	43	0	1	8	40	2	57	2	2	9	.458	.429
Harmon, Brian, Yakima	.254	22	73	59	4	15	18	3	0	0	8	0	2	0	12	0	9	0	0	3	.305	.370
Harris, Robert, S. Oregon	.252	63	272	230	31	58	77	14	1	1	16	3	4	3	32	0	32	9	5	5	.335	.346
Heams, Shane, Everett	.197	27	65	61	5	12	19	4	0	1	4	0	0	1	3	0	28	2	0	2	.311	.246
Hernaiz, Juan, Yakima	.278	50	167	158	23	44	57	9	2	0	16	1	1	1	6	0	30	9	3	1	.361	.307
Hilo, Johnny, Yakima*	.250	50	194	168	18	42	61	10	0	3	22	0	0	3	23	2	33	5	2	4	.363	.351
Hines, Pooh, Eugene	.242	44	152	124	26	30	49	7	3	2	13	4	1	3	20	1	27	13	2	3	.395	.358
Hodges, Randy, Eugene*	.291	61	229	206	29	60	83	7	5	2	28	3	1	7	12	1	35	10	6	3	.403	.350
Hutchins, Norm, Boise†	.250	45	198	176	34	44	60	6	2	2	11	4	1	2	15	0	44	10	6	2	.341	.314
Jimenez, Elvis, Portland	.179	37	132	123	8	22	29	0	2	1	9	1	0	0	8	0	36	7	4	4	.236	.229
Kane, Ryan, Boise	.276	74	318	283	39	78	138	14	2	14	59	0	5	5	25	4	57	0	0	10	.488	.340
Keifer, Greg, Bellingham	.278	10	42	36	6	10	18	1	2	1	3	0	1	1	4	1	14	0	1	0	.500	.357
Klostermeyer, Mike, S. Oregon*	.237	64	223	186	31	44	60	7	0	3	19	2	1	3	31	1	36	4	2	4	.323	.353
Knight, Bill, Southern Oregon	.206	48	163	136	21	28	43	7	1	2	19	3	2	1	21	0	43	5	4	3	.316	.313
Kortmeyer, Scott, Spokane	.141	21	74	64	6	9	11	2	0	0	2	0	2	3	5	0	26	0	0	2	.172	.230
Lewis, Dwayne, Spokane*	.208	46	183	149	24	31	38	2	1	1	8	1	0	3	30	0	55	8	8	2	.255	.352
Lombard, George, Eugene*	.252	68	293	262	38	66	92	5	3	5	19	2	1	5	23	0	91	35	13	0	.351	.323

Player, Team	Avg.	G	TPA	AB	R	H	TB	2B	3B	HR	RBI	SH	SF	HP	BB	IBB	SO	SB	CS	GDP	Slg.	OBP
Lunar, Fernando, Eugene	.244	38	142	131	13	32	44	6	0	2	16	2	0	0	9	0	28	0	1	2	.336	.293
Mahoney, Mike, Eugene	.241	43	132	112	14	27	36	6	0	1	15	1	1	3	15	1	17	6	2	5	.321	.344
Malave, Joshua, Yakima	.270	44	147	137	12	37	57	13	2	1	15	1	2	1	6	0	41	1	1	1	.416	.301
Markert, Jason, Yakima	.272	34	96	81	10	22	28	4	1	0	10	0	0	1	14	0	17	1	1	2	.346	.385
Mayber, Chan, Portland	.205	27	95	78	13	16	20	2	1	0	8	2	0	2	13	0	22	6	3	0	.256	.333
McAninch, John, Boise	.250	42	126	112	16	28	43	9	0	2	12	1	0	2	11	0	24	0	0	6	.384	.328
McClain, Terrance, Yakima	.204	33	70	54	12	11	13	2	0	0	2	1	0	3	12	0	23	7	3	1	.241	.377
Medrano, Teodoro, Everett	.333	1	3	3	0	1	1	0	0	0	0	0	0	0	0	0	1	0	0	0	.333	.333
Melito, Mark, Spokane	.250	61	240	200	24	50	68	7	1	3	20	5	2	6	27	0	30	2	2	3	.340	.353
Meskauskas, John, Portland	.345	9	38	29	4	10	16	3	0	1	9	0	0	1	8	1	7	2	2	0	.552	.500
Meyer, Travis, Yakima	.205	36	97	83	9	17	24	7	0	0	5	0	2	1	11	0	22	0	1	4	.289	.299
Miranda, Tony, Spokane	.271	71	306	266	53	72	95	17	0	2	22	3	2	7	28	1	36	15	10	8	.357	.353
Morales, Julio, Bellingham	.254	66	294	248	43	63	105	18	3	6	25	0	1	11	34	0	60	26	9	1	.423	.367
Moreno, Victor, Spokane	.167	7	27	24	3	4	5	1	0	0	0	0	0	1	2	0	10	0	0	0	.208	.259
Morimoto, Ken, Yakima	.270	55	202	178	27	48	56	4	2	0	14	3	2	0	19	1	40	19	4	1	.315	.337
Moschetti, Mike, S. Oregon	.241	39	168	141	21	34	40	4	1	0	15	0	1	6	20	0	27	13	1	4	.284	.357
Mota, Alfonso, Boise*	.288	51	128	104	25	30	41	5	0	2	16	2	0	1	21	1	11	4	0	1	.394	.413
Myers, Aaron, Portland	.201	57	209	184	25	37	60	5	0	6	24	0	0	2	23	1	44	1	3	6	.326	.297
Nathan, Joe, Bellingham	.232	56	208	177	23	41	61	7	2	3	20	5	2	2	22	1	48	3	2	5	.345	.320
Nations, Joel, Spokane	.214	40	161	140	15	30	38	6	1	0	16	0	0	1	20	0	26	1	1	2	.271	.317
Neubart, Garrett, Portland	.266	39	158	128	23	34	42	8	0	0	8	0	2	7	21	0	24	12	3	0	.328	.392
Newhan, David, S. Oregon*	.269	42	179	145	25	39	67	8	1	6	21	1	3	1	29	1	30	10	5	2	.462	.388
Norton, Andy, Bellingham	.218	25	67	55	3	12	13	1	0	0	5	2	0	2	8	2	15	0	0	3	.236	.338
Owen, Andy, Yakima*	.242	56	184	165	16	40	54	12	1	0	17	1	2	3	9	0	35	6	1	4	.327	.291
Paulin, Randy, Spokane	.204	54	210	191	14	39	54	6	0	3	22	0	2	3	14	0	49	0	1	8	.283	.267
Pena, Elvis, Portland†	.251	58	245	215	29	54	66	6	3	0	18	3	0	1	26	0	45	28	7	2	.307	.335
Person, Wilton, Eugene	.264	62	226	197	25	52	62	8	1	0	23	1	1	7	20	0	21	7	6	4	.315	.351
Pinoni, Scott, Spokane	.184	11	44	38	4	7	9	2	0	0	4	0	0	1	5	0	9	0	0	1	.237	.295
Pomierski, Joe, Everett*	.221	59	247	217	31	48	102	15	3	11	38	0	0	4	26	0	58	4	2	2	.470	.316
Prospero, Teodoro, Bellingham	.138	41	122	109	7	15	20	2	0	1	6	3	2	2	6	0	45	0	1	1	.183	.193
Quinn, Mark, Spokane	.284	44	185	162	28	46	80	12	2	6	37	0	3	5	15	0	28	0	1	5	.494	.357
Ramirez, Joel, Everett	.251	70	291	243	31	61	76	12	0	1	31	2	0	9	37	0	39	9	6	3	.313	.370
Rand, Ian, Bellingham	.128	23	53	47	4	6	6	0	0	0	1	0	0	2	4	0	25	0	0	0	.128	.226
Rasmussen, Nate, Yakima*	.234	44	133	128	12	30	35	3	1	0	5	0	0	1	4	1	43	1	1	4	.273	.263
Reynolds, Paul, Portland	.207	45	154	135	15	28	40	7	1	1	6	0	1	3	5	1	43	9	3	0	.296	.250
Robles, Juan, Spokane	.000	4	10	9	0	0	0	0	0	0	0	0	0	0	1	0	5	0	0	0	.000	.100
Rodriguez, Javier, Everett	.133	20	68	60	2	8	9	1	0	0	1	0	0	1	7	0	13	0	0	1	.150	.235
Roland, William, Spokane	.218	70	296	262	26	57	87	16	1	4	30	1	3	4	26	3	53	1	1	13	.332	.295
Rondon, Alex, S. Oregon	.359	14	49	39	7	14	18	4	0	0	7	1	1	4	4	0	12	0	1	0	.462	.458
Rust, Brian, Eugene	.204	53	170	157	18	32	53	7	1	4	19	2	2	2	7	0	43	2	1	2	.338	.244
Sachse, Matthew, Everett*	.230	59	227	191	34	44	53	6	0	1	14	2	1	4	29	1	76	5	4	3	.277	.342
Sasser, Rob, Eugene	.269	57	244	216	40	58	96	9	1	9	32	0	2	3	23	1	51	14	4	2	.444	.344
Saturnino, Sherton, Eugene	.238	8	22	21	4	5	8	0	0	1	1	0	0	0	1	0	7	2	0	0	.381	.273
Schafer, Brett, Spokane	.195	62	248	205	23	40	50	7	0	1	19	1	1	2	39	0	42	11	1	4	.244	.328
Sheffer, Chad, Everett†	.280	56	232	193	31	54	65	9	1	0	18	6	4	2	27	0	38	28	8	3	.337	.367
Shy, Jason, Eugene	.241	20	55	54	6	13	21	2	0	2	6	0	0	0	1	0	12	0	0	0	.389	.255
Simonton, Cy Leon, Everett*	.206	48	174	155	17	32	36	2	1	0	15	3	1	1	14	0	36	8	4	3	.232	.275
Slemmer, David, S. Oregon	.224	66	284	246	36	55	69	5	3	1	20	1	1	0	36	1	42	16	4	9	.280	.322
Sosa, Juan, Yakima	.235	61	239	217	26	51	78	10	4	3	16	4	2	1	15	2	39	8	1	4	.359	.285
Spiegel, Rich, Eugene	.143	7	17	14	0	2	2	0	0	0	0	0	0	1	2	0	3	0	0	1	.143	.294
Taylor, Matthew, Eugene*	.000	10	30	24	1	0	0	0	0	0	0	0	0	1	5	0	8	0	1	1	.000	.200
Tejada, Miguel, S. Oregon	.245	74	315	269	45	66	115	15	5	8	44	0	3	2	41	2	54	19	2	3	.428	.346
Thomasson, Shane, Everett	.210	40	106	100	10	21	23	0	1	0	3	2	0	2	2	0	23	7	2	1	.230	.240
Thompson, Bruce, Bellingham*	.232	66	285	241	49	56	73	7	2	2	13	1	0	0	43	1	75	18	6	1	.303	.349
Thompson, Karl, Everett	.246	54	211	187	29	46	76	13	1	5	26	2	2	4	16	0	39	4	0	9	.406	.316
Tinoco, Luis, Everett	.286	62	242	203	34	58	99	10	2	9	31	0	1	3	35	1	41	9	3	6	.488	.397
Tocco, Todd, Eugene*	.197	59	140	117	12	23	29	3	0	1	8	2	2	2	17	0	32	0	1	1	.248	.304
Topping, Dan, Bellingham	.267	57	203	180	15	48	68	5	0	5	31	0	1	8	14	4	24	0	0	6	.378	.345
Torrealba, Yolvit, Bellingham	.155	26	75	71	2	11	14	3	0	0	8	0	1	1	2	0	14	0	1	1	.197	.187
Trippy, Joe, Eugene*	.309	75	300	259	48	80	102	16	0	2	38	2	2	13	24	0	31	29	13	1	.394	.393
Tucker, Jonathan, Yakima*	.165	41	130	115	6	19	25	3	0	1	5	0	1	1	13	0	35	0	0	2	.217	.254
Twist, Jeffrey, Portland†	.139	27	90	79	6	11	14	3	0	0	6	0	1	1	9	0	18	0	2	2	.177	.233
Valenti, Jon, Southern Oregon	.209	35	122	110	13	23	34	5	0	2	16	1	2	1	8	0	18	2	0	1	.309	.264
Vallone, Gar, Boise†	.242	37	131	99	21	24	30	6	0	0	16	8	1	3	20	1	33	4	2	3	.303	.382
Vandergriend, Jon, Boise*	.287	56	186	157	30	45	62	8	0	3	24	0	0	3	26	1	32	7	3	3	.395	.398
Vickers, Randy, Everett	.256	68	289	266	35	68	121	13	2	12	37	0	0	3	20	2	102	5	2	6	.455	.315
Vida, James, Spokane*	.323	74	311	291	38	94	121	13	1	4	39	0	0	1	19	5	32	0	0	5	.416	.367
Wagner, Kyle, Boise	.141	36	103	78	14	11	15	1	0	1	14	0	1	7	17	0	18	1	4	1	.192	.340
Walkanoff, A.J., Yakima	.223	38	135	112	7	25	30	5	0	0	15	0	2	0	17	0	21	1	0	1	.268	.321
Wathan, Dusty, Everett†	.271	53	206	181	32	49	78	9	1	6	25	1	0	7	17	0	26	2	1	4	.431	.356
Watson, Jonathan, Bellingham	.299	65	262	231	42	69	84	9	0	2	27	4	3	4	20	2	41	16	9	3	.364	.360
Weathersby, Leon, Spokane	.229	37	131	118	13	27	40	4	3	1	12	0	0	4	9	0	42	2	3	4	.339	.305
Weaver, Terry, Bellingham	.250	37	126	116	24	29	40	2	0	3	13	0	0	1	9	1	30	2	1	0	.345	.310
Welch, Brandon, S. Oregon*	.147	39	119	102	6	15	18	3	0	0	11	1	0	1	15	0	30	1	0	3	.176	.263
Whitley, Bill, Portland	.230	64	282	230	40	53	67	10	2	0	20	3	1	13	35	1	33	8	3	5	.291	.362
Williams, Glenn, Eugene†	.224	71	296	268	39	60	100	11	4	7	36	0	2	5	21	1	71	7	4	4	.373	.291

GRAND SLAMS: Buxbaum, 3; Quinn, 2; Burrows, Calderon, Carpentier, Kane, Lombard, Myers, Pomierski, K. Thompson, Weathersby, Williams, 1 each.

AWARDED FIRST BASE ON CATCHER'S INTERFERENCE: Reynolds 6 (Lunar 2, Graves, Hallmark, Rondon, Walkanoff); Baughman 3 (Lunar 2, K. Thompson); Owen 3 (Arias, Mahoney, Rondon); Walkanoff 2 (Ardoin, Norton).

1995 PITCHING

TEAM

Team	W	L	Pct.	ERA	G	CG	ShO	Sv.	IP	H	TBF	R	ER	HR	SH	SF	HB	BB	IBB	SO	WP	Bk.
Bellingham	43	33	.566	3.05	76	0	8	21	685.1	618	2931	297	232	34	22	15	29	285	2	591	43	13
Portland	41	34	.547	3.06	75	4	4	23	662.1	531	2779	284	225	27	21	20	40	277	13	561	58	19
Eugene	37	39	.487	3.56	76	0	2	19	667.0	606	2955	372	264	39	26	21	44	313	19	635	53	11
Everett	37	39	.487	3.63	76	5	4	15	680.0	622	2919	346	274	55	15	14	44	294	14	572	54	15
Spokane	36	40	.474	3.65	76	1	4	20	680.2	653	2952	345	276	38	20	21	52	269	11	522	44	9
Southern Oregon	33	43	.434	3.72	76	0	3	13	669.1	667	2941	374	277	40	28	28	59	237	16	542	51	13
Boise	48	27	.640	3.90	75	4	5	20	653.2	575	2836	343	283	44	17	17	48	329	13	590	69	9
Yakima	28	48	.368	4.54	76	0	2	17	667.2	637	3039	426	337	34	19	37	40	396	12	537	95	16

INDIVIDUAL

TOP QUALIFIERS FOR EARNED-RUN AVERAGE TITLE

Minimum 61 innings. *Lefthanded pitcher.

Pitcher, Team	W	L	Pct.	ERA	G	GS	CG	ShO	GF	Sv.	IP	H	TBF	R	ER	HR	SH	SF	HB	BB	IBB	SO	WP	Bk.
Randall, Scott, Portland	7	3	.700	1.99	15	15	1	0	0	0	95.0	76	391	35	21	2	2	2	8	28	1	78	7	2
Blood, Darin, Bellingham	6	3	.667	2.54	14	13	0	0	0	0	74.1	63	315	26	21	2	4	0	3	32	0	78	6	1
Cruz, Charlie, Eugene*	6	7	.462	2.55	15	15	0	0	0	0	81.1	68	348	34	23	2	2	3	4	36	2	90	2	1
Niemeier, Todd, Everett*	4	3	.571	2.81	15	15	0	0	0	0	80.0	74	338	33	25	4	4	2	3	26	0	80	5	2
Villarreal, Modesto, Spokane	8	2	.800	2.90	16	11	0	0	1	0	80.2	73	330	30	26	4	2	3	3	23	2	57	5	2
McKnight, Chris, Eugene*	5	2	.714	2.92	13	13	0	0	0	0	64.2	63	282	31	21	4	6	4	1	21	1	30	6	0
D'Alessandro, Marc, Portland*	9	3	.750	2.96	16	15	2	0	0	0	97.1	85	397	41	32	9	0	4	3	28	0	64	2	3
Thurmond, Travis, Boise	9	3	.750	3.11	16	15	4	1	1	0	101.1	75	401	36	35	7	0	3	3	31	0	93	7	0
Kurtz, Danny, Everett	5	2	.714	3.12	14	12	1	0	1	0	69.1	60	293	27	24	6	1	2	6	32	1	43	4	2
Trawick, Tim, Everett	6	2	.750	3.14	16	13	3	1	1	0	86.0	66	350	34	30	11	0	0	9	30	1	63	1	2
Prihoda, Stephen, Spokane*	1	6	.143	3.25	14	13	1	0	0	0	69.1	65	293	36	25	7	3	1	5	18	0	63	4	0
Soden, Chad, Everett*	4	3	.571	3.38	13	12	0	0	0	0	61.1	55	256	30	23	3	0	0	1	17	1	52	3	1
Silva, Luis, Southern Oregon	4	3	.571	3.81	19	14	0	0	3	1	78.0	79	337	43	33	8	3	3	7	20	0	76	5	0
Garcia, Jose, Eugene	3	3	.500	3.86	14	14	0	0	0	0	70.0	64	307	43	30	7	1	0	0	35	0	62	2	2
Cooper, Brian, Boise	3	2	.600	3.92	13	11	0	0	1	1	62.0	60	264	31	27	5	4	1	6	22	1	66	4	1

DEPARTMENTAL LEADERS: W—Vermillion, 12; L—Wuestenhoefer, 9; Pct.—Vermillion, Villarreal, .800; G—Chrismon, 32; GS—Several pitchers tied with 15; CG—Thurmond, 4; ShO—Thurmond, Trawick, 1; GF—Emiliano, 22; Sv.—Scutero, 12; IP—Thurmond, 101.1; H—Wuestenhoefer, 88; TBF—Thurmond, 401; R—Blythe, 55; ER—Blythe, 41; HR—Trawick, 11; SH—McKnight, 4; SF—Hodge, 6; HB—Holden, 17; BB—S. Soto, 54; IBB—Butler, 5; SO—Thurmond, 93; WP—Several pitchers tied with 12; Bk.—Gonzalez, McNeely, Mitchell, 5.

ALL PITCHERS

*Lefthanded pitcher.

Pitcher, Team	W	L	Pct.	ERA	G	GS	CG	ShO	GF	Sv.	IP	H	TBF	R	ER	HR	SH	SF	HB	BB	IBB	SO	WP	Bk.
Abbott, Todd, S. Oregon	2	3	.400	2.96	17	5	0	0	2	1	48.2	39	199	22	16	3	1	1	0	18	0	41	2	1
Abreu, Jose, Bellingham	1	2	.333	4.63	13	0	0	0	5	1	23.1	17	99	12	12	0	1	0	1	12	0	29	2	0
Adam, Justin, Spokane	3	4	.429	5.29	15	8	0	0	2	1	49.1	45	220	34	29	2	0	0	4	31	0	35	2	0
Agosto, Stevenson, Boise*	6	2	.750	2.92	13	11	0	0	1	0	52.1	39	224	20	17	1	0	3	5	30	2	34	12	0
Albrecht, Jon, Spokane*	2	2	.500	3.38	17	0	0	0	13	6	21.1	14	89	8	8	1	0	0	3	12	1	15	2	0
Ali, Sam, Bellingham	0	2	.000	7.88	5	0	0	0	4	0	8.0	10	38	7	7	1	1	0	0	4	0	3	2	1
Alvarez, Juan, Boise*	0	0	.000	0.77	9	0	0	0	2	0	11.2	12	47	1	1	0	0	0	1	2	0	11	0	0
Avila, Edwin, Boise	1	1	.500	10.35	14	1	0	0	6	0	20.0	27	100	27	23	6	0	0	1	14	0	17	2	2
Babineaux, Darrin, Yakima	1	6	.143	3.64	12	10	0	0	2	0	59.1	53	251	33	24	3	1	3	4	18	1	36	0	1
Bailey, Philip, Bellingham*	6	1	.857	1.36	19	4	0	0	0	0	59.2	51	237	15	9	3	0	0	3	15	0	39	1	1
Barcelo, Lorenzo, Bellingham	3	2	.600	3.45	12	11	0	0	0	0	47.0	43	198	23	18	3	0	1	2	19	0	34	1	1
Batchelder, Bill, S. Oregon	1	4	.200	5.52	18	5	0	0	4	0	44.0	56	195	30	27	3	0	1	1	13	1	20	1	0
Bermudez, Manuel, Bellingham	1	2	.333	3.81	13	13	0	0	0	0	56.2	51	244	28	24	3	2	2	2	25	0	39	4	1
Bevel, Bobby, Portland*	2	3	.400	3.54	25	0	0	0	8	1	28.0	24	128	13	11	0	3	2	1	18	4	25	5	0
Blasingim, Joseph, Bellingham	1	1	.500	4.26	13	1	0	0	3	0	25.1	31	118	14	12	0	1	2	1	14	0	22	3	0
Blood, Darin, Bellingham	6	3	.667	2.54	14	13	0	0	0	0	74.1	63	315	26	21	2	4	0	3	32	0	78	6	1
Blythe, Billy, Eugene	1	6	.143	9.80	14	10	0	0	2	1	37.2	45	213	55	41	4	0	2	7	49	1	24	12	0
Bost, Allen, Portland	1	0	1.000	3.38	10	0	0	0	1	0	16.0	15	63	6	6	1	0	0	0	0	0	25	1	0
Brester, Jason, Bellingham*	1	0	1.000	4.13	8	6	0	0	0	0	24.0	23	104	11	11	3	0	0	1	12	0	17	0	0
Brizek, Seth, Everett	0	2	.000	6.97	8	0	0	0	3	1	10.1	13	55	10	8	1	0	0	2	8	0	16	1	0
Brooks, Antone, Eugene*	2	0	1.000	0.53	15	0	0	0	5	0	17.0	9	67	5	1	1	0	0	0	8	1	26	0	0
Brown, Darold, Eugene*	0	3	.000	4.24	3	3	0	0	0	0	17.0	18	77	16	8	3	1	0	0	6	1	13	1	0
Butler, Adam, Eugene*	4	1	.800	2.49	23	0	0	0	18	8	25.1	15	109	9	7	0	1	0	3	12	5	50	1	0
Cervantes, Peter, Yakima	3	5	.375	4.65	13	10	0	0	1	0	50.1	55	226	32	26	3	1	2	3	16	0	35	1	0
Chambers, Scott, Yakima*	1	2	.333	5.34	20	1	0	0	6	1	28.2	31	130	20	17	4	1	1	0	13	0	37	4	0
Charles, Israel, Spokane	1	0	1.000	4.50	4	0	0	0	1	0	6.0	6	28	3	3	0	0	0	0	3	0	5	1	1
Chrismon, Thad, Eugene	2	2	.500	2.61	32	0	0	0	13	3	38.0	31	165	15	11	3	0	4	5	21	1	28	5	0
Clifford, Eric, Everett	3	2	.600	2.40	28	0	0	0	11	4	45.0	39	183	17	12	2	2	3	2	11	1	39	4	1
Coe, Keith, Boise	2	5	.286	4.69	13	12	0	0	0	0	55.2	49	250	35	29	4	2	0	5	38	1	42	5	1
Collett, Andy, Everett	0	0	.000	0.00	1	0	0	0	0	0	0.1	1	4	0	0	0	0	0	0	2	0	0	1	0
Connelly, Steven, S. Oregon	2	4	.333	3.81	17	0	0	0	10	2	28.1	29	133	17	12	1	3	2	4	14	4	19	6	0
Conway, Robert, Everett	1	0	1.000	4.00	6	0	0	0	0	0	9.0	6	42	6	4	0	0	0	0	11	1	3	4	1
Cooper, Brian, Boise	3	2	.600	3.92	13	11	0	0	1	1	62.0	60	264	31	27	5	4	1	6	22	1	66	4	1
Cooper, David, Everett	1	2	.333	7.36	17	2	0	0	7	0	33.0	36	166	31	27	5	1	0	3	31	0	20	8	0
Costello, T.J., S. Oregon*	0	0	.000	6.23	3	0	0	0	0	0	4.1	8	25	4	3	0	0	0	1	2	0	5	0	0
Coyle, Bryan, Yakima	2	0	1.000	1.40	6	1	0	0	1	0	19.1	14	78	3	3	1	1	0	0	8	0	17	1	0
Crossley, Chad, Boise	0	0	.000	20.25	2	0	0	0	1	0	1.1	3	9	4	3	1	0	0	0	1	0	0	0	0
Cruz, Charlie, Eugene*	6	7	.462	2.55	15	15	0	0	0	0	81.1	68	348	34	23	2	2	3	4	36	2	90	2	1

Pitcher, Team	W	L	Pct.	ERA	G	GS	CG	ShO	GF	Sv.	IP	H	TBF	R	ER	HR	SH	SF	HB	BB	IBB	SO	WP	Bk.
Dafun, George, Boise	4	4	.500	5.31	16	12	0	0	2	1	59.1	57	271	40	35	5	4	1	8	33	1	61	4	0
D'Alessandro, Marc, Portland*	9	3	.750	2.96	16	15	2	0	0	0	97.1	85	397	41	32	9	0	4	3	28	0	64	2	3
Davis, Eddie, Yakima	2	3	.400	4.89	20	4	0	0	5	1	53.1	61	248	33	29	2	1	3	5	32	2	36	5	0
Deakman, Josh, Boise	1	1	.500	1.54	3	3	0	0	0	0	11.2	11	49	8	2	0	0	1	0	4	0	8	0	0
DeLaCruz, Fernando, Boise	0	0	.000	13.50	1	0	0	0	0	0	1.1	3	11	6	2	1	0	0	1	2	0	4	0	0
Dietrich, Jason, Portland	0	0	.000	0.00	10	1	0	0	5	4	13.1	5	48	0	0	0	0	0	0	5	0	24	0	0
Emiliano, James, Portland	4	1	.800	3.49	28	0	0	0	22	11	38.2	31	165	18	15	0	2	1	4	16	2	41	5	0
Epstein, Ian, Southern Oregon*	2	2	.500	2.90	23	0	0	0	19	1	40.1	32	163	17	13	1	2	5	2	9	2	36	2	1
Farfan, David, Boise	1	0	1.000	2.53	14	0	0	0	4	0	21.1	19	94	9	6	0	0	0	0	12	0	17	2	2
Fontenot, Joe, Bellingham	0	3	.000	1.93	6	6	0	0	0	0	18.2	14	77	5	4	0	0	0	0	10	0	14	0	2
Foster, Kris, Yakima	2	3	.400	2.89	15	10	0	0	5	3	56.0	38	241	27	18	2	2	4	2	38	3	55	8	1
French, Jon, Southern Oregon	1	2	.333	6.41	20	0	0	0	12	0	26.2	34	132	21	19	3	1	0	5	17	1	18	3	0
Garcia, Jose, Eugene	3	3	.500	3.86	14	14	0	0	0	0	70.0	64	307	43	30	7	1	0	0	35	0	62	2	2
Gerland, Greg, Eugene*	4	2	.667	2.16	19	2	0	0	2	1	41.2	39	180	18	10	1	3	1	1	15	1	33	2	1
Giard, Ken, Eugene	3	0	1.000	2.38	25	0	0	0	7	2	34.0	31	137	9	9	3	2	0	1	5	1	44	3	0
Gomez, Dennys, Bellingham	0	1	.000	7.50	4	0	0	0	2	1	6.0	8	31	6	5	2	0	0	0	3	0	6	1	0
Gonzalez, Laril, Portland	3	4	.429	4.06	15	11	0	0	2	2	57.2	44	258	31	26	4	1	1	7	43	0	48	9	5
Gryboski, Kevin, Everett	1	5	.167	3.50	25	0	0	0	14	2	36.0	27	156	18	14	2	3	1	3	18	2	25	3	0
Gunther, Kevin, S. Oregon	1	1	.500	1.42	5	5	0	0	0	0	19.0	14	71	6	3	0	0	0	0	2	0	11	2	0
Herrera, Ivan, Bellingham	0	0	.000	0.00	1	0	0	0	0	0	2.0	0	7	0	0	0	0	0	0	1	0	1	0	0
Hilton, Willy, Southern Oregon	1	4	.200	4.40	16	1	0	0	6	1	30.2	37	143	22	15	1	3	2	0	12	1	31	4	1
Hodge, Hal, Spokane*	3	1	.750	4.26	16	15	0	0	0	0	69.2	81	308	39	33	5	2	6	7	20	0	45	3	2
Holden, Jason, S. Oregon	2	6	.250	4.72	19	8	0	0	0	0	61.0	64	290	42	32	2	4	4	17	23	0	30	10	4
Hutzler, Jeff, Bellingham	2	2	.500	1.72	7	7	0	0	0	0	31.1	35	130	9	6	0	1	0	0	8	0	19	2	2
Iddon, Brent, Everett	3	5	.375	4.36	14	14	1	0	0	0	74.1	86	326	49	36	8	1	0	6	25	0	67	3	0
Judice, Bryan, Spokane	0	1	.000	7.91	14	0	0	0	4	1	19.1	29	101	18	17	0	1	1	4	10	2	14	4	0
Kammerer, James, Portland*	2	1	.667	1.53	11	5	0	0	0	0	35.1	24	135	8	6	0	1	1	0	11	0	17	1	0
Kaysner, Brent, Spokane	0	2	.000	1.56	19	0	0	0	11	4	34.2	15	147	7	6	1	1	0	7	24	0	37	4	0
Keehn, Drew, Portland	2	4	.333	3.80	20	0	0	0	6	0	42.2	38	182	22	18	3	4	1	1	17	1	30	1	1
Keppen, Jeffrey, Yakima	2	2	.500	5.66	20	3	0	0	6	0	41.1	46	210	35	26	1	1	5	6	32	0	32	7	1
Kjos, Ryan, Southern Oregon	2	0	1.000	2.45	9	0	0	0	4	2	11.0	9	47	4	3	2	0	0	0	5	0	16	2	0
Knoll, Brian, Bellingham	5	2	.714	2.05	22	2	0	0	5	0	57.0	44	232	22	13	1	4	1	3	17	0	35	2	1
Koehler, P.K., Eugene*	0	2	.000	22.50	2	2	0	0	0	0	4.0	4	27	10	10	1	0	0	1	12	0	5	0	1
Kurtz, Danny, Everett	5	2	.714	3.12	14	12	1	0	1	0	69.1	60	293	27	24	6	1	2	6	32	1	43	4	2
Leibee, Skye, S. Oregon*	0	0	.000	3.86	2	0	0	0	0	0	2.1	1	10	1	1	0	0	0	1	1	1	3	0	0
Lintern, Cory, Bellingham	2	0	1.000	0.87	3	0	0	0	1	1	10.1	6	41	2	1	0	1	0	0	2	0	6	0	0
Liz, Jesus, Spokane*	0	0	.000	7.11	9	0	0	0	4	0	12.2	19	70	15	10	0	0	2	0	12	0	11	3	0
Macca, Christopher, Portland	3	2	.600	3.28	24	0	0	0	16	5	35.2	25	152	15	13	1	2	2	6	17	1	41	6	0
Marte, Damaso, Everett*	2	2	.500	2.21	11	5	0	0	1	0	36.2	25	141	11	9	2	1	1	1	10	0	39	3	0
Martin, Chandler, Portland	4	1	.800	1.66	7	7	0	0	0	0	38.0	20	153	10	7	0	2	0	2	21	0	34	3	3
Masaoka, Onan, Yakima*	2	4	.333	3.65	15	7	0	0	5	3	49.1	28	225	25	20	2	1	0	4	47	0	75	12	4
Mayber, Chan, Portland	0	0	.000	0.00	1	0	0	0	1	0	1.0	0	4	0	0	0	0	0	0	1	0	0	0	0
Mayer, Aaron, Boise	3	1	.750	5.40	20	1	0	0	1	0	35.0	38	159	29	21	4	1	0	2	22	0	32	11	0
Mayhew, Keith, Eugene	0	1	.000	4.54	24	1	0	0	3	1	39.2	46	185	29	20	2	2	1	3	17	0	35	4	2
Mazzone, Tony, Eugene	3	1	.750	3.89	25	0	0	0	7	2	44.0	50	200	24	19	3	2	4	7	12	1	38	1	0
McDonald, Matt, S. Oregon*	3	2	.600	3.14	13	9	0	0	0	0	51.2	42	211	22	18	4	2	1	2	18	0	47	2	1
McKnight, Chris, Eugene*	5	2	.714	2.92	13	13	0	0	0	0	64.2	63	282	31	21	4	6	4	1	21	1	30	6	0
McMullen, Jerry, Eugene*	1	1	.500	1.47	22	0	0	0	8	1	30.2	28	128	7	5	0	4	0	1	8	2	31	3	0
McNeely, Mitch, Yakima*	3	4	.429	4.25	24	3	0	0	8	1	53.0	53	226	30	25	1	2	2	0	15	2	31	6	5
McWilliams, Matt, Eugene	2	3	.400	2.01	24	4	0	0	10	0	49.1	34	208	21	11	1	1	0	7	16	2	42	4	2
Medero, Gadiel, Bellingham	0	0	.000	6.35	4	0	0	0	0	0	5.2	10	33	7	4	1	0	1	0	4	0	4	3	0
Mimnaugh, Scott, S. Oregon	0	2	.000	3.24	3	3	0	0	0	0	8.1	10	43	8	3	1	1	0	2	4	0	8	0	1
Mitchell, Kelvin, Everett*	3	2	.600	4.62	25	0	0	0	6	1	37.0	41	171	26	19	2	0	3	2	23	4	24	6	5
Mlodik, Kevin, S. Oregon	2	2	.500	3.15	20	10	0	0	1	0	60.0	62	273	35	21	3	0	3	8	20	0	43	4	2
Morrison, Chris, S. Oregon	2	1	.667	2.40	6	0	0	0	2	0	15.0	14	56	4	4	0	1	0	0	1	0	11	1	0
Mosman, Marc, Bellingham	0	0	.000	5.81	12	3	0	0	1	0	26.1	38	122	21	17	4	1	0	0	8	0	21	2	0
Murphy, Sean, Portland	2	0	1.000	1.59	21	0	0	0	7	0	39.2	21	156	11	7	1	0	1	1	16	2	39	3	1
Nelson, Chris, S. Oregon	2	3	.400	3.48	16	6	0	0	3	1	54.1	43	218	25	21	5	3	3	3	13	1	52	1	1
Newman, Damon, S. Oregon	3	3	.500	3.61	14	7	0	0	1	1	47.1	51	221	32	19	1	1	0	4	24	0	35	4	1
Nied, David, Portland	0	0	.000	0.00	1	1	0	0	0	0	3.0	1	10	0	0	0	0	0	0	1	0	5	0	0
Niemeier, Todd, Everett*	4	3	.571	2.81	15	15	0	0	0	0	80.0	74	338	33	25	4	4	2	3	26	0	80	5	2
O'Quinn, James, Boise*	0	0	.000	4.84	23	0	0	0	9	0	22.1	22	106	12	12	1	1	2	3	18	2	26	6	0
Ortiz, Russell, Bellingham	2	0	1.000	0.52	25	0	0	0	20	11	34.1	19	131	4	2	1	0	1	0	13	0	55	2	1
Pearsall, J.J., Yakima*	2	3	.400	3.26	20	1	0	0	8	1	38.2	39	167	18	14	1	1	2	2	14	0	26	5	0
Petri, Tom, Boise	1	0	1.000	4.18	10	1	0	0	1	0	23.2	27	105	12	11	0	1	4	1	13	0	9	5	1
Prihoda, Stephen, Spokane*	1	6	.143	3.25	14	13	1	0	0	0	69.1	65	293	36	25	7	3	1	5	18	0	63	4	0
Randall, Scott, Portland	7	3	.700	1.99	15	15	1	0	0	0	95.0	76	391	35	21	2	2	2	8	28	1	78	7	2
Reitzenstein, Brad, Portland	0	1	.000	10.13	7	0	0	0	2	0	8.0	2	44	10	9	0	1	0	2	16	1	10	10	2
Renko, Todd, Boise	0	0	.000	7.36	5	0	0	0	2	0	3.2	6	20	8	3	3	0	0	0	3	0	2	0	0
Ritter, Jason, Spokane	3	1	.750	3.21	10	4	0	0	0	0	33.2	25	135	12	12	1	0	1	3	15	0	29	1	1
Rivette, Scott, Southern Oregon	2	0	1.000	0.95	9	1	0	0	3	2	19.0	16	83	5	2	0	1	1	1	11	2	22	1	0
Robbins, Mike, Spokane*	1	3	.250	2.33	5	5	0	0	0	0	27.0	23	109	9	7	1	1	0	2	6	0	16	1	1
Rocker, John, Eugene*	1	5	.167	5.16	12	12	0	0	0	0	59.1	45	260	40	34	4	1	1	2	36	0	74	7	2
Rodriguez, Luis, Bellingham*	0	0	.000	6.00	4	0	0	0	1	0	6.0	6	33	5	4	0	0	1	0	8	0	8	1	0
Rolish, Chad, Southern Oregon*	1	0	1.000	3.00	4	0	0	0	4	1	6.0	6	26	3	2	0	2	0	0	4	2	1	0	0
Romine, Jason, Portland	0	1	.000	6.39	4	3	0	0	0	0	12.2	14	58	9	9	0	0	2	0	7	0	5	0	0
Rose, Brian, Portland	1	1	.500	5.19	5	0	0	0	1	0	8.2	10	40	5	5	1	2	1	2	6	1	11	0	0
Ruskey, Jason, Everett*	0	3	.000	6.08	3	3	0	0	0	0	13.1	15	62	13	9	3	0	0	1	9	0	7	2	0
Saier, Matthew, Spokane	1	2	.333	3.31	16	0	0	0	9	4	35.1	24	138	14	13	2	2	1	2	12	0	41	4	0
Sanchez, Mike, Yakima	1	2	.333	0.95	18	1	0	0	11	5	28.1	16	121	4	3	0	2	1	4	20	2	27	5	1
Sanders, Allen, Spokane	4	5	.444	4.47	14	10	0	0	2	0	56.1	67	257	43	28	2	3	1	2	18	1	36	3	0
Sanders, Craig, Spokane	3	1	.750	1.94	22	0	0	0	12	3	46.1	32	197	11	10	2	2	1	2	24	0	32	2	1
Santiago, Jose, Spokane	2	4	.333	3.14	22	0	0	0	10	1	48.2	60	227	26	17	1	1	2	5	20	4	32	3	0

Pitcher, Team	W	L	Pct.	ERA	G	GS	CG	ShO	GF	Sv.	IP	H	TBF	R	ER	HR	SH	SF	HB	BB	IBB	SO	WP	Bk.
Scheer, Greg, Everett*	0	1	.000	4.15	18	0	0	0	5	1	21.2	16	102	12	10	0	1	2	3	19	2	23	2	0
Scheffer, Aaron, Everett	2	5	.286	3.74	24	0	0	0	9	1	43.1	44	185	23	18	4	1	0	2	16	1	38	2	1
Schiefelbein, Mike, Bellingham	0	0	.000	0.00	3	0	0	0	0	0	0.2	1	6	0	0	0	0	0	0	3	0	1	0	0
Scutero, Brian, Boise	1	2	.333	4.91	22	0	0	0	20	12	22.0	17	101	13	12	1	2	0	1	16	1	17	1	0
Silva, Luis, Southern Oregon	4	3	.571	3.81	19	14	0	0	3	1	78.0	79	337	43	33	8	3	3	7	20	0	76	5	0
Soden, Chad, Everett*	4	3	.571	3.38	13	12	0	0	0	0	61.1	55	256	30	23	3	0	0	1	17	1	52	3	1
Sosa, Helpis, Southern Oregon	0	1	.000	6.75	6	2	0	0	2	0	13.1	21	65	11	10	2	0	2	1	6	1	17	1	0
Soto, Daniel, Spokane	0	3	.000	5.06	3	2	0	0	1	0	10.2	11	45	6	6	1	0	1	1	4	0	10	0	0
Soto, Seferino, Yakima	0	2	.000	7.75	15	6	0	0	1	0	36.0	30	189	37	31	1	0	2	1	54	2	34	9	2
South, Carl, Yakima	3	6	.333	6.14	13	10	0	0	1	0	55.2	72	257	47	38	4	1	3	1	19	0	30	12	0
Stone, Ricky, Yakima	4	4	.500	5.25	16	6	0	0	7	2	48.0	54	213	31	28	5	2	2	2	20	0	28	4	1
Stoops, Jim, Bellingham	6	5	.545	3.43	24	0	0	0	14	4	42.0	32	178	23	16	1	2	1	5	17	0	58	2	0
Sumter, Kevin, Boise	0	1	.000	2.27	21	0	0	0	5	0	31.2	15	141	8	8	1	0	0	2	31	1	38	5	1
Szimanski, Tom, Everett	2	0	1.000	1.69	16	0	0	0	11	5	21.1	13	79	4	4	1	0	0	0	6	0	32	0	0
Takahashi, Kurt, Bellingham	1	2	.333	5.61	17	0	0	0	5	0	25.2	28	116	18	16	2	0	0	2	14	0	20	4	0
Tapia, Elias, Yakima	0	1	.000	5.40	13	1	0	0	3	0	23.1	23	111	20	14	3	1	1	2	13	0	15	8	0
Thomas, Robbie, Yakima*	0	1	.000	3.60	7	2	0	0	1	0	20.0	15	89	11	8	0	1	2	1	11	0	17	2	0
Thomasson, Shane, Everett	0	0	.000	9.00	2	0	0	0	2	0	2.0	5	10	2	2	1	0	0	0	0	0	1	2	0
Thurmond, Travis, Boise	9	3	.750	3.11	16	15	4	1	1	0	101.1	75	401	36	35	7	0	3	3	31	0	93	7	0
Trawick, Tim, Everett	6	2	.750	3.14	16	13	3	1	1	0	86.0	66	350	34	30	11	0	0	9	30	1	63	1	2
Tucker, Benjamin, Bellingham	2	1	.667	1.91	12	10	0	0	1	0	56.2	53	249	21	12	4	2	2	4	19	0	48	2	1
Upchurch, Wayne, Spokane	1	1	.500	6.39	7	0	0	0	5	0	12.2	22	64	12	9	2	2	0	0	5	1	7	2	0
Valdez, Ken, Boise	1	0	1.000	4.63	5	0	0	0	0	0	11.2	11	55	8	6	1	0	0	2	7	0	9	2	0
Vavrek, Mike, Portland*	0	0	.000	0.00	3	3	0	0	0	0	14.0	8	52	0	0	0	0	0	0	3	0	14	0	0
Vermillion, Grant, Boise	12	3	.800	1.96	30	0	0	0	15	6	59.2	49	244	19	13	2	2	1	5	16	4	50	2	1
Villarreal, Modesto, Spokane	8	2	.800	2.90	16	11	0	0	1	0	80.2	73	330	30	26	4	2	3	3	23	2	57	5	2
Vukson, John, Yakima	0	0	.000	16.71	11	0	0	0	5	0	7.0	9	57	20	13	1	0	4	3	26	0	6	6	0
Washburn, Jarrod, Boise*	3	2	.600	3.33	8	8	0	0	0	0	46.0	35	185	17	17	1	0	1	2	14	0	54	1	0
Williamson, Jeremy, Spokane*	3	1	.750	1.43	11	7	0	0	0	0	44.0	32	171	12	7	4	0	1	1	9	0	35	0	1
Winders, Brian, Spokane	0	1	.000	30.00	2	1	0	0	0	0	3.0	10	23	10	10	2	0	0	1	3	0	2	0	0
Woodrow, James, Bellingham	4	4	.500	3.65	27	0	0	0	14	3	44.1	35	192	18	18	3	2	3	2	25	2	34	3	1
Wuestenhoefer, Brady, Portland	1	9	.100	4.64	14	14	1	0	0	0	77.2	88	343	50	40	5	1	2	3	23	0	50	5	2
Zedalis, Craig, Eugene	0	0	.000	2.70	8	0	0	0	1	0	13.1	16	62	6	4	0	0	1	1	4	0	10	0	0

COMBINATION SHUTOUTS: **Bellingham (8)**—Barcelo-Knoll-Takahashi-Ortiz, Barcelo-Woodrow, Bermudez-Knoll-Ortiz, Blood-Woodrow, Brester-Bailey-Stoops, Brester-Bailey-Woodrow, Tucker-Abreu-Takahashi-Ortiz, Tucker-Ortiz. **Boise (4)**—Cooper-Sumter, Dafun-Sumter-O'Quinn-Mayer-Scutero, Deakman-Farfan-O'Quinn-Scutero, Thurmond-Vermillion. **Eugene (2)**—Gerland-McMullen-Butler, McKnight-Giard-Butler. **Everett (3)**—Kurtz-Marte-Gryboski-Scheer-Scheffer, Soden-Cooper-Clifford-Scheer, Trawick-Cooper-Scheer-Clifford. **Portland (4)**—Kammerer-Macca-Emiliano, Martin-Gonzalez, Randall-Macca-Dietrich, Randall-Rose-Dietrich. **Southern Oregon (3)**—Mlodik-Newman, Newman-Rivette-French, Silva-Abbott. **Spokane (4)**—Hodge-Albrecht, Hodge-Sanders, Villarreal-Adam, Villarreal-Adam-Kaysner. **Yakima (2)**—Babineaux-Chambers-Davis, Coyle-Foster.

NO-HIT GAMES: None.

1995 FIELDING

TEAM

Team	Pct.	G	PO	A	E	TC	DP	PB
Portland	.967	75	1987	909	100	2996	68	27
Boise	.965	75	1961	808	99	2868	66	7
Everett	.963	76	2040	874	112	3026	63	22
Spokane	.962	76	2042	920	117	3079	73	25
Bellingham	.958	76	2056	860	129	3045	55	21
Southern Oregon	.954	76	2008	915	140	3063	54	22
Yakima	.954	76	2003	878	139	3020	63	21
Eugene	.946	76	2001	844	161	3006	54	23

TRIPLE PLAYS: None.

INDIVIDUAL

FIRST BASEMEN

NOTE: All caps denotes fielding-percentage leader based on 38 games for catchers, 51 for all other non-pitchers and 76 innings for pitchers. *Throws lefthanded.

Player, Team	Pct.	G	PO	A	E	TC	DP
Amado, Jose, Everett	1.000	3	17	3	0	20	0
Buxbaum, Danny, Boise	.985	56	497	20	8	525	40
Calderon, Ricardo, Bellingham*	1.000	1	5	0	0	5	0
Castillo, Alberto, Bellingham*	.978	74	650	54	16	720	46
Dalton, Jed, Boise	.750	1	3	0	1	4	0
Dantzler, Eric, Bellingham	.917	3	10	1	1	12	1
DaSilva, Manny, S. Oregon	1.000	12	91	15	0	106	6
Daugherty, Keith, Eugene	.941	2	14	2	1	17	2
DRIZOS, Justin, Portland*	.992	71	668	45	6	719	57
Felix, Pedro, Bellingham	1.000	4	19	0	0	19	2
Filchner, Duane, S. Oregon*	.950	3	17	2	1	20	1
Hacker, Steve, Eugene	.966	12	81	5	3	89	8
Hallmark, Patrick, Spokane	1.000	2	18	2	0	20	4
Harmon, Brian, Yakima	.958	4	22	1	1	24	6
Klostermeyer, Mike, S. Oregon*	.989	57	474	45	6	525	28
Malave, Joshua, Yakima	.981	14	94	8	2	104	7
McAninch, John, Boise	.986	11	65	4	1	70	9
Moreno, Victor, Spokane	1.000	3	14	2	0	16	1
Paulin, Randy, Spokane	.986	14	129	15	2	146	18
Person, Wilton, Eugene	.980	50	423	27	9	459	27
Pinoni, Scott, Spokane	.979	4	46	1	1	48	0
Pomierski, Joe, Everett	.985	58	486	42	8	536	38
Rasmussen, Nate, Yakima*	.975	40	292	16	8	316	15
Rondon, Alex, S. Oregon	.900	2	8	1	1	10	1
Slemmer, David, S. Oregon	1.000	2	11	3	0	14	2
Spiegel, Rich, Eugene	1.000	1	2	1	0	3	0
Tinoco, Luis, Everett	1.000	4	8	0	0	8	1
Tocco, Todd, Eugene	.987	29	145	12	2	159	8
Tucker, Jonathan, Yakima*	.979	38	302	26	7	335	22
Twist, Jeffrey, Portland	.986	8	62	6	1	69	4
Valenti, Jon, Southern Oregon	.977	16	117	11	3	131	11
Vandergriend, Jon, Boise	.993	16	131	11	1	143	14
Vickers, Randy, Everett	.990	13	94	8	1	103	10
Vida, James, Spokane*	.987	57	545	42	8	595	46
Wathan, Dusty, Everett	.973	7	68	3	2	73	4

SECOND BASEMEN

Player, Team	Pct.	G	PO	A	E	TC	DP
Amado, Jose, Everett	.875	4	6	8	2	16	2
Backowski, Lance, Yakima	.947	16	26	46	4	76	11
Betten, Randy, Boise	.833	2	1	4	1	6	0
Carpentier, Mike, Yakima	.959	11	25	45	3	73	7
Cruz, Deivi, Bellingham	1.000	6	8	11	0	19	0
Davalillo, David, Boise	.950	24	33	62	5	100	18
Durrington, Trent, Boise	.979	37	52	90	3	145	19
Elam, Brett, Portland	.952	4	3	17	1	21	3
Ellison, Skeeter, Eugene	1.000	4	3	4	0	7	0
Griffin, Chad, Everett	.911	20	20	31	5	56	4
Groseclose, Harold, Portland	1.000	4	7	16	0	23	4

Player, Team	Pct.	G	PO	A	E	TC	DP
Harris, Robert, S. Oregon	.936	39	47	99	10	156	14
Hines, Pooh, Eugene	.954	29	42	61	5	108	10
Hodges, Randy, Eugene	.957	46	88	111	9	208	22
Lewis, Dwayne, Spokane	.892	13	27	39	8	74	6
Mayber, Chan, Portland	.966	17	32	52	3	87	15
Moschetti, Mike, So. Oregon	.931	29	45	89	10	144	12
Mota, Alfonso, Boise	1.000	9	7	11	0	18	0
Nations, Joel, Spokane	.971	37	67	103	5	175	23
Pena, Elvis, Portland	.954	52	92	137	11	240	24
Prospero, Teodoro, Bellingham	.944	36	65	88	9	162	16
RAMIREZ, Joel, Everett	.9591	67	142	163	13	318	36
Schafer, Brett, Spokane	.945	28	63	74	8	145	21
Slemmer, David, S. Oregon	.964	13	19	35	2	56	8
Sosa, Juan, Yakima	.9586	51	85	147	10	242	23
Taylor, Matthew, Eugene	1.000	6	10	16	0	26	3
Vallone, Gar, Boise	.987	21	29	46	1	76	14
Vickers, Randy, Everett	.500	3	1	0	1	2	0
Watson, Jonathan, Bellingham	.968	44	92	122	7	221	24
Whitley, Bill, Portland	1.000	4	9	15	0	24	4

THIRD BASEMEN

Player, Team	Pct.	G	PO	A	E	TC	DP
Amado, Jose, Everett	.919	44	44	104	13	161	14
Backowski, Lance, Yakima	.913	16	5	37	4	46	2
CRUZ, Deivi, Bellingham	.941	54	47	113	10	170	12
Dalton, Jed, Boise	.667	2	0	2	1	3	0
DaSilva, Manny, S. Oregon	.833	4	2	8	2	12	1
Davalillo, David, Boise	1.000	10	7	16	0	23	1
Elam, Brett, Portland	.914	14	9	23	3	35	3
Escandon, Emiliano, Spokane	.667	2	2	2	2	6	0
Felix, Pedro, Bellingham	.960	25	11	37	2	50	4
Griffin, Chad, Everett	1.000	4	1	6	0	7	1
Gross, Rafael, Yakima	.926	40	28	97	10	135	5
Harris, Robert, S. Oregon	.929	15	7	32	3	42	1
Hines, Pooh, Eugene	1.000	1	0	3	0	3	0
Hodges, Randy, Eugene	.800	10	6	10	4	20	1
Kane, Ryan, Boise	.917	69	42	135	16	193	19
Malave, Joshua, Yakima	.854	23	10	31	7	48	2
Mayber, Chan, Portland	.962	9	6	19	1	26	0
Myers, Aaron, Portland	.914	51	28	89	11	128	8
Pomierski, Joe, Everett	1.000	1	0	2	0	2	0
Quinn, Mark, Spokane	.837	13	8	33	8	49	3
Reynolds, Paul, Portland	.893	16	9	16	3	28	0
Roland, William, Spokane	.932	58	30	149	13	192	14
Rust, Brian, Eugene	.841	51	26	80	20	126	9
Sasser, Rob, Eugene	.833	4	3	7	2	12	0
Schafer, Brett, Spokane	.882	6	3	12	2	17	1
Slemmer, David, S. Oregon	.927	51	37	116	12	165	7
Sosa, Juan, Yakima	.810	7	3	14	4	21	1
Thomasson, Shane, Everett	.625	5	0	5	3	8	0
Tocco, Todd, Eugene	.846	28	14	52	12	78	3
Valenti, Jon, Southern Oregon	.942	16	11	38	3	52	1
Vickers, Randy, Everett	.874	32	20	70	13	103	6
Watson, Jonathan, Bellingham	.727	7	0	8	3	11	0

SHORTSTOPS

Player, Team	Pct.	G	PO	A	E	TC	DP
Baughman, Justin, Boise	.915	57	68	157	21	246	36
Carpentier, Mike, Yakima	.929	41	53	117	13	183	21
Cuevas, Trent, Yakima	.917	35	46	98	13	157	17
Durrington, Trent, Boise	.904	12	18	29	5	52	3
Elam, Brett, Portland	.909	15	14	56	7	77	11
Escandon, Emiliano, Spokane	.965	10	21	34	2	57	6
Groseclose, Harold, Portland	1.000	1	2	4	0	6	1
Harris, Robert, S. Oregon	.800	4	2	10	3	15	2
Hines, Pooh, Eugene	.881	12	23	29	7	59	4
Lewis, Dwayne, Spokane	.907	9	10	39	5	54	8
Mayber, Chan, Portland	.875	1	3	4	1	8	1
MELITO, Mark, Spokane	.967	61	100	189	10	299	36
Nathan, Joe, Bellingham	.897	54	76	150	26	252	23
Ramirez, Joel, Everett	.917	9	5	17	2	24	1
Rust, Brian, Eugene	1.000	2	0	1	0	1	0
Sasser, Rob, Eugene	.890	54	71	164	29	264	21
Sheffer, Chad, Everett	.948	53	81	139	12	232	19
Slemmer, David, S. Oregon	1.000	4	3	9	0	12	1
Sosa, Juan, Yakima	.900	3	5	13	2	20	2
Taylor, Matthew, Eugene	.952	4	10	10	1	21	4
Tejada, Miguel, S. Oregon	.930	72	129	214	26	369	39
Thomasson, Shane, Everett	.936	28	40	62	7	109	6
Vallone, Gar, Boise	.974	14	16	21	1	38	1
Weaver, Terry, Bellingham	.907	24	31	57	9	97	8
Whitley, Bill, Portland	.942	58	83	210	18	311	40
Williams, Glenn, Eugene	.905	9	15	23	4	42	5

OUTFIELDERS

Player, Team	Pct.	G	PO	A	E	TC	DP
BILDERBACK, Ty, Boise*	1.000	58	73	2	0	75	0
Bray, Notorris, Bellingham	1.000	1	3	0	0	3	0
Brown, Roosevelt, Eugene	.857	44	45	3	8	56	0
Bryan, Leonardo, Boise	.909	36	34	6	4	44	0
Brzozoski, Marc, Portland	.971	52	63	4	2	69	0
Burrows, Mike, Everett*	.992	67	127	4	1	132	1
Calderon, Ricardo, Bellingham*	.942	52	92	6	6	104	0
Choi, Kyung, Boise*	.920	20	22	1	2	25	0
Christenson, Ryan, S. Oregon	.978	48	84	3	2	89	1
Corujo, Rey, Bellingham	.946	35	49	4	3	56	0
Cruz, Jose, Everett	1.000	3	7	0	0	7	0
Dalton, Jed, Boise	.970	33	30	2	1	33	0
Davanon, Jeff, S. Oregon	.864	40	47	4	8	59	0
DeLeon, Reymundo, Eugene	.878	46	62	3	9	74	0
Ellison, Skeeter, Eugene	1.000	7	8	0	0	8	0
Feuerstein, David, Portland	.974	64	104	8	3	115	3
Filchner, Duane, S. Oregon*	.988	56	81	4	1	86	2
Finnieston, Adam, Spokane	.947	9	15	3	1	19	1
Frazier, Tyrone, Spokane	.963	50	73	4	3	80	1
Gibbs, Kevin, Yakima	.973	36	71	1	2	74	0
Granzow, Judd, Yakima	.944	36	47	4	3	54	3
Gross, Rafael, Yakima	1.000	1	1	0	0	1	0
Hallead, John, Portland*	.955	38	80	4	4	88	1
Ham, Kevin, Boise	.966	59	77	9	3	89	1
Hearns, Shane, Everett	.895	22	13	4	2	19	0
Hernaiz, Juan, Yakima	.914	39	52	1	5	58	0
Hilo, Johnny, Yakima	.974	40	72	3	2	77	0
Hodges, Randy, Eugene	.667	5	2	0	1	3	0
Hutchins, Norm, Boise*	.979	45	92	3	2	97	0
Jimenez, Elvis, Portland	.971	27	32	2	1	35	0
Keifer, Greg, Bellingham	.833	6	9	1	2	12	0
Klostermeyer, Mike, S. Oregon*	1.000	1	1	0	0	1	0
Knight, Bill, Southern Oregon	.926	45	60	3	5	68	0
Kortmeyer, Scott, Spokane	.941	21	30	2	2	34	0
Lewis, Dwayne, Spokane	.971	22	33	0	1	34	0
Lombard, George, Eugene	.962	65	71	5	3	79	2
McClain, Terrance, Yakima	.923	21	30	6	3	39	1
Miranda, Tony, Spokane	.980	60	94	3	2	99	0
Morales, Julio, Bellingham	.953	64	138	5	7	150	1
Moreno, Victor, Spokane	1.000	5	6	1	0	7	0
Morimoto, Ken, Yakima	.982	48	107	3	2	112	0
Neubart, Garrett, Portland	1.000	23	39	2	0	41	1
Newhan, David, S. Oregon	.964	39	50	4	2	56	0
Owen, Andy, Yakima*	.978	34	39	5	1	45	0
Person, Wilton, Eugene	1.000	10	9	0	0	9	0
Quinn, Mark, Spokane	.963	19	24	2	1	27	0
Rand, Ian, Bellingham	.962	22	25	0	1	26	0
Reynolds, Paul, Portland	.957	25	18	4	1	23	1
Sachse, Matthew, Everett*	.978	50	85	3	2	90	1
Saturnino, Sherton, Eugene	.778	6	7	0	2	9	0
Schafer, Brett, Spokane	.968	29	59	1	2	62	1
Shy, Jason, Eugene	.955	12	21	0	1	22	0
Simonton, Cy Leon, Everett*	.971	45	61	6	2	69	0
Thompson, Bruce, Bellingham	.952	64	96	3	5	104	0
Tinoco, Luis, Everett	.937	58	67	7	5	79	2
Trippy, Joe, Eugene*	.970	74	126	5	4	135	0
Valenti, Jon, Southern Oregon	1.000	2	1	0	0	1	0
Vandergriend, Jon, Boise	1.000	19	30	3	0	33	0
Vickers, Randy, Everett	1.000	10	9	2	0	11	0
Weathersby, Leon, Spokane	.961	34	45	4	2	51	0
Welch, Brandon, S. Oregon	.912	26	30	1	3	34	0

CATCHERS

Player, Team	Pct.	G	PO	A	E	TC	DP	PB
Alzualde, Daniel, Boise	.988	21	146	18	2	166	1	2
Ardoin, Danny, S. Oregon	.971	57	402	61	14	477	0	13
Arias, Rogelio, Portland	.990	13	92	11	1	104	1	8
Barthol, Blake, Portland	.986	47	333	26	5	364	2	12
DaSilva, Manny, S. Oregon	.964	16	99	9	4	112	1	6
Foote, Derek, Eugene	1.000	1	1	0	0	1	0	0
Graves, Bryan, Boise	.969	27	117	8	4	129	1	3
Hallmark, Patrick, Spokane	.970	51	334	51	12	397	2	20
Lunar, Fernando, Eugene	.977	37	298	41	8	347	2	7
Mahoney, Mike, Eugene	.981	41	265	38	6	309	3	13
Malave, Joshua, Yakima	1.000	3	1	0	0	1	0	0
Markert, Jason, Yakima	.994	30	156	15	1	172	2	1
McAninch, John, Boise	.993	20	117	20	1	138	0	1
Medrano, Teodoro, Everett	1.000	1	8	2	0	10	0	0
Meskauskas, John, Portland	1.000	7	57	6	0	63	0	2
Meyer, Travis, Yakima	.982	32	147	19	3	169	1	12
Norton, Andy, Bellingham	.970	24	136	23	5	164	1	5
Paulin, Randy, Spokane	.973	24	172	10	5	187	2	4

Player, Team	Pct.	G	PO	A	E	TC	DP	PB
Robles, Juan, Spokane	1.000	4	27	3	0	30	0	1
Rondon, Alex, S. Oregon	.938	10	54	7	4	65	0	3
Shy, Jason, Eugene	.933	9	40	2	3	45	0	2
Spiegel, Rich, Eugene	1.000	4	24	3	0	27	2	1
Thompson, Karl, Everett	.997	37	275	28	1	304	2	10
TOPPING, Dan, Bellingham	.988	47	291	46	4	341	2	10
Torrealba, Yolvit, Bellingham	.973	26	152	26	5	183	1	6
Twist, Jeffrey, Portland	.961	14	91	8	4	103	0	5
Wagner, Kyle, Boise	.996	36	221	27	1	249	1	1
Walkanoff, A.J., Yakima	.986	36	241	31	4	276	6	8
Wathan, Dusty, Everett	.984	41	307	53	6	366	4	12

PITCHERS

Player, Team	Pct.	G	PO	A	E	TC	DP
Abbott, Todd, S. Oregon	1.000	17	2	7	0	9	1
Abreu, Jose, Bellingham	.667	13	0	2	1	3	1
Adam, Justin, Spokane	.706	15	8	4	5	17	1
Agosto, Stevenson, Boise*	.857	13	2	10	2	14	0
Albrecht, Jon, Spokane*	1.000	17	5	2	0	7	0
Ali, Sam, Bellingham	1.000	5	0	3	0	3	0
Alvarez, Juan, Boise*	1.000	9	1	1	0	2	0
Avila, Edwin, Boise	1.000	14	0	2	0	2	0
Babineaux, Darrin, Yakima	.941	12	8	8	1	17	0
BAILEY, Philip, Bellingham*	1.000	19	2	21	0	23	2
Barcelo, Lorenzo, Bellingham	1.000	12	2	6	0	8	0
Batchelder, Bill, S. Oregon	1.000	18	9	5	0	14	0
Bermudez, Manuel, Bellingham	.947	14	7	11	1	19	0
Bevel, Bobby, Portland*	1.000	25	1	7	0	8	0
Blasingim, Joseph, Bellingham	1.000	13	3	4	0	7	0
Blood, Darin, Bellingham	.955	14	7	14	1	22	1
Blythe, Billy, Eugene	1.000	14	9	11	0	20	1
Bost, Allen, Portland	1.000	10	2	2	0	4	0
Brester, Jason, Bellingham*	1.000	8	1	5	0	6	0
Brizek, Seth, Everett	1.000	8	1	1	0	2	0
Brooks, Antone, Eugene*	.857	15	0	6	1	7	2
Brown, Darold, Eugene*	.900	3	1	8	1	10	0
Butler, Adam, Eugene*	1.000	23	1	1	0	2	0
Cervantes, Peter, Yakima	.800	13	10	6	4	20	1
Chambers, Scott, Yakima*	1.000	20	1	1	0	2	0
Charles, Israel, Spokane	1.000	4	1	1	0	2	0
Chrismon, Thad, Eugene	1.000	32	3	5	0	8	1
Clifford, Eric, Everett	1.000	28	3	9	0	12	1
Coe, Keith, Boise	.917	13	1	10	1	12	2
Connelly, Steven, S. Oregon	.889	17	4	4	1	9	0
Conway, Robert, Everett	.667	6	1	1	1	3	0
Cooper, Brian, Boise	.867	13	3	10	2	15	0
Cooper, David, Everett	.750	17	2	4	2	8	0
Coyle, Bryan, Yakima	.750	6	0	3	1	4	0
Cruz, Charlie, Eugene*	.962	15	6	19	1	26	0
Dafun, George, Boise	.842	16	6	10	3	19	0
D'Alessandro, Marc, Portland*	.971	16	11	23	1	35	1
Davis, Eddie, Yakima	1.000	20	3	8	0	11	0
Deakman, Josh, Boise	1.000	3	1	5	0	6	0
Dietrich, Jason, Portland	1.000	10	0	2	0	2	0
Emiliano, James, Portland	.889	28	4	4	1	9	0
Epstein, Ian, S. Oregon*	1.000	23	2	5	0	7	0
Farfan, David, Boise	1.000	14	1	4	0	5	0
Fontenot, Joe, Bellingham	.800	6	2	2	1	5	0
Foster, Kris, Yakima	.667	15	2	6	4	12	0
French, Jon, Southern Oregon	1.000	20	6	2	0	8	0
Garcia, Jose, Eugene	1.000	14	6	13	0	19	1
Gerland, Greg, Eugene*	1.000	19	2	8	0	10	1
Giard, Ken, Eugene	.857	25	1	5	1	7	0
Gonzalez, Laril, Portland	.929	15	2	11	1	14	0
Gryboski, Kevin, Everett	1.000	25	4	6	0	10	2
Gunther, Kevin, S. Oregon	1.000	5	2	2	0	4	0
Hilton, Willy, Southern Oregon	.667	16	6	0	3	9	0
Hodge, Hal, Spokane*	.929	16	1	12	1	14	0
Holden, Jason, S. Oregon	.950	19	5	14	1	20	0
Hutzler, Jeff, Bellingham	1.000	7	4	6	0	10	2
Iddon, Brent, Everett	1.000	14	6	7	0	13	1
Judice, Bryan, Spokane	1.000	14	3	2	0	5	0
Kammerer, James, Portland*	1.000	11	2	11	0	13	1
Kaysner, Brent, Spokane	1.000	19	1	5	0	6	0
Keehn, Drew, Portland	.692	20	3	6	4	13	1
Keppen, Jeffrey, Yakima	.500	20	0	3	3	6	0
Kjos, Ryan, Southern Oregon	1.000	9	0	1	0	1	0
Knoll, Brian, Bellingham	.889	22	2	6	1	9	0
Kurtz, Danny, Everett	1.000	14	6	7	0	13	0
Leibee, Skye, Southern Oregon*	1.000	2	0	1	0	1	0
Lintern, Cory, Bellingham	1.000	3	4	4	0	8	0
Liz, Jesus, Spokane*	.500	9	0	1	1	2	0
Macca, Christopher, Portland	1.000	24	3	6	0	9	0
Marte, Damaso, Everett*	.714	11	3	7	4	14	1
Martin, Chandler, Portland	1.000	7	2	8	0	10	1
Masaoka, Onan, Yakima*	.750	15	1	5	2	8	0
Mayer, Aaron, Boise	.900	20	3	6	1	10	0
Mayhew, Keith, Eugene	1.000	24	1	9	0	10	1
Mazzone, Tony, Eugene	.875	25	3	4	1	8	1
McDonald, Matt, S. Oregon*	1.000	13	6	10	0	16	2
McKnight, Chris, Eugene*	.929	13	3	10	1	14	2
McMullen, Jerry, Eugene*	1.000	22	1	9	0	10	0
McNeely, Mitch, Yakima*	.889	24	4	12	2	18	0
McWilliams, Matt, Eugene	.923	24	3	9	1	13	1
Medero, Gadiel, Bellingham	.000	4	0	0	1	1	0
Mimnaugh, Scott, S. Oregon	.667	3	0	2	1	3	0
Mitchell, Kelvin, Everett*	.818	25	1	8	2	11	0
Mlodik, Kevin, S. Oregon	.813	20	8	5	3	16	1
Morrison, Chris, S. Oregon	1.000	6	4	3	0	7	0
Mosman, Marc, Bellingham	.750	12	3	0	1	4	0
Murphy, Sean, Portland	.938	21	7	8	1	16	2
Nelson, Chris, S. Oregon	.769	16	6	4	3	13	1
Newman, Damon, S. Oregon	.895	14	6	11	2	19	0
Nied, David, Portland	1.000	1	0	1	0	1	0
Niemeier, Todd, Everett*	1.000	15	2	14	0	16	0
O'Quinn, James, Boise*	.750	23	0	3	1	4	0
Ortiz, Russell, Bellingham	1.000	25	3	6	0	9	1
Pearsall, J.J., Yakima*	.846	20	5	6	2	13	0
Petri, Tom, Boise	1.000	10	1	3	0	4	0
Prihoda, Stephen, Spokane*	1.000	14	2	12	0	14	0
Randall, Scott, Portland	.912	15	11	20	3	34	1
Reitzenstein, Brad, Portland	1.000	7	0	3	0	3	0
Ritter, Jason, Spokane	1.000	10	3	5	0	8	1
Rivette, Scott, S. Oregon	1.000	9	1	3	0	4	0
Robbins, Mike, Spokane*	1.000	5	2	4	0	6	0
Rocker, John, Eugene*	.900	12	3	6	1	10	0
Rolish, Chad, S. Oregon*	.750	4	0	3	1	4	0
Romine, Jason, Portland	1.000	4	0	1	0	1	0
Rose, Brian, Portland	1.000	5	0	2	0	2	0
Ruskey, Jason, Everett*	1.000	3	1	1	0	2	0
Saier, Matthew, Spokane	1.000	16	3	2	0	5	0
Sanchez, Mike, Yakima	1.000	18	0	6	0	6	1
Sanders, Allen, Spokane	.909	14	2	8	1	11	0
Sanders, Craig, Spokane	1.000	22	3	7	0	10	0
Santiago, Jose, Spokane	.750	22	3	6	3	12	1
Scheer, Greg, Everett*	1.000	18	3	8	0	11	0
Scheffer, Aaron, Everett	.818	24	0	9	2	11	1
Scutero, Brian, Boise	.900	22	4	5	1	10	0
Silva, Luis, Southern Oregon	1.000	19	8	9	0	17	0
Soden, Chad, Everett*	1.000	13	4	8	0	12	1
Sosa, Helpis, S. Oregon	1.000	6	4	1	0	5	0
Soto, Daniel, Spokane	1.000	3	0	2	0	2	1
Soto, Seferino, Yakima	1.000	15	3	4	0	7	0
South, Carl, Yakima	.889	13	3	13	2	18	1
Stone, Ricky, Yakima	.778	16	3	4	2	9	1
Stoops, Jim, Bellingham	1.000	24	2	5	0	7	0
Sumter, Kevin, Boise	1.000	21	0	3	0	3	0
Szimanski, Tom, Everett	1.000	16	3	3	0	6	0
Takahashi, Kurt, Bellingham	1.000	17	2	2	0	4	0
Tapia, Elias, Yakima	.833	13	0	5	1	6	0
Thomas, Robbie, Yakima*	1.000	7	0	3	0	3	0
Thurmond, Travis, Boise	.952	16	7	13	1	21	0
Trawick, Tim, Everett	1.000	16	8	9	0	17	3
Tucker, Benjamin, Bellingham	1.000	11	2	4	0	6	1
Upchurch, Wayne, Spokane	1.000	7	1	1	0	2	0
Valdez, Ken, Boise	1.000	5	1	0	0	1	0
Vavrek, Mike, Portland*	.750	3	0	3	1	4	0
Vermillion, Grant, Boise	.857	30	2	10	2	14	0
Villarreal, Modesto, Spokane	.963	16	6	20	1	27	2
Vukson, John, Yakima	.500	11	0	1	1	2	0
Washburn, Jarrod, Boise*	1.000	8	0	6	0	6	0
Williamson, Jeremy, Spokane*	1.000	11	3	5	0	8	0
Winders, Brian, Spokane	1.000	2	0	1	0	1	0
Woodrow, James, Bellingham	.900	27	5	4	1	10	0
Wuestenhoefer, Brady, Portland	.909	14	3	7	1	11	0
Zedalis, Craig, Eugene	1.000	8	3	3	0	6	0

The following players did not have any fielding statistics at the positions indicated or appeared only as a designated hitter, pinch-hitter or pinch-runner: Backowski, of; Benner, dh; R. Brown, 2b; Bryan, c; Collett, p; Costello, p; Crossley, p; Davalillo, of; DeLaCruz, p; Ellison, 1b; Gomez, p; Griffin, ss; Hearns, 3b; Herrera, p; Koehler, p; Lombard, c; Mayber, p; Meyer, of; Morimoto, ss; Mota, 3b, ss; Myers, 2b; Person, 3b, ss; Renko, p; J. Rodriguez, dh, ph; L. Rodriguez, p; Schiefelbein, p; Sheffer, 3b; Thomasson, 2b, of, p; Vallone, 3b; Vandergriend, c.

LEAGUE CHAMPIONS

Year	Team	Pct.
1901—	Portland	.675
1902—	Butte	.608
1903—	Butte	.578
1904—	Boise	.625
1905—	Vancouver	.586
	Everett*	.667
1906—	Tacoma	.600
1907—	Aberdeen	.625
1908—	Vancouver	.578
1909—	Seattle	.653
1910—	Spokane	.596
1911—	Vancouver	.628
1912—	Seattle	.600
1913—	Vancouver	.600
1914—	Vancouver	.632
1915—	Seattle	.564
1916—	Spokane	.622
1917—	Great Falls	.592
1918—	Seattle	.588
1919—	Seattle	.590
1920—	Victoria	.600
1921—	Yakima	.710
	Yakima	.660
1922—	Calgary‡	.600
1923-36—	Did not operate.	
1937—	Wenatchee	.603
	Tacoma*	.627
1938—	Yakima	.583
	Bellingham (2nd)†	.511
1939—	Wenatchee	.601
	Tacoma (2nd)†	.533
1940—	Spokane	.587
	Tacoma (4th)†	.500
1941—	Spokane	.669
1942—	Vancouver	.594
1943-45—	Did not operate.	
1946—	Wenatchee	.622
1947—	Vancouver	.566
1948—	Spokane	.614
1949—	Yakima	.660
	Vancouver (2nd)†	.615
1950—	Yakima	.613
1951—	Spokane	.655
1952—	Victoria	.631
1953—	Salem	.635
	Spokane*	.590
1954—	Vancouver*	.636
	Lewiston	.629
1955—	Salem	.646
	Eugene*	.639
1956—	Yakima	.691
	Yakima	.619
1957—	Eugene	.576
	Wenatchee*	.647
1958—	Lewiston	.621
	Yakima*	.594
1959—	Salem	.623
	Yakima*	.563
1960—	Yakima	.638
	Yakima	.562
1961—	Lewiston*	.621
	Yakima	.600
1962—	Wenatchee*	.574
	Tri-City	.580
1963—	Lewiston	.594
	Yakima*	.613
1964—	Eugene	.636
	Yakima*	.611
1965—	Lewiston	.667
	Tri-City*	.681
1966—	Tri-City	.679
1967—	Medford	.607
1968—	Tri-City	.600
1969—	Rogue Valley	.633
1970—	Lewiston§	.538
	Coos Bay-No. Bend	.563
1971—	Tri-City§	.625
	Bend	.538
1972—	Lewiston§	.675
	Walla Walla	.513
1973—	Walla Walla∞	.638
	Portland	.563
1974—	Bellingham	.619
	Eugene▲	.571
1975—	Portland	.545
	Eugene◆	.684
1976—	Portland	.556
	Walla Walla◆	.639
1977—	Bellingham■	.618
	Portland	.667
1978—	Grays Harbor▼	.671
	Eugene	.514
1979—	Central Oregon◆	.606
	Walla Walla	.571
1980—	Bellingham•	.643
	Eugene•	.529
1981—	Medford◆	.600
	Bellingham	.557
1982—	Medford	.757
	Salem◆	.486
1983—	Medford††	.735
	Bellingham	.588
1984—	Tri-Cities††	.622
	Medford	.608
1985—	Everett††	.541
	Eugene	.541
1986—	Bellingham††	.608
	Eugene	.608
1987—	Spokane▲	.711
	Everett	.653
1988—	Southern Oregon	.605
	Spokane◆	.553
1989—	Southern Oregon	.600
	Spokane◆	.547
1990—	Boise	.697
	Spokane◆	.645
1991—	Boise◆	.658
	Yakima	.579
1992—	Bellingham◆	.566
	Bend	.566
1993—	Bellingham	.579
	Boise◆	.539
1994—	Yakima	.645
	Boise◆	.579
1995—	Boise◆	.640
	Bellingham	.566

*Won split-season playoff. †Won four-club playoff. ‡League disbanded June 18. §League divided into Northern and Southern divisions, declared champion under league rules. ∞League divided into Eastern and Western divisions, declared champion under league rules. ▲League divided into Eastern and Western divisions; won two-team playoff. ◆League divided into North and South divisions; won two-team playoff. ■League divided into Affiliate and Independent divisions; won two-team playoff. ▼Declared league champion after winning one-game playoff. Balance of playoff canceled due to rain and wet grounds. •Declared co-champion after winning one game. Balance of playoff canceled due to rain and wet grounds. ††League divided into Washington and Oregon divisions; won two-team playoff. (NOTE—Known as Pacific Northwest League 1901-02, Pacific National League 1903-04, Northwestern League 1905-18, Pacific Coast International League 1919-22 and Western International League 1937-54.)

SOUTH ATLANTIC LEAGUE

LEAGUE OFFICE

President/secretary-treasurer
John Moss

Address
P.O. Box 38
Kings Mountain, NC 28086

Phone
704-739-3466

Teams (affiliation)
Asheville Tourists (Rockies)
Augusta Greenjackets (Pirates)
Capital City Bombers (Mets)
Charleston (S.C.) Riverdogs (Rangers)
Charleston (W.Va.) Alley Cats (Reds)
Columbus Redstixx (Indians)
Delmarva Shorebirds (Expos)
Fayetteville Generals (Tigers)
Greensboro Bats (Yankees)
Hagerstown Suns (Blue Jays)
Hickory Crawdads (White Sox)
Macon Braves (Braves)
Piedmont Bollweevils (Phillies)
Savannah Cardinals (Cardinals)

1995 FINAL STANDINGS

FIRST HALF

NORTHERN DIVISION

Team	W	L	T	Pct.	GB
Piedmont (Phillies)	45	25	0	.643	....
Fayetteville (Tigers)	42	27	0	.618	2
Hagerstown (Blue Jays)	36	33	0	.522	8½
Greensboro (Yankees)	35	34	0	.507	9½
Charleston (W.Va.) (Reds)	34	36	0	.486	11
Asheville (Rockies)	32	36	0	.471	12
Hickory (White Sox)	21	47	0	.309	23

SOUTHERN DIVISION

Team	W	L	T	Pct.	GB
Augusta (Pirates)	43	25	0	.627	....
Columbia (Mets)	38	32	0	.543	5½
Columbus (Indians)	37	33	0	.522	7
Macon (Braves)	35	34	0	.507	8
Savannah (Cardinals)	32	37	0	.464	11
Albany (Expos)	31	39	0	.443	12½
Charleston (SC) (Rangers)	24	47	0	.343	19½

SECOND HALF

NORTHERN DIVISION

Team	W	L	T	Pct.	GB
Asheville (Rockies)	44	27	0	.620	....
Fayetteville (Tigers)	44	28	0	.611	½
Charleston (W.Va.) (Reds)	43	29	0	.597	1½
Piedmont (Phillies)	37	33	0	.529	6½
Hagerstown (Blue Jays)	37	35	0	.514	7½
Greensboro (Yankees)	35	36	0	.493	9
Hickory (White Sox)	28	42	0	.400	15½

SOUTHERN DIVISION

Team	W	L	T	Pct.	GB
Columbus (Indians)	43	29	0	.597	....
Macon (Braves)	36	36	0	.500	7
Columbia (Mets)	34	36	0	.486	8
Augusta (Pirates)	33	37	0	.471	9
Albany (Expos)	31	39	0	.443	11
Charleston (SC) (Rangers)	26	42	0	.382	15
Savannah (Cardinals)	24	46	0	.343	18

COMPOSITE

Team	Fay.	Pie.	C'us	Aug.	Ash.	CWV	Hag.	C'ia	Mac.	Gbr.	Alb.	Sav.	CSC	Hck.	W	L	T	Pct.	GB
Fayetteville (Tigers)	....	7	7	2	9	11	10	5	3	10	6	5	4	7	86	55	0	.610	....
Piedmont (Phillies)	7	....	3	4	8	9	8	5	4	8	5	7	2	12	82	58	0	.586	3½
Columbus (Indians)	1	5	....	8	3	4	3	8	6	4	13	9	11	5	80	62	0	.563	6½
Augusta (Pirates)	6	4	6	....	3	3	3	8	12	6	5	7	8	5	76	62	0	.551	8½
Asheville (Rockies)	5	5	5	5	....	6	10	5	2	9	5	4	5	10	76	63	0	.547	9
Charleston (W.Va.) (Reds)	3	5	4	5	8	....	9	3	6	3	6	7	7	11	77	65	0	.542	9½
Hagerstown (Blue Jays)	4	6	5	4	4	7	....	6	5	10	4	6	4	8	73	68	0	.518	13
Columbia (Mets)	3	5	6	6	3	5	2	....	6	5	6	8	15	2	72	68	0	.514	13½
Macon (Braves)	5	4	8	4	6	2	3	8	....	6	8	2	9	6	71	70	0	.504	15
Greensboro (Yankees)	6	6	4	2	4	11	4	2	2	....	6	7	4	12	70	70	0	.500	15½
Albany (Expos)	2	3	3	9	3	2	4	7	6	2	....	10	7	4	62	78	0	.443	23½
Savannah (Cardinals)	3	1	5	6	4	1	2	6	11	1	4	....	9	3	56	83	0	.403	29
Charleston (SC) (Rangers)	4	1	3	4	3	1	4	3	5	4	7	7	....	4	50	89	0	.360	35
Hickory (White Sox)	6	6	3	3	5	3	6	2	2	2	3	4	4	....	49	89	0	.355	35½

Major league affiliations in parentheses.

PLAYOFFS: Augusta defeated Columbus, two games to none; Piedmont defeated Asheville, two games to one; Augusta defeated Piedmont, three games to none, to win league championship.

REGULAR-SEASON ATTENDANCE: Albany, 91,289; Asheville, 138,148; Augusta, 171,166; Charleston (S.C.), 101,280; Charleston (W.Va.), 106,530; Columbia, 152,207; Columbus, 128,816; Fayetteville, 121,051; Greensboro, 170,444; Hagerstown, 113,438; Hickory, 265,017; Macon, 113,825; Piedmont, 115,649; Savannah, 113,849. Total—1,902,709. Playoffs (8 games)—15,267. All-Star Game at Albany—4,102.

MANAGERS: Albany, Doug Sisson; Asheville, Bill McGuire; Augusta, Jeff Banister; Charleston (S.C.), Mike Berger; Charleston (W.Va.), Razor Shines; Columbia, Howie Freiling; Columbus, Jeff Datz; Fayetteville, Dwight Lowry; Greensboro, Trey Hillman; Hagerstown, Omar Malave; Hickory, Mike Rojas; Macon, Nelson Norman; Piedmont, Roy Majtyka; Savannah, Scott Melvin.

ALL-STAR TEAM: 1B—Daryle Ward, Fayetteville; 2B—Julio Zorrilla, Columbia; 3B—Wes Helms, Macon; SS—Hiram Bocachica, Albany; Utility IF—Dan Donato, Greensboro; OF—Derrick Gibson, Asheville; Vladimir Guerrero, Albany; Andruw Jones, Macon; Utility OF—Gus Kennedy, Macon; C—Julio Mosquera, Hagerstown; DH—Jeff Ladd, Hagerstown; RHP—Brent Crowther, Asheville; LHP—Larry Wimberly, Piedmont; Most Valuable Player—Andruw Jones, Macon; Most Outstanding Pitcher—Larry Wimberly, Piedmont; Most Outstanding Major League Prospect—Andruw Jones, Macon; Manager of the Year—Roy Majtyka, Piedmont.

1995 BATTING

TEAM

Team	Avg.	G	TPA	AB	R	H	TB	2B	3B	HR	RBI	SH	SF	HP	BB	IBB	SO	SB	CS	GDP	LOB	ShO	Slg.	OBP
Augusta	.256	138	5070	4531	628	1158	1579	203	37	48	539	33	32	60	411	23	940	215	108	74	871	11	.348	.324
Hagerstown	.255	141	5293	4678	638	1191	1788	244	34	95	557	29	34	90	461	15	1173	100	56	95	1014	7	.382	.331
Columbus	.254	142	5343	4748	630	1207	1797	221	45	93	551	31	32	50	480	24	918	134	65	102	1016	5	.378	.327
Albany	.254	140	5415	4757	633	1206	1743	251	44	66	550	23	39	84	510	24	1099	136	105	75	1026	7	.366	.334

Team	Avg.	G	TPA	AB	R	H	TB	2B	3B	HR	RBI	SH	SF	HP	BB	IBB	SO	SB	CS	GDP	LOB	ShO	Slg.	OBP
Fayetteville	.252	141	5270	4633	660	1169	1718	234	30	85	585	37	38	73	489	15	1025	158	79	84	955	6	.371	.331
Piedmont	.249	140	5307	4595	683	1146	1601	213	46	50	573	54	49	89	519	23	938	123	75	106	996	9	.348	.334
Greensboro	.249	140	5284	4632	645	1154	1687	223	26	86	557	49	28	49	525	30	1077	127	80	108	972	11	.364	.330
Charleston (W.Va.)	.249	142	5208	4551	633	1133	1588	206	57	45	549	44	41	56	513	17	1002	230	101	82	961	12	.349	.330
Macon	.245	141	5579	4876	739	1197	1871	231	31	127	651	24	34	73	571	26	1225	172	54	79	1030	7	.384	.331
Asheville	.243	139	5067	4477	578	1086	1587	210	24	81	488	45	37	65	438	19	928	130	82	78	876	9	.354	.317
Columbia	.241	140	5156	4619	571	1111	1581	183	34	73	481	54	36	57	387	27	1118	187	85	86	889	12	.342	.305
Charleston (S.C.)	.234	139	5147	4509	546	1054	1452	220	20	46	450	39	45	40	514	14	939	218	135	64	932	9	.322	.315
Hickory	.227	138	5061	4538	459	1030	1457	198	29	57	387	28	27	71	397	14	1047	118	101	92	883	13	.321	.298
Savannah	.215	139	5214	4534	448	977	1321	138	28	50	362	46	29	60	544	18	1243	124	71	102	1036	16	.291	.306

INDIVIDUAL

TOP QUALIFIERS FOR BATTING CHAMPIONSHIP

Minimum 383 plate appearances. *Lefthanded batter. †Switch-hitter.

Player, Team	Avg.	G	TPA	AB	R	H	TB	2B	3B	HR	RBI	SH	SF	HP	BB	IBB	SO	SB	CS	GDP	Slg.	OBP
Guerrero, Vladimir, Albany	.333	110	464	421	77	140	229	21	10	16	63	0	4	7	30	3	45	12	7	8	.544	.383
Fullmer, Brad, Albany*	.323	123	527	468	69	151	221	38	4	8	67	0	6	17	36	4	33	10	10	9	.472	.387
Donato, Dan, Greensboro*	.318	108	431	387	55	123	176	30	1	7	69	0	3	4	37	5	46	7	6	12	.455	.381
White, Eric, Columbus	.317	112	423	369	49	117	165	24	3	6	46	1	1	1	51	5	45	11	7	12	.447	.400
Ladd, Jeff, Hagerstown	.305	94	401	311	54	95	175	17	3	19	58	0	3	9	78	5	94	6	3	2	.563	.454
Tatis, Fernando, Cha. (S.C.)†	.303	131	556	499	74	151	247	43	4	15	84	1	4	7	45	4	94	22	19	5	.495	.366
Hall, Ronnie, Asheville	.299	130	518	448	64	134	174	20	4	4	46	1	4	17	44	4	78	26	13	7	.388	.380
Millan, Adam, Piedmont	.294	107	449	394	69	116	175	25	2	10	64	1	3	7	44	3	45	1	4	15	.444	.373
Rivers, Jonathon, Hagerstown	.294	123	480	429	54	126	172	16	6	6	48	1	4	6	40	0	104	18	5	9	.401	.359
Gibson, Derrick, Asheville	.292	135	561	506	91	148	280	16	10	32	115	1	6	19	29	5	136	31	13	10	.553	.350
Staton, T.J., Augusta*	.292	112	421	391	43	114	160	21	5	5	53	0	1	2	27	5	97	27	13	6	.409	.340
Northeimer, Jamie, Piedmont	.291	115	471	392	56	114	149	24	4	1	54	4	2	20	53	1	72	9	4	13	.380	.400
Mosquera, Julio, Hagerstown	.291	108	456	406	64	118	159	22	5	3	46	3	5	13	29	2	53	5	5	13	.392	.353
Cardenas, Epi, Columbus	.290	125	556	513	69	149	206	28	4	7	56	6	5	2	30	0	64	11	7	4	.402	.329
Darr, Mike, Fayetteville*	.289	112	463	395	58	114	154	21	2	5	66	0	6	4	58	2	88	5	2	5	.390	.380
Glass, Chip, Columbus*	.289	115	449	402	70	116	158	17	5	5	45	5	0	5	37	1	47	37	8	4	.393	.356

DEPARTMENTAL LEADERS: G—A. Jones, Morrow, 139; AB—Helms, 539; R—A. Jones, 104; H—Fulmer, Tatis, 151; TB—Gibson, 280; 2B—Tatis, 43; 3B—Guiliano, 12; HR—Gibson, R. Wright, 32; RBI—Gibson, 115; SH—Lobaton, 11; SF—A. Jones, 9; HP—Northeimer, 20; BB—Kennedy, 95; IBB—Ward, 11; SO—Schwab, 173; SB—A. Jones, 56; CS—Rutz, 26; GIDP—Friedrich, 16; Slg.—Ladd, .563; OBP—Ladd, .454.

ALL PLAYERS

*Lefthanded batter. †Switch-hitter.

Player, Team	Avg.	G	TPA	AB	R	H	TB	2B	3B	HR	RBI	SH	SF	HP	BB	IBB	SO	SB	CS	GDP	Slg.	OBP
Abell, Tony, Savannah	.122	17	55	49	1	6	7	1	0	0	2	1	0	1	4	0	18	1	1	0	.143	.204
Acosta, Ed, Albany	.152	51	122	105	9	16	17	1	0	0	9	2	2	5	8	0	30	1	3	2	.162	.242
Adolfo, Carlos, Albany	.243	57	234	214	31	52	87	13	5	4	33	1	0	2	17	0	65	5	6	4	.407	.305
Afenir, Tom, Columbus	.077	5	13	13	1	1	1	0	0	0	0	0	0	0	0	0	5	0	0	0	.077	.077
Aguila, Hector, Cha. (S.C.)	.152	13	39	33	4	5	6	1	0	0	3	1	0	0	5	0	13	0	1	2	.182	.263
Albert, Rashad, Hickory	.213	88	366	328	34	70	105	16	2	5	20	4	1	14	19	1	108	22	12	4	.320	.285
Alderman, Kurt, Albany*	.248	55	173	161	21	40	56	8	1	2	17	0	0	1	11	0	40	2	1	1	.348	.301
Allen, Marlon, Cha. (W.Va.)	.270	117	457	396	47	107	160	26	0	9	76	0	6	13	42	3	108	2	2	10	.404	.354
Almanzar, Richard, Fayetteville	.247	80	353	308	47	76	90	12	1	0	16	9	0	7	29	0	32	39	15	5	.292	.326
Almond, Greg, Savannah	.161	18	65	56	2	9	11	2	0	0	3	0	0	1	8	0	16	0	1	0	.196	.277
Amador, Manny, Piedmont†	.000	1	5	4	0	0	0	0	0	0	0	0	0	1	0	0	0	0	1	0	.000	.200
Ambrosina, Pete, Savannah†	.239	129	550	464	55	111	128	10	2	1	36	4	2	11	69	3	100	20	12	6	.276	.350
Antczak, Chuck, Hickory	.200	6	5	5	0	1	1	0	0	0	1	0	0	0	0	0	2	0	0	0	.200	.200
Arias, Rogelio, Asheville	.160	67	227	213	9	34	38	4	0	0	4	6	0	1	7	0	25	0	3	2	.178	.190
Arvelo, Tom, Columbia†	.125	8	19	16	4	2	2	0	0	0	0	0	0	0	3	0	7	2	0	0	.125	.263
Asche, Mike, Augusta	.266	106	423	376	62	100	147	17	6	6	59	3	3	5	35	1	60	21	5	6	.391	.334
Ashby, Chris, Greensboro	.274	88	359	288	45	79	131	23	1	9	45	2	2	6	61	2	68	3	3	9	.455	.409
Balfe, Ryan, Fayetteville†	.261	113	456	398	53	104	158	20	2	10	49	0	1	9	48	0	85	1	1	11	.397	.353
Balint, Rob, Fayetteville	.242	13	34	33	4	8	13	2	0	1	4	0	0	0	1	0	15	0	0	0	.394	.265
Barkett, Andy, Cha. (S.C.)*	.218	21	91	78	7	17	23	6	0	0	12	0	3	0	10	0	27	0	3	3	.295	.297
Bass, Jayson, Fayetteville*	.215	108	410	368	47	79	136	15	6	10	48	1	1	3	37	1	111	14	3	3	.370	.291
Bearden, Doug, Hickory	.156	44	149	141	9	22	35	5	1	2	12	2	0	1	5	1	44	1	1	6	.248	.190
Beeney, Ryan, Greensboro	.278	57	265	227	32	63	69	6	0	0	21	2	3	4	29	0	48	9	8	3	.304	.365
Bocachica, Hiram, Albany	.284	96	444	380	65	108	154	20	10	2	30	3	1	8	52	3	78	47	17	4	.405	.381
Boka, Ben, Columbia	.083	8	14	12	1	1	1	0	0	0	1	0	1	0	1	0	4	0	0	1	.083	.143
Borel, Jamie, Fayetteville	.244	86	325	279	60	68	83	9	3	0	20	1	2	2	41	0	43	36	14	2	.297	.343
Bowen, Glenn, Savannah	.231	16	52	52	1	12	15	3	0	0	2	0	0	0	0	0	17	0	1	0	.288	.231
Bragga, Matt, Cha. (W.Va.)*	.248	88	293	258	35	64	85	11	5	0	26	0	3	4	28	2	62	6	5	2	.329	.328
Branyan, Russell, Columbus†	.256	76	310	277	46	71	148	8	6	19	55	0	3	3	27	2	120	1	1	6	.534	.326
Brewer, Brett, Macon	.241	128	530	452	78	109	174	25	8	8	60	3	5	10	60	0	113	15	5	6	.385	.340
Brinkley, Josh, Albany	.174	22	75	69	8	12	18	3	0	1	5	0	0	3	3	0	11	2	2	1	.261	.240
Brooks, Eddie, Augusta	.273	67	272	238	40	65	94	13	5	2	37	2	3	1	28	0	61	3	5	2	.395	.348
Brown, Adrian, Augusta†	.300	76	326	287	64	86	121	15	4	4	31	3	2	1	33	0	23	25	14	2	.422	.372
Brown, Nate, Albany*	.254	117	441	397	34	101	142	23	3	4	49	4	3	5	32	1	112	4	8	6	.358	.316
Brown, Ray, Cha. (W.Va.)*	.118	6	21	17	3	2	3	1	0	0	0	0	0	0	4	0	3	0	0	0	.176	.286
Brown, Vick, Greensboro	.227	118	491	432	66	98	116	10	1	2	36	8	1	6	44	0	93	24	9	11	.269	.306
Brunson, Matt, Fayetteville†	.222	43	168	144	18	32	44	3	3	1	8	1	0	1	22	0	34	16	6	1	.306	.329
Buchanan, Brian, Greensboro	.302	23	106	96	19	29	41	3	0	3	12	0	0	1	9	1	17	7	1	1	.427	.368
Camilli, Jason, Albany	.188	53	224	181	28	34	48	5	0	3	16	0	2	3	38	0	50	13	10	0	.265	.335
Cancel, David, Hickory†	.288	76	254	240	24	69	82	3	2	2	13	2	1	0	11	0	37	11	10	3	.342	.317
Cardenas, Epi, Columbus	.290	125	556	513	69	149	206	28	4	7	56	6	5	2	30	0	64	11	7	4	.402	.329
Cardona, Javier, Fayetteville	.206	51	179	165	18	34	51	8	0	3	19	0	0	1	13	0	30	1	0	5	.309	.268
Carpenter, Matt, Ash.-C'bus	.143	11	30	28	2	4	9	2	0	1	6	0	0	1	1	0	4	0	0	0	.321	.200

Player, Team	Avg.	G	TPA	AB	R	H	TB	2B	3B	HR	RBI	SH	SF	HP	BB	IBB	SO	SB	CS	GDP	Slg.	OBP
Carranza, Pete, Asheville	.254	111	488	433	67	110	161	32	2	5	29	2	5	3	45	2	49	10	9	4	.372	.325
Caruthers, Clayton, Cha. (W.Va.)†	.000	29	0	0	1	0	0	0	0	0	0	0	0	0	0	0	0	0	0	0	.000	.000
Carvajal, Jhonny, Cha. (W.Va.)	.263	135	558	486	78	128	156	18	5	0	42	4	4	6	58	0	77	44	19	4	.321	.347
Chambers, Mack, Columbus	.000	2	5	4	0	0	0	0	0	0	0	0	0	0	1	0	1	0	1	0	.000	.200
Chapman, Eric, Columbus	.241	54	220	199	27	48	63	9	3	0	8	2	0	0	19	1	42	23	6	4	.317	.307
Coach, Calvin, Savannah*	.197	65	241	218	15	43	47	2	1	0	10	2	0	1	20	1	58	8	4	3	.216	.268
Collum, Gary, Columbia	.250	9	28	24	2	6	8	0	1	0	7	0	2	0	2	0	7	2	0	0	.333	.286
Colombino, Carlo, Columbus	.000	1	2	2	0	0	0	0	0	0	0	0	0	0	0	0	1	0	0	0	.000	.000
Comeaux, Edward, Cha. (S.C.)	.210	90	290	243	38	51	60	7	1	0	19	3	3	2	39	0	58	10	7	3	.247	.321
Conner, Decomba, Cha. (W.Va.)	.263	91	360	308	55	81	120	10	7	5	40	4	6	3	39	1	77	22	5	6	.390	.346
Cooney, James, Cha. (S.C.)	.087	18	49	46	2	4	7	0	0	1	2	0	0	0	3	0	14	1	0	1	.152	.143
Cooper, Steve, Savannah	.250	48	180	156	13	39	46	7	0	0	12	0	1	1	22	0	51	2	0	4	.295	.344
Coquillette, Trace, Albany	.269	128	541	458	67	123	167	27	4	3	57	4	6	9	64	2	91	17	16	8	.365	.365
Cossins, Tim, Cha. (S.C.)	.203	22	69	59	8	12	20	5	0	1	8	0	0	1	9	0	13	2	0	2	.339	.319
Darr, Mike, Fayetteville*	.289	112	463	395	58	114	154	21	2	5	66	0	6	4	58	2	88	5	2	5	.390	.380
Dawson, Charles, Macon	.246	42	142	122	19	30	45	6	0	3	13	0	2	0	18	0	27	1	0	3	.369	.338
DeBerry, Joe, Greensboro*	.400	12	54	45	14	18	36	3	0	5	11	0	0	0	9	3	6	0	0	1	.800	.500
Delafield, Wil, Greensboro	.208	107	407	384	37	80	106	14	0	4	29	5	1	1	16	0	107	3	7	12	.276	.241
Delgado, Jose, Macon†	.237	45	186	169	19	40	60	5	3	3	16	4	2	0	11	0	28	3	4	2	.355	.280
Diaz, Linardo, Piedmont	.083	9	12	12	0	1	2	1	0	0	0	0	0	0	0	0	2	0	0	0	.167	.083
Dishington, Nate, Savannah*	.214	124	529	444	56	95	155	17	5	11	44	0	6	17	62	4	154	13	7	14	.349	.329
Donato, Dan, Greensboro*	.318	108	431	387	55	123	176	30	1	7	69	0	3	4	37	5	46	7	6	12	.455	.381
Drent, Brian, Hickory	.188	24	80	69	8	13	23	5	1	1	5	0	1	4	6	0	28	0	4	0	.333	.288
Dukart, Derek, Greensboro*	.256	86	341	305	35	78	121	21	2	6	40	2	4	2	28	4	59	2	3	11	.397	.319
Eaglin, Mike, Macon	.266	129	607	530	82	141	170	15	4	2	30	5	1	7	64	0	94	41	13	8	.321	.352
Ealy, Tracey, Savannah†	.243	101	419	370	38	90	131	18	1	7	35	3	3	2	41	3	103	8	5	10	.354	.320
Eddie, Steve, Cha. (W.Va.)	.275	115	371	331	45	91	131	16	3	6	47	3	6	7	24	0	46	10	3	9	.396	.332
Edwards, Aaron, Augusta	.263	47	174	160	29	42	50	4	2	0	9	1	1	1	11	0	39	10	4	2	.313	.312
Elam, Brett, Asheville	.000	1	2	2	0	0	0	0	0	0	0	0	0	0	0	0	1	0	0	0	.000	.000
Encarnacion, Juan, Fayetteville	.282	124	498	457	62	129	222	31	7	16	72	1	2	8	30	0	113	5	6	10	.486	.336
Estrada, Josue, Albany	.213	70	264	235	27	50	69	11	1	2	17	3	0	2	24	3	70	2	3	7	.294	.291
Falciglia, Tony, Savannah	.169	23	82	71	4	12	14	2	0	0	5	0	1	1	9	0	17	1	1	1	.197	.268
Fantauzzi, John, Asheville*	.213	107	387	329	38	70	114	20	0	8	44	1	2	3	51	2	79	1	1	6	.347	.322
Ferrier, Ross, Columbia	.186	23	79	70	6	13	20	1	0	2	5	0	0	1	8	0	20	5	0	4	.286	.278
Figueroa, Danny, Asheville	.233	80	267	227	34	53	86	22	1	3	22	7	3	6	24	0	73	3	7	2	.379	.319
Fithian, Grant, Greensboro	.225	51	177	151	16	34	50	8	1	2	12	3	3	1	19	0	45	5	4	5	.331	.310
Flores, Jose, Piedmont	.263	61	222	186	22	49	56	7	0	0	19	5	4	3	24	0	29	11	8	6	.301	.350
Friedrich, Steve, Hickory	.252	136	559	532	56	134	188	24	6	6	50	2	4	5	16	0	107	19	16	16	.353	.278
Fullmer, Brad, Albany*	.323	123	527	468	69	151	221	38	4	8	67	0	6	17	36	4	33	10	10	9	.472	.387
Fussell, Denny, Cha. (W.Va.)*	.250	20	49	44	4	11	13	2	0	0	7	0	1	0	4	1	10	1	0	0	.295	.306
Gainey, Bryon, Columbia*	.243	124	489	448	49	109	181	20	5	14	64	0	2	9	30	1	157	1	3	7	.404	.303
Gambill, Chad, Asheville	.256	106	392	367	34	94	145	25	1	8	57	3	4	2	16	2	92	6	4	9	.395	.288
Gann, Steve, Cha. (W.Va.)	.208	15	55	48	3	10	11	1	0	0	4	0	1	0	6	0	7	1	1	1	.229	.291
Garcia, Neil, Fayetteville†	.231	88	326	251	46	58	93	12	1	7	33	2	4	10	59	0	49	3	6	5	.371	.392
Gatti, Dom, Cha. (S.C.)	.230	96	399	335	50	77	93	8	4	0	32	3	4	4	53	0	38	39	15	5	.278	.338
Giardi, Mike, Greensboro	.168	46	120	101	10	17	24	4	0	1	5	0	1	3	15	0	17	3	4	2	.238	.292
Gibson, Derrick, Asheville	.292	135	561	506	91	148	280	16	10	32	115	1	6	19	29	5	136	31	13	10	.553	.350
Gipner, Marcus, Greensboro†	.150	7	22	20	0	3	4	1	0	0	2	0	1	0	1	0	6	0	0	2	.200	.182
Glass, Chip, Columbus*	.289	115	449	402	70	116	158	17	5	5	45	5	0	5	37	1	47	37	8	4	.393	.356
Goldberg, Lonnie, Cha. (S.C.)	.218	100	375	340	29	74	94	12	1	2	31	2	4	1	26	1	54	17	11	3	.276	.272
Gomez, Paul, Columbia	.204	68	221	181	19	37	61	10	1	4	20	1	2	4	33	0	65	0	3	4	.337	.336
Gomez, Ramon, Hickory	.229	76	254	231	26	53	59	6	0	0	9	3	0	2	18	0	64	17	9	5	.255	.291
Gonzalez, Jhonny, Asheville*	.000	21	1	1	0	0	0	0	0	0	0	0	0	0	0	0	0	0	0	0	.000	.000
Gonzalez, Mario, Cha. (S.C.)†	.207	11	33	29	3	6	7	1	0	0	1	0	1	0	3	0	4	2	1	0	.241	.273
Gonzalez, Wikleman, Augusta	.241	84	313	278	41	67	93	17	0	3	36	2	5	2	26	0	32	5	4	7	.335	.305
Green, Bert, Savannah	.228	132	497	429	48	98	120	7	6	1	25	9	1	3	55	0	101	26	9	6	.280	.320
Guerrero, Rafael, Columbia	.277	116	448	415	47	115	160	18	3	7	56	2	6	0	25	1	63	13	8	15	.386	.314
Guerrero, Vladimir, Albany	.333	110	464	421	77	140	229	21	10	16	63	0	4	7	30	3	45	12	7	8	.544	.383
Guiliano, Matt, Piedmont	.226	129	524	451	67	102	160	22	12	4	59	9	6	7	51	1	114	6	8	7	.355	.311
Guillen, Jose, Augusta	.235	10	38	34	6	8	17	1	1	2	6	0	0	2	2	0	9	0	0	0	.500	.316
Haas, Matt, Albany*	.235	52	190	166	18	39	46	7	0	0	15	3	1	2	18	1	30	1	5	1	.277	.316
Hall, Ronnie, Asheville	.299	130	518	448	64	134	174	20	4	4	46	1	4	17	44	4	78	26	13	7	.388	.380
Hammell, Al, Columbia	.000	3	9	6	0	0	0	0	0	0	0	1	0	0	2	0	4	0	0	0	.000	.250
Hampton, Mike, Cha. (W.Va.)	.245	96	364	302	46	74	99	16	3	1	32	2	1	6	53	1	70	17	4	6	.328	.367
Harper, Rantie, Savannah	.208	91	359	318	34	66	91	12	2	3	31	2	3	2	34	0	114	13	3	6	.286	.286
Harris, G.G., Augusta	.245	100	395	368	38	90	119	23	0	2	46	2	4	4	17	1	50	2	6	9	.323	.282
Harriss, Robin, Columbus	.223	51	196	179	18	40	52	6	0	2	18	3	0	3	11	0	30	0	3	8	.291	.280
Hayes, Darren, Hickory	.245	58	220	196	18	48	73	12	2	3	19	1	1	6	16	1	53	7	2	6	.372	.320
Heller, Bradley, Cha. (S.C.)	.224	76	242	214	27	48	73	13	0	4	15	6	1	0	21	0	37	3	1	4	.341	.292
Helms, Wes, Macon	.276	136	602	539	89	149	216	32	1	11	85	0	3	10	50	0	107	2	2	8	.401	.347
Helton, Todd, Asheville*	.254	54	227	201	24	51	67	11	1	1	15	0	0	1	25	1	32	1	1	7	.333	.339
Henley, Bob, Albany	.281	102	432	335	45	94	125	20	1	3	46	1	2	11	83	3	57	1	2	11	.373	.436
Herider, Jeremy, Cha. (W.Va.)†	.133	8	17	15	2	2	2	0	0	0	0	0	0	0	2	0	6	0	0	0	.133	.235
Holley, Jack, Hagerstown	.203	23	84	79	6	16	20	4	0	0	7	1	0	1	3	0	18	0	2	4	.253	.241
Hooker, Kevin, Piedmont	.174	16	59	46	4	8	10	2	0	0	6	0	1	3	9	0	13	1	0	0	.217	.339
Houser, Kyle, Asheville	.211	112	404	361	43	76	93	11	0	2	32	6	2	1	34	0	43	5	4	7	.258	.279
Huff, Larry, Piedmont	.272	130	576	481	86	131	168	26	4	1	51	7	4	10	74	5	64	26	8	9	.349	.378
Hunter, Scott, Columbia	.250	12	45	40	2	10	10	0	0	0	1	1	1	1	2	0	13	2	1	2	.250	.295
Izquierdo, Sergio, Hickory	.146	45	135	123	6	18	20	2	0	0	4	3	1	0	8	0	20	0	0	4	.163	.197
Jarrett, Linc, Asheville†	.235	116	480	404	46	95	106	11	0	0	20	10	2	2	62	1	60	12	10	5	.262	.338
Jenkins, Dee, Cha. (W.Va.)*	.244	31	102	86	14	21	24	1	1	0	5	1	0	0	15	0	19	5	0	2	.279	.356
Johnson, Jeff, Hickory	.229	53	188	170	15	39	54	9	0	2	14	3	1	1	13	1	40	2	2	2	.318	.286
Johnson, Mark, Hickory*	.182	107	385	319	31	58	73	9	0	2	17	2	2	3	59	1	52	3	5	4	.229	.313

Player, Team	Avg.	G	TPA	AB	R	H	TB	2B	3B	HR	RBI	SH	SF	HP	BB	IBB	SO	SB	CS	GDP	Slg.	OBP
Jones, Andruw, Macon	.277	139	632	537	104	149	275	41	5	25	100	0	9	16	70	7	122	56	11	9	.512	.372
Jones, Pookie, Asheville	.349	16	65	63	16	22	32	6	2	0	8	0	0	0	2	0	14	3	0	1	.508	.369
Kelley, Erskine, Augusta	.218	105	380	349	47	76	111	13	5	4	32	1	1	7	22	2	86	24	7	10	.318	.277
Kennedy, Gus, Macon	.253	128	539	439	83	111	222	29	5	24	76	0	3	2	95	10	151	20	6	7	.506	.386
Key, Jeff, Piedmont*	.258	111	426	384	55	99	159	18	6	10	54	2	5	9	26	4	100	5	7	6	.414	.316
Koerick, Thomas, Hickory	.185	73	223	200	15	37	55	10	1	2	20	0	1	7	15	0	85	2	2	2	.275	.265
Lackey, Steve, Columbia	.191	67	199	178	21	34	45	8	0	1	21	5	3	2	11	1	42	9	2	2	.253	.242
Ladd, Jeff, Hagerstown	.305	94	401	311	54	95	175	17	3	19	58	0	3	9	78	5	94	6	3	2	.563	.454
Landry, Dan, Macon	.226	13	63	53	4	12	13	1	0	0	6	0	1	3	6	0	16	2	0	0	.245	.333
Lantigua, Eduardo, Columbus	.241	23	94	87	13	21	29	5	0	1	10	0	1	2	4	1	20	2	1	2	.333	.287
Larkin, Stephen, Cha. (S.C.)*	.255	113	432	369	50	94	130	19	1	5	45	3	5	1	54	2	80	18	10	7	.352	.347
Ledee, Ricky, Greensboro*	.269	89	390	335	65	90	160	16	6	14	49	0	1	2	51	6	66	10	4	3	.478	.368
Lee, Carlos, Hickory	.248	63	227	218	18	54	77	9	1	4	30	0	0	1	8	2	34	1	5	7	.353	.278
Leon, Geraldo, Savannah	.165	41	145	133	15	22	28	4	1	0	11	1	0	1	10	1	46	0	1	6	.211	.229
Lewis, Andreaus, Columbus†	.261	76	287	245	35	64	88	8	5	2	23	1	2	3	36	2	86	18	7	3	.359	.360
Lewis, Rob, Columbus	.152	20	77	66	6	10	17	1	0	2	8	0	1	1	9	0	18	0	1	3	.258	.260
Lidle, Kevin, Fayetteville	.142	36	135	113	15	16	34	4	1	4	13	3	2	1	16	0	44	0	1	1	.301	.250
Light, Tal, Asheville	.270	23	84	63	13	17	33	4	0	4	13	0	3	0	18	0	17	0	0	0	.524	.417
Llanos, Aurelio, Hagerstown	.251	106	421	378	54	95	173	25	1	17	63	0	3	11	29	2	115	9	7	5	.458	.321
Lobaton, Jose, Greensboro	.243	60	222	185	26	45	61	6	5	0	23	11	2	2	22	0	58	11	6	3	.330	.327
Lofton, James, Cha. (W.Va.)	.208	65	215	192	20	40	52	10	1	0	14	2	0	3	18	1	43	8	5	2	.271	.286
Lombard, George, Macon*	.206	49	214	180	32	37	54	6	1	3	16	1	0	5	27	3	44	16	4	4	.300	.325
Long, Terrence, Columbia*	.197	55	208	178	27	35	46	1	2	2	13	1	0	1	28	4	43	8	5	3	.258	.309
Lopez, Jose, Columbia	.232	82	328	280	37	65	105	17	4	5	38	2	7	4	35	3	76	7	2	7	.375	.319
Lopez, Victor, Cha. (S.C.)	.289	12	43	38	4	11	14	3	0	0	2	0	0	1	4	0	3	3	0	1	.368	.372
Luciano, Virgilio, Cha. (S.C.)*	.218	104	321	285	30	62	84	14	1	2	31	3	4	3	26	2	76	18	9	2	.295	.286
Lunar, Fernando, Macon	.179	39	150	134	13	24	26	2	0	0	9	3	0	3	10	0	38	1	0	3	.194	.252
Martinez, Dalvis, Fayetteville	.255	36	119	102	17	26	42	7	0	3	15	1	0	0	16	0	35	1	0	0	.412	.356
Matos, Julius, Columbus	.245	52	170	155	16	38	51	7	3	0	13	1	0	3	11	1	21	2	2	8	.329	.308
Matos, Pasqual, Macon	.185	72	250	238	23	44	72	11	1	5	26	0	0	1	11	0	86	2	2	4	.303	.224
Mayber, Chan, Asheville	.193	34	96	88	11	17	21	4	0	0	3	1	0	0	7	0	19	7	0	1	.239	.253
McClure, Craig, Hickory	.169	49	172	154	13	26	37	3	1	2	8	1	0	0	17	0	56	6	2	4	.240	.251
McDougal, Mike, Savannah	.080	15	52	50	2	4	4	0	0	0	4	0	0	0	2	0	17	1	1	1	.080	.115
McLamb, Brian, Greensboro†	.226	81	285	252	34	57	86	11	0	6	32	2	0	6	25	2	61	11	4	9	.341	.311
McMillan, Tom, Savannah	.214	85	304	262	21	56	87	8	1	7	21	3	2	2	35	2	91	5	4	3	.332	.309
McNally, Shawn, Savannah	.219	49	197	169	21	37	52	8	2	1	14	2	1	1	24	0	48	8	2	2	.308	.318
Mendoza, Jesus, Hickory	.251	116	485	434	49	109	161	24	2	8	49	2	4	9	36	3	53	2	7	11	.371	.319
Mercedes, Guillermo, Columbus†	.191	55	205	183	23	35	48	5	1	2	8	1	0	3	18	0	19	6	3	5	.262	.275
Meskauskas, John, Asheville	.278	30	86	79	11	22	35	4	0	3	13	0	2	1	4	0	16	0	1	4	.443	.314
Millan, Adam, Piedmont	.294	107	449	394	69	116	175	25	2	10	64	1	3	7	44	3	45	1	4	15	.444	.373
Millican, Kevin, Cha. (S.C.)	.215	88	306	270	27	58	90	17	0	5	28	1	2	2	31	1	81	2	4	3	.333	.298
Mobilia, Bill, Piedmont	.240	55	173	150	17	36	45	5	2	0	17	7	1	2	13	0	39	1	0	1	.300	.307
Monroe, Darryl, Fayetteville	.259	104	432	382	55	99	133	21	2	3	28	8	3	16	23	1	76	23	12	7	.348	.325
Morales, Eric, Columbia	.275	38	125	109	12	30	34	4	0	0	11	3	0	1	12	0	18	2	1	1	.312	.352
Morales, Francisco, Savannah	.147	19	81	75	3	11	20	3	0	2	4	0	1	1	4	0	23	0	2	2	.267	.198
Morgan, Dave, Hagerstown	.265	67	272	249	26	66	94	14	1	4	26	1	2	2	18	1	53	1	0	4	.378	.317
Morillo, Donald, Cha. (S.C.)	.000	19	1	1	0	0	0	0	0	0	0	0	0	0	0	0	0	0	0	1	.000	.000
Morrow, Nick, Cha. (W.Va.)	.251	139	549	467	67	117	188	28	8	9	54	2	1	2	77	2	123	41	17	5	.403	.358
Mosquera, Julio, Hagerstown	.291	108	456	406	64	118	159	22	5	3	46	3	5	13	29	2	53	5	5	13	.392	.353
Mota, Guillermo, Columbia	.243	123	443	400	45	97	139	24	3	4	45	6	1	4	32	1	127	8	3	5	.348	.304
Moyle, Mike, Columbus	.203	73	272	227	19	46	71	7	0	6	31	3	6	1	35	0	46	2	3	3	.313	.305
Mummau, Rob, Hagerstown	.257	107	431	366	63	94	132	17	3	5	42	6	3	14	42	1	74	6	1	7	.361	.353
Myers, Aaron, Asheville	.138	20	70	65	1	9	12	3	0	0	6	1	0	1	3	0	27	0	0	1	.185	.188
Navas, Jesus, Hickory†	.228	79	241	202	23	46	56	7	0	1	16	3	3	5	28	0	36	3	6	4	.277	.332
Newell, Brett, Macon	.256	76	322	285	39	73	84	9	1	0	29	5	1	7	24	0	72	5	1	5	.295	.328
Nitschke, Bear, Piedmont*	.000	2	4	4	0	0	0	0	0	0	0	0	0	0	0	0	3	0	0	0	.000	.000
Northeimer, Jamie, Piedmont	.291	115	471	392	56	114	149	24	4	1	54	4	2	20	53	1	72	9	4	13	.380	.400
Oakland, Mike, Asheville	.208	18	60	48	4	10	11	1	0	0	2	1	0	1	10	0	6	0	0	1	.229	.356
O'Brien, Joe, Piedmont	.217	60	217	189	27	41	50	4	1	1	31	1	2	6	19	0	38	2	5	6	.265	.306
Ocasio, Fred, Asheville	.308	14	42	39	3	12	12	0	0	0	2	0	0	0	3	0	7	0	2	0	.308	.357
Oram, Jon, Columbus	.217	64	220	198	20	43	61	6	3	2	19	1	4	4	13	1	40	2	5	9	.308	.274
Ordaz, Luis, Cha. (W.Va.)	.231	112	390	359	43	83	117	14	7	2	42	8	4	6	13	1	47	12	5	10	.326	.267
Ortman, Ben, Asheville	.158	14	43	38	7	6	10	1	0	1	4	0	1	0	4	0	9	1	1	0	.263	.233
Ozario, Yudith, Columbia	.217	123	504	456	59	99	121	12	2	2	33	9	2	3	34	3	113	40	15	8	.265	.275
Pearson, Cory, Cha. (S.C.)	.208	61	206	183	21	38	49	8	0	1	13	0	0	5	18	1	53	13	6	5	.268	.296
Pena, Elvis, Asheville†	.228	48	180	145	27	33	35	2	0	0	4	3	0	4	28	0	32	23	6	1	.241	.367
Perez, Joe, Cha. (S.C.)*	.272	67	266	243	24	66	93	14	2	3	29	0	2	3	18	2	55	10	3	2	.383	.327
Perez, Santiago, Fayetteville†	.238	130	470	425	54	101	130	15	1	4	44	7	7	1	30	0	98	10	9	6	.306	.285
Perry, Chan, Columbus	.285	113	472	411	64	117	182	30	4	9	50	2	4	2	53	1	49	7	2	6	.443	.366
Petillo, Bruce, Piedmont	.111	2	9	9	0	1	1	0	0	0	2	0	0	0	0	0	3	0	0	0	.111	.111
Pollock, Elton, Augusta	.234	26	105	94	8	22	29	5	1	0	10	2	2	0	7	0	23	8	3	5	.309	.282
Pond, Simon, Albany*	.213	23	86	80	4	17	22	5	0	0	7	0	0	2	4	0	25	1	0	3	.275	.267
Pozo, Yohel, Asheville	.216	40	145	139	7	30	36	3	0	1	15	1	1	0	4	0	32	0	3	7	.259	.236
Prensi, Dagoberto, Hagerstown	.208	104	387	361	40	75	115	18	5	4	33	1	1	5	18	0	106	10	6	10	.319	.255
Preston, Doyle, Cha. (W.Va.)*	.125	7	20	16	1	2	3	1	0	0	2	0	0	0	4	0	5	0	2	1	.188	.300
Prieto, Ricky, Columbus	.222	4	18	18	1	4	7	0	0	1	2	0	0	0	0	0	4	0	0	0	.389	.222
Pullen, Shane, Piedmont*	.251	118	479	435	65	109	164	26	4	7	57	2	5	3	34	3	70	4	2	12	.377	.306
Reilly, John, Hagerstown	.000	1	3	2	1	0	0	0	0	0	0	1	0	0	0	0	1	0	0	0	.000	.000
Resetar, Gary, Asheville*	.000	2	2	2	0	0	0	0	0	0	0	0	0	0	0	0	1	0	0	1	.000	.000
Reyes, Winston, Piedmont	.176	6	18	17	1	3	5	0	1	0	5	0	0	0	1	0	8	0	1	0	.294	.222
Reynolds, Chance, Augusta†	.215	24	81	65	8	14	19	2	0	1	6	0	0	4	12	1	11	0	2	1	.292	.370
Rice, Charles, Augusta†	.222	14	58	54	8	12	18	3	0	1	8	0	0	2	2	0	14	0	0	0	.333	.276
Rivera, Miguel, Savannah	.253	128	550	514	44	130	162	14	3	4	41	6	4	5	21	1	76	10	6	15	.315	.287

Player, Team	Avg.	G	TPA	AB	R	H	TB	2B	3B	HR	RBI	SH	SF	HP	BB	IBB	SO	SB	CS	GDP	Slg.	OBP
Rivers, Jonathon, Hagerstown	.294	123	480	429	54	126	172	16	6	6	48	1	4	6	40	0	104	18	5	9	.401	.359
Rives, Sherron, Fayetteville	.227	56	169	150	15	34	42	8	0	0	19	2	3	3	11	0	36	3	1	5	.280	.287
Robinson, Tony, Augusta	.229	96	348	297	34	68	83	9	0	2	37	1	1	11	38	1	60	21	11	4	.279	.337
Robles, Rafael, Savannah†	.197	56	185	142	15	28	32	2	1	0	7	3	0	1	39	2	43	2	4	2	.225	.374
Rodriguez, Adam, Fayetteville	.302	39	151	139	16	42	70	14	1	4	25	1	0	2	9	0	25	0	1	5	.504	.353
Rosado, Juan, Albany*	.182	5	11	11	0	2	3	1	0	0	3	0	0	0	0	0	4	1	0	0	.273	.182
Royster, Aaron, Piedmont	.264	126	539	489	73	129	182	23	3	8	58	0	4	7	39	1	106	22	9	16	.372	.325
Rutz, Ryan, Cha. (S.C.)	.220	133	557	491	60	108	133	20	1	1	22	7	2	2	55	0	88	36	26	6	.271	.300
Sanders, Anthony, Hagerstown	.232	133	583	512	72	119	173	28	1	8	48	9	5	5	52	0	103	26	14	8	.338	.307
Sanders, Rod, Cha. (W.Va.)	.204	81	168	152	22	31	45	7	2	1	11	3	0	1	12	0	45	4	8	3	.296	.267
Sanderson, David, Columbia*	.237	121	411	363	53	86	122	11	5	5	36	7	0	3	38	8	81	20	10	6	.336	.314
Santa, Roberto, Cha. (S.C.)*	.261	99	361	295	35	77	105	11	1	5	46	1	8	2	55	1	37	0	6	4	.356	.372
Saturnino, Sherton, Macon	.188	42	123	117	6	22	30	2	0	2	13	1	0	2	3	1	36	1	2	1	.256	.221
Schreimann, Eric, Piedmont	.174	7	25	23	1	4	5	1	0	0	1	0	1	0	1	1	4	0	0	0	.217	.200
Schwab, Chris, Albany	.227	122	537	484	60	110	153	22	3	5	43	0	4	1	48	1	173	4	6	4	.316	.296
Seguignol, Fernando, Albany†	.208	121	498	457	59	95	157	22	2	12	66	1	6	6	28	3	141	12	8	6	.344	.260
Segura, Juan, Augusta	.225	25	86	80	3	18	20	2	0	0	4	4	1	0	1	0	21	0	2	3	.250	.232
Sharp, Scott, Cha. (W.Va.)	.211	55	174	161	7	34	40	2	2	0	16	4	1	1	7	0	63	1	2	4	.248	.247
Shugars, Shawn, Cha. (S.C.)*	.227	8	24	22	2	5	6	1	0	0	3	0	0	1	1	0	3	0	2	0	.273	.292
Shumpert, Derek, Greensboro†	.216	56	180	153	21	33	38	3	1	0	14	7	0	2	18	0	41	4	2	2	.248	.306
Silvia, Brian, Savannah	.247	59	240	198	25	49	91	14	2	8	33	0	3	8	31	1	39	4	2	9	.460	.367
Simmons, Brian, Hickory†	.190	41	184	163	13	31	45	6	1	2	11	0	0	2	19	0	44	4	4	2	.276	.283
Smith, Jason, Asheville	.100	24	90	80	7	8	14	3	0	1	8	0	0	2	8	0	40	0	1	1	.175	.200
Smith, Rod, Greensboro†	.243	62	273	235	31	57	74	5	6	0	9	2	0	2	34	1	41	17	12	4	.315	.343
Staton, T.J., Augusta*	.292	112	421	391	43	114	160	21	5	5	53	0	1	2	27	5	97	27	13	6	.409	.340
Stingley, Derek, Piedmont	.179	39	96	84	20	15	20	2	0	1	5	1	1	4	6	0	24	13	2	2	.238	.263
Stone, Craig, Hagerstown	.276	96	402	355	47	98	150	20	4	8	52	0	5	8	34	0	104	3	2	6	.423	.348
Strange, Mike, Hagerstown	.234	96	357	290	51	68	84	9	2	1	27	2	0	4	61	0	92	13	3	7	.290	.375
Stumberger, Darren, Columbus	.270	127	520	448	62	121	181	27	0	11	57	0	5	9	56	2	72	3	3	13	.404	.359
Subero, Carlos, Augusta†	.186	31	102	97	8	18	20	2	0	0	6	3	0	0	2	0	24	1	0	2	.206	.202
Swafford, Derek, Augusta*	.253	119	497	447	69	113	147	15	5	3	48	6	2	8	33	1	101	52	16	4	.329	.314
Sweet, Jonathan, Augusta*	.285	87	295	267	28	76	90	9	1	1	22	2	2	5	18	2	31	5	4	6	.337	.339
Tatis, Fernando, Cha. (S.C.)†	.303	131	556	499	74	151	247	43	4	15	84	1	4	7	45	4	94	22	19	5	.495	.366
Taylor, Byron, Savannah*	.103	14	31	29	2	3	3	0	0	0	0	0	0	1	1	0	10	0	0	0	.103	.161
Thobe, Steve, Augusta	.299	84	325	291	43	87	121	12	2	6	38	0	0	5	29	6	71	1	3	2	.416	.372
Thomas, Rod, Cha. (W.Va.)	.146	29	91	82	8	12	18	3	0	1	6	0	2	0	7	1	25	3	0	3	.220	.209
Thompson, Andy, Hagerstown	.239	124	502	461	48	110	151	19	2	6	57	1	3	8	29	2	108	2	3	15	.328	.293
Thompson, Leroy, Columbus*	.214	82	294	248	34	53	95	15	3	7	35	1	0	5	40	4	78	1	2	4	.383	.334
Tidick, Michael, Hickory	.212	56	160	132	17	28	47	9	2	2	9	0	2	5	21	2	41	5	4	1	.356	.338
Torborg, Dale, Greensboro	.198	33	89	81	10	16	23	4	0	1	11	0	0	1	7	0	28	1	0	0	.284	.270
Torok, John, Piedmont*	.188	91	255	202	26	38	55	4	5	1	22	6	1	1	45	1	39	11	7	2	.272	.337
Towle, Justin, Cha. (W.Va.)	.268	107	395	343	54	92	142	22	2	8	60	1	3	1	44	0	95	3	6	6	.414	.350
Trimble, Rob, Greensboro*	.133	33	88	83	5	11	13	2	0	0	5	1	0	0	4	0	22	0	1	0	.157	.172
Troilo, Jason, Greensboro	.288	19	66	59	6	17	30	4	0	3	9	3	1	0	3	0	19	0	1	0	.508	.317
Turner, Rocky, Columbia	.176	12	21	17	2	3	3	0	0	0	1	2	0	0	2	0	5	0	2	0	.176	.263
Turrentine, Rich, Columbia	.000	26	1	1	0	0	0	0	0	0	0	0	0	0	0	0	1	0	0	0	.000	.000
Twitty, Sean, Greensboro	.283	80	330	293	49	83	140	25	1	10	58	0	2	6	29	1	83	6	2	9	.478	.358
Utting, Ben, Macon*	.218	21	62	55	5	12	14	2	0	0	6	0	0	0	7	0	13	1	1	0	.255	.306
Valdez, Mario, Hickory*	.272	130	516	441	65	120	193	30	5	11	56	0	3	5	67	2	107	9	7	5	.438	.372
Valera, Willy, Columbus	.163	31	108	104	8	17	28	3	1	2	6	0	0	0	4	0	35	0	1	3	.269	.194
Van Overen, Ryan, Albany†	.163	49	152	135	11	22	29	4	0	1	7	1	2	0	14	0	44	1	1	0	.215	.238
Vaske, Terry, Macon*	.169	53	166	148	14	25	47	7	0	5	18	0	0	0	18	2	58	0	1	1	.318	.259
Vasquez, Danilo, Cha. (S.C.)	.214	44	143	131	12	28	41	6	2	1	7	1	1	4	6	0	42	6	3	4	.313	.268
Veras, Juan, Cha. (S.C.)	.203	102	346	305	39	62	77	11	2	0	17	7	1	1	32	0	69	16	8	1	.252	.280
Waldrop, Tom, Macon*	.237	60	212	194	19	46	68	11	1	3	24	1	1	2	14	2	52	1	1	3	.351	.294
Walker, Shon, Augusta*	.229	110	431	358	49	82	120	20	0	6	51	1	4	0	68	3	127	10	9	3	.335	.349
Wampler, Sam, Piedmont†	.000	1	3	3	0	0	0	0	0	0	0	0	0	0	0	0	2	0	0	0	.000	.000
Ward, Daryle, Fayetteville*	.284	137	582	524	75	149	223	32	0	14	106	0	7	5	46	11	111	1	2	13	.426	.344
Warner, Bryan, Columbus*	.239	119	424	393	47	94	140	14	4	8	58	4	0	2	25	3	73	8	2	5	.356	.288
Watts, Josh, Piedmont*	.234	111	414	355	50	83	111	13	0	5	43	3	7	4	45	3	96	8	5	6	.313	.321
Weaver, Colby, Macon	.243	14	44	37	4	9	12	0	0	1	6	0	0	2	5	0	8	1	0	1	.324	.364
Wells, Mark, Asheville*	.287	40	128	115	21	33	69	6	3	8	23	1	2	1	9	2	38	1	3	1	.600	.339
White, Eric, Columbus	.317	112	423	369	49	117	165	24	3	6	46	1	1	1	51	5	45	11	7	12	.447	.400
White, Jimmy, Cha. (W.Va.)*	.169	20	74	65	7	11	19	3	1	1	8	1	1	1	6	0	27	1	1	0	.292	.247
Whitehurst, Todd, Columbia†	.164	21	77	61	10	10	16	3	0	1	1	1	0	4	11	0	19	2	1	0	.262	.329
Wilhelm, Brent, Hickory	.225	67	258	240	19	54	73	9	2	2	24	0	2	1	15	0	36	4	3	6	.304	.271
Williams, Curtis, Savannah*	.187	51	159	134	14	25	32	2	1	1	9	5	0	0	20	0	44	2	5	2	.239	.292
Williams, Glenn, Macon†	.175	38	141	120	13	21	25	4	0	0	14	1	3	1	16	0	42	2	1	3	.208	.271
Williams, Mark, Savannah	.154	64	240	201	19	31	45	2	0	4	13	5	1	0	33	0	57	0	0	10	.224	.272
Williamson, Matt, Piedmont	.235	88	330	285	44	67	84	10	2	1	25	6	2	2	35	0	67	3	4	5	.295	.321
Wilson, Brian, Cha. (W.Va.)	.308	5	15	13	3	4	5	1	0	0	1	2	0	0	0	0	1	3	0	0	.385	.308
Wilson, Preston, Columbia	.269	111	474	442	70	119	215	26	5	20	61	1	3	9	19	2	114	20	6	4	.486	.311
Wilson, Vance, Columbia	.250	91	354	324	34	81	110	11	0	6	32	1	2	8	19	1	45	4	3	6	.340	.306
Winterlee, Scott, Columbia	.429	4	9	7	0	3	3	0	0	0	0	0	0	0	2	0	0	0	0	0	.429	.556
Witt, Kevin, Hagerstown*	.232	119	514	479	58	111	190	35	1	14	50	3	0	4	28	2	148	1	5	5	.397	.280
Wright, Ron, Macon	.271	135	594	527	93	143	264	23	1	32	104	0	3	2	62	1	118	2	0	11	.501	.348
Wright, Terry, Cha. (W.Va.)*	.283	125	470	410	68	116	155	13	10	2	56	7	1	2	50	4	43	46	16	8	.378	.363
Wuerch, Jason, Greensboro*	.188	31	98	85	4	16	18	2	0	0	8	1	1	0	11	0	20	2	2	5	.212	.278
Yedo, Carlos, Greensboro*	.246	117	490	435	65	107	170	22	1	13	57	0	2	0	53	5	126	2	1	4	.391	.327
Zorrilla, Julio, Columbia†	.276	133	563	518	65	143	164	15	3	0	31	10	4	0	31	2	75	42	18	9	.317	.315
Zuniga, David, Columbia	.178	36	84	73	6	13	15	2	0	0	4	1	0	3	7	0	19	0	2	2	.205	.277

GRAND SLAMS: Gainey, Gibson, 2 each; A. Brown, Darr, Encarnacion, R. Guerrero, Hayes, A. Jones, Kennedy, A. Lewis, Luciano, McLamb, Mendoza, T. Sanders, Thobe, R. Wright, 1 each.
AWARDED FIRST BASE ON CATCHER'S INTERFERENCE: Hall 4 (W. Gonzalez, Lunar, Mosquera, Northeimer); Towle 3 (Morgan 2, P. Gomez); Goldberg 2 (Cardona, Dawson); V. Guerrero 2 (Fithian, M. Williams); Stumberger 2 (W. Gonzalez, Lunar); Asche (Boka); Fantauzzi (N. Garcia); Ledee (M. Johnson); Lombard (Henley); Prensi (V. Wilson); Swafford (Moyle); Sweet (Towle).

PLAYERS WITH TWO OR MORE TEAMS

Player, Team	Avg.	G	TPA	AB	R	H	TB	2B	3B	HR	RBI	SH	SF	HP	BB	IBB	SO	SB	CS	GDP	Slg.	OBP
Carpenter, Matt, Asheville	.095	9	22	21	0	2	3	1	0	0	3	0	0	0	1	0	2	0	0	0	.143	.136
Carpenter, Matt, Columbus	.286	2	8	7	2	2	6	1	0	1	3	0	0	1	0	0	2	0	0	0	.857	.375

1995 PITCHING

TEAM

Team	W	L	Pct.	ERA	G	CG	ShO	Sv.	IP	H	TBF	R	ER	HR	SH	SF	HB	BB	IBB	SO	WP	Bk.
Asheville	76	63	.547	3.14	139	7	13	42	1212.0	1060	5056	505	423	69	27	19	64	450	7	1011	104	30
Augusta	76	62	.551	3.14	138	4	8	36	1199.1	1059	5109	533	419	60	40	28	57	460	18	1000	93	10
Columbia	72	68	.514	3.16	140	13	11	30	1235.2	1067	5182	542	434	65	35	37	58	488	14	1045	99	20
Fayetteville	86	55	.610	3.22	141	3	10	54	1231.2	1035	5205	571	440	55	34	33	81	524	6	1183	105	17
Piedmont	82	58	.586	3.27	140	7	12	38	1218.1	1087	5150	574	442	62	38	37	59	460	7	1074	93	19
Columbus	80	62	.563	3.41	142	3	17	48	1242.1	1085	5300	598	471	66	38	29	78	569	39	1103	74	20
Hagerstown	73	68	.518	3.52	141	11	8	41	1216.0	1178	5152	599	476	76	39	31	56	391	9	906	97	11
Greensboro	70	70	.500	3.58	140	5	11	38	1226.0	1137	5204	595	488	79	34	40	52	450	19	1130	91	11
Charleston (W.Va.)	77	65	.542	3.60	142	10	11	42	1209.0	1166	5154	559	483	59	41	35	83	443	47	930	90	18
Savannah	56	83	.403	3.65	139	3	6	36	1228.2	1121	5307	608	498	79	38	43	54	492	25	1118	120	11
Albany	62	78	.443	3.90	140	6	5	31	1242.1	1282	5465	713	538	59	46	47	62	460	16	1016	82	12
Macon	71	70	.504	3.90	141	2	9	31	1269.2	1127	5548	699	550	89	39	32	79	627	9	1136	122	24
Hickory	49	89	.355	3.98	138	7	9	27	1222.0	1236	5315	712	541	106	48	45	62	436	46	988	89	26
Charleston (S.C.)	50	89	.360	4.11	139	7	4	23	1201.1	1179	5264	683	548	78	39	45	72	509	27	1032	104	19

INDIVIDUAL

TOP QUALIFIERS FOR EARNED-RUN AVERAGE TITLE

Minimum 114 innings. *Lefthanded pitcher.

Pitcher, Team	W	L	Pct.	ERA	G	GS	CG	ShO	GF	Sv.	IP	H	TBF	R	ER	HR	SH	SF	HB	BB	IBB	SO	WP	Bk.
Kusiewicz, Michael, Asheville*	8	4	.667	2.06	21	21	0	0	0	0	122.1	92	484	40	28	6	2	0	6	34	0	103	9	1
Jordan, Jason, Fayetteville	10	4	.714	2.28	24	24	0	0	0	0	138.0	128	575	48	35	5	0	3	8	43	0	103	13	1
Manning, Len, Piedmont*	10	10	.500	2.64	27	26	1	0	0	0	160.0	130	658	68	47	10	7	5	7	58	0	154	4	2
Wimberly, Larry, Piedmont*	10	3	.769	2.67	24	24	0	0	0	0	135.0	99	542	48	40	9	1	3	9	44	0	139	8	4
Herbert, Russell, Hickory	3	8	.273	2.67	18	18	1	1	0	0	114.2	83	474	48	34	9	3	3	8	46	0	115	5	2
Moraga, David, Albany*	8	8	.500	2.68	25	24	1	0	0	0	147.2	136	620	63	44	6	6	4	1	46	0	109	10	0
Atwater, Joe, Columbia*	9	6	.600	2.69	27	18	3	2	6	1	147.1	106	567	52	44	10	4	6	2	28	1	127	5	2
Allen, Cedric, Cha. (W.Va.)*	13	7	.650	2.85	27	27	5	2	0	0	170.1	143	690	64	54	8	6	4	14	46	4	108	6	4
Sievert, Mark, Hagerstown	12	6	.667	2.91	27	27	3	0	0	0	160.2	126	644	59	52	14	5	1	2	46	0	140	2	0
Gooch, Arnold, Ash.-C'bia	5	8	.385	2.94	21	21	1	1	0	0	128.2	111	541	51	42	8	3	3	4	57	0	117	13	0
O'Flynn, Gardner, Cha. (S.C.)*	9	10	.474	2.96	30	24	2	1	1	0	167.0	156	698	70	55	11	4	3	6	61	0	110	7	4
Meiners, Doug, Hagerstown	8	4	.667	2.99	18	18	3	0	0	0	117.1	121	477	52	39	5	2	2	3	14	0	73	4	1
Briggs, Anthony, Macon	8	5	.615	2.99	29	24	1	1	1	0	147.1	145	635	76	49	12	2	1	4	56	1	114	9	0
Wright, Jaret, Columbus	5	6	.455	3.00	24	24	0	0	0	0	129.0	93	554	55	43	9	3	6	13	79	0	113	11	3
Johnston, Sean, Columbia*	11	6	.647	3.03	23	22	2	0	0	0	148.1	132	621	60	50	6	4	4	11	63	2	105	15	1

DEPARTMENTAL LEADERS: W—Ebert, 14; L—Ramirez, 15; Pct.—B. Smith, .900; G—Golden, 64; GS—C. Smith, 29; CG—Allen, 5; ShO—B. Crowther, 3; GF—Reed, 53; Sv.—Reed, 41; IP—Ebert, 182.0; H—Ebert, 184; TBF—Ebert, 766; R—Hackman, 95; ER—Hackman, 85; HR—John Kelly, 16; SH—Culp, J. Ford, 8; SF—Durocher, 11; HB—C. Smith, 18; BB—Shumate, C. Smith, 87; IBB—Welch, 10; SO—Moss, Sanchez, 177; WP—C. Smith, 21; Bk.—Hackman, 7.

ALL PITCHERS

*Lefthanded pitcher.

Pitcher, Team	W	L	Pct.	ERA	G	GS	CG	ShO	GF	Sv.	IP	H	TBF	R	ER	HR	SH	SF	HB	BB	IBB	SO	WP	Bk.
Adair, Scott, Columbia	0	1	.000	10.38	3	0	0	0	0	0	4.1	10	26	8	5	0	0	1	1	0	0	4	0	0
Alazaus, Shawn, Greensboro*	3	1	.750	5.54	33	0	0	0	6	1	39.0	43	179	25	24	5	2	3	1	18	0	40	0	1
Allen, Cedric, Cha. (W.Va.)*	13	7	.650	2.85	27	27	5	2	0	0	170.1	143	690	64	54	8	6	4	14	46	4	108	6	4
Almanza, Armando, Savannah*	3	9	.250	3.92	20	20	0	0	0	0	108.0	108	476	62	47	13	5	4	3	40	1	72	6	1
Ambrose, John, Hickory	4	8	.333	3.95	14	14	0	0	0	0	73.0	65	314	41	32	6	2	3	3	35	0	49	9	2
Anderson, Jimmy, Augusta*	4	2	.667	1.53	14	14	0	0	0	0	76.2	51	305	15	13	1	1	0	4	31	0	75	9	1
Anez, Maycoll, Hickory	0	0	.000	2.25	2	0	0	0	1	0	4.0	3	19	2	1	0	0	0	0	4	0	4	1	0
Antonini, Adrian, Piedmont	2	0	1.000	3.80	6	5	0	0	1	0	21.1	19	85	10	9	1	0	0	2	2	0	26	1	1
Arias, Alfredo, Hagerstown	4	6	.400	4.16	35	1	0	0	17	1	71.1	67	308	37	33	6	6	2	3	35	2	59	8	1
Atwater, Joe, Columbia*	9	6	.600	2.69	27	18	3	2	6	1	147.1	106	567	52	44	10	4	6	2	28	1	127	5	2
Avrard, Corey, Savannah	1	6	.143	3.98	13	13	0	0	0	0	54.1	38	228	25	24	4	1	4	0	33	2	51	6	0
Aybar, Manuel, Savannah	3	8	.273	3.04	18	18	2	1	0	0	112.2	82	461	46	38	8	7	4	2	36	0	99	8	1
Bajda, Mike, Fayetteville	0	0	.000	3.00	4	0	0	0	1	0	9.0	8	41	5	3	1	0	0	0	10	0	4	2	0
Baker, Derek, Columbia	2	8	.200	3.30	36	0	0	0	24	6	62.2	52	267	25	23	5	2	4	6	35	0	44	5	1
Barbao, Joe, Piedmont	8	4	.667	3.38	43	0	0	0	14	1	66.2	70	288	34	25	2	4	5	7	12	1	24	2	1
Barnes, Keith, Asheville*	2	0	1.000	1.98	10	6	0	0	1	1	36.1	25	142	10	8	2	2	0	0	15	0	21	4	0
Beirne, Kevin, Hickory	0	0	.000	4.50	3	0	0	0	1	0	4.0	7	16	2	2	0	0	0	0	0	0	4	0	0
Bell, Mike, Albany*	3	3	.500	2.61	12	0	0	0	4	0	20.2	13	81	8	6	0	2	0	1	8	0	14	0	0
Benson, Jeremy, Greensboro*	0	0	.000	0.00	3	0	0	0	3	0	4.0	1	14	0	0	0	0	0	0	2	0	4	0	0
Beverlin, Jason, Greensboro	2	4	.333	2.65	7	7	1	1	0	0	51.0	49	198	15	15	1	0	0	0	6	0	31	4	0
Binversie, Brian, Greensboro	0	4	.000	4.96	31	0	0	0	12	0	45.1	53	206	30	25	7	0	5	2	18	1	32	2	0
Bledsoe, Randy, Savannah	2	1	.667	6.42	28	0	0	0	7	0	33.2	41	167	25	24	0	1	3	4	22	1	28	4	0
Blythe, Billy, Macon	0	2	.000	10.34	7	2	0	0	2	1	15.2	15	79	20	18	0	1	0	4	14	0	15	5	2
Bost, Heath, Asheville	4	1	.800	1.52	9	2	0	0	4	0	23.2	20	90	6	4	1	0	0	1	3	0	17	1	2
Bowie, Micah, Macon*	4	1	.800	2.28	5	5	0	0	0	0	27.2	9	104	8	7	1	0	0	3	11	0	36	1	0
Boyd, Jason, Piedmont	6	8	.429	3.58	26	24	1	0	1	0	151.0	151	638	77	60	8	5	3	4	44	0	129	18	2
Briggs, Anthony, Macon	8	5	.615	2.99	29	24	1	1	1	0	147.1	145	635	76	49	12	2	1	4	56	1	114	9	0
Broome, John, Hickory	0	1	.000	9.64	4	0	0	0	3	0	4.2	8	25	5	5	1	0	1	0	4	0	3	0	0
Brown, Charlie, Greensboro	4	4	.500	4.42	45	2	0	0	22	4	57.0	57	252	31	28	6	3	3	2	23	5	69	11	1

Pitcher, Team	W	L	Pct.	ERA	G	GS	CG	ShO	GF	Sv.	IP	H	TBF	R	ER	HR	SH	SF	HB	BB	IBB	SO	WP	Bk.
Brown, Darold, Macon*	3	1	.750	3.29	31	0	0	0	20	5	54.2	39	230	22	20	1	3	4	4	32	1	55	7	2
Brownson, Mark, Asheville	6	7	.462	4.01	23	12	0	0	4	1	98.2	106	422	52	44	12	2	2	4	29	0	94	4	2
Burdick, Morgan, Asheville	0	1	.000	4.39	17	0	0	0	7	0	26.2	26	110	13	13	1	0	0	0	10	1	19	2	0
Buteaux, Shane, Hickory	2	7	.222	7.29	13	13	0	0	0	0	66.2	90	316	63	54	10	4	5	3	32	2	30	2	1
Cain, Travis, Macon	1	2	.333	7.52	14	2	0	0	4	0	26.1	25	136	23	22	2	0	0	6	31	0	32	7	0
Caldwell, David, Columbus*	11	10	.524	4.40	27	27	0	0	0	0	151.1	162	655	87	74	12	4	2	4	58	0	104	6	2
Callahan, Damon, Cha. (W.Va.)	2	1	.667	6.12	6	6	0	0	0	0	25.0	33	120	22	17	1	0	1	2	14	2	17	4	0
Carlson, Garret, Hickory	0	0	.000	32.40	3	0	0	0	1	0	1.2	2	11	6	6	1	0	0	0	4	0	2	0	0
Caruthers, Clayton, Cha. (W.Va.)	11	7	.611	3.70	27	27	0	0	0	0	138.2	149	600	67	57	6	5	4	14	50	1	105	13	2
Castillo, Carlos, Hickory	5	6	.455	3.73	14	12	2	0	2	1	79.2	85	343	42	33	11	1	3	3	18	0	67	3	6
Censale, Silvio, Piedmont*	10	6	.625	3.15	22	21	0	0	0	0	120.0	96	507	54	42	6	5	4	5	54	0	123	10	3
Chavarria, David, Cha. (S.C.)	3	5	.375	3.92	52	0	0	0	22	6	62.0	55	277	33	27	5	2	5	1	38	3	68	16	0
Chaves, Rafael, Augusta	1	0	1.000	2.08	7	0	0	0	2	2	8.2	2	36	3	2	0	2	0	0	6	0	9	0	0
Civit, Xavier, Albany	2	3	.400	7.62	12	1	0	0	0	0	26.0	34	135	30	22	0	2	0	2	18	4	29	2	2
Clark, Doug, Fayetteville	0	1	.000	11.57	4	0	0	0	2	0	4.2	10	27	11	6	2	0	0	0	3	0	3	0	1
Cole, Jason, Albany	3	3	.500	4.37	32	4	0	0	11	1	57.2	67	257	33	28	3	2	2	4	22	2	51	2	1
Collins, Zach, Macon*	0	0	.000	5.40	4	0	0	0	2	0	3.1	7	20	4	2	0	0	0	1	2	0	3	0	0
Colmenares, Luis, Asheville	2	2	.500	2.29	45	0	0	0	38	21	55.0	37	223	15	14	1	2	2	1	29	1	74	11	2
Conway, Keith, Savannah*	7	2	.778	1.46	60	0	0	0	26	10	74.0	49	297	14	12	1	5	3	3	26	3	87	3	0
Cook, Rodney, Cha. (S.C.)	3	8	.273	2.53	60	0	0	0	36	11	96.0	83	415	32	27	3	5	4	9	39	5	88	8	1
Cooke, Steve, Augusta*	1	0	1.000	0.00	1	1	0	0	0	0	5.0	2	19	0	0	0	0	0	0	1	0	6	0	0
Cooney, James, Cha. (S.C.)	0	0	.000	0.00	1	0	0	0	0	0	0.0	0	0	0	0	0	0	0	0	0	0	0	0	0
Cooper, Steve, Savannah	0	1	.000	6.75	2	0	0	0	2	0	1.1	2	8	1	1	0	0	0	1	1	1	0	1	0
Cordero, Francisco, Fayetteville	0	3	.000	6.30	4	4	0	0	0	0	20.0	26	92	16	14	1	2	2	0	12	0	19	4	0
Corn, Chris, Greensboro	8	7	.533	1.76	49	0	0	0	39	24	82.0	54	317	20	16	3	1	2	2	22	0	101	5	1
Crine, Dennis, Hickory	3	6	.333	6.12	15	11	0	0	1	1	60.1	74	276	52	41	7	2	4	5	20	2	20	5	1
Crowther, Brent, Asheville	12	3	.800	2.28	15	15	3	3	0	0	98.2	79	393	31	25	4	0	1	3	25	0	72	11	1
Crowther, John, Hagerstown	1	3	.250	5.45	11	11	0	0	0	0	38.0	52	189	36	23	3	0	0	3	27	0	21	10	2
Cruise, Mark, Savannah	0	0	.000	3.68	6	0	0	0	0	0	7.1	8	37	5	3	1	0	0	0	1	0	5	1	1
Cruz, Nelson, Hickory	2	7	.222	2.70	44	0	0	0	29	9	66.2	65	285	31	20	6	3	1	4	15	2	68	5	0
Cubillan, Darwin, Greensboro	5	5	.500	3.62	22	14	1	1	3	0	97.0	86	409	50	39	5	3	1	4	38	1	78	5	0
Culp, Wes, Macon	4	6	.400	3.53	39	5	0	0	14	3	104.2	100	456	56	41	7	8	5	6	44	2	56	9	1
Davenport, Joe, Hagerstown	0	1	.000	6.11	13	0	0	0	2	0	17.2	22	91	19	12	3	0	0	1	13	0	13	6	0
Davey, Tom, Hagerstown	4	1	.800	3.38	8	8	0	0	0	0	37.1	29	167	23	14	2	1	1	2	31	0	25	9	0
Davis, Kane, Augusta	12	6	.667	3.75	26	25	1	0	0	0	139.1	136	602	73	58	4	3	4	9	43	0	78	10	1
Dinnen, Kevin, Columbus	2	7	.222	4.14	49	0	0	0	24	1	58.2	47	255	34	27	4	4	4	3	34	9	43	1	0
Dinyar, Eric, Fayetteville	4	3	.571	2.49	42	0	0	0	16	5	86.2	77	356	34	24	1	1	4	8	25	0	71	2	1
Dixon, Jim, Hickory	4	1	.800	1.93	35	0	0	0	17	5	51.1	43	220	23	11	1	4	2	1	16	5	56	6	1
Doman, Roger, Hagerstown	2	2	.500	4.41	14	6	0	0	3	1	51.0	65	233	32	25	0	0	1	3	13	0	24	4	0
Done, J.J., Columbus	0	3	.000	9.00	4	3	0	0	0	0	12.0	21	65	15	12	1	0	1	1	9	1	8	3	1
Donnelly, Brendan, Cha. (W.Va.)	1	1	.500	1.19	24	0	0	0	22	12	30.1	14	112	4	4	0	1	2	1	7	1	33	1	0
Donovan, Scot, Columbus	0	6	.000	4.81	40	0	0	0	31	10	48.2	53	238	38	26	6	3	0	3	36	4	38	6	1
Dougherty, Tony, Columbus	4	4	.500	4.72	27	10	0	0	3	0	87.2	85	405	61	46	5	2	4	8	50	4	78	4	1
Doyle, Tom, Cha. (W.Va.)*	6	4	.600	4.35	14	12	1	0	0	0	62.0	57	272	34	30	3	2	1	7	30	3	66	9	0
Durocher, Jayson, Albany	3	7	.300	3.91	24	22	1	0	1	0	122.0	105	526	67	53	5	4	11	5	56	1	88	11	1
Ebert, Derrin, Macon*	14	5	.737	3.31	28	28	0	0	0	0	182.0	184	766	87	67	12	5	4	7	46	0	124	3	2
Eden, Bill, Asheville	5	3	.625	2.14	33	0	0	0	17	9	67.1	55	269	22	16	4	1	0	1	14	0	80	7	2
Escamilla, Jaime, Cha. (S.C.)*	3	4	.429	4.42	32	5	0	0	10	2	71.1	59	305	38	35	8	3	3	2	38	1	76	8	1
Estavil, Mauricio, Piedmont*	3	5	.375	3.68	42	0	0	0	18	1	44.0	33	202	20	18	0	0	0	2	37	1	58	6	0
Evangelista, Alberto, Macon	4	4	.500	3.50	24	2	1	0	12	0	54.0	42	224	29	21	4	4	3	2	16	0	51	6	2
Fantauzzi, John, Asheville*	0	0	.000	18.00	1	0	0	0	1	0	1.0	2	8	2	2	0	0	0	0	4	0	1	0	0
Fereira, Marcos, Hickory	0	2	.000	16.88	4	0	0	0	1	0	2.2	6	20	6	5	0	2	1	1	4	2	1	2	3
Forbes, Adam, Hickory*	0	0	.000	9.82	2	0	0	0	1	0	3.2	5	19	5	4	1	0	1	2	0	0	1	1	0
Ford, Ben, Greensboro	0	0	.000	5.14	7	0	0	0	2	0	7.0	4	31	4	4	1	1	0	0	5	1	8	2	0
Ford, Jack, Hickory*	8	14	.364	3.89	27	27	3	0	0	0	173.2	174	738	86	75	14	8	5	6	66	3	157	5	0
France, Aaron, Augusta	6	6	.500	2.47	18	15	0	0	0	0	94.2	80	388	29	26	4	3	3	5	26	0	77	6	2
Franklin, Joel, Cha. (W.Va.)	3	3	.500	4.97	24	1	0	0	4	2	50.2	49	221	28	28	2	2	3	4	22	2	58	6	0
Gambs, Chris, Piedmont	0	0	.000	6.86	9	0	0	0	2	0	19.2	24	95	17	15	2	0	2	1	14	0	15	3	0
Garcia, Frank, Savannah	0	3	.000	3.16	34	0	0	0	32	24	37.0	26	156	17	13	3	0	1	2	15	0	41	8	0
Garcia-Luna, Francisco, Augusta	2	1	.667	2.86	14	10	1	0	0	0	63.0	57	263	31	20	3	1	2	3	17	0	48	5	0
Gardner, Scott, Fayetteville	6	3	.667	2.06	49	1	0	0	22	4	87.1	62	351	26	20	5	1	0	2	24	1	112	8	2
Genke, Todd, Piedmont	3	2	.600	3.91	31	1	0	0	4	1	53.0	50	227	30	23	3	3	1	2	18	3	37	4	0
Giard, Kenneth, Macon	1	0	1.000	0.68	5	0	0	0	3	0	13.1	7	51	1	1	0	1	0	0	5	0	19	2	0
Giron, Emiliano, Cha. (W.Va.)	0	0	.000	0.94	30	0	0	0	28	20	28.2	12	108	3	3	0	1	0	1	8	0	39	1	2
Glauber, Keith, Savannah	2	1	.667	3.73	40	0	0	0	3	0	62.2	50	277	29	26	2	2	3	5	36	3	62	9	1
Gogolewski, Chris, Cha. (S.C.)*	5	13	.278	4.23	30	19	2	0	5	0	140.1	169	627	93	66	5	4	5	12	38	1	84	12	2
Golden, Matthew, Savannah	7	3	.700	2.00	64	0	0	0	24	1	90.0	71	355	22	20	2	2	2	0	21	4	94	4	2
Gonzalez, Jhonny, Asheville*	4	3	.571	2.48	21	0	0	0	10	3	32.2	23	136	13	9	3	2	1	1	15	1	31	1	1
Gooch, Arnold, Ash.-C'bia	5	8	.385	2.94	21	21	1	1	0	0	128.2	111	541	51	42	8	3	3	4	57	0	117	13	0
Graham, Steve, Macon	1	1	.500	9.35	5	0	0	0	2	0	8.2	17	53	12	9	2	1	0	1	5	0	7	1	1
Granata, Chris, Columbus	11	5	.688	2.47	33	12	0	0	6	0	113.0	94	477	43	31	2	6	3	4	53	7	93	8	1
Grebe, Brett, Augusta	2	2	.500	3.62	32	0	0	0	15	2	37.1	42	165	19	15	3	1	2	0	16	1	36	2	1
Grundt, Ken, Asheville*	0	0	.000	0.30	20	0	0	0	11	1	30.1	18	111	1	1	0	1	1	1	7	1	38	2	0
Hackman, Luther, Asheville	11	11	.500	4.64	28	28	2	0	0	0	165.0	162	710	95	85	11	3	3	14	65	0	108	9	7
Halley, Allen, Hickory	2	1	.667	2.55	13	9	0	0	2	1	60.0	46	234	21	17	6	1	0	2	12	2	58	2	1
Hamilton, Paul, Piedmont	1	0	1.000	4.71	15	1	0	0	4	0	21.0	24	90	11	11	0	0	1	2	7	0	10	2	0
Hampton, Mark, Augusta	5	5	.500	4.13	39	0	0	0	15	0	56.2	46	255	32	26	8	4	1	1	38	2	45	6	0
Handy, Russell, Albany	2	7	.222	4.27	30	5	0	0	6	2	71.2	78	340	50	34	4	6	3	6	37	1	57	14	1
Hartmann, Rich, Savannah	1	2	.333	5.05	31	0	0	0	10	0	41.0	35	182	26	23	8	2	1	3	20	2	52	3	0
Hartshorn, Tyson, Hagerstown	3	4	.429	5.36	12	7	0	0	1	0	48.2	59	224	37	29	8	1	1	5	20	0	28	6	0
Harvell, Pete, Cha. (W.Va.)*	0	0	.000	2.93	27	0	0	0	9	0	27.2	25	114	11	9	2	1	1	3	10	1	17	5	0
Hausmann, Isaac, Cha. (S.C.)	0	0	.000	9.45	5	0	0	0	4	0	6.2	10	35	10	7	2	1	0	2	1	0	6	0	1
Helvey, Rob, Savannah*	2	1	.667	7.97	18	0	0	0	7	0	20.1	28	107	22	18	1	2	0	3	16	0	25	5	0

CLASS A *South Atlantic League*

Pitcher, Team	W	L	Pct.	ERA	G	GS	CG	ShO	GF	Sv.	IP	H	TBF	R	ER	HR	SH	SF	HB	BB	IBB	SO	WP	Bk.
Henderson, Chris, Asheville	1	1	.500	1.63	17	0	0	0	10	1	27.2	20	119	6	5	1	0	1	4	18	0	28	4	0
Herbert, Russell, Hickory	3	8	.273	2.67	18	18	1	1	0	0	114.2	83	474	48	34	9	3	3	8	46	0	115	5	2
Hibbard, Billy, Hagerstown	2	1	.667	3.89	16	0	0	0	5	0	34.2	42	149	16	15	1	0	1	1	6	1	20	2	0
Housley, Adam, Fayetteville	3	1	.750	2.37	19	0	0	0	6	1	38.0	26	156	14	10	0	0	1	1	11	1	43	1	0
Hower, Dan, Cha. (S.C.)*	4	7	.364	7.29	22	17	0	0	3	1	82.2	96	404	88	67	5	4	3	5	59	1	55	13	0
Humphry, Trevor, Piedmont	5	7	.417	3.62	28	20	2	0	4	0	119.1	122	532	67	48	7	2	4	6	63	0	102	13	0
Hunter, Rich, Piedmont	10	2	.833	2.77	15	15	3	2	0	0	104.0	79	404	37	32	9	1	1	2	19	0	80	0	0
Jacobson, Kelton, Fayetteville	5	7	.417	5.82	25	12	0	0	5	0	68.0	72	317	52	44	3	2	3	6	44	1	64	9	2
Jarvis, Jason, Gre.-Hag.	12	10	.545	3.19	30	24	0	0	2	0	160.2	152	678	74	57	8	6	9	4	51	4	124	20	2
Johnson, Jason, Augusta	3	5	.375	4.36	11	11	1	0	0	0	53.2	57	233	32	26	2	1	1	4	17	0	42	3	0
Johnston, Sean, Columbia*	11	6	.647	3.03	23	22	2	0	0	0	148.1	132	621	60	50	6	4	4	11	63	2	105	15	1
Jordan, Jason, Fayetteville	10	4	.714	2.28	24	24	0	0	0	0	138.0	128	575	48	35	5	0	3	8	43	0	103	13	1
Judd, Mike, Greensboro	0	0	.000	0.00	1	0	0	0	1	0	2.2	2	11	0	0	0	0	0	0	0	0	1	0	0
Karvala, Kyle, Piedmont*	5	1	.833	3.44	20	0	0	0	10	2	18.1	13	75	9	7	0	0	2	0	7	0	17	1	0
Kell, Rob, Cha. (S.C.)*	1	4	.200	3.48	7	7	0	0	0	0	44.0	38	184	20	17	2	3	1	2	9	0	47	3	0
Kelly, Jeff, Augusta*	6	11	.353	3.47	26	26	0	0	0	0	142.2	134	608	68	55	6	5	5	4	51	0	114	12	0
Kelly, John, Columbia	8	8	.500	3.88	28	28	3	0	0	0	167.0	148	691	80	72	16	2	5	10	65	0	124	11	2
Kindell, Scott, Columbia*	0	0	.000	0.00	1	0	0	0	1	0	0.1	0	1	0	0	0	0	0	0	0	0	0	0	0
Knight, Brandon, Cha. (S.C.)	4	2	.667	3.13	9	9	0	0	0	0	54.2	37	218	22	19	5	0	4	0	21	0	52	4	1
Knighton, Toure, Cha. (S.C.)	1	9	.100	4.88	22	19	1	0	1	0	107.0	121	482	64	58	5	2	3	8	46	0	100	8	1
Koppe, Clint, Cha. (W.Va.)	7	13	.350	3.37	30	22	2	0	1	0	157.2	144	653	66	59	10	4	5	6	47	5	119	8	1
Kosek, Kory, Piedmont	1	2	.333	0.00	15	0	0	0	7	3	20.1	13	83	8	0	1	2	0	3	5	2	24	0	0
Kramer, Scott, Columbus	2	2	.500	2.08	19	1	0	0	6	2	52.0	45	213	19	12	3	0	0	6	14	1	53	4	0
Kusiewicz, Michael, Asheville*	8	4	.667	2.06	21	21	0	0	0	0	122.1	92	484	40	28	6	2	0	6	34	0	103	9	1
LaPoint, Jason, Albany*	5	2	.714	3.52	33	0	0	0	12	0	61.1	72	272	34	24	1	1	2	1	15	0	52	3	0
Larson, Toby, Columbia	3	3	.500	2.63	8	8	0	0	0	0	51.1	43	224	24	15	2	1	2	1	19	0	53	5	1
Lasbury, Robert, Asheville	0	2	.000	8.64	6	0	0	0	1	0	8.1	10	43	11	8	1	0	0	0	6	0	5	1	0
Lavenia, Mark, Macon*	4	3	.571	2.14	24	3	0	0	16	4	46.1	38	195	17	11	2	3	0	1	14	1	45	1	1
Lee, Jeremy, Hagerstown	7	11	.389	4.20	26	26	1	0	0	0	148.0	160	626	82	69	11	1	8	8	29	0	118	4	0
Legrow, Brett, Piedmont	0	1	.000	5.14	8	2	0	0	4	1	14.0	16	64	10	8	2	0	0	0	5	0	8	2	0
Leiber, Zane, Hickory	1	0	1.000	5.60	14	0	0	0	7	0	17.2	19	78	13	11	3	0	1	0	5	0	13	5	1
Logan, Marcus, Savannah	3	6	.333	3.32	34	7	0	0	2	0	86.2	73	373	42	32	3	1	5	2	38	0	83	11	1
Lott, Brian, Cha. (W.Va.)	8	7	.533	3.46	28	20	0	0	3	1	138.0	155	586	56	53	9	4	1	6	33	3	96	3	3
Lovingier, Kevin, Savannah*	6	3	.667	1.34	38	0	0	0	18	1	47.0	35	195	14	7	1	3	1	1	21	5	54	3	0
Maberry, Louis, Cha. (W.Va.)	0	1	.000	0.00	4	0	0	0	2	0	5.0	2	21	1	0	0	1	0	0	3	1	0	0	0
Magre, Pete, Cha. (W.Va.)	2	1	.667	5.08	21	0	0	0	2	0	28.1	34	119	16	16	2	1	2	2	8	2	19	3	0
Manning, Len, Piedmont*	10	10	.500	2.64	27	26	1	0	0	0	160.0	130	658	68	47	10	7	5	7	58	0	154	4	2
Martin, Chandler, Asheville	4	3	.571	3.83	8	8	0	0	0	0	49.1	48	216	23	21	0	2	0	3	27	0	32	6	1
Martinez, Johnny, Columbus	6	1	.857	1.83	16	2	0	0	2	0	54.0	37	210	15	11	0	2	1	4	14	0	43	3	0
Martinez, Osvaldo, Fayetteville	0	0	.000	4.15	6	0	0	0	2	0	13.0	11	49	6	6	2	1	1	0	1	0	15	0	1
Maskivish, Joe, Augusta	2	1	.667	2.12	26	0	0	0	26	20	29.2	23	122	9	7	0	1	0	3	9	4	33	2	0
Mattes, Troy, Albany	0	2	.000	5.03	4	4	0	0	0	0	19.2	21	90	12	11	0	2	0	0	12	1	15	1	1
McAdams, Denny, Asheville	0	0	.000	3.86	5	0	0	0	3	0	7.0	7	29	4	3	1	0	0	0	2	0	7	0	0
McBride, Chris, Hagerstown	5	10	.333	4.29	19	19	2	0	0	0	107.0	121	461	61	51	4	5	3	5	27	1	52	3	1
McClinton, Patrick, Asheville*	1	2	.333	3.51	18	0	0	0	7	2	33.1	27	140	16	13	2	3	3	4	9	1	22	3	3
McEntire, Ethan, Columbia*	3	2	.600	3.34	6	6	1	1	0	0	32.1	26	146	14	12	4	3	0	0	23	0	31	3	0
McNeill, Kevin, Savannah*	3	7	.300	4.96	29	21	0	0	2	0	110.2	131	502	74	61	5	1	0	3	47	1	87	14	0
Medina, Rafael, Greensboro	4	4	.500	4.01	19	19	1	0	0	0	98.2	86	418	48	44	8	0	5	6	38	0	108	6	3
Meiners, Doug, Hagerstown	8	4	.667	2.99	18	18	3	0	0	0	117.1	121	477	52	39	5	2	2	3	14	0	73	4	1
Mejias, Fernando, Hickory	2	9	.182	4.59	30	16	0	0	4	0	111.2	128	497	78	57	6	3	3	5	38	4	76	11	2
Meyer, David, Greensboro*	8	4	.667	4.86	14	14	1	1	0	0	87.0	104	377	52	47	5	3	2	3	28	0	54	5	1
Mikkelsen, Lincoln, Albany	0	1	.000	1.93	12	0	0	0	5	5	23.1	24	107	14	5	0	1	0	3	8	0	17	1	0
Millwood, Kevin, Macon	5	6	.455	4.63	29	12	0	0	5	0	103.0	86	458	65	53	10	3	1	5	57	0	89	10	0
Minor, Tom, Savannah	1	1	.500	4.91	8	0	0	0	3	0	7.1	10	33	7	4	1	0	1	0	2	0	9	0	0
Mitchell, Courtney, Piedmont*	0	1	.000	10.38	5	0	0	0	2	0	4.1	7	22	5	5	0	0	0	0	5	0	3	1	0
Mittauer, Casey, Greensboro	3	6	.333	1.94	49	0	0	0	22	8	74.1	60	294	26	16	3	6	4	3	14	4	59	5	0
Montoya, Wilmer, Columbus	3	3	.500	3.12	51	0	0	0	41	31	80.2	65	337	33	28	4	1	0	2	36	1	91	6	2
Moore, David, Hickory	1	0	1.000	6.18	20	0	0	0	12	0	27.2	41	128	20	19	5	0	2	3	7	1	15	2	0
Moraga, David, Albany*	8	8	.500	2.68	25	24	1	0	0	0	147.2	136	620	63	44	6	6	4	1	46	0	109	10	0
Morillo, Donald, Cha. (S.C.)	1	4	.200	2.10	18	0	0	0	13	1	25.2	22	115	7	6	1	0	0	3	17	2	28	1	0
Mortimer, Mick, Cha. (S.C.)	0	0	.000	0.00	5	0	0	0	1	0	13.1	10	52	2	0	0	0	2	1	6	0	11	2	0
Moss, Damian, Macon*	9	10	.474	3.56	27	27	0	0	0	0	149.1	134	653	73	59	13	0	2	12	70	0	177	14	5
Najera, Noe, Columbus*	3	1	.750	3.38	43	0	0	0	15	1	42.2	34	189	20	16	3	2	1	6	24	3	53	4	2
Newton, Chris, Fayetteville*	0	0	.000	5.79	2	0	0	0	1	0	4.2	6	20	3	3	0	0	1	0	1	0	3	0	0
Nieto, Tony, Cha. (W.Va.)	3	4	.429	3.44	13	8	2	2	0	0	55.0	55	246	37	21	1	6	1	8	21	6	35	1	0
Nunez, Maximo, Hagerstown	1	1	.500	5.54	22	0	0	0	11	0	37.1	40	172	29	23	4	3	2	3	20	0	21	8	0
Nuttle, Jamison, Augusta	0	0	.000	1.17	6	0	0	0	0	0	7.2	5	38	3	1	0	0	0	0	8	0	10	0	0
Nyari, Pete, Piedmont	5	1	.833	4.52	35	1	0	0	12	1	61.2	58	279	40	31	0	3	2	5	39	0	49	8	6
Nygaard, Chris, Albany*	6	4	.600	2.86	41	0	0	0	18	1	56.2	60	241	25	18	5	3	0	2	8	0	43	3	0
Ocasio, Fred, Asheville	0	0	.000	0.00	1	0	0	0	1	0	0.2	0	2	0	0	0	0	0	0	0	0	0	0	0
O'Flynn, Gardner, Cha. (S.C.)*	9	10	.474	2.96	30	24	2	1	1	0	167.0	156	698	70	55	11	4	3	6	61	0	110	7	4
Olszewski, Eric, Macon	2	5	.286	3.76	35	1	0	0	15	5	81.1	54	351	37	34	3	1	1	8	50	1	103	11	3
Oropeza, Igor, Columbus	4	1	.800	1.48	9	8	0	0	0	0	48.2	39	200	13	8	1	2	0	3	13	0	46	2	2
Pace, Scott, Hagerstown*	4	2	.667	1.09	11	6	2	1	2	1	57.2	32	211	8	7	2	1	0	2	12	0	57	4	0
Pack, Steve, Columbia	2	7	.222	3.70	36	0	0	0	22	12	56.0	63	254	33	23	1	3	0	1	20	5	35	0	3
Parotte, Frisco, Greensboro	3	1	.750	2.80	22	0	0	0	8	0	35.1	40	161	20	11	3	2	1	2	16	1	35	3	0
Paugh, Rick, Augusta*	6	2	.750	2.59	52	0	0	0	25	2	59.0	60	252	23	17	3	4	1	0	17	5	61	6	1
Pauls, Matthew, Cha. (S.C.)	3	3	.500	4.22	16	0	0	0	14	2	21.1	22	103	20	10	0	3	2	2	10	4	19	2	0
Pelka, Brian, Augusta	1	3	.250	5.98	26	0	0	0	7	0	40.2	46	193	31	27	3	4	2	5	20	1	29	4	1
Perez, Joe, Cha. (S.C.)*	0	0	.000	0.00	1	0	0	0	1	0	1.0	0	3	0	0	0	0	0	0	0	0	0	0	0
Perez, Julio, Columbus	8	5	.615	4.02	22	17	0	0	5	1	109.2	109	461	53	49	4	2	3	4	39	5	100	5	5
Perpetuo, Nelson, Cha. (S.C.)*	6	4	.600	3.21	32	10	1	0	13	0	103.2	80	439	47	37	11	3	2	5	51	5	125	5	1
Peterman, Ernie, Hagerstown	0	1	.000	12.60	2	0	0	0	2	0	5.0	9	25	7	7	2	0	0	0	1	0	4	0	0

Pitcher, Team	W	L	Pct.	ERA	G	GS	CG	ShO	GF	Sv.	IP	H	TBF	R	ER	HR	SH	SF	HB	BB	IBB	SO	WP	Bk.
Phelps, Tommy, Albany*	10	9	.526	3.33	24	24	1	0	0	0	135.1	142	597	76	50	6	0	4	5	45	0	119	5	1
Phillips, Jason, Augusta	4	3	.571	3.60	30	6	0	0	3	0	80.0	76	354	46	32	2	2	2	0	53	1	65	10	0
Phipps, Chris, Piedmont	0	2	.000	1.96	11	0	0	0	3	0	23.0	24	101	9	5	0	0	2	2	8	0	10	3	0
Pickford, Kevin, Augusta*	7	3	.700	2.00	16	16	0	0	0	0	85.2	85	354	28	19	5	2	1	5	16	1	59	2	0
Portillo, Alex, Hickory*	0	3	.000	2.25	33	0	0	0	15	2	56.0	57	243	24	14	1	3	0	6	10	5	36	0	0
Powell, Brian, Fayetteville	4	0	1.000	1.61	5	5	0	0	0	0	28.0	15	111	5	5	0	1	1	2	11	0	37	2	0
Powell, Jeremy, Albany	1	0	1.000	1.59	1	1	0	0	0	0	5.2	4	20	1	1	0	0	0	0	1	0	6	1	0
Presley, Kirk, Columbia	1	2	.333	5.14	4	4	0	0	0	0	21.0	30	100	17	12	0	1	0	0	13	0	8	1	0
Raines, Ken, Macon*	1	1	.500	1.93	14	0	0	0	12	8	18.2	11	70	4	4	0	0	0	0	5	1	22	1	1
Ramirez, Rafael, Savannah	6	15	.286	3.91	26	25	0	0	0	0	147.1	160	645	81	64	8	4	9	7	42	1	91	9	2
Reames, Britt, Savannah	3	5	.375	3.46	10	10	1	0	0	0	54.2	41	227	23	21	7	0	0	5	15	0	63	9	1
Reed, Brandon, Fayetteville	3	0	1.000	0.97	55	0	0	0	53	41	64.2	40	252	11	7	1	1	0	3	18	1	78	8	0
Reid, Rayon, Augusta	2	5	.286	4.38	12	11	1	0	0	0	61.2	52	268	36	30	6	1	1	5	28	0	47	4	1
Reyes, Jose, Cha. (S.C.)	0	0	.000	18.00	4	0	0	0	2	0	4.0	10	25	8	8	2	0	0	0	3	0	5	1	0
Reynolds, Chance, Augusta	0	0	.000	0.00	1	0	0	0	1	0	0.1	1	2	0	0	0	0	0	0	0	0	0	0	0
Rhine, Kendall, Hagerstown	3	3	.500	2.60	42	0	0	0	36	13	55.1	41	230	20	16	2	4	0	3	28	1	49	8	0
Rhodriguez, Rory, Albany	3	4	.429	3.50	37	7	0	0	10	2	90.0	80	379	44	35	8	3	3	2	34	0	83	3	0
Ricken, Ray, Greensboro	3	2	.600	2.23	10	10	0	0	0	0	64.2	42	245	20	16	2	1	1	0	16	1	77	3	0
Roberts, Willis, Fayetteville	6	3	.667	2.70	17	15	0	0	0	0	80.0	72	339	33	24	2	1	2	6	40	0	52	15	3
Robinson, Martin, Greensboro*	1	0	1.000	7.56	2	1	0	0	0	0	8.1	8	44	7	7	0	1	0	0	12	0	5	1	0
Rocker, John, Macon*	4	4	.500	4.50	16	16	0	0	0	0	86.0	86	375	50	43	5	1	1	4	52	0	61	5	1
Rojano, Rafael, Greensboro	0	0	.000	6.58	19	1	0	0	9	1	26.0	35	134	24	19	5	0	0	7	13	0	38	5	2
Rose, Brian, Asheville	1	0	1.000	4.91	10	1	0	0	5	0	14.2	14	62	8	8	0	0	0	4	2	0	15	1	0
Ruiz, Rafael, Hickory*	1	0	1.000	15.75	5	0	0	0	1	0	4.0	7	25	8	7	0	0	0	1	5	0	5	2	0
Runion, Jeff, Cha. (S.C.)	1	1	.500	3.18	2	2	0	0	0	0	11.1	12	54	8	4	0	2	0	1	6	0	6	2	0
Runyan, Paul, Cha. (W.Va.)	6	2	.750	4.13	15	5	0	0	2	0	52.1	56	227	29	24	3	0	1	2	17	5	28	5	0
Rushworth, Jim, Albany	1	2	.333	8.31	6	0	0	0	4	1	8.2	10	44	9	8	0	1	0	1	6	3	5	3	0
Ryan, Reid, Cha. (S.C.)	0	4	.000	9.38	22	5	0	0	6	0	47.0	64	250	57	49	3	1	1	6	40	2	39	4	0
Sanchez, Jesus, Columbia*	9	7	.563	3.13	27	27	4	0	0	0	169.2	154	705	76	59	9	2	5	7	58	0	177	10	4
Sanders, Frankie, Columbus	1	1	.500	3.00	2	0	0	0	1	0	9.0	9	39	3	3	0	1	0	1	4	0	9	1	0
Sauerbeck, Scott, Columbia*	5	4	.556	3.27	19	0	0	0	13	2	33.0	28	139	14	12	2	2	0	1	14	1	33	3	1
Schaffner, Eric, Greensboro	0	1	.000	5.06	1	1	0	0	0	0	5.1	5	28	8	3	0	1	1	0	5	0	0	2	0
Schlomann, Brett, Greensboro	10	7	.588	3.90	25	25	1	0	0	0	147.2	144	639	76	64	10	2	1	9	54	1	140	8	1
Schneider, Jeff, Hagerstown	0	1	.000	27.00	2	0	0	0	1	0	0.2	1	8	2	2	0	0	0	1	4	0	0	0	1
Serna, Joe, Fayetteville	4	0	1.000	2.36	12	0	0	0	4	0	26.2	14	105	13	7	1	3	0	2	10	0	21	2	0
Sexton, Jeff, Columbus	6	2	.750	2.19	14	13	2	2	0	0	82.1	66	318	27	20	2	1	1	3	16	0	71	1	0
Sharp, Scott, Cha. (W.Va.)	0	0	.000	27.00	1	0	0	0	1	0	1.0	1	7	3	3	0	0	1	0	3	0	0	2	0
Shelby, Anthony, Greensboro*	3	8	.273	4.01	27	13	0	0	3	0	89.2	87	381	54	40	5	2	4	6	28	0	81	6	0
Shoemaker, Steve, Greensboro	4	4	.500	3.11	17	17	0	0	0	0	81.0	62	347	33	28	5	2	2	4	52	0	82	4	0
Short, Barry, Columbia	4	3	.571	1.97	40	1	0	0	15	4	77.2	63	319	22	17	1	2	0	2	22	2	56	5	2
Shumate, Jacob, Macon	0	8	.000	7.23	17	14	0	0	0	0	56.0	38	296	56	45	7	1	3	9	87	0	57	19	2
Sievert, Mark, Hagerstown	12	6	.667	2.91	27	27	3	0	0	0	160.2	126	644	59	52	14	5	1	2	46	0	140	2	0
Siler, Jeff, Fayetteville*	1	1	.500	0.40	21	0	0	0	4	1	22.2	16	86	2	1	0	2	0	1	11	0	25	1	1
Silva, Theodore, Cha. (S.C.)	5	4	.556	3.38	11	11	0	0	0	0	66.2	59	276	26	25	4	1	3	7	12	2	66	5	2
Skrmetta, Matt, Fayetteville	9	4	.692	2.71	44	2	0	0	15	2	89.2	66	371	36	27	9	6	1	3	35	2	105	2	0
Slamka, John, Asheville*	1	1	.500	4.09	6	1	0	0	2	0	11.0	9	46	5	5	0	0	1	1	4	0	7	1	1
Smith, Brian, Hagerstown	9	1	.900	0.87	47	0	0	0	36	21	104.0	77	402	18	10	1	5	0	5	16	1	101	2	2
Smith, Cam, Fayetteville	13	8	.619	3.81	29	29	2	2	0	0	149.0	110	652	75	63	6	3	3	18	87	0	166	21	1
Smith, Justin, Cha. (W.Va.)	4	5	.444	3.61	44	0	0	0	14	1	62.1	66	275	28	25	3	4	1	2	24	5	43	3	1
Sobik, Trad, Fayetteville	8	5	.615	4.16	18	18	0	0	0	0	101.2	100	430	68	47	4	2	6	3	43	0	58	1	2
Solomon, David, Cha. (W.Va.)*	1	2	.333	3.40	43	0	0	0	27	6	39.2	38	175	19	15	3	2	2	5	23	2	29	6	2
Spade, Matt, Augusta	6	5	.545	2.92	51	1	0	0	21	5	71.0	50	289	23	23	4	1	0	6	19	3	71	5	1
Spring, Josh, Hagerstown	1	4	.200	4.17	19	4	0	0	4	0	45.1	44	198	23	21	5	2	2	3	19	0	33	4	0
Stephens, Bill, Albany	1	3	.250	5.75	13	1	0	0	6	0	20.1	25	95	16	13	2	1	3	1	9	0	16	3	0
Stewart, Scott, Cha. (S.C.)*	1	7	.125	3.69	11	11	1	0	0	0	75.2	76	302	38	31	6	1	4	0	14	1	47	3	5
Stubbs, Jerry, Albany	3	2	.600	3.22	47	1	0	0	17	3	100.2	106	438	51	36	4	6	3	10	30	2	80	8	1
Stumpf, Brian, Piedmont	3	3	.500	2.34	55	0	0	0	47	28	61.2	59	258	20	16	2	5	2	0	19	0	66	7	0
Surratt, Jamie, Hickory	0	1	.000	1.76	12	0	0	0	9	3	15.1	13	69	8	3	1	1	1	0	8	4	19	1	0
Swanson, David, C'bia-Ash.*	8	1	.889	2.02	37	4	0	0	18	4	80.1	62	332	21	18	3	2	3	5	38	2	67	7	2
Tatis, Ramon, Columbia*	2	3	.400	5.63	18	2	0	0	9	0	32.0	34	141	27	20	1	2	1	1	14	0	27	5	0
Temple, Jason, Augusta	5	2	.714	2.26	51	0	0	0	18	5	71.2	45	297	26	18	6	4	2	3	28	0	84	5	1
Theodile, Robert, Hickory	6	9	.400	3.79	20	17	1	1	1	0	107.0	103	470	61	45	8	3	5	5	53	2	77	13	4
Thompson, Mark, Macon	3	2	.600	4.71	13	0	0	0	8	2	21.0	13	82	12	11	1	2	4	1	4	1	15	0	1
Thurman, Michael, Albany	3	8	.273	5.47	22	22	2	0	0	0	110.1	133	482	79	67	4	3	7	4	32	0	77	7	0
Tomko, Brett, Cha. (W.Va.)	4	2	.667	1.84	9	7	0	0	0	0	49.0	41	192	12	10	1	1	1	1	9	1	46	4	2
Toney, Mike, Hagerstown	3	3	.500	2.48	20	0	0	0	10	4	29.0	21	127	11	8	0	1	3	0	17	2	26	6	2
Trimble, Rob, Greensboro	1	1	.500	3.65	6	0	0	0	3	0	12.1	12	51	5	5	0	0	0	0	4	1	5	1	0
Turrentine, Rich, Columbia	4	4	.500	2.51	26	14	0	0	8	2	104.0	70	437	38	29	3	6	4	6	60	1	111	16	1
Tweedlie, Brad, Cha. (W.Va.)	2	4	.333	6.16	19	7	0	0	4	0	49.2	46	226	36	34	3	0	4	3	34	0	40	5	1
Tyner, Mark, Macon	2	2	.500	3.28	29	0	0	0	16	3	46.2	48	204	31	17	5	2	2	0	17	1	38	9	0
Van Overen, Ryan, Albany	0	1	.000	9.00	1	0	0	0	1	0	1.0	1	5	1	1	0	0	0	0	1	0	1	0	0
Vaske, Terry, Macon	0	1	.000	36.00	1	0	0	0	1	0	1.0	4	8	4	4	0	0	0	0	1	0	0	0	0
Vavrek, Mike, Asheville*	5	4	.556	2.00	12	12	1	0	0	0	76.2	64	322	24	17	3	0	1	5	25	0	54	4	5
Vazquez, Javier, Albany	6	6	.500	5.08	21	21	1	0	0	0	102.2	109	459	67	58	8	1	2	9	47	0	87	2	2
Vejil, Aaron, Cha. (W.Va.)*	2	0	1.000	0.00	6	0	0	0	3	0	3.1	2	15	0	0	0	0	0	0	3	1	5	0	0
Waldrep, Art, Asheville	0	3	.000	5.68	15	3	0	0	5	1	31.2	48	153	23	20	3	2	0	3	10	2	21	3	1
Warrecker, Teddy, Columbus	10	5	.667	4.13	24	24	1	1	0	0	130.2	104	559	76	60	10	3	3	13	80	1	125	6	0
Weber, Lenny, Columbus	4	0	1.000	1.84	17	0	0	0	5	2	29.1	19	113	6	6	0	2	0	0	10	3	32	3	0
Wehn, Kevin, Asheville	0	2	.000	6.30	5	0	0	0	3	1	10.0	9	42	7	7	1	0	0	0	4	0	5	1	0
Weidert, Chris, Albany	1	2	.333	7.84	3	3	0	0	0	0	10.1	16	55	14	9	3	0	1	0	5	0	17	0	0
Weiss, Marc, Cha. (W.Va.)	1	0	1.000	5.52	11	0	0	0	2	0	14.2	23	78	10	9	2	0	0	0	13	2	12	1	0
Welch, David, Hickory*	4	5	.444	2.67	60	0	0	0	19	5	77.2	68	328	39	23	5	6	2	3	21	10	82	7	1
Wells, David, Hickory	1	1	.500	5.17	17	1	0	0	4	0	38.1	44	167	28	22	4	2	2	1	13	2	30	2	1

Pitcher, Team	W	L	Pct.	ERA	G	GS	CG	ShO	GF	Sv.	IP	H	TBF	R	ER	HR	SH	SF	HB	BB	IBB	SO	WP	Bk.
Whiteman, Greg, Fayetteville*	6	8	.429	4.23	23	23	1	1	0	0	125.2	108	547	68	59	9	5	4	9	58	0	145	4	1
Whiteman, Tony, Fayetteville*	0	1	.000	3.96	28	0	0	0	4	0	25.0	25	117	16	11	1	2	1	2	18	0	23	2	0
Wilkerson, Steven, Cha. (W.Va.)	1	1	.500	5.49	16	0	0	0	8	0	19.2	21	97	13	12	0	0	0	2	18	0	15	4	0
Wilson, Mike, Fayetteville	4	3	.571	4.38	17	8	0	0	3	0	49.1	43	211	29	24	2	1	0	7	19	0	36	8	1
Wimberly, Larry, Piedmont*	10	3	.769	2.67	24	24	0	0	0	0	135.0	99	542	48	40	9	1	3	9	44	0	139	8	4
Windham, Mike, Savannah	6	9	.400	4.07	26	25	0	0	0	0	132.2	133	581	73	60	11	2	2	10	60	1	115	16	1
Wolff, Tom, Columbia	0	0	.000	4.37	15	0	0	0	13	0	22.2	21	99	13	11	0	0	1	3	8	0	16	3	0
Woodring, Jason, Albany	1	1	.500	2.66	48	0	0	0	39	16	50.2	46	222	19	15	0	2	2	5	20	2	50	3	2
Wright, Jaret, Columbus	5	6	.455	3.00	24	24	0	0	0	0	129.0	93	554	55	43	9	3	6	13	79	0	113	11	3
Young, Danny, Augusta*	1	0	1.000	2.51	6	2	0	0	1	0	14.1	9	66	6	4	0	0	1	0	16	0	11	2	0
Zedalis, Craig, Macon	1	1	.500	4.76	12	0	0	0	6	0	22.2	25	102	12	12	2	1	1	1	8	0	17	2	0
Zolecki, Mike, Asheville	3	2	.600	3.80	9	9	0	0	0	0	42.2	34	187	20	18	3	1	0	3	29	0	33	6	1
Zubiri, Jon, Columbus	0	0	.000	0.00	1	1	0	0	0	0	3.0	3	12	0	0	0	0	0	0	0	0	3	0	0

COMBINATION SHUTOUTS: **Albany (5)**—Moraga-Nygaard, Moraga-Woodring, Phelps-Handy-Woodring, Vazquez-Mikkelson, Vazquez-Rushworth. **Asheville (9)**—Barnes-Colmenares, Crowther-Grundt-Colmenares, Gooch-McClinton, Hackman-Bost, Kusiewicz-Barnes-Rose, Kusiewicz-Colmenares, Kusiewicz-Eden-Colmenares, Kusiewicz-Gonzalez-Colmenares, Vavrek-Colmenares. **Augusta (8)**—Anderson-Hampton, Anderson-Phillips-Hampton-Spade-Paugh, France-Grebe-Paugh, France-Paugh-Temple, Johnson-Temple-Paugh, Kelly-Temple-Maskivish, Pickford-Pelka-Phillips-Paugh, Pickford-Spade-Maskivish. **Charleston (S.C.) (3)**—Hower-Cook, O'Flynn-Cook, Silva-Hower. **Charleston (W.Va.) (7)**—Allen-Magre-Giron, Caruthers-Koppe-Solomon, Caruthers-Smith, Lott-Solomon, Runyan-Franklin, Tomco-Smith-Harvell-Magre, Tweedlie-Tomko-Giron. **Columbia (8)**—Atwater-Pack, Kelly-Baker, Johnston-Short-Baker, Kelly-Atwater-Baker, Sanchez-Atwater, Sanchez-Baker, Sanchez-Turrentine, Short-Sauerbeck. **Columbus (14)**—Granata-Montoya 2, Caldwell-Kramer-Donovan, Caldwell-Weber-Najera-Montoya, Granata-Donovan-Najera-Montoya, Oropeza-Najera-Montoya, Oropeza-Weber, Oropeza-Weber-Montoya, Perez-Najera, Sexton-Dinnen-Montoya, Warrecker-Najera-Montoya, Wright-Granata-Najera-Montoya, Wright-Kramer-Donovan, Wright-Perez. **Fayetteville (7)**—Jordan-Reed, Jordan-Whiteman-Dinyar-Gardner-Reed, Powell-Housley-Siler-Reed, Smith-Reed, Whiteman-Dinyar, Whiteman-Dinyar-Gardner, Whiteman-Skrmetta-Reed. **Greensboro (8)**—Jarvis-Mittauer, Medina-Shelby-Brown, Ricken-Binversie, Ricken-Binversie-Parotte-Brown, Ricken-Corn, Shelby-Parotte-Ford-Rojano-Benson, Shoemaker-Jarvis-Corn, Shoemaker-Mittauer-Corn. **Hagerstown (7)**—Davey-Smith, Meiners-Smith, Pace-Hartshorn-Smith, Pace-Hibbard-Rhine, Sievert-Davenport, Sievert-Pace, Sievert-Toney. **Hickory (7)**—Ambrose-Welch, Castillo-Dixon-Portillo, Crine-Cruz-Welch-Dixon, Crine-Portillo, Crine-Welch-Portillo, Herbert-Cruz, Theodile-Dixon. **Macon (8)**—Ebert-Raines 2, Bowie-Evangelista, Lavenia-Brown, Millwood-Olszewski, Moss-Shumate-Culp, Moss-Thompson, Moss-Zedalis. **Piedmont (10)**—Wimberly-Stumpf 2, Censale-Genke-Humphry, Censale-Stumpf, Hunter-Stumpf, Manning-Barbao-Gambs, Wimberly-Barbao, Wimberly-Genke-Stumpf, Wimberly-Kosek, Wimberly-Nyari-Stumpf. **Savannah (5)**—Almanza-Conway-Garcia, Almanza-Golden-Conway, Aybar-Glauber-Lovingier-Golden-Conway-Garcia, Reames-Conway, Windham-Lovingier-Garcia.

NO-HIT GAMES: None.

PITCHERS WITH TWO OR MORE TEAMS

Pitcher, Team	W	L	Pct.	ERA	G	GS	CG	ShO	GF	Sv.	IP	H	TBF	R	ER	HR	SH	SF	HB	BB	IBB	SO	WP	Bk.
Gooch, Arnold, Asheville	5	8	.385	2.94	21	21	1	1	0	0	128.2	111	541	51	42	8	3	3	4	57	0	117	13	0
Gooch, Arnold, Columbia	2	3	.400	4.46	6	6	0	0	0	0	38.1	39	169	25	19	3	0	1	2	15	0	34	5	0
Jarvis, Jason, Greensboro	8	7	.533	3.01	22	16	0	0	2	0	110.2	103	468	47	37	5	4	5	1	38	3	82	13	1
Jarvis, Jason, Hagerstown	4	3	.571	3.60	8	8	0	0	0	0	50.0	49	210	27	20	3	2	4	3	13	1	42	7	1
Swanson, David, Columbia*	7	1	.875	1.46	29	4	0	0	16	3	67.2	48	276	14	11	2	1	3	4	31	2	60	7	2
Swanson, David, Asheville*	1	0	1.000	4.97	8	0	0	0	2	1	12.2	14	56	7	7	1	1	0	1	7	0	7	0	0

1995 FIELDING

TEAM

Team	Pct.	G	PO	A	E	TC	DP	PB
Asheville	.971	139	3636	1584	156	5376	137	31
Charleston (W.Va.)	.968	142	3627	1525	169	5321	112	26
Columbus	.966	142	3727	1575	184	5486	146	31
Greensboro	.965	140	3678	1432	185	5295	100	31
Columbia	.962	140	3707	1525	206	5438	126	22
Savannah	.962	139	3686	1397	202	5285	105	35
Hagerstown	.961	141	3648	1517	208	5373	103	34
Piedmont	.961	140	3655	1467	208	5330	113	32
Charleston (S.C.)	.961	139	3604	1480	207	5291	120	31
Macon	.960	141	3809	1586	226	5621	122	23
Fayetteville	.960	141	3695	1508	218	5421	107	27
Hickory	.957	138	3666	1517	231	5414	104	21
Augusta	.955	138	3598	1484	239	5321	114	15
Albany	.945	140	3727	1519	303	5549	118	25

TRIPLE PLAY: Charleston (W.Va.).

INDIVIDUAL

FIRST BASEMEN

NOTE: All caps denotes fielding-percentage leader based on 71 games for catchers, 94 for all other non-pitchers and 142 innings for pitchers. *Throws lefthanded.

Player, Team	Pct.	G	PO	A	E	TC	DP
Allen, Marlon, Charleston (W.Va.)	.974	64	489	32	14	535	38
Balint, Rob, Fayetteville	1.000	5	32	1	0	33	1
Barkett, Andy, Charleston (S.C.)*	.986	16	127	10	2	139	11
Boka, Ben, Columbia	1.000	1	1	0	0	1	1
Bragga, Matt, Charleston (W.Va.)	.973	26	168	12	5	185	13
Brown, Nate, Albany*	.971	102	861	77	28	966	74
Brown, Ray, Charleston (W.Va.)	1.000	2	20	4	0	24	2
Carranza, Pete, Asheville	1.000	2	4	1	0	5	1
Cooney, James, Charleston (S.C.)	1.000	7	50	0	0	50	9
Cooper, Steve, Savannah	.997	36	306	16	1	323	27
DeBerry, Joe, Greensboro*	1.000	12	99	9	0	108	9
Dishington, Nate, Savannah	.986	85	713	44	11	768	48
Donato, Dan, Greensboro	1.000	6	40	5	0	45	4
Eddie, Steve, Charleston (W.Va.)	.995	76	504	56	3	563	47
Fantauzzi, John, Asheville*	.984	85	838	74	15	927	79
Friedrich, Steve, Hickory	1.000	1	1	0	0	1	0
Fullmer, Brad, Albany	.974	32	248	13	7	268	16
Fussell, Denny, Charleston (W.Va.)*	1.000	1	10	0	0	10	0
Gainey, Bryon, Columbia	.979	118	998	57	23	1078	90
Garcia, Neil, Fayetteville	1.000	6	41	1	0	42	3
Giardi, Mike, Greensboro	1.000	1	7	0	0	7	0
Gipner, Marcus, Greensboro	1.000	1	1	0	0	1	0
Goldberg, Lonnie, Charleston (S.C.)	.969	4	28	3	1	32	3
Gomez, Paul, Columbia	.957	6	21	1	1	23	2
Guerrero, Rafael, Columbia	.996	26	213	13	1	227	17
Haas, Matt, Albany	.958	12	109	6	5	120	14
Harris, G.G., Augusta	.985	70	600	40	10	650	49
Heller, Bradley, Charleston (S.C.)	1.000	1	12	1	0	13	0
Helton, Todd, Asheville*	.990	44	388	21	4	413	31
Izquierdo, Sergio, Hickory	1.000	1	1	0	0	1	0
Koerick, Thomas, Hickory	.986	26	205	14	3	222	12
Ladd, Jeff, Hagerstown	.987	15	146	11	2	159	12
Lantigua, Eduardo, Columbus	.970	4	31	1	1	33	2
Larkin, Stephen, Charleston (S.C.)*	.980	55	371	29	8	408	35
Lidle, Kevin, Fayetteville	1.000	1	11	2	0	13	1
Llanos, Aurelio, Hagerstown	.968	17	145	8	5	158	11
McDougal, Mike, Savannah	.970	12	93	4	3	100	8
McMillan, Tom, Savannah	1.000	1	1	0	0	1	0
Millan, Adam, Piedmont	.991	75	627	41	6	674	50
Millican, Kevin, Charleston (S.C.)	.935	8	54	4	4	62	1
Mobilia, Bill, Piedmont	1.000	15	94	5	0	99	6
Morgan, Dave, Hagerstown	.981	19	148	8	3	159	6
Mosquera, Julio, Hagerstown	1.000	1	4	0	0	4	0
Mota, Guillermo, Columbia	1.000	1	3	0	0	3	0
Moyle, Mike, Columbus	.947	2	17	1	1	19	2
Mummau, Rob, Hagerstown	1.000	1	1	0	0	1	1
Oakland, Mike, Asheville	.986	7	68	4	1	73	5
Perry, Chan, Columbus	.997	64	570	37	2	609	56
Pullen, Shane, Piedmont	.988	59	472	40	6	518	37
Reyes, Winston, Piedmont	1.000	3	19	1	0	20	2
Rice, Charles, Augusta	.971	10	92	8	3	103	9
Rives, Sherron, Fayetteville	.944	3	16	1	1	18	1

Player, Team	Pct.	G	PO	A	E	TC	DP
Robles, Rafael, Savannah	1.000	2	4	0	0	4	0
Rodriguez, Adam, Fayetteville	.990	13	86	10	1	97	7
Santa, Roberto, Charleston (S.C.)*	.993	64	521	42	4	567	46
Silvia, Brian, Savannah	.986	8	70	2	1	73	2
Smith, Jason, Asheville	.957	5	43	1	2	46	5
STONE, Craig, Hagerstown	.991	95	829	64	8	901	59
Stumberger, Darren, Columbus	.991	76	620	53	6	679	65
Thobe, Steve, Augusta	.979	61	562	33	13	608	39
Torborg, Dale, Greensboro	.967	14	59	0	2	61	2
Valdez, Mario, Hickory	.989	120	1040	67	12	1119	77
Vaske, Terry, Macon	.969	21	177	10	6	193	17
Ward, Daryle, Fayetteville*	.987	121	1009	77	14	1100	77
Whitehurst, Todd, Columbia	1.000	2	5	0	0	5	0
Wright, Ron, Macon	.984	120	1035	99	18	1152	85
Wuerch, Jason, Greensboro	.980	5	46	2	1	49	6
Yedo, Carlos, Greensboro*	.985	111	930	84	15	1029	68

TRIPLE PLAY: Eddie.

SECOND BASEMEN

Player, Team	Pct.	G	PO	A	E	TC	DP
Acosta, Ed, Albany	.920	13	20	26	4	50	4
Aguila, Hector, Charleston (S.C.)	1.000	1	2	2	0	4	1
Almanzar, Richard, Fayetteville	.971	79	170	226	12	408	40
Amador, Manny, Piedmont	1.000	1	0	6	0	6	1
Ambrosina, Pete, Savannah	.957	121	224	286	23	533	65
Arvelo, Tom, Columbia	.889	4	1	7	1	9	0
Bocachica, Hiram, Albany	1.000	2	4	3	0	7	1
Brinkley, Josh, Albany	1.000	1	1	2	0	3	0
Brooks, Eddie, Augusta	.931	24	40	54	7	101	12
Brown, Vick, Greensboro	.948	117	226	269	27	522	55
Brunson, Matt, Fayetteville	.973	33	71	71	4	146	15
Camilli, Jason, Albany	.951	18	38	39	4	81	5
CARDENAS, Epi, Columbus	.978	124	267	353	14	634	92
Carranza, Pete, Asheville	1.000	1	2	2	0	4	0
Carvajal, Jhonny, Charleston (W.Va.)	.969	106	206	270	15	491	60
Chambers, Mack, Columbus	1.000	1	2	2	0	4	1
Coquillette, Trace, Albany	.975	110	252	292	14	558	62
Delgado, Jose, Macon	.958	4	10	13	1	24	4
Eaglin, Mike, Macon	.954	128	274	354	30	658	74
Eddie, Steve, Charleston (W.Va.)	1.000	4	3	5	0	8	0
Flores, Jose, Piedmont	.931	9	13	14	2	29	4
Friedrich, Steve, Hickory	.963	89	180	238	16	434	29
Garcia, Neil, Fayetteville	1.000	2	2	1	0	3	0
Giardi, Mike, Greensboro	1.000	12	19	25	0	44	2
Goldberg, Lonnie, Charleston (S.C.)	.935	13	18	25	3	46	4
Herider, Jeremy, Charleston (W.Va.)	.500	1	0	1	1	2	1
Holley, Jack, Hagerstown	1.000	1	2	3	0	5	1
Hooker, Kevin, Piedmont	1.000	2	2	3	0	5	0
Huff, Larry, Piedmont	.953	127	252	292	27	571	78
Jarrett, Linc, Asheville	.991	80	128	185	3	316	44
Jenkins, Dee, Charleston (W.Va.)	.959	24	39	54	4	97	10
Lackey, Steve, Columbia	.909	4	4	6	1	11	0
Landry, Dan, Macon	1.000	2	5	4	0	9	0
Lofton, James, Charleston (W.Va.)	.986	22	22	47	1	70	10
Matos, Julius, Columbus	.963	6	14	12	1	27	4
Mayber, Chan, Asheville	1.000	7	8	25	0	33	6
McLamb, Brian, Greensboro	.952	21	37	43	4	84	9
Mendoza, Jesus, Hickory	.967	46	83	124	7	214	29
Mobilia, Bill, Piedmont	1.000	1	1	1	0	2	0
Mummau, Rob, Hagerstown	.980	54	103	144	5	252	18
Navas, Jesus, Hickory	.939	18	27	35	4	66	9
Newell, Brett, Macon	.976	9	19	22	1	42	8
Ocasio, Fred, Asheville	.976	10	19	22	1	42	4
Oram, Jon, Columbus	.957	9	23	21	2	46	6
Pena, Elvis, Asheville	.954	48	86	140	11	237	39
Rivera, Miguel, Savannah	1.000	1	2	1	0	3	0
Rives, Sherron, Fayetteville	.957	36	68	64	6	138	15
Robles, Rafael, Savannah	.959	18	32	38	3	73	8
Rutz, Ryan, Charleston (S.C.)	.963	131	274	330	23	627	77
Segura, Juan, Augusta	1.000	5	11	11	0	22	2
Smith, Rod, Greensboro	1.000	1	1	2	0	3	1
Strange, Mike, Hagerstown	.939	93	134	237	24	395	45
Subero, Carlos, Augusta	1.000	1	2	0	0	2	0
Swafford, Derek, Augusta	.941	115	207	290	31	528	53
Utting, Ben, Macon	1.000	1	0	1	0	1	0
Van Overen, Ryan, Albany	.900	6	10	8	2	20	2
Veras, Juan, Charleston (S.C.)	1.000	2	4	2	0	6	1
White, Eric, Columbus	.895	4	8	9	2	19	2
Williamson, Matt, Piedmont	.962	7	9	16	1	26	3
Zorrilla, Julio, Columbia	.961	128	257	285	22	564	68
Zuniga, David, Columbia	1.000	8	9	17	0	26	4

TRIPLE PLAY: Carvajal.

THIRD BASEMEN

Player, Team	Pct.	G	PO	A	E	TC	DP
Acosta, Ed, Albany	.769	26	11	29	12	52	4
Adolfo, Carlos, Albany	.000	1	0	0	1	1	0
Aguila, Hector, Charleston (S.C.)	.923	7	5	19	2	26	2
Ambrosina, Pete, Savannah	1.000	1	0	2	0	2	0
Asche, Mike, Augusta	.857	97	61	172	39	272	7
Balfe, Ryan, Fayetteville	.906	104	55	206	27	288	22
Balint, Rob, Fayetteville	1.000	2	2	6	0	8	0
Branyan, Russell, Columbus	.856	62	34	120	26	180	9
Brinkley, Josh, Albany	.815	20	12	32	10	54	4
Brooks, Eddie, Augusta	.882	27	14	46	8	68	3
CARRANZA, Pete, Asheville	.936	102	69	266	23	358	16
Colombino, Carlo, Columbus	1.000	1	0	1	0	1	0
Coquillette, Trace, Albany	.824	18	14	28	9	51	2
Donato, Dan, Greensboro	.965	54	31	106	5	142	9
Dukart, Derek, Greensboro	.945	73	60	130	11	201	11
Eddie, Steve, Charleston (W.Va.)	.953	31	18	43	3	64	5
Flores, Jose, Piedmont	.937	44	34	84	8	126	8
Friedrich, Steve, Hickory	.890	30	28	53	10	91	3
Fullmer, Brad, Albany	.763	41	21	53	23	97	3
Gann, Steve, Charleston (W.Va.)	.897	14	5	21	3	29	3
Garcia, Neil, Fayetteville	.833	3	1	4	1	6	2
Giardi, Mike, Greensboro	1.000	5	3	7	0	10	1
Goldberg, Lonnie, Charleston (S.C.)	.857	15	10	26	6	42	3
Gomez, Paul, Columbia	1.000	1	0	2	0	2	0
Haas, Matt, Albany	.800	2	2	2	1	5	0
Hampton, Mike, Charleston (W.Va.)	.885	94	56	167	29	252	14
Harper, Rantie, Savannah	1.000	1	1	2	0	3	0
Helms, Wes, Macon	.900	133	91	269	40	400	25
Holley, Jack, Hagerstown	.951	12	5	34	2	41	1
Hooker, Kevin, Piedmont	.852	10	3	20	4	27	2
Huff, Larry, Piedmont	1.000	1	1	0	0	1	0
Koerick, Thomas, Hickory	.774	13	3	21	7	31	1
Lackey, Steve, Columbia	.848	38	14	64	14	92	4
Landry, Dan, Macon	.667	2	1	3	2	6	0
Lantigua, Eduardo, Columbus	.962	9	6	19	1	26	2
Lee, Carlos, Hickory	.848	44	30	76	19	125	4
Leon, Geraldo, Savannah	.810	20	8	26	8	42	3
Lidle, Kevin, Fayetteville	.857	9	4	20	4	28	3
Lofton, James, Charleston (W.Va.)	1.000	9	3	17	0	20	0
Lopez, Jose, Columbia	.907	79	44	171	22	237	16
Martinez, Dalvis, Fayetteville	.942	26	20	45	4	69	7
Matos, Julius, Columbus	1.000	1	1	0	0	1	0
Mayber, Chan, Asheville	.912	22	14	38	5	57	3
McLamb, Brian, Greensboro	.875	13	5	16	3	24	0
Meskauskas, John, Asheville	1.000	1	0	2	0	2	0
Mobilia, Bill, Piedmont	.774	18	12	29	12	53	2
Mummau, Rob, Hagerstown	.939	12	8	23	2	33	1
Myers, Aaron, Asheville	.886	20	12	50	8	70	6
Newell, Brett, Macon	.880	8	7	15	3	25	1
O'Brien, Joe, Piedmont	.791	14	9	25	9	43	4
Ocasio, Fred, Asheville	1.000	3	0	2	0	2	0
Oram, Jon, Columbus	.850	15	13	21	6	40	1
Pond, Simon, Albany	.789	22	11	49	16	76	3
Preston, Doyle, Charleston (W.Va.)	.833	7	0	15	3	18	1
Reyes, Winston, Piedmont	.786	2	2	9	3	14	0
Rivera, Miguel, Savannah	.905	117	86	255	36	377	16
Rives, Sherron, Fayetteville	.778	10	2	12	4	18	2
Robles, Rafael, Savannah	.950	6	5	14	1	20	0
Segura, Juan, Augusta	.900	3	0	9	1	10	0
Tatis, Fernando, Charleston (S.C.)	.900	124	98	235	37	370	24
Thobe, Steve, Augusta	.917	15	5	28	3	36	2
Thompson, Andy, Hagerstown	.869	119	86	200	43	329	13
Van Overen, Ryan, Albany	.908	31	19	70	9	98	7
Vaske, Terry, Macon	.750	3	1	2	1	4	0
White, Eric, Columbus	.920	68	43	141	16	200	16
Whitehurst, Todd, Columbia	.970	20	19	46	2	67	1
Wilhelm, Brent, Hickory	.899	67	32	138	19	189	5
Williamson, Matt, Piedmont	.903	68	63	132	21	216	8
Wuerch, Jason, Greensboro	.818	3	2	7	2	11	0
Zuniga, David, Columbia	.854	20	4	31	6	41	2

SHORTSTOPS

Player, Team	Pct.	G	PO	A	E	TC	DP
Acosta, Ed, Albany	.786	6	5	6	3	14	0
Aguila, Hector, Charleston (S.C.)	1.000	2	0	4	0	4	0
Arvelo, Tom, Columbia	1.000	2	3	4	0	7	1
Bearden, Doug, Hickory	.880	44	47	114	22	183	20
Beeney, Ryan, Greensboro	.900	56	76	150	25	251	20
Bocachica, Hiram, Albany	.880	94	161	263	58	482	55
Brinkley, Josh, Albany	1.000	1	1	2	0	3	0

Player, Team	Pct.	G	PO	A	E	TC	DP
Brooks, Eddie, Augusta	.769	5	1	9	3	13	1
Brown, Vick, Greensboro	1.000	1	0	1	0	1	0
Brunson, Matt, Fayetteville	.943	10	5	28	2	35	1
Camilli, Jason, Albany	.902	37	48	99	16	163	19
Carvajal, Jhonny, Charleston (W.Va.)	.968	35	36	86	4	126	11
Chambers, Mack, Columbus	.750	1	2	1	1	4	1
Delgado, Jose, Macon	.924	41	59	112	14	185	18
Dukart, Derek, Greensboro	.800	1	3	1	1	5	0
Flores, Jose, Piedmont	.943	8	10	23	2	35	3
Giardi, Mike, Greensboro	1.000	2	0	3	0	3	0
Goldberg, Lonnie, Charleston (S.C.)	.922	46	53	124	15	192	20
Gonzalez, Mario, Charleston (S.C.)	.897	7	14	12	3	29	7
Green, Bert, Savannah	.917	132	205	358	51	614	58
Guiliano, Matt, Piedmont	.936	129	146	382	36	564	65
Herider, Jeremy, Charleston (W.Va.)	.813	5	2	11	3	16	3
HOUSER, Kyle, Asheville	.973	110	151	318	13	482	64
Jarrett, Linc, Asheville	.980	32	47	100	3	150	25
Johnson, Jeff, Hickory	.937	50	59	134	13	206	20
Lackey, Steve, Columbia	.976	25	27	54	2	83	13
Landry, Dan, Macon	.974	8	12	26	1	39	4
Lobaton, Jose, Greensboro	.928	58	62	170	18	250	33
Matos, Julius, Columbus	.914	30	43	96	13	152	18
Mayber, Chan, Asheville	.800	2	4	4	2	10	0
McLamb, Brian, Greensboro	.929	27	30	61	7	98	11
Mercedes, Guillermo, Columbus	.966	54	70	155	8	233	29
Mobilia, Bill, Piedmont	1.000	1	1	3	0	4	0
Mota, Guillermo, Columbia	.935	122	202	373	40	615	66
Mummau, Rob, Hagerstown	.960	26	49	72	5	126	15
Navas, Jesus, Hickory	.914	56	79	145	21	245	28
Newell, Brett, Macon	.933	47	69	155	16	240	32
Oram, Jon, Columbus	.921	33	37	91	11	139	18
Ordaz, Luis, Charleston (W.Va.)	.954	111	164	290	22	476	52
Perez, Santiago, Fayetteville	.916	129	176	327	46	549	58
Rives, Sherron, Fayetteville	.862	8	7	18	4	29	2
Robinson, Tony, Augusta	.930	93	131	281	31	443	53
Robles, Rafael, Savannah	.814	10	13	22	8	43	0
Rutz, Ryan, Charleston (S.C.)	.750	1	0	3	1	4	0
Segura, Juan, Augusta	.975	18	27	50	2	79	9
Subero, Carlos, Augusta	.948	29	53	93	8	154	21
Utting, Ben, Macon	.888	20	22	49	9	80	9
Valera, Willy, Columbus	.919	31	43	94	12	149	31
Van Overen, Ryan, Albany	1.000	12	7	26	0	33	6
Veras, Juan, Charleston (S.C.)	.951	94	126	245	19	390	45
Wilhelm, Brent, Hickory	.800	1	3	1	1	5	0
Williams, Glenn, Macon	.867	32	37	87	19	143	11
Williamson, Matt, Piedmont	.789	4	3	12	4	19	3
Wilson, Brian, Charleston (W.Va.)	1.000	5	8	13	0	21	2
Witt, Kevin, Hagerstown	.919	117	203	338	48	589	61
Zuniga, David, Columbia	1.000	1	1	0	0	1	0

TRIPLE PLAY: Ordaz.

OUTFIELDERS

Player, Team	Pct.	G	PO	A	E	TC	DP
Abell, Tony, Savannah	.826	17	17	2	4	23	0
Acosta, Ed, Albany	1.000	7	6	0	0	6	0
Adolfo, Carlos, Albany	1.000	50	96	6	0	102	2
Aguila, Hector, Charleston (S.C.)	1.000	1	0	1	0	1	0
Albert, Rashad, Hickory	.976	85	194	7	5	206	3
Barkett, Andy, Charleston (S.C.)*	1.000	5	8	1	0	9	0
Bass, Jayson, Fayetteville*	.932	95	133	4	10	147	1
Borel, Jamie, Fayetteville	.993	70	143	4	1	148	2
Bragga, Matt, Charleston (W.Va.)	.971	24	32	1	1	34	0
Brewer, Brett, Macon	.961	112	170	3	7	180	1
Brooks, Eddie, Augusta	1.000	1	1	0	0	1	0
Brown, Adrian, Augusta	.950	68	124	8	7	139	1
Brown, Nate, Albany*	.917	11	21	1	2	24	0
Buchanan, Brian, Greensboro	.970	23	31	1	1	33	0
Cancel, David, Hickory	.938	66	115	5	8	128	0
Carranza, Pete, Asheville	1.000	3	2	0	0	2	0
Carvajal, Jhonny, Charleston (W.Va.)	1.000	1	1	0	0	1	0
Chapman, Eric, Columbus	.967	51	88	1	3	92	0
Coach, Calvin, Savannah*	.985	63	121	7	2	130	1
Collum, Gary, Columbia*	1.000	5	5	0	0	5	0
Comeaux, Edward, Charleston (S.C.)	.966	80	137	7	5	149	1
Conner, Decomba, Charleston (W.Va.)	.989	90	184	3	2	189	2
Coquillette, Trace, Albany	1.000	5	3	0	0	3	0
Darr, Mike, Fayetteville	.939	97	123	15	9	147	2
Delafield, Wil, Greensboro	.965	105	208	11	8	227	3
Diaz, Linardo, Piedmont	.938	9	15	0	1	16	0
Donato, Dan, Greensboro	1.000	8	13	0	0	13	0
Drent, Brian, Hickory	.900	23	26	1	3	30	0
Ealy, Tracey, Savannah	.972	97	167	5	5	177	0
Eddie, Steve, Charleston (W.Va.)	.813	10	13	0	3	16	0
Edwards, Aaron, Augusta	.964	43	78	3	3	84	0
Encarnacion, Juan, Fayetteville	.956	102	143	10	7	160	0
Estrada, Josue, Albany	.989	61	87	5	1	93	0
Ferrier, Ross, Columbia	.955	13	19	2	1	22	0
Figueroa, Danny, Asheville	.968	49	87	4	3	94	1
Friedrich, Steve, Hickory	1.000	3	9	0	0	9	0
Gambill, Chad, Asheville	1.000	90	138	7	0	145	3
Gatti, Dom, Charleston (S.C.)	.978	96	176	2	4	182	0
Giardi, Mike, Greensboro	1.000	11	18	2	0	20	1
Gibson, Derrick, Asheville	.957	125	190	11	9	210	2
Glass, Chip, Columbus*	.984	111	178	11	3	192	2
Goldberg, Lonnie, Charleston (S.C.)	.909	16	18	2	2	22	0
Gomez, Ramon, Hickory	.976	72	147	13	4	164	1
Guerrero, Rafael, Columbia	.990	59	92	12	1	105	1
Guerrero, Vladimir, Albany	.953	94	207	15	11	233	4
Guillen, Jose, Augusta	1.000	6	5	0	0	5	0
Haas, Matt, Albany	1.000	1	1	0	0	1	0
Hall, Ronnie, Asheville	.948	130	209	11	12	232	3
Harper, Rantie, Savannah	.980	85	140	4	3	147	1
Hayes, Darren, Hickory	.946	56	81	6	5	92	0
Holley, Jack, Hagerstown	.857	2	5	1	1	7	0
Hunter, Scott, Columbia	.957	12	21	1	1	23	0
Jones, Andruw, Macon	.988	130	332	10	4	346	4
Kelley, Erskine, Augusta	.975	96	143	13	4	160	2
Kennedy, Gus, Macon	.978	109	169	10	4	183	0
Key, Jeff, Piedmont	.963	61	102	3	4	109	0
Lantigua, Eduardo, Columbus	.750	7	6	0	2	8	0
Larkin, Stephen, Charleston (S.C.)*	.903	28	53	3	6	62	1
Ledee, Ricky, Greensboro*	.982	87	160	7	3	170	2
Leon, Geraldo, Savannah	1.000	1	1	0	0	1	0
Lewis, Andreaus, Columbus	.973	75	103	4	3	110	0
Lidle, Kevin, Fayetteville	1.000	1	2	0	0	2	0
Llanos, Aurelio, Hagerstown	.958	70	133	5	6	144	3
Lofton, James, Charleston (W.Va.)	.913	20	18	3	2	23	0
Lombard, George, Macon	.958	35	44	2	2	48	1
Long, Terrence, Columbia*	.937	49	69	5	5	79	0
Luciano, Virgilio, Charleston (S.C.)*	.976	81	107	14	3	124	3
Martinez, Dalvis, Fayetteville	1.000	1	1	0	0	1	0
Matos, Julius, Columbus	1.000	14	18	0	0	18	0
McClure, Craig, Hickory	.963	46	74	4	3	81	0
McLamb, Brian, Greensboro	1.000	8	13	0	0	13	0
McMillan, Tom, Savannah	.938	67	103	3	7	113	1
McNally, Shawn, Savannah	.989	49	87	3	1	91	1
Millican, Kevin, Charleston (S.C.)	1.000	3	1	0	0	1	0
Monroe, Darryl, Fayetteville	.992	70	116	4	1	121	0
Morrow, Nick, Charleston (W.Va.)	.975	138	292	17	8	317	3
O'Brien, Joe, Piedmont	.978	31	43	1	1	45	0
Oram, Jon, Columbus	1.000	4	3	0	0	3	0
Ortman, Ben, Asheville	1.000	10	9	1	0	10	0
Ozario, Yudith, Columbia	.969	115	213	9	7	229	0
Pearson, Cory, Charleston (S.C.)	.953	50	77	4	4	85	1
Perez, Joe, Charleston (S.C.)*	.980	57	92	4	2	98	0
Perry, Chan, Columbus	1.000	17	28	0	0	28	0
Pollock, Elton, Augusta	.926	26	50	0	4	54	0
Prensi, Dagoberto, Hagerstown	.973	103	168	9	5	182	1
Prieto, Ricky, Columbus	1.000	4	11	0	0	11	0
Pullen, Shane, Piedmont	1.000	19	27	2	0	29	1
Rivers, Jonathon, Hagerstown	.958	122	212	14	10	236	1
Rives, Sherron, Fayetteville	1.000	1	1	0	0	1	0
Robles, Rafael, Savannah	.909	5	10	0	1	11	0
Rosado, Juan, Albany*	1.000	5	5	0	0	5	0
ROYSTER, Aaron, Piedmont	.991	123	204	6	2	212	2
Sanders, Anthony, Hagerstown	.990	133	274	15	3	292	1
Sanders, Rod, Charleston (W.Va.)	.979	62	85	10	2	97	2
Sanderson, David, Columbia*	.976	74	118	5	3	126	0
Saturnino, Sherton, Macon	.769	25	18	2	6	26	1
Schreimann, Eric, Piedmont	1.000	2	2	0	0	2	0
Schwab, Chris, Albany*	.949	106	142	6	8	156	1
Seguignol, Fernando, Albany	.964	110	205	7	8	220	1
Shumpert, Derek, Greensboro	1.000	51	77	1	0	78	0
Simmons, Brian, Hickory	.988	41	77	2	1	80	1
Smith, Rod, Greensboro	.948	62	89	3	5	97	1
Staton, T.J., Augusta*	.948	100	153	10	9	172	1
Stingley, Derek, Piedmont	.978	30	43	1	1	45	1
Taylor, Byron, Savannah	1.000	4	2	0	0	2	0
Thomas, Rod, Charleston (W.Va.)	.944	18	32	2	2	36	1
Thompson, Leroy, Columbus*	.976	37	37	4	1	42	1
Tidick, Michael, Hickory	.967	47	57	2	2	61	1

Player, Team	Pct.	G	PO	A	E	TC	DP
Torok, John, Piedmont	.966	89	130	11	5	146	1
Turner, Rocky, Columbia	1.000	8	12	0	0	12	0
Twitty, Sean, Greensboro	.918	66	116	7	11	134	0
Vasquez, Danilo, Charleston (S.C.)	.962	42	64	11	3	78	3
Waldrop, Tom, Macon*	1.000	24	38	1	0	39	0
Walker, Shon, Augusta*	.944	96	151	19	10	180	5
Warner, Bryan, Columbus*	.978	110	170	12	4	186	0
Watts, Josh, Piedmont	.987	106	144	11	2	157	2
Wells, Mark, Asheville	1.000	28	38	4	0	42	1
White, Eric, Columbus	.986	38	66	6	1	73	0
Williams, Curtis, Savannah*	.958	47	69	0	3	72	0
Williams, Mark, Savannah	.500	1	1	0	1	2	0
Wilson, Preston, Columbia	.961	104	189	10	8	207	3
Wright, Terry, Charleston (W.Va.)*	.985	115	180	13	3	196	3
Wuerch, Jason, Greensboro	.952	14	18	2	1	21	1

CATCHERS

Player, Team	Pct.	G	PO	A	E	TC	DP	PB
Afenir, Tom, Columbus	1.000	5	23	7	0	30	0	2
Alderman, Kurt, Albany	.954	23	136	9	7	152	1	5
Almond, Greg, Savannah	1.000	11	112	9	0	121	0	2
Arias, Rogelio, Asheville	.986	67	440	49	7	496	5	20
Ashby, Chris, Greensboro	.983	62	456	65	9	530	2	11
Balint, Rob, Fayetteville	1.000	2	16	0	0	16	0	1
Boka, Ben, Columbia	.903	7	27	1	3	31	0	1
Bowen, Glenn, Savannah	.982	16	100	8	2	110	1	6
Cardona, Javier, Fayetteville	.990	48	339	48	4	391	4	7
Carpenter, Matt, Ash.-C'bus	.960	11	38	10	2	50	0	0
Cooney, James, Charleston (S.C.)	1.000	4	15	0	0	15	0	0
Cossins, Tim, Charleston (S.C.)	.966	19	130	13	5	148	1	1
Dawson, Charles, Macon	.983	38	257	32	5	294	3	1
Donato, Dan, Greensboro	1.000	1	2	0	0	2	0	0
Eddie, Steve, Charleston (W.Va.)	1.000	2	3	0	0	3	0	0
Falciglia, Tony, Savannah	1.000	18	116	13	0	129	1	4
Fithian, Grant, Greensboro	.985	51	352	49	6	407	3	14
Garcia, Neil, Fayetteville	.981	52	386	38	8	432	0	16
Gomez, Paul, Columbia	.970	26	142	20	5	167	0	3
Gonzalez, Wikleman, Augusta	.985	49	345	43	6	394	5	6
Haas, Matt, Albany	.987	31	197	23	3	223	0	6
Hammell, Al, Columbia	.967	3	25	4	1	30	0	1
Harriss, Robin, Columbus	.981	51	397	68	9	474	6	9
Heller, Bradley, Charleston (S.C.)	.978	65	405	37	10	452	2	8
Henley, Bob, Albany	.983	94	684	111	14	809	9	14
Izquierdo, Sergio, Hickory	.979	44	276	50	7	333	4	9
Johnson, Mark, Hickory	.986	100	681	67	11	759	3	10
Koerick, Thomas, Hickory	.982	12	48	7	1	56	0	2
Ladd, Jeff, Hagerstown	.984	26	163	24	3	190	3	9
Lewis, Rob, Columbus	.990	20	178	18	2	198	2	3
Lidle, Kevin, Fayetteville	.985	23	219	36	4	259	0	3
Lopez, Victor, Charleston (S.C.)	1.000	12	95	8	0	103	1	3
Lunar, Fernando, Macon	.967	32	261	35	10	306	7	6
Matos, Pasqual, Macon	.985	72	498	76	9	583	1	16
Meskauskas, John, Asheville	.979	29	171	16	4	191	0	4
Millan, Adam, Piedmont	.989	31	243	26	3	272	0	4
Millican, Kevin, Charleston (S.C.)	.985	62	395	50	7	452	5	19
Morales, Eric, Columbia	.987	35	264	41	4	309	1	3
Morales, Francisco, Savannah	1.000	18	123	15	0	138	7	4
Morgan, Dave, Hagerstown	.969	23	112	15	4	131	0	9
MOSQUERA, Julio, Hagerstown	.991	98	637	103	7	747	6	16
Moyle, Mike, Columbus	.979	67	494	66	12	572	8	17
Nitschke, Bear, Piedmont	1.000	2	5	3	0	8	0	0
Northeimer, Jamie, Piedmont	.987	108	812	92	12	916	6	27
Petillo, Bruce, Piedmont	.900	1	9	0	1	10	0	0
Pozo, Yohel, Asheville	.970	40	322	39	11	372	2	6
Reynolds, Chance, Augusta	1.000	22	143	22	0	165	2	2
Rodriguez, Adam, Fayetteville	.988	24	214	39	3	256	1	0
Schreimann, Eric, Piedmont	.973	5	32	4	1	37	0	1
Sharp, Scott, Charleston (W.Va.)	.982	53	319	54	7	380	3	10
Silvia, Brian, Savannah	.976	24	185	19	5	209	3	4
Smith, Jason, Asheville	1.000	8	37	5	0	42	1	1
Sweet, Jonathan, Augusta	.985	77	534	51	9	594	4	7
Towle, Justin, Charleston (W.Va.)	.984	100	622	103	12	737	3	16
Trimble, Rob, Greensboro	.987	24	206	15	3	224	1	1
Troilo, Jason, Greensboro	1.000	16	98	13	0	111	0	5
Vaske, Terry, Macon	1.000	1	2	0	0	2	0	0
Weaver, Colby, Macon	.983	14	104	14	2	120	2	0
Williams, Mark, Savannah	.991	62	491	62	5	558	6	16
Wilson, Vance, Columbia	.981	85	605	99	14	718	4	12
Winterlee, Scott, Columbia	1.000	1	2	1	0	3	0	1

CATCHERS WITH TWO OR MORE TEAMS

Player, Team	Pct.	G	PO	A	E	TC	DP	PB
Carpenter, Matt, Asheville	.956	9	33	10	2	45	0	0
Carpenter, Matt, Columbus	1.000	2	5	0	0	5	0	0

PITCHERS

Player, Team	Pct.	G	PO	A	E	TC	DP
Adair, Scott, Columbia	.500	3	0	1	1	2	0
Alazaus, Shawn, Greensboro*	1.000	33	2	3	0	5	0
Allen, Cedric, Charleston (W.Va.)*	.980	27	17	31	1	49	2
Almanza, Armando, Savannah*	1.000	20	0	17	0	17	0
Ambrose, John, Hickory	.857	14	5	13	3	21	1
Anderson, Jimmy, Augusta*	.968	14	5	25	1	31	6
Anez, Maycoll, Hickory	1.000	2	0	1	0	1	0
Antonini, Adrian, Piedmont	.667	6	1	3	2	6	0
Arias, Alfredo, Hagerstown	.727	35	0	8	3	11	0
Atwater, Joe, Columbia*	.947	27	8	10	1	19	2
Avrard, Corey, Savannah	1.000	13	2	7	0	9	0
Aybar, Manuel, Savannah	1.000	18	16	17	0	33	1
Bajda, Mike, Fayetteville	1.000	4	2	0	0	2	0
Baker, Derek, Columbia	1.000	36	4	6	0	10	1
Barbao, Joe, Piedmont	.786	43	4	7	3	14	0
Barnes, Keith, Asheville*	1.000	10	4	5	0	9	0
Bell, Mike, Albany*	1.000	12	0	5	0	5	1
Benson, Jeremy, Greensboro*	1.000	3	0	1	0	1	0
Beverlin, Jason, Greensboro	1.000	7	2	7	0	9	1
Binversie, Brian, Greensboro	1.000	31	3	2	0	5	1
Bledsoe, Randy, Savannah	.833	28	1	4	1	6	0
Blythe, Billy, Macon	1.000	7	3	2	0	5	0
Bost, Heath, Asheville	.875	9	3	4	1	8	0
Bowie, Micah, Macon*	1.000	5	1	2	0	3	0
Boyd, Jason, Piedmont	.912	26	14	17	3	34	1
Briggs, Anthony, Macon	.935	29	19	10	2	31	0
Brown, Charlie, Greensboro	.909	45	4	6	1	11	0
Brown, Darold, Macon*	.882	31	5	10	2	17	0
Brownson, Mark, Asheville	.913	23	6	15	2	23	1
Burdick, Morgan, Asheville	.833	17	2	3	1	6	1
Buteaux, Shane, Hickory	.963	13	7	19	1	27	1
Cain, Travis, Macon	1.000	14	3	1	0	4	0
CALDWELL, David, Columbus*	1.000	27	6	28	0	34	2
Callahan, Damon, Charleston (W.Va.)	.714	6	2	3	2	7	0
Carlson, Garret, Hickory	1.000	3	0	1	0	1	0
Caruthers, Clayton, Char. (W.Va.)	.964	27	11	16	1	28	1
Castillo, Carlos, Hickory	.900	14	5	13	2	20	0
Censale, Silvio, Piedmont*	.810	22	5	12	4	21	1
Chavarria, David, Charleston (S.C.)	.923	52	3	9	1	13	0
Chaves, Rafael, Augusta	.000	7	0	0	1	1	0
Civit, Xavier, Albany	.889	12	3	5	1	9	0
Clark, Doug, Fayetteville	1.000	4	0	2	0	2	0
Cole, Jason, Albany	.800	32	2	10	3	15	0
Collins, Zach, Macon*	1.000	4	0	2	0	2	1
Colmenares, Luis, Asheville	.875	45	1	6	1	8	1
Conway, Keith, Savannah*	.909	60	3	7	1	11	1
Cook, Rodney, Charleston (S.C.)	.912	60	6	25	3	34	2
Cooke, Steve, Augusta*	1.000	1	0	1	0	1	0
Cordero, Francisco, Fayetteville	.625	4	2	3	3	8	0
Corn, Chris, Greensboro	.857	49	6	12	3	21	1
Crine, Dennis, Hickory	.857	15	3	9	2	14	1
Crowther, Brent, Asheville	.944	15	14	20	2	36	3
Crowther, John, Hagerstown	.667	11	1	5	3	9	0
Cruise, Mark, Savannah	1.000	6	2	3	0	5	0
Cruz, Nelson, Hickory	.909	44	1	9	1	11	0
Cubillan, Darwin, Greensboro	.933	22	3	11	1	15	1
Culp, Wes, Macon	1.000	39	7	17	0	24	0
Davenport, Joe, Hagerstown	.500	13	0	1	1	2	0
Davey, Tom, Hagerstown	1.000	8	5	4	0	9	1
Davis, Kane, Augusta	.929	26	9	30	3	42	3
Dinnen, Kevin, Columbus	1.000	49	4	10	0	14	0
Dinyar, Eric, Fayetteville	.893	42	3	22	3	28	3
Dixon, Jim, Hickory	1.000	35	5	7	0	12	0
Doman, Roger, Hagerstown	.933	14	3	11	1	15	0
Done, J.J., Columbus	1.000	4	0	2	0	2	0
Donnelly, Brendan, Char. (W.Va.)	.667	24	3	3	3	9	0
Donovan, Scot, Columbus	.833	40	3	7	2	12	0
Dougherty, Tony, Columbus	.800	27	3	5	2	10	0
Doyle, Tom, Charleston (W.Va.)*	.947	14	5	13	1	19	1
Durocher, Jayson, Albany	.970	24	13	19	1	33	2
Ebert, Derrin, Macon*	.946	28	9	44	3	56	3
Eden, Bill, Asheville*	.857	33	1	5	1	7	0
Escamilla, Jaime, Char. (S.C.)*	1.000	32	4	11	0	15	0
Estavil, Mauricio, Piedmont*	1.000	42	2	6	0	8	0
Evangelista, Alberto, Macon	.727	24	5	3	3	11	0

Player, Team	Pct.	G	PO	A	E	TC	DP
Fereira, Marcos, Hickory	1.000	4	0	1	0	1	0
Ford, Ben, Greensboro	1.000	7	0	2	0	2	0
Ford, Jack, Hickory*	.919	27	6	28	3	37	0
France, Aaron, Augusta	.957	18	6	16	1	23	0
Franklin, Joel, Charleston (W.Va.)	1.000	24	1	8	0	9	1
Gambs, Chris, Piedmont	.800	9	1	3	1	5	0
Garcia, Frank, Savannah	1.000	34	1	3	0	4	0
Garcia-Luna, Francisco, Augusta	.889	14	0	8	1	9	1
Gardner, Scott, Fayetteville	.923	49	8	16	2	26	0
Genke, Todd, Piedmont	1.000	31	3	7	0	10	0
Giard, Kenneth, Macon	1.000	5	2	1	0	3	0
Giron, Emiliano, Char. (W.Va.)	1.000	30	2	0	0	2	0
Glauber, Keith, Savannah	1.000	40	9	10	0	19	1
Gogolewski, Chris, Char. (S.C.)*	.892	30	7	26	4	37	4
Golden, Matthew, Savannah	.850	64	7	10	3	20	0
Gonzalez, Jhonny, Asheville*	1.000	21	0	6	0	6	0
Gooch, Arnold, Ash.-C'bia	.962	27	9	16	1	26	1
Graham, Steve, Macon	.750	5	0	3	1	4	0
Granata, Chris, Columbus	.944	33	7	10	1	18	2
Grebe, Brett, Augusta	.909	32	7	3	1	11	0
Grundt, Ken, Asheville*	1.000	20	1	2	0	3	0
Hackman, Luther, Asheville	.976	28	13	27	1	41	2
Halley, Allen, Hickory	.846	13	4	7	2	13	0
Hamilton, Paul, Piedmont	.800	15	2	2	1	5	1
Hampton, Mark, Augusta	1.000	39	6	10	0	16	0
Handy, Russell, Albany	.846	30	10	12	4	26	0
Hartmann, Rich, Savannah	.909	31	3	7	1	11	0
Hartshorn, Tyson, Hagerstown	.867	12	4	9	2	15	0
Harvell, Pete, Charleston (W.Va.)*	1.000	27	1	7	0	8	1
Helvey, Rob, Savannah*	.857	18	5	1	1	7	0
Henderson, Chris, Asheville	1.000	17	2	2	0	4	1
Herbert, Russell, Hickory	.852	18	6	17	4	27	0
Hibbard, Billy, Hagerstown	.900	16	5	4	1	10	0
Housley, Adam, Fayetteville	.917	19	6	5	1	12	0
Hower, Dan, Charleston (S.C.)*	.818	22	6	12	4	22	1
Humphry, Trevor, Piedmont	.941	28	3	13	1	17	0
Hunter, Rich, Piedmont	.943	15	6	27	2	35	2
Jacobson, Kelton, Fayetteville	.941	25	7	9	1	17	1
Jarvis, Jason, Gre.-Hag.	.951	30	14	25	2	41	1
Johnson, Jason, Augusta	1.000	11	1	6	0	7	0
Johnston, Sean, Columbia*	.974	23	9	29	1	39	5
Jordan, Jason, Fayetteville	.857	24	6	12	3	21	1
Karvala, Kyle, Piedmont*	1.000	20	0	1	0	1	0
Kell, Rob, Charleston (S.C.)*	1.000	7	2	6	0	8	0
Kelly, Jeff, Augusta*	.871	26	7	20	4	31	4
Kelly, John, Columbia	.875	28	9	19	4	32	0
Knight, Brandon, Charleston (S.C.)	.833	9	3	7	2	12	0
Knighton, Toure, Charleston (S.C.)	.933	22	4	10	1	15	1
Koppe, Clint, Charleston (W.Va.)	.958	30	9	14	1	24	1
Kosek, Kory, Piedmont	1.000	15	1	5	0	6	0
Kramer, Scott, Columbus	.846	19	6	5	2	13	1
Kusiewicz, Michael, Asheville*	.848	21	8	20	5	33	1
LaPoint, Jason, Albany*	.769	33	2	8	3	13	0
Larson, Toby, Columbia	.923	8	8	4	1	13	1
Lasbury, Robert, Asheville	1.000	6	1	2	0	3	0
Lavenia, Mark, Macon*	1.000	24	3	4	0	7	1
Lee, Jeremy, Hagerstown	1.000	26	10	12	0	22	0
Legrow, Brett, Piedmont	1.000	8	1	0	0	1	0
Logan, Marcus, Savannah	.933	34	4	10	1	15	0
Lott, Brian, Charleston (W.Va.)	.971	28	15	19	1	35	0
Lovingier, Kevin, Savannah*	.909	38	2	8	1	11	0
Maberry, Louis, Charleston (W.Va.)	1.000	4	1	1	0	2	0
Magre, Pete, Charleston (W.Va.)	1.000	21	2	2	0	4	0
Manning, Len, Piedmont*	.791	27	8	26	9	43	2
Martin, Chandler, Asheville	1.000	8	1	10	0	11	0
Martinez, Johnny, Columbus	.923	16	2	10	1	13	2
Martinez, Osvaldo, Fayetteville	1.000	6	2	3	0	5	1
Maskivish, Joe, Augusta	.714	26	2	3	2	7	1
Mattes, Troy, Albany	1.000	4	1	4	0	5	1
McAdams, Denny, Asheville	1.000	5	0	2	0	2	0
McBride, Chris, Hagerstown	.967	19	10	19	1	30	1
McClinton, Patrick, Asheville*	1.000	18	0	7	0	7	1
McEntire, Ethan, Columbia*	.938	6	5	10	1	16	0
McNeill, Kevin, Savannah*	.949	29	5	32	2	39	3
Medina, Rafael, Greensboro	.846	19	3	8	2	13	1
Meiners, Doug, Hagerstown	.931	18	7	20	2	29	0
Mejias, Fernando, Hickory	.840	30	6	15	4	25	3
Meyer, David, Greensboro*	.960	14	6	18	1	25	0
Mikkelsen, Lincoln, Albany	1.000	12	2	6	0	8	0
Millwood, Kevin, Macon	1.000	29	10	11	0	21	0
Minor, Tom, Savannah	.500	8	1	0	1	2	0
Mitchell, Courtney, Piedmont*	1.000	5	0	1	0	1	0

Player, Team	Pct.	G	PO	A	E	TC	DP
Mittauer, Casey, Greensboro	.920	49	8	15	2	25	1
Montoya, Wilmer, Columbus	.889	51	7	9	2	18	3
Moore, David, Hickory	1.000	20	0	2	0	2	0
Moraga, David, Albany*	.971	25	8	26	1	35	1
Morillo, Donald, Charleston (S.C.)	.750	18	1	2	1	4	0
Mortimer, Mick, Charleston (S.C.)	1.000	5	2	2	0	4	2
Moss, Damian, Macon*	.889	27	7	25	4	36	0
Najera, Noe, Columbus*	.833	43	0	5	1	6	0
Newton, Chris, Fayetteville*	1.000	2	0	2	0	2	0
Nieto, Tony, Charleston (W.Va.)	.882	13	2	13	2	17	3
Nunez, Maximo, Hagerstown	.900	22	1	8	1	10	0
Nuttle, Jamison, Augusta	1.000	6	0	1	0	1	0
Nyari, Pete, Piedmont	.846	35	6	5	2	13	1
Nygaard, Chris, Albany*	.867	41	2	11	2	15	0
O'Flynn, Gardner, Char. (S.C.)*	.930	30	11	42	4	57	1
Olszewski, Eric, Macon	.941	35	11	5	1	17	0
Oropeza, Igor, Columbus	.857	9	1	5	1	7	0
Pace, Scott, Hagerstown*	1.000	11	3	14	0	17	0
Pack, Steve, Columbia	.929	36	5	8	1	14	0
Parotte, Frisco, Greensboro	.900	22	1	8	1	10	1
Paugh, Rick, Augusta*	.818	52	2	7	2	11	0
Pauls, Matthew, Charleston (S.C.)	1.000	16	0	2	0	2	0
Pelka, Brian, Augusta	.875	26	1	6	1	8	1
Perez, Julio, Columbus	.963	22	11	15	1	27	1
Perpetuo, Nelson, Char. (S.C.)*	.941	32	2	14	1	17	0
Peterman, Ernie, Hagerstown	1.000	2	3	0	0	3	0
Phelps, Tommy, Albany*	.903	24	3	25	3	31	1
Phillips, Jason, Augusta	.929	30	5	8	1	14	0
Phipps, Chris, Piedmont	1.000	11	9	2	0	11	0
Pickford, Kevin, Augusta*	.957	16	3	19	1	23	0
Portillo, Alex, Hickory*	1.000	33	3	9	0	12	1
Powell, Brian, Fayetteville	1.000	5	2	2	0	4	0
Powell, Jeremy, Albany	1.000	1	0	1	0	1	0
Presley, Kirk, Columbia	.800	4	1	3	1	5	1
Raines, Ken, Macon*	1.000	14	1	5	0	6	0
Ramirez, Rafael, Savannah	.958	26	8	15	1	24	0
Reames, Britt, Savannah	.778	10	0	7	2	9	1
Reed, Brandon, Fayetteville	.750	55	1	5	2	8	0
Reid, Rayon, Augusta	.867	12	6	7	2	15	0
Reyes, Jose, Charleston (S.C.)	1.000	4	2	0	0	2	0
Rhine, Kendall, Hagerstown	.944	42	4	13	1	18	3
Rhodriguez, Rory, Albany	.857	37	5	7	2	14	0
Ricken, Ray, Greensboro	.941	10	8	8	1	17	0
Roberts, Willis, Fayetteville	.857	17	3	15	3	21	1
Robinson, Martin, Greensboro*	1.000	2	0	3	0	3	0
Rocker, John, Macon*	1.000	16	4	18	0	22	2
Rojano, Rafael, Greensboro	1.000	19	6	3	0	9	0
Rose, Brian, Asheville	1.000	10	1	2	0	3	0
Ruiz, Rafael, Hickory*	1.000	5	0	2	0	2	0
Runion, Jeff, Charleston (S.C.)	.857	2	2	4	1	7	0
Runyan, Paul, Charleston (W.Va.)	1.000	15	4	8	0	12	1
Rushworth, Jim, Albany	1.000	6	1	4	0	5	0
Ryan, Reid, Charleston (S.C.)	.643	22	2	7	5	14	0
Sanchez, Jesus, Columbia*	.978	27	9	35	1	45	2
Sanders, Frankie, Columbus	1.000	2	1	1	0	2	0
Sauerbeck, Scott, Columbia*	1.000	19	1	6	0	7	1
Schaffner, Eric, Greensboro	1.000	1	1	1	0	2	0
Schlomann, Brett, Greensboro	.875	25	4	10	2	16	0
Serna, Joe, Fayetteville	.875	12	1	6	1	8	0
Sexton, Jeff, Columbus	.913	14	12	9	2	23	0
Shelby, Anthony, Greensboro*	.957	27	5	17	1	23	1
Shoemaker, Steve, Greensboro	.944	17	6	11	1	18	2
Short, Barry, Columbia	.957	40	6	16	1	23	1
Shumate, Jacob, Macon	1.000	17	3	7	0	10	1
Sievert, Mark, Hagerstown	.973	27	9	27	1	37	2
Siler, Jeff, Fayetteville*	.889	21	0	8	1	9	0
Silva, Theodore, Char. (S.C.)	1.000	11	5	10	0	15	1
Skrmetta, Matt, Fayetteville	.941	44	4	12	1	17	0
Slamka, John, Asheville*	1.000	6	0	1	0	1	0
Smith, Brian, Hagerstown	.885	47	6	17	3	26	1
Smith, Cam, Fayetteville	.789	29	14	16	8	38	1
Smith, Justin, Charleston (W.Va.)	1.000	44	8	9	0	17	0
Sobik, Trad, Fayetteville	.805	18	10	23	8	41	2
Solomon, David, Charleston (W.Va.)*	.875	43	5	9	2	16	0
Spade, Matt, Augusta	.929	51	1	12	1	14	0
Spring, Josh, Hagerstown	1.000	19	4	5	0	9	1
Stephens, Bill, Albany	.800	13	0	4	1	5	0
Stewart, Scott, Charleston (S.C.)*	.952	11	2	18	1	21	0
Stubbs, Jerry, Albany	.935	47	5	24	2	31	1
Stumpf, Brian, Piedmont	.850	55	4	13	3	20	0
Surratt, Jamie, Hickory	1.000	12	1	2	0	3	0
Swanson, David, C'bia-Ash.*	1.000	8	2	1	0	3	0

Player, Team	Pct.	G	PO	A	E	TC	DP
Tatis, Ramon, Columbia*	.500	18	1	1	2	4	0
Temple, Jason, Augusta	.625	51	4	6	6	16	0
Theodile, Robert, Hickory	.900	20	7	20	3	30	1
Thompson, Mark, Macon	1.000	13	0	2	0	2	0
Thurman, Michael, Albany	1.000	22	10	14	0	24	1
Tomko, Brett, Charleston (W.Va.)	1.000	9	1	3	0	4	0
Toney, Mike, Hagerstown	.909	20	5	5	1	11	0
Trimble, Rob, Greensboro	1.000	6	3	1	0	4	0
Turrentine, Rich, Columbia	.920	26	8	15	2	25	2
Tweedlie, Brad, Charleston (W.Va.)	.833	19	1	9	2	12	0
Tyner, Mark, Macon	1.000	29	1	3	0	4	0
Vavrek, Mike, Asheville*	.917	12	3	8	1	12	0
Vazquez, Javier, Albany	.852	21	10	13	4	27	1
Waldrep, Art, Asheville	1.000	15	2	2	0	4	0
Warrecker, Teddy, Columbus	.800	24	6	10	4	20	2
Weber, Lenny, Columbus	1.000	17	2	5	0	7	0
Wehn, Kevin, Asheville	1.000	5	2	3	0	5	1
Weidert, Chris, Albany	1.000	3	1	1	0	2	0
Weiss, Marc, Charleston (W.Va.)	1.000	11	0	4	0	4	0
Welch, David, Hickory*	.889	60	2	14	2	18	0
Wells, David, Hickory	1.000	17	2	4	0	6	0
Whiteman, Greg, Fayetteville*	.952	23	4	16	1	21	1
Whiteman, Tony, Fayetteville*	.846	28	5	6	2	13	0
Wilkerson, Steven, Char. (W.Va.)	.857	16	3	3	1	7	0
Wilson, Mike, Fayetteville	.889	17	1	7	1	9	0
Wimberly, Larry, Piedmont*	.870	24	1	19	3	23	0
Windham, Mike, Savannah	.933	26	9	19	2	30	1
Wolff, Tom, Columbia	1.000	15	0	2	0	2	0
Woodring, Jason, Albany	1.000	48	4	12	0	16	1
Wright, Jaret, Columbus	.913	24	7	14	2	23	0
Young, Danny, Augusta*	1.000	6	0	3	0	3	0
Zedalis, Craig, Macon	1.000	12	3	5	0	8	0
Zolecki, Mike, Asheville	.818	9	3	6	2	11	0

PITCHERS WITH TWO OR MORE TEAMS

Player, Team	Pct.	G	PO	A	E	TC	DP
Gooch, Arnold, Asheville	1.000	21	9	13	0	22	1
Gooch, Arnold, Columbia	.750	6	0	3	1	4	0
Jarvis, Jason, Greensboro	.969	22	13	18	1	32	1
Jarvis, Jason, Hagerstown	.889	8	1	7	1	9	0
Swanson, David, Columbia*	1.000	29	4	16	0	20	2
Swanson, David, Asheville*	1.000	8	2	1	0	3	0

The following players did not have any fielding statistics at the positions indicated or appeared only as a designated hitter, pinch-hitter or pinch-runner: Antczak, of, c; Beirne, p; Broome, p; Cardona, of; Cooney, p; Cooper, p; Eddie, ss; Elam, 3b; Fantauzzi, p; Figueroa, 1b; Forbes, p; R. Gomez, 1b; Hausmann, p; R. Jones, dh; Judd, p; Key, 1b; Kindell, p; Lackey, 1b; C. Lee, ss; Leiber, p; Light, dh, ph; D. Martinez, ss; O'Brien, 1b; Ocasio, p; Oram, 1b; Jo. Perez, p; Reilly, dh; Resetar, ph; Reynolds, p; Rodriguez, of; Schneider, p; Sharp, p; Shugars, of; Silvia, of; Towle, 1b; Van Oeveren, p; Vaske, of, p; Vejil, p; Wampler, dh; J. White, dh; Zubiri, p.

LEAGUE CHAMPIONS

Year	Team	Pct.
1948—	Lincolnton*	.627
1949—	Newton-Conover	.667
	Rutherford Co. (2nd)†	.627
1950—	Newton-Conover	.627
	Lenoir (2nd)†	.626
1951—	Morganton	.645
	Shelby (2nd)†	.604
1952—	Lincolnton	.649
	Shelby (2nd)†	.645
1953-59—	League inactive.	
1960—	Lexington	.707
	Salisbury (2nd)†	.650
1961—	Salisbury	.627
	Shelby (4th)†	.481
1962—	Statesville	.563
	Statesville	.700
1963—	Greenville†	.576
	Salisbury	.631
1964—	Rock Hill	.672
	Salisbury‡	.631
1965—	Salisbury	.641
	Rock Hill‡	.603
1966—	Spartanburg	.682
	Spartanburg	.767
1967—	Spartanburg	.730
	Spartanburg	.567
1968—	Spartanburg	.597
	Greenwood‡	.597
1969—	Greenwood‡	.587
	Shelby	.565
1970—	Greenville	.576
	Greenville	.619
1971—	Greenwood	.631
	Greenwood	.759
1972—	Spartanburg‡	.788
	Greenville	.652
1973—	Spartanburg‡	.646
	Gastonia	.619
1974—	Gastonia	.606
	Gastonia	.672
1975—	Spartanburg	.543
	Spartanburg	.614
1976—	Asheville	.544
	Greenwood‡	.600
1977—	Greenwood	.557
	Gastonia‡	.590
1978—	Greenwood	.614
	Greenwood	.565
1979—	Greenwood‡	.565
	Spartanburg	.525
1980—	Greensboro	.590
	Charleston	.561
1981—	Greensboro‡	.695
	Greenwood	.549
1982—	Greensboro‡	.681
	Florence	.546
1983—	Columbia	.620
	Gastonia‡	.587
1984—	Charleston	.549
	Asheville‡	.510
1985—	Florence‡	.599
	Greensboro	.540
1986—	Columbia‡	.682
	Asheville	.643
1987—	Asheville	.655
	Myrtle Beach‡	.597
1988—	Charleston (S.C.)	.616
	Spartanburg‡	.500
1989—	Gastonia	.657
	Augusta‡	.535
1990—	Columbia	.580
	Charleston (W.Va.)‡	.538
1991—	Charleston (W.Va.)	.648
	Columbia‡	.614
1992—	Columbia	.572
	Myrtle Beach‡	.522
1993—	Savannah‡	.662
	Greensboro	.603
1994—	Columbus	.630
	Savannah‡	.599
1995—	Piedmont	.586
	Augusta‡	.551

*Won championship and four-club playoff. †Won four-club playoff. ‡Won split-season playoff. (NOTE—Known as Western Carolina League from 1948 through 1962 and known as Western Carolinas League through 1979.)

APPALACHIAN LEAGUE

LEAGUE OFFICE

President
Lee Landers

Address
20360 Carson Lane
Bristol, VA 24202

Phone
703-669-3644

Teams (affiliation)
Bluefield Orioles (Orioles)
Bristol White Sox (White Sox)
Burlington Indians (Indians)
Danville Braves (Braves)
Elizabethton Twins (Twins)
Johnson City Cardinals (Cardinals)
Kingsport Mets (Mets)
Martinsville Phillies (Phillies)
Princeton Reds (Reds)

1995 FINAL STANDINGS

NORTH DIVISION

Team	W	L	T	Pct.	GB
Bluefield (Orioles)	49	16	0	.754	....
Princeton (Reds)	31	32	0	.492	17
Martinsville (Phillies)	30	37	0	.448	20
Burlington (Indians)	26	38	0	.406	22½
Danville (Braves)	27	40	0	.403	23

SOUTH DIVISION

Team	W	L	T	Pct.	GB
Kingsport (Mets)	48	18	0	.727	....
Elizabethton (Twins)	33	31	0	.516	14
Johnson City (Cardinals)	35	33	0	.515	14
Bristol (White Sox)	28	39	0	.418	20½
Huntington (Co-op)	22	45	0	.328	26½

COMPOSITE

Team	Blu.	Kng.	Elz.	J.C.	Pri.	Mar.	Brs.	Bur.	Dan.	Hun.	W	L	T	Pct.	GB
Bluefield (Orioles)	....	1	5	3	6	6	4	8	8	8	49	16	0	.754	....
Kingsport (Mets)	2	....	6	6	6	4	7	3	5	9	48	18	0	.727	1½
Elizabethton (Twins)	0	4	....	7	3	3	5	2	4	5	33	31	0	.516	15½
Johnson City (Cardinals)	1	4	3	....	2	5	6	3	3	8	35	33	0	.515	15½
Princeton (Reds)	3	3	1	2	....	4	3	5	6	4	31	32	0	.492	17
Martinsville (Phillies)	4	1	1	5	5	....	2	3	6	3	30	37	0	.448	20
Bristol (White Sox)	1	3	4	4	2	2	....	6	1	5	28	39	0	.418	22
Burlington (Indians)	1	1	2	2	3	7	4	...	5	1	26	38	0	.406	22½
Danville (Braves)	2	0	5	2	4	4	3	5	....	2	27	40	0	.403	23
Huntington (Co-op)	2	1	4	2	1	2	5	3	2	....	22	45	0	.328	28

Major league affiliations in parentheses.

PLAYOFFS: Kingsport defeated Bluefield, two games to one, to win league championship.

REGULAR-SEASON ATTENDANCE: Bluefield, 45,127; Bristol, 29,691; Burlington, 32,648; Danville, 63,905; Elizabethton, 18,982; Huntington, 20,631; Johnson City, 41,449; Kingsport, 35,891; Martinsville, 46,155; Princeton, 29,021. Total—363,500. Playoffs (3 games)—2,524.

MANAGERS: Bluefield, Andy Etchebarren; Bristol, Chris Cron; Burlington, Harry Spilman; Danville, Max Venable; Elizabethton, John Russell; Huntington, Phillip Wellman; Johnson City, Steve Turco; Kingsport, John Gibbons; Martinsville, Ramon Henderson; Princeton, Brad Kelly.

ALL-STAR TEAM: 1B—Jarrod Patterson, Kingsport; 2B—Kevin Hooker, Martinsville; 3B—Carlos Lee, Bristol; SS—Eddy Martinez, Bluefield; Utility IF—Zach Elliott, Martinsville; OF—Johnny Isom, Bluefield; Jeramie Simpson, Kingsport; Darron Ingram, Princeton; Utility OF—Eugene Kingsale, Bluefield; C—A.J. Pierzynski, Elizabethton; DH—Tony Boyette, Princeton; RHP—Chris Fussell, Bluefield; LHP—Chris Murphy, Princeton; Relief Pitcher—Manuel Mendez, Johnson City; Most Valuable Player—Jarrod Patterson, Kingsport; Manager of the Year—John Gibbons, Kingsport.

1995 BATTING

TEAM

Team	Avg.	G	TPA	AB	R	H	TB	2B	3B	HR	RBI	SH	SF	HP	BB	IBB	SO	SB	CS	GDP	LOB	ShO	Slg.	OBP
Bluefield	.293	65	2493	2174	437	637	927	120	22	42	370	24	27	27	241	7	416	128	46	43	427	0	.426	.367
Elizabethton	.263	64	2466	2172	363	572	879	108	11	59	315	9	15	27	243	4	493	78	36	36	458	1	.405	.343
Kingsport	.263	66	2520	2199	402	578	819	98	22	33	327	23	18	33	247	7	458	113	39	29	440	3	.372	.344
Danville	.258	67	2526	2230	326	576	823	100	21	35	274	6	20	28	241	10	546	128	58	37	470	0	.369	.335
Bristol	.253	67	2495	2209	296	559	773	91	18	29	251	18	19	38	210	6	546	95	39	38	478	2	.350	.326
Johnson City	.249	68	2632	2261	357	562	811	119	23	28	300	14	20	33	304	4	583	70	51	37	506	4	.359	.343
Martinsville	.247	67	2477	2131	325	526	739	98	17	27	279	13	17	58	257	6	531	91	32	53	471	4	.347	.341
Burlington	.238	64	2384	2133	298	508	750	92	15	40	236	6	15	31	194	3	598	104	39	29	420	5	.352	.309
Princeton	.237	63	2362	2098	330	497	782	100	13	53	286	15	14	25	210	3	546	71	26	25	396	5	.373	.312
Huntington	.237	67	2461	2134	307	505	741	96	22	32	255	23	19	30	255	5	552	108	44	37	438	7	.347	.324

INDIVIDUAL

TOP QUALIFIERS FOR BATTING CHAMPIONSHIP

Minimum 184 plate appearances. *Lefthanded batter. †Switch-hitter.

Player, Team	Avg.	G	TPA	AB	R	H	TB	2B	3B	HR	RBI	SH	SF	HP	BB	IBB	SO	SB	CS	GDP	Slg.	OBP
Elliott, Zach, Martinsville	.358	45	193	151	46	54	78	10	4	2	19	1	2	7	32	1	30	13	5	3	.517	.484
Munoz, Juan, Johnson City*	.347	57	219	190	43	66	101	12	1	7	31	0	2	0	27	0	17	13	2	1	.532	.425
Lee, Carlos, Bristol	.346	67	282	269	43	93	133	17	1	7	45	0	3	2	8	3	34	17	7	6	.494	.365
Isom, Johnny, Bluefield	.344	59	247	212	47	73	113	14	4	6	56	2	7	1	25	0	27	9	2	5	.533	.404
Hooker, Kevin, Martinsville	.335	49	210	179	38	60	105	16	1	9	46	0	3	7	21	0	34	2	3	1	.587	.419
Pierzynski, A.J., Elizabethton*	.332	56	220	205	29	68	104	13	1	7	45	0	1	0	14	1	23	0	2	6	.507	.373
Mendoza, Carlos, Kingsport*	.328	51	228	192	56	63	75	9	0	1	24	4	2	3	27	0	24	28	6	3	.391	.415
Simpson, Jeramie, Kingsport*	.323	59	259	229	50	74	105	11	10	0	28	1	3	6	20	0	37	25	5	2	.459	.388
Rincones, Wuarnner, Bristol	.317	61	227	189	25	60	81	10	4	1	25	0	2	4	32	0	29	2	0	5	.429	.423
Kingsale, Eugene, Bluefield†	.316	47	209	171	45	54	69	11	2	0	16	4	2	5	27	0	31	20	8	0	.404	.420

Player, Team	Avg.	G	TPA	AB	R	H	TB	2B	3B	HR	RBI	SH	SF	HP	BB	IBB	SO	SB	CS	GDP	Slg.	OBP
Russin, Tom, Bluefield	.312	57	238	215	42	67	105	21	1	5	41	0	1	4	18	2	27	1	1	3	.488	.374
Martinez, Eddy, Bluefield	.308	57	215	185	42	57	77	11	3	1	35	1	1	5	23	0	42	5	5	1	.416	.397
Almonte, Wady, Bluefield	.307	51	201	189	37	58	90	12	1	6	30	0	2	1	9	2	49	6	5	4	.476	.338
Garcia, Carlos, Elizabethton	.306	62	262	235	42	72	104	15	1	5	34	3	4	4	16	0	41	27	8	5	.443	.355
Cross, Adam, Danville	.304	50	195	181	21	55	73	15	0	1	16	0	1	2	11	0	16	15	11	7	.403	.349

DEPARTMENTAL LEADERS: G—Haas, C. Lee, 67; AB—C. Lee, 269; R—Mendoza, 56; H—C. Lee, 93; TB—C. Lee, 133; 2B—Russin, 21; 3B—Simpson, 10; HR—Ingram, 14; RBI—Patterson, 57; SH—Mastrullo, 10; SF—Isom, 7; HP—Schreimann, 13; BB—Haas, 52; IBB—Hendricks, C. Lee, 3; SO—Haas, 93; SB—M. Anderson, 38; CS—Cross, 11; GIDP—Bryant, 10; Slg.—Hooker, .587; OBP—Elliott, .484.

ALL PLAYERS

*Lefthanded batter. †Switch-hitter.

Player, Team	Avg.	G	TPA	AB	R	H	TB	2B	3B	HR	RBI	SH	SF	HP	BB	IBB	SO	SB	CS	GDP	Slg.	OBP
Abell, Antonio, Johnson City	.258	55	222	190	27	49	63	10	2	0	16	2	3	5	22	1	76	8	8	0	.332	.345
Albert, Chernan, Bristol	.270	38	165	152	27	41	67	5	3	5	14	1	0	3	9	1	37	12	8	2	.441	.323
Almonte, Wady, Bluefield	.307	51	201	189	37	58	90	12	1	6	30	0	2	1	9	2	49	6	5	4	.476	.338
Anderson, Frank, Bristol	.222	46	163	153	10	34	49	7	1	2	16	0	2	0	7	0	52	2	3	0	.320	.253
Anderson, Milton, Burlington†	.257	58	256	210	45	54	76	7	3	3	19	0	1	4	41	1	44	38	6	2	.362	.387
Andino, Luis, Martinsville	.192	27	80	73	13	14	24	5	1	1	11	1	1	1	4	0	27	1	2	1	.329	.241
Andrews, Jeff, Huntington	.107	34	121	112	10	12	15	0	0	1	12	0	1	2	6	0	31	1	1	1	.134	.165
Anglen, Toby, Danville*	.253	63	249	221	32	56	76	11	0	3	35	0	3	1	24	1	33	14	4	5	.344	.325
Antczak, Chuck, Bristol	.305	24	73	59	11	18	25	4	0	1	10	0	1	7	6	0	16	2	0	1	.424	.425
Bagley, Sean, Bristol	.203	35	75	64	8	13	16	1	1	0	5	2	0	1	8	0	25	9	3	1	.250	.301
Bass, Jayson, Danville†	.224	64	302	268	38	60	85	17	4	0	17	0	2	4	28	2	61	24	8	2	.317	.305
Bates, Shawn, Bluefield*	.000	14	1	1	0	0	0	0	0	0	0	0	0	0	0	0	0	0	0	1	.000	.000
Bearden, Doug, Bristol	.234	46	181	167	26	39	60	10	1	3	22	3	2	3	6	0	40	5	0	1	.359	.270
Black, Brandon, Kingsport*	.292	31	118	106	17	31	45	5	0	3	20	0	1	3	8	0	23	7	1	3	.425	.356
Bogle, Bryan, Bluefield	.452	10	38	31	11	14	19	2	0	1	4	0	1	2	4	0	2	1	0	1	.613	.526
Bowness, Brian, Bristol	.223	54	217	202	20	45	52	4	0	1	23	0	1	2	12	0	37	0	1	5	.257	.272
Boyette, Tony, Princeton	.293	61	249	222	41	65	112	15	1	10	49	0	3	3	21	0	41	2	0	3	.505	.357
Bracho, Darwin, Princeton†	.207	31	87	82	5	17	22	5	0	0	7	0	0	1	4	0	16	0	2	2	.268	.253
Brito, Domingo, Martinsville	.148	29	93	81	8	12	12	0	0	0	3	1	0	0	11	0	32	1	0	0	.148	.250
Brown, Jerome, Elizabethton†	.183	17	77	71	10	13	15	2	0	0	1	0	0	1	5	0	25	5	0	2	.211	.247
Bryant, Chris, Bluefield	.287	58	227	195	39	56	83	10	1	5	37	1	3	3	25	0	30	6	4	10	.426	.372
Buckles, Matt, Martinsville*	.190	22	63	58	6	11	13	2	0	0	4	1	0	2	2	1	17	2	0	2	.224	.242
Cardona, Alex, Johnson City	.217	22	58	46	9	10	13	3	0	0	7	1	0	0	11	1	4	0	1	0	.283	.368
Cloud, Tony, Princeton	.000	12	1	1	0	0	0	0	0	0	0	0	0	0	0	0	1	0	0	0	.000	.000
Coats, Nathan, Burlington	.313	20	72	64	8	20	28	5	0	1	5	1	0	3	4	0	15	1	0	1	.438	.380
Coburn, Todd, Huntington	.281	62	251	228	37	64	94	12	3	4	39	0	0	1	22	1	47	7	1	5	.412	.347
Colburn, Brian, Elizabethton*	.175	11	45	40	3	7	7	0	0	0	4	0	0	2	3	0	8	2	0	1	.175	.267
Concepcion, David, Princeton†	.236	60	249	203	44	48	80	10	2	6	24	2	1	1	42	1	44	10	0	2	.394	.368
Conner, Decomba, Princeton	.125	6	20	16	2	2	4	2	0	0	5	0	1	0	3	0	3	2	0	0	.250	.250
Cox, Robert, Kingsport	.197	57	224	188	29	37	55	9	0	3	25	1	0	5	30	1	59	1	3	2	.293	.323
Cross, Adam, Danville	.304	50	195	181	21	55	73	15	0	1	16	0	1	2	11	0	16	15	11	7	.403	.349
Current, Jeremy, Johnson City	.254	23	76	63	5	16	19	3	0	0	6	1	1	3	8	0	23	0	0	0	.302	.360
Cushman, Dwayne, Princeton	.000	26	1	1	0	0	0	0	0	0	0	0	0	0	0	0	1	0	0	0	.000	.000
Daedlow, Craig, Bluefield	.000	5	18	13	1	0	0	0	0	0	1	0	1	0	4	0	3	0	1	0	.000	.222
Davidson, Cleatus, Elizabethton†	.296	39	166	152	27	45	64	6	2	3	27	0	0	3	11	0	31	10	4	2	.421	.355
Davis, James, Princeton	.276	58	243	225	40	62	89	10	4	3	29	1	2	1	14	0	33	8	0	2	.396	.318
Deck, Billy, Johnson City*	.259	59	245	205	27	53	68	12	0	1	30	1	2	7	30	0	52	4	6	4	.332	.369
Dellucci, David, Bluefield*	.333	20	77	69	11	23	36	5	1	2	12	0	1	1	6	1	7	3	1	1	.522	.390
Diaz, Ivan, Johnson City	.214	6	14	14	0	3	3	0	0	0	2	0	0	0	0	0	3	0	0	0	.214	.214
Dougherty, Keith, Danville	.294	25	90	85	14	25	47	5	1	5	14	0	1	1	3	0	14	1	1	2	.553	.322
Drent, Brian, Bristol	.242	49	206	161	31	39	67	13	0	5	26	0	3	3	39	1	58	16	2	5	.416	.393
Duncan, Robert, Danville*	.232	49	178	142	23	33	38	3	1	0	8	1	1	5	29	0	45	5	3	1	.268	.379
Edmondson, Tracy, Kingsport	.265	44	187	155	36	41	61	11	0	3	25	2	1	2	27	1	34	8	1	0	.394	.378
Edwards, Donald, Burlington	.169	43	149	130	20	22	24	2	0	0	5	0	0	2	17	0	35	5	2	2	.185	.275
Elliott, Zach, Martinsville	.358	45	193	151	46	54	78	10	4	2	19	1	2	7	32	1	30	13	5	3	.517	.484
Ennis, Wayne, Princeton	.048	10	22	21	4	1	1	0	0	0	2	1	0	0	0	0	8	0	0	1	.048	.048
Erickson, Corey, Kingsport	.333	2	9	9	1	3	6	0	0	1	4	0	0	0	0	0	3	0	0	0	.667	.333
Espada, Angel, Danville	.301	33	126	113	17	34	39	0	1	1	8	1	0	0	12	0	16	16	4	3	.345	.368
Falciglia, Tony, Johnson City	.314	33	134	118	18	37	63	14	0	4	26	0	3	1	12	0	34	0	1	4	.534	.373
Fernandez, Randy, Huntington*	.308	15	46	39	2	12	12	0	0	0	3	2	0	0	5	0	16	2	4	0	.308	.386
Foote, Derek, Danville*	.362	17	62	58	10	21	34	4	0	3	9	0	0	1	3	0	21	0	0	0	.586	.403
Franklin, James, Danville	.243	51	178	148	30	36	45	5	2	0	17	1	1	0	28	1	51	9	5	4	.304	.362
Fraser, Joseph, Elizabethton	.261	46	210	184	29	48	64	4	0	4	21	2	2	2	20	0	22	5	4	5	.348	.337
Frost, Robert, Kingsport	.333	11	33	30	3	10	12	2	0	0	7	1	0	1	1	0	5	1	0	0	.400	.375
Gabriel, Denio, Bluefield†	.289	53	213	180	39	52	59	4	0	1	24	6	1	1	25	0	36	31	8	1	.328	.377
Garcia, Carlos, Elizabethton	.306	62	262	235	42	72	104	15	1	5	34	3	4	4	16	0	41	27	8	5	.443	.355
Gargiulo, Mike, Bluefield*	.289	48	192	180	24	52	76	7	4	3	21	1	1	0	10	1	35	1	2	6	.422	.325
Gill, Sean, Kingsport	.000	8	19	18	2	0	0	0	0	0	0	0	0	0	1	0	10	0	1	0	.000	.053
Glavine, Mike, Burlington*	.245	46	180	155	28	38	81	10	0	11	28	0	2	1	22	0	37	1	0	0	.523	.339
Gunderson, Shane, Elizabethton	.309	37	162	139	32	43	79	11	2	7	30	0	1	2	20	0	24	4	0	3	.568	.401
Guthrie, David, Princeton†	.204	55	207	181	28	37	48	11	0	0	13	4	1	3	18	1	41	7	1	4	.265	.286
Haas, Chris, Johnson City*	.269	67	295	242	43	65	107	15	3	7	50	0	0	1	52	0	93	1	3	8	.442	.400
Hall, Darran, Princeton*	.120	9	32	25	3	3	3	0	0	0	1	1	1	0	5	0	10	1	2	0	.120	.258
Hardy, Brian, Burlington*	.200	29	91	80	15	16	35	4	0	5	12	0	0	1	10	0	40	1	0	1	.438	.297
Harmer, Francis, Bluefield†	.190	18	69	58	5	11	14	3	0	0	10	0	2	0	9	0	14	1	0	0	.241	.290
Harris, Rodger, Johnson City†	.182	45	143	121	26	22	29	5	1	0	7	1	0	2	19	0	44	5	2	3	.240	.303
Helms, Ryan, Bristol†	.164	48	162	146	16	24	28	2	1	0	9	2	1	2	11	0	33	3	1	3	.192	.231
Hendricks, Ryan, Huntington*	.258	58	226	178	38	46	91	12	0	11	36	0	2	0	46	3	50	8	1	2	.511	.407
Herdman, Eli, Elizabethton*	.212	62	254	217	36	46	86	10	0	10	36	0	2	1	34	1	60	1	2	4	.396	.319
Herrera, Jesus, Princeton†	.242	46	162	149	18	36	47	8	0	1	9	1	1	4	7	0	38	6	5	1	.315	.292

Player, Team	Avg.	G	TPA	AB	R	H	TB	2B	3B	HR	RBI	SH	SF	HP	BB	IBB	SO	SB	CS	GDP	Slg.	OBP
Higman, Joel, Blu.-Hun.	.246	24	76	69	6	17	18	1	0	0	7	0	0	1	6	0	26	3	0	4	.261	.316
Hobbie, Matt, Huntington*	.227	60	240	211	25	48	76	12	5	2	24	0	5	1	23	0	49	17	5	1	.360	.300
Hodges, Randy, Danville*	.250	2	9	8	1	2	5	0	0	1	1	0	0	1	0	0	2	0	1	1	.625	.333
Hollins, Darontaye, Bristol	.248	62	250	222	24	55	66	7	2	0	14	2	2	4	20	1	75	14	5	5	.297	.319
Hooker, Kevin, Martinsville	.335	49	210	179	38	60	105	16	1	9	46	0	3	7	21	0	34	2	3	1	.587	.419
Hoover, Will, Kingsport	.190	11	23	21	1	4	5	1	0	0	3	0	0	0	2	0	10	0	0	0	.238	.261
Hunter, Lanier, Huntington†	.250	62	260	216	36	54	82	12	2	4	18	2	2	8	32	0	64	15	10	2	.380	.364
Ingram, Darron, Princeton	.275	60	247	233	37	64	118	6	3	14	53	0	2	1	11	0	78	3	1	5	.506	.308
Isom, Johnny, Bluefield	.344	59	247	212	47	73	113	14	4	6	56	2	7	1	25	0	27	9	2	5	.533	.404
Janke, Jared, Martinsville	.242	46	178	149	24	36	56	11	0	3	27	0	0	3	26	0	25	5	1	6	.376	.365
Jensen, Blair, Burlington	.191	21	54	47	3	9	10	1	0	0	2	1	0	0	6	0	21	2	0	3	.213	.283
Jimenez, Ruben, Johnson City†	.164	41	139	116	13	19	27	0	4	0	20	1	3	3	16	0	27	5	6	2	.233	.275
Johnson, Heath, Elizabethton*	.209	59	246	201	31	42	55	10	0	1	16	0	1	3	41	1	51	4	5	3	.274	.350
Johnson, Travis, Elizabethton*	.341	14	49	44	6	15	28	5	1	2	4	0	0	0	5	0	10	2	1	0	.636	.408
Jones, Ivory, Elizabethton*	.199	47	161	136	21	27	39	4	1	2	11	3	0	0	22	0	43	6	5	0	.287	.310
Juarez, Raul, Elizabethton	.283	40	144	120	25	34	50	7	0	3	16	0	1	0	23	1	50	10	3	0	.417	.396
Kearney, Chad, Martinsville	.225	29	91	80	9	18	22	1	0	1	5	0	0	1	10	0	32	1	2	1	.275	.319
Kennedy, Justin, Martinsville*	.199	43	156	146	11	29	38	7	1	0	15	0	2	1	7	0	36	11	0	2	.260	.237
Kerr, Brian, Bluefield	.167	3	6	6	0	1	2	1	0	0	1	0	0	0	0	0	2	0	0	0	.333	.167
Kingsale, Eugene, Bluefield†	.316	47	209	171	45	54	69	11	2	0	16	4	2	5	27	0	31	20	8	0	.404	.420
Lakovic, Greg, Elizabethton*	.244	14	48	41	7	10	12	2	0	0	8	1	0	3	3	0	8	0	1	1	.293	.340
Langford, Derrick, Danville	.341	27	96	85	7	29	35	3	0	1	16	0	1	1	9	0	18	1	2	2	.412	.406
Lantigua, Miguel, Kingsport†	.125	6	18	16	0	2	2	0	0	0	1	0	1	0	1	1	6	0	0	0	.125	.167
LeCronier, Jason, Bluefield*	.246	21	81	69	11	17	29	4	1	2	10	0	1	0	11	1	17	1	1	1	.420	.346
Lee, Carlos, Bristol	.346	67	282	269	43	93	133	17	1	7	45	0	3	2	8	3	34	17	7	6	.494	.365
Lee, Jason, Johnson City*	.105	28	86	76	10	8	9	1	0	0	4	1	0	1	8	0	38	2	4	0	.118	.200
Livingston, Clyde, Martinsville*	.212	33	113	104	15	22	37	5	2	2	25	0	1	0	8	0	22	1	0	4	.356	.265
Lugo, Ursino, Burlington†	.245	32	98	94	13	23	23	0	0	0	5	1	0	0	3	0	20	9	4	6	.245	.268
Malin, Edgar, Huntington	.175	21	73	63	12	11	15	1	0	1	8	0	0	0	10	0	27	3	2	3	.238	.288
Mapp, Eric, Princeton†	.224	61	233	210	32	47	73	11	0	5	23	2	0	3	18	0	58	10	1	1	.348	.294
Martin, Ryan, Danville	.214	5	18	14	2	3	4	1	0	0	2	0	0	0	3	0	5	0	1	0	.286	.353
Martinez, Eddy, Bluefield	.308	57	215	185	42	57	77	11	3	1	35	1	1	5	23	0	42	5	5	1	.416	.397
Martinez, Tony, Johnson City	.234	24	105	77	18	18	26	0	1	2	8	1	0	1	26	0	14	3	2	2	.338	.433
Mason, Lamont, Princeton	.167	26	94	78	11	13	18	3	1	0	3	0	0	0	16	0	21	6	4	2	.231	.309
Mastrullo, Mike, Huntington	.179	46	176	134	20	24	33	5	2	0	14	10	4	3	25	0	43	5	4	4	.246	.313
Mata, Manuel, Martinsville*	.400	1	5	5	1	2	2	0	0	0	2	0	0	0	0	0	0	0	0	0	.400	.400
McCarthy, Kevin, Kingsport*	.132	26	109	91	11	12	19	2	1	1	4	0	0	1	17	1	18	1	2	0	.209	.275
McClure, Craig, Bristol	.233	64	253	223	26	52	74	6	2	4	26	4	1	3	22	0	65	7	8	3	.332	.309
McCroskey, Jackie, Huntington*	.288	49	186	156	26	45	73	12	5	2	27	0	1	3	26	1	31	12	3	0	.468	.398
McDougal, Mike, Johnson City	.175	32	103	97	8	17	31	3	1	3	12	0	0	0	6	0	27	0	2	2	.320	.223
McNeal, Pepe, Bur.-J.C.	.226	54	210	186	13	42	56	8	0	2	27	0	2	3	19	1	48	4	0	4	.301	.305
McWhite, Ray, Danville†	.260	64	253	231	37	60	114	16	1	12	53	1	2	3	16	0	76	8	4	5	.494	.313
Mejia, Miguel, Bluefield	.298	51	208	181	50	54	75	6	3	3	30	6	2	1	18	0	30	36	5	5	.414	.361
Mendoza, Carlos, Kingsport*	.328	51	228	192	56	63	75	9	0	1	24	4	2	3	27	0	24	28	6	3	.391	.415
Mepri, Sal, Princeton	.200	6	5	5	0	1	1	0	0	0	0	0	0	0	0	0	3	0	0	0	.200	.200
Messner, Jake, Burlington*	.222	46	164	144	17	32	42	2	4	0	9	0	1	1	14	0	40	8	5	0	.292	.294
Mifflin, Brian, Kingsport	.250	1	5	4	1	1	1	0	0	0	0	0	0	0	1	0	0	0	0	0	.250	.400
Milledge, Tony, Johnson City	.276	31	95	87	14	24	42	7	1	3	12	0	0	1	7	0	15	1	0	2	.483	.337
Mota, Christian, Burlington†	.282	59	244	234	37	66	95	17	3	2	36	0	2	2	6	1	55	7	3	4	.406	.303
Mota, Gleydel, Kingsport*	.000	1	4	3	1	0	0	0	0	0	0	0	0	1	0	0	2	0	0	0	.000	.250
Mullen, Adam, Danville	.137	17	57	51	2	7	9	0	1	0	3	1	1	0	4	0	17	1	1	0	.176	.196
Munoz, Juan, Johnson City*	.347	57	219	190	43	66	101	12	1	7	31	0	2	0	27	0	17	13	2	1	.532	.425
Murphy, Quinn, Burlington*	.175	40	142	126	12	22	33	5	0	2	9	1	0	1	14	0	56	2	5	0	.262	.262
Naples, Brandon, Kingsport	.275	32	122	109	22	30	36	1	1	1	23	0	1	1	11	0	11	2	0	0	.330	.344
Nolte, Bruce, Huntington	.220	61	238	209	30	46	65	6	2	3	21	5	1	2	21	0	46	16	5	3	.311	.296
O'Connor, Richard, Martinsville	.224	53	208	174	27	39	45	4	1	0	11	4	0	4	26	1	52	13	8	1	.259	.338
Oliveros, Leonardo, Martinsville	.284	48	173	155	17	44	59	9	0	2	18	0	2	2	14	1	18	0	0	8	.381	.347
Patellis, Anthony, Princeton	.253	46	181	166	21	42	84	7	1	11	32	0	1	3	11	1	58	4	2	1	.506	.309
Patterson, Jarrod, Kingsport*	.279	64	271	240	45	67	129	17	3	13	57	0	3	0	28	2	50	3	1	2	.538	.351
Pena, Francisco, Elizabethton	.190	10	23	21	4	4	6	2	0	0	2	0	0	0	2	0	10	0	0	0	.286	.261
Pena, Jose, Burlington	.200	23	73	70	7	14	22	2	0	2	6	0	1	1	0	0	21	0	1	2	.314	.208
Pennyfeather, William, Princeton	.000	1	3	3	0	0	0	0	0	0	0	0	0	0	0	0	1	0	0	0	.000	.000
Pickett, Eric, Danville*	.220	61	242	218	20	48	63	5	5	0	26	0	3	2	19	2	67	9	4	2	.289	.285
Pierzynski, A.J., Elizabethton*	.332	56	220	205	29	68	104	13	1	7	45	0	1	0	14	1	23	0	2	6	.507	.373
Pointer, Corey, Danville	.278	46	184	158	33	44	79	5	3	8	27	0	2	5	19	1	60	8	4	1	.500	.370
Polanco, Enohel, Kingsport	.229	62	231	205	28	47	62	5	2	2	21	3	3	2	18	0	60	7	6	5	.302	.294
Raio, Domenick, Martinsville	.214	6	16	14	1	3	3	0	0	0	1	1	0	0	1	0	4	0	0	0	.214	.267
Ramirez, Alonso, Burlington	.167	10	22	18	3	3	3	0	0	0	1	0	1	0	3	0	6	0	0	0	.167	.273
Ramirez, Daniel, Kingsport	.248	62	251	226	30	56	72	6	2	2	32	9	0	1	15	1	44	21	10	5	.319	.298
Ramos, Noel, Bluefield	.196	31	119	107	18	21	43	5	1	5	18	0	0	2	10	0	43	1	0	0	.402	.277
Raymondi, Mike, Huntington	.220	28	89	82	8	18	24	3	0	1	8	0	0	2	5	0	27	1	0	3	.293	.281
Reyes, Freddy, Elizabethton	.277	40	140	130	17	36	63	10	1	5	21	0	1	3	6	0	28	0	0	4	.485	.321
Reyes, Winston, Huntington	.265	20	72	68	5	18	22	4	0	0	8	1	0	0	3	0	17	3	2	4	.324	.296
Rincones, Wuarnner, Bristol	.317	61	227	189	25	60	81	10	4	1	25	0	2	4	32	0	29	2	0	5	.429	.423
Roberson, Gerald, Huntington	.213	52	210	188	28	40	62	11	1	3	14	2	2	5	13	0	31	12	4	3	.330	.279
Robinson, Kerry, Johnson City*	.296	60	271	250	44	74	105	12	8	1	26	3	2	0	16	1	30	14	10	3	.420	.336
Russin, Tom, Bluefield	.312	57	238	215	42	67	105	21	1	5	41	0	1	4	18	2	27	1	1	3	.488	.374
Salano, Manuel, Princeton	.216	30	83	74	12	16	23	4	0	1	14	1	0	1	7	0	20	2	2	0	.311	.293
Santiago, Arnold, Burlington	.285	35	129	123	15	35	42	5	1	0	11	0	2	0	4	0	22	3	1	1	.341	.302
Sasser, Rob, Danville	.319	12	52	47	8	15	19	2	1	0	7	0	1	0	4	1	7	5	1	1	.404	.365
Schofield, Andy, Johnson City	.227	40	141	119	22	27	35	8	0	0	11	0	0	3	19	0	30	6	1	0	.294	.348
Schreimann, Eric, Martinsville	.299	38	153	127	12	38	52	8	0	2	18	2	1	13	10	2	20	2	1	4	.409	.404
Schroeder, John, Elizabethton*	.263	62	259	236	44	62	103	7	2	10	39	0	2	3	18	0	59	2	1	0	.436	.320

Player, Team	Avg.	G	TPA	AB	R	H	TB	2B	3B	HR	RBI	SH	SF	HP	BB	IBB	SO	SB	CS	GDP	Slg.	OBP
Serafin, Ricardo, Martinsville	.189	22	56	53	8	10	14	1	0	1	4	0	0	2	1	0	20	4	0	2	.264	.232
Serbio, Carmen, Martinsville	.229	28	109	83	15	19	33	6	1	2	12	2	0	4	20	0	23	0	1	5	.398	.402
Short, Richard, Bluefield	.282	11	43	39	9	11	19	2	0	2	12	0	1	1	2	0	1	2	1	2	.487	.326
Shy, Jason, Danville	.231	8	15	13	1	3	3	0	0	0	0	0	0	0	2	0	3	0	0	0	.231	.333
Simpson, Jeramie, Kingsport*	.323	59	259	229	50	74	105	11	10	0	28	1	3	6	20	0	37	25	5	2	.459	.388
Smalley, Jevon, Princeton*	.258	39	115	97	17	25	38	5	1	2	14	0	0	2	16	0	31	3	2	1	.392	.374
Soriano, Juan, Kingsport	.262	40	130	107	29	28	35	5	1	0	12	0	1	2	20	0	21	7	2	1	.327	.385
Spry, Shane, Bristol*	.233	15	54	43	5	10	12	2	0	0	6	0	1	0	10	0	7	0	0	0	.279	.370
Stone, Matthew, Martinsville*	.252	40	143	111	15	28	36	8	0	0	13	0	1	2	29	0	37	3	0	5	.324	.413
Strasser, John, Bristol	.226	46	187	159	24	36	43	3	2	0	10	4	0	4	20	0	38	6	1	1	.270	.328
Sturges, Brian, Johnson City	.143	17	48	42	5	6	7	1	0	0	6	1	0	3	2	0	7	0	0	3	.167	.234
Taylor, Jerry, Burlington	.296	10	37	27	7	8	17	1	1	2	8	0	1	1	8	0	6	1	0	0	.630	.459
Taylor, Reggie, Martinsville*	.222	64	272	239	36	53	75	4	6	2	32	0	4	6	·23	0	58	18	7	5	.314	.301
Terry, Tony, Princeton†	.170	47	128	106	15	18	21	3	0	0	8	2	1	2	17	0	40	7	4	0	.198	.294
Tiller, Brad, Burlington	.236	55	213	195	24	46	61	10	1	1	23	2	2	3	11	0	49	11	5	2	.313	.284
Torbett, Hanes, Kingsport	.261	19	56	46	10	12	17	1	2	0	5	0	1	0	9	0	8	0	0	0	.370	.375
Townsend, Terric, Martinsville	.286	5	18	14	4	4	4	0	0	0	1	0	0	1	3	0	2	1	0	0	.286	.444
Utting, Ben, Danville*	.238	55	220	189	30	45	55	8	1	0	15	1	1	2	27	2	34	12	4	1	.291	.338
Valera, Yojanny, Kingsport	.294	56	223	204	30	60	82	13	0	3	36	2	1	5	11	0	33	2	1	6	.402	.344
Wampler, Sam, Martinsville†	.136	11	25	22	0	3	3	0	0	0	1	0	0	0	3	0	10	0	0	2	.136	.240
Whitaker, Chad, Burlington*	.238	47	197	181	20	43	73	13	1	5	27	0	1	1	14	1	59	2	3	1	.403	.294
Williams, Errick, Martinsville	.239	36	122	113	19	27	28	1	0	0	11	0	0	2	6	0	32	13	2	1	.248	.289
Williams, Jewell, Burlington	.219	46	167	146	20	32	52	6	1	4	15	0	0	8	13	0	52	11	4	3	.356	.317
Winn, Wess, Bluefield†	.224	24	64	49	4	11	13	2	0	0	9	3	0	0	12	0	12	2	2	0	.265	.377
Wood, Tony, Huntington	.268	56	224	205	26	55	64	5	2	0	19	1	1	2	15	0	55	5	2	4	.312	.323
Woolf, Jason, Johnson City†	.279	31	124	111	16	31	40	7	1	0	14	1	3	1	8	0	21	6	3	0	.360	.325

GRAND SLAMS: Ingram, 3; Coburn, McWhite, 2 each; Drent, Gargiulo, Gunderson, Jones, Munoz, Patellis, Pierzynski, Valera, 1 each.
AWARDED FIRST BASE ON CATCHER'S INTERFERENCE: Messner 4 (Foote 2, Antczak, Gargiulo); F. Anderson (Coats); Martin (Gunderson); J. Pena (McNeal); E. Williams (Boyette).

PLAYERS WITH TWO OR MORE TEAMS

Player, Team	Avg.	G	TPA	AB	R	H	TB	2B	3B	HR	RBI	SH	SF	HP	BB	IBB	SO	SB	CS	GDP	Slg.	OBP
Higman, Joel, Bluefield	.208	11	27	24	2	5	5	0	0	0	3	0	0	0	3	0	8	2	0	2	.208	.296
Higman, Joel, Huntington	.267	13	49	45	4	12	13	1	0	0	4	0	0	1	3	0	18	1	0	2	.289	.327
McNeal, Pepe, Burlington	.281	27	96	89	4	25	33	2	0	2	15	0	1	2	4	0	20	2	0	1	.371	.323
McNeal, Pepe, Johnson City	.175	27	114	97	9	17	23	6	0	0	12	0	1	1	15	1	28	2	0	3	.237	.289

1995 PITCHING

TEAM

Team	W	L	Pct.	ERA	G	CG	ShO	Sv.	IP	H	TBF	R	ER	HR	SH	SF	HB	BB	IBB	SO	WP	Bk.
Bluefield	49	16	.754	3.22	65	2	3	28	561.0	511	2381	269	201	41	14	10	36	227	4	531	50	10
Elizabethton	33	31	.516	3.41	64	4	5	13	551.0	550	2396	299	209	29	21	14	23	183	7	535	53	18
Kingsport	48	18	.727	3.49	66	5	6	20	574.1	480	2414	263	223	38	18	10	35	226	5	532	52	4
Princeton	31	32	.492	4.19	63	1	4	15	543.1	538	2434	339	253	29	6	18	24	267	16	506	73	13
Bristol	28	39	.418	4.24	67	2	2	10	566.1	552	2493	347	267	40	18	22	27	224	2	532	52	16
Danville	27	40	.403	4.35	67	2	2	18	570.2	540	2515	378	276	31	17	37	33	243	3	536	74	14
Martinsville	30	37	.448	4.58	67	0	1	17	557.2	582	2475	349	284	38	10	17	35	247	4	511	77	13
Johnson City	35	33	.515	4.75	68	2	3	20	589.0	599	2666	399	311	50	21	20	36	279	5	539	55	27
Burlington	26	38	.406	4.88	64	4	4	12	550.0	538	2491	373	298	38	12	12	35	272	7	582	57	9
Huntington	22	45	.328	5.49	67	6	1	11	560.1	630	2551	425	342	44	14	24	46	234	2	465	79	14

INDIVIDUAL

TOP QUALIFIERS FOR EARNED-RUN AVERAGE TITLE

Minimum 54 innings. *Lefthanded pitcher.

Pitcher, Team	W	L	Pct.	ERA	G	GS	CG	ShO	GF	Sv.	IP	H	TBF	R	ER	HR	SH	SF	HB	BB	IBB	SO	WP	Bk.
Garber, Joel, Bristol*	5	1	.833	1.20	19	6	0	0	4	0	60.0	37	229	13	8	3	1	2	1	12	0	66	4	1
Murphy, Chris, Princeton*	7	1	.875	1.55	10	10	1	1	0	0	63.2	51	266	23	11	4	0	2	2	19	0	52	6	0
Fussell, Chris, Bluefield	9	1	.900	2.19	12	12	1	1	0	0	65.2	37	265	18	16	4	1	1	7	32	0	98	3	1
Abreu, Winston, Danville	6	3	.667	2.31	13	13	1	0	0	0	74.0	54	277	29	19	5	0	4	1	13	0	90	2	0
Ojeda, Erick, Kingsport*	6	2	.750	2.40	14	5	0	0	3	0	60.0	47	240	18	16	3	2	0	1	12	0	60	4	1
Olson, Phillip, Kingsport	6	2	.750	2.42	12	10	2	1	1	1	67.0	47	271	24	18	1	1	1	8	23	0	45	4	1
Feliz, Bienvenido, Burlington	4	2	.667	2.71	12	12	1	1	0	0	73.0	55	296	29	22	8	1	0	1	20	0	78	2	2
Sanders, Frankie, Burlington	3	5	.375	2.96	12	12	3	0	0	0	70.0	48	292	31	23	2	1	0	3	32	0	80	2	1
Figueroa, Nelson, Kingsport	7	3	.700	3.07	12	12	2	2	0	0	76.1	57	304	31	26	3	3	2	5	22	1	79	5	0
Roberts, Randolph, Princeton	4	5	.444	3.16	15	9	0	0	2	0	62.2	51	281	35	22	3	1	2	6	33	3	74	14	2
Wagner, Ken, Burlington	5	5	.500	3.16	13	12	0	0	0	0	68.1	54	285	34	24	7	1	2	1	23	0	80	7	1
Splittorff, James, Elizabethton	5	4	.556	3.24	13	12	1	1	1	0	72.1	64	319	40	26	5	0	2	7	29	0	72	11	2
Mear, Rich, Johnson City*	7	3	.700	3.35	14	14	0	0	0	0	78.0	68	338	37	29	4	3	1	3	40	1	75	11	1
Mahaffey, Alan, Elizabethton*	5	6	.455	3.47	13	12	1	0	0	0	70.0	66	308	42	27	4	6	2	3	21	0	73	4	8
Jimenez, Jose, Johnson City	5	7	.417	3.49	14	14	1	1	0	0	90.1	81	380	48	35	3	3	1	5	25	0	85	7	1

DEPARTMENTAL LEADERS: W—Fussell, 9; L—Adair, 9; Pct.—Fussell, .900; G—S. Reed, 31; GS—Jimenez, Mear, Young, 14; CG—Sanders, 3; ShO—Figueroa, 2; GF—Mendez, 28; Sv.—Mendez, 19; IP—Jimenez, 90.1; H—Adair, 96; TBF—Jimenez, 380; R—Secoda, 57; ER—M. DeWitt, 49; HR—Roettgen, 11; SH—Mahaffey, 6; SF—Adair, Guiliano, Schnur, 5; HB—Oldham, Young, 9; BB—Pumphrey, 42; IBB—Roberts, 3; SO—Fussell, 98; WP—Roberts, Shumate, 14; Bk.—Mahaffey, 8.

ALL PITCHERS

*Lefthanded pitcher.

Pitcher, Team	W	L	Pct.	ERA	G	GS	CG	ShO	GF	Sv.	IP	H	TBF	R	ER	HR	SH	SF	HB	BB	IBB	SO	WP	Bk.
Abreu, Winston, Danville	6	3	.667	2.31	13	13	1	0	0	0	74.0	54	277	29	19	5	0	4	1	13	0	90	2	0
Adair, Scott, Huntington	2	9	.182	4.70	13	13	1	0	0	0	74.2	96	317	47	39	3	2	5	2	13	0	28	2	0
Aguiar, Douglas, Martinsville	2	2	.500	5.56	15	7	0	0	4	0	45.1	46	195	28	28	3	0	1	3	21	0	42	5	1
Alexis, Julio, Huntington	1	6	.143	4.74	14	13	0	0	0	0	81.2	89	352	55	43	9	2	2	3	21	0	65	5	1
Alvarado, Luis, Huntington	3	4	.429	3.68	11	5	1	0	1	0	44.0	43	195	28	18	4	1	1	1	12	0	43	4	0
Anderson, Eric, Elizabethton*	3	2	.600	2.95	21	2	0	0	5	0	39.2	48	185	21	13	0	4	0	2	19	1	31	1	1
Anderson, Gary, Burlington	1	2	.333	6.35	14	0	0	0	12	3	17.0	18	81	12	12	2	0	0	4	8	0	22	3	0
Anez, Maycoll, Bristol	0	2	.000	5.74	7	2	0	0	1	1	15.2	24	78	14	10	1	1	1	0	8	0	11	0	0
Angerhofer, Chad, Princeton*	2	4	.333	7.22	13	7	0	0	2	0	38.2	52	189	37	31	5	0	2	1	17	0	38	6	1
Barfield, Rodney, Johnson City	2	7	.222	9.82	10	10	0	0	0	0	36.2	52	199	50	40	3	3	2	8	30	0	18	4	2
Bartels, Todd, Elizabethton	6	2	.750	4.11	13	9	2	0	1	0	57.0	66	239	27	26	4	1	2	1	3	0	45	0	1
Bates, Shawn, Bluefield*	2	0	1.000	2.45	14	2	0	0	5	3	25.2	22	113	13	7	1	1	0	2	16	0	31	5	1
Beebe, Joey, Kingsport*	5	1	.833	3.25	9	7	0	0	1	0	44.1	43	182	16	16	3	2	1	1	12	0	34	5	0
Beirne, Kevin, Bristol	1	0	1.000	0.00	9	0	0	0	7	2	9.0	4	35	0	0	0	0	0	0	4	0	12	0	0
Blang, Michael, Kingsport	0	2	.000	3.18	23	0	0	0	15	7	28.1	19	111	10	10	3	0	1	1	7	1	18	3	1
Blank, John, Elizabethton*	3	0	1.000	4.54	15	5	0	0	2	0	35.2	40	159	21	18	3	0	0	0	16	1	32	5	2
Boggs, Harold, Elizabethton	3	5	.375	5.82	12	12	0	0	0	0	60.1	77	276	53	39	2	2	4	2	20	0	55	6	0
Bowser, Robert, Martinsville	2	2	.500	3.90	17	0	0	0	8	1	32.1	30	136	15	14	1	1	1	4	9	2	35	0	2
Burger, Rob, Martinsville	2	4	.333	4.65	9	9	0	0	0	0	40.2	47	188	25	21	1	0	2	3	23	0	54	5	0
Buteaux, Shane, Bristol	7	6	.538	4.26	13	13	1	0	0	0	74.0	72	337	45	35	9	0	4	8	41	0	49	9	4
Chapman, Walker, Elizabethton	0	1	.000	5.63	4	1	0	0	0	0	8.0	9	34	6	5	1	0	1	1	1	0	7	2	1
Chen, Bruce, Danville*	4	4	.500	3.97	14	13	1	0	0	0	70.1	78	310	42	31	3	1	4	3	19	1	56	4	1
Cloud, Tony, Princeton	4	5	.444	4.20	12	12	0	0	0	0	55.2	47	232	34	26	1	0	3	1	26	1	46	8	0
Cochrane, Andrew, Danville*	1	1	.500	4.63	6	0	0	0	0	0	11.2	14	57	11	6	0	0	1	0	6	0	10	2	0
Coggin, David, Martinsville	5	3	.625	3.00	11	11	0	0	0	0	48.0	45	209	25	16	1	1	1	5	31	0	37	8	1
Collins, Ken, Danville	1	0	1.000	4.18	18	1	0	0	10	0	32.1	36	153	31	15	2	2	2	4	15	0	29	7	0
Cooper, Chadwick, Kingsport	0	0	.000	3.03	22	1	0	0	14	6	29.2	21	123	12	10	3	0	0	2	12	0	38	1	0
Cooper, Keith, Danville	1	0	1.000	1.65	17	0	0	0	14	4	27.1	20	106	9	5	1	1	1	1	5	0	23	3	0
Cope, Craig, Kingsport*	0	0	.000	8.44	12	0	0	0	7	0	10.2	9	54	12	10	0	0	1	1	12	0	10	5	0
Corey, Mark, Princeton	1	1	.500	3.68	4	3	0	0	0	0	14.2	12	61	7	6	1	0	0	0	6	0	8	0	0
Crills, Brad, Bluefield	3	0	1.000	0.90	4	4	0	0	0	0	20.0	15	78	3	2	0	0	0	5	5	0	15	1	0
Cruz, Nelson, Bristol	0	0	.000	9.00	1	0	0	0	1	0	1.0	2	6	1	1	0	0	1	1	0	0	0	0	0
Cushman, Dwayne, Princeton	2	3	.400	3.09	26	0	0	0	21	8	35.0	33	159	21	12	1	0	1	1	15	2	40	2	0
Davis, Lance, Princeton*	3	7	.300	3.88	15	9	0	0	0	0	58.0	77	271	39	25	2	2	1	3	25	2	43	6	2
Dean, Greg, Bluefield	6	2	.750	3.89	10	6	0	0	3	1	37.0	34	159	22	16	3	1	1	2	17	0	33	4	1
Desrosiers, Erik, Bristol	0	2	.000	3.09	22	0	0	0	15	2	32.0	22	129	13	11	1	2	2	3	7	1	47	1	0
DeWitt, Chris, Kingsport	1	0	1.000	3.86	23	0	0	0	10	5	28.0	31	123	18	12	3	3	0	1	7	1	16	2	0
DeWitt, Matt, Johnson City	2	6	.250	7.04	13	12	0	0	0	0	62.2	84	305	56	49	10	0	3	1	32	0	45	5	6
Dunne, Brian, Martinsville*	2	3	.400	4.28	16	6	0	0	1	1	48.1	67	229	39	23	7	1	2	2	10	0	33	3	2
Edwards, Jon, Burlington	3	2	.600	5.30	19	1	0	0	5	1	37.1	44	172	28	22	2	0	0	1	16	1	31	3	0
Eibey, Scott, Bluefield*	3	1	.750	5.56	14	6	0	0	3	2	43.2	51	196	32	27	4	2	0	2	24	0	26	6	1
Feingold, Leon, Burlington	0	0	.000	216.00	1	0	0	0	0	0	0.1	2	11	8	8	0	0	0	0	8	0	1	0	0
Feliz, Bienvenido, Burlington	4	2	.667	2.71	12	12	1	1	0	0	73.0	55	296	29	22	8	1	0	1	20	0	78	2	2
Fereira, Marcos, Huntington	0	1	.000	15.63	5	1	0	0	3	0	6.1	9	45	16	11	0	0	2	2	14	0	3	3	1
Figueroa, Nelson, Kingsport	7	3	.700	3.07	12	12	2	2	0	0	76.1	57	304	31	26	3	3	2	5	22	1	79	5	0
Fleetwood, Tony, Burlington*	2	2	.500	4.71	18	0	0	0	9	0	28.2	25	131	18	15	5	0	1	2	14	0	34	2	1
Fonceca, Chad, Princeton	0	0	.000	7.25	11	1	0	0	3	0	22.1	27	107	19	18	4	0	1	1	10	2	21	2	0
Frace, Ryan, Martinsville	3	2	.600	2.17	14	0	0	0	7	1	29.0	20	121	14	7	1	0	0	1	9	1	31	4	1
Fussell, Chris, Bluefield	9	1	.900	2.19	12	12	1	1	0	0	65.2	37	265	18	16	4	1	1	7	32	0	98	3	1
Garber, Joel, Bristol*	5	1	.833	1.20	19	6	0	0	4	0	60.0	37	229	13	8	3	1	2	1	12	0	66	4	1
Giron, Roberto, Princeton	1	1	.500	5.50	24	0	0	0	12	4	36.0	33	159	23	22	3	1	3	4	14	1	41	6	1
Giuliano, Joe, Danville	2	5	.286	7.25	11	11	0	0	0	0	49.2	71	236	45	40	7	1	5	1	19	0	48	7	2
Gobert, Chris, Danville*	0	0	.000	0.00	3	0	0	0	0	0	5.2	1	23	0	0	0	0	0	0	3	0	3	1	0
Grife, Richard, Burlington	2	0	1.000	2.32	16	0	0	0	5	1	31.0	20	126	12	8	0	1	0	1	10	0	31	2	0
Hackett, Jason, Bluefield*	3	1	.750	3.02	13	6	0	0	4	1	50.2	45	226	28	17	3	1	1	3	28	2	54	13	1
Halley, Allen, Bristol	1	0	1.000	12.00	2	0	0	0	1	0	3.0	5	15	4	4	0	1	0	0	1	0	3	0	0
Harris, Jeffrey, Elizabethton	1	3	.250	3.82	21	0	0	0	10	0	33.0	42	154	15	14	2	1	0	4	13	1	27	6	1
Harrison, Scott, Burlington	0	1	.000	9.00	5	5	0	0	0	0	16.0	22	81	19	16	3	2	2	1	13	0	13	1	0
Hasselhoff, Derek, Bristol	7	3	.700	3.66	12	11	0	0	1	0	66.1	66	281	32	27	4	1	1	2	14	0	46	2	2
Herbison, Brett, Kingsport	1	0	1.000	7.20	1	1	0	0	0	0	5.0	6	23	4	4	2	1	0	0	2	0	4	1	0
Hoalton, Brandon, Huntington	1	3	.250	5.34	6	6	0	0	0	0	28.2	31	127	23	17	4	1	1	2	11	0	26	5	0
Hunt, Jon, Bristol*	2	4	.333	4.47	13	13	0	0	0	0	58.1	52	262	39	29	2	1	0	3	34	0	54	11	2
Jimenez, Jose, Johnson City	5	7	.417	3.49	14	14	1	1	0	0	90.1	81	380	48	35	3	3	1	5	25	0	85	7	1
Kershner, Jason, Martinsville*	4	2	.667	5.14	13	13	0	0	0	0	63.0	67	278	42	36	10	0	2	5	29	0	64	6	0
Kessel, Kyle, Kingsport*	4	0	1.000	1.80	5	5	0	0	0	0	30.0	33	134	11	6	1	0	0	4	10	1	23	0	0
King, Matt, Johnson City	0	0	.000	67.50	1	0	0	0	0	0	0.2	2	8	5	5	0	0	0	0	4	0	2	1	0
Knoll, Randy, Martinsville	0	3	.000	8.83	6	6	0	0	0	0	17.1	21	83	18	17	1	0	1	0	9	0	22	8	0
Knowland, Sam, Danville	4	2	.667	2.86	20	0	0	0	5	1	34.2	37	155	23	11	3	3	4	2	10	1	21	2	3
Koehler, P.K., Danville*	2	1	.667	3.54	11	6	0	0	2	1	40.2	39	178	25	16	2	1	2	1	16	0	46	4	1
Kosek, Kory, Martinsville	1	0	1.000	2.37	9	0	0	0	7	2	19.0	10	69	5	5	1	0	0	0	4	0	17	2	0
Kown, John, Johnson City	4	2	.667	2.65	16	4	1	0	1	0	51.0	41	220	31	15	2	2	0	2	18	1	42	7	4
Kraus, Tim, Bristol	0	1	.000	2.35	5	0	0	0	4	1	7.2	3	33	3	2	0	1	1	0	7	0	9	3	1
Kruse, Kelly, Bristol	0	1	.000	12.32	15	0	0	0	8	0	19.0	29	107	32	26	5	2	0	4	16	0	21	2	3
LaRocca, Todd, Bluefield	4	1	.800	3.05	8	6	1	1	0	0	44.1	38	181	17	15	5	0	0	3	14	0	38	1	0
Loewe, Kevin, Danville*	1	3	.250	3.79	20	0	0	0	9	5	38.0	24	151	20	16	1	2	0	1	10	0	43	3	0
Loudermilk, Darren, Burlington	2	2	.500	5.05	21	1	0	0	0	0	41.0	40	195	27	23	1	0	1	6	23	1	38	8	0
Lowry, Elliott, Burlington*	0	0	.000	5.85	10	0	0	0	0	0	20.0	26	95	15	13	1	1	1	0	10	0	15	8	0
Mahaffey, Alan, Elizabethton*	5	6	.455	3.47	13	12	1	0	0	0	70.0	66	308	42	27	4	6	2	3	21	0	73	4	8
Maine, Dalton, Bluefield	0	1	.000	11.25	1	0	0	0	1	0	4.0	7	18	5	5	2	0	0	1	0	0	2	0	0
Manon, Julio, Huntington	3	4	.429	3.65	16	8	2	0	3	1	74.0	75	319	34	30	4	0	3	2	30	2	77	10	0

Pitcher, Team	W	L	Pct.	ERA	G	GS	CG	ShO	GF	Sv.	IP	H	TBF	R	ER	HR	SH	SF	HB	BB	IBB	SO	WP	Bk.
Martinez, Dennis, Burlington	0	1	.000	7.90	15	2	0	0	6	0	27.1	35	139	31	24	1	0	1	2	18	1	22	7	1
Martinez, Willie, Burlington	0	7	.000	9.45	11	11	0	0	0	0	40.0	64	208	50	42	1	2	2	4	25	0	36	6	3
Mattox, Gene, Princeton	0	0	.000	11.32	11	0	0	0	4	0	10.1	13	56	13	13	0	0	0	1	12	1	10	3	2
McCaffrey, Dennis, Johnson City	2	0	1.000	4.78	24	0	0	0	7	0	32.0	36	148	24	17	3	0	1	2	17	1	24	7	1
McDougal, Mike, Johnson City	0	0	.000	0.00	1	0	0	0	0	0	0.0	0	1	0	0	0	0	0	0	1	0	0	0	0
McKnight, Chris, Danville*	0	1	.000	3.00	1	1	0	0	0	0	3.0	1	12	2	1	0	0	0	0	1	0	6	0	0
Mear, Rich, Johnson City*	7	3	.700	3.35	14	14	0	0	0	0	78.0	68	338	37	29	4	3	1	3	40	1	75	11	1
Mendez, Manuel, Johnson City*	3	0	1.000	3.08	30	0	0	0	28	19	38.0	33	158	13	13	2	1	0	1	12	0	61	2	3
Mercedes, Carlos, Bluefield	0	0	.000	9.00	1	0	0	0	1	0	1.0	2	6	1	1	0	0	0	0	1	0	0	1	0
Milledge, Tony, Johnson City	0	0	.000	18.00	2	0	0	0	1	0	2.0	5	11	4	4	1	0	0	0	0	0	1	0	0
Miller, Brian, Martinsville	6	4	.600	5.16	23	0	0	0	8	3	45.1	46	194	28	26	3	1	1	2	15	0	35	6	3
Montgomery, Joe, Princeton	3	0	1.000	2.38	13	3	0	0	4	0	45.1	45	190	19	12	1	0	1	2	14	0	27	5	3
Moore, David, Bristol	1	0	1.000	5.16	15	0	0	0	5	0	29.2	34	136	22	17	3	0	1	0	11	0	37	3	0
Moreno, Julio, Bluefield	4	3	.571	4.20	9	8	0	0	1	0	49.1	61	214	31	23	3	1	3	0	12	0	36	3	1
Morseman, Robert, Bluefield*	1	0	1.000	2.02	18	1	0	0	12	6	35.2	22	142	9	8	2	1	1	1	14	1	38	1	0
Mosquea, Alberto, Martinsville	0	0	.000	4.58	9	3	0	0	0	0	19.2	13	98	10	10	0	0	1	3	25	0	15	6	1
Murphy, Chris, Princeton*	7	1	.875	1.55	10	10	1	1	0	0	63.2	51	266	23	11	4	0	2	2	19	0	52	6	0
Niedermaier, Brad, Elizabethton	2	0	1.000	2.21	7	7	0	0	0	0	40.2	33	171	14	10	1	0	1	0	17	0	47	9	0
Noone, Bill, Martinsville	0	0	.000	2.08	1	1	0	0	0	0	4.1	3	17	1	1	1	0	0	0	1	0	5	0	0
Ojeda, Erick, Kingsport*	6	2	.750	2.40	14	5	0	0	3	0	60.0	47	240	18	16	3	2	0	1	12	0	60	4	1
Oldham, Bob, Burlington	3	6	.333	5.50	18	8	0	0	4	0	52.1	55	249	43	32	3	2	1	9	32	2	55	4	0
Olson, Phillip, Kingsport	6	2	.750	2.42	12	10	2	1	1	1	67.0	47	271	24	18	1	1	1	8	23	0	45	4	1
Olszewski, Tim, Bluefield	3	2	.600	3.06	16	0	0	0	9	3	35.1	34	155	19	12	2	3	1	4	19	0	29	4	1
Ortiz, Steve, Burlington*	1	3	.250	4.55	22	0	0	0	19	7	27.2	30	130	16	14	2	1	1	0	20	2	46	2	0
Osting, James, Danville*	2	7	.222	7.15	11	10	0	0	0	0	39.0	46	190	34	31	1	0	1	0	25	0	43	12	0
Peters, Tim, Elizabethton*	2	3	.400	1.65	27	0	0	0	7	0	32.2	27	134	16	6	1	0	0	0	5	2	36	4	0
Pierce, Drew, Huntington	2	4	.333	6.21	22	0	0	0	17	2	33.1	46	159	29	23	2	3	2	4	10	0	42	9	1
Pizarro, Melvin, Martinsville*	0	0	.000	6.23	10	0	0	0	4	0	17.1	20	79	13	12	1	0	3	4	5	0	17	0	2
Ponson, Sidney, Bluefield	6	3	.667	4.17	13	13	0	0	0	0	77.2	79	324	44	36	7	1	2	1	16	0	56	4	3
Poupart, Melvin, Kingsport	1	1	.500	5.06	18	0	0	0	4	1	26.2	27	119	17	15	5	1	0	1	10	1	32	4	1
Prejean, Alex, Huntington	3	2	.600	9.38	14	3	0	0	2	0	31.2	37	164	36	33	2	0	3	3	31	0	23	11	1
Pumphrey, Kenny, Kingsport	7	3	.700	3.86	12	12	0	0	0	0	65.1	50	283	32	28	3	3	0	6	42	0	76	7	0
Quintana, Urbano, Huntington	1	2	.333	5.71	19	1	0	0	11	3	34.2	43	162	26	22	4	1	1	5	12	0	35	6	5
Raines, Ken, Danville*	0	0	.000	0.71	11	0	0	0	11	6	12.2	8	47	4	1	0	0	2	0	1	0	14	0	1
Rath, Fred, Elizabethton	1	1	.500	1.35	27	0	0	0	25	12	33.1	20	134	8	5	2	2	0	1	11	1	50	3	0
Reed, Dan, Bluefield*	1	0	1.000	2.57	6	1	0	0	1	1	14.0	10	53	5	4	1	0	0	0	5	0	11	0	0
Reed, Kenny, Martinsville	0	1	.000	7.43	13	0	0	0	6	0	23.0	29	119	22	19	3	0	0	2	21	0	15	13	0
Reed, Steven, Johnson City	2	2	.500	4.43	31	0	0	0	19	1	42.2	48	194	24	21	2	0	1	0	15	0	41	3	2
Reynolds, Walker, Danville	1	3	.250	3.99	20	0	0	0	4	1	38.1	26	166	19	17	3	1	2	6	19	1	30	3	0
Richardson, Kasey, Elizabethton*	1	0	1.000	2.33	3	3	0	0	0	0	19.1	12	79	8	5	0	3	1	1	13	1	11	1	0
Roberts, Randolph, Princeton	4	5	.444	3.16	15	9	0	0	2	0	62.2	51	281	35	22	3	1	2	6	33	3	74	14	2
Roettgen, Mark, Johnson City	4	5	.444	5.59	13	13	0	0	0	0	66.0	63	302	48	41	11	4	3	6	40	0	60	4	4
Rogan, Sean, Johnson City*	1	0	1.000	5.65	12	0	0	0	6	0	28.2	30	134	22	18	4	2	3	3	17	0	22	2	0
Roque, Jorge, Johnson City	2	0	1.000	5.12	14	0	0	0	3	0	19.1	15	81	11	11	4	1	1	2	9	1	22	0	3
Ruiz, Rafael, Bristol*	1	2	.333	2.15	22	0	0	0	6	1	37.2	26	154	14	9	1	3	0	0	15	0	57	2	0
Sanders, Frankie, Burlington	3	5	.375	2.96	12	12	3	0	0	0	70.0	48	292	31	23	2	1	0	3	32	0	80	2	1
Santamaria, Bill, Kingsport	5	3	.625	4.18	13	13	1	0	0	0	71.0	62	303	37	33	8	1	3	3	29	0	55	3	0
Santos, Juan, Bluefield	0	0	.000	0.00	1	0	0	0	0	0	3.0	1	10	0	0	0	0	0	0	0	0	2	1	0
Sauritch, Chris, Bluefield	4	1	.800	3.72	13	0	0	0	8	3	19.1	18	91	13	8	3	2	0	2	11	1	16	2	0
Schleuss, Will, Princeton*	0	3	.000	4.50	23	0	0	0	5	1	32.0	29	142	20	16	1	1	1	1	22	2	34	9	0
Schnur, Curt, Danville	1	4	.200	5.74	18	0	0	0	7	0	31.1	34	159	24	20	0	3	5	4	22	0	31	5	3
Secoda, Jason, Bristol	2	8	.200	5.35	13	12	0	0	0	0	65.2	78	307	57	39	3	1	3	1	33	0	63	8	1
Sellner, Aaron, Elizabethton	1	2	.333	2.14	19	1	0	0	5	0	33.2	30	137	15	8	1	0	1	0	10	0	32	1	1
Shumaker, Anthony, Martinsville*	1	3	.250	4.50	6	4	0	0	0	0	28.0	31	120	16	14	1	2	0	1	8	0	26	3	0
Shumate, Jacob, Danville	1	2	.333	10.80	7	2	0	0	2	0	13.1	6	80	21	16	1	0	2	2	32	0	16	14	0
Sikes, Jason, Martinsville	0	3	.000	5.94	4	3	0	0	0	0	16.2	23	81	13	11	1	2	1	0	9	0	10	4	0
Snyder, Matt, Bluefield	0	0	.000	1.04	17	0	0	0	15	8	34.2	35	150	9	4	1	0	0	3	13	0	46	1	0
Spang, R.J., Huntington	1	2	.333	4.60	18	0	0	0	10	3	31.1	31	138	21	16	3	3	1	5	9	0	31	2	3
Sparks, Jeff, Princeton	2	0	1.000	3.23	16	2	0	0	7	2	39.0	32	172	19	14	2	0	1	0	27	2	49	2	1
Splittorff, James, Elizabethton	5	4	.556	3.24	13	12	1	1	1	0	72.1	64	319	40	26	5	0	2	7	29	0	72	11	2
Starling, Marcus, Huntington*	0	2	.000	15.19	13	3	0	0	4	0	21.1	36	130	39	36	2	0	1	6	25	0	22	11	0
Tanksley, William, Elizabethton	0	2	.000	4.11	11	0	0	0	4	1	15.1	16	67	13	7	3	2	0	1	5	0	17	0	1
Tebbetts, Scott, Martinsville	1	3	.250	2.25	22	0	0	0	20	9	32.0	31	133	15	8	0	1	0	0	7	1	30	1	0
Vejil, Aaron, Huntington*	1	0	1.000	5.95	14	0	0	0	10	2	19.2	19	91	15	13	2	1	1	2	10	0	21	5	1
Vicentino, Andy, Princeton*	2	2	.500	7.50	10	7	0	0	2	0	30.0	36	149	30	25	1	1	0	1	27	0	23	4	1
Villafuerte, Brandon, Kingsport	5	1	.833	5.63	20	0	0	0	6	0	32.0	28	144	21	20	0	1	1	1	26	0	42	8	0
Virchis, Adam, Bristol	0	7	.000	5.30	10	10	1	0	0	0	56.0	65	239	39	33	5	2	3	3	7	0	33	2	2
Vota, Michael, Bristol	1	2	.333	4.60	22	0	0	0	12	3	31.1	33	145	19	16	3	2	3	1	14	1	24	5	0
Wagner, Ken, Burlington	5	5	.500	3.16	13	12	0	0	0	0	68.1	54	285	34	24	7	1	2	1	23	0	80	7	1
West, Adam, Johnson City*	1	1	.500	2.85	18	1	0	0	1	0	41.0	41	187	26	13	1	2	4	3	19	1	41	2	0
Wise, James, Danville*	0	1	.000	15.43	2	0	0	0	1	0	2.1	3	14	6	4	0	0	0	0	4	0	3	1	1
Wise, William, Danville	0	3	.000	5.63	10	10	0	0	0	0	46.1	42	201	33	29	2	2	2	7	23	0	24	4	2
Yoder, Jason, Martinsville	1	2	.333	5.40	8	4	0	0	2	0	28.1	33	126	20	17	2	1	1	0	11	0	23	3	0
Young, Ty, Huntington	4	6	.400	4.67	14	14	2	1	0	0	79.0	75	352	56	41	5	0	1	9	36	0	49	6	1

COMBINATION SHUTOUTS: **Bluefield (1)**—Crills-Morseman. **Bristol (2)**—Garber-Desrosiers, Hunt-Desrosiers-Beirne. **Burlington (3)**—Feliz-Loudermilk-Ortiz, Oldham-Grife, Sanders-Edwards. **Danville (2)**—Abreu-Cochran-Loewe-Reynolds, Osting-Koehler. **Elizabethton (4)**—Blank-Sellner-Anderson, Niedermaier-Peters-Rath, Niedermaier-Splittorff, Splittorff-Chapman-Anderson-Harris. **Huntington (0)**—None. **Johnson City (2)**—Jimenez-Reed-Roque-Mendez, Mear-Mendez. **Kingsport (3)**—Beebe-Blang, Ojeda-Blang, Pumphrey-Blang. **Martinsville (1)**—Burger-Dunne-Miller-Tebbets. **Princeton (3)**—Corey-Schleuss, Davis-Cushman, Montgomery-Giron.

NO-HIT GAMES: Abreu, Danville, defeated Burlington, 7-1 (seven innings), July 2; Young, Huntington, defeated Elizabethton, 4-0 (seven innings), August 3.

1995 FIELDING

TEAM

Team	Pct.	G	PO	A	E	TC	DP	PB
Kingsport	.962	66	1723	687	94	2504	45	11
Bluefield	.956	65	1683	651	107	2441	56	18
Martinsville	.953	67	1673	682	115	2470	50	11
Danville	.949	67	1712	650	126	2488	49	29
Huntington	.948	67	1681	704	131	2516	40	16
Burlington	.947	64	1650	613	127	2390	42	21
Johnson City	.946	68	1767	685	141	2593	38	15
Princeton	.944	63	1630	657	136	2423	47	17
Bristol	.941	67	1699	691	151	2541	43	11
Elizabethton	.934	64	1653	741	168	2562	51	13

TRIPLE PLAY: Bristol.

INDIVIDUAL

FIRST BASEMEN

NOTE: All caps denotes fielding-percentage leader based on 34 games for catchers, 45 for all other non-pitchers and 68 innings for pitchers. *Throws lefthanded.

Player, Team	Pct.	G	PO	A	E	TC	DP
Anglen, Toby, Danville	1.000	1	1	0	0	1	0
Bowness, Brian, Bristol	.982	54	441	44	9	494	29
Boyette, Tony, Princeton	.971	39	313	22	10	345	24
Cardona, Alex, Johnson City	.500	2	1	0	1	2	0
Coburn, Todd, Huntington	.985	14	119	10	2	131	8
Davis, James, Princeton	.971	4	31	3	1	35	2
Deck, Billy, Johnson City*	.985	58	492	38	8	538	25
Dougherty, Keith, Danville	.972	19	125	15	4	144	8
Ennis, Wayne, Princeton	.958	8	44	2	2	48	8
Foote, Derek, Danville	1.000	1	7	0	0	7	0
Glavine, Mike, Burlington*	.990	38	278	19	3	300	15
Gunderson, Shane, Elizabethton	1.000	1	9	1	0	10	0
Hardy, Brian, Burlington	1.000	2	10	0	0	10	0
Hendricks, Ryan, Huntington	.985	52	434	35	7	476	27
Janke, Jared, Martinsville	.972	36	259	20	8	287	18
Lakovic, Greg, Elizabethton	.929	1	11	2	1	14	1
Lantigua, Miguel, Kingsport	1.000	1	2	0	0	2	0
Lee, Carlos, Bristol	1.000	5	26	3	0	29	2
Mastrullo, Mike, Huntington	1.000	1	5	0	0	5	0
Mata, Manuel, Martinsville*	.857	1	6	0	1	7	1
McDougal, Mike, Johnson City	.969	11	89	6	3	98	4
McWhite, Ray, Danville	.976	51	416	23	11	450	34
Naples, Brandon, Kingsport*	.982	15	103	7	2	112	8
PATTERSON, Jarrod, Kingsport	.992	54	463	35	4	502	28
Pierzynski, A.J., Elizabethton	1.000	1	4	1	0	5	0
Ramos, Noel, Bluefield	.996	27	231	19	1	251	18
Raymondi, Mike, Huntington	.933	2	14	0	1	15	1
Reyes, Freddy, Elizabethton	.981	18	147	12	3	162	9
Rincones, Wuarnner, Bristol	.929	13	80	11	7	98	5
Russin, Tom, Bluefield	.974	40	304	29	9	342	33
Santiago, Arnold, Burlington	1.000	31	222	15	0	237	17
Schroeder, John, Elizabethton	.958	47	440	36	21	497	36
Smalley, Jevon, Princeton	.972	20	135	6	4	145	9
Stone, Matthew, Martinsville*	.976	35	266	17	7	290	23
Torbett, Hanes, Kingsport	.857	1	5	1	1	7	1

TRIPLE PLAY: Bowness.

SECOND BASEMEN

Player, Team	Pct.	G	PO	A	E	TC	DP
Anglen, Toby, Danville	.978	11	16	29	1	46	6
Bracho, Darwin, Princeton	.938	6	4	11	1	16	2
Brito, Domingo, Martinsville	.778	2	2	5	2	9	0
Brown, Jerome, Elizabethton	1.000	2	3	5	0	8	1
Concepcion, David, Princeton	.941	36	65	110	11	186	16
Cross, Adam, Danville	.970	27	49	48	3	100	10
Daedlow, Craig, Bluefield	1.000	2	5	4	0	9	2
Diaz, Ivan, Johnson City	1.000	4	2	4	0	6	0
Edmondson, Tracy, Kingsport	.958	41	56	105	7	168	15
Erickson, Corey, Kingsport	1.000	1	6	2	0	8	2
Espada, Angel, Danville	.966	31	57	84	5	146	16
Fraser, Joseph, Elizabethton	.920	45	67	140	18	225	23
GABRIEL, Denio, Bluefield	.965	50	73	122	7	202	24
Garcia, Carlos, Elizabethton	.944	20	30	54	5	89	12
Guthrie, David, Princeton	.944	4	6	11	1	18	1
Harris, Rodger, Johnson City	.926	42	66	96	13	175	11
Helms, Ryan, Bristol	.922	47	79	111	16	206	19
Hodges, Randy, Danville	1.000	2	1	4	0	5	1
Hooker, Kevin, Martinsville	.963	43	67	88	6	161	21
Jimenez, Ruben, Johnson City	.956	22	38	49	4	91	13
Mason, Lamont, Princeton	.940	25	52	73	8	133	20
Mastrullo, Mike, Huntington	.950	24	36	60	5	101	4
Milledge, Tony, Johnson City	1.000	9	18	17	0	35	1
Murphy, Quinn, Burlington	.911	35	50	94	14	158	14
O'Connor, Richard, Martinsville	.964	23	40	68	4	112	11
Rincones, Wuarnner, Bristol	.957	5	6	16	1	23	3
Roberson, Gerald, Huntington	.952	39	47	110	8	165	16
Short, Richard, Bluefield	.962	7	9	16	1	26	3
Simpson, Jeramie, Kingsport	.800	4	1	3	1	5	0
Soriano, Juan, Kingsport	.943	21	36	46	5	87	10
Strasser, John, Bristol	.933	20	36	47	6	89	8
Sturges, Brian, Johnson City	1.000	1	0	3	0	3	0
Tiller, Brad, Burlington	.919	32	49	87	12	148	12
Torbett, Hanes, Kingsport	1.000	6	8	14	0	22	0
Winn, Wess, Bluefield	.956	15	21	22	2	45	7
Wood, Tony, Huntington	.969	6	10	21	1	32	7

THIRD BASEMEN

Player, Team	Pct.	G	PO	A	E	TC	DP
Anglen, Toby, Danville	.950	45	25	90	6	121	7
Bearden, Doug, Bristol	.800	3	1	3	1	5	0
Bogle, Bryan, Bluefield	.900	6	8	10	2	20	1
Brito, Domingo, Martinsville	.909	17	7	33	4	44	0
BRYANT, Chris, Bluefield	.923	58	48	96	12	156	9
Concepcion, David, Princeton	.854	20	9	32	7	48	3
Cox, Robert, Kingsport	.904	57	35	107	15	157	5
Cross, Adam, Danville	1.000	4	2	4	0	6	0
Daedlow, Craig, Bluefield	.667	1	1	1	1	3	0
Dougherty, Keith, Danville	.750	2	1	2	1	4	0
Elliott, Zach, Martinsville	1.000	1	3	1	0	4	0
Garcia, Carlos, Elizabethton	.917	5	2	9	1	12	0
Guthrie, David, Princeton	.857	8	3	9	2	14	2
Haas, Chris, Johnson City	.893	64	51	116	20	187	9
Herdman, Eli, Elizabethton	.850	58	39	114	27	180	8
Hooker, Kevin, Martinsville	.944	6	6	11	1	18	0
Jensen, Blair, Burlington	.750	11	2	10	4	16	0
Jimenez, Ruben, Johnson City	1.000	1	0	3	0	3	0
Lee, Carlos, Bristol	.900	58	58	104	18	180	10
Mastrullo, Mike, Huntington	.862	13	9	16	4	29	0
McWhite, Ray, Danville	.970	9	10	22	1	33	1
Milledge, Tony, Johnson City	.810	8	5	12	4	21	1
Mota, Christian, Burlington	.917	59	45	99	13	157	8
Murphy, Quinn, Burlington	.667	3	2	4	3	9	0
O'Connor, Richard, Martinsville	.916	25	23	53	7	83	5
Patellis, Anthony, Princeton	.868	41	31	61	14	106	4
Reyes, Freddy, Elizabethton	.600	2	2	1	2	5	1
Reyes, Winston, Huntington	.906	18	12	36	5	53	4
Rincones, Wuarnner, Bristol	.970	11	7	25	1	33	1
Sasser, Rob, Danville	.852	11	7	16	4	27	1
Serbio, Carmen, Martinsville	.873	19	16	32	7	55	1
Short, Richard, Bluefield	.941	4	3	13	1	17	2
Soriano, Juan, Kingsport	.970	14	6	26	1	33	4
Torbett, Hanes, Kingsport	1.000	3	2	5	0	7	1
Townsend, Terric, Martinsville	.857	2	1	5	1	7	1
Wood, Tony, Huntington	.869	40	19	67	13	99	3

TRIPLE PLAY: Lee.

SHORTSTOPS

Player, Team	Pct.	G	PO	A	E	TC	DP
Anglen, Toby, Danville	.950	6	5	14	1	20	1
Bearden, Doug, Bristol	.850	43	54	116	30	200	16
Brito, Domingo, Martinsville	1.000	10	14	30	0	44	7
Brown, Jerome, Elizabethton	.615	6	5	11	10	26	2
Cross, Adam, Danville	.786	10	8	14	6	28	2
Daedlow, Craig, Bluefield	1.000	2	1	4	0	5	1
Davidson, Cleatus, Elizabethton	.884	38	54	113	22	189	20
Edwards, Donald, Burlington	.897	42	60	97	18	175	16
Elliott, Zach, Martinsville	.937	43	63	115	12	190	27
Gabriel, Denio, Bluefield	1.000	3	5	8	0	13	2
Garcia, Carlos, Elizabethton	.876	24	29	63	13	105	6
Guthrie, David, Princeton	.902	47	65	119	20	204	19
Jimenez, Ruben, Johnson City	.838	19	16	41	11	68	3
Martinez, Eddy, Bluefield	.904	56	71	135	22	228	31

Player, Team	Pct.	G	PO	A	E	TC	DP
Martinez, Tony, Johnson City	.919	23	19	60	7	86	4
Milledge, Tony, Johnson City	.917	2	5	6	1	12	1
Nolte, Bruce, Huntington	.913	60	90	163	24	277	25
O'Connor, Richard, Martinsville	.773	7	6	11	5	22	1
POLANCO, Enohel, Kingsport	.922	61	81	155	20	256	28
Roberson, Gerald, Huntington	.857	2	3	3	1	7	0
Salano, Manuel, Princeton	.847	27	34	49	15	98	12
Serbio, Carmen, Martinsville	.958	8	6	17	1	24	1
Soriano, Juan, Kingsport	1.000	7	3	16	0	19	3
Strasser, John, Bristol	.887	29	35	59	12	106	8
Tiller, Brad, Burlington	.897	24	32	46	9	87	11
Townsend, Terric, Martinsville	.875	3	5	9	2	16	1
Utting, Ben, Danville	.894	55	68	151	26	245	29
Winn, Wess, Bluefield	.964	8	15	12	1	28	3
Wood, Tony, Huntington	1.000	9	15	16	0	31	2
Woolf, Jason, Johnson City	.810	28	49	62	26	137	15

OUTFIELDERS

Player, Team	Pct.	G	PO	A	E	TC	DP
Abell, Antonio, Johnson City	.918	52	87	2	8	97	1
Albert, Chernan, Bristol	.903	35	63	2	7	72	0
Almonte, Wady, Bluefield	.918	47	52	4	5	61	1
Anderson, Milton, Burlington	.938	57	102	3	7	112	1
Andino, Luis, Martinsville	.886	20	27	4	4	35	0
Bagley, Sean, Bristol	.750	11	6	0	2	8	0
Bass, Jayson, Danville	.966	62	141	2	5	148	0
Black, Brandon, Kingsport	.938	26	43	2	3	48	0
Bracho, Darwin, Princeton	.000	3	0	0	1	1	0
Brown, Jerome, Elizabethton	.909	8	9	1	1	11	0
Buckles, Matt, Martinsville	.931	15	26	1	2	29	0
Coburn, Todd, Huntington	1.000	1	1	0	0	1	0
Colburn, Brian, Elizabethton*	.900	10	9	0	1	10	0
Conner, Decomba, Princeton	1.000	6	18	2	0	20	0
Current, Jeremy, Johnson City	.960	20	22	2	1	25	0
Dellucci, David, Bluefield*	.846	12	11	0	2	13	0
Drent, Brian, Bristol	.909	44	57	3	6	66	1
Duncan, Robert, Danville*	.937	43	58	1	4	63	0
Fernandez, Randy, Huntington*	.778	11	14	0	4	18	0
Franklin, James, Danville	.922	34	45	2	4	51	0
Garcia, Carlos, Elizabethton	.957	17	21	1	1	23	0
Gunderson, Shane, Elizabethton	.862	25	23	2	4	29	0
Hall, Darran, Princeton*	1.000	9	18	0	0	18	0
Herrera, Jesus, Princeton	.872	37	39	2	6	47	0
Higman, Joel, Blu.-Hun.	.897	21	22	4	3	29	0
HOBBIE, Matt, Huntington*	.984	58	122	1	2	125	0
Hollins, Darontaye, Bristol	.980	56	95	5	2	102	2
Hunter, Lanier, Huntington	.936	59	96	7	7	110	2
Ingram, Darron, Princeton	.952	57	98	2	5	105	0
Isom, Johnny, Bluefield	.974	48	71	5	2	78	0
Johnson, Heath, Elizabethton	.892	56	70	4	9	83	1
Johnson, Travis, Elizabethton	1.000	13	12	2	0	14	0
Jones, Ivory, Elizabethton*	.985	41	58	6	1	65	1
Juarez, Raul, Elizabethton	.961	35	47	2	2	51	0
Kearney, Chad, Martinsville	.893	23	23	2	3	28	2
Kennedy, Justin, Martinsville*	.932	41	63	5	5	73	1
Kerr, Brian, Bluefield	1.000	1	2	0	0	2	0
Kingsale, Eugene, Bluefield	.899	44	95	3	11	109	1
Langford, Derrick, Danville	1.000	9	8	0	0	8	0
LeCronier, Jason, Bluefield	1.000	5	8	0	0	8	0
Lee, Jason, Johnson City	.905	19	19	0	2	21	0
Lugo, Ursino, Burlington	.897	22	25	1	3	29	1
Malin, Edgar, Huntington	.750	17	18	0	6	24	0
Mapp, Eric, Princeton	.959	61	115	3	5	123	0
Mastrullo, Mike, Huntington	1.000	1	2	0	0	2	0
McCarthy, Kevin, Kingsport*	.919	25	34	0	3	37	0
McClure, Craig, Bristol	.944	59	80	4	5	89	1
McCroskey, Jackie, Huntington*	.939	41	75	2	5	82	0
Mejia, Miguel, Bluefield	.940	45	74	5	5	84	1
Mendoza, Carlos, Kingsport*	.951	33	54	4	3	61	0
Messner, Jake, Burlington*	.985	43	63	3	1	67	1
Mifflin, Brian, Kingsport	1.000	1	1	0	0	1	0
Mota, Christian, Burlington	1.000	1	2	0	0	2	0
Mota, Gleydel, Kingsport*	.750	1	3	0	1	4	0
Munoz, Juan, Johnson City*	.983	55	101	14	2	117	0
Naples, Brandon, Kingsport*	.846	11	11	0	2	13	0
Pennyfeather, William, Princeton	1.000	1	3	0	0	3	0
Pickett, Eric, Danville	.956	57	103	6	5	114	1
Ramirez, Daniel, Kingsport	.947	62	122	3	7	132	0
Roberson, Gerald, Huntington	.929	9	23	3	2	28	0
Robinson, Kerry, Johnson City*	.938	51	86	5	6	97	1
Schofield, Andy, Johnson City	.933	25	26	2	2	30	0
Schreimann, Eric, Martinsville	1.000	3	4	1	0	5	0
Serafin, Ricardo, Martinsville	.909	19	28	2	3	33	0
Simpson, Jeramie, Kingsport	.976	46	80	2	2	84	0
Spry, Shane, Bristol*	1.000	2	1	0	0	1	0
Taylor, Reggie, Martinsville	.940	63	116	9	8	133	3
Terry, Tony, Princeton	.964	36	26	1	1	28	0
Whitaker, Chad, Burlington	.920	39	44	2	4	50	0
Williams, Errick, Martinsville	.949	33	51	5	3	59	0
Williams, Jewell, Burlington	.942	42	48	1	3	52	0

OUTFIELDERS WITH TWO OR MORE TEAMS

Player, Team	Pct.	G	PO	A	E	TC	DP
Higman, Joel, Bluefield	.800	8	3	1	1	5	0
Higman, Joel, Huntington	.917	13	19	3	2	24	0

CATCHERS

Player, Team	Pct.	G	PO	A	E	TC	DP	PB
Anderson, Frank, Bristol	.983	46	350	64	7	421	2	6
Andrews, Jeff, Huntington	.968	34	202	39	8	249	3	9
Antczak, Chuck, Bristol	.972	23	131	10	4	145	0	3
Bagley, Sean, Bristol	.977	12	37	5	1	43	0	2
Boyette, Tony, Princeton	.990	12	89	8	1	98	0	4
Bracho, Darwin, Princeton	.991	18	97	14	1	112	0	4
Cardona, Alex, Johnson City	.987	19	130	17	2	149	3	4
Coats, Nathan, Burlington	.982	19	145	16	3	164	1	6
Coburn, Todd, Huntington	.970	27	198	32	7	237	1	5
Davis, James, Princeton	.980	40	296	50	7	353	1	9
Falciglia, Tony, Johnson City	.981	20	130	24	3	157	1	3
Foote, Derek, Danville	.969	14	117	6	4	127	2	1
Frost, Robert, Kingsport	1.000	8	59	7	0	66	1	2
Gargiulo, Mike, Bluefield	.973	48	384	51	12	447	3	11
Gunderson, Shane, Elizabethton	.967	10	83	4	3	90	0	0
Harmer, Francis, Bluefield	.994	18	150	13	1	164	1	7
Hoover, Will, Kingsport	1.000	8	22	6	0	28	0	5
Lakovic, Greg, Elizabethton	1.000	4	27	2	0	29	0	1
Lantigua, Miguel, Kingsport	.974	3	36	2	1	39	0	0
Livingston, Clyde, Martinsville	.976	9	76	4	2	82	0	1
Martin, Ryan, Danville	1.000	3	25	4	0	29	0	1
McNeal, Pepe, Bur.-J.C.	.986	53	438	40	7	485	3	12
Mepri, Sal, Princeton	1.000	5	5	0	0	5	0	0
Mullen, Adam, Danville	.969	16	110	13	4	127	2	7
OLIVEROS, Leonardo, Martins.	1.000	40	270	52	0	322	3	7
Pena, Francisco, Elizabethton	1.000	7	38	6	0	44	0	1
Pena, Jose, Burlington	.979	21	175	10	4	189	0	8
Pierzynski, A.J., Elizabethton	.974	49	372	71	12	455	3	11
Pointer, Corey, Danville	.958	35	241	34	12	287	4	19
Raio, Domenick, Martinsville	1.000	3	20	2	0	22	1	0
Ramirez, Alonso, Burlington	.977	9	42	1	1	44	1	1
Raymondi, Mike, Huntington	.983	11	54	4	1	59	0	2
Schreimann, Eric, Martinsville	.982	14	98	11	2	111	1	3
Shy, Jason, Danville	.881	8	34	3	5	42	0	1
Sturges, Brian, Johnson City	.988	13	70	10	1	81	0	2
Valera, Yojanny, Kingsport	.989	53	409	58	5	472	4	4
Wampler, Sam, Martinsville	.975	9	37	2	1	40	0	0

CATCHERS WITH TWO OR MORE TEAMS

Player, Team	Pct.	G	PO	A	E	TC	DP	PB
McNeal, Pepe, Burlington	.992	27	229	21	2	252	2	6
McNeal, Pepe, Johnson City	.979	26	209	19	5	233	1	6

PITCHERS

Player, Team	Pct.	G	PO	A	E	TC	DP
Abreu, Winston, Danville	1.000	13	5	5	0	10	0
ADAIR, Scott, Huntington	1.000	13	7	13	0	20	0
Aguiar, Douglas, Martinsville	1.000	15	3	4	0	7	0
Alexis, Julio, Huntington	.810	14	9	8	4	21	0
Alvarado, Luis, Huntington	1.000	11	1	4	0	5	0
Anderson, Eric, Elizabethton*	.909	21	3	7	1	11	0
Anderson, Gary, Burlington	1.000	14	0	1	0	1	1
Anez, Maycoll, Bristol	1.000	7	2	3	0	5	0
Angerhofer, Chad, Princeton*	.800	13	2	2	1	5	0
Barfield, Rodney, Johnson City	1.000	10	0	2	0	2	0
Bartels, Todd, Elizabethton	.938	13	9	6	1	16	0
Bates, Shawn, Bluefield*	.875	14	1	6	1	8	1
Beebe, Joey, Kingsport*	.800	9	2	2	1	5	1
Beirne, Kevin, Bristol	1.000	9	1	2	0	3	1
Blang, Michael, Kingsport	1.000	23	7	6	0	13	1
Blank, John, Elizabethton*	.900	15	3	6	1	10	0
Boggs, Harold, Elizabethton	.875	12	3	4	1	8	0
Bowser, Robert, Martinsville	1.000	17	2	7	0	9	0
Burger, Rob, Martinsville	.500	9	1	1	2	4	0
Buteaux, Shane, Bristol	.857	13	4	2	1	7	0
Chapman, Walker, Elizabethton	1.000	4	3	2	0	5	1
Chen, Bruce, Danville*	1.000	14	1	9	0	10	0
Cloud, Tony, Princeton	1.000	12	5	9	0	14	0
Cochrane, Andrew, Danville*	.500	6	0	1	1	2	0

Player, Team	Pct.	G	PO	A	E	TC	DP
Coggin, David, Martinsville	.857	11	6	6	2	14	1
Collins, Ken, Danville	1.000	18	2	1	0	3	0
Cooper, Chadwick, Kingsport	1.000	22	0	3	0	3	0
Cooper, Keith, Danville	.800	17	1	3	1	5	0
Corey, Mark, Princeton	.750	4	2	1	1	4	0
Crills, Brad, Bluefield	1.000	4	1	5	0	6	1
Cushman, Dwayne, Princeton	.857	26	1	5	1	7	0
Davis, Lance, Princeton*	.857	15	5	7	2	14	0
Dean, Greg, Bluefield	1.000	10	2	3	0	5	0
Desrosiers, Erik, Bristol	.800	22	3	1	1	5	0
DeWitt, Chris, Kingsport	.833	23	5	5	2	12	0
DeWitt, Matt, Johnson City	.929	13	5	8	1	14	0
Dunne, Brian, Martinsville*	1.000	16	3	8	0	11	1
Edwards, Jon, Burlington	.889	19	3	5	1	9	0
Eibey, Scott, Bluefield*	.900	14	3	6	1	10	1
Feliz, Bienvenido, Burlington	.778	12	7	7	4	18	1
Fereira, Marcos, Huntington	.500	5	0	1	1	2	0
Figueroa, Nelson, Kingsport	.889	12	3	13	2	18	2
Fleetwood, Tony, Burlington*	.714	18	1	4	2	7	0
Fonceca, Chad, Princeton	1.000	11	3	0	0	3	0
Frace, Ryan, Martinsville	1.000	14	3	2	0	5	0
Fussell, Chris, Bluefield	.857	12	1	5	1	7	1
Garber, Joel, Bristol*	.944	19	7	10	1	18	0
Giron, Roberto, Princeton	.875	24	3	4	1	8	0
Giuliano, Joe, Danville	.800	11	1	3	1	5	1
Gobert, Chris, Danville*	1.000	3	1	1	0	2	0
Grife, Richard, Burlington	1.000	16	2	4	0	6	0
Hackett, Jason, Bluefield*	.917	13	5	6	1	12	1
Halley, Allen, Bristol	1.000	2	1	1	0	2	0
Harris, Jeffrey, Elizabethton	1.000	21	3	5	0	8	1
Harrison, Scott, Burlington	1.000	5	0	5	0	5	0
Hasselhoff, Derek, Bristol	.833	12	10	10	4	24	0
Hoalton, Brandon, Huntington	1.000	6	1	8	0	9	0
Hunt, Jon, Bristol*	.667	13	4	6	5	15	0
Jimenez, Jose, Johnson City	.943	14	12	21	2	35	1
Kershner, Jason, Martinsville*	.882	13	5	10	2	17	0
Kessel, Kyle, Kingsport*	1.000	5	1	5	0	6	1
Knoll, Randy, Martinsville	.571	6	1	3	3	7	0
Knowland, Sam, Danville	1.000	20	5	6	0	11	0
Koehler, P.K., Danville*	.750	11	1	2	1	4	0
Kosek, Kory, Martinsville	1.000	9	0	4	0	4	0
Kown, John, Johnson City	1.000	16	4	6	0	10	0
Kraus, Tim, Bristol	1.000	5	2	3	0	5	0
Kruse, Kelly, Bristol	1.000	15	0	2	0	2	0
LaRocca, Todd, Bluefield	1.000	8	4	11	0	15	1
Loewe, Kevin, Danville*	.917	20	5	6	1	12	0
Loudermilk, Darren, Burlington	.846	21	5	6	2	13	0
Lowry, Elliott, Burlington*	.875	10	0	7	1	8	0
Mahaffey, Alan, Elizabethton*	.833	13	0	10	2	12	0
Maine, Dalton, Bluefield	1.000	1	1	1	0	2	1
Manon, Julio, Huntington	.929	16	5	8	1	14	2
Martinez, Dennis, Burlington	.875	15	2	5	1	8	1
Martinez, Willie, Burlington	.692	11	1	8	4	13	1
Mattox, Gene, Princeton	1.000	11	0	1	0	1	0
McCaffrey, Dennis, Johnson City	1.000	24	3	0	0	3	0
McKnight, Chris, Danville*	1.000	1	0	1	0	1	0
Mear, Rich, Johnson City*	.905	14	4	15	2	21	1
Mendez, Manuel, Johnson City*	1.000	30	1	3	0	4	0
Miller, Brian, Martinsville	.900	23	5	4	1	10	0
Montgomery, Joe, Princeton	1.000	13	3	2	0	5	0
Moore, David, Bristol	1.000	15	2	4	0	6	1
Moreno, Julio, Bluefield	.625	9	4	1	3	8	0
Morseman, Robert, Bluefield*	1.000	18	0	8	0	8	0
Mosquea, Alberto, Martinsville	.750	9	2	1	1	4	0
Murphy, Chris, Princeton*	.895	10	3	14	2	19	0
Niedermaier, Brad, Elizabethton	1.000	7	4	5	0	9	1
Noone, Bill, Martinsville	1.000	1	2	0	0	2	0
Ojeda, Erick, Kingsport*	.944	14	6	11	1	18	1
Oldham, Bob, Burlington	.688	18	1	10	5	16	0
Olson, Phillip, Kingsport	.950	12	5	14	1	20	0
Olszewski, Tim, Bluefield	.833	16	1	4	1	6	1
Ortiz, Steve, Burlington*	1.000	22	0	1	0	1	0
Osting, James, Danville*	1.000	11	1	5	0	6	0
Peters, Tim, Elizabethton*	1.000	27	4	7	0	11	1
Pierce, Drew, Huntington	1.000	22	3	6	0	9	0
Pizarro, Melvin, Martinsville*	1.000	10	1	1	0	2	0
PONSON, Sidney, Bluefield	1.000	13	10	10	0	20	0
Poupart, Melvin, Kingsport	.500	18	1	0	1	2	0
Prejean, Alex, Huntington	.833	14	3	2	1	6	0
Pumphrey, Kenny, Kingsport	.933	12	5	9	1	15	0
Quintana, Urbano, Huntington	1.000	19	2	1	0	3	0
Raines, Ken, Danville*	1.000	11	1	3	0	4	0
Rath, Fred, Elizabethton	.833	27	2	3	1	6	1
Reed, Dan, Bluefield*	1.000	6	2	3	0	5	0
Reed, Steven, Johnson City	.750	31	0	3	1	4	0
Reynolds, Walker, Danville	.600	20	2	1	2	5	0
Richardson, Kasey, Elizabethton*	1.000	3	0	5	0	5	0
Roberts, Randolph, Princeton	.789	15	5	10	4	19	0
Roettgen, Mark, Johnson City	.917	13	2	9	1	12	0
Rogan, Sean, Johnson City*	.333	12	0	1	2	3	0
Roque, Jorge, Johnson City	1.000	14	1	4	0	5	0
Ruiz, Rafael, Bristol*	.667	22	2	2	2	6	0
Sanders, Frankie, Burlington	.938	12	2	13	1	16	1
Santamaria, Bill, Kingsport	.833	13	3	7	2	12	0
Sauritch, Chris, Bluefield	.875	13	3	4	1	8	0
Schleuss, Will, Princeton*	1.000	23	0	6	0	6	0
Schnur, Curt, Danville	.600	18	1	5	4	10	0
Secoda, Jason, Bristol	.846	13	8	3	2	13	0
Sellner, Aaron, Elizabethton	.833	19	1	4	1	6	0
Shumaker, Anthony, Martinsville*	1.000	6	3	3	0	6	0
Shumate, Jacob, Danville	.500	7	0	1	1	2	0
Sikes, Jason, Martinsville	.833	4	1	4	1	6	0
Snyder, Matt, Bluefield	1.000	17	0	5	0	5	0
Spang, R.J., Huntington	.750	18	4	5	3	12	0
Sparks, Jeff, Princeton	1.000	16	2	1	0	3	0
Splittorff, James, Elizabethton	.900	13	6	12	2	20	2
Starling, Marcus, Huntington*	.875	13	1	6	1	8	1
Tanksley, William, Elizabethton	.750	11	1	2	1	4	0
Tebbetts, Scott, Martinsville	.900	22	4	5	1	10	0
Vejil, Aaron, Huntington*	1.000	14	1	2	0	3	0
Vicentino, Andy, Princeton*	.833	10	0	5	1	6	0
Villafuerte, Brandon, Kingsport	1.000	20	4	6	0	10	1
Virchis, Adam, Bristol	1.000	10	7	8	0	15	1
Vota, Michael, Bristol	1.000	22	3	2	0	5	0
Wagner, Ken, Burlington	.818	13	1	8	2	11	1
West, Adam, Johnson City*	.818	18	4	5	2	11	0
Wise, William, Danville	.882	10	5	10	2	17	0
Yoder, Jason, Martinsville	.857	8	2	4	1	7	0
Young, Ty, Huntington	.792	14	7	12	5	24	0

The following players did not have any fielding statistics at the positions indicated or appeared only as a designated hitter, pinch-hitter or pinch-runner: Andino, 3b; Cope, p; Cruz, p; Feingold, p; Gill, of; Herbison, p; King, p; McDougal, p; Mercedes, p; Milledge, p; C. Mota, ss; Raio, of; K. Reed, p; Santos, p; Schroeder, of; Serbio, 2b; J. Taylor, dh, ph; Torbett, of; J. Wise, p.

LEAGUE CHAMPIONS

Year	Team	Pct.
1921—	Greenville	.608
	Johnson City*	.627
1922—	Bristol	.557
1923—	Knoxville	.635
1924—	Knoxville*	.642
	Bristol	.607
1925—	Greenville	.667
1926-36—	Did not operate.	
1937—	Elizabethton	.559
	Pennington Gap*	.580
1938—	Elizabethton	.664
	Greenville (3rd)†	.571
1939—	Elizabethton‡	.597
1940—	Johnson City§	.726
	Elizabethton	.750
1941—	Johnson City	.614
	Elizabethton*	.661
1942—	Bristol	.667
	Bristol∞	.660
1943—	Bristol	.755
	Bristol▲	.617
1944—	Kingsport‡	.575
1945—	Kingsport‡	.670
1946—	New River‡	.675
1947—	Pulaski	.648
	New River (3rd)†	.516
1948—	Pulaski‡	.680
1949—	Bluefield‡	.721
1950—	Bluefield	.600
	Bluefield◆	.745
1951—	Kingsport‡	.659
1952—	Johnson City	.595
	Welch (3rd)†	.509
1953—	Welch*	.705
	Johnson City	.672
1954—	Bluefield‡	.619
1955—	Salem■	.689
1956—	Did not operate.	
1957—	Bluefield	.701
1958—	Johnson City	.662
1959—	Morristown	.603
1960—	Wytheville	.614
1961—	Middlesboro	.591
1962—	Bluefield	.671
1963—	Bluefield	.652

Year	Team	Pct.
1964—	Johnson City	.662
1965—	Salem	.614
1966—	Marion	.623
1967—	Bluefield	.627
1968—	Marion	.583
1969—	Pulaski▼	.576
	Johnson City	.544
1970—	Bluefield	.638
1971—	Bluefield▼	.609
	Kingsport	.559
1972—	Bristol▼	.588
	Covington	.586
1973—	Kingsport	.757
1974—	Bristol▼	.754
	Bluefield	.536
1975—	Marion	.515
	Johnson City▼	.603
1976—	Johnson City▼	.714
	Bluefield	.600
1977—	Kingsport	.623
1978—	Elizabethton	.594
1979—	Paintsville	.800
1980—	Paintsville	.657
1981—	Paintsville	.657
1982—	Bluefield▼	.681
	Johnson City	.478
1983—	Paintsville	.653
1984—	Elizabethton•	.580
	Pulaski	.536
1985—	Bristol††	.638
1986—	Johnson City	.667
	Pulaski•	.621
1987—	Burlington•	.729
	Johnson City	.609
1988—	Kingsport•	.644
	Burlington	.529
1989—	Elizabethton•	.691
	Pulaski	.618
1990—	Elizabethton	.761
1991—	Pulaski•	.662
	Burlington	.597
1992—	Elizabethton	.742
	Bluefield•	.597
1993—	Burlington•	.647
	Elizabethton	.552
1994—	Princeton•	.621
	Johnson City	.618
1995—	Bluefield	.754
	Kingsport•	.727

*Won split-season playoff. †Won four-team playoff. ‡Won championship and four-team playoff. §Johnson City, first-half winner, won playoff involving six clubs. ∞Won both halves and defeated second-place Elizabethton in playoff. ▲Won both halves, but Erwin won four-team playoff. ◆Won both halves, but Bristol won two-club playoff. ■Salem and Johnson City declared playoff co-champions when weather forced cancellation of final series. ▼League was divided into Northern, Southern divisions; declared league champion based on highest won-lost percentage. •League was divided into North and South divisions; won playoff. ††Bristol declared league champion based on regular-season record.

ARIZONA LEAGUE

LEAGUE OFFICE

President/treasurer
Bob Richmond
Address
P.O. Box 4941
Scottsdale, AZ 85261
Phone
602-483-8224

Teams*
Angels
Athletics
Diamondbacks
Mariners
Padres
Rockies

*Teams play their games in Chandler, Mesa, Peoria, Scottsdale and other Arizona sites to be announced.

1995 FINAL STANDINGS

COMPOSITE

Team	Ath.	Ang.	Brw.	Pad.	Mar.	Rck.	W	L	T	Pct.	GB
Athletics	....	6	8	5	7	11	37	19	0	.661	....
Angels	5	....	6	10	6	8	35	21	0	.625	2
Brewers	4	6	....	8	7	9	34	22	0	.607	3
Padres	5	2	3	....	6	8	24	31	0	.436	12½
Mariners	5	4	4	5	....	6	24	32	0	.429	13
Rockies	0	3	1	3	6	....	13	42	0	.236	23½

Games played in Chandler, Mesa, Peoria and Scottsdale.

Club names are major league affiliations.

PLAYOFFS: No playoffs scheduled.

REGULAR-SEASON ATTENDANCE: No total official attendance figures reported.

MANAGERS: Angels, Bruce Hines; Athletics, Juan Navarette; Brewers, Ralph Dickenson; Mariners, Tommy LeVasseur; Padres, Dan Norman; Rockies, Jim Eppard.

ALL-STAR TEAM: 1B—David Arias, Mariners; 2B—Dionys Cesar, Athletics; 3B—Juan Polanco, Athletics; SS—Edward Lara, Athletics; OF—Richard Stuart, Angels; Juan Rodriguez, Angels; Salvadore Duverge, Rockies; C—Ramon Hernandez, Athletics; DH—Daryl Rutherford, Padres; LHP—Keith Volkman, Angels; RHP—Jose Paulino, Athletics; LH Reliever—Keith Volkman, Angels; RH Reliever—Robert Kazmirski, Athletics; Most Valuable Player—Ramon Hernandez, Athletics; Manager of the Year—Juan Navarette, Athletics.

1995 BATTING

TEAM

Team	Avg.	G	TPA	AB	R	H	TB	2B	3B	HR	RBI	SH	SF	HP	BB	IBB	SO	SB	CS	GDP	LOB	ShO	Slg.	OBP
Brewers	.265	56	2173	1899	315	504	643	68	28	5	254	13	19	38	203	2	376	106	45	40	391	2	.339	.345
Angels	.263	56	2121	1832	287	482	639	60	35	9	223	23	18	34	214	3	386	92	47	32	393	0	.349	.348
Mariners	.260	56	2241	1959	304	510	698	93	28	13	228	8	18	32	224	1	477	71	47	32	443	2	.356	.343
Padres	.257	55	2041	1822	254	469	655	78	27	18	212	9	12	21	177	4	482	69	45	36	372	2	.359	.328
Athletics	.256	56	2177	1847	329	473	682	61	44	20	253	8	28	31	262	5	481	134	65	27	395	3	.369	.353
Rockies	.230	55	2083	1819	237	418	536	60	17	8	182	8	18	42	194	1	503	63	33	46	385	5	.295	.315

INDIVIDUAL

TOP QUALIFIERS FOR BATTING CHAMPIONSHIP

Minimum 151 plate appearances. *Lefthanded batter. †Switch-hitter.

Player, Team	Avg.	G	TPA	AB	R	H	TB	2B	3B	HR	RBI	SH	SF	HP	BB	IBB	SO	SB	CS	GDP	Slg.	OBP
Hernandez, Ramon, Athletics	.364	48	194	143	37	52	85	9	6	4	37	0	4	8	39	1	16	6	2	3	.594	.510
Johnson, Duan, Mariners	.351	43	186	174	33	61	76	9	3	0	28	0	2	2	8	0	14	3	2	5	.437	.382
Rutherford, Daryl, Padres	.333	47	200	186	29	62	97	12	4	5	27	0	3	0	11	1	28	13	7	3	.522	.365
Arias, David, Mariners*	.332	48	211	184	30	61	99	18	4	4	37	0	3	1	23	1	52	2	0	2	.538	.403
Wilkerson, Adrian, Brewers	.331	54	184	160	22	53	56	1	1	0	28	3	3	2	16	0	28	18	7	82	.350	.392
Cesar, Dionys, Athletics†	.322	48	201	171	41	55	80	11	4	2	21	3	2	2	23	0	29	17	10	0	.468	.404
Rodriguez, Miguel, Brewers	.313	49	180	163	24	51	68	12	1	1	18	1	1	4	11	0	34	9	2	4	.417	.369
Barnes, Larry, Angels*	.310	56	232	197	42	61	84	8	3	3	37	1	2	5	27	0	40	12	5	1	.426	.403
Cruz, Cirilo, Mariners	.308	39	167	146	22	45	53	8	0	0	20	2	0	3	16	0	37	0	2	2	.363	.388
Stuart, Rich, Angels	.299	56	236	204	42	61	89	10	6	2	33	2	2	3	25	1	42	20	8	5	.436	.380
Rodriguez, Juan, Angels†	.298	54	228	215	27	64	91	8	8	1	31	1	2	3	7	0	49	4	7	1	.423	.326
Polanco, Juan, Athletics	.296	48	204	179	41	53	80	11	5	2	23	1	4	2	17	0	35	18	8	2	.447	.356
Harrison, Adonis, Mariners*	.290	45	199	155	31	45	65	7	5	1	14	0	4	3	37	0	37	7	9	0	.419	.427
Lara, Edward, Athletics†	.288	47	211	184	42	53	74	6	6	1	26	1	2	2	22	0	19	23	9	4	.402	.367
Vidal, Carlos, Rockies	.287	39	163	136	19	39	55	11	1	1	20	0	3	1	23	0	20	3	3	9	.404	.387
Duverge, Salvador, Rockies	.287	46	193	164	22	47	65	9	3	1	18	0	3	6	20	1	36	11	4	5	.396	.378

DEPARTMENTAL LEADERS: G—Barnes, Stuart, 56; AB—Ju. Rodriguez, 215; R—Barnes, Lara, Stuart, 42; H—Ju. Rodriguez, 64; TB—Arias, 99; 2B—Arias, 18; 3B—Ju. Rodriguez, 8; HR—Paciorek, Rutherford, 5; RBI—Arias, Barnes, R. Hernandez, 37; SH—Wardrop, 5; SF—Martinez, 7; HP—R. Hernandez, 8; BB—R. Hernandez, 39; IBB—Jacobo, 2; SO—Paciorek, 58; SB—R. Harris, 26; CS—Cesar, R. Harris, 10; GIDP—Vidal, 9; Slg.—R. Hernandez, .594; OBP—R. Hernandez, .510.

ALL PLAYERS

*Lefthanded batter. †Switch-hitter.

Player, Team	Avg.	G	TPA	AB	R	H	TB	2B	3B	HR	RBI	SH	SF	HP	BB	IBB	SO	SB	CS	GDP	Slg.	OBP
Acevedo, Juan, Rockies	.211	29	103	90	10	19	23	2	1	0	8	2	1	1	9	0	25	2	4	3	.256	.287
Alamo, Efrain, Rockies	.252	39	161	147	14	37	49	4	4	0	14	0	2	5	7	0	36	4	2	2	.333	.304
Allen, Tony, Brewers	.221	46	133	113	19	25	35	0	5	0	14	2	2	2	14	0	35	7	2	2	.310	.313
Arias, David, Mariners*	.332	48	211	184	30	61	99	18	4	4	37	0	3	1	23	1	52	2	0	2	.538	.403

Player, Team	Avg.	G	TPA	AB	R	H	TB	2B	3B	HR	RBI	SH	SF	HP	BB	IBB	SO	SB	CS	GDP	Slg.	OBP
Balcazar, Carlos, Angels*	.301	35	107	93	11	28	38	5	1	1	11	0	0	2	12	1	20	2	0	1	.409	.393
Barnes, Larry, Angels*	.310	56	232	197	42	61	84	8	3	3	37	1	2	5	27	0	40	12	5	1	.426	.403
Barrios, Esteban, Angels*	.211	28	90	71	11	15	18	1	1	0	2	1	1	0	17	0	9	3	1	4	.254	.360
Campusano, Carlos, Brewers	.249	54	194	173	25	43	52	4	1	1	15	1	1	5	14	1	27	7	3	6	.301	.321
Carmona, Cesarin, Padres†	.255	15	57	51	7	13	22	2	2	1	4	1	0	0	5	0	10	3	3	0	.431	.321
Castro, Nelson, Angels†	.195	55	226	190	34	37	42	1	2	0	22	4	1	4	27	0	50	15	7	2	.221	.306
Cesar, Dionys, Athletics†	.322	48	201	171	41	55	80	11	4	2	21	3	2	2	23	0	29	17	10	0	.468	.404
Cespedes, Angel, Rockies†	.211	19	68	57	11	12	15	1	1	0	11	0	1	3	7	0	12	1	4	4	.263	.324
Chambers, Victor, Athletics*	.309	34	126	110	11	34	42	2	3	0	16	0	1	1	14	1	17	12	4	3	.382	.389
Chavez, Steven, Padres*	.259	55	228	197	30	51	68	7	5	0	24	1	1	5	24	0	48	5	6	4	.345	.352
Clark, John, Rockies	.203	52	214	192	22	39	46	5	1	0	12	1	3	4	14	0	52	6	1	4	.240	.268
Cowsill, Brendon, Angels	.257	34	135	113	18	29	40	5	3	0	13	2	2	0	18	0	28	7	0	1	.354	.353
Cruz, Cirilo, Mariners	.308	39	167	146	22	45	53	8	0	0	20	2	0	3	16	0	37	0	2	2	.363	.388
Cruz, Francisco, Padres	.000	1	3	2	0	0	0	0	0	0	0	0	0	1	0	0	1	1	0	0	.000	.333
Darrell, Thomas, Angels	.000	18	1	1	0	0	0	0	0	0	0	0	0	0	0	0	1	0	0	0	.000	.000
Davis, Josh, Padres	.203	37	147	128	20	26	32	4	1	0	7	2	0	3	14	0	35	3	3	1	.250	.297
Delacruz, Jesus, Angels	.241	31	87	79	6	19	25	4	1	0	10	2	0	3	3	1	17	1	2	2	.316	.294
Delgado, Ariel, Angels*	.206	53	211	189	26	39	50	5	3	0	19	1	1	5	15	0	36	5	3	7	.265	.281
Ducasse, Luis, Athletics	.063	6	22	16	1	1	1	0	0	0	1	0	1	0	5	0	8	0	0	2	.063	.273
Duverge, Salvador, Rockies	.287	46	193	164	22	47	65	9	3	1	18	0	3	6	20	1	36	11	4	5	.396	.378
Ebbert, Chad, Padres	.315	35	138	127	18	40	57	5	3	2	21	0	1	1	9	0	29	2	2	4	.449	.362
Erstad, Darin, Angels*	.556	4	19	18	2	10	11	1	0	0	1	0	0	0	1	0	1	1	0	0	.611	.579
Figueroa, Luis, Mariners	.292	32	135	120	14	35	37	2	0	0	11	0	1	2	12	0	9	1	2	4	.308	.363
Fowler, Marvin, Mariners*	.258	26	108	97	13	25	35	4	3	0	8	0	0	4	7	0	29	4	4	0	.361	.333
Freeman, Terrance, Athletics†	.242	34	109	95	14	23	25	0	1	0	5	1	0	3	10	0	25	3	3	3	.263	.333
Gordon, Garfield, Rockies	.252	36	160	135	20	34	38	2	1	0	8	0	0	3	22	0	37	20	7	1	.281	.369
Groseclose, Harold, Rockies	.252	31	136	119	19	30	36	4	1	0	8	0	0	0	15	0	26	4	0	3	.303	.336
Guerrero, Diogene, Athletics	.228	41	168	136	27	31	48	4	5	1	13	0	1	2	29	1	48	11	7	0	.353	.369
Harris, Mike, Brewers*	.304	6	25	23	5	7	11	2	1	0	4	0	0	0	2	0	7	0	1	0	.478	.360
Harris, Rico, Brewers†	.279	48	214	172	40	48	60	6	3	0	22	0	1	4	37	1	22	26	10	2	.349	.416
Harrison, Adonis, Mariners*	.290	45	199	155	31	45	65	7	5	1	14	0	4	3	37	0	37	7	9	0	.419	.427
Hernandez, Ramon, Athletics	.364	48	194	143	37	52	85	9	6	4	37	0	4	8	39	1	16	6	2	3	.594	.510
Hernandez, Victor, Athletics	.152	21	52	46	5	7	7	0	0	0	3	0	0	1	5	0	21	0	2	1	.152	.250
Hunter, Andy, Padres	.208	35	124	106	14	22	28	2	2	0	11	0	0	1	17	0	39	2	1	2	.264	.323
Hutchins, Norm, Angels†	.271	14	67	59	9	16	19	1	1	0	7	2	1	1	4	0	10	8	4	1	.322	.323
Iapoce, Anthony, Brewers	.333	3	4	3	2	1	1	0	0	0	0	0	0	0	1	0	1	1	0	0	.333	.500
Isom, Daleon, Mariners	.258	28	111	89	17	23	32	4	1	1	8	1	1	2	18	0	19	11	8	2	.360	.391
Jackson, Rod, Padres	.253	45	162	150	16	38	44	6	0	0	6	1	0	2	9	0	39	11	3	3	.293	.304
Jacobo, Roberto, Padres†	.241	46	179	166	18	40	48	2	3	0	15	0	0	1	12	2	49	10	7	3	.289	.296
Jacobus, Brian, Padres*	.194	44	155	144	12	28	35	7	0	0	11	0	1	2	8	0	32	0	1	7	.243	.245
Johnson, Duan, Mariners	.351	43	186	174	33	61	76	9	3	0	28	0	2	2	8	0	14	3	2	5	.437	.382
Johnson, Jace, Athletics	.132	17	43	38	4	5	9	1	0	1	4	0	0	1	4	0	16	1	1	0	.237	.233
Jones, Ken, Padres	.500	1	4	4	0	2	3	1	0	0	1	0	0	0	0	0	1	0	0	1	.750	.500
Jones, Timothy, Athletics*	.198	32	103	96	7	19	25	2	2	0	10	1	0	0	6	0	36	5	3	1	.260	.245
Judge, Mike, Brewers	.293	16	52	41	8	12	16	2	1	0	6	0	0	3	8	0	9	2	1	2	.390	.442
Kirkpatrick, Brian, Rockies	.139	38	136	122	11	17	21	1	0	1	7	2	1	0	11	0	54	4	1	4	.172	.209
Lara, Edward, Athletics†	.288	47	211	184	42	53	74	6	6	1	26	1	2	2	22	0	19	23	9	4	.402	.367
Law, Khris, Athletics	.165	36	120	103	17	17	24	1	0	2	11	0	0	2	15	1	37	5	3	2	.233	.283
Lawrence, Mike, Angels†	.162	18	46	37	5	6	7	1	0	0	5	0	1	1	7	0	11	1	0	1	.189	.304
Lindsey, John, Rockies	.235	48	198	179	23	42	58	10	0	2	22	0	1	7	11	0	48	0	2	4	.324	.303
Llanos, Alexis, Angels†	.283	26	57	53	6	15	20	1	2	0	3	1	0	0	3	0	11	0	0	1	.377	.321
Marnell, Anthony, Padres	.400	1	5	5	1	2	3	1	0	0	3	0	0	0	0	0	2	0	0	1	.600	.400
Martinez, Hipolito, Athletics	.221	46	173	149	23	33	51	4	4	2	27	0	7	1	16	1	47	8	4	1	.342	.289
Maynard, Scott, Mariners	.236	21	84	72	6	17	22	2	0	1	12	1	2	0	9	0	21	0	0	0	.306	.313
McDavid, Ray, Padres*	.464	9	36	28	13	13	20	2	1	1	6	0	0	0	8	0	7	3	1	0	.714	.583
McDougall, Matt, Mariners	.238	27	114	101	17	24	27	3	0	0	9	0	0	1	12	0	21	9	4	0	.267	.325
McGuire, Brandon, Angels†	.250	4	5	4	0	1	1	0	0	0	1	0	0	0	1	0	1	0	0	0	.250	.400
McNally, Jason, Rockies	.213	41	165	141	18	30	38	2	0	2	18	1	1	4	18	0	39	2	1	3	.270	.317
Medrano, Teodoro, Mariners	.000	1	3	3	0	0	0	0	0	0	0	0	0	0	0	0	0	0	0	0	.000	.000
Moore, Donald, Brewers	.239	38	82	71	10	17	20	0	0	1	6	0	0	2	8	0	27	3	1	0	.282	.333
Moore, James, Padres	.320	15	57	50	7	16	25	4	1	1	9	1	1	1	4	0	17	1	2	2	.500	.375
Needham, Scott, Mariners	.177	21	79	62	12	11	18	5	1	0	10	0	1	2	14	0	22	0	1	0	.290	.342
Niles, David, Rockies*	.198	40	140	116	21	23	26	3	0	0	9	1	0	1	22	0	50	3	0	2	.224	.331
Paciorek, Peter, Padres†	.257	54	218	183	32	47	79	11	3	5	24	1	0	1	33	1	58	6	4	1	.432	.373
Paulino, Arturo, Athletics	.256	31	133	117	18	30	40	2	4	0	13	0	0	2	14	0	36	14	2	2	.342	.346
Pernell, Brandon, Padres	.247	48	196	174	22	43	62	11	1	2	29	2	3	1	16	0	54	8	2	2	.356	.309
Peters, Tony, Brewers	.244	51	204	172	25	42	60	8	2	2	24	1	0	2	29	0	55	9	3	2	.349	.360
Polanco, Juan, Athletics	.296	48	204	179	41	53	80	11	5	2	23	1	4	2	17	0	35	18	8	2	.447	.356
Randolph, Edward, Mariners†	.281	41	153	135	22	38	66	11	4	3	25	1	2	3	12	0	30	5	5	3	.489	.349
Rauer, Troy, Athletics	.160	30	115	100	13	16	25	2	2	1	12	0	2	1	12	0	43	3	3	1	.250	.252
Rendon, Miguel, Brewers	.259	48	181	162	23	42	51	5	2	0	25	0	5	5	9	0	18	4	2	5	.315	.309
Ritter, Ryan, Brewers	.200	4	15	15	1	3	6	3	0	0	2	0	0	0	0	0	0	0	0	1	.400	.200
Roche, Michael, Brewers	.255	47	191	161	33	41	56	11	2	0	31	2	3	7	18	0	42	9	3	3	.348	.349
Rodriguez, Franklin, Mariners	.298	16	66	57	14	17	19	0	1	0	1	1	0	0	8	0	18	3	0	1	.333	.385
Rodriguez, John, Padres	.202	31	99	94	12	19	25	1	1	1	11	0	2	1	2	0	27	0	3	2	.266	.222
Rodriguez, Juan, Angels†	.298	54	228	215	27	64	91	8	8	1	31	1	2	3	7	0	49	4	7	1	.423	.326
Rodriguez, Miguel, Brewers	.313	49	180	163	24	51	68	12	1	1	18	1	1	4	11	0	34	9	2	4	.417	.369
Rogue, Francisco, Brewers	.226	19	63	62	10	14	19	3	1	0	10	0	0	0	1	0	9	0	0	2	.306	.238
Rosario, Eliezer, Padres	.259	7	33	27	3	7	7	0	0	0	3	0	0	1	5	0	6	1	0	0	.259	.394
Rose, Carlos, Mariners	.152	27	97	92	10	14	18	1	0	1	6	0	0	2	3	0	33	4	1	5	.196	.196
Rowson, James, Mariners	.189	30	117	106	9	20	28	6	1	0	9	1	1	3	6	0	38	9	2	1	.264	.250
Rushdan, Rasheed, Rockies	.000	6	20	18	1	0	0	0	0	0	3	0	0	0	2	0	5	0	0	2	.000	.100
Rutherford, Daryl, Padres	.333	47	200	186	29	62	97	12	4	5	27	0	3	0	11	1	28	13	7	3	.522	.365

Player, Team	Avg.	G	TPA	AB	R	H	TB	2B	3B	HR	RBI	SH	SF	HP	BB	IBB	SO	SB	CS	GDP	Slg.	OBP
Saucedo, Robert, Angels	.280	30	90	75	13	21	27	1	1	1	9	0	2	1	12	0	11	3	1	1	.360	.378
Schaub, Greg, Brewers	.274	33	102	95	12	26	36	4	3	0	11	1	1	0	5	0	20	5	4	1	.379	.307
Scheker, Luis, Athletics	.250	16	74	60	9	15	23	3	1	1	11	0	3	0	11	0	16	1	1	2	.383	.351
Selga, Andres, Rockies	.179	21	75	67	7	12	14	2	0	0	5	1	1	1	5	0	29	1	1	0	.209	.243
Silverio, Richard, Rockies*	.272	35	151	136	19	37	52	4	4	1	19	0	1	6	8	0	34	2	3	0	.382	.338
Singleton, Samuel, Brewers*	.245	47	163	139	28	34	44	4	3	0	19	1	2	1	20	0	33	2	3	3	.317	.340
Soriano, Jacobo, Angels	1.000	12	1	1	0	1	1	0	0	0	0	0	0	0	0	0	0	0	0	0	1.000	1.000
Stewart, Keith, Mariners*	.196	15	58	46	12	9	14	0	1	1	6	1	0	0	11	0	23	3	0	0	.304	.351
Stuart, Rich, Angels	.299	56	236	204	42	61	89	10	6	2	33	2	2	3	25	1	42	20	8	5	.436	.380
Tolbert, Ernest, Mariners	.176	26	102	91	16	16	26	3	2	1	7	0	0	2	9	0	24	2	2	1	.286	.265
Vazquez, Ramon, Mariners*	.206	39	162	141	20	29	34	3	1	0	11	0	0	2	19	0	27	4	3	2	.241	.309
Ventura, Wilfredo, Athletics	.279	34	129	104	19	29	43	3	1	3	20	1	1	3	20	0	32	7	3	0	.413	.406
Veras, Illuminado, Angels	.253	32	95	87	9	22	31	4	1	1	9	1	2	0	5	0	13	2	2	2	.356	.287
Vidal, Carlos, Rockies	.287	39	163	136	19	39	55	11	1	1	20	0	3	1	23	0	20	3	3	9	.404	.387
Walther, Christopher, Brewers	.259	50	186	174	28	45	52	3	2	0	19	1	0	1	10	0	9	4	3	5	.299	.303
Wardrop, Adam, Angels†	.253	49	188	146	26	37	45	4	2	0	10	5	1	6	30	0	36	8	7	2	.308	.399
Wilkerson, Adrian, Brewers	.331	54	184	160	22	53	56	1	1	0	28	3	3	2	16	0	28	18	7	82	.350	.392
Williams, Marcus, Mariners	.227	22	89	88	6	20	29	7	1	0	6	0	1	0	0	0	23	4	2	4	.330	.225

GRAND SLAMS: Balcarzar, Paciorek, 1 each.
AWARDED FIRST BASE ON CATCHER'S INTERFERENCE: Groseclose 2 (Saucedo, Veras); D. Moore (Randolph); Polanco (Randolph).

1995 PITCHING

TEAM

Team	W	L	Pct.	ERA	G	CG	ShO	Sv.	IP	H	TBF	R	ER	HR	SH	SF	HB	BB	IBB	SO	WP	Bk.
Angels	35	21	.625	2.94	56	5	6	17	489.0	422	2073	222	160	5	10	14	47	193	7	429	57	21
Brewers	34	22	.607	3.28	56	5	2	16	493.2	444	2122	238	180	11	16	21	26	199	5	536	60	20
Athletics	37	19	.661	3.37	56	1	3	15	491.1	436	2073	238	184	17	7	10	26	190	2	496	42	25
Padres	24	31	.436	3.76	55	3	2	12	469.1	457	2083	292	196	14	11	18	43	205	0	406	49	20
Mariners	24	32	.429	4.30	56	1	1	10	493.2	528	2228	326	236	13	9	27	25	244	1	448	62	18
Rockies	13	42	.236	5.82	55	0	0	5	473.1	569	2257	410	306	13	16	23	31	243	1	390	72	28

INDIVIDUAL

TOP QUALIFIERS FOR EARNED-RUN AVERAGE TITLE

Minimum 45 innings. *Lefthanded pitcher.

Pitcher, Team	W	L	Pct.	ERA	G	GS	CG	ShO	GF	Sv.	IP	H	TBF	R	ER	HR	SH	SF	HB	BB	IBB	SO	WP	Bk.
Darrell, Thomas, Angels	4	3	.571	1.71	18	5	0	0	7	2	63.0	51	254	18	12	1	1	3	4	14	0	49	3	1
Plant, David, Athletics	4	2	.667	1.76	14	6	0	0	4	2	51.0	34	198	11	10	1	0	0	2	12	0	51	2	1
Clark, Chris, Padres	5	5	.500	2.10	13	12	1	0	0	0	73.0	52	313	30	17	1	1	1	7	38	0	82	5	0
Bishop, Joshua, Brewers	8	2	.800	2.16	14	13	3	1	0	0	96.0	64	382	34	23	4	3	1	1	29	0	134	9	3
DeLosSantos, Valerio, Brewers*	4	6	.400	2.20	14	12	0	0	1	0	82.0	81	341	34	20	3	5	4	6	12	2	57	6	2
Romero, John, Angels	7	3	.700	2.41	18	6	2	1	4	1	71.0	57	291	29	19	0	0	2	5	18	1	64	8	4
Blevins, Jeremy, Angels	5	1	.833	2.45	11	9	0	0	0	0	51.1	39	224	20	14	0	2	0	4	32	0	48	4	1
Volkman, Keith, Angels*	5	2	.714	2.53	13	10	0	0	0	0	67.2	61	279	30	19	0	1	0	4	25	0	49	5	1
Jacob, Russell, Mariners	6	2	.750	2.88	12	11	0	0	1	0	56.1	47	248	29	18	0	0	1	3	31	0	54	6	2
Walker, Kevin, Padres*	5	5	.500	3.01	13	12	0	0	0	0	71.2	74	295	34	24	1	1	3	2	12	0	69	1	3
Desabrias, Mark, Padres	2	1	.667	3.11	19	2	0	0	13	0	55.0	52	234	28	19	2	1	1	7	20	0	28	3	0
Duncan, Devohn, Padres	4	5	.444	3.12	11	10	0	0	0	0	52.0	47	231	39	18	2	1	3	4	22	0	40	12	5
Paulino, Jose, Athletics	9	2	.818	3.19	15	13	0	0	2	0	87.1	74	343	35	31	5	2	2	2	17	0	72	2	3
Baez, Benito, Athletics*	5	1	.833	3.34	14	11	1	0	0	0	70.0	64	303	35	26	2	2	2	4	28	0	83	2	0
Stahl, Anders, Rockies	3	5	.375	3.46	12	12	0	0	0	0	52.0	42	223	31	20	1	3	1	3	19	0	44	9	2

DEPARTMENTAL LEADERS: W—Ishee, Paulino, 9; L—Rosa, 9; Pct.—Ishee, Paulino, .818; G—Kazmirski, 28; GS—Bishop, Druckrey, Paulino, 13; CG—Bishop, 3; ShO—Bishop, Kolb, Romero, Stockstill, 1; GF—Kazmirski, 25; Sv.—Kazmirski, Pavlovich, 10; IP—Bishop, 96.0; H—DeLosSantos, 81; TBF—Bishop, 382; R—Podjan, 58; ER—Podjan, 45; HR—Paulino, 5; SH—DeLosSantos, 5; SF—Blanco, Ishee, 6; HB—Druckrey, 8; BB—Ishee, 41; IBB—DeLosSantos, Kazmirski, Soriano, 2; SO—Bishop 134; WP—Podjan, 14; Bk.—Douglas, 11.

ALL PITCHERS

*Lefthanded pitcher.

Pitcher, Team	W	L	Pct.	ERA	G	GS	CG	ShO	GF	Sv.	IP	H	TBF	R	ER	HR	SH	SF	HB	BB	IBB	SO	WP	Bk.
Abreu, Oscar, Athletics	1	2	.333	7.96	20	1	0	0	7	0	26.0	33	146	30	23	0	0	1	2	35	0	29	11	2
Agosto, Stevenson, Angels*	0	1	.000	5.40	1	1	0	0	0	0	5.0	3	22	5	3	0	2	1	1	2	0	2	3	0
Ashley, Antonio, Angels	0	0	.000	2.25	5	0	0	0	2	0	8.0	6	31	3	2	0	0	0	0	1	0	4	0	1
Baez, Benito, Athletics*	5	1	.833	3.34	14	11	1	0	0	0	70.0	64	303	35	26	2	2	2	4	28	0	83	2	0
Barnes, Larry, Brewers	0	1	.000	1.77	6	5	0	0	0	0	20.1	16	84	4	4	0	0	0	0	14	0	31	1	1
Bennett, Tom, Athletics	1	1	.500	2.72	11	6	0	0	0	0	36.1	20	150	16	11	1	1	1	2	16	0	46	4	0
Bishop, Joshua, Brewers	8	2	.800	2.16	14	13	3	1	0	0	96.0	64	382	34	23	4	3	1	1	29	0	134	9	3
Blanco, Roger, Mariners	1	6	.143	5.50	12	12	0	0	0	0	54.0	60	247	43	33	2	1	6	7	24	0	27	5	2
Blevins, Jeremy, Angels	5	1	.833	2.45	11	9	0	0	0	0	51.1	39	224	20	14	0	2	0	4	32	0	48	4	1
Bonilla, Denis, Mariners*	1	1	.500	3.06	21	0	0	0	10	2	35.1	39	155	21	12	0	0	3	1	9	0	39	2	0
Bowles, Matt, Brewers	0	1	.000	6.60	7	0	0	0	1	0	15.0	20	69	12	11	0	0	2	1	3	0	4	3	1
Burton, Isaac, Mariners	0	0	.000	3.00	2	0	0	0	0	0	3.0	1	15	2	1	0	1	0	1	4	0	2	0	1
Cesar, Dionys, Athletics	0	0	.000	0.00	2	0	0	0	2	0	2.0	0	6	0	0	0	0	0	0	1	0	2	0	0
Clark, Chris, Padres	5	5	.500	2.10	13	12	1	0	0	0	73.0	52	313	30	17	1	1	1	7	38	0	82	5	0
Contreras, Orlando, Rockies	2	2	.500	6.04	16	0	0	0	5	1	28.1	40	144	27	19	0	1	2	0	17	0	18	0	0
Costello, Terrance, Athletics*	2	3	.400	3.74	12	6	0	0	2	1	43.1	46	180	22	18	2	0	0	2	9	0	41	5	1
Craig, Casey, Mariners	1	0	1.000	6.00	2	0	0	0	0	0	3.0	5	14	2	2	0	0	0	0	2	0	0	1	0
Darrell, Thomas, Angels	4	3	.571	1.71	18	5	0	0	7	2	63.0	51	254	18	12	1	1	3	4	14	0	49	3	1
DeLosSantos, Valerio, Brewers*	4	6	.400	2.20	14	12	0	0	1	0	82.0	81	341	34	20	3	5	4	6	12	2	57	6	2

Pitcher, Team	W	L	Pct.	ERA	G	GS	CG	ShO	GF	Sv.	IP	H	TBF	R	ER	HR	SH	SF	HB	BB	IBB	SO	WP	Bk.
Derenches, Albert, Mariners*	1	2	.333	3.31	19	0	0	0	3	0	35.1	36	155	15	13	1	0	1	1	21	0	40	5	0
Desabrias, Mark, Padres	2	1	.667	3.11	19	2	0	0	13	0	55.0	52	234	28	19	2	1	1	7	20	0	28	3	0
Douglas, Reggie, Rockies	0	1	.000	9.33	15	0	0	0	9	1	27.0	37	135	29	28	1	2	0	2	19	0	17	11	11
Drewien, Dan, Padres	0	0	.000	0.00	1	0	0	0	0	0	2.2	2	11	1	0	0	0	0	1	0	0	2	0	0
Druckrey, Chris, Rockies	0	8	.000	5.04	14	13	0	0	1	0	69.2	75	330	54	39	1	0	1	8	38	0	65	13	3
Drysdale, Brooks, Angels	0	0	.000	8.10	4	0	0	0	3	1	3.1	4	16	4	3	0	0	0	0	1	1	7	0	0
Duncan, Devohn, Padres	4	5	.444	3.12	11	10	0	0	0	0	52.0	47	231	39	18	2	1	3	4	22	0	40	12	5
Estrada, Horacio, Brewers*	0	1	.000	3.71	8	1	0	0	3	2	17.0	13	73	9	7	1	1	1	0	8	0	21	4	2
Ettles, Mark, Padres	0	0	.000	5.79	3	0	0	0	0	0	4.2	6	24	6	3	1	0	0	1	4	0	2	2	1
Florentino, Osmil, Rockies	0	2	.000	6.85	19	0	0	0	11	2	43.1	55	208	42	33	2	3	3	2	17	0	27	1	5
Foster, Cliff, Athletics	0	0	.000	27.00	1	1	0	0	0	0	1.0	4	8	4	3	0	0	0	0	0	0	0	0	0
Glick, Dave, Brewers*	2	0	1.000	4.26	18	0	0	0	4	0	25.1	24	115	13	12	0	1	0	1	14	0	29	4	4
Gomez, Alex, Angels	4	3	.571	5.58	13	3	0	0	2	0	30.2	30	143	21	19	0	1	1	4	23	1	31	8	0
Gonzalez, Jose, Mariners	4	4	.500	5.30	12	10	0	0	0	0	56.0	56	250	40	33	1	1	2	2	31	0	66	8	5
Guerrero, Diogene, Athletics	0	0	.000	0.00	1	0	0	0	0	0	1.0	0	4	0	0	0	0	0	1	0	0	0	0	1
Gutierrez, Alfredo, Brewers	0	0	.000	6.48	7	0	0	0	4	0	8.1	10	44	9	6	0	0	1	2	8	0	7	1	0
Gutierrez, Javier, Mariners	1	4	.200	5.88	14	4	1	0	4	0	33.2	43	159	31	22	4	1	2	1	19	0	38	8	1
Guzman, Jonathan, Brewers*	0	0	.000	10.38	11	0	0	0	4	0	13.0	18	71	16	15	1	0	2	3	8	0	4	2	3
Hamada, Nori, Angels	0	0	.000	13.50	1	0	0	0	0	0	0.2	1	4	1	1	0	0	0	0	1	0	0	2	0
Henderson, James, Padres	0	1	.000	8.22	3	1	0	0	0	0	7.2	12	40	8	7	0	0	0	1	6	0	12	1	3
Hernandez, Victor, Athletics	0	0	.000	18.00	1	0	0	0	0	0	1.0	2	6	2	2	0	0	0	0	1	0	0	0	0
Hill, Tyrone, Brewers*	0	0	.000	3.18	4	4	0	0	0	0	11.1	8	48	4	4	0	0	0	0	5	0	9	1	0
Ishee, Gabe, Brewers	9	2	.818	3.63	15	12	2	0	1	0	79.1	78	344	41	32	0	1	6	5	41	1	90	12	2
Jacob, Russell, Mariners	6	2	.750	2.88	12	11	0	0	1	0	56.1	47	248	29	18	0	0	1	3	31	0	54	6	2
Jimenez, Jhonny, Mariners	1	2	.333	4.45	19	0	0	0	6	0	32.1	39	147	23	16	1	0	3	2	14	0	28	2	4
Johnson, Shelby, Mariners	1	1	.500	5.29	9	0	0	0	3	0	17.0	24	82	16	10	0	1	1	2	9	0	14	2	0
Kammerer, James, Rockies*	1	0	1.000	0.96	6	0	0	0	5	0	9.1	11	43	5	1	0	0	0	0	3	0	14	1	0
Kaye, Justin, Mariners	0	1	.000	10.71	12	0	0	0	4	0	19.1	33	111	28	23	1	0	2	1	19	0	13	4	0
Kazmirski, Robert, Athletics	4	0	1.000	2.13	28	0	0	0	25	10	38.0	36	155	13	9	0	0	1	1	6	2	32	2	7
Kjos, Ryan, Athletics	0	0	.000	19.64	3	0	0	0	0	0	3.2	9	23	10	8	1	0	0	1	1	0	5	2	0
Knickerbocker, Thomas, A's*	4	3	.571	3.92	17	7	0	0	1	1	43.2	39	193	27	19	0	0	0	5	25	0	40	7	0
Kolb, Brandon, Padres	1	1	.500	1.17	4	4	1	1	0	0	23.0	13	100	10	3	0	0	0	3	13	0	21	4	0
Law, Khris, Athletics	0	1	.000	6.00	2	0	0	0	0	0	3.0	2	15	3	2	0	0	0	0	3	0	3	0	0
Leftwich, Phil, Angels	1	1	.500	0.45	4	4	0	0	0	0	20.0	13	76	4	1	0	0	2	0	2	0	32	0	0
Lenhardt, Bruce, Brewers	1	0	1.000	3.86	2	0	0	0	0	0	4.2	8	23	2	2	0	1	0	2	1	0	3	1	0
Lopez, Jose, Angels	2	2	.500	2.40	11	7	0	0	0	0	41.1	45	178	18	11	0	0	0	6	13	0	36	5	2
Lopez, Rodrigo, Padres	1	1	.500	5.45	11	7	0	0	3	1	34.2	41	162	29	21	0	1	2	2	14	0	33	3	1
Lowe, Derek, Mariners	1	0	1.000	0.93	2	2	0	0	0	0	9.2	5	35	1	1	0	0	0	0	2	0	11	0	0
Mahlberg, John, Rockies	2	3	.400	4.38	10	7	0	0	0	0	39.0	44	178	27	19	3	2	2	1	21	0	52	3	1
Martinez, Hipolito, Athletics	0	0	.000	0.00	1	0	0	0	1	0	0.2	1	2	0	0	0	0	0	0	0	0	0	0	0
Martino, Wil, Rockies*	3	1	.750	5.32	16	3	0	0	6	0	44.0	48	203	27	26	2	0	2	4	23	0	44	7	2
Matlack, Dan, Padres	0	2	.000	3.58	16	0	0	0	5	0	27.2	20	122	15	11	1	1	2	3	14	0	16	0	1
Mays, Joseph, Mariners	2	3	.400	3.25	10	10	0	0	0	0	44.1	41	189	24	16	0	2	2	1	18	0	44	7	1
McDonald, Matt, Athletics*	0	0	.000	2.20	5	1	0	0	2	0	16.1	16	71	7	4	1	0	2	1	9	0	23	1	1
McGuire, Brandon, Angels	1	0	1.000	3.38	2	0	0	0	0	0	5.1	3	20	3	2	0	0	0	0	3	0	6	1	0
Moreno, Juan, Athletics*	6	2	.750	1.21	20	0	0	0	8	0	44.2	36	181	10	6	1	1	1	0	20	0	49	2	5
Nash, Damond, Padres	1	3	.250	7.31	15	3	1	0	2	0	44.1	55	212	42	36	2	2	2	3	27	0	32	4	0
Neiman, Joshua, Padres	0	1	.000	4.24	10	0	0	0	4	1	17.0	20	74	9	8	2	0	1	1	3	0	18	2	1
Niles, David, Rockies*	0	1	.000	4.50	2	0	0	0	2	0	2.0	2	8	1	1	0	0	0	0	0	0	1	0	0
Nivar, Amaury, Rockies	0	0	.000	11.12	6	0	0	0	1	0	11.1	14	63	18	14	0	0	1	2	14	0	10	4	1
Nix, Wayne, Athletics	0	2	.000	5.79	6	3	0	0	0	0	14.0	15	57	10	9	3	1	0	1	4	0	14	1	0
Nogowski, Brandon, Mariners*	0	2	.000	2.70	20	0	0	0	17	7	26.2	30	123	10	8	0	0	1	0	13	1	27	4	0
Norris, McKenzie, Brewers	1	0	1.000	0.61	2	2	0	0	0	0	14.2	7	60	4	1	0	0	0	0	6	1	14	3	0
Osteen, Gavin, Athletics*	0	0	.000	0.00	1	1	0	0	0	0	2.0	1	7	0	0	0	0	0	1	0	0	1	0	0
Palki, Jeromy, Mariners	0	0	.000	7.94	4	0	0	0	1	0	5.2	7	29	7	5	0	1	1	0	5	0	2	1	0
Patterson, Ken, Angels*	0	0	.000	0.00	1	1	0	0	0	0	3.0	0	10	0	0	0	0	0	0	1	0	3	0	0
Paulino, Jose, Athletics	9	2	.818	3.19	15	13	0	0	2	0	87.1	74	343	35	31	5	2	2	2	17	0	72	2	3
Pavlovich, Tony, Brewers	0	2	.000	4.00	19	0	0	0	18	10	18.0	20	78	10	8	0	2	1	0	3	0	20	1	0
Perez, Jayson, Padres	0	0	.000	9.00	2	0	0	0	1	1	2.0	3	11	2	2	0	0	0	0	2	0	1	1	0
Perez, Jesse, Brewers	2	2	.500	2.70	16	0	0	0	9	4	20.0	16	84	6	6	1	0	1	2	4	1	20	3	1
Plant, David, Athletics	4	2	.667	1.76	14	6	0	0	4	2	51.0	34	198	11	10	1	0	0	2	12	0	51	2	1
Podjan, James, Rockies	2	7	.222	9.00	17	5	0	0	3	0	45.0	71	231	58	45	3	2	3	3	27	0	30	14	1
Polanco, Juan, Athletics	0	0	.000	18.00	1	0	0	0	0	0	1.0	1	5	2	2	0	0	0	0	1	0	0	1	3
Prempas, Lyle, Brewers*	6	5	.545	4.09	13	6	0	0	2	0	50.2	49	226	33	23	1	2	2	1	28	0	67	4	0
Preston, George, Brewers	1	0	1.000	0.00	2	0	0	0	0	0	7.2	5	30	1	0	0	0	0	0	3	0	15	1	1
Quinteros, Steve, Angels	0	0	.000	4.38	7	1	0	0	1	0	12.1	19	63	10	6	1	0	0	4	3	1	13	2	2
Richmond, Terrance, Angels	0	0	.000	9.00	1	0	0	0	0	0	1.0	1	5	1	1	1	0	0	0	1	0	0	0	0
Riley, Brian, Angels	0	1	.000	3.00	17	0	0	0	17	9	15.0	11	63	5	5	0	1	0	1	10	0	16	2	1
Rodriguez, Hector, Angels	2	2	.500	2.92	9	2	1	0	2	0	24.2	21	99	9	8	1	1	1	2	9	0	21	8	0
Rojas, Miguel, Angels	1	0	1.000	4.66	9	0	0	0	4	0	9.2	10	47	6	5	0	0	2	6	5	0	7	3	4
Romero, John, Angels	7	3	.700	2.41	18	6	2	1	4	1	71.0	57	291	29	19	0	0	2	5	18	1	64	8	4
Rosa, Cristy, Rockies	0	9	.000	5.37	12	12	0	0	0	0	58.2	77	273	56	35	0	2	4	2	16	0	42	8	2
Schroeder, Scott, Padres	0	1	.000	7.36	2	2	0	0	0	0	7.1	12	38	7	6	0	0	0	2	2	0	8	1	0
Segura, Juan, Rockies*	0	1	.000	5.22	20	0	0	0	12	1	29.1	32	140	19	17	0	1	4	3	19	1	20	1	0
Smith, Josh, Padres*	1	2	.333	1.69	8	0	0	0	4	1	10.2	12	53	8	2	0	1	0	1	8	0	8	6	1
Soriano, Jacobo, Angels	0	1	.000	3.09	11	0	0	0	9	4	11.2	9	53	6	4	0	0	0	3	7	2	10	0	2
Stahl, Anders, Rockies	3	5	.375	3.46	12	12	0	0	0	0	52.0	42	223	31	20	1	3	1	3	19	0	44	9	2
Stockstill, Jason, Angels*	3	1	.750	5.08	12	7	2	1	0	0	44.1	38	195	29	25	1	1	2	3	22	1	31	3	2
Suazo, Rigoberto, Athletics	1	0	1.000	1.69	2	0	0	0	1	1	5.1	3	20	1	1	0	0	0	1	2	0	5	0	1
Suzuki, Mac, Mariners	1	0	1.000	6.75	4	3	0	0	0	0	4.0	5	19	4	3	1	0	0	1	0	0	3	0	0
Szimanski, Tom, Mariners	0	0	.000	4.15	4	0	0	0	2	0	4.1	2	18	2	2	0	0	0	0	3	0	5	1	1
Tijerina, Tano, Brewers	0	0	.000	4.50	1	1	0	0	0	0	2.0	3	10	1	1	0	0	0	0	2	0	1	1	0
Tisdale, Warren, Mariners	1	1	.500	1.64	13	0	0	0	3	1	22.0	17	88	5	4	0	0	1	0	10	0	9	3	0

Pitcher, Team	W	L	Pct.	ERA	G	GS	CG	ShO	GF	Sv.	IP	H	TBF	R	ER	HR	SH	SF	HB	BB	IBB	SO	WP	Bk.
Torres, Derek, Brewers	0	0	.000	1.69	6	0	0	0	3	0	5.1	2	21	1	1	0	0	0	2	2	0	7	1	0
Torres, Luis, Padres	4	3	.571	4.75	22	2	0	0	20	8	36.0	36	163	24	19	2	2	3	5	20	0	34	4	4
Updike, Jon, Brewers	0	0	.000	12.00	4	0	0	0	1	0	3.0	2	19	4	4	0	0	0	0	8	0	3	2	0
Volkman, Keith, Angels*	5	2	.714	2.53	13	10	0	0	0	0	67.2	61	279	30	19	0	1	0	4	25	0	49	5	1
Walker, Kevin, Padres*	5	5	.500	3.01	13	12	0	0	0	0	71.2	74	295	34	24	1	1	3	2	12	0	69	1	3
Weymouth, Martin, Mariners	2	3	.400	3.98	9	4	0	0	1	0	31.2	37	144	23	14	2	1	1	2	10	0	26	3	1
Williams, Patrick, Rockies	0	2	.000	5.65	5	3	0	0	0	0	14.1	21	78	16	9	0	0	0	1	10	0	6	0	0

COMBINATION SHUTOUTS: **Angels (4)**—Darrell-Rodriguez-Riley, Lopez-Romero-Riley, Volkman-Gomez-Soriano, Volkman-Romero. **Athletics (3)**—Baez-Costello, Osteen-Plant-Costello-Kazmirski, Paulino-Kazmirski. **Brewers (1)**—Ishee-DeLosSantos. **Mariners (1)**—Jacob-Johnson-Derenches-Kaye. **Padres (1)**—Clark-Smith-Torres. **Rockies (0)**—None.

NO-HIT GAMES: Stockstill, Angels, defeated Brewers, 3-0, July 11.

1995 FIELDING

TEAM

Team	Pct.	G	PO	A	E	TC	DP	PB
Angels	.955	56	1467	654	100	2221	53	20
Athletics	.949	56	1474	602	111	2187	54	17
Mariners	.945	56	1481	649	123	2253	49	28
Brewers	.944	56	1481	621	125	2227	37	22
Padres	.935	55	1408	571	137	2116	43	15
Rockies	.933	55	1420	628	146	2194	43	15

TRIPLE PLAYS: None.

INDIVIDUAL

FIRST BASEMEN

NOTE: All caps denotes fielding-percentage leader based on 28 games for catchers, 37 for all other non-pitchers and 56 innings for pitchers. *Throws lefthanded.

Player, Team	Pct.	G	PO	A	E	TC	DP
ARIAS, David, Mariners*	.989	46	436	27	5	468	36
Balcazar, Carlos, Angels	1.000	4	23	2	0	25	0
Barnes, Larry, Angels*	.987	55	494	19	7	520	49
Cruz, Cirilo, Mariners	1.000	1	16	0	0	16	0
Hernandez, Ramon, Athletics	.966	13	81	3	3	87	10
Jacobo, Roberto, Padres*	.980	4	47	2	1	50	4
Johnson, Jace, Athletics	1.000	1	5	1	0	6	0
Jones, Timothy, Athletics	1.000	1	1	0	0	1	0
Judge, Mike, Brewers	.947	5	32	4	2	38	2
Lindsey, John, Rockies	.964	26	209	8	8	225	15
McNally, Jason, Rockies	1.000	1	10	1	0	11	1
Niles, David, Rockies*	.983	34	267	24	5	296	17
Paciorek, Peter, Padres*	.988	53	462	26	6	494	37
Paulino, Arturo, Athletics	1.000	4	32	2	0	34	3
Peters, Tony, Brewers	.985	24	184	17	3	204	13
Polanco, Juan, Athletics	.989	11	89	3	1	93	5
Rauer, Troy, Athletics	.941	10	92	3	6	101	7
Rendon, Miguel, Brewers	.929	4	25	1	2	28	0
Rodriguez, Juan, Angels	1.000	2	3	0	0	3	0
Rogue, Francisco, Brewers	1.000	4	12	1	0	13	1
Scheker, Luis, Athletics	.970	16	123	8	4	135	19
Ventura, Wilfredo, Athletics	.979	5	43	3	1	47	1
Walther, Christopher, Brewers	.978	26	235	26	6	267	14
Williams, Marcus, Mariners	.950	11	92	4	5	101	6

SECOND BASEMEN

Player, Team	Pct.	G	PO	A	E	TC	DP
Campusano, Carlos, Brewers	.750	4	1	2	1	4	1
Cesar, Dionys, Athletics	.930	34	67	65	10	142	15
Cespedes, Angel, Rockies	.916	15	24	52	7	83	6
Clark, John, Rockies	.951	17	44	53	5	102	13
Davis, Josh, Padres	1.000	3	7	7	0	14	1
Delacruz, Jesus, Angels	.890	21	21	44	8	73	9
Figueroa, Luis, Mariners	1.000	2	1	3	0	4	0
Freeman, Terrance, Athletics	.925	25	43	43	7	93	8
Groseclose, Harold, Rockies	.934	23	44	69	8	121	9
Guerrero, Diogene, Athletics	1.000	1	1	0	0	1	0
Harris, Rico, Brewers	.936	40	82	79	11	172	12
Harrison, Adonis, Mariners	.950	43	83	88	9	180	23
Jackson, Rod, Padres	.916	44	79	117	18	214	23
Kirkpatrick, Brian, Rockies	1.000	3	5	6	0	11	1
Lara, Edward, Athletics	1.000	1	1	1	0	2	0
Llanos, Alexis, Angels	.913	10	9	12	2	23	2
Paulino, Arturo, Athletics	.750	2	3	3	2	8	1
Polanco, Juan, Athletics	1.000	2	5	5	0	10	2
Roche, Michael, Brewers	.918	20	33	57	8	98	9
Rodriguez, Franklin, Mariners	.889	14	23	33	7	63	4
Rodriguez, John, Padres	.960	7	12	12	1	25	3
Rosario, Eliezer, Padres	.786	2	4	7	3	14	2
Rutherford, Daryl, Padres	.889	3	4	4	1	9	1
Vazquez, Ramon, Mariners	1.000	1	5	2	0	7	2
WARDROP, Adam, Angels	.960	37	74	96	7	177	23

THIRD BASEMEN

Player, Team	Pct.	G	PO	A	E	TC	DP
Acevedo, Juan, Rockies	.804	15	8	33	10	51	4
Campusano, Carlos, Brewers	.854	36	17	65	14	96	1
Cesar, Dionys, Athletics	1.000	4	2	7	0	9	0
CHAVEZ, Steven, Padres	.871	51	44	111	23	178	13
Clark, John, Rockies	1.000	3	5	2	0	7	1
Cowsill, Brendon, Angels	.927	33	19	96	9	124	8
Cruz, Cirilo, Mariners	.864	22	13	38	8	59	3
Delacruz, Jesus, Angels	.867	5	2	11	2	15	1
Figueroa, Luis, Mariners	.921	24	9	61	6	76	3
Hernandez, Ramon, Athletics	.813	6	6	7	3	16	0
Johnson, Duan, Mariners	.923	8	9	15	2	26	1
Kirkpatrick, Brian, Rockies	.780	23	16	30	13	59	3
Lara, Edward, Athletics	.667	2	2	0	1	3	0
Lawrence, Mike, Angels	.900	17	10	26	4	40	3
McNally, Jason, Rockies	.870	17	8	32	6	46	0
Paulino, Arturo, Athletics	.881	16	16	36	7	59	0
Polanco, Juan, Athletics	.880	34	31	72	14	117	10
Roche, Michael, Brewers	.714	18	8	17	10	35	1
Rodriguez, Franklin, Mariners	1.000	2	0	2	0	2	0
Rodriguez, John, Padres	.556	4	1	4	4	9	0
Rutherford, Daryl, Padres	1.000	2	2	2	0	4	0
Schaub, Greg, Brewers	.933	11	6	8	1	15	1
Vazquez, Ramon, Mariners	.900	3	4	5	1	10	0
Wardrop, Adam, Angels	.852	10	7	16	4	27	2

SHORTSTOPS

Player, Team	Pct.	G	PO	A	E	TC	DP
Campusano, Carlos, Brewers	.921	19	15	43	5	63	5
Carmona, Cesarin, Padres	.865	14	17	28	7	52	7
Castro, Nelson, Angels	.939	55	106	173	18	297	32
Cesar, Dionys, Athletics	.920	8	8	15	2	25	6
Cespedes, Angel, Rockies	.889	4	5	11	2	18	3
Clark, John, Rockies	.883	32	51	92	19	162	12
Figueroa, Luis, Mariners	.857	1	0	6	1	7	1
Groseclose, Harold, Rockies	.955	8	15	27	2	44	7
Harrison, Adonis, Mariners	1.000	1	1	1	0	2	0
Johnson, Duan, Mariners	.897	20	29	67	11	107	11
Kirkpatrick, Brian, Rockies	.867	12	15	24	6	45	4
LARA, Edward, Athletics	.963	45	80	127	8	215	25
Llanos, Alexis, Angels	1.000	4	1	2	0	3	1
Paulino, Arturo, Athletics	.926	7	8	17	2	27	4
Polanco, Juan, Athletics	1.000	1	4	4	0	8	0
Ritter, Ryan, Brewers	.786	3	5	6	3	14	0
Rodriguez, John, Padres	.841	18	17	41	11	69	6
Rosario, Eliezer, Padres	.957	5	8	14	1	23	3
Rutherford, Daryl, Padres	.898	25	32	47	9	88	5
Singleton, Samuel, Brewers	.924	46	66	104	14	184	18
Vazquez, Ramon, Mariners	.940	35	51	107	10	168	20
Wardrop, Adam, Angels	.667	3	0	2	1	3	0

OUTFIELDERS

Player, Team	Pct.	G	PO	A	E	TC	DP
Acevedo, Juan, Rockies	.882	12	15	0	2	17	0
Alamo, Efrain, Rockies	.900	36	60	3	7	70	1
Allen, Tony, Brewers	.957	43	43	1	2	46	0
Barnes, Larry, Angels*	.750	2	2	1	1	4	0

Player, Team	Pct.	G	PO	A	E	TC	DP
Barrios, Esteban, Angels*	1.000	13	17	1	0	18	0
Chambers, Victor, Athletics	.893	29	23	2	3	28	0
Cruz, Cirilo, Mariners	.882	9	14	1	2	17	0
Cruz, Francisco, Padres	.000	1	0	0	1	1	0
Delgado, Ariel, Angels*	.949	51	69	6	4	79	1
Ducasse, Luis, Athletics	1.000	6	8	0	0	8	0
Duverge, Salvador, Rockies	.896	39	55	5	7	67	1
Erstad, Darin, Angels*	1.000	3	3	0	0	3	0
Fowler, Marvin, Mariners	.886	26	28	3	4	35	1
Gordon, Garfield, Rockies	.915	32	54	0	5	59	0
Guerrero, Diogene, Athletics	.935	38	51	7	4	62	0
Hernandez, Victor, Athletics	1.000	13	12	3	0	15	1
Hunter, Andy, Padres	.980	32	47	3	1	51	0
Hutchins, Norm, Angels*	.895	14	17	0	2	19	0
Iapoce, Anthony, Brewers*	1.000	2	3	0	0	3	0
Isom, Daleon, Mariners	.875	26	35	0	5	40	0
Jacobo, Roberto, Padres*	.797	39	50	5	14	69	0
Jacobus, Brian, Padres*	.915	41	58	7	6	71	0
Jones, Timothy, Athletics	.978	22	42	3	1	46	1
Law, Khris, Athletics	.976	32	37	4	1	42	1
Martinez, Hipolito, Athletics	.964	40	48	6	2	56	0
McDavid, Ray, Padres	1.000	1	1	0	0	1	0
McDougall, Matt, Mariners	.921	25	33	2	3	38	1
Moore, Donald, Brewers	.964	35	26	1	1	28	0
Moore, James, Padres	.944	13	17	0	1	18	0
Niles, David, Rockies*	.800	1	3	1	1	5	1
Pernell, Brandon, Padres	.950	44	69	7	4	80	2
Peters, Tony, Brewers	.970	26	32	0	1	33	0
Rauer, Troy, Athletics	1.000	8	7	1	0	8	0
Rendon, Miguel, Brewers	.944	18	16	1	1	18	1
Rodriguez, Juan, Angels	.959	40	68	3	3	74	1
Rose, Carlos, Mariners	.842	25	30	2	6	38	0
Rowson, James, Mariners	.947	28	36	0	2	38	0
Rushdan, Rasheed, Rockies	1.000	5	12	3	0	15	1
Schaub, Greg, Brewers	.955	20	21	0	1	22	0
Selga, Andres, Rockies	1.000	13	28	3	0	31	1
Silverio, Richard, Rockies*	.964	31	49	5	2	56	1
Stewart, Keith, Mariners	1.000	11	15	1	0	16	1
STUART, Rich, Angels	.976	51	76	5	2	83	0
Tolbert, Ernest, Mariners	.976	24	39	2	1	42	1
Walther, Christopher, Brewers	.963	23	26	0	1	27	0
Wilkerson, Adrian, Brewers	.973	53	64	8	2	74	1
Williams, Marcus, Mariners	.941	10	15	1	1	17	0

CATCHERS

Player, Team	Pct.	G	PO	A	E	TC	DP	PB
Balcazar, Carlos, Angels	.979	20	123	17	3	143	2	4
Davis, Josh, Padres	.963	24	194	15	8	217	0	7
Ebbert, Chad, Padres	.980	29	208	40	5	253	0	6
HERNANDEZ, Ramon, Athletics	.982	31	271	51	6	328	2	12
Jones, Ken, Padres	1.000	1	6	0	0	6	0	1
Marnell, Anthony, Padres	1.000	1	2	2	0	4	0	1
Maynard, Scott, Mariners	.978	21	152	25	4	181	0	12
McDougall, Matt, Mariners	1.000	3	8	3	0	11	0	0
McNally, Jason, Rockies	.970	23	138	24	5	167	1	7
Medrano, Teodoro, Mariners	1.000	1	4	1	0	5	0	0
Randolph, Edward, Mariners	.962	40	263	67	13	343	2	16
Rodriguez, Miguel, Brewers	.968	45	378	73	15	466	3	17
Rogue, Francisco, Brewers	.966	16	121	20	5	146	4	5
Saucedo, Robert, Angels	.972	20	89	17	3	109	0	11
Ventura, Wilfredo, Athletics	.979	29	216	19	5	240	2	5
Veras, Illuminado, Angels	.972	30	218	28	7	253	1	5
Vidal, Carlos, Rockies	.961	34	251	47	12	310	7	8

PITCHERS

Player, Team	Pct.	G	PO	A	E	TC	DP
Abreu, Oscar, Athletics	.000	20	0	0	1	1	0
Baez, Benito, Athletics*	.833	14	1	14	3	18	0
Barnes, Larry, Brewers	1.000	6	0	2	0	2	0
Bennett, Tom, Athletics	.875	11	1	13	2	16	0
Bishop, Joshua, Brewers	.962	14	3	22	1	26	0
Blanco, Roger, Mariners	.933	12	4	10	1	15	0
Blevins, Jeremy, Angels	.857	11	2	4	1	7	0
Bonilla, Denis, Mariners*	.889	21	4	4	1	9	0
Bowles, Matt, Brewers	.800	7	3	1	1	5	0
Burton, Isaac, Mariners	.500	2	1	0	1	2	0
Cesar, Dionys, Athletics	1.000	2	0	1	0	1	1
Clark, Chris, Padres	.778	13	1	6	2	9	0
Contreras, Orlando, Rockies	.833	16	2	3	1	6	0
Costello, Terrance, Athletics*	1.000	12	0	11	0	11	0
Craig, Casey, Mariners	1.000	2	0	1	0	1	1
Darrell, Thomas, Angels	.900	18	2	16	2	20	0
DeLosSantos, Valerio, Brewers*	.867	14	4	9	2	15	1
Derenches, Albert, Mariners*	.750	20	2	4	2	8	0
Desabrias, Mark, Padres	.846	19	0	11	2	13	0
Douglas, Reggie, Rockies	.857	15	2	4	1	7	0
Druckrey, Chris, Rockies	1.000	14	5	10	0	15	0
Drysdale, Brooks, Angels	.500	4	0	1	1	2	0
Duncan, Devohn, Padres	.909	11	3	7	1	11	0
Estrada, Horacio, Brewers*	.667	8	0	2	1	3	0
Florentino, Osmil, Rockies	.727	19	4	4	3	11	0
Foster, Cliff, Athletics	1.000	1	1	0	0	1	0
Glick, Dave, Brewers*	.875	18	0	7	1	8	0
Gomez, Alex, Angels	.500	13	0	1	1	2	0
Gonzalez, Jose, Mariners	.941	12	3	13	1	17	1
Gutierrez, Javier, Mariners	.889	14	3	5	1	9	0
Guzman, Jonathan, Brewers*	.750	11	1	2	1	4	0
Henderson, James, Padres	1.000	3	0	1	0	1	0
Hill, Tyrone, Brewers*	1.000	4	0	3	0	3	0
Ishee, Gabe, Brewers	.967	15	8	21	1	30	0
Jacob, Russell, Mariners	.875	12	5	9	2	16	2
Jimenez, Jhonny, Mariners	1.000	19	2	3	0	5	1
Johnson, Shelby, Mariners	.800	9	1	3	1	5	1
Kaye, Justin, Mariners	.333	12	0	1	2	3	0
Kazmirski, Robert, Athletics	1.000	28	1	5	0	6	0
Kjos, Ryan, Athletics	.000	3	0	0	1	1	0
Knickerbocker, Thomas, A's*	.714	17	0	5	2	7	0
Kolb, Brandon, Padres	1.000	4	2	3	0	5	0
Law, Khris, Athletics	1.000	2	0	1	0	1	0
Leftwich, Phil, Angels	.500	4	0	1	1	2	0
Lenhardt, Bruce, Brewers	1.000	2	0	1	0	1	0
Lopez, Jose, Angels	.889	11	2	6	1	9	0
Lopez, Rodrigo, Padres	.900	11	1	8	1	10	0
Lowe, Derek, Mariners	1.000	2	0	2	0	2	0
Mahlberg, John, Rockies	1.000	10	3	5	0	8	0
Martino, Wil, Rockies*	.833	16	0	5	1	6	0
Matlack, Dan, Padres	.800	16	1	3	1	5	0
Mays, Joseph, Mariners	.833	10	3	12	3	18	2
McDonald, Matt, Athletics*	.750	5	0	3	1	4	0
Moreno, Juan, Athletics*	.688	20	2	9	5	16	1
Nash, Damond, Padres	1.000	15	5	8	0	13	0
Neiman, Joshua, Padres	1.000	10	1	1	0	2	1
Niles, David, Rockies*	1.000	2	0	1	0	1	0
Nivar, Amaury, Rockies	1.000	6	1	0	0	1	0
Nix, Wayne, Athletics	1.000	6	1	0	0	1	0
Nogowski, Brandon, Mariners*	1.000	20	1	2	0	3	0
Norris, McKenzie, Brewers	.500	2	0	1	1	2	0
Palki, Jeromy, Mariners	1.000	4	1	1	0	2	0
Patterson, Ken, Angels*	1.000	1	2	0	0	2	0
Paulino, Jose, Athletics	.750	15	2	7	3	12	0
Pavlovich, Tony, Brewers	1.000	19	1	4	0	5	0
Perez, Jesse, Brewers	.889	16	4	4	1	9	0
PLANT, David, Athletics	1.000	14	6	12	0	18	0
Podjan, James, Rockies	.778	17	2	12	4	18	0
Polanco, Juan, Athletics	1.000	1	1	0	0	1	0
Prempas, Lyle, Brewers*	.750	13	5	7	4	16	0
Preston, George, Brewers	.333	2	0	1	2	3	0
Quinteros, Steve, Angels	1.000	7	0	2	0	2	1
Riley, Brian, Angels	1.000	17	1	2	0	3	0
Rodriguez, Hector, Angels	.625	9	1	4	3	8	0
Rojas, Miguel, Angels	1.000	9	0	1	0	1	0
ROMERO, John, Angels	1.000	18	3	15	0	18	2
Rosa, Cristy, Rockies	.850	12	5	12	3	20	0
Schroeder, Scott, Padres	.500	2	0	1	1	2	0
Segura, Juan, Rockies*	1.000	20	0	4	0	4	0
Smith, Josh, Padres*	1.000	8	0	2	0	2	0
Soriano, Jacobo, Angels	1.000	11	0	2	0	2	1
Stahl, Anders, Rockies	.938	12	3	12	1	16	0
Stockstill, Jason, Angels*	.875	12	1	6	1	8	0
Suzuki, Mac, Mariners	1.000	4	1	0	0	1	0
Szimanski, Tom, Mariners	1.000	4	1	2	0	3	0
Tisdale, Warren, Mariners	1.000	13	3	4	0	7	0
Torres, Derek, Brewers	1.000	6	1	0	0	1	0
Torres, Luis, Padres	.833	22	3	7	2	12	0
Volkman, Keith, Angels*	.900	13	2	16	2	20	0
Walker, Kevin, Padres*	.882	13	3	12	2	17	1
Weymouth, Martin, Mariners	.800	9	2	6	2	10	0
Williams, Patrick, Rockies	1.000	5	2	1	0	3	0

The following players did not have any fielding statistics at the positions indicated or appeared only as a designated hitter, pinch-hitter or pinch-runner: Agosto, p; Ashley, p; C. Cruz, 2b; Drewien, p; Ducasse, 2b; Ettles, p; Guerrero, 3b, p; A. Gutierrez, p; Hamada, p; M. Harris, dh; R. Harris, of; V. Hernandez, p; D. Johnson, 1b; Kammerer, p; Martinez, p; McGuire, p; Needham, dh, ph; Osteen, p; Ja. Perez, p; Randolph, of; Richmond, p; Suazo, p; Tijerina, p; Updike, p.

LEAGUE CHAMPIONS

Year	Team	Pct.
1988—	Peoria Brewers	.690
1989—	Peoria Brewers	.732
1990—	Peoria Brewers	.679
1991—	Scottsdale A's	.650
1992—	Scottsdale A's	.607
1993—	Scottsdale A's	.636
1994—	Chandler Cardinals	.607
1995—	Scottsdale A's	.661

DOMINICAN SUMMER LEAGUE

1995 FINAL STANDINGS

WEST DIVISION

Team	W	L	T	Pct.	GB
Toronto	44	24	0	.647	....
New York Mets	41	27	0	.603	3
New York Yankees	31	37	0	.456	13
Pittsburgh	30	36	0	.455	13
Kansas City/Colorado	24	40	1	.375	18

CENTRAL DIVISION

Team	W	L	T	Pct.	GB
Cleveland	48	20	1	.706	....
Oakland	44	21	1	.677	2½
Texas	39	28	0	.582	8½
Florida	26	42	0	.382	22
Chicago (N.L.)/San Diego	22	45	1	.328	25½

EAST DIVISION

Team	W	L	T	Pct.	GB
Seattle	45	21	0	.682	....
Detroit	34	34	1	.500	12
Dodgers I	28	36	0	.438	16
Philadelphia/St. Louis	25	44	0	.362	21½
Montreal	21	47	1	.309	25

SAN PEDRO DE MACORIS DIVISION

Team	W	L	T	Pct.	GB
Toyo Carp	58	13	0	.817	....
Dodgers II	44	25	0	.638	13
California	31	39	1	.443	26½
Baltimore/Chicago (A.L.)	30	40	0	.429	27½
Houston/Milwaukee	28	39	1	.418	28
San Francisco	27	44	0	.380	31
Atlanta	26	44	0	.371	31½

Club names are major league affiliations.

PLAYOFFS—Toyo Carp defeated Toronto, two games to one; Cleveland defeated Seattle, two games to one; Toyo Carp defeated Cleveland, two games to none, to win league championship.

MANAGERS—Atlanta, Pedro Gonzalez; Baltimore/Chicago (A.L.), Carlos Bernhardt; California, Charles Romero; Chicago (N.L.)/San Diego, Julio Valdez; Cleveland, Alejandro Taveras; Detroit, Felix Nivar; Dodgers I, Antonio Bautista; Dodgers II, Victor Horacio Nazario; Florida, Hilario Soriano; Houston/Milwaukee, Ricardo Aponte; Kansas City/Colorado, Oscar Martinez; Montreal, Arturo De Freites; New York Mets, Luis Natera; New York Yankees, Rafael Concepcion; Oakland, Luis Martinez; Philadelphia/St. Louis, Wilfredo Tejeda; Pittsburgh, Ramon Sambo; San Francisco, Mateos Rojas Alou; Seattle, Ramon De Los Santos; Texas, Manuel Batista; Toronto, Ignacio Javier-Mike Guerrero; Toyo Carp, Manuel Castillo.

ALL-STAR TEAM: 1B—Pablo Sencion, Toronto; 2B—Edwin Perez, Cleveland; 3B—Marco Scuttaro, Cleveland; SS—Alfonso Guilleard, Toyo Carp; OF—Jesus Hernandez, Cleveland; Juan Moreno, N.Y. Mets; Charlie Pena, Toyo Carp; C—Ignacio Suero, Toronto; DH—Ramon Pena, Toronto; RHP—Luis Vizcaino, Oakland; LHP—Ismel Zabala, Seattle; Player of the Year—Jesus Hernandez, Cleveland; Pitcher of the Year—Luis Vizcaino, Oakland; Manager of the Year—Manuel Castillo, Toyo Carp.

1995 BATTING

TEAM

Team	Avg.	G	TPA	AB	R	H	TB	2B	3B	HR	RBI	SH	SF	HP	BB	IBB	SO	SB	CS	GDP	LOB	ShO	Slg.	OBP
Toyo Carp	.296	71	2958	2439	587	721	1023	124	30	39	469	12	48	50	409	7	346	105	31	56	559	...	.419	...
Toronto	.293	68	2666	2294	409	671	955	103	11	53	339	19	19	43	291	15	391	143	72	60	517	...	.416	...
Cleveland	.291	69	2753	2399	461	699	956	130	38	17	366	21	27	51	255	11	305	124	44	58	517	...	.398	...
Seattle	.290	66	2592	2181	427	633	963	100	19	64	370	20	18	35	338	19	390	77	61	60	514	...	.442	...
Texas	.277	67	2613	2171	419	601	835	94	22	32	330	11	23	41	367	7	407	87	63	57	536	...	.385	...
N.Y. Mets	.271	68	2656	2260	420	613	957	102	10	74	345	12	25	39	320	6	433	85	53	45	517	...	.423	...
Dodgers II	.265	69	2719	2265	454	600	813	96	30	19	353	24	25	55	350	13	337	114	48	66	517	...	.359	...
N.Y. Yankees	.263	68	2577	2219	345	583	832	105	18	36	281	7	22	39	290	6	365	86	50	72	485	...	.375	...
Pittsburgh	.262	66	2529	2190	342	573	798	81	18	36	278	13	18	48	260	3	433	65	59	57	496	...	.364	...
Phil./St.L.	.258	69	2625	2306	372	595	815	108	29	18	283	13	30	31	245	9	439	114	68	60	462	...	.353	...
Oakland	.257	66	2553	2138	388	549	796	97	21	36	313	18	26	28	343	8	416	87	50	51	488	...	.372	...
Bal./Chi. AL	.256	70	2733	2323	376	595	810	82	18	33	299	21	22	40	327	5	491	145	63	50	511	...	.349	...
Dodgers I	.255	64	2502	2100	351	536	754	91	20	29	288	18	19	36	329	12	378	44	29	55	514	...	.359	...
Chi. NL/S.D.	.251	68	2576	2177	344	547	725	83	16	21	266	15	21	33	330	5	393	52	50	76	519	...	.333	...
Montreal	.248	69	2678	2306	319	573	757	95	16	19	260	19	27	50	276	15	367	117	63	59	531	...	.328	...
Florida	.243	68	2521	2186	295	532	721	83	14	26	238	25	16	34	260	6	516	91	51	49	486	...	.330	...
San Francisco	.243	71	2553	2224	333	540	726	94	16	29	266	15	8	57	249	5	412	114	44	69	488	...	.326	...
Hou./Mil.	.242	68	2659	2270	359	549	756	99	15	26	256	24	26	43	296	12	383	169	59	43	482	...	.333	...
K.C./Colo.	.240	65	2441	2121	312	508	657	63	19	16	234	11	21	29	259	7	357	72	69	65	413	...	.310	...
Atlanta	.238	70	2753	2245	360	534	725	93	22	18	288	28	25	64	391	6	449	128	48	59	574	...	.323	...
Detroit	.236	69	2742	2199	373	519	725	80	30	22	299	31	27	60	425	18	467	91	64	65	569	...	.330	...
California	.234	71	2708	2282	325	535	706	90	18	15	254	13	15	39	359	13	401	93	41	52	576	...	.309	...

INDIVIDUAL

TOP QUALIFIERS FOR BATTING CHAMPIONSHIP

Minimum 192 plate appearances.

Player, Team	Avg.	G	TPA	AB	R	H	TB	2B	3B	HR	RBI	SH	SF	HP	BB	IBB	SO	SB	CS	GDP	Slg.	OBP
Hernandez, Jesus, Cleveland	.406	66	294	251	60	102	138	22	7	0	53	0	4	2	37	2	15	20	3	2	.550	.480
Scuttaro, Marco, Cleveland	.393	66	296	262	71	103	133	18	6	0	38	2	4	8	20	1	11	32	11	4	.508	.446
Guilleard, Alfonso, Toyo Carp	.366	63	272	227	52	83	113	12	3	4	55	1	8	6	30	1	19	8	2	1	.498	.439
Pena, Ramon, Toronto	.366	59	242	213	22	78	95	11	0	2	34	0	5	8	16	3	20	3	4	6	.446	.421
Guerrero, Wascar, Seattle	.364	48	194	173	37	63	109	14	1	10	43	0	1	2	18	2	40	1	0	4	.630	.428
Moreno, Juan, N.Y. Mets	.360	58	264	228	59	82	137	14	1	13	36	1	1	2	32	1	24	15	10	2	.601	.441
Guzman, Martin, Toyo Carp	.349	58	270	229	58	80	119	16	1	7	54	0	7	5	29	0	29	0	1	3	.520	.422
Valera, Ramon, Seattle	.347	59	261	202	50	70	88	6	3	2	20	7	2	3	47	0	23	46	20	3	.436	.472
Encarnacion, Mario, Oakland	.345	64	278	229	56	79	124	11	5	8	44	1	4	4	40	0	36	17	8	3	.541	.444
Pena, Charlies, Toyo Carp	.336	68	321	241	80	81	132	27	0	8	66	0	5	9	66	2	30	17	2	4	.548	.486

ALL PLAYERS

Player, Team	Avg.	G	TPA	AB	R	H	TB	2B	3B	HR	RBI	SH	SF	HP	BB	IBB	SO	SB	CS	GDP	Slg.	OBP
Abreu, Dennis, Chi. (NL)/S.D.	.285	64	280	242	44	69	75	6	0	0	23	1	1	3	33	1	26	11	12	9	.310	.376
Abreu, Miguel, Florida	.171	60	239	210	26	36	43	4	0	1	11	2	1	5	21	1	45	4	2	8	.205	.262
Aguilar, Jose, Oakland	.357	6	16	14	2	5	6	1	0	0	2	0	0	0	2	0	2	0	0	1	.429	.438
Agustin, Filiberto, Houston	.244	42	188	168	26	41	59	13	1	1	23	1	3	1	15	2	32	18	4	1	.351	.305
Alcala, Juan F., Seattle	.164	25	71	61	5	10	13	1	1	0	7	0	1	0	9	0	18	0	1	1	.213	.268
Alfonzo, Iran, Toronto	.165	30	89	79	8	13	15	2	0	0	6	2	1	1	6	0	14	0	3	4	.190	.230
Almonte, Hector, Florida	.000	0	1	1	0	0	0	0	0	0	0	0	0	0	0	0	1	0	0	0	.000	.000
Alvarez, Carlos, Cleveland	.236	28	86	72	18	17	22	3	1	0	6	0	1	5	8	2	14	7	0	0	.306	.349
Amador, Juan, Atlanta	.130	36	89	77	9	10	11	1	0	0	2	0	0	0	12	0	21	2	1	3	.143	.247
Andujar, Eliezer, Atlanta	.228	62	264	206	35	47	54	7	0	0	33	2	7	2	47	0	29	23	5	9	.262	.366
Andujar, Juan, Florida	.253	44	169	154	15	39	46	1	0	2	16	2	1	3	9	0	37	1	1	5	.299	.305
Antonio, Junior, Houston	.259	22	29	27	2	7	11	1	0	1	3	1	0	1	0	0	10	0	1	1	.407	.286
Antunez, Javier, Montreal	.208	20	55	48	3	10	11	1	0	0	1	2	0	1	4	0	11	1	0	0	.229	.283
Araujo, Danilo, Phi./St.L.	.296	47	202	159	41	47	62	5	5	0	28	1	3	6	33	0	25	18	6	1	.390	.428
Arbornoz, Hernan, Montreal	.243	27	85	74	12	18	21	3	0	0	8	1	0	0	10	0	10	2	2	2	.284	.333
Arias, Jorge, Phi./St.L.	.188	28	85	80	6	15	19	2	1	0	6	0	1	0	4	1	11	1	0	4	.238	.224
Baez, Juan, Toronto	.250	4	5	4	0	1	1	0	0	0	1	0	0	0	1	0	2	0	0	0	.250	.400
Banci, Aaron, Florida	.200	50	186	170	18	34	54	9	1	3	19	0	1	1	14	0	37	2	4	2	.318	.263
Barreras, Rafael, Texas	.291	29	62	55	15	16	16	0	0	0	5	1	1	0	5	0	13	5	4	2	.291	.344
Basabe, Jesus, Oakland	.227	40	132	110	25	25	35	5	1	1	13	0	0	1	21	0	22	4	0	4	.318	.356
Bautista, Francisco, K.C./Colo.	.208	23	90	72	13	15	20	2	0	1	9	0	1	1	16	0	23	5	1	3	.278	.356
Bello, Gilberto, Bal./Chi.(AL)	.296	60	241	199	32	59	89	14	2	4	38	3	4	3	32	0	30	6	7	9	.447	.395
Belmonte, Jose, California	.182	36	106	88	12	16	18	2	0	0	9	0	0	4	14	0	25	3	4	3	.205	.321
Beltre, Adrian, Dodgers I	.307	62	279	218	56	67	112	15	3	8	40	0	2	5	54	2	26	2	1	8	.514	.452
Beltres, Manuel, N.Y. Yankees	.215	56	179	158	21	34	48	6	1	2	14	0	1	1	19	0	38	2	5	2	.304	.302
Benitez, Miguel, K.C./Colo.	.203	25	68	59	7	12	13	1	0	0	5	0	1	1	7	0	18	0	0	3	.220	.294
Betancourt, Romulo, Bal./Chi.(AL)	.245	34	115	94	21	23	27	4	0	0	9	0	1	3	17	0	28	11	3	1	.287	.374
Blanco, Billy, Oakland	.050	14	24	20	1	1	1	0	0	0	0	0	0	0	4	0	8	0	0	1	.050	.208
Blanco, Daniel, San Francisco	.216	28	97	88	4	19	22	3	0	0	7	0	0	3	6	0	14	0	1	3	.250	.289
Blanco, Danny, Cleveland	.155	35	99	84	9	13	18	5	0	0	7	0	1	0	14	0	10	1	0	4	.214	.273
Bracho, Didimo, Montreal	.248	61	233	202	23	50	70	12	1	2	30	0	1	2	28	3	34	8	9	4	.347	.343
Bravo, Eulis, Cleveland	.212	48	132	118	20	25	29	4	0	0	8	3	0	2	9	0	8	4	3	7	.246	.279
Brea, Rafael, Florida	.242	65	275	207	48	50	77	8	5	3	15	9	1	4	54	0	49	23	5	1	.372	.406
Briceno, Freddy, Montreal	.171	42	101	76	12	13	13	0	0	0	5	1	1	6	17	0	10	4	3	6	.171	.360
Brito, Felix, N.Y. Yankees	.209	21	57	43	7	9	15	1	1	1	6	0	0	2	12	0	6	0	0	2	.349	.404
Brito, Johan, San Francisco	.222	55	225	176	31	39	46	4	0	1	14	1	0	10	38	0	24	30	6	6	.261	.388
Cabrera, Danny, N.Y. Mets	.296	45	173	142	25	42	66	12	0	4	25	1	2	0	28	2	26	1	3	2	.465	.407
Cadet, Javier, Chi. (NL)/S.D.	.000	1	3	3	0	0	0	0	0	0	0	0	0	0	0	0	1	0	0	1	.000	.000
Caines, Franklin, Phi./St.L.	.285	62	264	246	38	70	104	14	4	4	38	0	1	0	17	2	52	6	3	9	.423	.330
Camacaro, Pedro, Texas	.159	14	51	44	7	7	9	0	1	0	3	0	0	0	7	0	9	0	0	0	.205	.275
Camacho, Wandy, California	.190	51	162	142	11	27	35	8	0	0	20	1	2	0	17	3	39	0	1	6	.246	.273
Carmona, Antonio, Bal./Chi.(AL)	.217	49	162	138	21	30	44	2	0	4	18	0	3	3	18	0	18	6	2	4	.319	.315
Carvajal, Hugo, Dodgers II	.078	28	65	51	4	4	4	0	0	0	2	1	0	1	12	0	6	0	1	3	.078	.266
Casimiro, Claudio, Bal./Chi.(AL)	.259	31	137	108	17	28	49	7	1	4	19	2	1	2	24	0	36	10	4	0	.454	.400
Castillo, Alex, Houston	.271	42	153	129	30	35	56	7	1	4	16	1	0	3	20	0	21	10	1	3	.434	.382
Castillo, Daniel A., Dodgers I	.000	7	0	0	1	0	0	0	0	0	0	0	0	0	0	0	0	0	0	0	.000	.000
Castillo, Geramel, Texas	.335	51	188	161	27	54	70	7	3	1	14	0	1	3	23	0	20	11	5	3	.435	.426
Castro, Cesar, California	.250	9	19	16	2	4	6	2	0	0	3	0	0	0	3	1	2	1	0	1	.375	.368
Castro, Jesus, Toronto	1.000	1	1	1	0	1	1	0	0	0	0	0	0	0	0	0	0	0	0	0	1.000	1.000
Castro, Jorge, Dodgers II	.238	39	129	105	14	25	31	3	0	1	16	1	2	2	19	1	19	1	3	4	.295	.359
Castro, Martirez, Texas	.307	67	273	225	35	69	102	14	2	5	44	0	4	6	38	1	44	3	10	7	.453	.414
Castro, Rafael, Phi./St.L.	.236	18	56	55	3	13	15	2	0	0	5	0	0	0	1	0	11	0	1	5	.273	.250
Cedeno, Ruddy, Houston	.317	51	197	161	41	51	65	10	2	0	14	0	3	0	33	1	14	12	7	1	.404	.426
Celedonio, Carlos, San Francisco	.262	55	215	183	33	48	70	13	0	3	14	1	0	5	26	0	38	11	4	5	.295	.369
Chavel, Ali, California	.250	5	14	12	2	3	6	0	0	1	3	0	0	0	2	0	5	0	1	1	.500	.357
Ciociola, Miguel, Dodgers I	.263	33	105	80	14	21	28	5	1	0	5	3	0	6	16	0	22	3	2	0	.350	.422
Collado, Hugo, Dodgers I	.283	38	135	106	21	30	34	2	1	0	17	1	1	1	26	1	15	5	3	2	.321	.425
Collado, Juan, N.Y. Yankees	.272	29	90	81	14	22	39	6	1	3	11	0	1	2	6	0	17	1	0	2	.481	.333
Compres, Miguel, N.Y. Yankees	.167	23	56	54	6	9	14	2	0	1	5	0	0	1	1	0	10	0	0	3	.259	.196
Cordero, Willie, Texas	.254	45	146	122	25	31	34	1	1	0	19	0	1	3	20	0	15	4	1	4	.279	.370
Corporan, Manuel, Bal./Chi.(AL)	.207	31	99	87	15	18	19	1	0	0	6	2	0	1	9	0	25	3	3	2	.218	.289
Cruz, Charlie, Dodgers I	.179	14	29	28	2	5	7	0	1	0	1	0	0	0	1	0	13	0	0	0	.250	.207
Cruz, Luis, Toyo Carp	.325	65	321	271	75	88	123	14	3	5	51	0	5	5	40	0	34	18	5	7	.454	.414
Cruz, Radhames, K.C./Colo.	.225	43	125	111	12	25	34	4	1	1	15	1	2	3	8	0	22	0	4	5	.306	.290
Cruz, Silvio, K.C./Colo.	.255	63	253	212	43	54	80	11	3	3	24	3	2	4	32	0	22	11	6	4	.377	.360
Dacosta, Samuel, Montreal	.269	27	65	52	5	14	17	3	0	0	11	0	1	1	11	0	6	0	0	1	.327	.400
DeJesus, Eddy, California	.242	50	175	153	22	37	55	12	0	2	20	2	0	2	18	0	36	6	3	3	.359	.329
DeJesus, Wilmer, Montreal	.178	38	102	90	6	16	20	1	0	1	9	1	0	2	9	0	16	0	0	4	.222	.267
DeLaCruz, Antonio, N.Y. Mets	.263	35	115	95	21	25	33	3	1	1	12	0	0	2	18	0	25	5	4	0	.347	.391
DeLaCruz, Henry, Chi. (NL)/S.D.	.181	38	123	94	12	17	25	5	0	1	10	0	1	1	27	0	44	2	3	2	.266	.366
DeLaCruz, Jose, Oakland	.248	41	154	125	26	31	43	6	0	2	12	0	1	2	26	0	29	4	0	2	.344	.383
DeLaCruz, Juan, San Francisco	.260	58	189	177	20	46	61	6	0	3	25	2	0	3	7	0	27	17	4	7	.345	.299
DeLaCruz, Pedro, Toronto	.205	15	40	39	5	8	12	2	1	0	2	0	1	0	0	0	8	1	1	1	.308	.200
DeLaCruz, Rafael, San Francisco	.175	24	60	57	2	10	12	2	0	0	2	1	0	1	1	0	15	0	2	3	.211	.203
DeLaCruz, Raul, Pittsburgh	.223	60	247	229	27	51	74	12	1	3	20	1	1	6	10	0	53	8	4	9	.323	.272
DeLaEspada, Miguel, Houston	.247	43	177	158	24	39	73	10	3	6	35	0	2	2	15	2	34	8	2	3	.462	.316
DeLaRosa, Erasmo, Houston	.206	33	115	102	13	21	31	3	2	1	13	1	1	2	9	0	25	5	5	2	.304	.281
DeLaRosa, Miguel, Texas	.259	56	209	158	36	41	66	7	0	6	26	4	2	3	42	0	57	10	11	1	.418	.420
DeLeon, Jose, Detroit	.280	35	117	100	12	28	30	2	0	0	14	0	2	2	13	2	22	4	2	3	.300	.368
DeLeon, Ricardo, Atlanta	.260	36	139	123	11	32	41	4	1	1	25	1	0	0	15	1	23	1	2	2	.333	.341
Delgado, Ramon, Seattle	.306	62	249	206	46	63	109	10	3	10	45	0	1	3	39	6	46	1	2	6	.529	.422

Player, Team	Avg.	G	TPA	AB	R	H	TB	2B	3B	HR	RBI	SH	SF	HP	BB	IBB	SO	SB	CS	GDP	Slg.	OBP
DeLosSantos, Aurelio, Phi./St.L.	.179	27	84	78	6	14	17	3	0	0	7	0	0	0	6	1	16	2	2	3	.218	.238
Del Valle, Carlos, Detroit	.266	66	275	222	35	59	78	12	2	1	28	2	1	0	50	4	26	2	1	9	.351	.399
Diaz, Emenegildo, San Francisco	.295	55	209	176	32	52	95	12	2	9	45	0	2	5	26	2	24	3	3	7	.540	.397
Diaz, Ivan, Phi./St.L.	.292	12	51	48	4	14	15	1	0	0	10	1	1	0	1	0	4	0	1	2	.313	.300
Diaz, Miguel, California	.217	53	212	198	28	43	58	12	0	1	23	1	1	5	7	0	37	5	2	5	.293	.261
Diaz, Welvis, Oakland	.274	57	228	168	31	46	65	7	3	2	19	2	1	3	54	2	49	3	5	4	.387	.456
D'Leon, Sandy, Seattle	.239	43	104	88	12	21	30	2	2	1	11	3	2	2	9	0	13	0	0	3	.341	.317
Dominguez, Enrique, Montreal	.202	50	126	109	18	22	24	2	0	0	10	1	1	7	8	0	16	9	3	4	.220	.296
Duncan, Jan Carlos, Phi./St.L.	.231	51	211	182	27	42	57	7	4	0	25	1	7	1	20	1	44	8	7	3	.313	.300
Duverge, Salvador, K.C./Colo.	.304	6	25	23	5	7	19	1	1	3	8	0	0	1	1	0	2	0	1	0	.826	.360
Ellis, Franklin, Houston	.239	29	103	92	10	22	30	5	0	1	13	2	4	0	5	0	19	5	1	1	.326	.267
Encarnacion, Edgardo, California	.226	51	174	159	22	36	48	8	2	0	15	1	1	1	12	0	16	4	2	7	.302	.283
Encarnacion, Mario, Oakland	.345	64	278	229	56	79	124	11	5	8	44	1	4	4	40	0	36	17	8	3	.541	.444
Encarnacion, Pedro, Bal./Chi.(AL)	.329	37	168	140	31	46	69	7	2	4	30	0	2	2	24	0	25	9	1	4	.493	.429
Encarnacion, Sonder, Seattle	.286	54	204	168	33	48	76	7	0	7	35	1	5	5	25	1	16	6	7	6	.452	.384
Espino, Fernando, Seattle	.335	62	242	203	41	68	103	15	1	6	33	0	1	6	32	5	23	3	7	7	.507	.438
Espino, Jose, Toyo Carp	.265	58	225	204	34	54	72	9	3	1	34	1	3	5	12	0	46	5	3	7	.353	.317
Estevez, Domingo, Toronto	.220	45	164	141	23	31	46	6	0	3	15	3	2	2	16	1	26	7	4	3	.326	.304
Eusebio, Ruben, Houston	.235	34	111	98	14	23	23	0	0	0	2	2	0	4	7	0	10	3	6	3	.235	.312
Fajardo, Alejandro, Phi./St.L.	.329	52	221	183	31	60	80	11	3	1	21	1	2	3	32	0	24	17	7	10	.437	.432
Farraez, Adel, Houston	.207	35	102	87	11	18	20	2	0	0	11	0	1	4	10	0	17	9	3	5	.230	.314
Farraez, Jesus, Houston	.227	40	139	119	15	27	35	5	0	1	12	0	0	0	20	0	17	18	2	0	.294	.338
Felix, Edgar, Pittsburgh	.230	35	147	135	13	31	43	3	0	3	11	0	0	2	10	0	32	0	1	4	.319	.293
Fernandez, Juan, Dodgers I	.233	41	108	86	13	20	28	2	3	0	8	1	0	0	21	0	18	3	3	0	.326	.383
Fernandez, Robert, Cleveland	.227	14	51	44	9	10	13	0	0	1	6	0	1	1	5	0	10	3	0	1	.295	.314
Fernandez, Winston, Texas	.229	50	156	109	41	25	36	3	4	0	19	1	1	3	42	0	11	21	7	2	.330	.452
Ferreiras, Luis, Cleveland	.230	27	65	61	3	14	23	3	0	2	14	0	0	0	4	1	15	0	1	4	.377	.277
Figueroa, Jose, Oakland	.212	39	134	113	19	24	41	8	0	3	17	2	3	2	14	1	21	2	0	3	.363	.303
Fischer, Carlos, California	.329	48	194	155	25	51	54	3	0	0	13	0	1	1	37	0	16	10	5	2	.348	.459
Flores, Carlos, Houston	.200	5	15	15	0	3	5	0	1	0	2	0	0	0	0	0	4	0	1	1	.333	.200
Flores, Julio, Montreal	.306	58	228	196	29	60	79	10	3	1	29	2	3	3	24	3	16	16	7	5	.403	.385
Font, Franklin, Chi. (NL)/S.D.	.312	64	285	237	50	74	90	8	4	0	30	2	1	2	43	1	25	8	7	6	.380	.420
Francisco, Frank, Atlanta	.236	64	266	229	29	54	77	10	5	1	23	1	1	4	31	0	73	18	6	2	.336	.336
Franco, Deyvi, Detroit	.256	23	56	43	9	11	12	1	0	0	6	0	0	3	10	0	13	3	2	3	.279	.429
Franco, Jorge, Montreal	.227	29	100	88	11	20	25	3	1	0	7	2	2	2	6	0	9	2	1	7	.284	.286
Galban, Elvis, Montreal	.307	64	268	231	42	71	97	14	3	2	37	0	6	6	25	1	20	24	8	6	.420	.381
Garcia, Eduardo, California	.276	17	71	58	11	16	22	4	1	0	8	1	0	0	12	0	13	2	1	0	.379	.400
Garcia, Juan, Atlanta	.292	64	295	240	54	70	102	15	7	1	40	0	4	5	46	1	45	16	8	4	.425	.410
Garcia, Juan, Detroit	.179	22	32	28	4	5	7	2	0	0	3	0	0	1	3	0	14	1	0	0	.250	.281
Garcia, Julio, N.Y. Yankees	.333	4	13	12	2	4	4	0	0	0	1	0	0	0	1	0	1	1	1	0	.333	.385
Garcia, Leoncio, California	.242	46	165	124	14	30	39	2	2	1	17	0	3	5	33	1	30	3	0	0	.315	.412
Garcia, Luis, Dodgers II	.297	53	240	185	56	55	83	8	7	2	24	2	0	5	48	2	29	10	7	3	.449	.454
German, Aris, N.Y. Mets	.256	22	52	43	6	11	13	2	0	0	2	1	0	2	6	0	10	1	0	1	.302	.373
German, Julian, Detroit	.214	59	195	154	26	33	42	4	1	1	14	1	0	6	34	1	34	13	11	5	.273	.376
Germosen, Julio, Pittsburgh	.231	62	268	238	32	55	79	9	3	3	38	4	1	4	21	1	61	3	3	7	.332	.303
Geronimo, Cesar, California	.246	61	245	211	29	52	71	9	2	2	24	3	2	2	27	1	16	8	5	7	.336	.335
Gil, Alberto, Cleveland	.306	61	233	196	36	60	90	7	7	3	30	1	4	2	30	2	32	7	4	1	.459	.397
Giron, Edilberto, Pittsburgh	.190	18	51	42	7	8	9	1	0	0	4	0	0	1	8	0	18	1	0	0	.214	.333
Giron, Isabel, Toronto	.250	36	124	120	14	30	42	4	1	2	13	0	0	1	3	0	34	2	3	5	.350	.274
Giron, Juan, Atlanta	.292	56	226	171	33	50	62	9	0	1	25	1	1	16	37	1	27	6	5	7	.363	.458
Gomera, Rafael, Dodgers I	.242	60	240	215	37	52	75	7	2	4	28	1	2	1	21	2	59	3	3	1	.349	.310
Gomez, Luis, Houston	.155	29	72	58	6	9	15	3	0	1	6	0	3	3	8	1	10	3	1	0	.259	.278
Gonzalez, Adalberto, Montreal	.214	24	59	42	7	9	10	1	0	0	0	1	0	2	14	1	11	5	1	0	.238	.431
Gonzalez, Cesar, Montreal	.194	23	75	62	7	12	14	2	0	0	9	3	1	2	7	0	9	4	4	1	.226	.292
Gonzalez, Franklin, Chi. (NL)/S.D.	.260	24	90	77	14	20	23	1	1	0	8	4	0	0	9	0	13	1	3	3	.299	.337
Gonzalez, Santo, Chi. (NL)/S.D.	.222	59	221	180	29	40	60	8	3	2	19	1	1	2	37	0	32	6	6	3	.333	.359
Guerra, Carlos, Cleveland	.150	10	22	20	2	3	4	1	0	0	1	0	0	1	1	0	2	0	0	1	.200	.227
Guerra, Hubert, California	.171	50	172	146	20	25	36	6	1	1	16	1	1	0	24	1	27	13	2	3	.247	.287
Guerrero, Frank, Houston	.187	39	136	123	16	23	28	3	1	0	15	1	1	2	9	0	24	2	2	4	.228	.252
Guerrero, Hamlet, N.Y. Mets	.285	61	249	214	37	61	110	10	0	13	43	0	4	4	27	1	30	7	2	3	.514	.369
Guerrero, Wascar, Seattle	.364	48	194	173	37	63	109	14	1	10	43	0	1	2	18	2	40	1	0	4	.630	.428
Guilleard, Alfonso, Toyo Carp	.366	63	272	227	52	83	113	12	3	4	55	1	8	6	30	1	19	8	2	1	.498	.439
Gutierrez, Victor, Pittsburgh	.247	51	170	150	19	37	51	3	1	3	20	0	2	1	17	0	21	6	3	5	.340	.324
Guzman, Carlos, Detroit	.202	31	101	84	13	17	23	2	2	0	12	0	2	2	13	0	14	5	3	2	.274	.317
Guzman, Cristian, N.Y. Yankees	.269	46	180	160	24	43	68	6	5	3	20	2	1	5	12	1	23	11	7	2	.425	.337
Guzman, Juan, Bal./Chi.(AL)	.200	37	128	120	12	24	30	6	0	0	12	1	0	1	6	0	20	2	2	1	.250	.244
Guzman, Juan, Phi./St.L.	.187	50	175	155	25	29	40	4	2	1	16	3	1	1	15	0	37	6	5	1	.258	.262
Guzman, Martin, Toyo Carp	.349	58	270	229	58	80	119	16	1	7	54	0	7	5	29	0	29	0	1	3	.520	.422
Guzman, Santos, Pittsburgh	.328	37	142	131	16	43	59	5	1	3	16	0	1	1	9	0	27	1	1	1	.450	.373
Haad, Yamid, Pittsburgh	.254	36	132	118	17	30	31	1	0	0	8	2	1	2	9	0	17	1	9	2	.263	.315
Heredia, Andres, K.C./Colo.	.150	25	62	60	2	9	9	0	0	0	4	0	0	0	2	0	15	0	1	2	.150	.177
Heredia, Rafael, Chi. (NL)/S.D.	.298	61	248	215	38	64	117	15	4	10	41	0	5	7	21	1	38	4	1	5	.544	.371
Hernandez, Darwin, Pittsburgh	.255	57	251	204	37	52	73	7	4	2	24	2	1	4	40	0	40	8	9	6	.358	.386
Hernandez, Jesus, Cleveland	.406	66	294	251	60	102	138	22	7	0	53	0	4	2	37	2	15	20	3	2	.550	.480
Hernandez, Jorgelio, Toyo Carp	.246	18	66	61	9	15	17	2	0	0	6	0	0	0	5	0	4	3	2	4	.279	.303
Hernandez, Leonardo, N.Y. Mets	.209	41	98	91	4	19	22	1	1	0	10	0	1	2	4	0	21	4	2	0	.242	.255
Hernandez, Rafael, Montreal	.317	56	245	218	34	69	103	16	3	4	32	1	5	1	20	1	30	7	3	5	.472	.369
Herrera, Alvaro, California	.228	61	236	184	34	42	55	7	3	0	16	0	2	12	38	4	36	10	2	2	.299	.390
Infante, Danny, Texas	.303	63	250	234	31	71	96	13	0	4	39	1	2	0	13	1	49	2	5	1	.410	.337
Infante, Julio, Dodgers I	.207	24	64	58	4	12	14	2	0	0	5	0	0	1	5	0	14	0	1	2	.241	.281
Iquerey, Rodney, Cleveland	.205	43	107	88	13	18	20	2	0	0	7	1	0	4	14	0	14	2	3	3	.227	.340
Jadagui, Carlos, Chi. (NL)/S.D.	.204	32	110	93	14	19	24	2	0	1	6	0	0	2	15	0	22	0	0	7	.258	.327
Javier, Jesus, Dodgers I	.246	46	165	126	20	31	36	5	0	0	11	3	0	1	35	0	30	1	2	2	.286	.414

Player, Team	Avg.	G	TPA	AB	R	H	TB	2B	3B	HR	RBI	SH	SF	HP	BB	IBB	SO	SB	CS	GDP	Slg.	OBP
Jimenez, Felipe, Chi. (NL)/S.D.	.209	45	174	148	23	31	36	2	0	1	18	2	1	4	19	0	28	9	6	8	.243	.314
Jimenez, Miguel, Seattle	.327	62	265	226	50	74	108	11	1	7	51	1	1	5	32	2	33	9	4	4	.478	.420
Jimenez, Ramon, N.Y. Yankees	.241	39	90	79	21	19	28	3	0	2	13	0	0	0	11	0	22	10	2	1	.354	.333
Jose, Leonardo, Oakland	.250	18	71	60	7	15	17	0	1	0	3	0	1	3	7	0	21	10	6	0	.283	.352
King, Cesar, Texas	.302	54	209	182	33	55	73	9	0	3	22	0	0	5	22	1	34	3	2	9	.401	.392
King, Daniel, Oakland	.238	27	100	80	13	19	26	4	0	1	16	1	0	2	17	0	18	1	0	1	.325	.384
Langagney, Shelwin, Toronto	.335	65	270	221	45	74	92	15	0	1	39	1	2	3	43	3	29	16	8	7	.416	.446
Lara, Balnes, Detroit	.213	57	203	160	26	34	50	6	2	2	22	3	5	5	30	1	65	5	2	5	.313	.345
Lara, Felix, Pittsburgh	.185	46	154	135	19	25	34	2	2	1	9	0	0	4	15	1	53	2	4	3	.252	.286
Ledesma, Felipe, Dodgers II	.306	63	261	235	43	72	90	10	4	0	53	0	5	4	17	1	15	12	6	8	.383	.356
Leidens, Misael, Montreal	.257	34	122	109	20	28	36	3	1	1	8	0	1	2	10	0	18	4	4	2	.330	.328
Lima, Jose, K.C./Colo	.217	8	27	23	4	5	8	1	1	0	2	0	0	0	4	0	4	2	0	0	.348	.333
Lina, Donald, K.C./Colo.	.179	39	128	112	17	20	22	0	1	0	5	1	0	1	14	0	12	3	1	5	.196	.276
Linares, Rafael, Bal./Chi.(AL)	.194	45	120	98	18	19	20	1	0	0	3	1	0	5	16	0	23	8	3	1	.204	.336
Linares, Sendry, Houston	.254	29	82	71	10	18	23	2	0	1	10	4	0	0	7	0	4	10	5	1	.324	.321
Loaisiga, Stanley, Montreal	.289	65	251	232	22	67	93	10	2	4	30	1	3	4	11	5	35	6	2	3	.401	.328
Lopez, Luis, San Francisco	.269	58	241	219	41	59	87	9	2	5	33	0	0	5	17	0	35	9	3	14	.352	.336
Lorenzo, Julio, Detroit	.173	46	103	81	9	14	21	3	2	0	6	1	1	2	18	0	19	0	2	2	.259	.333
Loyo, Oscar, Florida	.327	14	56	52	4	17	31	5	0	3	14	0	0	0	4	0	8	0	0	1	.596	.375
Maldonado, Franklin, Chi. (NL)/S.D.	.241	52	184	162	23	39	49	7	0	1	23	2	0	4	16	0	28	2	2	4	.302	.324
Marcano, Dennys, Chi. (NL)/S.D.	.250	46	176	152	28	38	50	9	0	1	15	0	1	4	19	1	37	4	0	2	.329	.347
Marte, Julian, Dodgers II	.307	49	195	163	23	50	57	3	2	0	33	1	3	4	24	0	13	3	5	5	.350	.402
Marte, Nestor, Detroit	.259	43	88	58	14	15	19	2	1	0	11	1	1	1	27	0	8	3	2	4	.328	.494
Martich, Juan, Dodgers I	.000	5	13	12	1	0	0	0	0	0	0	0	0	0	1	0	3	0	0	0	.000	.077
Martinez, Andres, N.Y. Mets	.240	48	147	129	21	31	48	7	2	2	11	2	1	2	13	0	45	2	3	0	.372	.317
Martinez, Claudio, Dodgers II	.000	6	0	0	2	0	0	0	0	0	0	0	0	0	0	0	0	0	0	0	.000	.000
Martinez, David, Toronto	.312	58	233	199	34	62	76	6	1	2	29	2	2	3	27	0	39	8	3	6	.382	.398
Martinez, Fausto, N.Y. Mets	.195	27	50	41	8	8	10	0	1	0	2	0	1	2	6	0	16	0	1	1	.244	.320
Martinez, Gregorio, Dodgers II	.189	60	211	159	36	30	40	6	2	0	15	2	1	1	48	0	54	13	4	3	.252	.378
Martinez, Jose, Cleveland	.317	61	244	218	35	69	92	20	0	1	38	1	1	11	13	0	25	2	1	13	.422	.383
Martinez, Winston, Detroit	.179	35	75	56	9	10	13	0	0	1	5	0	1	7	11	0	21	0	1	1	.232	.373
Mata, Felix, Toyo Carp	.000	7	7	5	1	0	0	0	0	0	1	0	1	0	1	0	2	0	0	0	.000	.143
Mateo, Amaury, Texas	.301	48	201	176	30	53	80	9	3	4	42	1	2	2	20	1	23	1	2	3	.455	.375
Mateo, Freddy, Dodgers II	.283	66	282	240	50	68	106	13	2	7	45	0	5	13	24	2	49	8	2	5	.442	.372
Mateo, Victor, N.Y. Yankees	.333	66	273	248	34	83	114	17	4	2	37	0	2	3	20	0	19	5	4	8	.460	.388
Matos, Wellington, N.Y. Yankees	.282	59	243	209	36	59	96	8	1	9	39	0	1	2	31	2	32	2	1	7	.459	.379
McDonald, Gabriel, San Fran.	.236	58	225	178	31	42	60	8	5	0	24	1	2	11	33	1	49	11	2	5	.337	.384
McFarlane, Ivan, K.C./Colo.	261	37	99	88	15	23	28	5	0	0	5	0	0	1	10	0	26	2	2	3	.318	.343
McLean, Guillermo, Dodgers II	.232	26	69	56	12	13	16	1	1	0	7	0	0	4	9	0	12	2	0	2	.286	.377
Medina, Richy, Detroit	.182	42	113	88	15	16	23	2	1	1	6	5	0	1	19	1	24	8	2	2	.261	.333
Mejia, Jose, Atlanta	.238	35	102	84	13	20	26	6	0	0	7	2	2	5	9	0	16	6	1	5	.310	.340
Mejia, Juan, Phi./St.L.	.284	54	235	218	30	62	85	12	1	3	26	1	6	3	7	0	43	14	4	6	.390	.308
Mejia, Luis, Houston	.275	28	108	80	22	22	32	2	1	2	15	0	2	1	25	0	18	8	3	0	.400	.444
Mejia, Oliver, Pittsburgh	.313	52	200	179	30	56	71	9	3	0	25	0	1	2	18	0	27	4	4	7	.397	.380
Mejia, Renato, Florida	.329	65	271	240	36	79	109	13	1	5	29	0	2	2	27	0	53	10	7	2	.454	.399
Mendez, Claudio R., Seattle	.174	26	54	46	8	8	9	1	0	0	5	0	0	2	6	0	9	0	1	0	.196	.296
Mento, Alfredo, N.Y. Mets	.228	51	188	158	29	36	67	11	1	6	24	0	0	3	27	0	42	4	3	2	.424	.351
Meran, Jorge, Detroit	.270	67	276	237	36	64	96	8	3	6	41	1	3	6	29	3	52	12	8	8	.405	.360
Mercado, Henry, Cleveland	.231	32	61	52	10	12	14	2	0	0	3	0	0	4	5	0	18	4	2	0	.269	.344
Mercedes, Luis, San Francisco	.142	37	127	113	14	16	23	1	0	2	8	1	0	0	13	0	28	2	1	2	.204	.230
Mercedes, Matias, Detroit	.283	58	251	198	48	56	78	3	2	5	27	5	1	7	40	1	24	12	11	3	.394	.419
Mijares, Robert, Dodgers II	.173	34	89	75	14	13	17	2	1	0	6	0	0	0	14	0	15	5	0	5	.227	.303
Molina, Alfredo, Dodgers II	.216	34	90	74	14	16	17	1	0	0	6	3	0	1	12	0	8	1	2	4	.230	.333
Morales, Anaximando, Atlanta	.207	38	147	116	23	24	40	4	0	4	12	4	0	8	19	0	31	1	1	4	.345	.357
Morales, Cesar, San Francisco	.250	33	102	92	10	23	35	4	1	2	8	2	1	1	6	1	16	0	0	1	.380	.300
Morales, Domingo, Bal./Chi.(AL)	.311	38	114	106	15	33	42	4	1	1	14	0	0	1	7	0	7	12	4	1	.396	.360
Morelo, Fulvio, N.Y. Yankees	.207	51	122	111	13	23	33	5	1	1	12	2	3	1	5	0	9	1	1	9	.297	.242
Moreno, Antony, Houston	.226	32	116	93	10	21	26	5	0	0	6	6	0	5	12	0	11	4	3	0	.280	.345
Moreno, Johnny, Bal./Chi.(AL)	.283	55	201	184	25	52	79	11	2	4	27	1	3	1	12	1	45	10	4	3	.424	.325
Moreno, Jose, Seattle	.237	53	181	152	28	36	48	10	1	0	24	1	0	2	26	0	13	4	6	5	.316	.356
Moreno, Juan, N.Y. Mets	.360	58	264	228	59	82	137	14	1	13	36	1	1	2	32	1	24	15	10	2	.601	.441
Moreno, Willy, N.Y. Yankees	.275	21	71	51	7	14	20	3	0	1	7	0	0	0	20	1	15	2	0	1	.392	.479
Moreta, Ramon, Dodgers II	.304	67	302	253	57	77	95	8	5	0	39	5	4	2	38	1	25	31	9	6	.375	.394
Mota, Pedro, San Francisco	.236	36	128	110	11	26	34	4	2	0	13	1	1	1	15	0	24	4	1	3	.309	.331
Mota, Victor, Detroit	.193	45	136	109	14	21	36	6	3	1	29	0	1	2	24	1	33	0	3	4	.330	.346
Mundo, Alberto, Atlanta	.239	66	308	230	51	55	62	3	2	0	11	2	3	4	69	0	43	25	9	6	.270	.418
Munoz, Eduardo, Seattle	.170	20	55	47	5	8	9	1	0	0	4	2	0	2	4	0	13	1	0	5	.191	.264
Nina, Amaury, Texas	.289	37	128	114	27	33	46	7	3	0	15	0	2	3	9	1	28	5	2	1	.404	.352
Nina, Jose, Toronto	.297	43	141	118	17	35	41	2	2	0	15	2	0	1	20	0	28	7	9	3	.347	.403
Nova, Joselin, Florida	.250	60	239	224	18	56	69	11	1	0	21	1	1	2	11	1	30	0	2	8	.308	.290
Nova, Kelvin, Oakland	.209	47	179	153	29	32	45	8	1	1	14	1	3	1	21	1	23	9	4	4	.294	.303
Nunez, Abraham, Toronto	.301	54	219	186	49	56	84	10	3	4	25	1	0	2	30	1	27	24	6	4	.452	.404
Nunez, Bienvenido, San Fran.	.284	29	87	74	7	21	30	4	1	1	12	0	0	3	10	1	15	1	1	2	.405	.391
Nunez, Euripides, Bal./Chi.(AL)	.207	46	132	111	8	23	25	0	1	0	12	2	1	0	18	0	35	7	5	2	.225	.315
Nunez, Jorge, Toronto	.133	13	16	15	1	2	5	0	0	1	4	0	0	0	1	0	5	0	0	0	.333	.188
Nunez, Jose, K.C./Colo	.236	64	239	203	29	48	61	4	3	1	30	0	3	1	32	0	33	5	4	3	.300	.339
Nunez, Jose, Oakland	.225	51	176	151	26	34	58	7	1	5	29	0	2	3	20	0	62	2	2	3	.384	.324
Oliva, Osvaldo, Atlanta	.213	67	297	240	37	51	95	14	0	10	58	0	5	7	45	2	69	7	4	6	.396	.347
Olivares, Melvin, N.Y. Mets	.326	64	260	236	39	77	121	12	1	10	54	1	5	3	15	0	21	3	4	8	.513	.367
Olivero, Ricardo, Montreal	.214	40	117	98	8	21	25	4	0	0	7	2	1	0	16	1	15	2	2	1	.255	.322
Oramas, Victor, Houston	.250	20	55	48	6	12	12	0	0	0	1	0	0	0	7	1	6	1	0	1	.250	.345
Ortiz, Jose, Oakland	.300	61	254	217	45	65	108	12	2	9	41	2	3	0	32	0	22	14	7	7	.498	.385
Otano, Delvin, Toyo Carp	.306	63	290	245	51	75	112	13	3	6	60	0	2	1	42	2	30	2	3	9	.461	.407

Player, Team	Avg.	G	TPA	AB	R	H	TB	2B	3B	HR	RBI	SH	SF	HP	BB	IBB	SO	SB	CS	GDP	Slg.	OBP
Ovalle, Jesus, Texas	.230	41	105	87	11	20	23	3	0	0	8	1	1	0	16	0	6	2	3	5	.264	.346
Ovalles, Albin, K.C./Colo.	.223	53	177	139	27	31	35	4	0	0	13	0	1	5	32	1	18	4	10	6	.252	.384
Ozuna, Pedro, N.Y. Yankees	.335	57	227	182	42	61	77	10	3	0	21	0	3	2	40	1	12	6	8	10	.423	.454
Paz, Richard, Bal./Chi.(AL)	.287	67	293	230	46	66	82	8	1	2	27	1	3	4	55	3	28	18	4	7	.357	.428
Pena, Charlies, Toyo Carp	.336	68	321	241	80	81	132	27	0	8	66	0	5	9	66	2	30	17	2	4	.548	.486
Pena, Elvi, Seattle	.258	41	115	97	16	25	36	2	0	3	13	1	2	0	15	0	16	1	2	2	.371	.351
Pena, Onesimo, N.Y. Mets	.215	50	127	107	31	23	42	1	0	6	21	1	1	4	14	0	34	8	1	4	.393	.325
Pena, Ramon, Toronto	.366	59	242	213	22	78	95	11	0	2	34	0	5	8	16	3	20	3	4	6	.446	.421
Pena, Reynaldo, Detroit	.255	69	307	255	50	65	101	13	7	3	28	6	2	9	35	2	27	14	11	5	.396	.362
Pena, Victor, Phi./St.L.	.148	28	88	81	12	12	22	4	0	2	4	0	0	1	6	0	29	4	2	1	.272	.216
Pena, Warren, N.Y. Yankees	.197	41	141	117	17	23	29	6	0	0	9	0	2	3	19	1	12	1	2	2	.248	.319
Penalver, Juan, N.Y. Mets	.295	65	270	200	58	59	74	4	1	3	16	1	0	3	66	0	25	15	7	6	.370	.476
Peralta, Santiago, Toyo Carp	.276	58	261	225	46	62	90	4	9	2	46	1	3	3	29	1	35	11	4	9	.400	.362
Perdomo, Roberto, San Francisco	.139	23	82	72	10	10	12	2	0	0	4	1	0	3	6	0	16	6	2	1	.167	.235
Perez, Angelo, Toronto	.306	67	280	255	39	78	115	7	0	10	35	4	2	4	15	0	43	26	12	6	.451	.351
Perez, David, Atlanta	.166	47	164	151	5	25	28	3	0	0	17	6	1	1	5	0	35	0	0	5	.185	.196
Perez, Edwin, Cleveland	.322	63	268	239	58	77	109	9	7	3	37	2	1	3	23	2	24	14	4	4	.456	.387
Perez, Jose, Cleveland	.111	7	19	18	0	2	2	0	0	0	4	0	1	0	0	0	8	1	0	1	.111	.105
Perez, Manuel, Phi./St.L.	.273	38	102	77	21	21	24	1	1	0	3	0	1	2	22	0	12	8	7	1	.312	.441
Perez, Richard, Bal./Chi.(AL)	.307	60	264	218	48	67	90	6	4	3	21	4	2	8	32	0	32	28	14	7	.413	.412
Perez, Stiwar, Dodgers I	.306	61	257	219	32	67	103	10	1	8	42	4	3	8	23	1	44	5	1	4	.470	.387
Perez, Wegner, Cleveland	.200	26	49	45	9	9	15	3	0	1	4	0	0	3	1	0	6	0	0	2	.333	.265
Perez, Wilman, Florida	.209	36	106	91	16	19	23	4	0	0	6	1	0	1	13	0	27	7	1	0	.253	.314
Pimentel, Jose, Dodgers II	.278	66	269	223	56	62	97	17	3	4	38	2	4	8	32	3	21	24	5	8	.435	.382
Pimentel, Marino, Florida	.278	46	196	169	23	47	55	8	0	0	18	6	0	2	19	2	42	18	7	3	.325	.358
Pinales, Victor, Houston	.208	24	89	77	13	16	22	1	1	1	7	1	0	5	6	1	17	7	1	0	.286	.307
Pineda, Luis, Texas	.000	1	0	0	0	0	0	0	0	0	0	0	0	0	0	0	0	0	0	0	.000	.000
Pinedo, Hector, Phi./St.L.	.186	36	126	113	15	21	24	0	0	1	9	1	2	0	10	0	31	3	2	2	.212	.248
Polanco, Julio, Texas	.182	12	25	22	2	4	4	0	0	0	3	0	0	1	2	1	6	0	0	2	.182	.280
Polanco, Raul, Chi. (NL)/S.D.	.274	56	236	197	23	54	75	11	2	2	26	0	5	2	32	1	33	1	4	5	.381	.373
Polonia, Israel, Florida	.188	66	241	191	29	36	50	6	1	2	19	1	4	3	42	2	68	8	11	6	.262	.338
Polonio, Enrique, Pittsburgh	.312	63	282	237	48	74	91	8	0	3	24	0	5	9	31	0	24	20	13	7	.384	.404
Preciado, Victor, N.Y. Yankees	.290	57	232	210	30	61	79	15	0	1	29	1	6	1	14	0	29	1	1	10	.376	.329
Pringle, Juan, N.Y. Yankees	.248	34	107	101	13	25	34	6	0	1	15	0	0	2	4	0	24	0	0	1	.337	.290
Pujols, Rafael, Oakland	.250	49	189	168	26	42	50	6	1	0	19	3	2	3	13	1	13	3	2	4	.298	.312
Quero, Pedro, Montreal	.183	37	115	109	9	20	28	2	0	2	7	1	1	0	4	0	19	0	1	7	.257	.211
Quezada, Adalberto, San Fran.	.289	34	107	90	24	26	26	0	0	0	4	0	0	0	17	0	24	14	7	2	.289	.402
Ramirez, Aramis, Pittsburgh	.294	64	271	214	41	63	109	13	0	11	54	1	4	10	42	0	26	2	4	3	.509	.426
Ramirez, David, Texas	.148	33	72	61	6	9	10	1	0	0	3	0	1	2	8	0	14	0	2	4	.164	.264
Ramirez, Jordy, Toyo Carp	.266	41	131	109	26	29	32	3	0	0	9	3	1	4	14	0	26	5	1	2	.294	.367
Ramirez, Juan, K.C./Colo.	.210	62	247	229	22	48	56	6	1	0	27	1	3	3	11	0	20	3	2	13	.245	.252
Ramirez, Narciso, Montreal	.150	54	172	140	26	21	28	4	0	1	9	0	0	5	27	0	68	12	8	0	.200	.308
Ramirez, Rafael, Detroit	.190	48	149	116	18	22	34	7	1	1	19	2	2	3	26	0	32	2	2	1	.293	.347
Ramos, Kelly, N.Y. Mets	.253	54	175	158	18	40	56	7	0	3	24	1	4	3	9	0	28	3	3	1	.354	.299
Rebolledo, Jairo, Chi. (NL)/S.D.	.225	53	202	173	23	39	45	4	1	0	19	1	2	2	24	0	23	4	3	12	.260	.323
Renteria, Everth, Atlanta	.260	52	215	181	26	47	52	5	0	0	14	4	0	5	25	0	12	14	2	4	.287	.365
Reyes, Cristian, Oakland	.045	11	31	22	3	1	1	0	0	0	2	1	0	0	8	0	3	1	0	0	.045	.300
Reynoso, Ismael, Florida	.247	21	95	85	16	21	25	2	1	0	12	0	1	0	9	0	12	2	2	3	.294	.316
Ricardo, Alfredo, Oakland	.255	51	188	165	22	42	54	3	0	3	30	3	2	2	16	1	28	6	4	6	.327	.324
Ricardo, Luis, Dodgers I	.200	30	100	95	10	19	22	3	0	0	9	0	0	2	3	0	11	1	4	7	.232	.240
Richardson, Elbin, Texas	.283	26	67	60	9	17	25	3	1	1	10	0	0	2	5	0	11	1	0	1	.417	.358
Rios, Carlos, Houston	.261	56	215	176	25	46	65	11	1	2	25	1	2	0	36	4	26	4	5	6	.369	.383
Rivera, Juan C., Chi. (NL)/S.D.	.174	13	55	46	3	8	10	2	0	0	7	1	1	0	7	0	11	0	2	2	.217	.278
Rivera, Santo, San Francisco	.244	64	255	234	37	57	81	13	1	3	30	1	0	5	15	0	36	4	3	6	.346	.303
Rivera, Yorki, Dodgers I	.201	53	214	169	33	34	45	7	2	0	13	3	2	1	39	0	32	10	1	3	.266	.351
Robles, Victor, Bal./Chi.(AL)	.208	40	117	101	17	21	32	1	2	2	13	1	0	3	12	0	39	2	1	0	.317	.310
Rodriguez, Alfredo, Dodgers II	.321	35	121	106	19	34	49	6	0	3	31	0	0	4	11	0	22	0	1	2	.462	.405
Rodriguez, Felipe, Toronto	.267	52	213	165	48	44	51	3	2	0	5	2	1	7	38	0	36	42	11	0	.309	.422
Rodriguez, Geremias, Toyo Carp	.243	66	312	235	71	57	78	9	3	2	25	5	5	8	59	0	22	16	2	5	.332	.404
Rodriguez, Jose, Florida	.201	46	152	134	18	27	41	3	1	3	13	2	0	3	13	0	56	8	0	2	.306	.287
Rodriguez, Juan, Pittsburgh	.270	58	214	178	36	48	74	8	3	4	25	3	1	2	30	1	34	9	4	3	.416	.379
Rodriguez, Miguel, Phi./St.L.	.375	40	170	144	31	54	75	13	1	2	28	1	3	2	20	1	16	11	5	1	.521	.450
Rodriguez, Nelson, Dodgers I	.197	49	157	127	23	25	33	4	2	0	11	1	0	2	27	0	23	5	2	10	.260	.346
Romero, Mario, Houston	.207	13	35	29	4	6	8	2	0	0	1	1	0	2	3	0	11	2	2	1	.276	.324
Romero, Robinson, N.Y. Yankees	.257	43	117	101	11	26	42	1	0	5	19	0	1	3	12	0	19	1	0	5	.416	.350
Rondon, Jhonny, Seattle	.309	40	72	55	20	17	25	4	2	0	5	0	0	1	16	1	15	2	2	2	.455	.472
Rosario, Carlos, K.C./Colo.	.313	61	249	217	31	68	85	8	3	1	32	0	1	1	30	6	43	6	10	4	.392	.398
Rosario, Ramon, Houston	.241	28	96	83	10	20	29	3	0	2	13	0	2	3	8	0	12	4	0	5	.349	.323
Ruiz, Francis, Toyo Carp	.257	60	265	218	52	56	75	9	2	2	38	1	2	2	42	0	38	15	3	4	.344	.379
Ruiz, Jose, Seattle	.260	54	177	150	28	39	69	7	1	7	27	2	1	1	23	0	50	2	4	4	.460	.360
Salazar, Oscar, Oakland	.271	53	194	166	29	45	57	10	1	0	23	2	3	1	22	0	23	5	5	4	.343	.354
Samuel, Yojairo, Texas	.000	1	1	1	0	0	0	0	0	0	0	0	0	0	0	0	0	0	0	0	.000	.000
Sanchez, Jose, Detroit	.171	25	43	35	6	6	8	0	1	0	2	1	0	1	6	0	9	0	0	1	.229	.310
Sanchez, Manuel, Atlanta	.249	57	241	197	34	49	75	12	7	0	21	5	1	7	31	1	25	9	4	2	.381	.369
Sanchez, Willington, Toronto	.100	12	22	20	3	2	2	0	0	0	0	0	0	0	2	0	4	2	1	1	.100	.182
Sanquintin, Alexis, Cleveland	.107	12	31	28	2	3	3	0	0	0	1	0	0	0	3	0	0	0	0	1	.107	.194
Santana, Juan, Dodgers II	.213	50	193	164	24	35	47	7	1	1	16	5	0	5	19	0	20	4	2	4	.287	.314
Santana, Luis, Dodgers II	.231	34	105	91	15	21	27	6	0	0	10	1	1	1	11	1	20	0	0	3	.297	.317
Santana, Mario, California	.240	57	230	183	22	44	51	2	1	1	24	0	0	2	45	1	16	9	3	4	.279	.396
Santana, Pedro, Houston	.288	52	221	184	39	53	67	6	1	2	14	2	1	3	31	0	29	34	4	1	.364	.397
Santana, Ramon, K.C./Colo.	.209	52	178	148	25	31	33	2	0	0	15	1	0	2	27	0	23	13	9	4	.223	.339
Santana, Richard, K.C./Colo.	.212	49	154	137	13	29	35	3	0	1	14	3	4	0	10	0	19	4	4	3	.255	.258
Santelise, Osvaldo, Bal./Chi.(AL)	.232	51	175	155	18	36	60	5	2	5	28	0	0	1	19	1	47	0	0	0	.381	.320

Player, Team	Avg.	G	TPA	AB	R	H	TB	2B	3B	HR	RBI	SH	SF	HP	BB	IBB	SO	SB	CS	GDP	Slg.	OBP
Santos, Jose, California	.320	12	27	25	5	8	11	0	0	1	5	0	0	0	2	0	9	0	0	0	.440	.370
Santos, Jose, Texas	.304	56	249	184	53	56	96	10	3	8	39	0	2	6	57	0	41	9	5	4	.522	.478
Saturria, Arturo, Phi./St.L.	.318	66	283	245	48	78	114	16	7	2	33	0	2	2	34	1	26	12	7	5	.465	.403
Scuttaro, Marco, Cleveland	.393	66	296	262	71	103	133	18	6	0	38	2	4	8	20	1	11	32	11	4	.508	.446
Segura, Winston, Texas	.292	37	103	89	14	26	31	5	0	0	11	0	1	1	12	1	13	8	3	4	.348	.379
Sencion, Pablo, Toronto	.297	68	299	249	58	74	137	22	1	13	53	0	0	3	47	4	49	3	2	6	.550	.415
Severino, Danny, Florida	.275	68	295	258	28	71	98	9	3	4	45	1	4	8	24	0	51	8	9	8	.380	.350
Shinozuka, Takeiro, Montreal	.286	4	14	14	1	4	4	0	0	0	0	0	0	0	0	0	0	0	0	0	.286	.286
Sierra, Henry, N.Y. Mets	.193	42	132	119	17	23	32	3	0	2	8	1	0	0	12	1	23	4	2	5	.269	.267
Silverio, Richard, K.C./Colo.	.211	5	19	19	2	4	6	0	1	0	1	0	0	0	0	0	4	1	0	0	.316	.211
Silvestre, Juan, Seattle	.287	59	234	209	38	60	103	4	3	11	43	0	1	1	23	2	46	0	3	7	.493	.359
Smith, Nestor, N.Y. Yankees	.220	56	240	182	31	40	44	4	0	0	12	1	0	11	46	0	51	42	17	4	.242	.406
Solano, Joel, Toronto	.042	20	30	24	6	1	1	0	0	0	2	1	1	1	3	0	6	0	2	0	.042	.172
Sosa, Henry, Florida	.000	1	0	0	0	0	0	0	0	0	0	0	0	0	0	0	0	0	0	0	.000	.000
Sosa, Jorge, K.C./Colo.	.253	32	100	91	10	23	26	3	0	0	1	0	0	1	8	0	26	1	6	4	.286	.320
Sosa, Leonel, Dodgers I	.253	31	82	79	10	20	22	2	0	0	9	0	0	0	3	1	8	1	1	0	.278	.280
Soto, Luis, Chi. (NL)/S.D.	.222	50	189	158	20	35	46	3	1	2	21	1	2	0	28	0	32	0	1	7	.291	.335
Suero, Ignacio, Toronto	.333	65	275	243	37	81	139	13	0	15	61	1	2	7	22	3	20	2	3	8	.572	.401
Suriel, Miguel, Dodgers I	.295	57	242	210	28	62	89	11	2	4	47	0	8	1	23	0	17	2	1	8	.424	.355
Tavarez, Carlos, Seattle	.235	41	114	98	10	23	28	5	0	0	4	2	0	0	14	0	16	1	2	1	.286	.330
Taveras, Frank, Cleveland	.254	65	270	236	42	60	88	11	7	1	45	6	4	1	23	1	46	9	6	0	.373	.318
Taveras, Jose, K.C./Colo.	.315	54	201	178	35	56	87	8	4	5	24	1	3	4	15	0	27	12	8	3	.489	.375
Taveras, Luis, Texas	.161	37	118	87	17	14	18	2	1	0	8	2	2	1	26	0	13	2	1	4	.207	.353
Thomas, Wilson, N.Y. Yankees	.233	41	139	120	16	28	48	6	1	4	11	1	1	0	17	0	26	0	1	3	.400	.326
Tobias, Enrique, Dodgers I	.235	28	95	85	9	20	29	6	0	1	6	1	1	4	4	0	20	0	0	3	.341	.298
Tolentino, Juan, California	.270	48	164	137	27	37	53	5	1	3	11	1	1	3	22	0	30	5	5	2	.387	.380
Torres, Jairo, Bal./Chi.(AL)	.229	13	44	35	4	8	8	0	0	0	3	0	1	1	7	0	4	0	0	3	.229	.364
Toussent, Andres, Toronto	.000	3	3	2	0	0	0	0	0	0	0	0	0	0	1	0	1	0	0	0	.000	.333
Trinidad, Cesar, San Francisco	.258	44	141	128	19	33	45	8	2	0	19	3	2	1	7	0	17	1	2	2	.344	.297
Ubiera, Nadin, Toyo Carp	.243	56	217	169	32	41	59	6	3	2	24	0	6	2	40	1	31	5	3	1	.349	.382
Ubiera, Vinicio, Dodgers II	.294	30	98	85	15	25	37	5	2	1	12	1	0	0	12	2	9	0	1	1	.435	.381
Urquiola, Edgar, Montreal	.241	47	145	116	24	28	39	4	2	1	11	0	0	4	25	0	14	11	5	1	.336	.393
Valderrama, Carlos, San Fran.	.228	22	63	57	7	13	14	1	0	0	4	0	0	0	6	0	10	1	2	0	.246	.302
Valdez, Alvaro, Cleveland	.273	42	146	132	23	36	44	4	2	0	17	3	0	0	11	0	11	4	1	4	.333	.329
Valdez, Jose, Phi./St.L.	.157	35	123	102	24	16	19	3	0	0	5	1	0	9	11	0	26	4	4	1	.186	.295
Valdez, Socrates, Dodgers I	.273	51	217	187	37	51	77	10	2	4	36	0	0	3	27	5	23	3	4	5	.412	.373
Valera, Ramon, Seattle	.347	59	261	202	50	70	88	6	3	2	20	7	2	3	47	0	23	46	20	3	.436	.472
Vals, Lucrecio, Bal./Chi.(AL)	.211	58	223	199	28	42	47	5	0	0	19	3	1	1	19	0	49	13	6	5	.236	.282
Vargas, Iankel, Detroit	.246	58	222	175	29	43	54	7	2	0	26	3	5	2	37	2	30	7	1	7	.309	.374
Vasquez, Alejandro, Houston	.174	31	105	92	12	16	21	5	0	0	8	0	1	2	10	0	12	2	0	3	.228	.267
Vasquez, Arnulfo, Cleveland	.333	17	62	51	8	17	27	4	0	2	13	1	1	1	8	0	14	1	0	1	.529	.426
Vasquez, Jose, Oakland	.243	56	205	177	28	43	65	9	5	1	29	0	1	1	26	2	36	6	7	4	.367	.341
Vasquez, Moises, California	.203	23	63	59	3	12	20	1	2	1	3	0	0	0	4	1	14	3	0	0	.339	.254
Velasquez, Geovanny, California	.221	32	117	95	18	21	28	3	2	0	12	1	0	0	21	0	8	4	1	5	.295	.362
Ventura, Frank, Cleveland	.266	59	218	184	33	49	72	12	1	3	34	1	4	3	26	0	22	13	5	5	.391	.359
Ventura, Jose, California	.232	24	67	56	12	13	19	1	1	1	5	0	0	1	10	0	16	3	2	1	.339	.358
Vilomar, Henry, N.Y. Mets	.250	54	221	188	33	47	83	7	1	9	38	2	3	3	25	1	43	11	7	7	.441	.342
Virgil, Marcus, California	.222	30	95	81	6	18	21	3	0	0	7	1	1	1	11	0	10	4	2	0	.259	.319
Williams, Johanny, Phi./St.L.	.193	44	149	140	10	27	43	10	0	2	19	2	0	1	6	2	32	0	5	5	.307	.231
Zamora, Junior, N.Y. Mets	.261	33	135	111	14	29	43	8	0	2	19	0	2	4	18	0	20	2	1	3	.387	.378

1995 PITCHING

TEAM

Team	W	L	Pct.	ERA	G	CG	ShO	Sv.	IP	H	TBF	R	ER	HR	SH	SF	HB	BB	IBB	SO	WP	Bk.
Cleveland	48	20	.706	2.84	69	2	5	23	605.1	512	2528	293	191	16	19	19	29	221	5	417	48	4
Toyo Carp	58	13	.817	2.95	71	19	5	20	617.0	524	2679	288	202	23	14	17	45	278	2	408	40	13
Oakland	44	21	.677	3.17	66	11	5	15	572.2	536	2493	286	202	22	20	21	20	250	6	393	55	5
Toronto	44	24	.647	3.54	68	2	2	25	589.1	533	2559	308	232	33	13	13	37	305	6	476	35	7
California	31	39	.443	3.62	71	15	0	13	604.1	543	2714	372	243	24	15	21	45	313	5	421	45	22
Detroit	34	34	.500	3.80	69	5	3	14	600.0	626	2711	353	253	22	25	20	37	292	27	448	55	12
Dodgers II	44	25	.638	3.81	69	5	5	14	592.1	564	2680	355	251	22	15	25	48	311	10	380	51	18
Texas	39	28	.582	3.94	67	5	4	14	556.2	542	2492	311	244	34	22	21	30	278	12	327	41	5
Seattle	45	21	.682	4.07	66	2	4	20	562.1	454	2513	329	254	47	18	26	47	386	7	477	55	12
Florida	26	42	.382	4.24	68	1	0	11	573.2	579	2630	372	270	30	18	18	57	352	4	411	91	12
N.Y. Mets	41	27	.603	4.26	68	5	1	19	581.1	646	2564	355	275	69	14	15	36	201	10	426	44	10
N.Y. Yankees	31	37	.456	4.31	68	1	2	11	580.2	522	2645	360	278	39	10	13	52	393	1	482	56	11
Hou./Mil.	28	39	.418	4.35	68	2	1	12	594.1	533	2728	390	287	16	25	19	55	395	15	430	99	30
Bal./Chi. (AL)	29	41	.414	4.59	70	10	0	9	594.1	594	2630	432	303	53	17	22	49	336	2	403	55	9
Pittsburgh	30	36	.455	4.82	66	12	3	9	557.0	578	2538	373	298	46	9	21	34	294	7	485	75	13
K.C./Colo.	24	40	.375	4.96	65	2	2	14	566.0	646	2616	446	312	27	15	30	46	236	12	281	77	8
Dodgers I	28	36	.438	4.99	64	1	2	10	542.2	613	2582	395	301	19	21	23	43	360	27	322	70	8
Montreal	21	47	.309	5.08	69	6	0	10	597.0	614	2769	435	337	38	14	30	51	398	16	429	54	10
Phil./St.L.	25	44	.362	5.10	69	1	0	14	586.1	680	2745	486	332	17	14	36	43	291	5	339	81	5
San Francisco	27	44	.380	5.23	71	6	0	10	588.1	650	2922	497	342	18	22	22	62	385	12	360	96	14
Atlanta	26	44	.371	5.30	70	6	0	14	600.1	664	2879	492	354	27	25	25	58	386	15	427	70	10
Chi. (NL)/S.D.	22	45	.328	5.72	68	4	1	9	561.1	651	2653	475	357	40	21	33	35	331	2	344	76	10

INDIVIDUAL

TOP QUALIFIERS FOR EARNED-RUN AVERAGE TITLE

Pitcher, Team	W	L	Pct.	ERA	G	GS	CG	ShO	GF	Sv.	IP	H	TBF	R	ER	HR	SH	SF	HB	BB	IBB	SO	WP	Bk.
Patino, Leonardo, California	5	4	.556	1.35	21	6	2	0	12	3	73.1	56	303	26	11	2	3	1	2	28	2	63	4	3
Guzman, Wilson, Pittsburgh	5	0	1.000	1.47	16	6	1	0	9	4	55.0	52	231	17	9	3	0	1	1	17	2	48	2	1
DeLaCruz, Francisco, Toyo Carp	11	1	.917	1.56	16	13	9	2	1	1	103.2	73	419	26	18	0	0	1	7	31	0	80	5	1
Petique, Marino, Toyo Carp	10	1	.909	1.61	16	12	3	1	2	2	84.0	65	350	29	15	2	4	4	3	32	0	41	1	4
Henriquez, Roman, Dodgers I	8	4	.667	1.81	37	0	0	0	33	8	59.2	56	271	21	12	0	8	3	8	31	5	40	3	1
Mota, Henry, Texas	6	3	.667	1.85	29	4	0	0	23	8	63.1	48	249	19	13	1	4	4	5	12	0	57	4	0
Baez, Miguel, Cleveland	7	2	.778	1.99	15	15	1	1	0	0	95.0	64	369	34	21	0	3	0	6	24	0	74	5	0
Garcia, Jose, Cleveland	6	2	.750	2.02	19	10	0	0	6	2	71.1	60	289	27	16	1	3	1	4	16	1	67	7	0
Ortiz, Ramon, California	8	6	.571	2.23	16	16	7	0	0	0	97.0	79	466	44	24	2	1	2	3	54	0	100	6	2
Zapata, Juan, Houston	5	4	.556	2.31	13	13	1	1	0	0	81.2	60	353	40	21	1	1	1	4	43	1	60	10	0

ALL PITCHERS

Pitcher, Team	W	L	Pct.	ERA	G	GS	CG	ShO	GF	Sv.	IP	H	TBF	R	ER	HR	SH	SF	HB	BB	IBB	SO	WP	Bk.
Aguilar, Henry, California	3	8	.273	3.77	17	15	2	0	2	2	88.1	85	391	64	37	4	3	3	10	40	1	49	3	3
Almonte, Aquiles, Oakland	0	0	.000	0.00	3	0	0	0	3	1	6.0	3	22	0	0	0	0	0	0	3	0	6	0	0
Almonte, Hector, Florida	1	2	.333	4.26	20	1	0	0	16	9	31.2	28	129	17	15	0	1	2	6	11	0	27	3	0
Alvino, Roger, Chi. (NL)/S.D.	2	5	.286	6.02	25	3	0	0	15	8	52.1	46	240	47	35	6	3	5	3	36	1	48	14	0
Andrade, Jensy, Bal./Chi.(AL)	2	1	.667	4.66	6	3	0	0	3	1	19.1	20	91	11	10	1	2	0	1	13	0	15	3	3
Andujar, Elias, Atlanta	2	7	.222	6.28	16	10	2	0	5	0	67.1	85	325	61	47	8	1	4	7	32	0	36	9	2
Aquino, Cleto, Seattle	1	2	.333	11.57	11	2	0	0	4	0	14.0	19	83	21	18	1	0	0	1	24	0	9	4	0
Aracena, Juan, Cleveland	6	2	.750	2.06	24	3	0	0	15	5	56.2	39	224	19	13	0	0	3	4	18	0	31	5	0
Aracena, Ramon, Toyo Carp	7	3	.700	3.68	24	7	2	0	16	6	63.2	66	289	33	26	5	2	1	1	31	1	58	5	1
Arias, Cesarin, Chi. (NL)/S.D.	3	3	.500	5.15	12	12	2	0	0	0	57.2	68	257	44	33	3	2	3	3	14	0	33	1	1
Arias, Jose, Phi./St.L.	7	7	.500	5.31	18	17	1	0	0	0	81.1	98	383	73	48	0	1	2	5	49	0	42	10	0
Arias, Jose, N.Y. Yankees	0	1	.000	13.51	6	1	0	0	2	0	7.1	6	42	13	11	1	0	0	1	16	0	4	3	0
Arias, Kelvin, N.Y. Mets	1	2	.333	5.28	13	4	0	0	3	1	30.2	32	134	21	18	5	1	0	2	12	0	18	4	2
Arias, Miguel, Dodgers II	3	1	.750	1.82	10	8	0	1	0	0	49.1	36	207	12	10	0	1	0	6	22	0	34	3	0
Arias, Rafael, Chi. (NL)/S.D.	0	3	.000	13.74	8	4	0	0	0	0	19.0	35	114	39	29	3	3	2	1	21	0	6	2	0
Arias, Rafael, San Francisco	6	2	.750	3.79	16	10	1	0	1	0	73.2	73	336	49	31	3	2	4	10	31	1	38	8	1
Arias, Roberto, N.Y. Mets	5	2	.714	5.12	13	13	1	0	0	0	63.1	76	279	40	36	9	0	1	4	23	0	43	8	0
Asencio, Eddy, Detroit	3	3	.500	3.06	19	7	1	0	9	1	70.2	76	309	36	24	7	4	2	2	19	3	49	4	1
Avila, Jose, Pittsburgh	6	4	.600	3.09	14	14	4	2	0	0	90.1	73	364	35	31	4	0	1	5	27	0	95	8	0
Baez, Jose, Pittsburgh	0	3	.000	6.62	17	1	0	0	6	0	34.0	47	171	35	25	3	1	0	2	16	2	25	4	3
Baez, Miguel, Cleveland	7	2	.778	1.99	15	15	1	1	0	0	95.0	64	369	34	21	0	3	0	6	24	0	74	5	0
Balbuena, Martin, K.C./Colo.	5	6	.455	3.66	19	9	1	1	3	0	83.2	95	367	51	34	2	3	1	3	34	5	46	8	1
Baruch, Jaime, Montreal	0	2	.000	5.65	8	2	0	0	4	0	14.1	10	70	10	9	0	2	0	2	16	0	11	2	1
Belliard, Carlos, Dodgers II	7	3	.700	3.08	15	13	1	3	2	0	79.0	68	327	35	27	6	2	1	1	31	0	54	4	2
Bello, Emerson, Seattle	7	2	.778	2.80	13	13	1	0	0	0	83.2	72	353	33	26	4	3	2	2	33	1	76	5	1
Betancourt, William, Cleveland	6	2	.750	3.21	13	13	0	0	0	0	67.1	61	285	35	24	1	1	0	1	28	0	48	5	1
Bezhodashvila, N., California	0	1	.000	11.77	8	1	0	0	4	1	13.0	19	74	20	17	1	0	3	1	25	0	12	4	2
Blanco, Daniel, San Francisco	0	0	.000	0.00	1	0	0	0	1	0	1.0	0	6	0	0	0	0	0	0	3	0	0	1	0
Blanco, Fabian, Dodgers II	4	3	.571	4.02	14	13	1	0	1	0	62.2	59	288	45	28	2	0	4	6	38	1	56	10	3
Blanco, Pablo, Florida	3	5	.375	5.36	11	8	0	0	0	0	50.1	48	235	40	30	2	2	4	6	39	0	32	14	1
Blanco Veras, Johanny, Cleveland	3	1	.750	2.91	21	0	0	0	11	6	43.1	36	179	19	14	3	1	1	1	14	1	32	8	0
Bracho, Alejandro, N.Y. Yankees	6	2	.750	2.83	11	11	0	0	0	0	60.1	48	247	22	19	5	1	1	1	30	0	49	0	1
Brand, Fausto, Atlanta	1	7	.125	6.79	12	12	0	0	0	0	51.2	62	258	59	39	0	0	2	6	31	1	38	4	3
Bravo, Luis, Cleveland	1	0	1.000	2.25	1	0	0	0	0	0	4.0	4	15	1	1	0	0	0	0	1	0	3	0	0
Brazoban, Melvin, Texas	3	2	.600	5.57	7	7	0	0	0	0	32.1	30	145	25	20	1	2	2	1	20	0	27	1	0
Brea, Ramsey, Detroit	2	2	.500	4.71	7	7	0	0	0	0	36.1	32	167	29	19	0	1	0	2	27	0	25	5	2
Brito, Jose, California	0	0	.000	6.75	3	1	0	0	0	0	8.0	8	40	8	6	2	0	0	1	3	0	6	4	0
Cabral, Martires, Toronto	2	0	1.000	2.61	15	0	0	0	8	0	20.2	15	89	9	6	1	0	1	2	13	0	20	0	1
Caceres, Antonio, Toronto	3	6	.333	4.72	13	13	0	0	0	0	68.2	75	311	45	36	7	2	6	2	30	0	32	6	0
Cadet, Javier, Chi. (NL)/S.D.	1	0	1.000	5.11	18	1	0	0	12	1	24.2	29	121	17	14	0	0	2	0	21	0	12	4	0
Calderon, Ramon, San Francisco	2	5	.286	3.51	19	7	1	0	3	1	59.0	66	274	40	23	0	4	1	6	25	2	19	6	1
Carela, Jesus, Oakland	0	0	.000	0.00	1	0	0	0	0	0	1.2	1	8	1	0	0	0	0	1	1	0	3	0	0
Cariolan, Roberto, N.Y. Yankees	3	4	.429	5.01	16	7	0	0	4	1	41.1	31	194	28	23	4	1	0	5	39	0	53	6	2
Carjaval, Tomas, California	1	0	1.000	1.80	3	0	0	0	3	1	5.0	3	18	1	1	1	1	0	0	2	0	2	0	0
Carrasquel, Alejandro, Montreal	0	4	.000	8.07	24	0	0	0	15	3	35.2	41	185	40	32	4	3	0	2	40	2	22	8	1
Carrion, Jorge, Houston	1	1	.500	9.52	5	0	0	0	3	0	5.2	6	28	6	6	0	1	0	1	5	1	5	1	0
Carty, Henry, Texas	0	0	.000	0.00	1	0	0	0	0	0	0.2	0	2	0	0	0	0	0	0	0	0	1	0	0
Castillo, Daniel A., Dodgers I	0	1	.000	3.68	3	3	0	0	0	0	7.1	11	36	7	3	0	0	0	0	2	0	1	0	0
Castillo, Jose, Detroit	2	1	.667	3.68	21	0	0	0	12	3	36.2	38	163	18	15	1	2	4	3	15	1	18	1	1
Castillo, Victor, Toronto	0	0	.000	4.50	1	0	0	0	1	0	2.0	3	11	3	1	0	0	0	0	1	0	2	0	0
Castro, Eleuterio, Toyo Carp	0	0	.000	3.86	5	0	0	0	3	2	9.1	8	42	4	4	2	0	0	1	5	0	4	0	0
Celta, Nicolas, Houston	3	8	.273	5.66	16	14	1	0	0	0	70.0	60	318	56	44	2	3	5	5	53	0	61	17	7
Cera, Aquiles, Dodgers II	3	1	.750	4.30	16	3	1	0	7	2	52.1	58	249	36	25	2	3	4	8	24	2	39	1	1
Coco, Pascual, Toronto	7	1	.875	2.78	11	11	0	0	0	0	58.1	51	265	30	18	2	0	1	8	36	0	38	2	1
Collado, Hugo, Dodgers I	0	0	.000	1.29	6	0	0	0	1	0	7.0	7	34	3	1	0	1	0	0	4	0	4	1	0
Contreras, Angel, Pittsburgh	1	2	.333	6.75	9	0	0	0	3	0	14.2	16	75	13	11	1	2	1	1	15	1	9	8	0
Corniell, Henry, Oakland	0	0	.000	13.50	2	1	0	0	0	0	4.0	7	23	6	6	0	0	1	0	4	0	1	0	0
Cornielle, Alex, Toyo Carp	1	0	1.000	6.41	15	0	0	0	7	2	26.2	39	138	24	19	1	1	3	1	13	0	9	1	2
Cota, Marino, Dodgers II	4	3	.571	4.24	22	0	0	0	20	8	34.0	30	154	21	16	0	4	3	2	10	1	23	0	1
Cruz, Charlie, Dodgers I	0	0	.000	7.59	7	1	0	0	3	0	10.2	11	57	11	9	0	0	2	1	13	0	2	3	0
Cruz, Raul, Oakland	1	1	.500	1.93	10	0	0	0	5	0	18.2	9	82	6	4	0	2	0	2	13	1	12	5	0
Cueto, Jose, Seattle	6	1	.857	3.06	13	13	0	0	0	0	67.2	56	292	36	23	4	2	5	8	31	0	56	4	3
Dacosta, Samuel, Montreal	0	1	.000	7.15	5	0	0	0	3	0	11.1	15	57	12	9	1	0	1	0	11	0	5	0	0
Davis, Melvin, San Francisco	0	2	.000	4.82	7	0	0	0	1	0	9.1	6	53	8	5	0	1	0	2	14	0	15	1	0
DeLaCruz, Fernando, California	3	5	.375	7.09	10	8	0	0	1	0	39.1	36	198	43	31	0	0	1	1	45	1	49	4	1

Pitcher, Team	W	L	Pct.	ERA	G	GS	CG	ShO	GF	Sv.	IP	H	TBF	R	ER	HR	SH	SF	HB	BB	IBB	SO	WP	Bk.
DeLaCruz, Francisco, Toyo Carp	11	1	.917	1.56	16	13	9	2	1	1	103.2	73	419	26	18	0	0	1	7	31	0	80	5	1
DeLaCruz, Inocencio, N.Y. Mets	5	1	.833	3.38	14	13	3	0	0	0	69.1	69	299	36	26	9	1	1	4	24	1	60	4	3
DeLeon, Jose, Detroit	0	1	.000	9.00	1	0	0	0	0	0	2.0	3	11	3	2	0	0	0	0	2	0	1	3	0
DeLeon, Jose, Phi./St.L.	2	3	.400	4.19	24	4	0	0	4	1	73.0	95	337	53	34	3	3	5	2	19	0	40	7	1
DeLeon, Julio, N.Y. Yankees	4	5	.444	5.61	12	12	1	0	0	0	59.1	63	271	47	37	5	1	1	5	31	0	43	6	1
Delgado, Manuel, Toronto	4	4	.500	2.36	25	2	0	0	17	9	53.1	34	212	19	14	2	1	1	2	15	1	60	2	0
Deliza, Angel, Chi. (NL)/S.D.	1	4	.200	6.47	14	0	0	0	7	0	32.0	45	157	29	23	3	0	3	3	18	0	17	5	1
Del Orbe, Wellington, Cleveland	3	2	.600	4.30	14	0	0	0	4	0	23.0	21	102	15	11	1	0	0	1	10	0	8	1	0
DeLosSantos, A., K.C./Colo.	2	3	.400	6.38	22	9	0	0	2	1	66.1	71	309	58	47	6	0	1	7	32	0	38	5	2
DeLosSantos, D., K.C./Colo.	3	4	.429	7.44	26	1	0	0	13	0	42.1	67	207	45	35	2	1	4	2	14	0	19	5	0
DeLosSantos, Luis, N.Y. Yankees	3	4	.429	3.92	12	11	0	0	0	0	64.1	64	288	41	28	1	1	3	5	27	0	40	6	1
Diaz, Esteban, Dodgers I	0	3	.000	4.31	12	10	0	0	2	0	48.0	47	213	28	23	1	2	0	1	31	1	28	2	2
Diese, Jose, Toyo Carp	6	1	.857	2.33	12	10	0	1	1	0	54.0	39	241	27	14	1	1	1	3	36	0	51	11	4
Disla, Francisco, N.Y. Yankees	2	3	.400	2.62	9	9	0	0	0	0	34.1	19	150	15	10	1	1	0	3	31	0	32	0	0
D'LaCruz, Ignacio, San Francisco	1	3	.250	8.33	20	3	0	0	7	0	31.1	39	160	33	29	1	0	2	2	29	1	15	4	2
Dotel, Melido, Dodgers II	4	5	.444	4.91	13	13	1	0	0	0	58.2	52	263	42	32	2	2	2	5	43	0	25	6	0
Ernesto, Hector, Florida	1	1	.500	5.59	16	1	0	0	6	0	46.2	60	217	35	29	5	1	1	6	19	0	22	5	1
Escarlante, Simon, Phi./St.L.	1	9	.100	5.35	19	11	0	0	7	1	72.1	86	345	74	43	4	4	4	1	41	1	39	18	0
Escobar, Kelvin, Toronto	0	1	.000	1.72	3	2	0	0	0	0	15.2	14	62	3	3	0	0	0	0	5	1	20	0	0
Espinal, Orlando, Montreal	0	3	.000	5.59	14	6	0	0	3	0	37.0	30	181	28	23	0	0	1	9	33	0	20	3	2
Esquea, Alvin, Texas	0	0	.000	....	1	0	0	0	0	0	0.0	0	3	2	2	0	0	0	0	3	0	0	0	0
Estrella, Leoncio, N.Y. Mets	2	4	.333	5.44	12	8	0	0	1	0	43.0	61	202	37	26	5	0	4	4	13	0	32	6	2
Felix, Miguel, Bal./Chi.(AL)	3	5	.375	4.94	15	14	1	0	1	0	82.0	77	380	61	45	4	2	4	13	49	0	47	10	0
Felix, Osvaldo, K.C./Colo.	0	0	.000	9.00	5	0	0	0	1	0	5.0	10	29	7	5	1	0	1	0	2	0	3	0	0
Fernandez, Robert, Cleveland	2	0	1.000	3.94	6	3	0	0	1	0	16.0	9	71	10	7	0	0	0	2	16	0	14	2	0
Fernandez, Winston, Texas	0	0	.000	0.00	1	0	0	0	1	0	0.1	1	3	1	0	0	0	0	0	0	0	0	1	0
Florentino, Osmil, K.C./Colo.	0	0	.000	7.36	2	0	0	0	0	0	3.2	5	18	5	3	0	1	0	0	3	0	2	2	0
Francisco, Norberto, Bal./Chi.(AL)	0	0	.000	4.82	5	1	0	0	0	0	9.1	8	48	8	5	1	0	1	2	12	0	6	1	0
Frias, Jovanny, Bal./Chi.(AL)	1	6	.143	4.67	13	12	0	0	1	0	71.1	86	318	52	37	7	1	0	4	28	0	34	0	2
Fructuoso, Jose, Seattle	2	2	.500	3.13	7	6	0	0	1	1	23.0	16	96	9	8	3	0	0	1	12	0	17	1	1
Galvez, Randy, Dodgers I	5	5	.500	4.27	32	0	0	0	13	2	65.1	67	285	38	31	3	1	4	3	31	6	48	4	4
Garcia, Espedy, Oakland	1	2	.333	9.15	8	5	0	0	3	0	19.2	16	102	26	20	2	1	1	1	24	0	28	4	0
Garcia, Jhoan, Seattle	1	2	.333	5.96	20	1	0	0	4	1	25.2	23	127	23	17	1	1	4	4	27	0	19	2	1
Garcia, Jose, Cleveland	6	2	.750	2.02	19	10	0	0	6	2	71.1	60	289	27	16	1	3	1	4	16	1	67	7	0
Garcia, Rafael, Seattle	3	1	.750	4.84	18	5	0	0	1	0	48.1	35	216	32	26	6	2	3	4	42	0	40	3	0
Genao, Henry, Cleveland	0	0	.000	8.38	8	0	0	0	4	0	9.2	13	58	14	9	1	0	0	1	16	0	5	1	0
Genao, Martin, Dodgers II	4	2	.667	3.29	17	3	0	0	8	2	52.0	58	233	26	19	0	0	0	5	19	1	30	3	2
German, John, N.Y. Mets	6	2	.750	4.99	18	9	0	0	3	2	52.1	65	243	34	29	8	0	2	5	23	1	32	4	0
German, Julio, Detroit	0	0	.000	0.00	1	0	0	0	0	0	1.0	0	4	0	0	0	0	1	0	1	0	0	0	0
Glaterol, Becker, Toronto	4	3	.571	4.00	23	6	0	0	14	10	65.1	61	274	33	29	2	1	0	2	23	1	69	3	0
Gomez, Domingo, California	0	1	.000	3.35	18	0	0	0	13	5	48.1	39	163	23	18	1	1	6	2	17	0	8	0	2
Gomez, Jose, Seattle	4	3	.571	4.60	23	1	0	0	4	0	45.0	37	208	36	23	6	1	2	5	35	0	19	5	3
Gomez, Luis, Detroit	2	1	.667	4.68	17	0	0	0	8	0	25.0	22	126	23	13	0	3	2	3	26	2	17	7	0
Gomez, Luis, Houston	0	0	.000	3.86	7	0	0	0	3	0	9.1	8	42	7	4	1	0	0	2	2	0	3	0	0
Gomez, Manuel, Detroit	3	4	.429	3.30	21	4	0	0	9	6	46.1	43	206	22	17	2	3	1	2	23	7	49	2	1
Gomez, Miguel, Toronto	2	0	1.000	1.23	3	3	2	0	0	0	22.0	14	81	6	3	2	0	0	2	5	0	19	1	0
Gomez, Rafael, N.Y. Mets	3	4	.429	4.01	17	2	0	0	8	2	42.2	49	177	21	19	3	0	2	3	6	1	39	2	0
Gomez, Ricardo, Pittsburgh	2	3	.400	8.14	11	3	0	0	3	1	24.1	32	115	24	22	4	1	1	1	15	0	20	6	0
Gondola, Roberto, N.Y. Yankees	1	2	.333	3.37	15	0	0	0	3	1	34.2	37	155	19	13	1	0	2	1	19	0	38	6	1
Gonzalez, Edwin, K.C./Colo.	3	1	.750	2.66	35	0	0	0	28	10	50.2	55	232	27	15	2	1	5	4	19	3	40	10	0
Gonzalez, Elin, K.C./Colo.	0	0	.000	32.34	1	1	0	0	0	0	1.2	7	15	6	6	1	0	0	0	4	0	0	0	0
Guerra, Robert, California	0	0	.000	0.00	2	0	0	0	2	0	0.2	1	2	0	0	0	0	0	0	0	0	0	0	0
Guerrero, Jose, Seattle	4	1	.800	2.09	29	0	0	0	28	15	38.2	23	155	12	9	3	3	0	2	17	2	57	1	0
Guevara, Carlos, Pittsburgh	1	2	.333	5.79	5	0	0	0	2	0	9.1	11	43	8	6	1	0	0	1	4	0	10	0	0
Guillen, Angel, San Francisco	3	4	.429	5.23	28	0	0	0	20	6	43.0	41	190	31	25	2	4	1	4	25	3	21	8	6
Guzman, Ambiorix, Texas	2	3	.400	5.21	19	1	0	0	11	3	38.0	37	176	25	22	3	3	4	4	19	3	17	1	1
Guzman, Leybi, Dodgers I	1	2	.333	6.59	9	8	0	0	0	0	27.1	38	137	28	20	0	0	2	0	17	0	13	10	0
Guzman, Toribio A., Phi./St.L.	3	3	.500	4.03	18	7	0	0	3	0	58.0	55	265	37	26	1	1	3	4	35	0	46	9	0
Guzman, Wilson, Pittsburgh	5	0	1.000	1.47	16	6	1	0	9	4	55.0	52	231	17	9	3	0	1	1	17	2	48	2	1
Henriquez, Hector, Florida	1	3	.250	3.16	13	13	0	0	0	0	57.0	50	257	26	20	2	3	0	5	46	0	51	6	2
Henriquez, Jovanny, Texas	1	4	.200	3.74	15	9	0	0	4	1	53.0	45	244	32	22	3	2	1	1	39	1	34	7	0
Henriquez, Roman, Dodgers I	8	4	.667	1.81	37	0	0	0	33	8	59.2	56	271	21	12	0	8	3	8	31	5	40	3	1
Heredia, Maximo, Bal./Chi.(AL)	4	7	.364	3.86	16	15	3	0	1	0	93.1	89	323	68	40	5	3	3	12	43	0	46	3	1
Heredia, Ruddy, Toronto	1	0	1.000	0.00	1	0	0	0	0	0	1.0	1	5	0	0	0	0	0	0	1	0	0	0	0
Heredia, Willy, Atlanta	2	2	.500	11.44	11	1	0	0	3	0	19.2	31	120	34	25	0	0	4	3	25	1	11	8	1
Hernandez, German, Texas	1	0	1.000	2.53	3	2	0	0	0	0	10.2	10	46	3	3	0	0	0	0	8	0	3	0	1
Hernandez, Jose, Montreal	5	2	.714	3.90	15	15	1	0	0	0	99.1	99	442	59	43	7	0	2	4	39	2	98	4	0
Hernandez, Julio, California	0	2	.000	7.71	3	2	0	0	0	0	14.0	16	68	13	12	0	0	2	0	10	0	9	2	1
Hernandez, Pedro, Dodgers II	5	4	.556	3.73	14	14	1	1	0	0	79.2	87	356	47	33	5	1	3	5	20	0	46	8	4
Herrera, Misael, Chi. (NL)/S.D.	4	6	.400	4.66	15	13	1	0	1	0	73.1	70	317	51	38	2	0	2	5	29	0	43	6	3
Hiraldo, Juan, Cleveland	4	2	.667	4.44	14	9	0	0	0	0	50.2	48	221	34	25	1	4	5	3	27	0	35	1	0
Javier, Elias, K.C./Colo.	0	0	.000	33.71	2	0	0	0	1	0	2.2	7	22	10	10	1	0	0	0	6	0	1	5	0
Javier, Frank, Florida	2	2	.500	3.05	15	0	0	0	6	0	20.2	18	93	12	7	1	2	0	1	14	0	12	2	0
Jimenez, Alejandro, Texas	0	3	.000	12.97	5	2	0	0	0	0	8.1	9	52	19	12	1	0	0	0	20	0	7	2	0
Jimenez, Denny, Oakland	8	3	.727	2.67	15	11	3	2	3	1	84.1	92	358	37	25	1	4	5	2	19	0	48	3	0
Jimenez, Jhonatan, Texas	0	0	.000	6.00	1	0	0	0	1	1	3.0	2	14	2	2	0	0	1	0	3	0	2	1	0
Jimenez, Johnn, Dodgers I	3	0	1.000	4.54	13	0	0	0	1	0	35.2	39	164	29	18	0	1	2	3	20	3	22	4	0
Jimenez, Kelly, K.C./Colo.	4	2	.667	3.62	16	13	0	0	0	0	77.0	75	311	38	31	3	1	2	2	5	0	32	4	0
Jimenez, Ricardo, Bal./Chi.(AL)	2	3	.400	7.43	15	7	0	0	5	2	40.0	45	207	41	33	4	0	5	3	40	0	27	1	0
Lara, Nelson, Florida	0	3	.000	8.10	5	5	0	0	0	0	20.0	26	103	24	18	2	0	2	3	17	0	8	2	0
LaReal, Guillermo, San Francisco	2	0	1.000	4.12	13	0	0	0	6	1	19.2	26	92	12	9	0	0	0	2	6	0	8	1	1
Lechler, Luis, Dodgers II	4	2	.667	4.94	16	1	0	0	3	0	27.1	22	134	20	15	1	0	1	3	31	2	20	5	1
Leon, Rafael, Florida	2	6	.250	3.31	17	5	0	0	7	1	49.0	52	231	34	18	4	3	1	3	28	1	45	8	2

Pitcher, Team	W	L	Pct.	ERA	G	GS	CG	ShO	GF	Sv.	IP	H	TBF	R	ER	HR	SH	SF	HB	BB	IBB	SO	WP	Bk.
Leyva, Edgar, California	4	2	.667	2.78	11	9	1	0	1	0	68.0	57	289	27	21	3	2	0	9	28	0	42	0	2
Linares, Edwin, Atlanta	1	3	.250	4.11	15	15	1	0	0	0	85.1	84	395	59	39	2	8	4	2	66	2	78	13	2
Linares, Mario, Toyo Carp	8	3	.727	4.02	15	13	3	0	0	0	87.1	87	397	54	39	4	1	1	16	36	0	45	8	0
Lizardo, Julio, San Francisco	4	5	.444	4.82	13	10	0	0	0	0	56.0	57	375	38	30	1	2	3	14	37	0	41	5	0
Lora, Edison, K.C./Colo.	1	6	.143	4.91	17	10	0	0	2	0	51.1	54	243	43	28	2	2	1	6	28	0	19	7	1
Lora, Freddy, Pittsburgh	3	6	.333	3.93	15	9	1	0	2	0	66.1	58	288	36	29	4	0	2	0	32	0	61	9	2
Lorenzo, Martin, Houston	2	7	.222	5.59	18	10	0	0	1	0	66.0	61	319	55	41	1	1	3	12	43	0	33	7	9
Luis, Cristain, Houston	0	0	.000	6.23	14	1	0	0	4	0	17.1	21	85	13	12	2	0	2	3	12	0	8	4	0
Maria, Alcibiades, Texas	2	1	.667	4.94	11	2	0	0	4	0	27.1	40	136	18	15	5	0	2	2	11	1	9	3	0
Marshall, Victor, N.Y. Yankees	4	3	.571	5.87	22	1	0	0	15	5	23.0	17	111	17	15	1	1	2	4	20	0	27	4	1
Marte, Julian, Dodgers II	1	0	1.000	0.00	4	0	0	0	2	0	8.0	6	35	3	0	0	0	0	0	4	0	1	2	0
Marte, Luis, K.C./Colo.	1	5	.167	2.82	11	6	0	0	2	0	38.1	33	173	27	12	1	1	1	4	15	1	27	4	0
Martinez, Claudio, Dodgers II	0	0	.000	5.58	6	0	0	0	0	0	9.2	8	46	10	6	1	0	0	0	8	0	5	2	1
Martinez, Frank, Houston	2	1	.667	3.90	17	9	0	0	2	0	60.0	56	267	35	26	1	1	1	3	33	0	31	10	2
Martinez, Gabriel, Chi. (NL)/S.D.	0	1	.000	8.10	7	1	0	0	4	0	10.0	12	50	9	9	1	0	1	0	12	0	5	7	0
Martinez, Jhonny, K.C./Colo.	0	0	.000	4.16	3	0	0	0	1	0	4.1	6	21	3	2	0	0	1	1	2	1	1	1	0
Martinez, Jose, Texas	6	3	.667	3.47	16	7	1	0	7	0	62.1	60	267	28	24	4	5	1	1	19	2	39	3	1
Martinez, Juan R., Texas	0	0	.000	9.00	1	0	0	0	1	0	1.0	2	5	1	1	0	0	0	0	0	0	0	0	0
Martinez, Romulo, Detroit	0	0	.000	7.73	1	1	0	0	0	0	2.1	3	12	3	2	0	0	0	0	3	0	2	0	0
Martinez, Sandy, Houston	1	2	.333	5.40	19	0	0	0	4	0	38.1	51	193	33	23	1	4	2	4	27	1	24	5	1
Martinez, Wander, California	3	5	.375	2.55	11	9	3	0	0	0	67.0	62	297	34	19	2	1	1	4	17	0	44	5	1
Matias, Hansell, Atlanta	5	5	.500	4.81	21	2	1	0	9	1	76.2	101	359	63	41	6	4	4	5	24	0	47	2	0
Matos, Dauris, N.Y. Mets	0	0	.000	4.43	21	1	0	0	11	2	40.2	44	187	24	20	8	2	0	2	25	0	25	2	0
McWellyng, Venien, California	0	0	.000	16.17	3	0	0	0	2	0	1.2	3	9	3	3	0	0	0	0	2	0	2	0	0
Medina, Carlos, Florida	2	3	.400	2.18	12	11	1	0	0	0	62.0	59	266	29	15	2	0	2	0	30	0	47	9	0
Medina, Edward, Detroit	0	2	.000	7.00	12	1	0	0	2	0	9.0	7	58	13	7	0	2	1	3	19	0	1	1	0
Mejia, Luis, N.Y. Yankees	2	2	.500	2.60	15	0	0	0	7	0	27.2	13	125	15	8	0	0	0	3	28	0	38	1	1
Melian, Jhonathan, Seattle	1	0	1.000	3.60	17	0	0	0	4	0	20.0	16	103	11	8	3	1	1	3	23	1	12	5	0
Mena, Eddy, Detroit	0	0	.000	0.00	1	0	0	0	0	0	3.2	7	18	1	0	0	0	0	0	0	0	1	0	0
Mendez, Lenin, Seattle	0	0	.000	5.68	8	0	0	0	3	0	12.2	11	62	12	8	1	0	2	2	10	1	6	0	0
Mercedes, Carlos, Bal./Chi.(AL)	2	4	.333	4.74	12	0	0	0	10	2	24.2	29	115	19	13	1	1	1	1	7	0	25	1	0
Mercedes, Daniel, Pittsburgh	0	0	.000	11.57	6	0	0	0	2	0	7.0	10	42	10	9	0	0	1	2	12	0	3	5	0
Mercedes, Jose, Oakland	2	6	.250	5.03	15	13	1	0	1	1	73.1	87	352	63	41	5	5	5	2	48	0	36	10	0
Mercedes, Matias, Detroit	0	0	.000	13.43	1	0	0	0	0	0	0.2	0	3	1	1	0	0	0	0	2	0	0	0	0
Mercedes, Tomas, Toronto	4	2	.667	4.24	13	3	0	0	5	0	40.1	38	186	24	19	3	2	2	5	25	0	25	5	1
Mesa, Willy, K.C./Colo.	0	0	.000	4.91	3	0	0	0	0	0	7.1	7	35	5	4	0	0	0	0	6	0	5	4	0
Mesina, Juan, Florida	4	1	.800	3.13	20	0	0	0	10	0	31.2	24	142	14	11	1	1	0	3	23	0	28	3	0
Minaya, Pablo, Florida	1	4	.200	5.23	14	11	0	0	0	0	51.2	54	254	36	30	1	0	3	9	50	0	28	16	2
Monero, Pablo, California	2	1	.667	4.91	19	1	0	0	8	0	36.2	36	181	32	20	3	0	1	10	12	0	21	6	4
Montanez, Johan, Toronto	6	2	.750	3.51	13	12	0	0	0	0	77.0	82	337	34	30	6	0	1	1	45	1	42	2	0
Montero, Agustin, Oakland	0	1	.000	11.59	1	0	0	0	0	0	2.1	7	17	6	3	1	0	1	0	2	0	2	3	0
Montero, Francisco, Phi./St.L.	4	2	.667	3.69	29	0	0	0	15	2	53.2	50	247	26	22	0	0	2	8	29	2	34	1	1
Morel, Jose, Pittsburgh	4	2	.667	4.36	9	7	0	0	0	0	41.1	47	185	26	20	2	0	4	0	14	0	31	7	0
Moreno, Willy, N.Y. Yankees	0	0	.000	0.00	1	0	0	0	1	0	1.0	0	4	0	0	0	0	0	0	1	0	1	1	0
Moris, Miguel, N.Y. Mets	0	2	.000	3.47	13	3	0	0	3	0	33.2	33	149	23	13	4	2	1	4	10	0	19	4	0
Morrobel, Juan, Pittsburgh	0	1	.000	7.20	7	2	0	0	1	0	15.0	18	84	13	12	3	0	0	2	21	0	15	1	0
Mota, Henry, Texas	6	3	.667	1.85	29	4	0	0	23	8	63.1	48	249	19	13	1	4	4	5	12	0	57	4	0
Mota, Leonardo, San Francisco	0	1	.000	5.86	23	2	0	0	4	0	43.0	47	211	41	28	6	2	0	6	41	1	21	9	1
Nina, Jose, Bal./Chi.(AL)	2	0	1.000	9.88	8	0	0	0	2	0	13.2	21	70	16	15	6	0	1	1	11	0	4	4	1
Nivar, Amaury, K.C./Colo.	1	0	1.000	7.73	3	0	0	0	0	0	2.1	3	15	7	2	0	0	1	0	5	0	2	2	0
Nunez, Enrique, Phi./St.L.	2	7	.222	4.59	15	15	0	0	0	0	80.1	87	362	62	41	2	0	8	10	29	0	44	4	1
Nunez, Franklin, Dodgers II	1	0	1.000	7.36	12	1	0	0	4	0	22.0	27	118	25	18	0	1	1	3	20	0	17	2	0
Oliver, Jose, Oakland	4	2	.667	3.10	19	3	0	0	11	2	49.1	51	214	24	17	4	4	2	1	13	1	36	6	1
Olivo, Gary, San Francisco	0	2	.000	11.17	8	7	0	0	0	0	19.1	20	113	32	24	0	1	1	0	33	1	7	12	1
Olivo, Juan, Toyo Carp	3	0	1.000	2.89	19	2	0	0	8	5	46.2	44	192	17	15	2	0	1	0	17	0	27	4	1
Orta, Carlos, Montreal	2	6	.250	6.71	22	5	0	0	6	0	61.2	83	317	57	46	5	1	7	10	55	4	38	8	1
Ortiz, Eusebio, Phi./St.L.	0	1	.000	7.49	16	1	0	0	6	0	39.2	58	206	46	33	2	2	4	2	19	1	16	6	0
Ortiz, Pedro, Dodgers I	0	0	.000	9.52	8	0	0	0	2	0	5.2	11	37	9	6	3	1	0	0	8	1	2	3	0
Ortiz, Ramon, California	8	6	.571	2.23	16	16	7	0	0	0	97.0	79	466	44	24	2	1	2	3	54	0	100	6	2
Oviedo, Alexander, Oakland	8	1	.889	2.95	14	13	2	1	0	0	82.1	73	346	37	27	1	0	2	4	34	0	65	6	0
Ozorio, Douglas, N.Y. Yankees	0	1	.000	8.31	5	0	0	0	4	1	4.1	6	23	5	4	1	1	0	2	4	1	2	1	0
Ozorio, Eric, Atlanta	1	6	.143	9.08	20	0	0	0	15	3	37.2	53	200	50	38	1	3	1	3	34	4	24	6	0
Ozuna, Carlos, Oakland	2	0	1.000	2.61	12	1	0	0	5	1	41.1	37	179	15	12	2	0	1	2	26	0	19	1	0
Padua, Gerardo, N.Y. Yankees	1	1	.500	3.79	14	0	0	0	8	1	19.0	16	88	9	8	2	0	0	3	13	0	12	4	0
Paniagua, Freddy, Florida	4	2	.667	3.46	21	0	0	0	14	1	26.0	26	120	15	10	1	1	1	3	16	2	15	5	1
Paraqueima, Jesus, N.Y. Yankees	1	2	.333	6.67	11	6	0	0	0	0	27.0	27	130	23	20	3	0	0	3	27	0	22	4	1
Paredes, Roberto, Cleveland	3	2	.600	1.99	29	0	0	0	19	7	45.1	36	184	14	10	3	3	2	3	15	2	30	1	1
Parra, Catalino, N.Y. Yankees	2	1	.667	3.60	15	1	0	0	3	0	45.0	45	199	22	18	1	1	0	4	23	0	31	3	0
Parra, Jesus, Houston	4	4	.500	3.03	13	12	0	0	0	0	68.1	49	298	30	23	0	5	1	6	41	2	74	6	2
Parra, Jorge, Texas	0	1	.000	4.78	21	1	0	0	5	0	37.2	44	177	23	20	4	1	2	2	20	2	17	0	0
Parra, Klisber, Florida	4	5	.444	4.23	12	11	0	0	1	0	66.0	61	281	41	31	5	1	0	3	20	0	46	8	2
Pascual, Roberto, Chi. (NL)/S.D.	0	0	.000	0.00	1	0	0	0	1	0	0.2	2	7	3	0	0	0	0	1	0	0	1	0	0
Pascual, Ubaldo, Chi. (NL)/S.D	1	5	.167	4.35	23	0	0	0	13	0	51.2	50	241	40	25	4	0	6	4	31	0	36	7	0
Patino, Leonardo, California	5	4	.556	1.35	21	6	2	0	12	3	73.1	56	303	26	11	2	3	1	2	28	2	63	4	3
Paulino, Arison, Pittsburgh	0	0	.000	10.29	7	0	0	0	2	0	7.0	15	47	11	8	0	0	3	1	8	1	6	0	3
Paulino, Manuel, Oakland	5	1	.833	1.09	17	0	0	0	17	8	33.0	25	133	6	4	0	1	0	1	7	3	28	2	0
Peguero, Americo, Bal./Chi.(AL)	8	3	.727	2.48	15	13	6	0	1	1	101.2	64	417	38	28	5	3	1	8	47	0	120	11	0
Pena, Domingo, Pittsburgh	0	2	.000	8.03	11	0	0	0	7	0	12.1	8	62	13	11	0	0	1	1	18	0	10	7	0
Perdomo, Roberto, San Francisco	1	1	.500	4.11	9	0	0	0	3	0	15.1	16	65	8	7	0	0	0	2	5	0	7	1	0
Perez, Jorge, N.Y. Yankees	0	1	.000	4.96	8	1	0	0	3	0	16.1	14	74	12	9	2	0	0	1	16	0	10	2	0
Perez, Samuel, Cleveland	4	2	.667	2.61	18	6	0	0	2	1	62.0	51	265	30	18	3	4	1	2	26	0	46	9	1
Perozo, Alberto, Atlanta	4	3	.571	4.03	25	0	0	0	23	9	38.0	46	179	22	17	1	1	0	4	22	1	20	5	0
Petique, Marino, Toyo Carp	10	1	.909	1.61	16	12	3	1	2	2	84.0	65	350	29	15	2	4	4	3	32	0	41	1	4

Pitcher, Team	W	L	Pct.	ERA	G	GS	CG	ShO	GF	Sv.	IP	H	TBF	R	ER	HR	SH	SF	HB	BB	IBB	SO	WP	Bk.
Pinales, Demetrio, Texas	0	1	.000	3.15	7	2	0	0	0	0	20.0	18	93	9	7	1	1	0	1	11	0	14	1	0
Pinales, Otilio, Seattle	0	1	.000	9.58	14	2	0	0	3	0	20.2	20	118	27	22	1	1	0	4	38	0	17	7	0
Pineda, Luis, Texas	6	1	.857	3.00	12	5	0	0	1	0	39.0	36	186	17	13	0	2	0	4	31	2	19	6	1
Polanco, Elvis, Chi. (NL)/S.D.	1	5	.167	8.12	15	13	1	0	0	0	57.2	90	307	65	52	5	2	2	8	43	0	60	9	0
Polanco, Julio, Texas	0	0	.000	6.75	3	1	0	0	0	0	5.1	2	30	6	4	0	0	1	0	12	0	0	6	1
Presinal, Gilberto, Chi. (NL)/S.D.	1	1	.500	5.18	12	0	0	0	3	0	24.1	24	115	16	14	4	0	1	0	20	0	15	0	3
Quezada, Anulfo, California	2	4	.333	4.00	14	3	0	0	5	1	36.1	36	171	27	16	3	2	1	2	16	0	12	4	1
Quezada, Edward, Montreal	0	1	.000	6.77	1	0	0	0	0	0	1.1	2	8	3	1	1	1	1	0	2	0	0	0	0
Quiroz, Misael, Pittsburgh	2	6	.250	4.00	15	14	3	0	1	0	81.0	83	368	49	36	9	2	2	6	34	0	64	13	2
Racero, Aramis, Toronto	1	1	.500	6.46	8	8	0	0	0	0	30.2	38	148	29	22	5	0	0	3	26	0	19	3	0
Rafael, Jorge, Toronto	5	1	.833	3.59	11	8	0	0	1	0	47.2	33	201	24	19	1	2	0	7	31	0	36	5	4
Ramirez, Antonio, Montreal	2	1	.667	3.95	11	7	0	0	1	0	43.1	41	184	22	19	6	1	1	1	18	0	44	0	0
Ramirez, Jose, Detroit	7	5	.583	2.49	17	14	1	0	1	1	94.0	100	405	45	26	1	2	2	4	36	1	82	5	1
Ramos, Fernando, Phi./St.L.	2	5	.286	6.27	15	8	0	0	3	0	56.0	75	254	49	39	4	0	2	6	16	0	31	5	0
Ramos, Jose, Dodgers I	3	2	.600	5.10	26	2	0	0	2	0	67.0	82	319	51	38	2	5	3	9	32	4	35	9	0
Ramos, Juan C., Montreal	3	6	.333	5.09	16	15	4	0	1	1	88.1	99	386	56	50	6	0	5	6	29	2	66	2	1
Ravelo, Carlos, San Francisco	0	0	.000	13.03	9	0	0	0	4	0	9.2	19	67	25	14	0	0	3	1	14	0	5	9	0
Regalado, Frank, Toyo Carp	3	1	.750	10.64	8	0	0	0	2	0	11.0	14	56	15	13	2	0	0	0	9	0	8	1	0
Regalado, Maximo, Dodgers I	0	2	.000	7.86	11	3	0	0	0	0	18.1	21	93	20	16	3	0	1	2	14	1	13	2	0
Reyes, Bernardo, Dodgers II	0	0	.000	4.82	6	0	0	0	1	0	9.1	6	51	8	5	0	0	1	3	13	0	1	1	0
Reyes, Jose Luis, N.Y. Mets	3	3	.500	5.44	21	0	0	0	13	4	48.0	64	217	38	29	6	4	1	2	11	1	45	3	0
Reyes, Juan, Montreal	1	9	.100	5.40	15	9	1	0	2	0	61.2	68	289	52	37	1	0	4	5	42	2	36	5	2
Reyes, Pedro, N.Y. Yankees	0	1	.000	5.04	14	0	0	0	5	0	25.0	27	127	18	14	3	0	1	5	14	0	12	2	1
Reyes, Santos, Detroit	2	1	.667	3.66	10	0	0	0	5	1	19.2	19	84	10	8	1	2	1	2	9	0	9	1	0
Richardson, Roberto, Phi./St.L.	0	2	.000	14.29	12	2	0	0	5	0	17.0	31	102	33	27	0	0	2	3	19	0	8	8	0
Rijo, Fernando, Dodgers I	3	6	.333	7.07	16	11	1	0	0	0	56.0	71	279	51	44	0	0	3	1	45	2	28	3	0
Rijo, Francisco, Toyo Carp	2	1	.667	3.06	15	1	0	0	10	1	35.1	20	146	15	12	2	2	0	3	19	1	26	1	0
Rijo, Jose, Houston	3	5	.375	3.92	28	0	0	0	24	7	43.2	40	187	22	19	1	0	0	4	25	3	37	8	0
Rincones, Gabriel, Seattle	4	3	.571	5.98	13	12	1	0	0	0	58.2	62	270	44	39	10	1	3	5	32	0	41	7	0
Rivera, Homero, Detroit	0	0	.000	4.44	16	2	0	0	7	0	26.1	26	119	14	13	1	0	0	4	12	1	21	1	0
Rivera, Juan C., Chi. (NL)/S.D.	0	0	.000	11.59	2	0	0	0	2	0	2.1	6	14	3	3	1	0	0	0	2	0	3	1	0
Rodriguez, Aron, Bal./Chi.(AL)	0	2	.000	6.75	10	0	0	0	4	0	17.1	17	88	22	13	2	0	0	0	19	0	3	2	1
Rodriguez, Franklin, Toronto	2	1	.667	2.82	19	0	0	0	5	0	38.1	37	170	24	12	2	3	1	2	24	0	39	3	0
Rodriguez, Henry, Bal./Chi.(AL)	3	5	.375	3.65	21	0	0	0	15	1	49.1	55	229	35	20	10	1	0	0	23	1	33	9	0
Rodriguez, Marcell, Oakland	1	0	1.000	9.00	2	0	0	0	1	0	2.0	2	10	2	2	0	0	0	0	2	0	1	0	0
Rodriguez, Nelson, Dodgers I	0	0	.000	0.00	1	0	0	0	1	0	0.2	1	4	0	0	0	0	0	0	1	0	0	1	0
Rodriguez, Pedro, Seattle	3	2	.600	3.57	13	11	0	0	0	0	53.0	39	241	24	21	4	1	2	5	45	0	25	6	3
Rodriguez, Rodney, Atlanta	0	0	.000	18.57	4	0	0	0	0	0	5.1	9	39	14	11	0	0	1	5	7	0	0	4	0
Rojas, Cesar, Texas	5	3	.625	4.30	13	10	2	0	1	1	67.0	74	292	38	32	7	1	2	5	14	0	29	2	0
Rojas, Francisco, Dodgers II	2	1	.667	3.21	16	0	0	0	7	2	28.0	29	130	14	10	0	1	1	1	23	3	20	2	3
Rojas, Juan P., Atlanta	4	2	.667	4.06	14	14	0	0	0	0	68.2	72	324	44	31	2	0	1	5	47	2	36	3	0
Romano, Manuel, San Francisco	3	5	.375	5.11	10	9	1	0	0	0	56.1	60	270	51	32	1	0	1	4	38	2	49	7	1
Romero, Mario, Houston	0	0	.000	9.00	11	0	0	0	5	0	12.0	16	67	13	12	0	0	1	4	11	0	8	7	0
Romero, Raumer, Montreal	5	4	.556	3.36	32	0	0	0	20	5	67.0	54	285	34	25	4	3	3	3	40	4	49	11	0
Rondon, Gabriel, Houston	2	2	.500	5.21	18	0	0	0	9	3	38.0	33	178	27	22	2	2	0	2	26	2	32	5	4
Rosario, Rafael, Detroit	0	3	.000	7.48	19	2	0	0	4	1	33.2	48	179	37	28	1	0	2	3	27	2	14	4	1
Rosario, Ramon, Oakland	2	2	.500	2.75	13	4	0	0	5	1	39.1	33	170	16	12	3	2	0	1	25	1	19	5	2
Rosario, Reynaldo, Detroit	2	3	.400	4.73	10	9	0	0	1	0	45.2	43	197	26	24	4	2	1	0	23	4	47	2	0
Rosario, Ruben, Phi./St.L.	1	1	.500	4.15	3	3	0	0	0	0	13.0	14	62	10	6	1	0	0	0	6	0	9	2	0
Samuel, Yojairo, Texas	6	3	.667	3.16	15	14	2	1	1	0	79.2	76	337	39	28	3	1	1	4	31	1	47	2	0
Sanchez, Jose, Detroit	0	0	.000	9.00	2	0	0	0	2	0	1.0	5	8	1	1	0	0	0	0	0	0	1	0	0
Sanchez, Jossys, Montreal	0	0	.000	2.45	8	0	0	0	3	1	11.0	5	51	4	3	0	2	1	3	8	0	12	1	0
Sanchez, Martin, Atlanta	4	4	.500	3.87	16	16	2	0	0	0	102.1	88	450	58	44	6	2	2	12	41	0	110	12	2
Sanchez, Wellington, Chi. (NL)/S.D.	3	5	.375	4.91	15	10	0	0	1	0	58.2	63	266	47	32	2	3	2	2	26	0	21	2	2
Santamaria, Juan, Detroit	0	1	.000	9.00	1	1	0	0	0	0	3.0	4	16	3	3	0	0	0	0	3	0	3	1	0
Santana, Alfredo, Detroit	4	3	.571	2.66	13	9	0	0	2	1	67.2	65	298	25	20	0	4	2	8	29	6	34	10	4
Santana, Aris, Bal./Chi.(AL)	1	4	.200	6.17	16	5	0	0	4	1	42.1	44	201	40	29	0	4	4	3	33	1	34	9	1
Santana, Humberto, N.Y. Mets	6	2	.750	3.16	11	10	1	1	1	0	57.0	46	233	26	20	4	2	1	2	13	1	41	1	2
Santana, Luis, Dodgers II	2	0	1.000	3.10	9	0	0	0	9	0	20.1	18	89	11	7	3	0	4	0	5	0	9	2	0
Santana, Orlando, Bal./Chi.(AL)	0	0	.000	4.67	11	0	0	0	7	1	17.1	25	90	11	9	7	0	0	1	6	0	5	1	0
Santiago, Cesar, Florida	1	4	.200	6.25	15	2	0	0	1	0	36.0	48	175	33	25	2	2	1	3	17	0	30	6	1
Santos, Ricardo, N.Y. Yankees	0	1	.000	3.97	12	0	0	0	8	1	22.2	20	101	11	10	4	1	1	1	13	0	19	2	0
Santos, Victor, Detroit	7	5	.583	3.72	15	12	3	2	2	0	77.1	88	339	46	32	4	0	1	1	18	0	75	11	1
Segura, Yodys, Dodgers I	3	3	.500	3.88	14	11	0	0	1	0	55.2	62	266	33	24	3	1	0	3	41	2	36	8	0
Selmo, Alexandre, Atlanta	2	5	.286	4.15	20	0	0	0	9	1	47.2	33	230	28	22	1	6	2	6	57	4	27	4	0
Serrano, Wascar, Chi. (NL)/S.D.	3	3	.500	3.11	12	7	0	0	1	0	46.1	63	210	24	16	2	5	2	0	15	0	23	9	0
Sido, Wilson, Toyo Carp	1	0	1.000	2.88	11	0	0	0	2	1	25.0	19	108	10	8	1	2	2	1	15	0	22	1	0
Sierra, Luis, Toronto	2	2	.500	3.57	21	0	0	0	10	3	40.1	28	172	20	16	0	1	0	1	21	2	46	2	0
Silva, Luis, Toronto	1	0	1.000	4.50	5	0	0	0	5	3	8.0	9	35	5	4	0	1	0	0	4	0	9	1	0
Solano, Darling, Dodgers I	0	2	.000	13.20	11	3	0	0	1	0	15.0	18	93	28	22	2	0	3	3	33	0	9	7	1
Soler, Miguel, N.Y. Yankees	0	1	.000	4.28	12	5	0	0	1	0	33.2	27	148	21	16	1	1	1	1	21	0	27	2	1
Soriano, Gabriel, Dodgers I	2	6	.250	4.83	15	12	0	0	2	0	63.1	71	294	38	34	2	1	0	9	37	2	41	10	0
Sosa, Henry, Florida	0	1	.000	3.96	16	0	0	0	6	0	25.0	25	127	16	11	2	1	1	6	22	1	20	4	0
Soto, Angel, K.C./Colo.	1	1	.500	6.50	14	0	0	0	2	0	18.0	19	98	20	13	1	2	2	3	20	0	7	8	0
Soto, Carlos, N.Y. Mets	6	1	.857	1.96	19	0	0	0	14	7	36.2	27	148	10	8	1	0	1	2	16	4	27	4	0
Suarez, Ramon, K.C./Colo.	1	4	.200	5.14	18	4	0	0	6	3	42.0	50	201	36	24	1	3	5	6	18	2	14	4	1
Tavares, Heriberto, Pittsburgh	3	1	.750	3.78	17	0	0	0	13	4	16.2	14	79	9	7	2	1	1	2	17	1	20	2	0
Terrero, Ruben, N.Y. Mets	1	2	.333	4.55	15	3	0	0	3	0	31.2	35	148	22	16	3	0	1	1	19	0	25	2	1
Tineo, Marcos, Phi./St.L.	3	3	.500	2.48	28	1	0	0	25	10	40.0	28	171	20	11	0	3	4	2	27	1	29	8	2
Torres, Jairo, Bal./Chi.(AL)	1	1	.500	4.26	8	0	0	0	6	0	12.2	14	53	10	6	0	0	2	0	5	0	4	0	0
Trejo, Ulises, Houston	2	3	.400	5.06	12	8	0	0	0	0	42.2	37	200	37	24	3	3	2	1	42	0	30	11	3
Urena, Pedro, Texas	1	0	1.000	4.69	5	0	0	0	2	0	7.2	8	35	4	4	1	0	0	0	5	0	5	1	0
Uribe, Maximo, California	0	0	.000	8.21	7	0	0	0	3	0	7.2	7	44	7	7	0	1	0	0	14	1	2	3	0

Pitcher, Team	W	L	Pct.	ERA	G	GS	CG	ShO	GF	Sv.	IP	H	TBF	R	ER	HR	SH	SF	HB	BB	IBB	SO	WP	Bk.
Valdez, Juan, Pittsburgh	0	1	.000	6.57	6	1	0	0	1	0	12.1	9	66	12	9	0	1	1	2	18	0	5	2	0
Valdez, Orlando, San Francisco	3	7	.300	4.37	24	8	1	0	15	2	82.1	92	385	65	40	1	4	3	6	44	1	49	5	0
Valdez, Wolkin, N.Y. Yankees	2	2	.500	3.93	14	3	0	0	1	1	34.1	42	168	22	15	3	0	1	4	20	0	22	3	0
Valenzuela, Jose, Chi. (NL)/S.D.	2	4	.333	6.04	17	4	0	0	4	0	50.2	48	237	41	34	4	3	2	5	43	1	21	9	0
Vanderhorst, F., K.C./Colo.	2	8	.200	5.32	17	12	1	0	2	0	69.1	82	320	58	41	4	0	5	8	23	0	25	8	3
Vargas, Francisco, Cleveland	3	3	.500	3.25	16	10	1	1	4	2	61.0	70	266	41	22	2	0	6	1	10	1	24	3	1
Vargas, Jose, Toyo Carp	6	2	.750	2.43	13	13	2	1	0	0	70.1	50	301	34	19	1	1	3	9	34	0	37	2	0
Vasquez, Cesar, Houston	3	2	.600	2.18	22	1	0	0	11	2	41.1	35	193	16	10	1	4	1	4	32	5	24	8	2
Vasquez, Luis, N.Y. Mets	3	2	.600	4.18	16	2	0	0	3	1	32.1	45	148	23	15	4	2	0	1	6	1	20	0	0
Vega, Juan, San Francisco	2	7	.222	5.84	15	15	2	0	0	0	69.1	88	325	64	45	3	2	3	3	40	0	65	19	0
Veras, Carlos, Pittsburgh	0	0	.000	24.91	8	0	0	0	2	0	8.2	19	56	25	24	5	0	0	1	12	0	3	0	1
Villar, Maximo, Pittsburgh	3	3	.500	4.23	9	9	3	0	0	0	61.2	66	262	37	29	5	1	2	6	14	0	60	1	1
Vizcaino, Luis, Oakland	10	2	.833	2.27	16	15	5	1	0	0	115.0	93	477	41	29	3	1	3	3	29	0	89	10	2
Zabala, Ismel J., Seattle	9	1	.900	1.05	30	0	0	0	12	3	51.1	25	189	9	6	0	2	2	1	17	2	83	5	0
Zapata, Juan, Houston	5	4	.556	2.31	13	13	1	1	0	0	81.2	60	353	40	21	1	1	1	4	43	1	60	10	0
Zapata, Rolando, Montreal	3	8	.273	5.54	19	10	0	0	3	0	65.0	67	314	58	40	3	1	4	6	65	0	28	10	2

1995 FIELDING

TEAM

Team	Pct.	G	PO	A	E	TC	DP	PB
Toronto	.956	68	1768	809	118	2695	51	4
N.Y. Mets	.950	68	1744	725	130	2599	47	16
Cleveland	.948	69	1816	838	145	2799	66	26
Detroit	.948	69	1800	785	143	2728	74	19
Seattle	.948	66	1687	692	131	2510	69	19
Texas	.947	67	1670	703	133	2506	50	10
Toyo Carp	.947	71	1851	692	143	2686	48	16
Montreal	.946	69	1791	765	145	2701	62	18
N.Y. Yankees	.945	68	1742	799	149	2690	66	23
Pittsburgh	.942	66	1671	685	144	2500	52	17
Dodgers II	.939	69	1777	718	161	2656	50	32
Oakland	.939	66	1718	778	163	2659	70	20
Dodgers I	.937	64	1628	769	161	2558	69	18
Bal./Chi.(AL)	.933	70	1676	698	170	2544	71	6
Hou./Mil.	.932	68	1783	823	191	2797	55	53
California	.931	71	1629	752	177	2558	57	10
San Francisco	.930	71	1671	737	180	2588	61	8
Chi.(NL)/S.D.	.929	68	1684	696	183	2563	55	12
Florida	.927	68	1721	776	197	2694	58	16
K.C./Colo.	.922	65	1698	737	206	2641	53	23
Atlanta	.915	70	1801	731	235	2767	56	27
Phil./St.L.	.911	69	1759	744	244	2747	50	36

INDIVIDUAL

Player, Team	Pos.	Pct.	PO	A	E	DP	PB
Abreu, Dennis, Chi. (NL)/S.D.	2B	.895	141	133	32	11	0
Abreu, Miguel, Florida	OF	.972	65	4	2	2	0
Aguilar, Henry, California	P	.800	1	3	1	0	0
Aguilar, Jose, Oakland	DH	1.000	6	1	0	0	0
Agustin, Filiberto, Houston	OF	.970	60	4	2	1	0
Alcala, Juan F. Seattle	C	.966	100	14	4	2	2
Alfonzo, Iran, Toronto	C	.987	56	20	1	0	1
Almonte, Hector, Florida	P	.750	1	5	2	0	0
Alvarez, Carlos, Cleveland	OF	.914	29	3	3	2	0
Alvino, Roger, Chi. (NL)/S.D	P	.778	6	8	4	0	0
Amador, Juan, Atlanta	IF	.764	22	62	26	9	0
Andujar, Elias, Atlanta	P	.842	5	11	3	1	0
Andujar, Eliezer, Atlanta	OF	.921	110	7	10	1	0
Andujar, Juan, Florida	1B	.981	237	17	5	0	0
Antonio, Junior, Houston	C	1.000	8	0	0	0	2
Antunez, Javier, Montreal	OF	.951	36	3	2	1	0
Aracena, Juan, Cleveland	P	.938	6	9	1	2	0
Aracena, Ramon, Toyo Carp	P	.909	2	8	1	0	0
Araujo, Danilo, Phi./St.L.	DH	.876	30	62	13	1	0
Arbornoz, Hernan, Montreal	2B	.952	30	29	3	3	0
Arias, Cesarin, Chi. (NL)/S.D.	P	.857	4	8	2	1	0
Arias, Jorge, Phi./St.L.	C	.955	108	19	6	0	0
Arias, Jose, Phi./St.L.	P	.656	8	13	11	0	0
Arias, Jose, N.Y. Yankees	P	1.000	1	2	0	0	0
Arias, Kelvin, N.Y. Mets	P	1.000	1	2	0	0	0
Arias, Miguel, Dodgers II	P	.929	3	10	1	0	0
Arias, Rafael, Chi. (NL)/S.D.	P	1.000	0	5	0	0	0
Arias, Rafael, San Francisco	P	.875	0	7	1	0	0
Arias, Roberto, N.Y. Mets	P	.625	1	4	3	0	0
Asencio, Eddy, Detroit	P	1.000	0	10	0	0	0
Avila, Jose, Pittsburgh	P	.913	6	15	2	1	0
Baez, Jose, Pittsburgh	P	.750	2	4	2	0	0
Baez, Miguel, Cleveland	P	.968	5	25	1	0	0
Balbuena, Martin, K.C./Colo.	P	.774	6	18	7	2	0
Banci, Aaron, Florida	2B	.953	227	59	14	3	0
Barreras, Rafael, Texas	OF	.925	37	0	3	0	0
Baruch, Jaime, Montreal	P	1.000	2	5	0	0	0
Basabe, Jesus, Oakland	OF	.979	45	1	1	0	0
Bautista, Francisco, K.C./Colo.	OF	.905	35	3	4	0	0
Belliard, Carlos, Dodgers II	P	1.000	5	9	0	1	0
Bello, Emerson, Seattle	P	.857	3	15	3	0	0
Bello, Gilberto, Bal./Chi.(AL)	IF	.972	424	30	13	1	0
Belmonte, Jose, California	IF	.775	19	60	23	6	0
Beltre, Adrian, Dodgers I	3B	.899	88	187	31	19	0
Beltres, Manuel, N.Y. Yankees	2B	.902	83	119	22	12	0
Benitez, Miguel, K.C./Colo.	C	.941	91	5	6	0	2
Betancourt, Romulo, Bal./Chi.(AL)	OF	.873	42	6	7	3	0
Betancourt, William, Cleveland	P	.929	1	12	1	0	0
Bezhodashvila, Nina, California	P	1.000	0	1	0	0	0
Blanco, Billy, Oakland	C	.971	29	4	1	0	0
Blanco, Daniel, San Francisco	C	.963	159	21	7	0	5
Blanco, Danny, Cleveland	DH	.951	39	0	2	0	0
Blanco, Fabian, Dodgers II	P	.727	3	5	3	0	0
Blanco, Pablo, Florida	P	.684	1	12	6	0	0
Blanco Veras, Johanny, Clev.	P	.900	1	8	1	0	0
Bracho, Alejandro, N.Y. Yankees	P	1.000	0	21	0	0	0
Bracho, Didimo, Montreal	OF	.917	74	3	7	1	0
Brand, Fausto, Atlanta	P	.857	2	4	1	0	0
Bravo, Eulis, Cleveland	SS	.927	50	114	13	12	0
Bravo, Luis, Cleveland	P	1.000	0	4	0	0	0
Brazoban, Melvin, Texas	P	1.000	0	6	0	0	0
Brea, Rafael, Florida	2B	.964	126	114	9	10	0
Brea, Ramsey, Detroit	P	.636	1	6	4	0	0
Briceno, Freddy, Montreal	SS	.939	54	85	9	11	0
Brito, Felix, N.Y. Yankees	C	.981	93	10	2	0	5
Brito, Johan, San Francisco	IF	.938	117	111	15	8	0
Cabral, Martires, Toronto	P	1.000	0	2	0	0	0
Cabrera, Danny, N.Y. Mets	1B	.991	292	21	3	0	0
Caceres, Antonio, Toronto	P	.750	2	7	3	0	0
Cadet, Javier, Chi. (NL)/S.D.	P	.750	0	3	1	0	0
Caines, Franklin, Phi./St.L.	1B	.959	419	29	19	0	0
Calderon, Ramon, San Francisco	P	.923	1	11	1	0	0
Camacaro, Pedro, Texas	2B	.923	36	12	4	2	0
Camacho, Wandy, California	IF	.953	114	8	6	0	0
Carela, Jesus, Oakland	P	.000	0	0	1	0	0
Cariolan, Roberto, N.Y. Yankees	P	.800	1	3	1	0	0
Carjaval, Tomas, California	P	1.000	1	0	0	0	0
Carmona, Antonio, Bal./Chi.(AL)	C/IF	.976	140	23	4	0	0
Carrasquel, Alejandro, Montreal	P	.692	1	8	4	0	0
Carrion, Jorge, Houston	P	1.000	0	3	0	0	0
Carvajal, Hugo, Dodgers II	C	.976	111	9	3	1	3
Casimiro, Claudio, Bal./Chi.(AL)	IF	.911	63	90	15	8	0
Castillo, Alex, Houston	3B	.902	41	124	18	10	0
Castillo, Daniel A., Dodgers I	P	.500	1	0	1	0	0
Castillo, Geramel, Texas	2B	.913	110	79	18	6	0
Castillo, Jose, Detroit	P	.833	1	4	1	0	0
Castro, Cesar, California	C/IF	.970	29	3	1	0	2
Castro, Eleuterio, Toyo Carp	P	.500	0	1	1	0	0

Player, Team	Pos.	Pct.	PO	A	E	DP	PB
Castro, Jesus, Toronto	OF	1.000	5	0	0	0	0
Castro, Jorge, Dodgers II	C	.966	203	25	8	0	18
Castro, Martirez, Texas	OF	.944	110	7	7	1	0
Castro, Rafael, Phi./St.L.	C	.933	64	19	6	0	0
Cedeno, Ruddy, Houston	SS	.872	67	103	25	9	0
Celedonio, Carlos, San Fran.	IF	.838	47	77	24	6	0
Celta, Nicolas, Houston	P	.864	4	15	3	1	0
Cera, Aquiles, Dodgers II	P	1.000	1	5	0	0	0
Chavel, Ali, California	OF	.846	9	2	2	0	0
Ciociola, Miguel, Dodgers I	OF	.951	35	4	2	1	0
Coco, Pascual, Toronto	P	1.000	0	6	0	0	0
Collado, Hugo, Dodgers I	OF-P	.944	47	4	3	0	0
Collado, Juan, N.Y. Yankees	OF	.971	33	0	1	0	0
Compres, Miguel, N.Y. Yankees	C	.962	90	11	4	0	5
Contreras, Angel, Pittsburgh	P	1.000	2	2	0	0	0
Cordero, Willie, Texas	SS	.876	43	106	21	4	0
Corniell, Henry, Oakland	P	1.000	1	2	0	0	0
Cornielle, Alex, Toyo Carp	P	.875	2	5	1	0	0
Corporan, Manuel, Bal./Chi.(AL)	IF	.936	70	64	9	4	0
Cota, Marino, Dodgers II	P	1.000	0	7	0	0	0
Cruz, Charlie, Dodgers I	1B	.950	52	5	3	0	0
Cruz, Luis, Toyo Carp	OF/IF	.949	97	51	8	3	0
Cruz, Radhames, K.C./Colo.	C	.947	138	24	9	0	16
Cruz, Raul, Oakland	P	.833	0	5	1	0	0
Cruz, Silvio, K.C./Colo.	2B	.932	131	129	19	12	0
Cueto, Jose, Seattle	P	.857	4	8	2	2	0
Dacosta, Samuel, Montreal	1B-P	.981	92	8	2	1	0
Davis, Melvin, San Francisco	P	1.000	0	3	0	0	0
DeJesus, Eddy, California	OF	.933	67	3	5	0	0
DeJesus, Wilmer, Montreal	C	.969	185	36	7	2	0
DeLaCruz, Antonio, N.Y. Mets	SS	.868	36	56	14	5	0
DeLaCruz, Fernando, California	P	.833	1	4	1	0	0
DeLaCruz, Fernando, Toyo Carp	P	.909	3	17	2	3	0
DeLaCruz, Henry, Chi. (NL)/S.D.	OF	.933	37	5	3	1	0
DeLaCruz, Inocencio, N.Y. Mets	P	.875	3	11	2	1	0
DeLaCruz, Jose, Oakland	3B	.872	75	61	20	11	0
DeLaCruz, Juan, San Francisco	IF	.880	68	5	10	4	0
DeLaCruz, Pedro, Toronto	OF	.923	12	0	1	0	0
DeLaCruz, Rafael, San Francisco	1B	.935	91	9	7	2	0
DeLaCruz, Raul, Pittsburgh	OF	.975	75	3	2	0	0
DeLaEspada, Miguel, Houston	OF	.931	53	1	4	0	0
DeLaRosa, Erasmo, Houston	OF	.888	31	1	4	1	0
DeLaRosa, Miguel, Texas	DH	.947	71	1	4	0	0
DeLeon, Jose, Detroit	OF	.941	12	4	1	0	0
DeLeon, Jose, Phi./St.L.	P	.917	2	9	1	0	0
DeLeon, Julio, N.Y. Yankees	P	.905	4	15	2	0	0
DeLeon, Ricardo, Atlanta	C	.986	63	6	1	0	3
Delgado, Manuel, Toronto	P	.750	1	2	1	0	0
Delgado, Ramon, Seattle	1B	.987	286	12	4	4	0
Deliza, Angel, Chi. (NL)/S.D.	P	1.000	1	2	0	0	0
Del Orbe, Wellington, Cleveland	P	.800	1	3	1	0	0
DeLosSantos, Americo, K.C./Colo.	P	.810	2	15	4	0	0
DeLosSantos, Aurelio, Phi./St.L.	C	.930	115	31	11	0	0
DeLosSantos, Domingo, K.C./Colo.	P	.500	2	1	3	0	0
DeLosSantos, Luis, N.Y. Yankees	P	.950	4	15	1	1	0
Del Valle, Carlos, Detroit	1B	.975	601	23	16	4	0
Diaz, Emenegildo, San Francisco	IF	.981	442	21	9	2	0
Diaz, Esteban, Dodgers I	P	.833	1	9	2	0	0
Diaz, Ivan, Phi./St.L.	DH	.902	33	4	4	0	0
Diaz, Miguel, California	OF	.905	81	5	9	0	0
Diaz, Welvis, Oakland	OF	.935	67	5	5	0	0
Diese, Jose, Toyo Carp	P	.929	2	11	1	0	0
Disla, Francisco, N.Y. Yankees	P	1.000	0	8	0	0	0
D'LaCruz, Ignacio, San Fran.	P	.571	0	4	3	0	0
D'Leon, Sandy, Seattle	C	.972	174	31	6	1	2
Dominguez, Enrique, Montreal	OF	.971	65	3	2	1	0
Dotel, Melido, Dodgers II	P	.722	2	11	5	0	0
Duncan, Jan Carlos, Phi./St.L.	3B	.841	52	96	28	11	0
Duverge, Salvador, K.C./Colo.	DH	.667	2	0	1	0	0
Ellis, Franklin, Houston	OF	.923	29	7	3	1	0
Encarnacion, Edgardo, California	IF	.854	60	98	27	10	0
Encarnacion, Mario, Oakland	OF	.945	112	9	7	4	0
Encarnacion, Pedro, Bal./Chi.(AL)	OF	.957	63	3	3	0	0
Encarnacion, Sonder, Seattle	2B	.940	63	77	9	5	0
Ernesto, Hector, Florida	P	.571	3	1	3	0	0
Escarlante, Simon, Phi./St.L.	P	.667	0	6	3	0	0
Escobar, Kelvin, Toronto	P	1.000	2	6	0	0	0
Espinal, Orlando, Montreal	P	.800	1	3	1	0	0
Espino, Fernando, Seattle	OF	.946	80	8	5	5	0
Espino, Jose, Toyo Carp	OF	.911	93	9	10	2	0
Estevez, Domingo, Toronto	OF	.917	42	2	4	0	0
Estrella, Leoncio, N.Y. Mets	P	1.000	4	3	0	0	0
Eusebio, Ruben, Houston	2B	.956	62	68	6	3	0

Player, Team	Pos.	Pct.	PO	A	E	DP	PB
Fajardo, Alejandro, Phi./St.L.	OF	.930	102	4	8	1	0
Farraez, Adel, Houston	OF	.895	32	2	4	0	0
Farraez, Jesus, Houston	OF	.915	70	5	7	2	0
Felix, Edgar, Pittsburgh	SS	.887	39	87	16	5	0
Felix, Miguel, Bal./Chi.(AL)	P	.706	1	11	5	0	0
Felix, Osvaldo, K.C./Colo.	P	1.000	1	1	0	1	0
Fernandez, Juan, Dodgers I	SS	.820	26	83	24	7	0
Fernandez, Robert, Cleveland	OF-P	.938	24	5	2	1	0
Fernandez, Winston, Texas	OF	.969	91	2	3	0	0
Ferreiras, Luis, Cleveland	C	.959	61	10	3	0	11
Figueroa, Jose, Oakland	C	.974	171	15	5	2	3
Fischer, Carlos, California	IF	.916	69	137	19	13	0
Florentino, Osmil, K.C./Colo.	P	1.000	0	1	0	0	0
Flores, Carlos, Houston	OF	1.000	3	1	0	0	0
Flores, Julio, Montreal	OF	.922	67	4	6	0	0
Font, Franklin, Chi. (NL)/S.D.	3B	.937	114	153	18	14	0
Francisco, Frank, Atlanta	OF	.884	104	10	15	2	0
Francisco, Norberto, Bal./Chi.(AL)	P	1.000	1	2	0	1	0
Franco, Deyvi, Detroit	DH	.667	2	0	1	0	0
Franco, Jorge, Montreal	C	.993	120	26	1	0	0
Frias, Jovanny, Bal./Chi.(AL)	P	1.000	0	8	0	0	0
Fructuoso, Jose, Seattle	P	1.000	0	5	0	0	0
Galban, Elvis, Montreal	2B	.928	96	109	16	7	0
Galvez, Randy, Dodgers I	P	.917	3	8	1	0	0
Garcia, Eduardo, California	IF	.926	21	29	4	1	0
Garcia, Jhoan, Seattle	P	.556	2	3	4	0	0
Garcia, Jose, Cleveland	P	.882	3	12	2	0	0
Garcia, Juan, Atlanta	OF	.954	122	3	6	1	0
Garcia, Juan, Detroit	OF	1.000	3	0	0	0	0
Garcia, Julio, N.Y. Yankees	2B	.818	5	4	2	0	0
Garcia, Leoncio, California	C	.964	121	14	5	0	5
Garcia, Luis, Dodgers II	OF	.944	48	3	3	1	0
Garcia, Rafael, Seattle	P	.833	1	4	1	0	0
Genao, Martin, Dodgers II	P	.875	4	3	1	0	0
German, Aris, N.Y. Mets	C	.985	59	8	1	0	4
German, John, N.Y. Mets	P	.857	1	5	1	1	0
German, Julian, Detroit	2B	.968	65	84	5	8	0
Germosen, Julio, Pittsburgh	2B	.951	109	163	14	14	0
Geronimo, Cesar, California	OF	.958	111	4	5	0	0
Gil, Alberto, Cleveland	OF	.967	84	3	3	1	0
Giron, Edilberto, Pittsburgh	DH	.800	4	0	1	0	0
Giron, Isabel, Toronto	SS	.927	38	102	11	7	0
Giron, Juan, Atlanta	3B	.801	51	78	32	4	0
Glaterol, Becker, Toronto	P	1.000	5	8	0	0	0
Gomera, Rafael, Dodgers I	OF	.926	116	22	11	5	0
Gomez, Domingo, California	P	.875	1	6	1	1	0
Gomez, Jose, Seattle	P	.750	3	9	4	1	0
Gomez, Luis, Detroit	P	1.000	0	4	0	0	0
Gomez, Luis, Houston	C	.952	127	14	7	0	10
Gomez, Manuel, Detroit	P	1.000	1	6	0	0	0
Gomez, Miguel, Toronto	P	1.000	2	4	0	1	0
Gomez, Rafael, N.Y. Mets	P	.875	3	4	1	0	0
Gomez, Ricardo, Pittsburgh	P	1.000	0	1	0	0	0
Gondola, Roberto, N.Y. Yankees	P	1.000	1	4	0	0	0
Gonzalez, Adalberto, Montreal	SS	.929	19	46	5	2	0
Gonzalez, Cesar, Montreal	3B	.918	20	36	5	0	0
Gonzalez, Edwin, K.C./Colo.	P	1.000	3	7	0	0	0
Gonzalez, Franklin, Chi. (NL)/S.D.	OF	.923	57	3	5	0	0
Gonzalez, Santo, Chi. (NL)/S.D	SS	.934	83	142	16	11	0
Guerra, Carlos, Cleveland	SS	.939	12	19	2	2	0
Guerra, Robert, California	IF	.895	56	115	20	9	0
Guerrero, Frank, Houston	3B	.816	29	92	27	9	0
Guerrero, Hamlet, N.Y. Mets	OF	.979	87	7	2	0	0
Guerrero, Jose, Seattle	P	1.000	0	4	0	0	0
Guerrero, Wascar, Seattle	1B	.984	303	13	5	4	0
Guevara, Carlos, Pittsburgh	P	1.000	1	2	0	0	0
Guilleard, Alfonso, Toyo Carp	SS	.892	103	178	34	15	0
Guillen, Angel, San Francisco	P	.889	0	8	1	0	0
Gutierrez, Victor, Pittsburgh	2B	.923	73	95	14	10	0
Guzman, Ambiorix, Texas	P	.857	2	4	1	1	0
Guzman, Carlos, Detroit	OF	.944	30	4	2	0	0
Guzman, Cristian, N.Y. Yankees	SS	.882	58	159	29	13	0
Guzman, Juan, Bal./Chi.(AL)	C/1B	.974	191	35	6	0	3
Guzman, Juan, Phi./St.L.	OF	.954	98	6	5	0	0
Guzman, Leybi, Dodgers I	P	.750	0	3	1	0	0
Guzman, Martin, Toyo Carp	C/1B	.973	365	25	11	1	7
Guzman, Santos, Pittsburgh	C	.969	231	18	8	0	12
Guzman, Toribio A., Phi./St.L.	P	643	3	6	5	0	0
Guzman, Wilson, Pittsburgh	P	.875	2	12	2	1	0
Haad, Yamid, Pittsburgh	C	.980	265	31	6	1	5
Henriquez, Hector, Florida	P	.647	2	20	12	1	0
Henriquez, Jovanny, Texas	P	.714	0	5	2	0	0
Henriquez, Roman, Dodgers I	P	.773	2	15	5	0	0

Player, Team	Pos.	Pct.	PO	A	E	DP	PB
Heredia, Andres, K.C./Colo.	C	.935	72	14	6	0	5
Heredia, Maximo, Bal./Chi.(AL)	P	1.000	1	11	0	0	0
Heredia, Rafael, Chi. (NL)/S.D.	1B	.956	229	11	11	2	0
Heredia, Ruddy, Toronto	P	1.000	1	0	0	0	0
Heredia, Willy, Atlanta	P	.667	3	1	2	0	0
Hernandez, Darwin, Pittsburgh	1B	.982	448	46	9	5	0
Hernandez, German, Texas	P	1.000	0	3	0	0	0
Hernandez, Jesus, Cleveland	OF	.943	95	4	6	0	0
Hernandez, Jorgelio, Toyo Carp	OF	.952	19	1	1	0	0
Hernandez, Jose, Montreal	P	.952	12	8	1	0	0
Hernandez, Julio, California	P	.600	0	3	2	0	0
Hernandez, Leonardo, N.Y. Mets	OF	.962	44	7	2	2	0
Hernandez, Pedro, Dodgers II	P	.826	3	16	4	1	0
Hernandez, Rafael, Montreal	3B	.923	53	78	11	10	0
Herrera, Alvaro, California	1B	.980	366	21	8	1	0
Herrera, Misael, Chi. (NL)/S.D.	P	.800	1	11	3	0	0
Hiraldo, Juan, Cleveland	P	.545	0	6	5	0	0
Infante, Danny, Texas	1B	.983	343	52	7	9	0
Infante, Julio, Dodgers I	OF	.962	21	4	1	1	0
Iquerey, Rodney, Cleveland	3B	.962	109	41	6	3	0
Jadagui, Carlos, Chi. (NL)/S.D.	C	.927	118	22	11	2	4
Javier, Frank, Florida	P	.909	5	5	1	1	0
Javier, Jesus, Dodgers I	SS	.934	57	98	11	11	0
Jimenez, Alejandro, Texas	P	.800	0	4	1	0	0
Jimenez, Denny, Oakland	P	.929	4	9	1	1	0
Jimenez, Felipe, Chi. (NL)/S.D.	OF	.925	83	3	7	1	0
Jimenez, Johnn, Dodgers I	P	.636	3	4	4	0	0
Jimenez, Kelly, K.C./Colo.	P	.857	5	13	3	1	0
Jimenez, Miguel, Seattle	3B	.908	62	145	21	16	0
Jimenez, Ramon, N.Y. Yankees	OF	.956	43	0	2	0	0
Jimenez, Ricardo, Bal./Chi.(AL)	P	1.000	0	4	0	0	0
Jose, Leonardo, Oakland	3B	.915	36	29	6	2	0
King, Cesar, Texas	C	.967	277	43	11	0	5
King, Daniel, Oakland	1B	.979	223	10	5	1	0
Langagney, Shelwin, Toronto	OF	.954	116	8	6	2	0
Lara, Balnes, Detroit	OF	.941	91	5	6	2	0
Lara, Felix, Pittsburgh	OF	.909	57	3	6	0	0
Lara, Nelson, Florida	P	.667	2	4	3	0	0
LaReal, Guillermo, San Francisco	P	1.000	0	6	0	0	0
Lechler, Luis, Dodgers II	P	.800	2	2	1	0	0
Ledesma, Felipe, Dodgers II	3B	.909	54	115	17	7	0
Leidens, Misael, Montreal	SS	.896	47	82	15	8	0
Leon, Rafael, Florida	P	.733	4	7	4	2	0
Leyva, Edgar, California	P	1.000	0	13	0	0	0
Lima, Jose, K.C./Colo.	2B	.852	9	14	4	1	0
Lina, Donald, K.C./Colo.	SS	.814	29	50	18	3	0
Linares, Edwin, Atlanta	P	.929	4	35	3	0	0
Linares, Mario, Toyo Carp	P	.929	3	10	1	0	0
Linares, Rafael, Bal./Chi.(AL)	OF	.962	44	8	2	1	0
Linares, Sendry, Houston	C	.973	120	25	4	0	16
Lizardo, Julio, San Francisco	P	.900	0	9	1	2	0
Loaisiga, Stanley, Montreal	1B	.990	467	37	5	7	0
Lopez, Luis, San Francisco	OF	.944	78	7	5	3	0
Lora, Edison, K.C./Colo.	P	.889	3	13	2	1	0
Lora, Freddy, Pittsburgh	P	.571	1	3	3	0	0
Lorenzo, Julio, Detroit	OF	.945	62	7	4	2	0
Lorenzo, Martin, Houston	P	1.000	4	10	0	0	0
Loyo, Oscar, Florida	3B	.881	10	27	5	1	0
Luis, Cristian, Houston	P	1.000	1	2	0	0	0
Maldonado, Franklin, Chi. (NL)/S.D.	OF	.944	88	14	6	3	0
Marcano, Dennys, Chi. (NL)/S.D.	3B	.852	78	37	20	1	0
Maria, Alcibiades, Texas	P	.444	0	4	5	0	0
Marshall, Victor, N.Y. Yankees	P	.800	2	2	1	0	0
Marte, Julian, Dodgers II	IF	.938	74	107	12	9	0
Marte, Luis, K.C./Colo.	P	.600	2	4	4	0	0
Marte, Nestor, Detroit	OF	.931	25	2	2	1	0
Martinez, Andres, N.Y. Mets	DH	.900	29	34	7	2	0
Martinez, Claudio, Dodgers II	P	.500	2	0	2	0	0
Martinez, David, Toronto	3B	.888	45	129	22	8	0
Martinez, Fausto, N.Y. Mets	OF	.917	22	0	2	0	0
Martinez, Frank, Houston	P	.750	2	10	4	0	0
Martinez, Gabriel, Chi. (NL)/S.D.	P	1.000	0	2	0	0	0
Martinez, Gregorio, Dodgers II	SS	.844	92	162	47	11	0
Martinez, Jose, Cleveland	1B	.978	437	14	10	2	0
Martinez, Jose, Texas	P	.917	4	7	1	0	0
Martinez, Sandy, Houston	P	.750	1	5	2	0	0
Martinez, Wander, California	P	1.000	5	5	0	0	0
Martinez, Winston, Detroit	3B	.903	26	30	6	5	0
Mateo, Amaury, Texas	OF	.982	55	1	1	0	0
Mateo, Freddy, Dodgers II	1B	.975	487	28	13	0	0
Mateo, Victor, N.Y. Yankees	3B	.933	80	129	15	9	0
Matias, Hansell, Atlanta	P	.857	2	16	3	1	0
Matos, Dauris, N.Y. Mets	P	.909	4	6	1	0	0
Matos, Wellington, N.Y. Yankees	1B	.976	494	27	13	1	0
McDonald, Gabriel, San Fran.	OF	.838	55	2	11	0	0
McFarlane, Ivan, K.C./Colo.	OF	.828	22	2	5	0	0
McLean, Guillermo, Dodgers II	OF	.833	12	3	3	1	0
McWellyng, Venzen, California	P	1.000	0	1	0	0	0
Medina, Carlos, Florida	P	.778	2	12	4	0	0
Medina, Edward, Detroit	P	1.000	0	1	0	0	0
Medina, Richy, Detroit	3B	.825	28	52	17	5	0
Mejia, Jose, Atlanta	C	.938	158	37	13	2	10
Mejia, Juan, Phi./St.L.	SS	.910	62	121	18	12	0
Mejia, Luis, Houston	OF	.846	21	1	4	0	0
Mejia, Luis, N.Y. Yankees	P	.750	0	3	1	0	0
Mejia, Oliver, Pittsburgh	SS	.935	94	64	11	6	0
Mejia, Renato, Florida	OF	.943	144	6	9	2	0
Melian, Jhonathan, Seattle	P	.750	0	3	1	0	0
Mena, Eddy, Detroit	P	1.000	1	0	0	0	0
Mendez, Claudio R., Seattle	OF	.950	18	1	1	0	0
Mendez, Lenin, Seattle	P	1.000	0	2	0	0	0
Mento, Alfredo, N.Y. Mets	3B	.897	114	77	22	3	0
Meran, Jorge, Detroit	C	.964	294	54	13	1	0
Mercado, Henry, Cleveland	DH	.889	15	1	2	0	0
Mercedes, Carlos, Bal./Chi.(AL)	P	1.000	0	3	0	1	0
Mercedes, Daniel, Pittsburgh	P	.667	1	1	1	0	0
Mercedes, Jose, Oakland	P	.769	0	10	3	0	0
Mercedes, Luis, San Francisco	IF	.960	38	105	6	7	0
Mercedes, Matias, Detroit	2B-P	.929	89	134	17	18	0
Mercedes, Tomas, Toronto	P	1.000	3	4	0	0	0
Mesa, Willy, K.C./Colo.	P	1.000	2	0	0	0	0
Mesina, Juan, Florida	P	.750	1	5	2	0	0
Mijares, Robert, Dodgers II	OF	1.000	35	3	0	1	0
Minaya, Pablo, Florida	P	.941	2	14	1	0	0
Molina, Alfredo, Dodgers II	IF	.938	33	58	6	5	0
Monero, Pablo, California	P	.600	0	3	2	0	0
Montanez, Johan, Toronto	P	.941	2	14	1	1	0
Montero, Francisco, Phi./St.L.	P	.857	5	13	3	0	0
Morales, Anaximando, Atlanta	3B	.778	40	30	20	1	0
Morales, Cesar, San Francisco	C	.932	157	22	13	0	0
Morales, Domingo, Bal./Chi.(AL)	OF	.938	29	1	2	0	0
Morel, Jose, Pittsburgh	P	.750	0	6	2	0	0
Morelo, Fulvio, N.Y. Yankees	3B	.935	31	55	6	7	0
Moreno, Antony, Houston	SS	.888	41	94	17	9	0
Moreno, Johnny, Bal./Chi.(AL)	OF	.944	145	7	9	2	0
Moreno, Jose, Seattle	2B	.932	89	102	14	9	0
Moreno, Juan, N.Y. Mets	OF	.977	77	8	2	2	0
Moreno, Willy, N.Y. Yankees	OF	.846	10	1	2	0	0
Moreta, Ramon, Dodgers II	OF	.960	141	4	6	0	0
Moris, Miguel, N.Y. Mets	P	.818	1	8	2	0	0
Morrobel, Juan, Pittsburgh	P	.500	0	1	1	0	0
Mota, Henry, Texas	P	.917	0	11	1	0	0
Mota, Leonardo, San Francisco	P	.583	1	6	5	0	0
Mota, Pedro, San Francisco	OF	.929	24	2	2	1	0
Mota, Victor, Detroit	OF	.971	59	9	2	1	0
Mundo, Alberto, Atlanta	OF/IF	.888	119	119	30	17	0
Munoz, Eduardo, Seattle	DH	1.000	18	2	0	1	0
Nina, Amaury, Texas	OF	.977	43	0	1	0	0
Nina, Jose, Toronto	SS	.929	67	128	15	10	0
Nova, Joselin, Florida	C	.977	359	75	10	0	14
Nova, Kelvin, Oakland	2B	.970	84	79	5	7	0
Nunez, Abraham, Toronto	2B	.962	80	97	7	6	0
Nunez, Bienvenido, San Francisco	C	.943	57	9	4	0	3
Nunez, Enrique, Phi./St.L.	P	.818	5	4	2	0	0
Nunez, Euripides, Bal./Chi.(AL)	IF	.867	13	65	12	8	0
Nunez, Franklin, Dodgers II	P	.500	0	1	1	0	0
Nunez, Jorge, Toronto	SS	1.000	0	1	0	0	0
Nunez, Jose, K.C./Colo.	3B	.902	58	162	24	12	0
Nunez, Jose, Oakland	C	.990	181	23	2	0	9
Oliva, Osvaldo, Atlanta	1B	.973	506	32	15	2	0
Olivares, Melvin, N.Y. Mets	SS	.936	82	167	17	18	0
Oliver, Jose, Oakland	P	.750	1	2	1	1	0
Olivero, Ricardo, Montreal	C	.968	160	21	6	0	0
Olivo, Gary, San Francisco	P	.800	0	4	1	0	0
Olivo, Juan, Toyo Carp	P	.889	3	5	1	0	0
Oramas, Victor, Houston	C	.980	84	13	2	0	4
Orta, Carlos, Montreal	P	.913	5	16	2	0	0
Ortiz, Eusebio, Phi./St.L.	P	.667	3	3	3	0	0
Ortiz, Jose, Oakland	SS	.885	110	182	38	17	0
Ortiz, Pedro, Dodgers I	P	1.000	1	2	0	0	0
Ortiz, Ramon, California	P	.944	3	14	1	1	0
Otano, Delvin, Toyo Carp	3B	.893	58	151	25	11	0
Ovalle, Jesus, Texas	SS	.926	52	85	11	11	0
Ovalles, Albin, K.C./Colo.	SS	.900	73	143	24	10	0
Oviedo, Alexander, Oakland	P	.958	5	18	1	2	0
Ozorio, Douglas, N.Y. Yankees	P	1.000	1	2	0	1	0

Player, Team	Pos.	Pct.	PO	A	E	DP	PB
Ozorio, Eric, Atlanta	P	.833	1	9	2	0	0
Ozuna, Carlos, Oakland	P	1.000	2	7	0	0	0
Ozuna, Pedro, N.Y. Yankees	2B	.923	64	91	13	11	0
Padua, Gerardo, N.Y. Yankees	P	.750	2	4	2	0	0
Paniagua, Freddy, Florida	P	.875	0	7	1	0	0
Paraqueima, Jesus, N.Y. Yankees	P	1.000	1	5	0	1	0
Paredes, Roberto, Cleveland	P	.800	3	5	2	0	0
Parra, Catalino, N.Y. Yankees	P	.875	2	12	2	0	0
Parra, Jesus, Houston	P	.857	2	10	2	1	0
Parra, Jorge, Texas	P	1.000	0	5	0	0	0
Parra, Klisber, Florida	P	.846	3	8	2	0	0
Pascual, Ubaldo, Chi. (NL)/S.D.	P	.750	1	2	1	0	0
Patino, Leonardo, California	P	.842	2	14	3	0	0
Paulino, Arison, Pittsburgh	P	1.000	0	1	0	0	0
Paulino, Manuel, Oakland	P	1.000	1	9	0	1	0
Paz, Richard, Bal./Chi.(AL)	SS	.949	89	211	16	23	0
Peguero, Americo, Bal./Chi.(AL)	P	1.000	4	10	0	0	0
Pena, Charlies, Toyo Carp	OF	.994	165	2	1	1	0
Pena, Domingo, Pittsburgh	P	.667	0	2	1	1	0
Pena, Elvi, Seattle	C	.978	187	33	5	0	7
Pena, Onesimo, N.Y. Mets	OF	.947	85	5	5	0	0
Pena, Ramon, Toronto	DH	1.000	26	4	0	1	1
Pena, Reynaldo, Detroit	SS	.946	140	229	21	25	0
Pena, Victor, Phi./St.L.	SS	.837	36	46	16	6	0
Pena, Warren, N.Y. Yankees	OF	.967	54	5	2	1	0
Penalver, Juan, N.Y. Mets	2B	.966	130	129	9	5	0
Peralta, Santiago, Toyo Carp	1B	.981	451	18	9	2	0
Perdomo, Roberto, San Fran.	OF	.943	30	3	2	1	0
Perez, Angelo, Toronto	OF	.958	120	16	6	4	0
Perez, David, Atlanta	C	.994	294	54	2	1	14
Perez, Edwin, Cleveland	2B	.963	170	139	12	11	0
Perez, Jorge, N.Y. Yankees	P	.750	0	4	1	0	0
Perez, Jose, Cleveland	C	.974	32	6	1	0	4
Perez, Manuel, Phi./St.L.	2B	.921	30	28	5	2	0
Perez, Richard, Bal./Chi.(AL)	OF	.900	77	4	9	0	0
Perez, Samuel, Cleveland	P	.880	7	15	3	1	0
Perez, Stiwar, Dodgers I	1B	.977	533	24	13	0	0
Perez, Wegner, Cleveland	SS	.847	20	30	9	4	0
Perez, Wilman, Florida	1B	.941	171	38	13	4	0
Perozo, Alberto, Atlanta	P	.833	1	4	1	1	0
Petique, Marino, Toyo Carp	P	.909	3	7	1	0	0
Pimentel, Jose, Dodgers II	OF	.974	110	3	3	1	0
Pimentel, Marino, Florida	OF	.897	91	5	11	0	0
Pinales, Demetrio, Texas	P	1.000	1	4	0	0	0
Pinales, Otilio, Seattle	P	.667	0	2	1	0	0
Pinales, Victor, Houston	C	.929	76	15	7	0	17
Pineda, Luis, Texas	P	1.000	0	9	0	0	0
Pinedo, Hector, Phi./St.L.	2B	.926	74	88	13	8	0
Polanco, Elvis, Chi. (NL)/S.D.	P	.773	3	14	5	1	0
Polanco, Julio, Texas	1B-P	.980	49	0	1	0	0
Polanco, Raul, Chi. (NL)/S.D.	OF	.915	80	6	8	1	0
Polonia, Israel, Florida	SS	.903	99	179	30	22	0
Polonio, Enrique, Pittsburgh	OF	.897	73	5	9	0	0
Preciado, Victor, N.Y. Yankees	OF	.953	121	21	7	3	0
Presinal, Gilberto, Chi. (NL)/S.D.	P	.833	1	4	1	0	0
Pringle, Juan, N.Y. Yankees	DH	.934	76	9	6	1	3
Pujols, Rafael, Oakland	3B	.966	176	49	8	2	0
Quero, Pedro, Montreal	OF	.865	30	2	5	0	0
Quezada, Adalberto, San Fran.	OF	.978	41	4	1	1	0
Quezada, Anulfo, California	P	.800	4	4	2	0	0
Quezada, Edward, Montreal	P	1.000	0	1	0	0	0
Quiroz, Misael, Pittsburgh	P	.842	6	10	3	0	0
Racero, Aramis, Toronto	P	.857	2	4	1	0	0
Rafael, Jorge, Toronto	P	.857	2	4	1	0	0
Ramirez, Antonio, Montreal	P	.900	3	6	1	0	0
Ramirez, Aramis, Pittsburgh	3B	.886	65	82	19	4	0
Ramirez, David, Texas	3B	.913	40	23	6	3	0
Ramirez, Jordy, Toyo Carp	IF	.867	34	51	13	4	0
Ramirez, Jose, Detroit	P	.882	1	14	2	0	0
Ramirez, Juan, K.C./Colo.	1B	.980	568	30	12	3	0
Ramirez, Narciso, Montreal	OF	.902	83	8	10	1	0
Ramirez, Rafael, Detroit	OF	.957	39	5	2	0	0
Ramos, Fernando, Phi./St.L.	P	.789	5	10	4	0	0
Ramos, Jose, Dodgers I	P	.870	4	16	3	0	0
Ramos, Juan C., Montreal	P	.813	6	7	3	0	0
Ramos, Kelly, N.Y. Mets	C	.994	296	43	2	0	4
Rebolledo, Jairo, Chi. (NL)/S.D.	1B	.975	328	16	9	0	0
Regalado, Frank, Toyo Carp	P	1.000	0	1	0	0	0
Regalado, Maximo, Dodgers I	P	.667	0	2	1	0	0
Renteria, Everth, Atlanta	2B	.889	72	56	16	4	0
Reyes, Bernardo, Dodgers II	P	1.000	0	2	0	0	0
Reyes, Cristian, Oakland	SS	.891	22	19	5	2	0
Reyes, Jose Luis, N.Y. Mets	P	.917	4	7	1	1	0

Player, Team	Pos.	Pct.	PO	A	E	DP	PB
Reyes, Juan, Montreal	P	1.000	3	6	0	0	0
Reyes, Pedro, N.Y. Yankees	P	1.000	1	1	0	0	0
Reyes, Santos, Detroit	P	1.000	2	2	0	0	0
Reynoso, Ismael, Florida	SS	.888	32	55	11	5	0
Ricardo, Alfredo, Oakland	C	.977	171	39	5	0	8
Ricardo, Luis, Dodgers I	OF	.935	25	4	2	0	0
Richardson, Elbin, Texas	DH	.966	14	14	1	0	0
Richardson, Roberto, Phi./St.L.	P	1.000	0	1	0	0	0
Rijo, Fernando, Dodgers I	P	1.000	2	10	0	0	0
Rijo, Francisco, Toyo Carp	P	1.000	1	5	0	1	0
Rijo, Jose, Houston	P	.800	3	1	1	0	0
Rincones, Gabriel, Seattle	P	1.000	1	2	0	0	0
Rios, Carlos, Houston	1B	.984	470	23	8	0	0
Rivera, Homero, Detroit	P	1.000	0	4	0	0	0
Rivera, Juan C., Chi. (NL)/S.D.	3B-P	.833	9	21	6	4	0
Rivera, Santo, San Francisco	IF	.955	169	127	14	5	0
Rivera, Yorki, Dodgers I	OF	.939	70	7	5	3	0
Robles, Victor, Bal./Chi.(AL)	OF	.852	40	6	8	3	0
Rodriguez, Alfredo, Dodgers II	C	.990	182	13	2	0	11
Rodriguez, Aron, Bal./Chi.(AL)	P	.000	0	0	1	0	0
Rodriguez, Felipe, Toronto	2B	.957	112	113	10	6	0
Rodriguez, Franklin, Toronto	P	.778	0	7	2	0	0
Rodriguez, Geremias, Toyo Carp	2B	.959	92	93	8	4	0
Rodriguez, Henry, Bal./Chi.(AL)	P	1.000	6	0	0	1	0
Rodriguez, Jose, Florida	3B	.891	36	79	14	4	0
Rodriguez, Juan, Pittsburgh	OF	.940	115	11	8	3	0
Rodriguez, Miguel, Phi./St.L.	2B	.873	63	68	19	3	0
Rodriguez, Nelson, Dodgers I	2B-P	.954	114	113	11	11	0
Rodriguez, Pedro, Seattle	P	.889	1	7	1	0	0
Rodriguez, Rodney, Atlanta	P	1.000	1	1	0	0	0
Rojas, Cesar, Texas	P	1.000	4	8	0	0	0
Rojas, Francisco, Dodgers II	P	.889	2	6	1	0	0
Rojas, Juan P., Atlanta	P	.909	2	8	1	1	0
Romano, Manuel, San Francisco	P	.857	5	13	3	2	0
Romero, Mario, Houston	OF	.850	16	1	3	0	0
Romero, Raumer, Montreal	P	.765	4	9	4	0	0
Romero, Robinson, N.Y. Yankees	C	.982	230	38	5	2	10
Rondon, Gabriel, Houston	P	.714	1	4	2	0	0
Rondon, Jhonny, Seattle	2B	.828	20	28	10	3	0
Rosario, Carlos, K.C./Colo.	OF	.934	120	7	9	2	0
Rosario, Rafael, Detroit	P	1.000	3	2	0	0	0
Rosario, Ramon, Houston	1B/C	1.000	150	13	0	1	2
Rosario, Ramon, Oakland	P	.947	2	16	1	1	0
Rosario, Reynaldo, Detroit	P	.833	1	4	1	0	0
Rosario, Ruben, Phi./St.L.	P	1.000	1	4	0	0	0
Ruiz, Francis, Toyo Carp	C	.975	284	26	8	0	9
Ruiz, Jose, Seattle	OF	.987	72	5	1	0	0
Salazar, Oscar, Oakland	SS	.888	94	159	32	16	0
Samuel, Yojairo, Texas	P	.938	4	11	1	2	0
Sanchez, Jose, Detroit	3B	.877	30	20	7	0	0
Sanchez, Jossys, Montreal	P	.800	0	4	1	0	0
Sanchez, Manuel, Atlanta	IF	.900	112	122	26	8	0
Sanchez, Martin, Atlanta	P	.833	3	17	4	0	0
Sanchez, Wellington, Chi. (NL)/S.D.	P	.950	5	14	1	0	0
Sanchez, Willington, Toronto	2B	.846	3	8	2	1	0
Sanquintin, Alexis, Cleveland	C	.958	39	7	2	0	3
Santamaria, Juan, Detroit	P	1.000	1	1	0	0	0
Santana, Alfredo, Detroit	P	.750	4	11	5	0	0
Santana, Aris, Bal./Chi.(AL)	P	.636	2	5	4	0	0
Santana, Humberto, N.Y. Mets	P	.813	6	7	3	0	0
Santana, Juan, Dodgers II	2B	.920	84	101	16	8	0
Santana, Luis, Dodgers II	OF	.986	66	6	1	2	0
Santana, Mario, California	C	.979	285	48	7	0	3
Santana, Pedro, Houston	2B	.933	110	126	17	4	0
Santana, Ramon, K.C./Colo.	OF	.885	112	3	15	0	0
Santana, Richard, K.C./Colo.	OF	.976	77	4	2	1	0
Santelise, Osvaldo, Bal./Chi.(AL)	1B	.955	162	7	8	1	0
Santiago, Cesar, Florida	P	1.000	1	6	0	0	0
Santos, Jose, California	C	.833	4	1	1	0	0
Santos, Jose, Texas	3B	.961	74	122	8	7	0
Santos, Ricardo, N.Y. Yankees	P	1.000	1	1	0	0	0
Santos, Victor, Detroit	P	.947	3	15	1	0	0
Saturria, Arturo, Phi./St.L.	OF	.864	126	14	22	3	0
Scuttaro, Marco, Cleveland	3B	.931	57	211	20	17	0
Segura, Winston, Texas	2B	.911	46	46	9	4	0
Segura, Yodys, Dodgers I	P	.833	7	13	4	0	0
Selmo, Alexandre, Atlanta	P	.813	4	9	3	0	0
Sencion, Pablo, Toronto	1B	.988	611	29	8	2	0
Serrano, Wascar, Chi. (NL)/S.D.	P	.846	1	10	2	0	0
Severino, Danny, Florida	OF	.862	96	10	17	1	0
Shinozuka, Takeiro, Montreal	SS	.909	10	10	2	1	0
Sido, Wilson, Toyo Carp	P	1.000	1	2	0	0	0
Sierra, Henry, N.Y. Mets	C	.980	211	31	5	0	8

Player, Team	Pos.	Pct.	PO	A	E	DP	PB
Sierra, Luis, Toronto	P	1.000	1	4	0	0	0
Silva, Luis, Toronto	P	1.000	0	1	0	0	0
Silverio, Richard, K.C./Colo.	OF	.909	10	0	1	0	0
Silvestre, Juan, Seattle	OF	.939	44	2	3	0	0
Smith, Nestor, N.Y. Yankees	OF	.968	86	5	3	2	0
Solano, Darling, Dodgers I	P	.667	1	1	1	0	0
Solano, Joel, Toronto	OF	.750	2	1	1	1	0
Soler, Miguel, N.Y. Yankees	P	1.000	1	7	0	0	0
Soriano, Gabriel, Dodgers I	P	.692	1	8	4	0	0
Sosa, Henry, Florida	P	.333	1	2	6	0	0
Sosa, Jorge, K.C./Colo.	SS	.797	13	46	15	3	0
Sosa, Leonel, Dodgers I	C	.982	96	13	2	0	0
Soto, Angel, K.C./Colo.	P	1.000	0	3	0	0	0
Soto, Carlos, N.Y. Mets	P	.750	1	8	3	0	0
Soto, Luis, Chi. (NL)/S.D.	C	.973	214	40	7	2	5
Suarez, Ramon, K.C./Colo.	P	.813	2	11	3	0	0
Suero, Ignacio, Toronto	C	.970	410	77	15	1	2
Suriel, Miguel, Dodgers I	DH	.972	143	29	5	3	0
Tavares, Heriberto, Pittsburgh	P	1.000	0	3	0	0	0
Tavarez, Carlos, Seattle	OF	.904	47	0	5	0	0
Taveras, Frank, Cleveland	DH	.922	162	52	18	2	0
Taveras, Jose, K.C./Colo.	OF	.991	103	4	1	1	0
Taveras, Luis, Texas	C	.975	163	29	5	0	5
Terrero, Ruben, N.Y. Mets	P	.500	1	1	2	0	0
Thomas, Wilson, N.Y. Yankees	DH	.959	69	2	3	1	0
Tineo, Marcos, Phi./St.L.	P	.889	3	5	1	0	0
Tobias, Enrique, Dodgers I	C	.974	127	22	4	0	0
Tolentino, Juan, California	OF	.921	31	4	3	1	0
Torres, Jairo, Bal./Chi.(AL)	IF	.824	9	33	9	4	0
Toussent, Andres, Toronto	3B	1.000	0	1	0	0	0
Trejo, Ulises, Houston	P	.765	1	12	4	1	0
Trinidad, Cesar, San Francisco	IF	.856	56	123	30	16	0
Ubiera, Nadin, Toyo Carp	OF	.930	68	7	5	1	0
Ubiera, Vinicio, Dodgers II	OF	.905	18	1	2	1	0
Urena, Pedro, Texas	P	1.000	1	0	0	0	0
Urquiola, Edgar, Montreal	2B	.942	41	56	6	3	0
Valderrama, Carlos, San Fran.	OF	1.000	32	0	0	0	0
Valdez, Alvaro, Cleveland	C	.989	217	60	3	3	5
Valdez, Jose, Phi./St.L.	OF	.892	50	8	7	0	0
Valdez, Juan, Pittsburgh	P	.750	0	3	1	0	0
Valdez, Orlando, San Francisco	P	.867	1	12	2	1	0
Valdez, Socrates, Dodgers I	2B	.949	52	59	6	3	0
Valdez, Wolkin, N.Y. Yankees	P	.800	0	4	1	0	0
Valenzuela, Jose, Chi. (NL)/S.D.	P	.692	2	7	4	0	0
Valera, Ramon, Seattle	SS	.928	108	148	20	16	0
Vals, Lucrecio, Bal./Chi.(AL)	IF	.799	60	51	28	10	0
Vanderhorst, Francisco, K.C./Colo.	P	.773	7	10	5	0	0
Vargas, Francisco, Cleveland	P	.857	4	8	2	1	0
Vargas, Iankel, Detroit	C	.970	185	39	7	2	0
Vargas, Jose, Toyo Carp	P	.909	2	8	1	0	0
Vasquez, Alejandro, Houston	OF	.955	60	3	3	1	0
Vasquez, Arnulfo, Cleveland	C	.960	64	8	3	0	3
Vasquez, Cesar, Houston	P	.900	3	6	1	1	0
Vasquez, Jose, Oakland	OF	.949	92	1	5	0	0
Vasquez, Luis, N.Y. Mets	P	.857	2	4	1	0	0
Vasquez, Moises, California	OF	.909	26	4	3	1	0
Vega, Juan, San Francisco	P	.800	2	6	2	0	0
Velasquez, Geovanny, California	IF	.946	74	85	9	10	0
Ventura, Frank, Cleveland	OF	.924	69	4	6	2	0
Ventura, Jose, California	OF	.857	14	4	3	0	0
Veras, Carlos, Pittsburgh	P	.500	0	1	1	0	0
Villar, Maximo, Pittsburgh	P	.857	2	10	2	1	0
Vilomar, Henry, N.Y. Mets	OF	.920	76	5	7	0	0
Virgil, Marcus, California	IF	.957	54	36	4	3	0
Vizcaino, Luis, Oakland	P	.846	8	14	4	0	0
Williams, Johanny, Phi./St.L.	1B	.964	262	29	11	1	0
Zabala, Ismel J., Seattle	P	1.000	1	8	0	0	0
Zamora, Junior, N.Y. Mets	3B	.919	57	56	10	7	0
Zapata, Juan, Houston	P	1.000	2	9	0	0	0
Zapata, Rolando, Montreal	P	.824	4	10	3	0	0

GULF COAST LEAGUE

LEAGUE OFFICE

President
Tom Saffell
Address
1503 Clower Creek Dr., H-262
Sarasota, FL 34231
Phone
813-966-6407

Teams*
Astros
Blue Jays
Braves
Cubs
Expos
Marlins
Mets
Orioles
Pirates
Rangers
Red Sox
Royals
Twins
White Sox
Yankees
*Teams play their games in Bradenton, Dunedin, Fort Myers, Kissimmee, Melbourne, Port Charlotte, Port St. Lucie, Sarasota, Tampa and West Palm Beach, Fla.

1995 FINAL STANDINGS

EASTERN DIVISION

Team	W	L	T	Pct.	GB
Marlins	40	16	0	.714	....
Mets	38	19	0	.667	2 1/2
Expos	21	35	0	.375	19
Braves	14	43	0	.246	26 1/2

NORTHERN DIVISION

Team	W	L	T	Pct.	GB
Tigers	33	24	0	.579	....
Yankees	32	26	0	.552	1 1/2
Astros	32	26	0	.552	1 1/2
Blue Jays	19	40	0	.322	15

NORTHWEST DIVISION

Team	W	L	T	Pct.	GB
White Sox	36	22	0	.621	....
Orioles	34	25	0	.576	2 1/2
Rangers	24	34	0	.414	12
Pirates	23	36	0	.390	13 1/2

SOUTHWEST DIVISION

Team	W	L	T	Pct.	GB
Royals	37	20	0	.649	....
Cubs	35	22	0	.614	2
Red Sox	21	36	0	.368	16
Twins	20	35	0	.364	16

COMPOSITE

Team	Mrl.	Mets	Ryl.	W.S.	Cubs	Tig.	Ori.	Yan.	Ast.	Rng.	Pir.	Exp.	R.S.	Twi.	B.J.	Brv.	W	L	T	Pct.	GB
Marlins	....	11	0	0	0	0	0	0	0	0	0	13	0	0	0	16	40	16	0	.714	....
Mets	8	....	0	0	0	0	0	0	0	0	0	13	0	0	0	17	38	19	0	.667	2 1/2
Royals	0	0	....	0	7	0	2	0	0	2	1	0	12	13	0	0	37	20	0	.649	3 1/2
White Sox	0	0	2	....	2	0	8	0	0	8	14	0	1	1	0	0	36	22	0	.621	5
Cubs	0	0	9	0	....	0	2	0	0	2	1	0	10	11	0	0	35	22	0	.614	5 1/2
Tigers	0	0	0	0	0	....	0	10	10	0	0	0	0	0	13	0	33	24	0	.579	7 1/2
Orioles	0	0	0	9	0	0	....	0	0	11	11	0	2	1	0	0	34	25	0	.576	7 1/2
Yankees	0	0	0	0	0	9	0	....	7	0	0	0	0	0	16	0	32	26	0	.552	9
Astros	0	0	0	0	0	9	0	12	....	0	0	0	0	0	11	0	32	26	0	.552	9
Rangers	0	0	0	9	0	0	6	0	0	....	7	0	2	0	0	0	24	34	0	.414	17
Pirates	0	0	1	3	1	0	6	0	0	10	....	0	1	1	0	0	23	36	0	.390	18 1/2
Expos	5	6	0	0	0	0	0	0	0	0	0	....	0	0	0	10	21	35	0	.375	19
Red Sox	0	0	4	1	7	0	0	0	0	0	1	0	....	8	0	0	21	36	0	.368	19 1/2
Twins	0	0	4	0	5	0	1	0	0	1	1	0	8	....	0	0	20	35	0	.364	19 1/2
Blue Jays	0	0	0	0	0	6	0	4	9	0	0	0	0	0	....	0	19	40	0	.322	22 1/2
Braves	3	2	0	0	0	0	0	0	0	0	0	9	0	0	0	....	14	43	0	.246	26 1/2

Games played in Bradenton, Dunedin, Fort Myers, Melbourne, Osceola, Port Charlotte, St. Lucie County, Sarasota, Tampa and West Palm Beach, Fla.

Club names are major league affiliations.

PLAYOFFS: Tigers defeated Marlins, one game to none; Royals defeated White Sox, one game to none; Royals defeated Tigers, two games to none, to win league championship.

REGULAR-SEASON ATTENDANCE: No official attendance figures reported.

MANAGERS: Astros, Bobby Ramos; Blue Jays, Rocket Wheeler; Braves, Jim Saul; Cubs, Sandy Alomar; Expos, Luis Dorante; Marlins, Juan Bustabad; Mets, John Stephenson; Orioles, Julio Garcia; Pirates, Woody Huyke; Rangers, Chino Cadahia; Red Sox, Felix Maldonado; Royals, Bob Herold; Tigers, Kevin Bradshaw; Twins, Mike Boulanger; White Sox, Mike Gellinger; Yankees, Hector Lopez.

ALL-STAR TEAM: 1B—Gary Coffee, Royals; 2B—Elinton Jasco, Cubs; 3B—Jose Cepeda, Royals; SS—Alex Gonzalez, Marlins; OF—Jose Camilo, Marlins; Carlos Delacruz, Tigers; Thomas Peck, Blue Jays; C—Brian Downs, White Sox; Starting Pitcher—Octavio Dotel, Mets; Relief Pitcher—Brent Stentz, Tigers; Manager of the Year—Bob Herold, Royals.

1995 BATTING

TEAM

Team	Avg.	G	TPA	AB	R	H	TB	2B	3B	HR	RBI	SH	SF	HP	BB	IBB	SO	SB	CS	GDP	LOB	ShO	Slg.	OBP
Marlins	.260	56	2105	1835	289	478	629	72	23	11	212	10	19	28	213	5	306	95	26	33	403	3	.343	.343
Mets	.260	57	2157	1875	306	487	706	92	26	25	256	12	35	30	205	8	360	63	23	33	417	3	.377	.337
Pirates	.256	59	2098	1899	245	487	661	72	21	20	211	8	13	15	163	3	331	39	19	47	371	6	.348	.318
Royals	.256	57	2100	1834	294	470	696	82	18	36	238	5	20	26	214	1	366	43	25	32	389	3	.379	.339
Cubs	.255	57	2055	1793	276	457	655	73	28	23	226	18	21	23	199	3	397	128	47	39	343	4	.365	.333
Astros	.252	58	2028	1784	268	449	600	68	19	15	205	26	13	31	173	4	381	114	58	37	342	6	.336	.326
Yankees	.246	58	2149	1883	285	463	636	74	21	19	229	20	14	28	202	10	409	52	22	36	404	5	.338	.326
Orioles	.241	59	2127	1856	260	448	601	85	13	14	198	10	20	28	212	1	375	59	31	44	410	5	.324	.325
White Sox	.241	58	2118	1858	271	448	628	83	14	23	218	12	12	33	203	11	418	48	26	36	411	4	.338	.325

Team	Avg.	G	TPA	AB	R	H	TB	2B	3B	HR	RBI	SH	SF	HP	BB	IBB	SO	SB	CS	GDP	LOB	ShO	Slg.	OBP
Tigers	.240	57	1970	1715	237	411	566	50	24	19	185	18	12	36	189	2	467	122	39	27	359	6	.330	.326
Rangers	.232	58	2005	1783	230	414	567	68	20	15	188	10	17	25	170	1	417	135	40	30	334	6	.318	.305
Twins	.222	55	1920	1709	169	380	500	71	8	11	138	15	15	35	145	4	363	73	31	28	365	6	.293	.294
Red Sox	.221	57	2041	1785	223	395	505	59	6	13	169	24	15	40	175	1	382	73	29	31	370	5	.283	.303
Blue Jays	.221	59	2171	1819	259	402	577	82	21	17	215	19	16	52	258	5	467	47	22	45	440	5	.317	.332
Expos	.217	56	1951	1727	195	375	504	75	15	8	137	16	9	24	175	1	425	62	57	25	332	4	.292	.297
Braves	.189	57	1920	1721	141	326	425	53	2	14	116	13	6	19	161	2	401	36	33	39	333	6	.247	.265

INDIVIDUAL

TOP QUALIFIERS FOR BATTING CHAMPIONSHIP

Minimum 162 plate appearances. *Lefthanded batter. †Switch-hitter.

Player, Team	Avg.	G	TPA	AB	R	H	TB	2B	3B	HR	RBI	SH	SF	HP	BB	IBB	SO	SB	CS	GDP	Slg.	OBP
Cepeda, Jose, Royals	.348	54	209	187	32	65	79	6	4	0	21	1	4	2	15	0	5	2	2	0	.422	.394
Gallagher, Shawn, Rangers	.338	58	233	210	34	71	111	13	3	7	40	0	3	1	19	0	44	17	4	7	.529	.391
Camilo, Jose, Marlins*	.335	48	200	155	37	52	79	5	5	4	22	2	1	1	41	1	28	19	6	2	.510	.475
DelaCruz, Carlos, Tigers	.329	47	175	155	24	51	66	7	1	2	17	0	0	0	20	1	45	28	4	1	.426	.406
Coffee, Gary, Royals	.328	52	217	189	30	62	110	9	3	11	45	0	0	0	28	0	38	2	0	3	.582	.415
Samboy, Nelson, Astros	.313	55	226	192	39	60	79	12	2	1	22	4	1	3	26	0	19	21	8	4	.411	.401
Barrett, Michael, Expos	.311	50	199	183	22	57	78	13	4	0	19	0	1	0	15	1	19	7	6	1	.426	.362
Mifflin, Brian, Mets	.306	51	206	193	29	59	89	13	1	5	40	0	7	1	5	0	43	1	1	7	.461	.316
Bunkley, Antuan, Twins	.298	49	205	181	24	54	81	9	0	6	23	0	0	9	15	0	35	11	4	3	.448	.380
Gonzalez, Alex, Marlins	.294	53	213	187	30	55	76	7	4	2	30	1	4	2	19	0	27	11	2	2	.406	.358
Saffer, Jeffrey, Yankees	.293	50	202	184	30	54	78	10	1	4	33	0	0	1	17	0	55	0	2	1	.424	.356
Rivera, Roberto, Orioles	.293	42	164	150	21	44	66	7	3	3	26	0	2	2	10	0	38	6	3	5	.440	.341
Velazquez, Jose, Yankees*	.287	58	245	209	33	60	82	9	2	3	34	0	3	1	30	2	20	3	4	3	.392	.374
Barnes, Kelvin, Cubs	.286	49	195	168	28	48	84	6	6	6	37	0	2	1	24	0	37	11	4	4	.500	.374
Kopacz, Derek, Tigers	.285	53	194	165	24	47	71	12	3	2	30	0	3	1	25	0	40	11	3	2	.430	.376

DEPARTMENTAL LEADERS: G—Peck, 59; AB—Peck, 215; R—Peck, 42; H—Gallagher, 71; TB—Gallagher, 111; 2B—Kehoe, 17; 3B—Jimenez, 8; HR—Coffee, 11; RBI—Coffee, 45; SH—Butler, 8; SF—Mifflin, 7; HP—Douglas, 18; BB—Camilo, Whitlock, 41; IBB—Strawberry, 5; SO—Barksdale, 61; SB—Jasco, 29; CS—Barksdale, 11; GIDP—Ad. Pena, 9; Slg.—Coffee, .582; OBP—Camilo, .475.

ALL PLAYERS

*Lefthanded batter. †Switch-hitter.

Player, Team	Avg.	G	TPA	AB	R	H	TB	2B	3B	HR	RBI	SH	SF	HP	BB	IBB	SO	SB	CS	GDP	Slg.	OBP
Abreu, Nelson, Cubs	.214	57	201	173	21	37	50	3	2	2	24	6	3	0	19	1	37	12	8	8	.289	.287
Adamson, Jason, Pirates	.255	42	165	145	20	37	49	9	0	1	16	0	0	3	17	0	21	1	1	6	.338	.345
Agnoly, Earl, Marlins	.272	55	234	213	39	58	65	5	1	0	20	0	2	3	16	0	18	19	5	3	.305	.329
Aguila, Hector, Rangers	.192	53	200	182	20	35	52	7	5	0	17	1	2	3	12	0	27	6	2	8	.286	.251
Akins, Carlos, Orioles	.283	42	165	138	35	39	59	9	1	3	20	0	2	3	22	0	28	9	3	1	.428	.388
Alayon, Elvis, Red Sox*	.200	25	91	85	7	17	20	3	0	0	5	0	1	2	3	0	10	4	1	2	.235	.242
Alfonzo, Edgar, Orioles	.167	6	19	18	1	3	3	0	0	0	1	0	0	1	0	0	0	0	0	0	.167	.211
Alley, William, Orioles†	.300	12	44	30	10	9	13	4	0	0	3	0	2	1	11	0	4	0	0	1	.433	.477
Alleyne, Roberto, Astros	.218	35	120	110	12	24	29	2	0	1	11	1	0	1	8	1	27	5	5	4	.264	.277
Alvarado, Basilio, Expos	.297	28	81	74	8	22	33	6	1	1	12	3	0	0	4	0	11	1	1	3	.446	.333
Amaya, Edilberto, White Sox	.192	26	82	78	9	15	21	3	0	1	9	0	0	1	3	0	20	0	1	0	.269	.232
Antigua, Nilson, Pirates	.242	27	102	99	6	24	29	3	1	0	9	0	1	0	2	0	19	0	1	5	.293	.255
Antrim, Patrick, Yankees†	.250	16	59	52	9	13	17	2	1	0	4	2	0	1	4	0	13	3	0	1	.327	.316
Astacio, Onofre, Twins†	.224	47	189	165	21	37	42	3	1	0	8	1	1	5	17	0	42	26	6	3	.255	.314
Aybar, Ramon, Tigers*	.241	38	141	112	22	27	31	2	1	0	10	4	2	5	18	0	38	16	5	2	.277	.365
Ayuso, Julio, Twins	.169	25	80	71	5	12	12	0	0	0	3	1	0	1	7	1	20	0	1	3	.169	.253
Bales, Taylor, Royals	.000	8	20	14	2	0	0	0	0	0	0	0	0	1	4	0	6	0	0	0	.000	.263
Balint, Rob, Tigers	.200	1	5	5	1	1	4	0	0	1	1	0	0	0	0	0	2	0	0	0	.800	.200
Barksdale, Shane, Astros*	.258	47	182	159	19	41	61	9	1	3	25	0	0	3	20	1	61	7	11	3	.384	.352
Barnes, Kelvin, Cubs	.286	49	195	168	28	48	84	6	6	6	37	0	2	1	24	0	37	11	4	4	.500	.374
Barrett, Michael, Expos	.311	50	199	183	22	57	78	13	4	0	19	0	1	0	15	1	19	7	6	1	.426	.362
Bartee, Kimera, Orioles†	.238	5	24	21	5	5	8	0	0	1	3	0	0	0	3	0	2	1	1	0	.381	.333
Bautista, Jorge, Marlins	.206	42	140	126	16	26	34	6	1	0	4	1	0	1	12	0	23	0	0	0	.270	.281
Beaumont, Hamil, Yankees	.104	18	54	48	6	5	8	0	0	1	3	0	0	1	5	0	22	1	0	1	.167	.204
Bejarano, Brian, Blue Jays	.254	52	187	173	20	44	67	6	4	3	25	0	1	2	11	0	53	1	1	3	.387	.305
Beltran, Carlos, Royals†	.278	52	200	180	29	50	59	9	0	0	23	1	3	3	13	0	30	5	3	1	.328	.332
Betancourt, Rafael, Red Sox	.256	51	189	168	18	43	48	5	0	0	19	4	3	1	13	0	31	8	5	3	.286	.308
Bishop, Tim, Mets	.237	47	175	156	31	37	59	6	5	2	15	0	3	3	13	0	38	4	2	0	.378	.303
Black, Brandon, Mets*	.352	30	117	105	16	37	58	12	3	1	25	0	1	1	10	0	11	1	1	2	.552	.410
Blosser, Douglas, Royals*	.255	50	196	161	18	41	74	10	1	7	33	0	2	1	32	0	39	0	0	3	.460	.378
Borges, Victor, Cubs*	.213	35	116	94	20	20	22	0	1	0	6	2	0	1	17	0	18	8	2	1	.234	.339
Bowers, Kevin, Mets	.220	36	146	123	20	27	39	4	1	2	19	0	1	1	21	1	38	1	0	2	.317	.336
Brown, Derek, Orioles	.233	49	171	146	15	34	39	5	0	0	11	0	1	1	23	0	32	3	3	5	.267	.339
Bunkley, Antuan, Twins	.298	49	205	181	24	54	81	9	0	6	23	0	0	9	15	0	35	11	4	3	.448	.380
Burns, Kevin, Astros*	.250	42	149	136	17	34	49	4	1	3	23	0	1	0	12	1	24	8	3	5	.360	.309
Butler, Garrett, Yankees†	.232	48	215	185	40	43	55	4	4	0	16	8	1	5	16	0	45	11	0	1	.297	.309
Camilo, Jose, Marlins*	.335	48	200	155	37	52	79	5	5	4	22	2	1	1	41	1	28	19	6	2	.510	.475
Campos, Miguel, Cubs	.209	36	128	115	21	24	39	6	0	3	13	2	0	3	8	0	37	5	1	2	.339	.278
Capallen, Rene, Tigers	.317	33	120	101	17	32	37	3	1	0	13	4	0	2	13	0	14	6	4	0	.366	.405
Cardona, Luis, Red Sox	.213	42	150	136	14	29	38	6	0	1	15	0	1	5	8	0	35	0	1	5	.279	.280
Carubelli, Gustavo, Braves	.196	49	174	148	13	29	43	8	0	2	6	1	0	1	24	0	31	3	3	6	.291	.312
Casimiro, Carlos, Orioles	.252	32	121	107	14	27	41	4	2	2	11	1	2	1	10	0	22	1	3	3	.383	.317
Cedeno, Jesus, Tigers	.255	40	132	110	20	28	43	2	2	3	14	1	1	4	16	0	26	2	2	1	.391	.366
Cepeda, Jose, Royals	.348	54	209	187	32	65	79	6	4	0	21	1	4	2	15	0	5	2	2	0	.422	.394
Chapman, Scott, Astros	.286	14	33	28	3	8	9	1	0	0	1	1	0	0	4	0	4	1	1	2	.321	.375

Player, Team	Avg.	G	TPA	AB	R	H	TB	2B	3B	HR	RBI	SH	SF	HP	BB	IBB	SO	SB	CS	GDP	Slg.	OBP
Charles, Curtis, Orioles	.159	25	72	63	6	10	12	2	0	0	3	0	0	0	9	0	29	1	1	0	.190	.264
Charles, Steve, Blue Jays*	.214	48	179	145	17	31	39	4	2	0	15	1	1	4	24	1	47	7	1	4	.269	.339
Chastain, Dan, Marlins	.200	4	10	10	0	2	2	0	0	0	0	0	0	0	0	0	1	1	0	1	.200	.200
Chick, Bruce, Expos	.235	15	57	51	4	12	20	5	0	1	9	0	0	1	5	0	8	1	2	1	.392	.316
Cisar, Ryan, Blue Jays	.153	35	95	72	10	11	12	1	0	0	5	1	0	2	20	0	24	0	0	1	.167	.351
Coffee, Gary, Royals	.328	52	217	189	30	62	110	9	3	11	45	0	0	0	28	0	38	2	0	3	.582	.415
Cole, Eric, Astros	.270	39	134	122	17	33	38	3	1	0	12	3	0	2	7	0	21	7	5	0	.311	.321
Colon, Ariel, Braves	.202	30	98	84	6	17	19	2	0	0	7	2	0	3	9	0	25	1	0	0	.226	.302
Colon, Jose, Cubs	.227	40	134	119	14	27	37	4	0	2	11	1	1	3	10	0	30	8	5	4	.311	.301
Colson, Jeremiah, Expos*	.063	23	52	48	4	3	5	0	1	0	4	1	0	1	2	0	24	1	2	0	.104	.118
Connell, Jerry, Cubs	.211	22	82	76	6	16	24	5	0	1	6	0	0	0	6	0	12	1	1	3	.316	.268
Cordero, Edward, Tigers	.214	49	145	126	17	27	33	2	2	0	11	2	1	4	12	0	23	11	5	2	.262	.301
Corzo, Beau, Braves	.207	27	95	87	7	18	30	3	0	3	7	0	1	2	5	0	22	0	0	1	.345	.263
Cossins, Tim, Rangers	.000	2	4	4	0	0	0	0	0	0	0	0	0	0	0	0	1	0	0	0	.000	.000
Crutchfield, David, Cubs*	.231	31	121	104	19	24	37	5	4	0	8	3	1	2	11	0	33	13	1	1	.356	.314
Cruz, Andres, Twins	.241	32	123	112	10	27	34	5	1	0	9	0	1	1	7	1	19	1	0	4	.304	.289
Culp, Randy, Expos	.152	10	34	33	2	5	7	2	0	0	1	0	0	0	1	0	9	0	1	0	.212	.176
Daedelow, Craig, Orioles	.259	49	198	170	35	44	56	9	0	1	11	1	0	3	24	0	19	7	2	5	.329	.360
Daniels, Ronny, Expos	.162	20	78	74	6	12	20	4	2	0	3	0	0	0	4	0	27	3	1	1	.270	.205
Dasher, Melvin, Royals	.200	16	36	35	3	7	12	2	0	1	5	0	0	0	1	0	15	0	0	1	.343	.222
Davenport, Jeff, Red Sox	.077	5	16	13	0	1	1	0	0	0	0	1	0	0	0	0	3	0	0	0	.077	.077
Davidson, Cleatus, Twins†	.200	21	85	75	11	15	19	2	1	0	5	0	0	0	10	0	17	8	3	0	.253	.294
Davis, Albert, Pirates	.302	10	44	43	8	13	25	3	0	3	9	0	0	0	1	0	6	1	0	0	.581	.318
Davis, Torrance, Expos	.273	45	162	139	19	38	41	1	1	0	5	6	1	4	12	0	25	13	7	2	.295	.346
DeLaCruz, Carlos, Tigers	.329	47	175	155	24	51	66	7	1	2	17	0	0	0	20	1	45	28	4	1	.426	.406
DeLaCruz, Wilfredo, Yankees	.195	43	138	118	17	23	24	1	0	0	7	1	0	4	15	0	36	6	2	2	.203	.307
Delgado, Daniel, Pirates	.179	33	122	106	15	19	21	2	0	0	7	0	0	1	15	0	16	6	0	1	.198	.287
Dent, Darrell, Orioles*	.280	36	149	125	24	35	48	7	3	0	6	0	1	2	21	0	22	6	2	2	.384	.389
Deshazer, Jeremy, Astros†	.245	38	119	106	13	26	34	6	1	0	11	0	1	4	8	0	19	6	1	2	.321	.319
DiSalle, Javier, Orioles	.333	4	12	12	0	4	4	0	0	0	1	0	0	0	0	0	1	1	1	0	.333	.333
DiSarcina, Glenn, White Sox*	.194	9	37	36	6	7	12	3	1	0	3	0	0	1	0	0	4	1	0	3	.333	.216
Domingo, Tyrone, Tigers	.206	35	115	107	18	22	27	1	2	0	1	0	0	3	5	0	25	20	4	1	.252	.261
Douglas, John, Blue Jays	.235	55	228	179	21	42	54	6	0	2	26	3	4	18	24	1	35	6	4	4	.302	.373
Downs, Brian, White Sox	.285	37	139	130	22	37	51	8	0	2	18	0	0	2	7	0	27	0	1	2	.392	.331
Elliott, Dawan, Pirates*	.220	34	115	109	8	24	29	1	2	0	9	0	0	0	6	0	30	2	0	2	.266	.261
Ellison, Skeeter, Braves†	.226	20	68	62	4	14	20	4	1	0	4	0	0	0	6	0	27	1	4	0	.323	.294
Encarnacion, Pedro, White Sox	.333	10	26	24	1	8	8	0	0	0	1	1	0	0	1	0	4	2	1	0	.333	.360
Engle, Beau, Mets	.179	10	31	28	3	5	9	2	1	0	1	1	0	0	2	0	3	0	0	2	.321	.233
Erickson, Corey, Mets	.281	53	224	178	38	50	79	6	1	7	35	0	5	4	37	3	40	10	3	2	.444	.406
Fagley, Daniel, Marlins	.182	16	38	33	4	6	6	0	0	0	4	0	0	1	4	0	8	0	0	0	.182	.289
Fauske, Joshua, White Sox	.257	33	121	105	18	27	46	7	0	4	18	1	1	3	11	1	22	1	0	1	.438	.342
Febles, Carlos, Royals	.282	54	219	188	40	53	85	13	5	3	20	1	0	4	26	0	30	16	8	5	.452	.381
Feliz, Edgar, Pirates†	.236	17	58	55	4	13	17	4	0	0	8	0	1	0	2	0	14	0	2	1	.309	.259
Ferguson, Dwight, Red Sox*	.194	22	83	62	10	12	15	3	0	0	6	0	0	4	17	0	24	4	3	0	.242	.398
Fitzpatrick, Rob, Expos	.200	9	32	25	5	5	8	3	0	0	4	0	0	0	7	0	4	0	0	1	.320	.375
Flores, Oswaldo, Red Sox†	.273	14	36	33	8	9	12	0	0	1	6	0	0	0	3	0	11	1	1	0	.364	.333
Fortin, Blaine, Blue Jays	.205	42	122	112	13	23	32	4	1	1	14	0	2	3	5	0	16	0	2	3	.286	.254
Franco, Raul, Marlins	.277	49	205	184	30	51	63	12	0	0	22	1	2	2	16	0	14	9	3	5	.342	.338
Frias, Ovidio, Pirates	.283	29	109	99	16	28	37	5	2	0	7	0	0	3	7	0	10	1	0	1	.374	.349
Gallagher, Shawn, Rangers	.338	58	233	210	34	71	111	13	3	7	40	0	3	1	19	0	44	17	4	7	.529	.391
Garcia, Julio, Yankees	.154	4	15	13	1	2	2	0	0	0	3	0	1	0	1	0	3	2	0	0	.154	.200
Garcia, Luis, White Sox	.230	45	187	161	33	37	46	5	2	0	12	3	3	0	20	0	29	9	3	3	.286	.310
Gil, Daniel, Cubs	.167	9	7	6	0	1	1	0	0	0	0	0	0	0	1	0	0	0	0	0	.167	.286
Gomez, Ramon, White Sox	.262	30	118	103	16	27	33	3	0	1	6	0	0	3	12	0	22	12	4	2	.320	.356
Gonzalez, Alex, Marlins	.294	53	213	187	30	55	76	7	4	2	30	1	4	2	19	0	27	11	2	2	.406	.358
Goodwin, Rawlin, Red Sox	.429	18	72	63	15	27	29	2	0	0	11	3	1	2	3	0	8	10	1	1	.460	.464
Gordon, Buck, Cubs	.100	4	12	10	0	1	1	0	0	0	2	0	0	0	2	0	2	0	0	1	.100	.250
Green, Raymond, Marlins	.000	3	6	5	0	0	0	0	0	0	0	0	0	1	0	0	0	0	0	2	.000	.167
Green, Ronald, Cubs	.319	34	141	119	28	38	59	7	4	2	12	1	2	1	18	0	33	13	7	0	.496	.407
Griffin, Juan, Astros	.172	26	76	64	11	11	14	1	1	0	10	3	0	3	6	0	22	5	1	2	.219	.274
Gruber, Nick, Red Sox	.111	13	29	27	1	3	3	0	0	0	1	0	0	0	2	0	5	0	0	1	.111	.172
Guillen, Carlos, Astros	.295	30	118	105	17	31	45	4	2	2	15	1	2	1	9	1	17	17	1	0	.429	.350
Hagge, Kirk, Tigers†	.177	43	112	96	8	17	17	0	0	0	3	0	0	0	16	1	32	3	2	5	.177	.295
Harrison, Jamal, Twins	.143	5	16	14	0	2	3	1	0	0	2	0	0	0	2	0	1	0	0	0	.214	.250
Hayes, Darren, White Sox	.300	6	23	20	2	6	6	0	0	0	2	0	0	1	2	0	1	0	0	0	.300	.391
Hermansen, Chad, Pirates	.304	24	102	92	14	28	49	10	1	3	17	0	1	0	9	1	19	0	0	2	.533	.363
Hernandez, Alexander, Pirates*	.269	49	207	186	24	50	64	5	3	1	17	1	2	1	17	1	33	4	4	3	.344	.330
Higman, Joel, Orioles	.143	6	24	21	2	3	3	0	0	0	1	0	1	0	2	0	7	1	0	1	.143	.208
Horn, Marvin, White Sox*	.240	38	144	129	13	31	45	7	2	1	14	1	2	1	11	2	38	0	1	3	.349	.301
Imrisek, Jason, Yankees	.283	15	57	53	5	15	21	3	0	1	8	0	0	2	2	0	12	2	2	1	.396	.333
James, Kennouth, Expos†	.212	43	179	156	20	33	34	1	0	0	3	0	0	3	20	0	43	11	8	1	.218	.313
Jaroncyk, Ryan, Mets	.276	44	193	174	31	48	59	5	3	0	14	3	2	1	13	1	28	7	2	3	.339	.326
Jasco, Elinton, Cubs	.379	34	148	124	28	47	62	6	3	1	17	2	4	2	16	1	18	29	9	1	.500	.445
Jelsovsky, Craig, Mets	.233	18	52	43	6	10	12	2	0	0	6	2	1	3	3	0	4	0	2	0	.279	.320
Jenkins, Corey, Red Sox	.145	35	137	124	12	18	22	1	0	1	6	0	0	2	11	0	43	5	2	1	.177	.226
Jimenez, D'Angelo, Yankees†	.280	57	245	214	41	60	96	14	8	2	28	3	4	1	23	1	31	6	3	4	.449	.347
Johnson, Carlisle, Twins	.180	19	62	50	2	9	10	1	0	0	4	0	0	1	11	0	13	1	1	1	.200	.339
Johnson, Rontrez, Red Sox	.254	52	228	193	37	49	57	4	2	0	11	3	1	1	30	0	30	25	5	1	.295	.356
Johnson, Travis, Twins*	.316	24	95	76	14	24	32	5	0	1	10	1	0	7	11	0	9	5	4	1	.421	.447
Jones, Bryan, Tigers	.247	33	107	93	13	23	25	2	0	0	7	2	1	0	11	0	34	7	1	2	.269	.324
Jones, Jamie, Marlins*	.222	5	23	18	2	4	4	0	0	0	3	0	0	0	5	1	4	0	0	0	.222	.391
Juarez, Raul, Twins	.346	7	27	26	3	9	15	1	1	1	6	0	1	0	0	0	5	0	0	1	.577	.333
Katayama, Daiki, Tigers	.180	28	54	50	5	9	16	1	0	2	4	1	0	0	3	0	13	0	0	1	.320	.226

Player, Team	Avg.	G	TPA	AB	R	H	TB	2B	3B	HR	RBI	SH	SF	HP	BB	IBB	SO	SB	CS	GDP	Slg.	OBP
Keech, Erik, Yankees*	.225	37	134	120	6	27	37	7	0	1	19	0	1	1	12	1	18	0	1	6	.308	.299
Kehoe, John, Blue Jays	.274	57	241	201	32	55	88	17	5	2	32	1	2	2	35	0	52	8	0	8	.438	.383
Kelly, Pat, Yankees	.000	1	5	2	2	0	0	0	0	0	1	0	0	2	1	0	0	0	0	0	.000	.600
Kerr, Brian, Orioles	.184	10	44	38	4	7	14	2	1	1	7	1	2	1	2	0	10	1	0	1	.368	.233
Kerr, James, Yankees	.241	26	93	83	12	20	22	2	0	0	6	2	1	2	5	0	24	0	0	2	.265	.297
King, Brian, Orioles	.277	17	50	47	4	13	15	2	0	0	4	0	1	0	2	0	12	1	0	0	.319	.300
King, Kevin, Expos	.263	14	41	38	6	10	13	3	0	0	0	0	0	1	2	0	19	3	0	0	.342	.317
Kinnie, Donald, Cubs	.250	35	136	120	20	30	44	6	4	0	14	0	1	3	12	0	36	12	1	1	.367	.331
Klee, Charles, White Sox	.213	44	178	155	24	33	41	8	0	0	19	0	2	2	19	0	41	3	2	3	.265	.303
Knabenshue, Chris, Pirates*	.176	4	17	17	1	3	6	0	0	1	2	0	0	0	0	0	1	0	0	2	.353	.176
Kofler, Eric, Yankees*	.246	19	73	69	11	17	33	3	2	3	13	0	0	1	3	0	8	1	1	2	.478	.288
Kopacz, Derek, Tigers	.285	53	194	165	24	47	71	12	3	2	30	0	3	1	25	0	40	11	3	2	.430	.376
Kuilan, Hector, Marlins	.248	48	175	153	14	38	46	8	0	0	27	2	2	1	17	1	20	4	1	4	.301	.324
LaForest, Pierre, Expos*	.000	2	8	6	1	0	0	0	0	0	0	0	0	0	2	0	4	0	0	0	.000	.250
Landry, Dan, Braves	.238	38	139	122	16	29	40	5	0	2	7	3	0	3	11	0	25	4	1	2	.328	.316
Lantigua, Miguel, Mets	.262	27	93	84	11	22	28	6	0	0	7	1	1	3	4	0	16	4	2	3	.333	.315
Lebron, Juan, Royals	.177	47	163	147	17	26	41	5	2	2	13	0	4	2	10	0	38	0	3	6	.279	.233
Leon, Donny, Yankees†	.171	16	44	41	3	7	8	1	0	0	5	0	0	0	3	0	14	0	1	0	.195	.227
Lignitz, Jeremiah, Tigers*	.232	30	94	82	9	19	25	1	1	1	7	0	0	3	9	0	27	1	3	1	.305	.330
Lima, Estivinson, Rangers	.180	31	101	89	10	16	24	5	0	1	7	0	0	4	8	0	19	0	1	3	.270	.277
Liniak, Cole, Red Sox	.266	23	86	79	9	21	31	7	0	1	8	2	0	1	4	0	8	2	0	2	.392	.310
Llanos, Francisco, Expos	.149	37	125	114	15	17	26	9	0	0	5	0	0	1	10	0	40	3	2	1	.228	.224
Llibre, Brian, Rangers	.269	24	71	67	4	18	20	2	0	0	8	0	2	0	2	0	21	1	0	0	.299	.282
Lomasney, Steven, Red Sox	.163	29	106	92	10	15	21	6	0	0	7	1	0	5	8	1	16	2	1	0	.228	.267
Long, Garrett, Pirates	.349	20	80	63	13	22	29	2	1	1	8	0	0	0	17	0	10	0	1	3	.460	.488
Longueira, Tony, Royals	.242	41	108	95	12	23	31	5	0	1	13	1	2	1	9	0	11	3	0	1	.326	.308
Lopez, Edgar, Braves	.214	38	138	117	14	25	29	4	0	0	5	1	0	0	20	0	13	5	5	3	.248	.328
Lorenzo, Juan, Twins†	.217	14	51	46	3	10	10	0	0	0	2	0	1	0	4	0	6	0	0	0	.217	.275
Lowery, Terrell, Rangers	.265	10	40	34	10	9	23	3	1	3	7	0	0	0	6	0	7	1	0	1	.676	.375
Lutz, Manuel, White Sox*	.281	46	183	160	23	45	70	10	3	3	31	0	2	2	19	2	42	0	0	3	.438	.361
Maas, Kevin, Yankees*	.444	2	9	9	1	4	7	0	0	1	3	0	0	0	0	0	0	0	0	0	.778	.444
Macero, Victor, Cubs	.234	41	146	128	17	30	41	5	0	2	11	1	2	1	14	0	25	4	2	2	.320	.310
Maloney, Jeff, Blue Jays	.163	29	101	92	9	15	20	5	0	0	12	0	1	2	6	0	24	2	1	4	.217	.228
Mateo, Henry, Expos†	.148	38	147	122	11	18	18	0	0	0	6	5	1	5	14	0	47	2	7	2	.148	.261
May, Freddie, Pirates*	.333	29	115	96	18	32	47	5	2	2	13	0	1	0	18	0	16	2	4	2	.490	.435
Maysonet, Jose, Blue Jays	.145	29	87	69	14	10	12	2	0	0	1	2	0	2	14	0	11	1	2	3	.174	.306
McCarthy, Kevin, Mets*	.133	22	80	75	5	10	14	1	0	1	5	0	2	1	2	0	13	0	0	2	.187	.163
McDonald, Donzell, Yankees†	.236	28	129	110	23	26	33	5	1	0	9	0	1	2	16	0	24	11	2	1	.300	.341
McHenry, Joseph, Twins*	.219	34	126	114	9	25	33	8	0	0	7	2	1	0	9	0	38	2	3	1	.289	.274
McLendon, Craig, Rangers	.242	25	72	66	7	16	18	2	0	0	4	0	0	1	5	0	10	1	0	2	.273	.306
McSparin, Paul, Pirates	.292	23	78	72	14	21	35	5	0	3	13	0	1	1	4	0	19	1	1	2	.486	.333
Medina, Alger, Cubs	.224	23	88	76	10	17	24	5	1	0	11	0	1	1	10	0	4	7	4	1	.316	.318
Medina, Robert, Blue Jays	.177	30	72	62	5	11	20	1	1	2	8	0	0	0	4	0	23	1	1	1	.323	.227
Mejia, Marlon, Astros	.235	34	114	98	19	23	24	1	0	0	5	6	0	2	8	0	21	2	3	5	.245	.306
Mercado, Julio, Rangers	.167	55	168	156	13	26	31	5	0	0	12	1	1	0	10	0	49	9	2	1	.199	.216
Mifflin, Brian, Mets	.306	51	206	193	29	59	89	13	1	5	40	0	7	1	5	0	43	1	1	7	.461	.316
Miles, Aaron, Astros*	.257	47	190	171	32	44	59	9	3	0	18	4	1	0	14	0	14	9	6	3	.345	.312
Millwood, Terry, Twins	.217	47	183	161	15	35	46	5	3	0	11	0	1	4	17	0	29	5	2	1	.286	.306
Miyauchi, Hector, Expos	.233	16	53	43	9	10	15	2	0	1	2	0	0	3	7	0	8	3	1	0	.349	.377
Monds, Wonderful, Braves	.133	4	16	15	1	2	2	0	0	0	1	0	0	0	1	0	8	2	1	0	.133	.188
Monroe, Craig, Rangers	.249	54	216	193	22	48	58	6	2	0	33	1	2	2	18	0	25	13	2	1	.301	.316
Montas, Ricardo, Royals	.071	22	32	28	2	2	5	0	0	1	3	0	0	1	3	0	6	0	0	1	.179	.188
Montilla, Julio, Royals†	.239	17	56	46	6	11	11	0	0	0	3	0	1	0	9	0	5	0	0	1	.239	.357
Morrison, Ryan, Mets*	.255	38	134	110	20	28	38	7	0	1	11	0	3	4	17	1	21	3	0	0	.345	.366
Mota, Gleydel, Mets*	.320	34	149	122	32	39	49	6	2	0	18	3	4	1	19	1	27	21	5	1	.402	.404
Nelson, Kevin, Twins	.145	45	152	138	7	20	31	8	0	1	11	1	2	0	11	1	36	1	1	3	.225	.205
Nobles, Ivan, Blue Jays	.143	36	125	105	14	15	20	3	1	0	12	2	1	4	13	0	40	2	1	1	.190	.260
Nova, Fernando, White Sox	.208	36	147	125	17	26	32	6	0	0	7	1	1	4	16	2	46	1	3	4	.256	.315
Nova, Geraldo, Red Sox†	.077	16	33	26	1	2	2	0	0	0	3	1	1	1	4	0	7	0	0	0	.077	.219
Nunez, Juan, Rangers†	.241	43	157	137	16	33	40	2	1	1	7	3	0	2	15	0	46	26	9	0	.292	.325
Olmeda, Jose, Red Sox†	.217	42	150	129	15	28	46	4	1	4	14	5	2	3	11	0	42	3	3	5	.357	.290
Orndorff, Dave, Twins	.209	23	82	67	12	14	17	0	0	1	3	0	0	2	13	0	11	5	0	1	.254	.354
Oropeza, William, Expos	.231	45	156	143	14	33	52	8	1	3	27	0	4	0	9	0	28	2	5	3	.364	.269
Ortiz, Asbel, Rangers†	.305	43	142	128	18	39	60	10	1	3	23	2	1	3	8	0	26	4	2	0	.469	.357
Ortiz, Pedro, Orioles	.217	14	49	46	1	10	12	2	0	0	3	0	0	0	3	0	13	1	0	2	.261	.265
Otero, Oscar, Braves	.128	29	91	86	3	11	11	0	0	0	2	0	1	1	3	0	16	1	2	3	.128	.165
Ovalle, Bonelly, Rangers	.000	18	0	0	0	0	0	0	0	0	0	0	0	0	0	0	0	1	0	0	.000	.000
Ovalles, Homy, Expos	.234	30	68	64	7	15	20	3	1	0	2	0	0	0	4	0	18	1	1	1	.313	.279
Owen, Tom, Marlins	.227	28	81	66	13	15	18	3	0	0	10	2	1	0	12	0	6	0	2	7	.273	.342
Parra, Jose, Rangers†	.156	45	165	135	16	21	29	4	2	0	7	2	0	4	24	0	41	12	6	1	.215	.301
Pascual, Edison, Pirates*	.228	41	151	136	19	31	47	3	2	3	18	2	3	0	10	0	26	3	0	1	.346	.275
Paxton, Chris, Orioles*	.226	11	34	31	1	7	10	1	1	0	6	0	0	2	1	0	4	0	0	0	.323	.294
Payano, Alexi, Cubs†	.297	29	108	91	20	27	39	4	1	2	14	0	1	5	11	1	16	1	0	1	.429	.398
Pearson, Eddie, White Sox*	.300	6	23	20	7	6	11	2	0	1	6	0	0	0	3	0	2	0	0	0	.550	.391
Peck, Thomas, Blue Jays*	.270	59	265	215	42	58	80	12	2	2	22	4	2	4	40	0	39	10	6	3	.372	.391
Pena, Adelis, Pirates	.282	54	210	202	27	57	68	7	2	0	23	1	1	3	3	1	26	6	1	9	.337	.301
Pena, Alex, Pirates	.238	48	179	172	15	41	57	7	3	1	20	1	0	0	6	0	26	3	3	4	.331	.264
Pena, Frank, Twins	.188	21	76	69	7	13	19	6	0	0	5	1	1	0	5	1	18	0	0	0	.275	.240
Pena, Jose, Rangers	.242	50	169	153	25	37	49	4	4	0	10	0	3	1	12	1	29	22	5	2	.320	.296
Pendergrass, Tyrone, Braves†	.181	52	204	188	19	34	41	4	0	1	7	0	0	1	15	0	51	8	4	5	.218	.245
Peniche, Fray, Tigers	.157	28	88	83	8	13	17	1	0	1	4	0	1	2	2	0	31	2	0	1	.205	.193
Phillips, Darren, Blue Jays†	.136	20	49	44	3	6	6	0	0	0	3	1	0	0	4	0	21	0	1	0	.136	.208
Pickering, Calvin, Orioles	.500	15	63	60	8	30	43	10	0	1	22	0	1	0	2	0	6	0	0	3	.717	.508

SUMMER CLASS A *Gulf Coast League*

Player, Team	Avg.	G	TPA	AB	R	H	TB	2B	3B	HR	RBI	SH	SF	HP	BB	IBB	SO	SB	CS	GDP	Slg.	OBP
Pinto, Rene, Yankees	.184	15	58	49	2	9	11	0	1	0	4	0	1	1	7	0	11	0	0	3	.224	.293
Pitts, Shedrick, Royals†	.253	36	96	79	25	20	27	1	0	2	6	1	1	2	13	0	23	11	1	0	.342	.368
Pond, Simon, Expos*	.150	45	156	133	13	20	28	6	1	0	12	0	0	1	22	0	34	2	3	3	.211	.276
Porter, Kedric, Orioles	.218	47	173	147	20	32	41	4	1	1	12	1	0	4	21	0	17	11	3	2	.279	.331
Prada, Nelson, Twins	.269	24	88	78	5	21	27	4	1	0	13	0	3	4	3	0	12	0	0	2	.346	.318
Pressley, Kasey, Cubs*	.236	39	153	140	12	33	39	4	1	0	16	0	2	0	11	0	47	1	1	5	.279	.288
Quezado, Dalmiro, Twins	.155	32	110	103	5	16	22	6	0	0	6	4	1	1	1	0	17	1	1	4	.214	.170
Radcliff, Victor, Royals	.260	38	143	123	25	32	56	8	2	4	15	0	1	7	12	0	24	3	6	3	.455	.357
Ramirez, Francisco, Tigers	.217	41	155	143	15	31	51	4	5	2	22	2	0	3	7	0	38	6	4	3	.357	.268
Ramirez, Julio, Marlins	.284	48	219	204	35	58	81	9	4	2	13	1	0	1	13	0	42	17	6	2	.397	.330
Ramos, Jeff, Royals*	.227	28	85	75	10	17	30	4	0	3	7	0	1	2	7	0	16	0	1	1	.400	.306
Ramos, Noel, Orioles	.200	4	18	15	1	3	4	1	0	0	5	0	1	0	2	0	6	0	1	1	.267	.278
Rengifo, Daliene, White Sox	.208	27	86	72	7	15	17	2	0	0	5	1	0	3	10	0	21	5	2	1	.236	.329
Reyes, Freddy, Twins	.238	6	24	21	2	5	9	1	0	1	4	0	2	0	1	0	6	0	0	0	.429	.250
Reynoso, Ismael, Marlins	.221	25	81	68	12	15	15	0	0	0	8	0	0	1	12	0	18	1	0	0	.221	.346
Ribaudo, Mike, Orioles	.244	16	46	41	3	10	11	1	0	0	4	0	1	1	3	0	10	0	0	1	.268	.304
Rivera, Juan, Rangers	.186	28	83	70	8	13	15	2	0	0	6	0	0	0	13	0	29	5	1	1	.214	.313
Rivera, Roberto, Orioles	.293	42	164	150	21	44	66	7	3	3	26	0	2	2	10	0	38	6	3	5	.440	.341
Robertson, Dean, Orioles	.156	28	109	90	18	14	18	4	0	0	6	0	1	2	14	1	18	4	4	2	.200	.280
Robles, Juan, Royals	.162	29	84	74	9	12	15	3	0	0	7	0	1	0	9	0	9	0	0	1	.203	.250
Roche, Marlon, Astros	.326	29	108	92	20	30	35	5	0	0	11	1	3	2	10	0	19	9	8	1	.380	.393
Rodriguez, Carlos, Red Sox†	.214	13	52	42	12	9	12	3	0	0	0	1	0	0	9	0	3	0	1	0	.286	.353
Rodriguez, Liubiemithz, W.S.†	.227	36	144	119	18	27	38	6	1	1	11	2	0	0	23	0	19	4	2	2	.319	.352
Rodriguez, Sammy, Mets	.278	6	20	18	1	5	5	0	0	0	1	0	0	0	2	0	4	0	1	0	.278	.350
Rojas, Moises, Red Sox	.207	42	171	140	22	29	37	5	0	1	16	2	3	5	20	0	34	5	3	3	.264	.321
Rolison, Nate, Marlins*	.276	37	158	134	22	37	54	10	2	1	19	0	1	8	15	1	34	0	0	1	.403	.380
Roman, Felipe, Red Sox	.227	50	187	176	14	40	55	8	2	1	17	1	1	2	7	0	38	1	0	3	.313	.263
Rosado, Luis, Yankees	.256	52	194	168	25	43	56	7	0	2	16	2	0	2	22	1	31	2	1	4	.333	.349
Rosario, Juan, Marlins	.000	5	11	7	1	0	0	0	0	0	0	0	0	0	4	0	2	1	0	1	.000	.364
Rose, Damian, Rangers	.097	13	38	31	5	3	3	0	0	0	2	0	0	3	4	0	16	3	1	2	.097	.263
Rose, Michael, Astros	.258	35	103	89	13	23	30	2	1	1	9	0	0	3	11	0	18	2	1	1	.337	.359
Ruiz, Cesar, Tigers†	.288	45	149	132	17	38	57	6	5	1	19	1	2	3	11	0	35	4	2	0	.432	.351
Saffer, Jeffrey, Yankees	.293	50	202	184	30	54	78	10	1	4	33	0	0	1	17	0	55	0	2	1	.424	.356
Salazar, Juan, Cubs†	.285	36	140	130	12	37	52	7	1	2	24	0	1	0	9	0	12	3	1	4	.400	.329
Samboy, Nelson, Astros	.313	55	226	192	39	60	79	12	2	1	22	4	1	3	26	0	19	21	8	4	.411	.401
Sanford, Chance, Pirates*	.211	6	21	19	2	4	7	0	0	1	1	0	0	0	2	0	2	0	0	0	.368	.286
Santos, Edgardo, Expos*	.221	23	73	68	4	15	19	2	1	0	4	1	1	0	3	0	6	2	2	2	.279	.250
Scharrer, Jim, Braves	.180	48	186	172	10	31	41	4	0	2	22	0	0	1	13	0	43	1	3	3	.238	.242
Schneider, Brian, Expos*	.227	30	112	97	7	22	25	3	0	0	4	0	0	1	14	0	23	2	4	1	.258	.330
Schreiber, Stan, Pirates	.258	38	155	128	16	33	38	1	2	0	10	3	1	2	21	0	23	8	1	1	.297	.368
Selivanov, Andrei, Braves*	.154	23	59	52	4	8	11	3	0	0	4	0	0	0	7	0	7	0	0	4	.212	.254
Serra, Joaquin, Orioles	.141	29	94	85	7	12	12	0	0	0	3	3	0	0	6	0	12	2	2	2	.141	.198
Shelton, Barry, White Sox	.282	33	121	103	10	29	40	5	0	2	13	1	0	7	10	0	16	0	1	2	.388	.383
Shipman, Thomas, Tigers†	.183	30	73	60	8	11	16	2	0	1	10	0	0	3	10	0	21	4	0	0	.267	.329
Shipp, Skip, Pirates	.130	18	61	54	4	7	7	0	0	0	4	0	1	1	5	0	13	0	0	2	.130	.213
Shirley, Al, Mets	.333	4	18	15	4	5	7	2	0	0	0	0	0	0	3	0	4	3	1	0	.467	.444
Sime, Rafael, Marlins*	.240	55	230	204	26	49	74	7	6	2	22	0	3	3	20	1	48	7	1	3	.363	.313
Simmons, Brian, White Sox†	.176	5	23	17	5	3	7	1	0	1	5	0	0	0	6	0	1	0	0	1	.412	.391
Smith, John, Astros	.149	23	75	67	9	10	20	3	2	1	5	0	2	3	3	0	23	2	2	0	.299	.213
Smith, Phillip, Braves	.123	38	120	114	5	14	15	1	0	0	5	2	0	0	4	0	37	0	1	2	.132	.153
Solano, Angel, White Sox	.232	44	161	151	20	35	45	5	1	1	13	0	1	0	9	1	23	7	3	0	.298	.273
Solano, Fausto, Blue Jays	.295	11	53	44	12	13	24	5	0	2	7	3	1	2	3	0	6	2	1	4	.545	.360
Soriano, Carlos, Mets	.263	47	187	167	25	44	76	11	3	5	24	1	2	2	15	0	24	1	2	4	.455	.328
Soriano, Juan, Mets	.219	10	36	32	5	7	12	2	0	1	3	0	0	0	4	0	9	3	0	1	.375	.306
Spencer, Jeffrey, Braves	.234	48	189	171	17	40	62	8	1	4	21	1	3	2	12	2	42	7	2	1	.363	.287
Springfield, Bo, Pirates*	.000	3	7	6	1	0	0	0	0	0	0	0	0	0	1	0	1	1	0	0	.000	.143
Stafford, Kimani, Royals	.164	39	79	67	13	11	14	1	1	0	4	0	0	0	12	0	30	0	0	1	.209	.291
Stephens, Joel, Orioles	.232	23	91	82	8	19	24	3	1	0	10	1	0	3	5	0	25	2	1	3	.293	.300
Stevens, Clayton, White Sox	.224	42	167	143	19	32	56	1	4	5	21	1	0	3	20	3	40	3	2	6	.392	.331
Stevenson, Chad, Tigers	.158	32	111	95	11	15	30	4	1	3	12	1	1	3	11	0	23	1	0	5	.316	.264
Strawberry, Darryl, Yankees*	.250	7	30	20	3	5	7	2	0	0	4	0	1	0	9	5	5	2	0	1	.350	.467
Suero, Rey, Rangers	.216	39	129	111	19	24	29	3	1	0	5	0	3	1	14	0	23	12	5	1	.261	.302
Sullivan, Davey, Orioles	.232	38	140	125	13	29	38	6	0	1	12	2	2	1	10	0	23	1	1	1	.304	.290
Tardiff, Jeremy, Red Sox	.130	10	24	23	2	3	8	0	1	1	4	0	0	0	1	0	2	0	0	1	.348	.167
Taylor, Avery, Orioles	.033	13	33	30	2	1	1	0	0	0	2	0	0	0	3	0	12	0	0	2	.033	.121
Taylor, Matthew, Braves*	.161	35	126	112	9	18	20	2	0	0	6	2	0	2	10	0	11	1	4	4	.179	.242
Terry, Reggie, Rangers	.294	5	17	17	3	5	5	0	0	0	0	0	0	0	0	0	4	2	0	0	.294	.294
Tessmar, Timothy, Mets*	.209	56	232	196	20	41	54	5	4	0	28	0	2	4	30	1	27	4	1	2	.276	.323
Tillero, Adrian, Royals	.252	36	111	103	14	26	33	4	0	1	11	0	0	0	8	1	33	1	1	3	.320	.306
Torrealba, Steve, Braves	.207	30	106	92	3	19	23	4	0	0	10	0	1	2	11	0	20	0	0	3	.250	.302
Truitt, Theron, Marlins	.179	24	80	67	8	12	12	0	0	0	8	0	3	3	7	0	13	6	0	0	.179	.275
Ubaldo, Nelson, Astros	.243	34	116	103	12	25	36	4	2	1	9	1	1	3	8	0	32	9	2	3	.350	.313
Valencia, Enrique, Red Sox*	.000	14	1	1	0	0	0	0	0	0	0	0	0	0	0	0	1	0	0	0	.000	.000
Valencia, Victor, Yankees	.241	25	64	58	5	14	18	1	0	1	8	0	0	0	6	0	22	0	0	1	.310	.313
Varriano, Mark, Red Sox	.163	18	57	49	4	8	9	1	0	0	6	0	0	2	6	0	10	0	0	1	.184	.281
Vecchioni, Gerald, Braves	.172	33	111	99	10	17	18	1	0	0	2	1	0	1	10	0	23	2	3	2	.182	.255
Velazquez, Jose, Yankees*	.287	58	245	209	33	60	82	9	2	3	34	0	3	1	30	2	20	3	4	3	.392	.374
Veras, Wilton, Red Sox	.264	31	101	91	7	24	25	1	0	0	5	0	0	3	7	0	9	1	2	2	.275	.337
Vilchez, Jose, Twins†	.225	45	147	142	14	32	38	6	0	0	6	4	0	0	1	0	29	7	5	0	.268	.231
Villa, Willie, Blue Jays	.181	40	154	138	20	25	35	6	2	0	11	1	0	1	14	0	28	2	1	2	.254	.261
Ware, Jeremy, Expos	.241	38	138	116	18	28	42	4	2	2	15	0	1	3	18	0	28	5	4	2	.362	.355
Weisner, Randy, White Sox*	.286	5	8	7	1	2	3	1	0	0	4	0	0	0	1	0	0	0	0	0	.429	.375
Welch, Coby, Royals	.279	16	46	43	7	12	14	2	0	0	9	0	0	0	3	0	8	0	0	1	.326	.326

Player, Team	Avg.	G	TPA	AB	R	H	TB	2B	3B	HR	RBI	SH	SF	HP	BB	IBB	SO	SB	CS	GDP	Slg.	OBP
Wesson, Barry, Astros	.188	45	160	138	14	26	38	2	2	2	18	1	1	1	19	0	40	4	0	2	.275	.289
West, Kenyon, Marlins	.000	13	1	1	0	0	0	0	0	0	0	0	0	0	0	0	0	0	0	0	.000	.000
White, Mickey, Astros	.000	1	4	4	1	0	0	0	0	0	0	0	0	0	0	0	0	0	0	0	.000	.000
Whitlock, Mike, Blue Jays*	.256	54	216	168	27	43	68	10	3	3	22	0	1	6	41	3	48	5	0	4	.405	.417
Winn, Wess, Orioles†	.222	5	21	18	2	4	6	2	0	0	5	0	0	0	3	0	3	0	0	1	.333	.333
Zambrano, Eddie, Red Sox	.000	1	5	5	0	0	0	0	0	0	0	0	0	0	0	0	2	0	0	0	.000	.000
Zambrano, Jose, Red Sox	.286	10	38	28	5	8	14	0	0	2	9	0	1	1	8	0	10	2	0	0	.500	.447
Zambrano, Victor, Yankees†	.205	27	86	78	10	16	21	3	1	0	5	2	0	1	5	0	15	2	3	2	.269	.262
Zamora, Junior, Mets	.232	20	64	56	9	13	19	2	2	0	4	1	1	1	5	0	10	0	0	2	.339	.302

GRAND SLAMS: Barnes, 2; Adamson, Coffee, Daedelow, Erickson, Fauske, Gallagher, Tardiff, 1 each.

AWARDED FIRST BASE ON CATCHER'S INTERFERENCE: R. Medina 4 (Keech 2, Stevenson 2); S. Charles 3 (Griffin 2, Keech); Velazquez 2 (Griffin, Stevenson); T. Bales (Campos); Borges (F. Pena); Cruz (Cardona); Je. Davenport (T. Bales); Robertson (Weisner); M. Rojas (Payano).

1995 PITCHING

TEAM

Team	W	L	Pct.	ERA	G	CG	ShO	Sv.	IP	H	TBF	R	ER	HR	SH	SF	HB	BB	IBB	SO	WP	Bk.
Cubs	35	22	.614	2.07	57	0	5	11	483.0	369	2015	184	111	11	20	22	29	189	6	344	31	15
Marlins	40	16	.714	2.30	56	2	4	16	481.2	367	1966	167	123	15	21	13	27	158	9	401	40	8
Mets	38	19	.667	2.53	57	3	4	17	490.2	381	2012	175	138	14	7	12	21	173	4	439	57	12
Orioles	34	25	.576	2.66	59	6	7	17	490.1	407	2073	223	145	16	9	19	21	190	5	377	28	10
Royals	37	20	.649	2.76	57	1	5	15	483.0	406	2011	223	148	16	15	16	45	142	1	423	46	9
Yankees	32	26	.552	2.89	58	2	8	13	489.1	372	2052	215	157	16	19	9	43	241	3	483	79	21
White Sox	36	22	.621	2.91	58	3	5	13	482.2	438	2021	217	156	21	6	17	18	155	3	400	34	14
Twins	20	35	.364	3.12	55	5	6	9	453.1	406	1982	244	157	16	18	16	32	232	1	357	52	16
Astros	32	26	.552	3.21	58	2	4	12	476.1	429	2066	228	170	16	23	12	29	199	6	492	59	13
Tigers	33	24	.579	3.39	57	3	5	23	462.0	406	2003	243	174	16	22	16	32	177	10	399	57	20
Rangers	24	34	.414	3.68	58	3	5	13	477.1	456	2082	274	195	18	8	18	32	196	3	385	51	7
Red Sox	21	36	.368	3.93	57	7	3	9	476.2	494	2084	287	208	37	12	14	18	181	4	400	42	7
Expos	21	35	.375	3.99	56	1	6	12	466.1	470	2056	275	207	18	13	24	26	179	2	310	51	16
Pirates	23	36	.390	4.22	59	2	3	9	488.0	523	2196	316	229	20	14	11	30	196	2	363	49	9
Braves	14	43	.246	4.34	57	2	2	7	467.0	448	2099	314	225	11	10	20	27	244	1	342	72	19
Blue Jays	19	40	.322	4.88	59	3	5	7	480.0	518	2196	363	260	22	19	18	43	205	2	350	86	20

INDIVIDUAL

TOP QUALIFIERS FOR EARNED-RUN AVERAGE TITLE

Minimum 48 innings. *Lefthanded pitcher.

Pitcher, Team	W	L	Pct.	ERA	G	GS	CG	ShO	GF	Sv.	IP	H	TBF	R	ER	HR	SH	SF	HB	BB	IBB	SO	WP	Bk.
Martin, Jeffrey, Royals	3	1	.750	1.47	11	10	1	1	0	0	55.0	35	216	12	9	1	0	2	7	11	0	53	2	3
Alicea, Patrick, Tigers	5	2	.714	1.93	12	8	2	1	2	1	51.1	45	211	21	11	1	1	2	3	14	0	43	5	1
Dace, Derek, Astros*	3	4	.429	1.95	11	10	2	1	1	0	69.1	60	274	20	15	2	3	1	1	6	0	77	5	2
Pena, Juan, Red Sox	3	2	.600	1.95	13	4	2	1	6	1	55.1	41	217	17	12	2	1	2	1	6	0	47	2	1
DeWitt, Scott, Marlins*	5	3	.625	1.98	11	10	1	0	0	0	63.2	48	245	15	14	1	3	2	2	9	0	70	1	1
White, Gary, Orioles*	5	4	.556	2.17	12	10	2	1	1	0	66.1	52	262	26	16	1	1	2	1	16	1	56	5	1
Dotel, Octavio, Mets	7	4	.636	2.18	13	12	2	0	1	0	74.1	48	293	23	18	0	1	0	5	17	1	86	9	0
Kolb, Daniel, Rangers	1	7	.125	2.21	12	11	0	0	0	0	53.0	38	219	22	13	0	0	2	3	28	0	46	8	2
Perez, Odaliz, Braves*	3	5	.375	2.22	12	12	1	1	0	0	65.0	48	264	22	16	0	3	0	3	18	0	62	7	3
Robinson, Martin, Yankees*	6	1	.857	2.48	11	8	2	2	0	0	61.2	54	236	20	17	4	2	0	3	13	0	56	7	2
Santiago, Derek, Marlins	5	1	.833	2.48	11	10	0	0	1	0	58.0	55	245	20	16	1	1	2	3	17	0	59	8	1
Pacheco, Delvis, Braves	1	8	.111	2.55	13	13	0	0	0	0	60.0	47	260	26	17	1	0	1	3	38	0	52	5	2
Prestash, J.D., Astros*	4	3	.571	2.63	11	11	0	0	0	0	51.1	48	225	18	15	0	2	1	5	24	0	56	4	6
Birsner, Roark, Cubs	3	2	.600	2.70	12	12	0	0	0	0	50.0	40	209	18	15	2	0	1	4	22	0	42	3	1
Nichols, James, White Sox	7	2	.778	2.89	11	10	0	0	1	0	65.1	64	257	31	21	4	0	2	2	12	0	38	3	0

DEPARTMENTAL LEADERS: W—Dotel, Nichols, 7; L—Pacheco, 8; Pct.—Carmano, Robinson, .857; G—Hernandez, Severino, Stentz, 24; GS—Pacheco, 13; CG—Black, 3; ShO—K. Richardson, Robinson, 2; GF—Stentz, 24; Sv.—Stentz, 16; IP—Dotel, 74.1; H—Black, 83; TBF—Rhodes, 311; R—R. Santos, 49; ER—R. Santos, 36; HR—Asher, Santana, 6; SH—Several pitchers tied with 5; SF—Villegas, 6; HB—Glover, 11; BB—Taylor, 54; IBB—Austin, R. Martinez, 3; SO—Dotel, 86; WP—T. Smith, 17; Bk.—Mejia, Prestash, 6.

ALL PITCHERS

*Lefthanded pitcher.

Pitcher, Team	W	L	Pct.	ERA	G	GS	CG	ShO	GF	Sv.	IP	H	TBF	R	ER	HR	SH	SF	HB	BB	IBB	SO	WP	Bk.
Aguilar, Alonzo, Royals	0	1	.000	3.76	15	1	0	0	5	1	26.1	26	116	14	11	2	0	3	7	10	0	24	4	0
Aguilar, Carlo, Yankees	6	0	1.000	2.08	18	0	0	0	6	1	39.0	36	159	11	9	0	3	0	0	13	1	34	8	1
Alicea, Patrick, Tigers	5	2	.714	1.93	12	8	2	1	2	1	51.1	45	211	21	11	1	1	2	3	14	0	43	5	1
Alvarado, Carlos, Pirates	0	0	.000	6.00	2	0	0	0	0	0	3.0	1	15	2	2	0	0	1	0	5	0	2	3	0
Alvarado, David, Pirates	1	0	1.000	4.80	9	2	0	0	4	1	15.0	15	66	8	8	1	0	0	2	4	0	15	3	2
Anderson, John, Astros	0	2	.000	3.00	2	0	0	0	1	0	3.0	3	13	3	1	0	0	0	0	1	0	5	2	0
Anez, Maycoll, White Sox	4	1	.800	0.93	7	1	0	0	3	1	29.0	19	109	6	3	0	0	0	1	4	0	21	3	0
Armas, Antonio, Yankees	0	1	.000	0.64	5	4	0	0	0	0	14.0	12	61	9	1	1	1	0	1	6	0	13	3	1
Arroyo, Bronson, Pirates	5	4	.556	4.26	13	9	0	0	3	1	61.1	72	275	39	29	4	2	0	4	9	0	48	5	0
Asher, Ray, Red Sox	0	3	.000	6.92	10	3	0	0	4	0	26.0	32	139	29	20	6	1	2	2	26	2	21	4	0
Austin, Swan, Marlins	0	2	.000	3.10	15	0	0	0	12	4	20.1	22	91	9	7	0	2	0	0	12	3	15	2	0
Bair, Wayne, Marlins*	2	2	.500	2.96	6	6	0	0	0	0	24.1	21	97	10	8	1	2	0	1	7	0	22	0	2
Bales, Joseph, White Sox	3	1	.750	3.97	11	9	1	0	0	0	45.1	44	213	27	20	0	1	2	2	31	0	44	3	1
Ballew, Preston, Mets*	3	0	1.000	1.75	14	2	0	0	6	4	36.0	27	143	8	7	0	1	0	2	6	0	42	5	1
Batista, Mario, Pirates	0	1	.000	5.40	1	1	0	0	0	0	5.0	7	23	4	3	1	0	0	0	3	0	2	2	0

Pitcher, Team	W	L	Pct.	ERA	G	GS	CG	ShO	GF	Sv.	IP	H	TBF	R	ER	HR	SH	SF	HB	BB	IBB	SO	WP	Bk.
Battaglia, Chuck, Rangers	4	3	.571	4.97	10	8	0	0	1	0	41.2	46	186	31	23	2	0	2	1	13	0	35	5	0
Bauldree, Joe, Braves	0	0	.000	7.09	12	0	0	0	3	0	26.2	26	129	21	21	1	0	0	4	26	0	19	2	0
Beckerman, Andy, Astros	0	0	.000	0.00	2	0	0	0	0	0	3.0	1	12	0	0	0	0	0	0	0	0	3	0	0
Beirne, Kevin, White Sox	0	0	.000	2.45	2	0	0	0	2	2	3.2	2	15	2	1	0	0	0	1	1	0	3	0	0
Bell, Rob, Braves	1	6	.143	6.88	10	8	0	0	0	0	34.0	38	154	29	26	2	0	2	2	14	0	33	7	0
Bernal, Manuel, Royals	3	0	1.000	1.36	6	6	0	0	0	0	33.0	29	130	9	5	1	0	1	1	4	0	25	3	0
Betti, Rich, Red Sox*	1	0	1.000	2.45	3	1	0	0	2	1	7.1	7	30	3	2	0	0	0	1	3	0	13	1	0
Birrell, Simon, Braves	2	3	.400	5.97	13	3	0	0	6	1	37.2	47	184	37	25	2	3	2	4	23	0	18	4	1
Birsner, Roark, Cubs	3	2	.600	2.70	12	12	0	0	0	0	50.0	40	209	18	15	2	0	1	4	22	0	42	3	1
Black, Jayson, Red Sox	4	5	.444	4.43	12	9	3	1	0	0	65.0	83	293	42	32	3	2	1	7	14	0	50	7	0
Boike, Todd, Expos	2	4	.333	3.94	23	1	0	0	13	2	48.0	54	220	32	21	1	1	2	6	13	1	35	6	2
Bonilla, Miguel, Pirates	0	0	.000	1.93	2	0	0	0	2	0	4.2	5	20	1	1	0	0	0	0	1	0	2	0	0
Booker, Chris, Cubs	3	2	.600	2.76	13	7	0	0	2	1	42.1	36	173	22	13	0	0	2	0	16	0	43	4	1
Borkowski, David, Tigers	3	2	.600	2.96	10	10	1	0	0	0	51.2	45	212	24	17	2	1	0	5	8	0	36	1	2
Borkowski, Robert, Mets	0	0	.000	2.25	5	0	0	0	1	1	8.0	6	31	2	2	0	0	0	0	3	1	1	2	0
Bowles, Brian, Blue Jays	0	1	.000	2.40	8	0	0	0	2	0	15.0	18	70	12	4	2	0	1	1	3	0	11	2	1
Boyd, Bradley, Expos	1	1	.500	5.01	17	0	0	0	9	1	23.1	27	111	17	13	0	1	2	1	13	0	10	5	1
Brand, Scott, Yankees	0	0	.000	0.90	4	0	0	0	0	0	10.0	5	37	1	1	1	0	0	0	3	0	8	1	0
Bray, Christopher, Orioles	3	2	.600	3.68	12	2	0	0	1	0	29.1	27	135	20	12	1	0	0	3	16	1	22	5	3
Brito, Juan, Mets*	3	2	.600	3.89	13	4	0	0	7	2	37.0	42	162	20	16	1	0	0	1	10	0	33	4	1
Brown, Brett, Astros*	0	0	.000	3.18	12	0	0	0	9	1	11.1	12	52	7	4	0	1	0	0	6	1	12	0	0
Brown, Tighe, White Sox	0	0	.000	1.17	3	0	0	0	1	0	7.2	3	28	1	1	0	0	1	0	2	0	12	1	0
Bruner, Clayton, Tigers	0	1	.000	3.94	5	4	0	0	0	0	16.0	15	77	12	7	1	3	0	3	10	0	15	1	0
Bryant, Chris, Cubs*	0	0	.000	4.91	6	0	0	0	2	0	11.0	11	49	6	6	0	1	2	0	5	1	13	0	0
Bryant, Scooter, Rangers	0	0	.000	0.00	1	0	0	0	1	0	1.0	0	4	0	0	0	0	0	0	1	0	1	0	0
Buckman, Thomas, W. Sox	1	2	.333	3.08	18	0	0	0	15	7	26.1	26	113	15	9	1	1	1	1	6	0	18	1	2
Burchart, Kyle, Blue Jays	1	3	.250	7.64	13	2	0	0	2	0	35.1	55	186	45	30	2	1	4	4	20	0	27	11	5
Burke, Ethan, Mets	1	2	.333	4.34	13	0	0	0	12	5	18.2	19	83	9	9	0	0	1	0	5	0	14	2	0
Burnett, Allan, Mets	2	3	.400	4.28	9	8	1	0	1	0	33.2	27	144	16	16	2	0	2	2	23	0	26	7	4
Burton, Jamie, Royals*	0	0	.000	8.25	6	1	0	0	1	0	12.0	13	60	11	11	1	0	1	1	10	0	14	5	1
Butler, Robert, Red Sox	1	4	.200	5.01	14	8	0	0	2	0	46.2	48	216	36	26	5	1	1	0	32	1	58	8	0
Cannon, Kevan, Red Sox*	2	1	.667	0.68	5	3	1	0	0	0	26.2	14	107	6	2	1	0	0	0	9	0	38	0	1
Carlson, Garret, White Sox	2	0	1.000	0.00	2	0	0	0	1	0	5.0	2	17	0	0	0	0	0	0	0	0	3	0	0
Carmano, Kevin, Royals	6	1	.857	2.12	15	0	0	0	7	2	34.0	25	140	18	8	0	5	0	8	9	0	16	4	1
Centeno, Jose, Expos*	1	0	1.000	2.45	15	0	0	0	7	1	25.2	18	105	7	7	1	1	1	2	6	0	17	1	1
Chantres, Carlos, White Sox	2	3	.400	3.21	11	11	2	0	0	0	61.2	65	257	32	22	2	1	1	1	14	0	47	1	2
Cobb, Trevor, Twins*	2	0	1.000	0.95	3	3	0	0	0	0	19.0	11	74	5	2	0	1	0	1	7	0	15	2	0
Coe, Brent, Blue Jays*	0	1	.000	3.38	2	2	0	0	0	0	8.0	8	35	4	3	0	1	0	0	3	0	6	2	0
Collins, Zach, Braves*	0	0	.000	2.57	3	0	0	0	3	1	7.0	6	27	2	2	0	1	0	0	1	0	2	0	0
Cook, O.J., Pirates	0	4	.000	3.63	12	7	0	0	4	2	34.2	33	154	24	14	1	0	1	1	22	0	25	4	0
Cooper, Keith, Braves	1	0	1.000	3.00	2	0	0	0	1	0	3.0	2	12	1	1	0	0	0	0	1	0	3	0	0
Corba, Lisandro, Braves	0	2	.000	1.06	6	3	0	0	0	0	17.0	9	63	5	2	0	0	0	1	1	0	18	1	4
Corrales, Rafael, Cubs	1	1	.500	2.42	12	0	0	0	5	2	22.1	23	97	8	6	2	1	0	1	8	0	10	3	1
Crawford, Christopher, Astros	1	0	1.000	3.62	10	5	0	0	1	0	32.1	29	147	15	13	0	2	1	3	25	0	22	3	0
Crawford, Paxton, Red Sox	2	4	.333	2.74	12	7	1	0	4	2	46.0	38	184	17	14	2	0	0	1	12	0	44	6	0
Cumberland, Chris, Yankees	0	1	.000	1.29	4	4	0	0	0	0	7.0	3	26	1	1	0	0	0	0	1	0	7	0	0
Dace, Derek, Astros*	3	4	.429	1.95	11	10	2	1	1	0	69.1	60	274	20	15	2	3	1	1	6	0	77	5	2
Davenport, Joe, Blue Jays	2	3	.400	5.66	15	10	1	0	1	1	55.2	67	267	47	35	2	3	2	3	30	0	29	9	3
DeLaRosa, Raul, White Sox	4	1	.800	1.67	11	2	0	0	5	0	27.0	22	116	9	5	0	1	2	1	16	1	22	4	0
DeLosSantos, Luis, Yankees	0	0	.000	0.00	2	0	0	0	1	0	5.0	5	23	2	0	0	0	0	1	2	0	6	0	0
Demorejon, Pedro, W. Sox	3	4	.429	3.60	12	0	0	0	5	1	30.0	28	125	14	12	3	1	0	2	5	1	34	1	4
Dempster, Ryan, Rangers	3	1	.750	2.36	8	6	1	0	0	0	34.1	34	154	21	9	1	0	1	2	17	0	37	2	1
Dessellier, Chris, Tigers	0	0	.000	0.00	1	0	0	0	1	1	1.0	0	5	0	0	0	0	0	0	1	0	3	0	0
Deutsch, Curry, Pirates*	2	4	.333	2.83	14	0	0	0	10	1	35.0	40	149	17	11	1	3	1	2	11	1	19	3	0
DeWitt, Scott, Marlins*	5	3	.625	1.98	11	10	1	0	0	0	63.2	48	245	15	14	1	3	2	2	9	0	70	1	1
Dickson, Lance, Cubs	1	0	1.000	0.00	2	1	0	0	0	0	3.0	2	14	0	0	0	0	0	0	3	0	3	0	0
Dotel, Octavio, Mets	7	4	.636	2.18	13	12	2	0	1	0	74.1	48	293	23	18	0	1	0	5	17	1	86	9	0
Dreyer, Steve, Rangers	0	1	.000	1.00	2	2	0	0	0	0	9.0	6	34	1	1	0	0	1	0	2	0	7	0	0
Duncan, Sean, White Sox*	0	0	.000	0.00	3	0	0	0	1	1	6.0	5	25	3	0	0	0	0	0	1	0	6	1	0
Dunn, Cordell, Pirates	1	1	.500	5.40	5	0	0	0	2	0	10.0	13	46	9	6	0	0	0	0	4	0	5	2	0
Duvall, Michael, Marlins*	5	0	1.000	2.22	16	1	0	0	10	1	28.1	15	120	8	7	1	0	0	2	12	1	34	4	2
Ellison, Austin, Twins	0	0	.000	3.78	11	0	0	0	6	2	16.2	17	78	10	7	0	0	0	1	15	0	11	3	1
Enloe, Mark, Mets*	2	1	.667	3.12	11	2	0	0	0	0	26.0	24	114	14	9	0	0	0	0	16	0	25	4	1
Espina, Randy, Twins*	0	1	.000	0.90	4	2	0	0	1	0	10.0	11	50	10	1	0	1	0	0	6	0	3	3	2
Eyre, Scott, White Sox*	0	2	.000	2.30	9	9	0	0	0	0	27.1	16	106	7	7	0	0	1	1	12	0	40	2	0
Farnsworth, Kyle, Cubs	3	2	.600	0.87	16	0	0	0	6	1	31.0	22	120	8	3	0	4	0	1	11	0	18	1	1
Farrell, Jim, Red Sox	1	0	1.000	1.50	1	1	0	0	0	0	6.0	2	20	1	1	1	0	0	0	1	0	3	0	0
Feliz, Jose, Cubs	3	2	.600	1.75	13	5	0	0	6	1	36.0	29	158	20	7	0	2	1	4	10	0	27	2	0
Fereira, Marcos, White Sox	0	1	.000	14.73	7	0	0	0	4	0	7.1	11	40	14	12	2	0	0	0	8	0	4	4	1
Figueroa, Julio, Expos	2	3	.400	3.08	10	10	0	0	0	0	49.2	44	211	27	17	5	4	2	0	20	0	37	2	1
Fisher, Louis, Orioles	4	3	.571	1.85	9	7	2	1	0	0	39.0	27	167	23	8	0	0	3	0	24	0	29	4	2
Fisher, Ryan, Pirates*	0	0	.000	0.00	1	0	0	0	0	0	1.0	1	4	0	0	0	0	0	0	0	0	1	0	0
Fleming, Dave, Royals*	0	0	.000	0.00	1	1	0	0	0	0	3.0	2	11	1	0	0	0	0	0	0	0	1	0	0
Forster, Peter, Twins*	2	5	.286	3.71	10	7	2	0	1	0	43.2	37	191	21	18	1	4	0	4	27	0	36	6	1
Fortune, Peter, Expos*	3	5	.375	4.69	11	11	1	0	0	0	48.0	46	209	33	25	1	2	1	2	18	0	27	3	0
Fowler, Benjamin, Braves	1	2	.333	1.09	12	0	0	0	6	1	24.2	17	106	13	3	0	0	2	0	13	0	23	4	0
Fuduric, Tony, Tigers	5	2	.714	2.97	16	0	0	0	7	0	30.1	25	136	13	10	1	2	2	1	21	0	21	4	3
Gaerte, Travis, Pirates	0	0	.000	6.00	6	0	0	0	1	0	12.0	14	57	9	8	2	0	0	3	2	0	5	1	1
Garcia, Freddy, Astros	6	3	.667	4.47	11	11	0	0	0	0	58.1	60	256	32	29	2	3	3	6	14	0	58	5	0
Garff, Jeffery, Twins	4	2	.667	1.77	15	6	0	0	6	1	45.2	34	175	12	9	3	1	0	4	5	0	30	1	0
Garsky, Brian, Expos	2	3	.400	3.12	14	6	0	0	2	1	43.1	48	199	25	15	1	1	3	2	19	0	43	6	3
Gaston, Ryan, Rangers	0	0	.000	1.99	10	1	0	0	5	2	22.2	19	95	9	5	0	0	2	2	6	0	9	1	0
Geraldo, Antonio, Blue Jays	0	0	.000	1.50	2	2	0	0	0	0	6.0	6	24	1	1	0	0	0	0	1	0	6	2	0

Pitcher, Team	W	L	Pct.	ERA	G	GS	CG	ShO	GF	Sv.	IP	H	TBF	R	ER	HR	SH	SF	HB	BB	IBB	SO	WP	Bk.
Gerland, Greg, Braves*	1	0	1.000	0.00	2	0	0	0	2	0	4.0	1	14	0	0	0	0	0	0	1	0	3	0	0
Getz, Rod, Marlins	1	1	.500	3.38	6	6	0	0	0	0	29.1	25	112	12	11	2	0	1	1	4	0	30	3	0
Gil, Daniel, Cubs	1	1	.500	3.46	7	0	0	0	2	2	13.0	9	59	7	5	0	0	1	2	8	0	9	4	0
Gillispie, Ryan, Pirates	0	1	.000	2.45	4	0	0	0	4	0	7.1	8	37	4	2	0	0	1	1	6	0	4	1	0
Glover, John, Blue Jays	3	7	.300	4.91	12	10	2	0	0	0	62.1	62	279	48	34	4	4	3	11	26	0	46	8	0
Goedde, Roger, Pirates	1	1	.500	2.61	6	6	1	0	0	0	31.0	31	130	12	9	0	1	0	2	7	0	25	0	0
Gonzalez, Generoso, Tigers	5	3	.625	3.89	16	4	0	0	2	1	39.1	29	163	19	17	1	2	1	1	16	0	45	8	1
Gosch, Grant, Astros*	0	0	.000	0.00	1	0	0	0	1	0	0.2	0	3	0	0	0	0	0	0	1	0	1	0	0
Gray, Jason, White Sox	4	2	.667	2.02	14	4	0	0	6	1	35.2	35	150	10	8	1	0	0	0	9	1	37	2	0
Gulin, Lindsey, Mets*	6	0	1.000	1.71	10	4	0	0	3	0	47.1	36	182	11	9	4	0	1	1	13	0	48	2	2
Guzman, Jose, Cubs	0	0	.000	1.50	2	2	0	0	0	0	6.0	5	24	1	1	1	0	0	0	0	0	3	0	0
Hacen, Abraham, Orioles	2	3	.400	2.54	13	8	0	0	2	2	46.0	34	201	21	13	2	1	3	4	32	0	37	3	1
Hale, Shane, Orioles	0	0	.000	1.29	2	2	0	0	0	0	7.0	6	32	2	1	0	0	0	0	4	0	6	0	0
Halladay, Roy, Blue Jays	3	5	.375	3.40	10	8	0	0	1	0	50.1	35	203	25	19	4	2	0	1	16	0	48	9	2
Hammons, Matt, Cubs	3	1	.750	2.35	10	8	0	0	1	0	46.0	35	186	14	12	1	1	3	2	16	0	32	2	1
Harris, Doug, Orioles	1	0	1.000	0.00	1	0	0	0	1	0	1.0	2	4	0	0	0	0	0	0	0	0	0	0	0
Hausmann, Isaac, Rangers	1	2	.333	2.67	18	0	0	0	15	6	30.1	24	128	11	9	0	1	1	2	9	0	23	0	0
Hecker, Doug, Red Sox	0	0	.000	5.40	2	0	0	0	1	0	1.2	4	11	2	1	0	0	0	0	0	0	4	0	0
Herbison, Brett, Mets	3	0	1.000	2.20	9	9	0	0	0	0	41.0	31	170	13	10	3	1	2	0	16	0	31	4	0
Hernandez, Francisco, Orioles	2	2	.500	1.32	24	0	0	0	20	11	27.1	18	105	4	4	1	0	1	1	6	0	23	2	1
Holobinko, Mike, Cubs*	3	2	.600	1.74	8	1	0	0	3	0	20.2	16	86	8	4	1	1	2	3	8	0	11	1	0
Hook, Jeff, Astros	1	0	1.000	0.00	2	0	0	0	0	0	6.0	4	24	0	0	0	0	0	0	2	0	4	0	0
Horton, Aaron, Yankees*	2	1	.667	1.57	8	6	0	0	0	0	23.0	17	93	7	4	0	0	1	5	6	0	21	3	1
Hundley, Chanin, White Sox	0	0	.000	6.23	3	0	0	0	0	0	4.1	7	22	5	3	1	0	3	0	2	0	2	0	0
Huntsman, Brandon, Orioles	6	3	.667	3.86	13	12	1	0	0	0	65.1	53	286	38	28	4	2	2	3	33	0	64	4	0
Hurtado, Victor, Marlins	3	1	.750	0.81	7	7	1	0	0	0	33.1	14	134	5	3	0	2	1	2	16	0	28	2	0
Izquierdo, Hansel, Marlins	0	0	.000	0.00	1	0	0	0	0	0	2.0	3	10	3	0	0	1	0	0	2	0	0	1	0
Jelsovsky, Craig, Mets	0	0	.000	0.00	1	0	0	0	1	1	1.0	0	3	0	0	0	0	0	0	0	0	0	0	0
Johnson, Joaquin, Braves*	0	0	.000	5.00	11	2	0	0	6	0	27.0	25	125	17	15	2	2	3	1	16	0	15	8	1
Johnson, Mike, Blue Jays	0	2	.000	7.20	3	3	0	0	0	0	15.0	20	74	15	12	1	0	0	3	8	0	13	7	0
Jolliffee, Brian, Braves*	0	2	.000	6.65	11	0	0	0	5	1	23.0	36	112	24	17	0	0	2	1	9	0	15	6	3
Judd, Mike, Yankees	1	1	.500	1.11	21	0	0	0	18	8	32.1	18	123	5	4	0	0	0	4	6	0	30	4	0
Kauflin, David, Tigers	2	1	.667	4.86	5	3	0	0	0	0	16.2	11	69	11	9	0	0	1	0	7	0	13	4	0
Kelley, Jason, Cubs	1	1	.500	0.70	7	5	0	0	1	0	25.2	10	110	11	2	0	0	0	5	19	0	20	2	2
Kessel, Kyle, Mets*	3	0	1.000	1.80	7	7	0	0	0	0	40.0	29	160	12	8	1	1	1	2	11	0	47	3	0
Key, Francis, Royals	1	2	.333	2.57	16	0	0	0	11	2	28.0	17	118	13	8	0	4	0	4	12	1	34	3	1
Kinney, Matt, Red Sox	1	3	.250	2.93	8	2	0	0	4	2	27.2	29	119	13	9	0	1	2	2	10	0	11	5	0
Knight, Brandon, Rangers	2	1	.667	5.25	3	2	0	0	0	0	12.0	12	54	7	7	0	0	1	0	6	0	11	2	0
Kolb, Daniel, Rangers	1	7	.125	2.21	12	11	0	0	0	0	53.0	38	219	22	13	0	0	2	3	28	0	46	8	2
Kruse, Kelly, White Sox	1	0	1.000	4.50	3	0	0	0	2	0	4.0	4	17	2	2	0	0	0	0	1	0	2	0	1
Lacey, James, Expos	1	1	.500	8.34	12	1	0	0	6	0	22.2	35	120	29	21	2	0	4	0	14	0	10	3	2
Lakman, Jason, White Sox	3	0	1.000	3.27	9	5	0	0	1	0	41.1	44	181	17	15	2	0	2	5	12	0	23	2	2
LaPlante, Michael, Pirates	0	0	.000	0.00	2	0	0	0	2	1	3.0	1	12	0	0	0	0	0	0	0	0	4	0	0
Lara, Nelson, Marlins	1	1	.500	3.74	11	0	0	0	4	1	21.2	21	101	13	9	1	0	1	2	11	1	9	2	1
Lara, Yovanny, Expos	1	2	.333	5.10	11	4	0	0	1	0	30.0	35	139	21	17	4	0	3	2	19	0	16	0	1
Lawrence, Clint, Blue Jays*	1	5	.167	4.57	12	9	0	0	3	0	45.1	40	202	33	23	1	0	1	1	26	0	40	9	1
Lawrie, Jason, Tigers	0	1	.000	4.50	4	4	0	0	0	0	12.0	10	59	8	6	0	0	0	1	12	2	12	0	0
Lebron, Jose, Expos	0	0	.000	0.00	2	0	0	0	1	0	2.0	0	9	0	0	0	0	0	0	3	0	0	0	0
Licciardi, Ronald, Cubs*	4	3	.571	2.43	17	1	0	0	7	0	33.1	24	141	13	9	1	1	0	1	16	2	22	3	4
Lynch, James, Astros	2	1	.667	1.56	17	1	0	0	12	4	34.2	14	148	12	6	1	0	0	0	26	0	49	10	2
Macero, Victor, Cubs	0	1	.000	5.40	1	1	0	0	0	0	5.0	3	19	3	3	1	0	0	0	1	0	5	0	0
Maine, Dalton, Orioles	1	0	1.000	2.08	18	0	0	0	6	2	30.1	24	122	7	7	0	0	1	0	9	1	32	1	0
Malko, Bryan, Twins	1	2	.333	2.73	10	4	0	0	3	1	33.0	23	142	14	10	1	3	1	4	23	0	29	5	0
Manley, Kevin, Mets	0	0	.000	6.75	2	0	0	0	0	0	1.1	1	8	1	1	0	0	0	0	3	0	0	1	0
Manser, Chris, Tigers	3	2	.600	2.45	6	5	0	0	1	0	29.1	24	120	10	8	1	1	2	0	5	0	26	6	0
Mansur, Jeff, Orioles*	0	0	.000	3.38	3	0	0	0	1	0	5.1	11	27	5	2	1	0	1	1	0	0	2	0	0
Markey, Barret, Cubs	4	1	.800	1.76	17	1	0	0	9	1	41.0	43	168	11	8	0	1	0	0	7	0	24	1	1
Marquez, Ralph, Twins	0	4	.000	4.09	11	0	0	0	11	1	22.0	19	103	13	10	1	1	1	0	18	1	19	2	3
Marriott, Michael, Marlins	0	0	.000	1.13	2	2	0	0	0	0	8.0	2	32	2	1	0	0	0	1	7	0	6	1	0
Marshall, Lee, Twins	0	1	.000	4.91	6	1	0	0	0	0	11.0	16	57	10	6	1	1	1	2	8	0	7	2	0
Martin, Cleburne, Expos	2	5	.286	4.85	17	4	0	0	5	2	42.2	43	187	26	23	1	0	4	0	22	1	26	10	1
Martin, Jeffrey, Royals	3	1	.750	1.47	11	10	1	1	0	0	55.0	35	216	12	9	1	0	2	7	11	0	53	2	3
Martinez, Humberto, R. Sox	0	3	.000	3.62	14	0	0	0	6	1	27.1	25	119	14	11	3	0	2	2	17	0	19	2	0
Martinez, Juan, Rangers	2	3	.400	5.40	12	6	0	0	5	0	38.1	43	166	28	23	5	0	0	0	11	1	27	1	0
Martinez, Ramulo, Tigers	0	0	.000	7.50	16	0	0	0	3	1	24.0	27	115	22	20	0	1	0	1	13	3	14	3	5
Martino, Jason, Cubs	0	0	.000	0.00	8	0	0	0	5	2	10.2	4	42	2	0	0	1	0	0	5	1	4	1	0
Mason, Roger, Pirates	1	0	1.000	0.00	1	0	0	0	0	0	1.0	2	5	0	0	0	0	0	0	0	0	1	0	0
Mattes, Troy, Expos	2	0	1.000	0.00	2	2	0	0	0	0	12.0	7	43	0	0	0	0	0	0	3	0	8	0	0
Maysonet, Jose, Blue Jays	0	0	.000	0.00	1	0	0	0	0	0	1.0	1	6	0	0	0	0	0	0	2	0	1	0	0
McBride, Rodney, Twins	3	7	.300	3.08	12	11	1	1	1	1	61.1	63	275	38	21	3	4	5	3	34	0	36	8	1
McCarter, Jason, Astros	1	0	1.000	2.86	16	0	0	0	9	2	22.0	16	97	8	7	2	5	0	2	16	0	21	6	0
McCaskey, Thomas, W. Sox	1	1	.500	3.00	6	1	0	0	0	0	18.0	17	77	6	6	1	0	0	0	7	0	16	4	1
McCormack, Andy, W. Sox*	1	0	1.000	1.50	1	1	0	0	0	0	6.0	4	21	1	1	1	0	0	0	0	0	4	0	0
McFarlane, Joseph, Tigers	0	0	.000	0.00	1	0	0	0	0	0	1.1	1	5	0	0	0	0	0	0	0	0	1	0	0
McFerrin, Chris, Astros	4	4	.500	2.86	20	0	0	0	12	5	34.2	28	153	20	11	0	3	0	5	17	2	39	6	1
McKnight, Tony, Astros	1	1	.500	3.86	3	3	0	0	0	0	11.2	14	48	5	5	0	0	2	0	2	0	8	1	0
Meady, Todd, Royals	3	3	.500	2.63	12	6	0	0	2	2	37.2	33	156	21	11	1	0	1	2	6	0	26	2	0
Medina, Tomas, Astros	1	0	1.000	8.46	11	1	0	0	0	0	22.1	37	115	26	21	0	1	0	1	14	0	23	7	0
Mejia, Felix, Yankees	2	0	1.000	3.45	9	0	0	0	3	0	15.2	11	68	6	6	0	0	2	2	13	0	21	6	6
Mendoza, David, Blue Jays	2	5	.286	4.99	12	10	0	0	0	0	48.2	58	225	37	27	0	2	1	4	14	0	39	4	3
Mendoza, Geronimo, W. Sox	0	1	.000	4.30	10	0	0	0	8	0	14.2	8	59	9	7	3	0	2	1	7	0	11	1	0
Mercedes, Carlos, Orioles	2	1	.667	2.55	10	1	0	0	2	0	24.2	22	96	8	7	2	0	0	0	2	0	10	0	0
Mesewicz, Mark, Pirates*	0	0	.000	3.86	3	0	0	0	0	0	4.2	5	21	2	2	0	0	0	0	1	0	6	0	0

Pitcher, Team	W	L	Pct.	ERA	G	GS	CG	ShO	GF	Sv.	IP	H	TBF	R	ER	HR	SH	SF	HB	BB	IBB	SO	WP	Bk.
Meyhoff, Jason, Twins*	0	0	.000	4.50	2	0	0	0	1	0	2.0	3	9	3	1	0	0	1	0	0	0	3	1	0
Mills, Al, Orioles	0	0	.000	0.00	1	1	0	0	0	0	2.0	3	11	0	0	0	0	0	0	2	0	1	0	1
Moody, Ritchie, Rangers	0	0	.000	2.70	2	2	0	0	0	0	10.0	10	46	3	3	0	0	0	0	6	0	10	1	0
Moore, David, Royals	2	2	.500	4.18	14	1	0	0	8	2	28.0	28	124	17	13	3	0	1	1	12	0	12	3	0
Moreno, Julio, Orioles	3	2	.600	1.59	5	5	1	1	0	0	34.0	17	131	9	6	0	1	2	1	7	0	29	1	1
Moreno, Orber, Royals	1	1	.500	2.45	8	3	0	0	1	0	22.0	15	89	9	6	0	0	0	2	7	0	21	2	0
Moreno, Ricardo, Rangers	1	0	1.000	1.80	4	1	1	0	2	1	15.0	13	56	3	3	1	2	0	0	1	0	8	0	1
Mota, Daniel, Yankees	2	3	.400	2.20	14	0	0	0	9	0	32.2	27	133	9	8	2	4	0	2	4	0	35	6	3
Mullis, Steven, Royals*	2	1	.667	2.92	8	1	0	0	3	1	12.1	7	52	6	4	0	0	1	0	7	0	13	2	0
Newell, Brandon, Mets	0	0	.000	0.00	1	0	0	0	1	0	1.0	1	7	2	0	0	0	1	0	2	1	2	0	0
Nezelek, Andy, Pirates	1	1	.500	7.71	4	0	0	0	4	1	7.0	12	34	7	6	0	1	0	0	2	1	6	2	0
Nichols, James, White Sox	7	2	.778	2.89	11	10	0	0	1	0	65.1	64	257	31	21	4	0	2	2	12	0	38	3	0
Ocando, Stewart, Twins	0	1	.000	5.96	14	0	0	0	8	0	22.2	26	118	25	15	2	1	4	4	22	0	20	7	4
O'Conner, Brian, Pirates*	2	2	.500	1.88	14	5	0	0	5	1	43.0	33	183	22	9	1	0	1	0	13	0	43	4	2
Olson, Philip, Mets	0	0	.000	4.50	1	0	0	0	0	0	2.0	1	10	1	1	0	0	0	0	3	0	3	0	0
Ovalle, Bonelly, Rangers	4	2	.667	3.72	17	5	1	1	3	1	58.0	51	243	29	24	1	2	3	6	20	1	58	5	0
Pacheco, Delvis, Braves	1	8	.111	2.55	13	13	0	0	0	0	60.0	47	260	26	17	1	0	1	3	38	0	52	5	2
Paredes, Carlos, Royals	4	2	.667	3.53	10	10	0	0	0	0	51.0	56	221	28	20	2	2	2	2	17	0	37	4	0
Parotte, Frisco, Yankees	0	0	.000	2.79	9	0	0	0	7	1	9.2	9	43	3	3	0	1	0	0	6	0	8	2	0
Pena, Jesus, Pirates*	0	0	.000	2.57	7	6	0	0	0	0	35.0	20	138	11	10	0	0	0	0	19	0	36	4	0
Pena, Juan, Red Sox	3	2	.600	1.95	13	4	2	1	6	1	55.1	41	217	17	12	2	1	2	1	6	0	47	2	1
Penny, Tony, Royals	2	0	1.000	5.06	10	0	0	0	4	0	16.0	17	66	9	9	4	0	0	0	4	0	7	0	0
Peraza, Jose, Cubs*	0	0	.000	0.00	3	0	0	0	1	0	2.1	0	8	0	0	0	0	1	0	1	0	2	0	0
Perez, Leonardo, Orioles	1	1	.500	4.41	8	0	0	0	4	0	16.1	14	76	13	8	1	0	3	3	7	0	7	0	0
Perez, Odaliz, Braves*	3	5	.375	2.22	12	12	1	1	0	0	65.0	48	264	22	16	0	3	0	3	18	0	62	7	3
Persails, Mark, Tigers	1	4	.200	4.41	11	10	0	0	0	0	51.0	50	237	37	25	4	5	3	4	25	0	30	8	1
Petcka, Joe, Mets	0	0	.000	0.00	1	0	0	0	1	0	2.0	1	7	0	0	0	0	0	0	0	0	0	0	0
Prestash, J.D., Astros*	4	3	.571	2.63	11	11	0	0	0	0	51.1	48	225	18	15	0	2	1	5	24	0	56	4	6
Puffer, Brandon, Twins	0	3	.000	2.88	14	5	0	0	6	1	40.2	29	175	21	13	0	0	0	2	21	0	35	5	0
Quezada, Edward, Expos	0	7	.000	4.99	12	10	0	0	2	0	52.1	52	221	36	29	2	1	1	5	10	0	36	10	1
Ramos, Edgar, Astros	0	1	.000	1.84	5	5	0	0	0	0	14.2	14	62	6	3	0	1	0	2	5	0	16	1	0
Randolph, Stephen, Yankees*	4	0	1.000	2.22	8	3	0	0	1	0	24.1	11	94	7	6	1	0	0	1	16	0	34	3	1
Rangel, Julio, Yankees	1	3	.250	4.40	14	0	0	0	5	2	28.2	20	123	18	14	2	1	0	4	16	1	30	2	0
Rauch, Robert, Red Sox	0	1	.000	4.76	7	0	0	0	6	2	5.2	8	27	4	3	0	2	0	0	2	1	6	0	0
Reilly, Sean, Twins*	0	1	.000	5.27	6	0	0	0	1	0	13.2	19	65	12	8	1	0	0	0	6	0	11	0	0
Reynolds, Mark, Rangers	0	2	.000	5.40	7	1	0	0	2	0	10.0	8	50	10	6	1	0	0	0	11	0	10	2	1
Rhodes, Joe, Orioles	4	2	.667	3.04	13	11	0	0	0	0	71.0	72	311	36	24	0	3	1	2	28	1	43	2	0
Richardson, David, Marlins	0	2	.000	2.30	9	0	0	0	6	1	15.2	8	62	5	4	1	0	1	2	5	0	8	1	0
Richardson, Kasey, Twins*	5	2	.714	1.15	7	7	2	2	0	0	47.0	38	190	10	6	1	0	0	3	11	0	35	1	0
Ricketts, Chad, Cubs	1	0	1.000	0.00	2	2	0	0	0	0	9.0	1	32	1	0	0	0	0	1	1	0	5	0	0
Ritter, Jason, Royals	0	0	.000	0.00	2	0	0	0	1	1	3.2	3	16	1	0	0	1	0	0	1	0	2	1	0
Robbins, Jake, Yankees	2	3	.400	5.54	14	3	0	0	3	0	37.1	32	159	26	23	2	2	1	1	18	1	17	4	0
Roberts, Franklin, Rangers	0	0	.000	27.00	1	0	0	0	0	0	0.2	1	7	2	2	0	0	0	0	4	0	0	0	0
Roberts, Grant, Mets	2	1	.667	2.15	11	3	0	0	4	0	29.1	19	121	13	7	1	1	1	3	14	1	24	4	1
Robinson, Martin, Yankees*	6	1	.857	2.48	11	8	2	2	0	0	61.2	54	236	20	17	4	2	0	3	13	0	56	7	2
Rodriguez, Tomas, Tigers	0	0	.000	2.53	14	0	0	0	8	1	21.1	14	93	13	6	0	0	1	5	8	0	21	5	1
Rojas, Euclides, Marlins	2	0	1.000	0.90	2	2	0	0	0	0	10.0	6	35	1	1	0	1	0	0	1	0	7	0	1
Romo, Greg, Tigers	3	1	.750	2.63	5	5	0	0	0	0	27.1	25	110	9	8	0	0	2	0	5	0	25	3	0
Rosario, Juan, Marlins	0	0	.000	13.50	1	0	0	0	0	0	1.1	4	10	2	2	0	0	0	0	1	0	3	1	0
Ross, Jeremy, Marlins	2	0	1.000	0.00	3	0	0	0	3	1	8.0	8	33	1	0	0	0	0	0	1	1	11	1	0
Ruch, Rob, Twins	1	3	.250	3.86	7	2	0	0	4	2	23.1	16	98	13	10	0	0	1	0	16	0	30	3	0
Ruffcorn, Scott, White Sox	0	0	.000	0.90	3	3	0	0	0	0	10.0	7	46	4	1	0	1	0	0	5	0	7	1	0
Ryan, Michael-Sean, Rangers	2	5	.286	2.35	17	0	0	0	8	2	38.1	36	159	15	10	1	1	2	2	8	1	22	0	0
Sacharko, Mark, Astros	1	2	.333	3.75	12	0	0	0	8	0	24.0	23	105	14	10	5	0	2	2	12	1	22	0	0
Samboy, Javier, Mets*	5	3	.625	2.98	12	4	0	0	4	1	48.1	40	196	17	16	0	0	2	3	17	0	31	3	0
Sanchez, Bienvenido, Expos	1	2	.333	1.46	16	1	0	0	9	5	37.0	27	153	7	6	0	2	0	3	12	0	29	4	3
Sanders, Allen, Royals	0	0	.000	0.00	1	0	0	0	1	1	2.0	1	6	0	0	0	0	0	0	0	0	3	0	0
Santamaria, Juan, Tigers	2	0	1.000	5.40	12	0	0	0	2	1	20.0	26	104	17	12	2	1	1	4	11	1	17	4	3
Santana, Pedro, Red Sox	2	4	.333	6.41	12	6	0	0	2	0	39.1	51	182	40	28	6	2	3	0	20	0	14	3	1
Santiago, Antonio, Red Sox*	2	2	.500	4.32	6	3	0	0	2	0	25.0	30	107	17	12	2	1	0	0	3	0	24	2	1
Santiago, Derek, Marlins	5	1	.833	2.48	11	10	0	0	1	0	58.0	55	245	20	16	1	1	2	3	17	0	59	8	1
Santos, Juan, Orioles	0	2	.000	3.20	21	0	0	0	15	2	25.1	25	107	11	9	3	1	0	2	4	1	16	1	0
Santos, Rafael, Pirates	2	5	.286	6.31	11	10	1	0	1	0	51.1	63	246	49	36	1	4	2	6	27	0	26	1	0
Schaffner, Eric, Yankees	2	2	.500	1.65	11	7	0	0	1	0	43.2	31	182	17	8	1	4	1	4	16	0	48	4	2
Schneider, Jeff, Blue Jays	0	2	.000	15.43	3	2	0	0	0	0	4.2	9	33	10	8	0	0	1	2	7	0	2	1	0
Schrenk, Steve, White Sox	0	1	.000	0.00	2	2	0	0	0	0	7.0	5	27	2	0	0	0	0	0	0	0	6	0	0
Scofield, Josh, Pirates*	0	0	.000	9.00	2	0	0	0	0	0	2.0	3	13	2	2	0	0	0	0	4	0	4	0	0
Seabury, Jaron, Blue Jays	3	0	1.000	3.18	15	0	0	0	5	1	39.2	35	164	16	14	2	2	1	7	17	0	18	6	1
Settle, Brian, Pirates	0	2	.000	8.27	11	0	0	0	5	0	20.2	25	105	22	19	4	2	3	1	20	0	11	4	1
Severino, Edy, Blue Jays	1	3	.250	5.63	24	0	0	0	12	1	24.0	31	121	25	15	0	2	2	2	13	0	13	8	2
Shannon, Bobby, Royals*	1	1	.500	3.25	16	0	0	0	9	2	27.2	28	112	11	10	0	1	2	3	3	0	26	4	0
Shiell, Jason, Braves	1	3	.250	4.43	12	0	0	0	9	2	22.1	23	101	16	11	0	0	0	2	10	1	13	3	0
Shurman, Ryan, Braves	1	6	.143	6.75	10	7	0	0	0	0	34.2	37	158	31	26	1	0	0	2	21	0	26	9	3
Simmons, Carlos, Rangers	4	3	.571	3.28	14	9	0	0	3	0	57.2	57	255	33	21	1	2	2	9	22	0	44	4	0
Smart, J.D., Expos	2	0	1.000	1.69	2	2	0	0	0	0	10.2	10	43	2	2	0	0	1	2	1	0	6	0	0
Smith, Dan, Rangers	0	3	.000	4.26	4	3	0	0	0	0	19.0	19	81	9	9	0	0	1	2	5	0	12	0	0
Smith, Tom, Rangers	0	0	.000	27.00	5	0	0	0	1	0	3.0	6	33	14	9	0	0	0	0	17	0	4	17	2
Sorzano, Ronnie, Expos	1	2	.333	5.21	4	4	0	0	0	0	19.0	24	86	13	11	0	0	0	1	6	0	10	1	0
Stading, Kris, Cubs*	0	0	.000	0.66	11	0	0	0	1	0	13.2	8	66	4	1	0	0	1	1	14	0	12	1	1
Stallings, Ben, Red Sox	0	1	.000	7.82	8	0	0	0	4	0	12.2	14	61	11	11	2	0	0	0	11	0	7	1	0
Stark, Zac, Marlins	3	1	.750	1.73	11	1	0	0	3	2	26.0	18	102	7	5	0	2	1	2	3	0	16	1	0
Stentz, Brent, Tigers	2	1	.667	2.36	24	0	0	0	24	16	26.2	21	107	7	7	1	1	1	1	12	2	28	4	1
Stewart, Scott, Twins	0	0	.000	6.35	3	1	0	0	0	0	5.2	7	29	4	4	0	0	0	1	4	0	9	0	1

Pitcher, Team	W	L	Pct.	ERA	G	GS	CG	ShO	GF	Sv.	IP	H	TBF	R	ER	HR	SH	SF	HB	BB	IBB	SO	WP	Bk.
Styles, Bobby, Rangers	0	0	.000	6.55	12	1	0	0	7	1	22.0	31	106	24	16	4	0	0	3	9	0	21	3	0
Suero, Rey, Rangers	0	1	.000	13.50	2	0	0	0	2	0	1.1	2	6	2	2	1	0	0	0	0	0	0	0	0
Symmonds, Mike, Pirates	1	1	.500	4.70	6	0	0	0	5	0	7.2	3	39	5	4	0	0	0	4	9	0	9	6	0
Tam, Jeff, Mets	0	0	.000	3.00	2	1	0	0	0	0	3.0	2	13	1	1	0	1	0	1	1	0	2	1	0
Taylor, Brien, Yankees*	2	5	.286	6.08	11	11	0	0	0	0	40.0	29	199	37	27	1	0	1	10	54	0	38	16	1
Tejera, Michael, Marlins*	3	1	.750	2.65	11	3	0	0	4	2	34.0	28	142	13	10	2	4	1	2	16	1	28	3	0
Tessmar, Timothy, Mets*	1	0	1.000	0.00	1	0	0	0	0	0	1.1	1	7	0	0	0	0	0	0	1	0	1	1	0
Thorn, Todd, Royals*	4	2	.667	3.23	11	10	0	0	0	0	47.1	43	201	23	17	1	1	1	6	14	0	58	4	1
Tillmon, Darrell, Red Sox*	1	0	1.000	1.13	3	1	0	0	0	0	8.0	4	29	2	1	0	0	0	0	0	0	5	0	0
Torres, Eric, Mets	0	2	.000	0.44	11	0	0	0	6	3	20.2	11	83	5	1	1	1	0	1	6	0	8	4	2
Trimble, Rob, Yankees	0	0	.000	0.57	11	0	0	0	2	1	15.2	12	62	2	1	0	0	1	0	4	0	14	0	0
Turley, Jason, Astros	5	0	1.000	5.63	11	0	0	0	2	0	16.0	14	79	13	10	0	0	1	2	13	1	13	1	2
Valencia, Enrique, Red Sox*	1	2	.333	4.76	14	4	0	0	7	0	34.0	51	154	25	18	3	0	1	0	9	0	19	0	2
Vanderbush, Matt, Twins*	2	3	.400	4.00	8	6	0	0	1	0	36.0	37	153	23	16	2	1	2	3	9	0	28	3	3
Vaninetti, Gene, Blue Jays	0	2	.000	4.98	20	0	0	0	20	2	21.2	25	98	14	12	3	1	0	0	6	1	7	1	2
Vardijan, Daniel, Marlins	5	0	1.000	1.64	9	8	0	0	1	0	44.0	21	164	11	8	2	0	1	5	10	0	34	2	0
Veniard, Jay, Blue Jays*	2	0	1.000	0.82	3	1	0	0	2	0	11.0	4	39	2	1	0	0	0	1	2	0	18	2	0
Verdin, Cesar, Yankees*	2	2	.500	3.46	11	5	0	0	0	0	26.0	26	114	15	10	1	0	0	1	10	0	35	1	0
Viegas, Randy, Pirates*	3	2	.600	2.54	6	4	0	0	2	0	28.1	28	119	13	8	0	0	0	1	5	0	24	0	0
Villar, Maximo, Pirates	1	1	.500	7.20	6	3	0	0	1	1	20.0	29	101	21	16	2	0	0	3	9	0	13	1	2
Villegas, Ismael, Cubs	3	2	.600	2.40	11	10	0	0	0	0	41.1	33	168	17	11	1	2	6	2	11	0	26	3	2
Vizcaino, Edward, Cubs	1	1	.500	2.70	14	0	0	0	6	1	16.2	15	77	10	5	1	5	2	2	6	2	11	0	0
Wallace, Jeff, Royals*	5	3	.625	1.23	12	7	0	0	3	1	44.0	28	177	20	6	0	1	1	1	15	0	51	3	2
Ward, Kerry, Pirates	2	6	.250	4.87	11	6	0	0	2	0	44.1	59	204	33	24	2	1	1	0	13	0	27	3	1
West, Kenyon, Marlins	2	1	.667	2.45	13	0	0	0	7	3	29.1	32	125	17	8	2	2	0	1	6	2	9	0	0
White, Eric, Braves	1	1	.500	6.75	13	1	0	0	8	0	32.0	39	161	37	24	1	1	3	1	22	0	10	9	0
White, Gary, Orioles*	5	4	.556	2.17	12	10	2	1	1	0	66.1	52	262	26	16	1	1	2	1	16	1	56	5	1
Wicks, Ross, Mets	0	1	.000	3.38	12	1	0	0	6	0	18.2	15	75	7	7	1	0	1	0	6	0	15	1	0
Widerski, Jonathan, Marlins	1	0	1.000	3.33	14	0	0	0	3	1	24.1	16	106	13	9	1	1	2	1	18	0	12	7	0
Williams, Bradford, Yankees*	0	3	.000	5.32	11	7	0	0	0	0	23.2	14	117	19	14	0	1	2	4	34	0	28	9	3
Wise, Willie, Braves*	0	2	.000	6.75	4	0	0	0	3	0	6.2	11	35	8	5	0	0	1	0	3	0	6	1	0
Wood, Kerry, Cubs	0	0	.000	0.00	1	1	0	0	0	0	3.0	0	9	0	0	0	0	0	0	1	0	2	0	0
Wyatt, Ben, Braves*	1	3	.250	2.98	12	8	1	0	3	1	42.1	36	194	25	14	1	0	4	3	27	0	24	6	2
Yanez, Luis, Astros	2	5	.286	2.95	11	11	0	0	0	0	61.0	52	253	29	20	4	2	1	0	15	1	63	8	0
Yonemura, Kazuki, Tigers	2	4	.333	2.32	14	4	0	0	4	1	42.2	38	180	20	11	2	4	0	3	9	2	49	1	2
Yount, Andrew, Red Sox	0	1	.000	2.76	5	5	0	0	0	0	16.1	13	69	8	5	1	1	0	2	6	0	17	1	1
Zavershnik, Mike, Blue Jays*	1	1	.500	5.45	19	0	0	0	8	2	36.1	44	170	29	22	1	1	2	3	11	1	26	5	0

COMBINATION SHUTOUTS: **Astros (3)**—Prestash-McCarter, Prestash-McFarrin, Yanez-Lynch. **Blue Jays (4)**—Halladay-Zavershnik 2, Lawrence-Severino-Vaninetti, Mendoza-Seabury-Vaninetti. **Braves (1)**—Shurman-Perille. **Cubs (5)**—Birsner-Markey, Hammons-Farnsworth-Licciardi, Hammons-Stading-Farnsworth, Ricketts-Farnsworth-Markey, Villegas-Stading-Licciardi. **Expos (6)**—Figueroa-Centeno-Boyd, Fortune-Garsky-Centeno, Garsky-Lacey-Boike, Mattes-Boike, Mattes-Garsky, Sanchez-Garsky. **Marlins (4)**—Duvall-Lara, Hurtado-Duvall-Stark, Rojas-Widerski-Austin, Vardijan-Richardson. **Mets (4)**—Dotel-Burke, Dotel-Samboy, Gulin-Ballew, Gulin-Wicks. **Orioles (4)**—Huntsman-Hacen-Bray-Santos, Mercedes-Hernandez, Rhodes-Hernandez, White-Huntsman-Hernandez-Santos. **Pirates (3)**—Goedde-Cook, Goedde-Viegas, Villar-Alvarado. **Rangers (4)**—Dempster-Ovalle-Kolb-Hausman, Knight-Ovalle, Reynolds-Ryan-Hausmann, Smith-Knight-Hausman. **Red Sox (1)**—Yount-Crawford. **Royals (4)**—Bernal-Meady-Key, Meady-Aguilar-Moore, Moreno-Key, Paredes-Carmano. **Tigers (4)**—Alicea-Yonemura-Stentz, Manser-Gonzalez-Rodriguez, Persails-Stentz, Romo-Yonemura-Gonzalez-Stentz. **Twins (3)**—Cobb-Ruch-Puffer, McBride-Malko, Richardson-Ruch. **White Sox (5)**—DeLaRosa-Mendoza, Eyre-Carlson, Nichols-Buckman, Nichols-Demorejon-Fereira, Ruffcorn-Demorejon-Buckman. **Yankees (6)**—Cumberland-Schaffner-Judd, Randolph-Judd-Parotte, Schaffner-Trimble-Mota-Rangel, Verdin-Brand-Robbins-Judd, Williams-Aguilar-Judd, Williams-Verdin-Horton-Trimble.

NO-HIT GAMES: None.

1995 FIELDING

TEAM

Team	Pct.	G	PO	A	E	TC	DP	PB
Mets	.966	57	1472	633	75	2180	28	6
Marlins	.961	56	1445	606	84	2135	39	5
Rangers	.957	58	1432	589	91	2112	47	25
Yankees	.956	58	1468	641	96	2205	57	15
White Sox	.955	58	1448	606	97	2151	49	12
Astros	.955	58	1429	600	96	2125	35	15
Royals	.954	57	1449	615	100	2164	54	18
Expos	.952	56	1399	622	101	2122	44	5
Tigers	.949	57	1386	574	105	2065	42	20
Red Sox	.948	57	1430	573	109	2112	40	31
Cubs	.947	57	1449	551	111	2111	40	17
Orioles	.947	59	1471	640	118	2229	46	13
Twins	.946	55	1360	621	113	2094	45	26
Pirates	.946	59	1464	638	120	2222	46	17
Braves	.942	57	1401	604	124	2129	41	15
Blue Jays	.939	59	1440	664	137	2241	47	26

TRIPLE PLAY: None.

INDIVIDUAL

FIRST BASEMEN

NOTE: All caps denotes fielding-percentage leader based on 30 games for catchers, 40 for all other non-pitchers and 59 innings for pitchers. *Throws lefthanded.

Player, Team	Pct.	G	PO	A	E	TC	DP
Agnoly, Earl, Marlins	.996	26	217	10	1	228	13
Alleyne, Roberto, Astros	.994	22	157	15	1	173	16
Amaya, Edilberto, White Sox	.991	25	208	13	2	223	20
Antigua, Nilson, Pirates	1.000	1	2	0	0	2	0
Balint, Rob, Tigers	1.000	1	8	2	0	10	1
Bejarano, Brian, Blue Jays	.981	15	138	14	3	155	11
Blosser, Douglas, Royals	.970	20	149	10	5	164	15
Brown, Derek, Orioles	.978	16	130	3	3	136	12
Bunkley, Antuan, Twins	.970	29	247	16	8	271	22
Burns, Kevin, Astros*	.982	39	301	21	6	328	14
Cardona, Luis, Red Sox	.906	3	28	1	3	32	4
Chastain, Dan, Marlins	1.000	1	5	1	0	6	0
Coffee, Gary, Royals	.983	34	285	10	5	300	25
Colon, Ariel, Braves	.979	23	173	13	4	190	14
Cruz, Andres, Twins	.988	21	163	6	2	171	15
Culp, Randy, Expos	1.000	5	49	2	0	51	7
Erickson, Corey, Mets	1.000	1	2	0	0	2	0
Gallagher, Shawn, Rangers	.986	57	478	19	7	504	42
Hagge, Kirk, Tigers	.981	42	284	26	6	316	25
Harrison, Jamal, Twins	1.000	4	28	3	0	31	2
Hernandez, Alexander, Pirates*	.952	9	77	3	4	84	6
Horn, Marvin, White Sox*	.986	36	272	14	4	290	21
Jelsovsky, Craig, Mets	1.000	2	5	0	0	5	0
Katayama, Daiki, Tigers	.917	4	20	2	2	24	1
Landry, Dan, Braves	1.000	1	9	0	0	9	0

Player, Team	Pct.	G	PO	A	E	TC	DP
Lima, Estivinson, Rangers	1.000	1	14	0	0	14	0
Llanos, Francisco, Expos	.966	32	265	16	10	291	22
Long, Garrett, Pirates	.986	14	134	6	2	142	12
Macero, Victor, Cubs	.971	28	222	9	7	238	15
Mifflin, Brian, Mets	.957	3	22	0	1	23	0
Montilla, Julio, Royals	.983	10	56	3	1	60	3
Oropeza, William, Expos	1.000	5	16	0	0	16	2
Pascual, Edison, Pirates*	.952	37	278	22	15	315	25
Pearson, Eddie, White Sox	1.000	2	12	0	0	12	2
Phillips, Darren, Blue Jays	1.000	2	15	1	0	16	1
Pickering, Calvin, Orioles	.968	11	86	6	3	95	2
Pressley, Kasey, Cubs	.955	23	166	2	8	176	15
Ramos, Jeff, Royals	1.000	3	6	0	0	6	2
Ramos, Noel, Orioles	1.000	4	30	3	0	33	2
Reyes, Freddy, Twins	1.000	5	42	4	0	46	1
Ribaudo, Mike, Orioles	1.000	4	16	0	0	16	1
Robertson, Dean, Orioles	.986	28	259	25	4	288	22
Rolison, Nate, Marlins	.984	30	283	20	5	308	20
Roman, Felipe, Red Sox	.974	48	358	21	10	389	27
Rose, Michael, Astros	.750	1	1	2	1	4	0
Ruiz, Cesar, Tigers	.985	26	184	13	3	200	11
Salazar, Juan, Cubs	.981	7	49	2	1	52	3
Santos, Edgardo, Expos*	.995	22	180	9	1	190	11
Scharrer, Jim, Braves	.973	36	304	25	9	338	23
Serra, Joaquin, Orioles	1.000	1	3	0	0	3	2
Shelton, Barry, White Sox	1.000	1	8	0	0	8	1
Smith, John, Astros	1.000	1	9	0	0	9	0
Soriano, Carlos, Mets	1.000	1	1	0	0	1	1
TESSMAR, Timothy, Mets*	.996	56	478	35	2	515	25
Velazquez, Jose, Yankees	.986	58	519	46	8	573	48
Veras, Wilton, Red Sox	.986	9	69	2	1	72	3
Welch, Coby, Royals	1.000	1	3	0	0	3	0
Whitlock, Mike, Blue Jays	.957	45	400	41	20	461	31

SECOND BASEMEN

Player, Team	Pct.	G	PO	A	E	TC	DP
Alayon, Elvis, Red Sox	.927	20	41	48	7	96	11
Alfonzo, Edgar, Orioles	.857	2	3	9	2	14	2
Antrim, Patrick, Yankees	.929	13	18	34	4	56	7
Astacio, Onofre, Twins	.953	17	38	43	4	85	14
Aybar, Ramon, Tigers	.959	33	38	80	5	123	10
Bautista, Jorge, Marlins	.971	11	14	19	1	34	3
Betancourt, Rafael, Red Sox	.950	22	46	49	5	100	12
Brown, Derek, Orioles	1.000	2	2	1	0	3	0
Campos, Miguel, Cubs	.875	9	13	15	4	32	4
Casimiro, Carlos, Orioles	.957	22	37	51	4	92	10
Cepeda, Jose, Royals	1.000	4	6	10	0	16	1
Daedelow, Craig, Orioles	1.000	1	3	3	0	6	1
Davidson, Cleatus, Twins	1.000	7	19	25	0	44	5
Delgado, Daniel, Pirates	.915	9	15	28	4	47	5
Douglas, John, Blue Jays	1.000	2	4	5	0	9	1
ERICKSON, Corey, Mets	.961	45	81	116	8	205	8
Febles, Carlos, Royals	.948	54	117	101	12	230	39
Franco, Raul, Marlins	.933	49	91	104	14	209	21
Frias, Ovidio, Pirates	.941	14	22	26	3	51	6
Garcia, Julio, Yankees	.955	4	13	8	1	22	4
Jasco, Elinton, Cubs	.937	34	77	57	9	143	13
Jelsovsky, Craig, Mets	1.000	1	2	3	0	5	0
Jones, Bryan, Tigers	.949	25	28	65	5	98	14
Kehoe, John, Blue Jays	.952	49	66	132	10	208	20
Kelly, Pat, Yankees	1.000	1	3	3	0	6	3
Kerr, Brian, Orioles	.932	9	19	22	3	44	6
Kerr, James, Yankees	.961	20	38	35	3	76	11
Kopacz, Derek, Tigers	1.000	3	5	8	0	13	2
Landry, Dan, Braves	1.000	3	1	5	0	6	0
Longueira, Tony, Royals	1.000	3	6	6	0	12	0
Lopez, Edgar, Braves	.955	36	66	103	8	177	19
Mateo, Henry, Expos	.949	37	69	98	9	176	22
Maysonet, Jose, Blue Jays	.981	12	25	27	1	53	2
Medina, Alger, Cubs	.971	17	35	31	2	68	7
Miles, Aaron, Astros	.934	21	35	50	6	91	9
Montas, Ricardo, Royals	.900	5	7	2	1	10	1
Montilla, Julio, Royals	1.000	2	5	4	0	9	2
Nova, Geraldo, Red Sox	.925	12	19	18	3	40	4
Nunez, Juan, Rangers	.953	31	57	84	7	148	16
Otero, Oscar, Braves	.813	4	7	6	3	16	2
Ovalles, Homy, Expos	.951	17	25	33	3	61	2
Pond, Simon, Expos	.944	12	14	20	2	36	4
Quezado, Dalmiro, Twins	.970	31	78	83	5	166	14
Reynoso, Ismael, Marlins	1.000	4	5	10	0	15	0
Rodriguez, Carlos, Red Sox	.933	8	14	14	2	30	3
Rodriguez, Liubiemithz, W. Sox	.971	36	63	102	5	170	19
Ruiz, Cesar, Tigers	.889	2	2	6	1	9	0
Samboy, Nelson, Astros	.977	39	86	85	4	175	15
Sanford, Chance, Pirates	.944	4	8	9	1	18	3
Schreiber, Stan, Pirates	.969	35	80	74	5	159	14
Serra, Joaquin, Orioles	.948	24	42	49	5	96	11
Solano, Angel, White Sox	.956	25	46	63	5	114	11
Soriano, Carlos, Mets	1.000	7	11	9	0	20	3
Soriano, Juan, Mets	1.000	8	14	30	0	44	5
Suero, Rey, Rangers	.968	27	59	61	4	124	15
Taylor, Avery, Orioles	.909	7	10	10	2	22	2
Taylor, Matthew, Braves	.976	20	36	44	2	82	7
Winn, Wess, Orioles	1.000	2	3	6	0	9	1
Zambrano, Victor, Yankees	.958	23	36	55	4	95	15

THIRD BASEMEN

Player, Team	Pct.	G	PO	A	E	TC	DP
Aguila, Hector, Rangers	.925	52	36	113	12	161	10
Alfonzo, Edgar, Orioles	1.000	1	0	1	0	1	0
Barnes, Kelvin, Cubs	.888	46	34	109	18	161	6
Barrett, Michael, Expos	1.000	1	0	2	0	2	0
Bautista, Jorge, Marlins	.855	31	15	50	11	76	2
Bejarano, Brian, Blue Jays	.771	12	10	17	8	35	2
Betancourt, Rafael, Red Sox	.940	19	14	33	3	50	0
Brown, Derek, Orioles	.909	33	23	77	10	110	8
Bunkley, Antuan, Twins	.904	24	18	48	7	73	0
Campos, Miguel, Cubs	.920	7	8	15	2	25	1
Capallen, Rene, Tigers	.667	3	0	2	1	3	0
CEPEDA, Jose, Royals	.955	52	45	123	8	176	14
Cole, Eric, Astros	.857	32	18	54	12	84	3
Culp, Randy, Expos	.333	1	1	0	2	3	0
Douglas, John, Blue Jays	.850	42	22	63	15	100	6
Frias, Ovidio, Pirates	.933	4	5	9	1	15	1
Jelsovsky, Craig, Mets	.800	4	1	3	1	5	0
Kehoe, John, Blue Jays	.889	9	6	18	3	27	0
King, Brian, Orioles	.737	17	5	23	10	38	1
Kopacz, Derek, Tigers	.838	47	32	87	23	142	10
Landry, Dan, Braves	.929	8	4	9	1	14	0
Leon, Donny, Yankees	.939	10	7	24	2	33	4
Liniak, Cole, Red Sox	.974	21	21	53	2	76	1
Long, Garrett, Pirates	.667	1	0	2	1	3	0
Longueira, Tony, Royals	.667	3	0	2	1	3	0
Lutz, Manuel, White Sox	.915	35	17	58	7	82	4
Medina, Alger, Cubs	.818	5	4	14	4	22	0
Montas, Ricardo, Royals	.828	9	11	13	5	29	2
Montilla, Julio, Royals	1.000	1	1	1	0	2	1
Nelson, Kevin, Twins	.890	36	18	63	10	91	6
Oropeza, William, Expos	.883	30	31	52	11	94	7
Ortiz, Asbel, Rangers	.792	10	7	12	5	24	3
Otero, Oscar, Braves	.750	6	6	9	5	20	1
Ovalles, Homy, Expos	1.000	1	0	1	0	1	0
Owen, Tom, Marlins	.833	20	12	33	9	54	1
Pena, Adelis, Pirates	.883	54	42	117	21	180	10
Pena, Alex, Pirates	1.000	1	2	2	0	4	2
Phillips, Darren, Blue Jays	.750	4	1	5	2	8	1
Pond, Simon, Expos	.908	31	18	81	10	109	1
Quezado, Dalmiro, Twins	1.000	1	1	2	0	3	0
Radcliff, Victor, Royals	.842	8	5	11	3	19	0
Reynoso, Ismael, Marlins	.893	14	6	19	3	28	2
Ribaudo, Mike, Orioles	.760	9	5	14	6	25	1
Rosado, Luis, Yankees	.935	51	16	84	7	107	12
Ruiz, Cesar, Tigers	.886	16	10	21	4	35	1
Samboy, Nelson, Astros	.886	14	13	26	5	44	1
Serra, Joaquin, Orioles	1.000	2	0	2	0	2	0
Shelton, Barry, White Sox	.795	26	9	53	16	78	4
Smith, John, Astros	.745	17	11	27	13	51	1
Solano, Angel, White Sox	1.000	1	2	2	0	4	0
Soriano, Carlos, Mets	.906	38	28	88	12	128	3
Spencer, Jeffrey, Braves	.839	42	38	82	23	143	6
Taylor, Avery, Orioles	1.000	1	1	1	0	2	0
Taylor, Matthew, Braves	1.000	2	0	2	0	2	0
Veras, Wilton, Red Sox	.885	22	11	35	6	52	1
Winn, Wess, Orioles	1.000	4	1	8	0	9	0
Zamora, Junior, Mets	.943	20	19	31	3	53	5

SHORTSTOPS

Player, Team	Pct.	G	PO	A	E	TC	DP
Abreu, Nelson, Cubs	.916	57	91	161	23	275	24
Alfonzo, Edgar, Orioles	1.000	1	1	2	0	3	1
Antrim, Patrick, Yankees	1.000	1	2	3	0	5	0
Astacio, Onofre, Twins	.890	30	30	75	13	118	10
Barrett, Michael, Expos	.892	48	65	141	25	231	26
Betancourt, Rafael, Red Sox	.960	13	16	32	2	50	6
Campos, Miguel, Cubs	.500	2	0	1	1	2	0
Capallen, Rene, Tigers	.899	21	28	43	8	79	8

Player, Team	Pct.	G	PO	A	E	TC	DP
Casimiro, Carlos, Orioles	.820	13	11	30	9	50	4
Cepeda, Jose, Royals	1.000	4	8	12	0	20	5
Cole, Eric, Astros	.842	4	3	13	3	19	1
Cordero, Edward, Tigers	.950	47	71	80	8	159	16
Daedelow, Craig, Orioles	.930	49	60	152	16	228	28
Davidson, Cleatus, Twins	.907	14	19	49	7	75	10
Delgado, Daniel, Pirates	.898	22	28	69	11	108	11
DiSarcina, Glenn, White Sox	.875	2	3	4	1	8	0
Douglas, John, Blue Jays	.857	8	14	16	5	35	3
Erickson, Corey, Mets	.903	6	8	20	3	31	4
Feliz, Edgar, Pirates	.885	16	12	34	6	52	3
Frias, Ovidio, Pirates	.941	6	9	23	2	34	3
Gonzalez, Alex, Marlins	.932	52	65	168	17	250	26
Hermansen, Chad, Pirates	.884	16	20	56	10	86	9
JARONCYK, Ryan, Mets	.952	43	59	121	9	189	8
Jelsovsky, Craig, Mets	.854	12	15	20	6	41	5
Jimenez, D'Angelo, Yankees	.927	56	95	173	21	289	31
Klee, Charles, White Sox	.935	42	46	126	12	184	26
Landry, Dan, Braves	.910	14	26	35	6	67	8
Longueira, Tony, Royals	.898	37	24	82	12	118	13
Lopez, Edgar, Braves	1.000	1	1	2	0	3	0
Lorenzo, Juan, Twins	.862	14	15	41	9	65	7
Maloney, Jeff, Blue Jays	.840	27	37	68	20	125	13
Mateo, Henry, Expos	1.000	2	2	7	0	9	0
Maysonet, Jose, Blue Jays	.907	15	34	34	7	75	7
Mejia, Marlon, Astros	.914	33	32	74	10	116	17
Miles, Aaron, Astros	.895	25	18	50	8	76	7
Montas, Ricardo, Royals	.750	6	1	8	3	12	2
Montilla, Julio, Royals	.905	5	9	10	2	21	3
Nova, Geraldo, Red Sox	.800	1	1	3	1	5	1
Olmeda, Jose, Red Sox	.900	42	60	111	19	190	23
Ortiz, Asbel, Rangers	.864	17	18	39	9	66	5
Otero, Oscar, Braves	.364	2	0	4	7	11	0
Ovalles, Homy, Expos	.942	11	15	34	3	52	5
Parra, Jose, Rangers	.939	43	58	141	13	212	20
Pena, Adelis, Pirates	1.000	1	1	0	0	1	0
Radcliff, Victor, Royals	.856	26	25	64	15	104	5
Reynoso, Ismael, Marlins	.944	8	12	22	2	36	6
Rodriguez, Carlos, Red Sox	1.000	3	6	10	0	16	2
Serra, Joaquin, Orioles	.800	2	3	1	1	5	0
Solano, Angel, White Sox	.908	16	26	43	7	76	9
Solano, Fausto, Blue Jays	.955	11	28	36	3	67	9
Soriano, Juan, Mets	1.000	1	1	1	0	2	0
Taylor, Matthew, Braves	.894	13	20	39	7	66	8
Vecchioni, Gerald, Braves	.929	30	36	68	8	112	10
Zambrano, Victor, Yankees	1.000	3	1	1	0	2	0

OUTFIELDERS

Player, Team	Pct.	G	PO	A	E	TC	DP
Adamson, Jason, Pirates	.966	28	54	2	2	58	0
Agnoly, Earl, Marlins	.966	20	26	2	1	29	0
Akins, Carlos, Orioles	.955	39	55	8	3	66	1
Alleyne, Roberto, Astros	1.000	13	22	1	0	23	0
Ayuso, Julio, Twins	1.000	15	15	2	0	17	0
Barksdale, Shane, Astros	.889	46	58	6	8	72	0
Barnes, Kelvin, Cubs	1.000	2	7	2	0	9	1
Bartee, Kimera, Orioles	1.000	5	15	0	0	15	0
Beaumont, Hamil, Yankees	1.000	10	12	1	0	13	0
Bejarano, Brian, Blue Jays	1.000	8	17	1	0	18	0
Beltran, Carlos, Royals	.977	51	79	6	2	87	0
Bishop, Tim, Mets	.973	47	71	2	2	75	0
Black, Brandon, Mets	.984	30	59	2	1	62	0
Borges, Victor, Cubs*	1.000	27	57	1	0	58	0
Butler, Garrett, Yankees	.933	48	67	3	5	75	1
Camilo, Jose, Marlins*	.984	34	63	0	1	64	0
Campos, Miguel, Cubs	.000	1	0	0	1	1	0
Capallen, Rene, Tigers	.955	13	20	1	1	22	0
Carubelli, Gustavo, Braves	.963	49	98	6	4	108	2
Cedeno, Jesus, Tigers	1.000	33	42	3	0	45	1
Charles, Curtis, Orioles	1.000	8	10	1	0	11	0
Charles, Steve, Blue Jays	.974	47	69	6	2	77	1
Chick, Bruce, Expos	.941	11	15	1	1	17	0
Coffee, Gary, Royals	1.000	2	2	0	0	2	0
Colon, Jose, Cubs	.987	38	73	4	1	78	3
Colson, Jeremiah, Expos*	.966	18	26	2	1	29	0
Connell, Jerry, Cubs	1.000	20	52	2	0	54	0
Crutchfield, David, Cubs	.959	28	66	4	3	73	1
Dasher, Melvin, Royals	.929	12	13	0	1	14	0
Davis, Albert, Pirates	1.000	9	8	1	0	9	0
Davis, Torrance, Expos	.986	41	67	6	1	74	1
DeLaCruz, Carlos, Tigers	.949	33	55	1	3	59	0
DeLaCruz, Wilfredo, Yankees	.976	34	40	1	1	42	0
Dent, Darrell, Orioles*	.975	31	75	2	2	79	0
Deshazer, Jeremy, Astros	.966	27	25	3	1	29	0
Domingo, Tyrone, Tigers	.980	29	49	1	1	51	0
Elliott, Dawan, Pirates*	.913	30	41	1	4	46	0
Ellison, Skeeter, Braves	.917	18	20	2	2	24	0
Encarnacion, Pedro, White Sox	1.000	10	14	0	0	14	0
Ferguson, Dwight, Red Sox*	.938	20	29	1	2	32	0
Flores, Oswaldo, Red Sox	1.000	13	15	2	0	17	0
Garcia, Luis, White Sox	.958	41	65	4	3	72	0
Gil, Daniel, Cubs	1.000	1	1	0	0	1	0
Gomez, Ramon, White Sox	.914	26	30	2	3	35	0
Goodwin, Rawlin, Red Sox	1.000	15	21	4	0	25	2
Green, Ronald, Cubs	.955	33	60	4	3	67	0
Hayes, Darren, White Sox	1.000	5	5	3	0	8	1
Hernandez, Alexander, Pirates*	.987	36	71	4	1	76	1
Higman, Joel, Orioles	.875	4	6	1	1	8	0
James, Kennouth, Expos	.976	41	80	3	2	85	1
Jenkins, Corey, Red Sox	.985	32	62	3	1	66	0
Johnson, Carlisle, Twins	.800	12	11	1	3	15	0
Johnson, Rontrez, Red Sox	.960	49	90	7	4	101	0
Johnson, Travis, Twins	.944	22	31	3	2	36	0
Jones, Jamie, Marlins*	1.000	4	3	0	0	3	0
Juarez, Raul, Twins	.941	7	16	0	1	17	0
Kerr, Brian, Orioles	1.000	1	1	0	0	1	0
King, Kevin, Expos	.963	14	26	0	1	27	0
Kinnie, Donald, Cubs	.984	30	59	4	1	64	0
Knabenshue, Chris, Pirates	1.000	3	6	2	0	8	1
Kofler, Eric, Yankees*	.885	18	21	2	3	26	1
Landry, Dan, Braves	.938	9	13	2	1	16	0
Lebron, Juan, Royals	.915	46	54	0	5	59	0
Lima, Estivinson, Rangers	.875	10	13	1	2	16	0
Lowery, Terrell, Rangers	1.000	3	7	0	0	7	0
Maas, Kevin, Yankees*	1.000	2	3	0	0	3	0
Macero, Victor, Cubs	1.000	1	1	0	0	1	0
May, Freddie, Pirates*	.963	25	50	2	2	54	0
McCarthy, Kevin, Mets*	.967	22	28	1	1	30	0
McDonald, Donzell, Yankees	.936	28	44	0	3	47	0
McHenry, Joseph, Twins	.920	33	42	4	4	50	3
Medina, Alger, Cubs	1.000	3	4	0	0	4	0
Mercado, Julio, Rangers	.973	55	102	6	3	111	4
Mifflin, Brian, Mets	.941	16	16	0	1	17	0
Millwood, Terry, Twins	.967	44	55	4	2	61	0
Miyauchi, Hector, Expos	.966	16	27	1	1	29	0
Monds, Wonderful, Braves	1.000	4	8	0	0	8	0
Monroe, Craig, Rangers	.962	53	94	7	4	105	1
Morrison, Ryan, Mets	.938	34	44	1	3	48	0
Mota, Gleydel, Mets*	.964	33	52	2	2	56	0
Nobles, Ivan, Blue Jays	.868	32	32	1	5	38	0
Nova, Fernando, White Sox	.958	30	67	2	3	72	2
Nunez, Juan, Rangers	1.000	1	2	0	0	2	0
Ortiz, Asbel, Rangers	1.000	4	4	0	0	4	0
Ortiz, Pedro, Orioles	1.000	5	1	0	0	1	0
Otero, Oscar, Braves	1.000	4	3	0	0	3	0
Pascual, Edison, Pirates*	1.000	3	5	0	0	5	0
PECK, Thomas, Blue Jays	1.000	58	107	6	0	113	0
Pena, Alex, Pirates	.968	45	86	6	3	95	0
Pena, Jose, Rangers	.944	47	62	5	4	71	0
Pendergrass, Tyrone, Braves	1.000	52	101	2	0	103	0
Peniche, Fray, Tigers	1.000	28	29	1	0	30	0
Pitts, Shedrick, Royals	1.000	32	35	3	0	38	0
Pond, Simon, Expos	1.000	3	1	0	0	1	0
Porter, Kedric, Orioles	.975	42	76	2	2	80	1
Ramirez, Francisco, Tigers	.902	26	36	1	4	41	0
Ramirez, Julio, Marlins	.983	46	109	7	2	118	1
Rengifo, Daliene, White Sox	.974	24	37	1	1	39	0
Rivera, Roberto, Orioles	.929	32	49	3	4	56	2
Roche, Marlon, Astros	.976	27	38	2	1	41	1
Rojas, Moises, Red Sox	.949	37	70	4	4	78	0
Rose, Damian, Rangers	.778	12	7	0	2	9	0
Saffer, Jeffrey, Yankees	.915	40	43	0	4	47	0
Selivanov, Andrei, Braves	.714	4	5	0	2	7	0
Shipman, Thomas, Tigers	.875	26	27	1	4	32	0
Shirley, Al, Mets	1.000	4	5	0	0	5	0
Sime, Rafael, Marlins*	.964	52	78	3	3	84	1
Simmons, Brian, White Sox	1.000	5	13	1	0	14	0
Smith, Phillip, Braves	.981	37	49	3	1	53	0
Springfield, Bo, Pirates	1.000	2	2	0	0	2	0
Stafford, Kimani, Royals	1.000	33	28	0	0	28	0
Stephens, Joel, Orioles	.958	16	23	0	1	24	0
Stevens, Clayton, White Sox	.986	36	69	1	1	71	1
Strawberry, Darryl, Yankees*	1.000	4	3	1	0	4	0
Suero, Rey, Rangers	1.000	2	2	0	0	2	0
Tardiff, Jeremy, Red Sox	.909	9	8	2	1	11	1
Terry, Reggie, Rangers	1.000	4	5	0	0	5	0

Player, Team	Pct.	G	PO	A	E	TC	DP
Tillero, Adrian, Royals	.971	36	31	2	1	34	0
Truitt, Theron, Marlins	1.000	15	13	0	0	13	0
Ubaldo, Nelson, Astros	.963	30	26	0	1	27	0
Vilchez, Jose, Twins	.964	44	73	8	3	84	0
Villa, Willie, Blue Jays	.962	36	47	3	2	52	1
Ware, Jeremy, Expos	1.000	37	57	8	0	65	2
Wesson, Barry, Astros	1.000	44	71	9	0	80	1
White, Mickey, Astros	1.000	1	1	0	0	1	0
Zambrano, Jose, Red Sox	1.000	8	13	1	0	14	0

CATCHERS

Player, Team	Pct.	G	PO	A	E	TC	DP	PB
Alley, William, Orioles	.971	12	61	6	2	69	0	1
Alvarado, Basilio, Expos	.987	28	143	13	2	158	0	0
Antigua, Nilson, Pirates	.980	25	159	33	4	196	1	4
Bales, Taylor, Royals	.973	8	30	6	1	37	0	5
Bowers, Kevin, Mets	.982	21	145	17	3	165	0	3
Campos, Miguel, Cubs	.963	20	117	14	5	136	4	8
Cardona, Luis, Red Sox	.943	20	124	8	8	140	0	15
Chapman, Scott, Astros	1.000	13	71	9	0	80	0	3
Chastain, Dan, Marlins	.938	2	12	3	1	16	0	0
Cisar, Ryan, Blue Jays	.974	20	62	13	2	77	1	5
Corzo, Beau, Braves	.981	25	128	27	3	158	2	7
Cossins, Tim, Rangers	.909	2	10	0	1	11	0	0
Davenport, Jeff, Red Sox	1.000	5	29	1	0	30	0	0
DiSalle, Javier, Orioles	.950	4	17	2	1	20	0	0
Downs, Brian, White Sox	.983	37	268	30	5	303	3	3
Engle, Beau, Mets	.985	10	55	10	1	66	0	1
Fagley, Daniel, Marlins	.965	15	75	8	3	86	4	1
Fauske, Joshua, White Sox	.951	25	131	6	7	144	2	9
Fitzpatrick, Rob, Expos	.923	2	11	1	1	13	0	0
Fortin, Blaine, Blue Jays	.993	31	109	30	1	140	2	10
Gordon, Buck, Cubs	1.000	2	4	1	0	5	0	0
Green, Raymond, Marlins	1.000	2	8	1	0	9	0	0
Griffin, Juan, Astros	.972	26	181	29	6	216	1	9
Gruber, Nick, Red Sox	.968	13	53	8	2	63	1	3
Imrisek, Jason, Yankees	.961	14	108	14	5	127	1	4
Katayama, Daiki, Tigers	.985	24	115	16	2	133	2	1
Keech, Erik, Yankees	.964	18	134	25	6	165	1	3
Kuilan, Hector, Marlins	.994	47	309	52	2	363	1	4
Lantigua, Miguel, Mets	.987	26	186	41	3	230	2	1
Leon, Donny, Yankees	.818	3	8	1	2	11	0	1
Lignitz, Jeremiah, Tigers	.968	22	105	16	4	125	0	11
Lima, Estivinson, Rangers	1.000	3	14	0	0	14	0	1
Llibre, Brian, Rangers	.986	11	63	8	1	72	0	11
Lomasney, Steven, Red Sox	.972	23	146	29	5	180	1	11
McLendon, Craig, Rangers	.981	25	144	15	3	162	1	4
McSparin, Paul, Pirates	.959	19	105	13	5	123	1	2
Medina, Robert, Blue Jays	.951	26	93	23	6	122	0	11
Orndorff, Dave, Twins	.966	20	133	11	5	149	1	8
Oropeza, William, Expos	.974	6	32	6	1	39	1	2
Paxton, Chris, Orioles	.957	11	56	10	3	69	2	2
Payano, Alexi, Cubs	.978	19	124	11	3	138	0	3
Pena, Frank, Twins	.960	14	106	15	5	126	1	5
Phillips, Darren, Blue Jays	.971	15	59	8	2	69	0	0
Pinto, Rene, Yankees	1.000	10	62	16	0	78	0	2
Prada, Nelson, Twins	.975	24	135	19	4	158	1	13
Ramos, Jeff, Royals	.980	25	134	15	3	152	1	3
Rivera, Juan, Rangers	.983	28	160	18	3	181	1	9
Robles, Juan, Royals	.985	28	177	24	3	204	2	8
Rodriguez, Sammy, Mets	.977	6	34	8	1	43	0	1
ROSE, Michael, Astros	1.000	33	214	44	0	258	0	3
Salazar, Juan, Cubs	.993	20	114	23	1	138	1	6
Schneider, Brian, Expos	.982	27	138	26	3	167	0	3
Selivanov, Andrei, Braves	.970	10	29	3	1	33	0	1
Shipp, Skip, Pirates	.984	18	109	15	2	126	2	11
Stevenson, Chad, Tigers	.969	28	165	20	6	191	3	8
Sullivan, Davey, Orioles	.968	38	249	25	9	283	1	10
Torrealba, Steve, Braves	.982	30	185	33	4	222	2	7
Valencia, Victor, Yankees	.978	25	148	27	4	179	0	5
Varriano, Mark, Red Sox	.948	12	44	11	3	58	3	2
Weisner, Randy, White Sox	.909	5	9	1	1	11	0	0
Welch, Coby, Royals	.976	14	78	4	2	84	0	2

PITCHERS

Player, Team	Pct.	G	PO	A	E	TC	DP
Aguilar, Carlo, Yankees	.889	18	3	5	1	9	1
Alicea, Patrick, Tigers	1.000	12	1	13	0	14	4
Alvarado, Carlos, Pirates	1.000	2	0	1	0	1	0
Alvarado, David, Pirates	1.000	9	1	2	0	3	0
Anderson, John, Astros	1.000	2	1	1	0	2	0
Anez, Maycoll, White Sox	.818	7	3	6	2	11	0
Armas, Antonio, Yankees	1.000	5	0	3	0	3	0
Arroyo, Bronson, Pirates	.857	13	3	9	2	14	2
Asher, Ray, Red Sox	.750	10	0	3	1	4	0
Austin, Swan, Marlins	1.000	15	1	0	0	1	0
Bair, Wayne, Marlins*	1.000	6	0	9	0	9	0
Bales, Joseph, White Sox	.833	11	2	8	2	12	1
Ballew, Preston, Mets*	1.000	14	1	4	0	5	0
Batista, Mario, Pirates	1.000	1	1	1	0	2	0
Battaglia, Chuck, Rangers	.778	10	1	6	2	9	0
Bauldree, Joe, Braves	.833	12	1	4	1	6	0
Beckerman, Andy, Astros	1.000	2	0	2	0	2	0
Beirne, Kevin, White Sox	1.000	2	0	1	0	1	0
Bell, Rob, Braves	.857	10	3	3	1	7	0
Bernal, Manuel, Royals	1.000	6	2	7	0	9	0
Betti, Rich, Red Sox*	1.000	3	0	1	0	1	0
Birrell, Simon, Braves	.875	13	4	3	1	8	0
Birsner, Roark, Cubs	1.000	12	1	8	0	9	1
Black, Jayson, Red Sox	.923	12	2	10	1	13	0
Boike, Todd, Expos	.917	23	5	6	1	12	0
Bonilla, Miguel, Pirates	1.000	2	0	1	0	1	0
Booker, Chris, Cubs	.667	13	0	2	1	3	0
Borkowski, David, Tigers	.905	10	5	14	2	21	0
Bowles, Brian, Blue Jays	.750	8	1	2	1	4	0
Boyd, Bradley, Expos	.800	17	0	4	1	5	1
Brand, Scott, Yankees	1.000	4	0	1	0	1	0
Bray, Christopher, Orioles	.875	12	1	6	1	8	0
Brito, Juan, Mets*	.750	13	1	5	2	8	0
Bruner, Clayton, Tigers	.833	5	1	4	1	6	0
Bryant, Chris, Cubs*	1.000	6	0	1	0	1	0
Buckman, Thomas, White Sox	.667	18	1	1	1	3	0
Burchart, Kyle, Blue Jays	.933	13	2	12	1	15	0
Burke, Ethan, Mets	1.000	13	1	1	0	2	0
Burnett, Allan, Mets	1.000	9	2	5	0	7	1
Burton, Jamie, Royals*	1.000	6	1	2	0	3	0
Butler, Robert, Red Sox	.846	14	4	7	2	13	0
Cannon, Kevan, Red Sox*	.625	5	2	3	3	8	0
Carlson, Garret, White Sox	1.000	2	0	1	0	1	0
Carmano, Kevin, Royals	.857	15	2	4	1	7	1
Centeno, Jose, Expos*	1.000	15	2	4	0	6	0
Chantres, Carlos, White Sox	.909	11	4	16	2	22	0
Cobb, Trevor, Twins*	1.000	3	3	5	0	8	1
Coe, Brent, Blue Jays*	1.000	2	1	0	0	1	0
Collins, Zach, Braves*	1.000	3	0	1	0	1	0
Cook, O.J., Pirates	1.000	12	3	4	0	7	0
Cooper, Keith, Braves	1.000	2	0	1	0	1	0
Corba, Lisandro, Braves	.750	6	1	5	2	8	0
Corrales, Rafael, Cubs	1.000	12	0	2	0	2	0
Crawford, Christopher, Astros	.818	10	6	3	2	11	0
Crawford, Paxton, Red Sox	.800	12	2	6	2	10	0
Cumberland, Chris, Yankees*	1.000	4	0	1	0	1	0
Dace, Derek, Astros*	1.000	11	4	17	0	21	0
Davenport, Joe, Blue Jays	.733	15	7	4	4	15	0
DeLaRosa, Raul, White Sox	1.000	11	1	5	0	6	0
DeLosSantos, Luis, Yankees	.250	2	1	0	3	4	0
Demorejon, Pedro, White Sox	.833	12	2	3	1	6	0
Dempster, Ryan, Rangers	.750	8	1	2	1	4	0
Deutsch, Curry, Pirates*	.933	14	7	7	1	15	0
DeWitt, Scott, Marlins*	1.000	11	3	15	0	18	0
Dickson, Lance, Cubs*	1.000	2	0	1	0	1	0
Dotel, Octavio, Mets	.944	13	7	10	1	18	0
Dreyer, Steve, Rangers	1.000	2	0	2	0	2	0
Duncan, Sean, White Sox*	1.000	3	2	1	0	3	0
Dunn, Cordell, Pirates	1.000	5	1	2	0	3	0
Duvall, Michael, Marlins*	1.000	16	1	3	0	4	0
Ellison, Austin, Twins	.000	11	0	0	1	1	0
Enloe, Mark, Mets*	.875	11	1	6	1	8	0
Espina, Randy, Twins*	1.000	4	1	1	0	2	0
Eyre, Scott, White Sox*	1.000	9	1	2	0	3	0
Farnsworth, Kyle, Cubs	1.000	16	0	9	0	9	0
Farrell, Jim, Red Sox	1.000	1	1	1	0	2	0
Feliz, Jose, Cubs	.667	13	0	2	1	3	0
Fereira, Marcos, White Sox	.333	7	0	1	2	3	1
Figueroa, Julio, Expos	1.000	10	3	9	0	12	0
Fisher, Louis, Orioles	.833	9	1	4	1	6	0
Fleming, Dave, Royals*	1.000	1	0	2	0	2	0
Forster, Peter, Twins*	.850	10	2	15	3	20	0
Fortune, Peter, Expos*	.833	11	2	3	1	6	0
Fowler, Benjamin, Braves	.444	12	3	1	5	9	1
Fuduric, Tony, Tigers	1.000	16	1	9	0	10	1
Gaerte, Travis, Pirates	1.000	6	0	3	0	3	0
Garcia, Freddy, Astros	1.000	11	9	12	0	21	1
Garff, Jeffery, Twins	.900	15	0	9	1	10	0
Garsky, Brian, Expos	1.000	14	2	4	0	6	0

Player, Team	Pct.	G	PO	A	E	TC	DP
Gaston, Ryan, Rangers	.667	10	1	3	2	6	0
Geraldo, Antonio, Blue Jays	1.000	2	2	1	0	3	0
Gerland, Greg, Braves*	1.000	2	1	2	0	3	0
Getz, Rod, Marlins	.750	6	2	1	1	4	0
Gil, Daniel, Cubs	.667	7	1	1	1	3	0
Gillispie, Ryan, Pirates	1.000	4	1	1	0	2	0
Glover, John, Blue Jays	.769	12	5	15	6	26	1
Goedde, Roger, Pirates	.900	6	3	6	1	10	0
Gonzalez, Generoso, Tigers	1.000	16	3	1	0	4	0
Gray, Jason, White Sox	.714	14	1	4	2	7	1
Gulin, Lindsey, Mets*	.900	10	1	8	1	10	0
Guzman, Jose, Cubs	1.000	2	1	1	0	2	0
Hacen, Abraham, Orioles	.800	13	1	7	2	10	0
Halladay, Roy, Blue Jays	.944	10	4	13	1	18	1
Hammons, Matt, Cubs	.933	10	3	11	1	15	0
Harris, Doug, Orioles	1.000	1	1	0	0	1	0
Hausmann, Isaac, Rangers	1.000	18	0	5	0	5	0
Herbison, Brett, Mets	1.000	9	4	7	0	11	0
Hernandez, Francisco, Orioles	.800	24	3	1	1	5	0
Holobinko, Mike, Cubs*	.500	8	0	3	3	6	0
Horton, Aaron, Yankees*	1.000	8	2	5	0	7	1
Hundley, Chanin, White Sox	1.000	3	0	1	0	1	0
Huntsman, Brandon, Orioles	.895	13	4	13	2	19	0
Hurtado, Victor, Marlins	1.000	7	2	4	0	6	1
Izquierdo, Hansel, Marlins	.000	1	0	0	1	1	0
Johnson, Joaquin, Braves*	.857	11	1	5	1	7	0
Johnson, Mike, Blue Jays	.750	3	1	2	1	4	0
Jolliffee, Brian, Braves*	.818	11	2	7	2	11	1
Judd, Mike, Yankees	1.000	21	4	7	0	11	2
Kauflin, David, Tigers	.667	5	0	2	1	3	0
Kelley, Jason, Cubs	.333	7	0	1	2	3	0
Kessel, Kyle, Mets*	.889	7	1	7	1	9	1
Key, Francis, Royals	1.000	16	0	3	0	3	0
Kinney, Matt, Red Sox	1.000	8	2	1	0	3	0
Knight, Brandon, Rangers	1.000	3	1	2	0	3	1
Kolb, Daniel, Rangers	1.000	12	0	6	0	6	1
Lacey, James, Expos	1.000	12	1	1	0	2	0
Lakman, Jason, White Sox	1.000	9	3	2	0	5	0
LaPlante, Michael, Pirates	1.000	2	1	0	0	1	0
Lara, Nelson, Marlins	1.000	11	2	4	0	6	0
Lara, Yovanny, Expos	.667	11	1	3	2	6	0
Lawrence, Clint, Blue Jays*	.867	12	3	10	2	15	0
Lawrie, Jason, Tigers	1.000	4	1	1	0	2	0
Lebron, Jose, Expos	1.000	2	0	1	0	1	0
Licciardi, Ronald, Cubs*	1.000	17	0	6	0	6	1
Lynch, James, Astros	1.000	17	1	5	0	6	0
Maine, Dalton, Orioles	1.000	18	3	2	0	5	0
Malko, Bryan, Twins	.750	10	5	4	3	12	0
Manser, Chris, Tigers	.800	6	2	2	1	5	0
Mansur, Jeff, Orioles*	1.000	3	0	2	0	2	0
Markey, Barret, Cubs	.833	17	0	5	1	6	1
Marquez, Ralph, Twins	.875	11	3	4	1	8	0
Marriott, Michael, Marlins	.500	2	0	1	1	2	1
Marshall, Lee, Twins	.333	6	0	1	2	3	0
Martin, Cleburne, Expos	.818	17	2	7	2	11	2
Martin, Jeffrey, Royals	.833	11	1	9	2	12	0
Martinez, Humberto, Red Sox	.900	14	3	6	1	10	0
Martinez, Juan, Rangers	1.000	12	1	3	0	4	1
Martinez, Ramulo, Tigers	1.000	16	4	2	0	6	0
Martino, Jason, Cubs	1.000	8	0	1	0	1	0
Mattes, Troy, Expos	1.000	2	0	1	0	1	0
McBride, Rodney, Twins	.938	12	3	12	1	16	0
McCarter, Jason, Astros	1.000	16	1	5	0	6	0
McCaskey, Thomas, W. Sox	1.000	6	2	3	0	5	0
McCormack, Andy, W. Sox*	1.000	1	0	1	0	1	0
McFerrin, Chris, Astros	1.000	20	4	11	0	15	0
McKnight, Tony, Astros	1.000	3	1	0	0	1	0
Meady, Todd, Royals	1.000	12	0	3	0	3	0
Medina, Tomas, Astros	.833	11	1	4	1	6	0
Mejia, Felix, Yankees	1.000	9	0	1	0	1	0
Mendoza, David, Blue Jays	.882	12	10	5	2	17	0
Mendoza, Geronimo, W. Sox	.500	10	0	1	1	2	0
Mercedes, Carlos, Orioles	.667	10	0	2	1	3	0
Moore, David, Royals	1.000	14	3	10	0	13	1
Moreno, Julio, Orioles	1.000	5	2	4	0	6	0
Moreno, Orber, Royals	1.000	8	0	2	0	2	0
Moreno, Ricardo, Rangers	1.000	4	2	4	0	6	0
Mota, Daniel, Yankees	.714	14	1	4	2	7	0
Nezelek, Andy, Pirates	.750	4	1	2	1	4	0
Nichols, James, White Sox	.957	11	5	17	1	23	3
Ocando, Stewart, Twins	1.000	14	1	6	0	7	1
O'Conner, Brian, Pirates*	.900	14	1	8	1	10	1
Ovalle, Bonelly, Rangers	.833	17	3	7	2	12	1

Player, Team	Pct.	G	PO	A	E	TC	DP
Pacheco, Delvis, Braves	.917	13	4	7	1	12	0
Paredes, Carlos, Royals	.900	10	3	15	2	20	0
Parotte, Frisco, Yankees	1.000	9	3	2	0	5	1
Pena, Jesus, Pirates*	.833	7	0	5	1	6	0
Pena, Juan, Red Sox	1.000	13	2	6	0	8	1
Penny, Tony, Royals	1.000	10	1	2	0	3	0
Perez, Leonardo, Orioles	1.000	8	0	2	0	2	0
Perez, Odaliz, Braves*	.880	12	4	18	3	25	0
Persails, Mark, Tigers	.842	11	5	11	3	19	0
Prestash, J.D., Astros*	.786	11	4	7	3	14	0
Puffer, Brandon, Twins	1.000	14	4	5	0	9	0
Quezada, Edward, Expos	.786	12	3	8	3	14	0
Ramos, Edgar, Astros	.800	5	0	4	1	5	0
Randolph, Stephen, Yankees*	.714	8	1	4	2	7	0
Rangel, Julio, Yankees	1.000	14	2	2	0	4	0
Reilly, Sean, Twins*	1.000	6	1	1	0	2	0
Rhodes, Joe, Orioles	1.000	13	2	17	0	19	2
Richardson, David, Marlins	.833	9	2	3	1	6	0
Richardson, Kasey, Twins*	.880	7	2	20	3	25	0
Ricketts, Chad, Cubs	1.000	2	0	1	0	1	0
Ritter, Jason, Royals	1.000	2	1	1	0	2	0
Robbins, Jake, Yankees	.900	14	1	8	1	10	0
Roberts, Grant, Mets	.917	11	3	8	1	12	1
ROBINSON, Martin, Yankees*	1.000	11	2	20	0	22	2
Rodriguez, Tomas, Tigers	.667	14	1	1	1	3	0
Rojas, Euclides, Marlins	1.000	2	0	3	0	3	0
Romo, Greg, Tigers	1.000	5	2	2	0	4	0
Ruch, Rob, Twins	.750	7	1	5	2	8	0
Ruffcorn, Scott, White Sox	1.000	3	1	2	0	3	0
Ryan, Michael-Sean, Rangers	.833	17	0	10	2	12	0
Sacharko, Mark, Astros	.667	12	0	2	1	3	0
Samboy, Javier, Mets*	.800	12	5	3	2	10	0
Sanchez, Bienvenido, Expos	1.000	16	3	5	0	8	0
Sanders, Allen, Royals	1.000	1	0	1	0	1	1
Santamaria, Juan, Tigers	.800	12	2	2	1	5	0
Santana, Pedro, Red Sox	.429	12	1	2	4	7	0
Santiago, Antonio, Red Sox*	.833	6	0	5	1	6	0
Santiago, Derek, Marlins	1.000	11	3	6	0	9	0
Santos, Juan, Orioles	.667	21	0	2	1	3	0
Santos, Rafael, Pirates	.929	11	2	11	1	14	1
Schaffner, Eric, Yankees	.857	11	2	10	2	14	0
Schrenk, Steve, White Sox	1.000	2	0	1	0	1	0
Seabury, Jaron, Blue Jays	1.000	15	4	13	0	17	1
Settle, Brian, Pirates	.667	11	0	2	1	3	0
Severino, Edy, Blue Jays	.800	24	4	4	2	10	0
Shannon, Bobby, Royals*	1.000	16	2	3	0	5	0
Shiell, Jason, Braves	.917	12	5	6	1	12	0
Shurman, Ryan, Braves	.833	10	0	10	2	12	1
Simmons, Carlos, Rangers	.917	14	5	6	1	12	1
Smart, J.D., Expos	.667	2	1	1	1	3	0
Smith, Dan, Rangers	1.000	4	0	1	0	1	0
Smith, Tom, Rangers	1.000	5	0	1	0	1	0
Sorzano, Ronnie, Expos	1.000	4	1	2	0	3	1
Stading, Kris, Cubs*	.000	11	0	0	1	1	0
Stallings, Ben, Red Sox	1.000	8	1	0	0	1	0
Stark, Zac, Marlins*	1.000	11	1	4	0	5	0
Stentz, Brent, Tigers	1.000	24	1	3	0	4	1
Stewart, Scott, Twins*	1.000	3	0	2	0	2	0
Styles, Bobby, Rangers	.750	12	1	2	1	4	0
Symmonds, Mike, Pirates*	.000	6	0	0	1	1	0
Tam, Jeff, Mets	1.000	2	0	2	0	2	0
Taylor, Brien, Yankees*	1.000	11	2	4	0	6	1
Tejera, Michael, Marlins*	1.000	11	0	7	0	7	0
Thorn, Todd, Royals*	1.000	11	0	8	0	8	0
Tillmon, Darrell, Red Sox*	1.000	3	0	3	0	3	0
Torres, Eric, Mets	.857	11	2	4	1	7	0
Trimble, Rob, Yankees	1.000	11	2	3	0	5	0
Turley, Jason, Astros	1.000	11	2	2	0	4	0
Valencia, Enrique, Red Sox*	1.000	14	1	7	0	8	0
Vanderbush, Matt, Twins*	.778	8	1	6	2	9	0
Vaninetti, Gene, Blue Jays	1.000	20	0	4	0	4	0
Vardijan, Daniel, Marlins	.867	9	2	11	2	15	1
Veniard, Jay, Blue Jays*	1.000	3	0	3	0	3	1
Verdin, Cesar, Yankees*	1.000	11	1	2	0	3	0
Viegas, Randy, Pirates*	1.000	6	2	5	0	7	0
Villar, Maximo, Pirates	.800	6	1	3	1	5	1
Villegas, Ismael, Cubs	.846	11	4	7	2	13	0
Vizcaino, Edward, Cubs	.750	14	1	2	1	4	0
Wallace, Jeff, Royals*	.778	12	3	11	4	18	0
Ward, Kerry, Pirates	1.000	11	5	6	0	11	1
West, Kenyon, Marlins	.714	13	4	1	2	7	0
White, Eric, Braves	.800	13	2	2	1	5	0
White, Gary, Orioles*	.893	12	6	19	3	28	2

Player, Team	Pct.	G	PO	A	E	TC	DP
Wicks, Ross, Mets	.600	12	1	2	2	5	0
Widerski, Jonathan, Marlins	1.000	14	1	2	0	3	0
Williams, Bradford, Yankees*	.500	11	0	2	2	4	0
Wood, Kerry, Cubs	1.000	1	0	1	0	1	0
Wyatt, Ben, Braves*	.818	12	4	5	2	11	0
Yanez, Luis, Astros	.818	11	4	5	2	11	0
Yonemura, Kazuki, Tigers	.789	14	4	11	4	19	1
Yount, Andrew, Red Sox	1.000	5	1	1	0	2	0
Zavershnik, Mike, Blue Jays*	1.000	19	1	8	0	9	1

The following players did not have any fielding statistics at the positions indicated or appeared only as a designated hitter, pinch-hitter or pinch-runner: Aguila, of; A. Aguilar, p; Bejarano, ss; R. Borkowski, p; B. Brown, p; T. Brown, p; B. Bryant, p; Cisar, of; Daniels, dh, pr; Dessellier, p; DiSarcina, of; Erickson, 3b; E. Feliz, 3b; R. Fisher, p; Gil, 3b; Gosch, p; Guillen, dh, ph; Hale, p; Hecker, p; Hook, p; Jelsovsky, p; Kruse, p; LaForest, 3b; Lantigua, 1b; Llanos, of; Llibre, 3b; Macero, p; Manley, p; Mason, p; Maysonet, p; McFarlane, p; Mesewicz, p; Meyhoff, p; Mills, p; Moody, p; Morrison, 3b; Mullis, p; Newell, p; Olson, p; A. Ortiz, 2b; Peraza, p; Petcka, p; Radcliff, of; Rauch, p; Reynolds, p; F. Roberts, p; Rosario, of, p; Ross, p; J. Schneider, p; Scofield, p; Shelton, c; Stafford, 2b; Suero, p; Tessmar, p; Wise, p; E. Zambrano, dh.

LEAGUE CHAMPIONS

Year	Team	Pct.
1964—	Sarasota Braves	.610
1965—	Bradenton Astros	.632
1966—	New York AL	.667
1967—	Kansas City	.614
1968—	Oakland	.650
1969—	Montreal	.585
1970—	Chicago AL	.600
1971—	Kansas City	.755
1972—	Chicago NL*	.651
	Kansas City*	.651
1973—	Texas	.732
1974—	Chicago NL	.702
1975—	Texas	.774
1976—	Texas	.704
1977—	Chicago AL	.731
1978—	Texas	.600
1979—	Houston	.635
1980—	Kansas City-Blue	.635
1981—	Kansas City-Gold	.688
1982—	New York AL	.667
1983—	Texas	.645
	Los Angeles†	.617
1984—	White Sox	.651
	Rangers†	.571
1985—	Yankees§	.705
	Rangers	.532
1986—	Reds	.548
	Dodgers†	.541
1987—	Dodgers†	.683
	Royals	.635
1988—	Yankees†	.714
	Royals	.619
1989—	Yankees‡	.651
	Dodgers	.635
1990—	Expos	.635
	Dodgers‡	.603
1991—	Orioles	.593
	Expos∞	.533
1992—	Royals∞	.695
	Expos	.593
1993—	Rangers▲	.667
	Astros	.593
1994—	Royals◆	.797
	Astros	.695
1995—	Royals■	.649
	Tigers	.579

*Declared co-champions; no playoff. †League divided into Northern and Southern divisions; won one-game playoff for league championship. ‡League divided into Northern and Southern divisions; won best-of-three playoff for league championship. §Yankees declared champion based on winning percentage when one-game playoff against Rangers was rained out. ∞League divided into Northern, Southern and Central divisions; won best-of-three playoff for league championship. ▲League divided into Eastern, Central and Western divisions; won three-team playoff. ◆League divided into Eastern, Northern and Western divisions; won three-team playoff. ■League divided into Eastern, Northern, Northwest and Southwest divisions; won four-team playoff. (Note—Known as Sarasota Rookie League in 1964 and Florida Rookie League in 1965.)

PIONEER LEAGUE

LEAGUE OFFICE

President
Jim McCurdy
Address
P.O. Box 2564
Spokane, WA 99220
Phone
509-456-7615

Teams (affiliation)
Billings Mustangs (Reds)
Butte Copper Kings (Tampa Bay Devil Rays)
Great Falls Dodgers (Dodgers)
Helena Brewers (Brewers)
Idaho Falls Braves (Braves)
Lethbridge Black Diamonds (Arizona Diamondbacks)
Medicine Hat Blue Jays (Blue Jays)
Ogden Raptors (Brewers)

1995 FINAL STANDINGS

FIRST HALF

NORTHERN DIVISION

Team	W	L	T	Pct.	GB
Billings (Reds)	25	8	0	.758	....
Great Falls (Dodgers)	18	15	0	.545	7
Medicine Hat (Blue Jays)	16	20	0	.444	10½
Lethbridge (Co-op)	15	21	0	.417	11½

SOUTHERN DIVISION

Team	W	L	T	Pct.	GB
Idaho Falls (Padres)	22	13	0	.629	....
Helena (Brewers)	20	15	0	.571	2
Ogden (Co-op)	14	20	0	.412	7½
Butte (Co-op)	8	26	0	.235	13½

SECOND HALF

NORTHERN DIVISION

Team	W	L	T	Pct.	GB
Billings (Reds)	24	12	0	.667	....
Medicine Hat (Blue Jays)	19	17	0	.528	5
Great Falls (Dodgers)	13	23	0	.361	11
Lethbridge (Co-op)	10	26	0	.278	14

SOUTHERN DIVISION

Team	W	L	T	Pct.	GB
Helena (Brewers)	29	7	0	.806	....
Idaho Falls (Padres)	20	16	0	.556	9
Ogden (Co-op)	18	18	0	.500	11
Butte (Co-op)	11	25	0	.306	18

COMPOSITE

Team	Bil.	Hel.	I.F.	M.H.	Ogd.	G.F.	Let.	But.	W	L	T	Pct.	GB
Billings (Reds)	....	4	3	10	3	10	15	4	49	20	0	.710	....
Helena (Brewers)	2	....	10	5	11	2	6	13	49	22	0	.690	1
Idaho Falls (Padres)	3	5	....	4	10	3	3	14	42	29	0	.592	8
Medicine Hat (Blue Jays)	6	1	2	....	3	9	10	4	35	37	0	.486	15½
Ogden (Co-op)	3	5	6	3	....	5	3	7	32	38	0	.457	17½
Great Falls (Dodgers)	3	4	3	7	1	....	7	6	31	38	0	.449	18
Lethbridge (Co-op)	1	0	3	6	3	9	....	3	25	47	0	.347	25½
Butte (Co-op)	2	3	2	2	7	0	3	....	19	51	0	.271	30

Major league affiliations in parentheses.

PLAYOFFS: Helena defeated Idaho Falls, two games to one; Medicine Hat defeated Billings, two games to one; Helena defeated Medicine Hat, two games to none, to win league championship.

REGULAR-SEASON ATTENDANCE: Billings, 103,758; Butte, 19,658; Great Falls, 62,312; Helena, 36,224; Idaho Falls, 57,620; Lethbridge, 47,607; Medicine Hat, 19,603; Ogden, 56,630. Total, 766,912. Playoffs (7 games), 7,480.

MANAGERS: Billings, Donnie Scott; Butte, Billy Gardner; Great Falls, John Shoemaker; Helena, Alex Morales; Idaho Falls, Mike Basso; Lethbridge, Dan Simonds; Medicine Hat, Darren Balsley; Ogden, Willie Ambos.

ALL-STAR TEAM: 1B—Sean Watkins, Idaho Falls; 2B—Ricardo Gama, Idaho Falls; 3B—Mike Kinkade, Helena; SS—Mickey Lopez, Helena; OF—Jamie Lopiccolo, Ogden; Christian Rojas, Billings; Manuel Gonzalez, Great Falls; C—Ben Davis, Idaho Falls; DH—(tie) Shane Jones, Ogden, and Gerry Parent, Helena; RHP—Damon Callahan, Billings; LHP—Justin Atchley, Billings; Relief Pitcher—John Mitchell, Medicine Hat; Player of the Year—Jamie Lopiccolo, Ogden; Manager of the Year—Mike Basso, Idaho Falls.

1995 BATTING

TEAM

Team	Avg.	G	TPA	AB	R	H	TB	2B	3B	HR	RBI	SH	SF	HP	BB	IBB	SO	SB	CS	GDP	LOB	ShO	Slg.	OBP
Helena	.304	71	2911	2428	558	739	1092	160	14	55	458	20	31	45	387	12	424	119	68	49	542	1	.450	.405
Idaho Falls	.293	71	2987	2525	519	741	1091	133	26	55	467	18	32	50	361	10	485	83	38	53	588	0	.432	.388
Ogden	.291	70	2866	2430	444	708	982	131	10	41	379	34	24	42	336	9	462	55	45	65	562	1	.404	.383
Billings	.289	69	2845	2426	463	702	1017	138	21	45	389	15	27	38	339	15	514	80	51	31	583	1	.419	.381
Great Falls	.272	69	2679	2326	399	632	915	118	33	33	335	12	32	40	268	8	536	97	49	51	484	4	.393	.353
Butte	.266	70	2778	2394	372	638	890	113	35	23	322	6	21	47	309	4	521	88	38	55	564	4	.372	.359
Medicine Hat	.261	72	2828	2434	415	636	939	130	19	45	351	13	27	36	317	16	611	84	35	58	539	1	.386	.351
Lethbridge	.241	72	2784	2404	340	580	788	92	28	20	261	22	19	49	290	13	531	98	46	62	517	4	.328	.333

INDIVIDUAL

TOP QUALIFIERS FOR BATTING CHAMPIONSHIP

Minimum 194 plate appearances. *Lefthanded batter. †Switch-hitter.

Player, Team	Avg.	G	TPA	AB	R	H	TB	2B	3B	HR	RBI	SH	SF	HP	BB	IBB	SO	SB	CS	GDP	Slg.	OBP
Lopiccolo, Jamie, Ogden	.388	70	326	260	74	101	154	11	3	12	55	0	3	8	55	4	40	15	7	7	.592	.503
Watkins, Sean, Idaho Falls*	.372	67	302	247	51	92	153	20	1	13	67	0	2	10	43	6	55	0	1	13	.619	.480

Player, Team	Avg.	G	TPA	AB	R	H	TB	2B	3B	HR	RBI	SH	SF	HP	BB	IBB	SO	SB	CS	GDP	Slg.	OBP
Gonzalez, Manuel, G. Falls†	.360	59	210	197	35	71	98	9	3	4	30	1	3	0	9	1	27	16	7	2	.497	.383
Lopez, Louis, Ogden	.357	46	205	182	36	65	101	15	0	7	39	3	2	2	16	0	20	1	1	5	.555	.411
Parent, Gerald, Helena*	.355	57	256	203	50	72	109	16	0	7	63	0	3	0	50	2	30	1	7	6	.537	.477
Kinkade, Mike, Helena	.353	69	325	266	76	94	127	19	1	4	39	0	6	10	43	2	38	26	9	6	.477	.452
Scott, Thomas, Billings	.353	67	304	252	68	89	142	24	4	7	43	2	3	3	44	0	65	17	9	0	.563	.450
Mealing, Al, Helena*	.349	55	195	169	35	59	90	11	4	4	31	2	0	1	23	1	43	17	7	3	.533	.430
Goodhart, Steven, Billings	.340	65	288	250	48	85	105	12	4	0	45	3	5	2	28	1	34	9	4	1	.420	.404
Barkett, Andy, Butte*	.333	45	202	162	33	54	90	11	5	5	51	0	4	3	33	2	39	1	0	1	.556	.446
Ozuna, Rafael, Great Falls†	.327	62	268	245	45	80	114	15	5	3	34	2	2	2	17	2	36	5	6	8	.465	.372
Lopez, Mickey, Helena†	.324	57	274	225	66	73	99	19	2	1	41	2	4	5	38	3	20	12	8	1	.440	.426
Jones, Shane, Ogden	.323	70	323	297	46	96	145	21	2	8	69	2	7	0	17	0	55	3	3	6	.488	.352
Gama, Ricardo, Idaho Falls	.320	70	336	266	71	85	129	16	2	8	58	3	10	2	55	1	29	17	4	2	.485	.426
Curl, John, Medicine Hat*	.319	69	304	270	47	86	135	26	1	7	63	0	3	0	31	8	61	5	1	11	.500	.385

DEPARTMENTAL LEADERS: G—Peeples, Woodward, 72; AB—Jones, 297; R—Kinkade, 76; H—Lopiccolo, 101; TB—Lopiccolo, 154; 2B—Curl, 26; 3B—Cropper, Kernan, 7; HR—Watkins, 13; RBI—Jones, 69; SH—Several players tied with 6; SF—Gama, 10; HP—Bray, J. Larue, 12; BB—McCormick, 64; IBB—Curl, 8; SO—Hinds, 87; SB—Hutchison, Levias, 33; CS—Coca, 13; GIDP—Peeples, 14; Slg.—Watkins, .619; OBP—Lopiccolo, .503.

ALL PLAYERS

*Lefthanded batter. †Switch-hitter.

Player, Team	Avg.	G	TPA	AB	R	H	TB	2B	3B	HR	RBI	SH	SF	HP	BB	IBB	SO	SB	CS	GDP	Slg.	OBP
Abernathy, George, Id. Falls*	.293	63	291	256	52	75	124	12	5	9	45	1	3	5	26	1	64	6	4	2	.484	.366
Allen, Dustin, Idaho Falls	.327	29	127	104	21	34	53	7	0	4	24	0	2	0	21	0	19	1	2	2	.510	.433
Amerson, Gordon, Id. Falls*	.305	46	208	167	40	51	80	16	5	1	22	0	0	2	39	0	33	8	7	4	.479	.442
Andreopoulos, Alex, Helena*	.556	3	13	9	3	5	11	0	0	2	7	0	0	0	4	0	0	0	0	0	1.222	.692
Arevalos, Ryan, Helena	.241	47	182	137	40	33	53	11	0	3	18	2	0	4	39	0	38	5	4	2	.387	.422
Arrollado, Courtney, Butte	.269	62	241	216	34	58	69	11	0	0	21	2	2	2	19	0	38	9	2	4	.319	.331
Aviles, Ronnel, Lethbridge†	.078	43	90	77	6	6	8	2	0	0	0	1	0	3	9	0	22	0	1	4	.104	.202
Baker, Jason, Great Falls	.260	55	122	104	17	27	42	3	0	4	22	0	0	7	11	0	23	2	1	3	.404	.369
Barkett, Andy, Butte*	.333	45	202	162	33	54	90	11	5	5	51	0	4	3	33	2	39	1	0	1	.556	.446
Barlock, Todd, Great Falls	.274	59	221	190	43	52	77	12	5	1	31	0	1	1	29	0	45	10	3	1	.405	.371
Benner, Brian, Butte	.302	67	296	245	42	74	105	15	5	2	40	0	3	4	44	1	83	5	2	3	.429	.412
Bethea, Larry, Great Falls	.172	21	31	29	2	5	5	0	0	0	3	0	0	1	1	0	7	0	0	2	.172	.226
Bledsoe, Jim, Ogden	.359	38	150	131	17	47	70	14	0	3	22	0	0	0	19	0	27	3	1	3	.534	.440
Bogle, Bryan, Butte	.333	2	10	9	0	3	4	1	0	0	2	0	0	0	1	0	4	0	0	0	.444	.400
Bramlett, Jeff, Great Falls	.145	32	70	55	5	8	12	2	1	0	5	0	2	1	12	0	23	1	2	1	.218	.300
Bray, Notorris, Butte	.255	60	248	188	50	48	62	9	1	1	14	1	1	12	46	0	35	27	10	4	.330	.429
Brown, Eric, Great Falls	.255	54	172	145	26	37	66	10	5	3	36	0	5	0	22	2	56	6	3	4	.455	.343
Bucci, Carmen, Idaho Falls	.186	50	134	113	22	21	23	2	0	0	7	0	2	5	14	0	32	7	2	1	.204	.299
Burks, Donny, Lethbridge	.155	62	221	181	19	28	35	3	2	0	6	2	0	4	34	0	40	4	2	6	.193	.301
Burress, Andrew, Billings	.262	35	113	103	17	27	46	9	2	2	18	0	1	3	6	0	16	0	2	4	.447	.319
Cancel, Robinson, Helena	.240	46	168	154	18	37	46	9	0	0	24	1	2	2	9	0	20	8	3	3	.299	.287
Carpentier, Mike, Great Falls	.263	6	20	19	4	5	7	2	0	0	2	0	0	0	1	0	3	0	0	0	.368	.300
Claybrook, Stephen, Billings*	.287	63	240	188	45	54	66	9	0	1	14	3	1	3	45	1	52	21	6	2	.351	.430
Coca, Mark, Ogden	.296	70	338	277	61	82	95	11	1	0	36	4	1	2	54	1	43	11	13	7	.343	.413
Cook, John, Lethbridge	.264	58	245	220	26	58	75	10	2	1	29	4	2	1	18	1	32	4	3	6	.341	.320
Cornish, Tim, Ogden	.119	13	46	42	3	5	6	1	0	0	2	0	0	0	4	0	19	1	0	0	.143	.196
Cropper, Roger, Lethbridge†	.284	65	281	243	38	69	97	11	7	1	24	6	4	4	24	1	53	16	5	4	.399	.353
Curl, John, Medicine Hat*	.319	69	304	270	47	86	135	26	1	7	63	0	3	0	31	8	61	5	1	11	.500	.385
Davis, Ben, Idaho Falls†	.279	52	219	197	36	55	84	8	3	5	46	3	1	1	17	1	36	0	0	3	.426	.338
Davis, Josh, Idaho Falls	.222	4	19	18	3	4	5	1	0	0	1	0	0	0	1	0	2	0	0	1	.278	.263
Demetral, Scott, Ogden*	.273	60	262	231	37	63	79	11	1	1	27	6	0	3	22	1	42	3	4	6	.342	.344
DeSensi, Craig, Butte	.208	29	82	72	10	15	19	2	1	0	5	0	0	4	6	0	14	2	0	3	.264	.305
Dillingham, Daniel, Lethbridge	.174	51	182	161	21	28	44	7	0	3	16	2	2	2	15	2	49	4	2	0	.273	.250
Ebbert, Chad, Idaho Falls	.333	1	4	3	0	1	1	0	0	0	0	0	0	0	1	0	1	0	0	1	.333	.500
Elliott, David, Helena	.262	54	213	172	35	45	79	11	1	7	37	1	4	3	33	1	29	3	5	3	.459	.382
Farner, Matt, Medicine Hat*	.275	45	169	142	28	39	54	3	3	2	24	0	0	1	26	3	48	9	5	3	.380	.391
Fehrenbach, Todd, Billings*	.094	15	37	32	2	3	3	0	0	0	0	0	0	0	5	0	13	1	0	0	.094	.216
Flores, Eric, Great Falls	.229	40	100	83	12	19	26	5	1	0	9	1	0	0	16	0	28	3	1	1	.313	.354
Gama, Ricardo, Idaho Falls	.320	70	336	266	71	85	129	16	2	8	58	3	10	2	55	1	29	17	4	2	.485	.426
Garcia, Miguel, Great Falls†	.222	59	197	171	32	38	52	7	2	1	20	2	1	5	18	0	47	22	4	2	.304	.313
Gavello, Tim, Ogden*	.269	8	34	26	3	7	10	3	0	0	4	0	0	0	8	0	5	0	0	0	.385	.441
Giallella, Brian, Butte†	.240	33	113	100	12	24	33	3	0	2	20	0	2	0	11	0	14	0	1	1	.330	.310
Gonzalez, Manuel, G. Falls†	.360	59	210	197	35	71	98	9	3	4	30	1	3	0	9	1	27	16	7	2	.497	.383
Goodhart, Steven, Billings	.340	65	288	250	48	85	105	12	4	0	45	3	5	2	28	1	34	9	4	1	.420	.404
Goodman, Herbert, Billings	.203	37	89	79	10	16	19	3	0	0	4	0	0	1	9	0	24	3	1	1	.241	.292
Gordon, Herman, Med. Hat†	.232	51	197	181	26	42	61	2	1	5	20	1	4	1	10	0	57	2	1	0	.337	.270
Gronowski, Craig, Ogden*	.333	10	48	36	11	12	13	1	0	0	3	0	0	0	12	1	5	4	2	0	.361	.500
Guerrero, Sergio, Helena	.302	41	148	129	26	39	63	10	1	4	17	3	1	2	13	0	12	5	1	6	.488	.372
Hall, Darran, Billings*	.148	15	35	27	11	4	6	0	1	0	2	0	0	0	8	0	3	1	1	2	.222	.343
Hampton, Robbie, Med. Hat	.235	55	206	187	28	44	81	14	1	7	27	0	2	6	11	0	73	2	3	2	.433	.296
Hills, Richard, Idaho Falls	.308	61	271	224	49	69	106	14	1	7	48	0	5	11	31	0	27	4	1	5	.473	.410
Hinds, Collin, Lethbridge	.186	69	246	220	26	41	60	7	0	4	27	0	1	4	21	1	87	5	5	9	.273	.268
Hokanson, Don, Lethbridge	.000	9	1	1	0	0	0	0	0	0	0	0	0	0	0	0	0	0	0	0	.000	.000
Hunt, Kenya, Idaho Falls	.219	32	90	73	13	16	24	2	0	2	15	0	0	1	16	1	32	1	0	0	.329	.367
Hutchison, Tom, Lethbridge	.276	62	257	217	43	60	76	7	3	1	17	4	0	4	32	1	21	33	6	3	.350	.379
Iapoce, Anthony, Helena	.301	39	180	146	43	44	51	7	0	0	13	2	2	2	28	0	24	19	3	2	.349	.416
Illig, Brett, Great Falls	.167	23	46	42	4	7	8	1	0	0	1	1	0	0	3	0	14	0	0	2	.190	.222
Jenkins, Geoff, Helena*	.321	7	32	28	2	9	11	0	1	0	9	0	1	0	3	0	11	0	2	0	.393	.375
Johnson, Anthony, Lethbridge	.297	61	256	229	30	68	90	10	3	2	41	1	2	6	18	2	33	6	8	9	.393	.361
Johnson, Brian, Helena	.247	32	100	85	24	21	29	2	0	2	10	3	2	1	9	0	17	3	4	1	.341	.320
Johnson, Ledowick, Helena*	.253	35	120	95	18	24	30	3	0	1	18	1	2	2	20	0	25	5	6	0	.316	.387

Player, Team	Avg.	G	TPA	AB	R	H	TB	2B	3B	HR	RBI	SH	SF	HP	BB	IBB	SO	SB	CS	GDP	Slg.	OBP
Jones, Shane, Ogden	.323	70	323	297	46	96	145	21	2	8	69	2	7	0	17	0	55	3	3	6	.488	.352
Judge, Mike, Helena	.348	30	130	112	28	39	54	13	1	0	25	1	0	6	11	0	12	1	2	4	.482	.434
Keighley, Chris, Ogden	.188	47	179	133	21	25	36	5	0	2	21	5	4	1	36	1	31	1	1	4	.271	.356
Kernan, Phil, Butte*	.275	59	232	200	24	55	90	9	7	4	39	0	2	4	26	0	57	0	2	5	.450	.366
King, Brian, Ogden*	.257	9	40	35	4	9	14	3	1	0	5	0	0	1	4	0	10	0	1	1	.400	.350
Kinkade, Mike, Helena	.353	69	325	266	76	94	127	19	1	4	39	0	6	10	43	2	38	26	9	6	.477	.452
Knight, Brook, Helena	.235	16	42	34	4	8	9	1	0	0	4	0	0	0	8	0	2	1	0	3	.265	.381
Kominek, Tobias, Helena	.333	13	53	48	7	16	28	1	1	3	18	0	1	1	3	0	9	2	1	0	.583	.377
Langdon, Trajan, Idaho Falls	.174	11	28	23	4	4	7	0	0	1	3	2	0	0	3	0	9	0	1	0	.304	.269
Larue, Michael, Billings	.273	58	215	183	35	50	75	8	1	5	31	2	2	12	16	2	28	3	5	2	.410	.366
LaRue, Shaun, Lethbridge*	.333	29	6	6	0	2	2	0	0	0	0	0	0	0	0	0	1	0	0	0	.333	.333
Levias, Andres, Butte†	.294	57	263	228	47	67	89	7	6	1	26	1	1	2	30	0	35	33	12	3	.390	.379
Lewis, Dwayne, Lethbridge*	.255	16	63	47	8	12	19	3	2	0	8	0	0	1	15	0	9	0	1	0	.404	.444
Lindsey, Rodney, Idaho Falls	.265	35	173	155	30	41	53	4	4	0	14	0	1	4	13	0	37	21	7	1	.342	.335
Lopez, Louis, Ogden	.357	46	205	182	36	65	101	15	0	7	39	3	2	2	16	0	20	1	1	5	.555	.411
Lopez, Mickey, Helena†	.324	57	274	225	66	73	99	19	2	1	41	2	4	5	38	3	20	12	8	1	.440	.426
Lopiccolo, Jamie, Ogden	.388	70	326	260	74	101	154	11	3	12	55	0	3	8	55	4	40	15	7	7	.592	.503
Manfredi, Joel, Great Falls	.219	33	79	73	6	16	21	2	0	1	10	0	0	0	6	0	14	0	0	3	.288	.278
Marnell, Anthony, Idaho Falls	.125	3	10	8	0	1	2	1	0	0	1	0	0	0	2	0	1	0	1	0	.250	.300
Martinez, Erik, Ogden	.259	34	140	116	21	30	42	9	0	1	13	6	1	6	11	0	26	1	0	4	.362	.351
Martinez, Matt, Ogden	.200	4	13	10	3	2	2	0	0	0	0	1	0	1	1	0	2	0	0	0	.200	.333
Martinez, Obed, Idaho Falls	.275	53	212	193	31	53	65	7	1	1	31	1	0	3	15	0	33	3	3	8	.337	.336
Martinez, Rafael, Great Falls*	.273	58	213	183	30	50	81	13	3	4	30	0	3	3	23	0	36	6	3	6	.443	.358
Mateo, Jose, Great Falls†	.245	40	128	110	20	27	29	2	0	0	3	3	0	2	13	0	30	4	3	2	.264	.336
Mauch, Dennis, Great Falls	.253	28	97	79	10	20	22	2	0	0	9	1	1	6	10	0	19	4	2	1	.278	.375
McCarty, Matt, G.F.-Let.	.294	54	180	163	30	48	62	3	4	1	15	0	1	3	13	0	35	6	3	5	.380	.356
McCormick, Andrew, Med. Hat	.295	69	328	258	64	76	113	18	2	5	37	1	1	3	64	0	67	15	5	3	.438	.439
Mealing, Al, Helena*	.349	55	195	169	35	59	90	11	4	4	31	2	0	1	23	1	43	17	7	3	.533	.430
Merila, Mark, Idaho Falls†	.284	56	255	197	42	56	63	7	0	0	39	6	3	5	43	0	21	5	3	5	.320	.419
Messick, J.T., But.-Let.	.215	46	176	149	18	32	41	7	1	0	20	1	3	0	23	0	27	0	0	6	.275	.314
Meyer, Bobby, Great Falls	.150	25	45	40	4	6	8	0	1	0	4	1	1	0	3	0	14	0	0	1	.200	.205
Montgomery, Andre, Billings	.254	44	134	122	18	31	38	2	1	1	9	1	2	1	8	0	20	4	4	0	.311	.301
Moore, James, Idaho Falls	.255	15	56	47	10	12	19	5	1	0	6	0	1	1	7	0	9	1	0	1	.404	.357
Moreno, Victor, Lethbridge	.280	46	180	157	25	44	72	10	3	4	24	0	1	4	18	2	43	7	2	2	.459	.367
Morrison, Gregory, G. Falls*	.323	55	183	164	29	53	71	8	2	2	30	0	5	2	12	1	15	1	3	4	.433	.366
O'Hearn, Paul, Ogden†	1.000	13	3	2	1	2	2	0	0	0	0	0	0	0	1	0	0	0	0	0	1.000	1.000
O'Neal, Troy, Let.-Hel.	.242	47	184	149	22	36	41	3	1	0	16	0	4	9	22	1	21	3	3	6	.275	.364
Ozuna, Rafael, Great Falls†	.327	62	268	245	45	80	114	15	5	3	34	2	2	2	17	2	36	5	6	8	.465	.372
Padilla, Roy, Butte*	.000	16	1	1	0	0	0	0	0	0	0	0	0	0	0	0	0	0	0	0	.000	.000
Parent, Gerald, Helena*	.355	57	256	203	50	72	109	16	0	7	63	0	3	0	50	2	30	1	7	6	.537	.477
Parsons, Jason, Billings	.315	60	264	222	47	70	105	20	0	5	48	1	4	5	32	0	41	3	1	2	.473	.407
Paul, Kortney, Lethbridge	.239	58	229	201	28	48	68	11	0	3	24	0	2	1	25	2	48	3	2	0	.338	.323
Peeples, Michael, Med. Hat	.312	72	330	285	55	89	120	14	4	3	50	2	3	5	35	1	46	27	5	14	.421	.393
Pena, Angel, Great Falls	.290	49	165	138	24	40	65	11	1	4	15	0	3	3	21	2	32	2	1	5	.471	.388
Perez, Nelson, Butte	.223	61	227	215	24	48	69	5	5	2	20	1	0	2	9	0	44	2	2	9	.321	.261
Phair, Kelly, Ogden	.250	62	230	188	35	47	58	7	2	0	25	5	4	7	26	0	28	8	5	5	.309	.356
Preston, Doyle, Billings*	.285	65	289	242	40	69	101	12	1	6	43	0	3	2	42	3	60	1	2	7	.417	.391
Prokopec, Luke, Great Falls*	.244	43	132	119	16	29	45	6	2	2	24	0	4	1	8	0	37	5	2	1	.378	.288
Ritter, Ryan, Helena	.281	47	184	167	32	47	83	7	1	9	38	2	0	1	14	0	50	10	2	3	.497	.341
Roche, Michael, Helena	.118	4	20	17	4	2	2	0	0	0	1	0	0	1	2	0	4	1	0	0	.118	.250
Rodriguez, Sammy, Butte	.246	17	61	57	7	14	18	1	0	1	6	0	0	0	4	0	13	2	1	0	.316	.295
Rojas, Christian, Billings	.263	68	308	270	48	71	125	11	5	11	56	0	1	2	35	5	57	6	6	3	.463	.351
Rosario, Eliezer, Idaho Falls	.246	20	74	69	9	17	22	3	1	0	7	1	1	0	3	0	9	4	2	1	.319	.274
Sanchez, Ismael, Ogden	.283	20	81	60	16	17	19	2	0	0	8	0	0	5	16	0	13	2	1	0	.317	.469
Sanchez, Marcos, Idaho Falls†	.327	42	178	165	35	54	78	8	2	4	33	1	1	0	11	0	36	5	0	3	.473	.367
Scheffer, Lawrence, Ogden	.283	61	250	233	34	66	98	11	0	7	41	0	2	5	10	1	43	1	3	8	.421	.324
Schock, Jared, Ogden	.091	7	12	11	1	1	1	0	0	0	0	0	0	0	1	0	3	0	0	2	.091	.167
Schultea, Matt, Ogden	.000	34	1	1	0	0	0	0	0	0	0	0	0	0	0	0	1	0	0	0	.000	.000
Scott, Thomas, Billings	.353	67	304	252	68	89	142	24	4	7	43	2	3	3	44	0	65	17	9	0	.563	.450
Shanks, Cliff, Butte	.279	42	158	147	19	41	57	8	1	2	22	0	0	6	5	0	37	0	1	7	.388	.329
Shapiro, Tony, Butte	.289	40	134	121	13	35	55	9	1	3	15	0	0	4	9	0	34	2	0	2	.455	.358
Shatley, Andy, Medicine Hat	.226	70	298	261	32	59	81	12	2	2	30	0	4	4	29	2	66	1	3	9	.310	.309
Smith, Ramon, Med. Hat†	.000	20	2	2	0	0	0	0	0	0	0	0	0	0	0	0	1	0	0	0	.000	.000
Smith, Rick, Helena*	.307	61	261	218	42	67	112	19	1	8	44	0	3	4	36	3	40	0	4	6	.514	.410
Snelling, Allen, Medicine Hat	.226	35	127	115	9	26	31	2	0	1	11	2	0	3	7	0	31	1	2	1	.270	.288
Sorg, Jay, Billings*	.296	67	277	247	42	73	110	14	1	7	40	0	1	3	26	3	52	4	3	5	.445	.368
Srebroski, Andrew, Ogden	.067	10	38	30	3	2	2	0	0	0	0	0	0	1	7	0	12	0	1	1	.067	.263
Stewart, Paxton, Med. Hat*	.248	50	186	161	30	40	57	13	2	0	17	1	1	0	23	0	34	4	2	6	.354	.341
Stuckenschneider, Eric, G.F.	.314	40	156	118	32	37	61	8	2	4	16	0	1	5	32	0	26	10	7	2	.517	.474
Timmons, Shayne, Med. Hat	.167	24	51	42	5	7	8	1	0	0	3	0	1	2	6	0	11	0	1	1	.190	.294
Underwood, Devin, Butte†	.237	55	226	190	22	45	57	12	0	0	17	0	2	4	30	0	31	0	4	6	.300	.350
Valdespino, Jose, Med. Hat	.190	35	127	105	14	20	36	3	2	3	13	1	1	2	18	0	34	1	1	6	.343	.317
Vallero, Rich, Ogden*	.228	46	145	127	17	29	35	6	0	0	9	2	0	0	16	0	35	1	2	6	.276	.315
Walker, Rodney, Lethbridge	.264	39	151	125	21	33	39	4	1	0	8	2	0	4	20	0	31	7	4	5	.312	.383
Ward, Jason, Lethbridge	.125	11	30	24	3	3	3	0	0	0	2	0	0	0	6	0	6	0	0	2	.125	.300
Watkins, Sean, Idaho Falls*	.372	67	302	247	51	92	153	20	1	13	67	0	2	10	43	6	55	0	1	13	.619	.480
Whitson, Eric, Ogden†	.000	22	2	2	0	0	0	0	0	0	0	0	0	0	0	0	2	0	0	0	.000	.000
Wilson, Brian, Billings	.287	62	252	209	32	60	76	14	1	0	36	3	4	1	35	0	49	7	7	2	.364	.386
Wilson, Craig, Med. Hat	.283	49	215	184	33	52	89	14	1	7	35	0	4	3	24	1	41	8	2	1	.484	.367
Woodward, Chris, Med. Hat	.232	72	288	241	44	56	73	8	0	3	21	5	3	6	33	1	41	9	4	1	.303	.336
Zumwalt, Rusty, Butte*	.274	41	129	113	19	31	40	5	2	0	10	0	1	0	15	1	20	5	1	2	.354	.357

GRAND SLAMS: Allen, Keighley, McCormick, Ritter, 2 each; Abernathy, Andreopoulos, Baker, Hills, Kernan, Lopiccolo, Moreno, Ozuna, Scheffer, Stuckenschneider, C. Wilson, 1 each.

AWARDED FIRST BASE ON CATCHER'S INTERFERENCE: Levias (C. Wilson); R. Martinez (Valdespino); McCormick (Vallero); Merila (C. Wilson).

PLAYERS WITH TWO OR MORE TEAMS

Player, Team	Avg.	G	TPA	AB	R	H	TB	2B	3B	HR	RBI	SH	SF	HP	BB	IBB	SO	SB	CS	GDP	Slg.	OBP
McCarty, Matt, Great Falls	.227	16	24	22	3	5	5	0	0	0	1	0	0	1	1	0	4	0	1	0	.227	.292
McCarty, Matt, Lethbridge	.305	38	156	141	27	43	57	3	4	1	14	0	1	2	12	0	31	6	2	5	.404	.365
Messick, J.T., Butte	.200	40	155	130	16	26	33	5	1	0	14	1	3	0	21	0	23	0	0	5	.254	.305
Messick, J.T., Lethbridge	.316	6	21	19	2	6	8	2	0	0	6	0	0	0	2	0	4	0	0	1	.421	.381
O'Neal, Troy, Lethbridge	.230	43	169	135	17	31	35	2	1	0	15	0	4	9	21	1	21	3	3	6	.259	.361
O'Neal, Troy, Helena	.357	4	15	14	5	5	6	1	0	0	1	0	0	0	1	0	0	0	0	0	.429	.400

1995 PITCHING

TEAM

Team	W	L	Pct.	ERA	G	CG	ShO	Sv.	IP	H	TBF	R	ER	HR	SH	SF	HB	BB	IBB	SO	WP	Bk.
Billings	49	20	.710	3.58	69	0	4	23	613.0	613	2670	316	244	20	12	20	29	239	22	474	48	14
Medicine Hat	35	37	.486	4.44	72	5	3	17	624.2	613	2816	422	308	46	27	26	44	312	5	510	70	14
Great Falls	31	38	.449	4.68	69	0	0	9	594.1	635	2748	426	309	37	13	29	37	309	16	485	61	12
Helena	49	22	.690	4.69	71	0	3	17	616.0	608	2854	388	321	44	16	16	61	411	4	559	69	21
Lethbridge	25	47	.347	4.90	72	5	2	14	632.0	710	2890	446	344	48	18	30	35	297	8	595	51	15
Idaho Falls	42	29	.592	5.25	71	1	3	17	634.2	669	2877	455	370	30	24	27	50	344	7	564	84	9
Ogden	32	38	.457	5.84	70	4	1	9	617.2	759	2893	506	401	51	15	30	53	313	10	443	57	16
Butte	19	51	.271	6.69	70	0	0	12	597.1	769	2930	551	444	41	15	35	38	382	15	454	76	23

INDIVIDUAL

TOP QUALIFIERS FOR EARNED-RUN AVERAGE TITLE

Minimum 58 innings. *Lefthanded pitcher.

Pitcher, Team	W	L	Pct.	ERA	G	GS	CG	ShO	GF	Sv.	IP	H	TBF	R	ER	HR	SH	SF	HB	BB	IBB	SO	WP	Bk.
Veniard, Jay, Medicine Hat	4	1	.800	2.71	11	10	0	0	0	0	63.0	67	280	34	19	2	2	3	3	21	0	43	6	2
Callahan, Damon, Billings	9	2	.818	2.91	14	14	0	0	0	0	80.1	82	347	36	26	1	2	3	4	30	2	50	7	0
Bailey, Ben, Billings	6	4	.600	2.96	13	13	0	0	0	0	79.0	74	340	32	26	2	2	3	3	29	2	68	11	0
Atchley, Justin, Billings*	10	0	1.000	3.51	13	13	0	0	0	0	77.0	91	327	33	30	4	2	1	2	20	2	65	2	1
Neal, Billy, G.F.-Let.	3	3	.500	3.72	16	9	1	0	3	0	65.1	74	290	42	27	1	1	2	4	24	1	55	6	3
Lapka, Rick, Billings	8	4	.667	3.76	14	14	0	0	0	0	79.0	66	334	36	33	2	2	2	6	43	3	46	7	2
Rodriguez, Victor, Med. Hat	4	1	.800	3.88	17	2	0	0	0	0	58.0	42	255	31	25	5	3	2	9	40	0	45	11	0
Novak, Troy, Ogden	5	1	.833	3.88	15	15	2	1	0	0	97.1	101	416	50	42	5	1	3	3	41	0	71	5	0
Reed, Jason, Great Falls*	2	5	.286	4.09	15	12	0	0	1	1	72.2	79	323	42	33	2	1	2	5	28	1	45	0	1
Gooda, David, Helena*	4	4	.500	4.17	10	10	0	0	0	0	58.1	54	267	32	27	3	4	2	7	33	1	33	1	5
Mann, James, Medicine Hat	5	4	.556	4.29	14	14	1	1	0	0	77.2	78	347	47	37	5	3	2	7	37	0	66	6	0
Clement, Matt, Idaho Falls	6	3	.667	4.33	14	14	0	0	0	0	81.0	61	349	53	39	3	6	3	13	42	0	65	19	2
Newman, Eric, Idaho Falls	8	4	.667	4.41	15	14	0	0	0	0	81.2	91	365	49	40	3	5	4	7	35	0	65	3	1
Kirkman, Casey, Lethbridge	5	6	.455	4.55	15	15	1	0	0	0	95.0	94	404	56	48	4	2	4	3	39	0	91	3	1
Flores, Ignacio, Great Falls	6	4	.600	4.72	16	12	0	0	1	0	68.2	66	301	42	36	3	0	1	4	38	0	76	4	2

DEPARTMENTAL LEADERS: W—Atchley, 10; L—Corral, Friedman, Justiniano, 8; Pct.—Atchley, 1.000; G—Schultea, 34; GS—Kirkman, Novak, Remington, D. Richardson, 15; CG—Corral, Novak, Porzio, 2; ShO—Several pitchers tied with 1; GF—Bryant, 26; Sv.—Bryant, Guzman, Mitchell, 11; IP—Novak, 97.1; H—Remington, D. Richardson, 106; TBF—Novak, 416; R—Corral, Spear, 65; ER—Justiniano, Remington, 50; HR—Martinez, 10; SH—Clement, 6; SF—Corral, 7; HB—O'Hearn, 14; BB—Collins, 63; IBB—Several pitchers tied with 4; SO—Kirkman, 91; WP—Clement, 19; Bk.—Justiniano, 7.

ALL PITCHERS

*Lefthanded pitcher.

Pitcher, Team	W	L	Pct.	ERA	G	GS	CG	ShO	GF	Sv.	IP	H	TBF	R	ER	HR	SH	SF	HB	BB	IBB	SO	WP	Bk.
Abreu, Juan, Butte*	1	4	.200	8.74	8	5	0	0	2	0	22.2	27	124	31	22	1	2	0	2	28	0	21	11	0
Alexander, Donald, Ogden	2	4	.333	6.40	19	1	0	0	6	0	32.1	43	164	32	23	0	4	1	3	26	1	30	7	3
Atchley, Justin, Billings*	10	0	1.000	3.51	13	13	0	0	0	0	77.0	91	327	33	30	4	2	1	2	20	2	65	2	1
Bailey, Ben, Billings	6	4	.600	2.96	13	13	0	0	0	0	79.0	74	340	32	26	2	2	3	3	29	2	68	11	0
Bales, Daniel, Idaho Falls	0	1	.000	10.67	10	1	0	0	3	1	14.1	26	85	24	17	0	0	0	2	13	0	8	3	0
Barnes, Larry, Helena	2	0	1.000	2.25	3	2	0	0	0	0	12.0	5	49	5	3	0	0	1	1	6	0	15	6	0
Baron, Jim, Idaho Falls*	2	3	.400	5.65	27	1	0	0	5	0	43.0	51	201	31	27	2	0	2	1	19	1	43	8	0
Battaglia, Chuck, Lethbridge	0	3	.000	3.98	4	3	0	0	0	0	20.1	24	90	11	9	2	1	1	0	6	0	9	1	0
Benny, Peter, Helena	5	0	1.000	3.88	11	7	0	0	1	0	46.1	48	205	25	20	2	0	0	4	24	0	47	4	1
Berninger, Darren, Helena	3	1	.750	7.71	21	0	0	0	4	0	28.0	45	159	28	24	4	1	1	2	34	2	11	2	0
Besser, Mike, Ogden*	1	1	.500	5.14	4	0	0	0	1	0	7.0	10	27	4	4	1	0	1	2	2	0	1	0	0
Bonilla, Welnis, Butte	2	2	.500	4.38	27	2	0	0	13	5	39.0	46	202	34	19	4	0	0	3	33	2	30	3	4
Bourbakis, Michael, G. Falls	1	2	.333	5.14	11	1	0	0	6	0	14.0	16	69	10	8	0	0	3	1	8	0	13	0	0
Bowles, Matt, Helena	1	0	1.000	15.19	6	3	0	0	0	0	10.2	17	66	18	18	2	0	0	5	18	0	10	7	0
Brabec, William, Med. Hat	0	1	.000	7.03	19	0	0	0	7	0	24.1	31	136	33	19	2	1	0	7	20	0	25	9	1
Bryant, Adam, Billings	4	2	.667	3.13	29	0	0	0	26	11	37.1	39	157	13	13	3	0	1	2	5	1	30	4	4
Bucci, Carmen, Idaho Falls	0	0	.000	27.00	1	0	0	0	1	0	1.0	3	7	3	3	0	0	0	0	1	0	0	0	0
Burge, Jason, Lethbridge*	2	4	.333	3.44	23	0	0	0	15	5	34.0	27	151	17	13	2	2	1	4	13	0	49	0	1
Callahan, Damon, Billings	9	2	.818	2.91	14	14	0	0	0	0	80.1	82	347	36	26	1	2	3	4	30	2	50	7	0
Camp, Jared, Helena	1	4	.200	8.65	8	8	0	0	0	0	34.1	44	166	39	33	1	1	3	3	20	0	26	6	2
Campbell, Tim, Idaho Falls	1	1	.500	5.20	18	0	0	0	5	1	36.1	37	162	21	21	0	1	1	2	17	1	38	5	0
Caravelli, Mike, Ogden*	1	2	.333	3.93	5	3	0	0	0	0	18.1	27	83	11	8	1	0	3	1	3	0	13	0	1
Cardona, Isbell, Butte	0	2	.000	7.04	3	3	0	0	0	0	15.1	26	73	13	12	1	0	0	0	7	0	9	0	0
Castillo, Vic, Medicine Hat	0	0	.000	0.00	2	0	0	0	0	0	2.0	5	14	5	0	0	0	0	0	1	0	2	0	1
Chapa, Javier, Great Falls	2	2	.500	5.69	13	9	0	0	1	0	49.0	54	217	36	31	4	0	3	2	17	0	37	5	0
Charbonneau, Marc, G. Falls*	4	1	.800	3.61	14	7	0	0	2	0	42.1	37	198	28	17	3	1	3	2	27	2	30	2	1
Clark, Chris, Idaho Falls	0	0	.000	4.50	1	1	0	0	0	0	6.0	3	24	3	3	1	0	0	0	4	0	9	1	0

Pitcher, Team	W	L	Pct.	ERA	G	GS	CG	ShO	GF	Sv.	IP	H	TBF	R	ER	HR	SH	SF	HB	BB	IBB	SO	WP	Bk.
Clement, Matt, Idaho Falls	6	3	.667	4.33	14	14	0	0	0	0	81.0	61	349	53	39	3	6	3	13	42	0	65	19	2
Collins, Edward, Helena	5	3	.625	5.86	14	13	0	0	0	0	55.1	50	274	44	36	2	0	2	7	63	0	33	6	1
Cooke, Alan, Ogden	0	5	.000	5.13	16	5	0	0	2	0	40.1	52	194	26	23	5	0	1	1	32	1	23	4	1
Corral, Ruben, Medicine Hat	4	8	.333	4.81	14	14	2	0	0	0	86.0	92	382	65	46	7	5	7	2	34	0	50	4	1
Davis, John, Great Falls	2	2	.500	2.81	11	1	0	0	3	0	32.0	24	137	20	10	6	0	0	3	19	2	26	5	1
Dawsey, Jason, Helena*	3	0	1.000	2.74	9	8	0	0	0	0	42.2	40	183	15	13	1	0	3	2	23	0	47	5	1
Dillon, Chad, Butte	0	5	.000	10.23	15	7	0	0	0	0	41.1	60	228	58	47	2	0	5	7	39	0	26	11	0
Done, Johnny, Medicine Hat	5	5	.500	4.59	22	1	0	0	13	1	33.1	35	156	25	17	1	4	1	2	15	3	29	6	2
Erdos, Todd, Idaho Falls	5	3	.625	3.48	32	0	0	0	20	1	41.1	34	185	19	16	1	3	2	5	30	2	48	8	0
Escobar, Kelvin, Med. Hat	3	3	.500	5.71	14	14	1	1	0	0	69.1	66	307	47	44	6	2	5	6	33	0	75	4	4
Estrada, Horacio, Helena*	1	2	.333	5.40	13	0	0	0	1	0	30.0	27	144	21	18	3	5	0	3	24	0	30	2	0
Falls, Curtis, Lethbridge	2	2	.500	3.71	24	4	1	0	5	1	53.1	56	238	27	22	3	2	3	3	19	1	49	3	2
Feliciano, Pedro, Great Falls*	0	0	.000	13.50	6	0	0	0	3	0	6.2	12	43	12	10	0	0	0	0	7	1	9	4	2
Fernandes, Jamie, Butte	4	4	.500	6.02	12	12	0	0	0	0	64.1	75	305	52	43	7	3	3	8	32	0	44	9	0
Fernandez, Omar, Great Falls	3	1	.750	4.84	19	2	0	0	6	0	35.1	39	166	28	19	4	0	3	1	21	2	27	8	0
Flores, Ignacio, Great Falls	6	4	.600	4.72	16	12	0	0	1	0	68.2	66	301	42	36	3	0	1	4	38	0	76	4	2
Fox, Ryan, Ogden	0	0	.000	7.71	2	0	0	0	1	0	2.1	7	16	6	2	1	0	0	1	0	0	2	1	0
Friedman, Matt, Lethbridge	0	8	.000	6.60	20	6	0	0	10	4	43.2	55	210	40	32	2	2	5	1	26	4	36	1	5
Gamez, Rene, Ogden	4	2	.667	6.29	10	10	0	0	0	0	54.1	53	247	41	38	1	1	5	5	30	1	42	7	3
Garcia, Eddy, Billings	3	2	.600	2.63	15	5	0	0	3	1	48.0	38	193	20	14	0	0	0	0	12	1	45	2	2
Gaskill, Derek, Helena	5	2	.714	3.70	31	0	0	0	10	3	56.0	50	243	30	23	3	0	1	4	23	0	59	10	0
Gomez, Miguel, Med. Hat	2	5	.286	5.10	14	14	1	0	0	0	72.1	79	326	55	41	10	2	1	6	32	0	46	5	2
Gooda, David, Helena*	4	4	.500	4.17	10	10	0	0	0	0	58.1	54	267	32	27	3	4	2	7	33	1	33	1	5
Graves, Jon, Idaho Falls	0	0	.000	13.50	4	0	0	0	0	0	4.0	5	26	7	6	0	0	1	1	12	0	0	2	0
Grote, Jason, Butte	2	5	.286	7.04	22	7	0	0	13	4	47.1	67	223	46	37	0	1	3	1	23	3	35	8	1
Guerrero, Sergio, Helena	0	0	.000	13.50	1	0	0	0	1	0	2.0	3	10	3	3	1	0	1	0	0	0	1	0	0
Gullard, Jack, Lethbridge*	0	2	.000	6.60	26	2	0	0	11	1	30.0	38	141	27	22	4	2	3	0	13	1	34	3	0
Guzman, Domingo, Id. Falls	2	1	.667	6.66	27	0	0	0	23	11	25.2	25	127	22	19	2	3	1	1	25	1	33	6	3
Harper, Terry, Ogd.-Let.	1	4	.200	8.33	23	1	0	0	8	0	31.1	35	163	36	29	6	4	0	7	25	1	39	4	1
Henderson, James, Id. Falls	3	0	1.000	2.25	4	4	0	0	0	0	20.0	19	81	6	5	0	0	1	3	9	0	16	4	1
Hibbard, Billy, Medicine Hat	1	1	.500	3.57	4	3	0	0	0	0	17.2	14	70	8	7	1	0	1	0	4	0	15	0	0
Hindy, Mark, Ogden*	2	3	.400	4.73	24	6	0	0	5	1	70.1	89	327	52	37	5	1	3	0	24	0	44	4	2
Hokanson, Don, Lethbridge	0	0	.000	7.98	8	0	0	0	1	0	14.2	32	81	21	13	0	0	1	0	7	0	7	1	0
Holding, Brook, Butte	4	3	.571	5.14	27	0	0	0	10	3	42.0	36	191	26	24	1	2	2	0	33	1	49	6	1
Hommel, Brian, Helena*	2	0	1.000	0.45	15	0	0	0	8	2	20.0	7	86	3	1	0	2	0	4	14	0	32	2	1
Irvine, Michael, Idaho Falls	2	1	.667	5.85	28	0	0	0	9	2	52.1	59	238	40	34	6	1	2	3	28	1	52	6	0
James, Jhon, Medicine Hat	0	0	.000	18.00	2	0	0	0	1	0	1.0	2	8	2	2	1	0	0	0	3	0	1	1	0
Jamie, Jorge, Ogden*	0	0	.000	4.32	10	0	0	0	6	1	16.2	22	74	8	8	1	1	0	1	4	0	12	1	0
Jenkins, Scott, Lethbridge	1	3	.250	6.51	15	6	0	0	4	0	47.0	56	239	49	34	8	0	2	7	40	0	43	9	1
Johnson, Mike, Med. Hat	4	1	.800	3.86	19	0	0	0	7	3	49.0	46	217	26	21	2	2	2	0	25	1	32	6	0
Johnson, Scott, Butte	0	2	.000	6.58	20	0	0	0	4	0	39.2	59	191	31	29	2	0	2	0	11	1	31	2	4
Jones, Matthew, Butte	0	1	.000	7.97	21	0	0	0	9	0	35.0	54	181	40	31	4	0	3	2	17	1	30	2	2
Judice, Bryan, Lethbridge	1	1	.500	3.00	7	0	0	0	7	3	6.0	5	27	4	2	0	1	1	0	3	0	8	0	0
Justiniano, Rene, Butte	0	8	.000	7.50	12	12	0	0	0	0	60.0	86	285	58	50	7	0	5	1	26	1	40	3	7
Kazama, Yuhito, Ogden	0	1	.000	14.04	6	1	0	0	1	0	8.1	16	48	17	13	4	0	0	2	8	0	4	2	0
King, Raymond, Billings*	3	0	1.000	1.67	28	0	0	0	15	5	43.0	31	169	11	8	1	2	0	0	15	3	43	1	1
Kirkman, Casey, Lethbridge	5	6	.455	4.55	15	15	1	0	0	0	95.0	94	404	56	48	4	2	4	3	39	0	91	3	1
Kline, Jason, Ogden*	3	4	.429	5.43	25	6	0	0	10	2	58.0	80	273	45	35	7	2	4	3	25	1	37	2	1
Kolb, Brandon, Idaho Falls	2	3	.400	7.04	9	8	0	0	0	0	38.1	42	181	33	30	1	2	2	2	29	0	21	5	0
Lapka, Rick, Billings	8	4	.667	3.76	14	14	0	0	0	0	79.0	66	334	36	33	2	2	2	6	43	3	46	7	2
LaRue, Shaun, Lethbridge	2	2	.500	2.97	26	0	0	0	8	0	36.1	30	163	13	12	1	1	2	2	24	2	42	3	0
Lawrence, Rich, Billings	0	1	.000	3.24	13	2	0	0	2	1	25.0	25	112	18	9	2	0	1	1	11	0	27	1	0
Lee, Calvin, Ogden	1	2	.333	7.52	5	5	0	0	0	0	20.1	21	102	23	17	1	0	0	2	21	0	15	3	0
Lenhardt, Bruce, Helena	0	1	.000	1.93	9	0	0	0	6	0	9.1	7	46	6	2	1	0	0	1	11	1	10	1	0
MacRae, Scott, Billings	0	1	.000	5.67	18	0	0	0	4	1	27.0	32	135	24	17	0	0	5	3	20	4	9	2	1
Mann, James, Medicine Hat	5	4	.556	4.29	14	14	1	1	0	0	77.2	78	347	47	37	5	3	2	7	37	0	66	6	0
Marine, Justin, Billings	1	0	1.000	1.75	18	0	0	0	7	2	25.2	20	114	14	5	0	1	1	4	11	0	20	2	0
Martin, Jeremy, Ogden*	1	1	.500	7.64	9	2	0	0	2	0	17.2	23	79	16	15	2	1	1	4	11	0	11	3	0
McMillan, Leonard, Butte	0	1	.000	9.88	10	0	0	0	1	0	13.2	18	78	17	15	2	1	0	1	18	1	15	2	1
Medero, Gadiel, Butte	0	0	.000	15.30	8	1	0	0	5	0	10.0	22	59	19	17	0	0	0	1	7	0	4	1	1
Mejia, Carlos, Butte*	2	1	.667	3.76	10	7	0	0	2	0	38.1	37	164	16	16	4	1	5	2	17	1	28	2	1
Merila, Mark, Idaho Falls	0	0	.000	45.00	1	0	0	0	1	0	1.0	5	9	5	5	0	0	0	1	1	0	0	0	0
Messick, J.T., But.-Let.	0	0	.000	9.00	1	0	0	0	1	0	1.0	2	5	1	1	1	0	0	0	0	0	2	0	0
Miller, Shawn, Helena	2	0	1.000	4.82	16	0	0	0	4	0	28.0	37	136	18	15	1	0	1	0	16	0	33	2	1
Mitchell, John, Medicine Hat	2	2	.500	2.50	25	0	0	0	23	11	36.0	20	150	15	10	1	3	1	1	17	1	50	5	1
Mullins, Greg, Helena*	4	0	1.000	2.74	4	4	0	0	0	0	23.0	22	98	7	7	0	0	0	2	6	0	14	0	2
Nakashima, Toni, Great Falls*	2	4	.333	5.60	20	3	0	0	4	2	35.1	39	171	25	22	1	1	0	2	20	0	32	2	0
Nate, Scott, Helena*	0	2	.000	9.00	3	0	0	0	2	1	2.0	4	10	3	2	1	1	0	0	0	0	2	0	0
Neal, Billy, G.F.-Let.	3	3	.500	3.72	16	9	1	0	3	0	65.1	74	290	42	27	1	1	2	4	24	1	55	6	3
Newman, Eric, Idaho Falls	8	4	.667	4.41	15	14	0	0	0	0	81.2	91	365	49	40	3	5	4	7	35	0	65	3	1
Novak, Troy, Ogden	5	1	.833	3.88	15	15	2	1	0	0	97.1	101	416	50	42	5	1	3	3	41	0	71	5	0
Ochsenfeld, Christopher, G.F.*	1	4	.200	6.86	14	7	0	0	2	1	42.0	50	209	45	32	1	0	4	1	33	0	32	5	0
O'Hearn, Paul, Ogden	1	4	.200	8.91	11	7	0	0	1	0	32.1	41	176	45	32	0	0	1	14	26	0	27	3	3
Padilla, Roy, Butte*	2	7	.222	5.91	15	14	0	0	0	0	70.0	80	340	60	46	1	2	4	7	54	0	49	11	0
Pasqualicchio, Michael, Helena*	3	0	1.000	3.16	8	7	0	0	0	0	31.1	30	142	14	11	2	0	1	1	20	0	21	1	3
Pavlovich, Tony, Helena	0	0	.000	0.93	9	0	0	0	9	4	9.2	4	37	1	1	1	0	0	1	3	0	14	1	0
Perez, Jayson, Idaho Falls	0	0	.000	0.00	1	0	0	0	0	0	1.0	1	4	0	0	0	0	0	0	0	0	2	0	0
Porzio, Mike, Ogden*	4	3	.571	6.38	8	8	2	0	0	0	48.0	66	220	39	34	4	0	3	2	15	0	26	6	0
Preston, George, Helena	1	0	1.000	8.10	3	2	0	0	1	0	6.2	11	36	9	6	3	0	0	2	2	0	9	0	0
Reed, Jason, Great Falls*	2	5	.286	4.09	15	12	0	0	1	1	72.2	79	323	42	33	2	1	2	5	28	1	45	0	1
Remington, Jake, Idaho Falls	5	5	.500	5.15	15	15	1	1	0	0	87.1	106	379	62	50	3	2	3	5	29	0	54	5	1
Richardson, Darrell, Let.	5	4	.556	5.00	15	15	1	0	0	0	84.2	106	393	63	47	6	1	1	5	38	0	85	10	1
Richardson, Jesse, Helena*	3	1	.750	4.62	25	0	0	0	6	2	39.0	44	182	23	20	6	2	0	2	27	0	34	1	0

Pitcher, Team	W	L	Pct.	ERA	G	GS	CG	ShO	GF	Sv.	IP	H	TBF	R	ER	HR	SH	SF	HB	BB	IBB	SO	WP	Bk.
Riedling, John, Billings	2	2	.500	7.04	13	7	0	0	2	1	38.1	51	192	38	30	4	0	3	1	21	2	28	8	0
Rivera, Oscar, Great Falls	2	1	.667	4.13	18	1	0	0	13	1	28.1	28	134	19	13	3	2	4	0	17	1	30	3	0
Robins, Doug, Lethbridge	2	2	.500	5.13	15	4	0	0	2	0	40.1	43	175	29	23	7	0	1	0	16	0	28	6	2
Rodriguez, Luis, Butte*	0	1	.000	9.49	7	0	0	0	2	0	12.1	12	61	14	13	1	0	1	1	12	0	10	2	0
Rodriguez, Sammy, Butte	0	0	.000	9.00	1	0	0	0	0	0	2.0	2	11	2	2	0	0	0	0	3	0	5	0	0
Rodriguez, Victor, Med. Hat	4	1	.800	3.88	17	2	0	0	0	0	58.0	42	255	31	25	5	3	2	9	40	0	45	11	0
Rosario, Nelson, Med. Hat*	0	1	.000	7.82	10	0	0	0	7	0	12.2	21	64	13	11	1	0	1	1	6	0	5	1	0
Sak, James, Idaho Falls	3	1	.750	1.65	13	0	0	0	3	1	32.2	15	123	9	6	1	1	0	0	12	1	55	1	1
Sangeado, Juan, Great Falls	1	3	.250	4.30	16	3	0	0	4	1	46.0	47	207	28	22	4	4	1	1	25	3	46	4	0
Schultea, Matt, Ogden	4	2	.667	4.67	34	0	0	0	10	1	54.0	59	244	37	28	1	3	3	4	18	4	43	3	1
Sheldon, Shane, Helena	0	0	.000	13.50	17	0	0	0	7	0	15.1	18	91	28	23	3	0	0	3	25	0	15	8	2
Smith, Ramon, Med. Hat*	1	4	.200	3.63	19	0	0	0	9	2	22.1	15	104	16	9	2	0	0	0	24	0	26	6	0
Smith, Travis, Helena	4	2	.667	2.41	20	7	0	0	11	5	56.0	41	224	16	15	4	0	0	7	19	0	63	4	2
Spear, Russell, Idaho Falls	3	2	.600	6.21	14	13	0	0	0	0	66.2	83	324	65	46	7	0	5	4	36	0	53	8	0
Sweezey, Gary, Great Falls	2	1	.667	3.21	17	0	0	0	11	2	28.0	34	125	22	10	4	1	3	2	6	0	18	5	1
Taczy, Craig, Great Falls*	0	4	.000	3.52	18	2	0	0	7	0	30.2	25	145	20	12	1	0	1	2	28	0	24	6	1
Torres, Jackson, Great Falls	3	3	.500	4.59	14	8	0	0	2	1	51.0	66	242	37	26	1	2	1	9	11	3	32	8	1
Torres, Luis, Idaho Falls	0	1	.000	27.00	1	0	0	0	0	0	1.0	3	7	3	3	0	0	0	0	2	0	2	0	0
Upchurch, Wayne, Lethbridge	2	6	.250	5.60	9	9	1	1	0	0	53.0	68	247	44	33	6	0	3	4	19	0	39	2	0
Veniard, Jay, Medicine Hat	4	1	.800	2.71	11	10	0	0	0	0	63.0	67	280	34	19	2	2	3	3	21	0	43	6	2
Waites, Steve, Butte	2	5	.286	4.78	28	0	0	0	8	0	43.1	60	209	33	23	3	3	2	2	22	4	26	3	1
Weiss, Marc, Billings	1	2	.333	7.62	18	1	0	0	6	1	26.0	36	127	26	22	0	0	0	1	15	2	14	1	1
Whitson, Eric, Ogden	2	1	.667	8.59	22	0	0	0	17	4	29.1	35	142	33	28	8	1	1	2	16	2	31	5	1
Wright, Scott, Billings	2	0	1.000	3.62	17	0	0	0	4	0	27.1	28	123	15	11	1	1	0	2	7	0	29	0	2

COMBINATION SHUTOUTS: **Billings (4)**—Callahan-King, Callahan-King-Wright-Weiss-Marine-Bryant, Callahan-Weiss, Lapka-MacRae. **Butte (0)**—None. **Great Falls (0)**—None. **Helena (3)**—Dawsey-Gaskill-Richardson-Smith, Gooda-Gaskill-Hommel, Smith-Gaskill-Pavlovich. **Idaho Falls (2)**—Clement-Bales, Henderson-Campbell-Guzman. **Lethbridge (1)**—Robins-Falls-Gullard-Friedman. **Medicine Hat (1)**—Hibbard-Smith. **Ogden (0)**—None.

NO-HIT GAMES: Remington, Idaho Falls, defeated Helena, 6-0 (first game), June 23; Escobar, Medicine Hat, defeated Ogden, 2-0 (first game), July 20.

PITCHERS WITH TWO OR MORE TEAMS

Pitcher, Team	W	L	Pct.	ERA	G	GS	CG	ShO	GF	Sv.	IP	H	TBF	R	ER	HR	SH	SF	HB	BB	IBB	SO	WP	Bk.
Harper, Terry, Ogden	1	2	.333	11.81	8	1	0	0	4	0	10.2	14	61	21	14	4	0	0	3	11	0	11	1	0
Harper, Terry, Lethbridge	0	2	.000	6.53	15	0	0	0	4	0	20.2	21	102	15	15	2	4	0	4	14	0	28	3	1
Neal, Billy, Great Falls	0	1	.000	5.84	6	1	0	0	3	0	12.1	19	61	12	8	0	1	0	2	4	1	8	0	2
Neal, Billy, Lethbridge	3	2	.600	3.23	10	8	1	0	0	0	53.0	55	229	30	19	1	0	2	2	20	0	47	6	1

1995 FIELDING

TEAM

Team	Pct.	G	PO	A	E	TC	DP	PB
Ogden	.959	70	1853	837	114	2804	72	24
Billings	.959	69	1839	780	112	2731	75	21
Helena	.958	71	1848	798	117	2763	78	20
Idaho Falls	.957	71	1904	861	123	2888	91	18
Lethbridge	.950	72	1896	786	142	2824	49	26
Butte	.948	70	1792	775	142	2709	60	15
Medicine Hat	.939	72	1874	732	170	2776	60	19
Great Falls	.938	69	1783	744	168	2695	55	19

INDIVIDUAL

FIRST BASEMEN

NOTE: All caps denotes fielding-percentage leader based on 36 games for catchers, 48 for all other non-pitchers and 72 innings for pitchers. *Throws lefthanded.

Player, Team	Pct.	G	PO	A	E	TC	DP
Allen, Dustin, Idaho Falls	1.000	3	39	1	0	40	3
Barkett, Andy, Butte*	.991	45	407	39	4	450	35
Bethea, Larry, Great Falls	1.000	8	19	2	0	21	1
Bramlett, Jeff, Great Falls	.992	27	112	13	1	126	16
Cook, John, Lethbridge	.993	46	379	32	3	414	22
Curl, John, Medicine Hat	.984	63	499	45	9	553	42
Dillingham, Daniel, Lethbridge	1.000	1	9	0	0	9	1
Hunt, Kenya, Idaho Falls	.939	9	30	1	2	33	4
Johnson, Anthony, Lethbridge	.987	28	213	20	3	236	13
JONES, Shane, Ogden	.989	70	656	46	8	710	68
Judge, Mike, Helena	.985	16	125	8	2	135	15
Kernan, Phil, Butte	.979	11	86	8	2	96	8
Kinkade, Mike, Helena	.995	21	174	14	1	189	26
Martinez, Rafael, Great Falls*	.984	58	449	39	8	496	30
Messick, J.T., But.-Let.	.962	4	24	1	1	26	1
O'Hearn, Paul, Ogden	1.000	1	5	0	0	5	0
Parent, Gerald, Helena	1.000	13	109	4	0	113	12
Parsons, Jason, Billings	.976	9	74	7	2	83	12
Sanchez, Marcos, Idaho Falls	1.000	3	25	3	0	28	6
Shanks, Cliff, Butte	.971	15	118	15	4	137	11
Smith, Rick, Helena	.992	27	218	25	2	245	19
Sorg, Jay, Billings	.987	62	567	30	8	605	54
Stewart, Paxton, Medicine Hat	.936	8	44	0	3	47	3
Timmons, Shayne, Med. Hat	.929	5	25	1	2	28	3
Valdespino, Jose, Med. Hat	1.000	2	16	0	0	16	2
Vallero, Rich, Ogden	1.000	1	2	0	0	2	0
Watkins, Sean, Idaho Falls*	.981	65	561	45	12	618	67

TRIPLE PLAY: Kinkade.

FIRST BASEMEN WITH TWO OR MORE TEAMS

Player, Team	Pct.	G	PO	A	E	TC	DP
Messick, J.T., Butte	.000	1	0	0	0	0	0
Messick, J.T., Lethbridge	.962	3	24	1	1	26	1

SECOND BASEMEN

Player, Team	Pct.	G	PO	A	E	TC	DP
Arevalos, Ryan, Helena	.921	12	21	37	5	63	9
Arrollado, Courtney, Butte	.933	58	133	185	23	341	41
Bramlett, Jeff, Great Falls	1.000	1	1	1	0	2	0
Bucci, Carmen, Idaho Falls	1.000	4	2	8	0	10	2
Burks, Donny, Lethbridge	.970	11	14	18	1	33	2
Carpentier, Mike, Great Falls	1.000	1	0	1	0	1	0
Coca, Mark, Ogden	.900	2	3	6	1	10	1
Demetral, Scott, Ogden	.973	38	84	95	5	184	33
Flores, Eric, Great Falls	1.000	4	1	4	0	5	0
Gama, Ricardo, Idaho Falls	.959	69	160	212	16	388	68
Giallella, Brian, Butte	.893	17	24	43	8	75	8
Goodhart, Steven, Billings	.957	65	128	187	14	329	47
Guerrero, Sergio, Helena	.977	7	17	26	1	44	9
HUTCHISON, Tom, Lethbridge	.972	53	106	137	7	250	23
Lewis, Dwayne, Lethbridge	.955	9	14	28	2	44	6
Lopez, Mickey, Helena	.968	26	56	66	4	126	20
Martinez, Erik, Ogden	.893	29	52	90	17	159	19
Martinez, Matt, Ogden	.750	2	4	2	2	8	1
Mateo, Jose, Great Falls	.833	4	3	2	1	6	1
Merila, Mark, Idaho Falls	1.000	2	5	9	0	14	4
Meyer, Bobby, Great Falls	.784	15	10	19	8	37	2
Ozuna, Rafael, Great Falls	.942	62	110	148	16	274	28
Peeples, Michael, Med. Hat	.873	45	88	90	26	204	14
Phair, Kelly, Ogden	.941	5	7	9	1	17	3
Ritter, Ryan, Helena	.940	27	53	57	7	117	15

Player, Team	Pct.	G	PO	A	E	TC	DP
Schock, Jared, Ogden	1.000	2	5	3	0	8	1
Snelling, Allen, Medicine Hat	.914	30	52	65	11	128	10
Walker, Rodney, Lethbridge	.857	8	14	16	5	35	4
Wilson, Brian, Billings	.976	8	17	23	1	41	2

THIRD BASEMEN

Player, Team	Pct.	G	PO	A	E	TC	DP
Arrollado, Courtney, Butte	.929	4	6	7	1	14	1
Barlock, Todd, Great Falls	.862	56	35	121	25	181	5
Bledsoe, Jim, Ogden	.850	5	4	13	3	20	0
Bucci, Carmen, Idaho Falls	.900	12	4	5	1	10	0
Burks, Donny, Lethbridge	.750	1	3	0	1	4	1
Demetral, Scott, Ogden	.979	13	15	32	1	48	7
DeSensi, Craig, Butte	.894	26	25	34	7	66	3
Guerrero, Sergio, Helena	.907	23	13	55	7	75	7
Hills, Richard, Idaho Falls	.951	32	16	62	4	82	3
Hutchison, Tom, Lethbridge	.818	8	6	12	4	22	3
Illig, Brett, Great Falls	.684	11	2	11	6	19	0
Judge, Mike, Helena	.750	1	2	1	1	4	0
Kinkade, Mike, Helena	.909	25	10	50	6	66	6
Kominek, Tobias, Helena	.909	6	4	16	2	22	2
Langdon, Trajan, Idaho Falls	.783	9	5	13	5	23	2
Lopez, Louis, Ogden	.930	44	33	114	11	158	11
Lopiccolo, Jamie, Ogden	.837	11	9	27	7	43	3
Manfredi, Joel, Great Falls	.900	19	8	28	4	40	3
McCarty, Matt, Lethbridge	.881	27	15	44	8	67	3
Merila, Mark, Idaho Falls	.867	36	23	75	15	113	7
Messick, J.T., But.-Let.	.921	31	12	46	5	63	4
Moreno, Victor, Lethbridge	.849	24	12	33	8	53	1
Parent, Gerald, Helena	.845	20	11	38	9	58	5
Peeples, Michael, Med. Hat	.667	1	2	0	1	3	0
PRESTON, Doyle, Billings	.929	64	48	136	14	198	18
Shanks, Cliff, Butte	.927	21	8	30	3	41	2
Shatley, Andy, Medicine Hat	.851	70	53	130	32	215	13
Timmons, Shayne, Med. Hat	.667	4	1	3	2	6	0
Walker, Rodney, Lethbridge	.931	10	6	21	2	29	3
Ward, Jason, Lethbridge	.897	11	10	16	3	29	0
Wilson, Brian, Billings	.885	11	4	19	3	26	3

THIRD BASEMEN WITH TWO OR MORE TEAMS

Player, Team	Pct.	G	PO	A	E	TC	DP
Messick, J.T., Butte	.933	29	12	44	4	60	4
Messick, J.T., Lethbridge	.667	2	0	2	1	3	0

SHORTSTOPS

Player, Team	Pct.	G	PO	A	E	TC	DP
Arevalos, Ryan, Helena	.922	35	44	98	12	154	22
Bucci, Carmen, Idaho Falls	.963	31	45	85	5	135	22
Burks, Donny, Lethbridge	.906	49	66	127	20	213	17
Carpentier, Mike, Great Falls	.917	6	9	13	2	24	2
Demetral, Scott, Ogden	1.000	7	8	23	0	31	4
DeSensi, Craig, Butte	1.000	1	1	2	0	3	1
Flores, Eric, Great Falls	.843	36	37	65	19	121	14
Giallella, Brian, Butte	.906	13	19	29	5	53	6
Guerrero, Sergio, Helena	.978	10	21	24	1	46	7
Hills, Richard, Idaho Falls	.947	30	58	103	9	170	28
Hokanson, Don, Lethbridge	1.000	1	0	3	0	3	0
Hutchison, Tom, Lethbridge	1.000	1	0	1	0	1	0
Illig, Brett, Great Falls	.833	10	9	6	3	18	2
Lewis, Dwayne, Lethbridge	.923	6	9	15	2	26	2
Lopez, Mickey, Helena	.899	31	54	88	16	158	20
Martinez, Erik, Ogden	.667	1	2	0	1	3	0
Martinez, Matt, Ogden	1.000	1	6	1	0	7	0
Mateo, Jose, Great Falls	.923	36	48	96	12	156	18
McCarty, Matt, G.F.-Let.	.838	14	6	25	6	37	3
Messick, J.T., Butte	.889	2	1	7	1	9	1
Meyer, Bobby, Great Falls	1.000	1	1	0	0	1	0
Montgomery, Andre, Billings	.878	33	41	81	17	139	15
Perez, Nelson, Butte	.893	61	84	176	31	291	36
PHAIR, Kelly, Ogden	.948	57	90	181	15	286	34
Ritter, Ryan, Helena	1.000	1	2	1	0	3	0
Rosario, Eliezer, Idaho Falls	.921	20	34	71	9	114	18
Srebroski, Andrew, Ogden	.895	10	18	33	6	57	5
Walker, Rodney, Lethbridge	.880	22	24	42	9	75	4
Wilson, Brian, Billings	.920	52	62	157	19	238	35
Woodward, Chris, Medicine Hat	.911	72	106	202	30	338	34

TRIPLE PLAY: Arevalos.

SHORTSTOPS WITH TWO OR MORE TEAMS

Player, Team	Pct.	G	PO	A	E	TC	DP
McCarty, Matt, Great Falls	.857	12	3	21	4	28	2
McCarty, Matt, Lethbridge	.778	2	3	4	2	9	1

OUTFIELDERS

Player, Team	Pct.	G	PO	A	E	TC	DP
Abernathy, George, Idaho Falls	.959	61	86	7	4	97	1
Allen, Dustin, Idaho Falls	1.000	12	12	1	0	13	0
Amerson, Gordon, Idaho Falls*	.951	45	70	7	4	81	0
Aviles, Ronnel, Lethbridge	.946	37	32	3	2	37	0
Baker, Jason, Great Falls*	.986	52	62	6	1	69	0
Barlock, Todd, Great Falls	1.000	1	1	0	0	1	0
Benner, Brian, Butte	.976	59	78	2	2	82	0
Bledsoe, Jim, Ogden	1.000	2	1	1	0	2	0
Bogle, Bryan, Butte	.000	2	0	0	1	1	0
Bramlett, Jeff, Great Falls	1.000	2	1	1	0	2	0
Bray, Notorris, Butte	.959	60	111	7	5	123	0
Brown, Eric, Great Falls	.978	36	45	0	1	46	0
Claybrook, Stephen, Billings	.975	63	110	6	3	119	1
Coca, Mark, Ogden	.953	69	109	12	6	127	0
Cornish, Tim, Ogden	.926	12	23	2	2	27	0
Cropper, Roger, Lethbridge	.961	64	94	5	4	103	1
Dillingham, Daniel, Lethbridge	.880	25	22	0	3	25	0
ELLIOTT, David, Helena	1.000	48	46	2	0	48	0
Farner, Matt, Medicine Hat*	.976	42	77	3	2	82	0
Garcia, Miguel, Great Falls	.942	55	109	5	7	121	2
Gonzalez, Manuel, Great Falls	.949	48	90	3	5	98	1
Goodman, Herbert, Billings	.900	32	26	1	3	30	0
Gordon, Herman, Med. Hat	.965	45	107	3	4	114	2
Gronowski, Craig, Ogden*	.917	10	10	1	1	12	0
Hall, Darran, Billings*	1.000	12	16	1	0	17	0
Hampton, Robbie, Med. Hat	.964	53	95	11	4	110	3
Hinds, Collin, Lethbridge	.937	69	124	10	9	143	1
Hunt, Kenya, Idaho Falls	1.000	8	3	1	0	4	0
Iapoce, Anthony, Helena*	.966	39	55	2	2	59	0
Jenkins, Geoff, Helena*	1.000	6	15	1	0	16	1
Johnson, Anthony, Lethbridge	.927	34	49	2	4	55	0
Johnson, Brian, Helena	.971	30	34	0	1	35	0
Johnson, Ledowick, Helena	.923	30	47	1	4	52	0
King, Brian, Ogden*	.929	8	13	0	1	14	0
Kominek, Tobias, Helena	1.000	6	4	1	0	5	0
Levias, Andres, Butte	.967	56	115	4	4	123	0
Lindsey, Rodney, Idaho Falls	.949	35	69	6	4	79	1
Lopiccolo, Jamie, Ogden	.983	58	112	7	2	121	0
Martinez, Erik, Ogden	1.000	1	1	0	0	1	0
Martinez, Obed, Idaho Falls	.893	51	48	2	6	56	0
McCormick, Andrew, Med. Hat	.961	67	112	11	5	128	2
Mealing, Al, Helena	.962	48	72	3	3	78	0
Moore, James, Idaho Falls	1.000	14	8	1	0	9	0
Morales, Rich, Ogden	1.000	1	1	0	0	1	0
Moreno, Victor, Lethbridge	.870	20	19	1	3	23	0
Morrison, Gregory, Great Falls*	.877	44	61	3	9	73	0
Parent, Gerald, Helena	.960	17	22	2	1	25	0
Peeples, Michael, Medicine Hat	1.000	8	22	0	0	22	0
Prokopec, Luke, Great Falls	1.000	34	30	4	0	34	0
Ritter, Ryan, Helena	1.000	17	13	3	0	16	0
Rojas, Christian, Billings	.980	68	140	8	3	151	2
Sanchez, Ismael, Ogden	.936	19	41	3	3	47	0
Sanchez, Marcos, Idaho Falls	1.000	2	1	0	0	1	0
Scheffer, Lawrence, Ogden	.938	41	42	3	3	48	0
Scott, Thomas, Billings	.990	66	94	6	1	101	0
Shapiro, Tony, Butte	.958	18	21	2	1	24	0
Smith, Ramon, Medicine Hat*	1.000	1	1	0	0	1	0
Stewart, Paxton, Med. Hat	.895	12	16	1	2	19	1
Stuckenschneider, Eric, G.F.	1.000	3	2	0	0	2	0
Zumwalt, Rusty, Butte*	.950	36	35	3	2	40	0

CATCHERS

Player, Team	Pct.	G	PO	A	E	TC	DP	PB
Andreopoulos, Alex, Helena	1.000	3	11	3	0	14	0	0
Burress, Andrew, Billings	.973	23	98	11	3	112	1	6
Cancel, Robinson, Helena	.978	45	349	53	9	411	5	7
Cook, John, Lethbridge	1.000	2	12	3	0	15	0	1
Davis, Ben, Idaho Falls	.985	48	362	44	6	412	0	1
Davis, Josh, Idaho Falls	.938	4	41	4	3	48	3	10
Ebbert, Chad, Idaho Falls	.889	1	7	1	1	9	0	0
Fehrenbach, Todd, Billings	.897	8	31	4	4	39	0	5
KEIGHLEY, Chris, Ogden	.987	44	260	33	4	297	1	9
Kinkade, Mike, Helena	.976	18	107	15	3	125	1	7
Knight, Brook, Helena	1.000	14	54	5	0	59	0	4
Larue, Michael, Billings	.980	54	346	46	8	400	7	10
Manfredi, Joel, Great Falls	1.000	12	26	1	0	27	0	3
Marnell, Anthony, Id. Falls	1.000	3	18	4	0	22	0	1
Mauch, Dennis, Great Falls	.947	28	163	15	10	188	1	6
Messick, J.T., Butte	.952	8	33	7	2	42	0	0
O'Neal, Troy, Let.-Hel.	.970	42	294	59	11	364	2	13
Paul, Kortney, Lethbridge	.967	38	305	44	12	361	5	14

Player, Team	Pct.	G	PO	A	E	TC	DP	PB
Pena, Angel, Great Falls	.980	45	297	42	7	346	3	9
Prokopec, Luke, Great Falls	1.000	2	10	1	0	11	0	1
Rodriguez, Sammy, Butte	.927	14	69	7	6	82	0	3
Sanchez, Marcos, Id. Falls	.968	19	132	19	5	156	1	6
Shanks, Cliff, Butte	1.000	2	1	0	0	1	0	0
Timmons, Shayne, Med. Hat	.986	13	64	9	1	74	0	1
Underwood, Devin, Butte	.969	54	344	35	12	391	1	12
Valdespino, Jose, Med. Hat	.980	31	220	27	5	252	3	4
Vallero, Rich, Ogden	.966	36	200	26	8	234	0	15
Wilson, Craig, Medicine Hat	.982	35	237	29	5	271	3	14

TRIPLE PLAY: Cancel.

CATCHERS WITH TWO OR MORE TEAMS

Player, Team	Pct.	G	PO	A	E	TC	DP	PB
O'Neal, Troy, Lethbridge	.967	38	263	55	11	329	2	11
O'Neal, Troy, Helena	1.000	4	31	4	0	35	0	2

PITCHERS

Player, Team	Pct.	G	PO	A	E	TC	DP
Abreu, Juan, Butte*	.667	8	5	3	4	12	1
Alexander, Donald, Ogden	.889	19	0	8	1	9	0
Atchley, Justin, Billings*	.846	13	1	10	2	13	1
Bailey, Ben, Billings	.867	13	4	9	2	15	1
Bales, Daniel, Idaho Falls	1.000	10	1	2	0	3	1
Barnes, Larry, Helena	.667	3	0	2	1	3	0
Baron, Jim, Idaho Falls*	1.000	27	0	4	0	4	0
Battaglia, Chuck, Lethbridge	.800	4	1	3	1	5	1
Benny, Peter, Helena	.846	11	5	6	2	13	1
Berninger, Darren, Helena	.857	21	3	3	1	7	0
Bonilla, Welnis, Butte	.909	27	6	4	1	11	0
Bourbakis, Michael, Great Falls	1.000	11	1	1	0	2	0
Bowles, Matt, Helena	1.000	6	0	4	0	4	1
Brabec, William, Medicine Hat	1.000	19	0	3	0	3	0
Bryant, Adam, Billings	1.000	29	0	4	0	4	0
Burge, Jason, Lethbridge*	1.000	23	0	4	0	4	0
Callahan, Damon, Billings	.857	14	6	6	2	14	0
Camp, Jared, Helena	1.000	8	4	4	0	8	0
Campbell, Tim, Idaho Falls	.875	18	3	4	1	8	0
Caravelli, Mike, Ogden*	1.000	5	0	1	0	1	0
Cardona, Isbell, Butte	1.000	3	2	1	0	3	0
Chapa, Javier, Great Falls	.909	13	5	5	1	11	0
Charbonneau, Marc, Great Falls*	.786	14	2	9	3	14	0
Clement, Matt, Idaho Falls	.960	14	10	14	1	25	0
Collins, Edward, Helena	.889	14	2	6	1	9	0
Cooke, Alan, Ogden	1.000	16	2	5	0	7	1
Corral, Ruben, Medicine Hat	.895	14	3	14	2	19	1
Davis, John, Great Falls	1.000	11	1	1	0	2	0
Dawsey, Jason, Helena*	1.000	9	1	9	0	10	1
Dillon, Chad, Butte	.600	15	4	2	4	10	0
Done, Johnny, Medicine Hat	1.000	22	4	6	0	10	0
Erdos, Todd, Idaho Falls	1.000	32	1	2	0	3	0
Escobar, Kelvin, Medicine Hat	.909	14	7	3	1	11	0
Estrada, Horacio, Helena*	.900	13	2	7	1	10	1
Falls, Curtis, Lethbridge	.818	24	2	7	2	11	0
Fernandes, Jamie, Butte	.944	12	9	8	1	18	0
Fernandez, Omar, Great Falls	.857	19	2	4	1	7	0
Flores, Ignacio, Great Falls	.875	16	3	11	2	16	0
Friedman, Matt, Lethbridge	.917	20	4	7	1	12	0
Gamez, Rene, Ogden	1.000	10	7	6	0	13	0
Garcia, Eddy, Billings	.875	15	4	3	1	8	1
Gaskill, Derek, Helena	.818	31	3	6	2	11	0
Gomez, Miguel, Medicine Hat	.909	14	6	14	2	22	2
Gooda, David, Helena*	.938	10	6	9	1	16	0
Graves, Jon, Idaho Falls	1.000	4	2	1	0	3	0
Grote, Jason, Butte	.909	22	5	5	1	11	1
Gullard, Jack, Lethbridge*	1.000	26	1	4	0	5	0
Guzman, Domingo, Idaho Falls	.667	27	0	2	1	3	0
Harper, Terry, Ogd.-Let.	1.000	23	2	4	0	6	0
Henderson, James, Idaho Falls	.833	4	2	3	1	6	1
Hibbard, Billy, Medicine Hat	1.000	4	0	5	0	5	0
Hindy, Mark, Ogden*	.857	24	6	6	2	14	0
Hokanson, Don, Lethbridge	1.000	8	1	4	0	5	0
Holding, Brook, Butte	1.000	27	7	6	0	13	1
Hommel, Brian, Helena*	1.000	15	0	4	0	4	0
Irvine, Michael, Idaho Falls	1.000	28	3	3	0	6	1
Jamie, Jorge, Ogden*	1.000	10	0	4	0	4	0
Jenkins, Scott, Lethbridge	.778	15	1	6	2	9	0
Johnson, Mike, Medicine Hat	.875	19	1	13	2	16	0
Johnson, Scott, Butte	1.000	20	2	5	0	7	0
Jones, Matthew, Butte	1.000	21	1	2	0	3	0
Judice, Bryan, Lethbridge	1.000	7	0	1	0	1	0
Justiniano, Rene, Butte	.900	12	6	12	2	20	0
Kazama, Yuhito, Ogden	1.000	6	0	1	0	1	0
King, Raymond, Billings*	.909	28	7	3	1	11	0
Kirkman, Casey, Lethbridge	.913	15	13	8	2	23	0
Kline, Jason, Ogden*	.917	25	3	8	1	12	1
Kolb, Brandon, Idaho Falls	.750	9	0	3	1	4	0
Lapka, Rick, Billings	1.000	14	7	8	0	15	0
LaRue, Shaun, Lethbridge	1.000	26	3	10	0	13	0
Lawrence, Rich, Billings	1.000	13	0	3	0	3	1
Lee, Calvin, Ogden	.800	5	0	4	1	5	0
Lenhardt, Bruce, Helena	1.000	9	0	1	0	1	0
MacRae, Scott, Billings	1.000	18	1	3	0	4	0
Mann, James, Medicine Hat	.737	14	6	8	5	19	0
Marine, Justin, Billings	.500	18	1	0	1	2	0
Martin, Jeremy, Ogden*	1.000	9	0	1	0	1	0
McMillan, Leonard, Butte	1.000	10	0	1	0	1	0
Medero, Gadiel, Butte	1.000	8	2	2	0	4	0
Mejia, Carlos, Butte*	1.000	10	4	4	0	8	0
Miller, Shawn, Helena	1.000	16	2	0	0	2	1
Mitchell, John, Medicine Hat	.833	25	1	4	1	6	0
Mullins, Greg, Helena*	.889	4	3	5	1	9	1
Nakashima, Toni, Great Falls*	.667	20	1	1	1	3	0
Nate, Scott, Helena*	1.000	3	0	1	0	1	0
Neal, Billy, G.F.-Let.	.905	16	8	11	2	21	1
Newman, Eric, Idaho Falls	.900	15	6	12	2	20	1
NOVAK, Troy, Ogden	1.000	15	8	9	0	17	0
Ochsenfeld, Christopher, G. Falls*	.714	14	2	3	2	7	0
O'Hearn, Paul, Ogden	.889	11	3	5	1	9	0
Padilla, Roy, Butte*	.972	15	7	28	1	36	0
Pasqualicchio, Michael, Helena*	.800	8	5	3	2	10	0
Pavlovich, Tony, Helena	1.000	9	1	0	0	1	0
Porzio, Mike, Ogden*	1.000	8	0	6	0	6	0
Preston, George, Helena	.000	3	0	0	1	1	0
Reed, Jason, Great Falls*	.941	15	0	16	1	17	0
Remington, Jake, Idaho Falls	.955	15	8	13	1	22	0
Richardson, Darrell, Lethbridge	.933	15	7	7	1	15	0
Richardson, Jesse, Helena*	.833	25	0	5	1	6	0
Riedling, John, Billings	1.000	13	1	3	0	4	0
Rivera, Oscar, Great Falls	1.000	18	1	7	0	8	0
Robins, Doug, Lethbridge	1.000	15	4	6	0	10	1
Rodriguez, Luis, Butte*	1.000	7	0	1	0	1	0
Rodriguez, Victor, Med. Hat	.850	17	4	13	3	20	1
Rosario, Nelson, Med. Hat*	1.000	10	0	1	0	1	0
Sak, James, Idaho Falls	.857	13	1	5	1	7	0
Sangeado, Juan, Great Falls	.700	16	5	2	3	10	1
Schultea, Matt, Ogden	1.000	34	4	6	0	10	0
Sheldon, Shane, Helena	1.000	17	3	0	0	3	1
Smith, Ramon, Medicine Hat*	.778	19	1	6	2	9	1
Smith, Travis, Helena	.941	20	7	9	1	17	0
Spear, Russell, Idaho Falls	.667	14	3	3	3	9	0
Sweezey, Gary, Great Falls	1.000	17	2	5	0	7	1
Taczy, Craig, Great Falls*	1.000	18	3	1	0	4	0
Torres, Jackson, Great Falls	.545	14	0	6	5	11	3
Upchurch, Wayne, Lethbridge	.938	9	4	11	1	16	0
Veniard, Jay, Medicine Hat*	.667	11	4	12	8	24	0
Waites, Steve, Butte	1.000	28	1	5	0	6	1
Weiss, Marc, Billings	1.000	18	4	4	0	8	1
Whitson, Eric, Ogden	1.000	22	3	3	0	6	1
Wright, Scott, Billings	1.000	17	1	1	0	2	0

TRIPLE PLAY: Collins.

PITCHERS WITH TWO OR MORE TEAMS

Player, Team	Pct.	G	PO	A	E	TC	DP
Harper, Terry, Ogden	1.000	8	1	1	0	2	0
Harper, Terry, Lethbridge	1.000	15	1	3	0	4	0
Neal, Billy, Great Falls	1.000	6	1	1	0	2	0
Neal, Billy, Lethbridge	.895	10	7	10	2	19	1

The following players did not have any fielding statistics at the positions indicated or appeared only as a designated hitter, pinch-hitter or pinch-runner: Barkett, 3b; Besser, p; Bucci, p; Castillo, p; Clark, p; Elliott, ss; Feliciano, p; Fox, p; M. Garcia, ss; Gavello, dh; Guerrero, p; Illig, 2b; James, p; Keighley, of; B. King, 3b; Lewis, of; E. Martinez, 3b; McCarty, 2b; Merila, p; Messick, p; Meyer, of; Montgomery, of; O'Hearn, of; Ozuna, ss; J. Perez, p; D. Preston, ss; S. Rodriguez, p; Schock, 3b, ss; Shapiro, c; Ri. Smith, ss, of; Snelling, 3b, ss; L. Torres, p; Walker, of; Whitson, of.

LEAGUE CHAMPIONS

Year	Team	Pct.
1939—	Twin Falls*	.581
1940—	Salt Lake City	.608
	Ogden (4th)*	.492
1941—	Boise	.623
	Ogden (2nd)*	.598
1942—	Pocatello†	.690
	Boise	.683
1943-44-45—	Did not operate.	
1946—	Twin Falls‡	.585
	Salt Lake City†	.585
1947—	Salt Lake City	.618
	Twin Falls†	.600
1948—	Pocatello	.611
	Twin Falls (2nd)*	.595
1949—	Twin Falls	.624
	Pocatello (3rd)*	.595
1950—	Pocatello	.635
	Billings (3rd)*	.571
1951—	Salt Lake City	.618
	Great Falls (3rd)*	.559
1952—	Pocatello	.595
	Idaho Falls (2nd)*	.573
1953—	Ogden	.679
	Salt Lake City (4th)*	.527
1954—	Salt Lake City	.595
	Great Falls (4th)*	.530
1955—	Boise	.588
	Magic Valley (4th)*	.489
1956—	Boise	.561
1957—	Salt Lake City	.650
	Billings†	.582
1958—	Great Falls	.582
	Boise†	.615
1959—	Boise	.633
	Billings (2nd)*	.523
1960—	Boise†	.686
	Idaho Falls	.650
1961—	Boise	.638
	Great Falls*	.571
1962—	Boise§	.565
	Billings†	.706
1963—	Idaho Falls	.702
	Magic Valley†	.643
1964—	Treasure Valley	.615
1965—	Treasure Valley	.530
1966—	Ogden	.591
1967—	Ogden	.621
1968—	Ogden	.609
1969—	Ogden	.620
1970—	Idaho Falls	.629
1971—	Great Falls	.643
1972—	Billings	.694
1973—	Billings	.629
1974—	Idaho Falls	.569
1975—	Great Falls	.577
1976—	Great Falls	.577
1977—	Lethbridge	.629
1978—	Billings∞	.735
1979—	Helena	.623
	Lethbridge▲	.559
1980—	Lethbridge▲	.743
	Billings	.629
1981—	Calgary	.657
	Butte▲	.557
1982—	Medicine Hat▲	.629
	Idaho Falls	.600
1983—	Billings▲	.614
	Calgary	.600
1984—	Billings	.691
	Helena▲	.647
1985—	Great Falls	.771
	Salt Lake City▲	.657
1986—	Salt Lake City◆	.643
	Great Falls	.571
1987—	Salt Lake City◆	.700
	Helena	.657
1988—	Great Falls◆	.754
	Butte	.629
1989—	Great Falls◆	.791
	Butte	.621
1990—	Great Falls◆	.706
	Salt Lake	.618
1991—	Salt Lake City◆	.700
	Great Falls	.657
1992—	Salt Lake	.697
	Billings◆	.697
1993—	Billings◆	.653
	Helena	.589
1994—	Billings◆	.694
	Helena	.611
1995—	Billings	.710
	Helena■	.690

*Won four-club playoff. †Won split-season playoff. ‡Ended first half in tie with Salt Lake City and won one-game playoff. §Ended first half in tie with Billings and Great Falls and won playoff. ∞Billings (first place) defeated Idaho Falls (second place) in first place-second place playoff. ▲League divided into Northern and Southern divisions; won two-club playoff. ◆Won two-club playoff. ■League divided into Northern and Southern divisions; won four-club playoff.

MINOR LEAGUE INDEX

TEAMS AND CITIES

Adelanto, Calif. (see High Desert) 462
Aguascalientes, Mexico 389
Aguila, Mexico 389
Albany, Ga. 537
Albuquerque, N.M. 404
Appleton, Wis. (see Wisconsin) 501
Arkansas 450
Asheville, N.C. 537
Auburn, N.Y. 516
Augusta, Ga. 537
Augusta, N.J. (see New Jersey) 516
Bakersfield, Calif. 462
Batavia, N.Y. 516
Battle Creek, Mich. (see Michigan) 501
Bellingham, Wash. 528
Beloit, Wis. 501
Billings, Mont. 599
Binghamton, N.Y. 421
Birmingham, Ala. 436
Bluefield, W.Va. 552
Boise, Idaho 528
Bowie, Md. 421
Bradenton, Fla. 584
Brevard County, Fla. 485
Bristol, Va. 552
Buffalo, N.Y. 359
Burlington, Ia. 501
Burlington, N.C. 552
Butte, Mont. 599
Calgary, Alberta 404
Campeche, Mexico 389
Canton/Akron, O. 421
Carolina 436
Cedar Rapids, Ia. 501
Chandler, Ariz. 562
Charleston, S.C. 537
Charleston, W.Va. 537
Charlotte, Fla. 485
Charlotte, N.C. 372
Chattanooga, Tenn. 436
Clearwater, Fla. 485
Clinton, Ia. 501
Colorado Springs, Colo. 404
Columbia, S.C. 537
Columbus, Ga. 537
Columbus, O. 372
Comstock Park, Mich.
(see West Michigan) 501
Danville, Va. 552
Davenport, Ia. (see Quad City) 501
Daytona, Fla. 485
Des Moines, Ia. (see Iowa) 359
Dunedin, Fla. (Florida St.) 485
Dunedin, Fla. (Gulf Coast) 584
Durham, N.C. 475
Edmonton, Alberta 404
Elizabethton, Tenn. 552
Elmira, N.Y. 516
El Paso, Tex. 450
Erie, Pa. 516
Eugene, Ore. 528
Everett, Wash. 528
Fayetteville, N.C. 537
Fishkill, N.Y. (see Hudson Valley) 516
Fort Myers, Fla. (Florida St.) 485
Fort Myers, Fla. (Gulf Coast) 584
Fort Wayne, Ind. 501
Frederick, Md. 475
Geneva, Ill. (see Kane County) 501
Great Falls, Mont. 599
Greensboro, N.C. 537
Greenville, S.C. 436
Hagerstown, Md. 537
Harrisburg, Pa. 421
Helena, Mont. 599
Hickory, N.C. 537
High Desert 462
Hudson Valley 516
Huntington, W.Va. 552
Huntsville, Ala. 436
Idaho Falls, Ida. 599
Indianapolis, Ind. 359
Iowa 359
Jackson, Miss. 450
Jacksonville, Fla. 436
Jalisco, Mexico 389
Jamestown, N.Y. 516
Johnson City, Tenn. 552
Kane County 501
Kingsport, Tenn. 552
Kinston, N.C. 475
Kissimmee, Fla. (Florida St.) 485
Kissimmee, Fla. (Gulf Coast) 584
Knoxville, Tenn. 436
Lake Elsinore, Calif. 462
Lakeland, Fla. (Florida St.) 485
Lakeland, Fla. (Gulf Coast) 584
Las Vegas, Nev. 404
Lethbridge, Can. 599
Little Rock, Ark. (see Arkansas) 450
Louisville, Ky. 359
Lynchburg, Va. 475
Macon, Ga. 537
Martinsville, Va. 552
Medford, Ore. (see S. Oregon) 528
Medicine Hat, Alberta 599
Melbourne, Fla. (Gulf Coast) 584
Memphis, Tenn. 436
Mesa, Ariz. 562
Mexico City, Red Devils 389
Mexico City, Tigers 389
Michigan 501
Midland, Tex. 450
Minatitlan, Mex. 389
Modesto, Calif. 462
Monclova, Mexico 389
Monterrey, Mexico 389
Nashville, Tenn. 359
New Britain, Conn. 421
New Haven, Conn. 421
New Jersey 516
New Orleans, La. 359
Norfolk, Va. 372
Norwich, Ct. 421
Nuevo Laredo, Mexico 389
Ogden, Utah 599
Oklahoma City, Okla. 359
Omaha, Neb. 359
Oneonta, N.Y. 516
Orlando, Fla. 436
Ottawa, Ont. 372
Pawtucket, R.I. 372
Peoria, Ariz. 562
Peoria, Ill. 501
Phoenix, Ariz. 404
Piedmont, N.C. 537
Pittsfield, Mass. 516
Port Charlotte, Fla. (Gulf Coast) 584
Port City 436
Portland, Me. 421
Portland, Ore. 528
Port St. Lucie, Fla. (Gulf Coast) 584
Prince William, Va. 475
Princeton, W.Va. 552
Puebla, Mexico 389
Quad City 501
Rancho Cucamonga, Calif. 462
Reading, Pa. 421
Reynosa, Mex. 389
Richmond, Va. 372
Riverside, Calif. 462
Rochester, N.Y. 372
Rockford, Ill. 501
St. Catharines, Ontario 516
St. Lucie, Fla. 485
St. Petersburg, Fla. 485
Salem, Va. 475
Saltillo, Mexico 389
Salt Lake, Utah 404
San Antonio, Tex. 450
San Bernardino, Calif. 462
San Jose, Calif. 462
San Pedro de Macoris, D.R. 569
Santo Domingo, D.R. 569
Sarasota, Fla. (Florida St.) 485
Sarasota, Fla. (Gulf Coast) 584
Savannah, Ga. 537
Scottsdale, Ariz. 562
Scranton/Wilkes-Barre, Pa. 372
Shreveport, La. 450
South Bend, Ind. 501
Southern Oregon 528
Spokane, Wash. 528
Springfield, Ill. 501
Stockton, Calif. 462
Syracuse, N.Y. 372
Tabasco, Mexico 389
Tacoma, Wash. 404
Tampa, Fla. (Fla. St.) 485
Tampa, Fla. (Gulf Coast) 584
Toledo, O. 372
Torreon, Mexico 389
Trenton, N.J. 421
Tucson, Ariz. 404
Tulsa, Okla. 450
Utica, N.Y. 516
Vancouver, British Columbia 404
Vermont 516
Vero Beach, Fla. 485
Visalia, Calif. 462
Watertown, N.Y. 516
West Michigan 501
West Palm Beach, Fla. (Florida St.) 485
West Palm Beach, Fla. (Gulf C.) 584
Wichita, Kan. 450
Williamsport, Pa. 516
Wilmington, Del. 475
Wilmington, N.C. (see Port City) 436
Winooski, Vt. (see Vermont) 516
Winston-Salem, N.C. 475
Wisconsin 501
Yakima, Wash. 528
Yucatan, Mexico 389
Zebulon, N.C. (see Carolina) 436